C000148772

ISBN 978-0-265-80272-4
PIBN 10891788

TWENTY PAGES.

BREEDER AND SPORTSMAN

Vol. XVI. No 1.
No. 313 BUSH STREET.

SAN FRANCISCO, SATURDAY, JAN. 4, 1890.

SUBSCRIPTION
FIVE DOLLARS A YEAR.

Storyettes.

HARVEY W. PECK.

I clip from the Chicago Horseman, of the 5th of Dec., the following:

"The tireless interviewer will at times make the most careful student and practical man say things that will not connect, and which look to those on the inside as if something were overlooked. This is very apparent in the interview with J. C. Sibley, published in an Eastern contemporary, where among other things the popular Pennsylvania breeder compares the relative merits of George Wilkes and Electioneer as follows:

"George Wilkes and Electioneer are sons of Hambletonian, and their dams are both by Clay horses. The dam of George Wilkes produced no other of note, but the dam of Electioneer, to the cover of Messenger Duroc and Middletown, neither of which are considered sires of the highest order, produced, besides Electioneer, seven with records better than 2:30, and another with a record of 2:31, with a strong probability that at least two others will enter the list. To me it seems a reasonable deduction that Electioneer may be expected to excel George Wilkes as a speed producer in about the same ratio as the dam of the one excelled the dam of the other."

To those knowing the facts it is plain that they will not admit of such an inference, for if individual blood lines are of any value George Wilkes was a better-bred horse than Electioneer. And aside from that who knows but that Dolly Spanker would have continued producing foals of as high class as George Wilkes proved had she been spared. The natural order of events, however, shows that she gave her life to her first foal, and that foal proved the greatest son of Hambletonian, both on the turf and in the stud. On the other hand, Green Mountain Maid had sixteen foals, only one of which was by Hambletonian. That seven of them should have entered the 2:30 list is remarkable, and places her in front of all other speed producers; but even with that brilliant array she cannot be pronounced the superior of a mare that produced but one colt, which after a turf career was retired to the stud and founded a greater family of successful performers than can be credited to Electioneer or any of his contemporaries.

George Wilkes has been dead seven years, and from nine seasons in Kentucky his greatness emanates. Electioneer has been twelve years in California, and while not in high favor at Palo Alto during all that time he was always used in the stud. The appearance of Fred Crocker brought him to the front, and since that time his get have been on the move. Time will eventually give him a longer list of performers than Dolly Spanker's son, but more of them will be asked to appear on the Eastern tracks and prove themselves better race horses on the wear-and-tear order like Harry Wilkes, Wilson, Ambassador, Baron Wilkes, Kentucky Wilkes and J. B. Richardson before the admirers of successful campaigners will admit that even in the first remove Electioneer can excel George Wilkes as a sire."

This is in some respects rather a singular Editorial. I am one of those who "know the facts" I think, and I am compelled to say that I do not consider Geo. Wilkes a better bred horse than Electioneer. In fact, I think I shall prove beyond controversy that Electioneer is the better bred of the two, performances and breeding of their immediate ancestors to be the test.

Neither do I consider Geo. Wilkes as great a sire as Electioneer! I mean by this statement his individual get, for all of Electioneer sons are as yet comparatively young, whether or no they will sire speed with the sons of Geo. Wilkes as time goes on, is a proposition that I do not, at this time, wish to enter into. It is sufficient to say that there could be no reason given why they should not. I am however, dealing with the immediate descendants of the two horses.

First, however, let us enter into an investigation of the breeding of these two great horses. (I will state parenthetically, that I am as warm an admirer of Geo. Wilkes as can be found upon any piece of sod that this earth turns to the sun! I shall deal only in facts and written history, which I think shows the preponderance of evidence to favor Electioneer, and the Horseman's editorial to be a mistake.)

Geo. Wilkes was sired by Rysdyks Hambletonian, his dam being Dolly Spanker by Henry Clay, 8, his second dam claimed to be by Baker's Highlander.

It is a well-known fact that the full breeding of this justly celebrated horse was not known until many years after his birth, and then after much tracing his second dam was discovered to be by Baker's Highlander. This point is immaterial at best, for Highlander has never contributed anything to the trotting turf, and so far as I am informed, his blood does not appear in the pedigree of any performer of note.

Electioneer was sired by Rysdyk's Hambletonian, his dam being Green Mountain Maid by Harry Clay 45; 2nd dam Shanghai Mary, breeding not known.

These two stallions then were sired by the same horse, thus being equal in point of breeding on the sire's side. The dam of Wilkes was by Henry Clay—the dam of Electioneer by Harry Clay, a great grandson of Henry Clay.

From the standpoint of breeding and individual merit, Harry Clay is certainly a superior horse to his great grandsire; just as Director is a better bred trotting horse than his grandsire; just as Guy Wilkes is a better bred trotting horse than his grandsire; just as Stamboul is a better trotting horse than his grandsire.

Henry Clay was sired by Andrew Jackson, a well-known old time trotter. His dam was a mare called Surry, a Canadian. To this mare Surry was attributed the faint-heartedness that for years kept the Clays in the background.

From Henry Clay came Cassius M. Clay, 18; dam Jersey Kate, (dam of the trotter John Anderson.) The horse sired George M. Patchen 2:23. He also sired Neavis Cassius M. Clay Jr., Amos' Cassius M. Clay Jr., Strader's Cassius M. Clay Jr., and Ballard's Cassius M. Clay Jr.

Neaves' Cassius M. Clay Jr. had for a mother a mare by Chancellor, a son of Mambrino. He sired four trotters, among them Harry Clay, 45. This horse Harry Clay made a record of 2:29, and was much the fastest of the Clays. His dam was by Imp. Bellfounder, the "Norfolk trotter," (sire of the dam of Rysdyk's Hambletonian.) Imp. Bellfounder was bred in England and imported in July, 1822. He was sired by Old Bellfounder, his dam being Velocity, by Haphazard, a racing bred horse. This mare Velocity was matched in the year 1806, to trot 16 miles on the Norwich road in an hour, the conditions being that every time the mare should make a break she should turn around. She broke 15 times in the 16 miles, but still won. Bellfounder himself when six years old is claimed to have been matched for 200 guineas to trot nine miles in thirty minutes, which he won easily by 22 seconds. His owner afterwards made a challenge to trot Bellfounder 17½ miles in an hour, but it was not accepted. Suffice it to say that the blood of Imp. Bellfounder is much prized and I consider it assisted Rysdyk's Hambletonian in rising to the summit of equine honors, in a very marked degree.

Harry Clay is one of the noted brood mare sires, having sired twelve mares that have produced twenty trotters. It is a fact that Harry Clay was a faster horse than Henry Clay, that his dam was a better mare, both in breeding and stamina than the Surry mare; Harry Clay's sire was a better bred horse than Henry Clay. He was in the stud but a short time, when he was destroyed in consequence of breaking his leg. He sired the mare Cora that obtained a three-year-old record of 2:37½, and was afterwards lost in a fire. This record was made many years ago, when a three-year-old that could go that fast was thought a wonder.

We have now reached the grandams of Electioneer and Geo. Wilkes. The latter's grandam has never been claimed to have been a mare of great superiority. It is alleged that she lived—that's all. The grandam of Electionner was Shanghai Mary, a very game mare. Writers of her day claim for her a trial in 2:28. This mare when coupled with Sayre's Harry Clay, produced Green Mountain Maid, a mare with seven 2:30 or better trotters in the list, one in 2:31, one with a one-half mile trial of 1:08. There are at least two others that will get there in time.

But, says the Horseman, the dam of Wilkes died and Green Mountain Maid was bred for many years.

True, but had Wilkes' dam lived and been bred the same as the other mare, would she have produced the trotters the Maid did? The fact that no other mare in the United States has done so, (though many of them are better mares by long odds than Wilkes' dam) is presumtive evidence that she would not!

Let me illustrate. Green Mountain Maid has produced seven trotters, two have died that would have entered the list, and more are knocking at the portal.

Has any other mare by Harry Clay approached this showing?

No! Has any mare by any other stallion approached this showing? No! When this mare then, can show such a list, in addition to Electioneer, what sort of mare are we naturally led to believe her dam must have been? A mare inferior to the grandam of Geo. Wilkes? Well hardly! Figs do not grow upon thistles, nor grapes upon hazel-brush!

If Shanghai Mary had not been a mare of very great excellence and strong individuality, her daughter would not have been the brood mare queen. Or is it a feasible proposition to consider that it "simply happened!"

We will now take the horses as sires.

After as careful a computation as can be had without having the exact facts at hand, it appears that Geo. Wilkes has sired almost twice as many foals as Electioneer. Wilkes stood for years as a public stallion and had access to the best blood of the country.

But very few men in California have bred to Electioneer, and but few outsiders own horses by him. Every one will understand that all of his produce being owned upon one farm precludes giving all his colts as good a chance as they would have were they universally owned throughout California, for various reasons.

Although such is the fact, Electioneer has sired fifty horses that have beaten 2:30, two two-year-olds that made records of 2:30½, while Wilkes, from public service, sired a dozen more from twice the number of colts. It must be remembered that one-third of Electioneer's colts are less than two years old, while the progeny of Wilkes are aged horses. When all the youngsters by Electioneer are developed there is no telling how far, numerically, he will surpass Wilkes.

Electioneer is a much greater sire of extreme speed than Wilkes. To not go too much into detail, he has sired a three year old with a faster record by three seconds than the fastest of Wilkes' offspring.

He has sired a horse with a record of 2:12½ from a thoroughbred mare. No other horse has been able to impart such speed under similar conditions.

He has sired a horse with a record of 2:20 from a thoroughbred mare. No other horse has been equal to the task.

One of his sons sired a yearling that went a mile in 2:31½, the best record for that age.

He has sired nine two-year-olds that have trotted to records from 2:18 to 2:30½.

He has sired eight three-year-olds that have made records from 2:10½ to 2:27¼.

As for campaigning, the very fact of nearly all his get being owned by one farm would naturally militate against them as against the get of a horse whose immediate get has been owned for years in almost every State in the Union. California is a comparatively young State—in years at least—and has but an insignificant circuit to trot horses through compared with the vast territory east of the Rocky Mountains, where horses are campaigned from New York to Texas, and for six months of the year.

Not every man can take trotters East, even were they very excellent campaigners, but when some of the Electioneers appear there in the future the Horseman may consider them very fair campaigners. Whenever a stallion's produce [illegible] speed enough to win in three straight heats there isn't much opportunity for the "wear and tear" kind to show their good qualities.

Some six years ago the Breeders' Gazette published a half column article on the greatness of George Wilkes. I excerpt the following:

"The fastest of the family, Wilson, 2:16½, is not by any means the best, and it should not be forgotten that his record was obtained in a race which he lost to Director at Cleveland last summer, and in which he had the help of all the other starters in the race, barring the black stallion. In appearance Wilson is a horse that strikes one favorably, having plenty of size, a well molded body, set on legs that are not bad, and in these respects he has greatly the advantage of most of the family, the chief fault with Wilkes as a sire being the fact that his get come in all sizes, and that none of them were particularly handsome or well proportioned. Lumps, 2:21, a mere pony, is probably the fastest trotter of his inches ever foaled. So-So, 2:17½, on the other hand, is a most ungainly animal, with a head that is almost a deformity. But in the great points of getting a uniform high rate of speed at an early age, Wilkes is, perhaps, the best of modern trotting sires, Electioneer always excepted."

If this was the opinion of the Breeders' Gazette six years ago, what would be its decision now?

A Vermont farmer and his wife on their first visit to the Capital at Montpelier, paused before the statute of Ethan Allen. They gazed long and thoughtfully, and then the silence was broken by the husband: "Gosh, mother, I allus thought Ethan Allen was a horse."

It would seem that Anteeo is pretty well thought of in the East. Mr. L. E. Simmons of Wilkes Lodge, Lexington, Ky., bred the following mares to him last season: Hattie Woodward, 2:15½, by Aberdeen; Eva 2:30½, by Geo. Wilkes; Anglia by Geo. Wilkes, Lizzie Tracey by Geo. Wilkes; Louise Wilkes by Geo. Wilkes; Bella by Geo. Wilkes; Sallie Jay by Jay Bird; Beulah by Beverly Wilkes.

These mares are among the gilt-edged matrons of the country.

I understand that the Litton's Springs property owned by Mervyn Donahue is to be converted into a horse farm. For the truthfulness of this rumor I will not vouch. In case it proves true, it is to be hoped that Mr. Donahue will endeavor to raise horses of sufficiently good class that he can utilize a portion of them by hitching them to the cars between this place and Point Tiburon. There would be numerous advantages in the new system. First, the horses would make less noise than an engine; second, they wouldn't have to stop to "wood up"; third, and more important than all, they would be faster.

The Science of Horse Breeding.

WRITTEN FOR THE BREEDER AND SPORTSMAN.

Few men who have any knowledge of pedigree of race horses will deny that there is a considerable amount of scientific skill required to bring together those strains or elements in the blood of male and female in such a fashion that the chances are greatly in favour of producing a first-class horse from the combination.

The laws of Nature work so mysteriously that the student of horse breeding continually finds himself "tripped up," and it is no exaggeration to say that the pages of the English Stud book fairly teem with blighted hopes and cruel disappointments, indeed, out of the 3,000 or so colts and fillies bred every year, the first-class ones may be counted on the fingers of one hand, while the 3rd, 4th, and 5th to 50th raters make up quite 90 per cent of the year's out-put. This is all the more remarkable, because in England the breeding of race horses is mostly the pastime of wealthy and intelligent men who have every facility for studying the shapes pedigrees and running of successful horses, to say nothing of scores of men of leisure who make it a study of the subject and are always willing to hand over the result of their investigations for experiment. Failures may be traced to many causes, notably a want of skill in *nicking*, as the hitting off of strains is generally designated amongst breeders, and in nicking the student can only be guided by closely studying the genealogy of celebrated horses, having also due regard to the shape, running, constitution, and temper of the animals. And the term nicking must by no means be taken in the general acceptation of the word as applied by breeders to the blending (through sire and dam) in the offspring of such fashionable strains as "Stockwell," "Touchstone," "Melbourne," etc. The breeder may very often discover that he has two much fashionable blood in his sire, and in such cases he will find it advisable to look around for mares through whose veins run a preponderance of blood considered the reverse of fashionable. The breeding of those two great race horses, "Navigator" and "Trident," is a singular confirmation of this.

"Robinson Crusoe's" blood teems with fashion, having a close double strain of Touchstone and one of Stockwell and Melbourne. The majority of the mares in the Terrara stud were bred on similar lines, therefore did not suit him. In the imported mare "Cocoanut" he was fortunate enough to get the extra nick he required. She had three or four strains of Whalebone in combination with such discredited blood as "Nutbourne," "Nabob," "The Nob," "Rattle," etc. To have mated her with a horse equally bred away from fashion would have been to court certain failure. Whereas in the "Robinson Crusoe" nick was found the happy blend which supplied to each those essential qualities which he or she lacked. It will be apparent, therefore, to those who have followed me so far that the very natural outcome of the breeders' experience is the golden rule: "When the right nick is found stick to it." The critic's answer to this will be —How do you account for so many cases of full brothers and sisters being so widely different in point of excellence? As the answer to this would occupy far more space than you could place at my disposal, I propose to touch slightly on only one or two reasonable suggestions as to why we see such brilliant and honest horses (over all distances) as "Chester" and "Richmond," succeeded by such indifferent animals from the same matings. In the case of "Maribyrnong"—Fawn cross—there can be no room for doubt that her 3rd foal, "Bosworth," although a very fair animal, was much inferior to his elder brother "Richmond," while "Palmyra," "Segenhoe," "Warwick," "Astute," "Superb," and "Genesta" and "Montem" dwindled down from second class to no class at all. "Chester's dam, "Lady Chester," may be said to have been, after her first foal, an absolute failure to "Yattendon," as neither "Roodee," "St. George," "Silver Bell," "Monmouth," "Grosvenor," or "Cleveden" ever showed anything better than third to sixth rate form. These two cases have been selected because they are so well impressed on the minds of racing and breeding men, and because, in both instances, the first foal was a pronounced success, the succeeding ones tapering off to absolute inferiority. These remarkable failures of Nature to sustain her representation may be traced to two likely causes, viz.—first, the failure in health of either sire or dam; or secondly, to the probability of *impregnation of dam with the sire strains through foal's circulation previous to birth*. This latter suggestion may not find acceptance with men who have not studied physiology, yet it is a well known fact amongst scientific men and practical breeders that the female is certainly tainted with the blood of her first mate as evidenced in the markings and peculiarities of the succeeding offspring. Medical evidence is forthcoming of numerous instances of the negro taint showing in the offspring of white men from women who have previously borne children to negroes; and in Blaine's Rural Sports there is a well-authenticated case of a blood mare having been put to a Quagga. The result was an animal with all the markings of the Quagga, and scarcely any mane; and when the dam was subsequently covered by a blood horse the progeny showed almost the same resemblance to the Quagga as her previous foal, and it took several crosses to eradicate the taint. In the face of such strong evidence as this, may it not be quite feasible to suppose that "Lady Chester" became considerabley impregnated with the blood of Yattendon," which filtered through her system from the yet unborn Chester.

If this is admitted, it becomes a comparatively easy matter to believe that each succeeding foal would be so saturated with the infusions of Yattendon as to be rendered far too inbred to race. Indeed, it is not stretching the comparison too far to say that Lady Chester, at the time of her last serving to Yattendon, stood as close in actual affinity to him as though she were his own daughter. How close the relationship might be; could only be determined by knowing the actual amount of his nature absorbed at each foal bearing; but Dame Nature so jealously guards her secrets, that the truth will remain a mystery until some Huxley of the future discovers a method of analysing the virgin blood, and afterwards testing for alien matter. "There are more things, Horatio," etc.

In support of the above theory, note the remarkable likeness often seen between man and wife, in old couples, where the wife has borne a large family. These ideas have been in my mind for some years, though never expressed in print; yet so long ago as 1878, I had a glimmering of what the consequences would be in Lady Chester's case, and wrote to the late E. K. Cox, pressing him to send her to Hawthornden for a change, as the flashy blood of that horse would tone her system down with those strains she (as well as "Yattendon") was very deficient in, viz., the brothers Castrel and Selem. That a dash of this blood was very essential to Yattendon may be noted by looking into the pedigree of First Lady, the dam of his greatest son Grand Flaneur." These strains have been always recognized by English writers (to wit, Nimrod) as soft and flashy; and following out my reasoning it will be seen that, as First Lady was persistently inbred to the two brothers (Castrel and Selem), she would predominate in her first two matings with Yattendon, and throw sprinters, until her system was invigorated and strengthened by the stout Yattendon impregnation, finally culminating in that galloping machine, Grand Flaneur. Thus we have similar causes working out opposite effects in two separate cases. Melos, who ran at the last V. R. C. Meeting in such first-class form, is another remarkable illustration of this interesting phase of breeding. His dam Melody (by the Barb from Mermaid by Fisherman) was put for four successive years to Goldsborough. One of the progeny, a chestnut colt The Broker, performed well as a two-year-old, and indeed won the Adelaide Leger; but, in point of racing excellence of good looks, he cannot be named in the same day with Melos, his full brother born after Melody had in the meantime thrown a colt and filly to The Drummer (imported). And I ask any impartial man to say whether Melos, in color and markings, is not more like that horse than his own sire Goldsborough. To my mind, the secret of his success lies in the strains deposited in the dam's system through The Drummer's stock, especially as Goldsborough's greatest success have always been with mares carrying a strain of Stockwell, so closely related to The Drummer.

In placing the foregoing remarks on paper, I do not profess to have made a discovery, because the physiological phase of the question has long been known to scientific men and observant studmasters, and yet, perhaps, have never properly realized its effects upon stock. I wish, therefore, to draw the attention of the individual engaged in the business of raising stud stock, to the fact that "things are not always what they seem;" or, to employ an illustration, it is quite probable that the Blair-Athol mare which has been bought expressly (and at a big figure) to nick with your stud horse, may, if previously covered by Kelpie for six or seven successive seasons, have retained only a very small fraction of that Blair-Athol force which you are seeking to utilise. And to the disappointed studmaster (as to myself) it may explain the cause of many a failure where all apparently necessary elements of success had been carefully brought together.

SIDNEY, Dec., 27, '89. C. BRUCE LOWE.

The Standard.

[AS REVISED AND ADOPTED BY THE NATIONAL ASSOCIATION OF TROTTING-HORSE BREEDERS, DECEMBER 14, 1887.]

IN order to define what constitutes a trotting-bred horse and to establish a BREED of trotters on a more intelligent basis, the following rules are adopted to control admission to the records of pedigrees. When an animal meets the requirements of admission and is duly registered, it shall be accepted as a standard trotting-bred animal;—

FIRST.—Any stallion that has himself a record of two minutes and thirty seconds (2:30) or better, provided any of his get has a record of 2:35 or better, or provided his sire or his dam is already a standard animal.

SECOND.—Any mare or gelding that has a record of 2:30 or better.

THIRD.—Any horse that is the sire of two animals with a record of 2:30 or better.

FOURTH.—Any horse that is the sire of one animal with a record of 2:30 or better, provided he has either of the additional qualifications: (1) A record himself of 2:35 or better. (2) Is the sire of two other animals with a record of 2:35 or better. (2) Has a sire or dam that is already a standard animal.

FIFTH.—Any mare that has produced an animal with a record of 2:30 or better.

SIXTH.—The progeny of a standard horse when out of a standard mare.

SEVENTH.—The female progeny of a standard horse when out of a mare by a standard horse.

EIGHTH.—The female progeny of a standard horse when out of a mare whose dam is a standard mare.

NINTH.—Any mare that has a record of 2:35 or better, and whose sire or dam is a standard animal.

Best Trotting Records.

1 mile—2:08¾, Maud S., against time, in harness, accompanied the distance by a running horse, Glenville, O., July 30, 1885......2:13¾, best time in a race between horses, Maud S., Chicago, Ills., July 24, 1880......2:12, Axtell, against time, accompanied by running horse—fastest stallion time, Terre Haute, Ind., Oct. 11, 1889......2:13¼, Phallas, fastest heat by a stallion against other horses, Chicago, July 14, 1884......2:12¾, Palo Alto, third heat in race at Stockton, Cal., Sept. 26, 1889......2:15½, Jay-Eye-See, half-mile track, Lincoln, Neb., Sept. 14, 1887......2:15¾, Great Eastern, under saddle, third heat, Morrisania, N. Y., Sept. 22, 1877......2:10¾, Jay-Eye-See, against time, best five-year-old record, Providence, R. I., Sept. 15, 1883......2:16, Manzanita, third heat, best four-year-old record, Lexington, Ky., Sept. 3, 1876......2:16, Edgemark, four-year-old stallion record, against time, Lexington, Ky., Oct. 18, 1889......2:10½, Sunol, against time, accompanied by a runner, best three-year-old record, San Francisco, Nov. 9, 1889......2:18, Sunol, 2 years, against time, San Francisco, Cal., Oct. 27, 1888......2:20½, Regal Wilkes, two-year-old stallion record, San Francisco, Nov. 9, 1889......2:31½, Norlaine, yearling, against time, San Francisco, Cal., Nov. 12, 1887......2:35, Faustino, yearling stallion record, San Francisco, Nov. 9, 1889.

2 miles—4:43 against time, Fanny Witherspoon, Chicago, Ill., Sept. 2, 1889.

3 miles—7:21¼, Huntress, harness, Brooklyn, L. I., Sept. 21, 1872.

4 miles—10:34½, Longfellow, wagon, California, Dec 31, 1869.

5 miles—13:00, Lady Mac, harness, San Francisco, Cal., April 2, 1874.

10 miles—27:23¼, Controller, harness, San Francisco, Cal., Nov. 23 1878.

20 miles—58:25, Captain McGowan, harness, half-mile track, Boston, Oct. 31, 1865,

Pacing Records at One Mile.

Johnston, harness, against time, Chicago, Ills., Oct 9, 1884, 2:06¼.

Brown Hal, best stallion record, Cleveland, Ohio, July 31, 1889, 2:12½.

Westmont, July 10, 1884, Chicago, Ills., with running mate, 2:01¾.

Ed Rosewater, two years old, Council Bluffs, Iowa, Nov. 3, 1888, 2:20½.

Yolo Maid, 3 years old, San Francisco, Oct. 13, 1888, 2:14.

Gold Leaf, four years old, 2:11½ on August 17, 1889, at Napa.

Arrow, five years old, 2:13½, made at Cleveland, Ohio, August 1, 1888.

Fastest Time on Record.

RUNNING.

MILES.		
¼	Jim Miller, 2, Deer Lodge (Mont.), Aug. 16, 1888 / †Sleepy Dick, a, Kiowa (Kan.), Nov. 24, 1888	0:21¼
[illegible]	Cyclone, a, 130 lbs., Helena (Mont.), Aug. 28, 1889	0:34¼
[illegible]	Geraldine, 4, 122 lbs., Westchester Course, Aug. 30, 1889	0:46
[illegible]	Britannic, 5, 122 lbs., Westchester Course, Aug. 31, 1889	0:59
[illegible]	Fordham, a, 115 lbs., Westchester Course, Oct. 4, 1889	0:59
[illegible]	El Rio Rey, 2, 126 lbs., Westchester Course, Aug. 31, 1889	1:11
[illegible]	Tipstaff, 3, 107, Westchester Course, Oct. 4, 1889	1:11
[illegible]	Britannic, 5, 110 lbs., Sheepshead Bay, Sept. 5, 1889	1:25 2-5
[illegible]	Ten Broeck, 5, 110 lbs., Louisville, May 24, 1877 (against time)	1:39¾
1	Maori 4, 105 lbs., Chicago, July 12, 1889, (in a race)	1:39 4-5
1 1-16	Wheeler T., 3, 98 lbs., St. Louis, June 1, 1888	1:47¼
1 1-16	Eyiton 4, 108, Chicago, Ill., June 28, 1889	1:47¼
1⅛	Terra Cotta, 4, 124 lbs., Sheepshead Bay, June 23, 1888	1:53
1 3-16	Joe Cotton, 5, 109¼ lbs., Sheepshead Bay, Sept. 7, 1887	2:00¼
1¼	Kingston, 5, 122 lbs., Gravesend, Sept. 24, 1889	2:06¼
1 m 500 yds.	Ben d'Or, 4, 116 lbs., Saratoga, July 25, 1882	2:10¼
1⅜	Triboulet, 4, 117 lbs., San Francisco, April 26, 1888 / Richmond, 6, 122 lbs., Sheepshead Bay, June 27, 1889	2:21¼
1½	Firenzi, 4, 113 lbs., Monmouth Park, Aug. 2, 1888 / Luke Blackburn, 3, 102 lbs., Monmouth Park, Aug. 17, '80 / Jim Guest, 4, 98 lbs., Chicago (Washington Park, July 24 '88)	2:34
1⅝	Hindoocraft, 3, 75 lbs., Westchester, Aug. 27, 1889	2:48
1¾	Glidelia, 5, 116 lbs., Saratoga, Aug. 5, 1882	3:01
1⅞	Enigma, 4, 90 lbs., Sheepshead Bay, Sept. 15, 1885	3:20
2	Ten Broeck, 5, 110 lbs., Louisville, May 29, 1877	3:27½
2¼	Monitor, 4, 110 lbs., Baltimore, Oct. 20, 1880	3:44½
2½	Springbok, 5, 114 lbs. / Preakness, a, 114 lbs. — Saratoga, July 29, 1875	3:56¼
2⅝	Aristides, 4, 104 lbs., Lexington, May 13, 1876	4:27½
2¾	Ten Broeck, 4, 104 lbs., Lexington, Sept. 16, 1876	4:58½
2⅞	Hubbard, 4, 107 lbs., Saratoga, Aug. 9, 1873	4:58¾
3	Drake Carter, 4 115 lbs., Sheepshead Bay, Sept. 6, 1884	5:24
4	Ten Broeck, 4, 104 lbs., Louisville, Sept. 27, 1876	7:15¾

HEAT RACES.

MILES.		
¼	Sleepy Dick, a, Kiowa (Kan.), Nov. 24, 1888	0:21½—0:22¼
½	Bogus, a, 115 lbs., Helena (Mont.), Aug. 24, 1888	0:48 —0:48
¾	Kittie Pease, 4, Dallas (Tex.), Nov. 2, 1887 / Sadie McNairy, 3, 98 lbs., Chicago, July 2, 1889	1:00 —1:00 / 1:02¼—1:02
⅞	Lizzie S., 5 118 lbs., Louisville, Sept. 28, 1888	1:13¼—1:12¾
1	Bounce, 4, 90 lbs., Sheepshead Bay, Sept. 7, 1881	1:42 —1:41½
1	3 in 5, L'Argentine, 6, 115 lbs., St. Louis, June 14, 1879	1:43—1:44 —1:47¼
1 1-16	Slipalong, 5, 115 lbs., Chicago (Wash. Park), Sept. 2, 1885	1:50½—1:48
1⅛	Gabriel, 4, 112 lbs., Sheepshead Bay, Sept. 22, 1888	1:56 —1:56
1¼	Glenmore, 5, 114 lbs., Sheepshead Bay, Sept. 25, 1880	2:10 —2:14
1½	Keno, 6, Toledo, Sept. 16, 1880 (1st and 3d heats)	2:43½—2:45
2	Miss Woodford, 4, 107½ lbs., Sheepshead Bay, Sept. 20, 1884	3:33 —3:31½
3	Norfolk, 4, 100 lbs., Sacramento, Sept. 23, 1861	5:27¼—5:29½
4	Ferida, 4, 105 lbs., Sheepshead Bay, Sept. 18, 1880	7:23½—7:41

†Made in a heat race.
*Doubtful, and made in a heat race.

Noonday.

EDITOR BREEDER AND SPORTSMAN:—I was in the East last fall with a view of buying a stallion to stand in place of Fallis (2:23), which I sold to the Riverside Farm, Bridgeport, Conn., but failing to find one that filled the requirements I thought a stallion should have for this coast, having in view more particularly an idea of getting one with a Belmont cross on his sire's side and a Pilot Jr. cross on his dam's side. My attention was called to the high-bred young trotting stallion Noonday, by Wedgewood (2:19), by Belmont, the sire of Nutwood (2:18¾), first dam Noontide (2:20½), by Harold, the sire of Maud S. (2:08¾), second dam Midnight, the dam of Jay Eye See (2:10), by Pilot Jr., third dam by Lexington, the sire of the dam of Ansel (2:20). I went to see him and found him just the stallion I had been looking for, being almost a fac-simile as regards size, color, form and gait of Goldleaf (2:19) by Nugget (2:26½), a son of Wedgewood (2:19) that I saw trot last fall at Lexington one of the best contested races I ever saw in a large field of horses, in which he won in 2:19¼ 2:19 and 2:19, but found Noonday was not for sale, so I have procured a lease of him for the season of 1890, after which he will return to Kentucky. I wish to call the particular attention of horsemen to this royal bred young trotting stallion, as his breeding is the cross we require on this coast, and it will be the only chance to breed to get this royal and game blood that a first-class racehorse requires. Yours,

SACRAMENTO, Jan. 1, 1890. F. P. LOWELL.

The Canon.

The canon is of great importance, in fact is the key note to the judging of the limbs of a horse, and too much attention cannot be paid to them when purchasing. Henry Tweedley, M. R. C. V. S. of Buffalo, had a very interesting description of the canon in the Horse World, which we herewith copy, giving a specially prepared plate showing good and bad limbs, so that the reader can understand the Doctor's instructive essay without any trouble:

It now remains to describe the examination of the canon as to soundness, concluding with a few remarks on the diseases that most frequently affect this part. In proceeding to the examination of a horse for soundness, the veterinary surgeon derives the greatest advantage from employing a method; that is to say, he follows a certain routine. It is only by employing a method that the various affections can be detected with the least chance of error.

The method usually employed is to begin at the head, on the near side; then the front of the fore limb is examined; the position is then reversed, and the back of the limb considered; proceeding along the trunk, down the front of the hind limb; then back of the limb, finishing at the hind foot. In examining these parts the fingers are chiefly employed. In all examinations of parts we must, first of all, be aware of the anomalies that are usually to be found there. To confine our remarks to the canon, the method of procedure is as follows: The examiner stands near the shoulder, looking toward the same direction as the horse; he then bends down and passes his thumb and fingers down the front of the canon bone, the thumb grasping one side and the two fore fingers the other. In this way any unevenness in the canon bone, even the slightest, can be detected; what we are looking for at this part is usually a splint; the slightest splint is easily detected, and it may be added that any unevenness on this part, of a bony nature, is termed a splint. Frequently, also, we find the entire canon bone enlarged and thickened, this being very frequent in young horses that have been worked excessively; this is an affection of the nature of splint, and consists of an inflammation of the covering of the bone (*periosteum*). In examining the front of the canon bone for splint, particular attention should be given to that part situated immediately below the knee, as a splint at that situation may be very easily passed over. Splints are more commonly found on the inner surface of the bone. On the front of the fetlock, and sometimes extending a considerable way up the canon, we observe a considerable swelling, soft and fluctuating in consistency; this is of the nature of a windgall, and consists of a distention of the mucous sac situated under the extensor tendon of the foot as it passes over the fetlock joint. The examiner then turns and faces the opposite direction and proceeds to examine the back of the canon. The previous anatomical description will show clearly the parts we have now to examine; these are the canon bone, the suspensory ligament and the back tendons. We invariably proceed to a second examination of the canon, as we can in this position examine more minutely the small canon bones, the parts where splints are more usually found. We proceed exactly in the same manner as before, but here I have to refer to my previous remarks on the button of the small canons which, as I said, when excessively developed may easily be mistaken for splints. Having examined the canon bones and found everything correct, we next pass our fingers down the suspensory ligament and observe that it is quite even, with no trace of thickening; also observe its tense, firm feel; consider how it stands in relation to the canon bones and back tendons. Lastly, we proceed to the examination of the back tendons, and it is probably here that most uncertainty will be felt. The back tendons, as I have previously mentioned, should stand out clearly and distinctly, and be, at least inferiorly, at a certain distance from the suspensory ligament; like this latter, in a sound state they should be perfectly clear and distinctly perceived by their feeling of denseness and rigidity to the touch; they should likewise be perfectly even from immediately below the knee, till they pass over the fetlock joint. While it is the very simplest matter to detect an extensive injury to the back tendons, it is not always easy to the novice to distinguish slight affections of this apparatus. A horse, for example, is placed before you for examination; you find him, perhaps, standing a little straighter on the limbs than you would like, and at the same time you find the back tendons are not so distinctly perceived, but possibly a little thickened or stocked. In this case, how are you to decide whether there is a serious defect in the tendons, or whether this connection is only transient, perhaps the result of excessive labor? In proceeding to examine the condition of the back tendons, the method we employ is as follows: As mentioned previously, we run our fingers down the tendons, and on observing any thickening present, we grasp the part firmly between the thumb and forefingers and compress the tendons as tightly as possible. When there is the least pain present, the animal at once shows it by elevating the limb, and when the pain is excessive and the pressure be continued, the animal rears off both fore limbs. In this manner we can detect the very slightest pain in the tendons, and according to the amount of pressure requisite to evince these symptoms, so great is the pain in the part. I may add that the part requiring most attention is that situated immediately below the knee, as a slight affection may there exist and not be easily noticed on examination. Of course any excessive pain in the tendons is accompanied by lameness. But even with the lameness present you may have some difficulty in telling whether the cause resides in the tendons or not.

A word of warning may be necessary. It does not follow that although the back tendons are swelled and pain is manifested on pressure, as above directed, that the back tendons are necessarily diseased; and here I may remark that the disease most affecting the back tendon is "sprain" or "strain," and it may be necessary to tell how this may be distinguished. The back tendons are sometimes swelled and painful on pressure, whilst in reality they are not at all diseased. This swelling may proceed from disease situated in quite another part. For instance, a horse may be pricked with a nail; this causes a considerable inflammatory effusion that may mount up along the back tendons and lead to the belief that the tendons are affected, whilst this is not so; or an animal may receive an injury to the region of the fetlock with similar results. How, then, are we to distinguish a sprain of the back tendons? In sprain of the tendons the swelling is limited to a certain part of the tendon and is frequently well circumscribed, the pain being only felt in the region of the affection, whilst in swelling of the back tendons symptomatic of disease residing in another part, the swelling is diffused all along the tendon, this latter being painful to pressure over all its extent. This simple distinction will, as a rule, be sufficient to differentiate these affections. If I might give a valuable hint to those who have followed me in these remarks, I would impress on you that in every case of lameness, no matter if you think you have discovered sufficient to point to the seat of disease, have the shoe taken off at once and the foot thoroughly examined. This is a rule that even veterinary surgeons frequently neglect, and a short story to show its importance may be of service. A horse whilst at work near a house that was being erected, fell over into some excavation that was proceeding. On being taken out he was found to be so excessively lame that he could not walk. The veterinary surgeon diagnosed an injury to the shoulder; the animal was taken to his infirmary, the shoulder fomented and afterwards a strong blister was applied to the shoulder. At the end of six weeks he was found to be as bad as ever, and on a more minute examination being made, a splinter of wood was found which had penetrated the sole of the foot and had remained there all the time. The splinter abstracted, with subsequent attention, he recovered immediately.

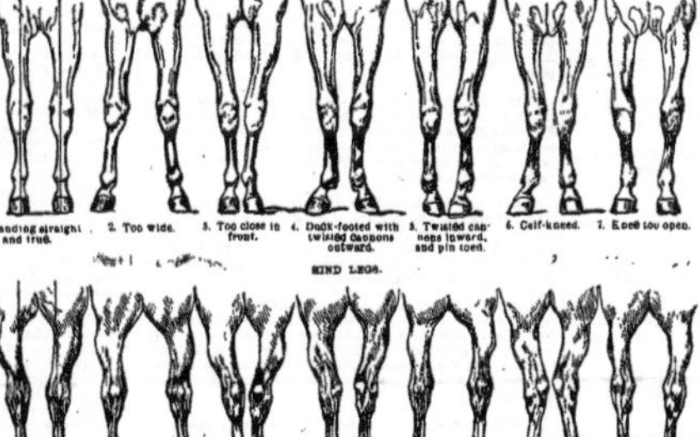

FORE LEGS.

1. Standing straight and true. 2. Too wide. 3. Too close in front. 4. Duck-footed with twisted Cannons outward. 5. Twisted cannons inward, and pin toed. 6. Calf-kneed. 7. Knee too open.

HIND LEGS.

1. Standing straight and correctly. 2. Too wide. 3. Too close behind. 4. Duck-footed behind. 5. Bow-legged and pin-toed. 6. Cow hock. 7. Too open.

As an adjunct to the above I have to say, do not believe too readily when you are told that your horse is lame in the shoulder; I care not who it may be that says it. This region, as I have elsewhere remarked, is the invariable resort of the ignorant, and hundreds of horses have been tortured for disease of the shoulder when no disease was there present. When teaching students, I have been in the habit of telling them not to believe in shoulder lameness. By this I do not mean it to be inferred that shoulder lameness does not exist; but I do say that when it does exist there is usually no difficulty in detecting it. Frequently people point to an atrophy, a wasting of the muscles of the shoulder, as evidence of disease existing at that part, but this is no proof that such is the case, as lameness of any part of the limb, if existing for any length of time, is invariably accompanied by this wasting of the muscles, due to diminished action of these muscles.

A still more common affection of the region of the canon is that commonly termed "windgall." At the present day, I need hardly say, this designation is entirely misleading. windgall being simply an exasperated collection of synovia in the sheaths of the tendons, This is in health the pathology of most of those soft, fluctuative swellings found on various parts of the frame, rejoicing in the names of thoroughpins, capped hock and elbow, etc. I will conclude the description of the region of the canon with a few remarks on the diseases most commonly affecting it. These, as I have said, are splint, sprain and windgalls.

Splints are characterized externally by the relief which they form under the skin. They are accompanied or not by lameness, according to the date of their origin and the sense in which they are developed. At the beginning of their formation they always cause manifest lameness, because then the bones are the seat of a pretty intense inflammatory action. But later this lameness may disappear, although the splint may have acquired a pretty large development. The lameness arising from a splint is usually only permanent when the bony tumor is situated on the margin of the articulation between the knee and canon bone. I have already pointed out the necessity of examining this part, more particularly for splint, as owing to the natural prominence of the knee, that formed by a splint is liable to be overlooked. Another position in which splint causes persistent and often obscure lameness, is when it is situated within or on the inside of the small splint bones, in which case, as will at once be observed by those who have studied the previous anatomical sketch, it produces pain by pressing on the suspensory ligament. In both of these cases even a very small splint may produce an intense and persistent lameness.

Splint is more commonly developed on young animals, owing to the fact that active growth is going on in the bones at that period; still, old horses are not exempt from it.

The treatment for splint is to apply cold applications for a few days, and afterwards blister with biniodide of mercury ointment, 1 part of mercury to 6 or 8 of lard, or vaseline. Should this not be successful, firing, by means of the pointed irons, may be resorted to.

To detect whether a splint is the cause of lameness, by pressing firmly with the fingers upon the part it will cause pain; when first forming, the splint has not the hard, bony feel it afterward possesses. The lameness of splint is also characteristic. A horse lame from a splint will be found to *walk* tolerably sound, but when he is forced to *trot* he is found very lame. In other words, the lameness observable in the trot is out of proportion to that noticed in the walk. Frequently also the horse points—a pretty good index that the lameness is situated under the knee.

I have already sufficiently indicated the means of detecting a sprain of the back tendons. The lameness from a newly produced sprain is very evident, but after the acute inflammation is passed, the lameness greatly lessens. With regard to the treatment of sprains, I have only to add—do not allow ignorant blacksmiths and farriers to apply their nostrums, rubbing the part with hot vinegar and such like, but at once have it attended to by the veterinarian, and this is the more urgent the longer the injury has existed. The reason of the above advice is this—if the horse be allowed to go for any considerable time suffering from a sprain, he will invariably end by becoming knuckled over at the fetlock, and when this takes place to any extent, the horse is almost useless. The cause of this is easily explained; owing to the pain of the tendons, the horse raises his heel and frequently stands on his toe, this continuing for some time; changes take place in the relations of the tendons, changes which become permanent and are equivalent to a shortening of the tendons, although this, contrary to what is frequently taught, does not, and, indeed, cannot actually take place.

Changes at the same time take place in the hoof, the heels not being used as before, grow much faster and deeper, thus they tend to contract, and the whole bearing in the foot being greatly altered changes take place in the hoof, which are likewise irremediable. These are the reasons why a sprain should be at once attended to, and those changes frequently do not require very long to be produced. If the owner wishes to undertake the treatment himself, let him apply cooling lotion for two days, such as Grulard's extract, and apply a Cantharides blister, one part of Cantharides to six of lard and vaseline. This blister may be repeated in a fortnight—six week's rest will be necessary to complete the cure. In very heavy draught horses suffering from sprain the application of the actual cautery, together with a blister, is followed by the happiest results. Innumerable means have been tried for the despersion of those swellings, termed windgall, counter-irritation in some form or other, forming the basis of them all. Knowning that such is the case, the application of the biniodide or the oleate of mercury should form the best of preparations, and this I hav little hesitation in say they do. The biniodide of mercury can be made as above directed for splint the oleate may be purchased in the oleate of mercury cum morphia 10 per cent. A small quantity of these may be applied daily until a scurf is formed; intermit for a few days until the parts regain their usual appearance applying lard or oil in the interim, then apply the treatment as before; this may be continued as long as the swelling exists. One of the best means of treating some of these synovial enlargements is to withdraw the excess of fluid by means of an aspirator, and afterwards apply the ointments as above directed. This however requires a competent vetinary surgeon as the operation requires knowledge which can only be applied by such.

TURF AND TRACK.

W. Lakeland is training Fordham at present.

£10,000 will be added to next year's Melbourne Cup.

King Crab broke a blood vessel last week at Guttenberg.

Longfish has been fired. He has a badly bowed tendon.

Mr. McLaughlin distributes fines and suspensions with a lavish hand.

Garrison is said to have refused an offer of $8,000 from the Dwyers.

Coney Island is practically deserted by horses and horsemen at present.

Capt. Franklin (Kennesaw Farm) is said to have a slashing sister to Stuyvesant.

R. Tucker, Nashville has bought the yearling brother to Madstone, for $2,500.

Jas. Carter, ex-trainer for J. K. Megibben, trains for Ruddy Bros. next season.

J. B. Haggin has no jockey engaged, and may possibly trust to disengaged riders.

Budd Doble, 2:13¼, will be offered for sale on Feb. 8th at Abdallah Park, Cynthiana.

Fitzpatrick is mentioned as McLaughlin's successor with the flag at Guttenberg.

Gracie B. 2:22½, won 20,000 francs in a race at Vienna among the imported brigade.

Axtell's apartments at Terra Haute when completed will be the most luxurious in America.

Dan Honig has leased from W. B. Jennings the running qualities of Frank Ward, Swift and Romp.

Alfy Lakeland has, it is rumored, purchased the racing qualities of Exile from his brother William.

Five hundred pounds even was bet on Surefoot, Le Nord, Heaume and Riviera, mixed for the English Derby.

E. J. Baldwin's $5,000 bet that he would not see a race on an Eastern track was probably less than 5,000 cents.

The old half-mile track at Clifton is being renovated and will be used to exercise on when the regular track is soft.

Naturally one hears of many fast yearlings (two year olds now). Barbee is said to have the best in New York State.

Secretary Brewster is elated. Washington Park has received 132 entries, to Coney Island's 129 for the Friendly Stakes.

Baron Alphonse de Rothschild has engaged Fred Barrett to ride on Sundays in France, next season, whenever he requires him.

Secretary Lawrence has attached a codicil to the Suburban to the effect that all horses handicapped at 126 lbs. and over escape all penalties.

Matt Feakes will probably train the Canadian Stable this season W. Hendrie Jr., having made a trip to New York to make arrangements with him.

The English sporting papers say, despite their looks, if Matt Dawson makes a move, tons of money will pour in on the Australian colts for the Derby.

E. Rossiter, who rode Robert the Devil, in his memorable Derby against Ben d'Or, died in an asylumn in Germany after riding there for the last two years.

Congressman W. L. Scott is looking out for another English stallion. Rayon d'Or has proved a success and Mr. Scott should secure another bargain.

Captain S. S. Brown will remove all his stock from Kentucky to Brownsville, La Fayette Co., where he has purchased 2,000 acres for a breeding farm.

August Sharpe, of Louisville, Ky., sells in the Woodard sale, Electrotype, five years old, by Electioneer out of Addie, dam of Woodnut 2:16½, and Manon 2:21.

The Hough Bros. have secured Day—who is rapidly recovering—for next season. It is said Garrison offered his services, but his terms were too exhorbitant.

Milton Young has paid James Galway $7,500, for the stallion Macduff, ten years old, by imp. Maccaroon out of Jersey Lass by imp King Ernest, grandam by Australian.

The American horse show lately held in Chicago was only a superficial success, resulting in a loss of $16,000. The Directors are said to have displayed very little business instinct.

Col. Stryker of Sprinfifield is in hard luck. Only a few weeks ago he lost two horses by fire at Louisville, and last week his stallion Monon (Nutwood—Verbena, by Princeps) died of lockjaw.

It is said that Chev. Ginistrelli has only to name a price for Signorina and the nitrate king (Col. North) will sign the cheque. But the Chevalier is thoroughbred and money cannot influence him.

George Kinney's book for 1890, is full at $150, consequent on the form shown by his youngsters last season. John Happy (his full brother), at Rancho Del Paso, is showing great promise as a sire.

Abercorn won the Metropolitan stakes at the A. J. C. meeting and on the same afternoon Mr. White ran one, two for the Derby and wound up by taking the Oaks with a sister to Abercorn called Spice.

August Belmont, W. L. Scott, Pierre Lorillard, Ben Ali Haggin, A. J. Cassatt, John Brewster and other prominent racing men, in a recent article in the N. Y. Spirit, are all in favor of more long distance races.

W. R. Brasfield & Co., among other stock, will offer Elected 7598, 5 years old, by Electioneer out of Cora by Don Victor, and Commoner, 4 year old stallion by Electioneer, dam Mollie Cobb by General Benton.

Senator Hearst and E. J. Baldwin head the list of entries to the Chicago end of the Friendly Stakes with six each, while Longfellow enjoys the pride of having nine of his get entered. Billet is second, with seven.

Rudolph, the winner of the Caulfield Cup, is by Martini Henry out of Rusk by Brown Bread out of Lady Sophia. Senator Hearst's imported Borbus is by Darebin, dam Sophietina, who is a full sister to Rusk.

Experiments are being made in Germany with paper horse shoes. Rubber has not been found practicable to replace metal horse shoes with, but paper is said to solve the puzzle. It wears rough for one thing, and is an assurance against slipping.

A new quadruple telegraph board was used for the first time at Kempton Park a few months ago. It indicates the placed horses on four sides, and worked so well that it is likely to become generally adopted on the English race-courses.

The winter edition of Ruffs Guide shows that the yearling sales in England last year had a greater average, greater total, more stallions bred, and more yearlings sold than in any of the past five years. 662 yearlings by 189 sires averaged 300 guineas.

The Langtry Farms' mare Miss Josephine, by Struan, dam Maid of Harris by Flageolet, granddam by Adventurer, slipped a colt foal by Friar Tuck (Imp). With the double Newminster also and treble Touchstone cross, the colt should have proved invaluable.

The Hon. T. J. Megibben has purchased imported Moccasin by Macaroni, dam Madam Straus by King Tom, and will use him in the stud. Moccasin covered a few mares at Rancocas prior to going to Canada and got several winners, among them being Amazon and Disdain.

Wilber Smith, who was in town last Monday, says Thapsin is improving but is not yet well enough to be removed. By the way, Wilber has charge of Al Farrow, who was attached by the Sheriff for a debt of $1600 owed by the new owner, W. H. E. Smith, to the Sonoma Bank.

Chinn & Morgan have leased from Charles H. Maguire of New York the services of the stallion Fond du Lac, by Glengarry—Hop (dam of Kirkman), and will use him in their stud near Harrodsburg, Ky. Fond du Lac was a horse of great speed, and should prove a very successful sire.

The Governor has appointed F. M. Loeber of St. Helena and L. W. Buck of Vacaville members of the District Board of Agriculture for District No. 25, vice themselves, terms expired: also, R. McKey of Placerville a Director of District Agricultural Society No. 8, vice A. T. Leachman, term expired.

Robt. Peck, the well known ex-trainer, has since giving up training, raced a good deal. His last venture was leasing Howbury Hall and the surrounding land on a long lease, and fitting up the most complete breeding establishment in England. It is situated near Bedford and will have room for sixty mares, yearlings, etc.

One of the most successful sales ever held was the Dwyer sale. 21 head sold for $43,950. Among them were: Kenwood (2), $6,150; Fordham (4), $5,900; Oregon (3), $4,000; Meriden (3), $3 500; Printer (2), $3,250; Folsom (2), $3,100; Taviston (3), $3,000. George Walbaum bought Oregon, Kenwood and Folsom, while S. Emery secured Fordham.

One of the best planned and well executed coups of the winter season was Peter Weber's Christmas handicap with Vendetta at Guttenberg. The four year old had been quietly worked along at Jerome Park and when he got in at 87 lbs. Peter and the Fordhamites thought it about time to cut loose, and though he went to the post at 30-1 every book was said to be a loser.

Lord Zetland, the Irish viceroy, should revive racing in the Emerald Isle, and certainly should not lose any popularity by his fondness for the sport of kings. He will probably run a horse or two with the famous Aske spots next season. Among his effects taken to Ireland were the gold cups and racing trophies, including those won by Voltiguer and Vedette.

The English Royal Commission after considering all the evidence offered with regard to hereditary diseases or malformations has decided that any of the following are sufficient for disqualification, roaring, whistling, ringbone, unsound feet, navicular disease, spavin and cataract. Curbs, as will be noted are not included in the list.

It is probable that the bookmakers who do business at the winter tracks, and especially those who have held stands at Elizabeth, will be forced to combine at an early date and fight a common enemy. They have sustained some heavy losses of late by the payment of forged or bogus tickets. The common enemy they are called upon to battle with is a gang who have evidently joined hands for the purpose of swindling the pencillers.

D. A. Honig recently selected out Jakie Toms as about the worst plug he had in his stable, and desiring to compliment his friend and fellow trainer renamed him James McCormick. Not to be outdone in these little delicate attentions, J. H. McCormick, in selling General Boulanger recently, stipulated as a clause of the sale that he should be renamed Dan Honig, and threw off $25 of the purchase money for the fulfillment of the agreement.

The list of winning jockeys in Austria-Hungaria is headed by Busby who was once attached to the Ashgill stable, and the rider of Thorn in some of his races. Rawlinson stands second, W. Smith third and H. Huxtable fourth, those immediately following the horsemen mentioned being C. Jones, G. Bell and W. Wyatt. E. Rossiter was successful on twelve occasions, and A. Lemaire, Goodway and C. Bowman scored nine, five and four wins respectively.

Would it not be a seasonable time for the various racing organizations, Los Angeles, Fresno, San Jose, Blood Horse, Sacramento and others to come to some arrangement by which the same starter could be employed and paid for the whole of next season. This would give the official a chance to effect good starts and obtain control of the boys and at the same time have some knowledge of the horses. As matters stand now anyone is starter pro-tempore, a state of things which exists nowhere but in California.

L. D. Parker, Secretary of the National Breeders' Association, is said to be very much against what are called "in-cup" records, and thinks the Board will decide to allow only horses that have trotted in 2:30 in an actual race to enter the standard list.

Ex-Governor Bowie, President of the Maryland Jockey Club, in a letter issued to the members of one of our oldest racing associations, states that there will be no more racing under their management at Pimlico. The reason given is that they could not afford money to draw large fields with so much racing going on all through the winter. Baltimore is not to be without a meeting though, for the Maryland Agricultural and Mechanical Association have decided to hold a spring meeting and have trotting in the fall.

An incident showing the power of memory in a horse is told of the great trotting stallion Almont. His disposition was of the most kindly nature, and he would permit any one to stroke his glossy hide and play with him. One day his groom struck him severely and was discharged for so doing. Almont showed no change, but more than two years after, when the groom returned, he suddenly became vicious and would not let the groom come near him. He evidently remembered the groom and the blow of two years before.

It has been calculated that the American turf gives employment to 50,000 people and indirectly assists 50,000 more to a livelihood. The thoroughbred stallions and brood mares on the great stock farms are valued at $6,000,000 and the sons and daughters of these stallions and brood mares earned above $2,000,000 more during the past season, the value of the stock now employed for racing being valued at $7,000,000 while the the capital invested in race tracks and stables is $6,000,000. The stock farms embrace 140,000 acres of the finest land in the country, and last year the yearlings sold footed up to $1,000,000, while the the attendance at race courses numbered over 3,500,000.

The Sporting Chronicle says: A great point of difference between English and Australian sportsmen is that the latter seldom, if ever, shoe their horses; and Mr. White's colts, Kirkham and Narellan, who are now at Newmarket, will run next season without shoes. Australian breeders aim at size, combining speed with strength. Remembering this, they invariably choose a limestone foundation for their pasture land. They are also believers in strong bracing air, and as a consequence the large racing establishments, Mordialloc and Williamstown, are close to the sea. Both are bright chestnuts, well grown, and possessed of all the qualities of racehorses. Narellan stands about 15¾ hands, while Kirkham, who is a more lightly-boned horse than Narellan, is fully half a hand taller. He was foaled on January 24, 1887, and is expected to turn out the best of the two.

Some interesting news about the "wintering" of the leading English jockeys is given by a London contemporary. Evidently they are sliding into society, for John Watts has been invited to have a week or two in Cheshire with Lord Dudley, who is hunting from the neighborhood of Tarporley this season. Fred Barrett will put in his off time with The Baron in the Vale of Aylesbury, with an occasional day with Mr. Lowndes; whilst George Barrett, when he is not with the Fitzwilliam or the Oakley on their best side, will hunt with the Pytchley and Quorn, and probably for a week or two in Yorkshire. Sam and Tom Loates, who share the same quarters in the Exeter-road, are hardly so aspiring in their tastes, and although they may have a day on the grass occasionally, they, like Warne and Rickaby, will do the principal part of their hunting with the Newmarket and Thurlow, a two-day a week pack that deserve supporting, and that so far this season have been showing excellent sport.

William Archer, the father of Fred Archer, the famous jockey, and Charlie Archer, the well known trainer, died on December 5th. William Archer was, in his younger days, a good rider himself. One of his first engagements was to Alderman Copeland for one year, renumeration for the year £6 and a suit of livery. In 1843, he went to Russia to ride for the Czar at a salary of £100 per annum and all expenses paid. He stayed two seasons and as the climate did not suit, returned. Between 1849 and 1858, he was in grand form across sticks and country, winning the Grand National in 1858, on Little Charlie. His death removes one of the old-time horsemen contemporary with Tom Oliver, Jack Mytton and others, while when he was born Sam Chifney, Buckle, Robinson and others were in full swing, his reminiscences of them being particularly interesting.

The New York Spirit of the times, in its carefully arranged and exceptionally interesting Christmas number has among other readable and instructive articles, one entitled "Some Foreign Horse Dealers." The London, Provincial French and German dealers are mentioned, but where is the Irishman? Certainly he is entitled to a place for his blarney, while as a horse trader he is about the deadest of the whole profession. At home his colts are all out of mares that were leppers sure, while one cannot get a horse that has not Irish Birdcatcher blood in him—if you believe Paddy. And when he gets to a fair—well, if you beat him, why, you will have earned it. All Yorkshire men have heard the tale of Paddy S——, who went to Howden fair with twenty head, and one long pedigree written out. A well known hunting and steeplechasing farmer bought (Paddy said he gave him them) a five and a six year old, own brothers, after two day's dickering, and put the pedigree in his pocket. "Hould on a bit," said Paddy, "How am I to sell the other eighteen if you take the bit of paper wid yez?"

"There is," says "Borderer," in Baily's Magazine, "one thing which now stares all breeders in the face, more clearly, perhaps, than it ever has done before, and this is that the value of a good sire is, in these days, something marvellous. It is suicide to allow the foreigners to buy and carry off a well-bred and sound horse before he has had a fairly good trial in his own country, where his value most certainly is double what it is in any other country in the world. We have suffered in years gone by from this haste to sell—Buccaneer and The Flying Dutchman to wit; and whether we have done wisely in parting with Ormonde, roarer though he be, has yet to be proved. Personally, I think the Duke of Westminister was right, for there will always be the possibility that the tendency may be reproduced in Ormonde's stock. Nothwithstanding this, I unhesitatingly say that there are fewer roarers among our fashionable sires of to-day than I have ever known before. This is a healthy sign. Let us stick to it." Borderer might have mentioned Glencoe, Leamington, Bonnie Scotland, Prince Charlie, Glenelg and several other stallions who have left their mark here, while Fisherman, Traducer and Musket in Australia have left undying traces of their merit, two of Traducer's sons, Sir Modred and Cheviot, being now in this country.

Hamilton is visiting St. Louis now.

Hindoocraft has undergone a slight blistering.

Kilkenny is another winner by George Kinney.

H. Blaylock has signed with the Beverwyck Stable.

Banker, 2:26½, is said to be ringing in South America.

The penalty for betting on a horse race in Vermont is $500.

F. Walbaum about won Oregon out last week at Guttenberg.

Firenzi is looking wonderfully well now, having wintered nicely.

Did Senaton Hearst ever say he would give $250,000 for Sunol?

The New York Jockey Club now has over eleven hundred members.

Mr. J. A. Morris has built a new stable of 28 stalls outside the Brooklyn Track.

S. W. Street has named the Powhattan—Call Duck, two-year-old Mohican.

The erstwhile Plunger, Walton, is back again in Philadelphia, hotel keeping.

Maud S. and Sunol are 15.3 in front, while Maud is 16 behind and Sunol 16.1.

Parson Lloyd has christened his two-year-old King Alfonso—Flirtation colt Sam Love.

Good pole horses are in great demand East. The record is liable to be lowered next season.

The Belair Jockey Club, Montreal, Canada, has decided to admit the public to the track free.

Robt. Steele of Philadelphia expects to give Antevolo a record of 2;14 or better next season.

The first regular meeting in New York State will begin on May 15th at the Brooklyn Jockey Club Track.

William McMahon has purchased his son-in-law Garrison's interest in all the horses jointly owned by them.

Rushville claims the second week in June for their Spring meeting, which is the next week to Terre Haute.

Lottie W. 2:21 is the latest purchase for the European market. Eight thousand dollars is the stated price.

Brown Dick has a two-year-old brother to Outbound, who is said to be better at his age than Protection was.

The latest report 'in re' Garrison is that he, Pittsburgh Phil and two or three of that ilk sail for Europe to-day.

Mr. Marcus Daly claims for his colors a copper colored jacket and cap, probably in memory of the Anaconda Mine.

The Running Meade Stud Farm, Ky., bought of D. D. Bell the two-year-old Hueneme (Billet—by Virgil) for $3,500.

Messrs. Weatherby say that Davenport was sold for export, price, 3,000 guineas, and not 4,000 as was generally circulated.

Mr. B. C. Murray still owns Pontico, the half brother to Pontiac, although he ran several times lately in J. J. Dwyer's name.

Johnny Corlett the well known editor of the 'Pink Un" has a high opinion of the Australian canditates for Classic honors.

The Chicago Stable removed to Lexington and were turned over by B. J. Johnson to Leigh & Kiley, Mr. Hankins' new partners.

A colt by Bermuda, 2:20½, dam Baby Mine, 2:27½, is said to have paced an eighth in 22½ seconds when five and a half months old.

Starter Caldwell set Horton down for the year, Lewis and Blaylock for the rest of the day, and Farren for life last week at Guttenberg.

J. B. Todd, a prominent Lexington horseman, took a lot of horses to Central America and thinks of staying there, the prospects are so encouraging.

Lottery, formerly Lothair, has been re-named Jim Irwin. His owner, Mr. E. R. Griffiths, has also changed Jack Homer's name (formerly Wheat) to Ed Cole.

Mr. W. Lakeland has returned Peg Woffington to her owner, Mr. George Clay, Balgowan Stock Farm, Ky. Mr. Lakeland had a lease of her running qualities.

Spokane got loose on the Louisville track, and while galloping about stepped on some broken glass, but is said to be not much worse, although the cuts festered.

H. R. H. the Prince of Wales has sent seven yearlings (two now) to John Porter, Kingsclere to be trained for next season. They were raised on the Sandringham estate.

While the horses were at the post for the first race at Clifton last Saturday, Cullen on King Arthur had his ankle fractured by Adonis, who let out savagely with both hind feet.

W. R. Brasfield and J. W. Samuels have leased four hundred acres near Lexington, Ky., and will have a trotting breeding farm with Bonnie McGregor, 2:13½, as premier stallion.

George Middleton, the well known Chicagoan, offers to match Jack 2;15, who is at present in Fresno in Doble's string, for from $5,000 to $15,000 against any trotter in the world.

Two well known English racing men, the Duke of Montrose and his brother-in-law, Lord Houghton, left England for the Cape of Good Hope. They will stay a short while there.

Walter Gilbey, who is one of the most extensive breeders of heavy draught horses in England, has had a heavy loss in the death of his Shire stallion Spark, who cost him 800 guineas a few years ago.

The New York Sportsman almost surpasses itself in its Christmas number. Among other interesting features is a striking portrait of J. H. Goldsmith, who was the leading driver out East last season.

C. W. Williams in his interesting article in the Chicago Horseman, on Axtell, says he could not show better than a four-minute gait as a yearling, further that he never trotted a trial and his best work-out was in 2:27.

The local pool rooms are said to have been done up again all round by the sure thing combination who tapped the wires last Tuesday and backed King William for the 4th race at Guttenberg at tens heavily after they received the result.

During 1889, Mr. William Astor has lost (dead) the stallion Baden Baden, a suckling by Kingston (imp)—Aranza, a suckling by Kingston (imp)—Pinde, a suckling Baden Baden—Naiad, and the mare Australind (Australian—Dolly Carter).

Wheelock, who was in F. J. Black's employ a few years ago out East, and a season ago ran a book which was supposed to be backed by E. J. Baldwin, is reputed to have won $150,000 bookmaking on his own account at Saratoga, West Side and Nashville this year.

Matt Allen, Senator Hearst's trainer, has a lot of the most promising yearlings—now two—in America on the Sheepshead Bay Track. He is particularly impressed with Warpath by Warwick or San Fox out of Second Hand and Fireworks, a slashing sister to Dewdrop.

Several yearlings were worked over the Kentucky Association Track last week. The best performance by far was by a brown colt imported in utero, by The Rake out of Flora McDonald, who worked three-eighths with his shoes on and 120 pounds up in 38 seconds. The colt was foaled at Woodburn.

Mr. John A. Morris, after a careful examination of Texas, has bought a ranch for a stud farm in Gillespie Co., 150 miles north of San Antonio, and will try the effect of the native grasses (mesquite, etc.,) upon young stock. The altitude is greater than most California ranches and the experiment will be carefully watched.

C. H. Nelson has three trotters working on the snow at Waterville, all of whom can beat 2:20. He is willing to match Nelson against Jack for any reasonable amount, the match to be two in three, one to take place at Buffalo, another at Fleetwood, and another at Mystic Park. Mr. Middleton says he is looking for a match with Jack. Why do not they put up?

Hearst, after many unsuccessful attempts, has at last earned a winning bracket, beating a field of eleven at Guttenberg in a five furlong dash with 103 lbs. up. Hearst is one of the Australians imported by Mr. Newton and later sold in New York. Another of the imported Australians, Gertrude by Somnus—Geraldine was sold to Senator Hearst on her arrival and has won a race at San Luis Obispo this fall.

Garrison's exalted opinion of himself is well known. Among many tales of the flattering comments on himself, the last is probably the best. After Raceland—Garrison up—defeated Firenzi— with Hayward in the saddle—a mile and a furlong, at Jerome, Mr. Belmont asked: "Did you win easily?" "Well, I had some to spare, but to tell you the truth, Mr. Belmont, if I had been on the mare I should have beaten your horse." One of our best posted California horsemen says old Bill has forgotten more than Garrison ever knew.

Senator Hearst will have a large enough stable at San Simeon to take out on the Western circuit. W. L. Donathan, who went down to the ranch last Monday, will have about twenty to work on including the imported horses, True Briton, Somnus—Geraldine filly, Somnus—Maid of the Hill colt, and Baggage, Almont, a sister to Joe Courtney, Evalita, and others as well as half a dozen promising two year olds. The stable will probably take in the Blood Horse prior to going East.

The Rosslyn Heights Farm, Pennsylvania, have bought in England the eight-year-old stallion Bonnie Charlie by Petrarch, dam Bonnie Leith by Rataplan, grandam Bonnie Bell (dam of Beauclerc) by Voltigeur, grandam Queen Mary. His breeding is something extraordinary; his sire, who was one of the handsomest horses in England, has a double Touchstone cross and is the sire of a host of clinkers, while Rataplan, besides being a successful sire is an own brother to Stockwell, and no one should inquire any further than Queen Mary.

There is said to be a large band of wild horses, led by a thoroughbred known to the stockmen as the "Outlaw Stud," ranging between Truckee, Nevada county, and Peavine, Nev. Years ago the stallion, a fine thoroughbred escaped to the mountains, and has since defied capture. By desperate riding stock men manage to get into the band every year and drive out the colts. The horses range on the highest peaks, beyond where cattle and sheep often go. They only go to water once a day, and then in single file down the mountain trail as fast as they can gallop. They go back at their leisure, feeding by the way.

The number of horses, remarks a British contemporary, that suffer from the disease of "roaring" seems unhappily to be on the increase. Certainly it is so among thoroughbreds; but it is painfully common at the first check, after a sharp burst with hounds, to hear the sound, and if one gets into a procession of carriages on the way to a race meeting, or elsewhere, the chance of the poor brute in the carriage behind roaring badly is very great. Statements as to an intra-laryngeal operation, which was said to be a perfect and permanent cure for roaring, were, therefore, received with much interest; but unhappily these statements are not borne out by an investigation of facts. The operation has been tried on several animals, and in each case without the least satisfactory result.

Jockey Stoval appears to have been demoralized by the example of the backsliding Brotherhood ball players and is likely to become a bone of contention between two owners of racing stables. Early last month he is alleged to have signed regular contract to ride for the Clover Stable in 1890. Now report has it that he has made another contract to ride next season for his old employer A. G. McCampbell. The report may be unfounded, but if it is true Stoval is likely to find himself in hot-water before the racing season opens, as jockey clubs have a straightforward fashion of enforcing agreements and are dead set against contract jumpers. Stoval made a fair record last year, and is a very capable jockey, very popular with western race-goers.

Mr. Jas. Galway has decided to sell Belvidere. The brother to Sir Dixon, by Billet out of Jaconet, who is a sister to Iroquois, should prove a success in the stud, for there is a Billet (Voltigeur), Leamington, Australian, Boston and Glencoe cross one on top of the other.

"What is the use of paying large prices for stallions and breeding horses for the sole purpose of staying a distance when there is so little opportunity for them to show their quality?" says Glen Cairn in the N. Y. S. In the case of short distances, such as half a mile or five or six furlongs, any common-bred stallion is liable to be the sire of a colt or filly that would prove a world-beater at these distances, but when asked to go a distance would be beaten off by 'selling platers.'" This is what some people say, and we agree with them if they mean to aver that there is no use breeding four-mile horses simply because there are no four-mile races; but, for goodness sake, is it not going a little too far to say that any common-bred horse is liable to sire a great winner of races at the present distances? Over 90 per cent. of the winning horses on the turf during the past season—these very no account sprinters, as they are called—are direct descendants of Boston and Lexington, long distance champions of the most approved strains of staying blood. This only leaves about 8 or 10 per cent. for the common-bred fellows, and research tells us that even they for the most part are from high-bred imported stock. Does not this prove conclusively that the old four-mile blood is just as necessary for the racehorse to-day as ever it was in the past? The horse that can run a mile in 1:40 or three-quarters of a mile in 1;11 needs something more substantial than the blood of a plebian sire. They tell us that it is the pace that kills. If such is the case, and we have always held that it is, does it not seem remarkable that these degenerate sprinters are cutting down, year after year, records at distances where pace, and keeping it up, is everything. So far, at least, the common-bred sire or dam have not figured prominently?

In a long article in the Fortnightly Review William Day the famous English racehorse trainer, who is also well known to American race goers as the trainer of Foxhall, has the following to say about the increasing value of thoroughbreds:

At Middle Park, about 1867, or soon after, yearlings fetched extraordinary prices, as much as 1,060 guineas and 2,400 guineas were given, and out of a lot one year the average price was 500 guineas, or 20 000 for the 40. Such prices no one thought would be exceeded, or even ever reached again. But prices have still gone up, and broodmares have increased in value as much as the yearlings, and, in fact, every sort of racehorse has augmented in value in like proportion, till now over 3,000 guineas are given for a brood mare and over 4,000 guineas for a yearling. Stallions have fetched 16,000 guineas, 20,000 guineas have been offered and refused for a horse in training, and 5,000 guineas was a sum not sufficiently attractive to secure a yearling that was offered for sale at private contract this year. But these facts and figures, gigantic and surprising as they are, dwindle into utter insignificance when compared with the value of Hermit. This wonderful and lucky horse stands alone as a racehorse and stallion, for Hermit has won in stakes and bets for his owner, Mr. Chaplin, somewhere about £150,000, and has since earned at the stud at least as much more, and may still further augment this almost incredible sum. Again, Donovan up to the present time, has won in stakes more than any horse ever did, and may, and most likely will add many more thousands to his record. He has already secured £39,963, and many yet even surpass the mighty deeds of Hermit at the stud, as he has triumphed over his performances on the racecourse. Ayrshire, another lucky horse, has won for the same ducal owner nearly as much as Donovan himself, having secured in stakes alone over £35,000 up to the present date, and may, like him, yet increase largely this magnificent sum before his racing career is terminated, and afterwards be at the stud as great a success as either of the two extraordinary horses just mentioned. These few cases, to which many other horses may be added, will show us the present value of our racehorse, and how greatly it exceeds the worth of those of any other age or country.

William of Wykeham is credited with the statement that "Manners maketh the man." So-called jockeys here are too ready made. A boy, after exercising for six months, feels injured if he is not put up in a race, and very soon suffers from the big head. In England, where boys have to undergo a regular apprenticeship, a jockey knows his position better, and as an instanc the N. Y. Sporting World says, speaking of the late Fred Archer: "Archer without doubt had amassed a considerable fortune by his riding, and at the time of his death was probably a five times richer man than most of those for whom he constantly rode. Should any owner, no matter who, ask him to ride his horse, Archer would raise his hat in reply and answer civily (without venturing to ask any such impertinent question as to whether the horse had any chance or not) 'Thank you, sir, I'm engaged for that race;' or, 'Thank you, sir, with pleasure.' Here was no idea of conferring a favor; the boot was on the other leg, and this man, too, a prince in his profession. The difference which apparently existed between him and many of our own Jockeys was that as he rose and got rich at his calling like many self-made men in business, his manners rose to the occasion. Another difference, too, in his case was that his mind was set wholly on his duties and not on betting. He recognized the fact that owners and trainers had been mainly instrumental in assisting him to the position he held, and had good sense enough always to bear it in mind." And in speaking of the modern American jockey the same journal says:—

At the present day it would seem as if the majority of jockeys, by reason of their successes in the saddle, and the money thus brought to them, considered themselves fully the equals, if not of a truth the superiors, of those who employ them. They become victims of that fell disease, which too frequently follows in the wake of success—the big head. Take the instance of an owner or trainer (who has no specially retained jockey) asking one of these professionals to ride for him. Does the boy consider it a compliment? Not much. Rather he will think he is confering a favor, and before accepting will want to know: "Has the horse a chance? How has he been working? Does the owner intend to back him, etc.? A list of impertinent questions, which by rights should not affect him in the slightest. They do affect him, and for this reason jockeys are not contented nowadays unless they can bet, and bet, too, in big money. It is a pity that it should be so, and that they should learn to think far more of their betting than they do of their duties, but some jockeys at the head of the profession have set the bad example, and the lesser lights must needs follow it. As a consequence, matters have come to such a pass that for an owner to ask a jockey to ride, unless it is a horse prominent in the betting, is tantamount to asking the jockey to do him a favor. Big head is rampant, and it seems difficult to know how to check the disease or make jockeys understand their position.

A Reminiscence.

A party of racing spirits were sitting talking horse in one of San Francisco's fashionable hotels a few evenings ago when a tall, powerful, athletic-looking man walked by. Every eye was turned on him and the question was asked:

"Who is he?"

"Why, that's Mr. C——, from Chicago."

"Boys, pass that decanter and I'll tell you something about that handsome man that would have turned any one's else hair gray."

The speaker filled his glass, held it up to the light as if trying the past through the sparkling fluid, swallowed the contents, and began:

"It was the 10th of July, 1886. Place: Washington Park, Chicago. I was sitting in the grand stand. I had had a good day, so I was going to have a good dinner, and let the other two races alone.

"The bell rang for the fifth race. I was making myself comfortable, when I saw the gentleman that just passed come into the stand and take a seat by the side of a beautiful woman. Strange, I thought to myself, I had not noticed her before. You all know my failing; I like to look at 'em—from a distance. She looked fit to run for a man's life Beautiful chestnut hair, brought smoothly back from a broad, intelligent forehead, and snugly tucked under a dark velvet Princess cap. Her forearms of snowy whiteness could be plainly seen through a pretty summer dress. Her barrel a little too small to be a good feeder; but her foot, neatly encased in racing plates, looked to belong to a pastern of beautifully modeled spring steel. Her foot was beating the devil's tattoo on the floor from evident nervousness when the gentleman came up. She looked the question she could not ask:

" 'What did you play?'

"He was very pale—but a forced calmness—that one could see he was highly excited.

"His answer was 'Hopedale.

"It was a mile heat race with eight starters, though from the betting there were only three in it; and so it proved. Hopedale, Irish Pat and Bootblack; Stoval, Murphy and West up, in the order named. The first words that I heard the lady speak, were: "My God, if Stoval will only ride to win!"

"They got the flag well bunched, and made a pretty race in the stretch. Stoval brought his mount to the front and won easy enough, but he did not see Murphy go to his whip. Pat was coming like a hurricane, and if Murphy had sat still he would have been second; but when he hit him Pat bolted to the inside, West getting second, Biddy Bowling third and Pat fourth. Time, 1:43.

"I looked at my neighbors. The gentleman's face was flushed with hope; but his fair companion was as pale as death.

" 'What's the matter, darling?' he whispered.

"She turned a pair of heavenly brown eyes to him, and answered: 'Irish Pat, or rather Murphy, will win the next heat.'

" 'Why do you think so?' he asked.

" 'You know that Hopedale does not like a distance, and that Irish Pat has as much speed when he'll run. Stoval did not see Murphy use his whip, and if Murphy ever gets near enough to collar Hopedale he'll win, for Murphy will not use his whip, for he knows Pat won't stand it. Stoval will not use his because Murphy won't."

"Then I fear we are lost, for I have played every cent that I could get hold of on Hopedale, and if Pat wins a heat I'm afraid he'll win the race.

"With a sigh of intense anguish on his handsome face he folded his arms across his magnificent chest.

It was then that I saw the most beautiful expression I ever saw on a woman's face. It was worth living a life for. With a quick move of her hand towards her breast she handed a bill to her (I was certain now he was) husband, and quietly asked him if he would try and put it on Irish Pat for the heat. Hopedale was a top-heavy favorite, so he soon returned and told her he got $500 to $100. I had become intensely interested in the pair before me and watched the race with unusual interest.

"Hopedale and Biddy Bowling was the order at the quarter. Pat had worked up to Hopedale at the half, and led into the stretch by a neck. Then commenced one of the most terrible finishes I have ever seen Murphy gave Pat a shake, but Stoval was after him and was soon alongside. They rode as I have never seen men ride before or since. At the eighth pole the entire stand rose to their feet. You could hear a pin drop in that immense structure. Some fellow spat on the floor and it sounded like a clap of thunder. On, on they came, as if riding for their lives. The others were out of it. Neither would take his whip, but rode it out with hands and legs. It was as the fair stranger had feared. Stoval would not use his whip, because Murphy didn't. There was the stillness of death all over the grounds. No one knew who had won, when Irish Pat's number was hung up. Then commenced one of the wildest scenes it was ever my fortune to witness. Could the noble red man or the cow-boys of the great and golden West have heard those yells, they would have died a death of agonized envy. My blood seemed on fire. The yelling was contagious. I rose from my seat and gave a yell as only a man who is half frantic with sympathy for a beautiful woman can give. As I started with a mad rush for the paddock, I gave one hasty glance at my fair stranger. I caught her eye and then I was mad. Never had I seen such soul-thrilling orbs in the head of a human being. That look burned into my brain and set it on fire. There was the one word written as in letters of gold in those glorious orbs—hope. Down three steps at a time I flew until I reached the paddock. I saw Irish Pat first, and could plainly see he was terribly distressed. Then Hopedale was closely scanned, and, while his sides were bleeding, I could see he was the freshest of the two. I started for the boys' dressing room, and found both men being as vigorously rubbed down as were the two horses. Both were fearfully tired. Great drops of perspiration were rolling off them Murphy was the strongest, as his condition was far superior to Stoval's. Little Eddie West was guying Stoval, and the first words that greeted my ears were:

" 'If you waits for Isaac to go to the bat, nigger, you'll git left. Why, Stokes, Pat'll bolt if you go to the bat. Isaac'll fool you, ha, ha!'

"It was evident that 'Stokes' was out to win. So, to relieve my own charged feelings, I bought all the auctions on old Hopedale I could get. Pat was a good favorite. When I got back to my seat my strangers were as I had left them—the lady hopeful, the gentleman seemed resigned to his fate for he was now certain Murphy could win. I took my seat, leaned over the shoulder of the big man and said:

" 'Hopedale's a cinch.'

"What his answer was I have never heard. Again those great brown eyes looked thanks at me, and I forgot the world and all its troubles until a yell from the spectators brought me to my senses and my feet at the same time. The two horses were coming into the stretch, and I did not know they had gone to the post. But now I saw what the howl meant. As they swung into the homestretch Stoval drew his whip, and with a couple of raps old Hopedale ran away from Pat, and as Isaac began to ride Pat, his tail went heavenward, and those who knew him knew he was done for, and was coming gamely on when a wail caught the air. He was seen to falter at the sixteenth pole. Murphy saw it and redoubled his efforts to catch him. But Stoval was not to be outdone so close to home. He had too much of a lead. He got home five lengths in front of Pat, but it was well he had not another quarter to go. Hopedale was bleeding at the nose, having burst a blood vessel. He ran the race in the slow time of 1:45. The track was like greased lightning.

"Though there was another race to be run, my handsome strangers got up as though they were leaving, and as they walked down from the stand and straight for the train, I have never laid eyes on either of them until to-night.

"The eyes of that beautiful woman have haunted me from that day. I have searched the world over for a pair like them and should I ever meet a woman to be won with eyes like those of my dream my name will be 'McGinty' if I don't win her."

With a nightcap of California's generous vintage we bade each good night and went to dream of a pair of eyes like those our friend wishes to possess.

Doc.

The National Trotting Association.

BOARD OF REVIEW—OFFICIAL REPORT.

In accordance with By-Law Article VII, Section 11, a regular meeting of the Board of Review was held in the City of New York, on Dec. 3, 1889, at the Fifth Avenue Hotel.

Present—Judge P. P. Johnston, President; Governor M. G. Bulkeley, of the Eastern District; George W. Archer, Esq., of the Atlantic District; L. G. Delano, Esq., of the Central District; Hon. John L. Mitchell, of the Western District, and the undersigned Secretary.

The President called the meeting to order at 7 P. M., and the following is a report of the proceedings during the several sessions held until adjournment at 5 P. M., on Thursday, the 5th.

The Secretary reported the resignation of Mr. J. McM. Shafter, of San Francisco, as second Vice-President.

The Treasurer's report of receipts and expenditures from May 1st to Nov. 1, 1889, with vouchers therefor approved by the Auditing Committee, was presented, showing a balance on hand of $19,526 90, which report was accepted and approved. A printed copy of the same has been mailed to all the members.

A list of suspensions for unpaid entrance dues was presented, which were ordered canceled on the records, as per By-Law XI, Sec. 2.

The Secretary also presented a list of new members enrolled since the last meeting in May, which was approved.

The cases on the docket were then considered and the following decisions rendered:

1568.—The National Trotting Association (by T. J. Vail, Sec'y) vs. W. B. Wright, Lachine, P. Q., Can. Application for an order.

At a former meeting on May 8, 1889, it was ordered that the respondent return unlawful winnings to the amount of $280, and himself and horse be suspended until the order was complied with and the case be continued. The order not having been complied with and the case as to violation of Rule 6, Section 4, and Rule 14, appearing clear, it is

Ordered, That W. B. Wright, of Lachine, P. Q., Can., be expelled.

1648.—Frank R. Hayden, alias John Smith, Island Pond, Vt., Ex-parte. Application for removal of expulsion.

Ordered, That the temporary re-instatement granted at the December meeting of 1887, be continued until the next meeting.

1763.—M. M. Morse, Secretary, vs. M. T. Downing, Boston, Mass., and Prince. Application for an order as to identity, eligibility and change of name.

At the meeting in May, 1889, the respondent was ordered to return unlawful winnings of the b g Champion John L., to pay a recording fee of $50, and a fine of $100, as per Rule 5, and to be suspended until the order was complied with. No attention having been paid to the above it is now

Ordered, That he and the horse be expelled.

1768.—Cleveland Driving Park Company, Cleveland, Ohio, vs. L. F. Hunter, Warren, Ohio. Complaint and application for an order to punish defendant for charging the company with falsifying time.

Referred back to the Cleveland Driving Park Company for initiatory action.

1828.—James H. Gilmore, Seneca Falls, N. Y., Ex Parte. Application for reward under Rule 15.

It appearing that applicant gave the first information leading to the detection of a fraudulent entry it is

Ordered, That he be paid the reward of $50.

1831—M. M. Morse, Sec'y, vs. Anderson and McIntosh, Marietta, Ga. Application for an order under Rule 13 for return of money wrongfully obtained.

Parties remain suspended until the order of the Board is complied with.

1839.—The National Trotting Association vs. A. M. Wilson, North Jackson, Ohio. Frank Jackson, C. C. Williams, St. Clairsville, Ohio, and br m Frank, alias Grandmother Grace, alias Grace. Application for an order under Rules 6 and 14.

Application dismissed.

1850.—W. H. McCarthy, et al, Lexington, Ky., vs. Hudson River Driving Park, D. B. Herrington, manager, Poughkeepsie, N. Y., C. J. Hamlin, Buffalo, N. Y., and ch m Mocking Bird. Application for an order under Rule 2, section 2, as to the eligibility of the ch m Mocking Bird in the 2:30 race August 21, 1889.

The plaintiffs protested the ch m Mocking Bird in the 2:20 class as not having been named in accordance with Rule 2, Section 2, her name not appearing on the list of published entries. The evidence of Mr. Herrington, the manager of the driving park, is to the effect that while at Buffalo, Mr. Hamlin read off his entries to him, and he copied them in writing on the regular entry blank, but failed to fill in the class for Mocking Bird, in consequence of which the acting Secretary failed to place her name on the list.

It is held that the nominator cannot be held responsible for the mistakes or neglect of the secretary, and therefore the application is dismissed.

1862.—L. R. Griffis, Andover, Ohio, ex-parte. Application for relief of the b s Ben Clifford, formerly Nicodemus, from payment of recording fee.

The applicant started his horse in a three-year-old race as Nicodemus, after which he applied to the editor of the trotting register to have him registered under that name, which was refused, the name having already been chosen. He was then registered under the name of Ben Clifford, and afterwards entered under the same name with the member at Orwell, Ohio, as formerly Nicodemus, and claim for recording fee sent from the office of the National Trotting Association.

While the Board is fully aware of the apparent hardship involved, yet Rule 6, Section 4, is absolute in its character, and any other interpretation would open the door to frauds without number. It is, therefore, decided that the recording fee must be paid before competing on members' grounds.

1884.—W. R. Brasfield & Co. (owners), W. R. Brasfield, (driver) Lexington, Ky., ex parte. Application for permanent relief of themselves and the b m Linnie from expulsion imposed by order of the Bourbon Trotting Club, Paris, Ky., July 1, 1889, under Rule 17.

All the papers and evidence in this case were sent to the President who granted temporary re-instatement under By-Law Article, and it is now upon recommendation of the member, made permanent.

1888.—Budd Doble, Chicago, Ills., vs. Driving Club of New York, Morrisania, N. Y. Application for release of himself and the b g Ed Annan (pacer) and the ch m Amy Lee from suspension imposed Oct. 3, 1889.

The application is granted upon the ground that the suspensions were not imposed within the time limited, as per Rule 3, Sec. 8.

1894.—Daniel De Noyelles, New York, N. Y., vs. Charter Oak Driving Park, Hartford, Conn. Application for an order.

It appears the plaintiff had a subscription in the $10,000 Stake race; that he paid up the subscription and named the b s Nelson by arrangement with the owner. The horse won second money, which was $2,500. The owner, Mr. Nelson, was paid $1,500 by the association, and they also paid De Noyelles $1,000. The plaintiff had previously notified the association in writing, through its Secretary, protesting against the payment of any part of the purse which the horse might win, except upon his written order.

It is claimed by the Association that the plaintiff and Mr. Nelson were virtually partners and therefore the payment to either one or a part to each was valid.

On the other hand it is claimed by De Noyelles that, as he made all the payments, refused to transfer the subscription and named the horse, the association had no right to pay any money to any one but himself. He also claims it is usual in such cases to divide the net profits and that he should, therefore, receive $750, out of the amount paid to Nelson. After an exhaustive hearing and examination it is

Ordered, That the Charter Oak Driving Park Association pay the plaintiff $750; that C. H. Nelson refund that amount to the Charter Oak Driving Park, and the Treasurer of the National Trotting Association is ordered to reserve said amount from any money in his hands belonging to Mr. Nelson and pay the same to Charter Oak Driving Park in satisfaction of this judgment.

1896.—James Linden, Sacramento, Cal., ex-parte. Application for permanent relief from expulsion imposed by order of the Capital Turf Club, Sacramento, Cal., July 30, 1889, under authority of Rule 46.

The applicant was temporarily re-instated by the President September 4, 1889, upon recommendation of the Judges who expelled him upon a suitable apology being made to them, and the re-instatement is now made permanent.

1915.—Hamilton Busbey, New York, N. Y., vs. C. W. Williams, Independence, Iowa, and br s Allerton. Application for an order as to the eligibility of said horse in the 2:27 stake race at Chicago, Ill., August 23, 1889.

The plaintiff protested the b s Allerton as not being eligible in the 2:27 Subscription Stake race of the Northwestern Association of Trotting and Pacing Horse Breeders, alleging that Lady Mack was named and appeared on the printed entry list, and that Allerton had no right to start in her place unless Mr. Williams or the Secretary could show a letter bearing post-mark on or before the day set for naming the horses. It is claimed by Williams that he bought the subscription from Wilson & Stanley and sent a letter in time, naming Allerton, but misdirected it to Janesville, Iowa, instead of sending it to Janesville, Wis., the residence of the Secretary. He sends press copy of letter, naming the horse, which is dated the 5th day of August, the date set for naming, and also a certificate from the cashier of a bank that he bought on that day a draft for $100 payable to the Secretary, as last payment on the subscription.

There is a discrepancy in the evidence as to the original misdirected letter. Mr. Williams states that after it was returned to him from Janesville, Iowa, he immediately forwarded it to Secretary McKinney at Janesville, Wis. The latter says he received the letter, but not the original misdirected envelope, which Mr. Williams had inadvertently destroyed. The original letter of entry with the envelope is the best evidence of the validity of the nomination, and these not having been furnished, the protest is sustained, as the defendant failed to produce legal evidence to sustain his entry.

1936.—The National Trotting Association vs. C. H. Nelson, Waterville, Me., and b s Nelson; F. L. Noble, George G. Robens, Grand Rapids, Mich., and gr s Alcryon. Application for an order in the matter of alleged fraud in the $10,000 Stallion Stake race, trotted at Beacon Park, Boston, Mass., on September 28, 1889.

After consideration, this case was continued at the request of the respondents, and they were ordered to be notified to appear at a special meeting of the Board, to be held at Buffalo, N. Y., on Tuesday, February 11, 1890, at 2 P. M.

No other business appearing, the Board adjourned.

M. M. Morse, Secretary

A Sensational Lot.

The Kentucky Stock Farm has the following in reference to the horses taken East by Col. R. S. Strader:—

We had the pleasure a day or two since of looking over the great consignment of Electioneer stock just received by Col. R. S. Strader from Palo Alto. Unless we greatly over-estimate its value it is destined to exercise a very potent influence upon the breeding of trotting horses in Kentucky. Col. Strader has long been identified with the breeding interest, and his recent venture proves that he has lost none of the enterprise for which he has always been remarkable.

The oldest horse in the lot is Clay, 2:25, by Electioneer; dam Maid of Clay (dam of Carrie C, four-year-old record 2:24, Clay, 2:25½, Capt. Smith, 2:29, and Clay, 2:25), by Henry Clay, sire of the dam of George Wilkes; second dam by Dey's Messenger: third dam by Bald-face Consul. Dey's Messenger, by Liberty (son of imp Messenger); dam by imp Messenger. Bald-face Consul by Bond's Consul; dam by Corlander (son of imp Messenger). Clay was foaled in 1879. He is a black horse, tan flanks and muzzle, 15 hands high, bred at Palo Alto. He has a Hambletonian top cross through Electioneer, and is inbred to Henry Clay through two mares whose 2:30 performers aggregate 11. He is himself a fast trotter and his sire and dam are great speed producers. Clay has very much the conformation and appearance of George Wilkes with higher finish. He is a horse with very remarkable bone, his legs being broad and flat, gaskins and forearms very strongly muscled, canon bones and pasterns short, stifles remarkably full, loins exceedingly strong, body very large for its height, shoulders sloping, back short, neck of good length, head finely finished. He is a very strongly-built horse, and his muscular development is something wonderful.

There are two fillies by Clay in the consignment, one a brown filly, dam Lady Ellen 2:28 (dam of Ella, four-year-old record 2:20), by Carr's Mambrino 1789, son of Mambrino Patchen; second dam Ida May Jr., by Owen Dale, son of California Belmont; third dam Ida May by Belmont. The other a bay filly dam Sallie Hamlet, by Hamlet; second dam Sal (dam of Coaster, 2:26½), by Canada Chief. This is a pair of very elegant weanlings, having fine size and quality and would be a credit to any sire.

Conrad 5381 is another of the horses in this consignment. He is a full brother to Anteeo, 2:16½, and Antevolo 2:19½, by Electioneer; first dam Columbine, by A. W. Richmond 1687, sire of Romero, 2:19½. Conrad was foaled in 1886 and is 15¾ hands high. He is a horse of elegant appearance and great substance. The fact that both Anteeo and Antevolo have shown such remarkable speed affords a strong presumption that the other members of the family will also be fast. Conrad is as yet unbroken to harness. He will make a model stock horse.

Another horse that will attract attention is Wellington, full brother to the great California filly Sunol, 2:10½. Wellington is a bay horse, five years old, and stands 15 hands 2 inches high. His pedigree is well known, and if it were not, the fact that he is a brother to Sunol would be pedigree enough. He is an excellent individual.

Warlock is a bay colt, foaled in 1885 by Whips son of Electioneer; 1st dam Nellie Walker (dam of Peruvian Bitters (pacer) 2:23½) by Thorndale, or a son of Alexander's Edwin Forrest; 2nd dam Rosalind, 2:21½ by Alexander's Abdallah; 3rd dam Burch mare (dam of Rosalind 2:21½, and Donald 2:27) by Parker's Brown Pilot. This fellow has a great deal of the thoroughbred finish combined with plenty of bone and muscle. He is 15 hands 3½ inches high. His pedigree is very rich in blood and speed lines.

Ellison is a black colt foaled in 1886 by Electioneer; dam Lady Ellen 2:28 by Carr's Mambrino; 2nd dam Ida May Jr., by Owen Dale, son of California Belmont, etc. He is 15 hands 2½ inches high, and in every-respect an excellent individual. While in California Col Strader saw a yearling sister to Ellison trot a quarter in 36 seconds. Ellison has not yet been handled for speed.

Del Mar, 2:30 (brother to Commotion, 2:30), is a bay colt, foaled in 1887, sired by Electioneer; dam Sontag Dixie (dam of Commotion, 2:30, and Sonnet, 2:24½), by Toronto Sontag; second dam Dixie by Billy Townes; third dam by Sir Charles.

Monica is a bay colt, dam half sister to Bonita, 2:18½, foaled in 1887, sired by Ansel, son of Electioneer; dam Mecca by Mohawk Chief (sire of Lot Slocum, 2:17½); second dam May Fly, 2:30½ (dam of Bonita, 2:18½), by St. Clair.

Col. Strader will keep Clay and Conrad in the stud. Their service fee, we understand, will be $150 each. We have no doubt their books will fill rapidly, as the breeding and individuality of the horses cannot but attract public attention, It will require no urging to induce the horsemen of this vicinity and visitors to the city to go to Col. Strader's place and examine this grand lot of California stock.

Grim's Gossip.

John Mackey who has been very ill at Sacramento is rapidly recovering.

What has become of the base ball Gala Day, that was to be held for the purpose of starting the California League Base Ball Stake?

Miss Josephine by Straun, dam Maid of Harris by Flageolet, slipped a horse colt by imp Friar Tuck December 23rd. She was owned by Mrs. Langtry.

C. H. Corey owner of Almont Patchen has repurchased the Lick House in San Jose and it will become as before the Garden City horsemen's headquarters.

C. H. Nelson says that the charge of fraud made against him in the Balch stallion race is a case of personal spite and will be seen in that light by the public before long.

Dr. C. W. Aby manager of the Guenoc Stock Farm, has been in town during the week, and has secured a number of mares to be bred to St. Savior and imp. Greenback.

Primrose, one of the brood mares at the Woodburn farm is now carrying her twentieth foal and yet the oldest of her family is but twenty. With a single exception they are all alive.

Wilbur F. Smith reports Thapsin 2:21½ as being considerably better than last reported. The horse is still at the Bay District track and will not be taken to Sacramento for some time.

Two stories. Scott Quinten has left the employ of Marcus Daly. Scott Quinton has not left the employ of Marcus Daly. Both reports are rumored in horse circles, so you can believe which you please.

Mina West, who has been at Village Farm, near Buffalo, N. Y., for some time past, has accepted a position as trainer for George Robinson of Los Angeles, and will leave for the Pacific Coast the first of the year.

A large influx of the Eastern Bookmakers may be expected in San Francisco almost any day. Some of them will remain over until the Spring meeting of the Blood Horse Association to have a go at the "Dear Public."

I am pleased to announce that the Valensin Stock Farm will have the services of Ed Bither as trainer and driver for the coming year. Mr. Bither telegraphed yesterday morning that he accepted the offer of Mr. Valensin.

Mr. E. Topham has at his Milpitas place a nice string of trotters that will be heard from next season on the California circuit. A good trainer and driver will be engaged, and the Topham colors will be carried to victory many a time.

J. L. McCord has a singlefooter that is the admiration of the residents of the capital City. Mr. McCord will bring the animal to San Francisco next week and surprise some of the Park equestrians who imagine their horses cannot be excelled.

Mr. R. Murphy of Santa Rosa was in the city last Thursday, and he says he feels confident that S. A. Brown & Co. of Kalamazoo will have to pay him $200 this year, for he has two Anteeo youngsters that will go into the list without fail.

Secretary Crickmore of the Monmouth Park Association says that the work on Monmouth's new track is progressing to the satisfaction of all, and that race goers will be delighted with the grounds that will be thrown open to them on Independence Day of next year.

Edwin C 2:15 by Elector 2:21½ is the fastest green pacer that appeared in 1889. He will now have to contend in the free for all class, but as he has got over his bad habit of breaking, Mr. Johnson feels confident that 2:15 will be cut down considerably next season.

C. V. Sass, for many years editor of the N. Y. Sporting World, but now Secretary of the Clifton Association, has earned the thanks of all race goers by inaugurating longer races than are now usual. One such contest is enjoyed as much as half a dozen five furlong dashes.

When the Sunny Slope horses are sent East for sale B. C. Holly will also send some good ones, and the Valensin Stock Farm will be represented by some choice Sidney youngsters. The eyes of the trotting world are now turned toward California and the three large consignments should bring top prices.

Adonis has been turned out to give him a needed rest prior to entering on an extensive campaign next season. When the Sidney gelding strikes the free for all class back East next summer, there will be weeping wailing and gnashing of teeth among the backers of Gossip, Jewett, etc., on more occasions than one.

Uncle Jim Guest, of Danville, Ky., has purchased from S. H. Baughman, of Stanford, Ky., a yearling by Conoregan, dam Olena (dam of Santaline) for $1,200. For the season of 1890, J. W. Guest Jr., will train his father's horses. There are many who wish that there may be another Terra Cotta in the stable.

P. A. Finigan, Treasurer of the Pacific Blood Horse Association felt annoyed at the vaporings of a reporter in one of the evening papers, and on going to the office of the paper in question, and showing the falsity of the report the writer was instantly discharged. Stick to facts, boys, and you will not get into trouble.

Gold Leaf 2:11½ will be bred next spring to the premier stallion of the Pleasanton Stock Farm, Director 2:17. It is probably needless to say that the progeny of such a union will command a "top of the tree" price whenever it is offered for sale, but Mr. Salisbury will want to develop that kind himself before he lets it go.

S. L. Akins, of Newman, Stanislaus Co., has sold to Holbert & Smith, of Indepenpence, Inyo Co., the magnificent, two year old colt Antare by Anteros, dam by Iowa Chief 528; 2nd dam by Tornado 502. This is a great addition to the fine horses of Inyo County and those having good mares in that section should not overlook him.

Mr. John W. Martin, of Yolo, Yolo County, offers this week for sale, the handsome young colt Alexander Button Jr. He is well bred and can show high speed. He can be bought at a reasonable figure and it is well worth while to read the advertisement containing his pedigree, and then write to Mr. Martin.

It is now in order for the new Directors of the Pacific Coast Blood Horse Association to meet and select a date for the opening of their spring meeting as there are several other associations who desire to make their announcements but wish to wait and see what fixture the older organization will take.

B. C. Holly, of Vallejo, has made an offer of $8,000 for Billy Thornhill 8707 by Bevelry Wilkes 8706; dam Emily by Geo. Wilkes 519; 2nd dam Sue Stout by Ashland 47; 3rd dam The Lear mare by Sir William, he by Sir Charles. James Boyd, the owner of Thornhill, is reported to have refused the amount. The horse is a well bred one, and as there is such a demand for Wilkes blood, should command a large number of mares.

Marcus Daly, who has appeared so prominently as a purchaser of trotters and thoroughbreds, during 1889, is at present in Philadelphia, having his eyes looked after by a prominent physician. There is a current rumor that he will not have his trotters trained in 1890, but several persons who claim to know the gentleman, say that he will have more of them out than ever.

In the Budd Doble String at Fresno, is the gray gelding Jack 2:15, which is owned by George Middletown of Chicago. Mr. Middletown is anxious to make a match for his horse against any trotter in the world for from $5,000 to $15,000 a side, and will trot almost anywhere. What a good chance this is for J. C. Hamblin to show what his mare Belle Hamblin can do, and from this far off point it looks as though Jack would be the favorite in a match race.

Samuel D. Prather sent me word from Forest Meadows, under date of December 20th, of the death of Imogene, by Norwood 522, dam by American Star 14, 2nd dam by Henry Clay 8. Imogene is the dam of Del Wood by Del Sur, Imona by Steinway, and Guide 2:28½ by Director, and three very promising colts by Admar, a son of Admiral. A. T. Hatch bought her from the Cook Stock Farm some years ago and he retained an interest in her till her death.

Who says that Wilbur Smith will not go back into the running business. When the sheriff attached Al Farrow a week or two ago at the instance of the Bank of Sonoma, that official placed the celebrated crack in the stable of Wilbur for safe keeping, and now the owner of Thapsin 2:21½ can be seen any morning at the Sacramento track, sitting on top of the fence with a split second watch in his hand, timing the handsome horse quarters and halves. The early love will crop out at times.

We have been asked quite a number of times if Stamboul 2:12½ would stand in public service during the coming spring. Mr. Hobart being asked the question, stated that positively no outside mares will be taken for Stamboul, and that he has had to refuse at least fifty mares from friends who wished to patronize the stallion. What the arrangements may be for another year the owner does not know, but it will save trouble and bother for this season, as the rule laid down will not be deviated from.

Mr. M. Salisbury, of Pleasanton Stock Farm, Pleasanton, Cal sold four head, two fillies, and two mares, one Echora 2:23½ the dam of Direct, at the Kidd, Edmonson & Morse Combination Sale at Chicago in November for almost $12,000 an average of nearly $3,000 each. Mr. Salisbury was so well pleased with the results of the sale that he told Kidd, Edmonson & Morse who hold a great sale commencing March 17 to 23rd at Chicago, that he would always sell in the future there, that it was preferable to either Kentucky or New York.

L. J. Rose Esq informs me that he will send every one of his brood mares, with the exception of Minnehaha and a few non-standard ones, to his sale which will take place in New York March 6th and 7th. He will also send on all the colts and fillies by Stamboul and Alcazar, which will make the Rose sale of 1890 one of the best ever given by a California breeder. No doubt there will be very lively competition when Alcazar is brought forward and Mr. Kellogg asks the question, "Now then, gentlemen, what am I bid for this great son of Sultan?"

Sam Gamble has taken full charge of the Hobart breeding establishment, and none better could have been selected for the responsible position. Sam is earnest and enthusiastic, still does not allow his enthusiasm to lead him astray in matters appertaining to the great problem of breeding. As a Christmas present, his employer Mr. Hobart, made him a present of an elegant split second time piece, of remarkably good workmanship and exquisite design. There is no truth in the rumor that a trainer and driver has been secured by Mr. Hobart.

Considerable correspondence has been indulged in relative to a match between Roy Wilkes and Almont Patchen but nothing has come of all the talk as yet. As a final proposition, Mr. Davies offers to pace Roy Wilkes against Almont Patchen, mile heats, three in five and wager $2,500 against $2,000. The race can come off on any track within one hundred miles of San Francisco any time up to February 15th. Mr. Davies suggests that if the offer is accepted that each of the parties select one person each, and those two select one other, the three to determine whether the track be fit to race on on the day appointed.

At the recent meeting of the New England Association of Trotting Horse Breeders, the question was raised in regard to the reduction of expenses at the annual fair usually held at Mystic Park. It was suggested by one of the members that the bill for advertising, which last year amounted to more than $1,000 be reduced, but Mr. J. S. Davis, the well-known soap manufacturer of Cambridge, Mass., was on his feet in an instant, and strenuously opposed anything of the sort. He said that he owed a greater part of his success to advertising, and thought that every class of business would profit by judicious advertising.

"I believe Stamboul is the greatest trotting stallion in the world," remarked the popular trainer, James Golden in the American Cultivator office a few days ago. "He is the best made one all over that I ever saw. California is a great country for horses," continued Golden. "I did not see a poor animal while there. It seems to me, however, that their climate and soil are not so conducive to sound, well-shaped feet as ours in New England. The finest mares that I ever saw," said Golden, "were at Palo Alto, got by Senator Stanford's trotting stallions, and out of thoroughbred dams. They have a finish and quality superior to any others that I ever saw."

The law with respect to racing in Vermont is absolutely prohibitive of betting. The act legalizes racing for stakes and premiums offered by individuals. The penalty for betting on a horse race in Vermont is $500.

Billy Vioget's picture, in a Montgomery st. store has attracted a good deal of attention, but it looks to the ordinary observer as if his trousers were too short, and what have you got on the bottom of them, Billy?

Orville Appleby a brother of W. L. Appleby has started a training stable on his own account and has already the runners belonging to T. F. Montgomery of San Jose. Orrie is a good careful man and should command a large run of trade.

I had a pleasant call from Willie Thornton this week and his report from the Rancho Resaca, is full of hope for the future. The yearlings are all in fine fettle, many of them showing extremely high form. The many friends of Col. Thornton will be pleased to see his colors again to the fore.

Sometimes a rather ungracious letter is received at this office from some one who has become tired of waiting for an answer to some query, and yet we are just as anxious to give them the information desired as they are to receive it. At times a dozen or more letters have to be sent out in order to get an answer to a single question.

The Du Bois Bros. of Denver, sustained a severe loss on Friday night of last week in the death of the brood mare Administratrix. She was by Administrator 357, dam by Nonpareil. This mare was highly prized by the Du Bois Bros., and what makes her loss doubly severe, she was heavy with foal to Superior, 2:19½.

The San Jose Blood Horse Association are bound to be early on the scene of action with their dates, and a meeting will be held on Tuesday, January 14th to elect officers for the ensuing years and also to fix the time for the spring meeting. The association is composed of energetic men and they will offer a brilliant programme with large enough purses to warrant the attendance of the best horses in the State.

Mr. Holly is keeping up the Vallejo end of the market in horse sales. During the week past he has sold to a Colonel Thompson of New Jersey the converted pacer San Diego (pacing record 2:21) by Victor, for $1,500, the br g J. R. by Elector, dam St. Lawrence, record 2:24½, for $2,000, the ch m Alaretta by Altoona, dam Nellie for $2,500. I do not know Col. Thompson, but there is one thing sure he has secured three very serviceable animals all of whom can beat their present records and should prove good winners during 1890.

An Arizona correspondent sends me the information that there will be three days racing between Christmas and New Years, at Phoenix A. T. He also encloses the following clipping from a local paper which shows the "hoss" knowledge of the Editor.

Mr. B. F. Baker, probably the smallest man in San Bernardino, brought in last week two of the largest stallions lately seen. "Bismarck" is a Hambletonian Clydesdale, about 16 hands high and weighing 1,435 pounds. "Drake" boasts of Norman Percheron descent from Black Hawk and Morgan. He is a splendid fellow, 17 hands one inch high, weighing 1800 pounds and aged eight years. His neck curves handsomely and he is as gentle as a lady school teacher.

It would seem that during the long winter months the wives of trainers who have been accustomed to the city, and are living partly isolated lives on a race track would find something of monotony therein says the N. Y. Sporting World. Not so, however, with Mrs. Allen, who has cultivated her artistic ability, and finds considerable pleasure with the brush and pallet. Although an amateur, and simply developing her gift for her own amusement, Mrs. Allen's efforts would put to blush the work of some of our professional artists. She has nearly completed a fine portrait of Gorgo, and is busy now portraying on canvas one of Joseph Cairn Simpson's trotting horses from a likeness produced in his paper. Should King Thomas make his name famous the coming season, the hand that has often patted him will probably paint his likeness.

One of my Australian correspondents sends word that Childe Harold 414 died on October 27, from the effect of bursting a blood vessel. He was by Harold 413 dam Young Portia by Mambrino chief, 2nd dam Portia by Rosebuck, 3rd dam by Whip etc. He was taken to England about 1877 and proved himself by performance to be one of the fastest trotters outside of America. He won the Intercolonial Stakes in Liverpool in 1878 winning in three straight heats of two miles each, in 5:05; 5:04, and 5:11, with a standing start. He also won the Handicap Sweepstakes at Alexandria Park in 1879 in which there were twenty four horses placed in front of him, some of them as much as 700 yards ahead, still he won easily. He was afterwards taken to Berlin where he won four races and then to Hamburg where he won three races. In 1880 he won the champion stallion race at Alexandria Park, and in 1882 was taken to Australia where he has stamped himself as a great producer of speed. Childe Harold was the property of Andrew Town of Hobartville, Richmond, N. S. W.

A letter from New York conveys the intelligence that the Hearst stable at Sheepshead Bay, are all in excellent condition and wintering in good shape. The three-year-old contingent certainly are very promising. Headed by that grand looking colt King Thomas, there are the colts Tournament by Sir Modred—Plaything; Ballarat, by Sir Modred—La Favorita, and Anaconda by Spendthrift—Maid of Athol; while specially strong is the stable with three year old fillies, with Golden Horn by Spendthrift—Constantinople; Gloaming, by Sir Modred—Twilight; Miss Belle, by Prince Charlie—Lincoet, and Everglade, by Iroquois—Agenoria. Another good looking one is the daughter of Isonomy, Gorgo. She seems to have grown materially, and her long, black, silken coat looks like a sealskin robe. Tournament is a big fellow, too. Mr. Allen also has several yearlings, just now coming to, including Sir Lancelot, War Path, by Warwick or Ban Fox, out of the dam of Exile, and an apparent gem in Fireworks, a full sister to the mighty Dew Drop. Then there are among the others Atlas, by Hyder Ali—Fidelity; Ægenon, a favorite with Mr. Allen, who knew his sire, Joe Hooker, so well in California. This colt is out of Faustina, and his half brother, Sir Lancelot, by Sir Modred, occupies a near by stall. Babicora, named after Senator Hearst's Mexican ranch, by Hyder Ali—Graciosa, is another of the yearlings. Besides Senator Hearst's string there are but few other horses at the track. J Shields has a few yearlings, but it is soon expected on with the full stable, and others are likely to arrive about Christmas time.

El Rio Rey.

The racing stable of Theodore Winters won $63,000 during the season just closed, says the Breeder's Gazette. Of course the bulk of this large sum came through the performances of the great two-year-old colt El Rio Rey, he having an unbeaten record and winning some of the most valuable stakes in the East and West. In spite of the fact that on several occasions when rich prizes were at his mercy, El Rio Rey was prevented by rain from starting, his trainer not caring to take any chances with such a valuable colt, his gross winnings for the season were $47,485, and had he been started in all his engagements irrespective of weather conditions, and won them, the amount to his credit would have been close to $60,000. Whether or not El Rio Rey will be of any account as a race horse next season is a question that will be discussed by horsemen all the winter. It is almost the universal experience that when a colt has lung troubles of the kind that attacked El Rio Rey a couple of months ago, and brought him so close to death's door, it is seldom the animal ever fully recovers its vigor, especially to the extent that it is again capable of running or trotting good races. On the showing made during the season of 1889, El Rio Rey should easily head the list of American three-year olds in 1890, and as he is entered in all the principle stakes for his age, including the American and Kentucky Derbies, the question of whether or not his lungs have been permanently injured is an important one to the owners of other colts that are nominated in the same events, but that if the Californian is in fix might as well be in the barn on the day of the race, so far as any chance they might have of beating him is concerned. It seems certain that from now until say the first of next June, by which time it will be possible to tell something about the real condition of the colt, the owner of El Rio Rey will have a chance to do as much thinking as any man in the country. If his colt has not been permanently injured it is practically certain that he will win $50,000 in stakes next season. If he has been permanently injured he won't win anything at all. It is quite like a lottery for Mr. Winters.

ATHLETICS.

Athletic Sports and Other Pastimes.

Edited by Arphippus.

SUMMARY.

The athletes are jubilant over the prospect of a dry spell. In a few days the ground will be sufficiently dry to allow the runners and walkers a chance to resume practice. From present indications it is safe to assert that the Spring of 1890 will be a memorable one in the history of amateur athletics on the Pacific Coast. Athletes, oarsmen and wheelmen are already beginning to make preparations for the coming season, and it is a foregone conclusion that many of the coast records will be lowered during the present year.

TO THE ATHLETES.

In this, the first issue of the BREEDER AND SPORTSMAN for 1890, we would like to address a few remarks to the athletes. This department is now several months old, and is generally acknowledged to be the best edited athletic department west of the Rocky Mountains. From the start it has been the aim of the editor to publish only such news as would interest the athletic readers of the BREEDER AND SPORTSMAN. Except under the headings of "Jottings from all Over," the notes that have appeared in this department from time to time have all been strictly original. The athletic, rowing and bicycling jottings have always been the chief feature of our athletic columns, and our readers can always rest assured that our notes are perfectly auth ntic, and can be relied upon as true facts. We have, through our large and universal acquaintance with the athletes, been able to obtain news that the reporters of the daily press have failed to gather. As a genuine proof of this assertion, we would like to call the readers' attention to the fact that fifty per cent of the athletic news appearing in these columns is utilized by the sporting editors of other local journals. The athletic prospect ahead is indeed very bright, and in the course of the present year there will be quite a large amount of news to publish. Our readers can rest assured that after they have perused the athletic department of this paper, they will have become acquainted with all the news worthy of attention. In the future, as in the past, it will be our chief aim to present our readers with such news as will particularly interest them, and they can rest doubly assured that when criticising any performance or exhibition, our opinion will be based on an upright and unprejudiced foundation, and we will make it our special duty to ferret out fraud and expose it to our readers.

ATHLETICS 1889—1890.

We are on the verge of a new season. The one just passed was anything but a pleasant one for the athletes. Fewer athletic meetings were held during the year 1889 than during any other year since athletics first began to creep into favor on the Pacific Coast. The cause is easily explained. In the first place, the athletic clubs, outside of the Olympic Club, took more interest in "slogging matches" than in amateur athletics. In comparison with the noble fistic gladiator, the amateur athlete was a mere nothing. It has been *fights, fights, fights* from one end of the year to the other. For the professional "sloggers" the amateurs have been cast aside as it were, but realizing the danger which threatened their pastimes, they have boldly struck out for themselves and the result of their uprising was the organization of the Alpine Amateur Athletic Club.

In forming this club the athletes did a very creditable piece of work. They proved that they were no longer willing to remain in bondage. They manifested their disapproval of being members of clubs run and *owned* by corporations. Taking, for instance, the Golden Gate Athletic Club as a criterion, what has it ever done in the interest of its out-door amateur members? True, a picnic was twice held under its auspices, but last year its *owners* were too much absorbed in prize-fighting to afford any of their time in the interest of amateur athletics. When the did hold a field day the medals awarded the winners were so wretched that the athletes vowed never again to compete in the club games. And yet the club, month after month, subscribes sums ranging from $500 to $1,500 for "fake" slogging matches. We are surprised that the P. C. A. A. ever permitted such an organization to become one of its associate clubs. There are many other clubs of the same description in San Francisco which are also *owned* by a body of men and run in *their* interests and not in the interests of the members. However, we are highly pleased to think that these bogus clubs will soon dwindle into insignificance. The citizens of San Francisco are beginning to grow heartily sick of prize-fighting.

Every morning at the breakfast table, on picking up the daily paper, the first item that attracts a person's notice is *prize-fighting*. Sometimes this branch of news is disguised under the heading of "Athletics." Be that as it may, our wives and daughters, as well as our sons, have their attention repeatedly called to nauseating reports of brutal fights.

Such newspaper articles are perfectly demoralizing to our youth. After the Sullivan-Jackson fight, if it *ever* takes place, the interest in fighting will suddenly die out, and with perhaps one exception the clubs will all break up.

Amateur athletics will then receive more attention and legitimate sports, both indoor and out-door, will soon be booming. With three first-class clubs in the field on May 30th next the battle for the Champion pennant should be a hot one. Each club will urge its representative to train—and many of the long standing records will possibly make room for better ones.

The club that will win the banner this year will certainly be a champion club. At present it would be hard to name the winner, but there is no telling what changes may occur during the months that will intervene between now and May. The athletic meetings during the present year will be numerous. There will be several in-door meetings in addition to the usual field days, so that the outlook for the amateurs is indeed very encouraging.

RUNNERS, WALKERS, JUMPERS, etc.

McDonald, the young Olympic sprinter, states that he will appear on the track in fine condition on February 22.

Jarvis should not compete in the Washington Birthday games unless he can spare time to get into good condition. A man out of condition who is heavily handicapped generally finds it a difficult task to win a race.

Charley Hill, the ex-champion walker, has informed us that he will never appear on the track again.

James Sexsmith of the Alpine Athletic Club, should make a new record in the pole vault at the championship games.

Charles Vultie of the Alpine Club, will try for second place in the high jump. With judicoius and faithful practice this promising young athlete should come next to Moffitt.

The amateurs of the California Athletic Club are still wondering if the club will ever do anything in their interest. Many of them have joined the Alpine Athletic Club.

Without Purcell and Schifferstein the Olympic Club will make but a poor showing at the championship games. The chances are that both men will train a little in order to keep their club out.

H. C. Cassidy, the mile runner, has made up his mind to returned to Woolland. He will visit the City every month in order to compete in the Alpine Athletic Clubs. Members handicap meetings at Harbor View.

The absurd report that the Olympic Club contemplated donating a prize of $1500 for a professional sprint race at its opening games on February 22nd, is deserving of ridicule. The club will find it hard enough to pay for the medals to be awarded the amateurs without throwing away $1500 on a couple of professional "fake" sprinters.

P. N. Gafney has been elected official handicapper of the Alpine Amateur Athletic Club.

J. J. Larkey has been elected field captain.

THE WHEELMEN.

The weather having modified somewhat, the wheelmen are commencing to get their wheels into shape for the coming season.

George P. Wetmore and Sanford Plummer, both of the Bay City Wheelmen, have joined the Alpine Athletic Club.

Henry M. Lichtenstein, of the San Francisco Bicycle Club, has also joined the Alpines.

The Alpine Athletic Club will probably add a bicycle race to their programme for February.

The coming carnival at the Mechanics Pavilion is causing great excitement in wheeling circles. A prize of $150 is offered by the Directors of the Mechanics Pavilion for a competitive drill among the wheelmen. Clubs from all over the State will be represented and the competition will most undoubtedly be close.

The Stockton Club is to send sixteen men to compete.

AT THE OARS.

H. O. Farrell has resigned from the Ariel Rowing Club. He has joined the Alpine Athletic Club.

Several other prominent members have joined the Alpine Club and will resign from the Ariel Club in the near future.

The Lurline Club gave an athletic and aquatic exhibition at their club house on Sunday last. The boat races were hotly contested and the indoor exhibition was unusually good. About 1,000 persons were present.

It is rumored that Long Bridge will be deserted by the rowing clubs before present season is over. For the regatta purposes the location is certainly out of the way and Alameda would be a much better locality for the clubs.

All the members of the Amateur Champion Crew have joined the Alpine Athletic club and Harbor View will be used as a training station for the present. When the club grows stronger the chances are that the S. P. Co. will build a boat house for the club at Alameda.

The charter of the Pacific Rowing Association is now open in order to give all the clubs a chance to join.

CLUB JOTTINGS.

There is but little chance now that the track at the Olympic clubs new out-door grounds will be in first class condition on Feb. 22. The ground is in a terrible condition and it will require at least two weeks drying before the track can be finished.

The Olympic club will give one of its enjoyable "Ladies Nights" about the end of the present month. The medals won at the late field day of the club held at Berkeley will be presented to the winners on that evening.

The California Athletic club appears to be followed by bad luck. Nearly every month one of its booked fighters gets disabled so that the exhibitions have to be constantly postponed. The same luck that attends the fighters appears to have overtaken the Amateur Champion Wrestler of the club, Gus Ungerman, who badly bruised his finger a couple of days ago. He was to wrestle a match in a few days but owing to his injury the match has been declared off.

Why does not the P. C. A. A. A. hold a business meeting?

Work was begun on the dressing rooms for the Alpine Athletic Club's members at Harbor View athletic grounds on Sunday last. Half a dozen carpenters, assisted by over twenty volunteers from amongst the members of the club worked like Trojans all day long. By sundown the main building was almost finished. The club members who were at the grounds when the work commenced attached their names to a sheet of paper, placed it in a bottle and buried it beneath the building. The following names were attached to the paper: E. H. Moody, T. J. Cunningham, J. J. McKinon, Charles Armbruster, M. C. Giry, F. Howard, Jas. Sheehan, P. N. Gafney, J. McLaughlin, C. A. Eldridge, George Simmonds and John D. Garrison. The grounds will be finished by January 15th.

The Modesto Athletic Club has disqualified itself as an amateur club by offering money as prizes for boxing matches. There are no strictly amateur clubs now on the Pacific Coast outside of San Francisco, barring the University Atheltic club.

JOTTINGS FROM ALL OVER.

T. P. Conneff, the crack runner, is lying dangerously ill. It is thought that he will not be strong enough to run again for many months.

H. H. Baxter of the New York Athletic Club, the holder of the outdoor and indoor records for pole vaulting, 11ft 5in, and 11ft 3in, respectively, has entirely recovered from the effects of the accident which befell him some months ago while competing at an athletic meeting. Owing to the injury to his arm he was obliged to refrain from competing during the summer months.

The annual election of officers of the Athletic Club of the Schuylkill Navy, Philadelphia, took place on December 14th, the regular ticket being carried by a large majority. The officers for 1890 are as follows: President, M W Phillips; vice-President, the Hon. John E Reyburn; Secretary, W E Wallace; Treasurer, Harry McMillan; Captain, John F Huncker; Directors, George R Crump, Joseph H Baker, William Carey Brown, Dr. Thomas H Fenton, J B Mingus, Edward Milligan, George W Grove, Walter Cunningham, James B McCutcheon, William M Beuerman, Dr. Bernard Berens, Brandon L Keys, H B Langworthy, Eugene Zieber, Alonzo R Parsons; Elective Committee, N L Toy, Walter Nagle, W E Jenks, J D Ferguson, Dr. Conrad Berens, H Y Mageoch, B L Robinson. The report of the retiring Board was a most satisfactory one. In the hands of the treasurer there is a fund of $20,000, saved from the receipts of the current year. The membership to date is 1,775, and when the list reaches 2,000 the initiation fee will be increased from $15 to $25. The question of an outdoor athletic grounds is certain to be solved ere long, and a location is now in view which has good facilities in regard to access.

A few figures concerning the Thanksgiving Day football game on the Berkeley oval between Yale and Princeton, may open the eyes of some who probably have not thought of the financial part of that great college event. Dr. John B White, president of the Berkeley Athletic Club, furnished the figures. He says the receipts from admission tickets and seats were $14,307, and from gate money and coaches $1,000 more, making a grand total of $15,307. The respective college teams received in the neighborhood of $6,000 each as their share.

The members of the Manhattan Athletic Club are anxiously looking forward to the completion of their new building on Madison avenue, New York City.

ALPINE AMATEUR ATHLETIC CLUB,

The second meeting of the Alpine Amateur Athletic Club was held at 539 California Street, on Friday evening, December 27th.

The committee on club rooms reported progress.

The committee on out-door training grounds reported that the Harbor View Athletic Grounds had been secured and would be ready for occupancy on January 15th. The committee were given power to have suitable bathing and dressing rooms built for the use of the members. It was decided to close the charter roll.

H. O Farrell made a long speech in which he stated that the club was now an assured success, and that the turning point had just been reached. His remarks im brief were these:

"Gentlemen, there is not a person in this room to-night who can say otherwise than that the Alpine Amateur Athletic Club is a success. What other club at present existing in San Francisco can claim to have started out on such a solid basis as this one has? Just think of it, we have over 150 members and yet we have been organized but two weeks. There remains now for us either to go ahead and prosper or remain stationary and perish. Let ambition carry us forward to victory. Rome was not built in a day, neither can we expect to build our reputation in a day. If we make ourselves known inside of one year, I think we will be doing well. If each and every member would only be ambitious, we will not only be known but feared inside of twelve months. The first stepping stone to success in a club like this one should be show. We have got to make a show or we will never succeed.

Let us hold a monster indoor athletic tournament in the Mechanics Pavilion, embracing all the in and outdoor past times. Let us offer valuable prizes for competition, and every amateur athlete on the Pacific Coast will help us out. The public will patronize us on account of the inducements offered and our treasury will be made richer.

The co-operation of the members is necessary to insure success, and I feel confident that every man who has signed his name to our charter roll will acquiesce in my ideas.

President Giry ably responded to Mr. Farrell's speech, and asked some of the members present to express their opinions on the subject. It was finally decided to appoint a committee of ten to make careful enquiries into the cost of holding the tournament proposed by Mr. Farrell. The following gentlemen were named by the president as a committee to investigate the matter and report back to the club at large: T. J. Cunningham (chairman), Charles Valtee, E P. Moody, J. P. Bean, P. N. Gafney, J. J. McKinnon, H. O'Farrell, E. Sullivan, John D. Garrison and Felix McKenna.

It was decided to hold a handicap meeting for members of the club only at the Harbor View training grounds about the second Sunday in February. Valuable medals will be presented to the winners. Only members of the club will be allowed to witness this exhibition.

The following investigation committee was appointed: J. P. Bean, T. J. Quinlan and Rudolph Brewer. The following athletes were nominated for Field Captain: E. P. Moody, J. J. Larkey and R. J. Luttringer. For the position of Official Handicapper, the following were nominated: P. N. Gafney, E. J. Goodwin and W. J. Jefferey.

The Board of Directors will make the appointments.

On the Charter roll are the names of several prominent oarsmen, wheelmen, and general athletes. The initiation fee for the next three months will be $2 50. The monthly dues have been fixed at $1.

Until such time as the rooms of the club on Tenth Street are finished, it will occupy temporary rooms.

The club will probably be admitted to the P. C. A. A. A. before Washington's Birthday.

THE FARM.

Breeding Herefords.

In his address before the American Hereford Association, Adams Earl, its president, urged his hearers not to be discouraged at the present low prices of beef or breeding stock. In his younger days, he said, even lower prices prevailed. Stock raising, the breeding of Hereford cattle in particular, he declared to be a good and profitable business. He urged a more frequent use of the knife, and that pure bred steers be exhibited more frequently. Of late steers had not taken so active a part in shows as they should, grades in particular, as they, above all others, showed what could be done by a good Hereford sire.—O. J. Farmer.

Shall Milch Cows Breed Annually?

Practically I find that where cows are kept in milk over eleven or twelve months, they are quite sure to convert more of their food into flesh, and less into milk than when bred to come in annually. The best of cows will often thus take on flesh and become dry before the close of the second year, though fed on the best of milk-producing rations. A good dairy cow, with proper food and care, will continue to yield a large amount of milk during nearly the entire year when in calf every twelve months. Without these conditions of food and care, she will dry off as when in her natural state, or if, by reason of a superior milking development, there should chance to be a continued flow, it would be at the cost of debility in the mother, and a weak and imperfect development in the calf. Under favorable treatment both the mother and progeny may be healthy and strong, though the former may continue to give a good flow of milk for eleven months out of the twelve and yield a much stronger aggregate amount of milk in two years than when in calf but once during the time. By allowing our cows to remain in milk so long after calving, we get too far from those natural conditions which underlie a large and healthy product of milk, which maternity alone supplies.—[F. D. Douglas, in Rural New Yorker.

Cattle Firms Join Issues.

It is now a settled fact that two of the biggest beef and cattle firms in the country, the Monroes of Boston, and the Hammond Co., of Hammond, Ind., have united, and that in the amalgamation the live cattle industry has lost one of the heaviest dealers, while the dressed beef industry has been increased by one. It was rumored Saturday that the Monroes had purchased a big amount of stock in the Hammond dressed meat corporation. Monday the story was to a certain extent verified by the fact that the stock purchased by W. H. Thompson, Jr., the Chicago representative of the Monroes, was weighed to Hammond & Co.

Mr. Thompson stated yesterday that the firms had consolidated and that he was sending his purchases to Hammond. Beyond that he could give no particulars. The change gave rise to considerable speculation in stock circles when it became known. The Monroe firm was one of the heaviest buyers at the Chicago yards to-day, having shipped stock on hoof to Albany and Boston. They have been engaged in the dressed beef business for about two years, but did all the slaughtering at Eastern points. The Boston dressed beef plant has, it is understood, been turned into the new company, and it is understood that the Monroes will be eastern representatives of the Hammond Company. The Hammond concern is one of the most extensive in the country. It is one of the alleged "Big Four."—Chicago Herald.

Ayrshire Cattle.

The Ayrshire breed has taken a well-defined place in American husbandry. While, on the one hand, no one expects from an Ayrshire cow any phenomenal records in the production of milk or butter, on the other she maintains a good average production, both in quality and quantity. The milk is less rich in butter-fats than that of Channel Island cattle, but shows on an average about thirteen per cent. of solids and four, to four and a half per cent. of butter-fats, and selected cows have far exceeded this. The yield of milk is never phenomenally great in quantity, but an average of five thousand to seven thousand pounds per year may be depended upon. While making no claims as a special beef breed, the Ayrshires "kill well," steers at two or three years old weighing twelve hundred and fifty to fourteen hundred pounds. The dressed carcass does not show so large a per cent. of weight compared with the total when alive, as the Short-horns, Herefords or Aberdeen-Angus. But the beef, when well fattened, is finely marbled, palatable and of good flavor. They are good feeders, and an Ayrshire bullock or dry cow will fatten on feed that would scarcely keep a pampered animal of the larger breeds alive. But the distinguishing excellence of the Ayrshire is that it is hardy, largely exempt from disease, and easily kept. It is this which makes it the "farmer's cow" all around the world.—American Agriculturist.

Diplomacy With Kickers.

It sometimes seems as if the horns and cloven hoofs of the cow were significant of a legacy of evil-mindedness from a personality generally pictured with such equipments. Every one knows that a cow always acts the meanest and most obstinate when one is in a hurry or out of patience. The obvious moral is—not to be in a hurry or out of patience in dealing with a nervous cow. One can always draw more milk from her than he can pound out. Cows have more than one reason for lifting a foot in protest against the milker. It may be fright, nervousness, real pain or an old habit. The last is the hardest to manage, but each cause needs to be studied and treated in its own peculiar way. With one cow that persistently started, stepped and kicked it was at last discovered that she did it when the teat was grasped high up in beginning to milk. The pressure of milk there caused pain. The milking at first with but two or three fingers on the end of the teat and drawing downward so as to elongate it and relieve the pressure above, the cow was got to stand perfectly quiet. This plan may mollify a number of "kickers." An old farmer's remedy is to strap a surcingle tightly around the cow's body just forward of the udder. Whether it is the feeling of restraint that it gives or some effect of the pressure at the upper extremity of the udder, or the constriction of the muscles that draw the leg forward is difficult to say, but the plan is often successful. There are, too, appliances for drawing back the leg and holding it, clamps to screw on the joint, etc. But half the battle will be ours if the confidence and good will of the animal can be won by kind treatment and such conciliatory advances as rubbing her neck and the offer of a handful of meal.—Charles H. Crandall in N. Y. Tribune.

Axioms for Beef Growers.

Some kinds of cattle will come to maturity sooner than others. Some cattle will return a larger amount of weight for a given quantity of food than others. Some cattle will give a larger percentage of desirable and valuable meat to the undesirable and invaluable than others. Some cattle will be eagerly sought after and greedily bought by butchers, while others, which have really cost more money to raise, will be shunned, and if bought at all, only at an unremunerative price. The present beef markets are the most eloquent advocates of intelligent improvement in beef production. The differences in prices of the desirable and undesirable types are too great to be longer ignored by our cattle raisers. A new fashion in beef animals has invaded our land, and in this as in everything else, fashion is a despot. Its mandates must be observed, its orders must be obeyed.

Breed in accordance with the requirements of the fashion, whether you like the fashion or not. Beef cattle are low in price, but poor beef cattle are much lower than good ones. It costs no more, nor as much to raise the good than the poor. Cattle we must have, our farms demand them, they are one of the foundation stones of fertility. The necessity acknowledged, it is folly to hesitate regarding the kind of cattle to grow. Breeders adapted to the present demands of the beef market are at hand, and of their capacity we need have no doubt. There never was a time when the desired blood could be so cheaply introduced into our herds as now, and probably will not be again for many years to come. This fact coupled with the almost positive assurance that the margin of price between the desirable and undesirable types is rapidly growing wider in our markets, pleads "trumpet tongued" for a universal improvement in beef cattle. I can not afford to buy a blooded bull, nor ever pay for the service of one while cattle are so low in price," is neither good logic nor good business. Better reasoning is this. "Cattle are low in price; the best are low enough; the poorer then are out of the question. The times demand the best, and if at present prices the best show no prospect of profit, why should I invite heavy loss by raising the poor?—Farm, Stock and Home.

New Blood in Poultry.

New blood in poultry is the basis of beauty, vigor and prolificness. It is more essential to successful poultry culture than all else combined. Fowls that are inbred, that have been bred in line several years without the addition or infusion of fresh blood from other strains of the same variety, but to which they are not directly related, become inactive, diminutive and unprofitable.

It has been said that inbred fowls breed true to feather, and that for this reason, because they all come alike and are therefore best suited to exhibition, inbreeding is desirable, and this is true to a very great extent, for we have tried it. They do come alike in more respects than one. They breed true to feather, it is true, but they also have the same inactive, stupid and unattractive appearance. Their very life seems to have been dulled. They are slow to develop in form and muscle, and they are slow to lay.

While inbred fowls may be suitable for exhibition purposes, they are certainly unprofitable, and for this reason, with the person who is keeping poultry for profit, they should have no part or lot.

Far more desirable is the fowl that by its very appearance, its very move and action manifests the fresh, new blood that it embodies. There is an activity, grace and vigor about it that is refreshing.

The male bird that comes of fresh blood is the one that is ever on the alert to make himself attractive and agreeable to his mates. Every choice bit of food that he finds he saves for them, and he calls them about him with a gallantry that is admirable. He leads them to the nest over which he crows with a satisfactory crow, that seems to manifest a knowledge of its value in the poultry world.

A male bird of this kind crows from the top of the fence with a flap of the wings that always gives notice of the bugle call that is to follow.

Equal to the male bird of fresh blood is the hen that comes of a similar parentage. She is keen and active, healthy and vigorous, and one of the best layers of her kind. In truth, in no way does new blood manifest itself more strongly than in the laying qualities of our hens.

It is absolutely necessary, in order to have our hens lay profitably, that is, to lay enough eggs to pay for their keep and a profit besides, that we introduce fresh blood in our flocks every year. The writer has kept a record for several years, and observed closely, and in every instance the pullets of the newest blood that come of the flock in which a male absolutely un-akin to the females had been introduced the spring previous, were always the first to lay, in point of age, and make the best layers generally.

To have healthy, vigorous and profitable poultry we must then, without any question, introduce new blood annually in our flocks.—Southern Cultivator.

A Study of Merinos.

For more than 2,000 years prior to the beginning of the present century the Spaniards bred the Merino sheep and kept the blood pure. The government did not allow any of them to go out of the country. The Napoleonic wars opened the way for their dissemination by confiscating the property of the nobles and princes, they owning the best flocks. It was then that importations of these sheep arrived in this country. Several flocks went to Vermont. The animals were wrinkly and somewhat greasy. These features being considered evidences of "royal blood" the subsequent breeding there was to that end. Wrinkles and weight of fleece (which in this case largely means grease) were bred for at the expense of size of body and vigor of constitution, and to-day "Vermont sheep" and "wrinkles and grease" are synonymous. These are properly the Spanish merinos. One lot of the earliest importation found its way to Ohio, where subsequent successful inbreeding from them has ever since been conducted with other ends in view—to breed off the wrinkles, to secure longer wool freer from grease, larger carcass and more vigorous constitution. Flocks of similar breeding have sprung up in Western Pennsylvania, West Virginia and other places. These improved sheep can be rightfully classed under the one general head of American Merinos. Some of the sub-divisions are the Dickinson, Blacktop, Delaine, and Mutton. Breeders of these different families claim direct descent from the Humphrey importation of 1802; whether this be really so or not, the animals of the various flocks appear alike and their powers of prepotency are well established.

It is rightly claimed for the American Merinos that they are the best combination of wool and mutton, with the quality of early maturity, herding, feeding, vigor of constitution and prepotent power of reproduction. The bucks are largely in demand in California, Texas, and on the Southwestern ranges for several reasons: Merinos will eat ten to twelve more kinds of herbage than any other breed; in a continuously warm climate nature goes to work at once to relieve them of their surplus fleeces, if Northern blood were not constantly introduced the average weight of fleece would soon shrink to a minimum. So long as sheep are grown for profit in the warmer sections of the United States, there will be required a constant in-pouring of Northern blood where nature provides the animals with a finer and denser coating their protection from the ever changeable weather. The sheep in warmer climate are shorn twice a year, principally because at the close of the hot dry season the wool takes a new start in growth and if not short then there will be a weak spot in the wool fibre, seriously imparing the value of the fleece. The American Merinos possessing so great a weight of fleece and length of fibre free from gum and surplus grease is found to be desirable in such season. An inch or even half an inch, increased length at the semi-annual clipping adds largely to the prices obtainable for the out-put of wool.—Galen Wilson in New York Tribune.

Grading Up.

If we realized how little it costs to have good animals we would certainly possess them. For the shambles, the dairy, or work, high grade are fully as good as pure bred animals. In fact a majority of feeders prefer high grade cattle, sheep or hogs to full blooded animals for feeding for flesh. They put on flesh as economically and rapidly as pure bred stock, and a touch of native blood makes them a little less fastidious about their food and a little better adapted to "rustling." But this touch of native blood should not exceed one-eighth. That is, for the animal to be as desirable as a full blood for all purposes other than breeding it must have at least seven-eighths good blood.

Now how long and how much money will it take to get this? Not a reader of this paper has perhaps a scrub animal; all our stock has at least a little improved blood. But to make the worst possible case for grading up, so that none can object, we will presume that our animals are scrubs. A full-blooded boar can be bought for ten dollars more than a scrub. He will not have a fancy pedigree, but he will have an undoubted and a good one—he will be a registered hog; and he will be a first-class animal in individual merits. This boar will, with fair care and feed, serve thirty sows in one season and get at least 250 live pigs. At the end of this season he will sell for more than a scrub; but we will not count this, and therefore the cost per pig of the improvement he has made is four cents. That is, a half blood pig costs four cents more than a scrub. Using a pure bred male on the half blood sows will produce three-quarters good blood pigs, at an additional cost of four cents per pig; and a further expense of four cents per pig will bring the pigs up to a seven-eighths grade. Thus the total cost of a seven-eighth grade pig above a scrub is only twelve cents, and the improvement can be made in about two years and a half. How very cheap this improvement! No sensible man can doubt that it would be highly profitable.

How much will a seven-eighths grade calf cost above a scrub? I can get a good Shorthorn, Holstein Friesian or Jersey bull for $40 more than a scrub will cost. This animal will not have a fancy pedigree, but it will be a good, registered one; and for our purpose such an animal is just as good as one having a fancy pedigree. During the season this bull will get fifty calves, and he may be used a second season. Hence the cost of the improvement he puts on each calf will be only forty cents. The first forty cents will make the calf a half blood; the second will make it a three-quarter blood, and the third forty cents will bring it up to our standard—seven-eighths improved blood. The total cost per calf is $1 20! The value of the improvement, when the animal is three years old, is not less than $12—at least ten times what it has cost. Certainly realizing one thousand per cent. on an investment is good business.

If a farmer has not fifty sows or fifty cows he can purchase a full blooded boar or bull in partnership with some neighbors. Likely a purchase on the co-operation plan is best. Let one of the purchasers be paid so much for taking care of the animals, and all parties pay so much per service; then at the close of the season the margin of receipts for services above expenditure for care is divided among the purchasers, in proportion to the amount of purchase money contributed by each. Of course it will be very desirable to purchase a full blooded female also. Her produce being full blooded can be used as breeders, thus keeping at home the money that otherwise would be sent elsewhere for pure bred males, while a herd of pure bred animals would be built up. The service of a male could be exchanged with some neighbor if necessary, to avoid too close in-and-in breeding.—Stockman and Farmer.

The annual meeting of the American Poland-China Record Company will be held at the Grand Hotel, Cedar Rapids, Iowa, beginning Wednesday, January 15, 1890.

Last year the December receipts at the Chicago stock yards were 211,861 cattle, 5,436 calves, 447,075 hogs, 135,833 sheep, and 3 287 horses. It is estimated that this month's receipts of hogs will be at least 200,000 head in excess of the number received last December.

There are in Great Britain this season 2,825 silos, being 158 more than last year, and representing an increase in the silo capacity of 658,789 cubic feet.

The New York Sun says that the following are standard quotations in the New York horse market: "Pairs of matched carriage horses from $800 to $1,600, pair of coachers $600 to $1,200, saddle horses $300 to $1,000, teams of truckers $600 to $900, express pairs $600 to $800, single drivers (or light roadsters) $250 to $750, business horses $175 to $250 roadsters $100 to $150.

The progress of Aberdeen-Angus cattle is indicated by the fact that 11,260 have been registered by the American Association having this breed in charge—1,396 during the last year.

The number of hogs packed between November 1st and December 17th at leading points is 2,190,000, against 1,785,000 a year ago, showing an increase of 405,000. As compared with two years ago there is a moderate decrease for the season.

The Cook ranch sent a grand polled Angus (1750 lbs.) to the California market for Christmas. Two hundred dollars was paid for him.

The Visalians combined and poisoned 4,700 acres of land which was infested with squirrels, and destroyed immense quantities. Buzzards are said to be growing fat on the carcasses.

Queen Victoria followed up her successes with her short-horns at the Birmingham Fat Stock Show, by taking a first prize at Smithfield, and has since sold him for £150 which is at the rate of two shillings and four pence a pound. [illegible] think of the advt for the butcher.

THE WEEKLY

Breeder and Sportsman.

JAMES P. KERR, PROPRIETOR.

The Turf and Sporting Authority of the Pacific Coast.

Office, No. 313 Bush St.

P. O. Box 2300.

TERMS—*One Year, $5; Six Months, $3; Three Months, $1.50.*
STRICTLY IN ADVANCE.

Money should be sent by postal order, draft or by registered letter, addressed to JAMES P. KERR, San Francisco, Cal.

Communications must be accompanied by the writer's name and address, not necessarily for publication, but as a private guarantee of good faith.

ALEX. P. WAUGH, - - - - - - Editor.

To Subscribers.

The date printed on the wrapper of your paper indicates the time to which your subscription is paid.

Should the BREEDER AND SPORTSMAN be received by any subscriber who does not want it, write us direct to stop it. A postal card will suffice.

Special Notice to Correspondents.

Letters intended for publication should reach this office not later than Wednesday of each week, to secure a place in the issue of the following Saturday. Such letters to insure immediate attention should be addressed to the BREEDER AND SPORTSMAN, and not to any member of the staff.

San Francisco, Saturday, Jan. 4, 1890.

A Breeding Theory.

On another page will be found a letter from C. Bruce Lowe, of Sidney, New South Wales, a gentleman who has paid a good deal of attention to the breeding problem; and is considered by Australians the peer of any man living in the knowledge which is so highly essential to those who study and carry out practically the various theories which are from time to time brought before the public by the many writers for the sporting press. Mr. Lowe advances a theory that is not altogether new, but presents it so forcibly that it is well worthy of the consideration of every breeder in this country. We should be pleased to hear from our readers what they think of Mr. Lowe's idea, as there cannot be too much said or written in regard to any new suggestion that will tend to enlighten those who are breeding to get the best.

P. C. T. H. B. A.

Next Wednesday evening is the time selected for the annual meeting of the Pacific Coast Trotting Horse Breeders' Association, and every member should make it a point to be present. The annual election for officers is the most important feature of the meeting, and it is to the interest of each and every one that a suitable Board of Directors be chosen. A Breeders' Association should not be one only in name, but should be controlled by those who have the interests of breeders at heart; in fact, should be directed by gentlemen actually in the business. There are plenty of live, wide-awake breeders who can be selected as Directors from among the following names. Leland Stanford, Wm. Corbitt, G. Valensin, M. Salisbury, F. H. Burke, F. W. Loeber, D. M. Reavis, S. N. Straube, R. Girl, W. Page, J. H. White, G W. Guerne, Irvin Ayres, E. Topham, A. Gonzalez and Gilbert Tompkins. These names are simply taken at random, and without having a list of the members to select from, gentlemen who are in the business to make money, and it is only natural to suppose that they would guard the interests of the association as they would any of the details of their own private affairs. It is from such as these that the Directors should be taken, and if this suggestion is acted upon, the breeder's meeting of 1890 will be the most successful ever held in California.

If a fair representation from various portions of the State should be present, it will be a favorable opportunity to start the Pacific Coast Trotting Association, which was talked so much about last Fall. In fact, there are so many important matters to be looked after, that every member should be present. Remember, Wednesday evening, January 8th, at the Palace Hotel, San Francisco.

The Breeder and Sportsman Futurity Stake.

As has been predicted in our columns for several weeks past, the Futurity Stake is a grand success. Every mail brings further additions to the already large list, and many are still expected from the southern portion of the State, the washouts preventing the arrival of the Los Angeles mail up to the time of our going to press. Every prominent breeding establishment has sent in a reasonable quota of nominations, and scores have sent in as entries the produce of one and two mares. In the next issue of the BREEDER AND SPORTSMAN the full list of entries will be given, so that all may know what there is in the stake.

A Meeting Necessary.

Some weeks ago we called attention to the fact that it was necessary in the near future to have a meeting of delegates from each of the associations in the State, to name dates for the fair season of 1890. Since the first mention was made of the matter several gentlemen have discussed it pro and con when visiting at the BREEDER AND SPORTSMAN's office, and one and all seem anxious to prevent the clashing that occurred last year. As is readily understood, each and every association cannot have a week all to itself, but arrangements can be made so that there will be various circuits formed which will not interfere one with another. There are now so many horses trained annually in California that there are plenty and to spare for all the meetings if the Directors of the same will only arrange them properly. We should like to hear from the Secretaries of the different associations as to the views of their Directors, and would also like to have suggestions made as to the most advantageous place of meeting for the delegates. From present appearances it seems highly plausible to suppose that there will be at least four circuits, two in the South and two in the North, and if due attention is paid to the fixing of dates no trouble should be experienced in making each of the meetings a financial success. There is no time to waste now; the dates must be arranged very soon, and it is to the interest of every association to take time by the forelock and have it understood what dates each city and town will claim. Letters bearing on this subject are now in order and we hope to hear from every section of the State, especially from the officers of the Agricultural Societies.

California vs. Kentucky.

For many years the Golden State has been recognized as the principal horse breeding State in the Union, and it does hurt the feelings of a Kentuckian to hear peons of praise raised in favor of California. The Eastern journalists, to a man, declare that the particular State in which they reside is the equal of the Pacific Coast States when the breeding of colts is called in question, and yet every now and again a wail goes forth from some one of the writers that tends to show that the shoe is pinching terribly. In a late number of the Kentucky Stock Farm the well known "Iconoclast" says.—

"Aurelius in a late communication intimates that the Californians trot their horses till half past eleven o'clock on the night of December 31. While this is rather a strong statement, it embodies the truth with substantial accuracy. Long after the season is past in which it is possible for Eastern people to trot or train their horses the work of record making and record breaking is proceeding on the Western Coast. This gives the Pacific breeder an undue advantage over those east of the Rockies, and enables them to obtain marks for their horses, particularly their youngsters, long after our trotting season is past."

Undue advantage, forsooth. You are trying on a child's method, taking advantage of the baby act, Mr. Iconoclast, and it is not manly. Come out openly and say to your readers that the climatic influences of California are such that Kentucky cannot hope to compete with California in horse breeding. Say also that the rich and succulent native grasses are so nutrative that a yearling in California is fully as large as a two year old raised in Kentucky, and do not take our word for the assertion, but ask any honest and fair-minded Kentuckian who has visited this glorious State during the winter that is now in progress. There is not a month in the year passes but what some Eastern breeder visits California and carries away, as the result of purchase, one or more of our native grown foals. Can you believe it possible, Iconoclast, that Col. Strader, W. H. Allen, Sibley & Miller, S. A. Brown, W. H. Wilson, R. Steele, J. I. Case, Robert Bonner and other well known breeders would come to this faraway State and buy horses if they could secure what they desired in Kentucky? No indeed; they recognize the fact that just what they want is raised in California, and as a consequence they come here to buy. When the Haggin yearlings are offered for sale annually in New York the prices realized are far larger than for those sent from any other section of the country. Why? Because the colts and fillies are so superior in size and hardiness that the eye of the expert is taken at once, and the conclusion is forced upon prospective purchasers that there is not the same element of chance in buying California yearlings that there is in bidding on those sent on from Kentucky. Every breeder who visits this State is a walking advertisement for California, and the day is fast approaching when breeders from the Eastern States will endeavor to secure eligible locations in this State to start stock farms, and thus enjoy the advantages which have made the name of California known from one end of the world to the other.

St. Louis Jockey Club.

Entry blanks and advance programmes of the June race meeting of the St. Louis Jockey Club may be had on application to this office or to the rooms of the leading pool sellers. Under the management of President Chas. Green and Secretary C. W. Bellairs the meetings of the Club are most successful, beside being very rich from a racing standpoint.

A Fight on Hand.

NATIONAL ASSOCIATION OF TROTTING HORSE BREEDERS, Secretary's Office, 1 Broadway, New York, Dec. 13, '89.

EDITOR BREEDER AND SPORTSMAN:—It becomes my official duty to notify you of the following action of this association:

Whereas, It appears that a certain agricultural paper published in Boston, Mass., called The American Cultivator, has assumed, without any authority, to administer a garbled and incorrect form of the standard of this association, and issue certificates of standard rank thereon; and

Whereas, These irregular and unauthorized certificates have conferred fictitious standard rank on many animals that are not standard, and cannot be registered as standard, thus encouraging dishonesty and inflicting a wrong upon the unwary; therefore

Resolved, That the compiler of Wallace's American Trotting Register be requested, as the most direct means of abating these evils, to decline to accept pedigrees from any breeder or dealer who knowingly or wilfully seeks the benefit of registration under an unauthorized and garbled standard, wherever sought to be administered.

L. D. PACKER, Secretary.

A Good Pedigree.

Many years ago the name of Nathan Coombs was known of all horsemen. His thoroughbreds were of the best, and at various times thousands have watched his colors come under the wire first. As time wore on, and the "Coombs Boys" grew to manhood's estate, Frank L. and Nathan contracted a fondness for the trotting division, and from the beginning have endeavored to breed only the very best. Their success, like that of many others, has been varied, but now they have one, that from the great producing blood lines shown, should prove a veritable wonder. We give below the tabulated pedigree of

LORD CLIVE 1127.

Silver Bow.

The stallion advertisements will from now out be a source of interest to all who own brood mares and from week to week the announcements will be read with intense eagerness as every one desires to breed to the best. In the proper column this week will be found the card of P. J. Williams, an old turfite, than whom there is no better judge of breeding and form for many a mile around. He has purchased the young stallion Silver Bow, one of the highest bred trotters in the State who comes from speed producing lines on both the top and bottom crosses. An examination of the pedigree will convince the most skeptical. His sire Robert McGregor, has a host in the "30" list and is also the sire of Bonnie McGregor 2:13½, and that surely should be recommendation enough for those who are looking for fast stock. Silver Bow is only three years old and Mr. Williams has very wisely limited his service to fifteen approved mares. Those who are looking for a gilt edged pedigree should not fail to examine the tabulation of Silver Bow.

Mr. H. P. Rennie, of Oakland, advertises cocker spaniels in another part of the paper. His dogs are of the best breeding and are winners.

Answers to Correspondents.

Answers for this department must be accompanied by the name and address of the sender, not necessarily for publication, but as proof of good faith. Write the questions distinctly, and on one side of the paper only. Positively no questions will be answered by mail or telegraph.

A. J.

Who owns the horse Baywood by Nutwood?

Answer—E. S. Smith, 119 Empire St. San Jose.

F. K. Lewis.

Please answer the following questions. Has Chieftain 721 any record? What is the address of the party to send to for blanks for registering horses.

Answer—No. We have forwarded the necessary blanks to you.

The other queries you sent will be answered in all probability next week.

Milton Medium.

Several week ago a subscriber asked whether Milton Medium was still alive and we said yes. This was a mistake as Milton Medium, died at Walla Walla in 1883.

E. W. C.

Has Arno any colts in the thirty class? What is his record?

Answer—Arno has none of his progeny in the 2:30 list. He has no record.

S. D. P.

Will you kindly give breeding of Grey Dale, dam of Silverthreads. Is she standard? Is Newlands Hambletonian standard?

Answer—Grey Dale by American Boy Jr., he by American Boy the sire of Belmont; dam Grey Poll by Winfield Scott, he by Edward Everett; 2nd dam Sorred Poll by Sir Henry; 3rd dam by Printer. She is not standard. Newland's Hambletonian is not standard.

Inquirer.

Will you kindly give me the pedigree and number of "Belvoir" and record, if he has any. I believe he is owned in Cheyenne, Wyoming

Answer.—Belvoir 6150, foaled 1880, by Belmont 64, dam Puss Prall, by Mark Time, son of Berthune, 2nd dam by Daniel Webster, son of Lance, etc. He is not in the 2:30 list. He is owned by G. B. Goodell, Cheyenne, Wyoming Territory.

A Subscriber.

Is a mare sired by Mambrino Wilkes, 6083, dam by Chieftain, 721, eligible to be registered?

Answer.—Yes.

San Jose.

Chieftain is the sire of Flora. with a record of 2:36 and trial 2:28. She campaigned against Ajax and others; her dam is by Wilson's Lemon. Is this the same Flora that is accredited to Chieftain with a mark of 2:30? If so, please state where and when she made the record, and oblige.

Answer.—The records do not show that the Flora you allude to has a record of 2:36, but 2:39½. The Flora accredited to Chieftain is a pacer with a record of 2:30, made at San Francisco August 29th, 1872.

J. H. O.

What qualifications does it require for a stallion to take a premium at a fair as a roadster, and what would bar him.

Answer.—According to the rule as laid down by the Directors of the State Fair Association, any carriage horse which is not standard bred, is eligible, for a roadster premium. Being standard bred would be a bar. However, different associations have different rules.

Horseman.

Please give the breeding of San Bruno and his record. Also the breeding of Algerine.

Answer:—San Bruno by Geo. M. Patchen Jr., dam not traced. Record 2:25½. Algerine, by Capt. Fisher, dam Maria Mink. Record 2:45.

J. L. W.

Will you please answer through your valuable columns the following questions: 1st. What is the number of Carr's Mambrino? 2nd. Give names and records of horses that he has sired. 3d. Is Dan Voorhees registered? If so, give number. Also give names and records of horses he has sired. 4th. Is the sire of Bella Alta, Williamson's Belmont, trotting bred or not?

Answer.—(1) 1789. (2) It would take too much space to give the names of the horses he has sired, but he has in the 2:30 list Lady Ellen 2:29½. and is also the sire of the dam of Ella 2:29. (4) Yes; Dan Voorhees 887. He has in the list Jim L. 2:20½. (4) Belmont was a thoroughbred.

Subscriber.

Please inform me of the pedigree of Silver King, bred by Alvinza Hayward.

Answer.—Silver King 3622 by Hambletonian 725, dam Harvest Queen, 2:29½, by Hambletonian 10, 2nd dam Dubois mare by American Star 14, 3rd dam by Abdallah 1.

S. C. J.

Will you please tell me what Alfalfa is.

Answer.—Lucern (Medicago Sativa), a forage plant of the family leguminosæ, and related to clover (trifolium) not only in its botanical characters but in its agricultural uses. The derivation of the word is obscure, but it is supposed by some to be from the Swiss canton of the same name; it is known in Spain as alfalfa, which name it bears also in Spanish American countries, and is still retained in California and New Mexico. The root of lucerne is perennial, from which arise erect, smooth, branching stems, two feet or more high; the leaves are triple, the flowers instead of being dense head as in clover, are erect and the corolla violet purple, and the many seeded pod spirally coiled. It was probably cultivated several centuries before Christ, and came into European agriculture through the south of France and Spain. Lucern has never been much grown in England or in the older parts of the United States, but on the continent of Europe and in our far Southern and Western States it is regarded as of great value—its reputation on the Pacific Coast has led agriculturalists at the East to experiment with it. The experiments of Chancellor Livingston near the close of the last century called the attention of farmers to lucern as a valuable forage plant, but our agriculture was not then sufficiently advanced to make its culture profitable; it is only when draining and improved tillage are practiced that its value is manifest. The plant has very long roots, sometimes penetrating to twelve feet or more, hence it is quite unsuited to light, thin soil, with a poor subsoil.

J. F. Merced.

Did Mr. S. Whipple have in 1879 a horse called Shafter and a mare called Harvest Queen? If so, can you give me the pedigree of the horse Shafter? I believe that he was bred by Mr McCracken of Consumne, Sacramento County, and was by David Hill.

Answer.—A letter sent to Mr. J. L. McCord has been replied to as follows:

SACRAMENTO, Dec. 28, 1889.

EDITOR BREEDER AND SPORTSMAN—DEAR SIR:—Yours of the 26th duly at hand, and in reply to the horse Shafter I don't know him by that name. He might have been named after leaving the ranch. Give me his age and description and I can tell you if any such horse was foaled there since 1875 as I have obtained the old Stud book that was kept by J. G. McCracken that far back.

We have every occasion to believe that the horse you refer to was originally called "Butte" and was owned at one time by Judge J. McM. Shafter of this city. He passed through several hands and was finally taken to your section of the country. If it is the same horse, we imagine he was by David Hill, dam a printer mare.

J. B. G.

Please inform me if my filly, sired by Fallis, dam by Tilton Almont, second dam a running mare, is standard. If so, what will I have to do to have her registered? What is the best method for laying out a mile track where you have plenty of room? Please answer in your columns.

Answer.—Your filly is standard. Send full address and we will forward you the necessary blanks.

For a mile track draw a line through an oblong center 440 yards in length, setting a stake at each end. Then draw a line on either side of the first line, exactly parallel with and 140 yards from it, setting stakes at either end of them. You will then have an oblong square 440 yards long and 280 yards wide. At each end of these three lines you will now set stakes. Now then fasten a cord or wire 140 yards long to the center stake of your parallelogram, and then describe a half circle, driving stakes as often as you wish to set a fence-post. This half circle, commencing at one side and extended to the other, will measure 440 yards. When the circle is made at both ends of your parallelogram you will have two straight sides that measure 440 yards each, and two circles of exactly the same length, which, measured three feet from the fence, will be exactly a mile. The turns should be thrown up an inch to the foot.

Lorena and Starlight.

I had occasion a few days ago to visit Capt. Harris' stable, corner of Turk and Steiner streets, and there I saw two of my favorites, Lorena and Starlight. The former is now three years old and the latter two, yet both of them are campaigners and earned laurels last year. Lorena has filled out wonderfully and gives every promise of being as speedy as a ghost. Only a few days ago her owner drove her half a mile in 1:08½, and the Captain feels sure that he has a coming world beater. There is no one that will begrudge him his luck, for he has been a persistent breeder for many years, and it seems that at last luck has smiled on him. Starlight has improved as much in proportion as has Lorena, and the chestnut filly shows every indication of great speed. As their names will appear prominently before the public this year, I herewith give their pedigrees:—

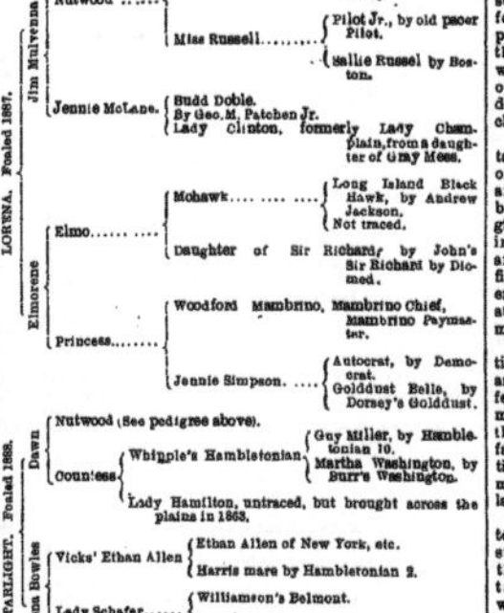

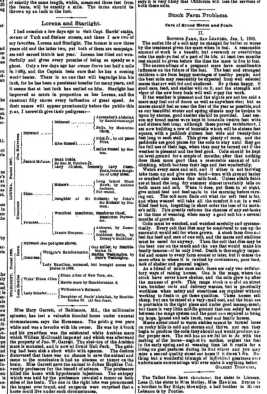

Miss Mary Garrett, of Baltimore, Md., the millionaire spinster, has lost a valuable blooded horse under unusual circumstances, says the Horseman. The gelding was pure white and was a favorite with his owner. He was by Adrock and his granddam was the celebrated white Arabian mare which William McDonald imported and which was afterward the property of Jno. W. Garrett. The skeleton of the Arabian mare is mounted, and is now at Druid Hall Park. The gelding had been sick a short while with spasms. The doctors discovered that there was no chance to save the animal and came to the conclusion it had an abscess or tumor on the brain. Miss Garrett gave the animal to Johns Hopkins University professors for the benefit of science. The professors killed the horse with hypodermic injections. The autopsy which was held by the professors revealed a tumor on both sides of the brain. The one in the right lobe was pronounced the largest ever found, and surgeons were surprised that a horse could live under such circumstances.

The Valensin Stock Farm.

As another year has rolled around, we again have to announce to our readers that the Valensin Stud Farm stallions, Sidney and Simmocolon are as usual to stand for the coming season, for a few select mares at the farm at Pleasanton. While the new arrival has not the reputation of the premier stallion, still he has many friends, those who have seen him in his work, and while it is highly probable that Sidney's book will fill very rapidly, still there is every reason to believe that Simmocolon will also have plenty of custom.

Mr. Valensin has tabulated the pedigree of Simmocolon so that breeders can see at a glance what grand blood flows through the veins of the late arrival. Simmons, his sire, is one of the most fashionable sires in Kentucky to-day, and he already has nine or ten in the 2:30 list. Simmocolon has a record of 2:29½, and in making that he actually walked under the wire, his mark being no criterion of his speed. Examine the advertisement and then select what mares you can spare to send to the Valensin Stock Farm stallions.

A Rumor Probably Founded on Fact.

Since the first of last year prominent breeders whose stock farms are in the Eastern States have been snapping up all the stallions in California that money could buy. There is not a horse of any note whatever but what someone has wanted the owner to price, and it has only been by the use of the emphatic NO that any of the better known are still retained in the State. And now comes a rumor, too late for verification this week, that Mr. Guerne of Santa Rosa is in negotiation with parties in Kentucky for the services of Alfred G, and also with the understanding that he shall put a purchasing price on the colt. His record of 2:19¾, made under the most adverse circumstances, stamped him as a horse of rare speed at the trot, and those who witnessed the performance are fully aware that the son of Anteeo can beat his present mark all to pieces.

The story as it is told, is, that J. W. Knox, who took Anteeo to Kentucky, is in negotiation for Alfred G., and that Mr. Guerne has put the price at $25,000. It seems that parties from the same State are also after Redwood, 2:24½, he another son of Anteeo, and the gossipy witch, Dame Rumor, says it is very likely that California will lose the services of both these colts.

Stock Farm Problems.

Care of Brood Mares and Foals.

II.

SOUTHER FARM, SAN LEANDRO, Jan. 1, 1890.

The entire life of a colt may be changed for better or worse by the treatment given the mare when in foal. A reasonable amount of work is a benefit; but overwork or overdriving robs the embryo foal of a part of its life. At least two months rest should be given before the time the mare is due to foal.

The surroundings of a pregnant mare have considerable influence on the future of the foal. The best and strongest children come from happy marriages of healthy people; and the best colts may reasonably be expected from well selected mares that are well fed and sheltered. Keep them happy, if good care, feed, and shelter will do it, and the strength and vigor of the new born foals will well repay the work.

If the weather is pleasant and the nights are not too cold a mare may foal out of doors as well as anywhere else; but as mares should foal as near the first of the year as possible, and as our beautiful winter and spring climate may be broken in upon by storms, good shelter should be provided. Last season my brood mares were kept in boxstalls twelve feet wide and sixteen feet long; although these proved satisfactory, I am now building a row of boxstalls which will be sixteen feet square, with a paddock sixteen feet wide and twenty-four feet long to each stall. This gives plenty of room, and the paddocks are good places for the colts to stay until they get the full use of their legs, when they may be turned out if the weather is pleasant and the feed good. Colts should be kept on level ground for a couple of months; after that nothing does them more good than a reasonable amount of hill-climbing, which hardens their legs and feet wonderfully.

Watch every mare and colt, and if either is not thriving take them up and give extra food—bran with ground barley or crushed oats makes fine milk food. Unless alfalfa fields are at hand the long dry summer almost invariably tells on both mare and colt. When it does, put them in at night, give mixed feed and feed again in the morning before turning out. The colt soon finds out what the soft feed is for, and when weaned will take all the comfort it can in a well filled feed box, forgetting in short order the loss of its mother's milk. This greatly reduces the chances of any set-backs at the time of weaning, when many a good colt loses several months of growth.

Colts must be watched, and watched carefully and systematically. Every colt that dies may be considered to use up the amount it would sell for when grown. A stock farm does not feel the feed and care of one colt, and the mares and stallions must be cared for anyway. Then the colt that dies may be the best one on the ranch and the one that would make his family famous—if he only lived. Death is thoroughly impartial and comes to every farm sooner or later, but it comes the more often to where it is invited by carelessness, poor food, lack of shelter and general neglect.

As a friend of mine once said, there are only two satisfactory ways of raising horses. One is the range, where the stock have never know shelter, and the colts grow up after the manner of goats. This range stock is useful on street cars, butcher carts and delivery wagons, but is practically worthless when safety and steadiness are required without working to death to get these qualities. These horses sell cheap, but can be raised at a very small cost, and the business is profitable in the right place and under good management; but there is very little middle ground that can safely be used between the range system and the good care required to bring up large, honest and safe track, road and family horses.

Mares accustomed to warm stables cannot be turned loose on rocky hills in cold and storms and thrive, nor can they begin to produce the colts they should and would produce, under proper care. The colt has an awful lot to do with the making of the horse—neglect its mother, neglect the foal in the early spring and at weaning time let it rustle for a living on goat pastures during its first winter and you may raise a second quality street car horse if it doesn't die. Nothing but a wonderful triumph of individual greatness over unfortunate surroundings will ever make it anything better.

GILBERT TOMPKINS.

The Talbot Bros. have christened the sister to Lioness, Lena C; the sister to Miss Motley, Miss Hawkins. Bruins is a brother to Bay Ridge; Mountjoy, a half brother to Mount Lebanon is by Pontiac.

THE KENNEL

Dog owners are requested to send for publication the earliest possible notices of whelps, sales, names claimed, presentations and deaths in their kennels, in all instances writing plainly names of sire and dam and of grandparents, colors, dates and breed.

Quarterly Meeting of the Executive Committee of the American Kennel Club, Held at 44 Broadway, New York.

NEW YORK, Dec, 10, 1889.

The meeting was called to order at 1:15 P. M., Vice-President Terry in the chair.

Present: Associates, Dr. Perry; Philadelphia Kennel Club, J. H. Winslow; Southern Field Trial Club, J. L. Anthony; Great Dane Club, G. Muss-Arnolt; Michigan Kennel Club, J. M. Taylor; Westminster Kennel Club, T. H. Terry; Collie Club of America, G. B. Cromwell; St. Paul Kennel Club, A. D. Lewis; Mascoutah Kennel Club, J. Mortimer; American Spaniel Club, J. Watson; New England Kennel Club, F. B Fay; New Jersey Kennel Club, A. C. Wilmerding; Fox Terrier Kennel Club, W. Rutherford; Beagle Club, H. F. Schellhass.

Minutes of the previous meeting read and approved.

The Secretary's report was read as follows by the Secretary:

To the Delegates of the American Kennel Club—Gentlemen:—Since my last report I have received an application from the Continental Kennel Club of Denver, Colorado, for admission to this Association. This application was duly forwarded and received in accordance with the rule laid down in your Constitution, and said applicant is eligible to membership and is hereby recommended. As this Club held its first Bench Show December 5th, and has complied with all the requirements of our rules, I would respectfully recommend the adoption of a resolution at this meeting by which the awards made at said show shall be recognized by the American Kennel Club. At the last meeting of this club the application of the California Kennel Club was laid on the table until your Secretary could correspond with the Pacific Kennel Club on the expediency of admitting another member from San Francisco. Your Secretary mailed communications to both the Committee of the California Kennel Club and the Secretary of the Pacific Kennel Club, to which he received in due course a reply from the latter, which will be laid before you at this meeting.

The Brooklyn Kennel Club was promptly notified of their rejection at our last meeting, and upon its order the dues forwarded to me with the application was returned, and the receipt for the same is on file in this office. The Southern California Kennel Club was duly notified of its election to membership, and of the fact that the awards at its show held prior to its admission would not be recognized, to which no reply has been received from any of its officers, but under date of December 6th President Belmont, Jr., forwarded me a communication from Mr. J. B. Martin of San Francisco, an exhibitor at said show, asking this club to reconsider its action, so far as the recognition of the awards is concerned, upon the ground that as the show was advertised to be held under A. K. C. rules, many entries were made by exhibitors from a great distance, expecting that wins would count, and that the action of this club is a hardship to innocent parties. And further, such action on the part of the American Kennel Club would encourage and assist dog shows on the Pacific Coast. This matter is now before you for further action if you deem it advisable. The special committee on the "revision of the rules," appointed at the last meeting, completed its labors and published its report and recommendations in the November Gazette. In this connection I would advise you that Mr James L. Anthony was appointed on said committee in the place of Mr. F. R. Hitchcock, who resigned on account of absence from the city. A communication from the German Mastiff or Great Dane Club of America, submits a copy of its Rule 29 as follows: "This Club adopts the Standard of points and the scale of measurements as approved September 4, 1889, as the correct standard and scale of points for judging in this country, and this club will not, through its membership, exhibit German Mastiff or Great Dane dogs at bench shows, unless they are to be judged by standard points and scale of values as adopted by this club." The German Mastiff or Great Dane Club requests the American Kennel Club to take action in this matter. The members feel that their standard is correct, and in order to make it effective in this country would respectfully ask this club to adopt the same for the judging of this breed of dogs at all shows held by members of the American Kennel Club. I have received from Dr. J. Frank Perry notice of proposed amendments to Article IV of the Constitution, and published same in the November issue of the American Kennel Gazette. It will be submitted for your action at this meeting. Charges have been preferred by Mr. Lorenzo Daniels against Mr. William Graham in the matter of the St. Bernard dog Visp II. Mr. Daniels claims that Mr. Graham misrepresented the dog, and owing to such misrepresentation said Daniels was put to an expense that should in his opinion be paid by Graham. In a letter following said charges Daniels states that he can produce witnesses to testify to the above mentioned misrepresentation. I also received a letter from Mr. Graham requesting the return of all papers deposited in this office as part of the testimony in a previous case between these gentlemen respecting the dog Visp II. This correspondence will be submitted to you at this meeting. Under the provision of Article XVIII of the Constitution, the annual dues of active members must be paid at or before January 1st of each year, under penalty of forfeiture of all right to representation in this club; and such delinquents may be suspended or dropped from the roll. I would respectfully request this meeting to adopt a resolution delegating the power to the Advisory Committee to suspend or drop such clubs as may be in arrears on January 2d next, if in the judgment of said committee it should be deemed proper. Your Secretary would recommend and urge the adoption of a resolution at this meeting, whereby the American Kennel Club shall donate at each show held by its members in the year 1890 a special prize, consisting of a *complete set of the Stud books*, to be competed for by members of the Specialty Clubs that are members in good standing of the American Kennel Club, and to be given to the best kennel of four owned by one exhibitor. The choice of club, to which this special shall be first awarded, to be determined by its date of membership in the American Kennel Club; that is, the oldest specialty member to compete at the first bench show of 1890, and as the shows progress the special to be designated according to seniority of membership.

As Treasurer of this club, I would say that I could see no good reason why I should depart from my usual custom in presenting the Treasurer's report and will submit the usual one, showing the gross amounts received and disbursed and the balance on hand, but would ask the adoption of a resolution at this meeting, directing the publication of a detailed financial statement of the club for the year ending December 31, 1889, and to appear in the Kennel Gazette of January, 1890. In conclusion, I have to advise you that I am just in receipt of the resignation of the Fort Schuyler Kennel Club of Utica, N. Y., which will be submitted to you for action. And by the same mail I received the application of the Duquesne Kennel Club of Pittsburg, Pa., for admission as an active member. The application enclosed the necessary papers and annual dues in proper form, and the club is eligible to membership. As this application did not reach me until 5 o'clock this day, that portion of the rule requiring it to be filed at this office at least ten days previous to election has not been complied with. I submit this application with the above remarks. Respectfully submitted,

A. P. VREDENBURGH, Secretary.

Adopted.

The Treasurer's report was read as follows:

NEW YORK, December 18, 1889.

The Treasurer begs to report as follows:

Receipts from all sources from January 11th to date	$7,649.41
Expenses for same period	6,482.30
Balance on hand	$1,167.11

Respectfully submitted,

A. P. VREDENBURGH, Treasurer.

Adopted.

Mr. Anthony—In connection with the recommendation made by the Secretary, I would like to offer, if it is in order at the present time, before any other business is proceeded with, the resolution that he has embodied in his report, namely, that he be required to prepare and publish in the January Gazette, a detailed statement of the financial condition of this club, and of every account upon his book, showing exactly the sources of revenue derived and the expenditures, on account not only of the club, but the Stud Book and all other accounts that the Secretary and Treasurer has charge of. I sincerely hope the resolution will prevail, because we desire the public and every delegate here to know exactly what has been done this year. I am at liberty to say to you, because I have examined the accounts, that after the items have been charged to their proper account, there is shown a surplus, a thing that I do not believe has been accomplished before by any club under similar circumstances.

The report of the Advisory Committee was read and adopted, and is as follows:

MEETING ADVISORY COMMITTEE, DECEMBER 19, 1889.

Present: T. H. Terry, Dr J. F. Perry, J. L. Anthony. Absent: A Belmont, Jr., J. S. Wise.

Meeting called to order at 11 o'clock. Mr. Terry in the chair.

In the matter of American Pet-Dog Club, the Secretary having advised us that at a meeting of said club, it was voted to abolish the entire list of dogs as now designated as Pet Dogs in their list. On motion said club was recommended for election.

In the matter of the non-payment of the prizes by the Albany Kennel Club, the Secretary was ordered to suspend said club, and to notify the officers that if the several amounts now due exhibitors are not paid within 30 days, that the penalty under Rule 28 will be enforced.

In the matter of the charge made by Andrew Laidlaw against H. P. Rennie, the society was ordered to notify said Rennie, that if proper explanation or defense be not made or the matter satisfactorily adjusted between the complainant and defendant within 60 days, the prayer of the petitioner will be granted.

In the matter of the appeal of Jas. Watson against the action of the Rochester Kennel Club in not allowing the protest against the entry of the collie Metchley Surprise in the challenge class, was laid over until such time as Mr. Watson produces evidence to sustain his appeal.

In the matter of Mr. Huntington's resolution asking the A. K. C. to pay the travelling expenses of their associate delegates to and from meetings, it was resolved that said resolution be referred back to the full ex committee of the A. K. C., to be acted upon by them.

The following resolution was offered and adopted:

Whereas evidence has been received from Mr. Wm. Graham, informing this club that Mr. L. Daniels has failed to pay the amount due said Graham as per decision of this committee of June 10, 1889, amounting to $50.10.

Resolved, that Mr. Lorenzo Daniels be and hereby is suspended. That he be given 60 days within which to pay the award as made by this committee to Mr. Graham; that if said award be not paid and evidence of said payment is not furnished this committee on or before the expiration of said 60 days, said Daniels shall be disqualified.

(Signed) T. H. TERRY.
J. FRANK PERRY.
J. L. ANTHONY.

Adopted.

The application of the California Kennel Club, which was laid over at the September meeting until advices were received from the Pacific Kennel Club, if in their judgment it would be advisable to admit two clubs from the same city, was submitted. The Secretary read a communication from the Pacific Kennel Club in reply to his communication on the subject, in which it was stated that there being a plan now on foot to consolidate the said California Kennel Club with the Pacific Kennel Club, in the opinion of the members of said Pacific Kennel Club it was deemed that it would be to the best interests of both the American Kennel Club and the doggy matters on the Pacific Coast to delay action on the application of the California Kennel Club, until further notice. On motion said application was laid over for future action, pending advices from the Pacific Kennel Club.

President Belmont Jr. arrived and took the chair.

The report of the Special Committee on Rules was made, and the matter laid on the table for a subsequent action.

Applications from the American Pet Dog Club and the Continental Kennel Club were read by the Secretary, and on motion, both clubs were admitted to membership in the American Kennel Club, and on motion the awards of the show held by the Continental Kennel Club on December 5th, were recognized.

A communication was read from an exhibitor requesting a reconsideration of the action taken at the last meeting in the matter of not recognizing wins at the Southern California Kennel Club Show.

Major Taylor moved to reconsider such action.

Motion lost.

The Secretary then read a communication by Mr. Lorenzo Daniels, preferring charges against Mr. William Graham, in regard to the St. Bernard dog Visp II, Mr. Daniels claiming that Mr. Graham misrepresented the dog, and owing to such misrepresentation, he (Daniels) was put to considerable expense.

On motion of Mr. Anthony the communication of Mr. Daniels was laid on the table.

The following resolution by Dr. Perry was adopted:

Resolved, That attested copies be made of all documentary evidence furnished by William Graham in the case of Lorenzo Daniels, and the original be returned to him, as he has requested.

A communication was read from the Great Dane Club, the Secretary stating that they had furnished a copy of their standard and scale of points adopted by that club, and also a copy of their rules, and that they requested the American Kennel Club to recognize that standard at their show.

Mr. Muss-Arnolt: I offer a resolution that only dogs which shall conform to the standard of the Great Dane Club shall be registered in the Stud Book, regardless of pedigree.

Motion lost.

The request of the Great Dane Club for the American Kennel Club to enforce their standard was refused.

The Secretary called attention to the resolution offered at the last meeting by Mr. Huntington in regard to the American Kennel Club paying the traveling expenses of the associate delegates, which resolution was referred to the Advisory Committee. The Secretary stated that that committee had decided to refer the matter back to the Executive Committee, refering that they should act upon the matter.

Mr. Anthony: It seems to me it would be proper for the Secretary to be instructed to make an appropriation of $100 per annum from money received from the associate members, which amount should be used to pay the expenses of the delegates coming here to attend any meeting on business, and I make a motion to that effect.

Motion seconded and carried.

The President: I think I shall have to leave you shortly, but before I go I should like to bring up a subject that seems to me of some importance. The Kennel Gazette is published under the auspices of the American Kennel Club, but its officers are responsible for it, and the form and the matter has been in a great measure left to their discretion, and they have acted as best they could. There has been some criticism made with respect to the editorials in the Gazette, and that criticism was of such a nature that I thought it best at the time to shoulder the blame personally, so as to put a stop to it, and then refer the matter to you, and ascertain whether in your judgment, it was best to eliminate that feature from the Gazette entirely, or continue it. If you look at the editorials I think you will find that they have never referred to any subject which did not concern the American Kennel Club itself, and I personally have felt that the Gazette ought at times to speak for the American Kennel Club. The Advisory Committee through its meetings, feels the pulse constantly of what is going on, and there are attacks made upon the club, or misinterpretations appear in the public print which the breeder and exhibitor desires to have cleared up. I do not see why it should be necessary for the Secretary or the President, or for any officer of the Kennel Club to go in print over his own signature in the way of sporting papers.

If the subject is to be treated from a club point of view, I don't see why it should not be treated in the Gazette. If other official organs speak for their organizations, I do not see why the Gazette should not. It need not be personal. I don't think any case was personal, although it seems to have been taken so. No names were used. The principle only was treated of, and I should like to ask the delegates for action on the subject. It has not been brought up before the Advisory Committee at all. The subject was discussed by letter to a certain extent, with the members of the Advisory Committee, and also talked over, and some were in favor of continuing the editorials, and others were not; but it was never settled, and really it was not in the province of the Advisory Committee to settle that question. Inasmuch as the matter has been made the subject of discussion, I should like to ask your action on the question, and if you will allow the matter to come up now so I can retire, I shall be obliged to you.

Maj. Taylor—I move, in order to get the views of the delegates here, that the action in this request in the past be approved, and continued in the same line.

Motion carried.

At this point Mr. Terry takes the Chair on the departure of Mr. Belmont.

Mr. Anthony—I move that the Treasurer be requested to make an itemized statement to be published in the January Gazette, showing the receipts and disbursements from all sources, and also showing the amount of credit on each account, the sources from which the revenue was derived—in other words, a complete itemized account, so that anybody who is familiar with figures can take it and see how we stand.

Mr. Watson thought before being published, the account should be carefully examined and verified.

The Secretary suggested that he should make out his statement for the year 1889 for publication, and that the Chair appoint a committee who would endorse on the bottom of his account that they had examined his accounts and found them correct, as stated.

Mr. Anthony—In order to comply with the suggestions made by Mr. Watson and Mr. Vredenburgh, I will add to my motion, that before publication, an auditing committee consisting of Messrs. A. C. Wilmerding, Major Taylor and F. B. Fay be appointed to audit the accounts. I name these gentlemen because they are ex-officio, and I ask that they be appointed to audit the accounts and to state whether they are correct, whether they have been correctly kept, etc.

Motion carried.

A communication was read from the Fort Schuyler Kennel Club, tendering their resignation from the American Kennel Club.

On motion the resignation was accepted.

The Secretary called attention to the recommendation contained in his report in regard to the matter of special prizes to be competed for by members of specialty clubs, and on motion of Mr. Anthony, his recommendation was adopted.

The Bench Show rules, as published in the Gazette, were then read and slightly amended, and on motion adopted.

The following amendment to the Constitution was adopted:

That all articles of the Constitution, and all rules and regulations affecting associate members or referring thereto, be cancelled, and that Article IV. of the Constitution read as follows:

ARTICLE IV.

Section 1—Any person vouched for in writing to the Secretary of the American Kennel Club by not less than two members of any club a member of this association, or by two associate members, shall upon payment of $5 annual dues, and the endorsement of his application by the Presidents of the American Kennel Club and of the associate members, become an associate member and be announced as such in the next issue of the Kennel Gazette.

Sec. 2—An associate member shall be entitled to the Kennel Gazette and Stud Book for one year, and to two free registrations in the Stud Book.

Sec. 3—The annual dues of $5 shall be payable on the first of January of each year to the Secretary of the American Kennel Club, and any person whose dues are not paid on or before January 30th, shall thereby forfeit his right to be included in the list of members eligible for election to office, and to vote for officers for the ensuing year; and if his dues shall remain unpaid at the next annual meeting of the associate members, his name shall be stricken from the roll, provided, however, that upon remitting the $5 dues with an application of membership, he shall be re-instated upon the endorsement of his application by the two Presidents as hereinbefore provided.

Sec. 4—The annual meeting of the associate members shall be held on the day preceding the annual meeting of the American Kennel Club, at which meeting the reports of the retiring officers shall be presented, which together with a copy of the official minutes of the meeting, shall be filed with the Secretary of the American Kennel Club.

Sec. 5—The officers of the Associate members shall be a President, vice-President and Secretary. The President shall be a member of the Advisory Committee. The Associate members shall have the right to be represented by three delegates, to which position the officers may be elected; and for every one hundred members over three hundred, they shall elect an additional delegate.

Sec. 6—No Associate member shall be eligible to hold office or sit as delegate who is a member of any club a member of this Association other than a specialty club.

Sec. 7—That all elections shall be by mail vote, and the annual election of officers and delegates shall be conducted as follows:

On January 21st. of each year the secretary of the American Kennel Club shall forward to each and every associate member in good standing a printed list of all members aligible to hold office, together with an addressed envelope for return, on which the word "vote" is legibly printed or written. The member receiving such printed list shall mark thereon his choice for president, vice-president, and secretary and the delegates to which the club is entitled, in such manner as may be indicated, and return the same in the envelope provided.

Fifteen full days after the mailing of such slips to the associate members the secretary of the American Kennel Club shall in the presence of the presidents of the American Kennel Club and Associate Members, or such person as either of them may deputize to represent him, open all such mail votes, and the result of the election shall be certified to by the three officials present.

Immediately upon the signing of such certificate the secretary of the American Kennel Club shall notify each and every person of his election and also send notice thereof to the president of the associate members.

In the case of a tie vote for any office the tie shall be decided by a majority vote of members present at the annual meeting, and in the event of an officer elected declining to serve, the member receiving the next highest number of votes shall at the annual meeting be declared elected.

Votes for additional members as each quota of one hundred additional members is filled shall be conducted upon the same principle as the annual mail vote for officers and delegates, the vote being taken as soon as the one hundred additional members have qualified. The same rule shall also hold good in event of a vacancy in the ranks of officials or delegates.

Adjourned.

A. P. VREDENBURGH, secretary.

Girls' Dogs.

One of our popular novelists writes up her heroine, a slender sylph of the Big Smoky country, as having for a companion and friend a large, gaunt, yellow dog with knobs for joints and a decided stamp of inferiority in his hulking movements.

This fair young girl, "loves Watch kin behave ez much like folks ez any dog kin," and she pleats his scraggy, yellow ears with as much pride as if he were of nobler blood, while another girl, trim, tailor-made, esthetic, cultured, is pictured in a farther part of the sunny South as tripping forth for her daily walk with two sleek, perfectly-proportioned mastiffs bounding at her side. It may be the Big Smoky girl loves Watch with that feminine sympathy women so often mistake for the nobler fire. It may be she would have a preference for him right under the very noses of the high-bred mastiffs were they her to have and to hold, but depend upon it, when you find a girl owning and caressing a mongrel cur of low degree, there is something soft in that girl's head as well as in her heart, for our girls are looking dogward these days with the eyes of connoisseurs.

They pity the abused and neglected, but when it comes to the point of possession, they are far more critical than boys rejecting the "poor man's dog" and preferring the animal of fine pedigree, beautiful parts and superior intelligence.

Boys are flattered by a dog's devotion, while their sisters love the beautiful and talented in dogs. It may be much after the same fashion that they will make any sacrifice for husbands they can be proud of, and who will serve to make the "other girls" envious.

Our grandmothers, those dear old ladies whose manners and customs are so often held up as a lasting reproach to us, gave their allegiance to lap dogs, insignificant little creatures that knew nothing above dainty bits to eat and an embroidered blanket to keep out the cold.

Is it not a sign of a stronger generation of women that those little dogs are no longer carried about in the pocket, fondled on the best sofa, or led through the streets by a string, but that the noble Newfoundlands, the colossal mastiffs or the graceful hounds have become the pets of the ladies?

Our own Matilda Lotz did not scorn to have herself photographed with her huge St. Bernard, and one of her best pictures is the painting of Offenbach's dogs.

An intelligent girl can judge correctly of the merits of any work of art and she ought to know how to tell a fine horse or a talented dog when she sees it, for truly do they bear the impress of the Divine hand

It is an exploded idea that it is vulgar for a woman to know a spaniel from a poodle, or a pug from a pointer. A woman who does, need not be a hoyden nor what is objectionably called "fast." All our finer judgments are the outgrowth of training.

Then train the girls to know a blooded dog when they see it. Take them to the dog shows, what harm? You take them to see the ballet, do you not?

Only let me beseech you, my dear brethren, to change the name. The man, woman or child who can invent and succeed in fastening upon not only the dog show, but the dog himself a new name shall be worthy a place in history, and some day, perhaps, a corner in Westminster Abbey, for despite our revered Shakespeare's flouting, there is much in a name, especially when it comes fraught with ugly tradition, and you know the dog is spoken of, in both the old and new testaments with abhorrence, being ranked among the unclean beasts, and the Mohammedam could not apply a more opprobrious epithet than "dog," "cur" or "hound."

Let us annihilate the curs, which alas! make up the majority of the canine population and are responsible for the spread of hydrophobia, and fill their places with beautiful dogs for which people will be willing to pay, instead of regarding each new dog as an additional burden to the family, being unwilling to receive him even as a gift.

Were dogs fewer and more precious, how many a boyish heart would be spared the anguish of "drowning the puppies."

When ladies become properly interested in the proper kinds of dogs, there will be less barbarous treatment of ears and tails, which practice is not only inhuman, but often injurious. Dogs are often made deaf from having the ears cropped in fanciful shapes. A lady in a natty little cart drawn by a fine dog, whose pleasure in her service is plainly to be seen, is one of the alluring pictures which we hope will soon materialize into a pleasing reality.

Leibnitz says dogs have been taught to speak. He says he heard a dog in Saxony articulate no less than thirty distinct words.

What a field for woman's tact and patience!

When a dear little pug puppy can be taught to talk, parrots will be banished from the boudoir—harsh voices, dirty ways and all.

Dogs have held their own in history. Alexander the Great built a city in honor of a dog. Emperor Hadrian buried a dog with imposing and solemn rites. Pythagoras caused a dog to be held to the mouths of the dying, saying, as a departing human soul must enter into some animal, a dog was the most worthy to receive it and to perpetuate its virtues.

Pliny wrote of people in Africa who elected a dog as their king, and were governed entirely by motions of his body which they interpreted by signs. Fancy being ruled by the wag of a dog's tail!

The favorite lap-dog of Mary Queen of Scots accompanied her to the scaffold, and continued to caress the body after the head had been cut off. The poor little creature died of grief a few days afterward.

Sir Walter Scott sings, in beautiful verse, the praise of a faithful dog found after three months, worn almost to a skeleton, still guarding the remains of his master, who had fallen over a precipice in the Helvellyn mountains.

The Dog-star is said to have been named from a star which appeared just before the inundations of the Nile as a signal to remove the flocks to higher ground.

The Romans fattened the dog for the table, and many people in Asia, Africa and Armenia still raise him expressly for food. Carts are drawn in Paris, sledges in Lapland, and timber in Newfoundland by dogs, and until forbidden by law, hauling was done by them to quite an extent in London.

In large cities valuable dogs are never safe from thieves, who break through and steal with an eye to large rewards. Narcotic balls thrown to the dogs soon silence objections.

One of the cleverest schemes for defeating the aims of the Pound took form in Virginia City, Nev., not long since. The arm of the law in a spasmodic attack of attention to duty, gathered the untagged dogs together in a large shed, or rather he paid the enterprising small boy (not of the county treasury) thirty-five cents per head for victims. When dogs became scarce on the streets, one youth let down a neatly sawed panel from the back of the shed, coaxed out and secured half a dozen of the poor, half-starved beasts with bits of meat, and promptly sent them around to the front by his "pardner," to be sold to the dozing official. The plan repeated at judicious intervals robbed Peter but paid Paul quite handsomely.

MISS KELLY.

December 31, 1889.

Visits.

California Spaniel Kennels (H. P. Rennie, Oakland) liver and white cocker bitch Fanny (Sprig—Nellie) to owner's black cocker stud dog Giffee, Sept. 24th, 1889.

Whelps.

California Spaniel Kennels, (H. P. Rennie, Oakland), liver and white cocker bitch Fanny (Sprig—Nellie), seven, six dogs and one bitch; two since dead. Color, two black dogs, one black and tan, one red dog and one red bitch, by California Spaniel Kennels stud dog "Giffee," November 14th, 1889.

Tigress, pure fawn colored mastiff bitch pop with black points whelps July 7, 1889, by mastiff dog Dick, A. K. A. (10549) and Juno, to Dr. J. H. Bayliss, San Bernardino.

Sale.

California Spaniel Kennels (H. P. Rennie, Oakland), has sold:

Red cocker dog puppy, by black cocker dog Giffee and Woodstock Belle, to Echo Spaniel Kennels, (Dr. A. C. Davenport, Stockton.)

Mr. L. L. Campbell has sold Irish red setters, whelped August 28, '89, by Barrymore, (Elcho Jr.—Maid) ex Belle C. (Mike—Lady Elcho T).

To Mr. W. B. Lafferty, San Francisco, a bitch.
To Dr. C F. Grant, Healdsburg, a dog.
To J. J. Bowen, San Francisco, a dog.
To R. J. Stenson, San Francisco, a bitch.
To George March, San Francisco, a bitch.

Names Claimed.

Echo Spaniel Kennels (Dr. A. C. Davenport, Stockton) claims the name of "Red Robin" for red cocker dog puppy whelped September 16, 1889, sired by Giffee and out of Woodstock Belle.

Mr. George March, San Francisco, claims the name Jennie for an Irish red setter bitch, whelped Aug. 28th by Barrymore—Belle.

Mr. R. J. Stenson claims the name Lady Mack for litter sister to preceding.

Mr. W. B. Lafferty claims the name Nora for litter sister to preceding

Dr. C. F. Grant claims the name Lou G. for litter brother to preceding.

Mr. L. L. Campbell claims the name L. B. Cooper for litter brother to preceding.

Two weeks only to field trial time, the best event of the year. The round trip to Bakersfield can be made for a fare and a third, the Southern Pacific Company having conceded so much to the club. To secure the reduced rates certificates must be procured from the Secretary of the club, at 313 Bush street, San Francisco, and presented to the ticket agents at the various starting points.

The Gopher Hole Dog.

Those who have had experience in sending out dogs for training, may recall a dozen form of weakness in their animals, as stated by breakers, but it has been left for Mr Ned Bosqui, of this city, to discover an erroneous impression in a dog returned as yard broken, which differs materially from any recorded hitherto. The dog had been eleven months in the hands of a trainer, and was then handed over to Mr. Bosqui at the trainer's instance as yard broken, and broken to the gun within the meaning of the terms "yard" and "broken" as ordinarily construed. Mr. Bosqui was very proud of his pointer, a handsome white and lemon, of rare breeding, and fine form, and soon after receiving the animal took it out to show his friends, Mr. Will Kittle and Harry Golcher, how elegantly the beast could perform. It ranged tastily over a lot of ground, flushed as many birds as any plug, and finally exhausted the patience of the owner, who shot at one of the birds flushed by the dog. The high-headed, free-sterned thing of beauty, was transformed in an instant to an apologetic, sneaky, slinking caricature of pointer style, which speeded like a ghost until it was hidden by cover. The owner strolled in that direction a little way, failed to discover his dog and was about to give up the search, when Mr. Kittle called his attention to something which looked like a dog's tail projecting from the earth a short distance away. Closer examination showed that Mr. Bosqui's fine pointer, in his eagerness to get away from the gun, had attempted to go down a gopher hole. The dog was soothed and encouraged and at last ranged freely until Mr. Bosqui again discharged his gun, when the gopher hole was again sought and no art could induce the dog to leave his shelter.

Mr. Geo. T. Allender left for Bakersfield on December 26th with nine dogs, of which five will go in the field trials. They all looked well and keen.

Mr. C. H. Kobicke of this city has sent his imported bloodhounds to Mr. F. L. Wilson, master of Mr Murphy's kennel of foxhounds, near Gilroy. Mr. Wilson is just the man to enter the hounds upon game or to train them to trail human scent. We hope they may thrive.

Messrs. Nelson, Aldrich and Pyle, chosen to judge the coming field trials, have accepted and will serve, bar the act of God or public enemies. We commend them and their judgments to the candid, considerate reception to which the honor and painstaking of the men entitle them, and hope the judging may cover all of the points suggested in the rules.

There are men and men, reporters and reporters, kennel editors and kennel editors, but there is only one Hammond, and we hope he may flourish like a bay tree and make Forest and Stream just what it should be in a doggy way. Friend Waters of the American Field calls a spade a spade, and when he had to describe the absurd judging at the Central Field Trials he did so in fervid terms, but Major Hammond damns the judges beyond redemption in this fashion:

"This was the last heat of the preliminary series, and the judges, in selecting the dogs to remain in, performed their duties in a praiseworthy manner, keeping in some that had shown considerable merit."

BILLIARDS.

Frank Ives does not believe he has been treated right by Frank Maggioli, who is now in Chicago, because the latter has seen fit to challenge him for a contest for the light weight medal which Carter won in the tournament held at the Madison Street Theater last fall, at balkline billiards, and which was forfeited to Ives by Carter. Ives claims that Maggioli challenged him at a time when he (Ives) has entered in two tournaments at balkline billiards, and has posted a forfeit of $500 to play in both New York and Chicago, with $7,500 in sight in prize money, and that he is now called upon by Maggioli to play for $250 a side at fourteen inch balkline billiards, and on an entirely different cushion than the one on which the two big tournaments are to be played. Ives further states he is so sure he can beat Maggioli that he will play a match with him within two weeks after he has played in the Chicago tournament, and that he will concede Maggioli 200 in 1,000 points up at eight inch balkline billiards for any part of $2,500 a side.

A correspondent of a contemporary, referring to the coming tournaments and the difficulty with the experts, writes as follows: "Professional billiard experts are essentially as thankless as they are ungrateful. They are selfish, jealous and vindictive; integrity and honor rarely, if ever, play any part in their professional life, and the story of woe is written on every billiard manufacturing firm that has ever depended on their friendship and sincerity." Whew!

Harvey McKenna, the phenomenal Western billiard player, died at the New York Hospital three weeks ago of consumption. Mr. McKenna was only 27 years old, but had already made a name for himself as a player of extraordinary ability.

Capt. B. E. Harris, the old time horseman, is an enthusiast at billiards and he takes especial delight in "downing" any of his old friends Cap never plays outside of his own residence, where he has an elegant Strable table, and many are the large runs that have been made on it,

The gentlemen who contributed toward the McCleery Christmas present were:—

P. W. Nahl.	A. Englehart.
H. Rothschild.	E. J. Baldwin.
F. A. Waterhouse.	P. A. Giannini.
E. Isaacs.	J. A. Crawford.
A. H Unruh.	Geo. S. Ingersoll.
H. H. Briggs.	J. W. Orndorff.
W. H. Parks.	R. Neumann.
C. G Jillson.	James P. Kerr.
Col. W. H. Barnes.	M. Heilbronner.

Brunswick, Balke & Collender Co.

Some persons have an idea that horsemen are of no account except when handling equines. Any one can have that notion disabused by watching Major Du Bois of Denver and L. A. Davies handle billiard cues. Both of them are experts and the Palace Hotel is frequently the scene of their contests.

THE GUN.

Taxing Deer.

EDITOR BREEDER AND SPORTSMAN:—Last week the Examiner published an absurd paragraph to the effect that, in violation of the Game law, at a butcher's shop on Market street, was the carcass of a deer dressed for the market and on sale; and that the deer was killed in Sonoma Country, not in violation of the law, but that it had been supplied by a man living in Sonoma who had authority of law for the out-of-season killing. It was thus: This man, every year, in giving in his assessment to the County Assesser, made statement to the ownership of "seventeen head of deer." The particulars as to where the deer were to be found were mentioned. The Assessor did not exact statement of locality. The man made no exact statement. All he claimed was that every year he returned statement of "seventeen head of deer" in his annual assessment, and paid thereupon—privileged, of course, to kill his deer, as he might see fit to kill his chickens or his turkeys at any time of year.

I have remarked that the story was absurd, but this is not quite enough. It is worse, and in a measure scandalous. The County Assessor is involved. To do that which is imputed in the paragraph on the part of that officer, would cause him to be regarded by any who do not know him as an incompetent in office.

William Longmore is County Assessor of Sonoma. He possesses the qualifications for office set forth by Thomas Jefferson—he is honest; he is competent. He has the respect and confidence of every citizen of Sonoma, without regard to difference of opinion on political matters. He is a faithful public servant, an estimable citizen. Assessor Longmore has not, in his term of office, accepted the assessment of deer, nor have any of his deputies in office done so. The proposition is too preposterous for consideration. Only the gullible will give credence to the story in the Examiner; but as it is the unexpected which always happens, it seems to be, nowadays, the gullible who make up a considerable sum of public sentiment. It is against the tendency of this sort of public sentiment that this communication is directed.

As to the game law this:—No pet deer are owned in Sonoma County, in defiance of the law. Assessor Longmore is a faithful steward of his official duties and a strict observer of the laws in protection of game, and in Sonoma "the goose hangs nigh" in the season.

ONE OF OLD SONOMA.

Payne Shafter's Idea.

EDITOR BREEDER AND SPORTSMAN:—We have had rain, rain, rain, until the reign of King Pluvius has been complete. Swollen streams, sodden plowed lands, slides on the county roads, all attest the fury of the storms. The hand of man is stayed; when the storm king rides the blast, he sits by his fire place, speculates and wonders at the fury of the storm, or airs his opinions

"When village statesmen talk with looks profound,
And news much older than their "beer" goes round."

As a rule, with the first heavy rains, salmon run up the streams to spawn. Boys and men with guns and spears patrol the banks, and what few eggs the salmon "deposit in the bank" they do on the sly; in the shades of night or very early in the morning. Coons, four-footed, patrol the streams by night for the eggs which they dearly love. King-fishers and cranes watch their chance to destroy the germs of commencing fish, and altogether they (the fish) have a hard time. Never have coons, foxes, wild-cats and coyotes been so abundant as now. Why? I will tell you.

The American pioneer has moved further away from settlements or grown old, like his pack of hounds. The demands of his family keep him busy to earn the fulfillment of prayer, this day our daily bread. On Point Reyes, next the ocean, hardly a hare or quail is left by the ravages of the coyote The cunning bandits often attack and kill freshly born calves. Now what will the result be so near San Francisco from the depredations of men and wild animals. Both of these are after food animals. The average hunter from the city has no time nor inclination to hunt bear, panther, wild-cats, foxes and coons; he wants roast duck, broiled quail, snipe, etc.; so do the predatory wild animals. Result in a few years without fearless, wise protection, no game birds, nor fish for the true sportsman who, out of what he earns, is willing to put up a reasonable amount to protect the wild game which gives him an outing with his dog and gun.

We are all children of the giant Anteus. We belong to mother earth, and must for health and strength of mind and body, leave the ease, surfeit and confinement of the great cities for the green fields, the ozone, oxygen, plain, wholesome food and early hours of the country. The freedom of America, the cry against restriction is all *rot* (excuse the expression) (*ne plus ultra*).

Liberty is not license, but the right to do as anyone chooses so long as he does not infringe on the rights of anyone else. Look at the Golden Gate Park (San Francisco). It is for the *free* enjoyment of the public. How free? Why so free as to keep and preserve it and its possessions for the use, not abuse, of all mankind. You may not drive very fast in the park; you must not pull flowers, nor drive upon the grass; you may not *shoot* the deer, quail, nor other wild animals; and still this park is for the free use of the people. Take the police away and let the dear people, "without restriction," have the free use of the park, and Sodom and Gomorrah would be a paradise compared with these results. Self control makes good and great men and women, and wise protection fosters all our industries, preserves our animal life, and in truth, makes us a nation.

P. J. SHAFTER.

With its current issue the Kern County Californian published at Bakersfield, owned by A. C. Maude and edited by C. E. Sherman, enters upon its twenty-fifth volume, twenty-fifth year, and the tenth year of its present management. The owner is a brisk, progressive business man, who makes a newspaper that people must have, by employing the most brilliant and conscientious editorial assistant and staff that money will procure. We wish lots of good wishes to the sterling journal and all connected with it.

Mr. Fred Watson of Colusa has had a challenge standing for a month to shoot any man in Colusa or Sutter Counties (John Clough preferred), any or all of the following matches at live pigeons for $100 a side.

25 pair double birds, 18 yards rise.

50 single birds, 21 yards rise.

California State Sportsman's Rules or 50 birds Hurlingham Rules.

Hurlingham match at 30 yards with 12 guage guns.

$40 forfeit to be put up with any reliable sportsman in Colusa.

Introduction of European Game.

I plead guilty to being a crank on at least one subject, viz., the introduction of foreign game. It seems to me that the New England States are neglecting so long, what must surely come to pass in time—the importation of hardy non-migratory birds and beasts, says a correspondent, writing to an exchange. And why should we not cull the cream from every land, so far as the circumstances of the case will permit? Is not Europe indebted to America for one of the most delicious birds that fly, the turkey? True, as we see the Thanksgiving gobbler strutting around the barnyard shortly before his untimely decease, we realize that now, however imposing in his splendor, he is, in many sections, no longer a game bird. Nevertheless, he was a very worthy gift from the New West to the Old East, and merits a return in kind.

The peculiarities of our climate, with its sudden and savage changes from balmy springlike weather to a temperature that makes the benumbed brain think almost impatiently of the practical advantages of Tophet as a winter retreat, renders the introduction of only the most hardy game desirable. Giving due weight to these considerations, I have narrowed the list of possible additions to our fauna, to the following animals and game birds: Beasts—wild boar, fallow deer, roe deer. Birds—capercailie, black game, partridge, ditto red leg, hazel hen, willow grouse, pheasant. This is but a small list, but what an increase it would make to our scanty total of non-migratory game.

We have now in New England practically the deer, ruffed grouse, American hare and fox. If we could double our available quadrupeds and increase the varieties of birds at present existing eight times, it would surely be a noble result. All these creatures are non-migratory, except that they, following the promptings of instinct, shift their ground a little with the seasons, seeking shelter and food adapted to the time of year, but to no greater extent than do our indiginous deer and grouse.

I shall briefly consider in turn the claims of each of the above enumerated beasts and birds to American citizenship, beginning with the fallow deer.

THE FALLOW DEER.—(*Cervus dama.*)

In olden days, when Robin Hood and his "merrie men" were making free with the deer in the royal forest of Sherwood, their game was the fallow buck. It was undoubtedly once a fine game animal, although at present, owing to confinement in paddocks and parks of limited area, it is hardly considered as such in England to-day. But I would risk a small sum that once this deer was acclimatized in New England, with scope to run, and increase, and multiply, he would become the sport-furnishing animal his ancestors were in the days of Cedric the Saxon.

In weight the bucks run from 100 lbs. to 120 lbs., although one was killed at Eastwell in Kent, in 1863, that tipped the beam at 176 lbs This was, however, an extraordinary weight. In Europe a fallow deer to one acre of rich grass land is considered a correct allowance, provided no sheep are permitted upon the same ground. Horses and cattle do little harm, as they feed on the coarser herbage rejected by the deer.

In stocking a ground a proportion of one-third bucks and two-thirds does has proved satisfactory when tried. The lay of the land must be carefully considered, as upon it the success of the effort will hinge. Shelter is necessary, even in England, hence it is hardly likely the deer would succeed north of Boston or away from the sea. Further south, say about the latitude of Maryland and Virginia, the climate would appear admirably adapted to the habits of the fallow deer.

Outside of the natural food produced by the ground the deer inhabit, it is well in hard weather to provide them with some extra food (this is supposing there is a very large stock for the size of the ground), and of artificial foods, hay is the best, say three tons to 100 deer per winter, and, after hay, the branches of deciduous trees cut down in the summer and dried with the leaves on like hay, and stacked in the forest, makes an excellent and cheap winter feed. It has been found best to surround each rick with a deer proof fence, which can be removed when the season has arrived to give artificial food.

"Ory" does are in season from November 1st to February 1st, and the bucks from July 15th to October 1st; hence it can be seen how the importation of this deer would extend the legal period for the use of the rifle.

The doe brings forth her young in the month of June, and in two days they can follow her about. The bucks lose their horns in April and run in October. The fallow buck never exceeds 20 years of age, and rarely lives as long unless carefully fed and sheltered in a paddock. The venison is delicious, as I can state from personal experience, having in years gone by, through the kindness of the "ranger", often partaken of a haunch from the royal herd that graze round Hampton Court Palace

It will be found that this deer will succeed best in a broken country, variety of surface being necessary. Wood and old pastures should succeed one another on a typical fallow deer range. Make it a rule never to kill a deer that is under six years of age, nor to allow them to live much after nine years if good venison is desired. New blood is requisite every few years in a closely preserved herd, but would probably not be required under the conditions that exist in this country.

The habit of this deer is to cease feeding about 11 A. M. and lie down in the open. About 5 o'clock P. M. they resume feeding, and feed all night long.

The fallow deer are gregarious, but the bucks and does keep apart except during the pairing season, and during cold weather when they assemble promiscuously.

It is stated by good authority that when the teams of experts that are to tour the country reach San Francisco, Messrs. Budd and Stice will shoot a match at 35 live birds each, and Messrs. McMurchy and Heikes at 25 birds each. The first of the inter-team matches will be shot at Dayton, Ohio, on January 27th.

The most pleasurable moments vouchsafed to us are those passed in listening to tales of sport in earlier days, from the lips of such vivid narrators as our friend Mr. John K. Orr, and men of like tastes.

The other day while Mr. Orr was sitting in our office, the name of Mr. C. S. Schenck was mentioned, and with the mention of the "Boss," Mr. Orr's face lighted up and he said: "Mention of that finest of shots and most thorough of sportsmen brings to mind a day we spent together when three hundred sharp-tailed grouse were bagged. It was in 1866, when on a visit to Portland, Oregon, that myself and "Boss" were invited out to the Dalles for a day's sport. We went and found the rest of the party ready, Messrs. Will Bradford, George Naggs, Frank Dodge, Lawrence E. Coe, Victor Trevet and Mr. Buchanan. Starting early one day in August, we drove out to Thirteen Mile Creek, and Frank Dodge, "Boss" Schenck and I were put down about three miles from Modes House, where we were to camp.

We shot along the creek lined by willows, and when we reached the house had about a hundred of the sharp-tails. I was using a little 13-bore Westley Richard muzzle loader, three drams of powder, and an ounce of sixes. With that outfit I scored forty seven grouse in fifty-one shots. Next day five of the party began shooting at early dawn and at three o'clock returned to camp and counted heads, the score being three hundred and twelve grouse, all fine fat birds.

The plan was for half of the party to walk along each side of a willow-lined creek and take the birds as they flushed from the trees or from corn stalks standing along the fields on either side.

The grouse would break cover with a rush that was embarrassing, but were easy marks after a few had been knocked over. In those days "Boss" Schenck had no equal on the Pacific Coast as a shot unless it was Tom Estey, of Nicasio.

As the birds were killed they were drawn, stuffed with dry grass and hung to the willows, to be gathered by the wagon later in the day. In the afternoon on returning to camp a royal dinner was prepared, Mr. Coe furnishing a pan of crisp brook trout, which together with unlimited baked grouse, and such little tumblers of something as "Boss" Schenck is famous for, made mere existence a delight.

After dinner the grouse were festooned about the wagon in half dozens, and when the Dalles were reached a large portion were distributed to acquaintances, the remainder going to friends in Portland. The grouse could then be found in packs of two or three hundreds, but now one is lucky if on that ground a day's tramping returns a dozen birds."

Duck shooters might as well clean up their guns and stow them away for the season. The rain it raineth every day and the duck disperseth so variously that the man who encompasses more than a half dozen in a day is thereby marked as of rare ability.

The additions recently made to Messrs. Clabrough, Golcher & Co.'s store-rooms at 630-632 Montgomery Street, city, have placed the firm in a most advantageous position, both as to carrying increased and more varied stock, and as to handling their very large and rapidly increasing trade. The latest feature of the store is a miniature gymnasium, fitted to show the exhaustive line of athletic appliances carried by the house. The idea is a brilliant one, and the room affords interesting study. The new lines of fishing tackle just beginning to come, are of such superb quality as even the Golcher's, for years the best tackle purveyors in America, have not had in other years. In fine gut and trout flies particularly, there is so much to be seen that hours do not suffice to exhaust interest.

The gun material of the firm remains at the high standard fixed many years ago by Mr. Clabrough and that prince of gun makers, William Golcher, now at rest.

On January 18th and 19th, at Traver, Tulare County, there will be held a real old-time shooting tournament. Live bird shooting, rifle shooting, bow and arrow shooting and everything else is to go. The time is just that at which the field trial men will be travelling toward Bakersfield, and President P. C. Jurgens of the Traver Gun Club especially invites the doggy men to visit the tournament, the invitation being joined in by Mr. E. Miles, the Secretary of the club.

This is the Manchester, Eng., idea: "A party of sportsmen set off from Bourbon, U. S. A., for a ten day's shoot, and being partial to the drink of their native town, took a good supply of whisky with them. But, unfortunately, the whisky gave out at the end of the fifth day, and great was the distress which was suffered by the gallant sportsmen. However, they determined not to return until the expiration of the ten days, and, when they did return, eager was the rush to the saloon, and loud the call for drinks. Then came the story of the privations they had undergone, when a stranger interrupted the narrative.

"Guess," said he, "you couldn't have suffered much. Why, there was a river alongside you all the time."

"Oh," replied one of the sportsmen, "don't show your derned ignorance. How do you expect a man to pay any attention to his personal cleanliness when he is suffering from such an infernal thirst?"

Says the Kentucky Stock Farm: It is worth a visit to W. H. Wilson's Abdallah Park to see the order and system with which all the operations of the farm are conducted. His office contains all the appliances for the rapid despatch of the vast business of the farm. On entering it the first picture that greets the eye is a portrait of Mr. L. J. Rose, the great California breeder. The walls are covered with handsome and finely executed pictures of distinguished horses. A telegraphic instrument connecting with the Western Union lines is one of the recent additions to the facilities in his office for the despatch of business.

The following statement comes from the Express, published at Terre Haute, the home of the unbeaten Axtell: "Our California friends are having a terrible time in their endeavor to beat the stallion record set by Axtell. When the weather was good their horses did not have the speed, but the weather is bad. Never mind, we will give you a new record next year, and your tracks will have to be made more like a toboggan slide than they are now to beat it." It was a fortunate thing for the Terre Haute reporters that Axtell was taken there to winter, as every third item in the local department has something to say about the great young stallion, which tends to fill space when there is no chance to get other news. Things are very dull in Terre Haute.

"Jefferson" writes from Hartford as follows: "Sunol may be the only trotter to have made a quarter in 30 seconds, but that is not the fastest quarter ever made by a trotter, as the brown gelding Dart, owned by Mr. M. B. Smith of New York City (formerly head of the R. G. Dunn Mercantile Agency), has trotted a quarter over the Fleetwood track in 29 seconds. The horse is known in New York as a phenomenal quarter and half mile horse, and has been trial miles in 2:16 and 2:17. He was put into John Turner's hands last season to further develop, but has never trotted races, as his owner would not consent to have him entered."

Congestion of the Lungs.

How Death of Horses by Suffocation May Be Averted

Congestion of the lungs is usually caused by over exertion, especially when the animal is out of condition, and sometimes by defective ventilation in the stable or by cold.

The distress is caused by the lungs becoming gorged with more blood than they can purify and return back to the heart. Death in this disease occurs from suffocation. Air is taken freely into the lungs, but the circulation almost ceases in them, and in spite of this hurried breathing, as shown by his panting sides, he is almost as completely suffocated as if a cord were tied around his neck. On examining his eyes and nostrils they are seen to be turgid and purple, the vessels being filled with carbonized blood, while the heart beats rapidly and feebly, and the countenance is expressive of anxiety and distress.

Another symptom is indicated by very rapid breathing, amounting in some cases to 50, 60, or 70 a minute, the nostrils being distended and cold air expired. Very rarely is there a decided beat of the pulse to be felt under the jaw; the artery is distended with blood and the fluid seems to creep through it by separate impulses. The animal stands with forelegs apart, and, nothwithstanding the distressed state of breathing, seems to object to fresh air, as they always select a corner furthest from an opening. This habit of seeking remote corners is observed in most cases of sickness among animals.

A proper treatment is to give a stimulant, such as a wine glassful of tincture of arnica, or a quarter of a pint of whiskey or brandy (if the arnica is not at hand) in water, or sweet spirits of nitre three ounces, which should be mixed with cold water. These stimulants may be repeated after fifteen or twenty minutes. Allow the horse plenty of fresh air to breathe and water to drink. Use warm fomentations to the sides, place the legs in warm water, hand rub the body and clothe comfortably, and if the symptoms be not relieved, bleed to the extent of about a gallon.

During convalescence give laxative food with half an ounce of nitre mixed in it daily.

Diffusable stimulants, by quickening the general circulation, tend to relieve congestion. Alcohol in small and repeated doses is a stimulant and diaphonetic (a medicine which increases the action of the skin); in large doses it is a narcotic. Arnica seems to have a special action in stimulating the small vessels of the surface of the body, hence its probable value in cases of congestion of the lungs.

I received a letter early in the week from an old friend in Yorkshire. Among other news, etc., he says: On Tuesday, December 10th, the Gimcrack Club held their 123rd anniversary dinner. A characteristic letter was received from the Hon. Jas. Lowther, usually known as Jimmy Lowther in which he regretted his inability to be present and congratulated the members on the beneficial effects of their last meeting. Lord Wenlock proposed the stewards and members of the Jockey Club which was replied to by Lord Downe. The 'piece de resistance' then followed. The Hon. Reginald Parker proposed the toast of Stewards and Patrons of York races, referring in highly eulogistic terms to Lord Durham, who responded to the toast in what has generally been described as an excellent, gentlemanly, frank, manly speech. He first of all spoke in high terms of all old and time honored institutions, such as York races, and truly said that Yorkshire men were showing their appreciation of and fondness for racing, and particularly Yorkshire racing by the tremendous crowds who always witnessed the meetings on Knavesmire. The speaker then in eloquent terms regretted the death of the late Lord Falmouth, whom all Yorkshire delighted to honor for his integrity and straightforward racing. Then referring to his last year's speech, Lord Durham said he made it with his eyes open, regardless of whether he gained or lost friends. The reason he spoke there instead of in the Jockey Club was because he was sure it would have more effect. His speech all through was a justification of his previous actions and wound up with many good suggestions for the future, among them being one that the Jockey Club should have among its active members, men more closely connected with turf pursuits, more racing men and men who were willing and not afraid to speak, and that the Stewards should in future hold their meetings with open doors, allowing reporters to be present and give a correct report of the proceedings.

Geo. D. Boynton of Ravenswood Stock Farm, Lexington, Ky., says that while he works with horses he will use the Boyce wash in preference to all other preparations.

CHICAGO, ILLS. -:- BREEDERS' SALE.

SECOND GRAND COMBINATION SALE OF

KIDD, EDMONSON & MORSE,

Will be held in Chicago, Ill., MARCH 17th to 23d, 1890.

Trotters, Pacers, Stallions, Brood Mares, Colts, Saddle and Harness Horses.

Those wishing to dispose of their stock to the best advantage should send for conditions and entry blanks at once, as the sale promises to be very large.

Entries to close January 24, 1890. Send in your entries at once.

Our first sale was a grand success, and was only a foreshadowing of what is to follow. Address,

KIDD, EDMONSON & MORSE, Lexington, Ky.

Or No. 806 West Madison St., Chicago, Ill.

New York Sales of Trotting Stock

PETER C. KELLOGG & CO.'S

CALIFORNIA COMBINATION SALE OF

-TROTTING STOCK-

in New York will commence

Tuesday, March 11,'90

At the American Institute Building.

For Contracts, giving terms and full particulars, and for Entry Blanks (state number of horses to be consigned) address the firm as below.

Buyers who desire to increase their lines of choicely bred brood mares, or to secure stallions suited to the mares of California, can, by spending the month of March in New York, have opportunity to select from hundreds of offerings in our sales, the choicest blood and the best assortment in the country. It should be borne in mind that the climatic crosses which have been most prolific of great results in California (and also in Kentucky) have been secured in the colder climates of the North and East. If you are to use a home-bred stallion, obtain mares that are bred and reared under radically different climatic influences. If you use home-bred mares get your stallions from widely different climatic sources. While there are exceptions to all rules the more you study this subject the more irresistable will be the conviction that the greatest success has most often resulted from this plan. It is just as important in breeding to obtain a proper climatic out-cross as to obtain a good blood out-cross.

One or the other seems absolutely necessary. To combine both is doubly effective

WHETHER YOU ARE BUYER OR SELLER NEW YORK IS THE PLACE TO BE NEXT MARCH.

Our first sale will contain much Mambrino Patchen and Almont blood from the highly successful Village Farm Stud, owned by Mr. C. J. Hamlin, Buffalo, New York.

Our second sale will close out the celebrated Rosemeade Stud belonging to Mr. L. J. Rose of Los Angeles, Cal., with its brood mares and its youngsters by Stamboul and Alcazar.

Both these sales will occur the first week of March, to be followed throughout the month by others of great importance; representing California and the most important Eastern States; concluding the last week of March with an extensive consignment from Palo Alto.

Bids executed without charge, in the interest of absent buyers who remit in advance; but we greatly prefer their presence or that of their agent.

Address all correspondence to

PETER C. KELLOGG & CO.,
107 John Street, New York.

SANMATEO STOCKFARM

HOME OF GUY WILKES,
Record, 2:15 1-4.

Guy Wilkes' Book is full for 1890, and positively no more mares will be received. Book now open for 1891, at $500 the Season.

Sable Wilkes, three-year-old record 2:18, will be allowed to serve 25 mares in addition to those already engaged at $250 the season of 1890. SABLE Wilkes, 15½ hands, black horse, by Guy Wilkes, first dam Sable by The Moor; second dam Gretchen by Mambrino Pilot; third dam Kitty Kirkman by Canada Chief; fourth dam by Fanning's Tobe; fifth dam by imp. Leviathan.

Leo Wilkes, brown horse, four years, 16 hands, full brother to Sable Wilkes, will be allowed to serve 30 mares at $100 the season

Mares not proving with foal may be returned the following season free of service fee. Parties engaging the services of any of the above horses must send a deposit of 10 per cent. of service money with engagement. Pasturage $6 per month, and when the condition of the animal requires it, hay or grain, or both, are fed, the charge will be $12 50 per month. Good care will be taken of all mares sent to the Farm, but no liability will be assumed for accidents or escapes.

All bills are due at time of service, but must be paid by August 1st of each year. No stock will be allowed to leave the place until all bills are paid.

WILLIAM CORBITT.
San Mateo Stock Farm.

The Washington Park Club,

CHICAGO,

Will close the following Stakes January 15th, 1890, to be run at their Summer Meeting of 1890, beginning Saturday, June 21st and ending Saturday, July 19th, for which a programme will be arranged for

TWENTY-FIVE DAYS' RACING,

—WITH—

$110,000

In Added Money to Stakes and Purses.

THE WHEELER HANDICAP.

A SWEEPSTAKES for three-year-olds and upward, $100 each, $25 forfeit, or only $10 if declared; $1,000 added; the second to receive $150, and the third $200 out of the stakes. Weights to be announced Saturday, July 5th; declarations to be made on or before Wednesday, July 9th. Starters to be named through the entry box Friday, July 18th. A winner of any race after the announcement of weights, of the value of $1,000, to carry 5 lbs. extra. To be run Saturday, July 19th. One mile and a quarter.

THE GREAT WESTERN HANDICAP.

A SWEEPSTAKES for all ages, $50 each, h. f., or only $10 if declared out on or before May 1st, 1890, $1,500 added; the second to receive $400, and the third $200 out of the stakes. Weights to be announced April 1st, 1890. A winner of any race after the publication of weights, of the value of $1,000, to carry 5 lbs., or $1,500, 7 lbs. extra. One mile and a half.

THE OAKWOOD HANDICAP.

A SWEEPSTAKES for all ages, $50 each, h. f., or only $10 if declared out on or before May 1st, 1890, $1,000 added; the second to receive $200, and the third $100 out of the stakes. Weights to be announced April 1st, 1890. A winner of any race after the publication of weights, of the value of $1,000, to carry 5 lbs. extra. One mile and a furlong.

THE BOULEVARD STAKES.

A SWEEPSTAKES for all ages, $25 each, $10 forfeit; $1,000 added; the second to receive $200, and the third $100 out of the stakes. A winner in 1890 of two races of any value to carry 5 lbs.; of three or more races of any value, 7 lbs. extra. Maidens allowed 10 lbs. One mile.

THE MAIDEN STAKES.

A SWEEPSTAKES for three-year-olds (foals of 1887) that have not won a race previous to January 1st, 1890; $50 entrance, $15 forfeit, with $1,000 added, of which $200 to the second horse and $100 to the third. Maidens at the time of starting allowed 5 lbs. One mile and a furlong.

THE DEARBORN HANDICAP.

A SWEEPSTAKES for three-year-olds (foals of 1887), $50 each, $15 forfeit, with $1000 added; the second to receive $200, and the third $100 out of the stakes. Weights to be announced by 12 m. two days before the day appointed for the race. Starters to be named through the entry box, at the usual time of closing, the day before the race. One mile and a furlong.

THE LAKE VIEW HANDICAP.

A SWEEPSTAKES for two-year-olds (foals of 1888), $50 each, $15 forfeit; with $1,000 added; the second to receive $200, and the third $100 out of the stakes. Weights to be announced by 12 m. two days before the day appointed for the race. Starters to be named through the entry box at the usual time of closing, the day before the race. Three-quarters of a mile.

THE QUICKSTEP STAKES.

A SWEEPSTAKES for two-year-olds (foals of 1888), $25 each, $10 forfeit; $1,000 added, the second to receive $200, and the third $100 out of the stakes. A winner of two races of any value to carry 7 lbs. extra. Maidens allowed 7 lbs. Half a mile.

All declarations in the above Stakes void unless accompanied with the money.
All Purses and Handicaps, $600 to $800.

Please observe that in the above stakes declarations are permitted for a small forfeit.
Turfmen failing to receive entry blanks can obtain them by applying to the Secretary.
Nominations and all Communications to be addressed to the Secretary, Room 32, Palmer House, Chicago, Illinois.

J. E. BREWSTER, Secretary.

For Sale by Pleasanton Stock Farm Co.

ONE STALLION COLT, 1 year old, by DIRECTOR, 2:17, dam Sweetness, record 2:21¼. This Colt is a half brother to Sidney, the great Sire of Pacers.

ONE STALLION COLT, 1 year old, by DIRECTOR, 2:17, dam Echora, record 2:23½. This Colt is a full brother to Direct, record 2:23 at Three Years Old.

ONE FILLY, 1 year old, by CLOVIS, dam Nettie, trial record to Wagon 2:36.

ONE STALLION, 2 Years old, by NUTMONT, he by Nutbourne, brother to Nutwood, dam by Electioneer. This Colt can trot very fast.

ONE STALLION, 2 years old, by SIDNEY, dam Fernleaf. This Colt is a full brother to Gold Leaf

ONE FOUR-YEAR-OLD FILLY, GOLD LEAF, pacing record 2:15.

ONE THREE-YEAR OLD FILLY, by DIRECTOR, dam by a son of Whipple's Hambletonian. This is a grand mare in looks and breeding, and is very fast.

ONE Filly, 2 years old, by MONROE CHIEF, full sister to Miss Gilmer, sold at auction when three years old for $1,700.

ONE PACING HORSE, 4 years old, by STEINWAY, dam by Nutwood. This horse is very stylish, and can show a 2:10 gait.

One Brown Mare, heavy in foal to DIRECTOR, by Gibraltar, dam May Day, by Cassius M. Clay. This Mare is very fast; showed a quarter in 34 seconds, and is a half sister to Margaret S., that got a record of 2:31 at twenty-four months old.

One Brown Mare, by DEL SUR, he by The Moor, heavy in foal to Director. This Mare is very fast.

For particulars call on or address M. SALISBURY, 320 Sansome Street, Room 96, San Francisco, or

ANDY McDOWELL, Pleasanton, Cal.

Stallion for Sale

AT A BARGAIN.

Full Brother to Fairmont.

By Piedmont, dam Queen by Garibaldi—see State Fair Edition of BREEDER AND SPORTSMAN, September 14, 1889, for description of Fairmont—three years old, solid bay. Can trot a 2:40 gait or better. Sound in every particular. Can be seen at Oakland Trotting Park, Oakland.

P. J. WILLIAMS.

THE BUCKINGHAM.
OLD STRAIGHT WHISKIES.
141 Montgomery Street.
303 Bush Street, S. F.
M. J. BALFE, Proprietor.

Singleton & Addington,
Bank Exchange,
3d and K Streets, Sacramento.
Superior Wines, Liquors and Cigars.

Breeders' Directory.

Advertisements under this heading 50c. per line per month.

HORSES AND CATTLE.

PAGE BROTHERS.—Penn's Grove, Sonoma Co. Cal. Breeders of Short-Horn Cattle; Draft, Roadster and Standard Bred Horses.

JAMES MADDOCK, Petaluma, Cal.—Trotters trained at reasonable prices. Stock handled carefully. Correspondence solicited.

SETH COOK, breeder of Cleveland Bay Horses, Devon, Durham, Polled Aberdeen-Angus and Galloway Cattle. Young stock of above breeds on hand for sale. Warranted to be pure bred, recorded and average breeders. Address, Geo. A. Wiley, Cook Farm, Danville, Contra Costa Co., Cal.

HAMBRINO WILKES COLTS and FILLIES, full brothers and sisters to Gus Wilkes 2:22, and Balkan 2:29¼, for Sale. Address SMITH HILL, Walnut Creek, Contra Costa County, Cal.

B. F. RUSH, Suisun, Cal., Shorthorns, Thoroughbred and Grades. Young Bulls and Calves for Sale.

PETER SAXE & SON, Lick House, San Francisco, Cal.—Importers and Breeders for past 18 years of every variety of Cattle, Horses, Sheep and Hogs.

HOLSTEIN THOROUGHBREDS of all the noted strains. Registered Berkshire Swine. Catalogues. F. H. BURKE, 401 Montgomery St., S. F.

CLEVELAND BAYS and Norman Horses, Jersey Cattle, and pure bred Poland China Hogs.—DR. W. J. PRATHER, Fresno, Cal.

HENRY C. JUDSON, Wild Idle Farm.—Breeder of Thoroughbred Horses. The home of "Wild Idle." P. O. Santa Clara; Box 223.

W. S. JACOBS, Sacramento, Cal. — Breeder of Thoroughbred Shorthorns and Berkshire Hogs.

J. H. WHITE, Lakeville, Sonoma County—Breeder of Registered Holstein Cattle.

EL ROBLAS RANCHO—Los Alamos, Cal., Francis T. Underhill, proprietor, importer and breeder of thoroughbred Hereford Cattle. Information by mail. C. F. Swan, manager.

FERGUSON & AUSTIN,
FRESNO, CAL.
Registered Polled Angus and Short-Horn Cattle.

Oysters.

M. B. MORAGHAN

Is the only importer, planter and wholesale dealer in the CALIFORNIA MARKET, Stalls 68, 69 to 71 and 47,48. All the choicest brands of Fresh Oysters constantly on hand. Prompt attention paid to hotel and country orders. Price List.

Large Eastern Oysters .... $1 00 per 100
Transplanted Eastern Oysters .... 1 70 per 100
California Oysters .... 2 00 " sack
Fresh Fresh Eastern Oysters at $7 00 per doz. cans.

Shoes For Comfort, Elegance and Durability.

Having my own factory, and giving my personal supervision to all work I am in a position to warrant perfect satisfaction. Inspection invited.

Gentlemen's Park Riding Boots made to Order.

FACTORY S. W. cor. Battery and Jackson Sts.
SALESROOM Pioneer Building, corner Stevenson and Fourth Streets.

A full line of **Boots and Shoes** constantly on hand, and rules for Self-Measurement by Mail.

JNO. T. SULLIVAN.

HORSES PURCHASED ON COMMISSION.

THOROUGHBREDS A SPECIALTY.

Will select and buy, or buy selected Animals for all desiring, for reasonable compensation

KEEPS PROMISING YOUNGSTERS IN VIEW.

L. M. LASLEY, Stanford, Ky.

References:—J. W. Guest, Danville, Ky.
B. G. Bruce, Lexington Ky.
S. H. Baughman, Stanford, Ky.
G. A. Lackey, Stanford, Ky.
Geo. McAllister, Stanford, Ky.
First National Bank, Stanford, Ky.

SAMUEL VALLEAU. JAS. R. BRODIE.

J. R. BRODIE & CO.,
Steam Printers,
—And Dealers in—
Poolseller's and Bookmaker's Supplies.
401—403 *Sansome Street, corner Sacramento, San Francisco.*

Old Hermitage Whiskies
"STEINER'S,"
No. 311 BUSH STREET,
San Francisco.
Under Breeder and Sportsman Office.

HEALD'S
Business College, 24 Post St.
—San Francisco.—
The most popular school on the Coast
E. HEALD, President. C. S. HALEY, Sec'y.
☞ Send for Circulars

The Wine that is held in HIGHEST ESTEEM by the LEADING CLUBS and in SOCIETY

IS

MOËT & CHANDON

-:- "WHITE SEAL," -:-

THE PERFECTION OF A DRY

Champagne

For Sale by all the Leading Grocers and Wine Merchants.

SHERWOOD & SHERWOOD,
PACIFIC COAST AGENTS.
212--214 Market Street, San Francisco, Cal.

TO HORSEMEN!

PREPARE!!

Your Stallion Advertisements for the

Breeder & Sportsman

For the Coming Season---1890.

We are pleased to announce that we have the best facilities for furnishing

Stallion Pictures,
Stallion Cards,
Pedigrees, Folders,
Contracts, Bills, Etc.

We make a specialty of this department of our business, and have UNRIVALED FACILITIES FOR LOOKING UP PEDIGREES and doing accurate and handsome work.

Promptness, Good Work, Low Prices.

TO REACH ALL
OF THE
Horsemen and Breeders on the Pacific Coast
ADVERTISE in the

Breeder & Sportsman,

313 Bush Street, S. F.

BOYCE TABLETS.

Leg and Body Wash.

THE BOYCE TABLETS are packed in a nicely decorated metal box with hinged lid—one hundred tablets in each box; directions for use plainly engraved upon the box; therefore, the convenience of the package—no liability to leakage and breakage—economy and ready solubility, together with the absolute certainty of their action, will at once commend the use of BOYCE'S TABLETS to the intelligent horsemen of the country. TABLETS sufficient to make one hundred pints of leg and body wash are conveniently carried in an inside coat pocket or in the hip-pocket of the trousers.

The BOYCE WASH can be applied ALL OVER THE BODY WITHOUT FEAR OF BLISTERING OR AFFECTING THE KIDNEYS.

The BOYCE WASH will cure CRACKED HEELS, PUFFS, STOCKINGS, SCRATCHES, INFLAMED TENDONS and FEVERED LEGS.

Price per Box of One Hundred Tablets, $2, sent postpaid to any part of the United States; **six boxes for $10.** A sample of BOYCE'S TABLETS will be mailed to any address on application. These TABLETS are warranted to keep in any climate. Address

BOYCE TABLET COMPANY,
600 Wabash Avenue, - - - Terre Haute, Indiana.

J. A. McKERRON, Pacific Coast Agent,
228-230-232 Ellis Street, San Francisco, Cal.

It is really surprising how people will suffer month after month and year after year with

CONSTIPATION,

when a regular habit of body can be secured without changing the diet or disorganizing the system, if they will only

A Simple but Effective Vegetable Compound.

"I have used Simmons Liver Regulator for Constipation, and always with decided benefit."—HIRAM WARNER, Late Chief Justice of Ga.

——Prepared by——
J. H. ZEILIN & CO., Philadelphia, Pa.

PACIFIC COAST
Trotting-Horse Breeders' Association.

The first Annual Meeting of the above Association for the election of officers for the ensuing year and for the transaction of such other business as may come before it, will occur on

Wednesday, January 8, 1890,
AT PARLOR A, OF THE
PALACE HOTEL, SAN FRANCISCO.
J. H. WHITE, President.
WILFRED PAGE, Secretary.

PASTURAGE
AND
FIRST-CLASS CARE
TAKEN OF
Gentlemen's Road Horses and Trotters.

Colts Broken and Trained to Harness or Saddle.

Twenty new Box Stalls. First-class Pasturage, and the best of care given to all horses. **Terms, $4 per month.** Satisfaction Guaranteed. Address,

K. O'GRADY,
Laural Creek Farm,
SAN MATEO, CAL.

GOLDEN EAGLE HOTEL

Corner SEVENTH and K STREETS, SACRAMENTO.
FIRST CLASS IN EVERY RESPECT.
The LARGEST and FINEST HOTEL in the City.
W. O. BOWERS, Proprietor.
Free 'Bus to and from the Hotel.
Telephone, Telegraph Office and Messenger Service at Hotel

Call and See the New

CRUISING BOOTS
E. T. ALLEN,
Fire Arms and Sporting Goods
416 Market St., S. F.

The Thoroughbred Stallion

INTRUDER

Will make the Season of 1890 at Agricultural Park, SACRAMENTO.

Bay Horse, foaled 1871, bred by Sir L. Newman, England. Imported by D. D. Withers, Esq., New York.

By Crater, Son of Orlando and Vesuvienne by Gladiator.

1st dam Lady Bountiful by Rataplan (Rataplan is own brother to Stockwell, and winner of 42 races, including the Doncaster Cup and 19 Queen's Plates, and proved himself the most distinguished race horse of his day in England).

2d dam Plentiful by Don John (the winner of St. Leger and Doncaster Cup).

3d dam Plenty by Bay Middleton (winner of the Derby and Two Thousand Guinea Stakes).

4th dam Plenary, own sister of Plenipotentiary, by Emilius. (Both Emilius and Plenipotentiary were Derby winners).

5th dam Harriet, dam of the renowned Plenipotentiary by Pericles.

6th dam by Selim, winner of the One Thousand Guinea Stakes.

7th dam by Pypilina, by Sir Peter.

8th dam Rally, by Trumpeter.

9th dam Fancy, by Florizel. Fancy was full sister to Diomed, the first Derby winner in England, and after his importation into this country, sired the illustrious Sir Archy, etc. See English Stud Book.

Imported INTRUDER is a beautiful bay, standing fully 16 hands high, of great length and substance, and descends through close and strong currents from the most illustrious winners and winning lines of blood of which the English Stud Book bears record.

A careful review of the first six crosses of the pedigree of INTRUDER will show nine Derby winners; five St. Leger winners; two winners of The Oaks; two winners of the Two Thousand Guineas; two winners of the One Thousand Guineas; one Goodwood Cup winner; one Cesarwich Cup winner; one Cambridgeshire Stakes winner, and four Doncaster Cups, in addition to a great number of steeplechases and other races of importance.

INTRUDER, at the great fair held at St. Louis, Mo., in 1876, was awarded the highest stallion honors—the blue ribbon and the $500 purse—in the sweepstakes ring for stallion of any age or blood. The list of competitors embraced the large number of thirty-three animals, and they represented England, Canada, Kentucky, Tennessee, and other states. He also took first premium in his class and in sweepstakes for the best stallion of any age or breed at the State Fair at Peoria, Ill., 1884. He is the sire of Tidal Wave, George Hakes, Bernice and April Fool.

INTRUDER is the sire of Interpose, who is the dam of Spokane, winner of the Kentucky Derby, in which he beat the great horse Proctor Knott and broke the record.

TERMS: $50 for the season. Mares not proving with foal can be returned the next season free of charge. Good pasturage at $4 per month. Mares cared for in any manner owners may desire, and fed on hay and grain, either or both, at reasonable rates. While every precaution will be taken, no responsibility will be assumed for escapes or accidents. Mares sent from a distance in care of the undersigned, will be met and taken to the park. For further particulars, address

T. J. KNIGHT.
Agricultural Park, Sacramento.

By-Laws

—AND—

Rules and Regulations

—OF THE—

NATIONAL

Trotting Association

ALSO THE

AMERICAN

Trotting Association,

AND THE

PACIFIC COAST BLOOD-HORSE ASSOCIATION.

With Betting Rules.

For Sale at the Office of the

Breeder and Sportsman,

313 Bush St., S. F., Cal.

Price, 25c. each.

By Mail, Postage Paid, 30c. each.

---

6 DOS

DO you bet?
DO you go to the races?
DO you know HOW to bet?
DO you know BEST system?
DO you want Good ADVICE?
DO as you ought to do:

SEND FOR PROSPECTUS TO

GOODWIN BROS.,

241 BROADWAY, NEW YORK

Who will mail you

FREE OF CHARGE,

one of their circulars showing the GREAT SUCCESS they have met with from the time they established the system of "Point" providing in this country in 1881; it also contains

MANY OTHER INTERESTING ITEMS

with which the general public is not familiar.

The Trotting Stallion

Silver Bow

Will make the season of 1890 at the Oakland Race Track.

Pedigree.

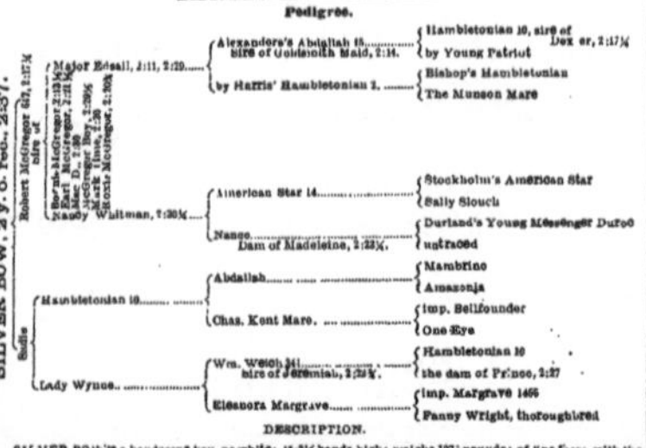

DESCRIPTION.

SILVER BOW is a handsome bay, no white; 15-3¼ hands high; weighs 1075 pounds; of fine form, with the best of legs and a clean cut, intelligent head. Is remarkably level headed, seldom making a break; wears 7-ounce shoes in front. His record 2:37, is no mark of his speed; he can beat 30 easy, and with his gilt-edge breeding, he is just what he ought to be, a trotter sired by a trotter whose dam was herself a trotter and his grandam the dam of two trotters. His dam Sadie being by Hambletonian 10, shows him to be bred from the cream of the trotting blood.

TERMS: $100 for the season. Mares not proving in foal returnable for the season of 1891 free of charge. Good pasturage and first-class care taken of mares for $5 per month. No responsibility assumed for escapes or accidents. For further particulars, address

Limited to 15 approved mares.
Season to end June 1st, 1890.

P. J. WILLIAMS.
Care Race Track, Oakland, Cal.

Valensin Stock Farm Stallions.

SIDNEY, 2:19 3-4.

At Eight Years of Age Sire of the following Fastest on Record:

FAUSTINO, yearling stallion, record of the world	2:35
FLEET, fastest yearling record in 1888	2:36
FLEET, fastest two-year-old filly in 1889	2:24
GOLD LEAF, fastest four-year-old Pacing record in the world	2:11¼
ADONIS, fastest three-year-old Pacing Gelding in the world	2:14¼
ADONIS, four-year-old Gelding Pacing record	2:14

—Also the Sire of—

LONGWORTH, four years old	2:19
SISTER V., four years old (trial 2:23)	2:27
SANTA RITA	2:39
MEMO, two-year-old (three-year-old trial 2:20½)	2:49

And many others.

SIDNEY is the sire of Faustino 2:35, and Fleet 2:36, the two fastest yearlings the world has ever known by one sire, and his slowest yearling is faster than the great Electioneer's fastest.

Terms, $250, with usual return privileges, for a limited number of approved mares. Book rapidly filling.

SIMMOCOLON, Four-year-old, 2:29 1-2.

Trial, 2:24; Half Mile in 1:08; Quarter in 33 1-2 Seconds.

Chestnut Horse, foaled 1885.

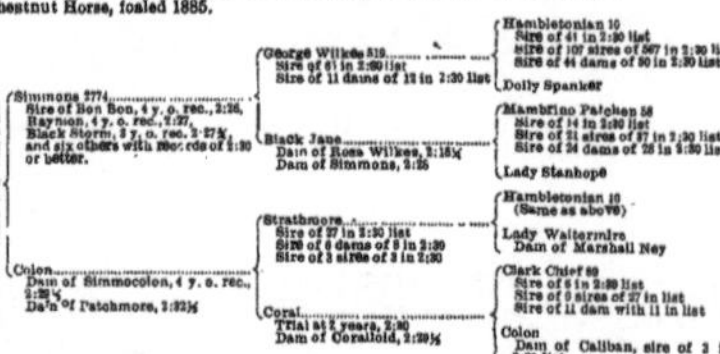

As will be seen, Simmocolon is by a performing and producing son of George Wilkes, 2:22. He has back of him three producing dams, and combines the blood of the great sire George Wilkes handsomely blended with the blood of the greatest broodmare families. On the dam's side Mambrino Patchen, Strathmore, Clark Chief and Clay. A fine individual himself, pure gaited and very fast.

Terms, $150, with usual return privileges, for a limited number of mares. Season to close JUNE 15th, when he will be prepared for track purposes. Pasturage $5 per month. Reasonable charges if fed hay and grain. Best of care taken of mares, but positively no responsibility assumed for accidents or escapes. For further particulars address

G. VALENSIN, Pleasanton, Cal.

TREES AND SEEDS.

Trumbull & Beebe's Nurseries

ESTABLISHED 1853.

500,000 **Fruit Trees** 500,000

FOR SALE.

Having added by purchase, to that of our own growing, the entire nursery stock grown at James Shinn's Nurseries, Niles, Cal., we are better prepared than ever before to meet the increasing demand for trees, and offer for the season of 1889-1890 the LARGEST AND MOST COMPLETE ASSORTMENT OF NURSERY STOCK ON THE PACIFIC COAST, embracing all the leading varieties of FRUIT, SHADE and ORNAMENTAL TREES, ROSES, PLANTS, Etc. BERRY BUSHES of all kinds in quantities to suit. GRAPE VINES (strong roots), also 60,000 OLIVE TREES (Mission and Picholine), ORANGE, LEMONS, NUT TREES, Etc., Etc.

NURSERIES—San Rafael, Alameda and Niles, Cal. Packing Grounds and Sales-yard at Niles R. R. Station. Catalogues sent upon application. Address all communications to

TRUMBULL & BEEBE, 419-421 Sansome St., San Francisco, Cal

Draught Horse Breeders,

Attention!

JUST ARRIVED! A Number of Fine Young Pure-bred

CLYDESDALE STALLIONS,

Imported from Scotland and registered in the Clydesdale Stud Book. Among them are:

BOGWOOD (5561), Vol. X, C. S. B.
BELTED CRUISER (6481), Vol. XI, C. S. B.
CANNY JAMIE (6574), Vol. XI, C. S. B.

They are of good dark colors with the Regular Clydesdale Markings, and are the finest Horses that have ever been imported to this State. They are the property of A. V. WILSON, Esq., North Yakima, W. T., and will be sold for a reasonable figure. They may be seen at the Mt. Eden Farm. For pedigrees and particulars, call on or address, A. V. WILSON, North Yakima, W. T., or H. P. MOHR, Mount Eden, Alameda Co., Cal.

Highland Farm,

LEXINGTON, KY.,

Home of Red Wilkes.

Standard-bred Trotting Stock

For Sale,

sired by Red Wilkes, Wilton, 2:19¼; Allandorf and Sentinel Wilkes, out of highly bred Standard Mares of the most fashionable blood of the day.

W. C. FRANCE, Proprietor.

Fiske's Vanes.

MADE OF

COPPER

And Gilded with

PURE

GOLD LEAF.

Manufacturer's Agent.

The HOWE SCALE CO.

411 & 413 Market Street, S. F.

Scales for Weighing of

Live Stock

SEEDS, FEED, Etc.

Write for Catalogue.

PERRIER-JOUET

& Co.

EPERNAY

CHAMPAGNE

W. B CHAPMAN,

Sole Agent for Pacific Coast.

For sale by all first-class Wine Merchants and Grocers.

Southern Pacific Co.

(PACIFIC SYSTEM.)

Trains leave and are due to arrive at San Francisco.

LEAVE (FOR)	FROM DECEMBER 1, 1889.	ARRIVE (FROM)
7.30 A M	Haywards, Niles and San Jose ...	*12.45 P M
7.30 A M	Sacramento and Redding, via Davis	7.15 P M
7.30 A M	Sacramento, Auburn, Colfax	5.45 P M
8.00 A M	Martinez, Vallejo, Calistoga and Santa Rosa	6.15 P M
8.30 A M	Los Angeles Express, Fresno, Bakersfield, Mojave and East and Los Angeles	11.15 A M
8.30 A M	Niles, San Jose, Stockton, Ione, Sacramento, Marysville, Oroville and Red Bluff	5.45 P M
10.30 A M	Haywards and Niles	2.15 P M
*12.00 M	Haywards, Niles and San Jose...	* 3.45 P M
*1.00 P M	Sacramento River Steamers..	**6.00 A M
3.00 P M	Haywards, Niles and San Jose....	9.45 A M
3.30 P M	2d Class for Ogden and East.	10.45 P M
4.00 P M	Stockton and §Milton; Vallejo, Calistoga and Santa Rosa........	9.45 A M
4.30 P M	Sacramento and Knight's Landing via Davis	10.45 A M
* 4.30 P M	Niles and Livermore.	* 8.45 A M
* 4.30 P M	Niles and San Jose........	‡ 4.15 P M
5.30 P M	Haywards and Niles........	7.45 A M
6.00 P M	Sunset Route, Atlantic Express, Santa Barbara, Los Angeles, Deming, El Paso, New Orleans and East........	8.45 P M
7.00 P M	Shasta Route Express, Sacramento, Marysville, Redding, Portland, Puget Sound and East........	7.45 A M
8.00 P M	Central Atlantic Express, Og- and East........	9.45 A M

SANTA CRUZ DIVISION.

LEAVE (FOR)		ARRIVE (FROM)
‡ 8.00 A M	Hunters train to San Jose, ...	‡ 7.20 P M
8.15 A M	Newark, Centerville, San Jose, Felton, Boulder Creek and Santa Cruz........	5.50 P M
* 2.15 P M	Centerville, San Jose, Felton, Boulder Creek and Santa Cruz	*11.50 A M
4.15 P M	Centerville, San Jose, Almaden, and Los Gatos	9.50 A M

Coast Division (Third and Townsend Sts.)

LEAVE (FOR)		ARRIVE (FROM)
7.25 A M	San Jose, Almaden and Way Stations........	2.30 P M
8.30 A M	San Jose, Gilroy, Tres Pinos; Pajaro, Santa Cruz; Monterey; Pacific Grove, Salinas, San Miguel, Paso Robles, Santa Margarita (San Luis Obispo) and principal Way Stations........	6.12 P M
10.30 A M	San Jose and Way Stations.	5.02 P M
12.01 P M	Cemetery, Menlo Park and Way Stations........	3.38 P M
* 3.30 P M	San Jose, Tres Pinos, Santa Cruz, Salinas, Monterey Pacific Grove and principal Way Stations........	*10.00 A M
* 4.20 P M	Menlo Park and Way Stations.	* 7.58 A M
5.20 P M	San Jose and Way Stations........	9.03 A M
6.30 P M	Menlo Park and Way Stations.....	6.35 A M
†11.45 P M	Menlo Park and principal Way Stations	†7.28 P M

A M for Morning. P M for Afternoon.
*Sundays excepted. †Saturdays only. ‡Sundays only.
**Mondays excepted. §Saturdays excepted.

KILLIP & CO.,

LIVE STOCK AND GENERAL AUCTIONEERS,

22 Montgomery Street, San Francisco

SPECIAL ATTENTION PAID TO SALES OF

High-Bred Horses and Cattle.

At auction and private sale.

Will Sell in All Cities and Counties of the State.

REFERENCES.

Hon. C. Green, Sacramento. • Hon. J. D. Carr, Salinas.
J. P. Sargent, Esq., Sargents. Hon. John Boggs, Colusa.
Hon. L. J. Rose, Los Angeles. Hon. A. Walrath, Nevada.
J. B. Haggin, Esq., San Francisco.

Represented at Sacramento by Edwin F. Smith secretary State Agricultural Society.

At San Jose by Messrs. Montgomery & Rea, Real Estate Agents.

Being the oldest established firm in the live-stock business on this Coast, and having conducted the important auction sales in this line for the past fifteen years, amounting to one half a million of dollars, we feel justified in claiming unequaled facilities for disposing of live stock of every description, either at auction or private sale. Our list of correspondents embraces every breeder and dealer of prominence upon the Pacific Coast, thus enabling us to give full publicity to animals placed with us for sale. Private purchases and sales of live stock of all descriptions will be made on Commission, and stock shipped with the utmost care. Purchases and sales made of land of every description. We are authorised to refer to the gentlemen whose names are appended.

KILLIP & CO., 22 Montgomery Street.

For any Kind of a

SORE THROAT

USE

McCLELLAN'S DIPHTHERIA REMEDY

An Unfailing Cure.

FOR SALE BY ALL DRUGGISTS

San Francisco and North Pacific Railway.

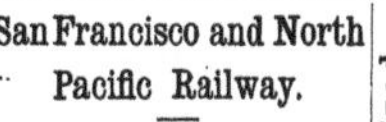

THE DONAHUE BROAD-GAUGE ROUTE.

COMMENCING SUNDAY, MARCH 17, 1889, AND until further notice, boats and trains will leave from and arrive at the San Francisco Passenger Depot, Market-street Wharf, as follows:

Leave San Francisco. Week Days.	Leave San Francisco. Sun-Days.	Destination	Arrive San Francisco. Sun-Days.	Arrive San Francisco. Week Days.
7.40 / 3.30 P M / 5.00 P M	8.00 A M / 5.00 P M	Petaluma and Santa Rosa	10.40 A M / 6.10 P M	8.50 A M / 10.31 A M / 6.05 P M
7.40 A M / 3.30 P M	8.00 A M	Fulton, Windsor, Healdsburg, Litton Spri'gs, Cloverdale, and way stations.	6.10 P M	10.30 A M / 6.05 P M
7.40 A M	8.00 A M	Hopland and Ukiah.	6.10 P M	6.05 P M
7.40 A M	8.00 A M	Guerneville	6.10 P M	6.05 P M
7.40 A M / 5.00 P M	8.00 A M	Sonoma and Glen Ellen.	10.40 A M / 6.10 P M	8.50 A M / 6.05 P M

Stage connects at Santa Rosa for White Sulphur Springs, Sebastopol and Mark West Springs; at Geyserville for Skaggs Springs, and at Cloverdale for the Geysers; at Hopland for Highland Springs, Kelseyville, Soda Bay, Lakeport and Bartlett Springs, and at Ukiah for Vichy Springs, Saratoga Springs, Blue Lakes, Willits, Cahto, Calpella, Potter Valley, Sherwood Valley and Mendocino City.

EXCURSION TICKETS from Saturdays to Mondays, to Petaluma, $1.50; to Santa Rosa, $2.25; to Healdsburg, $3.40; to Litton Springs, $3.60; to Cloverdale, $4.50; to Hopland, $5.70; to Ukiah, $6.75; to Guerneville, $3.75; to Sonoma, $1.50; to Glen Ellen, $1.80.

EXCURSION TICKETS, good for Sundays only, to Petaluma, $1; to Santa Rosa, $1.50; to Healdsburg, $2.25; to Litton Springs, $2.40; to Cloverdale, $3; to Guerneville, $2.50, to Sonoma, $1; to Glen Ellen, $1.20.

From San Francisco for Point Tiburon and San Rafael: Week Days—7.40, 9.20, 11.20, A. M.; 3.30, 5.00, 6.15 P. M. Sundays—8.00, 9.30, 11.00 A. M.; 1.30, 5.00, 6.20 P. M.

To San Francisco from San Rafael: Week Days—6.20, 7.55, 9.30 A. M.; 12.45, 3.40, 5.05 P. M. Sundays—8.10, 9.40 A. M.; 12.15, 3.40, 5.00 P. M.

To San Francisco from Point Tiburon: Week Days—6.50, 8.20, 9.55 A. M.; 1.10, 4.05, 5.30 P. M.; Sundays—8.40, 10.05 A. M.; 12.40, 4.05, 5.30 P. M.

On Saturdays an extra trip will be made from San Francisco to San Rafael, leaving at 1.40 P. M.

H. C. WHITING, General Manager.

PETER J. McGLYNN, Gen. Pass. & Tkt. Agt.

Ticket Offices at Ferry, 222 Montgomery Street and 2 New Montgomery Street.

KENNEL ADVERTISEMENTS.

Thoroughbred Pugs, $40 each.

PEDIGREE.

PUPPIES—
- Fido—
  - imp. Jumbo ..... { Marshall's Uno / Lady Bess
  - Fannie .... Rex / imp. Fly
- Budge—
  - Senator Fair's Fritz
  - McCleery's Mamma Snoots { Sam / imp. Alice

Can be seen daily from 9 A. M. to 3 P. M. at 411 Ellis Street, San Francisco.

J. F. B. McCLEERY.

Irish Setters & Pointers.

In the Stud, winner of 16 first and special prizes, CHAMPION MIKE T., 6435, A. K. S. B. Irish Setter puppies by Champion Mike T. 6435 A. K. S. B.—Champion Lady Elcho T. 6451 A. K. S. B., for sale. Two pointers, a year old, by Rush T. 10069 A. K. S. B.—Champion Patti Croxteth T. 10128 A. K. S. B. for sale. Yard broken. Address,

A. B. TRUMAN,
1425 Steiner St., S. F., Cal.

IF YOU WISH A GOOD REVOLVER PURCHASE ONE OF **SMITH & WESSON'S**

Finest small arms ever manufactured and the first choice of all experts. In calibres 32, 38 and 44-100. Single or double action, Safety Hammerless and Target models. Best quality wrought steel, carefully inspected for workmanship and stock. Unrivaled for finish, durability and accuracy. Do not be deceived by cheap *malleable iron imitations* often sold for the genuine article. They are unreliable and dangerous. The SMITH & WESSON REVOLVERS are stamped upon the barrels with firm's name, address and dates of patents, and are guaranteed perfect. Insist upon having them, and if your dealer cannot supply you, an order sent to address below will receive prompt attention. Descriptive catalogue and prices upon application.

SMITH & WESSON,
Springfield, Mass.

LAMBORN ROAD MACHINE

LIGHT DRAFT. MADE OF IRON. STRONG, SIMPLE, DURABLE. EASILY OPERATED.

TRUMAN HOOKER & CO,
SAN FRANCISCO. - - CALIFORNIA

DR. FISHERMAN'S

Carbolized Alkaline LOTION

Cures after all other Remedies have Failed.

Sprains, Sores, Bruises, Galls, Swellings, Scratches, Thrush, Grease Heels, Curb, Rheumatism. Restoring Weak Knees and Ankles to their original condition. As a wash it insures glossy manes and tails. Valuable as an internal remedy for Coughs, Colic, Congestion or Fever. You really get Half a Gallon of Remedy for $1.00, or Two Gallons for $3.00, after being adulterated as directed.

This Liniment has received the endorsement of some of our best horsemen. Recommended by Jos. Cairn Simpson. See BREEDER AND SPORTSMAN of November 10th, 1888.

LYNDE & HOUGH, Proprietors.

116 California St., S. F.

Or ask your Druggist for it.

THE B. & Y. HOOF OIL

GOOD FOR MAN OR BEAST.

Will positively destroy the effects of the "Cattle Fly."

A SURE CURE for Sores, Scratches, Cuts, Wounds, Bruises, Corns, Thrush, Foot Rot, Quarter Crack, Sand Crack, Dry, Brittle, Hard and Fevered Hoof, or any local trouble about the Horse.

Warranted to make the hoof grow without cause of complaint on the part of the horse-shoer for gumming his rasp.

B. & Y. New Process Neats Foot Oil, Best Leather Oil made.

CHEAP AND LASTING

Recommended by leading Harness Men, Drivers and Trainers. Is well adapted to wet weather, as it does not open pores like old process goods.

Ask your dealer for it, or send to

HUNT & DOREMUS,
99 FLOOD BUILDING, - San Francisco.

HORSE OWNERS!

TRY GOMBAULT'S

CAUSTIC BALSAM.

A Safe, Speedy and Positive Cure for Curb, Splint, Sweeny, Capped Hock, Strained Tendons, Founder, Wind Puffs, all Skin Diseases or Parasites, Thrush, Diphtheria, Pinkeye, all Lameness from Spavin, Ringbone or other Bony Tumors. Removes all Bunches or Blemishes from Horses and Cattle.

Supersedes all Cautery or Firing.

Impossible to Produce any Scar or Blemish.

Every bottle sold is warranted to give satisfaction. Price $1.50 per bottle. Sold by druggists, or sent by express, charges paid, with full directions for its use. Send for descriptive circulars. Address

LAWRENCE, WILLIAMS & CO., Cleveland, O.

BROU'S INJECTION

A PERMANENT CURE in from 3 to 6 days, of the most obstinate cases; guaranteed not to produce Stricture; no sickening doses; and no inconvenience or loss of time. Recommended by physicians and sold by all druggists. J. Ferré, (successor to Brou), Pharmacien, Paris.

California Horse Shoe Co's

I have used in my business the Steel and Iron Shoes made by the above Company, and take great pleasure in saying they are the best I have ever used in twenty-two years' practice. I have never seen anything like the STEEL SHOE made by this Company. I can fully recommend them to every practical Horseshoer in the country. Yours respectfully,

No. 8 Everett Street. JOHN GRACE.

OUR IMPROVED. ALL SIZES AND WEIGHTS. G.W. BOHANON. PATENTED, 1888.

THE BOHANON SULKY!

BEST MADE.
Perfect Riding Buggies.
Breaking Carts.
Fine Repairing, Reasonable Prices.

Bohanon Carriage Co., 161-163 Ogden Ave., CHICAGO.

Send for Catalogue.

VETERINARY.

DR. THOS. BOWHILL, M.R.C.V.S

VETERINARY SURGEON.

Graduate New Veterinary College, Edinburgh. Awarded the Highland and Agricultural Societies Medals for Horse Pathology, Anatomy, Physiology and Histology. The Williams' Prize, '84-'85, for highest works in professional examinations, and six first-class certificates of merit. Honorary Member Illinois State Veterinary Medical Association.

CENTENNIAL STABLES,

1523-25 California Street. Telephone No. 66.

Veterinary Infirmary and Residence, 2209 Jackson Street. Telephone 4128.

W. H. WOODRUFF.

Veterinary Dentist,

AT FASHION STABLES,

221 Ellis Street, San Francisco

Improved Instruments, Humane Methods, First-Class Work.

Dr. Wm. H. Jones, M.R.C.V.S.

Veterinary Surgeon,

(CLUB STABLES)

409–411 Taylor Street, San Francisco.

Consultations by letter, and cases of URGENT NECESSITY in the interior will receive prompt attention.

H. E. CARPENTER,

Veterinary Surgeon,

Graduate of Ontario Veterinary College, Toronto, Canada.

RESIDENCE AND VETERINARY INFIRMARY

331 Golden Gate Ave., San Francisco.

Telephone 3069.

OPEN DAY AND NIGHT.

No risk in throwing Horses. Veterinary Operating Table on the premises.

DR. C. MASOERO,

Veterinary Surgeon,

Successor to DR. A. DeTAVEL,

GRADUATE OF ROYAL VETERINARY COLLEGE, TURIN.

OFFICE AND INFIRMARY,

No. 811 HOWARD STREET,

Between Fourth and Fifth. SAN FRANCISCO.

Telephone, No. 457.

R. WATKINS,

Veterinary Dentist,

Of twelve years practice, is now permanently located in San Francisco, and may be found at C. S. Crittendens' Golden Gate Livery and Riding Academy, 24 to 28 Golden Gate Avenue.

Will treat ailments of the horse's mouth, and cure all such. Siderein Pullers and Tongue Lollers, etc.

Satisfaction guaranteed. Orders by mail will receive prompt attention. Examination Free.

Scientific Horse Shoeing

BOYD & MORGAN

Are now permanently located at

No. 106 Golden Gate Ave.,

A few doors above Crittenden's Stables.

Particular attention given to Track and Road Horse. Our Motto: "The Shoe to fit the foot vs. The foot to fit the shoe."

We have references from the leading Trainers, Drivers and Breeders of the Coast. Give us a trial.

E. J. O'ROUKE.

I have the honor to announce to my old patrons and the general public that I may be found at my old stand, where, as heretofore, the

Shoeing of Horses,

whether for the Track, Drive, or for general work, will receive my personal attention.

E. J. O'ROUKE,
211 Ellis Street

NOTICE.

C. BRUCE LOWE,

Pedigree Stock Agent,

19 Bligh Street,

SYDNEY, New South Wales.

Reference—J. B. HAGGIN, ESQ.

Brushes.

BUCHANAN BROS.,

Brush Manufacturers,

609 Sacramento Street, two doors above Montgomery.

Horse Brushes of every description on hand and made to order. Bristle Body Brushes our Specialty.

Everything for Trotter or Runner,

At J. A. McKERRON'S,

228, 230 and 232 Ellis St., San Francisco

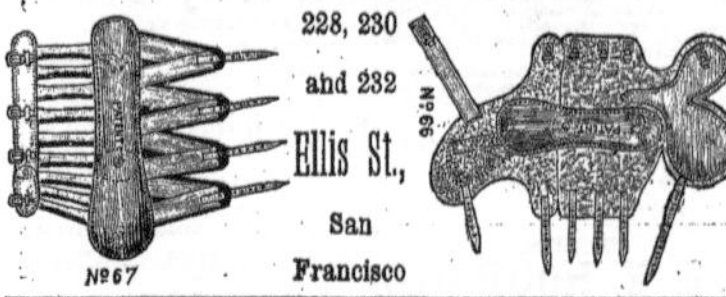

THE IMPROVED NOYES ROAD-CART,

PATENTED JULY 17, 1883, AND JUNE 8, 1886.

Some of the Advantages of the Noyes Cart Over All Others.

There is no bar for the rider to climb over in getting in or out. The horse can be hitched eighteen inches nearer than any other road-cart made. You can get in or out with perfect safety—no danger of being thrown into the wheel—a great advantage in breaking colts. THE EASIEST CART FOR ROAD OR TRACK. The only cart that a horse can be speeded to within one second as fast as to a sulky. All our carts are made of the very best materials and are warranted. Manufactured by the NOYES CART COMPANY, Kalamazoo, Mich.

They are indorsed by the following horsemen, all of whom are using them. Ask their opinion of the Noyes Cart: John Splan, who drove Guy a full mile in 2:17¾ and Chanter a half-mile in 1:10¾ to a Noyes Cart, says he would not take $250 for it if he could not get another; W. J. Gordon, Glenville, O.; W. B. Fasig, Cleveland, O.; Dave Muckel, Cleveland, O.; R. J. Moorehead, North East, Pa.; W. J. Chamberlain, Cleveland, O.; H. P. Malone, Bradford, Pa.; S. A. Brown & Co., Kalamazoo Stock Farm; Charles Marvin, Menlo Park, Cal.; W. H. Crawford, Lexington, Ky.; S. L. Caton, who gave Bell Boy a mark at Los Angeles, Cal., of 2:19¼, and drove Chanter a half mile in 1:06¾ and Lowland Girl a full mile in 2:22 to a Noyes Cart; Mike Bowerman, Lexington, Ky.; James Golden, Medford, Mass.; John E. Turner, Philadelphia, Pa.; T. L. Newton, Beaver Dam, Wis.; F. V. Johnston, Marshall, Mich.; W. H. McCarthy, Los Angeles, Cal.; A. W. Dennison, El Dorado, Kan.; P. O. Shank, Cleveland, O.; Charles Barnard, Boston, Mass.; Johnson Bros., Greenville, Mich.; John G. Avery, Buffalo, N. Y.; General R. L. Howard, Buffalo, N. Y.; Howard Conklin, Buffalo, N. Y.; W. D. Ham, Hennepin, Ill.; R. G. Henry, Waterbury, Conn; J. E. Hayer, Newburgh, O.; J. C. Hart, Jefferson, Tex.; A. W. Harbison, Rock Point, Pa.; Carl Hodges, Battle Creek, Mich.; Barney Treacy, Lexington, Ky.; George Forbes, Cleveland, O.; Gifford Dudley, Topeka, Kan.; William and J. L. Thompson, Lamont, Pa.; C. F. Emery, Forest City Stock Farm, Cleveland, O.; R. F. Jones, Minneapolis, Minn.; John Forbes, Elyria, O.; D. J. Downs Battle Creek, Mich.; Frank Caton, Randall Station, O.; Arthur D. Sutton, Ind., Pa.; W. F. Neely, Grand Ridge, Ill.; Walter Clark, owner of Pilot Medium, Battle Creek, Mich.; H. R. Kingman, Battle Creek, Mich.; Dr. Sutton and H. C. Reed, Kalamazoo, Mich.; Budd Doble, Chicago, Ill.

SOLE MANUFACTURERS OF STONE'S PATENT SULKY CASE.

They will more than save their cost in one season, and horsemen campaigning trotters cannot afford to do without them. Would refer to Samuel A. Brown, Kalamazoo Stock Farm, S. L. Caton and W. H. McCarthy. Address

NOYES CART COMPANY, Kalamazoo, Mich.

Office and Factory, corner Rose and Eleanor streets. R. ARTHUR STONE, Manager.

Poplar Grove Breeding FARM.

Standard-bred Trotters, Colts and Fillies.

The get of CLOVIS, 4909; PASHA, 2039; APEX, 2935.

For Sale.

Address S. N. STRAUBE, Poplar Grove Breeding Farm, **Fresno, Cal.**

Inspection by intending purchasers invited, and information by mail.

OSSIDINE

Results obtained at the well-known KALAMAZOO FARM.

KALAMAZOO, MICH., Sept. 15, 1888.

GENTLEMEN:—We have used OSSIDINE for the past two years, and consider it invaluable for Sprung Tendons, Curbs, Ringbone, and Spavins; there is nothing equals it: and for us it effected a permanent cure where firing failed, although performed by one of the most successful veterinarians on the continent. We have recommended it to others with like success, and believe it has more merit than any blister ever used.

Very respectfully yours,
S. A. BROWNE & CO., Prop's.

This scientific preparation is an absolute cure for all bony or callous lumps on horses, and is a more powerful absorbent than "firing," without creating the slightest blemish.

Acknowledged by leading horsemen of the world to be the ONLY preparation that will remove a Bone Spavin after it has become ossified.

We have authority also to refer to Mr. JEROME I. CASE, Mr. FRED. GEBHARD, Mr. JOHN PORTER (Trainer to H.R.H. the Prince of Wales), And hundreds of others from whom we have very flattering testimonials.

One Style Only. $3.00 per Bottle.

A. P. BUSH & CO., 149 Pearl St., BOSTON, MASS., Sole Agents for United States and Canada. *Beware of Imitations.*

SOLD BY C. N. Crittenton, A. R. Van Nest & Co., and C. M. Moseman & Bro., NEW YORK CITY. Morrisson, Plummer & Co., Peter Van Schaack & Sons. CHICAGO, ILL. John D. Park & Son, CINCINNATI, O.; Floyd & Foster, DETROIT, MICH.; F. S. Slosson, CLEVELAND, O.; Meyer Bros. Drug Co., ST. LOUIS, MO.; R. A. Robinson, LOUISVILLE, KY.; H. H. Moore & Sons, STOCKTON, CAL.

J. C. JOHNSON & CO.,

IMPORTERS, MANUFACTURERS, AND DEALERS IN

HARNESS & SADDLERY

☞ We carry a large assortment of goods in our line from the cheapest to the best made.

400 to 404 Market Street

Corner BATTERY STREET, San Francisco.

J. O'KANE, 767 MARKET STREET.

Horse Boots, Clothing and Furnishings, For Track, Driving Training and Stable. Every requisite for Horsemen. Harness, Medicines, Etc.

The PARKER Hammerless Shot Gun.

At the Annual Tournament of 1889, held at Cannes, France, the grand prize, consisting of 2000 Francs and a Valuable Cup, was won by The Parker Hammerless.

The first Parker Hammerless Gun made won the championship of America at Decatur Illinois.

SEND FOR ILLUSTRATED CIRCULAR.

PARKER BROS., Makers,

New York Salesroom, 97 Chambers St., Meriden Conn.

To Horse Breeders and Stockmen.

SPECIAL OFFER.

I offer for sale, title warranted, the best bargain in stock ranches on the Coast. The ranch contains 887 acres; one mile frontage on Clear Lake; 310 acres alfalfa land; 120 acres now seeded to alfalfa, cuts six tons per acre; 70 acres in timothy cuts four tons per acre, both without irrigation. The rest of the land is fine rolling pasture, or can be cultivated. There are two dwellings on the property, one new, cost $2,000; three barns, capacity 330 tons of hay; two artesian wells, with pipes laid to houses, barns and dairy house. Fine cold spring on premises. An orchard of apples, pears and cherries now in bearing. Peaches, prunes, apricots, strawberries and all other fruits do well. At option of purchaser with the property will be sold 600 head of sheep, 61 head of cattle, 22 horses, and 7 young brood mares in foal. Also wagons, harness, farming implements, etc.

This is a grand opportunity to establish a stock ranch. The S. F. & N. P. R. R. now runs within 35 miles of the property and will in a short time be extended quite to the place. Price $25,000, half cash. For further particulars, apply to

JOHN T. PETERS,
Agent for Sonoma Lake and Mendocino County Land.
29 New Montgomery St., in Grand Hotel.

MANHATTAN FOOD.

Keeps horses healthy, promotes digestion, fattens horses, loosens the hide, assists the appetite, prevents leg swelling, strengthens the kidneys, regulates the bowels and destroys worms. $7.50 per 100 lbs. Ask your dealer for it or send to

MANHATTAN FOOD CO., 206 Clay St., S. F.

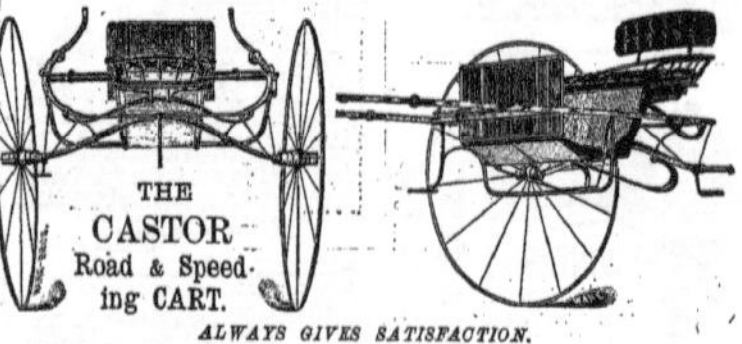

THE CASTOR Road & Speeding CART.

ALWAYS GIVES SATISFACTION.

Combining perfect riding qualities, proportions and balance, with genteel appearance.

No vehicle exhibits a horse to better advantage, and no Cart approaches them for speeding or training purposes.

A stylish vehicle for exercising or pleasure driving, at one-fourth the cost of a carriage. Have none of the horse jockey or objectionable features of other Road Carts.

They are the Leading Cart wherever introduced, and are in use by the most prominent breeders and pleasure drivers everywhere.

Elegant Shifting Top Carts.

Perfectly Balanced Stylish Pole Carts.

For Illustrated Catalogue, with Prices, address,

LEWIS F. CASTOR,
Frankford, Philadelphia, Pa.

JOHN PLAN, General Agent.

TWENTY PAGES.

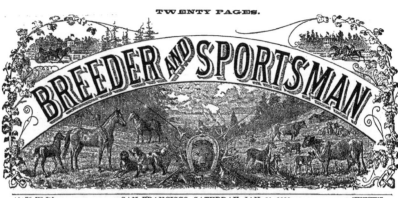

BREEDER AND SPORTSMAN

Vol. XVI. No. 2.
No. 313 BUSH STREET.

SAN FRANCISCO, SATURDAY, JAN. 11, 1890.

SUBSCRIPTION
FIVE DOLLARS A YEAR.

ALFRED G, 2:19¾.

Owned by G. E. Guerne. - - Santa Rosa.

It is hard to say farewell and almost as hard to write it, but from the present aspect of affairs, the horse-loving community of California will, within a few days, bid farewell to Alfred G., 2:19¾, the first trotting grandson of Electioneer to enter the 2:20 list. Last week we mentioned that it was extremely likely Alfred G. would be sent to Kentucky, and an interview with Mr. Guerne, the owner, verifies the report. The Sonoma County Stock Breeder's Association were the owners of Anteeo, and were prevailed upon to send their great young horse to the celebrated blue grass region of Kentucky, and that their advisers were not wrong in the estimate that the Eastern horse breeders would put upon the horse, it is only necessary to say that in less than six days his book was filled for the season of 1889 at a service fee of $200. J. W. Knox, who took Anteeo East, as is well known, finally sold him to the Kalamazoo Stock Farm, and to-day he is considered by many the greatest stock horse in the western States. It is only a few weeks ago that Peter V. Johnson, the well known trainer and driver, said in our presence that he fully expected to see Anteeo one of the greatest sires of the age. An opinion such as that, and coming from competent authority, carries sufficient weight to warrant the belief that Electioneer's son has a grand future before him.

Mr. Knox has made a contract with Mr. Guerne, by which he takes Alfred G. to Lexington, Ky., where he will stand for public service at $200, and the lessee also has the privilege of selling the horse, the price placed on him being $25,000. It is hardly to be presumed that a young horse like this will ever have a chance to return to California, as there are Eastern buyers always on the outlook for rare bargains, and this is as good a one as was ever offered.

Alfred G. is a handsome bay, with four white feet and a small star in forehead. He stands 15.2 in height, and weighs 1050 pounds. His conformation is exceedingly good to the eye, and he will please any judge of horse flesh. As a three-year-old he made two appearances, the first of which was at Santa Rosa on August 15th, where he met Ben Davis, Redwood and Anti-Coolie. He won the first and third heats, but was ultimately beaten out by Ben Davis. The next appearance of the colt was at Petaluma, where he had as antagonists Redwood, Ben Davis, Anti-Coolie and Alice, but he failed to do better than get third money, the largest end of the purse being taken by Redwood, another son of Anteeo.

Napa was the first of the circuit towns in 1889, and there we find him battling against his old opponent Redwood, Lookout, Nono Y. and Flora B. He won the first heat by a head in 2:31½, Redwood being second. Lookout, who had considerable local backing, won the second heat in 2:27¾, and the third and fourth heats were won by Redwood in 2:24½ and 2;27½. In the fifth heat a change of drivers was made, J. A. Dustin taking his place behind Alfred G., and from the start it was seen that the alteration was beneficial. Hickok, with his master hand, was driving Redwood, and it was all he could do to win the deciding heat in 2:25, Alfred G. being a good second. It was now evident that, barring accident, Alfred G. would make a name for himself on the circuit, as he had shown speed enough to beat his class if handled properly, and the colt was turned over to Dustin's management. The change was noticeable at San Rosa, where he won in straight heats, in 2:29¾, 2:23½ and 2:24¾. Again, at Petaluma, he repeated the trick in the District four-year-old race, where he again won as he pleased in 2:36½, 2:30½ and 2:27½. Oakland was the next objective point, and here we find Alfred G. pitted against Atto Rex, Lord Byron, Pink and Express. Atto Rex, the San Diego horse, had made such a showing on the circuit, that he sold favorite in the pools at $60, Lord Byron $55, Express $27, Pink $20, and Alfred G. was almost neglected, at $10 and $11. Rex won the race in straight heats, but Alfred G. was second in each; the first heat he was only beaten by a nose in 2;21¼.

At Sacramento the game young horse was overtaken with the prevailing disease, the epizootic, and was far from being in winning form, still he managed to get third place in four heats out of five, each of his miles being trotted inside of 2:21. When he appeared at Stockton the following week, he was a very sick horse, and it seemed a shame to turn him loose in the company he had to face, the field consisting of Hazel Wilkes, Emma Temple, Mary Lou, Pink, Lorita, and the subject of this sketch. Alfred G. won the first heat in 2:23½, but was beaten by Hazel Wilkes, by half a length, for the second heat in 2:20. Even the constitution of a horse could not stand the excessive strain, especially in view of his trouble, and he had to be content with third money, Emma Temple ultimately winning the race. At San Jose he was still under the weather, and was again unable to do better than get third money, in the 2:23 class, Hazel Wilkes proving the victor.

At the Pacific Coast Trotting Horse Breeder's Association meeting, we again find Alfred G. contending against Nono Y. and Balkan, he winning easily the first, second and fourth heats in 2:24, 2:23½ and 2:23. He was now sent back to Santa Rosa, where he was given an occasional jog, but the weather was so bad that he could not even be given a work out.

When the news was flashed over the wires that an attempt would be made to lower a lot of the records at Napa, Mr. Guerne's horse was sent overland, and there joined the great band of horses that were about to add another laurel to the wealth of California. Arriving on Saturday morning, Alfred G. was sent for a record that afternoon, Marvin driving the grandson of Electioneer, and notwithstanding the lack of necessary work, the celebrated Palo Alto driver had no difficulty in sending Alfred G. a mile in 2:19¾.

When the exhibition was concluded, the fifteen hundred spectators fairly made the welkin ring, as both owner and horse are very popular. It was another grand victory for the advocates of the Electioneer blood, and stamped the fact solidly, that Electioneer does breed on in generation after generation. We are extremely sorry to think that our neighbors further East are going to have the advantages of Alfred G.'s breeding, but what is a loss to California is a gain to Kentucky. The following is his pedigree;

ALFRED G., 2:19¾	Anteeo, 2:16¼	Electioneer	Hambletonian 10	Abdallah Chas. Kent Mare
			Green Mountain Maid	Harry Clay Shanghai Mary
		Columbine	A. W. Richmond	Blackbird by Rattler
			Columbia	Bonnie Scotland Young Fashion
	Rosa B.	Speculation	Hambletonian 10	Abdallah Kent Mare
			Martha Washington..	Burr's Washington by Abdallah
		Elizabeth..	Alexander 490........	Geo. M. Patchen Jr. Lady Crum
			Nora.....	Glencoe Thoroughbred.

Foals of 1889.

Trotting foals of 1889, property of Morse Stock Farm, Kewanna, Fulton County, Ind.:—

Aug. 7th, 1889, bay colt by Blue Vein 8466 (son of Blue Bull 75), dam Lily by Resolute, son of Alhambra, he by Mambrino Chief.

Aug. 8th, 1889, bay colt by Blue Vein 8466, dam by Queen, Daniel Lambert, 2nd dam by Young Columbus.

Aug. 19th, 1889, bay filly by Grenadeer (son of Princeps, dam Dawn, full sister to Nutwood) dam purity by Blue Bull 75, 2nd dam by Zoro, son of Boston.

May 22nd, 1889, bay filly by Blue Vein, dam Flora Leiter by Hickory, 2:27½, 2nd dam by Resolute by Alhambra.

May 31st, 1889, bay filly by Blue Vein, dam Mary Parks by Bonnie Scotland, 2nd dam by Knox Messenger.

Entries for the Friendly Stakes.

ENTRIES RECEIVED BY THE WASHINGTON PARK CLUB.

J. Q. Adams' b c Jack Star, by Day Star, dam Laraminta.
J. Q. Adams' b c Paymaster, by Onondaga, dam Vallisea.
T. W. Anderson's b c Ke-he-ma, by Hindoo, dam Bayadere.
Bashford Manor Farm's b f Cantatrice, by Falsetto, dam Sungleam.
Bashford Manor Farm's b c Gascon, by Falsetto, dam Mollie Wood.
Bashford Manor Farm's b f Caprice, by Leonatus, dam Belle Boyden.
August Belmont's b c Fritz, by imp. St. Blaise, dam Fillette.
August Belmont's b c Masher, by imp. The Ill Used, dam Magnetism.
August Belmont's blk or br g Adair, by Imp. St. Blaise, dam Imp. Adosinda.
August Belmont's ch f La Tosca, by Imp. St. Blaise, dam Imp. Toucques.
D. D. Bell's b c Hueneme, by Billet, dam Virgie D.
Bedford & Steele's br f Mignon, by Billet, dam Vienna.
Beverwyck Stable's br f Polly S, by Whisper, dam Amandine.
Beverwyck Stable's b f Bertha Campbell, by King Alfonso, dam Vulpine.
Beverwyck Stable's b c Craft, by Fellowcraft, dam Lady Himyar.
Otis Bowers' ch c Berndene, by Wawakus, dam Menetta.
T. D. Carter's b c Glen Rush, by Glengary, dam Pearlash.
T. D. Carter's b c Altair, by Blazes, dam Lizzie B.
Gentry Campbell's ch c Mirabeau, by Jils Johnson, dam Little Fannie.
W. L. Cassidy & Co.'s blk or br c Sir Abner, by Uhlan, dam Barbary.
W. L. Cassidy & Co.'s br c Liberty Bell, by Blazes, dam Belle.
W. L. Cassidy & Co.'s ch g The Major, by Glengarry, dam Lucia.
T. J. Clay's b c Balgowan, by Strathmore, dam Trinkitat.
Geo. H. Clay's b f Ace of Hearts, by Imp. Zorilla, dam Imp. Gardenia.
R. E. Campbell's b f Saxonette, by Imp. Saxon, dam Marionette.
Crit. Davis' b g Leader II., by Leonatus, dam Ell-See-Ess.
H. B. Durham's b c Long Fortune, by Longfellow, dam Misfortune.
Marcus Daly's br c Brown Fox, by San Fox, dam Illusion.
Marcus Daly's br f Virgin, by Miner, dam Virgie.
Marcus Daly's b f Audacity, by Imp. Darebin, dam Zozodont.
Eastin & Larabie's b c High Tariff, by Longfellow, dam Christine.
Eastin & Larabie's b c Post Scout, by Longfellow, dam Gypsy.
A. L. Ferguson's b f Mattie Allen, by Billet, dam Vassar.
Walter Gratz's b f Love in Idleness, by Glengarry, dam Bonnie Harold.
C. C. Graves' b c Running Brooch, by Ten Broeck, dam Isis.
J. O. Gray's br f Amy Robsart, by Stratford, dam Lady B.
Gray & Co.'s ch c Quarter Stretch, by Faustus, dam Tassel.
Gray & Co.'s b c Zender, by Faustus, dam Bank Stock.
Geo. Hake's ch c Bernard Fowler, by Versailles, dam Cousin Kate.
Geo. Hake's br c George Bomes, by Versailles, dam Nyanza.
Geo. Hake's ch f Maggie Jordan, by Versailles, dam Mollie Merrill.
John Hunter's blk f Oriawin, by Onondaga, dam Annette.
John Hunter's b f Mayflower, by Iroquois, dam Blue Gown.
John Hunter's ch c Hoodlum, by Joe Daniels, dam Miss Clay.
John Hunter's b c Dictum, by Iroquois, dam Bonnie Meade.
George Hearst's b c El Verano, by Hock Hocking, dam Vixen.
George Hearst's b c J. B., by Warwick, dam Maria F.
George Hearst's b c Yo Semite, by Hyder Ali, dam Nellie Collier.
George Hearst's ch c Anarchist, by Joe Hooker, dam Chestnut Belle.
George Hearst's ch c Snow Ball, by Joe Hooker, dam Laura Winston.
George Hearst's ch c Charley Brown, by Jim Brown, dam Viola.
George Hearst's ch c Primero, by Powhattan, dam Speed.
D. R. Harness' b g Equinox, by Grenada, dam Sunshine.
Highland Park Stable's b f Ella Blackburn, by Luke Blackburn, dam Amerique.
A. B. & S. P. Harlan's br c Ascot, by Vanderbilt, dam Nina Turner.
Hogg & McGuffin's b c Lancelot, by Longfellow, dam Lady Ringlet.
Ingleside Place's ch c The Kaiser, by imp Pizarro, dam Blomida.
Ireland Bro.'s b c Woodvale, by imp Deceiver, dam Lady Grafton.
Ireland Bro's ch f Marietta, by imp Deceiver, dam Silver Bell.
E. Johnson's c Wild Sunflower, by Zeta, dam Bingen.
W. P. Keegan's b c Jack Shelley, by Aristides, dam Odessa.
W. P. Keegan's b c Grand Duke Michael, by Uhlan, dam Rebecca.
Kentucky Stable's b c Ganges, by Hindoo, dam Emily Fuller.
Kentucky Stable's br f Mary McGowan, by Longfellow, dam Encore.
Kentucky Stable's b f St. Bridget, by Leonatus, dam Bettie Magruder.
W. H. Laudeman's ch c Palestine, by Powhattan, dam Cachuca.
M. J. Lennon's ch f Laura E., by Grenada, dam Alert.
W. R. Letcher's b c Caperton, by Longfellow, dam Rosemary.
W. R. Letcher's br c Harry Ray, by Longfellow, dam Indemnity.
W. R. Letcher's ch c Greenleaf, by Forester, dam Pixy.
W. R. Letcher's b f Mattie Mc, by Jils Johnson, dam Lizzie Stone.
A. McGuigan's ch c Chimes, by Onondaga, dam Fonwitch.
A. McGuigan's b c Linlithgow, by Duke of Montrose, dam Trinket.
A. McGuigan's ch f Annie Megrue, by Onondaga, dam Skylight.
W. M. Murry's blk c Power, by Powhattan, dam Lawn Tennis.
W. M. Murry's b c Parapet, by Bulwark, dam Nettie Brady.
W. M. Murry's ch c Gerald, by Powhattan, dam Geneva.
W. M. Murry's b f Lady Scoggan, by Little Ruffin, dam Hiawassee.
John Neil's ch c Toronto, by Fonso, dam Ætna.
Bryan Ubear's br g Leader, by Lead On, dam Mary J.
Palo Alto Stock Farm's ch f Glenlivet, by Flood, dam Glendew.
Palo Alto Stock Farm's ch f Tearless, by Wildidle, dam imp Teardrop.
Palo Alto Stock Farm's ch c Rinfax, by Argyle, dam imp Amelia.
Palo Alto Stock Farm's b c Scamper, by Shannon, dam Sallie Gardner.
Palo Alto Stock Farm's b c Jackson, by Flood, dam imp Queen Bess.
Wickliffe Preston's b f Marmoro, by Falsetto, dam Marmoset.
B. F. Pettit's b f Miss Bowling, by Glenelg, dam Katie Bowling.
B. F. Pettit's gr f Kittie H., by imp Deceiver, dam Grey Nell.
H. S. Payne's ch f Apex, by Buchanan, dam Ascension.
L. J. Rose's br c Conrad, by Flood, dam imp Gonia.
L. J. Rose's br c Oscar by Wildidle, dam imp. Petroleuse.
L. J. Rose's b f Flight by Flood, dam imp Flirt.
J. B. Ross' b f Hazel Hurst by Billet, dam Juanita.
Rutherford & Doxey's br f Laura Doxey by Iroquois, dam Sallie Norvall.
Santa Anita Stable's b f Blazeaway by Blazes, dam Dollie L.
Santa Anita Stable's b f Ogarita by Longfellow, dam Mission Belle.
Santa Anita Stable's b f La Cienaga by Grinstead, dam Jennie D.
Santa Anita Stable's ch c El Carmen by Gano, dam Grey Annie.
Santa Anita Stable's b c Encinado by Rutherford, dam Aritta.
Santa Anita Stable's b f Esperanza by Grinstead, dam Hermosa.
Scoggan Bros.' b c National by Leonatus, dam Brandoline.
Scoggan Bros.' b c Eli Kindig by George Kinney, dam Leona.
Scoggan Bros.' b f Lady Washington by Miser, dam Minnarette.
E. H. Storn's ch f Caroline by Forester, dam Albatross.
E. H. Storn's br f Nellie Whittaker by Sensation, dam Clara A.
E. H. Stern's b c John Shea by Outcast, dam Storm Angel.
Stony Point Stable's ch c Yale 91 by Onondaga, dam Zaidee.
S. Smith & Co.'s br c Tom Rogers by Falsetto, dam Ems.
S. Smith & Co.'s b c Sanford by Falsetto, dam Kitty
S. Smith & Co.'s b c Dickerson by Duke of Montrose, dam Billetta.
S. B. Stroud's b f Belle of Norwalk by Billy Lee, dam by Hardwood.
Talbot Bros.' ch c Mountjoy by Pontiac, dam Accidenta.
Talbot Bros.'s b c Villain by Barnes, dam Villa.
Talbot Bros.' b c Brutus by Billet, dam Hi.
Talbot Bros.' b f Mary O. by Billet, dam Vega.
Talbot Bros.' b f Miss Hawkins by Billett, dam Lady Motley.
Talbot & Rogers' b g Cossack by imp. Uhlan, dam Kate Claxton.
J. E. Taylor's ch c Sunrise by Tennyson, dam Agnes Dunlap.
H. A. Trowbridge's ch f Queenie Trowbridge by Aliunde, dam Ada Lambert.
R. Tucker's br f Too Sweet by Longfellow, dam Allegro.
D. Waldo's br or blk f Katie Foley by Falsetto, dam Little Casino.
Theo. Winters' b c Rey del Rey by Norfolk, dam Marion.
Theo. Winters' ch c San Juan by Norfolk, dam Ballinette.
Theo. Winters' ch c Judge Post by Joe Hooker, dam Countess Zeika.
Theo. Winters' ch f Belle Songer by Joe Hooker, dam Lou Spencer.
C. E. Winchell's b c Senor by Bersan, dam Sister to Joe Daniels.
C. Weatherford's ch f Miss Courtney by Blarney, dam Comet.
W. O. Wood's b c King Silver by imp. Silver Mine, dam Miss Mickey.
Woodford & Buckner's b c Bramblebush by Greenbush, dam Brambaletta.
R. N. Watts' b f Ella Mack by Wawekus, dam Red Bonnet.
J. M. Young & Co.'s b c Chance by Powhattan, dam Patula.
J. M. Young & Co.'s c f Lott by Powhattan, dam Lotta.

ENTRIES RECEIVED BY CONEY ISLAND JOCKEY CLUB.

P. Meaney's b c Sam Corey, by Longtaw, dam Algebra.
W. L. Scott's ch c Bolero, by Rayon d'Or, dam All Hands 'Round.
W. L. Scott's b c Versatile, by Rayon d'Or, dam Valleria.
W. L. Scott's ch c Florimor, by Rayon d'Or, dam Florence I.
W. L. Scott's ch f Miss Ransom, by Rayon d'Or, dam Nellie Ransom.
W. L. Scott's b or br f Amulet, by Rayon d'Or, dam Presto.
W. L. Scott's b f Exclusion, by Rayon d'Or, dam Monopoly.
W. L. Scott's b f Maywood, by Rayon d'Or, dam Belle of Maywood.
W. L. Scott's b c Vagabond, by Wanderer, dam Vivid.
W. L. Scott's b f Tulle, by Wanderer, dam Clemency.
W. L. Scott's ch f Millrace, by Wanderer, dam Santa Lucia.
M. Keller's b f Edith L., by Geo. Kinney, dam Midsummer.
M. Keller's ch g Woodford, by Hindoo, dam Theckla.
Clover Stable's blk f Margherita, by Rossifer, dam Certiorari.
Clover Stable's ch f Sarah Hall, by Stratford, dam Minnie Andrews.
Henry R. Levi's br c Baltimore, by Stratford, dam Gazelle.
Henry R. Levi's b c Annapolis, by Alarm, dam Blossom.
S. P. Knut's b c Tom Alms, by Charaxus, dam Latona.
W. C. Daly's ch f Liz, by St. Blaise, dam Feu Follet.
J. F. Donovan's blk c ——, by Hindoo, dam Uproar.
Davis & Hall's ch c, by Luke Blackburn, dam Janet Norton.
Davis & Hall's br c, by Gaberlunzie, dam Olive Branch.
Davis & Hall's br c, by Gaberlunzie, dam May D
Davis & Hall's ch f Euna, by Gaberlunzie, dam Eunice.
Auburndale Stable's b c, by Tympanum, dam Oreda.
Auburndale Stable's br c St. Crescent, by St. Blaise, dam Lorelle.
Labold Bros' b or br c, by Duke of Montrose, dam Patti.
John Crocker's b g, by Fonso, dam Madoline.
J. A. & A. H. Morris' b c Westchester, by Glenelg, dam Ann Fief.
J. A. & A. H. Morris' b c Key West, by Glenelg, dam Florida.
J. A. & A. H. Morris's ch c Dr. Hasbrack, by Sir Modred, dam Sweetbriar.
J. A. & A. H. Morris' b c Two Tips, by Darebin, dam Kiss-Me-Quick.
J. A. & A. H. Morris' b c Miletus, by Darebin, dam Melita.
J. A. & A. H. Morris' b c Mountain Deer, by Iroquois, dam Martica.
D. D. Wither's b c, by Uncas, dam Necromancy.
D. D. Withers' ch c, by Uncas, dam Abundance.
D. D. Wither's b f, by King Ernest, dam Laura Gould.
Jack Neil's c Toronto, by Fonso, dam Ætna.
Empire Stable's ch f Landscape, by Woodlands, dam Artifice.
Geo. Hearst's b f, by Falsetto, dam Explosion.
Geo. Hearst's b c, by Warwick, or San Fox, dam Second Hand.
Geo. Hearst's ch c, by Joe Daniels, dam Fostena.
Geo. Hearst's ch c by Hyder Ali, dam Fidelity.
D. T. Pulsifer's b c by Attila, dam The Squaw.
D. T. Pulsifer's ch c by Spendthrift, dam Piccadilly.
D. T. Pulsifer's ch c by Stratford, dam Heatherbelle.
Thos. N. Shreve's ch f by Volturno, dam Miss McGowan.
Thos N. Shreve's br f by Volturno, dam Merry Lass.
W. J. Spiers' b c War Duke by Duke of Montrose, dam War Over.
H. Theobald's br c imp. Douglass by Lowland Chief, dam imp. Restless.
Colaizzi & Fisher's b c by Duke of Montrose, dam Lizzie S.
August Belmont's b c Fritz by St. Blaise, dam Fillette.
August Belmont's b c Masher by Ill-Used, dam Magnetism.
August Belmont's blk or br g Adair by St Blaise, dam Adosinda.
August Belmont's ch f La Tosca by St Blaise, dam Toucques.
S. S. Brown's ch c by Richmond, dam Mayfield.
S. S. Brown's ch c by Richmond, dam Gladys.
S. S. Brown's ch f by Richmond, dam Ellen Alice.
S. S. Brown's ch f by Himyar, dam Jewel.
S. S. Brown's b c by Richmond, dam Alabama.
Rancocas Stable's br c Cyrus by Emperor, dam Cyrilla.
Rancocas Stable's b c Sirocco by Emperor, dam Breeze.
Rancocas Stable's b c Uncertainty by Emperor, dam Quandary.
Rancocas Stable's b f Killdeer by Darebin, dam Lou Lanier.
Rancocas Stable's b f Vanity by Rotherhill or Glenelg, dam Pride.
Rancocas Stable's ch f Lima by Pizarro, dam Gladiola.
Rancocas Stable's b f Arrogance by Emperor, dam Disdain.
Rancocas Stable's ch c imp. Catian by Cymbal, dam imp. The Cat.
R. A. Swigert's b f Marmose by Glenelg, dam Marmot.
Louis Stuart & Co.'s b c by Pickwick, dam Shamrock.
Louis Stuart & Co.'s b c by Pickwick, dam Maggie Hunt.
R. Tucker's b f Lizzie Sanier by Falsetto, dam Anxiety.
Preakness Stable's ch f Flavilla by Macduff, dam Vintage.
Kinzea Stone's b or br f Sister Linda by imp. Zorilla, dam Celinda.
Dudley Allen's b c Kingman by Glengarry, dam Patricia.
J. W. Turner's b c Gay Deceiver by Deceiver, dam Waifer.
J. W. Turner's ch c London Smoke by London, dam Etha.
Dwyer Bro.'s b c Baldwin by Enquirer, dam Bribery.
Dwyer Bro.'s b c Hannibal by Hindoo, dam Mercedes.
Dwyer Bro.'s b c Bay Chester by Luke Blackburn, dam Silver Maid.
Dwyer Bro.'s b c Envoy by Enquirer, dam Tom Boy.
Dwyer Bro.'s b c Blacklock by Billet, dam Jaconet.
Dwyer Bro.'s b c Hempstead by Hindoo, dam Emma Hanley.
Dwyer Bro.'s b c Long Shore by Longfellow, dam Sea Shell.
Dwyer Bro.'s ch c Bush Bolt by Himyar, dam Booty.
Dwyer Bros.' b c Rimlex, by Himyar, dam War Reel.
Dwyer Bros.' blk or br f ——, by Hindoo, dam Katie.
T. J. Megibben's ch c McKinley, by Springbok, dam Zoolite.
T. J. Megibben's ch c Eldorey, by Springbok, dam Astora.
T. J. Megibben's b c Pesarra, by Imp. Pizarro, dam Sister Monica.
T. J. Megibben's ch c Valliera, by Springbok, dam Valseco.
T. J. Megibben's gr c Hypolite, by Springbok, dam Jennie V.
T. J. Megibben's b c Claude Melnotte, by Audrain, dam Mademoiselle.
T. J. Megibben's b c Avalon, by Audrain, dam Venita.
T. J. Megibben's br c Silver Lake, by Imp. Silver Mine, dam Æolia.
T. J. Megibben's ch c Ufa, by Audrain, dam Aurelietta.
T. J. Megibben's ch c Tom Reed, by Audrain, dam War Lass.
T. J. Megibben's ch c Glendale, by Audrain, dam Zephyrus.
T. J. Megibben's ch c Richelieu, by Imp. Richmond, dam Bonairette.
T. J. Megibben's ch c Palmer, by Pizarro, dam Electrical
T. J. Megibben's ch c Onondagas, by Onondaga, dam Minnock.
T. J. Megibben's ch f Vesta, by Audrain, dam Venora.
T. J. Megibben's ch f Ethel, by Springbok, dam Lavena.
T. J. Megibben's ch f Birdella M., by Springbok, dam Ester Planet.
T. J. Megibben's b f Tube Rose, by Springbok, dam Fanny Hall.
T. J. Megibben's b f Silver Bell, by Imp. Silver Mine, dam Manilla.
T. J. Megibben's ch f Actress, by Springbok, dam Edith.
T. J. Megibben's b f Ezelea, by Barnes, dam Clipsa.
T. J. Megibben's blk f Ina B., by Pizarro, dam Zingarelli
T. J. Megibben's b c Major Thornton, by Springbok, dam Blue Bonnet.
Ed. Brown's b c Ben's Pet, by Himyar, dam Themis.
Ed. Brown's ch f Palerna, by Falsetto, dam Lerna.
Ed. Brown's b c King Edward, by King Alfonso, dam Ethel.
Hough Bros.' br c ——, by Stratford, dam Evelyn Carter.
Hough Bros.' b f Queer Girl, by Himyar, dam Queen Ban.
Hough Bros.' b c ——, by Bersan, dam——
Wm. Walker's blk f ——, by Pizarro, dam Lucy Jackson.
Wm. Walker's b c ——, by Spendthrift, dam Phœbe Mayflower.
Wm Walker's b c ——, by Spendthrift, dam Constantinople.
Wm. Walker's b f——, by Falsetto, dam Marshmallow.
G. B. Morris' b g Strathmeath, by Strathmore, dam Flower of Meath.
G. B. Morris' b g ——, by Luke Blackburn, dam Ogarita.
W. O. Scully & Co.'s br c Labold, by Sensation, dam Memento.
McClellan & Roche's b or br c ——, by The Rake, dam Imp. Flora Macdonald.
McClellan & Roche's ch f - , by Hindoo, dam Red and Blue.
B. G. Rhomas' b f Fannie S., by Himyar or Fellowcraft, dam Lula S.
B. G. Thomas, ch f Borka, by Himyar, dam The Sweeper.
Des Cognets, Simpson & Co.'s ch f Last Ban, by King Ban, dam Radha.
A. McGuigan's ch f Annie Megrue, by Onondaga, dam Skylight.

"Abe."

H. G. Crickmore relates a touching incident in the life of Abe, the colored jockey who rode Bayswater, the winner of the first race at the opening of Jerome Park in 1866. Abe was never known to have a surname. The world knew him only as Abe; he rode at New Orleans, Saratoga, and Jerome Park as Abe, and the turf reporters wrote of him as Abe. He was a clever jockey, his methods in the saddle being described as a combination of the methods of Garrison, Hamilton and Murphy. He was neither beautiful nor graceful, but had a knack of "getting there." In slavery days Abe was a chattel of Duncan F. Kenner, of New Orleans, the man after whom the Kenner Stake at Saratoga was named. When the war began Mr. Kenner went to Europe, where he remained till after the days of reconstruction. Abe became a freedman, and in 1866 journeyed to the North to pursue his calling as a jockey, riding wherever and whenever he could get a mount. His savings in a year or two amounted to some $4,000, which he deposited in a bank in New York. Already an old man when he left Dixie, he could not resist a longing to return; so one day, without saying a word to anybody, he set out for New Orleans. Going to the bank he presented his book and asked for $100. "Ise gwine away for good," he informed the teller; "gwine back to deplantashun." "Going away for good, eh?" said the teller, counting out $100 and entering the draft on Abe's book. "What are you going to do with the rest of your money?" "Leave that hyer for my ole marster. He mout need it w'en 'e gits back." When Abe died Mr. Kenner buried him at the head of the home-stretch on his private training-ground near New Orleans.

A young western horse which had evidently been pampered up and drugged for sale, was completely let down and suffering from much fever. Finding it necessary to employ an active purge, I, at the request of the owner, used Simmons Liver Regulator, giving one pint doses twelve hours apart, and as soon as he could eat giving it in powder form in bran. In one week he had fully recovered.—Geo. W. Rodfong, V. S. Germantown, Pa.

REDWOOD, 2:24½.

THE PROPERTY OF A. McFADYEN.

The fame of Anteeo has gone abroad, the splendid performances of his progeny last year, stamping him as a great producer of speed and as a natural consequence those of his sons who are in public service this season will receive a large number of mares. Parties in Kentucky wanted to secure a lease of Redwood, but the owner absolutely refused to allow him to go East, having determined to give the breeders of California a chance to avail themselves of Redwood's grand breeding. A look over the pedigree will prove to any one that Redwood should also transmit speed as he is fleet of foot himself and has not had a chance to get anything near a paper mark for himself. Year before last, as a three-year-old he appeared twice, first at Petaluma where he met Ben Davis, Alfred G., Anti-Coolie and Alice. He won the third, fourth and fifth with considerable ease in 2:35, 2:31 and 2:30½. His last work for 1888 was as a contestant in the Occident Stake at the State Fair Meeting at Sacramento. Sol Wilkes was the only other starter and both of the animals were dead lame. Sol Wilkes won the first heat in 2:47 but Redwood cut the matter short by taking the next heats in 2:39½, 2:36½ and 2:40½.

In 1889 he again appeared, the first time at Napa, where he faced a strong field of horses, and although his half brother won the first heat, and Lookout won the second, still, guided by O. A. Hickok, he won the third, fourth and fifth heats, repeating his performances of the year before, and winning a large sum of money for his backers. In this race he got his record, 2:24½, and it is no exaggeration in stating that he could have reduced that mark by a second or two. He only appeared once again, the epizootic having taken a strong hold of the young colt, and he was in no condition to do himself justice. Mr. McFadyen is positive that during this year he will make a very low record; in fact there are some that imagine he should almost touch his sire's mark. In color he is a beautiful bay, with black points, the relief being one white hind toot. His dam, Lou Medium, was a very fast trotter, being able to show a mile in 2:25 at almost any time; in fact she was one of the best of the progeny left in this State by Milton Medium. The grandam of Redwood was "Fly" the sorrel mare so well known in the Ralston team, The Late Banker, frequently showing the speed of his fast pair to the road frequenters. Fly was undoubtedly well bred, and it seems sheer nonsense that the pedigree of such a fast mare should never have been established. Mr. Ralston was very negligent in the matter, or the word "untraced" would not be there to-day. However, Redwood is as fast as a bullet and will stand for the season of 1890 at the Oakland Trotting Park, where the best of care and attention will be paid to all mares sent to the embrace of this great son of Anteeo.

P. C. T. H. B. A.

The Pacific Coast Trotting Horse Breeder's Association held their annual meeting on Thursday evening at the Palace Hotel, with J. H. White (Pres.) in the chair. Acting Sec'y, W. Page, read his report, showing the good financial status of the association, there being $1,354 to their credit. The treasurer and secretary's reports were adopted. A long discussion then took place as to whether the association should be incorporated, it being eventually referred to the Board. The election of officers resulted in the selection of J. H. White, F. W. Lober, G. Valensin, F. H. Burke, M. Salisbury, A. T. Hatch, W. Page, W. S. Hobart, Irvin Ayres, F. L. Coombs and G. Tompkins.

The newly elected Directors met immediately after the adjournment, and elected the following officers: President, J. H. White; vice-Presidents, F. H. Burke and F. W. Loeber; Treasurer, N. T. Smith. The election of a Secretary was deferred until after the revision of the by-laws.

The new Board of Directors met on Thursday morning, with President J. H. White, F. H. Burke, W. Page, I. Ayres, G. Valensin, F. L. Coombs, F. W. Loeber and G. Tompkins present. The morning session was devoted to the constitution and by-laws, the most noteworthy being the initiation fee which was fixed at $25 and the annual dues at $10. In electing officate no proxies are eligible; the Secretary was instructed to have a sufficient quantity of copies of the By-laws printed.

When the Board of Directors met for the afternoon session, the first and most important discussion took place over the Secretaryship. Mr. Wilfred Page, who was one of the originators and instigators of the association, had acted as temporary Secretary, but being unwilling, owing to his other engagements to continue, Mr. J. P. Kerr was after some discussion unanimously appointed Secretary, and the offices will in future be in the BREEDER AND SPORTSMAN office. The Directors decided to give at their next meeting, the date of which was not fixed, yearling, two-year-old, three and four-year-old stake races, purses for three-year-olds who have not beaten 3:00, four-year-olds that have not beaten 2:40, and also purses for the get of stallions who have no representatives in the 2:30 class, and a purse of $1,000 for 2:30 stallions.

The Stanford stakes were called up for rediscussion, and it was decided to accept the stakes. It will be trotted in 1892 by foals of 1889. The entrance was reduced from $175 to $100.

Pacific Coast Blood Horse Association.

The new Board of Directors met on Thursday evening Mr. Lathrop taking the chair. Messrs. Thornton, Williams, Gunst, Carrol, and Finigan, in fact all the Directors, were present. The Secretary, E. S. Culver, was duly reappointed without a dissenting vote, as was the Treasurer, P. A. Finigan. Mr. Lathrop then appointed the various committees, including several new ones, notably a Handicapping Committee of three, composed of Messrs. Thornton, Williams and Finigan, and another of Messrs. Williams and Gunst, to induce the tradesmen, hotels and railroads to give added money to several stakes in the fall.

Considerable discussion took place about fixing the date of the spring meeting. Saturday, April 12th, was eventually selected as the opening day. Whether the race would take place at the Bay District track or not could not be definitely stated, as probably it would be turned into building property at any time. If they could not secure it Oakland is almost sure to have the ta[illegible]es there. The Pres. then proposed that the Association should secure suitable offices. The Secretary presented an offer from Mr. James P. Kerr to provide them with office room free in the BREEDER AND SPORTSMAN offices. A vote of thanks to Mr. Kerr for his liberal offer was passed, but as some of the Directors were unwilling to accept the room on Mr. Kerr's terms, preferring to pay for the space, Mr. Lathrop was appointed a committee of one to c n with Mr. Kerr. The Board then adjourned.

TURF AND TRACK.

St. Blaise will only serve his owner's mares this season.

Dave Pulsifer thinks Tenny will be invincible next season.

Jim Clare took the flag when McLaughlin resigned at Clifton.

Billy Lakeland paid $3500 for his new stable on the Boulevard.

Kingston is red hot just now, i. e. will be when the flag drops.

Mark D. Hanover, the author of 'Laws of Horses' died last month.

Tucker & Cherry have engaged the light weight Fox for next season.

Frank McCabe trainer for Dywer Bros. at Gravesend has 46 horses in training.

S. P. Stroud, Los Angeles sent the last entry to the Chicago end of the Friendly Stakes.

John Watts, the well known English jockey, has started a stud farm at Exning, England.

D. B. Goff, New York, purchased from Lynn Bros. Stock Farm Ohio, Lynn 2:21½.

Sir Henry Hawkins was by acclamation elected a member of the English Jockey Club last month.

A mare is said to have dropped dead in Bangor, Maine, within six months of her 42nd birthday.

The blind pacing gelding William Newman, 2:27½, was sold at auction last month at New Orleans for $120.

The Indian Circuit includes Indianapolis, Rushville, Columbus, Peru, Edinburgh and Cambridge City.

They hold running and trotting races every Sunday afternoon on the half mile track at Audubon Park, New Orleans.

John Campbell, trainer and part owner of the Beverwyck stable, says he keeps his horses keyed up by liberal doses of quinine.

The spring meeting of the Hartford Trotting Association will take place at Charter Oak on June 24th and three following days.

There are employed in E. E Eagles coal yard at Lexington Ky., eight clerks who were formerly employed in the various pool rooms.

C. W. Williams, late owner of Axtell, and W. H. McHenry, a well known driver and colt handler, have gone into partnership in a stable of trotters.

Frank Patros, one of the smartest two-year-olds seen out in the north of England last season, has been sold privately for £2,000, his destination being Italy.

The Directors of the Sonoma and Marin Agricultural Association elected the well known veterinary surgeon, Dr. T. MacClay, Secretary for the ensuing year.

It is reported that T. J. Dunbar may handle Maud S. next season. Dunbar is head trainer at Fashion Farm, and his contract does not expire until next fall.

Gypsey Queen 2:19½ by Rushville, has been sold for $10,500 to A. J. Feek, of Syracuse, N. Y. Messrs. Johnson and Perry, of Nebraska, were the former owners.

Lisle Simpson's three-year-old colt Milton, (Onondaga Smilax) is said to have improved wonderfully. The Sire Bros. wanted to get a price on him, but failed.

D. G. Dolson of Arcata, Humboldt County, has lately purchased two splendid Percheron stallions (Country gentleman and New Orleans) from W. H. E. Smith.

The regular fee for registration of colors in England is five shillings a year or £5 for life. Under Grand National Rules five shillings per annum and £2 for life.

J. P. Starmu, New Mexico, has bought the two fillies Gertie and Ethel, foaled in 1886 and 1887 by Kinlock (by Cuyler) dam Mollie Douglass (sister to Fred Douglass 2:24½).

Ed. Corrigan is reported to have a speedy yearling in Connie Buckingham, a filly by Powhattan—Hattie Harris. She is wintering at Memphis, and is two years old now.

The Memphis races will commence on April 12. If there is a matinee day it will be ten days prior to their regular meeting, and horses that are in winter quarters only are eligible,

Numerous operations have been performed lately by English veterinaries to cure roaring by removing the arytenoid cartilage but the result is now officially declared to be a failure.

Last week Pike Barnes bought the speedy bay mare Mollie Hardy (6) by Jack Hardy—Tar River, from W. K. Cherry for $700 Barnes has placed the mare at the Avondale Stable to be trained.

The Brighton Beach Association some years ago purchased a full set of surgical instruments, bandages, etc. The case was removed to Clifton and proved very useful when Cullen was injured.

George E. Monroe, Massachusetts, is now sole owner (having bought Mr. Herrick's share) of Elmotwood, three years old, by Whips, 2:27½ (son of Electioneer) out of a sister to Woodnut 2:16½ and Manon 2:21.

The Leicester Royal Handicap did not prove such a success as was at first anticipated. Only 133 entries turned up instead of 250. The stakes were therefore reduce to £6,000. Col. North has eight nominations.

On account of the prolonged drought at New Orleans all the water tanks at the Fair Grounds have been emptied. The tables are supplied with water from the public fountain at a charge of twenty five cents a barrel.

There is still hope of a National Jockey Club. Mr. Withers has written to England for the rules govering the turf there, and when he receives them, the Eastern and Western clubs may unite in a set of rules that will be of benefit to racing.

Fred Barrett, one of Englands crack riders, sailed on Christmas eve for Buenos Ayres. He will ride a few races there and return to England in the latter part of February, expecting to be back by the 6th of March.

Maori, West & Co.'s imported filly by Poulet—imp. Queen of Cypress, who showed Saratogans such speed last summer is wintering well at Memphis, and her owners anticipate more speedy work from her another season.

The new English racing rules insist on horses being named at or before time of entry, and also partnerships, sales with engagements and leases are to be registered before the animal is eligible to be entered or run for a race.

Mr. John A. Morris has lost a fine yearling, a filly by Tom Ochiltree out of Faithless (the dam of Britannic), by Leamington. She recently broke away and injured herself so badly that it was found necessary to destroy her.

News has been received from Gabe S. Caldwell that his health is greatly improved and he is likely to thoroughly recover. He is now contemplating going North early in February to take the starter's flag again at Clifton.

The present trainer of the Union Stable, Frank West, has worked a revolution in the form of the horses since he has had charge of them. Wynwood and Ilma B both showed last week the effects of West's labors with them.

The local bookmakers have been in a sad plight for several days as owing to receiving no early betting reports they have had to figure the odds for themselves in the morning. I do not hear though of any of them being badly hurt.

The Grand Prix de Paris will this year probably take place on the 29th of June, a fortnight later than usual, which will give the English racing fraternity a chance to run their horses at Ascot, prior to taking chances across the channel.

Roseburg merchants subscribe $3200 to the capital stock of the Douglas county fair association. The association has purchased 100 acres of land for $5,000 and increased its capital stock to $20,000, in order to properly improve the grounds.

It is estimated that within the last six weeks 200 horses have been stolen from Middle Tennessee and taken into Kentucky. It is said they are then taken to Cincinnati. General Jackson, Col. Overton and the Cockerills will probably form a Farmers' Association and employ a strong force to rout them out of the wild, unsettled portion of Kentucky which they fly to.

The Duke of Westminster charges one shilling for the right of inspecting Eaton Hall, and forwarded last month from that source of revenue £500 to the Chester Infirmary, and £200 to the Grosvenor Museum and School of Arts in Chester.

District Agricultural Association No. 6 Los Angeles is to the fore in fixing the date of their spring meeting which will take place from April 14th to April 19th inclusive. There will be two running and one trotting (or pacing) race each day.

The Exposition Driving Park Association, Kansas, will hold their early trotting meeting the last week in May. Secretary R. W. Cunningham is hustling around to get up a good meeting, as it is the initial meeting of the Northwestern Circuit.

The Candian trotting faculty struck a bargain when they purchased Muscovite in Kentucky. He stood a season near Quebec, and has lately been sold to a gentleman near Chicago for $15,000. He leaves almost a dozen promising younsters in Canada.

The judges at Clifton made a blunder last week when they claimed that a horse was not in the starter's hands until he made a break away. To decide when a real break was made would indeed prove a difficult question even for judges to determine.

The annual meeting of the Santa Clara Valley Agricultural Association was held on Wednesday last week when reports were submitted and William Backley was elected President for the next term. Wm. Quin and T. S. Montgomery were elected directors.

R. Tucker has bought of *Lyle & Parmer*, of Nashville, the yearling Turner brother to Vermont by Vanderbilt out of Gertrude: price not stated. It is understood he was bought for a well-known Nashville turfman, for whom Mr. Tucker will train next season.

Polo Jim, the well known colored assistant to Starter Caldwell, died last week from pneumonia. He was one of the best known characters on the American race tracks and deserves a good deal of the credit given to Caldwell. His real name was Ambrose Jefferson.

Of the horses that have sold for $10,000 and over this year, John E. Madden of Lexington Ky. formerly a citizen of Pennsylvania, has owned three of them—Bosque Bonita, Bluegrass Hambletonian and Warlock. He also owned a half interest in the Wilkes stallion Macey.

Prince Charlie (dead), who stood second in the list of winning sires this year, only cost Mr. Swigert about $4 000. He was bought at the earnest solicitation of Mr. B. G. Bruce, who argued that although a failure in England he would be a success crossed on American-bred mares.

It is said that at the last meeting of the Kempton Park (England) Directors, a very large bonus was given to the shareholders, in order that the company should not declare too high a dividend. There is an income tax in England, which probably influenced the Directors.

1884 was Hammond's year in England. St. Gatien ran a dead heat for the Derby, and Florence wound up the season by carrying 127 pounds to the front in the Cambridgeshire Handicap. Last year Florence was bred to St. Gatien, but unfortunately slipped her foal last month.

Pepper and Riley have re-named their late purchase 'Elias Lawrence,' Melbourne. It looks a little late in life to change the old horse's name, and most certainly changing horses names should be stopped. The horse was originally named after the first Secretary of the Latonia Jockey Club.

Among the Tennessee thoroughbred stock farms are something over 200 youngsters, yearlings who will be sold at auction this spring. Belle Meade has sixty, Cliff Lawn twelve, all by Saxon; Fairview about 45, Richland fifteen, Bonaventura five, by Vanguard; Kennesaw ten and Peytona ten.

This office will pay Twenty-five Cents for copies of the Breeder and Sportsman of the following dates: January 26, 1889; April 6, 1889; July 27, 1889; and for two copies of August 10, 1889; and will deem it a favor if readers who do not care to preserve files will forward the numbers mentioned.

Alf Estill was in Nashville on the 27th, and arranged stable accommodations for the Winters' Stable Mr. Estill came on to Sacramento and will go to Reno in time to take the two-year-olds back to meet McCormick with El Rio Rey, Don Jose-Joe Courtney, and the rest of the Eastern stable in Nashville in the latter part of February.

The Governor has commissioned as Directors for District 12 C. W. Aby (the well known manager of the Guenoc & Langtry Stud Farms), vice Q. V. P. Day, resigned; David Alexander of Lake County, vice self, term expired. District No. 19—Charles P. Low of Santa Barbara County, vice self, term expired; A. Hayman of Santa Barbara County, vice F. M. Sextenny, removed from the district.

There is to be a new race course in the vicinity of Paris 318 lots having been purchased at Surrenes, near the Bois de Bolongue. The Chairman is W. G Craven, a well known member of the French and English jockey clubs, while two of the Kempton Park Directors are on the board. It is intended to have a club house, on the Sandown Park plan, fitted up for the members.

Jockey Bergen finds himself in a dilemma just now. The Dwyer Brother have increased their original bid, which was made for his services next year some time ago, several thousand dollars, but each time Walbaum has stood the raise. Now that both parties have reached the top figure Bergen is forced to name his future employer. All things being equal it is more than probable that Bergen will next year wear the red and blue sash.

The most popular races in India used to be the Hyderabad. Last year they were not so well patronized by the owners of the large Arab stables. The totalisator was very little used, the innovation not having nearly as much play as the old pari-mutuel, which was worked on the credit system. It has been suggested that a money lender be on hand to keep things on a cash basis. There were two firms of bookmakers who did great business.

On being asked if he anticipated a union of the National and American Associations, President Johnson said: "That, I cannot say, but a state of affairs now exists which leaves no obstacle in the way of union. The personal relationships between the leading members of the two bodies are of the most friendly character, and I believe that the breeders and the principal horsemen of the country realize that it would be to their advantage to be governed by one body."

The Kentucky Trotting Horse Breeders' Association opened four important stakes, which closed January 1, 1890. The Stallion Representative Stake of $5000 is for foals of 1889 the get of stallions which may be nominated in this stake to trot as three-year-olds at the autumn meeting of the association in 1892. The Lexington Stake of $1000 is for two year olds. The Kentucky Stake for three-year olds and the Blue Grass Stake for four-year-olds are also for $1000 each.

While talking to Wm. Coombs about Dolly McMann slipping her colt, he told me that he originally bought her and bred her to Nutwood, but being away from home when she was about due to foal, she got among some mares and colts and foaled all right, but not being taken up at once (owing to the neglect of the employes) the colts kicked and trampled on the chestnut colt, breaking his back. His brothers got the old mare then and bred her to Whippleton, the result being Lillie Stanley 2:17½.

The Passaic County Agricultural Society on Dec. 28th announced what will probably be the first race for two year olds of 1890. The race will be called the Early Blossom Stake, will be at three-eighths of a mile, and will be run on Feb. 14th next at Clifton, if the track and weather permit. Otherwise the race will be run on the first favorable day. The society will add $1000 to the stakes, entrance to which will be $10 each, with $15 extra for starters. The stakes will close Feb. 1st, and the cash entrance fee must accompany the nomination.

Arthur Lion and Tom Treacy on January 2nd matched their three year olds Mayor Nolan and Mayor Noonan for $500 a side at three-quarters of a mile, weight for age, the race to be run at the Fair Grounds early in the spring. Mayor Noonan is by Springbok, and although he only started but four times as a two year old he showed that he was a good one. He won one race and came in second twice. Mayor Nolan is by Great Tom and is named after Mayor Nolan of Albany, the head of the Beverwyck stable Mayor Nolan started 12 times and has one win to his credit.

Geo. G. White, proprietor of the Chicken Cock stud farm, near Paris, Ky., has bought at a high price the black stallion Clay Wilkes, 9, by George Wilkes, first dam by American Clay, second dam the dam of Howard, 2.27½, and Jeff Wilkes 2:29½. He was owned by the Prospect Hill farm in Pennsylvania. Besides this stallion Mr. White owns the celebrated Victor Von Bismarck, the sire of the great unbeaten Edgemark, 2:16 as a four year old, who won all his races as a yearling, a two year old and a three year old. Clay Wilkes will be campaigned next year after he serves a limited number of mares.

There are quite a number of men, defaulters in India, who are racing in England, and several prominent sporting journals in India have been commenting strongly on the action of the Premier Racing Club (the Calcutta Turf Club) in not sending official information to the racing authorities in England. If they do not do so, the same men will probably default there, and others will come here and eventually cast a reflection on the club in question. That they have the power has been proved last season when the Victoria Jockey Club prevented the irrepressible Mr. Weekes from racing in Melbourne on receipt of notice of his default in India.

The sons and daughters of Longfellow since the the year 1876 when they first appeared on the turf have won $650,000 in stakes and purses. For several years he has been standing at $500, but he is likely to be used only as a private stallion. He was the first horse to run a mile in 1:40 on the American soil.

There is one thing certain, says an Exchange, only horses with the most certain proof of having been entered should be allowed to start in trotting races even under protest. They are often serious disturbing elements and it is poor satisfaction for the winner of only portion of a race to have to wait months for his winnings.

Major Frank McLaughlin is once more in California and is full of things he's seen etc. etc. One peculiarly American institution remains to scare him, the sight of a reporter acts on him like a red flag on. a bull. The gallant major says that he had not time to unpack when he was attacked by a mob of the fighting reporters and how he got rid of them God and he alone know.

The stockholders of the Arizona Industrial Exposition Association last week elected a board of directors, six out of the thirteen new men. We may now look for increased effectiveness from so much fresh blood. The board includes: H. H. Logan, J. D. Monihon, T. J. Trask, L. Fowler, C. R. Hakes, H. E. Kemp, H. W. Ryder, D. H. Recarte, J. Harbert, O. H. Christy, C. W. Johnstone, K. E. Farrington, E. Ganz. The new board will organize January 6, 1890.

In building the road from the Hatfield Gate to the backstretch of the Westchester track several old coins have been found. Big pennies, which smack of past generations, when one got the worth of his money. One is clearly marked "1840," but there is another with "1300" inscribed below the profile of a man with a powdered wig and riband of a century back. And now the question is, Was American money made in 1300 or does this find indicate that John A. Morris has unearthed Capt. Kidd's treasure.

If John Mackey is unable to go East, as his present state of health, I am sorry to say, indicates, E. S. Culver, the erudite Secretary of the Blood Horse, will probably go East with the trotters next month. Mr. Haggin will send yearlings two, three, and four year olds and no better man than Ned Culver could be found for he knows almost as much about the old California trotters as John Mackey and is just as genial and full of general information which he imparts fully to cover one.

Dave Pulsifer is said to have brought off the largest coup of last year on December 28th. The rooms were reopened in Chicago and the West and all Saturday the wires were kept hot with messages to Louisville, Nashville, Chicago, Detroit, Kansas City, St. Paul, Denver and San Francisco bearing the legend "lay me fifty each way on Wynwood at post odds, answer," signed D. T. Pulsifer. In the local N. Y. pool rooms Mr. Pulsifer continued betting and on the track kept it up till the flag fell when he had $4000 on to win $32000 and pulled it off.

The Australian condidates for the English Derby have had very little work so far and no one can really know what their true form is. A well known racing man says: they are bigboned, sturdy-built colts somewhat coarse about their head and necks, and lack the quality so generally to be seen in the kind of animals which distinguish themselves in our classic races. Then again, the action of the colts—more particularly in their slow paces—strikes me as being heavy and somewhat coachy not at all adapted for the up-and-down hill course at Epsom.

Cridge, the well known New York bookmaker, claims to have the boss preventative to bogus tickets (duly patented). It is a "serrator" which has an irregular or serrate edge, and is used in detaching the ticket from the stub, and it has been found in practice that the line of tear produced by the use of the use of the implement will vary with each particular use, consequently that the ticket or other paper separated from the stub can be fitted only to its own particular stub.

Since the use of the patent Mr. Cridge says he has only paid on one bogus ticket, and then through an employee's carelessness.

During last season in England, horses running under Jockey Club Rules, have divided amongst their owners $2,400,000. This, of course, does not include prizes taken by hunters, handicap steeple chase horses and in hurdle races, and as during six months of the year the illegitimate sport is going on all over the country, and big money put up, there is a goodly sum to be added to the total. Last year shows an advance of $250 000 on the previous year, which was almost as much in advance of 1883. Evidently the Britishers are up with the times.

When Axtell and Allerton trotted their fast miles as three year olds they wore very light shoes, something like six ounces in front and a little less behind. When Sunol went in 2:10½ she wore nine ounce shoes in front and four ounces behind. Margaret S. wore only 8 ounces in front and about 3 ounces behind, and Lillian Wilkes was very evenly balanced. In fact, it is generally admitted that very fast colts must go with light shoes, since it is contrary to common sense to suppose that they can take up a great amount of weight on their feet and do the trick.

A mutual understanding between man and horse is necessary in order to insure the largest per cent. of profit to the stall-owner, says a leading writer. If friendly word and kindly act are sent as messengers, the equine nature moves in quick response; if angry tone and brutal blow be offered, they are treasured up in sullen, vengeful mind, and at the moment least expected are tendered back in most disastrous manner. The prudent stallioner is friendly with his horse. His nature is made the subject of careful study; his peculiarities of temper are learned; his faults are skillfully corrected, and his vices, if any unfortunately there be, are mitigated.

An invention likely to interest all breeders and horsemen, has just been brought out at the Vienna Military Veterinary Institute. Prof. Polanski and Dr. Schindelka have constructed an instrument admitting of the inspection by mirror of the horse's larynx. This apparatus is used with a tiny electric lamp, and the examination is made, not as heretofore, through the animal's mouth, but through its nostrils. Only three men have been required to hold the horses during the experiments which have been made at the Vienna Institute. The new method has the advantage of allowing the nostrils to be thoroughly examined at the same time as the larynx, which for certain diseases is all important.

The great trotting sire Wilton, by George Wilkes, dam Allie, by Rysdyk's Hambletonian, jointly owned heretofore by W. C. France and Bowerman Bros., was sold on Jan. 1st to the latter. The price is private, but said to be the largest for which a stallion has ever been sold in America.

Ione race track is in exceptionally good trim. The track is beautifully built, being several feet higher than the surrounding land, while the soil is such that in a couple of days the track is in good working order. As a proof of the excellence of the track, quite a number of horses have wintered there. C. F. Bunch has a big half dozen, while Waterman brought two from Stockton, and several other prominent trainers are in Ione. Last year, Amador and Sacramento counties gave preference to the runners, and judging from the satisfaction given all round, and the good racing shown, they will continue the programme this year, and should be extensively patronized by both runners and trotters; their liberality and general good management deserve it.

The Melbourne Cup will be run this year on November 4th. The following are the revised conditions as fixed by the Victoria Racing Club:—

"The Melbourne Cup, a handicap sweepstakes of 50 sovs. each, 10 forfeit, or only 5 if declared before August 4th, with 10,000 sovs. and a trophy, value 150 sovs., added. After the declaration of the weights the winner of any handicap flat race, value 100 sovs., to carry 3 lbs.; 200 sovs, 5 lbs.; 300 sovs, 7 lbs.: 500 sovs. or upwards, 14 lbs. extra, provided that the winner of the Jockey Club or Victoria Racing Club Derby of this year shall carry not less than 7 st. 6 lbs. Distance from stand, two miles. Entries, with 5 sovs., to be made before Monday, June 2nd, and the weights to appear on June 23rd. The second forfeit of 5 sovs. to be declared and paid on the Tuesday preceding the race."

I had a very chatty visit from Bruce Cockrill last Saturday. He says that the Salinas track is in very fair order. He has had a hard stroke of luck. The yearling filly by Milner out of Maggie O is dead, while Daisy D's colt has only just recovered from his accident—he fell down in front of a plough and cut his shoulder a month ago. Mr. Cockrill took down with him a recent purchase from Palo Alto, viz, the bay two year old colt Mero (Wildidle—Precious), brother to Philander and half brother to Peel and Pliny. Bruce gave $1,000 for the colt, who is a very promising youngster, heavily engaged on the coast. Among his engagements are the Racine Stakes (spring), Autumn Stakes (fall), at the Blood Horse this year, and in 1891 at the Blood Horse Spring Meeting he is entered for the Tidal Stakes and the Pacific Derby, and also in the Fame Stakes in the fall.

After all the credit the Jubilee Plunger received for writing "How I lost £250,000 in two years," it turns out that all he wrote was two words, "Ernest Benzon," which he put under his portrait on the title page. There is, after all, something in a name. The real writer was Vero Shaw, a well known sporting writer, who was engaged by two well known publishers, and as he only receiving £100 instead of £200 as agreed on, he sued the publisher and got a verdict for the extra £100. The facts were supplied by the Rev. Evelyn Burnaby, who knew the plunger during his minority, and Sir George Chetwynd. By the way, an exchange in re Benzon says Benzon, "the Jubilee Plunger" is again in a state of financial collapse, and is contemplating a lecture tour in this country. But Americans need no instruction on how to spend money. What they like to hear is how to earn it.

The now two-year-olds at Lexington were worked along the last few days of their yearlinghood. James Murphy worked the sister to Clay Stockton, and the grey colt by Longfellow out of Gray Helen, a quarter in 24¼ seconds, while the Silver Mine and Clarence G. filly, owned by Larry Hart, went the same distance in the fast time of 23 4-5 seconds. Byron McClelland's brown filly by Billet, dam Retreat by Virgil, handily beat a Duke of Montrose and Hindoo colt, three-eighths in 37 seconds, while a filly by Vauxhall, out of Silken Ban, served a Mr. Pickwick filly in the same style, in a dash of a quarter, which he ran in 25 seconds. The best performance of the week, and the season thus far, was done by Sister Linda, a daughter of imported Zorilla, who covered three furlongs in 36 seconds. Her feat was accomplished in the trial noted above, with shoes on and weight up. Trainers are astonished at her performance, and no youngster in training there is accorded as much attention, as she gives every indication of developing into a Miss Woodford or a Spinaway.

The Monterey District Trotting Association held their annual meeting in Salinas last week. The Treasurer's report showed that there had been paid out to the winners of the colt stakes of 1889, the sum of $400, and that there was on hand $105 paid in as entrance money for the twenty-one entries of 1890. The second payment of $10 was made on each of the following nominations to the stake of 1890: J. B. Iverson's filly Mambrita, Wm. Vanderhurst's filly Salinas Maid, Z. Hebert's colt Spokane, C. C. Allen's filly Pocahontas, Paris Kilburn's filly Aunty Wilkes, and J. D. Carr's Nina B. Second payment delinquent at 12 o'clock at night, Jan. 1, 1890. M. Lynn was unanimously elected President of the association for the ensuing year. Jas. B. Iverson, Treasurer, and S. Z. Hebert, Secretary. It was voted that the stake money for 1891, be divided as follows: 50 per cent. to first horse; 25 per cent. to second horse; 15 per cent. to third, and 10 per cent. to fourth; also that distance be waived.

The two-year-old stake for 1891 was opened and received nine entries on the spot; the stallions Antevolo, Junio, Mulvoorhees and St. Patrick having two of their get entered, while the ninth was a Sidney.

'Hiram Woodruff Howe died on January 2nd.' Very few among us noticed the announcement in the daily papers, and fewer still recognized that this was the celebrated driver of Lady Thorn 2:18½, American Girl 2:16½, Maggie Lambert 2:25½, Woodbridge Girl and a host of other well known trotters. Hiram Woodruff Howe was the nephew and adopted son of Hiram Woodruff, the driver among drivers, who died in 1867, leaving behind him an untarnished name and a reputation such as no man ever had in trotting circles. His well known sterling principles and ideas were early impressed on his relative who worthily upheld the reputation of the family. Hiram Woodruff's wife lived with Howe until her death in March, 1888. For the last fifteen years, Hiram Howe kept a road house on the Boulevard, Coney Island, which was a popular resort with all driving and sleighing parties, particularly the old school, who liked to chat of days of yore. He married one of the Misses Shaw; the other sister married John Murphy, 'the Red Prince,' who died only a few months ago. The death of these two grand drivers and trainers will be deeply regretted all over the country, but though dead they will never be forgotten among trotting men and lovers of the trotting horse.

The Rev. E. J. Saxton, while preaching at Barnsley on "Betting and Gambling," said that bookmakers all "lived in fine mansions," "have splended surroundings," "maintain their carriages" and "make as much as £50,000 in a day." Occasionally they lose, but of course the reverend minister did not figure on that; later on referring to Jubilee Juggins, concerning whom he quoted some chatty notes by that excellent writer of cheap sensationalism, Mr. Runciman. This writer had said that Benzon's £250,000 was robbed from him in the sight of all England, whereupon the Rev. Mr. Saxton in his righteous wrath exclaims: "Talk of brigands; we have an army of them in our midst. Had this robery taken place in Greece or Spain, all our newspapers and our Government would have cried that the men should be found and punished, yet the men who robbed this youth are honored in society, and probably contribute to religious and charitable objects some of the blood money." It looks as though the worthy minister of the gospel was wasting his sympathy on a boy who *would* break the books but did not. The only way to stop him was to put him in an asylum.

At the late Newmarket sale Mr. Edmond Tattersall, the premier auctioneer, was suffering from bronchitis, so his son, Somerville Tattersall, mounted the rostrum. The sale was a great success, and in future December sales will be a regular thing. On the first day Sir George Mar purchased for Hampton Court Stud (The Queens) Madam du Barry, 1875, (Favonius—Strategy) for 900 guineas and Luciennes, 1885, (Beauclerc—Madam du Barry) for 390 guineas. The Duke of Hamilton gave top price, 1,300 guineas for Mercy, 1886, (Barcaldine—Clemence) and John Porter (for Baron Hirsch) paid 1,250 guineas for Pinkbasket, 1883, (Hampton—Bercaunette). The late Lord Falmouth's racing stock were sold by Mr. Somerville Tattersall on Wednesday, Dec. 20th. Eight yearlings averaged 835 guineas, Captain Macheli paying 2,700 guineas for the Galliard—Madge Wildfire filly. Twelve weanlings averaged 446 guineas, Mr. Milnor paying 1,100 guineas for the Springfield–Darnaway weanling. Twenty brood mares averaged 998 guineas. Doncaster 1883 (Doncaster—Belle Agnes) brought top price, 2,300 guineas, the Duke of Hamilton purchasing her. Two Hermit mares sold for 2,200 guineas each, viz., Wharfedale, 1878 (Hermit—Bonnie Doon) and Pauline, 1883 (Hermit—Lady Masham) Labrynth, 1881 (Hampton—Pretence) was sold for 2,000 guineas. Merry-Go-Round, a thirteen-year-old stallion by Scottish Chief out of Spinaway, sold for only 420 guineas. Rada, a four-year-old mare by Speculum out of Nellie McGregor, in training, sold for 1,150 guineas. Taken altogether, the sale was one of the best ever held; over £50,000 was taken in on the whole day's sales, while Lord Falmouth's 42 head sold for £33,570 guineas.

The leading stallion for last season is Wm. L. Scott's imported horse Rayon d'Or. He is closely followed by the dead (imported) Prince Charlie, late the property of Daniel Swigert, while the third place is occupied by Frank B. Harper's great Longfellow. Rayon d'Or's get won the enormous sum of $172,897. Prince Charlie's $169,546 and Longfellow's $140,015. The biggest winner was Chaos, by Rayon d'Or, who won $63,550 in stakes and purses.

Rayon d'Or has, as will be seen below, a double cross of Glencoe, a treble cross of Diomed, and a double cross of Touchstone. He is racing-bred on both sides, Flageolet being a very high class race-horse; while his dam—a half sister to King Tom, Stockwell and Rataplan—has produced, among others, Chamant, winner of the 2,000 guineas, Camelia, winner of the 1,000 guineas and dead heat for the Oaks, and Wellingtonia, the sire of Plaisanterie. Rayon d'Or himself was a race-horse, winning, among others, the Leger, the Champion Stakes, 2 miles 73 yards, beating Placida (the Oaks winner), Exeter and five others, the Challenge Stakes, six furlongs, when he beat such well known horses as Lollypop, Placida and Parole. As a four-year-old he won two races in France, 2 miles 5 furlongs and 3 miles 1 furlong, and in England he walked over for the Post Stakes and Prince of Wales Stakes, and carried 132 pounds to the front in the Rous Memorial at Ascot. During his turf career he won $122,140.

It is no wonder, when one reads the horse's record and looks carefully into his blood lines, that he is at the head of all the stallions in use in America. Rayon d'Or was imported in 1882 by Congressman W. L. Scott after one short season in France, where he left nine colts, most of which have since raced well there.

PEDIGREE.

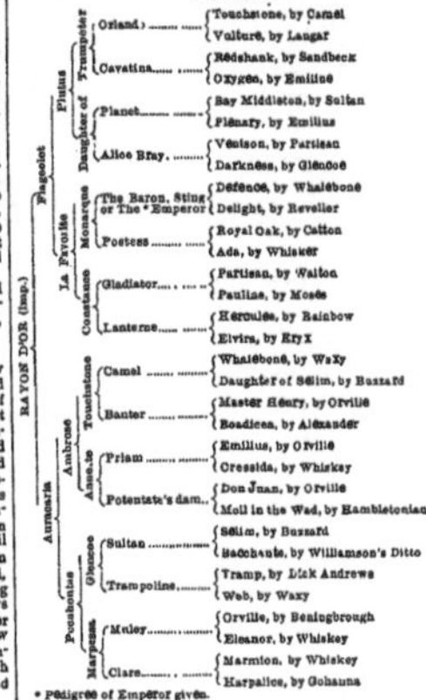

* Pedigree of Emperor given.

ATHLETICS.

Athletic Sports and Other Pastimes.

Edited by Arphippus.

SUMMARY.

Next week the athletes will commence to train for coming events. For the present the Olympic athletes will be compelled to train indoors, while the Alpine Amateurs will be able to use their outdoor grounds towards the end of next week.

Several rowing clubs not already in the Pacific Rowing Association have applied for admission.

RUNNERS, WALKERS, JUMPERS, ETC.

The cinder path at Berkeley is in a very wretched condition, and it will be some time before the students can resume practice.

The chief athletic meeting of the year will be the championship meeting on May 30th. Three clubs will compete for the flag, the Olympic, the University and the Alpine. The former club should certainly stand the best show of coming out ahead, as it has the largest number of athletes on its side. The University club is composed of but a few men, but its members are all athletes of the first order. A few men, such as Gallagher, Mays, Hill, Moffett and Rouse would prove more destructive to the enemy than fifty second-rate athletes. To meet these champions the Olympic Club will send Henderson, Jarvis, Purcell, Buchanan, McGee, Cassidy, Cooley, McArthur, Haley, and possibly Schifferstein. The Alpine Club has only three or four really first-class men, but these athletes will make a great effort to win first place in their different events. Cassidy has a very fair show to win the mile; McKinnon is liable to break the record in the hammer throwing event, while Sexsmith will possibly win the pole vault. Besides these three men there are two or three other athletes in the club who may capture some second medals. The Alpine boys would not attempt to meet either the Olympic or University clubs single-handed, their only hope being to win a sufficient number of points on the outside to capture the pennant or else to take second place. There is not a particle of doubt but that every athlete who takes part in the games will be in the very best of condition. The meeting will be well worth a day's journey to witness, and May 30th will certainly be a red letter day in the history of athletics on the Pacific Coast.

The athletes will find some very important news regarding the Amateur Athletic Union under the heading of "Jottings From All Over." Now that the Pacific Coast Amateur Athletic Association is a member of the Union, the athletic readers of this paper may find it to their interest to read the notes referred to.

We expect to be able to publish the Olympic programme of games for Washington's birthday in our next issue.

There still exists a doubt as to whether the outdoor grounds of the Olympic Club will be ready for February 22d or not.

The training grounds of the Alpine Amateur Athletic Club at Harbor View will be ready for use about the 15th. The dressing rooms are complete, and the track will soon be in first-class condition.

The University students will be assessed this year to defray the expenses of improving the track at Berkeley. Hot water baths will also be erected in the gymansium.

JOTTINGS FROM ALL OVER.

Thomas P. Conneff, the well known amateur runner is rapidly recovering from an attack of typhoid fever, and it is thought that he will soon be able to attend to his business duties as usual. It will be many months, however, before he can again appear on the cinder path.

G. M. L. Sachs, the well known patron of amateur athletic has decided to resign from all the clubs of which he is a member. There have been published so many unfounded rumors concerning Mr. Sacks' action that for the information of our readers we publish the following sample of his letters of withdrawal:

WINDSOR HOTEL, NEW YORK CITY, Dec. 21.—Wm. B. Curtis, President N. A. S. A.—MY DEAR SIR: Acting under the advice of my physician, that I must abstain from all active participation in business and athletic matters and sojourn for some time in the south of France (for which place I leave to-day). I am reluctantly compelled to send in my resignation as a member of the National Amateur Skating Association. I know my own nature too well, and if I did not resign from all athletic clubs and associations, I would at the first opportunity break all promises and endanger my health. With my best wishes for the future of the N. A. S. A.,

I remain, truly yours, GUS M. L. SACKS.

At the general meeting of the English Amateur Athletic Association, held in Birmingham, Dec. 14, the following records were passed: 200yds.—E. H. Pelling, 19 4-5s; 440yds.—H. C. L. Tindall, 48½s.; 600yds.—H. C. L. Tindall, 1m. 12s.; 1,000yds.—Pollock Hill, 2m. 15 4-5s.; three miles—J. Kibblewhite, 14m. 29 3-5s.; throwing the hammer—W. J. M. Barry, 130ft.; pole jump—E. L. Stones, 11ft. 7in. It was decided to include 250yds. as a new distance on the record list, and E H. Pelling's record of 24 4-5s. was accepted. The championships for 1890 were fixed for decision at Aston Lower Grounds, Birmingham.

Jake Gaudaur very sensibly refuses to row an important race on such water as is generally to be found at the Point of Pines; Boston Bay, but says that he is prepared to make a match to row John Teemer or Ned Hanlan, or both, for $1,000 a side for each race, at Lake Quinsigamond, Mass., any time before July 4 next.

The annual fencing championship meeting will be held at the New York Athletic Club house, 104 West Fifty-fifth Street, New York City.

The trials February 4th and 5th, and the finals, February 8th. The events will be given the same as last year, and an entrance fee of $2 will be charged for each event. Contestants will furnish their own implements. Five jurors or judges will be selected, three professionals and two amateurs. All communications should be addressed to J. E. Sullivan, P. O. Box 611, New York City.

About 800 persons were present at the Armory of the Thirteenth Regiment of Brooklyn, N. Y., on Saturday evening, December 28th, to witness the games at the joint meeting of Company K, of the regiment, and the Acorn Athletic Association, which were followed by terpsichorean exercises. Summary:

Fifty yards run—W. H. Morgan, New Jersey Athletic Club, 4ft start, first, in 5 4-5s; Percy Levy, Harlem Pleasure Club, 3ft, second.

One mile walk—W. Donaghy, Thirteenth Regiment Athletic Club, 25s. start, first, in 7m 25s; J. Lambert, Pastime Athletic Club, 20s, second.

Half mile run—C. M. Raymond, Manhattan Athletic Club, 14yds. start, first, in 2m 4 2-5s; E. Hjertberg, New Jersey Athletic Club, scratch, second.

Two mile bicycle race—J. A. Schoefer, Brooklyn, 45yds. start, first, in 6m 50 1-5s; J. W. Judge, Riverside Wheelmen, 65yds, second.

One mile run—Charles Britton, American Athletic Club, 60yds. start, first, in 4m 37 4-5s; Frank Kublike, Prospect Harriers, 100yds, second.

Two hundred and twenty yards run—F. F. Sliny, New Jersey Athletic Club, 5yds. start, first, in 25 1-5s; E. S. De Lahn, Pastime Athletic Club, 8yds, second.

Quarter mile run—C. M. Carbonell, New Jersey Athletic Club, 15yds. start, first, in 55s; C. J. Harvey, Star Athletic Club, 18yds, second.

Running high jump—Zach A. Cooper, Brooklyn, allowed 3in, first, 5ft 7in; H. L. Spencer, New Jersey Athletic Club, 3in, second, 5ft 7in. In tossing to decide the tie the former won.

There was the customary large crowd to witness the competitions at the annual tournament for the championships in boxing and wrestling, under the auspices of the Amateur Athletic Union, held at the Metropolitan Opera House, New York City, on Thursday evening, December 19th.

The management was, as usual, excellent, but the competitions cannot be said to have been up to the standard; consequently, the displays were lacking in interest to those who appreciate superior exhibitions. A summary follows:

SPARRING.

Class 105 lb.—Final bout: D. O'Brien, Pastime Athletic Club, beat Matt Rice, Varuna Boat Club, the judges disagreeing and the referee deciding.

Class 115 lb—Final bout: William Kenny, New Jersey Athletic Club, beat Andy Kelly, Bridge Athletic Club.

Class 125 lb., special—Final bout: W. McGarry, Star Athletic Club, beat E. B. Pyfer, Athletic Club of the Schuylkill Navy.

Class 158 lb.—Final bout: W. Stucky, West End Athletic Club, beat J. M. McAuliff, Bridge Athletic Club, the latter being disqualified for wrestling.

WRESTLING.

Class 105 lb.—Final bout: J. B. Riley, Schuylkill Navy Athletic Club, beat G. Pfortner, New Jersey Athletic Club in 7m 44s.

Class 115 lb.—Final bout: F. Miller, National Turnverein, Newark, N. J., beat J. K. Hyslop, Athletic Club of the Schuylkill Navy, in 2m 46s.

Class 135 lb.—Final bout: Max Luttberg, New York Turnverein, beat Charles Schneckenberg, New York Turnverein, in 4m 11s.

Class 158 lb.—Final bout: W. Law, Scottish American Athletic Club, beat J. Hughes, Pastime Athletic Club, in 9m 22s.

THE AMATEUR ATHLETIC UNION.

A meeting of the Board of Managers of the central body was held at the Astor House, New York City, on Saturday evening, December 28th, at which some important business was transacted by the following members: A. G. Mills, New York Athletic Club; Walter Storm, Manhattan A. C.; F. W. Janssen, Staten Island A. C.; J. E Sullivan, Pastime A. C.; Fred Gerow, American A. C.; and A. C. Stevens, New Jersey A. C. The Committee on Boxing and Wrestling reported that they had rejected the entry of Patrick Cahill, Scottish American A. C., for the recent championship meeting, for the reason that he had from indisputable evidence received by them, violated the spirit of the amateur law, and as it was foreign to the purposes of the Union to encourage such practices, they had taken the action they did. The report was adopted without dissent. The report of the Committee on Records, to whom had been referred back the application of George Schwegler, Staten Island Athletic Club, for the recognition as record of the time made in the 250 yards hurdle race on October 26th, recommended that the record be refused, owing to the hurdles having been improperly placed. Report adopted. The report of the Committee on Organization in favor of tabling the resignation of the Berkeley Athletic Club, handed in prior to the disbandment of the Old National Association, was also adopted. The applications of A. H. Howard, Boston Athletic Association; M. H. Berry, Young Men's Christian Association of Buffalo, N. Y., and W. Hourihan, Bridge Athletic Club, for reinstatement to the amateur ranks, were favorably considered, while that of H. A. Lannigan of the Caledonian Club, of Fall River, Mass., was rejected. The Reading (Pa.) Athletic Club was admitted to membership in the Union, and Eugene Van Schaich, Manhattan Athletic Club, was added to the Committee on Fencing. A plan for a series of amateur championship baseball contests during the season of 1890 was adopted, and after the transaction of some additional business of minor importance, the meeting adjourned.

A number of changes were made in the rules, the more important of which are as follows:

RULE 1, relating to officials, provides that all amateur meetings shall be under the direction of one referee, two or more inspectors, three judges at finish, three or more field judges, three timekeepers, one judge of walking, one starter, and one clerk of the course. If deemed necessary, one scorer, one marshal, and an official reporter may also be appointed.

2. The referee only shall have the power to change the order of events as laid down in the official programme. When in any but the final heat of a race a claim of foul or interference is made, he shall have the power to disqualify the competitor who is at fault if he considers the foul intentional, and shall also have the power to allow the hindered competitor to start in the next round of heats just as he had been placed in his trial. When in a final heat a claim of foul or interference is made he shall have the power to disqualify the competitor who is at fault if he considers the foul intentional, and he shall also have the power to order a new race between such of the competitors as he thinks entitled to such privilege.

3 Provides that the inspectors are merely assistants to the referee, and aids to him in detecting fouls.

4. A finish shall be counted when any part of the contestant's body, except his hands or arms, shall touch the tape at the finish line.

7. A false start shall prevent the man at fault from competing in that event. The starter shall also rule out of that event any competitor who attempts to advance himself from his mark prescribed in the official programme after he has given the warning to "get ready."

Protests against any entered competitor made verbally to the referee at or before the conclusion of any athletic meeting by any responsible person shall, if possible, be immediately decided by the referee. If it cannot be so decided, the protested competitor shall compete under protest and such protest be decided by the referee within forty-eight hours, unless its subject be the amateur standing of the competitor, in which case the referee must report such protest in writing within forty-eight hours to the secretary.

17. In making a hurdle record it shall be necessary for the competitors to jump over every hurdle in its proper position. This means that if a man knocks down several hurdles during the race, and by so doing makes faster time than he would have made if the hurdles were in their proper positions, it will not go on record.

18 Makes a fair jump, one that is made without the assistance of weights, diving, somersaults, or handsprings. It also provides that in all handicap jumps scratch man shall be entitled to try last.

19. In putting the shot the shot shall be a solid sphere made of metal and weighing at least sixteen or twenty-four pounds, or as the event may call for. It was formerly provided that iron should be used. It shall be put with one hand, and in making the attempt it shall be above and not behind the shoulder. The competitor shall stand in a circle seven feet in diameter, on two feet of the circumference of which shall be placed a board four inches high, at which the competitor shall stand when the shot leaves his hand. A fair put shall be one where no part of the person of the competitor shall touch in front of the circle or on the board. A put shall be counted foul if the competitor steps over the front half of the circle or on the board before the measurement of his put is made. Shot must be furnished by the club giving the game, but contestants may use their own private shots if they so desire, in which case the other contestants shall be allowed to use the private shot. This also applies to the fifty-six pound weight and the hammers.

After a session lasting till about three o'clock in the morning the Board adjourned to meet at the house of the Warren Athletic Club, Wilmington, Del., January 25th.

The plan must be submitted to a general meeting of all the clubs of the Union, thus assuring all clubs then members to have an equal voice in the amendment and final adoption of the plan. The attention of existing associations of clubs is also invited to the fact that, at the last annual meeting of the Amateur Athletic Union, its constitution was altered so as to prepare the way for this important reorganization, and, among other changes, provision was made for increasing the number of memberships of the Amateur Athletic Union Board of Managers to fifteen, with the understanding that the additional memberships should be reserved for representatives of existing associations of clubs desiring to participate with the Amateur Athletic Union in the proposed reorganization, and whose present affiliation therewith will thus make them co-workers in formulating the plan. The negotiation of the details of such affiliation has been delegated by the Amateur Athletic Union Board of Managers to its Committee on Organization.

Applications for or correspondence relating to club membership in the Amateur Athletic Union should therefore be addressed to J. E. Sullivan, Secretary Amateur Athletic Union, P. O. Box 611, New York, N. Y., and all correspondence relating to the affiliation with the Amateur Athletic Union by existing associations of clubs or otherwise designated athletic organizations should be addressed to A. G. Mills, Secretary Committee on Organization, Amateur Athletic Union, 38 Park Row, New York, N. Y.

Harry McMillan, Walton Storm, A. G. Mills, Committee on Organization A. A. U.

Cross country runs are very frequent in the vicinity of New York City. The participants nearly all agree in saying that a good cross country does an athlete more good than two weeks of ordinary training.

THE WHEELMEN.

The next regular meeting of the Oakland Bicycle Club will be held at the residence of Captain Drake, 1720 Seward St., Oakland, on Tuesday evening, January 14, at 8 o'clock. This club will not be represented at the competitive drill in the Mechanics Pavilion.

The Bay City Wheelmen will be represented by sixteen men at the drill, and it is thought that this club will carry off first honors.

The Alpine Athletic club will apply for admission to the L. A. W.

AT THE OARS.

Several of the crews were out for a spin on Sunday. The fine weather was a genuine surprise to the oarsmen.

Of late there appears to have been considerable dissension amongst the members of the Ariel Rowing Club. It was in consequence of this that so many of the members left and joined the Alpine Club.

The Alpine Athletic Club will apply for admission to the Pacific Rowing Association at the next regular meeting of that body. The following oarsmen have been elected delegates H. O. Farrell, Henry Tank and J. P. Bean.

On account of the charter being re-opened several rowing clubs not already in the Pacific Rowing Association have applied for admission. From present indications great interest will be taken in rowing during the coming season.

The Lurline Club is fast coming to the front and may prove a thorn in the sides of the older clubs before the year is out.

Captain George W. Jordan of the Olympic club is a very hard worker in the interest of his club. Already he has started in to urge his men to commence training for May 30. He claims to have a man on his team who can put the shot 40 feet, throw the 16lb. hammer 120 feet, and fling the 56lb. weight 28ft.

During the past few months we have received severl communications in regard to the P. C. A. A. A. Some of the letters we deposited in the editorial waste paper basket, simply because they were too exactly on the officers of the association. We will admit during the past year athletics were poorly patronized and can scarcely blame the officers of the P. C. A. A. A. for their want of interest in athletic matters. The new year, however, promises well and the P. C. A. A. A. will be called upon to transact some very important business during the coming season. There is no reason why the indoor tournament scheme should be abandoned. The associate clubs would most assurely take on active interest in the undertaking and the effort of the association would be highly successful. We hope the matter will be brought up again at the next meeting and pushed through.

The Alpine Amateur Athletic Club has leased a large hall and ante-rooms in the Murphy Building, corner of Market and Jones street. The hall will be converted into a gymnasium and the ante-rooms will be used for meeting, smoking and reading. Ober $600 worth of apparatus has already been placed in the gymnasium. Two professors will instruct the members in the art of boxing. There will also be fencing and wrestling instructors employed. Exhibitions to be followed by dancing will be held monthly at the club rooms. The first monthly members out-door games will be held at the clubs Athletic Grounds, Harbor View Park, on Sunday February 16, commencing at 1 o'clock P. M.

The following is the official programme as adopted at a meeting of the Board of Directors held January 7th:—

1. 100 yard run, handicap, 10 yards limit.
2. 150 yards run, handicap, 12 yards limit.
3. 220 yards run, handicap, 20 yards limit.
4. 880 yards run, handicap, 60 yards limit.
5. One mile run, handicap, 175 yards limit.
6. One-half mile novice walk, scratch.
7. One mile handicap walk, 1 mile limit.
8. Alpine race (original), ⅛ mile limit.
9. Throwing 12 lb. hammer, handicap 35 ft. limit.
10. Putting 16 lb. shot, handicap, 6 ft. limit.
11. Flinging 56 lb. weight, handicap, 3 ft. limit.
12. Running high jump, handicap, 6 ft. limit.
13. Running broad jump, handicap, 3 ft. limit.
14. Standing broad jump, handicap, 1½ ft. limit.
15. Pole vault, handicap, 2½ feet limit.
16. One-eighth mile hopping race, scratch.

Three prizes will be given for each event, and a special medal will be awarded the man who earns the greatest number of points. The games will be open only to members of the club. As this will be the initial out-door meeting no admission fee will be charged at the gate, each member being allowed two invitations. It is expected that over fifty athletes will take part in the games and the spectators will most undoubtedly be well repaid for their trouble in journeying to Harbor View. The following gentlemen will act as officers of the day: Referee, J. P. Bean; starter, H. C. Farrell; judges, Louis Thors, J. Bassett and Timothy J. Quinlan, timers, Harry Tank, Jacob Mutt and J. Hunton; clerks of course, Messrs Goodwin and Collins; official announcer T. J. Cunningham; call steward, J. H. Donohoe; judges of walking, P. H. Gafney, J. D. Garrison. The colors adopted by the club are garnet pants, white shirt trimmed with garnet. All contestants in out-door games must wear knee pants.

Grim's Gossip.

Cook the jockey is on a trip back east. He may return in time to ride at the spring meetings.

It is claimed that Andy McDowell is exercising five of Director's progeny, all of whom can beat 2:20.

N. J. Stone of Mountain View, has bought the standard mare Jennie, by Brigadier, dam by old Signal, from Dr. Latham.

Dr. H. Latham has purchased from J. H. Jewett, of Marysville, the standard bred mare Jennie by Brigadier, dam by Old Signal.

"Oregon Jimmy" has been at work at the Rancho Del Paso until lately, but he has now transferred his services to L. M. Morse, of Lodi.

F. W. Loeber has had a bit of hard luck lately, as his fine broodmare (dam of Lookout, 2:25) dropped a dead foal, to Whippleton, December 30th.

Alf Estill has returned from the East and is now preparing to take the two year olds from Mr. Winters Stock Farm to Nashville. He will again go East in February.

W. H. E. Smith of Eureka, writes me that Al Farrow was released from legal entanglements on Dec. 30th. We suppose that Wilbur Smith has lost his source of amusement.

If there are any breeders who wish to send horses back East between now and February 10th they can find a good opportunity by addressing G. Valensin, Pleasanton.

J. G. Fair, Jr, has secured the services of Humphrey Sullivan to look after his colts and fillies at the Knight's Ferry Farm, and no better man could have been got for the place.

A grand brood mare is offered for sale at a bargain by Mr. S. L. Goldstein, who has to go East. She is of the right kind, and should find a purchaser at once. Read the advertisement.

N. J. Stone of Mountain View, Santa Clara Co, has been offered $500, for his Hawthorne.—Abdallah Queen filly. The amount was tendered by a Kentucky breeder but was refused by Mr. Stone.

Allo has a record of 2:22½ and was owned by Dr. A. A. Davenport but a note informs me that the Doctor has sold the horse. However he does not say who the purchaser is nor does he give the price.

Knap McCarthy has to look after one hundred and thirty two thoroughbreds at Brookdale Farm, the breeding establishment of D. D Withers. He reports his horses in training as looking in superb condition.

James Corcoran, who trained his stable of horses at Petaluma last winter, has taken entire charge of the D. M. Reavis' Stable at Chico, and he is strongly inclined to the opinion that there are several fast youngsters on the ranch.

The Princess Lexington, formerly called Jessie C. has not benefited much by the change of name, she has just been declared out of all her engagements, an accident causing a dislocation of one of her ankles. She was at the Sacramento track when the accident happened.

O. A. Hickok will take a string of horses East next season, if the present outlook continues. He has several that warrant an appearance on the big circuit, and two or three of the dark ones will prove a surprise party to the talent before the season of 1890 is passed.

Owing to the fact that Dr. Thomas Bowhill will shortly leave for England, W. Henry Jones, M. R. C. V. S. will attend to the veterenary duties of the paper. The gentleman this week contributes an article on horseshoeing which should be read by all.

Mr John Scott who is one of our best known and most reliable importers is again with us. This time he has half a dozen pure bred Clydesdales, and judging from the excellence of his importations and well known integrity he should have a speedy sale. His card appears elsewhere.

The following telegram explains itself:

Received so far nine hundred and twenty-seven (927) entries for the Matron Stakes, the principal subscribers being J. B. Haggin 129, Milton Young 103, W. L. Scott 66, B. G. Thomas 50, D. D. Withers 48, A. Belmont 32, Clay & Woodford 30, D. Swigert 23, T. G. Megibben 20 G. A. and A. H. Morris 19, Rancocas Stable 18 Fleetwood Stud 18, Spendthrift Stud 17. Full particulars of entries in all stakes by mail.

T. H. Kock.
Secretary New York Jockey Club.

N. J. Stone of Mountain View, Santa Clara Co., has bought a half interest in Hazel Leaf from Senator Hearst for $500. That inbred Brigadier filly is now owned by Mr. Stowe & Dr. Latham who will have her trained and developed this season. She is as much like her dam, Hazel Kirke as can be.

It was quite a delightful sight to see the large number of breeders who were in the city Wednesday to attend the meeting of their association. It goes to show that there is a great deal of interest manifested among members, and that it will untimately be the leading organization of the west, there can be no doubt.

The citizens of Lodi have about finished their new race track, and good authorities say that it will be one of the best winter tracks in this State. If the committe have been fortunate enough to select what will prove a serviceable winter course, there should be a lot of money in the speculation.

Dr. J. P. Klench a prominent member of the California State Veterinary Society, has left his former residence, Santa Rosa and settled in Nashville, Tenn. It was the donors intention to take up his abode in New Orleans, but he found a better opening in Nashville. The many friends of Dr. Klench will wish him success in his new practise.

Among the stock at J. B. Haggin's ranch in California is a three year old colt called Florentin, that is a full brother to the famous race mare Firenzi. Just why he has not been brought out on the turf the California papers do not say, but they announce that he will be placed in the stud next spring.—(Breeders Gazette.)

Great Scott! A little knowledge is a dangerous thing.

Ed. Bither will start from Racine to join forces with the Valensin Stock Farm about the first of March. Mr. Bither is one of the close mouthed kind and all the gossipers could find out was that he had received a large offer from a California breeder. The Breeder and Sportsman was the first newspaper in the country to state positively that the noted reinsman would make his home in California.

Major Du Bois, of Denver purchased last Monday from Mr. L. A. Davis representative of the Calumet Stock Farm the br m Clara Belle 2:31½ (public trial at Chicago 2:22¼) by Masterlode, dam by Fisks Mambrino Chief Jr.: also the roan filly Azure, by Walkill Prince 2797, dam by Blue Bull 75, 2nd dam by Tom Crowder, 3rd dam by Tom Hal 3000. The price given for these two choice brood mares has not been stated.

William Archer, father of the famous jockey Fred Archer died lately in England aged sixty three years. The son's name eclipsed his senior's but William Archer was a well known cross country jockey in his day. He won the Grand National on Little Charley in 1858, and still earlier he was entrusted to convey a stud of horses to Russia to the late Emperor in whose service he afterwards held a favored place and won many races in the Imperial colors.

T. H. Griffin of San Francisco has purchased from J. W. Hartzell, of New Orleans, for $3,000 the three year old bay stallion Alfred D., by Robert McGregor, dam Bessie H., by Wyman's Logan; second dam by Ohio Eclipse. He has a good turn of speed, and has shown a mile inside of 2:30.—(Chicago Horseman.)

Our Chicago contemporary has been deceived; there is no such horse in existence.

I have received the following note which speaks for itself; "My mare Mollie McCarthy by Eugene Casserly foaled bay horse colt by Woodnut Dec 28th five days before her time. She was very old and paralyzed and was never able to get up after the birth so I distroyed her but saved the colt by putting it on another mare who has a colt 3 months old. She took to it at once and is as crazy after it as though it were her own. The Graves mare (owned by D. Minnie my neighbor) by Echo dam by Bell Alta foaled bay horse colt by Woodnut January 2nd, 1890."

B. C. Melly.

On the 21st ult., Mr. W. H. Wilson, of Abdallah Park, Cynthiana, Ky, received his two Guy Wilkes mares from California, one being Linda Wilkes, (dam of the weanling he sold a few weeks ago for $5 000,) by Guy Wilkes 2:15½, dam Atalanta (sister to Beautiful Bells 2:29½, dam of Bell Boy 2:19¼ and three others in 2:30) by The Moor 790; second dam Minnehaha (dam of five in 2:30) by Steven's Bald Chief; 3rd dam by Strader's Clay, etc. The other, Anteeo Wilkes by Guy Wilkes, dam by Anteeo 2:16½, son of Electioneer; 2nd dam by Alexander, record 2:31½; third dam by Naubuc (bro. to Thos. Jefferson 2:23) etc.

L. H. Hatch, of Hanibal, Mo. J. A. Dustin and C. W. Aby visited the stock Farms at Pleasanton on Thursday last. At different times Mr. Salisburg has owned some very fast animals and while the gentlemen were looking at those now to be seen there, the merits of the many fast ones were discussed, Gold Leaf 2:11½, Director 2:17, Corette 2:17, Nellie R. 2:17½, Monroe Chief 2:18¼, Direct 2:18½, Change 2:19, Margaret S. 2:19½, Sister 2:19½, Romero 2:19½, Sweetness 2:21, Gibralter 2:22, Bateman 2:22½, Maid of Oaks 2:23, Echora 2:23½, Nettie 2:26, Inca 2:27 and May Day 2:30, each had good words said for them. By the way there are very few breeders in the country that have had so many first class ones.

The advertisement of the Guenoc Stock Farm appears this week and the familar names of St. Savior and Greenback are once more seen in the columns. At the last state fair the farm was fortunate enough to obtain first prize for thoroughbred stallions and the adjoining farm of Mrs. Langtry, obtained second premium with Friar Tuck. Dr. C. W. Aby has the entire management of both farms and is thoroughly competent to take charge of such Mammoth possessions, having a great deal of experience. For years the doctor was at the Nonfans Stock Farm in Kentucky and is thoroughly conversant with every thing that appertains to such business. Read the advertisement and send word to the Guenoc Stock Farm how many mares you are going to send to the gilt edged stallions.

The common complaint among smaller breeders was that the P. C. T. H. B. A., in arranging their stakes last year, did so for the benefit of the larger breeding farms. Without admitting this to be a fact, we will say that this year no such complaints can be made. The new Board of Directors will offer colt stakes as follows:

Free for all.	Yearlings.	Mile dash.
"	2-year-olds	
"	3-year-olds	
"	4 year-olds	

3-year-olds that have not beaten 3 minutes.
4-year olds " " " " 2:40 "

And for the three and four-year-old colts of stallions who have no representatives in the 2:30 list.

Lookout for the advertisement next Saturday.

This office will pay Twenty-five Cents for copies of the Breeder and Sportsman of the following dates: January 26, 1889; April 6, 1889; July 27, 1889; and for two copies of August 10, 1889, and will deem it a favor if readers who do not care to preserve files will forward the numbers mentioned.

The Stanford Stakes.

The second payment, due January 2nd, 1890, on entries in Stanford Stake for 1891 have been made as follows:—

PALO ALTO STOCK FARM.

B c Commerce, by Electioneer.
B f Ellener, by Electioneer.
B f Mont Rosa, by Electioneer.
B f Mayfair, by Electricity.
B c Almoner, by Alban.
B f Norgirl, by Norval.
B f Maid, by Nephew.
B c Truman, by Electioneer.

BEN. E. HARRIS.

S c Brentwood, by Dawn

JOS. CAIRN SIMPSON.

B f Voliter, by Antevolo.
B or br g Vols, by son or imported Kelpie and Sprite.

WILBER F. SMITH.

Br f Felucca, by Guy wilkes.

JAS. P. KERR.

S f Grace, by Sidney.

ARTHUR L. WHITNEY.

Ch f Anna Belle, by Da

SAN MATEO STOCK FARM.

Ch f Vida wilkes, by Guy Wilkes.
B f Tasso Wilkes, by Guy Wilkes.

J. A. GOLDSMITH.

Ch f Eclipse, by Guy Wilkes.

WILFRED PAGE.

Bl c Gran Moro, by Le Grande.

The third payment, due January 2nd, 1890, for entries in the Stanford Stake for 1891, have been made as follows;—

PALO ALTO STOCK FARM.

B f Coral, by Electioneer.
Ch c Norris, by Ansel.
Br f Clarion, by Ansel.
B f Wildmont, by Piedmont.

BEN. E. HARRIS.

Br or bl f Lorena, by Jim Mulvenna.

JOS. CAIRN SIMPSON.

Br c Praevolo, by Antevolo.

G. VALENSIN.

Bl f Fleet, by Sidney.

Yours truly,
N. T. Smith.

THE FARM.

Ensilage for Sheep.

The London (Eng.) Farmer and Stock Breeder remarks that ensilage proves to be good food for ewes in lamb. Last year on the home farm of the Earl of Bective, at Underly the ewes were fed from early in December till February 1 on a few swedes on pasture, a little hay, and one-half pound of oats daily. The swedes then failed and 145 ewes received till March 1st 10 cwt, daily of chopped clover ensilage, with the same quantities of hay and oats. Then the lambs began to fall, and the ewes received the ensilage as before, mixed with four stones of bran, one pound of oats each, daily, and hay, of which last however they took very little. They did exceedingly well on this mixture, on which both ewes and lambs continued to be fed till they all went to the butcher fat.

The Physiology of Breeding.

Mr. James Howard, who was considered good authority on the physiology of breeding deemed the following cardinal points fully established in breeding.

1. That from the male parent is mainly derived the external structure, configuration and outward characteristics, also the locomotive system of development.

1. From the female parent is derived the internal structure, the vital organs, and in a much greater proportion than from the male, the constitution, temper and habit, in which endurance and "bottom" are included.

3. That the purer the race of the parent, the more certainty there is of its transmitting its qualities to the offspring: say two animals are mated, if one is of purer descent than the other, he or she will exercise the most influence in stamping the character of progeny, particularly if the greater purity is on the side of the male.

4. That apart from certain disturbing influences or causes the male if of pure race, and descended from a stock of uniform color, stamps the color of the offspring.

5. That the influence of the first male is not unfrequently protracted beyond the birth of the offspring of which he is parent, and his mark is left upon subsequent progeny.

6. That is the transmission of disease of the vital organs is more certain if on the side of the female, and diseases of the joints if on the side of the male parent.

The Poultry to Keep.

The breed to keep is what you need. We know the qualities of the Jersey, the Guernsey, the Alderney and the Hereford cattle. We know when we want butter what breed to select, and what is needed when merely a milk market is desired. We know the qualities of the Berkshire, the Poland China and the Chester White hogs. We know when we want pork what breed to get. In short, in all live stock we know the fitness of the one kind in preference to another.

So it is with poultry. We know that the Houdan, the Spanish, the Minorca, and the White Leghorn all lay large, white eggs and many of them. We know the Plymouth Rock the Langshan and the game lay brown eggs and many of them. If our market wants a white egg we have it. If it wants a brown egg we have it. If we want to furnish a table fowl, we know the qualities of an Asiatic class—the Brahmas the Cochins and the Langshans. And so we single out. Let there be an object for every poultry farm. Better have one good object and fully carried out than two objects and only half done. Keep one variety if possible. It will be more satisfactory. You will know your birds sooner. Success comes the quickest to the man who knows what he is about. Above all things, however, commence at the lowest round of the ladder and climb up.—[The Homestead.

Against Dehorning.

A correspondent of the Kansas City Drovers' Telegram writes:

The dehorning of cattle in this country appears to have met with general favor, judging from the popular vain which has recently spread all over the country, but in as much as the writer has ever contended that it was a cruelty imposed upon cattle that was not justified by the results, and that it is barbarous in the extreme. It subjects the animal to great pain and misery, from which no adequate results commensurate with the attending cruelty can possibly arise. It will no doubt be of interest to many of your readers to learn of some of the objectionable points urged against this barbarous practice, by an old and well known feeder and stock raiser, Mr. W. Edwards. His evidence being all the more valuable on account of being given from actual experience. I visited Mr. Edwards' farm to-day upon which he has a large number of cattle, several hundred of which he has on full feed. He has all the modern feeding arrangements and appliances, including the best of running and well water. Mr. Edwards had a large number of nice steers dehorned last Spring, mostly three year olds; others of the same age were allowed to retain their horns. These cattle were all used the same way, pastured the same and put on corn early in September. The cattle with horns are now fat, while those that were deprived of their horns are only in fair condition. One particular lot of these cattle Mr. Edwards bought last spring, which he says were extremely thin in flesh. At the time he had the others dehorned the thin cattle were not dehorned. They now have at least 100 pounds more fat than the cattle which were dehorned. Mr. Edwards declares it to be his belief that the process takes away the senses of the animal The gentleman above referred to says his cattle that were dehorned are hard to drive or handle. They appear to have lost their intelligence, common to ordinary cattle. In support of this theory I will offer Mr. I. G. Pryor's testimony. In conversation with him on the subject of dehorning at Arkansas City he had bought a drove of Texas cows, which had been dehorned. He said they did not appear to have a particle of sense about being driven or handled. Mr. P. seemed to think that the cutting off their horns and exposing a large cavity in each side of the head, affected their animal senses. The writer has no special desire to cast discredit on any system that will add to the wealth of the country or the community of the farmers, but when knowledge comes to his notice through the reliable channels of actual experience of practical feeders, demonstrating the fallacy of a cruel craze which has taken possession of the country, not only carrying with it a practice akin to the usages of barbarians, but brings with it untold losses to the cattle interests of the country. He feels that there can no harm grow out of the laying of these facts, as obtained from reliable sources, before the feeding and cattle raising public for their deliberate and close investigation.

Carelessness About Utensils.

One of the most dangerous germs that can infest milk is that found in old rotten milk in the seams, joints and corners of pails, and in and under the many patches of tinkered up milk fixings. Old butter bowls and old wooden churns are as a rule cooked full of fats that for ten or thirty years have been nests for the propagation of these bacteria The only plan to pursue is to have as little patching and mending done as possible in dairy utensils. Discard at once all suspicious machinery and get new. Thousands of tons of butter that now finds final sale at the soap-makers was well made, but the utensils were old and germ-laden with more or less of these enemies of good produce, and as soon as the butter was made they commenced their destructive fermenting and corroding, and went faster than freight or express trains, and when the butter reached the market it was worthless for food. Had this butter been made in new and well cared for apparatus it would have reached market a pride to the maker.

White Fowls.

We do not hear much of late years on the delicacy of white fowls, although stock breeders and farmers underrate white horses and cattle. This question of color has been handed down to us from ancient times, but whether there is a solid and unquestionable foundation for such a general opinion we cannot say. Early writers undervalued white fowls, white horses, white dogs, white cats and white cattle, and even modern naturalists have shared in the same discriminating belief. If the animals and domestic fowls of extremely cold countries naturally tend to gray or grayish white color the question arises, Is this a provision of nature to escape the sight and pursuit of enemies, or is it a warmer color for enduring cold? This question can be discussed pro and con; the information solicited would bring us back to the starting point. Many of our fanciers who held such a prejudice a few years ago would perhaps say to day that it is like many other things—an old fogy notion; that the proof is in our present white varieties of fowls, which for hardiness, constitutional vigor and other useful points are the equal of the colored varieties.

It matters not whether this old saying is true or false; ideas often become reversed by the force of circumstances. Irrepressible popularity has set in for the new white varieties. Fanciers and non-fanciers take up their breeding; they show all the good points of their colored relatives; give like satisfaction so far in their culture; they meet the demands of the trade; there is nothing specially noticeable about their vigor, hardiness, prepotent faculties and staying productiveness beside colored varieties. Then why ought they not to be as good for all practical purposes as the colored ones?

One sometimes says that white fowls are more easily seen by hawks, and for that reason they are not so well adapted to rural life. This may be true in general, but our experience with white fowls and hawks is the very reverse. Some years ago we lived in the suburbs, and were breeding White Leghorns, with four or five colored breeds. They had full range of eight acres, and hawks were very plentiful and destructive. In a troop of twenty to fifty, half and three-fourths grown chickens, white and colored, almost invariably the hawks selected the colored birds from the flocks. This was not for one season, but for four years. We often sat under the shade of a tree and watched the wily bandit pass over the white birds and snatch up a colored one. The black chickens also seemed to escape comparatively well. We reasoned thus: The white is an unusual color; it is not the color of birds that become the prey of hawks: seen at a distance the outline is not so marked; the reflection of light gives to the bird a large appearance, and the hawk naturally selects birds which come near to the color of the wild game. Of course we do not pretend to say there is much logic in this, but the facts as they came under our observation remain the same.

We do not encourage any one to quit breeding colored varieties in hope of profiting by getting white ones. It is a matter of taste or speculation to choose white in preference to other colors. In the white there is nothing artistic; no colors, shades or lines, markings, pencilings or lacings. The whole plumage is taken in at a glance, but still a white plumage leaves a pleasing impression on the mind. For lawns or nicely kept grass runs a flock of white fowls is a beautiful sight. When the plumage is in good condition they look clean and neat. The contrast of a rich red comb, face and wattles, yellow or flesh-colored beak and legs with the plumage and green grass, the shading trees and other natural surroundings commands admiration. In the matter of utility, the white birds will be found as valuable as the colored; in matter for breeding they are much preferred, and for market, either dressed or alive, they show to good advantage. In dressing they do not show the dark pin-feathers which detract much from the value of a market fowl.—National Stockman and Farmer.

Notes.

What the cause of it is cannot be stated, but it is an understood fact that the cattle and horse business of Nevada is on the decline and is being gradually superseded by the sheep industry. This is vouched for by a correspondent of the Reno (Nev.) Gazette, who says: "It will not be long until the bands of cattle and horses that have roamed over all eastern Nevada for the past thirty years or more as free commoners will only be known as a matter of history and that cattle raising will be chiefly confined to the home ranches and that hereafter eastern Nevada will be noted for its immense flocks of sheep, as it has been in the past for its immense bands of of cattle and horses."

The Las Vegas Stock Grower of the 28th, says: Dr Thornton, of the Perrin Land & Cattle Company, returned recently from San Francisco He thinks the California market for northern Arizona stock is getting better. His son G. P. is shipping 22 carloads from Williams to San Francisco. Stephen Ross, of Garland & Ross, is shipping from same place to Los Angeles. The Aztec Co. is shipping 12 cars to Jones & Co.

Several prominent cattle men in Southern Oregon have tried stall feeding this winter and are so satisfied with the results that there will be a greater number of stall fed cattle there in future

The council of the Smithfield Club England have adopted a rule that if dentition is inconsistent with the ages given in the form of entry the stewards must disqualify, and to meet the matter of forced dentition they have fixed a limit under which rule fourteen animals in the cattle classes were disqualified at their late show including some Birmingham prize winners.

Official receipts of cattle at Chicago for the first eleven months of the year were 2 773,615, or 374.000 head more than during the same period of 1888. The receipts at that point for the year will prove by far the greatest on record. So also of sheep with 1,674,506 received up to December 1.

Mason Valley, Lyon County, is suffering from a surplus of hay, very few cattle having come into the valley to feed this winter, owing to the low price of beef.

Cattle and sheep have suffered all over during the late storm. San Luis Obispo has been particularly unfortunate in that respect.

H. Abel, a prominent Milpitas butcher, killed a six-year-old Devon and Shorthorn steer, live weight 2,785 pounds, dressed 2,185 pounds The steer was raised and fed by Mr. Abel, and was probably the best and heaviest ever killed in that section of the country.

Del Norte is getting to be one of the best dairy counties in the State. During last year eighteen dairymen, who, according to the Record's account, milked 1336 cows during the past year, and made 199,095 pounds of butter. The 18 dairies occupy 1635 acres of land.

The loss of cattle at Dutton's Landing, Solano county, will probably be very large. Seven or eight hundred head of cattle are on the island, with very little chance of saving them, as about two miles of levee is washed away.

In 1889 there were 43 sales of Shorthorns in England, 2,323 head in all were sold for £76,571. In 1888, 1,594 head were sold for £44,013. The average in 1889 of £32,193 is the highest since 1885. The Duke of Devonshires, selections from his celebrated herd at Holker, had the best average, viz., £104.13. The highest price made in the year was £535 10, at the late Sir R. Loder's sale at Whittlebury.

There are about 27,000 sheep and 10,000 horses and cattle in Eagle Valley, Oregon, and the Oregon Blade says that there is only about 500 tons of hay left, the price for which is $6 a ton, and if the cold snap continues it will probably go up to $10 or $12.

According to the Live Stock Journal Almanac, thirty Short-horn sales were held at the residences of British breeders during 1889, at which a total of £46.532 was realized for 1348 head, being a general average of £24. The highest single price was 510 guineas; the lowest, 3 guineas.

A convenient arrangement for scalding hogs is a box with a sheet-iron bottom placed over a furnace; the top of the box should be on a level with the cleaning table, and the fire can be regulated to keep the water at the desired temperature. The box should be of sufficient length, depth and width to admit it to be turned from one side to the other without throwing out the water.

If it costs no more to feed blooded fowls than common, what economy is there in keeping the latter? Many imagine that the care bestowed upon the finer strains of poultry makes them much harder to breed and keep, and this extra labor never pays. You make a mistake if you think this way. Experience will teach you the wisdom of breeding choice blooded stock, and why it pays best. Farmers can do no better than test this matter thoroughly and be satisfied that this advice is worth heeding.

We are pleased to chronicle the fact as showing the growing market of all our finely bred stock, whether it be hogs, cattle, sheep or poultry, that by the last steamer to Japan, some $200 worth of finely bred Buff Cochins were shipped to Tokio.

Mr. Williams, the well-known Walnut Creek butcher, bought two Polled Angus cattle of the Cook Farm, a two-year-old steer and a three-year-old heifer, weighing 1,380 lbs each. The local ranchers are said to have been so impressed with the appearance of the cattle that they may be expected to join the pure bred brigade.

Texas is moving to corral if possible the "Big Four" in Chicago, who squeeze all profit out of beef and leave the stock grower nothing. Her cattle men have called an interstate convention to meet at Fort Worth March 14, 1890. Prices have declined 60 per cent., but consumers pay the same old rates. The Texans say that, estimating the annual consumption of meat in the United States at 10 000,000 head, which is equivalent to one animal for every six and a half of our population, we are losing the enormous sum of $200,000,000 annually, which goes to a very large extent into the hands of four men who are known as "The Big Four" of Chicago.

Among the many stockmen in the State who have suffered heavy losses from the rains, none have met with harder luck than Col. Irvin Ayres, who took twelve hundred head of cattle to Marysville in September and rented good pasturage, including alfalfa, at an exhorbitant price, only to have the river drive his cattle out of all the alfalfa and have to purchase hay, etc., besides retarding the feeding of the cattle.

Taking the whole area of the United States, the farm lands comprise 289 acres in every 1,000, leaving 711 acres unoccupied. Of the former quantity 153 acres are productive, 103 woodland, and 33 unproductive, though partly susceptible of improvement.

The Birmingham (England) Fat Stock Show was notable for the well bred cattle entered by the Upper Ten, who were very successful all round. Nearly all the highest honours were won by the Queen, who sent nine bullocks from Windsor, with which she won four first prizes and two seconds. Her Majesty's triumphs did not end here, as she also won the special prizes given for the best of the Hereford and Shorthorn breeds, while, crowning triumph of all, her Shorthorn then took the Elkington Challenge Cup of a hundred guineas, given for the best bullock in all the classes. This is the first time that Her Majesty has won this champion prize at Birmingham, although she has gained a similar distinction at the Smithfield Club Show, but the triumph would have been more complete if the animal had been bred at Windsor, for in this case it would also have won the prize of £25 given by Lord Burton, who is President for the year, to the best bullock bred and fed by the exhibitor. The Prince of Wales sent some cattle and sheep from Sandringham, but the only prize he won was a second with a pen of Southdown sheep. Among the other successful exhibitors were the Duke of Portland, whose Shorthorns seem to be as formidable as his racehorses; Lord Coventry, who is invariable bad to beat, with his Herefords; Colonel Henry Platt, who exhibits some splendid specimens of the Welsh breed; the Duke of Hamilton, who is to the front with his black pigs; and Lord Tredegar, and Sir John Swinburne, who, like the Duke of Portland, send Shorthorns of the purest type.

Entries for the BREEDER AND SPORTSMAN'S Futurity Stake.

Nominator.	Sire.	Dam.	Sire of Dam.
Adams, E. F.	Sidney	Daughter of	Linwood.
Archer, E. C.	Steve Whipple	Nellie.	Partisan.
Brown, Robt S	Secretary	Miss Pierce	Tom Hyer Jr.
" " "	"	Debonair.	Sultan.
Brook Dale Stock Farm	Director	Phaceola	Silver Threads.
" " " "	Sidney	An Tricks	Anteeo.
" " " "	Woodnut	Tricks	Whipple's Hambletonian.
" " " "	Memo	Lady Blanchard	Whipple's Hambletonian.
" " " "	Volo	Maud P	Nutwood.
Bartlett, W. T	Coligny	Molly	Eugene Casserly.
Bonner, Robt	St. Nicholas	Lady Bonner	American Union.
Bellingall, P. W	"	Bellingall's Road Mare.	Unknown.
Curtin, C	Clovis	Alice Clay	Alcona Clay.
Casey, W. J	Billy Thornhill	Flora Pierce	Black Hawk Comet.
" "	Eros	Maud Center	Imp. Hercules.
Chadbourne, Joshua	Director	Molly	Ben Allan.
Cook Stock Farm	Steinway	None Better	Allandorf.
" " "	Chas. Derby	Addie Ash	Indianapolis.
Clawson & Gamble	Noonday	Ellie C	Creson.
Carter, Martin	Director	Lida W	Nutwood.
Coombs Bros	"	Lillie Stanley	Whippleton.
Crousey, Geo	"	Alice R	Nauboc
Clawson, L. E	Memo	Brunette	Whipple's Hambletonian.
Chino Ranch	Woolsey	Easter	Billy Norfolk
" "	"	Nettie Norfolk	Billy Norfolk
" "	Albion	Susie Blair	Billy Norfolk.
" "	"	Indee	Inca.
" "	Will Crocker	Lady Inca	Inca.
" "	"	Queen	Echo.
Crabb, H. W	Grandissimo	Flora B	Whippleton.
" " "	"	Etta	Naubuc.
Duncan, F. L	Signal Wilkes	Gold Elsie	Sam Purdy.
Du Bois Bros	Superior	Magdalene	Magnet.
" "	"	Knoxie	Knox Boy.
" "	"	Ina	Dictator.
Drew, J. C	Adrian	Venus	Transit.
Davis & Endicott	Antee-up	Express	Bay Mac.
De Camp, E. A	McKinney	Bronco	The Moor.
Den, E. R	Alcazar	Carrie B	A. W. Richmond.
Evans, J. J	Mortimer	Miss Cottle	Victor.
" "	Leo Wilkes	Jennie Cottle	Victor.
Farnum, Dr. C. E	Director	Belle	Capt. Webster.
Frasier, D. S	Secretary	Daughter of	Anteeo.
" "	"	Emma	Whippleton.
Fortin, D. E	St. Nicholas	Bell A	Geo M Patchen Jr.
Fink, A. W	Guy Wilkes	Jennie McCarty	Patchen Vernon.
Funck Bros	Noonday	Grayson Lillie	Elector.
Gannon, Dennis	"	Miss Sidney	Sidney.
Galloway, Wm	Altamont	Hollywood	Hambletonian Mambrino.
Gamble, W. A	Noonday	Black Swan	Nephew.
" "	Mountain Boy	Mabel Echo	Echo.
Greene, Chas	Sidney	Queen	Sultan.
" "	"	Emma G	Elmo.
Gonsalez, Alfred	"	Kate Ewing	Berlin.
" "	Junio	Yum Yum	Elmo.
Grant, Frank	Prompter	Cauliflower	St. Jacob.
Greene, A. I	Sidney	Linda	Linwood.
" "	Simmocolon	Bessie Howard	Whipple's Hambletonian.
Goldsmith, Jno. A	Guy Wilkes	Manon	Nutwood
Gardner, Jno. W.	McKinney	Lady I	Billy Norfolk.
Griffin, Jno. S	Alcazar	Elwood	A. W. Richmond.
Guerne, Geo. E	Alfred G	Nellie	Alexander.
" "	"	Minnie Laughlin	Gen. Lee.
" "	"	Roseuburgh	Trusty Henry.
" "	"	Daisy	Nutwood.
" "	"	Zulu	Zulu Chief.
Harris & Harris	Secretary	Thursa D	Admiral.
" "	Stanford	Rose Abbot	Abbotsford.
" "	"	Echola	Echo.
Heald & Loeber	Whippleton	Kate Chapman	Naubuc.
Hatch, A. T	Guide	Primera	Admar.
" "	My Guy	La signa	Le Grande.
" "	Director	Daughter of	Irvington.
Helman, H. H	Strathway	Sealette	Pasha.
Haney, Free	"	Emeline Temple	Jackson Temple.
Huntley, L. L	Sidney	Idalette	Silver Threads.
Hicks, M. W	Prompter	Gazelle	Buccaneer.
" "	Sterling	Ripple	Prompter.
Hicks, L. B	Prompter	Valley Belle	Privateer.
Hoppin, Chas. R	Alexander Button	Molly	Dietz's St. Clair.
" "	Mountain Boy	Hattie H	Alexander.
Hewlett, L	Director	Brownie H	Priam.
Hallinan, J	Sidney	Grindelia	Gen. Benton.
Hobart, W. S	Stamboul	Trinket	Princeps.
" "	"	Kitty Wilkes	Geo. Wilkes.
" "	"	Alta Belle	Electioneer.
" "	"	Bon Bon	Simmons.
Head, R. G	Noonday	Nellie Steinway	Steinway.
Hall & Whitely	Director	Brainey	Echo.
Holly, B. C	Woodnut	Economy	Echo.
" "	Mountain Boy	Lissette	Abdallah Wilkes.
" "	Happy Prince	Aurelia	Albert W.
" "	Wildwood	Veronica	Alcona.
Jordan Rudolf, Jr	Alexander Button	Adeline Patti	Effingham.
Knox, J. W	Florida	Emily	Geo. Wilkes.
" " "	"	Patience	Young Jim.
" " "	"	Clarie	Bayard.
" " "	Anteeo	Hattie Woodard	Aberdeen.
" " "	"	Eva	Geo Wilkes.
Kemper M	Woodnut	Alice B	Admiral.
Kingsley, C. H	Sidney	Ruby	Norwood.
Kerr, Jas. P	Memo	Marguerite	Speculation.
Lamonreux, Theo	Director	Kate Gennette	Billy Roberts
Latham, B	Dexter Prince	Belta	Bell Alta.
Loeber, Fred W	Grandissimo	Whidana	Whippleton.
" " "	Director	Wisp	Whippleton.
La Siesta Ranch	Eros	Daughter of	Comet.
" " "	"	Nettie Nutwood	Nutwood.
" " "	"	Lady Alice	Nutwood.
" " "	"	Olita	Nutwood.
" " "	"	Morna	Brigadier.
" " "	"	Nerea	John Nelson.
" " "	"	Nerea Patchen	Geo. M. Patchen, Jr.
" " "	"	Queen Piedmont	Piedmont.
" " "	"	Ante	Anteeo.
" " "	"	Duchess	s. t. b. by Young Morrill
" " "	"	Stella S	s. t. b. by Young Morrill.
" " "	"	Lady Santa Claus	Santa Claus.
" " "	"	Rose	Erwin Davis.
" " "	"	Flora	Elmo.
" " "	"	Algonette	Algona.
" " "	"	Amaryllis	Woodburn.
" " "	"	Daughter of	Bob Wooding.
" " "	"	Lady Voorhees	Dan Voorhees.
Lynch, H. H	Memo	Grey Mare	Not given.
McCafferty, Wm	McCafferty's Nutwood	Maggie	Patchen Vernon.
" "	Noonday	Pansy	McCafferty's Nutwood.
Murphy, P. W	Gaviota	Lilly Vernon	Tom Vernon.
" " "	"	Mary O	Gladiator.
Mayhew, H. A	Arbitrator	Ethel Hayward	Billy Hayward.
McCord, J. L	Tom Benton	Brown Jennie	Dave Hill, Jr.
" " "	"	Fannie	McCracken's Black Hawk.
Malone, F. S	Son of Director	Kitty	Irvington.
Mansfeldt, Oscar	Sidney	Alborac	Naubuc.
Meese, Wm	Noonday	Steinie	Steinway.
Murphy, D. J	Soudan	Jane McLain	Budd Doble.
" " "	"	Patchen Molly	Geo. M. Patchen, Jr.
" " "	"	Molly	Son of Geo. M. Patchen, Jr.
" " "	"	Daughter of	Elmo.
Mendenhall, W. W	Grand Moor, Jr.	Alice H	Nutwood.
McIver, Chas. C	Linda Vista	Lillie S	Milton Medium.
" " "	Director	May M	Bentonian.
Murphy Rufus	Anteeo	Maud	Nutwood
" "	"	Fanny	Brigadier
Morse L. M	Dexter Prince	Ida	Abbotsford
McFadyen A	Redwood	Zulu Maid	Zulu Chief
" "	Mountain Boy	Lou Milton	Milton Medium
Murphy M. A	Woolsey	Bessie	Inca
Montgomery T. S	Antinous	Nettie Nutwood	Nutwood
Napa Stock Farm	Dexter Prince	Mollie Patten	Whippleton
" " "	Leo Wilkes	Norma	Arthurton
Newman R. O	Strathway	Elizabeth Basler	Bill Arp
" " "	"	Richmoor	Pasha
" " "	"	Ida May	Grosvenor
Needham C. E	Steve Whipple	Ze-Ette	Chrisman's Hambletonian
O'Brien Jno D	Sidney	Ale Bay	Alexander
Pleasanton Stock Farm Co	Director	May Day	Ballard's Cassius M. Clay
" " " "	"	Roxana	Gibraltar
" " " "	"	Brown Crockett	Overland
" " " "	"	Maid of Oaks	Duke McClellan
" " " "	"	Belle Echo	Echo
" " " "	"	Maude	Bertrand
" " " "	"	Belle S	Whipple's Hambletonian
" " " "	"	Misfortune	Monroe Chief
" " " "	"	Bonny	Echo
" " " "	"	Sister to Blue Bell	Greenback
" " " "	"	Daisy	Prompter
Pierce Ira	Memo	Flora Wilkes	Mambrino Wilkes
" "	Danger	Poscora Belle	Billy Hayward
Pinkham Chas. E	Sterling	Crescent	Prompter
Patery J. P	Alexander Button	Lucy	Hercules
Pardee S. H	Director	Nellie Grant	Santa Claus
Page, Wilfred	Eclectic	Reinette	Dexter Prince
" "	"	Leoline	Clovis
" "	"	Minnie Allen	Arthurton
" "	"	Reka Patchen	Alexander
" "	"	Bellasa	Elector
" "	Mortimer	Clara S	Nutwood
" "	"	Ida Walker	Curtis's Hambletonian
" "	"	Lady del Sur	Del Sur
" "	"	Sunny Slope Belle	The Moor
Palo Alto Stock Farm	Electioneer	Beautiful Bells	The Moor.
" " " "	"	Belle Campbell	General Benton
" " " "	"	Tillie	General Benton.
" " " "	"	Dame Winnie	Planet
" " " "	Nephew	Lorinne	General Benton
" " " "	"	Wildflower	Electioneer
" " " "	Piedmont	Maiden	Electioneer
" " " "	"	Thalia	Electioneer
" " " "	Azmoor	Bonnie	General Benton
" " " "	"	Emma Robson	Woodburn
" " " "	Palo Alto	Jennie Benton	General Benton
" " " "	"	Meta	Piedmont
Rodman A. B	Advocate	Patty P	Richmont
Rust W. R	Superior	Countess	Admir'l son Com Vanderbilt
Robinson W. J	Secretary	Jenny Lind	Ironclad
Rose L. J	Stamboul	Almeh	Sultan
" " "	Alcazar	Garred	Son of Dictator
Rea Jas. W	Nephew	Magdallah	Primus
Reuck J. M	Apex	Rosa	Pasha
Rose Dale Breeding Farm	Daly	Cygnet	Steinway
Rudisill H. T	Alcazar	Mollie	Not Given
Smith J. D	Sidney	Addie S	Steinway
San Miguel Stock Farm	Mambrino Wilkes	Annie Laurie	Echo
" " " "	"	Fanny Fern	Jack Hawkins
" " " "	"	Contra	Electioneer
" " " "	"	Fredolia	Fred Arnold
" " " "	"	Piracy	Buccaneer
" " " "	Balkan	Amy	Mambrino Wilkes
Shippee L. U	Hawthorne	Mord	Dan Lambert
" " "	Campaign	Old Tempest	Morgan Rattler
Spreckels A. B	Alcazar	Gracie S	Speculation
" " "	Aptos Wilkes	Erminie	Abbotsford
" " "	"	Ashcat's daughter	Speculation
" " "	Alcazar	Lillie S	Speculation
Stutz Jacob	St. Nicholas	Amelia S	Algerine
Stimpson C. W	Sidney	Maye	Newland's Hambletonian.
Striening M. J	Redwood	Dollie	Union
Smith, Thos	George Washington	Nancy R	Admiral.
Smith, Wilber Field	Albert W	Belle Blanche	The Moor.
Skinner, Mrs. Silas	Director	Fontana	Almont.
Starr, H. B	Noonday	Lillie C	Alcona Clay.
Snider, T. C	Director	Alice	Prompter.
Straube, S. N	Apex	Devotion	Dexter Prince.
" " "	"	Peggy	Whipple's Hambletonian.
" " "	Clovis	Mattie Consuella	Steinway.
" " "	"	Baby S	Nephew.
San Mateo Stock Farm	Guy Wilkes	Ruby	Sultan.
" " " "	"	Margaret	Sultan.
" " " "	"	Sweetness	Volunteer.
" " " "	"	Sister	Admiral.
" " " "	"	Blanche	Arthurton.
" " " "	"	Cora	Buccaneer.
" " " "	Sable Wilkes	Vixen	Nutwood.
" " " "	"	Mamie Comet	Nutwood.
" " " "	"	Minnie Princess	Nutwood.
" " " "	"	Molly Drew	Winthrop.
Tarpey, M. F	Clovis	Daughter of	Nutwood.
Tompkins, Gilbert	Jester D	Rosaline	Major Mono.
" "	"	Effie Deans	Whipple's Hambletonian.
" "	Figaro	Puss	Kentucky Hunter.
" "	"	Fanny Sinfoot	Erwin Davis.
Thornton, H. I	James Madison	Belle Allen	Ethan Allen, Jr
" " "	" "	Estelle	Elmo
" " "	" "	Lena	Berlin
" " "	Noonday	Betsy Trotwood	Abbotsford
" " "	Director	Adina	Electioneer
Varne, Thos. S	Alcona	Adamson's mare	Vick's Ethan Allen
Villegia, L	Sidney	May	John Nelson
Visher, P	Linwood	Maggie V	Nephew
Valensin Stock Farm	Simmocolon	Santa Rita	Sidney
" " "	"	Sybil	Sidney
" " "	"	Fern Leaf	Flaxtail
" " "	"	Lightfoot	Flaxtail
" " "	"	Ivy	Buccaneer
" " "	Sidney	Faustina	Crown Point
" " "	"	Flight	Buccaneer
" " "	"	Venus	Capt Webster
" " "	"	Flirt	Buccaneer
" " "	"	Nettie Lambert	Jno. Nelson
" " "	"	Alice C	Wilkes Boy
" " "	"	Patti	Nutwood
" " "	"	Variation	Allandorf
" " "	"	Maud V	Buccaneer
" " "	"	Highland Lass	Buccaneer
" " "	"	Juno	Buccaneer
" " "	"	Belle Grande	La Grande
" " "	"	Florence Wilkes	Red Wilkes
" " "	"	Ellen Tomlinson	Dictator
" " "	"	Mattie Strathmore	Strathmore
Wright, S. B	Alfred G	Ruth Whippleton	Whippleton.
Warfield, R. H. & G. H	Philosopher	Nellie	Grey McClellan.
Wattles, Wood	Director	Young Miami	Paul's Abdallah.
Watson, James E	Memo	Nellie	McClellan.
Weske, A	Prince Imperial	Amelia	Grey McClellan.
Welby Chas. W	Guy Wilkes	Bay View Maid	General Benton.
Woodard, Geo. W	Alex. Button	Viola	Flaxtail.
" "	"	Margaret	Fred Lowe.
" "	"	Sibble	Unknown.
Wilson, A. W.	Noonday	Nettie Scales	Steinway.
Wilson, W. H	"	Linda Wilkes	Guy Wilkes.
Wickersham, F. B	Apex	Maude	Whippleton.
" "	"	Stella	Kentucky Hunter.
Young, David	Dexter Prince	Emma	Nutwood.

THE WEEKLY

Breeder and Sportsman.

JAMES P. KERR, PROPRIETOR.

The Turf and Sporting Authority of the Pacific Coast.

Office, No. 313 Bush St.

P. O. Box 2300.

TERMS—*One Year, $5; Six Months, $3; Three Months, $1.50.* STRICTLY IN ADVANCE.

Money should be sent by postal order, draft or by registered letter, addressed to JAMES P. KERR, San Francisco, Cal.

Communications must be accompanied by the writer's name and address, not necessarily for publication, but as a private guarantee of good faith.

ALEX. P. WAUGH, - - - - - Editor.

To Subscribers.

The date printed on the wrapper of your paper indicates the time to which your subscription is paid.

Should the BREEDER AND SPORTSMAN be received by any subscriber who does not want it, write us direct to stop it. A postal card will suffice.

Special Notice to Correspondents.

Letters intended for publication should reach this office not later than Wednesday of each week, to secure a place in the issue of the following Saturday. Such letters to insure immediate attention should be addressed to the BREEDER AND SPORTSMAN, and not to any member of the staff.

San Francisco, Saturday, Jan. 11, 1890.

The Breeder and Sportsman Futurity Stake.

When the BREEDER AND SPORTSMAN Futurity Stake was first proposed, one or two of the timid breeders predicted that it would be a failure. "The State was too young to guarantee $3,000, and only misfortune could possibly arise to he who was foolhardy enough to attempt it," was one remark overheard, but we wanted to show to the breeders of other States that California is much more prolific in breeding farms than many are aware of. The number of well bred brood mares in California was what we figured on from the start, and the number of entries prove that our theory was correct. Those who only have two, three or four mares have responded nobly, and we assert without fear of contradiction that the BREEDER AND SPORTSMAN Futurity Stake is the most successful ever instituted. Four years ago the New York Spirit of the Times started one, and there were represented States from the Atlantic to the Pacific, and from the Gulf of Mexico to the Canadian border, the total number of entries being 307. A summing up shows a total of 284 entries in the BREEDER AND SPORTSMAN Stake, of which 273 are from the State of California alone, six being from Kentucky, four from Colorado, and one from Oregon. We are more than gratified at the result, and hasten to thank our many friends for their cordial support in making the stake a success.

By going over the list it will be seen that twenty-nine Sidneys are nominated, while the friends of Director follow closely with twenty-eight. Eros has nineteen representatives and Noonday has eleven, these being the only four to touch double figures. Guy Wilkes has nine and Alfred G., Alexander Button, Simmocolon, Alcazar, Secretary and Memo have six each. Those having five to their credit are Strathway, Mambrino Wilkes, Mortimer, Eclectic, Apex and Stamboul. The stallions having four each in the list are Soudan, St. Nicholas, Clovis, Superior, Sable Wilkes, Anteeo, Mountain Boy, Dexter Prince and Electioneer. Those having three are James Madison, Florida, Prompter, Nephew, Woodnut, Grandissimo and Woolsey. There are two each accredited to Steve Whipple, Albion, Will Crocker, McKinney, Leo Wilkes, Stanford, Sterling, Jester D., Figaro, Aptos Wilkes, Palo Alto, Azmoor, Piedmont, Redwood, Tom Benton and Gaviota. There are single entries of the progeny of Advocate, Volo, Coligney, Billy Thornhill, Steinway, Chas. Derby, Balkan, Hawthorne, Campaign, Danger, Antinous, Linda Vista, Grand Moor Jr., Son of Director, Arbitrator, Signal Wilkes, Adrian, Antee Up, Altamont, Junio, Whippleton, Guide, My Guy, Happy Prince, Wildwood, McCafferty's Nutwood, Prince Imperial, George Washington, Albert W., Alcona, Linwood, Philosopher and Daly. The most fashionable families are represented, and speed is firmly implanted in each and every entry. The reader can easily imagine what the produce from Trinket 2:14, and Stamboul 2.12½ should be. There has never been an entry in the world to equal that, and it is with pardonable pride that we call attention to it.

The first entry was received from Wilbur Field Smith of Sacramento, and the last from H. T. Rudisill of Los Angeles, the terrible storms having delayed the mail from that section. We congratulate those who have entries in the first BREEDER AND SPORTSMAN Futurity Stake, and trust that the winner may be fast enough to add additional laurels to the wreath of our glorious State.

The State Agricultural Society.

The parent organization of all the California Agricultural Societies has branched out, and will give an early spring meeting for the running brigade, the entries for which are so large that a most successful meeting is assured. In the present issue the declarations made on January 1st are given, and there is also an advertisement asking for entries in the new stakes. The first is named after the well known president of the association, Christopher Green, and is an all aged handicap, $50 entrance, half forfeit, with $500, added. The distance is a mile and a quarter, and with the liberality displayed by the society should have a large list of entries. The second of the new events, has been christened the Spring Stakes, for three-year-olds $50 entrance half forfeit and there is $400 added. The distance is a mile and should also bring out a large field, the many two-year-olds of last season, insuring a plentiful supply of three-year-olds.

The secretary Mr. Edwin F. Smith has also forwarded to this office a list of the entries for the Occident Stakes of 1892, as well as a list of those who have made second and third payments in the same stake for 1891 and 1890. The effect of the Breeder and Sportsman's Futurity Stake is apparent in the large list entered for the 1892 Occident Stake, breeders realizing the fact that these colt stakes are productive of immense good and they have sent in the nominations with a lavish hand. All of the principal farms are represented and a number of new names are also seen on the roll.

The Hamlin Sale.

Among the new advertisements this week is one from Peter C. Kellogg & Co. of New York, in which they announce to our readers that they will shortly offer for sale a consignment from the breeding establishment of J. C. Hamlin. That gentleman has been one of the foremost breeders of later days, and has always been progressive. In offering a large number to the public at auction he has judgment enough to know that only the very best will pass muster from Village Farm.

The catalogue will include brood mares in foal, young stallions, colts and fillies of high winning and campaigning strains, bred for beauty, style, finish and soundness, as well as for speed. The owner especially invites a comparison of the animals of his own breeding offered in this sale with any lot that has been placed upon the market by any other noted breeding centre.

The brood mares to be sold are stinted to Hamlin's Almont Jr, Mambrino King and Chimes (son of Electioneer and Beautiful Bells), and some of them are so good in quality that the buyer will have a reasonable chance of securing in the prospective foal, if a stallion, the equal of his sire, or if a trotter developed for speed, a Belle Hamlin, a Prince Regent or a Sunol.

The colts and fillies by Almont Jr. and Mambrino King will not suffer in comparison with any corresponding lot that can be found in the Almont and Mambrino Patchen families. Those stallions may justly claim to have surpassed their distinguished sires in the stud and to mark a stage of improvement in the progress of their respective families. The colts and fillies offered in this sale, therefore, give every promise of enriching their buyers in the future, as the colts and fillies of Almont and Mambrino Patchen have in the past.

Send to the auctioneer for one of the catalogues.

Kidd, Edmonson and Morse Sale.

At the request of a large number of prominent breeders and to avoid dates claimed by other sales, Kidd, Edmonson and Morse have changed the dates of their great Chicago sale to March 17th to 23rd inclusive, entries for which close Feb. 20th. This is destined to be the greatest sale on earth, because Chicago is so centrally located and accessable from every direction, that every body who will buy a horse will go to Chicago.

F. L. Goulding, V. S., of Mt. Clemens, Mich., says that he used the Boyce Wash freely over the body of his horse and that it makes the joints limber and relieves the tendons and ligaments from soreness and fever.

CORRESPONDENCE.

Willows, Cal. January 8th, 1889.

EDITOR BREEDER AND SPORTSMAN.—Your article headed "A Meeting Necessary," in issue of Jan'y 4th meets with the hearty approval of the Directors of the association. The constant conflicting and clashing of dates between the associations and the different portions of the state, has always resulted to the detriment, and also to the finacial detriment, of all. We think that the only thing to be done is to do as you suggest in your article. My idea would be to form what might be termed "The Northern Circuit," to consist of say Glenbrook, Marysville, Chico, Redding and Willows, (and also Red Bluff) as they will have an association there ready for meeting this year). I have already, by order of board of directors of this association, corresponded with the above named associations relative to the formation of such a circuit.

Yours very turly,
H. V. FREEMAN.
Secretary, Willows Agricultural Association.

This office will pay Twenty-five Cents for copies of the Breeder and Sportsman of the following dates: January 26, 1889; April 6, 1889; July 27, 1889; and for two copies of August 10, 1889, and will deem it a favor if readers who do not care to preserve files will forward the numbers mentioned.

Answers to Correspondents.

Answers for this department must be accompanied by the name and address of the sender, not necessarily for publication, but as proof of good faith. Write the questions distinctly, and on one side of the paper only. Positively no questions will be answered by mail or telegraph.

INFORMATION WANTED.

Santa Barbara.

Subscribers asks the following question and it is just possible that some of our readers may be able to give the needed information.

About the year 1867 a bay mare ran several races in Paradise Valley and in Stockton she was entered by a man by the name of Kline, and in Stockton ran against a mare known as Stockton filly, she is reported to have won every race she started in, and if you can give us any information as to the time she made, other particulars of the race or races, you will much oblige several subscribers here. Please answer through the columns of your paper.

Reader.

Please give breeding of the dam of Governor Stanford four year old record 2:23¼ made at Cleveland Ohio, October 5th, 1889.

Answer.—Barnes ch m by Whipple's Hambletonian 725. 1st dam by Chieftain 721; 2nd dam by Jim Crow.

J, P. S.

What kind of hay did they feed Sunol at the time she got her mark? Which is the best to feed a horse in training wet or dry oats?

Answer.—"Sunol" in her work was fed on oat and barley hay mixed, and her feed dry oats which is better then wet during training.

San Jose.

Kindly give the record of Laundry Boy by imp Hercules. It was made I think in the neighborhood of Sacramento or Maryeville some eight or ten years ago, driven by Chancey Kane.

Answer.—We cannot find that he has any record.

Boston, Mass.

The American Cultivator, Horse Department, writes for the full pedigree of Maud H. 2:30 by Mambrino Jr. 1789, (Carr's) the name of owner and breeder of her dam as much as can be certified to, and the name of the gentleman that drove her to her record of 2:30, and place where made. Can any reader give the information.

G. Santa Rosa.

Please let me know the pedigree of Glencoe; was he thoroughbred?

Answer.—Imp Glencoe by Sultan, 1st dam Trampoline by Tramp; 2nd dam Web by Waxy; 3rd dam Penelope by Trumpator; 4th dam Prunella by Highflyer; 5th dam Promise by Snap; 6th dam Julia by Blank, etc. He was thoroughbred.

Knight's Landing.

Will you kindly inform me through your valuable paper the pedigree (and record if any) of the horse Overland, imported by Mr Rose, I think.

Answer.—Overland by Bald Chief (Stevens) he by Bay Chief, a son of Mambrino Chief II, dam Madam Botts by John M. Botts. He is not in the 2:30 list.

W. F. J.

Please give pedigree of Silverthread raised by L. J. Rose, and sold to Fred Arnold, of Stockton. Is he registered and what is his number? Also the best performance of his half brothers and sisters, or their produce. 2. The pedigree of Winthrop by old Drew Horse and whether he is standard, and if registered, what is his number?

Answer.—Silverthread by The Moor 870, dam Gray Dale by Hollenback's American Boy Jr., 2nd dam Grey Poll by Winfield Scott. He is not registered. The only one of his half brothers that has a record is Longworth (pacer) 2:19.

Winthrop registered number 505, by Drew Horse 114, dam by the Eaton Horse 122, 2nd dam the Niles mare by Stone or Simpson Messenger.

EDITOR BREEDER AND SPORTSMAN:—The address of Dr. H. M. Pratt asked for in the late issue of the BREEDER AND SPORTSMAN, was at a recent date, Oakdale, Cal. The Patchen stallion asked for was owned at the time of his death by a Mr. Milliken, who resides near Santa Clara.

LIVERMORE, Cal. WM. MCDONALD,

Now then, L. A. Davis, the owner of Roy Wilkes is hot. He has deposited $500 with the BREEDER AND SPORTSMAN and asks the owner of any pacer in this neck of woods to cover it. He is after Hickok, and means to draw him out of his winter slumber. Now then Orrin, what do you say to that? Step up and make a match; the deposit is here in the office and you can be accommodated, provided you make the race to take place before Feb. 15th.

State Agricultural Association.

ENTRIES OCCIDENT STAKE 1892.

Jas. A. Bowers names br f Sadie B, Tom Benton—Brown Jennie.
La Siesta Ranch names br c Cupid, Eros—Margarita by Christmas Hambletonian.
La Siesta Ranch names br c Sancelita, Eros—Olita by Nutwood.
F. L. Duncan names blk c Purdy Wilkes, Sable Wilkes—Gold Elsie by Sam Purdy.
I. De Turk names dk b in Nathan Coombs, Anteeo—by Abbottsford.
I. De Turk names dk b c Antietam, Anteeo—by Nutwood.
W. F. Smith names blk f Semora, Guy Wilkes—Belle Branch by The Moor.
W. F. Smith names ch c Le Roy, Le Grande—Santa Rita by Sidney.
Thos. Smith names br c Columbus, McDonald—Fannie Rose by Ethan Allen Jr.
Chas. E. Sibber names br c Lippo Ti, Mambrino Wilkes—Narka by Nephew.
G. W. Woodard names b f Violet B, Alex Button—Viola.
G. W. Woodward names b c Frank B, Alex Button—Gazelle.
Sunny Knoll Stock Farm, (J. L. McCord) names b c Dave Benton, Tom Benton—Young Jennie by Dave Hill Jr.
C. E. Pinkham names b c Thuja, Sterling—Olive by Prompter.
Palo Alto Stock Farm names b f Bellflower, Electioneer—Beautiful Bells by The Moor.
Palo Alto Stock Farm names b f Lulu, Electioneer—Lula Wilkes by George Wilkes.
Palo Alto Stock Farm names b f Helena, Electioneer—Lady Ellen by Carr's Mambrino.
Palo Alto Stock Farm names br f Starlight, Electioneer—Sallie Benton by General Benton.
Palo Alto Stock Farm names ch f Captive, Piedmont—Clariurso by Electioneer.
Palo Alto Stock Farm names b f Tiny, Electioneer—Telle by General Benton.
Palo Alto Stock Farm names b f Jet, Piedmont—Bess by General Benton.
Palo Alto Stock Farm names b f Sylvia, Piedmont—Ash by Electioneer.
Palo Alto Stock Farm names br f Elden, Nephew—Eleanor by Electioneer.
Palo Alto Stock Farm names b f Wildbud, Nephew—Wildflower by Electioneer.
Palo Alto Stock Farm names b f Laurel, Nephew—Laura C. by Electioneer.
Palo Alto Stock Farm names br f Leola, Nephew—Lilly by Electioneer.
M. J. Striening names b c Willits, Anteeo—Dollie.
Ed. W. Berry names b f Viola, Antevolo—Prussima Damsel by Whipple's Hambletonian.
Wilfred Page names br c Loriliad (11182), Admont (5349)—Lorilee by Glasgow.
Wilfred Page names b f Mortrica, Mortimer—Reka Patchen by Alexander.
Hollywood Stock Farm (B. C. Holly), names b c Hollywood, Woodnut—Aurelia by Albert W.
Hollywood Stock Farm (B. C. Holly), names ch f Extravagant, Woodnut—Economy by Echo.
Pleasanton Stock Farm Co. names b f Diana, Director—Roxana by Gibraltar.
L. H. Titus names br f, Director—Belle Echo.
J. F. English names br f Rosetta, Tempest—Kittie Dubois.
Harris & Harris name b c Sirocco, Tempest, Carr's Mambrino—Daisy by General Taylor.
Harris & Harris name blk c Acorn, Seven Oaks, Nutwood—Elmorene by Elmo.
Harris & Harris name b f Gleam, Dawn, Nutwood—Sweetwood by Nutwood.
Harris & Harris name br f Belle Abbot, Stanford, Electioneer—Rose Abbot by Abbotsford.
Harris & Harris name br f Stanly, Stanford, Electioneer—Belle Brown by Whipple's Hambletonian.
Harris & Harris name b f Sidena, Sidney, Santa Claus—Lena Bowles by Ethan Allen Jr.
Jos. Cairn Simpson names ch f Del Paso, Con Moony, dam by Red Boy.
Napa Stock Farm names b f Wood Nymph, Woodnut—Belle Irvington by Irvington.
Napa Stock Farm names br f Grandissimo, Grandissimo (by Le Grande)—Belle Thorne by Whippleton.
San Mateo Stock Farm names dk b f Rubina Wilkes, Guy Wilkes—Ruby by Sultan.
San Mateo Stock Farm names blk f Mabel Wilkes, Guy Wilkes—Sable by The Moor.
San Mateo Stock Farm names b f Lucina Wilkes, Guy Wilkes—Hattie by Electioneer.
San Mateo Stock Farm names dk b c Legal Wilkes, Guy Wilkes—Margaret by Sultan.
San Mateo Stock Farm names br f Thora, Sable Wilkes—Theo by Le Grande.
San Mateo Stock Farm names blk c Macleay, Sable Wilkes—Mamie Comet by Nutwood.
San Mateo Stock Farm names b f Princessa, Sable Wilkes—Minnie Princess by Nutwood.
San Mateo Stock Farm names b c Veto, Sable Wilkes—Vixen by Nutwood.
J. A. Goldsmith names blk c Milroy, Guy Wilkes—Marion by Nutwood.
Irvin Ayres names b c Baikal, Mambrino Wilkes—Fanny Fern by Jack Hawkins.
Irvin Ayres names b c Gondar, Mambrino Wilkes—Piracy by Buccaneer, Louise by G. N. Patchen Jr.
Irvin Ayres names blk f Nevassa, Mambrino Wilkes—Fedolia by Fred Arnold.
Irvin Ayres names b c Saragon, Mambrino Wilkes—Contra by Electioneer.
W. H. Lumsden names dk br c Isaac D., Anteeo—Gypsey by Echo.
A. T. Hatch names s f ——— by Sidney—by Irvington.
A. T. Hatch names blk f ———, Guid —Mollie by Admar by Admiral.
E. McLees names b f Lady Thorn, Thornhill—Lady Nutwood by Nutwood.
L. J. Shippee names b c Storm King, Hawthorne—Old Tempest by Morgan Rattler.
L. U. Shippee names b c Native Son, California Lambert, dam by Hawthorne.
L. U. Shippee names b c New Edition, Red Thorne—Maud by California Lambert.
Geo. E. Guerne names dk b c Lee Anteeo, Anteeo—Minnie by Gen. Lee.
Geo. E. Guerne names b c Nut Anteeo, Anteeo—Daisy by Nutwood.
Valensin Stock Farm names b c Mountaineer, Sidney—Highland Lass by Buccaneer.
Valensin Stock Farm names br c Sid Fleet, Sidney—Flight by Buccaneer.
Valensin Stock Farm names ch f Smilax, Sidney—Ivy by Buccaneer.
Rufus Murphy names b f Addie M, Anteeo—Maud by Nutwood.
Chino Ranch names b f Nettie Woolsey, Woolsey—Nettie Norfolk by Billy Norfolk.
Chino Ranch names b f Oka Crocker, Will Crocker—Lady Garner by Overland.
Chino Ranch names blk f Alba, Albion—Helen by Billy Norfolk.
J. A. Aguirre names b c Rango, Raymond—Mollie by Sacramento

LIST OF ENTRIES THAT MADE SECOND PAYMENT IN OCCIDENT STAKE 1891.

J. A. Goldsmith, ch f Eclipse by Guy Wilkes—Marion by Nutwood.
Palo Alto Stock Farm, gr c Commerce, Electioneer—Sallie Benton by Gen. Benton.
Palo Alto Stock Farm b f Rusencle by Electioneer—Rebecca by Gen. Benton.
Palo Alto Stock Farm, b f Mayfair by Electricity—Mayflower by St. Clair.
Palo Alto Stock Farm, br c Almoner by Alban—America by Rysdyk's Hambletonian.
Palo Alto Stock Farm, b f Norgirl by Norval—American Girl by Toronto Sontag.
Palo Alto Stock Farm, br f Norhawk by Norval—Sontag Mohawk by Mohawk Chief.
Palo Alto Stock Farm, b f Ellener by Electioneer—Lady Ellen by Carr's Mambrino.
Palo Alto Stock Farm, br c Advertiser by Electioneer—Lulu Wilkes by Geo. Wilkes.
Palo Alto Stock Farm, b f Mont Rose by Electioneer—Rosemont by Piedmont.
Otto Hansen, ch f Promptbird by Prompter—Lucy H. by Blackbird.
I. De Turk, br f Myrtle by Anteeo—Luella by Nutwood.
I. De Turk, b c Ransom by Anteeo—Marion by Nutwood.
I. De Turk, b c Hodiac by Mambrino Wilkes—Fanny Fern by Bonner.
Irvin Ayres, blk c Chaldean by Mambrino Wilkes—Fredalia by Fred Arnold.
Irvin Ayres, b f Mylitta by Mambrino Wilkes—Molly Fern by Capt. Cole.
Irvin Ayres b f Istar by Mambrino Wilkes—Narka by Nephew.
Lot D. Slocum, dk ch f Pirah by Dexter Prince—Princess by Nutwood.
B. E. Harris, ch c Brentwood by Dawn—Sweetwood by Nutwood.
B. E. Harris, ch f Starlight by Dawn—Lena Bowles by Ethan Allen.
J. U. Hastings, b c Sidney Foster by Sidney—Belle Foster.
G. W. Hancock, b c Easter Wilkes by Guy Wilkes—Zepher by Nutwood.
Nathan Coombs, b c The Dane by Stamboul—Dolly McMann.
Wilfred Page, blk c Gran Moro by Le Grande—Sunny Slope Belle by The Moor.
La Siesta Ranch, br f Clovewood by Clovis—Olita by Nutwood.
Hallinan & McDowell, b c Contraband by Clovis—Crazy by Steinway.
Pleasanton Stock Farm Co., b c Pleasanton by Director—May Day.
M. C. Hogan, b c Jigg by Fallis—Belle by Roe Allen.
San Mateo Stock Farm, blk c Cognac by Guy Wilkes—Lottie by Alexander's Belmont.
San Mateo Stock Farm, b c Nabob by Guy Wilkes—Hattie by Electioneer.
San Mateo Stock Farm, ch f Vida Wilkes by Guy Wilkes—Vixen by Nutwood.
San Mateo Stock Farm, b f Tasso Wilkes—Tabbie Rosebaum by Nutwood.
L. U. Shippee, br f Rosethorne by Hawthorne, dam by Priam.
C. A. Durfee, b f Sue King by Ramon—Leonor by Dashwood.
J. W. Gardner b f Lady Gossip by Gossiper—Lady T. by Billy Norfolk
Martin G. Aguirre, b f Ala by Stamboul—Molly by Sacramento.

LIST OF ENTRIES THAT MADE PAYMENT IN OCCIDENT STAKE, 1890.

Palo Alto Stock Farm, b f Wild May, by Electioneer—May by Wildidle.
Palo Alto Stock Farm, b f Corval by Electioneer—Columbine by A. W. Richmond.
Palo Alto Stock Farm, br f Clarion by Ansel—Consolation by Dictator.
Palo Alto Stock Farm, ch c Norris by Ansel—Norma by Alexander's Norman.
Palo Alto Stock Farm, b f Wildmont by Piedmont—Wildflower by Electioneer.
Jos. Cairn Simpson, b f A· by Antevolo—Lady Del Sur by Del Sur.
B. E. Harris, br or blk f Lorena by Jim Mulvenna—Elmorene by Elmo.
Lot D. Slocum, b f Moss Rose by Anteeo—Luella by Nutwood.
H. H. Helman, g c Richmond Chief by Monroe Chief—Ella by A. W. Richmond.
G. Valensin, blk f Fleet by Sidney—Flight by Buccaneer.
F. Fitzgerald, b c Kill Ross by Killarney—by Cal. Dexter.

RUNNING EVENTS, STATE AGRICULTURAL SOCIETY.

Declarations made January 1, 1890, in fixed events (Running) at State Fair, 1890.

CALIFORNIA BREEDERS' STAKE.

El Rio Rey, Rascal, Barret, Chan Haskell, Novette, Evelina, Jessie C., Kid Kid, Elsie S., Falsalara, Whisban, Bonnie Brook, Stella S. and Riverside.

CAL. AUTUMN STAKE.

Rey del Rey, San Juan, Average Oscar, Sinfax, Peri and Loma.

CAL. ANNUAL STAKE.

Judge Post, Black Bart, Uno Grandi, Sinfax, Oscar and Memnon.

SUNNY SLOPE STAKE.

Bell Songer, Hettie Humphreys, Queen High and Dancing Eyes.

Third payments in President Stake, 1890, were made January 1st, on the following entries:

Glenloch, Floren, Herzog, Major Ban, Fellowcharm, Take Notice, Mabel F. and Sacramento.

Second payments in President Stake, 1891:

Joe Harding, Power, Rinfax, Mero, Conrad, Lodowic, The Drake, White Oak, May H. and False Queen.

Declarations in Spring events, 1890, were made as follows:

NORFOLK STAKES.

Onti Ora, Romeetta, Judge Terry, Rey del Rey, San Juan, Uno Grandi, Parapet, Power, Lakeview, Sinfax, Oscar, Austrian, Memnow.

MATACENO STAKES.

Onti Ora, Romeetta, Judge Terry, Parapet, Sinfax and Oscar.

WESTERN HOTEL STAKES.

Bell Songer, Nettie Humphreys, Otelia, Marinette, Dancing Eyes and Loma.

GOLDEN EAGLE HOTEL HANDICAP.

Average, Judge Post, Uno Grandi, Black Bart, Parapet, Lakeview, Sinfax, Oscar, Peri, Austrian and Memnow.

WEINSTOCK, LUBIN & CO.'S STAKE.

Abdiel, Rover and Whisban.

THE HALL, LUHRS & CO. HANDICAP.

Abdiel, Rover and Elsie S.

THE CALIFORNIA OAKS.

Novette, Florance A., Stella S., Elsie S., Whisban and Falsalara.

THE CAL. DERBY.

Abdiel, El Rio Rey, Novette, Rover, Mabel F., Whisban and Elsie S.

VETERINARY.

Conducted by W. Henry Jones, M. R. C. V. S.

Subscribers to this paper can have advice through this column in all cases of sick or injured horses or cattle by sending an explicit description of the case. Applicants will send their name and address that they may be identified. Questions requiring answers by mail should be accompanied by two dollars, and addressed to W. Henry Jones, M. R. C. V. S., Club Stables, Taylor Street, San Francisco.

Horse Shoeing.

EDITOR BREEDER AND SPORTSMAN:—This is a subject which has been so well ventilated that I am afraid it will be somewhat stale to the readers of your valuable paper.

I have often wondered why owners of valuable horses do not pay more personal attention to the manner in which their animals are shod. It is a well known fact that the majority of owners of horses do not know anything about the way their horses are ill-treated and abused by the persons entrusted to shoe them.

If they only took the trouble and time to look into the matter they would be better off as far as horse-flesh is concerned and also for the welfare of their horses.

The majority of horse-shoers look upon the horse's foot as a block of wood, entirely devoid of sensibility. They little think that it is supplied with a large amount of blood vessels and nerves. Did they but take the trouble to ascertain something about the anatomy and physiolology of the foot, they would benefit themselves and also their clients.

In the removal of shoes, which should be done once every month, the clinches should be cut clean and the shoes carefully removed, and not with force, as is usually done. In the case of a horse with thin and brittle wall the nails should be drawn separately, so as not to damage the external wall.

The foot should then be taken down to its natural size by the rasp. The soles and frog should be left intact, removing only the ragged portion of the frog, to prevent the accumulation of dirt. The sole should not be pared out, except in cases of injury or disease, as nature will remove the exfoliations as they become necessary.

In fitting the shoe, the shoe should be made to fit the foot, and not the foot the shoe, as is done in the majority of cases.

It is the common practice of smiths to shun the necessary labor required to get an equal bearing for the shoe, to apply the shoe almost if not quite in a red hot condition, and keep it there sufficiently long to remove any irregularity on the wall of the foot which may exist.

Little do they imagine the injury they are doing by such negligence, little do they think what the future result will be; if they did, the probability is they would desist from this injurious and pernicious practice.

The shoe, in being fitted, should be applied at a black heat, and kept on only sufficiently long to ascertain where the inequalities exist on the wall, and then remove with the rasp. It is a too frequent practice to use more nails than are necessary. Five to seven are in the majority of cases all that are necessary, provided they are properly placed. Toe clips are necessary, and should be made of a decent size, not too small, for in that case they are nearly useless. The clip, when properly drawn up, should supply the place of two nails.

After the shoes have been fitted and nailed on, on no account should the external wall be allowed to be touched, except for the purpose of putting down the clinches. The rasping of the external wall by the smith, who will remove more of the crust in one shoeing than nature can produce in six months, should be prevented. The result of this free use of the rasp is that in a few months the wall has become so thin that it becomes almost impossible to keep a shoe on. This then becomes a nuisance to the owner, and finally terminates in a lame horse.

A few suggestions may be of service to your readers. Never allow a red-hot shoe to be applied to the foot in fitting it.

Never permit the sole to be pared out.

Never allow the foot to be cut and carved out, as is so frequently done, in a most artistic manner.

Permit no more nails to be driven than are absolutely necessary, and above all, never let the smith apply the rasp to the external wall.

On a subsequent occasion we may make some other remarks on this important subject, as I consider it is one which is to the interest of all horse owners.

Apologizing for occupying so much of your valuable space I am yours respectfully,

W. HENRY JONES.
M. R. C. V. S.

Club Stables, Taylor Street, San Francisco.

ROD.

Fish Commission.

The monthly meeting of the Board of Fish Commissioners was held at 220 Sutter street, room 13, on Saturday last. President Joseph Routier and Secretary J. Downey Harvey were present. After approval of the minutes the report of the Chief of Patrol was read and accepted. It was as follows:—

To the Honorable the Board of Fish Commissioners.

GENTLEMEN:—The report of the Chief of Patrol for the month of December is submitted with the prefatory remark that the exceeding inclemency of the weather during all of the period covered by the report has almost prevented both illegal fishing and patrolling. Such cases as were in hand at the time of the last report have been closely followed up and no effort spared to secure convictions, and it is gratifying to record that public sentiment has so far changed under the active administration of your Honorable Board, that in some portions of the state the prosecutors of game and fish cases receive fair treatment from Courts and juries. The experience of your deputies is that more justice is to be had in non-metropolitan courts than in those of the large cities.

The vigorous action of the Board during September and October, with reference to deer skins from which evidence of sex had been removed has completely broken up the trade in skins of that description.

Neither the railway, steamship nor sailing lines will receive or transport such skins.

Deputy Thomas Tunstead, to whom has been assigned the duty of looking for such deer hides, has been unvarying in faithfulness and has closely watched both the city front and the commission houses, beside occasional visits to tanneries and other places where hides are handled.

I feel safe in reporting that not one deer skin from which evidence of sex has been removed, nor one doe skin or fawn skin has been received at San Francisco during the month last passed.

This result has been reached without antagonizing either tanners or commission merchants.

In every case where arrests and prosecutions have been ordered by the Board, the outcome has been assurances of abstinence in future from illegal trade and proffers of assistance in carrying out the purposes of the Board of Fish Commissioners.

In no case has malice, nor an undue desire for pecuniary reward been allowed to influence the action of your deputies in pushing prosecutions.

Strictly legitimate efforts only have been permitted and the fact that principle alone moved the Board has at all times been impressed.

On December 5th, with three deputies I went to Martinez to prosecute 3 Chinese arrested on Nov. 21st. for catching small-fish with bag-nets. After considerable trouble in securing a jury, because of technical objections interposed by the attorneys for the defense, the cause went to trial before Justice M. W. Ballhache and a very thorough investigation which occupied three days was had. On December 9th Judge Ballhache fined the men $100 each, on the first charge, using bag-nets.

On December 11th before Justice Joachimsen in San Francisco the case of John H. Wise accused of having in possession deer skins from which evidence of sex had been removed was tried and submitted. Mr. Wise strenuously disclaimed all intention to violate the game law, and knew nothing of the deer skins which were the immediate cause of prosecution. Judge Joachimsen in dismissing the case remarked that he felt disposed to be lenient for the reason that only recently had any systematic effort been made to break up what he believed was an illegal trade in deer skins, but he added that if Mr. Wise was again brought before him upon a similar charge and the evidence was such as to warrant conviction the penalty imposed would be a very heavy one.

The case of the People against Clayburgh & Waldeck, hide dealers, for having deer skins from which evidence of sex had been removed was tried before Judge Rix at San Francisco on December 12th.

The evidence was clear and conclusive, but the Judge dismissed the case with the remark that he thought "the men who killed the deer and removed the evidence of sex should be prosecuted rather than merchants who merely handled the hides in the way of trade."

It might be remarked in this connection that possession was made a misdemeanor for the very purpose of securing convictions; it being impossible to detect any hide-hunter in the actual killing and skinning of deer.

Fortunately, few judges coincide with Judge Rix in his interpretation of the section of the Penal Code in question.

The work of some of your deputies in outlying districts merits especial mention.

In Humboldt County Deputy A. T. Smith has been very active. His especial province is the prevention of the illegal killing of deer and during the month he has made thirteen arrests of which but three have been acquitted. Two of the acquittals were for killing a doe. The sex of the animal and the killing were acknowledged, but the evidence was that the animal was shot while running, at a range of three hundred and fifty yards and the jury evidently thought there was a lack of wilfullness.

The other acquittal was for reasons best known to the jury, and was not based on the evidence.

On December 11th, at Rohnerville, Humboldt County, Deputy Smith convicted E. S. Philips, a commission merchant, for having skins without evidence of sex, and Justice Cloud, of Fortuna, fined him $50.

On the 13th the same deputy convicted a man named Elliott on a similar charge, and Justice Cloud fined him $50 also.

Deputy Smith now has Davis & Davis of Fortuna under arrest upon a like charge, and anticipates a conviction.

Justice Cloud, in deciding one of the cases, said, "When dealers who unguardedly purchase deer skins which the law prohibits them from handling are made to know that they are paying the penalty for the vandal and illegal acts of those who kill the deer, an end will be put to the traffic and the unwarranted slaughter of deer will cease. The only recourse the dealer has is to enter complaint against the parties from whom he purchases."

In Mendocino County, Deputy C. C. Johnson is rapidly breaking up illegal fishing, and is also devoting especial attention to stopping the running of sawdust into the salmon and trout streams. Deputy Johnson has the warm support of the various influential newspapers of Mendocino County, and will, beyond doubt, soon be able to report a clean bill for his county.

At Arcata, Justice Truesdale fined Martin Olsen and M. Neilson $50 each on December 19th for catching salmon with a seine. The prosecution was made by Thomas H. Selvage.

On December 14th five Chinese were fined $150 each at Martinez for fishing with bag-nets and having small fish in possession.

December 18th four Chinese were tried at Martinez on a similar charge and fined $150 each, both trials being before Judge Ballhache, and being attended by myself and three Deputies.

On the 24th three Chinamen were fined $75 each by Judge Rix in San Francisco for using Chinese sturgeon lines.

If in proper form, I would like to suggest the making of a rule by the Board, requiring all Deputies to send to the Chief of Patrol monthly reports of the work done, giving full details, names, etc. The reports should be in hand on a date not later than the first day of the succeeding month, in order to permit their collation into proper form for presentation to the Board. Respectfully submitted,

F. P. CALLUNDAN,
Chief of Patrol.

SAN FRANCISCO, Jan. 4th, 1890.

A Deputy reported that at the instance of the Board two hundred dozens of Bob White quail had been ordered from Arkansas, to be delivered about March 1st, and to be distributed as ordered by the Board. The matter of introducing wild turkeys was mentioned but no action taken, although it was stated that acclimated birds could be purchased at Vallejo. It was stated that Mr. La Motte of Glen Ellen, Sonoma County, had asked permission to take fish from Sonoma River for hatching purposes and the request had been granted. Mr. Ramon E. Wilson inquired whether Mr. La Motte desired merely to stock a private preserve or public waters. The Board was in doubt whether the fish were to be placed in some part of Sonoma River or some other stream. It was known that Mr. La Motte was interested in a trout preserve near Ukiah, and the impression was that the fish were to be taken from Sonoma River to stock the Ukiah waters.

Mr. Wilson then said that there existed an infamous dam in Sonoma River, upon which there was no effective fish ladder, and the popular impression was that Mr. La Motte claimed ownership in the dam. If he proposed to stop breeding fish at his dam on their way up the river, take them from the river and to private waters, Mr. Wilson was opposed to granting him the permit to do so. He feared that interest in fish on the part of one who maintained a dam over which spawning fish could not pass was not sincere.

The Board then ordered Deputy Woodbury to visit Glen Ellen and report upon the condition of the La Motte dam or dams.

The Board then adjourned to meet the first week in February.

There is a fish pond at Dieano, Cal., which is supplied from an artesian well. The fish are spurted out every day, and belong to the same species as those at Owen's Lake, on the other side of the coast range.

The North Pacific Land and Improvement Company does not intend to let the storms of the past two months prevent them from stocking the streams near the Ukiah part of Mendocino County with trout. It was their intention to have had their fish hatchery on Robinson Creek erected and in running order by the first of January, but the stormy weather, which has now lasted for six weeks, has kept work there at a standstill, and the hatchery cannot be completed in time for this season's hatching. It is now the intention of the company to hatch their fish this season at Glen Ellen, and ship them to Ukiah for distribution in the streams. In the meantime work will be completed on their hatchery at Robinson Creek, so as to be in readiness for the next hatching season.

A notable addition to local angling society is Mr. George P. Goff, a lawyer, relative of Captain Harry N. Morse. Mr. Goff has done some very vivid writing about fishing for current journals, and contributed to Captain Thomas Chubb's catalogue for 1888. He is welcomed and commended to the friendliness of the guild.

THE KENNEL.

Dog owners are requested to send for publication the earliest possible notices of Whelps, sales, names claimed, presentations and deaths in their kennels, in all instances writing plainly names of sire and dam and of grandparents, colors, dates and breed.

The Southern California Bench Show.

Mr. C. M. Munhall sends from Cleveland, Ohio, the following letter received by him from J. H. Winslow, of Philadelphia, with reference to the effort recently made to have the wins at the first show of the Southern California Kennel Club recognized by the American Kennel Club. Mr. Winslow writes:

PHILADELPHIA, Dec. 24, 1889.

C. M. MUNHALL ESQ., CLEVELAND O.—DEAR SIR:—I suppose you will see in the paper a full account of the meeting of the American Kennel Club, and if not in the paper, will see it in the American Kennel Gazette. Major Taylor and I did all we could to make the delegates understand that the Southern California Club held a good show and their award should be recognized, but they voted us entirely down. Major Taylor made the motion to reconsider and I seconded it, although with the true facts before me, I could not conscientiously do it, as the club had clearly ignored the American Kennel Club, and still ignores it up to this time. The facts in the case are these: They made their application and Mr. Vredenburg wrote the Secretary a full letter telling him that he had thought no doubt they would be admitted, and that their remarks would be recognized by the American Kennel Club if they held a show under their rules. He particularly pointed out Rule 2 and several others. Instead of holding their show under the Kennel Club rules, they changed the rules to suit themselves: they did not require exhibitiors to register their dogs, and have not since sent a marked catalogue and several other things which the rules require them to do. However, as you desired me to do this, I took great pleasure in taking your views of the case and assisting you all I could. Major Taylor's note and mine were the only two votes cast in favor of recognizing their remarks.

Yours truly, J. H. WINSLOW.

Mr. Munhall adds:

You will see by the above that my efforts to have the awards of the Southern California Kennel Club recognized by the American Kennel Club were not successful. They should have carried out the rules to the letter. The club is to blame. I am sorry for the exhibitors. I did all I could. Yours,

C. M. MUNHALL.

[We have not felt at liberty to urge any particular course of action with reference to the Southern California Kennel Club Show wins for personal reasons, but now that the matter has been finally disposed of, may be permitted to ask whether there was any such departure from the spirit of the American Kennel Club rules as could vitiate the results of a show to which men went hundreds of miles to exhibit, solely in the hope of having the wins if they were successful, stand as records? We shall be very pleased to hear from the officers of the Southern California Kennel Club, in order that their precise position may be generally known and like errors, if any there were, avoided in future.—KEN. ED.]

Sales.

Mr. L. L. Campbell has sold to Mr. F. A. Dillingham, Honolulu, the Irish Red Setter L. B. Cooper, whelped August 28, 1889, by Barrymore—B ll C.

Deaths.

J. C. Nattrass' Irish Red Setter bitch Judith by Champion Brush—Lucille, December 24, 1889; cause, salmon eating.

CLEARBROOK, WASH., Dec. 30, 1889.

EDITOR BREEDER AND SPORTSMAN:—I have just sustained a loss in the death of my beautiful Irish Setter Bitch Judith, which I will never be able to replace. She was a perfect specimen and a grand breeder, a bitch of exquisite nose and great hunting experience, having bred her myself, hunted her in Illinois, Iowa, Kansas, Nebraska and Washington Territory. Three years' companionship made her an almost inseparable companion, but salmon feeding got away with her.

J. C. NATTRASS.

We are pleased to note that our versatile and energetic friend, Mr. Harry A. Weaver, of Stockton, on January 2nd, became a partner in the business of The Miner Publishing Company; principal office, Bodie, Mono County, California. branch house, Stockton, San Joaquin County, Cal. Mr Weaver will manage the Stockton end of the business and we wish him distinguished success.

The Westminster Kennel Club's premium list for its Fourteenth Annual Bench Show is at hand. One hundred and seventy-one classes are listed, the regular prizes in about half the classes being $20. $10 and $5, and in the rest $10, $5 and $3. The specials are many and very rich. Success to Superintendent Mortimer and the crack club of the world.

Sam Meriwether cannot act as Marshal at the coming field trial, but a vicarious sacrifice has been found in the person of that herculeam gentleman, Mr. P. D. Linville, who served with such spirit and ability in '88. Linville announces that he is going down, they "can't stop him'" and the affair is to a finish. He desires Joe Bassford, Nick White and the other frisky boys to understand that he is up to all manner of tricks and will arrest and tie to a fence post with barbed wire any spectator caught doing anything without inviting the participation of the Marshall. He will watch Fred Taft especially, whenever that amateur astronomer drives through a slough below the horizon and if Taft attempts to observe any through that peculiar black equatorial, the Marshall will make "the punishment fit the crime."

Walter L. Wilder in the New York Sun: In a recent number of the Sun I saw a statement that a grey-hound is probably the swiftest quadruped. But there is an animal on the Colorado plains which is much swifter. It is the small red prairie fox, commonly known as "the swift." A good greyhound will pull down two or three from a bunch of antelopes but "the swift" escapes readily from him. In the chase the fox will stop still and wait until the hound is near him and then easily distance, and repeat the same maneuver. It does not jump like a hound, but runs with a peculiar gliding motion. I to legs are of medium length and muscular.

Quite a number of the young men of Lower Lake, Lake County on Monday last shouldered arms, collected the town dogs and sallied forth in regular Quixotic style in quest of adventures. They formed in line of battle on the Konocti Vineyard about one dozen boys and four dogs on one side pitted against about half that number of rabbits on the other. After many skirmishes and such maneuvering on the part of the rabbits they were finally routed and four of them brought home in triumph as prisoners of war. A reinforcement of rabbits appearing in the Wrey Vineyard the battle was renewed the next day resulting in the loss of two of their number and a complete rout of the remainder. A truce has been declared pending negotiations of peace.

Local fanciers of pointing dogs and field trials, who desire certificates entitling them to a reduced fare for the trip to Bakersfield, can obtain them at 630 Market Street from Mr. E. W. Briggs, who has kindly consented to keep some for distribution. "Ned's" place of business is quite the center of the shooting and kennel world, in the evening hours particularly, and many a rich story of flood and field is recited there.

If all of the men who profess an intention to visit Bakersfield during field trial week do so, the hospitable town will be taxed to entertain them. Interest in the trials has grown year by year, and taken firm hold of a good many, but this year numbers of sportsmen who have not before manifested the slightest concern about the trials, are asking for information about them, and declaring they will attend.

Thomas Bennett, albeit a man of affairs, and at the head of a business which ramifies throughout the continent, can yet find time now and then to shoot over his fine English setter Sirius, and both Mr Bennet and that irrepressible cashier of his, Mr. Jack Kilgarif, will pervade Bakersfield week after next.

A number of people rescued a fine deer hound on Sunday last from death by either drowning or starvation at Santa Cruz. The dog was discovered in a cove along the cliffs near the light-house point. It is said that the dog was thrown over there by some one. After discovering hound several people coaxed it to swim out from its dangerous position Once swimming it kept out in the bay some distance, but finally turned back and came ashore in another larger cove by the residence of James Phelan and where some steps lead down from the cliffs above. A young man went down and brought the dog up.

This office will pay Twenty-five Cents for copies of the Breeder and Sportsman of the following dates: January 26, 1889; April 6, 1889; July 27, 1889; and for two copies of August 10, 1889; and will deem it a favor if readers who do not care to preserve files will forward the numbers mentioned.

THE GUN.

Recently Philip Hegerman living on the Cuffey's Cove and Anderson Valley County Road, Mendocino, while out hunting encountered a large panther, measuring eight feet, which he quickly disposed of. It had been a terror to surrounding stockmen for a long time, even extending its stealthy and rapacious trips to neighbor's house yards.

Two Sonoma duck hunters nearly lost their lives while hunting in the marshes, south of that place, last week. They were caught by the tide and had to swim several deep sloughs to reach terra firma. In this connection the Sonoma Index-Tribune recalls that a few years ago a young man living near Glen Ellen visited the Sonoma marshes near Embarcadero for a day's shooting. He was alone, but was seen to enter the marsh near Green's Landing. He never returned, and from that day to this his fate has been an impenetrable mystery. It is supposed, however, that the unfortunate young man became mired down in one of the many treacherous blind sloughs that wend their sinuous way through the labyrinth of the land bordering the shores of San Pablo bay, and being unable to extricate himself was slowly strangled to death by the incoming tide and eventually sank out of sight in the soft mud

Blue Bills in numbers have been driven to the marshes about Mount Eden and Alvarado by recent storms. Mr. Chris. Gading of Mount Eden, one of the cracks of that town of shooters, has been making big bags.

Miss Lillian F. Smith, "The California Girl" gave an exhibition at Woodland on New Years Day, breaking 50 glass balls in 51 seconds, using two repeating rifles.

Lake Margarita, the beautiful little sheet of water adjoining the town of Santa Margarita on the east, is becoming a popular resort for pleasure strolls, as well as a frequent haunt of the local sportsman. There should be a boat put on the lake, by all means, for general use and pleasure. The only means of securing the ducks killed any distance from shore, at present, is to let them float in or swim out after them.

English hares are becoming so numerous in sections of New Jersey that farmers there fear they will soon be as great a nuisance as the sparrow.

The Dixon Tribune is authority for this: A Solano man who spent the fall months in Del Norte County, is said to have killed 200 deer during his stay. Such indiscriminate slaughter will in a few years exterminate this noblest of game. There are many hunters in that section of the country who slaughter hundreds of deer in a year for their hides only, leaving the carcasses to rot.

[The above, from the Breeder and Sportsman of December 7th, will be read with great interest and curiosity by the readers of the Record, who would like to know the man who killed that amount of deer during his visit to Del Norte County. He probably killed three or four deer during his stay, and has drawn on his imagination for the rest.—Del Norte Record.]

[We hope the Record is right in believing the stories about the killing of great numbers of deer false, but in face of the fact that deer-hides by thousands come from Northern California, we submit that an ordinary observer is justified in believing that many more deer are killed than are taken to market or consumed by the hunters.—Field Ed.]

In another column can be found the advertisement of Messrs. Clabrough, Golcher & Co., 630-632 Montgomery St., city, offering "Blue Rock" targets. The firm holds the sole agency for the "Blue Rocks" of which more are used than of all others together. No more profitable hour can be passed than one spent in the store rooms of Clabrough, Golcher & Co.

Mr. W. S. Ferguson, proprietor of the American Hotel, at Arbuckle, Colusa Co., called at this office on Wednesday last, with the cheering news that on February 20th, an open shooting tournament will be given at Arbuckle. The first day the shooting will be open only to Sutter and Colusa counties, at 12 birds, Hurlingham style, entrance $10, three monies. The next day the matches will be open to the State; purse $35, entrance $15, three monies. Colusa County is famous for hospitality and those who take part in the tournament at Arbuckle will have reason to remember their visit with pleasure.

The California Academy of Science, of which our friend, Mr. Walter E. Bryant, is the Curator, elected its officers for '90 on January 6th, the following gentlemen being chosen, all of them being in office for the year last passed: President, H. W. Harkness; 1st Vice-President, H. H. Behr; 2nd Vice-President, George Hewston; Corresponding Secretary, Frederick Gutzkow; Recording Secretary, J. R. Scupham; Treasurer, I. E. Thayer; Librarian, Carlos Trover; Director of Museum, J. G. Cooper; Trustees, Charles F. Crocker, D. E. Hayes, S. W. Holladay, George C. Perkins, E. J. Molera, Irving M. Scott, John Taylor.

That most debonnaire of traveling gun salesmen Mr. Harvey McMurchy, writes us that he will not change his business relations as to the "L. C. Smith" gun, but will continue to represent the gun on the road. The news is good news, and we congratulate the firm which is to manufacture the gun, upon the retention of so universally liked and useful a representative as friend McMurchy.

The latter adds to his note:

"Mr. Smith sold his business to the Hunter-Comstock Arms Co. of Fulton, N. Y., retaining an interest. They have erected a new and much larger plant in Fulton, and retained all the skilled workmen, who have recently been employed by L. C. Smith, and with the improved machinery and increased facilities, we shall in the future be able to fill orders promptly, which you are well aware we were not able to do in the past year. The finish of the gun will be greatly improved.

"I have been called upon to be one of the Eastern team on the shooting trip given by Mr. C. W. Dimmick of the U. S. Cartridge Co., which will take possibly until the latter part of March, and I may be a few weeks late in calling on you, but will have the pleasure of doing so in time for spring trade.

"The name of the new firm for the manufacture of the famous L. C. Smith gun will be 'The Hunter Arms Co.'; Mr. Harry Comstock's interest having been purchased, he is in no way connected with the new firm. The L. C. Smith gun only will be made by them. We have now over two thousand guns in stock and are ready to receive orders at once."

A Detroit dog fancier who was acquainted with a farmer in Taylor township coaxed him to take home a young dog and encourage him to hunt. In about a week the farmer came in with the dead body of the dog in his wagon and calmly observed:

"Here is your dog."

"But he is dead!" exclaimed the owner.

"Yes."

"Who or what killed him?"

"He was out in the field and a rabbit took after him and run him to death. I was afraid of it when you sent it out. If you want me to take another, you'd better select an old dog—one with lots of teeth and used to dodging."

"But, great Scott, man! what sort of rabbits do you have out there?"

"Not as large as they ought to be, as the locomotives keep 'em pretty badly scared. Run about the size of yearling hogs, I guess, and us farmers have to carry our revolvers into the field with us. Expect, any day, when my children will be carried off and eaten alive."—Detroit Free Press.

Some birds are used medicinally, and it is well known what strange ideas native East Indian doctors have of the virtues of bird flesh. Both the flesh and the brains of the common sparrow, especially the cock-sparrow, are in great repute for certain diseases; so a cageful of these familiar clatterers is never missing in the market. Certain species are used in making love potions, and are administered by rejected suitors to the objects of their adoration. On the other hand, the blood or the flesh of the owl is supposed to make a person insane who drinks or eats it. On this account, men who are devoured by jealousy of a rival or hatred of an enemy come furtively to the market, and, purchasing an owl, in silence carry it home secretly and prepare a decoction which an accomplice will put into the food or drink of the object of their malignant designs.

The list of uses for bird flesh is not exhausted yet Eating a crow is supposed to prolong life by keeping the hair black and preventing it from turning gray. The common roller, often called a bluejay, has certain rites performed over it, and is then set free after one feather has been plucked from it. This feather is then worn as an amulet, and is supposed to have great potency in averting the evil eye. Another purpose for which birds are purchased every morning is to be set free again. This is done by Hindoos as a work of merit, and by Mohammedans, after certain rites have been performed, as an atonement in imitation of the Jewish scapegoat. It is essential that a bird used for this purpose should be strong enough to fly away, but that does not induce the cruel dealers to feed their birds or to refrain from dislocating their wings or breaking their legs. They put down everything to good or bad luck, and leave the customers to choose a strong bird if he can find one, and to go away if he cannot.

The merit obtained by setting a bird free is not attributed to the Deity, but is supposed to come in a large measure from the bird itself or from its attendant spirit, and hence birds of good or bad omen, and especially kites and crows, are in much demand, and are regularly caught to be sold for that purpose.

BASE BALL.

A big fine looking specimen of manhood jumped up on a downtown bootblack stand last Sunday night and in a tone that nearly tore the shivering "shiner" apart, ordered the dirt removed from his clothes and shoes. "My name is M. U. D., and that's enough to carry without taking away any of your California soil", remarked the individual. The party proved to be the renowned "Mike" Kelly, who made a monkey of himself and played some pretty good baseball for the Boston League Club last year. 'Kel' came out here years ago with the New York Giants and made a small pot of money, and an unenviable name for himself. He was so much thought of before leaving town on his last visit that a large delegation were at the ferry landing to throw shoes—filled ones— at him; before he departed. Besides Kelly, the rest of the Boston Club which has wintered here in reality have left for their eastern homes. Most of them arrived in town with good fat purses but as they only played enough games here to settle their board bills and as their original stakes went against draw, they will have to get down to opening oysters or following some other healthy vocation on their return home.

Some one must have been practicing handwriting last week and accidentally touched on Brotherhood affairs for a practice specimen. In doing so, he unconsciously touched upon California baseball affairs. After completing the penmanship exercise the writer threw the paper away and some person evidently picked it up and shipped it to an Eastern paper, whose editor must have had an off day, for he published it. The spasm went on to say that there was to be a pocket edition of the Players' League organized here. May-be there is. The Bangups of Cow Hollow ain't goin' to stan' enny more guff from dere man'ger. He only got dem tree games las' Sunday, an' dey ain't goin' to have dat enny more. See?" While in the Beauty Brights of North Beach there is even more discontent. This oppression the clubs of California will not stand. There is too strong a spirit for right in this glorious State, and these great players would stand up in their might—and spiked shoes—and fight against the rule of tyranny. Probably this is where the idea of where a "pocket edition" of the Brotherhood came from. There is certainly no more chance for an independent players' league in California than there is for finding gold watches in bakers' pies, or any other kind of pies for that matter. The California League people have got a neck hold on the baseball interests here that would take more than the combined efforts of the handful of players here to shake off. And even though there was a possible chance for the players to combine in some way, they are one and all in such fear of losing their sit's that they dare not open their mouths for fear of being replaced by imported or amateur talent.

Someone has suggested that Johnny Mone begin right away and sign the staff of umpires for next season. What is the matter with giving himself the preference? Johnny would make a good umpire. He knows all about the game up to the present time, and what he does not know he can probably pick up in the flag-leaf of Bellamy's Looking Backwards."

A good story is told on Mone's knowledge of the national game. It was several seasons ago, and the battle for first place in the league race was close between the Pioneers and Haverlys, as they were then called. The season was fast drawing to a close, and great interest was manifested in the games between the two leading clubs. One Sunday the clubs met in the presence of a large throng. The Pioneers had the game well in hand, and Mone was kept busy recording the runs as they came in from the shrill sounding gong. At last the Haverleys came in for their half of the seventh inning. It was their lucky inning, and everyone knew it. Several lucky hits filled the bases, and with one hand out, Levy came to the bat. He caught the first ball, pitched on the handle of his bat, and the sphere sailed backwards over his head and landed in the press-box. "Whew, that was a good hit," yelled Mone. "That was a daisy, and it will win the game for the Haverlys, sure." When he saw that Levy didn't run, and stood at the plate waiting for the ball to be returned, Johnny relapsed into silence. After the game he made the inquiry, and was told that a man doesn't run on a foul. "Oh, yes; why of course. Ha! ha! Well, will you—will you have a smile?" And they smile.

Sacramento has got Zeagler in the East digging up players for the coming season. He is making great headway, and if his selections are of any account, the capital city team will be a good, healthy one.

Here is a pointer for some of the managers. This man Wilmot, of last year's Washington team, is looking for an engagement. He is a good fielder, a hard hitter, and would be willing to play out here.

Sheridan will undoubtedly be calling off balls and strikes in the California league the coming season. He has had the offer of an Eastern engagement, and held that out for a raise. Mone will come to his terms and Sheridan will stay.

The last game of the winter between the Bostons and St. Louis Browns, was played off last Sunday, and won by the Missourians. The Beaneaters were crippled by the absence of three of their valuable players, whose places were filled by local talent. The score of the game is as follows;

St. Louis	AB.	R.	BH.	SH.	PO.	A.	E.
Latham, 3 b	5	1	1	1	1	6	0
Ryan, r f	1	1	0	0	2	0	0
Crooks, 2 b	5	2	1	0	1	1	0
O'Neill, l f	3	2	1	0	2	0	0
Comiskey, 1 b	4	0	1	0	10	0	0
O'Brien, c f	4	0	2	1	4	0	0
Tebeau, s s	4	2	1	0	3	2	1
Boyle, c	4	1	2	0	4	0	0
Baldwin, p	4	0	2	0	0	3	0
Totals	34	9	11	2	27	12	1

Bostons.	AB.	R.	BH.	SH.	PO.	A.	E.
Brown, l f	1	1	0	0	1	0	1
Kelly, r f	1	0	0	0	1	0	0
Clarkson, p & c f	4	1	0	0	0	2	1
Smalley, 3 b	3	1	1	0	3	4	2
Richardson, 2 b	4	1	1	1	2	4	1
Hurley, c	5	0	1	0	2	4	0
Smith, s s	5	1	1	0	2	3	0
Morrill, 1 b	3	0	0	0	13	1	1
Radbourne, c f & p	4	1	1	1	0	0	0
Totals	20	6	5	2	24	16	6

SCORE BY INNINGS.

St. Louis	2	5	0	0	1	0	1	0	*—9
Bostons	0	0	1	0	1	1	3	0	0—6

Summary: Earned runs—Bostons 4, St. Louis 2. Three-base hit—Smith. Two-base hits—O'Brien, Baldwin 2, Richardson, Tebeau, Boyle. Stolen bases—Clarkson, Kelly, Ryan, Latham, Crookes, Boyle, Smith, Brown 2. First base on errors—Bostons 0, St. Louis 3. First base on called balls—Bostons 9, St. Louis 5. Left on bases—Bostons 10, St. Louis 6. Struck out—By Baldwin 2, by Radbourne 1, by Clarkson 1. Hit by pitcher—Smalley, Kelly 2. Double plays—Latham, Tebeau and Comisky, Richardson, Smith and Morrill. Passed ball—Boyle 1. Wild pitch—Bald[illegible]. Balk—Radbourne 1.

Langtry Farms' Stud

Imp. FRIAR TUCK

By the Immortal HERMIT

DAM ROMPING GIRL BY WILD DAYRELL,

AT $50 THE SEASON.

Mares not proving with foal may be returned the following season. Good care taken of mares, but no liabilities for accidents or escapes.

Good Pasturage at $5 per month.

Mares shipped to ST. HELENA, care CHARLES WILLIAM ABY, St. Helena Stables, will be cared for. For further particulars address,

CHAS. WILLIAM ABY,
Middletown, Lake County, Cal.

2:08 3-4 2:10 2:12

MAMBRINO WILKES, 6083.

SIRE OF

GUS WILKES, 2:22; ALPHEUS, 2:27; CLARA P, 2:29½; BALKAN, 2:29½ (3-year-old) and timed separately 2:22½ in 4-year-old Stake, Bay District Track, October 14, 1889.

DESCRIPTION.

Black; sixteen hands; weighs, in exercise, 1,200 lbs. For style, finish, symmetry and proportion, comparison is challenged with any trotting bred horse. His colts follow in size, style and beauty. Balkan, for instance, being "facile princeps" of trotters in these particulars.

PEDIGREE.

Sired by Geo. Wilkes, sire of Harry Wilkes, 2:13½, Guy Wilkes, 2:15¼, and 80 other trotters in the 2:30 list, in addition to 6 pacers, and of the sire of Axtell, 2:12 (three-year-old), beating all stallions of any age, and the sire of Regal Wilkes, 2:20¾, best two-year-old stallion record.

First dam Lady Chrisman by Mambrino (Todhunter's), son of Mambrino Chief 11, sire of Lady Thorn, 2:18¼; Woodford Mambrino, 2:21½, and four others in 2:30, and of the dams of Director, 2:17, Piedmont, 2:17¼, Onward, 2:25¼, etc.

Second dam by Pilot Jr. 12, sire of nine in the 2:30 list, and of the dams of Maud S., 2:08¾, Jay-Eye-See, 2:10, Nutwood, 2:18¾, Viking, 2:19¼, Pilot Boy, 2:20, Naiad Queen, 2:20¾, etc.

TERMS.

Mares from a distance will be received at the Dexter Stables, Oakland, or Livery Stable, Martinez, the owner notifying Smith Hill, Superintendent at the farm. Good pasture and plenty of water. For the purpose of placing the service of a Wilkes within reach of breeders, the same rate will be maintained as last year, to wit, $75 for the season. Although it is not admitted thereby that this horse is inferior as a producer to the horses whose fees are placed at from $150 to $500. Address

SMITH HILL,
San Miguel Stock Farm,
Walnut Creek, Contra Costa Co., Cal.

2:12¾ 2:13½ 2:15¼

Thoroughbred Stallion

Prince of Norfolk.

Will Make the Season of 1890, from Feb 1st to July 1st, at Sacramento.

Prince of Norfolk, chestnut horse, foaled 1881, by Norfolk; first dam Marion by Malcolm; second dam Maggie Mitchell by imp. Yorkshire; third dam Charmer by imp. Glencoe; fourth dam Betsy Malone by Stockholder; fifth dam by Potomac, sixth dam by imp. Diomed; seventh dam by Pegasus, etc. Norfolk, the unbeaten son of Lexington, is the sire of Winters, Twilight, Connor, Ballot Box, Trade Dollar, Flood, Duchess of Norfolk, Lou Spencer, the Great Emperor of Norfolk, the unbeaten El Rio Rey, and many others. Marion's sire, Malcolm, was one of the first horses to bring Bonnie Scotland into notice. Through the Maggie Mitchell cross comes the blood of two of the most celebrated racemares of their day, Charmer and Betsy Malone. The combined speed of these great families seem to be concentrated in the get of Norfolk and Marion, as is instanced in the case of the Emperor of Norfolk, and El Rio Rey, who are full brothers to the Prince of Norfolk.

The blood lines here displayed cannot be surpassed in the world, there not being a single cross that has not been celebrated for speed and endurance, and it is fair to assume that the get of this stallion will show equally well with those of past generations.

TERMS: $50 for the season. We offer first-class pasturage on our own ranch, at $3 per month, and the best of care will be taken of mares sent to us, but no responsibility can be incurred. *For further particulars,* address by mail or wire,

DAN DENNISON.
or, W. P. TODHUNTER, Sacramento.

ROME HARRIS. JOHN MERIGAN.

"Laurel Palace,"

N. W. corner Kearny and Bush Streets
SAN FRANCISCO.

2:19 **NOONDAY** 2:20½

STANDARD No. 10,000.

This celebrated trotting bred stallion will make the season of 1890 at the stable of the undersigned at Sacramento, Cal., at $75 for the season and $100 to insure a mare in foal. Payable on or before July 1st, 1890. Money will be refunded on mares bred by insurance as soon as the fact becomes known that they are not in foal.

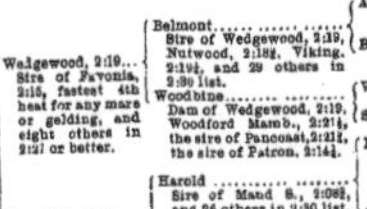

NOONDAY.
- Wedgewood, 2:19... Sire of Favonia, 2:15, fastest 4th heat for any mare or gelding, and eight others in 2:21 or better.
  - Belmont... Sire of Wedgewood, 2:19, Nutwood, 2:18¾, Viking, 2:19½, and 29 others in 2:30 list.
    - Alexander's Abdallah, sire of Goldsmith Maid, 2:14; Almont, with 36 horses in 2:30 list, etc.
    - Belle, dam of Hambletonian, 2:26½; B'cara, dam of Pancoast, 2:21¾, the sire of Patron, 2:14¼.
  - Woodbine... Dam of Wedgewood, 2:19, Woodford Mamb., 2:21½, the sire of Pancoast, 2:21¾, the sire of Patron, 2:14¼.
    - Woodford.
    - Singleton Mare.
- Noontide, 2:20½... (Trial, 2:13¼).
  - Harold... Sire of Maud S., 2:08¾, and 26 others in 2:30 list.
    - Hambletonian (Rysdyk's), sire of George Wilkes, 2:22, the sire of Guy Wilkes, 2:15¼; Electioneer, the sire of Sunol, 2:10½, and scores of noted trotters and producers.
    - Enchantress, by Abdallah 1.
  - Midnight... Dam of Jay-Eye-See, 2:10, Noontide, 2:20½.
    - Pilot Jr., sire of dams of Maud S., 2:08¾, Jay-Eye-See, 2:10, Nutwood, 2:18¾, etc.
    - Twilight, by Lexington, sire of the dam of Ansel, 2:20.

NOODAY is a dark seal brown, foaled 1884, 15 hands 1½ inches high. Individually he is equal to his royal breeding. He is all that can be desired in conformation, intelligence, color and trotting action, and no stallion now in public service can show a pedigree with such fast records and royal game trotting blood as Noonday.

DON MARVIN,

Record 2:28 as a five-year-old. Standard by Breeding and Performance

Standard No. 7927.

Don Marvin 2:28.

Don Marvin is a beautiful seal brown, foaled 1881, bred by Hon. Leland Stanford, Palo Alto, Cal., standing 15 hands, and weighs, in ordinary condition, 1200 lbs. He is a fine individual, good style and form, combined with great substance, and good temper. Is very level headed; in his first race the past season he only made one break in five closely contested heats. He has great speed and endurance, with the pure, rapid Electioneer gait. He trots without toe weights, and wears only 8 oz. shoes in front. He gained his record the past season in the third heat, on a slow track, after making a season (serving over 60 mares), with scarcely any preparation. His record is no mark of his speed. He was a natural born trotter, and Mr. Charles Marvin considered him the fastest two year old at Palo Alto that season.

By FALLIS, 2:23, - - by Electioneer, sire of
Sire of Don Marvin, 2:28. — Sunol, three-year-old, 2:10-1-2, Palo Alto, 2:12¾, and 47 others in 2:30 list.

Dam CORA, by Don Victor by Belmont, sire of
Dam of Don Marvin, 2:28. — Ventura, 2:27¾, and sire of the dam of Bell Echo, 2:20, and six others in 2:30 list.

2d dam CLARABEL, - by Abdallah Star,
Dam of Clifton Bell, 2:24 1-2, and grandam of Rexford, three years, 2:24. — Sire of Hattie Maples, 2:33.

3d dam FAIRY, - - by Rysdyk's Hambletonian,
Sister of Sweepstakes, sire of 16 in 2:30 list. — Sire of Electioneer, George Wilkes, and many other noted sires and trotters.

4th dam EMMA MILLS, by Seely's American Star,
Dam of 4 horses that have 2:30 performers. — The great broodmare sire of the world.

The above pedigree should show every intelligent breeder that Don Marvin is "high" bred though very strong in trotting blood. All the comment it is deemed necessary to make as to the value of "thoroughbred blood" in the trotter is simply to refer to the very significant fact that the first and second dams of Maud S., 2:08¾, Jay-Eye-See 2:10, Sunol, three years 2:10 1-2, Palo Alto 2:12¾, Anteeo 2:16¼, Nutwood 2:18¾, Wedgewood 2:19, and many other successful sires and sensational trotters of the day are thoroughbred.

TERMS—Don Marvin will make the ensuing season from February 1st to July 1st, 1890, at $40 the season, with the usual privilege of returning the mare next season if not proving in foal. Mares from a distance met at the cars or boats on notification, and carefully handled, but no responsibility assumed for accidents or escapes. Good alfalfa pasture furnished (free from barb wire fence) at $4 per month. For further particulars or complete circulars address

F. P. LOWELL,
1520 F Street, Sacramento, Cal.

The Thoroughbred Stallion

INTRUDER

Will make the Season of 1890 at Agricultural Park, SACRAMENTO.

Bay Horse, foaled 1871, bred by Sir L. Newman, England. Imported by D. D. Withers, Esq., New York.

By Crater, Son of Orlando and Vesuvienne by Gladiator.

1st dam Lady Bountiful by Rataplan (Rataplan is own brother to Stockwell, and winner of 42 races, including the Doncaster Cup and 19 Queen's Plates, and proved himself the most distinguished race horse of his day in England).

2d dam Plentiful by Don John (the winner of St. Leger and Doncaster Cup).

3d dam Plenty by Bay Middleton (winner of the Derby and Two Thousand Guineas Stakes).

4th dam Plenary, own sister of Plenipotentiary, by Emilius. (Both Emilius and Plenipotentiary were Derby winners).

5th dam Harriet, dam of the renowned Plenipotentiary by Pericles.

6th dam by Selim, winner of the One Thousand Guineas Stakes.

7th dam by Pypilina, by Sir Peter.

8th dam Rally, by Trumpeter.

9th dam Fancy, by Florizel. Fancy was full sister to Diomed, the first Derby winner in England, and after his importation into this country, sired the illustrious Sir Archy, etc. See English Stud Book.

Imported INTRUDER is a beautiful bay, standing fully 16 hands high, of great length and substance, and descends through close and strong currents from the most illustrious winners and winning lines of blood of which the English Stud Book bears record.

A careful review of the first six crosses of the pedigree of INTRUDER will show nine Derby winners; five St. Leger winners; two winners of The Oaks; two winners of the Two Thousand Guineas; two winners of the One Thousand Guineas; one Goodwood Cup winner; one Cesarwich Cup winner; one Cambridgeshire Stakes winner, and four Doncaster Cups, in addition to a great number of Steeplechases and other races of less import.

INTRUDER, at the great fair held at St. Louis, Mo., in 1876, was awarded the highest stallion honors—the blue ribbon and the $500 purse—in the sweepstakes ring for stallion of any age or blood. The list of competitors embraced the large number of thirty-three animals, and they represented England, Canada, Kentucky, Tennessee, and other states. He also took first premium in his class and in sweepstakes for the best stallion of any age or breed at the State Fair at Peoria, Ill., 1883. He is the sire of Tidal Wave, George Hakes, Bernice and April Fool.

INTRUDER is the sire of Interpose, who is the dam of Spokane, winner of the Kentucky Derby, in which he beat the great horse Proctor Knott and broke the record.

TERMS: $50 for the season. Mares not proving with foal can be returned the next season free of charge. Good pasturage at $4 per month. Mares cared for in any manner owners may desire, and fed on hay and grain, either or both, at reasonable rates. While every precaution will be taken, no responsibility will be assumed for escapes or accidents. Mares sent from a distance in care of the undersigned, will be met and taken to the park. For further particulars, address

T. J. KNIGHT.
Agricultural Park, Sacramento.

CANNON BALL, 8820

BY SIMMONS 2744.

RECORD 2:28, (Full Brother to Rosa Wilkes, 2:18 1-4), Sire of Nine in 2:30 List at 10 Years Old.

First dam Gurgle, pacing record 2:20; trial of 2:15½ for W. H. Crawford; by Pocahontas Boy, sire of Buffalo Girl, 2:12½; Raven Boy, 2:15½, and ten others in the list.

Second dam Matlock by Grey Diomed.

Third dam by Tom Hal.

DESCRIPTION.

Brown bay, right hind foot and left inside hind heel white. Foaled May 20, 1887. Bred by W. H. Wilson, Abdallah Park, Cynthiana, Ky.

He is a grand individual, large boned, fine size and appearance. When fully matured will probably be 16 hands, and weigh 1200 lbs.

Is of speedy conformation and level headed. His blood lines are stout and fashionable, being the Wilkes and Mambrino Patchen on pacing and thoroughbred foundations, and from a family of producers on both sides.

Can be seen until February 1st at Agricultural Park, Los Angeles, in charge of C. A. Durfee, after which he will serve ten approved mares at $40 the season, with usual privilege of return in 1891, at Lockhaven Stock Farm, Burbank, Cal. Mares kept on grass $1 per month, and extra charge where grain and alfalfa are fed. For further particulars, address

O. H. LOCKHART, Proprietor,
Lockhaven Stock Farm,
Burbank, Cal.

Nine Miles from Los Angeles.

NOTICE.

C. BRUCE LOWE,

Pedigree Stock Agent,

19 Bligh Street,
SYDNEY, New South Wales.

Reference—J. B. HAGGIN, ESQ.

2:08 3-4 2:10 2:12

BALKAN

By Mambrino Wilkes.

(See that Horse's Advertisement.)

DAM FANNY FERN BY JACK HAWKINS
Son of Boston.

The grandam of Maud S. (2:08¾) was by Boston and the grandam of Jay-Eye-See (2:10) was by Lexington, son of Boston. So Balkan is the same remove from Boston that Maud is, and one remove nearer than Jay-Eye-See.

Fanny Fern has produced Molly Drew, Onyx, Fred Arnold, Molly Fern and Balkan, all by different sires.

Balkan's sire and dam both being producers, and he being a trotter himself, it is but fair to presume that he will get trotters of the highest order.

DESCRIPTION.

He is seal brown, 16-1 hands high, in style rivalled by few, and excelled by none with as pure a gait as has yet been exhibited in public—bar none.

Balkan will be at Oakland Trotting Park for the season of 1890, and will be limited to ten mares, at $100 fee, in order to be put in training early, as it is morally certain that if given a reasonable opportunity he will be fast enough to compete with the best of his age. For further particulars, address

A. L. HINDS,
Dexter Stables, Oakland.

2:12¾ 2:13½ 2:15¼

GROVER CLAY.

Bay Stallion, Black Points,
15 3-4 hands high.

Bred by W. W. Traylor, San Francisco.

BY ELECTIONEER.

First dam Maggie Norfolk by Norfolk, son of Lexington, he by Boston. Second dam Tilda Quill by Billy Cheatham he by Cracken, and he by Boston. Third dam by Dorsey's Golddust.

TERMS.

Will make the season of 1890 at the Training Stables of Denis Gannon, near Oakland Trotting Park, at $50 the season, payable at time of service. Season to commence February 1st and ending July 1st. Proper care of mares will be taken, but no responsibility incurred for accidents or escapes. Address,

DENIS GANNON, Oakland, Cal.

The Fast Trotting Stallion

REDWOOD.

Four-Year-Old Record 2:24 1-2

Will make the season of 1890—February 1st to July 1st—at the

OAKLAND RACE TRACK.

REDWOOD is a dark bay colt, 15.2½ hands high, weighs 1[illegible] lbs. Foaled in 1886, by Anteeo, 2:16¼, sire of Alfred G., 2:19¾. Anteeo is by Electioneer. First dam Lou Milton by Milton Medium; second dam Old Nelly, a thoroughbred mare brought from the East in 1871 by W. C. Ralston, Esq.

Redwood's sire was out of Columbine by A. W. Richmond, the sire of the pacers Arrow 2:13¾, and Elwood 2:2[illegible], and the trotters Romero, 2:19¾, and Len Rose, 2:3[illegible]. Redwood has shown a quarter in 33 seconds.

Terms $100

For the season. Mares not proving with foal may be returned next season free of charge, provided Redwood remains the property of the present owners. Good pasturage at $5 per month. No responsibility assumed for escapes or accidents. Service fees payable before removal of the mare. Limited to 40 approved mares. For further particulars address

A. McFAYDEN.
Race track, Oakland, Cal.

The Trotting Stallion

G & M

FULL BROTHER TO

ALFRED G, 2:19¾,

(Who has been taken to Kentucky to stand at $250)

Will make the season of 1890 from FEBRUARY 1st to JULY 1st, at

SANTA ROSA.

G. & M. is by Anteeo, 2:16¼; was foaled 1886; first dam Rosa B. by Speculation (son of Hambletonian 10); 2d dam Elizabeth by Alexander 490; 3d dam Nora by imp. Glencoe. Anteeo is by Electioneer, out of Columbine by A. W. Richmond 1687.

G. & M. is a handsome dark bay; stands 15-2 1-2 hands high, and weighs 1061 pounds. Gameness, stoutness, speed and stamina are indelibly impressed in every line of the pedigree of G. & M. Owners of brood-mares in search of these qualities, will do well to patronize this promising colt.

PHILOSOPHER,

Foaled 1886 by Pilot Wilkes 2987; first dam Bella by George Wilkes 519; second dam by Bell Morgan 61.

Philosopher's sire, Pilot Wilkes 2987, is by George Wilkes 519, dam Grace (the dam of Alice Woodburn, etc.), by Pilot Jr. 12, grandam by Orphan Boy.

Will make the season of 1890, from FEBRUARY 1st to JULY 1st, at Santa Rosa.

TERMS for the season:

G. & M., $50.

PHILOSOPHER, $30,

with privilege of returning mares that do not prove in foal the next season free of charge, provided the horse bred to remains the property of the present owners. Good pasturage at $3 per month. No responsibility assumed for accidents or escapes. Service fees payable before removal of the mare. For further particulars, address

GEO. E. GUERNE,
Santa Rosa Cal.

"TOBEY'S,"

214 Post Street,

Between Grant Avenue and Stockton Street,

Adjoining New Hamman Baths.

D. J. TOBIN, Proprietor.

CHICAGO, ILLS. -:- BREEDERS' SALE.

SECOND GRAND COMBINATION SALE OF

KIDD, EDMONSON & MORSE,

Will be held in Chicago, Ill., MARCH 17th to 23d, 1890.

Trotters, Pacers, Stallions, Brood Mares, Colts, Saddle and Harness Horses.

Those wishing to dispose of their stock to the best advantage should send for conditions and entry blanks at once, as the sale promises to be very large.

Entries to close February 20, 1890. Send in your entries at once.

Our first sale was a grand success, and was only a foreshadowing of what is to follow. Address,

KIDD, EDMONSON & MORSE, Lexington, Ky.

Or No. 806 West Madison St., Chicago, Ill.

New York Sales of Trotting Stock

PETER C. KELLOGG & CO.'S

CALIFORNIA COMBINATION SALE OF

-TROTTING STOCK-

in New York will commence

Tuesday, March 11, '90

At the American Institute Building.

For Contracts, giving terms and full particulars, and for Entry Blanks (state number of horses to be consigned) address the firm as below.

Buyers who desire to increase their lines of choicely bred brood mares, or to secure stallions suited to the mares of California, can, by spending the month of March in New York, have opportunity to select from hundreds of offerings in our sales, the choicest blood and the best assortment in the country. It should be borne in mind that the climatic crosses which have been most prolific of great results in California (and also in Kentucky) have been secured in the colder climates of the North and East. If you are to use a home-bred stallion, obtain mares that are bred and reared under radically different climatic influences. If you use home-bred mares get your stallions from widely different climatic sources. While there are exceptions to all rules the more you study this subject the more irresistable will be the conviction that the greatest success has most often resulted from this plan. It is just as important in breeding to obtain a proper climatic out-cross as to obtain a good blood out-cross.

One or the other seems absolutely necessary. To combine both is doubly effective

WHETHER YOU ARE BUYER OR SELLER NEW YORK IS THE PLACE TO BE NEXT MARCH.

Our first sale will contain much Mambrino Patchen and Almont blood from the highly successful Village Farm Stud, owned by Mr. C. J. Hamlin, Buffalo, New York.

Our second sale will close out the celebrated Rosemeade Stud belonging to Mr. L. J. Rose of Los Angeles, Cal., with its brood mares and its youngsters by Stamboul and Alcazar.

Both these sales will occur the first week of March, to be followed throughout the month by others of great importance; representing California and the most important Eastern States; concluding the last week of March with an extensive consignment from Palo Alto.

Bids executed without charge, in the interest of absent buyers who remit in advance; but we greatly prefer their presence or that of their agent.

Address all correspondence to

PETER C. KELLOGG & CO.,
107 John Street, New York.

THE "BLUE ROCK" TARGET.

Quotations furnished F. O. B. at Cleveland, Ohio, or San Francisco.

CLABROUGH, GOLCHER & CO.,
630 and 632 Montgomery Street, S. F., Cal.
SOLE AGENTS for the Pacific Coast

THE BRUNSWICK BALKE COLLENDER COMPANY,

MANUFACTURERS OF

Standard Billiard and Pool Tables, Saloon and Bank Fixtures,
653--655 Market Street, San Francisco, Cal.

The Washington Park Club,

CHICAGO,

Will close the following Stakes January 15th, 1890, to be run at their Summer Meeting of 1890, beginning Saturday, June 21st and ending Saturday, July 19th, for which a programme will be arranged for

TWENTY-FIVE DAYS' RACING,

—WITH—

$110,000

In Added Money to Stakes and Purses.

THE WHEELER HANDICAP.

A SWEEPSTAKES for three-year-olds and upward, $100 each, $25 forfeit, or only $15 if declared; $1,500 added; the second to receive $750, and the third $250 out of the stakes. Weights to be announced Saturday, July 5th; declarations to be made on or before Wednesday, July 9th. Starters to be named through the entry box Friday, July 18th. A winner of any race after the announcement of weights, of the value of $1,500, to carry 5 lbs. extra. To be run Saturday, July 19th. One mile and a quarter.

THE GREAT WESTERN HANDICAP.

A SWEEPSTAKES for all ages, $50 each, h. f., or only $10 if declared out on or before May 1st, 1890; $1,500 added; the second to receive $400, and the third $100 out of the stakes. Weights to be announced April 1st, 1890. A winner of any race after the publication of weights, of the value of $1,000, to carry 5 lbs., of $1,500, 7 lbs. extra. One mile and a half.

THE OAKWOOD HANDICAP.

A SWEEPSTAKES for all ages $50 each, h. f., or only $10 if declared out on or before May 1st, 1890; $1,000 added; the second to receive $200, and the third $100 out of the stakes. Weights to be announced April 1st, 1890. A winner of any race after the publication of weights, of the value of $1,500, to carry 5 lbs. extra. One mile and a furlong.

THE BOULEVARD STAKES.

A SWEEPSTAKES for all ages, $15 each, $1 forfeit; $1,000 added; the second to receive $200, and the third $100 out of the stakes. A winner in 1890 of two races of any value to carry 5 lbs.; of three or more races of any value, 7 lbs. extra. Maidens allowed 10 lbs. One mile.

THE MAIDEN STAKES.

A SWEEPSTAKES for three-year-olds (foals of 1887), that have not won a race previous to January 1st, 1890; $50 entrance, $15 forfeit, with $1,000 added, of which $200 to the second horse and $100 to the third. Maidens at the time of starting allowed 5 lbs. One mile and a furlong.

THE DEARBORN HANDICAP.

A SWEEPSTAKES for three-year-olds (foals of 1887), $50 each, $15 forfeit, with $1000 added; the second to receive $200, and the third $100 out of the stakes. Weights to be announced by 12 M. two days before the day appointed for the race. Starters to be named through the entry box, at the usual time of closing, the day before the race. One mile and a furlong.

THE LAKE VIEW HANDICAP.

A SWEEPSTAKES for two-year-olds (foals of 1888), $50 each, $15 forfeit; with $1,000 added; the second to receive $200, and the third $100 out of the stakes. Weights to be announced by 12 M. two days before the day appointed for the race. Starters to be named through the entry box at the usual time of closing, the day before the race. Three-quarters of a mile.

THE QUICKSTEP STAKES.

A SWEEPSTAKES for two-year-olds (foals of 1888), $25 each, $10 forfeit; $1,000 added; the second to receive $200, and the third $100 out of the stakes. A winner of two races of any value to carry 5 lbs. extra. Maidens allowed 7 lbs. Half a mile.

All declarations in the above Stakes void unless accompanied with the money.

All Purses and Handicaps, $600 to $800.

Please observe that in the above stakes declarations are permitted for a small forfeit.

Turfmen failing to receive entry blanks can obtain them by applying to the Secretary.

Nominations and all communications to be addressed to the Secretary, Room 72, Palmer House, Chicago, Illinois.

J. E. BREWSTER, Secretary.

For Sale by Pleasanton Stock Farm Co.

ONE STALLION COLT, 1 year old, by DIRECTOR, 2:17, dam Sweetness, record 2:21¼. This Colt is a half brother to Sidney, the great Sire of Pacers.

ONE STALLION COLT, 1 year old, by DIRECTOR, 2:17, dam Echora, record 2:23½. This Colt is a full brother to Direct, record 2:23 at Three Years Old.

ONE FILLY, 1 year old, by CLOVIS, dam Nettie, trial record to Wagon 2:26.

ONE STALLION, 2 years old, by NUTMONT, he by Nutbourne, brother to Nutwood, dam by Electioneer. This Colt can trot very fast.

ONE STALLION, 2 years old, by SIDNEY, dam Fernleaf. This Colt is a full brother to Gold Leaf.

ONE FOUR-YEAR-OLD FILLY, GOLD LEAF, pacing record 2:15.

ONE THREE-YEAR OLD FILLY, by DIRECTOR, dam by a son of Whipple's Hambletonian. This is a grand mare in looks and breeding, and is very fast.

ONE Filly, 2 years old, by MONROE CHIEF, full sister to Miss Gilmer, sold at auction when three years old for $1,700.

ONE PACING HORSE, 4 years old, by STEINWAY, dam by Nutwood. This horse is very stylish, and can show a 2:10 gait.

One Brown Mare, heavy in foal to DIRECTOR, by Gibraltar, dam May Day, by Cassius M. Clay. This Mare is very fast; showed a quarter in 34 seconds, and is a half sister to Margaret S., that got a record of 2:31 at twenty-four months old.

One Brown Mare, by DEL SUR, he by The Moor, heavy in foal to Director. This Mare is very fast.

For particulars call on or address M. SALISBURY, 320 Sansome Street, Room 96, San Francisco, or

ANDY McDOWELL, Pleasanton, Cal.

Stallion for Sale

AT A BARGAIN.

Full Brother to Fairmont.

By Piedmont, dam Queen by Garibaldi—see State Fair Edition of BREEDER AND SPORTSMAN, September 14, 1889, for description of Fairmont—three years old, solid bay. Can trot a 2:40 gait or better. Sound in every particular. Can be seen at Oakland Trotting Park, Oakland.

P. J. WILLIAMS.

THE BUCKINGHAM.
OLD STRAIGHT WHISKIES.
141 Montgomery Street.
308 Bush Street, S. F.
M. J. BALFE, Proprietor.

Singleton & Addington,
Bank Exchange,
2d and K Streets, Sacramento.
Superior Wines, Liquors and Cigars.

Breeders' Directory.

Advertisements under this heading 50c. per line per month.

HORSES AND CATTLE.

EL ROBLAS RANCHO—Los Alamos, Cal., Francis T. Underhill, proprietor, importer and breeder of thoroughbred Hereford Cattle. Information by mail. C. F. Swan, manager.

PAGE BROTHERS.—Penn's Grove, Sonoma Co. Cal. Breeders of Short-Horn Cattle; Draft, Roadster and Standard Bred Horses.

JAMES MADDOCK, Petaluma, Cal.—Trotters trained at reasonable prices. Stock handled carefully. Correspondence solicited.

SETH COOK, breeder of Cleveland Bay Horses, Devon, Durham, Polled Aberdeen-Angus and Galloway Cattle. Young stock of above breeds on hand for sale. Warranted to be pure bred, recorded and average breeders. Address, Geo. A. Wiley, Cook Farm, Danville, Contra Costa Co., Cal.

MAMBRINO WILKES COLTS and FILLIES, full brothers and sisters to Gus. Wilkes 2:22, and Balkan 2:29¼, for Sale. Address SMITH HILL, Walnut Creek, Contra Costa County, Cal.

B. F. RUSH, Suisun, Cal., Shorthorns, Thoroughbred and Grades. Young Bulls and Calves for Sale.

PETER SAXE & SON. Lick House, San Francisco, Cal.—Importers and Breeders for past 18 years of every variety of Cattle, Horses, Sheep and Hogs.

HOLSTEIN THOROUGHBREDS of all the noted strains. Registered Berkshire Swine. Catalogues. F. H. BURKE, 401 Montgomery St., S. F.

CLEVELAND BAYS and Norman Horses, Jersey Cattle, and pure bred Poland China Hogs.—DR. W. J. PRATHER, Fresno, Cal.

HENRY C. JUDSON. Wild Idle Farm.—Breeder of Thoroughbred Horses. The home of "Wild Idle." P. O. Santa Clara; Box 223.

W. S. JACOBS. Sacramento, Cal. — Breeder of Thoroughbred Shorthorns and Berkshire Hogs.

J. H. WHITE, Lakeville, Sonoma County—Breeder of Registered Holstein Cattle.

FERGUSON & AUSTIN,
FRESNO, CAL.
Registered Polled Angus and Short-Horn Cattle.

Oysters.

M. B. MORAGHAN

Is the only importer, planter and wholesale dealer in the CALIFORNIA MARKET, Stalls 68, 69 to 71 and 47, 48. All the choicest brands of Fresh Oysters constantly on hand. Prompt attention paid to hotel and country orders. Price List.

Large Eastern Oysters .... $1 00 per 100
Transplanted Eastern Oysters .... 1 50 per 100
California Oysters .... 2 00 " sack
Fresh frozen Eastern Oysters at $7 00 per doz. cans.

SAMUEL VALLEAU. JAS. R. BRODIE.

J. R. BRODIE & CO.,
Steam Printers,
—And Dealers in—
Poolseller's and Bookmaker's Supplies.
401—403 *Sansome Street, corner Sacramento, San Francisco.*

Old Hermitage Whiskies
"STEINER'S,"
No. 311 BUSH STREET,
San Francisco.
Under Breeder and Sportsman Office.

"DICKEY'S,"
SIXTH AVENUE AND D ST.
Near entrance to Bay District Track.
Choicest Brands of
WINES AND CIGARS.
A Delightful Resort.
Telephone 1488. J. R. DICKEY, Propr.

PHIL J. CRIMMINS. JOHN C. MORRISON.

"Silver Palace,"
36 Geary Street,
San Francisco, Cal.

John D. Gall. Jas. P. Dunne

"The Resort,"
No. 1 Stockton Street, cor. Ellis,
San Francisco.

HEALD'S
Business College, 24 Post St.
—San Francisco.—
The most popular school on the Coast
P. HEALD, President. C. S. HALEY, Sec'y.
☞ Send for Circulars

The Wine that is held in HIGHEST ESTEEM by the LEADING CLUBS and in SOCIETY
IS
MOËT & CHANDON
-:- "WHITE SEAL," -:-
THE PERFECTION OF A DRY
Champagne

For Sale by all the Leading Grocers and Wine Merchants.

SHERWOOD & SHERWOOD,
PACIFIC COAST AGENTS,
212--214 Market Street, San Francisco, Cal.

TO HORSEMEN!

PREPARE!!

Your Stallion Advertisements for the

Breeder & Sportsman

For the Coming Season---1890.

We are pleased to announce that we have the best facilities for furnishing

Stallion Pictures,
Stallion Cards,
Pedigrees, Folders,
Contracts, Bills, Etc.

We make a specialty of this department of our business, and have UNRIVALED FACILITIES FOR LOOKING UP PEDIGREES and doing accurate and handsome work.

Promptness, Good Work, Low Prices.

TO REACH ALL
OF THE
Horsemen and Breeders on the Pacific Coast
ADVERTISE in the
Breeder & Sportsman,
313 Bush Street, S. F.

BOYCE TABLETS.
Leg and Body Wash.

THE BOYCE TABLETS are packed in a nicely decorated metal box with hinged lid—one hundred tablets in each box; directions for use plainly engraved upon the box; therefore, the convenience of the package—no liability to leakage and breakage—economy and ready solubility, together with the absolute certainty of their action, will at once commend the use of BOYCE'S TABLETS to the intelligent horsemen of the country. TABLETS sufficient to make one hundred pints of leg and body wash are conveniently carried in an inside coat pocket or in the hip-pocket of the trousers.

The BOYCE WASH can be applied ALL OVER THE BODY WITHOUT FEAR OF BLISTERING OR AFFECTING THE KIDNEYS.

The BOYCE WASH will cure CRACKED HEELS, PUFFS, STOCKINGS, SCRATCHES, INFLAMED TENDONS and FEVERED LEGS.

Price per Box of One Hundred Tablets, $2, sent postpaid to any part of the United States; six boxes for $10. A sample of BOYCE'S TABLETS will be mailed to any address on application. These TABLETS are warranted to keep in any climate. Address

BOYCE TABLET COMPANY,
600 Wabash Avenue, - - - Terre Haute, Indiana.

J. A. McKERRON, Pacific Coast Agent,
228-230-232 Ellis Street, San Francisco, Cal.

RUB YOUR HORSES

In cases of SWELLING or STIFFNESS OF THE JOINTS, with

DARBYS FLUID.

If you value your Horses, Dogs and Cattle always keep it on hand.

IT HAS NO EQUAL

For Cuts, Scratches, Bruises, Bites, Sores, Etc.

It gives immediate relief, and prevents Poison, Gangrene and Proud Flesh.

J. H. ZEILIN & CO., - Philadelphia, Pa.
SOLD BY ALL DRUGGISTS.

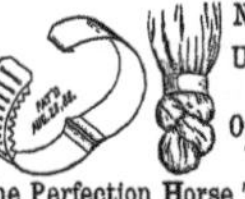

NOVEL, USEFUL and Ornamental.

The Perfection Horse Tail Tie,
Saves Time and the Tail.
Send 25 cents for Sample,
BREEDER AND SPORTSMAN,
313 Bush Street, San Francisco.
or to BARNES & PARKER, Des Moines, Ia., Manufrs.

PASTURAGE
AND
FIRST-CLASS CARE
TAKEN OF
Gentlemen's Road Horses and Trotters.

Colts Broken and Trained to Harness or Saddle.

Twenty new Box Stalls. First-class Pasturage, and the best of care given to all horses. Terms, $4 per month. Satisfaction Guaranteed. Address,

K. O'GRADY,
Laural Creek Farm,
SAN MATEO, CAL.

GOLDEN EAGLE HOTEL

Corner SEVENTH and K STREETS, SACRAMENTO.
FIRST CLASS IN EVERY RESPECT.
The LARGEST and FINEST HOTEL in the City.
W. O. BOWERS, Proprietor.
Free 'Buss to and from the Hotel.
Telephone, Telegraph Office and Messenger Service at Hotel

BERGEZ'S
RESTAURANT.
FIRST-CLASS. *Charges Reasonable.*
Private Rooms for Families,
332—334 Pine St., below Montgomery St.
JOHN BERGEZ, Propr.

R. LIDDLE & SON
538 Washington St., S. F.,
Wholesale and Retail Dealers in
Guns, Rifles and Pistols.
A Full Line of FISHING TACKLE and SPORTSMAN'S GOODS.
Orders by mail receive prompt attention.

For any Kind of a
SORE THROAT
USE
McCLELLAN'S
DIPHTHERIA REMEDY
An Unfailing Cure.
FOR SALE BY ALL DRUGGISTS

The Trotting Stallion

Silver Bow

Will make the season of 1890 at the Oakland Race Track.

Pedigree.

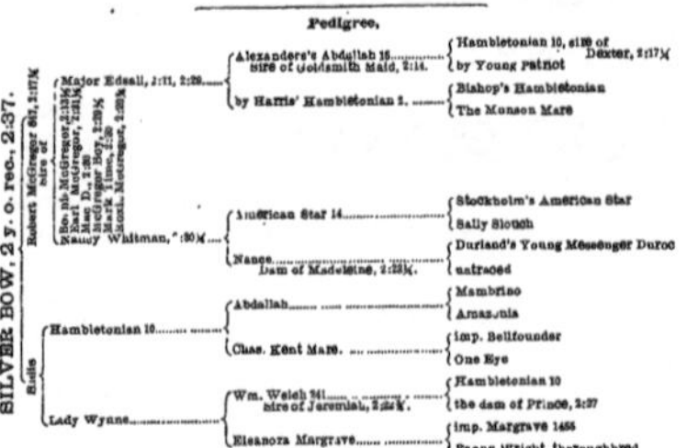

DESCRIPTION.

SILVER BOW is a handsome bay, no white; 15-3¼ hands high; weighs 1071 pounds; of fine form, with the best of legs and a clean cut, intelligent head. Is remarkably level headed seldom making a break; wears 7-ounce shoes in front. His record 2:37, is no mark of his speed; he can beat 30 easy, and with his gilt-edge breeding, he is just what he ought to be, a trotter sired by a trotter whose dam was herself a trotter and his grandam the dam of two trotters. His dam Sadie being by Hambletonian 10, shows him to be bred from the cream of the trotting blood.

TERMS: $100 for the season. Mares not proving in foal returnable for the season of 1891 free of charge. Good pasturage and first-class care taken of mares for $5 per month. No responsibility assumed for escapes or accidents. For further particulars, address

Limited to 15 approved mares.
Season to end June 1st, 1890.

P. J. WILLIAMS.
Care Race Track, Oakland, Cal.

Valensin Stock Farm Stallions.

SIDNEY, 2:19 3-4.

At Eight Years of Age Sire of the following Fastest on Record:

FAUSTINO, yearling stallion, record of the world 2:35
FLEET, fastest yearling record in 1888 .... 2:36
FLEET, fastest two-year-old filly in 1889 .... 2:24
GOLD LEAF, fastest four-year-old Pacing record in the world 2:11½
ADONIS, fastest three-year-old Pacing Gelding in the world 2:14¼
ADONIS, four-year-old Gelding Pacing record 2:14

—Also the Sire of—

LONGWORTH, four years old 2:19
SISTER V., four years old (trial 2:23) 2:27
SANTA RITA 2:39
MEMO, two-year-old (three-year-old trial 2:20½) 2:49

And many others.

SIDNEY is the sire of Faustino 2:35, and Fleet 2:36, the two fastest yearlings the world has ever known by one sire, and his slowest yearling is faster than the great Electioneer's fastest.

Terms, $250, with usual return privileges, for a limited number of approved mares. Book rapidly filling.

SIMMOCOLON, Four-year-old, 2:29 1-2.

Trial, 2:24; Half Mile in 1:08; Quarter in 33 1-2 Seconds.

Chestnut Horse, foaled 1885.

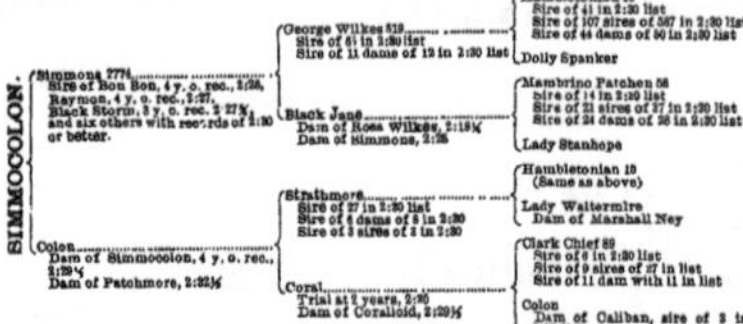

As will be seen, Simmocolon is by a performing and producing son of George Wilkes, 2:22. He has back of him three producing dams, and combines the blood of the great sire George Wilkes handsomely blended with the blood of the greatest broodmare families. On the dam's side Mambrino Patchen, Strathmore, Clark Chief and Clay. A fine individual himself, pure gaited and very fast.

Terms, $150, with usual return privileges, for a limited number of mares. Season to close JUNE 15th, when he will be prepared for track purposes. Pasturage $5 per month. Reasonable charges if fed hay and grain. Best of care taken of mares, but positively no responsibility assumed for accidents or escapes. For further particulars address

G. VALENSIN, Pleasanton, Cal.

Poplar Grove Breeding FARM.

Standard-bred Trotters, Colts and Fillies.

The get of CLOVIS, 4909; PASHA, 2039; APEX, 2935,

For Sale.

Address S. N. STRAUBE, Poplar Grove Breeding Farm,

Fresno, Cal.

Inspection by intending purchasers invited, and information by mail.

Guenoc Stud Farm, Lake Co., Cal.

Imp. GREENBACK

(Sire of the English winners Greenlight, Greenjacket, Greenshank, Greenwave and Greenhorn)

By Dollar, dam Music, by Stockwell. $100 the Season

ST. SAVIOR,

(FULL BROTHER TO EOLE)

By Eolus, dam War Song, by War Dance. $100 the Season.

PASTURAGE, $5 PER MONTH.

with right to return the following year if mare does not prove with foal. The best of care taken, but no liability for accidents or escapes. Mares shipped to C. W. ABY, care ST. HELENA STABLES, St. Helena Napa County, will be taken in charge by competent men.

For further information write to

DR. C. W. ABY, Middletown, Lake County, Cal.

SOUTHER FARM

P. O. Box 208. San Leandro, Cal.

1½ miles northwest of San Leandro; 8 miles southeast of Oakland. Turn off County road between above places at "Stanley Road," ½ mile north of San Leandro.

Horses boarded at all times in any manner desired. Best of care but no responsibility for accidents. Colts broken and handled for the road or track. Terms Reasonable.

Glen Fortune,	Jester D,	El Benton,	Figaro,
By Electioneer.	By Almont.	By Electioneer.	Hambletonian 725
$50 for 1889.	$50 for 1890.	Limited to 5 mares.	Limited to 12 mares
		Book Full.	Book Full.

If horses are to last for a profitable time they must occasionally have a change from hard pavements, wooden floors, and dry, hard feed.

THE SOUTHER FARM

Has Green Feed the Year Round,

and feeds Hay in connection with the green feed, which a horse must have if he is to thrive. Every animal is given

A Dry, Warm Place to Sleep,

No matter how stormy the weather. All Stock under cover when it rains.

VISITORS WELCOME ANY DAY EXCEPT SUNDAY.

Write to the above address for references, circulars and price lists. Terms reasonable.

GILBERT TOMPKINS, Proprietor.

SAN MATEO STOCK FARM

HOME OF GUY WILKES,
Record, 2:15 1-4.

Guy Wilkes' Book is full for 1890, and positively no more mares will be received. Book now open for 1891, at $500 the Season.

Sable Wilkes, three-year-old record 2:18, will be allowed to serve 25 mares in addition to those already engaged at $250 the season of 1890. SABLE Wilkes, 15½ hands, black horse, by Guy Wilkes, first dam Sable by The Moor; second dam Gretchen by Mambrino Pilot; third dam Kitty Kirkman by Canada Chief; fourth dam by Fanning's Tobe; fifth dam by imp. Leviathan.

Leo Wilkes, brown horse, four years, 16 hands, full brother to Sable Wilkes, will be allowed to serve 30 mares at $100 the season

Mares not proving with foal may be returned the following season free of service fee. Parties engaging the services of any of the above horses must send a deposit of 10 per cent. of service money with engagement. Pasturage $6 per month, and when the condition of the animal requires it, hay or grain, or both, are fed, the charge will be $12 50 per month. Good care will be taken of all mares sent to the Farm, but no liability will be assumed for accidents or escapes.

All bills are due at time of service, but must be paid by August 1st of each year. No stock will be allowed to leave the place until all bills are paid.

WILLIAM CORBITT.
San Mateo Stock Farm.

2:20 1-2 (Half Mile Track) at 5 Years. — Fastest Record (in a Race) of any Wilkes — 2:14 1-2 at 5 Years

ROY WILKES, 2:12¾,

THE GREATEST CAMPAIGNER OF 1889.

Handsome, Game, Pure Gaited. Level Headed.

Will make a season at the PLEASANTON STOCK FARM, PLEASANTON, CAL. Service Fee $150, with return privilege. Season ends April 1st., 1890.

For further information, address

L. A. DAVIES, Hotel Pleasanton,
SUTTER AND JONES STREETS, San Francisco, Cal.

Southern Pacific Co.

(PACIFIC SYSTEM.)

Trains leave and are due to arrive at San Francisco.

LEAVE (FOR)	FROM DECEMBER 1, 1889.	ARRIVE (FROM)
7.30 A M	Haywards, Niles and San Jose	*12.45 P M
7.30 A M	Sacramento and Redding, via Davis	7.15 P M
7.30 A M	Sacramento, Auburn, Colfax	5.45 P M
8.00 A M	Martinez, Vallejo, Calistoga and Santa Rosa	6.15 P M
8.30 A M	Los Angeles Express, Fresno, Bakersfield, Mojave and East and Los Angeles	11.15 A M
8.30 A M	Niles, San Jose, Stockton, Ione, Sacramento, Marysville, Oroville and Red Bluff	5.45 P M
10.30 A M	Haywards and Niles	2.15 P M
*12.00 M	Haywards, Niles and San Jose	* 3.45 P M
*1.00 P M	Sacramento River Steamers	**6.00 A M
3.00 P M	Haywards, Niles and San Jose	9.45 A M
3.30 P M	2d Class for Ogden and East	10.45 P M
4.00 P M	Stockton and Milton; Vallejo, Calistoga and Santa Rosa	9.45 A M
4.30 P M	Sacramento and Knight's Landing via Davis	10.45 A M
* 4.30 P M	Niles and Livermore	* 8.45 A M
* 4.30 P M	Niles and San Jose	‡ 4.15 P M
5.30 P M	Haywards and Niles	7.45 A M
6.00 P M	Sunset Route, Atlantic Express, Santa Barbara, Los Angeles, Deming, El Paso, New Orleans and East	8.45 P M
7.00 P M	Shasta Route Express, Sacramento, Marysville, Redding, Portland, Puget Sound and East	7.45 A M
8.00 P M	Central Atlantic Express, Ogden and East	9.45 A M

SANTA CRUZ DIVISION.

LEAVE (FOR)		ARRIVE (FROM)
‡ 8.00 A M	Hunters train to San Jose	‡ 7.20 P M
8.15 A M	Newark, Centerville, San Jose, Felton, Boulder Creek and Santa Cruz	5.50 P M
* 2.15 P M	Centerville, San Jose, Felton, Boulder Creek and Santa Cruz	*11.50 A M
4.15 P M	Centerville, San Jose, Almaden, and Los Gatos	9.50 A M

Coast Division (Third and Townsend Sts.)

LEAVE (FOR)		ARRIVE (FROM)
7.25 A M	San Jose, Almaden and Way Stations	2.30 P M
8.30 A M	San Jose, Gilroy, Tres Pinos; Pajaro, Santa Cruz; Monterey; Pacific Grove, Salinas, San Miguel, Paso Robles, Santa Margarita (San Luis Obispo) and principal Way Stations	6.12 P M
10.30 A M	San Jose and Way Stations	5.02 P M
12.01 P M	Cemetery, Menlo Park and Way Stations	3.38 P M
* 3.30 P M	San Jose, Tres Pinos, Santa Cruz, Salinas, Monterey, Pacific Grove and principal Way Stations	*10.00 A M
* 4.20 P M	Menlo Park and Way Stations	* 7.58 A M
5.20 P M	San Jose and Way Stations	9.03 A M
6.30 P M	Menlo Park and Way Stations	6.35 A M
†11.45 P M	Menlo Park and principal Way Stations	†7.38 P M

A M for Morning. P M for Afternoon.
*Sundays excepted. †Saturdays only. ‡Sundays only.
**Mondays excepted. §Saturdays excepted.

KILLIP & CO.,

LIVE STOCK AND GENERAL AUCTIONEERS,

22 Montgomery Street, San Francisco

SPECIAL ATTENTION PAID TO SALES OF

High-Bred Horses and Cattle.

At auction and private sale.

Will Sell in All Cities and Counties of the State.

REFERENCES.

HON. C. GREEN, Sacramento. — HON. J. D. CARR, Salinas.
J. P. SARGENT, ESQ., Sargents. — HON. JOHN BOGGS, Colusa.
HON. L. J. ROSE, Los Angeles. — HON. A. WALRATH, Nevada.
J. B. HAGGIN, ESQ., San Francisco.

Represented at Sacramento by Edwin F. Smith Secretary State Agricultural Society.

At San José by Messrs. Montgomery & Rea, Real Estate Agents.

Being the oldest established firm in the live-stock business on this Coast, and having conducted the important auction sales in this line for the past fifteen years, amounting to one half a million of dollars, we feel justified in claiming unequaled facilities for disposing of live stock of every description, either at auction or private sale. Our list of correspondents embraces every breeder and dealer of prominence upon the Pacific Coast, thus enabling us to give full publicity to animals placed with us for sale. Private purchases and sales of live stock of all descriptions will be made on commission, and stock shipped with the utmost care. Purchases and sales made of land of every description. We are authorized to refer to the gentlemen whose names are appended.

KILLIP & CO., 22 Montgomery Street

IRON TURBINE
P.P. MAST & Co.
31 MARKET ST. SAN FRANCISCO
WINDMILL
THE MOST Powerful and Durable Combination For RAISING WATER IN THE WORLD.
& BUCKEYE PUMP

LAMBORN ROAD MACHINE
LIGHT DRAFT.
MADE OF IRON. STRONG, SIMPLE, DURABLE.
EASILY OPERATED.
TRUMAN HOOKER & CO.
SAN FRANCISCO, - - CALIFORNIA

San Francisco and North Pacific Railway.

THE DONAHUE BROAD-GAUGE ROUTE.

COMMENCING SUNDAY, MARCH 17, 1889, AND until further notice, boats and trains will leave from and arrive at the San Francisco Passenger Depot, Market-street Wharf, as follows:

Leave San Francisco. Week Days.	Leave San Francisco. Sundays.	Destination	Arrive San Francisco. Sundays.	Arrive San Francisco. Week Days.
7.40 3.30 P 5.00 P M.	8.00 A M 5.00 P M	Petaluma and Santa Rosa	10.40 A M 6.10 P M	8.50 A M 10.30 A M 6.05 P M
7.40 A M 3.30 P M	8.00 A M	Fulton, Windsor, Healdsburg, Litton Spr'gs, Cloverdale, and way stations.	6.10 P M	10.30 A M 6.05 P M
7.40 A M	8.00 A M	Hopland and Ukiah,	6.10 P M	6.05 P M
7.40 A M	8.00 A M	Guerneville	6.10 P M	6.05 P M
7.40 A M 5.00 P M	8.00 A M	Sonoma and Glen Ellen.	10.40 A M 6.10 P M	8.50 A M 6.05 P M

Stage connects at Santa Rosa for White Sulphur Springs, Sebastopol and Mark West Springs; at Geyserville for Skaggs Springs, and at Cloverdale for the Geysers; at Hopland for Highland Springs, Kelseyville, Soda Bay, Lakeport and Bartlett springs, and at Ukiah for Vichy Springs, Saratoga Springs, Blue Lakes, Willits, Cahto, Calpella, Potter Valley, Sherwood Valley and Mendocino City.

EXCURSION TICKETS from Saturdays to Mondays, to Petaluma, $1.50; to Santa Rosa, $2.25; to Healdsburg, $3.40; to Litton Springs, $3.60; to Cloverdale, $4.50; to Hopland, $5.70; to Ukiah, $6.75; to Guerneville, $3.75; to Sonoma, $1.50; to Glen Ellen, $1.80.

EXCURSION TICKETS, good for Sundays only, to Petaluma, $1; to Santa Rosa, $1.50; to Healdsburg, $2.25; to Litton Springs, $1.40; to Cloverdale, $3; to Guerneville, $2.50, to Sonoma, $1; to Glen Ellen, $1.20.

From San Francisco for Point Tiburon and San Rafael: Week Days—7.40, 9.20, 11.20, A. M.; 3.30, 5.00, 6.15 P. M. Sundays—8.00, 9.30, 11.00 A. M.; 1.30, 5.00, 6.20 P. M.

To San Francisco from San Rafael: Week Days—6.20, 7.55, 9.30 A. M.; 12.45, 3.40, 5.05 P. M. Sundays—8.10, 9.40 A. M.; 12.15, 3.40, 5.00 P. M.

To San Francisco from Point Tiburon: Week Days—6.50, 8.20, 9.55 A. M.; 1.10, 4.05, 5.30 P. M.; Sundays—8.40, 10.05 A. M.; 12.40, 4.05, 5.30 P. M.

On Saturdays an extra trip will be made from San Francisco to San Rafael, leaving at 1.40 P. M.

H. C. WHITING, General Manager.

PETER J. McGLYNN, Gen. Pass. & Tkt. Agt.

Ticket Offices at Ferry, 222 Montgomery Street and 2 New Montgomery Street.

KENNEL ADVERTISEMENTS.

Thoroughbred Pugs, $40 each.

PEDIGREE.

PUPPIES:
- Fido
  - imp. Jumbo — Marshall's Uno / Lady Bess
  - Fannie — Rex / imp. Fly
- Budge
  - Senator Fair's Fritz
  - McCleery's Mamma Snoots — Sam / imp. Alice

Can be seen daily from 9 A. M. to 3 P. M. at 411 Ellis Street, San Francisco.

J. F. B. McCLEERY.

Irish Setters & Pointers.

In the Stud, winner of 16 first and special prizes, CHAMPION MIKE T., 6435, A. K. S. B. Irish Setter puppies by Champion Mike T. 6435 A. K. S. B.—Champion Lady Elcho T. 6461 A. K. S. B., for sale. Two pointers, a year old, by Rush T. 10069 A. K. S. B.—Champion Patti Croxteth T. 10128 A. K. S. B. for sale. Yard broken. Address,

A. B. TRUMAN,
1425 Steiner St., S. F., Cal.

CALIFORNIA SPANIEL KENNELS.

Oakland, California, H. P. RENNIE, Prop; Breeder and importer of typical COCKER SPANIELS. Winner of first prizes at S. F. and Los Angeles, 1889; also, Columbus, 1889, New York, 1887. In the stud, solid Black Cocker dog, GIFFEE, won 1st and Gold Medal at S. F., 1889. Fee, $25. Puppies and grown dogs at reasonable prices. My dogs can neither talk nor climb a tree, but are fielders and prize winners.

IF YOU WISH A GOOD REVOLVER PURCHASE ONE OF SMITH & WESSON'S

Finest small arms ever manufactured and the first choice of all experts. In calibres 32, 38 and 44-100. Single or double action, Safety Hammerless and Target models. Best quality wrought steel, carefully inspected for workmanship and stock. Unrivaled for finish, durability and accuracy. Do not be deceived by cheap *malleable iron imitations* often sold for the genuine article. They are unreliable and dangerous. The SMITH & WESSON REVOLVERS are stamped upon the barrels with firm's name, address and dates of patents, and are guaranteed perfect. Insist upon having them, and if your dealer cannot supply you, an order sent to address below will receive prompt attention. Descriptive catalogue and prices upon application.

SMITH & WESSON,
Springfield, Mass.

SELBY STANDARD 10 — THE BEST IS THE CHEAPEST — STANDARD CHAMBERLIN SHOTGUN CARTRIDGES

DR. FISHERMAN'S Carbolized Alkaline LOTION

Cures after all other Remedies have Failed.

Sprains, Sores, Bruises, Galls, Swellings, Scratches, Thrush, Grease Heels, Curb, Rheumatism, Restoring Weak Knees and Ankles to their original condition. As a wash it insures glossy manes and tails. Valuable as an internal remedy for Coughs, Colic, Congestion or Fever. You really get Half a Gallon of Remedy for $1.00, or Two Gallons for $3.00, after being adulterated as directed.

This Liniment has received the endorsement of some of our best horsemen. Recommended by Jos. Cairn Simpson. See BREEDER AND SPORTSMAN of November 10th, 1888.

LYNDE & HOUGH, Proprietors.

116 California St., S. F.

Or ask your Druggist for it.

THE B. & Y. HOOF OIL

GOOD FOR MAN OR BEAST.

Will positively destroy the effects of the "Cattle Fly."

A SURE CURE for Sores, Scratches, Cuts, Wounds, Bruises, Corns, Thrush, Foot Rot, Quarter Crack, Sand Crack, Dry, Brittle, Hard and Fevered Hoof, or any local trouble about the Horse.

Warranted to make the hoof grow without cause of complaint on the part of the horse-shoer for gumming his rasp.

B. & Y. New Process Neats Foot Oil, Best Leather Oil made.

CHEAP AND LASTING

Recommended by leading Harness Men, Drivers and Trainers. Is well adapted to wet weather, as it does not open pores like old process goods.

Ask your dealer for it, or send to

HUNT & DOREMUS,
99 FLOOD BUILDING, - San Francisco.

HORSE OWNERS! TRY GOMBAULT'S CAUSTIC BALSAM.

A Safe, Speedy and Positive Cure for Curb, Splint, Sweeny, Capped Hock, Strained Tendons, Founder, Wind Puffs, all Skin Diseases or Parasites, Thrush, Diphtheria, Pinkeye, all Lameness from Spavin, Ringbone or other Bony Tumors. Removes all Bunches or Blemishes from Horses and Cattle.

Supersedes all Cautery or Firing. Impossible to Produce any Scar or Blemish.

Every bottle sold is warranted to give satisfaction. Price $1.50 per bottle. Sold by druggists, or sent by express, charges paid, with full directions for its use. Send for descriptive circulars. Address

LAWRENCE, WILLIAMS & CO., Cleveland, O.

BROU'S INJECTION

A PERMANENT CURE in from 3 to 6 days, of the most obstinate cases; guaranteed not to produce Stricture; no sickening doses; and no inconvenience or loss of time. Recommended by physicians and sold by all druggists. J. Ferré, (successor to Brou), Pharmacien, Paris.

California Horse Shoe Co's

STEEL SHOE

Light, Strong and Perfect.

Superior to all others for Speed Horses.

ALSO

The Celebrated GOODENOUGH Pattern Shoe.

OFFICE: 202 Market St., San Francisco, Cal.

I have used in my business the Steel and Iron Shoes made by the above Company, and take great pleasure in saying they are the best I have ever used in twenty-two years' practice. I have never seen anything like the STEEL SHOE made by this Company. I can fully recommend them to every practical Horseshoer in the country. Yours respectfully,

No. 8 Everett Street. JOHN GRACE.

OUR IMPROVED. ALL SIZES AND WEIGHTS. G.W. BOHANON. ESTAB. 1868.

THE BOHANON SULKY!

BEST MADE.
Perfect Riding Buggies.
Breaking Carts.
Fine Repairing, Reasonable Prices.

Bohanon Carriage Co., 161-163 Ogden Ave., CHICAGO.

Send for Catalogue.

VETERINARY.

DR. THOS. BOWHILL, M.R.C.V.S

VETERINARY SURGEON.

Graduate New Veterinary College, Edinburgh. Awarded the Highland and Agricultural Societies Medals for Horse Pathology, Anatomy, Physiology and Histology. The Williams' Prize, '84-'85, for highest works in professional examinations, and six first-class certificates of merit. Honorary Member Illinois State Veterinary Medical Association.

CENTENNIAL STABLES,

1523-25 California Street. Telephone No. 66.

Veterinary Infirmary and Residence, 2209 Jackson Street. Telephone 4128.

W. H. WOODRUFF. Veterinary Dentist,

AT FASHION STABLES,

221 Ellis Street, San Francisco

Improved Instruments, Humane Methods, First-Class Work.

Dr. Wm. H. Jones, M.R.C.V.S. Veterinary Surgeon,

(CLUB STABLES)

409—411 Taylor Street, San Francisco.

Consultations by letter, and cases of URGENT NECESSITY in the interior will receive prompt attention.

H. E. CARPENTER, Veterinary Surgeon,

Graduate of Ontario Veterinary College, Toronto, Canada.

RESIDENCE AND VETERINARY INFIRMARY

331 Golden Gate Ave., San Francisco.

Telephone 3069.

OPEN DAY AND NIGHT.

No risk in throwing Horses. Veterinary Operating Table on the premises.

DR. C. MASOERO, Veterinary Surgeon,

Successor to DR. A. DeTAVEL,

GRADUATE OF ROYAL VETERINARY COLLEGE, TURIN.

OFFICE AND INFIRMARY,

No. 811 HOWARD STREET,

Between Fourth and Fifth. SAN FRANCISCO.

Telephone, No. 457.

R. WATKINS, Veterinary Dentist,

Of twelve years practice, is now permanently located in San Francisco, and may be found at C. S. Crittendens' Golden Gate Livery and Riding Academy, 24 to 28 Golden Gate Avenue.

Will treat ailments of the horse's mouth, and cure all such. Siderein Pullers and Tongue Lollers, etc.

Satisfaction guaranteed, Orders by mail will receive prompt attention. Examination Free.

E. J. O'ROUKE.

I have the honor to announce to my old patrons and the general public that I may be found at my old stand, where, as heretofore, the

Shoeing of Horses,

whether for the Track, Drive, or for general work, will receive my personal attention,

E. J. O'ROUKE,
211 Ellis Street

6 DOS

DO you bet?
DO you go to the races?
DO yon know HOW to bet?
DO you know BEST system?
DO you want Good ADVICE?
DO as you ought to do:

SEND FOR PROSPECTUS TO

GOODWIN BROS.,

241 BROADWAY, NEW YORK,

Who will mail you

FREE OF CHARGE,

one of their circulars showing the GREAT SUCCESS they have met with from the time they established the system of "Point" providing in this country in 1881; it also contains

MANY OTHER INTERESTING ITEMS

with which the general public is not familiar.

Brushes.

BUCHANAN BROS.,

Brush Manufacturers,

609 Sacramento Street, two doors above Montgomery.

Horse Brushes of every description on hand or made to order. Bristle Body Brushes our Specialty.

Everything for

Trotter or Runner.

At J. A. McKERRON'S,

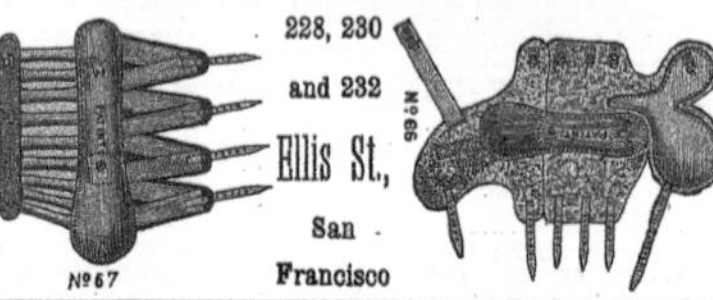

228, 230 and 232 Ellis St., San Francisco

THE IMPROVED NOYES ROAD - CART.

PATENTED JULY 17, 1883, AND JUNE 8, 1886.

Some of the Advantages of the Noyes Cart Over All Others.

There is no bar for the rider to climb over in getting in or out. The horse can be hitched eighteen inches nearer than any other road-cart made. You can get in or out with perfect safety—no danger of being thrown into the wheel—a great advantage in breaking colts. THE EASIEST CART FOR ROAD OR TRACK. The only cart that a horse can be speeded to within one second as fast as to a sulky. All our carts are made of the very best materials and are warranted. Manufactured by the NOYES CART COMPANY, Kalamazoo, Mich.

They are indorsed by the following horsemen, all of whom are using them. Ask their opinion of the Noyes Cart: John Splan, who drove Guy a full mile in 2:17¼ and Chapter a half-mile in 1:10¾ to a Noyes Cart, says he would not take $200 for it if he could not get another; W. J. Gordon, Glenville, O.; W. B. Fasig, Cleveland, O.; Dave Muckel, Cleveland, O.; R. J. Moorehead, North East, Pa.; W. J. Chamberlain, Cleveland, O.; H. P. Malone, Bradford, Pa.; S. A. Brown & Co., Kalamazoo Stock Farm; Charles Marvin, Menlo Park, Cal.; W. H. Crawford, Lexington, Ky.; S. L. Caton, who gave Bell Boy a mark at Los Angeles, Cal., of 2:19¾, and drove Chanter a half mile in 1:06¾ and Lowland Girl a full mile in 2:[illegible] to a Noyes Cart; Mike Bowerman, Lexington, Ky.; James Golden, Medford, Mass.; John E. Turner, Philadelphia, Pa.; T. L. Newton, Beaver Dam, Wis.; F. V. Johnston, Marshall, Mich.; W. H. McCarthy, Los Angeles, Cal.; A. W. Dennison, El Dorado, Kan.; P. O. Shank, Cleveland, O.; Charles Barnard, Boston, Mass.; Johnson Bros., Greenville, Mich.; John G. Avery, Buffalo, N. Y.; General R. L. Howard, Buffalo, N. Y.; Howard Conklin, Buffalo, N. Y.; W. D. Ham, Hennepin, Ill.; R. G. Henry, Waterbury, Conn; J. E. Hayer, Newburgh, O.; J. C. Hart, Jefferson, Tex.; A. W. Harbison, Rock Point, Pa.; Carl Hodges, Battle Creek, Mich.; Barney Treacy, Lexington, Ky.; George Forbes, Cleveland, O.; Gifford Dudley, Topeka, Kan.; William and J. L. Thompson, Lamont, Pa.; C. F. Emery, Forest City Stock Farm, Cleveland, O.; R. F. Jones, Minneapolis, Minn.; John Forbes, Elyria O.; D. J. Downs, Battle Creek, Mich.; Frank Caton, Randall Station, O.; Arthur D. Sutton, Ind., Pa.; W. F. Neely, Grand Ridge, Ill.; Walter Clark, owner of Pilot Medium, Battle Creek, Mich.; H. R. Kingman, Battle Creek, Mich.; Dr. Sutton and H. C. Reed, Kalamazoo, Mich.; Budd Doble, Chicago, Ill.

SOLE MANUFACTURERS OF STONE'S PATENT SULKY CASE.

They will more than save their cost in one season, and horsemen campaigning trotters cannot afford to do without them. Would refer to Samuel A. Brown, Kalamazoo Stock Farm, S. L. Caton and W. H. McCarthy. Address

NOYES CART COMPANY, Kalamazoo, Mich.

Office and Factory, corner Rose and Eleanor streets. H. ARTHUR STONE, Manager.

TREES AND SEEDS.

Trumbull & Beebe's Nurseries

ESTABLISHED 1859.

500,000 **Fruit Trees** 500,000

FOR SALE.

Having added by purchase to that of our own growing, the entire nursery stock grown at James Shinn's Nurseries, Niles, Cal., we are better prepared than ever before to meet the increasing demand for trees, and offer for the season of 1889-1890 the LARGEST AND MOST COMPLETE ASSORTMENT OF NURSERY STOCK ON THE PACIFIC COAST, embracing all the leading varieties of FRUIT, SHADE and ORNAMENTAL TREES, ROSES, PLANTS, Etc. BERRY BUSHES of all kinds in quantities to suit. 200,000 GRAPE VINES (strong roots), also 60,000 OLIVE TREES (Mission and Picholine), ORANGES, LEMONS, NUT TREES, Etc., Etc.

NURSERIES—San Rafael, Alameda and Niles, Cal. Packing Grounds and Sales yard at Niles R. R. Station. Catalogues sent upon application. Address all communications to

TRUMBULL & BEEBE, 419-421 Sansome St., San Francisco, Cal

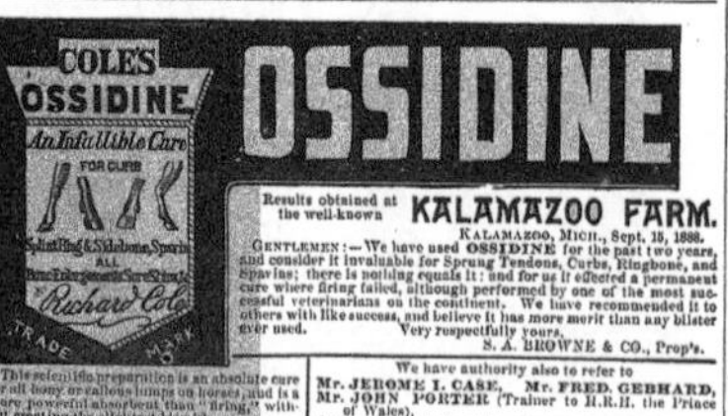

OSSIDINE

Results obtained at the well-known **KALAMAZOO FARM.**

KALAMAZOO, MICH., Sept. 15, 1888.

GENTLEMEN:—We have used OSSIDINE for the past two years, and consider it invaluable for Sprung Tendons, Curbs, Ringbone, and Spavins; there is nothing equals it: and for us it effected a permanent cure where firing failed, although performed by one of the most successful veterinarians on the continent. We have recommended it to others with like success, and believe it has more merit than any blister ever used.

Very respectfully yours,
S. A. BROWNE & CO., Prop's.

This scientific preparation is an absolute cure for all bony or callous lumps on horses, and is a more powerful absorbent than "firing," without creating the slightest blemish.

Acknowledged by leading horsemen of the world to be the **ONLY** preparation that will remove a Bone Spavin after it has become ossified.

We have authority also to refer to
Mr. JEROME I. CASE, Mr. FRED. GEBHARD, Mr. JOHN PORTER (Trainer to H.R.H. the Prince of Wales),
And hundreds of others from whom we have very flattering testimonials.

One Style Only. $3.00 per Bottle.

A. P. BUSH & CO.,
149 Pearl St.,
BOSTON, MASS.,
Sole Agents for United States and Canada.
Beware of Imitations.

SOLD BY C. N. Crittenton, A. R. Van Nest & Co., and C. M. Moseman & Bro., NEW YORK CITY.
Morrisson, Plummer & Co., Peter Van Schaack & Sons. CHICAGO, ILL.
John D. Park & Son, CINCINNATI, O.; Floyd & Foster, DETROIT, MICH.; F. S. Slosson, CLEVELAND, O.; Meyer Bros. Drug Co., ST. LOUIS, MO.; R. A. Robinson, LOUISVILLE, KY.; H. H. Moore & Sons, STOCKTON, CAL.

J. C. JOHNSON & CO.,

IMPORTERS, MANUFACTURERS, AND DEALERS IN

HARNESS & SADDLERY

☞ We carry a large assortment of goods in our line from the cheapest to the best made.

400 to 404 Market Street

Corner BATTERY STREET, San Francisco.

J. O'KANE, 767 MARKET STREET.

Horse Boots, Clothing and Furnishings,
For Track, Driving Training and Stable.
Every requisite for Horsemen.
Harness, Medicines, Etc.

The PARKER Hammerless Shot Gun.

At the Annual Tournament of 1889, held at Cannes, France, the grand prize, consisting of 2000 Francs and a Valuable Cup. was won by The Parker Hammerless.

The first Parker Hammerless Gun made won the championship of America at Decatur Illinois.

SEND FOR ILLUSTRATED CIRCULAR.

PARKER BROS., Makers,

New York Salesroom, 97 Chambers St. Meriden Conn.

To Horse Breeders and Stockmen.

SPECIAL OFFER.

I offer for sale, title warranted, the best bargain in stock ranches on the coast. The ranch contains 657 acres; one mile frontage on Clear Lake; 210 acres alfalfa land; 120 acres now seeded to alfalfa, cuts six tons per acre; 70 acres in timothy cuts four tons per acre, both without irrigation. The rest of the land is fine rolling pasture, or can be cultivated. There are two dwellings on the property, one new, cost $2,000; three barns, capacity 310 tons of hay; two artesian wells, with pipes laid to houses, barns and dairy house. Fine cold spring on premises. An orchard of apples, pears and cherries now in bearing. Peaches, prunes, apricots, strawberries and all other fruits do well. At option of purchaser with the property will be sold 800 head of sheep, 60 head of cattle, 23 horses, and 7 young brood mares in foal. Also wagons, harness, farming implements, etc.

This is a grand opportunity to establish a stock ranch. The S. F. & N. P. R. R. now runs within 35 miles of the property and will in a short time be extended quite to the place. Price $35,000, half cash. For further particulars, apply to

JOHN T. PETERS,
Agent for Sonoma Lake and Mendocino County Land.
29 New Montgomery St., in Grand Hotel.

keeps horses healthy, promotes digestion, fattens horses, loosens the hide, assists the appetite, prevents leg swelling, strengthens the kidneys, regulates the bowels and destroys worms. $7.50 per 100 lbs. Ask your dealer for it or send to

MANHATTAN FOOD CO., 206 Clay St., S. F.

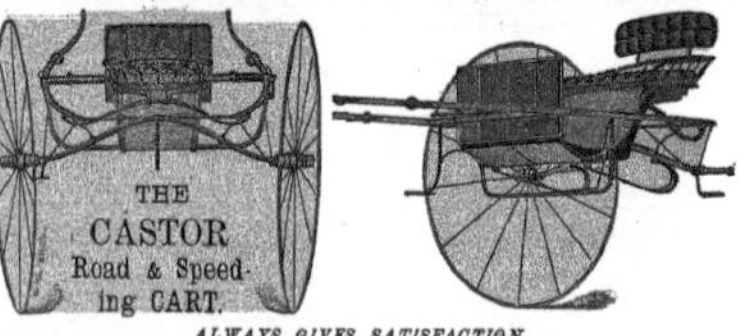

ALWAYS GIVES SATISFACTION.

Combining perfect riding qualities, proportions and balance, with genteel appearance.

No vehicle exhibits a horse to better advantage, and no Cart approaches them for speeding or training purposes.

A stylish vehicle for exercising or pleasure driving, at one-fourth the cost of a carriage. Have none of the horse jockey or objectionable features of other Road Carts.

They are the Leading Cart wherever introduced, and are in use by the most prominent breeders and pleasure drivers everywhere.

Elegant Shifting Top Carts.

Perfectly Balanced Stylish Pole Carts.

For Illustrated Catalogue, with Prices, address,

LEWIS F. CASTOR,
Frankford, Philadelphia, Pa.

JOHN SPLAN, General Agent.

TWENTY PAGES.

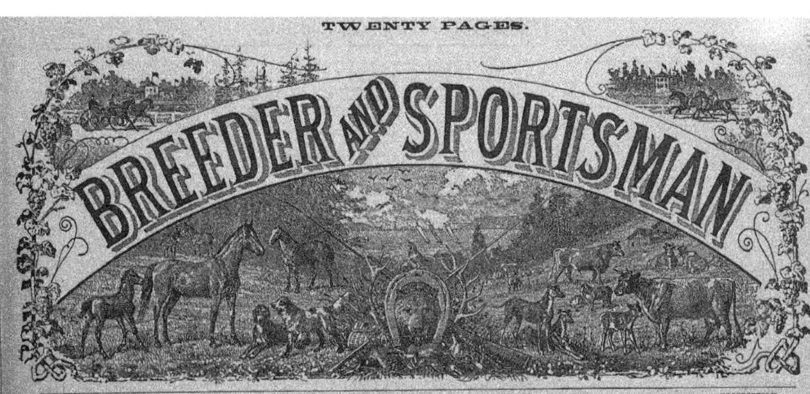

Vol. XVI. No. 3.
No. 313 BUSH STREET.

SAN FRANCISCO, SATURDAY, JAN. 18, 1890.

SUBSCRIPTION
FIVE DOLLARS A YEAR.

ANTINOUS,

The Property of James W. Rea, Esq., San Jose.

It is with a feeling of pride we this week draw attention to the happy effort of our artist who has depicted a son of the great Electioneer in his best style. Antinous was foaled in 1882, on Senator Stanford's Palo Alto Ranch, and was bought by his present owner, Mr. Rea, last May. He is a good dark bay, standing 15.2½ hands high, with an almost perfect head, good neck, nice sloping shoulders, with good back well ribbed up and powerful quarters, long muscular thighs, short cannon bones and good feet; his forelegs show signs of wear and tear having evidently been severely blistered.

His breeding is exceptional. Electioneer is the sire of Sunol 2:10½ at three years old; Palo Alto 2:12¾, Manzanita 2:16, Anteeo 2:16¾, Adair 2:17¼, Lot Slocum 2:17¼, Norval 2:17½, Bonita 2:18¾, Bell Boy at three years 2:19½, Hinda Rose 2:19½ at three years old, Antevolo 2:19½, and many others; in fact, Electioneer is the sire of forty-eight trotters and one pacer, and grandsire of nine trotters in the 2:30 list, including Alfred G. 2:19¾, and the pacer Edwin C. 2:15.

Toronto Sontag is by Toronto Chief, record 2:31, sire of three and of the dams of four in the 2:30 list.

Laura Keene is a sister to Alban 2:24, by Hambletonian 10, sire of 41 in the 2:30 list, and grandsire of 721 in the 2:30 list, including Maud S. 2:08¾, Jay Eye See 2:10, Sunol 2:10½, St. Julien, 2:11¼, and Axtell 2:12. Fanny is by Exton Eclipse, sire of the dam of Billy Denton, who is the sire of two and grandsire of three in the 2:30 list.

Such a trotting pedigree is rarely seen, and when backed up with such good shape and make as Antinous has is bound to tell in the stud as well as on the track. Referring to his speed, Mr. Chas. Marvin, the courteous Superintendent of the Palo Alto Stock Farm—than whom there should be no better judge—says he was very promising in yearling and two-year-old form, having shown quarters in 0:36 at two years old, and would, no doubt, have trained on with improving speed, but his legs failed him somewhat in his two-year-old season; hence, we let up on his work. Mr. Marvin also says that his older sisters showed corresponding speed in 2, 3, and 4-year-old form, and winds up by saying Antinous should prove an A 1 sire. Antinous will make the season at San Jose race track at the low price of $75 per mare, and should be extensively patronized. He is at present being jogged on the Oakland track by J. W. Gordon, and will be driven for a record after the season.

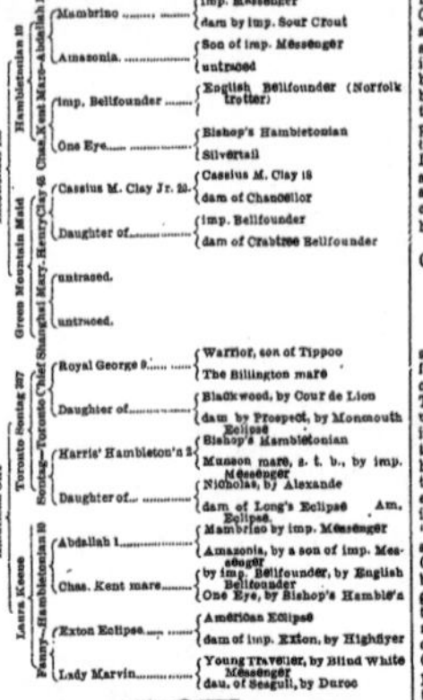

Abdallah (15) Alexander's.

WRITTEN FOR THE BREEDER AND SPORTSMAN.

Since this horse is of National reputation, conceded by all as the best 'breeding on" son of Hambletonian, a few facts hitherto unpublished will be of interest.

January, 1859, Mr. James Miller, then of Cynthiana, now of Paris, Ky.—well known as a breeder of trotters—accompanied by Joel F. Love, went to New York to buy a trotting bred stallion. They went direct to Goshen, Orange County, and stopped at the hotel of John Edsall, then owner of Abdallah (15). The horse was then seven years old.

On first sight both men, especially Mr. Miller, were pleased, for Abdallah looked every inch the *king* he was, They tried to get a price, but were told that the horse was not for sale. Mr. Edsall had also a livery stable, and was wintering a great many horses owned in New York City. He furnished the gentlemen from Kentucky his best horses and went with them to see all the stallions of any note in the county. On their return he was again asked to price Abdallah, but refused.

As they were starting the second time on a more extended tour, Mr. Miller said: "I notice that the best mares here are by your horse's sire, and since you cannot cross him with his sisters, would it not be well to sell him and buy a horse you can?" This speech was the means of bringing Abdallah to Kentucky. After two weeks spent in vain search for something to suit, Miller and Love gave up the hunt and turned their faces homeward.

Miller said: "let us go by Goshen and try again to buy Edsall's horse" Love answered: "it is of no use, he will not sell. Miller insisted and Love finally consented. Edsall was glad to see them and asked: "What luck?" The same as before, we have looked this country over and found nothing to suit but your horse and we are going home without buying." Edsall said: "This will never do; the idea of coming all the way from Kentucky and getting nothing is too bad. While you were away I have been thinking of what you said to me about not being able to breed to the best mares here, and have concluded to sell the horse. "Price him at what he is worth, and we will buy him." "$2,500 is my price." "We will take the horse" We want you to blanket and get him in shape, and bring him yourself by the middle of March to Kentucky." This Edsall agreed to do and fulfilled his contract, spending several weeks in the blue grass country. Abdallah stood that season (1859) and three others at Cynthiana.

In August of 1862 Messrs. Miller and Love fearing that he would be taken by soldiers, took him to Woodburn, thinking that there he would be safe as Lord R. A. Alexander was a citizen of Great Britain. In the spring of 1863 Mr. Alexander gave in exchange for him $2,500 in money and a son of Edwin Forrest and Flora Temple.

His subsequent history is well known. How he was taken by soldiers, overheated by excessive riding, made to swim a river, being allowed to cool suddenly, and chilling to death.

Like the mothers of most great horses, his dam, "Katy Darling," was more than an ordinary mare. We propose to look up her history and pedigree more fully, this much is now known:—She was by a horse called "Roman", and was a noted road mare of her day. In 1850, while being driven across a railroad track, caught her foot and broke her ankle. Her owner was about to kill her when a gentleman well acquainted with her great excellence, begged for her life, saying that there were plenty of worthy men who would be glad to get her, and that he would see that she fell into good hands. Her ankle got well, but was always crooked, she was bred to Hambletonian. There was a race trotted on the ice for a new set of fine harness. The owner of "Katy Darling" rode her (while Abdallah was in utero) to witness it.

There was lacking one entry to fill, her owner proposed trotting her if they would allow her to start under saddle. She won the race with the greatest ease.

Mr. Miller says that Abdallah in motion was one of the grandest looking horses that he has ever seen, and that his record of 2:42 is no measure of his speed, even for these days, when 2:42 was equal to 2:20, or better at the present time.

W. E. BEAN.

Anteeo De Turk.

Among the fine Anteeo colts in Sonoma County which merit mention is one bred by Robert Crane, ex-Supervisor, whose farm is on Crane's Creek, seven miles south of Santa Rosa. The colt is named Anteeo De Turk, and was foaled February 9, 1889. He is a handsome dark brown, similar to his sire, with a white star in forehead. His dam was Minnie D, by Alexander; second dam Shoo Fly, by General McClellan; third dam by Niagara. The colt is nearly 15 hands, and the arm measures 17 inches. He is of perfect form, with a fine head and very fine eyes, denoting good disposition and intelligence. He has been carefully handled on the farm, but has not been subjected to studious training and is merely broken to halter. He has remarkable power and shows thorough action, with docility and ease of motion. All the points which denote speed and endurance are apparent, and the promise is that he will prove a record breaker. Anteeo De Turk is in every respect a model colt from his noted sire, and his dam is a square trotter of good speed. Mr. Crane is a painstaking breeder, fond of superior stock of every specie, and his management of his large farm is evidence of his skill and thrift.

Comparison of the 2:30 Trotters of George Wilkes and Electioneer.

BY J. C. SIBLEY.

If any apology may seem necessary for giving you the result of several weeks of patient research, it arises from the frequent innuendoes from those owning none of the blood of Electioneer, that, as a family, they are not race-horses. Those who seem to be most persistent in decrying their value are generally those who have never possessed one. An intimate knowledge of the Electioneer family, and a desire to inform myself of the true facts, led me to a task, which, had I known its magnitude, would never have been undertaken. To answer those who have stated that the Electioneers were not race-horses, and who seem to desire to give the impression that most of their records have been made against "Father Time," I have selected for comparison that noted sire, George Wilkes. Not to demonstaate by any means that George Wilkes was not the sire of a family of race-horses, but rather because he is to-day recognized as one of the grandest sires that the world has yet produced, induced me to select him for comparison, and also because he was recognized as preeminently the sire of race-horses of speed and courage. The fact that no one denies the greatness of George Wilkes led me to believe that if Electioneer in comparison would show a fair mark it could not but redound to the latter's credit.

This table has not been prepared with any reference to the injury of any horse or family, for I doubt from a causal inspection, if any family would stand the comparison with Electioneer as close as the Wilkes family. The tables are published with no view of provoking controversy or calling out apologies or explanations. I simply publish the result of investigation, and with that my labor ends. It becomes then subject matter for the student who without prejudice, desires to know the the truth. The tables have been prepared from both "Chester's Manual" and "Wallace's Year-Book" and while there may be inaccuracies owing to the hundreds of columns of figures which have been necessary in its preparation, yet a careful recompilation leads me to believe in their substantial accuracy. I prefer to publish the tables complete merely for the reason that each one who may own any individual named, if a wrong has been done by me in the preparation of the figures, can easily right it. These summaries are so surprising that were I to publish them merely as summaries their accuracy would be doubted. In this compilation of the races lost and won no accounts have been taken, either with the George Wilkes family or that of Electioneer in contests against time. The contests have all either been with fields of horses or walkovers for purses in regular events and in the race average which is made up of the heats won by each horse in each seperate contest, no figures are taken into account where the time made was against the watch. The Years-Books" of 1889 performances not yet having been published will lead undoubtedly to some omissions of contests of this year.

ELECTIONEER.

Lost.	Won.	Name.	Record.	Average
1	6	Sunol	2:10½	2:22¾
7	3	Junio	2:22	2:35 5-12
8	4	Fallis	2:23	2:70 9-10
1	12	Bell Boy	2:19¼	2:33 5-6
2	5	St. Bel	2:24½	2:32 37-48
1	3	Palo Alto Belle	2:22½	2:31 4-15
2	6	Hinda Rose	2:19½	2:20 7-15
20	9	Adair	2:17¼	2:27 6-7
3	3	Bonita	2:18¾	2:20 5-12
7	20	Lot Slocum	2:17½	2:24 8-15
0	1	Maiden	2:23	2:26
2	4	Old Nick	2:23	2:26
2	3	Manzanita	2:16	2:24 2-9
0	1	Aroi	2:24	2:24½
1	4	Campbell's Electioneer	2:72½	2:35 1 15
0	2	Grace Lee	2:29½	2:34½
3	0	Stella	2:30	
		Egotist	2:29	
0	1	Emmaline	2:27½	2:31½
0	2	Ansel	2:20	2:23 1-5
2	6	Sphinx	2:28	2:30 1:14
0	1	Gertrude Russell	2:23½	2:24½
0	3	Wildflower	2:21	2:32¾
1	14	Palo Alto	2:12¾	2:22 26-37
11	8	Antero	2:16½	2:27 5-22
11	6	Antevolo	2:19½	2:28 3-5
17	11	Albert W	2:20	2:32½
2	1	Governor Stanford	2:29¾	2:30 7-12
0	6	Hattie D	2:26¾	2:42 43-44
2	2	Norval	2:17½	2:24¾
2	1	Pedlar	2:27¾	2:31½
6	1	Express	2:31	2:29 11-12
4	1	Amnoor	2:24¾	2:26¼
8	13	Morea	2:26	2:30½
1	0	Fred Crocker	2:26¼	
		Whips	2:27½	
3	1	Rexford	2:24	2:24¾
0	1	Clifton Bell	2:24½	2:26 7-12
0	1	Clay	2:25	2:31 11-12
0	4	Carrie C	2:24	2:35¾
0	2	Eros	2:29½	2:33¼
8	2	Arbutus	2:25½	2:31 1-16
4	1	Elector	2:21¼	2:33
1	3	Ella	2:29	2:32 31-3
0	1	Cubic	2:28½	2:30 1-6
1	1	Del Mar	2:30	2:32⅝
140	184		2:22 43-46 Average Record.	2:29 19-21 Average Race Rec'd

Percentage lost, 43:21-100, Percentage won, 56:79-100.

GEORGE WILKES.

Lost.	Won.	Name.	Record.	Average.
10	2	Baron Wilkes	2:18	2:29¾
16	6	J. B. Richardson	2:17½	2:29 3-10
14	6	So So	2:17¾	2:30½
7	16	Joe Bunker	2:19½	2:24½
6	4	Wilton	2:19¼	2:31 5-12
32	20	Tom Rogers	2:20	2:32 5-6
13	28	Rosa Wilkes	2:18¼	2:31 5-12
5	21	Guy Wilkes	2:15¼	2:23 1-11
22	12	Wilson	2:16¼	2:23 7-13
10	44	Harry Wilkes	2:13½	2:20 1-5
7	2	Simmons	2:28	2:31 1-24
20	5	Sister Wilkes	2:22½	2:33 3-5
8	2	Wilkes Boy	2:24½	2:30½
35	7	Young Wilkes	2:28½	2:35 3-7
14	5	Lumps	2:21	2:26 6-13
17	5	Magna Wilkes	2:29½	2:35 1-20
		Mambrino Wilkes	2:28¾	
37	27	May Bird	2:21	2:18 1-30
1	2	Miss Wilkes	2:29	2:36
7	3	Nelly L	2:28¾	2:29 5-12
6	3	Onward	2:25¾	2:31 8-9
20	5	Prospect Maid	2:18¾	2:33 1-15
2	4	Queen Wilkes	2:23¾	2:30½
13	17	Richard Wilkes	2:29¼	2:32 2-5
0	1	Rowena	2:24¾	2:31 1-6
8	5	St. Gothard	2:27	2:33 8-15
5	1	Sherman	2:23½	2:31 5-6
30	7	Albert France	2:20½	2:26 13-20
3	5	Alcantara	2:23	2:30 2:15
18	4	Alcyone	2:27	2:36 11-12
20	5	Anglin	2:27½	2:37 1-5
4	4	Blondine	2:24¾	2:49 5-8
7	1	Bob's Jug	2:22¾	2:38½
		Bonny Wilkes	2:29½	
35	16	Busbey	2:29¼	2:35
4	3	Carrie	2:29¾	2:40 5-8
24	6	Cuba	2:27¾	2:33
15	2	Daisy Wilkes	2:20	2:31 3-5
8	3	Defender	2:26	2:34 7-9
25	8	Brown Wilkes	2:21¾	2:34 19-23
8	21	Ambassador	2:21¼	2:31 5-87
9	6	Abbie	2:26¾	2:36 10-17
7	4	General Wilkes	2:21¾	2:27¾
11	2	Georgiana	2:16¾	2:31¼
6	1	Howard	2:27½	2:33¾
8	2	Kitty Wilkes	2:30	2:27½
18	3	Lizzie Wilkes	2:22½	2:31 7-9
31	12	Kentucky Wilkes	2:71¼	2:29 1-11
8	2	The King	2:29¼	2:19
30	4	King Wilkes	2:22¾	1:26 1-20
1	1	Ira Wilkes	2:28	2:34½
11	4	Isaac	2:25½	1:37
10	1	Jeff Wilkes	2:29¼	2:42
7	4	Early Dawn	2:21¼	2:24½
7	1	Ellerslie Wilkes	2:28¾	2:31½
11	8	Fanny Wilkes	2:26¾	2:40 8-9
11	0	Favorita	2:25½	
5	3	Favorite Wilkes	2:25½	2:29½
5	0	Gambetta Wilkes	2:26	
735	389		2:24 14-59 Average Record.	2:32 28-55 Average Race Re'd.

Percentage lost, 65.40 100. Percentage won 34,60 100.

The analysis of the above show that the 2:30 trotters of George Wilkes won 34,60-100 per cent. of all their races.

The Electioneer won 56,79-100 and lost 43 21-100 per cent. of all their races.

The average recods of the George Wilkes is 2.24.14-59.

The average record of the Electioneer is 2 22.24 46.

The average race time of the George Wilkes is 2 32 28 55.

The average race time of the Electioneer is 2.29.19-21.

Had the Electioneers won a large percentage of their races against inferior horses in slow time their manifest superiority would not be so great, but the table shows that in order to win a race the Electioneer had to trot nearly three seconds faster in every race than was requisite for the Wilkes to win theirs. In spite of this fact the summaries show that the get of Electioneer win 56 79 100 per cent. of all theirs.

In comparison with Electioneer my judgment is no family of great prominence will stand the test so close as the Geo. Wilkes. However as a student in horse breeding, I should be extremely grateful to any one who will publish the complete race summaries of other prominent families for the purpose of instituting comparisons, which are based alone upon absolute contests when the money is up. In this manner we can most easily determine the value of the racing abilities of any given family.—N. Y. Spirit of the Times.

Communication for Trainers and Drivers.

EDITOR BREEDER AND SPORTSMAN:—I have for several years thought that there would be saved to breeders and owners of trotting bred colts much time and expense, and to drivers in races much annoyance if, between those who break the colts and those who train and drive them in their races, there were an agreement or consistency as to the use of the words "get up," "whoa," "go on," "slack up," "take care," the "chirup," the "cluck," etc. Doubtless all agree that any one of these words should have but one meaning to the colt or horse, and that whether being broken to drive or being driven in a race it should have to him at all times the same meaning; that if the word "whoa" means that the horse stop to a standstill while walking, it does not mean that he merely go slower while trotting or walking, or that he go steadier while trotting. But if the man who breaks the colt attach to it one meaning and use it for one purpose, and the one who trains or drives him in races attach to it a different or several different meanings, the colt is hardly blamable for becoming confused in unlearning what has been taught.

I would like to ask the opinion of the BREEDER AND SPORTSMAN and also of trainers and drivers in races as to the best word to be used to a colt in breaking him for a trotter when the word is to be used for each of the following purposes: To start the colt from a standstill to a walk; to urge him from a walk to a trot; to increase his speed at the trotting or walking gait; to decrease his speed at the trotting or walking gait; to bring him from a trot to a walk; to bring him from a walk to a standstill? Also to quiet or allay his excitement while speeding; to prevent him from breaking? Hoping that I do not trouble you too much, I am yours respectfully,

C. E. FARNUM, M. D.

Dec. 26, 1889.

Horses, Cattle and Chickens.

For colic and grubs, for lung fever, cough or hide-bound, I give Simmons Liver Regulator (liquid) in one ounce doses; or, one teaspoonful of the powder in a mash twice a day. You can recommend it to any one having stock as the best medicine known for the above complaints. In using it with my chickens for cholera or gapes I mix it with the dough and feed it to them once a day. By this treatment I have lost none where the Regulator was given promptly and regularly.—E. T. TAYLOR, Agt. for Grangers of Ga.

GILROY RACES.

Ida, One of Jim Mulvena's Colts Scores a Victory.

The races which were to have been trotted the day succeeding Thanksgiving, but which were postponed on account of the inclemency of the weather, were trotted at Sargent's Driving Park, Saturday, Jan. 11th. Though there were a large number on the grounds, the crowd was evidently not in a mood for betting as very few pools were sold.

The track was heavy and a stiff breeze was blowing down the backstretch, which accounts for the comparatively slow time.

In the race for the 2:40 class, there were three entries, viz: Ida, sired by Jim Mulvena, entered by Chas. Lynch; Harry, sired by John Seven Oaks and entered by Hecox; Sutter Maid, Brigadier and entered by Jack Cocheran.

First Heat—Was won by Harry with Ida a neck in the rear and Sutter Maid third.

Second Heat—Ida first, Sutter Maid second, Harry third. Time, 2:50.

Third Heat—Ida first, Sutter Maid second and Harry third. Time, 2:51.

Fourth Heat—Ida first, Harry second, Sutter Maid third. Time, 2:46.

SUMMARY.

Ida	Chas. Lynch	2	1	1	1
Harry	Hecox	1	3	3	2
Sutter Maid	Cocheron	3	2	2	3

SECOND RACE.

The free-for-all race, for a purse of $150 closed with three entries, viz: Acrobat, Maud H. and Argent,

Maud H. won the first, second and third heats. Time, 2:37, 2:42 and 2:49; Acrobat second. Argent was withdrawn on account of sickness.

L. Loupe, Secretary.

The Doble Stable at Fresno.

During the past sixty days, travel has been almost at a standstill, the Californians displaying a most strenuous objection to making visits during the unprecedented weather with which we have been afflicted during the past two months. And it cannot be wondered at, rain almost continuously has endangered the road-bed in quite a number of places, but the company have had a small army of men at work to repair the damages as fast as the water would recede.

Taking advantage of two spare days, the writer paid a visit to Fresno, and paid a personal visit to the stable of Budd Doble, which is wintering at that superb winter training ground. Geo. Starr is Budd's right bower with the California contingent, and an able master he proves. George has been at the business for a long time, and under the best mentor in the country, so that it is not to be wondered at that "he knows a thing or two." He has gained his experience by hard knocks, and by brushing down the homestretch with Gen. Turner, Knap McCarthy, John Splan, Jimmy Goldsmith, and others of the "ilk" that are tough enough to drive an ordinary judge crazy by simply looking at the stand, and it is from the ranks of such as these that Starr has graduated until now he is a "scratch" man; able to give points to most of the Eastern drivers, and ranking with the best. He has quite a number of stalls at the Fresno Fair grounds, and many a well known favorite can be seen daily taking a "constitutional."

There is probably no place in the wide world where the fame of Johnson, 2:06¼, has not extended; at least wherever the English language is spoken, the speedy pacer is known of. His stall is fitted up as becomes the king of the side-wheel fraternity; pictures and bric-a-brac lending a charm to the eye of the visitor. Of a kindly disposition, he makes no objection to the entry of those who wanted to see him, but rather seems to enjoy the amazement of the strangers who pass remarks about his ungainly head. He may not look as handsome as Roy Wilkes or Yolo Maid, but he stands at the head of the lateral motion division as the fastest in the world.

Ed Annan is one of the curios of the Doble collection, and should have been called "Hop o' My Thumb," that is, unless the original Ed Annan is a dwarf in some dime museum. Ed Annan, 2:16½, is a rough, shaggy little creature, standing only 14.2 in height, with full rotund belly, and to all intents and purposes, enjoying the climatic change from the extreme colds of the northwestern States where he was, to the more congenial and salubrious air of Fresno, where he gets plenty of sunshine, no snow, and but little exercise. Eight times did he start during the past season, and six times did he land first money for his owner. He has been a perfect mint since he was first placed in Mr. Doble's hands, his gameness and stubborn fighting ability enabling him to win many a seemingly hopeless race. Next year he will be again to the fore in the 2:17 class, and benefited by the winter's rest, should once more repeat his victories.

The grey gelding Jack is not the model of a trotting horse, and he would not be selected by an artist to represent the ideal light harness horse of America. Still he has a record of 2:15 made in 1889, and his owner George Middleton, of Chicago has issued a challange that he will match Jack against any trotter in the world for from $5,000 to $15,000 a side.

Maria Jansen is a trim little mare, and great things are expected of her before the season of 1890 closes. The long price of $10,000 was paid for her ladyship, and it was fully expected that she would win herself out during the past season. However she will be reserved for the class where she belongs, and the trotting world may expect to hear of a big clean up with her this year.

Reina is a black mare, five years old, who has reduced her record this year from 2:27¾ to 2:22½, and there is plenty of speed still latent in her little body. She is by St. Arnaud 1519, dam Mabel L. by Victor 1963; second dam by Volunteer 55. Reina is a useful animal, and as she will be entered throughout the great circuit, we fully expect to hear good reports about her when she returns.

Faustino, the yearling son of Sidney, who cut down the stallion record for that age, has been turned over to Mr. Starr's care, and all of the hands around the stable are delighted with the young gentleman. He is a favorite, and the "boys" all claim that the two-year-old record will be in danger next season.

Maudlen is closely related to Maud S., being by Harold, 413, dam Nutala by Belmont; second dam Miss Russell: W. R. Allen, of Pittsfield, Mass., paid $15,000 for this queenly-bred mare, and although she has a record now of 2:25¾, her owner is not satisfied with that, and she will be sent for a mark commensurate with her royal breeding.

Lady Bullion is another of those bred in the purple, being by Pilot Medium 1597, dam Hattie Hoyer by Bullion 6030; second dam Gipsey Maid by Stephen A. Douglas 422. She is a good campaigner, and reduced her 1888 record of 2:21½ to 2:18¾ during last year. There are several others unknown to fame in the stable, and all of them are doing well. Mr. Starr is well satisfied with the track and its surroundings, and is quietly waiting until the weather settles so that he can move the horses at a little speedier gait than they have been asked to show lately.

Pacific Coast Horses for Circuits of 1890.

The subjoined list comprises horses with records of 2:35 and better liable to start in the several circuits on this coast during the next season. Mares retired to the harem and horses badly injured (so far as known) are not included herein. The list is printed for the benefit and convenience of the managers of fairs and trotting meetings. If, more than likely, there be omissions or mistakes in either records or breeding, we shall be thankful for any corrections that may be pointed out; or, if any of the horses herein named have been shipped away, relegated to the breeding stud, or injured, so that they will assuredly *not* start this year, we shall be grateful for information to that effect. Figures between brackets (where given) denote ages *this* year.

NAME.	SIRE.	DAM.	SIRE OF DAM.	REC.
Sunol 4	Electioneer	Waxana	Gen Benton	2:1[illegible]
Palo Alto	Electioneer	Dame Winnie	Planet	2:12
Stamboul	Sultan	Fleetwing	Hambleto'nian 10	2:12
†Favonia	Wedgewood	Federte	Abdallah 15	2:15
Lot Slocum	Electioneer	Glencora	Mohawk Chief	2:17
Lillian Wilkes 4	Guy Wilkes	Flora	Untraced	2:17
Alfred S	Elmo	Nora Marshall	Untraced	2:18
†Lord Byron	Gen Benton	May Day	Wissahickon	2:18
Sable Wilkes	Guy Wilkes	Fable	The Moor	2:18
†Faust 4	Florida	Claire	Bayard	2:18
Direct	Director	Echora	Echo	2:18
Wells Fargo	G M Patchen, Jr		Gen. Taylor	2:18
Margaret S 4	Director	May Day	C. M. Clay, Jr.	2:19
Maggie E	Nutwood		G M Patchen, Jr	2:19
Alfred G	Anteeo	Rosa B	Speculation	2:19
†Conde	Steinway	Katy Tricks	The Colonel	2:20*
Don Tomas	Del Sur	Vasuti	Mam'o Patch'n	2:20
Hazel Wilkes	Guy Wilkes	Blanche	Arthurton	2:20
Jim L	Dan Voorhees		Untraced	2:20
Franklin	Gen. Reno		Untraced	2:20
†Wanita	Aberdeen	Wyoming Belle	Lowe's Pilot	2:20
†Col. Bradshaw	Messenger Chief	Jewel	Vermont	2:20
Regal Wilkes	Guy Wilkes	Margaret	Sultan	2:20
Emma Temple	Jackson Temple		Emigrant	2:21
Express	Electioneer	Esther	Express	2:21
Mount Vernon	Nutwood		Chieftain	2:21
Alto Rex	Attorney		Brougham	2:21
Ben Ali	G M Patchen, Jr.		Untraced	2:22
Gracie S	Speculation	Jenny	Bull Pup	2:22
Gus Wilkes	Mamb'o Wilkes	Peny	Bonner	2:22
Junio	Electioneer		Granger	2:22
†Senator	Echo	Sen. Jones' Mare	Untraced	2:22
Valentine	Kent'y Clay, Jr.	Queen	Untraced	2:22
Victor	Echo		Woodburn	2:22
Carlisle	Piedmont	Isabella		2:22
Ha-Ha	Nephew	Ryan Mare	Blackhawk	2:22
†Palatina	Milton Medium	Snowflake	Snowstorm	2:22
Addie S	Algona			2:22
Alto	Altoona	Nelly	Untraced	2:22
Lorita	Piedmont	Lady Lowell	St. Clair	2:22
Richmond Jr.	A. W. Richmond		Untraced	2:22
Sport	Piedmont	Sontag Mohawk	Mohawk Chief	2:22
Steve Whipple	Chrisman's Hambletonian		Whipple Hambletonian	2:23
†Antelope	Nutwood			2:23
Gertrude Russell	Electioneer	Dame Winnie	Planet	2:23
Grandee	Le Grande	Norma	Arthurton	2:23
Arol	Electioneer	Aurora	Jno. Nelson	2:24
Fleet (3)	Sidney	Flight	Buccaneer	2:24
Rabe	Strader	Little Rose		2:24
Wanda	Eros		Elmo	2:24
†Gipsy Queen	Rushville			2:24
†Louetta	Romulus			2:24
†Spartan	Strathmore	Alla	Almont	2:24
Geronimo	Inca		Sacramento	2:24
Hazel Kirke	Brigadier	Fanny	Jim Brown	2:24
Ira	Piedmont	Irene	Mohawk Chief	2:24
J. R. (4)	Elector		St. Lawrence	2:24
Redwood	Anteeo		Milton Medium	2:24
†Uncle Jack				2:24
†Harry Velox	Velox	Albosa	Untraced	2:24
Almonta	Tilton Almont			2:25
Argent	Sterling	Madam Buckner		2:25
†Fantasia	Ranchero	Lady Kate	Toronto Chief	2:25
Lookout	Stanford		John Nelson	2:25
Nona Y.	Admiral	Flora	Black Prince	2:2[illegible]
Perihelion	Admiral	Flora	Black Prince	2:25
Pink	Inca		Echo	2:25
Ross S.	Nutwood		Naubuc	2:25
†Geo. Moshier	Strathmore			2:25
†Little Joe	Joe Bates		Untraced	2:25
Mary Lou	Tom Benton			2:25
†Stemwinder	Altamont			2:25
†Hunter	Jerry Ladd		Untraced	2:25
Alta	Altamont			2:26
Bon-Bon	Simmons	Bonnie Wilkes	Geo. Wilkes	2:26
†Gloster	Tempest			2:26
Mista	Alcazar			2:26
Little Doc				2:26
Albion	Gen. Benton	Amy	Messenger Duroc	2:26
Allorita	Altoona			2:26
Artist	McCracken's Golddust		Dave Hill, Jr.	2:26
Belle B.	Jim Hawkins		Mormon Chief	2:26
†Danger	Odd Fellow			2:2[illegible]
Eva W.	Nutwood		Naubuc	2:26
Florence R.	Nutwood		Erwin Davis	2:26
Wallace G.	Plumas		Untraced	2:26
Liliena	Altamont			2:2[illegible]
Idaho Patchen	H. B. Patchen			2:26
John Henry	Pilot Mambrino		Dan Lambert	2:26
†Lady Maxim	Maxim			2:26
Transit	Prompter	Venus	California Dexter	2:26
Old Sport				"
Blaine	Pathfinder		untraced	2:26
†Hattie D.*	Electioneer	Maple	Nutwood	2:26
Marion	Piedmont	Lady Morgan	Hambleto'n 10	2:26
Alpheus	Mamb. Wilkes	Rose	Major Mono	2:27
†Bishop Hero	Bishop	Lida Kendall	Hero of Thorndale	2:27
Flora B.	Whippleton			2:27
John'y Hayward	Poscora Ha'ward		untraced	2:27
†Lady Beach	Altamont			2:27
Moro	Pasha		Mess'n Duroc	2:27
Mortimer	Electioneer	Marin	Whip's Hamb.	2:27
Redwood	Nutwood			2:27
†Sister V.	Sidney	Nettie Lambert		2:27
Waterford	Abbotsford	Lady Softly	Speculation	2:27
Melrose	Sultan			2:27
Scandinavian	Vt. Blk. Hawk Jr.		untraced	2:27
Barney B.	Budd Doble		untraced	2:27
Lohengrin	Echo			2:27
Raymon	Simmons			2:2[illegible]
†Blondie (4)	Lemont			2:2[illegible]
Carrie F.	Erwin Davis			2:27
Jim Mulvenna	Nutwood	Jane McClane	Budd Doble	2:27
Pasha	Echo			2:27
Pedlar (3)	Electioneer	Penelope	Mohawk Chief	2:27
Don Marvin	Fallis	Cora	Don Victor	2:28
Dubec	Sultan	Madam Dey	Calif. Dexter	2:28
†James F.	Reporter			2:28
Sargent	Brown Jug			2:28
†Bertie M.				2:28
Blaine (?)	Wm's Bellfounder (?)			2:28
Daisy Gardner	Hawkeye	Peerless	Defiance	2:28
Ned Lock	Antelope			2:28
Wm. Agnew	[illegible] Franklin			2:28
Lucilla	Nephew	Lucinda	Gen. McClellan	2:28
[illegible]	Electioneer	Cuba	Imp. Austral'n	2:28
Fred B.	Tyler's Blk. Ha[wk]		untraced	"
Geranium (4)	Clm. Belmont			"
Guide	Director	Imogene	American Star	"
Hugh Patrick	unknown			"
Cora C.	Whippleton			2:28
Ed	Erwin Davis		untraced	2:2[illegible]
†Magnet*	Magnolia	Mischief	Abdallah 15	2:27
Spry	Gen. Benton	Sprite	Belmont	2:2[illegible]
Acrobat	Sterling			2:29
Dora	Gibraltar	Nelly	Black Warrior	2:29
El Monte	Echo	Lightfoot	Hubbard	2:29
Lady	Billy Norfolk			2:29
Ross	Gladiator		Consternation	2:29
Centre	Sultan	Belleview Maid	Peck's Idol	"
Col. Hawkins	Echo		untraced	"
Flora G.	Altoona	Susie	Conway's Patchen	"
Tramp	unknown			"
Balkan	Mamb'o Wilkes	Fanny Fern	Jack Hawkins	2:29
Barbero	Len Rose		Creighton	2:29
Bonanza	Arthurton	Fister	John Nelson	2:29
Clara P	Mamb'o Wilkes		Coralcon	2:29
Gossiper	Simmons	Lady Bryan	Smuggler	2:29
Lady Maud	Rockwood			2:29
Ontario				2:29
Pond Lily	G.M.Patchen Jr.			2:29
Simmocolon	Simmons	Colon	Strathmore	2:29
Vesolia (4)	Stamboul	Mez	The Moor	2:29
What Ho	A. W. Richmond			2:2[illegible]
J. C. Shelly	Hawthorne		Morgan Rattler	2:29
†Oneca	Altamont	Belle Price	Doble	2:29
Del Mar	Electioneer	Sonntag Dixie	Toronto Sonntag	2:30
Don Angus				2:30
Frank				2:30
Glendine	Judge Salisbury			2:30
I. Jay. S.				2:30
Lorena	Jim Mulvenna		Echo	2:30
Maud H	Carr's Mambrino		Dan Voorhees	2:30
G Washington (4)	Mamb'o Chief Jr	Fanny Rose		2:30
Fedora	Brigadier			2:3[illegible]
Maud Knox	Winthrop Knox			2:30
San Diego	Victor			2:30
†Altao (4)	Altamont			2:31
Stoneman	Priam			2:31
Patch Allen	G.M. Patchen Jr.			2:31
Directa (4)	Director			2:31
Jaggers (4)	Dexter Prince			"
Lee	Gen Lee			"
Mambrino Boy	Carr's Mamb'o			"
†Hailstorm	Vict's Bismarck			2:31
Bella A	Tilton Almont			2:32
†George K.	Rob't McGregor			2:32
Topsy	Brigadier			2:32
†Helen (4)	Dan Lambert			2:32

†Do not belong in the California Circuits.
*Went through California Circuits last season.

Kidd, Edmonson & Co.'s Sale.

Editor Breeder and Sportsman:—The prospect for the Great Combination Sale at Chicago of Kidd, Edmonson & Morse is exceedingly encouraging, as a great many entries are already at hand from some of the leading establishments of the country, but many of our patrons have expressed a desire that we defer our sale on account of the lateness of the season in the West, wanting more time to prepare their stock and not wishing to conflict with the Kentucky sales, and (as we hope to have everybody at the Chicago sale that attends the Kentucky sales) we have determined to change the dates, to commence March 17th and continue six days.

We hope that everyone that has entered stock with us or intends to do so, will make note of the change. If we cannot get the Exposition Building, we will sell at the Battery as before.

Buyers will likely be on hand as usual from all parts of the country; indeed, orders are coming in daily for catalogues and those wishing to enter their stock *good ones*, should do so at once.

Remember, it is the place to sell your stock and your best bred ones. Chicago is the center of demand; the money is there, the people will be there. Will you have your best stock there?

The following persons have sent entries (with many more to hear from) to the Lexington Office of Kidd, Edmonson & Morse's Great Horse Sale, to be held at Chicago, March 17th to 21st inclusive:

Mr. S. A. Brown, Kalamazoo, Mich.
Mr. F. T. Waters, Chicago, Ill.
Mr. M. L. Hare, Indianapolis, Ind.
Mr. Tom Taggarth, Indianapolis, Ind.
Mr. T. W. Browning, Indianapolis, Ind.
Mr. H. D. McKenney, Janesville, Wis.
Mr. T. C. Chadwick, Juda, Wis.
Mr. E. Remington, Fenton, Wis.
Mr. Granger Smith, Waukegan, Ill.
Mr. Lewis Cook, Lexington, Ky., one car load.

Our list will be continued next week with those from Chicago. Entries will close February 20th.

Lexington, Ky. Kidd, Edmonson & Morse.

Crawford in Kentucky.

In conversation with Mr. W. H. Crawford, soon after his return from California, he appeared well satisfied with both the horses he saw there and their owners. I remarked to Mr. Crawford that he had a close call as to losing his money, says "Hopeful" in the Spirit.

"Yes" said he, "if Stamboul has trotted as fast as he did and it had been over any one of several of our Eastern tracks my money would have been lost, as there are several managers of trotting east of the Rockies stuck on having fast records made on their tracks, and as a rule, sqeeze off a fraction but out in California they are both accurate and just timers."

"Well," said he "I don't think Stamboul can beat his previous record, 2:12½?"

"Yes" said he, "no doubt he can, and had the weather held favorable he would have done it, and I would have lost my money. I really thought I was going to lose, and when I learned that Mr Hickok was to get $9,000 if he did the trick, I said to a gentleman 'It is a consolation to know that my friend Orrin gets the money if I lose.'"

I then asked him to give me his opinion of Sunol.

"Well" said he, "she fooled me once and may do so again, but no doubt she is a most wonderfully great filly, and when she comes East next season I shall not be so ready to bet that she won't beat all records as I was to bet she would not beat 2:12. The day she trotted in 2:10½, I offered to bet $1,000 to $400 that she could not beat 2:12. Luckily no one would take so large a bet, although I lost quite well on it at that, but if the backers of time had bet freely I would have lost more than I won on the match against time. In fact, I felt confident (knowing as I did that she was not ready for such a trial), that she could not beat 2:12, and would have went broke on the result, which once for all satisfies me that truly great horses are not to be measured by the same scale that common horses are."

"Then take it all together, Mr. Crawford, you are well satisfied with your California trip are you not?" I asked.

"Well, yes I am, but there as in most places (with a wink to his friend Bowerman) those newspaper barnacles, sharks or whatever you please to call them (present company excepted) don't correctly quote an outsider. The newspapers out there stated that I said things I never had thought of."

TURF AND TRACK.

Father Bill Daly is on the sick list.

Ed. Corrigan has gone "in hibernia" at Memphis.

Allo, 2:22½, has been sold for $5,000, to go to Australia.

Five mile dash ice races in Canada will become very popular.

Jimmy McLaughlin, after all, turned out a failure as a starter.

Scott Quinton will resume business in Trenton, N. J., this season.

The first foal dropped on the Rancho Del Paso was a John Happy.

Mr. M. F. Dwyer will make a trip to England and France this winter.

The Beverwyck stable have purchased Once Again and Long Dance.

June, full sister to Nelson, 2:14½, has been bred to Antevolo, 2:19½.

'Piccolo' Jones, the well-known old time cross country jock, is dead.

W. M. Murry will send Jessie C. to be bred to imported Greenback.

Starter Caldwell had to resign the flag at Guttenberg, owing to La Grippe.

Egmont and Terra Cotta will both be used in the stud this coming season.

The Jockey Club gave at Paris, Fontainbleau and Chantilly £66,800 in added money.

When the Grand Prix de Paris was run last year $78,800 was taken in at the gate.

B. C. Holly has purchased Flora G., 2:29¼, by Altoona, dam by Conway's Patchen.

Surefoot, the favorite for the English Derby, is by Wisdom, out of a Galopin mare.

The Lexington Turf Club held a swell New Years reception and banquet on the first.

M. Bergen rode second in the first race, and won the next five last Tuesday at Guttenberg.

Hindoocraft's leg is very pronounced, and it is extremely probable he has run his last race.

Ed. Corrigan has bought from F. B. Harper the well known racehorse *Libretto*. Price, $1,500.

The shares of the Manchester (England) Race Course Company, par value £100, sell for £650.

C. M. C. Weedman has sold to W. A. Collins, of Long Island, the pacer Monkey Rollo 2:15¼.

The Italian Government has purchased Elwood Medium, 2:24¾, by Happy Medium, for $12,000.

Major Doswell, one of the old-time turfmen in America, is dangerously ill at his home in Virginia.

It is said that Marcus Daly is in such bad health that none of his horses will be trained this season.

Mr. William Rockefeller is said to have a nailing double team to go for the record at Fleetwood.

Maclure, four year old stallion, brother to Miss Leland 2:25¼, has been sold to go to Buenos Ayres.

Dr. Maclay, the new Secretary of the Sonoma and Marin Agricultural Association, is doing good work.

C. H. Todd, Dan McCarty's lucky Derby winner, died recently of blood poisoning at Sheepshead Bay.

Mr. Walton has Argent, 2:24½, at San Jose race track. He is rounding to in good shape after a sick spell.

Sorrento, Dan McCarty's unlucky cast off, is being worked again and will be in good trim in about a month.

Secretary Brewster, of the Washington Park, is again on deck. Luckily it was only a cold that troubled him.

Gregory, who won upwards of $15,000 last season, cost a few hundred dollars as a yearling, being very undersized.

The most promising yearling trotter in Kentucky is Fly Wheel, by Onward out of the dam of Nancy Hanks 2:24½.

Jas. Lee has left Mr. Charles Reed. It is said Mr. Reed was annoyed at Lee showing the horses to newspaper men.

Every one will be pleased to hear that John Mackey, the Rancho Del Paso superintendent, is rapidly regaining health.

Noah Armstrong, the owner of Spokane, is going to sell his trotting stock and breed nothing but thoroughbreds in future.

Superintendent Jim Clare will, it is said, be the permanent starter at Clifton. He has often held the flag, temporarily.

G. & C. P. Cecil, Danville, Ky., have sold Mambrino Maid, 2:23¾, for $6,000, to Messrs. Fox & Moore, Philadelphia.

Mr. Shepard of Boston has offered Knap McCarthy and the Edgewood farm, the owners of Geneva S., $10,000 for the mare.

W. Lakeland is doing well with Fordham, although the horse is said to be showing signs of the work he has undergone.

The Hermitage Stud Farm near Nashville will build a covered track this spring to exerise colts under during wet weather,

Pacers are in great favor as road horses in Hartford, Conn. During the recent sleighing half the horses used were side wheelers.

Pittsburgh Phil, accompanied by two friends, sailed on the Etruria. Garrison did not go on account of the McMahon affair.

Reno's Baby was the first Texas bred two-year-old to beat 2:30, which he did the last week in December, trotting in 2:28½.

Capt. S. S. Brown, in a recent interview, says that Troubadour is laid up for good on his farm in Oldham County, Kentucky.

Alcryon, 2:15¼, Jack, 2:15, Hendrix, 2:24¼, Ketch, 2:18½, Baroness, 2:30, Wanita, 2:24½, Frenzy, 2:27½, and Sport, 2:22¾, are all grays.

The Hon. Jas. White's health is very bad. His death would, of course, disqualify Narellan and Kirkham for the English Derby.

Buenos Ayres racing public are at a disadvantage now, the Government having put a tax of 25 per cent. on all importations of racing stock.

Orville Appleby has in training at San Jose Alfarata and Juanita, both thoroughbred, and Mr. Montgomery's highly bred trotter Boodle.

The Hon. W. F. Cody, better known as Buffalo Bill, is breeding pure bred Cleveland bays on a large scale, on his ranch in Nebraska.

In 1889, eight of the descendants of Mr. Watt's Blacklock (or as Dr. Shorthorse said "that accursed Blacklock)" have won $200,000 in England.

W. L. Boots has eight horses exercising at the San Jose race track. Nerva, Nabean, Installation, Vinco, two three-year-olds and two two-year-olds.

J. B. Perry, of Lexington, has sold for $1,000 the weanling b c Ellerton, by Eagle Bird, dam by Simmons, to T. Pollock & Son, of Bloomington, Ill.

Charles Reed's string of 19 two-year-olds, now at the Westchester race track, are said to be the finest lot of green youngsters ever seen in the East.

A mare in India was bitten by a dog and went mad. Before the mare was destroyed she tore all the flesh off her legs and sides, being raving mad.

Dan McCarty returned from Fresno last Saturday and says he shall take more of his trotters there as he was very pleased with the track and environs.

Messrs. Beck and Fisher, the owners of Florida, are having her jogged along all winter, and hope to beat the Montana three-year-old record this season.

The New Jersey Trotting Horse Breeders' Association will petition the State Legislature for an appropriation of $2,000, to be added to the premium list.

The Garrison-McMahon trouble does not get settled in a hurry. Garrison says it is a family affair. It is also rumored that the Snapper is flat broke.

Wilcox, 2:16½, will probably end his days in the South. Not long ago he won a pacing race in Alabama, stepping off three heats in 2.22, 2:18¾, 2:18¾.

In Australia bookmakers have to show a bank roll of $5,000, and get security for $5,000 more before they can get in the ring. This is compulsory.

Hiram G. Smith is much impressed with Drew Wilkes, a son of Guy Wilkes, owned in Newark, N. J., and thinks he can drive him in 2:25 next season.

Middleway, who got a record of 2:22½ at Colon, Michigan, last year, was so mean looking when young that his owner was glad to get rid of him for $100.

The Guttenberg pet, H. Penny, is rapidly discovering that Guttenberg style (get away in front and keep your whip and spurs going) is not exactly *the thing*.

Green B. Morris, who is one of the oldest and most successful trainers in the country, has moved into a new house near the Brooklyn Jockey Club track.

McCabe has 46 horses of the Dwyers at Gravesend, Albert Cooper has 13, W. Cavill 6, Ryan 5, Sweeney 6, and there are several others at the Gravesend track.

W. L. Appleby has part of his horses at San Jose and the rest at Santa Clara. Among them are Steve Stroud, Wild Oats, Raindrop, Odette and White Cloud.

W. T. Withers, o Fairlawn Farm, Lexington, has sold for $750 the weanling b c Idaho, by Almont Wilkes, dam by C. M. Clay Jr., to S. J. Odell, of Lincoln, Neb.

One of August Belmont's stables at the Nursery Stud, near Lexington, Ky., was burnt down last week; four brood mares who occupied the stable were rescued.

Patsy Duffy, the once famous Haggin jockey, is in New Orleans, a mere wreck of the brilliant horseman who rode Ben Ali and Tyrant with such rare judgment.

Oregon, who was purchased by George Walbaum at the Dwyer sale, has seriously injured himself (wrenched his fetlock joint), and probably will be unable to race again.

It is understood that one of the mares to be bred by Mr. Bonner to his new stallion Ansel, is Lucy Cuyler, who pulled a wagon in 2:15½ over Fleetwood Park track several years ago.

W. K. Vanderbilt's stables on Long Island have just been erected and fitted up at a cost of $400 000. They are English in every respect, i. e., men, boys and nearly all the furnishings.

Knapsack McCarthy says if he doesn't make a success out of Mr. Withers' cracks, it won't be for lack of opportunities. Mr. Withers has everything a trainer needs to make a horse out of.

Mr. Sibley, of Miller & Sibley, Franklin, Pa., says that Senator Stanford spent the $12,500 they gave for Electric Bell as a yearling, on the destitute children of New York and Boston.

Frank A. Jones is training three two-year-olds for Mr. Jas. Murphy, Chicago, three for Mr. Donovan, St. Louis, and several for Major B. G. Thomas. The stable is at present at Latonia.

Goldseeker, who was sent to Messrs. Tattersall's sales at Newmarket last month, had a reserve price of 250 gs placed on him, and Clairvaux 3500 gs, but no offer was made for either horse.

C. M. C. Weedman of Farmer City, Ill., Jan. 3, sold to W. A. Collins of the Fleetwood stables, Long Island, his celebrated pacer, Monkey Rollo, record 2:15¼ made at Terre Haute last summer.

Matt Dawson is said to be the first trainer in England to give short sharp spins every once and again to the horses in training, instead of the old plan of long, slow work and frequent sweats.

J. E. McDonald has concluded to sell the following named horses who are now in active training and ready to race: Bill Barnes, Brac a-Ban, Spring Eagle and a chestnut filly 5 years old by King Ban, dam Hazem.

One of the oldest and most successful stock breeders on Long Island is Mrs. Sarah A. Barnum, who ownes and manages 2000 acres. Her pride and boast is that she has never sold a colt for less than $600,

There is some discussion going on in the East as to the advisability of inviting some representative English owners to send a stable to New York, to test the relative merits of the English and American horses.

The talent seem to think that Aurania will bear watching because the Dwyers did not sell her when they weeded out the stable. She is a sister to Tremont, which may possibly be the reason she was retained.

An attempt is being made to make another Eastern trotting association comprised of Hornersville, Elmira, Binghampton, Syracuse, Phœnix and Oswego Each city has agreed to give an average of $500 a race in purses.

One of the most promising two-year-olds now in training is owned by George Waulbaum, the bookmaker. It is a gray colt by Blazes–Emma H., was purchased from D. J. McCarthy which he sold out his racing stable.

Egbert has furnished seventeen 2:30 performers this year. Belmont 11, Onward 10, Electioneer and Happy Medium nine each; Governor Sprague and Nutwood eight each, and Red Wilkes and Simmons have seven each.

It is said that Maud S 2:08¾, has 42 per cent. of thoroughbred blood; Jay-Eye-See 2:10, 40½; Sunol 2:10½ 39; Guy 2:10½, 40½; St. Julien 2:11¼, 17; Axtell 2:12, 38½; Stamboul 2:12½, 30; Palo Alto 2:12¾ 69½; Belle Hamlin 2:12¾ 18.

Senator Stanford has repurchased from the Elsmeade Stud, Elsmere foaled 1888, by Electioneer, out of Winona by Almont 33, out of Dolly, the dam of Director, 2:17; Thorndale, 2:22¼; Onward, 2:25¼, and Czarina, 2.27½.

The committee appointed by the representatives of the clubs forming the Ohio and West Virginia Fair Circuit have recommended that the circuit employ expert judges of trotting races or adopt the single judge system.

Secretary Lawrence of the Coney Island Jockey Club has issued notices that all races closing on January 2, 1890 and thereafter, at six furlongs, will be run over the Futurity course, which is now three-quarters of a mile.

The increased number of horses owned by bookmakers is getting to be a serious detraction to racing in the East; here they own and have a controlling interest in many stables, but not so openly as in the East, which is still worse.

The Brooklyn Jockey Club starts racing on May 15th, on which day the Brooklyn Handicap of $10,000 is to be run. Already there have been received more entries than last year, and everything indicates a very successful meeting.

The Hudson County Jockey Club paid the bets of the defaulting books on Wynwood, and issued a notice that in future, although they will use every precaution to prevent welching, they will only repay the original investment.

The managers of the West Side Park, Chicago, are trying to induce Joseph J. Burke, the presiding judge at Guttenberg, to serve in a like capacity at the Western track. If they succeed in getting Mr. Burke they will secure a good man.

Michael F. Dwyer, President of the New Jersey Jockey Club, and one of the owners of the famous Brooklyn racing stable, is confined to his house by a severe attack of la grippe. His European trip has been indefinitely postponed in consequence.

Mr. David Bonner says Sunol's time-killing gait is the most deceptive he ever saw. He was present when she worked a mile in California on a bad track recently in 2:17½ and he could have sworn she was not going in 2:27 till he saw the watch.

B. C. Holly took his recent purchase, Reveille, up to Vallejo last Saturday. He was very well pleased with the grey son of Shiloh, who has already got one good racehorse in Tycoon. Reveille will have a few good mares of Mr. Holly's this season.

Hernanni, 2:32½, property of J H. White, President, P C. T. H. B. A., Susie S, 2:15½, Houri, 2:17, Lunette, 2:25½, Thalia, 2:26, Count Wilkes, 2:25½ and The King, 2:29½, are among the select lot to be sold at the Woodard sale on February 17th.

Major B. G. Thomas, the veteran turfman and proprietor of the famous Dixiana Stud, has endowed a bed in the Protestant Hospital at Lexington. The ladies having charge of the institution have named the Major's gift "The B. G. Thomas Cot."

The Messrs. Du Bois and Luke Du Bois all reside in Denver, Colorado, but the veteran Luke (not the Du Bois Bros) is the owner of Muskova, 2:28½, although W. S. Hobart and W. H. Crawford are said to have tempted him with a good deal of hard cash.

C. C. Cook, of Canton, Ohio, has bought of A. Kitzmiller, of Lexington, for $4,000, these two brood mares: Mambrino Maid, fourteen years by Mambrino Patchen, dam by Mambrino Chief, and Curlew, nine years, by Almont, dam by American Clay.

Henry Walsh left for Senator Stanford's Vina Ranch last Thursday. Several well bred brood mares have been from time to time sent up there and bred to trotters. It is probable Mr. Walsh will select six or seven mares to bring back and use to breed thoroughbreds from instead of trotters.

There should most decidedly be more weight for age races. After a horse is four years old there is very little future before him except in handicaps, and by that time, if he is in honest hands, his form is so exposed that he has very little chance against the well-kept brigade.'

The grounds and property of the National Fair Association of the District of Columbia, including the Ivy City race-course, were advertised to be sold at public auction on Jan. 14th. This means that another famous race course will share the fate of Jerome and Pimlico.

During the past season at the Westchester track of the New York Jockey Club fifteen races were run over the straight course of three-quarters of a mile in 1:14 or better, and the same number were run at five-eighths of a mile in 1:01 or better, a record never before equalled.

The Helena Fair Association intend having this season, a two and three-year-old trotting stake exclusively for Montana bred colts. The association will also have a four-year-old trotting stakes, free-for-all, and intends to have a four-year-old trotting stake for Montana colts.

Mr. J. W. Gordon has at the San Jose race track, eleven head of trotters. Among them are the old stallion Henry Patchen, a brother to Big Lize 2;24½, Bismarck 2;29½, a chestnut stallion by Index, one of the last of Nutwood's California colts, and several others including Antinous.

Lord Byron 2:18 will enjoy a season in the stud, while the famous pacer, Yolo Maid 2:12½ will run out and Favonia 2:15 with others will be bred to Mascot, is the latest news of the Daly trotters. Owing to Mr. Daly's continued bad state of health none of the trotters will be campaigned.

The question of long distance racing seems settled for this year, judging from the forthcoming subscriptions. While the Toboggan Slide handicap at six furlongs received 103 entries, the Westchester Cup at a mile and a half received only 28. As a rule the shorter the race the longer the list of nominations.

Auctioneer Kellogg is lost in wonder at the magnitude of the trotting horse interest. Breeders, he says, are no longer afraid to send in their best and take chances under the hammer. G J. Hamlin is to take this course in February, and the California consignments this year will be better than ever.

Lockjaw caused the death last week, in Kentucky, of M. Walker's b c Champagne Charley three years by imported Prince Charlie, dam Triangle by Gilroy. He was a good performer, his total winnings being $14,630 in the two years he was on the turf. At one time his owner refused $8,000 for him.

George Walbaum whose success as a bookmaker has been phenomenal and who has made still more fame as one of the managers of the Hudson County Jockey Club, has recently blossomed out as the owner of quite a large stable of thoroughbreds, he believes in securing the best horses and engaging them well.

The Marquis of Ailesbury, famous or rather infamous on the English turf, has at last reached the end of his tether. His splendid estate of 40,000 acres is up for sale. He has been ruled off every race course for crookedness and is noted as a drunkard and for vicious characteristics of the most unmentionable kind.

Mr. Hogoboom has agreed not to enter Sacramento Girl for the two year old stake at the ninth annual district fair, because if she had been entered it is probable she would have frightened the rest out of the race. Last year at Rhonerville, as a yearling, the daughter of Alcazar and Viola, by Flaxtail, easily trotted in 2:56, on a slow track.

The total value of races won under Newmarket Rules in 1889 was broadly 480,000 sovs. The corresponding amounts of late years were as follows: In 1888, 413 000 sovs; in 1887, 415,000 sovs; in 1886, the same; in 1885, 426,000 sovs; in 1884, 393,000 sovs; and in 1883, 391,000 sovs. It will thus be seen that the figures have rapidly increased.

A glance at the English Racing Calendar shows that 1,623 races were run in Great Britain and Ireland in 1889, which is the largest number since 1885. At five furlongs and under six there were 793 races; six furlongs and under a mile 256; one mile 345; over one mile and under two 176, two miles and under three 42; three miles and under four 8, and at four miles 3.

Mr. John A. Morris says he has six or eight stallions and about 35 mares in Texas; he expects to have 100 thoroughbred mares there shortly. Mr. Morris also has about 20 mares in England, 15 of which are in foal to English stallions. The foals will be imported as yearlings. Most of the mares are American bred, and four had foals last year by Barnes or Tom Ochiltree.

At the meeting of the Eureka Jockey Club, held at the Western Hotel on January 8th, the following officers for the ensuing year were elected: H. M. Devov, President; J. A. Livington, Vice-president; C. G. Taylor, Treasurer; R W. Ridcout, Secretary. Directors: H. M. Devoy, W. S. Clark, T. F. Ricks, Dan Murphy, J. Livingston, R. Gross, P. H. Quinn, S. F. Pine and F. A. Cutler.

Mr. Corlett in the 'Pink Un' says that Ormonde will be put into training again at Buenos Ayres, prior to going into the stud. It is to be hoped this is not correct, for the magnificent race horse whose escutcheon was never tarnished, might possibly suffer defeat under the circumstances. Horses who have enjoyed stud life have rarely proved successful when put back on the turf.

Edward Laferty is at Pleasanton with Mr. Kirkendall's trotters, which he brought from Montana. Among them are Lady Maxim 2:26, and several promising green horses. Mr. Laferty also brought Mary Eagle (the dam of Ranchero 2:21½) by American Clay 34, Dolly 2:32 by Mambrino Diamond 2:26, out of a mare by Clark Chief Jr., the dam of Rolla 2:24, and several other brood mares to be stinted to Director.

European buyers of fast horses are finding out that it pays to have competent trainers and drivers, as well as blooded stock. It is necessary to have a handler who knows not only how to drive horses but also to balance, feed and do them up after their races. Barney Stanford, who is now on the Atlantic with Gypsy Queen and Lottie W, two of last season's prominent performers, is likely to impress the lesson even more thoroughly.

Theodore Winters has not entered his famous colts, El Rio Rey and Rey del Rey, in any of the stakes to be run in the East this spring, though he has entered them largely for the Fall meetings. The stable will begin racing in the West at Nashville and Memphis, where stake races are of no more value that the purse races of the East. The policy of Mr. Winters in starting his youngsters in the West under the circumstances is one of the mysteries of the turf.

Glanders is an infectious, incurable disease, which the horse may even communicate to man and other animals. In England, it is less common than it was once, probably owning to the better application of the laws that forbid the sale of a glandered horse, and make his owner liable for damages caused by his existence. In this country there is no law in this direction, any man being allowed to harbor a glandered horse.

Professor Brewer of New Haven, in a recent lecture on the horse, denies that the English thoroughbred is an Oriental horse. Since 1790, the beginning of pedigrees and pure breeding, it is the horses of known pedigree that have raked in the most money. Old King Hamet begot 494 winners and won over £200,000 for his owners. One-forty seems to be about the time limit, and the most we can do now is to increase the number and improve the general all-round horse.

George Walbaum, the well known bookmaker, who has been getting together a fine stable of race horses, has secured the services of Martin Bergen as his chief jockey for this year. It is said that Bergen will receive a retainer of $5,000 besides pay for his mounts. James McLaughlin, the erstwhile famous jockey, has assumed his duties as trainer at Pierre Lorillard's Jobstown farm. He has a string of thirty-eight two-year-olds to begin work with, many of them being well bred. Most of them have been tried with George Taylor and "Spider" Anderson in the saddles.

A good deal of correspondence is going on just now in some of our British sporting contemporaries anent the cause, apparent or imaginary, of the unpopularity of steeplechasing, and the falling off in the class of horses entered. All sorts of suggestions have been made, and there is no doubt that this branch of sport requires a thorough remodelling. *Apropos* of the discussion, it turns out that of the thirty-nine members of the G. N. H., only five own cross-country horses, and of these five gentlemen, only one owns horses of any importance.

The annual meeting of the Sonoma County Agricultural Park Association was held last week. The indebtedness of the Association was announced as $900; the property is valued at $25,000. The following directors were elected: Guy E Grosse, B. M. Spencer, J. H Laughlin, I. de Turk, Julius Ort, S. I. Allen and C. A. Wright. The following officers were elected: President, Guy E Grosse; Vice-President, J. H. Laughlin; Treasurer, W. L. Borris; Secretary, B. M. Spencer. The Directors were not in favor of holding races this season unless the citizens show more appreciation and a livelier interest in them than they have heretofore.

The trainers and jockeys employed in the various racing stables have organized a society for mutual benefit. The object of the association is to raise a fund for the care of jockeys or trainers who may be injured in the discharge of their business, so that appeals for charity will not have to be made to race-goers. The officers of the association are James McLaughlin, President; William Lakeland, Vice President; W. P. Ward, Treasurer; A. H. Langley, Secretary; and John H. Smith, Recording Secretary. In order to make a good starting fund, the association will give a ball at Tammany Hall on Friday evening, Feb. 7, tickets for which are now being sold in goodly numbers at $1 each. The society is one with an excellent purpose and deserving of the encouragement of all racing people.

It is probable that H. R. H. the Prince of Wales will next season race on a far larger scale than he has hitherto done, and his interests will in all probability be closely connected with those of his friend Baron de Hirsch. As a matter of fact, the Prince of Wales and Baron de Hirsch are on terms of great intimacy, and whether the Duke of Westminster's horses are removed to Newmarket or not, it may be safely wagered that the Prince and the Baron will henceforth race on a more extensive scale. In the place of two or three horses each has hitherto had under the care of John Porter, some ten or a dozen will represent each owner next season. Early in January the Prince visits Baron de Hirsch at Merton Hall, Thetford, which the Baron has taken on a short lease from Lord Walsingham.

The claim made by the admirers of the Pacific Slope for perfect development of horses has says the Sporting World, received another indorsement from the lips of Robert Bonner, who recently paid his first visit there. Speaking of the development of horses in California he says: "The youngsters can grow there from Jan. 1 to Dec. 31 and there is no drawback on account of the weather. Up at my farm for several months in each year the cold weather retards the growth of young stock very materially, no matter how liberal the feed may be or how much care is bestowed. In California on the contrary, the weather favors the growth of stock continually, and a yearling there is like ours here at two years old."

Most Pacific Coast athletes and sporting men know McComb, Skinner and Kittleman. Archie Mccomb is stated to have cleared about seven thousand dollars on the job race said to have been run by M. Kittleman and Ed. Skinner at Wichita, Kansas, recently. It appears that "Kit" agreed to lose, and thereupon a sporting man named Stirling, who thought he had both ends and the middle safe, wagered about ten thousand on the certainty. But the ways of the sprinter are not always straight, and as Kittleman ran the race out on Skinner, Stirling was done out of his good money, which was probably whacked up by the principals. Billy Trenane is said to have lost about $5,000 and John McFarlane $4,000, but as both were willing to profit by what they thought was a squared race, the public of that section do not feel much sympathy for them.

The argument against long distance racing is put in a nutshell by a well-known turfman: "In order that the betting privileges of our race tracks may be made salable, they must be made valuable; in order to make them valuable, we must bring large fields to the post. Large fields make heavy betting, and consequently big profits for the bookmakers. In races under a mile we have no trouble in getting from 12 to 20 starters. As the distances increase, the fields decrease, the betting falls off, business is dull in the ring, and the bookmakers growl, turn their slates and threaten to retire. With big fields a stand is worth $100 a day; with small fields in which there is usually a top-heavy favorite, it is not worth half as much. There's the rub. The clubs must encourage big fields, in order to keep the bookmakers."

"Bras de Fer," in the London World, says: "I do not share in Lord Durham's fears that the large gate-money meetings may one day shake off the authority of the Club and become a law unto themselves; for I believe that that authority is too firmly established to be shaken, unless by some ill-judged action or abandonment of duty on the part of the Club not likely to occur. His plea for their meetings being held in public, so far as the admission of representatives of the Press to them, will probably meet with general approval outside the Club. I have grave doubts, however, about the inside. His little remark about the fear lest the Jockey Club should become a 'mutual admiration society', was distinctly good, and I can only hope that what he and Lord Downe said as to the atmosphere of the Turf having never been purer or healthier than now is true."

James B. McMasters, Secretary of the Deer Lodge Fair and Racing Association, Deer Lodge, Montana, writes: The Deer Lodge Fair and Racing Association is now upon a firm footing. All necessary additions to the present buildings will be made. The track, which is a full mile, will be put in excellent condition, and it is the intention of the management to spare no expense to make the meeting of 1890 the the most successful one ever held in the county.

Directors: J[illegible] F. Strauhal, W. N. Aylesworth, N. J. Bielenberg; John Bielenberg, President, Joseph Lodge, Vice-President; C D. Joslyn, Treasurer; James B. McMasters, Secretary.

The Directors meet and set the dates for meeting of 1890 as follows: July 14, 15, 16, 17, 18 19. Messrs. Bielenberg and Lodge were appointed a committee to get up the speed programme. It is expected that the purses will be worth $6,000 altogether.

News from the various racing associations having stakes closing on January 1, indicates a falling off in the number of entries received, except for those of the Brooklyn Jockey club, which just about holds its own, although for each club there is still time for more nominations at different points to be heard from. Quite a well grounded opinion appears to exist among secretaries and others who have to do with the management of the larger racing meetings in this part of the country, that a falling off in entries for the fixed events is only a natural result of the times. Not so much because of their multiplied number although that might reasonably be supposed to have some influence, as because of the greatly increased value of the purses. As the secretary of one of the most prominent jockey clubs said: "Why should owners enter in advance for these stakes when they can run for purses of $1,000, the entrance money added to which makes them worth nearly that amount to the winner alone, while second receives $200, and the third $100 in many instances?"

Garrison's legal troubles with the McMahon family caused him to postpone his departure for England. It is generally understood that Garrison is short of money, a condition of affairs due no doubt to plunging on the races at Clifton and Guttenburg. In the summer the "Snapper" landed on many good things, and prospered amazingly. A friend inquired one day why he did not ride oftener, and the reply was: "Oh, I don't need to ride; I can beat 'em on the outside." This beating 'em on the outside has at last beat him. Jockeys who play the races pick about as many losers as the average bettor. No jockey should bet except on his own mounts. Garrison's admirers supposed he was making at least $20,000 a year, and the statement that on a recent occasion he was obliged to borrow pocket money to attend the races caused great surprise. The only jockey in America who has held fast to any considerable part of his earnings is the colored rider Isaac Murphy, who is said to own property valued at over $100,000. W. Donohue, not the least thrifty person in the world, could draw a check for $10,000 without wiping out his bank account. McLaughlin was rich once, but if report be true, is now, comparatively speaking, a poor man. Hamilton made a great deal of money last year, but squandered most of it. Hayward has a comfortable home near Eatontown, N. J., and lives well, but is not excessively rich. As a rule, jockeys earn their money so easily that they do not know its value.

The Hon. James White, who is striving to win the English Derby, is deserving of great commendation for his enterprise. A few lines about his turf career may not be out of place. Mr. White, as a young man, although fond of a bit of sport, did not take any active part in the racing of his native colony, New South Wales, and it was not until about twelve or thirteen years ago that he commenced racing in a small way with a steeplechaser named Hotspur, who more than once carried the blue and white to victory. With Goulburn, too, he was successful in steeplechases; and on the flat he gained triumphs with Democrat and The Pontiff; but it was with Chester that his name became well known in connection with racing in Victoria. The success of the great son of Yattendon in the V. R. C. Derby and Cup whetted Mr. White's appetite, and he longed for further triumphs. He then determined to establish a stud for himself, and selected a most suitable spot near Kirkham, close to the town of Camden, where in the old days the famous Macarthur flocks and herds occupied the pastures in the vicinity. When Chester retired from the turf he was selected as the lord of the harem, and Mr. White, having made a trip to England, selected there a few mares for his stud. In choosing the mares that were to form the nucleus of the Kirkham stud, Mr White displayed splendid judgment. He stuck to the good old plan of making his selections from families that had proved successful in the home of the thoroughbred, and the successes which have attended the descendants of these mares are sufficient corroboration of the wisdom of the colonial sportsman's action. In other ways Mr. White displayed admirable judgment. His purchase of Martini-Henry, Trident, Matchlock, Nordenfeldt, etc., showed that he had an eye for a good yearling, and his double triumph with the first named in Derby and Cup resulted in the addition to his exchequer of something over £25 000, while the victories of Trident, Matchlock and Nordenfeldt also brought plenty of grist to the mill. His successes on the turf have been too numerous to recapitulate; suffice it to say that nearly every important race in Australia has been won at some time or other by horses carrying his colors. The Australasian, from which the above is taken, adds, "His determination to beard the British lion in his den has aroused the enthusiasm of his countrymen, who admire his pluck in sending horses to England to prove that we can breed them as well here as they can in the old country. All going well, Mr. White will, after next year, have them trained and ridden by Australians, and he has, I believe made arrangements for Tom Peyton to go to England to prepare the colts for their Derby of 1891. Every Australian will, I am sure join with me in wishing him success in his patriotic venture."

ATHLETICS.

Athletic Sports and Other Pastimes.

EDITED BY ARPHIPPUS.

SUMMARY.

Unfortunately for the out-door athletes, the storm has commenced again, and as we go to press the indications for a prolonged spell are very pronounced. One hope, however, lurks in the breast of the athlete, and that is that when the weather really settles a very dry and pleasant season may be anticipated. The continued rain will sadly interfere with the arrangements of the Olympic and Alpine Clubs for their coming out-door meetings.

RUNNERS, WALKERS, JUMPERS, ETC.

Owing to the inclement state of the weather it has been an utter impossibility for the runners and walkers to take out door exercise. Two very important field meetings will take place within five weeks, and the amateurs will be compelled to enter the games in an untrained condition unless the weather modifies within the next few days.

Captain Jordan of the Olympic Club, is apparently satisfied that Buchanan, the latest addition to the club's roll of champions, will easily defeat McKinnon of the Alpine Club in the championship games on May 30th.

S. V. Cassidy is determined to duplicate his victory of last year by winning the two hundred and twenty yards run on May 30th. With proper training, there is no reason why this popular young sprinter should not be successful in his undertaking.

Owing to press of business, Walter A. Scott will be unable to train during the coming season. He holds the one mile running record, and the athlete who beats Scott's time will certainly prove himself to be a good man.

Carpenter, who took second place in the high jump at the championship meeting two years ago, has retired from the athletic world. He has a record of 5 feet 8 inches.

Owing to ill health William Zephus will not train for the coming games.

Foster, the hurdle racer, has resigned from the California Athletic Club and applied for admission to the Olympic Club. He should take second place on May 30th.

F. L. Holland, also of the California Athletic Club, will resign in the near future and lend his valuable aid to the Alpines.

The California Club is now without an out-door amateur, and the probabilities are that the annex will disband. In selecting Philo Jacoby as President, the amateurs of the club made a grave error. As a marksman Mr. Jacoby is certainly a success, but as President of an amateur athletic club he is not. No person can dispute the fact that Philo Jacoby possesses average ability and that he is ambitious, but he has painfully proven to the young athletes whom he governed that his thoughts were in the neighborhood of the targets at Harbor View when they should have been in the California Club, in the midst of its amateur athletes. The athletes looked up to him for aid but he was powerless to help them, as he was satisfied to be ruled himself by the regular directors of the club. This is where the Golden Gate and California Clubs are at fault, in allowing the officers of their professional branches to have full jurisdiction over their amateur annexes.

H. C. Cassidy, of the Alpine Amateur Athletic Club, is highly pleased at the introduction of a two-mile handicap run at the Olympic games which will take place Feb. 22nd Those who have seen him run in private say that he is fully able to lower the existing coast record without training an hour.

John D. Garrison, of the Alpine Athletic Club, promises to do well in the next games. In the running broad jump and in the one hundred yards run he will be heard from especially.

Phil Moody and M. C. Giry will train hard for the half mile run, and both men will be well up at the finish.

In the person of James Jarvis, the Olympic Club has a splendid athlete, and on Decoration Day his valuable assistance will be of much account. The position which he holds at present, and which he did not obtain through the influence of his club, renders it impossible for him to train owing to the long hours which he is compelled to work, and if the rich and influential members who pretend to take such an active interest in the athletic welfare of their club, would only exert themselves just a little bit, they might be able to procure a much better and easier position for Mr. Jarvis, who is a perfect stranger in the city, and whose absence at the championship games might mean defeat to the Olympic Club.

E. Sullivan, of the Alpine Club, promises to develop into a first-class hammer thrower.

The Acme Athletic Club, of Oakland, will be represented by two or three good men at the championship games.

The friends of C. B, Hill regret that they will not have a chance to see him compete against Jarvis, as Mr. Hill has fully made up his mind to remain off the cinder track.

The field captain of the Olympic Club through the medium of a local daily paper gave it as his opinion that without the aid of John Purcell and Victor E. Schifferstein, the Olympic Club would have no trouble in winning the championship pennant of 1890. While admitting that Mr. Jordan is a hard worker in the interest of his club, we will say that he might be somewhat less positive about the ability of his team. It is very poor policy on the part of Mr. Jordan to affirm that the club could get along without the aid of Purcell and Schifferstein. Further argument on the subject is unnecessary, as it is generally known that without the assistance of the two athletes in question, the Olympic Club would have been badly defeated last May. Moreover, Mr. Jordan seems to think that only one athletic club should exist, as he evidently ignores the existence of the Alpine Amateur Athletic Club. Good natured rivalry amongst the athletes is all very well in its way, but when it comes to bad feelings, then the line should be drawn. The Alpine Club was not organized to down the Olympic Club as a club; it was started solely for the purpose of downing prize-fighting institutions, and for upholding amateur athletics. We hope the ill-feeling at present existing will blow over, and that on February 22d all the athletes will join hand in hand, and in a manly and good-natured way strive to defeat each other in the different events.

A local illustrated weekly sporting paper, lately sprung into existence, in its last issue censures the officers and members of the Alpine Athletic Club for not opening their games which are announced to take place on February 16th. A senseless argument is no argument at all, and the editor of the paper referred to used very poor judgment when he wrote the article. How can it be expected that a new club only three or four weeks organized, could offer prizes for an open athletic competition? Irrespective of this, the editor must have been fully aware of the fact that the main object of the club was to offer to its members inducements which no other club on the Pacific Coast ever dared to do. In offering prizes for monthly competition amongst its members, the Alpine Amateur Athletic Club had a two-fold object in view. In the first place, monthly games are likely to keep the members in constant practice, so that in open competition they will be in first class trim. In the next place it will benefit athletes who are too modest to compete against cracks, but who are willing to contest with their fellow members. Having interviewed the officers of the Alpine Club, we are able to state that the club intends to be more liberal than either the University or Olympic Clubs. After the initial games, which will take place on Sunday, February 16th, the Alpine Club will open three or four events each month to members of clubs belonging to the P. C. A. A. A.

The old-time athletes will regret to learn that the "dear old" Bay District track is about to be cut up into building lots. The memory of many pleasant evenings spent on the good old track will never die out, and in years to come the boys will smoke their pipes and talk of the good old times when they trained at the Bay District track.

AT THE OARS.

The Alpine Amateur Athletic club was admitted into the Pacific Rowing Association at the last meeting of that body. A grand jollification will be held at the club grounds at Harbor View about the end of April.

Owing to the wet weather the boats at the different club houses remained dry on Sunday last. The crews remained in-doors and discussed future events.

The Lurline club elected several new members at its last meeting.

The Pacific Rowing Association held its annual meeting in Irish-American Hall last Wednesday evening. Representatives of the Ariel, Alpine, Dolphin, Lurline and Pioneer Clubs were present. As officers for the year Leo Heringi was elected President; W. H. Growney, first Vice-President; P. J. Burnam, second Vice-President; H. O. Farrell, Secretary; and G. W. Van Gueiph, Treasurer. The committee on regatta was named as follows: Ariel Club, E. Flanders; Alpine, L. P. Bean; Dolphin, A. P. Rathkoff; Lurline, M. Hanley; Pioneer. W. C. Espy; South End, John Trainor. An Executive Committee was appointed, consisting of W. H. Growney, Ariel Club; Tony Russell, Dolphin; Fred Tauffenbach, Lurline; John Doherty, South End; B. Tank, Alpine; P. H. McDonnell, Pioneer. Some alterations were made in the constitution and by-laws and the association adjourned.

THE WHEELMEN.

Like the runners and walkers, the wheelmen are disgusted at the weather. Should the rain continue much longer several new "house trainers" will have to be ordered as the ones now in use are getting worn out.

The different teams are now ready for the drill. It is expected that the affair will be a grand success

The ladies cycling club will be organized early in the spring.

The medals awarded the winners at the races at the race meet which was held at the Napa on Thanksgiving Day are splendid specimens of the Jewelers art.

A regular meeting of the Bay City Wheelmen will be held on Monday evening next.

UNIVERSITY JOTTINGS.

A pair of parallel bars has been erected in the gymnasium.

A horizontal steel bar, 54 feet long, has been erected extending from one end of the room to the other.

There is a large attendance at the gymnasium daily, as the majority of the outdoor men are already reducing their fat, preparatory to regular training for the coming Olympic games.

The students, knowing that the O. A. C. will not have the assistance of Purcell and Schefferstein at the next champion games, are fully bent on the carrying of the flag. Every student who is anything of an athlete will train for the occasion, and it is an assured fact that the college yell will be heard many times during the day.

It is expected that the inter-collegiate record of 22 ft. 6 in. for the running broad jump will be broken during the season.

The athletic editor of "The Occident," a paper published weekly for the benefit of the students at Berkeley, thus speaks of the Olympic Club: "According to one of the city papers, the O. A. C. rejoices at the formation of another athletic club, as it promises to give them some opposition in the coming games. It is very well for the O. A. C. to pretend to ignore the existence of the U. C., but they cannot hide this fact, that they morally fear us in the coming championship, and they are ready to move heaven and earth to prevent us from securing the pennant this year. We gave them all the opposition they desired last year, and if our men will only make sufficient effort we will certainly defeat them this time."

The Olympic Club will possibly hold its Washington Birthday games on the campus, as the rain will prevent the club from having its own grounds ready by that date.

An effort will be made to have the fence enclosing the tennis court removed while athletic games are being held.

The cinder track is in a terrible condition.

JOTTINGS FROM ALL OVER.

We clip the following from the New York Sun:—

An idea is prevalent that trained athletes are shortlived. Whether this be true or not, the case of T. P. Conneff, the amateur five-mile champion of America, would, from this point of view, be a subject for interesting investigation to physicians. A Sun reporter called at St. Vincent's Hospital yesterday morning and was admitted to Mr. Conneff's room. He found the patient suffering somewhat from difficulty in breathing. He seemed to be in a sort of lethargic state, and found it troublesome to talk. He was also quite deaf, and the reporter was obliged to talk in a loud voice to make him hear. Upon asking him if there was anything he would like to say about his sickness, he said: "I have nothing to say except that I feel much better, and hope it won't be long before I am out again, but it will probably be a long time before I can run in races. When I was taken sick about the first of this month, I became deaf, and I find it very hard to hear anything. I don't know what the trouble is, but I think it is in the lungs; the doctors won't tell me anything about it. The trouble came on gradually; and I don't know what the cause was." From his appearance Conneff looks as though there was a good chance of his recovery. He did not appear to be wasted, and his face was no thinner than is usually the case with a trained athlete, but his voice was very weak, and not to annoy him further the reporter said good-by and departed. Tommy Conneff is very popular among his club mates and much interest is taken in his condition. He came to this country from Ireland in the spring of 1881 and joined the Manhattan Athletic Club. In 1886 he won the one mile championship of Ireland in 4 minutes 32 3-5 seconds. In 1887 he won the four mile championship of Ireland in 2[illegible] minutes 55 4-5 seconds. In 1888, as a member of the M. A. C., he won the same championship in 20 minutes 46 seconds and in the same year he won the English one mile championship in 4 minutes 31 3-5 seconds, the N. A. A. A. A. championship at the same distance in 4 minutes 32 2-5 seconds and also the five-mile championship of the N. A. A. A. A. After the amalgamation of the two associations last summer he won the five mile championship in 26 minutes 42 seconds.

The third annual midwinter indoor games of the Athletic Association of the University of Pennsylvania, to be held at the Philadelphia Academy of Music on February 1st, will include the following events: Forty yards dash, scratch. 440 yards dash, handicap, 20 yards limit. Half mile run, handicap, 40 yards limit. Mile run, handicap, 80 yards limit. Running high jump, handicap, 6 inches limit. 220 yards hurdle race, 8 flights, 2 feet 6 inches, handicap, 15 yards limit. tug-of-war, 625 pound teams. 440 yards dash, scratch for Interacademic Athletic Association of Philadelphia, and Interscholastic Athletic Association of New York. There will also be several bouts of wrestling. All members of the Amateur Athletic Union will be allowed to compete. E. C. Carter of the New York Athletic Club will act as handicapper, and George Turner of Philadelphia as starter. Entries will close with Thomas G. Hunter, Drexel Building, Fifth and Chestnut streets, on January 23rd.

Albert Beers of Boston, who won the Adams mileage medal, is credited with having ridden 9,000 miles this season up to date. These figures surpass the record of George Nesbitt of the New York Club, who held the record previously with 8,-261 miles to his credit for one year's riding.

W. P. Page, the champion high jumper of the world, states that a man can clear two or three inches higher in the open air than he can in the gymnasium. On two different occasions Page cleared 6 feet on boards, and in a day or two after he jumped 6 feet 3 inches at an open air athletic meeting.

OLYMPIC GAMES.

The following is the programme of games to take place on Washington's Birthday:

1. 100 yds novice race, O A C members.
2. 100 yds, handicap, run, open.
3. 100 yds, handicap, run, open.
4. 220 yds, handicap, run, open.
5. 440 yds, handicap, run, open.
6. 880 yds, handicap, run, open.
7. 2 miles, handicap, run, open.
8. 1 mile, handicap, walk, open.
9. 120 yards, handicap, hurdle, open.
10. 100 yards, handicap, run for Directors of the O A C.
11. 100 yards handicap, run for Juvenile members of O A C.
12. Tug of war between married and single members. 850 lbs limit.
13. Running high jump, handicap, open.
14. Pole vault, handicap, open.
15. 440 yards run for Hammersmith medal.
16. 100 yards partnership race, open.

The programme is subject to change. Entries will close at the Olympic club rooms on Feb. 12, 1890 at 8 o'clock P. M. sharp.

Only members of clubs belonging to P. C. A. A. A. will be allowed to compete in the games.

Two very important events putting the 16lb. shot and throwing the hammer have been omitted from the programme why we are unable to say. We hope that when the athletic committee meets again they will include the two events mentioned.

BLUB JOTTINGS.

The Alpine Amateur Athletic Club has applied for admission to the Pacific Coast Amateur Athletic Association.

Great preparations are being made for the "Ladies Night" which will take place at the Olympic club rooms towards the end of the present month.

Over two tons of seats were shipped to Harbor View on Tuesday last for the grounds of the Alpine Athletic club. A grand stand suitable for the accommodation of 1500 people will be built at once.

We are in receipt of the following communication:

ARPHIPPUS, BREEDER AND SPORTSMAN—

Dear Sir: Through your valuable and influential columns, I would like to state that the Pacific Athletic Club applied to Mr. J. J. Jameson, Secretary of the P. C. A. A. A. to be allowed to see the copy of its Constitution and By-Laws in his possession, but Mr. Jamison stated that he was unable to find the copy. Now I think it is high time that some action was taken by the different clubs in regard to the management of the P. C. A. A. Of what use is the association if its officers fail to attend to their duties? At present only one or two meetings a year are held, whereas at least one meeting a month should be held. Respectfully yours,

M. C. GIRY.
President P. A. C.

ANSWERS TO CORRESPONDENTS.

G. H. L.

What salary does the official handicapper of the American Athletic Union receive, and what is his name?

Does the official handicapper of the Olympic Athletic Club of this city receive any remuneration?

Answer.—Mr. E. C. Carter, the official handicapper of the American Athletic Union, is paid a salary of $1,500 per annum.

2. Mr. George W. Jordan, the official handicapper of the Olympic Club of San Francisco, so we have been informed, receives about $30 a month remuneration.

Wire fences, although not constructed of barbed wire, are the cause of a great deal of complaint among the fox hunters of England. Lord Willoughby de Brake, master of the Warwickshire Hunt, has informed the Southern Farmer's Club that unless the wire fences are taken down in winter the hunting will be stopped Since the present season began his wife has been nearly killed, his first whip injured and two horses severely torn in consequence of this objectionable system. Other masters of the hunt have announced in different countries that there can be no hunting where the wire fences are kept up in winter.

The bay colt Champagne Charlie, foaled 1888, by imported Prince Charlie, dam Triangle, by Gilroy, property of M. Walker, died in Fayette County, Ky., from lockjaw, on the night of December 31st. He was a good two-year-old but failed to sustain his reputation at three.

Grim's Gossip.

There will be racing at the Oakland track to-morrow. I wonder if Stover and his gang have caught another of the sucker brigade.

James D. Snowden died at St. Mary's Hospital, San Francisco, on the 9th of last month. He was known to nearly all the horsemen of the State.

Mr. Baldwin's wonderful little race mare Los Angeles has been entered in all the principal Eastern events, and 1890 will again see her battling with the giants of the turf.

Owing to the excessive weight of snow on the grand stand at Glenbrook Park, Nevada County, that building broke down a few days ago, entailing a serious loss on the association.

In order to increase the entry list in the three-year-old trotting stake offered by W. P. Fine, of Petaluma, Captain Ben E. Harris has agreed not to enter his black filly Lorena therein.

The Sire Bros. have been trying to purchase some of the Irvin Ayres stock, but wished to exact a condition that the horses should be landed in New York. Mr. Ayres would not accede to the demand so the sale is off.

Alfred G. will stand during the season of 1890 at the farm of R. B. Metcalf on the Harrodsburg Pike, about one mile from the Lexington Fair Grounds. He will be under the charge of J. W. Knox, and the service fee will be $200.

I see by an exchange that Dr. Aby has been made a director of the Lake County Agricultural Association It is about time that one horseman was a member, for in the past there has been a lamentable amount of ignorance shown up there.

I saw a fine-appearing young colt in Fresno last week called Buccaneer Jr. He is the property of James Waterman, and can show a full mile in 2:25. His pedigree is given as by Buccaneer, dam Mountain Maid by Kentucky Gold Dust.

Mr. Sibley, of Miller & Sibley, Franklin, Ia., is authority for the statement that the $12,500 they gave Hon. Leland Stanford for the yearling colt Electric Bell, was spent by the California millionaire on the homeless children of New York and Boston.

We have to acknowledge the receipt of a very fine lithograph of Nutwood 2:18¾ which has been sent to this office by the Stout Bros of Dubuque, Iowa It is a faithful representation of the old horse and has been given a position of honor in the BREEDER AND SPORTSMAN picture gallery.

Colonel R. S. Strader, Lexington, Ky., has sold to W. S. Hobart of this city, at a long price, the four-year-old chestnut filly Nola by Nutwood, 2;18¾, dam Belle Bowman, by Bowman's Clark Chief; second dam Belle Hook, by Almont; third dam by Alexander's Bay Chief; fourth dam by Davy Crockett, pacer.

In the list of horses with trotting records better than 2:20, we find that The Pleasanton Stock Farm Company own five head Director, 2:17; Nellie R. 2:17½; Monroe Chief, 2:18¼; Direct. 2:18½; and Margaret S., 2:19½, which is more than is owned by anyone man or company in the United States. They also own the pacers Gold Leaf 2:11½, and Corette 2:19.

Mr. Peter Wood, the well know driver and trainer from Chicago is now in this city, and is open for engagements to train, and drive. He is well recommended by well known horsemen in the East and can be heard of by calling at the BREEDER AND SPORTSMAN office. Having had about twenty years experience, he would be invaluable on this coast.

I am well pleased to hear that Contention, J. H. White's Director colt, stands a very fair show of going inside the "twenty" list next season. He was taken some time ago to Pleasanton, and Andy McDowell has been giving him a sort of special preparation, and the effect of education is beginning to show. He can rattle off quarters very fast, and is taking kindly to his work.

As almost everyone knows Billy Donothan has taken charge of the thoroughbreds at Senator Hearst's ranch and will prepare a number of them for a Western campaign. If the Blood Horse meeting is not delayed too late, Billy will in all likelihood bring a number of racers to the Bay District track, and there pick out the best of the lot and take them back to St. Louis, Louisville, Memphis, Nashville etc.

Lillian Wilkes 2:17½ was a great favorite, for the short time she was on the circuit last year, and there can be no reasonable doubt but that she would have reduced her mark considerably if accident had not overtaken her. Mr. Corbitt informs me that the great young filly is once more all right, and that she will be seen again this year ready to give anything on the circuit a fight for first honors.

Scott Quinton has returned to Trenton, N. J., from Montana, where he handled Mark Daly's trotters the past season. M. Daly's health continues bad, and it has been decided not to start any of his horses in 1890. Mascot will be bred to a few mares, one of which will probably be Favonia, and Lord Byron, who took a four-year-old record of 2:18, will also be given a chance in the stud. Yolo Maid, the great pacer, will enjoy a run at grass.

The great California filly Margaret S will again be seen on the Eastern circuit next year, She is entered in the Great Expectation Stake at Chicago, and also in the Four-year-old Stake at Independence. Iowa, which Axtell Williams has instituted. In both of these races she will have to meet Allerton, 2:18¼ and then there will be a race, California against Iowa, 2:19½ against 2:18¼. May the best and fastest win.

There seems to be a dangerous disease among the horses in some portions of Indian Valley. It is reported that about two weeks ago Mr. Droge lost a couple of animals. Mr. Cadie has lost two and has more sick. Word comes from Taylorsville, also, that Mr. Hardgrave has lost his fine Norman stallion, "Dodu." This loss is quite serious, perhaps $1,000. The disease appears to be some kind of a distemper which has a marked effect on the nervous system.

Harrison Jones and Charles Kerr on Monday made up a stallion race to be run for $500 a side on January 27th, either at the Stockdale ranch or on the old race track between the two towns, says the Kern County Californian. There is to be a half mile and a mile dash with not more than 30 minutes wait between each. Harrison Jones names Kit Carson and Charles Kerr names Apache. Forfeit money was placed in bank upon the day the race was agreed upon.

Not one of the pacing contingent has been in to see whether the $500 left by L. A. Davis as a deposit for a match is in Gold, Silver or paper. They evidently do not want to win $2,500 or they have come to the conclusion that Roy Wilkes is too hard a game for them to beat.

The sudden death of Bell Boy has caused his owners, Messrs Clark and Hepper, to look carefully over the young horses of the country, to see if one could be secured to fill the place of Bell Boy, and their choice fell on the grand youngster at the San Mateo Stock Farm, Regal Wilkes, two-year-old record 2:20¼ A telegram was sent to Mr. Corbitt asking him to place a price on his pet, but Regal is not for sale. A price will not be put on the colt, and California will retain the services of the greatest two-year-old stallion that ever lived.

A proclamation has been issued by the Southern Pacific R. R. and no doubt many will avail themselves of the chance offered. A special fast train will leave San Francisco February 12th at 5 P. M. for New Orleans, so that those who wish to can take part in the Mardi Gras festival. The special train will be only three days and eighteen hours on the road, and will be composed of Pullman sleepers and dining car. Tickets and sleeping car berth reservations can be secured in advance. Winter racing will be at its height, so that horsemen who go can have a good time.

D Scott Quintin says of the stallion Palo Alto: "This horse has been complaining in one of his forward feet all summer. Whenever he struck an uneven place in the track, the pain was so great that the stallion was compelled to break, and yet he would catch quickly and go right on." Mr. Quinlan adds: "This furnished me the highest evidence of the intensity of the trotting disposition of Palo Alto. A horse that will not leave the trot, except to avoid the sharpest pain, is gaited right for harness battles. If Palo Alto's trouble is relieved, he will find it an easy task to beat 2:12."

Messrs. W. H. Bradford, M. E. Burgess and F. H. Burgess of Bennington, Vt., passed the most of New Year's Day at Allen Farm, and spoke in high praise of the excellence of the horses they had seen. Mr. Bradford is one of Bennington's wealthy manufacturers. He took a strong fancy to the yearling brown colt, Gotha. Gotha is by Mambrino Wilkes, dam by Guy Wilkes, a royally bred fellow, and a born trotter. Mr. Bradford made what he considered a good offer, but while the offer was appreciated, it fell short of the price, and no sale was made.—Berkshire Eagle.

A mutual understanding between man and horse is necessary in order to insure the largest per cent. of profit to the stallioner, says a leading writer. If friendly word and kindly act are sent as messengers, the equine nature moves in quick response; if angry tone and brutal blow be offered, they are treasured up in sullen, vengeful mind, and at the moment least expected are tendered back in most disastrous manner. The prudent stallioner is friendly with his horse. His nature is made the subject of careful study; his peculiarities of temper are learned; his faults are skillfully corrected, and his vices, if any unfortunately there be, are mitigated.

The following are the names of the gentlemen and farms that have booked mares to Axtell at $1 000 each: Woodburn Farm, Spring Station, Ky.; R S. Veech, Indian Hill Farm, St. Matthews, Ky.; A. H. Moor, Cloverdale Farm, Colmar, Pa.; John Dupee, Chicago, Ill; C B Weiser Chicago, Ill.; John S. Clark, New Brunswick, N. J.; W. E. Speir, Glens Falls, N. Y.; Ed. Pyle, Humbolt, Neb.; S A. Browne & Co., Kalamazoo Farm, Kalamazoo, Mich.; McFerran & Clancy, Louisville, Ky.; C. B. Gillman, Waterville, Me.; W. H. Hill, Worcester, Mass.; W. R. McKeen, Edgewood Stock Farm, Terre Haute, Ind.; B. G Cox, Mar Park, Terre Haute, Ind; D. J Campau, Detroit, Mich.; and A. B. Darling, Darlington Farm, Ramseys, N. Y.

Red-clover hay is nutritive and puts on flesh, but it is bad for wind and condition; and mixed hay is better without sweet scented vernal, which gives that delicious smell we often find in hay, but has little nutriment. If meadowed pasture cannot be procured, then the most available of the above grasses reared from seed should be used. This is a matter where the judgment must be guided by local experience, which, after all, is the only sure test. Pasture hay should be moderately fine, somewhat hard and a year old, unheated and with a green tinge. All hay should be cut early in the season, before the seed has matured. It then contains more nourishment. Needless to say, it should be well saved. A sweet smell is no object. That comes from sweet smelling grasses as vernal, and horses will often reject such hay for that which is almost scentless.

A decidedly novel innovation in pool selling has been started in St. Louis, pools being sold on the site of the World's Fair. Donovan's pool room has the credit of making this innovation. The betting is quite lively, indicating that the idea has struck the chord of popular approval, although the amounts are small, the majority of bets averaging from $10 to $50.

New York City is the site as a strong favorite, 5 to 4 on, being the ruling odds. Chicago ranks next, at even money, while 8 to 1 is offered against St. Louis, and 40 to 1 Washington. At the opening 50 to 1 was laid against Washington as the site, but a few bets caused a reduction of that price.

Mr. Ariel Lathrop informs me that Palo Alto, 2:12¼, will be bred to about ten or a dozen mares this spring, most of which will be thoroughbreds. Positively no outside mares will be taken for him, he being reserved for the farm brood mares. It only seems like yesterday that Seneca Daniels started in to breed trotters from thoroughbreds, and yet that must be a quarter of a century ago. How time does fly! The Sonoma County breeder did not make a magnificent success of his attempts, but Governor Stanford has secured two first-class performers, and now the world looks to Palo Alto for a further development of the thoroughbred theory in trotters.

Some of the Eastern sporting papers have given a record to Una Wilkes of 2:30, but the following note from her owner shows that she is not entitled to one:—

"Some over zealous friend of Guy Wilkes, in a letter to Mr. Balch of Boston, and not intended for publication, gave Una Wilkes, a three year old filly by Guy Wilkes, credit for having made a record of 2:30. Such was not the case. She was entered and started in but one race, and that with aged horses at San Jose. There were six heats in the race, and some of the horses showed their ability to trot close to 2:20, and have since made a record of 2:22¼ Una took fourth money, but got no record, but, barring accidents, she will be well inside the 2:30 list next fall, but I want no credit that I am not justly entitled to for any of my stock.

WM. CORBITT.

Henry A. Couse, who has spent the past year in Southern California, speaks very highly of the horses in that locality, says the Kansas City Referee. As Hank is something of a horseman, it is safe to say that his ideas may prove to be somewhat of a "tip." Some of the boys will remember his predictions on C. A Todd two years ago. Hank says that should Mikado, Odette or the Tycoon colt come this way it would be well for the boys to keep an eye on them. They were the property of Ben Hill of San Diego, who lately sold them to Mr. Rose, and are capable of holding their own with the best of them. Mr. Hill has a number of highly bred yearlings, and as he is generally ready to sell, parties visiting that section of the country will do well to give him a call if they are looking for good ones. San Diego can boast of several good trotters and as good a mile track as can be found in the State. Doc. Burke generally has a string of ten or a dozen trotters, among them the famous Atto Rex. Bell Boy wintered there last year. Joseph Brophey of San Diego, who, by the way, is a jolly good fellow, can give the Eastern tenderfoot visiting that section of the country all the pointers necessary.

The Standard.

[AS REVISED AND ADOPTED BY THE NATIONAL ASSOCIATION OF TROTTING-HORSE BREEDERS, DECEMBER 14, 1887.]

IN order to define what constitutes a trotting-bred horse and to establish a BREED of trotters on a more intelligent basis, the following rules are adopted to control admission to the records of pedigrees. When an animal meets the requirements of admission and is duly registered, it shall be accepted as a standard trotting-bred animal:—

FIRST.—Any stallion that has himself a record of two minutes and thirty seconds (2:30) or better, provided any of his get has a record of 2:35 or better, or provided his sire or his dam is already a standard animal.

SECOND.—Any mare or gelding that has a record of 2:30 or better.

THIRD.—Any horse that is the sire of two animals with a record of 2:30 or better.

FOURTH.—Any horse that is the sire of one animal with a record of 2:30 or better, provided he has either of the additional qualifications: (1) A record himself of 2:35 or better. (2) Is the sire of two other animals with a record of 2:35 or better. (3) Has a sire or dam that is already a standard animal.

FIFTH.—Any mare that has produced an animal with a record of 2:30 or better.

SIXTH.—The progeny of a standard horse when out of a standard mare.

SEVENTH.—The female progeny of a standard horse when out of a mare by a standard horse.

EIGHTH.—The female progeny of a standard horse when out of mare whose dam is a standard mare.

NINTH.—Any mare that has a record of 2:35 or better, and whose sire or dam is a standard animal.

Best Trotting Records.

1 mile—2:08¾, Maud S., against time, in harness, accompanied the distance by a running horse, Glenville, O., July 30, 1885......2:13¾, best time in a race between horses, Maud S., Chicago, Ills., July 24, 1880......2:12, Axtell, against time, accompanied by running horse—fastest stallion time, Terre Haute, Ind., Oct. 11, 1889......2:13½, Phallas, fastest heat by a stallion against other horses, Chicago, July 14, 1884......2:13¾, Palo Alto, third heat in race at Stockton, Cal., Sept. 26, 1889......2:15½, Jay-Eye-See, half-mile track, Lincoln, Neb., Sept. 14, 1887......2:16¾, Great Eastern, under saddle, third heat, Morrisania, N. Y., Sept. 22, 1877......2:10½, Jay-Eye-See, against time, best five-year-old record, Providence, R. I., Sept. 15, 1883......2:16, Manzanita, third heat, best four-year-old record, Lexington, Ky., Sept. 3, 1876......2:16, Edgemark, four-year-old stallion record, against time, Lexington, Ky., Oct. 18, 1889......2:10½, Sunol, in Stanford Stake, accompanied by a runner, best three-year-old record, San Francisco, Nov. 9, 1889..2:18, Sunol, 2 years, against time, San Francisco, Cal., Oct. 27, 1888......2:20¼, Regal Wilkes, two-year-old stallion record, San Francisco, Nov. 9, 1889......2:31½, Norlaine, yearling, against time, San Francisco, Cal., Nov. 12, 1887......2:35, Faustino, yearling stallion record, San Francisco, Nov. 9, 1889.

2 miles—4:43 against time, Fanny Witherspoon, Chicago, Ill., Sept. 25, 1885.

3 miles—7:21¼, Huntress, harness, Brooklyn, L. I., Sept. 21, 1872.

4 miles—10:34½, Longfellow, wagon, California, Dec 31, 1869.

5 miles—13:00, Lady Mac, harness, San Francisco, Cal., April 2, 1874.

10 miles—27:23¼, Controller, harness, San Francisco, Cal., Nov. 23, 1878.

20 miles—58:25, Captain McGowan, harness, half-mile track, Boston, Oct. 31, 1865.

Pacing Records at One Mile.

Johnston, harness, against time, Chicago, Ills., Oct 9, 1884, 2:06¼.

Brown Hal, best stallion record, Cleveland, Ohio, July 31, 1889, 2:12½.

Westmont, July 10, 1884, Chicago, Ills., with running mate, 2:01¾.

Ed Rosewater, two years old, Council Bluffs, Iowa, Nov. 9, 1888, 2:20½.

Yolo Maid, 3 years old, San Francisco, Oct. 13, 1888, 2:14.

Gold Leaf, four years old, 2:11½ on August 17, 1889, at Napa.

Arrow, five years old, 2:13½, made at Cleveland, Ohio, August 1, 1888

Fastest Time on Record.

RUNNING.

Miles.		
¼	Jim Miller, 2, Deer Lodge (Mont.), Aug. 16, 1888 / †Sleepy Dick, a, Kiowa (Kan.), Nov. 24, 1888	0:21¼
⅜	Cyclone, a, 120 lbs., Helena (Mont.), Aug. 28, 1889	0:34¼
½	Geraldine, 4, 122 lbs., Westchester Course, Aug. 30, 1889	0:46
⅝	Britannic, 5, 122 lbs., Westchester Course, Aug. 31, 1889	:59
⅝	Fordham, a, 115 lbs., Westchester Course, Oct. 4, 1889	0:59
¾	El Rio Rey, 2, 126 lbs., Westchester Course, Aug. 31, 1889	1:11
¾	Tipstaff, 3, 107, Westchester Course, Oct. 4, 1889	1:11
⅞	Britannic, 5, 110 lbs., Sheepshead Bay, Sept. 5, 1889	1:26 2-5
1	Ten Broeck, 5, 110 lbs., Louisville, May 24, 1877 (against time)	1:39¾
1	Maori 4, 105 lbs, Chicago, July 12, 1889, (in a race)	1:39 4-5
1 1-16	Wheeler T., 3, 98 lbs., St. Louis, June 1, 1888	1:47¾
1 1-16	Kelton 4, 106, Chicago, Ill., June 24, 1889	1:17¾
1⅛	Terra Cotta, 4, 124 lbs., Sheepshead Bay, June 23, 1888	1:53
1 3-16	Joe Cotton, 5, 109½ lbs., Sheepshead Bay, Sept. 7, 1887	2:00¾
1¼	Kingston, 5, 122 lbs., Gravesend, Sept. 24, 1889	2:06¼
1 m 500 yds.	Ben d'Or, 4, 115 lbs., Saratoga, July 25, 1882	2:10¾
1⅜	Triboulet, 4, 117 lbs., San Francisco, April 26, 1882 / Richmond, 6, 122 lbs., Sheepshead Bay, June 27, 1888	2:21¾
1½	Firenzi, 4, 113 lbs., Monmouth Park, Aug. 2, 1888 / Luke Blackburn, 3, 102 lbs., Monmouth Park, Aug. 17, '80 / Jim Guest, 4, 98 lbs., Chicago, (Washington Park, July 24 '86)	2:34
1⅝	Hindoocraft, 3, 75 lbs., Westchester, Aug. 27, 1889	2:48
1¾	Glidelia, 5, 118 lbs., Saratoga, Aug. 5, 1882	3:01
1⅞	Enigma, 4, 90 lbs., Sheepshead Bay, Sept. 15, 1885	3:20
2	Ten Broeck, 5, 110 lbs., Louisville, May 29, 1877	3:27½
2⅛	Monitor, 4, 110 lbs., Baltimore, Oct. 20, 1880	3:41½
2¼	Springbok, 5, 114 lbs. / Preakness, a, 114 lbs., Saratoga, July 29, 1875	3:56¼
2½	Aristides, 4, 104 lbs., Lexington, May 13, 1876	4:27½
2⅝	Ten Broeck, 4, 104 lbs., Lexington, Sept. 16, 1876	4:58½
2¾	Hubbard, 4, 107 lbs., Saratoga, Aug. 9, 1873	4:58¾
3	Drake Carter 4 115 lbs., Sheepshead Bay, Sept. 6, 1884	5:24
4	Ten Broeck, 4, 104 lbs., Louisville, Sept. 27, 1876	7:15¾

HEAT RACES.

Miles.		
¼	Sleepy Dick, a, Kiowa (Kan.), Nov. 24, 1888	0:21¼—0:22¼
½	Bogus, a, 112 lbs., Helena (Mont.), Aug. 21, 1886	0:48 —0:48
⅝	Kittie Pease, 4, Dallas (Tex.), Nov. 2, 1887	1:00 —1:00
⅝	Sodie McNairy, 3, 98 lbs., Chicago, July 2, 1883	1:02½—1:03
¾	Lizzie S., 5, 118 lbs., Louisville, Sept 28, 1883	1:13¾—1:13¾
1	Bounce, 4, 90 lbs., Sheepshead Bay, Sept. 7, 1881	1:42 —1:41¾
1	3 in 5. L'Argentine, 6, 115 lbs., St. Louis, June 14, 1879	1:43—1:44 —1:47¾
1 1-16	Slipalong, 5, 115 lbs., Chicago (Wash. Park), Sept. 2, 1885	1:50½—1:48
1⅛	Gabriel, 4, 112 lbs., Sheepshead Bay, Sept. 23, 1890	1:56 —1:56
1¼	Glenmore, 5, 114 lbs., Sheepshead Bay, Sept. 25, 1880	2:10 —2:14
1½	Keno, 5, Toledo, Sept. 16, 1887 (1st and 3d heats)	2:43¼—2:45
2	Miss Woodford, 4, 107½ lbs., Sheepshead Bay, Sept. 20, 1884	3:33 — 3:31¾
3	Norfolk, 4, 100 lbs., Sacramento, Sept. 23, 1865	5:27¼—5:29½
4	Ferida, 4, 105 lbs., Sheepshead bay, Sept. 18, 1880	7:23½—7:41

†Made in a heat race.
*Doubtful, and made in a heat race.

THE GUN.

At Colton.

Mr. A. W. Bruner, champion wing shot of California, kindly sends us the scores of the match for the Selby Medal for Southern California, shot at Colton on January 4th. The beastly weather and washouts on the railroad prevented a large attendance. The match was at 50 single "Blue Rock" targets and twenty-five pairs, and the scores of the match for the medal were:

Gus Knight............	0	1	1	1	1	1	1	1	1	1	1	1	1	
	1	1	1	1	1	1	0	0	0	1	1	1		—21
Parker, No. 10, 1½, No 7	1	0	0	1	1	1	1	0	1	1	1	0	1	
	1	0	0	1	1	1	1	1	1	1	1	1		—19
5 Ds. F F G, 19 yds....	10	00	10	11	11	10	11	11	11	11	10	00	01	
	11	10	10	01	11	11	10	11	11	11	11	10		—36—76
M. E. Taber............	1	1	1	1	1	0	1	1	1	0	1	1	1	
	1	0	1	1	1	1	1	1	1	1	1	1		—22
Smith, 12 G 3½ Ds Schultz	1	1	1	1	1	1	1	1	1	1	1	1	1	
	1	1	1	1	1	1	1	1	1	1	0	1		—24
1½, No. 8................	11	10	11	01	11	01	11	01	01	11	01	11	10	
	11	10	10	10	11	11	10	01	11	00	00	10		—32—78
Jas. Meckam............	0	0	0	1	0	1	0	1	0	0	1	0	1	
	0	1	1	1	0	0	1	1	0	1	0	1		—12
Smith, 12 G, 3½ Ds, F F G	1	1	1	1	0	0	0	1	1	1	1	1	1	
	0	1	1	1	1	1	1	1	0	1	1	1		—20
1½ No. 7, 16............	10	11	10	10	10	10	10	11	10	00	00	01	00	
	11	10	00	10	11	10	11	01	10	00	10	10		—25—57

Doctor Aby Shoots.

Editor Breeder and Sportsman:—I send you by express this A. M. three brace of snipe, a part of my last evening's bag.

The weather has been so beastly bad since my return from the city it has been impossible to get out of doors.

About four o'clock last evening Old Sol poked out from behind a cloud. The sight was so unusual that R–, my Irish setter, got up from the hearth rug and made a rush at the door, with a bark of evident delight.

As I opened the door he made a rush towards the meadows, which are only a short walk from the house, stopped and looked back, as if he expected me to follow.

The invitation was too strong to be refused. as all my inclinations were meadowards bent. I got into my high-water boots and chose the Colt hammerless as my companion, and with twenty-five shells I started.

I had not gone 500 yards before yak, whirr! up went a beauty, and away went Red on a hot chase.

A "Come in, you red devil" brought him back, and, with an admonition to take care, enforced with my pocket whip, brought him to his work.

A few yards further, and I knew work was in store for me. One moment I waited to see the impatient dog stand, and as the speckled beauties rose with their peculiar twist, bang! bang! in quick succession went my gun.

Only one; it should have been two. Before my next shells were in place up went three more.

Again did one only bite the mud as the dog was coming in with the dead bird. He flushed four, and then my very soul was on fire with enthusiasm, one to the right and one on the left.

I hugged myself in my delight [an armful.—Ed.]. Out of twelve shots I got seven birds and had not moved ten steps. A little farther on I walked into a regular covey of snipe. Up they went in all directions. Then I did get wild. Thrice did I empty my gun and not a feather. For once I was *rattled*. After talking to the dog in the most forcible Spanish that I am master of, I wiped out my gun, took a drink of water to cool my nerves, etc.

I had only seven more shells and only seven birds. The sun hid himself again, and the birds were slow. I had marked down some singles, and as I walked them up I simply waited for my shot and put in five straights to my credit and bag.

While hunting in my jacket pockets for tobacco, I dug up six No. 7 shells (had been shooting 8's). Eight more shots.

As the dog was hunting for a dead bird, I happened to look up, and as straight and swift as an arrow a cock bird was crossing over me about 60 feet high. Up went my piece of destruction, and as the charge of No. 7's went to meet the king of game birds there was a collision, and down came the king at my feet.

Mingled with my yell of "Good boy, Doc," was a thought "a small bottle on me if my editor could have seen that shot!"

With three more easy kills and one miss, and with 15 birds for 30 shells, I came on back to the genial hot fire, in the old open fire place. With slippers, cap and pipe, I leaned back in my comfortable chair and pitied you fellows fastened up in town. My last thought was, "Won't I make those snipe howl to-morrow evening!"

To-morrow evening came, and with it the same desire for murder of the snipe. I was some little time finding the birds, as it was a bright sunshiny afternoon and they were in the heavy grass. When I did find them, they went up all at once. I went around banging away, with as little damage to the birds as the rankest of Salvation Army fiends could wish; 12, then two more shots, and not a bird. It was then that plain every-day English could only inadequately express my feelings. They were simply flying in every direction, and in the most provokingly slow and easy way, as when they are going to feed.

After a five minutes rest, and with a clean gun, I re-opened the charge. Ah! Richard is himself again; first a single and then a double. Seven straights, and all on the ground. As the dog was bringing them in, two cowards were run up out of the grass, and immediately bit it again. I began to be encouraged. I got a couple of flyers that it took the second barrel to stop.

Twenty-eight shots and only 13 birds! Would I ever get half? It was getting cold and late. I started homewards and picked up a nice easy pair across the brook.

I did get half, and with them was coming home, well content, with my average when just as I was feeling my best, up went a sky scraper. Bang, bang, and not a feather.

I didn't have courage enough left to swear at the dog, simply told him to go to the devil, as he went scampering away after a very lively bird.

Fifteen out of thirty-two.

Well, if I don't improve, I can't prevent you and Chief Callundan wiping my eye, when you come up next month.

I am tired with my tramps, and it is bedtime, so good-night, with good luck to the boys. Aby.

Middletown, Lake Co., Jan. 10th, 90.

[Doctor Aby's average on snipe and every thing else is high, even at story telling. Now that he has established himself in print as a charming raconteur, we shall rely upon him for notes at short intervals.—Ed.]

Canonical Sportsmen.

California, just past its formative period, can recall the services rendered to the State by the grand men in sacred functions, who, nevertheless, did not fail to meet popular errors and who preserved the faith in times that were next to anarchistic. Name after name comes to mind as we write. Men first, then clergymen, those heroes of the fifties, many of them were sportsmen of the keenest type, fishermen, shots and lovers of Nature.

The recent arrest and fine of Rev. Dr. Rainsford, of New York, for killing game illegally prompted a reporter to interview some of the prominent persons of that town, about their notions with respect to field sports, and these are the results:

The magazine articles of the Rev. Dr. Henry van Dyke, pastor of the Brick Church in Fifth Avenue, have made the public familiar with that gentleman's passion for fishing. Izaak Walton was not a more ardent angler than this enthusiastic disciple, who has wet his line in a thousand lakes and streams. Dr. van Dyke has an unusually large head and a very small foot, and his body strikes a happy average between the two extremities. The writer has noticed that men with big heads; men who think a great deal, whose brains are more active than their bodies, make the most successful fishermen. Walton was such a man. Daniel Webster another. Dr. van Dyke has an enormous back head, an abundance of brown hair, a full beard of the same color, blue eyes, a prominent nose, and the ruddy complexion of a man much in the sun. In every capacity but that of fisherman, he seems nervous and high strung. When the writer spoke to him on the subject of recreation, he answered bluntly; "The way in which I amuse myself is nobody's business but my own. The world has no more business to concern itself with the recreations of clergymen than with the recreations of any other class of men. Every clergyman has the right to say, in the words of the poet:

"I dare do all that may become a man."

He does not fish or shoot in his clerical capacity, but as a human being. Some of the best ministers that the world has ever known have been enthusiastic lovers of out door sports, and since the day when Peter cast a hook in the sea and took out a fish, angling has been a familiar apostolic occupation. I have no particular concern to defend shooting as a sport, but I have fished for trout and salmon and grayling in many parts of the world, and my conscience does not give me a single qualm upon the subject. I am only sorry for the fish that I didn't catch, and grateful for the happy days that God has permitted me to spend in fishing in his beautiful lakes and rivers. If any one doesn't like my angling, I advise him to consider the example of the man in New Jersey, who made a large fortune by minding his own business. But, of course, a minister has no more right to break the game laws than any other man, and, if he does, the law must first prove it and then punish him."

Reverend George H. McGrew, of St. Paul's Methodist Episcopal Church, was next interviewed, and said:—

"I am passionately fond of fishing and hunting, and would as soon shoot quail over a good dog as wade in water up to my thighs casting for trout. I can see no harm in either. Though partial to quail shooting, I do not object to hunting bigger game. When in India I used to go tiger hunting, and found it royal sport."

The next call was upon Rev. Wm. M. Taylor, of the Broadway Tabernacle.

"The recreations of a clergyman," he said, "depend largely on the time at his disposal. If he can find the time to fish, let him fish; if he can find the time to hunt, let him hunt. Any sport that is good for a member of my congregation is good for me. I cannot see the necessity for any distinctions. Let a man be controlled by his conscience. I don't try to control other men's consciences, because I have as much as I can do to control my own."

"Do you fish?"

"Not now; but I used to be very fond of it. My last fishing was done in Moosehead Lake several years ago."

"Do you shoot?"

"No. I fear if I should go shooting I should break my neck."

Rev. Dr. Charles H. Parkhurst of the Madison Square Presbyterian church was the next to speak.

Dr. Parkhurst takes the broad ground that what is proper for the layman is proper for the clergyman, and what is improper for the clergyman is improper for the layman. Said he:—

"I think there is a little meanness on the part of the laymen, who seem to believe that because they are laymen they can do things that a clergyman ought not to do. A woman of my congregation said to me the other day, after describing the performance at a theater she had visited the night before: 'Oh, I wish you could have seen it, but then I should have been sorry to see you there.'"

"Do you shoot or fish, doctor?"

"I do not. They are sports that never appealed to me, but I see no harm in them. If a clergyman wants to do either the one of the other, or both, I say let him. It's nobody's business but his."

A Baptist clergyman who goes a-fishing whenever he gets a chance, but wouldn't shoot a quail for all the world, may be regarded as a novelty. Such a man is the Rev. W. H. P. Faunce, the new pastor of the Fifth Avenue Baptist Church. Mr. Faunce is a young man of nervous-sanguine temperament—sandy hair, sandy mustache, sandy complexion. He is exceedingly affable, and "makes friends" with a man in short order. When the writer asked him to explain how he could have scruples against shooting and none against fishing, he said:

"In shooting birds or larger game we often take the life of creatures whose organization is as high as our own, or even higher, whereas in fishing we only destroy a much lower order of creation. I have no objection to killing an insect, and see no harm in taking a fish."

Dr. Robert Collyer was next called upon.

Being invited to enter, the first question, as usual was:—

"Do you shoot?"

The answer was long in coming. It was easy to see that the Doctor, taken somewhat by surprise at the absurdity of the question, had suddenly gone back in the recesses of his memory to something stowed away there more than fifty years ago. The discovery of it caused him to smile away down below the belt. When a man like Dr. Collyer smiles he smiles all over.

"I never shot a gun but once in my life," he said, "and that was by accident. It came near killing another boy. I was fifteen years old at the time."

"Of course you follow the example of St. Peter and Izaak Walton?"

"Fishing is my favorite sport, though I have not practiced it since I was in Colorado."

"You see nothing objectionable, then, in either hunting or fishing?"

"I think it is wrong to hunt as hares are hunted—by coursing. That is a species of cruelty which I cannot approve. As for fishing, where lies the harm? When you throw in your hook and pull out a fine trout, and lay him down on the fresh grass, and he wriggles and wriggles, and jumps about flapping his tail on one side, then rolling over and flapping it on the other, I think he enjoys it twice as much as you do. He seems perfectly happy, doesn't he? He seems to thank you for taking him out of the water and letting him frolic in the grass. Anyway, that is the view I try to take of it."

Accompanying his visitor to the elevator, the Doctor suddenly broke out with:—

"Oh by-the-by that was too bad about poor Rainsford wasn't it. To think that he should have got into such trouble! Poor fellow. I'm sorry it happened."

"But doctor, he broke the game law, and the general impression is that he got off light. Only $25 and costs you know. Dr. Rainsford is very popular in Southampton, and the judge didn't want to fine him at all."

"Yes, yes, they all like sporting parsons, and we fellows do manage to get off very easy, I admit."

"Go talk with Dr. Bridgman; you'll find him a capital fellow," said a well known member of the Madison Avenue Baptist Church, over which Dr. Bridgman presides.

He was right. The doctor is a charming man, bubbling over with wisdom, wit and allegory, and therefore good natured, cheerful and full of the milk of human kindness.

"I have hardly time to think of recreation during the work year," he said. "When vacation time arrives in the summer I rush across the water and bury myself in the heart of London where I loaf. Yes, literally loaf. Last summer I went to Holland and still enjoy thinking about those delightful old Dutch pictures that I saw. I hardly think I shall go abroad next year, however. I have an idea I should like to go a-fishing."

"Ah, you fish?"

"It is the only sport for which I have an attachment. I can play fool at one end of a fishing pole for four hours with the expectation of getting a bite at the end of that time."

"And if the bite doesn't come?"

"Why, I'm willing to play the fool four hours longer."

Do you shoot."

"In the matter of shooting I think I may say that I have an unbeaten record. In the course of my life I have shot a gun four times. My trophies were a robin, two deer and a hole through my shoe."

"Then you never missed a shot."

"Never missed a shot. When I was a boy I borrowed a gun from another boy and went hunting. As I had never seen anybody load a gun, it was but natural that I should be extravagant with my shot and prodigal with my powder. The charge that I put in must have filled the barrel about half full. When everything was ready and primed, I espied a robin sitting in a tree and crept stealthily upon him. Being ambitious of success, I continued to creep till the muzzle of my gun was within ten feet of the unfortunate creature, then, taking long and careful aim, I pulled the trigger. The effect was disastrous at both ends. I remember turning two somersaults backward, and getting up with my jaw in my hands, while blood streamed from my mouth. But I went for the bird, and found it, or what was left of it. My aim had been perfect. The entire load had passed through its body, taking everything with it except the two wings and a shred of skin. That was my first shot. My second was very humiliating. We were out deer hunting, and it fell to my lot to stand in a certain spot and do the shooting, while the rest of the fellows did the driving. They got up several fine deer, which galloped by me in easy range, but their movements were so graceful, and I was so delighted with watching them, as to forget entirely my great responsibility. Suddenly, however, the gun went off, I must have pulled the trigger unconsciously, and the load passed through the toe of my shoe. But that wasn't the worst of it. Pretty soon the boys came running up, and the first question they fired at me was: 'Did you hit him, Charley?' My other two shots were made in the Adirondacks, where I was camping with Dr. Loomis, and each brought down a deer."

Rev. Ensign McChesney, pastor of the Madison Avenue Methodist Episcopal Church, said his favorite pastime was fishing, but he did not shoot. Many other clergymen were interviewed but their opinions are reflected in the responses given and the consensus, was strongly in favor of free practice of field sports.

During the recent floods at Anaheim every hummock was swarming with hares and rabbits that were driven from the plains. They were slaughtered by thousands by boys and men, who used sticks, and when tired of the sport they would run the poor beasts off their dry places into the raging waters.

A prominent citizen of Woodland went out robin shooting the other day and was ordered out of almost every field he got into. He does not want to shoot in a man's field when the owner objects, and finally gave up the sport and returned to town. People who have vineyards, orchards and stock do not care to take the chances of reckless hunters, but seldom fail to accord permission to shoot when properly approached.

Wm. Nattress killed a large California lion on his ranch, near San Lucas, on Sunday. At a rough estimate the animal was considered to be eight feet from tip to tip. Several more of these destructive animals have their dens in the hills, and make midnight excursions to the ranches in the vicinity. Young calves, sheep and hogs suffer considerably from the attacks of these vicious beasts.

Martin Stryker and a friend known as "Fred" were hunting on Sunday near Henley, Siskiyou County. They took different ridges to cover more ground, and Fred seeing Stryker's head above the opposite ridge, shot thinking it was a head of a deer. The ball entered in front and below the ear and it is feared that the wound is fatal.

The recklessness with which riflemen turn loose at every moving thing is appalling, but will probably continue until the race of fools becomes extinct.

Blue Rock Club.

The club met on January 7th last, and decided to continue its existence for another season. Its annual meeting occurs on February 28th. The prizes for '89 together with the total scores and donors, are given as follows:

CLASS A.

Winner.	Score.	Prize.	Presented By.
S. L. Kellogg	127	Hunting Shoes	Dr. S. E. Knowles
J. O. Cadman	116	Silver Match Box	H. A. Tubbs.
A. F. Adams	110	Golcher Shooting Coat	W. J. Fox.
F. B. Norton	106	Leather Cartridge Case	W. J. Golcher.
W. A. Beck	97	Box of Cigars	M. A Newell.
W. E. Mayhew	91	100 Cartridges	S. L. Kellogg.
J. H. Maynard	90	Bamboo Rod	J. O. Cadman.

CLASS B.

Winner.	Score.	Prize.	Presented By.
F. R. Noyes	99	Sole Leather Gun Case	W. J. Golcher.

CLASS C.

Winner.	Score.	Prize.	Presented By.
A. L. Abbott, Jr	76	Case of Fine Wine	F. H. Putzman.

"Please don't shoot the cows" is a sign on the premises of a Pennsylvania farmer, placed there for the benefit of city sportsmen who go out after rabbits. The farmer means well, but he will have his trouble for his pains. Hunters who mistake cows for rabbits couldn't see such a sign.

The rooms of the Students and Sportsmen's Club at Bakersfield have been elegantly furnished by Mr. Truxton Beale, who seems to have done a great deal toward it as a labor of love. He has sent from this city, two oil paintings by M. Valencia, two valuable etchings, one showing the water front of Warwick Castle and the other a view of Windsor, with the castle in bold relief; two very handsome engravings of dogs, and three delightful pictures which seem to be steel engravings imprinted upon satin. Added to this for the adornment of the walls, is a set of furniture both handsome and comfortable. Altogether it makes as fine a club room as can be found outside of any large city and it will become the choice place of resort for the Bohemian contingent. All members of the Knights of the Trigger are ex-officio Students and Sportsmen and all other males who were members of the other clubs have an opportunity to become members by paying the difference between their former initiation fee and $5 the former fee for becoming a Knight. Doubtless a full set of by-laws will soon be adopted, as there is every indication that the new club with its elegant rooms, will become a central resort.

Last week while riding up a creek about eight miles above Caliente, J. E. Miller, of Bakersfield, came upon a golden eagle. The bird had killed a yearling lamb and had so gorged itself that it was not active in rising and Miller lassoed it with a bit of cotton rope. He then watched his chance and caught one wing and then the other and by using a good deal of patient strategy managed to tie its feet without getting clawed, or torn by its vicious bill. Then he had it so secure that be carried it home under his arm, as handily as Brudder Bones would tote a more eatable bird home from a neighbor's hen roost. He made a cage and the noble bird can now be seen at the Caliente depot It is full grown, has tremendous claws and looks at one steadily with clear untameable, unconquerable eyes. It is really a prize, but then, so is a white elephant, and what to do with him is a puzzling question.—C. E. Sherman, in Kern County Californian.

[Keep that bird alive at all hazards until field trial time, and permit us to feed Mr. Fred A. Taft to him. Taft agrees with eagles when administered in small doses, plain,—Ed.]

BASE BALL.

Make-up of the Clubs for Next Season—Harris Thrown Out.

Henry Harris has been counted out, and the brains of the California League declares that he will not again have anything to do with that organization. The job was consummated at Sacramento last Saturday night, when, after it was decided not to increase the league to six clubs, the Directors voted to retain Stockton, and rejected the application of San Jose. Harris had worked up the people of the Garden city to such a pitch, that he had been guaranteed plenty of capital to carry a club through at least one season, and under his management it would probably have become a paying and permanent member of the league. On the other hand, Stockton never has and never will support a ball club, and it is silver to copper that the Slough city club will not finish the season; or if it does, it will be with a team of fourth class men that will not attract 300 people to a Sunday game. The moneyed men of Stockton have grown tired of putting up their coin to support a ball club, and even if the team plays the string out, it will be the last season for some time that the city of wind-mills will have a professional ball team. Possibly the league Directors know their business, but there are few outsiders who would gamble on it.

We are not to get much of a rest from base ball after all. The players in this city have formed a three team League and will play Thursdays, Saturdays and Sundays at Central Park. If the venture is a success, the boys say they will carry out their proposed Brotherhood scheme and establish a permanent League in opposition to the old organization. The players are getting frightened at the large number of Eastern men who are signing with the California League, and have at last awakened to the fact that something must be done immediately to save themselves from being left out in the cold. Among the men who will play at Central Park are Van Haltren, Brown, Nick Smith and nearly all the favorites of last seasons League Clubs.

The make up of the Oakland team for next season so far as can be ascertained will be: Homer and Warner, of New Haven, for one battery; Mehrle, pitcher; Cartwright, of St. Joseph, first base; Jim McDonald, second base; Tom Forster, of the Western Association, short stop; Norris O'Neill, third base; Charles O'Neil, of the Tri-State League, left field; Danny Long, center field. A change catcher and right fielder is yet to be signed.

George Zeigler, of the Sacramento team, has returned from the East and announces the following players as having been secured: Borchers and Zeigler, pitchers; William Bowman, of Wheeling, W Va., catcher; Ed Stapleton, of Detroit, first base; Henry P. Reitz, of Chicago, second base; John Godar, Cincinnati, third base; Jack Daly, Chicago, short stop; Goodenough, center field. An effort has been made to secure Roberts, but the youngster wants a National League salary.

Borchers is at liberty to sign with any club in the country. When he was blacklisted by the California League that body was not a member of the National agreement, consequently the black list does not now hold. As Borchers was only suspended by the Eastern clubs, a suspension only holding for a single season, the glass-eating track walker has a perfect right to sign a Sacramento contract.

Bill Smalley and Charlie Dooley have both signed with the Cleveland League team. The latter and his wife have left for New York.

Stallings has gone to Jacksonville, Fla. He was anxious to have Coughlan accompany him, but Roscoe preferred to remain in this city until he has to report for duty with the Chicago League team.

Harris will transfer the men signed for his San Jose Club to Manager Finn. The San Francisco Club will probably include Meegan and Incell, pitchers; Power, first base; Howard, second base; Stickney, third base; Shea, short stop; Levy, left field; Hanley, right field, with two catchers to alternate in right field.

So far the Stockton management has made no move towards securing any men for the coming season, which opens March 23rd and closes November 23rd.

THE KENNEL.

Dog owners are requested to send for publication the earliest possible notices of whelps, sales, names claimed, presentations and deaths, in their kennels, in all instances writing plainly names of sire and dam and of grandparents, colors, dates and breed.

Name Claimed.

Mr. J. M. Bassford, Jr., claims the name Nick White for a white and lemon pointer dog by Scout Croxteth—Blossom.

A Notable Death.

Editor Breeder and Sportsman:—The Bay View Kennel mourns the death of Lady Elaine by Romeo out of Rural Nellie, whelped Oct. 2, 1889, one of the most promising pups I ever bred. She had the speed of her dam and the nose and sense of her sire. I had begun shooting over her and her little sister Lynnette owned by Dr. Foulkes, of San Francisco, and it was a pretty sight to see the pair point and back like old dogs and retrieve without ruffling a feather. Only two days before we found her dead in the kennel, I noticed her pick up a small piece of coal and before I could get to her she swallowed it which I feel sure caused her death. She was growing to be a very handsome bitch with black ears, fine tan markings over eyes and under jaws, with body handsomely blue ticked. So one more noble Llewellin has passed to the happy hunting grounds. C. A. Loud.

Pacific Beach, Jan. 12, 1890.

George T. Allender is located on the Wible Rancho, about thirteen miles from Bakersfield with his string of dogs for the field trials.

Judge C. N. Post went down to Bakersfield last week to overlook the final preparation of his dogs for the field trials. He undoubtedly has some good ones, and his dogs are always sent to win if it lies within their hides.

Mr. Joe Bassford's Scout Croxteth—Blossom pointer is bred to run, if there is anything in blood. Bow, Sleaford, Vandevort's Don, Croxteth, Bang, Hamlet, and a score of other names as notable, appear in the pedigree. The dog is a fine looker, and promises as well as any pup ever bred by Mr. Bassford.

Mr. Geo. T. Allender wrote from Bakersfield early in the week that his dogs were shaping up well. Mr. Schreiber's Nestor, which showed such superior natural quality last year, is particularly promising on single birds. No news has come from either Mr. Walter, Mr. Geo. W. Bassford or Mr. De Mott, so that it may be concluded that everything is well with them.

When this issue reaches the homes of our leading sportsmen the heads of the families will not receive it—they will have left on their yearly pilgrimage to that Mecca of all who truly love the most refined phase of field sport, the field trial. The article in another column about the sportsmanly tastes of reverend gentlemen is couched in moderate terms. If those men could participate in one field trial there would be more vividness in their phrasing.

A dainty pamphlet indeed is that prepared by Mr. W. E. Houghton of Bakersfield, in which the articles recently published in this paper about the trip to the top of Mount Whitney are reprinted. In writing the articles, Mr. C. E. Sherman interwove a vast deal of information about early times in Kern that will grow more valuable as time passes, and the footprints of the sturdy pioneers come to be properly esteemed.

President Ramon E. Wilson of the Pacific Kennel Club, has appointed Messrs. William Schreiber, Thomas J. O'Keeffe, Clarence A. Haight and H. H. Briggs a committee to confer with a committee from the California Kennel Club for the purpose of devising some plan to amalgamate the clubs. Such an end is most desirable and we hope the committees will be guided solely by regard for the best interests of the doggy world, and not by any personal prejudices.

This is for Kern County shooters by an effete Eastern enthusiast. "Take him all round, and designate him what you will—game or vermin—the rabbit is about the most satisfactory bird or beast or insect or reptile, whatever he may really be to pursue in any shape or form. You can hunt him with dogs of all sort, sizes and breeds. You can stalk him with a small bore rifle and pot him (or otherwise) when you consider you are within range of him. You can track him in the snow to his lair, and proceed as seemth best to you to endeavor to achieve his destruction. You can oust him from the bowels of the earth with the co-operation of the insidious and insinuating ferret and smite him hip and thigh as he scurries away, metaphorically laughing in his sleeve, to think how easily he has fooled his keen scented but slow footed detective. He keeps you busily employed all the time in a good days' covert shooting, and last, but not least, he is succulent and toothsome (when not too ripe in years), no matter how you have introduced him to the cooks."

A prominent sportsman of Bakersfield, Mr. Truxton Beale, son of General E. F. Beale, is projecting great improvements upon the property owned in that city by the General. Among other schemes is one to build up a great sportsman's club and shooting preserve, and Mr. Beale says of the scheme:—

"It is not generally known as it should be that a number of gentlemen who are interested in preserving the game in our section of the State have organized a club to which we have given the name of 'The Knights of the Trigger.'

"There are already about 100 members, and when the purposes for which the club was organized become more generally known we hope to enlist the interest of naturalists and gentlemen fond of field sports in every part of the State.

"It is a well known fact that years ago antelope, deer and game of all kinds were remarkably abundant in the section of the country embraced in the Haggin & Carr and Miller & Lux ranches. The pot-hunters had pretty nearly exterminated the larger game when we took hold of the matter and determined that the same thing should not happen to the antelope that has to the buffalo, namely, an almost complete extermination of this beautiful and characteristic American animal.

"So far as the right to take game of any kind on the 600,000 acres of land comprising the three ranches above named is concerned, it has been confided to the Knights of the Trigger, and all complaints are sworn out by and all prosecutions pushed by the club.

The purpose is not to create a monopoly of sport, or to exclude proper persons from hunting in a sportsman-like manner, but to so regulate affairs on this immense preserve that the greatest amount of rational sport may be enjoyed by the greatest number of lovers of true sport.

There is a club house at Bakersfield for the accommodation of the members, and the dues have been placed at the low figure of $6 per annum, so as to be within the means of anyone desiring to join us.

We think there are enough public-spirited men in the State who will cooperate with us to create an interest in the subject of game preserving in other sections.

We thought once we had timber enough to last for all time, but no thoughtful man believes it now. And it was just so with the game, so plentiful on our hills and in our valleys. The wasteful and wanton destruction of everything that could be shot at has nearly exterminated certain kinds—the most interesting. There are older communities than ours where the sportsman may enjoy a day with the gun and dogs with less trouble and expense than he can in California.

It is to be hoped that our example will be followed by others, and that game districts will be formed and regulated with the same wisdom that always manifests itself when our people take hold of any matter in earnest.

Its value to the State at large can hardly be estimated, for when you add to the climate of the State the attraction of splendid shooting, it will draw thousands of people of means and leisure, many of them will come to stay."

ROD.

Oregon Fish Commission.

The third annual report of F. C. Reed, E. P. Thompson and R. C. Campbell, constituting the Oregon State Fish Commission, in relation to salmon, states that the total value of salmon packed and consumed in home markets shows a grand total of $2,700,000. Great stress is laid upon the importance of hatcheries and the Commission cites statistics of work in that direction carried on prior to this year in the Fraser river. Since 1882 and up to 1889 there had been a steady decrease of salmon, but 14,646,000 of fry planted in 1885-6-7 8 has resulted in the packing on Fraser river in the season of 376 000 cases, the largest pack in the history of the river. The value of the product of the U. S. is $6,054,000 and that of British Columbia $2,119,000. Besides, in 1888, $47,236 is to be credited to shad, smelt and tom cod. It is expected that the fry of 1887 will return and swell the catch of next year. The salaries and expenses of the Commissioners were $1,925.

What is a Fishing Privilege?

In 1859, the legislature of California passed a law to regulate the salmon fisheries of Eel river, in Humboldt County. By the terms of this law the sole and exclusive right to catch fish went with the title to lands bordering on the river. If Mr. Smith's land lay along the river he was supposed by the law to control the right to salmon fishing between the eastern and western boundaries of his line as absolutely as he controlled his fields or timber lots. When he sold the land he also conveyed the fishing privilege.

Fishing seems, for a time at least, to have been carried on within the intent of the law, and property has from time to time changed hands, the "privilege" going with the property. Mr. E. M. Heckman is now in possession of one of these privileges, but of late years other fishermen on the river have set up a claim to the greater privilege of fishing wherever they can find water enough to float a salmon—even on Mr. Heckman's "privilege." To this he objects, and a month ago brought suit to quiet title to his water lot. Alberto Robertson, Smith Fulmore and others being joined as defendants in the suit.

The case was heard by Judge Hunter last week, when he sustained defendant's demurrer, but allowed plaintiff fifteen days to file an amended complaint.

The case involves nice questions of law—the constitutionality of the act under which the "privilege" is sought to be maintained, and the right of injunction, the effect of subsequent legislation under which State lands were disposed of, etc. No damage was asked; the plaintiff simply wants judicial opinion as to whether the exclusive right and privilege which he bought is a privilege in fact, or whether he is expected to maintain it for the use and benefit of his neighbors to the detriment of himself.

At the regular monthly meeting of the Sacramento River Fishermen's Protective Union held at Benicia on Tuesday of last week 300 members being present, the price of salmon for the coming season was fixed at 5 cents a pound for spring and 4 cents for fall. Eastern capital has been enlisted at Martinez and the old steel works is being converted into a cannery. Several other other new canneries will run the coming season.

Private Robert Ward writes to the Ferndale Enterprise from Fort Gaston as follows: "We are to have a full-fledged fish hatchery in this valley, Lieutenant-Commander Brice, of the U. S. Navy, and a fish expert have been here superintending the construction of the buildings and tanks. They expect to turn many thousands of young salmon, as well as other varieties of fish, loose in the rivers before the close of the coming season. This piece of news will undoubtedly be cheerfully received by those interested in the fishing industry on Eel river."

THE WEEKLY

Breeder and Sportsman.

JAMES P. KERR, PROPRIETOR.

The Turf and Sporting Authority of the Pacific Coast.

Office, No. 313 Bush St.

P. O. Box 2300.

TERMS—One Year, $5; Six Months, $3; Three Months, $1.50.
STRICTLY IN ADVANCE.

Money should be sent by postal order, draft or by registered letter, addressed to JAMES P. KERR, San Francisco, Cal.

Communications must be accompanied by the writer's name and address, not necessarily for publication, but as a private guarantee of good faith.

ALEX. P. WAUGH, - - - - - Editor.

Advertising Rates

Per Square (half inch)

One time	$1 50
Two times	2 50
Three times	3 25
Four times	4 00

And each subsequent insertion 75c. per square.

Advertisements running six months are entitled to 10 per cent. discount.

Those running twelve months are entitled to 20 per cent. discount.

Reading notices set in same type as body of paper, 50 cents per line each insertion.

To Subscribers.

The date printed on the wrapper of your paper indicates the time to which your subscription is paid.

Should the BREEDER AND SPORTSMAN be received by any subscriber who does not want it, write us direct to stop it. A postal card will suffice.

Special Notice to Correspondents.

Letters intended for publication should reach this office not later than Wednesday of each week, to secure a place in the issue of the following Saturday. Such letters to insure immediate attention should be addressed to the BREEDER AND SPORTSMAN, and not to any member of the staff.

San Francisco, Saturday, Jan. 18, 1890.

Stallions Advertised

IN THE
BREEDER AND SPORTSMAN.

Thoroughbreds.

FRIAR TUCK, Hermit—Romping Girl............C. W. Aby, Middletown.
GREENBACK, Dollar—Music............C. W. Aby, Middletown.
INTRUDER, Crater—Lady Bountiful............T. J. Knight, Sacramento.
PRINCE OF NORFOLK, Norfolk—Marion............Dan Dennison, Sacramento.
ST. SAVIOR, Eolus—War Song............C. W. Aby, Middletown.

Trotters.

ALEXANDER BUTTON, Alexander—Lady Button............Cache Creek Farm, Yolo.
APEX, Prompter—Mary............Poplar Grove Breeding Farm, Wildflower.
BALKAN, Mambrino Wilkes—Fanny Fern............A. L. Hinds, Oakland.
CLOVIS, Sultan—Sweetbriar............Poplar Grove Breeding Farm, Wild flower.
CANNON BALL, Simmons—Gurgle............Lockhaven Stock Farm, Burbank.
DIRECTOR, Dictator—Dolly............Pleasanton Stock Farm, Pleasanton.
EL BENTON, Electioneer—Nellie Benton............Souther Farm, San Leandro.
FIGARO, Hambletonian—Emblem............Souther Farm, San Leandro.
GROVER CLAY, Electioneer—Maggie Norfolk............Denis Gannon, Oakland.
G. & M., Anteeo—Rosa B............George E. Guerne, Santa Rosa.
GUY WILKES, George Wilkes—Lady Bunker............San Mateo Stock Farm, San Mateo.
GLEN FORTUNE, Electioneer—Glenna............Souther Farm, San Leandro.
JESTER D, Almont—Hortense............Souther Farm, San Leandro.
JUNIO, Electioneer—by Granger............S. N. Straube, Fresno.
LEO WILKES, Guy Wilkes—Sable............San Mateo Stock Farm, San Mateo.
MEMO, Sidney—Flirt............Valensin Stock Farm, Pleasanton.
MAMBRINO WILKES, George Wilkes—Lady Christman............San Miguel Stock Farm, Walnut Creek.
NOONDAY, Wedgewood—Noontide............F. P. Lowell, Sacramento.
PLEASANTON, Director—May Day............Pleasanton Stock Farm, Pleasanton.
PHILOSOPHER, Pilot Wilkes—Belle............George E. Guerne, Santa Rosa.
ROY WILKES, Adrian Wilkes—Nellie B............Pleasanton Stock Farm, Pleasanton.
REDWOOD, Anteeo—Lou Wilton............A. McFayden, Oakland.
SILVER BOW, Robert McGregor—Sadie............P. J. Williams, Oakland.
SIDNEY, Santa Claus—Sweetness............Valensin Stock Farm, Pleasanton.
SIMMOCOLON, Simmons—Colon............Valensin Stock Farm, Pleasanton.
SABLE WILKES, Guy Wilkes—Sable............San Mateo Stock Farm, San Mateo.
ST. NICHOLAS, Sidney—Towhead............John Rowen, Oakland Trotting Park.

Antevolo Sold Again.

When Antevolo was sold his former owner claimed that the horse was worth $40,000, and it is evident that others think so as well as Joseph Cairn Simpson, for the telegraph informs us that R. Steele, of Philadelphia, has sold the California colt to parties in Michigan for $40,000. Antevolo is one of the best colts that ever left this State and that it was one of the improving kind is evident in the fact that only a few weeks ago, Mr. Steele announced through the sporting press that he would endeavor to give Antevolo a low mark next season, and the figure was placed at 2:13 or 2:14. His owner must have had some grounds for the belief in his speed or that story would never have been sent broadcast to the trotting horse world. However, it is to be hoped that the new owners will give him a chance, for his present mark is no measure of his speed.

Santa Rosa.

An item under the heading of Turf and Track, informs the public that the Directors of the Santa Rosa Association have had their annual meeting and elected new officers for the ensuing year. So far so good, but there is a line or two at the end of the item which calls for comment. "The sentiment of the Board is opposed to holding a fair or races this year, unless a disposition different from that of former years is manifested by the people in this part of the country." It seems a shame that such a resolution was passed, and yet the Directors were compelled in justice to themselves to let the people of Santa Rosa know that there would be no more racing at that point, unless the citizens are willing to financially assist the gentlemen who usually have to put their hands in their pockets and pay a deficiency each year. During the year 1889, Napa made money, and Petaluma scored a financial success, but Santa Rosa lost. There were more Santa Rosa people at the Petaluma race-track on one certain day, than there were Santa Rosa residents on any day at the track during the late Santa Rosa Meeting. They seem to have lost all interest in their own town and are all looking for the almighty dollar, without giving the requisite support to those who are trying to keep up the sport of the kings at that point. From the present outlook, Santa Rosa will be dropped from the circuit and it is nothing more than is due to the Santa Rosans for the lukewarm manner in which they have supported the late Directors in their efforts to secure good sport.

The San Jose Stakes.

The Agricultural Society of the Garden City is the first to advertise their yearling stakes to the country. The stake is a peculiar one; it is for certain stallions which are mentioned in the advertisement, and the owners of each stallion must pay into the society $100, or the get of the stallion is not eligible. The other conditions are as follows:

The colts from the horses that make the deposit must pay $15 on March 1, 1890; $15 on June 1, 1890, and $20 on August 1, 1890; $300 added by the Society.

The conditions are as follows: To be trotted during fair week of 1890, one-half mile heats.

Stake deposit and added money divided 66 per cent. to first, 30 per cent. to second and 10 per cent. to third.

National Association rules to govern except as herein stated.

For a walk-over the colt will take the whole stake, but no added money.

If two colts start they must contest for the deposit and stake money only, divided two-thirds and one-third.

A colt distancing the field will take the whole stake, but no added money.

Declarations are void unless accompanied by the money.

Nominations not making payments when due forfeit previous payments.

All colts properly entered in this stake if sold will be entitled to start. If it is the opinion of the judges before starting this race that it cannot be finished on the closing day of the fair, it may be continued.

Entries for the stallions close February 1st. Entries for the colts close March 1st.

The Stake is worthy of the support of all breeders, and should receive liberal patronage.

A Sad Loss.

Last Saturday night we received a telegram from our Kentucky correspondent, stating that Bell Boy, 2:19¼, and all of the Macy Stable at Versailles, Ky., had been destroyed by fire. Of course the report created considerable excitement, and calls were frequent at this office to learn the latest particulars. The more valuable of the horses that were burned beside Bell Boy were:—

Arden, a bay stallion three years old, by Nutwood, dam Adele Clark, $6,000; owned by O. T. Mackey of New York.

A bay filly two years old, by Red Wilkes, $2,000; owned by Judson H. Clark.

Forward, a bay stallion four years old, by Onward, $4,000; owned by H. H. Culbertson of Versailles.

Cookey, a bay filly three years old, by Messenger Chief, dam Cuckoo, $2,500; owned by Stewart Brumsfield of Danville, Ky.

Buckner, Belmont stallion, $2,500; owned by T. W. Hendry of Chicago.

You and I, two year old twin fillies, $4,000.

Fannie Fern and Lena D., $2,000 each.

Three Messenger Chief Colts, two year olds, were also lost, besides other horses valued at $2,000, or less.

In all, forty head, worth $125,000 were burned, Bell Boy being placed at $51,000. It is said that $102,000 was recently refused for him.

Other property losses aggregated $25,000; insurance, $20,000. This includes $13,000 on Macey's stable. A $2,500 dwelling belonging to ex-Governor Thomas Porter was also destroyed.

Such a frightful disaster always carries dismay to the heart of the ordinary reader, and at once the query is asked, What precautions have been used by the proprietors to prevent such a loss of equine life? In the present instance the fire occured at four o'clock in the morning, and the entire stable must have been in flames before the alarm was given, as it was impossible to save any of the valuable animals. Messrs. Clark and Hopper paid $51,000 for Bell Boy, the greatest price ever paid for a horse at public auction, because they were satisfied that the investment was a good one, and yet, after paying this enormous sum, it can hardly be said they exercised due caution in the choice of a place to keep the horse. There should be no chance whatever to lose such a life, for money cannot replace it, and his services are gone for all time. Too much care cannot be taken; stallion stalls should always have more than one exit, and the doors should only be fastened in such a way that the first person present could remove the inmates. See that every precaution is taken against the devastating element.

The Field Trials.

The man who suggested that racing was the "sport of kings," turned a pretty phrase, but if he could have seen a well conducted field trial under favorable conditions the sport with fine setters and pointers would have been given preference. That there is excitement of the most intense sort in coursing or horse racing cannot be denied, but in both sports there are but few qualities, comparatively, to be tested. Given speed, stamina and heart, and the race with either horses or hounds is generally a mere matter of a run. But when men go afield with dogs and guns to compete under field trial rules the competitions present multiform points of interest to every reflective mind. Primarily the contests are between dogs, but in course of training the magnificent animals become so knowing and so fully in sympathy with their masters that dog and man come to be rather complements, then entities and the races are fair measures both of the natural pointing instinct and other attributes of the good field dog, and of the quickness of perception, patience and sportsmanly habits of the handler. Mere speed avails little in a field trial. Stamina alone is valueless. High pointing instinct by itself is inimical to success. Any and all natural qualities conduce only slightly to winning if they be not thoroughly refined, confirmed and developed by studious, judicious care on the part of man. The earlier stages of a field trial are interesting, but as heat after heat is run and the poorer dogs are weeded out, the interest intensifies to such a degree as to become absorbing, even to veterans in other lines of sport.

Poplar Grove Breeding Farm.

S. N. Straube of Fresno is one of the progressive breeders of the San Joaquin Valley, and has improved his stock so much that a visit to Fresno is never considered complete unless a call is made at Mr. Straube's place. He has over seventy brood mares, many of them standard bred, and he is continually adding to their number. His stallions are the grandly bred Clovis 4909, Apex 8935, and Junio, who is eligible to registration, but has not been numbered yet. The latter horse, has been leased by Mr. Straube to cross with his Clovis, Apex and Pasha fillies. Mr. John Donahoo has several of the Poplar Grove Farm youngsters in training at the Fresno Fair Grounds, all of whom are showing up to the satisfaction of owner and trainer. Junio is looking better than he ever was in his life, and should make a very successful season in the stud. An unnamed two year old colt by Electioneer, dam Fanny by Romulus, is of exceedingly great promise, and as Fanny is the dam of Lizzie Thorne, there are grounds for the belief that the new comer will be speedy. Elsie, by Clovis, is another of those threatened with speed, and although only at work a short time is giving satisfaction to the handler.

A three-year-old brown colt by Clovis has been nicknamed "Nick" for the time being, but will have a more high sounding name when it becomes necessary. His dam is Fleetwing by Winthrop 505, 2nd dam Sallie Ward by Pacific, he by Niagara. This would be a grand young stock horse for anyone who desires the services of a young stallion, and as he is for sale at a reasonable figure, should be snapped up eagerly by some of the younger breeders. Mr. Straube has also several good brood mares and fine young stock which can be had at a bargain. The advertisement of the stallions will be found under the proper heading. Junio will stand at the Fair Ground, Fresno, while Clovis and Apex will serve mares at the farm.

Wonderful, isn't it, how some people manage to hide their light under a bushel? Mr. F. F. Kerr of Newman, Stanislaus County, owns a bay stallion sired by Anteros [full brother to Anteeo, 2:16½ (sire of Alfred G., 2:19¾, and Redwood, 2.24½), and to Antevolo, 2:19½]. His dam was sired by Nutwood, 2:18¾ (half brother to Maud S., 2:08¾), and his grandam by Roodhouse's St. Lawrence, who has twice proved himself the begetter of sires of producing dams. Mr. Kerr is not a horseman, or he would have let us know what sort of a horse he had hidden away in his alfalfa fields.

Answers to Correspondents.

Answers for this department must be accompanied by the name and address of the sender, not necessarily for publication, but as proof of good faith. Write the questions distinctly, and on one side of the paper only. Positively no questions will be answered by mail or telegraph.

Oregon George.

GREENVILLE, PLUMAS COUNTY, CAL., Dec. 30, 1889.

EDITOR BREEDER AND SPORTSMAN:—I saw an inquiry in regard to Oregon George, and I will give you all the information I can for the benefit of the inquirer. John M. Shaw says that in 1854 Luke Savage owned old Oregon George at Salem, Oregon, who was a quarter horse, and there were frequent races between the George stock and the Veto stock, owned by English. The Oregon George which sired the dam of Ashley came to Indian Valley, Plumas County, in about 1865. He was a large sorrel horse with white feet and bald face; he ran here in half mile races and also the full mile heats; could go a mile in from 1:56 to 2 minutes. Wm. Bolinger brought some running bred horses to this valley. His brother Charley gambled off a small mare, one of the lot, to a party who sold her to James Wesley, who bred her to Oregon George and got the dam of Ashley. Jack Cochran ought to know who brought Oregon George to Indian Valley. C. M. Lawrence and Jack Cochran gave $71 for the dam of Ashley after Ashley began to show some speed. She bred several colts by Plumas, one or two mares, and Jack Hathaway drives a full brother to Ashley in a buggy here. He is a sorrel, with bald face and white legs, and has trotted in 3:17. One of the fillies was a bay, and could trot in about 3 minutes; the other I never saw. Yours, etc.,

D. S. HAUN.

INFORMATION WANTED.

Can any of our readers answer the following questions?

1. Breeding of Ben Franklin, sire of Kate Agnew 2:28¼.

2. Breeding of General Lee, sire of Lee 2:31½. There was a General Lee that used to stand in Sonoma Co. He was sired by Union, son of Stockbridge Chief Jr. We are informed he is the sire of the dam of Ned Lock 2:28½.

Concord.

Please give the correct time that Axtell took to make each quarter in his 2:12 mile.

Answer.—The telegraph gave a slight variation from the following when the feat was accomplished, but now we give the quarters as taken from the official books: 33, 32¼, 32½, 34¼.

T. S.

Please answer the following questions: Has Mambrino Belmont a record? What is the breeding of Berthune?

Answer.—(1) No. (2) Berthune, by Sidi Hamet, dam Susette by Aratus, 2nd dam Jenny Cockracy by Potomac, 3rd dam by imp Saltram, 4th dam by Symme's Wildair, 5th dam by Driver, 6th dam by imp Fallower, etc.

E. W. Cæsar.

Please give the pedigrees of the following horses: Fisk's, Mambrino Chief Jr., Magna Charter and Vermont Hero.

Answer.—Mambrino Chief Jr., 214, by Mambrino Chief 11, dam by Birmingham, 2nd dam by Bertrand. 3rd dam by Sumpter, 4th dam by Buzzard, etc. Magna Charta 105, by Morgan Eagle, son of Morgan Eagle, by Woodbury, a son of Justin Morgan. Dam a sorrel mare from Indiana, breeding unknown. There are two Vermont Heros; the first by Sherman Black Hawk, dam by Liberty, son of Bishop's Hambletonian, and the other by Hales Green Mountain Morgan, dam by Black Hawk 5, 2nd dam by Hambletonian 2.

L. C. W.

Please inform me if my filly is standard, and if she is eligible to be registered. She is by Mount Vernon 2:21 (he by Nutwood 2:18¾). First dam by Chieftain, second dam by Kentucky Whip.

Answer.—Your filly can be registered if Mount Vernon has been registered, and he is eligible. Send to J. A. McCloud, Stockton, for further information.

G. F., Fresno.

If we answered your question, it would simply be an advertisement for a stallion. We cannot answer such.

Porter Mickle.

Please inform me through the columns of your valuable paper if Altimont, "a dark bay horse bred by Wm. T. Withers, of Lexington, Ky., foaled April 24th, 1878, sired by Almont, 1st dam Belle Miller by Blackwood, 2nd dam by Mambrino Chief, etc., is a standard or registered horse. 2nd. Please give me correct breeding of horse known as Shylock; stood in Sonoma and San Luis Obispo Counties, and is owned by Dr. Hugh Isham; said to be a thoroughbred.

Answer.—Altimont is standard and registered. (2.) Do not know the breeding of Shylock.

A. C. C.

Will you kindly tell me, through your valuable paper, the record of Ben Allen, owned by Mr. Alexander, of Stockton? 2d. If any of his get has a record? 3d. If a colt by him out of an Hamiltonian mare is standard bred?

Answer.—2:38. (2) No. (3) No.

L. W. H.

Will you kindly send me the pedigree of Strathmore and the names of one or two of his get outside of Santa Claus and Steinway?

Answer.—We do not send answers by mail. Strathmore 408, foaled 1866 by Hambletonian 10, dam Lady Waltermire (dam of Marshal Ney) by North America; second dam said to be by Hambletonian 2. He has 30 trotters in the 2:30 list and 2 pacers. In addition to those you mention, he has Cyprus, 2:22½, Skylight Pilot, 2:19, Secret, 2:20½, and Tucker, 2:19.

Gilbert Tompkins.

I claim and have advertised that my colt El Benton (by Electioneer, out of Nellie Benton by Gen. Benton) is a brother in blood to Sunol, 2:10½, who is by Electioneer, out of Waxana by Gen. Benton; and base my claim on the fact that El Benton carries 75 per cent. of the blood of Sunol, 50 per cent. of the blood of the sire Electioneer, and 25 per cent. of the blood of the sire of the dam Gen. Benton. My understanding of the meaning of the term brother or sister in blood is the possession of from 65 to 90 per cent. of identical blood; the best use of the term is to denote a degree of relationship between half sister or brother and full sister or brother. Please tell me if I am correct, as one or two people have argued the point with me.

Answer.—The term brother in blood is commonly used to denote a relationship, which is intermediate between half brother and full brother, and is used to classify a horse bred as is yours when spoken of in conjunction with a mare bred as is Sunol.

W. S. Enos.

Can you tell me where I can find the pedigree of Oregon Nell, and has she a record?

Answer.—We do not know her pedigree, and she has no record. Fill out the blanks which we have sent you by mail and forward them to the Wallace Register Co., 280 Broadway, New York, and then they will determine what to accept and what to reject.

VETERINARY.

Conducted by W. Henry Jones, M. R. C. V. S.

Subscribers to this paper can have advice through this column in all cases of sick or injured horses or cattle by sending an explicit description of the case. Applicants will send their name and address that they may be identified. Questions requiring answers by mail should be accompanied by two dollars, and addressed to W. Henry Jones, M. R. C. V. S., Club Stables, Taylor Street, San Francisco.

SCRATCHES IN HORSES.

This is not a disease, but merely the result of negligence on behalf of grooms intrusted with the care of horses. Horses when coming in from work should have their legs well washed and then thoroughly dried, either with a sponge or a dry rubber.

Answer.—The treatment should be as follows: If the case is a bad one poultice with flaxseed poultices until the inflammation and pain has become reduced. After, apply oxide of zinc ointment. If the legs swell very much give a dose of cathartic medicine. To prevent this complaint I would advise that horses which have to work during the wet and muddy weather; vaseline or pure lard rubbed into the legs will have the desired effect.

WM. HENRY JONES, M. R. C. V. S.,
Club Stables, Taylor Street, S. F.

DR. W. HENRY JONES, VETERINARY EDITOR BREEDER AND SPORTSMAN:—I have a valuable bitch which was hurt in one eye about six weeks ago. The eye is quite closed and she suffers considerable pain. Can you do anything for her?

Answer.—Foment with warm water until the inflammation has subsided. Then apply a lotion of nitrate of silver, 5 grains to the ounce of distilled water. If there is no improvement, consult some veterinary surgeon.

DR WM. H. JONES, VETERINARY EDITOR BREEDER AND SPORTSMAN — DEAR SIR: — Will you please explain the following? I have got a bay mare, three years old, and she was shod last week for the first time. Ever since that she has been lame in both legs. Will you please give the reason? Very respectfully, GEO. N. WILLIAMSON, City.
Jan. 14, 1890.

Answer.—Your inquiry with reference to bay mare is rather ambiguous. What I would suggest is that you have the shoes removed and the feet poulticed. The probability is that the shoes are badly fitted, and hence the cause of lameness. In the event of the mare not becoming sound, I would advise you to call in a duly qualified veterinary surgeon.

W. HENRY JONES, M. R. C. V. S.,
Club Stables, Taylor St., S. F.

Improvements at Morris Park.

Mr. John A. Morris, the owner of this handsome property, is not satisfied with it to remain idle 335 days in the year. Rightly and justly unwilling is he that its employments should be limited to the thirty days allowed by the laws of New York for horse racing, for that would scarcely repay for the immense amount of time, labor, and capital that has been expended in its construction. A million and a half dollars has already been used in buying the land for Morris Park and fitting it up for a race track, and now another half million will be spent in so completing it that it may be used for some purpose or other a hundred or two hundred, or perhaps every day in the year.

Briefly, the present scheme is as follows: In the great inner field, opposite the grand stand and the paddock, and bounded by the Eclipse course, the lower turn and the backstretch of the race track, grounds will be laid out specially adapted for games of baseball, football, lacrosse, athletic contests of all kinds, lawn tennis and croquet, a cinder track will be constructed and special stands will be erected for the accommodation of spectators. On the knoll, just below the grand stand and between it and the secretary's office, will be built a clubhouse, surpassing in architecture, size and appointment anything of its kind to be found on any race track in the world, and superior for club purposes to anything outside of the great cities.

GOOD NEWS FOR ATHLETES.

I met Mr. Morris at the rooms of the New York Jockey Club, Fifth avenue and Twenty second street, one day last week and found him very enthusiastic over the proposed plans, says a reporter.

"In the matter of constructing our new athletic grounds," said he, "we shall be governed entirely by expert opinion as to what is best fitted for the purposes in view. We are now in communication with the leading athletic associations in this city and with members of similar organizations at the leading colleges throughout the country, and in this way we hope to so perfect our plans that as soon as the frost is out of the ground, in the spring we can go on with the work immediately and without any delay complete it before summer."

Delegations from the New York and Manhattan Athletic Clubs were to have visited the grounds at Westchester last week, but the prevailing bad weather prevented it, so that Mr. Morris could give me no exact idea as to the minor details of the plan. He said, however, that it would be left to leading athletes to determine whether the cinder path should be three laps, or four laps, or five laps to the mile. A straightway track will be constructed long enough to provide for the sprint races and the hurdle contests, so that all of them may be run without a turn.

"It is our intention," said Mr. Morris, "if the plan shall prove acceptable, to organize great athletic meetings to occur on public holidays of the year. There are hundreds and thousands of people in New York and Brooklyn who have no desire to go to the race track on Decoration Day, or Fourth of July, or Labor Day, but who would gladly avail themselves of an opportunity to witness athletic contests on these days. Outdoor sports, in which the strength, the power and the energy of men are engaged, are just as popular as the contests of horses, and if it is possible to provide the people with these we shall certainly do so."

A WELL DRAINED FOOTBALL FIELD.

The grounds which will be devoted to football and baseball will surpass anything now existing in this vicinity. People who were present at the recent games between the Princeton and Yale football elevens at Berkeley Oval on Thanksgiving Day undoubtedly have a most vivid recollection of the execrable condition of the grounds, due to the heavy rain of the night before, added to the absence of anything approaching proper drainage. These same people also remember the exceedingly bad means of handling a big crowd furnished at the Oval. Any such troubles as these will be completely obviated at Morris Park. The extensive and almost perfect drainage system at Westchester, when directed to its football field will render it of use on almost any occasions. There will be no disagreeable puddles for the kickers to splash through after a season of rain, no need of adoring the grounds with patches of water-soaked sawdust. Then the capacity of Morris Park for handling a big crowd would be almost unlimited. With the new railroad communication, which will be ready next spring 30,000 or 40,000 people could get into the grounds within an hour, and could get away again at the end of the day in even less time. Such facts as these are bound to commend themselves to the management of any affairs like the big college footfall games.

The same features that will be obtained as to football will apply to the baseball contests. The diamond will be laid out in the most approve style, nothing that will add to making it as perfect as possible being omitted.

NEW STANDS FOR SPECTATORS.

In addition to the mammouth grand stand, from which the horse races are now viewed, Mr. Morris will have new stands erected directly overlooking the athletic grounds. These will be built at the lower end of the field, just inside of the fence along the race track turn. Whether they shall be permanent structures or only temporary, to be taken down when not in use, has not yet been decided. They will be arranged to accommodate 5000 or 6000 spectators, and will make the seating capacity of Morris Park on any great athletic occasion fully 15,000.

For winter sport, if the summer affairs prove successful, the club will have toboganing and skating. The latter will be on a pond or reservoir, which is to be constructed in the grove just beyond the free field.

THE CLUBHOUSE.

But the greatest feature of Morris Park when all the plans shall have been completed, will be the clubhouse. This structure is to be of brick and wood and will be 150 feet long, and 120 deep, with a tower 30 feet square and 130 feet high. These dimensions, however, scarcely give an adequate idea of what the building will be.

The view from the tower will be surpassingly grand, overlooking, as it will, the whole property of the club, the surrounding portions of Westchester, upper New York and Long Island Sound in the distance. The tower will have a large clock, which can be seen for miles around, and which will serve as a worthy successor to the broken-down timepiece of the Catholic Protectory, which for many years regulated the rising of the sun on Westchester.

The exterior of the clubhouse will be imposing. The approach to the building from the driveway in front will be a massive flight of stone steps leading up to the threshold under an immense arch, with a span of twenty-four feet, and adorned with carvings in modern Pompeian terra cotta. Directly over the centre arch on the second and third floors will be two balconies, giving character and detail to the facade.

Passing through the doorway in front the visitor will find himself in a spacious vestibule, with the club office on the right, and at the left a hugh open fireplace. Beyond the office will be a large smoking room for gentlemen, opposite which, across the wide hallway, will be a ladies' parlor and retiring room.

The dining rooms will be on the race track side of the house and will all overlook the course, their whole west side to be of glass and opening on a large piazza. The main dining room, which is to be one of the chief features of the club house, will be 60 feet by 88 feet long, with a ceiling 20 feet high and decorated magnificently. On both sides will be smaller dining rooms, all to be decorated by old fashioned fireplaces.

The second floor of the building will be laid out in small dining rooms, which will be so arranged that they can either be used separately or be thrown together on the occasion of a banquet or a ball. On the third floor will be sleeping apartments, with bathrooms and all the modern improvements of a well appointed clubhouse. The fourth floor will be for the use of the attaches of the club.

The clubhouse will be open every day in the year.

IMPROVED RAILROAD FACILITIES.

Mr. Morris told me that he had already conferred with the management of the New York, New Haven and Hartford and the Suburban Railroad Companies, and he was assured that by next spring matters would be so arranged that people might go to the track direct by train over one of the roads without having to make the troublesome change at Harlem river.

The membership of the club is rapidly increasing, and although it is now less than six months old it has already over 1100 members. The fact that until further notice by the governing committee the regular initiation fee of $100 will not be charged is attracting many to the club, the present expense for a member being simply the annual dues of $25 for resident members and $15 to those residing over 100 miles from New York.

With the membership of 2,000, which the management expects to have by the time the clubhouse is opened, the New York Jockey Club will, indeed, be an organization powerful to do good racing and for the many other sports which it is its plan to foster.

The pool-rooms in New York were all tightly closed on Thursday and Friday of last week. There was no raid, nor, as far as is known, any police interference publicly. An order to put up the shutters must have been privately promulgated, however, judging from the unanimity with which all the resorts shut down business. On Saturday there were no betting transactions, ostensibly, but privileged parties had little difficulty in investing their money on animals of their choice, and the same was true of Monday and Tuesday, when there was not quite such an air of secrecy. Most of the pool-room owners declared at first that the charges of the Western Union Telegraph Company was the cause of the lock-out; that the tax had become unbearable, $50 and 60 being charged a day by the company for telegraphic service. The pool-room owners therefore decided that there was no use trying to conduct business for the benefit of a telegraph company, and agreed to stop business to see if some more equitable arrangement could not be effected. The renewal of business on the quiet, however, seems to favor the belief that the police are really at the bottom of the closing.—(Turf, Field and Farm).

THE FARM.

Salt as a Preventive of Fluke.

Referring to your reply to a question on salt for cattle, in the Mark Lane of October 28th, will you kindly inform me if I may securely trust to rock salt as a preventive of fluke or rot in sheep? I should be much obliged if you would answer in your next issue. ONCE BITTEN.

There is no agent that can be securely trusted to prevent fluke or liver-rot—you can only prevent it by avoiding the cause. You are probably aware that rot in sheep is caused by the invasion of the liver, or bile ducts, by parasites in greater or less numbers. The parasites (*Fasciola hepatica*) are picked up in embryotic form in the pastures. Low-lying, marshy land, adjacent to water-courses liable to flooding, are the most dangerous.

Leaving sheep on these lands during a very wet season, or after the summer has passed, will cause them to rot. Certain years are remarkable for outbreaks, and you will doubtless remember only too well the disastrous consequences to sheep-masters of the rotting year at the beginning of the present decade.

Salt will do a great deal to prevent this and other parasitic invasions, but you cannot "securely trust" it, either as a preventive or accurative agent. For the reasons already stated in the paragraph, to which you refer, salt may be usefully allowed to all domestic animals, but in the treatment of rot it is best administered alternately with sulphate of iron. No great amount of success can be claimed for it, but experience has taught us that it is the best that can be done, and the "bad is the best," unfortunately.

Security there is none, except to keep the animals off rotting land. Talking about prevention of parasitic and dietic diseases in sheep is easy enough, but commercial and economic considerations are always obtruding themselves in a manner most inconvenient to the theorist. Give the salt by all means, but do not trust it so securely as to leave sheep exposed to danger.—M. R. C. V. S., in Mark Lane Express.

The Humboldt Creamery.

The creamery is now in operation, having started up last week. The machinery of the new institution works like clock work, and Mr. Stewart, under whose general supervision the new establishment was erected and equipped, has established the fact beyond the possibility of dispute that he thoroughly understands and has completely mastered the business he has chosen to follow. This is the first real creamery on the Eastern plan in California, and Ferndale may well be proud of starting an enterprise that promises a most important forward step in one of California's leading industries. The Humboldt Creamery is second to but two out of two thousand in the United States, and for arrangement and equipment second to none. The main creamery building is 30x80 feet, and rests on a solid brick foundation. Half of the building is used for manufacturing butter and the other half for cold storage purposes, to store butter, eggs and other perishables. The capacity of the creamery is estimated at three thousand pounds of butter per day, two patent cream separators, two churns and two butter-workers operated by steam, being necessary to perform the work. The cold storage apartments are sufficiently large to store 60,000 dozen of eggs, which can be kept from spring to winter in a perfect condition. The ice factory is 30x30 feet, and is operated by the same power as runs the creamery. Ice will be manufactured in ample quantities to not only supply the storage rooms, but the county demand for that article as well. Those interested in the creamery feel confident that their investment will prove a profitable one, and expect by the time spring fairly opens to receive milk in sufficient quantities to keep the creamery in steady operation. We understand that Mr. S. H. Paine is to act as manager of the new institution, and a more competent, reliable and trustworthy gentleman could not have been selected.

In connection with this notice it is but justice to state that J. W. Blackmore superintended the construction of the creamery building, and C. I Fuller the placing of the machinery, all of which was executed in a manner most satisfactory to those interested.

The officers of the Creamery Association are as follows: President, Ira A. Russ; Vice-President, N. Hurlbutt; Secretary and Manager, S. H. Paine; Treasurer, F. G. Williams, who, with P. Calanchini, compose the Board of Directors. The stockholders in the corporation are. Z. Russ & Sons, Russ, Early & Williams, Russ, Sanders & Co., Mrs. M. Henry, C. A. Doe, P. Calanchini, N. Hurlbutt and S. H. Paine.—Enterprise.

Advantages of the Creamery System.

A subscriber interested in dairy matters would ask some of the contributors to The Stockman to write an article stating clearly the advantage of the creamery system, or cold setting of milk, over the old plan of setting milk in small or large shallow pans without the use of water or ice, for the benefit of those dairymen who still claim they can obtain more cream by allowing the milk to stand 24 or 36 hours, and some even a longer period; and why, after allowing the milk to stand in small pans 24 or 36 hours in a temperature of 60 or 63 degrees, more cream can then be raised by setting pans on the stove and heating up to higher temperature.

The advantage of the creamery or cold deep setting of milk over the old plan consists in the uniformity and certainty of the results, the saving of labor, time and storage room, ease of management, and, as a result of all these, economy. Set fresh, warm milk in a deep can in ice water and raise all its cream in from 8 to 12 hours, and the cream and skimmed milk will be sweet the cream always of the same consistency and if the after-treatment is the same the butter will be of uniform quality. Milk set in open, shallow pans is affected by changes of the weather, and is liable to sour and thicken before all the cream is up, while that set in the creamery has a climate of its own, and where ice water is used the skimming can be done regularly before each milking.

We have used shallow pans, pots, crocks, tin pails, covered and uncovered; have scalded the milk after straining into the pails and have set it warm from the cow; have set the pails on the cellar floor and on shelves in cellar and pantry, and finally tried the deep setting, first submerging in ice water and now setting in a creamery with ventilated covers to the cans, and this gives the best results of all. With deep setting, if you sell cream, you are sure of always having it sweet, and can calculate on having a certain quantity from a given amount of milk, and you have the benefit of sweet skimmed milk for house use or for feeding, while in open shallow setting you are not certain what you will have until the milk is skimmed. There are a large number of pots and pans to be handled every day, and these must be carefully scalded and aired to prevent the next setting of milk from being soured before all the cream is up. With a creamery there are only two or three cans to be washed and scalded; they need no sunning, nor need they be lifted from the creamery.

The creamery yields much the larger bulk of cream, but it is thinner than that raised in shallow pans, though that will make just as good butter as cream raised in deep cans. As for the "why" milk, after standing in shallow pans for 24 to 36 hours in a temperature of 60 to 65 degrees, will raise more cream if set on stove and heated to higher temperature, I don't believe it will. A yellow scum rises, as I have often noticed, but it is claimed that it will not make butter if it is churned. I have never tried it, as the scum was too thin to warrant experiments.

Skimmed milk from a creamery has been analyzed and found to have practically no cream in it; this was where all the conditions were complied with, milk set as soon as drawn from the cow, plenty of ice used, etc; and the experience of thousands seems to prove that the cold deep setting method is the best yet discovered.

A. L. C.

Hampshires and Oxfordshire Downs.

These are the largest in size of any of the Down varieties, and it is the boast of the breeders that they come to earlier maturity than any others. They admirably suit the large chalk farms of the southwestern counties that are possessed of artificial water-meadows, the latter giving abundant food for the ewes and lambs in the critical month of April, when in other districts the farms are very barren after all the turnips have been consumed. The race originated by crossing the old Berkshire knot and the Wiltshire horn with the Southdown, by which means early in the century a characteristic variety, with gaunt frames, coarse heads, and black faces had been created, termed at first West Country Downs. When about 1845, the late Mr. Humphry set himself to improve this race by the employment of some of the finest and thickest-fleshed of Jonas Webb's Southdown rams, the improved Hampshire came into existence, and has had truly marvellous development ever since. The extension of the breed has certainly not been so great as that of the Shropshire, from the fact probably of the latter being adapted to a more extended set of soils and circumstances. Hampshires are, however, popular not only in the counties of Hants, Wilts, and Dorset, but further eastward and northward, as there is every reason why they should be, whenever the conditions of early maturity can be supplied. Hampshires were entered for the Royal Show to the number of 78.

The Oxfordshire variety is closely allied with the Hampshire, having originally been derived from ewes of that breed, tupped by Cotswold rams. The alliance proved an extremely happy one, for the progeny of long wool and short wool parents is one of the best for grazing property, and there was a combination of size to admirable quality, which from the first gave this particular cross a high reputation. There happened at first some diversity of type when efforts were made to perpetuate a new variety, but by studious selections and skillful matings, all evils were eventually overcome, and long before the R. A. S. Council gave the Oxfordshire Downs special classes—which was in 1862, at Battersea—a distinctive character with tolerable uniformity of type had been attained to.

This has been concentrated very much since that period, the general effort, as with the Shropshires, apparently being after a higher quality. They are fine, handsome-looking sheep, that will graze heavy weights, their mutton being as highly esteemed as that of the Hampshires. Rams from the leading flocks not only are in demand for the north of England and Scotland to cross other sheep with, but a great many are exported every year to Germany and America. They are well adapted for mixed soils and tolerably fertile, arable sheep farms, and have extended themselves very much out of their native districts. They stand third highest in the list for the Windsor Show, the number of their entries being 82 Not often have they been brought out to anything like the extent of this, and it is highly creditable to the breeders that they will be so admirably represented.—Mark Lane Express.

Thoroughbred Poultry.

My experience for the last fifteen years fully satisfies me that the high bred fowl is the fowl for all purposes. And what intelligent person would not discard the so-called old-fashioned or mongrel breed for pure bred fowls that it has taken years of the most careful breeding by some of the most intelligent and competent men of both continents to bring to their now high standard of excellence. If all could take their choice at the same price, I dare say they would not be long in making a selection, and it would be in favor of the high bred fowl. There are many of our farmers who are not yet acquainted with the merits of pure bred poultry and still cling to the mongrels. To any one who has had experience with both kinds the difference is quite apparent. The ratio is the same as with thoroughbred cattle and scrubs.

The real mongrels are so small in size that it does not pay to raise them for market, and for egg production they are but little better, for they lay but few eggs, and those mostly during the spring, when eggs are cheap. If you chance to find a large, well formed mongrel, you may be sure it is the result of crossing to some pure bred variety. If, then, a few crosses so vastly improve the stock, the pure bred fowls themselves must necessarily be far superior to the mongrels both in point of size and egg production.

There are a great many people among us who are always sighing for the good old-fashioned breed of fowls—those with big bodies and short legs, non scratches and everlasting layers—oblivious of the fact that if the same motherly old hens that live so pleasantly in their memories were suddenly resurrected they would cut a sorry figure by the side of our modern Brahmas, Plymouth Rocks, etc.

It is a very general and very harmless delusion that the sun shone brighter and the grass grew a brighter green when we talk of the past glories of our domestic stock, we are confronted by the stern and undeniable fact that there has been constant and steady improvement in their useful as well as their ornamental qualities, and among the modern breeds and varieties now kept by fanciers are fowls that will outweigh, outlay and outshow anything produced in the days of "Auld Lang Syne." It is ridiculous for people to be so slow to acknowledge that there is any difference between one kind of fowl and another. They may say a chicken is a chicken, whether it weighs two pounds at maturity or ten pounds; whether it is tender and juicy or tough, dry and stringy; and an egg is an egg, whether large or small, delicate in flavor or tough and rank.

But every one who has had the opportunity for observation will acknowledge the superiority of good Southdown mutton over a mongrel carcass. And to which is the preference to be given, a Shorthorn bullock or a steer, the offspring of a hundred generations of mongrel stock? Almost any farmer of ordinary intelligence will answer the above and tell you how much more profitable for every purpose is the thoroughbred stock over the native. Because a mongrel chicken was good enough for you, stage coaches were good enough for the present generation, surely we do not refuse the benefits conferred by steam and electricity simply because our ancestors had no such blessings. You are not satisfied to breed horses that can trot a mile in three and one half minutes because that was the highest speed attained in your grandfather's time, and why not carry the same idea of improvement into the poultry yard? As fondly as some may hug the delusion, they cannot resist the testimony to the fact that our modern fowls show the effect of persistent effort toward improvement, as the present breeds of cattle, sheep or swine, and the offspring of the common or mongrel hen by a thoroughbred cock will show as much improvement as that of the common cow by the Jersey bull.

Those of my farmer friends who have not already given thoroughbred poultry a trial I would advise that they at once do so. If you do not feel able to buy both thoroughbred hens and cocks, get a few cocks and let them run with your common hens. You will find that as a result your poultry another year will be of larger size, better layers, and will give increased pleasure and profit.

Leghorns, Plymouth Rocks Brahmas, Wyandottes, Langshans and Games are among the best for the farmers' use.—Southern Fancier.

Notes.

A contemporary says: The cattlemen of Scotts River and Trinity Valley, Siskiyou County, have to use snow-shoes to herd their stock.

The snow is quite deep in Eastern Nevada and Idaho, as well as on the Sierra Nevada. The News-Miner says it is about three and a half feet deep on the level at Hailey, and the White Pine News says it is seven feet deep at Hamilton.

The Vermont Chronicle speaks of a dairyman who makes 30 cent butter for less trouble and expense than are bestowed on their product by those who make 16 cent butter. It is less work and costs less to make butter in the right way than it does to do everything out of time and order and thus turn out a poor article.

The only way to improve the dairy stock of the country is to raise better, and it is the duty of every dairyman to raise his share. It is also for his interest to do it, for it will bring him both money and intellectual development. He cannot improve his stock without thinking, and cannot think without improving his mind.

Always have a rack of nice hay or a lick of meal in the manger, each night and morning for the cows and there will be no need of sending a dog or tired and cross hired man after them. They will be on hand at milking time, ready to hurry into their places, and they will express their satisfaction by increasing the contents of the pail.

Secretary Rusk, in the report of the department of agriculture for the United States, says "no less than 6,000,000 dozen eggs were imported at a first cost of over 15 cents a dozen, or nearly $2,500,000, while the average annual value of such importation during the past four years has been $2,216,320." Nearly all these eggs come from Canada.

An Exchange says some people wonder why the Maine farmers are raising so many horses. An old farmer who came into Bangor the other morning with a well dressed four-year old steer which he forced to sell for $27, explains it. "I raise no more beef steers," he said, "for it don't pay. This critter has eaten as much as would raise a colt to the same age, and a good four-year-old colt of good size is worth $150. From now out you'll find me raising horse-flesh."

A new process of butter-making is reported from Australia. Air is introduced into the cream in the churn through an intermediate vessel, in which is stored water and a harmless solution, which purifies the air and otherwise renders it suitable for producing the desired effect upon the cream. The air-pipe opens into the churn near the bottom, through which the gases are driven out. The butter runs off from a tap at the bottom. The process lasts from twenty to forty or sixty minutes' according to the conditions of the cream and other circumstances.

If you have a litter of choice fat pigs and have doubt about wintering them properly about the best hint that can be given is to have an occasional roast, on the principle that when you have a good thing try to save it. Some of the old folks who dined off this toothsome morsel half a century ago can give you old-time directions as to the roasting and preparation for the table. Our own opinion is that roast pig is about as expensive a dish as the farmer can sit down to in the way of meat of his own production, but to the genuine epicure this only adds zest to his appetite.

As one country after another opens up to settlement and progress, new fields open for the introduction of improved breeds of stocks. South America has been the source of a good deal of profit to the breeders of Great Britain for the last few years, and now that the market in that quarter has been pretty well stocked, or at least will be at an early date, they are looking about industriously for new patrons. An English journal just at hand is of the opinion that the next country to buy pedigree stock freely, will be South Africa, the colonization of many parts of which has given its agriculture and stock raising a most progressive turn.—National Stockman.

The Mirror and Farmer says: Dr. Horne thinks cottonseed meal in any form unfit food for cattle. But Prof. Hunter Nicholson, the dairy editor of the Jersey Bulletin, says: "Cottonseed meal is an exceedingly valuable cow food, but it needs to be fed with discrimination and judgment." We think the professor is right. Cottonseed meal is a very strong nitrogenous food, and therefore must be fed lightly and duly balanced with other foods, both as to bulk and carbonaceous material. It is from excessive feeding or from a lack of attention in balancing the ration, that some have got an unfavorable impression of it. The fact that it has to be fed with care is to us an evidence of its value.

Prof. H. W. Conn, professor of biology in the Wesleyan University, Conn., reiterates what other scientists have said before, that all the changes which occur in milk are the result of the growth of bacteria. Practically this has been acknowledged for a long time, it having been discovered that if the atmosphere is entirely excluded from contact with the milk it will keep sweet and limpid for a long time. But the peculiar development, whether bacteria or fungi, is of comparatively recent discovery. With such facility do the germs of bacteria get into milk from the air, from the body of the cow, the hands of the milker and the vessels used for holding milk, that it is declared that pure milk is unknown except to the experimenting scientist.

FOR SALE

AT

Vineland Stock Farm

STALLIONS, BROODMARES AND FILLIES

ONE STALLION FIVE YEARS OLD, SEAL-BROWN, by WHIPPLETON (sire of Lily Stanley, 2:17 1-2 Homestakes 2:18 1-2, etc.), dam Sally Gorham by Werner's Rattler. This horse is scarcely 15 1-2 hands high, but very compactly built. He breeds exceptionally large and well finished colts. Any one understanding the business could clear him in one season, or he would make a No. 1 road horse, as he can trot a 40 gait any time.

ONE THREE-YEAR-OLD, SEAL-BROWN, by WHIPPLETON (sire of Lilly Stanley, 2:17 1-2, Homestakes 2:18 1-2, etc.), dam Sally Gorham, etc. This ought to make a great General Purpose sire, and with opportunities get trotters, as he is compact, strong-boned, and will measure when grown about 16 hands and weighs 1,250 lbs. With a little road work last fall he developed a wonderful burst of speed.

ONE THREE-YEAR-OLD, BLACK, by WHIPPLETON (sire of Lilly Stanley, 2:17 1-2, etc.), dam by Nanbuc (sire of the dam of Eva W., 2:23 1-2, etc.), full brother to Thomas Jefferson, 2:23. This horse will be fully 16 1-2 hands high. He is smooth, rapid gaited and from size and conformation should breed, like his sire, large, fancy, finished colts.

ONE TWO-YEAR-OLD, BRIGHT CHESTNUT, sired by DAWN 2:18¾, dam Alida (dam of Directa, three-year-old record 2:21¾, trial 2:26) by Admiral (sire of sister 2:19 1-2, Nona Y 2:25, etc.). This colt is the making of an extraordinary horse. He is large boned and will be over sixteen hands high when grown; he is of the true Nutwood type, is clean gaited and can land a piece as fast as any man's colt.

ONE TWO-YEAR-OLD, BLOOD BAY, (full brother to Alcona Jr. sire of Silas Skinner, trial 2:22) sired by ALCONA (sire of Flora Belle 2:24, etc.), dam Madonna by Cassius M. Clay Jr. This colt will make a trotter and a great stock horse if developed; he has the combined blood of Almont, Mambrino Chief, Cassius M. Clay Jr. and Joe Downing.

These colts are all sound and promising. The only reason I offer them for sale is, that I have three aged stallions in use, and the surplus is growing on me. If I were starting a breeding business for profit, I should consider either of these colts a representative to commence with. Also brood mares and fillies for sale. Correspondence solicited.

FRED. W. LOEBER, St. Helena, Napa Co., Cal.

By-Laws

—AND—

Rules and Regulations

—OF THE—

NATIONAL Trotting Association

ALSO THE

AMERICAN Trotting Association,

AND THE

PACIFIC COAST BLOOD-HORSE ASSOCIATION.

With Betting Rules.

For Sale at the Office of the

Breeder and Sportsman,

313 Bush St., S. F., Cal.

Price, 25c. each.

By Mail, Postage Paid, 30c. each.

Valensin Stock Farm Stallions,

SIDNEY, 2:19 3-4.

At Eight Years of Age Sire of the following Fastest on Record:

FAUSTINO, yearling stallion, record of the world.................2:35
FLEET, fastest yearling record in 1888.................2:36
FLEET, fastest two-year-old filly in 1889.................2:24
GOLD LEAF, fastest four-year-old Pacing record in the world.................2:11½
ADONIS, fastest three-year-old Pacing Gelding in the world.................2:14½
ADONIS, four-year-old Gelding Pacing record.................2:14

—Also the Sire of—

LONGWORTH, four years old.................2:19
SISTER V., four years old (trial 2:23).................2:27
SANTA RITA.................2:30
MEMO, two-year-old (three-year-old trial 2:20½).................2:49

And many others.

SIDNEY is the sire of Faustino 2:35, and Fleet 2:36, the two fastest yearlings the world has ever known by one sire, and his slowest yearling is faster than the great Electioneer's fastest.

Terms, $250, with usual return privileges, for a limited number of approved mares. Book rapidly filling.

SIMMOCOLON, Four-year-old, 2:29 1-2.

Trial, 2:24; Half Mile in 1:08; Quarter in 33 1-2 Seconds.

Chestnut Horse, foaled 1885.

SIMMOCOLON.

- Simmons 2774. Sire of Bon Bon, 4 y. o. rec., 2:26, Raymon, 4 y. o. rec., 2:27, Black Storm, 3 y. o. rec. 2:27¾, and six others with records of 2:30 or better.
  - George Wilkes 519. Sire of 61 in 2:30 list. Sire of 11 dams of 12 in 2:30 list
    - Hambletonian 10. Sire of 41 in 2:30 list. Sire of 107 sires of 587 in 2:30 list. Sire of 44 dams of 50 in 2:30 list
    - Dolly Spanker
  - Black Jane. Dam of Rose Wilkes, 2:18¾. Dam of Simmons, 2:28
    - Mambrino Patchen 58. Sire of 14 in 2:30 list. Sire of 21 sires of 37 in 2:30 list. Sire of 24 dams of 28 in 2:30 list
    - Lady Stanhope
- Colon. Dam of Simmocolon, 4 y. o. rec., 2:29½. Dam of Patchmore, 2:32¾
  - Strathmore. Sire of 27 in 2:30 list. Sire of 4 dams of 5 in 2:30. Sire of 3 sires of 3 in 2:30
    - Hambletonian 10 (Same as above)
    - Lady Waltermire. Dam of Marshall Ney
  - Coral. Trial at 2 years, 2:30. Dam of Coralloid, 2:29¾
    - Clark Chief 89. Sire of 6 in 2:30 list. Sire of 9 sires of 27 in list. Sire of 11 dam with 11 in list
    - Colon. Dam of Caliban, sire of 3 in 2:30 list

As will be seen, Simmocolon is by a performing and producing son of George Wilkes, 2:22. He has back of him three producing dams, and combines the blood of the great sire George Wilkes handsomely blended with the blood of the greatest broodmare families. On the dam's side Mambrino Patchen, Strathmore, Clark Chief and Clay. A fine individual himself, pure gaited and very fast.

Terms, $150, with usual return privileges, for a limited number of mares. Season to close JUNE 15th, when he will be prepared for track purposes. Pasturage $5 per month. Reasonable charges if fed hay and grain. Best of care taken of mares, but positively no responsibility assumed for accidents or escapes. For further particulars address

G. VALENSIN, Pleasanton, Cal.

ST. NICHOLAS,

A Son of the World Renowned

SIDNEY,

Will Make the Season of 1890, at the Oakland Trotting Park.

ST. NICHOLAS was bred by Mr. G. Valensin at the Arno Stock Farm, Sacramento Co., California, in 1885. He is a beautifully-proportioned bright bay horse, 15.3 hands high; is well muscled, lengthy, and lots of bone, with splendid natural action and a phenomenal turn of speed. As a three-year-old he easily worked three heats on the Oakland Track in 2:32, 2:28 and 2:27¾. His breeding is just what one would expect from such a highly formed bloodlike horse. Sidney, his sire, is the most successful young stallion—whether for getting pacers or trotters—America has ever seen, and no wonder for his blood lines are exceptional fine and are all trotting lines, Santa Claus, Strathmore, Rysdyk's Hambletonian and Abdallah, while Sweetness again runs back through that great sire Volunteer, to Rysdyk's Hambletonian and also through her dam to Rysdyk's Hambletonian and Harry Clay 45, the sire of Electioneer's dam. St. Nicholas' dam is by Echo, an exceptionally prepotent son of Hambletonian thus giving St. Nicholas four Rysdyk's Hambletonian crosses and further back a Harry Clay cross which with his grand dam's thoroughbred cross should make him invaluable in the stud.

TERMS: Fifty dollars the season, which will commence on the 5th of February and close on the 1st of July. Due care will be taken of mares, but no responsibility for accidents or escapes.

Mares taken and kept as desired by the owners, and at reasonable rates.

JOHN ROWEN.

Oakland Trotting Park.

PERRIER-JOUËT & Co.

EPERNAY

CHAMPAGNE

W. B CHAPMAN,

Sole Agent for Pacific Coast.

For sale by all first-class Wine Merchants and Grocers.

Poplar Grove Breeding FARM.

Standard-bred Trotters, Colts and Fillies.

The get of CLOVIS, 4909; PASHA, 2039; APEX, 2935,

For Sale.

Address S. N. STRAUBE, Poplar Grove Breeding Farm,

Fresno, Cal.

Inspection by intending purchasers invited, and information by mail.

"TOBEY'S,"

214 Post Street,

Between Grant Avenue and Stockton Street,

Adjoining New Hamman Baths.

D. J. TOBIN, Proprietor.

Brushes.

BUCHANAN BROS.,

Brush Manufacturers,

609 Sacramento Street, two doors above Montgomery.

Horse Brushes of every description on hand and made to order. Bristle Body Brushes our Specialty

The Poodle Dog "Rotisserie,"

FIRST-CLASS IN EVERY RESPECT.

Elegant Family Dining Rooms.

S. E. cor. GRANT AVE. and BUSH STREET.

ANDRE POTENTINI, Proprietor.

Old Hermitage Whiskies

"STEINER'S,"

No. 311 BUSH STREET,

San Francisco.

Under Breeder and Sportsman Office.

"DICKEY'S,"

SIXTH AVENUE AND D ST.

Near entrance to Bay District Track.

Choicest Brands of

WINES AND CIGARS.

A Delightful Resort.

Telephone 1485. J. R. DICKEY, Propr.

John D. Gall. Jas. P. Dunne

"The Resort,"

No. 1 Stockton Street, cor. Ellis,

San Francisco.

How Is This for a Race?

We recently received from that progressive breeder of New York, Mr. A. E. Whyland, a card which contained beside the several high prices paid for horses, a table showing the time by quarters made by the eight fastest horses by the record. A queer "if" suggested by this card, says L. C. Baker in the Horse World, is that if Jay-Eye-See had trotted his first quarter as fast as he did his last, his record would now be 2:07½ as he went to the quarter at a 2:14 gait, making the last quarter to the tune of 2:04.

Mr. Whyland's card above mentioned suggested to me how the eight fastest horses would appear together in a race, each one trotting as he or she did when they made their best records and each one having an exactly even chance, viz: each one have to travel but a mile, instead of being scattered from the pole to eighth position. Below is the account:

From an excellent start, Sunol gradually drew away, and was leading at the quarter, with Guy and Palo Alto at her wheel, Maud S. lapping them, St. Julien at her wheel with Axtell and Stamboul, neck and neck lapping him, a clear length ahead of Jay-Eye-See. Time, 32 seconds.

At the half Maud S. had forged ahead, with Sunol, St. Julien and Palo Alto neck and neck a length behind, Axtell and Stamboul still head and head at their wheels, Guy lapping them while Jay-Eye-See still brought up the rear, a clean length of daylight being visible between he and Guy. The watches clicked at this point at 1:04¾.

At the three-quarters Maud had increased her lead so that there were two lengths of daylight between her and Sunol who was second, with Axtell on her wheel. Guy and St. Julien in turn lapping the stallion, neck and neck. Jay-Eye-See had moved up and was now head and head with Palo Alto, but a clean length behind Guy and St. Julien. Stamboul bringing up the rear, a clean length behind. Time, 1:35½. If it can be kept up 2:07½ will be recorded. As they sweep into the homestretch Jay-Eye-See comes up with a marvelous flight of speed, cuts his competitors down one by one until he reaches second place, Sunol making a tired break near the wire, but he cannot reach Maud S., who goes under the wire in 2:08¾, two open lengths in advance of Jay-Eye-See, who in turn is a length in advance of Sunol, lapped by Guy, who in turn is about a length in advance of St. Julien, who is a clean length ahead of Axtell, lapped by Stamboul and Palo Alto, neck and neck.

Long Distance Races.

Owners and trainers are anxious for long distant races at weights which will permit of a jockey (not a little boy who is a beginner and no judge of pace) riding. The reason of the entries in the cup races proving so light is not hard to find. The fault lies with the conditions of such races. Take any of the cups, with the exception of the Coney Island Cup, and you will find the penalties are ridiculously small, and in most cases there are no allowances. It does not take much of a prophet, therefore, to write out a list of the horses which will be entered for these cups long before the entries close. Who, then, but a born fool, would waste his dollars in entering his horse when he knows full well that he will have to meet Raceland, Kingston, Firenzi, etc., at a difference only of seven pounds or less outside of weight for age. If the cups are to be a success some other horses besides those at the top of the tree must be given a chance.

Putting aside the cup races, let Secretaries give us purses—say at least one each day—at distances from a mile and a half upward. Let them make conditions, with adequate penalties and allowances. They will then find out whether or not owners and trainers like long distance races. They will receive big entries, and the public, too, will be interested. It is a stupid theory to claim that long distance races are not popular because the cups receive poor entries. I, for one, should consider any man an idiot who would enter a moderate horse for a cup, looking at the conditions of these races. You need go no further back than the recent long distance races at Clifton to find out that they are popular. The best horse there has proved to be Eleve. Yet, Eleve was a maiden at the big tracks, simply because Secretaries never gave a race far enough to give him a show. The same may be said of plenty of other horses. At the present rate of procedure, without doubt, we shall soon revert to the old time quarter dashes, for nothing but sprinting is nowadays considered in the conditions. Breeders naturally will breed to suit the market, and by degrees we shall come to consider a horse who can compass a mile and a quarter a horse of wonderful stamina. You may claim that the thoroughbred of to-day is the superior of the thoroughbred of olden days. True. I grant he is speedier; but I don't think he has the same stamina, and for the reason that breeders look nowadays only for speed, and with that object alone in view. Yours truly,

A TRAINER.

The Undine Stable has one of their colts entered in part of the Eastern events as Homer, and in others as Scamper. Under which name is the colt going to run?

Synopsis of SIXTY HEAD of

VILLAGE FARM TROTTING STOCK,

THE PROPERTY OF

Mr. C. J. HAMLIN.

To be Sold at Auction, in New York,

THE FIRST WEEK OF MARCH, 1890,

AT THE

AMERICAN INSTITUTE BUILDING,

Third Ave., bet. 63d and 64th Sts., New York, by

PETER C. KELLOGG & CO., Auctioneers.

Office, 107 John Street, New York.

This consignment contains 18 Colts and 14 Fillies by Mambrino King, the handsomest horse in the world, the greatest stallion by Mambrino Patchen (whom he has exceeded in the stud), and the sire of "the bull-dog four-year-old of the grand circuit of 1889," Prince Regent 2:21¼. Also, 9 Colts and 9 Fillies, by Hamlin's Almont, Jr., sire of Belle Hamlin 2:12¾, and the greatest Stallion left by Almont, having proved himself superior to his sire. Also numerous Brood Mares, stinted to Almont, Jr., Mambrino King and Chimes (son of Electioneer and Beautiful Bells).

Name.	Color and Sex.	Year.	Sire.	Dam's Family.
Bona	ch. m.	1884	Mambrino King.	Bright Eyes, by Blackwood Chief (by Blackwood, dam by Dictator). Stinted to Almont, Jr.
Peaches	b. m.	1888	Mambrino King.	Dolores, by Almont, Jr.; 2d dam by Mambrino Patchen.
Queen Bess	b. m.	1888	Mambrino King.	Bessie Hamlin, by Almont, Jr.; 2d dam, by Mambrino Patchen; 3d dam, by Tom Crowder.
Senorita	b. m.	1887	Mambrino King.	Toilet, by Almont, Jr.; 2d dam, by Dictator.
Exquisite	b. m.	1888	Mambrino King.	Toilet, by Almont, Jr.; 2d dam, by Dictator.
Medea	bl. m.	1884	Mambrino King.	Mink, by Hamlin's Patchen; 2d dam (dam of Henrietta 2:23¼), by Rysdyk's Hambletonian. Stinted to Almont, Jr.
Lassie	bl. m.	1887	Mambrino King.	Olive, by Plato, son of Mam. Patchen; 2d dam, Mink (above).
Chicadee	b. m.	1887	Mambrino King.	Chicory, by Mambrino Dudley 2:19¾; 2d dam, Emilia (dam of Orpheus 2:30), by Rysdyk's Hambletonian.
Roxie	b. m.	1885	Mambrino King.	Lady Barnes, by Hamlin Patchen; 2d dam, by Field's Royal George. Stinted to Almont, Jr.
Daylight	ch. m.	1887	Mambrino King.	Lady Barnes. See above.
——	b. m.	1889	Mambrino King.	Beloved, by Almont, Jr. 2:26; 2d dam, Nellie Mac (dam of Beauregard 2:21½).
Queen	b. m.	1885	Mambrino King.	Favorite, by Dunn's Star 9417, son of Seely's American Star. Stinted to Chimes.
Buttercup	b. m.	1885	Mambrino King.	Hawkeye, by Hamlin Patchen. Stinted to Almont, Jr. 2:26.
Patience	bl. m.	1887	Mambrino King.	Corinne, by Almonarch 2:24¾; 2d dam, Grandmother 2:20¾ (p), by Almont, Jr. 2:26.
Automatic	b. s.	1888	Mambrino King.	Topaz, by Strathmore; 2d dam, by Albion; 3d dam, Ned, dam of Clemmie G. 2:15¼ and 4 others in the list.
Delmar	b. s.	1888	Mambrino King.	Homora, by Almonarch 2:24¾; 2d dam, by Almont, Jr. 2:26; 3d dam, by Hamlin Patchen.
Patrician	b. s.	1888	Mambrino King.	Clarice, by Almont, Jr. 2:26; 2d dam, by Hamlin Patchen; 3d dam, by Field's Royal George.
Houghton	bl. s.	1887	Mambrino King.	Gerty Smith, by Mambrino Patchen; 2d dam, thoroughbred, by Lancaster, son of imp. Glencoe.
General Riley	b. s.	1888	Mambrino King.	Gerty Smith, by Mambrino Patchen (see above).
Germaine	b. s.	1888	Mambrino King.	Verdant, by Almont, Jr. 2:26; 2d dam, by Hamlin Patchen; 3d dam, Mermaid, by Dictator.
Carleton	b. s.	1885	Mambrino King.	Barbara, by Kentucky Prince; 2d dam (dam of Bergen 2:26¾), by Rysdyk's Hambletonian.
——	b. s.	1889	Mambrino King.	Amanda, by Almont Dictator 2:37¼; 2d dam, by Hamlin Patchen.
——	ch. s.	1889	Mambrino King.	Lady Barnes, by Hamlin Patchen; 2d dam, by Field's Royal George.
Pardee	ch. s.	1888	Mambrino King.	Nelly Mac (dam of Beauregard 2:21½).
Gail King	b. s.	1888	Mambrino King.	Gail Mare, by Almont, Jr. 2:26; 2d dam, by C. J. Wells, son of Royal George.
Autocrat	ch. s.	1887	Mambrino King.	Coquette, imported French Coaching Mare.
Astonish	b. s.	1887	Mambrino King.	Dictotrice, imported French Coaching Mare.
Clarice	b. m.	1884	Almont, Jr. 2:26.	Daisy, by Hamlin Patchen; 2d dam, by Field's Royal George. Stinted to Mambrino King.
Brilliant	b. m.	1884	Almont, Jr. 2:26.	Topaz, by Strathmore; 2d dam, by Albion; 3d dam, Ned (5 from 2:15¼ to 2:28¼). Stinted to Mambrino King.
Senora	b. m.	1887	Almont, Jr. 2:26.	Sateene, by Mambrino King; 2d dam, Miranda (dam of W. H. Nichols 2:23¼), by Mambrino Patchen.
Verdant	b. m.	1881	Almont, Jr. 2:26.	Mollie O., by Hamlin Patchen; 2d dam, Mermaid, by Dictator. Stinted to Mambrino King.
Hostess	b. m.	1888	Almont, Jr. 2:26.	Maple Leaf, by Mambrino King; 2d dam, by Waverly; 3d dam, by Field's Royal George.
Chastina (sister to Justina 2:23¼.)	b. m.	1887	Almont, Jr. 2:26.	Black Golddust, by Hamlin Patchen; 2d dam, by Golddust; 3d dam, by imp. Glencoe.
Caprice	b. m.	1887	Almont, Jr. 2:26.	Nathalie, by Mambrino King; 2d dam, by Dunn's Star 9417.
Miss Kerr	b. m.	1888	Almont, Jr. 2:26.	Molly, by Bartlett Morgan; 2d dam, by McCracken's Black Hawk.
Gail Mare	b. m.	1879	Almont, Jr. 2:26.	Daughter of C. J. Wells son of Royal George. Stinted to Mambrino King.
Aspirant	b. s.	1888	Almont, Jr. 2:26.	Satory, by Almonarch 2:24¾; 2d dam, by Hamlin Patchen; 3d dam, by Dictator.
Hollister	b. s.	1887	Almont, Jr. 2:26.	Miranda (dam of W. H. Nichols 2:23¼), by Mambrino Patchen; 2d dam, by Tom Crowder.
Hudson	b. s.	1888	Almont, Jr. 2:26.	Miranda, by Mambrino Patchen (see above).
Albert Fink	b. s.	1888	Almont, Jr. 2:26.	Goldie, by Mambrino King; 2d dam, by Hamlin Patchen; 3d dam by Golddust.
Methodical	b. s.	1886	Almont, Jr. 2:26.	Medea, by Mambrino King; 2d dam, by Hamlin Patchen; 3d dam, by Rysdyk's Hambletonian; 4th dam, by Golddust; 5th dam by imp. Glencoe.
Hollander	b. s.	1886	Almont, Jr. 2:26.	Sister to Elda B. 2:21, by Wood's Hambletonian; 2d dam, by Dandy, son of L. I. Black Hawk; 3d dam, dam of Midge 2:27¾.
Depew	b. s.	1887	Almont, Jr. 2:26.	Betty Mac, by Red Wilkes; 2d dam, dam of Fanny Witherspoon 2:16¼, by Gough's Wagner.
Knight Errant	b. s.	1888	Almont, Jr. 2:26.	Nathalie, by Mambrino King; 2d dam, by Dunn's Star.
Osborne	b. s.	1888	Almont, Jr. 2:26.	Louisa (dam of Lucretia 2:29¾ at 4 years, and Blaine 2:31), by Hamlin Patchen; 2d dam, Mermaid, by Dictator.
Furoline	bl. m.	1881	Kentucky Prince.	Lady Dexter (sister to Dexter 2:17¼), by Hambletonian; 2d dam, by Seely's American Star; 3d dam, dam of Shark 2:27¾ (s). Stinted to Chimes.
Mary Weston	b. m.	1887	Mohican, 608.	Merry Lass 2:40, by Rysdyk's Hambletonian; 2d dam, by Voorhees' Abdallah. Stinted to Mambrino King.
Electa	b. m.	1885	Almont Dictator.	Mandrake, by Blackwood Chief; 2d dam, by Hamlin Patchen; 3d dam, by Field's Royal George. Stinted to Chimes.
Amanda	b. m.	1885	Almont Dictator.	Nettie Murphy, by Hamlin Patchen. Stinted to Mam. King.
Brooch	b. m.	1887	Almont Dictator.	Lady Clay, dam of Actor 2:29¼ (p.)
Hobart H.	b. s.	1887	Almont Dictator.	Maple Leaf, by Mam. King; 2d dam, Belle B., by Waverly.
Balmoral	b. m.	1882	Blackwood Chief.	Thornhedge, by Almont, Jr. 2:26; 2d dam (dam of Henrietta 2:23¼), by Hambletonian; 3d dam, by Golddust. Stinted to Mambrino King.
Corning	b. s.	1885	Shawmut 2:26.	Jenny Bate, by Cuyler; 2d dam, by Shelby Chief 223; 3d dam, by Pilot, Jr.
Erastus	b. s.	1886	Shawmut 2:26.	Jenny Bate, by Cuyler (see above).
Chicory	b. m.	1883	Mambrino Dudley 2:19¾	Emilia (dam of Orpheus 2:30), by Rysdyk's Hambletonian; 2d dam, by Tom Thumb. Stinted to Chimes.
Myrtle (sis. to Elda B. 2:21)	b. m.	1881	Wood's Hambletonian	May, by Dandy, son of L. I. Black Hawk; 2d dam, dam of Midge 2:27¾. Stinted to Chimes.
Ursula	b. m.	1876	Lagow 7912.	Vic (dam of Mattie Graham 2:21¼ and Dainty 2:26¾), by Mambrino Chief. Stinted to Mambrino King.
Favorite	b. m.	1879	Dunn's Star 9417.	Daughter of Harry Clay 2:29; 2d dam, by Balsora. Stinted to Chimes.
Halsie	b. m.	1887	Gen. Riley 7873.	Halcie B., by Charley B. 812; 2d dam, by Monroe Morgan.
Fanny French	b. m.	1888	Silver King 2:25¼.	Fanny B., by Maj. Greenwood.

CATALOGUES SENT ONLY ON APPLICATION. Address all correspondence to

PETER C. KELLOGG & CO.,
107 John St., New York.

Langtry Farms' Stud

Imp. FRIAR TUCK

By the Immortal HERMIT

DAM ROMPING GIRL BY WILD DAYRELL,

AT $50 THE SEASON.

Mares not proving with foal may be returned the following season. Good care taken of mares, but no liabilities for accidents or escapes.

Good Pastnrage at $5 per month.

Mares shipped to ST. HELENA, care CHARTES WILLIAM ABY, St. Helena Stables, will be cared for. For further particulars address,

CHAS. WILLIAM ABY,
Middletown, Lake County, Cal.

2:08 3-4 2:10 2:12

MAMBRINO WILKES, 6083.

SIRE OF

GUS WILKES, 2:22; ALPHEUS, 2:27; CLARA P, 2:29½; BALKAN, 2:29½ (3-year-old) and timed separately 2:22½ in 4-year-old Stake, Bay District Track, October 14, 1889.

DESCRIPTION.

Black; sixteen hands; weighs, in exercise, 1,260 lbs. For style, finish, symmetry and proportion, comparison is challenged with any trotting bred horse. His colts follow in size, style and beauty. Balkan, for instance, being "facile princeps" of trotters in these particulars.

PEDIGREE.

Sired by Geo. Wilkes, sire of Harry Wilkes, 2:13¼, Guy Wilkes, 2:15¼, and 60 other trotters in the 2:30 list, in addition to 6 pacers, and of the sire of Axtell, 2.12 (three-year-old), beating all stallions of any age, and the sire of Regal Wilkes, 2:20¾, best two-year-old stallion record.

First dam Lady Chrisman by Mambrino (Todhunter's), son of Mambrino Chief 11; sire of Lady Thorn, 2:18¼; Woodford Mambrino, 2:21½, and four others in 2:30, and of the dams of Director, 2:17, Piedmont, 2:17¼, Onward, 2:25¼, etc.

Second dam by Pilot Jr. 12, sire of nine in the 2:30 list, and of the dams of Maud S., 2:08¾, Jay-Eye-See, 2:10, Nutwood, 2:18¾, Viking, 2:19¼, Pilot Boy, 2:20, Naiad Queen, 2:20¼, etc.

TERMS.

Mares from a distance will be received at the Dexter Stables, Oakland, or Livery Stable, Martinez, the owner notifying Smith Hill, Superintendent at the farm. Good pasture and plenty of water. For the purpose of placing the service of a Wilkes within reach of breeders, the same rate will be maintained as last year, to wit, $75 for the season. Although it is not admitted thereby that this horse is inferior as a producer to the horses whose fees are placed at from $150 to $500. Address

SMITH HILL,
San Miguel Stock Farm,
Walnut Creek, Contra Costa Co., Cal.

2:12¾ 2:13½ 2:15¼

Thoroughbred Stallion

Prince of Norfolk.

Will Make the Season of 1890, from Feb 1st to July 1st, at Sacramento.

Prince of Norfolk, chestnut horse, foaled 1881, by Norfolk; first dam Marion by Malcolm; second dam Maggie Mitchell by imp. Yorkshire; third dam Charmer by imp. Glencoe; fourth dam Betsy Malone by Stockholder; fifth dam by Potomac, sixth dam by imp. Diomed; seventh dam by Pegasus, etc. Norfolk, the unbeaten son of Lexington, is the sire of Winters, Twilight, Connor, Ballot Box, Trade Dollar, Flood, Duchess of Norfolk, Lou Spencer, the great Emperor of Norfolk, the unbeaten El Rio Rey, and many others. Marion's sire, Malcolm, was one of the first horses to bring Bonnie Scotland into notice. Through the Maggie Mitchell cross comes the blood of two of the most celebrated race mares of their day, Charmer and Betsy Malone. The combined speed of these great families seem to be concentrated in the get of Norfolk and Marion, as is instanced in the case of the Emperor of Norfolk, and El Rio Rey, who are full brothers to the Prince of Norfolk.

The blood lines here displayed cannot be surpassed in the world, there not being a single cross that has not been celebrated for speed and endurance, and it is fair to assume that the get of this stallion will show equally well with those of past generations.

TERMS: $50 for the season. We offer first-class pasturage on our own ranch, at $3 per month, and the best of care will be taken of mares sent to us, but no responsibility can be incurred. For further particulars, address by mail or wire,

DAN DENNISON.
or, W. P. TODHUNTER, Sacramento.

ROME HARRIS. JOHN MERIGAN,

"Laurel Palace,"

N. W. corner Kearny and Bush Streets
SAN FRANCISCO.

2:19 NOONDAY 2:20½

STANDARD No. 10,000.

This celebrated trotting bred stallion will make the season of 1890 at the stable of the undersigned at Sacramento, Cal., at $75 for the season and $100 to insure a mare in foal. Payable on or before July 1st, 1890. Money will be refunded on mares bred by insurance as soon as the fact becomes known that they are not in foal.

NOONDAY.

- Wedgewood, 2:19... Sire of Favonia, 2:15, fastest 4th heat for any mare or gelding, and eight others in 2:27 or better.
  - Belmont... Sire of Wedgewood, 2:19, Nutwood, 2:18¾, Viking, 2:19¼, and 29 others in 2:30 list.
    - Alexander's Abdallah, sire of Goldsmith Maid, 2:14; Almont, with 35 horses in 2:30 list, etc.
    - Belle, dam of Hambletonian, 2:26½; B'cars, dam of Pancoast, 2:21¾, the sire of Patron, 2:14¼.
  - Woodbine... Dam of Wedgewood, 2:19, Woodford Mamb., 2:21½, the sire of Pancoast, 2:21¾, the sire of Patron, 2:14¼.
    - Woodford.
    - Singleton Mare.
- Noontide, 2:20½.... (Trial, 2:13½).
  - Harold ... Sire of Maud S., 2:08¾, and 26 others in 2:30 list.
    - Hambletonian (Rysdyk's), sire of George Wilkes, 2:22, the sire of Guy Wilkes, 2:15¼; Electioneer, the sire of Sunol, 2:10½, and scores of noted trotters and producers.
    - Enchantress, by Abdallah 1.
  - Midnight ... Dam of Jay-Eye-See, 2:10, Noontide, 2:20½.
    - Pilot Jr., sire of dams of Maud S., 2:08¾, Jay-Eye-See, 2:10, Nutwood, 2:18¾, etc.
    - Twilight, by Lexington, sire of the dam of Ansel, 2:20.

NOODAY is a dark seal brown, foaled 1884, 15 hands 1¼ inches high. Individually he is equal to his royal breeding. He is all that can be desired in conformation, intelligence, color and trotting action, and no stallion now in public service can show a pedigree with such fast records and royal game trotting blood as Noonday.

DON MARVIN,

Record 2:28 as a five-year-old. Standard by Breeding and Performance

Standard No. 7927.

Don Marvin 2:28.

Don Marvin is a beautiful seal brown, foaled 1884, bred by Hon. Leland Stanford, Palo Alto, Cal., standing 14 hands, and weighs, in ordinary condition, 1,210 lbs. He is a fine individual, good style and form, combined with great substance and good temper. Is very level headed; in his first race the past season he only made one break in five closely contested heats. He has great speed and endurance, with the pure, rapid Electioneer gait. He trots without toe weights, and wears only 8 oz. shoes in front. He gained his record the past season in the third heat, on a slow track, after making a season (serving over 40 mares), with scarcely any preparation. His record is no mark of his speed. He was a natural born trotter, and Mr. Charles Marvin considered him the fastest two year old at Palo Alto that season.

By FALLIS, 2:23, - - by Electioneer, sire of
Sire of Don Marvin, 2:28. — Sunol, three-year-old, 2:10 1-2, Palo Alto, 2:12¾, and 47 others in 2:30 list.

Dam CORA, by Don Victor by Belmont, sire of
Dam of Don Marvin, 2:28. — Ventura, 2:27¼, and sire of the dam of Bell Echo, 2:20, and six others in 2.30 list.

2d dam CLARABEL, - by Abdallah Star,
Dam of Clifton Bell, 2:24 1-2, and grandam of Rexford, three years, 2:24. — Sire of Hattie Maples, 2:33.

3d dam FAIRY, - - by Rysdyk's Hambletonian,
Sister of Sweepstakes, sire of 16 in 2.30 list. — Sire of Electioneer, George Wilkes, and many other noted sires and trotters.

4th dam EMMA MILLS, by Seely's American Star,
Dam of 4 horses that have 2:30 performers. — The great broodmare sire of the world.

The above pedigree should show every intelligent breeder that Don Marvin is "high" bred, though very strong in trotting blood. All the comment it is deemed necessary to make as to the value of "thoroughbred blood" in the trotter is simply to refer to the very significant fact that the first and second dams of Maud S., 2:08¾, Jay-Eye-See 2:10, Sunol, three years 2:10 1-2, Palo Alto 2:12¾, Anteeo 2:16¼, Nutwood 2:18¾, Wedgewood 2:19, and many other successful sires and sensational trotters of the day are thoroughbred.

TERMS—Don Marvin will make the ensuing season from February 1st to July 1st, 1890, at $40 the season, with the usual privilege of returning the mare next season if not proving in foal. Mares from a distance met at the cars or boats on notification, and carefully handled, but no responsibility assumed for accidents or escapes.

Good alfalfa pasture furnished (free from barb wire fence) at $4 per month. For further particulars or complete circulars address

F. P. LOWELL,
1520 F Street, Sacramento, Cal.

The Thoroughbred Stallion

INTRUDER

Will make the Season of 1890 at Agricultural Park, SACRAMENTO.

Bay Horse, foaled 1871, bred by Sir L. Newman, England. Imported by D. D. Withers, Esq., New York.

By Crater, Son of Orlando and Vesuvienne by Gladiator.

1st dam Lady Bountiful by Rataplan (Rataplan is own brother to Stockwell, and winner of 42 races, including the Doncaster Cup and 19 Queen's Plates, and proved himself the most distinguished race horse of his day in England).

2d dam Plentiful by Don John (the winner of St. Leger and Doncaster Cup).

3d dam Plenty by Bay Middleton (winner of the Derby and Two Thousand Guineas Stakes).

4th dam Plenary, own sister of Plenipotentiary, by Emilius. (Both Emilius and Plenipotentiary were Derby winners).

5th dam Harriet, dam of the renowned Plenipotentiary by Pericles.

6th dam by Selim, winner of the One Thousand Guineas Stakes.

7th dam by Pypilina, by Sir Peter.

8th dam Rally, by Trumpeter.

9th dam Fancy, by Florizel. Fancy was full sister to Diomed, the first Derby winner in England, and after his importation into this country, sired the illustrious Sir Archy, etc. See English Stud Book.

Imported INTRUDER is a beautiful bay, standing fully 16 hands high, of great length and substance, and descends through close and strong currents from the most illustrious winners and winning lines of blood of which the English Stud Book bears record.

A careful review of the first six crosses of the pedigree of INTRUDER will show nine Derby winners; five St. Leger winners; two winners of The Oaks; two winners of the Two Thousand Guineas; two winners of the One Thousand Guineas; one Goodwood Cup winner; one Cesarwich Cup winner; one Cambridgeshire Stakes winner, and four Doncaster Cups, in addition to a great number of Steeplechases and other races of less import.

INTRUDER, at the great fair held at St. Louis, Mo., in 1876, was awarded the highest stallion honors—the blue ribbon and the $500 purse—in the sweepstakes ring for stallion of any age or blood. The list of competitors embraced the large number of thirty-three animals, and they represented England, Canada, Kentucky, Tennessee, and other states. He also took first premium in his class and in sweepstakes for the best stallion of any age or breed at the State Fair at Peoria, Ill., 1884. He is the sire of Tidal Wave, George Hakes, Bernice and April Fool.

INTRUDER is the sire of Interpose, who is the dam of Spokane, winner of the Kentucky Derby, in which he beat the great horse Proctor Knott and broke the record.

TERMS: $50 for the season. Mares not proving with foal can be returned the next season free of charge. Good pasturage at $4 per month. Mares cared for in any manner owners may desire, and fed on hay and grain, either or both, at reasonable rates. While every precaution will be taken, no responsibility will be assumed for escapes or accidents. Mares sent from a distance in care of the undersigned, will be met and taken to the park. For further particulars, address

T. J. KNIGHT.
Agricultural Park, Sacramento.

CANNON BALL, 8820

BY SIMMONS 2744.

RECORD 2:28, (Full Brother to Rosa Wilkes, 2:18 1-4), Sire of Nine in 2:30 List at 10 Years Old.*

First dam Gungle, pacing record 2:21; trial of 2:15¼ for W. H. Crawford; by Pocahontas Boy, sire of Buffalo Girl, 2:12¼; Raven Boy, 2:15¼, and ten others in the list.

Second dam Matlock by Grey Diomed.

Third dam by Tom Hal.

DESCRIPTION.

Brown bay, right hind foot and left inside hind heel white. Foaled May 20, 1887. Bred by W. H. Wilson, Abdallah Park, Cynthiana, Ky.

He is a grand individual, large boned, fine size and appearance. When fully matured will probably be 16 hands, and weigh 1200 lbs.

Is of speedy conformation and level headed. His blood lines are stout and fashionable, being the Wilkes and Mambrino Patchen on pacing and thoroughbred foundations, and from a family of producers on both sides.

Can be seen until February 1st at Agricultural Park, Los Angeles, in charge of C. A. Durfee, after which he will serve ten approved mares at $60 the season, with usual privilege of return in 1891, at Lockhaven Stock Farm, Burbank, Cal. Mares kept on grass $4 per month, and extra charge where grain and alfalfa are fed. For further particulars, address

O. H. LOCKHART, Proprietor,
Lockhaven Stock Farm,
Burbank, Cal.

Nine Miles from Los Angeles.

NOTICE.

C. BRUCE LOWE,
Pedigree Stock Agent,
19 Bligh Street,
SYDNEY, New South Wales.

Reference—J. B. HAGGIN, ESQ.

POPLAR GROVE

Breeding Farm

STALLIONS.

CLOVIS, 4909,

CLOVIS is a beautiful black, Eight Years Old, 16 1-2 Hands High, and weighs 1260 lbs.

He is a horse of beautiful symmetry and magnificent action.

PEDIGREE.

CLOVIS was sired by Sultan, 2:24, sire of Stamboul, 2:12 1-4, Ruby, 2:19¼, and fifteen others with records of 2.30 or better.

First dam Sweetbriar by Thorndale 2:22 1-2, sire of Edwin Thorne, 2:16 1-2, Daisy Dale, 2.19, and May Thorne, 2:24.

Second dam Ulster Queen, dam of Volmer, 2:24¼, by Hambletonian 10. Sire of Dexter, 2:17¼, George Wilkes, 2:22.

Third dam by Thomas Jefferson, he by Toronto Chief, he by Royal George.

Fourth dam by Mambrino Paymaster, sire of Mambrino Chief.

Sultan, by The Moor, sire of Beautiful Bells, dam of Hinda Rose, 2:19 1-2, and Sable, dam of Sable Wilkes, three year old record 2:18.

First dam of Sultan, Sultana, by Delmonico, Sire of Darby, 2:16 1-2, by Guy Miller, sire of Whipple's Hambletonian.

Second dam by Mambrino Chief.

Third dam by Downing's Bay Messenger.

Fourth dam Mrs. Caudle, dam of Ericsson, four year old record 2.30 1-2.

Clovis will make the season of 1890 at Poplar Grove Breeding Farm, near Wildflower, Fresno County, commencing February 1st and ending July 1st.

Terms, $75, due at time of service.

Mares cared for in any manner owners may desire; pasturage $2 per month. Every care exercised, but no liability for escapes or accidents. Mares not proving with foal can be returned next season, providing I still own this stallion.

APEX, 8935.

FOUR-YEAR-OLD RECORD, FOURTH HEAT, 2:26.

Will make the present season at the Poplar Grove Breeding Farm, near Wildflower, Fresno Co., season commencing Feb. 1st, and ending July 1, 1890. Terms, $50 the season, due at time of service. Apex is eight years old, a beautiful bay, 15 1-2 hands high, and weighs 1100 lbs. He is a horse of fine disposition, and his gait is faultless.

PEDIGREE.

Apex was sired by Promptor 2305, he by Blue Bull 75; first dam Mary by Flaxtail, he by Pruden's Blue Bull. Flaxtail being the sire of the dams of Buccaneer, five-year-old record, 2:24 1-2; Pride, yearling record, 2:44 1-2, and Shamrock, two-year old record, 2:25, third heat. Second dam by Bright Eyes, son of Boanarages. Prompter (sire of Apex, record 2:26, and Transit, 2:26 1-2), by Wilson's Blue Bull, by Pruden's Blue Bull, son of Merring's Blue Bull. Prompter's dam Prairie Bird, by Flaxtail; second dam by John the Baptist, son of Tally Ho Morgan, by Sherman Morgan; third dam Fannie Fern by Irwin's Tuckaho.

Apex made his appearance in the circuit as a two-year-old, and obtained a record of 2:42. As a three-year-old he reduced this in a race at Santa Rosa against Stamboul to 2:31, it taking six heats to decide the contest, which was won by Apex. As a four-year-old he gained his present record of 2:26.

Mares cared for in any manner owners may desire. Pasturage $2 per month. Every care exercised, but no liabilities for escapes or accidents. Mares not proving with foal can be returned next season, providing I still own this stallion.

The Standard Stallion

JUNIO,

RECORD 2:22.

WILL MAKE THE PRESENT SEASON OF 1890 AT FRESNO FAIR GROUNDS.

Season Commencing Feb. 1st and ending July 1st

TERMS—$100 the season, due at time of service.

JUNIO is eight years old, a handsome dark bay 16 hands high, and weighs 1250 pounds. He is the personification of the light harness horse, and his trotting action is superb. At the State Fair of 1888 he took first premium over forty of the finest trotters in the State.

PEDIGREE.

*Junio, by Electioneer, premier stallion of Palo Alto (sire of Sunol 2:10 1-2, Palo Alto 2:12 1-4, and 47 others in the 2:30 list. Dam by Granger by imp. Hercules.

Granger, by imp. Hercules, dam Jenny Lind, by Stockbridge Chief, Jr., he by Stockbridge Chief, he by Vermont Black Hawk. Second dam by Kentucky Whip.

Imp. Hercules, by Kingston, first dam daughter of Tuscar, by Bay Middleton, second dam Malvina, by Oscar; 3rd dam Spotless by Walton; 4th dam by Trumpator (see Bruce's American Stud Book, Vol. I, page 28). Hercules is the sire of the dam of Ansoor 2:2[illegible]; also sire of Can of Men 2:21 1-2.

Mares not proving in foal may be returned next year free of charge, providing I still have the horse. Pasturage $3 per month. While every care will be taken of horses, no liability will be assumed for accidents or escapes.

For further particulars address

S. N. STRAUBE, Fresno, Cal.
Poplar Grove Breeding Farm.

CHICAGO, ILLS. -:- BREEDERS' SALE.

SECOND GRAND COMBINATION SALE OF

KIDD, EDMONSON & MORSE,

Will be held in Chicago, Ill., MARCH 17th to 23d, 1890.

Trotters, Pacers, Stallions, Brood Mares, Colts, Saddle and Harness Horses.

Those wishing to dispose of their stock to the best advantage should send for conditions and entry blanks at once, as the sale promises to be very large.

Entries to close February 20, 1890. Send in your entries at once.

Our first sale was a grand success, and was only a foreshadowing of what is to follow. Address,

KIDD, EDMONSON & MORSE, Lexington, Ky.

Or No. 806 West Madison St., Chicago, Ill.

THE "BLUE ROCK" TARGET.

Quotations furnished F. O. B. at Cleveland, Ohio, or San Francisco.

CLABROUGH, GOLCHER & CO.,

630 and 632 Montgomery Street, S. F., Cal.

SOLE AGENTS for the Pacific Coast

THE BRUNSWICK BALKE COLLENDER COMPANY,

MANUFACTURERS OF

Standard Billiard and Pool Tables, Saloon and Bank Fixtures,

653--655 Market Street, San Francisco, Cal.

The Trotting Stallion

G & M

FULL BROTHER TO

ALFRED G, 2:19¾.

(Who has been taken to Kentucky to stand at $200)

Will make the season of 1890 from FEBRUARY 1st to JULY 1st, at

SANTA ROSA.

G. & M. is by Anteeo, 2:16¼; was foaled 1886; first dam Rosa B. by Speculation (son of Hambletonian 10); 2d dam Elizabeth by Alexander 490; 3d dam Nufa by imp. Glencoe. Anteeo is by Electioneer, out of Columbine by A. W. Richmond 1687.

G. & M. is a handsome dark bay, stands 16-2 1/2 hands high, and weighs 1060 pounds. Gameness, stoutness, speed and stamina are indelibly impressed in every line of the pedigree of G. & M. Owners of brood-mares in search of these qualities, will do well to patronize this promising colt.

PHILOSOPHER,

Foaled 1886 by Pilot Wilkes 2987; first dam Bella by George Wilkes 519; second dam by Bell Morgan 81.

Philosopher's sire, Pilot Wilkes 2987, is by George Wilkes 519, dam Grace (the dam of Alice Woodburn, etc.), by Pilot Jr. 12, grandam by Orphan Boy.

Will make the season of 1890, from FEBRUARY 1st to JULY 1st, at Santa Rosa.

TERMS for the season:

G. & M., $50.

PHILOSOPHER, $30,

with privilege of returning mares that do not prove in foal the next season free of charge, provided the horse bred to remains the property of the present owners. Good pasturage at $3 per month. No responsibility assumed for accidents or escapes. Service fees payable before removal of the mare. For further particulars, address

GEO. E. GUERNE,
Santa Rosa Cal.

2:08¾ 2:10 2:12

BALKAN

By Mambrino Wilkes.

(See that Horse's Advertisement.)

DAM FANNY FERN BY JACK HAWKINS

Son of Boston

The grandam of Maud S, (2:08¾) was by Boston and the grandam of Jay-Eye-See (2:10) was by Lexington, son of Boston. So Balkan is the same remove from Boston that Maud is, and one remove nearer than Jay-Eye-See.

Fanny Fern has produced Molly Drew, Onyx, Fred Arnold, Molly Fern and Balkan, all by different sires.

Balkan's sire and dam both being producers, and he being a trotter himself with a record of 2:29 1-2 three-year-old) and timed separately 2:22 1-2 in 4-year-old Stake, Bay District Track, October 14, 1889—it is but fair to presume that he will get trotters of the highest order.

DESCRIPTION.

He is seal brown, 16-1 hands high, in style rivalled by few, and excelled by none with as pure a gait as has yet been exhibited in public—bar none.

Balkan will be at Oakland Trotting Park for the season of 1890, and will be limited to ten mares, at $100 fee, in order to be put in training early, as it is morally certain that if given a reasonable opportunity he will be fast enough to compete with the best of his age. For further particulars address

A. L. HINDS,
Dexter Stables, Oakland.

2:12¾ 2:13½ 2:15¼

Singleton & Addington,

Bank Exchange,

2d and K Streets, Sacramento.

Superior Wines, Liquors and Cigars.

The Fast Trotting Stallion

REDWOOD.

Four-Year-Old Record 2:24 1-2

Will make the season of 1890—February 1st to July 1st—at the

OAKLAND RACE TRACK.

REDWOOD is a dark bay colt, 15.2¾ hands high, weighs 1100 lbs. Foaled in 1885, by Anteeo, 2:16¼, sire of Alfred G., 2:19¾. Anteeo is by Electioneer. First dam Lou Milton, by Milton Medium; second dam Old Fly, a thoroughbred mare brought from the East in 1871 by W. C. Ralston, Esq.

Redwood's sire was out of Columbine by A. W. Richmond, the sire of the pacers Arrow 2:13¾, and Elwood 2:2[illegible], and the trotters Romero, 2:19½, and Len Rose, 2:3[illegible]. Redwood has shown a quarter in 33 seconds.

Terms $100

For the season. Mares not proving with foal may be returned next season free of charge, provided Redwood remains the property of the present owners. Good pasturage at $5 per month. No responsibility assumed for escapes or accidents. Service fees payable before removal of the mare. Limited to 40 approved mares. For further particulars address

A. McFAYDEN.

Race track. Oakland, Cal.

GROVER CLAY.

Bay Stallion, Black Points,
15 3-4 hands high.

Bred by W. W. Traylor, San Francisco.

BY ELECTIONEER.

First dam Maggie Norfolk by Norfolk, son of Lexington, he by Boston. Second dam Tilda Quill by Billy Cheatham he by Cracken, and he by Boston. Third dam by Dorsey's Golddust.

TERMS.

Will make the season of 1890 at the Training Stables of Denis Gannon, near Oakland Trotting Park, at $50 the season, payable at time of service. Season to commence February 1st and ending July 1st. Proper care of mares will be taken, but no responsibility incurred for accidents or escapes. Address,

DENIS GANNON, Oakland, Cal.

Fine Hats,

Latest Styles and Colors.

Meussdorffer & Hubner

8 Kearny Street, San Francisco.

Next to New Chronicle Building

SAMUEL VALLEAU. JAS. R. BRODIE.

J. R. BRODIE & CO.,

Steam Printers,

—And Dealers in—

Poolseller's and Bookmaker's Supplies.

401—403 *Sansome Street, corner Sacramento, San Francisco.*

Pleasanton Stock Farm Co.'s Stallions,

DIRECTOR, 2:17.

Director's book is open for 15 good mares more than already booked for the season of 1890, at $300 each.

This is the cheapest service fee ever charged for a stallion, taking into consideration his BREEDING and RACE RECORD and the RACE RECORDS OF HIS COLTS.

Season to commence February 15th and close August 1st.

PLEASANTON.

Sire Director 2:17. Dam May Day 2:30.

PLEASANTON is a light bay, 16 hands high, and is full brother to Margaret S, three year old record 2:19½.

His book is now open for 10 good mares at $100 for the season, which will commence March 1st and end June 1st.

Mares not proving with foal may be returned next season free of charge of service fees to the same stallion, if he is still in our possession; if not, to some other stallion equally as good, or money will be refunded at option of the company.

Pasturage $4 per month; hay and grain extra. Accidents and escapes at owner's risk.

Service fees due at time of service, and must be paid, together with pasturage, etc., before mares are taken away, or a good approved note given, payable August 1st, 1890, at which date all bills must be settled.

For further information call or address M. SALISBURY, 320 Sansome Street, Room 26, San Francisco, or

PLEASANTON STOCK FARM CO.;
Pleasanton, Alameda Co., Cal.

DISTRICT COLT STAKES

TO BE TROTTED FOR ON

Petaluma Track

Under the auspices of the

Sonoma and Marin District Agricultural Association.

1890.

STAKE FOR YEARLINGS.

Half mile and repeat for $30 each, $10 of which must be paid February 1st, 1890, to W. P. Fine, when the colt must be named and described, giving sire and dam. The second payment of $10 must be made on or before April 1st, 1890, and the third payment of $10 for starters must be paid on the evening before the race. One-third of the gate money to be added to this stake.

STAKE FOR TWO YEAR OLDS.

The stake for two year olds will be $50 each, $10 to be paid February 1st, 1890, when the colt must be named and described, giving sire and dam. The second payment of $10 must be made on or before April 1st, 1890; the third payment of $10, June 1st, 1890, and the fourth payment of $20 to be paid on the evening before the race. Mile heats, best two in three. One-third of the gate money added to this stake.

STAKE FOR THREE YEAR OLDS.

The stake for three year olds will be $50 each and one third of the gate money. The terms, payments and conditions will be the same as in the two year old stake, except that the race will be mile heats, three in five.

These races are to be trotted over the Petaluma track on the day and date indicated by a majority of the nominators in the stakes, at the time of making second payments, but all three are to be trotted on the same day, and not later than the first Saturday in August, 1890.

The stakes and added money will be divided as follows in each of the races:—

To the first colt sixty per cent., to the second colt twenty-five per cent., to the third colt fifteen per cent.

Entries close positively February 1st, 1890, and all parties failing to make subsequent payment; forfeit, amounts already paid. Address all communications to

W. P. FINE,
Lessee Agricultural Park, Petaluma.

BERGEZ'S

RESTAURANT.

FIRST-CLASS. Charges Reasonable.

Private Rooms for Families,

332—334 Pine St., below Montgomery St.

JOHN BERGEZ, Propr.

R. LIDDLE & SON

538 Washington St., S. F.,

Wholesale and Retail Dealers in

Guns, Rifles and Pistols.

A Full Line of FISHING TACKLE and SPORTSMAN'S GOODS.

Orders by mail receive prompt attention.

THE BUCKINGHAM.

OLD STRAIGHT WHISKIES.

141 Montgomery Street.

308 Bush Street, S. F.

M. J. BALFE, Proprietor.

The State Agricultural Society

Spring Meeting 1890.

(The week following the P. C. B. H. A.)

The Chris. Green Handicap

The Spring Stakes

To Close FEBRUARY 1st, 1890.

THE CHRIS. GREEN HANDICAP.

A Sweepstakes for all ages, of $50 each, h f, or $10 if declared, with $500 added; second horse to receive $100 out of stakes. Weights announced March 1st. Declarations due by 6 P. M. April 1st. A winner of any race after publication of weights, of one mile or upwards, to carry 3 lbs; of two races, 5 lbs; of three or more, 7 lbs. extra. This will not apply to horses handicapped at 125 lbs. or over. One and one quarter miles.

THE SPRING STAKES.

A Sweepstakes for three year olds (foals of 1887) that have not won a race previous to January 1st, 1890; $50 entrance, h f, or $15 if declared April 1st, 1890; $400 added, second to receive $75 from stakes. Maidens at time of starting allowed 5 lbs. One mile.

The general conditions of the race meeting as to postponements and track discipline will apply to these stakes.

All declarations are void unless accompanied by the money.

CHRIS. GREEN, President.

EDWIN F. SMITH, Secretary.

SAN JOSE

Yearling Colt Stakes

Foals of 1889.

The get of the following stallions: Jim L, Argent Eros, Bismarck, J. Weatherhead's horses (3), Guy Davis, Nutwood Boy, Orion, King William, Tommy T., Stranger, John Sevenicks, Col. Benton, Wilmington, Dick Patchen, Baywood, Fleetwood, Sultan Jr., Billy Thornhill, Ampersand, Magic, Chancellor, Monte, Christmas Hambletonian, Brentwood, Nut Fore, Prince Albert, Alex Graham, Designer, Cyrus R., Harry Almont, Rea's Nutwood, Boodle, Parnell, Robin Adair, Fred Grant, Elect, Mambrino Jr., California Nutwood, Soudan, Jim Mulvenna, Brown Jug, Menlo Almont Patchen, Antinous, Electric Light, May Boy, C. W. S. Henderson's Henry, S. B. Emerson, Carr's Mambrino, Designer, Prince Warwick, Henry Burr, J. Dunn's horses (3).

Each owner of the above named stallions must deposit $10 each on or before February 1, 1890, otherwise their colts will not be eligible to enter.

The colts from the horses that make the deposit must pay $15 on March 1, 1890, $15 on June 1, 1890; and $20 on August 1, 1890; $300 added by the Society.

The conditions are as follows: To be trotted during fair week of 1890, one-half mile heats.

Stake deposit and added money divided: 60 per cent. to first, 30 per cent. to second and 10 per cent. to third.

National Association rules to govern except as herein stated.

For a walk-over the colt will take the whole stake, but no added money.

If two colts start they must contest for the deposit and stake money only, divided two-thirds and one-third.

A colt distancing the field will take the whole stake, but no added money.

Declarations are void unless accompanied by the money.

Nominations not making payments when due forfeit previous payments.

All colts properly entered in this stake if sold will be entitled to start. If it is the opinion of the judges before starting this race that it cannot be finished on the closing day of the Fair it may be continued.

Entries for the stallions close February 1st. Entries for the colts close March 1st.

G. H. BRAGG, Secretary,
San Jose, California.

Breeders' Directory.

Advertisements under this heading 50c. per line per month.

HORSES AND CATTLE.

J. H. WHITE, Lakeville, Sonoma County—Breeder of Registered Holstein Cattle.

EL ROBLAS RANCHO—Los Alamos, Cal., Francis T Underhill, proprietor, importer and breeder of thoroughbred Hereford Cattle. Information by mail. C. F. Swan, manager.

PAGE BROTHERS.—Penn's Grove, Sonoma Co Cal- Breeders of Short-Horn Cattle; Draft, Roadster and Standard Bred Horses.

JAMES MADDOCK, Petaluma, Cal.—Trotters trained at reasonable prices. Stock handled carefully. Correspondence solicited.

SETH COOK, breeder of Cleveland Bay Horses, Devon, Durham, Polled Aberdeen-Angus and Galloway Cattle. Young stock of above breeds on hand for sale. Warranted to be pure bred, recorded and average breeders. Address, Geo. A. Wiley, Cook Farm, Danville, Contra Costa Co., Cal.

MAMBRINO WILKES COLTS and FILLIES, full brothers and sisters to Gus Wilkes 2:22, and Balkan 2:29¾, for Sale. Address SMITH HILL, Walnut Creek, Contra Costa County, Cal

B. F. RUSH, Suisun, Cal., Shorthorns, Thoroughbred and Grades. Young Bulls and Calves for Sale.

PETER SAXE & SON Lick House, San Francisco, Cal.—Importers and Breeders for past 18 years of every variety of Cattle, Horses, Sheep and Hogs.

HOLSTEIN THOROUGHBREDS of all the noted strains. Registered Berkshire Swine. Catalogues. F. H. BURKE, 471 Montgomery St., S. F.

CLEVELAND BAYS and Norman Horses, Jersey Cattle, and pure bred Poland China Hogs.—DR. W. J. PRATHER, Fresno, Cal.

HENRY C. JUDSON, Wild Idle Farm.—Breeder of Thoroughbred Horses. The home of "Wild Idle." P. O. Santa Clara; Box 223.

W. S. JACOBS, Sacramento, Cal.—Breeder of Thoroughbred Shorthorns and Berkshire Hogs.

FERGUSON & AUSTIN,
FRESNO, CAL.
Registered Polled Angus and Short-Horn Cattle.

Oysters.

M. B. MORAGHAN

Is the only importer, planter and wholesale dealer in the CALIFORNIA MARKET, Stalls 68, 69 to 71 and 47, 48. All the choicest brands of Fresh Oysters constantly on hand. Prompt attention paid to hotel and country orders. Price List.

Large Eastern Oysters .... $2 00 per 100
Transplanted Eastern Oysters .... 1 50 per 100
California Oysters .... 2 00 " sack
Fresh frozen Eastern Oysters at $7 00 per doz. cans.

PASTURAGE
AND
FIRST-CLASS CARE
TAKEN OF
Gentlemen's Road Horses and Trotters.

Colts Broken and Trained to Harness or Saddle.

Twenty new Box Stalls. First-class Pasturage, and the best of care given to all horses. **Terms, $4 per month.** Satisfaction Guaranteed.

Address,
K. O'GRADY,
Laural Creek Farm,
SAN MATEO, CAL

Fiske's Vanes.

MADE OF
COPPER
And Gilded with
PURE
GOLD LEAF.

Manufacturer's Agent.

The HOWE SCALE CO.
411 & 413 Market Street, S. F.

Scales for Weighing of
Live Stock
SEEDS, FEED, Etc.
Write for Catalogue.

PHIL J. CRIMMINS. JOHN C. MORRISON.

"Silver Palace,"
36 Geary Street,
San Francisco, Cal.

The Wine that is held in HIGHEST ESTEEM by the LEADING CLUBS and in SOCIETY
IS
MOËT & CHANDON
"WHITE SEAL,"
THE PERFECTION OF A DRY
Champagne

For Sale by all the Leading Grocers and Wine Merchants.

SHERWOOD & SHERWOOD,
PACIFIC COAST AGENTS;
212-214 Market Street, San Francisco, Cal.

TO HORSEMEN!

PREPARE!!

Your Stallion Advertisements for the
Breeder & Sportsman
For the Coming Season---1890.

We are pleased to announce that we have the best facilities for furnishing

Stallion Pictures,
Stallion Cards,
Pedigrees, Folders,
Contracts, Bills, Etc.

We make a specialty of this department of our business, and have UNRIVALED FACILITIES FOR LOOKING UP PEDIGREES and doing accurate and handsome work.

Promptness, Good Work, Low Prices.

TO REACH ALL
OF THE
Horsemen and Breeders on the Pacific Coast
ADVERTISE in the
Breeder & Sportsman,
313 Bush Street, S. F.

BOYCE TABLETS.
Leg and Body Wash.

THE BOYCE TABLETS are packed in a nicely decorated metal box with hinged lid—one hundred tablets in each box; directions for use plainly engraved upon the box; therefore, the convenience of the package—no liability to leakage and breakage—economy and ready solubility, together with the absolute certainty of their action, will at once commend the use of BOYCE'S TABLETS to the intelligent horsemen of the country. TABLETS sufficient to make one hundred pints of leg and body wash are conveniently carried in an inside coat pocket or in the hip-pocket of the trousers.

The BOYCE WASH can be applied ALL OVER THE BODY WITHOUT FEAR OF BLISTERING OR AFFECTING THE KIDNEYS.

The BOYCE WASH will cure CRACKED HEELS, PUFFS, STOCKINGS, SCRATCHES, INFLAMED TENDONS and FEVERED LEGS.

Price per Box of One Hundred Tablets, $2, sent postpaid to any part of the United States; **six boxes for $10.** A sample of BOYCE'S TABLETS will be mailed to any address on application. These TABLETS are warranted to keep in any climate. Address

BOYCE TABLET COMPANY,
600 Wabash Avenue, - - - Terre Haute, Indiana.

J. A. McKERRON, Pacific Coast Agent,
228-230-232 Ellis Street, San Francisco, Cal.

The Park Training Stable.

CHAS. DAVID, PROPRIETOR.

Corner Grove and Baker Streets, near Entrance to Golden Gate Park.

EVERY FACILITY FOR TRAINING COLTS and taking care of Gentlemen's Roadsters.

Finely appointed stable with every convenience and sixteen roomy box stalls.

The best care given all horses by experienced help, under the personal superintendence of the proprietor.

Convenient to the Park Speed Drive, and Accessible to Six Lines of Cable Cars.

THE TRAINING OF COLTS AND ROADSTERS A SPECIALTY.

TROTTERS AND ROADSTERS FOR SALE.
HORSES SOLD ON COMMISSION.

The proprietor trained and brought out the following well known horses "Sister, Huntress," "Perihelion," "Nona Y," and others.

NOVEL, USEFUL and Ornamental.

The Perfection Horse Tail Tie,
Saves Time and the Tail.

Send 25 cents for Sample,
BREEDER AND SPORTSMAN,
313 Bush Street, San Francisco.
or to BARNES & PARKER, Des Moines, Ia., Manufrs.

GOLDEN EAGLE HOTEL

Corner SEVENTH and K STREETS, SACRAMENTO.

FIRST CLASS IN EVERY RESPECT.
The LARGEST and FINEST HOTEL in the City.
W. O. BOWERS, Proprietor.
Free 'Buse to and from the Hotel.
Telephone, Telegraph Office and Messenger Service at Hotel

---

6 DOS

DO you bet?
DO you go to the races?
DO yon know HOW to bet?
DO you know BEST system?
DO you want Good ADVICE?
DO as you ought to do:

SEND FOR PROSPECTUS TO
GOODWIN BROS.,
241 BROADWAY, NEW YORK,

Who will mail you
FREE OF CHARGE,
one of their circulars showing the GREAT SUCCESS they have met with from the time they established the system of "Point" providing in this country in 1881; it also contains
MANY OTHER INTERESTING ITEMS
with which the general public is not familiar.

Call and See the New

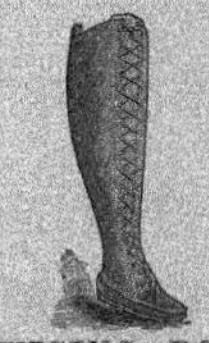

CRUISING BOOTS
E. T. ALLEN,
Fire Arms and Sporting Goods
416 Market St., S. F.

Southern Pacific Co.

(PACIFIC SYSTEM.)

Trains leave and are due to arrive at San Francisco.

LEAVE (FOR)	FROM JANUARY 1, 1890.	ARRIVE (FROM)
7.30 A M	Haywards, Niles and San Jose...	*12.45 P M
7.30 A M	Sacramento and Redding, via Davis...	7.15 P M
7.30 A M	Sacramento, Auburn, Colfax...	5.45 P M
8.00 A M	Martinez, Vallejo, Calistoga and Santa Rosa...	6.15 P M
8.30 A M	Los Angeles Express, Fresno, Bakersfield, Mojave and East and Los Angeles...	11.15 A M
8.30 A M	Niles, San Jose, Stockton, Ione, Sacramento, Marysville, Oroville and Red Bluff...	5.45 P M
10.30 A M	Haywards and Niles...	2.15 P M
*12.00 M	Haywards, Niles and San Jose...	* 3.45 P M
*1.00 P M	Sacramento River Steamers...	**6.00 A M
3.00 P M	Haywards, Niles and San Jose...	9.45 A M
3.30 P M	2d Class for Ogden and East...	10.45 P M
4.00 P M	Stockton and Milton; Vallejo, Calistoga and Santa Rosa...	9.45 A M
4.30 P M	Sacramento and Knight's Landing via Davis...	10.45 A M
* 4.30 P M	Niles and Livermore...	* 8.45 A M
* 4.30 P M	Niles and San Jose...	‡ 4.15 P M
5.30 P M	Haywards and Niles...	7.45 A M
6.00 P M	Sunset Route, Atlantic Express Santa Barbara, Los Angeles, Deming, El Paso, New Orleans and East...	8.45 P M
7.00 P M	Shasta Route Express, Sacramento, Marysville, Redding, Portland, Puget Sound and East...	7.45 A M
8.00 P M	Central Atlantic Express, Ogden and East...	9.45 A M

SANTA CRUZ DIVISION.

‡ 8.00 A M	Hunters train to San Jose...	‡ 7.20 P M
8.15 A M	Newark Centerville, San Jose, Felton, Boulder Creek and Santa Cruz...	5.50 P M
* 2.15 P M	Centerville, San Jose, Almaden, Felton, Boulder Creek and Santa Cruz...	*11.50 A M
4.15 P M	Centerville, San José, and Los Gatos...	9.50 A M

Coast Division (Third and Townsend Sts.)

7.25 A M	San Jose, Almaden and Way Stations...	2.30 P M
8.30 A M	San Jose, Gilroy, Tres Pinos; Pajaro, Santa Cruz; Monterey; Pacific Grove, Salinas, San Miguel, Paso Robles, Santa Margarita (San Luis Obispo) and principal Way Stations...	6.12 P M
10.30 A M	San Jose and Way Stations...	5.02 P M
12.01 P M	Cemetery, Menlo Park and Way Stations...	3.38 P M
* 3.30 P M	San Jose, Tres Pinos, Santa Cruz, Salinas, Monterey, Pacific Grove and principal Way Stations...	*10.00 A M
* 4.20 P M	Menlo Park and Way Station...	* 7.58 A M
5.20 P M	San Jose and Way Stations...	9.03 A M
6.30 P M	Menlo Park and Way Stations...	6.35 A M
†11.45 P M	Menlo Park and principal Way Stations...	†7.23 P M

A M for Morning. P M for Afternoon.
*Sundays excepted. †Saturdays only. ‡Sundays only.
**Mondays excepted. §Saturdays excepted.

OCEANIC STEAMSHIP CO.

Carrying United States, Hawaiian and Colonial Mails.

WILL LEAVE THE COMPANY'S WHARF, foot of Mission Street, No. 1,

For Honolulu.

SS. AUSTRALIA (3,000 tons) January 31, 1890, at 12 M

For Honolulu, Auckland and Sydney,

WITHOUT CHANGE,

The Splendid New 3,000-ton Iron Steamer.

ALAMEDA ....Saturday, January 11, 1890, at 12 M., Or immediately on arrival of the English mails.

☞ For freight or passage, apply at office, 327 Market Street. JOHN D. SPRECKELS & BROS. General Agents.

KILLIP & CO.,

LIVE STOCK AND GENERAL AUCTIONEERS,

22 Montgomery Street, San Francisco

SPECIAL ATTENTION PAID TO SALES OF

High-Bred Horses and Cattle.

At auction and private sale.

Will Sell in All Cities and Counties of the State.

REFERENCES.

Hon. C. Green, Sacramento. Hon. J. D. Carr, Salinas.
J. F. Sargent, Esq., Sargents. Hon. John Boggs, Colusa.
Hon. L. J. Rose, Los Angeles. Hon. A. Walrath, Nevada.
J. B. Haggin, Esq., San Francisco.

Represented at Sacramento by Edwin F. Smith secretary State Agricultural Society.

at San Jose by Messrs. Montgomery & Rea, Real Estate Agents.

Being the oldest established firm in the live-stock business on this Coast, and having conducted the important auction sales in this line for the past fifteen years, amounting to one half a million of dollars, we feel justified in claiming unequaled facilities for disposing of live stock of every description, either at auction or private sale. Our list of correspondents embraces every breeder and dealer of prominence upon the Pacific Coast, thus enabling us to give full publicity to animals placed with us for sale. Private purchases and sales of live stock of all descriptions will be made on commission, and stock shipped with the utmost care. Purchases and sales made of land of every description. We are authorized to refer to the gentlemen whose names are appended.

KILLIP & CO., 22 Montgomery Street

LAMBORN ROAD MACHINE

LIGHT DRAFT. MADE OF IRON. STRONG, SIMPLE, DURABLE.

TRUMAN HOOKER & CO.
SAN FRANCISCO, - - - CALIFORNIA

San Francisco and North Pacific Railway.

THE DONAHUE BROAD-GAUGE ROUTE.

COMMENCING SUNDAY, MARCH 17, 1889, AND until further notice, boats and trains will leave from and arrive at the San Francisco Passenger Depot, Market-street Wharf, as follows:

Leave San Francisco.		DESTINATION	Arrive San Francisco.	
WEEK DAYS.	SUNDAYS.		SUNDAYS.	WEEK DAYS.
7.40 A M 3.30 P M 5.00 P M	8.00 A M 5.00 P M	Petaluma and Santa Rosa	10.40 A M 6.10 P M	8.50 A M 10.30 A M 6.05 P M
7.40 A M 3.30 P M	8.00 A M	Fulton, Windsor, Healdsburg, Litton Springs, Cloverdale, and way stations.	6.10 P M	10.30 A M 6.05 P M
7.40 A M	8.00 A M	Hopland and Ukiah.	6.10 P M	6.05 P M
7.40 A M	8.00 A M	Guerneville	6.10 P M	6.05 P M
7.40 A M 5.00 P M	8.00 A M	Sonoma and Glen Ellen.	10.40 A M 6.10 P M	8.50 A M 6.05 P M

Stage connects at Santa Rosa for White Sulphur Springs, Sebastopol and Mark West Springs; at Geyserville for Skaggs Springs, and at Cloverdale for the Geysers; at Hopland for Highland Springs, Kelseyville, Soda Bay, Lakeport and Bartlett Springs, and at Ukiah for Vichy Springs, Saratoga Springs, Blue Lakes, Willits, Cahto, Calpella, Potter Valley, Sherwood Valley and Mendocino City.

EXCURSION TICKETS from Saturdays to Mondays, to Petaluma, $1.50; to Santa Rosa $[illegible]; to Healdsburg, $3.40; to Litton Springs, $3.60; to Cloverdale, $4.50; to Hopland, $5.70; to Ukiah, $6.75; to Guerneville, $3.75; to Sonoma, $1.50; to Glen Ellen, $1.80.

EXCURSION TICKETS, good for Sundays only, to Petaluma, $1; to Santa Rosa, $1.50; to Healdsburg, $2.25; to Litton Springs, $2.40; to Cloverdale, $3; to Guerneville, $2.50, to Sonoma, $1; to Glen Ellen, $1.20.

From San Francisco for Point Tiburon and San Rafael: Week Days—7.40, 9.20, 11.20, A. M.; 3.30, 5.00, 6.15 P. M. Sundays—8.00, 9.30, 11.00 A. M.; 1.30, 5.00, 6.20 P. M.

To San Francisco from San Rafael: Week Days—6.20, 7.55, 9.30 A. M.; 12.45, 3.40, 5.05 P. M. Sundays—8.10, 9.40 A. M.; 12.15, 3.40, 5.00 P. M.

To San Francisco from Point Tiburon: Week Days—6.50, 8.20, 9.55 A. M.; 1.10, 4.05, 5.30 P. M.; Sundays—8.40, 10.05 A. M.; 12.40, 4.05, 5.30 P. M.

On Saturdays an extra trip will be made from San Francisco to San Rafael, leaving at 1.40 P. M.

H. C. WHITING, General Manager.
PETER J. McGLYNN, Gen. Pass. & Tkt. Agt.

Ticket Offices at Ferry, 222 Montgomery Street and 2 New Montgomery Street.

KENNEL ADVERTISEMENTS.

Thoroughbred Pugs, $40 each.

PEDIGREE.

PUPPIES
- Fido
  - imp. Jumbo — Marshall's Uno, Lady Bess
  - Fannie — Rex, imp. Fly
- Budge
  - Senator Fair's Fritz
  - McCleery's Mamma Snoots — Sam, imp. Alice

Can be seen daily from 9 A. M. to 5 P. M. at 411 Ellis Street, San Francisco.

J. F. B. McCLEERY.

Irish Setters & Pointers.

In the Stud, winner of 16 first and special prizes, CHAMPION MIKE T., 6435, A. K. S. B. Irish Setter puppies by Champion Mike T. 6435 A. K. S. B.—Champion Lady Elcho T. 8451 A. K. S. B., for sale. Two pointers, a year old, by Rush T. 10169 A. K. S. B.—Champion Patti Croxteth T. 10126 A. K. S. B. for sale. Yard broken. Address,

A. B. TRUMAN,
1425 Steiner St., S. F., Cal.

CALIFORNIA SPANIEL KENNELS,

Oakland, California. H. P. Rennie, Prop. Breeder and importer of typical COCKER SPANIELS. Winner of first prizes at S. F. and Los Angeles, 1889; also, Columbus, 1889, New York, 1887. In the stud, solid Black Cocker dog, GIFFEE, won 1st and Gold Medal at S. F., 1889, Fee, $25. Puppies and grown dogs at reasonable prices. My dogs can neither talk nor climb a tree, but are fielders and prize winners.

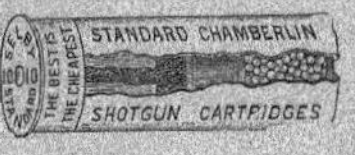

THE GREAT

STABLE DISINFECTANT.

Many horses and cattle become diseased and die from the impure atmosphere of their stables. And even though stables may be kept clean and the foul air be unnoticeable, it may still exist.

DARBYS FLUID

IS GOOD FOR CUTS, BRUISES, ETC., WARDS OFF DISEASE, PURIFIES THE AIR AND PREVENTS CONTAGION AMONG ANIMALS.

It is cheap and never wasted by free use; should be sprinkled about the stalls and stable as a safeguard against Influenza, Pink-eye, Epizooty, etc.

If you value your horses and stock never be without Darbys Prophylactic Fluid.

J. H. ZEILIN & CO., Philadelphia, Pa.

SOLD BY ALL DRUGGISTS.

DR. FISHERMAN'S

Carbolized Alkaline

LOTION

Cures after all other Remedies have Failed.

Sprains, Sores, Bruises, Galls, Swellings, Scratches, Thrush, Grease Heels, Curb, Rheumatism. Restoring Weak Knees and Ankles to their original condition. As a wash it insures glossy manes and tails. Valuable as an internal remedy for Coughs, Colic, Congestion or Fever. You really get Half a Gallon of Remedy for $1.00, or Two Gallons for $3.00, after being adulterated as directed.

This Liniment has received the endorsement of some of our best horsemen. Recommended by Jos. Cairn Simpson. See BREEDER AND SPORTSMAN of November 10th, 1888.

LYNDE & HOUGH, Proprietors.

116 California St., S. F.

Or ask your Druggist for it.

THE

B. & Y. HOOF OIL

GOOD FOR MAN OR BEAST.

Will positively destroy the effects of the "Cattle Fly."

A SURE CURE for Sores, Scratches, Cuts, Wounds, Bruises, Corns, Thrush, Foot Rot, Quarter Crack, Sand Crack, Dry, Brittle, Hard and Fevered Hoof, or any local trouble about the Horse.

Warranted to make the hoof grow without cause of complaint on the part of the horse-shoer for gumming his rasp.

B. & Y. New Process Neats Foot Oil,

Best Leather Oil made.

CHEAP AND LASTING

Recommended by leading Harness Men, Drivers and Trainers. Is well adapted to wet weather, as it does not open pores like old process goods.

Ask your dealer for it, or send to

HUNT & DOREMUS,
99 FLOOD BUILDING, - San Francisco.

HORSE OWNERS!
TRY GOMBAULT'S

CAUSTIC BALSAM.

A Safe, Speedy and Positive Cure for Curb, Splint, Sweeny, Capped Hock, Strained Tendons, Founder, Wind Puffs, all Skin Diseases or Parasites, Thrush, Diphtheria, Pinkeye, all Lameness from Spavin, Ringbone or other Bony Tumors. Removes all Bunches or Blemishes from Horses and Cattle.

Supersedes all Cautery or Firing.

Impossible to Produce any Scar or Blemish.

Every bottle sold is warranted to give satisfaction. Price $1.50 per bottle. Sold by druggists, or sent by express, charges paid, with full directions for its use. Send for descriptive circulars. Address LAWRENCE, WILLIAMS & CO., Cleveland, O.

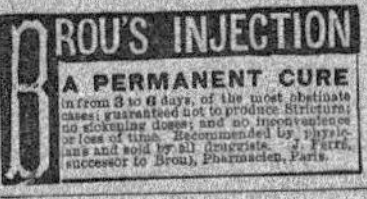

For any Kind of a
SORE THROAT
USE
McCLELLAN'S
DIPHTHERIA REMEDY
An Unfailing Cure.
FOR SALE BY ALL DRUGGISTS

VETERINARY.

Dr. Wm. H. Jones, M.R.C.V.S.

Veterinary Surgeon,

(CLUB STABLES)

409-411 Taylor Street, San Francisco.

Consultations by letter, and cases of URGENT NECESSITY in the interior will receive prompt attention.

W. H. WOODRUFF.

Veterinary Dentist,

AT FASHION STABLES,

221 Ellis Street, San Francisco

Improved Instruments, Humane Methods, First-Class Work.

H. E. CARPENTER,

Veterinary Surgeon,

Graduate of Ontario Veterinary College, Toronto, Canada.

RESIDENCE AND VETERINARY INFIRMARY

331 Golden Gate Ave., San Francisco.

Telephone 3069.

☞ OPEN DAY AND NIGHT. ☜

No risk in throwing Horses. Veterinary Operating Table on the premises.

DR. C. MASOERO,

Veterinary Surgeon,

Successor to **DR. A. DeTAVEL,**

GRADUATE OF ROYAL VETERINARY COLLEGE, TURIN.

OFFICE AND INFIRMARY,

No. 811 HOWARD STREET,

Between Fourth and Fifth. SAN FRANCISCO.

Telephone, No. 457.

R. WATKINS,

Veterinary Dentist,

Of twelve years practice, is now permanently located in San Francisco, and may be found at **C. S. Crittendens'** Golden Gate Livery and Riding Academy, **24 to 28 Golden Gate Avenue.**

Will treat ailments of the horse's mouth, and cure all such. Siderein Pullers and Tongue Lollers, etc.

Satisfaction guaranteed. Orders by mail will receive prompt attention. Examination Free.

E. J. O'ROUKE.

I have the honor to announce to my old patrons and the general public that I may be found at my old stand, where, as heretofore, the

Shoeing of Horses,

whether for the Track, Drive, or for general work, will receive my personal attention.

Telephone 2011.

E. J. O'ROUKE,
209 Ellis Street

California Horse Shoe Co's

I have used in my business the Steel and Iron Shoes made by the above Company, and take great pleasure in saying they are the best I have ever used in twenty-two years' practice. I have never seen anything like the STEEL SHOE made by this Company. I can fully recommend them to every practical Horseshoer in the country. Yours respectfully,

No. 8 Everett Street. JOHN GRACE.

Bohanon Carriage Co., 101-103 Ogden Ave., CHICAGO.

Send for Catalogue.

HEALD'S

Business College, 24 Post St.

San Francisco.

The most popular school on the Coast

E. P. HEALD, President. C. S. HALEY, Sec'y.

☞ Send for Circulars

TWENTY PAGES.

Vol. XVI. No. 4
No. 313 BUSH STREET.
SAN FRANCISCO. SATURDAY, JAN. 25, 1890.
SUBSCRIPTION
FIVE DOLLARS A YEAR.

ALEXANDER BUTTON, 2:26 1-2.

The property of G. W. WOODARD, Woodland, Yolo County, Cal.

Alexander Button 2:26 1-2.

Among the notable horses of California Alexander Button 2:26½ can safely be said to take high rank, not alone for his own performances, but from the remarkable speed shown by his progeny. His record should have been much lower than it is, for he has frequently gone miles in 2:16 and better, and he would have been sent for a low mark, but a "leg" has interfered and necessitated a let up in his work. Large in stature, yet of good conformation, he is a horse to please the eye of the visitor when seen for the first time. As our artist has given ad exquisite representation of Alexander Button, the reader can at once detect the excellent proportions and beautiful lines of this justly celebrated stallion. It is a great pity that his record is not where it should be, but as a horse is judged by the speed that he produces in his foals, so the fame of Alexander Button has gone forth to the world by the performances of his sons and daughters. Yolo Maid, by many thought to be the fastest pacer in the world, not even barring Johnson, brought him into great prominence in 1888, by pacing as a three year old in 2:14, which she further reduced to 2:12¼ last season. Belle Button was another of the improving kind, and easily made a record of 2:29, while Thomas Ryder, another son of Alexander Button, got a record of 2:20½. Rosa Mac made her record of 2:20¾ prior to being taken back East, and if we are creditably informed, can materially lower that mark now. Harry Mac, a full brother to Rosa Mac, can show a "twenty" clip and can be seen almost any day on the Park roads, where he is being driven by Capt. B. E. Harris. All of Alexander Button's colts are noted for their speed, and in sending mares to him the breeder is always sure to get a fast foal. The sire of Alexander Button was Alexander 490, who had himself a record of 2:31½, and a three mile record of 7:54½. He was one of Geo. M. Patchen Jr.'s best sons, and is noted as the sire of Nellie Patchen 2:27½, Reliance 2:22½, Tommy Dodd 2:24, in addition to Alexander Button; it will therefore be seen that he is entitled to his speed producing power and that he comes from a family that have all been endowed the same way. Mr. Geo. W. Woodard, the owner of Alexander Button, is a breeder of the progressive type, and has secured a number of first class mares which were bred to Alexander Button last season. As a result Mr. Woodward will have a fine lot of foals, and we shall expect to hear that they are all "threatened with speed." The following is Alexander Button's pedigree, by Alexander 490, dam Lady Button by Napa Rattler. Alexander by Geo. M. Patchen Jr. 31, dam Lady Crum, said to be by Brown's Bellfounder.

The Standard.

[AS REVISED AND ADOPTED BY THE NATIONAL ASSOCIATION OF TROTTING-HORSE BREEDERS, DECEMBER 14, 1887.]

IN order to define what constitutes a trotting-bred horse and to establish a BREED of trotters on a more intelligent basis, the following rules are adopted to control admission to the records of pedigrees. When an animal meets the requirements of admission and is duly registered, it shall be accepted as a standard trotting-bred animal:—

FIRST.—Any stallion that has himself a record of two minutes and thirty seconds (2:30) or better, provided any of his get has a record of 2:35 or better, or provided his sire or his dam is already a standard animal.

SECOND.—Any mare or gelding that has a record of 2:30 or better.

THIRD.—Any horse that is the sire of two animals with a record of 2:30 or better.

FOURTH.—Any horse that is the sire of one animal with a record of 2:30 or better, provided he has either of the additional qualifications: (1) A record himself of 2:35 or better. (2) Is the sire of two other animals with a record of 2:35 or better. (3) Has a sire or dam that is already a standard animal.

FIFTH.—Any mare that has produced an animal with a record of 2:30 or better.

SIXTH.—The progeny of a standard horse when out of a standard mare.

SEVENTH.—The female progeny of a standard horse when out of a mare by a standard horse.

EIGHTH.—The female progeny of a standard horse when out of mare whose dam is a standard mare.

NINTH.—Any mare that has a record of 2:35 or better, and whose sire or dam is a standard animal.

Best Trotting Records.

1 mile—2:08¾, Maud S., against time, in harness, accompanied the distance by a running horse, Glenville, O., July 30, 1885......2:13¾, best time in a race between horses, Maud S., Chicago, Ills., July 24, 1880......2:12, Axtell, against time, accompanied by running horse—fastest stallion time, Terre Haute, Ind., Oct. 11, 1889......2:13¾, Phallas, fastest heat by a stallion against other horses, Chicago, July 14, 1884......2:13¾, Palo Alto, third heat in race at Stockton, Cal., Sept. 26, 1889......2:15½, Jay-Eye-See, half-mile track, Lincoln, Neb., Sept. 14, 1887......2:15¾, Great Eastern, under saddle, third heat, Morrisania, N. Y., Sept. 22, 1877......2:10¾, Jay-Eye-See, against time, best five-year-old record, Providence, R. I., Sept. 15, 1883......2:16, Manzanita, third heat, best four-year-old record, Lexington, Ky., Sept. 5, 1876 ...... 2:16, Edgemark, four-year-old stallion record, against time, Lexington, Ky., Oct. 18, 1889......2:10½, Sunol, in Stanford Stake, accompanied by a runner, best three-year-old record, San Francisco, Nov. 9, 1889..2:18, Sunol 2 years, against time, San Francisco, Cal., Oct. 27, 1888......2:20½, Regal Wilkes, two-year-old stallion record, San Francisco, Nov. 9, 1889......2:31½, Norlaine, yearling, against time, San Francisco, Cal., Nov. 12, 1887......2:35, Faustino, yearling stallion record, San Francisco, Nov. 9, 1889.

2 miles—4:46 against time, Fanny Witherspoon, Chicago, Ill., Sept. 25, 1885.

3 miles—7:21¼, Huntress, harness, Brooklyn, L. I., Sept. 21, 1872.

4 miles—10:34½, Longfellow, wagon, California, Dec 31, 1869.

5 miles—13:00, Lady Mac, harness, San Francisco, Cal., April 2, 1874.

10 miles—27:23¼, Controller, harness, San Francisco, Cal., Nov. 23, 1878.

20 miles—58:25, Captain McGowan, harness, half-mile track, Boston, Oct. 31, 1865.

Pacing Records at One Mile.

Johnston, harness, against time, Chicago, Ills., Oct 9, 1884, 2:06¼.

Brown Hal, best stallion record, Cleveland, Ohio, July 31, 1889, 2:12½.

Westmont, July 10, 1884, Chicago, Ills., with running mate, 2:01¾.

Daisy, yearling, Sacramento, Dec. 31, 1885, 2:28¼.

Ed Rosewater, two years old, Council Bluffs, Iowa, Nov. 8, 1888, 2:20½.

Yolo Maid, 3 years old, San Francisco, Oct. 13, 1888, 2:14.

Gold Leaf, four years old, 2:11½ on August 17, 1889, at Napa.

Arrow, five years old, 2:13½, made at Cleveland, Ohio, August 1, 1888

Fastest Time on Record.

RUNNING.

MILES.		Time
¼	Jim Miller, 2, Deer Lodge (Mont.), Aug. 16, 1888 / †Sleepy Dick, a, Kiowa (Kan.), Nov. 24, 1888	0:21¼
⅜	Cyclone, a, 120 lbs., Helena (Mont.), Aug. 28, 1889	0:34¼
½	Geraldine, 4, 122 lbs., Westchester Course, Aug. 30, 1889	0:46
⅝	Britannic, 5, 122 lbs., Westchester Course, Aug. 31, 1889	0:59
⅝	Fordham, a, 115 lbs., Westchester Course, Oct. 4, 1889	0:59
¾	El Rio Rey, 2, 126 lbs., Westchester Course, Aug. 31, 1889	1:11
¾	Tipstaff, 3, 107, Westchester Course, Oct. 4, 1889	1:11
⅞	Britannic, 5, 110 lbs., Sheepshead Bay, Sept. 5, 1888	1:26 2-5
	Ten Broeck, 5, 110 lbs., Louisville, May 24, 1877 (against time)	1:39¾
1	Maori 4, 105 lbs., Chicago, July 12, 1889, (in a race)	1:39 4-5
*1 1-16	Wheeler T., 3, 98 lbs., St. Louis, June 1, 1888	1:47¼
1 1-16	Eyrlton 4, 108, Chicago, Ill., June 28, 1889	1:47¼
1⅛	Terra Cotta, 4, 124 lbs., Sheepshead Bay, June 22, 1888	1:53
*1 3-16	Joe Cotton, 5, 109¼ lbs., Sheepshead Bay, Sept. 7, 1887	2:00¼
1¼	Kingston, 5, 123 lbs., Gravesend, Sept. 24, 1889	2:08¼
1 m 500 yds.	Bend d'Or, 4, 115 lbs., Saratoga, July 25, 1882	2:10¼
1⅜	Triboulet, 4, 117 lbs., San Francisco, April 26, 1888 / Richmond, 6, 122 lbs., Sheepshead Bay, June 27, 1888	2:21¼
1½	Firenzi, 4, 113 lbs., Monmouth Park, Aug. 2, 1888 / Luke Blackburn, 3, 102 lbs., Monmouth Park, Aug. 17, '80 / Jim Guest, 4, 98 lbs., Chicago, (Washington Park, July 24 '85)	2:34
1⅝	Hindoocraft, 3, 73 lbs., Westchester, Aug. 27, 1889	2:48
1¾	Glidelia, 5, 118 lbs., Saratoga, Aug. 5, 1882	3:01
1⅞	Enigma, 4, 90 lbs., Sheepshead Bay, Sept. 15, 1885	3:20
2	Ten Broeck, 5, 110 lbs., Louisville, May 29, 1877	3:27¼
2¼	Monitor, 4, 110 lbs., Baltimore, Oct. 20, 1880	3:44¼
2½	Springbok, 5, 114 lbs. / Preakness, a, 114 lbs. — Saratoga, July 29, 1875	3:56¼
2⅝	Aristides, 4, 104 lbs., Lexington, May 13, 1876	4:27¼
2¾	Ten Broeck, 4, 104 lbs., Lexington, Sept. 16, 1876	4:58¼
2⅞	Hubbard, 4, 107 lbs., Saratoga, Aug. 9, 1873	4:58¾
3	Drake Carter 4, 115 lbs., Sheepshead Bay, Sept. 6, 1884	5:24
4	Ten Broeck, 4, 104 lbs., Louisville, Sept. 27, 1876	7:15¼

HEAT RACES.

MILES.		Time
¼	Sleepy Dick, a, Kiowa (Kan.), Nov. 24, 1888	0:21¼—0:22¼
½	Bogus, a, 112 lbs., Helena (Mont.), Aug. 21, 1888	0:48 —0:48
⅝	Kittie Pease, 4, Dallas (Tex.), Nov. 2, 1887	1:00 —1:00
⅝	Sudie McNairy, 3, 95 lbs., Chicago, July 2, 1888	1:02¼—1:02
¾	Lizzie S., 5, 118 lbs., Louisville, Sept. 28, 1883	1:13¼—1:13¼
1	Bounce, 4, 90 lbs., Sheepshead Bay, Sept. 7, 1881	1:42 —1:41¼
1	3 in 5. L'Argentine, 6, 115 lbs., St. Louis, June 14, 1879	1:43—1:44 —1:47¼
*1 1-16	Slipalong, 5, 115 lbs., Chicago (Wash. Park), Sept. 2, 1885	1:50¼—1:49
1¼	Gabriel, 4, 112 lbs., Sheepshead Bay, Sept. 28, 1880	1:56 —1:56
1¼	Glenmore, 5, 114 lbs., Sheepshead Bay, Sept. 25, 1880	2:10 —2:14
1½	Keno, 6, Toledo, Sept. 16, 1887 (1st and 3d heats)	2:43¼—2:45
2	Miss Woodford, 4, 107¼ lbs., Sheepshead Bay, Sept. 20, 1884	3:33 —3:31¼
3	Norfolk, 4, 100 lbs., Sacramento, Sept. 23, 1865	5:27¼—5:29½
4	Ferida, 4, 105 lbs., Sheepshead Bay, Sept. 18, 1880	7:23¼—7:41

†Made in a heat race.

*Doubtful, and made in a heat race.

Short Stories.

BY HARVEY W. PECK.

Some three years ago two gentlemen named William Jones and Ezekial Robbins were partners in a running horse called Robert Lamont.

The affinity of the trio was so well known that they were familiarly style "Bill," "Zeke" and "Bob." These three were a precious gang. The antecedents of Bill and Bob were buried in obscurity, while the pedigree of their runner was immured in the dim and distant past. Bill however always persisted that Boby—as he invariably called the horse—was sired by Glencoe, while Zeke stated, quite confidentially, that his dam had run a half in 46½! In fact these two gentlemen were noted for the joyous manner with which they toyed with the truth, while some people satirically said the horse could not run fast enough to head a cow in a lane!

The first thing that shook my faith in Bill Jones' truthfulness happened in this wise: Bill was a person of varied experiences in life having served in the Mexican war 8 years, as a scout 12 years, was in the jungles of Central Africa 7 years, during which sojourn he killed several elephants and hundreds of wilder—beasts; was at Cape Colony and in the diamond mines for 11 years, etc., etc.

Aside from the above localites, Bill had been in Brazil for several years; in Buenos Ayres a few years, in short had been most everything in most every clime. Bill told me these things at different *seances*. I kept an account of the number of years he had served in his different capacities and made a list of them. This list showed Bill to be 135 years old. One day I confronted Bill with this list expecting him to collapse. I was mistaken. He snatched his head meditatively and said there must be some mistake.

"Did you not say you were in Africa so long?"

"I was" he replied.

"And in Brazil so long?"

"Yes!"

"And in Cape Colony so long?"

"Yes, sir."

"And served in the Mexican War eight years?',

"For a fact."

"You were in Buenos Ayres several years?"

"I was!"

Thus I went through every item of the list and then said: "Well, Bill, that makes you 135 years old according to your own statement!"

Bill said he'd be hanged of he could see how it was, it looked right, but really couldn't be, of course, but he positively swore that he had been in all the places he told me about for exactly the number of years he claimed! I will state that Bill was probably 40 years of age.

Zeke was hardly Bill's equal as a liar—he was worse! It can be seen that when this pair was united they made a strong combination.

Robert Lamont, the horse could run any distance from a quarter to a derby route, and was first-class at all, so Zeke said! For over a year they kept this horse, took good care of him; occassionally galloped him, but never tried to get a race for him. They finally took him to Round Valley and made a race with a horse owned by a resident, the alleged stakes being $1000 a side. This was of course a mistake, as Bill and Zeke did not have that amount of money. The real purpose of the race was to skin the Indians upon the reservation, which thing they successfully accomplished, the Indians losing three or four hundred dollars and two or three ponies. The race was a half mile and "Boby" won in 54½ seconds, being badly punished and sadly wearied. That night one of the Indian braves stuck a big knife into Boby's anatomy and in the morning Zeke and Bill found him dead! They mourned long and loud declaring him "one of the most valuable horses" in existence.

In a paper published in the principle town of the valley, there appeared the following:

SAD FATE OF A GREAT HORSE.

"The night following the race at Simpson's ranch, between Messrs. Jones and Robbins' horse Robert Lamont, by imp. Glencoe, and Nat Collin's mare Red Mary, with the particulars of which all our readers are familiar, some miscreant, presumably an Indian, killed Messrs. Jones and Robbins' horse! This was a very valuable animal, they having been offered $8000 for him, which they indignantly refused. His loss to this country is irreparable. His owners have the sympathy of the entire community. As Mr. William Jones said in our presence, "his like will not be seen for many a day." It can be said of great horses as of great men, '*requieat in pace*'!"

I witnessed a race many years ago upon the plains of Utah, that was productive of more betting, louder shouting and more vigorous kicking than any race I have seen since.

I was spending a few months in Ogden, and had about become used to the various Mormon customs; thus the sight of six or seven women with one man evoked no surprise, while the running brooks beside she roadway and the vast array of things in the "tithing-yard" had lost their charm.

In order that the reader may understand the true inwardness of the race, I will give, very briefly, a little sketch of the Mormon customs and of my individual experience. Ogden is a town of about 8,000 inhabitants, the Mormons being in the majority. They style all outsiders either Gentiles or "the ungodly." The two classes do not mingle together very much, and cordially dislike each other. There are some exceptions, of course. Some of the better class of Mormons will invite one to their houses and entertain him royally, but the subject of polygamy is invariably tabooed.

I attended a ball in Salt Lake City one night. Three carloads of Gentiles left Ogden on a special train, upon invitation of the ball committee, arriving in the Mormon stronghold about 8.30 P. M. Some three hundred people were in attendance, principally Mormons. An elegant band was discoursing selections from Wantafel and Strauss, and the music was being interspersed in many ways by many dancers. That was before my hair was white and my brow furrowed, and I took an active part in the gaiety. While the revelry was at its height I was dancing with a young lady named Young. I had been introduced to many by the same name. While we were promenading I launched into a satirical tirade against some of the alleged tenets of the Mormon faith. I noticed that while the lady had been a good conversationalist on all other topics, she seemed peculiarly stupid upon this subject. After the number was finished I explained to a friend what I had done. He laughed and said: "That girl is Brigham Young's daughter; so are all the others here of the same name." I met a score of Brigham's daughters that night, and they were not a bad lot either. They were fairly well educated, moderately informed, and endeavored to be as nice as possible.

I noticed that the "ungodly" were not viewed favorably by the younger Mormons, and in many ways the class prejudice was evinced.

Several miles from Ogden there nestles a little hamlet called Eden. In appearance it is not what its namesake of long ago was popularly supposed to be. One of the Saints informed me that from that place the "chosen of the Lord" would rise to meet him in the sky. In this sequestered nook there was owned a Cayuse dubbed Wahoo. He was about 14½ hands high, roan in color, diabolical in conformation, uncertain in disposition, and could run 600 yards very fast. At that date there flourished a man whom I will call Parsons. He lived in Ogden. For a long time he had been looking for a pony that could beat the Eden production. One day an Indian—true blue, feathers in his hair, bow and quiver slung across his back, scarlet blanket over his shoulders—rode into town upon a disreputable pony, which he was anxious to sell. The Indian said his horse could outrun anything among his tribe, and could beat anybody's horse five or six hundred yards. Parsons tried the horse, concluded he would do, and bought him. Within thirty days he made a race with the Eden horse for $50 a side. The usual method of procedure was to make a match for a small amount, and then the opposing parties would bet all they could raise.

About seventy-five of us went to the race. It was held in a narrow valley between two spurs of the Wasatch Range. Parson's horse was ridden by a sharp-featured Indian boy, while Wahoo's saddle was decorated by a little tow-headed Edenite. The distance was 550 yards, and Parson's horse won in the last jump. The Edenites were broke to almost a man. Money, sugar-cane and everything else was gone. Considerable tact was required to keep a free fight from taking place. Everybody yelled from start to finish, and they badly scared the tow-headed boy that rode Wahoo by threats to hang him for not winning.

There can be nothing truer than the saying, "Nothing succeeds like success!" The practical exemplication of this axiom is constantly witnessed in every walk of life. If a man amasses wealth in any mercantile pursuit, he is very generally voted "smart," which term is used to express intelligence, keenness and sagacity! Very many men of this kind are entitled to none of these encomiums, being naturally ignorant and thick-headed, having been unfortunate enough to receive no education in their youth.

Thus it is in the horse world. Every turf writer now comes to the front and says, "That Axtell could not help being the great horse he is—forsooth, look at his breeding; by William L., dam by a horse with a record of 2:26, and that horse a son of Mambrino Patchen, the great broodmare sire; again, he is inbred just right," etc.

The above quotation works are my own, but the words express in substance about the general tenor of the reasons given.

These same writers well know that if a man had told them he was going to breed a mare by Mambrino Boy to William L., and expected the produce to beat 2:15 as a three-year-old, they would have considered him crazy.

Everybody—meaning all horsemen—know that very many colts are bred throughout these United States every year that are the equal, and in many instances the superior of Axtell in breeding, but they don't trot in 2:12 at three years, nor in 2:25 for that matter, though the dam may have been a great broodmare of tested quality, and the sire a trotter and producer.

What, then, is the reason that one young horse will turn out thus phenominally, far surpassing the other 999 equally well bred, and with equal opportunity? Can any one tell? Very many reasons can be adduced looking to an explanation, but are they true? Do they represent the actual reasons?

We may all hold theories more or less tenable, but my opinion is that none of us can tell the exact reasons, else the problem of breeding fast horses would not have the same degree of fascination it now possesses.

Were all horses very fast, the high figure now obtainable for a horse of extreme speed would fade like a mist before the sun. I presume the degree of uncertainty encountered in rearing fast horses gives it the highest flavor—there is always a certain fascination in chance!

But that inate something, that indescribable factor within the blood and brain, which renders one horse so vastly superior in speed to all others of equal age and breeding, what is it? Plenty of men think they know, but do they?

The issue of the BREEDER AND SPORTSMAN of January 4th, contained an article by C. Bruce Lowe, which is worthy of consideration. The fact that the produce of a mare, by a certain horse, will sometimes bear a striking resemblance to some other stallion, which she was bred to the season before, is so well known, that it will not be refuted by any intelligent man. But that it goes farther than outside resemblance can not be proven.

The mare bred to a Quagga, that afterward produced colts with stripes upon them—when bred to stallions—is undoubtedly true, but no proof has been given to show that they partook of the disposition of the Quagga.

To my mind, the reason for the stripes appearing in after produce is found in the fact that the nervous organism and sensative brain of the mare were so strongly affected at time of breeding as to produce the apparent phenomena at two or three subsequent breedings.

A mare once bred to a jackass will sometimes afterward have a colt by a stallion marked with a stripe down the back, or in some other way resembling the jack. This is not to be wondered at, for the appearance and tone of voice of a jack is sufficient to render life unbearable, and the only wonderment is that all the mares' subsequent colts do not resemble the jackass in all particulars.

Mr. Lowe says that there is such a thing as "*impregnation of dam with the sire strains through foal's circulation previous to birth.*" To this fact he attributes the workings above mentioned, instead of to the effect the singular appearance of such a sire might have upon a highly organized mare.

If this theory be true, men have made most wonderful mistakes for many years past in the choice of broodmares. It would be far better if this "impregnation of the dam with sire strains" is an existent fact, to buy a mare that had been bred, we will say to Geo. Wilkes, for several years, than to purchase a daughter of his, for in case the first mare was stinted to Wilkes six or seven consecutive years, she ought to be about fifteen-sixteenths Wilkes at the end of the time—that is, as a producer.

This would be a good thing, financially, for breeders, as daughters of Wilkes are held very high.

The Los Angeles Races.

[By our Special Commissioner.]

Los Angeles, Jan. 13th.

The promoters of the winter race meeting have played in hard luck. The rain first necessitated a postponement, and the cold spell which has prevailed for a week past has seriously interfered with the attendance. The fields have been large, and the racing on the whole has been good. The talent has not fared very well, several rank outsiders knocking out their calculations in a most aggravating manner. The judges who officiated were Clifton Bell of Denver, A. W. Barret and Hank McGregor. They have been kept busy watching out for jobs. Los Angeles never before enjoyed the presence of so many sprint racehorses.

Saturday morning, January 11th, it was discovered that some miscreant had given Kitty Van a dose of aconite. The fiend gave the speedy mare more than he intended, and her life was despaired of for several hours. This despicable act has caused considerable feeling in a certain quarter, and a well known character on many California race tracks is accused of being the guilty party. The two prominent starters against Kitty Van were Rondo and Painkiller. The judges very sapiently declared the race off. A few people made a vigorous protest, but it is always well to protect the betting public. The poisoning of Kitty Van demonstrated that a job had been contemplated in the interest of either Rondo or Painkiller, but unfortunately there is nothing but a little circumstantial evidence to guide any one in finding out the guilty party. Another disagreeable feature of the meeting was the wretched starting in several races.

The writer holds that a winter racing in Los Angeles can be made to pay, but it is out of reason to expect people to shiver with the cold while watching the races. Enthusiasts will turn out, but the general public can hardly be blamed for not putting in an appearance.

The first day of January was admirably adapted for racing, and those who journeyed to Agricultural Park enjoyed a capital day's sport. It will be remembered that the programme run off was arranged for Christmas Day. This will account for three year olds running in the dash for two year olds. Atalanta won the five furlongs from Gambo and Rosemeade.

SUMMARY.

First Race.—Five furlongs; two year olds.

E. J. Baldwin's b f Atalanta .... L. Brown, 117 lbs 1
N. A. Covarrubias' b c Gambo .... J. Clifford, 122 2
L. H. Vignolo's b f Rosemeade .... Scofield, 117 3

Time—0:16.

Pools sold—Atalanta $10, Gambo $4, Rosemeade $3.

The next race was a surprise party. McGuinnis and Winona were thought to be the only two in the race, but Louise M. upset all calculations and won cleverly.

SUMMARY.

Second race—One mile; for all ages.

T. Hazlet's b f Louise M, 4 .... Hazlet 114 1
Kelly & Samuels' b h Ed McGinnis 4 .... Marshall 124 2
E. J. Baldwin's b m Winona, 4 .... Brown, 119 3
Matt Storn's ch g Forrester, 5 .... Pierce, 109 0
J. D. Dunn's s h Four Acres, 4 .... Dunn, 119 0

Time—1:46

Pools sold—Ed McGinnis $15; Winona $9; Louise M $4; and the field $2. Paris Mutuals paid, Ed McGinnis $7.50 and Louise M. $6.60.

The selling race was easily captured by Tom Daly, Kildare just defeating Ida Glenn for the place.

SUMMARY.

Third race—Seven furlongs: selling.

S. Mulkey's ch g Tom Daly, 6 .... L. Newhall, 112 1
Matt Storn's ch g Kildare, 4 .... Pierce, 120 2
H. D. Miller's ch m Ida Glenn, a .... J. Roach, 98 3
H. E. Rose's b c Dan Murphy, 3 .... Clifford, 119 0
E. J. Baldwin's b g Gladiator, 2 .... G. West, 115 0
J. B. Ross' ch h Sir Ladd, 4 .... Hazlet, 100 0
C. A. Davis' ch h Jack Brady, 5 .... J. Device, 109 0
J. Abit's b g Jack Pot, 3 .... Ward, 100 0
Kelly & Samuels' br m Welcome, 4 .... Marshall, 12[illegible] 0

Time—1:32½.

Pools sold—Tom Daly $20; Kildare $6; Dan Murphy $2; and the field $5. Paris mutuals paid—Tom Daly $5.75, Kildare $6.20.

In the last race Painkiller led for considerable of the distance, but Sunday won handily.

SUMMARY.

Fourth race—Nine sixteenths of a mile; for all ages.

T. F. Lynch's br g Sunday, a .... Davis, 1[illegible] 1
G. Lyman's b h Painkiller, a, 120 2
J. B. Ross' b f Kitty Van, 3 .... Hazlett, 111 3
D. F. Able's ch h Rondo, a, 130 0

Pools sold—Sunday $10; Kitty Van $6; Rondo $4; Painkiller $5.

On Thursday, Jan. 9, the first event on the card was the one and one-sixteenth dash for all ages. Atlanta was made a hot favorite at $20, with Fannie F second choice for $10, and the field for $8. Atalanta was never in the race, and coming down the straight Fannie F looked all over the winner, but Naicho B came up on the outside full of running, and under the clever manipulation of Hazlett won Cleverly. Hazlett displayed his wisdom by running on the outside, as the footing was very much better than on any other part of the track. The Paris mutuals, which were sold for $2, paid $9.85.

SUMMARY.

First race—One mile and a sixteenth; for all ages.

John Forster's s g Naicho B. 3 .... Hazlett 119 1
Matt Storn's b m Fannie F, 5 .... Narvice 2
Kelly & Samuel's b m Welcome, 5 .... Marshall 119 1
E. J. Baldwin's b f Atalanta, 3 .... L. Brown 99 0
L. H. Vignolo's b f Rosemeade, 3 .... Scofield 99 0

Time—1.56½.

The favorite was again defeated in the "Possible Case" handicap. Louise M sold for $25, Ed McGinnis $20 and the field $5. The son of Grinstead captured the event rather handily. Dan Murphy cut out a terrific pace and Haslett very injudiciously rushed Louise M along with Dan Murphy. The other starters were strung out for a dozen lengths. The pace told on the mare, and when Marshall made his effort on Ed McGinnis the race was all over.

SUMMARY.

Second race—One mile and a quarter: for all ages.

Kelly & Samuel's b h Ed McGinnis, 5 .... Marshall, 112 1
T. Hazlett's b f Louise M, 4 .... Hazlett, 107 2
H. E. Rose's b h Dan Murphy, 4 .... Clifford, 107 3
Matt Storn's ch g Forester, 5 .... Pierce, 112 0
J. D. Dunn's s h Four Aces, 4 .... Dunn, 107 0

Time—2.17½.

The last event on the programme was the seven-eights mile heats.

Oro was made a red hot favorite, and he justified the confidence reposed in him by winning in straight heats. There were many people who thought, however, that the judges erred in giving the first heat to Oro. A dead heat would have about hit the nail on the head.

SUMMARY.

Third race—Seven furlongs; heats; for all ages.

T. B. Ross' b g Oro, 6 .... Hazlett, 117 1 1
C. A. Davis' b h Jack Brady, 6 .... Narvice, 117 2 2
E. B. Denn's b h Othello, 4 .... Hennessy, 114 3 3
O. Walters' b c Reno, 3 .... Clifford, 99 dis
P. Donalech's s g Naicho B, 4 .... Hazlett, 117 dis

Time—1.32 and 1.35½.

Pools sold—Oro $15, Jack Brady $7, and the field $3.

The track was slow and heavy when the bell was rung for the first race on Friday. In fact, the slow time made in all the races during the entire meeting is due to the condition of the track. Sunday, Painkiller, Rondo, Fannie F. and Sidlaw sported silk for the five-eighths mile dash. Sunday was installed a hot favorite. Rondo and Painkiller had a few supporters. Sunday romped home an easy winner. Just before the start of this race the judges put up new riders on Rondo and Painkiller.

SUMMARY.

First race—Five furlongs, for all ages.

T. F. Lynch's b g Sunday, a, 120 .... Davis 1
G. Lyman's b h Painkiller, 5, 120 .... Brown 2
D. F. Abel's s g Rondo, a, 120 .... West 3
M. Storn's b m Fannie F., 5, 115 .... Pierce 0
E. B. Den's b g Sid Law, 5, 120 .... Hennessy 0

Time, 1:04.

Pools sold: Sunday, $25; Rondo, $11, and the field $7.

Everybody wanted Oro in the next race, and there was a rush to get a pool ticket on the son of Norfolk. The talent again received a hard knock, as Oro failed to get a slice of the money. It was a great race down the straight between Oro, Gladiator and Othello, but the Santa Anita entry captured the event, and the few who backed the Maltese Cross were jubilant.

SUMMARY.

Second race—One mile and seventy yards, for all ages.

E. J. Baldwin's b g Gladiator, 4, 119 .... West 1
E. B. Den's b h Othello, 4, 119 .... Hennessy 2
T. B. Ross's b g Oro, 5, 124 .... Hazlett 3
L. H. Vignolo's b f Rosemeade, 3, 99 .... Roache 0
M. Stornn's ch g Forester, 5, 107 .... Pierce 0
J. D. Dun's ch h Four Aces, 4, 112 .... Riley 0
Kelly & Samuels' br m Welcome, 5, 119 .... Marshall 0

Time, 1:53½.

Pools sold. Oro, $15; the field, $5; Gladiator, $2.

The talent called the turn in the next race. Tom Daly packed his terrific weight and easily defeated his field. Adam ran gamely and at one time looked dangerous:

SUMMARY.

Third race—One mile, for all ages, welter weights.

C. Mulkey's ch g Tom Daly, 6, 162 .... Hill 1
C. A. Davis' ch g Adam, a, 162 .... Foster 2
G. Walters' b h Reno, 3, 132 .... Clifford 3
C. A. Davis' b h Jack Brady, 6, 162 .... Smith 0

Time, 1:52.

Pools sold: Tom Daly, $2[illegible]; Davis' stable, $17; Reno, $3. Paris mutuals paid: No. 2161, $2 70.

The weather was cold and disagreeable on Saturday which interfered with the attendance. Nine faced the starter in the seven furlong dash.

Tom Daly was a red-hot favorite with Louise M. second choice. Dan Murphy looked as fit as a fiddle and had a few staunch admirers. Welcome cut up at the start and the flag was eventually lowered to an admirtble start. Atlanta was left behind and Welcome crowded into Tom Daly thus making the favorite lose fully eight lengths. It was any one's race coming down the stretch but Othello gained the verdict by a head.

SUMMARY.

First race—Seven furlongs; for all ages.

E. B. Den's b h Othello, 119 lbs .... Hennessy 1
T. Haslett's b m Louise M, 114 lbs .... Hazlett 2
N. A. Covarrubias' b h Dan Murphy, 119 lbs .... Clifford 3
Cy Mulkey's ch g Tom Daly, 6, 124 lbs .... Narvice 0
E. J. Baldwin's b m Atalanta, 3, 99 lbs .... Brown 0
L. K. Vignolo's b m Rosemeade, 3, 99 lbs .... Roach 0
S. D. Dunn's ch h Four Aces, 4, 119 .... Dunn 0
M. Storn's b m Fannie F., 5, 117 lbs .... Pierce 0
Kelly & Samuels' b m Welcome, 5, 117 lbs .... Marshall 0

Time, 1:32½.

Pools sold—Tom Daly, $10; Louise M., $7; the field, $7 and Dan Murphy $6.

Ed McGinnis, Winona and Kildare came to the post for the owner's handicap. Mr. McGinnis sold a hot favorite. There was a quiet tip out on Winona but Ed McGinnis captured the race in easy style. McGinnis and Kildare broke away and ran a mile before the race, but this little exercise appeared to agree with Ed McGinnis.

SUMMARY.

Second Race—One mile and one-eighth, owners to handicap.

Kelly & Samuels' d h Ed. McGinnis, 5, 80 .... Marshall 1
E. J. Baldwin's b m Winona, 5, 99 .... Brown 2
M. Storn's ch g Kildare, 5, 82 .... Pierce 3

Time, 1:57½.

Pools sold: McGinnis, $10; Kildare, $4; Winona, $3. Paris mutuals paid $4.30.

The last event of the day, the five-eighths mile heats, was declared off, owing to the attempt made to poison Kitty Van.

The last day of the winter meeting took place on Tuesday. The weather was much more pleasant than on the preceding days and capital sport was provided. The opening mile dash proved to be a capital betting race. Old John Treat sold favorite at first, but as the betting settled down, Tom Daly sold first choice with Treat, Oro and Winona in the order named. This resulted in a big boil over and the backers of the field again reaped a harvest. Davis on Painkiller sent the Joe Hooker representative to the front at the fall of the flag, and he kept him there throughout the race. It was a whipping finish between Painkiller, Oro, Tom Daly and Winona but the first named gained the verdict with but little to spare.

SUMMARY.

First race—One mile, for all ages, at 100 pounds.

G. Lyman's b h Painkiller, 4, 100 .... Davis 1
J. B. Ross' b g Oro, 6, 100 .... Haslett 2
Cy. Mulkey's ch g Tom Daly, 6, 100 .... Narvice 3
E. J. Baldwin's b m Winona, 4, 100 .... Brown 0
E. B. Den's b h Othello, 3, 100 .... Hennesey 0
J. D. Dunn's s h. Four Aces, 3, 100 .... Bilay 0
Al. Moran's g g John Treat, 6, 100 .... Roach 0

Time, 1:46½.

Pools sold: Tom Daly, $11; J. Treat, $10; Oro, $6; Winona, $5, and the field $5.

The January Handicap proved a gift to Ed McGinnis, who easily defeated Naicho B., Jack Brady and Forester.

SUMMARY.

Second Race—January handicap. One mile and one-quarter; for all ages.

Kelly & Samuels' b h Ed McGinnis, 4, 124 lbs .... Marshall 1
C. A. Davis' b h Jack Brady, 6, 112 lbs .... Narvice 2
J. Forster's b g Naicho B., 3, 115 lbs .... Roach 3
M. Storn's ch g Forester, 5, 95 lbs .... Pierce 0

Time, 2:16.

Pools sold: Ed McGinnis $30, Brady $10, the field $15.

The last race of the meeting was a cinch for Louise M. Welcome sulked as usual at the start, and delayed matters.

SUMMARY.

Third Race—One mile and forty yards; for all ages.

T. Hazlet's b m Louise M., 4, 99 lbs .... Hazlet 1
Kelly & Samuels' b m Welcome, 4, 104 lbs .... Marshall 2
N. A. Covarrubias' b c Dan Murphy, 3, 104 lbs .... Clifford 3
M. Storn's b m Fannie F., 4, 104 lbs .... Pierce 0

Time, 1:48½.

Pools sold: Louise M. $10, Murphy $6, the field $4.

Dagworth.

Sporting Gossip From Australia.

C. Bacon Lowe.

Editor Breeder and Sportsman:—I send you by this mail some news from this side of the world. You will, of course, long ago have heard through the wires of the sad death of our young champion sculler, Searle. He took ill on the voyage from England, and was dangerously so when he reached Adelaide, where the doctor pronounced it typhoid. He came on with the steamer as far as Melbourne, and died there after a few days in the hospital. The body was brought up to the residence of his trainer, Neil Matheson, in Sidney, and taken through the main street of Sidney to the Cathedral, where a short service was performed, and the cortege then proceded to the circular quay, where the coffin was taken on board a steamer to be buried at the residence of his parents at his native place on the Clarence River, over whose placid bosom our young champion developed his magnificent powers. The procession was attended by the representatives of all the rowing and athletic clubs, members of Parliament, and thousands of citizens, who assembled to do honor for the last time to one of the most phenominal pullers this or any country has ever produced. The streets through which the procession marched were lined with spectators, and it is computed that not less than 200,000 witnessed the ceremony. He retained his senses up to the last few hours of his life, and met the approach of grim death with the same fortitude that he showed when pitted against the flower of your great continent, O'Conner.

It is very sad that one so gifted by nature with such glorious powers of muscular skill should be cut off before he had attained the full vigor of life, and to Australia (viewed in the light of sport) it is quite a national calamity. It was the fashion of English writers a few years back to argue that Australians would necessarily degenerate, owing to the climate, but the feats of our teams of cricketters, followed by Laycock, Beach, Kemp and Searle in the water, and inside the ropes such men as Slavin and Jackson, go a long way to prove that these pessamists were "barking up the wrong tree."

While I write there is a squabble about the championship of the world, to which O'Connor has put in a big claim, but by all unprejudiced judges it must be acceded that Kemp has a far more valid claim. The latter was champion of the world until Searle beat him, whereas O'Conner never won the championship. Certain it is that Searle brought it back and laid it upon the shores of his native country, and if the English or Americans would win it they must come over here, where they will find several hard nuts to crack.

So much for acquatics. Since I sent you our files of newspapers there has not been any racing worth chronicling, but the coming week will usher in the first of a series of first class meetings, at which most of our best New South Wales horses will compete. I send you a further instalment of a series of articles I have been writing on "The Science of Horse Breeding." This one only slightly touches on that, to breeders, important phase, the law of sex, and while I do not profess to have made any discoveries, the cases I adduce to bear me out in the theory may be of service to breeders, and it was more with a view to provoke a controversy on the subject that I published my observations. I feel convinced that no breeder will succeed over a term of years without a close knowledge of physiology, as well as a reliable gallery of the principal landmarks in the stud. There is nothing which indicates so clearly the tend of heredity as color and shape, and with the portraits of his ancestors before you, the nick of blood required by your sire will be less a matter of chance than the present haphazard method of going to work.

The prices of horse stock are absurdly low down here at present, and any of your stud men who require a change of blood should take advantage of the bad times to make their purchases. The Hon. Jas. White, our premier racing (and stud) man, has hitherto been chary of parting with any of his choice blood, but seeing that his stud is not big enough to absorb all the high class and well performed colts he breeds, he has placed in my hands two of his best performers. These stallions are by his renowned Chester from imported mares, and are inbred to the emperor of stallions, English Stockwell. The success achieved by Mr. J. B. Haggin with the handsome Sir Modred has made an old friend of mine gnash his teeth with envy because his offer of $6,300 was refused only a few months before the horse was sent by me to America. He has, however, some balm to his feelings in being the owner of Anteous, a very brilliant colt and one of the few sons left by the expatriated hero. The Victorians are determined that the Melbourne Cup will maintain its prestege and this year they give $50,000 added money. Of this rich prize $10,000 go to second and $5,000 to third horse. This is more valuable to the winner than the Lancashire Plate of $60,000, because the latter is made up in a great measure by the racing men in entrances and sweeps. In our race the club add this big sum. It would be well worth the while of some of your big owners to run down and win this and they may be quite certain of a right royal welcome and the fairest play if they do come.

We are looking forward with much interest to the match between Jackson and Sullivan to come off in your city, and from the good feeling shown by your State to Jackson, we have every confidence he will get a fair show and dress the knots off Sullivan who must be getting rather blaze.

TURF AND TRACK.

C. N. King has sold Bonnie King to Sam Hildreth.

Brooke Hardy has sold Monica Hardy to Jake Johnson for $5000.

The new course at Randwick, Sydney, is one mile and three furlongs.

John Mackey has been steadily improving, and is expected in the city shortly.

Australia claims a very low percentage of roarers among their thoroughbreds.

Lord Calthorpe was offered $5,000 for Satiety, by Isonomy, out of Wifey, but refused it.

The first thoroughbred foal on the Palo Alto Ranch was by (imp) Cyrus out of (imp) Amelia.

The Australian St. Blaize is by St. Albans, a son of Blair Athol. He has won a few races lately.

James Murphy will handle Teuton, Penn P, Estelle and others this year. He is located at Lexington.

On November 27th at Dunedin, New Zealand, £12,983 passed through the totalisator on the race course.

The Queensland Turf Club at Brisbane have contracted for a new grandstand of iron and bricks to cost $30,000.

Byron McClelland has offered J. E. Madden $2,500 for the brown two-year-old colt by imp The Rake out of Flora Macdonald.

The Turf Congress of the National Trotting Association will meet at the Iroquois Hotel, Buffalo, on Wednesday, February 12.

Lyle Simmons has returned Queen of Trumps to Mr. B. M. Cole, owing, it is said, to a break in their friendship. She won $4,420 last year.

Dick Havey, like all thoroughbreds, cannot forget the old love, and will probably have two or three well bred two-year-olds of his own next season.

The Australians have discovered another market for their thoroughbred stock. The steamer Matapedia took 100 horses to Colombo for Mr. C. H. Pate.

Mr. Kelly, ex-trainer of Moorebank, sues Mr. Gill, a prominent turfman, for $5,000 damages for stating that he fraudulantly treated or stuffed Moorebank.

Mr. J. A. Morris says that Westchester will continue all the historic races as far as practicable. The Belmont, Withers, etc., will not be allowed to die out.

Owing to the bad weather and a slight indisposition, Henry Walsh did not go to Vina last week but one of his Aides fetched down a carload of thoroughbred mares.

It is said the new San Diego track, which will be built on Coronado Beach, adjacent to the hotel, will be one of the finest in California, with every Eastern convenience.

It is rumored that the Dwyers are really the owners of Hueneme, the crack two-year-old at Lexington. He is very heavily engaged in the Futurity among other stakes.

The Lindsleys, father and son, have clipped over 12,000 horses and mules this season in St. Louis. This is great work and hardly excelled, as speed goes, in a saw mill.

At the Rawal Haidi (India) meeting Landshark, an Australian bred gelding, was ridden by Lord William Beresford, winning the Amateurs' Purse, one mile, carrying 154 lbs.

Hickenbotham, the well known Australian trainer of Carbine, Oakleigh and Moorebank, says if the latter would run in the afternoon as he does in the morning he would be almost invincible.

Barnes is due at the Santa Anita Ranch on the first of February, it being deemed advisable for him to get used to the horses before starting out for the East. His salary is said, on good authority, to be $8,000.

The settling over the V. R. C. meeting was very slow, Bravo evidently not suiting the public. Many of the backers have not yet settled, and the bookmakers will probably make an example of one or two of the *gentlemen*.

They are becoming Americanized in race track methods in Russia. At Moscow after a race an attempt was made to mob a driver, concerning the old question between losers and winners as to the honesty of the gait of the winner.

At Clifton last Monday Father Bill Daly treated the boys to a surprise, Glory beating Telie Doe and Juggler one mile in 1:47½. Evidently the price suited the estate owner, who is said to be in the habit of waiting until it does.

The stakes of the spring meeting of the Memphis Jockey Club closed January 16th with about 150 entries for the eight stakes. There are probably a large number of other entries on the way, having been mailed on the 14th and 15th.

Guy Wilkes (2:15¼) and his daughter Lillian Wilkes (2:17½) have the fastest combined record for sire and daughter in the world. Robert McGregor (2:17½) and Bonnie McGregor (2:13½) have the fastest combined record for sire and son.

Occident, the winner of the Exhibition Cup at Dunedin, N. Z., was bred in Tasmania by Mr. John Field, the breeder of Malua, Sheet Anchor, and many other well known performers. Mr. Field will use Arsenal, the 1886 Cup winner, in his stud.

The Australian turf has suffered a severe loss in the death of the two imported mares Petroleuse and Rosette; the latter, was a half sister to Bend Or, the Derby winner in 1880. He was by the triple crowned Lord Lyon out of Rouge Rose by Thormanby.

The Australian Jockey Club will probably in future, in order to keep pace with the times, have to add £5,000 to the Gold Cup, which is a two mile handicap, run on the Randwick course, Sydney. The Australian papers say the New South Wales Government should declare a holiday on the day, and thus have a large gate; the grand stands, course, etc., have been enlarged and renovated, the intention being to make Randwick a second Flemington.

M. E. Ragan of Hanford is the owner of Addie E, the Algona mare, who obtained a record of 2:22½ last season at Chico, he has a four-year-old stallion by Bay Rose out of Addie E., who should prove pretty good. I hear he shows plenty of speed. Mr. Ayres originally owned the dam of Addie E.

A. F. Newland, a prominent steeplechase rider, was killed on November 28th. He cut out the pace for a mile, and then took second place, but his horse (Salford) fell heavily at the stone fence, killing the rider instantaneously. Ten or twelve jockeys have been killed during the last few years in Australia.

The annual meeting of the stockholders of the Ukiah Park Association was held last week. The following directors were elected for the ensuing year: J. S. Reed, W. A. Hagans, J. M. Mannon, L. T. Day, Sam Wheeler. Subsequently the Directors elected J. S. Reed, President, and L. T. Day, Secretary.

The new kind of track with one turn, of which we hear so much, may prove fast if properly built, but the people may not take kindly to it. The general public like to see as much as possible of a race, in this case the greater part of the mile will be trotted so far from the grand stand that the contest will look tame.

The Elmendorff yearlings are said to be very fine specimens of what a thoroughbred should be. Among them are brothers to J. B. Haggin's Firenzi, E. J. Baldwin's Grisette, and to Dry Monopole; while there is a sister to Los Angeles who will only be leased for her racing career, and a host of others who should be clinkers.

The local pool rooms have been very late this week receiving their returns from Clifton, etc. Owing to the storms the telegraph system has been very inactive for some time. If it lasts we shall possibly hear of the wires being tapped again. Is there anything in that old gag? One hears it so often a slight suspicion is admissable.

The V. A. T. C. stewards in Australia held an investigation into the running of Moorebank last November, and followed their usual practice (English precedent), i. e. not having any reporters present, consequently there has been a good deal of discussion which will be heightened when they receive Lord Durham's Gimcrack speech.

The Canterbury Jockey Club Derby of 1891 has 81 nominations, twenty-two are from the New Zealand Stud Company, most of them being by Nordenfeldt, a slashing son of Musket. This is quite a good showing for the New Zealanders. By the way, one of the entries is by St. George (brother to Chester) out of Idalia, the dam of Sir Modred and Cheviot.

B. C. Holly has purchased of B. R. Crocker the fine six-year-old stallion Election for the sum of $5,000. Election is a son of Senator Stanford's Electioneer, first dam Lizzie H. by Whipple's Hambletonian; second dam Lizzie Harris by Comus, son of Green's Bashaw; third dam by Arnold Harris, he by Whalebone, dam Sportsmistress by American Eclipse.

The number of horses in European Russia is 21,000,000, including six government studs, besides a large number of private ones. The Russian government devotes annually $80,000 to the purchase of stallions and so widespread has been the interest of late years in improving this stock, that races, trotting matches and shows have been largely increased all over the country.

Carbine, the phenomenal Australian four-year-old, who carried his weight so nobly under difficulties to second place in the last Melbourne Cup, is doing good work again. His foot is all right and he is being specially prepared for the Champion Stakes run next March, in which he will meet Abercorn and other cracks at weight for age, without any penalties or allowances.

Reno's Baby trotted in December 26th in 2:25½ and on December 30th paced in 2:24½ in Texas. It may be of interest to horsemen to know this feat was accomplished by simply taking off a toe weight of four ounces, and that so evenly is he balanced at either gait, a simple removal of a four ounce toe-weight changes him from the trot to the pace. In trotting he wears thirteen ounces forward and in pacing nine ounces.

$250,000 is said to be the most money ever put up for two horses to race for. This sum was wagered at Natchez, Miss., in 1836, Walker Thurston matching his horse, Rodolph, against Hon. J. F. Claybourne's mare, Susan Yandell, for 2500 bales of cotton a side, it being equal to $250,000. Susan Yandell had a walk over for the money, as Rodolph was taken sick shortly before the time set for the contest.

A certain class of Australian racing men, have of late, caused a good deal of trouble and annoyance by appealing against the decision of the stewards. It is hinted that in several instances the objections were made on the off chance that money might be made by betting that the horse objected to would get the race. It is suggested that the introduction of a rule to increase the deposit to £50 to be forfeited if objection is frivolous.

Justice Higinbotham at the Ballarat Circuit Court sentenced John Stewart to twelve months imprisonment for welshing Mr. Jenkins of £9. It appears that at the Ballarat Miners' Races, on the 28th of November, Mr. Jenkins backed Hard Times with Stewart, but when the horse won and Mr. Jenkins went for his money, Stewart had gone, but was arrested at the Ballarat East station, with the result before mentioned.

The Australasian paid Myers the foot racer a compliment when it said he is a gentlemanly fellow, far above the general run of professional pedestrians, and was probably equally as correct when it said that he, Myers, was painting thickly when he said half a million could be won on the Melbourne Cup. The Australasian says if the amount, presumably in American money, were landed, there would be a poor show of getting it all. Ante-post betting is loosing ground and eventually cash betting will be the prevailing system of Australia.

The work on the improvements at the Kentucky Association course have been begun, the first thing thus far done being the tearing down of the betting shed, which will be built large enough to make it capable of accommodating thirty stands. The public stand has also been torn down. The old lumber will be utilized in building several additional stables, containing from fifteen to twenty stalls each. It is thought by taking advantage of the open winter, that by the spring meeting all the contemplated improvements will be finished, and on the opening day in May this historic course will present a modern appearance.

Arsenal, who won the Melbourne Cup in 1886, has been sold for 600 guineas, and his purchaser, Mr. Field, has taken him to his stud farm in Tasmania. The son of Goldsbrough and Powder should nick well with the Whalebone mares which Mr. Field has there.

The Australasian makes a very good suggestion which might be applicable to other countries as well as Australia: — In these degenerate days, when "reversal of form" is so much the rule, it would not be a bad idea if the V. R. C. were to appoint two or three paid stewards to attend the various suburban meetings. At present it is always difficult to get honorary stewards to act, and most daring deeds are performed without the slightest notice being taken of them. If this suggestion were carried out, probably we should not hear so much of suspicious running.

Many of the old-time champion geldings have passed away, such as Dexter, 2:17¼, Great Eastern, 2:18, Judge Fullerton, 2:18, Red Cloud, 2:18, Col. Lewis, 2:18½, is now 19, Midnight, 2:18½ is 17, and still has a great flight of speed, being one of John D. Rockefeller's favorite pair of blacks. Of the old-timers that were performing in the '70s, Comee, 2:19¼; Iron Age, 2:19¼, Troubadour, 2:19¼, Camors, 2:19¾, are dead, while Deck Wright, 2:19½, Bodine, 2:19¼, Driver, 2:19¼, and possibly Moose, 2:19½, Thomas L. Young, 2:19½, Captain Emmons, 2:19½, and Albemarle, 2:19, are still alive.

Isaac Murphy, the celebrated jockey, is spending his winter quietly at his home in Lexington. He rarely ever goes down town, and spends most of his time hunting, of which sport he is not only very fond, but he is also a crack shot with either rifle or shotgun. He has a passion for guns and has a choice collection of all kinds of rifles and shotguns. A few nights ago, Isaac was initiated into a local colored lodge of Masons, and he is therefore probably the only jockey in this country to become a member of that ancient order. Murphy will ride this season principally in the East, where he will probably be in the service of the well-known Dwyer Brothers.

The Winter's two year olds which Alf Estill will take East will probably include Rey Del Rey, a full brother to The Emperor of Norfolk and El Rio Rey; Judge Post, a full brother to Don Jose, Pocatello and Ed Corrigan, by Joe Hooker—Countess Zeika: Black Bart, by Three Cheers—Bonita; Uno Grande, a half sister to Lady Helen, by Joe Hooker—Jessie R; San Juan, brother to Alta, by Norfolk—Ballinette; Blizzard, by Blazes—Trade Wind; Belle Songer, by Joe Hooker—Lou Spencer; Hettie Humphries, by Joe Hooker—Alice N, dam of Applause; Average, by Joe Hooker—Avail, dam of Laura Gardner; Aletia, sister to Bonanza, by Joe Hooker—Mattie Glenn. They will leave here late in February.

A correspondent in Spirit of the Times says that in Salem, N. J., there are two short pieces of road which were covered with oyster shells about 10 inches deep. The tops have been ground fine by continued driving, presenting a very smooth, compact surface which is slightly elastic. The roads, where the shells end, are made of loam and gravel, and are comparatively smooth. Now, it has been noticed by all in speeding over these roads, as soon as the shell portion is reached, the horse increases his stride and action, and therefore goes much faster. The gentleman suggests that a track built on that principle, i. e., an eight or ten-inch covering of pulverized oyster shells, should prove invaluable, particularly during frost and wet weather.

The Australian Jockey club has made a new departure with regard to its young stakes which cannot but meet with the approval of racing men generally, and buyers of yearling in particular. In place of the present Sires' produce stakes and Foal stakes, which will lapse in three years it has decided to establish several new races styled Biennial Stakes, the first of which will be run at the A. J. C Autumn Meeting of 1892. According to the prevailing custom, horses are entered for produce races while they are yet foals, but under the new order of things entries will not be taken until they are yearlings, so that it will be optional with the buyers of this class of blood stock to nominate their purchases as they may think fit, instead of allowing the breeder to do so, as has hitherto been the practice.

The Lucknow (India) meeting was noticeable for the fact that several English and Australian racers competed. In the Trial Stakes the expatriated Australian Moorhouse, by Moorthorpe, won handily, five furlongs in 1:04. The Little Gochase was won by Lord W. Beresford's Australian mare Nellie, who beat five Arabs and two Indian breds. The Bar Cup was won by Fitz-William, an imported English horse, while the Grand Annual was won by an Australian, Harvester. At the Sonepore meeting Midas won the Doomraon Cup and Beltiah Cup, Charlton won the Hutwa Cup, Erbank the Durbhunga Cup, Little Sister the Merchants' Cup, Spray the Beck Cup, Saleyard the Indian Planter's Gazette Purse, Charlton the Civilians' Cup, The Ghost the Jaintpore Plate and Gold Jessop's Cup, all the winners being Australians.

Secretary Brewster, of the Washington Park Jockey Club, says the Times Democrat, reports forty entries to the stakes of the club have been received with just exactly half of the hoped for number in, and the Californian and other far Western stables, the Tennessee stables, those now at New Orleans, a number in Kentucky and others to hear from, it appears that Secretary Brewster's desire will be realized.

When the rich Wheeler handicap was instituted it was anticipated that the event would be recognized as the most important handicap of the West, and on a par with the Suburbad and Brooklyn in the East. Heretofore the Oakwood has always received the greatest number of entries but it is already evident that the Wheeler has supplanted it and taken the place it was designed to fill in the estimation of Western owners. He has already received sixty-two entries for this race.

Judge, starter and every racing official comes in for censure and adverse comment every now and again, but of late, that much abused official, the handicapper, has been catching it right and left in England and the Colonies. In England, Major Egerton's work was so criticised that there will be probably two handicappers in future. In New Zealand, the Dunedin handicapper has so offended the northern horse owners that they (owners of seventeen of the best horses) have written to the Dunedin Jockey Club asking for a change in the handicapping, and requesting that a new handicapper be appointed; otherwise they would not send their horses to the autumn meeting. The Dunedin Jockey Club sent a circular letter to each of the protesting owners declining to make a change, but saying that they would as heretofore, carefully consider the fitness of their officials at the proper time, when the annual appointments were made.

We all probably have read the soul stirring lines of Adam Lindsay Gordon the Australian poet. His 'Sick Stock-rider' and 'How we beat the favorite' with many other hunting and racing poems are so vivid and realistic that after reading them one could almost swear he witnessed the scenes. It is therefore with pleasure we read that in Ballarat, where the poet first distinguished himself in Victoria, is to be erected a statue of him, the expense is to be defrayed by Mr. & Mrs. Jas. Macpherson, the latter of whom is one of the well known brilliant horsewomen of the Colonies.

The Ione Valley Echo has assumed quite a sporting aspect since the race track has drawn so many horses to their handy locality. Among other racing items it says: John Waterman, of Farmington, is training two very promising young horses at the Ione track. One is the stallion John W., owned by himself, and the other a two-year-old filly owned by L. L. Huntley of Oakland, and later on says that T. H. Rae and T. J. Drais, of Farmington, visited Ione a couple of days last week. Both gentlemen are interested in breeding thoroughbreds. They visited the Ione track Wednesday morning and saw Ajax, John W., Lynnette and several other trotters speeded, and were much pleased. They were of the opinion that the Ione track is without doubt the best winter track in the State.

In an interview with a St. Louis reporter President Charlee Green says: There is a new movement on foot, too, for the government of the trotting meetings. It is suggested that no prospectus be issued until nearly the end of the Grand Circuit; then have an agent on the ground at Buffalo and Rochester with power to make and fill races. Trotting horses shift so rapidly that a prospectus arranged any length of time before a meeting is almost useless. Thus, last year the free for all pace had to be changed to a 2:16 class and the free for all trot did not fill at all. The trouble could be obviated by an agent being on the ground where the performers and owners are and offering no race which he did not feel certain would fill and fill well. Thus a programme could be arranged which would bring here almost every horse on the Grand Circuit.

Ed. Corrigan will school his recent purchase, Libretto, over hurdles, he being unsound; it is believed he could not stand preparation for flat racing. He says racing will commence at West Side Park, Chicago, this spring on May 15, and continue without interruption (save during the summer meeting of the Washington Park Club) until late in the month of October. His stable is now quartered at Memphis, Tenn., where his horses will remain until the racing at that point is over, then they go to Nashville and then to Chicago. Riley, his great three-year-old, is doing well, and his owner believes he has in him the making of another Freeland. He, with several others of Mr Corrigan's horses, will not be sent to West Side Park, but will go to Louisville, Latonia, St. Louis and other points, where they are engaged in important stakes.

W. R. Wilson, a well known Australian who is starting a breeding farm, has imported from England two stallions, three brood mares and a St. Simon filly. Of the stallions, Eridispord, who was a fair racehorse, is royally bred. He is by Isonomy, dam Sousie Queen by Musket from Highland Lassie by Caterer or Stockwell, from Glengowrie by Touchstone. Such a pedigree is rarely seen, while the other stallion, Castor, is almost as well bred, being by Zealot out of Lady Yardley by Stirling out of Leda by Weatherbit out of Wish by Touchstone. Zealot is by Hermit, dam by Stockwell. Castor was a good performer, winning nineteen races in his two, three and four-year-old career. As a five-year-old, he ran once as the property of Plunger Benzon. Mr. Wilson will most assuredly be heard from in racing circles in years to come, as he has some good mares to mate with these highly bred stallions.

Trainer McLaughlin, having given up his position as starter at Clifton, has entered upon his duties as the ruling spirit at Pierre Lorillard's Rancocas Stud, Jobstown, N. J. James H. McCreery, who has had charge for a year, was offered the position of assistant trainer, but desired to sever his connection with Rancocas. He says he left behind him as fine a lot of youngsters as has been at that establishment for years. There are now over twenty two-year-olds on the farm, and a handsome lot they are—sound, healthy and beautifully made, with hardly an exception. Among the finest is the Emperor colt Cyrus, who has gone to the quarter pole in 0:23 with 118 pounds up. He has lots of endurance, and weight seems to give him no concern whatever. The mile straightaway track on the Rancocas Farm is now nearly completed, and is one of the finest private tracks to be found. George Taylor will be first jockey.

A Cincinnati paper some time ago said:

"A patrol judge is a practical necessity, and it will be interesting to note the clubs that will evade the use of such an official. Another thing that the jockey clubs must come to is to watch the fluctuation of the odds in the betting ring. Many a job is uncovered in the betting ring, and the talent are all posted, but the judges mount their box and see the scheme go through in total ignorance of the fact that the race was fixed. With a well posted man in the betting ring to note what was going on, they could have had advance knowledge enough to have watched the actions of certain horses closely, and thereby understand what they were doing."

Our contemporary is quite right. A patrol judge is getting to be quite necessary, and the betting should also be watched, while the starter should have as keen an eye on boys who *do not want to get away*, as on those who are too anxious.

The Australian says: In England, America, and Australia cash betting is daily becoming more general upon racecourses and with the increase of stakes no doubt the system will become more popular. There was a time, not so very long ago, that ante-post betting was all the rage in Australia, and no sooner was one Melbourne Cup decided than wagering commenced on the one that was to follow. In this way the leading bookmakers entered thousands in their books and the amount of "dead" money which they raked in fairly crippled the public, while it enriched the wielders of the metallic pencil. All that is changed now, and after watching the game closely for a year or two, we have come to the conclusion that cash betting is preferable to ante-post betting. In America the cash system is largely in vogue, and the press and the public prefer it, because, it is alleged, it has the effect of reducing the number of "stiff" horses that are supposed to run at various meetings. Probably our contemporary is right it may reduce, but does not do away with stiffs for many a horse runs to swell the field and prevent some other horse from winning.

A patched up horse is hardly ever of much value. One dare not back him as he is liable to break down any time, and what races he will win will hardly repay one for the trouble. Dick Havey, the old rider of Norfolk and other cracks, gave me a good illustration of the uncertainty of backing a patched up horse. Some twelve or thirteen years ago Ballot Box, who had run out in the snow in Nevada for a couple of winters, after breaking down badly, was patched up and entered in a two mile and repeat at Reno. He won the first heat easily, and after it, Dick slipped into his box and felt his leg, which was very hot and feverish, and going straight back bought the other end for little or nothing, despite the solicitation and urging of his friends who had also examined the horse's leg, when the second heat was run Ballot Box shut up like a jackknife at the head of the stretch, breaking down badly, and then it turned out that Havey had unwittingly felt of what was supposed to be his sound leg, but in which he had broken down, while the others had examined the old leg which stood up well. It was the old story, the horse had used his game leg so tenderly that he broke down on the other.

Gurney C. Gue, editor of the North West, writes to W. P. Ijams, of Terre Haute, in regard to the dam of Axtell as follows: "In a sketch of Axtell, which I wrote at the time of the Northwestern Breeders' Meeting, which you may have seen, I said, upon information gained from a gentleman in whom I had a good deal of confidence, and who claimed to know all about Lou, that she was a fair average mare, except for a suspicious bunch on one of her hocks. My informant put it stronger and said she was spavined. Now after having seen Lou, I am satisfied beyond all doubt, that the gentleman had in mind some other mare. There is nothing that could be rated 'average' about the dam of Axtell. She is a magnificent individual; large, shapely, stylish and very substantial, with just as clean and perfect set of limbs as I ever saw. She has plenty of bone, and it is of Mambrino Patchen quality. Her joints, both knees and hocks, are broad and strong and perfectly formed; in my humble judgment, all in all, I never saw Lou's better in physical structure." This but confirms the statement recently made by the lady who now owns the mare.

The New Louisiana Jockey Club has retired from the Turf Congress. Col. Simmons, when spoken to on the subject, said that the club had retired from the congress because it could not conform to the new regulations adopted"

"They have," said he, "prohibited the giving of purses for races of less than one mile for three year olds and upward, and while we approve of their efforts to discourage sprinting and encourage long distance racing, we cannot possibly conform to this rule, as we are now situated. It would be impossible for us to run our winter meeting in conformity with this rule, and therefore, while we wish them well in their efforts toward turf reform we feel that the only course open to us is to resign our membership in the congress."

"Will the decisions of the New Louisiana Jockey Club be hereafter recognized and upheld by members of the Turf Congress?"

"I cannot say as yet of course, but I presume they will be. We recognize the rulings of all clubs and racing organizations of every sort and I suppose that they will hold that when we rule off a man or boy we have had good and sufficient reasons for doing so."

The Santa Anita Stable has great expectations from The Emperor this season. Mr. Baldwin says he hopes to start him in several of the thousand dollar purse races in the East, and will get him into a few stakes if possible. He has for the last two weeks worked steadily on the ranch, his best work being a quarter in 0:25½. and five furlongs in 1:05½, in which he showed his well known speed, and finished as sound as a bell. I have not seen the horse since he left the Bay District track, and shall have grave doubts of his racing until he gets to the post, for it is always the last few gallops that find out the weak spot in a dicky horse. Mr. Baldwin does not expect anything big this year from any of his others except Los Angeles, and possibly Honduras, both of whom are in good trim. Of the two-year-olds, the best is probably a colt by Gano out of Grey Annie, but they are all rather undersized—perhaps the *soupcon* of inbreeding, which is noticeable among the youngsters, has something to do with it. Mr. Baldwin says if he pays expenses he will be satisfied this season, and as he will have less forfeits to pay than usual, owing to skipping the Western meetings, the Maltese cross will in all likelihood be seen at Coney Island for the first time this season. Among other news, Mr. Baldwin said that Mollie's Last and a couple more mares, would be bred to The Emperor. Grisette is expected to be in foal to the same horse, while Miss Ford was bred on the 18th of *June* to Verano (Grinstead—Jennie D. by Glenelg). Mr. Baldwin, by the way, has serious intentions of purchasing Bravo, the winner of the Melbourne Cup. The price will probably be stiff, but of course that is immaterial to the Santa Anita millionaire, and the horse should be invaluable as an outcross, having three Touchstone and two Bay Middleton crosses in his truly racing pedigree.

There are two race course officials who should be paid in California, and as far as practicable should be employed throughout the State; *they are one judge and the starter*. Jobs have been, and probably will be, plentiful. A judge has an exceptional chance—being posted in a coign of vantage—of seeing how horses run and comparing notes at the various meetings, while the starter is in an equally good position; he sees many things also that a Judge cannot see, and if of an observing turn of mind—as he should be—will have a reminiscence the next time a jockey attempts to get left, or in other ways, tries to beat the public. There is another reason, too, against trusting too much to local talent in the judge's stand and with the flag, viz.: They with very few exceptions, lack the necessary racing knowledge. I do not mean for one moment to insinuate that the local management is not honest and trustworthy, but that the mistakes which occur daily through the circuit are the result of an almost total lack of racing knowledge. I recollect several cases where I was personally interested; one occurred in the northern part of the State, a three-year-old and an aged horse were among the competitors, distance five furlongs; the aged horse, a gelding, carried 118 *because his rider could just ride that weight*; the three-year old carried 120 for the same reason. When I inquired the reason I was duly informed that judges were allowed a certain amount of latitude, t'was interesting and rather amusing. In another instance a repeat race was run; the first heat was won by, say Maud, the second a dead heat between Maud and a gelding, Bob; a false start, during which both ran the entire course, was the next phase of the race. Joe won the next heat and the run off, distancing the mare. The owner of the horse who finished third in the second heat claimed second money; the winner claimed it; the owner of the mare who ran in the final claimed it, and last but not least, the judges asserted that it reverted to the association. Rules 84 and 85 P. C. B. H. A. settled the association and the owner of the first horse; the original claimant, who was third in the second heat, argued for a long time, but eventually the money was duly adjusted after some explanatory remarks in re rule 85. I could give many more instances, all of which tend to show that it is for the better interests of racing to have a paid judge and starter, and the sooner the various agricultural districts and racing associations unite in a judge and starter who shall attend wherever possible, the better every one will be pleased.

A good deal has been written about the ancestry of the racehorse, and it is generally claimed to be the Arabian blood that gives stamina and fine form to the thoroughbred. The Australasian says on that subject:

Hitherto it has been the custom of many modern writers on the subject to give the Arab all the credit for the excellence of the English thoroughbred. We must confess that we have labored under the impression that we owed everything to the Eastern horse for providing England with an animal which by years of judicious breeding has become the most wonderful the world has ever produced. The best living authority on the breeding of the thoroughbred, Mr. Joseph Osborne, has, however, exploded this oft-repeated dictum, and proved by the production of many facts that long before the importation of the Byerly Turk, Darley Arabian, or the Godolphin Arabian, the English racehorse was far superior to the Arab, and while giving due credit to the good done by the infusion of the Arab blood, he successively combats the idea that to the Arab, and the Arab alone, are we indebted for all the excellence of the English thoroughbred. He tells us in the Horse-breeder's Handbook that on the particular subject of the original ancestry of the British thoroughbred it is singular how writers, though particularly careful in other genealogical topics of less importance, are evasive, vague, and often misleading. Most of these writers have told us that the origin of the thoroughbred is "traced back to three Oriental ancestors," and pretty well all who have touched upon the subject of horse-breeding and its history have followed suit.

But Mr. Osborne is at issue with them, and in support of his argument he says:—"In the first place, as evidence and argument have already been adduced to show, the English race horse of the seventeenth century (that is, the horse that had been breeding for coursing and running in the matches of speed dating back to the days of King John) has already proved himself superior to the best Eastern horses that had been imported, and continued to maintain this priority up to the time of the Restoration, after which, of course, we can no longer trace the 'early English' racer as a distinct breed. This in itself, however, is an important point, as showing, and I think conclusively, that the English thoroughbred of to-day is no 'creation' of the Arab and other Eastern importations, but simply a manufacture which they had improved. But the improvement had no more commenced with them than it has ceased to continue since. Then, as regards the relative influence of the imported sires, it must be borne in mind that a considerable period intervened—a century, more or less—between the great majority (numbering considerably more than 150) and the one sire to whom the chief share of merit is justly awarded, viz., The Godolphin; and it would be absurd to ignore the direct and indirect bearing which these have upon the three great channels (Matchem, Herod and Eclipse) through which all the composite qualities of the thoroughbred have reached us. But in the female lines there are undeniable proofs of important influence, outside and anterior to the known Eastern sires—and here I maintain that in considering the origin of the 'thoroughbreds,' as distinct from his stud book genealogy, it is most unreasonable, nay even preposterous, to set aside the female sources. Indeed, if the investigation be pursued logically, that side must be the most interesting in this instance, because the sires being admittedly Eastern, it becomes imperative to trace, if possible, the blood of their mates. If a potent average of the dams at the roots is found to be not Eastern, then it becomes obvious that any restrictive claim for purely Arab descent has no authentic basis in fact." In analysing the pedigrees of Eclipse, Herod and Matchem, Mr. Osborne shows pretty conclusively that both Eclipse's sire Marske and his dam Spiletta were full of pure English blood, and deals in turn with each of the long divisions or sixteen sections which begin with the fourth remove. He points out that the first and second sections apply to the Darley Arabian and Betty Leedes the sire and dam of Bartlet's Childers both of pure Eastern decent. The third and fourth sections refer to Snake and Grey Wilkes, the sire and dam of sister to, Old Country Wench, in both of which there are flaws. The first is found in the dam of Snake, of whom nothing further is known than that she was the daughter of Hautboy, from which it is quite reasonable to infer that her dam was not of Eastern descent, but rather of English origin; for it is quite certain that had she been an Arabian, Barb, or Royal mare, it would have been stated, as in the case of Betty Leedes's grandam. Further instances are adduced of the English descent of Marske, and it is also pointed out that Spiletta, the dam of Eclipse, is not altogether of Eastern descent and the extravagant conclusions which have been arrived at respecting the descent of Matchem and Herod are not at all agreed with by Mr. Osborne who quotes an ancient authority, Gervase Markham, to prove that the English horse had attained great excellence before the importation of Arabs or Turks. Markham says:—"Again what nation hath brought forth that horse which hath exceeded the English.

When the best Barbaries that ever were in their prime, I saw them over-runne by a black hobbie at Salisbury, yet that hobbie was more overrunne by a horse called Valentine, which Valentine neither in hunting nor running was ever equalled, yet was a plain bred English horse both by syre and dam. Again, for infinite labour and long endurance, which is to be desired in our hunting matches, I have not seen any horse to compare with the English. He is of tolerable shape, strong, valiant, and durable." In corroboration of this, an American authority says:—"As the progenitors of our Narragansett pacers and others were brought to this country (America) before the first Arabian ever reached England, and as running, pacing and trotting races had become so common as to be suppressed by the law before a thoroughbred ever reached this continent, we must conclude there was something good in the original English horse for which he has hitherto not been credited." As other nations besides England used Arab sires, but never produced anything to compare with the English thoroughbred, it is plain that the hunting and running horse of England previous to the advent of the Arabs was an animal of great excellence, though the union with horses of Eastern descent doubtless had the effect of producing a breed which commands the admiration of the civilized world, and brings into England so much of the wealth of other nations.

San Jose Agricultural Park.

The Erection of a Pavilion Proposed—Jas. Boyd's Miniature Track under Cover—The Leading Stallions there and in the Vicinity—A Marked Advance in Trotting-horse Breeding worthy of Comment.

San Jose has been noted for having one of the best mile tracks on the coast and the records show that some of the fastest time and record breaking have been done there. In the last few years the trotting-horse-breeding industry has advanced a hundred-fold, there being now several breeding farms in the vicinity. There are at the Park and about San Jose as grand representatives of the Wilkes, Mambrino Patchen, Hambletonian, Nutwood families as can be found in the State, and all doing service in the stud at moderate fees, individuality and breeding considered. The progress is due to the integrity of the officers of the Agricultural Society, their combined labor never being spared, giving liberal purses and premiums, the result of which has been a marked improvement in such enterprises as add to the breeding up of the horse. In the last few years there have been selected for directors some of the most energetic young men in the country, and most of them are directly interested in trotting or running horses, thereby placing themselves in the capacity to plan means to the benefit of the horse owners, and consequently to the success of the meetings of the association. In the present year the district will show for itself, and undoubtedly will do its share in bringing forth successfull competitors for honors which will add laurels to the crown of our already far-famed Golden State. Mr. Topham, the ex-President of the Agricultural Society, is agitating the erection of a pavilion in the grounds, an edifice that has been wanted for years, and is indispensable. A committee has been appointed to carry out plans and means to build such a structure, and there is no doubt but that the members of the association will each and all unite their influence to have the same under way of construction at an early date and by all means completed by the coming Fair.

Mr. James Boyd's miniature track is one of the leading attractions; it is under cover in the same plan as that of the Palo Alto, one-sixteenth of a mile around with 80 foot stretches. This means business, and all modern arts and facilities for the development of the colt trotters will be adopted. The knowing ones will undoubtedly benefit by it, and liberally patronize it. Colts from any part of the State will be taken and given the primary lessons at the trot, and in due time they are turned over to the further training of the skillful drivers.

By the way, the San Jose Yearling Colts' Stakes, as per announcement in the advertising columns, for the foals of 1889, is one of the wisest schemes yet placed before the breeders. It insures in the first place a means of inducing the owners of colts by the respective stallions to bring them into prominence, as the purse will be in proportion to the co-operation of the stallion owners, and it is to their interest to have as many of the produce experimented on, as that is the only way they can find out what they are made of, and most assuredly this will bring enough $100 checks to make up something to compensate for the wear and tear, time and expense of bringing up the young things to their best condition to compete for the prize; and those that fail to contribute towards the success of this enterprise are neglecting one of the chief points that lead to a successful stock breeder. The value of a stallion fee before the estimation of the public is in proportion to his success as a producer, as it is evident that all can't own the stallions, but we are all desirous of possessing a grand individual, a performer sired by a performer whose ancestors trace back to the great families through performing channels, etc. Now is the chance of San Joseans to put up your $100 and call around to your patrons and encourage them to develop the colts, that the link which connects your stallion to those illustrious ancestors and brought them to fame may be continued on through him and propagated till McGinty is raised. The following are the names of a few of the stallions and their owners, from which our readers may choose, their announcements, are duly advertised in other columns, and the fees are very moderate, everything considered.

Billy Thornhill 8707, is the property of Jas. Boyd Esq., San Jose. He may well congratulate himself in owning this piece of horse flesh. His sire, Beverly Wilkes, was a very promising young horse, and unfortunately met with premature death from injuries received by a kick when three years old. He was a full brother to Prospect Maid 2:23, Walsingham (sire of Latitude in the 2:30 list) Georgia Wilkes, (sire of Billy Wilkes 2:30) all young sires coming into prominence by the Great George Wilkes 2:22, and out of Wilson by Mambrino Pilot 2:27.

Thornhill's dam Emily also by George Wilkes, is the dam of Fortuna, two-year-old record 2:31, three-year-old record 2:23, and out of sire Stout by Surplus, son of Ashland by Mambrino Chief. Second dam the Lear mare, dam of Jim Irving 2:23, Young Jim (sire of Butterfly 2:19¾), Garnett 2:19, and others by Lear's Sir William, the whole combining to make one grand individual, and that he will prove himself as good as his breeding is conclusive, or we must put aside the fundamental rule that like produces its like or the likeness of some ancestor. Which ever side we analize we find a Wilkes—Mambrino Chief cross through producers and a remove further is the Pilot Jr. on one side and thoroughbred in the other. He is the stock horse of breeding and type we want in California, and hard to beat anywhere. The colts (the oldest here only being yearlings) are all bays after a smooth Wilkes pattern, being inbred to that royal family. Billy Thornhill possesses its marked characteristic, and he is specially noted for transmitting the same to his progeny. At the horse show of our last fair, the group, representing his get, was acknowledge by all horsemen as being the best ever seen from any one sire anywhere.

These youngsters will be heard from in the near future; they are all very promising. Mr. Boyd places the service fee at only $50 with usual privileges, and that moderate figure is indeed within the reach of everybody.

Mambrino Jr. 1789, (Carr's) the property of George P. Bull, San Jose, is inbred to Mambrino Chief 11, his sire Mambrino Patchen 58 by Mambrino Chief 11, and his dam by Mambrino Chief 11. There are few stock farms without this strain of blood in their stallions or brood mares, and well may they be sought after when the Hambletonian-Mambrino Chief union have established such prepotent sires as Belmont, Almont, Piedmont, Director, Onward, Red Wilkes, Thorndale, etc., and still they breed on with distinction from one generation to another, and with a renewed impetus do they improve when the daughters of Mambrino Patchen and of his sons are used; the advance into prominence of the Mambrino Patchen family is so recent (only about ten years since), that the public will not be taxed to see it in print so repeatedly. I will conclude by prophesying that the fame of Guy Wilkes, William L. Alcantara, Simmons, etc, though decidedly wonderful, are only in their infancy, their future greatness is yet to be seen. So much may well be claimed as the success of the family to which Mambrino Jr. 1789 belongs. As to himself he never was given any opportunity, having been brought as a two and a half-year-old to a district where the industry of the community was anything but that of improving the breed of the trotter or developing the speed of a promising youngster. Yet under these circumstances he obtained a record of 2.45 as a three-year-old, and it is a well known fact that he was capable of trotting close to 2:30, but was not allowed to distance the competitor's horse, who was at the time, President of the association; he was only asked to win the race which he did, and was never put in training again. As a sire, in spite of all disadvantages, there have sprung up Lady Ellen 2:28, (out of a thoroughbred mare) dam of Ella 2:29, and a yearling that trotted quarters in 36 seconds last fall at Palo Alto; also Maud H. 2:30 and several others knocking at the door, amongst which is Merchant, trial 2:25. As a stock horse Mambrino Jr. should not be overlooked on this coast, possessed of such stout breeding and backed as Dr. L. Herr, his breeder, says by a strictly thoroughbred grandam of the ne-plus-ultra stamina. See ad in advertising columns.

Chrisman's Hambletonian 10178 is a mahogany bay, the property of Jesse Chrisman, Esq., San Jose. He is one of the most attractive stallions in the vicinity. He was sired by Whipple's Hambletonian 725. First dam Flora 2:39½, by Chieftain 721; second dam by Wilson's Leamon.

His pedigree combines one of the best trotting strains ever on this coast, based on a pacing foundation and backed by thoroughbred. Through his sire he traces to Hambletonian 10, founder of our trotting families, and through his sire's dam, Martha Washington, a double infusion of Mambrino strains predominate, coming from Burr's Washington, an inbred Mambrino, and a second Abdallah 1 flow from Martha's dam, she being by Abdallah 1, sire of Hambletonian 10. Martha Washington is worthy of special comment, as she is one of the great brood mares, having produced besides Whipple's Hambletonian, Speculation (sire of Crown Point 225, he sire of Valensin, 3 year old record 2:23; Ontano 2:28; Oakland Maid 2:22, Gracie S 2:22, and the dams of Waterford 2:27). She is also the dam of Young Martha, the dam of Crown Point 2:20, sire of Faustine, the dam of the champion yearling colt Faustino 2:35. Mr. Chrisman has a great future for his horse who has such grand ancestors, and with the limited opportunities depending entirely on transient patronage, taking all sorts of mares, he has shown the wonderful potency of reproducing in his get the grand characteristics of the family whose name he bears. He has sired Steve Whipple 2:23, Kate Agnew 2:28½, and others very promising.

Chrisman's Hambletonian's dam was a campaigner of her days, having obtained a record of 2:29½ and showed capacity to trot well in the twenties, and being a daughter of Chieftain 721, sire of Defiance 2:17¾ (pacing), 2:24 trotting, and others, possesses a pacing out cross of the Histoga type, that will be undoubtedly of benefit to the quickening of the Hambletonian long stride. His services are within the reach of all. See card in advertising columns.

Baywood, the property of E. C. Smith, Esq., of San Jose, is a magnificent trotting stallion, bay with black points, excellent limbs and resolute carriage. He represents a Hambletonian—Clay combination, with thoroughbred backing. Such crosses have produced George Wilkes, Electioneer, St. Julien through other branches of the Hambletonian and Clay, and in this Nutwood—Clay cross will be found Maggie E., 2:19½, Jim Mulvenna, 2:27, and others; and by Speculation (by Hambletonian 10) we have Crown Point, 2.24, from Young Martha by George M. Patchen 31. Crown Point in turn produced Faustine, the dam of Faustino, yearling record 2:35, best colt record to date. George M. Patchen 31 never failed to show his produce where an opportunity was given him; and he is to California what Harry Clay, 2:29, is to Kentucky, a great brood mare sire. Every year we see some of his daughters producing speed both at the trot and pace. The same can be said of the progeny of his sons and daughters and grandchildren; they breed on with uniformity, and what they can do only needs the master hand of man to develop. When these facts are taken in consideration, and noting that Baywood is a performer himself, it follows that his services are of great value to the trotting horse breeders. He has shown his capacity to trot a mile in 2:26 in his work, but owing to an injured tendon had to be withdrawn from his engagements the past season; he will be prepared for a record the coming fall, and barring further accident he will be placed in the list of the performing sons of his sire, the great Nutwood 33. See his card in the advertising column.

Woodnut, (Weatherhead's) the property of Jas. Weatherhead, of San Jose, is a solid bay, black points, 15½ hands high and weighs 1050 lbs. He has the Hambletonian conformation, a rapid trotting action, well able to trot in the forties, though never handled for speed. He has shown himself an excellent stock horse, his colts all being of commanding appearance, good carriage and prompt drivers of unsurpassed road qualities. The few that have been handled for speed have shown in very short time satisfactory evidence that Woodnut (Weatherhead's) is a sire of trotters from the great Nutwood 2:18¾. Few branches of the Hambletonian families have shown the capacity to breed on to the remotest generation with as decided uniformity as that founded by Alexander's Abdallah 15, and the subject of this paragraph has the potency of transmitting a well defined, yet smooth Hambletonian conformation to all his get. That he will make a sire of fast trotters only time is needed, as he is drawing to his embrace some very choice daughters of Tilton Almont, Geo. M. Patchen Jr, and others of equal merits. Enough is said when his sire is Nutwood 2:18¾, and his dam Flora 2:39½, trial 2:26, dam of Chrisman's Hambletonian, sire of Steve Whipple 2:23, Kate Agnew 2:28½ by Chieftain 721. Further comment would be useless. See column of advertisements.

Queer Racing Characters.

Men Who Act and Talk Irrationally Under Betting Excitement

"I believe I enjoy my visits to the race track as much as any person who attends such places regularly," says the Sporting World. This remark was made on the return journey from Clifton only a day or two ago by an individual whose face has become so familiar to track patrons that he would be classed among regular racegoers. The remark rather surprised his listeners, and for a moment they were inclined to believe he was jesting. The young man quickly assured his friends that he was in earnest, while other listeners became interested in the conversation. "I do, for a fact, enjoy my visits to a race track at all times, even aside from the excitement which betting affords," he continued. "Of course there may no doubt be many people who go racing who enjoy the sport itself quite as much as myself. Aside from the racing I can find as much divertisement at a track as at the opera or at other entertainments in which I am much interested. I find it an exceptional place to study characters. People on the track and off it look and act to me like different individuals. At the races I notice that a man appears to be controlled by a sort of impulse. His mind, I presume, is kept so actively at work that he does not observe his surroundings even in a general way. He moves about as though his mind was absorbed in some foreign subject, and acts as though he did not realize what was going on about him. Friends appear anxious to avoid each other, except at times when the bands which appear to bind the mind down so closely become relaxed at intervals for a short space of time.

"Even when meetings take place under these circumstances the conversation which usually lasts but a few minutes is made up of commonplace remarks which lack thought. The mind flies back between the imaginary bands again, and so the parties go mosing about as before they met. Now and again one may see one friend dash through a group of people with his face beaming in smiles and grasp the hand of some old chum he has not met in a long while.

"If you will carefully observe such a party you will notice that the greeting is not natural, and besides he will hardly talk rationally. For the time being he tries to resume his ordinary politeness and every day actions, but away they fly in a few moments and back will go his thoughts to those he experiences when his mind appears clasped in the bands. In fact a majority of the people imply by their looks and actions that they desire to be left to their own thoughts. Again, one will notice that the action of the people appear to imply that they go through certain stages in their movements. One can almost discover from an individual's actions just how far he has advanced in his career on the turf.

First of all the beginner can be signalled out from the throng without difficulty. He would remind one of some of the people from this city who attended the Centennial Exhibition at Philadelphia. They arrived at the Quaker City on a cattle train shortly before noon, and to get home again on their excursion tickets they were required to be on board their train at 3 o'clock. During the time that intervened between the arrival and departure of the train they made an effort to inspect everything that was to be seen at the big show. These people cannot understand the fascination of racing or betting. They act more like themselves than any other people on a course, but their time is so taken up in watching the horses, the betting and other sights which interest them that they have no time to spend standing about.

"After a few visits, however, the novice becomes controlled by the same impulse which appears to take possession of his more experienced companions. Old time betting men and bookmakers are as easily signalled out from other people on a track as a chestnut horse is discernible from a bay or brown. The expression of their faces is about alike when they labor under the excitement incident to a race. They, of course, make every effort to hide the real thoughts like the average poker player. In their efforts to appear contended and at ease, their faces assume an intensely serious expression. Besides, they keep as quiet as possible and seldom speak. Of course they cannot hide their nervousness, although they try in every way to avoid any betrayal of it by their actions. It is not probable that these people ever think of how they act when laboring under great excitement on a race track, but it is evident to a close observer that they intuitively do all in their power to appear naturel and at ease.

Every race-goer has noticed people turn their backs to the horses after a start has been effected. These people belong to the betting class, and they cannot stand the effect of the excitement which is brought about by watching the movements of the horse they are interested in. Were they to follow their horse as he competed, they would betray their real feelings, and to avoid so doing they turn their backs to the track proper. These people, however, will listen attentively to the remarks of bystanders who call out the positions of the competing horses. They can fortify themselves against the effects of the excitement while listening which they could not do if they witnessed the contests themselves. As a rule, the people who do not watch the races cannot afford to sustain loss if their investments do not turn out profitable. In fact, lack of experience in turf matters and continued losses tend to make them act in the way they do.

The people who shout and scream at the top of their voices during a race are made up of novices and those who do not bet. If they do invest on the results they wager small amounts and can afford to lose without becoming distressed. There is but little difference in the actions of the women as compared with the men on a race track. The women find more fault, however than the men. They "kick" frightfully and express themselves in plain terms, but of course to their acquaintance only. The women who attend the races regularly and bet do not invest to any great extent except in a small way. Some few women however, have at times bet heavily, but they lived a short time. A two dollar mutuel ticket is about the extent of the investment made by the average female track visitor. During a close finish between horses in which a number of women are interested their actions would remind one of a chicken flying about with its head cut off.

The fastest three-year-old trotter thus far bred in Canada is Albani, a chestnut filly that this season made a record of 2:29½, lowering the best previous Canadian record by nine seconds. She is by Hermit, a son of Harold, her dam being by American Clay. Hermit, although by a trotting sire and himself the sire of speed at the trot, is a pacer, and this year made a record of 2:29¾ at that gait. He is but six years old, and to have a three-year-old that has beaten 2:30 to his credit is quite a feather in his cap. Of late years there has been a great influx of American trotting stallions into Canada, and the results have been more then satisfactory. The number of trotting tracks has increased wonderfully, and as trotting meetings have become popular the runners have gone down hill until now the interest in the thoroughbred has about died out.

Grim's Gossip.

Matt Storn has returned from Los Angeles and reports having had a pleasant trip to the city of the Angles.

Last year Overland Park, Denver, was the first to claim a new 2:30 performer, but owing to the bad weather, we have not had a chance to record any such performance as yet.

We have to thank Dr. Thomas Maclay of Petaluma for a copy of one of the early reports of the State Agricultural Society several volumes of which were missing from our set.

Mr. A. B. Speckles entered the produce of Lillie S., by Alcazar in the BREEDER AND SPORTSMAN Futurity Stake which closed on the first. January 16th she dropped twin foals, both dead.

John W. Martin, of Yolo, has sold his well bred young stallion Alex Button Jr., 7085 to G. W. Woodard, of Woodland. He is by Alexander Button, dam by John Nelson. The price was $1,500.

In the list of horses published last week, as likely to start this year, the names of Clay Duke 2:31½ and Eros 2:29½ were unintentionally omitted. We will be pleased to receive any further corrections.

The stallion advertisements are flocking in, and owners of broodmares will find little or no trouble in being able to select the exact kind of animal they may want from the columns of the BREEDER AND SPORTSMAN.

Petaluma has claimed the old date two weeks before the State fair. San Jose claims the same week, and the Breeder's Association claims the week following Stockton. This looks as though complications may arise.

In another column there is a letter from F. W. Loeber of St. Helena in reference to the pedigree of the fast trotting mare Lorena. It will now be in order for Capt. Harris to reply and tell where he got the pedigree.

Of all the interior papers, the Petaluma Argus is the only one that pays proper attention to the horse interest of its section. Editor McNabb has a keen appreciation of a good horse, and is happy in the ownership of several.

Mr. J. P. Kerr has purchased from Mrs. Wheeler of St Helena a pair of Whippleton colts. They are nicely matched and make a handsome road team C. David of the park training stables will handle the team for a month or two.

The railroad blockade has caused a great scarcity of news and the "Gossip" page is not up to what I should like to see, but when the weather clears up and the roads are passable items will come in more rapidly, and the department look better.

The racing contingent who have returned from Los Angeles claim that the attendance was miserable, hardly a corporal's guard being out on any of the days. Nothwithstanding the bad weather, the racing was good and those who attended had first class sport.

Col. H. I. Thornton and John Mackey, Superintendent of the Rancho Del Paso, will start for Fresno to-morrow, the former gentleman having an intention to purchase a stock farm in that neighborhood. Mr. Mackey is recovered from his late illness, and is once more able to be around.

J. H. White, the President of the Breeder's Association, has the honor to own the first colt born in California this year. One of his brood mares to the cover of Hernani, had a foal on January 1st. What a time there will be naming him! One friend of Mr. White's suggests "Just in Time."

Are we going to have another Margaret S? A note from the Secretary of the Pleasanton Stock Farm Co. informs me that May Day foaled a fine bay filly (by Director) on the morning of January 21st. The many friends of Mr. Salisbury will wish him even a faster filly than is Margaret S.

Reno's baby a two year old has made a reputation that is ringing from one side of the country to the other. On December 26th, he trotted at Dallas, Texas, making a record of 2:25½ and on the 31st of the same month he paced over the same track a full mile in 2:24¼. As Californians we will have to keep our eye on Texas.

The directors of the San Jose race track have had a miniature track built on which to speed young colts. It is completely covered and the spectators have to stand on the inside of the track to watch the youngsters. The idea is a good one and should be adopted by all the other tracks where colts are in the habit of being trained.

I had the pleasure of examining early in the week, a magnificent book which has lately been presented to Col. Harry I. Thornton, by Judge Garber. The work contains hand painted portraits of all the celebrated horses of France and England from the year 1760 up to and including 1887. It is a rare work of art and is highly appreciated by Colonel Thornton.

Mr. Irvin Ayers reports that he will have out his new catalogue in the course of a few days. The San Mateo Stock Farm will shortly issue a new one, as will the Pleasanton Stock Farm Co. Catalogues are very useful, and many a sale has been consummated by the breeding of a horse, catching the attention of some one who without the catalogue would never have heard of him.

Daniel Brown says that if a Jackson Temple colt wins one of the stakes opened by W. P. Fine, he will add $100 to the winner, says the Petaluma Argus. J. H. White will do the same for a Hernanni or Marco colt, and A. L. Whitney will put in a like sum for a Dawn colt. Mr. Brown will also give a premium of $50 to each Jackson Temple colt that gets into the 2:30 class during the present year.

Mr. A. T. Hatch of Livermore has as good an idea of a horse as almost any man. He reports Guide as being in fine trim, and if he continues so I fully expect the colt to beat 2:20 this year. He is of the improving sort and favorably impressed many who saw him on the circuit last year. Primera has dropped a dead foal by Guide, from which Mr. Hatch expected a first class animal.

Dan McCarty, he of White Hatk Fame, called to see me a few days ago, and he was just the same old Dan, with horse talk enough to fill a book. He reports a successful season back East, and says he has enjoyed the best of health. He has a lot of brood mares which he has brought back with him, and he claims that if he does not sell them that he will breed them all to California stallions.

G. W. Hancock, of Sacramento, has sold to D. C. Braid of this city the two year old standard bred stallion Fred Hawthorne, brother in blood to Tempest, record 2:19. Both are by Hawthorne, son of Nutwood, and out of dams by Chieftain, sire of Defiance, 2:17¼ pacing, and 2:24 trotting. The purchase price is not stated, but Mr. Hancock says that he valued him at $1000 when a yearling. Fred Hawthorne will be mated this season to a handsome five year old bay mare by Albert W, 2:20, son of Electioneer.

The next steamer from Honolulu will bring over Harry J. Agnew. To use his own words he has sold out lock, stock and barrel, and is now prepared to purchase a breeding farm and settle down to raising high class horses. He says in his letter that a number of inquiries have been made, asking him to put a price on Emma Temple, and the figure he has named is a very large one, so that the man who buys her will have to dig down deep in his pocket to get the mare.

The catalogue of Irwin Ayres made its appearance yesterday, and is a credit to the compiler. The list of stallions is of course headed with that grand representative of the Wilkes family, Mambrino Wilkes, and is followed by Alpheus, Balkan and Kaulbar, all sons of Mambrino Wilkes. The pedigrees of a score of brood mares are also given, and then the breeding of a lot of youngsters. The pamphlet is a valuable addition to the horse lore of the State and is a credit to the San Miguel Stock Farm. Mr. Ayres will gladly forward a catalogue to any breeder who may desire one, by sending him a letter addressed to 30 Fremont Street, San Francisco.

Los Angeles. Fresno and San Jose are among those who will hold spring meetings. Last Friday night the Directors of the San Jose Blood Horse Association met, and it was decided to hold their meeting commencing Saturday, April 5th. The Monday and Wednesday following will also be devoted to racing. three days only being given. A committee consisting of T. S. Montgomery, W. J. Casey and G. W. Bragg, was appointed, with instructions to frame a speed programme. It was decided to give three dash races and a heat race on each successive day. Fresno is also agitating for a spring meeting, but they will have mixed racing, trotting and pacing as well as running. Mr. Baldwin has been confined to his room or the programme would have been out before this.

In an interview with Mr. Joe Battell, compiler of the Morgan Register, Mr. Joseph Van Cott, West 58th street, New York, who is 65 years old and well posted on old time trotters, says: "Surry (the dam of Henry Clay) belonged to Jacob S. Platt, who built Platt Street, New York, about 1830. He owned three small mares—Surrey, Bet and Rose—and drove together and alternately. Surry was a little bay mare, 14 2, all bay, pricked and docked; trotted on the old Central course, beating Cato and Black Kate in 2:40. Wallace persists in calling her a pacer; she was as square gaited a mare as ever struck a trot in the world. She afterwards fell into the hands of George M. Patchen. She was not mixed gaited; no pacing when she started. May Day was out of Bet by Eclipse."

The directors of the Agricultural Park Association held a meeting at Captain Grosse's office on Monday afternoon says the Santa Rosa Republican. The principal business coming before the directors' meeting was in regard to what should be done with the grounds the present season. On account of the failure, financially, of last season's program and the lack of interest displayed, not only by those interested in such an association, but also by the people generally, it was decided expedient—and, in fact, found necessary—to close the grounds for the season, or at least until a better support of the organization can be assured. In view of this condition of things the following resolution was passed unanimously by the directors: That the gates of the Agricultural Park grounds, both outside and in, be locked until some satisfactory disposition of the property can be made, and that some one be put in charge of the buildings and grounds until that time, free of charge upon the society.

The Cook Stock Farm is the first to issue an 1890 catalogue, and it tells a good story on the outer cover, "Standard bred trotting stock." That is what purchasers are after now-a-days, they want standard bred stock, and that sort is always saleable. The preface reads as follows:

"In presenting our catalogue for 1890, we call the attention of horsemen to the grand selection of brood-mares now on the Cook Stock Farm. No expense has been spared to secure the best blood it is possible to get, combined with good size and colors, natural speed and absolute soundness. The pedigrees are extended only so far as to show what the trotting blood lines are, without going into remote extensions.

The sires in use are too well known to require description. Steinway, 2:25¾, continues to sire style and speed. In Cresco 4908, we get a double top cross of Hambletonian blood through Strathmore 408, and that great progenitor Almont 33. In Chas. Derby 4907, we get much of the same Hambletonian blood through a different channel—that of the great Electioneer.

That we have reason to expect first-class results, all horsemen will readily accord."

A sanguinary battle took place on Christmas Day at Cairo, Ill., in the Illinois Central stockyards, between a fierce, large black horse and a mule, the two having been on exceptionally good terms with one another up to a few months previous to the conflict, says the Indiana Horseman. Suddenly the mule made a dash at the horse with his teeth, and whirling about, planted both feet against the horse's body with a resonant thud which could be heard throughout the yards. Then began the battle in earnest. The horse promptly resented the kicks by rounding to and returning them with rapid precision, both animals squealing with rage, biting and kicking one another until the blood flowed in rivulets from every portion of their bodies, the fight lasting an hour without intermission. The yards contained many horses and mules, which appeared much excited during the row, herding and trembling in one corner and exhibiting every evidence of fear. The yardmen who witnessed the singular affair used every effort to part the crazy beasts, but without success, indeed running much personal risk in their efforts. Copious applications of cold water with the hose and a liberal use of clubs were entirely unavailing, the fight raging until the mule ignominiously fled, bleeding and lame from the severe punishment. Both animals are badly used up, being hardly able to walk, the mule faring the worst.

A New Invention.

A new horse detacher has just been patented by Mr. George Amos, of Point Pleasant, West Va. It is not the first device invented for the same purpose; several others have been patented heretofore but have, as yet, not been taken into use. Mr. Amos' device may possibly fare better in this regard, as it is much less complicated than its forerunners.

In cases where horses become so badly frightened as to be wholly unmanageable, or where the lines break and the animal dashes ahead, it is certainly better that the vehicle and the occupants be safely left behind, rather than be strewn promiscuously along the route, and perhaps severely injured. Mr. Amos' invention consists of detaching devices in connection with a system of operating them at the required moment. The detacher proper consists of a small oblong block or sleeve of metal, in one end of which is a hook pivotally attached. This hook is so arranged that when turned into normal engagement a slide bar or bolt in the aperture of the detacher will press forward by a coil spring, and the point of the bar will enter an aperture in the hook. On one side face of the block is a strong hook to which is to be attached the harness tug. The hook end of the block is to be attached to the hame hook, so that in effect the trace or tug is forwardly finished or terminated with a detacher device. The rear end of the slide bolt is provided with a ring, to which the cords are attached for withdrawing the bolt at the proper time. It may be well at this point to state that this detacher differs from most others in releasing the tugs from the forward part or hame hook. A cord, being attached to each device, is extended rear-wardly upward and joined over the back of the animal, and thence extended singly to the buggy dash and disposed for convenient seizure.

A similar detaching block is attached to the back band and its bolt is connected to the joined cords, so as to be operated also when the pull is made. When the horse becomes frightened, the cord being pulled, the bolts release the hook forward, and the horse glides out of the thills, the tugs and pull cords with the detachers, remaining with the vehicle. In or- that the thills may not drop and catch into the ground, there are cords attached to staples and lead to the vehicle body, so that when the horse has departed the thill will be hung clear of the ground.

News From Santa Barbara.

Santa Barbara is waking up from a long sleep, and she wakes up alive to the interests of the breeders of fine horses. On the 15th of January some of the principle owners of stock farms got together and made preparations for a grand race for yearling trotters owned in this district. The race will take place at the Fall meeting of the Agricultural Association, which will be held at the city of Santa Barbara. Each owner of a stallion subscribes $25, and yearlings sired by stallions whose owners have subscribed $25 will be elegible. The entrance will close April 1, 1890, at which date the colt must be entered. The entrance money of $30 each, and the $25 of each stallion, and $100 added by the Agricultural Association, will be divided into three moneys for the first, second, and third colt. The race will be one-half mile and repeat to harness.

The following have subscribed, and all those having yearlings from their stallions should enter: J. R. Roobin, of Los Alamos, $25, his stallion Antioch, by A. W. Richmond; Glenwood by Nutwood, owned by A. W. McPhail; R. Bennet, of Lowfre, has subscribed for his stallion Bashaw by Wapsie; Merritt & Murray have subscribed for their stallion Electro by Electioneer: J. R. Fisher for his stallion Don Patricio by A. W. Richmond; H. W. Lawrence for his handsome bay stallion by Bashaw; C. A. Storke for his grey stallion Roswall by A. W. Richmond, and N. W. Johnston for his beautiful bay stallion by Sultan.

It is hoped that the owner of Stamboul will subscribe $25 so that his handsome son, out of Carrie B., she by A. W. Richmond; second dam by Crighton, will contest for first money. The colt is named Harry Stamboul, and he is as handsome a yearling as ever trotted. He is very large and powerfully made up. The purse for this yearling race will amount to nearly $1,000. At the Fall meeting there will be also a sweepstake for two-year-olds, five-eighths of a mile dash. This purse will amount to $600.

The Santa Barbara Agricultural Association is determined to have the greatest meeting ever held in this country. They propose to give very liberal purses, so that horses coming from other counties can well afford to make the journey, and the winners be well repaid. Santa Maria, in this county, will offer liberal purses and attractive premiums.

There are so many young trotters and runners in the district, that the races this Fall will be a great success. Ventura will come to the front and offer liberal purses, and also Hueneme in Ventura County. The new track at the latter place will be a fast one. The little town of Hueneme is growing rapidly. The farmers around that vicinity have fine horses, and the farms are most productive.

In looking over the list of the Futurity Stakes of the Breeder and Sportsman, we are disappointed not to find Merritt & Murray, of this county, represented. They have several standard-bred mares in foal by Electro, and we expected to find them entered. Mr. Den, of this city, has entered Carrie B., and he is already willing to bet that if his colt does not win the race, that the colt will be well in the front at the finish of each heat. Our sympathies are with him. Mr. Den's handsome stallion Othello, by Hock-Hocking, won the seven-eighths mile dash at Los Angeles January 12th. There were eight horses against him. We congratulate P. Monchaen, Othello's trainer. Othello is a very fast stallion, and when he is out for a race, he will make the best of his age take a back seat.

We earnestly hope that some subscriber of the Breeder and Sportsman will be able to give information about the bay mare that ran several races in Paradise Valley and Stockton. If any one remembers Stockton filly, perhaps he may recall some of the horses that ran against her. This bay mare is now owned in Santa Barbara, and she has foaled as fine a colt as ever ran a race. Her owner is justly proud of this handsome bay colt, and he is very anxious to trace the mother's pedigree. The colt is very large for his age, and very muscular. He runs close to the ground, and his propelling powers are wonderfully developed. If Mr. Arrellanes, of Santa Maria, can down this colt with his brother, he can carry many a dollar from the Santa Barbara boys who will bet their sack on their handsome bay colt. T. M.

THE KENNEL.

Dog owners are requested to send for publication the earliest possible notices of whelps, sales, names claimed, presentations and deaths, in their kennels, in all instances writing plainly names of sire and dam and of grandparents, colors, dates and breed.

Coursing at Newark.

Despite the inclement elements, about a hundred and fifty came up to time at Newark on Sunday, to witness the long talked of coursing meeting. The weather was fairly good, that is, rain kept off, but the ground was wet and muddy, while the coursing ground was dotted with little sheets of water which were not conducive to good healthy trials, the dogs slipping and floundering about in a very disastrous fashion. A 16 dog stake with several old favorites (Nipper, Snowflake, Tipperary Girl and Flight W.) was run through with the veteran, Mr. John Dickson, acting as judge in his usual straightforward fashion. There was nothing unusual in the first two rounds, that is to those who are used to coursing under difficulties. The celebrated McGinty after a tie went down below, being handsomely beaten by Catherine Hayes. In the third round Catherine Hayes again had a tie, and in the run off her previous exertions told and she hung fire a little being beaten by Rambler who was made a hot favorite for the final only to be beaten cleverly by Tipperary Girl.

First round—M. Tiernan's Tipperary Girl beat P O'Connel's Bellflower, J. Barry's Trip the Daisy beat T. J. Brady's unknown, J. Barry's Prairie Clipper beat P. O'Connell's Mission Boy, P. Canty's Whip beat J. Grace Jr.'s Teeney, J. Shea's Juanita beat T. Brady's Nipper, J. Shea's McGinty beat J. O'Leary's Mayflower, T. J. Cronin's Rambler beat M. Tiernan's Flight W. and M. Tiernan's Catherine Hayes beat T. J Cronin's Snowflake.

First ties—Tipperary Girl beat Trip the Daisy, Prarie Clipper beat Whip, Rambler beat Juanita and Catherine Hayes beat McGinty.

Second ties—Tipperary Girl beat Prairie Clipper and Rambler beat Catherine Hayes.

Final—Tipperary Girl beat Rambler and won the stake, $30. Rambler took second money, $20; Prairie Clipper and Catherine Hayes, $7 each.

ATHLETICS.

Athletic Sports and Other Pastimes.

EDITED BY ARPSIPPUS.

SUMMARY.

The wet weather is still with us, and the majority of the athletes have given up the idea of attempting to train for next month's games. The Olympic and Alpine Athletic Clubs, however, are determined to hold their sports at all costs, and after all perhaps some of the athletes may make a decent showing.

RUNNERS, WALKERS, JUMPERS, ETC.

T. Buchanan of the Olympic team is training hard in the gymnasium, and some good performances may be expected of him next month.

Cooley, Cassidy, Haley and McArthur will compete in the two mile run on February 22d. All four will probably be placed at scratch.

Horace Coffin will not be in good trim for the coming games, and will possibly postpone his reappearance on the cinder path until Decoration Day.

It is claimed that Little of the Alpine Athletic Club will prove a dangerous man in the quarter and half at the championship games.

Leon has resigned from the California Club, because its directors would not allow him to wrestle Ed. Kolb at the Olympic Club rooms. In losing this valuable young athlete, the California Club has lost it best indoor amateur, and now the amateur annex consists of about half a dozen third-rate boxers and runners. If these men have any spirit they will also withdraw and apply for admission to some club that will appreciate their services.

Weather permitting, the Olympic runners will take their postponed cross country run to-morrow morning.

Several members of the Alpine Club will take a spin to the Cliff House, and return early to-morrow morning.

S. V. Cassidy of the O. C. is particularly interested in cross country runs, as he considers that kind of sport to be of the greatest help in reducing of superfluous flesh.

The out-door athletes all agree that this season's rain deserves the championship medal.

The track in the O. C. gymnasium is nightly thronged with runners and walkers, who take indoor exercise with the hope that the weather will clear up a few days before Washington's Birthday, so that they may be able to enter the games in half condition.

Billy Kenealley states that he is done with fighting, but that he has no intention of retiring from the cinder path. Up to date he has succeeded in winning over fifty medals for running, and the chances are that before the present year is out he will have added a few more to his collection.

R. J. Lattringer, one of the old time athletes, will represent the Alpine Club in the Sprint races on May 30th.

An effort will be made this year to induce the Caledonian and Thistle Clubs to add a list of amateur events to their programme. In the past it has been proven that the amateur races excited much more interest than the professional ones.

For the information of our readers we wish it to be understood that these columns are always open to athletes. All communications properly authenticated will be gladly published, as the Breeder and Sportsman makes no discrimination.

UNIVERSITY JOTTINGS.

The athletes have been obliged to abandon the cinder track on account of its wretched condition.

Night and day the gymnasium is filled with students desirous of reducing their fat.

A field day will probably be held in April.

The championship team will commence training in March, so that they will be in first class condition on May 30th.

It is whispered that two or three "dark horses" will strengthen the team.

THE WHEELMEN.

Several of the Wheelmen who have become disgusted with the weather have decided to sell their machines.

Unusual interest is taken in the whist tournament now going on at the club rooms of the Bay City wheelmen.

It will not be many weeks before the roads will be in order again for travelling, and the long distance men will be entirely out of practice by the time the rain has taken its departure.

R. M. Thompson Chief Consul has been very ill with La Grippe which has settled in one eye causing him much trouble.

The Bay City Wheelmen have abandoned their idea of holding an in-door evening tournament at the Mechanics Pavilion.

On account of increased business Frank D. Elwell has resigned from the Bay City Wheelmen. His name has been placed on the honorary list.

After the wet spell it is thought that there will be a boom in bicycling. It is proposed to hold several race weeks during the coming season.

The competitive drill at the carnival which was postponed from last Saturday will be held this evening. Probably only two teams will enter:—the Garden City wheelmen of San Jose and the Bay City wheelmen of San Francisco. The Garden City wheelmen have been steadily drilling while the Bay City wheelmen with their long experience should be able to make a most interesting competetion. The trophy will cost $150.

AT THE OARS.

In making the rounds of the boat clubs last Sunday, we noticed unusual activity displayed. The Ariel club members are anxiously awaiting fair weather to enable them to begin the construction of their elegant club house, which will cost in the neighborhood of $3000.

The Regatta Committee appointed at the last meeting of the Pacific Rowing Association will hold a meeting early in the month of February when preparations will be made for the holding of their annual regatta.

The Pioneer Club members take great pleasure in rowing to the five mile house where they generally have a good time. Dinner interspersed with sparkling wit is always in order, and the boys generally return home fully satisfied with their trip and its incidents.

Last Sunday a crew from the Pioneer Club braved the weather and paid a visit to the Lurline Club at North End.

The following challenge has been handed us for publication:

Athletic Editor Breeder and Sportsman:—Dear Sir:—I hereby challenge Henry Henceman of the Union Rowing [illegible], of Stockton, Cal., to row me a three mile single scull race in best and best shells on the three mile course at the Alameda mole. Race to be rowed four [illegible] after signing articles, stake to be $1,000 a side. Signed,

[C]harles Long,
San Francisco, Jan. 22, 1890. 20 Fourth St.

JOTTINGS FROM ALL OVER.

W. H. Rocap, one of the brightest athletic lights of the athletic club of the Schuylkill Navy, is dangerously ill with typhoid-pneumonia.

A prominent Eastern sporting paper recently asserted that next spring, Victor E. Schifferstein, of the Olympic Club, of San Francisco, would attempt to beat the world's record for the running broad jump of 23 feet, 3in, held by Malcom W. Ford. The report appears to be without foundation, as we understand that Mr. Schifferstein has retired from the athletic world.

Thayer, of Cornell, who played half-back against Yale so effectively is probably the best all-round athlete in his college. He holds the University record for the running broad jump, is champion single sculler, and has rowed in two 'Varsity crews, is a good man on a wheel, one of the best sprinters, holds the second best record of the college in lifting weights, and is put down as winner of the hammer and shot events on next field day.

Vassar's new gymnasium just completed is the pride of Poughkeepsie and the largest one connected with any women's college. The building is in the form of two parrallelgrams, one 200x47 feet and two stories high, the other 67x40 feet, the whole topped by a tower.

Amherst's new athletic field, the gift of Mr. Fred. B. Pratt, of Brooklyn, when finished will be one of the most complete and picturesquely located in New England. It will be provided with a 100 and 220 yards straightaway, a quarter-mile track and a grand stand of the most improved pattern. The baseball diamond will occupy the center of the field, while west of the track several tennis courts will be located. With a gymnasium second to none, and the increased facilities for training which the new field will furnish, Amherst should make her name formidable in intercollegiate athletics.

Several of the Eastern crack athletes are laid up with La Grippe.

The annual championship meeting of the New Zealand Amateur Athletic Association was successfully held at Dunedin on Saturday, December 14th. Over 3 000 persons were in attendance. The track (396 yards to the lap) was small and badly laid off, but it was well packed, rolled and marked. The standards fixed for the different events were rather severe, and were equalled only in a few instances. The following is a summary of the results:

100 yards Flat. Standard 10 1-5 seconds.

FIRST HEAT.

J. H. Hempton, Southland 1
H. F. Greenwood, Canterbury 2

Time, 10 seconds.

B. Owen (Auckland) and F. Meenan (Dunedin) also ran.

Second Heat.

H. M. Reeves, Canterbury 1
H. Schwartzkoff, Sydney 2

Time, 10 seconds.

G. F. Williamson (Sydney) also ran.

Half-mile Flat. Standard 2min 5sec.

J. F. Grierson, Canterbury 1
R. F. Cook, Dunedin 2

Time, 2 min 5 2-5 seconds.

A. J. M'Credy (Dunedin), G. T. Spencer (Sydney), P. J. Ness (Dunedin), and J. W. Winks (Auckland) also ran.

100 yards Flat.

Final Heat.

J H Hempton, Southland 1
H M Reeves, Canterbury 2

Time, 9 3-5 second.

H F Greenwood (Canterbury) and H Schwartzkoff (Sydney) also ran.

One-mile Walk. Standard 7min 15sec.

E J M'Kelvey, Dunedin 1
H S Cocks, Canterbury 2

Time, 7min 13sec.

A Findlay (Dunedin) and C E Smith (South Canterbury) also competed.

Long Jump. Standard 20ft.

T D Harman, Canterbury, 20ft 6½in 1
L A Cuff, Canterbury, 19ft 8½in 2
J T Prain (Dunedin, 19ft 1½in), also competed.

250 yards Flat. Standard 27sec.

First Heat.

J H Hempton, Southland 1
H M Reeves, Canterbury 2

Time, 28½ seconds.

G F Williamson (Sydney) also ran.

Second Heat.

H F Greenwood, Canterbury 1
B Owen, Auckland 2

Time, 27 4-5 seconds.

R F Cook (Dunedin) and F J O'Meara (Dunedin) also ran.

High Jump. Standard 5ft 4in.

J M'Naught, Dunedin, 5ft 3½in 1
J W F Thompson, Southland, 4ft 11½in 2
D M Robertson (Canterbury) 4ft 11in, and E M M'Lauchlan (Dunedin) 4ft 10in, also competed.

One Mile Flat. Standard 4min 40sec.

P Morrison, South Canterbury 1
R F Cook, Dunedin 2

Time, 4min 41 seconds.

J F Grierson (Canterbury) and J W Winks (Auckland) also ran.

120yds Hurdles. Standard 17sec.

First Heat.

H W Batger, Wellington 1
W J Moir, Canterbury 2

Time, 16 3-5 seconds.

J F Prain (Dunedin) also ran. Batger, who took his hurdles in beautiful style, led all the way, and won by half a dozen yards from Moir,

Second Heat.

G. B. Shaw (Canterbury) walked over. Shaw was allowed a walk over in this heat, but covered the distance at top speed.

Time, 16 3-5 seconds.

Putting the weight, 16lb, 10ft run. Standard 35ft.

R J Malcolm (Wellington), 34ft 9¾in........................ 1
W J Moir, Canterbury, 33ft 11in........................ 2

W J Strong (Dunedin) 31ft 11in, also competed. Malcolm won with his first put, and in a subsequent trial reached 36ft 7in:

120 yards Hurdles..

Final Heat.

H W Batger, Wellington........................ 1
G B Shaw, Canterbury........................ 2

Time, 16 1-5 seconds.

W J Moir (Canterbury) also ran.

Three-mile Walk. Standard 23 min.

E J M'Kelvey, Dunedin........................ 1
H S Cocks, Canterbury........................ 2

Time, 24 min. 18 2-5 sec.

A Findlay (Dunedin) also competed.

Quarter-mile Flat. Standard 52 sec.

H M Reeves, Canterbury........................ 1
J M King, Wellington........................ 2

Time, 54 2-5 seconds.

J C Hutchinson (Auckland) and P J Ness (Dunedin) also ran.

Pole Jump. Standard 10ft.

D M Robertson, Canterbury. 9ft 5½in, walked over.

Three-mile Flat. Standard 15 min. 30 sec.

P Morrison, South Canterbury........................ 1
D Wood, Canterbury........................ 2

Time, 16 min. 3 2-5 sec.

L Spencer (Sydney) and A J M'Credie (Dunedin) also started.

250 yds. Flat.

Final Heat.

J H Hempton, Southland........................ 1
H F Greenwood, Canterbury........................ 2

Time, 27 2-5 seconds.

J B Owen (Auckland) also ran.

Tommy Conneff's family are sorely distressed over his illness, and the Manhattan Athletic Club has received three cablegrams from his father since the popular little runner was taken ill. Conneff Sr. is a well to do farmer in Ireland and it is not at all improbable that Tommy may seek convalescence on his native heath.

One of the most curious pedestrian events contested in England is the weight carrying race. In this game the runners carry heavy weights while competing and it becomes a question of strength and endurance as well as fleetness. A recent match was made between Jack Kelly and Jack Davis for £50 aside. The conditions are to race two miles, each carrying 200 pounds.

Tommy O'Neill, the popular little trainer, has obtained the position of instructor to the athletes of the Columbia Athletic Club, of Washington, D. C., and will soon start for the capital. In a letter to Secretary Sullivan of the A. A. U., Howard Perry, the Secretary of the Columbia A. C.. states that the Board of Directors at a special meeting, resolved to accept O'Neill's terms for a year, and if mutually satisfactory, the situation will be a permanent one. Tommy was the trainer of the defunct Brooklyn Athletic Association, and is probably the most efficient trackmaster in the country.

The swimming match in London between Charles Beckwith and D. Dalton came to somewhat an abrupt termination on the morning of the third day, Dalton refusing to swim, giving as his reason that the water was too hot. Beckwith, however, entered the water at the time announced for the start and swam in 8min 30sec, when Dalton notified the referee that he resigned the contest. The match was for £50 a side, and the conditions were to swim on the back five hours each day for six days, and the one traversing the greatest distance to be declared the winner. Beckwith was over two miles in the lead when the match came to the unsatisfactory conclusion. Dalton claims to be champion of America, but sporting men here do not know who he is.

Here is what an Eastern Contemporary says in regard to the opening of the Olympic out-door grounds: The Olympic Athletic Club of San Francisco will have a grand opening of their new grounds on Washington's Birthday. In considering the programme to be presented the directors resolved to introduce a number of professional events in addition to the amateur games. It is thought that this plan will attract a larger attendance of the sport loving public than a programme of amateur events only The club have received an offer from Harry Bethune the companion sprinter to take part in the Club's games. He says that if the Olympic will offer a purse of $1,500 he will guarantee to have on the grounds in addition to himself, the well known runners Skinner, Harry Johnson and Gibson. He is willing also that the race should be for the championship. The proposition looks tempting on the face.

CLUB JOTTINGS.

A. H. Lean and E. A. Kolb are to wrestle for a $200 trophy on March 6th.

Should the weather clear up the outdoor grounds of the Alpine Amateur Athletic Club at Harbor View will be ready for use by next Sunday.

The Olympic Club is determined to hold its games at its own grounds on Washington's Birthday. Even if the track should not be in good condition the club would act very wisely in using their own grounds in preference to those of the University at Berkeley.

When the Olympic grounds are entirely furnished they will be second to none in the United States. The only fault to be found with the grounds is the size of the track. The bicycle men are virtually shut out as the track, six laps to the mile, is not at all suitable for wheel racing.

The Alpine Amateur Athletic Club is seriously thinking about moving from its present quarters in the Murphy building to more spacious rooms on Powell St. Owing to the large increase in the membership, this step is necessary.

A splendid programme will be arranged for the Olympic Clubs' "Ladies Night" which will take place Jan. 30. The medals won at the last gala day and the prizes won at the late boxing tournament will be distributed on that evening.

ROD.

Gen. John F. Sheehan, in his Redwood Times Gazette, pertinently says:

"The Deputy Fish Commissioners have been bestirring themselves recently, and as a result several arrests have been made within the past few months. The unlawful killing of the grandest of food fishes—the salmon—in and out of season by market fishermen bids fair to receive a black eye henceforth. The deputies, with the assistance rendered them by honest Judges and jurymen, should be able to protect an industry from ruin which is to this State worth thousands of dollars annually. If, however, they continue to meet with the opposition which has been recently directed against their untiring efforts to bring the offenders of the fish laws to justice by ignorant or prejudiced jurors, then poaching will be carried on to an unlimited extent until fresh salmon will be as scarce a commodity in the San Francisco markets as buffalo meat.

It is the indiscriminate slaughter of salmon during the close and breeding season by netters and others, who use giant powder and spears, that should be put a stop to before the fish become entirely extinct. It is hoped that the Deputy Fish Commissioners will be encouraged in the good work they have set a-going by the judges and jurors of the country towns who hear and act upon these cases which are brought to their notice."

Fish are said to be in abundance in the lower Russian river and the smaller northern streams, and owing to the heavy raids and consequent rushing streams, they have been comparatively safe.

Salmon have begun to run in the Pescadero and coast rivers, consequently the fishermen have been on the alert for the last few days.

The Petaluma Imprint of last week says: "A fishing party left this city yesterday morning and on their return reported that they had struck a "bonanza." To verify their statement they produced two very large and handsome specimens of salmon trout, which they caught in Petaluma creek about two miles out of town."

It is perhaps as well for the party that the Fish Commission had none of their patrol on hand when the fish were exhibited.

THE GUN.

Game is said to be very plentiful in the neighborhood of Prohibition flat, Tulare County, deer having been driven down by the snow.

The snow in Black Mountain Valley, Tulare County, is much lower and more plentiful this year than usual, but deer are very scarce, and quail scarcer, although quite a number of ducks have been seen along the river, principally teal.

A meeting of the Forester Gun Club, Sacramento, was held last week to arrange preliminaries for the reception of the teams of shotgun experts of the Eastern States; soon to start for this coast and Sacramento. A contest at live birds at this unfavorable season was not deemed advisable with the cracks but a committee consisting of F. F. Tibbets, W. E. Gerber and E. C. Chapman was appointed to confer with the other gun clubs to outline an exhibition shoot and arrange for the proper reception of the shooters.

The San Luis Obispo Mirror says:—Messrs. J. H. Hollister and Fred Branch, about Feb. 1st, will take a trip to Arizona. At Tuscon they expect to be joined by a party of gentlemen, and will visit the White Mountains on a hunting expedition, and Johnny says he will have the hides of two grizzleys before he returns. The grizzleys he will flank by wild turkeys, wild hogs, deer, and probably an Apache or two. They go loaded for bar.

Good luck to 'em; beware of the bar, though.

We have often insisted on the almost culpable negligence displayed in allowing youths—almost infants—to carry shot-guns or rifles, and last Sunday we received intelligence of the unfortunate accident to Mr. Adams of Madison, Yolo County It seems his son was carrying a 32 rifle over his shoulder, full cocked, and, sad to say, owing to some jar, it was discharged, the ball lodging in his father's leg. As Mr. Adams is not a young man he will probably feel the effects of the wound for the rest of his life. And last Sunday George Gilbert, a boy of fourteen years, and his brother were out shooting rabbits near Sonoma. The brother shot George in the arm, and though no serious results are anticipated, it will probably be very annoying to the boy for some time. Parents should most distinctly refuse to allow boys of doubtful age to carry firearms of any kind.

Many a man has felt better and happier after a bottle of Burgundy and a good canvas-back (16 minutes), but it seems there is a great risk of that delectable bird disappearing altogether—at any rate in the East. Many suggestions have been made, and it is quite on the cards that Chesapeake Bay will be strictly protected for a year or two. According to the American Cultivator, the canvas-back duck has been growing scarce for years, and this season especially there has been a notable falling off from the Chesapeake Bay region, where the finest flavored specimens have always been found. Those which undoubtedly come from that locality lack their accustomed flavor. The great floods last spring buried under sand and mud the beds of wild celery on which the canvas-back of those localities feeds, and to which its flavor is due. Driven by hunger and the scarcity of its favorite food, these canvas-backs have taken to feeding on fish and water insects, and their flavor is abominable. It is said that in Canada, where the canvas-back goes to breed in summer, the people in their neighborhood have taken to eating their eggs. This, and the warfare made on them elsewhere, threaten this variety with total extinction Perhaps with the hint that the excellence of the canvas-back duck is due to eating celery, the feeders of other ducks may improve their quality, if not make them equal to the canvas-back, by giving them similar rations, at least while preparing for market.

THE WEEKLY

Breeder and Sportsman.

JAMES P. KERR, PROPRIETOR.

The Turf and Sporting Authority of the Pacific Coast.

Office, No. 313 Bush St.

P. O. Box 2300.

TERMS—One Year, $5; Six Months, $3; Three Months, $1.50. STRICTLY IN ADVANCE.

Money should be sent by postal order, draft or by registered letter, addressed to JAMES P. KERR, San Francisco, Cal.

Communications must be accompanied by the writer's name and address, not necessarily for publication, but as a private guarantee of good faith.

ALEX. P. WAUGH, - - - - - Editor.

To Subscribers.

The date printed on the wrapper of your paper indicates the time to which your subscription is paid.

Should the BREEDER AND SPORTSMAN be received by any subscriber who does not want it, write us direct to stop it. A postal card will suffice.

Special Notice to Correspondents.

Letters intended for publication should reach this office not later than Wednesday of each week, to secure a place in the issue of the following Saturday. Such letters to insure immediate attention should be addressed to the BREEDER AND SPORTSMAN, and not to any member of the staff.

San Francisco, Saturday, Jan. 25, 1890.

Stallions Advertised

IN THE

BREEDER AND SPORTSMAN.

Thoroughbreds.

FRIAR TUCK, Hermit—Romping Girl..........C. W. Aby, Middletown.

GREENBACK, Dollar—Music..........C. W. Aby, Middletown.

INTRUDER, Crater—Lady Bountiful..........T. J. Knight, Sacramento.

PRINCE OF NORFOLK, Norfolk—Marion..........Dan Dennison, Sacramento.

ST. SAVIOR, Eolus—War Song..........C. W. Aby, Middletown.

Trotters.

ALEXANDER BUTTON, Alexander—Lady Button..........Cache Creek Farm, Yolo.

APEX, Prompter—Mary..........Poplar Grove Breeding Farm, Wildflower.

ALCONA, Almont—Queen Mary..........Fred W. Loeber, St. Helena

BALKAN, Mambrino Wilkes—Fanny Fern..........A. L. Hinds, Oakland.

BONANZA, Arthurton—Sister..........Richard Havey, Oakland

CLOVIS, Sultan—Sweetbriar..........Poplar Grove Breeding Farm, Wildflower.

CUPID, Sidney—Venus..........C. O. Thornquest, Oakland

CHRISMAN'S HAMBLETONIAN 10178, Whipple's Hambletonian—Flora..........Jesse Chrisman, San Jose

CANNON BALL, Simmons—Gurgle..........Lockhaven Stock Farm, Burbank.

DIRECTOR, Dictator—Dolly..........Pleasanton Stock Farm, Pleasanton.

DON MARVIN, Fallis—Cora..........F. P. Lowell, Sacramento

ELECTO, Antevolo, dam by Capt. Webster..........G. W. Stimpson, Oakland

ELEGANCE..........G. W. Stimpson, Oakland

EL BENTON, Electioneer—Nellie Benton..........Souther Farm, San Leandro.

ECLECTIC, Electioneer—Manette..........Wilfred Page, Sonoma County

FIGARO, Hambletonian—Emblem..........Souther Farm, San Leandro.

GROVER CLAY, Electioneer—Maggie Norfolk..........Denis Gannon, Oakland.

G. & M., Anteeo—Rosa B..........George E. Guerne, Santa Rosa.

GUY WILKES, George Wilkes—Lady Bunker..........San Mateo Stock Farm, San Mateo.

GLEN FORTUNE, Electioneer—Glenna..........Souther Farm, San Leandro.

GRANDISSIMO, LeGrande—Norma..........Fred W. Loeber, St Helena

JESTER D, Almont—Hortense..........Souther Farm, San Leandro

JUNIO, Electioneer—by Granger..........S. N. Straube, Fresno.

LEO WILKES, Guy Wilkes—Sable..........San Mateo Stock Farm, San Mateo.

MEMO, Sidney—Flirt..........Valensin Stock Farm, Pleasanton.

MAMBRINO WILKES, George Wilkes—Lady Chrisman..........San Miguel Stock Farm, Walnut Creek.

MAMBRINO JR 1789, Mambrino Patchen, dam by Mambrino Chief..........Geo. P. Bull, San Jose.

MORTIMER, Electioneer—Marti..........Wilfred Page, Sonoma County

NOONDAY, Wedgewood—Noontide..........F. P. Lowell, Sacramento.

PLEASANTON, Director—May Day..........Pleasanton Stock Farm, Pleasanton.

PHILOSOPHER, Pilot Wilkes—Belle..........George E. Guerne, Santa Rosa.

ROY WILKES, Adrian Wilkes—Flora..........Pleasanton Stock Farm, Pleasanton.

REDWOOD, Anteeo—Lou Wilton..........A. McFayden, Oakland.

SILVER BOW, Robert McGregor—Sadie..........P. J. Williams, Oakland.

SHAMROCK, Bucaneer—Fernleaf..........G. W. Stimpson, Oakland

SIDNEY, Santa Claus—Sweetness..........Valensin Stock Farm, Pleasanton.

SIMMOCOLON, Simmons—Colon..........Valensin Stock Farm, Pleasanton.

ABLE WILKES, Guy Wilkes—Sable..........San Mateo Stock Farm, San Mateo.

ST. NICHOLAS, Sidney—Towhead..........John Rowen, Oakland Trotting Park.

WOODNUT, Nutwood—Flora..........Jas. Weatherhead, San Jose

WHIPPLETON 1883, Hambletonian Jr.—Lady Livingston..........Fred W. Loeber, St. Helena

Kennel Work.

The lovers of the dog and those who take an interest in our kennel work, will be disappointed this week in the dog department, as the kennel editor has been all week at Bakersfield attending the field trials there. The telegraphed account has been very meagre and rather than give results, we will await his return and then give a report in full of the pleasant week that has been had by the host of good fellows who have been there in attendance.

Woodside to be Sold.

In the advertising columns will be found an announcement that Mrs. Silas Skinner has determined to sell Woodside Farm and all the well bred stock. There are standard bred mares, young stallions, fillies and any number of non-standard horses that will answer for roadsters. The Almont blood is largely represented in the catalogue, and there should be lively competition for the Almont mares, and, in fact, for any of the mares in which there is any of the Almont blood, for breeders now recognize the fact that the greatest brood mares of the present day are thickly impregnated with Almont blood. We are sorry to lose Mrs. Skinner from the list of the breeders, and trust that some energetic person will secure Woodside and carry on the business.

P. C. T. H. B. A.

The Directors of the Breeder's Association have had a meeting, and this week announce a series of colt stakes, some of which have been prepared in the interests of the smallers breeders, and also to give the progeny of stallions, whose names are not now enrolled in the great table, a chance to distinguish themselves. There are four stakes for yearlings two, three and four-year-olds, to all of which there is a liberal allowance of added money. The payments are easy, extending over a number of months. There are also two purses offered for three and four-year-old class horses, those eligible in the three minute class being the three-year-olds, while the four-year-olds are given a 2:40 class trot. Three purses are also offered for the get of stallions who at present have no representatives in the 2:30 list, restricted to two, three and four year olds. All of these should have large entries, as there are many good stallions who as yet have none of their progeny in the charmed circle. A 2:30 stallion purse is also offered, the amount given being $1,000. The Stanford Stake is again advertised, this time under the auspicies of the Breeder's Association, and entries to that stake will close at the same time, as will all the stakes and purses offered, March 1st. When the proper time arrives, the entire programme will be announced. Taken all in all, the stakes and purses are such that they should command the attention of every breeder on the coast. The Directors have been extremely liberal, and there is every reason to believe that the breeders will be just as liberal in their entries.

A Clash.

Some weeks ago we called the attention of Directors and Secretaries to the fact that a meeting of representatives would be advisable, as there was a prospect of a clash. Two associations have already claimed dates, they being Petaluma and San Jose, and both claim the same week. The Trotting Horse Breeders have selected the week after Stockton, presumedly as San Jose claimed another date.

Now it seems that this could have been easily avoided if delegates from each of the associations had met and compared notes. Fresno will probably want to claim the same date they had last year, but that will conflict with the Breeder's meeting. Santa Rosa dropping out from the circuit, is probable the cause of San Jose claiming an early date, and yet, by the way, it is no sure thing that Santa Rosa will be on the shelf in 1890. The Directors there say they will give a week of racing if certain inducements are held out by the citizens of the town.

Now if the race loving people of Santa Rosa will give the necessary assurances, there will, in all likelihood, be another week to fill in. As at present claimed, the clash is inevitable unless one of the associations will give way. The Petaluma folks say they have had the date, two weeks before the State Fair, for a long number of years, and they are not going to change now, and the San Joseans say they have been knocked around from pillar to post by all of the associations for a number of years, and that now they are going to choose their own date irrespective of whom they clash with. It is presumed that the State Fair Directors will claim the two weeks beginning September 8th, and the other societies will arrange accordingly. It seems that with that date taken for a basis, a good circuit could have been arranged as follows:

Napa August 11th to 16th, Petaluma 18th to 23rd, San Jose 25th to 30th, Oakland Sept. 1st to 6th, Sacramento 8th to 20th, Stockton 22nd to 27th, Breeders Meeting 29th to Oct. 4th, Fresno 6th to 11th of October. This would have given all a chance and each of the associations would make money. As it is now, there is a prospect of more than one of them making financial failures. With a little friendly feeling displayed, there may still be a chance to over come the trouble, and it will be for the best interests of all concerned to give and take a little in this important matter.

The Pedigree of Lorena.

EDITOR BREEDER AND SPORTSMAN:—In your paper of January 4th you published a tabulated pedigree of Capt. Harris' filly Lorena, and gave the breeding of her granddam Princess as follows: Sired by Woodford Mambrino, son of Mambrino Chief, dam Jennie Simpson by Autocrat, he by Democrat, dam Golddust Belle, by Dorsey's Golddust. In 1880 I got Princess from Capt. Harris, and the enclosed tag was attached to her, which is in Capt. Harris' handwriting; he herein gives her a record of 2:27½, and she is credited to Mambrino Chief instead of Woodford Mambrino.

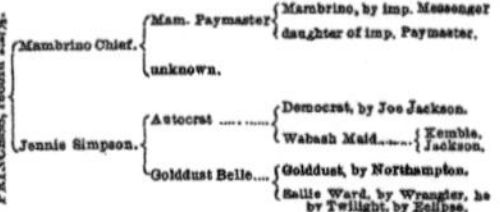

I sent a copy of this pedigree to J. H. Wallace, and enclosed find his answer:

NEW YORK, Sept. 6, 1880.

MR. FRED W. LOEBER, ST. HELENA, CAL.—DEAR SIR:—Yours of 30th ult. is to hand, and the pedigree of Princess does not strike me favorably. It is impossible to tell whether it is right, without knowing who bred the mare and through what hands she passed to her present owners. If she is by Mambrino Chief, she cannot be less than 17 years old, and may be a good deal more. It is a thousand to one that the pedigree of the dam is made up to suit. Some of the elements I know to be wrong. Yours truly, J. H. WALLACE per J. S. C.

I sent Capt. Harris a copy of Wallace's letter, and received the following reply: "In regard to the pedigree of Princess and Wallace's reference to it in answer to your communication to him, I can only say, the pedigree as recorded in my book, is as it was given by Mr. Moses Alma, a gentleman well known in his life by all acquaintances for truth and veracity. He has repeatedly stated in my presence that he purchased her from the man who raised her, the sire being Mambrino. After his death, and when I got hold of the mare, I learned from a friend of Wm. F. Williamson, who had all of his old papers after the death of Alma, that such was her pedigree, and I so made the memorandum at the time. This is the whole story of Princess and her breeding. There was another Princess on this coast known as the Edmonson mare; they may have become confounded."

BEN E. HARRIS.

After "Hark Comstock's" return from California in writing up the leading two-year-olds in an article which was copied in your paper, October 19th., he gives Lorena the following pedigree: "Sired by Jim Mulvenna, dam Elmo, second dam by Cassius M. Clay, third dam by Harris' Hambletonian.

The true history of the mare, Princess, as near as known is—Mr. Moses Alma (now deceased) formally connected with the firm of Wilmerding, Kellogg & Co., of San Francisco, bought her in Maraga Valley, and kept her a number of years for a road mare. He used to keep his horses at Bridge's stable. After his death, Mr. Bridge kept Princess in livery for several years, until she got lame. Mr. Bridge then disposed of her to Captain Harris. Mr. Bridge asserts that Captain Harris knew her history. I went to see Mr. Kellogg, of the firm of Wilmerding, Kellogg & Co., to ascertain whether Mr. Alma had ever been to Kentucky in the interest of the business, and whether he ever purchased any horses while there. Mr. Kellogg assured me that Mr. Alma had never been East from the time he first came to California until he died. The only way to perpetuate the breeding interests successfully is stick to correct pedigrees. Yours truly,

FRED W. LOEBER.

The editor of the Indiana Horseman says: "Great is Adonis, swift is this son of Sidney; nevertheless there are plenty of people East who believe that Roy Wilkes, properly conditioned and in the right hands, can beat any pacer on earth except Johnston." Well, Mr. Editor, there are people here who believe that Adonis can beat Johnston.

Answers to Correspondents.

Answers for this department must be accompanied by the name and address of the sender, not necessarily for publication, but as proof of good faith. Write the questions distinctly, and on one side of the paper only. Positively no questions will be answered by mail or telegraph.

KATE AGNEW'S BREEDING.

Mr. Chrisman sends the following which explains itself: The sire of Kate Agnew 2:28½ is Chrisman's Hambletonian by Whipple's Hambletonian 725 and not Ben Franklin. The breeding of Ben Franklin (who is dead about 10ys.,) was sired by David Hill Jr., son of Vermont Black Hawk, dam a Washingtonian mare. JESSE CHRISMAN.

E. R. D.

Please be kind enough to let me know what was the name of the horse that won the La Rue stakes at Sacramento, in 1885, 2¼ miles and what time?

Answer.—Arthur H. 4.00½.

G H. K

Please inform me what is the best time ever made by Pliny for three quarters of a mile.

Answer.—1:14¾ at Eureka, last July.

S. L. O.

Can you let me know the breeding, performance and present owner of young Niagara, who, I believe, is now called Pacific? Did he ever sire a trotter; if so, give name and time made.

Answer—He has no representative in the 2:30 list. Can any of our readers supply the other information asked for?

J. W. D.

Will you kindly give through the columns of your valuable paper the breeding of the grand and great grandams of the standard bred mare Francine foaled in 1881 bred by Martin McCabe Springboro Pa. Registered in American Trotting register Vol. 6 as standard.

Answer.—The American Turf Register does not give the names any of the grandams of Francine. You had better write to Mr. McCabe.

Subscriber.

Please inform me whether the horse called Fred Drake, owned by J. P. Sanborn of Port Huron, Mich., is standard. Give his pedigree if practicable.

Answer.—He is standard, and registered 4834. He is by Joe Gavin, 564, dam Minnie Drake by Louis Napoleon, 207, 2nd dam Julia Drake by Endorser.

A. B. R.

Will you please inform me if Richmont by Almont, dam Minnie by Simon Kenton, is standard?

Answer.—If Minnie has been registered, Richmont is standard by breeding, but she is not in the Register up to Vol. 7. You had better write to the Wallace Register Co., 280 Broadway, N. Y., and find out if she is in Vol. 8 or 9. She is the dam of Kitty Wilkes, who is registered.

Subscriber.

Is a mare sired by Priam, sire of Honesty, record 2:24¼, dam by Chieftain 721, standard bred?

Answer.—Yes.

T. W. B.

Was San Bruno 2:25½ by George M Patchen Jr. ever in the Stud, or was there a San Bruno by David Hill and had he a record below 3 minutes.

Answer.—San Bruno 2:25½ was a gelding, we do not know of any other San Bruno with a record. There was a son of David Hill by the name of San Bruno, that some years ago stood at Fairfield in Solano County.

J. W. Murphy.

What is the correct pedigree of Sam Purdy? (2nd.) Is or was he a pacer or a trotter? (3rd) Where was he bred? (4th) Was there any full brothers to Sam Purdy ever raised on J. B. Haggin's ranch?

Answer.—(1) Sam Purdy by Geo M. Patchen Jr., dam Whiskey Jane, pedigree not traced. (2) Trotter. (3) San Francisco. (4) Not that we know of.

T. A. B.

Please give the pedigree of Brown's Bellfounder and number if he is registered; has he a record? Is there any of his get in the 30 list?

Answer. Browns Bellfounder was by Bellfounder Morgan dam Lady Allport by Mambrino. He is not registered, has no record and none of his get are in the 2:30 list.

A subscriber.

Sir, please inform through your paper the following information. (1) Whether a filly sired by "St. Elmo", dam by Chieftain is standard? also, (2) If a stallion by St. Elmo dam by Whipples Hambletonian is standard?

Answer. (1) If you mean Elmo 891, sometimes called St. Elmo, yes. (2) Not unless the dam is standard.

E. A. P.

Alfred G. and G. & M. were bred by Guerne & Murphy of Santa Rosa. Alfred G. is now owned by G. E Guerne, and we believe he also owns G. & M. Col. Lewis was a gelding, foaled 1870, by Rifleman, dam not traced. The other questions will be answered as soon as we receive answers to letters sent out.

Robbery Boy.

Can you give me the pedigree of Robbery Boy formerly owned in Santa Barbara?

Answer.—A letter sent to Mr. Den has elicited the following reply:

SANTA BARBARA, Cal., Jan. 19, 1890.

EDITOR BREEDER AND SPORTSMAN:—With regard to Robbery Boy's pedigree, I can safely state that it is entirely unknown, but will give you all the information that we know about him. In the spring of 1873, some emigrants coming from Oregon stopped at the ranch, and our foreman took a fancy to a bay colt, a yearling then, and bought him for $50, they being short of money. They stated to us that he was a well bred horse by a running horse in Oregon, and that is all we know about his pedigree. We began training him as a three-year-old, and showed a great deal of speed, won several good races and we had him entered against Walking John and Eleclar, half mile at Los Angeles, in 1875, and a few days before the race, on a trial, he split both front hoofs from the hair to the ground, and that was the last of his running days as he could never stand training again. The old horse shows a great deal of breeding, and all his colts out of nothing but pure mustang mares show speed. I have a saddle horse that can run a quarter in twenty-three seconds, and another that runs half miles better than fifty. Robbery Boy never had but one thoroughbred mare, that was Lillian by Creighton, who is the dam of Sid Lew. Yours truly,

E. B. DEN.

Maud H.

A couple of weeks ago, we asked for information regarding the record of Maud H. by Carr's Mambrino, and have received the following from our Salinas correspondent. Maud H. trotted in the 2:30 class at Sherwood Park during the district fair races held here during the week, beginning October 7, 1889. Her record was made in the second heat of the race and was thus described by the Salinas Morning Journal, Oct. 10th, the day following the race:

Second heat—Auction pools: Field $12, Maud H. $6, Allen L. $4. This was a good start. Maud H made play for the pole and took it from Mambrino Boy at the quarter. She soon opened up a gap and was never caught, finishing first by a short length from Allen L., Mambrino Boy third at Allen L's wheel, and Acrobat just inside of the distance flag. Time, 2:30.

Names Claimed.

W. P. Todhunter claims the name of McGinty for sorrel colt sired by Prince of Norfolk, dam Lizzie Idle, foaled March 20th, 1889, marked one fore white leg and one white hind leg a white stripe in his forehead.

Yours respectfully,
W. P. TODHUNTER.

EDITOR BREEDER AND SPORTSMAN:—I claim the name Nova for bay filly, foaled March 27th, 1880, by General Hamilton, dam Nellie S. J. A. SOWELL.

WHEATLAND, January 22, 1890.

Our Australian Letter.

EDITOR BREEDER AND SPORTSMAN:—In a recent number of your paper, an Australian correspondent remarked upon the number of race meetings held near Melbourne, Victoria, and the pernicious effect it had upon the sport. Sydney is just as bad, as may be Judged from the fact that there are never less than six race meetings a month in the immediate vicinity of Sydney. There are now three proprietory clubs, Rosehill, Canterbury Park and Warwick Farm, who push business very closely, and go in for cut-throat business.

On a recent public holiday two of them held meetings, and as there were various other attractions, the pair, to use a new colonial sporting vulgarism, "fell in the soup," so they are not likely to again give the racing public a surfeit of good things. With so many "rat" meetings, it may be imagined owners of the shady type play the game pretty "low down."

It is not so long since that a horse went out to the start with shoes on and his rider minus spurs. These are considered pretty sure signs out here that a horse is not "on the job," and his stock went down to zero. However, the shoes, which were only *glued* on, were wrenched off at the back of the course before the race started, and the "books" were duly affixed to the jockeys heels. But the *coup* did not come off after all this trouble, and the smart party missed a big thing by a head.

Boxing day will see the first big two-year-old event of the year at Randwick, the course of the Australian Jockey Club, the premier body of New South Wales. This is naturally looked forward to by racing men with interest, as showing where we are to look to for next years' cracks. Correeze, owned by our sporting barrister Mr. "Jack" Want, showed great speed when first asked to race, but he showed poor form when asked to race in the big event, the Maribyrnong Plate, and it would appear the young 'un has gone completely off.

The American trotter is making himself felt in the colonies, not so much on the track as in the improved class of buggy horses now seen on our streets. So far, trotting on the track has not taken a big hold of the public, more particularly in Sydney, where trotting events are generally run in conjunction with pony and galloway races, and shady as our legitimate turf morals are, they are clear as sunlight compared with the doings of the trotters, ponies and galloways.

Breeding trotters is a paying game, as at the last sale of the Hobartville stock, the young trotters averaged more than the fashionably-bred running youngsters. The colony recently suffered a big loss in the sudden death of the trotting stallion Childe Harold, whose get are remarkable for style and kindness of temper. In New Zealand, however, the trotter appears to be getting a better grip, as they were recently at Canterbury able to run off seven handicap trotting events in the one afternoon.

I may be pardoned a little bit of "blow," when I state that Australia is not altogether in the back-ground of the world's sports. We have shown the universe we can raise a fair sculler, pugilist, and cricketer. Sheffield, in its palmiest days, could not hold a candle to our running tracks, and now it seems we are going to lead the world in the "sport of kings," by giving the enormous sum of £10 000 for the next Melbourne Cup. Donovan received £12,000 for his win of the Lancashire Plate (Eng.), certainly, but as the £10,000 for the Melbourne Cup will be in addition to the sweepstakes of nominators, there is not much doubt the Victorian Racing Club will score a best on record next November. The growth of the Melbourne Cup has been phenomenal. The first cup was in 1861, when the added money was £200. This was raised in 1868 to £300, and it was not till 1876 that it reached £500, in which year "the Cup" was won by a mare, Briseis, for the only time in the history of the race. 1883 saw £1,000; 1886, £2,000; £1887, £2,500; 1888, £3,000; 1889, £5,000, and now with a gigantic stride the Cup of 1890 will be for the plum of $10,000 added money.

The death of Searle and the rather complicated condition in which he has left the aquatic championship must be my excuse for inserting an aqueous item in my usual turf letter. Searle died in Melbourne, but his body was brought to Sydney, where he was accorded a public funeral, when the biggest crowd yet known to gather together in Sydney turned out, as may be judged from the fact that it took the procession five hours to force its way a distance of some two miles. With regard to the shoulders upon which the championship mantle is to descend, Searle, on his death-bed, expressed a wish that the honor should be competed for by colonial scullers. Old England, who certainly dies hard, expresses the opinion through its press, that O'Connor is entitled to it, but it seems to me that the trouble rests between America and Australia, both of whose second or third class-men could beat England's best. The general opinion in Australia is that it should revert to Peter Kemp, from whom Searle wrested it, but in any case without a contest, the title is an empty one. However, Searle went to the other side of the world to give you a chance for it, so it only seems fair your best man—O'Connor, I suppose—should come over here and return the compliment. Stansbury, the young fellow who rowed Searle, the only hard race the latter ever pulled, is our most likely man, but Searle improved to a vast extent by the time he met O'Connor, but it remains to be seen "how Stansbury has gone ahead." THE JUNGLE.

SYDNEY, N. S. WALES, Australia, Dec. 24. '89.

VETERINARY.

Conducted by W. Henry Jones, M. R. C. V. S.

Subscribers to this paper can have advice through this column in all cases of sick or injured horses or cattle by sending an explicit description of the case. Applicants will send their name and address that they may be identified. Questions requiring answers by mail should be accompanied by two dollars, and addressed to W. Henry Jones, M. R. C. V. S., Club Stables, Taylor Street, San Francisco.

Question.

My mare is lame; has been so for four weeks; very sore in both fore feet, and can hardly stand. The feet are very hot.

Answer.—In all probability your mare has laminitis. Remove the shoes, cut down the soles, and poultice the feet. Give the mare one dose of physic containing Barb Aloes, six drams, and one dram of ginger. I would advise you to call in a veterinary surgeon.

J. T. J.

In reference to your enquiry for a recommendation to a horse-shoer, I would suggest that you look at the advertisements in BREEDER AND SPORTSMAN.

J. P. Shafter.

I cannot possibly advise you with reference to your colt without first seeing him. It is one of those cases that a veterinary surgeon cannot diagnose without an examination.

The Science of Horse Breeding.

The Law of Sex.

WRITTEN FOR THE BREEDER AND SPORTSMAN.

With regard to natural laws regulating sex, many theories have been promulgated from time to time, but the one most likely to approach the solution of this (to breeders) most important question is that of the American writer, Starkweather. His valuable work on "The Law of Sex" was published in 1883, but so far back as 1878 I find notes of my own observations which are corroborated by his book. He bases his theory (in human beings) on the intellectual and physical superiority of either male or female. Thus, if the male is superior in intellect and health to his mate, he fixes the sex, making it opposite to his own, and *vice versa*. This is sound reasoning in the main, or else why do we so rarely see brilliant sons following brilliant fathers. If marriages were polygamous this would be obviated, but as it is the exception for a man to marry twice the opportunity of reversing a mistake is remote. By way of illustration of the above theory, and applying it to horses, I take from my note book of 1878, the case of Kelpie (imp). This stallion came into possession of the late Mr. George Wyndham of Dalwood and Bukulla, about 1862, and presided (at the latter property) over as choice a harem as then existed in the country, sireing such undeniably good racehorses as Stockwell and Cyclone, both a stone better than Kingfisher (winner of the Sydney Cup), Kareola, Cronstadt, Trump Card, Tommy Dodd, Brolga, Plover, Mariner, and a score of lesser lights, who "swept the boards" in the northern districts of New South Wales for many years. In all that time, however, he never sired a filly up to the commonest selling plate form, and as a matter of fact the mares threw a very large proportion of colts. The knowledge of this set me thinking, and I put it down to two causes: First, the excessively bad care taken of the horse both between and during the seasons. To save trouble in exercising, the stable door leading into a black-soil yard was invariably open all day, and in wet weather that same yard was a caution to stallions. Grooming he rarely got, and as the growth of green stuff depended on the spring weather, as often as not he was stinted in proper food. Not so the mares running out on excellent box country, and rarely foaling until the spring grass was forward. On the one side want of exercise, condition, and careful grooming; on the other, natural free life on the hills with excellent pasture. According to Starkweather, the mares would in such a case fix the sex opposite to their own, and my reasoning led me to a similar conclusion. Starkweather has, however, missed an important factor in this "law of sex," and while the foregoing causes tend very largely to decide the matter, I am convinced that the sex and excellence of same depends as much, or more, on the potency of strains of blood as on health. Consequently, the blood of the mares of the Bukulla stud, rich with infusions of the Darley-Arabian through Cap-a pie, Plover, Scratch, Snake, Whisker (imp), grafted on to branches of the old imported mares Penelope, Miss Lane, Mancipe, and many others, succeeded in carrying the sway against the weatherbit, St. Francis, Taurus and Zinganee strains of Kelpie—and hence the preponderance of (excellent) sons.

Now mark the difference in results when Kelpie was installed at Gordon Brook. Few breeders in New South Wales treat their stallions so wisely as Mr. T. H. Smith, and with the combined advantages of ample exercise, comfortable stabling, grooming, and the best of food, he was far more potent than the mares, which were as a rule covered early (for racing purposes) and before shedding their coats. Moreover, the flashy, speedy strains of blood in their veins such as Pitsford, Livingston, Sir Richard, Glaucus, etc., were as much inferior to Kelpie as he had been to the stout Bukulla blood. As a natural sequence his fillies raced well, and in proof of this I have only to instance Thyra (winner of £1,000 Cup Glen Innes), Maude (a remarkably good mare), Atalanta (dam of Melanion), The Nun, and a dozen others.

While in England in 1882-3 Captain Machell showed me over Lord Calthorpe's stud at Newmarket, where Petrarch was then "lord of the harem." Chatting over his probabilities as a first-class sire, I remarked that his fillies would probably be better than his colts, because he strained so much away from the Darley-Arabian, and to the Byerley Turk and Godolphin, through flashy blood, like Orlando, Alarm, and further back, Castral and Selim and Reubens. I need scarcely say that he was too polite to ridicule the idea, but it was quite too apparent that he did not believe there was anything in it. Nevertheless, I had the satisfaction, after returning to the colony, to see two Oak winners accredited to Petrarch in Busybody and Miss Jummy, against only one really brilliant colt in the person of The Bard, and I cannot recall since Priam any instance of a stallion pulling off the Oaks twice within so short a time of his going to the stud.

C. BRUCE LOWE.

THE FARM.

Imported Mutton.

An article in the Journal of the Royal Agricultural Society of England says the National Stockman points out that the frozen mutton trade which only comenced in 1880 has attained very large dimensions. In 1882 only 9 400 tons were imported, while the amount brought in 1888 equaled 49,450 tons, which represents three pounds for each man, woman and child in the United Kingdom. The mutton represented by the live sheep importations in 1888 did not exceed one and a half pounds per head. This makes the total amount of mutton imported both of live and frozen or fresh mutton only four and a half pound per head per annum. Largely, therefore as the new imports have increased the quantity of imported mutton is not yet enough to supply each unit of population with a single ounce of mutton per week, while the produce of English pastures is still sufficient to provide each one with nearly an ounce a day. Foreign mutton supplies are now nearly half a pound more for each of our population than is provided by the much longer established beef. The problem, therefore which anyone who is calculating the chances of the further growth of the newer trade must try to face is whether the course of events already seen in the check of fresh beef imports is to be paralleled or not in the case of mutton.

Cattle Without Horns.

Many breeders have been annoyed and had their valuable horses and brood mares injured by cattle. The Holstein Freisian Register says: The experiment of breeding off the horn is nothing new, says Field and Farm. There is no question but in the case of the Red Polls the horns have been dispensed with by breeding hornless cattle to hornless cattle for generations. Editor Cheever, of the New England Farmer, during years of successful breeding, eliminated horns from his dairy cows at Pine Hedge farm, and another Massachusetts man has nearly thirty head descended from this original herd. An Ohio agriculturist has polled Jerseys, now in the third generation, the result of crossing a "mooly" and a Jersey bull. From the same State comes report of a breed or family of "polled Durhams," to the development of which perhaps a dozen patient men have been faithfully devoted for a considerable time. Last year specimens of this stock were publicly exhibited, and this season also (at the State and several local fairs) where it attracted favorable comment.

Mr. Morse, of the Windsor Farm Denver, Col., is confident that he will be able by the fourth or fifth generation to produce a family of hornless Holsteins, and bring about the result by persistent dehorning. Says he: "If I fail, then I shall conclude that the theory of breeding as understood at the present day is a delusion and an uncertainty. If from a curby hock in a horse I can get a curby hock, why not from a hornless bovine get a hornless calf? If not the first generation continue it on until you get it. I am a believer in hereditary defect and in hereditary improvement. At all events I am out for the trial, and shall keep the horns going until they are gone."

American Steers in Germany.

A short time ago the attention of the Department of Agriculture was called to a recent shipment of American cattle sold in the Rhenish province. Through the Department of State, the Department of Agriculture was placed in possession of a consul at Cologne, in which this gentleman reported the sale of some thirty head of American cattle in that market in reference to which he made the following statement:

"The quality of these oxen was good, but too fat, which, however, can be remedied. The price obtained per 100 lbs. of the dressed meat, that is, exclusive of the head, hide, feet and entrails, which fall to the butcher, was Marks 70 being the same price paid for the home stock. Therefore, American cattle can compete with the home production.

"There is a difference among oxen fattened on pastures and those fattened in stables. The latter are preferred here, especially the red and checked ones, which might command a higher price, say Marks 72 per 100 pounds. Both kinds are readily marketed here. There being rather a scarcity of cattle here this year and a consequent rise in the price of beef meat, it is thought that a considerable number of American cattle can be sold here, and I am informed that another large shipment is on its way from America for the German market."

In order to be able to give to our American stock raisers full information on this subject, the Secretary of agriculture addressed a communication to the Department of State, requesting information in regard to the laws now in force in Germany with reference to cattle imported from the United States, and in a recent communication from the Department of State, enclosing the report on this subject of the American Consul at Hamburg, the Secretary of State promises to obtain further information which shall include the law on the subject of the exclusion of pork and any efforts that may have been made recently to secure its repeal, allusion to which was made in American papers in the form of a press dispatch, purporting to have been sent from Berlin, under date of Nov. 20th.

In the meantime, for the information of those interested, the substance of the correspondence between the Department of State and the American consuls at the points referred to, is here given. It would appear from the report of the consul at Hamburg and the enclosures forwarded with his communication, that cattle imported into any of the German States and Provinces from the United States, South America or Great Britain, are subject to a four week's quarantine, and furthermore, that there is no likelihood of such quarantine being either abolished or modified. It should also be stated, that the cattle sold in Cologne, formed part of a shipment of 160 head sold in the Rhenish Provinces, and that the data in regard to them was obtained from Messrs. Salm & Whil, one of the largest cattle dealing firms in Cologne. It appears further, that during the early part of last fall, some six or seven hundred head of cattle were landed in the port of Toening, from the United States, and that these were subjected to only five or six days' quarantine, but that this was due to a special permit from the imperial chancellor, which was granted in view of the fact, that the persons interested had entered into contracts for the delivery of said cattle, without a knowledge of the existence of the quarantine regulations, and would consequently have sustained heavy pecuniary loss had the cattle been subjected to the regular four weeks' quarantine. At the same time, however, strict orders were issued, that henceforth the regulations must be rigidly enforced. The consul at Hamburg also informs the Department of State, that until recently, large quantities of American beef have been used in the Province of Schleswig in Prussia, for the consumption of the German army. An order has since been issued, however, prohibiting its further use for that purpose.

The above is substantially all the formation of the Department of Agriculture has been able to procure on this subject up to date. THE STOCK GROWER.

Red Polled Cattle.

When a demand for these Norfolk and Suffolk cattle began to spring up in America the English breeders in most instances wisely refused to part with their best, even at advanced high prices. They said they would keep them for ten years to breed from, after this, obtaining an abundant produce, they would sell a part of them for exportation. The ten years have about expired, so we suppose our breeders can now import from the choicest of Red Polls, which we trust they will do abundantly, for they are among the most profitable of all cattle to bring up to maturity. The absence of horns makes considerable difference in the economy of their rearing, it is calculated as six to five of equal weights over horned stock; and then they are not wounding and even killing horses and other cattle pasturing and yarded with them; men also occasionally.

An objection was first made by Americans to these cattle on account of their size, they not being large enough, but many of the English breeders have been increasing them for a few years past, cows often weighing at present 900 to 1,000 pounds, and bulls 1,200 to 1,600. Indeed, well fattened at three to four years old some have attained still heavier weights, and bullocks over 1,700 to 1,900 pounds.

The average milk from fairly selected cows for eight months after calving, on pasture only, is from 10 to 15 quarts per day, and for six to seven months 16 to 20 quarts per day. This milk is generally of superior quality, commonly showing 15 to 20 per cent. of cream, and occasionally 30 to 35 per cent. Taking these things into consideration, and that they are hardy, thrifty and cheaply fattened, making beef of superior quality, we think the general run of our farmers would find it advantageous to stock their acres with a majority of these Red Polls. By using bulls to their native cows their half-bred calves would be found a decided improvement over their dams, and those three-fourths bred, for utility would be nearly as good as the full bred.—Stockman & Farmer.

Cattle Judging by Decimal Scale.

Many a good standard has been made abortive through the scale of points by which it was applied. I hold that the application of all standards should be by the use of a single scale of points, and that the decimal scale, being one of ten sections, each section consisting of ten points. Perfection then becomes of equal value in each section, and ten the synonym of it; 100 points become the grand total of perfection in the whole animal.

This necessitates that each animal be divided into ten equal sections, and to describe in the printed text minutely and clearly each of these sections, and the principle laid down that perfection must result from points of as equal value in head as in back or loin; that defects which destroy perfection shall be determined by computation of the percentage by which perfection is marred: To wit, if judgment determines a head be damaged 25 per cent., that it be cut 2½ points, and if back and loin 25 per cent. defective, that it shall be cut 2½ points. The mean value of the section has nothing to do with it; it is the percentage that perfection is damaged in such sections.

All standards serve two purposes—development and punishment of defects. A would-be Solomon, who desires special development in a certain section, demands that a large proportion of the points in the scale be apportioned to said section. He forgets that these points are never used except to punish; therefore has he, by this disproportionate number of points, only secured an unequal and more severe punishment for all defects found to exist in his hobby section. Perfection is next to a miracle, and defects the universal rule; therefore has he established the rule of an unjust cut for his hobby section. There is no equality except as development and punishment for want of it are in harmony, and this we can have only when we divide our animal up into equal sections, and give each section the same numerical value, and this we see most strongly demonstrated by the use of the decimal scale. It metes out exact Justice to each section of a cow, equal justice to each breed, as competing with other breeds, and equal justice to species as compared and competing with other species. So long as each kind is divided into ten sections of ten each, and each breed and species be accurately described, then all, no matter what—cattle, horses, dogs, fowls, beasts of prey, or man—all can compete for prizes with equal chances to win, and by any other standard or scale of points they cannot.

Let us make the scale of points by which the standard is to be applied, and I can secure the prizes, for by so doing I will make the cow I am competing with the standard by which all the others must be cut, by simply making the sections in which my cow is comparatively perfect those of large value in points, while to those in which she is faulty I would give but a few points in value. But suppose we made for the Jersey and Ayrshire cattle the following scale of points:

BULLS.

Head and ears	10
Neck and brisket	10
Shoulders and legs	10
Back and loins with tail	10
Barrel and flanks	10
Hips and rumps	10
Escutcheon and rowels	10
Scrotum with rudimentary teat and milk vein	10
Color of hair, color and handling of skin	10
Typical appearance and condition	10
	100

FEMALES.

Head and ears	10
Neck and brisket	10
Shoulder and legs	10
Back and loin, with tail	10
Barrel and flanks	10
Hips and rump	10
Forward udder	10
Rear udder	10
Escutcheon, teats and milk veins	10
Color of hair, color and handling of skin	10
	100

As these several sections are improved by condition and typical appearance, we say: In case of ties, typical appearance and condition shall break the tie and demand the first award. Ossified joints or any unsoundness detrimental to breeding or loss in practical points, should disqualify from competition, as should also cows not having had calves inside of two years, or three-year-old heifers not having had calves.

One will see that by such a scale, and an accurate description in the text of the structure, all can compete on an equality, irrespective of sex, breed or species, simply from the fact that each standard is applied by the same scale of points. The judge can readily select five of a class competing, to be scored, in which surely the best three of a class are to be found, when the scoring would take but a few moments, the highest score to win. The law becoming a law, intelligent judges' scores would go a long way in determining the worth of the animals. One could, by consulting these, determine to a great extent the species, beauty and quality. I believe the day not far distant when cattle will be sold on their score, as poultry is now being sold.

Such a standard and scale would secure prime all-round specimens. It is useless to deny that beauty is quality, so long as beauty in a horse, cow, dog or chicken brings a larger price in the market than equal weight without beauty. In this age, then, beauty is of practical worth and has a cash value to the farmer and breeder. The judge in open judging does not ignore this law, for he will every time give beauty with fair quality the first place, extra quality lacking beauty the second place. Standards are keen-edged knives that are used only to slay and discount.

Many are carried away by the mere shape of the udder, and they have placed the value of the fore udder at 13 points. That feature is faulty all of 49 times in 50 of the cows exhibited, and not one cow in five hundred out of all the females of the race will pass uncut. To give one cow in 500 a large value for this merit, the making of their standard cuts the other 499 in an unjust ratio for their defects, and it takes one of little intelligence to see that the Jersey standard, as now applied by their scale of points, militates against the best cows whenever scoring is resorted to, and for this reason good judges fight shy of its use.

I have written out a scale, but were I to come close to my own sense of fitness of things, I should say—forward udder, with milk veins, 10; rear udder, with teats, 10; and making a section of typical appearance and condition, 10 for the female, instead of, as now, placing thirty points in the udder and adjuncts. The present standard of the Jersey Club has 39 points; but I defy any judge to tell anything about the quantity of milk a cow will give by the mere shape of her udder. The color and handling of the hide, the wedge shape of body and milk-vein development are ten times more reliable as a means of determining the quality and quantity of the product. It matters not in what kind of a storehouse we place our wares, any more than the shape of the bag that holds the milk. To place 13 points in the fore udder secures a cut of from 1½ to 8 points in nineteen-twentieths of all the exhibited animals. A cow may be equally faulty in five other sections and perfect in this one, and win over them, if the defects are computed on a fair percentage of their effect on the perfection of said section.

In the judging of the future, is it not worth considering the feasibility of—1. Securing a division of the animal into 10 just and equal sections, giving each the same value in points; 2. To demand perfections of equal value, and determine its defects by this percentage plan; 3. Demanding that males be judged on 100 points as well as females?

To-day we are told to judge the males, omitting all milk adjuncts. Will any breeder deny the fact that a bull with a smooth scrotum, having no rudimentary teats and no indication of milk vein, will get heifers with fawn shape and large-sized teats? Will any breeder deny the fact that bulls of high degrees of excellence, coming from the fine cows of the day, have not well-defined teats and rudimentary milk veins? As a breeder, I would not keep or own a bull of the acknowledged dairy breeds that did not show well developed teats and the ordinary course of the milk vein.

But I have said enough to set the ball in motion. Let us hear from others. A radical change in our standard and scale of points in cattle, and the promulgation of more correct ones, and then their general use, is a demand of the times.—I. K. FELCH, in Country Gentleman.

Notes.

Russell & Bradley, Elko county, have gathered about 1,200 head of cattle off their range in the last week, and will ship them to California or ship hay for them from California.

Five Union county! (Oregon) farmers have butchered 450 hogs his winter that averaged 317lbs. At 4 cents the pork would be worth $5706. That's a good way to farm. It pays, and keeps that much money from going back East.

Kirman & Bickey are feeding 10,000 head of cattle on hay at their Douglas county ranch. The firm has 20,000 head of cattle in Humboldt County, nearly all of which they expect to lose on account of the heavy snowfall in that region.

The Argentine Republic has recently granted a bounty of five per cent on capital of companies exporting dressed beef. This has led to several establishments exporting on a very large scale, fitting up special steamers with machinery for freezing and stowing cargoes.

Canadian cattle foreign trade is decidedly on the increase, the present season being the largest on record. It is stated that in the future all beasts from Canada will be shipped to the ports on the west coast of Ireland, and there pastured for a few weeks before being sent to market.

George Russell says that his advices from his Idaho and Snake river ranges are that the cattle are all right, but he is anticipating quite a loss on his Elko county range. He has ordered 200 tons of hay shipped from California to Elko, and will feed all the poorer cattle and in that way save them.

The outbreak of foot-and-mouth disease at Steinbruck, Hungary, the great cattle depot, compelled the slaughter of 1,509 head of cattle. According to the congress of veterinarians recently held at Paris, tuberculosis is spreading in Continental Europe. Over one per cent. of animals slaughtered in Paris are affected by this disease.

Editor Kelly, of the Winnemucca Silver State is quite frosty, he says: The cold weather, deep snow and scarcity of feed is severe on stock, and many poor cattle are dying. Some say if cattle could get water out in the sagebrush they would weather it through. When a poor animal lies down hungry in the snow these cold nights, the chances are against it getting on its legs again.

The cold snap has been very severe in Nevada and many cattle have suffered severly. The Truckee Republican says: The train men on the west-bound overland express reported at Reno that 1000 head of cattle had frozen to death on a range near Carlin in Elko county, and that stockmen say that not a hoof will be left on Eastern Nevada ranges if the cold wave lingers much longer. The depth of snow is too great to admit of the cattle browsing on sagebrush.

WoodsideFarm

IMPORTANT SALE OF

Standard Trotting Mares Young Stallions and Fillies,

ROAD AND DRIVING HORSES

Farming Implements, Etc.

By direction of MRS. SILAS SKINNER.

Mrs. Skinner having determined to retire permanently from the breeding of Fine Stock, has decided to offer at

PUBLIC AUCTION

Thursday, March 6, '90,

at 12 M., on the Premises.

THE WELL-KNOWN

WOODSIDE FARM,

Near Napa,

together with all the highly bred trotting stock thereon.

The brood mares at Woodside are among the choicest in the State. Among them are mares by Almont, dam by Alexander's Abdallah; by Cassius M. Clay Jr., dam by Joe Downing; by Cassius M. Clay Jr., dam by Richelieu son of Mambrino Chief; by Duke of Orange Jr., dam by Cassius M. Clay Jr.; by Almont Mambrino, dam by Blood's Black Hawk; by Alcona—dam Fontana, dam of Flora Belle, 2:24, and Silas Skinner, trial 2 29¼—by Almont; by Alcona Clay—dam Metamora, dam of Clay Duke, 2:31¼—by Duke of Orange Jr. These mares have been bred to Director, Noonday, Mountain Boy and Wildwood, and are with foal. The young stallions are by Sitka, son of Alaska, by Electioneer, Whippleton, sire of Lillie Stanley, 2:17¼, Alcona Clay, etc. About twenty head well-bred trotting and driving animals will be sold in addition to the standard bred horses.

Catalogues giving extended pedigrees and full information are being prepared, and will be forwarded upon application.

At the conclusion of sale of horses,

WOODSIDE FARM

will be sold.

WOODSIDE FARM is situated three and a half miles from Napa City, up the river, upon what is known as the middle or big ranch road. It contains 87 1-2 acres of the choicest quality of land for alfalfa or any kind of grain, 40 acres being now in alfalfa over a foot high. The land produces from four to six tons of hay to the acre, of choice quality. Five of the fields are in pasture, four in alfalfa, one in timothy, the other kept in hay or grain necessary for stock, though well adapted for alfalfa. There is a nice orchard, small vineyard, and comfortable dwelling house of nine rooms. There is a good school house directly opposite, the best in the county. As to its adaptability as a stock ranch: There is living water in every field, and plenty of it, corrals and stock yards, stable room for forty horses, besides seven good box stalls two good stables, granery, etc. It is within two miles of the Napa Agricultural Society's race track, the finest constructed in the State for years. Should there not be sufficient land, 62 acres adjoining can be purchased at reasonable figures.

There is no more eligible location in the State for a small stock farm, and this affords a rare opportunity, with the stock, to at once engage in this remunerative pursuit.

The sale will be positive, Mrs. Skinner having large interests in Oregon which will require her personal attention during the greater portion of the year, compels the sale of the Woodside Farm.

Parties are invited to visit the farm and look over the stock. The undersigned will be glad to give any information required, either as to stock or ranch.

KILLIP & CO.
Live Stock Auctioneers,
22 Montgomery St., S. F.

For Sale

A FIRST-CLASS

Napa County Farm

—OR—

STOCK RANCH,

800 Acres Improved,

SITUATED TWO AND A HALF MILES FROM NAPA CITY, with good roads leading thereto, a good hard finished house of nine rooms, with all modern improvements, streams running all summer, a great amount of live oak and black oak timber. It lies in a fruit belt, surrounded by fine vineyards and orchards growing upon the same quality of soil, and originally a part of this tract. About one-half hill, and one-half rolling land, but none of it is steep and all easily cultivated, splendidly situated for the breeding of fine horses. Price, $65 per acre. Further particulars given at this office.

BREEDER AND SPORTSMAN,
313 Bush St.

R. LIDDLE & SON

538 Washington St., S. F.,

Wholesale and Retail Dealers in

Guns, Rifles and Pistols.

A Full Line of FISHING TACKLE and SPORTSMAN'S GOODS.

Orders by mail receive prompt attention.

SEASON 1890.

The Great Son of Buccaneer

SHAMROCK,

Two-Year Old Record of 2:25, beating the World's Record 4 1-2 Seconds when made.

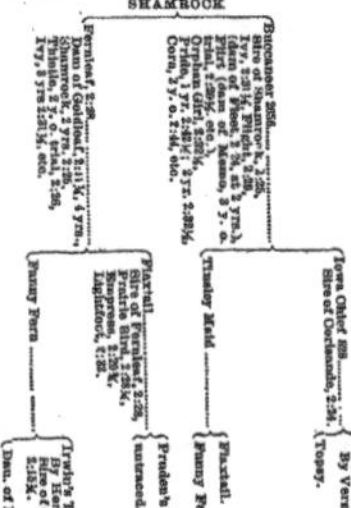

As will be seen from the tabulated pedigree and performances above, Shamrock is not only a phenomenal horse himself, but his ancestors on both sides have shown themselves to be uniformly producers of GREAT and PARTICULARLY early speed, and his record like many others of his family was made in a hotly contested race, instead of a trial against time.

HE IS NOW IN SPLENDID FORM, AND I TRULY BELIEVE WILL LOWER HIS RECORD TO 2:15 THIS YEAR.

TERMS, $100, with usual return privilege, for a limited number of CHOICE mares, season ending June 1st.

Electo.

By Anteevolo 2:19¼ by Electioneer, dam Captain Webster (sire of dam of Adonis 2:15), by Williamson's Belmont.

Electo, while but three years old this spring, is, as well as being grandly bred, a great individual.

TERMS, $50, with the usual return privilege, limited to 15 approved mares. Season to end June 1st.

Imported Cleveland bay stallion

Elegance.

(Registered in Cleveland Bay Stud Book No. 75.) Prize winner over twenty of his own breed in the GREAT YORKSHIRE SHOW OF ENGLAND.

The Cleveland Bays are the most prepotent coach horses in the world, and their get from ordinary mares makes the most stylish and serviceable horses for that purpose that can be raised. Rich bays with black points having the preference over ALL OTHERS.

TERMS, $25, with usual return privilege, season ending July 1st.

Care taken but no responsibility assumed for accidents or escapes. Pasturage, $5 per month. For further particulars call at or address me at my hospital, where horses will make the season.

G. W. STIMPSON, V. S.
Veterinary Hospital, 19th St., near San Pablo Ave, Oakland, Cal.

For Sale.

The Standard bred Stallion

Anteeo Button,

sire Anteeo, 2:16¼, sire of Alfred G. 2:19¾; Redwood, 2:24¼, etc. Dam Mollie Button, dam of Alexander Button, sire of Yolo Maid, 2:14; Rosa Mac, 2:20¾; Belle Button, 2:30¼, etc.

ANTEEO BUTTON is a dark bay 15¾ hands high, four years old, and weighs 1025 lbs. In style and action he is all that could be desired, and can trot a mile with ease in 2:40 to a cart.

This colt must be seen to be appreciated.

Apply to

I. DE TURK,
Santa Rosa, Cal.

Highland Farm,

LEXINGTON, KY.,

Home of Red Wilkes.

Standard-bred Trotting Stock

For Sale,

Sired by Red Wilkes, Wilton, 2:19¼; Allandorf and Sentinel Wilkes, out of highly bred Standard Mares of the most fashionable blood of the day.

W. C. FRANCE, Proprietor.

SAMUEL VALLEAU. JAS. R. BRODIE.

J. R. BRODIE & CO.,

Steam Printers,

—And Dealers in—

Poolseller's and Bookmaker's Supplies.

401—403 Sansome Street, corner Sacramento, San Francisco.

The Trotting Stallion

BONANZA 2:29½

Will make the season of 1890, from February 1st to July 1st, at the

OAKLAND TROTTING PARK.

PEDIGREE.

BONANZA, 2:29½.
- Arthurton 365 — Sire of Arab, 2:15, Joe Arthurton 2:20¼, Lady Escot, 2:28¼. Dams of Grandee, 2:23¼, Hidalgo, 2:27.
  - Hambletonian 10 — Sire of 41 in 2:30 list. Sires of 147 of the sires of 567 in 2:30 list.
  - Imogene, by Am. Star 14 — Dam of Leland 1900 Sire of Clara, 2:21, Miss Leland, 2:25¼, Hades, 2:27¼.
- Sister — Dam of Albert W., 2:20.
  - John Nelson 187 — Sire of Nerea, 2:31¼, Gov. Stanford, 2:27¼, Aurora, 2:27, Nemo, 2:30.
  - Lamott Mare — Dam of Aurora, 2:27; g d of Arol, 2:24¼.

DESCRIPTION.

BONANZA is a very handsome chestnut of commanding form and splendid proportions. He stands nearly 16 hands high, is remarkably intelligent, level headed and pure gaited. His record is no mark of his speed. He is a great foal getter, and his colts are handsome fancy animals.

TERMS, $40 for the season, with the usual return privileges. Excellent pasturage near the track at $5 per month. The best of care taken of mares, but no responsibility assumed for accidents or escapes.

For further particulars, address

RICHARD HAVEY,
Oakland Trotting Park, Oakland.

THE MAMBRINO Patchen Stallion.

MAMBRINO JR., 1789 (formerly Carr's), Sire of Lady Ellen 2:28 (dam of Ella 2:29), Maud H. 2:30, Mambrino Boy (Carr's) 2:31 1 2.

Will stand at my farm, 2 1-2 miles north of San José, on the Milpitas road. Season to commence February 1st, 1890, at $60, with return privilege 1891. Fifteen mares of approved breeding, besides my own, will be given him. Parties owning good mares, performers or out of producing dams, will find an opportunity to breed them on shares, and the best of care taken of them till colt is weaned, if so desired.

PEDIGREE.

MAMBRINO JR., 1789, by Mambrino Patchen 58 [full brother of Lady Thorne 2:18 1-4] by Mambrino Chief 11. First dam by Mambrino Chief 11; 2nd dam by imp. Jordan [thoroughbred]; 3rd dam by Bertrand, son of Sir Archy; 4th dam by Chewkees, son of Sir Archy.

For further particulars address

GEO. P. BULL.
San José, Cal.

Box 1067.

The Hambletonian Stallion 10178.

CHRISMAN'S HAMBLETONIAN, Sire of Steve Whipple, 2:22, Kate Agnew 2:28¼, etc.
- Whipple's Hambletonian — Sire of 14 trotters and 1 pacer from 2:19 to 2:30, and 7 sons with 8 performers from 2:21¼ to 2:30, and dams of 6 from 2:19½ to 2:30.
  - Guy Miller — By Hambletonian 10.
  - Martha Washington — Dam of Speculation 928 Sire of Crown Pt. 2 24 Oakland Maid, 2:22, Gracie S., 2:28¼, and dam of Waterford, 2:27
- Flora, 2:39¼, trial, 2:26. Dam of Chrisman's Hambletonian, sire of Steve Whipple, 2 22 Kate Agnew, 2:28¼.
  - Chieftain 721 — Sire of Defiance, 2:24 and 2 17¼, pacing; Cairo, 2:26, and Onward, 2:24, pacer.
  - daughter of Wilson's Leamon.

Stud season now on till the 1st of August, 1890, at $40 each mare, with return privilege in 1891, provided stallion and mare, or either, do not change owners. Good pasture at hand, and comfortable accommodation for brood mares and colts. For further particulars, address

JESSE CHRISMAN, Proprietor.
San José, Cal.

The Trotting Stallion

CUPID,

Full Brother to Adonis 2:14,

—Sired by—

The Celebrated SIDNEY 2:19 3-4, and out of Venus.

Will make the season of 1890 at the OAKLAND TROTTING PARK.

PEDIGREE.

CUPID is by Sidney out of Venus by Capt. Webster 10173, record 2:30, and sire of Freestone 2:19. Second dam by Skenandoah 936, sire of Daisy Burns 2:29¾, Erwin Davis (sire of two in the 30 list) and dams of four in the 30 list.

DESCRIPTION.

Cupid is a handsome bright bay 15.2¾ hands high, weighs 1100 lbs.; was foaled in 1885. As a yearling, with very little work he showed quarters in 42 seconds, and at 2 years old, quarters in 38 seconds. As a three year old he has not been worked, but he shows the speed and endurance that must come from his excellent blood lines.

TERMS $50 for the season, with the usual return privilege. Good pasturage near the track at $5 per month. The best of care taken of mares in any way that owners may desire, but no responsibility assumed for accidents or escapes.

For further particulars address

C. O. THORNQUEST,
Oakland Trotting Park, or
C. BAAB, 9?3 Broadway, Oakland.

Vineland Stock Farm

Whippleton 1883,

Sire of

LILY STANLEY	Record	2:17½
HOMESTAKE	"	2:16½
FLORA B.	"	2:27
CORA C.	"	2:31½
BLACK PRINCE	"	2:36½
RACHEL	"	2:38
PRINCE W.	"	2:40

WHIPPLETON is not only the sire of trotters, but he is the greatest sire of Carriage Horses on the Pacific Coast. Some of the best carriage and road teams in San Francisco are sired by Whippleton. A carriage team by Whippleton received First Premium at Napa, Petaluma, Oakland, Sacramento, Stockton and San Jose. Whippleton and his colts have never been beaten in the show ring.

DESCRIPTION.

WHIPPLETON is black, tan muzzle and flanks, 17 hands, and weighs 1,400 lbs. Most of his colts are 16 hands or over, and with a few exceptions, bay, brown or black. He never sired a sorrel or white face colt. (If he does, I agree to refund service money.)

PEDIGREE.

WHIPPLETON, sired by Hambletonian Jr. (sire of Hancock 2:29), by Whipple's Hambletonian (sire of Graves, 2:19, Westfield, 2:20¼, Express, 2:24, and 12 others in the 2:30 list), dam Lady Livingston (dam of Lady Blanchard, 2 26¼, Bloomfield Maid, trial 2:22), by General Taylor (sire of the dams of Wells Fargo, 2:18¼, Nerea, 2:18¼, Bickford, 2:29¼, Lady Blanchard, 2:26¼, etc., and sire of grandam of Hazel Wilkes, 2:20) by the Morse Horse 6, sire of Norman 25 (sire of Lulu, 2:14¾, May Queen 2:20, etc.).

TERMS at $40, limited to 20 mares, for the season, usual return privileges. I would like to get about ten well bred mares with the proper combination of blood to breed to Whippleton on shares this season.

Alcona 730.

Sire of

FLORA BELLE	Record	2:24
CLAY DUKE	"	2:31½

ALCONA will be a great sire, but four of his colts have ever been trained, and all have shown full miles better than 2:30, and two of them as good as 2:20. Two of his first sons each sired a colt as a two-year-old, and last season one as a four-year-old trotted a full mile in 2:22¼, and the other, a three-year-old, a mile in 2:31. With opportunities, Alcona is destined to be one of Almont's best sons. Almont, for his opportunities, is beyond doubt the most prepotent sire of his age. He has 36 representatives in the 2:30 list; 49 sons and 21 daughters that have already produced 2:30 performers. Almont died five years ago at 20 years old. If he lived he would be but 25 years old.

PEDIGREE.

ALCONA sired by the great Almont (sire of Westmont 2:13¾, Fanny Witherspoon 2:17¼, Piedmont 2:17¼, and 34 others with records better than 2:30, and grandsire of Belle Hamlin 2:13¾, etc.); by Alexander's Abdallah (sire of Goldsmith Maid 2:14), he by Rysdyk's Hambletonian. Alcona's dam, Queen Mary, by Mambrino Chief (sire of Lady Thorne 2 18 1-4, and 5 others in the 2:30 list, and sire of the dams of Director 2:17, Piedmont 2:17¼, Onward 2:25 1-4, Red Wilkes, Almont, Belmont and many other noted sires).

DESCRIPTION.

Alcona is a beautiful chestnut 16 3 1-2 hands high, and weighs 1300 lbs. His colts possess speed, style, finish and beauty, and if they don't trot they command the highest prices for carriage horses.

$40 for the season. Usual return privilege.

Grandissimo,

Full Brother to GRANDEE, Three Year Old Record 2:23 1-2.

Sired by Le Grande [son of Almont and out of Jessie Pepper, by Mambrino Chief. Jessie Pepper is the dam of Ione 2:17 1-2, Alpha 2:23 1-2, and granddam of Montezuma 2:19¾. First dam Norma [dam of Grandee 2:23 1-2], by Arthurton [sire of Arab 2:15, Joe Arthurton 2:20 1-2, etc.]; second dam Nourmahal 2:39 [full sister to A. W. Richmond, sire of Arrow 2:13¾, Romero 2:19, and sire of the dams of Anteevolo 2:19 1-4, and Anteeo 2:16 1-4, sire of Alfred G 2:19¾; and Redwood 2 24 1-2.

GRANDISSIMO, with limited training as a three year old last year showed 1-4 mile in 37 seconds, and, barring accidents, will trot fast next fall.

Limited to 20 mares at $50 each; usual return privilege.

Season on Grandissimo ends June 1st, 1890.

Season on Whippleton and Alcona ends July 1st, 1890.

Best kind of pasturage at $4 per month. Mares kept in any manner desired.

For further particulars send for circular or call at stables, one mile south of St. Helena.

FRED W. LOEBER.
St. Helena, Napa Co., Cal.

WOODNUT

(Weatherhead's) by Nutwood 600

Sire of Belmont Boy, 2:15, pacer, Woodnut, 2:16¼, Felix, 2:18¾, Dawn, 2:18¾, Maggie E., 2 19¾, Irma, 2:18¾, and 26 others in 2 30 or better; 1st dam Flora, 2:39¾, trial 2 26, dam of Chrisman's Hambletonian, sire of Steve Whipple, 2:22, Kate Agnew, 2:28¼, by Chieftain 721, sire of Defiance 2:17¼ pacing and 2 24 trotting, Cairo, 2:26, Onward, 2:24, pacer; second dam by Wilson's Leaman.

Woodnut is a beautiful bay with black points, 15¾ hands high weighing 1,075 pounds. His colts are all larger than himself, and sell readily for road and carriage purposes, being of good color and very docile, yet prompt to obey, and always ready.

Service fee, $25, with usual privileges. Colts and fillies from Tilton Almont, Patchen, Stockbridge Chief, and other desirable crosses, FOR SALE. For further particulars, pedigrees, or any communication in horse matters, address

JAS. WEATHERHEAD, Prop.
San Jose, Cal.

GROVER CLAY.

Bay Stallion, Black Points, 15 3-4 hands high.

Bred by W. W. Traylor, San Francisco.

BY ELECTIONEER.

First dam Maggie Norfolk by Norfolk, son of Lexington, he by Boston. Second dam Tilda Quill by Billy Cheatham he by Cracken, and he by Boston. Third dam by Dorsey's Golddust.

TERMS.

Will make the season of 1890 at the Training Stables of Denis Gannon, near Oakland Trotting Park, at $50 the season, payable at time of service. Season to commence February 1st and ending July 1st. Proper care of mares will be taken, but no responsibility incurred for accidents or escapes. Address,

DENIS GANNON, Oakland, Cal.

Pacific Coast Trotting - Horse Breeders Ass'n

Stakes and Installment Purses for 1890.

Entries close March 1st, 1890.

STAKES.

YEARLINGS—FOALS 1889.

ONE MILE DASH, $50 entrance, payable $5 March 1, 1890, $10 May 1, 1890, $10 July 1, 1890 and $25 on the fifth day preceding the first advertised day of the meeting.

TWO-YEAR OLDS—FOALS 1888.

ONE MILE AND REPEAT; $75 entrance, $25 added, payable $10 on March 1, 1890, $10 May 1, 1890, $15 July 1, 1890, and $40 on the fifth day preceding the first advertised day of the meeting.

THREE-YEAR-OLDS—FOALS 1887.

MILE HEATS best three in five; entrance $100, with $200 added, payable $10 on March 1, 1890, $10 on May 1, 1890, $30 on July 1, 1890, and $50 on the fifth day preceding the first advertised day of the meeting.

FOUR-YEAR-OLDS—FOALS 1886.

MILE HEATS best three in five; $100 entrance, $100 added, payable $10 on March 1, 1890, $10 May 1, 1890, $30 on July 1, 1890, and $50 on the fifth day preceding the first day of the meeting.

PURSES.

$500. THREE YEAR OLDS. Foals of 1887. Eligible to 2:50 minute Class. Mile heats; three in five.

$500. FOUR YEAR OLDS. Foals of 1886, eligible to 2:40 Class. Mile heats; three in five.

Purses open to the get of Stallions with no Representatives in the 2:30 List.

$500. TWO YEAR OLDS. Foals of 1888. Mile and repeat.

$500. THREE YEAR OLDS. Foals of 1887. Mile heats; three in five.

$500. FOUR YEAR OLDS. Foals of 1886. Mile heats; three in five.

Stallion Purse $1,000.

Open to stallions eligible to 2:20 Class. Mile heats, three in five.

ENTRANCE—On all purses—10 per cent.; payable: 2 per cent. March 1st 1890; 2 per cent. May 1st, 1890; 2 per cent. July 1st, 1890; and 4 per cent. on the fifth day preceding the first advertised day of the meeting.

The Stanford Stakes for 1892.

FOALS OF 1889.

OPEN TO THE WORLD.

MILE HEATS.—Three in five. Entrance $100, with $100 added for each starter over two and up to five head, and $25 for each additional starter up to ten head. Payments: $10 on March 1st, 1890; $10 on January 2nd, 1891; $10 on January 2nd, 1892; $20 on May 1st 1892; and $50 on the fifth day preceding the first advertised day of the meeting at which the stake shall be trotted.

CONDITIONS.

First payment, whether for purses payable in installments or for stakes, MUST ACCOMPANY NOMINATIONS, or they will not be considered.

Neglect to provide payments on the dates stipulated will incur forfeiture of all previous payments.

No horses and Colts owned on the Pacific Coast by others than members of the P. C. T. H. B. A. are eligible to the above purses and stakes (excepting the Stanford stake), but horses and colts OWNED outside of the Pacific Coast are eligible thereto.

All States and Territories lying in whole or in part west of the Rocky Mountains are held to be part of the Pacific Coast.

The Directors reserve the right to change the hour and day of any race except when it becomes necessary to ante-date a race, in which instance the nominator will receive three days notice of change by mail to address of entry.

Entries not declared out by 6 P. M. of the day preceding the race, shall be required to start.

When there is more than one entry to a purse or stake by one person or in one interest, the horse to be started must be named by 6 P. M. of the day preceding the race.

Purses and stakes will be divided into four moneys, viz., 50 per cent. to the winner, 25 per cent. to the second horse, 15 per cent. to the third horse, and 10 per cent. to the fourth horse.

No added money will be paid for a walk-over. If only three horses start in a stake race, only first, second and third money shall be paid—if but two start, the Directors reserve the right to call it a walk-over, and divide the stake money paid in, two thirds to the winner and one-third to the second horse. In case of a walk-over, only the money received from entries to said stake will be paid. In purse races, three horses will be required to start.

A horse distancing the field shall only be entitled to first and third moneys.

The Board of Directors reserve the right to declare any purse or stake filled or not filled without binding itself to any specified number of entries.

Trotting and racing colors shall be named by six o'clock on the day preceding the race, and MUST be worn upon the track.

Otherwise than the above, National or American Trotting Association Rules—as this Association may select—will govern the stake and purse races offered.

Persons desirous of making entries in the above purses and stakes, and who have not as yet joined the P. C. T. H. B. A., should make application for membership to the Secretary, and remit the sum of $25 to cover membership fee before March 1, 1890.

THE PROGRAMME FOR

Aged Horses—Trotters and Pacers,

AND FOR SPECIAL EVENTS,

will be announced at the proper time.

J. H. WHITE, President.

JAS. P. KERR, Secretary,

313 Bush Street, S. F.

DISTRICT COLT STAKES

TO BE TROTTED FOR ON

Petaluma Track

Under the auspices of the

Sonoma and Marin District Agricultural Association.

1890.

STAKE FOR YEARLINGS.

Half mile and repeat for $30 each, $10 of which must be paid February 1st, 1890, to W. P. Fine, when the colt must be named and described, giving sire and dam. The second payment of $10 must be made on or before April 1st, 1890, and the third payment of $10 for starters must be paid on the evening before the race. One-third of the gate money to be added to this stake.

STAKE FOR TWO YEAR OLDS.

The stake for two year olds will be $50 each, $10 to be paid February 1st, 1890, when the colt must be named and described, giving sire and dam. The second payment of $10 must be made on or before April 1st, 1890; the third payment of $10, June 1st, 1890, and the fourth payment of $20 to be paid on the evening before the race. Mile heats, best two in three. One-third of the gate money added to this stake.

STAKE FOR THREE YEAR OLDS.

Capt. Harris' LORENA Barred.

The stake for three year olds will be $50 each and one third of the gate money. The terms payments and conditions will be the same as in the two-year old stake, except that the race will be mile heats three in five.

These races are to be trotted over the Petaluma track on the day and date indicated by a majority of the nominators in the stakes, at the time of making second payments, but all three are to be trotted on the same day, and not later than the first Saturday in August, 1890.

The stakes and added money will be divided as follows in each of the races—

To the first colt sixty per cent., to the second colt twenty-five per cent., to the third colt fifteen per cent.

Entries close positively February 1st, 1890, and all parties failing to make subsequent payment; forfeit amounts already paid. Address all communications to

W. P. FINE,

Lessee Agricultural Park, Petaluma.

SAN JOSE Yearling Colt Stakes

Foals of 1889.

The get of the following stallions: Jim L, Argent Eros, Bismarck, J. Wetherbead's horses (3), Guy Davis, Nutwood Boy, Orion, King William, Tommy T., Stranger, John Sevenicks, Col. Benton, Wilmington, Dick Patchen, Baywood, Fleetwood, Sultan Jr., Billy Thornhill, Simpson, Magic, Chancellor, Monte Christo, Hambletonian, Boxwood, Nut Cove, Prince Albert, Alex Graham, Designer, Cyrus R., Harry Almont, Hea's Nutwood Boodle, Parnell, Robin Adair, Fred Grant, Elect, Mambrino Jr., California Nutwood, Soudan, Jim Mulvenna, Brown Jug, Menlo Almont Patchen, Antinous, Electric Light, May Boy, C. W. S. Henderson's Henry, S. B. Emerson, Carr's Mambrino, Designer, Prince Warwick, Henry Burr, J. Dunn's horses (3).

Each owner of the above named stallions must deposit $10 each on or before February 1, 1890, otherwise their colts will not be eligible to enter.

The colts from the horses that make the deposit must pay $15 on March 1, 1890, $15 on June 1, 1890; and $30 on August 1, 1890; $250 added by the Society.

The conditions are as follows: To be trotted during fair week of 1890, one-half mile heats.

Stake deposit and added money divided; 60 per cent. to first, 30 per cent. to second and 10 per cent. to third.

National Association rules to govern except as herein stated.

For a walk-over the colt will take the whole stake, but no added money.

If two colts start they must contest for the deposit and stake money only, divided two-thirds and one-third.

A colt distancing the field will take the whole stake, but no added money.

Declarations are void unless accompanied by the money.

Nominations not making payments when due forfeit previous payments.

All colts properly entered in this stake if sold will be entitled to start. If it is the opinion of the judges before starting this race that it cannot be finished on the closing day of the Fair it may be continued.

Entries for the stallions close February 1st. Entries for the colts close March 1st.

G. H. BRAGG, Secretary,

San Jose, California.

By-Laws

—AND—

Rules and Regulations

—OF THE—

NATIONAL

Trotting Association

ALSO THE

AMERICAN

Trotting Association,

AND THE

PACIFIC COAST BLOOD-HORSE ASSOCIATION.

With Betting Rules.

For Sale at the Office of the

Breeder and Sportsman,

313 Bush St., S. F., Cal.

Price, 25c. each.

By Mail, Postage Paid, 30c. each.

The State Agricultural Society

Spring Meeting 1890.

(The week following the P. C. B. H. A.)

The Chris. Green Handicap

The Spring Stakes

To Close FEBRUARY 1st, 1890.

THE CHRIS. GREEN HANDICAP.

A Sweepstakes for all ages, of $50 each, h f, or $10 if declared, with $300 added; second horse to receive $100 out of stakes. Weights announced March 1st. Declarations due by 4 P. M. April 1st. A winner of any race after publication of weights, of one mile or upwards, to carry 3 lbs; of two races, 5 lbs; of three or more, 7 lbs. extra. This will not apply to horses handicapped at 125 lbs. or over. One and one quarter miles.

THE SPRING STAKES.

A Sweepstakes for three year olds (foals of 1887) that have not won a race previous to January 1st, 1890; $50 entrance, h f, or $15 if declared April 1st, 1890; $400 added, second to receive $75 from stakes. Maidens at time of starting allowed 5 lbs. One mile.

The general conditions of the race meeting as to postponements and track discipline will apply to these stakes.

All declarations are void unless accompanied by the money.

CHRIS. GREEN, President.

EDWIN F. SMITH, Secretary.

1890.

Petaluma Colt Stakes

TO BE TROTTED AT THE

Fall Meeting

OF THE

Sonoma and Marin Agricultural Society

District No. 4.

FREE-FOR-ALL COLTS.

1st. For two-year-olds, foals of 1888, Purse $400, entrance 10 per cent. of the purse, of which 2½ per cent. must accompany the nomination, to be made on March 1st; 2½ per cent., be paid on May 1st, and 5 per cent. on August 1st. Four colts to make the last payment, and three to start.

2nd. For three-year-olds, foals of 1887. Purse $500, entrance ten per cent of the purse, of which 2½ per cent. must accompany the nomination to be made on March 1st, 2½ per cent to be paid on May 1st, and 5 per cent. on August 1st. Four colts to make the last payment, and three to start.

All moneys in the above races to be divided as follows: 60 per cent. to the first horse, 30 per cent. to the second, and 10 per cent. to the third.

Balance of Conditions as per District Stakes.

The following Stakes and Purses open to the Counties of Sonoma, Marin, Napa, Solano, Lake, Mendocino, Yolo and Colusa.

YEARLING STAKE.

For foals of 1889. Mile dash. $30 entrance, of which $10 must accompany the nomination March 1st; $10 be paid on May 1st and $10 on July 1st; $100 added.

TWO-YEAR-OLD STAKE.

For foals of 1888. Mile and repeat. $60 entrance, of which $10 must accompany the nomination March 1st; $30 be paid on May 1st and $20 on July 1st; $200 added.

THREE-YEAR-OLD PURSE.

Three in five. Purse $300. Entrance fee 10 per cent. of the purse of which five per cent. must accompany the nomination March 1st, and five per cent. paid on August 1st. Four colts to make the last payment.

In the above stakes and purses, five to enter and three to start. But the Board reserves the right to hold entries, and start a race with a less number.

All moneys in the above races to be divided as follows: 60 per cent. to the first horse, 30 per cent. to the second and 10 per cent. to the third. If only two start they must contest for the stakes paid in, and one-half the added money to be divided, 66⅔ per cent. to the first and 33⅓ per cent. to the second.

If, in the opinion of the judges, any race cannot be finished on the closing day of the fair it may be continued or declared off at the option of the judges.

Entries to all the above races to close on March 1, 1889, with the Secretary.

J. H. WHITE, President.

DR. THOS. MACLAY, Secretary.

FOR SALE

AT

Vineland Stock Farm

STALLIONS, BROODMARES AND FILLIES

ONE STALLION FIVE YEARS OLD, SEAL-BROWN, by WHIPPLETON (sire of Lilly Stanley, 2:17 1-2 Homestakes 2:16 1-2, etc.), dam Sally Gorham by Werner's Rattler. This horse is scarcely 15 1-2 hands high, but very compactly built. He breeds exceptionally large and well finished colts. Any one understanding the business could clear him in one season, or he would make a No. 1 road horse, as he can trot a 40 gait any time.

ONE THREE-YEAR-OLD, SEAL-BROWN, by WHIPPLETON (sire of Lilly Stanley, 2:17 1-2, Homestakes 2:16 1-2, etc.), dam Sally Gorham, etc. This ought to make a great General Purpose sire, and with opportunities get trotters, as he is compact, strong-boned, and will measure when grown about 16 hands and weighs 1,300 lbs. With a little road work last fall he developed a wonderful burst of speed.

ONE THREE-YEAR-OLD, BLACK, by WHIPPLETON (sire of Lilly Stanley, 2:17 1-2, etc.), dam by Naubuc (sire of the dam of Eva W., 2:23 1-2, etc.), full brother to Thomas Jefferson, 2:23. This horse will be fully 16 1-2 hands high. He is smooth, rapid gaited and from size and conformation should breed, like his sire, large, rangy, finished colts.

ONE TWO-YEAR-OLD, BRIGHT CHESTNUT, sired by DAWN 2:18¾, dam Alida (dam of Directa, three-year-old record 2:21¼, trial 2:26) by Admiral (sire of sister 2:10 1-2, Nona Y 2:25, etc). This colt is the making of an extraordinary horse. He is large boned and will be over sixteen hands high when grown; he is of the true Nutwood type, is clean gaited and could ad a piece as fast as any man's colt.

ONE TWO-YEAR-OLD, BLOOD BAY, (full brother to Alcona Jr. sire of Silas Skinner trial 2:23) sired by ALCONA (sire of Flora Belle 2:24, etc.,) dam Madonna by Cassius M. Clay Jr. This colt will make a trotter and a great stock horse if developed; he has the combined blood of Almont, Mambrino Chief, Cassius M. Clay Jr. and Joe Downing.

These colts are all sound and promising. The only reason I offer them for sale is, that I have three aged stallions in use, and the surplus is growing on me. If I were starting a breeding business for profit, I should consider either of these colts a representative to commence with. Also brood mares and fillies for sale. Correspondence solicited.

FRED. W. LOEBER, St. Helena,

Napa Co., Cal.

Draught Horse Breeders,

Attention!

JUST ARRIVED: A Number of Fine Young Pure-bred

CLYDESDALE STALLIONS,

Imported from Scotland and registered in the Clydesdale Stud Book. Among them are:

BOGWOOD (5561), Vol X, C. S. B.
BELTED CRUISER (6481), Vol. XI, C. S. B.
CANNY JAMIE (6574), Vol XI, C. S. B.

They are of good dark colors with the Regular Clydesdale Markings, and are the finest Horses that have ever been imported to this State. They are the property of A. V. WILSON, Esq., North Yakima, W. T., and will be sold for a reasonable figure. They may be seen at the Mt. Eden Farm. For pedigrees and particulars, call on or address, A. V. WILSON, North Yakima, W. T., or H. P. MOHR, Mount Eden, Alameda Co., Cal.

Langtry Farms' Stud

Imp. FRIAR TUCK

By the Immortal HERMIT

DAM ROMPING GIRL BY WILD DAYRELL,

AT $50 THE SEASON:

Mares not proving with foal may be returned the following season. Good care taken of mares, but no liabilities for accidents or escapes.

Good Pastorage at $5 per month.

Mares shipped to ST. HELENA, care CHARTES WILLIAM ABY, St. Helena Stables, will be cared for. For further particulars address,

CHAS. WILLIAM ABY,
Middletown, Lake County, Cal.

2:08 3-4 2:10 2:12

MAMBRINO WILKES, 6083.

SIRE OF

GUS WILKES, 2:22; ALPHEUS, 2:27; CLARA P, 2:29½; BALKAN, 2:29½ (3-year-old) and timed separately 2:22½ in 4-year-old Stake, Bay District Track, October 14, 1889.

DESCRIPTION.

Black; sixteen hands; weighs, in exercise, 1,260 lbs. For style, finish, symmetry and proportion, comparison is challenged with any trotting bred horse. His colts follow in size, style and beauty. Balkan, for instance, being "facile princeps" of trotters in these particulars.

PEDIGREE.

Sired by Geo. Wilkes, sire of Harry Wilkes, 2:13¼, Guy Wilkes, 2:15¼, and 60 other trotters in the 2:30 list, in addition to 8 pacers, and of the sire of Axtell, 2:12 (three-year-old), beating all stallions of any age, and the sire of Regal Wilkes, 2:20½, best two-year-old stallion record.

First dam Lady Chrisman by Mambrino (Todhunter's), son of Mambrino Chief 11; sire of Lady Thorn, 2:18¼; Woodford Mambrino, 2:21½, and four others in 2:30, and of the dams of Director, 2:17, Piedmont, 2:17¼, Onward, 2:25¼, etc.

Second dam by Pilot Jr. 12, sire of nine in the 2:30 list, and of the dams of Maud S., 2:08¾, Jay-Eye-See, 2:10, Nutwood, 2:18¾, Viking, 2:19¾, Pilot Boy, 2:20, Naiad Queen 2:20¾, etc.

TERMS.

Mares from a distance will be received at the Dexter Stables, Oakland, or Livery Stable, Martinez, the owner notifying Smith Hill, Superintendent at the farm. Good pasture and plenty of water. For the purpose of placing the service of a Wilkes within reach of breeders, the same rate will be maintained as last year, to wit, $75 for the season. Although it is not admitted thereby that this horse is inferior as a producer to the horses whose fees are placed at from $150 to $500. Address

SMITH HILL,
San Miguel Stock Farm,
Walnut Creek, Contra Costa Co., Cal.

2:12¾ 2:13½ 2:15¼

Thoroughbred Stallion

Prince of Norfolk.

Will Make the Season of 1890, from Feb 1st to July 1st, at Sacramento.

Prince of Norfolk, chestnut horse, foaled 1881, by Norfolk; first dam Marion by Malcolm; second dam Maggie Mitchell by imp. Yorkshire; third dam Charmer by imp. Glencoe; fourth dam Betsy Malone by Stockholder; fifth dam by Potomac, sixth dam by imp. Diomed; seventh dam by Pegasus, etc. Norfolk, the unbeaten son of Lexington, is the sire of Winters, Twilight, Connor, Ballot Box, Trade Dollar, Flood, Duchess of Norfolk, Lou Spencer, the Great Emperor of Norfolk, the unbeaten El Rio Rey, and many others. Marion's sire, Malcolm, was one of the first horses to bring Bonnie Scotland into notice. Through the Maggie Mitchell cross comes the blood of two of the most celebrated race-mares of their day, Charmer and Betsy Malone. The combined speed of these great families seem to be concentrated in the get of Norfolk and Marion, as is instanced in the case of the Emperor of Norfolk, and El Rio Rey, who are full brothers to the Prince of Norfolk.

The blood lines here displayed cannot be surpassed in the world, there not being a single cross that has not been celebrated for speed and endurance, and it is fair to assume that the get of this stallion will show equally well with those of past generations.

TERMS: $50 for the season. We offer first-class pasturage on our own ranch, at $2 per month, and the best of care will be taken of mares sent to us, but no responsibility can be incurred. For further particulars, address by mail or wire,

DAN DENNISON.
or, W. P. TODHUNTER, Sacramento.

[J]ROME HARRIS. JOHN MERIGAN,

"Laurel Palace,"

[N.] W. corner Kearny and Bush Streets

2:19 NOONDAY 2:20½

STANDARD No. 10,000.

This celebrated trotting bred stallion will make the season of 1890 at the stable of the undersigned at Sacramento, Cal., at $75 for the season and $5.00 to insure a mare in foal. Payable on or before July 1st, 1890. Money will be refunded on mares bred by insurance as soon as the fact becomes known that they are not in foal.

NOONDAY.
- Wedgewood, 2:19. Sire of Favonia, 2:15, fastest 4th heat for any mare or gelding, and eight others in 2:27 or better.
  - Belmont. Sire of Wedgewood, 2:19, Nutwood, 2:18¾, Viking, 2:19½, and 29 others in 2:30 list.
    - Alexander's Abdallah, sire of Goldsmith Maid, 2:14; Almont, with 36 horses in 2:30 list, etc.
    - Belle, dam of Hambletonian, 2:26½; B'cara, dam of Pancoast, 2:21¾, the sire of Patron, 2:14¼.
  - Woodbine. Dam of Wedgewood, 2:19, Woodford Mamb., 2:21½, the sire of Pancoast, 2:21¾, the sire of Patron, 2:14¼.
    - Woodford.
    - Singleton Mare.
- Noontide, 2:20½. (Trial, 2:13¾).
  - Harold. Sire of Maud S., 2:08¾, and 26 others in 2:30 list.
    - Hambletonian (Rysdyk's), sire of George Wilkes, 2:22, the sire of Guy Wilkes, 2:15¼; Electioneer, the sire of Sunol, 2:10½, and scores of noted trotters and producers.
    - Enchantress, by Abdallah 1.
  - Midnight. Dam of Jay-Eye-See, 2:10, Noontide, 2:20½.
    - Pilot Jr., sire of dams of Maud S., 2:08¾, Jay-Eye-See, 2:10, Nutwood, 2:18¾, etc.
    - Twilight, by Lexington, sire of the dam of Ansel, 2:20.

NOODAY is a dark seal brown, foaled 1884, 15 hands 1½ inches high. Individually he is equal to his royal breeding. He is all that can be desired in conformation, intelligence, color and trotting action, and no stallion now in public service can show a pedigree with such fast records and royal game trotting blood as Noonday.

DON MARVIN,

Record 2:28 as a five-year-old. Standard by Breeding and Performance

Standard No. 7927.

Don Marvin 2:28.

Don Marvin is a beautiful seal brown, foaled 1884, bred by Hon. Leland Stanford, Palo Alto, Cal., standing 16 hands, and weighs, in ordinary condition, 1200 lbs. He is a fine individual, good style and form, combined with great substance, and good temper. Is very level headed; in his first race the past season he only made one break in five closely contested heats. He has great speed and endurance, with the pure, rapid Electioneer gait. He trots without toe weights, and wears only 8 oz. shoes in front. He gained his record the past season in the third heat, on a slow track, after making a season (serving over 30 mares), with scarcely any preparation. His record is no mark of his speed. He was a natural born trotter, and Mr. Charles Marvin considered him the fastest two year old at Palo Alto that season.

By FALLIS, 2:23, - - by Electioneer, sire of
Sire of Don Marvin, 2:28. — Sunol, three-year-old, 2:10 1-2, Palo Alto, 2:12¾, and 47 others in 2:30 list.

Dam CORA, by Don Victor by Belmont, sire of
Dam of Don Marvin, 2:28. — Ventura, 2:27¼, and sire of the dam of Bell Echo, 2:20, and six others in 2:30 list.

2d dam CLARABEL, - by Abdallah Star,
Dam of Clifton Bell, 2:24 1-2, and grandam of Rexford, three years, 2:24. — Sire of Hattie Maples, 2:38.

3d dam FAIRY, - - by Rysdyk's Hambletonian,
Sister of Sweepstakes, sire of 16 in 2:30 list. — Sire of Electioneer, George Wilkes, and many other noted sires and trotters.

4th dam EMMA MILLS, by Seely's American Star,
Dam of 4 horses that have 2:30 performers. — The great broodmare sire of the world.

The above pedigree should show every intelligent breeder that Don Marvin is "high" bred though very strong in trotting blood. All the comment it is deemed necessary to make as to the value of "thoroughbred blood" in the trotter is simply to refer to the very significant fact that the first and second dams of Maud S. 2:08¾, Jay-Eye-See 2:10, Sunol, three years 2:10 1-2, Palo Alto 2:12¾, Antevo 2:16¾, Nutwood 2:18¾, Wedgewood 2:19, and many other successful sires and sensational trotters of the day are thoroughbred.

TERMS—Don Marvin will make the ensuing season from February 1st to July 1st, 1890, at $40 the season, with the usual privilege of returning the mare next season if not proving in foal. Mares from a distance met at the cars or boats on notification, and carefully handled, but no responsibility assumed for accidents or escapes.

Good alfalfa pasture furnished (free from barb wire fence) at $4 per month. For further particulars or complete circulars address

F. P. LOWELL,
1520 F Street, Sacramento, Cal.

The Thoroughbred Stallion

INTRUDER

Will make the Season of 1890 at Agricultural Park, SACRAMENTO.

Bay Horse, foaled 1871, bred by Sir L. Newman, England. Imported by D. D. Withers, Esq., New York.

By Crater, Son of Orlando and Vesuvienne by Gladiator.

1st dam Lady Bountiful by Rataplan (Rataplan is own brother to Stockwell, and winner of 42 races, including the Doncaster Cup and 19 Queen's Plates, and proved himself the most distinguished race horse of his day in England).

2d dam Plentiful by Don John (the winner of St. Leger and Doncaster Cup).

3d dam Plenty by Bay Middleton (winner of the Derby and Two Thousand Guinea Stakes).

4th dam Plenary, own sister of Plenipotentiary, by Emilius. (Both Emilius and Plenipotentiary were Derby winners).

5th dam Harriet, dam of the renowned Plenipotentiary by Pericles.

6th dam by Selim, winner of the One Thousand Guinea Stakes.

7th dam by Pypilina, by Sir Peter.

8th dam Rally, by Trumpeter.

9th dam Fancy, by Florizel. Fancy was full sister to Diomed, the first Derby winner in England, and after his importation into this country, sired the illustrious Sir Archy, etc. See English Stud Book.

Imported INTRUDER is a beautiful bay, standing fully 16 hands high, of great length and substance, and descends through close and strong currents from the most illustrious winners and winning lines of blood of which the English Stud Book bears record.

A careful review of the first six crosses of the pedigree of INTRUDER will show nine Derby winners; five St. Leger winners; two winners of The Oaks; two winners of the Two Thousand Guineas; two winners of the One Thousand Guineas; one Goodwood Cup winner; one Cesarwich Cup winner; one Cambridgeshire stakes winner, and four Doncaster Cups, in addition to a great number of Steeplechases and other races of less import.

INTRUDER, at the great fair held at St. Louis, Mo., in 1876, was awarded the highest stallion honors—the blue ribbon and the $500 purse—in the sweepstakes ring for stallion of any age or blood. The list of competitors embraced the large number of thirty-three animals, and they represented England, Canada, Kentucky, Tennessee, and other states. He also took first premium in his class and in sweepstakes for the best stallion of any age or breed at the state Fair at Peoria, Ill., 1881. He is the sire of Tidal Wave, George Hakes, Bonnie and April Fool.

INTRUDER is the sire of Interpose, who is the dam of Spokane, winner of the Kentucky Derby, in which he beat the great horse Proctor Knott and broke the record.

TERMS: $50 for the season. Mares not proving with foal can be returned the next season free of charge. Good pasturage at $4 per month. Mares cared for in any manner owners may desire, and fed on hay and grain, either or both, at reasonable rates. While every precaution will be taken, no responsibility will be assumed for escapes or accidents. Mares sent from a distance in care of the undersigned, will be met and taken to the park. For further particulars, address

T. J. KNIGHT.
Agricultural Park, Sacramento.

CANNON BALL, 8820

BY SIMMONS 2744.

RECORD 2:28, (Full Brother to Rosa Wilkes, 2:18 1-4), Sire of Nine in 2:30 List at 10 Years Old.

First dam Guigle, pacing record 2:20; trial of 2:15¼ for W. H. Crawford; by Pocahontas Boy, sire of Buffalo Girl, 2:12¼; Raven Boy, 2:15¼, and ten others in the list.

Second dam Matlock by Grey Diomed.

Third dam by Tom Hal.

DESCRIPTION.

Brown bay, right hind foot and left inside hind heel white. Foaled May 20, 1887. Bred by W. H. Wilson, Abdallah Park, Cynthiana, Ky.

He is a grand individual, large boned, fine size and appearance. When fully matured will probably be 16 hands, and weigh 1200 lbs.

Is of speedy conformation and level headed. His blood lines are stout and fashionable, being the Wilkes and Mambrino Patchen on pacing and thoroughbred foundations, and from a family of producers on both sides.

Can be seen until February 1st at Agricultural Park, Los Angeles, in charge of C. A. Durfee, after which he will serve ten approved mares at $60 the season, with usual privilege of return in 1891, at Lockhaven Stock Farm, Burbank, Cal. Mares kept on grass $3 per month, and extra charge where grain and alfalfa are fed. For further particulars, address

O. H. LOCKHART, Proprietor,
Lockhaven Stock Farm,
Burbank, Cal.

Nine Miles from Los Angeles.

NOTICE.

C. BRUCE LOWE,
Pedigree Stock Agent,
19 Bligh Street,
SYDNEY, New South Wales.

Reference—J. B. HAGGIN, ESQ.

POPLAR GROVE

Breeding Farm

STALLIONS.

CLOVIS, 4909,

CLOVIS is a beautiful black, Eight Years Old, 16 1-2 Hands High, and weighs 1260 lbs.

He is a horse of beautiful symmetry and magnificent action.

PEDIGREE.

CLOVIS was sired by Sultan, 2:24, sire of Stamboul, 2:12 1-4, Ruby, 2:19¾, and fifteen others with records of 2.30 or better.

First dam Sweetbriar by Thorndale 2:22 1-2, sire of Edwin Thorne, 2:16 1-2, Daisy Dale, 2:19, and May Thorne, 2:24.

Second dam Ulster Queen, dam of Volmer, 2:24¾, by Hambletonian 10, sire of Dexter, 2:17¼, George Wilkes, 2:22.

Third dam by Thomas Jefferson, a son of Mambrino Paymaster, Jr.

Fourth dam by Mambrino Paymaster, sire of Mambrino Chief.

Sultan, by The Moor, sire of Beautiful Bells, dam of Hinda Rose, 2:19 1-2, and Sable, dam of Sable Wilkes, three year old record 2:18.

First dam of Sultan, Sultana, by Delmonico, sire of Darby, 2:16 1-2, by Guy Miller, sire of Whipple's Hambletonian.

Second dam by Mambrino Chief.

Third dam by Downing's Bay Messenger.

Fourth dam Mrs. Caudle, dam of Ericsson, four year old record 2.30 1-2.

Clovis will make the season of 1890 at Poplar Grove Breeding Farm, near Wildflower, Fresno County, commencing February 1st and ending July 1st.

Terms, $75, due at time of service.

Mares cared for in any manner owners may desire; pasturage $2 per month. Every care exercised, but no liability for escapes or accidents. Mares not proving with foal can be returned next season, providing I still own this stallion.

APEX, 8935.

FOUR-YEAR-OLD RECORD, FOURTH HEAT, 2:26.

Will make the present season at the Poplar Grove Breeding Farm, near Wildflower, Fresno Co., season commencing Feb. 1st, and ending July 1, 1890. Terms, $50 the season, due at time of service. Apex is eight years old, a beautiful bay, 15 1-2 hands high, and weighs 1140 lbs. He is a horse of fine disposition, and his gait is faultless.

PEDIGREE.

Apex was sired by Promptor 2305, he by Blue Bull 75; first dam Mary by Flaxtail, he by Pruden's Blue Bull. Flaxtail being the sire of the dams of Buccaneer, five-year-old record, 2:24 1-2; Pride, yearling record, 2:44 1-2, and Shamrock, two-year old record, 2:25, third heat. Second dam by Bright Eyes, son of Boanarges. Prompter (sire of Apex, record 2:26, and Transit, 2:26 1-2), by Wilson's Blue Bull, by Pruden's Blue Bull son of Merring's Blue Bull. Promptor's dam Prairie Bird, by Flaxtail; second dam by John the Baptist, son of Tally Ho Morgan, by Sherman Morgan; third dam Fannie Fern by Irwin's Tuckaho.

Apex made his appearance in the circuit as a two-year-old, and obtained a record of 2:42. As a three-year-old he reduced this in a race at Santa Rosa against Stamboul to 2:31, it taking six heats to decide the contest, which was won by Apex. As a four year-old he gained his present record of 2:26.

Mares cared for in any manner owners may desire. Pasturage $2 per month. Every care exercised, but no liabilities for escapes or accidents. Mares not proving with foal can be returned next season, providing I still own this stallion.

The Standard Stallion

JUNIO,

RECORD 2:22.

WILL MAKE THE PRESENT SEASON OF 1890 AT FRESNO FAIR GROUNDS.

Season Commencing Feb. 1st and ending July 1st

TERMS—$100 the season, due at time of service.

JUNIO is eight years old, a handsome dark bay 16 hands high, and weighs 1250 pounds. He is the personification of the light harness horse, and his trotting action is superb. At the State Fair of 1888 he took first premium over forty of the finest trotters in the State.

PEDIGREE.

Junio, by Electioneer, premier stallion of Palo Alto (sire of Sunol 2:10 1-2, Palo Alto 2:12 1-4, and 47 others in the 2:30 list). Dam by Granger by imp. Hercules.

Granger, by imp. Hercules, dam Jenny Lind, by Stockbridge Chief, Jr., he by Stockbridge Chief, he by Vermont Black Hawk. Second dam by Kentucky Whip.

Imp. Hercules, by Kingston, first dam daughter of Tuscar, by Bay Middleton, second dam Malvina, by Oscar; 3rd dam Spotless by Walton; 4th dam by Trumpator (see Bruce's American Stud Book, Vol. 1, page 28). Hercules is the sire of the dam of Anteeo 2:16¾; also of dam of Menlo 2:21 1-2.

Mares not proving in foal may be returned next year free of charge, providing I still have the horse. Pasturage $2 per month. While every care will be taken of horses, no liability will be assumed for accidents or escapes.

For further particulars address

S. N. STRAUBE, Fresno, Cal.

Poplar Grove Breeding Farm.

CHICAGO, ILLS. -:- BREEDERS' SALE.

SECOND GRAND COMBINATION SALE OF

KIDD, EDMONSON & MORSE,

Will be held in Chicago, Ill., MARCH 17th to 23d, 1890.

Trotters, Pacers, Stallions, Brood Mares, Colts, Saddle and Harness Horses.

Those wishing to dispose of their stock to the best advantage should send for conditions and entry blanks at once, as the sale promises to be very large.

Entries to close February 20, 1890. Send in your entries at once.

Our first sale was a grand success, and was only a foreshadowing of what is to follow. Address,

KIDD, EDMONSON & MORSE, Lexington, Ky.

Or No. 806 West Madison St., Chicago, Ill.

THE BRUNSWICK BALKE COLLENDER COMPANY,

MANUFACTURERS OF

Standard Billiard and Pool Tables, Saloon and Bank Fixtures,

653--655 Market Street, San Francisco, Cal.

2:20 1-2 (Half Mile Track) at 4 Years. Fastest Record (in a Race) of any Wilkes 2:14 1-2 at 5 Years.

ROY WILKES, $2{:}12\frac{3}{4}$,

Seal brown; 15¾ hands; foaled 1882; by Adrian Wilkes 6560, son of Geo. Wilkes; 1st dam by Blue Bull 75; 2d dam by grandson of American Eclipse; 3d and 4th dams thoroughbred.

THE GREATEST CAMPAIGNER OF 1889.

Handsome, Game, Pure Gaited. Level Headed.

Will make a season at the PLEASANTON STOCK FARM, PLEASANTON, CAL. Service Fee $150, with return privilege. Season ends April 1st., 1890.

For full record of performances, extended pedigree, etc., address

L. A. DAVIES, Hotel Pleasanton,

SUTTER AND JONES STREETS, San Francisco, Cal.

The Trotting Stallion

G & M

FULL BROTHER TO

ALFRED G, $2{:}19\frac{3}{4}$.

(Who has been taken to Kentucky to stand at $500)

Will make the season of 1890 from FEBRUARY 1st to JULY 1st, at

SANTA ROSA.

G. & M. is by Anteeo, 2:16¼; was foaled 1886; first dam Rosa B. by Speculation (son of Hambletonian 10); 2d dam Elizabeth by Alexander 490; 3d dam Nora by imp. Glencoe. Anteeo is by Electioneer, out of Columbine by A. W. Richmond 1687.

G. & M. is a handsome dark bay; stands 15.2 1.2 hands high, and weighs 1061 pounds. Gameness, stoutness, speed and stamina are indelibly impressed in every line of the pedigree of G. & M. Owners of broodmares in search of these qualities, will do well to patronize this promising colt.

PHILOSOPHER,

Foaled 1886 by Pilot Wilkes 2087; first dam Bella by George Wilkes 519; second dam by Bell Morgan 61.

Philosopher's sire, Pilot Wilkes 2087, is by George Wilkes 519, dam Grace (the dam of Alice Woodburn, etc.), by Pilot Jr. 12, grandam by Orphan Boy.

Will make the season of 1890, from FEBRUARY 1st to JULY 1st, at Santa Rosa.

TERMS for the season:

G. & M., $50,

PHILOSOPHER, $30,

with privilege of returning mares that do not prove in foal the next season free of charge, provided the horse bred to remains the property of the present owners. Good pasturage at $3 per month. No responsibility assumed for accidents or escapes. Service fees payable before removal of the mare. For further particulars, address

GEO. E. GUERNE,

Santa Rosa Cal.

ST. NICHOLAS.

A Son of the World Renowned

SIDNEY,

Will Make the Season of 1890, at the Oakland Trotting Park.

ST. NICHOLAS was bred by Mr. G. Valensin at the Arno Stock Farm, Sacramento Co., California, in 1885. He is a beautifully proportioned bright bay horse, 15.3 hands high; is well muscled, lengthy, and lots of bone, with splendid natural action and a phenomenal turn of speed. As a three-year-old he easily worked three heats on the Oakland Track in 2:32, 2:29 and 2:27¾. His breeding is just what one would expect from such a highly formed bloodlike horse. Sidney, his sire is the most successful young stallion—whether for getting pacers or trotters—America has ever seen, and no wonder for his blood lines are exceptional fine and are all trotting lines, Santa Claus, Strathmore, Rysdyk's Hambletonian and Abdallah, while Sweetness again runs back through that great sire Volunteer, to Rysdyk's Hambletonian and also through her dam to Rysdyk's Hambletonian and Harry Clay 45, the sire of Electioneer's dam. St. Nicholas' dam is by Echo, an exceptionally prepotent son of Hambletonian thus giving St. Nicholas four Rysdyk's Hambletonian crosses and further back a Harry Clay cross which with his grand dam's thoroughbred cross should make him invaluable in the stud.

TERMS: Fifty dollars the season, which will commence on the 5th of February and close on the 1st of July. Due care will be taken of mares, but no responsibility for accidents or escapes.

Mares taken and kept as desired by the owners, and at reasonable rates.

JOHN ROWEN.

Oakland Trotting Park.

The Fast Trotting Stallion

REDWOOD.

Four-Year-Old Record 2:24 1-2

Will make the season of 1890—February 1st to July 1st—at the

OAKLAND RACE TRACK.

REDWOOD is a dark bay colt, 15.2½ hands high, weighs 1100 lbs. Foaled in 1885, by Anteeo, 2:16¼, sire of Alfred G., 2:19¾. Anteeo is by Electioneer. First dam Lou Milton, by Milton Medium; second dam Old Fly, a thoroughbred mare brought from the East in 1871 by W. C. Ralston, Esq.

Redwood's sire was out of Columbine by A. W. Richmond, the sire of the pacers Arrow 2:13¼, and Elwood 2:21, and the trotters Romero, 2:19½, and Len Rose, 2:2'. Redwood has shown a quarter in 33 seconds.

Terms $100

For the season. Mares not proving with foal may be returned next season free of charge, provided Redwood remains the property of the present owners. Good pasturage at $5 per month. No responsibility assumed for escapes or accidents. Service fees payable before removal of the mare. Limited to 40 approved mares. For further particulars address

A. McFAYDEN.

Race track. Oakland, Cal.

$2{:}08\frac{3}{4}$ 2:10 2:12

BALKAN

By Mambrino Wilkes.

(See that Horse's Advertisement.)

DAM FANNY FERN BY JACK HAWKINS

Son of Boston.

The grandam of Maud S, (2:08¾) was by Boston and the grandam of Jay-Eye-See (2:10) was by Lexington, son of Boston. So Balkan is the same remove from Boston that Maud is, and one remove nearer than Jay-Eye-See.

Fanny Fern has produced Molly Drew, Onyx, Fred Arnold, Molly Fern and Balkan, all by different sires.

Balkan's sire and dam both being producers, and he being a trotter himself with a record of 2:29 1-2 (three-year-old) and timed separately 2:22 1-4 in 4-year-old Stake, Bay District Track, October 14, 1889—it is but fair to presume that he will get trotters of the highest order.

DESCRIPTION.

He is seal brown, 16-1 hands high, in style rivalled by few, and excelled by none with as pure a gait as has yet been exhibited in public—bar none.

Balkan will be at Oakland Trotting Park for the season of 1890, and will be limited to ten mares, at $100 fee, in order to be put in training early, as it is morally certain that if given a reasonable opportunity he will be fast enough to compete with the best of his age. For further particulars address

A. L. HINDS,

Dexter Stables, Oakland.

$2{:}12\frac{3}{4}$ $2{:}13\frac{1}{2}$ $2{:}15\frac{1}{4}$

THE BUCKINGHAM.

OLD STRAIGHT WHISKIES.

141 Montgomery Street.

303 Bush Street, S. F.

M. J. BALFE, Proprietor.

"TOBEY'S,"

214 Post Street,

Between Grant Avenue and Stockton Street,

Adjoining New Hamman Baths.

D. J. TOBIN, Proprietor.

Pleasanton Stock Farm Co.'s Stallions,

DIRECTOR, 2:17.

Director's book is open for 15 good mares more than already booked for the season of 1890, at $300 each.

This is the cheapest service fee ever charged for a stallion, taking into consideration his BREEDING and RACE RECORD and the RACE RECORDS OF HIS COLTS.

Season to commence February 15th and close August 1st.

PLEASANTON.

Sire Director 2:17. Dam May Day 2:30.

PLEASANTON is a light bay, 16 hands high, and is full brother to Margaret S, three year old record 2:19½.

His book is now open for 10 good mares at $100 for the season, which will commence March 1st and end June 1st.

Mares not proving with foal may be returned next season free of charge of service fees to the same stallion, if he is still in our possession; if not, to some other stallion equally as good, or money will be refunded at option of the company.

Pasturage $4 per month; hay and grain extra. Accidents and escapes at owner's risk.

Service fees due at time of service, and must be paid, together with pasturage, etc., before mares are taken away, or a good approved note given, payable August 1st, 1890, at which date all bills must be settled.

For further information call or address M. SALISBURY, 320 Sansome Street, Room 26. San Francisco, or

PLEASANTON STOCK FARM CO.;

Pleasanton, Alameda Co., Cal.

BAY STALLION

ECLECTIC

11,321

By ELECTIONEER, dam MANETTE (full sister to Woodnut 2:16½,) Manon 2:21 and Maple, dam of Hattie D. (three-year-old record 2:26½) by Nutwood 2:18¾, etc., etc.

Terms $100 for the Season.

BROWN STALLION

MORTIMER

5,346

Four-year-old Record 2:27

By ELECTIONEER, dam MARTI, by Whipple's Hambletonian (sire of 15 in 2:30, and of dams of eight in 2:30). Second dam Ida Martin by Rifleman (son of Col. Lewis 2:18¾).

Terms $60 for the Season.

Season closes JULY 15, 1890. Usual return privileges.

For further particulars address owner,

WILFRED PAGE, Penns Grove,

Sonoma County, Cal

Valensin Stock Farm Stallions,

SIDNEY, 2:19 3-4.

At Eight Years of Age Sire of the following Fastest on Record:

FAUSTINO, yearling stallion. record of the world 2:35
FLEET, fastest yearling record in 1888 .... 2:36
FLEET, fastest two-year-old filly in 1889 .... 2:24
GOLD LEAF, fastest four-year-old Pacing record in the world .... $2{:}11\frac{1}{2}$
ADONIS, fastest three-year-old Pacing Gelding in the world .... $2{:}14\frac{1}{2}$
ADONIS, four-year-old Gelding Pacing record 2:14

—Also the Sire of—

LONGWORTH, four years old 2:19
SISTER V., four years old (trial 2:23) 2:27
SANTA RITA 2:39
MEMO, two-year-old (three-year-old trial $2{:}20\frac{1}{2}$) 2:49

And many others.

SIDNEY is the sire of Faustino 2:35, and Fleet 2:36, the two fastest yearlings the world has ever known by one sire, and his slowest yearling is faster than the great Electioneer's fastest.

Terms, $250, with usual return privileges, for a limited number of approved mares. Book rapidly filling.

SIMMOCOLON, Four-year-old, 2:29 1-2.

Trial, 2:24; Half Mile in 1:08; Quarter in 33 1:2 Seconds.

Chestnut Horse, foaled 1885.

SIMMOCOLON.
- Simmons 2774. Sire of Bon Bon, 4 y. o. rec., 2:26, Raymon, 4 y. o. rec., 2:27, Black Storm, 3 y. o. rec. 2:27¾, and six others with records of 2:30 or better.
  - George Wilkes 519. Sire of 61 in 2:30 list. Sire of 11 dams of 12 in 2:30 list
    - Hambletonian 10. Sire of 41 in 2:30 list. Sire of 107 sires of 567 in 2:30 list. Sire of 44 dams of 50 in 2:30 list
    - Dolly Spanker
  - Black Jane. Dam of Rosa Wilkes, 2:18¼. Dam of Simmons, 2:28
    - Mambrino Patchen 58. sire of 14 in 2:30 list. Sire of 21 sires of 37 in 2:30 list. Sire of 24 dams of 28 in 2:30 list
    - Lady Stanhope
- Colon. Dam of Simmocolon, 4 y. o. rec., 2:29½. Dam of Patchmore, 2:32¾
  - Strathmore. Sire of 27 in 2:30 list. Sire of 6 dams of 8 in 2:30. Sire of 3 sires of 3 in 2:30
    - Hambletonian 10 (Same as above)
    - Lady Waltermire. Dam of Marshall Ney
  - Coral. Trial at 2 years, 2:30. Dam of Coralloid, 2:29¾
    - Clark Chief 89. Sire of 6 in 2:30 list. Sire of 9 sires of 27 in list. Sire of 11 dam with 11 in list
    - Colon. Dam of Caliban, sire of 3 in 2:30 list

As will be seen, Simmocolon is by a performing and producing son of George Wilkes, 2:22. He has back of him three producing dams, and combines the blood of the great sire George Wilkes handsomely blended with the blood of the greatest broodmare families. On the dam's side Mambrino Patchen, Strathmore, Clark Chief and Clay. A fine individual himself, pure gaited and very fast.

Terms, $150, with usual return privileges, for a limited number of mares. Season to close JUNE 15th, when he will be prepared for track purposes. Pasturage $5 per month. Reasonable charges if fed hay and grain. Best of care taken of mares, but positively no responsibility assumed for accidents or escapes. For further particulars address

G. VALENSIN, Pleasanton, Cal.

Breeders' Directory.

Advertisements under this heading 50c. per line per month.

HORSES AND CATTLE.

J. H. WHITE, Lakeville, Sonoma County—Breeder of Registered Holstein Cattle.

EL ROBLAS RANCHO—Los Alamos, Cal., Francis T. Underhill, proprietor, importer and breeder of thoroughbred Hereford Cattle. Information by mail. C. F. Swan, manager.

PAGE BROTHERS.—Penn's Grove, Sonoma Co. Cal. Breeders of Short-Horn Cattle; Draft, Roadster and Standard Bred Horses.

JAMES MADDOCK, Petaluma, Cal.—Trotters trained at reasonable prices. Stock handled carefully. Correspondence solicited.

SETH COOK, breeder of Cleveland Bay Horses, Devon, Durham, Polled Aberdeen-Angus and Galloway Cattle. Young stock of above breeds on hand for sale. Warranted to be pure bred, recorded and average breeders. Address, Geo. A. Wiley, Cook Farm, Danville, Contra Costa Co., Cal.

MAMBRINO WILKES COLTS and FILLIES, full brothers and sisters to Gus. Wilkes 2:22, and Balkan 2:29¾, for Sale. Address SMITH HILL, Walnut Creek, Contra Costa County, Cal.

B. F. RUSH, Suisun, Cal., Shorthorns, Thoroughbred and Grades. Young Bulls and Calves for Sale.

PETER SAXE & SON, Lick House, San Francisco, Cal.—Importers and Breeders for past 18 years of every variety of Cattle, Horses, Sheep and Hogs.

HOLSTEIN THOROUGHBREDS of all the noted strains. Registered Berkshire Swine. Catalogues. F. H. BURKE, 401 Montgomery St., S. F.

CLEVELAND BAYS and Norman Horses, Jersey Cattle, and pure bred Poland China Hogs.—DR. W. J. PRATHER, Fresno, Cal.

HENRY C. JUDSON, Wild Idle Farm.—Breeder of Thoroughbred Horses. The home of "Wild Idle." P. O. Santa Clara; Box 223.

W. S. JACOBS, Sacramento, Cal. — Breeder of Thoroughbred Shorthorns and Berkshire Hogs.

SITUATION WANTED.

AN INDUSTRIOUS AND CAPABLE MAN wants to secure a situation as Stallion Groom. Can give good references. Address,

GROOM, This Office.

FERGUSON & AUSTIN,
FRESNO, CAL.
Registered Polled Angus and Short-Horn Cattle.

Oysters.

M. B. MORAGHAN

Is the only importer, planter and wholesale dealer in the CALIFORNIA MARKET, Stalls 68, 69 to 71 and 47, 48. All the choicest brands of Fresh Oysters constantly on hand. Prompt attention paid to hotel and country orders. Price List.

Large Eastern Oysters .... $2 00 per 100
Transplanted Eastern Oysters .... 1 50 per 100
California Oysters .... 2 00 " sack
Fresh frozen Eastern Oysters at $7 00 per doz. cans.

PASTURAGE
AND
FIRST-CLASS CARE
TAKEN OF
Gentlemen's Road Horses and Trotters.

Colts Broken and Trained to Harness or Saddle.

Twenty new Box Stalls. First-class Pasturage, and the best of care given to all horses. **Terms, $4 per month.** Satisfaction Guaranteed.

Address,

K. O'GRADY,
Laural Creek Farm,
SAN MATEO, CAL

Fiske's Vanes.

MADE OF
COPPER
And Gilded with
PURE
GOLD LEAF.

Manufacturer's Agent.

The HOWE SCALE CO.
411 & 413 Market Street, S. F.

Scales for Weighing of
Live Stock
SEEDS, FEED, Etc.
Write for Catalogue.

TO HORSEMEN!

PREPARE!!

Your Stallion Advertisements for the

Breeder & Sportsman

For the Season---1890.

We are pleased to announce that we have the best facilities for furnishing

Stallion Pictures,
Stallion Cards,
Pedigrees, Folders,
Contracts, Bills, Etc.

We make a specialty of this department of our business, and have UNRIVALED FACILITIES FOR LOOKING UP PEDIGREES and doing accurate and handsome work.

Promptness, Good Work, Low Prices.

TO REACH ALL
OF THE
Horsemen and Breeders on the Pacific Coast
ADVERTISE in the
Breeder & Sportsman,
313 Bush Street, S. F.

BOYCE TABLETS.
Leg and Body Wash.

THE BOYCE TABLETS are packed in a nicely decorated metal box with hinged lid—one hundred tablets in each box; directions for use plainly engraved upon the box; therefore, the convenience of the package—no liability to leakage and breakage—economy and ready solubility, together with the absolute certainty of their action, will at once commend the use of BOYCE'S TABLETS to the intelligent horsemen of the country. TABLETS sufficient to make one hundred pints of leg and body wash are conveniently carried in an inside coat pocket or in the hip-pocket of the trousers.

The BOYCE WASH can be applied ALL OVER THE BODY WITHOUT FEAR OF BLISTERING OR AFFECTING THE KIDNEYS.

The BOYCE WASH will cure CRACKED HEELS, PUFFS, STOCKINGS, SCRATCHES, INFLAMED TENDONS and FEVERED LEGS.

Price per Box of One Hundred Tablets, $2, sent postpaid to any part of the United States; **six boxes for $10**. A sample of BOYCE'S TABLETS will be mailed to any address on application. These TABLETS are warranted to keep in any climate. Address

BOYCE TABLET COMPANY,
600 Wabash Avenue, - - - - Terre Haute, Indiana.

J. A. McKERRON, Pacific Coast Agent,
228-230-232 Ellis Street, San Francisco, Cal.

HORSES PURCHASED ON COMMISSION.

THOROUGHBREDS A SPECIALTY.

Will select and buy, or buy selected Animals for all desiring, for reasonable compensation.

KEEPS PROMISING YOUNGSTERS IN VIEW.

L. M. LASLEY, Stanford, Ky.

References:—J. W. Guest, Danville, Ky.
B. G. Bruce, Lexington Ky.
S. H. Baughman, Stanford, Ky.
G. A. Lackey, Stanford, Ky.
Geo. McAlister, Stanford, Ky.
First National Bank, Stanford, Ky.

Shoes For Comfort, Elegance and Durability.

Having my own Factory, and giving my personal supervision to all work I am in a position to warrant perfect satisfaction. Inspection invited.

AGENT for the VISCALIZED SHOES.

FACTORY—S. W. cor. Battery and Jackson Sts.
SALESROOM—Pioneer Building, corner Stevenson and Fourth Streets.

A full line of **Boots and Shoes** constantly on hand, and rules for Self-Measurement by Mail.

JNO. T. SULLIVAN.

Old Hermitage Whiskies
"STEINER'S,"
No. 311 BUSH STREET,
San Francisco,
Under Breeder and Sportsman Office.

BERGEZ'S
RESTAURANT.

FIRST-CLASS. Charges Reasonable.

Private Rooms for Families,

332–334 Pine St., below Montgomery St.

JOHN BERGEZ, Propr.

The Poodle Dog
"Rotisserie,"

FIRST-CLASS IN EVERY RESPECT.

Elegant Family Dining Rooms.

S. E. cor. GRANT AVE. and BUSH STREET.

ANDRE POTENTINI, Proprietor.

The Park Training Stable.

CHAS. DAVID, PROPRIETOR.

Corner Grove and Baker Streets, near Entrance to Golden Gate Park.

EVERY FACILITY FOR TRAINING COLTS and taking care of Gentlemen's Roadsters.

Finely appointed stable with every convenience and sixteen roomy box stalls.

The best care given all horses by experienced help, under the personal superintendence of the proprietor.

Convenient to the Park Speed Drive, and Accessible to Six Lines of Cable Cars.

THE TRAINING OF COLTS AND ROADSTERS A SPECIALTY.

TROTTERS AND ROADSTERS FOR SALE.
HORSES SOLD ON COMMISSION.

The proprietor trained and brought out the following well known horses: "Sister, Huntress," "Perihelion," "Nona Y," and others.

NOVEL, USEFUL and Ornamental.

The Perfection Horse Tail Tie,

Saves Time and the Tail.

Send 25 cents for Sample,

BREEDER AND SPORTSMAN,
313 Bush Street, San Francisco,
or to BARNES & FABBER, Des Moines, Ia., Manufrs.

GOLDEN EAGLE HOTEL

Corner SEVENTH and K STREETS, SACRAMENTO.

FIRST CLASS IN EVERY RESPECT.

The LARGEST and FINEST HOTEL in the City.

W. O. BOWERS, Proprietor.

Free 'Buss to and from the Hotel.

Telephone, Telegraph Office and Messenger Service at Hotel

6 DOS

DO you bet?
DO you go to the races?
DO you know HOW to bet?
DO you know BEST system?
DO you want Good ADVICE?
DO as you ought to do:

SEND FOR PROSPECTUS TO

GOODWIN BROS.,
241 BROADWAY, NEW YORK,

Who will mail you

FREE OF CHARGE,

one of their circulars showing the GREAT SUCCESS they have met with from the time they established the system of "Point" providing in this country in 1881; it also contains

MANY OTHER INTERESTING ITEMS

with which the general public is not familiar.

Call and See the New

CRUISING BOOTS

E. T. ALLEN,
Fire Arms and Sporting Goods
416 Market St., S. F.

The Trotting Stallion

Silver Bow

Will make the season of 1890 at the Oakland Race Track.

Pedigree.

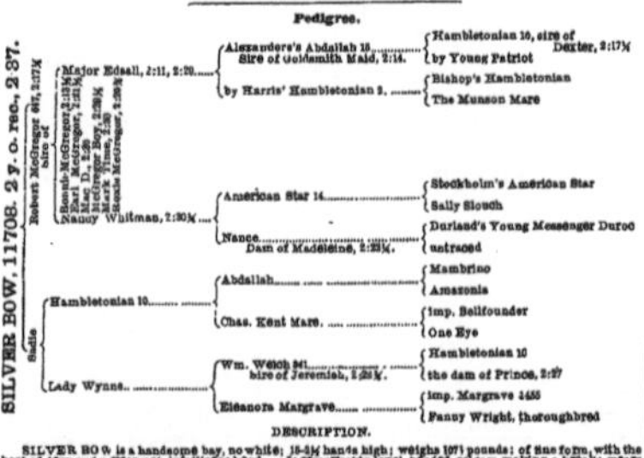

DESCRIPTION.

SILVER BOW is a handsome bay, no white; 15-3¼ hands high; weighs 1071 pounds; of fine form, with the best of legs and a clean cut, intelligent head. Is remarkably level headed, seldom making a break; wears 7-ounce shoes in front. His record 2:37, is no mark of his speed; he can beat 30 easy, and with his gilt-edge breeding, he is just what he ought to be, a trotter sired by a trotter whose dam was herself a trotter and his grandam the dam of two trotters. His dam Sadie being by Hambletonian 10, shows him to be bred from the cream of the trotting blood.

TERMS: $100 for the season. Mares not proving in foal returnable for the season of 1891 free of charge. Good pasturage and first-class care taken of mares for $5 per month. No responsibility assumed for escapes or accidents. For further particulars, address

Limited to 15 approved mares.
Season to end June 1st, 1890.

P. J. WILLIAMS.
Care Race Track, Oakland, Cal.

MEMO.

The Best Son of SIDNEY

Will Make the Season of 1890 at the VALENSIN STOCK FARM

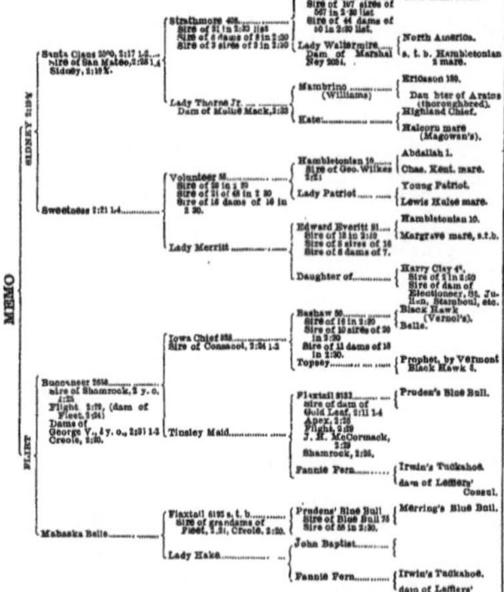

MEMO is, as can be seen at a glance, one of the best bred young stallions in service, having three crosses of Rysdyk's Hambletonian and one of Harry Clay, the sire of Green Mountain Maid (dam of Electioneer, etc.), while Long Island Black Hawk and Flaxtail also contribute to his blood. Sidney (Memo's sire) is universally known as the best young sire in the world, a producer of extreme speed at an early age.

PERFORMANCES.

MEMO trotted in public in his two year-old form, obtaining a record of 2:49, though he was close to Grandee in a race on the Bay District Track, the second heat of which was made in 2:31 1-2, the first in 2:21. He exhibited phenomenal speed when three years old, and had it not been for a slight strain of his fore fetlock, there is little question that he would have shown in public very close to the best record. On the Oakland track he was timed a mile in 2:20 1-2, and frequently trotted quarters in from 32 1-2 to 31 seconds.

As a four-year-old Memo only started once—at Sacramento—when, although out of condition, he showed great speed, and improving as he went on, great hopes were entertained of his going well down in the 'teens at the P. C. T. H. B. A. meeting, but after showing several very fast miles his leg filled and he was laid up for the season. He is sixteen hands high, and of powerful build throughout. His color is a glossy black, with both fore-feet white. His disposition is all that could be desired, and his action superb. He is a sure foal getter, only one mare being reported not in foal during his last season.

TERMS, $ 50, with usual return privileges, for a limited number of mares. Season to close JUNE 15th, when he will be prepared for track purposes. Pasturage $5 per month. Reasonable charges if fed hay and grain. Best of care taken of mares, but positively no responsibility assumed for accidents or escapes. For further particulars address

J. P. KERR, 313 Bush Street, San Francisco,
or, G. VALENSIN, Pleasanton, Cal.

Guenoc Stud Farm, Lake Co., Cal.

Imp. GREENBACK

(Sire of the English winners Greenlight, Greenjacket, Greensbank, Greenwave and Greenhorn)

By Dollar, dam Music, by Stockwell. $100 the Season

ST. SAVIOR,

(FULL BROTHER TO EOLE)

By Eolus, dam War Song, by War Dance. $100 the Season.

PASTURAGE, $5 PER MONTH.

With right to return the following year if mare does not prove with foal. The best of care taken, but no liability for accidents or escapes. Mares shipped to C. W. ABY, care ST. HELENA STABLES, St. Helena Napa County, will be taken in charge by competent men.

For further information write to

DR. C. W. ABY, Middletown, Lake County, Cal.

SOUTHER FARM

P. O. Box 208. San Leandro, Cal.

1½ miles northwest of San Leandro; 8 miles southeast of Oakland. Turn off county road between above places at "Stanley Road," ½ mile north of San Leandro.

Horses boarded at all times in any manner desired. Best of care but no responsibility for accidents. Colts broken and handled for the road or track. Terms reasonable.

Glen Fortune,	Jester D,	El Benton,	Figaro,
By Electioneer.	By Almont.	By Electioneer.	Hambletonian 725
$50 for 1889.	$50 for 1890.	Limited to 5 mares.	Limited to 12 mares
		Book Full.	Book Full.

If horses are to last for a profitable time they must occasionally have a change from hard pavements, wooden floors, and dry, hard feed.

THE SOUTHER FARM

Has Green Feed the Year Round,

and feeds Hay in connection with the green feed, which a horse must have if he is to thrive. Every animal is given

A Dry, Warm Place to Sleep,

No matter how stormy the weather. All Stock under cover when it rains.

VISITORS WELCOME ANY DAY EXCEPT SUNDAY.

Write to the above address for references, circulars and price lists. Terms reasonable.

GILBERT TOMPKINS, Proprietor.

SAN MATEO STOCK FARM

HOME OF GUY WILKES,
Record, 2:15 1-4.

Guy Wilkes' Book is full for 1890, and positively no more mares will be received. Book now open for 1891, at $500 the Season.

Sable Wilkes, three-year-old record 2:18, will be allowed to serve 25 mares in addition to those already engaged at $250 the season of 1890. SABLE Wilkes, 15½ hands, black horse, by Guy Wilkes, first dam Sable by The Moor; second dam Gretchen by Mambrino Pilot; third dam Kitty Kirkman by Canada Chief; fourth dam by Fanning's Tobe; fifth dam by imp. Leviathan.

Leo Wilkes, brown horse, four years, 16 hands, full brother to Sable Wilkes, will be allowed to serve 30 mares at $100 the season

Mares not proving with foal may be returned the following season free of service fee. Parties engaging the services of any of the above horses must send a deposit of 10 per cent. of service money with engagement. Pasturage $6 per month, and when the condition of the animal requires it, hay or grain, or both, are fed, the charge will be $12 50 per month. Good care will be taken of all mares sent to the Farm, but no liability will be assumed for accidents or escapes.

All bills are due at time of service, but must be paid by August 1st of each year. No stock will be allowed to leave the place until all bills are paid.

WILLIAM CORBITT.
San Mateo Stock Farm.

Poplar Grove Breeding FARM.

Standard-bred Trotters, Colts and Fillies.

The get of CLOVIS, 4909; PASHA, 2039; APEX, 2935,

For Sale.

Address S. N. STRAUBE, Poplar Grove Breeding Farm,
Fresno, Cal.

Inspection by intending purchasers invited, and information by mail.

Southern Pacific Co.

(PACIFIC SYSTEM.)

Trains leave and are due to arrive at San Francisco.

LEAVE (FOR)	FROM JANUARY 1, 1890.	ARRIVE (FROM)
7.30 A M	Haywards, Niles and San Jose ...	*12.45 P M
7.30 A M	Sacramento and Redding, via Davis	7.15 P M
7.30 A M	Sacramento, Auburn, Colfax...	5.45 P M
8.00 A M	Martinez, Vallejo, Calistoga and Santa Rosa	6.15 P M
8.30 A M	Los Angeles Express, Fresno, Bakersfield, Mojave and East and Los Angeles	11.15 A M
8.30 A M	Niles, San Jose, Stockton, Ione, Sacramento, Marysville, Oroville and Red Bluff	5.45 P M
10.30 A M	Haywards and Niles	2.15 P M
*12.00 M	Haywards, Niles and San Jose...	* 3.45 P M
*1.00 P M	Sacramento River Steamers	**6.00 A M
3.00 P M	Haywards, Niles and San Jose...	9.45 A M
3.30 P M	2d Class for Ogden and East	10.45 P M
4.00 P M	Stockton and Milton; Vallejo, Calistoga and Santa Rosa	9.45 A M
4.30 P M	Sacramento and Knight's Landing via Davis	10.45 A M
* 4.30 P M	Niles and Livermore	* 8.45 A M
* 4.30 P M	Niles and San Jose	‡ 4.15 P M
5.30 P M	Haywards and Niles	7.45 A M
6.00 P M	Sunset Route, Atlantic Express. Santa Barbara, Los Angeles, Deming, El Paso, New Orleans and East	8.45 P M
7.00 P M	Shasta Route Express, Sacramento, Marysville, Redding, Portland, Puget Sound and East	7.45 A M
8.00 P M	Central Atlantic Express, Ogden and East	9.45 A M

SANTA CRUZ DIVISION.

LEAVE		ARRIVE
‡ 3.00 A M	Hunters train to San Jose	‡ 7.20 P M
8.15 A M	Newark, Centerville, San Jose, Felton, Boulder Creek and Santa Cruz	5.50 P M
* 2.15 P M	Centerville, San Jose, Almaden, Felton, Boulder Creek and Santa Cruz	*11.50 A M
4.15 P M	Centerville, San Jose, and Los Gatos	9.50 A M

Coast Division (Third and Townsend Sts.)

LEAVE		ARRIVE
7.25 A M	San Jose, Almaden and Way Stations	2.30 P M
8.30 A M	San Jose, Gilroy, Tres Pinos; Pajaro, Santa Cruz; Monterey; Pacific Grove, Salinas, San Miguel, Paso Robles, Santa Margarita (San Luis Obispo) and principal Way Stations	6.12 P M
10.30 A M	San Jose and Way Stations	5.02 P M
12.01 P M	Cemetery, Menlo Park and Way Stations	3.38 P M
* 3.30 P M	San Jose, Tres Pinos, Santa Cruz, Salinas, Monterey Pacific Grove and principal Way Stations	*10.00 A M
* 4.30 P M	Menlo Park and Way Station	* 7.58 A M
5.30 P M	San Jose and Way Stations	9.03 A M
6.30 P M	Menlo Park and Way Stations	6.35 A M
†11.45 P M	Menlo Park and principal Way Stations	†7.38 P M

A M for Morning. P M for Afternoon. *Sundays excepted. †Saturdays only. ‡Sundays only. **Mondays excepted. ‖Saturdays excepted.

San Francisco and North Pacific Railway.

THE DONAHUE BROAD-GAUGE ROUTE.

COMMENCING SUNDAY, MARCH 17, 1889, AND until further notice, boats and trains will leave from and arrive at the San Francisco Passenger Depot, Market-street Wharf, as follows:

Leave San Francisco. Week Days.	Leave San Francisco. Sundays.	Destination	Arrive San Francisco. Sundays.	Arrive San Francisco. Week Days.
7.40 A M 3.30 P M 5.00 P M	8.00 A M 5.00 P M	Petaluma and Santa Rosa	10.40 A M 6.10 P M	8.50 A M 10.30 A M 6.05 P M
7.40 A M 3.30 P M	8.00 A M	Fulton, Windsor, Healdsburg, Litton Springs, Cloverdale, and way stations.	6.10 P M	10.30 A M 6.05 P M
7.40 A M	8.00 A M	Hopland and Ukiah.	6.10 P M	6.05 P M
7.40 A M	8.00 A M	Guerneville	6.10 P M	6.05 P M
7.40 A M 5.00 P M	8.00 A M	Sonoma and Glen Ellen.	10.40 A M 6.10 P M	8.50 A M 6.05 P M

Stage connects at Santa Rosa for White Sulphur Springs, Sebastopol and Mark West Springs; at Geyserville for Skaggs Springs, and at Cloverdale for the Geysers; at Hopland for Highland Springs, Kelseyville, Soda Bay, Lakeport and Bartlett Springs, and at Ukiah for Vichy Springs, Saratoga Springs, Blue Lakes, Willits, Cahto, Calpella, Potter Valley, Sherwood Valley and Mendocino City.

EXCURSION TICKETS from Saturdays to Mondays, to Petaluma, $1.50; to Santa Rosa, $2.25; to Healdsburg, $3.40; to Litton Springs, $3.60; to Cloverdale, $4.50; to Hopland, $5.70; to Ukiah, $6.75; to Guerneville, $3.75; to Sonoma, $1.50; to Glen Ellen, $1.80.

EXCURSION TICKETS, good for Sundays only, to Petaluma, $1; to Santa Rosa, $1.50; to Healdsburg, $2.25; to Litton Springs, $2.40; to Cloverdale, $3; to Guerneville, $2.50, to Sonoma, $1; to Glen Ellen, $1.20.

From San Francisco for Point Tiburon and San Rafael: Week Days—7.40, 9.20, 11.20, A. M.; 3.30, 5.00, 6.15 P. M. Sundays—8.00, 9.30, 11.00 A. M.; 1.30, 5.00, 6.20 P. M.

To San Francisco from San Rafael: Week Days—6.20, 7.55, 9.30 A. M.; 12.45, 3.40, 5.05 P. M. Sundays—8.10, 9.40 A. M.; 12.15, 3.40, 5.00 P. M.

To San Francisco from Point Tiburon: Week Days—6.50, 8.20, 9.55 A. M.; 1.10, 4.05, 5.30 P. M.; Sundays—8.40, 10.05 A. M.; 12.40, 4.05, 5.30 P. M.

On Saturdays an extra trip will be made from San Francisco to San Rafael, leaving at 1:40 P. M.

H. C. WHITING, General Manager.

PETER J. McGLYNN, Gen. Pass. & Tkt. Agt.

Ticket Offices at Ferry, 222 Montgomery Street and 2 New Montgomery Street.

KENNEL ADVERTISEMENTS.

FOR SALE.

2 English Bloodhound Bitches

(PEDIGREED). Also

Two Well Broken Foxhounds

(GOOD DEER DOGS.)

Apply to CAYOTE KENNELS, Gilroy, Cal.

BULL TERRIERS FOR SALE.

Some fine BULL TERRIER PUPS, from game stock. These are fancy.

Call on or address, J. P. McKENNA, No. 20 Bonita Street, off Polk, near Green.

Thoroughbred Pugs, $40 each.

PEDIGREE.

PUPPIES
- Fido
  - Imp. Jumbo — Marshall's Uno / Lady Bess
  - Fannie — Rex / Imp. Fly
- Budge
  - Senator Fair's Fritz
  - McCleery's Mamma Snoots — Sam / imp. Alice

Can be seen daily from 9 A. M. to 3 P. M. at 411 Ellis Street, San Francisco.

J. F. B. McCLEERY.

Irish Setters & Pointers.

In the Stud, winner of 16 first and special prizes, CHAMPION MIKE T., 6435, A. K. S. B. Irish Setter puppies by Champion Mike T. 6435 A. K. S. B.—Champion Lady Elcho T. 6451 A. K. S. B., for sale. Two pointers, a year old, by Rush T. 10069 A. K. S. B.-Champion Patti Croxteth T. 10128 A. K. S. B. for sale. Yard broken. Address,

A. B. TRUMAN, 1425 Steiner St., S. F., Cal.

CALIFORNIA SPANIEL KENNELS.

Oakland, California, H. P. RENNIE, Prop; Breeder and importer of typical COCKER SPANIELS. Winner of first prizes at S. F. and Los Angeles, 1889; also, Columbus, 1889, New York, 1887. In the stud, solid Black Cocker dog, GIFFEE, won 1st and Gold Medal at S. F., 1889. Fee, $25. Puppies and grown dogs at reasonable prices. My dogs can neither talk nor climb a tree, but are fielders and prize winners.

VETERINARY.

Dr. Wm. H. Jones, M.R.C.V.S.

Veterinary Surgeon,

(CLUB STABLES)

409–411 Taylor Street, San Francisco.

Consultations by letter, and cases of URGENT NECESSITY in the interior will receive prompt attention.

W. H. WOODRUFF.

Veterinary Dentist,

AT FASHION STABLES,

221 Ellis Street, San Francisco

Improved Instruments, Humane Methods, First-Class Work.

H. E. CARPENTER,

Veterinary Surgeon,

Graduate of Ontario Veterinary College, Toronto, Canada.

RESIDENCE AND VETERINARY INFIRMARY

331 Golden Gate Ave., San Francisco.

Telephone 3069.

☞ OPEN DAY AND NIGHT. ☜

No risk in throwing Horses. Veterinary Operating Table on the premises.

DR. C. MASOERO,

Veterinary Surgeon,

Successor to DR. A. DeTAVEL,

GRADUATE OF ROYAL VETERINARY COLLEGE, TURIN.

OFFICE AND INFIRMARY,

No. 811 HOWARD STREET,

Between Fourth and Fifth. SAN FRANCISCO.

Telephone, No. 457.

R. WATKINS,

Veterinary Dentist,

Of twelve years practice, is now permanently located in San Francisco, and may be found at C. S. Crittendens' Golden Gate Livery and Riding Academy, 24 to 28 Golden Gate Avenue.

Will treat ailments of the horse's mouth, and cure all such. Sidereln Pullers and Tongue Lollers, etc. Satisfaction guaranteed. Orders by mail will receive prompt attention. Examination Free.

E. J. O'ROUKE.

I have the honor to announce to my old patrons and the general public that I may be found at my old stand, where, as heretofore, the

Shoeing of Horses,

whether for the Track, Drive, or for general work, will receive my personal attention.

Telephone 2011.

E. J. O'ROUKE, 209 Ellis Street

California Horse Shoe Co's

I have used in my business the Steel and Iron Shoes made by the above Company, and take great pleasure in saying they are the best I have ever used in twenty-two years' practice. I have never seen anything like the STEEL SHOE made by this Company. I can fully recommend them to every practical Horseshoer in the country. Yours respectfully,

No. 8 Everett Street. JOHN GRACE.

Everything for

Trotter or Runner.

At J. A. McKERRON'S,

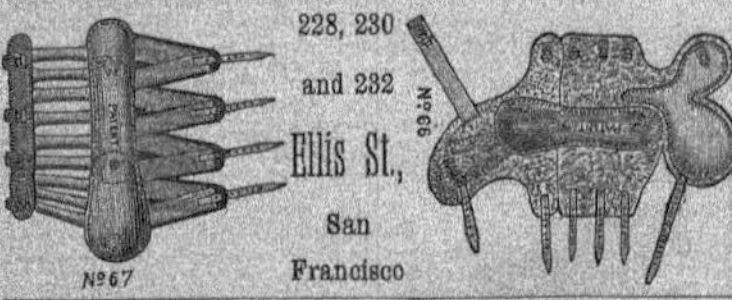

228, 230 and 232 Ellis St., San Francisco

THE IMPROVED NOYES ROAD - CART.

PATENTED JULY 17, 1883, AND JUNE 8, 1886.

Some of the Advantages of the Noyes Cart Over All Others.

There is no bar for the rider to climb over in getting in or out. The horse can be hitched eighteen inches nearer than any other road-cart made. You can get in or out with perfect safety—no danger of being thrown into the wheel—a great advantage in breaking colts. THE EASIEST CART FOR ROAD OR TRACK. The only cart that a horse can be speeded to within one second as fast as to a sulky. All our carts are made of the very best materials and are warranted. Manufactured by the NOYES CART COMPANY, Kalamazoo, Mich.

They are indorsed by the following horsemen, all of whom are using them. Ask their opinion of the Noyes Cart: John Splan, who drove Guy a full mile in 2:17¾ and Chanter a half-mile in 1:10¾ to a Noyes Cart, says he would not take $250 for it if he could not get another; W. J. Gordon, Glenville, O.; W. B. Fasig, Cleveland, O.; Dave Muckel, Cleveland, O.; R. J. Moorehead, North East, Pa.; W. J. Chamberlain, Cleveland, O.; H. P. Malone, Bradford, Pa.; S. A. Brown & Co., Kalamazoo Stock Farm; Charles Marvin, Menlo Park, Cal.; W. H. Crawford, Lexington, Ky.; S. L. Caton, who gave Bell Boy a mark at Los Angeles, Cal., of 2:19¼, and drove Chanter a half mile in 1:08¾ and Lowland Girl a full mile in 2:22 to a Noyes Cart; Mike Bowerman, Lexington, Ky.; James Golden, Medford, Mass.; John E. Turner, Philadelphia, Pa.; T. L. Newton, Beaver Dam, Wis.; F. V. Johnston, Marshall, Mich.; W. H. McCarthy, Los Angeles, Cal.; A. W. Dennison, El Dorado, Kan.; P. O. Shank, Cleveland, O.; Charles Barnard, Boston, Mass.; Johnson Bros., Greenville, Mich.; John G. Avery, Buffalo, N. Y.; General R. L. Howard, Buffalo, N. Y.; Howard Conklin, Buffalo, N. Y.; W. D. Bam, Hennepin, Ill.; R. G. Heury, Waterbury, Conn.; J. E. Hayer, Newburgh, O.; J. C. Hart, Jefferson, Tex.; A. W. Harbison, Rock Point, Pa.; Carl Hodges, Battle Creek, Mich.; Barney Treacy, Lexington, Ky.; George Forbes, Cleveland, O.; Gifford Dudley, Topeka, Kan.; William and J. L. Thompson, Lamont, Pa.; C. F. Emery, Forest City Stock Farm, Cleveland, O.; H. F. Jones, Minneapolis, Minn.; John Forbes, Elyria, O.; D. J. Downs, Battle Creek, Mich.; Frank Caton, Randall Station, O.; Arthur D. Sutton, Ind., Pa.; W. F. Neely, Grand Ridge, Ill.; Walter Clark, owner of Pilot Medium, Battle Creek, Mich.; H. R. Kingman, Battle Creek, Mich.; Dr. Sutton and H. C. Reed, Kalamazoo, Mich.; Budd Doble, Chicago, Ill.

SOLE MANUFACTURERS OF STONE'S PATENT SULKY CASE.

They will more than save their cost in one season, and horsemen campaigning trotters cannot afford to do without them. Would refer to Samuel A. Brown, Kalamazoo Stock Farm, S. L. Caton and W. H. McCarthy. Address

NOYES CART COMPANY, Kalamazoo, Mich.

Office and Factory, corner Rose and Eleanor streets. R. ARTHUR STONE, Manager.

TREES AND SEEDS.

Trumbull & Beebe's Nurseries

ESTABLISHED 1857.

500,000 **Fruit Trees** 500,000

FOR SALE.

Having added by purchase, to that of our own growing, the entire nursery stock grown at James Shinn's Nurseries, Niles, Cal., we are better prepared than ever before to meet the increasing demand for trees, and offer for the season of 1889-1890 the LARGEST AND MOST COMPLETE ASSORTMENT OF NURSERY STOCK ON THE PACIFIC COAST, embracing all the leading varieties of FRUIT, SHADE and ORNAMENTAL TREES, ROSES, PLANTS, Etc. BERRY BUSHES of all kinds in quantities to suit. 250,000 GRAPE VINES (strong roots), also 60,000 OLIVE TREES (Mission and Picholine), ORANGES, LEMONS, NUT TREES, Etc., Etc.

NURSERIES—San Rafael, Alameda and Niles, Cal. Packing Grounds and Sales-yard at Niles R. R. Station. Catalogues sent upon application. Address all communications to

TRUMBULL & BEEBE, 419-421 Sansome St., San Francisco, Cal

OSSIDINE

Results obtained at the well-known **KALAMAZOO FARM.**

KALAMAZOO, MICH., Sept. 15, 1888.

GENTLEMEN:—We have used OSSIDINE for the past two years, and consider it invaluable for Sprung Tendons, Curbs, Ringbone, and Spavins; there is nothing equals it; and for us it effected a permanent cure where firing failed, although performed by one of the most successful veterinarians on the continent. We have recommended it to others with like success, and believe it has more merit than any blister ever used.

Very respectfully yours,
S. A. BROWNE & CO., Prop's.

This scientific preparation is an absolute cure for all bony or callous lumps on horses, and is a more powerful absorbent than "firing," without creating the slightest blemish.

Acknowledged by leading horsemen of the world to be the **ONLY** preparation that will remove a Bone Spavin after it has become ossified.

We have authority also to refer to
Mr. JEROME I. CASE, Mr. FRED. GEBHARD, Mr. JOHN PORTER (Trainer to H.R.H. the Prince of Wales),
And hundreds of others from whom we have very flattering testimonials.

One Style Only. $3.00 per Bottle.

A. P. BUSH & CO.,
149 Pearl St.,
BOSTON, MASS.,
Sole Agents for United States and Canada.
Beware of Imitations.

SOLD BY C. N. Crittenton, A. B. Van Nest & Co., and C. M. Moseman & Bro., NEW YORK CITY. Morrisson, Plummer & Co., Peter Van Schaack & Sons, CHICAGO, ILL. John D. Park & Son, CINCINNATI, O.; Floyd & Foster, DETROIT, MICH.; F. S. Slosson, CLEVELAND, O.; Meyer Bros. Drug Co., ST. LOUIS, MO.; R. A. Robinson, LOUISVILLE, KY.; H. H. Moore & Sons, STOCKTON, CAL.

J. C. JOHNSON & CO.,

IMPORTERS, MANUFACTURERS, AND DEALERS IN

HARNESS & SADDLERY

☞ We carry a large assortment of goods in our line from the cheapest to the best made.

400 to 404 Market Street

Corner BATTERY STREET, San Francisco.

J. O'KANE, | Horse Boots, Clothing and Furnishings, For Track, Driving Training and Stable. Every requisite for Horsemen. Harness, Medicines, Etc.

The PARKER Hammerless Shot Gun.

At the Annual Tournament of 1889, held at Cannes, France, the grand prize, consisting of 2000 Francs and a Valuable Cup, was won by The Parker Hammerless.

The first Parker Hammerless Gun made won the championship of America at Decatur Illinois.

SEND FOR ILLUSTRATED CIRCULAR.

PARKER BROS., Makers,

New York Salesroom, 97 Chambers St., Meriden Conn.

MANHATTAN FOOD.

keeps horses healthy, promotes digestion, fattens horses, loosens the hide, assists the appetite, prevents leg swelling, strengthens the kidneys, regulates the bowels and destroys worms. **$7.50 per 100 lbs.** Ask your dealer for it or send to

MANHATTAN FOOD CO., 206 Clay St., S. F.

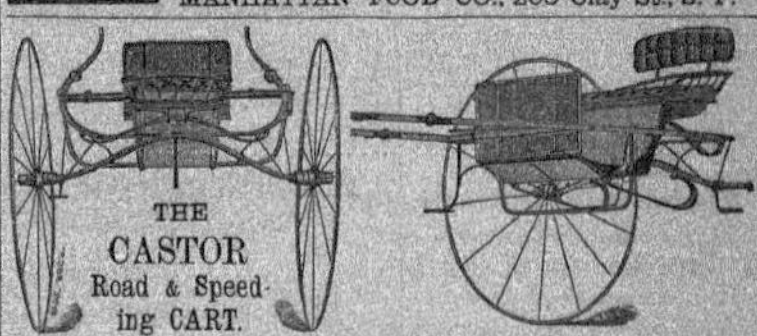

ALWAYS GIVES SATISFACTION.

Combining perfect riding qualities, proportions and balance, with genteel appearance.

No vehicle exhibits a horse to better advantage, and no Cart approaches them for speeding or training purposes.

A stylish vehicle for exercising or pleasure driving, at one-fourth the cost of a carriage. Have none of the horse jockey or objectionable features of other Road Carts.

They are the Leading Cart wherever introduced, and are in use by the most prominent breeders and pleasure drivers everywhere.

Elegant Shifting Top Carts.

Perfectly Balanced Stylish Pole Carts.

For Illustrated Catalogue, with Prices, address,

LEWIS F. CASTOR,
Frankford, Philadelphia, Pa.

JOHN SPLAN, General Agent.

THE "BLUE ROCK" TARGET.

Quotations furnished F. O. B. at Cleveland, Ohio, or San Francisco.

CLABROUGH, GOLCHER & CO.,
630 and 632 Montgomery Street, S. F., Cal.

SOLE AGENTS for the Pacific Coast.

TWENTY PAGES.

BREEDER AND SPORTSMAN

Vol. XVI. No. 5.
No. 313 BUSH STREET. SAN FRANCISCO. SATURDAY, FEB. 1, 1890. SUBSCRIPTION FIVE DOLLARS A YEAR.

Wherein Lies the Disgrace?

EDITOR BREEDER AND SPORTSMAN:—I clip the following from a contribution by Mr. Jos. Cairn Simpson. "The letters received. * * * * Criticise the programme adopted, especially in regard to limiting contests to a presumably inferior class of horses, in this way encouraging the breeding of a lower rate of animals, and also having a direct tendency to limit attendance. * * * * Three-year-olds that have not beaten three minutes, four-year-olds that have not achieved 2:40, and the "get" of sires, the progeny of which have not shown merit enough to obtain a place in "the list" will not be "drawing cards," and the stallion purse, with eligibility depending on so slow a rate as 2:30, will hardly entice many people to witness *the big event of the meeting. Taken as a whole, the programme can be termed a disgrace to the Pacific Coast.* Occupying the position of the greatest horse breeding country on the continent, especially in the line of fast trotters, an association which adopts the name, and formulates a bill with six of the ten events hampered with conditions which do not encourage the breeding of the best type of horses, takes a narrow view of the position." (The italics are mine).

The breeders of the Pacific Coast owes no thanks to Mr. Simpson for the foregoing misleading statement of the action regarding stakes and purses offered by the Board of Directors of the P. C. T. H. B. A.

I have no objection to, and sincerely hope that everything the Board may do will receive fair criticism, but I doubt very much if such articles as the above are written in the right spirit, or will tend to benefit any breeder or the breeding interests on this coast.

Mr. Simpson in the first place condemns a programme, which he does not so much as care to publish and which, if published, would have placed his sharp criticism in a very peculiar light before the majority of our breeders.

Before passing any further comments, therefore, on the extracts above quoted, I will give, *so far as it has been at present decided on*, the programme that has called forth Mr. Simpson's very terse condemnation:

1.—Free-for-all Yearling Trotting Stakes; $50 entrance.
2.— " " 2-year-old Trotting Stakes: $75 " $250 added.
3.— " " 3-year-old Trotting Stakes; $100 " $300 "
4.— " " 4-year-old Trotting Stakes; $100 " $400 ".
5.—3:00 Class: 3-year-old Trotting: Purse $500.
6.—2:40 Class; 4-year-old Trotting; Purse $500.
7.— Open to the get of stallions with no representatives in 2:30 list. 2-year-old Trotting: Purse $500.
8.— " 3-year-old Trotting; Purse $500.
9.— " 4-year-old Trotting; Purse $500.
10—2:30 Class, Stallion Trotting; Purse $1,000.

Mr. Simpson, on authority that he does not quote, refers to No. 10 as *the big event* of the meeting. I trust it may prove such, but if he intended to convey the meaning, and had himself inferred that this is the annual "National Stallion Race" that has become a feature of our meetings, all I have to say is that he owes the association an apology for a most egregious blunder which he has gratuitously published to the world on no better authority than his own hasty conclusions.

Mr. Simpson also criticises the programme, especially in regard to *limiting* contests to a *presumably* inferior class of animals!

If trotting colts are inferior, why then there is a "limit," but otherwise there is nothing to bar any lunatic, if he so desire, from entering Clydesdales, Normans or thoroughbreds (if they will only trot) in stakes 1 to 4 against such a class of colts as Sunol, Lillian Wilkes, Margaret S., or Regal Wilkes. As the Board was somewhat of the opinion that there would not be a superabundance of contestants against these phenomena, they decided to offer two other classes (5 and 6) for the ages in which these exceptional colts would appear. Do Mr. Simpson and his correspondents maintain that the Board should have told these breeders: "You must either start against Sunol and Regal Wilkes or stay out!"

Had the "bar record" been set somewhat lower, in Nos. 5 and 6, it might have done as well, but at the same time, it would have brought out the old complaint: "I see you just cut me out, but let so and so in." Placed where it is, it will come pretty near giving us "green" colts altogether, and as, aside from the bar named, there is nothing to prevent full brothers and sisters, *to the above*, starting in one stake or the other (for none of them have records of any kind), I fail to see wherein purses 5 and 6 are a disgrace to the State, or wherein they discourage the breeding of the best type of horses; nor is there any reason why the colts should not trot as fast for purses 5 and 6 and the contests proved as good "drawing cards," as those that are offered under stakes 1 to 4.

It was on my motion that purses Nos. 7, 8 and 9 were offered for the get of stallions that have no representatives in the 2:30 list. In his condemnation of the purses and stakes offered, Mr. Simpson has thought it necessary to put in a disclaimer of his being actuated by personal motives or self-interest, perhaps it will be as well for me to do as much. I have no colts of my own breeding, sired by my own stallions, that are older than yearlings, and have only two of these that are likely to be worth training. The association has not offered a purse or stakes for yearlings under this seemingly obnoxious and "disgraceful" condition.

Mr. Simpson dubs Nos. 7, 8 and 9 purses for the get of sires, the progeny of which *have not showed merit enough to obtain a place in the list.* Correct, Mr. Simpson, *in a measure*, but they also admit foals of such *inferior* stallions as Antevolo, 2:19½ (sold by you for $18,000; re-sold for $40,000); Anteros (full brother to Antevolo); Palo Alto, 2:12¾; Norval, 2:17½ (sire of Norlaine, one-year-old, 2:31½); Albert W., 2:20; Ansel, 2:20; Woolsey (full brother to Sunol, 2:10½); Elector, 2:21¼ (sire of Edwin C., pacer, 2:15); Clay, 2:25; Azmoor, 2:24½; Bentonian, Benton Frolic, Benefit, Alfred, Alban, (sires by Gen. Benton in use at Palo Alto); Clovis (son of Sultan); Bay Rose (son of Sultan); Soudan, 2:27½ (son of Sultan); Dexter Prince (son of Kentucky Prince and a sister of Dexter); Alpheus, 2:27 (by Mambrino Wilkes); Sable Wilkes, 2:18 (by Guy Wilkes); Napa Wilkes (by Guy Wilkes); Dawn, 2:18¾ (by Nutwood); Mount Vernon, 2:21 (by Nutwood); Menlo, 2:21½ (by Nutwood), etc., and a host of other well-bred sons of Electioneer, Director, Gen. Benton, Guy Wilkes, Piedmont, Nutwood, Sidney, Sultan, and others, scattered throughout the length and breadth of the Pacific Coast, many of which are owned by small breeders who depend upon the incomes their stallions bring them, to defray the expense of training *one or two* of the few colts they themselves raise.

These small breeders are, or should be, members of the P. C. T. H. B. A. They have been repeatedly invited to join it. Is there any inducement for them to belong when Mr. Simpson commences by pronouncing their stallions 'inferior,' unless they are willing to pit the foals of such stallions against the phenominal produce of Electioneer, Guy Wilkes, Sidney and other proved producers of speed?

Let me try to draw a parallel between one colt and the other. On the one hand we have (1) for sire Electioneer, the greatest sire of *early* speed living, or that ever did live; (2) for dam any one of forty mares that have already thrown speed, and extreme speed, to the cover of Electioneer or some other stallion; (3) for trainer and driver, Charles Marvin; (4) colts trained from yearlings up; (5) every convenience in the shape of kindergarten, track, stalls, feed, etc., conceivable; (6) a selection of ten or more in at least forty to make entries from; (7) a selection of one in ten to fifteen to start.

On the other hand we have (1) an untried son of Electioneer; (2) one half dozen or a dozen mares, usually of uncertain breeding, none of which was ever known to throw a 2:30 horse to the cover of anything; (3) for trainer Mr. Forty or Mr. Sixty Dollars Amonth; (4) colts taken up in April or May, sometimes at two years old, generally not before three years old; (5) for kindergarten a square cow corral, no box-stall, a draughty stable, no track until he goes to Mr. So Much Amonth; (6) a selection of one in six down to one in one to make entries from; (7) one in one to start or pay forfeit on.

Now add to this handicap a repetition of favorable circumstances similar to those at Palo Alto, as enjoyed by the entries made by San Mateo, Rosemeade, Pleasanton, and Valensin stock farms. What I should like to know is the odds against colt number two getting a share of the purse. Admitting even that the owner of the latter has no one but himself to blame and that he adopts all the measures used at these farms, is not the produce of his untried sire out of an untried mare still unreasonably handicapped?

Palo Alto usually enters in stakes foals by two or three stallions other than Electioneer, and *usually*, also, the starter to represent the stable is by Electioneer. Does this brand the sires of the other entries as "inferior?" Certainly inferior to Electioneer. They and their get may not hold a candle to the old horse and his produce, yet the former may be great horses. These other stallions also have the use of these "producing" mares, and yet they are seldom started. Why then ask still more heavily handicapped stallions on the outside either to come in and compete with the best of Palo Alto, San Mateo, Pleasanton, etc., or stay out altogether, when, as a rule, Palo Alto itself dare not start any but the best foal of its best stud?

Palo Alto is run on business principles and to pay its way; when we see its trainer behind a horse we all know he is out for the stuff and for the fame of its great stallions; we do not see Mr. Marvin bring out an Electioneer when there is a moral certainty of his being distanced by a phenomenal colt like Regal Wilkes, that happened along last fall.

Did Marvin acknowledge Electioneer to be an 'inferior,' stallion to Guy Wilkes by staying in the stable on this occasion? Of course not. Why then expect the small breeder to put himself in that position with the odds ten times greater against him than against Palo Alto or any other great breeding farm.

Did Marvin disgrace this coast, the Palo Alto Farm and the great Electioneer when he entered Palo Alto in the 2:20 class, and not in the free-for-all in the early part of last fall's circuit, or Express in the 2:30 class and not in the 2:20 class, after he had shown them 2:18 on the farm?

Certainly not: he entered them where they had a right to enter and where they had a *reasonable chance to win their share of the money*, and that is all that the smaller breeders are asking and that the Board of Directors have offered to them in purses 7, 8 and 9.

A great many small breeders own sons of Electioneer, Guy Wilkes, Sultan, etc., and although they may all hope, there are but few who expect them to prove as great producers as their sires. A little encouragement will go a long way with them as with most horsemen. Trotting a close second to Palo Alto, San Mateo or Pleasanton in 2:20 or even 2:16 *may* be glory, but it does not so much as give one a record of 2:30, and is most decidedly encouraging. It is *the record that tells.*

Alfred G. trotted a most wonderful race at Oakland against Atto Rex, Express and others, and I believe another great race at Stockton; but, so far as his fame in Kentucky is concerned, the mark he achieved at Napa *against time*, is worth five hundred such races as the one at Oakland in which he never won a heat, and therefore got no record. In the former instance he proved to a few spectators that he was a fast and game horse. In the latter he proved to the world what rate of speed he could and did carry, and the mark set opposite his name becomes part of that name.

The smaller breeders have no desire to go in for 'tin cup' marks, but they want a chance to get records and to get them honestly in fair contests. It is not for an association the P. C. T. H. B. A. to turn up its nose at these small breeders and say, 'Look here, gentlemen, we want your annual and membership dues, but if you expect us to return any part of it to your 'inferior' horses or their scrub produce, you have come to the wrong shop.'

The small breeders, the beginners and purchasers of the sons of the great stallions fully appreciate that whatever is beneficial to the owners of the great speed producers is more or less beneficial to them.

The owners of stallions of established reputation should keep in mind, that those reputations will be still further entranced of their sons be given the opportunity to prove that they also will breed speed, six grandsons and daughters of Electioneer last year fought their way into the 2:30 list. Not a single one of them was placed there by Palo Alto; nor did any of them get there in free for all colt stakes.

The sires of every one of these six were prior to last year 'inferior' horses whose progeny were not of sufficient merit to obtain a place in the list. To-day their produce are being sought after for shipment to the East.

If the P. C. T. H. B. A. was gotten up for the sole purpose of exhibiting Sunols, Regal Wilkes, Faustinos, Directs, Palo Altos, Stambouls and their equals and condemning everything else as inferior and 'a disgrace to the Pacific Coast,' we might as well close out the small breeders and the Association at once.

I have given my reasons at length for offering this class of colt stakes, and I trust that Mr. Simpson's correspondents will do as much for opposing them. I believe that in suggesting colt stakes Nos. 7, 8, and 9, I met the desires of a majority of the large and small breeders who belong to the association; I therefore invite them to express their views through the press or by letters addressed to the secretary with or without permission to print them over their signatures. I know that it is not my intention to go counter to the general desires of the members and I have no reason to believe any of my fellow directors to feel differently to myself in that respect.

Certainly, if the members view the programme as Mr. Simpson does, as a disgrace to the Pacific Coast, the action of the Board will necessarily reflect on the Association and indirectly on the individual members.' I trust therefore they will make their opinions known as above suggested.

Respectfully, yours, WILFRED PAGE.

A Hundred Years Ago.

Stud Fees of the Olden Time in Contrast With Those of To-day.

The advertisements of stallions in the old Kentucky Gazette of 1789, just a hundred years ago, furnish curious reading in this day of high priced stud fees. Now we are standing horses at a thousand, five hundred and down to a hundred dollars, and a few below these figures, says the Live Stock Record. In looking over the Kentucky Gazette of 1789 we find the following list of stallions, their pedigrees and the fees asked for their services. The stud fees at the present times, $500 and $1,000, are more than these horses of a hundred years ago cost, judging by service fees.

Don Carlos, bay, 15 hands, foaled 1772, by imp Figaro, dam Primrose by imp Dove, stood at Gen. Charles Scott's at 40 shillings a mare, payable in corn, beef, bacon, cows, calves, sheep, hogs, butter or lard.

Don Careless, bay, 15½ hands, by Old Don Careless, said to have been imported by Col. Taylor of Virginia, dam by Tom Jones, stood at Francis Keene's at $5 the season, payable in corn, calves, neat cattle, sheep, pork, wheat, rye or oats, at their cash value.

Dolphin, bay, 15 hands, foaled 1782, by Godolphin, dam Kitty Fisher, by Fitzhugh's Regulus, grandam imp. Lady Northumberland, by Northumberland, etc., stood at Samuel Beeler's at $4, or 10 shillings a leap, payable in cash or country produce at market rates.

Ferguson's Guy, gray, by Simm's Wildair, dam by Skipworth,s Comus, grandam by Imp. Jolly Roger, etc., stood at Bryant Ferguson's at 20 shillings, or country produce at cash prices.

Laburnain, chestnut, 15 hands, by Imp. Lath, dam Imp. Kitty Fisher, by Cade, at $10 the season, or 400 pounds of tobacco, or 10 barrels of corn, or 400 pounds of pork, or 20 bushels of rye, or any merchantable produce.

Mogul, bay, by imp Lath, at $4, payable in corn, rye, wheat, bacon, etc. Arabian, gray, but his breeding is not given. They were advertised by John Crittenden to stand at Horatio Turpin's.

The Godolphin, bay, 15 hands by Godolphin Arabian, dam imp Kitty Fisher. This horse is not recorded and we give it as stated in the advertisement. He stood at Nicholas Lafon's at 30 shillings or 200 pounds of tobacco.

Tippoo Saib, gray, foaled 1871, by imp Lath, dam Brandon, dam of Meade's Celer, Pilgrim, Clodius, etc., by imp Aristotle, etc., stud at S. Johnson's near mouth of Hickman at 50 shillings the season, with a proviso that the season might be discharged by the payment of 40 shillings in cash, or in beef, young cattle, tobacco, pork, hemp, butter, etc., at market rates.

Union, bay, foaled 1772, by Shakespeare, dam by Nonpareil, grandam by imp. Traveller, &c., stood at George Blackburn's in Woodford County at 3 pounds, or 5 pounds to insure. It is well to state a Kentucky shilling was worth 16⅔ cents, and a Kentucky pound was $3.33. It will be seen by the above that in those times a hundred years ago stud horses in Fayette County and that immediate neighborhood were extremely well bred, and doubtless from the figures asked for their service can be explained to a great extent the good foundation laid for Kentucky stock. Without exception they were well bred and no other kind were advertised, so farmers and breeders had to use them or nothing. Only ten were advertised when we have hundreds at this day, and the highest priced fee was $10, while ours are up to $500 and in some cases $1000.

Its Wonderful Mechanism.

The Horse's Heart a Great Double Force Pump.

The ablest physiologist cannot tell what is life, though he can give a thousand proofs that stagnation is death; the chemist cannot tell how oxygen and carbon combine so as to maintain heat with such unerring regularity in any climate; the mechanic cannot discover how a fluid so thick as blood is passed so rapidly through tubes too fine to pass the purest water, nor can he show us where the motive power originates. The most elaborate, complete and delicate machine ever constructed by the skill of man is a clumsy, bungling, wasteful piece of mechanism compared to the organization that circulates, warms and invigorates the blood of the horse —the heart, the great double force pump which appears to keep all in motion.

To the right side of the heart comes a stream of dark fluid, composed of blood, that has gone the round of the system, and of newly made chyle, selected and extracted by very fine lacteals from the food passing through the bowels. This mixture is immediately pumped out of the heart into the lungs to be warmed, purified, and supplied with new oxygen. It there gets rid of its load of poisonous carbonic acid gas, and is changed from a dull dark to a bright red color. How is all this done in a few seconds? The lungs are a beautiful sight under the microscope, and would be far more so if it were possible to see them at work. They contain millions of cells, too minute to be seen by the eye, yet each cell receives its particle of blood or its particle of air, and without confusing them together allows the air to get near enough to the blood to give it oxygen and to take away carbonic acid gas, to burn up waste material and to effect all the known and unknown changes necessary to fit it to carry new life and heat and vigor to every part of the body.

Every particle of blood is made to meet the fresh air, not only without cooling it, but heating it in the process, and heating it most when the air introduced is coldest. Having been thus fitted for its work, the blood goes back to the heart, entering it now on the left side, and is immediately pumped into the arteries which carry it all over the system, delivering the required quantity as fresh and pure at the feet as at the heart itself, pulling down and building up wherever and whatever is necessary, carrying nerves, brain, muscles, hair, hoofs, skin, or bones, through vessels too small to carry water and flowing into the veins comes back again to the right side of the heart to be again passed through the warming and purifying fire in the lungs. All this is done so rapidly that the whole of the blood in the body passes through the heart in a time varying from one to three minutes, and the faster it is kept going by reasonable exercise the more completely does it accomplish its work

Fire is the rapid combination of carbon with oxygen. Wherever this combination takes place, either quickly or slowly, heat is produced in exact proportion to the amount of carbon and oxygen mixed together. It is seen going in hearth fires fast enough to produce a destructive flame, and still faster in the smith's fire, where the oxygen is rapidly forced into contact with the carbon by the smith's bellows.

The same thing goes on slowly in the lungs, restrained and regulated by a strictly limited supply of oxygen. One principal reason why the blood is heated most in cold weather is because cold air lies in less compass than warm air, so that the same pipes can convey more of it, and consequently more oxygen at each inspiration.

The lungs are a wonderful self regulating furnace that warms the blood just as much and no more than is needed, while the warm blood, by its rapid circulation through a beautiful system of pipes, warms every inch of the body, and with the help of a good, healthy clean skin, will preserve a uniform temperature of about 100 degrees, whether surrounded by a temperature 20 degrees below zero or 260 degrees above it. Thus the blood is always kept warm enough to circulate through tubes too small to be seen, yet never warm enough to injure the inconceivably fine texture that composes the millions of cells in which the blood meets, without mingling with, the air in the lungs.

There is a beautiful and wonderful feature in connection with circulation which cannot be understood without going a little into the composition of the blood itself. The greater part of the blood is greasy water, but about 13 per cent. of it consists of minute onion shaped particles, or little soft, tough, flattened circles, about the three-thousandth part of an inch through their greatest diameter, and the ten-thousandth of an inch between their flatter sides.

These are called blood corpuscles, or blood cells, and consist of a material called cruor, which has the property of attracting oxygen from the air, and of parting with it to the various tissues of the body, or, in other words, of picking it up in the lungs and carrying it to any part of the body that wants it.

These little cells go out from the lungs loaded with oxygen, which they take to combine with carbon in the distant tissues of the body. They return with their color changed from red to black and loaded with carbonic acid gas, produced by the combination of the oxygen with the carbon, in the exhausted tissues of the body.

Thus while the purely liquid part of the blood gathers heat in the lungs and carries it to every part of the body, just as warm water would do passing through a furnace and running back through the pipes of a hot house, these little blood cells go out, not only warmed themselves, but carrying out the material with which to keep up a little fire at the extremities and bring back the poisonous products of that fire, to be sent out with the warm, moist air from the lungs. They thus keep up heat by burning away waste material at the extremities, just as it is kept up on a larger scale in the lungs. They are so tough that they will squeeze through a space smaller than themselves and recover their original form. They are smaller in the horse than in man, and are still smaller in the deer, probably smallest in those liable to be called on for the most rapid circulation or most remarkable for speed and endurance.

Blood corpuscles compose 13 per cent. of the blood, but that is only a rough average estimate. They vary from something like 5 to 20 per cent., and the cause of their variation is a most important consideration in connection with the subject of this chapter. The smallest percentage is found in the blood of poor needle women, or of any females poorly fed, getting little active exercise, and above all shut up in close rooms. The largest percentage is found in the blood of man or any other animal constantly at work in the cold open air, with enough good nutritious food. With women shut up from the open air the blood cells are usually so few that their feet are kept warm with difficulty, if at all. With too much hard work in the cold open air the blood cells may get so large a percentage of the blood as to give a tendency to inflammation when food or drink of an inflammatory character are indulged in. Poor blood can only be made good blood by good food and plenty of exercise in the open air; high feeding without the exercise in the open air will only do mischief, and especially endanger the lungs. The blood cells can be slowly increased by the open air exercise, they can be rapidly decreased by shutting up in bad air, they can be instantly lessened by bleeding, and the corpuscles so lost cannot be restored for some weeks or month under the very best treatment."

Thus Mrs. Heman's allusion to the "rich blood" of the Arab is as pyhsologically correct as it is poetically beautiful, and such rich blood must be cultivated in any animal that is to be capable of any extraordinary exertion. In other words, if the horse is to be fit for much he must both be taken into the open air and the pure air must be taken into him, if he is to be shut up at all. He must not breathe air that has already parted with its free oxygen and become loaded with carbonic acid gas, or with the ammonia arising from stones reeking with the excretions of his own body.

The Standard.

(AS REVISED AND ADOPTED BY THE NATIONAL ASSOCIATION OF TROTTING-HORSE BREEDERS, DECEMBER 14, 1887.)

IN order to define what constitutes a trotting-bred horse and to establish a BREED of trotters on a more intelligent basis, the following rules are adopted to control admission to the records of pedigrees. When an animal meets the requirements of admission and is duly registered, it shall be accepted as a standard trotting-bred animal:—

FIRST.—Any stallion that has himself a record of two minutes and thirty seconds (2:30) or better, provided any of his get has a record of 2:35 or better, or provided his sire or his dam is already a standard animal.

SECOND.—Any mare or gelding that has a record of 2:30 or better.

THIRD.—Any horse that is the sire of two animals with a record of 2:30 or better.

FOURTH.—Any horse that is the sire of one animal with a record of 2:30 or better, provided he has either of the additional qualifications: (1) A record himself of 2:35 or better. (2) Is the sire of two other animals with a record of 2:35 or better. (3) Has a sire or dam that is already a standard animal.

FIFTH.—Any mare that has produced an animal with a record of 2:30 or better.

SIXTH.—The progeny of a standard horse when out of a standard mare.

SEVENTH.—The female progeny of a standard horse when out of a mare by a standard horse.

EIGHTH.—The female progeny of a standard horse when out of mare whose dam is a standard mare.

NINTH.—Any mare that has a record of 2:35 or better, and whose sire or dam is a standard animal.

Best Trotting Records.

1 mile—2:08¾, Maud S., against time, in harness, accompanied the distance by a running horse, Glenville, O., July 30, 1885......2:13¾, best time in a race between horses, Maud S., Chicago, Ills., July 24, 1880......2:12, Axtell, against time, accompanied by running horse—fastest stallion time, Terre Haute, Ind., Oct. 11, 1889......2:13¼, Phallas, fastest heat by a stallion against other horses, Chicago, July 14, 1884......2:12¾, Palo Alto, third heat in race at Stockton, Cal., Sept. 26, 1889......2:15¼, Jay-Eye-See, half-mile track, Lincoln, Neb., Sept. 14, 1887......2:15¼, Great Eastern, under saddle, third heat, Morrisania, N. Y., Sept. 22, 1877......2:10¾, Jay-Eye-See, against time, best five-year-old record, Providence, R. I., Sept. 15, 1883......2:16, Manzanita, third heat, best four-year-old record, Lexington, Ky., Sept. 8, 1876 ...... 2:16, Edgemark, four-year-old stallion record, against time, Lexington, Ky., Oct. 18, 1889......2:10½, Sunol, in Stanford Stake, accompanied by a runner, best three-year-old record, San Francisco, Nov. 9, 1889..2:18, Sunol 2 years, against time, San Francisco, Cal., Oct. 27, 1888......2:20½, Regal Wilkes, two-year-old stallion record, San Francisco, Nov. 9, 1889......2:31½, Norlaine, yearling, against time, San Francisco, Cal., Nov. 12, 1887...... 2:36, Faustino, yearling stallion record, San Francisco, Nov. 9, 1889.

2 miles—4:43 against time, Fanny Witherspoon, Chicago, Ill., Sept. 25, 1885.

3 miles—7:21¼, Huntress, harness, Brooklyn, L. I., Sept. 21, 1872.

4 miles—10:34½, Longfellow, wagon, California, Dec 31, 1869.

5 miles—13:00, Lady Mac, harness, San Francisco, Cal., April 2, 1874.

10 miles—27:23½, Controller, harness, San Francisco, Cal., Nov. 23, 1878.

20 miles—58:25, Captain McGowan, harness, half-mile track, Boston, Oct. 31, 1865.

Pacing Records at One Mile.

Johnston, harness, against time, Chicago, Ills., Oct 8, 1884, 2:06¼.

Brown Hal, best stallion record, Cleveland, Ohio, July 31, 1889, 2:12½.

Westmont, July 10, 1884, Chicago, Ills., with running mate, 2:01¾.

Daisy, yearling, Sacramento, Dec. 31, 1885, 2:38¼.

Ed Rosewater, two years old, Council Bluffs, Iowa, Nov. 3, 1888, 2:20½.

Yolo Maid, 3 years old, San Francisco, Oct. 13, 1888, 2:14.

Gold Leaf, four years old, 2:11¼ on August 17, 1889, at Napa.

Arrow, five years old, 2:13¼, made at Cleveland, Ohio, August 1, 1888.

Fastest Time on Record.

MILES.	RUNNING.	
¼	Jim Miller, 2, Deer Lodge (Mont.), Aug. 16, 1888 ......; †Sleepy Dick, a, Kiowa (Kan.), Nov. 24, 1888 ...... *	0:21¼
⅜	Cyclone, a, 120 lbs., Helena (Mont.), Aug. 28, 1889	0:34½
½	Geraldine, 4, 122 lbs., Westchester Course, Aug. 30, 1889	[illegible]
⅝	Britannic, 5, 122 lbs., Westchester Course, Aug. 31, 1889	0:59
⅝	Fordham, a, 115 lbs., Westchester Course, Oct. 4, 1889	0:59
¾	El Rio Rey, 2, 126 lbs., Westchester Course, Aug. 31, 1889	1:11
¾	Tipstaff, 3, 107, Westchester Course, Oct. 4, 1889	1:11
⅞	Britannic, 5, 110 lbs., Sheepshead Bay, Sept. 5, 1889	1:26 2-5
	Ten Broeck, 5, 110 lbs., Louisville, May 24, 1877 ...... (against time)	1:39¾
1	Maori 4, 108 lbs., Chicago, July 12, 1889, (in a race)	1:39 4-5
1 1-16	Wheeler T., 3, 98 lbs., St. Louis, June 1, 1888	1:47¼
1 1-16	Eyton 4, 106, Chicago, Ill., June 28, 1889	1:47¼
1⅛	Terra Cotta, 4, 124 lbs., Sheepshead Bay, June 23, 1888	1:53
1 3-16	Joe Cotton, 5, 109½ lbs., Sheepshead Bay, Sept. 7, 1887	2:00¼
1¼	Kingston, 8, 122 lbs., Gravesend, Sept 24, 1889	2:06¼
1 m 500 yds.	Ben d'Or, 4, 115 lbs., Saratoga, July 25, 1882	2:10¼
1⅜	Triboulet, 4, 117 lbs., San Francisco, April 26, 1888; Richmond, 6, 122 lbs., Sheepshead Bay, June 27, 1888	2:21¾
1½	Firenzi, 4, 113 lbs., Monmouth Park, Aug. 2, 1888; Luke Blackburn, 3, 102 lbs., Monmouth Park, Aug. 17, '80; Jim Guest, 4, 98 lbs., Chicago, (Washington Park, July 24 '88)	2:34
1¾	Hindoocraft, 3, 73 lbs., Westchester, Aug. 27, 1889	2:48
1⅞	Gildelia, 6, 116 lbs., Saratoga, Aug. 5, 1882	3:01
1⅞	Enigma, 4, 90 lbs., Sheepshead Bay, Sept. 15, 1885	3:20
2	Ten Broeck, 5, 110 lbs., Louisville, May 29, 1877	3:27¼
2¼	Monitor, 4, 110 lbs., Baltimore, Oct. 20, 1880	3:44½
2½	Springbok, 5, 114 lbs.; Preakness, a, 114 lbs. — Saratoga, July 29, 1875	3:56¼
2½	Aristides, 4, 104 lbs., Lexington, May 13, 1876	4:27¼
2⅝	Ten Broeck, 4, 104 lbs., Lexington, Sept. 16, 1876	4:58½
2¾	Hubbard, 4, 107 lbs., Saratoga, Aug. 9, 1873	4:58¾
3	Drake Carter, 4 115 lbs., Sheepshead Bay, Sept. 6, 1884	5:24
4	Ten Broeck, 4, 104 lbs., Louisville, Sept. 27, 1876	7:15¾

MILES.	HEAT RACES.	
¼	Sleepy Dick, a, Kiowa (Kan.), Nov. 24, 1888	0:21½—0:22¼
½	Bogus, a, 115 lbs., Helena (Mont.), Aug. 21, 1888	0:48 —0:48
⅝	Kittie Pease, 4, Dallas (Tex.), Nov. 2, 1887 ......; Sudie McNairy, 2, 98 lbs., Chicago, July 2, 1889	1:00 —1:00; 1:02¾—1:03
¾	Lizzie S., 5 118 lbs., Louisville, Sept. 28, 1882	1:13¾—1:13¼
1	Bounce, 4, 90 lbs., Sheepshead Bay, Sept. 7, 1881	1:42 —1:41¾
1	3 in 5, L'Argentine, 6, 115 lbs., St. Louis, June 14, 1879	1:43—1:44 —1:47¼
1 1-16	Slipalong, 5, 115 lbs., Chicago (Wash. Park), Sept. 2, 1885	1:50½—1:48
1⅛	Gabriel, 4, 112 lbs., Sheepshead Bay, Sept. 23, 1880	1:56 —1:56
1¼	Glenmore, 5, 114 lbs., Sheepshead Bay, Sept. 25, 1880	2:10 —2:14
1½	Keno, 4, Toledo, Sept. 18, 1889 (1st and 3d heats)	2:43½—2:46
2	Miss Woodford, 4, 107½ lbs., Sheepshead Bay, Sept. 20, 1884	3:33 —3:31½
3	Norfolk, 4, 100 lbs., Sacramento, Sept. 23, 1865	5:27½—5:29½
	Ferida, 4, 105 lbs., Sheepshead Bay, Sept. 18, 1880	7:23½—7:41

†Made in a heat race.
*Doubtful, and made in a heat race.

CORRESPONDENTS WANTED.

We want a correspondent and agent in every town on the Pacific Coast where Horses are Bred, Trained or Raced.

Also correspondence relating to Hunting, Fishing and the Kennel.

Reasonable compensation will be paid to those who send NEWS.

For particulars, address,

BREEDER AND SPORTSMAN,
313 Bush Street, S. F.

Grim's Gossip.

The noted turf writer "Aurelius" says that he never attended a dozen trotting meetings in his life.

It is now stated on what should be good authority that G. S. Davis paid Mr. Steele of Philadelphia $35,000 for Antevolo.

C. F. Emery of the Forest City Farm has engaged Caton, the driver, and will have a string of trotters on the circuit this year.

It is reported that T. J. Dunbar may handle Maud S. next season. Dunbar is head trainer at Fashion Farm, but his term does not expire until next fall.

Last week I mentioned that R. Steele of Philadelphia had sold Antevolo for $40,000. It now turns out that Geo. S. Davis of the Clairview Stock Farm, near Detroit is the purchaser.

We have been asked quite a number of times when Goodwin's Annual Turf Guide would appear. From information received from the office, we can state that they will be out inside of ten days.

L. J. Rose will have eighty six head of horses in the coming New York Auction Sale and the Valensin Stock Farm will be represented with twenty head. The sale is set for March 5th and 6th.

John Faylor has accepted a position with E. J. Baldwin and left for the Santa Anita ranch yesterday. He will have full charge of the breeding department at which he has had many years of experience.

R. Porter Ashe will have seven racers in his stable this year, including, of course, the now famous Geraldine. Letters from the East assure the owner that the great sprinter is better than ever before.

Mike Kelly paid the city a flying visit a few days ago. He reports the stock at the Ashe Farm in splendid condition, and also thinks he can show up a number of speedy two year olds this year that will be hard to beat.

Fred Barrett one of England's crack riders, sailed on Christmas eve for Buenos Ayres. He will ride a few races there and return to England in the latter part of February, expecting to be back by the 6th of March.

J. H. White, of Lakeville, Sonoma County, is unfortunate in the death of Accident, one of his best broodmares. She was by Frank McClellan, out of the Ralston mare. Her death resulted from an injury which she received several weeks ago.

It is with a great deal of pleasure that I contradict the statement made last week about the damage to the grand stand at Glenbrook Park. It seems that the only damage done by the snow, was to some temporary buildings and the stand is uninjured.

Some of the turfmen around Louisville have made a proposition to have a farm for horses that have been successful racers in which to spend their old age. The project appears to be a good one, and will probably be carried out by those that are interested in it.

The Leonard Bros., Elemeade Stud, Lexington Ky. has sold to Governor Leland Stanford, Palo Alto Stock Farm, a bay yearling colt by Electioneer, dam Winona, by Almona, by Almont; second dam Dolly, dam of Onward, 2:20½; Director, 2:17, and Thorndale 2:22¼.

Work on the new Monmouth Park race track is progressing steadily and enough has now been done to indicate that long before the Monmouth Park racing season begins the grandest race track surely on the American continent, and most likely on any other continent will be ready for occupancy.

Seth Griffin, who has prepared all the fast tracks over which Maud S has made her records, has written Robert Bonner from Philadelphia to come and see the soil and material put on Belmont track; and if Maud S. can ever beat her record, she should be able to do it over that track.

Judson H. Clark, of Elmira, but well-known in this city, refused a bonafide offer of $102,000 for the great Bell Boy, a few days before he was burned to death. The income from the horse this year would have been $32,500. Mr. Hopper owned a half interest in the nag.—Buffalo Commercial Advertiser.

A few weeks ago I mentioned in Gossip that Geo. Middleton of Chicago was willing to match Jack 2:15 against any trotter in the country. In an interview recently held with the gentleman he stated that he was convinced that his grey gelding would make a mark of 2:10 or better during the season of 1890.

Philadelphia has a pair of car horses which for sagacity are wonderful, if the story is true. They say that if these horses, on nearing a crossing at night, see a man standing on a corner of a street with a lighted cigar in his hand, and at the approach of the car he throws it into the street, the horses will come to a full stop at the crossing.

Mr. L. J. Rose is talking in a confident manner about Stamboul making a record of 2:10 sometime this year. There were many who thought he was too enthusiastic when he made the wager with Crawforn last year. But there is not a person who saw the mile made at Napa but what knows perfectly well that only the elements prevented the accomplishment of the allotted task.

A number of the horsemen who live in and around Petaluma have contributed toward a common fund and will purchase a set of Wallace's Register and year books, Chester's Trotting and Pacing Records, and also a set of Bruce's American Stud books. This will be a great convenience, for there are questions coming up continually that can only be answered by having the authorities at hand.

The Pleasanton Stock Farm is not going to be out done by the other large producers who have annual sales, so Mr. Salisbury has made arrangements with Mr. Peter C. Kellogg & Co, and will sell a consignment from the home of Director on March 7th, the day following the conclusion of the Rose and Valensin sale.

An Eastern contemporary states that W. Mulkey, Kansas City, Mo., has sold to California parties the bay filly Mary M., foaled 1887, by Lucifer, dam Lady Veto, by Veto, out of Julia Howard's Glencoe; Lela, brown mare, foaled 1884, by Virginius, dam Lady Veto, and the chestnut horse War Sign, foaled 1880, by War Dance, dam Louisa by imp Australian, out of Luileme by Lexington.

Next year's Derby in England will be run under entirely new conditions. It will be a stake of £6,000, the winner taking £5,000, the nominator of the winner £500, and the owners of the second and third horses £300 and £200 respectively. The subscription is £50 each, or £25 forfeit if declared by January 7th. Probably no animal will be left in that will not be prepared for the race.

A letter received from the Valensin Stock Farm, notifies me that Venus (dam of Adonis, 2:14) gave birth to a beautiful chestnut filly, by Sidney, on the morning of January 28th. The only white on this valuable foal is a white diamond on the nose. A full sister to Adonis should be a very valuable animal, and there will be plenty of fanciers who will be willing to pay a long price for this little damsel.

"In discussing the point why thoroughbreds are unable to maintain for a mile their best speed for a quarter," says Robert Bonner, "I think many men overlook the fact that it is the pace that kills. The ox never tires because, although he keeps constantly at work, he doesn't move fast enough to drain his strength. Even with machinery, to obtain high speed, the power must be increased in greater ratio."

Mike McManus has again assumed command of a string of trotters for D. M. Reavis of Chico, Mike has altogether about twenty head at the race track, and he confidently believes that he has a number of good ones among them. It is now many years since Mike last worked for Mr. Reavis, and it is to be hoped that he will bring out prominently some of the old Blackbird stock of which there are so many on the ranch.

With Kingstone, Firenzi, Tenny, Hanover, Salvator, Britannic, Geraldine, Volunteer, Prince Royal, Badge, Blue Rock Cracksman, Proctor Knott, Los Angeles. Come to Taw, Belle d'Or, Tipstaff and exactly 100 others on his hand, the adjuster of the Toboggan Slide handicap, at three-quarters of a mile, will have something to keep him busy for a week. The New York Jockey club did wisely in giving the sprinters a chance.—New York Mail and Express.

Beautiful Bells, dam of Bell Boy 2:19¼, and Hinda Rose 2:19½, is the only mare that ever threw two foals that at 3 years old had records of 2:20 or better. She also has the honor of being the dam of the highest price horse ever sold at auction in America, her son Bell Boy, brining $51,000 at public sale. The highest price ever paid for a horse in the world at auction was given for Blair Athol, in England, he being knocked down at a bid of $62,500.—(Kentucky Stock Farm.)

The race horse has often the advantage of very accomplished teachers. Men from whom much can be learned. The innumerable vices, so often conspicuous on the public racecourse, are little seen in the private training stable and those who judge the one from the other and think that everything connected with the race horse must be depraved, would be surprised to witness the command of temper, the high character, and the noble self control of some of the men who are entrusted with the care of the most valuable race horses.

F. A. Lovecraft, Secretary of the American Jockey Club, has sent to all interested, the following circular:

In accordance with "Racing Rule" No. 10, the following stakes for 1890 and 1891, already closed, will be run over the course of the New York Jockey Club, Westchester, New York, under the control of the American Jockey Club, viz.:

The Juvenile, Withers, Belmont, Ladies, for the Spring, and the Jerome, Mosholu, Hunter, Nursery and Titan for the Fall of 1890.

The Wither, Ladies, Belmont, for the Spring and the Jerome, Hunter and Mosholu for the Fall of 1891.

The daily press of San Francisco yesterday received the following dispatch:—"The Times-Index will this evening publish a statement on the authority of Governor Waterman that Richard Gird of this county will be appointed a director of the State Agricultural Society, to succeed G. W. Hancock, whose term has expired. Mr. Gird will also be appointed the Manager of the State Citrus Fair for Southern California, which is to be held at Los Angeles in March, in place of Mr. Hancock. The appointment is satisfactory to every one, and the fruit growers in San Bernardino County will assist in the State Citrus Fair."

After pronouncing El Rio Rey the greatest two-year-old the country has ever seen, the Week's Sport says: "If the sickness he suffered from last fall has not interfered with him, he promises to be the most perfect three-year-old America has yet produced, good enough to win the English Derby any year, and to be a "world-beater" indeed. If, however, the attack was as severe as represented, it is quite probable he may take a year to get over it, as has often been found to be the case. From El Rio Rey it is a long step to the next one, whichever one takes that to be, whether Reclare or Gregory. In either case there is a most curious contrast in the surroundings. El Rio Rey is essentially a lordly colt, the property of a millionaire, racing for glory as much as for money, though his winnings are so great while Reclare and Gregory are animals that have had to earn their daily bread."

A week or two ago mention was made in this column about a race that had been arranged to take place at Bakersfield between horses owned by Harrison Jones and Charles Kerr. The match was for two races, one, a mile dash and the second a half mile dash, there to be only twenty minutes intervening between the two races. Well, the event has been decided, Mr Kerr winning with his stallion Apache both races easily. Those who were acquainted with the running qualities of the Jones horse, fancied that it was impossible to lose, and as a consequence were early on the scene of action to place their money as best they could. Mr. Kerr, so we are informed wagered $3 200 on the result and the backers of Harrison Jones' horse are trying to borrow money enough to get home. Apache is a beautiful chestnut by imp Mortemer, dam The Bashee by Lexington. He was taken in hand by Hanger Jones to prepare for the last meeting of the Blood Horse Association but failed to show form enough to warrant his owner in starting him. The chances are that he may be seen at the Bay District Track in April,

The most remarkable performer ever foaled was the Hungarian thoroughbred mare Kincsem (pronounced Keen-chem). She won fifty-four races, and was never beaten. In one of her races Prince Giles the First, the best horse of his day in Germany, was pitted against her The Prince got much the best of the start, but the mare ran him to a dead heat and then easily beat him in the run-off. Her races were run in Austria, Germany, England and other countries, and she won $96,634 in stakes and purses She met with an accident which caused her death, thus losing her to the stud.

As was told my readers last week, Harry J. Agnew, of Honolulu, arrived on the steamer which arrived on Saturday. He has brought over with him a green pacer called Boswell Jr., by Boswell, a son of Almont. The dam is Maude, 2:20, by Black Hawk Bertrand; 2d dam by Hamilton Chief. He is a neat turned horse, and can show a good, lively mile even now. Mr. Agnew has also brought with him two two-year-old fillies, one called Angie Wilkes, by Guy Wilkes, dam Maude (the dam of Boswell Jr.), and she is as pretty a little trotter as one would wish to see. When I was present, Mr. Wm. Corbitt offered $1,500 for her, but Harry values the daughter of Guy at a much higher figure. The second of the fillies is a tall, stately miss by Doncaster, son of Elmo, dam Kitty Malone by Patchen Vernon. Mr. Agnew will now look around for a stock farm, and prepare to start in the breeding business on an extensive scale.

I find the following rather peculiar proposition in a late copy of the N. Y. Spirit of the Times:

I have received numerous letters in regard to the bay gelding Diamond, 2:21¼, and many have made offers less than our catalogue price, which is useless, as we have only one price to all, and if changed will be changed to all alike. I will now make this proposition (and I am still outside of an insane asylum): I will sell Diamond for $10 000 cash, and will then bet any man $2,500 against $10,000 (which is 1 to 4) that I can and will, within six months from March 1, 1890 give him a record of 2:10 or better, I to have entire control of horse and the selecting of his groom, and all other matters, the same as if he was my own, the owner paying all expenses of horse and groom, which I will guarantee shall not exceed $150 per month for the six months. This will make anyone a very cheap horse from any standpoint. If he fails to make the time specified he will then stand his owner not over $8,400, and if he does make the specified time the cost to his owner will be $18,400. I have within the last ten days refused more than the first amount for him, so that I have not got this up as a scheme to reduce the price, but the reverse, as I think it very probable that with the above arrangement I would realize more than our catalogue price.

Yours, DELL BARKER, Agent.
Richlawn Farm, Greenwood, Mo.

L. M. Lasley, writing to me from Nashville, says:

Not much fast work has been done here yet, though just prior to the close of the stakes some few were sent short spins, and were generally satisfactory. A three-year-old, Burford, by Boulevard, and a two-year-old by the same sire, were thought to have shown the best. The latter, to my thinking, is a little coarse, but has lots of stamina and driving power, yet not so even turned and symmetrical as I like; still a large chestnut and very much like his sire. El Rio Rey is expected here about the 1st of February, and will meet an ovation, for everybody is on tiptoe to see the great champion. His stable may be glad he is not here now, for it has rained continually up to a day or two since, and, without warning, turned very cold and froze up tight and hard; still I saw some horses galloping this morning on a very hard, frozen track. No objection to that, as they were not mine; perhaps it was better they did. There are now about one hundred quartered here, and mostly seem to be doing well. The stakes just closed have filled well beyond expectation, which, by the way, is just and due the liberal management pursued by the officers in charge. The track is a good one indeed, having been recently—as one old gentleman told me—"*hosstiled*," and other needful work done. A great meeting the one next April will be and should be. The Belle Meade and other sales will bring the largest crowd ever seen here.

Capt. B. C. Harris on the Pedigree of Lorena.

EDITOR BREEDER AND SPORTSMAN:—In the last issue of your paper, under the head of Grim's Gossip, it is suggested that I should tell where I got the pedigree of the mare Princess 2:27½. The facts, in brief, are simply these: When I purchased Princess I also got another mare Lady Loud of Mr. Bridge, and upon asking him concerning their breeding, his reply was that he did not know how they were bred, but that one of them was known as the Loud mare, and the other, Princess, was the well known fast roadster, formerly owned and driven by Moses Alma then deceased. Upon this information, (designing the mare for brood purposes) and having often heard Mr. Alma speak of his "Mambrino mare," her breeding, etc., besides having some personal knowledge of her speed as a roadster, I set about the work of tracing up their pedigrees, as best I could. Of Mr. Warren Loud, who bred Lady Loud, I easily obtained her pedigree; while in regard to that of Princess I found much trouble, as, in those days, pedigrees of animals on the Pacific Coast were not as carefully preserved as they are now. Upon making further inquiry of several persons concerning their knowledge of Princess, I chanced to meet with Mr. Albert Whipple, who was, at the time, also looking after some breeding items for his brother S. B. Whipple. From him I obtained the information that (while looking over some files of papers, pedigrees and books belonging to W. F. Williamson, who had for a long time been the turf writer for the Alta and reporter for the California Spirit of the Times, and who was, in his day the accepted authority on all horse matters in the State of California) he came across the pedigree of the Alma mare, and as he was going to send the books and papers, among other things to some one in the East, I obtained the data which I then copied in my book. In regard to the discrepancy in the name of sires, I made a note of the names Mambrino Chief or Woodford Mambrino, which accounts for it as shown in the pedigrees published. As to the writings of that popular authority Hark Comstock, I can only say, that while the fair was in progress at Petaluma last fall, he asked me the breeding of Lorena's sire and dam, to which I replied as follows: "Sired by Jim Mulvenna, a son of Nutwood, dam Elmorene by Elmo. In his writing of the California two-year-olds, she has sometimes been called Loretta. Such mistakes are trivial and quite common, and are frequently typographical. Mr. Bridge who truthfulness is not to be questioned, assures me that he never said that I knew the pedigree of the old mare when I got her! And what could have prompted such a promulgation, unless it be a proneness to falsehood or egotism for appearing in print, I cannot see.

BEN E. HARRIS,
SAN FRANCISCO, Jan. 28, '90. 1626 Turk St.

TURF AND TRACK.

D. A. Honig's brother is seriously ill.

Will Cody 2:19½ died recently in Iowa.

Ansel stands at $200 at Mr. Bonners farm.

The Cleveland race track is being improved at a great cost.

J. H. McCormick has purchased the well known five-year old mare Belinda.

The New York winter tracks have been asked to give more half mile and repeat races.

The Governor has appointed John Harney and A. J. Stice Directors of Agricultural District No. 22.

Millard Sanders, the Canadian trainer, will open a public training stable in New York this month.

Superintendent Van Keuren has been confined to his house for the past few days with influenza.

It was Glory all the way at Clifton on the 20th, distance and going seeming to have no terrors for the Daly filly.

The Macey Brothers have closed up their large livery business in Lexington, and will attend strictly to educating trotting horses.

Mr. R. S. Veech of Indian Hill farm, who sends 17 mares to Axtell, has taken the vacant places in the book of Phallas, whose fee is $250.

The talk of Monmouth County last week was a rumor that Mr. Littlefield's Pardee filly, Penitent, showed three furlongs recently in 36 seconds.

It is said Frank Whitney the well known equine artist has decided to give up newspaper work and devote his time to color work which is more profitable.

Had Bell Boy lived through this season his stud fees would have left a balance of $11,000; $51,000 was given for him and his fees would have amounted to $62,000.

Morton, who rode for Palo Alto until the last Blood Horse meeting, has—or is going—to San Simeon to ride in the coming season for Senator Hearst's Western contingent.

An Eastern contemporary says the best matched team in New York State is probably the one in Matt Byrnes' stable at Monmouth, which Mr. B. A. Haggin took from California.

Dan McCarty has changed his mind and will fetch his horses from Fresno to San Francisco, in order to give the public a chance to see his trotters work quarters and halves in ——?

The Patterson New Jersey fanciers have tumbled to the fact that racehorsemen are bad to beat at a cock fight. When they win a battle they will have a chance to crow, but it is said they never will.

David, 2:19¼, who was shipped to England a while ago, should have a picnic in the pony classes there, as he is nicely under 16 hands, and should have almost a minute in hand with the English ponies.

Bither says Jay Eye See, his pet and pride, will not be seen again in public, when out here Bither had great hopes of his standing another season's work, but it is now decided he will not face the music again.

J. H. Walters, who has purchased the Lakeport Fair Grounds from the Lakeport Agricultural Park Association, purposes renovating and improving the track and grounds so that it will be the equal of any in the State.

Mr. E. B. Muir, a well known trotting horse breeder, residing in Donerail, Ky., is improving in health and will soon be out again. Mr. Muir is the owner of Nellie Burns 2:20¾ and Burns McGregor two-year-old record 2:29¾.

The condition of the local pool rooms has been peculiar for several days. Last Saturday they obtained no returns, but on Monday morning they received the winners, but were left in the same predicament with regard to Monday's races.

Six thoroughbred foals already at Palo Alto speak volumes for the careful management exercised by Superintendent Henry Walsh. Racine's dam Fairy Rose has a filly by imp. Cheviot while Flirt dam of Gorgo and Flambeau has a colt by Flood.

Samuel Gamble has purchased (presumably for Mr. Hobart) of Hart Boswell, Lexington, Ky., Nancy Lee, bay mare, foaled 1868, by Dictator—Sophy, by Alexander's Edwin Forest, for $6,000. She is the dam of the famous Nancy Hanks 2:24¾, who was never beaten.

Mr. Baldwin will attempt to raise some January foals next season, and in pursuance of that object several of his younger mares, including probably Mollie's Last, Viente, Rosebud and Atalanta, will be bred this month to The Emperor, Gano, Verano and the other stallions.

Eighteen heavy gray horses were consigned to A. L. Tiplin, Newark, by a dealer in Basto, Pennsylvania, on January 10th. On their arrival at the freight yards of the New Jersey Central Railroad, fifteen were suffocated, there being no ventilation except through the doors.

At a meeting of the Directors of the Coney Island Jockey Club held a fortnight ago, it was resolved that members of the American Jockey Club in good standing, who may apply and be elected to the Coney Island Jockey Club prior to March 1st, shall be admitted without initiation fee.

At the last Stanford sale in New York about a year ago, Lecturer—then 3 years old—by Electioneer, dam Mamie C., dam of Azmoor, 2:24½, was sold to Professor F. C. Fowler for for $1100; about a fortnight ago Lecturer was resold to Messrs. Rundle and White, Danbury; price, $6,500.

Among the mares book to Axtell for next season is Butterfly 2:19¾. She is by Young Jim, son of George Wilkes, dam Tansey, daughter of George Wilkes, and as Axtell is a grandson of George Wilkes, there will be in Butterfly's foal about as much George Wilkes as it is possible to get. Is it not possible to get too much of a good thing in breeding?

At a meeting of the life members of the Monterey Agricultural Association—District No. 7—held in the City Hall last week, it was agreed to recommend the following named gentlemen to Governor Waterman for appointment as Directors of the association. Dr. Thomas Flint, of San Juan, vice self, term expired; J. H. McDougall, vice Paris Kilburn, resigned.

Capt. Franklin, on his return to New Orleans a fortnight ago, took with him a two-year-old bay colt by Vanderbilt—Eva S; a three-year-old chestnut colt by Plenipo—Jaconet, and Vatican, a four-year-old black colt by Vanderbilt—Minnie Rogers. He purchased others, including Miss Leon, b f, 4, by Longfellow—Jennie M., which he has left at Nashville.

Clifton race goers and trainers are said to agree that the colt by Stratford out of Gazelle, the dam of Gallus Dan, is the best looking on the track. He will probably be saved for the great American stakes at the Brooklyn Jockey Club meeting in May. The colt was bought by Mr. Levy with another by Alarm out of Blossom by Saxon at the Chesterbrook sale.

A sporting contemporary says: If Red Elm had been well handled in his races this winter what a coup his people could have made. Within his distance he is one of the fastest horses in training. The Montana horse keeps winning every now and again, and last Saturday earned another winning bracket. Montana has several other sprinters who would probably astonish the Easterners.

That well-known turfman and breeder, Mr. Ben F. Pettit, is reported to be at the point of death at his home in Kentucky, from the effects of a severe attack of pneumonia Mr. Pettit is a part owner of the well-known Prince Charlie filly, Princess Bowling, and he also, jointly with Mr. Sanford Lyne, owns the imported stallion Deceiver, who cost his owner $10,000, and who is considered one of the most promising untried sires now in Kentucky.

The well-known performer, Duke of the Highlands, has been broken to harness by his trainer, Brown Dick, who drives him now to a buggy around Lexington every day. The horse's legs are shaky, and Dick, fearing he will not be able to stand training, has concluded to put him into a service, which, while it might appear ignoble to a high mettled racer, at least gives him a chance to earn his oats.

Prince Wilkes was driven but one English mile in 1889, and that he trotted in 2:15¾, which his trainer, Chambers, considers equal to 2:10, the track at Buenos Ayres being that much slow. Chambers, who has recently returned to his home in Kentucky, says the reputation of Prince Wilkes is so great in the Argentine that it will be difficult for him to be raced successfully hereafter on account of the long distances he will be handicapped.

The only horses of Mr. Haggin's that Byrnes has are cared for by his hinchman L. Cummings, in Mr. Byrnes' absence. These are Firenzi and Salvator, also Hawkstone, Ransom Kern, Fitzjames, Fernwood, Rosetta and Schoolboy, a four-year-old maiden half brother to Troubadour, being by King Alfonso—Glenluine. Mr. Cummings thinks Mr. Byrnes will will dispose of him. He is simply a giant in stature, being by far the largest horse at the track.

The managers of the new Linden course have begun to make preparations for a meeting at their track, to be held at the same time as the meeting at Elizabeth. It is possible that the officers of the two clubs may arrange matters so that there will not be a conflict between them. Again, it is said that the Elizabeth course will be kept open for the entire month, from April 15th to May 15th, regardless of the movements of the management of other tracks.

Lucien Appleby (late Appleby & Johnson) although not generally credited with owning any horses at present, has by no means abandoned the sport he loves. Mr. Apppleby is now living in a handsome cottage just opposite the Little Silver station, near Monmouth Park. The cottage, palatial in size, is fitted up with every improvement, and Mr. Appleby enjoys his suburban residence. More than that, Builder Decker is now erecting for him a two story barn and stable with twelve box stalls, and it is being built in the best possible manner.

Reports from Cynthiana say that Hon. T. J. Megibben, the famous breeder and President of the Latonia Jockey Club, still continues in a most dangerous condition, and fears are entertained that he will never arise from his sick bed. His death would not only be a loss to his immediate section, but to the entire turf world, he being honored and esteemed by turfmen all over the United States. It is understood that in the event of his death he has made provisions for the future carrying on of his famous establishment, Edgewater Stud Farm.

Mr. W. G. Withers, Jr., is enthusiastic over his yearling filly by Maximus (son of Almont, dam by Sentinel), and he thinks she is one of the best youngsters ever raised at the famous Fairlawn farm. Though she will not be twelve months old until May 11th, she showed the other day, the third time she was ever hooked up, a quarter in fifty-nine seconds. She is blessed with a faultless gait, and appears to be perfectly level headed. Her young owner thinks she is a wonder, and believes she will show it by the end of the season.

Robert Walden, son of Wyndham Walden, once Mr. Geo. L. Lorillard's famous trainer, and since then breeder, owner and trainer for himself, was at New Orleans last week. The Waldens train Mr. John A. Morris's horses for him, and young Walden, who was in New Orleans on a visit to Mr. Morris, says he has been over to the Morris Breeding Farm in Texas, and thinks the climate and soil are better adapted to breeding farm purposes than California. He thinks the three colts sent on to his father are the finest he ever saw and will make a name for the Texas blue grass belt. Mr. Walden left for home last week.

The following celebrated trotters and pacers are among the 1200 head of horses which will be sold at auction here, at the Brasfield and other sales during February: Susie S., 2:15¼; Houri, 2:17; Bud Crook, 2:18½; Protection, 2:19½; Hinder Wilkes, 2:20½; Cognac, 2:20¼, Emulation, 2:21; Elgin Girl, 2:20½; Calinda, 2:22½; Thalia, 2:26; Lunette, 2:25½; The King, 2:29½; Count Wilkes 2:29¼; Egbertha, 2:29½; Elkhorn, 2:28¾; Woodford Pilot, 2:23½; Susette, 2:26¼; Danville Wilkes, 2:27; Bessie Wingate, 2:28; Problem, 2:24½, and Rene, 2:26. Never in the history of breeding have so many trial performers been offered at public sale in a single month in the same county.

In England the education of a horse often and wisely begins on the first day of its existence. The little long legged animal is brought into a loose box with its mother, and if not actually haltered and taught to lead, is gently handled from head to foot which has a great effect in making it ever after fearless of the approach of man. The more often this is repeated the better. When two or three months old it is often fed from a manger with its mother, and frequent opportunities taken to handle it. It is sometimes shut up in a loose box during the forced absence of its mother and at others follows her through the roads, over the bridges, and among the sights and scenes of its future life.

The stable of Megibben & Co., including Laura Davidson, Sportsman, that trio of good three-year olds, Avondale, Eberles and W. G. Morris, and a number of promising two-year-olds, among the latter a brother to Avalon and a sister to Huntress, will race in the East principally this year. The stable will leave the West immediately after the close of the Latonia spring meeting. Avondale is said to be the most improved colt of the lot, although Eberles and W. G. Morris both show the benefits of their let-up, and Sportsman, it is thought, will be a much better horse than he was last year, and his owners have entered him in the Suburban handicap, believing that, if properly weighted, he will have a chance to carry off that rich prize, for which event he will be especially prepared.

The following horses with records better than 2:30 are booked to stand in Kentucky this season: Bonnie McGregor 2:13½, Phallas 2:13¾, Don Pizarro 2:14¾, Jerome Turner 2:15¾, Anteeo 2:16½, Robert McGregor 2:17½, Norval 2:17¾, Duquesne 2:17¾, Baron Wilkes 2:18, C. F. Clay 2:18, Wilton 2:19½, Alfred G 2:19¾, Abbotsford 2:19½, Blue Grass Hambletonian 2:20¾, Eagle Bird 2:21, Hambletonian Mambrino 2:21¼, Bermuda 2:20½, Artillery 2:21½, General Wilkes 2:21¾, King Wilkes 2:22¼, Cyclone 2:23¼, Sultan 2:24, Hylos 2:24¼, Wilkes Boy 2:24½, Nutbreaker 2:24¼, Onward 2:25¼, Shawmut 2:26, Gambetta Wilkes 2:26, Alcantre 2:26½, McAllister 2:27, Simmons 2:28, Ellerslie Wilkes 2:28¾, and Macy 2:29½. A modest valuation of these horses would make them worth more than half a million dollars.

The track at Monmouth Park has been in exceptionally good order this winter, and horses are very forward. Among the trainers located there is Mr. Littlefield, who has 19 head in training, most of which could be put in racing trim in three weeks or less, among them are a good-looking two-year-old My Craft (Fellow Craft—Hegira), Heeltaps, who is a brother to Monopole, Adventure, by Miser, out of Peradventure, Simrock (Fellow Craft—Elmira), a very promising two-year-old, having shown better form than any yearling previously handled by Littlefield, and Joe, a two-year-old by Joe Daniels, out of Vestella, purchased at the Haggin yearlings of 1889. The older horses are all doing well, and should give an account of themselves.

Firenzi is in grand order for the time of year, being at present at Monmouth Park; she is enjoying the best of health, far better than a year ago. Indeed, this is a fact as regards all the horses at the track, they are eating well, filling out, and caring nothing about the epidemic grip that has laid so many human beings low. Firenzi was always a slow mare in the spring, but from present indications she may be seen this year in the Suburban. That is, providing the handicapper doesn't ask her to carry several of the other horses the Journey before she throws them away and beats them. Salvator has also grown and thickened out well, and all the others in the Haggin string are in good fettle.

It is a mistaken notion that M. Byrnes has a lot of Mr. Haggin's 2-year-olds. He has ten 2-year-olds altogether, two on the Monmouth track and eight at his own farm. The first two are his own property, the latter eight the property of Mr. Marcus Daly. Mr. Byrnes' two are both George Kinneys and good looking, one being the chestnut colt out of Bijou Mr. Byrnes, purchased at the Hurstbourne sale. The Marcus Daly lot were all bought at Mr. Haggin's sale in July and are as follows: Silver King, ch c, by St. Blaise—Maud Hampton, and consequently half brother to King Thomas; Montana, b c, by Ben Fox—imp Queen, the other six are all by Sir Modred, as follows: Prince Charming, b c, dam Carissima; Gold Dollar, ch c, dam Trade Dollar; Mistletoe and Namouna, bay fillies, dams Lafole and La Favorita, and Lenora and Bonnie Lass, chestnut fillies, dams Lizzie Lucas and Bonnie Kate. The entire lot are youngsters of size, conformation and apparent quality.

Mike Kelly, the Maltese Villa Stable trainer, has been in town for several days arranging for transportation for three two-year-olds, viz., King Alta, Romiata and Judge Terry. They will probably go on the Valensin car to New York and join the stable at Westchester. King Alta is by that good race-horse Alta out of Geraldine's dam, Cousin Peggy; Judge Terry is by Alta out of Pet, by Norfolk, while Romiata is by (imp.) Woodlands out of Dizzy Blonde. Cousin Peggy has a yearling filly by Alta, but is not in foal this year, and will be bred back to Alta. Mike will have half a dozen horses East this season, viz., Geraldine, Flood Tide, Abdiel, and the three two-year-olds previously mentioned. J. Wall, Kelly's lieutenant, is in charge of the three at present in the East. Kelly, whose leg is all right now, not having bothered him for some time, says that El Rio Rey will be better than ever this season, while their half-bred mare (for so he says they call her at Westchester), Geraldine, will be pretty hot goods in a sprint or two, and if lightly weighted in the Brooklyn Flood Tide, should give a good account of himself.

Eugene Leigh, the well known trainer, was in Lexington last week inspecting the stables preparatory to choosing one for the accommodation of his own horses and the Hankins string, which is in his charge. Twenty of Hankins' horses will be trained here, while the rest, in charge of Tom Kiley, will go to Memphis to take part in the early spring southern racing It is understood that Terra Cotta, Egmont and Little Minch will all three be placed in the stud this winter, and not be trained again. The latter horse could doubtless stand another campaign, but his owner is of the opinion he has done enough on the turf. He is now ten years old, and since Mr. Hankins purchased him in the winter of 1886 for $6,000, he has won a total of thirty-seven races, and $29,765 in stakes and purses. As to Egmont and Terra Cotta, they are both badly bowed, and while they might be good for a race or two, it is almost certain neither one of them could make a long campaign. Terra Cotta cost his present owner $17,500, and he has won for him $19,065 in stakes and purses, while Egmont since entering the Hankins stable at a cost of $10,500, has won the neat sum of $15,494. Thus Mr. Hankins is several thousand ahead on his stallions.

Marcus Daly's Thoroughbreds.

We have been asked many times what thoroughbreds Marcus Daly has at Riverside Farm on the Bitter Root, Montana. An old correspondent of the BREEDER AND SPROTSMAN visited the ranch just before the first consignment started East, and sends us his opinion of the different bangtails which he saw there:—

Missoula County to-day boasts the possession of twenty-two of the handsomest thoroughbred yearling colts and fillies owned by any one man in the United States. This seems like a broad assertion, but a visit to Mr. Marcus Daly's Riverside Farm at Charlo station on the Bitter Root branch of the Northern Pacific, will be enough to convince the most skeptical. The BREEDER AND SPORTSMAN reporter went out there last Monday, and in a stay of three hours saw enough to convince him that there was nothing to equal it either at Woodburn or Belle Meade, and nothing to surpass it at the famous St. Alban's Stud Farm near Geelong in Australia. These youngsters were all bred at Mr. J. B. Haggin's Rancho del Paso, near Sacramento and were sold at auction near New York in July last. The prices paid were the heaviest average per head ever known in America, and the New Yorkers made Mr. Daly pay liberally for all he got. Two of the colts were turned out in a paddock and will not be galloped till next year. One of these is by Ban Fox out of the imported mare Queen, and the other is by Darebin out of Agenoria, dam of Pontico and Pontiac. The others are as follows:

1. Vergie, br f by Milner, out of a mare by Virgil. Has Star and off heel white. A very racy looking mare.

2. Bay filly by Hyder Ali, out of Pandora by Spendthrift. this is a racy mare with big driving power.

3. Bay filly by Darebin, out of Katy Darling by Longfield. Has a star and two white heels, and is a very pretty mare.

4. Brown filly by Darebin out of Sozodont. Very large and highly formed.

5. Bay filly by Joe Daniels out of Nonage by King Ernest. Long and low, but looks more speedy than enduring.

6. Bay filly by Sir Modred out of Letola. This is one of the most shapely mares in the world and is very mature in her outlines.

7. Bay filly, own sister to Ballarat, winner of the Surf Stakes at Coney Island.

8. Bay colt, by John Happy out of Susan by California Warwick, son of Hubbard. This colt shows the Bonnie Scotland stock all over and may be safely set down as a good and useful horse.

9. Bay colt by Ban Fox, out of the imported mare Queen. This is one of the highest finished colts in America and has no end of quality.

10. Chestnut colt by St. Blaise, out of Maud Hampton, the dam of Ban Fox and King Fox, the best two-year-olds of their day. This youngster is a very rangy fellow, with a narrow blaze in his face and both off legs white. He cost Mr. Daly $22,000 at auction.

11. Bay colt by Sir Modred, out of Carissma by Kingfisher. This colt has a large star and two white heels, and reminds us something of the noted campaigner Volante, behind the saddle, save that he is already a bigger horse.

12. Chestnut colt, without white, by Sir Modred out of Trade Dollar by Norfolk. Here is one of the most beautiful colts in America. His mother was one of the best of Norfolk's daughters, and we believe he will prove himself a goer in good company.

13. Chestnut filly by Sir Modred out of Bonny Kate by Bonnie Scotland. A large and highly formed mare, a trifle leggy but very highly finished.

14. Bay filly by Sir Modred, out of Wanda by Norfolk; a very pretty mare but small as compared with the others.

15. Bay colt by Joe Daniels—long and large in every way. Has a few flexen hairs in his tail and mane. This is the hardiest and highest strung horse in the bunch.

16. Chestnut filly by Warwick, out of Eliza by Norfolk. Has three white legs and a blaze face. This filly has been sick, and has been given little or no work.

17. Chestnut filly by Sir Modred, out of Lizzie Lucas. Has broad blaze and white heels. This is a very compact mare and looks like a dangerous customer under a mile.

18. Chestnut filly by Hyder Ali, out of Assyria by Lever. She has two white heels, and is a very pretty mare in any country.

19. Chestnut filly by Joe Daniels out of Bessie by Onondaga. Has a blaze and two white heels. She shows her Australian blood plainly.

Our pick of the colts is the bay one by Sir Modred, out of Carissima, with the Ban Fox—Queen colt next. That high priced St. Blaise colt is our third choice and the Trade Dollar colt fourth. Of the fillies, the one out of Letola is the best to our eye, with the Milner filly, Vergie, as second choice, and the sister to Ballarat third. We shall see how these predictions turn out when they come to be trained and face the starter. These youngsters are cantered slowly each day, over a track three-quarters of a mile in circumference, under supervision of Joseph Nelson, who was for a long time in the employ of Mr. Haggin at the Rancho del Paso. He is a very quiet young man, and seems to be thoroughly familiar with his duties. These colts are fed ten quarts of oats per day and all the hay they can eat. They will not be speeded till next year.

Mr. Daly has just completed the handsomest barn in Montana for his young racers. It consists of two tiers of boxes, twenty eight in number, with big double doors. Between them and the outer walls of the barn is an open passage way of twenty-three feet, to be used for slow trotting exercise in rainy weather. The upper stories are for hay and grain. The outer walls of the barn are built in sections so they can be moved in hot weather, and the stables are rendered cooler for the summer months. This is 360x120 feet over all and gave employment to sixty odd carpenters during its construction.

When a bridle has been taken off a young horse without unfastening a curb chain, or in such a way as to twist the bit in his mouth, hitch it in his teeth, or in any way to inflict serious pain upon him, he will often repeat the mischief, in his impatience to avoid it, until it becomes a habit dangerous to himself, and to those who handle him, from the violence with which he will throw up his head, rush back, rear, and sometimes even strike with his forelegs. When it comes to this it is a very serious business, and one that will get worse if the horse continues to hurt himself at it. The safest and quickest way to get over such habit is to put the horse down, and hobbling his legs so that he can only rise to a natural lying position, put the bridle carefully on and off him for an hour. After that, use a bridle on him in which the bit can easily be unbuckled, and dropped quietly out of his mouth, before the bridle is taken off his head. A tall horse that will not let you quietly handle his ears, his eyes, or any part of his head or body, should be put down in the same way, and kindly, but perseveringly handled until he loses all fear of your hand or your brush upon him.

"The Science of Horse Breeding."

In reading C. Bruce Lowe Esq.'s letter to the BREEDER AND SPORTSMAN on "The Science of Horse Breeding," I was forcibly impressed with his ideas on the influence of the sire's blood upon the dam through the foal while in embryo, or, as he puts it, "impregnation of dam with the sire strain through the foal's circulation previous to birth." That there is much truth in the theory no breeder can doubt if he follows the business by close observation. When I first commenced the breeding business, before I had gained practical experience, through reading and what I might term natural inferences, I formed the idea that whichever, sire or dam, had the strongest physical conformation would control the character and general qualities of the offspring, but in this I found many disappointments. When I first got Whippleton, about eight years ago, and noticed the uniformity of his colts in makeup and color, I began to study and observe the character of his colts each succeeding year closer, and found that in most instances (with few exceptions), as he was bred to a mare continuously, that colts were more like him each year. I have a mare by Dennison's Jack Hawkins; she is bright chestnut in color, with white spot in face, about 14½ hands high. The first colt she had by Naubuc Prince, a black horse with star and both hind feet white, was a chestnut colt, white strip in face, one white foot. Her next two were by Naubuc, a black horse; they were chestnut fillies, white strip and one white foot each. Next she was bred to Whippleton (I will here state that Whippleton is a horse of peculiar makeup and individuality, differs from any other sire I know of; he is fully 17 hands high, very high crested, deep through the heart, with long, slim neck, and large boney head, and there is a similarity in all of his colts that is very marked). Her produce was a seal brown colt, no white, a little longer and more of Whippleton type. Next was a bay filly, no white; she is a true Whippleton type, long head, slim neck, and all the leading points. The last, now three years old, is a black colt, and any one can see that he is his sire all over. I had another mare, said to be by John Nelson, about 15 hands high, bright chestnut, no white. Her first colt from Whippleton was a light bay; next a light bay; next seal brown, and her last, now four years old, a black filly a true model of her sire's family. I could cite a great number of cases that have come under personal observation, where small mares were bred successively to Whippleton, where the first colts were small (that is for Whippletons), modelled something like the mare or her stock, and possessed much of the same temperament and general characteristics of the dam; then each succeeding colt would be larger and more like its sire. While the above instances go to show that the "*influence of the sire's blood becomes intensified in the dam through the consecutive foals while in embryo*," there are instances which have come under my observation that work directly opposite. Some years ago a black mare sired by McCracken's Black Hawk, was bred to Naubuc, a black horse, and the produce was a black colt, an exact copy of his sire, black, a slim tail, and even the gait was just like the old horse's. She was bred the next season and foaled a sorrell filly (the color of her second dam), with heavy main and tail, and low, straight gaited, just the opposite of the sire of the other colts. I could name other instances, but this is sufficient for illustration. Now the question for the observer to answer is, "how to account for the differences above cited?"

I believe it is a law of nature that in most instances the sire, or in fact the male of all nature is the most prepotent of the two sexes, and therefore exerts a controlling influence over the offspring. The stronger the prepotency of the sire, the more uniform will be his progeny. But in all of nature we will find *antagonistic elements*; we will find mares with certain combinations of blood, temperament and qualities that resist the influences of the most prepotent sire, and continue to produce an offspring entirely different from the sire's average progeny when we take this same mare and breed her to an inferior horse, one generally known to be less prepotent, it strikes a happy union and reproduces the sire successively.

Past experiences of breeding the trotting horse have taught us that a certain amount of inbreeding has proven successfully, and that the reuniting of certain strains of blood has intensified the instinct to trot and perfected the physical qualities necessary to carrying and maintaining a high rate of speed.

It is this kindly blending of similar blood elements in sire and dam that result in harmonious and successful unions. When this method of breeding is judiciously carried out, and not carried to extremes, we get the most uniform results. When we cross sires and dams of entirely dissimilar blood elements, and go to entire outcrosses, we then strike the *antagonistic elements* of nature, and the results are uncertain. We are likely to get either extreme.

Since writing the above, the BREEDER AND SPORTSMAN has come to hand, and looking it over I see Mr. Harvey W. Peck's comments on C. Brube Lowe Esq. article on "Science of Horse Breeding." He seems to ridicule the idea "impregnation of the dam with sire's strains, etc., and gives very decided opinions upon a mare producing a foal resembling a stallion to which she had been bred several seasons before. He attributes the resemblance to *the effect the singular appearance of such a sire might have upon a highly organized mare.*

I will say that years ago I was an advocate of that theory, but by observation and experiment, I have become thoroughly convinced that there is nothing in it. As a matter of test, and an evidence of my disbelief in the theory, I will allow Mr. Peck, or any other gentleman, to select five or ten mares, sorrel or chestnut, with any white markings (not pintoes, as they are an entire outcross; a fixed, individual type of horse, and according to my theories, the result would be uncertain); take regular broodmares; we will breed them to Whippleton; we will never let them see the horse; blindfold them when being bred, and I will breed the entire number free if they are not all bay brown or black in color.

I do not doubt that some of the colts may possess something in make up and character of the stallions that have previously been bred to the mares, but if there is any foundation for the theory *the effect of appearances* the sire may have upon a mare, certainly the first and most notable feature would be the color.

I will even go farther; these mares can be brought in contact and associated with any other sire before and after breeding to Whippleton, and the result will be the same. I only use Whippleton as an illustration. The result would be the same with many other sires, inbred to imp. Messenger strains through Hambletonian, Clays, Mambrino Chief, etc.

Electioneer breeds solid color, as did Rysdyk's Hambletonian, Volunteer, Happy Medium, and I am informed that Sable Wilkes colts thus far are all bay, brown or black. These sires were bred to all classes of mares, and if there was anything in the visionary theory, some of them would have lost their control. Another notable feature with all these sires is, that none of them can control the grey. I believe that all of them sire a grey occasionally; this simply proves the *hereditary influence of fixed qualities in the blood carried down through generations of inbreeding.*

Imp. Messenger, the founder of the Hambletonians and many other noted trotting families, was a grey, and when any of his inbred descendants are coupled with grey mares, the original color frequently predominates. I do not use the argument that color breeding has any particular influence upon the production of speed or endurance, as the great Nutwood was a chestnut in color, and that same color predominates in most of his descendants, but I do maintain that any sire that breeds strictly after his own color (no matter what that color is), proves his individual merit as a uniform producer of his own qualities.

FRED W. LOEBER.

Old Reminiscences.

One of the oldest horsemen now on the Pacific Coast is undoubtedly Thomas Clark, Esq., of Springville, Ventura county. The gentlemen is seventy-five years of age, and has been interested in horses for over sixty years. His memory is of the best, and it is a delightful experience to sit and listen to the old gentleman recall old races and historical horses whose names will always be known to the turf loving public. He left England many years ago, but can recall with vivid distinctness any number of contests which he witnessed at Newmarket, and he can also give the pedigrees and history of many of the old horses which were brought to this coast in the "early days." Having asked Mr. Clark to give an account of the old Lummex horse, he writes as follows:

I got acquainted with John and Jerry Welch in Oregon in 1854, they having arrived in 1851 or 2, and settled eight miles south of Eugene City, in Lane County, on Donation Claims. They brought out with them a fine black mare by imp. Consternation who was a son of Confederate, out of Curiosity by Figaro. About the same time the Welch boys arrived, there came across the plains two brothers named Bailey who originally lived in Missouri and they brought with them a colt by Leviathan Jr., whose dam was a Stockholder mare. Leviathan Jr. was by imp. Leviathan, and was also out of a stockholder mare. The Bailey colt was also called Leviathan. He was bred by a Mr. Weaver in Missouri who brought his horses from Virginia.

I mention particularly about the colt brought over by the Bailey Bros. as the Welchs bred the Consternation mare to Leviathan twice and secured two foals, the oldest of which was a grey. like the sire, and was sold when about five years old to Mr. Cornelius Hill who resided on the Willamette River, some seven or eight miles above Eugene City. The other was a bay with a white stripe in the face, and I think, one hind foot, (however, I only saw him once) he was named Gilpatrick and afterwards came to California, as Mr. Winfield Wright of Santa Rosa, informed me in 1862 that he had been breeding to a horse of that name that came from Oregon. A near neighbor of ours, Mr. Henry Hadley, claimed to me, however, that Gilpatrick was sired by a two year old colt of his, by "Old Lummax" (called at one time "Old Celer." The name, I think, was a corruption of Selim). This Lummax. Celer or Selim, was a horse brought to Oregon by an old gentleman named Owensby, who lived near Corvallis. The Owensby horse was the sire of old Dan, who was the sire of Sim Oldham's Comet, a noted quarter mile and six hundred yard horse, and many other fast ones, including a large over grown colt bred by Mr. Jenkins, on Long Tom, Lane County, Oregon. This colt was named Jo, but from his monstrous size was nicknamed Lummux, and it is from this horse that the Lummax breed of horses first originated. The last I heard of this horse he was at or near Clear Lake in the northern part of California. The horse Gilpatrick was more like a Lummux than a Leviathan, and they all run out loose together on the range. The big colt Lummux ran a race as a three year old against a horse with a very bad name (not fit for publication), sired by Lute Savage's horse Old George, but Lummux was beaten easily, although during the following season he beat the same horse quite readily for a wager of $600. After John Welch sold the gray colt, which I have spoken about before, to Mr. Hill, he started East and rented old Consternation, standing him two years in Kentucky, if my memory serves me aright. In the first year he bought Rifleman and sent him to Oregon by a friend named Ralph Geer, who lived in the Waldo Hills, several miles northeast from Salem, and the following year he returned, bringing with him the mare Mary Chilton, and then the two brothers followed their profession of surveyors. Their horse Rifleman was not very popular in Oregon, as the neighbors were taken up with the Lute Savage horse, Old George, the Lummux horse, Little Tom (Whip and Printer) and Walnut Bark, owned by John Edmonson.

Rifleman covered a few mares, mostly on shares, as the people did not feel like paying $100 for something that they did not know anything about. Then reports were circulated that Rifleman was only a half breed, and that his dam was a Spanish horse and that he had never been further East than California, and any quantity of other derogatory rumors were started. Consequently his patronage was not extensive. After keeping him in Oregon about two years John Welch took him to California, and also Gilpatrick and the filly Mary Chilton, and, my impression is, ran them with poor success, finally selling Rifleman to a man named Doll, who afterwards transferred him to J. C. Tyler of Tehama. The filly was sold to John Boggs of Princeton, and it was from her that came the great son of Langford, Thad Stevens. It was after this sale that he started East to purchase something in the thoroughbred line that would surpass anything we had here then, but poor fellow, he lost his life returning. At about this same time Felix Scott, ex-Lieutenant Governor of Missouri, was killed by the red devils in the Modoc country, He had gone back to Virginia and purchased five fine fillies, but the Indians killed him and his two men, and that was the last heard of the blooded stock.

Yours respectfully,

THOS. CLARK.

Valuable Dogs Drowned.

EDITOR BREEDER AND SPORTSMAN:—When I arrived home from San Francisco, I found misfortune awaiting me in the shape of a flood. The flood came at 1 A. M. Sunday night, and the water rose so suddenly that my wife's family barely had time to get up stairs, losing their clothing, etc. The water stood three feet in my house, and five feet in the kennels. Everything we have is ruined. Mr. Jas. E. Watson's Jet (black pointer bitch), Mr. William Curlett's *Leo* (Point—Blossom), and my dog Roscoe (Don—Sal) were drowned, the remaining two dogs were saved. My man came very near being drowned trying to reach the kennels, having been swept several hundred yards by the current.

Very truly yours, GEO. T. ALLENDER.

Big Racers.

Studying the Eccentricities of the Horse—Busy Scenes About the Stables.

There is a charm about racing life that the casual visitor in the grand stand never tastes, and that the anxious, dusty betting crowd that has only the hope of striking a winner in view knows nothing of. This is the life around the stables where the horses are in training. From the grand stand one gets a glimpse, now and then, of long, low, weather-beaten buildings in the distance, with here and there a boy moving about lazily, or a procession of muffled-up horses, each led by a boy, walking solemnly in a circle. But it is only through rare good luck that closer inspection is obtained, for trainers do not court attention, but guard their stable secrets religiously. In those rambling buildings the horses are housed, and to every track during its racing season a colony of men and boys follow the horses and do nothing but take care of them.

I went down to Monmouth Park on an off-day when there was no racing to see for myself just how the horses spend their time when they are not tearing madly around the track for a lot of money; and also to find out how such glossy, shining, spirited beauties that prance and cavort at the starting post are evolved from the shaggy, long-legged shy little creatures that I've seen kicking up their heels in pastures. The place looked as pleasant as a village forty miles from a railroad station. Here and there were strings of horses walking about, and at the stables the horses that had been out were indolently nodding their heads out of the open stall doors. The boys who had finished their morning work were lying, heels up, in the feed-rooms, or basking like puppies in the sun. Occasionally I caught a glimpse of a Jockey looking strangely stuffed, with his coat buttoned to his chin over his sweater, swinging along at a strong pace, stick in hand, and a companion in short sleeves at his side, blowing and perspiring.

Talk about the care and attention given to babies, it isn't a circumstance to that given to race horses. Trainers hold as varied opinions as mothers on the right way to attain the greatest perfection in their charges, and they have to be just as careful and study as closely the dispositions they have to deal with. Successful trainers, like poets and good mothers, are born, not made, for sometimes it is only their horse instinct that will guide them. I asked some of the trainers who have developed the racing qualities of famous horses how they selected yearlings; what points they noted.

"It is a pretty hard thing to select a yearling," I was told. "It is like buying a ticket in a lottery. It may turn out well, and it may not. Many owners, especially proprietors of large stables, are influenced by a youngster's pedigree, and it's a right good thing to go by. Then, if a brother or a sister has turned out well, the yearling is considered very desirable on account of the hope that he has the same qualities. Blood will tell, especially in horse flesh. Good legs and feet to accomplish the hard work that they are asked to do in their two or three-year-old forms, broad jowl and plenty of heart room that promises good breathing power, and a back not too long, well ribbed back, leaving no weak spots, showing a good weight carrier, are the points eagerly looked for. Sometimes we get familiar with the characteristics and peculiarities of a certain strain of horses, and prefer handling them. The Bonnie Scotlands are notoriously strong and hardy; the Leamingtons all suffer more or less from contracted feet, and the Billet colts, of which Raceland is one, are very delicate."

"What do you call a large horse?"

"About sixteen hands, while fifteen hands is a small horse."

"How about the size of race horses? Do you like big horses best?"

"Not always. Big horses are generally preferred on account of their superior weight-carrying powers. But occasionally you find a small horse that can pick up the same weight and walk away from a big horse. This is on account of his perfect action. Perfect action is one of the most desirable possessions of a horse. You have seen horses that, when they run, seemed to run all over; their hoofs thundered on the track and they lifted their feet high and bent their knees as much as if they were trying to walk upstairs. A climber like this will soon tire himself out, and he will have no chance with a nice, smooth-going horse that seems to skin over the ground and scarcely lift his feet. Perfect action in a horse is like the work of finely adjusted machinery—the movement of each is just enough to accomplish the task imposed without any waste, while too much action in a horse is like the 'false motion' of a compositor—he makes unnecessary movements, which retard his progress and tire him.

"A horse's age is reckoned from the first day of the year he is foaled. For instance, if he was foaled the last day of December 1888, or the 1st of January, 1889, he is officially counted a year old, although he is but a day old in reality. In June of the year following their birth they are taken up from the paddock, where they have been allowed to disport themselves and fight each other, and are sold at the annual sale of yearlings. These little untried animals, with untold possibilities hidden in their lively bodies, bring all sorts of prices, from a hundred to many thousand dollars; but the highest price ever paid for a yearling was given by Senator Hearst for King Thomas, the last of the King Bans. He and Lucien Appleby, of Appleby & Johnson, ran the bids up from $5,000 to $38,000, at which figure the colt was knocked down to Mr. Appleby. A short time after the public sale it was announced that the costly colt had passed into Senator Hearst's possession, and $40,000 of the Senator's money was resting snugly in Mr. Appleby's wallet. The excitement caused by the purchase at that figure has not even yet died away.

"The youngsters are broken in July, and during August and September they are exercised and worked. Then in October they are given their first trial on their owner's private track, or at whatever race track they are. When their training begins they are handled like a baby learning to walk, trying a little more day by day. They are worked short distances, which are gradually increased as they grow stronger and hardier, till the trial, which is three-eighths of a mile. This they run with full weight up, 115 pounds, and if a yearling accomplishes the distance on the Sheepshead Bay track in thirty-six seconds he is considered well worthy of further attention. After this trial, which is to determine if there is a racer in him, his work is gradually lessened when the stable goes into winter quarters and finally ceases. In January he is again taken up and gradually prepared for his career as a two-year-old.

In training these young things the greatest care and patience is required, and many a horse's disposition has been irretrievably ruined by the viciousness and stupidity of bad stable boys, while at the same time hereditary bad tempers have been overcome by judicious handling.

The horses' legs always receive the greatest care, and it is while they are yearlings that their shins are "bucked"—that is, made sore from much work. I suppose it on the same principle that unusual exercise causes soreness and inflammation in persons' legs. Sometimes their shins get bucked in the natural course of events and sometimes trainers buck them on purpose, then blister them and get it over with. For if they don't get sore while they are yearlings they will later on, and possibly interfere with some of their engagements as two-year-olds.

The same methods will not succeed with every horse, nor can any rule be laid down prescribing the amount of work. What would scarcely affect one horse would wear another one out. Some horses are of a sluggish nature and require continual work to get them in racing condition, while others are so exceedingly nervous and excitable that they fret themselves thin. They differ greatly about their eating, too. Some horses are hearty and will eat all that is given them, but the delicate ones need a deal of humoring and fussing over. Careful trainers give such animals only a handful of oats at a time, and when that is eaten another handful is given, until a sufficient amount has been eaten. Where a good deal depends on a horse feeling all right the trainer will often get up at night and feed him daintily. They frequently become track-weary, and do not perform so well when they exercised on the track all the time.

Frequently horses that have been raced several seasons grow cunning and turn rogues. They refuse to work and can't be extended at trials in order to find out what they can do. All sorts of expedients are resorted; they are sent out to work in the company of other horses, sometimes even a boy in racing colors is put up to make them think they are in a race. They get so shrewd that they will not try in a race and on that account are often started at steeplechasing. Some horses can tell when they are going to be raced, and get nervous about it, and don't eat or sleep well and cause the trainer anxiety and trouble.

During the winter months, when there is no racing except at little tracks, the horses are put into winter quarters and given a rest. Many of the horsemen have breeding farms to which they are sent. On such a farm there is a track measuring from half a mile to a mile; the stables are on the most approved plan; there are quarters for the boys, and there is a straw track under cover on which to exercise the horses in inclement weather. The Belmont farm at Babylon, L. I., has a mile track and the straw track is a sixteenth of a mile. Those who have not farms winter at some of the race tracks

When racing is done they gradually cease exercising them, and then turn them out after taking off their shoes. They are taken up every night and fed, but as little as possible is done to them in order to let them have a good rest, to tone up and take on flesh. In January they begin to prepare them for the spring racing, and then the sporting writers begin to send news about the progress of this filly or that colt, or the whereabouts of a popular mare or fate of some broken-down horse with a stirring history that reads for all the world like society notes. The horses are at first led around the straw track and given very gentle exercise. On fine days they are taken out, and as the spring advances their work is gradually increased to the distance they are expected to run, and the muscles are hardened till they are like steel and every superfluous ounce of flesh is worked off.

This work has to be gradually done as to make the change scarcely perceptible from day to day, and the muscles are hardened by hours of rubbing as well as by exercise. When an exercise boy takes a horse on the track the trainer watches with practiced eye every movement of the horse. If his work tires him it is not increased. If he does it with ease he gets more to do next day, and so on till he is "wound up and thoroughly clean inside, and fit to run for a man's life." The most difficult thing to discover is when a horse is "fit." When his muscles are hard he eats well and when he can run the distance of a race in which he is entered in good shape and time, his trainer feels safe about starting him. Before a race a horse is generally tried over the distance at his full speed, but this is not always done with nervous, delicate horses that, as the saying goes, "have to be trained around a pocket handkerchief." Their powers are reserved for the final test. Even when a horse does well at a trial he may not redeem his promise in the race, and a horse may run well one day and fail utterly the next. This is called running in and out.

When the horses are fit then comes the bustle and excitement of the opening racing season, when every man's heart is full of hope from the promising work of his beauties and he is on the qui vive for any signs of improvements or retrogression on his rival's string, and the voice of the bookmaker is heard in the land. Then the big tracks echo with the sound of hammer and saw, plows and harrows are busy, the big frame stables are opened and fresh straw put in the roomy boxes, the horses arrive from all directions and are walked up and down and admired, the stable boys are filled with glee and deviltry at meeting old friends again, and the ball is started rolling for the summer.

That's when life on a race track is pleasant.

The trainer fixes up his quarters in a box adjoining the pride of the stable, and makes it look like a bower with the pretty things his wife and sisters and cousins and aunts have filled his trunks with. The boys decorate their quarters over the boxes with play bills and advertising cards, and in the stalls of their favorite horses put up the colored lithographs of actors and actresses, and the cook sets out his dishes and pots and pans in fancy piles on the kitchen shelves, and almost covers the walls with highly colored pictures, generally of fair burlesquers, and the pretty advertising bills of jockey clubs. To be sure all these things have to be taken down and moved and put up again every few weeks, but it is done with never a thought that it is any trouble. The trainer sleeps at the stable, usually with one eye open, and there is always a faithful canine attached that keeps both eyes open during the night to guard the jewels of the turf. For every two horses there are two attendants, a man and an exercise boy, and often the horses get so accustomed to having the same attendance that they will not allow any others to come near them.

At the track each horse has a nice large box-stall in which he can move around easily. His several suits of clothing are hung against the walls of the box on a line stretched from corner to corner, and the floor is covered with clean fresh straw. At the door are all the toilet articles, including brushes, towels, chamois skin, sponge, etc., his bandages, his water-bucket, and his feed-box. His day begins at dawn, which, in summer, begins about 4 o'clock. He is given a hasty rub, sometimes a quart of oats, and is led out for a walk. Then he is taken on the track and trotted and cantered with an exercise boy on his back. Perhaps his trainer will let him work a certain distance at racing speed while he sits on the fence, watch in hand, with his eyes fastened on the horse. These early morning trials are eagerly watched for by the touts, who resort to all sorts of stratagems to learn something definite of a horse's movements, but the trainers are just as acute in frustrating their attempts. After the horse is taken off the track several boys go to work on him to dry him out by rubbing him with towels. He is given a few sups of water, his legs are washed, rubbed and bandaged, a linsey is put on him, and he is walked around for awhile longer until he has cooled out and the excitement incident to his exercise has passed away. Then he goes through another stage of his elaborate toilet, being rubbed and brushed and polished until he shines like richest satin and there isn't a speck of dirt on him as big as the head of a pin. Then comes food and rest and quiet in his box. If the day is cool the box is closed and he has a chance to meditate in the dark, and if it is warm the upper half of the door is left open and he can thrust his head out and take note of events or amuse himself nipping at passers-by. Here he stays in placid comfort, while his trainer sees that he doesn't suffer from any change of temperature, and the stable boys busy themselves in cleaning saddles and bridals and scouring stirrups and bits till they shine like silver. This morning exercise and toilet last for about an hour and a half; at 4 o'clock he is taken out again and walked and cared for, fed and put up for the night.

This is the day's programme during the racing season when the horse is in condition and has not a race to run. The night before he runs a race he is not fed so much, and if he is a glutton a muzzle is put on him to keep him from eating his bedding. Every precaution is taken to afford him a good night's rest, and he is given very little to do in the morning. Before the race he is "warmed up" to feel like running, and after it is over he is cooled out gradually and carefully guarded from taking cold, and if he fails he is not, unlike a human contestant for a prize, given hard knocks and abuse, but the good care and the good feeding go on as before.

In a stable there are always some horses that need attention beyond this. Some horse is ailing and needs the care of a fever patient, and generally there is one that has to have his legs or feet doctored. There are soaking-tubs for the horse's feet, which they stand in while a boy with a tin cup sits near dipping up water and pouring it on their legs. Sometimes the feet must be soaked in oiled meal, or the legs rubbed with liniment and bandaged.

The stable boys are a queer lot, and many of them as improvident as a traveling tinker. They are sometimes very troublesome, too. "Where do they all come from?" I asked. "They seem foot-loose, with no other ties than those that bind them to their stable, and they are with it winter and summer."

Some of them are obtained from charitable institutions, from villages, from parents who are ambitious to see them successful jockeys, and some, darkies especially, just drift into the work because they couldn't be happy away from the atmosphere of a stable. They are all bound to their employers. Some of the large stables provide teachers and have a night-school for the boys during the winter. The apprentice boys are obliged to attend, and the larger boys are at liberty to do so if they wish. They all bet more or less, and if a stable boy has just a hundred dollars in the world and likes a horse he will put it on him as coolly as he will five. The darkies buy sweetmeats, watermelons, or anything particularly toothsome, bet on the horses, play cards and shoot craps, but rarely spend their money for clothes. I asked an ebony attendant of a $10,000 mare, The Lioness, what he would rather do than be in a racing stable.

"Nothing I know of," he said, with a grin. "This suits me well enough."

"How do you amuse yourself?"

"Play ball, play cards and go boating."

"Shoot craps!"

"Only about the first of the month. Don't take long to lose all my money."

A horseshoer who makes a specialty of shoeing race horses follows from track to track, as does a veterinary surgeon. Each stable has its own kitchen outfit and cook, which it carries with it, and there are kitchens built at every track for the stables. Even the cooking stove is packed up and carried from place to place. Some stables, however, that visit the same tracks year after year, and occupy the same stables, buy a stove for each place and so avoid the necessity of moving such a cumbersome article.

Horsemen are famous as good livers. They have good cooks and buy the best in the market. They are hospitality itself, and I treasure pleasant memories of some delightful track dinners.

The expenses of a racing stable are enormous. The feed for the horses is of the best; nothing is too good for them, and what was said about an old English trainer is true of many a one here: "That he would give his horses gold to eat if he thought they would eat it and that it would do them good." The oats are of the finest quality, and before fed to the horses are sifted and cleaned of every bit of dust. The racing plates cost $4 a set, and a horse needs not less than four or five sets in a season, and frequently as many as eight or ten. The clothing of different weights for a horse costs from $20 to $30 and each has his own outfit. Bridles cost $8 or $9, martingales about $3, saddles from $25 to $50, racing colors from $10 to $75. A jockey gets a retainer of from $1,000 to $12,000 a year, and in addition he is entitled to $10 for every losing mount and $25 for every winning mount. For every two horses a man and a boy must be kept. It costs on an average $4 a week to feed each person. Then there are heavy traveling expenses, entrance fees and sundries, that pile up mountain high, and when all this is added up and subtracted from the winnings it makes a mighty big hole in them.

The trainers and many of the boys entertain the warmest affection for the horses. They know them like a book, and with their eyes shut they can sometimes distinguish them coming down the stretch by the beat of their hoofs.—Horse Review.

THE FARM.

To Cure Barb Wire Injuries.

If the cuts are on the limbs the parts should be poulticed with linseed meal having a little weak solution of carbolic acid mixed in the poultice Change poultices twice daily, and when removed bathe the part well with warm water. Continue poulticing so long as discharge continues to issue from the wound. When it ceases a solution of two drachms of carbolic acid and one of glycerine in a pint of water should be applied twice daily, after cleansing the wound. If a fungous outshoot should appear, apply a little of a solution of two ounces of sulphate of zinc in a pint of water twice daily.

What to Avoid in Swine Breeding.

Perhaps of all things in connection with swine breeding there is none which is more necessary to avoid than that of in-breeding. The Chicago Market Review says: It is a question which has for ages been discussed, both by those who are opposed to it and those who have been compelled to resort to it in order to produce the ideal type which they had set up. In these days of so many different strains of blood, together with so many family types, we do not believe it is necessary either to cross parent with offspring or even the males and females of that offspring together. To one of knowledge and judgment it cannot be difficult to procure the type of animal he requires, whereas the extra trouble and expense which it may likely give him to find and purchase it, can in no way be compared with the trouble and loss which is certain to ensue from the very pernicious habit of in breeding.

First Impressions.

Experienced breeders claim that with the majority of stock the first impression influences to a greater or less extent the future offspring. Hence the importance of being very careful in the selection of the breeding animals, especially so of males, using nothing but the very best full-blooded animals which have been well matured. This is applicable to all kinds of stock, but more especially to hogs.

Under present conditions no farmer can afford to keep anything but the best stock, and in breeding care must be taken to select good animals. It is too often the case that in breeding farm hogs considerable carelessness is shown with the young sows. Pains are not taken to castrate the young boars as soon as they should be, and the pigs are allowed to run together, and in consequence more or less of the young sows will get with pig before they are sufficiently matured to breed properly and before the boars are old enough to use as breeders. Such a plan will not give the best pigs for breeding, nor will it be an advantage to the sows in the future.

It is of course necessary to use young sows for breeding, and if the standard of the herd is kept up it will be necessary to take good care in the selection and then in the mating and breeding. It is a settled fact that carefully selected sows, even though they are only common stock, mated with thoroughbred, well matured males, will bring about a very rapid improvement in the quality of the hogs; with good stock it is especially true. But the stock must be well matured. A very good plan of management is to use the older boars upon the young sows. If kept in a proper condition for breeding better, stronger and thriftier pigs will be secured than by using all young stock for breeding. With the young sows that are being used for breeding the first time good care should be taken to use a well matured thoroughbred male, which is in good condition, healthy and vigorous

It is best to select the breeding stock early and feed them especially for this purpose. A good development of bone and muscle are important things, and the feed is an important item in this respect. By selecting early and feeding for this especial purpose a better quality of animals for breeding, may be secured, and then with good care in the management the herd may be kept up to the standard.—Aaron in Stockman and Farmer.

Border Leicester Sheep.

Professor Wrightson, who has contributed to the Live Stock Journal a series of articles on sheep and their management in Britain, devoted the fifteenth of the series to Border Leicesters. In his introductory notice he says:

"The Border Leicester sheep is full of interest to north-country farmers. Not only has it achieved an independent position as a breed, but it has out-rivalled in its distribution, as well as in its value, the original Dishley stock from which it is descended. It is not too much to say that the Border Leicester is the mainstay of Border counties' farming. It is constantly crossed both with Cheviots and Blackfaces for the purpose of breeding wether lambs, and it is also well maintained as pure-bred stock over many large districts, and its improvement has been, and is, carried on with great enthusiasm."

The professor, after reciting the early history of the breed, proceeds to notice the prevalent ideas regarding its origin, thus:—'The idea which has been expressed that Border Leicesters were produced by crossing Cheviotes and Leicesters is not accepted by their breeders, and Mr. Archibald, who has been already quoted, rebuts it as untrue. The well-known history of such flocks as the Mertoun, Mongoswalls, Mellendean, Bonnington, Mersington, and The Rock are sufficient guarantee that Dishley was the original home of both English and Border Leicesters, and that the brothers Culley brought out the Border Leicesters by repeated crossings of Dishley rams upon Teeswater ewes. In Northumberland, which is the native county of the breed, they found patrons in the Bosanquets at the Rock, in the Greys of Millfield, and, later, in the Messrs. Dinning, the late Mr. John Atkinson, of Bywell-hall (Peepy), and Andrew Wood on the banks of the Tyne. Among the most noted breeders of Border Leicesters, Lord Polwarth stands prominently forward. The late A. R. Melvin is now represented by executors, who exhibited specimens of the Bonnington flock last June at Windsor. The Crichton Mains flock, owned by Mr. Samuel Jack, is of genuine old blood, as is well known to those who are versed in Border Leicesters. The Right Hon. Arthur James Balfour, M. P., breeds exceptionally good sheep at Whittinghame, Prestonkirk, and secured the first prize at Windsor for his shearling ram. Mr. George Simson, of Courthill, Kelso, is another well-known breeder, who realized an average of £10 17s over 42 rams, and £75 for one in 1888. In Cumberland we may mention Mr. John Twentyman, of Hawkrigg-house, Wighton, as a successful breeder. The Earl of Dalhousie, Mr. T. Clarke, Miss Stark, Mr. Bain, Mr. Marks, Mr. W. S. Ferguson, the Earl of Morton, Mr. G. Robeson, and many others are distinguished in the ranks of breeders of Border Leicester sheep. Others ought no doubt to be mentioned, but it would be impossible to do full justice to the many farmers who hold genuine Border Leicester flocks."

The Butcher Steer of the Future.

Every year, in view of his Christmas show of meat, Mr. John Jones, Central Buildings, Llandudno, Wales, issues a circular of a unique character, bearing upon his experience as an agriculturist, purveyor of meat, and student of the market and the general requirements of the public. This year he has enunciated some new and what might be called startling theories, which may cause some consternation among breeders of cattle, sheep and pigs, and to lead to much controversy.

We reprint the salient points. "For several years I have exhibited to the public at my Christmas show the fattest animals in the United Kingdom, the great majority of them being prize winners at the leading shows. Each succeeding Christmas I found that the taste of my customers increased against over-fat and unprofitable meat, and such was the disinclination of the public last Christmas to purchase fat meat, that, although I exhibited probably the finest collection of show animals I ever had, the meat was so unsaleable that I had the greatest difficulty in disposing of it, and my experience has led me to the conclusion that the interest of the public ceases in over-fat show animals, when asked to purchase the meat. It is noticeable that the days of fat show animals are drawing to a close with the public and exhibitors, and in the near future will disappear as prize winners in our great fat stock shows. They have served the purpose of the breeder in proving the possibility of breeding and rearing animals almost to any size and fatness, and the conclusions of to-day are based upon the experience of the past as to the feeding properties and development of meat of the various breeds. The breeder of the ideal butcher's beast of the future, from a consumer's point of view, will have to be guided more by the standard of value, realized by his fat stock, than to the purity of their breed."—London Live Stock Journal.

Age of Cattle.

The subject of dentition has long been a vexed one in relation to young pigs at shows. With a view to promote uniformity in Judging, the Smithfield Club has compiled and issued the following code of regulations:—

Cattle having their central permanent incisors cut will be considered as exceeding one year and six months. Cattle having their central permanent incisors fully up will be considered as exceeding one year and nine months. Cattle having their second pair of permanent incisors fully up will be considered as exceeding two years and three months. Cattle having their third pair of permanent incisors cut will be considered as exceeding two years and eight months. Cattle having their fourth pair (corner) of permanent incisors fully up and their anterior molar showing signs of wear, will be considered as exceeding three years. Sheep having their central Permanent incisors cut will be considered as exceeding ten months. Sheep having their central permanent incisors fully up will be considered as exceeding 12 months. Sheep having their third pair of permanent incisors cut will be considered as exceeding 19 months. Sheep having their third pair of permanent incisors fully up and the temporary molars shed will be considered as exceeding 24 months. Sheep having their corner permanent incisors well up and showing marks of wear will be considered as exceeding three years. Pigs having their corner permanent incisors cut will be considered as exceeding six months. Pigs having their permanent tusks more than half up will be considered as exceeding nine months, Pigs having their central permanent incisors up and any of the first three permanent molars cut will be considered as exceeding 12 months. Pigs having their lateral temporary incisors shed and the permanents appearing will be considered as exceeding 15 months. Pigs having their lateral permanent incisors fully up will be considered as exceeding 18 months.

The Ayrshire Cow.

The Ayrshire cow now ranks very high as to both the quality and quantity of its produce. A fair average of herds of, say 50 cows, not especially selected, runs from 640 to 680 gallons of milk per annum, according to as excellent authority as The Mark Lane Express, which furnishes an interesting account of the recent development of this breed.

An Ayrshire cow generally shows 13 per cent. of solids, 13 to 16 per cent. of cream, and 3½ to 4½ per cent. of butter fat. In the milking competitions of the London dairy show and the Oxfordshire and other shows, the Ayrshires have stepped far ahead of the Shorthorns, Guernseys, etc., in the quantity and quality of the milk they yielded.

The milk of the Ayrshire is pre-eminently suited for cheese making. All samples of milk under the microscope are seen to be composed of a homogeneous fluid, in which float little globules of butter fat. These globules vary in size, and while in the Jersey they are comparatively large, in the Ayrshire they are small and not rising quickly, but, mixing with the curd butter, make an evenly rich cheese. The quantity of cheese yielded by such animal is about six hundredweight, estimated in so many stones of twenty-four pounds each.

As to the butter yielding properties of the Ayrshire dairy cow, the ordinary milk shows about 4 to 4½ per cent. of butter fat, while selected animals come up to, if they do not exceed, the Jerseys. The average yield, so far as records go, ought to be something about 240 pounds per annum. The writer has had recently tested a 4-year-old Ayshire cow, which is yielding fifteen pounds of butter per week.

It is customary with some breeders of cattle to speak disparagingly of the Ayrshire from a butcher's point of view. We venture, however, to maintain that of all the races of milk producing animals, she dies best and most profitably when no longer desired for the milk Pail.

The devolpment of this breed within the past fifty years has been very marked and rapid. The Ayrshire cow is fast superseding other dairy races in England. She graces innumerable dairy farms in Holland, has crossed the wide Atlantic, and feeds along the northern as well as the southern shores of the river St. Lawrence, and rests beneath the shadow of the Rocky mountains. Possessed of the finest and nicest woolly coat of any breed of cattle, she has lately been extensively imported to the stormy regions of Russia, and at present she is unquestionably the favored dairy animal of Australia and New Zealand.

The English Shropshire Society has 245 life and 130 annual members, and a cash balance of $5 700. "Export trade" says the report, "has been well sustained during the past season, and some countries had taken Shropshires for the first time Exporters now confine their purchases to registered flocks entirely, and this is to a certain extent much the same with the home buyers, the difference in price between registered and unregistered flocks being very marked."

Pleuro-Pneumonia.

The health of farm live stock, and the best methods of preserving it, are subjects of never-failing interest in Great Britain and its numerous dependencies. On the question whether a country can be safely regarded as free from pleuro-pneumonia wide differences of opinion are still found to exist, and some difficulties which present themselves have been brought to the surface of late. In the Netherlands, some years ago, an outbreak of pleuro occurred amongst cattle grazing in a gentleman's park. "This," states a veterinary surgeon, through the Live Stock Journal, "was followed by the slaughter of the entire herd, except one or two milking-cows, who, having been attacked lightly, had quickly been restored to health; but, singular to say, time after time, as fresh stock was introduced, although the neighborhood was free, outbreaks again occurred that necessitated their slaughter. Every precaution was adopted, and the sanitary condition of the premises was carefully attended to, but still the disease hung around the place. At last the two cows that had been attacked, and recovered some years previously, were fattened and slaughtered, and in the lungs of the one was found a large cyst, or agglomeration of decayed organic matter almost like cheese, and in this the germs of the disease were supposed to have lurked, and have been occasionally given off with the breath, to the infection of the cattle that came in contact with it. At least, after her death, from that time to this, the locality has been free from every symptom of the disease." This is justly regarded as an exemplification of the hidden dangers of pleuro.

Notes.

The Griffin Bros. have purchased the Levi Morris Rancho, four miles north of Winters, for $60,000.

The celebrated racehorse Ormonde is to be followed to Buenos Ayres by one of the finest of the Queen's bulls at Windsor. Favourite is his name; he is one of the famous Court House breed, and he lately took the first prize at the Windsor show.

It is said that Pedro Altube of Independence valley has turned out 3,000 head of cattle to shift for themselves or die in the attempt, as he has not feed sufficient to carry them through. It is not likely that many of the poor brutes will survive the winter.

The Humboldt Creamery Company evidently finds business good, for they have rented the Vedder cheese factory at Coffee Creek for one year. It is the intention of the company to put in a couple of separators and receive milk at that place. The cream will be hauled to the Arlynda Creamery to be made into butter.

A Tacoma dispatch says at least ten human beings and thousands of cattle and sheep have perished in the blizzards which have raged over the State of Washington since the first of the year. Reports from Colville Reservation are that the cattle are dying by hundreds from starvation and thirst. Cattlemen believe they will lose half their herds.

A sale of American bred Merino sheep at Sydney, New South Wales, is reported in the English papers. The animals were specially picked and imported by Messrs. E D. Morrison and Laymond D. Clark, of Vermont. The highest price for a ram was 455 gs. The average made by sixty-seven rams was £103 12s, and on eighteen ewes £107 18s. 4d.

Foot-and-mouth disease continues to rage among the live stock in various districts of the Continent of Europe. The authorities are doing their best to deal with the disease, but its progress seems to be unchecked. In Hungary over 1,000 farms were effected when the last government statistics were published, and there are also many cases in both Upper and Lower Austria.

The loss of young stock this winter in Humboldt County has already been unprecedented. Even the dairymen and stockraisers on bottom lands, who are accustomed to sheltering and feeding a portion of the time in winter, report a considerable loss in yearling calves. Among the stockmen on the ridges, where snow has remained for nearly a month, the loss must be even greater. The sheepmen, however, will probably be the greatest losers.

At the Birmingham (Eng.) Fat Stock Show, in which the Queen was particularly successful, there were the following entries, as compared with the last five years.

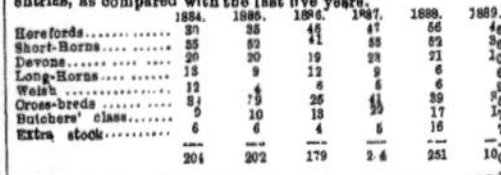

	1884.	1885.	1886.	1887.	1888.	1889.
Herefords	30	35	45	47	56	46
Short-Horns	55	52	41	55	52	36
Devons	20	20	19	23	21	10
Long-Horns	13	9	12	9	6	6
Welsh	12	4	5	5	6	9
Cross-breds	81	79	25	41	39	85
Butchers' class	9	10	13	20	17	17
Extra stock	6	6	4	5	16	7
	204	202	179	2·4	251	100

At a recent meeting of the live-stock commissioners and veterinary, held in Springfield, Ills., big-jaw was, among other subjects, under discussion. The conference resolved as follows:

"*Whereas*, It is the expressed opinion of leading scientists that *actino-mycosis*, or big-jaw, is a contagious disease, capable of communication from one animal to another, and from animals to mankind.

Resolved, That it is the sense of this conference that animals affected with this disease should be destroyed, and that the carcasses thereof should not be used for human food."

A correspondent in Australia sent the London Fanciers' Gazette the following: "A few weeks back a certain vessel arrived at a port which shall be nameless with a pen of fine fowls (of a clean-legged breed) for a well known poultry fancier. The intimation of the birds' presence on board was notified in the Fanciers' Gazette, and consequently several persons went to inspect them, the new arrivals meeting with considerable praise. When the question was asked the official in charge as to whether the hens had laid recently, with a wink he replied, 'Well, yes, I think I've got an egg or two stowed away somewhere.' This evidently greatly interested the visitors, who evinced a desire to have a look at them; and the official went off, returning very shortly with five eggs! 'Why, they're quite fresh looking' 'Of course they are,' replied the wily official. 'Will you sell them? What price?' After a few moments' thought the answer came in the affirmative, and the visitors left with the five eggs the vendor enriched to the tune of one guinea sterling. Very carefully were those eggs placed under a hen, and the result eagerly looked forward to; but, consternation! three eggs only proved fertile, and these three chicks feather legged. More consternation! And the wily official scored considerably, for the eggs had been purchased at the previous port of call for the ship's supply!"

ATHLETICS.

Athletic Sports and Other Pastimes.

EDITED BY ARPHIPPUS.

SUMMARY.

The athletes have abandoned all hopes of being able to get in condition for the coming field days. The prospects for a dry spell at present are no brighter than they were a month ago. Even if the sun should shine continually for the next couple of weeks the tracks would not be dry enough for good performances.

It is more than probable that the Olympic Club will not give a full programme of games on Washington's Birthday. If at all possible some races will be held but the chances are they will be open only to members of the club. The formal opening of the grounds will not take place until such time as the weather will be favorable for out-door training.

RUNNERS, WALKERS, JUMPERS, ETC.

The cross country run of the Olympic Club will not come off until after Washington's Birthday.

Several of the Alpine athletes took advantage of the fine weather on Sunday last and exercised mildly on their new track at Harbor View Park.

The New York Clipper Annual for 1890, contains an account of the Pacific Coast Amateur Athletic Association championship games from 1886 up to the present time. This is the first time that these games have been recorded in the Annual.

T. Buchanan, the Australian amateur shot and weight performer, will take part in the exhibition on "Ladies Night" at the Olympic Club rooms.

Since the storm began the Bay District track has undergone a complete transformation. The surface of the track at present looks like a skating rink, the coarse clay having been washed completely away. On Sunday, Monday and Tuesday last a party of athletes exercised on the track, and one of the party, an old time amateur runner, said that the Bay District, in its present condition, was as fast for foot racing as any track in the United States. Between showers a good many of the amateurs will take their spins out there until the other new tracks are finished.

Victor E. Schifferstein, the amateur sprinter and long jumper, is engaged in the real estate business at San Jose, Cal. His health is very poor at present and it will be impossible for him to train for the coming championship games.

John Purcell is undecided whether he will enter the championship games or not. If he can afford time to train he will compete in the pole vault and shot putting events.

A. H. Lean is seriously thinking about competing in the championship games on Decoration Day. He has fully recovered from his recent illness.

F. C. Philips, the well known amateur pedestrian, has joined the Alpine Club.

Several of the local professional runners and walkers are strongly advocating the organization of a professional annex in connection with one of the leading amateur clubs. They claim that it is just as proper to have a professional annex attached to an amateur club as it is to have an amateur annex in connection with a professional club.

Through being defeated by Billy Smith at the Occidental Club rooms on Monday evening last, Joe Bowers, according to the opinions of a good many of the sporting fraternity, dropped from the pinnacle of victory to the level of disgrace. It may be true that Mr. Bowers in all his fights was fortunate enough not to have met his match, but at all events there is no denying that he has defeated some really good men, and if he was guilty of showing the white feather on Monday evening that was no reason why the sporting reporters should have taken away his credit for past victories. The old proverb that "when a man is down his enemies will try to keep him down," was painfully illustrated in this instance. In all of his previous battles Bowers made a good showing, and it was very unkind of certain local papers to try and shatter his reputation.

A. H. Lean and E. A. Kolb met at the Olympic Club on Monday evening, and signed articles to wrestle for the amateur middle weight championship of the Pacific Coast and a $200 trophy. The match will come off in the Olympic Club gymnasium on the evening of March 6th. The following rules of the Pacific Coast Amateur Athletic Association will govern the contest:

That neither competitor shall exceed 154 pounds in weight at 8 P. M., on March 5, 1890, nor exceed 158 pounds at 8 P. M., on the evening of the contest, at both of which times they shall submit themselves to be weighed by the leader of the Olympic Club at its rooms, both to have the privilege of weighing stripped.

Should both contestants exceed 158 pounds in weight on the night of the contest no championship or trophy shall be competed for. Should one be overweight, and the other be within weight, and the former win, he will not be awarded either the championship or the trophy; but in the event of the latter winning under those conditions he shall be declared the victor.

A rest of one-half hour will be allowed between falls, but, aside from that, the contest shall be prosecuted to a finish without delay.

Greasing the body, pulling hair, biting, gouging, digging finger nails into the flesh, clutching by the throat or twisting the fingers shall constitute a foul.

The winner must get two out of three falls.

H. C. Moffet, of the University Athletic Club, may possibly be sent East this summer to represent his club in the Intercollegiate championship games. He would certainly win three first prizes, viz., the hurdle race, the long and high jumps.

THE WHEELMEN.

Chief Consul R. M. Thompson, has almost entirely recovered from an attack of La Grippe.

The competitive drill did not take place at the Mechanic's Pavilion as announced on Saturday evening last, owing to the fact that several members of the Stockton and San Jose teams were suffering from the effects of La Grippe.

The Bay City wheelmen team, however, gave an excellent exhibition drill which they repeated last evening. The $150 trophy will be given to this team.

Several of the members who are interested in the whist tournament which is in progress at the Bay City Wheelmen's club rooms are down with La Grippe and the attendance during the week has been unusually small.

The introduction of safety tandem races at future race meets would certainly prove a novelty. A couple of good men such as Cook, Elwell, Davis, Plummer or Wetmore mounted on one of these machines would very easily beat the Eastern record which is somewhere in the neighborhood of 2:37.

JOTTINGS FROM ALL OVER.

Owing to the delayed mails we are unable this week to present our readers with the usual Eastern news.

The seventy two hours go as-you-please race at Waterbury, Conn., ended at midnight January 18th, with the following announced score: Davis 391 miles, Golden 375, Hughes 372, Tracey fourth and Curley fifth. Davis received about $280, Golden $175, Hughes $105, Tracey and Curley $56.

Thomas Howarth was the winner of the seventy-two hours go-as-you-please race that ended at the rink in Detroit, Mich., January 18th. Score: Howarth 374 miles, Hart, 341, Noremac 337, Smith 329, Horan 323.

The Manhattan Athletic Club of New York City will have to vacate their grounds at Eighty-sixth street and Eighth avenue this year, as a considerable portion of the property on the Eighty-sixth street side has already been disposed of for building purposes, and more will soon go. A committee has been appointed to secure an eligible site for a new outdoor headquarters, but they find great difficulty in obtaining what they want. The club may have to cross the Harlem River, or perhaps go to Staten Island.

The Staten Island Athletic Club a few days ago passed a resolution that hereafter the club should not pay the entrance fees and traveling expenses of members to athletic games other than those for the championship. While there may not be any reasonable objection, so far as the amateur law is concerned, to the club defraying such expenses, athletes cannot find good and sufficient reasons to find fault with this action, which at most can only necessitate a curtailment of their sphere of action. Therefore, it is a matter of regret that, as reported, some members of the island club feel so much aggrieved at the course pursued by the organization, that they threaten to withdraw therefrom and offer their more or less valuable services to some other club. Under such circumstances, the fact of such disgruntled members having joined could hardly be regarded as an acquisition to the club or clubs to which their allegiance was transferred.

IN THE SURF.

It would be well for those who are unacquainted with the art of swimming to take lessons at once, for there is no telling when the city will be under water.

Oarsman P. H. McDonnell fell overboard on Sunday last last at Long Bridge, dressed in his new Sunday clothes. Unlike McGinty, however, he did no go to the bottom but quietly swam ashore. After witnessing the performance Mr. Long stated that he was willing to wave his right to the "Swimming Championship."

AT THE OARS.

A dispatch from Toronto says that O'Connor was shown some remarks made by Hanlan in a New York paper to the effect that O'Connor would tire at the end of a mile if pushed. O'Connor is rather annoyed at the constant disparagement of his staying powers by Hanlan, and says he is willing to row the latter any distance from 100 yards to 100 miles, and will bet him $10,000 to $5,000 or any amount at 2 to 1 that he can beat him. If Hanlan will make a match, O'Connor says he will return from San Francisco and row him on any water in America.

Sunday was the first good day this season for the rowing men, but the storm had left the adjuncts to the boat houses in such a terrible condition that the majority of the club men devoted the entire forenoon in replacing their floats. The Pioneer and Ariel boat houses were damaged most, and in each case new floats will be required before the boats can be launched with safety.

Ed. Finley, L. F. Nunan, H. Plese and Johnson Hardy, all of the Ariel Club, visited the Lurline Club at North Beach in the afternoon.

Eugene Flanders, Henry Whitkopp and E. Phelan of the Ariels took the whitehall and went to the other side of the oil wharf in search of a better site for the new club house. They will lay the application before the Harbor Commissioners at their next meeting.

The Lurline Club has some very ambitious oarsmen. A. C. Ronard takes exercise daily in his canoe, the "Ho-bo". He has acquired such skill with the paddles that his many challenges to his club-mates remain unanswered.

E. Heenan of the Pioneer Club has just finished a new shell, and he deserves great credit for his initial effort. The The boat is a model of the mechanic's art. He has a contract with his club to build three new shells during the coming season.

Charley Long accompained by his club mate, E. Heenan, took a spin to the sugar refinery.

The Alpine Club will have its new barge before the regatta, which will be held under the auspices of the Pacific Rowing Association.

When Charley Long of the Pioneer Club was defeated by Henry Henceman at Stockton, the former was not at all in enjoyment of good health. Some of the local oarsmen think that Mr. Long acted foolishly in challenging Henceman again but the "knowing ones" only smile and say, "If at first you don't succeed etc." So far the challenge remains unanswered, and perhaps Mr. Henceman will take time for consideration before deciding whether he will accept or not.

One of the daily papers made an error in announcing that the Dolphin Club would hold its high jinks on Sunday last. As a consequence several persons visited the boat house only to be disappointed in their expectations. The affair will not come off until about the 23 of next month.

CLUB JOTTINGS.

Director Dally's *expose* of the doings of the officers of the California Athletic Club was by no means a startling revelation. For some time past it has been generally known that at least twenty five per cent. of the persons who attend the fight of the club were admitted on "dead head" tickets. If the members are satisfied with this kind of management so much the better for the directors who are hardly to be blamed for feathering their own nests. But why did not Mr. Dally make his accusations long ago?

The regular monthly exhibition of the Occidental Athletic Club was held on Monday evening last.

The P. C. A. A. A. will hold its next meeting on Feb. 6, and will hold meetings every two weeks after that date until after May 30.

The Olympic Club "Ladies Night" has been postponed to February 13, on account of several of the members who were to take part in the exhibition being affected with La Grippe.

After all the Golden Gate Athletic Club is likely to remain in the P. C. A. A. A.

Secretary J. J. Jamison informs us that the G. G. A. C. will be represented at the championship games on May 30. In a brief interview Mr. Jamison said: "Why so many persons are down on the Golden Gate Athletic Club I cannot for the life of me see. Up to about a year and a half ago we had in our Amateur Annex some of the finest athletes on the Pacific Coast, including runners, walkers, jumpers and weight performers. At the annual championship meetings of the P. C. A. A. A. the Golden Gate Athletes were always feared. A couple of years ago our team would have won the flag had not one of its members been ill. Immediately after these games the Directors of the California Club came to the conclusion that such an excellent team of Amateurs would help to boom their club and they accordingly set about capturing our champions. They were offered free entrance into the California Club, and with the numerous other inducements which were held out to them they could scarcely stand the temptation, and so they bolted. After waiting a year they were convinced that the inducements which had drawn them from their own club were merely "air bubbles", and now the same party of athletes have resigned from the California Club in order to identify themselves with clubs that will better appreciate their services. Several of our old athletes have wandered back to us and I can confidently assure you that the amateur annex of the Golden Gate Athletic has no idea of disbanding. Persons who share in the opinion that the club lives only for prize fighting are grossly mistaken, and during the coming year we hope to be able to prove to our amateurs that they are not entirely forgotten.

THE KENNEL.

Dog owners are requested to send for publication the earliest possible notices of whelps, sales, names claimed, presentations and deaths, in their kennels, in all instances writing plainly names of sire and dam and of grandparents, colors, dates and breed.

Another Dog Lost.

EDITOR BREEDER AND SPORTSMAN:—How little did I think when I reported the sad death of "Lady Elaine" that I should so soon report the death of "Countess Lynnette" which occurred on Saturday, the 18th. She was taken the same way that "Lady Elaine" was, cramps in the bowels. We did all we could for her, but nothing seemed to relieve her. I did not dissect Lady Elaine, being satisfied it was the coal ashes that killed her at the time she swallowed it. Countess also got a piece in her mouth, but I ran and took it from her as I thought before she had swallowed any, but in this I was mistaken as I found three or four hard bunches that had grown in the small intestines, completely stopping the passage, which being opened, showed signs of a hard, gritty substance, which I think must have been the coal ashes. It was a hard blow to us, and I am afraid it will be a long day before their place can be filled in our kennel. They were a remarkably fine brace. Now side by side they rest in peace.

C. A. LOUD.

Spaniels.

America and California seem to have a hazy idea of what a spaniel really is. The Fanciers' Gazette says: "There is probably no variety of the canine race which differs so much in type as the spaniel—leaving out the English and Irish water spaniel, it has four distinct varieties—the Clumber, the Sussex, the Field and the Cocker. In some points, however, they are all similar, such as flatness of coat, and length of ears and feathering. The three first-named are built on the same lines, important properties being great length of body and shortness of legs, as distinct from the Cocker, which is shorter in body in comparison to its height. It is in the shape at the head, which is the indicator of type in every breed of dogs, that the whole four differ. Taking the Clumber first the predominant color is white, with lemon patches on head and body. It should have a large square head with a deep stop, the upper lip slightly overhanging the lower, and the eyes showing the haw; the nose flesh-color, length from tip of nose to set on of stern up to 45in., or more if possible; weight up to 65lb; height, 15in. to 18in. The Sussex spaniel is golden-liver in color, the head more square and shorter than the field spaniel, but with less stop than the Clumber, more liver-color; weight from 26lb. to 46lb.; length from tip of nose to set on of stern up to 35in.; height from 13in. to 15in. The field spaniel (in which we include black, black and-white, liver, liver-and-white, black-and-tan, liver-and-tan, and roan) has a longer and narrower head than either the Clumber or the Sussex, but must not be at all snipey in muzzle, and, like the Sussex, must not show the haw in the eyes; the ears are also set rather lower; weight from 26lb. to 56lb; length from tip of nose to set on of stern up to 40in., and sometimes more; height 13in. to 15in.; nose black in all but the livers, when it is the same as the body color. The Cocker is smaller, weighing not more than 26lb, and is more sprightly in action, the head, like the body, is not so long, nor the muzzle so broad as the other varieties, and the skull is not so flat, the ears being set rather higher; height from 10in. to 12in; length from tip of nose to set on of tail up to 29in. Small field spaniels are sometimes exhibited in the Cocker class, and have won prizes, but the disposition is now to send them back to their own class."

The Best All-Round Sporting Dog.

The Australasian, which is the best all-round sporting paper published in the colonies, has had a series of letters in regard to which is the best sporting dog for their country. Several of their correspondents have so much instructive matter in their letters, that we publish some of them in extenso.

TO THE EDITOR OF THE AUSTRALASIAN—

Sir: The shooting season will be opened in another month, and as a good dog is as necessary to good shooting almost as much as a good gun, I trust you will allow me to ask, through your columns, which is the best dog for all-round shooting in this colony?

The spaniel, retriever, pointer, setter, and even the fox-terrier, all have champions, as they all have been shot over, and if sportsmen who have tried them will give their experiences, it will assist those who have not yet got a dog to decide which breed to go in for.

I am surprised that the English setter has not more admirers in Victoria. He has the best record as a field dog in America and in England, and if trained according to "Kennelman's" instructions, he cannot be beaten in the field for all-round work, from retrieving a duck to pointing a quail. The English setter makes a capital water-dog, and cannot be improved upon much as a companion. Yet, there are not, I believe, 50 first-class English setters in Victoria. I cannot understand why this is, unless the idea that they are headstrong and hard to train frightens sportsmen from them. To show how erroneous an impression of this sort is, I may mention that I have an English setter pup, which at three months old retrieves land and water, and goes down to hand and shot readily. I am, etc. ENGLISH SETTER.

North-eastern District, November 13th.

To the Editor of the Australasian—

Sir: "English Setter" inquires through your columns of November 30th, which is the best dog for all-round shooting? I presume he is aware that a setter taught to retrieve will not be first-class at either setting or retrieving, but will become unsteady when in the field and flush his birds—especially if birds are at all wild. I should not advise "English Setter" to train a dog all-round, but obtain a good setter and a retriever; he will then have a dog, each adapted to its own particular business.

Your correspondent is altogether wrong in his ideas as to the English setter being headstrong and hard to train. My experience is that this class of dog cannot be beaten for nose or steadiness in the field, and is not at all difficult to break in. I find the Gordon the most headstrong and hard to break, and far too much inclined to range wide. A good pointer comes next to the English setter for steadiness—in fact, too steady, or, I should say, slow, because if birds are inclined to run, which they will very often do, the pointer is not so quick in following up as the English setter. A Gordon makes a better all-round dog than the English, being fonder of the water, and with patience and careful training can be made a useful dog; but a true sportsman likes to own a dog well trained to its own legitimate business, and "English Setter" will find much more satisfaction in keeping a setter and a retriever, instead of one imperfect "all-round dog." I am, etc., POINTER.

To the Editor of the Australasian—

Sir: In answer to the letter, signed "English Setter," which appeared in your issue of Saturday last, I beg to make a few remarks on the subject of the heading of this epistle. The best all-round sporting dog, in my opinion, is not to be found in any of the dogs mentioned by "English Setter," but in a cross between the pointer and retriever. By this cross you get a dog with a nose good enough for all purposes. He can be made to stand to game, either feather or fur, just as well as setter or pointer; and as a retriever, either on land or water, he is all that can be desired. Other points in his favor are that he travels at a pace that enables his olfactory powers to be used to the best advantage, and that, whilst the possessor, as a rule, of plenty of courage, he is an easy dog to break. He is also capable of great endurance.

Whilst conceding all these good points, it is only fair to state that in the matter of carriage, he is not to be compared to either pointer or setter, nor is his attitude, whilst pointing, so finely marked as the above. He also has a strong tendency to hunt low, and it requires some trouble to cure him of this habit, if, indeed, it can be accomplished at all. I have had both the English and Irish setter, and have paid some attention to their education, but in neither case was I satisfied that, for all-round work, very great excellence could be attained. I have now a highly-bred Gordon setter and a crossbred in hand, and intend to give them a good trial in the field as soon as the close season for quail terminates; and whichever dog shows the greatest superiority in nose (this being the most important natural quality we look for), will have the fact credited in his favor. Although I am partial to the crossbred as an all-round performer, I do not expect, nor do I intend it, that my praises in his behalf will induce shootists (the majority of whom are dog fanciers) to select him in preference to a pure-bred dog of any breed. I take it that most sportsmen like either a setter, pointer, spaniel, or retriever. If not, perhaps, the best all-round dogs, we know that they each have specialties which, under good tuition, can be brought out to perfection, while in appearance they have much to recommend them to either the shooter or non-shooter. Besides, they can always be placed on the show-bench, when, if beaten, we can take consolation in the "pastime" of condemning the judge or judges as incompetent; or, if good-natured enough to take our gruel kindly, can hope for better "luck next time." With the crossbred there is none of this, although in intelligence and sagacity he stands second to none.

"English Setter" laments the fact that the English setter has so few admirers in the colony, and speaks of him as being a good all-round dog. I am not prepared to deny this latter assertion, any more than I would if he had mentioned the Irish or Gordon, as I feel that the making of the dog, except in the matter of nose, depends wholly upon the breaker. Whether the pointer is a better quail dog than a setter (including the several breeds) is a point about which few of us in the colonies can speak with authority. Before this can be done we must have field trials, the institution of which I was pleased to observe, has recently been advocated in your columns. Our estimate of these breeds is arrived at in something after the following fashion: Jones, on a good scenting day, and probably favored with a good supply of birds and a clear eye, kills (say) 10 brace over his pointer; while Jenkins, who finds himself all abroad with his Purdey (caused probably by an over-indulgence in a whisky manufactured in the Isle of Skye), and birds none too plentiful, bags only five brace on a still day to his setter. Without considering anything beyond the size of the bag, the pointer-fancier at one concludes that he is the better-dog and that therefore, all setters are inferior to pointers. From experience I am not prepared to speak with any weight on this question, although I have repeatedly heard it argued that the pointer is superior to the setter on quail. In the old country of recent years the setter invariably beats the pointer in the trails, and for my own part I should prefer him (the setter) as a quail dog, provided he is properly broken. I must confess to having digressed from the main question, but in a measure I did it purposely, in the hope that any future discussion on the subject of "The Best All-round Sporting Dog" may be generalised after the fashion I have adopted; only, let us hope by more competent authorities. Yours, etc., CROSSBRED.

BENALLA, December, 2.

BASE BALL.

The Opening Game At Central Park—A Victory for the Brotherhood.

The first game of the California Players' League was contested last Sunday at Central Park, the protracted storm having prevented the playing of the games previously scheduled. If the rain holds off some interesting contests may be looked for during the next two months.

Stockwell has signed with the Cleveland League team for the season of 1890 at a salary of $2,400. Californians will take quite an interest in the "Spiders" now, for in addition to Stockwell, Smalley and Veach will be in that club.

Judge O'Brien of New York has decided the injunction suit of the New York Ball Club vs. John M. Ward in favor of the latter. This is virtually a victory for the Brotherhood, yet bets are freely offered that the new Players' League will never pitch a ball over the plate.

The wet weather has knocked the life out of base ball matters on the Coast, and there has been absolutely nothing to record in the shape of news. Even the managers have been too disgusted to slosh around after players, and but few contracts have been signed.

The Stockton management has raised the $2 000 necessary for them to hold their franchise, and this week a certified check for that amount was deposited with President Moore. This settles Harris' chances of having a team in the California League during the coming season.

Henry Harris will take a team of professional ball players to Oregon and Washington next May, and if practicable will establish a league composed of the principal cities of the northwest. The venture ought to be a success, and the BREEDER AND SPORTSMAN wishes the gentleman all the good luck he deserves.

Hen Moore will again don a Stockton uniform this season Fudger will play third base for the Slough City's and Selna has been signed to guard the initial. Truly, there is a good foundation for a team of pennant winners.

Charlie Sweeney has attached his autograph to a 'Frisco contract. He will play first base. The home team is now complete with the exception of a second baseman, and a rattling good team it is.

Power has got the Eastern fever in a violent form and it looks as though "Smiling Tom" will not grace a California diamond this season. For heaven's sake don't let him go; we need him right here.

Another illustration of Johnny Mone's business capabilities. For the sake of saving a few dollars he has refused to accede to Jack Sheridan's terms, and the best umpire that ever stepped behind a plate will go to the Brotherhood. Well, Mone can rattle his dollars for a while, but it's silver to copper that he will find it dear economy before the season is half over.

It is doubtful if Danny Long will play with Oakland this season. Too many week day games interfere with his business and he prefers to devote his attention to law.

THE GUN.

A good deal has been written and spoken in regard to ruffed grouse. The Forest and Stream of January 2nd has in its correspondence the following letter which gives one a good idea of the weight of that picturesque bird:

Editor Forest and Stream:

I note in the issues for Dec. 12 and Dec. 19 what two correspondents say in regard to the weight of ruffed grouse I have probably weighed more grouse than any other man living, it having been my practice for years to weigh all the birds coming to my hand, and as I handled them largely for several years I must have weighed a good many thousands of them all told; and the result of my weighing is this. The average weight varies from year to year, according to circumstance—food, weather, etc. It also varies in different localities; for instance, birds shot in a territory covered with beech trees, in a year when beechnuts are plenty, are always heavy, while birds in an oak and chestnut territory always run smaller. Then again, a large crop of blackberries means an addition of at least 3oz. average over a year when there are no berries.

The smallest average I ever took was of 20oz. This was very unusual and happened eight or nine years ago. The birds were very poor and were evidently ill fed. With the exception of this one season the average has been pretty regular at 23oz., which corresponds with Dr. Morris's opinion, until this year, when it was 24oz.

Now a word as to the big birds. Out of the tens of thousands that I have weighed the heaviest bird weighed 29oz., while the same year I killed two or three that weighed 28oz., and altogether I have weighed probably five or six, not more than that number, weighing 28oz., probably twenty-five weighing 27oz., 100 or probably more weighing 26oz., and so on down. Now I have heard of these phenomenally large birds weighing 2¼lbs., 2½lbs., and 2¾lbs, "as large as a hen," "as large as a turkey," and even as large "as an old Tom turkey." I bunch these stories all together and simply "want to weigh the bird myself." At this moment there comes to me the recollection of a story told me of a bird killed in Litchfield, Conn. It ended something like this: "And what do you think that bird weighed? Well, sir, that partridge weighed just 2lbs. and ¾." Now the man was drunk when he told the story, he was probably in the same condition when he weighed the bird; and all that I believe was, that it was a lie pure and simple. I do not wish Mr. Obl to think that I discredit his story of the 2 1-16lbs grouse, nor Dr. Morris's account of half a dozen 2lbs. grouse, but I look at it this way: There is a chance that the scales might vary on that, possibly a mistake was made by the weigher. NOLTIKS.

THE WEEKLY

Breeder and Sportsman.

JAMES P. KERR, PROPRIETOR.

The Turf and Sporting Authority of the Pacific Coast.

Office, No. 313 Bush St.

P. O. Box 2300.

TERMS—*One Year, $5; Six Months, $3; Three Months, $1.50.* STRICTLY IN ADVANCE.

Money should be sent by postal order, draft or by registered letter, addressed to JAMES P. KERR, San Francisco, Cal.

Communications must be accompanied by the writer's name and address, not necessarily for publication, but as a private guarantee of good faith.

ALEX. P. WAUGH, - - - - - Editor.

Advertising Rates

Per Square (half inch)

One time	$1 50
Two times	2 50
Three times	3 25
Four times	4 00

And each subsequent insertion 75c. per square.

Advertisements running six months are entitled to 10 per cent. discount.

Those running twelve months are entitled to 20 per cent. discount.

Reading notices set in same type as body of paper, 50 cents per line each insertion.

To Subscribers.

The date printed on the wrapper of your paper indicates the time to which your subscription is paid.

Should the BREEDER AND SPORTSMAN be received by any subscriber who does not want it, write us direct to stop it. A postal card will suffice.

Special Notice to Correspondents.

Letters intended for publication should reach this office not later than Wednesday of each week, to secure a place in the issue of the following Saturday. Such letters to insure immediate attention should be addressed to the BREEDER AND SPORTSMAN, and not to any member of the staff.

San Francisco, Saturday, Feb. 1, 1890.

Stallions Advertised

IN THE

BREEDER AND SPORTSMAN.

Thoroughbreds.

FRIAR TUCK, Hermit—Romping Girl..........C. W. Aby, Middletown.
GREENBACK, Dollar—Music..........C. W. Aby, Middletown.
INTRUDER, Crater—Lady Bountiful..........T. J. Knight, Sacramento.
PRINCE OF NORFOLK, Norfolk—Marion..........Dan Dennison, Sacramento.
ST. SAVIOR, Eolus—War Song..........C. W. Aby, Middletown.

Trotters.

ANTEEOP, Anteeo—Bessie G..........Guy E. Grosse, Santa Rosa.
ANTEEOP, Anteeo—Nance..........Guy E. Grosse, Santa Rosa.
ADMIRO, Admiral—dam by San Bruno..........Smith & Sutherland, Pleasanton.
ANTEROS NUTWOOD, Anteros—Newark Belle..........T. W. Barstow, San Jose.
ALEXANDER BUTTON, Alexander—Lady Button..........Cache Creek Farm, Yolo.
APEX, Prompter—Mary..........Poplar Grove Breeding Farm, Wildflower.
ALCONA, Almont—Queen Mary..........Fred W. Loeber, St. Helena
BALKAN, Mambrino Wilkes—Fanny Fern..........A. L. Hinds, Oakland.
BONANZA, Arthurton—Sister..........Richard Havey, Oakland
CLOVIS, Sultan—Sweetbriar..........Poplar Grove Breeding Farm, Wildflower.
CUPID, Sidney—Venus..........C. O. Thornquest, Oakland
CHRISMAN'S HAMBLETONIAN 10176, Whipple's Hambletonian—Flora Jesse Chrisman, San Jose
CANNON BALL, Simmons—Gurgle..........Lockhaven Stock Farm, Burbank.
DIRECTOR, Dictator—Dolly..........Pleasanton Stock Farm, Pleasanton.
DON MARVIN, Fallis—Cora..........F. P. Lowell, Sacramento
ELECTO, Antevolo, dam by Capt. Webster..........G. W. Stimpson, Oakland
ELECTION, Electioneer—Lizzie H..........B. C. Holly, Vallejo.
ELEGANCE..........G. W. Stimpson, Oakland
EL BENTON, Electioneer—Nellie Benton..........Souther Farm, San Leandro.
ECLECTIC, Electioneer—Manette..........Wilfred Page, Sonoma County
EROS, Electioneer—Sontag Mohawk..........W. H. Vioget, Menlo Park
FIGARO, Hambletonian—Emblem..........Souther Farm, San Leandro.
GROVER CLAY, Electioneer—Maggie Norfolk..........Denis Gannon, Oakland.
G. & M., Anteeo—Rosa B..........George E. Guerne, Santa Rosa.
GUY WILKES, George Wilkes—Lady Bunker..........San Mateo Stock Farm, San Mateo.
GLEN FORTUNE, Electioneer—Glenna..........Souther Farm, San Leandro.
GUIDE, Director—Imogene..........Smith & Sutherland, Pleasanton.
GRANDISSIMO, Le Grande—Norma..........Fred W. Loeber, St Helena
ILLUSTRIOUS, Happy Medium—Abdalletta..........George A. Stone, Santa Rosa.
JESTER D, Almont—Hortense..........Souther Farm, San Leandro
JUNIO, Electioneer—by Granger..........S. N. Straube, Fresno.
KAFIR, Alcazar—Flower Girl..........B. C. Holly, Vallejo.
LEO WILKES, Guy Wilkes—Sable..........San Mateo Stock Farm, San Mateo.
LYNWOOD, Nutwood—Hattie Morrison..........P. Visher, Stockton.
MEMO, Sidney—Flirt..........Valensin Stock Farm, Pleasanton.
MOUNTAIN BOY, Kentucky Prince—Elsie..........B. C. Holly, Vallejo.
MAMBRINO WILKES, George Wilkes—Lady Chrisman..........San Miguel Stock Farm, Walnut Creek.
MART BOORHEM, Sidney—Towhead..........B. C. Holly, Vallejo.
MAMBRINO JR 1789, Mambrino Patchen, dam by Mambrino Chief Geo. P. Bell, San Jose.
MORTIMER, Electioneer—Marti..........Wilfred Page, Sonoma County
NOONDAY, Wedgewood—Noontide..........F. P. Lowell, Sacramento.
PLEASANTON, Director—May Day..........Pleasanton Stock Farm, Pleasanton.
PILOT NUTWOOD, Nutwood—Belle..........T. W. Barstow, San Jose.
PHILOSOPHER, Pilot Wilkes—Belle..........George E. Guerne, Santa Rosa.
REVEILLE, Shiloh—Norfolk..........B. C. Holly, Vallejo.
ROY WILKES, Adrian Wilkes—Flora..........Pleasanton Stock Farm, Pleasanton.
REDWOOD, Anteeo—Lou Wilton..........A. McFarden, Oakland.
SILVER BOW, Robert McGregor—Sadie..........P. J. Williams, Oakland.
SUNSET, Anteeo—Bessie G..........Guy E. Grosse, Santa Rosa.
SHAMROCK, Buccaneer—Fernleaf..........G. W. Stimpson, Oakland
SIDNEY, Santa Claus—Sweetness..........Valensin Stock Farm, Pleasanton.
SIMMOCOLON, Simmons—Colon..........Valensin Stock Farm, Pleasanton.
SABLE WILKES, Guy Wilkes—Sable..........San Mateo Stock Farm, San Mateo.
ST. NICHOLAS, Sidney—Towhead..........John Rowen, Oakland Trotting Park.
WOODNUT, Nutwood—Flora..........Jas. Weatherhead, San Jose
WHIPPLETON 1883, Hambletonian Jr.—Lady Livingston..........Fred W. Loeber, St. Helena
WOODSIDE, Woodnut—Veronica..........B. C. Holly, Vallejo.

The Kennel Department.

We have to apologize to our readers for not having a full and complete report of the field trials, but the kennel editor is at present confined to his bed, and it was impossible to get the copy in time for this week's issue. We trust that next week we will be able to make up for the deficiency.

The Clash Continues.

The conflict of dates seems no nearer an end than when the last number of the BREEDER AND SPORTSMAN was issued. No word has been received from San Jose, and the Directors at Petaluma are determined to hold to the week which they have taken for so many years. It would seem that irrespective of the selection of dates by the Trotting Horse Breeders Association, Fresno has also resolved to claim the same dates they had last year as the following letter shows:

FRESNO, Cal., Jan. 27, '90.

EDITOR BREEDER AND SPORTSMAN:—DEAR SIR:—I see by your paper that the Breeders Meeting comes after Stockton. Would like to have you change to some other dates for we will have our meeting the next week after Stockton, irrespective of any other association's claims on that week.

Yours respectfully, N. I. BALDWIN, Sec'y.

Whether the Directors of the Breeders Association will give way and take some other date remains to be seen. However, at present, things are in a perfect muddle.

Sacramento Colt Stakes Association.

Once more the association, who has for a name the caption of this article, appear before the public with an exceptionally good list of colt stakes, entries for which are solicited. Considerable interest has already been manifested by those owning promising youngsters in the section from which entries may be made, and it is confidently believed that there will be a generous representation from all points north of Stockton.

As the conditions of the different stakes vary somewhat, we give each in detail, so that there may be no misunderstanding as to payments by those who desire to contend for the stakes.

The first is the yearling trotting event, for which the entrance is $75, of which $10 must accompany nomination; $15 to be paid May 1, 1890; $25 August 1, 1890, and $25 on the Saturday before the race. To be trotted at Sacramento during the State Fair of 1890. One mile dash. First colt to receive 50 per cent., second colt 30 per cent., and third colt 20 per cent. of stake.

The second is the trotting stake for two-year-olds. $75 entrance, of which $10 must accompany nomination; $15 to be paid April 1, 1890; $25 May 1, 1890, and $25 June 9, 1890. To be trotted at Sacramento June 10, 1890, good day and track. One mile and repeat. First colt to receive 50 per cent., second colt 30 per cent., and third colt 20 per cent. of stake.

Then comes the stake for three-year-old trotters. $75 entrance, of which $10 must accompany nomination; $15 to be paid April 1, 1890; $25 to be paid May 1, 1890, and $25 June 9, 1890. To be trotted at Sacramento June 10, 1890, good day and track. Mile heats, three in five. First colt to receive 50 per cent., second colt 30 per cent., and third colt 20 per cent. of stake.

The sidewheel fraternity are also afforded splendid opportunities to show what they can do, the Association fixing a stake for yearling pacers as follows: $75 entrance, of which $10 must accompany nomination; $15 to be paid May 1st, 1890; $25 August 1st, 1890; and $25 on the Saturday before the race. To be paced at Sacramento the first Monday in November, 1890, good day and track. One mile dash. First colt to receive 50 per cent., second colt 30 per cent. and third colt 20 per cent. of stake.

The two year old pacers are taken care of as follows: $75 entrance, of which $10 must accompany nomination; $15 to be paid May 1st, 1890; $25 August 1st, 1890, and $25 on the Saturday before the race. To be paced at Sacramento the first Monday in November, 1890, good day and track. Mile and repeat. First colt to receive 50 per cent., second colt 30 per cent. and third colt 20 per cent. of stake.

The last of the stakes is for the three year olds, the conditions being the same as in the other pacing stakes: $75 entrance, of which $10 must accompany nomination; $15 to be paid May 1st, 1890; $25 August 1st, 1890 and $25 on the Saturday before the race. To be paced at Sacramento the first Monday in November, 1890, good day and track. Mile heats, three in five. First colt to receive 50 per cent., second colt 30 per cent. and third colt 20 per cent. of stake.

As stated before, entries are eligible to all horses owned north of and including the city of Stockton. Failure to make payment in any of the stakes when due forfeits all previous payments. Entries to all of the stakes close Feb. 15th, 1890, with the Secretary. Those having nominations to make should read the advertisement.

Foals of 1890.

PLEASANTON, Jan. 26, 1890.

EDITOR BREEDER AND SPORTSMAN:—On the night of Tuesday, January 21st, Faustina (dam of Faustino, yearling record 2:35) dropped a filly by Sidney. As you will see, she is a full sister to Faustino; color, a beautiful bay with black points and star in forehead; good size, and magnificently framed. I herewith claim for her the name of "Fausta." She was the first foal of the season on the ranch. Yours, etc.,

G. VALENSIN.

EDITOR BREEDER AND SPORTSMAN:—The following colts and fillies have been dropped at Palo Alto since January 1st:

TROTTERS.

Jan. 24th, b c by Electioneer—Belle Campbell, by General Benton.

THOROUGHBREDS.

Jan. 10th, ch c by Imp. Cyrus—Imp. Amelia, by Lowlander.
Jan. 18th, b f by Flood—Imp. Flirt, by The Hermit.
Jan. 19th, b f by Argyle—Biglin, by Imp. Glengary.

The following characteristic letter came to hand on Tuesday last:—

"The winner of the B. & S. Futurity Stake arrived this morning (Monday) early. She is a chestnut filly by Woodnut out of Economy (record 2:30) by Echo.

B. C. HOLLY.

News From Ventura.

The late storms have done a great deal of damage in Ventura County. A great deal of the vineyard at Carmelos has been destroyed by the floods of the Santa Clara river, and all along the river banks many acres of alfalfa have been carried away. Farmers have not been able to plow, and the weeds have grown so that cultivating the lands will be no easy matter. The many fine horses at Carmelos are doing well. A yearling by Hockhocking that Ulpicarea Del Valle of Carmelos bought last fall at auction in Los Angeles is growing and he looks all over a runner.

The A. W. Richmond fillies and mares in Ventura County are all finely gaited and promising, and they command a good price for brood mares. L. J. Rose, Jr., has a string of mares and geldings in his stables at Ventura worth looking at and as fine as you can find in any stable. Mr. Rose is jogging Richmond Jr, brown gelding by A. W. Richmond. Last year as a four-year-old, he obtained a record of 2:22¼, which he trotted in the sixth heat of a race, which he won. Richmond Jr. is so speedy and so gamey that he will make another Jack. It is not saying too much that he will trot in 2:18 or better this year.

Richmond Jr. has a plain head, but pleasing to the eye, and a remarkable feature of this speedy gelding is his prominent eye, which betrays a keen intelligence, and added to this he has a mild and kind disposition. His shoulders are oblique and very muscular, and his loins denote much power, his hips are well elevated and his legs have plenty of bone and without blemishes. Mr. Rose has also a brown gelding not named, by A. W. Richmond, and a dead mate to Richmond Jr. He is five years old, and although he has no record, he has shown the ability to beat 2:30. He has a two-year-old filly by Stamboul, dam by A. W. Richmond, second dam by Rifleman, he by imp Glencoe. Mr. Rose said of this filly: "This one is the sweetest gaited one I have ever seen." The famous Inez, 2:30, dam of Vesolia, 2-year-old record 2:29½, is also in Mr. Rose's barn and is in foal to Stamboul—San Mateo Maid—by Whipple's Hambletonian, with foal to Alcazar. The latter three will leave on the 25th of February next for New York in their consignment of 84 head to be sold by Peter Kellogg & Co., March 6th and 7th.

L. J. Rose, Jr., has also in his stable at Ventura a three-year-old by A. W. Richmond, dam by Ben Wade, and a three year old by Le Grande, dam by Arthurton.

Were I at the sale of Peter Kellogg and Co. on March 6th and 7th, I should certainly want to purchase the two-year-old filly by Stamboul, dam by A. W. Richmond. She is bred just as I would want my mares to be bred. She has lots of thoroughbred in her, and she is so evenly gaited that she should be a great broodmare. A colt out of her by the famous Palo Alto would make a colt that would endanger all records of trotters. She is certainly a most handsome filly, and will command a fashionable figure.

The handsome brown mare Inez, by The Moor, is as handsome a broodmare as ever adorned any fashionable stock farm. Just think, she has a record of 2:30, the dam of Vesolia, two-year-old record of 2:29½, and she is with foal by Stamboul.

The farmers around Santa Paula have many fine horses, and many young ones are being trained, as this summer will be a most propitious one to the owners of trotters and runners for the purses that will be given in Ventura City. Hueneme, Ventura County, and Santa Barbara will be very liberal. When the rain gives up, and gentle Spring dethrones old Winter, the tracks will be put in condition, and all the youngsters will be put to work.

J. M. Kaiser, W. R. Willoughby, Chrisman Bonestel, L. J. Rose, Jr., and others, are doing a great deal towards improving the stock of horses in the county of Ventura. The half-mile track of the little city can be made a fast track if properly worked. It wants to be widened, and the turns well thrown up so that the horses trotting around them can be well balanced.

They need stables on the track very much, and a high fence along the seashore side to break the cold winds in the afternoon. It is to be hoped that the people of Ventura will offer inducements for horses from the surrounding counties. In the past they have had too many races opened restricted to horses of their county. They have fast and promising horses and they should be allowed to compete with outsiders. Let Santa Barbara, San Luis Obispo and Los Angeles have an opportunity to compete next summer and fall. If they can not win they will give you good sport, and your horses will have a good opportunity to show their speed and endurance. That county has bred and reared one good trotter and a very fast running mare, and many new ones will come in for honors this year. This year will be a great season for records. It is an even bet that Sunol will lower Maud S.'s record, and one of the pacers, perhaps Roy Wilkes, will lower Johnstone's record.

T. M.

VETERINARY.

Conducted by W. Henry Jones, M. R. C. V. S.

Subscribers to this paper can have advice through this column in all cases of sick or injured horses or cattle by sending an explicit description of the case. Applicants will send their name and address that they may be identified. Questions requiring answers by mail should be accompanied by two dollars, and addressed to W. Henry Jones, M. R. C. V. S., Club Stables, Taylor Street, San Francisco.

Questions and Answers.

F. R. I.

Have got a bay mare which has a split on her off fore foot. My blacksmith says the split can be united by the application of a steel band. Please give me your opinion.

Answer.—In answer to your inquiry with reference to your mare, I beg to inform you that a steel band will not bring about a reunion. The best thing for you to do is to cut the fissure down to the bottom, then blister round the coronet, and after a time turn out to pasture, and allow time for the foot to grow down.

W. Henry Jones, M. R. C. V. S.

J. H.

Two years ago the "big-jaw," so called, made its appearance among range cattle, a few solitary cases appearing before. We have always thrown the animal (mostly two-year-olds or over), cut the swelling and pressed out the bad swelling matter. The animal apparently recovers, with seldom a recurrence of the swellings. Swellings are always on the head—generally back of the lower jaw-bone. Through the country one sees a case here and there. Is this disease actinomycosis? Is there any remedy to prevent its spreading? Say an animal with it is cut, etc., to-day, and—as far as looks go—recovers, with the exception of a slight swelling round the scar; two years hence, is this animal as meat, dangerous to handle?

Answer.—By your description, I do not consider the disease "actinomycosis." If you find any trace of contagion, I would advise you to destroy the animals affected, and also those that show any trace of the disease. It would be dangerous to handle the meat, and it would be unfit for human consumption. If you get an opportunity to send up a specimen, I would be able to give you more information on the subject.

W. Henry Jones, M. R. C. V. S.

Answers to Correspondents.

Answers for this department must be accompanied by the name and address of the sender, not necessarily for publication, but as proof of good faith. Write the questions distinctly, and on one side of the paper only. Positively no questions will be answered by mail or telegraph.

Shylock.

Editor Breeder and Sportsman:—There was an inquiry in a late number of your paper in regard to the pedigree of Shylock, and so many others desire the same information I will give what heresay evidence I have in the hope it may lead to something more tangible.

Shylock was bred by the late Dr. Hugh Isom, then of Bloomfield, Sonoma County, and later of Moro, San Luis Obispo County, where Shylock made two or three seasons about 1873 or 1874. The horse was afterwards taken to Lemoore, Tulare County.

He was a chestnut stallion sired by Boston Jr., dam variously given, generally as the dam of Orphan Boy, sometimes as Kate by Medoc, again as by Imp. Lawyer. Dr. Isom was prominently identified with the race horse interests of Sonoma County in the sixties, and there should be no trouble in tracing Shylock's pedigree through information obtained among the old residents of that county.

Yours truly,

T. H. K.

Oakland, January 28th, 1889.

THE BEN HOLLIDAY MARE.

Can any of our readers furnish information about a bay mare owned and driven by the late Ben Holliday, who is said to have imported her. The mare was subsequently owned by Benjamin Fish and was sold by him to S. C. Talcott, of San Francisco. We wish, if possible, to trace the mare to the person from whom Mr. Holliday bought her, and ascertain her breeding. Anyone knowing the mare will confer a favor by writing, and although the information might not be considered material by the writer, it might lead to the knowledge of persons names who might, upon correspondence, furnish valuable information. So please give the names (and address if known) of all persons who might know the mare or her breeding.

J. A. H.

Will you please give me the pedigree of old Milton Meditim and his record, if he has any? Is he still alive?

Answer—Milton Medium was foaled 1871, by Happy Medium 400, dam (the dam of Hattie 2:29¾) by Hambletonian 1727 (Sacket's). His record is 2:25½. He died at Walla Walla, W. T.

D. & E.

Please give the pedigree of Elmo, both sire and dam; also please state how many colts Elmo has in the 2:30 list and their names.

Answer.—By Mohawk 604, dam untraced. He has in the list Alfred S., Como, Emma G., Overman, Sunflower and the pacer Elma.

P. M. Hanford.

Is Revolution, a black horse owned by a Mr. Dudley at or near Stockton, four or five years ago, registered: if so give pedigree and number.

Answer.—He does not appear in the register. The only horse of the name registered is owned in Maine.

G. J., San Jose.

Please give pedigree of the stallion Director; also of a horse called Contention. Is he stallion or gelding?

Answer.—By Dictator 113, dam Dolly by Mambrino Chief 11, 2nd dam said to be by a son of Potomac, 3rd dam by Saxe Weimar. Contention is a stallion by Director, dam Helen Benton by Gen. Benton, 2nd dam Nettie George by Norfolk.

A Reader.

The rule as laid down for the measurement of a track is as near correct as can possibly be given by simple figures. There is probably no track in the world that is *exactly* one mile in length, and if you had thought for an instant that fact might have occurred to you. The rule as given is the best that can be devised without going into fractions, and saves hiring a surveyor.

A Subscriber.

Kindly inform me through your valuable paper what the best 100 yard record is, made by any amatuer or professional, foot racer.

Answer—H. M. Johnson, Cleveland, O., July 31st, 1886, 9 4 5 seconds, the same time was also made by Harry Bethune, Oakland, Cal., Feb. 22d, 1888. We do not credit Geo. Seward with the 9¼ seconds usually attributed to him.

J. A. A.

Will you please inform me what is the best time made by the running horse Moses B. in one mile and one mile and a half.

Answer.—The horse has not won at either one mile or one mile and a half.

Snipe Hunter.

Can you tell me anything about the breeding of Arab Massoud, who sired Old Transylvania, and was imported to America by A. Keene Richards, of Scott Co., Ky.; also, Roger Hanson, by imp. Sythian, who sired the dam of Cousin Judy, by Beacon, son of Lexington?

Answer.—Arab Massoud, chestnut horse, an Arab stallion from the Anayza tribe, foaled 1844, imported by Mr. Richards in 1853, died 1859. Roger Hanson by imp. Scythian, dam Doty by Denmark; 2d dam Polly C. by Wagner; 3d dam Cinderella by Kosciusko; 4th dam by Kennedy's Diomed, etc.

Southern California News.

Los Angeles, Jan. 29th.

The wet weather has interfered with the work of the Palo Alto youngsters recently purchased by L. J. Rose. I watched a half dozen being put through their facings the other morning. The track was too heavy for fast work, so I did not produce the chronometer borrowed for the occasion. Mr. Rose tells me that he will breed several of the fillies to Dr. Ross' Australian stallion Cheviot. A trial will be made in a few days, and the fillies which show the least speed will be stinted. It is anticipated that the string to make the Eastern journey will not contain more than a dozen horses. It will surprise me if Racine and Flambeau are not in the string, notwithstanding that it was an oversight not to have had the matter arranged so that these crack California youngsters could have measured strides with the Eastern article in some of the big stakes for three-year-olds.

Will Alcazar be sold outside of this State? That is the question agitating the minds of several of the local breeders. It is whispered around in horse circles that Senator Stanford has an eye on the son of Sultan and Minnehaha. Another gentleman desirous of securing Alcazar is Mr. Bachman, the breeder of Electioneer.

There is a two-year-old filly at Santa Anita that is reported to be very speedy. I rather think it is Esperanza. The following is a full list of those now in training at Santa Anita:

Emperor of Norfolk, b h, 5, Norfolk—Marion.
Los Angeles, ch m, 5, Glenelg-La Polka.
Gannymede, b h, 4, Grinstead—Jennie B.
Honduras, ch c, 3, Grinstead—Jennie B.
Olio, b c, 3, Grinstead—Glenita.
Amigo, ch c, 3, Prince Charley—Mission Belle.
Santiago, b c, 3, Grinstead—Clara D.
Sinaloa, ch f, 3, Grinstead—Maggie Emerson.
St. Cecilia, ch f, 3, Grinstead—Sister Anne.
Magdalena, b f, 3, Glenelg—Malta.
Guadaloupe, ch c, 3, Grinstead—Josie C.
San Joaquin, b c, 2, Longfellow—Santa Anita Belle.
Ensenada, b c, 2, Rutherford—Arreta.
Silverado, ch c, 2, Rutherford—Josie C.
San Rafael, ch c, 2, Gano—Glenita.
San Gabriel, b c, 2, Rutherford—Santa Anita.
El Carmen, ch c, 2, Geno—Gray Anna.
Esperanza, b f, 2, Grinstead—Hermosa.
Cleopatra, b f, 2, Grinstead—Maggie Emerson.
Santa Ana, b f, 2, Grinstead—Clara D.
Ogrita, b f, 2, Longfellow—Mission Belle.
Blazeaway, b f, 2, Blazes—Dolly L.
La Cienga, b f, 2, Grinstead—Jennie D.

The following above are all in training at Santa Anita except Guadaloupe, who will be prepared in the East. I should expect Sinaloa to develop into the best three-year-old, and it is my opinion that Sinaloa will be the stable favorite for the American Derby, but prognostications are a trifle premature at this stage of the game.

QUARTER STRETCH GOSSIP.

Gladiator is now being driven in a buggy at Santa Anita.

Two Stamboul youngsters arrived at Rosemeade on the last day of the year.

Pike Barnes and Graham West will ride for Santa Anita this year. Barnes was expected here Wednesday.

L. J. Rose will breed two mares to Stamboul this season.

Sam Caton, the well known driver, who has a string of trotters at the Agricultural Park, has been confined to his bed with the prevailing epidemic.

Tom Rodman has just recovered from an attack of the la grippe.

The Santa Anita flyers make their debut at the Brooklyn meeting this year.

Mr. Outhwaite, a Cleveland capitalist, is about to establish a breeding farm in close proximity to Rosemeade.

Emperor of Norfolk continues to show up well in his work. The chances are that he will be seen on several Eastern tracks this season.

W. J. Robinson, the owner of Edgemont, the new breeding farm established near Rosemeade, is visiting the East.

Welcome is to be bred to Ed McGinnis.

Rico and Los Angeles are the Los Angeles entries for the suburban.

There is some talk of another race-track for Los Angeles.

Santa Barbara, San Bernardino, Long Beach, Santa Ana, San Diego, Coronado, Escondido, Downey and Los Angeles, are the towns in Southern California which can boast of race-tracks.

There are several right-smart youngsters in Rose's string at the Agricultural Park. The most of them are well entered at the Blood Horse meeting.

Cy Mulkey will winter his horses here. He will shortly receive from Bakersfield several brothers and sisters of Gladstone.

Mr. Ross says that he will take Oro and Kitty Van East this season.

Fallen Leaf and Grisette are in foal to Emperor of Norfolk. Miss Ford who was beaten by a head by C. H. Todd for the American Derby is also in foal.

It is the general impression that Dave Bridges will be the trainer for the Rose string which will be sent East.

John Treat is hopelessly broken down. He was a great race horse and has given the talent a black eye on divers occasions. The son of Shiloh has won a mint of money for the betting men of this city.

Dagworth.

CORRESPONDENCE.

Noonday.

Editor Breeder and Sportsman:—I have been asked what is to be done with the mares that proved not in foal to Noonday last season? I will say to those who bred to Noonday in 1889 that if the same mare prove not in foal and the service bill is paid up, they will have a return privilege free on said mare. I find quite a number on my books that have not paid their bills. I have sent to F. P. Lowell, Esq., 1520 F street, Sacramento, a list of all that have paid the service fee for last season, and they can send the mare to him if she proves not with foal. I will also send him a list of those who have not paid the service fee, so that he may know whom to refuse.

Yours respectfully,

Samuel Gamble.

San Mateo, January 13th, 1890.

The Pure Trotting-bred Stallion

ILLUSTRIOUS

STANDARD No. 4178

DESCRIPTION.

Dark bay, black points, 15 1-2 hands high, weight 1000 pounds, foaled May 30, 1880; bred by General W. T. Withers, Lexington, Ky.

PEDIGREE.

By Happy Medium, sire of Maxey Cobb 2:13¼ and 82 with records of 2:30 or better. First dam Abdalletta by Cassius M. Clay Jr., sire of Durango 2:23¼, Harry Clay 2:23¼ and sire of the dams of Minnehaha, Bertha 2:27¾, Charley West 2:28¼, Grandmont 2:25 1-2, Lottie K 2:26½, Mambrino Diamond 2:26, Richwood 2:28 1-2, Topsy 2:24½, Happy Thought 2:22 1-2, Pequot 2:23 1-2, Fairlawn Medium 2:27 1-2, Polley 2:27¼ and Mambrino Boy 2:26 1-2; second dam Laura Crockett by Almont, sire of Westmont 2:13¾, Puritan 2:16, Fanny Witherspoon 2:16¾, Piedmont 2:17¼, Aline 2:18¼ and 27 with records better than 2:30; third dam Sally Tee by Alexander's Abdallah, sire of Goldsmith Maid 2:14; fourth dam Kate Crockett, the dam of Lulu 2:14¾, by imp Hooton.

Illustrious is a horse of extra fine finish, large clean bone, good feet, back short and strong, loins and quarters well muscled, and powerful. He has a kind disposition and splendid trotting action, and is as handsome and bloodlike in form and finish as any trotting stallion in the land.

He is pronounced by his breeder, General Withers, to be the best bred son of Happy Medium living, and is undoubtedly one of the very best bred trotting stallions in the State. He has had but six weeks' regular training and a part of that time was sick with epizootic, but was trotted quarters in 39 1-4 seconds, and barring accidents will certainly trot better than 2:30 this season.

TERMS—$50 the season. Mares not proving with foal may be returned next year free.

Good pasturage at $3 per month.

Season to begin February 1st and end June 15th.

GEO. A. STONE,
Santa Rosa, Cal.

HOLLYWOOD BREEDING FARM.

MOUNTAIN BOY 4841.

Br s MOUNTAIN BOY, 4841, bred by Charles Backman, Orange County, New York, foaled 1882, sire Kentucky Prince 2470, dam Elise, sister to Elaine, by Messenger Duroc 106; grandam Green Mountain Maid, 3d dam, Shanghai Mary, will serve a limited number of mares at $100 the season.

ELECTION.

Bay stallion ELECTION, bred at Senator Stanford's Palo Alto Stock Farm, foaled 1884, sire Electioneer, dam Lizzie H. by Whipple's Hambletonian 725, grandam Lizzie Harris (by Comus son of Green's Bashaw 50), great grandam by Arnold Harris, thoroughbred.

Election is one of the handsomest bloodlike sons of Electioneer and with his thoroughbred cross through Arnold Harris should prove invaluable as a sire. TERMS, $100 the season.

KAFIR.

B c KAFIR, bred by L. J. Rose, Los Angeles, foaled 1887, sire Alcazar, 2:20½, dam Flower Girl by Arthurton, sire of Arab, 2:15, grandam Flora by General McClellan, 144, sire of three in 2:30 list, great grand dam by Langford, he by Williamson's Belmont, will serve a limited number of mares at $50 the season.

WOODSIDE.

Ch c WOODSIDE, sire Woodnut, 2:16½; 1st dam Veronica by Alcona, 730; 2nd dam Fontana by Almont, 33; 3rd dam Fannie Williams by Alexander's Abdallah, 15. Book full.

MART BOORHEM.

B c MART BOORHEM, by Sydney, 2:19¾; 1st dam Towhead by Echo. This Colt is a full brother to St. Nicholas who showed a mile in 2:27½ at three years old. TERMS, $25 the season.

REVEILLE.

The well known thoroughbred stallion REVEILLE, by Shiloh, dam by Norfolk. Reveille is a brother to John Treat and is the sire of Tycoon and Gladstone. TERMS, $25 the season.

Hollywood is nicely situated three miles from Vallejo on the Napa road. Good pasturage and every care will be taken of mares at reasonable rates. For further particulars, apply,

B. C. HOLLY, Vallejo.

WoodsideFarm

IMPORTANT SALE OF

Standard Trotting Mares

Young Stallions and Fillies,

ROAD AND DRIVING HORSES

Farming Implements,

Etc.

By direction of MRS. SILAS SKINNER.

Mrs. Skinner having determined to retire permanently from the breeding of Fine Stock, has decided to offer at

PUBLIC AUCTION

Thursday, March 6, '90,

at 12 M., on the Premises.

THE WELL-KNOWN

WOODSIDE FARM,

Near Napa,

together with all the highly bred trotting stock thereon.

The brood mares at Woodside are among the choicest in the State. Among them are mares by Almont, dam by Alexander's Abdallah; by Cassius M. Clay Jr., dam by Joe Dowling; by Cassius M. Clay Jr., dam by Richelieu son of Mambrino Chief; by Duke of Orange Jr., dam by Cassius M. Clay Jr.; by Almont Mambrino, dam by Blood's Black Hawk; by Alcona—dam Fontana, dam of Flora Belle, 2:24, and Silas Skinner, trial 2:23½—by Almont; by Alcona Clay—dam Metamora, dam of Clay Duke, 2:31¼—by Duke of Orange Jr. These mares have been bred to Director, Noonday, Mountain Boy and Wildwood, and are with foal. The young stallions are by Sitka, son of Alaska, by Electioneer, Whippleton, sire of Lillie Stanley, 2:17½, Alcona Clay, etc. About twenty head well-bred trotting and driving animals will be sold in addition to the standard bred horses.

Catalogues giving extended pedigrees and full information are being prepared, and will be forwarded upon application.

At the conclusion of sale of horses,

WOODSIDE FARM

will be sold.

WOODSIDE FARM is situated three and a half miles from Napa City, up the river, upon what is known as the middle or big ranch road. It contains 87 1-4 acres of the choicest quality of land for alfalfa or any kind of grain, 40 acres being now in alfalfa over a foot high. The land produces from four to six tons of hay to the acre, of choice quality. Five of the fields are in pasture, four in alfalfa, one in timothy, the other kept in hay or grain necessary for stock, though well adapted for alfalfa. There is a nice orchard, small vineyard, and comfortable dwelling house of nine rooms. There is a good school house directly opposite, the best in the County. As to its adaptability as a stock ranch: There is living water in every field, and plenty of it, corrals and stock yards, stable room for forty horses, besides seven good box stalls, two good stables, granery, etc. It is within two miles of the Napa Agricultural Society's race track, the finest constructed in the State for years. Should there not be sufficient land, 67 acres adjoining can be purchased at reasonable figures.

There is no more eligible location in the State for a small stock farm, and this affords a rare opportunity, with the stock, to at once engage in this remunerative pursuit.

The sale will be positive. Upon all sales of Live Stock and personal property, one years' credit will be given on approved notes. Interest 10 per cent. per annum. Three per cent. discount for cash.

Upon Land, one-half cash; balance can remain upon mortgage for a term of years to suit purchasers. Interest eight per cent. per annum.

Vehicles will be in attendance at Napa Depot to convey parties to the farm. Lunch will be served upon the ground.

Mrs. Skinner having large interests in Oregon which will require her personal attention during the greater portion of the year, compels the sale of the Woodside Farm.

Parties are invited to visit the farm and look over the stock. The undersigned will be glad to give any information required, either as to stock or ranch.

KILLIP & CO.
Live Stock Auctioneers,
22 Montgomery St., S. F.

Attention Stockmen!

FOR SALE

At Chowchilla Ranch,

Thoroughbred Durham Cattle

Three Hundred Young DAIRY COWS, 2000 graded SHE CATTLE, Yearlings and up; a fine lot of high grade Durham Bulls; also have Mares, Horses, Mules and Norman Colts.

For particulars, apply to

ISAAC BIRD, JR., Supt.,
Merced, California.

For Sale.

A First-Class.

BREEDING FARM.

Of 800 Acres.

Four hours' ride from the city. Good roads to a first class track. Climate unexcelled. Plenty of wood and running water.

For further information apply to the office of the

BREEDER AND SPORTSMAN,
818 Bush Street. San Francisco.

THOROUGHBRED

Clydesdale Horses and Mares

FOR

Sale

Sixth Annual Importation by MR. JOHN SCOTT.

Four Pure-bred Clydesdale

HORSES

AND

2 Thoroughbred Clyde Mares

Can be seen at the Bay District Track.

For particulars apply to

KILLIP & CO., Auctioneers,
22 Montgomery Street, S F.

For Sale.

The Bay Stallion

AFTERNOON, 6543.

AFTERNOON was foaled in 1884, sired by Almont McGregor 1:75, dam Minnie by General Hatch '29; second dam Lucy by Prophet [Weed's], son of Prophet. He is a very gentle, intelligent, level headed and pure gaited trotter. He is a remarkable foal getter, and his colts are handsome, game and speedy. He will be sold at a reasonable price. Reason for selling, ill health of the owner.

ALSO

A Handsome Brown Road Mare.

Can trot easily better than 2:40 to a Chicago cart or light buggy. Stands 15½ hands high, weighs about 1060 lbs. She is by Green's Bashaw, and is very handsome, tough and speedy. Will be sold at a reasonable price.

Address

JACOB STEFFEN,
Vallejo, Cal.

For Sale.

AT A BARGAIN.

NETTIE B.

(Half-sister to Emma Temple, 2:21).

In Foal to Free Trade.

Nettie B. was foaled 1884, and is by Altimont 985, dam Lizzie B. (dam of Emma Temple, 2:21), by Emigrant. Nettie B. is heavy in foal to Free Trade 2477, he by Princeps 536 (sire of Trumpet, 2:14, and twenty others in the list), dam Dawn by Belmont 64 (sire of 23 in the list); second dam Midnight (dam of Jay-Eye-See, 2:10, and Noontide, 2:20 1-2), etc.

Nettie B. is about 16 hands high. Is a handsome bay, and is warranted sound in every particular by the owner.

Must be Sold.

as the owner is about to move from the State. For price and particulars, apply at the office of the

BREEDER AND SPORTSMAN,
313 Bush Street.

For Sale.

The Standard bred Stallion

Anteeo Button,

sire Anteeo, 2:16¼, sire of Alfred G. 2:19¼; Redwood, 2:24½, etc. Dam Mollie Button, dam of Alexander Button, sire of Yolo Maid, 2:14; Rosa Mac, 2:20¾; Belle Button, 2:30¾, etc.

ANTEEO BUTTON is a dark bay 15¾ hands high, four years old, and weighs 1025 lbs. In style and action he is all that could be desired, and can trot a mile with ease in 2:40 to a cart.

This Colt must be seen to be appreciated.

Apply to

I. DE TURK,
Santa Rosa, Cal.

For Sale

A FIRST-CLASS

Napa County Farm

—OR—

STOCK RANCH,

800 Acres Improved,

SITUATED TWO AND A HALF MILES FROM NAPA CITY, with good roads leading thereto, a good hard finished house of nine rooms, with all modern improvements, streams running all summer, a great amount of live oak and black oak timber. It lies in a fruit belt, surrounded by fine vineyards and orchards growing upon the same quality of soil, and originally a part of this tract. About one-half hill, and one-half rolling land, but none of it is steep and all easily cultivated, splendidly situated for the breeding of fine horses. Price, $65 per acre. Further particulars given at this office.

BREEDER AND SPORTSMAN,
313 Bush St.

Have Arrived.

Six Head of Finely Bred and Registered

CLYDESDALE HORSES

Two Stallions! Four Mares!

Being the second importation from Melbourne, Australia, of

JOHN BURNS.

Mr. Burns, having had the advantage of a previous trip here, and knowing the demands and requirements of the California market, has in this importation brought six head of the finest and soundest horses ever brought to the market.

THESE CLYDES ARE ALL REGISTERED,

—And are the—

Finest of their Class

Ever brought to this Coast. They may be seen at the

BAY DISTRICT TRACK.

Prices, Terms, etc., will be furnished by

KILLIP & CO.,
22 Montgomery Street S. F., Cal.

FOR SALE

AT

Vineland Stock Farm

STALLIONS, BROODMARES AND FILLIES

ONE STALLION FIVE YEARS OLD, SEAL-BROWN, by WHIPPLETON (sire of Lilly Stanley, 2:17 1-2 Homestakes 2:16 1-2, etc.), dam Sally Gorham by Werner's Rattler. This horse is scarcely 15 1-2 hands high, but very compactly built. He breeds exceptionally large and well finished colts. Any one understanding the business could clear him in one season, or he would make a No. 1 road horse, as he can trot a 40 gait any time.

ONE THREE-YEAR-OLD, SEAL-BROWN, by WHIPPLETON (sire of Lilly Stanley, 2:17 1-2, Homestakes 2:16 1-2, etc.) dam Sally Gorham, etc. This ought to make a great General Purpose sire, and with opportunities get trotters, as he is compact, strong-boned, and will measure when grown about 16 hands and weighs 1,250 lbs. With a little road work last fall he developed a wonderful burst of speed.

ONE THREE-YEAR-OLD, BLACK, by WHIPPLETON (sire of Lilly Stanley, 2:17 1-2, etc.), dam by Naubuc (sire of the dam of Eva W., 2:23 1-2, etc.), full brother to Thomas Jefferson, 2:23. This horse will be fully 16 1-2 hands high. He is smooth, rapid gaited and from size and conformation should breed, like his sire, large, rangy, finished colts.

ONE TWO-YEAR-OLD, BRIGHT CHESTNUT, sired by DAWN 2:18¾, dam Alida (dam of Directa, three-year-old record 2:31¼, trial 2:26) by Admiral (sire of sister 2:19 1-2, Nona Y 2:25, etc). This colt is the making of an extraordinary horse. He is large boned and will be over sixteen hands high when grown; he is of the true Nutwood type, is clean gaited and can lead a piece as fast as any man's colt.

ONE TWO-YEAR-OLD, BLOOD BAY, (full brother to Alcona Jr., sire of Silas Skinner, trial 2:23) sired by ALCONA (sire of Flora Belle 2:24, etc.,) dam Madonna by Cassius M. Clay Jr. This colt will make a trotter and a great stock horse if developed; he has the combined blood of Almont, Mambrino Chief, Cassius M. Clay Jr. and Joe Downing.

These colts are all sound and promising. The only reason I offer them for sale is, that I have three aged stallions in use, and the surplus is growing on me. If I were starting a breeding business for profit, I should consider either of these colts a representative to commence with. Also brood mares and fillies for sale. Correspondence solicited.

FRED. W. LOEBER, St. Helena,
Napa Co., Cal.

Stallion for Sale

AT A BARGAIN.

Full Brother to Fairmont.

By Piedmont, dam Queen by Garibaldi—see State Fair Edition of BREEDER AND SPORTSMAN, September 14, 1889, for description of Fairmont—three years old, solid bay. Can trot a 2:10 gait or better. Sound in every particular. Can be seen at Oakland Trotting Park, Oakland.

P. J. WILLIAMS.

Draught Horse Breeders,

Attention!

JUST ARRIVED! A Number of Fine Young Pure-bred

CLYDESDALE STALLIONS,

Imported from Scotland and registered in the Clydesdale Stud Book. Among them are:

BOGWOOD (5561), Vol. X, C. S. B.
BELTED CRUISER (6481), Vol. XI, C. S. B.
CANNY JAMIE (6574), Vol. XI, C. S. B.

They are of good dark colors with the Regular Clydesdale Markings, and are the finest Horses that have ever been imported to this State. They are the property of A. V. WILSON, Esq., North Yakima, W. T., and will be sold for a reasonable figure. They may be seen at the Mt. Eden Farm. For pedigrees and particulars, call on or address, A. V. WILSON, North Yakima, W. T., or H. P. MOHR, Mount Eden, Alameda Co., Cal.

Anteros Nutwood

——ONE OF THE——

Best Bred Young Stallions in the State.

DESCRIPTION.

Bay horse; black points; no white. Foaled in 1887. Bred by M. Carter, at the Nutwood Stock Farm, by Anteros 6020, by Electioneer, and full brother to Anteeo, 2:16¼, and Antevolo, four-year-old, record 2:19½.

First dam Newark Belle by Nutwood, 2:18¾, and half-brother to Maud S., 2:08¾—Queen of the Turf.

Second dam Tilly, 2:40, by San Bruno, by David Hill, by Vermont Blackhawk. This colt is very large of his age, and looks enough like Sunol to be her full brother.

If there is anything in breeding, this horse ought to make a good one.

Electioneer and Nutwood are his grandsires, both serving mares at $50 each. Nutwood is half-brother to the fastest trotter in the world—Maud S., 2:08¾; Electioneer, the sire of the fastest three-year-old, Sunol, 2:10½.

TERMS.

This colt will be limited to ten mares, outside of my own, for $50 the season.

Mares not proving in foal can be returned the following season by paying difference in price, if any.

The National Trotting Stallion

PILOT NUTWOOD (Cyrus R.)

Will make the season of 1890 at the stable of T. W. Barstow, corner of San Fernand Street and Wilson Avenue, San Jose.

TERMS.

$50 for the season, with usual return privileges, by paying difference in price. No fee if this horse does not secure a record of 2:30 or better in 1890, barring accidents. Limited to 15 outside mares. Season from February 1st to July 1st, 1890. The best care and attention given to mares, but no responsibility assumed for accidents or escapes. Good pasturage at $3 per month. 100 acres of the best feed in Santa Clara County.

DESCRIPTION.

Pilot Nutwood, 2:42, black horse; small star; foaled 1881; 15¾ hands; was worked five weeks, and got a record of 2:42 as a three-year-old; he was not worked again until 1888; after having six weeks work, showed his owner a mile in 2:26, and the last half in 1:10½. Sired by the mighty Nutwood, 2:18¾, half-brother to Maud S., 2:08¾—Queen of the Turf.

First dam Belle by Jack Roberts, half-brother to Ed St. Clair; 2d dam by Shakespeare, thoroughbred. Jack Roberts by Eclair or Leck, and he by old pacing Pilot, and his dam by Copperbottom.

This gives Pilot Nutwood two crosses of the great Pilot blood, coming through both sire and dam. This is the kind of breeding that breeders should be looking after in order to get to the front.

CHALLENGE.

To back my assertion made in the San Jose Mercury in December last, I will match this horse against any trotting stallion in San Jose, one or two-mile heats, any time after July 1st. The parties accepting this challenge can set the time and track, and I the right to name the amount. For further particulars, address,

T. W. BARSTOW,

P. O. Box 1268. San Jose, Cal.

ST. NICHOLAS.

Son of the World Renowned

SIDNEY,

Will Make the Season of 1890, at the Oakland Trotting Park.

ST. NICHOLAS was bred by Mr. G. Valensin at the Arno Stock Farm, Sacramento Co., California, in 1885. He is a beautifully proportioned bright bay horse, 15.3 hands high; is well muscled, lengthy, and lots of bone, with splendid natural action and a phenomenal turn of speed. As a three-year-old he easily worked three heats on the Oakland Track in 2:32, 2:29 and 2:27½. His breeding is just what one would expect from such a highly formed bloodlike horse. Sidney, his sire is the most successful young stallion—whether for getting pacers or trotters—America has ever seen, and no wonder for his blood lines are exceptional fine and are all trotting lines, Santa Claus, Strathmore, Rysdyk's Hambletonian and Abdallah, while Sweetness again runs back through that great sire Volunteer, to Rysdyk's Hambletonian and also through her dam to Rysdyk's Hambletonian and Harry Clay 45, the sire of Electioneer's dam. St. Nicholas' dam is by Echo, an exceptionally prepotent son of Hambletonian thus giving St. Nicholas four Rysdyk's Hambletonian crosses and further back a Harry Clay cross which with his grand dam's thoroughbred cross should make him invaluable in the stud.

TERMS: Fifty dollars the season, which will commence on the 5th of February and close on the 1st of July. Due care will be taken of mares, but no responsibility for accidents or escapes.

Mares taken and kept as desired by the owners, and reasonable rates.

JOHN ROWEN.

Oakland Trotting Park.

THE MAMBRINO Patchen Stallion.

MAMBRINO JR., 1789 (formerly Carr's) Sire of Lady Ellen 2:28 (dam of Ella 2:29), Maud H. 2:30, Mambrino Boy (Carr's) 2:31 1-2.

Will stand at my farm, 2 1-2 miles north of San Jose, on the Milpitas road. Season to commence February 1, 1890, at $40, with return privilege 1891. Fifteen mares of approved breeding, besides my own, will be taken him. Parties owning good mares, performers or out of producing dams, will find an opportunity to breed them on shares, and the best of care taken of them till colt is weaned, if so desired.

PEDIGREE.

MAMBRINO JR., 1789, by Mambrino Patchen 58 (full brother of Lady Thorne 2:18 1-4) by Mambrino Chief 11. First dam by Mambrino Chief 11; 2nd dam by imp. Jordan [thoroughbred]; 3rd dam by Bertrand, son of Sir Archy; 4th dam by Chewkees, son of Sir Archy.

For further particulars address

GEO. P. BULL.

San Jose, Cal.

Box 1067.

THE BUCKINGHAM.

OLD STRAIGHT WHISKIES.

141 Montgomery Street.

303 Bush Street, S. F.

M. J. BALFE, Proprietor.

SEASON 1890.

The Great Son of Buccaneer

SHAMROCK,

Two-Year Old Record of 2:25, beating the World's Record 4 1-2 Seconds when made.

SHAMROCK

- Buccaneer 2656 — Sire of Shamrock, 2:25, Ivy, 2:21½, Flight, 2:29, (dam of Fleet, 2:21, at 2 yrs.), Flirt (dam of Memo, 3 y. o. trial, 2:29½, etc.), Orphan Girl, 2:26½, Pride, 1 yr. 2:42½, 4 yr. 2:26½, Cora, 2 y. o. 2:46, etc.
  - Iowa Chief 528 — Sire of Oorlamande, 2:24
    - Green's Bashaw — 10 in 2:30 or better
    - By Vernol's Black Hawk
    - Topsy.
  - Tinsley Maid
    - Flaxtail.
    - Fanny Fern.
- Fernleaf, 2:28 — Dam of Guildleaf, 2:11½, 4 yrs., Shamrock, 2 yrs. 2:25, Thistle, 2 y. o. trial, 2:28, Ivy, 3 yrs. 2:21½, etc.
  - Flaxtail — Sire of Fernleaf, 2:28, Prairie Bird, 2:28½, Empress, 2:28½, Lightfoot, 2:32.
    - Pruden's Blue Bull.
    - unknown.
  - Fanny Fern
    - Irwin's Tuckahoe — By Herod's Tuckahoe — Sire of dam of Smuggler, 2:15¼.
    - Dau. of Leffler's Consul.

As will be seen from the tabulated pedigree and performances above, Shamrock is not only a phenomenal horse himself, but his ancestors on both sides have shown themselves to be uniformly producers of GREAT and PARTICULARLY early speed, and his record like many others of his family was made in a hotly contested race, instead of a trial against time.

HE IS NOW IN SPLENDID FORM, AND I TRULY BELIEVE WILL LOWER HIS RECORD TO 2:18 THIS YEAR.

TERMS: $100, with usual return privilege, for a limited number of CHOICE mares, season ending June 1st.

Electo.

By Antevolo 2:19½ by Electioneer, dam Captain Webster (sire of dam of Adonis 2:14), by Williamson's Belmont.

Electo, while but three years old this spring, is, as well as being grandly bred, a great individual.

TERMS, $50, with the usual return privilege, limited to 15 approved mares. Season to end June 1st.

Imported Cleveland bay stallion

Elegance.

(Registered in Cleveland Bay Stud Book No. 75.)

Prize winner over twenty of his own breed in the GREAT YORKSHIRE SHOW OF ENGLAND.

The Cleveland Bays are the most prepotent coach horses in the world, and their get from ordinary mares make the most stylish and serviceable horses for that purpose that can be raised. Rich bays with black points having the preference over ALL OTHERS.

TERMS $25, with usual return privilege, season ending July 1st.

Care taken but no responsibility assumed for accidents or escapes. Pasturage, $5 per month. For further particulars call at or address me at my hospital, where horses will make the season.

G. W. STIMPSON, V. S.

Veterinary Hospital, 19th St., near San Pablo Ave, Oakland, Cal.

WOODNUT

(Weatherhead's) by Nutwood 600

Sire of Belmont Boy, 2:16, pacer, Woodnut, 2:16½, Felix, 2:18½, Dawn, 2:18½, Maggie E., 2:19½, Irma, 2:18½, and 26 others in 2:30 or better; 1st dam Flora, 2:29½, trial 2:26, dam of Chrisman's Hambletonian, sire of Steve Whipple, 2:22, Kate Agnew, 2:28½, by Chieftain 721, sire of Defiance 2:17½ pacing and 2:24 trotting, Cairo, 2:26, Onward, 2:24, pacer; second dam by Wilson's Leamon.

Woodnut is a beautiful bay with black points, 15¼ hands high weighing 1,075 pounds. His colts are all larger than himself, and sell readily for road and carriage purposes, being of good color and very docile, yet prompt to obey, and always ready.

Service fee, $25, with usual privileges. Colts and fillies from Tilton Almont, Patchen, Stockbridge Chief, and other desirable crosses, FOR SALE. For further particulars, pedigrees, or any communication in horse matters, address

JAS. WEATHERHEAD, Prop.

San Jose, Cal.

The Fast Trotting Stallion

REDWOOD.

Four-Year-Old Record 2:24 1-2

Will make the season of 1890—February 1st to July 1st—at the

OAKLAND RACE TRACK.

REDWOOD is a dark bay colt, 16.2¼ hands high, weighs 1100 lbs. Foaled in 1885 by Anteeo, 2:16¼, sire of Alfred G., 2:19¾. Anteeo is by Electioneer. First dam Lou Milton, by Milton Medium; second dam (old Fly, a thoroughbred mare brought from the East in 1871 by W. C. Ralston, Esq.

Redwood's sire was out of Columbine by A. W. Richmond, the sire of the pacers Arrow 2:13¾, and Elwood 2:20, and the trotters Romero, 2:19¾, and Len Rose, 2:27. Redwood has shown a quarter in 33 seconds.

Terms $100

For the season. Mares not proving with foal may be returned next season free of charge, provided Redwood remains the property of the present owners. Good pasturage at $5 per month. No responsibility assumed for escapes or accidents. Service fees payable before removal of the mare. Limited to 40 approved mares. For farther particulars address

A. McFADYEN.

Race track, Oakland, Cal.

The Trotting Stallion

BONANZA 2:29½

Will make the season of 1890, from February 1st to July 1st, at the OAKLAND TROTTING PARK.

PEDIGREE.

BONANZA, 2:29½.
- Arthurton 365 — Sire of Arab, 2:15, Joe Arthurton 2:20½, Lady Escot, 2:28½. Dams of Grandee, 2:23½, Hidalgo, 2:27.
  - Hambletonian 10 — Sire of 41 in 2:30 list. Sires of 107 of the sires of 567 in 2:30 list.
  - Imogene by Am. Star 14 — Dam of Leland 1319. Sire of Clara, 2:21, Miss Leland, 2:23½, Hades, 2:27½.
- Sister — Dam of Albert W., 2:20.
  - John Nelson 187 — Sire of Neres, 2:23½, Gov. Stanford, 2:27½, Aurora, 2:27, Nemo, 2:30.
  - Lamott Mare — Dam of Aurora, 2:27; g d of Arol, 2:24½.

DESCRIPTION.

BONANZA is a very handsome chestnut of commanding form and splendid proportions. He stands nearly 16 hands high, is remarkably intelligent, level headed and pure gaited. His record is no mark of his speed. He is a great foal getter, and his colts are handsome fancy animals.

TERMS. $40 for the season, with the usual return privileges. Excellent pasturage near the track at $5 per month. The best of care taken of mares, but no responsibility assumed for accidents or escapes.

For farther particulars, address

RICHARD HAVEY,

Oakland Trotting Park, Oakland.

The Hambletonian Stallion 10178.

CHRISMAN'S HAMBLETONIAN — Sire of Steve Whipple, 2:22, Kate Agnew, 2:28½, etc.
- Whipple's Hambletonian — Sire of 14 trotters and 1 pacer from 2:19 to 2:30, and 7 sons with 8 performers from 2:21¼ to 2:30, and dams of 6 from 2:19½ to 2:30.
  - Guy Miller — By Hambletonian 10.
  - Martha Washington — Dam of Speculation 928. Sire of Crown Pt., 2:24, Oakland Maid, 2:22½, Gracie S., 2:24½, and dam of Waterford, 2:27.
- Flora, 2:29½, trial, 2:26, Dam of Chrisman's Hambletonian, sire of Steve Whipple, 2:23, Kate Agnew, 2:28½.
  - Chieftain 721 — Sire of Defiance, 2:24 and 2:17¼, pacing; Cairo, 2:26, and Onward, 2:24, pacer.
  - daughter of Wilson's Leamon.

Stud season now on till the 1st of August, 1890, at $40 each mare, with return privilege in 1891, provided stallion and mare, or either, do not change owners. Good pasture at hand, and comfortable accommodation for brood mares and colts. For further particulars, address

JESSE CHRISMAN, Proprietor.

San Jose, Cal.

The Trotting Stallion

CUPID,

Full Brother to Adonis 2:14,

——Sired by——

The Celebrated SIDNEY 2:19 3-4, and out of Venus.

Will make the season of 1890 at the OAKLAND TROTTING PARK.

PEDIGREE.

CUPID is by Sidney out of Venus by Capt. Webster 10173, record 2:30, and sire of Firestone 2:19. Second dam by Skenandoah 998, sire of Daisy Barns 2:29½, Erwin Davis (sire of two in the 30 list) and dams of four in the 30 list.

DESCRIPTION.

Cupid is a handsome bright bay 15.2½ hands high, weighs 1100 lbs.; was foaled in 1886. As a yearling, with very little work he showed quarters in 42 seconds, and at 2 years old, quarters in 38 seconds. As a three year old he has not been worked, but he shows the speed and endurance that must come from his excellent blood lines.

TERMS $50 for the season, with the usual return privileges. Good pasturage near the track at $5 per month. The best of care taken of mares in any way that owners may desire, but no responsibility assumed for accidents or escapes.

For further particulars address

C. O. THORNQUEST,

Oakland Trotting Park, or

C. BAAR, 9 2 Broadway, Oakland.

"TOBEY'S,"

214 Post Street,

Between Grant Avenue and Stockton Street,

Adjoining New Hamman Baths.

D. J. TOBIN, Proprietor.

ROME HARRIS. JOHN MERIGAN.

"Laurel Palace,"

N. W. Corner Kearny and Bush Streets

SAN FRANCISCO

HENRY J. COX. W. S. JOHNSON

The "EDWIN C."

40 EDDY STREET.

Cor. of Mason. San Francisco.

(Private Entrance Mason Street.)

Vineland Stock Farm

Whippleton 1883,

Sire of

LILY STANLEY	Record 2:17½
HOMESTAKE	" 2:16½
FLORA B.	" 2:27
CORA C.	" 2:31½
BLACK PRINCE	" 2:36½
RACHEL	" 2:38
PRINCE W.	" 2:40

WHIPPLETON is not only the sire of trotters, but he is the greatest sire of Carriage Horses on the Pacific Coast. Some of the best carriage and road teams in San Francisco are sired by Whippleton. A carriage team by Whippleton received First Premium at Napa, Petaluma, Oakland, Sacramento, Stockton and San Jose. Whippleton and his colts have never been beaten in the show ring.

DESCRIPTION.

WHIPPLETON is black, tan muzzle and flanks, 17 hands, and weighs 1,400 lbs. Most of his colts are 16 hands or over, and with a few exceptions, bay, brown or black. He never sired a sorrel or white face colt. (If he does, I agree to refund service money.)

PEDIGREE.

WHIPPLETON, sired by Hambletonian Jr. (sire of Hancock 2:29), by Whipple's Hambletonian (sire of Graves, 2:19, Westfield, 2:20½, Express, 2:24, and 12 others in the 2:30 list), dam Lady Livingston (dam of Lady Blanchard, 2:26¼, Bloomfield Maid, trial 2:22), by General Taylor (sire of the dams of Wells Fargo, 2:18¾, Neres, 2:23½, Bickford, 2:23½, Lady Blanchard, 2:26½, etc., and sire of grandam of Hazel Wilkes, 2:20) by the Morse Horse 6, sire of Norman 25 (sire of Lulu, 2:14¾, May Queen, 2:20, etc.).

TERMS at $40, limited to 20 mares, for the season, usual return privileges. I would like to get about ten well bred mares with the proper combination of blood to breed to Whippleton on shares this season.

Alcona 730.

Sire of

FLORA BELLE	Record 2:24
CLAY DUKE	" 2:31½

ALCONA will be a great sire, but four of his colts have ever been trained, and all have shown full miles better than 2:30, and two of them as good as 2:20. Two of his first sons each sired a colt as a two-year-old, and last season one as a four-year-old trotted a full mile in 2:23½, and the other, a three-year-old, a mile in 2:31. With opportunities, Alcona is destined to be one of Almont's best sons. Almont, for his opportunities, is beyond doubt the most prepotent sire of his age. He has 36 representatives in the 2:30 list; 49 sons and 22 daughters that have already produced 2:30 performers. Almont died five years ago at 20 years old. If he lived he would be but 25 years old.

PEDIGREE.

ALCONA sired by the great Almont (sire of Westmont 2:13¾, Fanny Witherspoon 2:16¾, Piedmont 2:17¾, and 34 others with records better than 2:30, and grandsire of Belle Hamlin 2:12¾, etc.); by Alexander's Abdallah (sire of Goldsmith Maid 2:14), he by Rysdyk's Hambletonian. Alcona's dam, Queen Mary, by Mambrino Chief (sire of Lady Thorne 2:18 1-4, and 5 others in the 2:30 list, and sire of the dams of Director 2:17, Piedmont 2:17¾, Onward 2:25 1-4, Red Wilkes, Almont, Belmont and many other noted sires).

DESCRIPTION.

Alcona is a beautiful chestnut 16 2 1-2 hands high, and weighs 1290 lbs. His colts possess speed, style, finish and beauty, and if they don't trot they command the highest prices for carriage horses.

$40 for the season. Usual return privilege.

Grandissimo,

Full Brother to GRANDEE, Three Year Old Record 2:23 1-2.

Sired by Le Grande (son of Almont and out of Jessie Pepper, by Mambrino Chief. Jessie Pepper is the dam of Ione 2:17 1-2, Alpha 2:23 1-2, and granddam of Montezuma 2:29½. First dam Norma (dam of Grandee 2:23 1-2), by Arthurton (sire of Arab 2:15, Joe Arthurton 2:20 1-2, etc.); second dam Nourmahal 2:39 (full sister to A. W. Richmond, sire of Arrow 2:13¾, Romero 2:19, and sire of the dams of Antevolo 2:19 1-4, and Anteeo 2:16 1-4, sire of Alfred G 2:19¾) and Redwood 2:24 1-2.

GRANDISSIMO, with limited training as a three year old last year showed 1-4 mile in 36 seconds, and, barring accidents, will trot fast next fall.

Limited to 20 mares at $50 each; usual return privilege.

Season on Grandissimo ends June 1st, 1890.

Season on Whippleton and Alcona ends July 1st, 1890.

Best kind of pasturage at $4 per month. Mares kept in any manner desired.

For further particulars send for circular or call at stables, one mile south of St. Helena.

FRED W. LOEBER.

St. Helena, Napa Co., Cal.

The Trotting Stallion

G & M

FULL BROTHER TO

ALFRED G, 2:19¾.

(Who has been taken to Kentucky to stand at $200)

Will make the season of 1890 from FEBRUARY 1st to JULY 1st, at

SANTA ROSA.

G. & M. is by Anteeo, 2:16¼; was foaled 1886; first dam Rosa B. by Speculation (son of Hambletonian 10); 2d dam Elizabeth by Alexander 490; 3d dam Nora by imp. Glencoe. Anteeo is by Electioneer, out of Columbine by A. W. Richmond 1687.

G. & M. is a handsome dark bay; stands 15-2 1-2 hands high, and weighs 1060 pounds. Gameness, stoutness, speed and stamina are indelibly impressed in every line of the pedigree of G. & M. Owners of brood mares in search of these qualities, will do well to patronize this promising colt.

PHILOSOPHER,

Foaled 1886 by Pilot Wilkes 2857; first dam Bella by George Wilkes 519; second dam by Bell Morgan 61.

Philosopher's sire, Pilot Wilkes 2857, is by George Wilkes 519, dam Grace (the dam of Alice Woodburn, etc.) by Pilot Jr. 12, grandam by Orphan Boy.

Will make the season of 1890, from FEBRUARY 1st to JULY 1st, at Santa Rosa.

TERMS for the season:

G. & M., $50,

PHILOSOPHER, $30,

with privilege of returning mares that do not prove in foal the next season free of charge, provided the horse bred to remains the property of the present owners. Good pasturage at $3 per month. No responsibility assumed for accidents or escapes. Service fee payable before removal of the mare. For further particulars, address

GEO. E. GUERNE,

Santa Rosa, Cal.

Breeders' Directory.

Advertisements under this heading 50c. per line per month.

HORSES AND CATTLE.

W. S. JACOBS, Sacramento, Cal. — Breeder of Thoroughbred Shorthorns and Berkshire Hogs.

J. H. WHITE, Lakeville, Sonoma County—Breeder of Registered Holstein Cattle.

EL ROBLAS RANCHO—Los Alamos, Cal., Francis T. Underhill, proprietor, importer and breeder of thoroughbred Hereford Cattle. Information by mail. C. F. Swan, manager.

PAGE BROTHERS.—Penn's Grove, Sonoma Co Cal. Breeders of Short-Horn Cattle; Draft, Roadster and Standard Bred Horses.

JAMES MADDOCK, Petaluma, Cal.—Trotters trained at reasonable prices. Stock handled carefully. Correspondence solicited.

SETH COOK, breeder of Cleveland Bay Horses, Devon, Durham, Polled Aberdeen-Angus and Galloway Cattle. Young stock of above breeds on hand for sale. Warranted to be pure bred, recorded and average breeders. Address, Geo. A. Wiley, Cook Farm, Danville, Contra Costa Co., Cal.

MAMBRINO WILKES COLTS and FILLIES, full brothers and sisters to Gus. Wilkes 2:22, and Balkan 2:29¾, for sale. Address SMITH HILL, Walnut Creek, Contra Costa County, Cal.

S. F. RUSH, Suisun, Cal., Shorthorns, Thoroughbred and Grades. Young Bulls and Calves for Sale.

PETER SAXE & SON Lick House, San Francisco, Cal.—Importers and Breeders for past 18 years of every variety of Cattle, Horses, Sheep and Hogs.

HOLSTEIN THOROUGHBREDS of all the noted strains. Registered Berkshire Swine. Catalogues. F. H. BURKE, 401 Montgomery St., S. F.

CLEVELAND BAYS and Norman Horses, Jersey Cattle, and pure bred Poland China Hogs.—DR. W. J. PRATHER, Fresno, Cal.

HENRY C. JUDSON, Wild Idle Farm.—Breeder of Thoroughbred Horses. The home of "Wild Idle." P. O., Santa Clara; Box 223.

SITUATION WANTED.

AN INDUSTRIOUS AND CAPABLE MAN wants to secure a situation as Stallion Groom. Can give good references. Address,

GROOM, This Office.

FERGUSON & AUSTIN,
FRESNO, CAL.
Registered Polled Angus and Short-Horn Cattle.

Oysters.

M. B. MORAGHAN

Is the only importer, planter and wholesale dealer in the CALIFORNIA MARKET, Stalls 68, 69 to 71 and 47, 48. All the choicest brands of Fresh Oysters constantly on hand. Prompt attention paid to hotel and country orders. Price List.

Large Eastern Oysters .... $2 00 per 100
Transplanted Eastern Oysters .... 1 50 per 100
California Oysters .... 2 00 " sack
Fresh frozen Eastern Oysters at $7 00 per doz, cans.

PASTURAGE

AND

FIRST-CLASS CARE

TAKEN OF

Gentlemen's Road Horses and Trotters.

Colts Broken and Trained to Harness or Saddle.

Twenty new Box Stalls. First-class Pasturage, and the best of care given to all horses. Terms, $4 per month. Satisfaction Guaranteed.

Address,

K. O'GRADY,
Laural Creek Farm,
SAN MATEO, CAL.

The HOWE SCALE CO.
411 & 413 Market Street, S. F.

Scales for Weighing of
Live Stock
SEEDS, FEED, Etc.
Write for Catalogue,

THE BRUNSWICK BALKE COLLENDER COMPANY,

MANUFACTURERS OF
Standard Billiard and Pool Tables, Saloon and Bank Fixtures,
653--655 Market Street, San Francisco, Cal.

BOYCE TABLETS.

Leg and Body Wash.

THE BOYCE TABLETS are packed in a nicely decorated metal box with hinged lid—one hundred tablets in each box; directions for use plainly engraved upon the box; therefore, the convenience of the package—no liability to leakage and breakage—economy and ready solubility, together with the absolute certainty of their action, will at once commend the use of BOYCE'S TABLETS to the intelligent horsemen of the country. TABLETS sufficient to make one hundred pints of leg and body wash are conveniently carried in an inside coat pocket or in the hip-pocket of the trousers.

The BOYCE WASH can be applied ALL OVER THE BODY WITHOUT FEAR OF BLISTERING OR AFFECTING THE KIDNEYS.

The BOYCE WASH will cure CRACKED HEELS, PUFFS, STOCKINGS, SCRATCHES, INFLAMED TENDONS and FEVERED LEGS.

Price per Box of One Hundred Tablets, $2, sent postpaid to any part of the United States; six boxes for $10. A sample of BOYCE'S TABLETS will be mailed to any address on application. These TABLETS are warranted to keep in any climate. Address

BOYCE TABLET COMPANY,
600 Wabash Avenue, - - - Terre Haute, Indiana.

J. A. McKERRON, Pacific Coast Agent,
228-230-232 Ellis Street, San Francisco, Cal.

ADVERTISE YOUR STALLIONS

—IN THE—

Breeder & Sportsman

For the Season---1890.

We are pleased to announce that we have the best facilities for furnishing

Stallion Pictures,
Stallion Cards,
Pedigrees, Folders,
Contracts, Bills, Etc.

We make a specialty of this department of our business, and have UNRIVALED FACILITIES FOR LOOKING UP PEDIGREES and doing accurate and handsome work.

Promptness, Good Work, Low Prices.

BREEDER AND SPORTSMAN,
313 Bush Street, S. F.

R. LIDDLE & SON
538 Washington St., S. F.,
Wholesale and Retail Dealers in

Guns, Rifles and Pistols.

A Full Line of FISHING TACKLE and SPORTSMAN'S GOODS.

Orders by mail receive prompt attention.

By-Laws

—AND—

Rules and Regulations

—OF THE—

NATIONAL
Trotting Association

ALSO THE

AMERICAN
Trotting Association,

AND THE

PACIFIC COAST BLOOD-HORSE ASSOCIATION.

With Betting Rules.

For Sale at the Office of the

Breeder and Sportsman,
313 Bush St., S. F., Cal.

Price, 25c. each.
By Mail, Postage Paid, 30c. each.

PERRIER-JOUET & Co.

EPERNAY

CHAMPAGNE

W. B. CHAPMAN,
Sole Agent for Pacific Coast.

For sale by all first-class Wine Merchants and Grocers.

HORSES PURCHASED ON COMMISSION.

THOROUGHBREDS A SPECIALTY.

Will select and buy, or buy selected Animals for all desiring, for reasonable compensation.

KEEPS PROMISING YOUNGSTERS IN VIEW.

L. M. LASLEY, Stanford, Ky.

References:—J. W. Guest, Danville, Ky.
B. G Bruce, Lexington Ky.
S. H. Baughman, Stanford, Ky.
G. A. Lackey, Stanford, Ky.
Geo. McAlister, Stanford, Ky.
First National Bank, Stanford, Ky.

Old Hermitage Whiskies

"STEINER'S,"
No. 311 BUSH STREET,
San Francisco.
Under Breeder and Sportsman Office.

The Park Training Stabl[e]

CHAS. DAVID, PROPRIETOR.
Corner Grove and Baker Streets, near E[n]trance to Golden Gate Park.

EVERY FACILITY FOR TRAINING COLTS a[nd] taking care of Gentlemen's Roadsters.

Finely appointed stable with every convenience a[nd] sixteen roomy box stalls.

The best care given all horses by experienced h[elp] under the personal superintendence of the propri[etor].

Convenient to the Park Speed Drive, a[nd] Accessible to Six Lines of Cable Cars.

THE TRAINING OF COLTS AND ROADSTE[RS] A SPECIALTY.

TROTTERS AND ROADSTERS FOR SALE.
HORSES SOLD ON COMMISSIO[N].

The proprietor trained and brought out the follo[wing] well known horses: "Sister, Huntress," "Perihelio[n]," "Nona Y," and others.

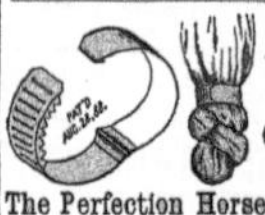

NOVEL, USEFU[L] and Ornamental.

The Perfection Horse Tail Ti[e]

Saves Time and the Tail.
Send 25 Cents for Sample,
BREEDER AND SPORTSMAN,
313 Bush Street, San Francisco
or to BARNES & PARKER, Des Moines, Ia., Manufrs.

GOLDEN EAGLE HOTE[L]

Corner SEVENTH and K STREETS,
SACRAMENTO.
FIRST CLASS IN EVERY RESPECT.
The LARGEST and FINEST HOTEL in th[e] City.
W. O. BOWERS, Proprietor.
Free 'Buss to and from the Hotel.
Telephone, Telegraph Office and Messenger Servi[ce] at Hotel

---

6 DOS

D O you bet?
D O you go to the races?
D O you know HOW to bet?
D O you know BEST system
D O you want Good ADVICE
D O as you ought to do

SEND FOR PROSPECTUS TO

GOODWIN BROS.,
241 BROADWAY, NEW YORK

Who will mail you
FREE OF CHARGE,
one of their circulars showing the GREAT SUCCESS they have met with from the time they established the system of "Point" providing in th[e] country in 1881; it also contains

MANY OTHER INTERESTING ITEMS

with which the general public is not familiar.

Call and See the New

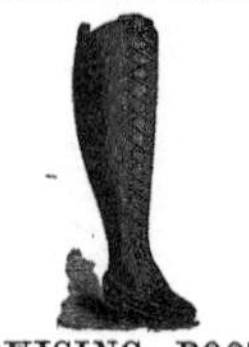

CRUISING BOOTS

E. T. ALLEN,
Fire Arms and Sporting Good[s]
416 Market St., S. F.

The Trotting Stallion
Silver Bow
Will make the season of 1890 at the Oakland Race Track.

Pedigree.

- Robert McGregor 647, 2:17½, Sire of Bonnie McGregor, 2:13½, Earl McGregor, 2:21½, Mac D., 2:20, McGregor Boy, 2:28¼, Mark Time, 2:30, Roxie McGregor, 2:28¾
  - Major Edsall, 2:11, 2:29
    - Alexanders's Abdallah 15, Sire of Goldsmith Maid, 2:14.
      - Hambletonian 10, sire of Dexter, 2:17¼
      - by Young Patriot
    - by Harris' Hambletonian 2.
      - Bishop's Hambletonian
      - The Munson Mare
  - Nancy Whitman, 2:30¼
    - American Star 14
      - Stockholm's American Star
      - Sally Slouch
    - Nance, Dam of Madeleine, 2:23½.
      - Durland's Young Messenger Duroc
      - untraced
- Sadie
  - Hambletonian 10
    - Abdallah
      - Mambrino
      - Amazonia
    - Chas. Kent Mare.
      - imp. Bellfounder
      - One Eye
  - Lady Wynne
    - Wm. Welch 341, sire of Jeremiah, 2:22½.
      - Hambletonian 10
      - the dam of Prince, 2:27
    - Eleanora Margrave
      - imp. Margrave 1455
      - Fanny Wright, thoroughbred

DESCRIPTION.

SILVER BOW is a handsome bay, no white; 15-2¼ hands high; weighs 1071 pounds; of fine form, with the set of legs and a clean cut, intelligent head. Is remarkably level headed, seldom making a break; wears ounce shoes in front. His record 2:37, is no mark of his speed; he can beat 30 easy, and with his gilt-edge breeding, he is just what he ought to be, a trotter sired by a trotter whose dam was herself a trotter and a grandam the dam of two trotters. His dam Sadie being by Hambletonian 10, shows him to be bred from the cream of the trotting blood.

TERMS: $100 for the season. Mares not proving in foal returnable for the season of 1891 free of charge. Good pasturage and first-class care taken of mares for $5 per month. No responsibility assumed for escapes or accidents. For further particulars, address

Limited to 15 approved mares.
Season to end June 1st, 1890.

P. J. WILLIAMS.
Care Race Track, Oakland, Cal.

MEMO.
The Best Son of SIDNEY
Will Make the Season of 1890 at the VALENSIN STOCK FARM

- SIDNEY 2:19¾
  - Santa Claus 2000, 2:17 1-2, Sire of San Mateo, 2:28 1-4, Sidney, 2:19¾.
    - Strathmore 408, Sire of 31 in 2:30 list, Sire of 6 dams of 8 in 2:30, Sire of 3 sires of 3 in 2:30
      - Hambletonian 10, Sire of 41 in 2:30 list, Sire of 107 sires of 567 in 2:30 list, Sire of 44 dams of 40 in 2:30 list.
        - Abdallah 1.
        - Chas. Kent mare.
      - Lady Waltermire, Dam of Marshal Ney 2081.
        - North America.
        - s. t. b. Hambletonian 2 mare.
    - Lady Thorne Jr., Dam of Mollie Mack, 2:33
      - Mambrino (Williams)
        - Ericsson 130.
        - Daughter of Aratus (thoroughbred).
      - Kate
        - Highland Chief.
        - Halcorn mare (Magowan's).
  - Sweetness 2:21 1-4
    - Volunteer 55, Sire of 29 in 2:30, Sire of 21 of 48 in 2:30. Sire of 16 dams of 16 in 2:30.
      - Hambletonian 10, Sire of Geo. Wilkes 2:22
        - Abdallah 1.
        - Chas. Kent. mare.
      - Lady Patriot
        - Young Patriot.
        - Lewis Hulse mare.
    - Lady Merritt
      - Edward Everitt 81, Sire of 13 in 2:30, Sire of 8 sires of 16, Sire of 6 dams of 7.
        - Hambletonian 10.
        - Margrave mare, s.t.b.
      - Daughter of
        - Harry Clay 45, Sire of 2 in 2:30, Sire of dam of Electioneer, St. Julien, etc.
- FLIRT
  - Buccaneer 2656, sire of Shamrock, 2 y. o., 2:25, Flight, 2:29, (dam of Fleet, 2:24), Dams of George V., 2 y. o., 2:31 1-2, Creole, 2:20.
    - Iowa Chief 528, Sire of Consasol, 2:24 1-2
      - Bashaw 50, Sire of 16 in 2:30, Sire of 10 sires of 20 in 2:30, Sire of 11 dams of 18 in 2:30.
        - Black Hawk (Vernol's).
        - Belle.
      - Topsey
        - Prophet, by Vermont Black Hawk 5.
    - Tinsley Maid
      - Flaxtail 8132, sire of dam of Gold Leaf, 2:11 1-4, Apex, 2:26, Flight, 2:29, J. H. McCormack, 2:29, Shamrock, 2:25.
        - Pruden's Blue Bull.
      - Fannie Fern
        - Irwin's Tuckahoe.
        - dam of Leffiers' Consul.
  - Mahaska Belle
    - Flaxtail 8132 s. t. b., Sire of grandams of Fleet, 2:24, Creole, 2:20.
      - Prudens' Blue Bull, Sire of Blue Bull 75, Sire of 58 in 2:30.
        - Merring's Blue Bull.
    - Lady Hake
      - John Baptist
      - Fannie Fern
        - Irwin's Tuckahoe.
        - dam of Leffiers' Consul.

MEMO is, as can be seen at a glance, one of the best bred young stallions in service, having three crosses of Rysdyk's Hambletonian and one of Harry Clay, the sire of Green Mountain Maid (dam of Electioneer, etc.), while Long Island Black Hawk and Flaxtail also contribute to his blood. Sidney (Memo's sire) is universally known as the best young sire in the world, a producer of extreme speed at an early age.

PERFORMANCES.

MEMO trotted in public in his two year-old form, obtaining a record of 2:49, though he was close to 30 in a race on the Bay District Track, the second heat of which was made in 2:31 1-2, the first in 2:32. He exhibited phenomenal speed when three years old, and had it not been for a slight strain of his fore fetlock, there is little question that he would have shown in public very close to the best record. On the Oakland track he was timed a mile in 2:20 1-2, and frequently trotted quarters in from 32 1-2 to 34 seconds. As a four-year-old Memo only started once -at Sacramento -when, although out of condition, he showed great speed, and improving as he went on, great hopes were entertained of his going well down in the 'teens at the P. C. T. H. B. A. meeting, but after showing several very fast miles his leg filled and he was laid up for the season. He is sixteen hands high, and of powerful build throughout. His color is a glossy black, with both fore-feet white. His disposition is all that could be desired, and his action superb. He is a sure foal getter, only one mare being reported not in foal during his last season.

TERMS, $100, with usual return privileges, for a limited number of mares. Season to close JUNE 15th, when he will be prepared for track purposes. Pasturage $5 per month. Reasonable charges if fed hay and grain. Best of care taken of mares, but positively no responsibility assumed for accidents or escapes. For further particulars address

J. P. KERR, 313 Bush Street, San Francisco,
or, G. VALENSIN, Pleasanton, Cal.

Guenoc Stud Farm, Lake Co., Cal.

Imp. GREENBACK
(Sire of the English Winners Greenlight, Greenjacket, Greensbank, Greenwave and Greenhorn)

By Dollar, dam Music, by Stockwell. $100 the Season

ST. SAVIOR,
(FULL BROTHER TO EOLE)

By Eolus, dam War Song, by War Dance. $100 the Season.

PASTURAGE, $5 PER MONTH.

With right to return the following year if mare does not prove with foal. The best of care taken, but no liability for accidents or escapes. Mares shipped to C. W. ABY, care ST. HELENA STABLES, St. Helena Napa County, will be taken in charge by competent men.

For further information write to

DR. C. W. ABY, Middletown, Lake County, Cal.

SOUTHER FARM

P. O. Box 208. San Leandro, Cal.

1½ miles northwest of San Leandro; 3 miles southeast of Oakland. Turn off County road between above places at "Stanley Road," ½ mile north of San Leandro.

Horses boarded at all times in any manner desired. Best of care but no responsibility for accidents. Colts broken and handled for the road or track. Terms reasonable.

Glen Fortune,	Jester D,	El Benton,	Figaro,
By Electioneer.	By Almont.	By Electioneer.	Hambletonian 725
$50 for 1889.	$50 for 1890.	Limited to 5 mares.	Limited to 12 mares
		Book Full.	Book Full.

If horses are to last for a profitable time they must occasionally have a change from hard pavements, wooden floors, and dry, hard feed.

THE SOUTHER FARM
Has Green Feed the Year Round,

and feeds Hay in connection with the green feed, which a horse must have if he is to thrive. Every animal is given

A Dry, Warm Place to Sleep,

No matter how stormy the weather. All Stock under cover when it rains.

VISITORS WELCOME ANY DAY EXCEPT SUNDAY.

Write to the above address for references, circulars and price lists. Terms reasonable.

GILBERT TOMPKINS, Proprietor.

SAN MATEO STOCK FARM
HOME OF GUY WILKES,
Record, 2:15 1-4.

Guy Wilkes' Book is full for 1890, and positively no more mares will be received. Book now open for 1891, at $500 the Season.

Sable Wilkes, three-year-old record 2:18, will be allowed to serve 25 mares in addition to those already engaged at $250 the season of 1890. SABLE Wilkes, 15½ hands, black horse, by Guy Wilkes, first dam Sable by The Moor; second dam Gretchen by Mambrino Pilot; third dam Kitty Kirkman by Canada Chief; fourth dam by Fanning's Tobe; fifth dam by imp. Leviathan.

Leo Wilkes, brown horse, four years, 16 hands, full brother to Sable Wilkes, will be allowed to serve 30 mares at $100 the season.

Mares not proving with foal may be returned the following season free of service fee. Parties engaging the services of any of the above horses must send a deposit of 10 per cent. of service money with engagement. Pasturage $6 per month, and when the condition of the animal requires it, hay or grain, or both, are fed, the charge will be $12 50 per month. Good care will be taken of all mares sent to the Farm, but no liability will be assumed for accidents or escapes.

All bills are due at time of service, but must be paid by August 1st of each year. No stock will be allowed to leave the place until all bills are paid.

WILLIAM CORBITT.
San Mateo Stock Farm

Poplar Grove Breeding FARM.
Standard-bred Trotters, Colts and Fillies.

The get of CLOVIS, 4909; PASHA, 2039; APEX, 2935,

For Sale.

Address S. N. STRAUBE, Poplar Grove Breeding Farm,
Fresno, Cal.

Inspection by intending purchasers invited, and information by mail.

CHICAGO, ILLS. -:- BREEDERS' SAL

SECOND GRAND COMBINATION SALE OF

KIDD, EDMONSON & MORSE,

Will be held in Chicago, Ill., MARCH 17th to 23d, 1890

Trotters, Pacers, Stallions, Brood Mares, Colts, Saddle and Harness Hors

Those wishing to dispose of their stock to the best advantage should send for conditions and entry blanks at once, as the sale promises to be very large.

Entries to close February 20, 1890. Send in your entries at once.

Our first sale was a grand success, and was only a foreshadowing of what is to follow. Address,

KIDD, EDMONSON & MORSE, Lexington, K

Or No. 806 West Madison St., Chicago, Ill.

2:20 1-2 (Half Mile Track) at 4 Years. — Fastest Record (in a Race) of any Wilkes — 2:14 1-2 at 5 Years

ROY WILKES, $2:12\frac{3}{4}$,

Seal brown; 15¾ hands; foaled 1883; by Adrian Wilkes 6660, son of Geo. Wilkes; 1st dam by Blue Bull 75; 2d dam by grandson of American Eclipse; 3d and 4th dams thoroughbred.

THE GREATEST CAMPAIGNER OF 1889.

Handsome, Game, Pure Gaited. Level Headed.

Will make a season at the PLEASANTON STOCK FARM, PLEASANTON, CAL. Service Fee $150. Money refunded if mare does not get in foal. Season ends April 1st, 1890.

For full record of performances, extended pedigree, etc., address

L. A. DAVIES, Hotel Pleasanton,
SUTTER AND JONES STREETS, San Francisco, Cal.

The Trotting Stallion

Guide 2:29

(At Four Years)

Will make the season of 1890 at the SANTA RITA RANCH, about one mile North of Pleasanton.

DESCRIPTION.

GUIDE is a handsome seal brown, five years old, stands 15¾ hands high, and weighs 1035 pounds. He is of fine form, level headed, intelligent and comes from blood lines that are noted for the qualities of speed and gameness.

PEDIGREE.

GUIDE, 2:29.
- Director, 2:17. Sire of Direct, 2 18¾, Margaret S., 2:19½.
  - Dictator 113. Sire of 23 trotters and 3 pacers in 2:30.
    - Hambletonian 10.
    - Clara, by American Star 14.
  - Dolly. Dam of Onward, 2:25¾, Thorndale, 2:22¾.
    - Mambrino Chief 11.
    - Fannie, by Ben Franklin.
- Imogene.
  - Norwood 522. Sire of Tommy Norwood, 2:26½.
    - Hambletonian 10.
    - Lady Fallis, by American Star 14.
  - daughter of
    - American Star 14.
    - daughter of Henry Clay 8.

The attention of breeders is especially called to the above pedigree as showing 3 crosses of American Star. GUIDE trotted into the 2 30 list last season with little training, and he will trot into the 2:20 list the coming season barring accidents.

Guide's sire has a record of 2:17, made in a five heat race, and Guide is closely related to Phallas, who made a record of 2:13¾ in a fourth heat, and to Jay-Eye-See, record 2:10.

TWO HUNDRED AND FIFTY DOLLARS will be given to the owner of the first of the produce of Guide put in the 2:30 list, and $100 to each one after the first.

TERMS—$75 for the season, with the usual return privileges.

Admiro,

Sire Admiral; dam by San Bruno, by Easton's David Hill.

This magnificent horse is a handsome bay, eight years old; stands 17 1-2 hands high, and weighs 1470 pounds. He is very speedy for a large horse, and breeds fine large carriage horses. His produce possess every qualification of the Cleveland Bay, with the added qualities of speed and endurance resulting from his high trotting breeding.

TERMS—$35 for the season, with usual return privileges.

Will stand three days each week at Santa Rita Ranch, Pleasanton, and at A. T. Hatch's Ranch "Almono," Alamo, Contra Costa County, alternately. All mares sent care of SMITH & SUTHERLAND, Pleasanton, will be taken in charge of on arrival, and will receive the best care and attention in any manner the owners may desire. Good pasturage at $4 per month. Only a limited number of approved mares will be served by this horse this season.

No responsibility assumed for escapes or accidents. For further particulars, address

SMITH & SUTHERLAND, Pleasanton.

or A. T. HATCH, care Palace Hotel, San Francisco.

1890 Three Anteeo Stallions 1890

SUNSET, 5 years old, by Anteeo
ANTEEOF, 4 years old, by Anteeo
ANTEEOP, 3 years old, by Anteeo

ANTEEO. Standard 7868. Record, 2:16 1-4. He by Stanford's Electioneer, and dam Columbine.

DESCRIPTIONS, PEDIGREES AND CONDITIONS.

"SUNSET" is a rich, dark bay, small star on forehead, portion of hind left foot white; was foaled March 11, 1885; is by ANTEEO and the inbred HAMBLETONIAN mare, BESSIE G, she by KING PHILLIP, son of WHIPPLE'S HAMBLETONIAN. He is 16 1 2 hands high, and weighs 1,200 lbs. He is of perfect build and splendid action cool headed and great speed for his size, having trotted a trial mile as a three-year-old in 2:36. He then entered heavy in the stud and was matched against Whalebone at the Healdsburg races November 7, 1889, winning just as he pleased in three straight heats: time, 2:47, 2:46 1-2, 2:42 1-2. He was then matched for a race to come off last Thanksgiving Day at Petaluma, but owing to the heavy rains the event did not take place. A few days previous to Thanksgiving Day Mr. Lawrence worked Sunset out and then he trotted three square miles and heats in 2:39¼, 2:34 and 2:37.

SUNSET will be bred to 40 mares only, at $67 each, no colt no pay.

"ANTEEOF" is a jet black, was foaled April 13, 1886, is 16¼ hands high, and weighs 1,200 lbs., has a very fine, heavy black mane and tail; is well proportioned, moves majestically, is of easy, lofty carriage; is symmetrical, in fact is a beautiful horse. He was sired by Anteeo and the O. A. Taylor mare "Nance," her dam, was raised by Dr. Oliver Plummer, of Consumnes, Cal., and sired by "Napoleon"; Napoleon was foaled May 20, 1852, and raised by James Kyle of Butler County, Ohio. He was sired by Benj. Sweet's horse Hellfounder, and he by Old Hellfounder, his dam was sired by Doc. Daniel Mulligan's horse, Cadmus, G. G. sire the celebrated Eclipse; his G. dam was sired by Big Shakespeare, G. G., sires dam by Messenger and Expedition.

ANTEEOF will be bred to 25 mares only, at $50 each. No colt, no pay.

"ANTEEOP" is a rich seal brown; was foaled March 7, 1887; by Anteeo and the inbred Hambletonian mare Bessie G., also dam of Sunset, his full brother and Midget his full sister; he is 15 1-2 hands high and weighs 95? lbs, and measures 22 inches around the arm, good head, fine neck, full, broad breast; withers and rump on nearly equal line, well proportioned bones, ankle, shoulders, loins and hips; strong legs all around, with great muscular development and splendid sinews; wirey pasterns and sound, compact feet; the lines from hip to hoof show power and speed; stands square and has excellent action, has a superb lustrous coat of rich deep brown fur of seal color without defect; an even, honest trotter, and has gone the mile as a two-year-old in 2:48, the last quarter in 38 seconds; is intelligent and of high spirit, with much temper, but is not vicious, has very fine eyes, is a handsome, showy colt; attractive in harness.

ANTEEOP will be bred to 15 mares only, at $35. No colt, no pay.

SEASON to commence February 1st, ending July 1, 1890. Book now ready. Apply to John H. Lawrence, "Manager and Trainer," on my fruit and hop ranch, 1 mile east of Court House, on Sonoma road. Excellent pasture furnished with running water, also dry knolls with oak shelter, at $3 per month for mares. Two of the above stallions will be for sale after the expiration of the their stud season.

GUY E. GROSSE,
SANTA ROSA, SONOMA CO., CAL.

Pleasanton Stock Farm Co.'s Stallions

DIRECTOR, 2:17.

Director's book is open for 15 good mares more than already booked for the season of 1890, [illegible] each.

This is the cheapest service fee ever charged for a stallion, taking into consideration his BRE[EDING] and RACE RECORD and the RACE RECORDS OF HIS COLTS.

Season to commence February 15th and close August 1st.

PLEASANTON.

Sire Director 2:17, Dam May Day 2:30.

PLEASANTON is a light bay, 16 hands high, and is full brother to Margaret S, three year old 2:19½.

His book is now open for 10 good mares at $100 for the season, which will commence March [illegible] and June 1st.

Mares not proving with foal may be returned next season free of charge of service fees to the stallion, if he is still in our possession; if not, to some other stallion equally as good, or money refunded at option of the Company.

Pasturage $4 per month; hay and grain extra. Accidents and escapes at owner's risk.

Service fees due at time of service, and must be paid, together with pasturage, etc., before ma[res are] taken away, or a good approved note given, payable August 1st, 1890, at which date all bills [must be] settled.

For further information call or address M. SALISBURY, 320 Sansome Street, Room [illegible] San Francisco, or

PLEASANTON STOCK FARM CO.;
Pleasanton, Alameda Co., C[al.]

BAY STALLION

ECLECTIC

11,321

By Electioneer, dam Manette (full sister to Woodnut 2.16 1-2)

Mason 2:21 and Maple, dam of Hattie D. (three year-old record 2.28¾) by Nutwood 2:18¾, etc., etc.

Terms $100 for the Season.

BROWN STALLIO[N]

MORTIME[R]

5,346

Four-year-old Record 2:2[illegible]

By ELECTIONEER, dam MARTI, by Wh[illegible] Hambletonian (sire of 15 in 2:30, and of dams o[f illegible] in 2:30). Second dam Ida Marti, by Rideman [illegible] of Col. Lewis 2:18¾).

Terms $60 for the Season.

Horses shipped via San Francisco may be consigned to J. W. MORSHEAD, City Front Stables, w[ho will] attend to their forwarding.

Season Closes JULY 1st, 1890. Usual return privileges.

For further particulars address owner,

WILFRED PAGE, Penns Grove,
Sonoma County.

Valensin Stock Farm Stallions

SIDNEY, 2:19 3-4.

At Eight Years of Age Sire of the following Fastest on Record;

FAUSTINO, yearling stallion, record of the world........
FLEET, fastest yearling record in 1888........
FLEET, fastest two-year-old filly in 1889........
GOLD LEAF, fastest four-year-old Pacing record in the world........
ADONIS, fastest three-year-old Pacing Gelding in the world........
ADONIS, four-year-old Gelding Pacing record........

—Also the Sire of—

LONGWORTH, four years old........
SISTER V., four years old (trial 2:23)........
SANTA RITA........
MEMO, two-year-old (three-year-old trial 2:20½)........

And many others.

SIDNEY is the sire of Faustino 2:35, and Fleet 2:36, the two fastest yearlings the world ha[s] known by one sire, and his slowest yearling is faster than the great Electioneer's fastest.

Terms, $250, with usual return privileges, for a limited number of approved mares. Book r[apidly] filling.

SIMMOCOLON, Four-year-old, 2:29 1-2.

Trial, 2:24; Half Mile in 1:08; Quarter in 33 1-2 Seconds.

Chestnut Horse, foaled 1885.

As will be seen, Simmocolon is by a performing and producing son of George Wilkes, 2:22. B[ehind the] back of him three producing dams, and combines the blood of the great sire George Wilkes hand[somely] blended with the blood of the greatest broodmare families. On the dam's side Mambrino Patchen, [Strath]more, Clark Chief and Clay. A fine individual himself, pure gaited and very fast.

Terms, $150, with usual return privileges, for a limited number of mares. Season to close [illegible] 15th, when he will be prepared for track purposes. Pasturage $5 per month. Reasonable charges [for] hay and grain. Best of care taken of mares, but positively no responsibility assumed for accide[nts or] escapes. For further particulars address

G. VALENSIN, Pleasanton, Ca[l.]

Pacific Coast Trotting - Horse Breeders Ass'n

Stakes and Installment Purses for 1890.

Entries close March 1st, 1890.

STAKES.

YEARLINGS—FOALS 1889.

ONE MILE DASH, $50 entrance, payable $5 March 1, 1890, $10 May 1, 1890, $10 July 1, 1890 and $25 on the fifth day preceeding the first advertised day of the meeting.

TWO-YEAR-OLDS—FOALS 1888.

ONE MILE AND REPEAT; $75 entrance, $250 added, payable $10 on March 1, 1890, $10 May 1, 1890, $15 July 1, 1890, and $40 on the fifth day preceding the first advertised day of the meeting.

THREE-YEAR-OLDS—FOALS 1887.

MILE HEATS best three in five; entrance $100, with $300 added, payable $10 on March 1, 1890, $10 on May 1, 1890, $20 on July 1, 1890, and $60 on the fifth day preceding the first advertised day of the meeting.

FOUR-YEAR-OLDS—FOALS 1886.

MILE HEATS best three in five; $100 entrance, $400 added, payable $10 on March 1, 1890, $10 May 1, 1890, $30 on July 1, 1890, and $50 on the fifth day preceding the first day of the meeting.

PURSES.

$800. THREE YEAR OLDS. Foals of 1887. Eligible to three minute class. Mile heats; three in five.

$800. FOUR YEAR OLDS. Foals of 1886, eligible to 2:40 class. Mile heats; three in five.

Purses open to the get of Stallions with no Representatives in the 2:30 list.

$500. TWO YEAR OLDS. Foals of 1888. Mile and repeat.

$600. THREE YEAR OLDS. Foals of 1887. Mile heats; three in five.

$800. FOUR YEAR OLDS. Foals of 1886. Mile heats; three in five.

Stallion Purse $1,000.

Open to stallions eligible to 2.30 class. Mile heats, three in five.

ENTRANCE to all purses—10 per cent.; payable: 2 per cent, March 1st 1890; 2 per cent. May 1st, 1890; 2 per cent. July 1st, 1890; and 4 per cent. on the fifth day preceding the first advertised day of the meeting.

The Stanford Stakes for 1892.

FOALS OF 1889.

OPEN TO THE WORLD.

MILE HEATS.—Three in five. Entrance $100, with $100 added for each starter over two and up to five head, and $25 for each additional starter up to ten head. Payments: $10 on March 1st, 1890; $10 on January 2nd, 1891; $10 on January 2nd, 1892; $20 on May 1st, 1892; and $50 on the fifth day preceding the first advertised day of the meeting at which the stake shall be trotted.

CONDITIONS.

First payment, whether for purses payable in installments or for stakes, MUST ACCOMPANY NOMINATIONS, or they will not be considered.

Neglect to provide payments on the dates stipulated will incur forfeiture of all previous payments.

No horses and colts owned on the Pacific Coast by others than members of the P. C. T. H. B. A. are eligible to the above purses and stakes (excepting the Stanford stake), but horses and colts OWNED outside of the Pacific Coast are eligible thereto regardless of membership.

All States and Territories lying in whole or in part west of the Rocky Mountains are held to be part of the Pacific Coast.

The Directors reserve the right to change the hour and day of any race except when it becomes necessary to ante-date a race, in which instance the nominator will receive three days notice of change by mail to address of entry.

Entries not declared out by 6 P. M. of the day preceding the race, shall be required to start.

When there is more than one entry to a purse or stake by one person or in one interest, the horse to be started must be named by 6 P. M. of the day preceding the race.

Purses and stakes will be divided into four moneys, viz., 50 per cent. to the winner, 25 per cent. to the second horse, 15 per cent. to the third horse, and 10 per cent. to the fourth horse.

No added money will be paid for a walk-over. If only three horses start in a stake race, only first, second and third money shall be paid—if but two start, the Directors reserve the right to call it a walk-over, and divide the stake money paid in, two-thirds to the winner and one-third to the second horse. In case of a walk-over, only the money received from entries to said stake will be paid. In purse races, three horses will be required to start.

A horse distancing the field shall only be entitled to first and third moneys.

The Board of Directors reserve the right to declare any purse or stake filled or not filled without binding itself to any specified number of entries.

Trotting and racing colors shall be named by six o'clock on the day preceding the race, and MUST be worn upon the track.

Otherwise than the above, National or American Trotting Association Rules—as this Association may select—will govern the stake and purse races offered.

Persons desirous of making entries in the above purses and stakes, and who have not as yet joined the P. C. T. H. B. A., should make application for membership to the Secretary, and remit the sum of $25 to cover membership fee before March 1, 1890.

THE PROGRAMME FOR

Aged Horses--Trotters and Pacers,

AND FOR SPECIAL EVENTS,
will be announced at the proper time.

J. H. WHITE, President.

JAS. P. KERR, Secretary.
313 Bush Street, S. F.

1890.

Petaluma Colt Stakes

TO BE TROTTED AT THE

Fall Meeting

OF THE

Sonoma and Marin Agricultural Society

District No. 4.

FREE-FOR-ALL COLTS.

1st. For two-year-olds, foals of 1888, Purse $400, entrance 10 per cent. of the purse, of which 2½ per cent. must accompany the nomination, to be made on March 1st; 2½ per cent., be paid on May 1st, and 5 per cent, on August 1st. Four colts to make the last payment, and three to start.

2nd. For three-year-olds, foals of 1887. Purse $500, entrance ten per cent. of the purse, of which 2½ per cent. must accompany the nomination to be made on March 1st, 2½ per cent to be paid on May 1st, and 5 per cent. on August 1st. Four colts to make the last payment, and three to start.

All moneys in the above races to be divided as follows: 60 per cent. to the first horse, 30 per cent. to the second, and 10 per cent. to the third.

Balance of conditions as per District Stakes.

The following Stakes and Purses open to the Counties of Sonoma, Marin, Napa, Solano, Lake, Mendocino, Yolo and Colusa.

YEARLING STAKE.

For foals of 1889. Mile dash. $30 entrance, of which $10 must accompany the nomination March 1st; $10 be paid on May 1st and $10 on July 1st; $100 added.

TWO-YEAR-OLD STAKE.

For foals of 1888. Mile and repeat. $50 entrance, of which $10 must accompany the nomination March 1st; $20 be paid on May 1st and $20 on July 1st; $200 added.

THREE-YEAR-OLD PURSE.

Three in five. Purse $300. Entrance fee 10 per cent. of the purse of which five per cent. must accompany the nomination March 1st, and five per cent. paid on August 1st. Four colts to make the last payment.

In the above stakes and purses, five to enter and three to start. But the Board reserves the right to hold entries, and start a race with a less number.

All moneys in the above races to be divided as follows: 60 per cent. to the first horse, 30 per cent. to the second and 10 per cent. to the third. If only two start they must contest for the stakes paid in, and one-half the added money to be divided, 66⅔ per cent. to the first and 33⅓ per cent. to the second.

If, in the opinion of the judges, any race cannot be finished on the closing day of the fair it may be continued or declared off at the option of the judges.

Entries to all the above races to close on March 1, 1889, with the Secretary.

J. H. WHITE, President.

DR. THOS. MACLAY, Secretary.

The State Agricultural Society

Spring Meeting 1890.

(The week following the P. C. B. H. A)

The Chris. Green Handicap

The Spring Stakes

To Close FEBRUARY 1st, 1890.

THE CHRIS. GREEN HANDICAP.

A Sweepstakes for all ages, of $50 each, h f, or $10 if declared, with $500 added; second horse to receive $100 out of stakes. Weights announced March 1st. Declarations due by 6 P. M. April 1st. A winner of any race after publication of weights, of one mile or upwards, to carry 3 lbs; of two races, 5 lbs; of three or more, 7 lbs. extra. This will not apply to horses handicapped at 125 lbs. or over. One and one quarter miles.

THE SPRING STAKES.

A Sweepstakes for three year olds (foals of 1887) that have not won a race previous to January 1st, 1890; $50 entrance, h f, or $15 if declared April 1st, 1890; $400 added, second to receive $75 from stakes. Maidens at time of starting allowed 5 lbs. One mile.

The general conditions of the race meeting as to postponements and track discipline will apply to these stakes.

All declarations are void unless accompanied by the money.

CHRIS. GREEN, President.

EDWIN F. SMITH, Secretary.

SACRAMENTO COLT STAKES ASSOCIATION

TROTTING AND PACING COLT STAKES FOR 1890.

N. B—Horsemen in the localities eligible will please note the conditions of each Stake.

SACRAMENTO YEARLING STAKE FOR 1890.

Open to all foals of 1889, owned in California on a line all north of and including the city of Stockton.

$75 entrance, of which $10 must accompany nomination; $15 to be paid May 1, 1890; $25 August 1, 1890, and $25 on the Saturday before the race. To be trotted at Sacramento during the State Fair of 1890. One mile dash. First colt to receive 50 per cent, second colt 30 per cent, and third colt 20 per cent. of stake. Failure to make payments when due forfeits all previous payments.

TWO-YEAR-OLD STAKE.

Open to all foals of 1888, owned in California, on a line all north of and including the city of Stockton.

$75 entrance, of which $10 must accompany nomination; $15 to be paid April 1, 1890; $25 May 1, 1890, and $25 June 9, 1890. To be trotted at Sacramento, June 10, 1890, good day and track. One mile and repeat. First colt to receive 50 per cent. second colt 30 per cent. and third colt 20 per cent. of stake. Failure to make payments when due forfeits all previous payments.

THREE YEAR OLD STAKE.

Open to all foals of 1887, owned in California on a line all north of and including the City of Stockton.

$75 entrance, of which $10 must accompany nomination: $15 to be paid April 1st, 1890; $25 to be paid May 1st, 1890; and $25 June 9th, 1890. To be trotted at Sacramento June 10th, 1890, good day and track. Mile heats, three in five. First colt to receive 50 per cent., second colt 30 per cent., and third colt 20 per cent of stake. Failure to make payments when due forfeits all previous payments.

PACING STAKES.

YEARLING STAKE FOR 1890.

Open to all foals of 1889, owned in California, on a line all north of and including the City of Stockton.

$75 entrance, of which $10 must accompany nomination: $15 to be paid May 1st, 1890; $25 August 1st, 1890; and $25 on the Saturday before the race. To be paced at Sacramento the first Monday in November, 1890, good day and track. One mile dash. First colt to receive 50 per cent., second colt 30 per cent., and third colt 20 per cent. of stake. Failure to make payments when due forfeits all previous payments.

TWO-YEAR-OLD PACING STAKE.

Open to all foals of 1888, owned in California, on a line all north of and including the city of Stockton.

$75 entrance, of which $10 must accompany nomination; $15 to be paid May 1, 1890; $25 August 1, 1890, and $25 on the Saturday before the race. To be paced at Sacramento the first Monday in November, 1890, good day and track. Mile and repeat. First colt to receive 50 per cent., second colt 30 per cent., and third colt 20 per cent. of stake. Failure to make payments when due forfeits all previous payments.

THREE YEAR-OLD PACING STAKE.

Open to all foals of 1887, owned in California on a line all north of and including the city of Stockton.

$75 entrance, of which $10 must accompany nomination; $15 to be paid May 1, 1890; $25 August 1, 1890, and $25 on the Saturday before the race. To be paced at Sacramento the first Monday in November, 1890, good day and track. Mile heats, three in five. First colt to receive 50 per cent., second colt 30 per cent., and third colt 20 per cent. of stake. Failure to make payments when due forfeits all previous payments.

Entries to all these stakes to close February 15, 1890, with

F. P. LOWELL, Secretary,
1020 F Street, Sacramento, Cal.

WILBER FIELD SMITH.
President Sacramento Colt Stake Association.

Season of 1890.

February 15 to June 15

LYNWOOD,

(STANDARD 3017.)

AT WOLF'S (RUSSELL'S) STABLES, STOCKTON, CAL.

TERMS.

$50 for the season, payable at the close of season. Pasturage at $3 per month. Accidents or escapes at owner's risk.

PEDIGREE.

LYNWOOD 3017, trial 2:28.

- Nutwood 600, 2:18¾. Sire of—Woodnut, 2:16½, 28 in 2:30 list.
  - Belmont 64. Sire of—29 in 2:30 list, 17 sires and 11 dams of trotters in 2:30 list.
    - Abdallah 15. Sire of—Goldsmith Maid, 2:14, 8 in 2:30 list, 13 sires and 21 dams of trotters in 2:30 list.
    - Belle, by Mambrino Chief 11. Dam of—Hambletonian 1:44, 2:28¾, the sire of 4 in 2:30 list.
  - Miss Russell. Dam of—Maud S., 2:08¾, Nutwood, 2:18¾, Cora Belmont, 2:24½.
    - Pilot Jr. 12. Sire of—3 in 2:30 list, 7 sires and 12 dams of trotters in 2:30 list.
    - Sally Russell. By Boston.
- Hattie Morrison. Fast Road Mare. Trial 2:32½.
  - Ethan Allen Jr. 2903. Sire of—Prince Allen, 2:27.
    - Ethan Allen 43, 2:25½. Sire of—7 in 2:30 list, 18 sires and 11 dams of trotters in 2:30 list.
    - Daughter of Hambletonian 2. Sire—4 in 2:30 list.
  - Grigsby Mare.
    - Sir Charles, thoroughbred.
    - Hosting Mare. S. t. b. of Messenger and Duroc blood.

DESCRIPTION.

Dark bay, 16 hands, weighs 1050 pounds, form stout and elegant, gait pure and rapid. He was foaled July 15, 1870, has done but little work in the stud, but enough to demonstrate that he is one of the best foal getters in the State. Only one of his get has had any systematic handling, and that could have gone into the 2:30 list last year as a two-year-old, had the owner desired.

It will be observed from an examination of Lynwood's pedigree, that he is one of the best bred sons of the GREAT NUTWOOD, who commands a service fee of $500 for the season.

P. VISHER, Stockton.

$2{:}08\frac{3}{4}$ 2:10 2:12

BALKAN

By Mambrino Wilkes.

(See that Horse's Advertisement.)

DAM FANNY FERN BY JACK HAWKINS Son of Boston.

The grandam of Maud S. (2:08¾) was by Boston and the grandam of Jay-Eye-See (2:10) was by Lexington, son of Boston. So Balkan is the same remove from Boston that Maud is, and one remove nearer than Jay-Eye-See.

Fanny Fern has produced Molly Drew, Onyx, Fred Arnold, Molly Fern and Balkan, all by different sires.

Balkan's sire and dam both being producers, and he being a trotter himself with a record of 2:29 1-2 (three-year-old) and timed separately 2:22 1-4 in 4-year-old stake, Bay District Track, October 14, 1889—it is but fair to presume that he will get trotters of the highest order.

DESCRIPTION.

He is seal brown, 16-1 hands high, in style rivalled by few, and excelled by none with as pure a gait as has yet been exhibited in public—bar none.

Balkan will be at Oakland Trotting Park for the season of 1890, and will be limited to ten mares, at $100 fee, in order to be put in training early, as it is morally certain that if given a reasonable opportunity he will be fast enough to compete with the best of his age. For further particulars, address

A. L. HINDS,
Dexter Stables, Oakland.

$2{:}12\frac{3}{4}$ $2{:}13\frac{1}{2}$ $2{:}15\frac{1}{4}$

GROVER CLAY.

Bay Stallion, Black Points, 15 3-4 hands high.

Bred by W. W. Traylor, San Francisco.

BY ELECTIONEER.

First dam Maggie Norfolk by Norfolk, son of Lexington, he by Boston. Second dam Tilda Quill by Billy Cheatham he by Cracker, and he by Boston. Third dam by Dorsey's Golddust.

TERMS.

Will make the season of 1890 at the Training Stables of Denis Gannon, near Oakland Trotting Park, at $50 the season, payable at time of service. Season to commence February 1st and ending July 1st. Proper care of mares will be taken, but no responsibility incurred for accidents or escapes. Address,

DENIS GANNON, Oakland, Cal.

Sire of Yolo Maid, $2{:}12\frac{1}{2}$

Alexander Button 1197.

FOUR YEAR-OLD RECORD, 2:26 1-2.

SIRE OF

YOLO MAID, 2:12½, BELLE BUTTON, 2:20, TOM RIDER, 2:20½, ROSA MAC, 2:20½, J. H. (seperately timed in a race) 2:22½, KEHOE, 2:34½, ALEX. BUTTON (3), 2:35½, BURBANK S. (2 y. o., ½-mile track), 2:53.

PEDIGREE.

Alex. Button was Sired by Alexander 490, Record, 2:31 1-4.

First dam Lady Button by Napa Rattler; 2d dam pacing mare (S. T. B.) by a Copperbottom horse.

ALEXANDER (490), record, 2:31½.

Sire of Alex. Button, 2:26 1-2, Reliance, 2:22 1-2, Tommy Dodd, 2:24, Nelly Patchen, 2:27 1-4, by Geo. M. Patchen Jr. (31), record 2:27; first dam Lady Crum by Brown's Bellfounder.

GEO. M. PATCHEN JR (31), rec., 2:27.

Sire of Wells Fargo, 2:18¾, Sam Purdy, 2:20 1-2, Vanderlynn, 2:21, Star King, 2:22, Ben Ali, 2:21, and five others in the 30 list, by Geo. M. Patchen (30), 2:23 1-2; first dam Bell by Top Bellfounder, son of imp. Bellfounder; 2d dam Hout's Laddie mare.

GEO. M. PATCHEN (30). RECORD 2:23½.

Sire of Lucy, 2:18¾; Chas. E. Low, 2:25¾; Geo. M. Patchen, Jr., 2:27; Mary, 2:2-; by Cassius M. Clay (18); 1st dam by Head'em, son of imp. Trustee; 2nd dam Itaska, by American Eclipse.

CASSIUS M. CLAY (18).

Sire of Geo. M. Patchen, 2:23½, etc.; by Henry Clay (8). 1st dam Jersey Kate, the dam of John Anderson.

HENRY CLAY (8).

Sire of Black Douglass, 2:30; Centerville (w), 2:32; by Andrew Jackson (4); 1st dam Surry.

ANDREW JACKSON (4).

By Young Bashaw; dam an Ohio mare of unknown blood.

YOUNG BASHAW.

By imp. Grand Bashaw; 1st dam Pearl, by First Consul; 2nd dam Fancy, by imp. Messenger; 3rd dam by imp. Rockingham.

NAPA RATTLER.

By Biggart's Rattler; 1st dam Poll, by imp. Consternation; 2nd dam Betsy Baker, by Mambrino.

BIGGART'S RATTLER.

Grandsire of Joe. Brown, 2:22; Lady Snell, 2:23¾; Mary Davis, 2:2¾; Nellie Webster, 2:28½, by old Henry, son of the Garrett Horse, by imp. Leonidas; 1st dam by the Hyde Horse, son of Long's Magnum Bonum; 2nd dam of Messenger blood.

BROWN'S BELLFOUNDER.

By imp. Bellfounder; 1st dam Lady Alport, by Mambrino; 2nd dam by Tippo Saib, son of imp. Messenger; 3rd dam by imp. Messenger.

DESCRIPTION.

ALEXANDER BUTTON is a dark bay with fine flowing mane and tail; stands 15-3¾ hands high; weighs 1,200 pounds, and is of excellent disposition. He is a natural trotter, inherited through the speed lines of his ancestors, and imparts his speed to his offspring with uniform certainty. His colts show him to be a wonderful producer—and with his breeding and terms of service, he is the cheapest and most wonderful horse in the State.

TERMS.

TERMS.—$100, payable at end of season. Mares not proving with foal may be returned next season free of charge. Good pasturage furnished at $2 per month, and due care taken to prevent accidents or escapes, but no liability whatever assumed.

Will stand at Cache Creek Farm, which is situated about one and one-half miles west of Yolo Station.

All mares sent to Yolo in my care will be forwarded free of charge.

G. W. WOODARD, Proprietor.
Yolo, Yolo Co., Cal.

Southern Pacific Co.

(PACIFIC SYSTEM.)

Trains leave and are due to arrive at San Francisco.

LEAVE (FOR)	FROM JANUARY 1, 1890.	ARRIVE (FROM)
7.30 A M	Haywards, Niles and San Jose	*12.45 P M
7.30 A M	Sacramento and Redding, via Davis	7.15 P M
7.30 A M	Sacramento, Auburn, Colfax	5.45 P M
8.00 A M	Martinez, Vallejo, Calistoga and Santa Rosa	6.15 P M
8.30 A M	Los Angeles Express, Fresno, Bakersfield, Mojave and East and Los Angeles	11.15 A M
8.30 A M	Niles, San Jose, Stockton, Ione, Sacramento, Marysville, Oroville and Red Bluff	5.45 P M
10.30 A M	Haywards and Niles	2.15 P M
*12.00 M	Haywards, Niles and San Jose	* 3.45 P M
*1.00 P M	Sacramento River Steamers	**6.00 A M
3.00 P M	Haywards, Niles and San Jose	9.45 A M
3.30 P M	2d Class for Ogden and East	10.45 P M
4.00 P M	Stockton and Milton; Vallejo, Calistoga and Santa Rosa	9.45 A M
4.00 P M	Sacramento and Knight's Landing via Davis	10.45 A M
*4.30 P M	Niles and Livermore	*8.45 A M
*4.30 P M	Niles and San Jose	‡4.15 P M
5.30 P M	Haywards and Niles	7.45 A M
6.00 P M	Sunset Route, Atlantic Express, Santa Barbara, Los Angeles, Deming, El Paso, New Orleans and East	8.45 P M
7.00 P M	Shasta Route Express, Sacramento, Marysville, Redding, Portland, Puget Sound and East	7.45 A M
8.00 P M	Central Atlantic Express, Ogden and East	9.45 A M

SANTA CRUZ DIVISION.

‡8.00 A M	Hunters train to San Jose	‡7.20 P M
8.15 A M	Newark, Centerville, San Jose, Felton, Boulder Creek and Santa Cruz	6.50 P M
*2.15 P M	Centerville, San Jose, Almaden, Felton, Boulder Creek and Santa Cruz	*11.20 A M
4.15 P M	Centerville, San Jose, and Los Gatos	9.50 A M

Coast Division (Third and Townsend Sts.)

7.25 A M	San Jose, Almaden and Way Stations	2.30 P M
8.30 A M	San Jose, Gilroy, Tres Pinos; Pajaro, Santa Cruz; Monterey; Pacific Grove, Salinas, San Miguel, Paso Robles, Santa Margarita (San Luis Obispo) and principal Way Stations	6.12 P M
10.30 A M	San Jose and Way Stations	5.02 P M
12.01 P M	Cemetery, Menlo Park and Way Stations	3.38 P M
*3.30 P M	San Jose, Tres Pinos, Santa Cruz, Salinas, Monterey Pacific Grove and principal Way Stations	*10.00 A M
*4.20 P M	Menlo Park and Way Station	*7.58 A M
5.20 P M	San Jose and Way Stations	9.03 A M
6.30 P M	Menlo Park and Way Stations	6.35 A M
†11.45 P M	Menlo Park and principal Way Stations	†7.28 P M

A M for Morning. P M for Afternoon.
*Sundays excepted. †Saturdays only. ‡Sundays only.
**Mondays excepted. ‡Saturdays excepted.

OCEANIC STEAMSHIP CO.

Carrying United States, Hawaiian and Colonial Mails.

WILL LEAVE THE COMPANY'S WHARF, foot of Mission Street, No. 1,

For Honolulu, Auckland and Sydney,

WITHOUT CHANGE,

The Splendid New 3,000-ton Iron Steamer.

MARIPOSA ... Saturday, February 8, 1890, at 12 M., Or immediately on arrival of the English mails.

For Honolulu.

SS. AUSTRALIA (3,000 tons), January 21, 1890, at 12 M

For freight or passage, apply at office, 327 Market Street. JOHN D. SPRECKELS & BROS. General Agents.

KILLIP & CO.,

LIVE STOCK AND GENERAL AUCTIONEERS,

22 Montgomery Street, San Francisco

SPECIAL ATTENTION PAID TO SALES OF

High-Bred Horses and Cattle.

At auction and private sale.

Will Sell in All Cities and Counties of the State.

REFERENCES.

HON. C. GREEN, Sacramento.
J. P. SARGENT, ESQ., Sargents.
HON. L. J. ROSE, Los Angeles.
HON. J. D. CARR Salinas.
HON. JOHN BOGGS Colusa.
HON. A. WALRATH Nevada.
J. B. HAGGIN, ESQ., San Francisco.

Represented at Sacramento by Edwin F. Smith secretary State Agricultural Society.

At San Jose by Messrs. Montgomery & Rea, Real Estate Agents.

Being the oldest established firm in the live-stock business on this Coast, and having conducted the important auction sales in this line for the past fifteen years, amounting to one half a million of dollars, we feel justified in claiming unequaled facilities for disposing of live stock of every description, either at auction or private sale. Our list of correspondents embraces every breeder and dealer of prominence upon the Pacific Coast, thus enabling us to give full publicity to animals placed with us for sale. Private purchases and sales of live stock of all descriptions will be made on commission, and stock shipped with the utmost care. Purchases and sales made of land of every description. We are authorized to refer to the gentlemen whose names are appended.

KILLIP & CO., 22 Montgomery Street.

LAMBORN ROAD MACHINE

LIGHT DRAFT. MADE OF IRON. STRONG, SIMPLE, DURABLE.

TRUMAN HOOKER CO.
SAN FRANCISCO, - - CALIFORNIA

San Francisco and North Pacific Railway.

THE DONAHUE BROAD-GAUGE ROUTE.

COMMENCING SUNDAY, MARCH 17, 1889, AND until further notice, boats and trains will leave from and arrive at the San Francisco Passenger Depot, Market-street Wharf, as follows:

Leave San Francisco.		DESTINATION	Arrive San Francisco.	
WEEK DAYS.	SUNDAYS.		SUNDAYS.	WEEK DAYS.
7.40 A M 3.30 P M 5.00 P M	8.00 A M 5.00 P M	Petaluma and Santa Rosa	10.40 A M 6.10 P M	8.50 A M 10.30 A M 6.05 P M
7.40 A M 3.30 P M	8.00 A M	Fulton, Windsor, Healdsburg, Litton Springs, Cloverdale, and way stations.	6.10 P M	10.30 A M 6.05 P M
7.40 A M	8.00 A M	Hopland and Ukiah.	6.10 P M	6.05 P M
7.40 A M	8.00 A M	Guerneville	6.10 P M	6.05 P M
7.40 A M 5.00 P M	8.00 A M	Sonoma and Glen Ellen.	10.40 A M 6.10 P M	8.50 A M 6.05 P M

Stage connects at Santa Rosa for White Sulphur Springs, Sebastopol and Mark West Springs; at Geyserville for Skaggs Springs, and at Cloverdale for the Geysers; at Hopland for Highland Springs, Kelseyville, Soda Bay, Lakeport and Bartlett Springs, and at Ukiah for Vichy Springs, Saratoga Springs, Blue Lakes, Willits, Cahto, Calpella, Potter Valley, Sherwood Valley and Mendocino City.

EXCURSION TICKETS from Saturdays to Mondays, to Petaluma, $1.50; to Santa Rosa, $2.25; to Healdsburg, $3.40; to Litton Springs, $3.60; to Cloverdale, $4.50; to Hopland, $5.70; to Ukiah, $6.75; to Guerneville, $3.75; to Sonoma, $1.50; to Glen Ellen, $1.80.

EXCURSION TICKETS, good for Sundays only, to Petaluma, $1; to Santa Rosa, $1.50; to Healdsburg, $2.25; to Litton Springs, $2.40; to Cloverdale, $3; to Guerneville, $2.50, to Sonoma, $1; to Glen Ellen, $1.20.

From San Francisco for Point Tiburon and San Rafael: Week Days—7.40, 9.20, 11.20, A. M.; 3.30, 5.00, 6.15 P. M. Sundays—8.00, 9.30, 11.00 A. M.; 1.30, 5.00, 6.20 P. M.

To San Francisco from San Rafael: Week Days—6.20, 7.55, 9.30 A. M.; 12.45, 3.40, 5.05 P. M. Sundays—8.10, 9.40 A. M.; 12.15, 3.40, 5.00 P. M.

To San Francisco from Point Tiburon: Week Days—6.50, 8.20, 9.55 A. M.; 1.10, 4.05, 5.30 P. M.; Sundays—8.40, 10.05 A. M.; 12.40, 4.05, 5.30 P. M.

On Saturdays an extra trip will be made from San Francisco to San Rafael, leaving at 1.40 P. M.

H. C. WHITING, General Manager.

PETER J. McGLYNN, Gen. Pass. & Tkt. Agt.

Ticket Offices at Ferry, 222 Montgomery Street and 2 New Montgomery Street.

KENNEL ADVERTISEMENTS.

Thoroughbred Pugs, $40 each.

PEDIGREE.

PUPPIES:
- Fido:
  - imp. Jumbo ... Marshall's Uno / Lady Bess
  - Fannie ... Rex / imp. Fly
- Budge:
  - Senator Fair's Fritz
  - McCleery's Mamma Scoots ... Sam / imp. Alice

Can be seen daily from 9 A. M. to 3 P. M. at 411 Ellis Street, San Francisco.

J. F. B. McCLEERY.

Irish Setters & Pointers.

In the Stud, winner of 16 first and special prizes, CHAMPION MIKE T., 6435, A. K. S. B. Irish Setter puppies by Champion Mike T. 6435 A. K. S. B.—Champion Lady Elcho T. 6451 A. K. S. B., for sale. Two pointers, a year old, by Rush T. 10,069 A. K. S. B.—Champion Patti Croxteth T. 10128 A. K. S. B. for sale. Yard broken. Address,

A. B. TRUMAN,
1425 Steiner St., S. F., Cal.

CALIFORNIA SPANIEL KENNELS,

Oakland, California. H. P. RENNIE, Prop. Breeder and importer of typical COCKER SPANIELS. Winner of first prizes at S. F. and Los Angeles, 1889; also, Columbus, 1889, New York, 1887. In the stud, solid Black Cockerdog, GIFFEE, won 1st and Gold Medal at S. F., 1889. Fee, $25. Puppies and grown dogs at reasonable prices. My dogs can neither talk nor climb a tree, but are fielders and prize winners.

STANDARD CHAMBERLIN SHOTGUN CARTRIDGES
THE BEST IS THE CHEAPEST

IF YOU WISH A GOOD REVOLVER PURCHASE ONE OF SMITH & WESSON'S

Finest small arms ever manufactured and the first choice of all experts. In calibres 32, 38 and 44-100. Single or double action, Safety Hammerless and Target models. **Best quality wrought steel**, carefully inspected for workmanship and stock. Unrivaled for **finish, durability and accuracy.** Do not be deceived by cheap *malleable iron imitations* often sold for the genuine article. They are unreliable and dangerous. The SMITH & WESSON REVOLVERS are stamped upon the barrels with firm's name, address and dates of patents, and are guaranteed perfect. Insist upon having them, and if your dealer cannot supply you, an order sent to address below will receive prompt attention. Descriptive catalogue and prices upon application.

SMITH & WESSON,
Springfield, Mass.

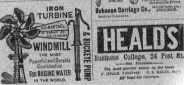

RUB YOUR HORSES

In cases of **SWELLING** or **STIFFNESS** OF **THE JOINTS**, with

DARBYS FLUID.

If you value your Horses, Dogs and Cattle always keep it on hand.

IT HAS NO EQUAL

For Cuts, Scratches, Bruises, Bites, Sores, Etc.

It gives immediate relief, and prevents Poison, Gangrene and Proud Flesh.

J. H. ZEILIN & CO., - Philadelphia, Pa

SOLD BY ALL DRUGGISTS.

DR. FISHERMAN'S Carbolized Alkaline LOTION

Cures after all other Remedies have Failed.

Sprains, Sores, Bruises, Galls, Swellings, Scratches, Thrush, Grease Heels, Curb, Rheumatism. Restoring Weak Knees and Ankles to their original condition. As a wash it insures glossy manes and tails. Valuable as an internal remedy for Coughs, Colic, Congestion or Fever. You really get Half a Gallon of Remedy for $1.00, or Two Gallons for $3.00, after being adulterated as directed.

This Liniment has received the endorsement of some of our best horsemen. Recommended by Jos. Cairn Simpson. See BREEDER AND SPORTSMAN of November 10th, 1888.

LYNDE & HOUGH, Proprietors,
116 California St., S. F.

Or ask your Druggist for it.

HORSE OWNERS! TRY GOMBAULT'S CAUSTIC BALSAM.

A Safe, Speedy and Positive Cure for Curb, Splint, Sweeny, Capped Hock, Strained Tendons, Founder, Wind Puffs, all Skin Diseases or Parasites, Thrush, Diphtheria, Pinkeye, all Lameness from Spavin, Ringbone or other Bony Tumors. Removes all Bunches or Blemishes from Horses and Cattle.

Supersedes all Cautery or Firing. **Impossible to Produce any Scar or Blemish.**

Every bottle sold is warranted to give satisfaction. Price **$1.50** per bottle. Sold by druggists, or sent by express, charges paid, with full directions for its use. Send for descriptive circulars. Address

LAWRENCE, WILLIAMS & CO., Cleveland, O.

BROU'S INJECTION

A PERMANENT CURE in from 3 to 6 days, of the most obstinate cases; guaranteed not to produce Stricture; no sickening doses; and no inconvenience or loss of time. Recommended by physicians and sold by all druggists. J. Ferré, (successor to Brou), Pharmacien, Paris.

For any Kind of a

SORE THROAT

USE

McCLELLAN'S

DIPHTHERIA REMEDY

An Unfailing Cure.

FOR SALE BY ALL DRUGGISTS

IRON TURBINE WINDMILL & BUCKEYE PUMP
P. P. MAST & Co. 31 MARKET ST., SAN FRANCISCO
THE MOST Powerful and Durable Combination For RAISING WATER IN THE WORLD.

VETERINARY.

Dr. Wm. H. Jones, M.R.C.V.S.

Veterinary Surgeon,

(CLUB STABLES)

409—411 Taylor Street, San Francisco.

Consultations by letter, and cases of URGENT NECESSITY in the interior will receive prompt attention.

W. H. WOODRUFF.

Veterinary Dentist,

AT FASHION STABLES,

221 Ellis Street, San Francisco

Improved Instruments, Humane Methods, First Class Work.

H. E. CARPENTER,

Veterinary Surgeon,

Graduate of Ontario Veterinary College, Toronto, Canada.

RESIDENCE AND VETERINARY INFIRMARY

331 Golden Gate Ave., San Francisco.

Telephone 3069.

OPEN DAY AND NIGHT.

No risk in throwing Horses. Veterinary Operating Table on the premises.

DR. C. MASOERO.

Veterinary Surgeon,

Successor to **DR. A. DeTAVEL,**

GRADUATE OF ROYAL VETERINARY COLLEGE, TURIN.

OFFICE AND INFIRMARY,

No. 811 HOWARD STREET,

Between Fourth and Fifth. SAN FRANCISCO.

Telephone, No. 467.

R. WATKINS,

Veterinary Dentist,

Of twelve years practice, is now permanently located in San Francisco, and may be found at **C. S. Crittendens'** Golden Gate Livery and Riding Academy, **24 to 28 Golden Gate Avenue.**

Will treat ailments of the horse's mouth, and cure all such. Sidereiu Pullers and Tongue Lollers, etc.

Satisfaction guaranteed. Orders by mail will receive prompt attention. Examination Free.

E. J. O'ROUKE.

I have the honor to announce to my old patrons and the general public that I may be found at my old stand, where, as heretofore, the

Shoeing of Horses,

whether for the Track, Drive, or for general work, will receive my personal attention.

Telephone 2011.

E. J. O'ROUKE,
209 Ellis Street

California Horse Shoe Co's

STEEL SHOE

Light, Strong and Perfect.

Superior to all others for Speed Horses.

ALSO

The Celebrated GOODENOUGH **Pattern Shoe.**

OFFICE:

203 Market St.

San Francisco, Cal.

I have used in my business the Steel and Iron Shoes made by the above Company, and take great pleasure in saying they are the best I have ever used in twenty-two years' practice. I have never seen anything like the STEEL SHOE made by this Company. I can fully recommend them to every practical Horseshoer in the country.

Yours respectfully,
No. 8 Everett Street. JOHN GRACE.

OUR IMPROVED. THE BOHANON SULKY! BEST MADE.

ALL SIZES AND WEIGHTS. G. W. BOHANON.

Perfect Riding Buggies. Breaking Carts.

Fine Repairing, Reasonable Prices.

Bohanon Carriage Co., 161-163 Ogden Ave., CHICAGO.

Send for Catalogue.

HEALD'S

Business College, 24 Post St.

—San Francisco.—

The most popular school on the Coast

P. HEALD, President. C. S. HALEY, Sec'y.

Send for Circulars

TWENTY PAGES.

BREEDER AND SPORTSMAN

Vol. XVI. No. 6.
No. 313 BUSH STREET.

SAN FRANCISCO, SATURDAY, FEB. 8, 1890.

SUBSCRIPTION
FIVE DOLLARS A YEAR.

Hollywood Farm.

The old race track is situated about three miles from Vallejo on the Napa railroad, and being one of the few railroads in the State which were open last week, a representative of the BREEDER AND SPORTSMAN was carefully put down within four hundred yards of the track, which, with an additional six hundred acres of land, was purchased by B. C. Holly four years ago. Mr. Holly or By Holly, as he is generally known, is one of the most noted trotting and men in America, equally facile and adept at either game, holding the reins over a trotter or training a runner.

Starting out years ago (born in 43) as a small light weight boy in a racing stable, by perseverance and careful attention to business, combined with a still tongue and a level head, the astute Easterner has, besides acquiring a little of this world's gear, proved himself on either a running or trotting track able to hold his own with the best in the country. He drove his first race in 1859 at Kalamazoo, Michigan. On the day Flora Temple trotted in 2:19¾, Holly drove a horse in the four-year-old class, and among his opponents was our late visitor, Luke DuBois, and since then his reputation has increased, so that now no man can say he is his superior in judgment and cool quiet style or in conditioning a horse. Mr. Holly's ranch includes about 700 acres of good land well inclosed and split up into suitable paddocks, while the race track, which is a ver ygood one, is of a good width, so that the outside may be used for runners.

There are a hundred box-stalls, and a covered oblong drive about a furlong will be in full use before next season; at present only about half of it is under cover.

Last year Mr. Holly sold Woodnut, 2:16½, for $20,000, a sale he has probably regretted ever since, although his place is worthily filled by one of the highest bred horses money could procure, viz., the brown stallion Mountain Boy, 4841, bred by Charles Backman, Orange County, New York, foaled 1882, sire Kentucky Prince, dam Elise, by Messenger Duroc; grandam Green Mountain Maid by Harry Clay 45, 3rd dam Shanghai Mary.

Mountain Boy has no record, owing to bad usage, as a youngster, but he can show an exceptional turn of speed, quarters in 35, being easily negotiated by him. His speed lines are so well known that it is almost superfluous to explain that Elise is a sister to Elaine, 2:20, Prospero, 2:20, and four others in the 2:30 list, while she is more than half sister to Electioneer. Kentucky Prince is the sire of Guy, 2:10¾, and a host of others. Election, a bay son of Electioneer, was the next horse to face us, and a handsomer high class trotter has never been seen; from his beautifully shaped head and neck and good back, down to the ground no fault can be found with him unless it were that he shows almost too much quality, evidently brought about in part through Arnold Harris, the sire of his great grandam. Election was purchased a fortnight ago from Mr. Crocker, who bought him at Palo Alto as a yearling. Election will make a season in the stud, and then be taken through the circuit. A good looking, short-legged, nicely topped bay, three year old, looking fit to compete in any company, was brought out for inspection, but his head gave him away at once, a true Sultan head, and Kafir, as the colt is called, carried it well, as his lineage would indicate. He is by Alcazar, 2:20½, dam Flower Girl by Arthurton, sire of Arab, 2:15; grandam Flora, double team record 2:33, by General McClellan 144, sire of three in the 2:30 list, great-grandam by Langford, he by Williamson's Belmont.

The next youngster was a beautifully turned chestnut, uncommonly like his renowned sire; he was Woodside, sire Woodnut, 2:16½, dam Veronica by Alcona 730, grandam Fontana by Almont 33, great-grandam Fannie Williams by Alexander's Abdallah 15.

Mr. Holly should in time forget his loss of Woodnut in his handsome son, for he moves in the same free, easy style, and is bound to trot fast. Mart Boorham is a useful looking bay son of Sydney, 2:19¾, first dam Towhead by Echo; he is a full brother to St. Nicholas, John Rowen's colt, who showed a mile in 2:27½ at three years old.

The above mentioned will, with the exception of Woodside whose book is full, take a few outside mares at a figure which places them within reach of anyone. Mr. Holly also has Reveille the sire of Tycoon and Gladstone—the fast sprinter taken east by Albert Cooper. Reveille is a big powerful gray and evidently is a good producer, his stud fee is like the rest of Mr. Holly's horses low enough to suit anyone.

There were three foals on the ranch, the oldest being the bay colt Premature, who came on the 28th of December. He is by Woodnut, dam Mollie McCarthy by Eugene Casserly; his mother unfortunately died, but strange to say, a work-mare who had a three months old colt, took him quite naturally, and he is thriving well, except a wound caused by running into a fork.

The second colt is a fortnight old, by Woodnut, out of Alice by Admiral, grandam by John Nelson. He is a fine slashing chestnut, with plenty of quality, good, big knees and hocks, and very stylish.

Economy, 2:30, by Echo, dam by Muldoon, has a very neat taking filly, only two days old, when she was seen, but as active and sprightly as a kitten. She is entered in the BREEDER AND SPORTSMAN Futurity Stakes, and her owner says, has a mortgage on it.

San Diego, Allorita and J. R. were all on view looking particularly well. As soon as the weather clears up they will go to their Eastern home. Pink, 2:25, has wintered very well, and will be put in trim for next season. Senator, 2:22, was under saddle, leading colts as handily as could be, single-footing in nice, easy style, looking himself as sound and fresh as a two-year-old. A black two year-old stallion by Alcona, out of Pansy by Cassius M. Clay Jr., was jogged on the road; he has a smooth way of going.

Mr. Holly also has two horses, the property of D. D. Streeter, Esq., President Denver Driving Club. One is a useful-looking gelding, and the other a rattling-bred three-year-old stallion by Sentinel, dam by Startle, grandam Flora Temple, 2:19¾. Mr. Streeter sent them to get the benefit of a California winter. Flora G., 2:29¼, a trim-looking brown mare by Altoona 8850, dam Susie by Patchen (Conway's) was recently purchased by Mr. Holly, who will campaign her this season, and probably breed her later on.

A whole host of yearlings were looked over, the most taking-looking being Hollywood 11778, by Woodnut, 2:16½, dam Aurelia by Albert W., 2:20, grandam Pacific Maid by Elmo, next dam by David Hill, out of a General Taylor mare, whose dam was by Williamson's Belmont. The colt is worthy of his illustrious lineage, a brilliant bay, with splendid head and neck, grand shoulders and good back, with good muscular thighs, big, clean hocks and knees, good feet, and a grand, free, easy, natural trotting action. No wonder his owner refused a few months ago to be tempted, although offered $2,800 for him. Extravagant is a neatly turned daughter of Woodnut and Economy, 2:30. Extravagant already has almost a record, for Economy obtained her mark, 2:30, at Santa Rosa six months before the filly was foaled. She is entered in the Occident Stake of 1892, and should render a good account of herself, for she has her sire's resolute, frictionless style of going. Several other Woodnuts were looked over, all of whom showed so much quality and style, that we could understand how sorry Mr. Holly feels for parting with the horse.

A whole host of rattling-bred, good-looking broodmares were looked over, the first being a strong, neat, grey mare, Jennie H. (sister to El Monte, 2:29), by Echo 462, dam Lightfoot by Hubbard, grandam Brunette by Rifleman, out o Fannie Frazier by Bertrand. She was bred to Mountain Boy last season, and will be bred back to him. Lisette, a good-looking daughter of Abdallah Wilkes 7562, and Musette, by Startle, was bred to Mountain Boy.

Annie Almont is a black mare by Tilton Almont out of Madam Nelson by John Nelson. Violette (in foal to Happy Prince) a grey mare 6 years old by George M. Patchen Jr., out of Viola by Echo grand dam by Woodbine. Clara Belle (in foal to Happy Prince) is by Alaska out of the Dooley filly by Muldoon, grand dam by McCracken's Black Hawk, great grand dam the Hedge mare.

Lady Patchen by George M. Patchen Jr. dam by Nutwood is in foal to Happy Prince.

Hattie W 7 years old by Alaska out of Sallie Coward by Mayboy grand dam Young Molly by Lodi; is in foal to Happy Prince.

Phyllis by imp Admirable, out of Daphne by Whipple's Hambletonian out of Phœbe Carey by Chieftain, next dam by Jim Crow. Phyllis had a filly last year by Woodnut which was sold for $1,000. She is in foal this year to Mambrino Eclipse. Economy 2:30 by Echo 462, out of Lady Berkey by Muldoon, grandam by St. Clair. She obtained her record at Santa Rosa, two years ago, in the fourth heat when heavy in foal. She has shown several miles better than 2:25, and is as sound as a bell; her produce have already been mentioned. Aurelia or 'the twin filly' was one of the twins by Albert W., out of Pacific Maid. She showed tremendous pace in Goldsmith's hands, but was not driven for a record, and evidently will produce well for her yearling has been mentioned as the best looking yearling on the ranch. She is in foal to Happy Prince.

A bay mare by Victor, dam by Echo, is in foal to Redwood 2:24½. Belle by Gus 2:26¾, dam by Mambrino Eclipse, is in foal to Kafir. A good looking mare by Bedouin, dam by Milton Medium was purchased from H. S. Hogoboom. Lou Medium, the dam of Redwood 2:24½ by Milton Medium was bred to Mountain Boy by the owners and will probably be bred back. She looked wonderfully well. A whole host of other well bred mares were seen and then some of the thoroughbred brood mares were looked over, the first being Ninena, who is heavy in foal to Sid. The daughter of Jim Brown and Nanny Hubbard by Hubbard was a good race mare in her day, winning five races as a two-year-old in 1886 and nine in 1887, and although rather lightish built should make a good brood mare with the right cross. A useful looking four-year-old chestnut mare is by Milner out of Mollie Ward by imp Intruder out of Kate Ward by Lexington. She was bred late last season to Kafir. Another four-year old chestnut mare (in foal to Tyrant) was by Joe Daniels out of Amanda L. by Shannon out of Eva Ashton by Ashland; Fusillades Last was heavy in foal to Sid.

She was a fine race mare, winning six races at two and three years old, and is exceptionally well bred, being by John W. Norton (a Bonnie Scotland) out of Fusillade, by War Dance, her dam by Planet. Old Fusillade was Mr. Holly's favorite mare, winning over $7,000 in races for him, and eventually, when well in the lead, broke her leg. Mr. Holly had her put in slings, and she recovered. He got two foals from her, but when Fusillade's Last was at her side the mother was struck by lightning, and the pet was raised on the bottle. Irish Lass, by Kyrle Daly out of Daisy Miller by Revolver, won seven races as a two year old in 1884, and seven as a three year old in 1885. She was covered the day Woodnut left for his Eastern home, and was due to foal last Sunday. Why Not, by Three Cheers, out of Nellie Collier, a sister to the well known racehorse, Fred Collier, is a three year old filly purchased by Mr. Holly from Mr. Hogoboom, who bought her of her breeder, Mr. Winters. She, despite having a hip down, won several good races, and should prove an acquisition to the stud.

As the day was rapidly waning, we wended our way to the railroad and were soon back in the city after, despite the weather, a very pleasant visit to one of the handiest and best breeding farms of the State.

A Race Track for San Francisco.

SAN FRANCISCO, Feb, 5, 1890.

EDITOR BREEDER AND SPORTSMAN—DEAR SIR:—Knowing the importance to the racing interests of California that a good and convenient race track should be established in the immediate vicinity of San Francisco, I have ventured to send you my views upon the subject. First of all, it should be understood without the shadow of a doubt, that such a track must be upon this side of the Bay. This is demonstrated by the fact that when the Blood Horse Association held its meeting at Oakland, the takings of the gate were far below the expenses, while the meetings of the same association at the Bay District track have for several years past paid fairly. The growth of the suburb of Richmond will soon absorb the Bay District Track, and even if it did not, the nature of the track causes it to be almost useless for winter work. It has long been the boast of Californians that their State is the best in the Union in which to winter race horses, whether runners or trotters, because good exercising and training can be had with but little interruption during the winter months. For these reasons a site should be chosen for a track where the nature of the soil, facilities for drainage, etc., insure the quick drying of the earth. Under these circumstances I venture to think that there is no spot so well adapted for a race track in this city and county as the site of the old Ocean House track. It has manifold advantages, as the climate is always mild; there is little wind and fog, and the soil is a light, sandy loam, easily drained, and can be kept in fine condition at slight expense. The space formerly occupied by the old track is now surrounded by trees, some forty feet high, making a great change in the climate for the better. The old track has been rendered historical by the great races held on it in early days, notably the contest between Norfolk and Lodi, and the great four mile and repeat race won by Thad Stevens. Its superior facilities for winter work can be easily proved by reference to many old drivers and trainers, among whom may be named Hickok, De Poyster, Albert Cooper, Henry Welch, and many others. The old track is already graded, and by carting a little sand on one quarter, could be easily put in order, so that if this plan is adopted it will save great expense, as the work required to level the old track would be very inconsiderable as compared with the work of grading, top dressing, draining, etc., a new piece of ground.

The most serious question in regard to the choice of the old Ocean House track for the new track is the means of getting there. At present the track can be reached by five roads, viz., by Golden Gate Park to Ocean House road; Golden Gate Park via Almshouse road to Ocean House road; Mission road and by Industrial School to Ocean House road; by Market St. Extension and 17th Street to Ocean House road and by the Golden Gate Park and along the beach to Ocean House road. It may, and no doubt will be said, that while the means of reaching the track mentioned above would prove sufficient for those who own or can afford to hire buggies, visiting the track would necessite a delightful drive; it would not meet with those who depend upon the street cars to reach the race track. While there is some truth in this objection, it may be argued that the formation of a new track is not so much for the present as for the future. At present visitors can easily, and at a small expense, be carried to and from the track from the Industrial School station, and in a very few years the means of reaching the track will be as numerous, convenient and cheap as now enjoyed by the Bay District.

The Great Highway, as the grand boulevard along the Ocean Beach from the Cliff House to the county line is called, must be constructed soon. The improvements going on south of the park and the demands of the public require this.

To that splendid section of the city lying south of the park, this highway is necessary as a bulkhead to prevent the sea sand drifting inland, and the property owners in this locality are now clamoring to have it built. The Park Commissioners are also in favor of it, and all that is wanted is a proper appropriation for the purpose which should be granted at the next session of the Legislature. Once let the Great Highway be built, and it will become the favorite holiday resort of all classes. The present Haight St. R. R. will be insufficient to meet the wants of the public, and other roads will be built south of the park. If 16th Street is not graded through, 17th Street will be, and sooner or later a road will run direct from the Miss on to park and ocean.

The building of the Great Highway and a railroad down I or J Street would wonderfully improve communications with the track, but what would most benefit it would be the extension of Market Street, which would meet the track itself. The fact that the grade of the street between Valencia and Castro Streets is about to be equalized and the old reservoir hill removed are signs that Market street is to be carried further West, and the matter is now receiving considerable attention. It has not yet been decided whether the street shall run over the Twin Peaks or round them, but that Market Street will one day be continued to the ocean there can be no doubt. The racing interests of this State are increasing year by year, and would be fostered by the construction of a good track near this city. Once let the track be built and races of sufficient interest arranged, and there will be found no difficulty in making the track; the demand for transportation facilities are sure to produce them.

Therefore, Mr. Editor, taking into consideration climate, soil and location, I honestly believe that the best place for the new track is upon the same ground as where Thad Stevens and Norfolk obtained their great victories.

There are other places in the same neighborhood admirably suited for a race track. The Spring Valley Water Company own land upon the peninsula between the two lakes which would do well for this purpose. This land is close to the Ocean House road, and also to the proposed continuation of that road to Ocean View and Colma, which will make a saving of three miles. The land in question would be surrounded by water on three sides. All that would be required would be to fence it where it joins the land, and to plant trees round it. The soil is the same as on the old track.

Another location, owned by Adolph Sutro must be mentioned It is a beautiful spot, sheltered by hills, covered by trees, and only half a mile from the San Jose railroad. A switch line from Industrial School station running westerly, would reach the track in this distance and at little expense. Mr. Sutro has done so much to beautify and improve this neighborhood by planting trees, etc., that there is little doubt that he would do all in his power to facilitate the building of a race track. The soil is the same as at the other places described, and a race track here would be sure to be popular with horse-owners and trainers. It should be mentioned that there is splendid winter grazing all through this neighborhood, which would add to the attractions of a race track.

I have written to you at length upon this subject, because I have noticed that all the newspaper articles published on the subject, ignore the neighborhood above described for the purposes of a speed track. Such articles invariably hint at locating such a track either across the bay or in San Mateo County. I consider the distance of all such locations too far from this city for race-meetings to pay, and as before stated, San Franciscans will not cross the bay to witness races. Any point upon the Ocean House road would be sure to be popular with owners of horses, who are the main supporters of racing, and livery-stable keepers would be greatly benefitted thereby. Altogether, I believe the above described places to be the best suited for a race track of any situated within an easy distance of the city, and in this matter I have no doubt that E. J. Baldwin, Budd Doble, Orrin Hickok, and all the principal owners and trainers will agree with me. C. S.

Blood Horse Programme.

At a meeting of the programme committee of the Blood Horse Association which met last Tuesday, the following programme was arranged for the four days' racing which they have announced to commence April 12th:—

FIRST DAY—SATURDAY, APRIL 12TH.

No. 1—Introduction Purse $400, of which $50 to second, $25 to third; for three year olds and upwards. Beaten maidens of three years old allowed 5 lbs.; if four years old or over, 10 lbs. One mile and a sixteenth.

No. 2—The California Stakes for two year olds. Half a mile. Closed.

No. 3—Selling purse, $350; of which $50 to second; for three year olds and upwards. Horses entitled to be sold for $1200 to carry rule weights; 3 lbs. allowed for each $100 less down to $800; then 3 lbs. for each $100 less down to $300. Horses entered not to be sold to carry 10 lbs. above the scale. Three quarters of a mile.

No. 4—The Tidal Stakes for three year olds. One mile and a quarter. Closed.

No. 5. Purse $350, of which $50 to second; for all ages. Weights 10 lbs. below the scale. Seven furlongs.

SECOND DAY—TUESDAY, APRIL 15th.

No. 6—Purse $400, of which $50 to second, $25 to third for three-year-olds and upwards. Winner of No. 1 at this meeting to carry five pounds extra. Horses starting and not placed in that race allowed three pounds. One mile.

No. 7—Free Handicap Sweepstakes for two-year-olds $10 each if not declared out, with $300 added. First horse to take the added money; second to receive 70 per cent, and the third 30 per cent. of the stakes. Weights announced Monday, April 14th, at 10 o'clock, A. M. Declarations due at 5 P. M. the same day. Five furlongs.

No. 8—Selling Purse $350, of which $50 to second for all ages. Horses entered to be sold for $1,500 to carry mile weights; three pounds allowed for each $100 less down to $1,000, then one pound for each $100 less down to $500. Horses entered not to be sold to carry eight pounds above the scale: One mile and a sixteenth.

No. 9—The Pacific Derby for three-year-olds. One mile and a half. Closed.

THIRD DAY—THURSDAY, APRIL 17TH.

No. 10—Selling purse $350, of which $50 to second, for 3-year-olds and upwards, Horses entered to be sold for $1,000 to carry rule weights; three pounds allowed for each $100 less down to $500, then two pounds for each $100 down to $300. Horses entered not to be sold to carry ten pounds above the scale. Fifteen-sixteenths of a mile.

No. 11—The Racine Stakes for two-year-olds. Three-quarters of a mile.

No. 12—Purse $400, of which $50 to second and $25 to third; for all ages. Mile heats.

No. 13—The Sequel Stakes for all ages; $25 each, half forfeit; $5 if declared out, with $500 added, second horse to receive $75, third to save stakes. Weights announced Wednesday, April 16th, at 10 o'clock A. M. Declarations at 5 P. M. the same day. One mile and three-eighths.

FOURTH DAY—SATURDAY. APRIL 19th.

No. 14—Purse $350, of which $50 to the second horse. A handicap for two year olds. Entrance fee for starters: declaration $5, to go to the racing fund. Weights announced Friday, April 18th, at ten o'clock A. M. Declarations due at five P. M. same day. Eleven-sixteenths of a mile.

No. 15—Selling Purse $350, of which $50 to the second. For all ages. Horses entered to be sold for $100 to carry rule weights; 3 lbs. allowed for each $100 less. Three fourths of a mile.

No. 16—Purse $400, of which $50 to second; $25 to third. For three year olds and upwards. Winners of any race at this distance or more at this meeting when carrying weights for age or more, to carry 5 lbs. extra; of two such races, 8 lbs. Horses beaten at this distance once allowed 3 lbs.; twice, 5 lbs. One mile.

No. 17—Purse $350, of which $50 to second horse. An owners' handicap for horses that have started and not won at this meeting. Weights to be given through the entry box at five o'clock P. M. the day before the race. Ten pounds over weight allowed; winners excused without penalty. One and one-sixteenth miles.

No. 18—The Ocean Handicap; a sweepstake; for all ages; $20 entrance; $10 forfeit, $5 if declared; with $600 added, of which $75 to the second, third to save stake. Weights announced Thursday, April 17th, at six o'clock P. M. Declaration due Friday, April 18th, at five o'clock P. M. One mile and five-eighths.

Lynwood.

Among the many horses standing for public service in Stockton and the immediate vicinity, there is none of which we have heard so much in the last few weeks as Lynwood; the bay stallion has several times shown that he could readily obtain a record low down in the twenties, and his breeding is superexcellent. Sire Nutwood 2:18¾, sire of Woodnut 2:16½, Dawn 2:18¾, Belmont Boy (pacer) 2:15, and thirty others in the 2:30 list; dam Hattie Morrison, a well known road mare, who trotted in 2:36½, by Ethan Allen Jr. (a son of old Ethan Allen and a Hambletonian two-year-old mare), out of the Grigsby mare, through whom he gets a thoroughbred cross. Lynwood's colts all take after their sire, being racey, game, trotting looking youngsters. One of them, Lynnette, won a two year old race at Sacramento in easy style, and was so good later on in the season that Worth Ober said she could easily trot in 2:30, if necessary. Another of his colts is in Oakland, the property of Judge Greene. The colt was seen last Sunday, and if only Lynwood gets all his colts like the Judge's, his fame will last, as the bay colt is as neatly turned, and shapely looking as any one's, and has a real trotting look all over. Lynwood will make the coming season at Stockton at the low price of $50.

Cattle are prevented from taking Epizooty, Pink-eye, etc., by using Darbys Fluid.

Norfolk.

BY GRIM.

There is a certain amount of fascination to all lovers of the sports of the turf, in reading anything that appertains to the old celebrities who have achieved honor on the track, and certainly, to residents of California, the name of Norfolk will be ever green, and reminiscences about the great unbeaten horse are always in order, and it is a source of satisfaction to me to add another good word for the horse that has tended so much to bring the merits of California as a breeding State before the world at large. His progeny have been of the best, and the fame of El Rio Rey is only compassed by the bounds of the earth. Yet even with the wonderful career of the great two-year-old so vividly before us, we are promised a still greater wonder in his younger brother, who has shown already some really marvelous performances. It is only a few days ago that I happened to cross the bay, and on the boat met Dick Havey, who came out to California with the unbeaten Norfolk shortly after his purchase by Mr. Winters. As we were both going in the same direction, a great deal of the time was spent in discussing old racing stories, and it was only natural that Norfolk and his career should occupy most of our conversation. Dick recalled the day when Norfolk started at the Abbey racecourse, the day when he stamped himself as the superior of any racehorse in the country, winning in a common gallop from such a grand thoroughbred as Tipperary, in addition to a large field of horses. Notwithstanding he ran away before the race and completed a full mile in 1:47, he was brought back and the judges allowed the trainer five minutes to prepare him for the start. When the word was given he cut out the work and again the mile was compassed, in 1:46, Norfolk winning as he pleased. After the race Mr. Winters looked him carefully over, as did also Jim Eoff, who was with the party.

As will be remembered, there was a spirit of rivalry existing between C. H. Bryan and Theodore Winters. The former owned Lodi, and he had beaten a favorite mare of Mr. Winters, and the latter determined to go back East and buy the best horse that money could procure, for he wanted to get even with Mr. Bryan for past losses. It was with this object in view that caused him to visit St. Louis, and as before stated, he examined Norfolk thoroughly when the race was over. Mr. Alexander was asked what he would take for the colt and he answered $15,000. Mr. Winters agreed to take him, and the gentleman were to meet next morning and complete the sale. When the buyer and seller met next day Mr. Alexander told Mr. Winters that he could not have the horse, and gave as his reason the wager he had made that he would sell a colt by Lexington for more money than he paid for the old horse. Mr. Winters then asked what would purchase Norfolk. Mr. Alexander answered, "I will have to raise you a dollar." Eoff began laughing, and said he would pay the extra dollar, whereupon the money was paid and the great horse changed owners. He was entered in several races in the North, among others the first Derby ever instituted in this country. The race was to take place at Paterson, N. J., but as Mr. Winters had business in Washington the horse was sent to New Jersey under the guidance of Mr. Eoff. John Morrissey was then a prominent feature of the turf, and it was not long before he and Eoff met, and discussed the probability of Norfolk winning. The outcome of the interview was that Eoff bet the noted gambler $1,000 that Norfolk would not start in the Derby. He also wagered him $3,000 that if Norfolk started the colt would win. Before the race the two men again met and many more thousands were bet. There were thirteen starters in the race, and it is now historical with what ease the son of Lexington and Novice won. Morrissey's losses made him very much annoyed, and he manipulated things so that Norfolk and Eoff were ruled off prior to the second day's racing, in which Norfolk was entered in a two mile and a quarter dash. As it is reasonable to suppose, Eoff was "mad all over." He knew perfectly well whose hand had managed one of the greatest wrongs ever perpetrated on a race track. It was a diabolical outrage and was so characterized by all lovers of fair play. Norfolk could not possibly have lost, but it did not suit the schemers to allow him to start. Morrissey and Eoff met, the former trying to induce the latter to match Norfolk, but the interview only resulted in talk and nothing came of it.

On July 13th Norfolk was shipped, there being on the same vessel Messrs. Winters, Eoff, Pickett, Barker, Marsh and Havey, he having been engaged to come to California immediately on the conclusion of the Derby, he having rode one of the horses in that race. The voyage was a very tempestuous one, and it was thought by many that they would never see land again. Thirty-one days were consumed on the trip, Norfolk landing in good shape. What he accomplished after his arrival in the State is too well known to need recapitulation here. Mr. Winters was amply repaid for his outlay, as he accomplished what he desired, viz, to beat Lodi.

A Desirable Colt.

In another column will be found an advertisement of an Antevolo colt for sale. It will well repay any person in search of a colt to look at Rex Volo. In appearance and disposition, he is all that the most fastidious could desire, in fact, a more gentle colt is but seldom seen. His dam Catchup, by Rustic, is a very speedy road mare, and her owner says can now show better than a forty gait in the park. She won the Petaluma Yearling Colt Stakes, but meeting with an accident when two years old, was thrown out of training. Everything considered, the price asked for Rex Volo is low. He can be seen any time at the corner of 24th and Castro Streets, opposite the car house.

California Nutwood.

The Nutwood Stock Farm is beautifully situated one mile from Irvington, with plenty of good, moderately-sized paddocks. The crack stallion on the ranch, California Nutwood, is one anyone would be proud to own. He is a dark chestnut, 16½ hands high, weighs (when in condition) 1250 lbs.; his action, like his appearance, is a counterpart of his sire's free, easy, frictionless movement, and when handled for speed, there is no doubt he will add even more lustre to his worthy father. Nutwood, 2:18¾, is the sire of Woodnut, 2:16½ (money cannot buy him now), and 27 other trotters in the 2:30-list, also of Belmont Boy, 2:15, and four other pacers. California Nutwood is out of Fanny Patchen by Geo. M. Patchen Jr., sire of Wells Fargo, 2:18¾, and a host of other well known performers, and is great grandsire of Yolo Maid, the invincible pacer. California Nutwood will stand at the extremely low figure of $40, and should be invaluable among some of our well-bred mares, having through Nutwood and Patchen some almost improvable strains of blood, viz., Belmont on Clay, which should be stout, hard and fast.

Grim's Gossip.

Ed. Bither will work this season at the Allen Stock Farm.

The well-known stallion Bay Rose 2:20½ is at the Oakland track.

Dolly McMann and her daughter, Lillie Stanley, 2:17½, will both visit the harem of Director, 2:17, this season.

Mr. B. Allison of Oakland, is the proud possessor of a fine young horse named Abdol. He has splendid action and can show a very fast clip even now.

John Rowen is jogging St. Nicholas preparatory to getting him ready for a heavy stud season. This son of Sidney is very popular, and mares are being booked to him at a lively rate.

James A. Dustin has decided to forego his Eastern trip for the present and will now stay here until next fall. His Dexter Prince youngster gives indication of being as fast as J. R.

Dr. Carpenter was called by telegraph to attend "Alta" which is at R. P. Ashe's Merced Stock Farm. The noted stallion had a severe attack of colic, but has now recovered.

David Bonner, than whom there is no better judge of trotters, says that Guy Wilkes reminds him more of old Hambletonian over the back and loins than any horse he has seen in a long time.

Redwood 2:24½, has arrived at the Oakland Track from Petaluma, and is greatly admired by the visitors. He will stand during the season over there, and already a number of mares are booked to him.

Maj. Dubois is happy as all his horses are in fine condition. He blistered the coronets of all four of Superior's feet, and now they are much improved. The stable will remain some time before they go back to Denver.

In a note from Mr. Kemper of Oakland, he informs me that B. C. Holly has offered $500, for the Alice B. colt by Woodnut. He is a handsome chestnut and full of promise. The mare will be bred this year to Election.

Billy Johnson, who drove Longworth 2:19, and Ringwood last season, is now training a thoroughbred which A. C. Dietz bought at one of Killip & Co.'s auction sales at Sacramento last fall. It is reported that he is showing up well.

To show the dimensions to which the trotting interests of California has grown, it is only necessary to say that 109 second payments were made from this state alone, to the N. Y. Spirit of the Times Purse. Verily California is in the van.

John Woods, who formerly assisted J. A. Dustin, has accepted a situation with Capt. Drake of Vallejo, and will handle the horses at the home of Admiral. He is a careful, conscientious man, and should do well with those placed under his charge.

John F. English of 313 Davis street, this city, has purchased from Henry Voorman a yearling filly by Harris's Tempest, dam Kitty Dubois. The filly is entered in the Occident Stake, and will also be in the Stanford. She is a beautiful brown and can trot a streak.

About a week from to-morrow there will be a race at the Oakland track between Chas. Nathan's trotter, Encinal, Wm. Schulte's grey pacer and Mr. Lapin's grey pacer. Some little interest is manifested in the three cornered contest, as all of the horses have many personal admirers.

Killip & Co. announced this week that they will sell on March 1st, 1890, for account of Capt. Ben E. Harris, twenty-five superior roadsters and saddle horses of all gaits. Catalogues can be had on application at the office 22 Montgomery St.

Several leading Australian bookmakers talk of coming to New York to ply their trade, feeling convinced that Australia has seen its best day. Joe and Barney Thompson have concluded to stay in England bookmaking, and if business is not renumerative they will then lay siege to New York.

From a carefully prepared table in an Eastern contemporary, it is shown that Yolo Maid paced a faster quarter than any other of the noted sidewheelers who heard the bell ring during the season of 1889. Her time is 30 seconds, while Gold Leaf and Johnston are each accredited with 31 seconds.

R. H. Newton writes me from Woodland that his fast young pacer Tom Ryder 2:20½ has wintered well, and that his lameness has entirely disappeared. Good reports also come from Belle Button and John H., and it is extremely likely that those of the lateral motion will be in high feather this year.

Mr. Irwin Ayres had fully expected to send back East several of his well bred Mambrino Wilkes representives, but as two of them were taken ill, the owner of San Miguel Stock Farm decided to cancel the entries to the sale and await for some other favorable opportunity to dispose of first-class stock at auction prices.

A would be sporting paper published in this city had the following last week: "The thoroughbred stallion Apache, gave a telling exhibition at Haggin's farm this week. Taking in consideration the state of the track, the time 2:15 for a mile is wonderful. Lorillard will undoubtedly be pleased to hear of this performance as the stallion was bred by him."

Dr. Thomas Bowhill, formerly veterinary editor of the BREEDER AND SPORTSMAN, has delayed his visit to Europe for a couple of weeks so that he might accompany the large consignment of trotters to be sent East by J. B. Haggin, Esq. The doctor had established a fine practice in this State, and his many clients will be sorry to lose the services of such a good "vet."

Leamar, the property of A. T. Hatch, has been taken to the Oakland track, where he will be prepared for the coming campaign. He is a good colt, and should make a low mark this year. Guide 2:29 is also reported as being in fine fettle. He will stand during the season for a few approved mares at Pleasanton. If there is anything in signs Guide will be another Director to enter the "twenty list" in 1890.

The effect of the severe weather can plainly be seen at the Oakland track, the two bridges having been carried away by the storms. The loss is considerable, but Mr. Hinchman will have them put in proper order at once, so that there will be no interference with the horses in training. The Bay District track is in much better condition than could be expected under the circumstances, and the harrow was put on, a week ago yesterday.

Cupid, a full brother to Adonis 2:14 will stand at the Oakland Track during the present stallion season. The terms are only $50, and it will be marvelous if his book does not fill rapidly. Unlike his brother, he is a natural trotter and as a two year old showed quarters in 36 seconds. He was not worked last year, but will be at the conclusion of the present season.

The Oakland Driving Club consists of some forty members all of them enthusiastic horsemen, and owners of horses. As soon as the track at the Park is repaired the members propose to give several matinees open only to those who belong to the club, and for which valuable prizes will be given to the winners. In the course of a few days a meeting will be held to elect permanent officers at which time a programme will be arranged for racing days.

The trotting stallion Bonanza has been domiciled at the Oakland track and is receiving gentle exercise every day. As yet his record is only 2:29½, but I have seen him go many a better mile, and the probabilities are strong that he will materially lower that mark this year. The son of Arthurton and sister (dam of Albert W. 2:20) never looked better in his life, and there are many who will feel pleased for his owner's sake if he touches 2:20 this season.

Brasfield & Co. of Lexington, Ky., have forwarded to this office a list of the animals which will be sold by them at their great sale commencing next Monday. There is not a celebrated sire in the country but what is represented in the catalogue. The list is a very extensive one, and animals have been entered from half the States in the union. If there are any of my readers who care about telegraphing a commission back to buy any of those offered for sale, the catalogue is at their service.

Baltimore reports are to the effect that Professor Ward has at his infirmary a horse with a clearly defined case of la grippe. The symptoms of la grippe in a horse are similar to those of human beings who have it, beginning with sneezing. Then a high fever sets in, which is the forerunner of pneumonia, and which sometimes ends fatally. During the epidemic of influenza which swept over Europe in 1729 and 1730 horses were attacked with a disease having all the symptoms of the human influenza.

La Grippe has played sad havoc with many of the horsemen. J. L. Hinds has been confined to his residence for several weeks, and Jimmy Hamilton has been exercising the Irving Ayres string during Mr. Hinds' absence. L. M. Smith who has charge of the Du Bois Bros.' stable, has also been confined to his bed for two weeks, but is able to be up and around once more. Mr. Valensin put in an appearance for the first time in ten days during the early part of the week.

I had the pleasure of taking a look at P. J. Williams' beautiful bay colt Silver Bow a few days ago, and he is worth a visit from any one. Perfect in every point, he is a grand individual, and is justly entitled to all the praise showered on him by the owner. Mr. Williams intends to take the colt through the Montana Circuit, after which he will be brought back to Stockton and participate in all the meetings which take place after that. Silver Bow will serve fifteen mares at the Oakland track before he is prepared for the campaign. The pedigree of Silver Bow can be found on another page.

It is very rarely that a race track fully equipped is advertised for sale, but in this issue the Directors of the Sonoma County Agricultural Park Association offer for sale their one mile track and grounds, consisting of eighty four acres. There are 300 box and cattle stalls, a two story pavilion 60 by 120, commodious grand stand and many out buildings. There is a lovely park of fifteen acres, a good wind break, and an abundance of water. Sealed bids will be received for the same up to February 17th 1890. The purchaser can be put in immediate possession.

The Los Angeles Herald last Sunday published a turf article in which the Santa Anita policy in breeding is severlly criticized. Here is an extract: "The prevailing idea is that Mr. Baldwin made a great mistake in not leaving this famous colt and Volante at the East, where they could stand for larger figures than in California, and fill the Santa Anita stud with an importation either from England or Australia. The latter horses are preferable, as having better bones, generally speaking, besides which they are matured in a dry climate and not addicted to "roaring." Mr. Haggin has already led the way by importing one stallion from Australia and another from New Zealand, and the fact that out of six Sir Modred colts tried last year four proved to be stake-winners, should have set the millionaire of Santa Anita to studying which foreign cross would be most desirable to succeed the once famous Grinstead, now slowly waning into senility, with Rutherford a downright failure."

I saw the original telegram sent by Ed. Bither to Mr. Valensin in which the former accepted the terms offered by the latter and it also stated that the contract had been forwarded. Evidently Mr. Bither is of a changeable mind for he has sent a second telegram to the Valencin Stock Farm in which he abrogates his previous acceptance and now states that he cannot come. Mr. Valensin is much put out and he has decided to send several horses to the New York sale that would have been kept here for trotting purposes on the next circuit. Kellogg & Co. have been telegraphed to and in addition to the horses already catalogued, there will also be sent, Fleet 2:24: full sister to Longworth 2:19, which was expected to beat 2:20 this year; Habibi, two year old has shown quarters in 36 seconds. The stable will not have any horses in training this season, and the colts engagements will all be canceled. The consignment will start on the 18th of this month and will be sold at public auction on March 7th at the American Institute building, New York City.

There has been a meeting of delegates from all of the Montana Associations with the exception of Helena, which was not represented. According to the programme laid out at the meeting the season will begin in July at Missoula, where the meeting will last six days. Another six-day meeting will immediately follow at Deer Lodge. Next in order comes Anaconda with a ten days meeting, beginning on July 30. Last will be the Butte meeting, which will also continue for ten days, beginning August 14.

The purses will aggregate $56,00 or more. The sum of $15,000 will be given in Anaconda and a like sum in Butte. The totals in Missoula and Deer Lodge are not quite so large, as the meetings there are not quite so long. The programme for each place will be prepared and announced in due time. The season chosen for the circuit will come in between the meetings of the Salt Lake and Salem associations, and there is every indication of very numerous and very important entries. Encouraged by past successes, a grand season is anticipated the coming summer.

On the first of the present month, entries closed to the two handicaps which are given below for the Sacramento Spring meeting and the showing is a good one.

The Chris. Green Handicap—A sweepstakes for all ages, of $50 each, h f or $10 if declared; with $500 added; second horse to receive $100 out of stakes. Weights announced March 1st. Declarations due by 6 P. M. April 1st. A winner of any race after publication of weights of one mile or upwards, to carry 3 pounds: of two races, 5 pounds; of three or more, 7 pounds. This will not apply to horses handicapped at 125 or over. One and one-quarter miles.

A. P. Hill, Santa Clara, b g Steve Stroud (3) by Bill Lee, dam by Woodburn.

W. L. Appleby, Santa Clara, b f Raindrop (3) by Wildidle, dam imp Teardrop.

W. L. Appleby, Santa Clara, ch f Odette (4) by Shiloh, dam Margery.

L. J. Rose, Los Angeles, b. g. Mikado (6), by Shiloh, dam Margery.

Matt Storn, San Francisco, ch. m. Lurline (4), by Longfield, dam Katy Pease.

Dennison Bros., Sacramento, b. h. Hotspur (4), by Joe Daniels, dam Sister to Jim Douglass.

Dennison Bros., Sacramento, b. g. G. W. (4), by Kyrle Daly, dam Elizabeth.

Kelley & Samuels, San Francisco, b. h. Ed. McGinnies (5) by Grinstead, dam Jennie T.

W. H. E. Smith, Eureka, b. h. Al. Farrow (5), by Conner, dam Della Walker.

J. F. McBride, Sacramento, ch. c. Longshot (4), by Duke of Norfolk, dam Langford.

L. U. Shippee, Stockton, br. m. Picnic (4), by Mr. Pickwick, dam Countess.

Elmwood Stables, Milpitas, b. g. Nabeau (5), by Nathan Coombs, dam Beauty.

H. D. Miller, Fresno, b. m. Daisy D. (aged), by Wheatley, dam Black Maria.

The Spring Stakes.—A sweepstakes for three-year-olds (foals of 1887) that have not won a race previous to January 1, 1890; $50 entrance, h. f., or $15 if declared April 1, 1890; $400 added; second to receive $75 from stakes. Maidens at time of starting allowed five pounds. One mile.

L. J. Rose, Los Angeles, s. h. Rover, by Wildidle, dam imp. Rosetta.

L. J. Rose, Los Angeles, b. f. Glenlock, by Flood, dam Glendew.

Matt Storn, San Francisco, ch f Marigold, by Milner' dam Katy Pease.

H. Howard, Sacramento, br f Mayetta, by Joe Daniels, dam Amanda.

W. M. Murry, Sacramento s h Kiro, by Joe Hooker, dam by Foster.

W. M. Murry, Sacramento, b g Leland, by Flood dam Amelia.

P. Herzog, Sacramento, b h Mohawk, by Norfolk dam Irene Harding.

Dennison Bros., Sacramento, ch h Prince's First, by Prince of Norfolk, dam Lizzie Idle.

Owen Bros., Fresno, b m Carona, by Norfolk, dam sister to Lottery.

L. U. Shippee, Stockton, b c Take Notice, by imp Prince Charles, dam Nota Bene.

L. U. Shippee, Stockton b f Mabel F. by Longfellow, dam Carrie Phillips.

L. Menenhall, Ione, ch m Maggie B.

A jockey club has been inaugurated by the young men visiting Santa Barbara and is called the Arlington Jockey Club: The following are the officers: President, H. E. Duryea; Secretary and Treasurer, W. S Barnes; Board of Stewards: H. B. Duryea, Chairman ex-officio; W. S. Barnes, Secretary ex-officio, Bayard Thayer, C. E. Bigelow, P. H. Duryea, R. H. Kissel, C. S. Fay. Among their rules and regulations are the following, self explanatory: The object of the club shall be: 1. To encourage racing and sports in general in Santa Barbara. 2. To promote the racing of native bred horses to the exclusion of thoroughbreds. 3. To rent the track of the Santa Barbara Association for the purpose of leveling and carrying on races, tournaments and such other sporting events as may be desirable. 4. All blooded horses, except in special and in announced events, shall be barred from contesting in any races which may be held under the auspices of this club. 5. Any horse entering any race may be subjected to a handicap which shall be arbitrary and from which there can be no appeal. 6. The club reserves the right to reject any and all entries that may be made for any event held under its auspices. 7. The club will conduct its events subject to the rules of the Blood Horse Association of California; but in special cases reserves the right to make its own rulings, which shall be decisive and final. These meetings will be very popular in Santa Barbara, as the officers and members of the Arlington Jockey Club are prominent, fond of equine sports, and are anxious to amuse themselves as well as the public. The races should be well contested and the meetings should be patronized. They purpose to hold two meetings a week. Next Saturday will be their inaugural meeting. The track will be in good condition and the following programme will be run off: First event—The Commercial Stakes open to all cold blooded horses; distance, one quarter of a mile; purse $30, of which $25 to first horse and $5 to second. Entrance fees $2 50. Weight 165 pounds. Second event—Mexican Fancy riding. Sweepstakes of 50 cents each; $20 added, 80 per cent given to first, 20 per cent to second. Third event—The Thayer Stakes, open to all cold blooded horses; half mile heats, best two in three; sweepstakes of $3 each; $50 added by Bayard Thayer Esq. 70 per cent given to the first horse, 20 per cent to second, and 10 per cent to third. Weight 165 pounds. Overweight allowed. Winners of Commercial Stakes five pounds extra. The second event should prove a very interesting one, for there are many very fine riders here who have horses that are very well trained. What the Spanish riders can do on their well trained horses is almost incredible. They ride with grace and perform intricate maneuverings with ease and confidence. And some of the native bred horses have shown an ability to run well and carry the weight that will be alloted to them in the races. The officers of the jockey club are gentlemen of experience and judgment. They realize the importance of fair play in all races and they will be always on the alert that all races should be conducted on the square. They have betrayed their acuteness and good judgment in their selection of a starter. S. P. Stow, Esq., of Santa Barbara, will be official starter for the season. Good starts are assured for Mr. Stow's ability to start a lot of unprofessional jockeys can not be questioned.

TURF AND TRACK.

Baylock will ride for the Beverwyck stable.

Allen will ride for Brown Dick again this season.

Palmer is engaged to ride for McMahon this season.

Freeman will ride for Dave Pulsifer in the coming season.

Alf Estill has been duly dubbed Capt. Estill by the Eastern press.

The New York Spirit seems to think Hanover's racing days are numbered.

Mr. August Belmont will have a new 24 stall stable erected at Westchester.

"Father Bill" Daly bought Lemon Blossom for $1,050 a fortnight ago.

Cruiser is said to be looking hoise at New Orleans, and also in the best trim.

Proctor Knott is wintering well and will be in good order for an early start this season.

John Dickerson will have a select stable round the big circuit in the East this coming season.

J. H. Thomas has sold the three year old trotter Elite by Ambassador for $11,000 to Hipple & Co.

According to Col. Chester's compilation, 782 horses entered the 2:30 list of trotters and pacers.

George Noble, who won the City and Suburban in England in 1863 on Adventurer, the well-known Newminster horse, is at Richmond, Yorks, horse-breaking for a living.

Christopher Green, Esq., was unanimously re-elected President of the State Board of Agriculture last week.

It was rumored at Clifton last week that Garrison had signed to ride for the Dywer Stable next season.

Geneva and Elista, with respective records of 2:19½ and 2:22½, are being driven to pole at the Allen Farm.

The Buffalo Express says Mr. Hamlin wishes to trot Belle Hamlin against either Palo Alto or the peerless Sunol.

Isaac Murphy says he can ride at 112 pounds with 24 hours notice. He has not been so light for several seasons.

Secretary Brewster is on deck again, wonderfully pleased with the satisfactory list of entries at Washington Park.

Harry Hill will have a tavern and chop-house near the Westchester race track if he can procure suitable property.

The Chicago Stable (George Hankins, Eugene Leigh and Tom Kiley) will have thirty-five head of horses this season.

Directors La Rue and Hancock were reappointed Superintendents of the Sacramento Pavilion and Park respectively.

The best of F. B. Harper's two-year-olds is reported to be St. August by St. Blaise out of Secret; he is 15.2 and well developed.

A few weeks ago Lion started a pool room at Hot Springs, and has been so successful that probably there will be another in full swing.

The Matron Stakes at Westchester for 1892 closed with 979 nominations, the largest number ever made for any American stake.

Johnny Osborne, the well-known English rider, was 57 years old on the 7th of January, and *the pusher* is almost as good as ever.

The imported horse Earl Clifden 11, by Blair Athol out of Curiosity, is said to have worked a half mile at Clifton in 49½ seconds last week.

A well known horseman sent among his Washington Park entries three well bred trotters. Is he hoping to beat Gov. Stanford's theory?

The Hon. J. C. Sibley, of Prospect Hill Farm, left New York last week for California, on the lookout for invigorating climate and trotters.

William Angel, who was for a time with the Chicago stable, is now in charge of Charles Reed & Son's string of racers at the Westchester track.

The well known owner and trainer Byron McClelland was the last runner up for the Brook Farm in Kentucky purchased by Col. Pepper.

That excellent colt Gregory is reported to be in fine fettle just now, and will make some of the three-year-olds hustle to beat him this Summer.

Sallie Hagan, the four-year old filly who injured herself in her stall at New Orleans, is in a bad way. It is feared she will never wholly recover.

Jack Sheehan, the well-known tipster, applied for the position as starter at Clifton, but when Mr. Caldwell put in an appearance the wizard quit.

W. B. Cheatham's thoroughbred yearlings this year are all by Saxon and number nine colts and seven fillies. They will be sold at auction in Nashville.

Jockey French who was injured recently by a fall with Sunshine of the Excelsior Stable, has so far recovered that he will probably ride again next week.

Green B Morris has sold the sulky Barrister to Abe Carson of the Excelsior stable for $1,200 with the understanding that he has the first stake Barrister wins.

Thos. P. Raymond, Louisville, Ky., recently lost the gray mare Hiawasse (dam of Cuban Queen) by War Dance, dam Sallie Knight by imp Knight of St. George.

G. R. Bohannon & Co, Midway, Ky., have sold to Beard Bros., of Ohio, the bay horse Procrastinator foaled 1884, by Bulwark, dam Bessie Lee by Hunter's Lexington.

Field Bros, Lexington, Ky., have sold to J. B. Davis, agent for Jesse Armstrong, a bay filly two years old, by Harry O'Fallon, dam Fleta (Chandler's dam) by imp Hurrah.

It's about worn threadbare, but still good, viz: "blood will tell." Breed to a good stallion with a well authenticated pedigree, and it is also just as well to have a racing bred one too.

J. B. Perry of Lexington, Ky., has sold his roan yearling colt by St. Bel, full brother to Bell Boy, out of a Mambrino Gift mare, to Thomas Weiser of Bethlehem, Penn., for $1,500

Tudor, Jack Cocks, Leman, T. J. Rush, Clara Moore and other well known race horses, are wintering at Galveston, Texas, and are said to be enjoying the salt water baths.

Checkmate the celebrated old racehorse after doing menial service in an omnibus at Versailles, Ky., has been turned out on Capt. Franklin's farm for the rest he so well has earned.

Alec Waugh, son of the Newmarket trainer, has been appointed official starter to the Hungarian and Austrian Jockey Club, and will go to Vienna this month to take up his duties.

Col. R. S. Strader, of Lexington, Ky., has sold to James Cox, Liverpool, England, for $3500, the six year old bay stallion Belview, by Belmont dam Lady Simmons by Volunteer.

B. J. Tracy, Ashland Park, Lexington, Ky., has sold to J. B. Davis, agent for Jesse Armstrong, a black filly two years old by imp The Rake, dam imp Scrubbing Brush by Saunterer.

Tulare County is gradually going in more and more for racing, especially Porterville. They will probably have a day or two of racing in the latter part of February at Kelley's Track.

L U. Shippee of Stockton will send to the Peoria Fair Grounds, Illinois, two car loads of trotters, principally youngsters by Hawthorne 10,935. The sale takes place on the 7th of March.

George Barbee's two-year-old colt Eblis (Iroquois—Evandine), broke down in the off fore-leg a fortnight ago; he was well thought of, having worked 7 furlongs in 1:31 with 125 pounds up.

St. Blaise the very successful imported stallion belonging to the Hon. August Belmont will be used as a private stallion hereafter and will be kept at his Nursery Stud Farm in Kentucky.

Minnehaha, the famous brood mare was bought for $200, and has directly and indirectly returned her owner $100,000. Green Mountain Maid returned even a greater amount to Stony Ford.

Knap McCarthy has to look after one hundred and thirty-two thoroughbreds at Brookdale Farm, the breeding establishment of D. D. Withers. He reports his horses in training as looking in superb condition.

Provision has been made in Charles Backman's will that the plot of ground on which stands the monument erected to the memory of Green Mountain Maid shall always be kept for the purpose for which it is now used.

Baron Hirsch the well known millionaire banker and racing man was black balled by the Paris Jockey Club, several prominent members including one of the Rothschilds have threatened to resign in consequence.

A. A. Jackson has been elected as delegate to represent the Willows Agricultural Association at the Annual Congress of the National Trotting Association, to be held at Buffalo, New York, on the 12th of February next.

Waldo Olney owner and trainer of the horses running in the name of the Clifton Stable, was married last week at Kreyer's Hotel on the King's Highway, Coney Island, to Adeline the oldest daughter to Mr. and Mrs. Kreyer.

James B. Clay, Iroquois Stud, Lexington, Ky., lost on January 9th, from the effects of slipping a foal the bay mare Taloolah, foaled 1886, by Dudley, dam Wahtawah by John C. Breckenridge, her dam Adele by imp Albion.

The Lamasney Brothers, finding the company in the East too "hot" for them, have decided to race only in the West this year, where there seems to be a better chance for their rather second class lot of horses to win some money.

The Governor last week reappointed George W. Hancock and Frederick Cox as members of the State Board of Agriculture, their terms having expired. Also Richard Gird of San Bernardino to succeed Charles F. Swan, term expired.

The fine farm of the late John G. Brooks, near Midway, Ky., containing 406 acres were sold at auction, 16th inst., to Colonel R. P. Pepper, of Frankfort, Ky, for $108 50 per acre, and will be used by him hereafter for a stock farm.

It is said Garrison has been retained to ride A. G. Newsome's gelding, Mt. Lebanon, in the Derby. The chestnut son of George Kinney and Accidenta must have improved on his two-year-old form of eleven starts without a bracket.

M. Danmas, Municipal Councillor of Paris, says in his report, that by the suppression of bookmakers, Paris loses a revenue of £50,000, and gets instead a rent of £18,000 from the Paris mutuel offices, a dead loss of £22,000 to the city.

Trainer M. T. Donovan has purchased of Mr. J. A. Morris the chestnut colt, three years old, by imp Pizarro—Pinafore. Mr. Donovan now has some twenty-two horses in his charge, including the Issaquena filly and all of the Western Union Stable.

To show how much Mr. Z. E. Simmons, formerly one of the owners of George Wilkes, thinks of Anteeo, it may be said that last season he bred to him Hattie Woodward, 2:15½; Eva 2:30½, by George Wilkes, and four other daughters of the same horse.

The Beverwyck stables have returned to F. B. Harper. Annie Blackburn, the half sister to Freeland. They were given her running qualities to recompense them for the loss of Valuable; owing to a leg, however, Annie was returned and will be bred to Rossington.

The Warnkes, who made a snug little fortune of $20,000 with their filly Reclare last year, have another filly, who looks enough like Reclare to be her sister, though not related to her. She is said to be very fast, and even more promising than was Reclare at her age.

Frank McCabe has had excellent luck with the Dwyer string this winter; there are no sick horses in the stable. Inspector B, Bella B., and several others of the cripples are at W. Daly's Hartford farm, and will not be worked until just before the Monmouth meeting.

The only mare whose ten first foals were all winners is Mariposa, the foals being Helmsman, Beatitude, Boulevard, Bliss, Beatrice, Swift, Glideaway, Emmet, Ada D. and Marshall Luke. She is the property of the Belle Meade stud, is 21 years old, and won but one race.

Prices for trotters that should improve in form are now ruling high. C. J. Hamlin says that he has refused $25,000 for the five-year-old Mocking Bird, whose record is 2:17½. Knapsack McCarty says: "Put Mocking Bird and Geneva S. together, and they can beat the double team record."

Dave Gideon's French Park is said to be standing up excellently through this trying weather. His legs appear to be all right now, and if they will stand some good, fast gallops he should be a great handicap horse this coming season, for his two year old form was remarkably brilliant.

H. D. Bowman, of Louisville, has purchased a two-year-old colt by a brother to Clingstone, dam by Kentucky Prince; 2nd dam by Hambletonian; 3d dam by American Star; also, a black filly by Pretender, son of Dictator, dam Miss Ada by Almont; 2d dam Mother Hubbard by Johnston's Toronto.

Matt Allen has been giving Senator Hearst's horses a lot of work of late and Gorgo is almost in racing condition. Golden Horn and King Thomas are also in fine fettle and look as if they should do as good work this year as was expected of them last year. The lot are at the Sheepshead Bay track.

While here, Mr. Bonner made Senator Stanford an offer for the now three-year-old filly by Woolsey (brother to Sunol, 2:10½) out of Belle by Kentucky Prince 2470, out of Belle of Richmond (dam of Bergen, 2:27), by Hambletonian, and has since purchased her, Senator Stanford having accepted his offer.

The bay horse Gunner, foaled 1879, by Alarm, out of War Reel by War Dance, her dam Dixie by imp. Sovereign out of St. Mary by Hamlet, etc., died January 16th of colic, at Meadowthorpe Stock Farm, Lexington, Ky. Gunner was a promising young sire, and was the sire of Gunwad and Gunshot.

John H. Shults is greatly pleased with the improved condition of his famous stallion, Pancoast. Parkville, another of Mr. Shults' stallions, will command attention this spring. He is a bay 15.2 hands, and was foaled in 1884, being by Electioneer out of Aurora 2:27, by John Nelson, son of imp. Trustee.

John Faylor, the well known old time rider and erstwhile trainer, has gone down to Santa Anita to superintend the breeding department. Johnny should soon have the breeding end of the business in much improved shape, that it has been neglected of late is evinced by the small inbred two-year-olds.

Mr. G. Valensin received a telegram from Bither last Monday, saying the contract drawn up did not suit, and all negotiations are finished between them. In consequence, Fleet and several more of Mr. Valensin's horses will be sold in New York which would otherwise have been trained and campaigned next season.

Green Morris's old racer, Favor, will begin his services in the stud this year at the McGrathiana farm of Milton Young, near Lexington, Ky., at $50 the season. His companions on the farm are Onondaga, Macduff, Duke of Montrose, Woodland, and Strathmore. Favor ought to prove as good a sire as any of them.

Steel Gray, probably the best trotter England ever produced, died the other day. She had a ten mile record of 26 min 56½ sec. I recollect years ago seeing her at Manchester, when crowds were round her box in the show grounds all day. When out in the ring her action was almost the perfection of pure trotting.

To name a thoroughbred after a Kentucky Senator appears to be bad luck, as neither Joe Blackburn nor Jim Beck earned any turf distinction. On the other hand, to be named for a Governor of that commonwealth seems to be an earnest of success, for both Luke Blackburn and Proctor Knott made national reputations on the turf.

William E. Weeks, who not long ago went to France to show the Frenchmen how to ride a trotting horse, writes that he did not find the French capital a very inviting field for his labor, and that he has crossed to London, and was preparing to return home. Weeks is a great favorite on the grand circuit, and will be seen there again.

Mr. Allen, the well known proprietor of the Allen Farm, Pittsfield, among other purchases in California bought from Palo Alto, Electrite 10878, (brother to Sphinx 2:23) by Electioneer, dam Sprite by Belmont out of Waterwitch by Pilot Jr. A few weeks ago, he refused $50,000 for the two-year-old, saying he was not for sale.

Dick Roche, the well-known Western racing man, bookmaker, etc., and owner of Lioness and other crack horses, arrived here last Tuesday with W. Donohue, the Eastern jockey. They will stay here some few weeks. Donohue has several relatives here. He and Roche will have a look at some of the large breeding farms in the State.

George Hankins of the Chicago Stables has just bought a twelve hundred dollar pair of carriage horses from A. M. Spellman of Minerva, O. The team is expected to make a sensation on Chicago boulevards in fine weather. They are dark chestnuts, five years old, stand 16 hands, high knee action, are matched to a hair and drive as one horse.

Committees on Revision of the Premium List for the State Fair were appointed as follows: Park—Directors Hancock, Cox and Singleterry. Pavilion—Directors Shippee, LaRue and Delong. Speed Programme—Directors Chase, Shippee, LaRue, Delong and Hancock, (President Green added). The date of the Fair was fixed for September 8th to 20th.

David Waldo and G. W. Poole will combine forces, with Soden as their principal jockey, this season, and race under the firm name of Waldo & Poole. Racegoers believe they have been doing that at the winter tracks already. Spaulding, Hamlet, Steve Jerome, Sayre, Irma H., Zulu, Lewis Clark, Gold Bond, Cassandra, St. Nick, Autumn Leaf, and others will make up their stable.

Dave Pulsifer's horses are at Westchester with Trainer Donovan in charge. Tenny is the crack and pride of the lot, and has filled out well, having great muscular development, and is expected to turn out in better form than last year if that were possible. The black Onaway is in the pink of condition; he has filled out into a grand looking horse, while the rest of the stable look equally well.

Barnes leads the winning jockeys with 170 wins out of 661; Bergan is second with 147 out of 633; Taylor third with 123 out of 463; Hamilton fourth with 113 out of 419; De Long is next with 106 out of 463 and Gerhardy follows close with 105 out of 444. Among the heavy weight cracks Garrison has 70 wins out of 236; Murphy 58 out of 195, Hayward 39 out of 174; McLaughlin 21 out of 50.

C. J. Hamlin has offered to match Chimes against any son of Beautiful Bells. Chimes showed up indifferently as a three year old, on account of a quarter crack; and was not trained at either four years or five years. He is being jogged now on the roads about Buffalo, and is going perfectly. Chimes will be sent for a record next autumn, barring accident.

The colors of the Dwyer Brothers. August Belmont, and other owners of large racing stables who have not heretofore raced at Clifton, will probably be seen in the Early Blossom Stakes, for two-year-olds, at three furlongs, which is to be run Feb. 14, weather permitting. The entries will close Feb. 1. and William Lakeland thinks he has a mortgage on it with one of his California bred youngsters.

The young Earl of Dudley has already commenced realizing by selling the gallery of paintings collected by his father. Among the most valuable in the collection was Turner's "Grand Canal Venice," which was said to be that great master's *chef d' oeuvre.* Cornelius Vanderbilt has paid £20,000 for the painting. The young Lord is evidently finding racing or something else rather expensive.

W. B. Jennings, the well-known owner and trainer, will relegate eighteen mares to his stock farm at Teesburg, Va. Among them will probable be Swift, Telie Doe, Romp, Utility, Biggonet, Yorkshire Lass and Temptation. The premier stallion is imp. Superior by Petrarch, out of Thoughtless by The Hermit, grandam Salamanca by Student, etc. Superior is therefore half-brother to Senator Stanford's (imp.) Amalie.

The stables quartered at the Memphis track last week were Mr. Tucker, with 11; Mr. King, with 3; Mr. Mahone, with 3; Mr. Duke, with 3; Mr. Spink, with 2; Mr. Weidner, with 9; W. McGuigan, with 15; Messrs. Roody Bros., with 12; E. Corrigan, with 21; P. Corrigan, with 6; Mr. McClouddem, with 6; Messrs. Cassidy & Co., with 12; Messrs. Dougherty & Co., with 11; Mr. Simmons, with 2; Messrs. Newsum & Co., with 15.

Friends of the Western Turf Congress do not attatch any importance to the withdrawal of the Louisiana Jockey Club, or believe it indicates popular sentiment against the rule forbidding races for three-year-olds and upward less than a mile. They say that, as a matter of fact, the club was practically out of the congress before the rule was passed, as it had not paid its dues for the past year, and was not represented at the last meeting.

It is extremely probably that Hindoocraft will never face the starter again. He hurt his right leg before his last race at the Brooklyn track, when he ran third to Badge and Bronzomarte and that accounts for the poor showing he made. Dr. Shepherd was called in and gave it as his opinion that with a good winter's rest the horse would be as good as ever He has had the rest, but the leg is not improved, and he will very likely be retired.

J. C. Sibley of Franklin, Penn., is one of the converts to the theory that an infusion of good thoroughbred blood in good racing families will alone produce the very highest rate of speed. So he has mated his stallion St. Bel, who is a son of Electioneer and Beautiful Bells, to thoroughbred mares, and has in their offspring a lot of youngsters who have as much speed, at least, and are as level-headed as are the sons and daughters of standard-bred mares.

"The English Hackney," says a well-known horseman who has just returned from abroad, "is a grand little animal, closely resembling the old-time Morgan. They are hardy and plucky, making excellent long-distance roadsters when not too high in their knee-action. They are rather small, though, for this country, being only from 14½ to 15½ hands, but no doubt would breed some fine light carriage-drivers, where high action is a desideratum."

The Monmouth Park Racing Association has announced its list of sweepstakes opened for the current year. They are 38 in number, two more than those opened at a corresponding period last year. Twelve of the lot are for two year olds, all at three-quarters of a mile; ten are for three year olds, all at a distance over a mile, and the balance, for all ages, mostly handicaps, at distances varying from a mile to the cup, at a mile and a quarter.

Racing for big stakes is not to be confined entirely to the United States, England and Australia. Italy steps into the game with the Roman Grand Prize of £3,200 to the winner, £480 to the second, £200 to the third and £120 to the fourth. The race is for three-year-olds, to be run at the Rome spring meeting in May. The meeting will be under a distinguished directorate, which includes Prince John Baptist Borghese, Marquis Roccagiovine and Baron Michael Lazzaroni.

The fiat has gone forth that the Homewood Driving Park, Pittsburg, shall be no more. The property is now placed upon the market, and before spring opens up it will probably be staked off in "town lots." Although this race course has had a short and checquered career, it has many associations which will keep it fresh in the minds of horsemen. Here Maud S. lowered her record from 2:10¾ to 2:10¼ on the 13th of July, 1881. Bonesetter, 2:19, dropped dead on this track after a hard fought heat.

Edward Moser the very gentlemanly and competent young jockey who was under Father Bill Daly's tuition during the past year has been secured by the Dwyer Brothers as their chief light-weight jockey next season. He is a very bright boy, a son of Mr. Moser, the Superintendent of J. H. Shults's stock farm at Parkville and one of the most promising youngsters seen in the saddle in late years. Above all he is thoroughly honest, and so Frank McCabe will find in him an able assistant in trying to place the Dwyer Brothers once more at the top of list of winning stables. Moser is about nineteen years old, and can easily ride at 100 pounds. He begins work with the Dwyers April 1.

The entries to the June running meeting of the Kansas City Jockey Club which have closed last week are very flattering. There are 365 entries to the nine stakes and among the horses entered are Riley, Milliken, Dollikens, English Lady, Wrestler, Robespierre, Cruiser, Kitty Cheatham, Huntress, Kaloolah, Macbeth, Swifter, Lepremier, Pilgrim, Joe, Ja-Ja, Morse and other cracks. The average is forty dollars to each stake race.

Among the foals on hand at Palo Alto up to last Thursday were eight thoroughbreds, Aurelia (imp) having a Cyrus colt; Cornelia (imp) by Isonomy has a Flood colt, Fairy Rose (imp), a Cheviot filly. Flirt (imp) a filly by Flood, Getaway (imp) a Cyrus colt, Goula (imp) a filly by Flood, Laelia (imp) a colt by Cyrus, and Regina a filly by Argyle. "Example is better than precept," and Senator Stanford's superintendent sets an example to the whole world.

The Winter racing at New Orleans this year has been of a peculiarly shady character, and as a result of Abbas's peculiar riding on Little Bess he has been ruled off the track. Little Ray, the colored jockey, is at New Orleans, but is not permitted to ride there, because he was ruled off at Louisville last Fall. He is the jockey who, Mr. Scoggan declares, pulled Hindoocraft at Sheepshead Bay in the race won by Bronzomarte. Ray is a fairly clever jockey, but has the reputation of being "in" with a bad lot of speculators.

Among the many California trotters and pacers to be sold to New York this spring will be Gold Leaf 2:11¼. Mr. Salisbury's crack Sidney pacer. A good deal of curiosity has been evinced as to who will buy her. One well known Californian said in the Grand Hotel the other day that he would make some of them pay high for her as he had never seen a mare he would rather have for the road. She is easy to handle, with a smooth, quiet style of going, does not wear a boot or weight, is level headed, and with her exceptional burst of speed no one could pass her on the road.

Homer Saxe is one of our best known purchasers of cattle and trotting stock. Of the latter he generally has a few on hand for private use. Last week he was persuaded by the Conkling Bros, Inyo County, to part with his well known three year old stallion Mount Vernon Prince by Mount Vernon, 2:21, out of a sister of Molly Drew by Winthrop, out of Fanny Fern by Jack Hawkins. The son of Mount Vernon should give a good account of himself in Inyo, if breeding and appearance are any criterion of a stallion.

Fox has signed again this season to ride the horses in the stable of the Richmond, Ky., turfman, Mr. W. R. Letcher, who, in addition to Longalight, Kate Malone and Rosemont, his well known tried performers, will have in his string some well bred and promising two-year-olds. Although Fox's name is omitted from Goodwin Bros.' list of winning jockeys, he won quite a number of good races last season, his taking of numerous long shot events at Washington Park, Chicago, being one of the features there. He rides with good judgment and is a fine finisher.

Pike Barnes and his valet, Horace Jackson, have left for California, the famous lightweight having engaged to ride for E. J. Baldwin this season at a salary of $8000. Barnes will appear at the Memphis, races where he will ride for E. S. Gardner, who has the second call on his services. The Times Democrat of the 26th ult. makes the above remarks. Evidently the colored crack lightweight is getting the bighead. There is an old Latin saying familiar to most people: *Facilis est decensus averni.* Barnes might with advantage study it. The end does not seem far distant.

As the dam of El Rio Rey, Emperor of Norfolk, The Czar, Duchess of Norfolk, and a number of other less famous but all good racers, Marian is beyond question the most famous broodmare living, and is priceless so far as her owner is concerned. And yet her sire, Malcolm, by Bonnie Scotland, perished meanly in a cellar in Chicago not so very long ago. Neglected and forgotten, the grandsire of El Rio Rey on the maternal side was kept in this hole a long time before death came to his relief. With any chance he might have been one of the famous sires of the age.

The Live Stock Record has the following:

Wanted.—I am commissioned to buy a horse that can run half mile heats in fifty seconds or less on half mile track (not an association track), not over six years, gelding preferred, no blemishes, must be cheap. Address, TOM WALLACE, Shelbyville, Ky.

That above should suit plenty of our short-horsemen who could sell a few of that kind and would probably have a better left if the purchaser wished to match him.

The Waldo Racing Park, Kansas City, has been sold under a deed of trust by William H. Lucas, trustee, to John I. Blair for $11,000. The deed of trust was given to secure notes given by David Waldo and others for money loaned. At one time a fabulous sum was offered for this tract of land, but the Waldos refused it, demanding $2,000 an acre for the property, which is six miles southeast of Westfort. In May, 1887, an option was given on this land for $1,500,000. The deal afterwards went through. John I. Blair has also purchased the Kansas City, Mastin Park and Westfort Railroad, which leads to Waldo Park, at trustee's sale for $5,600.

Dr. George Beerman, of Berlin, and Mr. Tappan, an American trainer, who has been with H. Moessinger, of Frankfort on-the-Main, are in the States, intending to buy twenty or thirty high stepping roadsters and ten trotters with records better than 2:30 and one able to beat 2:20. Only stallions and mares are wanted, as geldings have no chance for the richest prizes. Fashionable pedigree is not appreciated in Germany as in this country. Speed, staying qualities and good behavior in the animal are all the foreigners are up to yet. Dr. Beerman offered $10.000 for Geneva S. but "Knap" wants $15,000. This great mare is enjoying a let up, unblanketed, under her owner's care at Red Bank, N. J.

The Hon. T. J. Megibben, President of the Latonia Jockey Club, died after only a fortnight's illness, and was buried last week. his funeral at Cynthiana being attended by most of Kentucky's celebrated racing men. The late Mr. Megibben was 59 years old. He was one of Kentucky's wealthiest men, and also one of the most popular. Some years ago he started his breeding farm near Cynthiana, and purchased Springbok as lord of the harem. He had a lot of good broodmares, and besides racing a few horses with his brother James, sold yearlings for large figures every year. Audrain, who won the second Hindoo Stake at Latonia, now the Latonia Derby, was one of his best horses, but when at his best, went blind and was retired.

It looks now as though Aubine and Geneva S., would practically have the big 2:20 purses at their mercy next season, as they can surely trot in 2:17, and there seems to be nothing else in their class capable of beating them both being game as well as fast. Geneva S., is still owned by "Knap" McCarthy and will be trained next season. McCarthy thinks a great deal of this mare, believing her to be good for a record of 2:16, or better, and this was well illustrated a short time since when he refused a cash offer of $10,000 for her from Mr. John Shepard of Boston. McCarthy cannot train the mare himself on account of his being trainer of the runners belonging to Mr. D. D. Withers, he will let some friend do this, but he will appear behind her on race days when the purses are large, and handle the ribbons himself.

Last week a friend of the well-known pool seller, Lowry, who was Ira E. Bride's partner last year, has been staying in Lexington. He says in the Times Democrat that Lowry cleared no less than $70,000 last year, although he commenced the season with only $3000. His profits were principally derived from his commissions, but he also struck several "good things" during his rounds, which paid him handsomely. He is now at his home in Pittsburg, but will be with Bride again this year. The most successful meeting he attended last season was that of the Kentucky Horse Breeders' Association, when, during its five days' trotting, he sold $500,000 worth of pools. Lowry is only thirty years old, and his career promises to be fully as successful as that of either Dr. Underwood, or the late lamented Rob Cathcart.

The other day, Mr. Ed Graves, a well known gentleman rider of Lexington, and Isaac Murphy, the noted colored jockey, got into a dispute at the association track over two colts, one owned by Graves and the other by Murphy. It was finally agreed to run them a quarter of a mile, although the track was deep with mud. They each rode his own colt, and the race was on at once. It was a close contest every foot of the way, Graves winning in a desperate fight by a short head. Both riders were literally covered with mud, and Murphy was deeply chagrined at being defeated by an amateur rider, while, of course, Graves was correspondingly elated. Murphy is not at all satisfied with the result of the race, and when the track gets good another match between his colt and Graves' will possibly come off.

Among the horses that take a turn out South every day those that frequent the roads recognize the Electioneer four-year-old Electwood, with Charles Stiles holding the reins. He is a smooth-going young horse, and will be out for the money after his season. In conversation with his owner a few days ago says the Horseman he told why he put some money in the get of Electioneer. "A few years ago," he said, "I bought three Sultan colts and sent them to Kentucky. While they were eating their heads off Marvin came over with a stable of Electioneers, Manzanita being in the party. I played against her a couple of times, and when she came back again the following year it looked to me as if Patron could throw her down at St. Louis. You know the result, Palo Alto also made it interesting for me when he defeated C. F. Clay, Charley Hogan, Albert France, and Libby S. I was advised to take my money out, but could not believe that a four-year-old could upset such a field. Now I know different, and have a horse I think pretty well of, by the same sire."

One of the busiest men in town is Dr. Harry Carpenter. Last Sunday, I glanced through his well appointed infirmary on Golden Gate Avenue and was surprised to see how neatly and carefully the stable had been supplied with all the latest appliances and surgical instruments, etc., necessary in such a commodious establishment. A well arranged operating table is so made that with no trouble a horse can be safely and securely laid on it without throwing the horse, or running any other risk while the city ambulance wagon which is in Dr. Carpenter's care would insure no unnecessary risks while bringing horses to his stable. Dr. Carpenter last Sunday had in his stables several horses well known to racegoers, viz., Bay Rose whose leg is so far improved that he will be able to stand a season, Jim Duffy the chestnut sprinter who has been artistically fired, Elwood now used as Dr. Harry Carpenter's hack, and (imp.) Cheviot (a brother to Sir Modred) who has wintered there. Cheviot has since gone to his stud duties at Sacramento, Bay Rose to Oakland, and Jim Duffy to San Jose. The Doctor says he never keeps horses long, speedy cures procure quick payments.

The Roslyn Heights farm did not take imported Bonnie Charlie owing to his being unable to pass the Vet. Their agent has however bought Regent who is on his way out now, he is by Statesman (Young Melbourne dam by Orlando) out of The Orphan by Newminister. He was bred by T. E. Walker, Studley Castle Warwick, foaled 1877 and under John Dawson's handling he won 9 races out of 39 during his six seasons on the turf, he never started as a two year old being a biggish overgrown colt. His pedigree is a particularly good one having two Touchstone crosses through Orlando and Newminster while his grand dam was a full sister to Weathergage a Czarewich winner, and eventually runs back to a Barb mare. Regent has been used as a hunting sire for the last few seasons in Warwickshire and should be suitable for that purpose as he is a powerful good looking bay horse with black points while his having stood training for seven seasons is proof of his soundness. His pedigree as I said is exceptionally good in fact for that reason he should get more than hunters though he himself was never more than moderate second class.

Buenos Ayres is always buying high priced horses, and their local sales were said to be very heavy, yearlings being exceptionally dear. One sale, which took place the latter part of last year, gives some idea of the prices, but the final lines spoil the high priced illusion. The animals were the property of Mr. W. Kemmis, of Las Rosas, province of Santa Fe, and made the highest average yet obtained in that, or perhaps any other country. Thirty-five lots were offered for sale—twenty five colts and ten fillies. They realized the enormous total of $305,600, or an average of $8,731. Nine of the colts and two of the fillies were thoroughbreds, the remainder having in them three or four crosses of thoroughbred blood. Balmoral, a pure-bred colt by Phœnix, out of Blood Royal, topped the market with the magnificent price of $32,500. Mr. Bonoau, who will be well remembered in this country as the buyer of the unbeaten Ormonde and many other famous English horses, was the purchaser. Rockstone, a colt by Phœnix out of Faiks, fetched $25,000, and Bothwell, a colt by Phœnix out of Marie Seton, [illegible] $12,000. It may be mentioned that Marie Seton, the dam of the last named, is out of Blood Royal by Cult[illegible], and was foaled in Buenos Ayres. A half-bred filly Heart's Delight, by Phœnix, out of Blissful, sold for $13,500. It should be added in connection with these prices, that the dollar, which a few years ago was at par, is now only worth 2s.

VETERINARY.

Conducted by W. Henry Jones, M. R. C. V. S.

Subscribers to this paper can have advice through this column in all cases of sick or injured horses or cattle by sending an explicit description of the case. Applicants will send their name and address that they may be identified. Questions requiring answers by mail should be accompanied by two dollars, and addressed to W. Henry Jones, M. R. C. V. S., Olympic Stables, Sutter Street, San Francisco.

Navicular Disease in Horses.

My attention having been drawn to a paragraph in the Examiner with reference to the above disease, I deem it advisable to make a few remarks to the readers of the BREEDER AND SPORTSMAN. The remarks of our contemporary are likely to mislead the majority of horse-owners. It is a well-known fact, both to veterinary surgeons and horse-owners and trainers, that navicular disease does not occur in the hind feet, hence the absurdity of dividing the nerve above the hock. Any veterinarian knows perfectly well that the division of the nerve above the hock could not possibly affect the foot, owing to various sources with which it is supplied with nerve power.

Navicular disease may be produced by hereditary pre-disposition, and from the result of hard work over hard metalled roads; also from the result of bad shoeing.

The first indications of the disease are, a disinclination of the animal to travel with his usual freedom; the feet become hot, and the horse shows febrile symptoms. The lameness, when it has become apparent, shows itself more in going down an incline or a hill. In the stable he will point one foot then the other, endeavoring to take the weight off and so relieve himself from pain.

It is very seldom curable by any external remedy. Should the horse be a young one, it would be advisable to keep him on soft ground, and by so doing avoid concussion. Having tried for several years all sorts of remedial treatment, I have come to the conclusion that "neurotomy" (the division of the meta-carpal nerve) is the best remedy.

The only risk after the operation, is that the foot below the division of the nerves is devoid of all sensation, and that the animal may be pricked by the smith and would not feel any pain. The probable result will be suppuration will supervene, and in a few days the hoof will slough off. Many cases are put down to navicular disease which do not exist. I would advise all horse-owners before having their horses operated upon, to have them examined by a duly qualified veterinary surgeon, and not rely on the word of the charlatan, whose name is legion.

W. HENRY JONES,
Olympic Stables, Sutter St., S. F. M. R. C. V. S.

Dr. Stimpson's Veterinary Infirmary.

Last Saturday, being in Oakland, I called at Dr. Stimpson's Infirmary, 19th St., Oakland, and luckily found the doctor at home, and was courteously conducted through his well appointed infirmary and stables. The infirmary was, of course, fitted out with all the latest improvements and devices suitable and necessary for medical purposes. Dr. Stimpson, who is quite a trotting horseman, had in his stables among other patients, Longworth, the well known Sidney pacer, who obtained a four-year-old record of 2:19 last year. He has been fired on his fore legs and the job has been done in Dr. Stimpson's best style, for though, of course, the traces of the iron are plainly visible, the work has been very effectively done and it is only a few days before he will be in work again. Dr. Stimpson is now the owner of Shamrock (a black son of Buccaneer) who obtained his record of 2:25 when two years old, and with ordinary luck will assuredly go well down in the "teens" whenever asked. His legs and feet are as sound and fresh as the day he was foaled, while his glossy black coat indicates his good healthy condition. He will serve a few mares at $100 and judging from the extreme speed produced at an early age by his sire, Buccaneer, and especially with the Flaxtail cross below it, the Doctor will be inundated with mares. Electo, another of Stimpson's horses, a beautifully shaped three year old Antevolo, having all the racy, thoroughbred appearance of his sire, with just the same easy, pure gait. On his dam's side Electo is by Capt. Webster, sire of the dam of Adonis 2:14 Dr. Stimpson has wisely limited the youngster to 15 mares at $50. The last horse seen was a powerfully built pure bay, with short black legs. He is one of the most stylish Cleveland Bays ever seen in California. He was imported from Yorkshire, the home of the Cleveland, after a successful career in the show ring at the Yorkshire and other big shows (fairs) there. His color and size, combined with his brilliant shape and gentle disposition, should make him worth his weight in gold for getting good, honest, gentle carriage horses. Dr. Stimpson is breeding, among others, two mares to his horse Shamrock, which should produce flyers, one of which is Jenny O. Jones, record 3:30, trotting; one-half mile running 51 seconds. She is by Hubbard (a son of Planet, sire of Dame Winnie) out of a Gen. Taylor mare, she out of a Belmont mare; and the other is by Newland's Hambletonian, out of a Langford mare.

A Daniel Come to Judgment.

EDITOR BREEDER AND SPORTSMAN—I clip the following from the Mirror and Farmer:

"I fear," says a practical horseman, "some breeders will go wrong on this thoroughbred nonsense, and until Gov. Stanford produces trotters from other stallions than Electioneer, it will be better not to use thoroughbred blood. Piedmont, 2:18½, is better bred than Electioneer, but his success in this line is not assured."

It will be of interest to breeders to learn that Piedmont is a better bred horse than Electioneer, but the funny part of it is that the discovery has been made by a man who is down on "thoroughbred foolishness." As Hambletonian sired one and Almont the other, it won't require much argument to show that on the side of his sire, at least, Electioneer will not have to take a back seat. Now as to their dams, this genius, who is afraid of thoroughbred blood in the trotter, declares that Mag Ferguson, by Mambrino Chief, out of a *thoroughbred mare*, when bred to Almont, produced a better bred foal than was the son of Hambletonian and Green Mountain Maid. The man who can swallow Mag Ferguson and not gag at the thoroughbred in her, can come pretty near to taking Dame Winnie for a trotter. Her dam being entirely thoroughbred, and her sire a son of Mambrino Paymaster, out of a common mare, it would be interesting to know where the dam of Piedmont gets the blood that makes her a better bred trotting mare than Green Mountain Maid. As a fact, according to Wallace's Trotting Register, Mag Ferguson was just 11-16 thoroughbred and 5-16 unknown.

To add to the absurdity of the "practical horseman's" position, we should note the fact that Piedmont's paternal grandam, Kate Darling, belonged to the unknowns. To a man up a tree, it would look as though the fact that Electioneer can get trotters from thoroughbreds, and Piedmont can't, were due to some other cause than Piedmont's superior breeding.

DENVER.

The Chicago Sale.

Chicago January, 15, 1890.

EDITOR BREEDER AND SPORTSMAN:—Among the many entries received during the past week to the Kidd, Edmonson and Morse great fine horse combination sale at Chicago, March 17 to 23, is Judge Hayes 4429, by Robert McGregor 2:17½; dam Luna (record 2:39½) by Almont 33; 2nd dam Sallie Tee by Alexander's Abdallah; 3rd dam Kate Crockett (the dam of Lula 2:14¾) by imp Hooton. Judge Hayes is owned by Col. Crockett of Waukegan, Ill., and is a horse of remarkable finish and beauty. He has never been trained, but undoubtedly has the ability or capacity to trot very fast. His breeding entitles him to rank as one of the best and most prepotent bred horses in America. It is seldom so fine an individual and so stout a bred horse is offered to the public. In the show ring he has the best record of any horse in Illinois. Col. Crockett will also sell at the same time Flaxman 10148 by Lexington Wilkes 4878 (recently bought by J. I. Case, Racine, for $10,000); dam Sallie Tee by Alexanders' Abdallah, 15; 2nd dam Katie Crockett, dam of Lula 2:14¾, by imp Hooton.

The sale now promises to be very large, both of light harness and draft horses. Several large importers of draft horses have expressed their intention of making consignments to the sale, and this department as well as the trotting is enjoying a boom.

Yours truly,
KIDD, EDMONSON & MORSE.

THE KENNEL.

Dog owners are requested to send for publication the earliest possible notices of whelps, sales, names claimed, presentations and deaths, in their kennels, in all instances writing plainly names of sire and dam and of grandparents, colors, dates and breed.

Pacific Coast Field Trials.

The seventh field meeting of the Pacific Coast Field Trial Club held at Bakersfield, on January 20th, 21st, 22nd and 23rd was different in some respects from preceding gatherings of the club. The generally prevalent influenza had placed several of the most prominent members of the club upon their backs in bed. Others were not sufficiently recovered to make it safe for them to attend. Still others, though present, were yet suffering from the weakness and general bad feeling which follows "la grippe." Many familiar faces were missed, some of them being those of men who have always attended the trials, and whose presence has been most enjoyable. Joe and Henry Bassford could not be present. The former because of the prevalent malady—the other because there are now six in his family instead of five. William Schreiber, most anxious to attend, did not dare set at defiance the orders of his physician.

N. E. White, in universal demand, was detained by death in the family. W. W. Foote could not forsake important interests in a case on trial. L. J. Rose Jr. was also kept away by business interests. Sam Meriwether, living in far away New York, was present only in spirit, and the list might be greatly prolonged if it was not pleasanter to write of the sunshiny side of the affair than of the glowering aspects. If some rare ones were away, some of those who did attend partially atoned for the absentees by an exhuberance of spirits and hearty enjoyment of all the sport offered, that helped to lift all their friends to a plane upon which enthusiasm was possible.

That magnificent specimen of manly development, P. D. Linville, was careering about on a fine black horse, giving vent to screeches that could be heard for miles, ordering people about in an imperious way that was superb, and generally filling the office of marshal in incomparable style.

Lots of new men were on hand, and it is no discredit to the old timers to write that the new hands are keen as briars both at shooting and with dogs. Porter Ashe, with all his bonhomie, pervaded two days. Austin B. Sperry could not help being sardonic, even though his pointer puppy Count Dick did make a brilliant race. Andrew Jackson forsook his Napa soda heaven, and proved himself a rare pedestrian—walking for several days with that easy carriage and springy step which indicates an accomplished tramper. F. B. Dexter, from Fresno, smooth, pretty as a picture and shrewd as anybody, amused himself in the daytime, and in the evening sang "Annie Rooney." J. W. Harper from Suisun, not the shortest man in the company, had one eye out for points and the others alert for cotton-tails, of which several were in sight all the time. Harper hired out as driver to a reporter for nothing in particular, and it is only his meed to write that he is a crack driver as well as splendid company.

Clarence A. Haight, after many years of threats, did actually attend the trials, and in future years will be in demand both for his general jollity, and the dainty tenor voice. J. M. Kilgarif, au fait in most sports, is now an authority on field trials. Ramon E Wilson, after repeated failures in attempts to see a trial, at last can say that he knows what they are. A. B. Truman insouciant as ever, kept up a hot pace.

M. H. Drummond left Davisville to mourn while he watched with keen eyes every movement of dogs and judges. John Hughes from Capay, not obtrusive, but as courteous as possible, impressed himself upon all whom he met as a rare good 'un. The list of new men is a long one, and of each it may be written that he is a sportsman, a gentleman and the best of company. Of such were C. Binnse from New York, J. S. Dunham from Stockton, Wm. Dormer and Horace Lawrence from this city, Uncle Robert Liddle, John Lakeman from London, Eng., H. L. Love, L. J. Miller and W. E Saunders from Fresno, Charles Studarus from Routiers, P. W. Treat from Davisville, and others. The judges, Messrs. W. C. Nelson, D. M. Pyle and I. N. Aldrich, did their best, and it was a good attempt. Mr. Nelson showed himself the keen, thoroughly posted, cool hand. He saw everything, knew what it was worth, and was unreserved in his judgments. His associates were quite as painstaking, and the judgments, as a whole, met general approval.

The field trialers were accommodated by Mr. A. O. Thoms in his newly finished and beautiful hotel, the Ingleside. Nice rooms, scrupulously kept, a fine table, every convenience and the jolliest most engaging of landlords make the Ingleside the ideal hotel. As usual the rates were kept at a most moderate figure, as were the livery charges by that quaintest of characters, Mr. Dan A. Leonard, who has always provided the horses and carriages for the club. Adjacent to friend Thoms' Hotel, and communicating with it by sundry electric wires, is the hall of the Students and Sportsman's Club, a very handsome, large, elegantly furnished apartment where the gentlemen of Bakersfield meet in nightly vigils, and to which all visitors were welcomed during trial week. There by a huge brick fireside, the stories were told, the triumphs re-enacted, and unlimited numbers of Thoms' dainty rejuvenators absorbed.

Bakersfield is not yet rebuilt, and a few of the visitors had perforce to cast themselves upon the hospitality of citizens. It need not be said that the draft was honored. Mr. W. E. Houghton sheltered several. Mr. Richard Seymour resigned his elegant rooms to the Marshal. Mrs. Webb was fortunate in sheltering Clarence Haight and Mr. Broder, and so it went.

The usual cordial welcome was extended by Mr. Houghton, Mr. Henry Borgwardt, Messrs. Ed and Harry Lechner, Richard Seymour and Dan Miller, Dan Leonard, I. L. Miller, and the other noblemen to whose good graces the club is indebted for so much, and whose hearty sympathy and kindly co-operation makes a visit to Bakersfield a time to be remembered.

On Tuesday evening of field-trial week, the Trials Club held its annual meeting in the hall of the Students and Sportsman's Club, and after the transaction of routine business, the following officers were chosen for the current year; J. G. Edwards, President; Austin B. Sperry, first vice-President; M. H. Drummond, 2d vice-President; H. H. Briggs, 313 Bush Street, S. F., Secretary; J. Kilgarif, Treasurer. Executive Committee—C. N. Post, D. M. Pyle, J. S. Dunham, J. M. Bassford and William Schrieber.

The club decided to hold next year's field trials in Bakersfield, beginning on the third Monday of January, 1891, and voted their thanks to the citizens of Bakersfield and to the members of the Student and Sportsman's Club for the courteous treatment extended. The following new members were elected: R. Porter Ashe of San Francisco, Andrew Jackson of Napa, A. M. Wilder of Honolulu, J. M. Kilgarif of San Francisco, Robert Liddle of San Francisco, Austin B. Sperry of Stockton, Charles W. Binsse of New York, Fred B. Dexter of Fresno, and William Dormer of San Francisco.

Of the dogs which were run, several are familiar to readers. In the Derby the winner Salina showed herself a rarely keen, quick, tasty and independent animal. Her breaker was necessarily absent during her race, and Judge Post, but slightly acquainted with the animal, was compelled to handle her. She is a medium weight, nicely coated, pretty bitch and fit for any Derby Company. Second went to Sankey a pretty mover, free and merry and showing much bird sense. Sankey had had most of his handling at the hands of his owner Mr. Hughes, but as Geo. W. Bassford owned his field trial qualities he preferred to handle the dog, rather to his disadvantage it was thought. The winner of third, Stephanie, has not the rare caution and high tension of Salina, but will doubtless develope into a cracker.

Of the non-winners, the choice was Mr. Auerbach's beautiful Lissome—not yet at herself. Lissome is a pretty worker, and with work on birds will make a fine hunting dog.

In the aged stake the average quality of performance was high.

Sunlit, the winner, ran almost faultlessly, being positive yet cautious, showing nice style, good pace in the open and the rarest judgment when on birds. Her work in her two latter heats was unexceptionable in every respect, and would have beaten ninety-nine good dogs in every hundred.

Second went to Patti Croxteth T., probably the best pointer, bar Old Black Joe, that has run in California recently. Patti works like an English setter, cuts her ground up systematically, in fine style, is fast, uniform in range and independent, an animal to be proud of anywhere.

The surprise of the stake was Mr. A. B. Sperry's pointer puppy Count Dick, fifteen months old. Uncertainty about his age prevented his entry to the Derby where he should have run. Count Dick, despite his youth and the exceedingly warm company in which he was placed, divided third with credit. A few more months will give him courage and independence. He now has pretty much everything else he needs.

Half of third went to Sirius, a grand dog, perfectly trained, with fine nose, style, range and pace. In his first heat Sirius was perfect, but he then let down, went off in nose, became rank and wholly unlike himself, and got all he deserved. The two unplaced dogs did not meet expectations. Nestor, as grand a mover as any dog, finely trained, in fine condition, raced about like a winner, but was deficient in nose. He should have pointed more birds—had fair opportunities and failed to do it. Dick Foote, upon whose showing in training high hopes had been predicted, was careless; off in nose and nothing like so fast as last year. It was hoped that President J. G. Edwards would be present both because he is a splendid presiding officer and because he has a way of keeping things moving wherever he is. The field trial grounds were in splendid condition and birds were plenty enough. The grounds have often been described, and are, as Judge Nelson often remarked, "the best in America."

The first stake run was

THE DERBY—MONDAY, FIRST SERIES.

SANKEY—LISSOME.—G. W. Bassford's pointer Sankey, handled by owner, and R. H Auerbach's setter Lissome, handled by M. D. Walter, were put down at 11.08 on Section 18, not far from the Red House in a willow-lined slough. After a little spin Sankey found a bevy, and was steady to shot, Walter also shooting, and Lissome being steady. On a back cast Lissome made two flushes across what little wind there was, and Sankey pointed one of the birds killed when the bevy flushed, and to order retrieved. Lissome, a little rank, flushed a pair and drew to a pretty point, was steady to wing and gun, moved on and again pointed, Sankey a little distance away, also finding a bird and pointing it. Both dogs were growing wild. Soon on a salt grass ridge, Sankey drew up on point; Liss refused to back, ran in and pointed the same bird, but left the point and cast away. Sankey remained steady, and when Bassford killed, the dog was staunch. Through the few remaining minutes of the heat, Lissome scored two inexcusable flushes and two good points; Sankey three points, a refusal to back and a chase. Sankey had the pace, range, better style, and more bird sense. Up at 12.25, Sankey winning.

STEPHANIE—BEN HARRISON.—Stephanie, owned by the California Kennels and handled by M. D. Walter; Ben Harrison, owned and handled by Charles Studaurs. Down at 1:20 after lunch. Neither was up to a very high mark. Stephanie was over-cautious, and had almost to be lifted along. Ben Harrison hunted close to his handler, and did not seem to have a first rate nose. A bevy soon flushed wild from scrubby willows, and on the trail Stephanie pointed a single bird, and then another, being steady to wing both times. After a long round without finding in low alkali grass, Ben Harrison scored two pretty points and behaved nicely to wing and gun. Stephanie then drew up on a single, Ben backing to order, and both being steady to wing. Sent along, Ben flushed two birds, and at 2:30 the dogs were ordered up, Stephanie winning The heat might well have been shortened.

SALINA—ROSE.—Salina owned and handled by Judge C. N. Post and Rose handled by her owner, George W. Bassford, were cast off at 2 50. The race was highly interesting, although one sided. Salina instantly demonstrated herself to be one of the phenomenons of the year. Clean cut, spirited, always looking for birds, a tasty mover, although without stern action, high headed and it must be admitted hard headed. Salina showed herself almost a second Sweetheart. Rose was a little rank, although a very handsome worker.

Birds were scarce, Salina being able to score but one good point and being unsteady to wing. Rose made game once but when the bird ran the little bitch broke in. Running together in low grass several birds flushed wild by the dogs and at 3:35 Salina was given the heat.

TUESDAY—SECOND SERIES.

SANKEY—STEPHANIE.—Stephanie was given her head by her handler Walter and did excellently. She went squarely up to two covey points and picked up three singles nicely. Sankey was better handled than in his first heat, and nailed five single birds handily. Sankey was better in pace, range and style, but on the score it was anybody's race, the judges deciding in favor of Sankey after fifty minutes' work.

SALINA a bye, being the odd dog in the order of running.

THIRD SERIES.

SANKEY—SALINA.—At 1:30, after a luncheon enlivened by all the deviltry that Marshal Linville, Judge Nelson, and the other small boys could think of, Sankey and Salina were cast off to run for first money. Both were brilliant, but reckless. Salina cut out her work in splendid wide casts, and stayed out, after a long round, pinning a single prettily, moved on and nailed another, Sankey refusing to back, running in and pointing the same bird. Then Sankey pointed a single bird, and stood to game. Sent along, Sankey pointed uncertainly, but was staunch when the bird was flushed. After a riotous race down wind, during which a dozen birds flushed before the dogs, the brace was taken up and Salina given the heat at 1.53.

FOURTH SERIES.

SANKEY—ROSE.—At 2:13 after the rulable rest second money was run off. Sankey being so clearly superior, and scouring three nice points in such snappy fashion as to win out of hand. Rose did some nice backing in the heat. The brace ran thirty two minutes when Sankey was given the race and second money.

WEDNESDAY—FIFTH SERIES.

STEPHANIE—ROSE.—At 10:30 A. M. on Wednesday third was settled, Stephanie showing the caution and not making errors or being rank. In twenty five minutes of pretty work, Stephanie established a clear lead and was given the heat and rhird.

SUMMARY.

Bakersfield, Cal, Jan. 21, 1890. Derby.—Pacific Coast Field Trial Club's seventh annual Derby. Open to all setters and pointers whelped on or after January 1, 1888. Entrance $20. Forfeit $5. Closed May 1, 1890, with twenty-one nominations.

Geo. W. Bassford's white and lemon pointer dog Sankey, by Point—Blossom,	beat	R. H. Auerbach's white and black English setter bitch Lissome, by Loadstone—Janet.
California Kennel's orange Belton English setter bitch Stephanie, by Harold—Sweetheart,	beat	Charles Studarus' white and red cross-bred setter dog Ben Harrison, by Sport—Fanny.
California Kennel's orange Belton English setter bitch Salina, by Harold—Sweetheart,	beat	Geo. W. Bassford's white and lemon pointer bitch Rose, by Point—Blossom.

II.

Sankey beat Stephanie.

III.

Salina beat Sankey and won first.

IV.

Sankey beat Rose and won second.

V.

Stephanie beat Rose and won third.

1st. Salina.
2nd. Sankey.
3rd. Stephanie.

PREVIOUS WINNERS.

Walltown Timber, 1883	Butte Bow (pointer)	1
	Beatrice (Red setter)	2
	Bow Jr. (pointer)	3
White Rock, 1884	Trix (cross bred setter)	1
	Sweetheart (Enslish setter)	2
	Lemmie B. (pointer)	3
Point Reyes, 1885	Tom Pinch (pointer)	1
	Solano B. (pointer)	2
	Victor II (pointer)	3
Hanford, 1886	Shot (English setter)	1
	Climax (pointer)	2
	But two starters in stake.	
Bakersfield, 1888	Sunlit (English setter)	1
	Point (pointer)	2
	Haroldine (English setter)	3
	Blossom (pointer)	3
Bakersfield, 1889	Old Black Joe (pointer)	1
	Lottie B. (pointer)	2
	Nestor (pointer)	3

ALL-AGE STAKE.

SIRIUS—NESTOR.—Sirius handled by Wm. DeMott, and Nestor by Geo. T. Allender. Sirius ran a faultless race, although Nestor had the better pace and style. Nestor's range, though wide at times, was not uniform, and when in cover, he did not slow down sufficiently to enable him to keep his nose well ahead of him. Sirius soon pointed, and then again, Nestor backing to order, and both being steady, Sirius retrieving perfectly. Sent along in sedge where birds were running about, Sirius did some grand work in trying to head the birds, but could not stop them, and Nestor running in, flushed several. Nestor then made a swing along the edge of the sedge, and pointed nicely. Ordered on, Nestor again drew to point, moved on when the bird ran, and finally located it and stood to wing. Sirius, meanwhile, was working out a lot of cover, but could find no birds. At 11.40 Sirius was given the heat. Few dogs could have beaten his work.

PATTI CROXTETH T.—SUNLIT.—The race was the sensation of the trials. Patti was handled by Allender and Sunlit by Post. Both men were keen to win, and soon saw there was little choice between the dogs. The handlers lost their tempers, cross-fired at one another, the judges and everybody else. The heat really began at 1:24 after lunch, although the dogs ran twenty minutes before lunch, in nice cover, where scattered birds were plenty, and such a rattling succession of points has rarely been seen. Sunlit was marvellous in her certainty and judgment, two points in which she had the better of Patti. The work was so lively that no detailed report of each point could be kept. Sunlit found a bevy and rolled up eleven points on singles. Patti scored eleven good points on singles. Sunlit backed honestly; Patti at times had to be steadied on back by her handler. Sunlit made a slow, bad find on a dead bird. Patti's handler refused to kill a bird, and the bitch was ordered to retrieve a bird killed by Post, which she did indifferently. Both were quick and snappy among birds. The race was a close thing. At 2 o'clock, after one hour and forty minutes of actual running, Sunlit was given the heat.

DICK FOOTE—COUNT DICK.—Dick Foote handled by De Mott and Count Dick by Walter were cast off at 2:20. Dick Foote was heedless, rank, careless in cover, off in nose and not worth a cent in the early part of the heat. Count Dick moved about tastily, but was puppyish and lacked judgment. After twenty minutes of flushing by Dick Foote, a false point and a refusal to back, during which time Count Dick picked up three nice points and showed steadier to wing and gun Dick Foote settled down a little but could not over come the lead gained by his opponent. At three o'clock Dick was given the heat.

THURSDAY.—SECOND SERIES.

SIRIUS—SUNLIT.—A prettier pair is rarely seen, but as soon as the dogs were started it was seen that Sunlit was maintaining her extraordinary form, while Sirius had gone off at all points, slowed down and lost his caution and much of his nose, forgotten his bird sense, and was in all respects a different dog to what he was in the first series.

At 10.20, upon the bevy used on the first morning, the dogs were cast off. Lit had the foot of the race, and brave old Si was compelled to do more backing than he is accustomed to. Sirius is a perfectly honest dog, honors a back at any distance, and was handicapped by the fact. Lit soon scored a covey point, and then scored eight singles and a pretty retrieve. Sirius was credited with five good single points and perfect brace work. At 11:15 Sunlit was given the heat.

COUNT DICK a bye because he was the odd dog.

THIRD SERIES.

SUNLIT—COUNT DICK.—Count Dick was like the historic character who fell out of the balloon, he "wasn't in it." Sunlit had her mind with her, worked smartly and with perfect judgment, and won hands down. Count Dick made a nevy stand, but the only way he could catch Sunlit was to go the other way. Down at 12 and up at 12.14, with Sunlit a winner.

FOURTH SERIES.

COUNT DICK—PATTI CROXTETH T.—After a side treat to select a dog to run with Count Dick for second, in which Patti Croxteth T. beat Sirius, Patti and Count Dick were sent off for second.

Patti was all herself, worked as daintily and with as much dash as a dog could and although Count Dick held on bravely for an hour and a half, he could not level the scores, and Patti was given the heat and second money.

FIFTH SERIES.

COUNT DICK—SIRIUS.—The last race for third between Count Dick and Sirius was run for fifty minutes and then suspended. The dogs were about even, Count Dick perhaps having a shade the best of it. In the evening the judges placed the dogs equal third and the trials ended.

SUMMARY.

Bakersfield, January 27, 1890.—All-Age Stake. Pacific Coast Field Trial's Seventh Annual All-Age Stake; open to all setters and pointers. Entrance $20. Closed January 21st, with six nominations.

Thos. Bennet's orange and white English setter Sirius, by Sportsman—Sweetheart	beat	William Schreiber's white and lemon pointer dog Nestor, by Gladsome—Forest Queen II.
California Kennel's orange belton English setter bitch Sunlit by Sportsman—Sweetheart	beat	A. B. Truman's white and liver pointer bitch Patti Croxteth T., by Croxteth—Patti M.
A. B. Sperry's white and liver pointer dog Count Dick by James K.—Donna	beat	W. W. Foote's black, white and tan English setter dog Dick Foote, by Royal Duke II.—Adam's Nelly.

II.

Sunlit beat Sirius.

III.

Sunlit beat Count Dick and won first.

IV.

Patti Croxteth T. beat Count Dick and won second.

V.

Count Dick and Sirius placed equal third by the judges.

1st Sunlit.
2d Patti Croxteth T.
3d Count Dick. / Sirius

PREVIOUS WINNERS.

Walltown Timber, 1883	Dôre (Gordon setter)	1
	Beautiful Queen (pointer)	2
	Belle (red setter)	3
White Rock, 1884	Bow Jr. (pointer)	1
	Beautiful Queen (pointer)	2
	Ola (English setter)	
	Mountain Boy (pointer)	3
	Lemme B. (pointer)	
Point Reyes, 1885	Royal Duke II. (English setter)	1
	Beautiful Queen (pointer)	2
	Janet (English setter)	3
Hanford, 1886	Sweetheart (English setter)	1
	Lassie (pointer)	2
	Tom Pinch (pointer)	3
Bakersfield, 1888	Point (pointer)	1
	Harold (English setter)	2
	Royal Duke II. (English setter)	3
	Frail (pointer)	3
Bakersfield, 1889	Old Black Joe (pointer)	1
	Sirius English setter)	2
	Sunlit English setter)	3

Sunlit Forever!

Hurrah! for little Sunlit. To be Sirius! She is the dog star. I am Posted if I am no judge! Last year at Bakersfield I looked on Sunlit as the greatest natural hunter on trial, but Black Joe was a born pointer—a diamond of the first water. Allender, that prince of trainers, had him fit to run for a king's ransom. The bitch Sunlit lacked the bird sense. If told last year to look in likely places for birds to range, no barren plains he would cover with his eyes, his educated brain taught him to use his nose except in cover. He did not range away from, but to cover. On a point was as staunch as iron.

All that Sunlit wanted then, I could see, was experience, the great and sometimes cruel master. Last year "Lit", as the jovial judge calls his treasure, was not steadfast in a point, but would leave her point, no doubt to relocate the moving bird, which to my mind is the acme of dog sense. Some dogs hunt for themselves, others for their masters. Those dogs who keep track of the game command the situation.

I am glad the rain did not dampen that ardor of men and dogs. In front of my roaring fire, I longed to see you all and grasp you by the hands; all hands afield grow young again, and discuss the merits of dogs, horses and men, and feel that touch of Dame Nature's hand which makes the whole world akin.

For precocity, as a rule (not *to* rule), give me a fair representative of the sex. Sunol holds the trotting scepter among horses, Sunlit holds it among dogs. Hurrah! for Sunlit! May many sons and daughters light up "our friend," the judges house and hearth, as did in bygone days, Sweethearts!

P. J. SHAFTER.

OLEMA, January 28, 1890.

A joint meeting of committees from the Pacific Kennel Club and the California Kennel Club was held on Wednesday evening last at 436 Montgomery street. those present being Messrs. J. B. Lewis, Chairman; Clarence A. Haight, Secretary; Thomas J. O'Keeffe, J B. Martin, A. B. Truman and J. M. Crane. Some desultory discussion of the financial condition of the clubs was had, but no conclusion reached. Another meeting will be held on Monday evening next at the same place.

Names Claimed.

J. C. Nattrass, Clearbrook, Wash., claims the name Glaucus for red Irish setter dog puppy, whelped Nov. 6, 1889, by Nat Glencho (Champion Glencoe—Maid)—Judith (Champion Brush—Lucille).

Aurora, for bitch puppy, same litter.
Diana, for bitch puppy, same litter.
Judy Jr., for bitch puppy, same litter.

Fred A. Taft.

Mr. Fred A. Taft, of Truckee, after eight or nine years of uninterruptedly pleasant intercourse with his fellow sportsmen of California, has returned to his home in Dedham, Mass., to remain. Mr. Taft was called from Dedham to Truckee to manage the Pacific Wood and Lumber Company, an institution controlling a vast territory of timber land, and having connections all over the coast. The call implied great executive ability in Mr. Taft, and the outcome has much more than justified the wisdom of the choice. His rigid business methods, tireless activity and incessant forethought, have contributed largely to the success of the company, beside making him a marked man in business circles, and a leader in the community where he made his home. He has longed for years to leave the hardships of his position for the comforts of his staid Massachusetts home, and we congratulate him upon bringing about the change, even though we lose the wise counsel, keen perception and deep knowledge of the life-long sportsman. Few better dog trainers have ever lived, and none more enthusiastic. We hope to hear of many years spent in sunshine by our friend.

Dr. I. W. Haze'e', San Bernardino, claims the name Strictly Business for a while and lemon pointer dog whelped Aug. 9th, 1889, by Scout Croxteth—Blossom.

H. T. Payne, of Los Angeles, President of the State Sportsman's Association and the Southern California Kennel Club, has been seriously ill with the *grippe*, but under date, January 30th, writes that he is convalescent.

Virtue is not always without its tangible reward. Last Tuesday we found Port Warden Charles B. Smith in Mr. E. T. Allen's store selecting a handsome collar for Mr. Austin B. Sperry's nervy little pointer Count Dick, which divided the All-Aged Stake with Sirius. Count Dick showed himself a grand puppy, and as he is only just too old for the next puppy stake, great things may be expected from him.

THE GUN.

Postponed.

The pigeon shoot at Arbuckle has been postponed until further notice.

Trouble Bruin.

EDITOR BREEDER AND SPORTSMAN:—Cougar, wild cats and "bar" are unusually plentiful in Whatcom County, Or., this fall. Old Bruin has retired now for his winter's snooze. Next spring he will be "mosyin erreound," gaunt and hungry, in goodly numbers, and will afford the sportsmen some great "wing shooting." One or more bears are holed up near by and Sillilicum and Jay will be after them to-morrow morning. Will send the BREEDER AND SPORTSMAN an account. Over a dozen cougars have been seen and killed in this vicinity within the last month. They are hunting the deer incessantly (the congars are), making our always wild and cunning black tail deer, if possible, even more cunning.

We have only a few more days open for deer. A number of wild cats and bears have been killed this fall. Hope to send you a description of some of our cougar and other big game hunts soon.

JAY SEE EN.

The Selby Smelting and Lead Company is sending out its price lists of Standard shotgun cartridges for 1890. The list covers about all peculiarities in loading that are likely to be met, and throughout all the variations one invariable rule is met, namely, that the utmost accuracy shall prevail. For evenness, excellence, convenience and cheapness the Standards have no equals.

Says the Redwood Times-Gazette, "Uncle Nate Comstock has two deer to his credit already this year."

Our exchange should use its most virulent language in characterizing Comstock's departure from right doing. He has no right to kill deer until July 1st.

Information comes from Jackson, Amador County, that irresponsible men are slaughtering the deer driven down by the snow in numbers. One hundred and sixty does are said to have been killed within a few miles of West Point bridge in two weeks, the carcasses being left to rot. If the District Attorney and officers of Amador are so incompetent or so careless as to overlook flagrant violations of the game laws, why do not some of the sterling citizens, of who so many are to be found in that favored section, take the law into their own hands, and penalize a few of the deer killers in such manner as is likely to suggest itself to a body of indignant citizens.

There will be a grand pigeon shoot at Lathrop on Wednesday, February 12th. The first match will be at fifteen single live birds, Hurlingham style. Entrance fee $7.50 Money to be divided into 40, 30, 20 and 10 per cent. prizes. The second match will be at ten single birds, 21 yards rise, use of one barrel only. Entrance fee $5. Money to be divided into 40, 30, 20 and 10 per cent. prizes. The third match will be at ten single birds, 30 yards rise, Hurlingham style. Entrance fee $5. Money to be divided into 40, 30, 20 and 10 per cent. prizes. The fourth match will be a team shoot between three members of the Stockton Club and three members of the Lathrop Club. Loosers to pay for a supper. The fifth match will be at fifteeen single clay birds and five pairs of doubles. Entrance fee $2.50. Money to be divided into 40, 30, 20 and 10 per cent. prizes. Plenty of live and clay birds will be on hand, and the public are assured of a good day's sport. Shooting to begin at 10 o'clock. Messrs. Scarlett & Howland are managers, and their success with former tournaments is sufficient guarantee that the present venture will be all that can be desired.

ATHLETICS.

Athletic Sports and Other Pastimes.

EDITED BY ARCHIPPUS,

SUMMARY.

At last the storm is at an end, but the time between now and Washington's Birthday is too short to allow the runners and walkers to get in good condition. The Athletic Committee of the Olympic Club very wisely postponed the opening of the new grounds until such time as everything will be in tip-top condition for the grand initial tournament. The Alpine Club, however, will hold its first out-door meeting on Sunday, February 16th, as the track at Harbor View, owing to its being protected by the trees, suffered but little from the effects of the heavy rains. The wheelmen and oarsmen have started in to practice, and in less than a month out door athletics will be in full blast once more. The postponed "Ladies' Night" of the Olympic Club, which will be celebrated next week, is attracting unusual interest.

RUNNERS, WALKERS, JUMPERS, ETC.

William Zehfuss, the amateur walker, has developed into a first-class boxer.

The postponed cross-country run of the Olympic Club, will take place at Milbrae to-morrow. The athletes who intend taking part in the run are requested to take the 10.30 A. M. train at Fourth and Townsend Streets. A splendid lunch will be provided by the club.

Fair's Athletic Park at Alameda will shortly be divided up into building lots. The grounds have been unoccupied for some time past owing to the new law which requires all persons giving exhibitions to take out a yearly license of $500. The owner is willing to rent the grounds very cheap, and it is a great pity that some of the flourishing Athletic clubs across the bay do not jump at the chance and lease the place. By being properly managed, the park is bound to pay, as there is every prospect of a boom in amateur athletics during the coming season.

President M. C. Giry, of the Alpine Amateur Athletic Club, has just recovered from an attack of *la grippe*.

The five-mile handicap run, which will take place in the gymnasium of the Olympic Club on Thursday evening, February 27th, promises to attract a large field of competitors. Only members of the club will be allowed to enter. Three valuable medals will be awarded. Scott and McArthur will probably not enter, which fact will cause Cooley to be placed at scratch.

It is rumored that the championship games will not come off until July 4th, as the Olympic Club intends opening its new grounds on Decoration Day.

During the coming season the O. C. will probably hold a complimentary members out-door meeting once a month.

Several runners and walkers practice daily at the Bay District track.

After this month the Alpine Club will add a couple of open events to its regular monthly programme.

There is at Present residing in the city a young Irish amateur athlete who is credited with having thrown the 16 pound hammer a distance of 110 feet. He will possibly represent one of the clubs at the next open out-door meeting.

A very large number of entries have been received for the Alpine games, which will come off at Harbor View Park on Sunday, February 16th, commencing at 1 P. M. The list will close at the club rooms, Murphy Building, at 10 o'clock this evening. Next week we will present the full list, with the handicaps attached.

A. Cooke, the champion heel and toe walker, of the Los Angeles Athletic Club, has applied for admission to the Alpine Club.

Espinosa will enter the five mile run at the Olympic Club on the 27th inst. He has been practicing hard for some weeks past and should make things warm for Cooley.

In the half and one mile runs at the coming Alpine games good time will most unquestionably be made. Cassidy, Little, Moody, Garrison, Larkey, Tank and Eldridge will be amongst the starters.

For the half mile novice walk there are a dozen entries and the judge will need to keep his eyes open.

An individual all round championship meeting will probably be held under the auspices of the P. C. A. A. A. during the coming season.

The cinder path at Berkeley is getting into good shape again and the students will soon be able to resume out-door practice.

In a few weeks the members of the Alpine Club will hold their first cross country run from the athletic grounds at Harbor View across the Presidio to the Cliff House and return. Members of other clubs will be invited to join in the run.

Frank O'Kane, of the O C, indulges in an occasional spin and he should certainly win a medal at the next open meeting.

Dave Egan informs us that he may appear on the cinder path again. He is thinking about joining the Olympic Club.

John W. Flynn thinks of entering the sprint events at the championship games.

It is thought that Lucas, the old time amateur, will make his appearance again this year. Many are of the opinion that he would beat Purcell in an all round contest.

The interest in amateur athletics is evidently increasing and before the close of 1890, many of the Pacific Coast records will have fallen by the way side.

J. W. Geoghan and V. Hancock, two well known local athletes are at present giving exhibitions of boxing, club swinging and wrestling up north. They are under engagement to appear at several theatres in Oregon and Washington Territory.

The following is the definition of novice according to the rules of the Amateur Athletic Union:

A "novice" is one who has never won a prize in any athletic competition open to the members of two or more clubs, and his status shall be determined by his record when the entries for such event closed.

According to this ruling several amateurs who have heretofore been barred out of "novice" races will in future be eligible to compete.

Several of the leading Eastern sporting journals at the present time are presenting their readers with full lists of American and English athletic records. The Turf, Field and Farm and The Spirit of the Times have been devoting considerable space to this kind of matter for some weeks past.

Professors Watson, Zellner and Johansen have been engaged by the Occidental Club to instruct the members in boxing, wrestling and gymnastics. The class nights will be Monday, Wednesday and Friday.

It is to be hoped that Professor Corbett will not be too hasty in arranging matches with some of the Eastern crack fighters. Mr. Corbett is still a very young man, and although he is possessed of considerable science and grit, he should not be too ambitious in the start. His friends regret that he ever went into the fighting business, for a pugilist is certainly an enemy to society. When Jim Corbett was engaged as boxing instructor to the Olympic Club, his social standing was never questioned, but now that he has actually descended to the level of a prize fighter it can hardly be expected that he will be received with the same *eclat* among his former society friends. Mr. Corbett is far above the calling of a common fighter, and we earnestly hope that his career as a pugilist will not be of long duration. There is still a chance for him to return to his more honorable profession.

A good many of our local athletes are unaware of the fact that a good rubbing down after exercising is just as beneficial as the exercise itself. When a man rushes into a dressing room sweating and out of breath he should always, if possible, have a friend to rub him down. No man, no matter how experienced he may be, can get into first class condition without the aid of a rubber.

IN THE SURF.

Albert Sundstrom, the champion all distance swimmer of America, died at the German Hospital on Saturday last of typhoid pneumonia, brought on by a cold contracted while giving exhibitions in the surf at the Cliff House. He has been residing on the coast about two years, during which time Pinckham, the ex-Pacific Coast champion, met with defeat at his hands on more than one occasion. Sundstrom was born in New York and was twenty-six years old at the time of his death.

It is safe to predict that an active interest will be taken in swimming during the coming year. The Terrace Club was re-organized a couple of months ago and the present members are determined to make a good showing while the season lasts. There are quite a number of excellent swimmers connected with the Lurline and Alpine Clubs, and as both organizations have their own bathing quarters, many exciting contests will doubtless be witnessed during the summer months. The three clubs will no doubt join hands and give exhibitions at intervals during the season.

AT THE OARS.

Henry Peterson, the champion oarsman of California, has commenced training and is seriously thinking about going to Australia in company with William O'Connor.

The newspaper war between Hanlan and O'Connor will most likely bring about a match between the two men at the Alameda Mole course before O'Connor sails for Australia.

Charley Long, the single sculler of the Pioneer Club, has had his shell repaired in anticipation of a match being arranged between himself and Henry Henceman of Stockton.

The Comyns Amateur four have commenced to take regular exercise in order to prepare themselves thoroughly for the coming regatta of the Pacific Rowing Association.

The Lurlines certainly deserve credit for their push and ambition. Even while the storm was at its heighest the young Lurline members were busy making preparations for coming events. Their first annual regatta will come off on Richardson's Bay during the month of May.

The Columbia Club of Oakland will enter an amateur barge four at the regatta this summer, and the knowing ones say that the crew will stand an excellent chance of carrying the championship to Oakland.

Since the split up in the crew representing the Ariel Club it is very hard to get a crew together who will train as faithfully as Shitkoff, Phelan, Coffy and Hanraham of last season's crew.

The Pacific Rowing Association will hold a monster regatta and picnic at the grounds of the Alpine Club at Harbor View during the coming summer. The matter will come before the regatta committee next week.

The Alameda Boat Club was organized on Tuesday evening last. The course will be located on the estuary, with headquarters at the foot of Chestnut St.

Oarsmen Henry Tank is training for the sprint runs of the Alpine Amateur Athletic Club. He is in splendid condition and recently ran 100 yards inside of 11 seconds.

I. I. Larkey of the Ariel Club is also a good runner and will oppose Tank on February 16th.

THE WHEELMEN.

Affairs in the wheeling world at the present time are very quiet. The boys are just beginning to realize that the rain has actually stopped, and are making preparations to wipe the rust off their wheels.

The local riders will make an effort to secure a track and training grounds of their own this season. With so many wheelmen in the field there is no reason why they should not be successful in their efforts.

The next regular meeting of the Oakland Bicycle Club will be held at the residence of J. F. Revalk, 1789 William St., Oakland, on Tuesday evening next.

LAWN TENNIS

The California Lawn Tennis Club, will hold an open handicap tournament, doubles only, on Saturday, February 22, 1890, commencing at 10 A. M., at the club grounds, southeast corner Bush and Scott streets. The first prize will be the "Gogging's Trophy" and a prize given by the club. A second prize will also be given to be played for by those defeated by the winning team. Entries close February 16, 1890. Entrance fee $1 each player. Friends of the club are cordially invited to witness these games. Luncheon will be served. Entries may be made to E. N. Bee, Secretary, 208 California street.

JOTTINGS FROM ALL OVER.

The proposed Armory of the Thirteenth Regiment, Brooklyn, N. Y., according to specifications issued, will be 400 feet long by 250 wide, and render a fifth of a mile track as well as well as a 125 yard straightaway possible.

The following list shall constitute a championship programme for associations which belong to the Amateur Athletic Union:

RULE VI.—CHAMPIONSHIP EVENTS.

Sec. 1. The annual championship events shall be as follows, unless changed by authority of the Board of Managers.

Sec. 2. Out-door field meeting.

100-yard run.
220-yard run.
440-yard run.
880-yard run.
1-mile run.
5-mile run.
1-mile walk.
3-mile walk.
2 miles, bicycle.
Pole vault for height.
Running high jump.
Running broad jump.
Throwing 16-lb. hammer.
Throwing 56-lb. weight for distance.
Putting 16 lb. shot.
120 yard hurdle, 10 flights, 3ft 6in high.
220-yard hurdle, 10 flights, 2ft 6in high.
Individual tug-of-war, unlimited weight.
Tug-of-war, 4 men, unlimited weight.

For the benefit of our readers we print a few of the most important rules recently adopted by the American Athletic Union:

RULE VII.—RECORDS.

A new record at any distance in swimming, walking, running or hurdling, in order to stand shall be timed by at least three timekeepers, and a new record at jumping, pole vaulting, or in the weight competitions shall be measured by at least three measurers.

The Amateur Athletic Union will not recognize any new record, unless a report of it is made to the Secretary of the Union, properly supported by the affidavits of the referee, timekeepers, scorers, starter or measurers, as the case may be, as to the correctness of the time, measurement, weather, hour of day and place, with signatures of at least six witnesses, including officials.

RULE XV.—TRACK MEASUREMENT.

All distances run or walked shall be measured upon a line eighteen inches outward from the inner edge of the track, except that in races on straightaway tracks the distance shall be measured in a direct line from the starting mark to the finishing line.

RULE XVI.—THE COURSE.

Each competitor shall keep in his respective position from start to finish in all races on straightway tracks, with one or more turns he shall not cross to the inner edge of the track, except when he is at least six feet in advance of his nearest competitor.

The referee shall disqualify from that event any competitor who willfully pushes against, impedes, crosses the course of, or in any way interferes with another competitor.

The referee shall disqualify from further participation in the games any contestant competing to lose, to coach, or in any way impede the chances of another competitor, either in a trial or final contest.

The finish of the course shall be represented by a line between two finishing posts, drawn across and at right angles to the sides of the track, and three feet above which line shall be placed a tape, attached at either end to the finishing posts.

The tape is to be considered the finishing line, and the order of finishing across the track line shall determine the positions of the competitors.

The rules for jumping will be given next week.

RULE XXIII—SWIMMING.

Section 1. Officials shall consist of one referee, three judges at the finish, three timekeepers, one starter, one clerk of the course, with assistants, if necessary.

Sec. 3. Duties and powers of these officials shall be the same as is prescribed for them in the foregoing rules.

Sec. 3. In the 100 yard swimming race each competitor shall stand with one or both feet on the starting line, and when the signal is given shall plunge. Stepping back either before or after the signal will not be allowed.

Sec. 4. The half-mile and one mile start shall be the same as the 100 yards, except that competitors may start in the water (tread water start) from an imaginary line.

Sec. 5. A competitor shall keep a straight course, parallel with the courses of the other competitors, from his starting station to the opposite point in the finish line. Competitors will be started ten feet apart, and each one is entitled to a straight lane of water ten feet wide from start to finish. Any contestant who when out of his own water shall touch another competitor, is liable to disqualification for that event, subject to the discretion of the referee.

Sec. 6. Each competitor shall have finished the race when any part of his person reaches the finish line.

CLUB JOTTINGS.

An important meeting of the Pacific Coast Amateur Athletic Association, was held on Thursday evening last, particulars of which will appear in our next issue.

A general meeting of the Alpine Amateur Athletic Club was held at the club rooms, Murphy Building, on Thursday evening. Final preparations were made for the coming games, and it was decided to lease the Eureka Turn Verein Hall on Powell Street, between Pine and California Streets, as permanent headquarters for the club The gymnasium is 110 feet by 44, and is 30 feet high. Several new members were elected. The club will move to its new rooms early next week.

The California Athletic Club still exists, despite Mr. Dally's effort to "break it up." The members would have attached more importance to the ex-Director's bombas had he spoken earlier in the day. To say the least, it was contemptible of Dally to prefer the charges after he discovered that he was not wanted any more on the "Board."

A very successful athletic entertainment was given by the Acme Club of Oakland on Tuesday evening last. The rooms were crowded to their utmost capacity, and perfect order prevailed throughout the entire evening. At 8 30 Tom Cleary, of the Acme Club, and Will Hogarthy, of East Oakland, stepped into the ring and opened the fun with a four-round exhibition. There were several knock-downs during the bouts. Hogarty proved himself to be cleverest of the two. Billy Gallagher, of the Acme Club, and Hugh Gallagher, of the Olympic Club of San Francisco, next gave a clever exhibition in a three-round sparring contest, in which both won considerable applause for scientific displays. J. Kitchen, Jr., the amateur heavy-weight champion boxer of the Pacific Coast, and a blacksmith from East Oakland named Mike Sullivan, followed in an exhibition of science vs. strength. Kitchen merely played with his muscular opponent, much to the amusement of the audience. W. Sharp and L. Wolf, both light-weights of the Acme Club, sparred three rather tame rounds, and when they left the ring the Master of Ceremonies announced that the next contest would be the event of the evening, which was to be a six-round match between Fred Irvin and Walter Smith for the feather-weight championship of the club, and a $50 trophy. R. McArthur, of the Olympic Club of San Francisco, acted as referee, and his club mates, Eugene Van Court and Tom McCord, as judges. The men shook hands at 9 30. The battle was a hot one from the start, and during the three first rounds Irvin was knocked down several times, and it looked as though the affair would end in a "knock out." In the fourth round Irvin recovered his wind, and attempted to do up Smith in short order. He was too weak, however, and at the end of the sixth round, referee McArthur decided that Smith had fairly won the match.

THE FARM.

Dehorning Cattle at Windsor Farm, Denver Col.

There has been and is a great controversy as to the cruelty (or otherwise) of Dehorning cattle and also as to the benefits produced by it, and lastly whether a race of polled cattle can be produced by dehorning for a few generations. In regard to the two former propositions, the experiments conducted at the Windsor farm, would tend to prove there is no pain, while a Kansas Stockman says every one wanted dehorned cattle. We quote a full description of the experiments at Denver from the Denver Republican which says:

"Windsor Farm, lying seven miles Southeast of Denver, is perhaps the model farm in Colorado if not in the West. It embraces over 1000 acres under a high state of cultivation. Stockmen and agriculturists travel for hundreds of miles to witness the remarkable system of farming and stock raising which is there carried on under the management of Mr. Willard F. Morse, of the firm of Bush & Morse, who own and conduct the wonderful ranch.

Among the celebrated features of the Windsor farm, not the least is its herd of Holstein-Friesian cattle. Including pure bloods and high grades there are over 200 head of these cattle on the farm, of which number 103 are milkers, furnishing the favorite product of the Windsor dairy, the net profit during the past season of which was nearly $20,000. These 100 spotted beauties are carefully stabled and each one of them averages 2 lbs. of butter per day. The first impression of a visitor who walks down the long aisles and observes the cows quietly feeding, is that they are muleys. In one respect they are. They have been dehorned. The horns of every one of the 103 cows have been sawed off close to the head. It is claimed that the dehorning makes them more tractable and quiet, and less liable to injure their companion cows; that in consequence they become better milkers and heavier animals for market. The good effects are no longer disputed, but a great deal of discussion has been going on for years over the question as to whether the practice was not cruel and should not be suppressed by law.

So warm has the debate become that the Humane Society of this city, learning of the practice of dehorning cattle at Windsor place, took the matter up and even threatened to take legal steps to put a stop to what the society conceived to be cruelty to animals, and it was this state of feeling which induced Manager Morse to give a public test of his method and its results, and if it was decided that the method was inhuman and cruel he would hold himself amenable to the law.

In pursuance of this intention Mr. Morse issued invitations to a number of prominent citizens, stockmen and a well-known veterinary surgeon, also to Secretary G. H. Thompson of the Colorado Humane Society, and members of the press, to visit Windsor farm and witness the dehorning process, with a view of determining whether the method was cruel and inhuman, as its opponents claimed.

The invitation was accepted by all the gentlemen with exception of Secretary Thompson or any representative of the Humane Society. About 25 gentlemen drove out to the farm and found everything in readiness to dehorn 25 head of cows and a two year old thoroughbred Holstein bull. The cows had recently been purchase by Mr Morse in Nebraska, and are all high bred Holstein-Friesians, in fair condition, though not up to the flesh carried by the oldest resident of the ranch. Among those present were General William L Campbell, Judge Amos Steck. Charles Limburg, a prominent stock raiser of Western Colorado; Mr. Stokes, a large Montana ranchman; Dr. Charles Cresswell memoer of the Royal College of Veterinary Surgeons, London, and manager of the Colorado Veterinary Hospital; Mr. Gooding; a Republican representative, and others.

The modus operandi of dehorning a cow is extremely simple. Only three things are necessary: A cow, a stock and a sharp meat saw such as is used by butchers in cutting steaks. The animal is driven into a narrow stall or chute and its head fastened between two upright posts or bars which are opened and closed at the top by means of pulleys and rachets. A halter is thrown over the head, which is then pulled to one side, when an able-bodied man can saw the horns off in from eight to ten seconds.

The first animal, a fine young Holstein cow three years old, was driven into the stall at three o'clock. She was quickly fastened, and Superintendent Hunt sawed both horns off in nine seconds. The animal was somewhat restive, but made no outcry. When released she shook her head and walked to a trough and began licking salt. The stump bled to some extent, but the hemorrhage soon ceased. Nothing at all was applied to the wound, and the animal seemed to take no notice of it after the first few minutes following the operation.

The second cow was dehorned in ten seconds, the third in twelve and the fourth in eight seconds. A young heifer was made a muley in five seconds. She bawled once while the operation was being performed, and then walked off chewing her cud. It was evidently like pulling a tooth; there was momentary pain and it was all over. Sometimes a stump suppurates for a few days, but stockmen present said they never heard of a case resulting fatally. One cow was drinking at the water tank when driven into the stocks. Her horns were amputated in seven seconds. She kicked and plunged at a lively rate, but when released walked placidly to the tank and finished quenching her thirst.

The most interesting features of the operation were the observations taken by Dr. Cresswell, who made minute tests as the operation proceeded. He found that while the horns were being sawn off the animal's respiration and pulse each rose from four to six degrees, but subsided within ten minutes after the subject was released. There was also a proportionate rise of temperature during the operation, but this, too, became normal in a short time. In order to ascertain whether it was pain which caused the increase in respiration and pulse, a cow was driven into the box, her neck fastened and tied in the usual manner. At the end of ten seconds—the length of time required to saw her horns off—it was found by actual test with instruments that the respiration had risen from 46 to 52, and the pulse in the same proportion, showing, as Dr. Cresswell maintained, that the increase was due to excitement and restraint and not to pain.

Dr. Cresswell is of the opinion that sawing the horn itself is comparatively painless, and that whatever acute pain occurs is caused by the saw cutting through the skin which surrounds the base of the horn and that it is but momentary or lasts only as long as the operation of sawing continues. He does not believe that the operation is near as painful as the cruel practice of pressing a red hot branding iron against the side or hip of a cow; neither does the pain continue so long. When a cow is branded it almost invariably bawls in agony. Out of the 26 head of cattle dehorned at Windsor farm recently but two gave way to an expression of pain. One was a heifer who was thoroughly frightened and the other was the bull. He was not in pain, but he was mad.

Manager Morse, who has closely watched the result of dehorning, says that it renders the animals as docile as sheep. There is no bully in the crowd and no bulldozed animal covered with gashes caused by the horns of the bully. The dehorned animals flock together like sheep, eat and drink contentedly and consequently are more cheaply kept and take on flesh more rapidly than a herd of horned cattle In regard to to the ultimate effects of dehorning, a Kansas stockman says;

"Last March we had 1046 head of yearling steers; of that number we dehorned 800. We pastured them through the season. All did well. Could see no difference in the growth of those that had horns and of those that had none The past two months we sold the entire lot in bunches of 50 and 100 head to feeders. Now here is the difference: Men in looking over our steers to get a bunch, all wanted dehorned cattle. There are other very important reasons we discovered for dehorning. We kept all our steers in pastures fenced, some fenced with wire some with Osage hedge. We kept the hornless ones separate from those that had horns, except a few that had horns we put in with 250 without horns. These steers were in pasture fenced with hedge. Those steers that had horns in the latter part of the season gave us trouble breaking through the hedge, while the dehorned ones were much more quiet and gave us no trouble in that way. We had the same experience with those confined within our pastures. We kept 450 head, all dehorned, on one pasture during the season; saw no disposition at all with them to huddle in bunches, tramp each other's feet and produce mud holes. I would say, dehorn everything—cows, steers and bulls."

The Windsor farm is devoting its dairy department entirely to Holsteins. A small herd of Galloways are still on the farm, but it is the intention to dispose of these and keep none but Holstein. These are dehorned when about two years old. It is the opinion of scientific breeders that the system of dehorning if kept up will result in a breed of polled cattle superior in all respects to their horned ancestors.

Good Jersey Beef.

Whether it ever will be possible to select a strain of Jerseys whose surplus male calves will make either veal or beef cheaply we cannot tell. We think it to be quite possible. But there is no doubt about the power of the Kerry to produce such beef and veal makers as well as prime dairy cows. There was no more perfect beef steer in the whole of the classes than Mr. M. J. Sutton's Dexter-Kerry steer No. 251. He weighed 10 cwt. 1 qr. 3 lb. at forty months old, and was prime beef everywhere; and would probably dress 66 per cent. to 68 per cent. of carcass. Animals cannot, in these classes, be got ready for competition at only a year's notice. We do not at all doubt that Jersey breeders will do more in these classes in future years. Still, it must be chronicled that, so the first year's experience goes, the small breeds at Smithfield Club in 1889 go not to either of the Channel Islands breeds, but to the Dexter-Kerry. To the merit of producing wonderful little milch cows must be added that of producing finished Christmas beeves holding their own with the very finest English and Scotch beef cattle.—London Live Stock Journal.

Changing the Color of Birds.

Starting with the observed fact that canaries fed with cayenne pepper acquire a ruddy plumage, Dr. Sauermann, of the Berlin Physiological society, has based upon it a scientific investigation of canaries, fowls, pigeons and other birds. From these he obtained the following results: Feeding with pepper only produces an effect when given to young birds before they molt; the color of the feathers of older birds cannot be affected. Moisture facilitates the change of color to a ruddy hue, which is again discharged under the influence of sunlight and cold. A portion of the constituents of cayenne pepper is quite inactive, as, for instance, piperin and several extractives, similiarly the red coloring matter alone of the pepper has no effect on the color of the feathers.

It is rather the triolein, which occurs in the pepper in large quantities, together with the characteristic pigment which brings about the change of color by holding the red pigment of the pepper in solution. Glycerine may be used instead of triolein to bring about the same result. The same statement holds good with regard to the feeding of birds with aniline colors. The red pigment of the pepper is also stored in the egg yolk as well as in the feathers. The first appearance of the pigment in the yolk may be observed as a colored ring four days after the commencement of feeding with the pigment dissolved in fat. After a further two days' feeding the whole yolk is colored.—Ex.

"Meat" for the Veterinarians.

Capt. I. G. Heaps, of Annawan, Ill., came up to get points on a lump jaw question and succeeded in finding at Hess Bros., where the 109 head were killed a remarkably good specimen of a jaw-bone that was enlarged by the disease. At the lumpy part the bone was nearly twice the normal size, and there were tubes leading into the marrow. Capt. Heaps thinks that the disease is not communicable to the human family and quotes Prof. Williams of England and Prof. Jennings of Phildelphia as his authorities. He says there is no recorded evidence that any sickness ever proceeded from eating the flesh of cattle with lumps on their jaws, and believes that the veterinarians who have lately raised such a hobbub about it have taken it up as an eligible fad after they have worn the "pleuro-pneumonia racket" about thread-bare.

Lump jaw, or actinomycosis, he declares, can be cured easily with the pen knife, before the bone becomes affected. He has removed hundreds of tumorous formations on the jaws of cattle, and says that after washing the wound with carbolic acid it heals up so thoroughly that no one could tell that anything had been the matter with the animal. Capt. Heaps thinks that while there is no real danger from eating the flesh of lumpy jaws, it is best to be on the safe side and condemn such stock, especially where the bone or saliva gland have become affected.

Before the veterinarians found that actinomycosis was a good thing for their business there were just as many lump jaws as now, and as the animals fattened and thrived as well as others, people used them for food purposes without any thought of danger. The captain admitted that he would not knowingly eat the flesh of such an animal, but at the same time said it was more prejudice than anything else and was about on a par with the prejudice which would prevent him from eating horse flesh, though he knew it would not hurt him.—Drovers' Journal.

THE WEEKLY

Breeder and Sportsman.

JAMES P. KERR, PROPRIETOR.

The Turf and Sporting Authority of the Pacific Coast.

Office, No. 313 Bush St.

P. O. Box 2300.

TERMS—One Year, $5; Six Months, $3; Three Months, $1.50. STRICTLY IN ADVANCE.

Money should be sent by postal order, draft or by registered letter, addressed to JAMES P. KERR, San Francisco, Cal.

Communications must be accompanied by the writer's name and address, not necessarily for publication, but as a private guarantee of good faith.

ALEX. P. WAUGH, - - - - - Editor.

Advertising Rates

Per Square (half inch)

One time	$1 50
Two times	2 50
Three times	3 25
Four times	4 00

And each subsequent insertion 75c. per square.

Advertisements running six months are entitled to 10 per cent. discount.

Those running twelve months are entitled to 20 per cent. discount.

Reading notices set in same type as body of paper, 50 cents per line each insertion.

To Subscribers.

The date printed on the wrapper of your paper indicates the time to which your subscription is paid.

Should the BREEDER AND SPORTSMAN be received by any subscriber who does not want it, write us direct to stop it. A postal card will suffice.

Special Notice to Correspondents.

Letters intended for publication should reach this office not later than Wednesday of each week, to secure a place in the issue of the following Saturday. Such letters to insure immediate attention should be addressed to the BREEDER AND SPORTSMAN, and not to any member of the staff.

San Francisco, Saturday, Feb. 8, 1890.

Stallions Advertised

IN THE

BREEDER AND SPORTSMAN.

Thoroughbreds.

FRIAR TUCK, Hermit—Romping Girl..........C. W. Aby, Middletown.
GREENBACK, Dollar—Music..........C. W. Aby, Middletown.
INTRUDER, Crater—Lady Bountiful..........T. J. Knight, Sacramento.
ST. SAVIOR, Eolus—War Song..........C. W. Aby, Middletown.

Trotters.

ANTEEOP, Anteeo—Bessie G..........Guy E. Grosse, Santa Rosa.
ANTEEOP, Anteeo—Nance..........Guy E. Grosse, Santa Rosa.
ADMIRO, Admiral—dam by San Bruno..........Smith & Sutherland, Pleasanton.
ANTEROS NUTWOOD, Anteros—Newark Belle..........T. W. Barstow, San Jose.
ALEXANDER BUTTON, Alexander—Lady Button..........Cache Creek Farm, Yolo.
APEX, Prompter—Mary..........Poplar Grove Breeding Farm, Wildflower.
ALCONA, Almont—Queen Mary..........Fred W. Loeber, St. Helena
BALKAN, Mambrino Wilkes—Fanny Fern..........A. L. Hinds, Oakland.
BONANZA, Arthurton—Sister..........Richard Havey, Oakland
CLOVIS, Sultan—Sweetbriar..........Poplar Grove Breeding Farm, Wildflower.
CUPID, Sidney—Venus..........C. O. Thornquest, Oakland
CHRISMAN'S HAMBLETONIAN 10178, Whipple's Hambletonian—Flora Jesse Chrisman, San Jose
CANNON BALL, Simmons—Gurgie..........Lockhaven Stock Farm, Burbank.
CHARLE DERBY, Steinway—by Electioneer. Cook Stock Farm, Contra Costa Co.
CRESCO, Strathmore—Spartan..........Cook Stock Farm, Contra Costa Co
CALIFORNIA NUTWOOD, Nutwood—Fanny Patchen..........Martin Carter, Alameda Co.
DAWN, Nutwood—Countess..........A. L. Whitney, Petaluma
DIRECTOR, Dictator—Dolly..........Pleasanton Stock Farm, Pleasanton.
DON MARVIN, Fallis—Cora..........F. P. Lowell, Sacramento
ELECTO, Antevolo, dam by Capt. Webster..........G. W. Stimpson, Oakland
ELECTION, Electioneer—Lizzie H..........B. C. Holly, Vallejo.
ELEGANCE..........G. W. Stimpson, Oakland
EL BENTON, Electioneer—Nellie Benton..........Souther Farm, San Leandro.
ECLECTIC, Electioneer—Manette..........Wilfred Page, Sonoma County
EROS, Electioneer—Sontag Mohawk..........W. H. Vioget, Menlo Park
FIGARO, Hambletonian—Emblem..........Souther Farm, San Leandro.
GROVER CLAY, Electioneer—Maggie Norfolk..........Denis Gannon, Oakland.
G. & M., Anteeo—Rosa B..........George E. Guerne, Santa Rosa.
GUY WILKES, George Wilkes—Lady Bunker..........San Mateo Stock Farm, San Mateo.
GLEN FORTUNE, Electioneer—Glenna..........Souther Farm, San Leandro.
GUIDE, Director—Imogene..........Smith & Sutherland, Pleasanton.
GRANDISSIMO, LeGrande—Norma..........Fred W. Loeber, St Helena
ILLUSTRIOUS, Happy Medium—Abdalletta..........George A. Stone, Santa Rosa.
JESTER D, Almont Hortense..........Souther Farm, San Leandro
JUNIO, Electioneer—by Granger..........S. N. Straube, Fresno.
KAFIR, Alcazar—Flower Girl..........B. C. Holly, Vallejo.
LEO WILKES, Guy Wilkes Sable..........San Mateo Stock Farm, San Mateo.
LYNWOOD, Nutwood—Hattie Morrison..........P. Visher, Stockton.
MEMO, Sidney Flirt..........Valensin Stock Farm, Pleasanton.
MOUNTAIN BOY, Kentucky Prince Elsie..........B. C. Holly, Vallejo.
MAMBRINO WILKES, George Wilkes—Lady Chrisman..........San Miguel Stock Farm, Walnut Creek.
MART BOORHEM, Sidney—Towhead..........B. C. Holly, Vallejo.
MAMBRINO JR 1789, Mambrino Patchen, dam by Mambrino Chief Geo. P. Bull, San Jose.
MORTIMER, Electioneer Marti..........Wilfred Page, Sonoma County
NOONDAY, Wedgewood—Noontide..........F. P. Lowell, Sacramento.
PLEASANTON, Director—May Day..........Pleasanton Stock Farm, Pleasanton.
PASHA, Sultan—Madam Baldwin..........D. Bryson, Linden
PILOT NUTWOOD, Nutwood—Belle..........T. W. Barstow, San Jose.
PHILOSOPHER, Pilot Wilkes—Belle..........George E. Guerne, Santa Rosa.
REVEILLE, Shiloh—Norfolk..........B. C. Holly, Vallejo.
ROY WILKES, Adrian Wilkes—Flora..........Pleasanton Stock Farm, Pleasanton.
REDWOOD, Anteeo—Lou Wilton..........A. McFayden, Oakland.
SILVER BOW, Robert McGregor—Sadie..........P. J. Williams, Oakland.
STEINWAY, Strathmore—Abbess..........Cook Stock Farm, Contra Costa Co
SUNSET, Anteeo—Bessie G..........Guy E. Grosse, Santa Rosa.
SHAMROCK, Buccaneer—Fernleaf..........G. W. Stimpson, Oakland
SIDNEY, Santa Claus—Sweetness..........Valensin Stock Farm, Pleasanton.
SIMMOCOLON, Simmons—Colon..........Valensin Stock Farm, Pleasanton.
ABLE WILKES, Guy Wilkes—Sable..........San Mateo Stock Farm, San Mateo.
ST. NICHOLAS, Sidney—Towhead..........John Rowen, Oakland Trotting Park.
WOODNUT, Nutwood—Flora..........Jas. Weatherhead, San Jose
WHIPPLETON 1883, Hambletonian Jr.—Lady Livingston..........Fred W. Loeber, St. Helena
WOODSIDE, Woodnut—Veronica..........B. C. Holly, Vallejo.

Dates Claimed.

CALIFORNIA STATE FAIR	Sept. 8th to 20th
FRESNO (Spring Meeting)	March 18th to 29th
FRESNO (Fall Meeting)	Sept. 29th to Oct. 4th
PETALUMA	Aug. 25th to 30th
NAPA	Aug. 18th to 23rd

Saratoga Association.

The large number of entries from California to all the principal events in the programmes of the Eastern Associations show that more horses will be raced on the Atlantic Coast representing owners from this State this year, than ever before. Already the columns of the BREEDER AND SPORTSMAN have contained the advertisements of the leading jockey clubs, and now that old reliable body, the Saratoga Association, proclaim to our readers this week, their list of stakes for both the first and second meetings of 1890.

More money is offered this year than ever before, and there will be many endeavors made to pluck the rich plums offered so freely by the Saratogians. After a heavy campaign at Latonia and Chicago, there is no place in the East where horses will recuperate so fast as they do at the "City of the Springs," and it is a well known fact that horses show higher average form at Saratoga than at any other point on the circuit. The course is one of the best graded, and surely one of the safest, in the country, which, when taken into consideration with the salubrious climate, freedom from mosquitoes, and the purity of the water, makes it one of the most desirable places East to take race-horses. The usual thirty days racing will be given, and already the association has secured the services of Furman T. Nutt, Esq., as presiding judge and Mr. James Sheridan as starter. The Californians who are going to take horses back, or who have horses already in the East, should read the announcement carefully and make entries at once.

Overland Park.

The Overland Park Club Association, of Denver, Col., held their annual meeting on Saturday, Jan. 11th. The report of Superintendent Hall showed the affairs of the club to be in a very satisfactory condition, with a handsome profit on the year's business. The following Directors were elected for the ensuing year: James H. Carille, Joseph K. Choate, William Daniels, B. H. DuBois, Edward Eddy, George H. Estabrook, Phil Feldbauser, A. P. Fowler, Wm. R. Mygatt, D. D. Streeter, N. M. Tabor, J. H. P. Voorhees, and Henry R. Wolcott. The club will hold two meetings during the year 1890, in May and October. The club will also give matinee races once each week during the summer. Both the regular meetings and the weekly race days will provide for trotting, pacing and running races. As will be seen in the advertising columns, the Association announce their stakes for the spring meeting, and with their accustomed liberality have added to the stakes with a bountiful hand. There are two stakes for two year olds, two for three year olds, and two for the all aged horses. The distances are from half a mile to a mile and a half, and it is pleasant to note that neither of the three year old events are at less than a mile. The Denver Trotting Stake is also announced for colts and fillies three years old and under, that have never beaten 2.30. The nominating fee is very light, and this should warrant a large entry list. There has been such an interest manifested in superior breeding throughout Colorado, Utah and Montana that the meeting should be one of the best ever held in Denver. The officers elected are all energetic men, and no effort will be spared to provide for the comfort of those who may become patrons of the Overland Park Club.

Goodwin's Guide.

The annual edition of the now indispensible Goodwin's Guide arrived by mail on Thursday morning, too late for more than a passing notice this week. As usual, it contains the result of every running race which took place during 1889 of which authentic information could be obtained; racing fixtures for 1890; winners of stakes in 1889; scale of weights for the United States; Jockey mounts during 1889; "fastest time" made last year; some of the largest paying mutual pools; fastest time on record; running horses that have died since January 1, 1889; list of horses whose names have been changed during the year; jockeys' lowest weights and to whom engaged for 1890; race track terms and phrases; betting rules and interesting turf events; in fact, it is a perfect encyclopedia of racing matters, and no one can afford to be without it. The Guide is issued by Goodwin Bros., 241 Broadway, N. Y.

On a Trip.

The proprietor of the BREEDER AND SPORTSMAN, Mr James P. Kerr, has gone East as a delegate to attend the National Trotting Association, which convenes at Buffalo, N. Y., on the 12th inst. Before his return he will visit many of the principal cities of the East, and as many of the large breeding farms as time will admit of.

New York Jockey Club Entries.

The new club located at Westchester will have very successful meetings this year if the entries are any criterion to go by. Although in their infancy as yet, the association made such a bid for public favor last year that the assurance was given that they had come to stay, and the horsemen seemingly realize that fact, for the best horses in the country have been entered, and almost every State in the Union is represented. The following is the complete total received in each stake:

SPRING MEETING, 1890—Galliard, 138; Larchmont, 111; Anticipation 106; Van Nest, 101; Debutante, 117; Casanova, 92; Trial, 55; Bowling Brook Handicap, 85; Baychester, 86; Throgg's Neck, 60; Toboggan Slide Handicap, 117; New York Jockey Club Handicap, 68; Westchester Cup, 34; All Breeze, 74; Fort Schuyler, 50.

FALL MEETING, 1890—White Plains Handicap, 270; Dunmow, 230 Fashion, 141; Farewell, 93; Pelham Bay Handicap, 89; Protectory, 114; Echo, 56; Peytona, 58; Country Club Handicap, 97; New Rochelle 88.

FALL MEETING, 1892—Matron Stakes, 979.

The following stakes will also be run at Morris Park, under the supervision of the American Jockey Club:

SPRING MEETING, 1890—Belmont, Withers, Ladies, Juvenile.

FALL MEETING, 1890—Hunter, Jerome, Titan, Mosholu, Nursery.

California is well represented in all the events, Mr. Haggin alone having almost 130 entries in the Matron Stakes. The Bowling Brook Handicap for three-year-olds, one mile and a furlong, have entries from the Golden State, as follows:

Haggin, J. B., blk c Fernwood, Falsetto—Quickstep; b c Hawkstone, Hindo—imp Queen Maud; ch f Rosette, Joe Hooker—Rosa B
Hearst, Geo., b c King Thomas, imp King Ban—Maud Hampton; br c Tournament, imp Sir Modred—Plaything; b c Anaconda, Spendthrift imp—Maid of Athol; b c Ballarat, imp Sir Modred—La Favorita; br f Miss Bell, imp Prince Charlie—Linnet; b f Gloaming, imp Sir Modred—Twilight; b f Golden Horn, Spendthrift imp—Constantinople; b c Sir Lancelot, imp Sir Modred—Faustina; ch c Baggage, Warwick —Mafia F.
Maltese Villa S. F., b c Abdiel, Jocko—Cousin Peggy;
Palo Alto Stock Farm, b c Racine, Bishop—imp Fairy Rose; ch c Flambeau, Wildidle imp—Flirt.
Santa Anita Stable, b f Magdalena, imp Glenelg—Malta; b c Santiago, Grinstead—Clara D; b c Clio, Grinstead—Glenita; ch c Amigo, imp Prince Charlie—Mission Belle.
Shippee L. U. b c Fellowcharm, Longfellow—Trinket.

The Toboggan Slide Handicap was especially gotten up for the sprinters, and every good one is represented. As usual, a fair percentage of the entries are from this coast, the well known ones being:

Daly, Marcus, ch f Leonora, imp Sir Modred—Lizzie Lucas; b c Prince Charming, imp Sir Modred—Carissima.
Haggin, J. B., b m Firenzi, imp Glenelg—Florida; br c Fitz James, imp Kyrle Daly—Electra; blk c Fresno, Falsetto—Cachuca; ch c Salvator, imp Prince Charlie—Salina.
Hearst, George, blk m Gorgo, Isonomy—imp Flirt; b c Ballarat, imp Sir Modred—La Favorita; b c King Thomas, imp King Ban—Maud Hampton; b f Gloaming, imp Sir Modred—Twilight; b c Sir Lancelot, imp Sir Modred—Faustina; ch c imp Del Mar, Somnes—Maid of the Hills; ch f Cosette, Joe Hooker—Abbie W; b c Almont, Three Cheers—Question.
Maltese Villa Stock Farm, ch m Geraldine, Grinstead—Cousin Peggy.
Rose, L. J., b g Rico, Shannon—Fanny Lewis
Ross, J. R., b f Kitty Van, Vanderbilt—April Fool.
Santa Anita Stable, ch m Los Angeles, imp Glenelg—La Polka; ch f Sinaloa, Grinstead—Maggie Emerson; ch c Amigo, imp Prince Charlie—Mission Belle; b c Clio, Grinstead—Glenita; ch c Honduras, Grinstead—Jennie B.

A Current Falsehood Exposed.

LEXINGTON, Ky., January 18, 1890.

EDITOR BREEDER AND SPORTSMAN:—It is due to parties concerned that the following correspondence be made public:

NATIONAL TROTTING ASSOCIATION,
OFFICE OF THE PRESIDENT,
LEXINGTON, KY., Jan. 4, 1890.

MR. CHARLES GREENE, ST. LOUIS, MO.—DEAR SIR:—I have received from a correspondent a clipping from a Chicago paper, which had before escaped my notice, in which you are reported as saying:

"The overtures for consolidation came from the National some time ago, and so eager were the officers of that body to bring about such a result that they offered to step down and out and offered to accept the officers of the American as the governing board of the proposed association. We refused to accept the proposition for several reasons. I am firmly convinced that this country is entirely too large to be governed by one body with central organization. The only plan on which the National and American Associations could combine would be for each to retain its present staff of officers and appoint an executive board from the two associations to confer together. This is hardly necessary, as it would not bring the two bodies much nearer together. We work in perfect harmony now, and any horse ruled off by either party is debarred from races given under the auspices of the other. I think that is the nearest we will ever come to consolidation."

These statements require a response at my hands, and I do not feel authorized to assume that you are correctly quoted without first calling your attention to the language and asking you to inform me if you are. Trusting you will favor me with an early reply, I am very respectfully,

P. P. JOHNSTON.

ST. LOUIS, January, 6, 1890.

JUDGE P. P. JOHNSTON, LEXINGTON, KY.—DEAR SIR:—Yours of the 4th inst. to hand. The clipping referred to in your letter, and reported as emanating from me is not true.

Very truly yours, CHARLES GREEN.

It is a matter of regret that currency should have been given to an irresponsible statement that carried on its face evidence of a reckless regard of truth, conclusive to the mind of every well-informed horseman; especially when the aim of the fabrication was to arouse antagonism hurtful to the horse interest.

Very many thoughtful breeders and horsemen believe that the existence of two independent powers, administering law on the same subject matter in the same territory, is a misfortune that ought to be remedied. The personal business relations of the enlightened breeders and horsemen throughout the country are of a cordial character, and they work together harmoniously for the advancement and elevation of trotting interests. When anything of an irritable character, calculated to perpetuate the differences that unfortunately occurred a few years ago, is thrust before the public, it is, as a rule, without respectable paternity, and may be traced to some parasite on the trotting interest, who hopes to fatten on the disease he creates.

Personally, I would have no hesitation about making overtures to gentlemen engaged as I am in trying to promote the same general purposes, if I was authorized and the occasion seemed opportune. In so far as we differ now, the difference is an error of judgment on the part of one or the other. When we can agree upon what is right, we will have found the common ground where all will meet.

P. P. JOHNSTON.

Answers to Correspondents.

Answers for this department must be accompanied by the name and address of the sender, not necessarily for publication, but as proof of good faith. Write the questions distinctly, and on one side of the paper only. Positively no questions will beanswered by mail or telegraph.

Los Angeles.
A horse sired as you state would not be standard. He has not a single qualification.

J. F., Merced.
The pedigree of Butte was given in the BREEDER AND SPORTSMAN of January 4th. Judge J. McM. Shafter, of this city, might furnish you with further information.

W. P. F.
1. I wish you would find out for me how many races Vashti trotted and what is her best record. 2. Who bred her? 3. Is this right or not: Vashti, by Chieftain, dam by Nena Shaib (thoroughbred(, grandam by Jim Crow (thoroughbred)?

Answer.—Five races, as far as we can find out. Her record is 2:32½. We do not know who bred her, but she was formerly owned by J. C. Pray of Stockton. You have the sire and first dam right, but we cannot verify the second dam.

T. G. D.
Is Muldoon a standard horse, and was he sired by George M. Patchen, Jr?

Answer.—Give his breeding as far as you know it, and also his owner or the breeder.

E. H. C.
Oblige by giving the full breeding of Dexter Prince, also of Peerless by Gen. Knox. Can you inform me where they now stand?

Answer.—Dexter Prince is by Kentucky Prince, dam Lady Dexter; 2d dam Dexter's dam by Seeley's American Star. We cannot place the other horse. Dexter Prince is standing in this State.

J. R. E.
Please give the records of Emma G. and Sunflower, sired by Elmo; also, please give the sire of L. C. Lee, pacer record 2:15.

Answer—Emma G., 2:27½. Sunflower 2:28. While L. C. Lee has been credited to Elmo for several years, it is now generally accepted that his sire was Walker's Elmo.

Jas. M. Givern, Saint John, N. B.:
On page 532 in your paper, in answer to correspondence, you mention January's St. Lawrence's 2nd dam by Williamson's Belmont. Can that be the St. Lawrence horse that sired the Mackey mare now owned by L. J. Rose? If you can tell me I would be much obliged.

Answer.—The St. Lawrence to which you allude was probably a son of January's St. Lawrence and was called Roadhouse's St. Lawrence, but it is almost impossible to prove that he was the sire of the Mackey mare.

Laurel Dale.
The picture you allude to appeared March 2nd 1889. Have forwarded copy.

J. W. H.
Please let me know the pedigree of the horse Bummer and also that of Buccaneer, the first was owned at Rincon, and the other made two season there.

Answer.—We do not know either horse,

Playboy.
Kindly answer the following queries through your valuable columns. (1) Has McCracken's Black Hawk any record? (2) Did McCracken's Black Hawk get any trotters, if so, enumerate and give record. (3) Also pedigree and record of Jim Monroe.

Answer.—(1) No. (2) Sisson Girl, 2:28½. (3) Jim Monroe by Abdallah 15, dam Lizzie Peebles, said to be by Wagner. He has no record.

R. S.
Have the goodness to answer through your query column what registered number the stallion Kentucky has. He is owned by J. B. Haggin, is by Whipple's Hambletonian 725, out of Mossmare, she by Kentucky Hunter (sire of Borneo 2:23, Wormwood 2:25) and is claimed to be standard.

Answer.—Kentucky has no number; he is not standard.

R. A. R.
Will you please give, through the columns of your valuable paper, the breeding of Reveille, recently owned by Ben Hill of El Cajon? It is the general opinion here that he was sired by Shiloh, but there is a man here that says he knew the colt when John Treat bought him, and that he was not sired by Shiloh. This man, J. Green by name, says he has forgotten his pedigree, but he is sure that Shiloh was not his sire.

Answer—See answer to Los Angeles.

F. W. H.
Please inform me if the stallion Pick Pocket is a registered thoroughbred; if so send me the number of his registry, with his pedigree; also his record. I think he ran on the Bay District track and at Stockton in 1886; also what his position was in the races.

Answer—Horses are not registered by numbers in the Stud Book. He is entered on page 500, Vol. 5 Bruce's American Stud Book. He is by Joe Daniels, dam Mattie C. by Specter, 2nd dam Pet by Melbourne Jr., etc. He was owned by Col. C. Dorsey, and started four times as a three year old; he did not win a race that year (1886). He was last in each of two races at Glenbrook Park and third in a race at Stockton.

Los Angeles.
1. Give extended pedigree of Dan M. Murphy. 2. Is he of a racing family? 3. What near relations has he of note? 4. What is the pedigree of Shiloh by Cosmo? 5. What is the pedigree of Margery, dam of Shiloh? 6. What is the pedigree of Reville?.

Answer.—(1.) Dan M. Murphy, foaled 1886 by Imp. Speculator, dam Leona by Prolific; 2nd dam Peri by Hurricane; 3rd dam by Glencoe Jr.; 4th dam by imp. Onus: 5th dam said to have been by American Eclipse. (2.) As far as the records show, no. (3.) None of note. (4.) Shiloh foaled 1862 by Cosmo, dam Fanny Harper by Grey Eagle; 2nd dam Julia Ann by Medoc; 3rd dam by Imp. Eagle; 4th dam by Gallatin; 5th dam by Albert; 6th dam by Union, etc. (5.) Margery is not the dam of Shiloh, as you will see by the above. (6.) The pedigree of Reville is given as by Shiloh, dam by Norfolk.

J. W. M.
Please give the breeding in full of Jim Hawkins (sire of Tamarack 2:28, and Belle B 2:26½). He was bred and owned by Judge Hutton of Yolo, now deceased, and sold by him to Captain Johnson of Southern Calfiornia. Jim Hawkins is now standard under rule 3. and it will be of interest to many who have some of his descendants to know his breeding. He was certainly a remarkable horse. Living in comparative obscurity, with little or no opportunity in the stud, with nothing in his pedigree to induce any one to train his offspring, yet he has two fast trotters to his credit.

Answer.—Jim Hawkins is a son of Jack Hawkins, son of Boston. His pedigree and history is not recorded in any of the authorities.

Enquirer.—Can you give me the pedigree of the horse known as Dietz's St. Clair.

Answer.—Mr. Dietz was asked to answer and the following is his reply.—

EDITOR BREEDER AND SPORTSMAN:—In reply to your favor of January 28th, the following is as correct a statement as I can give you as to the breeding of Deitz's St. Clair. The grandam was brought to this State from Kentucky, by James Hornet in 1859. She was of Diomed stock; color, blood-bay; height about 15½ hands. In crossing the plains she got in foal by a Black Hawk stallion. The get was a black mare foal. At three years old I bred her to Miller's St. Clair. The get was a black horse colt, foaled in 1864, May 2d, I named him Young St. Clair, but within the last ten or twelve years he was known only as Deitz's St. Clair. His color was jet black, with heavy mane and tail; left hind foot white; solid built. His height was 15 hands and 3 inches, well coupled, fine disposition, rather high strung, good bottom and a square trotter. I drove him to a heavy buggy in three minutes. He died one year ago last Fall at Vacaville, Solano County. He was then the property of Mr. Hawkins.

In your issue of September 14, 1889, was a cut of Junio; it is a true picture of Deitz's St. Clair. I remain,

Yours truly, L. DIETZ.

WOODLAND, February 1, 1890.

Names Claimed.

EDITOR BREEDER AND SPORTSMAN:—I claim the name Stammoor for my two-year-old black colt by Stamboul, dam Moormaid by The Moor.

Rayannette for brown filly foaled April 29, '89, by Anteeo, dam Debonair by Sultan.

Sparrow Wilkes for bay colt foaled March 1889, by Guy Wilkes, dam Birdie by Pelmere. ROBT. S. BROWN, Petaluma.

Foals of 1890.

On January 16th Alice B., by Admiral, foaled a chestnut colt by Woodnut. The only white is a small star. I have named him Alwood. M. KEMPER, Oakville.

EDITOR BREEDER AND SPORTSMAN:—Following foals since last advice, viz.:

B c by Wildnut, dam Victoria by Don Victor.
B c by Nephew, dam Wildflower by Electioneer.

THOROUGHBREDS.

Br f by Flood, dam imp. Goula by Exminster.
B f by imp. Cheviot, dam imp. Fairy Rose by Kisber.
Ch c by imp. Cyrus, dam imp. Laelia by Carnelian.
B c by Flood, dam imp. Rosetta by Struan.
B f by imp. Cyrus, dam imp. Getaway by Balfe.

Yours truly, S. C. FERGUSON.

PALO ALTO, February 5, 1890.

Quarter Stretch Gossip From the South.

Santa Ana is the smallest two year old at the Santa Anita Ranch. She is a May foal, which probably accounts for her diminutive stature.

Here is a piece of news: Los Angeles can trot a mile any day in three minutes, and Bob Campbell thinks she could do 2:40 with a little training.

Ed Ryan, the popular lessee of the Agricultural Park track, now drives one of the finest teams in the State.

Horsemen here are anxiously awaiting the weights for the Brooklyn and Suburban handicaps.

St. David, one of the greatest stallions ever seen on a track in this part of the State, is kept in obscurity at the ranch of Machado Brothers. He has only been bred to one thoroughbred mare.

Mayor Hazard drives Don Tomas every day in his buggy. He is the owner of the Del Sur gelding. Your correspondent enjoyed a drive behind Don several days since.

Jockey Moneghan is here. He expects to ride for the Rose string.

Magdalene is the only horse under the weather at Santa Anita.

It is on the tapis that Lucky Baldwin will breed a number of his mares to Cheviot.

George Vignola has sold Rosemeade, the Wildidler—Dutchess filly, to Stover & Davis.

Ex-Senator Del Valle is one of the staunchest admirers of fast stock in this section of the country.

A stallion who will be seen on the California circuit this season is Radcliff. His breeding is right for a good campaigner, being by Pilot Medium out of Fury by Durango. Ed Smith imported this stud last year.

Capt. T. B. Merry has been enjoying the balmy air of Southern California, but has returned to San Francisco.

A match is on the tapis between Charley Durfee's Leonora by Dashwood and Dr. K. D. Wise's mare Semi Tropic, and the first time he drove her the circuit was made in 2:32½.

Dal Williams, formerly under trainer for Lucky Baldwin, is now located at Latonia. He has a select string of three racehorses in training, one of which is Bob Campbell's Protection, the winner of the Junior Championship.

Genial Tom Rodman has sold out his pool rooms to Fitzgerald & Co. Mr. Rodman will in all probability locate in San Francisco. He will be missed in Los Angeles.

Lee Brown, the jockey, is no longer connected with the Santa Anita flyers. The youngster, who is a promising rider, has secured a good berth with a Kentucky stable.

Ogrita is the tallest two year old at the Baldwin Ranch.

The misses at Santa Anita are principally those who were stinted to Emperor of Norfolk.

Mr. Len Bush, who is shortly to retire from the Santa Anita Ranch, is of the opinion that Verano will make one of the best stallions at Santa Anita.

"Kentucky" John, who came down here with the Palo Alto horses purchased by L. J. Rose, is a great admirer of Argyle, whom he says is the greatest young stud in the West.

DASWORTH.

LOS ANGELES, Feb. 5th.

The Pure Trotting-bred Stallion

ILLUSTRIOUS

STANDARD No. 4178.

DESCRIPTION.

Dark bay, black points, 15 1-2 hands high, weight 1000 pounds, foaled May 10, 1885; bred by General W. T. Withers, Lexington, Ky.

PEDIGREE.

By Happy Medium, sire of Maxey Cobb 2:13¼ and 82 with records of 2:30 or better. First dam Abdallah by Cassius M. Clay Jr., sire of Durango 2:[illegible], Harry Clay 2:23½ and sire of the dams of Minnehaha, Bertha 2:27½, Charley West 2:26½, Grandmont 2:25 1-2, Lottie K 2:26½, Mambrino Diamond 2:26, Richwood 2:28 1-2, Topsy 2:29½, Happy Thought 2:22 1-2, Pequot 2:23 1-2, Fairfawn Medium 2:27 1-2, Polley 2:27¼ and Mambrino Boy 2:26 1-2; second dam Laura Crockett by Almont, sire of Westmont 2:13¾, Puritan 2:16, Fanny Witherspoon 2:16¾, Piedmont 2:17¼, Altine 2:19½ and 37 with records better than 2:30; third dam Sally Tee by Alexander's Abdallah, sire of Goldsmith Maid 2:14; fourth dam Kate Crockett, the dam of Lulu 2:14¾, by imp Hooton.

Illustrious is a horse of extra fine finish, large clean bone, good feet, back short and strong, loins and quarters well muscled, and powerful. He has a kind disposition and splendid trotting action, and is as handsome and bloodlike in form and finish as any trotting stallion in the land.

He is pronounced by his breeder, General Withers, to be the best bred son of Happy Medium living, and is undoubtedly one of the very best bred trotting stallions in the State. He has had but six weeks' regular training, and a part of that time was sick with epizootic, but was trotted quarters in 39 1-4 seconds, and barring accidents will certainly trot better than 2:30 this season.

TERMS—$50 the season. Mares not proving with foal may be returned next year free.

Good pasturage at $3 per month.

Season to begin February 1st and end June 15th.

GEO. A. STONE,
Santa Rosa, Cal.

HOLLYWOOD BREEDING FARM.

MOUNTAIN BOY 4841.

Br s MOUNTAIN BOY, 4841, bred by Charles Backman, Orange County, New York, foaled 1882, sire Kentucky Prince 2470, dam Elise, sister to Elaine, by Messenger Duroc 106; grandam Green Mountain Maid, 3d dam, Shanghai Mary, will serve a limited number of mares at $100 the season.

ELECTION.

Bay stallion ELECTION, bred at Senator Stanford's Palo Alto Stock farm, foaled 1884, sire Electioneer dam Lizzie H. by Whipple's Hambletonian 725, grandam Lizzie Harris (by Comus son of Green's Bashaw 50), great grandam by Arnold Harris, thoroughbred.

Election is one of the handsomest bloodlike sons of Electioneer, and with his thoroughbred cross through Arnold Harris should prove invaluable as a sire. TERMS, $100 the season.

KAFIR,

B c KAFIR, bred by L. J. Rose, Los Angeles, foaled 1887, sire Alcazar, 2:20½, dam Flower Girl by Arthurton, sire of Arab, 2:15, grandam Flora by General McClellan, 144, sire of three in 2:30 list, great grand dam by Langford, he by Williamson's Belmont, will serve a limited number of mares at $50 the season.

WOODSIDE.

Ob c WOODSIDE, sire Woodnut, 2:16½; 1st dam Veronica by Alcona, 730; 2nd dam Fontana by Almont 33; 3rd dam Fannie Williams by Alexander's Abdallah, 15. Book full.

MART BOORHEM.

B c MART BOORHEM, by Sydney, 2:19¾; 1st dam Towhead by Echo. This colt is a full brother to St. Nicholas who showed a mile in 2:27½ at three years old. TERMS, $25 the season.

REVEILLE.

The well known thoroughbred stallion REVEILLE, by Shiloh, dam by Norfolk. Reveille is a brother to John Treat and is the sire of Tycoon and Gladstone. TERMS, $25 the season.

Hollywood is nicely situated three miles from Vallejo on the Napa road. Good pasturage and every care will be taken of mares at reasonable rates. For further particulars, apply,

B. C. HOLLY, Vallejo.

PASHA,

Registered No. 2039.

RECORD 2:36.

SIRE OF MORO 2:27.

Will make the present season at Linden, twelve miles east of STOCKTON.

Season commencing FEBRUARY 1st and ending JULY 1, 1890.

Terms $50 the season, due at time of service.

PASHA is ten years old; a beautiful black; 16½ hands high, and weighs 1,240 pounds. He is a horse of beautiful symmetery and magnificent action.

PEDIGREE.

PASHA was sired by Sultan 1513; first dam Madam Baldwin by The Moor 870; second dam by Ben Lippincott by Belmont. Pasha is a full brother to Bay Rose, record 2:20½.

Sultan, by The Moor, sire of Beautiful Bells, dam of Hinda Rose, 2:19½, and Sable, dam of Sable Wilkes, three-year-old record 2:18.

First dam of Sultans, sire of Delmonica. Sire of Darby 2:16½, by Guy Miller, sire of Whipple's Hambletonian.

Second dam by Mambrino Chief.

Third dam by Downing's Bay Messenger.

Fourth dam Mrs. Candle, dam of Ericsson, four-year-old record 2:30½.

Good pasturage at $3 per month.

For further particulars, address

D. BRYSON,
Linden Cal.

For Sale.

AT A BARGAIN.

NETTIE B.

(Half-sister to Emma Temple, 2:21).

In Foal to Free Trade.

Nettie B. was foaled 1884, and is by Altimont 986, dam Lizzie R. (dam of Emma Temple, 2:21), by Emigrant. Nettie B. is heavy in foal to Free Trade 2477, he by Princeps 536 (sire of Trumpet, 2:14, and twenty others in the list), dam Dawn by Belmont 64 (sire of 21 in the list); second dam Midnight (dam of Jay-Eye-See, 2:10, and Noontide, 2:20 1-2), etc.

Nettie B. is about 16 hands high. Is a handsome bay, and is warranted sound in every particular by the owner.

Must be Sold,

as the owner is about to move from the State. For price and particulars, apply at the office of the

BREEDER AND SPORTSMAN,
313 Bush Street.

THOROUGHBRED

Clydesdale Horses and Mares

FOR Sale

Sixth Annual Importation by MR. JOHN SCOTT.

Four Pure-bred Clydesdale HORSES

AND

2 Thoroughbred Clyde Mares

Can be seen at the Bay District Track.

For particulars apply to

KILLIP & CO., Auctioneers,
22 Montgomery Street, S. F.

FOR SALE

AT

Vineland Stock Farm

STALLIONS, BROODMARES AND FILLIES

ONE STALLION FIVE YEARS OLD, SEAL-BROWN, by WHIPPLETON (sire of Lily Stanley, 2:17 1-2 Homestakes 2:16 1-2, etc.), dam Sally Gorham by Werner's Rattler. This horse is scarcely 15 1-2 hands high, but very compactly built. He breeds exceptionally large and well finished Colts. Any one understanding the business could clear him in one season, or he would make a No. 1 road horse, as he can trot a 40 gait any time.

ONE THREE-YEAR-OLD, SEAL-BROWN, by WHIPPLETON (sire of Lilly Stanley, 2:17 1-2, Homestakes 2:16 1-2, etc.) dam Sally Gorham, etc. This ought to make a great General Purpose sire, and with opportunities get trotters, as he is compact, strong-boned, and will measure when grown about 16 hands and weighs 1,300 lbs. With a little road work last fall he developed a wonderful burst of speed.

ONE THREE-YEAR-OLD, BLACK, by WHIPPLETON (sire of Lilly Stanley, 2:17 1-2, etc.), dam by Naubuc (sire of the dam of Eva W., 2:21 1-2, etc.), full brother to Thomas Jefferson, 2:28. This horse will be fully 16 1-2 hands high. He is smooth, rapid gaited and from size and conformation should breed, like his sire, large, rangy, finished Colts.

ONE TWO-YEAR-OLD, BRIGHT CHESTNUT, sired by DAWN 2:18¾, dam Alida (dam of Directa, three-year-old record 2:31½, trial 2:26) by Admiral (sire of sister 2:19 1-2, Nona Y 2:25, etc). This colt is the making of an extraordinary horse. He is large boned and will be over sixteen hands high when grown; he is of the true Nutwood type, is clean gaited and can lead a piece as fast as any man's Colt.

ONE TWO-YEAR-OLD, BLOOD BAY, (full brother to Alcona Jr. sire of Silas Skinner, trial 2:22) sired by ALCONA (sire of Flora Belle 2:24, etc.,) dam Madonna by Cassius M. Clay Jr. This colt will make a trotter and a great stock horse if developed; he has the combined blood of Almont, Mambrino Chief, Cassius M. Clay Jr. and Joe Downing.

These colts are all sound and promising. The only reason I offer them for sale is, that I have three aged stallions in use, and the surplus is growing on me. If I were starting a breeding business for profit, I should consider either of these colts a representative to commence with. Also brood mares and fillies for sale. Correspondence solicited.

FRED. W. LOEBER, St. Helena.
Napa Co., Cal.

Have Arrived.

Six Head of Finely Bred and Registered

CLYDESDALE HORSES

Two Stallions! Four Mares!

Being the second importation from Melbourne, Australia, of

JOHN BURNS.

Mr. Burns, having had the advantage of a previous trip here, and knowing the demands and requirements of the California market, has in this importation brought six head of the finest and soundest horses ever brought to the market.

THESE CLYDES ARE ALL REGISTERED,

—And are the—

Finest of their Class

Ever brought to this Coast. They may be seen at the

BAY DISTRICT TRACK.

Prices, Terms, etc., will be furnished by

KILLIP & CO.,
22 Montgomery Street S. F., Cal.

WoodsideFarm

IMPORTANT SALE OF

Standard Trotting Mares Young Stallions and Fillies,

ROAD AND DRIVING HORSES

Farming Implements, Etc.

By direction of MRS. SILAS SKINNER.

Mrs. Skinner having determined to retire permanently from the breeding of Fine Stock, has decided to offer at

PUBLIC AUCTION
Thursday, March 6, '90,

at 12 M., on the Premises.

THE WELL-KNOWN

WOODSIDE FARM,

Near Napa,

together with all the highly bred trotting stock thereon.

The brood mares at Woodside are among the choicest in the State. Among them are mares by Almont, dam by Alexander's Abdallah; by Cassius M. Clay Jr., dam by Joe Downing; by Cassius M. Clay Jr., dam by Richelieu son of Mambrino Chief; by Duke of Orange Jr., dam by Cassius M. Clay Jr.; by Almont Mambrino, dam by Blood's Black Hawk; by Alcona—dam Fontana, dam of Flora Belle, 2:24, and Silas Skinner, trial 2 20½—by Almont; by Alcona Clay—dam Metamora, dam of Clay Duke, 2:31½—by Duke of Orange Jr. These mares have been bred to Director, Noonday, Mountain Boy and Wildwood, and are with foal. The young stallions are by Sitka, son of Alaska, by Electioneer, Whippleton, sire of Lillie Stanley, 2:17¾, Alcona Clay, etc. About twenty head well-bred trotting and driving animals will be sold in addition to the standard bred horses.

Catalogues giving extended pedigrees and full information are being prepared, and will be forwarded upon application.

At the conclusion of sale of horses,

WOODSIDE FARM

will be sold.

WOODSIDE FARM is situated three and a half miles from Napa City, up the river, upon what is known as the middle or big ranch road. It contains 67 1-2 acres of the choicest quality of land for alfalfa or any kind of grain, 40 acres being now in alfalfa over a foot high. The land produces from four to six tons of hay to the acre, of choice quality. Five of the fields are in pasture, four in alfalfa, one in timothy, the other kept in hay or grain necessary for stock, though well adapted for alfalfa. There is a nice orchard, small vineyard, and comfortable dwelling house of nine rooms. There is a good school house directly opposite, the best in the County. As to its adaptability as a stock ranch: there is living water in every field, and plenty of it. Corrals and stock yards, stable room for forty horses, besides seven good box stalls two good stables, granery, etc. It is within two miles of the Napa Agricultural Society's race track, the finest constructed in the State for years. Should there not be sufficient land, 67 acres adjoining can be purchased at reasonable figures.

There is no more eligible location in the State for a small stock farm, and this affords a rare opportunity, with the stock, to at once engage in this remunerative pursuit.

The sale will be positive. Upon all sales of Live Stock and personal property, one years' credit will be given on approved notes. Interest 10 per cent. per annum. Three per cent. discount for cash.

Upon Land, one-half cash: balance can remain upon mortgage for a term of years to suit purchasers. Interest eight per cent. per annum.

Vehicles will be in attendance at Napa Depot to convey parties to the farm. Lunch will be served upon the ground.

Mrs. Skinner having large interests in Oregon which will require her personal attention during the greater portion of the year, compels the sale of the Woodside Farm.

Parties are invited to visit the farm and look over the stock. The undersigned will be glad to give any information required, either as to stock or ranch.

KILLIP & CO.
Live Stock Auctioneers,
22 Montgomery St., S. F.

Antevolo Colt

For Sale.

AVOIO REX, foaled February 22, 1888; dam Catchup by Rustic; grandam Huntress by Don Victor; g g dam Betty Denice by American Boy Jr. Is 16.1 hands high, well developed, muscular, and without a blemish. Has a very gentle disposition, and shows speed and a good gait. Apply

HOME FURNISHING CO,
118 Fifth Street, S. F., Cal.

For Sale

A HALF BROTHER TO

ALMONT PATCHEN,

(2:25, trial 2:13 3-4).

JUANITA JR. is a beautiful bright bay, black points, with no white, foaled 1886. As a colt he has given much more promise than did Almont Patchen at the same age. Instead of being a pacer, he is a good, square trotter, with every indication of great speed, and is so gentle and kind, that a lady can drive him. The owner's only reason for selling him is that business calls him away from this section of the State. He will be sold at a reasonable figure. This is a splendid opportunity for a gentleman to secure a first-class trotter at a very low figure.

The pedigree of Juanita Jr. is by Juanita (sire of Almont Patchen), dam Nettie Moore by Old Tom Moore. For further particulars, address

JUANITA JR.,
Santa Clara P. O., Cal.

For Sale.

The Bay Stallion

AFTERNOON, 6543.

AFTERNOON was foaled in 1884, sired by Almont McGregor 1 [illegible], dam Minnie by General Hatch 39; second dam Lucy by Prophet (Weed's), son of Prophet. He is a very gentle, intelligent, level headed and pure gaited trotter. He is a remarkable foal getter, and his colts are handsome, game and speedy. He will be sold at a reasonable price. Reason for selling, ill health of the owner.

ALSO

A Handsome Brown Road Mare.

Can trot easily better than 2:40 to a Chicago cart or light buggy. Stands 15¾ hands high, weighs about 1050 lbs. She is by Green's Bashaw, and is very handsome, tough and speedy. Will be sold at a reasonable price. Address

JACOB STEFFEN,
Vallejo, Cal.

Stallion for Sale

AT A BARGAIN.

Full Brother to Fairmont.

By Piedmont, dam Queen by Garibaldi—see State Fair Edition of BREEDER AND SPORTSMAN, September 14, 1889, for description of Fairmont—three years old, solid bay. Can trot a 2:40 gait or better. Sound in every particular. Can be seen at Oakland Trotting Park, Oakland.

P. J. WILLIAMS.

For Sale!

A First-Class.

BREEDING FARM.

Of 800 Acres.

Four hours' ride from the city. Good roads to a first class track. Climate unexcelled. Plenty of wood and running water.

For further information apply to the office of the

BREEDER AND SPORTSMAN,
San Francisco.
313 Bush Street.

Attention Stockmen!

FOR SALE

At Chowchilla Ranch,

Thoroughbred Durham Cattle

Three Hundred Young DAIRY COWS, 2000 graded SHE CATTLE, Yearlings and up; a fine lot of high grade Durham Bulls; also have Mares, Horses, Mules and Norman Colts.

For particulars, apply to

ISAAC BIRD, Jr., Supt.,
Merced, California.

For Sale.

The Standard bred Stallion

Anteeo Button,

sire Anteeo, 2:16¼, sire of Alfred G. 2:19¾; Redwood, 2:24½, etc. Dam Mollie Button, dam of Alexander Button, sire of Yolo Maid, 2:14; Rosa Mac, 2:[illegible]; Belle Button, 2:20¾, etc.

ANTEEO BUTTON is a dark bay 15¾ hands high, four years old, and weighs 1125 lbs. In style and action he is all that could be desired, and can trot a mile with ease in 2:40 to a cart.

This colt must be seen to be appreciated.

Apply to

I. DE TURK,
Santa Rosa, Cal.

First Special Auction Sale

—OF—

HORSES,

For account of CAPT. BEN. E. HARRIS,

On Saturday, March 1,'90

At the Cor. TURK and STEINER STS.,

WE WILL SELL AT

Public Auction

A CATALOGUE OF 25 HEAD OF SUPERIOR ROADSTERS AND SADDLE-HORSES OF ALL GAITS.

Also a few select colts, mares and fillies of royal breeding, most all of which have been bred, raised and broken by Captain Harris, whose reputation for the culture of swift roadsters and saddle horses to high degree, is sufficient to warrant the public a rare opportunity for supplying their wants without the risk of disappointment. Among the lot there are several pairs of roadsters, one of which can trot in 2:30, besides a number of extra fine single flyers.

☞ The attention of ladies is particularly called to this sale, as many of the animals have been prepared especially for their use and safety.

This stock may be seen at the owner's stable corner of Turk and Steiner Streets, from now until day of sale.

TERMS cash, or an equivalent in approved paper. Catalogues at our office.

KILLIP & CO.,
Live Stock Auctioneers.
22 Montgomery St., S. F.

Anteros Nutwood

—ONE OF THE—

Best Bred Young Stallions in the State.

DESCRIPTION.

Bay horse; black points; no white. Foaled in 1887. Bred by M. Carter, at the Nutwood Stock Farm, by Anteros 6020, by Electioneer, and full brother to Anteeo, 2:16¼, and Antevolo, four-year-old, record 2:19¼.

First dam Newark Belle by Nutwood, 2:18¾, and half-brother to Maud S., 2:08¾—Queen of the Turf.

Second dam Tilly, 2:40, by San Bruno, by David Hill, by Vermont Blackhawk. This colt is very large of his age, and looks enough like Sunol to be her full brother.

If there is anything in breeding, this horse ought to make a good one.

Electioneer and Nutwood are his grandsires, both serving mares at $500 each. Nutwood is half-brother to the fastest trotter in the world—Maud S., 2:08¾; Electioneer, the sire of the fastest three-year-old, Sunol, 2:10½.

TERMS.

This colt will be limited to ten mares, outside of my own, for $50 the season.

Mares not proving in foal can be returned the following season by paying difference in price, if any.

The National Trotting Stallion

PILOT NUTWOOD (Cyrus R.)

Will make the season of 1890 at the stable of T. W. Barstow, corner of San Fernand Street and Wilson Avenue, San Jose.

TERMS.

$50 for the season, with usual return privileges, by paying difference in price. No fee if this horse does not secure a record of 2:30 or better in 18.0, barring accidents. Limited to 15 outside mares. Season from February 1st to July 1st, 1890. The best care and attention given to mares, but no responsibility assumed for accidents or escapes. Good pasturage at $3 per month on 100 acres of the best feed in Santa Clara County.

DESCRIPTION.

Pilot Nutwood, 2:42, black horse; small star; foaled in 1881; 15¾ hands; was worked five weeks, and got a record of 2:42 as a three-year-old; he was not worked again until 1888; after having six weeks work, showed his owner a mile in 2:26, and the last half in 1 10½. Sired by the mighty Nutwood, 2:18¾, half-brother to Maud S., 2:08¾—Queen of the Turf.

First dam Belle by Jack Roberts, half-brother to Old St. Clair; 2d dam by Shakespeare, thoroughbred, Jack Roberts by Eclair or Leck, and he by old pacing Pilot, and his dam by Copperbottom.

This gives Pilot Nutwood two crosses of the great Pilot blood, coming through both sire and dam. This is the kind of breeding that breeders should be looking after in order to get to the front.

CHALLENGE.

To back my assertion made in the San Jose Mercury in December last, I will match this horse against any trotting stallion in San Jose, one or two-mile heats, any time after July 1st. The parties accepting this challenge can set the time and track, and I the right to name the amount. For further particulars, address,

T. W. BARSTOW,

P. O. Box 1268. San Jose, Cal.

ST. NICHOLAS.

A Son of the World Renowned

SIDNEY,

Will Make the Season of 1890, at the Oakland Trotting Park.

ST. NICHOLAS was bred by Mr. G. Valensin at the Arno Stock Farm, Sacramento Co., California, in 1885. He is a beautifully proportioned bright bay horse, 15.3 hands high; is well muscled, lengthy, and lots of bone, with splendid natural action and a phenomenal turn of speed. As a three-year-old he easily worked three heats on the Oakland Track in 2:32, 2:29 and 2:27½. His breeding is just what one would expect from such a highly formed bloodlike horse. Sidney, his sire is the most successful young stallion—whether for getting pacers or trotters—America has ever seen and no wonder for his blood lines are exceptional fine and are all trotting lines, Santa Claus, Strathmore, Rysdyk's Hambletonian and Abdallah, white Sweetness again runs back through that great sire Volunteer, to Rysdyk's Hambletonian and also through her dam to Rysdyk's Hambletonian and Harry Clay 45, the sire of Electioneer's dam. St. Nicholas' dam is by Echo, an exceptionally prepotent son of Hambletonian thus giving St. Nicholas four Rysdyk's Hambletonian crosses and further back a Harry Clay cross which with his grand dam's thoroughbred cross should make him invaluable in the stud.

TERMS: Fifty dollars the season, which will commence on the 5th of February and close on the 1st of July. Due care will be taken of mares, but no responsibility for accidents or escapes.

Mares taken and kept as desired by the owners, and at reasonable rates.

JOHN ROWEN.

Oakland Trotting Park.

THE MAMBRINO Patchen Stallion.

MAMBRINO JR., 1789 (formerly Carr's) Sire of Lady Ellen 2:28 (dam of Ella 2:29), Maud H. 2:30. Mambrino Boy (Carr's) 2:31 1 2.

Will stand at my farm, 2 1-2 miles north of San Jose, on the Milpitas road. Season to commence February 1st, 1890, at $60, with return privilege 1891. Fifteen mares of approved breeding, besides my own, will be given him. Parties owning good mares, performers or out of producing dams, will find an opportunity to breed them on shares, and the best of care taken of them till colt is weaned, if so desired.

PEDIGREE.

MAMBRINO JR., 1789, by Mambrino Patchen 58 [full brother of Lady Thorne 2:18 1-4] by Mambrino Chief 11. First dam by Mambrino Chief 11; 2nd dam by imp. Jordan [thoroughbred]; 3rd dam by Bertrand, son of Sir Archy; 4th dam by Chewkees, son of Sir Archy.

For further particulars address

GEO. P. BULL.

Box 1067. San Jose, Cal.

THE BUCKINGHAM.

OLD STRAIGHT WHISKIES.

141 Montgomery Street.

303 Bush Street, S. F.

M. J. BALFE, Proprietor.

SEASON 1890.

The Great Son of Buccaneer

SHAMROCK,

Two-Year Old Record of 2:25, beating the World's Record 4 1-2 Seconds when made.

SHAMROCK

- Buccaneer 2656, Sire of Shamrock, 2:25; Ivy, 2:31¼; Flight, 2:29; (dam of Fleet, 2:24, at 2 yrs.); Flirt (dam of Memo, 3 y. o. trial, 2:20¼, etc.); Orphan Girl, 2:22¼; Prima, 1 yr. 2:42¾; 2 yr. 2:32¾; Cora, 2 y. o. 2:44, etc.
  - Iowa Chief 528, Sire of Corisande, 2:24.
    - Green's Bashaw, Min 2:30 or better. By Vernol's Black Hawk
    - Topsy.
  - Tinsley Maid
    - Flaxtail.
    - Fanny Fern.
- Fernleaf, 2:28, Dam of Goldleaf, 2:11¼, 4 yrs.; Shamrock, 2 yrs. 2:25; Thistle, 2 y. o. trial, 2:28; Ivy, 3 yrs 2:31¼, etc.
  - Flaxtail, Sire of Fernleaf, 2:28; Prairie Bird, 2:28¼; Empress, 2:29¼; Lightfoot, 2:28.
    - Pruden's Blue Bull.
    - untraced.
  - Fanny Fern
    - Irwin's Tuckahoe, By Herod's Tuckahoe, Sire of dam of Smuggler, 2:15¼.
    - Dam, of Leffler's Consul.

As will be seen from the tabulated pedigree and performances above, Shamrock is not only a phenomenal horse himself, but his ancestors on both sides have shown themselves to be uniformly producers of GREAT and PARTICULARLY early speed, and his record like many others of his family was made in a hotly contested race, instead of a trial against time.

HE IS NOW IN SPLENDID FORM, AND I TRULY BELIEVE WILL LOWER HIS RECORD TO 2:18 THIS YEAR.

TERMS, $100, with usual return privilege, for a limited number of CHOICE mares, season ending June 1st.

Electo.

By Antevolo 2:19¼ by Electioneer, dam Captain Webster (sire of dam of Adonis 2:15), by Williamson's Belmont.

Electo, while but three years old this spring, is, as well as being grandly bred, a great individual.

TERMS, $50, with the usual return privilege, limited to 15 approved mares. Season to end June 1st.

Imported Cleveland bay stallion

Elegance.

(Registered in Cleveland Bay Stud Book No. 75.) Prize winner over twenty of his own breed in the GREAT YORKSHIRE SHOW OF ENGLAND.

The Cleveland Bays are the most prepotent coach horses in the World, and their get from ordinary mares makes the most stylish and serviceable horses for that purpose that can be raised. Rich bays with black points having the preference over ALL OTHERS.

TERMS $25, with usual return privilege, season ending July 1st.

Care taken but no responsibility assumed for accidents or escapes. Pasturage, $5 per month. For further particulars call at or address me at my hospital, where horses will make the season.

G. W. STIMPSON, V. S.

Veterinary Hospital, 19th St., near San Pablo Ave, Oakland, Cal.

WOODNUT

(Weatherhead's) by Nutwood 600

Sire of Belmont Boy, 2:15, pacer, Woodnut, 2:16½, Felix, 2:14¾, Dawn, 2:18¾, Maggie E., 2:19¾, Irma, 2:18¾, and 26 others in 2:30 or better; 1st dam Flora, 2:39¼, trial 2:26, dam of Chrisman's Hambletonian, sire of Steve Whipple, 2:22, Kate Agnew, 2:28¼, by Chieftain 721, sire of Defiance 2:17¾ pacing and 2:24 trotting, Cairo, 2:26, Onward, 2:24, pacer; second dam by Wilson's Leamon.

Woodnut is a beautiful bay with black points, 16¼ hands high, weighing 1,075 pounds. His colts are all larger than himself, and sell readily for road and carriage purposes, being of good color and very docile, yet prompt to obey, and always ready.

Service fee, $25, with usual privileges. Colts and fillies from Tilton Almont, Patchen, Stockbridge Chief, and other desirable crosses, FOR SALE. For further particulars, pedigrees, or any communication in horse matters, address

JAS. WEATHERHEAD, Prop.

San Jose, Cal.

The Fast Trotting Stallion

REDWOOD.

Four-Year-Old Record 2:24 1-2

Will make the season of 1890—February 1st to July 1st—at the

OAKLAND RACE TRACK.

REDWOOD is a dark bay colt, 15.2¼ hands high, weighs 110 lbs. Foaled in 1885, by Anteeo, 2:16¼, sire of Alfred G., 2:19¾. Anteeo is by Electioneer. First dam Lou Milton, by Milton Medium; second dam Old Fly, a thoroughbred mare brought from the East in 1871 by W. C. Ralston, Esq.

Redwood's sire was out of Columbine by A. W. Richmond, the sire of the pacers Arrow 2:13¾, and Elwood 2:25, and the trotters Romero, 2:19¾, and Len Rose, 2:27. Redwood has shown a quarter in 33 seconds.

Terms $100

For the season. Mares not proving with foal may be returned next season free of charge, provided Redwood remains the property of the present owners. Good pasturage at $5 per month. No responsibility assumed for escapes or accidents. Service fees payable before removal of the mare. Limited to 40 approved mares. For further particulars address

A. McFADYEN.

Race track, Oakland, Cal.

The Trotting Stallion

BONANZA 2:29½

Will make the season of 1890, from February 1st to July 1st, at the OAKLAND TROTTING PARK.

PEDIGREE.

BONANZA, 2:29½.

- Arthurton 365, Sire of Arab, 2:15, Joe Arthurton 2:20½, Lady Escot, 2:28¼. Dams of Grandee, 2:23½, Hidalgo, 2:27.
  - Hambletonian 10, Sire of 41 in 2:30 list, Sires of 107 of the sires of 567 in 2:30 list.
  - Imogene, by Am. Star 14, Dam of Leland 1310, Sire of Clara, 2:21, Miss Leland, 2:25½, Hades, 2:27¼.
- Sister, Dam of Albert W., 2:20.
  - John Nelson 187, Sire of Nerea, 2:23¼, Gov. Stanford, 2:27¼, Aurora, 2:27, Nemo, 2:30.
  - Lamott Mare, Dam of Aurora, 2:27; g d of Arol, 2:24¼.

DESCRIPTION.

BONANZA is a very handsome chestnut of commanding form and splendid proportions. He stands nearly 16 hands high, is remarkably intelligent, level headed and pure gaited. His record is no mark of his speed. He is a great foal getter, and his colts are handsome rangy animals.

TERMS, $40 for the season, with the usual return privileges. Excellent pasturage near the track at $5 per month. The best of care taken of mares, but no responsibility assumed for accidents or escapes.

For further particulars, address

RICHARD HAVEY,

Oakland Trotting Park, Oakland.

The Hambletonian Stallion 10178.

CHRISMAN'S HAMBLETONIAN, Sire of Steve Whipple, 2:22, Kate Agnew, 2:28¼, etc.

- Whipple's Hambletonian, Sire of 14 trotters and 1 pacer from 2:19 to 2:30, and 7 sons with 8 performers from 2:21¼ to 2:30, and dams of 6 from 2:19¼ to 2:30.
  - Guy Miller, By Hambletonian 10.
  - Martha Washington, Dam of Speculation 928, Sire of Crown Pt. 2:24, Oakland Maid, 2:22¼, Gracie S., 2:26¼, and dam of Waterford, 2:27
- Flora, 2:39¼, trial, 2:26. Dam of Chrisman's Hambletonian, sire of Steve Whipple, 2:22, Kate Agnew, 2:28¼.
  - Chieftain 721, Sire of Defiance, 2:24 and 2:17¾, pacing; Cairo, 2:26, and Onward, 2:24, pacer.
  - daughter of Wilson's Leamon.

Stud season now on till the 1st of August, 1890, at $40 each mare, with return privilege in 1891, provided stallion and mare, or either, do not change owners. Good pasture at hand, and comfortable accommodation for brood mares and colts. For further particulars, address

JESSE CHRISMAN, Proprietor.

San Jose, Cal.

The Trotting Stallion

CUPID,

Full Brother to Adonis 2:14,

—Sired by—

The Celebrated SIDNEY 2:19 3-4, and out of Venus.

Will make the season of 1890 at the OAKLAND TROTTING PARK.

PEDIGREE.

CUPID is by Sidney out of Venus by Capt. Webster 10173, record 2:30, and sire of Prestone 2:23. Second dam by Skenandoah 926, sire of Daisy Burns 2:29¾, Erwin Davis (sire of two in the 20 list) and dams of four in the 30 list.

DESCRIPTION.

Cupid is a handsome bright bay 15.2¾ hands high, weighs 1100 lbs.; was foaled in 1886. As a yearling, with very little work he showed quarters in 42 seconds, and at 2 years old, quarters in 38 seconds. As a three year old he has not been worked, but he shows the speed and endurance that must come from his excellent blood lines.

TERMS $50 for the season, with the usual return privileges. Good pasturage near the track at $5 per month. The best of care taken of mares in any way that owners may desire, but no responsibility assumed for accidents or escapes.

For further particulars address

C. O. THORNQUEST,

Oakland Trotting Park, or

C. BAAB, 972 Broadway, Oakland.

GROVER CLAY.

Bay Stallion, Black Points, 15 3-4 hands high.

Bred by W. W. Traylor, San Francisco.

BY ELECTIONEER.

First dam Maggie Norfolk by Norfolk, son of Lexington, he by Boston. Second dam Tilda Quill by Billy Cheatham he by Cracken, and he by Boston. Third dam by Dorsey's Golddust.

TERMS.

Will make the season of 1890 at the Training Stables of Denis Gannon, near Oakland Trotting Park, at $50 the season, payable at time of service. Season to commence February 1st and ending July 1st. Proper care of mares will be taken, but no responsibility incurred for accidents or escapes. Address,

DENIS GANNON, Oakland, Cal.

HENRY J. COX | W. S. JOHNSON

The "EDWIN C."

40 EDDY STREET.

Cor. of Mason. San Francisco.

(Private Entrance Mason Street.)

Vineland Stock Farm

Whippleton 1883,

Sire of

LILY STANLEY	Record 2:17½
HOMESTAKE	" 2:16½
FLORA B.	" 2:27
CORA C.	" 2:31½
BLACK PRINCE	" 2:36½
RACHEL	" 2:38
PRINCE W.	" 2:40

WHIPPLETON is not only the sire of trotters, but he is the greatest sire of Carriage Horses on the Pacific Coast. Some of the best carriage and road teams in San Francisco are sired by Whippleton. A carriage team by Whippleton received First Premium at Napa, Petaluma, Oakland, Sacramento, Stockton and San Jose. Whippleton and his colts have never been beaten in the show ring.

DESCRIPTION.

WHIPPLETON is black, tan muzzle and flanks, 17 hands, and weighs 1,400 lbs. Most of his colts are 16 hands or over, and with a few exceptions, bay, brown or black. He never sired a sorrel or white face colt. (If he does, I agree to refund service money.)

PEDIGREE.

WHIPPLETON, sired by Hambletonian Jr. (sire of Hancock 2:29), by Whipple's Hambletonian (sire of Graves, 2:19, Westfield, 2:20½, Express, 2:24, and 12 others in the 2:30 list), dam Lady Livingston (dam of Lady Blanchard, 2:26½, Bloomfield Maid, trial 2:22), by General Taylor (sire of the dams of Wells Fargo, 2:18¾, Nerea, 2:23¼, Bickford, 2:29½, Lady Blanchard, 2:26¼, etc., and sire of grandam of Hazel Wilkes, 2:20) by the Morse Horse 6, sire of Norman 25 (sire of Lulu, 2:14¾, May Queen 2:20, etc.).

TERMS at $40, limited to 20 mares, for the season, usual return privileges. I would like to get about ten well bred mares with the proper combination of blood to breed to Whippleton on shares this season.

Alcona 730.

Sire of

FLORA BELLE	Record 2:24
CLAY DUKE	" 2:31½

ALCONA will be a great sire, but four of his colts have ever been trained, and all have shown full miles better than 2:3', and two of them as good as 2:20. Two of his first sons each sired a colt as a two-year-old, and last season one as a four-year-old trotted a full mile in 2:23¼, and the other, a three-year-old, a mile in 2:31. With opportunities, Alcona is destined to be one of Almont's best sons. Almont, for his opportunities, is beyond doubt the most prepotent sire of his age. He has 36 representatives in the 2:30 list; 49 sons and 22 daughters that have already produced 2:30 performers. Almont died five years ago at 20 years old. If he lived he would be but 25 years old.

PEDIGREE.

ALCONA sired by the great Almont (sire of Westmont 2:13¾, Fanny Witherspoon 2:17¼, Piedmont 2:17¼, and 31 others with records better than 2:30, and grandsire of Belle Hamlin 2:12¾, etc.); by Alexander's Abdallah (sire of Goldsmith Maid 2:14), he by Rysdyk's Hambletonian. Alcona's dam, Queen Mary, by Mambrino Chief (sire of Lady Thorne 2:18 1-4, and 5 others in the 2:30 list, and sire of the dams of Director 2:17, Piedmont 2:17¼, Onward 2:25 1-4, Red Wilkes, Almont, Belmont and many other noted sires).

DESCRIPTION.

Alcona is a beautiful chestnut 16 3 1-2 hands high, and weighs 1300 lbs. His colts possess speed, style, finish and beauty, and if they don't trot they command the highest prices for carriage horses.

$40 for the season. Usual return privilege.

Grandissimo,

Full Brother to GRANDEE, Three Year Old Record 2:23 1-2.

Sired by Le Grande [son of Almont and out of Jessie Pepper, by Mambrino Chief. Jessie Pepper is the dam of Ione 2:17 1-2, Alpha 2:23 1-2, and granddam of Montezuma 2:29¾. First dam Norma [dam of Grandee 2:23 1-2], by Arthurton [sire of Arab 2:15, Joe Arthurton 2:20 1-2, etc.]; second dam Nourmahal 2:39 [full sister to A. W. Richmond, sire of Arrow 2:13¾, Romero 2:19, and sire of the dams of Antevolo 2:19 1-4, and Anteeo 2:16 1-4, sire of Alfred G 2:19¾] and Redwood 2:24 1-2.

GRANDISSIMO, with limited training as a three year old last year showed 1-4 mile in 37 seconds, and, barring accidents, will trot fast next fall.

Limited to 20 mares at $50 each; usual return privileges.

Season on Grandissimo ends June 1st, 1890.

Season on Whippleton and Alcona ends July 1st, 1890.

Best kind of pasturage at $4 per month. Mares kept in any manner desired.

For further particulars send for Circular or call at stables, one mile south of St. Helena.

FRED W. LOEBER.

St. Helena, Napa Co., Cal.

The Trotting Stallion

G & M

FULL BROTHER TO

ALFRED G, 2:19¾.

(Who has been taken to Kentucky to stand at $200)

Will make the season of 1890 from FEBRUARY 1st to JULY 1st, at

SANTA ROSA.

G. & M. is by Anteeo, 2:16¼; was foaled 1886; first dam Rosa B. by Speculation (son of Hambletonian 10); 2d dam Elizabeth by Alexander 97; 3d dam Nora by imp. Glencoe. Anteeo is by Electioneer, out of Columbine by A. W. Richmond 1687.

G. & M. is a handsome dark bay; stands 15-2 1-2 hands high, and weighs 1050 pounds. Gameness, stoutness, speed and stamina are indelibly impressed in every line of the pedigree of G. & M. Owners of brood-mares in search of these qualities, will do well to patronize this promising colt.

PHILOSOPHER,

Foaled 1886 by Pilot Wilkes 2967; first dam Bella by George Wilkes 519; second dam by Bell Morgan 61.

Philosopher's sire, Pilot Wilkes, 2967, is by George Wilkes 519, dam Grace (the dam of Alice Woodburn, etc.), by Pilot Jr. 12, grandam by Orphan Boy.

Will make the season of 1890 from FEBRUARY 1st to JULY 1st, at Santa Rosa.

TERMS for the season:

G. & M., $50.

PHILOSOPHER, $30,

with privilege of returning mares that do not prove in foal the next season free of charge, provided the horse bred to remains the property of the present owners. Good pasturage at $3 per month. No responsibility assumed for accidents or escapes. Service fees payable before removal of the mare. For further particulars, address

GEO. E. GUERNE,

Santa Rosa, Cal.

Breeders' Directory.

Advertisements under this heading 50c. per line per month.

HORSES AND CATTLE.

W. S. JACOBS, Sacramento, Cal.—Breeder of Thoroughbred Shorthorns and Berkshire Hogs.

J. H. WHITE, Lakeville, Sonoma County—Breeder of Registered Holstein Cattle.

EL ROBLAS RANCHO—Los Alamos, Cal., Francis T. Underhill, proprietor, importer and breeder of thoroughbred Hereford Cattle. Information by mail. C. F. Swan, manager.

PAGE BROTHERS.—Penn's Grove, Sonoma Co. Cal. Breeders of Short-Horn Cattle; Draft, Roadster and Standard Bred Horses.

JAMES MADDOCK, Petaluma, Cal.—Trotters trained at reasonable prices. Stock handled carefully. Correspondence solicited.

SETH COOK, breeder of Cleveland Bay Horses, Devon, Durham, Polled Aberdeen-Angus and Galloway Cattle. Young stock of above breeds on hand for sale. Warranted to be pure bred, recorded and average breeders. Address, Geo. A. Wiley, Cook Farm, Danville, Contra Costa Co., Cal.

MAMBRINO WILKES COLTS and FILLIES, full brothers and sisters to Gus. Wilkes 2:22, and Balkan 2:29¼, for Sale. Address SMITH HILL, Walnut Creek, Contra Costa County, Cal.

B. F. RUSH, Suisun, Cal., Shorthorns, Thoroughbred and Grades. Young Bulls and Calves for Sale.

PETER SAXE & SON, Lick House, San Francisco, Cal.—Importers and Breeders for past 18 years of every variety of Cattle, Horses, Sheep and Hogs.

HOLSTEIN THOROUGHBREDS of all the noted strains. Registered Berkshire Swine. Catalogues. F. H. BURKE, 401 Montgomery St., S. F.

CLEVELAND BAYS and Norman Horses, Jersey Cattle, and pure bred Poland China Hogs.—DR. W. J. PRATHER, Fresno, Cal.

HENRY C. JUDSON, Wild Idle Farm.—Breeder of Thoroughbred Horses. The home of "Wild Idle." P. O., Santa Clara; Box 223.

FERGUSON & AUSTIN,
FRESNO, CAL.
Registered Polled Angus and Short-Horn Cattle.

Oysters.

M. B. MORAGHAN

Is the only importer, planter and wholesale dealer in the CALIFORNIA MARKET, Stalls 68, 69 to 71 and 47, 49. All the choicest brands of Fresh Oysters constantly on hand. Prompt attention paid to hotel and Country orders. Price List.

Large Eastern Oysters .... $2 00 per 100
Transplanted Eastern Oysters .... 1 50 per 100
California Oysters .... 2 00 " sack
Fresh frozen Eastern Oysters at $7 00 per doz. cans.

PASTURAGE

AND

FIRST-CLASS CARE

TAKEN OF

Gentlemen's Road Horses and Trotters.

Colts Broken and Trained to Harness or Saddle.

Twenty new Box Stalls. First-class Pasturage, and the best of care given to all horses. Terms, $4 per month. Satisfaction Guaranteed.
Address,

K. O'GRADY,
Laural Creek Farm,
SAN MATEO, CAL.

Fiske's Vanes.

MADE OF
COPPER
And Gilded with
PURE
GOLD LEAF.

Manufacturer's Agent.

The HOWE SCALE CO.
411 & 413 Market Street, S. F.

Scales for Weighing of
Live Stock
SEEDS, FEED, Etc.
Write for Catalogue.

PHIL J. CRIMMINS. JOHN C. MORRISON.

"Silver Palace,"

36 Geary Street,
San Francisco, Cal.

SARATOGA ASSOCIATION.

STAKES TO CLOSE MARCH 1st, 1890.

FOR FIRST MEETING, 1890.

THE FLASH STAKES, for two-year-olds; $100 each, half forfeit, or only $15 if declared by July 1st; with $700 added; the second to receive $200 out of the stakes. Winner of more than one sweepstakes race of the value of $2,000 each, to carry three pounds extra. Horses not having won a sweepstakes allowed seven pounds. Maidens allowed twelve pounds. Half a mile.

THE CALIFORNIA STAKES, for all ages; $50 entrance, $25 forfeit, with $750 added; the second horse to receive $200, and the third $100 out of the stakes. Non winners, this year, of $2,000 allowed five pounds; of $1,000, eight lbs.; or not having won a race this year, (selling races not counted,) allowed fourteen pounds. Maidens allowed, if three years old, eighteen pounds; if four years, 22 pounds; if five years, or upwards, 26 pounds. One mile.

THE ADIRONDACK HANDICAP, a handicap sweepstakes for all ages; $50 each, or only $15 if declared out; with $7.0 added; of which $200 to the second horse, and the third to save his stake. Weights to be announced by July 15th, and declarations to be made by July 25th. Winner after announcement of weights, of $1,500, to carry four pounds; of $2,500, or twice of $1,000, seven pounds extra. One mile and a furlong.

THE SPINAWAY STAKES, for fillies two year old; $100 each, half forfeit, or only $15 if declared out by June 15th; with $ 00 added; of which $200 to the second, and the third to save her stake. To carry 110 lbs. Winner of any sweepstakes race of the value of $2,000, to carry three pounds; of two or more such races, or one of $4,000, seven pounds extra. Non-winners of $1,000 allowed five pounds. Maidens allowed ten pounds. Five furlongs.

THE AMERICAN HOTEL STAKES, for three-year-olds; $50 each, $20 forfeit; with $600 added by Mr. Geo A. Farnham, proprietor of the American Hotel, the association to give $150 to the second horse. Horses not having won this year a race of the value of $2,000, allowed five pounds; of $1,500 seven pounds; or not having won a race of $1,000 in 1889 or 1890, allowed twelve pounds; or if the latter have not won a race this year, 17 pounds. Maidens allowed eighteen pounds. One mile.

THE EXCELSIOR STAKES, for all ages; $50 each half forfeit, or only $10 if declared by July 1st; with $1,000 added, of which $200 to the second horse, and the third to receive $100 out of the stakes. Non-winners, this year, of $2,000 allowed five pounds; of $1,000 eight lbs., or not having won a race this year, allowed thirteen pounds. Maidens allowed if four years old, eighteen pounds; if five years or upward, twenty-four pounds. One mile and a quarter.

THE VIRGINIA STAKES, for two-year-olds; $25 entrance, play or pay, with $700 added; the second to receive $150, and the third $50 out of the stakes. Colts and geldings to carry 118 pounds. Fillies 115 pounds. Those not having won a sweepstakes race of the value of $1,500 allowed five pounds. Maidens allowed ten pounds, or if beaten at this meeting, and never having been placed second for a sweepstakes, allowed thirteen lbs. Five furlongs.

THE KEARNEY STAKES, a handicap sweepstakes of $50 each, or only $15 if declared out by July 25th; with $1,000 added; the second horse to receive $250, and the third, $100 out of the stakes. Weights to be announced by July 15th. Winner, after announcement of weights, of a race of the value of $1,500, to carry four pounds; of two such races; or of one of the value of $2,500, seven pounds extra. One mile and a half.

THE FOSTER MEMORIAL, a sweepstakes of $50 each, half forfeit, or only $10 if declared out by July 1st; with $800 added; of which $200 to the second horse. For three-year-olds. Horses not having won a sweepstakes for that age, the value of $2,000; nor of two or more such stakes of the value of $2,000 each, allowed four pounds. Those not having won in 1890, a race of the value of $1,500 allowed seven lbs.; of $750, ten lbs. Non-winners this year, [selling races not counted] allowed fifteen lbs. Maidens allowed twenty lbs. One mile and half a furlong.

THE MERCHANTS STAKES, a sweepstakes for all ages; $100 each, half forfeit, or only $15 if declared out by July 1st; the merchants of Saratoga Springs to add $1,400, of which $300 to the second, and $100 to the third horse. Winner in 1889 or 1890, of two races of the value of $1,500 each, or one of $7,000, to carry five lbs. extra, of three of $4,000 or one of $10,000, seven lbs. extra. Winners, this year, of two races of the value of $2,000 each, to carry three lbs extra. Other horses non-winners this year of $1,500, allowed five lbs.; of $1,000 eight lbs.; or not having won a race this year, [selling races excepted,] fourteen lbs. Maidens allowed, if three years old, eighteen lbs.; if four years, twenty-two lbs.; if five or upwards, twenty-six lbs. One mile and five furlongs.

FOR SECOND MEETING, 1890.

THE UNITED STATES HOTEL STAKES, a sweepstakes for three year olds. $50 entrance, half forfeit, or only $10 if declared out by July 1st; with $1,000 added by the proprietors of the United States Hotel; the second horse to receive $200, and the third $100 out of the stakes. Winner, in 1890, of two or more races of the value of $2,000 each, or of one of $5,000, to carry 3 lbs. extra. Those not having won in 1890 a race of the value of $1,500 allowed 5 lbs. Non-winners this year allowed 10 lbs. Maidens allowed 15 lbs. One mile and a half.

THE HOTEL BALMORAL, MOUNT McGREGOR STAKES, a light-weight handicap sweepstakes, of $50 each, half forfeit, or only $10 if declared out by July 1st. Mr. W. J. ARKELL, proprietor of the Balmoral Hotel, to add $1,000, of which $200 to the second horse. Weights to be announced two days before the race. One mile and a half.

THE TENNESSEE STAKES, a sweepstakes for two year olds; $25 each, p. p., with $750 added; the second to receive $150, and the third $50 out of the stakes. Those not having won a sweepstakes race of the value of $1,000 allowed 5 lbs. Maidens allowed 12 lbs.; or if beaten at Saratoga this season, and never having been placed second in a race of the value of $1,500, allowed 15 lbs. Three-quarters of a mile.

THE CONGRESS HALL STAKES, a sweepstakes for all ages; $25 entrance p. p., the proprietors of Congress Hall to add $800, of which $200 to the second horse, and the third to receive $100 out of the stakes. Horses not having won this year a race of the value of $1500 allowed 5 lbs.; of $1000, 8 lbs. Those not having won a race this year (selling races excepted) allowed 14 lbs. Maidens allowed, if four years old, 18 lbs; if 5 years or upward 22 lbs. Heats of three-quarters of a mile. Time between heats 20 minutes. Distance 60 yards.

THE MISSES STAKES, a sweepstakes for fillies two years old; $50 each, $10 forfeit, with $750 added; the second filly to receive $150 and the third $75 out of the stakes. To carry 110 lbs. Winner of any race of the value of $1500 to carry 3 lbs.; of two or more such races, or of one of $3000, 5 lbs. extra. Maidens allowed 7 lbs; or if beaten in a maiden race at Saratoga this season, 10 lbs. Three-quarters of a mile.

THE BEVERWYCK STAKES, a sweepstakes of $50 each, half forfeit, or only $10 if declared out by July 1st; with $1000 added by HON. M. N. NOLAN, proprietor of the Beverwyck Brewery; the second horse to receive $200, and the third $100 out of the stakes. Winner this year of two races of the value of $2,000 each to carry 4 lbs. extra; of two of $4000, or of one of $10,000 in 1889 or 1890, 7 lbs extra. Other horses not having won this year a race of the value of $1500 allowed 5 lbs; of $1000, 8 lbs; of $700, 12 lbs; or not having won a race this year (selling races not counted) allowed 5 lbs. Maidens allowed, if four years old, 20 lbs; if five years or upward, 26 lbs. One mile and five hundred yards.

THE POCAHONTAS STAKES, a sweepstakes for fillies three years old; $50 each, half forfeit, with $1000 added; of which $200 to the second filly, and the third to receive $75 out of the stakes. To carry 118 lbs. Winner in 1890 of any race of the value of $2,000, or of two of $1500 each, to carry 4 lbs extra. Those not having won in 1890 a race of the value of $1000 allowed 5 lbs; or not having won a race this year, 10 lbs. Maidens allowed 15 lbs. One mile and three-sixteenths.

THE EQUITY STAKES, a sweepstakes for two year olds; $25 each, p. p., with $750 added, of which $150 to the second, and the third to save his stake. Colts and geldings to carry 118 lbs. Fillies 110 lbs. Winner of any race of the value of $1000 to carry 3 lbs; of two such races, or one of $2000, 5 lbs extra. Non-winners of $1000 allowed 5 lbs. Maidens allowed 10 lbs. Three quarters of a mile.

THE MORRISSEY STAKES, a handicap sweepstakes for all ages; $50 each, half forfeit, or only $10 if declared out by July 25th, with $1,000 added; the second horse to receive $250, and the third $100 out of the stakes. Weights to be announced by Aug. 20th. Winner after announcement of weights, of $1,500, to carry 4 lbs. extra; or of a handicap of that value, 7 lbs extra. One and three-quarter miles.

THE RELIEF STAKES, a sweepstakes for three year olds; $50 entrance, h. f., with $1000 added, of which $200 to the second horse, and the third to receive $100 out of the stakes. Colts and geldings to carry 118 lbs. Fillies 110 lbs. Winners in 1890 of any race of the value of $2000 to carry 3 lbs. extra; of two races of the value of $2000 each, or one of $4000, in 1889 or 1890, 5 lbs. extra. Other horses not having won a race this year of the value of $1000 allowed 5 lbs.; or not having won a race this year, 10 lbs. Maidens allowed 15 lbs. One mile and five hundred yards.

The usual 30 days racing (regular and extra) will be given. Dates will be announced in due time.

NOT LESS THAN FIVE RACES EACH DAY THROUGHOUT THE SEASON

When there are more than fifteen entries for one or more purse races, the race for which there is the largest number of entries will be "split" in the usual way, and an extra purse will be given by the Association; or if two races have an equal number of entries above fifteen, the one to be split will be determined by lot.

MR. FURMAN T. NUTT has been engaged as Presiding Judge for the season.

MR. JAMES SHERIDAN has been engaged as Starter.

STABLING FREE OF CHARGE, and all possible accommodations extended to turfmen.

Nominations for the stakes to close March 1st, to be addressed to the Secretary, at Fordham, Station T, New York City.

Errors: The Secretary, with the approval of the Executive Committee, is authorized to correct palpable errors in entries, if promptly reported.

☞ Turfmen failing to receive entry blanks will be supplied on application by letter or otherwise to the Secretary.

JAMES M. MARVIN, President.

C. WHEATLY, Secretary.

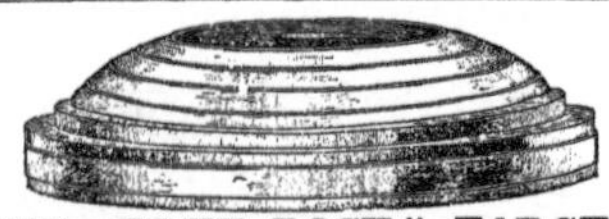

THE "BLUE ROCK" TARGET.

Quotations furnished F. O. B. at Cleveland, Ohio, or San Francisco.

CLABROUGH, GOLCHER & CO.,

630 and 632 Montgomery Street, S. F., Cal.

SOLE AGENTS for the Pacific Coast.

SAMUEL VALLEAU. JAS. R. BRODIE.

J. R. BRODIE & CO.,
Steam Printers,
—And Dealers in—
Poolseller's and Bookmaker's Supplies.
401—403 *Sansome Street, corner Sacramento, San Francisco.*

Brushes.

BUCHANAN BROS.,
Brush Manufacturers,
609 Sacramento Street, two doors above Montgomery.

Horse Brushes of every description on hand and made to order. Bristle Body Brushes our Specialty.

KENNEL ADVERTISEMENTS

Thoroughbred Pugs,

$40 each.

PEDIGREE.

PUPPIES { Fido... { Imp. Jumbo ..... { Marshall's Un / Lady Bess; Fanni .... Rex / Imp. Fly } ; Budge. { Senator Fair's Fritz; McCleery's Mamma Snoots { Sam / Imp. Alice } }

Can be seen daily from 9 A. M. to 3 P. M. at 411 Ell Street, San Francisco.

J. F. B. McCLEERY.

Irish Setters & Pointers

In the Stud, winner of 16 first and special prizes CHAMPION MIKE T., 6435, A. K. S. B. Irish Setter puppies by Champion Mike T. 6435 A. K. S. B.—Champion Lady Elcho T. 6451 A. K. S. B., for sale. Two pointers, a year old, by Rush T. 10069 K. S. B.—Champion Patti Croxteth T. 10128 A. K. S. B. for sale. Yard broken. Address,

A. B. TRUMAN,
1425 Steiner St., S. F., Cal.

CALIFORNIA SPANIEL KENNELS

Oakland, California. H. P. RENNIE, Prop. Breeder and importer of typical COCKER SPANIELS. Winner of first prizes at S. F. and Los Angeles, 18[illegible] also, Columbus, 18[illegible] New York, 1887. In the stud, solid Black Cocker dog, GIFFE[illegible] won 1st and Gold Medal at S. F., 18[illegible] Fee, $25. Puppies and grown dogs at reasonable prices. My dogs can neither talk nor climb a tree, but are fielders and prize winners.

Highland Farm,

LEXINGTON, KY.,

Home of Red Wilkes.

Standard-bred Trotting Stock

For Sale,

Sired by Red Wilkes, Wilton, 2:19¼; Allandorf and Sentinel Wilkes, out of highly bred Standard Mares of the most fashionable blood of the day.

W. C. FRANCE, Proprietor

The Park Training Stable

CHAS. DAVID, PROPRIETOR.

Corner Grove and Baker Streets, near Entrance to Golden Gate Park.

EVERY FACILITY FOR TRAINING COLTS and taking care of Gentlemen's Roadsters.

Finely appointed stable with every convenience and sixteen roomy box stalls.

The best care given all horses by experienced help under the personal superintendence of the proprietor.

Convenient to the Park Speed Drive, and Accessible to Six Lines of Cable Cars.

THE TRAINING OF COLTS AND ROADSTERS A SPECIALTY.

TROTTERS AND ROADSTERS FOR SALE.
HORSES SOLD ON COMMISSION.

The proprietor trained and brought out the following well known horses: "Sister, Huntress," "Perihelion," "Nona Y," and others.

NOVEL USEFUL and Ornamental.

The Perfection Horse Tail Tie

Saves Time and the Tail.

Send 25 cents for Sample,
BREEDER AND SPORTSMAN,
313 Bush Street, San Francisco,
or to BARNES & PARKER, Des Moines, Ia., Manufrs.

GOLDEN EAGLE HOTEL

Corner SEVENTH and K STREETS, SACRAMENTO.

FIRST CLASS IN EVERY RESPECT.

The LARGEST and FINEST HOTEL in the City.

W. O. BOWERS, Proprietor

Free 'Buss to and from the Hotel.

Telephone, Telegraph Office and Messenger Service in Hotel.

The Trotting Stallion

Silver Bow

Will make the season of 1890 at the Oakland Race Track.

Pedigree.

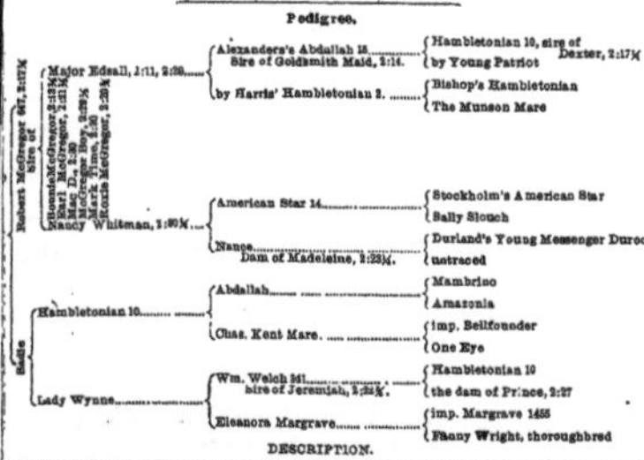

DESCRIPTION.

SILVER BOW is a handsome bay, no white; 15-2¾ hands high; weighs 1071 pounds; of fine form, with the set of legs and a clean cut, intelligent head. Is remarkably level headed, seldom making a break; wears ounce shoes in front. His record 2:37, is no mark of his speed; he can beat 30 easy, and with his gilt-edge breeding, he is just what he ought to be, a trotter sired by a trotter whose dam was herself a trotter and his grandam the dam of two trotters. His dam Sadie being by Hambletonian 10, shows him to be bred from the cream of the trotting blood.

TERMS: $100 for the season. Mares not proving in foal returnable for the season of 1891 free of charge. Good pasturage and first-class care taken of mares for $5 per month. No responsibility assumed for escapes or accidents. For further particulars, address

Limited to 15 approved mares.
Season to end June 1st, 1890.

P. J. WILLIAMS.
Care Race Track, Oakland, Cal.

1890 Three Anteeo Stallions 1890

SUNSET, 5 years old, by Anteeo
ANTEEOF, 4 years old, by Anteeo
ANTEEOP, 3 years old, by Anteeo

ANTEEO. Standard 7868. Record, 2:16 1-4. He by Stanford's Electioneer, and dam Columbine.

DESCRIPTIONS, PEDIGREES AND CONDITIONS.

"SUNSET" is a rich, dark bay, small star on forehead, portion of hind left foot white; was foaled March 1 1885; is by ANTEEO and the inbred HAMBLETONIAN mare, BESSIE G, she by KING PHILLIP, son of WHIPPLE'S HAMBLETONIAN. He is 16 1 2 hands high, and weighs 1,150 lbs. He is of perfect build and splendid action, level headed and great speed for his size, having trotted a trial mile as a three-year-old in 2:38. He then entered heavy in the stud and was matched against Whalebone at the Healdsburg races November 2, 1889, winning just as he pleased in three straight heats; time, 2:47, 2:46 1-2, 2:52 1-2. He was then matched for a race to come off last Thanksgiving Day at Petaluma but owing to the heavy rains the event did not take place. A few days previous to Thanksgiving Day Mr. Lawrence worked Sunset out and then he trotted three square miles and heats in 2:33½, 2:34 and 2.37.

SUNSET will be bred to 40 mares only, at $50 each, no colt no pay.

"ANTEEOF" is a jet black, was foaled April 13, 1886, is 16¼ hands high, and weighs 1,200 lbs., has a very fine, heavy black mane and tail; is well proportioned, moves majestically, is of easy, lofty carriage; is symmetrical, in fact is a beautiful horse. He was sired by Anteeo and the O. A. Taylor mare "Nance," her dam, was raised by Dr. Oliver Plummer, of Consumnes, Cal., and sired by "Napoleon"; Napoleon was foaled May 1, 1833, and raised by James Kyle of Butler County, Ohio. He was sired by Benj. Sweet's horse Bellfounder, and he by Old Bellfounder, his dam was sired by Doc. Daniel Melligan's horse, Cadmus, G. G. sire the celebrated Eclipse; his G. dam was sired by Big Shakespeare, G. G., sires dam by Messenger and Expedition.

ANTEEOF will be bred to 25 mares only, at $50 each. No colt, no pay.

"ANTEEOP" is a rich seal brown; was foaled March 7, 1887; by Anteeo and the inbred Hambletonian mare Bessie G., also dam of Sunset, his full brother and Midget his full sister; he is 15 1-2 hands high and weighs 950 lbs, and measures 22 inches around the arm, good head, fine neck, full, broad breast; wethers and rump on nearly equal line, well proportioned bones, ankle, shoulders, loins and hips; strong legs all around, with great muscular development and splendid sinews; wirey pasterns and sound, compact feet; the lines from hip to hoof show power and speed; stands square and has excellent action, has a superb lustrous coat of rich, deep brown fur of seal color without defect; an even, honest trotter, and has gone the mile as a two-year-old in 2:43, the last quarter in 38 seconds; is intelligent and of high spirit, with much temper, but is not vicious, has very fine eyes, is a handsome, showy colt; attractive in harness.

ANTEEOP will be bred to 15 mares only, at $50. No colt, no pay.

SEASON to commence February 1st, ending July 1, 1891. Book now ready. Apply to John H. Lawrence, "Manager and Trainer," on my fruit and hop ranch, 1 mile east of Court House, on Sonoma road, excellent pasture furnished with running water, also dry knolls with oak shelter, at $4 per month for mares. Two of the above stallions will be for sale after the expiration of the their stud season.

GUY E. GROSSE,
SANTA ROSA, SONOMA CO., CAL.

MANHATTAN FOOD.

keeps horses healthy, promotes digestion, fattens horses, loosens the hide, assists the appetite, prevents leg swelling, strengthens the kidneys, regulates the bowels and destroys worms. **$7.50 per 100 lbs.** Ask your dealer for it or send to

MANHATTAN FOOD CO., 206 Clay St., S. F.

THE BRUNSWICK BALKE COLLENDER COMPANY,

MANUFACTURERS OF

Standard Billiard and Pool Tables, Saloon and Bank Fixtures,
653--655 Market Street, San Francisco, Cal.

J. O'KANE, Horse Boots, Clothing and Furnishings,
For Track, Driving Training and Stable.
Every requisite for Horsemen.
Harness, Medicines, Etc.

Guenoc Stud Farm, Lake Co., Cal.

Imp. GREENBACK

(Sire of the English winners Greenlight, Greenjacket, Greenshank, Greenwave and Greenhorn)

By Dollar, dam Music, by Stockwell. $100 the Season

ST. SAVIOR,

(FULL BROTHER TO EOLE)

By Eolus, dam War Song, by War Dance. $100 the Season.

PASTURAGE, $5 PER MONTH.

With right to return the following year it mare does not prove with foal. The best of care taken, but no liability for accidents or escapes. Mares shipped to C. W. ABY, care ST. HELENA STABLES, St. Helena Napa County, will be taken in charge by competent men.

For further information write to

DR. C. W. ABY, Middletown, Lake County, Cal.

SOUTHER FARM

P. O. Box 208. San Leandro, Cal.

1½ miles northwest of San Leandro; 8 miles southeast of Oakland. Turn off county road between above places at "Stanley Road," ½ mile north of San Leandro.

Horses boarded at all times in any manner desired. Best of care but no responsibility for accidents. Colts broken and handled for the road or track. Terms reasonable.

Glen Fortune,	Jester D,	El Benton,	Figaro,
By Electioneer.	By Almont.	By Electioneer.	Hambletonian 725
$50 for 1889.	$50 for 1890.	Limited to 5 mares.	Limited to 12 mares
		Book Full.	Book Full.

If horses are to last for a profitable time they must occasionally have a change from hard pavements, wooden floors, and dry, hard feed.

THE SOUTHER FARM

Has Green Feed the Year Round,

and feeds Hay in connection with the green feed, which a horse must have if he is to thrive. Every animal is given

A Dry, Warm Place to Sleep,

No matter how stormy the weather. All Stock under cover when it rains.

VISITORS WELCOME ANY DAY EXCEPT SUNDAY.

Write to the above address for references, circulars and price lists. Terms reasonable.

GILBERT TOMPKINS, Proprietor.

SAN MATEO STOCK FARM

HOME OF GUY WILKES,
Record, 2:15 1-4.

Guy Wilkes' Book is full for 1890, and positively no more mares will be received. Book now open for 1891, at $500 the Season.

Sable Wilkes, three-year-old record 2:18, will be allowed to serve 25 mares in addition to those already engaged at $250 the season of 1890. SABLE Wilkes, 15½ hands, black horse, by Guy Wilkes, first dam Sable by The Moor; second dam Gretchen by Mambrino Pilot; third dam Kitty Kirkman by Canada Chief; fourth dam by Fanning's Tobe; fifth dam by imp. Leviathan.

Leo Wilkes, brown horse, four years, 16 hands, full brother to Sable Wilkes, will be allowed to serve 30 mares at $100 the season

Mares not proving with foal may be returned the following season free of service fee. Parties engaging the services of any of the above horses must send a deposit of 10 per cent. of service money with engagement. Pasturage $6 per month, and when the condition of the animal requires it, hay or grain, or both, are fed, the charge will be $12 50 per month. Good care will be taken of all mares sent to the Farm, but no liability will be assumed for accidents or escapes.

All bills are due at time of service, but must be paid by August 1st of each year. No stock will be allowed to leave the place until all bills are paid.

WILLIAM CORBITT.
San Mateo Stock Farm.

Poplar Grove Breeding FARM.

Standard-bred Trotters, Colts and Fillies.

The get of CLOVIS, 4909; PASHA, 2039; APEX, 2935,

For Sale.

Address S. N. STRAUBE, Poplar Grove Breeding Farm,
Fresno, Cal.

Inspection by intending purchasers invited, and information by mail.

CHICAGO, ILLS. -:- BREEDERS' SALE

SECOND GRAND COMBINATION SALE OF

KIDD, EDMONSON & MORSE,

Will be held in Chicago, Ill., MARCH 17th to 23d, 1890.

Trotters, Pacers, Stallions, Brood Mares, Colts, Saddle and Harness Horses

Those wishing to dispose of their stock to the best advantage should send for conditions and entry blanks at once, as the sale promises to be very large.

Entries to close February 20, 1890. Send in your entries at once.

Our first sale was a grand success, and was only a foreshadowing of what is to follow. Address,

KIDD, EDMONSON & MORSE, Lexington, Ky.

Or No. 806 West Madison St., Chicago, Ill.

Brothers of the Angle.

OUR NEW EIGHT-STRIP SPLIT BAMBOO is the "King" of all fishing-rods. Chubb's New Catalogue for 1890 is now ready. In addition to a complete list of anglers' supplies, it containsarticles from the pens of Dr. James A. Henshall, Petronella, W. H. Murray, Geo. P. Goff Norman, Brother Gardner, and others.

These papers are by the best writers on angling subjects, and are very interesting.

Send 25 cents, and receive Catalogue, post-paid. This amount will be deducted from first order (if accompanied with Coupon in book) for one dollar's worth or more of our goods. Address

THOS. H. CHUBB.

The Fishing-Rod Manufacturer,

POST MILLS, VT.

Please mention BREEDER AND SPORTSMAN.

2:20 1-2 (Half Mile Track) at 4 Years. — Fastest Record (in a Race) of any Wilkes — 2:14 1-2 at 5 Years.

ROY WILKES, 2:12 3/4,

Seal brown; 15¾ hands; foaled 1883; by Adrian Wilkes 6660, son of Geo. Wilkes; 1st dam by Blue Bull 75; 2d dam by grandson of American Eclipse; 3d and 4th dams thoroughbred.

THE GREATEST CAMPAIGNER OF 1889.

Handsome, Game, Pure Gaited. Level Headed.

Will make a season at the PLEASANTON STOCK FARM, PLEASANTON, CAL Service Fee $150. Money refunded if mare does not get with foal. Season ends April 1st, 1890

For full record of performances, extended pedigree, etc., address

L. A. DAVIES, Hotel Pleasanton,

SUTTER AND JONES STREETS, San Francisco, Cal.

The Trotting Stallion

Guide 2:29

(At Four Years)

Will make the season of 1890 at the SANTA RITA RANCH, about one mile North of Pleasanton.

DESCRIPTION.

GUIDE is a handsome seal brown, five years old, stands 15¼ hands high, and weighs 1035 pounds. He is of fine form, level headed, intelligent, and comes from blood lines that are noted for the qualities of speed and gameness.

PEDIGREE.

GUIDE, 2:28¼.
- Director, 2:17. Sire of Direct, 2:18¼. Margaret S., 2:19¼.
  - Dictator 113. Sire of 28 trotters and 3 pacers in 2:30.
    - Hambletonian 10.
    - Clara, by American Star 14.
  - Dolly. Dam of Onward, 2:25¼. Thorndale, 2:22¼.
    - Mambrino Chief 11.
    - Fannie, by Ben Franklin.
- Imogene.
  - Norwood 522. Sire of Tommy Norwood, 2:26¼.
    - Hambletonian 10.
    - Lady Fallis, by American Star 14.
  - daughter of
    - American Star 14.
    - daughter of Henry Clay 8.

The attention of breeders is especially called to the above pedigree as showing 3 crosses of American Star.

GUIDE trotted into the 2:30 list last season with little training, and he will trot into the 2:20 list the coming season barring accidents.

Guide's sire has a record of 2:17, made in a five heat race, and Guide is closely related to Phallas, who made a record of 2:13¾ in a fourth heat, and to Jay-Eye-See, record 2:10.

TWO HUNDRED AND FIFTY DOLLARS will be given to the owner of the first of the produce of Guide put in the 2:30 list, and $100 to each one after the first.

TERMS—$75 for the season, with the usual return privileges.

Admiro,

Sire Admiral; dam by San Bruno, by Easton's David Hill.

This magnificent horse is a handsome bay, eight years old; stands 17 1-2 hands high, and weighs 1400 pounds He is very speedy for a large horse, and breeds fine large carriage horses. His produce possess every qualification of the Cleveland Bay, with the added qualities of speed and endurance resulting from his high trotting breeding.

TERMS—$35 for the season, with usual return privileges.

Will stand three days each week at Santa Rita Ranch, Pleasanton, and at A. T. Hatch's Ranch "Almono," Alamo, Contra Costa County, alternately. All mares sent care of SMITH & SUTHERLAND, Pleasanton, will be taken in charge of on arrival, and will receive the best care and attention in any manner the owners may desire. Good pasturage at $4 per month. Only a limited number of approved mares will be served by this horse this season.

No responsibility assumed for escapes or accidents. For further particulars, address

SMITH & SUTHERLAND, Pleasanton.

or A. T. HATCH, care Palace Hotel, San Francisco.

Fine Hats,

Latest Styles and Colors.

Meussdorffer & Hubner

8 Kearny Street, San Francisco,

Next to New Chronicle Building.

John D. Gall. Jas. P. Dunne

"The Resort,"

No. 1 Stockton Street, cor. Ellis,

San Francisco.

'TOBEY'S,"

214 Post Street,

Between Grant Avenue and Stockton Street,

Adjoining New Hamman Baths.

D. J. TOBIN, Proprietor.

ROME HARRIS. JOHN MERIGAN,

"Laurel Palace,"

N. W. corner Kearny and Bush Streets

SAN FRANCISCO.

Pleasanton Stock Farm Co.'s Stallions.

DIRECTOR, 2:17.

Director's book is open for 15 good mares more than already booked for the season of 1890, at $200 each.

This is the cheapest service fee ever charged for a stallion, taking into consideration his BREEDING and RACE RECORD and the RACE RECORDS OF HIS COLTS.

Season to commence February 15th and close August 1st.

PLEASANTON.

Sire Director 2:17. Dam May Day 2:30.

PLEASANTON is a light bay, 16 hands high, and is full brother to Margaret S, three year old record 2:19½.

His book is now open for 10 good mares at $100 for the season, which will commence March 1st and end June 1st.

Mares not proving with foal may be returned next season free of charge of service fees to the same stallion, if he is still in our possession; if not, to some other stallion equally as good, or money will be refunded at option of the company.

Pasturage $4 per month; hay and grain extra. Accidents and escapes at owner's risk.

Service fees due at time of service, and must be paid, together with pasturage, etc., before mares are taken away, or a good approved note given, payable August 1st, 1890, at which date all bills must be settled.

For further information call or address M. SALISBURY, 320 Sansome Street, Room 96 San Francisco, or

PLEASANTON STOCK FARM CO.;

Pleasanton, Alameda Co., Cal.

BAY STALLION	BROWN STALLION
ECLECTIC	**MORTIMER**
11,321	5,346
By Electioneer, dam Manette (full sister to Woodnut 2.16 1-2) Manon 2:21 and Maple, dam of Hattie D. (three year-old record 2:26¼) by Nutwood 2:18¾, etc., etc.	Four-year-old Record 2:27. By ELECTIONEER, dam MARTI, by Whipple's Hambletonian (sire of 15 in 2:30, and of dams of eight in 2:30). Second dam Ida Martin by Rifleman (sire of Col. Lewis 2:18¾).
Terms $100 for the Season.	Terms $60 for the Season.

Horses shipped via San Francisco may be consigned to J. W. MORSHEAD, City Front Stables, who will attend to their forwarding.

Season closes JULY 1st, 1890. Usual return privileges.

For further particulars address owner,

WILFRED PAGE, Penns Grove,

Sonoma County, Cal

Valensin Stock Farm Stallions.

SIDNEY, 2:19 3-4.

At Eight Years of Age Sire of the following Fastest on Record;

FAUSTINO, yearling stallion, record of the world	2:35
FLEET, fastest yearling record in 1888	2:36
FLEET, fastest two-year-old filly in 1889	2:24
GOLD LEAF, fastest four-year-old Pacing record in the world	2:11
ADONIS, fastest three-year-old Pacing Gelding in the world	2:14
ADONIS, four-year-old Gelding Pacing record	2:14

—Also the Sire of—

LONGWORTH, four years old	2:19
SISTER V., four years old (trial 2:23)	2:27
SANTA RITA	2:39
MEMO, two-year-old (three-year-old trial 2:20½)	2:49

And many others.

SIDNEY is the sire of Faustino 2:35, and Fleet 2:36, the two fastest yearlings the world has ever known by one sire, and his slowest yearling is faster than the great Electioneer's fastest.

Terms, $250, with usual return privileges, for a limited number of approved mares. Book rapidly filling.

SIMMOCOLON, Four-year-old, 2:29 1-2.

Trial, 2:24; Half Mile in 1:08; Quarter in 33 1-2 Seconds.

Chestnut Horse, foaled 1885.

SIMMOCOLON.
- Simmons 2774. Sire of Bon Bon, 4 y. o. rec., 2:26, Raymon, 4 y. o. rec., 2:27, Black Storm, 3 y. o. rec. 2:27¾, and six others with records of 2:30 or better.
  - George Wilkes 519. Sire of 61 in 2:30 list. Sire of 11 dams of 12 in 2:30 list
    - Hambletonian 10. Sire of 41 in 2:30 list. Sire of 107 sires of 567 in 2:30 list. Sire of 44 dams of 50 in 2:30 list.
    - Dolly Spanker
  - Black Jane. Dam of Rosa Wilkes, 2:18¼. Dam of Simmons, 2:28
    - Mambrino Patchen 58. Sire of 14 in 2:30 list. Sire of 21 sires of 37 in 2:30 list. Sire of 24 dams of 28 in 2:30 list.
    - Lady Stanhope
- Colon. Dam of Simmocolon, 4 y. o. rec., 2:29½. Dam of Patchmore, 2:23¼
  - Strathmore. Sire of 27 in 2:30 list. Sire of 4 dams of 5 in 2:30. Sire of 3 sires of 3 in 2:30
    - Hambletonian 10 (Same as above)
    - Lady Waltermire. Dam of Marshall Ney
  - Coral. Trial at 2 years, 2:50. Dam of Coralloid, 2:29¼
    - Clark Chief 89. Sire of 6 in 2:30 list. Sire of 9 sires of 27 in list. Sire of 11 dam with 11 in list
    - Colon. Dam of Caliban, sire of 2 in 2:30 list

As will be seen, Simmocolon is by a performing and producing son of George Wilkes, 2:22. He has back of him three producing dams, and combines the blood of the great sire George Wilkes handsomely blended with the blood of the greatest broodmare families. On the dam's side Mambrino Patchen, Strathmore, Clark Chief and Clay. A fine individual himself, pure gaited and very fast.

Terms, $150, with usual return privileges, for a limited number of mares. Season to close JUNE 15th, when he will be prepared for track purposes. Pasturage $5 per month. Reasonable charges if fed hay and grain. Best of care taken of mares, but positively no responsibility assumed for accidents or escapes. For further particulars address

G. VALENSIN, Pleasanton, Cal.

Pacific Coast Trotting - Horse Breeders Ass'n

Stakes and Installment Purses for 1890.

Entries close March 1st, 1890.

STAKES.

YEARLINGS—FOALS 1889.

ONE MILE DASH, $50 entrance, payable $5 March 1, 1890, $10 May 1, 1890, $10 July 1, 1890 and $25 on the fifth day preceeding the first advertised day of the meeting.

TWO-YEAR-OLDS—FOALS 1888.

ONE MILE AND REPEAT; $75 entrance, $250 added, payable $10 on March 1, 1890, $10 May 1, 1890, $15 July 1, 1890, and $40 on the fifth day preceding the first advertised day of the meeting.

THREE-YEAR-OLDS—FOALS 1887.

MILE HEATS best three in five; entrance $100, with $300 added, payable $10 on March 1, 1890, $10 on May 1, 1890, $30 on July 1, 1890, and $50 on the fifth day preceding the first advertised day of the meeting.

FOUR-YEAR-OLDS—FOALS 1886.

MILE HEATS best three in five; $100 entrance, $400 added, payable $10 on March 1, 1890, $10 May 1, 1890, $30 on July 1, 1890, and $50 on the fifth day preceding the first day of the meeting.

PURSES.

$500. THREE YEAR OLDS. Foals of 1887. Eligible to three minute class. Mile heats; three in five.

$500. FOUR YEAR OLDS. Foals of 1886, eligible to 2:40 class. Mile heats; three in five.

Purses open to the get of Stallions with no Representatives in the 2:30 list.

$400. TWO YEAR OLDS. Foals of 1888. Mile and repeat.

$500. THREE YEAR OLDS. Foals of 1887. Mile heats; three in five.

$500. FOUR YEAR OLDS. Foals of 1886. Mile heats; three in five.

Stallion Purse $1,000.

Open to stallions eligible to 2:30 class. Mile heats, three in five.

ENTRANCE to all purses—10 per cent.; payable: 2 per cent. March 1st 1890; 2 per cent. May 1st, 1890; 2 per cent. July 1st, 1890; and 4 per cent. on the fifth day preceding the first advertised day of the meeting.

The Stanford Stakes for 1892.

FOALS OF 1889.

OPEN TO THE WORLD.

MILE HEATS.—Three in five. Entrance $100, with $100 added for each starter over two and up to five head, and $25 for each additional starter up to ten head. Payments: $10 on March 1st, 1890; $10 on January 2nd, 1891; $10 on January 2nd, 1892; $20 on May 1st, 1892; and $50 on the fifth day preceding the first advertised day of the meeting at which the stake shall be trotted.

CONDITIONS.

First payment, whether for purses payable in installments or for stakes, MUST ACCOMPANY NOMINATIONS, or they will not be considered.

Neglect to provide payments on the dates stipulated will incur forfeiture of all previous payments.

No horses and colts owned on the Pacific Coast by others than members of the P. C. T. H. B. A. are eligible to the above purses and stakes (excepting the Stanford stake), but horses and colts OWNED outside of the Pacific Coast are eligible thereto regardless of membership.

All States and Territories lying in whole or in part west of the Rocky Mountains are held to be part of the Pacific Coast.

The Directors reserve the right to change the hour and day of any race except when it becomes necessary to ante-date a race, in which instance the nominator will receive three days notice of change by mail to address of entry.

Entries not declared out by 6 P. M. of the day preceding the race, shall be required to start.

When there is more than one entry to a purse or stake by one person or in one interest, the horse to be started must be named by 6 P. M. of the day preceding the race.

Purses and stakes will be divided into four moneys, viz., 50 per cent. to the winner, 25 per cent. to the second horse, 15 per cent. to the third horse, and 10 per cent. to the fourth horse.

No added money will be paid for a walk-over. If only three horses start in a stake race, only first, second and third money shall be paid—if but two start, the Directors reserve the right to call it a walk-over, and divide the stake money paid in, two thirds to the winner and one-third to the second horse. In case of a walk-over, only the money received from entries to said stake will be paid. In purse races, three horses will be required to start.

A horse distancing the field shall only be entitled to first and third moneys.

The Board of Directors reserve the right to declare any purse or stake filled or not filled without binding itself to any specified number of entries.

Trotting and racing colors shall be named by six o'clock on the day preceding the race, and MUST be worn upon the track.

Otherwise than the above, National or American Trotting Association Rules—as this Association may select—will govern the stake and purse races offered.

Persons desirous of making entries in the above purses and stakes, and who have not as yet joined the P. C. T. H. B. A., should make application for membership to the Secretary, and remit the sum of $25 to cover membership fee before March 1, 1890.

THE PROGRAMME

FOR

Aged Horses--Trotters and Pacers,

AND FOR SPECIAL EVENTS,

will be announced at the proper time.

J. H. WHITE, President.

JAS. P. KERR, Secretary.

313 Bush Street, S. F.

1890.

Petaluma Colt Stakes

TO BE TROTTED AT THE

Fall Meeting

OF THE

Sonoma and Marin Agricultural Society

District No. 4.

FREE-FOR-ALL COLTS.

1st. For two-year-olds, foals of 1888, Purse $400, entrance 10 per cent. of the purse, of which 2½ per cent. must accompany the nomination, to be made on March 1st; 2½ per cent., be paid on May 1st, and 5 per cent. on August 1st. Four colts to make the last payment, and three to start.

2nd. For three-year-olds, foals of 1887. Purse $500, entrance ten per cent. of the purse, of which 2½ per cent. must accompany the nomination to be made on March 1st, 2½ per cent to be paid on May 1st, and 5 per cent. on August 1st. Four colts to make the last payment, and three to start.

All moneys in the above races to be divided as follows: 60 per cent. to the first horse, 30 per cent. to the second, and 10 per cent. to the third.

Balance of conditions as per District Stakes.

The following Stakes and Purses open to the Counties of Sonoma, Marin, Napa, Solano, Lake, Mendocino, Yolo and Colusa.

YEARLING STAKE.

For foals of 1889. Mile dash. $30 entrance, of which $10 must accompany the nomination March 1st; $10 be paid on May 1st and $10 on July 1st; $100 added.

TWO-YEAR-OLD STAKE.

For foals of 1888. Mile and repeat. $50 entrance, of which $10 must accompany the nomination March 1st; $10 be paid on May 1st and $30 on July 1st; $200 added.

THREE-YEAR-OLD PURSE.

Three in five. Purse $500. Entrance fee 10 per cent. of the purse, of which five per cent. must accompany the nomination March 1st, and five per cent. paid on August 1st. Four colts to make the last payment.

In the above stakes and purses, five to enter and three to start. But the Board reserves the right to hold entries, and start a race with a less number.

All moneys in the above races to be divided as follows: 60 per cent. to the first horse, 30 per cent. to the second and 10 per cent. to the third. If only two start they must contest for the stakes paid in, and one-half the added money to be divided, 66⅔ per cent. to the first and 33⅓ per cent. to the second.

If, in the opinion of the judges, any race cannot be finished on the closing day of the fair it may be continued or declared off at the option of the judges.

Entries to all the above races to close on March 1, 1890, with the Secretary.

J. H. WHITE, President.

DR. THOS. MACLAY, Secretary.

CALIFORNIA

NUTWOOD

Will stand for mares the season of 1890, commencing February 15th, and ending July 15th, at the NUTWOOD STOCK FARM, one mile from Irvington.

DESCRIPTION AND PEDIGREE.

He is a dark chestnut, with star in forehead; foaled September 18th, 1881; is 16 hands 1½ inches high and weighs 1250 pounds. Has a beautiful flowing mane and tail, with remarkable style and lofty carriage, a bold, open movement like his sire, but has never been handled for speed. He moves and looks like his sire, except that he is a larger horse.

CALIFORNIA NUTWOOD by Nutwood, record 2:18¾, has 32 trotters and pacers with records from 2:15 to 2:30, and put 8 in the 2:30 list in 1889. He is the only horse that ever lived with a record under 2:20 that produced five under 2:20. He is now serving mares at Dubuque, Iowa, at $500 for the season, and his colts at yearlings sell from $2500 to $5000 each. He is out of the dam of Maud S., record 2:08¾.

Nutwood, by Alexander's Belmont, sire of 32 with records from 2:15½ to 2:30. Alexander's Belmont by Alexander's Abdallah, sire of Goldsmiths Maid, record 2:14, and 5 others in 2:30 list. Alexander's Abdallah, by Rysdyk's Hambletonian, sire of 41 with records from 2:17¼ to 2:30, and is the founder of the Hambletonian family.

FANNY PATCHEN, dam of California Nutwood, by George M. Patchen Jr., record 2:27, and sire of Wells Fargo, 2:18¼, Sam Purdy 2:20½, Ben Ali 2:20¼, and 7 others from 2:21 to 2:30. He has 7 sons who together produced 12 trotters in 2:30 list, and 6 daughters who together produced 8 trotters and 1 pacer in 2:30 or better. He sired Alexander 2:31½. Alexander sired Alex. Button 2:26½; Alex. Button sired Yolo Maid, pacing record 2:14 at 4 years old, the fastest on record; George M. Patchen Jr., by George M. Patchen 2:23½, is sire of Lucy 2:18¼, and 3 others in the 2:30 list; he has 12 sons who together produced 40 trotters from 2:14¾ to 2:30, and 6 daughters who together produced 6 trotters in 2:30 list or better, he is grand sire of Hopeful 2:14¾, and best wagon record 2:16½, and sire of the granddam of Stamboul 2:12½.

George M. Patchen, by Cassius M. Clay, and he by Henry Clay, founder of the Clay family.

Laura, second dam of California Nutwood, was a fine large bay mare, a very fast roadster brought from Chicago by Wm. Wilson, of San Jose, and is said to have made a record of 2.35 in Chicago. Pedigree not traced.

TERMS.

$40 for the season, payable invariably before the animal is removed. Mares not proving in foal can be returned free next season. Pasturage $3 per month, but no liability for accidents or escapes. For further particulars address the owner,

MARTIN CARTER,

Newark, Alameda Co., Cal., or Irvington, Alameda County, Cal.

SACRAMENTO

COLT STAKES ASSOCIATION

TROTTING AND PACING COLT STAKES FOR 1890.

N. B—Horsemen in the localities eligible will please note the conditions of each Stake.

SACRAMENTO YEARLING STAKE FOR 1890.

Open to all foals of 1889, owned in California on a line all north of and including the city of Stockton.

$75 entrance, of which $10 must accompany nomination; $15 to be paid May 1, 1890; $25 August 1, 1890, and $25 on the Saturday before the race. To be trotted at Sacramento during the State Fair of 1890. One mile dash. First colt to receive 50 per cent, second colt 30 per cent, and third colt 20 per cent. of stake. Failure to make payments when due forfeits all previous payments.

TWO-YEAR-OLD STAKE.

Open to all foals of 1888, owned in California, on a line all north of and including the City of Stockton.

$75 entrance, of which $10 must accompany nomination; $15 to be paid April 1, 1890; $25 May 1, 1890, and $25 June 9, 1890. To be trotted at Sacramento, June 10, 1890, good day and track. One mile and repeat. First colt to receive 50 per cent. second colt 30 per cent. and third colt 20 per cent. of stake. Failure to make payments when due forfeits all previous payments.

THREE YEAR OLD STAKE.

Open to all foals of 1887, owned in California on a line all north of and including the City of Stockton.

$75 entrance, of which $10 must accompany nomination; $15 to be paid April 1st, 1890; $25 to be paid May 1st, 1890; and $25 June 9th, 1890. To be trotted at Sacramento June 10th, 1890, good day and track. Mile heats, three in five. First colt to receive 50 per cent., second colt 30 per cent., and third colt 20 per cent of stake. Failure to make payments when due forfeits all previous payments.

PACING STAKES.

YEARLING STAKE FOR 1890.

Open to all foals of 1889, owned in California, on a line all north of and including the City of Stockton.

$75 entrance, of which $10 must accompany nomination; $15 to be paid May 1st, 1890; $25 August 1st, 1890; and $25 on the Saturday before the race. To be paced at Sacramento the first Monday in November, 1890, good day and track. One mile dash. First colt to receive 50 per cent., second colt 30 per cent., and third colt 20 per cent. of stake. Failure to make payments when due forfeits all previous payments.

TWO-YEAR-OLD PACING STAKE.

Open to all foals of 1888, owned in California, on a line all north of and including the city of Stockton.

$75 entrance, of which $10 must accompany nomination; $15 to be paid May 1, 1890; $25 August 1, 1890, and $25 on the Saturday before the race. To be paced at Sacramento the first Monday in November, 1890, good day and track. Mile and repeat. First colt to receive 50 per cent., second colt 30 per cent., and third colt 20 per cent. of stake. Failure to make payments when due forfeits all previous payments.

THREE YEAR-OLD PACING STAKE.

Open to all foals of 1887, owned in California on a line all north of and including the city of Stockton.

$75 entrance, of which $10 must accompany nomination; $15 to be paid May 1, 1890; $25 August 1, 1890, and $25 on the Saturday before the race. To be paced at Sacramento the first Monday in November, 1890, good day and track. Mile heats, three in five. First colt to receive 50 per cent., second colt 30 per cent., and third colt 20 per cent. of stake. Failure to make payments when due forfeits all previous payments.

Entries to all these stakes to close February 15, 1890, with

F. P. LOWELL, Secretary,

1320 F Street, Sacramento, Cal.

WILBER FIELD SMITH.

President Sacramento Colt Stake Association.

Season of 1890.

February 15 to June 15

LYNWOOD,

(STANDARD 3017.)

AT WOLF'S (RUSSELL'S) STABLES, STOCKTON, CAL.

TERMS.

$50 for the season, payable at the close of season. Pasturage at $3 per month. Accidents or escapes at owner's risk.

PEDIGREE.

LYNWOOD 3017, trial 2:28.

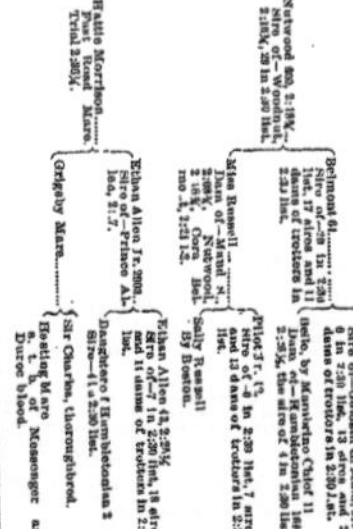

DESCRIPTION.

Dark bay, 15 hands, weighs 1050 pounds, form stout and elegant, gait pure and rapid. He was foaled July 17, 1886, has done but little work in the stud, but enough to demonstrate that he is one of the best foal getters in the State. Only one of his get has had any systematic handling, and that could have gone into the 2:30 list last year as a two-year-old, had the owner desired.

It will be observed from an examination of Lynwood's pedigree that he is one of the best bred sons of the GREAT NUTWOOD, who commands a service fee of $500 for the season.

P. VISHER, Stockton.

COOK STOCK FARM.

Season of 1890.

STEINWAY 1808.

Three-Year Old Record 2:25 3-4.

Sire of STRATHWAY, three year old record 2:26, and sire of the dam of BOURBON RUSSELL 2:30.

By STRATHMORE 408; sire of 31 in the 2:30 list; sire of 6 dams of 8 in the 2:30 list, and sire of 3 sires of 3 in 2:30 list

1st dam ABBESS (dam of Solo 2:28, and Soprano, dam of C. F Clay 2:18, Eminence 2:27 and Strathbridge, 3 year old record 2:29½) by ALBION, sire of VANITY FAIR 2:24½, and of the dam of FAVORITE 2:28¼.

2nd dam by MARSHALL NEY.

3rd dam by BERTRAND, a son of SIR ARCHY.

TERMS—$100 for the season.

CHARLES DERBY 4907

Brown Horse. Foaled 1885.

By STEINWAY 1808.

1st dam by the great ELECTIONEER, sire of SUNOL 3 year old record 2:10½, Palo Alto 2:12¼, etc., etc.

2nd dam FANNY MALONE, by NIAGARA.

3rd dam FANNY WICKHAM, by HERALD.

4th dam by Imp. TRUSTEE.

TERMS—$100 for the season.

CRESCO 4908.

(BROTHER TO SPARTAN, 2,24.)

By STRATHMORE 408, sire of 31 in the 2:30 list, etc.

1st dam the dam of SPARTAN 2:24, by ALMONT 33; sire of 71 with performers in the 2:30 list

2nd dam the dam of HENDERSON 2:27, by BRIGNOLI 77, sire of the dam of KING WILKES 2:22.

3rd dam by CRIPPLE, a son of MEDOC.

4th dam by AMERICAN ECLIPSE.

TERMS—$50 for the season.

Pasturage $5 per month. Accidents and escapes at owner's risk. Mares consigned to the farm should be sent to Fashion Stables, Oakland; Geary & Grindle's Stable, Haywards; or to Bennett's Stable, Martinez; from and to which places they will be delivered free of charge. Address

COOK STOCK FARM,

Danville, Contra Costa, Co., Cal.

The Thoroughbred Stallion

INTRUDER

Will make the Season of 1890 at Agricultural Park, SACRAMENTO.

Bay Horse, foaled 1871, bred by Sir L. Newman, England. Imported by D. D. Withers, Esq., New York.

By Crater, Son of Orlando and Vesuvienne by Gladiator.

1st dam Lady Bountiful by Rataplan (Rataplan is own brother to Stockwell, and winner of 42 races, including the Doncaster Cup and 16 Queen's Plates, and proved himself the most distinguished race horse of his day in England).

2d dam Plentiful by Don John (the winner of St. Leger and Doncaster Cup).

3d dam Plenty by Bay Middleton (winner of the Derby and Two Thousand Guineas Stakes).

4th dam Plenary, own sister of Plenipotentiary, by Emilius. (Both Emilius and Plenipotentiary were Derby winners).

5th dam Harriet, dam of the renowned Plenipotentiary by Pericles.

6th dam by Selim, winner of the One Thousand Guineas stakes.

7th dam by Pipylina, by Sir Peter.

8th dam Rally, by Trumpeter.

9th dam Fancy, by Florizel. Fancy was full sister to Diomed, the first Derby winner in England, and after his importation into this country, sired the illustrious Sir Archy, etc. See English Stud Book.

Imported INTRUDER is a beautiful bay, standing fully 16 hands high, of great length and substance, and descends through close and strong currents from the most illustrious winners and winning lines of blood of which the English Stud Book bears record.

A careful review of the first six crosses of the pedigree of INTRUDER will show nine Derby winners; five St. Leger winners; two winners of The Oaks; two winners of the Two Thousand Guineas; two winners of the One Thousand Guineas; one Goodwood Cup winner; one Cesarwich Cup winner; one Cambridgeshire Stakes winner, and four Doncaster Cups, in addition to a great number of Steeplechases and other races of less import.

INTRUDER, at the great fair held at St. Louis, Mo., in 1876, was awarded the highest stallion honor—the blue ribbon and the $500 purse—in the sweepstakes ring for stallion of any age or blood. The list of competitors embraced the large number of thirty-three animals, and they represented England, Canada, Kentucky, Tennessee, and other states. He also took first premium in his class and in sweepstakes for the best stallion of any age or breed at the State Fair at Peoria, Ill. 1882. He is the sire of Tidal Wave, George Hakes, Sorrento and April Fool.

INTRUDER is the sire of Interpose, who is the dam of Spokane, winner of the Kentucky Derby, in which he beat the great horse Proctor Knott and broke the record.

TERMS: $50 for the season. Mares not proving with foal can be returned the next season free of charge. Good pasturage at $1 per month. Mares cared for in any manner owners may desire, and fed on hay and grain, either or both, at reasonable rates. While every precaution will be taken, no responsibility will be assumed for escapes or accidents. Mares sent from a distance in care of the undersigned, will be met and taken to the park. For further particulars, address

T. J. KNIGHT.

Agricultural Park, Sacramento.

Shoes For Comfort, Elegance and Durability.

Having my own Factory, and giving my personal supervision to all work I am in a position to warrant perfect satisfaction. Inspection invited.

AGENT for the VISCALIZED SHOES.

FACTORY S W. cor. Battery and Jackson Sts.

SALESROOM - Pioneer Building, corner Stevenson and Fourth Streets.

A full line of Boots and Shoes constantly on hand, and rules for Self-Measurement by Mail.

JNO. T. SULLIVAN.

Langtry Farms' Stud

Imp. FRIAR TUCK

By the Immortal HERMIT

DAM ROMPING GIRL BY WILD DAYRELL,

AT $50 THE SEASON.

Mares not proving with foal may be returned the following season. Good care taken of mares, but no liabilities for accidents or escapes.

Good Pasturage at $5 per month.

Mares shipped to ST. HELENA, care CHARTES WILLIAM ABY, St. Helena Stables, will be cared for. For further particulars address,

CHAS. WILLIAM ABY,
Middletown, Lake County, Cal.

2:08 3-4 2:10 2:12

MAMBRINO WILKES, 6083.

SIRE OF

GUS WILKES, 2:22; ALPHEUS, 2:27; CLARA P, 2:29½; BALKAN, 2:29½ (3-year-old) and timed separately 2:22½ in 4-year-old Stake, Bay District Track, October 14, 1889.

DESCRIPTION.

Black; sixteen hands; weighs, in exercise, 1,260 lbs. For style, finish, symmetry and proportion, comparison is challenged with any trotting bred horse. His colts follow in size, style and beauty. Balkan, for instance, being "facile princeps" of trotters in these particulars.

PEDIGREE.

Sired by Geo. Wilkes, sire of Harry Wilkes, 2:13¾, Guy Wilkes, 2:15¼, and 60 other trotters in the 2:30 list, in addition to 8 pacers, and of the sire of Axtell, 2:12 (three-year-old), beating all stallions of any age, and the sire of Regal Wilkes, 2:20¾, best two-year-old stallion record.

First dam Lady Chrisman by Mambrino (Todhunter's), son of Mambrino Chief 11; sire of Lady Thorn, 2:18¼; Woodford Mambrino, 2:21½, and four others in 2:30, and of the dams of Director, 2:17, Piedmont, 2:17¼, Onward, 2:25¼, etc.

Second dam by Pilot Jr. 12, sire of nine in the 2:30 list, and of the dams of Maud S., 2:08¾, Jay-Eye-See, 2:10, Nutwood, 2:18¾, Viking, 2:19¼, Pilot Boy, 2:30, Naiad Queen, 2:20¾, etc.

TERMS.

Mares from a distance will be received at the Dexter Stables, Oakland, or Livery Stable, Martinez, the owner notifying Smith Hill, Superintendent at the farm. Good pasture and plenty of water. For the purpose of placing the service of a Wilkes within reach of breeders, the same rate will be maintained as last year, to wit, $75 for the season. Although it is not admitted thereby that this horse is inferior as a producer to the horses whose fees are placed at from $150 to $500. Address

SMITH HILL,
San Miguel Stock Farm,
Walnut Creek, Contra Costa Co., Cal.

$2:12\frac{3}{4}$ $2:13\frac{1}{2}$ $2:15\frac{1}{4}$

$2:08\frac{3}{4}$ 2:10 2:12

BALKAN

By Mambrino Wilkes.

(See that Horse's Advertisement.)

DAM FANNY FERN BY JACK HAWKINS
Son of Boston.

The grandam of Maud S, (2:08¾) was by Boston and the grandam of Jay-Eye-See (2:10) was by Lexington, son of Boston. So Balkan is the same remove from Boston that Maud is, and one remove nearer than Jay-Eye-See.

Fanny Fern has produced Molly Drew, Onyx, Fred Arnold, Molly Fern and Balkan, all by different sires.

Balkan's sire and dam both being producers, and he being a trotter himself with a record of 2:29 1-2 (three-year-old) and timed separately 2:22 1-4 in 4-year-old Stake, Bay District Track, October 14, 1889—it is but fair to presume that he will get trotters of the highest order.

DESCRIPTION.

He is seal brown, 16-1 hands high, in style rivalled by few, and excelled by none with as pure a gait as has yet been exhibited in public—bar none.

Balkan will be at Oakland Trotting Park for the season of 1890, and will be limited to ten mares, at $100 fee, in order to be put in training early, as it is morally certain that if given a reasonable opportunity he will be fast enough to compete with the best of his age. For further particulars, address

A. L. HINDS,
Dexter Stables, Oakland.

$2:12\frac{3}{4}$ $2:13\frac{1}{2}$ $2:15\frac{1}{4}$

JESSE E. MARKS & CO.,

Wholesale and Retail Dealers of Choice Brands

Havana & Key West Cigars

922 MARKET ST., S. F.

2:19 NOONDAY $2:20\frac{1}{2}$

STANDARD No. 10,000.

This celebrated trotting bred stallion will make the season of 1890 at the stable of the undersigned at Sacramento, Cal., at $75 for the season and $100 to insure a mare in foal. Payable on or before July 1st, 1890. Money will be refunded on mares bred by insurance as soon as the fact becomes known that they are not in foal.

NOONDAY.

- Wedgewood, 2:19. Sire of Favonia, 2:15, fastest 4th heat for any mare or gelding, and eight others in 2:27 or better.
  - Belmont. Sire of Wedgewood, 2:19, Nutwood, 2:18¾, Viking, 2:19¼, and 29 others in 2:30 list.
    - Alexander's Abdallah, sire of Goldsmith Maid, 2:14; Almont, with 35 horses in 2:30 list, etc.
    - Belle, dam of Hambletonian, 2:26½; B'cars, dam of Pancoast, 2:21¾, the sire of Patron, 2:14¼.
  - Woodbine. Dam of Wedgewood, 2:19, Woodford Mamb., 2:21½, the sire of Pancoast, 2:21¾, the sire of Patron, 2:14¼.
    - Woodford.
    - Singleton Mare.
- Noontide, 2:20½ (Trial, 2:13¼).
  - Harold. Sire of Maud S., 2:08¾, and 26 others in 2:30 list.
    - Hambletonian (Rysdyk's), sire of George Wilkes, 2:22, the sire of Guy Wilkes, 2:15¼; Electioneer, the sire of Sunol, 2:10½, and scores of noted trotters and producers.
    - Enchantress, by Abdallah 1.
  - Midnight. Dam of Jay-Eye-See, 2:10, Noontide, 2:20½.
    - Pilot Jr., sire of dams of Maud S., 2:08¾, Jay-Eye-See, 2:10, Nutwood, 2:18¾, etc.
    - Twilight, by Lexington, sire of the dam of Ansel, 2:20.

NOODAY is a dark seal brown, foaled 1884, 15 hands 1½ inches high. Individually he is equal to his royal breeding. He is all that can be desired in conformation, intelligence, color and trotting action, and no stallion now in public service can show a pedigree with such fast records and royal game trotting blood as Noonday.

DON MARVIN,

Record 2:28 as a five-year-old. Standard by Breeding and Performance

Standard No. 7927.

Don Marvin 2:28.

Don Marvin is a beautiful seal brown, foaled 1881, bred by Hon. Leland Stanford, Palo Alto, Cal., standing 16 hands, and weighs, in ordinary condition, 1200 lbs. He is a fine individual, good style and form, combined with great substance, and good temper. Is very level headed; in his first race the past season he only made one break in five closely contested heats. He has great speed and endurance, with the pure, rapid Electioneer gait. He trots without toe weights, and wears only 8 oz. shoes in front. He gained his record the past season in the third heat, on a slow track, after making a season (serving over 60 mares), with scarcely any preparation. His record is no mark of his speed. He was a natural born trotter, and Mr. Charles Marvin considered him the fastest two year old at Palo Alto that season.

By FALLIS, 2:23, - - by Electioneer, sire of
Sire of Don Marvin, 2:28. — Sunol, three-year-old, 2:10 1-2, Palo Alto, 2:12¾, and 47 others in 2:30 list.

Dam CORA, by Don Victor by Belmont, sire of
Dam of Don Marvin, 2:28. — Ventura, 2:27¼, and sire of the dam of Bell Echo, 2:20, and six others in 2:30 list.

2d dam CLARABEL, - by Abdallah Star,
Dam of Clifton Bell, 2:24 1-2, and grandam of Rexford, three years, 2:24. — Sire of Hattie Maples, 2:28.

3d dam FAIRY, - - by Rysdyk's Hambletonian,
Sister of Sweepstakes, sire of 16 in 2:30 list. — Sire of Electioneer, George Wilkes, and many other noted sires and trotters.

4th dam EMMA MILLS, by Seely's American Star,
Dam of 4 horses that have 2:30 performers. — The great broodmare sire of the world.

The above pedigree should show every intelligent breeder that Don Marvin is "high" bred, though very strong in trotting blood. All the comment it is deemed necessary to make as to the value of "thoroughbred blood" in the trotter is simply to refer to the very significant fact that the first and second dams of Maud S, 2:08¾, Jay-Eye-See 2:10, Sunol, three years 2:10 1-2, Palo Alto 2:12¾, Antevo 2:16¾, Nutwood 2:18¾, Wedgewood 2:19, and many other successful sires and sensational trotters of the day are thoroughbred.

TERMS—Don Marvin will make the ensuing season from February 1st to July 1st, 1890, at $40 the season, with the usual privilege of returning the mare next season if not proving in foal. Mares from a distance met at the cars or boats on notification, and carefully handled, but no responsibility assumed for accidents or escapes.

Good alfalfa pasture furnished (free from barb wire fence) at $4 per month. For further particulars or complete circulars address

F. P. LOWELL,
1580 F Street, Sacramento, Cal.

The Produce of Eros Averaged $2,200 Each at New York Auction Sale in 1889.

THE ELECTIONEER TROTTING STALLION,

5326 EROS 5326

Will make the season of 1890—February 1st to July 15—at LA SIESTA RANCH, MENLO PARK.

PEDIGREE.

EROS (5326)
Standard by his sire
" " dam
" " record
" " produce
" under all rules

EROS (5326)

- Electioneer. Grandsire of Norlaine, 1 yr., 2:31 1-2, Sire of Sunol, 2 yrs., 2:18, Sunol, 3 yrs., 2:10 1-2, Hinda Rose, 4 yrs., 2:16, Palo Alto, 2:12¾.
  - Hambletonian 10. Sire of Dictator, George Wilkes, Happy Medium, and 40 others in 2:30 list, and grandsire of 728 in list.
    - Abdallah 10. Sire of the dams of Goldsmith Maid, 2:14, and 7 other producing dams.
    - Charles Kent mare. By imp. Bellfounder.
  - Green Mountain Maid. Dam of Prospero, 2:20, Elaine, 2:20, Dame Trot, 2:22, Eliste, 2:22¾, Storm, 2:26¾, Antonio, 2:28¾, Miranda, 2:31, Mansfield, 2:26.
    - Harry Clay. Sire of the dams of St. Julian, 2:11¾, Bodine, 2:19¼, and 17 more in 2:30 list.
    - Shanghai Mary.
- Sontag Mohawk. Dam of Eros, 2:29 1-2, Sport, 2:22¾, Sallie Benton, 2:17¾, Conductor, trial, 2:28, Colma, 3-y-o trial, 2:21.
  - Mohawk Chief. Sire of the dams of Lot Slocum, 2:17¾, Sallie Benton, 4 yrs., 2:17¾, Pedlar, 2 yrs., 2:27¾, Stanford, 4 yrs., 2:30, Eros, 6th heat, 2:29 1-2.
    - Hambletonian 10. Sire of the dams of Stamboul, 2:12¾, Wilton, 2:19¾, and 20 other trotters.
    - Lady Perrine.
  - Sontag Nellie.
    - Toronto Sontag. By Toronto Chief.
    - Nellie Gray. 5-mile record, 13:45.

Produce of Eros
Wanda, 4 yrs., 2:21.
Solita, 3 yrs., 2:41 1-2.
Merjquita, 2 yrs., 2:42.
Daylight, 2 yrs., 2:56.
Hiram B., trial, 2:28.

These are the only colts alive by him that have ever had a harness on except one in New York that went a trial last July, and Hiram B. (dead) 2:28 (trial).

DESCRIPTION.

EROS is a rich seal brown stallion, bred by Hon. Leland Stanford at Palo Alto, and is the nearest living likeness of his celebrated sire, Electioneer. Stands 15.2 hands high, and weighs 1020 pounds.

In breeding to Eros, the owners of mares will strictly follow the great rule of breeding, viz., breed to a stallion by a producer and out of a sure producer of great speed. Eros is by the stallion that has produced more 2:30 trotters that any living horse, and is also the sire of more 2:20 performers than any horse living or dead.

EROS is out of the dam of Sally Benton, four years old, record 2:17¾, Sport 2:22¾, and Eros 2:29½ in the sixth heat, against a field of nine horses. He is from a family that is endowed with great natural speed, trot fast at an early age, train on, throw trotters from all classes of mares, are of good substance, bone, style and action, and breed solid colors.

TERMS.

$100 for the season, with the privilege of return next season should mares not be in foal and horse and mare still remain in the same hands.

Good pasturage can be obtained at $5 per month, but no responsibility for accidents or escapes. There are a large number of box stalls, and animals can be kept up and fed on hay and grain at reasonable rates if required. Mares already in foal can be sent to the ranch for foaling, and will receive all the attention bestowed upon our own mares. Mares left with Mr. Peter Pomyea, Broadway Street Stable, Oakland, or with Mr. F. H. Burke, 401 Montgomery Street, San Francisco, will be forwarded to the ranch free of charge. For further particulars apply to

W. H. VIOGET,
LA SIESTA RANCH, MENLO PARK, CAL.

EROS is the only stallion offered to the public on this Coast that has a dam that has three in the 2:30 list.

POPLAR GROVE Breeding Farm

STALLIONS.

CLOVIS, 4909,

CLOVIS is a beautiful black, Eight Years Old, 16 1-2 Hands High, and weighs 1260 lbs.

He is a horse of beautiful symmetry and magnificent action.

PEDIGREE.

CLOVIS was sired by Sultan, 2:24, sire of Stamboul, 2:12 1-4, Ruby, 2:19¾, and fifteen others with records of 2:30 or better.

First dam Sweetbriar by Thorndale 2:22 1-2, sire of Edwin Thorne, 2:16 1-2, Daisy Dale, 2:19, and May Thorne, 2:24.

Second dam Ulster Queen, dam of Volmer, 2:24¾, by Hambletonian 10, sire of Dexter, 2:17¼, George Wilkes, 2:22.

Third dam by Thomas Jefferson, a son of Mambrino Paymaster, Jr.

Fourth dam by Mambrino Paymaster, sire of Mambrino Chief.

Sultan, by The Moor, sire of Beautiful Bells, dam of Hinda Rose, 2:19 1-2, and Sable, dam of Sable Wilkes, three year old record 2:18.

First dam of Sultan, Sultana, by Delmonico. Sire of Darby, 2:16 1-2, by Guy Miller, sire of Whipple's Hambletonian.

Second dam by Mambrino Chief.

Third dam by Downing's Bay Messenger.

Fourth dam Mrs. Caudle, dam of Ericsson, four year old record 2:30 1-2.

Clovis will make the season of 1890 at Poplar Grove Breeding Farm, near Wildflower, Fresno County, commencing February 1st and ending July 1st.

Terms, $75, due at time of service.

Mares cared for in any manner owners may desire; pasturage $2 per month. Every care exercised, but no liability for escapes or accidents. Mares not proving with foal can be returned next season, providing I still own this stallion.

APEX, 8935.

FOUR YEAR-OLD RECORD, FOURTH HEAT, 2:26.

Will make the present season at the Poplar Grove Breeding Farm, near Wildflower, Fresno Co., season commencing Feb. 1st, and ending July 1, 1890. Terms, $50 the season, due at time of service. Apex is eight years old, a beautiful bay, 15 1-2 hands high, and weighs 1110 lbs. He is a horse of fine disposition, and his gait is faultless.

PEDIGREE.

Apex was sired by Promptor 2305, he by Blue Bull 75; first dam Mary by Flaxtail, he by Pruden's Blue Bull, Flaxtail being the sire of the dams of Buccaneer, five-year-old record, 2:24 1-4; Pride, yearling record, 2:44 1-2, and Shamrock, two-year old record, 2:25, third heat. Second dam by Bright Eyes, son of Busnarages. Prompter (sire of Apex, record 2:26, and Transit, 2:28 1-4), by Wilson's Blue Bull, by Pruden's Blue Bull, son of Merring's Blue Bull. Promptor's dam Prairie Bird, by Flaxtail; second dam by John the Baptist, son of Tally Ho Morgan, by Sherman Morgan; third dam Fannie Fern by Irwin's Tuckaho.

Apex made his appearance in the circuit as a two-year-old, and obtained a record of 2:42. As a three-year-old he reduced this in a race at Santa Rosa against Stamboul to 2:21, it taking six heats to decide the contest, which was won by Apex. As a four year-old he gained his present record of 2:26.

Mares cared for in any manner owners may desire. Pasturage $2 per month. Every care exercised, but no liabilities for escapes or accidents. Mares not proving with foal can be returned next season, providing I still own this stallion.

The Standard Stallion

JUNIO,

RECORD 2:22.

WILL MAKE THE PRESENT SEASON OF 1890 AT FRESNO FAIR GROUNDS.

Season Commencing Feb. 1st and ending July 1st.

TERMS—$100 the season, due at time of service.

JUNIO is eight years old, a handsome dark bay 16 hands high, and weighs 1250 pounds. He is the personification of the light harness horse, and his trotting action is superb. At the State Fair of 1886 he took first premium over forty of the finest trotters in the State.

PEDIGREE.

Junio, by Electioneer, premier stallion of Palo Alto (sire of Sunol 2:10 1-2, Palo Alto 2:12 1-4, and 47 others in the 2:30 list. Dam by Granger by imp. Hercules.

Granger, by imp. Hercules, dam Jenny Lind, by Stockbridge Chief, Jr., he by Stockbridge Chief, he by Vermont Black Hawk. Second dam by Kentucky Whip.

Imp. Hercules, by Kingston, first dam daughter of Tuscar, by Bay Middleton, second dam Malvina, by Oscar; 3rd dam Spotless by Walton; 4th dam by Trumpeter (see Bruce's American Stud Book, Vol. 1, page 26). Hercules is the sire of the dam of Asmoor 2:24¾; also sire of dam of Menlo 2:21 1-2.

Mares not proving in foal may be returned next year free of charge, providing I still have the horse. Pasturage $2 per month. While every care will be taken of horses, no liability will be assumed for accidents or escapes.

For further particulars address

S. N. STRAUBE, Fresno, Cal.

Poplar Grove Breeding Farm.

Southern Pacific Co.

(PACIFIC SYSTEM.)

Trains leave and are due to arrive at San Francisco.

LEAVE (FOR)	FROM JANUARY 1, 1890.	ARRIVE (FROM)
7.30 A M	Haywards, Niles and San Jose	*12.45 P M
7.30 A M	Sacramento and Redding, via Davis	7.15 P M
7.30 A M	Sacramento, Auburn, Colfax	5.45 P M
8.00 A M	Martinez, Vallejo, Calistoga and Santa Rosa	6.15 P M
8.30 A M	Los Angeles Express, Fresno, Bakersfield, Mojave and East and Los Angeles	11.15 A M
8.30 A M	Niles, San Jose, Stockton, Ione, Sacramento, Marysville, Oroville and Red Bluff	5.45 P M
10.30 A M	Haywards and Niles	2.15 P M
*12.00 M	Haywards, Niles and San Jose	* 3.45 P M
*1.00 P M	Sacramento River Steamers	**6.00 A M
3.00 P M	Haywards, Niles and San Jose	9.45 A M
3.30 P M	2d Class for Ogden and East	10.45 P M
4.00 P M	Stockton and Milton; Vallejo, Calistoga and Santa Rosa	9.45 A M
4.30 P M	Sacramento and Knight's Landing via Davis	10.45 A M
*4.30 P M	Niles and Livermore	* 8.45 A M
*4.30 P M	Niles and San Jose	‡ 4.15 P M
5.30 P M	Haywards and Niles	7.45 A M
6.00 P M	Sunset Route, Atlantic Express, Santa Barbara, Los Angeles, Deming, El Paso, New Orleans and East	8.45 P M
7.00 P M	Shasta Route Express, Sacramento, Marysville, Redding, Portland, Puget Sound and East	7.45 A M
8.00 P M	Central Atlantic Express, Ogden and East	9,45 A M

SANTA CRUZ DIVISION.

LEAVE (FOR)		ARRIVE (FROM)
‡ 8.00 A M	Hunters train to San Jose	‡ 7.20 P M
8.15 A M	Newark, Centerville, San Jose, Felton, Boulder Creek and Santa Cruz	5.50 P M
* 2.15 P M	Centerville, San Jose, Almaden, Felton, Boulder Creek and Santa Cruz	*11.50 A M
4.15 P M	Centerville, San Jose, and Los Gatos	9.50 A M

Coast Division (Third and Townsend Sts.)

LEAVE (FOR)		ARRIVE (FROM)
7.25 A M	San Jose, Almaden and Way Stations	2.30 P M
8.30 A M	San Jose, Gilroy, Tres Pinos; Pajaro, Santa Cruz; Monterey; Pacific Grove, Salinas, San Miguel, Paso Robles, Santa Margarita (San Luis Obispo) and principal Way Stations	6.12 P M
10.30 A M	San Jose and Way Stations	5.02 P M
12.01 P M	Cemetery, Menlo Park and Way Stations	3.38 P M
* 3.30 P M	San Jose, Tres Pinos, Santa Cruz, Salinas, Monterey, Pacific Grove and principal Way Stations	*10.00 A M
* 4.20 P M	Menlo Park and Way Station	* 7.58 A M
5.20 P M	San Jose and Way Stations	9.03 A M
6.30 P M	Menlo Park and Way Stations	6.35 A M
†11.45 P M	Menlo Park and principal Way Stations	†7.28 P M

A M for Morning. P M for Afternoon.
*Sundays excepted. †Saturdays only. ‡Sundays only.
**Mondays excepted. §Saturdays excepted.

OCEANIC STEAMSHIP CO.

Carrying United States, Hawaiian and Colonial Mails.

WILL LEAVE THE COMPANY'S WHARF, foot of Mission Street, No. 1,

For Honolulu, Auckland and Sydney,

WITHOUT CHANGE,

The Splendid New 3,000-ton Iron Steamer.

MARIPOSA ..... Saturday, February 8, 1890, at 12 M., Or immediately on arrival of the English mails.

For Honolulu,

SS. AUSTRALIA (3,000 tons), February 28, 1890, at 12 M

For freight or passage, apply at office, 327 Market Street.
JOHN D. SPRECKELS & BROS.
General Agents.

KILLIP & CO.,

LIVE STOCK AND GENERAL AUCTIONEERS,

22 Montgomery Street, San Francisco

SPECIAL ATTENTION PAID TO SALES OF

High-Brod Horses and Cattle.

At auction and private sale.

Will Sell in All Cities and Counties of the State.

REFERENCES.

Hon. C. Green, Sacramento.
Hon. J. D. Carr, Salinas.
J. P. Sargent, Esq., Sargents.
Hon. John Boggs, Colusa.
Hon. L. J. Rose, Los Angeles.
Hon. A. Walrath, Nevada.
J. B. Haggin, Esq., San Francisco.

Represented at Sacramento by Edwin F. Smith Secretary State Agricultural Society.
At San Jose by Messrs. Montgomery & Rea, Real Estate Agents.

Being the oldest established firm in the live-stock business on this Coast, and having conducted the important auction sales in this line for the past fifteen years, amounting to one half a million of dollars, we feel justified in claiming unequaled facilities for disposing of live stock of every description, either at auction or private sale. Our list of correspondents embraces every breeder and dealer of prominence upon the Pacific Coast, thus enabling us to give full publicity to animals placed with us for sale. Private purchases and sales of live stock of all descriptions will be made on commission, and stock shipped with the utmost care. Purchases and sales made of land of every description. We are authorized to refer to the gentlemen whose names are appended.

KILLIP & CO., 22 Montgomery Street

LAMBORN ROAD MACHINE

LIGHT DRAFT. MADE OF IRON STRONG, SIMPLE, DURABLE. EASILY OPERATED.

TRUMAN HOOKER CO.
SAN FRANCISCO. - CALIFORNIA

San Francisco and North Pacific Railway.

THE DONAHUE BROAD-GAUGE ROUTE.

COMMENCING SUNDAY, MARCH 17, 1889, AND until further notice, boats and trains will leave from and arrive at the San Francisco Passenger Depot, Market-street Wharf, as follows:

Leave San Francisco. Week Days.	Leave San Francisco. Sundays.	Destination	Arrive San Francisco. Sundays.	Arrive San Francisco. Week Days.
7.40 A M 3.30 P M 5.00 P M	8.00 A M 5.00 P M	Petaluma and Santa Rosa	10.40 A M 6.10 P M	8.50 A M 10.30 A M 6.05 P M
7.40 A M 3.30 P M	8.00 A M	Fulton, Windsor, Healdsburg, Litton Spri'gs, Cloverdale, and way stations.	6.10 P M	10.30 A M 6.05 P M
7.40 A M	8.00 A M	Hopland and Ukiah.	6.10 P M	6.05 P M
7.40 A M	8.00 A M	Guerneville	6.10 P M	6.05 P M
7.40 A M 5.00 P M	8.00 A M	Sonoma and Glen Ellen.	10.40 A M 6.10 P M	8.50 A M 6.05 P M

Stage connects at Santa Rosa for White Sulphur Springs, Sebastopol and Mark West Springs; at Geyserville for Skaggs Springs, and at Cloverdale for the Geysers; at Hopland for Highland Springs, Kelseyville, Soda Bay, Lakeport and Bartlett Springs, and at Ukiah for Vichy Springs, Saratoga Springs, Blue Lakes, Willits, Cahto, Calpella, Potter Valley, Sherwood Valley and Mendocino City.

EXCURSION TICKETS from Saturdays to Mondays, to Petaluma, $1.50; to Santa Rosa, $2.25; to Healdsburg, $3.40; to Litton Springs, $3.60; to Cloverdale, $4.50; to Hopland, $5.70; to Ukiah, $6.75; to Guerneville, $3.75; to Sonoma, $1.50; to Glen Ellen, $1.80.

EXCURSION TICKETS, good for Sundays only, to Petaluma, $1; to Santa Rosa, $.150; to Healdsburg, $2.25; to Litton Springs, $2.40; to Cloverdale, $3; to Guerneville, $2.50, to Sonoma, $1; to Glen Ellen, $1.20.

From San Francisco for Point Tiburon and San Rafael: Week Days—7.40, 9.20, 11.20 A. M.; 3.30, 5.05, 6.15 P. M. Sundays—8.00, 9.30, 11.00 A. M.; 1.30, 5.00, 6.20 P. M.

To San Francisco from San Rafael: Week Days—6.20, 7.55, 9.30 A. M.; 12.45, 3.40, 5.05 P. M. Sundays—8.10, 9.40 A. M.; 12.15, 3.40, 5.00 P. M.

To San Francisco from Point Tiburon: Week Days—6.50, 8.20, 9.55 A. M.; 1.10, 4.05, 5.30 P. M.; Sundays—8.40, 10.05 A. M.; 12.40, 4.05, 5.30 P. M.

On Saturdays an extra trip will be made from San Francisco to San Rafael, leaving at 1.40 P. M.

H. C. WHITING, General Manager.
PETER J. McGLYNN, Gen. Pass. & Tkt. Agt.

Ticket Offices at Ferry, 222 Montgomery Street and 2 New Montgomery Street.

6 DOS

DO you bet?
DO you go to the races?
DO you know HOW to bet?
DO you know BEST system?
DO you want Good ADVICE?
DO as you ought to do:

SEND FOR PROSPECTUS TO

GOODWIN BROS.,
241 BROADWAY, NEW YORK,

Who will mail you FREE OF CHARGE, one of their circulars showing the GREAT SUCCESS they have met with from the time they established the system of "Point" providing in this country in 1881; it also contains

MANY OTHER INTERESTING ITEMS with which the general public is not familiar.

Call and See the New

CRUISING BOOTS

E. T. ALLEN,
Fire Arms and Sporting Goods
416 Market St., S. F.

STANDARD CHAMBERLIN SHOTGUN CARTRIDGES — THE BEST IS THE CHEAPEST

THE GREAT

STABLE DISINFECTANT. DARBYS FLUID.

Many horses and cattle become diseased and die from the impure atmosphere of their stables. And even though stables may be kept clean and the foul air be unnoticeable, it may still exist.

DARBYS FLUID

IS GOOD FOR CUTS, BRUISES, ETC., WARDS OFF DISEASE, PURIFIES THE AIR AND PREVENTS CONTAGION AMONG ANIMALS.

It is cheap and never wasted by free use; should be sprinkled about the stalls and stable as a safeguard against Influenza, Pink-eye, Epizooty, etc.

If you value your horses and stock never be without Darbys Prophylactic Fluid.

J. H. ZEILIN & CO., Philadelphia, Pa.
SOLD BY ALL DRUGGISTS.

DR. FISHERMAN'S Carbolized Alkaline LOTION

Cures after all other Remedies have Failed.

Sprains, Sores, Bruises, Galls, Swellings, Scratches, Thrush, Grease Heels, Curb, Rheumatism. Restoring Weak Knees and Ankles to their original condition. As a wash it insures glossy manes and tails. Valuable as an internal remedy for Coughs, Colic, Congestion or Fever. You really get Half a Gallon of Remedy for $1.00, or Two Gallons for $3.00, after being adulterated as directed.

This Liniment has received the endorsement of some of our best horsemen. Recommended by Jos. Cairn Simpson. See BREEDER AND SPORTSMAN of November 10th, 1888.

LYNDE & HOUGH, Proprietors.
116 California St., S. F.
Or ask your Druggist for it.

HORSE OWNERS! TRY GOMBAULT'S CAUSTIC BALSAM.

A Safe, Speedy and Positive Cure for Curb, Splint, Sweeny, Capped Hock, Strained Tendons, Founder, Wind Puffs, all Skin Diseases or Parasites, Thrush, Diphtheria, Pinkeye, all Lameness from Spavin, Ringbone or other Bony Tumors. Removes all Bunches or Blemishes from Horses and Cattle.

Supersedes all Cautery or Firing. Impossible to Produce any Scar or Blemish.

Every bottle sold is warranted to give satisfaction. Price $1.50 per bottle. Sold by druggists, or sent by express, charges paid, with full directions for its use. Send for descriptive circulars. Address

LAWRENCE, WILLIAMS & CO., Cleveland, O.

BROU'S INJECTION

A PERMANENT CURE in from 3 to 6 days, of the most obstinate cases; guaranteed not to produce Stricture; no sickening doses; and no inconvenience or loss of time. Recommended by physicians and sold by all druggists. J. Ferré, (successor to Brou), Pharmacien, Paris.

For any Kind of a

SORE THROAT

USE

McCLELLAN'S
DIPHTHERIA REMEDY

An Unfailing Cure.
FOR SALE BY ALL DRUGGISTS

IRON TURBINE WINDMILL & BUCKEYE PUMP

F. P. MAST & Co. 31 MARKET ST. SAN FRANCISCO

THE MOST Powerful and Durable Combination For RAISING WATER IN THE WORLD.

VETERINARY.

Dr. Wm. H. Jones, M.R.C.V.S.

Veterinary Surgeon,
(CLUB STABLES)
409—411 Taylor Street, San Francisco.

Consultations by letter, and cases of URGENT NECESSITY in the interior will receive prompt attention.

W. H. WOODRUFF.

Veterinary Dentist,
AT FASHION STABLES,
221 Ellis Street, San Francisco

Improved Instruments, Humane Methods, First-Class Work.

H. E. CARPENTER,

Veterinary Surgeon,
Graduate of Ontario Veterinary College, Toronto, Canada.

RESIDENCE AND VETERINARY INFIRMARY
331 Golden Gate Ave., San Francisco.
Telephone 3069.

OPEN DAY AND NIGHT.

No risk in throwing Horses. Veterinary Operating Table on the premises.

DR. C. MASOERO,

Veterinary Surgeon,
Successor to DR. A. DeTAVEL,
GRADUATE OF ROYAL VETERINARY COLLEGE, TURIN.

OFFICE AND INFIRMARY,
No. 811 HOWARD STREET,
Between Fourth and Fifth. SAN FRANCISCO.
Telephone, No. 457.

R. WATKINS,

Veterinary Dentist,

Of twelve years practice, is now permanently located in San Francisco, and may be found at C. S. Crittendens' Golden Gate Livery and Riding Academy, 24 to 28 Golden Gate Avenue.

Will treat ailments of the horse's mouth, and cure all such. Sidetein Pullers and Tongue Lollers, etc. Satisfaction guaranteed. Orders by mail will receive prompt attention. Examination Free.

E. J. O'ROUKE.

I have the honor to announce to my old patrons and the general public that I may be found at my old stand, where, as heretofore, the

Shoeing of Horses,

whether for the Track, Drive, or for general work, will receive my personal attention.

Telephone 2011.

E. J. O'ROUKE,
209 Ellis Street

California Horse Shoe Co's

STEEL SHOE

Light, Strong and Perfect.

Superior to all others for Speed Horses.

ALSO

The Celebrated GOODENOUGH Pattern Shoe.

OFFICE: 202 Market St., San Francisco, Cal.

I have used in my business the Steel and Iron Shoes made by the above Company, and take great pleasure in saying they are the best I have ever used in twenty-two years' practice. I have never seen anything like the STEEL SHOE made by this Company. I can fully recommend them to every practical Horseshoer in the country.

Yours respectfully,
No. 8 Everett Street. JOHN GRACE.

OUR IMPROVED. ALL SIZES AND WEIGHTS. G. W. BOHANON.

THE BOHANON SULKY!

BEST MADE.
Perfect Riding Buggies.
Breaking Carts.
Fine Repairing, Reasonable Prices.

Bohanon Carriage Co., 161-163 Ogden Ave., CHICAGO.
Send for Catalogue.

HEALD'S

Business College, 24 Post St.
—San Francisco.—
The most popular school on the Coast
P. HEALD, President. C. S. HALEY, Sec'y.
Send for Circulars

The PARKER Hammerless Shot Gun.

At the Annual Tournament of 1889, held at Cannes, France, the grand prize, consisting of 2000 Francs and a Valuable Cup, was won by The Parker Hammerless.

The first Parker Hammerless Gun made won the championship of America at Decatur Illinois.

SEND FOR ILLUSTRATED CIRCULAR.

PARKER BROS., Makers,

New York Salesroom, 97 Chambers St. Meriden Conn.

J. C. JOHNSON & CO.,

IMPORTERS, MANUFACTURERS, AND DEALERS IN

HARNESS & SADDLERY

☞ We carry a large assortment of goods in our line from the cheapest to the best made.

400 to 404 Market Street

Corner BATTERY STREET, San Francisco.

Everything for Trotter or Runner,

At J. A. McKERRON'S,

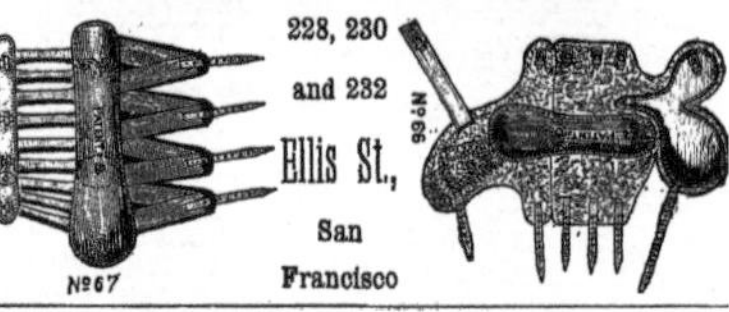

228, 230 and 232 Ellis St., San Francisco

1890. DENVER, COLORADO. 1890.

The Spring Racing and Trotting Meeting

OF THE

Overland Park Club Association

WILL BE HELD

MAY 30 and 31, JUNE 3, 4, 5 and 7, 1890.

The following Racing Stakes are now open to Close Saturday February 15th.

THE PRAIRIE STAKES.

A SWEEPSTAKES for two-year-olds, foals of 1888; $10 entrance to accompany the nomination; $15 additional to start, with $500 added by the Club, of which $100 to the second horse, $50 to the third. Winners of any race of the value of $750 or more to carry 3 pounds extra; of two or more such races, 5 pounds extra. Maidens, at time of starting—allowed 5 pounds. Five furlongs. To be run on the second day of the meeting.

THE FAR WEST STAKES.

A SWEEPSTAKES for two-year-olds, foals of 1888; $10 entrance to accompany the nomination; $15 additional to start, with $500 added by the Club, of which $100 to the second horse, $50 to the third. Colts and fillies bred, raised and owned in Colorado, Wyoming, New Mexico, Utah, Montana or Idaho allowed 5 pounds. The winner of two races of any value to carry 5 pounds extra. The winner of the Prairie Stakes to carry 7 pounds extra. Maidens—at time of starting—allowed 5 pounds. Half a mile. To be run on the fifth day of the meeting.

NOTE.—The allowance to colts and fillies bred, raised and owned in States and Territories named, to be allowed in addition to the maiden allowance, if any, also in taking up penalties, if any.

THE COLORADO DERBY.

A SWEEPSTAKES for three-year-olds, foals of 1887; $10 entrance to accompany the nomination; $15 additional to start, with $600 added by the Club, of which $100 to the second horse, $50 to the third. Winners of any stake race to carry 3 pounds extra; of any three-year-old stakes, 5 pounds extra. Maidens on February 15th allowed 5 pounds; if maidens at time of starting, allowed 7 pounds. One mile and a quarter. To be run on the first day of the meeting.

THE MOUNTAIN STAKES.

A SWEEPSTAKES for three-year-olds, foals of 1887; $10 entrance to accompany the nomination; $15 additional to start, with $500 added by the Club, of which $100 to the second horse, $50 the third. Non-winners of $1,000 in two-year-old form allowed 5 pounds. Maidens on February 15th allowed 7 pounds, if maidens at time of starting, allowed 10 pounds. The winner of the Colorado Derby to carry 5 pounds extra. One mile. To be run on the fourth day of the meeting.

THE MERCHANTS' STAKES.

A SWEEPSTAKES for all ages; $10 entrance to accompany the nomination; $15 additional to start, with $570 added by the Club, of which $100 to the second horse, $50 to the third. Winners of any race of the value of $1,000 or more, to carry three pounds extra; of two or more such races, 5 pounds extra. Non-winners in 1889 allowed 3 pounds. Maidens on February 15th, allowed 5 pounds; if maidens at time of starting, allowed 7 pounds. One mile and a half. To be run on the third day of the meeting.

THE OVERLAND HANDICAP.

A HANDICAP SWEEPSTAKES for all ages; $5 entrance to accompany the nomination; $20 additional to start, with $500 added by the Club, of which $100 to the second horse, $50 to the third. Weights to appear at 1 o'clock P. M., the first day of the meeting. Acceptances to be made through the entry box at the usual time of closing, the day before the race. Winners of a race after publication of weights to carry 3 pounds additional; of two or more such races, 5 pounds additional. One mile and a quarter. To be run on the last day of the meeting.

All the above stakes governed by the rules of the American Racing Association.

A liberal purse programme will be prepared and issued with the nominations in stakes about March 10, 1890.

Entrance free to all purse races, unless otherwise specified in the conditions.

All the above stakes close on Saturday, February 15th. Nominations to be addressed to D. L. HALL, Superintendent Overland Park Club, 13 Opera House, Denver, Colo.

TROTTING STAKE.

The Overland Park Club Association also announce the following stake to be trotted during their Spring Racing and Trotting Meeting, May 30th to June 7, 1890.

THE DENVER TROTTING STAKE.

FOR COLTS AND FILLIES three years old or under, that have never beaten 2:30. Mile heats, best three in five, in harness and to the rules and regulations of the American Trotting Association; $10 entrance, which must accompany the nomination, on Saturday, February 15th $10 on Thursday, May 1st—when the entries for trotting purses will close; and $10 from those who declare to start at 5 o'clock P. M., the night before the race; with $500 added by the Club. The stakes, forfeits and added money to be put together and divided—50 per cent. to first horse; 25 per cent. to second; 15 per cent. to third, and 10 per cent. to fourth. In case of an entry distancing the field, or any part thereof, it shall be entitled to the stakes and forfeits, with 50 per cent. of the added money, and no more. A walkover shall be entitled to all the stakes and forfeits, and 25 per cent. of the added money. Nominations are only liable for the first payment, but failure to make either of the subsequent payments, when due, shall be considered a forfeiture, and debar the entry from competing in the race.

Nominations Close on Saturday, February 15th.

THE TROTTING PROGRAMME will be issued about March 10th, and will provide for twelve or more Trotting and Pacing Races. The classes will be arranged to suit the records of horses expected at the meeting, and owners and trainers of Trotting and Pacing horses are invited to correspond with the Club, in order that this arrangement may be fully carried out. Nominations in purses will close May 1st.

Address all entries and communications to

D. L. HALL, Superintendent,
13 Opera House, Denver, Colo.

TREES AND SEEDS.

Trumbull & Beebe's Nurseries

ESTABLISHED 1853.

500,000 **Fruit Trees** 500,00C

FOR SALE.

Having added by purchase, to that of our own growing, the entire nursery stock grown at James Shinn's Nurseries, Niles, Cal., we are better prepared than ever before to meet the increasing demand for trees, and offer for the season of 1889-1890 the LARGEST AND MOST COMPLETE ASSORTMENT OF NURSERY STOCK ON THE PACIFIC COAST, embracing all the leading varieties of FRUIT, SHADE and ORNAMENTAL TREES, ROSES, PLANTS, Etc. BERRY BUSHES of all kinds in quantities to suit. 200,000 GRAPE VINES (strong roots), also 60,000 OLIVE TREES (Mission and Picholine), ORANGE-, LEMON-, NUT TREES, Etc., Etc.

NURSERIES—San Rafael, Alameda and Niles, Cal. Packing Grounds and Sales-yard at Niles R. R. Station. Catalogues sent upon application. Address all communications to

TRUMBULL & BEEBE, 419-421 Sansome St., San Francisco, Ca

OSSIDINE

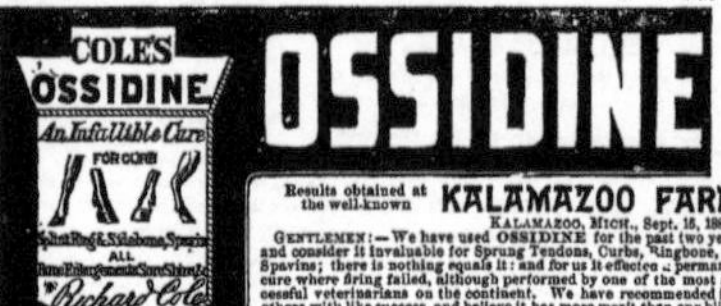

Results obtained at the well-known KALAMAZOO FARM

KALAMAZOO, MICH., Sept. 15, 1888.

GENTLEMEN:—We have used OSSIDINE for the past two years and consider it invaluable for Sprung Tendons, Curbs, Ringbone, and Spavins; there is nothing equals it: and for us it effected a permanent cure where firing failed, although performed by one of the most successful veterinarians on the continent. We have recommended it to others with like success, and believe it has more merit than any blister ever used.

Very respectfully yours,
S. A. BROWNE & CO., Prop's.

This scientific preparation is an absolute cure for all bony or callous lumps on horses, and is a more powerful absorbent than "firing," without creating the slightest blemish.

Acknowledged by leading horsemen of the world to be the **ONLY** preparation that will remove a Bone Spavin after it has become ossified.

We have authority also to refer to Mr. JEROME I. CASE, Mr. FRED. GEBHARD, Mr. JOHN PORTER (Trainer to H.R.H. the Prince of Wales),

And hundreds of others from whom we have very flattering testimonials.

One Style Only. $3.00 per Bottle

A. P. BUSH & CO., 149 Pearl St., BOSTON, MASS., Sole Agents for United States and Canada. *Beware of Imitations.*

SOLD BY C. N. Crittenton, A. R. Van Nest & Co., and C. M. Moseman & Bro., NEW YORK CITY. Morrisson, Plummer & Co., Peter Van Schaack & Sons, CHICAGO, ILL. John D. Park & Son, CINCINNATI, O.; Floyd & Foster, DETROIT, MICH.; F. S. Slosson, CLEVELAND, O.; Meyer Bros. Drug Co., ST. LOUIS, MO.; R. A. Robinson, LOUISVILLE, KY.; H. H. Moore & Sons, STOCKTON, ...

Nutwood 2:22¾ / 2:21 / 2:18¾ } Sire **DAWN 6407** Dam Countess { DAM OF Strathway (2-y-o) 2:2[illegible] / " trial 2:2[illegible] / Placida } Morna } Double team / Trial 2:2[illegible]

2:18¾; 2:20; 2:19½.

$100 Popular Price for season of 1890. $10(

Not having a breeding farm, and being dependent on the public for patronage, I have set the above low price in order to be within the reach of any one desiring to breed.

Good pasturage $3 per month.

For further particulars, address

A. L. WHITNEY, Petaluma.

TWENTY-FOUR PAGES.

BREEDER AND SPORTSMAN

Vol. XVI, No. 7.
No. 313 BUSH STREET.

SAN FRANCISCO, SATURDAY, FEB. 15, 1890.

SUBSCRIPTION
FIVE DOLLARS A YEAR.

started in mercantile pursuits in Stockton, and rapidly made a fortune, and although the sale of merchandise has been given up for a long time, the gentleman is still heavily interested in many of the manufacturing interests which make the name of Stockton famous.

From his youth, he was always an ardent admirer of live stock of all kinds, and although we only propose to speak of the horses in the present article, still he has pigs, sheep, cattle and fowls of the very choicest blood and strains that money can procure. It has for many years been his aim and ambition to have a gentleman's stock farm, not for the purpose of making money, but to which he might look as one of the pleasures and amusements of his life. Although he has been breeding for the last twenty-five years, it is only within the last ten that his fame has become known throughout California.

Some eight years ago he was fortunate enough to purchase a well-bred son of Nutwood which is called Hawthorne. This was long before the time that the name of his sire was so celebrated as it is at the present day, and simply goes to show the judgment which is used by Mr. Shippee in nearly all of his stock-buying transactions. Hawthorne in himself is a most magnificent individual, standing about sixteen hands in height, a beautiful bay in color, with black points, one hind foot white, and a few white hairs on the forehead. He is all that could be desired in disposition, looks and perfect make-up. He is as "clean as a whistle," and will compare favorably with any stallion in the State to-day. His get are very uniform, their legs being particularly good, for while we looked over a large number of his yearlings and two-year-olds, we failed to detect a single one in which there was spot or blemish: that he is a producer of speed, has already been testified to by the performances of Tempest, 2:19, J. C. Shelly, 2:29½, Moses S., 2:29½, and although this record is not very low, he was timed during the last season in a race, in which he came in second to Direct, in 2:21½. The following is Hawthorne's pedigree:

HAWTHORNE 10935	Nutwood 600	Belmont 64.
		Miss Russell, Dam of Maud S.
	Fidelia. Dam of St. Just, he by Electioneer, dam of Nutwood Chief.	Volunteer 55
		by Roe's Abdallah Chief, By Abdallah 1.

Mr. Shippee is confident that he can put at least eight of Hawthorne's get, now owned on the ranch, in the 2:30 list during the coming year, and making due allowances for the ordinary number of accidents which are liable to happen while horses are being prepared for campaign work, without such accidents, it is altogether probable that fully double that number could go in during the season.

A few days ago a visit was made to what is known as French Camp Farm, at which are located at present a number of youngsters which will be taken East between the 20th and 22d of the present month, to be sold one-half at Peoria and the remainder at Kidd, Edmonson & Morse's combination sale at Chicago.

When we arrived at Lathrop, a carriage was in waiting, and we found the genial Harry Whiting ready to drive us to the farm. As we journeyed along, the time was pleasantly consumed in narrating old horse anecdotes, in which Harry is a perfect mint of information; and it seemed but a few minutes for us to make the drive of 4½ miles. The proprietor was in waiting to receive the scribe, and after a pleasant salutation, the business of the day began. Colts and fillies were brought out in vast profusion, and comments were made on them as they passed under the eye of those present; one of the number, Judge Bennet of Stockton, proved himself a good judge of the equine race, his idea of the make-up of the little ones being first rate, and when we came to inspect the more aged ones, he seemed equally well at home.

A bay filly, two years old by Hawthorne 10935 was the first shown; her dam by Bonner, he by Gen. Knox 140; 2nd dam thoroughbred. She is a high spirited little Miss and a trotter.

Sheriff Thorne 11332 is a chestnut colt two years, old with white feet; his sire Hawthorne, dam, sister to dam of Tempest 2:19. He is a fine compact colt, splendid back and loins, and is well put up all over. This will be a rare prize for whoever may purchase him.

Attention was now called to a ch f two years old by Hawthorne, dam by Motion, he by Daniel Lambert 102; 2nd dam by Williamson's Belmont. This is a standard filly and has fine action, showing unmistakeable signs of being a natural trotter.

A perfect beauty, two years old, was next examined; she is by Abby, a son of Abbotsford, her dam being by Hawthorne; 2d dam by Chieftain; 3d dam by Belmont. This is a very racy-looking filly, and should bring a good price.

A black filly by Hawthorne was next led out; her dam is by Dan Lambert, which is guarantee enough of her excellence. The filly has an exceedingly fine gait, good knee action, and is fit to grace the stable of any owner of trotters.

The next was a bay colt two years old, by California Lambert, he a son of Addison Lambert, a son of Daniel Lambert. The colt's dam is the grandam of Tempest, 2:19, second dam being by Coburn's Jim Crow, a son of the thoroughbred Jim Crow; J. C. Shelly, 2:29½, and Brightlight are both out of the colt's first dam. This fine individual will be disposed of in the Peoria lot.

Another of the youngsters to be taken to Peoria is a two-year-old chestnut filly with white star, by California Lambert, and her dam is by Nutwood, the second dam being known as the Trustee Mare. She is a fine, rangy filly, with plenty of substance, and is very taking to the eye.

We now come to a black colt by Hawthorne, dam by Morgan Rattler, grandam by Belshazzer (thoroughbred); he has a small white strip in face; is a beautifully turned horse with fine quarters, good legs, and is double gaited. He should make, if properly handled, a trotter far above the average, although if trained to pace, he will undoubtedly be very fast.

Our attention was next called to a two-year-old bay filly by Hawthorne, her first dam being by Echo 462; 2d dam by Don Victor. This is a fine filly; solid colors, very clean out, and will be a gem for whoever may purchase her.

We now come to another bay colt with two hind feet white, faint star; he is a level-headed animal, and was trotted up and down, so that we might see what he was capable of doing; he is very nicely gaited, a good size for a two-year-old, plenty of bone, well muscled, and should prove a very fast horse. He is by Hawthorne, dam by Reuben, he a son of Black Hawk 5; Reuben is the sire of Alice Garret, 2:31, and Skylark; 2d dam by Chieftain, and the third dam by Skenendoab.

One of the three-year-old fillies was now brought out, a bay in color, with black points, and without a single white hair on her; she is by Hawthorne, dam by Chieftain; 2d dam by Belmont, the second dam being the dam of Nellie Grattan, 2:32. This is a fine individual, full-sized for her age, and a very quiet disposition, still, at the same time, with plenty of life and spirit when being exercised. From her blood lines she should prove a first-class brood mare, if whoever may purchase her does not wish to put her on the track.

Another of the three-year-olds was a dark bay colt by Long Island, he by New York 524, dam by Nutwood; 2d dam the Trustee mare spoken of above. She is another of those that may be ranked with the best, her conformation being perfect.

Our attention was next called to a chestnut filly two years old, by Hawthorne, dam Overshot by Chieftain, the dam being a full sister to the dam of Tempest; 2d dam Old Tempest by Morgan Rattler. This filly has been sick for some time, but has almost recovered. She is built on speed lines, and will prove, barring accidents, a very fast mare, or appearances go for nothing.

A beautiful brown colt, two years old, was now brought for examination, he being by Hawthorne, dam by Tilton Almont; 2d dam the Boggs mare by Lodi; 3d dam by Norfolk. This is a splendid type of the trotter, with plenty of thoroughbred blood; he has any quantity of nerve power; has been worked single and double, and gives every indication of proving himself a very fast trotter.

The next brought out, was a chestnut with one white hind foot, by Hawthorne, dam by Hambletonian 725, she being a full sister to Kilrain, which was timed as a three-year-old, the second horse in a race in 2:28, this filly will make a trotter sure.

Another of the 3-year-old colts which will be sent to Peoria, is a solid bay in color by Hawthorne, dam by Echo; 2nd dam by Don Victor, he is a perfect model of the ideal trotter, and will without doubt bring a very long price.

We were rather taken with the 3 year-old brown filly by Hawthorne, dam by Chieftain; 2nd dam by Belmont, who acted as though she knew she were on inspection and trod the ground with the air of a queen; her disposition is of the best, her action more than good and she can show, even thus early in the season, a merry clip.

A yearling filly, brown in color was next looked at, she has two hind feet white, with a white star, she is also by Hawthorne, dam Gen. Dana; 2nd dam by Belmont, this 2nd dam is the one mentioned above as being the dam of Nellie Gratten, 2:32.

A yearling colt which will be sent to the Chicago sale, was next brought out. He is by Breastplate 11,392 (full brother to Moses S., 2-year-old record 2:29½), he by Hawthorne; the dam of this colt is by John Nelson Jr., a son of John Nelson 187, grandam by Deitz's St. Clair. This is a very racy looking animal, and when offered for sale should be productive of much competition.

When Mr. Shippee purchased the horse known as Campbell's Electioneer 2:22½, he also bought at the same time the horse Campaign, a horse that for beauty and conformation cannot be surpassed in the country; he is by Electioneer, dam Lilly B., by Homer 1235, 2nd dam Maggie Lee by Blackwood 74, 3rd dam Lucille by Alexander's Abdallah, 4th dam by Pilot Jr. This young horse Campaign, is particularly mentioned, as he is the sire of a beautiful yearling brown filly, which for its age is very large and racy looking. The dam of the filly is by Motion 1544, he by Dan Lambert 102. She is a great big, fine animal, and shows beyond doubt the same conformation as do all the Electioneers, if she does not bring a handsome figure, we will be much mistaken.

A very handsome yearling, bay in color, now came trotting down the road, led by one of the assistants. He is by Henry Thorne 10,997, a son of Hawthorne. The dam of the colt is Daisy (dam of Mt. Vernon 2:21), 2nd dam Old Beauty. Like most of those carrying Nutwood blood, he is solid in color, and has an easy way of going that is particularly striking, and as he is bred in such speed line, both top and bottom, he should be invaluable as a stock horse; in addition to what he may do at the trot.

We now come to a shapely little fellow, brown in color, one year old, by Hawthorne, dam by Tilton Almont, 2nd dam the Boggs Mare. He is very evenly turned, and already shows his trotting inheritance.

The next shown is a yearling, black in color, by Hawthorne, dam by Harry Lambert, he a son of Addison Lambert; 2nd dam Ellen Douglas. We again see in this colt the strong evidences of the thoroughbred showing up. He is a perfect picture, and at the same time a good square trotter.

Hawthorne is once more represented in a yearling bay colt whose dam is by Harry Lambert, 2nd dam Yorktown by Chieftain. He is another built on the racy order, and should give a good account of himself.

Still another of the unnamed ones is a bay yearling by Hawthorne, dam by Joe Daniels, 2nd dam by the Burrow's horse, he by the McKinney Horse.

We now come to a bay colt, one year old, by Hawthorne, dam by Harry Lambert, 2nd dam by Don Victor. His color is relieved by one white hind foot. Like all the balance of the Hawthornes, he has plenty of bone and muscle, is high spirited and has very good action.

The last of the yearlings at the French Camp Farm was a chestnut filly with two hind coronets white, and a small star. She is by Abby, dam by Hawthorne; 2d dam by Chieftain. This is a high-finished animal, with an excellent way of going; if she does not make a trotter we will be sadly disappointed.

One of the young stallions which we looked at was a bay colt which was particularly admired, not only on account of his form, but also on account of his pedigree, and he should prove a good stock horse; he is by Hawthorne, dam by Sultan; 2d dam by Hambletonian 725; 3d dam by Bonner, he by Hambletonian 725; 4th dam by Williamson's Belmont. This is another of the double gaited animals, but his exquisite form and fine points was the cause of many exclamations of pleasure. When going at ordinary speed he seems a trotter pure and simple, but when urged, he strikes a very fast pace.

Major Thorne 11328, is a four-year-old black horse by Hawthorne, dam the dam of Tempest, and also dam of Shelly, 2:29½, and Brightlight, 2:40; 2d dam by Coburn's Jim Crow, he by Jim Crow, thoroughbred. Mr. Shippee has had several offers for this exceedingly fine horse, but has as yet refused all temptations to sell him.

Chestnut Thorne 11330, as his name would indicate, is a chestnut in color, with white stripe in face; he is by Hawthorne, dam Mocking Bird (full sister to Honesty, 2:25½); 2d dam by Chieftain; 3d dam by Coburn's Jim Crow. This grandly-bred individual will be disposed of at the Chicago sale.

Another one of those to be taken East for sale is a black filly by Hawthorne, dam Priam 1798; 2d dam by Black Hawk 767; 3d dam by Remley's Royal Oak.

When on a visit to the Stockten race track in the early portion of last year, some time before the circuit began, we had occasion to mention the good-looking Kilrain, which is as fine a specimen of the trotting horse as one could care to see; he is a bay with black points, and although at present high in flesh, looks as though he would like to be back at hard track work. Kilrain is by Hawthorne, dam by Hambletonian 725; 2d dam by Bonner, he by Hambletonian 725; 3d dam by Williamson's Belmont. Mr. Shippee has every confidence that before the close of the present season, the fame of Hawthorne will be still further augmented by Kilrain beating 2:20; he is fully 16 hands high, with plenty of spirit, and has an exceedingly fine gait. Kilrain will be sent to Stockton for active work as soon as the track will permit of it.

When Director commenced to prove how he was capable of breeding on, Mr. Shippee decided to procure the very best Dictator colt that could be purchased, and with that object in view, commenced corresponding with the prominent breeders of the East to find out where a choice representative of that family could be bought; after months of delay he finally selected one, and his choice proved that the animal was all that could be desired.

When Mr. Stemler started back East last summer, he was instructed to go and take a look at the colt which Mr. Shippee thought would suit him, with instructions to buy if he was a perfect animal. Mr. Stemler, after an examination, purchased the youngster, then only a yearling, and brought him back to California. This royal representative of the best blue blood of Kentucky has been named Dictator Wilkes; he is by Dictator, dam Manola by Geo. Wilkes; 2d dam Lizzie Brinker (dam of Budd Crook, 2:18½, Adjutant, 2:27½, Lucy Fleming, 2:24½, etc.), she by Drennan's Brinker; 3d dam by Million's Copper Bottom; 4th dam by a son of Blackburn's Whip; 5th dam by Bishop's Hambletonian. If this two-year-old does not make a mark in the breeding annals of this State, it will be very much of a surprise to all who have ever seen him; he is as perfect as can be, without spot or blemish, and is a kingly looking fellow. Mr. Shippee will breed him this year to four or five mares, then he will be gently exercised, and probably sent for a record before the season of 1890 ends.

We now come to a full fledged pacer, chestnut in color, called Chief Thorne 11331 by Harry Thorne, dam Daisy, 2:31½ (the dam of Mt. Vernon, 2:21); 2d dam Beauty by Old Doc. This colt has a regular pacing conformation, and is very speedy; he will be worked among others during the coming season.

Moses S. 11009 is so well known that it is hardly necessary to say much about him, he having made a name for himself and his sire in races, both in 1888 and 1889; he is by Hawthorne, dam the dam of Ha-Ha, 2:22½; 2d dam Billing's mare, sometimes known as the Jim Eoff mare. Moses S. has improved very much in form since he made his two-year-old record of 2:29½, and although his mark was not lowered last season, he was timed separately when he came in second to the great Direct, Moses S.'s time being 2:21½; he is another of the Hawthorne colts which it is confidently believed will be able to trot this season better than 2:20.

Pedro, a bay gelding six years old, by Hawthorne, is a full brother to Moses S., and has a mark of 2:36; he will also receive work before long, and if he shows any inclination to take his work kindly, will be sent among the 2:25 pacers on the coming circuit.

Where there are so many choice animals to look at, it is a hard matter to select one which seems to show better than the others, but there was one bay pacer, two years old, that caught our eye, as he seems to be built on very speedy lines; he is by Hawthorne, dam June Second by Ben Franklin 753; 2d dam Kitty Harris by Dan Lambert; 3d dam Gazelle. This is a very fine colt, and should go down the line at a rattling rate of speed.

Thornewood is a full brother to Kilrain, and is a very promising colt.

The stable boys have a great liking for the fine bay gelding, five years old, by Hawthorne, dam by Gen McClellan 145; 2d dam Lady Fine. He shows up well, and has evidently inherited a vast amount of speed.

Allen Thorne is a bay colt, three years old, by Hawthorne, dam by Dan Lambert; 2d dam Kitty Harris. We cannot help remarking that this colt resembles in a striking degree the old trotter Ethan Allen as we saw him many years ago, back in "Old York State."

Another of the likely looking colts is the chestnut horse Princewood; he has three white feet and strip in face; he is by Dexter Prince, dam by Nutwood; 2d dam Maud, the dam of Reliance, record 2:22½, and Magdallah, 2:23½; Princewood has evidently a great amount of speed, and it will require but little work to develop what there is latent in him.

As time was limited, and we had to return, it was impossible to examine the score of youngsters to be seen in the various paddocks; however, we hope in the near future to be able to give a more extended account of the horses at the French Camp Farm. A large majority of the above will be shipped between the 20th and 22d of this month, and forwarded to the East for sale.

It was well toward the evening hour before we finished the inspection, but not before a good look had been taken at the stable and barns, everything at which appeared in apple pie order. The entire consignment is under the charge of Mr. Jas. Thompson, who has lately arrived in this State, from Kansas, where he formerly worked for Mr. Campbell, the gentleman who now owns Campbell's Electioneer 2:22½, and Mr. Thompson is the driver who at Abilene, Kansas, on September 12th, drove Mr. Campbell's horse to his record. He is thoroughly posted in his business, a good judge of a horse, a splendid judge of gait and action, and should prove a most valuable man for Mr. Shippee. He will return immediately after the Chicago sales, and prepare some of Hawthorne's get, for records this year.

A short drive was made to French Camp where we took the evening train, and in a few minutes we were safely ensconced in the well known Yosemite Hotel in Stockton; after a bountiful repast, a visit was made to the bank, of which Mr. Shippee is President, and in his private office, horses, their pedigrees, their performances and prospective performances were fully talked over. Mr. Shippee is an enthusiast in horse breeding, as may readily be seen when it is stated that within a very short time he has spent about $200,000 for first-class stock. It is not only the trotters that he adheres to, but his stable of runners are also well known throughout the State, and while he has but very few as in comparison with the trotters, the thoroughbreds that he possesses are of the very best strains known to American breeders.

Having a desire to see some of the thoroughbred brood mares, we determined to remain over another day, and visit a second of the ranches, which is known as the Oaklawn Stock Farm, situated midway between Stockton and the flourishing little town of Lodi, on the old Cherokee Lane. When Mr. Shippee first bought this thousand acres, in 1865, he set out, around the entire allotment, a number of fir trees, at an equal distance apart, and also planted the same specie of trees in all the roads and lanes running through the farm. The sight to-day to a stranger, who is visiting that portion of the San Joaquin Valley for the first time, is very striking, as the handsome trees are a pleasing change to the eye, from the monotony of the ordinary fencing, which becomes tiresome to him who drives through the San Joaquin.

When we arrived at Oaklawn, Mr. Miller, the manager was at hand to show us his favored pets, and as paddock after paddock was gone through, it was with pardonable pride that he pointed out, first trotter and then thoroughbred, a large majority of whom are in foal to the very best bred stallions in this State. It would take up more room than the BREEDER AND SPORTSMAN can possibly spare, to enumerate each individual that was shown to us, yet it seems only right that mention should be made of a few of those that particularly struck us as being splendid individuals. The great storms of the past three months has not affected in any serious manner, the great paddocks which are here to be seen, and it was with no difficulty that we traversed some eight or ten of them, and viewed the royally bred matrons.

It might be just as well to state here that Mr. Shippee owns quite a number of stallions in addition to "Hawthorne" previously mentioned; one of which, "Long Island" was purchased in the East for Mr. Shippee by Chas. Marvin, the manager of Palo Alto Stock Farm. "Long Island" is a son of "New York" 524, a splendid specimen of equine beauty. He is a rich brown in color, with three white feet and a little white over the coronet of the fourth foot; his second dam was by "Bonnie Scotland", and his neck and head strongly shows the thoroughbred blood that runs through his veins. His get are all that could be desired, showing plenty of substance and stamina, and good trotting inheritance, he is a grand addition to Mr. Shippee's trotters, and will without doubt make a name for himself.

"California Lambert" is a son of "Addison Lambert" 744, he a son of "Daniel Lambert" 102, and an inbred Morgan, for those who like this out-cross, he is one of the best that could have been secured. Mr. Shippee has always had a great deal of faith in the Morgan Stock, and some few years ago, purchased in Vermont, an entire carload of the very best that could be purchased; that he made no mistake can readily be seen, when one looks over their descendants now running at large over the acreage of Oaklawn.

Mr. Shippee has also a very well formed colt by "Hawthorne" out of a "Nutwood" mare, which particularly pleased the writer, he showing plenty of bone and muscle, great substance, and is a perfect picture of the horse now idolized at the Stout Bros.' Stock Farm at Dubuque, Iowa.

As the beautiful creatures passed us, notes were made of the following, which constitute but a very small portion of the animals now at Oaklawn.

Continued in our next issue.

Communication.

YOLO, YOLO Co; Cal.

EDITOR BREEDER AND SPORTSMAN:—I must beg your indulgence while I give expression to my admiration of the masterly manner in which Mr. Wilfred Page defends the excellent programme lately adopted by the Board of the P. C. T. H. B. A. and advocates equal rights among the horse breeders of this coast.

It has been the fear of the very condition of things which Mr. Page so ably denounces and condemns, and which the lately adopted programme is designed to avoid that has deterred many small breeders from joining the association. There has been a seeming tendency toward the establishment of a kind of horse aristocracy in this State.

It has been claimed, and perhaps not without good reason, that discriminations are made against small breeders at fairs in the awarding of premiums, and that the representatives of certain farms and horse families are often the recipients of undeserved favors to the injury and disparagement of less prominent breeders and sires. I do not assert these things as facts, but inasmuch as they are quite current among horsemen, there must be some foundation for them. If Mr. Page and the rest of the directors of the Association continue to govern their actions by a policy of equal rights among breeders they will have the hearty endorsement and co-operation of all fair minded horsemen, their membership will become greatly augmented, and it will become a still more potent factor for promoting the horse breeding interests of this coast. Let the Association discountenance any policy that tends to foster the growth of an aristocracy, and let it be governed by principles purely democratic, and its success is assured.

J. W. M.

Salinas Colt Stakes.

Montery County has evidently determined not to be outdone by the more Northern districts, and has just closed a colt Stake which has received the support it so richly merited. Our correspondent forwards the following list of entries, and from the breeding there should be some rare good youngsters among those nominated.

Wm. Robson's sorrel c Harrison by St. Patrick, dam Maggie by Belmont.

Wideman & Kelly's br f Hazel L. by Junio, dam unknown.

H. P. Brown's b f by Sidney, dam by Belmont.

Jas. B. Iverson's b f Ivola by Antevolo, dam Salinas Belle by Vermont, 322.

Jas. B. Iverson's br c Baramark by Mul-Vorhees, dam Jennie by Kingston, a son of imp Hercules.

Jas. Dwain's br f Florine by Mul-Vorhees, dam Flora G. 2:29½ by Altoona 8850.

Z. Hebert's b c Bruno by Junio, dam Dolly by Mozart.

M. Lynn's gr c Violante by Antevolo dam by Pirate a son of Buccaneer.

M. Lynn's sorrel f Lucy by St. Patrick, dam Kitty Patchen.

Robt. Garside's b f by St. Patrick, dam by Mambrino 1789.

John Kalar's br c by Junio, dam by Mambrino 1789.

E. P. Iverson's sorrel f Cinderella by St. Patrick dam by Anderson's Abdallah.

Jas. H. Harris' blk c Charley A. by Erwin Davis, dam Kitty by De Groat's Starr King

D. G. McLean's b c by J. L J., a son of Del Sur, dam unknown.

J. E. Hiserman's ch c Elmo, sire unknown, dam Hildy, thoroughbred.

Chas. Moulton's b f Lady M. by St Patrick, dam Gipsey, by Belmont.

Jas. C. Storms' br f Juniora by Junio, dam Minnie by General Taylor

Z. Hebert's b c by St. Patrick, dam Laura H. by Altoona.

To the above list is to be added three entries by Hon. Jesse D. Carr which were received in time but names and pedigrees omitted.

The Doctrine of "Impregnation by Sire Strains" and the Theory of the "Control of Sex."

HARVEY W. PECK.

Mr. Fred W. Loeber, in the issue of this paper dated February 1st, refers to my comments upon the theory of Mr. C. Bruce Lowe, as advanced by him some weeks since. The slight attention I paid to Mr. Lowe's idea was done in a spirit of good-natured raillery, though I consider what I stated to be truth.

Mr. Loeber does not seem to just comprehend what I meant. I shall now enter into a discussion of the subject, of sufficient length, and I trust of sufficient clearness, to have my position definitely understood.

Mr. Lowe quoted the instance of a thoroughbred mare that was bred to a thoroughbred horse. The mare, we are given to understand, was the stoutest and best bred of the two, the stallion being considered as second class. Mr. Lowe says the first colt was a racehorse; the second one not quite so good; the third inferior to the second, until when the fourth, fifth and sixth foals were reached, it is said they were only common plugs, in point of speed, ranking even below ordinary selling platers. The reason ascribed for all this is that the mare controlled the characteristics of the first colt, but when continuously bred to this horse she lost her prepotency, the horse gradually assuming control, the horse being inferior to the mare, the colts kept growing worse. The reason of the mare's losing her prepotency, Mr. Lowe says, is that she was gradually 'impregnated by the sire's strains through the foal's circulation previous to birth." According, then, to this theory, this mare was inoculated by this horse (through the foal's circulation previous to birth) to such an extent that she lost her own individuality; no longer showed her line of ancestry or her own racing proclivities, but her offspring were an exact counterpart of the stallion.

Now, presuming this mare, after having been bred to this horse, and having become so impregnated with his inferiority as to be unable to produce a good colt, should be bred to a good horse, a horse of great excellence, what then? Simply this, she would be unable to bear a good colt to the cover of this horse—at least for two or three years. Why? Because it would take that length of time to overcome the inferior impregnation derived from the first stallion. Neither could this mare exert any of her own individuality in the first or second colts by the second stallion. Why? Because her own characteristics would have received an overlay of inferiority from the first horse that would preclude the exercisal of her own good qualities, until this inferiority was gradually dispelled and absorbed by the impregnation of the second horse.

Does anybody believe this? I certainly do not! Yet it is a reasonable deduction, so plain as to not even invite criticism. That this theory is not true, I have every reason to believe, as I have witnessed a practical demonstration of its imperfections dozens of times.

I have followed the "impregnation of sire strains idea" for several years, and have made it a point to get all that has been written upon the subject, for Mr. Lowe is not the first man to advance the idea.

I have followed the idea of "controlling sex at will," my experiments and the experiences of others tending to show conclusively that the man does not live that can contol sex in horses.

I may therefore, with out egotism, claim some little knowledge regarding both of these alleged theories.

I may say that no such thing as Mr. Lowe claims is ever witnessed in the human family—with possibly a few exceptions.

We have all heard the saying that very smart men seldom have very smart sons! If Mr. Lowe's theory was applicable to the human race, that saying would be reversed, for if a man of great learning and intellectuality were to have say six children, the sixth being a son, that son should be the father right over, in personal appearance, mannerisms and intellect.

Mr. Loeber does not believe that the appearance of a Jack or a Zebra or a Quaggy could affect the brain and organism of a mare at copulation, to such extent that the strangeness of their appearance would come to her mind at some subsequent breeding.

To carry out this thought he says that I may pick five or ten mares of any "off" color, barring pintoes, and breed them too Whippleton, and if all the colts are not bay, brown or black, he will charge nothing for the horses' service.

Well, does that prove the idea I advanced to be incorrect? Certainly not, for it is simply a side issue. Does Mr. Loeber see no difference between a stallion and a Jack, in the effect left upon a mare? The horse is of her own kind, the Jack is not. I have seen mares so badly scared when a Jack would attempt to cover them that it took three or four men to hold them. These mares were not young either, had been bred before, and if a horse had come up to them they would not have moved out of their tracks.

Now, let me give a practical illustration of the "impregnation with sire strains" theory. I will presume a certain mare bred to Director for seven years! She might not be worth $7 to start with. Her first colt would not be much good, for Director could not do it all; the second would be a trifle better; the third quite a trotter; but when we got the seventh we had a sure enough race horse, of high speed and courage. Why? Because the mare had become thoroughly impregnated with Director's strains by the time the seventh foal saw the light. She was in effect inoculated with the blood of Director, the word "blood" signifying the trotting instinct, the courage and the ability to train on possessed by Director. As a breeder, then, this mare would be essentially Director, having acquired, through constant service by him for a number of years, a perpotency stronger than would be possessed by one of his own daughters!

At this juncture we will switch off and breed the mare to some fairly bred young sire that has no record and has never sired a trotter. The result of this cross, I will assume, is a great young trotter. Where does the speed come from? From this young sire directly, or from Director indirectly? The "impregnation" theory would tend to prove that Director was the source.

It would therefore appear that no stallion could be tested, as a speed producer, if bred to a mare that had previously had a colt! To secure an accurate test he would, of necessity, have to be coupled with a mare that had never been bred, or he would have to cover a mare a sufficient number of years to invalidate any tendency previously implanted by some other horse. It would seem unnecessary to pursue this subject farther.

As for superiority of pretotency, in either sire or dam, I believe the following rules, which were published some years ago, for the first time I think, in an Eastern horse paper, to be as nearly correct, and to embody as much truth as could be got into the same space. It will be understood that there are occasionally exceptions to all rules.

THE LAWS OF HEREDITY.

1. That from the male parent is mainly derived the external structure, configuration and outward characteristics, also the locomotive system of development.

2. From the female parent is derived the internal structure, the vital organs, and in a much greater proportion, than from the male, the constitution, temper and habits, in which endurance and bottom are included.

3. That the purer the race of the parent, the more certainty there is of its transmitting its qualities to the offspring; say two animals are mated, if one is of purer descent than the other, he or she will exercise the influence in stamping the character of the progeny, particularly if the greater purity is on the side of the male.

4. That, apart from certain disturbing influences or causes, the male, if of pure race, and descended from a stock of uniform color, stamps the color of the offspring.

5. That the influence of the first male is not infrequently protracted beyond the birth of the offspring of which he is the parent and his mark is left upon subsequent progeny.

6. That the transmission of diseases of the vital organs is more certain if on the other side of the female, and diseases of the joints if on the side of the male parent.

The above six laws are in the great majority of cases, correct. We have all seen horses of great speed eminate from the coupling of a fast and game stallion and a mare of neither speed nor gameness. This shows that Rule 2 is open to exception, but all of them represent the facts of the case in nearly all instances.

Several years ago I bred a brown mare to a bay horse. The produce was a perfectly black filly. I bred the same mare to a grey horse. The produce was a light bay filly! Every horseman has seen, and probably in many instances had the same experience. It was simply an exemplification of the law of reversal. I do not believe that a mare can give anything to a colt that she herself does not possess. She might be "impregnated" from time immemorial, but the offspring would still represent in appearance, disposition and speed, its sire and dam or their ancestors.

If Mr. Lowe's theory be correct, a mare could be bred to a jack sufficiently long to become thoroughly inoculated, each succeeding foal resembling the jack more and more, until the last foal would be a little jackass instead of a mule.

Every man who knows much concerning horse breeding is well aware that some stallions impress their own image and characteristics upon their progeny in a much more marked manner than do others. This trait we term prepotency. This prepotency arises from several different causes, such as extreme vigor and strength, strong inbreeding; certain traits that have been handed down from sire to son, generation after generation, until they become a fixed attribute, etc., etc. This is also applicable of mares under similar conditions. When therefore, one of the above described stallions is bred to any ordinary mare the offspring will be a miniature of him. When a mare of similar discription is coupled with any ordinary stallion, she controlls the appearance and disposition of the progeny. Lady Patriot, dam of Volunteer; Sentinel 2:29¼, Marksman, Hertzel's Hambletonian, Heroine, etc., practically verifies this statement. Her influence upon Volunteer was very marked, and not only upon him, but his descendants as well. It is claimed that in all her produce and most of their descendants could be seen the impress of this truly great mare. Most of her colts were sired by Rysdyk's Hambletonian, and strange to say none of them resembled the old horse as much as her grandson, Shawmut 2:26. Shawmut was sired by Harry Clay 45, his dam being Heroine, by Hambletonian out of Lady Patriot. Every line of Shawmut shows Rysdyk's Hambletonian, from ears to tail. This is again the law of reversal.

I shall briefly notice the "controlling of sex" theory. The most ingenious writer upon this subject that I have read is Thomas B. Armitage. His theory is that the germ of the male is always female and the germ of the female always male, therefore, the one of the parents that was in the highest state of vigor and strength would control the sex. Thus he said a horse that was kept idle while in the stud, fed highly, allowed to get fat and gross, would certainly beget fillies, with rare exceptions, as the mares to whom he was bred were in likelihood used as road horses, and were consequently much "harder and in better physical health than the horse." To raise fillies, the dam should be reduced to a state of "innocuous dissuetude," made as week and flabby as possible, and the foal would certainly be a female. He was clever in his illustrations and forcible in his arguments, but for all that, who does not know that his control of sex theory is a myth, a chimeres, that is reflected by the imagination of man, as a mirage is reflected through refraction of the lower strata of the atmosphere upon the desert? Who has not seen this theory controverted under exactly the conditions Mr. Armitage mentions? But so long as the world stands just so long will men have "theories." This, I presume is as it should be, for the world owes more to theorists than to those who are content to move along year after year in the same groove, having nothing and wanting nothing, content as long as the blue vault hangs overhead, the sun and stars shine, birds sing, and flowers blow, for all these conditions whisper to them that this "plane between two eternities" dons the same grab year after year, and why should they aspire to superiority.

VETERINARY.

Conducted by W. Henry Jones, M. R. C. V. S.

Subscribers to this paper can have advice through this column in all cases of sick or injured horses or cattle by sending an explicit description of the case. Applicants will send their name and address that they may be identified. Questions requiring answers by mail should be accompanied by two dollars, and addressed, to W. Henry Jones, M. R. C. V. S., Olympic Stables, Butler Street, San Francisco.

O. L. C.

I wish to avail myself of the privilege of a subscriber to obtain through your Veterinary Department advise as to the best method of treatment of saddle sores over the kidneys on cow ponies.

Answer.—If the wounds are in a suppurative condition, I would advise you to poultice or foment with warm water; afterwards dress with carbolic acid and glycerine, one part of the former to five parts of the latter. In the meantime give the animals perfect rest as far as riding is concerned.

Names Claimed.

On February 6th, Fusillade's Last, dropped a chestnut colt with star in forehead and both hind ankles white by Sid. I hereby claim the name of Fusilier for him.

On February 7th, Irish Lass dropped a brown colt with star in forehead by Woodnut 2:16½. I claim the name of Marcus Daly for him.

B. C. HOLLY.

TURF AND TRACK.

Umpire is now the property of Jas. Clare.

Dictator is 27 years old and in good healthy condition.

H. D. Miller's Ida Glenn will be bred to Prince of Norfolk.

The Pimlico track at Baltimore will be used solely as a trotting track henceforth.

Rancho Del Paso's Mabel (sister to Beautiful Belle) will be bred to Stamboul this season.

A two-year-old brother to Madstone, called Ascot, is said to be showing speed at Nashville.

Montana Regent, the once well-known race horse, is making a season in the stud at Denver, Colo.

H. D. Miller will take Daisy D., Captain Al, and probably other two, East this season, staying off at Denver en route.

While Favonia, Marcus Daly's crack mare, was being campaigned, a $10,000 insurance policy was always carried on her.

Charlie Johnson, of Denver, Colo., has in his string two fine Jim Douglass two-year-olds that are said to rival their sire in speed.

Dr. S. A. Browne has a $20,000 insurance each on Anteeo, Ambassador and Warlock, and all his mares and foals are insured at less rates.

Captain W. H., more generally known as Billy Boyce, now holds the position of superintendent at the stock farm of W. C. France, Lexington Ky.

Louis Grabenstatter, who made his reputation behind Balsora Wilkes 2:17½ will assist in training C. J. Hamlin's Village Farm flyers the coming season.

The ten English Shire and Clydesdales sold at Springfield, Ill., last month, at auction, realized $7,500. $1,150 was the highest price for a single animal.

It is said that the Montana Agricultural, Mineral & Mechanical Association will confine its 2 and 3 year old trotting races to Montana-bred youngsters.

J. R. Ross will be seen on the Western circuit with Oro and Kitty Van. The latter should run a merry five furlongs with 105 pounds or thereabouts on her back.

The Hermitage Stock Farm declined an offer of $25,000 for Bow Bells, the three-year-old brother to Bell Boy. Bow Bells will leave Palo Alto shortly for Nashville.

There are only three pacers that have beaten 2:12 one of them Gold Leaf, Mr. Salisbury's filly will be put up at the Pleasanton Stock Farm's coming New York Sale.

A colt by Bermuda, 2:20½, dam Baby Mine 2:27¼, property of N. T. Kirby, Jerseyville, Ill., paced an eighth of a mile in 22¼ seconds, a 2:58 gait, when five and a half months old.

Jessie C., the two-year-old, who showed such promise last year, winning several races and was injured in her stall after the Blood Horse Meeting, has been bred to imp Intruder.

The Tuolumne County Fair Directors held a meeting last Saturday. Tom Hender was made Treasurer, and it was decided that the first fair be held in September of next year.

Charley Kerr, the owner of Apache, the sensational winner, in Bakersfield a few weeks, has sent Ona, a five-year-old mare by Onondaga out of Virgie, to Harry Howard to be trained.

George Middleton of Chicago owner of Jack 2:15 has another star performer he having puchase the gray gelding Pilot H. 3-year-old record, 2:19½ by Pilot Medium, dam by Tom Hunter.

D. D. Plummer, Gorham, Me., has an English thoroughbred broodmare weighing nearly 1,000 pounds, from which he has a nineteen months old filly, estimated to weigh 800 pounds.

Darby, record 2:16½, was started as a ringer under the name of June in a slow class on Long Island last season, but did not win. He struck himself, came near being distanced, and was drawn.

Colts cannot be reared like hot-house plants. They must have exercise to develop the muscular tissue, as on their strength and quality of bone the future supply of stamina depends.

A Southerner, who is a breeder, recently asked W. S. Bailey of Vermont to put a price on Cobden 2:28½, sire of Helen M., two-year-old record 2:28. It is said that the price was $10,000.

"Plunger" Walton's imported horse Richmond has a remarkably fine lot of youngsters. The first of his get will race this year, and their appearance on the turf is looked forward to with much interest.

The first thoroughbred foal reported in the east for 1890 is from August Belmont's nursery shed near Lexington, Ky. The youngster is a bay colt by The Ill-used, dam Madcap by Matador. He was foaled January 16th.

W. McCormick resigned the trainership of the Winters' Stable about three weeks ago and is at present in Sacramento. Mr. Winters will train his own stable, assisted by Joe Courtney. The two-year-olds will shortly go East.

Johnny Campbell, who brought out the pacer Rich Ball, 2:12½, says that quinine is a first-class tonic for horses, and should be given to horses that are kept in training for a long period and that naturally become a little stale.

Abe Perry, the well known colored trainer, who last year handled Penn P., and in his time had under his care such horses as Checkmate, Vera Cruz and Joe Cotton, will train for E. C. Hopper, the popular Latonia Secretary.

Brown Dick who furnished Eastern racing men so many surprises last season at the New York tracks has a promising filly called Fonsetta by Fonso-Aileen with which he expect to astonish Eastern turfmen this summer.

E. C. Walker ("Veritas") thinks that Harry Wilkes 2:13½ and Miss Alice 2:20½ hooked double would just about lower the double team record of 2:15¾ Mr. Walker drove Miss Alice in her successful campaign last season.

Marcus Daly, Anaconda, Montana, recently lost at his Missoula County ranch, the bay colt St. Val, foaled 1888, by Electioneer, dam by George Wilkes out of a mare by Clark Chief. Mr. Daly paid $5,000 for St. Val when a wealing.

Galatea 2:24¾, by Fearnaught 2:23¼, will be bred to Edgemark 2:16, next summer. She is already the dam of Grand Duchess 2:26½, and has produced colts besides by Alcantara and Viking. Her produce this year will be by Lumps 2:21.

President Phillip J. Dwyer, of the Brooklyn Jockey Club, is now at New Orleans enjoying what they call racing down that way. He will remain in the Crescent City until after Mardi Gras festival and its accompanying jollities are ended.

Lexington Wilkes 4878 one of the best bred sons of George Wilkes is the horse recently purchase by J. I. Case of Racine for $1000,00 one of the best bred sons will go to the highest bidder at the Kidd Edmonson & Morse, Chicago March Sale.

The stallion Red Cross, a son of Brignoli who made a record of 2:21½ several years ago under the management of G. J. Fuller, is to be sold at auction in New York City before long. He is well advanced in years, but is still a remarkably handsome horse.

Mr. Abington the English racing millionaire it is said intends in future to go in extensively for breeding bloodstock. As a purchaser of yearlings, Mr. Abington has been prominent of late years, but his luck with them in racing has been far from good.

The real estate on the National Fair Association, which included the Ivy City race track, was sold at auction for $133,500. James Lansburgh, of Washington, representing a syndicate, was the purchaser. The property will be divided into building lots.

Jas. A. Dustin the well known driver and trainer, who in his day has driven many cracks, went down to Palo Alto last Wednesday under engagement for the rest of the season. Presumably Dustin will handle the stable while Marvin goes East with Sunol, Palo Alto, etc.

George Hankins, one of the principals of the Chicago Stable confederacy, has been indicted by a Chicago grand jury for keeping a gambling house. There were two former indictments recorded against him, and to secure his liberty he was required to give bail in $5,000.

A number of horse dealers in this country are doing a great deal of injury to the foreign demand for American horses by sending abroad a lot of played out and unsound trotters. This is a shortsighted policy that injures not only the rogues but unfortunately the reputable honest breeder and dealers as well.

Chas. Marvin the well known Palo Alto Superintendent will have his book on training trotters in print next month. It should have any amount of valuable matter, the result of careful experience and long practice in the art of training trotters, in which business Marvin has proved himself facile princeps.

The month of March promises the greatest outpouring of richly bred trotting stock upon the New York auction market that has ever before been seen in a single month in any locality. California is better represented than any state in the Union, and the Rancho Del Paso entries will astonish even the California Breeders.

Many, horsemen—and they are horsemen in other respects—will insist in describing horses by the same sire as half brothers. *It does not* go. In just the same way they say he will be three years old (or whatever age it may be) in June, the first of January settles the age of a colt, and to be half brothers they must be out of one and the *same mare*.

The English, Germans, French, Italians and South Americans, have become regular patrons of our trotting markets. The American trotting horse will be in greater demand than ever, and the immense sums invested in breeding interests will pay as handsome dividends as almost any other legitmate business enterprise. The trotters hold the "age" and there is no limit to the game.

How is this for high? At the recent Melbourne Agricultural Show, Spondulix, a bay gelding, won the 12st hunters' prize with a jump of 6ft. 3½in Last year the same horse secured the same award with 6ft., and in 1887 also won with a leap of 6ft. ½in. At the Chicago Horse Show last November, Roseberry, a four year old chestnut gelding, cleared a bar 6ft 11½ in., high. The performances of both these animals are authenticated.

"What they want here in England," writes John Splan," is a 'cobby' built horse or mare; must be good gaited, able to draw weight, wear no boots or toe weights; for that kind of a horse that can step a 2:40 gait or better there are plenty of customers at long prices. They want sound horses, and are much better judges of sound horses than we are. One or two of the most influential newspapers are intending to make a strong effort to have trotting introduced here. What the newspapers here endorse is bound to succeed."

Reveille, B. C. Holly's son of Shiloh is well known as the sire of Gladstone, one of the crack sprinters taken east by Albert Cooper, Tycoon and other well known raceborses. Last week Reveille inadvertently appeared among trotting sires. If his trotters (have not heard of any) should turn out as speedy and reliable as his runners, racing men would soon have several, for his fee is only $25, and forgetting runners he is the cheapest sire in the list. Mr. Holly should raise to $75, for he has proved himself a sire among sires.

A Chicagoan intimates to the St. Louis Sporting News that Budd Doble will have Maud S. out for exhibition miles next season, and that the peerless queen will accompany his stable through a grand circuit, and if just right at any of the fast tracks will be sent to beat her own record 2:08¾. It is believed that Mr. Bonner while owning both of the great mares, Sunol and Maud S., would very much prefer that the latter should remain the world's fastest trotter, and to this end every chance will be given her.

Miss Russell is twenty-six years old, and is in foal this season to King Wilkes, 2:22½. Her two-year-old colt by Electioneer, who will do his first stud service this year, has been appropriately named Re-election. Like his dam his color is gray, and he resembles her in other ways, in fact he is more like her than any foal she ever dropped. After remaining in the stud for several seasons, he will be handled and driven to a record. He is highly prized at Woodburn, and will never be sold, as only recently his owner refused to set a price on him.

The gray gelding Jack is not the model of a trotting horse, and he would not be selected by an artist to represent the ideal light harness horse of America. Still he has a record of 2:15, made in 1889, and his owner, George Middleton, has issued a challenge that he will match Jack against any trotter in the world for from $5,000 to $15,000 a side.

Trainer McCabe appears to take even more interest in the horses in his charge than their owners. He spends his entire time at work and seldom leaves his stable. When his horses are taken out for exercise McCabe will be found riding a tailender and watching the movements of those in front. The Dwyers' entire string may be seen on parade along the Brooklyn Boulevard from the Park to Coney Island every day at this season.

To change the name of a horse having a record requires a fee of $50 to be paid to the American Trotting Horse Association, and when the same horse trots or paces under the National Association the owner again has to pay a fee of $50. It would seem to be the fair thing that a rule should be adopted so that to pay $50 in either association would make the animal eligible to both. By the way, it seems to me the racing associations, if ever they have a governing body, should insist on a big fee for changing names.

In regard to native half-bred horses, very evident does it appear that there are no grounds for the alarmist feeling that prevailed not long since as to their alleged scarcity. The Right Hon. E. Stanhope, in a speech recently delivered in Lincolnshire, was compelled to admit that Great Britain and Ireland can supply ample material for cavalry mounts, and that there will be no need in future to look abroad for available horses to serve that object. A register was some time since established for owners of British horses for sale to enter them, with their prices, on condition that the Army authorities may take them at any time they may be needed, and, according to Mr. Stanhope, no fewer than 14,000 have been registered.

The British Board of Trade returns show that during the eleven months of last year, ending with November, 13,255 horses of the value of £932,508 were exported, against 12,045 valued at £793,731, for the corresponding period of 1888. During the past eleven months British North America took from us 1384 stallions and 1188 mares; the United States 624 stallions and 418 mares; Belgium 15 stallions and 884 mares; Holland 31 stallions and 700 mares; France 79 stallions and 434 mares; and other countries 846 stallions and 1733 mares. Imports of horses have increased likewise, the numbers received in the eleven months of this year being 13,335, valued at £263,111, against 11,123, of the value of £186,737, for the corresponding period of 1888.

George Kinney who has made such a mark in the stud last year, (his first season's foals which have raced) is the property of N. T. Harris, Kentucky. Mr. Haggin who sold Kinney has an elder brother in John Happy, whose colts have the true Scotland appearance. Mr. Harris who has been in New Orleans says he has 22 yearlings which will be sold in New York. Eighteen are by Geo. Kinney, two by Neptune, one by Leonatus and one by Saracen. The latter has not been given much chance in the stud, but Mr. Harris is confident of his ability to get race horses, and will give him more opportunity to prove it hereafter. Among the Kinneys are a sister to Flyaway, a brother to Grayson, a colt out of Batchelor's Princess, a filly out of Olivette, a filly out of Princess Ban, a colt out of a sister to Blazes, a filly out of the grandam of Dew Drop and others. They are a handsome lot.

Mr. Harris last spring purchased a filly by Longfellow, out of Augusta, a sister to Persimmons. She has shown so well that Mr. Harris has named her Louisiana, in honor of his native State. She is now two years old and is well entered. Sam Bryant is training her.

The stakes of the Louisville Jockey Club which will be run at the Spring meeting, commencing May 14th, are as follows: The Hurstbourne Stake, five-eighths of a mile, for two-year-old fillies, 53 entries; the Alexander stake, five-eighths of a mile, for two-year old colts, 43 entries; the Runnymede stake, three-quarter mile dash, for two-year-old colts and fillies, 47 entries; the Delbech handicap, for three-year-olds and upwards, one and one-sixteenth miles, closed with 30 entries; the Merchants' handicap, for three-year-olds and upwards, closed with 27 entries; the Kentucky Jack Pot stakes, for three-year-olds and upwards, 14 entries; the Kentucky Derby, for three-year-old colts and fillies, has 111 entries; the Kentucky Oaks, for three-year-old fillies, has 87 entries; the Clark stakes, for three-year-old colts and fillies, has 100 entries. The meeting last nine days, and $30 000 will be added in stakes and purses. Spokane and Proctor Knott, with Maori, Fairy Queen, Brandolette, Clara, Nevada, Hypocrite, Bettina and Ballyhoo, Famine, Unite and Milton, appear in the handicaps. There are many stables training there, and by March 1st, nearly 200 horses will be quartered at the track.

While in Sacramento last week after looking at several of the runners I took a glance through W. Field Smith's stable which is suitably located close to the main entrance to the track and includes a long stable, neatly filled up with several box stalls, and two or three adjacent lots in which some of the youngsters are occasionally turned out. The Stable was a model of neatness and order, indicating at once that a careful supervision was exercised over everything. Mr. Smith who was disengaged kindly showed me round the stables and expatiated on the horses which looked in very good trim, a neat racy looking two-year-old filly Felucca, is by Guy Wilkes 2:15½ out of Cora by Buccaneer, grand dam Pearl by Blue Bull. Mr. Smith sold Cora to Mr. Corbitt last year. The three year old Kalibar with a true Sultan head is in every respect a grand looking three year old having good shoulders and a strong back with splendid legs and feet. He is a powerful bay colt and has done some fastwork. He is by Guy Wilkes 2:15½, dam by Sultan, grand dam Inez 2:30 by the Moor. Mr. Smith who is one of our most successful trainers is well known all over the State for his straightforward driving, while having been almost bred in the business, he should certainly not lack experience, and is reputed—and worthily so—one of the most careful enlightened trainers of either old or young horses; Thapsin, and many others having been successfully campaigned by him for several seasons. Owing to Thapsin's break up at the Bay District last fall, from which place he has never been fit to be removed, Mr. Smith has not yet a horse fit to start in the 2:20 class but it is dollars to cents that he has one or two in his string when the bell rings that will bear watching, and the public will be pleased to hear it, for they always have a saver on Wilbur's entry because, as a well known bettor and owner said "*we know him and consequently can rely on him.* '*Multum in parvo*' it expressed everything, implicit belief in his ability and also in his integrity, and don't you forget it; it is not misplaced.

Messrs. Clay & Woodford, of the Runnymede Stud Farm, Ky., will breed ten high class thoroughbred mares to Col. R. G. Stoner's noted trotting stallion Mambrino Russell. The event is an important one in the trotting horse world, and will be watched with great interest by all horse breeders.

W. M. Murry's three-year-old Kiro is moving in grand style now, and should be a good colt by the time racing starts. He worked a mile on the extreme outside of the Sacramento track in better than two minutes, which is about equivalent to 1:49, a little fast for this time of year.

B. C. Holly writes me that Fusillade's Last foaled a racy looking chestnut colt by Sid, while Irish Lass (with a mile record of 1:44½) foaled a brown colt by Woodnut 2:16½. The latter is called Marcus Daly, and the former Fusilier.

George Walbaum the eastern bookmaker has evidently determined to have a select stable. Already he has purchased Badge, Blue Rock, Sorrento, Kenwood, Folsom, Bradford, Mayor Nolan, and about a dozen others. Bergen is his jockey for this season.

Steps have been taken to form a driving club in St. Paul. There are to be 100 charter members, most of whom now belong to the Minnesota Club. The new organization, which will be modelled after the Washington Park Club, proposes to hang up $20,000 for a Fourth of July trotting meeting.

R. A. Swigert proposes to take his yearling colt by Glenelg, out of Lady Wayward, and called Carlsbad, to Europe this Fall or next Spring and try to capture fame and fortune in English races with him. He considers him the best thoroughbred yearling he ever saw, and expects him to be a "world beater," in every way equal to Donovan.

The employes of the Dwyer Brothers' racing stable, who make up what is called the Red and Blue Social Club held their annual ball at the Town Hall in Gravesend last week. Hardy Campbell, the trainer of the Dwyers second division is the president of the club and Jockey Neumeyer is its Financial Secretary.

A deed from the Maryland Jockey club to Oden Bowie, Robert C. Hall and John S. Gittings, conveying all of its property to them was recorded in the Clerk's office of the Superior Court at Baltimore, Md., Jan. 28. The property will be sold and the proceeds divided among the members.

The old trotting track at Saugus, Mass., known as Franklin Park was sold on Jan. 29 to Edward Heffernan, of Lynn, Mass., for the small sum of $17,650. The track is a full mile in circumference, and is one of the fastest in New England. It was built in 1855 and has been the scene of some important match trots.

The following three highlybred trotters have recently died in Montana: St. Val b c 2 by Electioneer, dam by Geo. Wilkes Marcus Daly paid $5000 for him as a weanling; Maximus b c 2 by Maxim, dam by Smuggler, being a full brother to Lady Maxim, 4, 2:26; he was owned by Huntley & Clark, as was also b f Montana Maid 2 by Maxim, dam by Mambrino Patchen.

W. B. Carr, in conjunction with several other well known local land owners, purpose building a race track at Bakersfield. The land is already selected and is beautifully located about a mile from town. Their motto is *nulli secundus* and they will act up to it in furnishing and adorning their track with fine shade trees and ornate grand stands.

It has been a doubtful point whether the New Jersey Jockey Club would have a stake race at its spring meeting to begin April 15th. Although no programme has yet been formulated, stakes for two year olds and older horses will be prepared, and Secretary McIntyre will announce them about March 1st, the stakes to close probably about April 1st.

Horsemen are devoting a good deal of time to the worship of Terpsichore just now. The Dwyer Brothers' employees had their annual ball last week at Gravesend, and later in the week the United Trainers and Jockeys' Association, of which James McLaughlin, the famous jockey, is President, danced at Tammany Hall. On the evening of March 7th the Clifton Club of horsemen, known as the C. W. Primrose Association, will dance at Washington Hall in Paterson.

Mr. W. R. Allen, proprietor of the Southern Hotel in St. Louis, and the great Allen Stock Farm, Pittsfield, Mass., writes: "I would have preferred and would have so ordered if I could that my name did not appear in connection with the monument to Green Mountain Maid. It was Mr. Backman's idea, and to him belongs all the honor that may be in it. I hope he understands the matter. Friendly feeling for him induced me to do it and not any desire to secure notoriety for myself."

A sad case of the downfall of a thoroughbred evinced at the last English Derby, when a cabman was summoned for driving a horse to this event which was in a totally unfit state for work, the poor animal being so weak he could hardly crawl. In the evidence it came to light that he had run in the Derby of 1874 under the name of The Hopeful Dutchman. True, he was last, but this does not lighten the sadness of the story.

If Spokane's leg does not give way this season, it is thought that he will add to his record made as a three year old in the Kentucky Derby and the Latonia and Clark stakes. A great feature about this horse is his even temper, and to this may be added his intelligence and obedience. Spokane does not get nervous if several false starts are made, but takes things as coolly and unconcerned as though he were not in a race.

Messrs. Huntley & Clark, Riverside Farm, Toston, Montana, recently lost the bay colt Maximus (full brother to Lady Maxim 2.26), foaled 1888, by Maxim, dam Lady Graves, (dam of Lady Maxim 2:26, Hailstorm 2:31, and Vera 2:34) by Smuggler 2:15¼, also the bay filly Montana Maid, foaled 1888, by Maxim (sire of Ida D. 2:27 and Lady Maxim 2:26, dam Mary Patchen, her dam Susie (dam of Lemonade 2:27) by Melbourne Jr. out of Kate (dam of Talavera 2:30) by Alhoit.

Agent Brodhead, of Woodburn Farm, has reached the conclusion that thoroughbred blood does more than sustain the trotting action: it also intensifies it, and is really to some extent also a trotting cross. "Our consideration of this fact," observes the Sportsman, "has led us to believe the point well taken for it is a matter of fact that the thoroughbred knows only two ways of going, he trots or runs, and does not required to be converted to either."

It is reported that Wm. Rockefeller has decided to sell his entire stud and plough up his track, one of the best half mile speeding places in New England. Independence (2.21½), by Gen Knox, and Wild Rake (three year old record 2:22¾), are at the head of Mr. Rockefeller's stud. The broodmares include Kate Sprague (2:18), Cleora (2:18¾), Urvanna Belle (2:20¼), Calamus (2:24½), Enchantress (2:26½), and others.

While the trotting and light harness entries do not abate in the Kidd Edmonson & Morse sale, the draft horse entries are still booming. Many large importers of Clydesdale, Shire, Percheron and French Coach Horses have already made liberal consignments, with many more to hear from. Parties having any class of draft horses to dispose of should embrace this opportunity and make their entries, while on the other hand any one requiring draft horses should be present and purchase.

The breaking up of the Rosemeade stud brings under the hammer in New York next month one of the best lot of horses, from a breeders' standpoint, that was ever sold in one sale. The Rosemeade mares are by Guy Wilkes, Kentucky Prince, Alcyone, Sweepstakes, Director, Electioneer, Nutwood, Arthurton, The Moor, etc., and many of them are in foal to Stamboul, 2:12½, and Alcazar, 2:20½. The latter himself will be sold, and also a full brother to the noted Mascot, the youngest foal of Minnehaha.

The money record made by the Dwyers since they left their butcher's stand in Washington Market to go on the turf, says a correspondent in the Richmond Times, is curious. Inside of fourteen years their best horses have won them in stakes $960,593. There is no account of bets in this amount. Hanover alone won $121,102: Miss Woodford $118 365; Geo. Kinney $64,660; Hindoo $62,075; Kingston $57,335; Inspector B. $56,837; Luke Blackburn $47,475; Tremont $40 450; Longstreet $38,390; Sir Dixon $37,740; Kingfish $36,6-0; Dew Drop $28,170; Bella B. $27,785; Bessie June $27,705.

It is said that while these stupendous efforts are being made to accomplish record breaking speed results with the light harness horse, an equally lucrative branch of horse breeding is being neglected—that of fine coach and carriage horses. Where there are thousands of men glad to pay for a trotter just for fun on the road, there are tens of thousands who want style instead of speed. One of the first things a traveller notices in England is the grand equipages that can be seen in and about London. Speed is not the aim there: style, action, quality and durability are what is sought and what they will have at any cost.

People, and even racegoers, seem not to notice the difference between December 31st and January 1st. For at least two months before the 1st of January fully 50 per cent. of the races contested over the winter tracks in the East were won by two year olds. Since the youngsters have become three year olds, however, they have changed form to such an extent that but few of them can win even place money. With an advantage of twenty-three pounds in weight, to which they were not entitled, it was not surprising that they showed such wonderful winning form; but where is their great form now when carrying their proper weight?

The stallion Mambrino Startle, full brother to Majolica, 2:15, and who has already sired several 2:30 trotters, is being jogged on the road by his owner, Mr. David Bonner of New York City. He is equally clever in single harness or to the pole, and will be trained next spring for the purpose of giving him a record better than 2:30, after which he will again enter the stud. His brother Majolica is to be sold at auction in New York before long. It is a good many years since he made his record of 2:15, and now one of his legs is in such a condition that he can never be trained again.

The thoroughbred stallions now doing service at the principal breeding establishments in Kentucky are nearly all getting well along in years. Pat Malloy is 25 years old, Glenelg 24, Longfellow and Kingfisher 23 each, Glen Athol and Harry O'Fallon 21 each, The Ill-Used, Springbok and Fellowcraft 20 each, King Alfonso, Woodland and Lelaps 18 each, Bullion 17, Lisbon, Outcast and Moccasin 16 each, Blue Eyes and Himyar 15 each, Falsetto, Jils Johnson, Strathmore, Spendthrift and Volturno 14 each, Elias Lawrence and Duke of Montrose 13 each, Hindoo 12, Powhattan, Onondaga and Macduff 11 each, and George Kinney, Leonatus and St. Blaise 10 each.

Henry Brown, one of the most widely known colored trainers of the race-horses in America, died on the 31st of Jan., after a short illness. He was for years the late James A. Grinstead's trainer, and with that gentleman handled many noted horses, among them being such famous performers as Lilatunah, Bradamante, (dam of The Bard), Pinafore, Jack Haverly, Mistake and many others well known on the turf. Of late years he has been training a public stable and in this line he was most distinguished for the campaign he made in 1888 was that good horse Autocrat In his early days he was a jockey of by no means small distinction. He was about 70 years old.

The leading editorial in the Montreal, P. Q., Sporting Life, of Jan. 27, is as follows: "With this present number the issue of the Sporting Life under the present management comes to a close. Negotiations are now pending for its sale, and we trust will be concluded in time to permit of its continuing to come out without a break. We once more desire to thank our readers for their kindness and courtesy to us all round, although more than two thirds of their subscriptions never reached our hands, having been embezzled by our absconding collector, W. A. *Daniels*. We may say that we would not extradite this miserable swindler if we could. All the horse editor yearns for is a quiet and uninterrupted quarter of an hour with him. At the close of that period he states he would offer a prize of $10 to any one who could identify him".

A carload of horses arrived from Hartford, Conn., last week, in charge of "Father Bill" Daly, had as passengers the Dwyer Brothers' well known racers Hanover, Sir Dixon and Bessie June. They were all in prime condition, having recovered from the effects of the blisters applied to their legs by Mr. Daly personally, to whom the Dwyers intrusted the delicate work. Mr. McCabe will at once take them in hand and get them in condition for the early spring races. Inspector B., Long Island and Congress will remain on the Hartford farm until about the 1st of April. Mr. Daly expects his horses The Bourbon and Urbana to arrive in New York from Hartford to-day. Father Bill thinks he has a couple of good two-year-olds in Best Boy, by Ten Broeck—Highflyer, and Lizzie, a filly, by St. Blaise—Feu Follet. The latter ran a quarter with Wynne, weighing 142 pounds, in the saddle, in 0:24½. Best Boy is said to have beaten Glory a head in a three-eighths of a mile trial at Hartford in 0:35½.

I see no reason why a thoroughbred should not be as level headed as a cold blooded fellow. They are apt to have more courage, endurance and spirit, but if properly handled will act just as well as their half or quarter bred compeers. I had in 1854 a bay gelding, says C. W. Kennedy of Montgomery, Ala., by imp. Riddlesworth, out of imp. Allegrante, bred by Mr. Clay, who could trot in three minutes only, but he could go all day. He was kind and level headed as any horse I ever broke to harness, but I did not undertake, as a great many drivers do, to make him do just as I wished. No; I listened to him when he spoke (by his actions) as any sensible trained horse should do. The man who will not notice what his horses say to him should never undertake to train either a runner or trotter. When I visit a stable and see a horse fighting the curry-comb I make up my mind at once that the manager is not the man for his place.

There are fourteen daughters of Lexington among the 83 broodmares now in the celebrated Woodburn stud. The oldest of these mares is in her 26th year, and the youngest 18 years old. The following is a list of these highly prized matrons: Bonita (dam of Apothecary and Bannach Lath), Cracitix (dam of Fair Play, Blanche J., Quito, St. Albans and St. Augustine), Geneva (dam of Silvio, Greystone and Blue Stone, Hester (dam of Springbok, Aspinwall and Panama), India (dam of Cathcart, Calcutta and Gallifet), Jamaica (dam of Foxhall), Lilly Duke (dam of Water Lilly, Lizzie Dwyer and Rose), Marguerite (dam of Katie Creel, Macola and Lizzie E.), Miranda (dam of Little Minnie, Carey and Miracle), Mollie Wood (dam of Sagamore, Golden Gate, Woodlark and Falcon), Queen Victoria (dam of Albert, Queen's Own, Infanta and Jennie T.), Quickstep (dam of Cromwell and False Step), Verites (dam of Lady Prewitt and Vera), and Zephyr (dam of Edwin Adams, Westwind, Falsehood and Cyclone). Of the other mares at Woodburn fifteen are granddaughters of Lexington and eighteen are his great-granddaughters.

Jimmy McLaughlin has acknowledged that he was a failure as a starter, says the St. Louis Republic. It seems to be very difficult to find a man who can throw the flag or tap the drum wisely and well. Men of worth who are above suspicion, and likewise possessed of vast turf experience, have gone to the post and made signal failures. Col. Bob Simmons, now the presiding officer at New Orleans, threw up the position in disgust. Col. Clark, president of the Louisville Jockey Club, has made several ineffectual trials. Capt. W. E. Conner probably did better than most men who have essayed the task of controlling jockeys at the post and getting the steeds away in good shape, but he pronounced himself a rank failure. Jacob Pincus never could start horses, and made but very few trials. Mr. Ferguson, of Lexington, did fair work here and in other Western cities, but was berated soundly at Jerome Park. Mr. Caldwell frequently comes in for an indignant outburst from the press and public, while Mr Sheridan frequently makes some wretched starts. Mr. Caldwell has probably stood the test better than any other man who has ever filled the unpleasant position of starter. It is stated that, though he is far from perfect and does not seem to have so much hold on the jockeys as he should, he is the only man available for the Eastern tracks. Perhaps Mr. Sheridan comes next, but he is a bad second, and it is fair to presume that Mr. Ferguson, in spite of his dismal failure at Jerome last year, is third.

Since the weights for the Suburban and Brooklyn handicaps came out the World has interviewed many well known racing men. Among those who expressed their views are,—

Starter Caldwell—Raceland should win either the Brooklyn Handicap or Suburban He could have won the latter event last year even with 128 pounds up.

Polo Jim—Raceland has a chance for the Brooklyn Handicap, but my choice for the Suburban is Retrieve or Firenzi.

Jim McGowan—I like Badge for the Brooklyn Handicap, though he is not over fond of going a mile and a quarter.

Billy Lakeland—Raceland will beat any horse in the Brooklyn Handicap, and if he stays my money will go on him.

Trainer James McCormick—Lakeland's horse Exile will win the Brooklyn Handicap and Senorita the Suburban.

James Daly—I like Proctor Knott for the Suburban, and when the Winter books open I am going to play him.

Jockey Taylor—Hanover for the Brooklyn, if he stands training, and Proctor Knott for the Suburban.

Trainer *Dumas*—If Fresno gets his two year old form back the one that beats him for the Suburban will know it has been in a race.

C. Satler—Major *Domo* will take some beating for the Brooklyn Handicap

Major Wheeler—It is too difficult this year for me to select a choice.

Sixty six entries were made for the City of Suburban in England, which is just half a dozen ahead of last year, when Goldseeker scored a runaway victory and gave the ring such a turn up. The horse has not been entered upon the present occasion, but such smart animals as Amphion, Veracity, Danbydale Philomel, Laureate, Friday, Quartus and Shall We Remember are a host in themselves. The Duke of Beaufort, Mr Henry Milner and Mr. Abington are each responsible for four entries, while Prince Soltykoff has entered a trio. Harry Hall has nominated Friday and Quartus, so that it would seem as though one or other of these horses is expected to do something this year. Friday, it may be mentioned, has not been seen in public since he broke down after running in the Lincolnshire Handicap of 1888. The weights may be expected on the 30th inst.

Never since the Lincolnshire Handicap was brought up to its present value, sixteen years ago, has it closed with such a small entry as on the present occasion. The subscribers number only 48, or 16 less than last year and in 1888, but class is well represented. The hero of last March, Wise Man, appears in the entry again, as does The Baron, who was third to him, but Acme, who separated the pair, was expatriated to Buenos Ayres, where he recently had to be destroyed, having broken his leg. Veracity, who was successful two years ago, although still in training, has not again been entered, but Weever's Stable is represented by Danbydale, who has so far been a disappointment. Sheen, Laureate, Mortaigue, Claribelle, The Rejected, Ormuz, Evergreen, The Turcophone, Juggler, Pioneer, Aperse, Theophilus, Nunthorpe, L'Abbesse de Jouarre, Star, and Whitelegs, are all well known performers and of the veterans Tommy Tittlemouse and Greenwich are not strangers to the Lincoln course. Crowberry, who has not run for eighteen months, is entered, another that has been on the shelf for a long time is Friday, whose last appearance in public was for the Lincolnshire Handicap, won by Veracity. Mr. Hall has also nominated Quartus, and the Spigot Lodge Stable is further represented by Dauntless. The latter is one of the five three-year-olds engaged, and the others are not of high class. Still, taken on the whole, the entry is a good one so far as quality is concerned, and if the field is not so large as usual, the race ought to prove as interesting as ever.

ROD.

Board of Fish Commissioners.

The February meeting, held on February 4th, at 220 Sutter street, Room 13, was one of the liveliest yet held by the Board; Hon. Joseph Routier and J. Downey Harvey present. After approval of the minutes, the monthly report of Chief of Patrol F. P. Callundan was then read, as follows:

THE HONORABLE THE BOARD OF FISH COMMISSIONERS—GENTLEMEN:—The adversities which hampered the work of your deputies during the month of December, as detailed in the last monthly report from the Chief of Patrol, were more numerous, if possible, during the month last passed. In every portion of the State extreme high water has prevented illegal salmon fishing, and has made the pursuit of small fish hardly worth the while, even of Chinese. Such general rules as have been laid down by the Board have been observed, particularly with reference to regular inspections of the various warehouses which handle deer skins, and the docks where such skins are received.

It is gratifying to be able to repeat the statement made in the December report, namely, that not one doe or fawn skin has been delivered at San Francisco during the month. It is not believed that the killing of does and fawns has been entirely stopped, but the market for the skins has been destroyed through the efforts of your Honorable Board, and if rigid watching of the tanneries and other avenues of entrance is maintained, there seems reason to believe that within a very few months there will be no reason for the slaughtering of does except the brutality of a few men who chance to live in sections where deer are plenty, and such men can readily be detected and punished.

Complaint has come during the month that certain persons claiming to be deputies of the Board have used their commissions as a shield to protect them in fishing the minor streams adjacent to San Francisco for salmon trout. It has not been within my power to investigate fully the charges made, but in a general way it is recommended that any one detected in stream fishing for "trout, salmon trout or any variety of trout," be at once placed under arrest, and if the offending person holds a commission as deputy from your Honorable Board, that such commission be recalled. The moral effects resulting from violations of what this Commission believes to be the law, by its deputies, is most disastrous both to the public standing of the Board and to successful work by such of your deputies as are guided by your wishes.

If your Honorable Board desires names and data, they can be furnished. Another complaint has reached the Chief of Patrol to the effect that Mr. La Motte of Glen Ellen, to whom this Board granted permission to take fish from Sonoma River for breeding purposes, has completely obstructed that river by a system of set nets, preventing the passage of fish either up or down the river, and practically insuring the taking of every fish of breeding size which may attempt either to go up or down.

The precise scope of the permission given Mr. La Motte I do not know, and the complaint is stated as received, with the remark that Mr. La Motte is one of the oldest and most noted fish breeders in the country, and presumably a man who would not commit any breach of the law or overstep the bounds of propriety.

At the last meeting of the Board a rule was made requiring each deputy to file a monthly report with the Chief of Patrol. I am not advised whether notice of the rule has been sent to the deputies, but not one such report has been received.

It is believed that such monthly reports will be most useful, both in enabling the Board to present to the public from time to time some statement of the work done and also in accumulating matter to be embodied in the biennial report of the Commission to His Excellency the Governor.

On January 31, before Hon. Hale Rix, in this city, the case of Antoine, a fish dealer, for having the young of fish in his possession, came up for trial, a jury being demanded. After ten minutes' deliberation the jury brought in a verdict of guilty, and the judge imposed a fine of one hundred dollars. The case is now on appeal to the Superior Court.

January 6th was spent in visiting the various transportation companies. In every place mention of the purpose of the visit secured the utmost freedom to inspect all hides on hand, and also elicited the highest commendations of the Board of Fish Commissioners and its policy.

January 9th was spent in the Police Court before Judge Rix, a Chinese being on trial for having the young of fish in possession. The man was fined and paid fifty dollars.

On the 13th, 14th and 15th, in response to urgent demands, I visited Cazadero, at the head of Austin Creek to break up a salmon fishery in which the seines extended from bank to bank. The fishery and apparatus were found, but the high water prevented use of the seines and no arrest could be made. The place is being watched, however, and a conviction is anticipated.

On January 24th, in the Police Court of this city, Judge Rix fined four Chinese fifty dollars each for violations of the fish law, and they paid their fines.

The conviction on December 24th of three Chinese before Judge Rix, was mentioned in my last report. The men were fined seventy-five dollars each or as many days in jail. After serving twenty-five days they paid fifty dollars each into the City and County Treasury.

Deputy Thomas Tunstead is especially mentioned for faithfulness in the discharge of his duties.

With settled weather, your deputies expect to resume hostilities, and hope to present a more satisfactory resume of work done, at the next meeting of your Honorable Board

Respectfully submitted, F. P. CALLUNDAN,
SAN FRANCISCO, Feb. 4, 1890. Chief of Patrol.

The complaints mentioned in the report were taken up one by one and disposed of. Two deputies, Messrs. C. H. Ohm and C. F. Precht, accused of catching trout in Sonoma River during the close season, were examined, and upon admitting that they had killed fish in that river recently, their commissions as deputies were withdrawn. A general discussion of the fish which run up coast streams to spawn was then entered upon. Messrs. Obm and Precht insisted that the fish were true salmon. The Commissioners and Messrs. Woodbury and Lamotte, two experts, coincided in believing the fish were salmon trout.

Being invited to address the Board upon the matter, Mr. Ramon E. Wilson, attorney for the Board, laid it down as sound doctrine that whether the fish which inhabit the coast streams are trout, salmon trout or salmon, they were the fish held in mind by the Legislature when it prohibited catching them, and the law was undoubtedly capable of enforcement. Mr. Wilson considered it advisable to arrest and prosecute actively all who were found fishing in the small streams for trout.

In answer to a complaint that Mr. Lamotte at Glen Ellen had entirely obstructed Sonoma River with fish traps, that gentleman replied that, acting under permission of the Board at certain hours of the day, he did obstruct the river, as was necessary to secure spawning fish, but the traps were lifted out for many hours each day so that fish might ascend the river.

Mr. Walter E. Bryant of the Academy of Science, was present to advise as to proper game birds to be imported. He thought Bob Whites and wild turkeys best.

Mr. C E. Stout of Arkansas, from whom Bob Whites had been ordered, was unable to meet the order, and the Board decided to address C. C. Reynolds at Converse Station, Texas, in that behalf. The Board then adjourned, to meet on the first Tuesday of March.

Mr. Totty's Day Fishing.

FOR THE BREEDER AND SPORTSMAN BY MISS KELLY.

Con knew when Mr. Totty intended to spend a day at the lake as well as a Llewellin setter ever can know anything, and the way he jumped and coaxed and cavorted about, asking to go was a sight to see.

Mr. Totty always set his starting time very early. "Call me at four o'clock in the morning" he would say, though he knew very well no one would be stirring at that hour, and he himself had no compunctions about dozing Holy Time away—'twas Sabbath time he chose for his sport, of a necessity, though, be it said to his credit, for the rest of the week, thus unholily begun, he devoted to bringing forth bread by the sweat of his brow.

Mrs. Totty never arose before her usual time, and generally had the satisfaction of seeing her lord well provisioned, as far, at least, as breakfast could go before he set forth for the day's victories.

I tell you frankly that Mrs. Totty had an objection to putting up lunches. She held that all members of all families should be present at all meals or go without. Besides, when Mr. Totty was absent from Sunday dinner it necessitated, in her mind, the saving of the leg of mutton, the regular bill of fare for this day, till Monday.

So, as you may imagine, the Totty family, there being but Mrs. Totty and a young Totty, looked with much disfavor upon these excursions.

Con being the only supporter, it sometimes took considerable courage for Mr. Totty, brave man as he was, to announce his intention of being called at four o'clock, but after he was once up and his preparations made none were braver than he. He could swear about his rubber boots not being in their proper place—(as he was not what you might call a particularly orderly man, *proper place* with him meant any place where he could readily lay his hand upon them)—he could heap abuses upon the little pail of bread and butter, flanked by a boiled egg and a dry doughnut which Mrs. Totty had hastily gathered from odds and ends in the pantry. He could kick Con out from under the little brown nag's feet with savage grace, and then tell him he could go along, poor fellow, as a salve for his wounds.

And may be you think Con did not understand these things. If you could have seen him lift up a paw scarcely grazed by the kick, and go around on three legs, howling woefully and looking the very picture of suffering doghood, and if you could have seen him recover at the magic words about going and jump all over and under the little brown horse, and then race from the barn to the house and back again just to show how very well and strong the injured leg had become, if you could have seen him cut around for a few minutes you would have concluded that Con had his tricks as well as most of us.

All this time, Mr. Totty has been busy getting his boat, The Belva Lockwood, rolled up on the frame of the buck board, where he secures it with ropes and straps And when he gets the small horse hitched to this remarkable combination and gets in himself, he is a picture worth seeing.

He sits well toward the middle of the boat, and must lean forward and crane his neck a great deal to see if all is well with the little animal, who guided by the reins coming up over the bright red prow of the boat, goes much as she pleases, But she goes. There seems to be an understanding between Mr. Totty and herself that she is to go when he holds the reins.

Mrs. Totty says she would drive out oftener if that little beast did not go so much like a soap-peddler's cart, and, indeed, at these outings the little nag squares up accounts, as it were, by indulging in a lame sort of walk, which often merges into a stop, and she kicks up in such stiff-legged resentment to the whip, that Mrs. Totty is really afraid to use it.

Con has taken his stand under the vehicle, where he trots along in a most contented fashion, feeling himself the king pin of the concern, of course.

Mr. Totty's hat, a big panama, is tipped far back upon his head so that there is a well-defined semi-circle of brim across his broad shoulders.

The fish poles and the oars nodding out of the stern of the boat keep up a merry chatter of the sports they have had before, and Mr. Totty, when he is well upon the road, the sunshine warming him through and through, the birds and bushes seeming to say to him in unscriptural verse how good it is for man to be alone, forgets the turbulent sentiments about being "treated like a d——d Chinaman" which had been rankling in his bosom.

Just as he had been about to start, there had been a little domestic scene, from which, as the novelists say, we will not lift the curtain, further than to say that the new flies had been mislaid by Mrs. Totty, so Mr. Totty said, and that she refused to become excited and hunt for them.

They were found all safe in the pocket of his hunting jacket, where he, himself, had put them, and you would think peace might have settled upon the scene, and so I suppose it would, had not a rent in this same jacket been found to gape, though Mr. Totty had asked his wife to mend it a week ago. Then he remembered that a button was off his shirt, too, and he expressed himself in his favorite phrase which was his sole remnant of Anti-Chinese League fervor.

An hour's soothing ride brought him to a desolate sheet of water, plumped down in the midst of desolation.

Mr. Totty drives through the tules down to the water's edge, the little nag backs the backboard into the lake, the boat is rolled off, the stead is loosed, picketed and fed, Con is coerced into playing guard, and Mr Totty, taking the oars is already in the midst of pure enjoyment, for the black bass are plentiful, though shy, and the catfish may some days be snared with a piece of red flannel and other days a catfish can not be caught with the fat of the land.

Besides the flies, Mr. Totty has on hand a can of angle worms, a bottle of grasshoppers and a can of shrimps. He is proud of catching fish when others fail and as soon as those other fishers are far enough away (Mr. Totty is not the only sinner from Bun City) he will try a shrimp and see how that will go. Go? They go like a charm and for half an hour Mr. Totty pulls in bass almost as fast as he can bait his hook.

What has he for bait? Oh, a few worms and hoppers. Its just skill that's all, and Mr. Totty very deceitfully changes his bait with his back to the enemy.

Now a lull. He gets a catfish now and then but fishing from a boat becomes slow.

He pulls in to shore and would eat his lunch with the unsuccessful spread out on the sand but that he remembered the meager lunch he has, (every man has a pride in his wife's cookery) and he strolls off to a little cove, puts on his rubber boots, wades out and begins the attack afresh, taking a mouthful of lunch occasionally from his pocket.

Mr. Totty often says his rubber boots would be three inches too short if they came up to his neck, and true it is he always comes home more or less wet from these trips, and is constantly taking port wine and horse radish for sciatica.

Something must be the matter with the fishing. They have ceased to bite. All the hot afternoon with the sun beating fiercely down upon him he keeps telling himself that they will bite again after the sun down—they always do. Then they might take a notion to bite just before dark. Some of the largest fish he ever caught in his life he got just before starting for home.

He knows very well that Mrs. Totty will sit up till he comes home, keeping his supper hot for him and that she will not forget to tell him of her sacrifice, but he seems in no haste. He finally counts out fifty-four shining bass and stows them carefully in a sack, then seventeen catfish, four of which are large, ugly looking monsters, are placed in another sack

Con, who feels the sharpness of an empty stomach, seems more delighted now than earlier in the day at the prospect of going. Besides, he is always a coach passenger on return trips.

Soon the little party is well under way, vague remembrance of oats in the manger lending speed to the little horse's heels, and Mr. Totty's tuneful whistle making music fitting for the trot.

What is this? As I live Mr. Totty drawing up in front of a saloon and taking out the bag containing the bass, when he is not four blocks from his own house. He may be going to guard against sciatica, but why take in the fish?

There he is amid a crowd of admirers displaying the beauties. Vanity and love of being thought a good fellow, how many have ye ruined!

Mr. Totty you make me weep. I would I had not chosen you for my hero, for with the story tellers power over time and place, I can see Mrs. Totty the next day, seated upon the wood-house steps driving nails into the flat heads of wriggling catfish, giving one turn with Mr. Totty's pocket knife (sharpened up to a proper edge on the stove pipe) around their necks, and then peeling the skins with both hands. One more slit with the knife and a writhing catfish is plumped into a pan of salted water.

Mrs. Totty often says these "pesky" things jump out of the frying pan, even after soaking all night, and she doesn't see why people can't catch something worth catching. It's precious seldom he brings home a bass. She wouldn't call herself a fisher, and spend days and nights at the lake if she had to come home with a few catfish, so small one could scarcely take hold of them to clean them. Besides, she would never clean another catfish, so there!

Mr. Totty with Monday meekness wanted to know why she didn't use the big fellows and leave the little ones in the tub to grow.

And hadn't she taken them all, big and little to make a mess? But he had brought seventeen catfish and—that is, he counted them himself and he guessed he could count, if his wife did know so much.

To have his fishing ability aspersed sat ill upon Mr. Totty's proud achievement and guilty conscience, but he experienced nothing, and went to the tub to see if he could solve the mystery.

That there was another fisher with great skill in the family did not occur to him until he heard the young Totty relate how she had watched Puss that morning sitting near the tub, licking her paws and seeming most unwilling to put them into the water until a big fish appeared at the surface, when quick as a flash he was speared in the back by the claws of Puss, and landed on the grass to struggle there till the black paws were well polished again, and then began the task of biting off her head without being stung by his wicked spines. Puss was far too careful a little mother to provide her kittens with food that had pins in it.

Puss has patience, too, another proof that she stands side by side with Mr. Totty as a fisher, for in the loft of the barn were found the mutilated bodies of nine large catfish.

Mr. Totty vows that if she ever fishes the cream of his fishing again he will hang her higher than Haman, kits and all.

The Sutter City Enterprise says: During the last high water fish were found in Willow Creek, which comes down through the Pass of Buttes. This is something never before known by the oldest settlers hereabouts.

A more open, keen and attractive face than that of Captain Thomas H. Chubb, as shown in his fishing tackle advertisement in another column one would need go far to seek. All the honesty in the face is backed up by the excellence of the rods and tackle sent out by the Captain. Send to him for his '90 catalogue, which contains articles by our peerless Petronella, Dr. Henshall, Rev. W. H. H. Murray, Geo. P. Goff and other classic writers.

The Salinas Democrat is authority for the statement that during a recent storm a shower of fish fell near Blanco, Monterey County. The fact of fish falling from the cloud is not an unheard of occurrence, but fish such as fell at Blanco were never heard of before. They were of a bright silvery color about two inches in length, and instead of fins they had sharp spines about one-fourth of an inch long where the pectoral and dorsal fins should be. Mr. W. H. Crowe of Blanco, has preserved a couple of them as specimens of great curiousity, as they are unlike any fish he has ever seen or heard of.

THE GUN.

Still Hunting vs. Hounding Deer.

EDITOR BREEDER AND SPORTSMAN:—Still hunting vs. Hounding has been a much mooted question among sportsmen of late, both methods of securing the wily deer having plenty of advocates, the supporters on both sides denouncing their opponent's tactics as unsportsmanlike. They may both be right or both wrong under different circumstances, conditions and surroundings.

The Virginia deer should be found and killed in most instances by the still hunter in comparatively open timber.

The black tail deer of our northwest country is a bird of another feather, possessing wonderful intelligence, of an extremely shy and timid disposition, frequently hunted by the cougar, lynx and wild cat. In our heavily timbered country he is never seen unless on rare occasions. Having an extraordinarily keen ear and eye, he knows well how to keep out of sight in his almost impassable forest home. Tracks may be seen by the dozen, but seeing tracks does not mean by any means seeing the maker of them. Very few black tail are killed in this country, and most of them are killed with dogs, although our forests contain vast herds of them.

I met an old hunter on a ferry boat on the Nuoksack River lately. He had come to our State from the East, where he had hunted for the market since his boyhood, coming here on the same errand. He was through with our State, he said, having spent four months constantly in the mountains. He had killed in that time only one deer, the only one he had seen in that time. He had seen a few bears and plenty of cougars, but he wasn't out for them. The meat was what he was after. He didn't believe there were any deer in the mountains, or he'd have seen them, as he had hunted early and late, and could always find and kill deer in any locality where he had been heretofore East of the Missouri. He was tired of it, and was returning home disgusted.

I smiled a smile quietly up my sleeve, always feeling glad to lose a neighbor who killed game for a living. I could have to him a tale unfolded, but "ignorance being bliss 'tis surely great folly to be wise." 'Tis an old saw, truly, but contains a wonderful amount of truth in it. So he went his way and I mine, never to see each other again.

I was reading an account of some of the early day hunts the other day, when Ohio, Kentucky and many other now thickly settled States were in their infancy and considered to be then the "wild wooly West," and was much amused at the idea of the wonderful changes which have occurred.

The railways have wiped all such hunting grounds out of existence most completely. An account of a hunt in Kentucky, where a band of fifty deer are quietly feeding within a stone's throw of a pair of hunters and a dog, who refrained from shooting (the hunters did), as they had already seen and killed more deer than they could use. The usual method of hunting being to "jist knock eround and blaze away when one got near enough," a track being seen, it is followed a short way, and the deer found standing, feeding quietly or rubbing his horns against a tree. Such easy chances would never be offered by our deer, for even if overrun with deer who never saw a hunter nor heard the rifle crack, nor heard the ping of a bullet, they instinctively keep out of sight and possess the faculty of concealment and noiseless movements on all occasions in a wonderful degree.

Many descriptions of deer hunting in Eastern States where deer (one naturally would suppose) would be wilder from being hounded and hunted more, and far more wily, tell how the boys went out and jumped a deer out of a thicket and broke him down, or trailing one to thick timber, they ran into him as he stood watching and listening, or may be "jest ran acrost a ole buck as he stud rubbin his pair of six prong antlers against a limb." Perhaps a bunch of five or six are walked into like walking into a bunch of girls coming home from school, who, timid, shy, but coy, would like to run, but, inquisitive, stay.

Gentlemen, such things, though maybe possible with the Virginia, are impossible with the Columbia deer. You can't go out before breakfast and bring in a deer in time for the daylight meal, like you would go and fetch in a quail or prairie chicken, or go into the hen-house, catch and kill a chicken. Oh, no; if you do go out before breakfast, and won't return till you get your deer, perhaps you will sleep out in the woods on an empty stomach that night.

No wonder the market hunter, who was broken on Eastern deer, weakened at the prospects of a fat living on our Columbia's, and considered it a long time "'tween drinks" The latter animal is a great discourager for the market hunter. Now although still hunting results in very little killing, with a hound we can get a deer within an hour in any direction. I can put a hound into a dozen patches of heavy timber within a mile of my home, and get from one to eight deer from each place. Thank goodness! hounding is prohibited!

Our impenetrable forests and thick undergrowths, heavy and close brush and tangle, keep the hunter out of half of the territory in most of our forests. The deer can multiply and increase for countless ages if not hounded. The deerhound can enter anywhere and bring the game out where it can be slaughtered with comfort. The scared, affrighted animal running anywhere to get away from the dreaded bay of the dog, paying no heed to danger in front; all his senses excited to get as far as possible from the keen-nosed hound.

There is little danger of our deer being thinned out by still hunting, and if not driven out by hounds, or railways, or the encroachments of civilization among our mountain fastnesses, he will last long beyond the ages of our great grandchildren's children.

The cougar, wolf and lynx hunt them, and kill many of their number, but they do not compare with the numbers that would be killed by hounding, and in the majority of cases the cunning deer will outwit the feline or lupine marauder.

Still hunting is a pleasure to the lover of nature, a fascinating, healthy pastime. To out wit the cunning of the most timid game in existence, to match human reasoning and experience against his cunning, affords the sportsman great delight, but when it comes to a question of meat, why then we can't get along without canine assistance.

That hounding is far more destructive to the game, must be evident; that the same skill or experience is not required, must be acknowledged. Skill with the rifle is the main consideration, aside from the knowledge of proper stands and ability to keep quiet.

Great sport and comfort are to be derived from this style of hunting, also the certainty of getting a deer if a good shot and deer are in the neighborhood, makes the pleasure sweeter, less work and wear and tear are certainties. I will give a brief description of the two styles of getting the wily animal in our county.

Six or eight deer having been located over the line in British Columbia in the heavy timber near Boundary line lake, while still hunting we repaired there with three good deer-hounds who understood their business.

A is placed on a stand on a runway making towards Section One lake, B is placed on a deer trail near the head of Lake Leman, C is placed in an open place in the timber commanding a view of a run or stream which meandered through its bed in the valley, while D takes up his stand in a meadow near a burn along another lake.

The dogs are separated and put onto three different trails, hunting individually. A deer is soon started by one of the dogs, and is run into Boundary lake, crossing the open, flying wildly for the water, a long running shot is made by B, an excellent shot which wounds the deer, and a second shot breaks it down, the 50-calibre bullet killing it instantly.

Another deer is started and run into the burn and meadow near D, who also scores a kill after firing four shots from his Winchester repeater, a 45-60. A doe soon appears to D, as it, frightened and bewildered, emerges from the timber upon the burn, a long shot, but he succeeds in killing it.

The bay of the hounds is heard, one hound in particular, an old veteran, has a deep, rich, musical voice; he roars on in full sight of the quarry, which he drives out, and down the bed of the stream it is vainly looking for a hiding place in the latter, but nothing can escape the nose of the approaching hound, who trails on in full cry, putting the deer out of the shallow stream in full view of C, who is ready, but being an indifferent shot, he misses it as it dashes by and disappears in the brush.

The dogs start several more deer, but fail to drive them out. The hunters not being bloodthirsty, are satisfied with three deer, call the dogs in, and getting a horse from a rancher, pack their game home, two fine buck and one doe.

Four deer having been seen and shot at, several more started, all in the course of two hours, if a day had been devoted to the sport and three different localities worked, two or three times as many deer would have been killed by the four men.

Now the two best shots of that party put in an entire day still hunting where a larger band of deer were wont to roam, and not a deer was seen, although both are as good stalkers as there are in the country, and if deer can be got by still hunting, they can get them. Not only one day, but many days, and parts of days, have they returned home empty handed, having trailed many deer, but failed to get a sight of them.

I will relate a day, when a fine buck was killed, as being one of the best; other bucks and does they have brought in at different times from a still hunt, but the one mentioned will fairly describe any.

A fresh snow had fallen, covering the ground with a soft white mantle, rendering tracking easy and the footfall silent. Much cold and snow having occurred for the past two weeks, the lakes are all frozen over, and surrounded on all sides by deep snow, the deer, therefore, do not go near the lakes. The open places and burns being buried deep under snow, those places are avoided. Wind, snow and storm have put the deer down off the mountains into the green timber, where but little snow is on the ground, and fine shelter from wind and cold afforded. The deer will lie close and hide in the thick jungles and windfalls, penetrating where the hunter cannot.

Three fresh tracks are discovered upon penetrating the thick timber east of section 1 lake. The trail is taken up and followed some distance to the highland or upland. Here are fresh droppings and evidences of having fed in the vicinity. The snow is now tramped down all around. . A rabbit jumping in the brush brings our rifles to our faces, but the mistake discovered they are lowered. There is a cougar's track, a hunter ahead of us, it will make hunting still doubly difficult.

There is a lynx track. He also wants to get his share of the meat.

Under a low lying tree trunk goes the trail so low that we wonder the deer could pass under. We follow, but now the deer have separated; the big track goes to our left while the other two keep to the right. We follow the big fellow, but soon it is joined by the others.

The trail approaches nearly to the edge of the heavy timber, then circles around clean back within a few yards of where we first started to trail, but keeps more east. We keep along quiet as two Indians trailing a coon. Now the track enters the thick brush where we can't get in without making noise enough to scare all the deer out of the county.

As we imagine they are hiding there, we separate, one passing around the jungle (which appears to be some 200 yards through) to the west, while the other goes east agreeing to circle clean around if possible, and meet on the other side, to discover if the track comes out anywhere.

We soon meet again, having found no track out. Now it is settled to a certainty that the deer are hid in the midst of the close underbrush and jungle.

Whether they have discovered us or are hiding from four footed hunters we know not, but know they will not stir unless driven out.

We select a rather promising place for an entrance being more open than the rest of jungle, one goes in while the other passes around to where the deer entered, taking up his stand there as the most likely place for them to come out if they do so at all.

Each cautioning the other not to shoot unless the deer is plainly seen, as accidents frequently happen where two hunters are separated, one mistaking a movement or dark object for game, when possibly it may be the other creeping or crouching hunter.

Now entering a thick windfall or jungle of 200 yards in extent seems easy enough in print, but the reality is a stern hardship, a slow, laborious process, hard on the clothing and cuticle, and very trying to the patience.

It is needless to tire the reader with a description of the big trunks buried in snow to be climbed over, or the thick growth of vine maples covered with snow, a touch shaking the damp article all over one, filling coat, collar, boot-tops, sleeves, etc., the encounters with "devil's clubs, miserable weeds covered with sharp needle like spines which break off and stay in the flesh like the festive cactus. Thorns with sharp strong points which made things very warm for a silent man, and many other unpleasant obstacles, suffice it to say these things were overcome after about an hour's hard scrambling and the thickest of the jungle reached. Here or very close by should be the deer, but as nothing is to be seen for a foot on any side of us, we can't use our rifle any way, so we will just make a grand racket and a hideous pow wow and try and give our partner a shot, and will drop down in this soft bed of snow out of the way of any flying bullets, as he shoots like lightning, and the whole chamber can be emptied into a band of deer so quick that it will make ones head swim. If we can scare the deer enough some of them may rush out with a racket, or again they may not get out at all, or may go out as quietly as they came in, so quietly that not a sound will be heard. However, we jump upon a log so the noise will reach further, and seem louder, distending our broad bosom to the utmost, till the healthy full sized lungs are full of wind. We take a young tree in each hand, and roar at the top of our lungs, at the same time stamping like mad on the dead, hollow trunk with both feet, which we had previously cleaned of snow, snapping the two young trees violently together, we flatter ourselves we made a champion noise. A rush like that of a pheasant whirring is heard, as one deer which doubtless had been very close to us at the time of our outburst, makes direct for our Tillicum.

Down with a dull and sickening thud we drop into the "white, beautiful snow" which envelopes us in its cold and clammy embrace, compelling us to rear our head aloft to get our wind, which one sudden immerson had caused to forsake our former boasted powerful lungs.

Bang goes the rifle of our Tillicum, a 50-110 Winchester Express, which has a beautiful sonorous voice, which rings sharp and clear with a peculiar roar.

No more shots following, we know that only one deer has gone his way and that one lies dead before him, or more shots would have followed.

We pick ourselves up, shake the beautiful show off our person, pick a peck of stuff out of each boot leg, a same amount imperial measure out of our coat collar, our pockets are emptied one after the other, our hat picked up and scraped out with a young maple.

When we notice our Tillicum's merry voice telling us to come out and see the "boss buck," when we have got enough snow out of our ears to hear plainly and freed our mouth sufficiently to answer, our joy is exhibited by means of a yell, which threatens to dislocate our collar bone, or blow up another lung as we solemnly declared to the partner afterward that we had exploded one lung when yelling, to scare out the deer.

But privately we don't mind stating now our last joyful yell was not so much one of joy at the success of his shot as for the termination of our travel in the thick jungle and snow banks. We get out after repeating our experiments upon entering but somewhat easier and faster as all restraint is now removed and noise is no object.

Tillicum is seated upon a splendid big buck, his arms crossed upon his chest, his gun carelessly reclined against his shoulder, he indifferently looks around at everything but the buck. His pose and general bearing denoting an absolute carelessness, such fine bucks one would infer to be a regular thing to kill most any time, same as you would pick your teeth, a matter of extreme small moment.

But his grand attitude not striking us dumb or "speechless", we enjoy a hearty laugh over our tribulations in the wilderness, and fall to admiring and discussing the merits of our noble quarry.

The other two deer had acted differently from this one, and had as they usually do when alarmed, quietly got out without giving a months notice.

This one had as luck would have it rushed headlong out in Tillicums arms, where he almost had to jump aside to escape its rush.

His 50 caliber ball had pierced its brain square between the eyes, but about 1½ inches higher than the line of the eyes, the most fatal shot of all, and most satisfactory, instant and sudden death being always the result.

The head being well back at the time (as it rushed beneath the limbs) to prevent striking the branches overhead the ball broke up inside the skull, the brain being scattered completely, some pieces of bullet came out back of the ears, while others came out back of the neck. Truly, a terrible wound. This ended one of many similar still hunts.

Tillicum many times since has chaffed us in the presence of others about our style of driving out deer, and diving into snow banks.

But we always loftily reply in our superior way, "That we are the only truly original deer driver."

The above process of getting deer out of a jungle is not patented, and while I would not recommend it to others as being the most sportsmanlike, still they are at liberty to use it if they can find no other way. If they are satisfied I surely ought to be.

Still hunting, as seen from the above, has more hardships attached and a smaller percentum of chances than hounding, and in our country in particular, if hunted in no other way, deer will mostly live happily till they die at a good old age, surrounded by a large and interesting family. JAY SEE EN.

A New Oliver in the Field.

EDITOR BREEDER AND SPORTSMAN:—I suppose field trial week was a gala week for all lovers of setters and pointers. It was a hard blow to me in not being able to attend, family sickness preventing. I eagerly await the reports of the trials, and I do hope the best dog won and that you all had a very pleasant week. I saw a letter written by you last week to Mr. Will Howard, now a resident of San Diego, formerly from the Western States. I formed the acquaintance of Mr. Howard since my return here, and I find him to be a sportsman of the first water, a jolly good fellow and one of the best posted men on the Llewellin setters I have had the pleasure to meet, and another thing, I have found out that a quail goes into his bag most every time his butt plate strikes his shoulder. I have had several pleasant hunts with him in the hills near our home.

I will tell you of a little hunt I had with him last Friday. The early train from San Diego brought friend Howard and his new 7½ 12 guage Parker hammerless. After a morning salute he took from his pockets a book, and pointing to some writing on a leaf said, "Read this," and here is what it said: "I bet Mr. McCarty $5 that I can go to Pacific Beach tomorrow and bring back thirty-six quail killed on the wing between the first and last trains to and from the beach."

"Well," I said, "I will be ready and with you in a jiffy."

It took but a few moments to lace up my hunting boots, don my coat with a good supply of shells, and open the kennel door and call out my old standby Romeo, and we sallied out for the foothills. We soon found a small covey which flushed and flew over a hill and we expected to find them in a small canyon, but we were disappointed, not a trace could we find of them, and after one hour's hard work we gave them up and struck out to find a second covey, which we found after a long hunt. It was a good large covey, and the birds were very wild, getting up at long range and going like a bullet, but we succeeded in bagging a few. We hunted hard till one o'clock, when we retired for refreshments beside a cool running stream and counted our bags, which netted only eighteen.

"It is no use," said Howard. "Luck is against me. McCarty will 'set 'em up' on my $5."

"Don't be too sure," said I. We have two long hours yet before we start for the station."

Well, after we took a good rest and washed our throats down with a nice drink from the cool stream we started out again. The writer took the side hill with Romeo, and Howard preferred the level ground. I soon heard Howard's voice saying "Look out. Romeo is froze stiff just ahead of you." And sure enough. I was soon beside him, when up went a brace and they both went to grass. When I ordered Romeo to fetch dead bird a few jumps brought him up stiff again, and two more quail bit the dust I will not tell you here how many quail were bagged on that side hill; modesty prevents. Then again, my old friend, J. K. Orr, might see this article and he would know I was singing the old "chestnut," but I will say that Romeo made some beautiful points and every bird killed was nicely retrieved. Friend Howard stood in the canyon below and said he enjoyed the sport, and one of the first questions he asked after we started for the station was. "What will you take for Romeo?" My answer was, "That question has been asked me many times. My only answer is, 'Not for sale.'"

Oh I almost forgot to to tell you that Mr. Howard went to San Diego with a fine bag of quail, and counted out enough to satisfy the referee that Howard would "set 'em up" on McCarty's $5.

C. A. Loud.

A Candidate for Field Trial Judge.

Editor Breeder and Sportsman:—We had just emerged from the brush and tangle surrounding Elk Lake on to the trail, with our guns and dogs, each of us carrying on our back a goodly load of ducks, when we ran across a specimen, in fact a genius, the specimen being one of the neighboring ranchers' help.

Standing over six feet in height, dressed in a suit of homespun, faded, patched and frayed, the pants reaching to high water mark, a pair of twinkling bead like eyes shone forth from a mass of fiery red hair which covered the entire face, projecting out in front and on either side of his face in wild disorder, a coon skin cap covering a shock of hair of the same firey hue.

Upon perceiving us he dropped the butt of his rulu into soft mud, which ancient piece of ordnance stood at full cock, fondly resting one huge palm upon the muzzle, then the other palm upon it, he scraped the ground with his foot.

"How do, strangers."

"Good day."

"Bin huntin?"

"Yes, sir."

"Got right smart o' ducks."

"Yes, fair."

"You live hyur?"

"No."

"You've got a right pert gun."

"Yep."

"Taint got no hammers, nuther."

"Nop."

"Kill fur?"

"Yep"

"Them bird dawgs?" pointing to the setters.

"Yep."

"Do they uns bark?"

"Nop."

"No good; you want a dawg as will bark at the birds. Si Willis has the best bird dawg in this hull kentry; he went aout last night and killed twenty-nine pheasants; he got five at one shot. "Oh, yes, Si is the Jim dandy shot, and he's jest got the boss gun, too. I seen him kill a pheasant on the very top of the highest tree in that timber yonder. Si won't sell that gun for love or money."

"But what good are them red dawgs if they don't bark?"

"They point the birds."

"They what."

They find the birds and point them with their noses.

"Eh! What's yer givin' us," neighbor?

Sure.

"Honest injin."

You bet.

"Wall, I never," by gum, I kin hardly b'lieve you uns. Lem Weiser would give five dollars for a dawg thet will do thet, then he could kill em all a heap, thet's what he would.

But you musn't shoot birds sitting or standing, and only on the wing when they are flying.

"Eh!"

A barking dog is a pot hunter's dog, and no true sportsman will shoot a bird when sitting.

"Kin you uns do thet? cos ef yer kin hit will be a new wrinkle in these parts. Let's hunt up a bird and you fellers shoot it a flyin.

Suiting the action to the words, we sent the dogs ahead, and one of them soon stiffened on a point into the brush, backed by the other dog, moving up, up, whirred with a great roar a cock grouse.

The choke bore boomed, and down like a wet rag the bird fell, limp and lifeless, a cloud of feathers floating off on the breeze. At a wave of the hand the obedient dog brings the bird in.

"Wall naouw, ef thet wan't the slickest piece o' work I ever did see Ye'r chained lightnin' stranger."

After looking carefully at the bird he took the hammerless gun in hand and examined carefully every particular, squinting along the rib and into the barrels. He next turned to the dog, we expecting to see him look down their nostrils to see if they too were choke bored.

"Wall, boys, ef thet don't beat all," ejaculates the now thoroughly puzzled rancher. "sech doin's not havin' been heard tell on in the experience of the oldest setter.

As he turned to leave us after a pressing invitation to go down to the store with him, the engineer asked him if there were many bears around.

"Wall, yes; thar's right smart o' bars mosyin eround on the Korduroy. I seen several tracks thar this mornin'.

"Jim Bowman had a narrer escape from a old she a few days ago. He wus a slashin' in thet piece o' timber acrost the tel graf road a-thinkin' o' nuthin' except what he wus a-workin' at, when a big ole she bar riz right up alongside o' him, and reached for him.

"Wall, as Jim says, says he, 'Ef I wan't took all of a heap. My har riz up on my ole scalp and I got es weak es I did the time I had the typhoid fever. Yer could hev erknocked me over with a straw.'

"Wall, I jest climbed aout o' thar in a hurry, I tell yer, and no mistake. After a-runnin' till I got to the edge o' the slashin', and jest as I wus a-climbin' eround a big root of a old fir I'll be gol darned ef I didn't run kerpluuk into another big bar, the he, I guess it wus; anyhow, he wus jest as surprised as I wus, but I didn't know it at the time. In course I went one way end he went the other, but I didn't stop a-runnin' till I got home, all aout o' breath, and all the time I kerried my ax in my hand.

"Wall, I used to hev lots o' grit, but sence that encounter with those ole 'no count' bars I've bin no good.

"Yaas, neighbor, there's a power o' bars all through the kentry, and don't you go and forget it, nuther," remarked the six-foot "innocent" mass of humanity as he shambled off.

Not till his shock of magenta hued hair, surmounted by the coon skin cap, had disappeared over a ridge like a setting sun did we recover our equanimity and proceed on our homeward way.

Jay See En.

The Weight of Grouse.

Notes in your issues of Dec. 12 and 19, also "Notlike" in issue Jan. 2, have called my attention to weight of ruffed grouse. Have handled grouse for the market for the past ten years and spend a few days each season for recreation in hunting them Have noticed as "Notlike" says that the weight "varies from year to year according to circumstances, food, weather, etc." The past two seasons having very open weather, little or no snow during the months of October. November and December, the grouse are found in the neighborhood of grain fields, especially those of buckwheat, where they find a quantity of easily procured rich feed. The weights this season with us have averaged unusually heavy, partly owing to the lateness in gathering the buckwheat crop. We purchased of A. P. LaPlant, a market-hunter of this place, among other birds, a cock grouse that weighed 30 plump ounces; it was a very large bird and from appearances a very old one. Its crop contained no unusual amount of food and was not distended as were many at times that we bought. Have had grouse brought in, their crops being so filled with buckwheat that you would imagine they were fed in a poultry yard with tame fowl. Others not in the neighborhood of grain fields had fed on the young and tender shoots of clover leaves, and one bird had at least a pint of wintergreen berries in its crop, showing they accustomed themselves to their surroundings and fed on whatever was in that neighborhood that pleased them best. On my shooting trip this season where I found a buckwheat stubble adjoining timber or brush lots so sure was I to find grouse if they were in that locality, and it took mighty quick work to bring one to bag, being strong and quick on the wing from well filled crops twice each day. For a table bird the grouse that feeds on buckwheat cannot be beaten.—Forest and Stream.

The Gun Club.

Editor Breeder and Sportsman:—The regular annual meeting of the S F. Gun Club took place on the 6th inst. at the club rooms, Nevada Block, which was attended by a majority of the members.

The following gentlemen were elected as Club Officers to serve for 1890:—President, A. W Havens; Vice-president, Howard Black; Secretary and Treasurer, Jno. K Orr, re-elected.

The various executive and membership committees on grounds, will be appointed by the President hereafter. It was decided to have the first shoot of the season on the 22nd of this month, provided. The Inter State match—Eastern and Western teams vs. The California team did not come off on same day.

Very truly yours,
J. K. Orr, Secy.

Mr. Lem Wilson of Porterville knocked over a fish eagle a few days since that measured nine feet from tip to tip.

C. C. Drake, of Price Creek, Humboldt County, killed a three-hundred pound black bear last week that yielded ten gallons of oil.

Forty odd dozens of duck were killed about Mt. Eden, Alameda County, on Sunday last—a revival of the days of seven or eight years ago.

Up Trinity and Lassen way half the able bodied men and boys are out deer hunting on the crusty snow. They should be overhauled by the authorities without delay.

A few days ago at Turlock S. J Allen of Turlock and Ed. Ducker shot a match at twenty live birds each for $20 a side. Allen scored twelve out of thirteen to Ducker's seven out of thirteen, when the latter threw up the match.

George B Hoag and A. J. Tufts of Davisville are in Fresno on a grand hunting trip We commend them to the hospitality of Mr. F. B. Dexter at the Grand Central They should hunt him first, and he will make their way smooth if any one can.

Reverend J. T. Anderson, of Biggs, had an annoying experience last Thursday A youth named Henshaw was popping small birds with a 22 rifle, and shot through a fence toward Mr. Anderson, the ball entering his side. The wound was not serious.

Warren Stephens and William Lewis were out hunting in the hills west of Scott & Lowe's stock farm, Mendocino Co., on Monday last, and succeeded in killing a California lion. A mass meeting of sheepmen, held the same day, returned thanks to the lucky hunters.

Messrs. Knapp of New York and McAllister of Philadelphia shot a match at Babylon, L. I., on February 6th, for $800 a side, 100 live birds to the man Hurlingham style. McAllister won with 92 kills to 79 by Knapp. If the men had average California birds at San Bruno or anywhere else in the State their scores would not have been so high.

In destroying the robins which have been driven out of the mountains by the snow, orchardists and vinyardists should not go to excess. This year many robins may not be too much, but at other seasons they are valuable, for they feed on insects and pests that eat foliage and destroy fruit. This bird is not called and counted a game bird anywhere else, and he deserves a bit of hospitality and a good deal of mercy.

The leading game bird of the season has been the robin. From all sections come reports of monstrous bags of them and the markets have at all times been full. At Livermore the other evening, John Worth killed 1421 robins, using 122 cartridges. Near Dixon William Wolfskill killed 1350 robins at 66 shots and sold them for 40 cents per dozen. On the following night he and his brother were out all night and in the morning they shipped 125 dozens, receiving 35 cents per dozen. At Winters two men killed one day 1500 robins from the fruit trees on their premises. A night or two before one of them bagged 1692 of the birds.

Some time ago a pair of hungry coyotes came down from the mountains and sought refuge in the tule and the fringe of the forest that skirts the river near Rio Vista. High water drove them out of their retreat, and they are committing serious depredations on the flocks in that vicinity. E. C. Dozier and others have devoted a great deal of time to an unavailing search for them. As a last resort there is talk of procuring a pack of hounds to run them down.

There are 992 gun clubs in America, distributed as follows:—

Alabama	17	Kentucky	59
California	24	Massachusetts	[illegible]
Colorado	27	Michigan	22
Connecticut	57	Minnesota	12
Dakota	23	Missouri	[illegible]
Delaware	7	Nebraska	16
Florida	7	New Jersey	[illegible]
Georgia	10	New York	77
Illinois	16	Ohio	[illegible]
Indiana	[illegible]	Pennsylvania	[illegible]
Iowa	86	Texas	16
Kansas	[illegible]	Canada	24

J. M. White of the Biggs Argus—better known as "Mississip,"—is one of the crack rifle shots of the world, says the Argus. In fact it is doubtful whether his equal can be found, His father was an expert marksman as were also his three brothers, and the faculty seems to be hereditary in the family. When only three years of age Jim made seventeen consecutive bull's eyes with a Colt's dragoon revolver and he has been shooting ever since. A week ago last Sunday, while hunting feathered game along Feather river near Hamilton, he entertained a number of companions with an exhibition of his skill by shooting at the small bird commonly called "chippy." Out of 23 shot at while they were flying, at distances ranging from twenty to forty yards he killed—with his rifle—21 and shot the wing off another one. This is extraordinarily good shooting, but "Mississip" does not think so. He has frequently thrown a short bit in the air and then hit it with a rifle bullet before it fell to the ground. It is very probable that a match will be arranged between him and Miss Lillian F Smith, who claims to be the champion rifle shot of the world, in which event Jim will be backed by big money by the sporting men of Butte.

[That story won't do. If "Mississip" is a veritable printer of the Argus crowd, where does he get "short bits" to throw in the air. Tell another one, but respect the verities.—Ed.

THE KENNEL

Dog owners are requested to send for publication the earliest possible notices of whelps, sales, names claimed, presentations and deaths, in their kennels, in all instances writing plainly names of sire and dam and of grandparents, colors, dates and breed.

Names Claimed.

Mr. M D. Walter, at Galt claims names for English setter dog puppies, by Rodney—Phyllis II, all black, white and tan, Lee R., France R , and Dandy R.

J. B. Martin, San Francisco, Cal., claims the name Golden Lilly for white foxterrier bitch, whelped July 16, 1889, by Clover Turk (Mixture—Spite), out of Beatrice (Champion Bacchanal—Blemton Arrow).

Whelps.

Mr. J. Martin Barney's (Dutch Flat) pointer bitch Galatea (Nick of Naso—Temptation), whelped January 18, 1890, ten, five dogs, to owner's Tom Pinch.

Visits.

J. B. Martin, San Francisco, Cal., has bred Beatrice (Champion Bacchanal—Blemton Arrow), foxterrier bitch, to Blemton Vesuvian (Champion Lucifer—Blemton Vesta), on February 4, 1890.

Count Dick.

Mr. Austin B. Sperry's pointer Count Dick which showe so brilliantly at the field trials, but whose age and breedin were not then known, turns out to be as suspected, but a fi teen months old puppy In breeding he is "way up" bein by Sam C. Hare's James K., a son of General Cosby' Bow Jr. out of Geo. W. Bassford's Josie Bow. Count Dick dam was Mollie Ashe owned by H. C. Brown at Sacramento Mollie Ashe was by Boyd (Sleaford—Jessie Belle) out of Jessi Belle (Sancho—Baker's Queen) Count Dick was bred by H C. Brown and was whelped on Oct. 4th 1888 If he train on he will be a dangerous competitor next year.

The English Kennel Club has resolved that hereafter an Irish terrier that has been cropped will not be eligible t compete at any kennel club show.

Editor C. E. Sherman, of the Kern County Californian brightest and best of country papers could not resist Patt and came up from Bakersfield on Monday last to revel i opera.

It is worth the while of English setter fanciers to study th blood lines of the dogs which are being bred by Mr. M. I Walter, at Galt, Sacramento county. They are particularl strong in the blood of Bergundthal's Rake and Fanny, an should be valuable no end

Mr. M. D. Walter thinks of locating somewhere near Sa Francisco, and we hope will do so, both because it will be good business move for that very pleasant trainer and b cause we can have more frequent visits from him.

It was particularly unfortunate that Mr. Allender shou have been called away from Bakersfield just before the tri because he left his dogs without his skillful care. Mr. Tr man informs us that his pointer Patti Croxteth T. on the d before her race was actually stuffed with food and only a fi teen mile run behind a buggy served to bring her down something like form.

Mr. George T. Allender intends as soon as the weather pe mits to move to some location more convenient to San Fra cisco than Watsonville. Several of his friends have advis the change and it appears wise to us. Owners prefer to a should see their dogs from time to time when in a traine hands, and if a trip can be made in a few hours at slight e pense, so much the better. A good location is not easy find and Mr. Allender will be thankful for suggestions.

ATHLETICS.

Athletic Sports and Other Pastimes.

EDITED BY ARPHIPPUS.

SUMMARY.

The athletes are enjoying the fine weather, and many of them are already in active training for the coming field days. On Wednesday evening the Golden Gate Athletic Club gave its regular monthly exhibition. On the following evening the Olympic Club held a very enjoyable "Ladies Night." To-morrow afternoon the members of the Alpine Athletic Club will hold their first out-door exhibition at Harbor View Park, when twenty events will be contested. Altogether the athletic outlook is very bright, and for some months to come the amateurs will have their hands full preparing for the numerous contests that will take place. Now that the three leading amateur clubs have their own training grounds, there will be no further room for kicking on the part of the out-door men, and this fact, coupled with the other inducements offered, cannot help but bring out all the amateur athletes, even the old-timers who have laid on the shelf for years.

RUNNERS, WALKERS, JUMPERS, ETC.

To-morrow the Alpine Club will make its initial bow to the public.

In a couple of weeks the new track of the Olympic Club will be finished. Already it is pronounced a success. When the grounds are opened on Decoration Day, many of the coast records will be considerably improved.

The University athletes are getting into trim for their Spring field-day.

The Alpine Club will hold its first cross-country run from Harbor View on Sunday, March 2d.

Cross-country runs are bound to become popular on the Pacific Coast during the coming season. The Olympic, University and Alpine clubs can always, at short notice, place good teams in the field, and there is no reason why an open cross-country championship should not be held during the summer. The public would be more than pleased to witness such an exhibition, and it would be an easy task to select a suitable course where the spectators could catch a glimpse of the contestants as they sped over the ground.

The amateur annex of the Golden Gate Athletic Club has in it several promising young boxers who will make their *debut* at the next boxing tournament.

The running track of the Olympic Club is continually occupied with the runners who intend competing in the five-mile run on February 26th.

Peter Schumacher, Champion Wrestler of the Pacific Coast was defeated at Milwaukee on Tuesday evening last by Tom Connors. The match was for the middle weight championship and $300 a side.

Owing to an accident which befell E. A. Kolb while training, the match between himself and A. H. Lean has been postponed to April 29th. Lean's friends are anxious to have the match come off, as they feel confident that their champion will win.

J. J. McKinnon, the amateur hammer thrower, will shortly take unto himself a wife.

Eugene Hulcombe of the O. C. promises to develop into a first-class heel and toe walker.

Charles Vultee of the Alpine Club will be heard from in the sprint events at the next open games. He is also a promising high jumper.

Sexsmith, Cassidy, Garrison, Luttringer, Tank and Eldridge will possibly make good records to-morrow at Harbor View.

THE WHEELMEN.

There will be no race meeting on Washington's Birthday, the wheelmen claiming that the wet weather prevented them from training.

H. A. Matthews will shortly begin his long rides through the interior. He has a long programme made out for the coming season.

On Monday evening next the Bay City Wheelmen will give a very select ball at Union Square Hall. Only a limited number of invitations will be issued, and everything possible will be done to insure the guests a pleasant evening. The club is about to adopt a new constitution and by-laws.

JOTTINGS FROM ALL OVER.

The second winter meeting of the Riverside Athletic Club of Newark, N. J., was held Wednesday, Jan. 22nd, at the Bellville Avenue Park. The following is a summary;

50-yard run, handicap—Final heat, M Bemmington, 1st. Time, 5 4 5secs. T Fay, 2nd.

300-yard novice run, scratch.—A Werner, 1st. Time, 43 1-5 seconds; B Van Cliff Jr. 2nd.

880-yard run, handicap—E Billings, 1st. Time, 2min. 10 seconds. A. Baier, 2nd.

250-yard run. handicap—W H Morgan (7yds) 1st time, 33 2-5 secs., J T Norton (4yds) 2nd.

One mile walk, handicap—J C Forbes (30secs) 1st. Time, 8min 4 4-5 secs. S Blumenthal (30 secs) 2nd.

Two-mile run, handicap—W D Daly, (scratch) 1st time, 10 min 43½secs; C Britton, (90yds) 2nd.

Running high jump, handicap—E W Goff (6in) 1st, 5ft 5½ in.; E E Barnes (4in) 2nd, 5ft 4½in.

A committee on revision of rules of the Amateur Athletic Union held a meeting on Feb. 3rd. at which their work was completed. During the evening F. W. Janssen, of the Staten Island Athletic Club, offered a resolution to the effect that the Union would further the best interests of amateur athletics by passing a law prohibiting any club from paying the expenses of its athletes to any competitive meeting other than that for the championship of the A A U. This resolution was passed, and it is not improbable that a law to the effect will be adopted, despite the opposition offered by a number of athletes, who, while burdened with ambition, prefer not to go down to their pockets to gratify their desires.

The third winter meeting of the University of Pennsylvania Athletic Association was held at the Academy of Music, Philadelphia, on Saturday evening, Feb. 1st, with the following results:

Half mile run—P D Skellman, N Y A C, 1st, time, 2min 17 sec.; J H Terry, U of Pa., 2nd.

Quarter-mile dash—J W Rutter, Y M C A (14yds) 1st. Time, 60secs.

Mile walk—C L Nicoll, M A C (scratch) 1st. Time, 8min 21½ secs.

Interacademic 440-yard dash—M G Rosengarten, 1st. Time, 1min 7½secs.

Forty-yard dash—L Cary, 1st. Time, 4 4 5sec; C S Amwake, 2nd.

Running high jump—H L Clark, 1st, 5ft 8½ in. D C Clegg, 2nd.

Two hundred and twenty yards hurdle race—J T Norton, 1st. Time, 31sec.

One mile run—P D Skellman, N Y A C, 1st. Time. 4min 45sec.; J H McKay (80yds) 2nd.

Duncan C. Ross and Captain E. N. Jennings are working Australia for gold by means of the mounted sword combat game.

The National Cross Country Association of America will hold an eight mile cross country handicap from either Fleetwood Park, on March 15th. It is the intention of the committee to make this handicap run the biggest affair of the kind ever held in America. The prizes will be both costly and handsome. The first ten men to reach home will be presented with prizes. The club being the first to have six men finish will be presented with a magnificent silk banner. The committee will give each starter a solid silver souvenir medal, all of which will be struck from the National Association standard die, and will each alone be a valuable prize. Entrance fee, $1. Entrance fees must accompany the entries, or entries will be rejected. It is estimated that there will be at least three hundred starters, and that all the leading colleges, schools, cross country and athletic clubs, will be represented in this gigantic cross country run. For particulars, address B. C. Williams, President and Chairman, Entertainment Committee, 104 West Fifty-fifth Street, New York City.

T. P. Conneff, of the M A C of New York, is rapidly recovering and there is some possibility that he may be strong enough to run in the championship games.

The following are the rules for jumping as recently adopted by the American Athletic Union.

RULE XVIII.—JUMPING.

Sec. 1: All jumps shall be made without any assisting devices.

A fair jump shall be one that is made without the assistance of weights, diving, somersets, or handsprings of any kind.

In all handicap jumps the scratch man shall be entitled to try last.

Sec. 2. The Running High Jump.—The measurers shall decide the height at which the jump shall commence, and shall regulate the succeeding elevations.

Each competitor shall be allowed three trial jumps at each height, and if on the third trial he shall fail he shall be declared out of the competition.

Competitors shall jump in order as placed in the programme then those failing, if any, shall have their second trial jump in a like order; after which those having failed twice shall make their third trial jump.

he jump shall be made over a bar resting on pins, projecting not more than 3 inches from the uprights, and when this bar is removed from its place it shall be counted as a trial jump.

Running under the bar in making an attempt to jump shall be counted as a "balk," and three successive "balks" shall be counted as a trial jump.

The distance of the run before the jump shall be unlimited.

A competitor may decline to jump at any height in his turn, and by so doing forfeits his right to again jump at the height he declined.

Sec 3. The Standing High Jump.—The feet of the competitor may be placed in any position, but shall leave the ground only once in making an attempt to jump. When the feet are lifted from the ground twice, or two springs are made in making the attempt, it shall count as a trial jump without result.

With this exception the rules governing the running high jump shall also govern the standing high jump.

Sec. 4. The Running Broad Jump.—When jumped on earth, a joist five inches wide shall be sunk flush with it. The outer edge of the joist shall be called the scratch line, and the measurements of all jumps shall be made from it at right angles to the nearest break in the ground made by any part of the person of the competitor.

In front of the scratch line the ground shall be removed to the depth of three and the width of twelve inches outward.

A foul jump shall be one where the competitor, in jumping off the scratch line, makes a mark on the ground immediately in front of it, and shall count as a trial jump without result.

Each competitor shall have three trial jumps, and the best three shall each have three more trial jumps.

The competition shall be decided by the best of all the trial jumps of the competitors.

The distance of the run before the scratch line shall be unlimited.

IN THE SURF.

Several swimmers look a dip in the surf on Sunday last. The bath proprietors think that the season will open early this year. They also predict a very warm season.

Wm. Greer Harrison ex-President of the Olympic Club and several other prominent business men have decided to open a first-class salt water bathing estableshment at the corner of Sutter and Stockton streets on the lot now occupied by the old Vienna Garden Building.

AT THE OARS.

There will be a meeting of the "Jolly Land Lubbers" at the house of the Triton Swimming and Boating Club Leavenworth and Bay Streets to-morrow afternoon at 1:30 for the purpose of re-organizing for the season of 1890. A fine lunch will be served at 2:20.

Sunday was another fine day for the oarsmen. The Pioneer Club sent out four crews and seven single scullers.

The most important event during the week was the acceptance of Charley Long's challenge by Henry Henceman of Stockton. The race will come off on Sunday March 16 at the Alameda Mole course and will be started at 11 o'clock. The principal attraction will be the starting and finishing of the race at the end of the mole, thereby doing away with the long and tiresome walk of over a mile and a half down the bridge.

Long has improved over a minute in the past year and he has plenty of friends who are willing to rish their last cent on the result of the race.

The Pless Bros. with Phelan and Finley of the Arie's rowed around to Harbor View Park last Sunday, and after having some clam chowder and "wet goods" returned to their boat house.

The Columbia Club of Oakland have a committee out making arrangements for the holding of a regatta on the waters in front of their boat house. The committee expects to be able to get some of the San Francisco clubs to help them out.

Mr. Ferry of the Union Club of Sacramento says that his club will join the Pacific Rowing Association after it receives a copy of the constitution. He says that there is an increased activity amongst the members of the club.

A committee of the Alpine Club will make an effort to rent the Yale boat house in Oakland for the use of the Amateur champion crew, consisting of Henry Tank, John J. Larkey, and H. O. Farrell. The crew will begin training at once and will make a big effort to carry the championship back to their club mates.

CLUB JOTTINGS.

The members of the Golden Gate Athletic Club were treated to a first-class exhibition of boxing at their club rooms on Stevenson street, on Wednesday evening. The chief event of the evening was a contest to a finish between Charles Gleason and Peter McCoy. The match lasted six rounds and was won by McCoy.

A full account of the "Ladies' Night" exhibition of the Olympic Club which was given on Thursday evening last will appear in our next issue.

A meeting of the Pacific Coast Amateur Athletic Association was held at the Club rooms of the Olympic Club on Thursday evening, February 6th. Secretary J. J. Jamison of the G. G. A. C. was unable to attend, and E. P. Moody of the Pacific Athletic Club was appointed temporary Secretary. George W. Jordan of the O. C. made charges against the G. G. A. C., and a committee was appointed to inquire into the standing of the club. A committee was also appointed to investigate the standing of the Alpine Amateur Athletic Club which had applied for admission into the Association. The meeting adjourned to Friday evening February 14th, when the application of the Alpine Club would be acted upon.

Several athletic clubs from the interior have applied for admission into the P. C. A. A. A.

The proposed indoor tournament of the Alpine Club has been postponed until April. The first indoor exhibition of the club will be given at the new club rooms, Eureka Turn Verein Hall, 806 Powell street, in about two weeks. A first-class programme will be given.

The Alpine Amateur Athletic club will move to its new Club rooms 806 Powell St. on Monday next.

The Alameda Olympic Club will shortly hold a "Ladies Night."

The Acme Club of Oakland is at present in a very flourishing condition. The membership is increasing rapidly.

The cross country run of the O. C. at Milbrae on Sunday last was well attended and the athletes all enjoyed a splendid days outing. The following well known amateurs were noticed amongst the startes: Captain George W. Jordan, Walter A. Scott, Horace Coffin, Frank L. Cooley, A. S. Henderson, N. J. Haberly, W. F Bouton, A. D. Carroll, C. Schlingheyde, J. B. Coe, Frank G. O'Kane, C. A. Fletcher, George Hicks, S. Mendelisohn, M. L. S. Espinoza, S. F. McDonald, N. L. Williams, J. S. J. Otts, R. Y. Cole, E. Gros, E. Thomas and D. W. Donnelly. The old time runner Peter McIntyre also took part in the fun. The pace very moderate and the distance about five miles. On their return to Milbrae, the boys enjoyed a bath after which they sat down to a fine lunch.

The following is a list of the handicaps with the order of events of the Alpine Amateur Athletic club games which will take place at the club grounds, Harbor View Park to-morrow afternoon commencing at 1 o'clock sharp:

1—100 yards run.—E. P. Moody, 2 yards; W. Kramer, 5 yards; T. Kelly, 2 yards; J. W. Creagh, 2 yards; G. W. Armbruster 4 yards; C. Armbruster, 4 yards; C. A. Eldridge, 2 yards; J. Sexesmith, scratch; D. Barry, 5 yards; C. Little, scratch; H Tank, 2 yards; C. Vultee, 2 yards; R. J. Luttrenger, 1 yard.

2—Half mile run.—H. C. Cassidy, 10 yards; C. Little scratch; M. C. Giry, 60 yards; J. W. Creagh 40 yards; J. D Garrison, 30 yards; E Goodman, 40 yards; C. A. Eldridge, 25 yards; E. P. Moody, 15 yards; G. W. Armbruster, 50 yards; J. R. Collins, 50 yards.

3—One mile walk.—P. N. Gaffney, scratch; M. C. Giry, 60 secs.; C. A. Eldridge 20 secs.; J. McLaughlin, 50 secs.

4—Pole Vault.—C. Meyer, 1 foot; C. A. Eldridge, 2 feet; J. Sheehan, 9 inches; J. Sexsmith, scratch.

5—Final 100 yard run.

6—Putting 16 lb. shot.—I. Sheehan, 2 feet; J. Sexsmith, scratch; P. N. Gaffney, 3 feet; F. M. Howard, 4 feet; C. Meyer, 3 feet; C. A. Eldridge, 3 feet; R. J. Luttrenger, 2 feet.

7—440 yards run.—H. C. Cassidy, 10 yards; C. Little, scratch; J. D. Garrison, 5 yards; E. P. Moody, 15 yards; R. J. Luttringer, 5 yards.

8—Standing broad jump—C A Eldridge, scratch; C. Meyer, 1 foot; J. Sheehan, 1 foot; J. Sexsmith, 6 inches; H. Tank, 1 foot; F M Howard, 1 foot.

9—Flinging 56 lb. weight—P N Gafney, 1 foot; T J Cunningham, 2 feet; J Sexsmith, scratch; R J Luttringer 6 in.

10—220 yards run—J D Garrison, 5 yards; H C Cassidy, 4 yards; T Kelly, 5 yards; C A Eldridge, 3 yards; M C Giry, 10 yards; R J Latinger, 2 yards; G W Armbruster, 9 yards; C Little, scratch, H Tank, 7 yards.

11—Half mile novice walk scratch—M C Giry, T J Gallagher, J Sheehan, J McLaughlin, H C Cassidy, J Nicholson, C Meyer, G W Armbruster, F M Howard, C Armbruster, John D Garrison, J W Creagh.

12—Running high jump—J Sheehan, 2 inches; C A Eldridge, 2in; P N Gafney, scratch; C Meyer, 2in; C Vultie, scratch; J Sexsmith, scratch; E P Moody, 1in.

13—220-yard run, final heat.

14—Throwing 12 lb hammer—J J McKinnon, scratch; J Sheehan, 35ft; P N Gafney, 30 ft; C A Eldridge, 35ft; C Vultie, 35ft; J Sexsmith, 20ft; E Sullivan, 29ft; T J Cunningham, 35ft.

14—120-yards run—J D Garrison, 2yds; G W Armbruster, 6yds; E P Moody, 4yds; H Tank, 2yds; T Kelly, 3yds; R J Luttringer, scratch; C A Eldridge, 2yds; C Little, scratch; H C Cassidy, 5yds.

15—Running broad jump—J D Garrison, 1 foot; H C Cassidy, 1½ feet; C A Eldridge, 1½ feet; C Meyer 1½ feet; H Tank; 1½ feet; J Sexmith, scratch.

16—Final heat, 120-yard run.

17—One mile run—H C Cassidy, scratch; C Little, 500ds; M C Giry, 175yds; E Goodman, 80yds; C A Eldridge, 75yds; J R Collins, 125yds; J McLaughlin, 175yds; C Vultee, 80yds; R J Luttringer 50yds.

18—Alpine race one mile scratch—H C Cassidy, M C Giry, J McLaughlin, J D Garrison, C A Eldridge, P N Gafney.

The amateurs of the California Club received another slap in the face when they were told that they would be "fired" if they got too fresh. Great Scott, is there no spirit amongst the crowd.

RANCHO DEL PASO TROTTERS.

Albert W., 2:20, Echo (462), 2:37 1-2, Sire of 12 in 2:30 List; Alcona 11543, Sire of Addie E. 2:22 1-2, the Produce of Mabel, Sister to Beautiful Bells, 2:29 1-2.

(Dam of Bell Boy, 3 y. o., 2:19 1-4, Hinda Rose, 3 y. o., 2:19 1-2, St. Bel, 2:24 1-2, and Palo Alto Belle, 2 y. o., 2:28 1-2) Sisters to Ben Ali, 2:22, Ha-Ha, 2:22 1-4—Dams of Wells Fargo, 2:18 3-4, Senator, 2:23 3-4, Pasha 2:27 3-4 Monarch 2:28 1-2, etc. etc.

Kentucky was for years conceded the premier position as the most suitable location in America for raising thoroughbred stock, but in the course of the last few years, Mr. Haggin has been so successful—both as an owner and breeder—that the fame of Rancho del Paso has spread all over the known world, and is universally acknowledged to be *the* breeding farm in America. Of course this could not be brought about without a lavish expense of money and time. "Rome was not built in a day," but was the result of years of patient labor, and in a similar way the ranch near Sacramento has been gradually, but surely, placed on a firm basis. While the fame of Rancho del Paso was spreading—as a thoroughbred stud farm—John Mackey, the superintendent, than whom there is no better authority in California on old-time trotters, having been a driver and trainer of trotting horses years ago, was carefully picking up well-bred trotting mares and relegating them to the Sacramento or Kern county ranch, and at the same time Echo 462, a son of Rysdyk's old horse, was purchased for a sire; while later on Algona 11543 (bred at Fairlawn), a son of Almont 33, was secured, and last of all Albert W., 2:20, was purchased to cross with the fashionable strains of blood already secured.

Owing to the universal interest taken in thoroughbred stock the trotters were not educated, but were allowed an easy existence until five years old, and the geldings were then sold unbroken, but having secured a son of Electioneer, and with a mark of 2:20, it was determined to inaugurate yearling trotting sales as well as the thoroughbred sales. This year there will necessarily be quite a large number of older horses sold, but in order that it should not be said that the best were being saved, *every one* of Albert W.'s get will be offered by Messrs. Easton in March.

When the first announcement of the sale was made most of our breeders scouted the idea of taking what they called unknown colts to New York to sell. Little did they know what they were talking of, and many a one will rue the day he said it, when he sees the 92 head in New York. One of our oldest and most prominent breeders was in Sacramento last week, and since his return said to me that he had no conception, and he was sure no one in California had, of the quantity of regally bred and grand looking youngsters located on the Rancho Del Paso. The consignment are nearly all unbroken. The yearlings have in a few instances gone through a little kindergarten exercise, having been exercised a few weeks, but otherwise nothing has been done.

The stallions whose get will be offered are Albert W (11333) 2:20, Echo 462, Algona 11543, Del Paso 11807, Western 11334, Cornelius 11335, and Bob Lee.

Albert W, foaled 1878, is a beautiful hard bay, with black points (one hind pastern white.) He has an almost perfect thoroughbred intelligent head and neck, with good sloping shoulders, neat strong back, with great muscular development behind, having very fine powerful quarters, while he has plenty of bone, good clean hocks and good feet. He is by Electioneer 125, dam Sister (sister to Aurora 2:27) dam of Bonanza 2:29½, by John Nelson 185, grandam the Lamott mare.

John Nelson 187, was by imported Trustee, out of the Redmond mare by Abdallah 1, and was the sire of Neres 2:23½, and three others in the 2:30, besides being grand sire of a host in 2:30. The Lamott mare although nothing was definitely known about her, was evidently an exceptionally well bred mare for she was the dam of Aurora 2:27 and grand dam of Albert W 2:20 and Bonanza 2:29½. Albert W has therefore a double Abdallah cross with a thoroughbred cross, through John Nelson, of Trustee one of our best imported horses. As a race horse Albert W was a grand success. As a three year old, he won three races out of four, and as a four year old, he won five hard races and was only beaten once (by Sweetness. In his race at Oakland he displayed great endurance and gameness, seven heats being trotted with Sweetness 2:21¼, Nellie R 2:17¼, and Poscora Hayward 2:23¼ Sweetness took the first two heats, Nellie R the third and fifth, and Albert the fourth, sixth and seventh, outstaying the others. He wound up the season of 1882 by easily winning a two mile race 5:04½ and 4:51, it being generally acknowledged that he could have beaten the two mile record if necessary. Albert went into winter quarters with a four year old mark of 2:22.

In 1884 Albert reduced his record to 2:20½ and beat Manon at Petaluma, winning the first, third and fifth in 2:22½, 2:22½ and 2:26. In 1885 Albert beat Sister at San Francisco, taking the first, third and fifth in 2:23¼, 2:24 and 2:26 In 1886 he took the first heat at Nevada City in 2:20. McConnell (Buster) who drove him when he made his record, 2:20, and also when he trotted in 2:20½, says he could easily have trotted in 2:15, the day he went in 2:20½, and he several times drove him in his work at Oakland in 2.17, while the day he went in 2:20 he was dead lame and only his sheer gameness carried him through. He was then retired for good and was afterwards purchased for Mr. Haggin. His colts are like the horse, wonderfully docile, and intelligent. Only two of his colts have been trained, the twin filly (Aurelia) and Little Albert; the latter at two years old showed a 2:28 gait, but never recovered from an attack of cerebro spinal meninginitis, and was not worked afterwards. Aurelia showed tremendous pace and would probably have trotted in 2:22 had she been persevered with, as she several times showed a 2:20 gait at Oakland

ECHO 462, RECORD 2:37½.

Bay horse; foaled 1866. Bred by Jesse T. Seely, Warwick, Orange Co., New York.

As will be seen from the pedigree below, Echo is royally bred. He is a son of Rysdyk's old horse, and on his dam's side he is a grandson of Magnolia, a son of Seely's American Star; the combination of the Star and Hambletonian blood being invaluable. Echo was a good performer himself, beating The Moor and Vaughn a two mile heat race, and among the other performances of his daughter Echora, in 1875 when three years old, she distanced Beautiful Bells and Arabia, and was the only horse in California to beat Director, which she did in 1882 at Santa Rosa, never allowing the black horse to get a heat.

Among others of Echo's get Victor is probably as grand as most horses at present on the track, having proved his staunchness many a time as did Gibraltar, Echora and in fact all of his get that have been trained. Echo is also the sire of the dams of Direct 2:18½ and Pink 2:25.

ECHO, SIRE OF

Belle Echo	2:20	Lohengrin	2:27½
Senator	2:21½	Pasha	2:27¾
Victor	2:22	Elmonte	2:29
Gibraltar	2:21¼	Col. Hawkins	2:29½
Echora	2:23½	Annie Laurie	2:30
Tippie	2:25¾	Economy	2:30

Sam Lewis (pacer) 2:25.

AND SIRE OF THE DAMS OF

Direct (4 years old)	2:18½	Pink	2:25

ECHO 462, rec. 2:37½.			
	Hambletonian 10	Abdallah 1	Mambrino
			Amazonia
		Chas. Kent Mare	*Bellfounder
			One Eye
	Fanny Felter	Magnolia 68	American Star 14
			Jenny Lind
		Daughter of	Kentucky Whip (Webber's)
			Dau. of Shakespeare

Algona 11543 was foaled in 1876, at General W. T. Wither's celebrated Fairlawn Farm in Kentucky. He is by Almont 33, dam Emma Kincaid by Conscript, grandam Effie Dean by Mambrino Chief 11, great grandam by Powell's Bertrand. Almont was the sire of Fanny Witherspoon 2:16½ and 31 others better than 2:30; also of Westmont pacer 2:13¾ and grandsire of innumerable others, Algona therefore a son of one of the best stallions in America and has a double infusion of the invaluable Mambrino Chief blood. Algona is a rich chestnut and Addie E., the only one of his get that has been trained, obtained a record of 2:22½ at Chico, taking the 1st, 4th and 5th heats in 2:22½, 2:25 and 2:26¾.

Cornelius 11,335 is a handsome bay horse, a Nutwood all over, and but for an accident would have had a low mark. He is one of the handsomest horses in California, and has a pure square gait, while his breeding of course is exceptional. He is by Nutwood 600, 2:18¾, dam Jennie G. by Echo 462, grandam Jenny Noyes, 2:40 (dam of Gus 2:26¾), Cornelius' colts are like himself, handsome and powerful, with good legs and feet and rapid action.

Western 11,334 is a full brother to Whippleton 1883, sire of Lillie Stanley 2:17½, Homestake 2:16½, etc. He is by Hambletonian Jr. 1882, dam Lady Livingstone (dam of Lady Blanchard 2:26½) by General Taylor, son of the Morse Horse 6, grandam the Lou Mills mare.

Hambletonian Jr. is by Hambletonian 725, out of Aschat by Hambletonian 10, grandam by American Star 14, great grandam by Abdallah.

Western's breeding is wonderfully good, and Whippleton has proved that it reproduces itself, for he added two more to his list of 2:30 performers last season, and is now the sire of five in the 2:30 list.

Bob Lee is by Nutwood 600, first dam Blackbird (the Singleton mare) by Blackbird 482, out of a Morgan mare Bob Lee is grand looking, neat, short backed, powerful chestnut horse and is getting good stock, useful as well as ornamental.

The yearlings which will be offered in New York were all looked over. They are, with only one or two exceptions, branded under the mane, and in mentioning them I will use these brands. They were a remarkably clean limbed, good looking lot, none of them having any blemishes and being particularly healthy looking and big and strong. The first looked at was of course Mabel's (sister to Beautiful Bells) foal by Albert W. It is branded 18 under the mane, and is a grand looking bay filly with black points. The head is well shaped, though rather spoiled by the drooping ears derived from The Moor blood, while the filly has a beautiful neck and good shoulders, with a good back well ribbed up, and a remarkable length from the hip to the stifle, with good hard, clean legs and sound feet. When out in the miniature exercising ring the youngster's action was so taking that it was useless to speculate on what will be the price bid when Mr. Easton enquires, "What am I offered for a daughter of Albert W, 2:20—by Electioneer, the greatest living sire—out of Mabel, a sister to Beautiful Bells, the dam of Bell Boy, etc. Such a chance will not occur again for years, and bidders will be as thick as flies on molasses. The colt and filly by Albert out of Maud and Ma Belle, daughters of Echo and Mabel, were then looked over. The colt, branded 6, was brought out into the ring. In appearance he is a lengthy bay colt with black legs, very highly finished and racy looking, has a beautiful thoroughbred head and neck, with an almost perfect set of legs and feet. When starred going in the ring he seemed to know no gait but trotting, and went down the hundred yards of straight like an old horse, with a low, easy, frictionless, rapid, resolute action, which was very deceptive, for he was going at quite a 40 clip then, and as one of the spectators (who should know, having seen him often) said he had never seen a horse square off and trot so much like old George Wilkes. The filly out of Ma Belle is branded 20, and is almost a counterpart of the colt, though hardly as rangy. Her action is a little higher than his, but is very rapid. The more one looked at the two the more one wondered what a colt and filly bred as they were would fetch. No. 22 was then brought out at Mr. Hendrickson's (the one time owner of G. M. Patchen Jr. 31) request. She was another bay filly with a splendid Albert head and neck, nice sloping shoulders, a good back, beautifully ribbed up, and a rather straight but speedy looking hind leg. Her action is as much like her sire's as it is possible to be. She is by Albert W, dam Echota, by Echo, grandam Lady Grey by Algona, great grandam by Odd Fellow, a son of Jack Hawkins.

No. 3 was next brought out. He is a magnificent looking chestnut colt with a star and hind fetlock white; he is a powerful compact sturdy looking colt, almost a horse now, and when started up round the ring; was in my opinion the best of the lot. He moves in a resolute, determined way, stepping a little too high in front perhaps, for some captious critics, but moving very rapidly and bending his knees and hocks well, getting his hind legs well under him, and seeming to know no gait but trotting, and as fast as a bullet. Irrespective of racing, as a sire he should be worth his weight in gold, for even the hypercritical cannot find a flaw in his breeding, by Albert W, dam Galena, by Nutwood, grand dam Eudora by Volunteer 55, next dam by Seely's American Star, out of a Seagullion (son of Duroc) mare.

No. 1 is a big lengthy chestnut colt with a good long back, big knees and hocks, nice short cannon bones and a pure natural gait. He is by Albert W, out of Rosa Clay by Sayres Henry Clay 45 out of Lady Winfield by Edward Everitt 81, out of a daughter of Rattler, son of Abdallah

No 9 is a big rangy looking bay colt, with black legs and a game wear and tear look about him. He is by Albert W. out of a mare by Exile (son of Echo and Belle Mason by Williamson's Belmont) out of Rosa Clay.

No. 11 is a roundish gentlemanly looking bay colt with a snip and one fetlock white. His looks alone should sel him while his breeding is equally good—racing too; he is by Albert W. out of a sister to El Monte 2:29 by Echo out of Lightfoot by Hubbard (son of Planet) out of Brunelle by Rifleman, out of Fannie Frasier by Bertrand.

No. 15 is a strong, rangy, muscular, brown colt, white snip and hind pastern, has a fearless way of going, easily traceable to his sire. He is by Albert W., dam by Hambletonian 725, out of Young Lady Vernon by Easton's David Hill.

No. 30 is a good bay, a highly formed colt by Cornelius out of Susie Allen by Ethan Allen Jr. (son of old Ethan Allen); 1st dam Santa Clara by Owen Dale out of Ida May by Red Buck, out of Old Mary by Red Bill.

No. 8 is a blocky, thick set colt, close to the ground, a dashing mover, and fast with every indication of extreme speed. He is by Albert W., out of Nellie Doon by Echo, out of Nellie by Muldoon (son of George M Patchen Jr. 31 and Victress, dam of Monarch 2:23½, by Williamson's Belmont), 3rd dam by McCracken's Black Hawk 767, 4th dam by Williamson's Belmont.

No. 12 is a big, strong colt with a good girth and powerful hind quarters. He is by Albert W. out of Marie Roze by Inca 557 (by Woodford Mambrino) 2nd dam Cecelia Clark by Clark Chief 89, 3rd dam by Captain Baird out of a daughter of imp Envoy and the Sister to the dam of Vandal by Tranby.

No. 10 is a big, strong, brown colt, with speedy looking hind quarters by Albert W, out of Jeannette by Kentucky Prince 2470, out of Wayward by Volunteer 55, out of the Jones mare

The next stripling interviewed was a filly—half sister to Cornelius, by Albert W, dam Jennie G by Echo, out of Jennie Noyes, dam of Gus 2 26¾. She is a big, lengthy, rather leggy filly, with slightly crooked hind legs, but built on speedy lines and is a sweet mover.

No. 14 is a chestnut colt with three white stockings and a star. He is a sturdy built, rather undersized, but neat colt, by Albert W., out of Nan, by Echo out of Nancy, who was well known as a race mare, but her pedigree could never be traced.

No. 13 is a thick set, dark brown colt, taking more after The Moors than the Electioneers. He is a very rapid gaited colt with plenty of style. He is an inbred Moor by Albert W, dam by Sultan, grandam by The Moor.

No. 5 is a brilliant bright bay colt by Albert W, out of the Jones mare (dam of Senator 2:21½) by Winthrop Morrell 373. He is a good stout built, loose gaited colt, with a very taking action, and should be one of the high priced colts at the sale.

The Jones mare was bred at Winthrop, Maine, and was purchased from Wesley & Balch for Senator John P. Jones of Nevada, but nothing is known of her dam, though anyone can tell from her appearance, even without taking into consideration her produce, that she is a well bred mare.

No. 4 is one of the gems of the catalogue; he is a big brown colt, the biggest in the lot; a loose limbed, rangy customer, with a grand top and beautiful clean legs and feet, and square, straightforward action. He is by Albert W., out of Augusta by Gus, 2:26¾: 2d dam Mollie by Speculation 928; 3d dam Ashcat (dam of Ajax, 2:29, and Hambletonian Jr. 1882) by Hambletonian 10; 4th dam by American Star 14; 6th dam by Abdallah 1. Breeding will tell, and there are in this colt, as can readily be seen, unparalleled strains of blood, and any quantity of the blood of Rysdyk's old horse close up.

No. 17 is a rich red chestnut filly with a white ratch in her face; she is a nice filly, with exceptionally fine bone, and a lengthy, muscular stifle; is by Albert W. out of Cecelia by Poscora Hayward 2889; 2d dam Creole by The Moor 870; 3d dam Madam Gibson by California Ten Broeck.

A white-faced filly attracted a good deal of attention; she is a big, lengthy, rather leggy filly, with wonderfully good hind quarters, and is exceptionally well gaited; can show a fifty gait any time; she is by Cornelius, out of the Hathaway mare (dam of Tippie, 2:25¾) by Hambletonian 725, out of the Denmark mare, by Williamson's Belmont.

No. 19 is a neat brown filly showing lots of quality and shape, and moving in a free natural attractive style. She is by Albert W out of Miss Ryan (sister to Ha Ha 2:22½) by Nephew 1220; 2nd dam Ryan, mare by Black Hawk 767, by grand dam Billings, mare by Royal Oak, son of Black Hawk 5. No. 66 is a big solid good looking, chestnut filly with a grand head and neck, nice sloping shoulders, good girth and close to the ground. She is by Bob Lee out of Dido by Hambletonian 725, 2nd dam by Chieftain 721 grand dam by Billy Wallace, pacer.

No. 31 is a chestnut with a blaze face; excepting his face he is the image of Nutwood, a big strong colt with a deep wide chest and wonderfully imposing when in motion. He is by Robert Lee out of Daphne by Hambletonian 725, 2nd dam Phœbe Carey (a well known trotter) by Chieftain 721, 3rd dam by Jim Crow.

No. 2 is an all brown colt; a big, heavyish topped colt with good shoulders, a long back and with lots of power behind. He is by Albert W. out of Alice Brown by Hambletonian 725, 2nd dam Alice Daniels by Geo. M. Patchen Jr., 3rd dam by Nevada Chief, 4th dam by Shakespeare out of the Robinson mare.

No. 27 is a very promising looking chestnut filly, with perfect shoulders and splendid barrel and a good set of legs. Her action would please the most critical observer, while her breeding equals her looks. She is by Albert W, dam Silica, by Algona; 2nd dam Galena by Nutwood; 3rd dam Eudora by Volunteer 55; 4th dam by American Star 14; 5th dam by Seagullion, son of Duroc.

No. 32 is a stout looking light bay filly with a level topped, solid appearance and exceptionally good sound legs and feet, big knees and clean hocks. She is by Cornelius out of Vixen (dam of Lohengrin 2:27½) by G. M. Patchen Jr, 31; 2nd dam Victress (dam of Monarch 2:28½), by Williamson's Belmont; 3rd dam a Louisiana thoroughbred mare. With the speedy horses already produced by Vixen and Victress, the filly should sell high.

No. 52 is a lively chestnut filly with beautiful clean limbs and good feet. She is by Del Paso 11807 out of Vic by Echo; second dam Victoria by G. M Patchen Jr, 31; 3rd dam Victress (the dam of Monarch 2:28½) by Williamson's Belmont.

No. 39 is a bay filly with a racy looking forehand, by Cornelius, dam by Monday; second dam Ida Martin by Rifleman, etc.

No. 56 is a well bred chestnut filly by Cornelius, dam by Longfield, grandam by Langford.

No. 62 is a dark bay filly with a very good back and shoulders, and on good short legs. She is by Cornelius out of Young Maggie O'Neil, by Echo out of Maggie O'Neil by St. Louis (Bruce's Stud Book).

No. 58 is a powerful short legged light bay filly with splendid shoulders and barrel. She is by Cornelius out of Circly, by Gus 2:26¾; second dam Reta by Geo. M. Patchen Jr, 31; third dam Molly by Speculation 928; fourth dam

Ashcat (dam of Ajax 2:29) by Hambletonian 10, etc., etc. The filly should be hard to buy, with breeding like hers and good looks to back them up.

No. 33 is a useful looking bay filly, a little on the leg, but speedy looking withal, and racy-looking, too. She is by Cornelius, out of Woodbine by Woodburn (thoroughbred son of Lexington), grandam Victress (a well known race mare) by Williamson's Belmont; grandam a Louisiana thoroughbred mare.

No. 23 is a big powerful bay filly with a white star in forehead; she is a Hambletonian all over, and has a grand trotting gait; is by Albert W. out of Reta by Geo. M. Patchen Jr. 31, out of Mollie by Speculation, great grand dam Ashcat (dam of Ajax, 2:29) by Hambletonian 10; next dam by American Star 13, and fifth dam by Abdallah, etc. Hambletonian blood is in the highest place now, and what should a filly like the above be worth? No price could be too dear.

A chestnut filly, unbranded, is very stylish looking, with a remarkably long, muscular stifle and general speedy look; she is by Albert W., dam by Alexander 490; 2d dam by Lancaster, son of Owen Dale; 3d dam Little Blossom by Billy Bell's Blossom.

No. 24 is a very handsome bay, a little light, but wonderfully highly finished; she is by Albert W., dam Ruth by Kentucky Hambletonian; 2d dam Sister to Ruth Ryan, a thoroughbred daughter of Lodi.

No. 28 is a slashing trotter, bay filly, with one white hind pastern; she is by Albert W., out of A Rose by The Moor 870; grandam Cecelia Clark by Clark Chief 89; third dam by Captain Baird, out of a mare by imp. Envoy, etc. See Bruce

No 29 is a medium sized, light bay filly, with white fetlocks, and is a very trim racy looking Electioneer; she is by Albert W dam Young Woodbine by Electioneer, grand dam Woodbine by Woodburn, (son of Lexington) g g d Victress by Williamson Belmont etc. The filly is as can readily be seen an inbred Electioneer and should be almost priceless.

No 26 is a particularly racy looking neat bay filly, by Albert W, out of the Middletown mare, by Middletown 152, 2nd dam Sister to Voltaire 2:20½, by Tattler 300, 3rd dam Young Portia by Mambrino Chief 11, etc. etc.

No 21 is a powerful bay filly, with any quantity of muscle and bone, liable to make a grand roomy broodmare. She is by Albert W, dam Ella, by Speculation 928 grand dam a sister to Hiram Woodruff.

No. 25 is a blocky strongly built bay filly with plenty of quality and bone by Albert W. 2:20, out of Sweet Home 2:30 by Bellfounder 62.

No. 38 is a strong stout looking chestnut filly by Del Paso 11807 out of Kate Brittain by Hambletonian 725 grandam by Grey Messenger Great West. Del Paso is by Algona out of Nettie by Nutwood, second dam by Tattler son of Pilot Jr., third dam Young Portia by MambrinoChief, etc.

No. 16 is a big, lengthy, rangy-looking, brown filly by Albert W. out of Walla Walla Maid by Milliman's Bellfounder 62.

Among the older animals to be sold, none of which have been worked, are some mares which are bound to make good broodmares, and should certainly make good track horses, for they have remarkably clean legs and feet. Among them is a four-year-old brown filly Cordelia by Cornelius out of Mollie by Speculation 928, second dam Ashcap (dam of Ajax 2 29 and by Hambletonian Jr. 1882) Hambletonian 10, etc. The great quantity of Hambletonian blood close is especially noticeable in this mare, and through great sons of his, while further back Seely's American Star and old Abdallah are to be found. A two year-old chestnut filly which was next viewed, was an exceptionally good looking, well bred filly. She is by Albert W out of Marie Roze by Inca 557, second dam Cecilia Clark by Clark Chief 89, etc.

Genevieve a six-year-old bay mare with a deep wide chest, good back and a good set of legs is by Algona out of Jennette by Kentucky Prince, 2nd dam Wayward by Volunteer, etc. A two-year-old bay filly, is particularly handsome, a little high behind and reminds one uncommonly of Norlaine. She is very fast and has been worked a few times and can show a forty gait now. She is by Albert W. out of Echo Queen by Young Echo, 2nd dam Queen of Hearts by Samson 276, 3rd dam Lady Crawford by American Star 14, etc.

Alberta a big strong bay 2-year-old filly with a racy appearance, should sell well; she is by Albert W. out of the Jones mare (dam of Senator 2:23½) by Winthrop Morrill 373.

The grey two year-old is a very shapely neat looking filly, though not as big as some of the others. She is by Albert W., dam by Hambletonian 725, grandam Young Lady Vernon by Easton's David Hill.

A handsome bay mare, four years old, is nicely gaited and fast, should make a wonderful brood mare. She is Cora by Echo out of Rosa Clay by Sayres Henry Clay 45, out of Lady Winfield by Henry Clay 45, 3rd dam by Rattler, son of Abdallah.

Another bay, 4-year-old mare is also by Echo. Her dam Alice Brown is by Hambletonian 725 out of Alice Daniels by G. M. Patchen Jr., 31.

A bay brown filly with a plainish head but otherwise good looking all over, has only been halter broken. She is by Cornelius out of Miss Ryan (sister to Ha Ha 2:22½) by Nephew 220, etc).

A four-year-old gray filly is a full sister to Elmonte 2:29, by Echo, dam Lightfoot by Hubbard (son of Planet, sire of Dame Winnie).

The four-year-old daughter of Algona and Victoria by G. M. Patchen Jr., 31, out of Victress, dam of Monarch 2:28½, a big, rangy chestnut with very powerful but rather ragged looking hind quarters.

A rich red chestnut filly three years old, is a little heavy shouldered, but well muscled and powerful all over; she is called Gussie Hamilton, by Victor, out of Young Lady Hamilton by Western, out of Lady Hamilton (dam of Arab 2:15).

Teacher, a three-year-old sister to Senator, 2:21½, is a bay mare with an Echo head, a wide chest, good flat knees and hocks; she is unbroken, and should prove fast; she is by Echo out of the Jones mare by Winthrop Morrill 373.

The three-year-old Alaska fillies out of Galena by Nutwood and Cicely by Gus 2:26¾, should sell remarkably well, for they are both good lookers, and of unparalled breeding.

Mollie Hamilton by Victor Patchen, half brother to Monarch 2:28½, out of Young Lady Hamilton by Western, out of dam of Arab 2:15, reminds one uncommonly of Arab, and should be invaluable for any purpose.

A two year old chestnut stallion is by Albert W out of Cecilia by Poscora Hayward 2839, grandam Creole by The Moor 870; third dam Madam Gibson by California Ten Broeck. He is a good dark chestnut with a nicely shaped head, good neck, sloping shoulders, and muscular back he is on good sound short legs and particularly well gaited.

There are a host of other well bred mares, but lack of space prevents their being gone through. The geldings are one of the grandest collections that have ever left the stall, and among them should be several fast trotters. None of them have been tried, some few only having been broken, but all are wonderfully gentle,

Grim's Gossip.

June, the full sister to Nelson 2:14½, has been bred to Antevolo 2:19½. The result should be a rare good trotter.

Scott Quinton is authority for the statement that the storms prevent the early education of colts in Montana.

"The Northern King" is a pet name used by the breeders of Maine, Vermont, and New Hampshire, when speaking of Nelson 2:14½.

I have received word from John A. Goldsmith that Mamie Comet 2:23½, foaled on the 9th inst, twins, by Sable Wilkes 2:18; both dead.

J. C. Sibley of Franklin, Pa., has been in town for a few days. He has examined a good many horses, and purchased two from Mr. Ariel Lathrop, for which he paid $15,000.

In the list of horses published Jan. 18th as likely to start on the circuit during 1890 the name of Soudan 2:27½ was omitted. If in good condition he should make a much lower mark.

J. F. Maguire, who has lately been located at Fresno, has decided to stand his well bred horse Fresno at Suisun for the coming season "Jim" has been made a handsome offer for the colt, but has refused to sell.

W. J. Prather of Fresno has lately purchased from Jesse Harris of Fort Collins, Col., Cleveland Rosuleaf, a bay mare by Sportsman. She is claimed to be the finest Cleveland bay ever brought to the State and is registered in both England America'

"Big Jim" Garland and W McCormick has purchased from Theodore Winters the colt Black Bart by Three Cheers The price given is not stated, but he is cheap at any reasonable figure, for I have received positive assurance that he is a first class colt.

Monroe Salisbury Esq. of Pleasanton has sold to D. M. Reavis of Chico the well known stallion Monroe Chief 2:18½, by Jim Monroe, dam Madam Powell. He has also purchased from Mr. Reavis two Director fillies for which he paid $6,000.

D. Scott Quinton is paying a visit to his many friends in San Francisco. He reports that Marcus Daly will not have any trotters on the track this year, and although he has had several flattering offers for some of his horses, he positively refuses to sell any of them.

James Corcoran, well and favorably known to all horsemen of the State, has located at the Oakland track, where he will be prepared to take horses to train. Jim is a good, capable man, sober and industrious, and will give satisfaction to any one who may patronize him.

In the list of horses likely to start on the circuit this year, published in our issue of Jan. 18th, Belle A. was credited as having a record of 2:32. This was an oversight of the compiler as Belle A. made a mark of 2:29 at Sacramento, on Thursday, the second week of the fair.

Joe Courtney has started East with the Winters' two year olds, the destination being Nashville. Alf Estill, the stable manager, will leave Reno on Sunday to take charge. Now that McCormick has resigned his position as trainer for Mr. Winters, Courtney will in all probability train the horses for the present.

A dispatch from Monrovia, Los Angeles county, says: An alarming disease prevails among horses. The symptoms are those of cholera. Veterinarians believe they have been poisoned. E C. Valentine's valuable sorrel horse died in the early part of the week. He had a record of 2:40½

At a meeting of the Directors of the Sonoma and Marin Agricultural Society, held at Petaluma last Saturday, they decided to add Contra Costa county to the list of Counties from which horses are eligible for all district races. As Contra Costa has several breeding farms, there should be large additions to the usual entry list.

Now that the figures are being made up, it seems Onward, 2:25¼, leads all the sons of George Wilkes in the number of trotters to his credit. He has twenty six 2:30 performers in the list, twenty-three trotters and three pacers. Red Wilkes is a close second, with twenty trotters and six pacers. Onward was foaled in 1875, and Red Wilkes in 1874.

The newly elected officers of the Seventeenth District Agricultural Association: M. L. Marsh, President; Charles L. Mitchell, Vice-President; I. J. Rolfe, Secretary; Senator E. M. Breston, Treasurer. The races will be held at Glenbrook Park, in the week beginning August 19 h. This makes another clash in the northern circuit. The associations all seem at loggerheads this year.

From the weights announced for the Brooklyn Handicap it would seem that Sir Dixon has a pretty good cinch on first money. The Suburban weights are far from being equitable, and already complaints are being heard. In the Volunteer Handicap Flambeau and Fellowcharm are both in very favorably, but many changes could be advantageously made, that is if a close finish would add to the attractiveness of racing.

The Californians who are planning a summer campaign either in Montana, or father East, should not forget the Overland Club of Denver. The directors are offering liberal inducements to horse owners, the betting is always good there, the accommodations are of the best and the track is a first class one, so that a lay off at Denver may prove a profitable investment for those contemplating an Eastern trip. Read the advertisement.

From Bruce Cockrill, who came down from the ranch on the Arroyo Seco Thursday, we learn that the grand old thoroughbred stallion Ironclad, property of the Cockrill Bros., died Jan. 27th, from the rupture of a blood vessel in the brain, says the Salinas Democrat. This is a sad loss as the animal was very valuable, and was greatly prized by the owners. Ironclad was 21 years old but spry as a colt up to the day of his death.

'Aurelius' in a communication to the New York "Sportsman" refers to that branch of the Mambrino family represented by Gen. Benton. Come to think of it, Aurelius is right. Hambletonian 10 stands first as a speed producer in that line, General Benton 1755 second, and Mambrino Chief 11 third. Who dare predict that General Benton's 'branch' will not in breeding overhaul the great Mambrino Chief in the course of time? and possibly press hard upon Hambletonian's heels.

James A. Dustin has accepted a position at Palo Alto, being second in command to Chas. Marvin. This will be a great relief to Mr. Marvin, who in the past has had to do both training and finishing as well as the driving, but now that he has "Jimmy's" master hand to assist him, the work should prove less arduous.

My old friend Daniel Geary, who for the last five years has been associated with Wallace's Monthly and the American trotting register, has joined forces with the N. Y. Sportsman having severed his connections with the former publications. Mr. Geary is one of the best catalogue compilers in the country and is at present getting up a very complete one for Wm. Corbitt of the San Mateo Stock Farm.

L. M Lasby has bought of G. A. Lackey, of Lincoln Co., Ky., one three-year-old ch f by St. Martin, dam by Harry O'Fallon; 2nd dam by Bayonette, etc., for $300 Also, of Jas. B. Gentry, of Lincoln Co., Ky, one two-year-old b f by Leonatus, dam Trumpetta by Trumpington (son of Leamington and the Gloaming by Glencoe) for $400, and has shipped them to Nashville to join the rest of his string. The Leonatus filly is a full sister to Chinn Music, who will soon be heard from.

Some weeks ago we acknowledged the receipt of a handsome picture of Nutwood 2:18¾ from his owners, the Stout Bros. of Dubuque, Iowa. Since then we have received a companion portrait from the Woodburn Farm, of the late stallion Belmont 64, which is a very handsome striking likeness of the great horse. He is the sire of Nutwood, 2:18¾; Wedgewood, 2:19; Viking 2:19½, and twenty-nine others in the 2:30 list. There is a very marked resemblance between Belmont and his great son Nutwood.

Many of the sporting papers of this country has made the assertion that the Melbourne Cup of 1890 will be the richest event ever contested for, but I am inclined to the belief that this is a mistake. A little figuring, part of which will have to be guessing, will tend to show that the cup will not be worth as much as the Futurity of 1890. The owner of Chaos received more money for winning the Futurity last year than will the owner of the next Melbourne Cup.

Speaking of the Melbourne Cup, the N. Y. Spirit says: "We ought to have such a handicap here, one like it at two miles, not the miserable little quarter horse cocktail affairs which are so common. Ben Bruce in his Live Stock Record advocates long distance handicaps, and his idea is worth adoption," and I heartily concur. The much despised Clifton association, under the able management of Mr. C. V. Sass, has inaugurated a series of the old time long races and they have been highly successful Let the good work go on.

P. J. Phillips, a prominent farmer and well known horseman who recently purchased the Jirah Luce ranch in Mendocino township, died at Mrs. Patterson's boarding house, in this city, at an early hour Monday morning. He had been sick only nine days and his symptoms were not regarded as serious until a day or two before his death. For some months past he had been giving personal supervision to the training of his trotting stock at Agriculture Park. Being of a genial, jovial disposition, he made many friends here by whom his death will be much regretted. The deceased was a native of New York and aged 59 years. The remains were taken charge of by his son from Healdsburg, where his wife and two sons reside, and in which community he was well known and highly respected.—(Santa Rosa Republican.)

There are a great number of mares, trotters and thoroughbreds, who have slipped foals in this vicinity, and breeders are at a loss to account for their number and frequency, says the Live Stock Record of Lexington, Ky. It has been a remarkable open winter and the grass is green and succulent. Some are inclined to think that the action of frost on the green and succulent grass is the cause of the miscarriages, the bowls becoming relaxed from the improper nature of the food. Besides the nature of food Stonehenge, says: 'Excitement of any kind is a fertile source of 'slipping' the foal, and anything which is at all likely to have that effect should be carefully avoided. The smell of blood is said to have a very prejudical influence in this way, and there is no doubt that one mare miscarrying will in some mode affect others in proximity to her. Possibly the same cause may act on all, but it seems to be generally concluded that the act is really contagious, either from what is called sympathy or in some other as inexplicable way."

Mr. Sibley's comparative tables between the race records of Geo. Wilkes' and Electioneer's produce seems to have raised a hornet's nest around that gentleman's head, the very best proof that the Wilkes' camp has been taken by surprise. The most amusing part is the claim now made that Electioneer had the very best mares that money could procure; whereas two or three years ago Eastern visitors would return from Palo Alto commenting on the 'inferior' class of mares that were used and owned at that establishment. The toughest thing to get over is the fact that, as regards 'fashionable' breeding, the majority of them were 'inferior', but have been made 'great' and 'fashionable' through the potency of Electioneer himself.

'Primus' in the N. Y. '*Spirit of the Times*' loses his temper and forgets his manners, closing his article as follows:

"After carefully studying the outline of Electioneer, etc. etc, etc."

Fie! Primus! Fie! Go look at William L's leg! But leg or nor leg, his son Axtell held a pretty long pole, when it came to knocking the persimmons! But Sunol held a longer one!

A new correspondent writes me as follows.

Noticing in a recent number of your valuable journal a call for correspondents, and realizing that we of Lake County are almost unknown in horse annals, I will contribute from time to time what I can to assist you in your efforts for the advancement and progress of horse breeding, and at the same time give your readers some idea of our county and its horses.

Lake County is adapted as is no other portion of the State for the growth and constant development of the horse throughout the year. Its climate being neither too warm to weaken by rapid growth nor too cold to retard, produces strong, hardy animals. Its combination of mountain and valley and timely rains, secure the necessary variety of feed. As a result of these advantages we have already several breeding farms. The lovers of horse flesh, though few, make up in enthusiasm, what is lacking in numbers, and are determined to put themselves right to the front. Of our horses, pedigrees and further information, more anon,

THE WEEKLY

Breeder and Sportsman.

JAMES P. KERR, PROPRIETOR.

The Turf and Sporting Authority of the Pacific Coast.

Office, No. 313 Bush St.

P. O. Box 2300.

TERMS—*One Year, $5; Six Months, $3; Three Months, $1.50.* STRICTLY IN ADVANCE.

Money should be sent by postal order, draft or by registered letter, addressed to JAMES P. KERR, San Francisco, Cal.

Communications must be accompanied by the writer's name and address, not necessarily for publication, but as a private guarantee of good faith.

ALEX. P. WAUGH, - - - - - Editor.

Advertising Rates

Per Square (half inch)

One time	$1 50
Two times	2 50
Three times	3 25
Four times	4 00

And each subsequent insertion 75c. per square.

Advertisements running six months are entitled to 10 per cent. discount.

Those running twelve months are entitled to 20 per cent. discount.

Reading notices set in same type as body of paper, 50 cents per line each insertion.

To Subscribers.

The date printed on the wrapper of your paper indicates the time to which your subscription is paid.

Should the BREEDER AND SPORTSMAN be received by any subscriber who does not want it, write us direct to stop it. A postal card will suffice.

Special Notice to Correspondents.

Letters intended for publication should reach this office not later than Wednesday of each week, to secure a place in the issue of the following Saturday. Such letters to insure immediate attention should be addressed to the BREEDER AND SPORTSMAN, and not to any member of the staff.

San Francisco, Saturday, Feb. 15, 1890.

Stallions Advertised

IN THE

BREEDER AND SPORTSMAN.

Thoroughbreds.

FRIAR TUCK, Hermit—Romping Girl.........C. W. Aby, Middletown.
GREENBACK, Dollar—Music.........C. W. Aby, Middletown.
INTRUDER, Crater—Lady Bountiful.........T. J. Knight, Sacramento.
ST. SAVIOR, Eolus—War Song.........C. W. Aby, Middletown.
REVEILLE, Shiloh—Norfolk.........B. C. Holly, Vallejo.

Trotters.

ARBITRATOR, Director—Lady Earnest.........H. A. Mayhew, Niles.
ANTEEOP, Anteeo—Bessie G.........Guy E. Grosse, Santa Rosa.
ANTEEOP, Anteeo—Nance.........Guy E. Grosse, Santa Rosa.
ADMIRO, Admiral—dam by San Bruno.........Smith & Sutherland, Pleasanton.
ASHLAND ALMONT, Almont—Pauline.........T. J. Whitehead, Oakland.
ANTEROS NUTWOOD, Anteros—Newark Belle.........T. W. Barstow, San Jose.
ALEXANDER BUTTON, Alexander—Lady Button.........Cache Creek Farm, Yolo.
APEX, Prompter—Mary.........Poplar Grove Breeding Farm, Wildflower.
ALCONA, Almont—Queen Mary.........Fred W. Loeber, St. Helena
BALKAN, Mambrino Wilkes—Fanny Fern.........A. L. Hinds, Oakland.
BONANZA, Arthurton—Sister.........Richard Havey, Oakland
BAY ROSE, Sultan—Madam Baldwin.........W. W. Ayres, Oakland.
CLOVIS, Sultan—Sweetbriar.........Poplar Grove Breeding Farm, Wildflower.
CUPID, Sidney—Venus.........C. O. Thornquest, Oakland
CHRISMAN'S HAMBLETONIAN 10178, Whipple's Hambletonian—Flora Jesse Chrisman, San Jose
CANNON BALL, Simmons—Gurgie.........Lockhaven Stock Farm, Burbank.
CHARLES DERBY, Steinway—by Electioneer. Cook Stock Farm, Contra Costa Co.
CRESCO, Strathmore—Spartan.........Cook Stock Farm, Contra Costa Co
CALIFORNIA NUTWOOD, Nutwood—Fanny Patchen.........Martin Carter, Alameda Co.
DEXTER PRINCE, Kentucky Prince—Lady Dexter.........L. Mc Morse, Lodi.
DAWN, Nutwood—Countess.........A. L. Whitney, Petaluma
DIRECTOR, Dictator—Dolly.........Pleasanton Stock Farm, Pleasanton.
DON MARVIN, Fallis—Cora.........F. P. Lowell, Sacramento
ELECTO, Antevolo, dam by Capt. Webster.........G. W. Stimpson, Oakland
ELECTION, Electioneer—Lizzie H.........B. C. Holly, Vallejo.
ELEGANCE.........G. W. Stimpson, Oakland
EL BENTON, Electioneer—Nellie Benton.........Souther Farm, San Leandro.
ECLECTIC, Electioneer—Manette.........Wilfred Page, Sonoma County
EROS, Electioneer—Sontag Mohawk.........W. H. Vioget, Menlo Park
FIGARO, Hambletonian—Emblem.........Souther Farm, San Leandro.
GROVER CLAY, Electioneer—Maggie Norfolk.........Denis Gannon, Oakland.
G. & M., Anteeo—Rosa B.........George E. Guerne, Santa Rosa.
GUY WILKES, George Wilkes—Lady Bunker.........San Mateo Stock Farm, San Mateo.
GLEN FORTUNE, Electioneer—Glenna.........Souther Farm, San Leandro.
GEORGE WASHINGTON, Mambrino Chief—Fanny Rose.........Thos. Smith, Vallejo.
GUIDE, Director—Imogene.........Smith & Sutherland, Pleasanton.
GRANDISSIMO, LeGrande—Norma.........Fred W. Loeber, St Helena
ILLUSTRIOUS, Happy Medium—Abdalletta.........George A. Stone, Santa Rosa.
JESTER D, Almont—Hortense.........Souther Farm, San Leandro
JUNIO, Electioneer—by Granger.........S. N. Straube, Fresno.
KAFIR, Alcazar—Flower Girl.........B. C. Holly, Vallejo.
LEO WILKES, Guy Wilkes—Sable.........San Mateo Stock Farm, San Mateo.
LYNWOOD, Nutwood—Hattie Morrison.........P. Visher, Stockton.
MEMO, Sidney—Flirt.........Valensin Stock Farm, Pleasanton.
MOUNTAIN BOY, Kentucky Prince—Elsie.........B. C. Holly, Vallejo.
MAMBRINO WILKES, George Wilkes—Lady Chrisman.........San Miguel Stock Farm, Walnut Creek.
MART ROORHEM, Sidney—Towhead.........B. C. Holly, Vallejo.
MAMBRINO JR. 1789, Mambrino Patchen, dam by Mambrino Chief Geo. P. Bull, San Jose.
MAMBRINO CHIEF, McDonald Chief—Venus.........Thos. Smith, Vallejo.
MORTIMER, Electioneer—Marti.........Wilfred Page, Sonoma County
NOONDAY, Wedgewood—Noontide.........F. P. Lowell, Sacramento.
PLEASANTON, Director—May Day.........Pleasanton Stock Farm, Pleasanton.
PASHA, Sultan—Madam Baldwin.........D. Bryson, Linden
PILOT NUTWOOD, Nutwood—Belle.........T. W. Barstow, San Jose.
PHILOSOPHER, Pilot Wilkes—Belle.........George E. Guerne, Santa Rosa.
ROY WILKES, Adrian Wilkes—Flora.........Pleasanton Stock Farm Pleasanton.
REDWOOD, Anteeo—Lou Wilton.........A. McFayden, Oakland.
SILVER BOW, Robert McGregor—Sadie.........P. J. Williams, Oakland.
STEINWAY, Strathmore—Abbess.........Cook Stock Farm, Contra Costa Co
SUNSET, Anteeo—Bessie G.........Guy E. Grosse, Santa Rosa.
SHAMROCK, Bucaneer—Fernleaf.........G. W. Stimpson, Oakland
SIDNEY, Santa Claus—Sweetness.........Valensin Stock Farm, Pleasanton.
SIMMOCOLON, Simmons—Colon.........Valensin Stock Farm, Pleasanton.
SABLE WILKES, Guy Wilkes—Sable.........San Mateo Stock Farm, San Mateo.
ST. NICHOLAS, Sidney—Towhead.........John Rowen, Oakland Trotting Park.
WOODNUT, Nutwood—Flora.........Jas. Weatherhead, San Jose
WHIPPLETON 1883, Hambletonian Jr.—Lady Livingston.........Fred W. Loeber, St. Helena
WOODSIDE, Woodnut—Veronica.........B. C. Holly, Vallejo.

Dates Claimed.

FRESNO (Spring Meeting)	March 15th to 29th
SAN JOSE (Blood Horse Meeting)	April 5th, 7th and 9th
NAPA	Aug. 18th to 23rd
SAN JOSE (Fall Meeting)	Aug 25th to 29th inclusive
PETALUMA	Aug. 25th to 30th
OAKLAND (District No. 1)	Sept. 1st to Sept. 6th
CALIFORNIA STATE FAIR	Sept. 8th to 20th
FRESNO (Fall Meeting)	Sept. 29th to Oct. 4th

The Sale of a Race Track.

The BREEDER AND SPORTSMAN contains an advertisement of the offer for sale of the race track and grounds of the Sonoma County Agricultural Park Association, in Santa Rosa. The sale is announced to be made by sealed bids, and not by public auction. Bids will be received until Monday, February 17th.

The sale of an established race track of wide and popular reputation is an unusual event in the records of the turf; still sales of the kind have been made in California and in the older States of the East, owing to circumstances and conditions. But the offer of sale of a leading race track, finely equipped, with ample and handsomely arranged and carefully cultivated grounds, fitted equally for local annual Agricultural Fairs and stated seasonable racing meetings, is in California an extraordinary circumstance.

The property offered for sale consists of eighty four acres of choice land eligibly situated within one mile of Santa Rosa. To it an elegant drive extends from the railroad depots and from the principal points of the city, by cleanly roads and pretty suburban homes. These grounds comprise the handsome Pavilion, built in 1883, the capacious grand stand, the stands for the judges, officers, reporters and turfmen; the long lines of stables for horses and sheds for cattle; the sheep pens and departments for swine and poultry, etc. These buildings are in good condition. The track is reputed one of the best in the State, with good turns and a fine home stretch. A secure high fence is built all about the track, and is well shaded and protected by a dense green hedge. An unfailing supply of water is assured. Adjoining the track and pavilion site is an area of delightful rides and strolls, of indigenous trees of shade and beauty, and of nut-bearing trees of choice variety—black walnut and other kinds.

More interesting to any who contemplate the purchase of this class of property is the character of the track and its history. The Association was organized in 1878 as an Agricultural Park and Fair Association. Since that year, until 1889, annual fairs and exhibitions have been held, with varying success, but generally with gratifying measure of prosperousness and brighter hopes. The Association has, first and last, expended in the purchase of the grounds, the erection of buildings, in securing permanent water supply, in improvements of every kind, a total of $40,000. Lands in the vicinity, with simply ordinary farm improvements, command from $175 to $275 per acre. A sale at $300 per acre is of record. The buildings of all kinds have cost above $12,000. A line of street railway runs between the track and the principal streets, near the Court House. A fashionable and favorite drive is out to the Park grounds, from the city.

Among the noted breeders who were early patrons of the Santa Rosa track the names of Judge James Mc M. Shafter and Theodore Winters are recalled. During later years the foremost of the turf regularly attended the annual fairs and meetings. Careful management, good order and pleasant association, gained reputation for the place and drew large attendance. Noble sport was cultivated. Leading horsemen visited and raced their best horses. Santa Rosa was duly assigned a favorable place in the ranking circuit—Santa Rosa, Petaluma, Napa, Oakland, Sacramento, Stockton and San Jose. The track and arrangements had advanced to prominent popularity.

With its records of the past to its recommendation, it is at first glance unaccountable that a property so eligible and so valuable as this Santa Rosa race track property is, is now offered for sale. The people in and about Santa Rosa will be much affected by a sale unless the track and grounds are to be continued in their present use. It will be a mistake in much consequent effect if the ground and track shall be abandoned and diverted to other uses.

Santa Rosa is in the fronting category of Fairs and Turf meetings, and to drop out of this prospering line will be equivalent to a recession of her former and fitting consideration. Sonoma County cannot afford to allow a sacrifice of the property to carry with it the abandonment of the annual fairs which have so worthily distinguished Santa Rosa in past years. The greatest events of the turf are expected to occur in California, with California bred horses, in the year now opened, and Sonoma, with Santa Rosa, occupies pridefu l position in the reckoning. The merits of Anteeo, of Dawn, of Albert G., of Button, and of others of high speed, are remembered and should not be forgotten nor neglected. The Santa Rosa race track should belong to Sonoma citizens, and be held by them to its accustomed uses.

The P. C. T. H. B. A.

The Pacific Coast Trotting Horse Breeders Association has advertised the colt stakes and purses for its fall meeting of 1890. Its first was the most memorable and phenomenal trotting meeting in the history and annals of the trotting turf and in its benefits to the trotting horse interests and breeders of this coast, it fairly eclipsed the great advertisement and impetus that those interests received through the great National Trotting Stallion Race of the preceding year between Stamboul, Woodnut and Antevolo.

After the great race alluded to, each of the competitors therein sold for what were then considered exceptional prices, Stamboul bringing $50,000, Woodnut $20,000, and Antevolo $18,000. It will be noted therefore, that a good horse may be beaten and still bring a small fortune. There is no doubt but that in the main, these handsome figures were the result of that one great race.

Mr. Bonner doubtless gave between $40,000 and $50,000 for Sunol and did this, before she had, and when but few, if any, believed that she could publicly prove her ability to beat Axtell's record of 2:12. Does any one doubt (had the 'dicker' not been made in such good time) Mr. Bonner would not have willingly added 25 or even 50 per cent. to the higher sum named to have become her owner after she had achieved 2:10½?

We know that $35,000 was offered and refused for Regal Wilkes. Here then are two three-year-olds and one of them a filly, that would have sold for about as much as the three aged stallions brought as the fruits of the preceding year's race. The prestige that Faustino gained by his remarkable mile (on the same day that Sunol and Regal Wilkes made their records), would, had he been placed under the hammer after that achievement undoubtedly have balanced the values of the three stallions without a cent's allowance over the actual sale price of Sunol.

There is not a breeder of trotting horses among us, even though he own only one good broodmare but was benefited by the prices obtained or offered to fortunate possessors of these wonderful colts. The prices and the remarkable achievements of the colts are a standing advertisement of the valuable and productive blood strains that are used on the coast, and are an advertisement which will annually bring hundreds of purchasers from the East in search of a few slices of the good things we are so lucky as to own.

The fact that the opportunity for these great things are afforded by and are under the management of an association controlled by reputable breeders and lovers of the trotting horse, intent upon reviving and building up the public interest and confidence, in fair and honest speed contests on the trotting turf, is a guarantee that nothing so much as savoring of a 'job' is or will be permitted, and it therefore becomes the duty and the interest of every breeder on the coast to lend his aid, financial as well as moral, to strengthen and support that association.

We regret to say that last year many a breeder excused himself from joining the association at that time, on the grounds that he had no colts to start at its first meeting. Others, again, gave as a reason for not supporting it, the fact that the Directors had failed to offer any stakes in which they might enter the produce of their untried stallions other than against the get of such phenomenal speed producers as Electioneer, Sidney, Director and Guy Wilkes.

Those giving the first excuse we would remind that, had the one hundred or less gentlemen who gave their time, labor and money and took the risk of meeting with financial disaster, looked upon the formation of the association in as narrow a light and with an eye solely to immediate self-interest, there would not have been to exceed two dozen members, and the grandest of trotting meetings would not have been held in this State.

To those who decline to risk defeat by measuring the speed of their colts against those of Electioneer, Guy Wilkes, etc., etc., we would say that the present Board of Directors have offered fair purses, entrance whereto is payable in easy installments, and to which only the produce of stallions that have no representatives in the 2:30 list are eligible.

The breeders do not, as a rule, look to money making as the prime purpose in entering their colts in purses and stakes. Their main idea is to advertise their stallions by the public performances of their produce, and with this belief in view the Directors have wisely restricted the amounts of purses and stakes, and have made the payments lighter and easier than they were last year to those whose entries may be injured or otherwise incapacitated from starting.

The stakes and purses already advertised will close on March 1st next, and with the exception of the Stanford Stakes, are, so far as horses owned on this coast are concerned, confined to those owned by members of the association.

The membership or initiation fee is $25; the annual dues $10. Surely there is no man owning a stallion standing for as small a sum even as $35, but what can afford to give the value of one stallion service in the interest of such an association. It cannot but be returned to him an hundred fold within three years and perhaps less time, and will certainly go further to help him than the offering of $100 apiece for any and every colt by his horse that may be placed in the 2:30 list.

The P. C. T. H. B. Association should number between four and five hundred members, and if it does not show at least two hundred names of reputable breeders and owners of trotting horses on its roll *from this State alone* before its next meeting, all we can say is that they cannot or do not appreciate and realize the benefits that accrue from an association of its character, and with its objects and purposes.

Probably the greatest and most popular of trotting meetings held in this country is the Breeders' Annual Meeting, at Lexington, Ky., under the management of just such a society as was organized here last year, and whose name is at the head of this article.

In Kentucky, second only to California as a producer of great trotting horses, and way ahead of it so far as numbers bred are concerned, there are neither bickerings nor jealousies between the great breeders, nor as between the great and the small breeders; they hang together, swear by each other's horses, and help one another, knowing that in so doing *each one is helping himself*.

Of course it is not, and cannot be, every breeder's luck to own a great sire—a phenomenal producer of speed; neither can everybody afford to pay $50,000, or even $5,000 for a stallion, but there is money—big money—in trotting horses at far lower figures than those named, and for every man who seeks a $50,000 stallion, there are a thousand who will choose the purchase of a well-bred one at $1,000, and a still greater proportion seeking individuals at $500; and who dare predict that the modest $500 stallion will not out-trot, out-last, and out-breed the $50,000 fashionable aristocrat? Such things have happened before, and they will continue to happen as long as breeders use their brains and the "proved" trotting strains. To-day fashion sells; to morrow blood tells, and, presto! blood becomes a new fashion, and fashion again sells!

There is no telling whose well bred, but untried stallion, is on the brink of fame; nor whose $20,000 or $50,000 stallion may not be tottering over the precipice of oblivion. Like breeds like, *or the likeness of some ancestor*, is the corner-stone of the breeder's beliefs and theories, but unfortunately the ancestors are sometimes very disheartening material, and when the colt of to-day turns out to be the likeness of one of *such* ancestors, his $50,000 purchaser, on the strength of fashion and individual performance only, is apt to bitterly rue his haste.

The least known stallion on the coast to-day, if bred right and bred on, may three years hence be commanding $250 or $300 per mare; therefore it is that we say the interests and benefits of the great and prominent breeding farms are those of every breeder on the coast, and in no way can all breeders better uphold, strengthen and advertise those interests and share in its benefits, than by encouraging and supporting, or, to use plain English, joining the Pacific Coast Trotting Horse Breeder's Association, and swelling the list of entries to and of starters in its colt stakes and purses.

Persons desirous of fully informing themselves as to the purposes and objects of the association, should apply to the secretary, Jas. P. Kerr, Secretary, 313 Bush St., San Francisco, for a copy of the By-Laws and Constitution now in the printer's hands.

A German Horse Exposition.

After the many horse expositions that we have had in the United States within the past two years, and also the annual horse fairs held in Great Britain, it would seem that Germany is about to follow in the footsteps of the countries named, as we have received a notice from the German Consul, which as it is self-explanatory, we copy in full.

San Francisco, Feb. 5, 1890.

Editor Breeder and Sportsman:—The Union Club in Berlin is arranging for a general exposition of German horses to take place at Berlin during the time from the 12th to the 22nd of June, 1890. It will be the task of the enterprise to show the development of horse breeding in Germany, and to manifest that the product there is not inferior to that of other countries.

Being aware that California holds a high rank in the production of fine horses, and assuming that the readers of your esteemed paper will take some interest in the matter, I beg to ask you to advise them of the exposition at Berlin through the columns of the Breeder and Sportsman. I am, sir, yours most respectfully,

Adolph Rosenthal,
Consul for the German Empire.

D. Scott Quintin's Interview.

"Great Scott! What yer givin' us?" The exclamation naturally rose to our lips on perusing the interview of D. Scott Quintin by the Horseman's representative. "In California, even the rubbers get $60 a month!" Good enough (for the rubbers, if they only got it)!

Scott Quintin did not strike us as 'that sort of a fellow' when out here, and we are afraid that either he must have been indulging in Jersey apple-jack or the other chap must have had something stouter aboard when that interview was held.

"We were preparing to go back home (with Yolo Maid) when there were propositions for matches."

Every body here knows that Yolo Maid was 'off' after the great race she raced at Sacramento; everybody also knows that Adonis was just working into form when he came against her there and that there was no day after that race until rain fell, but that he would have forced the gallant mare to badly beat the 2:12½, she then put to her credit three consecutive times to have won the race from the speedy son of Sidney.

We all saw Yolo Maid work out two heats in the Bay District Track during the Breeder's Meeting better than 2:16, the last quarters in 31½ and 31½; but still friend Quintin claimed his mare not to be 'at herself' and was unwilling to start against Adonis. We take as much pride in Yolo Maid as in Adonis, possibly more, friend Quintin, but Mr. Daly was not lying at the point of death during the Breeder's Meeting, at which his horse, *Lord Byron*, started in the free-for-all.

"Favonia scared them all, however, for when I entered in the California Circuit everybody else drew out. When we crossed the mountains there was one class in which I had made an entry, and promised not to name Favonia."

We will wager a big red apple that Scott Quintin never said any such thing; nor that he made any such promise. We are perfectly willing to acknowledge that one of our breeders publicly stated that he would not start his five-year-old stallion against Favonia; but as to Palo Alto, Alfred S., Lot Slocum or Lillie Stanley being afraid to start against Favonia, that is all 'in my eye.'

Before Mr. Quintin started for his mountain home (aside from the Breeders' Meeting) for his fast and game mare, as an inducement to bring her along, and if I am not misinformed, the same promise was accompanied by the supplementary one, to send her back home 'beaten' by one, if not two of her competitors.

"When we went to California with Mr. Daly's string we found the local talent intrenched in the good graces of the race managers."

We hope that D. S. Quintin will publicly disavow having made any such innuendo against the 'race managers' on this coast. Those same managers or some of them under whom Mr. Quintin trotted his races, 'managed' to do pretty fair justice to Mr. Crawford in his $10,000 bet against one of our most popular horsemen, when as Mr. Crawford has himself said, the time as it *would have been* announced anywhere in the *East*, would have lost him that bet. The 'fact' in the latter and the 'innuendo' in the former instance seem rather ill-mated—*they don't hitch!*

Mr Quintin now has the floor!

Challenges.

O. A. Hickok, Esq., City:—

Dear Sir: As you would not accept my proposition to make a race between Adonis and Roy Wilkes, to take place Feb. 15th [proposition made the first week in Dec.], I have concluded to match Roy Wilkes against Adonis at the time you wanted to go last Dec., viz., the first week in April. I will make this match for $2,500 a side, to take place at the Bay District track on April 5th, 1890. We can arrange regarding the gate receipts, starting judge and judges later on. I shall expect you to reimburse my expenses as per your telegram to me at Chicago, before I started, viz. transportation for myself, horse and man to and from Chicago, with any incidental expenses appertaining, all of which are close to $400; to be ascertained, however.

I have deposited $500 with the Breeder and Sportsman, as forfeit, where I will meet you at any time to arrange further particulars.

Roy is, and will continue to be, in stud service. I shall leave for the East with him the second week in April, and hope you will agree to the above date. I arrived here, you will remember, Nov. 4th; will have been here five months, surely long enough to make a race. I want an early reply.

Respectfully,
L. A. Davies.

Hotel Pleasanton, San Francisco, Feb. 10th, 1890.

Mr. C. H. Cory, San Jose, Cal :—

Dear Sir: I noticed in a San Francisco weekly paper of Feb. 8th, also in the issue of same paper of Feb. 1st, that you had expressed a willingness to match your horse against Roy Wilkes 2:12½.

I have several times offered to make this match, and have deposited a forfeit of $500 for a match from $1,000 to $5,000 a side without avail. You have *never* in any of your letters offered to *make* a match for *any* sum, but have always been quite non-committal, you expressing yourself thus in answer to my challenge to go for $1,000 a side: "$1,000 a side is too small a sum for two such great horses to compete for. Ask Mr. Davies if he will go for $5,000 a side;" to which I promptly replied through our mutual friend, Mr. Alex Waugh, "Yes." You did not appear to cover the forfeit, but evaded the point, and replied that you were very busy, etc.

For the last time I will say that I will match Roy Wilkes against your horse [Almont Patchen], and I sincerely hope you will accept one of the propositions made herein.

1st. I will match Roy Wilkes against your horse for $2500 a side, best three in five, to harness.

2nd. If you will bet $3,000 to $1,500, I will match Roy Wilkes *to go to wagon*, your horse to go to *sulky;* best three in five.

The race to take place on March 29th, at the Bay District track, the winner to take all the net receipts.

I have deposited with the Breeder and Sportsman a certified check on the Pacific Bank for $500 forfeit, for either of the above propositions, and will meet you there at any time to arrange further details.

Roy Wilkes is now doing stud service and will continue in that capacity up to the first of April; he will cover from twenty to twenty-four mares.

Thus handicapped, you should not hesitate in making one of the above matches.

Roy Wilkes will be taken East the second week in April, and can not go later [in a race] than the time mentioned. We shall have nearly two months for preparation, so there will be no advantage gained by either horse on that score. I hope to hear from you promptly. Very respectfully yours,

San Francisco, Feb. 10th, 1890. L. A. Davies.

Answers to Correspondents.

Answers for this department must be accompanied by the name and address of the sender, not necessarily for publication, but as proof of good faith. Write the questions distinctly, and on one side of the paper only. Positively no questions will be answered by mail or telegraph.

Who Can Answer This Query?

I am very desirous of finding out the whereabouts of the running mare Dewdrop, formerly owned by Lawrence Fray Genoa, Nev. she was purchased by J. W. Dowell in October at Carson City races. Lawrence Fray.

Genoa, Douglas Co., Nev.

A. C. C.

Will you kindly give through the Breeder and Sportsman the pedigree and record of Mr. R. Richard's Elector.

Answer—Elector 2:31 by Electioneer, dam Gilberta by Fred Lowe 655; 2nd dam Lady Gilbert (grandam of Lot Slocum 2:17½.)

Robert Christie.

I have a two-year-old stud colt, sire Sterling, dam Oberiss by Prompter, 2nd dam Etelka by Sultan, for which I want to claim and register the name of Allright. Will you kindly inform me through the columns of your valuable paper, of the necessary steps to be taken to accomplish the same—the expense, etc.

Answer.—The registration fee is $2. We have forwarded you the necessary blank.

F. P. Lowell.

Did the Emperor of Norfolk win a half mile dash at Jerome Park when he was a two-year-old. If so, what were the names of the colts that ran 1st, 2nd and 3rd, and what time did they make.

Answer.—He won the Free Handicap Sweepstakes, distance half a mile, as a two-year-old at Jerome Park, on Friday, Oct. 14, 1887; Leo H. was second and Cascade third. Time 49½ seconds.

A Subscriber.

Please inform me through the columns of your paper what course to pursue in order to have an animal registered and numbered. I also wish to know the breeding of the horse Chieftain and his record, if he has any. What was his reputation as a producer?

Answer.—Give your name and address in full, and we will send you blanks. Chieftain 721, by Hiatoga (Old Togue), dam by Trimbull's Eclipse. Above the average.

Pacific Coast Blood-Horse Association.

SPRING MEETING '90.

Entries Close Wednesday, March 5, 1890.

PROGRAMME.

First Day—Saturday, April 12th.

No. 1—Introduction purse $400, of which $50 to second, $25 to third; for three-year-olds and upward. Beaten maidens of three years old, allowed 5 pounds; if four years old or over, 10 pounds. One mile and a sixteenth.

No. 2—The California Stakes; for two-year-olds. Half a mile. Closed.

No. 3—Selling purse $350, of which $50 to second; for three-year-olds and upward. Horses entered to be sold for $1,200 to carry rule weights; 3 pounds allowed for each $100 less down to $800, then 3 lbs. for each $100 less down to $800. Horses entered not to be sold to carry 10 pounds above the scale. Three-quarters of a mile.

No. 4—Purse $350, of which $50 to second; for all ages. Weights, 10 pounds below the scale. Seven furlongs.

No. 5—The Tidal Stakes; for three-year-olds. One mile and a quarter. Closed.

Second Day—Tuesday, April 15th.

No. 6—Purse $400, of which $50 to second, $25 to third; for three-year-olds and upward. Winner of No. 1 at this meeting to carry 5 pounds extra. Horses starting and not placed in that race allowed 3 lbs. One mile.

No. 7—Free handicap sweepstakes; for two-year-olds. $10 each if not declared out, with $300 added. First horse to take the added money, second to receive 70 per cent., and the third 30 per cent. of the stakes. Weights announced Monday, April 14th, at 10 o'clock A. M. Declarations due at 5 o'clock P. M. the same day. Five furlongs.

No. 8—Selling purse $350, of which $50 to second; for all ages. Horses entered to be sold for $1,500, to carry rule weights; 3 pounds allowed for each $100 less down to $1,000, then 1 pound for each $100 less down to $500. Horses entered not to be sold to carry 5 pounds above the scale. One mile and a sixteenth.

No. 9—The Pacific Derby; for three-year-olds. One mile and a half. Closed.

Third Day—Thursday, April 17th.

No. 10—Selling purse $350, of which $50 to second, for three-year-olds and upward. Horses entered to be sold for $1,000 to carry rule weights; 3 pounds allowed for each $100 less down to $500, then 2 pounds for each $100 down to $300. Horses entered not to be sold to carry ten pounds above the scale. Fifteen-sixteenths of a mile.

No. 11—The Racine stakes; for two-year-olds. Three-quarters of a mile. Closed.

No. 12—Purse $400, of which $50 to second and $25 to third; for all ages. Mile heats.

No. 13—The Sequel stakes; a handicap for all ages; $25 each, half forfeit, $5 if declared out, with $500 added; second horse to receive $75, third to save stakes. Weights announced Wednesday, April 16th, at 10 o'clock in the morning. Declarations at 5 o'clock in the afternoon the same day. One mile and three-eighths.

Fourth Day—Saturday, April 19th.

No. 14—Purse $300, of which $50 to the second horse. A handicap for two-year-olds. Entrance free for starters; declarations $5, to go to the racing fund. Weights announced Friday, April 18th, at 10 o'clock in the morning. Declarations due at 5 o'clock in the afternoon the same day. Eleven-sixteenths of a mile.

No. 15—Selling purse $350, of which $50 to the second. For all ages. Horses entered to be sold for $1,000 to carry rule weights; 3 pounds allowed for each $100 less. Three-quarters of a mile.

No. 16—Purse $400, of which $50 to second; $25 to third. For three-year-olds and upward. Winners at this distance or more at this meeting when carrying weight for age or more, to carry 5 pounds extra; of two such races 8 pounds. Horses beaten at this distance once allowed 3 pounds; twice, 5 pounds. One mile.

No. 17—Purse $450, of which $50 to second horse. An owners' handicap, for horses that have started and not won at this meeting. Weights to be given through the entry-box at 5 o'clock in the afternoon, the day before the race. Ten pounds over weight allowed; winners excused without penalty. One and a sixteenth miles.

No. 18—The Ocean handicap; a sweepstake for all ages; $20 entrance; $10 forfeit, $5 if declared, with $600 added, of which $75 to the second, third to save stake. Weights announced Thursday, April 17th, at 5 o'clock in the evening. Declarations due Friday, April 18th, at 5 o'clock in the afternoon. One and five-eighths miles.

REMARKS AND CONDITIONS.

These races will be run under the revised rules of this Association adopted February 4th, 1887. Owners and trainers will be supplied with copies on application to the Secretary.

In all stakes starters must be named to the Secretary or through the entry box at the track on or before 5 o'clock P. M. of the day before the race.

In all stakes the right to forfeit ceases at 10 o'clock A. M. of the day on which the race is run.

Entrance fee for starters in purses. Non-starters can be declared out at 5 o'clock P. M. of the day before the race by paying five per cent of the amount of the purse.

All horses not so declared out will be required to start.

All declarations void unless accompanied by the money.

In all selling races the winner to be sold at auction but the right of the owner of a beaten horse to claim is not barred.

The Association reserves the right to postpone races on account of unfavorable weather or other sufficient cause.

Parties not having registered colors will be required to name their colors with their entry.

Entries close with the Secretary March 5th, 1890. Entry blanks will be supplied on application to the office, 313 Bush Street, San Francisco.

ARIEL LATHROP, President.

E. S. CULVER, Secretary.

Solano and Napa Agricultural Society.

Trotting Colt Guarantee Stakes for 1890.

The Solano and Napa Agricultural Society have opened the following Colt Stakes for Trotters:

NO. 1. TWO YEAR OLDS.—Free for all; $400 guaranteed. $50 entrance, payable as follows: $10 April 1st, when entries close; $10 May 1st, $10 June 1st, $10 July 1st, $10 August 1st, when colts must be named. Nominations transferable any time before colts are named. If the payments amount to more than the amounts guaranteed the additional amount to be added to the stake. All moneys divided as follows: 60, 30 and 10 per cent; in case of only two starting, 60 and 40 per cent; and in case of one horse walking over the whole amount to go to such horse. A failure to make any payment when due shall be considered a withdrawal and forfeiture of the amounts paid in. National or American Rules to govern, as the Society may elect. The right reserved to refund the first payment in case the stakes do not fill reasonably well.

No. 2. FOR THREE YEAR OLDS.—Free for all. $500 guaranteed. $100 entrance, payable as follows: $20 April 1st, when entries close; $20 May 1st, $20 June 1st, $20 July 1st, $20 August 1st, when colts must be named. Conditions same as in No. 1.

District Colt Stakes for districts comprising Counties of Solano, Napa, Sonoma, Marin, Lake, Colusa, Yolo, Mendocino and Butte.

No. 3. FOR YEARLINGS.—$250 guaranteed. District. $40 entrance, payable as follows: $10 April 1st, when entries close; $10 June 1st, $10 July 1st, $10 Aug. 1st, when colts must be named. Conditions same as in No. 1.

No. 4. FOR TWO YEAR OLDS.—$300 guaranteed. District. $50 entrance, payable as follows: $10 April 1st, when entries close; $10 May 1st, $10 June 1st, $10 July 1st, $10 August 1st when colts must be named. Conditions same as in No. 1.

No. 5. FOR THREE YEAR OLDS.—$400 guaranteed. District. $50 entrance, payable as follows: $10 April 1st when entries close; $10 May 1st, $10 June 1st, $10 July 1st, $10 August 1st, when colts must be named. Conditions same as in No. 1.

Yearling Stake. Single dash; one mile. Two Year Olds.—Mile heats, two in three. Three Year Olds Three in five, to harness. Parties entering colts will be notified by mail when payment becomes due.

The Society also offers the following stakes for class horses.

TROTTING STAKES.—Free for all.

2:30 CLASS—Trotting; purse $1500.

2:24 CLASS—Trotting; purse $1500.

2:20 CLASS—Trotting; purse $1500.

Horses eligible January 1st, 1890. Entrance $150, payable as follows: $25 April 1st, when entries close; $25 May 1st, $25 June 1st, $25 July 1st $50 August 1st, when horses must be named. Nominations transferable any time before August 1st. Right reserved to refund entrance fee in any of the stakes should they not fill reasonably well. Money divided, 50, 25, 15 and 10 per cent. National or American Association Rules to govern, as the Society shall elect. To be trotted at our regular summer meeting, upon days to be hereafter arranged.

Entries to Close April 1st, 1890, with

A. H. CONKLING, Secretary, Napa City, Cal.

L. L. JAMES, President.

STATE AGRICUL'L SOCIETY

State Fair, 1890.

TROTTING COLT SWEEPSTAKES

TO CLOSE MARCH 15, 1890.

No. 1. For Two-Year-Olds.

$50 entrance, of which $10 must accompany nomination; $15 payable July 1st, and remaining $25 payable August 10th, 1890. $300 added by the Society.

No. 2. For Three Year-Olds.

$100 entrance, of which $25 must accompany nomination; $25 payable July 1st, and remaining $50 payable August 10th, 1890. $400 added by the society.

No. 3. For Four-Year-Olds

[Conditions same as for three year olds.]

In all stakes failure to make payments as they become due forfeits entry and money paid in. Five to enter; three or more to start. Money in each stake to be divided as follows: To winning colt all the stakes and 60 per cent of added money; second colt, 33⅓ per cent; third colt, 16⅔ per cent of added money. Two year old stake, mile heats; three and four year olds three in five, to harness. No added money for a walkover. If only two start, they must contest for the stakes paid in, and divide two-thirds and one-third. Otherwise National Rules to govern.

CHRISTOPHER GREEN, President.

EDWIN F SMITH, Secretary.

BAY ROSE

REGISTERED No. 9814

Record 2:20½, third Heat.

Will make the season of 1890 from March 1st to July 1st at the race track, Oakland.

DESCRIPTION.

BAY ROSE is a dark bay or brown, with black points, is 16 hands high and weighs 1150 pounds. He is remarkably intelligent, of good disposition and a pure gaited trotter. He was foaled in 1881. His colts are large, stylish, rangy animals and inherit the qualities of speed and endurance.

PEDIGREE.

BAY ROSE 9814

- Sultan, 2:24, Sire of 18 in the 2:30 list.
  - The Moor, 870, Sire of Beautiful Bells, 2:29 1-2; Del Sur, 2:24 1-2; Inez, 2:30; Sir Guy, 2:28 1-2; Sultan, 2:24; Tommy Gates, 2:24.
  - Sultana.
- Madam Baldwin
  - The Moor, 870, Sire of 6 in the 2:30 list
  - By Ben Lippincott by Williamson's Belmont.

TERMS: $100 FOR THE SEASON.

Good pasturage near the track, and first-class care taken of mares for $5 per month. No responsibility assumed for escapes or accidents.

For further particulars, address

W. W. AYRES,

Care of Jas. Corcoran, Race Track, Oakland, Cal.

Race Track for Sale,

The One Mile Track & Grounds

—OF THE—

Sonoma County Agricul'l Park Association,

Situated at

SANTA ROSA, CALIFORNIA,

Consisting of 84 acres fine agricultural land, 100 Box and Cattle Stalls, a two story Pavilion 60x120, commodious grand stand, and many out-buildings, a lovely Park of 15 acres, rolling ground, ornamental, nut and native oak trees; a fine cypress "windbreak" hedge ¾ mile around the track, and abundant water facilities. This elegant property will be sold at a great bargain, and possession given immediately if required. Sealed bids for same will be received up to February 11th, 1190.

B. M. SPENCER, Secretary.

GUY E. GROSSE, President.

PASHA,

Registered No. 2039.

RECORD 2:36.

SIRE OF MORO 2:27.

Will make the present season at Linden, twelve miles east of STOCKTON.

Season commencing FEBRUARY 1st and ending JULY 1, 1890.

DESCRIPTION.

PASHA is a beautiful black; 16½ hands high, and weighs 1,260 pounds. He is a horse of beautiful symmetry and magnificent action.

PEDIGREE.

PASHA was sired by Sultan 1513, sire of Stamboul 2:12½, Ruby 2:18½, Alcazar 2:20½, Bay Rose 2:20½, and sixteen others with records below 2:30. First dam Madam Baldwin by The Moor 870; second dam Ben Lippincott by Belmont. Pasha is a full brother to Bay Rose, record 2:20½.

Sultan, by The Moor, sire of Beautiful Bells, dam of Hinda Rose, 2:19½, Bell Boy 2:19¼, and Sable, dam of Sable Wilkes, three-year-old record 2:18. First dam Sultana, by Delmonico, sire of Derby 2:16, by Guy Miller, sire of Whipple's Hambletonian. Second dam by Mambrino Chief. Third dam by Downing's Bay Messenger. Fourth dam Miss Caudle, dam of Ericsson, four-year-old record 2:30½.

Terms for the season, $50.

With privilege of returning mares that do not prove in foal next season free of charge.

Good pasturage at $2 per month. No responsibility will be assumed for accidents or escapes. Service fee payable before the removal of the mare.

For further particulars, address

D. BRYSON, Linden Cal.

The Trotting Stallion

ARBITRATOR

Will make the Season of 1890 at NILES, Alameda County.

PEDIGREE.

ARBITRATOR

- Director 1989, 2:17 in a race, Sire of Direct, 4 yrs., 2:18½ in a race, Margaret S., 3 yrs., 2:19½ in a race, Guide, 4 yrs., 2:28½ in a race.
- Lady Earnest.
  - Speculation 918, sire of Oakland Maid, 2:22 in a race, Gracie S., 2:22 in a race, Crown Point, 2:24 in a race, He the sire of Valensin, 3 yrs., 2:23 in a race, Sire of Dam of Alfred G., 2:19¾.
  - Lady Hibbard, dam of Lou Whipple, 2:26½ in a race.

Speculation's dam was Martha Washington, dam of Whipple's Hambletonian, sire of 15 in 2:30 and granddaughter of Burr's Napoleon, sire of Black Harry, who in 1850 won two miles in 5:14½. He sired Smith Burr, sire of Gen. Butler, 2:21, Wagon, 4:56½. He sired the dam of Fanny Mapes, dam of Jerome Eddy, 2:16½. He sired Telegraph, sire of dam of Rarus, 2:13¼.

DESCRIPTION.

ARBITRATOR was foaled 1885. He is of good size, fine conformation, and a beautiful seal brown.

TERMS.

Non-standard mares	$45
Standard mares by inheritance	35
Standard mares by performance or produce	25

For further particulars, address

H. A. MAYHEW, owner, Niles, Alameda Co.

AXTELL'S PICTURE FREE.

Do not waste a minute, the supply will not last forever. These pictures are a genuine work of art. Good judges do not hesitate to say they are the finest likeness yet seen of the fastest stallion in the world. They are in size 18x25 inches, finished in nine colors, and in the highest style of the lithographer's art. The rich bay color of the horse is set off by the dark back ground of the box stall, around the walls of which are arranged in proper form and colors the boots, bits, muzzles, brushes, blankets, cloths, etc., usually found in the quarters of "crack trotters." The colored attendant stands near the horse, carelessly holding the blanket which has been removed to show AXTELL to an admiring group of ladies and gentlemen present.

These pictures will literally "knock your eye out." You want one for your house, office or stable. Send at once. They will go fast and you will regret not having secured one when they are all gone. Sent to any address upon receipt of 15 cents in stamps to pay postage and packing.

Send in your name and address at once to Jas. B. Campbell & Co., Chicago, Ill., and get by return mail AXTELL'S picture in nine colors 18x25, suitable for framing.

NOTICE: Stamps will be returned and orders refused from parties failing to mention the paper they saw the advertisement in.

ST. NICHOLAS.

A Son of the World Renowned

SIDNEY,

Will Make the Season of 1890, at the Oakland Trotting Park.

ST. NICHOLAS was bred by Mr. G. Valensin at the Arno Stock Farm, Sacramento Co., California, in 1885. He is a beautifully proportioned bright bay horse, 15.3 hands high; is well muscled, lengthy, and lots of bone, with splendid natural action and a phenomenal turn of speed. As a three-year-old he easily worked three heats on the Oakland Track in 2:32, 2:29 and 2:27¾. His breeding is just what one would expect from such a highly formed bloodlike horse. Sidney, his sire is the most successful young stallion—whether for getting pacers or trotters—America has ever seen and no wonder for his blood lines are exceptional fine and are all trotting lines, Santa Claus, Strathmore, Rysdyk's Hambletonian and Abdallah, while Sweetness again runs back through that great sire Volunteer, to Rysdyk's Hambletonian and also through her dam to Rysdyk's Hambletonian and Harry Clay 45, the sire of Electioneer's dam. St. Nicholas' dam is by Echo, an exceptionally prepotent son of Hambletonian thus giving St. Nicholas four Rysdyk's Hambletonian crosses and further back a Harry Clay cross which with his grand dam's thoroughbred cross should make him invaluable in the stud.

TERMS: Fifty dollars the season, which will commence on the 5th of February and close on the 1st of July. Due care will be taken of mares, but no responsibility for accidents or escapes.

Mares taken and kept as desired by the owners, and at reasonable rates.

JOHN ROWEN. Oakland Trotting Park.

GEO. WASHINGTON,

11,623.

RECORD 2:30.

Bay colt, bred by Thomas Smith of Vallejo, Cal. Foaled 1886 by Mambrino Chief, Jr., 11,622, record 2:34 1-2. 1st dam Fanny Rose by Vick's Ethan Allen Jr. 2,903, sire of Prince Allen 2:27. 2nd dam Jenny Lind, thoroughbred, dam of Prince Allen 2:27. Will serve a limited number of mares at $60 for the season. Mares not proving with foal may be returned next season free.

Mambrino Chief, Jr.

11,622.

RECORD 2:34 1 2.

Sire of George Washington, record 2:30 at three years old. Bay horse bred by Rufus Ingalls of Belvedere, Ill. By McDonald Chief 3,583. First dam Venus by Mambrino Patchen 58, 2nd dam by Wardlow's Shakespeare. 3rd dam Lone Gold 4th dam by Silver Heels. Has not been in the stud before. He was 5 years old when he served a few mares, and his colts all show good style and form.

Terms for the season $50. For further particulars see or address

THOMAS SMITH, Vallejo, Cal.

"TOBEY'S,"

214 Post Street,

Between Grant Avenue and Stockton Street,

Adjoining New Hamman Baths.

D. J. TOBIN, Proprietor.

The Poodle Dog

"Rotisserie,"

FIRST-CLASS IN EVERY RESPECT.

Elegant Family Dining Rooms.

S. E. cor. GRANT AVE. and BUSH STREET.

ANDRE POTENTINI, Proprietor.

BERGEZ'S RESTAURANT.

FIRST-CLASS. Charges Reasonable.

Private Rooms for Families.

332-334 Pine St., below Montgomery St.

JOHN BERGEZ, Propr.

Breeders' Directory.

Advertisements under this heading 50c. per line per month.

HORSES AND CATTLE.

CLEVELAND BAYS and Norman Horses, Jersey Cattle, and pure bred Poland China Hogs.—DR. W. J. PRATHER, Fresno, Cal.

W. S. JACOBS, Sacramento, Cal. – Breeder of Thoroughbred Shorthorns and Berkshire Hogs.

J. H. WHITE, Lakeville, Sonoma County—Breeder of Registered Holstein Cattle.

EL ROBLAS RANCHO—Los Alamos, Cal., Francis T. Underhill, proprietor, importer and breeder of thoroughbred Hereford Cattle. Information by mail. C. F. Swan, manager.

PAGE BROTHERS.—Penn's Grove, Sonoma Co. Cal. Breeders of Short-Horn Cattle; Draft, Roadster and Standard Bred Horses.

JAMES MADDOCK, Petaluma, Cal.—Trotters trained at reasonable prices. Stock handled carefully. Correspondence solicited.

SETH COOK, breeder of Cleveland Bay Horses, Devon, Durham, Polled Aberdeen-Angus and Galloway Cattle. Young stock of above breeds on hand for sale. Warranted to be pure bred, recorded and average breeders. Address, Geo. A. Wiley, Cook Farm, Danville, Contra Costa Co., Cal.

MAMBRINO WILKES COLTS and FILLIES, full brothers and sisters to Gus. Wilkes 2:22, and Balkan 2:29¾, for Sale. Address SMITH HILL, Walnut Creek, Contra Costa County, Cal.

B. F. RUSH, Suisun, Cal., Shorthorns, Thohoughbred and Grades. Young Bulls and Calves for Sale.

PETER SAXE & SON, Lick House, San Francisco, Cal.—Importers and Breeders for past 18 years of every variety of Cattle, Horses, Sheep and Hogs.

HOLSTEIN THOROUGHBREDS of all the noted strains. Registered Berkshire Swine. Catalogues. F. H. BURKE, 401 Montgomery St., S. F.

HENRY C. JUDSON, Wild Idle Farm.—Breeder of Thoroughbred Horses. The home of "Wild Idle." P. O. Santa Clara; Box 223.

FERGUSON & AUSTIN,

FRESNO, CAL.

Registered Polled Angus and Short-Horn Cattle.

Oysters.

M. B. MORAGHAN

Is the only importer, planter and wholesale dealer in the CALIFORNIA MARKET, Stalls 68, 69 to 71 and 47, 48. All the choicest brands of Fresh Oysters constantly on hand. Prompt attention paid to hotel and country orders. Price List.

Large Eastern Oysters .... $1 00 per 100
Transplanted Eastern Oysters .... 1 50 per 100
California Oysters .... 2 00 " sack
Fresh frozen Eastern Oysters at $7 00 per doz, cans.

PASTURAGE

AND

FIRST-CLASS CARE

TAKEN OF

Gentlemen's Road Horses and Trotters.

Colts Broken and Trained to Harness or Saddle.

Twenty new Box Stalls. First-class Pasturage, and the best of care given to all horses. Terms, $4 per month. Satisfaction Guaranteed.

Address,

K. O'GRADY,

Laural Creek Farm,

SAN MATEO, CAL.

Brushes.

BUCHANAN BROS.,

Brush Manufacturers,

609 Sacramento Street, two doors above Montgomery.

Horse Brushes of every description on hand and made to order. Bristle Body Brushes our Specialty.

R. LIDDLE & SON

538 Washington St., S. F.,

Wholesale and Retail Dealers in

Guns, Rifles and Pistols.

A Full Line of FISHING TACKLE and SPORTSMAN'S GOODS.

Orders by mail receive prompt attention.

"DICKEY'S,"

SIXTH AVENUE AND D ST.

Near entrance to Bay District Track.

Choicest Brands of

WINES AND CIGARS.

A Delightful Resort.

Telephone 1486. J. R. DICKEY, Propr.

PHIL J. CRIMMINS. JOHN C. MORRISON.

"Silver Palace,"

36 Geary Street,

San Francisco, Cal.

2:10¾ 2:13¾ 2:10

DEXTER PRINCE.

This Royally-bred Stallion will make the Season of 1890 at the LIVE OAKS Breeding Farm, 2 miles from Lodi, San Joaquin County, Cal.

DESCRIPTION.

DEXTER PRINCE is a blood bay, 16 hands high, weighs over 1100 pounds; has great power and substance, and the highest finish. When two years old, at Palo Alto, he was timed quarters by Gov. Stanford in 36½ seconds, and he was driven eighths by Mr. Marvin at a faster rate of speed than that. He is a sure foal getter, and invariably sires foals of good size, of fine form and finish, and the highest rate of speed.

PEDIGREE.

By KENTUCKY PRINCE, the sire of Guy, 2:10¾, Spofford, 2:18¾, Company, 2:19¾, Bayonne Prince 2:21 1-4, Fred Folger, 2:20¾, and a score more in the 2:30 list.

First dam LADY DEXTER, full sister of the greatest of trotters, Dexter, and the greatest of sires, Dictator, the sire of Director, 2:17, Phallas, 2:13¾, in a fourth heat, and Jay-Eye-See, 2:10.

Second dam Clara, the dam of Dexter, 2:17 1-4, Dictator, Astoria 2:29 1-4, and Almah, 2:28¾. Clara was by American Star, that has 31 daughters that have produced 2:30 or better trotters.

Third dam the McKinstry mare, the dam of Shark, 2:27¾. HAMBLETONIAN, the grandsire of DEXTER PRINCE, has 40 trotters in the 2:30 list, 44 daughters that have produced 2:30 trotters, and more than 100 sons that have sired 2:30 trotters.

CLARK CHIEF, the grandsire on the sire's side, was the sire of performing and producing sons and daughters.

DEXTER PRINCE has faster blood lines, on both sides, than any other stallion in the world—Guy, 2:10¾, and Jay-Eye-See, 2:10.

TERMS.

$100 for the season, with usual return privileges. Payable before mares are removed. Good pasture, and the best care furnished, but no responsibility assumed for accidents.

PREMIUM.

$250 will be given to the first of the produce of DEXTER PRINCE put in the 2:30 list, and $100 each after the first. Address

L. M. MORSE, Lodi, Cal.

A SON OF ALMONT 33.

Only $25 for the Season.

ASHLAND ALMONT 3481.

PEDIGREE.

ASHLAND ALMONT 3481

- Almont 33, sire of 34 in 2:30 or better of 21 daughters and of 49 sires that have produce in 2:30 or better.
  - Abdallah 15, Sire Goldsmith Maid, 2:14; 6 in 2:30 list; 13 sires and 25 dams of trotters in 2:30 list.
    - Hambletonian 10, sire of 41 in 2:30 list; sire of 107 sires of 567 in 2:30 list.
    - Katy Darling.
  - Sally Anderson
    - Mambrino Chief 11
    - Lady Thorn, 2:18¼.
    - Kate, by Pilot Jr. 12.
- Pauline, Dam of Sapho.
  - Ashland Chief, Sire Black Cloud, 2:17¾.
    - Mambrino Chief 11
    - Lady Thorn, 2:18¼.
    - dau. of imp. Yorkshire, (thoroughbred).
  - Rosina, Dam Almonia, the dam of Sally Cossack, 2:22¼, dau. Mamb. Abdallah, sire Mam. Prince, 2:23, and of Mamb. Bashaw, sire of Graham's Mambrino, 2:23.
    - Abdallah 15, Sire Goldsmith Maid, 2:14.
    - Prof. Smith's Sir William.

DESCRIPTION.

ASHLAND ALMONT 3481 is a handsome chestnut; stands 16 hands; was foaled 1882, and bred by Gen. Withers, of Lexington, Ky. He is of fine form, and remarkably intelligent, sweet-tempered and absolutely sound. His oldest foal may be seen with him, and while he has never served a standard mare or one that was a producer of speed, all of his colts are large, sound, fast and handsome.

TERMS: $25 for the season, with usual return privileges. The best of care taken of mares in any manner that the owner may desire, but no responsibility assumed for escapes or accidents. This horse will make the season at the corner of 9th and Brush Streets, Oakland. For further particulars, address

T. J. WHITEHEAD, Manager.

or, W. H. ASHBY, Oakland, Cal.

Cor. 9th and Castro Streets, Oakland, Cal.

Trotting Stallion

Guide 2:29

(At Four Years)

Will make the season of 1890 at the SANTA RITA RANCH, about one mile North of Pleasanton.

DESCRIPTION.

GUIDE is a handsome seal brown, five years old, stands 15¾ hands high, and weighs 1095 pounds. He is of fine form, level headed, intelligent, and comes from blood lines that are noted for the qualities of speed and gameness.

PEDIGREE.

GUIDE, 2:28½.

- Director, 2:17, Sire of Direct, 2:18¾, Margaret S., 2:19¾.
  - Dictator 113, Sire of 23 trotters and 3 pacers in 2:30.
    - Hambletonian 10.
    - Clara, by American Star 14.
  - Dolly, Dam of Onward, 2:17¾, Thorndale, 2:22¾.
    - Mambrino Chief 11.
    - Fannie, by Ben Franklin.
- Imogene
  - Norwood 522, Sire of Tommy Norwood, 2:26¾.
    - Hambletonian 10.
    - Lady Fallis, by American Star 14.
  - daughter of
    - American Star 14.
    - daughter of Henry Clay 8.

The attention of breeders is especially called to the above pedigree as showing 3 crosses of American Star.

GUIDE trotted into the 2:30 list last season with little training, and he will trot into the 2:20 list the coming season barring accidents.

Guide's sire has a record of 2:17, made in a five heat race, and Guide is closely related to Phallas, who made a record of 2:13¾ in a fourth heat, and to Jay-Eye-See, record 2:10.

TWO HUNDRED AND FIFTY DOLLARS will be given to the owner of the first of the produce of Guide put in the 2:30 list, and $100 to each one after the first.

TERMS—$75 for the season, with the usual return privileges.

Admiro,

Sire Admiral; dam by San Bruno, by Easton's David Hill.

This magnificent horse is a handsome bay, eight years old; stands 17 1-2 hands high, and weighs 1470 pounds. He is very speedy for a large horse, and breeds fine large carriage horses. His produce possess every qualification of the Cleveland Bay, with the added qualities of speed and endurance resulting from his high trotting breeding.

TERMS—[illegible] for the season, with usual return privileges.

Will stand three days each week at Santa Rita Ranch, Pleasanton, and at A. T. Hatch's Ranch "Almono," Alamo, Contra Costa County, alternately. All mares sent care of SMITH & SUTHERLAND, Pleasanton, will be taken in charge of on arrival, and will receive the best care and attention in any manner the owners may desire. Good pasturage at $4 per month. Only a limited number of approved mares will be served by this horse this season.

No responsibility assumed for escapes or accidents. For further particulars, address

SMITH & SUTHERLAND, Pleasanton.

or A. T. HATCH, care Palace Hotel, San Francisco.

J. O'KANE, Horse Boots, Clothing and Furnishings, For Track, Driving Training and Stable. Every requisite for Horsemen. Harness, Medicines, Etc.

THE BRUNSWICK BALKE COLLENDER COMPANY,

MANUFACTURERS OF

Standard Billiard and Pool Tables, Saloon and Bank Fixtures,

653--655 Market Street, San Francisco, Cal.

KENNEL ADVERTISEMENTS.

Thoroughbred Pugs,

$40 each.

PEDIGREE.

PUPPIES

- Fido
  - imp. Jumbo
    - Marshall's Uno
    - Lady Bess
  - Fanni
    - Rex
    - imp. Fly
- Budge
  - Senator Fair's Fritz
  - McCleery's Mammi Snoots
    - Sam
    - imp. Alice

Can be seen daily from 9 A. M. to 3 P. M. at 411 Ellis Street, San Francisco.

J. F. B. McCLEERY.

Irish Setters & Pointers.

In the Stud, winner of 16 first and special prizes, CHAMPION MIKE T., 6436, A. K. S. B. Irish Setter puppies by Champion Mike T. 6436 A. K. S. B.—Champion Lady Elcho T. 6451 A. K. S. B., for sale. Two pointers, a year old, by Rush T. 10069 A. K. S. B.—Champion Patti Croxteth T. 10128 A. K. S. B. for sale. Yard broken. Address,

A. B. TRUMAN,

1426 Steiner St., S. F., Cal.

CALIFORNIA SPANIEL KENNELS,

Oakland, California, H. P. RENNIE, Prop; Breeder and importer of typical COCKER SPANIELS. Winner of first prizes at S. F. and Los Angeles, 1889; also, Columbus, 1889, New York, 1887. In the stud, solid Black Cocker-dog, GIFFEE, won 1st and Gold Medal at S. F., 1889, Fee, $25. Puppies and grown dogs at reasonable prices. My dogs can neither talk nor climb a tree, but are fielders and prize winners.

Highland Farm,

LEXINGTON, KY.

Home of Red Wilkes.

Standard-bred Trotting Stock

For Sale,

Sired by Red Wilkes, Wilton, 2:19¾; Allandorf and Sentinel Wilkes, out of highly bred Standard Mares of the most fashionable blood of the day.

W. C. FRANCE, Proprietor.

The Park Training Stable.

CHAS. DAVID, PROPRIETOR.

Corner Grove and Baker Streets, near Entrance to Golden Gate Park.

EVERY FACILITY FOR TRAINING COLTS and taking care of Gentlemen's Roadsters.

Finely appointed stable with every convenience and sixteen roomy box stalls.

The best care given all horses by experienced help, under the personal superintendence of the proprietor.

Convenient to the Park Speed Drive, and Accessible to Six Lines of Cable Cars.

THE TRAINING OF COLTS AND ROADSTERS A SPECIALTY.

TROTTERS AND ROADSTERS FOR SALE.

HORSES SOLD ON COMMISSION.

The proprietor trained and brought out the following well known horses: "Sister, Huntress," "Perihelion," "Nona Y," and others.

NOVEL, USEFUL and Ornamental.

PAT'D AUG. 28, 88.

The Perfection Horse Tail Tie,

Saves Time and the Tail.

Send 25 cents for Sample,

BREEDER AND SPORTSMAN,

313 Bush Street, San Francisco.

or to BARNES & PARKER, Des Moines, Ia., Manufrs

GOLDEN EAGLE HOTEL

Corner SEVENTH and K STREETS, SACRAMENTO.

FIRST CLASS IN EVERY RESPECT.

The LARGEST and FINEST HOTEL in the City.

W. O. BOWERS, Proprietor.

Free 'Buss to and from the Hotel.

Telephone, Telegraph Office and Messenger Service at Hotel

1890 Three Anteeo Stallions 1890

SUNSET, 5 years old. by Anteeo
ANTEEOF, 4 years old, by Anteeo
ANTEEOP, 3 years old, by Anteeo

ANTEEO. Standard 7868. Record, 2:16 1-4. He by Stanford's Electioneer, and dam Columbine.

DESCRIPTIONS, PEDIGREES AND CONDITIONS.

"SUNSET" is a rich, dark bay, small star on forehead, portion of hind left foot white; was foaled March 11, 1885; is by ANTEEO and the inbred HAMBLETONIAN mare, BESSIE G., she by KING PHILLIP, son of WHIPPLE'S HAMBLETONIAN. He is 16 1-2 hands high, and weighs 1,170 lbs. He is of perfect build and splendid action cool headed and great speed for his size, having trotted a trial mile as a three-year-old in 2:38. He then entered heavy in the stud and was matched against Whalebone at the Healdsburg races November 2, 1889, winning just as he pleased in three straight heats; time, 2:37, 2:36 1-2, 2:32 1-2. He was then matched for a race to come off at Thanksgiving Day at [illegible], but owing to the heavy rains the event did not take place. A few days previous to Thanksgiving Day Mr. Lawrence worked Sunset out and then he trotted three square miles and heats in 2:33, 2:34 and 2:37.

SUNSET will be bred to 40 mares only, at $50 each, no colt no pay.

"ANTEEOF" is a jet black, was foaled April 13, 1886, is 16¼ hands high, and weighs 1,200 lbs., has a very fine, heavy black mane and tail; is well proportioned, moves majestically, is of easy, lofty carriage; is symmetrical, in fact is a beautiful horse. He was sired by Anteeo and the O. A. Taylor mare "Nance," her dam, was raised by Dr. Oliver Plummer, of Cosumnes, Cal., and sired by "Napoleon"; Napoleon was foaled May 29, 1833, and raised by James Kyle of Butler County, Ohio. He was sired by Benj. Sweet's horse Bellfounder, Bellfounder, his dam was sired by Doc. Daniel Mehigan's horse Cadmus, G. G. sire the celebrated Old [illegible]; his G. dam was sired by Big Shakespeare, G. G., sires dam by Messenger and Expedition.

ANTEEOF will be bred to 25 mares only, at $30 each. No colt, no pay.

"ANTEEOP" is a rich seal brown; was foaled March 7, 1887; by Anteeo and the inbred Hambletonian mare Bessie G., also dam of Sunset, his full brother and Midget his full sister; he is 15 1-2 hands high and weighs 95[illegible] lbs., and measures 21 inches around the arm, good head, fine neck, full, broad breast; withers and rump on nearly equal line, well proportioned bones, ankle shoulders, loins and hips; strong legs all around, with great muscular development and splendid sinews; wirey pasterns and sound, compact feet; the lines from hip to hock show power and speed; stands square and has excellent action, has a superb lustrous coat of rich deep brown full of seal color without a defect; an even, honest trotter, and has gone the mile as a two-year-old in 2:43, the last quarter in 36 seconds; is intelligent and of high spirit, with much temper, but is not vicious, has very fine eyes, is a handsome, showy colt; attractive in harness.

ANTEEOP will be bred to 15 mares only, at $40. No colt, no pay.

SEASON to commence February 1st, ending July 1, 1890. Book now ready. Apply to John H. Lawrence, "Manager and Trainer," on my fruit and hop ranch, 1 mile east of Court House, on Sonoma road. Excellent pasture furnished with running water, also dry knolls with oak shelter, at $4 per month for mares. Two of the above stallions will be for sale after the expiration of the their stud season.

GUY E. GROSSE,
SANTA ROSA, SONOMA CO., CAL.

Valensin Stock Farm Stallions,

SIDNEY, 2:19 3-4.

At Eight Years of Age Sire of the following Fastest on Record:

FAUSTINO, yearling stallion, record of the world 2:35
FLEET, fastest yearling record in 1888 .... 2:36
FLEET, fastest two-year-old filly in 1889 .... 2:24
GOLD LEAF, fastest four-year-old Pacing record in the world 2:11½
ADONIS, fastest three-year-old Pacing Gelding in the world 2:14¼
ADONIS, four-year-old Gelding Pacing record 2:14

—Also the Sire of—

LONGWORTH, four years old 2:19
SISTER V., four years old (trial 2:23) 2:27
SANTA RITA 2:39
MEMO, two-year-old (three-year-old trial 2:20½) 2:49

And many others.

SIDNEY is the sire of Faustino 2:35, and Fleet 2:36, the two fastest yearlings the world has ever known by one sire, and his slowest yearling is faster than the great Electioneer's fastest.

Terms, $250, with usual return privileges, for a limited number of approved mares. Book rapidly filling.

SIMMOCOLON, Four-year-old, 2:29 1-2.

Trial, 2:24; Half Mile in 1:08; Quarter in 33 1-2 Seconds.

Chestnut Horse, foaled 1885.

SIMMOCOLON.
- Simmons 2774. Sire of Bon Bon, 4 y. o. rec., 2:26, Raymon, 4 y. o. rec., 2:27, Black Storm, 3 y. o. rec. 2:27¾, and six others with records of 2:30 or better.
  - George Wilkes 519. Sire of 61 in 2:30 list. Sire of 11 dams of 12 in 2:30 list
    - Hambletonian 10. Sire of 41 in 2:30 list. Sire of 107 sires of 567 in 2:30 list. Sire of 44 dams of 50 in 2:30 list
    - Dolly Spanker
  - Black Jane. Dam of Rosa Wilkes, 2:18¼. Dam of Simmons, 2:28
    - Mambrino Patchen 58. Sire of 14 in 2:30 list. Sire of 21 sires of 37 in 2:30 list. Sire of 24 dams of 25 in 2:30 list
    - Lady Stanhope
- Colon. Dam of Simmocolon, 4 y. o. rec., 2:29½. Dam of Patchmore, 2:22¼
  - Strathmore. Sire of 27 in 2:30 list. Sire of 4 dams of 5 in 2:30. Sire of 3 sires of 3 in 2:30
    - Hambletonian 10 (Same as above)
    - Lady Waltermire. Dam of Marshall Ney
  - Coral. Trial at 2 years, 2:30. Dam of Corallold, 2:29¼
    - Clark Chief 89. Sire of 6 in 2:30 list. Sire of 9 sires of 27 in list. Sire of 11 dam with 11 in list
    - Colon. Dam of Caliban, sire of 3 in 2:30 list

As will be seen, Simmocolon is by a performing and producing son of George Wilkes, 2:22. He has back of him three producing dams, and combines the blood of the great sire George Wilkes handsomely blended with the blood of the greatest broodmare families. On the dam's side Mambrino Patchen, Strathmore, Clark Chief and Clay. A fine individual himself, pure gaited and very fast.

Terms, $150, with usual return privileges, for a limited number of mares. Season to close JUNE 15th, when he will be prepared for track purposes. Pasturage $5 per month. Reasonable charges if fed hay and grain. Best of care taken of mares, but positively no responsibility assumed for accidents or escapes. For further particulars address

G. VALENSIN, Pleasanton, Cal.

Old Hermitage Whiskies

"STEINER'S,"
No. 311 BUSH STREET,
San Francisco,
Under Breeder and Sportsman Office.

John D. Gall. Jas. P. Dunne

"The Resort,"

No. 1 Stockton Street, cor. Ellis,
San Francisco.

THE HICKS-JUDD CO.

Successors to
HICKS & JUDD, Bookbinders,
and Women's Co-operative Printing Office.
Printers, Bookbinders,
Publishers,
23 First St., San Francisco.
BREEDERS' CATALOGUES A SPECIALTY.

NOTICE.

C. BRUCE LOWE,
Pedigree Stock Agent,
19 Bligh Street,
SYDNEY, New South Wales.
Reference—J. B. HAGGIN, ESQ.

Guenoc Stud Farm, Lake Co., Cal.

Imp. GREENBACK

(Sire of the English winners Greenlight, Greenjacket, Greensbank, Greenwave and Greenhorn)

By Dollar, dam Music, by Stockwell. $100 the Season

ST. SAVIOR,

(FULL BROTHER TO EOLE)

By Eolus, dam War Song, by War Dance. $100 the Season.

PASTURAGE, $5 PER MONTH.

With right to return the following year if mare does not prove with foal. The best of care taken, but no liability for accidents or escapes. Mares shipped to C. W. ABY, care ST. HELENA STABLES, St. Helena Napa County, will be taken in charge by competent men.

For further information write to

DR. C. W. ABY, Middletown, Lake County, Cal.

SOUTHER FARM

P. O. Box 208. San Leandro, Cal.

1¼ miles northwest of San Leandro; 8 miles southeast of Oakland. Turn off county road between above places at "Stanley Road," ¼ mile north of San Leandro.

Horses boarded at all times in any manner desired. Best of care but no responsibility for accidents. Colts broken and handled for the road or track. Terms reasonable.

Glen Fortune,	Jester D,	El Benton,	Figaro,
By Electioneer.	By Almont.	By Electioneer.	Hambletonian 725
$50 for 1889.	$50 for 1890.	Limited to 5 mares.	Limited to 12 mares
		Book Full.	Book Full.

If horses are to last for a profitable time they must occasionally have a change from hard pavements, wooden floors, and dry, hard feed.

THE SOUTHER FARM

Has Green Feed the Year Round,

and feeds Hay in connection with the green feed, which a horse must have if he is to thrive. Every animal is given

A Dry, Warm Place to Sleep,

No matter how stormy the weather. All Stock under cover when it rains.

VISITORS WELCOME ANY DAY EXCEPT SUNDAY.

Write to the above address for references, circulars and price lists. Terms reasonable.

GILBERT TOMPKINS, Proprietor.

SAN MATEO STOCK FARM

HOME OF GUY WILKES,
Record, 2:15 1-4.

Guy Wilkes' Book is full for 1890, and positively no more mares will be received. Book now open for 1891, at $500 the Season.

Sable Wilkes, three-year-old record 2:18, will be allowed to serve 25 mares in addition to those already engaged at $250 the season of 1890. SABLE Wilkes, 15½ hands, black horse, by Guy Wilkes, first dam Sable by The Moor; second dam Gretchen by Mambrino Pilot; third dam Kitty Kirkman by Canada Chief; fourth dam by Fanning's Tobe; fifth dam by imp. Leviathan.

Leo Wilkes, brown horse, four years, 16 hands, full brother to Sable Wilkes, will be allowed to serve 30 mares at $100 the season.

Mares not proving with foal may be returned the following season free of service fee. Parties engaging the services of any of the above horses must send a deposit of 10 per cent. of service money with engagement. Pasturage $6 per month, and when the condition of the animal requires it, hay or grain, or both, are fed, the charge will be $12 50 per month. Good care will be taken of all mares sent to the Farm, but no liability will be assumed for accidents or escapes.

All bills are due at time of service, but must be paid by August 1st of each year. No stock will be allowed to leave the place until all bills are paid.

WILLIAM CORBITT.
San Mateo Stock Farm.

Poplar Grove Breeding FARM.

Standard-bred Trotters, Colts and Fillies.

The get of CLOVIS, 4909; PASHA, 2039; APEX, 2935,

For Sale.

Address S. N. STRAUBE, Poplar Grove Breeding Farm,
Fresno, Cal.

Inspection by intending purchasers invited, and information by mail.

Anteros Nutwood

—ONE OF THE—

Best Bred Young Stallions in the State.

DESCRIPTION.

Bay horse; black points; no white. Foaled in 1887. Bred by M. Carter, at the Nutwood Stock Farm, by Anteros 6030, by Electioneer, and full brother to Anteeo, 2:16¼, and Antevolo, four-year-old, record 2:19¼.

First dam Newark Belle by Nutwood, 2:18¾, and half-brother to Maud S., 2:08¾—Queen of the Turf.

Second dam Tilly, 2:40, by San Bruno by David Hill, by Vermont Blackhawk. This colt is very large of his age, and looks enough like Sunol to be her full brother.

If there is anything in breeding, this horse ought to make a good one.

Electioneer and Nutwood are his grandsires, both serving mares at $500 each. Nutwood is half-brother to the fastest trotter in the world—Maud S., 2:08¾; Electioneer, the sire of the fastest three-year-old, Sunol, 2:10½.

TERMS.

This colt will be limited to ten mares, outside of my own, for $50 the season.

Mares not proving in foal can be returned the following season by paying difference in price, if any.

The National Trotting Stallion

PILOT NUTWOOD (Cyrus R.)

Will make the season of 1890 at the stable of T. W. Barstow, corner of San Fernand Street and Wilson Avenue, San Jose.

TERMS.

$50 for the season, with usual return privileges, by paying difference in price. No fee if this horse does not secure a record of 2:30 or better in 1890, barring accidents. Limited to 15 outside mares. Season from February 1st to July 1st, 1890. The best care and attention given to mares, but no responsibility assumed for accidents or escapes. Good pasturage at $3 per month on 100 acres of the best feed in Santa Clara County.

DESCRIPTION.

Pilot Nutwood, 2:18, black horse; small star; foaled in 1881; 15¾ hands; was worked five weeks, and got a record of 2:42 as a three-year-old; he was not worked again until 1888; after having six weeks work, showed his owner a mile in 2:26, and the last half in 1:10¾. Sired by the mighty Nutwood, 2:18¾, half-brother to Maud S., 2:08¾—Queen of the Turf.

First dam Belle by Jack Roberts, half-brother to Old St. Clair; 2d dam by Shakespeare, thoroughbred. Jack Roberts by Eclair or Leck, and he by old pacing Pilot, and his dam by Copperbottom.

This gives Pilot Nutwood two crosses of the great Pilot blood, coming through both sire and dam. This is the kind of breeding that breeders should be looking after in order to get to the front.

CHALLENGE.

To back my assertion made in the San Jose Mercury in December last, I will match this horse against any trotting stallion in San Jose, one or two-mile heats, any time after July 1st. The parties accepting this challenge can set the time and track, and I the right to name the amount. For further particulars, address

T. W. BARSTOW,

P. O. Box 1268. San Jose, Cal.

THE MAMBRINO Patchen Stallion.

MAMBRINO JR., 1789 (formerly Carr's) Sire of Lady Ellen 2:28 (dam of Ella 2:29), Maud H. 2:30, Mambrino Boy (Carr's) 2:31 1-2.

Will stand at my farm, 2 1-2 miles north of San Jose, on the Milpitas road. Season to commence February 1st, 1890, at $50, with return privilege 1891. Fifteen mares of approved breeding, besides my own, will be given him. Parties owning good mares, performers or out of producing dams, will find an opportunity to breed them on shares, and the best of care taken of them till colt is weaned, if so desired.

PEDIGREE.

MAMBRINO JR., 1789, by Mambrino Patchen 58 [full brother of Lady Thorne 2:18 1-4] by Mambrino Chief 11. First dam by Mambrino Chief 11; 2d dam by imp. Jordan [thoroughbred]; 3rd dam by Bertrand son of Sir Archy; 4th dam by Chewkees, son of Sir Archy.

For further particulars address

GEO. P. BULL.

Box 1067. San José, Cal.

The Trotting Stallion

CUPID,

Full Brother to Adonis 2:14,

—Sired by—

The Celebrated SIDNEY 2:19 3-4, and out of Venus.

Will make the season of 1890 at the OAKLAND TROTTING PARK.

PEDIGREE.

CUPID is by Sidney out of Venus by Capt. Webster 10178, record 2:30, and sire of Freestone 2:19. Second dam by Skenandoah 928, sire of Daisy Burns 2:29¾, Erwin Davis (sire of two in the 30 list) and dams of four in the 30 list.

DESCRIPTION.

Cupid is a handsome bright bay 15.3¼ hands high, weighs 1100 lbs.; was foaled in 1886. As a yearling, with very little work he showed quarters in 42 seconds, and at 2 years old, quarters in 38 seconds. As a three year old he has not been worked, but he shows the speed and endurance that must come from his excellent blood lines.

TERMS $50 for the season, with the usual return privileges. Good pasturage near the track at $5 per month. The best of care taken of mares in any way that owners may desire, but no responsibility assumed for accidents or escapes.

For further particulars address

C. O. THORNQUEST,

Oakland Trotting Park, or

C. BAAB, 972 Broadway, Oakland.

THE BUCKINGHAM.

OLD STRAIGHT WHISKIES.

141 Montgomery Street.

308 Bush Street, S. F.

M. J. BALFE, Proprietor.

SEASON 1890.

The Great Son of Buccaneer

SHAMROCK,

Two-Year Old Record of 2:25, beating the World's Record 4 1-2 Seconds when made.

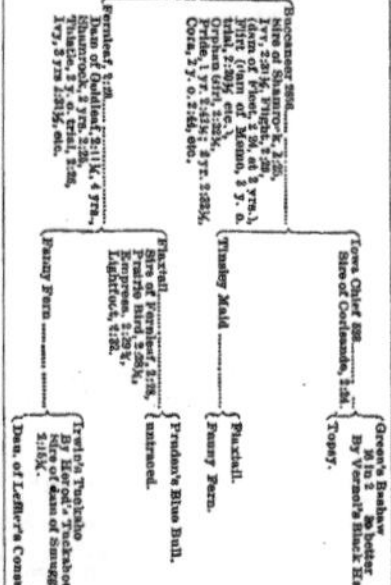

As will be seen from the tabulated pedigree and performances above, Shamrock is not only a phenomenal horse himself, but his ancestors on both sides have shown themselves to be uniformly producers of GREAT and PARTICULARLY early speed, and his record like many others of his family was made in a hotly contested race, instead of a trial against time.

HE IS NOW IN SPLENDID FORM, AND I TRULY BELIEVE WILL LOWER HIS RECORD TO 2:18 THIS YEAR.

TERMS, $100, with usual return privilege, for a limited number of CHOICE mares, season ending June 1st.

Electo.

By Antevolo 2:19¾ by Electioneer, dam Captain Webster (sire of dam of Adonis 2:14), by Williamson's Belmont.

Electo, while but three years old this spring, is, as well as being grandly bred, a great individual.

TERMS, $50, with the usual return privilege, limited to 15 approved mares. Season to end June 1st.

Imported Cleveland bay stallion

Elegance.

(Registered in Cleveland Bay Stud Book No. 75.) Prize winner over twenty of his own breed in the GREAT YORKSHIRE SHOW OF ENGLAND.

The Cleveland Bays are the most prepotent coach horses in the world, and their get from ordinary mares makes the most stylish and serviceable horses for that purpose that can be raised. Rich bays with black points having the preference over ALL OTHERS.

TERMS $25, with usual return privilege season ending July 1st.

Care taken but no responsibility assumed for accidents or escapes. Pasturage, $5 per month. For further particulars call at or address me at my hospital, where horses will make the season.

G. W. STIMPSON, V. S.

Veterinary Hospital, 19th St., near San Pablo Ave, Oakland, Cal.

WOODNUT

(Weatherhead's) by Nutwood 600

Sire of Belmont Boy, 2:15, pacer, Woodnut, 2:16¾, Felix, 2:18¾, Dawn, 2:18¾, Maggie E., 2:19¾, Irma, 2:18¾, and 26 others in 2:30 or better; 1st dam Flora, 2:29¾, trial 2:26, dam of Chrisman's Hambletonian, sire of Steve Whipple, 2:23, Kate Agnew, 2:28¾, by Chieftain 721, sire of Defiance 2:17¼ pacing and 2:24 trotting, Cairo, 2:26, Onward, 2:24, pacer; second dam by Wilson's Leaman.

Woodnut is a beautiful bay with black points, 15¾ hands high weighing 1,075 pounds. His colts are all larger than himself, and sell readily for road and carriage purposes, being of good color and very docile, yet prompt to obey, and always ready.

Service fee, $25, with usual privileges. Colts and fillies from Tilton Almont, Patchen, Stockbridge Chief, and other desirable crosses, FOR SALE. For further particulars, pedigrees, or any communication in horse matters, address

JAS. WEATHERHEAD, Prop.

San José, Cal.

The Fast Trotting Stallion

REDWOOD.

Four-Year-Old Record 2:24 1-2

Will make the season of 1890—February 1st to July 1st—at the

OAKLAND RACE TRACK.

REDWOOD is a dark bay colt, 15.2¾ hands high, weighs 1100 lbs. Foaled in 1885, by Anteeo, 2:16¼, sire of Alfred G., 2:19¾. Anteeo is by Electioneer. First dam Lou Milton, by Milton Medium; second dam Old Bly, a thoroughbred mare brought from the East in 1871 by W. C. Ralston, Esq.

Redwood's sire was out of Columbine by A. W. Richmond, the sire of the pacers Arrow 2:13¾, and Elwood 2:23, and the trotters Romero, 2:19¾, and Len Rose, 2:27. Redwood has shown a quarter in 33 seconds

Terms $100

For the season. Mares not proving with foal may be returned next season free of charge, provided Redwood remains the property of the present owners. Good pasturage at $5 per month. No responsibility assumed for escapes or accidents. Service fees payable before removal of the mare. Limited to 40 approved mares. For further particulars address

A. McFADYEN.

Race track, Oakland, Cal.

The Trotting Stallion

BONANZA $2:29\frac{1}{2}$

Will make the season of 1890, from February 1st to July 1st, at the OAKLAND TROTTING PARK.

PEDIGREE.

BONANZA, 2:29½.
- Arthurton 365 — Sire of Arab, 2:15, Joe Arthurton 2:20¾, Lady Scout, 2:26½. Dams of Grandee, 2:23½, Hidalgo, 2:27.
  - Hambletonian 10 — Sire of 41 in 2:30 list. Sires of 107 of the sires of 537 in 2:30 list.
  - Imogene by Am. Star 14 — Dam of Leland 1390. Sire of Clara, 2:21, Miss Leland, 2:25½, Hades, 2:27¾.
- Sister — Dam of Albert W., 2:20.
  - John Nelson 187 — Sire of Neres, 2:23¾, Gov. Stanford, 2:27¾, Aurora, 2:27, Nemo, 2:30.
  - Lamott Mare — Dam of Aurora, 2:27; g d of Arol, 2:24¾.

DESCRIPTION.

BONANZA is a very handsome chestnut of commanding form and splendid proportions. He stands nearly 16 hands high, is remarkably intelligent, level headed and pure gaited. His record is no mark of his speed. He is a great foal getter, and his colts are handsome fancy animals.

TERMS. $40 for the season, with the usual return privileges. Excellent pasturage near the track at $5 per month. The best of care taken of mares, but no responsibility assumed for accidents or escapes.

For further particulars, address

RICHARD HAVEY,

Oakland Trotting Park, Oakland.

The Hambletonian Stallion 10178.

CHRISMAN'S HAMBLETONIAN — Sire of Steve Whipple, 2:23, Kate Agnew, 2:28¾, etc.
- Whipple's Hambletonian — Sire of 14 trotters and 1 pacer from 2:19 to 2:30, and 7 sons with 8 performers from 2:21¾ to 2:30, and dams of 6 from 2:18¾ to 2:30.
  - Guy Miller — By Hambletonian 10.
  - Martha Washington — Dam of Speculation 928. Sire of Crown Pt. 2:24, Oakland Maid, 2:22¼, Gracie S., 2:22¼, and dam of Waterford, 2:27
- Flora, 2:29¾, trial, 2:26. Dam of Chrisman's Hambletonian, sire of Steve Whipple, 2:23, Kate Agnew, 2:28¾.
  - Chieftain 721 — sire of Defiance, 2:24 and 2:17¼, pacing; Cairo, 2:26, and Onward, 2:24, pacer.
  - daughter of Wilson's Leamon.

Stud season now on till the 1st of August, 1890, at $40 each mare, with return privilege in 1891, provided stallion and mare, or either, do not change owners. Good pasture at hand, and comfortable accommodation for brood mares and colts. For further particulars, address

JESSE CHRISMAN, Proprietor.

San Jose, Cal.

CALIFORNIA

NUTWOOD

Will stand for mares the season of 1890, commencing February 15th, and ending July 15th, at the NUTWOOD STOCK FARM, one mile from Irvington.

DESCRIPTION AND PEDIGREE.

He is a dark chestnut, with star in forehead; foaled September 16th, 1881; is 16 hands 1½ inches high and weighs 1260 pounds. Has a beautiful flowing mane and tail, with remarkable style and lofty carriage, a bold, open movement like his sire, but has never been handled for speed. He moves and looks like his sire, except that he is a larger horse.

CALIFORNIA NUTWOOD by Nutwood, record 2:18¾, has 32 trotters and pacers with records from 2:15 to 2:30, and put 8 in the 2:30 list in 1889. He is the only horse that ever lived with a record under 2:20 that produced five under 2:20. He is now serving mares at Dubuque, Iowa, at $500 for the season, and his colts at yearlings sell from $2500 to $5000 each. He is out of the dam of Maud S., record 2:08¾.

Nutwood, by Alexander's Belmont, sire of 32 with records from 2:15½ to 2:30. Alexander's Belmont by Alexander's Abdallah, sire of Goldsmiths Maid, record 2:14, and 5 others in 2:30 list. Alexander's Abdallah, by Rysdyk's Hambletonian, sire of 41 with records from 2:17¼ to 2:30, and is the founder of the Hambletonian family.

FANNY PATCHEN, dam of California Nutwood, by George M. Patchen Jr., record 2:27, and sire of Wells Fargo, 2:18½, Sam Purdy 2:20½, Ben Ali 2:20½, and 7 others from 2:21 to 2:30. He has 7 sons who together produced 12 trotters in 2:30 list, and 5 daughters who together produced 5 trotters and 1 pacer in 2:30 or better. He sired Alexander 2:31½. Alexander sired Alex. Button 2:26½; Alex. Button sired Yolo Maid, pacing record 2:14 at 4 years old, the fastest on record; George M. Patchen Jr., by George M. Patchen 2:23½, is sire of Lucy 2:18¼, and 3 others in the 2:30 list; he has 12 sons who together produced 40 trotters from 2:14¾ to 2:30, and 6 daughters who together produced 6 trotters in 2:30 list or better, he is grand sire of Hopeful 2:14¾, and best wagon record 2:16½, and sire of the granddam of Stamboul 2:12½.

George M. Patchen, by Cassius M. Clay, and he by Henry Clay, founder of the Clay family.

Laura, second dam of California Nutwood, was a fine large bay mare, a very fast roadster brought from Chicago by Wm. Wilson, of San José, and is said to have made a record of 2:35 in Chicago. Pedigree not traced.

TERMS.

$40 for the season, payable invariably before the animal is removed. Mares not proving in foal can be returned free next season. Pasturage $5 per month, but no liability for accidents or escapes.

For further particulars address the owner,

MARTIN CARTER,

Newark, Alameda Co., Cal., or Irvington, Alameda County, Cal.

HENRY J. COX — W. S. JOHNSON

The "EDWIN C."

40 EDDY STREET.

Cor. of Mason, San Francisco.

(Private Entrance Mason Street.)

Vineland Stock Farm

Whippleton 1883,

Sire of

LILY STANLEY	Record	2:17½
HOMESTAKE	"	2:16½
FLORA B.	"	2:27
CORA C.	"	2:31½
BLACK PRINCE	"	2:36½
RACHEL	"	2:38
PRINCE W.	"	2:40

WHIPPLETON is not only the sire of trotters, but he is the greatest sire of Carriage Horses on the Pacific Coast. Some of the best carriage and road teams in San Francisco are sired by Whippleton. A carriage team by Whippleton received First Premium at Napa, Petaluma, Oakland, Sacramento, Stockton and San Jose. Whippleton and his colts have never been beaten in the show ring.

DESCRIPTION.

WHIPPLETON is black, tan muzzle and flanks, 17 hands, and weighs 1,400 lbs. Most of his colts are 16 hands or over, and with a few exceptions, bay, brown or black. He never sired a sorrel or white face colt. (If he does, I agree to refund service money.)

PEDIGREE.

WHIPPLETON, sired by Hambletonian Jr. (sire of Hancock 2:29), by Whipple's Hambletonian (sire of Graves, 2:19, Westfield, 2:20¾, Express, 2:24, and 12 others in the 2:30 list), dam Lady Livingston (dam of Lady Blanchard, 2:26¾, Bloomfield Maid, trial 2:22), by General Taylor (sire of the dams of Wells Fargo, 2:18¾, Neres, 2:23¾, Bickford, 2:29¾, Lady Blanchard, 2:26¾, etc., and sire of grandam of Hazel Wilkes, 2:20) by the Morse Horse 6, sire of Norman 25 (sire of Lulu, 2:14¾, May Queen 2:20, etc.).

TERMS at $40, limited to 20 mares, for the season, usual return privileges. I would like to get about ten well bred mares with the proper combination of blood to breed to Whippleton on shares this season.

Alcona 730.

Sire of

FLORA BELLE	Record	2:24
CLAY DUKE	"	2:31½

ALCONA will be a great sire, but four of his colts have ever been trained, and all have shown full miles better than 2:30, and two of them as good as 2:20. Two of his first sons each sired a colt as a two-year-old, and last season one as a four-year-old trotted a full mile in 2:23¾, and the other, a three-year-old, a mile in 2:31. With opportunities, Alcona is destined to be one of Almont's best sons. Almont, for his opportunities, is beyond doubt the most prepotent sire of his age. He has 36 representatives in the 2:30 list; 48 sons and 22 daughters that have already produced 2:30 performers. Almont died five years ago at 20 years old. If he lived he would be but 25 years old.

PEDIGREE.

ALCONA sired by the great Almont (sire of Westmont 2:13¾, Fanny Witherspoon 2:16¾, Piedmont 2:17¾, and 3 others with records better than 2:30, and grandsire of Belle Hamlin 2:12¾, etc.); by Alexander's Abdallah (sire of Goldsmith Maid 2:14), he by Rysdyk's Hambletonian. Alcona's dam, Queen Mary, by Mambrino Chief (sire of Lady Thorne 2:18 1-4, and 5 others in the 2:30 list, and sire of the dams of Director 2:17, Piedmont 2:17¾, Onward 2:25 1-4, Red Wilkes, Almont, Belmont and many other noted sires).

DESCRIPTION.

Alcona is a beautiful chestnut 16 3 1-2 hands high, and weighs 1200 lbs. His colts possess speed, style, finish and beauty, and if they don't trot they command the highest prices for carriage horses.

$40 for the season. Usual return privilege.

Grandissimo,

Full Brother to GRANDEE, Three Year Old Record 2:23 1-2.

Sired by Le Grande (son of Almont and out of Jessie Pepper, by Mambrino Chief. Jessie Pepper is the dam of Ione 2:17 1-2, Alpha 2:23 1-2, and granddam of Montezuma 2:29¾. First dam Norma (dam of Grandee 2:23 1-2), by Arthurton (sire of Arab 2:15, Joe Arthurton 2:20 1-2, etc.); second dam Nourmahal 2:30 (full sister to A. W. Richmond, sire of Arrow 2:13¾, Romero 2:19, and sire of the dams of Antevolo 2:19 1-4, and Anteeo 2:16 1-4, sire of Alfred G 2:19¾ and Redwood 2:24 1-2.

GRANDISSIMO, with limited training as a three year old last year showed 1-4 mile in 35 seconds, and, barring accidents, will trot fast next fall.

Limited to 20 mares at $50 each; usual return privilege.

Season on Grandissimo ends June 1st, 1890.

Season on Whippleton and Alcona ends July 1st, 1890.

Best kind of pasturage at $4 per month. Mares kept in any manner desired.

For further particulars send for circular or call at stables, one mile south of St. Helena.

FRED W. LOEBER.

St. Helena, Napa Co., Cal.

The Trotting Stallion

G & M

FULL BROTHER TO

ALFRED G, $2:19\frac{3}{4}$.

(Who has been taken to Kentucky to stand at $200)

Will make the season of 1890 from FEBRUARY 1st to JULY 1st, at

SANTA ROSA.

G. & M. is by Anteeo, 2:16¼; was foaled 1886; first dam Rosa B. by Speculation (son of Hambletonian 10); 2d dam Elizabeth by Alexander 490; 3d dam Nora by imp. Glencoe. Anteeo is by Electioneer, out of Columbine by A. W. Richmond 1687.

G. & M. is a handsome dark bay; stands 15-3 1-2 hands high, and weighs 1050 pounds. Gameness, stoutness, speed and stamina are indelibly impressed in every line of the pedigree of G. & M. Owners of brood-mares in search of these qualities, will do well to patronize this promising colt.

PHILOSOPHER,

Foaled 1886 by Pilot Wilkes 2087; first dam Bella by George Wilkes 519; second dam by Bell Morgan 61.

Philosopher's sire, Pilot Wilkes 2087, is by George Wilkes 519, dam Grace (the dam of Alice Woodburn, etc.), by Pilot Jr. 12, grandam by Orphan Boy.

Will make the season of 1890, from FEBRUARY 1st to JULY 1st, at Santa Rosa.

TERMS for the season:

G. & M., $50.

PHILOSOPHER, $30,

with privilege of returning mares that do not prove in foal the next season free of charge, provided the horse bred to remains the property of the present owners. Good pasturage at $3 per month. No responsibility assumed for accidents or escapes. Service fees payable before removal of the mare. For further particulars, address

GEO. E. GUERNE,

Santa Rosa, Cal.

For Sale.

AT A BARGAIN.

NETTIE B.

(Half-sister to Emma Temple, 2:21).

In Foal to Free Trade.

Nettie B. was foaled 1884, and is by Altimont 885, dam Lizzie B. (dam of Emma Temple, 2:21), by Emigrant. Nettie B. is heavy in foal to Free Trade 2477, he by Princeps 536 (sire of Trumpet 2:14, and twenty others in the list), dam Dawn by Almont 33 (sire of 33 in the list); second dam Midnight (dam of Jay-Eye-See, 2:10, and Noontide, 2:20 1-2), etc.

Nettie B. is about 16 hands high. Is a handsome bay, and is warranted sound in every particular by the owner.

Must be Sold.

as the owner is about to move from the State. For price and particulars, apply at the office of the

BREEDER AND SPORTSMAN,
313 Bush Street.

FOR SALE
AT
Vineland Stock Farm
STALLIONS, BROODMARES AND FILLIES

ONE STALLION FIVE YEARS OLD, SEAL-BROWN, by WHIPPLETON (sire of Lily Stanley, 2:17 1-2, Homestake 2:16 1-2, etc.), dam Sally Gorham by Werner's Rattler. This horse is so fully 15 1-2 hands high, but very compactly built. He breeds exceptionally large and well finished colts. Any one understanding the business could clear him in one season, for he would make a No. 1 road horse, as he can trot a 40 gait any time.

ONE THREE-YEAR-OLD, SEAL-BROWN, by WHIPPLETON (sire of Lilly Stanley, 2:17 1-2, Homestake 2:16 1-2, etc.) dam Sally Gorham, etc. This ought to make a great General Purpose sire, and with opportunities get trotters as he is compact, strong-boned, and will measure when grown about 16 hands, and weighs 1,100 lbs. With a little road work he'll be developed a wonderful burst of speed.

ONE THREE-YEAR-OLD, BLACK, by WHIPPLETON (sire of Lilly Stanley, 2:17 1-2, etc.), dam by Nambec (sire of the dam of Eva W., 2:26 1-2, etc.), full brother to Thomas Jefferson, 2:23. This horse will be fully 16 1-2 hands high. He is smooth, rapid gaited and from size and conformation should breed, like his sire, large, rangy, finished colts.

ONE TWO-YEAR-OLD, BRIGHT CHESTNUT, sired by DAWN 2:18¾, dam Alida (dam of Direeta, three-year-old record 2:21¾, trial 2:20) by Admiral (sire of sister 2:19 1-2, Nona Y 2:26, etc). This Colt is the making of an extraordinary horse. He is large boned and will be over sixteen hands high when grown; he is of the true Nutwood type, is clean gaited and can ... as fast as any man's Colt.

ONE TWO-YEAR-OLD, BLOOD BAY, (full brother to Alcona Jr. sire of Silas Skinner trial 2:20) sired by ALCONA (sire of Flora Belle 2:24, etc.,) dam Madonna by Cassius M. Clay Jr. This Colt will make a trotter and a great stock horse if developed; he has the combined blood of Almont, Mambrino Chief, Cassius M. Clay Jr. and Joe Downing.

These colts are all sound and promising. The only reason I offer them for sale is, that I have three aged stallions in use, and the surplus is growing on me. If I were starting a breeding business for profit, I should consider either of these colts a representative to commence with. Also brood mares and fillies for sale. Correspondence solicited.

FRED. W. LOEBER, St. Helena.
Napa Co., Cal.

For Sale

A FIRST-CLASS

Napa County Farm

—OR—

STOCK RANCH,

800 Acres Improved,

SITUATED TWO AND A HALF MILES FROM NAPA CITY, with good roads leading thereto, a good hard finished house of nine rooms, with all modern improvements, streams running all summer, a great amount of live oak and black oak timber. It lies in a fruit belt, surrounded by fine vineyards and orchards growing upon the same quality of soil and originally a part of this tract. About one-half hill, and one-half rolling land, but none of it is steep and all easily cultivated, splendidly situated for the breeding of fine horses. Price, $06 per acre. Further particulars given at this office.

BREEDER AND SPORTSMAN,
313 Bush St.

Stallion for Sale

AT A BARGAIN.

Full Brother to Fairmont.

By Piedmont, dam Queen by Garibaldi—see State Fair Edition of BREEDER AND SPORTSMAN, September 14, 1889, for description of Fairmont—three years old, solid bay. Can trot a 2:40 gait or better. Sound in every particular. Can be seen at Oakland Trotting Park, Oakland.

P. J. WILLIAMS.

Attention Stockmen!

FOR SALE

At Chowchilla Ranch,

Thoroughbred Durham Cattle

Three Hundred Young DAIRY COWS, 2000 graded SHE CATTLE, Yearlings and up; a fine lot of high grade Durham Bulls; also have Mares, Horses, Mules and Norman Colts.

For particulars, apply to

ISAAC BIRD, Jr., Supt.,
Merced, California.

Woodside Farm

IMPORTANT SALE OF

Standard Trotting Mares Young Stallions and Fillies,

ROAD AND DRIVING HORSES
Farming Implements,
Etc.

By direction of MRS. SILAS SKINNER.

Mrs. Skinner having determined to retire permanently from the breeding of Fine Stock, has decided to offer at

PUBLIC AUCTION
Thursday, March 6, '90,

at 12 M., on the Premises.

THE WELL-KNOWN

WOODSIDE FARM,

Near Napa,

together with all the highly bred trotting stock thereon.

The brood mares at Woodside are among the choicest in the State. Among them are mares by Almont, dam by Alexander's Abdallah; by Cassius M. Clay Jr., dam by Joe Downing; by Cassius M. Clay Jr., dam by Richelieu son of Mambrino Chief; by Duke of Orange Jr., dam by Cassius M. Clay Jr.; by Almont Mambrino, dam by Blood's Black Hawk; by Alcona—dam Fontana, dam of Flora Belle, 2:24, and Silas Skinner, trial 2:22¾—by Almont; by Alcona Clay—dam Metamora, dam of Clay Duke, 2:31¾—by Duke of Orange Jr. These mares have been bred to Director, Noonday, Mountain Boy and Wildwood, and are with foal. The young stallions are by Sitka, son of Alaska, by Electioneer, Whippleton, sire of Lillie Stanley, 2:17¾, Alcona Clay, etc. About twenty head well-bred trotting and driving animals will be sold in addition to the standard bred horses.

Catalogues giving extended pedigrees and full information are being prepared, and will be forwarded upon application.

At the conclusion of sale of horses,

WOODSIDE FARM

will be sold.

WOODSIDE FARM is situated three and a half miles from Napa City, up the river, upon what is known as the middle or big ranch road. It contains 87 1-2 acres of the choicest quality of land for alfalfa or any kind of grain. 40 acres being now in alfalfa over a foot high. The land produces from four to six tons of hay to the acre, of choice quality. Five of the fields are in pasture, four in alfalfa, one in timothy, the other kept in hay or grain necessary for stock, though well adapted for alfalfa. There is a nice orchard, small vineyard, and comfortable dwelling house of nine rooms. There is a good school house directly opposite, the best in the county. As to its adaptability as a stock ranch: There is living water in every field, and plenty of it, corrals and stock yards, stable room for forty horses, besides seven good box stalls, two good stables, granery, etc. It is within two miles of the Napa Agricultural Society's race track, the finest constructed in the State for years. Should there not be sufficient land, 61 acres adjoining can be purchased at reasonable figures.

There is no more eligible location in the State for a small stock farm, and this affords a rare opportunity, with the stock, to at once engage in this remunerative pursuit.

The sale will be positive. Upon all sales of Live Stock and personal property, one years' credit will be given on approved notes. Interest 10 per cent. per annum. Three per cent. discount for cash.

Upon Land, one-half cash: balance can remain upon mortgage for a term of years to suit purchasers. Interest eight per cent. per annum.

Vehicles will be in attendance at Napa Depot to convey parties to the farm. Lunch will be served upon the ground.

Mrs. Skinner having large interests in Oregon which will require her personal attention during the greater portion of the year, compels the sale of the Woodside Farm.

Parties are invited to visit the farm and look over the stock. The undersigned will be glad to give any information required, either as to stock or ranch.

KILLIP & CO.
Live Stock Auctioneers,
22 Montgomery St., S. F.

Antevolo Colt
For Sale.

AVOLO REX, foaled February 22, 1888; dam Catchup by Rustic; grandam Huntress by Don Victor; g g dam Betty Denice by American Boy Jr. Is 16.1 hands high, well developed, muscular, and without a blemish. Has a very gentle disposition, and shows speed and a good gait. Apply

HOME FURNISHING CO.,
118 Fifth Street, S. F., Cal.

For Sale

A HALF BROTHER TO

ALMONT PATCHEN,

(2:25, trial 2:13 3-4).

JUANITA JR. is a beautiful bright bay, black points, with no white, foaled 1886. As a colt he has given much more promise than did Almont Patchen at the same age. Instead of being a pacer, he is a good square trotter, with every indication of great speed, and is so gentle and kind, that a lady can drive him. The owner's only reason for selling him is that business calls him away from this section of the State. He will be sold at a reasonable figure. This is a splendid opportunity for a gentleman to secure a first-class trotter at a very low figure.

The pedigree of Juanita Jr. is by Juanita (sire of Almont Patchen), dam, Nettie Moore by Old Tom Moore. For further particulars, address

JUANITA JR.,
Santa Clara P. O., Cal.

For Sale.

The Bay Stallion

AFTERNOON, 6543.

AFTERNOON was foaled in 1884, sired by Almont McGregor 1775, dam Minnie by General Hatch 39; second dam Lucy by Prophet [Weed's], son of Prophet. He is a very gentle, intelligent, level headed and pure gaited trotter. He is a remarkable foal getter, and his colts are handsome, game and speedy. He will be sold at a reasonable price. Reason for selling, ill health of the owner.

ALSO

A Handsome Brown Road Mare.

Can trot easily better than 2:40 to a Chicago cart or light buggy. Stands 15¾ hands high, weighs about 1050 lbs. She is by Green's Bashaw, and is very handsome, tough and speedy. Will be sold at a reasonable price.

Address

JACOB STEFFEN,
Vallejo, Cal.

For Sale!

A First-Class.

BREEDING FARM.

Of 800 Acres.

Four hours' ride from the city. Good roads to a first class track. Climate unexcelled. Plenty of wood and running water.

For further information apply to the office of the

BREEDER AND SPORTSMAN,
San Francisco.
313 Bush Street.

For Sale.

The Standard bred Stallion

Anteeo Button,

sire Anteeo, 2:16¼, sire of Alfred G. 2:19½; Redwood, 2:21¼, etc. Dam Mollie Button, dam of Alexander Button, sire of Yolo Maid, 2:14; Rosa Mac, 2:2.¾; Belle Button, 2:20¾, etc.

ANTEEO BUTTON is a dark bay 15¾ hands high, four years old, and weighs ... lbs. In style and action he is all that could be desired, and can trot a mile with ease in 2:40 to a cart.

This colt must be seen to be appreciated.

Apply to

I. DE TURK,
Santa Rosa, Cal.

First Special Auction Sale

—OF—

HORSES,

For account of CAPT. BEN. E. HARRIS,

On Saturday, March 1, '90

At the Cor. TURK and STEINER STS.,

WE WILL SELL AT

Public Auction

A CATALOGUE OF 25 HEAD OF SUPERIOR ROADSTERS AND SADDLE-HORSES OF ALL GAITS.

Also a few select colts, mares and fillies of royal breeding, most all of which have been bred, raised and broken by Captain Harris, whose reputation for the culture of swift roadsters and saddle horses to a high degree, is sufficient to warrant the public a rare opportunity for supplying their wants without the risk of disappointment. Among the lot there are several pairs of roadsters, one of which can trot in 2:30, besides a number of extra fine single flyers.

☞ **The attention of ladies is particularly called to this sale, as many of the animals have been prepared especially for their use and safety.**

This stock may be seen at the owner's stables, corner of Turk and Steiner Streets, from now until day of sale.

TERMS cash, or an equivalent in approved paper. Catalogues at our office.

KILLIP & CO.,
Live Stock Auctioneers.
22 Montgomery St., S. F.

ARGONAUT HERD.

POLLED ABERDEEN—ANGUS CATTLE.

Thirty head choice pure bred and high grade (Cross bred) HEIFERS and a few grand young BULLS for sale at reasonable prices. A fine opportunity for persons wishing to establish choice herds or change their bulls. Representatives from this herd were grand prize winners at the last California State Fair.

Address DR. G. M. DIXON,
Sacramento, Cal.

HORSES PURCHASED ON COMMISSION.

THOROUGHBREDS A SPECIALTY.

Will select and buy, or buy selected Animals for all desiring, for reasonable compensation.

KEEPS PROMISING YOUNGSTERS IN VIEW.

L. M. LASLEY, Stanford, Ky.

References:—J. W. Guest, Danville, Ky.;
B. G. Bruce, Lexington, Ky.
S. H. Baughman, Stanford, Ky.
G. A. Lackey, Stanford, Ky.
Geo. McAlister, Stanford, Ky.
First National Bank, Stanford, Ky.)

HOLLYWOOD BREEDING FARM.

MOUNTAIN BOY 4841.

Brown MOUNTAIN BOY, 4841, bred by Charles Backman, Orange County, New York, foaled 1882, sire Kentucky Prince 2470, dam Elise, sister to Elaine, by Messenger Duroc 106; grandam Green Mountain Maid, 3d dam, Shanghai Mary, will serve a limited number of mares at $100 the season.

ELECTION.

Bay stallion ELECTION, bred at Senator Stanford's Palo Alto Stock farm, foaled 1884, sire Electioneer, dam Lizzie H. by Whipple's Hambletonian 725, grandam Lizzie Harris (by Comus son of Green's Bashaw 50), great grandam by Arnold Harris, thoroughbred.

Election is one of the handsomest bloodlike sons of Electioneer, and with his thoroughbred cross through Arnold Harris should prove invaluable as a sire. TERMS, $100 the season.

KAFIR.

Bay KAFIR, bred by L. J. Rose, Los Angeles, foaled 1887, sire Alcazar, 2:20½, dam Flower Girl by Arthurton, sire of Arab, 2:15, grandam Flora by General McClellan, 144, sire of three in 2:30 list, great grand dam by Langford, he by Williamson's Belmont, will serve a limited number of mares at $50 the season.

WOODSIDE.

Ch c WOODSIDE, sire Woodnut, 2:16½; 1st dam Veronica by Alcona, 730; 2nd dam Fontana by Almont 33; 3rd dam Fannie Williams by Alexander's Abdallah, 15. Book full.

MART BOORHEM.

B c MART BOORHEM, by Sydney, 2:19¾; 1st dam Towhead by Echo. This colt is a full brother to St. Nicholas who showed a mile in 2:27½ at three years old. TERMS, $25 the season.

REVEILLE.

The well known thoroughbred stallion REVEILLE, by Shiloh dam by Norfolk. Reveille is a brother to John Treat and is the sire of Tycoon and Gladstone. TERMS, $25 the season.

Hollywood is nicely situated three miles from Vallejo on the Napa road. Good pasturage and every care will be taken of mares at reasonable rates. For further particulars, apply,

B. C. HOLLY, Vallejo.

CANNON BALL, 8820

BY SIMMONS 2744.

RECORD 2:28, (Full Brother to Rosa Wilkes, 2:18 1-4), Sire of Nine in 2:30 List at 10 Years Old

First dam Gurgle, pacing record 2:20; trial of 2:15¼ for W. H. Crawford; by Pocahontas Boy, sire of Buffalo Girl, 2:12¼; Raven Boy, 2:15¼, and ten others in the list.

Second dam Matlock by Grey Diomed.

Third dam by Tom Hal.

DESCRIPTION.

Brown bay, right hind foot and left inside hind heel white. Foaled May 20, 1887. Bred by W. H. Wilson, Abdallah Park, Cynthiana, Ky.

He is a grand individual, large boned, fine size and appearance. When fully matured will probably be 16 hands, and weigh 1200 lbs.

Is of speedy conformation and level headed. His blood lines are stout and fashionable, being the Wilkes and Mambrino Patchen on pacing and thoroughbred foundations, and from a family of producers on both sides.

Can be seen until February 1st at Agricultural Park, Los Angeles, in charge of C. A. Durfee, after which he will serve ten approved mares at $60 the season, with usual privilege of return in 1891, at Lockhaven Stock Farm, Burbank, Cal. Mares kept on grass $4 per month, and extra charge where grain and alfalfa are fed. For further particulars, address

O. H. LOCKHART, Proprietor,
Lockhaven Stock Farm,
Burbank, Cal.

Nine Miles from Los Angeles.

The Pure Trotting-bred Stallion

ILLUSTRIOUS

STANDARD No. 4178

DESCRIPTION.

Dark bay, black points, 15 1-2 hands high, weight 1000 pounds, foaled May 20, 1886; bred by General W. T. Withers, Lexington, Ky.

PEDIGREE.

By Happy Medium, sire of Maxey Cobb 2:13¼ and 52 with records of 2:30 or better. First dam Abdallatta by Cassius M. Clay Jr., sire of Durango 2:21¾, Harry Clay 2:23½ and sire of the dams of Minnehaha, Bertha 2:27¼, Charley West 2:26¾, Grandmont 2:25 1-2, Lottie K 2:28¾, Mambrino Diamond 2:26, Richwood 2:28 1-2, Topsy 2:29¾, Happy Thought 2:21 1-2, Pequot 2:23 1-2, Fairlawn Medium 2:27 1-4, Folley 2:27¾ and Mambrino Boy 2:26 1-2; second dam Laura Crockett by Almont, sire of Westmont 2:13¾, Puritan 2:16, Fanny Witherspoon 2:16¾, Piedmont 2:17¼, Aline 2:19¾ and 37 with records better than 2:30; third dam Sally Tee by Alexander's Abdallah, sire of Goldsmith Maid 2:14; fourth dam Kate Crockett, the dam of Lulu 2:14¾, by imp Hooton.

Illustrious is a horse of extra fine finish, large clean bone, good feet, back short and strong, loins and quarters well muscled, and powerful. He has a kind disposition and splendid trotting action, and is as handsome and bloodlike in form and finish as any trotting stallion in the land.

He is pronounced by his breeder, General Withers, to be the best bred son of Happy Medium living, and is undoubtedly one of the very best bred trotting stallions in the State. He has had but six weeks' regular training, and a part of that time was sick with epizootic, but was trotted quarters in 39 1-4 seconds, and barring accidents will certainly trot better than 2:30 this season.

TERMS—$60 the season. Mares not proving with foal may be returned next year free.

Good pasturage at $3 per month.

Season to begin February 1st and end June 15th.

GEO. A. STONE,
Santa Rosa, Cal.

Pacific Coast Trotting-Horse Breeders Ass'n

Stakes and Installment Purses for 1890.

Entries close March 1st, 1890.

STAKES.

YEARLINGS—FOALS 1889.

ONE MILE DASH, $50 entrance, payable $5 March 1, 1890, $10 May 1, 1890, $10 July 1, 1890 and $25 on the fifth day preceeding the first advertised day of the meeting.

TWO-YEAR-OLDS—FOALS 1888.

ONE MILE AND REPEAT; $75 entrance, $250 added, payable $10 on March 1, 1890, $10 May 1, 1890, $15 July 1, 1890, and $40 on the fifth day preceding the first advertised day of the meeting.

THREE-YEAR-OLDS—FOALS 1887.

MILE HEATS best three in five; entrance $100, with $300 added, payable $10 on March 1, 1890, $10 on May 1, 1890, $30 on July 1, 1890, and $50 on the fifth day preceding the first advertised day of the meeting.

FOUR-YEAR-OLDS—FOALS 1886.

MILE HEATS best three in five; $100 entrance, $400 added, payable $10 on March 1, 1890, $10 May 1, 1890, $30 on July 1, 1890, and $50 on the fifth day preceding the first day of the meeting.

PURSES.

$500. THREE YEAR OLDS. Foals of 1887. Eligible to three minute class. Mile heats; three in five.

$500. FOUR YEAR OLDS. Foals of 1886, eligible to 2:40 class. Mile heats; three in five.

Purses open to the get of Stallions with no Representatives in the 2:30 list.

$500. TWO YEAR OLDS. Foals of 1888. Mile and repeat.

$500. THREE YEAR OLDS. Foals of 1887. Mile heats; three in five.

$500. FOUR YEAR OLDS. Foals of 1886. Mile heats; three in five.

Stallion Purse $1,000.

Open to stallions eligible to 2.30 class. Mile heats, three in five.

ENTRANCE to all purses—10 per cent.; payable: 2 per cent. March 1st 1890; 2 per cent. May 1st, 1890; 2 per cent. July 1st, 1890; and 4 per cent. on the fifth day preceding the first advertised day of the meeting.

The Stanford Stakes for 1892.

FOALS OF 1889.

OPEN TO THE WORLD.

MILE HEATS.—Three in five. Entrance $100, with $100 added for each starter over two and up to five head, and $25 for each additional starter up to ten head. Payments: $10 on March 1st, 1890; $10 on January 2nd, 1891; $10 on January 2nd, 1892; $20 on May 1st, 1892; and $50 on the fifth day preceding the first advertised day of the meeting at which the stake shall be trotted.

CONDITIONS.

First payment, whether for purses payable in installments or for stakes, MUST ACCOMPANY NOMINATIONS, or they will not be considered.

Neglect to provide payments on the dates stipulated will incur forfeiture of all previous payments.

No horses and colts owned on the Pacific Coast by others than members of the P. C. T. H. B. A. are eligible to the above purses and stakes (excepting the Stanford stake), but horses and colts OWNED outside of the Pacific Coast are eligible thereto regardless of membership.

All States and Territories lying in whole or in part west of the Rocky Mountains are held to be part of the Pacific Coast.

The Directors reserve the right to change the hour and day of any race except when it becomes necessary to ante-date a race, in which instance the nominator will receive three days notice of change by mail to address of entry.

Entries not declared out by 6 P. M. of the day preceding the race, shall be required to start.

When there is more than one entry to a purse or stake by one person or in one interest, the horse to be started must be named by 6 P. M. of the day preceding the race.

Purses and stakes will be divided into four moneys, viz., 50 per cent. to the winner, 25 per cent. to the second horse, 15 per cent. to the third horse, and 10 per cent. to the fourth horse.

No added money will be paid for a walk-over. If only three horses start in a stake race, only first, second and third money shall be paid—if but two start, the Directors reserve the right to call it a walk-over, and divide the stake money paid in, two-thirds to the winner and one-third to the second horse. In case of a walk-over, only the money received from entries to said stake will be paid. In purse races, three horses will be required to start.

A horse distancing the field shall only be entitled to first and third moneys.

The Board of Directors reserve the right to declare any purse or stake filled or not filled without binding itself to any specified number of entries.

Trotting and racing colors shall be named by six o'clock on the day preceding the race, and MUST be worn upon the track.

Otherwise than the above, National or American Trotting Association Rules—as this Association may select—will govern the stake and purse races offered.

Persons desirous of making entries in the above purses and stakes, and who have not as yet joined the P. C. T. H. B. A., should make application for membership to the Secretary, and remit the sum of $15 to cover membership fee before March 1, 1890.

THE PROGRAMME FOR

Aged Horses—Trotters and Pacers,

AND FOR SPECIAL EVENTS, will be announced at the proper time.

J. H. WHITE, President.

JAS. P. KERR, Secretary.

313 Bush Street, S. F.

1890.

Petaluma Colt Stakes

TO BE TROTTED AT THE

Fall Meeting

OF THE

Sonoma and Marin Agricultural Society

District No. 4.

FREE-FOR-ALL COLTS.

1st. For two-year-olds, foals of 1888, Purse $400, entrance 10 per cent. of the purse, of which 2½ per cent. must accompany the nomination, to be made on March 1st; 2½ per cent., be paid on May 1st, and 5 per cent. on August 1st. Four colts to make the last payment, and three to start.

2nd. For three-year-olds, foals of 1887. Purse $500, entrance ten per cent. of the purse, of which 2½ per cent. must accompany the nomination to be made on March 1st, 2½ per cent. to be paid on May 1st, and 5 per cent. on August 1st. Four Colts to make the last payment, and three to start.

All moneys in the above races to be divided as follows: 60 per cent. to the first horse, 30 per cent. to the second, and 10 per cent. to the third.

Balance of Conditions as per District Stakes.

The following Stakes and Purses open to the Counties of Sonoma, Marin, Napa, Solano, Lake, Mendocino, Yolo and Colusa.

YEARLING STAKE.

For foals of 1889. Mile dash. $30 entrance, of which $10 must accompany the nomination March 1st; $10 be paid on May 1st and $10 on July 1st; $100 added.

TWO-YEAR-OLD STAKE.

For foals of 1888. Mile and repeat. $60 entrance, of which $10 must accompany the nomination March 1st; $20 be paid on May 1st and $30 on July 1st; $200 added.

THREE-YEAR-OLD PURSE.

Three in five. Purse $300. Entrance fee 10 per cent. of the purse of which five per cent. must accompany the nomination March 1st, and five per cent. paid on August 1st. Four Colts to make the last payment.

In the above stakes and purses, five to enter and three to start. But the Board reserves the right to hold entries, and start a race with a less number.

All moneys in the above races to be divided as follows: 60 per cent. to the first horse, 30 per cent. to the second and 10 per cent. to the third. If only two start they must contest for the stakes paid in, and one-half the added money to be divided, 66⅔ per cent. to the first and 33⅓ per cent. to the second.

If, in the opinion of the judges, any race cannot be finished on the closing day of the fair it may be continued or declared off at the option of the judges.

Entries to all the above races to close on March 1, 1890, with the Secretary.

J. H. WHITE, President.

DR. THOS. MACLAY, Secretary.

THE

Montana Agricultu'l, Mineral —AND— Mechanical Association

Announce the following stakes, to close March 1st 1890; to be run and trotted at the first annual State Fair, beginning at Helena, August 20th and ending August 30th, for which a programme will be arranged for ten days' racing with

$15,000

OR MORE IN ADDED MONEY TO STAKES AND PURSES.

THE LAST CHANCE HANDICAP.—A handicap sweepstake for all ages of $50 each; $400 added, $10 to accompany the nomination, $40 additional to start, weights to appear two days before the race, starters to be named in the usual manner through the entry box the evening preceding the race. One mile and a quarter.

THE DERBY STAKES.—A sweepstake for three year olds (foals of 1887) of $50 each; $500 added; guaranteed value of stake $1,000. Winner of any race this season of the value of $500 to carry 5 pounds extra; of two such races, 7 pounds. Maidens allowed 5 pounds. One mile and a half.

THE PIONEER STAKES.—A sweepstake for two year olds (foals of 1888) of $50 each; $500 added; guaranteed value of stake $1,000. Winner of a race of the value of $500 to carry 5 pounds extra; of two such races 7 pounds. Maidens allowed 5 pounds. Six furlongs.

THE NURSERY TROTTING STAKES.—A stake for two year olds bred and raised in Montana, of $50 each; $500 added; two in three.

THE JUVENILE TROTTING STAKES.—A stake for three year olds bred and raised in Montana; of $50 each; $500 added; three in five.

CONDITIONS.

Nominations close March 1st. Each nomination must be accompanied with $15, and shall plainly state age, color and sex of horse, name of sire and dam, and name of owner. A second payment of $15 is due and payable on or before June 1st. The remaining $20 for starters must be paid through the entry box before six o'clock P. M. of the day preceding that upon which the race is to take place.

A failure to make any one of the payments as above specified declares the nomination out of the stake.

All stakes divided into three moneys, 70, 20, and 10 per cent.

Blanks can be obtained at the office of this paper.

For further information address

FRANCIS POPE, Secretary,
Helena, Montana.

ROME HARRIS. JOHN MERIGAN.

"Laurel Palace,"

N. W. corner Kearny and Bush Streets

SAN FRANCISCO.

COOK STOCK FARM,

Season of 1890.

STEINWAY 1808.

Three-Year-Old Record 2:25 3-4.

Sire of STRATHWAY, three year old record 2:26, and sire of the dam of BOURBON RUSSELL 2:30.

By STRATHMORE 408; sire of 31 in the 2:30 list; sire of 6 dams of 8 in the 2:30 list, and sire of 3 sires of 8 in 2:30 list.

1st dam ABBESS (dam of Solo 2:28, and Soprano, dam of C. F. Clay 2:18, Eminence 2:27 and Strathbridge, 3 year old record 2:29½) by ALBION, sire of VANITY FAIR 2:24½, and of the dam of FAVORITE 2:35½.

2nd dam by MARSHALL NEY.

3rd dam by BERTRAND, a son of SIR ARCHY.

TERMS—$100 for the season.

CHARLES DERBY 4907

Brown Horse, Foaled 1885.

By STEINWAY 1808.

1st dam by the great ELECTIONEER, sire of SUNOL 3 year old record 2:10½, Palo Alto 2:12¼, etc., etc.

2nd dam FANNY MALONE, by NIAGARA.

3rd dam FANNY WICKHAM, by HERALD.

4th dam by Imp. TRUSTEE.

TERMS—$100 for the season.

CRESCO 4908.

(BROTHER TO SPARTAN, 2.24.)

By STRATHMORE 408, sire of 31 in the 2:30 list, etc.

1st dam the dam of SPARTAN 2:24, by ALMONT 33; sire of 71 with performers in the 2:30 list.

2nd dam the dam of HENDERSON 2:27, by BRIGNOLI 77, sire of the dam of KING WILKES 2:22.

3rd dam by CRIPPLE, a son of MEDOC.

4th dam by AMERICAN ECLIPSE.

TERMS—$50 for the season.

Pasturage $5 per month. Accidents and escapes at owner's risk. Mares consigned to the farm should be sent to Fashion Stables, Oakland; Geary & Grindle's Stable, Haywards; or to Bennett's Stable, Martinez; from and to which places they will be delivered free of charge. Address

COOK STOCK FARM,
Danville, Contra Costa. Co., Cal.

Sire of Yolo Maid, 2:12½

Alexander Button 1197,

FOUR YEAR-OLD RECORD, 2:26 1-4.

SIRE OF

YOLO MAID, 2:12½, BELLE BUTTON, 2:20,
TOM RIDER, 2:20½, ROSA MAC, 2:20½,
J. H., (seperately timed in a race) 2:22½,
KEHOE, 2:34½; ALEX. BUTTON (3), 2:35½,
BURBANK S. (2 y. o., ½-mile track), 2:53.

PEDIGREE.

Alex. Button was Sired by Alexander 490. Record, 2:31 1-4.

First dam Lady Button by Napa Rattler; 2d dam a pacing mare (S. T. B.) by a Copperbottom horse.

ALEXANDER (490), record, 2:31½.

Sire of Alex. Button, 2:26 1-2, Reliance, 2:22 1-2 Tommy Dodd, 2:24, Nelly Patchen, 2:27 1-4, by Geo. M. Patchen Jr. (31), record 2:27; first dam Lady Crum by Brown's Bellfounder.

GEO. M. PATCHEN JR (31), rec., 2:27.

Sire of Wells Fargo, 2:18¾, Sam Purdy, 2:20 1-2, Vanderlynan, 2:21, Star King, 2:22, Ben Ali, 2:21, and five others in the 30 list, by Geo. M. Patchen (30), 2:23 1-; first dam Bell by Top Bellfounder, son of imp. Bellfounder; 2d dam Hoot a Laddie mare.

GEO. M. PATCHEN (30). RECORD 2:23½.

Sire of Lucy, 2:18¾; Chas. E. Low, 2:25¾; Geo. M. Patchen, Jr., 2:27; Mary, 2:2-; by Cassius M. Clay (18) 1st dam by Head'em, son of imp. Trustee; 2nd dam Itaska, by American Eclipse.

CASSIUS M. CLAY (18).

Sire of Geo. M. Patchen, 2:23¾, etc., by Henry Clay (8). 1st dam Jersey Kate, the dam of John Anderson.

HENRY CLAY (8).

Sire of Black Douglass, 2:30; Centerville (w), 2:32; by Andrew Jackson (4); 1st dam Surry.

ANDREW JACKSON (4).

By Young Bashaw; dam an Ohio mare of unknown blood.

YOUNG BASHAW.

By imp. Grand Bashaw; 1st dam Pearl, by First Consul; 2nd dam Fancy, by imp. Messenger; 3rd dam by imp. Rockingham.

NAPA RATTLER.

By Biggart's Rattler; 1st dam Poll, by imp. Consternation; 2nd dam Betsy Baker, by Mambrino.

BIGGART'S RATTLER.

Grandsire of Joe. Brown, 2:22; Lady Snell, 2:23¾; Mary Davis, 2:2¾; Nellie Webster, 2:23¾, by Sir Henry, son of the Garrett Horse, by imp. Leonidas; 1st dam by the Hyde Horse, son of Long's Magnum Bonum; 2nd dam of Messenger blood.

BROWN'S BELLFOUNDER.

By imp. Bellfounder; 1st dam Lady Allport, by Mambrino; 2nd dam by Tippo Saib, son of imp. Messenger; 3rd dam by imp. Messenger.

DESCRIPTION.

ALEXANDER BUTTON is a dark bay with fine flowing mane and tail; stands 15-3¾ hands high; weighs 1,200 pounds, and is of excellent disposition. He is a natural trotter, inherited through the speed-lines of his ancestors, and imparts his speed to his offspring with uniform certainty. His colts show him to be a wonderful producer—and with his breeding and terms of service, he is the cheapest and most wonderful horse in the State.

TERMS.

TERMS.—$100, payable at end of season. Mares not proving with foal may be returned next season free of charge. Good pasturage furnished at $2 per month, and due care taken to prevent accidents or escapes but no liability whatever assumed.

Will stand at Cache Creek Farm, which is situated about one and one-half miles west of Yolo Station.

All mares sent to Yolo in my care will be forwarded free of charge.

G. W. WOODARD, Proprietor,
Yolo, Yolo Co., Cal.

Season of 1890.

February 15 to June 15

LYNWOOD,

(STANDARD 3047.)

AT WOLF'S (RUSSELL'S) STABLES, STOCKTON, CAL.

TERMS.

$50 for the season, payable at the close of season. Pasturage at $3 per month. Accidents or escapes at owner's risk.

PEDIGREE.

LYNWOOD 3047, trial 2:28.

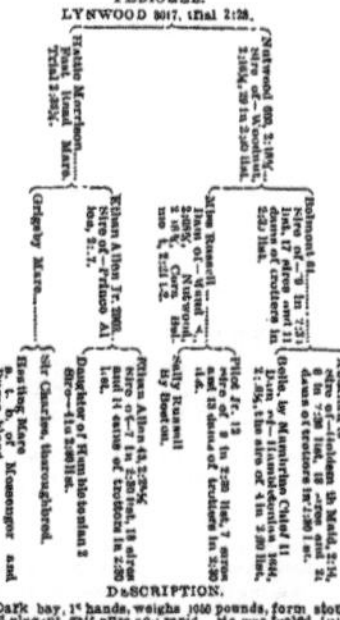

DESCRIPTION.

Dark bay, 16 hands, weighs 1050 pounds, form stout and elegant, gait pure and rapid. He was foaled July 13, 1880, has done but little work in the stud, but enough to demonstrate that he is one of the best foal getters in the State. Only one of his get has had any systematic handling, and that could have gone into the 2:30 list last year as a two-year-old, had the owner desired.

It will be observed from an examination of Lynwood's pedigree, that he is one of the best bred sons of the GREAT NUTWOOD, who commands a service fee of $500 for the season.

P. VISHER, Stockton.

The Thoroughbred Stallion

INTRUDER

Will make the Season of 1890 at Agricultural Park, SACRAMENTO.

Bay Horse, foaled 1871, bred by Sir L. Newman, England. Imported by D. D. Withers, Esq., New York.

By Crater, Son of Orlando and Vesuvienne by Gladiator.

1st dam Lady Bountiful by Rataplan (Rataplan is own brother to Stockwell, and winner of 42 races, including the Doncaster Cup and 18 Queen's Plates, and proved himself the most distinguished race horse of his day in England).

2d dam Plentiful by Don John (the winner of St. Leger and Doncaster Cup).

3d dam Plenty by Bay Middleton (winner of the Derby and Two Thousand Guinea Stakes).

4th dam Plenary, own sister of Plenipotentiary, by Emilius. (Both Emilius and Plenipotentiary were Derby winners).

5th dam Harriet, dam of the renowned Plenipotentiary by Pericles.

6th dam by Selim, winner of the One Thousand Guinea Stakes.

7th dam by Pypilina, by Sir Peter.

8th dam Rally, by Trumpeter.

9th dam Fancy, by Florizel. Fancy was full sister to Diomed, the first Derby winner in England, and after his importation into this country, sired the illustrious Sir Archy, etc. See English Stud Book.

Imported INTRUDER is a beautiful bay, standing fully 16 hands high, of great length and substance, and descends through close and strong currents from the most illustrious winners and winning lines of blood of which the English Stud Book bears record.

A careful review of the first six crosses of the pedigree of INTRUDER will show nine Derby winners; five St. Leger winners; two winners of The Oaks; two winners of the Two Thousand Guineas; two winners of the One Thousand Guineas; one Goodwood Cup winner; one Cesarwich Cup winner; one Cambridgeshire stakes winner, and four Doncaster Cups, in addition to a great number of Steeplechases and other races of less import.

INTRUDER, at the great fair held at St. Louis, Mo., in 1876, was awarded the highest stallion honors—the blue ribbon and the $500 purse—in the sweepstakes ring for stallion of any age or blood. The list of competitors embraced the large number of thirty-three animals, and they represented England, Canada, Kentucky, Tennessee, and other states. He also took first premium in his class and in sweepstakes for the best stallion of any age or breed at the State Fair at Peoria, Ill., 1882. He is the sire of Tidal Wave, George Hakes, Bernice and April Fool.

INTRUDER is the sire of Interpose, who is the dam of Spokane, winner of the Kentucky Derby, in which he beat the great horse Proctor Knott and broke the record.

TERMS: $50 for the season. Mares not proving with foal can be returned the next season free of charge. Good pasturage at $4 per month. Mares cared for in any manner owners may desire, and fed on hay and grain, either or both, at reasonable rates. While every precaution will be taken, no responsibility will be assumed for escapes or accidents. Mares sent from a distance in care of the undersigned, will be met and taken to the park. For further particulars, address

T. J. KNIGHT.
Agricultural Park, Sacramento.

Shoes For Comfort, Elegance and Durability.

Having my own Factory, and giving my personal supervision to all work I am in a position to warrant perfect satisfaction. Inspection invited.

AGENT for the VISCALIZED SHOES.

FACTORY—S. W. cor. Battery and Jackson Sts.
SALESROOM—Pioneer Building, corner Stevenson and Fourth Streets.

A full line of Boots and Shoes constantly on hand, and rules for Self-Measurement by Mail.

JNO. T. SULLIVAN.

Second Grand Combination Sale of Kidd, Edmonson & Morse.

CHICAGO, ILL; MARCH 17 to 21, in Battery D, adjoining Exposition Building.

Waters Stock Farm, Genoa Junction, Wis., a lot of their best bred ones.
S. A. Browne & Co., Kalamazoo, Mich., a grand pick of their choicest.
W. D. Crockett, Waukegan, Ill., one of Robert McGregor's best sons; Lexington Wilkes 4878, Star Hambletonian 2:28½.
H. D. McKinney, Janesville, Wis., sons of Phallis, 2:15½.
Granger Smith, Waukegan, Ill., grandsons and daughters of Dictator.
Ebin Remington, Fenton, Mich., stallions by Louis Napoleon 207.
M. L. Hair, Indianapolis, Ind., Hambrinos and a selection never excelled.
Rock River Stock Farm, Dixon, Ill., twenty-five head of choice ones.
Wildwood Stock Farm, Janesville, Wis., a picked consignment.
Charles M. Smith, Earlville, Ill., some good ones.

IMPORTED AND GRADE.
Percherons, Shires and Clydesdales.

W. L. Ellwood, De Kalb, Ill., car-load Percherons.
J. D. Beckett, Western Springs, Ill., Percherons and Coachers.
Evans & Bluett, Oregon, twenty-five imported Percherons.
D. J. Nicely. Union City, Ind., imported Clydesdales.
Henry Ives Cobb and J. V. Farwell, Lake Forest, Ill., seventeen imported Shires. Both sexes.
Havens Stock Farm, Alma, Neb., stallions, mares and geldings.
Marsh Black, Knoxville, Iowa, stallions.
R. D. Lowell, Sharon, Wis., Clydesdale stallions and mares.
Degan Bros., Ottawa, Ill., imported Percherons and French Coachers.
Morse Stock Farm, Kewanna Ind., imported Percherons.

JUDGE HAYES 4426,
By Robert McGregor, 2:17½, dam Luna, 2:39½, by Almont; second dam by Abdallah 15; third dam dam of Lula 2:14½.

BASSENGER BOY.
2:24 1-4, (trial 2:18) A game raceborse and campaigner.

KENTUCKY.
By Princeps, dam sister, by Volunteer; second dam by American Star.

FLAXMAN, 10,148.
By Lexington Wilkes, 4878, dam by Alexander's Abdallah 15; second dam Kate Crockett, dam of Lu a 2:14½.

LLEWELEN, 3229.
By Satellite 2500, dam by Volunteer 55; second dam by Seely's American Star 14

LADY ALLENDALE.
By The King 1917, 2:29½, son of George Wilkes

Chicago is the great horse centre and the best place to sell all kinds of horses in the world. A dirt track will be fixed on the lake front to show horses with speed. This sale will enjoy the largest and wealthiest audience that ever faced an auctioneer. ENTRIES CLOSE FEBRUARY 20. Address

KIDD, EDMONSON & MORSE, 806 West Madison Street, Chicago, Ill., or Lexington, Ky.

2:20 1-2 Half Mile Track) at 4 Years. | Fastest Record (in a Race) of any Wilkes | 2:14 1-2 at 5 Years

ROY WILKES, 2:12¾,

Seal brown; 15½ hands; foaled 1883; by Adrian Wilkes 6560, son of Geo. Wilkes; 1st dam by Blue Bull 75; 2d dam by grandson of American Eclipse; 3d and 4th dams thoroughbred.

THE GREATEST CAMPAIGNER OF 1889.

Handsome, Game, Pure Gaited. Level Headed.

Will make a season at the PLEASANTON STOCK FARM, PLEASANTON, CAL Service Fee $150. Money refunded if mare does not get with foal. Season ends April 1st, 1890

For full record of performances, extended pedigree, etc., address

L. A. DAVIES, Hotel Pleasanton,
SUTTER AND JONES STREETS, San Francisco, Cal.

MEMO.

The Best Son of SIDNEY

Will Make the Season of 1890 at the OAKLAND RACE TRACK

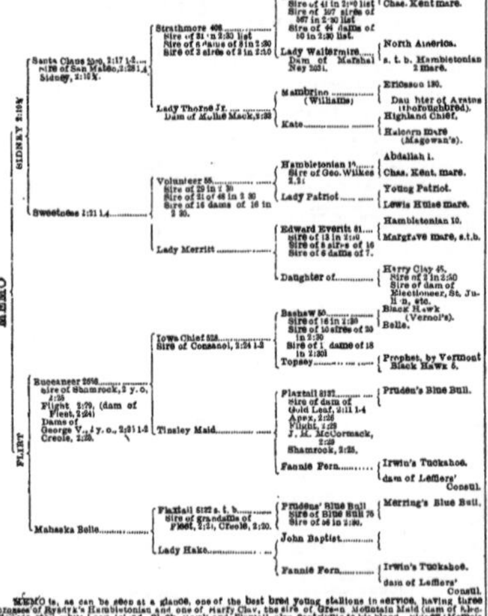

MEMO is, as can be seen at a glance, one of the best bred young stallions in service, having three crosses of Rysdyk's Hambletonian and one of Harry Clay, the sire of Green Mountain Maid (dam of Electioneer, etc.), while Long Island Black Hawk and Flaxtail also contribute to his blood. Sidney (Memo's sire) is universally known as the best young sire in the world, a producer of extreme speed at an early age.

PERFORMANCES.

MEMO trotted in public in his two year-old form, obtaining a record of 2:40, though he was close to Grandee in a race on the Bay District Track, the second heat of which was made in 2:31 1-2, the first in 2:3-. He exhibited phenomenal speed when three years old, and had it not been for a slight strain of his fore fetlock, there is little question that he would have shown in public very close to the best record. On the Oakland track he was timed a mile in 2:20 1-2, and frequently trotted quarters in from 42 1-2 to 34 seconds.

As a four-year-old Memo only started once at Sacramento when, although out of condition, he showed great speed, and improving as he went on, great hopes were entertained of his going well down in the 'teens at the P. C. T. H. B. A. meeting, but after showing several very fast miles his leg filled and he was laid up for the season. He is sixteen hands high, and of powerful build throughout. His color is a glossy black, with both fore-feet white. His disposition is all that could be desired, and his action superb. He is a sure foal getter, only one mare being reported not in foal during his last season.

TERMS, $100, with usual return privileges, for a limited number of mares. Season to close JUNE 15th, when he will be prepared for track purposes. Pasturage $5 per month. Have leased the cricket ground adjoining the track for pasturage, where there is fine feed. Reasonable charges if fed hay and grain. Best of care taken of mares in any manner owners may desire, but positively no responsibility assumed for accidents or escapes. For further particulars address

J. P. KERR, 313 Bush Street, San Francisco,
or, JOHN ROWEN, Race Track, Oakland, Cal.

Pleasanton Stock Farm Co.'s Stallions.

DIRECTOR, 2:17.

Director's book is open for 15 good mares more than already booked for the season of 1890, at $300 each.

This is the cheapest service fee ever charged for a stallion, taking into consideration his BREEDING and RACE RECORD and the RACE RECORDS OF HIS COLTS.

Season to commence February 15th and close August 1st.

PLEASANTON.

Sire Director 2:17. Dam May Day 2:30.

PLEASANTON is a light bay, 16 hands high, and is full brother to Margaret S, three year old record 2:19½.

His book is now open for 10 good mares at $100 for the season, which will commence March 1st and end June 1st.

Mares not proving with foal may be returned next season free of charge of service fees to the same stallion, if he is still in our possession; if not, to some other stallion equally as good, or money will be refunded at option of the company.

Pasturage $4 per month; hay and grain extra. Accidents and escapes at owner's risk.

Service fees due at time of service, and must be paid, together with pasturage, etc., before mares are taken away, or a good approved note given, payable August 1st, 1890, at which date all bills must be settled.

For further information call or address M. SALISBURY, 320 Sansome Street, Room 26, San Francisco, or

PLEASANTON STOCK FARM CO.;
Pleasanton, Alameda Co., Cal.

BAY STALLION	BROWN STALLION
ECLECTIC	**MORTIMER**
11,321	5,346
By Electioneer, dam Manette (full sister to Woodnut 2.16 1-2) Manon 2:21 and Maple, dam of Hattie D. (three-year-old record 2:26¾) by Nutwood 2:18¾, etc., etc.	Four-year-old Record 2:27. By ELECTIONEER, dam MARTI, by Whipple's Hambletonian (sire of 18 in 2:30, and of dams of eight in 2:30). Second dam Ina Martin by Rifleman (sire of Col. Lewis 2:18¾).
Terms $100 for the Season.	Terms $60 for the Season.

Horses shipped via San Francisco may be consigned to J. W. MORSHEAD, City Front Stables, who will attend to their forwarding.

Season closes JULY 1st, 1890. Usual return privileges.

For further particulars address owner,

WILFRED PAGE, Penns Grove,
Sonoma County, Cal

The Trotting Stallion

Silver Bow

Will make the season of 1890 at the Oakland Race Track.

Pedigree.

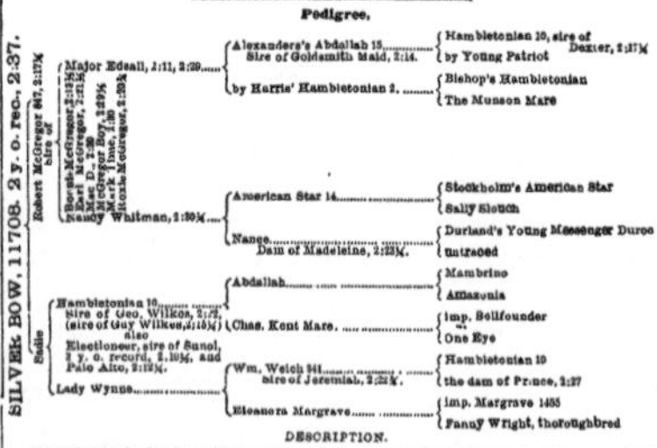

DESCRIPTION.

SILVER BOW is a handsome bay, no white; 15-2¾ hands high; weighs 1071 pounds; of fine form, with the best of legs and a clean cut, intelligent head. Is remarkably level headed seldom making a break; wears 7-ounce shoes in front. His record 2:37, is no mark of his speed; he can beat 30 easy, and with his gilt-edge breeding, he is just what he ought to be, a trotter sired by a trotter whose dam was herself a trotter and his grandam the dam of two trotters. His dam Sadie being by Hambletonian 10, shows him to be bred from the cream of the trotting blood.

TERMS: $100 for the season. Mares not proving in foal returnable for the season of 1891 free of charge. Good pasturage and first-class care taken of mares for $5 per month. No responsibility assumed for escapes or accidents. For further particulars, address

Limited to 15 approved mares.
Season to end June 1st, 1890.

P. J. WILLIAMS.
Care Race Track, Oakland, Cal.

Langtry Farms' Stud

Imp. FRIAR TUCK

By the Immortal HERMIT.

DAM ROMPING GIRL BY WILD DAYRELL,

AT $50 THE SEASON.

Mares not proving with foal may be returned the following season. Good care taken of mares, but no liabilities for accidents or escapes.

Good Pasturage at $5 per month.

Mares shipped to ST. HELENA, care CHARTES WILLIAM ABY, St. Helena Stables, will be cared for. For further particulars address,

CHAS. WILLIAM ABY,
Middletown, Lake County, Cal.

2:08 3-4 2:10 2:12

MAMBRINO WILKES, 6083.

SIRE OF

GUS WILKES, 2:22; ALPHEUS, 2:27; CLARA P, 2:29½; BALKAN, 2:29½ (3-year-old) and timed separately 2:22¼ in 4-year-old Stake, Bay District Track, October 14, 1889.

DESCRIPTION.

Black; sixteen hands; weighs, in exercise, 1,280 lbs. For style, finish, symmetry and proportion, comparison is challenged with any trotting bred horse. His colts follow in size, style and beauty. Balkan, for instance, being "facile princeps" of trotters in these particulars.

PEDIGREE.

Sired by Geo. Wilkes, sire of Harry Wilkes, 2:13½, Guy Wilkes, 2:15¼, and 60 other trotters in the 2:30 list, in addition to 8 pacers, and of the sire of Axtell, 2:12 (three-year-old), beating all stallions of any age, and the sire of Regal Wilkes, 2:20¾, best two-year-old stallion record.

First dam Lady Chrisman by Mambrino (Todhunter's, son of Mambrino Chief 11; sire of Lady Thorn, 2:18¼; Woodford Mambrino, 2:21½, and four others in 2:30. and of the dams of Director, 2:17, Piedmont, 2:17¼, Onward, 2:25¼, etc.

Second dam by Pilot Jr. 12, sire of nine in the 2:30 list, and of the dams of Maud S., 2:08¾, Jay-Eye-See, 2:10, Nutwood, 2:18¾, Viking, 2:19¼, Pilot Boy, 2:20, Naiad Queen, 2:20¾, etc.

TERMS.

Mares from a distance will be received at the Dexter Stables, Oakland, or Livery Stable, Martinez, the owner notifying Smith Hill, Superintendent at the farm. Good pasture and plenty of water. For the purpose of placing the service of a Wilkes within reach of breeders, the same rate will be maintained as last year, to wit, $75 for the season. Although it is not admitted thereby that this horse is inferior as a producer to the horses whose fees are placed at from $150 to $500. Address

SMITH HILL,
San Miguel Stock Farm,
Walnut Creek, Contra Costa Co., Cal.

$2:12\frac{3}{4}$ $2:13\frac{1}{2}$ $2:15\frac{1}{4}$

$2:08\frac{3}{4}$ 2:10 2:12

BALKAN

By Mambrino Wilkes.

(See that Horse's Advertisement.)

DAM FANNY FERN BY JACK HAWKINS
Son of Boston.

The grandam of Maud S, (2:08¾) was by Boston and the grandam of Jay-Eye-See (2:10) was by Lexington, son of Boston. So Balkan is the same remove from Boston that Maud is, and one remove nearer than Jay-Eye-See.

Fanny Fern has produced Molly Drew, Onyx, Fred Arnold, Molly Fern and Balkan, all by different sires. Balkan's sire and dam both being producers, and he being a trotter himself with a record of 2:29 1-2 (three-year-old) and timed separately 2:22 1-4 in 4-year-old Stake, Bay District Track, October 14, 1889—it is but fair to presume that he will get trotters of the highest order.

DESCRIPTION.

He is seal brown, 16-1 hands high, in style rivalled by few, and excelled by none with as pure a gait as has yet been exhibited in public—bar none.

Balkan will be at Oakland Trotting Park for the season of 1890, and will be limited to ten mares, at $100 fee, in order to be put in training early, as it is morally certain that if given a reasonable opportunity he will be fast enough to compete with the best of his age. For further particulars, address

A. L. HINDS,
Dexter Stables, Oakland.

$2:12\frac{3}{4}$ $2:13\frac{1}{2}$ $2:15\frac{1}{4}$

JESSE E. MARKS & CO.,

Wholesale and Retail Dealers of Choice Brands

Havana & Key West Cigars

922 MARKET ST., S. F.

2:19 NOONDAY $2:20\frac{1}{2}$

STANDARD No. 10,000.

This celebrated trotting bred stallion will make the season of 1890 at the stable of the undersigned at Sacramento, Cal., at $75 for the season and $100 to insure a mare in foal. Payable on or before July 1st, 1890. Money will be refunded on mares bred by insurance as soon as the fact becomes known that they are not in foal.

NOONDAY.
- Wedgewood, 2:19 .. Sire of Favonia, 2:15, fastest 4th heat for any mare or gelding, and eight others in 2:27 or better.
  - Belmont .... Sire of Wedgewood, 2:19, Nutwood, 2:18¾, Viking, 2:19½, and 29 others in 2:30 list.
    - Alexander's Abdallah, sire of Goldsmith Maid, 2.14; Almont, with 35 horses in 2:30 list, etc.
    - Belle, dam of Hambletonian, 2:26½; B'cars, dam of Pancoast, 2:21¾, the sire of Patron, 2:14½.
  - Woodbine .... Dam of Wedgewood, 2:19, Woodford Mamb., 2:21½, the sire of Pancoast, 2:21¾, the sire of Patron, 2:14½.
    - Woodford.
    - Singleton Mare.
- Noontide, 2:20½ ... (Trial, 2:18¾).
  - Harold .... Sire of Maud S., 2:08¾, and 26 others in 2:30 list.
    - Hambletonian (Rysdyk's), sire of George Wilkes, 2:22, the sire of Guy Wilkes, 2:15¼; Electioneer, the sire of Sunol, 2:10½, and scores of noted trotters and producers.
    - Enchantress, by Abdallah 1.
  - Midnight .... Dam of Jay-Eye-See, 2:10, Noontide, 2:20½.
    - Pilot Jr., sire of dams of Maud S., 2:08¾, Jay-Eye-See, 2:10, Nutwood, 2:18¾, etc.
    - Twilight, by Lexington, sire of the dam of Ansel, 2:20.

NOODAY is a dark seal brown, foaled 1884, 16 hands 1¼ inches high. Individually he is equal to his royal breeding. He is all that can be desired in conformation, intelligence, color and trotting action, and no stallion now in public service can show a pedigree with such fast records and royal game trotting blood as Noonday.

DON MARVIN,

Record 2:28 as a five-year-old. Standard by Breeding and Performance

Standard No. 7927.

Don Marvin 2:28.

Don Marvin is a beautiful seal brown, foaled 1881, bred by Hon. Leland Stanford, Palo Alto, Cal., standing 15 hands, and weighs, in ordinary condition, 1200 lbs. He is a fine individual, good style and form, combined with great substance, and good temper. Is very level headed; in his first race the past season he only made one break in five closely contested heats. He has great speed and endurance, with the pure, rapid Electioneer gait. He trots without toe weights, and wears only 8 oz. shoes in front. He gained his record the past season in the third heat, on a slow track, after making a season (serving over 60 mares), with scarcely any preparation. His record is no mark of his speed. He was a natural born trotter, and Mr. Charles Marvin considered him the fastest two year old at Palo Alto that season.

By FALLIS, 2:23, - - by Electioneer, sire of
Sire of Don Marvin, 2:28. — Sunol, three-year-old, 2:10 1-2, Palo Alto, 2:12¾, and 47 others in 2:30 list.

Dam CORA, by Don Victor by Belmont, sire of
Dam of Don Marvin, 2:28. — Ventura, 2:27¾, and sire of the dam of Bell Echo, 2:20, and six others in 2:30 list.

2d dam CLARABEL, - by Abdallah Star,
Dam of Clifton Bell, 2:24 1-2, and grandam of Rexford, three years, 2:24. — Sire of Hattie Maples, 2:33.

3d dam FAIRY, - - by Rysdyk's Hambletonian,
Sister of Sweepstakes, sire of 16 in 2:30 list. — Sire of Electioneer, George Wilkes, and many other noted sires and trotters.

4th dam EMMA MILLS, by Seely's American Star,
Dam of 4 horses that have 2:30 performers. — The great broodmare sire of the world.

The above pedigree should show every intelligent breeder that Don Marvin is "high" bred though very strong in trotting blood. All the comment it is deemed necessary to make as to the value of "thoroughbred blood" in the trotter is simply to refer to the very significant fact that the first and second dams of Maud S, 2:08¾, Jay-Eye-See 2:10, Sunol, three years 2:10 1-2, Palo Alto 2:12¾, Anteeo 2:16¼, Nutwood 2:18¾, Wedgewood 2:19, and many other successful sires and sensational trotters of the day are thoroughbred.

TERMS—Don Marvin will make the ensuing season from February 1st to July 1st, 1890, at $40 the season, with the usual privilege of returning the mare next season if not proving in foal. Mares from a distance met at the cars or boats on notification, and carefully handled, but no responsibility assumed for accidents or escapes.

Good alfalfa pasture furnished (free from barb wire fence) at $4 per month. For further particulars or complete circulars address

F. P. LOWELL,
1520 F Street, Sacramento, Cal.

The Produce of Eros Averaged $2,200 Each at New York Auction Sale in 1889.

THE ELECTIONEER TROTTING STALLION,

5326 EROS 5326

Will make the season of 1890—February 1st to July 1st—at LA SIESTA RANCH. MENLO PARK, adjoining Palo Alto.

PEDIGREE.

EROS (5326)
Standard by his sire
" " dam
" " record
" " produce
" under all rules

EROS (5326) ..
- Electioneer .... Grandsire of Norlaine, 1 yr., 2:31 1-2, Sire of Sunol, 2 yrs., 2:18, Sunol, 3 yrs., 2:10 1-2, Hinda Rose, 4 yrs., 2:16, Palo Alto, 2:12¾.
  - Hambletonian 10 .... Sire of Dictator, George Wilkes, Happy Medium, and 40 others in 2:30 list, and grandsire of 728 in list.
    - Abdallah 10 Sire of the dams of Goldsmith Maid, 2:14, and 7 other producing dams.
    - Charles Kent mare By imp. Bellfounder.
  - Green Mountain Maid .... Dam of Prospero, 2:20, Elaine, 2:20, Dame Trot, 2:22, Elista, 2:22¾, Storm, 2:26¾, Antonio, 2:29¾, Miranda, 2:31, Mansfield, 2:26.
    - Harry Clay Sire of the dams of St. Julian, 2:11¾, Bodine, 2:19¼, and 17 more in 2:30 list
    - Shanghai Mary.
- Sontag Mohawk .... Dam of Eros, 2:29 1-2, Sport, 2:22¾, Sallie Benton, 2:17¾, Conductor, trial, 2:26, Colma, 3-y-o trial, 2:24.
  - Mohawk Chief .... Sire of the dams of Lot Slocum, 2:17¼, Sallie Benton, 4 yrs., 2:17¾, Pedlar, 2 yrs., 2:27¾, Stanford, 4 yrs., 2:30, Eros, 6th heat, 2:29 1-2.
    - Hambletonian 10 Sire of the dams of Stamboul, 2:12¼, Wilton, 2:19¼, and 20 other trotters.
    - Lady Perrine
  - Sontag Nellie ....
    - Toronto Sontag By Toronto Chief.
    - Nellie Gray Amile record, 12:45.

Produce of Eros
Wanda, 4 yrs., 2 24,
Solita, 2 yrs., 2 41 1-2,
Meriquita, 2 yrs., 2:42,
Daylight, 2 yrs., 2:54,
Hiram B., trial, 2:28.

These are the only colts by him that have ever had a harness on except one in New York that went a trial last July in 2:26 1:2.

DESCRIPTION.

EROS is a rich seal brown stallion, bred by Hon. Leland Stanford at Palo Alto, and is the nearest living likeness of his celebrated sire, Electioneer. Stands 15.2 hands high, and weighs 1060 pounds.

In breeding to Eros, the owners of mares will strictly follow the great rule of breeding, viz., breed to a stallion by a producer and out of a sure producer of great speed. Eros is by the stallion that has produced more 2:30 trotters than any living horse, and is also the sire of more 2:20 performers than any horse living or dead.

EROS is out of the dam of Sally Benton, four years old, record 2:17¾, Sport 2:22¾, and Eros 2:29½ in the sixth heat, against a field of nine horses. He is from a family that is endowed with great natural speed, trot fast at an early age, train on, throw trotters from all classes of mares, are of good substance, bone, style and action, and breed solid colors.

TERMS.

$100 for the season; with the privilege of return next season should mares not be in foal and horse and mare still remain in the same hands.

Good pasturage can be obtained at $5 per month, but no responsibility for accidents or escapes. There are a large number of box stalls, and animals can be kept up and fed on hay and grain at reasonable rates if required. Mares already in foal can be sent to the ranch for foaling, and will receive all the attention bestowed upon our own mares. Mares left with Mr. Peter Pomyea, Broadway Street Stable, Oakland, or with Mr. F. H. Burke, 401 Montgomery Street, San Francisco, will be forwarded to the ranch free of charge. For further particulars apply to

W. H. VIOGET,
LA SIESTA RANCH, MENLO PARK, CAL.

EROS is the only stallion offered to the public on this Coast that has a dam that has three in the 2:30 list.

POPLAR GROVE

Breeding Farm

STALLIONS.

CLOVIS, 4909,

CLOVIS is a beautiful black, Eight Years Old, 16 1-2 Hands High, and weighs 1260 lbs.

He is a horse of beautiful symmetry and magnificent action.

PEDIGREE.

CLOVIS was sired by Sultan, 2:24, sire of Stamboul, 2:12 1-4, Ruby, 2:19¾, and fifteen others with records of 2:30 or better.

First dam Sweetbriar by Thorndale 2:22 1-2, sire of Edwin Thorne, 2:16 1-2, Daisy Dale, 2:19, and May Thorne, 2:22

Second dam Ulster Queen, dam of Volmer, 2:24¾, by Hambletonian 10. Sire of Dexter, 2:17¼, George Wilkes, 2:22.

Third dam by Thomas Jefferson, a son of Mambrino Paymaster, Jr.

Fourth dam by Mambrino Paymaster, sire of Mambrino Chief.

Sultan, by The Moor, sire of Beautiful Bells, dam of Hinda Rose, 2:19 1-2, and Sable, dam of Sable Wilkes, three year old record 2:18.

First dam of Sultan, Sultana, by Delmonica. Sire of Darby, 2 16 1 2, by Guy Miller, sire of Whipple's Hambletonian.

Second dam by Mambrino Chief.

Third dam by Downing's Bay Messenger.

Fourth dam Mrs. Caudle, dam of Ericsson, four year old record 2.30 1-2.

Clovis will make the season of 1890 at Poplar Grove Breeding Farm, near Wildflower, Fresno County, commencing February 1st and ending July 1st.

Terms, $75, due at time of service.

Mares cared for in any manner owners may desire; pasturage $2 per month. Every care exercised, but no liability for escapes or accidents. Mares not proving with foal can be returned next season, providing I still own this stallion.

APEX, 8935.

FOUR - YEAR - OLD RECORD, FOURTH HEAT, 2:26.

Will make the present season at the Poplar Grove Breeding Farm, near Wildflower, Fresno Co., season commencing Feb. 1st, and ending July 1, 1890. Terms, $50 the season, due at time of service. Apex is eight years old, a beautiful bay, 15 1-2 hands high, and weighs 1140 lbs. He is a horse of fine disposition, and his gait is faultless.

PEDIGREE.

Apex was sired by Promptor 2305, he by Blue Bull 75; first dam Mary by Flaxtail, he by Pruden's Blue Bull. Flaxtail being the sire of the dams of Buccaneer, five-year-old record, 2:24 1-4; Pride, yearling record, 2:44 1-2, and Shamrock, two-year old record, 2:25, third heat. Second dam by Bright Eyes, son of Boanarages. Prompter (sire of Apex, record 2:26, and Transit, 2:26 1-4), by Wilson's Blue Bull, by Pruden's Blue Bull, son of Merring's Blue Bull. Promptor's dam Prairie Bird, by Flaxtail; second dam by John the Baptist, son of Tally Ho Morgan, by Sherman Morgan; third dam Fannie Fern by Irwin's Tuckahoe.

Apex made his appearance in the circuit as a two-year-old, and obtained a record of 2:42. As a three-year-old he reduced this in a race at Santa Rosa against Stamboul to 2:31, it taking six heats to decide the contest, which was won by Apex. As a four year-old he gained his present record of 2:26.

Mares cared for in any manner owners may desire. Pasturage $2 per month. Every care exercised, but no liabilities for escapes or accidents. Mares not proving with foal can be returned next season, providing I still own this stallion.

The Standard Stallion

JUNIO,

RECORD 2:22.

WILL MAKE THE PRESENT SEASON OF 1890 AT FRESNO FAIR GROUNDS.

Season Commencing Feb. 1st and ending July 1st.

TERMS—$100 the season, due at time of service.

JUNIO is eight years old, a handsome dark bay 16 hands high, and weighs 1250 pounds. He is the personification of the light harness horse, and his trotting action is superb. At the State Fair of 1886 he took first premium over forty of the finest trotters in the State.

PEDIGREE.

"Junio, by Electioneer, premier stallion of Palo Alto (sire of Sunol 2 10 1-2, Palo Alto 2:12 1-4, and 47 others in the 2 30 list." Dam by Granger by imp. Hercules.

Granger, by imp. Hercules, dam Jenny Lind, by Stockbridge Chief, Jr., he by Stockbridge Chief, he by Vermont Black Hawk. Second dam by Kentucky Whip.

Imp. Hercules, by Kingston, first dam daughter of Tuscar, by Bay Middleton, second dam Malvina, by Oscar; 3rd dam Spotless by Walton; 4th dam by Trumpator (see Bruce's American Stud Book, Vol. 1, page 26). Hercules is the sire of the dam of Azmoor 2 2¾; also sire of dam of Menlo 2:21 1-2.

Mares not proving in foal may be returned next year free of charge, providing I still have the horse. Pasturage $3 per month. While every care will be taken of horses no liability will be assumed for accidents or escapes.

For further particulars address

S. N. STRAUBE, Fresno, Cal.

Poplar Grove Breeding Farm.

Southern Pacific Co.

(PACIFIC SYSTEM.)

Trains leave and are due to arrive at San Francisco.

LEAVE (FOR)	FROM JANUARY 1, 1890.	ARRIVE (FROM)
7.30 A M	Haywards, Niles and San Jose	*12.45 P M
7.30 A M	Sacramento and Redding, via Davis	7.15 P M
7.30 A M	Sacramento, Auburn, Colfax	5.45 P M
8.00 A M	Martinez, Vallejo, Calistoga and Santa Rosa	6.15 P M
8.30 A M	Los Angeles Express, Fresno, Bakersfield, Mojave and East and Los Angeles	11.15 A M
8.30 A M	Niles, San Jose, Stockton, Ione, Sacramento, Marysville, Oroville and Red Bluff	5.45 P M
10.30 A M	Haywards and Niles	2.15 P M
*12.00 M	Haywards, Niles and San Jose	* 3.45 P M
*1.00 P M	Sacramento River Steamers	**6.00 A M
3.00 P M	Haywards, Niles and San Jose	9.45 A M
3.30 P M	2d Class for Ogden and East	10.45 P M
4.00 P M	Stockton and ‡Milton; Vallejo, Calistoga and Santa Rosa	9.45 A M
4.30 P M	Sacramento and Knight's Landing via Davis	10.45 A M
* 4.30 P M	Niles and Livermore	* 8.45 A M
* 4.30 P M	Niles and San Jose	‡ 4.15 P M
5.30 P M	Haywards and Niles	7.45 A M
6.00 P M	Sunset Route, Atlantic Express, Santa Barbara, Los Angeles, Deming, El Paso, New Orleans and East	8.45 P M
7.00 P M	Shasta Route Express, Sacramento, Marysville, Redding, Portland, Puget Sound and East	7.45 A M
8.00 P M	Central Atlantic Express, Og- and East	9.45 A M

SANTA CRUZ DIVISION.

‡ 8.00 A M	Hunters train to San Jose	‡ 7.20 P M
8.15 A M	Newark, Centerville, San Jose, Felton, Boulder Creek and Santa Cruz	5.50 P M
* 2.15 P M	Centerville, San Jose, Almaden, Felton, Boulder Creek and Santa Cruz	*11.50 A M
4.15 P M	Centerville, San Jose, and Los Gatos	9.50 A M

Coast Division (Third and Townsend Sts.)

7.25 A M	San Jose, Almaden and Way Stations	2.30 P M
8.30 A M	San Jose, Gilroy, Tres Pinos; Pajaro, Santa Cruz; Monterey; Pacific Grove, Salinas, San Miguel, Paso Robles, Santa Margarita (San Luis Obispo) and principal Way Stations	6.12 P M
10.30 A M	San Jose and Way Stations	5.02 P M
12.01 P M	Cemetery, Menlo Park and Way Stations	3.36 P M
* 3.30 P M	San Jose, Tres Pinos, Santa Cruz, Salinas, Monterey, Pacific Grove and principal Way Stations	*10.00 A M
* 4.20 P M	Menlo Park and Way Station	* 7.58 A M
5.20 P M	San Jose and Way Stations	9.03 A M
6.30 P M	Menlo Park and Way Stations	6.35 A M
†11.45 P M	Menlo Park and principal Way Stations	†7.28 P M

A M for Morning. P M for Afternoon.
*Sundays excepted. †Saturdays only. ‡Sundays only.
**Mondays excepted. §Saturdays excepted.

OCEANIC STEAMSHIP CO.

Carrying United States, Hawaiian and Colonial Mails.

WILL LEAVE THE COMPANY'S WHARF, foot of Mission Street, No. 1,

For Honolulu, Auckland and Sydney,

WITHOUT CHANGE,

The Splendid New 3,000-ton Iron Steamer.

MARIPOSA ..... Saturday, February 8, 1890, at 12 M., Or immediately on arrival of the English mails.

For Honolulu,

SS. AUSTRALIA (3,000 tons), February 28, 1890, at 12 M

☞ For freight or passage, apply at office, 327 Market Street. JOHN D. SPRECKELS & BROS. General Agents.

KILLIP & CO.,

LIVE STOCK AND GENERAL AUCTIONEERS,

22 Montgomery Street, San Francisco

SPECIAL ATTENTION PAID TO SALES OF

High-Bred Horses and Cattle.

At auction and private sale.

Will Sell in All Cities and Counties of the State.

REFERENCES.

HON. C. GREEN, Sacramento. — HON. J. D. CARR, Salinas.
J. P. SARGENT, ESQ., Sargents. — HON. JOHN BOGGS, Colusa.
HON. L. J. ROSE, Los Angeles. — HON. A. WALRATH, Nevada.
J. B. HAGGIN, ESQ., San Francisco.

Represented at Sacramento by Edwin F. Smith secretary State Agricultural Society. At San Jose by Messrs. Montgomery & Rea, Real Estate Agents.

Being the oldest established firm in the live-stock business on this Coast, and having conducted the important auction sales in this line for the past fifteen years, amounting to one half a million of dollars, we feel justified in claiming unequaled facilities for disposing of live stock of every description, either at auction or private sale. Our list of correspondents embraces every breeder and dealer of prominence upon the Pacific Coast, thus enabling us to give full publicity to animals placed with us for sale. Private purchases and sales of live stock of all descriptions will be made on commission, and stock shipped with the utmost care. Purchases and sales made of land of every description. We are authorized to refer to the gentlemen whose names are appended.

KILLIP & CO., 22 Montgomery Street

TRUMAN HOOKER & CO.
SAN FRANCISCO, - - CALIFORNIA

San Francisco and North Pacific Railway.

THE DONAHUE BROAD-GAUGE ROUTE.

COMMENCING SUNDAY, MARCH 17, 1889, AND until further notice, boats and trains will leave from and arrive at the San Francisco Passenger Depot, Market-street Wharf, as follows:

Leave San Francisco. Week Days.	Leave San Francisco. Sundays.	DESTINATION	Arrive San Francisco. Sundays.	Arrive San Francisco. Week Days.
7.40 A M 3.30 P M 5.00 P M	8.00 A M 5.00 P M	Petaluma and Santa Rosa	10.40 A M 6.10 P M	8.50 A M 10.30 A M 6.05 P M
7.40 A M 3.30 P M	8.00 A M	Fulton, Windsor, Healdsburg, Litton Springs, Cloverdale, and way stations.	6.10 P M	10.30 A M 6.05 P M
7.40 A M	8.00 A M	Hopland and Ukiah.	6.10 P M	6.05 P M
7.40 A M	8.00 A M	Guerneville	6.10 P M	6.05 P M
7.40 A M 5.00 P M	8.00 A M	Sonoma and Glen Ellen.	10.40 A M 6.10 P M	8.50 A M 6.05 P M

Stage connects at Santa Rosa for White Sulphur Springs, Sebastopol and Mark West Springs; at Geyserville for Skaggs Springs, and at Cloverdale for the Geysers; at Hopland for Highland Springs, Kelseyville, Soda Bay, Lakeport and Bartlett Springs, and at Ukiah for Vichy Springs, Saratoga Springs, Blue Lakes, Willits, Cahto, Calpella, Potter Valley, Sherwood Valley and Mendocino City.

EXCURSION TICKETS from Saturdays to Mondays, to Petaluma, $1.50; to Santa Rosa $2.25; to Healdsburg, $3.40; to Litton Springs, $3.60; to Cloverdale, $4.50; to Hopland, $5.70; to Ukiah, $6.75; to Guerneville, $3.75; to Sonoma, $1.50; to Glen Ellen, $1.80.

EXCURSION TICKETS, good for Sundays only, to Petaluma, $1; to Santa Rosa, $1.50; to Healdsburg, $2.25; to Litton Springs, $2.40; to Cloverdale, $3; to Guerneville, $2.50, to Sonoma, $1; to Glen Ellen, $1.20.

From San Francisco for Point Tiburon and San Rafael: Week Days—7.40, 9.20, 11.20, A. M.; 3.30, 5.00, 6.15 P. M. Sundays—8.00, 9.30, 11.00 A. M.; 1.30, 5.00, 6.20 P. M.

To San Francisco from San Rafael: Week Days—6.20, 7.55, 9.30 A. M.; 12.45, 3.40, 5.05 P. M. Sundays—8.10, 9.40 A. M.; 12.15, 3.40, 5.00 P. M.

To San Francisco from Point Tiburon: Week Days—6.50, 8.20, 9.55 A. M.; 1.10, 4.05, 5.30 P. M.; Sundays—8.40, 10.05 A. M.; 12.40, 4.05, 5.30 P. M.

On Saturdays an extra trip will be made from San Francisco to San Rafael, leaving at 1.40 P. M.

H. C. WHITING, General Manager.
PETER J. McGLYNN, Gen. Pass. & Tkt. Agt.

Ticket Offices at Ferry, 222 Montgomery Street and 2 New Montgomery Street.

CHICAGO, MILWAUKEE AND ST. PAUL RAILWAY.

Steam Heated and Electric Lighted Vestibuled Trains between Chicago, St. Paul and Minneapolis.
Electric Lighted and Steam Heated Vestibuled Trains between Chicago, Council Bluffs and Omaha.
Finest Dining Cars in the world.
Free Reclining Chair Cars between Chicago and Omaha.
Fast Mail Line between Chicago, Milwaukee, St. Paul and Minneapolis.
Transcontinental Route between Chicago, Council Bluffs and Omaha, or St. Paul.
Great National Route between Chicago, Kansas City and St. Joseph, Mo.
5,700 miles of road in Illinois, Wisconsin, Minnesota, Iowa, Missouri, South and North Dakota.
Everything First-Class.
First-Class People patronize First-Class Lines.
Ticket Agents everywhere sell Tickets over the Chicago, Milwaukee and St. Paul Railway.

W. T. ALLEN,
Pacific Coast Passenger Agent
Office, No 138 Montgomery St., San Francisco, Cal.
Under Occidental Hotel

6 DONTS

DON'T own a racehorse.
DON'T be a breeder.
DON'T be a trainer.
DON'T be a jockey.
DON'T bet on the races.
DON'T go to a race track.

WITHOUT HAVING IN YOUR POCKET ONE OF

Goodwin's ANNUAL OFFICIAL TURF GUIDES.

Price, in cloth.....$7.00
Price, in half morocco..... 3.00
Price, in half calf..... 4.00
If sent by mail.....10 cents extra

SUBSCRIBE TO IT FOR 1890.

It is published semi-monthly during the racing season, and is but **$10 per year.** Address

GOODWIN BROS.,
241 Broadway, New York City.

Business College, 24 Post St.
—San Francisco.—
The most popular school on the Coast
E. HEALD, President. C. S. HALEY, Sec'y.
☞ Send for Circulars

FOR HORSES,

DOGS AND CATTLE.

Simmons Liver Regulator, a strictly vegetable compound and general Condition Powder, is

A SAFE AND SURE REMEDY FOR

COLIC,
GRUBS,
LUNG FEVER,
HIDE-BOUND.

No Stable or Kennel should be without it: it gives new life to a lazy or drooping horse, and is a positive preventive and cure for **Distemper** or **Mange** in Dogs.

J. H. ZEILIN & CO.,
Proprietors, Philadelphia, Pa.

DR. FISHERMAN'S

Carbolized Alkaline

LOTION

Cures after all other Remedies have Failed.

Sprains, Sores, Bruises, Galls, Swellings, Scratches, Thrush, Grease Heels, Curb, Rheumatism. Restoring Weak Knees and Ankles to their original condition. As a wash it insures glossy manes and tails. Valuable as an internal remedy for Coughs, Colic, Congestion or Fever. You really get Half a Gallon of Remedy for $1.00, or Two Gallons for $3.00, after being adulterated as directed.

This Liniment has received the endorsement of some of our best horsemen. Recommended by Jos. Cairn Simpson. See BREEDER AND SPORTSMAN of November 10th, 1888.

LYNDE & HOUGH, Proprietors.
116 California St., S. F.
Or ask your Druggist for it.

HORSE OWNERS
TRY GOMBAULT'S

CAUSTIC BALSAM.

A Safe, Speedy and Positive Cure for Curb, Splint, Sweeny, Capped Hock, Strained Tendons, Founder, Wind Puffs, all Skin Diseases or Parasites, Thrush, Diphtheria, Pinkeye, all Lameness from Spavin, Ringbone or other Bony Tumors. Removes all Bunches or Blemishes from Horses and Cattle.

Supersedes all Cautery or Firing. Impossible to Produce any Scar or Blemish.

Every bottle sold is warranted to give satisfaction. Price $1.50 per bottle. Sold by druggists, or sent by express, charges paid, with full directions for its use. Send for descriptive circulars. Address LAWRENCE, WILLIAMS & CO., Cleveland O.

BROU'S INJECTION

A PERMANENT CURE in from 3 to 6 days, of the most obstinate cases; guaranteed not to produce Stricture; no sickening doses; and no inconvenience or loss of time. Recommended by physicians and sold by all druggists. J. Ferré, (successor to Brou), Pharmacien, Paris.

For any Kind of a

SORE THROAT

USE

McCLELLAN'S

DIPHTHERIA REMEDY

An Unfailing Cure.

FOR SALE BY ALL DRUGGISTS

VETERINARY.

Dr. Wm. H. Jones, M.R.C.V.S.

Veterinary Surgeon,
(OLYMPIC CLUB STABLES)
503 Sutter Street, San Francisco.
Telephone, No. 1404.

Consultations by letter, and cases of URGENT NECESSITY in the interior will receive prompt attention.

W. H. WOODRUFF.

Veterinary Dentist,

AT FASHION STABLES,
221 Ellis Street, San Francisco
Improved Instruments, Humane Methods, First-Class Work.

H. E. CARPENTER,

Veterinary Surgeon,
Graduate of Ontario Veterinary College, Toronto, Canada.
RESIDENCE AND VETERINARY INFIRMARY
331 Golden Gate Ave., San Francisco.
Telephone 3069.
☞ OPEN DAY AND NIGHT. ☜
No risk in throwing Horses. Veterinary Operating Table on the premises.

DR. C. MASOERO.

Veterinary Surgeon,

Successor to **DR. A. DeTAVEL,**
GRADUATE OF ROYAL VETERINARY COLLEGE, TURIN.
OFFICE AND INFIRMARY,
No. 811 HOWARD STREET,
Between Fourth and Fifth. SAN FRANCISCO.
Telephone, No. 457.

R. WATKINS,

Veterinary Dentist,

Of twelve years practice, is now permanently located in San Francisco, and may be found at **C. S. Crittenden's** Golden Gate Livery and Riding Academy, **24 to 28 Golden Gate Avenue.**

Will treat ailments of the horse's mouth, and cure all such. Sidereín Pullers and Tongue Lollers, etc. Satisfaction guaranteed. Orders by mail will receive prompt attention. Examination Free.

E. J. O'ROUKE.

I have the honor to announce to my old patrons and the general public that I may be found at my old stand, where, as heretofore, the

Shoeing of Horses,

whether for the Track, Drive, or for general work, will receive my personal attention.

Telephone 2011.

E. J. O'ROUKE,
209 Ellis Street

California Horse Shoe Co's

I have used in my business the Steel and Iron Shoes made by the above Company, and take great pleasure in saying they are the best I have ever used in twenty-two years' practice. I have never seen anything like the STEEL SHOE made by this Company. I can fully recommend them to every practical Horseshoer in the country. Yours respectfully,

No. 8 Everett Street. JOHN GRACE.

The PARKER Hammerless Shot Gun.

At the Annual Tournament of 1889, held at Cannes, France, the grand prize, consisting of 2000 Francs and a Valuable Cup. was won by The Parker Hammerless.

The first Parker Hammerless Gun made won the championship of America at Decatur Illinois.

SEND FOR ILLUSTRATED CIRCULAR.

PARKER BROS., Makers,

New York Salesroom, 97 Chambers St., Meriden Conn.

1890. DENVER, COLORADO. 1890.

The Spring Racing and rotting Meeting

OF THE

Overland Park Club Association

WILL BE HELD

MAY 30 and 31, JUNE 3, 4, 5 and 7, 1890.

The following Racing Stakes are now open to Close Saturday February 15th.

THE PRAIRIE STAKES.

A SWEEPSTAKES for two-year-olds, foals of 1888; $10 entrance to accompany the nomination; $15 additional to start with $600 added by the Club, of which $100 to the second horse, $50 to the third. Winners of any race of the value of $750 or more to carry 3 pounds extra; of two or more such races, 5 pounds extra. Maidens - at time of starting—allowed 5 pounds. Five furlongs. To be run on the second day of the meeting.

THE FAR WEST STAKES.

A SWEEPSTAKES for two-year-olds, foals of 1888; $10 entrance to accompany the nomination; $15 additional to start, with $600 added by the Club, of which $100 to the second horse, $50 to the third. Colts and fillies bred, raised and owned in Colorado, Wyoming, New Mexico, Utah, Montana or Idaho allowed 5 pounds. The winner of two races of any value to carry 5 pounds extra. The winner of the Prairie Stakes to carry 7 pounds extra. Maidens—at time of starting—allowed 5 pounds. Half a mile. To be run on the fifth day of the meeting.

NOTE.—The allowance to colts and fillies bred, raised and owned in States and Territories named, to be allowed in addition to the maiden allowance, if any, also in taking up penalties, if any.

THE COLORADO DERBY.

A SWEEPSTAKES for three-year-olds, foals of 1887; $10 entrance to accompany the nomination; $15 additional to start, with $600 added by the Club, of which $100 to the second horse, $50 to the third. Winners of any stake race to carry 3 pounds extra; of any three-year-old stakes, 5 pounds extra. Maidens on February 15th allowed 5 pounds; if maidens at time of starting, allowed 7 pounds. One mile and a quarter. To be run on the first day of the meeting.

THE MOUNTAIN STAKES.

A SWEEPSTAKES for three-year-olds, foals of 1887; $10 entrance to accompany the nomination; $15 additional to start, with $500 added by the Club, of which $100 to the second horse, $50 the third. Non-winners of $1,000 in two-year-old form allowed 5 pounds. Maidens on February 15th allowed 7 pounds, if maidens at time of starting, allowed 10 pounds. The winner of the Colorado Derby to carry 5 pounds extra. One mile. To be run on the fourth day of the meeting.

THE MERCHANTS' STAKES.

A SWEEPSTAKES for all ages; $10 entrance to accompany the nomination; $15 additional to start, with $600 added by the Club, of which $100 to the second horse, $50 to the third. Winners of any race of the value of $1,000 or more, to carry three pounds extra; of two or more such races, 5 pounds extra. Non-winners in 1889 allowed 3 pounds. Maidens on February 15th, allowed 5 pounds; if maidens at time of starting, allowed 7 pounds. One mile and a half. To be run on the third day of the meeting.

THE OVERLAND HANDICAP.

A HANDICAP SWEEPSTAKES for all ages; $5 entrance to accompany the nomination; $20 additional to start, with $600 added by the Club, of which $100 to the second horse, $50 to the third. Weights to appear at 1 o'clock P. M., the first day of the meeting. Acceptances to be made through the entry box at the usual time of closing, the day before the race. Winners of a race after publication of weights to carry 3 pounds additional; of two or more such races, 5 pounds additional. One mile and a quarter. To be run on the last day of the meeting.

All the above stakes governed by the rules of the American Racing Association.

A liberal purse programme will be prepared and issued with the nominations in stakes about March 16, 1890.

Entrance free to all purse races, unless otherwise specified in the conditions.

All the above stakes close on Saturday, February 15th. Nominations to be addressed to D. L. HALL, Superintendent Overland Park Club, 13 Opera House, Denver, Colo.

TROTTING STAKE.

The Overland Park Club Association also announce the following stake to be trotted during their Spring Racing and Trotting Meeting, May 30th to June 7, 1890.

THE DENVER TROTTING STAKE.

FOR COLTS AND FILLIES three years old or under, that have never beaten 2:30. Mile heats, best three in five, in harness and to the rules and regulations of the American Trotting Association; $10 entrance, which must accompany the nomination, on Saturday, February 15th $10 on Thursday, May 1st—when the entries for trotting purses will close; and $30 from those who declare to start at 8 o'clock P. M., the night before the race; with $500 added by the Club. The stakes, forfeits and added money to be put together and divided—50 per cent. to first horse; 25 per cent. to second; 15 per cent. to third, and 10 per cent. to fourth. In case of an entry distancing the field, or any part thereof, it shall be entitled to the stakes and forfeits, with 50 per cent. of the added money, and no more. A walkover shall be entitled to all the stakes and forfeits, and 25 per cent. of the added money. Nominations are only liable for the first payment, but failure to make either of the subsequent payments, when due, shall be considered a forfeiture, and debar the entry from competing in the race.

Nominations Close on Saturday, February 15th.

THE TROTTING PROGRAMME will be issued about March 10th, and will provide for twelve or more Trotting and Pacing Races. The classes will be arranged to suit the records of horses expected at the meeting, and owners and trainers of Trotting and Pacing horses are invited to correspond with the Club, in order that this arrangement may be fully carried out. Nominations in purses will close May 1st.

Address all entries and communications to

D. L. HALL, Superintendent,
13 Opera House, Denver, Colo.

J. C. JOHNSON & CO.,

Importers, Manufacturers, and Dealers in

Harness and Saddlery

Just received an elegant line of special patterns of fine Robes, Blankets, and Whips.

400 to 404 Market Street,

Corner BATTERY STREET, - - San Francisco.

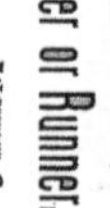

At J. A. McKERRON'S,

228, 230 and 232 Ellis St., San Francisco

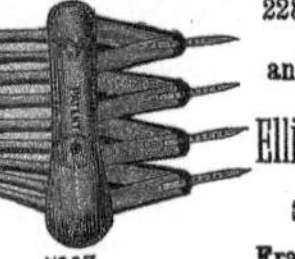

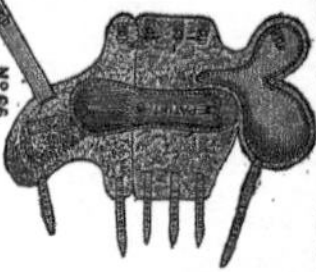

Brothers of the Angle,

OUR NEW EIGHT-STRIP SPLIT BAMBOO is the "King" of all fishing-rods. Chubb's New Catalogue for 1890 is now ready. In addition to a complete list of anglers' supplies, it contains articles from the pens of Dr. James A. Henshall, Petronella, W. H. Murray, Geo. P. Goff Norman, Brother Gardner, and others.

These papers are by the best writers on angling subjects, and are very interesting

Send 25 cents, and receive Catalogue, post-paid. This amount will be deducted from first order (if accompanied with Coupon in book) for one dollar's worth or more of our goods. Address

THOS. H. CHUBB.

The Fishing-Rod Manufacturer,

POST MILLS, VT.

Please mention BREEDER AND SPORTSMAN.

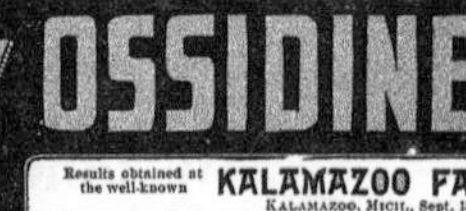

OSSIDINE

Results obtained at the well-known **KALAMAZOO FARM.**

KALAMAZOO, MICH., Sept. 15, 1888.

GENTLEMEN:—We have used OSSIDINE for the past two years, and consider it invaluable for Sprung Tendons, Curbs, Ringbone, and Spavins; there is nothing equals it: and for us it effected a permanent cure where firing failed, although performed by one of the most successful veterinarians on the continent. We have recommended it to others with like success, and believe it has more merit than any blister ever used.

Very respectfully yours,
S. A. BROWNE & CO., Prop's.

This scientific preparation is an absolute cure for all bony or callous lumps on horses, and is a more powerful absorbent than "firing," without creating the slightest blemish.

Acknowledged by leading horsemen of the world to be the **ONLY** preparation that will remove a Bone Spavin after it has become ossified.

We have authority also to refer to
Mr. JEROME I. CASE, Mr. FRED. GEBHARD,
Mr. JOHN PORTER (Trainer to H.R.H. the Prince of Wales),
And hundreds of others from whom we have very flattering testimonials.

One Style Only. $3.00 per Bottle.

A. P. BUSH & CO.,
149 Pearl St.,
BOSTON, MASS.,
Sole Agents for United States and Canada.
Beware of Imitations.

SOLD BY C. N. Crittenton, A. R. Van Nest & Co., and C. M. Moseman & Bro., NEW YORK CITY.
Morrisson, Plummer & Co., Peter Van Schaack & Sons, CHICAGO, ILL.
John D. Park & Son, CINCINNATI, O.; Floyd & Foster, DETROIT, MICH.; F. S. Slosson, CLEVELAND, O.; Meyer Bros. Drug Co., ST. LOUIS, MO.; R. A. Robinson, LOUISVILLE, KY.; H. H. Moore & Sons STOCKTON, CAL.

Nutwood 2:22¾ / 2:21 / 2:18¾ } Sire

DAWN 6407

Dam Countess } DAM OF: Strathway (2-y-o) 2:26, " trial 2:21; Placida } Morna } Double team Trial 2:26

2:18¾; 2:20; 2:19½.

$100 **Popular Price for season of 1890.** $100

Not having a breeding farm, and being dependent on the public for patronage, I have set the above low price in order to be within the reach of any one desiring to breed. Good pasturage $3 per month.

For further particulars, address

A. L. WHITNEY, Petaluma.

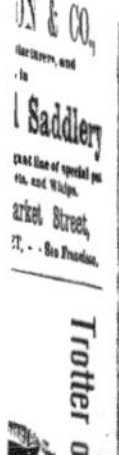

TWENTY-FOUR PAGES.

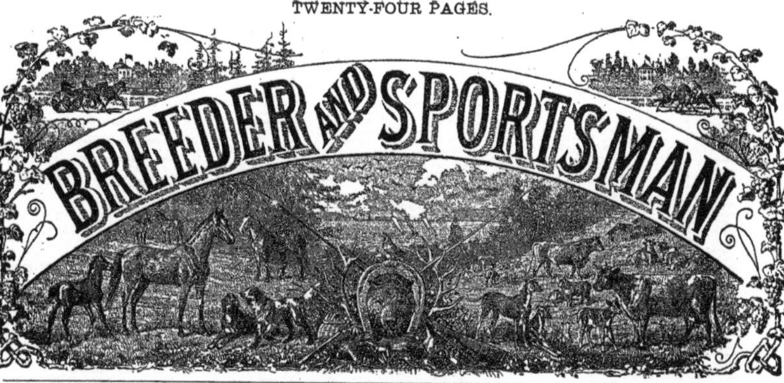

Vol. XVI. No. 8.
No. 313 BUSH STREET.

SAN FRANCISCO, SATURDAY, FEB. 22, 1890.

SUBSCRIPTION
FIVE DOLLARS A YEAR.

DEXTER PRINCE.

The property of L. M. Morse, Lodi, California.

We present to our readers a likeness of the royally bred horse, Dexter Prince. In blood and speed lines he has no superior. He is by Kentucky Prince, the sire of Guy 2:10¾, Spofford 2:18¾, Company, 2:19¾, Bayonne Prince 2.21½, Fred Folger 2:20½, and many others. Kentucky Prince was himself one of the speediest horses, and could trot at a phenomenal rate of speed. In the presence of Governor Stanford, Mr. David Bonner timed him quarters at a 2:10 gait. DexterPrince's dam is Lady Dexter, full sister to Dexter 2:17¼, Dictator, the greatest sire of speedy and staying trotters, Astoria 2:29½, and Alma 2:28¾. On the dam's side there is Jay Eye See 2:10. There is no stallion in the world that has such speed on both sides; 2:10¾ and 2:10. Dexter Prince had the highest rate of speed as a two year old. Governor Stanford timed him quarters in 32½ seconds, and Mr. Marvin drove him eighths at a faster rate of speed than that. Dexter Prince has size, conformation and power to a marked degree. He is a sure foal getter, and his services are put at such low figures as to put his blood and speed lines within reach of everybody.

National Trotting Congress.

[By our Special Commissioner.]

The 13th biennial congress of the National Trotting Association was held in one of the parlors of the Iroquois Hotel on Wednesday of last week. Among those present were David Bonner of New York, Peter P. Johnson of Lexington, Ky; Cicero J. Hamlin of Buffalo, Hamilton Busby of New York; Dr. J. W. Day of Waterloo, N. Y., C. A. Emery, W. E. Edwards and W. B. Fasig of Cleveland; W. H. Wilson of Cynthiana, Ky.; T. O. King of Hartford, Jesse D. Carr, California, C. H. Page of Philadelphia, J. F. Holmes of Carthage, J. L. Mitchell of Milwaukee, U. C. Blake of Iowa, R. B Conover of Patterson, N. J., William McDonald of Hoosic Falls, George M. Robinson of Elmira, John R. Graham of Boston, George W. Archer of Rochester, J. Wood Martin of Philadelphia, John E. Green of Kentucky, and many others.

The congress was presided over by Judge Peter P. Johnston of Lexington, Ky. Secretary Moore and Treasurer Powers were also present. The calling of the roll occupied considerable time.

Mr. John E. Green of Louisville, Ky, moved to appoint a committee of five to nominate officers for the ensuing two years. The motion was carried, and the Chair appointed Messrs. Green of Kentucky, Page of Pennsylvania, Kerr of California, Blake of Iowa, and King of Connecticut as such committee.

Mr. Page of Philadelphia spoke very feelingly of the great loss sustained by an esteemed member of the association, the Hon. Benjamin F. Tracy, Secretary of the Navy. He said Mr. Tracy was largely interested in turf matters, and was mentioned for President of the association at the last meeting. He said the hearts of all were in sympathy with Secretary Tracy.

He offered the following resolution.

Resolved, That the members of the National Trotting Association, assembled at Buffalo, N. Y., February 12, 1890, hereby tender their deepest and most sincere sympathy to the Hon. Benjamin F. Tracy, Secretary of the Navy, and to each of the surviving members of his family in their terrible affliction.

Mr. H. M. Whitehead, of New York, also added a few words, praising Mr. Tracy's efforts to elevate horse breeding, etc., and said he was held in high esteem in trotting circles. The resolution was adopted unanimously.

Mr. Page next offered the following, which was adopted with unmistakable alacrity.

Whereas, The Board of Review has been restrained by the court from investigating the charges of fraud pending against C. H. Nelson, F. L. Noble and George G. Bobson and the horses Nelson and Alcryon, therefore be it

Resolved, By the Congress of the National Trotting Association, that the said parties and horses are hereby suspended from all privileges on the courses in membership with this association until such injunction is dissolved and the said charges are legally investigated by the Board of Review.

Later in the session Mr. Nelson appeared before the convention and made an apology for invoking the aid of the court in the matter, and promised to have the injunction dissolved at the earliest opportunity. He also said he would accept whatever penalty the Board of Review might impose, with resignation.

President Johnson said he was glad to see Mr. Nelson take this action, and he promised that the case would be disposed of justly and as rapidly as possible.

Secretary Morse then presented his report, from which we cull the following:

The number of persons and horses remaining under penalty December 31, 1889, is as appended:

Persons suspended	2,705
Persons expelled	209
Horses suspended	1,405
Horses expelled	128
Whole number	4 447

The secretary's report of two years ago will show that the number of persons and horses suspended were:

Persons suspended	3,317
Persons expelled	178
Horses suspended	1,974
Horses expelled	111
Whole number	5,580
Deducting the number of men and horses under penalty of suspension and expulsion, as above, December 31, 1889	4,447
Shows a decrease in the aggregate of	1,133

It also shows that the Board, under a rigid construction and administration of the rules, has increased the number of expulsions of men and horses by 48, while at the same time the number of men and horses under suspension has been diminished, notwithstanding the entries have been much more numerous in consequence of the aggregate increase of the trotting interest. It is firmly believed that the rigid enforcement of the rules as to the discovery and punishment of frauds will in the near future show a corresponding decrease in their attempted perpetration. In this connection it may be said that at the commencement of the trotting season of 1890, a special circular was sent to the members, calling attention to Rule 7, Section 3, and giving specific instructions thereunder, and there is no reason to doubt that many fraudulent contestants have been detected thereby.

The following is a condensed report of receipts and disbursements for each of the years 1888 and 1889, the vouchers for the latter as audited by the committee being on file in the office:

Cash on hand Jan. 1, 1888 (as per previous report	$10,740 56
Receipts for 1888	16,861 64
	$27,602 20
Disbursements for 1888	13 341 77
	$14,260 43
Receipts for 1889	16,888 13
	$31,148 56
Disbursements for 1889	14,316 27
Leaving balance on hand Jan. 1, 1890	$16,833 29

The Treasurer's statement, appended hereto, will show the receipts and expenditures in detail of both the association and general accounts, including the trust fund.

To show the vast interests controlled by our members, it may be stated that in 1889 they offered in stakes and purses, in round numbers, more than $1,000,000.

In conclusion, the Secretary desires to congratulate the members on the fact that the association was never in a more flourishing condition, financially and otherwise,

Treasurer Powers of Hartford submitted a financial statement for the years 1888 and 1889. The receipts for 1888 were $27,602 20, of which $9,920 was from members' fees and $3,065 from fines. The receipts for 1889 were $31,148.56, of which the membership fees netted $10,014 and fines $2,085. The disbursements for 1888 were $13,341.77 and for 1889, $14,316 27. The balance on hand on January 1, 1890, was $16,833.29.

President Johnston, in behalf of Mr. C. J. Hamlin, invited the officers, members, and newspaper representatives to be his guests at a banquet at the Hotel Iroquois in the evening. On motion of William E. Edwards of Cleveland the invitation was accepted and a vote of thanks given Mr. Hamlin.

The committee on rules presented a long report, read by G. M. Fogg of Nashville, Tenn. A large number of changes in phraseology, etc., was submitted.

Dr. J. W. Day of Waterloo, N. Y., offered an amendment to one rule in relation to the identification of horses. He suggested that certificates be issued to owners and drivers of horses. "There are too many 'ringers' traveling around the country, and some such means should be adopted to put a stop to the disreputable practice."

He offered the following amendment:—

Any association may require of any nominator in case of doubt and identity or eligibility of any entry a certificate signed by two reputable citizens of the place where the horse is owned with the county clerk's certificate of the county where the horse is owned, giving a complete description of the horse, age, pedigree, if known, color, size and particular marks.

Mr. Hamlin and others strenuously objected, and when the motion was put it was lost by a large majority.

The report was adopted, and the committee was given a vote of thanks. Thanks were also bestowed on the officers and members of the Board of Review.

A communication was received from the general Secretary of the Union Clubs of Berlin, Germany, in reference to the issuance of certificates for the importation of trotting horses, introduced in Germany. The rule committee asked that the subject matter be referred to the Board of Review with power to act. This was adopted.

The nominating committee reported the following list of officers for the next two years, and the report was unanimously adopted: For President, the Hon. Peter P Johnston of Lexington, Ky.; first Vice-President, David Bonner, of New York; second Vice-President, W. W. Stow, of San Francisco. Division Boards: Eastern District, George M. Stearns, Chicopee, Mass.; M. G. Bulkeley, Hartford; William H. Strickland, Bangor, Me; Western District, U. C. Blake, Cedar Rapids, Ia.; John L. Mitchell, Milwaukee, Wis.; A. J. Caton, Chicago; Atlantic District, George W. Archer, Rochester; Frank Brown, Baltimore; J. C. Sibley, Franklin, Pa; Pacific District, N. T. Smith, San Francisco: Jesse D. Carr, Salinas; Frank L. Coombs, Napa, Cal.; Central District, G. M. Fogg, Nashville; William E. Edwards, Cleveland; Wm. Russell Allen, St. Louis.

President Johnston briefly returned thanks for the honor conferred.

The president was authorized to appoint a new committee on rules.

Mr. Edwards moved that the next convention be held in New York City. This excited a pleasant strife. Mr. Vail named Hartford, Mr. Green urged the claims of Lexington.

Mr. Page—"New York and Kentucky wants the earth." He nominated Philadelphia. Mr. Blake proposed Cedar Rapids and San Francisco, Kansas City, St. Louis, Nashville, and Rochester were also named. The first vote settled the matter in favor of New York, and the president was authorized to name the hotel.

The congress adjourned *sine die* at 6 P. M.

Petaluma Park Colt Stakes.

Gen. W. P. Fine the lessee of the Petaluma track has had splendid good fortune with his initial Stakes, and it only goes to prove what a large number of gentlemen in that district are now interest in the light harness horse.

The following are the entries:

YEARLINGS—HALF MILE AND REPEAT.

P. J. Shafter, Olema, gr c Rustic King by Rustic, dam Gazelle by Gen McClellan.

J. H. White, Lakeville, b c George W. by Hernanni, dam Katie by Bellfounder.

Perry Sears, Sonoma, b f El Verano Maid by Dawn, dam Elaine by Booth.

I. M. Proctor, Petaluma Vesper Bells, roan f by Dawn, dam Gypsy by Nameless, he by Belmont.

B. C. Holly, Vallejo b c Hollywood by Woodnut, dam Aurelia by Albert W.

R. S. Brown, Petaluma br f Bayannetta by Anteeo, dam Debonair by Sultan.

J. McBrown, Petaluma, b c Daniel by Mambrino Chief Jr. dam—— by Levi.

W. J. Frost, Petaluma ch f Roseolema by Gen. McPherson, dam Olema by Whipple's Hambletonian.

Wm. Fitch, Petaluma, s f Addie L. by Whalebone.

H. G. Comstock, Petaluma, blk f Nellie Bly by Alcona Jr., dam Kate by Venture.

W. B Sanborn, Santa Rosa, b c Claude by Daly, dam Lady S. by Smuggler.

A. L. Whitney, Petaluma, blk —— by Dawn, dam Jennie Offut by McClellan.

TWO-YEAR-OLDS—MILE AND REPEAT.

T. J. Beggs, Petaluma, s f Elaine R. by Rafael, dam Lady Clair by Irvington.

T. J. Beggs, Petaluma, br f Marion R. by Rafael, dam Josie W. by Hambletonian 725.

J. H. McNabb, Petaluma, blk c Early Bird by Dawn, dam Avis by Gen. McClellan Jr.

Fred W. Lober, St. Helena, blk c Almoniton by Alcona, dam Pansy by Richelieu, he by Mambrino Chief.

R. H. Warfield, Healdsburg, iron gray —— Warde by Capri, dam Kate by son of Bell Alta.

Robert Crane, Petaluma, blk c Alcona C. by Alcona Jr., dam Minnie D. by Alexander 490.

Isaac De Turk, Santa Rosa, dk br f Myrtle by Anteeo, dam —— by Nutwood.

B. C. Holly, Vallejo, b c Mart Boorheim by Sidney, dam —— by Echo 462.

J. H. White, Lakeville, b f Ida Franklin by Hernanni, dam Annie by Gen. McClellan 144.

W. P. Fine, Petaluma, ch c Examiner by Dawn, dam Vashti by Chieftain 721.

A. L. Whitney, Petaluma, s f Anna Belle by Dawn, dam Pacheco by Hubbard.

D. McGovern, Petaluma, b c Dennis by Dawn, dam —— by Don Juan.

Edwards & Hinkle, Petaluma, b c Whaler by Whalebone, dam Queen by Gen. McClellan, 144.

Mrs. Silas Skinner, Napa, ch c Woodside by Woodnut, dam Veronica by Alcona 730.

Perry Sears, Sonoma, s c Cleveland by Dawn, dam Elaine by Booth.

Wilfred Page, Penn's Grove, blk c Gran Moro by Le Grande, dam Sunny Slope Belle by The Moor.

J. Mc. Brown, Petaluma, blk c Stammoor by Stamboul, dam Moor Maid by The Moor.

R. S. Brown, Petaluma, s f Nelly K by Dawn, dam Nelly by Brown's McClellan.

W. B. Sanborn, Santa Rosa, s c by Daly, dam Lady S. by Smuggler.

STAKE FOR THREE-YEAR-OLDS.

J. H. Lawrence, Santa Rosa, br c Anteeop by Anteeo, dam Bessie G. by King Philip.

M. O'Reilly, Petaluma, b f Emavolo by Antevolo, dam Emma Taylor by Alexander.

Geo. E. Guerne, Santa Rosa, b f Eva G. by Anteeo, dam Daisy by Nutwood.

J H. White, Lakeville, b s Joe by Marco, dam Kate by Bellfounder.

Geo. M. Saul, Petaluma, b f Daisy S. by Rustic, dam Sunflower by Alexander.

R Murphy, Santa Rosa, b f Maude by Anteeo, dam—— by Nutwood.

J. S. Wisecarver, Geyserville, blk f Antelulu by Anteeo, dam —— by Bell Alta.

Wm. P. Edwards, Petaluma, ch f Dolly H. by A. P., dam Queen by Gen. McClellan.

B C. Holly, Vallejo, b c Kafir by Alcazar, dam Flower Girl by Arthurton.

P. J. Shafter, Olema, b c Antevenio by Antevolo, dam Pastime by Rustic.

A. P. Whitney, Petaluma, s g Dor by Dawn, dam Jennie Offutt by Gen. McClellan.

The Arlington Jockey Club's Inaugural Meeting.

SANTA BARBARA, Feb. 10th, 1890.

The meeting of the Jockey Club was a decided success. The attendance was more than expected, and the events of the afternoon were interesting. In the first event, one quarter of a mile dash, there were sixteen horses entered, fourteen of which started. The race was run in heats and the first and second horse of each heat ran a final heat for the purse. The first heat was easily won by the favorite. The following horses ran in the first heat:

Grimbo, sorrel gelding, entered by H. B. Dwyer and ridden by him. Lovely, brown gelding, entered by J. O Minot and Blue Rock, roan, gelding, entered by Bayard Thayer. The favorite Grimbo won easily, time 27 seconds. Mr. Dwyer surprised all by his shrewdness and good horsemanship. He rode Grimbo with judgment, saving the gelding and still winning the heat. Lovely was second.

The second heat had the following starters: Nellie B., b f, entered by Bennett; Billy s g, entered by Mr. Carter; Laro b g, entered by W. W. Hollister. This heat was won by Laro, Billy 2nd. Time 27½ seconds.

Third Heat—The following horses ran: Bob, br g entered by C. Divers; Nellie Grey, g f, entered by Bradford; Nellie Bly, b f, entered by Clancy. This heat was interesting. The horses got off to a splendid start and they ran like a team, but under the wire Bob got his nose first in :25½. Nellie Grey 2nd. Mr. Divers who entered and rode Bob handled his yearling so cleverly that the sports were surprised, and admired his style of handling the gelding. It was soon learned that Mr. Divers was of "jockey reputation," and that he had ridden and won many a grand race in his younger days.

The fourth heat was run in slow time and the favorite won easily. Domino, s g, entered by C. Gates; Flay, b g, entered by W. S. Barnes; Jane, b f, entered by H. Doulton. Domino, 1st; Jane, 2nd. Time, :24½.

The sports came around the pool box and the pool sellers were kept busy. The eight horses that were to run the final heat were the first and second of each heat. In the pools Grimbo sold for $6; Bob, $4; Domino, $3 and the field for $2. A great many pools were sold and the favorite had money left when the eight horses went for the starting point. The eight horses were soon at their post and the official starter, S. P. Stow, soon dropped the flag to a most beautiful start. It was a hard struggle, for every inch of the distance was desperately fought by Grimbo and Bob. Duryea on Grimbo and Divers on Bob. The result was a surprise to the talent. Bob won the first heat and race by the shortest of necks in 25½ seconds. Grimbo was defeated, but it was no disgrace to the gelding or his rider, for the horse did his best and his rider did all that a jockey could do to land him first, but Bob had a little more speed. The admirers of Charlie Divers and Bob were very much elated over the victory. The winner is a brown gelding, seven years old, out of a sorrel mare, pedigree untraced and by the speedy quarter horse Robbery Boy, sire of Comet, half mile record 50, 5-8 of a mile in 1:02. Also the sire of E R. Den's Bobby, record one-quarter dash :22½. Sid Law half mile record :50 and other sprinters.

The next event was the Thayer Stakes, half mile and repeat. The following horses came to face the starter: El Semito entered by Seth Loomis; Captain Jinks entered by Sid Law; Charlie K. entered by Kissel; Mary entered by Doulton; Lima Beans entered by Stoddard; Pete entered by Bradford; Lightfoot entered by Duryea.

In the pools Lightfoot sold for $5, Pete for $3 and the field for $2. The talent thought it was impossible for Lightfoot to lose the race. The horses were given the word go to an even start. Lima Beans took the lead immediately after leaving the post and was never headed, winning the heat by a length, Lightfoot second, Pete third and Captain Jinks fourth; time, 56½ seconds. After the usual time between heats the horses came out for the second trial. It was a repetition of the first heat, Lima Beans winning easily, Captain Jinks second, Pete third, Lightfoot fourth; time, 57½. Frank Stoddard, who rode the winner of the Thayer Stakes, reminded one of Don Quixote attacking the windmills which he took for enchanted giants. He swung his arms as though getting up a strong breeze, and his legs kept time with his arms, and his sonorous voice was distinctly heard as he rode Lima Beans in, a winner. His friends shouted themselves hoarse. This race ended the day's sport, and the six hundred people present came away fully satisfied with the meeting. The officers of the Arlington Jockey Club are satisfied with their success, and on the 22nd of February they will give a series of events which will draw a large crowd and many horses, for the purses will be increased and all horses in the county can compete. W. S. Barnes and H. B. Duryea worked indefatigably, and the success of the meeting was largely due to their efforts, which are thoroughly appreciated by the public.

From Ventura came J. G. Hill to look at the native horses run. Mr. Hill owns the stock Farm in Ventura county called Los Palmas. He has many fine bred horses which he will sell at a low figure, as he wishes to retire from the business. He has a beautiful sorrel, three year old by Guy Wilkes 2:15½, out of a mare by Ulster Chief; 2nd dam May Queen 2 26. Also Fayett King by The King he by George Wilkes, dam by Beecher. Mr. Hill has a beautiful stock farm, and many fine horses. At Los Palmas A. W. Richmond past his last years and from there came Dotty Dimple, Ella Hill, Wildidler, and many others. I shall in the near future, give a full list of horses at the Las Palmas Breeding Farm.

T. M.

The Race Track Question.

Editor Breeder and Sportsman:—In my last week's letter advocating the building of a speed track in the neighborhood of the Ocean House Road, I stated that the building of the Great Highway would soon be commenced. I have now the pleasure of informing you that work upon it was commenced last Saturday by the Park Commissioners. The State Legislature, foreseeing that one day or another this city was bound to extend from bay to ocean, wisely reserved a strip of land, 200 feet broad, lying between high water mark and the boundary of private property, extending from the Cliff House southerly to the County line, for the purpose of a grand boulevard. This driveway when completed will form a marine parade unsurpassed in the world. The Park Commissioners have commenced upon the strip bordering the Park, and work will be pushed through as fast as the funds of the Commissioners will allow. The strip of land belongs to the State, and is all under the jurisdiction of the Park Commissioners; considering the great extent of the Park still unimproved, it is extremely doubtful if the appropriation for its improvement will prove sufficient to push the completion of the Great Highway as rapidly as the wants of the city require. Therefore it is to be hoped the Legislature will make a special appropriation for this purpose, and such a course should be advocated by the press.

In my last letter I pointed out the benefit that the construction of a speed track in the immediate vicinity of the city would be to owners of race horses, trainers, livery stable keepers and horsemen generally. Now let us look at the subject as it effects the general public. A fine race track furnished with all the conveniences of good stabling, etc., so situated, would give a great impetus to racing, and it would not be necessary for horses to go East to earn a reasonable profit for their owners. A good track easily drained and kept in good condition during the winter months, would naturally increase the number of meetings held during that period, and if once the interest of the public was aroused, the attendance would prove sufficient to guarantee liberal purses. There is no State in the Union where horses can winter so well as in California, and if once such a track was in running order and the purses sufficient to give horses a chance to "earn their oats," Eastern flyers would be brought across the Rockies and the interest in home racing be thereby greatly increased. Let it be understood that in transportation facilities, as in everything else, the demand creates the supply, and that, therefore, as soon as the public wanted to go to such a race track, say to the old Ocean House track, the various roads would make extensions to supply the necessary transportation. With the presence of Eastern horses the various events on the card would draw large crowds and lovers of horses from all parts of the State would visit the city for such race meetings. The money spent by such visitors could not fail to benefit all branches of business and it would naturally follow that the more attractive such meetings were made, the larger the profit gained. Unless the railroad companies both in and out of the city, the hotels and leading restaurants and saloons are blind to their own interests, they would at once subscribe toward purses and stakes to be offered. The merchants, who would find their country customers brought to town by a large and successful race meeting, would naturally follow suit, and it would not be many years after the establishment of such a track before the winter meetings at San Francisco would vie in interest with the most important meetings now held in spring, summer and fall in the Eastern and Western States. The anxiety of race horse owners that their stables should gain something during the winter months is fully shown by the numbers of horses of a good class which have been running since the close of the regular racing season at the Elizabeth, Clifton and Guttenberg tracks. It is unnecessary to point out the difficulties which exist in racing on Eastern tracks during the winter, or to compare the attractions of such tracks in an intensely cold climate with the advantages which would be offered by an equally well arranged track here. If owners will run their horses through the winter in New Jersey, they would certainly do so in San Francisco, providing, of course, if the same money inducements were held out. The bright sunshine and green grass which usually characterize a California winter, would not be without their attractions, and greatly add to the inducements to winter horses here. It appears to me that the matter lies entirely in the hands of the people of this city. If they choose to establish a good race track and offer liberal purses during the winter months, a very large number of Eastern horses would come here, many thousands of visitors from the interior, Oregon and Nevada, would be attracted to the city, and business would be duly improved thereby.

If the right men take hold of this business in a right way, it cannot fail to succeed. It is not a speculation, but a purely business proposition. Remove such a track beyond the limits of this city and county, however, and the support of the majority of San Franciscoans would be lost. I therefore believe, Mr. Editor, that the site of the old Ocean House track or some other piece of this light, sandy loam country bordering the Ocean House road is the locality which should be selected for a race track. The old track is but a short distance from the Great Highway, which is bound to become the fashionable driveway and great pleasure resort of this city. Its construction is bound to cause railroads other than the H Street road, now running south of the Park, to be built to the beach, and there is therefore no reason to suppose that by the time the track has sufficient attractions to induce the general public to visit it, any difficulty as regards transportation will exist.

You may think, Mr. Editor, that I am unduly interested in this matter, but allow me to state that I have been a resident of California for forty years, and love it dearly and firmly believe in its great future. I am thoroughly acquainted with the racing business of this coast, and have during my sojourn here owned some of the best trotters. Under these circumstances you can understand the interest I take in this matter of a race track, which should, if properly placed and managed, directly and indirectly benefit and develop this city. Why, with our usually fine winters, should not San Francisco become a pleasure resort? Why should it not be made a clean, handsome city, whose attractions, including several important race meetings, would bring thousands of Eastern people to pass the winter season here? Why should it not become a pleasure as well as a business city? Certainly nature has done all in her power to make it one. Can we not have well paved streets, clean sewers, fine buildings, beautiful driveways and successful race meetings as well as any other city in the world? I believe we can if we try, and a great step toward supplying amusement for our guests would be a fine race track. Let the silurian days be wiped out, and in racing and everything else a new and successful era be commenced. Will not the daily press take up this matter and thoroughly ventilate it? The breeding of race-horses has become of so much importance to California that anything which effects the wellbeing of the breeding interest like the want of a proper race track, is certainly worthy of public consideration. I sincerely hope the press in general will take up and agitate the question for the benefit of the entire community of this city. There can be no doubt that every line of business here would be financially benefitted by the holding of important race meetings, and such meetings cannot be held without a well appointed and properly located track.

C. S.

Morris Park Handicaps.

The entries and weights in two important handicaps to be run at Morris Park this season are as follows:

TOBOGGAN SLIDE HANDICAP:

For all ages; a sweepstake of $100 each, half forfeit or only $20 if declared, the club to guarantee the gross value of the stakes to be $10,000, of which $2,000 to second and $1,000 to third; weights to be announced February 1st and declarations to be made by February 20th, winners after April 1st of two races of any value or one of $15,000 to carry 4 lbs. extra; of one of $3,000 or two of $2,000, 7 pounds extra; of two of $3,000 or one of $6,000, 10 pounds extra. Six furlongs.

Names.	Age	Weight.	Names.	Age	Weight.
Kingston	6	126	Tormentor	3	108
Hanover	5	132	Starlight	3	108
Salvator	4	132	Vengeur	4	108
Tenny	4	130	Holiday	4	108
Prince Royal	5	130	Lady Reel	4	108
Firenzi	6	128	Druidess	3	108
Brittanic	5	127	Seymour	4	07
Volunteer II	5	24	Serenader	5	107
Proctor Knott	4	124	Kasson	4	107
Badge	5	124	Retrieve	4	107
Geraldine	5	122	Chesapeake	3	107
Strideaway	6	22	King Thomas	3	07
Gorgo	5	122	Maggie K	3	107
Bradford	6	122	Kate Bensberg	5	106
Reporter	4	122	Homoeopathy	3	106
Sam Harper Jr	a	122	Fresno	4	106
Los Angeles	5	120	Jersey Pat	3	106
Buddhist	4	120	English Lady	3	106
Cracksman	4	120	Punster Jr	3	106
Come-to-Taw	4	118	Leck	4	106
Gregory	3	118	Little Ella	3	106
Chaos	3	118	Bavarian	3	106
Blackburn	3	118	Paradox	3	106
Torso	3	118	Rainbow	3	106
French Park	4	118	Boodler	4	106
Loantaka	4	118	Stately	4	106
Madstone	4	118	Trestle	3	106
Fides	4	116	Persuader	4	106
Magnate	3	116	Culprit	4	106
Reclare	3	115	Red Elm	a	106
Tipstaff	4	116	Amazon	3	106
Cartoon	4	116	Sinaloa II	3	105
Cortez	4	116	King Hazem	3	105
Blue Rock	4	116	Roseberry	3	100
Patrocles	a	115	Sir Lancelot	3	100
Defaulter	5	114	Varius	3	100
Belle d'Or	5	114	Clio	3	100
G. W. Cook	5	112	Cosette	3	100
Castaway II	4	112	Laurentia	3	100
Aurania	4	112	Gloaming	3	100
Brown Princess	4	112	Dr. Helmuth	3	100
My Fellow	4	112	Pembe	3	100
Protection	3	112	Winfield	4	100
Ballarat	3	112	Imp Del Mar	4	100
Successor	3	112	Kitty Van	4	100
Rico	3	112	Isaac Lewis	3	100
Cassius	4	112	Granite	3	100
Stonington	4	112	Amigo	3	100
Bess	a	111	Ban Chief	3	100
Leighton	3	111	Good-Bye	3	100
Fitz James	5	110	Martha	3	100
Volta	5	110	Franco	3	100
St. John	a	110	Worth	3	100
Sunday	4	110	Coots	4	100
Sallie Hagan	4	110	Ofalece	6	100
Cynosure	4	110	Prince Charming	2	90
Forest King	4	109	Leonora	2	87
Almont	4	109	Amulet	2	87
Honduras	3	109	Seashore	2	87
Sir John	3	108			

BOWLING BROOK HANDICAP FOR THREE YEARS OLD.

A sweepstake of $100 each, h. f., or only $20 if declared, with $2,000 added, of which $500 to second and $200 to third. Weights to be published Feb. 1st, and declarations to be made by Feb. 20th. One mile and a furlong.

Name.	Weight.	Name	Weight.
Cayuga	128	Houston	105
Torso	122	Experience	105
Padisha	12[illegible]	Mr. Pelham	105
Racine	119	Bavarian	105
Blackburn	119	Punster, Jr.	105
Chaos	119	Rafter	105
Reclare	118	Golden Horn	104
June Day	118	Favorite	104
Devotee	118	Chieftain	103
Drizzle	118	Flossie	103
Flambeau	116	Fellowcharm	100
Onaway	116	Sir Lancelot	100
Riley	116	Longford	100
Ballarat	116	Martina colt	100
Tournament	116	Varius	100
Successor	115	Clio	100
Protection	115	King Thomas	100
Banquet	114	Magdalena	100
Fanfan colt	114	Mohican	100
Sir John	113	Village King	100
Tormentor	113	Clarendon	200
Miss Belle	113	Sam Doxey	100
Caldwell	112	Masterlode	100
Ralph Bayard	112	Dr. Helmuth	100
Leighton	112	Leda	100
Cyclone colt	110	Gloaming	100
Starlight	110	Amigo	95
Rancocas	110	Lady Jane colt	95
Gramercy	109	Fernwood	95
Druidess	108	Hawkstone	95
Santiago	108	King's Own	95
Eocola colt	108	Dundee	95
Lisimony	108	Abdell	95
Urbanna	107	Can Can	95
Maggie K	107	Jennie V. filly	95
Paradox	106	Bluebird	90
Flatbush	106	Foxmede	90
Anaconda	106	Franco	90
Little Ella	106	Jim Wasson	90
Amazon	106	B. B. Million	90
Baggage	106	Rosette	90
Maximus	106	Isaac Lewis	90
Homoeopathy	106		

Yolo County News.

Woodland, Feb. 9th, 1890.

Breeder and Sportsman:—Turf and horse matters generally have been greatly hampered and circumscribed by wind and flood the past winter but now that the glad sunshine has dispelled the clouds and dried up the mud, horsemen are again beginning to assume their usual animation and energy so that Yolo still promises to maintain her position in the front ranks as a producer of fast horses. Among the pacing contigent of Yolo, Tom Rider, Belle Button and J. H. are most prominent.

Each of these has its particular friends and admirers. One has seen Tom Rider go an eighth in 15½ seconds.

Another speaks of the fast miles Belle went last year when out of condition, and another of what J. H. might have done if handled differently.

There are other races coming to the front here among which may be mentioned a brown mare by Tilton Almont, dam by Odd Fellow owned by Mr. Barry of this place. She showed well last year for her chances, and there is no apparent reason why she should not make a good one.

Sheriff Weaver has a three year old pacing stallion by Alex Button, dam by Dietz's St. Clair, of whom much is reasonably expected. G. W. Woodard has other young pacers beside Belle, and it is currently reported that he has the material with which to lower the yearling pacing record.

The trotters of Yolo are altogether too numerous to mention. Dr. Boucher has had his stable quartered here this winter. In addition to J. H. he has Gen. Logan, four year old stallion by Alex Button, dam full sister to dam of Yolo Maid. This colt trotted as a yearling in the Sacramento colt stakes, winning second place, and was timed separately in 2:59. He has not been worked much, but will be given a show this season. The genial doctor has also Silver King, by Mulvenna, that showed a mile last year as a two year old close to :40, and other good ones. There are some excellent colts here by Caliph, a finely bred son of Sultan, some of which will be worked this season.

Mr. Woodard, who has a fine array of colts, is beginning to marshal his force for the season's work. The Johnstown flood, which recently swept through his part of the country, greatly retarded his work this season, as it damaged his farms to the extent of several thousand dollars.

Alex Button Jr., a recent purchase of Mr. Woodard's, is a colt that, barring accidents, will do great honor to the name of his illustrious sire.

Mr. R. H. Newton, ex-director of the State Agricultural Society, is one of our most enthusiastic horsemen. He is a fine judge of the individual merit of a horse, but can criticise a pedigree with equal acceptance.

The lightening pacer Tom Rider is at present his star, but he has some fine colts besides, one by Clay Duke and another by Del Rey that are especially promising.

On the other side of the creek, neighbors of Mr. Woodard, are Hoppin Brothers, who have fine landed estates, and are somewhat extensively engaged in breeding trotters. C. B. Hoppin, who has achieved a world wide fame as the breeder of the peerless pacing queen, Yolo Maid, has many fine colts by Alex Button and his own well bred stallion Cubit. Last year Mr. Hoppin rested upon his laurels, but it is understood that this season he contemplates going out again "among the boys."

Last, but by no means least, among the horsemen of this country is J. W. Martin, of Yolo, sometimes a contributor to the columns of your excellent paper. He is said to have many colts that are no discredit to his handsome, fast and well-bred stallion Clay Duke. He has also Del Rey, son of Clay Duke, that trotted miles last year in his races close to 30 with very scant preparation. These two horses are fast enough and well enough bred to contribute largely to the trotting horse history of the future. By the way, new impetus has been given to the trotting interest here by Mr. Martin, having leased the half-mile track at this place. He will use it for the training and development of his own horses, and for the use of the public. It will no doubt be kept in first-class order. It is a good half mile track, and fast when in condition.

I am not here for the purpose of attempting to create a boom in real estate, but it is my honest conviction that there is no part of this great horse-breeding State better adapted to the business than Yolo County. The air and soil and water is suited for the finest quality of hoof bone and muscular fibre. The native grasses, wild oats and filariee, so noted as forage grasses of this State, grow here in the greatest luxuriance upon the untilled pastures, while the alfalfa pastures afford the most effective means of promoting rapid growth and early maturity. The cool, dry weather in haying time insures perfect curing, so that Yolo's hay cannot be beaten the world over.

There are portions of California that are too hot or too dry, and other portions that represent the other extremes of coldness or dampness, but here in Yolo is the happy medium between all extremes. Here the winters, with occasionally a rare exception, such as the present, are mild and equable, the summers dry and cool. Here is the horseman's paradise, where the horse can be brought to the highest degree of perfection, and where doubtless on some of the great horse farms of the future will the horsemen's dream—the two-minute trotter—be realized. Yours truly, Jerd.

The Kidd, Edmonson and Morse Sale.

Editor Breeder and Sportsman:—The following is a partial list of the names and addresses of those that have entered horses to be sold in Kidd, Edmonson and Morse sale at Chicago, Ill., March 17th to 21st inclusive. The list will probably double in the next ten days.

Trotting horse owners—S. A. Brown, Kalmazoo, Mich.; W. D. Crockett, Waukegan, Ill.; L. U. Shippee, Stockton, Cal.; M. L. Hare, Indianapolis, Ind.; H. D. McKinney, Janesville, Wis.; Mortimer McRoberts, Dixon, Ill.; John Mescall, Chicago, Ill.; H. F. Wood, Indianapolis, Ind.; J. M. Wood, Indianapolis, Ind.; T. Taggart, Indianapolis, Ind.; L. D. Puett, Rockville, Ind.; W. P. Swain, Bellmore, Ind.; P. C. Kidd, Lexington, Ky.; R. C. Church, Frankfort, Ky.; Lewis Cook, Lexington, Ky.; Wildwood Stock Farm, Janesville, Wis.; B. H. Reed, Genoa, Neb.; W. W. Parrish, Momence, Ill.; O. E. Bennett, Jackson, Mich.; M. Piggott, Salina, Kansas; Glencove Stock Farm, Quincy Ill.; George W. Stoner, La Place, Ill.; A. J. Baker, Gridley, Kansas; John Rugles, Trenton, Mich.; Ebin Rennington, Trenton, Mich.; J. Friesenstice, Chicago, Ill.; C. A. Friendenburg, Chicago, Ill., A. C. Thomas, Chicago, Ill.; Granger Smith, Waukegan; Marsh Black, Knoxville, Iowa; Ira C. Williams, Muncie, Ind.

Draft horse owners—Evens & Bluett, Oregon; J. D. Beckett, Western Springs, Ill.; W. L. Ellwood, De Kalk, Ill.; E. D. Lowell, Walworth, Wis.; Harvins Stock Farm, Alma, Neb. Yours Resp'y, Kidd, Edmondson & Morse.

TURF AND TRACK.

Lee Rose went East yesterday.

Walter Rollins will train for J. T. Stewart when racing starts.

The Beverwick stable pays Bergen $2300 for second claim.

An attempt will be made this season for Norval to lower his record of 2:17½.

Gallatin 6, by imp. Glengarry, out of Dora, has been sold for export to Bermuda.

Mr. James Sheridan has been engaged to start at the Kansas City summer meeting.

W. C. Daly has purchased Fitzroy from D. D. Withers and has removed him to Clifton.

Grimaldi bled at the nose in his last race at Clifton, and is consequently not very reliable now.

Seventeen teams and a large force of men are at work on the new racetrack at Coronado, San Diego.

Clayton, who had his first winning mount on Swift, at Clifton, on the 13th, can ride at sixty-six pounds.

Grass Valley fair will be held this year on August 19th and following days and will precede Chico and Marysville.

Amos McCampbell's colt Grayson, by George Kinney, is being favorably mentioned as a Kentucky Derby candidate.

A subscription is being started in New York to erect a monument over the grave of that prince of drivers, John Murphy.

It is said that Charles Wood, who was refused a licence for his suspicious riding, purposes sending his sons to Cambridge University.

Isaac Woodruff, the well known trainer, will drive and train this season for Mr. Robert Steel of the Cedar Stock Farm, Philadelphia.

W. McCormick, El Rio Rey's trainer all through last season, says Tournament is the best three-year-old in America, *bar El Rio Rey*.

Matt Storn has been in town for several days, but the weather does not suit his delicate state of health and he has to return to Sacramento.

It is said that half the boys at Clifton would be glad to take 25 per cent. for the money owing to them by the swell owners who patronize the races.

Hypodermic injections of cocaine are being used to nullify the roguish propensities of some of the runners, and are the regular thing at Clifton and Guttenberg.

Orrin Hickok says San Diego is the best wintering place in America for trotters or runners. The new track at Coronada should have a large patronage in the winter.

Mr. Jeter Walden visited the Guttenberg track on the 12th but was politely informed that the association would enforce the Clifton ruling and Mr. Walden retired.

It is said the Darebin-Agenoria and the Ban Fox-Queen two-year-olds will not be raced this season, it being deemed advisable to give them more time to grow out.

Maud S. 2:08¾, whose shoes were taken off has been tramping around with bare feet on a bed of peat moss. She will be taken up and jogged on the road next week.

E D. Morgan, the New York banker, has recently purchased some valuable land at Wheatley, in Oyster Bay, L. I. and will establish a large thoroughbred breeding farm.

Mr. Elmore (Spokane's trainer) says that with Kiley, who understands the horse, in the saddle, he will back Spokane against Proctor Knott any weight and any distance.

Ontario Jockey Club stakes show seventeen entries for the Queen's Plate, fifteen in the Woodstock Plate, and eight in the Breeders' Stakes, for three-year-olds, to be run in 1891.

Judge McM Shafter was so pleased with Louise M's performances last fall and with Hazlitt's careful handling that he has sent several more thoroughbreds to him to be trained.

Governor Waterman has appointed as Agricultural Directors for the Fourteen District, P. I. Stribling, W. H. Aiken, R. C. Kirby' S. M. Locke, Martin Kinsley and A. Noble, all of Santa Cruz County.

The Rancho Del Paso trotters will leave on their special train to-morrow, weather permitting. Mr. Salisbury's two cars will also be attached to Mr. Haggin's train which will run straight through to New York.

Jeter Walden was, on the 10th of February, ordered by the Clifton Association to take himself and his horses off the track for using insulting language to Starter Caldwell and refusing to apologize to him.

By Holly and John Splan resemble each other closely in build and feature. Holly has not the oratorical powers of John, being sententious, cool and matter of fact, but like him is one of the king pins of the sulky.

Mr. E. L. Israels Thorndale Stud, Lexington, Ky., has purchased from J. F. Caldwell the bay mare Full Sail, foaled 1885, by Flood, dam Florence Anderson by Enquirer. Full Sail was bred at Palo Alto Stock Farm.

C. I. Hood, who recently paid $9000 for the sensational trotting mare Star Lily, 2:20, will retire her from the turf, but will drive her on the road double with Maggie Whitney, the very fast daughter of Lambert Chief.

The New Zealand Stud Company held their annual sale at Auckland last month, disposing of 41 yearlings for 6,158 guineas. The Nordenfeldt (son of Musket), Nelly Moore colt, fetched the highest figure, 1,025 guineas.

In addition to Wentworth and Nepean, bred to English time, and entered in the Derby of 1891, it is said that probably Abercorn and one or two other well-known performers on the Australian turf, will be sent to England.

Protection, the winner of the Junior Champion stakes last year, wintered at Latonia. He has grown and thickened at a great deal, is in high flesh and good health. He should be among the crack 3-year-olds this season.

The first of the get of old Strathspey, the speedy son of Glenelg and La Polka, consequently brother to Los Angeles, E. J. Baldwin's crack, was dropped 2 weeks ago at Mr. William Hendrie's Valley Farm, in Hamilton, Canada.

A bill has been introduced into the New York legislature limiting the time of racing on each track in that state to ten days in any one year. There is no danger of its passage, it being considered merely an effort to exact money from the clubs.

John Marrs, who trained for Scoggan Bros., last year, has retired and is succeeded by Wheeler, who trained Wheeler & Fairea last season. The stable has 23 horses, including Good Bye, who is the favorite of the stable for the Kentucky Derby.

Mr. Ariel Lathrop last week sold to Mr. Miller, of New York, the four-year-old stallion Monterey by Electioneer, out of Minx by Don Victor, second dam Minnie by Sparkle, son of Hambletonian 10. Also a four-year-old sister to Adair, 2:17¼.

Messrs Fred McEvoy and O'Shanassy, Australian racing men, have sent their well known race horse Chicago to England. J. E. Savill will train him and as he handled Ringmaster so successfully, he should make a good showing with Chicago.

Mr. A. T. Hatch has been singularly unfortunate in his entries for the Breeder and Sportsman Futurity Stakes. Out of his three entries two of the mares have slipped their foals, the last being La Signa by Le Grand. She was in foal to My Guy.

The London Sporting Times contains an interesting letter from Buenos Ayres, in which the tragical death of Acme is announced, Annamite being previously poisoned, 'Truth' says. The South American turf appears to be a vile welter of blackguardism and rascality.

The Macy brothers have purchased Wellington, the six-year-old brother to Sunol and will put him in Bell Boy's place in their breeding farm in Woodford County Kentucky. John E. Madden of Lexington, Ky., who owned Wellington will probably have made a big profit on him.

W. H. Wilson, of Abdallah Park, Cynthiana, has engaged the well-known Steve Philips, of Washington, Court House, O, to drive his campaigners this year. Mr. Philips has developed such noted performers as Sleepy Tom (pacer), 2:12¼ Lottie W. 2:21½, Lady Rolfe and other good ones.

Mr. Clark Maxwell, the former owner of Galore, paid Gravesend a flying visit to look over his stable which includes the Australian racer Fergus II and a two-year-old by Voltigeur. A three year old filly by Romney will be sent on from Virginia to join his horses in training in a few days.

Several leading Australian bookmakers talk of coming to New York to ply their trade, feeling convinced that Australia has seen its best day. Joe and Barney Thompson have concluded to stay in England bookmaking, and if business is not remunerative they will then lay siege to New York.

J H. Goldsmith, who is at his home in Washingtonville, N. Y., writes that all of his horses have wintered well, and are looking fine. Gene Smith is fat and strong, and acts like a colt. Barring accidents Goldsmith claims that the close of the season will see 2:12 opposite this trotter's name.

Mr. G. Valensin's two carload of trotters left for New York last Wednesday On the cars were several thoroughbred youngsters of R. P. Ashe's. Mr. Valensin took with him his well known stallion Simmocolon 2:29½ to be turned over to Jimmy Goldsmith who will train him next season for the Count.

J. E. Brewster, the Washington Park Secretary, is in New York on a visit of two or three weeks. He will try to bring over the Eastern racing officials to the adoption of a mile rule (forbidding running of any races under a mile for three-year-olds and upwards) similar to the one recently passed in the West.

The early Blossom Stakes for two-year-olds was won by an unnamed Pizarro-Una filly who was at once christened Early Blossom. The favorite Madge L. was only beaten a head after making all the running. She is by Darebin or Warwick, out of Altitude, and was sold at the last Haggin sale for $400 to A. Lakeland,

Wood Wattles who was down from his new Healdsburg ranch which he calls Millbrook Farm, says that the trotting prospects are good up there, his Anteeo.—Young Miami colt is very promisng, while the old mare is this year in foal to Director 2.17, Sweetbriar 2.26 will be properly bred to Col. Thornton's fast Anteeo stallion, James Madison.

William Hendrickson, who in 1862, brought Geo. M. Patchen 31 to California, has been in the city the last few days after spending a week or two at Sacramento talking over old times with the veteran John Williams. Mr. Hendrickson is as lively and entertaining as ever, so his friends say, while his reminiscences are both interesting and amusing.

Among the Pleasanton Stock Farm's select consignment to New York are Saccharine, a bay two year old colt by Director 2:17, out of Sweetness 2:21¼. Goldleaf 2:11¼, the famous five year old pacer, and Thistle, a three year old brother to Goldleaf; he is a good looking colt and paces like the wind. There should be rapid bidding when either of the three above are under the hammer.

The Buenos Ayres Standard says: "Just previously to the big race Ormonde was brought on the course, his appearance eliciting volley after volley of applause. An opportunity of comparison was thus afforded as he remained in front of the stand whilst the competitors for the International passed. I may add that he pricked up his ears and seemed to ask for a run with them."

After all it turns out that Henry Walsh will not take Peel, Racine, Flambeau and the other Palo Alto horses East in the coming season, but will race them in the California circuit. It is a great pity that two such slashing three-year-olds do not get a chance to show their mettle on an Eastern track where they would most assuredly make a good showing. D. Bridges will, it is said, train the Rose stable.

As yet the Baker County Stock and Agricultural Association in Oregon have taken no steps toward holding a race meeting next fall, but a meeting will probably soon be held to arrange a programme and fix the date for holding the fair.

The rule of the Board of Censors of the National Association of Trotting-Horse Breeders in regard to the names of trotting-bred horses is: "That every stallion and colt entire should be registered a name distinctly his own, and that a name of a distinguished ancestor of sire, or any material part thereof, should not be repeated in any form when naming animals further removed than the immediate progeny of said ancestor or sire."

The exodus of California trotting stock to New York began last Wednesday with Mr. Valensin in the lead, Pleasanton Stock Farm, Rancho Del Paso and Rosemeade (ready to start) are close up for second place and Palo Alto last. It will be interesting to watch the race. The railroad is not in a good state and one or the other may be side-tracked. Which will make the best average at the sale is almost as hard a conundrum.

The great daughter of Princeps, Femme Sole, 2:20, now owned by William Rockefeller, the Standard oil king, is to be sold, together with the entire stable belonging to this gentleman. Few mares in all America have so much speed and stamina united to so many desirable traits for the road or track as Femme Sole. Her owner says—and he is so enormously rich that he can hardly care for a few thousand dollars one way or the other—that this mare can trot in 2:15, and all posted turf men fully agree with him.

The Rancho Del Paso trotting stock are astonishing all the California breeders by their good looks and high breeding, the Albert W's being of an exceptionally high order. Orrin Hickok, who handled Albert W for a while, says of him that his record of 2:20 is no estimate of his speed and gameness, and that he worked him a half in 1:07, and could assuredly have finished the mile in 2:15, which was an exceptional performance when one considers that at the time Albert was dead lame, but his courage was such that he never flinched until he was pulled up.

The Duke of Westminster had a couple of yearling colts by Ormonde. One of these is from Angelica who is closely related to St. Simon, and the dam of Blue Green. The other is from Shotover, and thus presents the very extraordinary combination of having a Derby winner for his sire and a Derby winner for his dam. Only three fillies have won the Derby, and one of these has Blink Bonny, who was covered only by St. Leger winners, in all Ormonde has eight foals in the list, one of which is dead. These foals are respectively the property of the Duke of Westminster, Mr. Marshall, Mr. Snarry Lord Gerard, Lord Alington, and Mr. Simons Harrison.

Frank Van Ness entered Bolero in a race at Guttenberg, on Feb. 11th, for maidens, but was not permitted to start him because the Guide says he won a race at Oakland, on Sept. 10th. Frank Van Ness protested and is correct for the summary of the race in question should read:

Laurelwood Stables' ch m Laura Gardner, 3, Jim Brown—Avail.... ....Appleby 1
D. J McCarty's b c Bolero, 2, Norfolk—Neapolitan........Narvais 2
Jas. Garland's ch c Elwood, 3, Norfolk—Ballinette........Stewart 3
Time, 1:57½.

The Guide erroneously says:

Bolero, 2, 86 ....Navais 1
Elwood, 3, 104........Stewart 2
Laura Gardner, 3, 115........Appleby 3
Time, 1:57½.

The Directors of the Kansas City Jockey Club have decided to adhere to the new rule fixed at the last turf congress barring horses three years old and upwards from purse races where the distance is less than a mile. There was some doubt as to whether all the Western clubs would stick to this rule an account of the dissatisfaction with it expressed by owners whose stables are largely made up of sprinters, but notification was received from Latonia and St. Louis that these clubs would stick to the rules and the Kansas Club decided to do so also. In order to accomodate the sprinters, however, and satisfy the horsemen the club has decided to place on the programme a number of heat purses at five-eights or three-quarters of a mile. This is permitted under the turf congress rule, and will at the same time give the sprinters a chance and add to the interest of the meeting.

Mr. Wm. Hendrie of Hamilton, Ont., has purchased the following stallions: From Mr. Hetterick the chestnut horse Tornado, foaled 1881 by imp Glenlyon, dam Estella, by Australian. From M. J. Daly the bay horse Stripling, 5 years by imp Stonehenge, dam Minority by Narragansett: 2nd dam Minnie Minor by Lexington. From E. A. Cattereau, the chestnut horse Kingsford, foaled 1885 by imp Rayon d'Or, dam Ione by imp Eclipse. From F. Sasson the chestnut horse Prospect, foaled 1885 by Hindoo, dam imp Lady Stockwell by Knowsley. From T. Barratt the bay colt Hemlock, foaled 1886 by Hindoo or imp Billet, dam Mattie Amelia by King Alfonso; also the chestnut horse Costello, foaled 1884 by Sensation, dam Gulnare imp Glen Athol. The stallions will be used for breeding half-breds and hunters in Canada, as well as race-horses. They are all large, Mr Hendrie says, and have great bone and substance with quality enough.

The statement of Thomas, the ex Santa Anita trainer in re—The Emperor of Norfolk has been copied in almost every paper in America without comment. It seems a very peculiar statement for a man professing to be an expert trainer to make. The Emperor, he said, was at his best shortly before his breakdown, and, by the way, he averred that the breakdown was caused by being *yanked* and pulled in his races so that he might not make a show of his company, and thus let the public see what the colt was capable of. Isaac Murphy who rode him is one of the best riders in America, especially noted for his delicate handling, and no one would suppose that he would have to *yank* a horse like the Emperor in order to keep him well in hand. Later on Mr. Thomas said: A week or so before his breakdown, the Emperor, with Murphy up, and carrying 125 lbs., worked a mile in 1.38¾, and was not fully extended at that. The *veteran trainer* must have learned his business in a peculiar school, if after training and racing a horse as long as he had the Emperor, it was necessary to have a special trial. It looks rather as though the gallop a week before his breakdown, might have had something to do with breaking down. Thomas must have been threatened with an attempt of la grippe, and have passed the evening sampling the only cure (whisky our Field editor says), or else have been having a six-furlong trial for the new Veritas handicap when he said that the *mile with* 125 *lbs.* in 1.38¾ was done without the Emperor being *fully extended*. As a matter of fact no one but those *who saw* the trial will believe he ever did it, good horse though he was.

Matt Feakes, W. Hendrie's trainer, will be married to W. Hayward's daughter very shortly.

John McConnell (Buster) is going to Carson to work and drive Mr. Sweeny's horses. He will probably be seen on the California Circuit behind Mr. Sweenys' four year old pacer by Gibraltar 2:22½. Buster is as good a driver and trainer as any of our Californians, and the pacer is said to be as fast as greased lightning.

Veterinary surgeons in New York have been kept busy for the past week with firing irons and blisters. Letretia was blistered a few days ago and Mattie Locram also received a dose of the same treatment. The Warnkes called in a surgeon to alter a pair of their two year old who are at their Coney Island stable.

The Australian entries for their two big races, the Newmarket handicap and Australian Cup, were very satisfactory; there are 110 in the handicap, 26 in excess of last year. The cup also shows an increase 45 being nominated. Carbine the crack, son of Musket is in both, but Abercorn is not entered in either.

The Hon. James White's entries for the next year's English Derby include a royally bred colt in Wentworth, a brother to the well known racehorse Dreadnought. He is by Chester, out of Trafalgar, by Blair Athol (winner of the Derby in 1864.) His grandam is Mosquito, a sister to Musket, the sire of Carbine.

The Directors of the 12th District Agricultural Association will meet in Lakeport Feb. 24th, at 7 P. M., for the purpose of organizing and making preparations for the next Fair to be held in Lakeport. The new Directors from Lake County are Dr. C. W. Aby and D. Alexander. Mr. Hildreth takes the place of Hon. S. H. Long in Mendocino.

It seems while R. C. Church, North Elkhorn Stud, has sold to G. Conkin, New York city, for $20,000 the bay colt Elkhorn, three year old record 2:28¼, by Onward—Long Lane, by Long Island Patchen, that it does not become a transfer unless Mr. Wallace accepts the record and permits the colt to be registered in the American Trotting Register.

It is reported that after the Warnkes have finished racing Reclaire, the speedy daughter of Reform and imp. Clara, will join Mr. August Belmont's broodmares in Kentucky. The Banker is said to have paid $5,000 cash, and is to pay $5,000 more when she is delivered at the end of her turf career. She was originally bought at the Erdenheim sale for $475.

The Clifton statistics for the year show that Dan Hoenig heads the list of winning owners for the year, having the sum of nearly $19,000 to his credit, earned with horses like Capulin, Carnegie, Hilda, Can't Tell, Endurer, and others. Mr. Hoenig is now a strong upholder of Clifton and Brighton, and his success is likely to stimulate other Western owners to emulate his example.

On February 11th, at Lexington, among other horses sold, were Commoneer, br g, 4, by Electioneer, dam Mollie Cobb by Gen. Benton; A. H. Moore, Philadelphia, $5,600. Elected, br f, 5, by Electioneer, dam Cora by Don Victor; Richfield & Leathers, Lexington, $5,600 Directorine, blk, 2, by Director, dam Geraldine by Mambrino Patchen; McHenry & Williams, Independence, Io., $1,775.

M. T. Downing, owner of Mamie Hay, has been notified by the Hudson County Racing Association that they will receive no more of his entries at the Guttenberg track. He seemed to have backed his horse with the Argo Club at Boston, but the fact that all these tickets were for bets made in one room, a couple of hundred miles away, gave that backing a peculiar appearance, and so the club acted as stated.

Of the 362 stakes reported in Goodwin's Guide as being run on the American turf last season, over one-half (183 in number) were won by horses bred in Kentucky. Those foaled in California won 52 of these events, while Pennsylvania comes next with forty to her credit. The other States appear in this order: Tennessee 26, New Jersey and New York 18 each, Missouri 9, Virginia 7, Montana 3, Maryland 2, and Alabama and Georgia 1 each.

One of the most useful looking among the maidens at Coney Island is a Chestnut filly 3 years by St. Blaise, and is now in the Hough Bro., stable, but is owned by Albert Cooper the trainer. She was purchased from Mr. Belmont by Mr. Bernard through Jimmy McCormick. When she fell into Cooper's hands through a trade she had a bad splint. Now her legs are perfectly clean, and the filly cannot fail to make her mark if she reaches the starting post fit and well.

The two new stables being built at the Elizabeth track have twenty-four single stalls, each facing the track. An overhanging roof permits an inclosure, thus insuring a capital winter stable, with an exercise path at least a furlong in circumference. The only difference between the two stables will be that the one for which the foundation only is laid has a roadway in the center, while the one on which the roof is being put has not that accommodation.

A week ago last Sunday at the Rancho del Paso, Rosa May (by Sayres' Henry Clay 45, out of Lady Winfield by Edward Everitt 81, out of a daughter of Rattler, son of Abdallah 1) foaled a chestnut colt with white up to his hocks and knees, and a bald face. He was a big, strong colt, sired by Albert W., 2:20. His color and markings are traceable to Albert W.'s dam, and her sire, John Nelson. A yearling, full brother to the youngster, leaves to-morrow for New York to be sold.

The following stables have applied for quarters at the Memphis meeting: Wm. Amacker 4, R. Williams 5, Avondale stable 9, Charlie Brown 1, J. W. Richcreek 5, H. H. Brown 4, J. K. Johnson 4, S. C. Hildreth 8, W. P. Maxwell, John Huffman 2, W. C. Vivell 5, Gilford stable 7, L. Lamb, Ed. Trotter 2, W. O. Scully 12, Buckland stables 2, J. M. Brown & Co. 16, Louis Long 5, Price & West 8, Lone-Star stable 10, Darley & Hurns 8, A. Stude 2, Lamasney Bros. 14, Cumberland stables 5.

The famous stallion Homer, owned by the Messrs. Jewett, died on Feb. 12th at their stock farm in Buffalo, N. Y., of internal complaint. Homer was by Mambrino Patchen, dam Sally Chorister (dam of Belle Brassfield), by Mambrino Chorister, granddam by Blood's Black Hawk (son of Vermont Black Hawk), great-granddam by Moore's Pilot, son of Pilot. Homer's death was announced at the National Association banquet on the 12th, and a toast in his honor was drunk in silence. Homer is the sire of Palo Alto's Lilly B., the dam of L. U. Shippee's well known Electioneer stallion Campaign and Lelah H., 2:24½.

The three mile race to be decided at Clifton will, no doubt prove a grand success from a racing point of view. Owners from out side courses have already engaged boxes at Clifton for horses to take part in the contest, and from present indications a number of entries will be made. If owners wish to encourage Secretary Saas to continue to give big purses for such races they should enter liberally for them. Purses of $1,000 are not given every day, especially at this season of the year.

Antevolo, 2:19½, one of Electioneer's best sons, arrived at Detroit on January 31st, where he was exhibited for a few hours, and greatly admired by the leading horsemen of the city. Late in the afternoon he was driven out to the Claireview Stock Farm, his future home. The Claireview Stock Farm also bought from Robert Steel the bay mare Muriel, by Kentucky Prince, dam Bess by Hambletonian 10; 2d dam Jessie Sayre (dam of James Howell Jr., record 2:24), by Henry Clay 45; 3d dam by Liberty, son of Trance. In foal to Antevolo.

The following mares from Palo Alto will be bred to imp. Cheviot, brother to Sir Modred, this season: Imp. Mutiny by Adventurer; imp. Queen Bess by Strathconan; Glendew, dam of Guenn; Lady Evangeline, dam of Flood Tide; Shannon Rose by Shannon, out of Fairy Rose, dam of Racine; and Phœbe Anderson by Monday. It will be interesting to breeders to note the results of the doul ls cross of the great Newminster, who is close up in the pedigrees of Cheviot, Mutiny and Queen Bess. The mares were sent to Sacramento last week, and several of them have already taken the horse.

A good starter is invaluable and no time should be lost in securing a competent man for the Blood Horse Spring meeting, and if possible several of the circuit fairs. Perhaps it might be an inducement to a qualified man if an adequate amount of remuneration were attatched to the office. The Blood Horse starter gets $10 a day, which is certainly not enough. The State Fair Directors come nearer the mark, they according to their last report paid Dr. Aby $5 a race. San Jose, The Blood Horse and the State Fair should combine and engage a suitable man and pay him enough to make it an object.

E. J. Baldwin has sent eight mares to Sacramento, to be bred to imported Cheviot. They are Santa Anita, the dam of Gano (by Virgil out of Mary Martin by Lexington out of Alice Jones by Glencoe); Santa Anita Belle, a sister to Gano and a good race horse herself; Winona 5 by Grinstead, out of that grand mare Clara D; Viente 4, a sister to Volante; Aloha 4 (Grinstead—Experiment) is a sister to Silver Cloud, winner of the American Derby in 1886; Atalanta 3, Grinstead—Blossom; Molly McGurn, Joe Hooker—Kitten by imported Eclipse and Janova 4 by Grinstead out of Jennie D, dam of Ligero.

Augur, the brilliant turf writer, in the Australasian says that the pick of the yearlings of the veteran breeder Mr. Andrew Towne, which were to be sold in January, was a colt by Sardonyx out of Geraldine. He is, therefore, half-brother to Senator Hearst's imported Gertrude, who made her debut at Louisville and afterwards was successful a $150, local race at San Luis Obispo, and figures in Goodwin with a winner's bracket for it. The Guide makes a mistake in stating that she is by Soma, dam unknown, and also that she is a gelding by Iamony out of Geraldine, she is in reality a chestnut mare foaled 1886, by Somnus out of Geraldine dam of Moorehouse, by Yattendon.

The poolroom proprietors in St. Louis assert that they were beaten out of a total of $18,000 by a gang of conspirators on the 8th of February. The "killing" was made on the fifth race at Guttenberg, and fully ten rooms were mulcted. My Own was second choice in the betting at 5 to 2, and the money was not put on until the horses had been at the post for some time. The "bookies" charge that the conspirators had the race in then. The money went up simultaneously in all the rooms and while the tickets were being written the race came in. Over $18,000 was paid out, and now they propose to take no more bets after the horses are at the post.

A meeting of the Directors of the Dixon Driving Park Association was held last week. The resignation of Peter Timm was read and accepted and P. R. Willott was elected as his successor. The park was leased to Messrs. Watson & Tietjens, (the well known driver and trainer) of Sacramento, for a term of one year. B. F. Newby was appointed Superintendent of the park. It was decided to have one day's racing on the 1st day of May, and Wm. Ames, G. Wright and P. R. Willott were appointed a committee to consider the number and kind of races and the amount of the purses to be offered. An assessment of $2 50 per share was levied on the capital stock. The Board adjourned subject to the call of the President.

That well known authority on breeding, the late Dr. Shorthouse, was much given to inveighing against the Blacklock blood—"that accursed Blacklock blood." What would he think were he to see a horse, inbred to his accursed strain, at the head of English sires, after proving himself a great racehorse, winning the Derby in 1875. Galopin is by Voltigeur's son Vedette, who was in his time the best horse in England. Voltigeur, the sire of Vedette, was by Voltaire (son of Blacklock), and Vedette's dam, Mrs. Ridgway, was by Birdcatcher from Nan Darrell, by Inheritor from Nell, by Blacklock. Then Flying Duchess, the dam of Galopin, was by Flying Dutchman from Merope, by Voltaire (son of Blacklock). St. Simon was one of the best sons of Galopin, and would most assuredly have been a Derby had not the death of his nominator, Prince Batthyany prevented his starting. As it was he won; he beat Tristan, Ossian, the Leger winner, and all the cracks of his year, and last season was third in the list of winning sires.

The owner of the Madison Stable decided to close up his farm at Madison, N. Y., and has made arrangements to have his mares bred and cared for at Erdenheim, the old home of Parole and Iroquois. Among the mares are:

Atalanta, b m, 1879, by John Morgan—Clara L.
Carola, br m, 1884, by Algerine—imp Belle of Eltham.
Delaware, br m, 1883, by Lisbon—Austria.
Edisto, ch m, 1884, by Enquirer—Babee.
Hilda, ch m, 1873, by imp Eclipse—Jessie Dixon.
Hutoka, b m, 1886, by Reform—Maggie B.B.
Lackawanna, ch m, 1884, by Glenelg—Ems.
Leeda, b m, 1884, by Cape Race—Beware.
Medusa, br m, 1885, by Sensation—Hilde.
Mollie Carew, b m, 1873, by Narragansett—Chignon.
Ranee, b m, 1881, by Reform—Sue Ryder.
Tuscaloosa, br m, 1879, by imp Leamington, or Reform—La Rose.
Greenland, b h, by Glengarry—Nevada.

The Melbourne Sportsman says Australians are gnashing their teeth, etc., because Darebin, Sir Modred and his brother Cheviot, have gone to America. A winner by one or the other crops up every now and again in the colonies, the last being Sir William, a three-year-old Sir Modred who, in one day, won two races, a seven furlong handicap and a mile and a quarter handicap, at the A. J. C. meeting held at Randwick, and at the Sydney Tattersall's meeting at Randwick, with 102 pounds up, was beaten two lengths for the Carrington stakes, six furlongs, by The Gift, 4, 104 pounds; the *other 38 starters* were beaten off. Time, 1:16½. On the following Monday, in the Tattersall's Sale Cup, 2 miles, with 15 starters, Sir William turned into the straight in front, and won by a length and a half in 3:36½, which shows that the Australians have good cause for regretting the loss of his sire, Sir Modred.

The executive committee of the Washington Jockey Club held a meeting at Willard's on the 10th, and officially announced its decision to give a spring meeting at the Benning's track in May. A full and enthusiastic attendance was present. The details of a programme were discussed, but that will not be made public until the next meeting.

A movement is also on foot to establish a spring trotting circuit, to take in the Benning's track, Belmont and Point Breeze Driving Park in Philadelphia, and Pimlico and the gentlemen's Driving Park of Baltimore. Mr. Joseph A. Winderath, President of the Point Breeze Association, during a recent visit to Washington, when this place was proposed, said the Belmont people had set their dates for the first week in May, and will give $5,000 in purses, to be equally divided among ten events, eight for trotting and two for pacing, to include performers, from 3 00 to 2.20 horses. The people in Washington propose holding their meeting later in the same month.

The thirteenth biennial congress of the National Trotting Association was convened on February 12th by President P. P. Johnson, of Lexington. A large number of horsemen were present. The number of persons and horses remaining under penalty December 31, 1889, according to Secretary M. M. Morse's report, is as follows: Persons suspended, 2,705; persons expelled, 209; horses suspended, 1,405; horses expelled, 128. Total, 4447. The report for two years shows: Persons suspended, 3317; persons expelled, 176; horses suspended, 1,974; horses expelled, 111. Total, 5,580. Deducting the number of men and horses under penalty of suspension and expulsion December 21, 1889 (4,447) shows a decrease in the aggregate of 1,133.

Treasurer Lewis J. Powers, of Springfield, Mass., reported as follows: Cash on hand January 1, 1888 (as per previous report), $10,740 56; receipts for 1888 $16,861 64. Total, $27,602 20. Disbursements for 1888, $13,341 77. Balance for 1888, $14,260 43. Receipts for 1889, $16,888 13. Disbursements for 1889, $14,315 28. Balance on hand January 1, 1890, $16,833 29.

The Duke of Portland has twelve two-year-olds in training at Newmarket, including a colt by St. Simon, out of Wheel of Fortune (Simon Magnus) a colt by Barcaldine out of Rattlewings (Flutterwings), a colt by St. Gatien out of Modwena (Molina), a filly by Bend Or out of Atalanta, dam of Ayrshire (Caithness), an own sister to Semolina (Koorah), and a filly by St. Simon out of Ulster Queen (St. Bridget). It will be singular if the last four of those animals do not race, but Simon Magnus and Flutterwings are doubtful quantities. Wheel of Fortune is full of running blood, and she was probably the best animal ever bred by the late Lord Falmouth, being when extended the personification of easy, frictionless action, but she has been nearly as hopeless a failure at the stud as Marie Stuart, and since the Duke of Portland gave 5 100 gs. for her at the sale of Lord Falmouth's breeding stud in July, 1886, she has produced nothing that could win a race. Rattlewings is another Mereworth-bred mare, being an own sister to Galliard. She was bought by the Duke as a yearling at Lord Falmouth's sale for 2100 gs., but never won a race, and it may be hoped that she will prove more successful at the stud.

The New York Times after commenting on the Dwyer's entries in the Suburban and Brooklyn, and speaking wonderfully favorable of Sir Dixon says: As to the rest of the lot in the two handicaps, one-third in each might as well be declared out by the 20th as to remain in until the day of the race so far as any chance of winning goes. Why they were ever entered no one but their owners can ever tell. Had the handicappers taken a margin of 75 pounds to work on, instead of limits of 38 and 42 pounds, as they did in the Brooklyn and Suburban respectively, it would even then have left about 50 per cent. of the entries without the remotest chance of winning. Such cattle as Ofalece, Fresno, Rico, Gloster, Maggie K., Elkton, Glendale, Loontaks, Juggler, Quesal, St. Luke, and a lot of other Winter track "skates," have about as much chance of winning such races as they have of flying. It would take a house and lot planted in the saddle of real racers to bring them down to anything like a level with these cattle. Yet bookmakers and touts may succeed in creating some such furor about one of them as was created over Juggler, last Spring, when people actually backed the horse with good United States money to beat a field of racers. Probably most of these will be stricken from the list of nominations by the day on which declarations are due. Of the lot left in about a dozen will probably go to the post for each race.

Rolf Boldrewood" in an Australian paper tells how, in the old days, when a filly named Hellcat, the property of Mr. John Hunter, won on Flemington race course the Sir Charles' purse, furnished by a generous stud patron for the owners of descendants of that forgotten courser, it was objected by a well known horse-coper of the day known as "Hopping Jack" that she was no true descendant of Sir Charles. However, the stewards concluded otherwise, and her owner received the stakes. It afterwards happened that the two Jacks went to sea in the same ship on a voyage to their native Scotia. A great storm arose and the ship was wrecked. As they clung gloomily and despairingly to the uplifted deck, fast on a reef. "Hopping Jack" approached Hunter with a grave and resolved air, and in that solemn hour, "the ruling passion strong in death," he thus adjured his turf acquaintance: "Look here, Mr. Hunter, we shall be all in —— in twenty minutes; it can't matter much *now*. Was Hellcat *really* a Sir Charles?" Which recalls the story of Fauntleroy, the fashionable banker, who, much to the annoyance of his guests, kept strictly to himself the source from which he obtained a certain much-admired liqueur. On the day before his execution for forgery, a number of men waited upon the doomed banker in the condemned cell. "Now, Fauntleroy," said one of their number, "in fourteen hours you'll be at the bar of God. It won't hurt you now if you will well and truly answer me a question." "What is it?" asked the miserable banker. "Where did you get that curacoa?"

L. U. Shippee's Horses.

(Continued from last Week)

In the last number of the BREEDER AND SPORTSMAN we gave a list of the trotting stallions now owned by Mr. Shippee, and also a partial list of the exceedingly fine colts and fillies which are to be seen at his ranch. We now come to the brood mares, all of which have been selected for their grand individuality as well as for pedigree. It would be a hard matter to go anywhere and find as large a number of brood mares all of which are in such perfect order; the best of care is taken of them at all seasons of the year, and it is only natural that they should present a better appearance than the average of those seen on the ordinary stock farm. It would be impossible to enumerate all we looked at, but among them may be mentioned Nellie F., by Daniel Lambert, 102; dam Jennie by Columbus; Nellie F., is a bay mare with star and right hind pastern white, foaled in 1887.

Daisy, record 2:34½, is by Chieftain 721, dam Beauty by old Doc, Daisy was foaled in 1869, is a bay mare and is noted as being the dam of Mt. Vernon 2.21, and Chief Thorne who as a yearling paced a quarter in 38 seconds.

Nellie Sigh is by Hawthorne 10935, dam Nellie F., by Daniel Lambert, Nellie is a bay mare foaled in 1887.

Sally Ry is by Hawthorne, dam Ryan mare [the dam of Ha Ha 2.22½], by Black Hawk 787. Sally Ry is a [black mare, foaled in 1883, full sister to Moses S., Maggie S. and Breastplate.

Maggie S. is a bay mare foaled in 1886, has yearling record of 2.58½, and is full sister to Sallie Ry.

Brown Priam is a brown mare foaled in 1879, by Priam 1798, dam the Ryan mare, dam of Ha Ha.

Old Tempest is by Morgan Rattler, dam the Page mare by Coburn's Jim Crow, he a son of Jim Crow [thoroughbred]; Old Tempest is a brown mare foaled in 1867, and her roll of honor does her justice, she has produced many foals, among which may be mentioned Bright Light, record 2.40, J. C. Shelly 2.29½, Beauty Sister of the dam of Tempest 2.19, and many others which were all trotters if they had an opportunity; her younger foals of 1887-88 and 89, will be worked this season.

Brown Tempest, is, as her name would indicate, a brown mare standing fully 16 hands high, with star and left hind foot white, foaled in 1878, and has already proved herself a producer both of quality and speed; naturally the best known of her produce is Tempest 2.19, which was sold last year by Mr. Shippee to go to South America where to-day she is acknowledged to be one of the handsomest race animals in the Argentine Republic. Brown Tempest is by Chieftain 721, out of Old Tempest mentioned above, by Morgan Rattler, She is in foal to Hawthorne.

Overshot and Beauty are both out of Old Tempest and are built on very speedy lines, they should prove very valuable in the brood-mare ranks at Oaklawn.

Clouds is a brown mare with two small stars, foaled in 1886, she is by Abby 10915, he a son of Abbotsford, Cloud's dam is Brown Tempest, she by Chieftain.

Ida May, a brown mare with star and left hind foot white, is a 4-year-old, and when in her 3-year-old form made a public trial in 2.34, she is by Hawthorne, dam Brown Tempest, dam of Tempest 2.19.

Hilda is a chestnut mare, the only white on her being a small star in forehead. She is four years old, by Hawthorne, dam Hose, she by Echo 462.

Hulda, a bay mare with star, both hind feet white, is a five year old, and full sister to Hilda.

Emotional, a bay filly foaled in 1887, is by Hawthorne, dam Right Motion, she by Motion 1544

We were particularly well pleased with Maud, a bay mare with star and right hind ankle white, foaled in 1877, by Dan Lambert 102, dam Columbia by Columbus 95, the second dam being by Harris's Hambletonian. Maud is a great road mare, and can do better than 2:40 without any track work whatever.

Undershot is a bay mare standing about 15 hands and 3 inches, and is three years old. She is by Hawthorne, dam Overshot (full sister to dam of Tempest) by Chieftain 721.

Storm is another of the three year old mares by Hawthorne, dam Beauty (sister of Tempest's dam) by Chieftain 721.

We now come to a very beautiful black mare six years old, named Haughty, who can pace at a very speedy gait. She is by Hawthorne, dam Maggie McClellan by General McClellan 144.

Flower, a bay mare almost 16 hands in height, is eight years old, by Hawthorne, dam Daisy, the dam of Mt. Vernon, and should be a great producer.

A handsome chestnut mare 15 hands three inches, foaled in 1886, is called the Jade, by Hawthorne, dam Wanton by Chieftain 721.

Laurel is a bay mare 7 years old, a small white star being her only distinguishing mark. She is by Hawthorne, dam Potter's Chieftain, she by Chieftain 721.

Bailey Nutwood is a bay mare, black points, small star, approaches close to 16 hands. She is by Nutwood, dam Noyse Bailey mare, she by Chieftain 721.

Amy, a bay mare, left hind foot white, was foaled in 1886, is by Hawthorne, dam Jennie Miller by John Nelson 187.

June Second, 7 years old, is a chestnut mare with star and right hind ankle white, by Ben. Franklin 753 (record 2:29) dam Kitty Harris by Dan. Lambert 102.

Helen Mar is another chestnut mare, 5 years old, by Hawthorne, dam Fanny Hughson, by Chieftain 721.

Maria H, bay mare with black points, eight years old, is by Sultan 1513, dam March Fourth by Hambletonian 725.

Miss Hubbard is a chestnut mare with star and snip, left hind ankle white; she was foaled in 1887, and is by Hawthorne, dam Maria H, whose pedigree precedes this.

Fifty is a brown mare with black points, 5 years old, by Hawthorne, dam March Fourth by Hambletonian 725.

Mistake, a bay mare, two white hind pasterns, foaled in 1884, is by La Rocke 10334, dam Laura Second by Chieftain 721.

Alice Cary, chestnut mare, narrow strip in face, two hind feet white, foaled in 1882, is by Hawthorne, dam Phoebe Cary (three year old record 2:52) by Chieftain.

Mockingbird, a chestnut mare with white stripe, 16 hands high, foaled in 1881, has a two year old record of 2:38½; she is by Priam 1798, dam Western Girl (dam of Honesty 2:25½) by Chieftain.

To the cover of Hawthorne, Mockingbird has produced several fillies, in 1885 Mertie, in 1886 Mavis, both of these being chestnut in color; in 1888 she produced a black filly which has been named Maybird.

Posey, a six year old bay mare with small star, is by Hawthorne, dam Bouquett by Chieftain.

La Roe is a chestnut mare 5 years old, by La Rocke 10834, dam Golddust by McCracken's Golddust.

Ida Thorne is a bay mare with black points, foaled in 1885, by Hawthorne, dam Belmont Mary Jr, she by Chieftain 721; Ida Thorne's second dam being Belmont Mary, dam of Nellie Grattan 2:32.

Mary Cole, chestnut mare by Hawthorne, dam Etta Russell by General Dana 1757.

Mary Ann, bay mare 7 years old, is by Chieftain 721, dam Mary Clay by Henry Clay.

May second is a bay mare with star and left hind ankle white, is 8 years old, by Hawthorne, dam May First by Hambletonian 725.

There were scores of others to be seen, but time would not admit of noticing more of the trotters, as time was limited. A few of the thoroughbred mares and stallions were glanced at, but only in a hurried manner. They all look well and are a credit to the wealthy owner, who has spared no expense in securing the best that could be had.

John A. will be so well remembered, that it is hardly necessary to speak of him. He is a beautiful black, nine years old, by Monday, dam Lady Clare by Norfolk; 2d dam Versalia by imp. Sovereign; 3d dam Cottage Girl by imp. Ainderby; 4th dam Princess Anna, by imp. Leviathan; 5th dam Sally Kirby by Stockholder. As a two-year-old John A. started five times, winning once only, but as a three-year-old he was unbeaten, winning, among other races, the Pacific Cup, 2¼ miles on a very muddy track in the creditable time of 4:13½. As a four-year-old he faced the starter twelves times, and was victorious in eight races. He did not start after that, but has had two race-horses to perpetuate his name, he being the sire of Hubert Earl and Emma Nevada, both of whom have proved winners.

Alameda, ch m, foaled 1882 by Springbok, dam Alme by Planet; 2d dam Edina by imp. Knight of St. George; 3d dam Edith (dam of Aerolite, Eleanor, Bellair and Judy) by imp. Sovereign; 4th dam Judith by imp. Glencoe; 5th dam Fandango by imp. Leviathan, etc

Agnes B., ch m, foaled 1886 by imp. Glengarry, dam Ensue by Enquirer; 2d dam Sue Walton by Jack Malone; 3d dam Wenonah by Capt. Elgee; 4th dam by imp. Albion, 5th dam by Pacific, etc.

Acquito, b m, foaled 1886 by Long Taw (sire of Come to Taw), dam Acquittal by Calvin; 2d dam Jury (dam of Passiac) by Lexington; 3d dam Roxana (dam of Tippecanoe, Susan Ann and Chesapeake) by imp. Chesterfield; 4th dam Levia by imp. Tranby; 5th dam Tolevia by imp. Contract, etc.

Boggs' mare, b m, foaled 1877 by Lodi, dam Ariadne by Belmont; 2d dam Susie Hawkins by Jack Hawkins; 3d dam Lola Montez by Grey Eagle; 4th dam Covinna by Trumpetor; 5th dam Directress by Director, etc.

Bonnie Brook, b f, foaled 1887 by Ten Broeck, dam Bonnie Kate (dam of Ella T., the dam of Tea Tray, Virgie Hearne, etc.) by imp. King of St. George; 2d dam Eagle by Zenith; 3d dam Eagletta by Grey Eagle; 4th dam Mary Howe by Tiger; 5th dam Lady Robin by Robin Grey, etc.

Decoy Duck is a bay mare foaled 1881, by Longfellow, dam Call Duck by Gilroy; 2d dam Wild Duck by imp. Eclipse; 3d dam Slipper by imp. Yorkshire; 4th dam Clipper by American Eclipse; 5th dam Eliza Jenkins by Sir William of Transport.

Earnestine, ch m foaled 1886, somewhat took my fancy, she presenting a good appearance in addition to her superb breeding. She is by Bertram, dam Kitty H. by imp King Ernest or Macaroon, 2nd dam Miss Bassett (sister to Harry Bassett) by Lexington; 3rd dam Canary Bird by imp Albion; 4th dam Panola (dam of Penelope) by imp Ainderby; 5th dam imp Sweetbriar by Recovery, etc.

Early Rose is an inbred Bonnie Scotland and is a finely put up young lady of five summers, having been foaled in 1885. In color she is brown and a splendid individual. She is by Duke of Montrose, he by Waverly and the Duke's dam was Kelpie by imp Bonnie Scotland. Early Rose's dam was Talega by imp Bonnie Scotland, and Talega was the dam of Talaria and Helen Blazes; 2nd dam Lady Taylor by imp Glencoe; 3rd dam Occidenta by Bertrand; 4th dam Diamond by Turpin's Florizel; 5th dam by Lewis's Eclipse.

Elsie S. is a chestnut filly foaled 1887, by imp Glenelg, dam Myriad by imp King Ban; 2nd dam Myra by Marion, son of Lexington; 3rd dam Florac by imp Mickey Free; 4th dam Dixie by imp Sovereign; 5th dam St. Mary by Hamlet.

Falsalara, ch f, foaled 1887 by Falsetto, dam Salara by Salvator, (winner of the Grand Prix de Paris, and French Derby, etc.) 2nd dam imp Lady Stockwell by Knowsley; 3rd dam Bab-at-the Bowster (sister to Balrownie) by Annandale, a son of Touchstone; 4th dam Queen Mary (dam of Bonnie Scotland) by Gladiator; 5th dam by Plenipotentiary.

Free Love is a big mare foaled 1886 by Luke Blackburn; dam Janet Norton by imp. Leamington; 2nd dam Carrie Atherton by Lexington; 3rd dam Glycera by imp. Sovereign, 4th dam Sister to Pryor, by imp. Glencoe; 5th dam Gipsey (sister to Medoc) by American Eclipse.

Gazelia, br. m. foaled 1886, by imp Glengarry, dam Azalea by King Alfonza; 2nd dam Marguerite, by Lexington; 3rd dam, My Lady, by imp Glencoe; 4th dam Motto, by imp Barefoot; 5th dam Lady Thompkins by American Eclipse, etc.

Glencola, b m foaled 1886 by imp Glengarry, dam Marcola by Monarchist; 2nd dam Tuscola by Enquirer; 3rd dam Bourbon Belle, by Bonnie Scotland; 4th dam Ella D. by Vandal; 5th dam Falcon by Woodpecker, etc.

Josie D. ch f foaled 1887, by Joe Daniels, dam Boggs Mare whose pedigree is given above.

Kathlene, ch m foaled 1886, by Long Taw, dam Athlene by Pat Malley; 2nd dam Anna Travis by imp Yorkshire; 3rd dam Margaret Wood (dam of Maria Wood, Wade Hampton, Capt. Travis and Heraldry) by imp Priam; 4th dam Maria West (dam of Wagner, Fannie, Childe Harold etc.) by Marion; 5th dam Ella Crump by imp Citizen.

If it were not for her name how I would admire Libbertiflibbet, for she is a magnificent creature and as the pedigree will show, she is all that can be desired. She (I cannot spell her name again) is by Bullion, a son of War Dance, and her first dam is Flibbertigibbet by Kingfisher; 2nd dam, imp Filagree, by Stockwell; 3rd dam, Extasy, by Touchstone; 4th dam, Miss Wilfred, by Lottery; 5th dam (Royal Oak's dam) by Smolensko and so on through the most noted families of England.

Tillie C. is a bay mare foaled 1877, by Wildidle, dam Abbie W. by Don Victor; 2nd dam Mary Chilton (dam of Thad Stevens) by imp Glencoe; 3rd dam by American Eclipse; 4th dam Queen Mary, by Bertrand; 5th dam Lady Fortune by Brimmer, etc.

A daughter of Tillie C. may also be seen; her name is Louisa D. by Norfolk. She was foaled in 1883, and is a beautiful bay.

Miss Douglas is another of the mares with good American top crosses, well backed up with imported blood. She is a bay, foaled 1885, by Joe Daniels, dam Ellen Douglas by Wildidle; 2nd dam Lady Clare by Norfolk; 3rd dam Versalia by imp Sovereign; 4th dam Cottage Girl by imp Ainderby; 5th dam Princess Ann by imp Leviathan, etc.

Napa Queen, (dam of Nighthawk) bay mare, foaled 1872, by Norfolk, dam Sweetwater by Volscian, 2nd dam Lady Letty by Argyle; 3rd dam by Duke of Bedford; 4th dam by Cherokee; 5th dam by Top Gallant, etc.

Nina Woodburn, dark bay mare, foaled 1876 by Woodburn, dam by imp Nina Sahib; 2nd dam by Jack Hawkins.

Seat is a bay mare, foaled 1886, by Joe Hooker, dam Kitten (dam of Sabrina and Ezza) by imp Eclipse; 2nd dam imp Pussy by Diophantus; 3rd dam Agapemone by Bay Middleton; 4th dam Venus by Sir Hercules; 5th dam Echo by Emilius, etc.

Stella S., bay filly, foaled 1887, is still another daughter of Tillie C., the sire being Joe Hooker.

The Teal, b m, foaled 1884, by Hindoo, dam Mundane (dam of Blue Wing) by Lexington, 2nd dam Sally Brown by imp Hooton; 3rd dam Quiz by Bertrand; 4th dam by Brimmer; 5th dam, dam of Woodpecker by Buzzard, etc

The last of the thoroughbred mares to be inspected was Whisban, the chestnut filly foaled in 1887, and well known to all our race goers. She is by imp King Ban, dam Whisperine by Whisper; 2nd dam Matella by imp Australian; 3rd dam La Grande Duchesse by Lexington; 4th dam Ann Innis by American Eclipse; 5th dam Miss Obstinate by Sumpter.

Being just in time to catch the train, we hurried back to town and started at once for Sacramento to view Mr. Shippee's thoroughbreds which are in training for the coming season's work. We were met by Ab Stemler, the well known trainer, who has the horses in charge and it was with pardonable pride that he led each of the beauties out for inspection. The first to claim attention was Major Ban, a chestnut colt, foaled 1887 by imp King Ban, dam Hearsay by imp Australian; 2nd dam Dixie by imp Sovereign; 3rd dam St. Mary by Hamlet; 4th dam imp Vamp by Langar; 5th dam Wire by Waxy, etc.

Take Notice is a royally bred fellow, foaled 1887, by imp Prince Charlie, dam Nota Bene by imp Glenelg; 2nd dam Notice by Lexington; 3rd dam Novice by imp Glencoe; 4th dam Chloe by Rodolph; 5th dam Belle Anderson by Sir William of Transport, etc. This colt has a little white on near fore coronet, and off hind pastern white, and also a star in forehead. As will be seen his second dam is a full sister to Norfolk and with the Glenelg cross above that. Take Notice should prove a race horse of the first water, especially as his sire was such a progenitor of speed.

I was more than pleased with the bay colt Lodowic, which will, bar accident, make his first appearance this year. He is by Longfellow, dam Carrie Phillips by Pat Malloy (an old favorite of mine); 2d dam Florita by Enquirer; 3d dam Florac (dam of Minus, May D., Warfield, Ella Warfield, Flit, Sour Mash and Florimore) by imp. Mickey Free; 4th dam Dixie (dam of Herzog, Aureola, War Jig, War Reel, Heretog, Hearsay, etc.) by imp. Sovereign, 5th dam St. Mary by Hamlet, etc. This colt has been entered in a large number of stakes, and I will be more than surprised if he does not give a good account of himself.

Fellowcharm, b c, foaled 1887, is by Longfellow, dam Trinket by Great Tom; 2d dam Bobinet (dam of Biggonet, Bigoeyet, etc.) by Brown Dick; 3d dam Alentia by Childe Harold; 4th dam Talma by imp. Glencoe; 5th dam Delta by imp. Priam, etc. Fellowcharm is a strapping good colt, who ran last fall second to Flambeau in the California Annual Stakes, but he has improved so much that he should be able to hold his own this year with any of them.

Picnic, foaled 1886, the brown mare which has raced quite a number of times in the colors of Mr. Shippee, is so well known that it is almost needless to speak of her, but as a matter of record, give her pedigree. She is by imp. Mr. Pickwick, dam imp. Countess by Theobald; 2d dam Romula by King Caradoc; 3d dam Miss Bower by Record; 4th dam by Righton or Romulus; 5th dam Selina by Fitz Teazle, etc.

Songstress, b m, is another well known performer, foaled 1886 by Luke Blackburn, dam imp. Malibran by Cathedral; 2d dam Melodious by Forrester or Peppermint; 3d dam Harp by Kremlin; 4th dam Harmony by Reveller; 5th dam by Orville, etc.

False Queen, b f foaled 1888 by Falsetto, dam Queen Victoria (dam of Jennie T. Albert, Queenstown, and Infanta) by Lexington; 2nd dam Magenta (dam of Duke of Magenta) by imp Yorkshire; 3rd dam Miriam (dam of Mamona, Magenta, Merrill, Marion, Hollywood, Necy Hale, Grecian Bend, etc.) by imp Glencoe; 4th dam Minerva Anderson, by imp Luzborough; 5th dam by Sir Charles etc. Is there any feature in the above pedigree that the most captious critic would have rubbed out? If there is any such thing as being bred in the purple, False Queen is certainly entitled to that distinction.

May H., b f, foaled 1888 by Falsetto, dam Glenluine (dam of Troubadour) by imp. Glenelg; 2d dam Lute (dam of Virginus) by Lexington; 3d dam Lulu Horton (dam of Spartan, Pequot and Kildare) by imp. Albion; 4th dam Martha Dunn by imp. Sovereign; 5th dam (dam of Laura, Lilly Ward and Fanny Cheatham) by Stockholder, etc.

Mable F. is a bay filly foaled 1887 by Longfellow, dam Carrie Phillips by Pat Malloy; 2d dam Florita by Enquirer; 3d dam Florac by imp. Mickey Free; 4th dam Dixie by imp. Sovereign; 5th dam St. Mary by Hamlet, etc.

In among the younger division, there is The Drake by Leonatus, dam The Teal by Hindoo; 2d dam Mundane by Lexington; 3d dam Sally Bowen by imp. Hooten; 4th dam Quiz by Bertrand, etc. He is a racy-looking fellow, and should give a good account of himself.

White Oak is another of the foals of 1888 by Joe Hooker, dam Lillie C., whose pedigree has already been given.

There is also a two-year-old by Joe Hooker, dam Nina Woodburn, of whom mention has already been made.

Mr. Shippee is entitled to great credit for his enormous outlay, and it is to be sincerely hoped that he may win many of the valuable stakes, in which his trotters and thoroughbreds are entered for, during the racing season of 1890.

Judson H. Clark Buys Alcazar.

The Kentucky Stock Farm says that Mr. Judson H. Clark, of Elmira, New York, one of the owners of the unfortunate Bell Boy, the horse that was destroyed in the fire at Macey's stable a few weeks ago, has purchased of Mr. L. J. Rose, his great young stallion Alcazar, 2:20½, by Sultan, dam Minnehaha (dam of Beautiful Bells, 2:29½, Eva, 2:23½, Sweetheart, 2:22½, Alcazar, 2:20½, etc), by Stevens' Bald Chief. Mr. Clark has written the Macey Brothers to ask if they can take charge of his purchase. It is probable that he will take the place of Bell Boy. Alcazar has the reputation of being one of the best young horses in America. He is the sire of the two-year-old filly, Mista, 2:26, and the yearling Reverie, 2:35.

We can hardly believe that the report is true, for while we have had no notice of the sale from Mr. Rose, it seems hardly probable that he would dispose of the star of his collection which are to be sold soon in New York. Inquiry among the more prominent horsemen fails to elicit any information in regard to the sale, and therefore we are inclined to doubt the Kentucky story.

THE FARM.

Fertile Eggs for Hatching.

After selecting your stock, weeding out all those that are too old, too small, or afflicted with any disease or deformity, then the food for the remainder should be carefully regulated in quantity and quality, in order that the eggs for hatching may be both abundant and fertile. A very fat hen will not lay many eggs, and a large percentage of those she does lay will prove infertile: consequently the proportion of those foods rich in carbon, which go to produce heat and fat, should be diminished, and those containing a preponderance of nitrogen and albumen should be increased.

Meat, contrary to the usually accepted opinion, contains none of the fattening elements. Lean meat is largely composed of albumen, which enters to a considerable extent into the white of an egg; therefore it is an excellent food at this time, and milk, for the same reason, is also valuable, while linseed meal and cottonseed meal are both fattening because they contain much carbon as well as nitrogen. Indian corn and potatoes also belong to this class, and therefore, as spring approaches, they should be fed in smaller quantities, while the ration of wheat and oats which furnish a larger propor' of albuminoids, should be increased.

I have been surprised lately at the avidity with which my flock continues to relish wheat bran; they never seem to grow tired of it. If there is any special food of which they are not particularly fond, but of which I should like to have them eat, I have only to mix wheat bran with it in order to have it eagerly devoured. They prefer a warm mess of mashed potatoes, hot milk and wheat bran to the same mixed with corn meal, and as the flock never appeared in better con tir did better work, I suppose it must be good for them. Wheat bran contains more of the requisites for renewing animal tissues, bones and feathers, as well as the constituents for egg-making, than does corn meal. Shorts is also good used in this direction, and better still is the whole grain of wheat coarsely ground into what we call graham or brown flour. The use of corn, however, should not be discontinued altogether, at letst not until warm weather, but I prefer the whole grains of corn given dry as an evening food.

Special care must also be taken at this time to providing a healthy regimen for the fowls. One of my neighbors had a pen of handsome Black Langshans which she yarded last spring in order to keep their eggs pure for hatching purposes, but as she failed to furnish them the necessary variety of food, their eggs, much to her sorrow, proved entirely infertile.

As the weather becomes milder, hens should be fed more sparingly in order to compel them to take more exercise; as a rule the active breeds and the most energetic foragers belonging to those breeds, not only produce the greatest number of eggs, but their eggs will hatch better. This is no doubt owing to the greater healthfulness produced by their active habits, and because the hen by taking a wider range is thus enabled to secure a greater variety of food.

While the color of egg shell is not affected by the food consumed by the hen, yet contents are. Confine a hen to a dry lot, and if she lays eggs at all the yolk will be pale and thin with an insipid flavor, while the white will be almost too poor to froth, but give her plenty of suitable grain with a liberal supply of green food, and in a very short time the contents of her eggs will assume a different color, flavor and consistency.

Just now my chickens are rejoicing over some winter turnips that I pulled up, tops and all, and scattered about over the poultry yard; they seem to prefer the greens fed in this way to having them cut off, as they like to think they are getting something green and growing. I should be glad to let my flock have the range of the vegetable garden at this season of the year, but the housekeeper thinks it would be a bad precedent; so I never exactly turn them in, but when I see an enterprising little Leghorn scale the five-foot palings I never drive her out. They are such indefatigable little forgers.

A fresh supply of ground oyster shells, broken crockery, ground bone, or sharp gravel, should be supplied them; and as lime enters largely into the composition of the egg-shell, plenty of it should be placed within sight of the laying hens so that we may not be troubled with soft-shelled eggs. Fresh lime is too caustic; fill an old crock or an iron vessel with lime and pour on a sufficient quantity of water to slake it. Place this in a corner of the yard, and every now and then you will see a hen go near and take a peck at it. Lime water added to their soft food, in the proportion of one gill to a gallon, will not only be found an efficient corrective of disordered digestion, but will give them the lime in solution when it may be readily assimilated.—A Farmer's Daughter in Country Gentleman.

Hornless Cattle.

At the annual Convention of the Breeders of Ohio a plea for hornless cattle was made by Dr. W. W. Crane, who said that a hundred thousand men in this country would dishorn their cattle at once if it could be done without pain. In all the world there is not a man, the owner of polled herds, who would if he could by a wish crown his mooleys with horns. It is often said, if nature wants her cattle smooth, polled, why did she not so create them? It needs no argument to show the necessity of those great weapons on aboriginal herds. The enemies no longer exist, and now the ox should go unarmed. I have with me to-day an argument against horn-breeding cattle which is greater than all the consideration of economy, convenience and profit. It consists of a catalogue of some of the cruel deeds of horns. It is the argument of humanity. It is a list of fifty persons who have been fearfully mangled and many of them mortally wounded. Beside, there are ten thousand unproved cases. At the slaughter yards are thousands of damaged hides; on butcher's blocks are inflamed and impure roasts; among many herds there are quivering, bleeding, lacerated flanks, an aggregate of damage amounting to hundreds of thousands of dollars, all traceable to horns. The edict of banishment for horns is issued and the horns are going. There being no supply of hornless cattle at hand for the wide demand, dishorning has come into vogue. The fact is, there are comparatively few feeders among our Western stockmen who are not fully convinced that the practice is economical and every way advantageous where cattle are being handled for butcher purposes.

Hornless cattle, as the Angus, Galloways and Red Polls already exist as it were, ready made to order; but they are as a drop in the bucket. The Polled Durhams are also coming rapidly into favor; yet in the presence of this inadequate supply the dishorning saw is largely used, and within two years the enormous number of 10,000,000 steers have been shorn of their horns. Instead of trying to create a new breed, the simpler method is to cross the pure Short-Horn with native hornless cows, and then breed back to the pure blood, thus establishing a sub-family of Durhams, having dropped the horns and added to and revived strong milk-giving characteristics.—Cultivator.

Cattle Prospects in Texas, Arizona and New Mexico.

George B. Loving, in the Texas Live-Stock Journal, says: "There is little doing in cattle business through the section of country tributary to El Paso. Our ranchmen expect in the near future to make quite a number of sales to Northern buyers. No contracts have as yet, so far as I know, been closed. There seems, as usual at this time of year, to be a difference of about $2 per head as to values in the ideas of ranchmen here and the Northern buyers. Two-year-old steers brought last spring through Southern Arizona and New Mexico from $9 to $12 per head, while three-year-olds brought from $13 to $16 per head, the price varying according to quality. Our ranchmen express themselves as being satisfied to sell at the same figure again this spring, while the buyers contend that in view of the low market for the past twelve months they should have their supply for the coming season at fully $2 per head less than the prices paid last year. The cattle through this section of the country are in fine flesh—in fact are in better condition than they have been for several years; our young steers can be turned off in May in splendid flesh and fine trim for making the long shipment to Northern ranches. A few good lots of two year old steers in Southern Arizona are now being offered at $9 per head. A majority of them, however, in that locality are being held at about $11, while in Southern New Mexico the best herds are being held at from $11 to $12 per head for two year olds. Yearling steers through the territory referred to held at from $7 50 to $9 per head, the price varying not so much on account of the quality of the cattle as the financial necessity of the owners. A majority of the ranchmen in Western Texas between El Paso and the Pecos River are preparing to make an early drive to the Indian Territory. As near as I can estimate, this drive from the section referred to will amount to fully 40,000 head. * * * Considering the fact that the present year will wind up the depression in the cattle business, and that a better and more prosperous era will dawn on the cattle industry with the beginning of 1891, this is certainly the proper time for investment by those who have money and desire to reap a rich harvest during the next few years."

Highland Cattle.

Twenty years ago, Mr. Allen in his work on "American Cattle," remarked: "The vast plains west and north of the Missouri as well as the wide mountain ranges which traverse them, must mainly be occupied in breeding and grazing cattle, if anything. These lands will be admirably adapted to a class like the West Highland. * * * This is looking somewhat into the future, we admit." He adds, in conclusion: "We hope yet to see the Highland cattle introduced into the country. Their introduction could be no bar to the other valuable breeds we have now among us, as these latter must always occupy our good soils, on which, if the Highland cattle were placed, they would soon lose their distinctive qualities."

What seemed a long look into the future has now become reality. The vast plains and mountains ranges of the west and northwest are no longer given up to the herds of wild buffaloes and equally untamed red men, but are divided into farms, or grazed by millions of domestic cattle. But with the advance of civilization and the settling up of the regions beyond the Mississippi, has come a great disillusionizing. A large proportion of the land which it was rather doubtfully supposed must be "occupied in breeding and grazing cattle, if anything," has sprinkled over with the homes of the thrifty settlers, standing amid waving fields of grain. It is, therefore, "the wide mountain ranges," only, which are eminently suitable as breeding places for these hardy cattle. Bred on the heights which have hitherto been trodden only by the wild goat and bighorns, the Highland cattle may be brought down to the plains for fattening, and shipped thence to the beef markets. As a recent British writer remarks: "To propagate Highlanders, and maintaintain the characteristics of the breed, they must be allowed to live wildly and much alone on natural pastures, mountainous and cold, if possible, with no shelter, summer or winter, beyond a shed, that they may go into or leave at pleasure. They are so picturesque in appearance that noblemen and gentlemen like to see them in the parks surrounding their mansions. But that is not their natural habitation. They must not be brought down from the hills if they are to maintain the attributes of true Highlanders. Most excellent beef for the table they make, beef that, when it reaches the London market, fetches the very highest prices of the day.

The virtual extinction of the American bison has created a pressing demand for robes, in place of those formerly supplied by their skins. For this purpose no domestic cattle are equal to the Highlanders. The thick coat of hair which nature has furnished them as a protection again Highland blasts, gives their hides, if slaughtered at the proper season, a value scarcely, if at all, inferior to that of the bison. With a carcass of the finest quality of beef, and a hide fit for a fine carriage robe, a well-fattened Highland steer should possess an extra value in the market.—American Agriculturist.

American Devon Cattle Club.

We are indebted to J. Buckingham, Secretary of the American Devon Cattle Club, Zanesville, Ohio, for his courteousy in sending us a copy of the transfers of pure bred Devons for the quarter ending December 31st. The Devon is an animal suitable for California, being a good rustler, very active, short legged and a rapid feeder. We have several good Devon breeders in the State and the breed only needs to be better known to be more appreciated. Among the transfers in the Secretary's list are Petaluma Boy 4896, sold by J. W. Morse & Son to M. D. Hopkins, Petaluma and Bellota 8271, sold by the estate of S. Cook to N. Saito, Nishibara, Japan, and two sales in Utah by Sarah G. Elridge.

Cotswolds.

Pedigreed sheep are not to be bred with a view to slaughtering as such breeding stock cost too much money for that purpose; but their value lies in the improvement on the common or non-registered sheep of the farmer. To get this it is necessary to procure the breed that will shear the most wool and the most mutton; and to do this successfully it is in my opinion best for the breeder of common sheep to procure the Cotswold; as it is an established fact that no other sheep shear such heavy fleeces of fine lustrous wool as do the Cotswolds; besides no other sheep attain such heavy weights at six or twelve months old, the lamb frequently weighing 100 pounds at 90 days of age. I had one lamb dropped last April that tipped the beam at 107 at 90 days old. The rams frequently attain the enormous weight of from 250 to 350 pounds at 12 months old.

The Cotswolds have won more sweepstakes prizes, both in England and America, than all other breeds combined. As breeders they are superior to any other sheep, stamping their fine qualities on everything they come in contact with. The ewes are more prolific than any other sheep, frequently dropping 2 or 3 lambs, and giving milk enought to raise them successfully. We will however, in this respect except the horned Dorset. For the production of more wool and mutton the breeders can do no better than to use a Cotswold ram on his common or grade ewes. The Cotswolds is of all others the wool mutton sheep of the world, from the oft-repeated testimony of early days and all the way down through the last 60 years. The sheep with the most wool and the most mutton, or in other words the model sheep, is in my opinion a Cotsworld, and besides all this he is superior in hardiness and vigor of constitution to any other sheep on earth. —Leonard Bryan, in Stockman and Farmer.

Sheep in Bad Shape.

Ed Yoxall and Sam Kurtz, the Denver mutton buyers who have been out south of the Galisteo buying sheep for ten days, came in yesterday, says the New Mexican. To-day they are at Lamy loading 1,500 head of mutton for the Denver market. They expected to purchase some 8,000 or 20,000 head on this trip, but secured less than half the desired number. A pitiful story of lack of water on the sheep range is told by them. The range is fair, but there is no water, no rains or snow worth noting having fallen for eight months in that region south of the Galisteo as far down as the Gallinas mountains. Western Bernalillo, southeastern Santa Fe and southwestern San Miguel counties, also part of Valencia county, cover the region affected. Over 20,000 head of sheep are on these ranges, but most of them are without water. Mr. Yoxall saw droves of sheep that had had no water for twenty-seven days and they were little better than mere hide and bones The queer thing about it is that water may be had by sinking wells twenty feet, but none of the flock owners seem inclined to put down wells. One man at Pino's Wells has a windmill and tank and an abundance of water, and he is growing rich watering his poor Mexican neighbor's flocks. He gets three sheep in payment for every 1,000 head watered at his well and he has accumulated a drove of several thousand by this means. Wells and windmills are what the flock owners need. Perhaps this experience will prove a blessing in disguise and force them to sell some of their sheep and put the proceeds into water development.

Great Turkeys.

A flock of turkeys reared by Mrs. B. Cady, of Dutchess county, New York, averaging twenty-six pounds dressed meat per pair when sold this fall. Some brood turkeys are used until three years old, but the majority of the birds sold are young ones. As the eggs are laid they are placed in oats with their small ends down, and covered with cloth, being kept in a warm, dry place. When the turkey is ready to sit, a barrel is placed on its side in some shady nook and the nest made of dry hay, or shavings, with a generous addition of onion skins as a preventative against lice.

After the poults are hatched, they are allowed to remain in the nest as long as they will stay there. When removed, the hard substance on the end of each of their beaks is removed, and the top of the head annointed with a little oil to destroy the vermin. They are first fed custard, made from four eggs and three quarts of milk. The loose soil is swept away, and they are fed upon the ground, never from a board. If the wings droop their ends are clipped. This is believe to allow bone and muscle to develop faster. While growing they are given plenty of burned bone, pulverized, and a little red pepper mixed in the food. As they increase in age they are fed with pot cheese, Irish oatmeal soaked over night, dry bread soaked in milk, and wheat middlings scalded, and still later on, treated to cracked corn.—[F. D. Ladd in Home and Farm.]

Brown Leghorns in the South.

I have been breeding brown Leghorns for over six years, and though I also breed several other varieties, had I to give up all but one my choice would be the brown Leghorn. I consider them particularly adapted to the South. First, health is to be considered. The Leghorn seems to stand our long heated term better than most other breeds, and during our damp and rainy season the larger breeds are more subject to the roup and other diseases caused by dampness. I have never had a Leghorn with the roup, nor have I ever seen one with it. Second, the color of the plumage suffers very much from our hot suns. White fades out, and black becomes rusty to a certain extent, while the brown Leghorn retains its color all the way through. Third, of course it is known the whole world over that they are not excelled as layers. It is also said that in cold climates the Asiatics are the best winter layers, but in our coldest weather even the Leghorn will shell out the eggs just the same as her larger cousins.—Ex.

Butter.

The old fashioned average, fifteen or twenty years ago, of the number of pounds of milk required to make a pound of butter was 25. This was the assumed average, and the records of the first butter factories that practiced deep, cold setting showed it to be nearly correct. That average has been considerably reduced within the last ten or fifteen years. Of 57 herds—whose average of milk for a pound of butter, as given by their owners who had butter on exhibition at the late meeting of the Vermont Dairy Association—the general average was 19 2 pounds of milk for a pound of butter. The lowest average for the herd was 14.1-2 pounds, and the highest 23.

THE GUN.

Golcher Trophy.

The cut shows to advantage the exceedingly rich and tasteful trophy presented for competion among the United States Cartridge Company's teams of shooters. The design originated with Messrs. W. J. and H. C. Golcher and is unique. A heavy tankard of beaten silver, having for a lid a blue rock target worked out in oxidized silver and gold, surmounted by a miniature blue rock target forms the design, and is most appropriate. On one side a perfect pair of hammerless guns and on the other a shield properly engraved, relieve the weighty app arance of the tankard and lend grace and elegance to what will certainly be one of the most valued of the many souvenirs of Colonel Dimmick's great tour.

San Diego Chat.

Editor Breeder and Sportsman:—The heavy rains up North seem to have delayed the Northern flight of ducks and geese, so that we have had very little water fowl shooting so far this season; but I notice the past week that our markets are fairly well stocked with both ducks and geese, and the local sportsmen report very good success near our Bay region. A number of the boys are planning hunting excursions inland, and we may hear of some good bags of game in the near future. Thousands of geese are seen every day winging their way northward, and as a great many stop a day or so with us to feed, we expect some good sport yet this spring.

Henry Seibold, of this city, keeps our markets fairly supplied with black brant (*Bernicla Nigricans*), and now I would like to inquire of your numerous readers whether this bird is found anywhere on the Pacific Coast north of San Diego Bay. It is one of the shyest waterfowls in the world, and to successfully hunt this bird one must be well supplied with sneak boat, battery, decoys, and above all, a full choked, hard shooting gun. They are on San Diego Bay now by the thousands, but excepting those killed by Seibold, it is safe to say that there are not more than a dozen killed weekly. One curious feature about black brant is that they are never found inland and never on fresh water. They are esteemed very highly here for delicacy of flavor, and find a ready sale.

Judge J. J. Henderson of this city, returned from a short visit to Eugene City, Oregon, last week bringing with him a pair of those beautiful birds the mongolian pheasant, which he has presented to E. S. Babcock Esq. of Coronado Beach, who proposes to introduce them on North Island, (part of Coronado Beach,) and preserve them for a year or so. The birds were introduced into Oregon less than eight years ago, and now number many thousands, so we may look for this country to be well supplied in the next ten years, if they are protected. Judge Henderson claims they are very gamey, and afford excellent sport in the fields, and as the Judge was a resident of China for some eight years and hunted them continually while there, he ought to know. There has been a great deal of controversy about this bird on this coast, regarding their introduction here, and from all reports from there, our Oregon friends seem to feel that this pheasant is about as undesirable a guest as the Chinaman is to our average Californian.

I was exceedingly sorry to hear of friend Louds' bad luck, in losing "Countess Linette," sister to "Lady Elaine" who died a week or so ago. Captain Loud is an ardent dog lover, as every thoroughbred sportsman is, and he always has a kennel of the best, and it is a source of regret that he should be so unfortunate in losing as fine a pair of dogs in one season as "Lady Elaine" and Countess Linette."

It will certainly be a long time before he can fill their places.

The poison fiend has been at work here, and a number of fine dogs have been poisoned in consequence, but it is a slight source of gratification that Mr. C. Hinman, whose fine pointer dog "Sport" was poisoned last week, apprehended the miscreant who did it, and made him pay him the sum of $50 for the pleasure of throwing the dog a bit of "doctored" meat. It is bad enough for a man to lose a highly-prized dog by natural causes, but when he finds his valuable and loved pointer, or setter, who has been his companion on so many an outing, dying in all the agony that only poison can inflict, it gets right to the bottom of his heart. I am glad that the legislature of our State passed a law making dogs personal property, a year or so ago, as it will prove some slight protection to sportsmen who keep them.

I understand M. Chick of this place has been invited to make one of a team of ten to meet the Eastern team in a trophy shoot. No worthier man than Mr. Chick can be selected in California for the honor of representing the shooters of this state and he ought to feel proud of the honor conferred on him.

Let us hope that "our boys" will meet our Eastern friends at the trap, and that the Selby trophy will remain right where it will be manufactured, in California. Ad. B. P.

San Diego, Cal., Feb. 10th 1890.

[The San Francisco markets are supplied with Bernicla Nigircans from Humboldt Bay and Sir Francis Drake's Bay, but not abundantly.—Ed.]

Miss Lillian F. Smith writes:—I am making a very successful tour of California. On the 14th of Feb., I gave an exhibition at this place Oroville in the present of a large and enthusiastic audience and I succeeded in breaking all my previous rifle records, I broke fifty balls in forty-five seconds.

Trap at Lathrop.

Some very lively races were shot at Lathrop on February 12th under the management of Messrs. Scarlett and Howland. Mr. Austin B. Sperry won the first match with a clean score, then went to pieces in the most approved style. Messrs. C. J. Haas and C. A. Merrill shot steadily as usual, and were always in the money. Dr. S. N. Cross killed nine out of ten three times, but fell down in the other races.

Messrs. Scarlett and Howland were attentive and effective in conducting the shoot, and we are indebted to Mr. Scarlett for the scores.

The first match was at 15 single live birds, Hurlingham style. Entrance $7.50, with four prizes of 40, 30, 20 and 10 per cent. of the entrance money. The score:

Name	Score	Total
Scarlett, F.	2 1 1 1 1 1 0 1 1 1 2 1 1 1 1	14
Sperry	1 1 1 1 1 1 2 1 1 2 1 2 2 1 1	15
Cross	0 2 1 0 1 0 w	3
Haas	1 1 1 1 1 2 1 1 2 2 2 1 0 0 1	13
Merrill	0 1 1 1 1 2 21 1 1 1 1 1 2 1	14

The second match was at ten single live birds, 21 yards rise, use of one barrel only; entrance 5, with four prizes. The score:

Name	Score	Total
Haas	1 1 1 1 1 1 1 1 1 1	10
Cross	1 1 1 1 1 1 1 1 0 1	9
Scarlett, F.	1 1 1 1 1 0 1 1 1 1	9
Merrill	1 1 1 1 1 0 0 1 1 1	8
Sperry	1 0 0 1 1 0 w	3
Briggs	1 0 1 1 1 1 0 1 0 w	6
Sutherland	1 1 0 1 1 0 1 1 1 0	7
Knight	1 1 1 0 1 1 0 1 0 0	6

The third match was at ten single live birds, Hurlingham style; entrance $5, with four prizes.

SCORE.

Name	Score	Total
Haas	0 1 1 1 1 1 2 1 1 1	9
Burnett	0 1 0 1 0 w	2
Cross	0 1 1 0 1 0 w	3
Knight	0 1 0 w	1
Sperry	1 1 0 1 0 2 0 w	4
Melton	1 0 0 1 0 w	2
Lee	1 0 1 0 1 1 1 1 2 1	8
Hutchinsom	0 1 2 2 1 1 0 0 w	5
Briggs	1 0 2 2 2 0 2 1 0 w	6
Merrill	0 1 0 1 1 1 1 2 1 1	8
Judy	2 0 2 1 1 1 2 2 1 2	9
Scarlett, W.	2 2 0 1 2 1 2 2 0 1	8
Scarlett, F.	1 2 2 1 2 2 2 2 1 1	10

The next shoot was a supper match between Stockton and Lathrop teams, the losers to pay for a spread for the crowd. The Lathrop boys lost and royally feasted their friends at the Shannon House. The match was at ten single live birds, Hurlingham Rules, $5 entrance, with three prizes of 50, 30 and 20 per cent. The scores were as follows:—

STOCKTON.

Name	Score	Total
Merrill	1 2 1 1 1 1 1 1 2 1	10
Cross	2 1 1 0 2 1 1 1 1 1	9
Sperry	1 1 0 0 1 2 1 1 2 1	8
Haas	1 0 1 1 1 1 1 1 1 1	9
Total		36

LATHROP.

Name	Score	Total
Scarlett, F.	1 2 1 2 1 1 2 1 1 1	10
Sutherland	1 2 2 2 1 1 1 2 0 1	9
Scarlett, W.	0 1 2 1 1 1 1 1 0 1	8
Knight	0 0 0 1 1 0 1 0 0 0	3
Total		30

The day's sport closed with a match at clay pigeons, fifteen singles and five pairs of doubles. The entrance fee was $2 50, with four prizes of 40, 30, 20 and 10 per cent. of the money. The score was as follows:

Name	Singles	Doubles	Total
Scarlett, F.	0 1 1 0 1 1 1 1 1 1 0 1 0 0 1	11 00 01 10 10	15
Haas	0 1 0 1 1 0 1 0 1 w		
Burnett	1 1 1 0 1 0 0 1 1 0 0 1 0 0 1	10 01 10 10 11	14
Melton	0 1 1 1 1 0 1 0 0 1 0 1 0 0 0	00 01 11 10 11	13
Hutchinson	1 1 1 1 1 1 0 1 1 0 1 0 0 1 1	00 11 10 10 11	17
Judy	1 1 1 1 1 1 1 1 1 1 1 0 1 1 1	11 11 11 11 00	27
Allen	1 1 0 1 0 1 0 0 0 0 0 1 0 0 1	10 11 01 01 11	13
Sperry	1 1 0 1 1 1 0 0 1 1 0 1 1 1 0	01 10 11 01 10	16
Knight	1 1 1 1 1 0 1 1 1 1 1 1 0 0 1	11 00 10 10 r0	16
Cross	0 0 1 1 0 1 0 0 0 w	00 11 00 00 10	
Lane	1 0 0 1 1 1 1 1 1 1 0 0 0 0 1	10 10 10 00 00	12
Briggs	1 0 1 0 1 1 0 w	10 11 00 00 10	

From Santa Barbara.

Santa Barbara, Feb. 16th.

Editor Breeder and Sportsman. It is a proverbially winter day at this writing, the rain coming down in good old-fashioned style, with the wind in the direct rainy quarter. I find it pretty hard to kill time, being too wet to go anywhere, outside, and almost every one either quietly resting in his room, or loafing around the reading room.

I am wondering why I have not had a line from any one since I left, especially from you, on matters connected with the proposed pigeon contest, between the Eastern and California team, nor have I been able to get hold of a San Francisco paper, thus far, which contains any reference to it. I wrote to Mr. Allen a few days since, on the subject, and fully expect an answer by to-morrow or Tuesday next. I am afraid that at this writing Mr. Editor, I cannot see my way clearly enough ahead to be able to state *with certainty*, what day I can get away from this place, and in this uncertainty, you had better, if you can do so; select some one in my place, on the team? It was my intention to leave Santa Barbara on the 20th instant, so as to give me one good night's rest at my home before the 22nd, as I am but a miserable sleeper on the cars; but I am compelled to remain one day longer, and start from here on the 21st, which would find me utterly unfit to take part *in good form*, in so important a match as that between the United States team and ourselves. This is a matter of great regret to me, but as I am entirely at the disposition of Mrs. Orr, and my children on this trip, I cannot now see how I can avoid disappointing you, if, indeed it shall prove any disappointment to you or any other interested party in the coming contest, therefore, under all circumstances, you had better elect some one in my stead, but if I should be able to be on hand, *on time*, I shall be pleased to bear my part, if called upon.

Up to yesterday the weather has been simply charming; no one could desire more, with the bright sunny days and cool tempered nights, and a delicious, balmy air pervading everything, a welcome exchange to us of the northern portion of the State, after the trying ordeal of the past, or rather passing winter.

I wish that my family and self could remain here for another month, we are so pleased with the climate and surroundings, and the accommodations at this hotel are as good as any I have experienced anywhere, and I do not except our best San Francisco hostelries. Then one meets such a lot of nice people, the majority being cultured, well bred Eastern residents, with a few Europeans, and I find considerable sporting taste developed among the young men visitors. A jockey club has been formed, several races having taken place, and another is in prospective for the 22nd inst., Washington's Birthday. Also a good deal of sporting element is met with, and there are several very prominent New Yorkers here, whose names are well known in sporting circles at the East and whom I have had the pleasure of being introduced to—names you would easily recognize did I mention them, but delicacy forbids me, in a letter. There is some talk of getting up a big pigeon contest in the near future, and I fancy that I shall carry up to San Francisco big orders to Purveyor Murphy for pigeons and cartridges from the gun stores, etc., etc.

As to field shooting in the vicinity it is but poor, and a very rough, hilly country, with a scarcity of birds and all with the unfortunate tendency to take to the trees when flushed. The sport is therefore precarious and disappointing.

Drop me a line or two and give me some of the on dits of the times, but do not write later than the 19th. The Eastern team must be now in this vicinity to-day en route for the North. J. K. Orr.

The visiting teams of shooters have been making good scores as will be seen by inspection of the appended table: The party consists of H. McMurchy, captain; W. H. Wolstencroft, W. E. Perry, H. B. Whitney and W. S. Perry composing the Eastern team; C. W. Budd, captain; J. R. Stice, R. O Heikes, C. E. Cahoon and R. A. Ruble composing the Western team; Col. C. W. Dimick, manager; W. Fred Quinby, substitute with the Eastern team; S. A. Tucker, substitute with the Western team, and E. Hough, representing Forest and Stream. All of the matches were at thirty singles and five pairs of Blue Rock targets, American Association Rules.

All along the route they have been presented with handsome trophies, among which were $25 cash by Mr. Dimick at Dayton, won by the Westerns; at Cincinnati five handsome silver cups by the Laflin and Rand Powder Company and Bandle Arms Company, won by the Easterns; at St Louis five elegant shaving cups by the Meacham Arms Company, won by the Western boys; at Memphis five silver match boxes by Mr. Dimick, won by the representative of the frigid East. At Houston, Mr. Dimick seeing that the Western boys felt so bad over the loss of the match boxes at Memphis, put up five more of a similar kind, and the cowboys as they are called in their special Pullman car, the Iolanthe, braced up and gathered them in, so that match boxes at least are easy. In Texas the party was presented with a genuine Texas wildcat, the tamest thing in the car, that is if one should believe half the stories told on the party by the members of the opposing teams.

The scores to date have been:—

DAYTON.	Western team	180
	Eastern team	166
CINCINNATI.	Eastern team	186
	Western team	176
LOUISVILLE.	Western team	176
	Eastern team	171
ST. LOUIS.	Western team	182
	Eastern team	178
MEMPHIS.	Eastern team	168
	Western team	167
NEW ORLEANS.	Western team	178
	Eastern team	177
HOUSTON.	Western team	175
	Eastern team	172
DALLAS.	Eastern team	176
	Western team	174
AUSTIN.	Eastern team	167
	Western team	167
SAN ANTONIO.	Eastern team	167
	Western team	170
EL PASO.	Eastern team	164
	Western team	162
LOS ANGELES.	Eastern team	178
	Western team	165

Of the individual scores Mr. Wolstencroft stands credited with a clean 40 on two occasions, while Stice, Budd, Ruble, McMurchy and Whitney have each scores of 39. The trophy, which is to be presented by the United States Cartridge Company to the winning team when the contest is over, is an elegant silver plate 19x20 inches, on which is engraved a representation of the palace car Iolanthe and the two teams standing by it, with appropriate inscriptions and ornamentations.

A happy-go-lucky lot of pilgrims are those inhabiting the Pullman car Iolanthe, under guidance of Colonel C. W. Dimmick, Manager of the United States Cartridge Company. The car was especially fitted up for the use of the sportsmen and they use the whole of it, including the roof and the cellar. It was Colonel Dimmick's original idea to open each day's duties with appropriate oblations by that saintly man Parson W. F. Quimby, but the jarring of continuous travel has entirely obscured the Parson's recollection of the beautiful language acquired in his earlier days, along about 1836, and instead of invocations to the several deities supposed to succor trap shots, the Parson pours out strange oaths, the like of which are only heard in Flanders.

Parson Quimby is on the probationer's list for the trip. Of the other sojourners, not one is named Truth. S. A. Tucker and Harvey McMurchy are full of guile as the sparks fly upward. J. R. Stice and C. W. Budd look as fierce as the nasty clawing wild-cat carried along as a mascot, but in point of fact neither has a single redeeming vice. Wolstencroft, Whitney and Heikes are too young to be trusted alone in a strange city with J. A. Ruble. Ruble may mean well, but it is impossible to understand him. The Perrys are nice men, even if they are systematically maligned by all the others of the party. The whole trip, so far, has been one unending lark, and for enjoyment leaves nothing to guess. Colonel Dimmick, in addition to being a keen man of business, is one of the heartiest, most engaging of cosmopolitans, and makes sunshine wherever he camps. All of the team have our sincerest sympathy.

Colonel Dimmick's Menagerie.

The collection of solitaires travelling in the interest of the United States Cartridge Company showed a degree of pluck on Wednesday last that would do credit to a nerveless man. The day opened rainy and the water came down in increasing volumes up to 1 o'clock, the hour at which the teams were called to the score.

Colonel Dimmick was urged to postpone the shoot, but remarked in his peculiar, snappy way, "We have not missed a date and cannot begin to do so now."

Messrs. W. J. Golcher and Sheldon I. Kellogg acted as judges, and Colonel Dimmick as referee in the only match shot, that at Blue Rock targets, the second match listed having to be deferred because of lack of daylight in which to shoot. The teams were:

West—Captain, C W Budd, Des Moines, Ia.; R O Heikes, Dayton, O.; J. R. Stice, Omaha, Neb; C. E. Cahoon, Freeport, Ill.; J. A. Ruble, Beloit, Wis.

East—Captain, H. McMurchy, Syracuse, N. Y.; W. H. Walstencroft, Philadelphia, Pa.; W. E. Perry, Boston, Mass., H. B. Whitney, Phelps, N. Y.; W. S. Perry, Worcester, Mass.

The styles of the visiting experts at the traps were as many as there are men, but every one proved himself a master of the shot gun. The match was won by the Eastern team. When all were so masterly close criticism by anyone but one equally versed in the art of wing shooting is valueless. The attendance was limited, and at the end of the race Colonel Dimmick presented tickets for the great match of to-day to each spectator. The event of the day was Mr. H. B. Whitney's brilliantly made clean score. Walstencroft gave a fine exhibition of brilliant shooting, and won repeated applause. Heikes, of the Westerners and W. S. Perry, of the Easterners, were both sorely under the weather, Heikes especially falling considerably below his average. Ruble had a very keen eye during the early part of the match, and on the single birds had a clean score, but on the doubles he seemed to have lost his nerve completely, killing but two of the ten birds. Captains McMurchy and Budd held their own fairly well, but hardly sustained their former averages. Stice was simply himself—cool, steady and reliable. On the single shoot he missed the second bird, but did not let another one escape him. The Easterners had the best of the single match, and also of the doubles, notwithstanding the Westerners spurted considerably toward the end.

The prizes won by the Eastern team in yesterday's match consist of a handsome silver trophy presented by Clabrough, Golcher & Co., and gold chain keyrings presented by the Selby Smelting and Lead Company. The following is the score:

EASTERN TEAM.

		Total
H. McMurchy, captain—		
Singles	111111111111111111111111011011—28	36
Doubles	11 11 11 10 10— 8	
W. H. Walstencroft—		
Singles	111111111111111111110111011111—18	35
Doubles	10 11 10 11 11— 7	
W. E. Perry—		
Singles	111111111111101111111011111111—28	36
Doubles	10 11 10 11 11— 8	
W. S. Perry—		
Singles	111001011110100000111011101101—18	24
Doubles	10 10 10 11 10— 6	
H. B. Whitney—		
Singles	111111111111111111111111111111—30	40
Doubles	11 11 11 11 11—10	

Team totals—Singles, 132; doubles, 39; grand total, 172.

WESTERN TEAM.

		Total
C. W. Budd, captain—		
Singles	111111111111111111110111011101 1—27	32
Doubles	10 10 11 10 10— 6	
J. A. Ruble—		
Singles	111111111111111111111111111111—30	32
Doubles	00 10 01 00 11— 2	
R. O Heikes—		
Singles	101101011101111011110111101001—21	30
Doubles	10 10 11 11 11— 8	
C. A. Cahoon—		
Singles	010101011110011111001111011111—21	26
Doubles	11 10 10 00 10— 5	
J. R. Stice—		
Singles	101111111111111111111111111111—29	37
Doubles	11 11 10 10 11— 8	

Team totals—Singles, 1[illegible]8; doubles, 29; grand total, 167.

On Wednesday evening the visiting team of experts were entertained by local sportsmen, at the Press Club. The usual supper, and accompaniments were destroyed, and then in response to urgent entreaties, Colonel Dimmick and his men all told their little stories in the peculiar dialect characteristic of aborigines of the wilderness east of the Rocky Mountains. Pleasant speeches of welcome and congratulation were made by Colonel S. I. Kellogg, W. J. Golcher, E. T. Allen, Robert Liddle Doctor C. W. Aby, Clarence A. Haight, H. T. Payne, W. S. Kittle and others. Everybody was eloquent, except Reverend W. F. Quimby, of Newark, N. Jersey, chaplain-in-ordinary to Colonel Dimmick. After supper Captain Jules Callundan and his brother, Mr. F. H. Callundan escorted the party through Chinatown visiting all the slummy places usually shown, and some that do not appear in the guide books.

In the match shot at Stockton on Monday last by the U. S. Cartridge Company aggregation the Eastern team won by a score of 177 to 161.

The supervisors of Kern County offer $1.50 for every coyote scalp, and $5.00 for the scalp of each California lion.

Ducks are thick in the tules at present but the trouble with hunters is, the water is so high that it is almost impossible to get into their flights. A party consisting of Stony Campbell, Charlie Laugenour, M. Diggs and T. Plummer, went one mile up the river from Knights Landing, on Saturday last and report many ducks about, but they only succeeded in bagging twenty five.

This afternoon at Height-street base ball park, a match will be shot at live birds between ten Californians and ten of the United States Cartridge Company's peripatetic sharpshooters. The California team will be J. K. Orr, Captain, and nine men from the following list: Jos. Delmas, O. J. Hass, C. A. Merrill, H. A. Bassford, Sheldon I. Kellogg, H. C. Golcher, Martinez Chick, Dr. S. E. Knowles, C. B. Smith, F. B. Norton and Ed Fay. The 10 from Colonel Dimmick's rodeo have not been announced, but it is certain that they will be as good as any to be found outside of California. The match begins at 1 o'clock P. M., and is at 15 live birds per man; Revised Rules of the American Shooting Association. The birds are good, the grounds easily reached by cable car, the seating comfortable, and the prospect of an interesting test of skill most flattering. Every shooter in or near San Francisco should be on hand. The trophy to be shot for is pictured elsewhere in the paper.

Cut of Allen Trophy.

The above is an illustration of a Sterling Silver Trophy which is offered by Mr. E. T. Allen, to the winning team in the live bird match between the United States Cartridge's Co.'s team and the California team, to be shot for on February 22nd, 1890. The design is original with Mr. Allen. It is of solid sterling silver, seventeen inches high, and seven inches in diameter at the base. Against the sides of the Trophy there rest three silver guns, eight inches in length. They are the exact models of the Parker hammerless. The drawing was made by Mr. P. B. Beakert, and is in mathematical proportions to one of the $200 grade Parker's of Mr. Allen's stock. The working models for the Silversmith were made by the well known gunsmith, Mr. David Thom.

Messrs. Vanderslice & Co., who are the manufacturers of this Trophy, cast the butt, frame and forend of the guns in solid silver; the barrels are made of silver tubes which were given the proper shape and welded together; then the upper and under ribs were soldered to the barrels, which are joined to the stock.

The urn is surmounted by the characteristic emblem of California, a grizzly bear, modeled after Nahl's great painting; the action of the bear is perfect.

Messrs. Vanderslice & Co. informs us that one hundred ounces of pure silver were used in the manufacture of this trophy, and both design and workmanship reflect credit upon local skill. Mr. Allen has interested himself in behalf of the visiting teams in most effective fashion, and is well entitled to the consideration shown him by Colonel Dimmick and his experts.

THE KENNEL.

Dog owners are requested to send for publication the earliest possible notices of whelps, sales, names claimed, presentations and deaths, in their kennels, in all instances writing plainly names of sire and dam and of grandparents, colors, dates and breed.

Whelps.

Mr. E. Martin's fox terrier Folly, whelped one dog and two bitches to C. A. Sumner's Blemton Vesuvian (14290) by Champion Lucifer, on Feb. 16, '90.

New Cockers.

I wish to report to your valuable paper the purchase of three fine cocker spaniels for my Kennel, from the celebrated Woodstock Cocker Spaniels Kennels, Woodstock Canada. One solid black dog, black Bronta by Champion Brant, dam McDougal's Moller. He has won three first prizes on the bench. One solid dark, orange bitch, a prize winner also, by Robin A K. C. S. B. (8535) dam Devon Beauty. One solid dark, liver bitch by Bob dam Pearl. Also 4 fine puppies by Blk. Bonita, dam Woodstock Maids, three fine dogs, one black bitch to sell. A. C. Davenport.

Stockton, Feb. 18, 1890.

How to Report.

Editor Breeder and Sportsman:—The Breeder and Sportsman report of the trials was at last read. It was good but could have been better. When a beautiful point is made, why does not the reporter dwell on it? When a dog wags his tail and works in a pleasing, merry fashion, why does he not tell about it? When a dog works with his tail about half bent like a hoop and never is known to wag it, and never had any tail action, he should tell about it. When a dog makes a long, beautiful point, tell about it. It is all these little things put together that make a report of this kind pleasing to read. The heats run in the last trials were entirely too short. Thirty minutes does not amount to anything. A good high-strung dog will not more than get down to his work in that time. Thirty minutes is no trial anyhow if the dogs are any good. It is like running a four mile horse a quarter of a mile. I would like to see a good trial once that was a trial, a test: say six hour heats. That would amount to something. It would test something.

Well' won't the rain ever stop? It rains all day and snows all night; there was more snow on the hills the last week than ever before. I am afraid I can not go quail hunting but once more this season, but I will go once if I have to go in the snow. I am going to Capay Valley next Monday and I wager Hughes and I will kill them, as he knows where they live, and when that old gun butt of his goes to his shoulder something goes "ker flop."

J. M. Bassford, Jr.

Vacaville, Feb. 19th, 1890.

Count Dick Again.

Editor Breeder and Sportsman:—In publishing the pedigree of Mr. A. B. Sperry's pointer Count Dick in your paper of February 15th, you have made an error. At the request of Mr. Sperry (when we were at the last field trials), I obtained Count Dick's pedigree of Mr. Jno. C. Lombard, the gentleman who bred him.

Count Dick is by S. C. Hare's James K. (Bow Jr.—Mollie Ashe), out of Donna, imported by John C. Lombard in 1888.

Donna is by Wm. Arkwright's Eldon Don (17635 E. K. C. S. B.), out of his Lady Olive (13433 E. K. C. S. B.), own sister to Champion Graphic by Bonus Sancho (10000 E. K. C. S. B.)—Furedon Juno, own sister to Champion Ponto, and herself a great winner. Mr. Arkwright writes that Eldon Don is first rate in the field, and has won a prize each time shown.

Count Dick's litter sister won first in the puppy class at the last Bench Show in San Francisco, May, 1889, shown by Wm. Lombard, of Wheatland, Yuba County.

Ike N. Aldrich.

[A worse mess than the pedigree of Count Dick as it appeared in this paper last week, we have rarely seen. The pedigree as given by Mr. Aldrich is right, and it was our intention to publish a correction, a pleasure which is precluded by Mr. Aldrich's kindness. Pointer fanciers should not lose sight of Dick when planning breeding schemes.—Ken. Ed.]

The Occidental Coursing Club has postponed its meeting advertised for to day until March 8th. The draw will be made on the evening of March 5th at No. 21 Kearney Street, Mr. William Schreibers.

Mr. E. K. Benchley, of Los Angeles, owner of Kan Koo, the winning pointer at the Los Angeles dog show, has purchased from R. T. Vandevort a pointer bitch, litter sister to Baron von Schroeder's Point, and has bred her to Kan Koo. Kan Koo is by Rush T.—Patti Croxteth T., and as the bitch is by Vandevort's Don—Drab, the cross should produce some field cracks.

We shall feel obliged if Dr. Edmonds and Mr. Fout will send us the pedigrees of their dogs.

Southern California is fast forging to the front in sporting dogs as it has in other lines. A grandly-bred pointer bitch has recently been brought to Dr. M. E. Taber at San Bernardino. The bitch is by Mainspring out of Maud by Croxteth—Trinket, a hard combination to beat. An old pointer bitch by Sensation is owned in the same town by Dr. Edmonds. Mr. A. W. Bruner at Colton owns a fine rangy, black pointer by Maximus—Lady Pepe, bred by John Drees in Arkansas. The dog is said by Mr. H. T. Payne and other good judges to be a clinker. Mr. Blake, also of San Bernardino, has recently imported from the kennels of J. B. Dilley in Wisconsin, a fine young pointer by Ranger Croxteth. Mr. C. E. Fout at Los Angeles, has bought a good young pointer from Mr. George W. Bassford.

A hundred keen coursers gathered at Ocean View Park on Sunday last, the attraction being a match for eight dogs. The ground was soft and the hares not particularly quick, because of the continued wet werther. The day was raw and gusty and showers fell at short intervals. T. J. Cronin owns the winner old Jack Dempsey a dog that has killed many a hare, yet runs true as ever.

Messrs. Eagan, Beehan and Tiernan were the judges, and gave satisfaction, except in the course between Sport and Ballyvourney, the latter dog as seen from the stand, doing by far the greatest amount of work, but the judges gave the course to Sport, which called forth considerable unfavorable comment from the owner of Bally. The following is the result of the running:

T. J. Cronin's Jack Dempsey beat J. Shea's McGinty; P. Canavan's Sport beat P. Brophy's Ballyvourney; P. Carty's Whip beat P. Canavan's Chronicle, and N. Nolan's Sam Nash beat B. Baxter's Daisy.

First Ties—Jack Dempsey beat Spot, Sam Nash beat Whip.

Final—Jack Dempsey beat Sam Nash and won the stakes, $20; Sam Nash second, $12.

BILLIARDS.

The coming Schaffer-McCleery contest naturally overshadows all other billiard news.

The match is made for $2,000 a side. The Examiner is the stakeholder, and it will come off about April 1st. Game 3,000 points up, to be played in three nights, 1,000 points each evening.

The original agreement was game to be for $2,500 a side. We called on Prof. McCleery for an explanation. Here it is: "The game or games said Mc, grew out of a remark Schaffer made that he could discount me at billiards, any game on the table." In answer, I said I will make the game and in addition will play Schaffer a match at pin pool for the world's championship and $2,500 a side.

Mr. Roche on Schaffer's part called on me about a week ago to make both games—an engagement was made for the next evening to settle the details.

I found that two of my friends were out of the city and I could not make the games; then Mr. Roche put up a forfeit giving me a week to cover it, (which I have done) to secure the billiard match—but for $2,000 a side, at the same time I have the privilege of putting up the other $500, and will do so before the game comes off. On account of not having the coin I cannot make the pool match at present." Now you have it straight.

Mc has a table in the ladies billiard-room of the Baldwin hotel, and will begin practice at once. As he is the manager, he plays almost every afternoon or evening in the public room; quite a treat for admirers of the game.

Jim Orndorff has not been well of late, but easily knocks off fifty or more as a light exercise.

A spirited contest, 100 points up for $20, took place at the Baldwin Tuesday afternoon between two of our well-known amateurs.

"How times change," remarked a gentleman as a party from the opera strolled into the Baldwin billiard room and were courteously shown through by an attendant. On enquiring, we found that hardly a day or evening passed without from one to a dozen parties paying the room a visit. "It gives tone to the house," says Manager McCleery, "and I am sure the patrons like it."

Saylor could make a match and get good odds from McCleery. Brace up, Ben.

ATHLETICS.

Athletic Sports and Other Pastimes.

EDITED BY ARPHIPPUS.

SUMMARY.

The weather has once more turned traitor and the outdoor athletes are worse off than ever. The members of the Alpine Club were compelled to postpone their initial field games on account of the muddy condition of the track at Harbor View. The regular monthly exhibition of the Occidental Club was held on Monday evening last, and on the following evening the California Club gave one of the best entertainments witnessed in its rooms for a long time. In our columns below will be found a report of the Olympic Clubs' "Ladies Night."

RUNNERS, WALKERS, JUMPERS, ETC.

The rain, the rain, the awful rain, has knocked the athletes out again.

The weather is simply terrible and the runners and walkers are about as badly off as they were a month ago. At the present time it is hard to guess how long the bad weather is going to remain with us. The storm is liable to continue for weeks yet.

Buchanan, the Australian athlete is a man of mighty muscle and the Olympic Club will do well in securing him as a member. Judging from the feats which he performed on "Ladies Night" he should be well able to land the shot-putting and hammer-throwing events on May 30.

J. J. McKinnon of the Alpine Club is in good trim and will make an excellent record in the hammer event at his clubs games.

A. H. Lean will shortly become a member of the Olympic Club. He will compete in the opening games on May 30.

The Alpine Amateur Athletic Club will hold its first indoor exhibition at the club rooms, 706 Powell street, next week.

Several of the Olympic Club runners took a spin on their new track on Sunday last. Cooley ran one and a half miles in 8:04.

What has become of Haley, the crack long distance runner?

A good many of the runners who are to compete in the five mile run of the Olympic Club on the 26th inst., would much prefer to have the race come off at the new grounds instead of at the club rooms. It is thought that some of the best runners will petition the Board of Directors to make the change. Cooley and Espinoza are both in fine condition, and if they had a chance to run on the new track both of them would certainly improve the present record

McDonald is looked upon as the winner of the "Novice" one hundred yards run on Decoration Day.

Mr. Victor E. Schifferstein was seen at San Jose one day last week, and in an interview stated positively that he has retired from the cinder path.

Owing to the sudden change in the weather, the games of the Alpine Amateur Athletic Club were not held on Sunday last. The rain which fell for two days previous had left the track in such a slippery condition that it was considered dangerous for the runners and walkers to attempt to do their best. In order not to disappoint the couple of hundred spectators present, about a dozen of the athletes volunteered to give exhibitions, and between the showers which fell all the afternoon the following events were given:

100-yards run—John D. Garrison, R J. Luttringer, E. P. Moody.

880 yards run—Charles Little, R. J. Luttringer, M. C. Giry, I. R. Collins, E. P. Moody, John D. Garrison.

Running High Jump—P. N. Gafney, Charles Vultee.

Flinging 56lb. weight—J. R. Collins, P. N. Gafney, J. J. McKinnon, C. Vultee, J. W. Creugh.

Half mile walk—P. N. Gafney, Charles Vultee.

Amongst the audience were many ladies who enjoyed the sport immensely. The games will come off, weather permitting, on Sunday, March 2nd.

The first cross-country run of the Alpine Club has been postponed to Sunday, March 16th.

C. A. Eldridge and W. L. Jeffery of the Alpine Club have been matched to run a one hundred yards race on March 2nd.

I. McLaughlin gave an exhibition two mile run at Harbor View on Sunday, covering the distance in 13 minutes and 10 seconds, which, considering the muddy state of the track, was remarkably good time.

The Acme Club of Oakland has a membership of over 250

THE WHEELMEN.

The Garden City Wheelmen of San Jose, Cal., have applied for admission into the P. C. A. A. A.

The complimentary party given by the Bay City Wheelmen at Union Square Hall on Monday evening last was a great success. Only 150 tickets were issued which fact made the ball a very select one. Dancing was enjoyed from 9 P. M. to 1 A. M. A fine orchestra performed during the evening.

Arthur Wright, Vice Consul of California and a member of the Oakleaf Wheelmen was in town last Saturday to attend the Patti Matinee. He reported everything lovely and expressed a hope that the weather would turn out fine on Washingtons Birthday.

Captain Richardson of the Bay City Wheelmen had called a club run far Saturday and Sunday February 22 and 23 to Healdsburg, through Sonoma Co., but on account of the rain the run has been indefinitely postponed.

Reports from the interior say that the present storm has played sad havoc with the roads.

JOTTINGS FROM ALL OVER.

At the games of the Forty-seventh Regiment held recently in New York City, W. D. Day, of the New Jersey A. C., broke the three mile indoor running record, covering the distance in 15min 12sec. On the same evening C. L. Nicoll, of the Manhattan A. C., broke the indoor board-floor record for the one mile walk. His time was 6min 5s against E. D. Lange's record of 6m 55s.

The indoor joint meeting of the Nautilus Boat Club and Company H, Thirteenth Regiment, N G S N Y, took place at the Armory in Hanson Place, Brooklyn, N. Y., on Wednesday evening, Feb. 5th. The assemblage was large enough to occupy all the seats in the hall, and the competition awakened at times considerable enthusiasm. Especially was this the case in the final heat of the fifty yards run, which resulted in a dead heat for first place, and when the dead heaters ran it off the result was the same. They tried it again, when M. Remington, of the Nautilus B C, won by six inches only. Return:

Fifty yards run—Final heat: M Remington, Nautilus Boat Club, 4ft start, first, after twice running off a heat with T I Lee, New York Athletic Club, scratch, the time of the first heat being 5 4-5s; A H Hutchings, Staten Island Athletic Club, 5ft, third.

Quarter mile run—Final heat: C R Thomas, Orange Athletic Club, 2yds start, first, in 55 1-5s; C M Carbonell, New Jersey Athletic Club, 11yds second; W C Johnson Varuna Boat Club, 13yds, third.

Half mile run, novice—Final heat: F Clark, Bayonne Rowing and Athletic Association, first, in 2min 15s; G Fitzgerald, Star Athletic Club, second; C B Gardiner, N Y C, third.

One mile walk—O E Paynter, West End Athletic Association, 35s start, first, in 7m 19 2-5s; C E Nicolls, Prospect Harriers, 30s, second; J C Korth, New York Athletic Club, 25 s, third; C L Nicol, Manhattan Athletic Club, scratch, fourth his time being 6m 58s.

Two mile bicycle race—L A Schafer, Prospect Harriers, 50 yds start, first, in 6m 41s; F Sternberg, Pastime Athletic Club, 75yds, second; J W Judge, Rutherford Wheelmen, 75 yds, third.

One mile run—W D Day, New Jersey Athletic Club, scratch, first, in 4m 31 2-5s; H Hjertberg, New Jersey Athletic Club, 35yds, second.

Running high jump—F J Hoep, National Turnverein, allowed 2½in first, 5ft 8½in; E E Barnes, New Jersey Athletic Club allowed 3in second, 5ft 7¾in; F F Siiney, New Jersey Athletic Club, allowed 4in third, 5ft 6in.

R C Chadsey, Company E, Ninth Regiment, N G S N Y in an attempt to beat the three mile running record of the National Guard, 16m 35s, completed the distance (provided the measurement was correct, which appeared uncertain,) in 16m 18 4-5s. The banner offered as a prize to the club scoring the greatest number of points was won by the New Jersey Athletic Club with 16 points; Prospect Harriers second with 8 points.

An elegant trophy has been offered by a member of the New York Athletic Club for a general competition among lightweights, the events to be included in the programme being as follows: Putting the 12-pound shot, standard 32 feet; 35 weight, standard 18 feet; 12-pound hammer, standard 75 feet; high jump, standard 4 feet 8 inches; broad jump, standard 16 feet; pole vault, standard 7 feet 6 inches; 100 yards run, standard 12 seconds; 1 mile run, standard 6 minutes; half-mile walk, standard 5 minutes; 120 yards, hurdle race, 3 feet hurdles, standard 20 seconds.

A half-mile track, with very easy turns, is to be constructed at the grounds of the New York Jockey Club, within the regular horse-racing track, under the supervision of the veteran, George Goldy, instructor to the New York Athletic Club. It will be built of cinders, and it is intended to make it superior in all respects to any other path in the country. There will also be facilities within the new track for the practice of field sports, and, when completed, the new grounds will be the spot for the decision of the principal athletic and 'cycling fixtures, as the accommodations, which are to include a new and commodious club house, etc., will be superior to others.

AT THE OARS.

The oarsmen have been forced to abandon practice once more on account of the change in the weather. Only a couple of crews were out on Sunday, the bay being unusually rough and the weather cold and wet.

Henry Henceman, of Stockton will train from the Columbia boat house for his coming race with Charles Long on Sunday March 16.

William H. Growney has written to Brown of Boston making enquiries as to the latest style of boat and will probably send for the latest improvement. Mr. Growney is determined to make a good showing in the coming regattas.

Eugene Flanders of the Ariel Rowing Club says he would like to see the big crews of the clubs belonging to the Pacific Rowing Association compete in a four oared shell race and settle the question what club is really entitled to the championship.

Richmond J. Luttringer of the Alpine Club will represent the after waist in the Amateur Crew of this club the coming summer.

Charley Long has secured the services of Walter Blake to train him for his race with Henry Henceman. He has taken up headquarters at the Yall boat house.

The Lurline Club has offered a fine silk banner, to be contested for during the season, to the member winning the greatest number of events.

The Dolphin Club will hold open house on Sunday, March 2nd. All the clubs belonging to the Rowing Association have been invited to attend. During the afternoon, a fine programme of boat and swimming races will be given.

The Alpine Club will shortly purchase a boat for their crew.

CLUB JOTTINGS.

The following prizes will be presented to the runners of the five mile run which will come off at the Olympic Club on February 26th. First prize, diamond locket; second prize, diamond ring; third prize, gold watch charm. There will be over a dozen starters.

At a meeting of the Pacific Coast Amateur Athletic Association, held on Friday evening, February 14th, the Alpine Amateur Athletic Club was admitted to membership.

The members of the G. G. A. C. annex are confident that their club will be allowed to remain in the P. C. A. A. A.

The California Club would do well in giving up some of their club rooms. Judging from the number of members that take exercise in the gymnasium, that branch of the club does not appear to be paying. Very few of the members care to visit New Montgomery street except on "fight" nights, and it would certainly be a great saving of money to the club if it decided to give up all its rooms except the hall where the fights are now held.

The Alpine Club moved to its new rooms, 706 Powell street, on Monday evening. The building, formerly occupied by the Eureka Turn Verein, is admirably suited for an amateur club, and the Alpines did well in selecting the place for their headquarters. The gymnasium which is furnished with all the necessary apparatus, is 110 feet long by 44 feet wide; besides, there are large dressing-rooms, with lockers attached, showers, officers' rooms, reading and card rooms, hat-room, and large store-rooms. The class nights will be Monday, Wednesday and Friday of each week. Persons desiring to visit the rooms must procure visitor's cards from the President of the club. Ladies will be allowed to visit the rooms on Friday nights. An indoor exhibition will be given once a month.

The enthusiasm over the proposed new building of the Olympic Club appears to have died out.

Bakersfield is to have an Athletic Club. A preliminary meeting of those interested was held in the Courthouse of that city on Friday evening of last week. S. L. Blodget was appointed temporary chairman, and J. J. Early Secretary. A list of about sixty-five was read, being the names of those who had already signified their desire to join the new club, and it was thought that the number could easily be increased to 100. On motion, the chairman appointed T. J. Packard, Alex. Heyman, J. J. Earley, J. F. O'Boyle and M. Goldberg, a committee on permanent organization. By unanimous vote the chairman was added to the committee. It was then authorized to solicit membership and requested to fully inform itself about a fitting place for the club. With that business foresight so characteristic of the man, Mr. W. E. Houghton convened the members of the Students and Sportsman's Club on Saturday evening to consider the mat. of inviting the co-operation of the Athletes in forming one large, sound and reliable Club rather than two or three lesser institutions. With all its progressiveness, it must be admitted that Bakersfield is hardly large enough as yet to sustain a properly equipped amateur Athletic Club. But if social features are added and the whole clubbable element of the city interested, an organization can be founded which will do credit to the city and become a notable feature of Southern California.

"Ladies Night" at the Olympic Club.

A "Ladies Night" exhibition was given at the Olympic Club-rooms on Thursday evening, February 18th. The spacious gymnasium was comfortably filled with ladies and gentlemen, who thoroughly enjoyed the athletic feast prepared for them. The opera kept a good many of the members away, otherwise there would not have been so many unoccupied seats in the gallery. The exhibition began at precisely 8:30 o'clock.

The first event of the evening was the five performances on the parallel bars by P. P. Bernharat, Clement J. Schuster, George S. Michling, W. J. Zeiner, J. M. Brewer, Jr., John Schuster, Arthur Ketter and J. S. J. Otto. All the athletes, without exception, showed a careful training, and their different acts earned loud applause.

The second number was pyramids by the juvenile class. The following youngsters under the directions of Prof. W. Smyth and P. P. Bernhardt, took part in the exhibition: H. S. Russ, Eddie Winterburn, Willie Smith, Otto Hasslinger, Thomas Pike, Edmond Lyons, Harry Kennedy, Alex. Ensbury, Willie Ensbury, J. H. McCallough, Walter N. Hogg. A fine arrangement of calcium lights helped to show the different groupings to perfection.

The third event was wrestling, and the following members proved themselves to be well up in the art: Jeff Martin and Eugene Van Court, C. J. Largen and W. T. Haberly. Four pupils of the juvenile class also entertained the audience with clever displays of their ability and strength. They were W. N. Hogg and J. Woolrich, Eddie Diggins and Fred Knight. The last pair looked like Hlypats, and their comical antics kept the spectators in a constant war of laughter.

Messrs F. A. Grim, J. H. Marshall, P. P. Cernharat and Prof. W. Smith followed in gladiatorial groupings. This exhibition was a combination of grace, strength and careful practice and each time the athletes appeared under the calcium lights they received their share of applause.

Henry B. Russ, the treasurer of the club who presided in the absence of the President and Vice President next announced that the medals won at the last field day of the Club and the prizes won at the late boxing tournament were ready for distribution, and he proceeded to call out the names of the winners whom he requested to step forward and receive their prizes. As each man crossed the floor to where Mr. Russ was seated at a table he was greeted with unbounded applause. The prizes for the boxing tournament were very costly, while the medals for the field games were unusually handsome.

The second part of the programme began with an exhibition on the horizontal bar by Messrs. Ben Bogner and Thomas S. Dale (clown). The former appeared to have lost none of his old time grace and skill while the latter was encored at least half a dozen times. He announced that owing to an accident his partner was unable to appear. In a short speech he said that in all his travels in Germany, England, France, etc., he had never seen a club as nicely fitted up as the Olympic club of San Francisco. His imitation of a boy learning to smoke was highly amusing. The club presented him with a handsome basket of flowers.

J B Buchanan, a young amateur athlete lately arrived from Australia, showed the fair sex how he could handle 50, 75 and 100 lb dumb bells. He also swung a pair of very heavy Indian clubs. G H Famerely and F A Chapins gave an exhibition of fencing which was rather tame.

The following appeared in sparring bouts: E M Brown and Joseph T Healy, juvenile class; M G Fenn and E Stracham, juvenile class; A J Treat and J P Jackson Jr; Tom McCord and Eddie Graney.

The bouts between the two latter were particularly interesting. Tug of war by Juveniles closed the entertainment. The contest was for the championship of the Juvenile class. The following is a list of the contestants:

Invincible—N Eckart, F Downing, Eddie Diggins, A Nelson, W D Leahy, E Smith, A Ensbury, A McCarthy.

Nonpareil—Walter N Hogg, J Woolrich, Willie Smith, J H McCullough, Willie Ensbury, Herbert Meyer, Harry Kennedy, Henry Newmark.

The Nonpareils pulled their opponents twice out of three times across the line and won a very even contest. An excellent string band added much to the pleasure of the evening.

Foals of 1890.

The following foals have been dropped at Palo Alto ranch since last advice, viz:

B c by Nephew—America by Rysdyk's Hambletonian.
Ch f by Palo Alto—Juanita by General Benton.
Br c by Mac Benton—Extra by Electioneer.

THOROUGHBREDS.

B c by Flood—Imp. Cornelia by Isonomy.

AT VINA RANCH, TEHAMA COUNTY, CAL.

B c by Electioneer—Dora by Don Victor.
B c by Nephew—Miss Peyton by Imp Glengarry.

Property of Robert Crane, Penns Grove, Cal.

January 21st, ch f by Mortimer 5346, dam Minnie D. by Alexander 490; grandam Shoo Fly by Gen. McClellan 144.

The following foals, propoperty of Mrs. S. B. Wolfskill, were dropped on the 9th instant, Sorrel filly, white face, hind feet white, by Wildidle, dam, Yolona.

On the 12th instant, Bay filly, stripe in face, hind foot and near fore foot, white; by Wildidle, dam Edelweiss.

Yours respectfully,
M. WOLFSKILL.

Grim's Gossip.

Abdallah, means the servant of God.

Many a bargain will be picked up at Capt. Ben Harris's sale next Saturday.

Write to Killip & Co. for a catalogue of the Mrs. Silas Skinner sale which will take place March 6th.

The Hicks-Judd Co. of 23 First street, San Francisco, will in future make a specialty of breeders' catalogues.

Mr. Skinner's Woodside Farm should bring a good round price from some of the gentlemen who are looking for stock farms.

Egbert, who put seventeen into the list last year, has his book full already. Well, no wonder, such a grand showing was enough to warrant plenty of patronage.

Breeders should look carefully over the colt stakes offered by the different associations in this issue. There are many of them, and entries may prove profitable.

1. DeTurk has returned from his Eastern trip, and will now receive offers for Anteeo Button which he desires to sell. This colt can show far better than a "forty gait."

Mr. Ijam's mare Myra, trial 2:21, own sister to Adair, 3.17½, and Grace Lee, 2:29½, by Electioneer, dam Addie Lee by Culver's Black Hawk, have been bred to Axtell.

Marcus Daly, of Anaconda, Mont., has lost by death the stallion St. Val by Electioneer, dam by George Wilkes; second dam by Clark Chief. Mr. Daly paid $5,000 for him as a weanling.

Several Eastern parties are trying to purchase Woodnut from Robert Steele, of Philadelphia. He states that the horse can be bought for $50,000 but that the offer holds good for two weeks only.

When the compiler arranged the catalogue of Irvin Ayres, Esq., he made a mistake with the mare Daisy. Instead of being bred to Daly, as is stated, she was bred to Mortimer, the property of W. Page.

Adonis is eating the rich and succulent grasses at Palo Alto Stock Farm. Mr. Hickok will keep him there for some time yet unless a match is made with Roy Wilkes, which event seems in the far distant future at present.

Peter Woods, of Chicago has determind to make California his future home, and will establish a training stable at the Oakland track. He has already been promised several gilt edged trotters. "Pete" is a good driver and comes highly recommended.

A few days ago, Yolo Maid, who is now quartered at Mr. Daly's Montana Ranch, received an injury which may incapatiate her from further track work. If such should prove to be the case, the wonderfully fast pacer will be bred to Roy Wilkes, in all probability.

The Solano and Napa Agricultural Colt Stakes, with amounts guaranteed, are a new departure in this line and should be a move in the right direction. Since the young blood was infused in this society, it has proven one of the most progressive in the State.

Jacob Steffen of Vallejo will sell at a bargain the bay stallion Afternoon 6543, by Almont McGregor 1775, dam Minnie by Gen Hatch 130; also a handsome brown road mare, which can trot easily to a cart in 2:40 or better. Who wants to pick up a couple of cheap animals?

It is not known generally that Orrin A. Hickok was the first man in the United States to make a stallion net. He had had a great deal of trouble with Elmo, and his ingenuity finally brought forth the net, which, if he had patented, would no doubt have made him a fortune.

Mr. Charles Marvin, telegraphed Mr May Overton, Nashville, Tenn., two weeks ago that he had found a purchaser for Bow Bells, own brother to Bell Boy, at $25,000. Mr. Overton declined the offer and Bow Bells who is at Palo Alto, will be shipped to Nashville, Tenn., next week.

While many newspapers have stated that Orrin A. Hickok would go East with a string of horses this year, the "Tallyrand of the Turf" has not determined yet whether he will invade the big circuit or not. As he says himself "it all depends on what kind of tools I have to work with."

T. B. Merry, who is now on his way to Australia to buy thorougbred horses for L. J. Rose, of Los Angeles, will arrive in Sydney Saturday, March 8th. Some of the newspapers have stated that he might possibly buy Bravo for Mr. Baldwin; he will not buy Bravo—at least for Mr. Baldwin.

To many inquiries I will state that the BREEDER AND SPORTSMAN is put into the San Francisco post-office every Friday evening between six and seven o'clock. If there are any subscribers who do not get their paper on time, the fault lies with the postal authorities, who of late have been very negligent.

When Axtell was formerly announced as being in the stud, only a short time elapsed before his book was full. The syndicate who own the noted stallion are in receipt of letters offering a large bonus above the advertised price ($1,000) if more mares can be taken. One enthusiast offers $1,300 for a service for his mare.

W. H. McCarthy has refused an offer of $13,000 for his chestnut mare, Geneva S. She showed her ability to trot very fast last summer by driving a horse out to his throatlatch in 2:15, and she was a close second to another in 2:14½. Her record is 2:19½. Many prominent horsemen predict that she will trot in 2:12 or better the coming summer.

Charles Sampson of San Francisco, has purchased from Morgan Hill, Madrone Station, Santa Clara County, the very promising stallion Prince Warwick, by Alcona 730; dam Warwick Maid by Mambrino Almont, etc. The price paid was $6,000. Prince Warwick is very speedy, and was handled by Mr. Hickok last fall, the veteran driver thinking very highly of the horse.

I took a look at imp Intruder a few days ago, and found him in the pink of condition. His superbly royal breeding has called the attention of prominent horsemen to the sire of the dam of Spokane, the Kentucky Derby winner, and Mr. Knight, his owner, has wisely decided to stand him at Sacramento during the present season.

Many of the Eastern associations are talking of large stakes with only five per cent. entrance money. Which will be the first of the "Slope" associations to start such an inovation?

At Irvington a disease resembling the grip has broken out among the horses. The horses first snuffle and discharge a thin fluid from the nostrils, which is followed with symptoms of foundering, the hind legs being subject to the severest attacks. The breathing is short and jerky, and actual panting or gasping sometimes occurs. The disease lasts about one week.—Mercury.

As will be seen by the report of our special correspondent at Buffalo, Mr. Frank L. Coombs of Napa has been selected as the new member of the Board of Review for the Pacific Coast. A good judge of horse flesh, familiar with all the horsemen of the coast, and thoroughly well posted on all the rules, he is the right man in the right place.

At the N. T. A. Congress several amendments were made to the present rules, among others, Section 2 of Rule I. now makes it obligatory with owners, drivers and trainers entering and competing over National Association tracks to formally recognize the jurisdiction of said tracks. The rule is to avoid similar defenses as made by Nelson and Noble.

Mr. Valensin reported, before he started East, that Sidney's book only required eight more mares to fill. The success of this horse is not to be wondered at, when it is considered what a sire of speed he is. Simmocolon, who was going to make the season at the Valensin Farm, has been shipped back East, and will be placed in James Goldsmith's hands for a low record.

Fred. W. Loeber, of St. Helena, has been under the weather lately, but is able to be around once more. He reports Whippleton, 1883, Alcona 730, and Grandissimo, all in fine fettle, with the prospect of a heavy stud season before each of them. Prospective purchasers should bear in mind that good horses can always be purchased for reasonable figures at the Vineland stock farm.

Wm. Corbitt, of the San Mateo stock farm, informs me that the book of Guy Wilkes 2:15¼, is full, both for 1890 and 1891. This announcement would have been made in the advertisement but was received to late to change the forms. The premier stallion of San Mateo is well worthy of this liberal patronage, especially as he is now acknowledged to be the very best of the Wilkes family.

There are many who think that the trotting boom is at its height, but we venture to predict that what is called a "boom," is really no false inflation, but the market value of stallions and prices will remain for years to come as high as they are at present. It is only a few months ago that F. P. Lowell, of Sacramento, sold to Crittenden and Barri of Bridgeport, Conn., the Electioneer stallion, Fallis, 2:23 for the stated price of $12,000. A few days ago the new owners refused $25,000 for the horse.

William Witzel of Oshkosh, Wis., has been ill for some time with what was supposed to be laryngitis. His physician, Dr. Gudden, after due examination, declares the case to be glanders, and his diagnosis is coincided in by other physicians. For three weeks prior to the illness Witzel was employed on a farm where, last summer, several glandered horses were shot by order of the State Veterinarian, and is supposed to have been inoculated with the disease by contact with some infected substance.

The proprietor of the San Mateo Stock Farm has had a good deal of his time taken up this week with a lawsuit which has given him a great deal of annoyance. It seems that when Mr. Keogh of San Francisco died, one of the persons in charge sold a mare and two fillies to Mr. Corbitt for $1,000. The claim is now made that a larger price can be secured for the stock, and that the sale was irregular as the probate court had not passed on the status of the executors. The case is still on.

On Tuesday, March 4th, Messrs. Killip & Co. will sell by auction at the Bay District Track a consignment of eight Clydeskale stallions and seven mares of the same breed. They have all been especially selected for the California market by such good judges as J. Trestrail, J. Burns and J. Scott. This is a rare opportunity for those who fancy the heavy draft horses to secure bargains. Stockmen are requested to call and examine them before the day of sale at the track and Villa stables, where they are now quartered.

Last week an article appeared in our columns taking Scott Quintin to task for a reported interview which appeared in a Chicago paper. Mr. Quintin made me a pleasant call during the early part of the week, and showed conclusively where the writer of the original article had misquoted him. We thought at the time that the reporter must have been mistaken, and are glad to think that the article as written were not his statements. Mr. Quintin says he will return East in a day or two.

At the combination sale shortly to be held in this city, Mr. Irvin Ayres will offer a superior lot of trotters by Mambrino Wilkes 6082 and several brood mares in foal to Balkan 8848. If other breeders will come forward and make entries liberally in this great sale it should prove a red letter day in the annals of horse breeding in this state. Almost every day persons come to this office, asking if we know of purchasers for their horses, this is the very opportunity for them. Enter with Killip & Co and try to make the annual combination sale a grand success.

Dr. C. W. Aby, manager of the Guenoc stud farm, reports that his grand old mare, Leverett, has thrown to the cover of imp. Greenback, a fine filly. "Doc." is very enthusiastic over the new-comer, and predicts a great future for her. Mares are being rapidly booked to Greenback and St. Savior; the two noted stallions, being two of the best in the State. The breeding in both are excellent, and as grand outcrosses for the mares of this State, have no superiors. Terms, etc., can be found in another column. The genial Doctor sent his two-year-old, Rodman, on with the Valensin horses, and Mr. Pincus will prepare him for a summer campaign.

Not to be outdone by the other Montana Associations, the Agricultural, Mineral and Mechanical Association of Helena are out with a list of stakes, three of which are for runners and two for trotters. The meeting will be held from August 20th to 30th inclusive, and $15,000 will be given in stakes and purses. Many improvements have been made in the grounds and buildings, and it is confidently asserted that the association grounds as they now are, beat anything west of Chicago. To those contemplating a visit through the Montana circuit, we would suggest taking a glance at the advertisement. Entries close March 1st.

Senator Stanford had intended serving a large number of mares to Palo Alto this year, but has of late left the matter in the hands of Mr. Marvin, who will select a few choice ones only, and then prepare Palo Alto for a hot campaign.

Daniel Donnelly, of Amador Co., was instantly killed while crossing Sutter Creek, on the bridge, near Ione last Thursday. He was on his way home from San Francisco, and stepped out on the platform to take a look at the swollen stream. While leaning over he was struck on the head by one of the bridge timbers, the body falling into the creek. At last accounts the corpse had not been recovered. Mr. Donnelly leaves a wife and two children, who have the heartfelt sympathy of the entire community. "Dan," as he was familiarly called, was a genial whole-souled man, and a great lover of horses, he having owned many good ones since he came to the Pacific Coast in the early "sixties." He was a native of New York City, and was a few days over fifty years old.

In last week's issue of the BREEDER AND SPORTSMAN there were two challenges from L. A. Davis, owner of Roy Wilkes, one to O. A. Hickok, and the other to C. H. Corey of San Jose. The latter gentleman has replied as follows, which, of course, prevents a match between the Wilkes representative, and Almont Patchen, as Roy must be taken East in April.

EDITOR BREEDER AND SPORTSMAN: There has been a great deal of talk about the fast pacing stallion, Roy Wilkes, record 2:12½, and I don't propose for him to come out here and not get a race, for I will pace Almont Patchen against Roy Wilkes and all other pacers now in California, that have a desire to enter in the race for one or two thousand dollars a corner, mile heats, three in five, to rule. Race to take place on the Bay District, or on San Jose tracks, on or about May 20th, 1890. Entries to be sent to the BREEDER AND SPORTSMAN. Now this will give all the fast pacing stock a chance to show what they can do. Yours truly, C. H. COREY.

In answer to an editorial which appeared in the BREEDER AND SPORTSMAN two or three weeks ago, "Iconoclast" says in the Kentucky Stock Farm: "When it comes to aged horses, California has never been able to do anything with the record of the Kentucky-bred Maud S., Jay-Eye-See, or the stallion record of Axtell. If there is any place on the foot-stool where better horses are made than in the Blue Grass region of Kentucky, that place has yet to be discovered. We admire the enterprise and energy of our California friends, but judging the future by the past, Kentucky will continue for some time to come to furnish them marks to shoot at in the records of her aged horses. When they want to improve their stock we will still furnish them with the best we have. We believe in giving them a fair chance." Many thanks, Iconoclast, for the offer of the best you have, but the "best you have" are evidently inferior to ours, as is proven by the fact that so many of your neighbors come to California to purchase our stock. By the way, have you kept count of how many Kentucky mares have been sent to this State to breed to California stallions? Come to think of it, just shoot for a little while at 2:12½ and 2:12¼ by aged stallions, and then we will give you a fresh mark to exercise at.

When the Directors, stockholders and members of the Santa Rosa Agricultural Park Association met last Monday there was only one bid found presented for the grounds of the society, and that was from G. A. Tupper, the amount offered being $15,000. The gentleman afterwards tendered $16,000, but on motion he was allowed to withdraw the offer. The Republican says:

W. P. Thompson, Esq., representing Rufus Murphy, interposed an objection to all the proceedings, and offered a protest against the same, asserting that the proceedings of the meeting were not in accordance with the provisions of the statute, and denied the power of the Board of Directors to sell the property under such proceedings.

J. N. Bailhache moved that the Board of Directors be empowered by the stock-holders to sell the property at as satisfactory price as can be obtained.

The proposition was carried by a vote of 1,847 shares to 150 in the negative, Mr. Thompson protesting on behalf of Mr. Murphy to the roll call.

John Strong asked for thirty days time to form an organization to purchase the property for agricultural ground purposes.

S. I. Allen then moved that the matter be left open until the first day of March to give the people an opportunity to form an agricultural organization and purchase the property, which motion prevailed.

Death of Lorena.

Capt. Ben E. Harris has suffered a serious loss in the death of his very fast mare Lorena 2:30 (made as a two year old) which occurred sometime during Sunday night at the stable corner of Turk and Stiner streets. When the closed box-stall was open on Monday morning by the attendant, Lorena was found lying on her right side dead, and she evidently had been for several hours. In several corners of the stall there were quantities of blood, there being at the head of the poor animal great clots of coagulated blood, and a mass of froth tinctured, with red, attached to the nostrils.

Captain Harris was negotiating with an Eastern horseman for the sale of the mare, but the price asked was considered excessive, still her owner was aware that she was phenomenably fast, and considered that he has a mortgage on every stake in which she was entered. This opinion was shared by all who knew anything about the filly, and there are many who credited her with being able to beat 2:20 easily, this year. The following certificate has been issued.

SAN FRANCISCO, Feb. 17, 1890.

This is to certify that at the request of Capt. B. E. Harris of San Francisco, we, this day, held a postmortem examination on the brown mare Lorena, and found that the immediate cause of death was due to rupture of one of the large pulmonary veins of the right lung. At the point of rupture the vein was in a morbid state, being much dilated, and from all appearances such condition had existed for a considerable period.

We also found that the same vein was varicosed at the entrance of the left auricle of the heart.

The right lung itself was in a state of chronic congestion, which must have existed some time previous to death.

The stomach was particularly healthy, and contained a quantity of food partially digested; also blood, which had evidently been swallowed during the profuse hemorrhage.

H. E. CARPENTER, M. O. C. V. S.,
A. E. BUZARD, M. R. C. V. S. L.

THE WEEKLY

Breeder and Sportsman.

JAMES P. KERR, PROPRIETOR.

The Turf and Sporting Authority of the Pacific Coast.

Office: No. 313 Bush St.

P. O. Box 2300.

TERMS—One Year, $5; Six Months, $3; Three Months, $1.50.

STRICTLY IN ADVANCE.

Money should be sent by postal order, draft or by registered letter, addressed to JAMES P. KERR, San Francisco, Cal.

Communications must be accompanied by the writer's name and address, not necessarily for publication, but as a private guarantee of good faith.

ALEX. P. WAUGH, ... Editor.

Advertising Rates

Per Square (half inch)

One time $1 50
Two times 2 50
Three times 3 25
Four times 4 00

And each subsequent insertion 75c. per square.

Advertisements running six months are entitled to 10 per cent. discount.

Those running twelve months are entitled to 20 per cent. discount.

Reading notices set in same type as body of paper, 50 cents per line each insertion.

To Subscribers.

The date printed on the wrapper of your paper indicates the time to which your subscription is paid.

Should the BREEDER AND SPORTSMAN be received by any subscriber who does not want it, write us direct to stop it. A postal card will suffice.

Special Notice to Correspondents.

Letters intended for publication should reach this office not later than Wednesday of each week, to secure a place in the issue of the following Saturday. Such letters to insure immediate attention should be addressed to the BREEDER AND SPORTSMAN, and not to any member of the staff.

San Francisco, Saturday, Feb. 22, 1890.

Stallions Advertised

IN THE

BREEDER AND SPORTSMAN.

Thoroughbreds.

FRIAR TUCK, Hermit—Romping Girl..........C. W. Aby, Middletown.
GREENBACK, Dollar—Music..........C. W. Aby, Middletown.
INTRUDER, Crater—Lady Bountiful..........T. J. Knight, Sacramento.
REVEILLE, Shiloh—Norfolk..........B. C. Holly, Vallejo.
ST. SAVIOR, Eolus—War Song..........C. W. Aby, Middletown.
THREE CHEERS, Imp. Hurrah—Young Fashion..........E. S. Culver, San Francisco.

Trotters.

ARBITRATOR, Director—Lady Earnest..........H. A. Mayhew, Niles.
ANTEEOP, Anteeo—Bessie G..........Guy E. Grosse, Santa Rosa.
ANTEEOP, Anteeo—Nance..........Guy E. Grosse, Santa Rosa.
ADMIRO, Admiral—dam by San Bruno..........Smith & Sutherland, Pleasanton.
ASHLAND ALMONT, Almont—Pauline..........T. J. Whitehead, Oakland.
ANTEROS NUTWOOD, Anteros—Newark Belle..........T. W. Barstow, San Jose.
ALEXANDER BUTTON, Alexander—Lady Button..........Cache Creek Farm, Yolo.
APEX, Prompter—Mary..........Poplar Grove Breeding Farm, Wildflower.
ALCONA, Almont—Queen Mary..........Fred W. Loeber, St. Helena
BALKAN, Mambrino Wilkes—Fanny Fern..........A. L. Hinds, Oakland.
BONANZA, Arthurton—Sister..........Richard Havey, Oakland
BAY ROSE, Sultan—Madam Baldwin..........W. W. Ayres, Oakland.
CLOVIS, Sultan—Sweetbriar..........Poplar Grove Breeding Farm, Wildflower.
CUPID, Sidney—Venus..........C. O Thornquest, Oakland
CHRISMAN'S HAMBLETONIAN 10178, Whipple's Hambletonian—Flora Jesse Chrisman, San Jose.
CANNON BALL, Simmons—Gurgle..........Lockhaven Stock Farm, Burbank.
CHARLES DERBY, Steinway—by Electioneer. Cook Stock Farm, Contra Costa Co.
CRESCO, Strathmore—Spartan..........Cook Stock Farm, Contra Costa Co
CALIFORNIA NUTWOOD, Nutwood—Fanny Patchen..........Martin Carter, Alameda Co.
DEXTER PRINCE, Kentucky Prince—Lady Dexter..........L. M. Morse, Lodi.
DAWN, Nutwood—Countess..........A. L. Whitney, Petaluma
DIRECTOR, Dictator—Dolly..........Pleasanton Stock Farm, Pleasanton.
DON MARVIN, Fallis—Cora..........F. P. Lowell, Sacramento
DESIGNER, Director—May Queen..........H. Scott, Oakland.
ELECTOR, Electioneer—Gilberta..........L. A. Richards, Grayson.
ELECTO, Antevolo, dam by Capt. Webster..........G. W. Stimpson, Oakland
ELECTION, Electioneer—Lizzie H..........B. C. Holly, Vallejo.
ELEGANCE..........G. W. Stimpson, Oakland
EL BENTON, Electioneer—Nellie Benton..........Souther Farm, San Leandro.
ECLECTIC, Electioneer—Manette..........Wilfred Page, Sonoma County
EROS, Electioneer—Sontag Mohawk..........W. H. Vioget, Menlo Park
FIGARO, Hambletonian—Emblem..........Souther Farm, San Leandro.
GROVER CLAY, Electioneer—Maggie Norfolk..........Denis Gannon, Oakland.
G. & M., Anteeo—Rosa B..........George E. Guerne, Santa Rosa.
GUY WILKES, George Wilkes—Lady Bunker..........San Mateo Stock Farm, San Mateo.
GLEN FORTUNE, Electioneer—Glenna..........Souther Farm, San Leandro.
GEORGE WASHINGTON, Mambrino Chief—Fanny Rose..........Thos. Smith, Vallejo.
GUIDE, Director—Imogene..........Smith & Sutherland, Pleasanton.
GRANDISSIMO, LeGrande—Norma..........Fred W. Loeber, St Helena
ILLUSTRIOUS, Happy Medium—Abdalletta..........George A. Stone, Santa Rosa.
JESTER D, Almont—Hortense..........Souther Farm, San Leandro
JUNIO, Electioneer—by Granger..........S. N. Straube, Fresno.
KAFIR, Alcazar—Flower Girl..........B. C. Holly, Vallejo.
LEO WILKES, Guy Wilkes—Sable..........San Mateo Stock Farm, San Mateo.
LYNWOOD, Nutwood—Hattie Morrison..........P. Visher, Stockton.
MEMO, Sidney—Flirt..........Valensin Stock Farm, Pleasanton.
MOUNTAIN BOY, Kentucky Prince—Elsie..........B. C. Holly, Vallejo.
MAMBRINO WILKES, George Wilkes—Lady Chrisman..........San Miguel Stock Farm, Walnut Creek.
MART BOORHEM, Sidney—Towhead..........B. C. Holly, Vallejo.
MAMBRINO JR. 1789, Mambrino Patchen, dam by Mambrino Chief Geo. P. Bull, San Jose.
MAMBRINO CHIEF, McDonald Chief—Venus..........Thos. Smith, Vallejo.
MORTIMER, Electioneer—Marti..........Wilfred Page, Sonoma County
NOONDAY, Wedgewood—Noontide..........F. P. Lowell, Sacramento.
PLEASANTON, Director—May Day..........Pleasanton Stock Farm, Pleasanton.
PASHA, Sultan—Madam Baldwin..........D. Bryson, Linden
PILOT NUTWOOD, Nutwood—Belle..........T. W. Barstow, San Jose.
PHILOSOPHER, Pilot Wilkes—Belle..........George E. Guerne, Santa Rosa.
ROY WILKES, Adrian Wilkes—Flora..........Pleasanton Stock Farm Pleasanton.
REDWOOD, Anteeo—Lou Wilton..........A. McFayden, Oakland.
SILVER BOW, Robert McGregor—Sadie..........P. J. Williams, Oakland.
STEINWAY, Strathmore—Abbess..........Cook Stock Farm, Contra Costa Co
SUNSET, Anteeo—Bessie G..........Guy E. Grosse, Santa Rosa.
SHAMROCK, Buccaneer—Fernleaf..........G. W. Stimpson, Oakland
SIDNEY, Santa Claus—Sweetness..........Valensin Stock Farm, Pleasanton.
SIMMOCOLON, Simmons—Colon..........Valensin Stock Farm, Pleasanton.
SABLE WILKES, Guy Wilkes—Sable..........San Mateo Stock Farm, San Mateo.
ST. NICHOLAS, Sidney—Towhead..........John Rowen, Oakland Trotting Park.
WOODNUT, Nutwood—Flora..........Jas. Weatherhead, San Jose
WHIPPLETON 1883, Hambletonian Jr.—Lady Livingston..........Fred W. Loeber, St. Helena
WOODSIDE, Woodnut—Veronica..........B. C. Holly, Vallejo.

Dates Claimed.

FRESNO (Spring Meeting)..........March 18th to 29th
SAN JOSE (Blood Horse Meeting)..........April 5th, 7th and 9th
IONE..........Aug 5th to 8th,
NAPA..........Aug. 18th to 23rd
SAN JOSE (Fall Meeting)..........Aug. 25th to 29th inclusive
PETALUMA..........Aug. 25th to 30th
OAKLAND (District No. 1)..........Sept. 1st to Sept. 6th
CALIFORNIA STATE FAIR..........Sept 8th to 20th
FRESNO (Fall Meeting)..........Sept. 29th to Oct. 4th

To All Interested in the Growth and Development of the Pacific Coast Trotting Horse Industry.

The Pacific Coast Trotting Horse Breeders Association wishes to do everything that can be done to advance the legitimate interest of the trotting horse, his owner, and his breeder. In order to work effectively, it must have liberal support and an invitation to join the association is hereby given to everyone who wishes to help on this work.

With the exception of the Stanford Stakes, the purses and stakes that will close on March 1st, are open only to members of the association. These races are arranged so as to give colts of all classes a fair chance to earn their oats, and it is hoped that the number of entries will encourage the association to offer still more purses for young stock.

Particular attention is asked for the purses given for two, three and four-year olds, the produce of stallions that have never produced a 2:30 performer. The Directors of the association feel that there are many young stallions of great merit on this coast, whose produce will not have a fair show while they are compelled to enter and start against the developed produce of the large breeding farms. The fact that a young stallion has no 2:30 performers is nothing discreditable, as his colts may have had no possible opportunity of showing their merit. Consider that several stallions which are now among the best in the land, were not long ago without representatives in the list. Anteeo, who will make a large season at a fee of $300, was up to a comparatively short time ago, without 2:30 performers. William L. was one of the great unknown up to the appearance of Axtell. Who knows how many young horses there are who would compare well with any if they but had a chance. As an example we quote the following from an article by Mr. Jos. Cairn Simpson, who writes as follows:

"Should nothing happen in the interval to change our views, entries will certainly be made in all of them (the two, three and four-year-old purses for colts sired by horses who have not produced a 2:30 performer) whereas, in the open stakes for three and four-year-olds there will have to be an unexpected display of speed to warrant engaging in stakes where Regal Wilkes, Pedlar, Lorena and Mista are likely to appear, and in that where Margaret S., Lilian Wilkes and some others are sure to be in. There could not be a bill which would be more to our individual wants than that offered, as with the exception of these named and the yearling stake we will enter in all the purses and the two-year-old stake, this if the entries close March 1st, or sooner, for if later may be disappointments to change the plan. Now there is no question that the arrangement agreed upon is a boon to the small breeders as it is fair to infer that many are in the same situation."

Mr. Simpson has stated the case very strongly and there seems to be no shadow of a doubt but that the entries to the purses for the produce of stallions who have no 2:30 performers will be very many. It is the wish of the association that Colt Stakes may become one of the most popular features of our trotting meetings.

In the past they have resulted far too often in walk-overs, but this may be laid to the entire lack of proper classification. It is just as reasonable to expect horses to enter against Stamboul and Palo Alto as it is is to expect breeders to enter their untried colts against such world beaters as Sunol, Regal Wilkes, Margaret S and Faustino. Men will not only refuse to enter in the face of sure defeat, but even if they are rash enough to enter, they will never make the second or third payment when such formidable names are in the list of possible starters.

While the Directors have thus endeavored to provide for the interests of the small breeder, the great breeding farms that have made California famous as the greatest country in the world for the production of early stock have by no means been neglected. Stakes have been opened for yearlings, two year olds, three year olds and four year olds, which are absolutely free to all. Then the three minute class for three year olds and the 2:40 class for four year olds gives the large breeding farms an opportunity to start any of their already tried and proved colts.

The entries to these stakes and purses and also to the 2:30 stallion race will close on March 1st. At the same date the entries for the Stanford Stakes for 1890 will close. Every man who ownes a horse that he considers worthy of any patronage whatsoever should see to it that some of the progeny of the horse be entered in as many of these purses and stakes as possible. All breeders should also consider the additional value given a promising colt by the fact of an entry in a valuable stake. Every one who has or expects to have good colts should make a personal matter of adding to the list of members and to the entries in the purses and stakes, as with proper support the Association can greatly increase the value of every good colt on the coast by opening up opportunities to such colts to earn money. When classified colt purses become as popular as they will become under proper management, the opportunisies for profit will be so greatly increased that good gaited, well bred colts that are entered in the valuable stakes and purses that the Association intends to give will be worth large sums of money. It is especially desired that these stakes and purses that close on March 1st receive the entry of every good colt in the State. If the purses for the produce of untried stallions fill as largely as it now seems probable that they will, there is little doubt but that the various Agricultural Associations will offer similar purses, and thus increase the opportunities for a colt to earn money. The first payment in all these entries is very reasonable, so reasonable, in fact, that any one who has several colts can well afford to enter them in all, and make second and third payments on those that train on in the most satisfactory manner.

Make every entry that you possibly can, as a few months' work frequently brings the colt that at the beginning of the year was considered the slowest of the lot to the very front rank at the time the race is trotted. In addition to giving your colts every opportunity, you will be helping the Association, and thereby helping yourself.

The Practical Horseshoer.

Being a collection of articles on horseshoeing in all its branches which have appeared from time to time in the columns of The Blacksmith and Wheelright, including a chapter on ox shoeing and another on horse physiognomy. Compiled and edited by M. T. Richardson. Profusely illustrated. New York, M. T. Richardson, publisher, 1890.

Numerous works on horseshoeing have been published, but each one from the brain of a single individual and representing only his experience and theories. The work before us embraces the varying views of a large number of horseshoers located in all parts of the United States, and as such is unique in its conception. Nearly, or quite every, phase of this intricate subject is treated in some shape or other. In the introductory portion there are illustrations of different styles of foreign nails and an engraving of an Arabian horseshoe. Chapter I. discusses horseshoeing in a general way. Chapter II. comprises a variety of styles of special tools used by horseshoers. Chapter III. gives Devices with illustrations for shoeing ugly horses and mules. There is another chapter on Hot and Cold Fitting; one on Contracted Feet and how to treat them; another on corns and the best methods of treatment; another on Interfering and Overreaching; another on Quarter Cracks and Split Hoofs; still another tells how to shoe knee sprung, fat footed or club footed horses. There is a chapter on Docking, telling just how to do it. Another on the use of tips for trotters, winding up with a chapter on horse physiognomy, and another on ox shoeing. The book in many respects is the most valuable contribution to the art of horseshoeing which has been published up to this time.

Ground for a Race Track.

Our readers will have noticed in the issue before last, a long communication from a correspondent who mentions a number of places where land may be obtained within San Francisco County, for the purpose of building a race track. It is essentially necessary for the welfare of the Pacific Coast Blood Horse Association, and for the Pacific Coast Trotting Horse Breeders Association, that the track should be located in San Francisco. There are many who are willing to assume that a track located in Alameda County or in the vicinity of Tiburon would be accessible for the residents of this city, but it has already been proven in a great number of instances, that the race-loving community of the Pacific Coast Metropolis will not cross the bay, except to witness very sensational performances. It therefore becomes the duty of all who are interested in advancing the horse-breeding interests of this Coast to take early action, so that land may be secured before the Bay District Track is finally cut up into building lots.

The correspondent alluded to lays particular stress on the fact that the Ocean House Course is still in existence, although it has been deserted as a race track for many years. We are led to believe that if the matter is brought properly before the present owners, that possession can be obtained of the old track for racing purposes and at a very moderate rental. It would seem to the best interests of all concerned, that this matter should be looked into at once; and if the two principal associations of the State will work hand in hand together, that the citizens of San Francisco would be willing to assist them very materially in finishing a first class course for this city; and it would be the means of bringing a great deal of money here annually. The hotels, the livery stable men, merchants, cable-car companies and the better class of saloon keepers would, beyond a doubt, be willing to subscribe liberally toward the fund for the purpose of putting the old track in proper condition. From the apathy at present shown, it would seem as though no action would be taken until the Bay District Track becomes a thing of the past.

It is to be hoped that a committee from both of the associations may be appointed to act in harmony, to try to secure at the earliest possible day, a suitable place for a race track in San Francisco.

San Jose Blood Horse Association.

There will be found in its proper place the advertisement of the "Garden City" Blood Horse Association Stakes, entries to which will close March 5th. They include the Introduction Stakes for all ages, with $300 added. The Vendome Stake for three year olds has $175 added, the distance being a mile. A half-mile dash for two year olds is called The Dubut Stake, and has $150 added. One of the stakes is named after the St. James Hotel; it is for all ages, one mile, with $175 in addition. For the second day there is the Santa Clara Stake. Another all aged event is seven furlongs, and has $175 added thereto. The Laurelwood Farm Stake is one mile and an eighth, for the aged division, and has $200 added. The Lamolle House Stake is for three year olds, one mile, with added money amounting to $175. The Milpitas Stake will call out the aged horses for a race of half-mile heats, to which $175 will be added. The third and last day will be opened with the entries for the Al Farrow Stake, which has been named after the noted racer, the stake to be renamed if Al Farrow's time of 1:40 is beaten. This is an owners' handicap. Weights to be announced the night before the race. The Lick House Stake follows, for two year olds, the distance being five furlongs. Still another of the all aged events is the Hobson Stake, one mile and a quarter, with $175 added, and the firm of T. W. Hobson & Co. will present the winning jockey with a fine suit of clothes made to order. The Sprinter Stakes is for short horses, quarter mile and repeat. Read the conditions.

Volume 8, American Trotting Register.

We have to acknowledge the receipt of volume 8 of Wallace's Trotting Register from the Wallace Trotting Register Co., of 280 Broadway, New York. It is uniform with the others that have preceded it, and now carries up the number of registered stallions to 11,422. There are a number of corrections and alterations, and a large list of standard mares and non-standard animals. Announcement is also made that volumes 1 and 2 will shortly be republished, they being at present out of print.

Our Australian Letter.

SYDNEY, N. S. Wales, Australia, Jan. 22, '90.

EDITOR BREEDER AND SPORTSMAN:—It will bring joy to the hearts of the admirers of Sir Modred to hear of the doings of one of his progeny, Sir William, at our recent big summer meetings. Sir William is a bay, three-year-old colt by Sir Modred from Vesper, a symmetrical but not by any means a large horse. Sir William first showed what he could do at Rosehill, near Sydney, where in anything but first rate trim he ran Leichhardt a close race. He then came like a flash at Randwick, where at the Australian Jockey Club Summer Meeting on December 26th, he won the opening race, the Flying Handicap, 6 furlongs, with 7 stone, 2 lbs., and on the same day, with 7 stone, 12 lb. He had no difficulty in winning the Australian Jockey Club Handicap of a mile and a quarter. On the following Saturday at the Tattersall's Club Annual Race Meeting, also held at Randwick, Sir William with 8 stone ran second to The Gift, a four-year-old weighted at 7 stone, 6 lb., but he made up for the disappointment on the second day by appropriating Tattersall's Club Cup, two miles, with 6 stone 5 lbs. Sir William is plucky to the backbone and great things are expected from him in the near future.

The midsummer reunion of the Australian Jockey Club held at Randwick on December 26th, proved a most successful meeting, fully 20,000 people putting in an appearance. For the Flying Handicap the Hon. James White's filly Sequel was most fancied and started at 2 to 1, but she was never in it, and the winner turned up in Sir William, who won easily from Second Thought. For the December Stakes, a two-year-old race, Wilga, a filly by the imported Epigram from Nellie was thought such a good thing that she started at 6 to 4, but the speedy Correze, a colt by Newminster from Ouida, of whom I have spoken in former letters, was in great form and beat the favorite by a neck. For the big event, the Summer Cup, the Hon. James White's five-year-old mare, Lava, by the owner's crack sire Chester from Etna, went out favorite with 7 stone, 6 lb. up and won with ease from Bonnie Spec, and the Hon. White also secured the next race, the Nursery Handicap, a five furlongs flutter for two-year-olds with Prelude, a filly by Martini—Henry from Phillina, who carried 8 stone. 3 lbs., and won in a canter from Golden Fleece, a filly owned by Mr. Sam Hordern. Mr. Hordern is the sportsman who owns Judge Belden and other tip-top imported American trotting stock. Sir William brought the meeting to a close by winning the Australian Jockey Club Handicap.

At Tattersall's Club meeting at Randwick on New Year's Day, the principal event was Tattersall's Club Cup, two miles, for which the Hon. James White's Lava, 8 st., started first favorite at even money, but Sir Modred's son, Sir William, with 6 st 5 lbs, landed first in the straight, and staving off a big run by the favorite, won by sheer pluck. In this race a horse called Syndey fell, and when he rose it was seen that his jockey was hanging by a stirrup, but Sydney, for a wonder, stood perfectly still until he was extricated. Poor Wilkins, the jockey, has since died from the effects of the fall. This race also proved disastrous to a former captain of one of the Australian Cricketing Elevens, who "went down" on Lava to the extent of over a couple of thousand pounds, which he was unable to meet on settling-up day.

On January 4th the racing men of the colony tendered a complimentary meeting at Randwick to Mr. Andrew Town. Mr. Town and his father before him have been intimately connected with racing in the colonies for a lifetime, and the annual sale of racing, and latterly trotting stock, at the beautiful Hobartville Estate has long proved a red letter day for colonial sportsmen from all the colonies. However, Andrew Town has somehow made a mess of his affairs, and it has been for some time an open secret that Hobartville has been his on sufferance only. Recently the crash came, and the genial Andrew was tendered the complimentary meeting under notice, the result of which was the handing over to Mr. Town the other day of a substantial check for £1,830.

I am not aware whether Yankee trainers are so great believers as ours in whiskey as a medium of Dutch courage to weak hearted animals. About this time last year a horse called Southerly Buster had no less than three bottles of whiskey poured into him just before starting in a race. It made the horse tight as a lord, and during the running he got mixed up with the paling fence, and his jockey was rather badly hurt. When the Buster got up he was staggering all over the course and started wagging his head with a ludicrous, drunken leer. Australian horses often have stiff "nips" given them, but the Buster is the first horse I have seen properly drunk and winking at the crowd.

A story is going the rounds of the colonial papers in connection with an American trotter which some of your old-time sports may remember. At a recent meeting at Breakfast Creek, Queensland, a horse was entered in the trot under the modest name of Jack, and his appearance was fully in keeping with his cognomen. His knees showed signs of frequent application to his prayers, and he looked so haggard and cast down that a funny man in the crowd admonished the starter to get them quickly away, before Jack fell down. But Jack managed to keep his legs until the flag fell and a bit longer, as he rattled his old bones and the sulky in a long way ahead of his field. It turned out that the old hatrack was 30 years old, and was identical with the once famous Yankee trotter, Commodore, who had in the States in his prime hung up a record of 2:26, when he was sold to an Australian dealer for 500 guineas. THE JUNGLE."

Sacramento Colt Stakes.

EDITOR BREEDER AND SPORTSMAN:—I enclose you the entries in the races that filled for the Sacramento Colt Stakes. The other stakes did not have the required number of entries to fill.

YEARLING TROT.

W. J. O'Brien, Sacramento, gray colt ——, sired by Albert W 2:20, dam Maggie A by Hack's Tecumseh.

B. C. Holly, Vallejo, bay colt Hollywood, sired by Woodnut, dam Avrella by Albert W.

E. Pickett, Elk Grove, sorrel colt Hicory Nut, by Ross S 2:25, dam by John Nelson.

Wilber F. Smith, Sacramento, black filly Remora, by Guy Wilkes, dam Belle Blanche, by The Moor.

Wilber F. Smith, Sacramento, bay colt Algiers, by Alcazar, dam Yerba Santa by Santa Claus.

C. P. Malcolm, Sacramento, sorrel filly Minnie C, by Ross S, dam Minnie S.

TWO-YEAR-OLD TROT.

T. J. Drais, Farmington, b c Farmington Boy by Dexter Prince, dam by Chieftain.

Pete Sullivan, Sacramento, b c Beacon, sire Sterling, dam Rachel by Edwin Forrest.

Wilber F. Smith, Sacramento, br f Felucca by Guy Wilkes, dam Cora by Buccaneer.

N. B. Whittaker, Stockton, b g Amot, sire Duke Altimont, dam ——

B. C. Holly, Vallejo, b c Mart Boorhem, sire Sidney, dam Towhead by Echo.

Mrs. Silas Skinner, Napa, ch c Woodside by Woodnut, dam Veronica by Alcona.

F. W. Loeber, St. Helena, blk c Almonition by Alcona, dam Pansy by C. M. Clay Jr.

N. Overhalster, Petaluma, b f Duchess by Sidney, dam Young Countess.

Fred Bean, Vallejo, b f Blanche by Woodnut, dam by Eugene Casserly.

N. Overhalster, Petaluma, bay c, Commodore by Sidney, dam Newland mare.

A. L. Whitney, Petaluma, chestnut filly Annie Bell by Dawn, dam Hubbard mare.

THREE-YEAR-OLD PACING STAKE.

S. H. Hoys, Winters, blue filly Brilliantine by Brilliant, dam by Prompter.

Thos. C. Snider, Washington, brown filly Adelia by Brilliant, dam Madam Buckner by Tom Hal.

F. P. Lowell, Sacramento, bay c Falrose by Fallis 2:23, dam Roseleaf by Buccaneer.

C. M. Robinson, Sacramento, chestnut colt Bozero by Prompter, dam Mary by Flaxtail.

W. C. Harlan, Winters, bay colt Vigor by Sterling, dam by Prompter. Yours, F P. LOWELL, Secretary.

SACRAMENTO, Cal., Feb. 18th, 1890.

Names Claimed.

I claim the name of Nellie B. for brown filly—by Clovis, dam by Mambrino Wilkes. Foaled Feb. 15 1890.

D. BRYSON.

LINDEN, San Joaquin Co., February 18th, 1890.

Among the many trotting stallions in the State none should command greater attention than Illustrious 4178. He is happily named, being a grand looker with a royal pedigree, a son of the prepotent Happy Medium, sire of Maxey Cobb, 2:13¼, and forty others in the 2:30 list, while his dam is by Cassius M. Clay Jr. 22, out of a well known Almont 33 mare. Illustrious is making the season at Santa Rosa at the particularly low figure of $80, and Mr. Stone will take exceptional care of every mare sent to him.

Answers to Correspondents.

Answers for this department must be accompanied by the name and address of the sender, not necessarily for publication, but as proof of good faith. Write the questions distinctly, and on one side of the paper only. Positively no questions will be answered by mail or telegraph.

Subscriber.

Please give in your next number how many horses Electioneer has with records better than 2:20. How many trotters has California in the 2:20 list?

Answer.—Eleven. Do you mean bred in this State, or those brought here and then trotted to their records?

C. P. C.

I own a bay stallion that I bought from E. S. Daniels. He was sired by Hernanni, property of J. H. White, President of the P. C. T. H. B. A. The stallion's pedigree is as follows: Bay colt, foaled April 19, 1887, sired by Hernani, dam Kitty Dean. Hernani by Electioneer, dam Gipsy by Paul's Abdallah. Kitty Dean by Fred Lowe, dam by Jack Hawkins. Fred Lowe by St. Clair. Jack Hawkins by Boston, is he eligible to registration.

Answer.—He is not eligible to registration.

T. T. D.

Please give me decision. Did Mattie Howard trot 20 miles in the hour, and was it not on the old half mile track of Jim Eoff, in San Francisco?

Answer.—Yes, on December 7, 1871, time, 59:30½.

Inquirer.

Will you kindly inform me through the column of "Answers to Correspondent" if the mare "Mollie McCarthy" bred by Mr. Winters ever left any colts in the East. I make this request because I surmise that certain parties in Illinois are seeking to defraud an acquaintance, and he has asked me for advice.

Answer.—Mollie McCarty never had but three foals and they were all born on this coast. In 1881 she had br f Fallen Leaf by Grinstead, in 1882 br c Brandywine by Lexington, in 1883 b f Mollie McCarty's last by Rutherford; the mare died 15th of March in that year.

D. S. H.

What are the dams of Admiral, Ulster Chief, and Rose's Abdallah?

Answer.—Admiral's dam was Lady Pierson by Cassius M. Clay 20. Ulster Chief's dam was Lady Ulster. We do not know the dam of Rose's Abdallah, in fact do not know the horse.

Playboy.

Please give the pedigrees of the following horses, viz., (1) Rifleman, (2) Bertrand, (3) Wagner.

Answer.—Rifleman, by imp Glencoe, dam Rudolph mare, 2nd dam Butterfly by Sumpter, 3rd dam by imp Buzzard, etc. Bertrand by Sir Archy, dam Eliza by imp Bedford, 2nd dam Mambrina by Mambrino, 3rd dam by Flank, 4th dam by Ward, etc. Which Wagner do you mean?

Los Angeles.

In the issue of February 8th, in answer to the questions, "What is the pedigree of Dan M. Murphy, is he of a racing family and what relations has he of note?" We said that as far as the records show he was not from a racing family, and that he had no relatives of note. A Los Angeles gentleman suggests the name of Wheeler T., as being one of note, the Chicago horse being by the sire of Dan M. Murphy. We had overlooked the fact that Wheeler T was by imp Speculator, but even so, as one swallow does not make a summer, one sprinter does not make a racing family.

Reader.

Please inform me whether the horse called Fred Arnold, owned by H. D. Albright of San Luis Obispo, is standard, and what is his record. What is the pedigree of Magic, owned in San Jose, and what is his record?

Answer.—Fred Arnold is standard, but we will not have his number until Volume 8 of the American Trotting Register is issued. His record is 2:33½. We do not know the pedigree of Magic. Later. Vol. 8 has been received. Fred Arnold's number is 11,084.

Subscriber.

1st. Please give the breeding on the dam's side of the stallion Bonner by Whipple's Hambletonian? 2nd. What year did the stallion John Nelson made a season in Stockton. When and where did he die and who owned him at the time of his death?

Answer.—(1) Maria Mink, there is nothing positive known of her breeding. (2) Wallace says that he died in 1871, but we have every reason to believe that he is mistaken. Will be able to answer positively within a week or two. As to when he stood in Stockton you can fine that out by examining the files of Stockton papers.

T. M.

Will you please let me know the record of Eagan's old Sport.

Answer.—2.26½, made February 22nd, 1889.

"Music in the Air."

CHALLENGE.

To back my assertion made in the San Jose Mercury in Dec. last, I will match this horse (Cyrus R) against any trotting stallion in San Jose, one or two mile heats, any time after July 1st. The parties accepting this challenge can set the time and track, and I the right to name the amount. For further particulars, address. T. W. BARSTOW, San Jose, Cal.

In answer to the above, which appeared in last week's BREEDER AND SPORTSMAN we have received an acceptance accompanied by a draft for $500 from R. H. Walton, of San Jose. It is now in order for Mr. Barstow to make known his wishes in the matter. The letter from Mr. Walton is as follows:

SAN JOSE, February 18th, 1890.

MR. T. W. BARSTOW, Dear Sir—In the BREEDER AND SPORTSMAN of February 13th, 1890, your challenge to match your stallion Cyrus R. against any stallion in San Jose, I accept I have to-day deposited with the BREEDER AND SPORTSMAN five hundred dollars as a forfeit for a purse of one thousand dollars a side. I name my stallion Argent, race to take place on San Jose race track, July 14th, 1890, race, mile heats three in five to harness and to rule; under the management of the officers of the San Jose Agricultural Society. Your forfeit of five hundred dollars to be deposited with BREEDER AND SPORTSMAN by March 1st, 1890. Balance, five hundred dollars aside to be deposited by each of us with BREEDER AND SPORTSMAN, by July 1st, 1890.

R. H. WALTON.

Our Southern California Letter.

The people who play the winter books are just about this time looking for the winner of the Brooklyn and Suburban Handicaps. I have not as yet had a chance to study over the lists. The handicapper has let Kingston down light with 128 pounds in the Brooklyn and he is sure to be the favorite in the winter books. Who can beat Kingston in that race? That is the question. After a casual glance over the lists I must say that I like the following the best: Raceland 124, Tenny 123, Hanover 122, Exile 122, Sir Dixon 118, Proctor Knott 118, Los Angeles 116, Badge 114, Gorgo 110 and Diablo 110. The distance might be a little too far for Badge but he should be dangerous with only 114 pounds to pack. Los Angeles should be hot property on a muddy track. Sir Dixon should not be overlooked. He was a greater three-year-old than Raceland, and I like his chances very much at 118 pounds. Stick a pin right here. Proctor Knott will be one, two or three when the numbers go up. "The three-year-old failure" as he has been contemptuously dubbed is going to carry some of my money and if the first Futurity winner comes to the scratch in good condition it will take a Kingston to beat him for the Brooklyn. Exile is an uncertain horse but it will not be policy to neglect him altogether, especially if long odds are obtainable. Exile has overthrown the talent on many a memorable occasion, but I think that 122 pounds is a trifle too much for Billy Lakeland's horse.

Raceland is fairly weighted, but I do not think the suburban winner of last year can capture the Brooklyn. Tenny will hardly be able to pack 123 pounds to the front in such fast company. If Gorgo can be gotten on an edge, the daughter of Isonomy should be in the hunt with 110 pounds. There are a couple of three-year-olds in the race that I fancy, of which more anon. In a nutshell, I like Kingston, Proctor Knott and Badge the best at the present writing.

The Suburban appears to be a more open event than the Brooklyn. Kingston will have a merry crowd to beat. What is the matter with Proctor Knott and Prince Royal in that race? They have both been leniently treated by the handicapper. Salvator has been given plenty of weight. Last season Raceland and Prince Royal, who were both crack three year olds of their year, were only asked to carry 120 pounds in these events as four year olds; yet Salvator is given 127 pounds. Salvator performed brilliantly as a three-year-old, but before the end of the season it will probably be discovered that he is not ten pounds better than Proctor Knott. Tea Tray will need watching in this event. Billy Lakeland knows how to fit a horse for a race. If Hindoocraft is all right, and I am not inclined to believe the reports now in circulation, he should be hot stuff.

QUARTER STRETCH GOSSIP.

Charlie Durfee has sold his stallion Raymon to Ab. Cole, of San Bernardino. The consideration was $4,800. Raymon is by Simmons, the coming young son of George Wilkes. The dam is Lady Raymond by Carlisle.

Six mares have been sent north from Santa Anita to be stinted to Cheviot. Atlanta, Queinte, Winona, Ahalo and Santa Anita Belle. L. J. Rose has also sent three of the fillies recently purchased from Palo Alto to be bred to the imported Australian stallion.

A stallion who will be seen on the California track this season is Larco by A. W. Richmond. He is sixteen hands high. Joe Romero told the writer that he has already shown him a 2:20 gait.

When Bonny McGregor was wintered in Los Angeles he was bred to several mares. Hancock Johnston is the lucky possessor of a filly out of a mare by Del Sur. George Carson, of Compton, has a stallion colt out of an A. W. Richmond mare. He is reported to be remarkably well-developed for his age.

The Rosemeade consignment of trotters to be sold in New York early in March will be shipped on Saturday.

On Saturday afternoon Feb 8th, a number of horsemen assembled at the Agricultural Park to witness Semi Tropic's attempt for a record. Walter Maben was in the sulky and he gave the mare a record of 2:24. She made the first half in 1:11. Semi Tropic is by Sultan, dam Lady Mackay, by Silver Threads. Dr. K. W. Wise who owns Semi Tropic, will keep the mare in training in the expectation of still further reducing his records. The judges were Waldo Johnston, N. A. Covarrubias and L. Rickenbaugh. The gentlemen who held the watches were Clifton Bell and B. B. Woods.

Mr. Kennedy, a well known driver in these parts, has just recovered from a severe illness. He is the owner of Danger and other trotters.

B. Benjamin has been appointed Secretary of the Sixth District Agricultural Association.

The Los Angeles Tribune scooped all the big San Francisco dailies in the publication of the weights for the Brooklyn and Suburban Handicaps.

Eugene Hahn, sporting reporter of the San Francisco Examiner, arrived in this city on Sunday.

Clifton Bell, of Denver, is still rusticating in Los Angeles.

The only mare to be bred to Emperor of Norfolk this year is Orange Leaf. The original plan was to breed fifteen mares to the older brother of El Rio Rey.

Los Angeles never looked better in her life. "Pike" Barnes gallops her daily.

I do not think that Pike Barnes has the big head as intimated in the last issue of the BREEDER AND SPORTSMAN, and no one else would think so if they would only drop down to Santa Anita and watch Barnes discuss Lucky Baldwin's mutton and beans with the rubbers and exercise boys every day. He is a very uncommunicative little cuss, however, and believes in the maxim, "Silence is golden."

The Mahoney brothers, the celebrated bookmakers of New York, have been visiting in Southern California. They looked in Baldwin's ranch last week.

A match is on the tapis for $1,000 between Gossiper and Glendine.

DAGWORTH.

Auction Sales.

Two very important auction sales of horses will take place under the management of Killip & Co., on March 1st and 6th. The first comprises a superior lot of roadsters and saddle horses of all gaits, most all of which have been bred and raised by Captain Harris, whose reputation for cultivating fast roadsters and saddle horses to a high degree is sufficient to warrant the public a rare opportunity for supplying their wants without the risk of disappointment. Among these horses there are several pairs of fast roadsters and some extra fine single driving horses. One team Harry Mc and Mate can trot in 2:30 or better.

The attention of ladies is particularly called to this selection of fine horses, as Captain Harris has spent much time in preparing them especially for their use. This stock may be seen at the R. R. Stables, corner Turk and Steiner Sts., from now until day of sale. Terms, cash or an equivelent in approved paper.

The second sale is that of Mrs. Silas Skinner at Woodside Farm, Napa County, on Thursday, March 6th. Catalogues for the same have been distributed broadcast, but those who have not received them, may do so by applying to Killip & Co., 22 Montgomery St.

Anteros Nutwood

—ONE OF THE—

Best Bred Young Stallions in the State.

DESCRIPTION.

Bay horse; black points; no white. Foaled in 1887. Bred by M. Carter, at the Nutwood Stock Farm, by Anteros 2000, by Electioneer, and full brother to Anteeo, 2:16¼, and Antevolo, four-year-old, record 2:19½.

First dam Newark Belle by Nutwood, 2:18¾, and half-brother to Maud S., 2:08¾—Queen of the Turf.

Second dam Tilly, 2:40, by San Bruno, by David Hill, by Vermont Blackhawk. This colt is very large of his age, and looks enough like Sunol to be her full brother.

If there is anything in breeding, this horse ought to make a good one.

Electioneer and Nutwood are his grandsires, both serving mares at $500 each. Nutwood is half-brother to the fastest trotter in the world—Maud S., 2:08¾; Electioneer, the sire of the fastest three-year-old, Sunol, 2:10½.

TERMS.

This Colt will be limited to ten mares, outside of my own, for $50 the season.

Mares not proving in foal can be returned the following season by paying difference in price, if any.

The National Trotting Stallion

PILOT NUTWOOD (Cyrus R.)

Will make the season of 1890 at the stable of T. W. Barstow, corner of San Fernand Street and Wilson Avenue, San Jose.

TERMS.

$50 for the season, with usual return privileges, by paying difference in price. No fee if this horse does not secure a record of 2:30 or better in 1890, barring accidents. Limited to 15 outside mares. Season from February 1st to July 1st, 1890. The best care and attention given to mares, but no responsibility assumed for accidents or escapes. Good pasturage at $3 per month on 100 acres of the best feed in Santa Clara County.

DESCRIPTION.

Pilot Nutwood, 2:42, black horse; small star; foaled in 1881; 15¾ hands; was worked five weeks, and got a record of 2:42 as a three-year-old; he was not worked again until 1888, after having six weeks work, showed his owner a mile in 2:36, and the last half in 1:16½. Sired by the mighty Nutwood, 2:18¾, half-brother to Maud S., 2:08¾—Queen of the Turf.

First dam Belle by Jack Roberts, half-brother to Old St. Clair; 2d dam by Shakespeare, thoroughbred. Jack Roberts by Eclair or Leok, and he by old pacing Pilot, and his dam by Copperbottom.

This gives Pilot Nutwood two crosses of the great Pilot blood, coming through both sire and dam. This is the kind of breeding that breeders should be looking after in order to get to the front.

CHALLENGE.

To back my assertion made in the San Jose Mercury in December last, I will match this horse against any trotting stallion in San Jose, one or two-mile heats, any time after July 1st. The parties accepting this Challenge can set the time and track, and I the right to name the amount. For further particulars, address,

T. W. BARSTOW,
P. O. Box 1288, San Jose, Cal.

THE MAMBRINO Patchen Stallion.

MAMBRINO JR., 1789 (formerly Carr's) Sire of Lady Ellen 2:28 (dam of Ella 2:29), Maud H. 2:30, Mambrino Boy (Carr's) 2:31 1-2.

Will stand at my farm, 2 1-2 miles north of San Jose, on the Milpitas road. Season to commence February 1st, 1890, at $60, with return privilege 1891. Fifteen mares of approved breeding, besides my own, will be given him. Parties owning good mares, performers or out of producing dams, will find an opportunity to breed them on shares, and the best of care taken of them till colt is weaned, if so desired.

PEDIGREE.

MAMBRINO JR., 1789, by Mambrino Patchen 58 [full brother of Lady Thorne 2:18¼] by Mambrino Chief 11. First dam by Mambrino Chief 11; 2nd dam by imp. Jordan [thoroughbred]; 3rd dam by Bertrand, son of Sir Archy; 4th dam by Chewkees, son of Sir Archy.

For further particulars address

GEO. P. BULL,
Box 1067. San Jose, Cal.

The Trotting Stallion

CUPID,

Full Brother to Adonis 2:14,

—Sired by—

The Celebrated SIDNEY 2:19 3-4, and out of Venus.

Will make the season of 1890 at the OAKLAND TROTTING PARK.

PEDIGREE.

CUPID is by Sidney out of Venus by Capt. Webster 10173, record 2:30, and sire of Firestone 2:19. Second dam by Skenandoah 235, sire of Daisy Burns 2:29¾, Erwin Davis (sire of two in the 30 list) and dams of four in the 30 list.

DESCRIPTION.

Cupid is a handsome bright bay 15.3¾ hands high, weighs 1100 lbs.; was foaled in 1886. As a yearling, with very little work he showed quarters in 42 seconds, and at 2 years old, quarters in 38 seconds. As a three year old he has not been worked, but he shows the speed and endurance that must come from his excellent blood lines.

TERMS $50 for the season, with the usual return privileges. Good pasturage near the track at $5 per month. The best of care taken of mares in any way that owners may desire, but no responsibility assumed for accidents or escapes.

For further particulars address

C. O. THORNQUEST,
Oakland Trotting Park, or
C. BAAB, 972 Broadway, Oakland.

THE BUCKINGHAM.
OLD STRAIGHT WHISKIES.
141 Montgomery Street.
303 Bush Street, S. F.
M. J. BALFE, Proprietor.

SEASON 1890.

The Great Son of Buccaneer

SHAMROCK,

Two-Year Old Record of 2:25, beating the World's Record 4 1-2 seconds when made.

SHAMROCK

- Buccaneer 2656, sire of Shamrock, 2:25, 1 yr, 2:29¼, Flight, 2:29, (dam of Fleet, 2:24, at 3 yrs), Flirt (dam of Memo, 3 y. o. trial, 2:22¾, etc.), Orphan Girl, 2:32¾, Prida, 1 yr. 2:43¾; 3 yr. 2:23¾, Cora, 2 y. o. 2:44, etc.
  - Iowa Chief 533, Sire of Cortmanda, 1:26.
    - Green's Bashaw, 2:30 or better. By Vernol's Black Hawk
    - Topsy.
  - Tinsley Maid
    - Flaxtail.
    - Fanny Fern.
- Fernleaf, 2:28, Dam of Goldleaf, 2:11¾, 4 yrs., Shamrock, 2 yrs. 2:25, Thistle, 2 y. o. trial 2:24, 1 y. 3 yrs 2:21¼, etc.
  - Flaxtail, Sire of Fernleaf, 2:28, Prairie Bird, 2:28¾, Empress, 2:29¾, Lightfoot, 2:22.
    - Pruden's Blue Bull.
    - untraced.
  - Fanny Fern
    - Irwin's Tuckahoe, By Harod's Tuckahoe, Sire of dam of Smuggler, 2:15¼.
    - Dau. of Leffler's Consul.

As will be seen from the tabulated pedigree and performances above, Shamrock is not only a phenomenal horse himself, but his ancestors on both sides have shown themselves to be uniformly producers of GREAT and PARTICULARLY early speed, and his record like many others of his family was made in a hotly contested race, instead of a trial against time.

HE IS NOW IN SPLENDID FORM, AND I TRULY BELIEVE WILL LOWER HIS RECORD TO 2:18 THIS YEAR.

TERMS, $100, with usual return privilege, for a limited number of CHOICE mares, season ending June 1st.

Electo.

By Antevolo 2:19¼ by Electioneer, dam Captain Webster (sire of dam of Adonis 2:16), by Williamson's Belmont.

Electo, while but three years old this spring, is, as well as being grandly bred, a great individual.

TERMS, $50, with the usual return privilege, limited to 15 approved mares. Season to end June 1st.

Imported Cleveland bay stallion

Elegance.

(Registered in Cleveland Bay Stud Book No. 75.) Prize winner over twenty of his own breed in the GREAT YORKSHIRE SHOW OF ENGLAND.

The Cleveland Bays are the most prepotent coach horses in the world, and their get from ordinary mares makes the most stylish and serviceable horses for that purpose that can be raised. Rich bays with black points having the preference over ALL OTHERS.

TERMS, $25, with usual return privilege, season ending July 1st.

Care taken but no responsibility assumed for accidents or escapes. Pasturage, $5 per month. For further particulars call at or address me at my hospital, where horses will make the season.

G. W. STIMPSON, V. S.
Veterinary Hospital, 19th St., near San Pablo Ave, Oakland, Cal.

WOODNUT

(Weatherhead's) by Nutwood 600

Sire of Belmont Boy, 2:15, pacer, Woodnut, 2:16¼, Felix, 2:18¾, Dawn, 2:18¾, Maggie E., 2:19¾, Irma, 2:18¾, and 26 others in 2:30 or better; 1st dam Flora, 2:29¾, trial 2:26, dam of Chrisman's Hambletonian, sire of Steve Whipple, 2:23, Kate Agnew, 2:29¼, by Chieftain 721, sire of Defiance 2:17¾ pacing and 2:24 trotting, Cairo, 2:26, Onward, 2:24, pacer; second dam by Wilson's Leaman.

Woodnut is a beautiful bay with black points, 15½ hands high, weighing 1,075 pounds. His colts are all larger than himself, and sell readily for road and carriage purposes, being of good color and very docile, yet prompt to obey, and always ready.

Service fee, $25, with usual privileges. Colts and fillies from Tilton Almont, Patchen, Stockbridge Chief, and other desirable crosses, FOR SALE. For further particulars, pedigrees, or any communication in horse matters, address

JAS. WEATHERHEAD, Prop.
San Jose, Cal.

The Fast Trotting Stallion

REDWOOD.

Four-Year-Old Record 2:24 1-2

Will make the season of 1890—February 1st to July 1st—at the

OAKLAND RACE TRACK.

REDWOOD is a dark bay colt, 15.2¾ hands high, weighs 1150 lbs. Foaled in 1884, by Anteeo, 2:16¼, sire of Alfred G., 2:19¾. Anteeo is by Electioneer. First dam Lou Milton, by Milton Medium; second dam Old Ely, a thoroughbred mare brought from the East in 1871 by W. C. Ralston, Esq.

Redwood's sire was out of Columbine by A. W. Richmond, the sire of the pacers Arrow 2:13¾, and Elwood 2:23, and the trotters Romero, 2:19¾, and Lou Rose, 2:27. Redwood has shown a quarter in 33 seconds.

Terms $100

For the season. Mares not proving with foal may be returned next season free of charge, provided Redwood remains the property of the present owners. Good pasturage at $5 per month. No responsibility assumed for escapes or accidents. Service fees payable before removal of the mare. Limited to 40 approved mares. For further particulars address

A. McFADYEN.
Race track, Oakland, Cal.

The Trotting Stallion

BONANZA 2:29½

Will make the season of 1890, from February 1st to July 1st, at the OAKLAND TROTTING PARK.

PEDIGREE.

BONANZA, 2:29¾.

- Arthurton 365, Sire of Arab, 2:15, Joe Arthurton 2:20¾, Lady Rascol, 2:26½. Dams of Grandee, 2:23½, Hidalgo, 2:27.
  - Hambletonian 10, Sire of 41 in 2:30 list, Sires of 117 of the sires of 567 in 2:30 list.
  - Imogene, by Am. Star 14, Dam of Leland 1930, Sire of Clara, 2:21, Miss Leland, 2:25½, Hades, 2:27¾.
- Sister, Dam of Albert W., 2:20.
  - John Nelson 187, Sire of Nerea, 2:24½, Gov. Stanford, 2:27¾, Aurora, 2:27, Nemo, 2:30.
  - Lamott Mare, Dam of Aurora, 2:27; g d of Arol, 2:24¾.

DESCRIPTION.

BONANZA is a very handsome chestnut of commanding form and splendid proportions. He stands nearly 16 hands high, is remarkably intelligent, level headed and pure gaited. His record is no mark of his speed. He is a great foal getter, and his colts are handsome rangy animals.

TERMS. $40 for the season, with the usual return privileges. Excellent pasturage near the track at $5 per month. The best of care taken of mares, but no responsibility assumed for accidents or escapes.

For further particulars, address

RICHARD HAVEY,
Oakland Trotting Park, Oakland.

The Hambletonian Stallion 10178.

CHRISMAN'S HAMBLETONIAN, Sire of Steve Whipple, 2:23, Kate Agnew, 2:29¾, etc.

- Whipple's Hambletonian, Sire of 14 trotters and 1 pacer from 2:19 to 2:30, and 7 sons with 8 performers from 2:21¼ to 2:30, and dams of 6 from 2:19½ to 2:30.
  - Guy Miller, By Hambletonian 10.
  - Martha Washington, Dam of Speculation 928, Sire of Crown Pt. 2:24, Oakland Maid, 2:22¾, Gracie S., 2:23¾, and dam of Waterford, 2:27.
- Flora, 2:29¾, trial, 2:26. Dam of Chrisman's Hambletonian, sire of Steve Whipple, 2:23, Kate Agnew, 2:29¾.
  - Chieftain 721, sire of Defiance, 2:24 and 2:17¾, pacing; Cairo, 2:26, and Onward, 2:24, pacer.
  - daughter of Wilson's Leamon.

Stud season now on till the 1st of August, 1890, at $40 each mare, with return privilege in 1891, provided stallion and mare, or either, do not change owners. Good pasture at hand, and comfortable accommodation for brood mares and colts. For further particulars, address

JESSE CHRISMAN, Proprietor.
San Jose, Cal.

CALIFORNIA

NUTWOOD

Will stand for mares the season of 1890, commencing February 15th, and ending July 15th, at the NUTWOOD STOCK FARM, one mile from Irvington.

DESCRIPTION AND PEDIGREE.

He is a dark chestnut, with star in forehead; foaled September 16th, 1881; is 16 hands 1½ inches high and weighs 1250 pounds. Has a beautiful flowing mane and tail, with remarkable style and lofty carriage, a bold, open movement like his sire, but has never been handled for speed. He moves and looks like his sire, except that he is a larger horse.

CALIFORNIA NUTWOOD by Nutwood, record 2:18¾, has 31 trotters and pacers with records from 2:15 to 2:30, and put 8 in the 2:30 list in 1889. He is the only horse that ever lived with a record under 2:20 that produced five under 2:20. He is now serving mares at Dubuque, Iowa, at $500 for the season, and his colts at yearlings sell from $2500 to $5000 each. He is out of the dam of Maud S., record 2:08¾.

Nutwood, by Alexander's Belmont, sire of 82 with records from 2:15½ to 2:30. Alexander's Belmont by Alexander's Abdallah, sire of Goldsmiths Maid, record 2:14, and 5 others in 2:30 list. Alexander's Abdallah, by Rysdyk's Hambletonian, sire of 41 with records from 2:17¼ to 2:30, and is the founder of the Hambletonian family.

FANNY PATCHEN, dam of California Nutwood, by George M. Patchen Jr., record 2:27, and sire of Wells Fargo, 2:18½, Sam Purdy 2:20½, Ben Ali 2:20¾, and 7 others from 2:21 to 2:30. He has 7 sons who together produced 12 trotters in 2:30 list, and 5 daughters who together produced 5 trotters and 1 pacer in 2:30 or better. He sired Alexander 2:31½. Alexander sired Alex. Button 2:26½; Alex. Button sired Yolo Maid, pacing record 2:14 at 4 years old, the fastest on record; George M. Patchen Jr., by George M. Patchen 2:23½, is sire of Lucy 2:18¼, and 3 others in the 2:30 list; he has 12 sons who together produced 40 trotters from 2:14½ to 2:30, and 6 daughters who together produced 8 trotters in 2:30 list or better, he is grand sire of Hopeful 2:14¾, and best wagon record 2:16½, and sire of the granddam of Stamboul 2:12½.

George M. Patchen, by Cassius M. Clay, and he by Henry Clay, founder of the Clay family.

Laura, second dam of California Nutwood, was a fine large bay mare, a very fast roadster brought from Chicago by Wm. Wilson, of San Jose, and is said to have made a record of 2.36 in Chicago. Pedigree not traced.

TERMS.

$40 for the season, payable invariably before the animal is removed. Mares not proving in foal can be returned free next season. Pasturage $3 per month, but no liability for accidents or escapes.

For further particulars address the owner,

MARTIN CARTER,
Newark, Alameda Co., Cal., or Irvington, Alameda County, Cal.

HENRY J. COX — W. S. JOHNSON

The "EDWIN C."

40 EDDY STREET.

Cor. of Mason, San Francisco.

(Private Entrance Mason Street.)

Vineland Stock Farm

Whippleton 1883,

Sire of

LILY STANLEY	Record	2:17½
HOMESTAKE	"	2:16½
FLORA B.	"	2:27
CORA C.	"	2:31½
BLACK PRINCE	"	2:36½
RACHEL	"	2:38
PRINCE W.	"	2:40

WHIPPLETON is not only the sire of trotters, but he is the greatest sire of Carriage Horses on the Pacific Coast. Some of the best carriage and road teams in San Francisco are sired by Whippleton. A carriage team by Whippleton received First Premium at Napa, Petaluma, Oakland, Sacramento, Stockton and San Jose. Whippleton and his colts have never been beaten in the show ring.

DESCRIPTION.

WHIPPLETON is black, tan muzzle and flanks, 17 hands, and weighs 1,400 lbs. Most of his colts are 16 hands or over, and with a few exceptions, bay, brown or black. He never sired a sorrel or white face colt. (If he does, I agree to refund service money.)

PEDIGREE.

WHIPPLETON, sired by Hambletonian Jr. (sire of Hancock 2:29), by Whipple's Hambletonian (sire of Graves, 2:19, Westfield, 2:20¼, Express, 2:24, and 11 others in the 2:30 list), dam Lady Livingston (dam of Lady Blanchard, 2:26¾, Bloomfield Maid, trial 2:22), by General Taylor (sire of the dams of Wells Fargo, 2:18¾, Nerea, 2:23¾, Bickford, 2:29¾, Lady Blanchard, 2:26¾, etc., and sire of grandam of Hazel Wilkes, 2:20) by the Morse Horse 6, sire of Norman 25 (sire of Lulu, 2:14¾, May Queen 2:20, etc.).

TERMS at $40, limited to 20 mares, for the season, usual return privileges. I would like to get about ten well bred mares with the proper combination of blood to breed to Whippleton on shares this season.

Alcona 730.

Sire of

FLORA BELLE	Record	2:24
CLAY DUKE	"	2:31½

ALCONA will be a great sire, but four of his colts have ever been trained, and all have shown full miles better than 2:30, and two of them as good as 2:30. Two of his first sons each sired a colt as a two-year-old, and last season one as a four-year-old trotted a full mile in 2:22¾, and the other, a three-year-old, a mile in 2:31. With opportunities, Alcona is destined to be one of Almont's best sons. Almont, for his opportunities, is beyond doubt the most prepotent sire of his age. He has 36 representatives in the 2:30 list; 49 sons and 22 daughters that have already produced 2:30 performers. Almont died five years ago at 20 years old. If he lived he would be but 26 years old.

PEDIGREE.

ALCONA sired by the great Almont (sire of Westmont 2:13¾, Fanny Witherspoon 2:16¾, Piedmont 2:17¼, and 34 others with records better than 2:30, and grandsire of Belle Hamlin 2:12¾, etc.); by Alexander's Abdallah (sire of Goldsmith Maid 2:14), he by Rysdyk's Hambletonian. Alcona's dam, Queen Mary by Mambrino Chief (sire of Lady Thorne 2:18 1-4, and 5 others in the 2:30 list, and sire of the dams of Director 2:17, Piedmont 2:17¼, Onward 2:25 1-4, Red Wilkes, Almont, Belmont and many other noted sires).

DESCRIPTION.

Alcona is a beautiful chestnut 16 3 1-2 hands high, and weighs 1300 lbs. His colts possess speed, style, finish and beauty, and if they don't trot they command the highest prices for carriage horses.

$40 for the season. Usual return privilege.

Grandissimo,

Full Brother to GRANDEE, Three Year Old Record 2:23 1-2.

Sired by Le Grande (son of Almont and out of Jessie Pepper, by Mambrino Chief. Jessie Pepper is the dam of Ione 2:17 1-2, Alpha 2:23 1-2, and granddam of Montezuma 2:29¼. First dam Norma (dam of Grandee 2:23 1-2), by Arthurton (sire of Arab 2:15, Joe Arthurton 2:20 1-2, etc.); second dam Nourmahal 2:[illegible] (full sister to A. W. Richmond, sire of Arrow 2:13¾, Romero 2:19, and sire of the dams of Antevolo 2:19 1-4, and Anteeo 2:16 1-4, sire of Alfred G 2:19¾ and Redwood 2:24 1-2.

GRANDISSIMO, with limited training as a three year old last year showed 1-4 mile in 37 seconds, and barring accidents, will trot fast next fall.

Limited to 20 mares at $50 each; usual return privileges.

Season on Grandissimo ends June 1st, 1890.

Season on Whippleton and Alcona ends July 1st, 1890.

Best kind of pasturage at $4 per month. Mares kept in any manner desired.

For further particulars send for circular or call at stables, one mile south of St. Helena.

FRED W. LOEBER,
St. Helena, Napa Co., Cal.

The Trotting Stallion

G & M

FULL BROTHER TO

ALFRED G, 2:19¾.

(Who has been taken to Kentucky to stand at $200)

Will make the season of 1890 from FEBRUARY 1st to JULY 1st, at

SANTA ROSA.

G. & M. is by Anteeo, 2:16¼; was foaled 1886; first dam Rosa B. by Speculation (son of Hambletonian 10); 2d dam Elizabeth by Alexander 490; 3d dam Nora by imp. Glencoe. Anteeo is by Electioneer, out of Columbine by A. W. Richmond 1687.

G. & M. is a handsome dark bay; stands 15-2 1-4 hands high, and weighs 1080 pounds. Gameness, stoutness, speed and stamina are indelibly impressed in every line of the pedigree of G. & M. Owners of brood mares in search of these qualities, will do well to patronize this promising colt.

PHILOSOPHER,

Foaled 1886 by Pilot Wilkes 2987; first dam Bella by George Wilkes 519; second dam by Bell Morgan 81.

Philosopher's sire, Pilot Wilkes 2987, is by George Wilkes 519, dam Grace (the dam of Alice Woodburn etc.), by Pilot Jr. 12, grandam by Orphan Boy.

Will make the season of 1890, from FEBRUARY 1st to JULY 1st, at Santa Rosa.

TERMS for the season:

G. & M., $50,

PHILOSOPHER, $30,

with privilege of returning mares that do not prove in foal the next season free of charge, provided the horse bred to remains the property of the present owners. Good pasturage at $3 per month. No responsibility assumed for accidents or escapes. Service fee payable before removal of the mare. For further particulars, address

GEO. E. GUERNE,
Santa Rosa, Cal.

Race Track for Sale.

The One Mile Track & Grounds

—OF THE—

Sonoma County Agricul'l Park Association,

Situated at

SANTA ROSA, CALIFORNIA.

Consisting of 84 acres fine agricultural land, 700 Box and Cattle Stalls, a two story Pavilion 60x120, commodious grand stand, and many out-buildings, a lovely Park of 16 acres, rolling ground, ornamental, nut and native oak trees; a fine cypress "wind break" hedge ¾ mile around the track, and abundant water facilities. This elegant property will be sold at a great bargain, and possession given immediately if required. Sealed bids for same will be received up to February 11th, 1890.

B. M. SPENCER, Secretary.

GUY E. GROSSE, President.

For Sale

A FIRST-CLASS

Napa County Farm

—OR—

STOCK RANCH,

800 Acres Improved,

SITUATED TWO AND A HALF MILES FROM NAPA CITY, with good roads leading thereto, a good hard finished house of nine rooms, with all modern improvements, streams running all summer, a great amount of live oak and black oak timber. It lies in a fruit belt, surrounded by fine vineyards and orchards growing upon the same quality of soil, and originally a part of this tract. About one-half hill, and one-half rolling land, but none of it is steep and all easily cultivated, splendidly situated for the breeding of fine horses. Price, $65 per acre. Further particulars given at this office.

BREEDER AND SPORTSMAN,

313 Bush St.

Stallion for Sale

AT A BARGAIN.

Full Brother to Fairmont.

By Piedmont, dam Queen by Garibaldi—see State Fair Edition of BREEDER AND SPORTSMAN, September 14, 1889, for description of Fairmont—three years old, solid bay. Can trot a 2:40 gait or better. Sound in every particular. Can be seen at Oakland Trotting Park, Oakland.

P. J. WILLIAMS.

Attention Stockmen!

FOR SALE

At Chowchilla Ranch,

Thoroughbred Durham Cattle

Three Hundred Young DAIRY COWS, 2000 graded SHE CATTLE, Yearlings and up; a fine lot of high grade Durham Bulls; also have Mares, Horses, Mules and Norman Colts.

For particulars, apply to

ISAAC BIRD, JR., Supt.,

Merced, California.

FOR SALE

AT

Vineland Stock Farm

STALLIONS, BROODMARES AND FILLIES

ONE STALLION FIVE YEARS OLD, SEAL-BROWN, by WHIPPLETON (sire of Lily Stanley, 2:17 1-2, Homestake 2:16 1-2, etc.), dam Sally Gorham by Werner's Rattler. This horse is scarcely 15 1-2 hands high, but very compactly built. He breeds exceptionally large and well finished colts. Any one understanding the business could clear him in one season, or he would make a No. 1 road horse, as he can trot a 40 gait any time.

ONE THREE-YEAR-OLD, SEAL-BROWN, by WHIPPLETON (sire of Lilly Stanley, 2:17 1-2, Homestake 2:16 1-2, etc.) dam Sally Gorham, etc. This ought to make a great General Purpose sire, and with opportunities get trotters, as he is compact, strong-boned, and will measure when grown about 16 hands and weighs 1,300 lbs. With a little road work last fall he developed a wonderful burst of speed.

ONE THREE-YEAR-OLD, BLACK, by WHIPPLETON (sire of Lilly Stanley, 2:17 1-2, etc.), dam by Nauboc (sire of the dam of Eva W., 2:23 1-2, etc.), full brother to Thomas Jefferson, 2:23. This horse will be fully 16 1-2 hands high. He is smooth, rapid gaited and from size and conformation should breed, like his sire, large, rangy, finished colts.

ONE TWO-YEAR-OLD, BRIGHT CHESTNUT, sired by DAWN 2:18¾, dam Alida (dam of Directa, three-year-old record 2:31¼, trial 2:26) by Admiral (sire of sister 2:19 1-2, Nona Y 2:26, etc.). This colt is the making of an extraordinary horse. He is large boned and will be over sixteen hands high when grown; he is of the true Nutwood type, is clean gaited and can lead a piece as fast as any man's colt.

ONE TWO-YEAR-OLD, BLOOD BAY, (full brother to Alcona Jr. sire of Silas Skinner, trial 2:23) sired by ALCONA (sire of Flora Belle 2:24, etc.,) dam Madonna by Cassius M. Clay Jr. This colt will make a trotter and a great stock horse if developed; he has the combined blood of Almont, Mambrino Chief, Cassius M. Clay Jr. and Joe Downing.

These colts are all sound and promising. The only reason I offer them for sale is, that I have three aged stallions in use, and the surplus is growing on me. If I were starting a breeding business for profit, I should consider either of these colts a representative to commence with. Also brood mares and fillies for sale. Correspondence solicited.

FRED. W. LOESER, St. Helena, Napa Co., Cal.

Woodside Farm

IMPORTANT SALE OF

Standard Trotting Mares Young Stallions and Fillies,

ROAD AND DRIVING HORSES

Farming Implements, Etc.

By direction of MRS. SILAS SKINNER.

Mrs. Skinner having determined to retire permanently from the breeding of Fine Stock, has decided to offer at

PUBLIC AUCTION

Thursday, March 6, '90,

at 12 M., on the Premises.

THE WELL-KNOWN

WOODSIDE FARM,

Near Napa,

together with all the highly bred trotting stock thereon.

The brood mares at Woodside are among the choicest in the State. Among them are mares by Almont, dam by Alexander's Abdallah; by Cassius M. Clay Jr., dam by Joe Downing; by Cassius M. Clay Jr., dam by Richelieu son of Mambrino Chief: by Duke of Orange Jr., dam by Cassius M. Clay Jr.; by Almont Mambrino, dam by Blood's Black Hawk; by Alcona—dam Fontana, dam of Flora Belle, 2:24, and Silas Skinner, trial 2 23¼—by Almont; by Alcona Clay—dam Metamora, dam of Clay Duke, 2:31¼—by Duke of Orange Jr. These mares have been bred to Director, Noonday, Mountain Boy and Wildwood, and are with foal. The young stallions are by Sirka, son of Alaska, by Electioneer, Whippleton, sire of Lillie Stanley, 2:17¼, Alcona Clay, etc. About twenty head well-bred trotting and driving animals will be sold in addition to the standard bred horses.

Catalogues giving extended pedigrees and full information are being prepared, and will be forwarded upon application.

At the conclusion of sale of horses,

WOODSIDE FARM

will be sold.

WOODSIDE FARM is situated three and a half miles from Napa City, up the river, upon what is known as the middle or big ranch road. It contains 87 1-2 acres of the choicest quality of land for alfalfa or any kind of grain, 40 acres being now in alfalfa over a foot high. The land produces from four to six tons of hay to the acre, of choice quality. Five of the fields are in pasture, four in alfalfa, one in timothy, the other kept in hay or grain necessary for stock, though well adapted for alfalfa. There is a nice orchard, small vineyard, and comfortable dwelling house of nine rooms. There is a good school house directly opposite, the best in the County. As to its adaptability as a stock ranch: there is living water in every field, and plenty of it, corrals and stock yards, stable room for forty horses, besides seven good box stalls two good stables, granery, etc. It is within two miles of the Napa Agricultural Society's race track, the finest constructed in the State for years. Should there not be sufficient land, 61 acres adjoining can be purchased at reasonable figures.

There is no more eligible location in the State for a small stock farm, and this affords a rare opportunity, with the stock, to at once engage in this remunerative pursuit.

The sale will be positive. Upon all sales of Live Stock and personal property, one years' credit will be given on approved notes. Interest 10 per cent. per annum. Three per cent. discount for cash.

Upon Land, one-half cash: balance can remain upon mortgage for a term of years to suit purchasers. Interest eight per cent. per annum.

Vehicles will be in attendance at Napa Depot to convey parties to the farm. Lunch will be served upon the ground.

Mrs. Skinner having large interests in Oregon which will require her personal attention during the greater portion of the year, compels the sale of the Woodside Farm.

Parties are invited to visit the farm and look over the stock. The undersigned will be glad to give any information required, either as to stock or ranch.

KILLIP & CO.

Live Stock Auctioneers,

22 Montgomery St., S. F.

For Sale

A HALF BROTHER TO

ALMONT PATCHEN,

(2:15, trial 2:13 3-4),

JUANITO JR. is a beautiful bright bay, black points, with no white, foaled 1886. As a colt he has given much more promise than did Almont Patchen at the same age. Instead of being a pacer, he is a good square trotter, with every indication of great speed, and is so gentle and kind, that a lady can drive him. The owner's only reason for selling him is that business calls him away from this section of the State. He will be sold at a reasonable figure. This is a splendid opportunity for a gentleman to secure a first-class trotter at a very low figure.

The pedigree of Juanita Jr. is by Juanita (sire of Almont Patchen), dam Nettie Moore by Old Tom Moore. For further particulars, address

JUANITA JR.,

Santa Clara P. O., Cal.

Antevolo Colt

For Sale.

AVOLO REX, foaled February 22, 1888; dam Catchup by Rustic; grandam Huntress by Don Victor; g g dam Betty Denice by American Boy Jr. Is 15.1 hands high, well developed, muscular, and without a blemish. Has a very gentle disposition, and shows speed and a good gait. Apply

HOME FURNISHING CO.,

118 Fifth Street, S. F., Cal.

For Sale

A First-Class.

BREEDING FARM.

Of 800 Acres.

Four hours' ride from the city. Good roads to a first class track. Climate unexcelled. Plenty of wood and running water.

For further information apply to the office of the

BREEDER AND SPORTSMAN,

San Francisco.

313 Bush Street.

First Special Auction Sale

—OF—

HORSES,

For account of CAPT. BEN. E. HARRIS,

On Saturday, March 1,'90

At the Cor. TURK and STEINER STS.,

WE WILL SELL AT

Public Auction

A CATALOGUE OF 25 HEAD OF SUPERIOR ROADSTERS AND SADDLE-HORSES OF ALL GAITS.

Also a few select colts, mares and fillies of royal breeding, most all of which have been bred, raised and broken by Captain Harris, whose reputation for the culture of swift roadsters and saddle horses to a high degree, is sufficient to warrant the public a rare opportunity for supplying their wants without the risk of disappointment. Among the lot there are several pairs of roadsters, one of which can trot in 2:30, besides a number of extra fine single flyers.

☞ **The attention of ladies is particularly called to this sale, as many of the animals have been prepared especially for their use and safety.**

This stock may be seen at the owner's stables, corner of Turk and Steiner Streets, from now until day of sale.

TERMS cash, or an equivalent in approved paper. Catalogues at our office.

KILLIP & CO.,

Live Stock Auctioneers.

22 Montgomery St., S. F.

For Sale.

14

Pure bred

PERCHERONS.

Stallions and Mares.

OF ALL AGES.

Part Imported, and all Registered Proof.

For further information, address

E. J. TURNER, Hollister, Cal.

Well bred Stallions

FOR SALE.

SATINWOOD

Is 3 years old, stands 16.1 hands high and weighs 1150 pounds; is a beautiful dark chestnut; was sired by Wormwood, a full brother to Eva W (2:25) and Redwood (2:27). First dam by John Nelson; second dam by Argyle; third dam Blackhawk Wormwood by Nutwood 2 18 3-4, sire of Woonut 2:16 1-4; dam the Cropsy Mare by Nauboc, dam Gipsy Queen by George M. Patchen; second dam Capt. Roberts Mare. Nutwood 2:18 3-4, by Belmont, dam Miss Russell (dam of Maud S, 2:08 3-4. Belmont, by Abdallah (sire of Goldsmith Maid) dam Belle by Mambrino Chief. Miss Russell, by Pilot Jr. dam Sally Russell by Boston.

Full pedigree and all particulars on application.

J. A. C.

Sorrell stallion, foaled April 22nd, 1887. Bred by Wm. Jeffries of San Francisco, Cal. sired by C. C. Bemis' Lancelot. First dam Bay Mare Nellie, sired by Ulster Chief he by Rysdyk's Hambletonian, her dam by Kentucky Hunter, noted for his speed and endurance (see Stud Book).

For further particulars apply to

J. A. CARLETON,

1302 Broadway, Oakland, Cal.

ARGONAUT HERD.

POLLED ABERDEEN—ANGUS CATTLE.

Thirty head choice pure bred and high grade (cross bred) HEIFERS and a few grand young BULLS for sale at reasonable prices. A fine opportunity for persons wishing to establish choice herds or change their bulls. Representatives from this herd were grand prize winners at the last California State Fair. Address

DR. G. M. DIXON,

Sacramento, Cal.

NOTICE.

C. BRUCE LOWE,

Pedigree Stock Agent,

19 Bligh Street,

SYDNEY, New South Wales.

Reference—J. B. HAGGIN, ESQ.

HOLLYWOOD BREEDING FARM.

MOUNTAIN BOY 4841.

Br s MOUNTAIN BOY, 4841, bred by Charles Backman, Orange County, New York, foaled 1882, sire Kentucky Prince 2470, dam Elise, sister to Elaine, by Messenger Duroc 106; grandam Green Mountain Maid, 3d dam, Shanghai Mary, will serve a limited number of mares at $100 the season.

ELECTION.

Bay stallion ELECTION, bred at Senator Stanford's Palo Alto Stock Farm, foaled 1884, sire Electioneer, dam Lizzie H. by Whipple's Hambletonian 725, grandam Lizzie Harris (by Comus son of Green's Bashaw 50), great grandam by Arnold Harris, thoroughbred.

Election is one of the handsomest bloodlike sons of Electioneer, and with his thoroughbred cross through Arnold Harris should prove invaluable as a sire. TERMS, $100 the season.

KAFIR.

B c KAFIR, bred by L. J. Rose, Los Angeles, foaled 1887, sire Alcazar, 2:20½, dam Flower Girl by Arthurton, sire of Arab, 2:15, grandam Flora by General McClellan, 144, sire of three in 2:30 list, great grand dam by Langford, he by Williamson's Belmont, will serve a limited number of mares at $50 the season.

WOODSIDE.

Ch c WOODSIDE, sire Woodnut, 2:16½; 1st dam Veronica by Alcona, 730; 2nd dam Fontana by Almont 33; 3rd dam Fannie Williams by Alexander's Abdallah, 15. Book full.

MART BOORHEM.

B c MART BOORHEM, by Sydney, 2:19¾; 1st dam Towhead by Echo. This colt is a full brother to St. Nicholas who showed a mile in 2:27¼ at three years old. TERMS, $25 the season.

REVEILLE.

The well known thoroughbred stallion REVEILLE, by Shiloh, dam by Norfolk. Reveille is a brother to John Treat and is the sire of Tycoon and Gladstone. TERMS, $25 the season.

Hollywood is nicely situated three miles from Vallejo on the Napa road. Good pasturage and every care will be taken of mares at reasonable rates. For further particulars, apply,

B. C. HOLLY, Vallejo.

CANNON BALL, 8820

BY SIMMONS 2744.

RECORD 2:28, (Full Brother to Rosa Wilkes, 2:18 1-4), Sire of Nine in 2:30 List at 10 Years Old.

First dam Gurgle, pacing record 2:20; trial of 2:15¼ for W. H. Crawford; by Pocahontas Boy, sire of Buffalo Girl, 2:12¼; Raven Boy, 2:15¼, and ten others in the list.

Second dam Matlock by Grey Diomed.

Third dam by Tom Hal.

DESCRIPTION.

Brown bay, right hind foot and left inside hind heel white. Foaled May 20, 1887. Bred by W. H. Wilson, Abdallah Park, Cynthiana, Ky.

He is a grand individual, large boned, fine size and appearance. When fully matured will probably be 16 hands, and weigh 1200 lbs.

Is of speedy conformation and level headed. His blood lines are stout and fashionable, being the Wilkes and Mambrino Patchen on pacing and thoroughbred foundations, and from a family of producers on both sides.

Can be seen until February 1st at Agricultural Park, Los Angeles, in charge of C. A. Durfee, after which he will serve ten approved mares at $40 the season, with usual privilege of return in 1891, at Lockhaven Stock Farm, Burbank, Cal. Mares kept on grass $5 per month, and extra charge where grain and alfalfa are fed. For further particulars, address

O. H. LOCKHART, Proprietor,

Lockhaven Stock Farm,

Burbank, Cal.

Nine Miles from Los Angeles.

The Pure Trotting-bred Stallion

ILLUSTRIOUS

STANDARD No. 4178.

DESCRIPTION.

Dark bay, black points, 15 1-2 hands high, weight 1000 pounds, foaled May 30, 1886; bred by General W. T. Withers, Lexington, Ky.

PEDIGREE.

By Happy Medium, sire of Maxey Cobb 2:13¼ and 62 with records of 2:30 or better. First dam Abdallietta by Cassius M. Clay Jr., sire of Durango 2:23¼, Harry Clay 2:23½ and sire of the dams of Minnehaha, Bertha 2:27¼, Charley West 2:28¼, Grandmont 2:25 1-2, Lottie K 2:26¼, Mambrino Diamond 2:26, Richwood 2 28 1-2, Topsy 2:26¼, Happy Thought 2:22 1-2, Pequot 2:23 1-2, Fairlawn Medium 2:27 1-2, Folley 2:27¼ and Mambrino Boy 2:28 1-2; second dam Laura Crockett by Almont, sire of Westmont 2:13¾, Puritan 2:16, Fanny Witherspoon 2:16¼, Piedmont 2:17¼, Aldine 2:19¼ and 37 with records better than 2:30; third dam Sally Tee by Alexander's Abdallah, sire of Goldsmith Maid 2:14; fourth dam Kate Crockett, the dam of Lulu 2:14¾, by imp Hooton.

Illustrious is a horse of extra fine finish, large clean bone, good feet, back short and strong, loins and quarters well muscled, and powerful. He has a kind disposition and splendid trotting action, and is as handsome and bloodlike in form and finish as any trotting stallion in the land.

He is pronounced by his breeder, General Withers, to be the best bred son of Happy Medium living, and is undoubtedly one of the very best bred trotting stallions in the State. He has had but six weeks' regular training, and a part of that time was sick with epizootic, but was trotted quarters in 39 1-4 seconds, and barring accidents will certainly trot better than 2:30 this season.

TERMS—$50 the season. Mares not proving with foal may be returned next year free.

Good pasturage at $3 per month.

Season to begin February 1st and end June 15th.

GEO. A. STONE,

Santa Rosa, Cal.

Guenoc Stud Farm, Lake Co., Cal.

Imp. GREENBACK

(Sire of the English winners Greenlight, Greenjacket, Greenshank, Greenwave and Greenhorn)

By Dollar, dam Music, by Stockwell. $100 the Season

ST. SAVIOR,

(FULL BROTHER TO EOLE)

By Eolus, dam War Song, by War Dance. $100 the Season.

PASTURAGE, $5 PER MONTH.

With right to return the following year if mare does not prove with foal. The best of care taken, but no liability for accidents or escapes. Mares shipped to C. W. ABY, care ST. HELENA STABLES, St. Helena Napa County, will be taken in charge by competent men.

For further information write to

DR. C. W. ABY, Middletown, Lake County, Cal.

SOUTHER FARM

P. O. Box 208. San Leandro, Cal.

1½ miles northwest of San Leandro; 3 miles southeast of Oakland. Turn off county road between above places at "Stanley Road," ¼ mile north of San Leandro.

Horses boarded at all times in any manner desired. Best of care but no responsibility for accidents. Colts broken and handled for the road or track. Terms reasonable.

Glen Fortune,	Jester D,	El Benton,	Figaro,
By Electioneer.	By Almont.	By Electioneer.	Hambletonian 725
$50 for 1889.	$50 for 1890.	Limited to 5 mares.	Limited to 12 mares
		Book Full.	Book Full.

If horses are to last for a profitable time they must occasionally have a change from hard pavements, wooden floors, and dry, hard feed.

THE SOUTHER FARM

Has Green Feed the Year Round,

and feeds Hay in connection with the green feed, which a horse must have if he is to thrive. Every animal is given

A Dry, Warm Place to Sleep,

No matter how stormy the weather. All Stock under cover when it rains.

VISITORS WELCOME ANY DAY EXCEPT SUNDAY.

Write to the above address for references, circulars and price lists. Terms reasonable.

GILBERT TOMPKINS, Proprietor.

SANMATEO STOCKFARM

HOME OF GUY WILKES,

Record, 2:15 1-4.

Guy Wilkes' Book is full for 1890, and positively no more mares will be received. Book now open for 1891, at $500 the Season.

Sable Wilkes, three-year-old record 2:18, will be allowed to serve 25 mares in addition to those already engaged at $250 the season of 1890. SABLE Wilkes, 15½ hands, black horse, by Guy Wilkes, first dam Sable by The Moor; second dam Gretchen by Mambrino Pilot; third dam Kitty Kirkman by Canada Chief; fourth dam by Fanning's Tobe; fifth dam by imp. Leviathan.

Leo Wilkes, brown horse, four years, 16 hands, full brother to Sable Wilkes, will be allowed to serve 30 mares at $100 the season

Mares not proving with foal may be returned the following season free of service fee. Parties engaging the services of any of the above horses must send a deposit of 10 per cent. of service money with engagement. Pasturage $6 per month, and when the condition of the animal requires it, hay or grain, or both, are fed, the charge will be $12 50 per month. Good care will be taken of all mares sent to the Farm, but no liability will be assumed for accidents or escapes.

All bills are due at time of service, but must be paid by August 1st of each year. No stock will be allowed to leave the place until all bills are paid.

WILLIAM CORBITT.
San Mateo Stock Farm.

Poplar Grove Breeding FARM.

Standard-bred Trotters, Colts and Fillies.

The get of CLOVIS, 4909; PASHA, 2039; APEX, 2935,

For Sale.

Address S. N. STRAUBE, Poplar Grove Breeding Farm,

Fresno, Cal.

Inspection by intending purchasers invited, and information by mail.

1890 Three Anteeo Stallions 1890

SUNSET, 5 years old, by Anteeo
ANTEEOF, 4 years old, by Anteeo
ANTEEOP, 3 years old, by Anteeo

ANTEEO. Standard 7868 Record, 2:16 1-4 ... by Stanford's Electioneer, and dam Columbine.

DESCRIPTIONS, PEDIGREES AND CONDITIONS.

"SUNSET" is a rich, dark bay, small star on forehead, portion of hind left foot white; was foaled March 11, 1885; is by ANTEEO and the inbred HAMBLETONIAN mare, BESSIE G., she by KING PHILLIP, son of WHIPPLE'S HAMBLETONIAN. He is 16 1-2 hands high, and weighs 1,300 lbs. He is of perfect build and splendid action, cool headed and great speed for his size, having trotted a trial mile as a three-year-old in 2:3–. He then entered heavy in the stud and was matched against Whalebone at the Healdsburg Races November 1, 188–, winning just as he pleased in three straight heats; time, 2:47, 2:46 1-2, 2:52 1-2. He was then matched for a race to come off at Thanksgiving Day at Petaluma but owing to the heavy rains the event did not take place. A few days previous to Thanksgiving Day Mr. Lawrence worked Sunset out and then he trotted three square miles and heats in 2:33½, 2:34 and 2:37.

SUNSET will be bred to 40 mares only, at $50 each, no colt no pay.

"ANTEEOF" is a jet black, was foaled April 13, 1886, is 16¼ hands high, and weighs 1,200 lbs., has a very fine, heavy black mane and tail; is well proportioned, moves majestically, is of easy, lofty carriage; is symmetrical, in fact is a beautiful horse. He was sired by Anteeo and the O. A. Taylor mare "Nance," her dam, was raised by Dr. Oliver Plummer, of Consumnes, Cal., and sired by "Napoleon"; Napoleon was foaled May 20, 1858, and raised by James Kyle of Butler County, Ohio. He was sired by Benj. Sweet's horse Bellfounder, and he by Old Bellfounder, his dam was sired by Doc. Daniel Melligan's horse, Cadmus, G. G. sire the celebrated Eclipse; his G. dam was sired by Big Shakespeare, G. G., sires dam by Messenger and Expedition.

ANTEEOF will be bred to 25 mares only, at $50 each. No colt, no pay.

"ANTEEOP" is a rich seal brown; was foaled March 7, 1887; by Anteeo and the inbred Hambletonian mare Bessie G., also dam of Sunset, his full brother and Midget his full sister; he is 15 1-2 hands high and weighs 950 lbs, and measures 22 inches around the arm, good head, fine neck, full, broad breast; withers and rump on nearly equal line, well proportioned bones, ankle, shoulders, loins and hips; strong legs all around, with great muscular development and splendid sinews; wirey pasterns and sound, compact feet; the lines from hip to hoof show power and speed; stands square and has excellent action, has a superb lustrous coat of rich deep brown fur of one color without defect; an even, honest trotter, and has gone the mile as a two-year-old in 2:43, the last quarter in 38 seconds; is intelligent and of high spirit, with much temper, but is not vicious, has very fine eyes, is a handsome, showy colt; attractive in harness.

ANTEEOP will be bred to 15 mares only, at $50. No colt, no pay.

SEASON to commence February 1st, ending July 1, 1890. Book now ready. Apply to John H. Lawrence, "Manager and Trainer," on my fruit and hop ranch, 1 mile east of Court House, on Sonoma road. Excellent pasture furnished with running water, also dry knolls with oak shelter, at $4 per month for mares. Two of the above stallions will be for sale after the expiration of the their stud season.

GUY E. GROSSE,
SANTA ROSA, SONOMA CO., CAL.

Valensin Stock Farm Stallions,

SIDNEY, 2:19 3-4.

At Eight Years of Age Sire of the following Fastest on Record:

FAUSTINO, yearling stallion, record of the world.....2:35
FLEET, fastest yearling record in 1888.....2:36
FLEET, fastest two-year-old filly in 1889.....2:24
GOLD LEAF, fastest four-year-old Pacing record in the world.....2:11¼
ADONIS, fastest three-year-old Pacing Gelding in the world.....2:14¼
ADONIS, four-year-old Gelding Pacing record.....2:14

—Also the Sire of—

LONGWORTH, four years old.....2:19
SISTER V., four years old (trial 2:23).....2:27
SANTA RITA.....2:39
MEMO, two-year-old (three-year-old trial 2:20½).....2:49

And many others.

SIDNEY is the sire of Faustino 2:35, and Fleet 2:36, the two fastest yearlings the world has ever known by one sire, and his slowest yearling is faster than the great Electioneer's fastest.

Terms, $250, with usual return privileges, for a limited number of approved mares. Book nearly full.

Only eight more mares can be taken for Season of '90.

Pasturage $5 per month. Reasonable charges if fed hay and grain. Best of care taken of mares, but positively no responsibility assumed for accidents or escapes. For further particulars address

G. VALENSIN, Pleasanton, Cal

The Trotting Stallion

Guide 2:29

(At Four Years)

Will make the season of 1890 at the SANTA RITA RANCH, about one mile North of Pleasanton.

DESCRIPTION.

GUIDE is a handsome seal brown, five years old, stands 15¾ hands high, and weighs 1055 pounds. He is of fine form, level headed, intelligent, and comes from blood lines that are noted for the qualities of speed and gameness.

PEDIGREE.

GUIDE, 2:28½.
- Director, 2:17, Sire of Direct, 2:18¾, Margaret S., 2:19¼.
  - Dictator 113, Sire of 23 trotters and 3 pacers in 2:30.
    - Hambletonian 10.
    - Clara, by American Star 14.
  - Dolly, Dam of Onward, 2:25¼, Thorndale, 2:22¼.
    - Mambrino Chief 11.
    - Fannie, by Ben Franklin.
- Imogene
  - Norwood 522, Sire of Tommy Norwood, 2:26¼.
    - Hambletonian 10.
    - Lady Fallis, by American Star 14.
  - daughter of
    - American Star 14.
    - daughter of Henry Clay 8.

The attention of breeders is especially called to the above pedigree as showing 3 crosses of American Star.

GUIDE trotted into the 2:30 list last season with little training, and he will trot into the 2:20 list the coming season barring accidents.

Guide's sire has a record of 2:17, made in a five heat race, and Guide is closely related to Phallas, who made a record of 2:13¾ in a fourth heat, and to Jay-Eye-See, record 2:10.

TWO HUNDRED AND FIFTY DOLLARS will be given to the owner of the first of the produce of Guide put in the 2:30 list, and $100 to each one after the first.

TERMS—$75 for the season, with the usual return privileges.

Admiro,

Sire Admiral; dam by San Bruno, by Easton's David Hill.

This magnificent horse is a handsome bay, eight years old; stands 17 1-2 hands high, and weighs 1400 pounds. He is very speedy for a large horse, and breeds fine large carriage horses. His produce possess every qualification of the Cleveland Bay, with the added qualities of speed and endurance resulting from his high trotting breeding.

TERMS—$35 for the season, with usual return privileges.

Will stand three days each week at Santa Rita Ranch, Pleasanton, and at A. T. Hatch's Ranch "Almono," Alamo, Contra Costa County, alternately. All mares sent care of SMITH & SUTHERLAND, Pleasanton, will be taken in charge of on arrival, and will receive the best care and attention in any manner the owners may desire. Good pasturage at $4 per month. Only a limited number of approved mares will be served by this horse this season.

No responsibility assumed for escapes or accidents. For further particulars, address

SMITH & SUTHERLAND, Pleasanton.

or A. T. HATCH, care Palace Hotel, San Francisco.

J. O'KANE, Horse Boots, Clothing and Furnishings, For Track, Driving Training and Stable. Every requisite for Horsemen. Harness, Medicines, Etc.

PASHA,

Registered No. 2039.

RECORD 2:36.

SIRE OF MORO 2:27.

Will make the present season at Linden, twelve miles east of STOCKTON.

Season commencing FEBRUARY 1st and ending JULY 1, 1890.

DESCRIPTION.

PASHA is a beautiful black; 16½ hands high, and weighs 1,240 pounds. He is a horse of beautiful symmetry and magnificent action.

PEDIGREE.

PASHA was sired by Sultan 1513, sire of Stamboul 2:12½, Ruby 2:19¼, Alcazar 2.20½, Bay Rose 2:20½, and sixteen others with records below 2:30. First dam Madam Baldwin by The Moor 870; second dam Ben Lippincott by Belmont. Pasha is a full brother to Bay Rose, record 2:2½.

Sultan, by The Moor, sire of Beautiful Bells, dam of Hinda Rose, 2:19½, Bell Boy 2:19½, and Sable, dam of Sable Wilkes, three-year-old record 2:18. First dam Sultana, by Delmonico, sire of Derby 2:16, by Guy Miller, sire of Whipple's Hambletonian. Second dam by Mambrino Chief. Third dam by Downing's Bay Messenger. Fourth dam Miss Caudle, dam of Ericsson, four-year-old recor 2:30½.

Terms for the season, $50.

With privilege of returning mares that do not prove in foal next season free of charge.

Good pasturage at $2 per month No responsibility will be assumed for accidents or escapes. Service fee payable before the removal of the mare.

For further particulars, address

D. BRYSON,
Linden Cal.

DESIGNER, 11,157

Son of Director 2:17.

Sire of DIRECT, 2:18½, as a four year-old, (lapping out PALO ALTO in 2:16½), and MARGARET S., 2:19½, as a three-year-old, and GUIDE, 2:28½, as a three-year-old. DIRECTOR is brother to JAY-EYE-SEE, 2:10, and PHALLAS, 2:13¾.

At the State Fair of 1889, he received the Gold Medal as the best producer of averaged speed in colts of two, three and four years of age. He is the only sire with two performers in the 2 20 list, when his oldest colts were only four years old; his services are eagerly sought by breeders, with a fee of $300.

Designer's dam is May Queen, by Abbotsford, 2:19 1-4, sire of Co de, 2:19¼; Abbotsford by Woodford's Mambrino, 2:21¼, and brother to Mambrino Dudley, 2:19 1-4, and Pancoast, 2:21 3-4, sire of Patron, 2:14 1-4. Woodford's Mambrino by Mambrino Chief, sire of Lady Thorne, 2:18 1-4, and of the dam of Director, 2:17, (dam) the dam of Wedgewood 2:19, sire of Favonia, 2:15.

May Queen was never trained. When two years old was driven over the road three weeks, and trotted to a cart two miles in six minutes. A few days after she paced a quarter in 40 seconds bare-footed; after being shod she trotted a quarter in 37 seconds.

Second dam by Elmo, full sister in blood to Overman, 2:19 1-4, sister to Alfred S., 2:22¾ as a four-year-old, and to the sire of L. C. Lee, 2:1o. Only two of her produce were handled very little, and one trotted as a three-year-old, with three weeks' work early in the spring, a mile in 2:35, last quarter in 35 seconds; the other, as a three-year-old, trotted a mile in 2:27¾, quarters in 33 seconds, with seven weeks' work. If her produce had been given proper training, she would surely have had three in the 2:30 list.

Third dam by David Hill, sire of Geo. Treat, 2:23 1-4, and Black Swan, 2:28¾.

Fourth dam by Gen. Taylor, sire of the dam of Wells Fargo, 2:18¾.

Fifth dam by Williamson's Belmont.

Designer is a rich bay horse, 5 years old, 15¾ hands high, weighs 1,050 pounds, evenly balanced and handsome, disposition the very best, has a perfect gait, and shows every indication of being very fast. He has never been trained, but will be given a low record, barring accidents. He is a horse of great substance and high finish; his family on both sides are producers of great speed. He can not fail to make a great producer, as his colts all inherit these qualities—the same disposition and natural trotting action. His colts are but few, but those who have them are highly pleased with them, and all returned the mares to him the following season but two.

Breeders will see by carefully examining his pedigree, that his blood lines are invaluable for the production of high breeding and great speed. No stallion now in public service can show a pedigree with such fast records as enrich the blood of Designer. Considering his breeding, he is by far the cheapest horse in California. This is a rare opportunity to get the service of a good horse for little money, as within a short period his price will be four times that amount.

Limited to 20 mares, at $50 for the season, commencing February 15th, ending June 15th. Mares can be returned next season if not with foal, provided mares or horse have not changed hands. Fee due at time of service, and must be paid before mares are removed. Pasturage $5 per month. All mares at owners' risk.

H. SCOTT,
Race Track, Oakland, Cal.

Highland Farm,

LEXINGTON, KY.,

Home of Red Wilkes.

Standard-bred Trotting Stock

For Sale,

Sired by Red Wilkes, Wilton, 2:19¾; Allandorf and Sentinel wilkes, out of highly bred Standard Mares of the most fashionable blood of the day.

W. C. FRANCE, Proprietor.

HORSES PURCHASED ON COMMISSION.

THOROUGHBREDS A SPECIALTY.

Will select and buy, or buy selected Animals for all desiring, for reasonable compensation.

KEEPS PROMISING YOUNGSTERS IN VIEW.

L. M. LASLEY, Stanford, Ky.

References:—J. W. Guest, Danville, Ky.
B. G Bruce, Lexington, Ky.
S. H. Baughman, Stanford, Ky.
G. A. Lackey, Stanford, Ky.
Geo. McAlister, Stanford, Ky.
First National Bank, Stanford, Ky.]

GEO. WASHINGTON.

11,623.

RECORD 2:30.

Bay colt, bred by Thomas Smith of Vallejo, Cal. Foaled 1886 by Mambrino Chief, Jr., 11,622, record 2:34 1-2. 1st dam Fanny Rose by Vick's Ethan Allen Jr. 2,903, sire of Prince Allen 2:27, 2nd dam Jenny Lind, thoroughbred, dam of Prince Allen 2:27. Will serve a limited number of mares at $60 for the season. Mares not proving with foal may be returned next season free.

Mambrino Chief, Jr.

11,622.

RECORD 2:34 1 2.

Sire of George Washington, record 2 30 at three years old. Bay h bred by R. fu Ingalls of Belvedere, Ill. By McDonald Chief's 3rd First dam Venus by Mambrino Patchen 58. 2nd dam by Wardlow's Shakespeare. 3rd dam Lone Gold 4th dam by Silver Heels. Has not been in the stud before. He was 5 years old when he served a few mares, and his colts all show good style and form.

Terms for the season $40. For further particulars see or address

THOMAS SMITH,
Vallejo, Cal.

Elector 2170.

Sire of J. R.

Three-Year Old Record 2:24.

Sired by Electioneer 125, sire of Sunol, three-year-old, 2:10½, Palo Alto, 2:12½, etc.; dam Gilberta by Fred Low 686, sire of Clay, 2:25½, etc.

Second dam Lady Gilbert (grandam of Lot Slocum, 2:17½) by General Knox 140 (sire of Lady Maud, 2:18½, and many others).

TERMS.

$150 for the season. Book full for 1890.

L. A. RICHARDS,
Grayson, Stanislaus Co., Cal.

The Thoroughbred Stallion

Three Cheers

Will make the season of 1890 at

Sacramento.

PEDIGREE.

THREE CHEERS
- imp. Hurrah
  - Newminster
    - Touchstone, by Camel
    - Beeswing, by Dr. Syntax
  - Jovial
    - Bay Middleton, by Sultan
    - Sister to Grey Momus, by Comus
- Young Fashion
  - imp. Monarch
    - imp. Priam, by Emilius
    - imp. Delphine, by Whisker
  - Fashion
    - imp. Trustee, by Catton
    - Bonnets o' Blue, by Sir Charles

Hurrah was imported by John Reber, of Lancaster, Ohio, a locality where there were but few breeders of thoroughbreds. Under these disadvantages he sired a long list of winners. His sire Newminster, won the St. Ledger 1851, and his dam, Jovial by Bay Middleton, winner of the Derby 1836. Newminster by Touchstone, winner St. Ledger 1834. Dam Beeswing, winner of 54 races out of 64 starts, by Dr. Syntax, winner of the Doncaster Cup, 1837—40—41—42, the only horse that ever accomplished that feat.

On the side of the dam Three Cheers is equally well related. Young Fashion was the dam of Surprise, Scotland (the only horse that ever beat Asteroid a heat), Liverpool, Columbia, and Bonnie Kate, the dam of Little Buttercup, and the flying Bonnie Lizzie. His grandam, Fashion was the greatest race mare of her day and beat Boston in that historical match at four mile heats, which is recorded as one of the greatest events in the annals of the turf.

Horsemen who are qualified to judge, pronounce Three Cheers to be the finest type of the Newminster line in America.

LOCATION.

THREE CHEERS will be located at the Arcade Training Stable, Rancho del Paso. This place has been selected for the reason that first class pasturage has been secured there for the exclusive use of these mares, and the other facilities to be obtained there for the care of mares (especially mares in foal) are better than can be found elsewhere in the locality.

TERMS.

$50 for the season with the usual return privileges. Pasturage $5 per month. Mares cared for as owners may desire at bottom rates for grain and hay. All bills payable before the mare is removed.

Mares shipped care of WM. IRVINE, Pacific Stables, Sacramento, will be properly cared for and sent to the ranch without delay.

Three Cheers will be in charge of one of the most experienced and competent stud grooms in the State, who will exercise every care, but no reponsibility assumed for accidents or escapes.

For further particulars apply to Louis Crissler, at the ranch; Wm. Irvine, Pacific Stables, Second St., Sacramento; or to the owner,

E. S. CULVER,
313 Bush St., San Francisco.

GROVER CLAY.

Bay Stallion, Black Points, 15 3-4 hands high.

Bred by W. W. Traylor, San Francisco.

BY ELECTIONEER.

First dam Maggie Norfolk by Norfolk, son of Lexington, he by Boston. Second dam Tilda Quill by Billy Cheatham, he by Cracken, and he by Boston. Third dam by Dorsey's Golddust.

TERMS.

Will make the season of 1890 at the Training Stables of Denis Gannon, near Oakland Trotting Park, at $50 the season, payable at time of service. Season to commence February 1st and ending July 1st. Proper care of mares will be taken, but no responsibility incurred for accidents or escapes. Address,

DENIS GANNON, Oakland, Cal.

COOK STOCK FARM,

Season of 1890.

STEINWAY 1808.

Three-Year-Old Record 2:25 3-4.

Sire of STRATHWAY, three year old record 2:26, and sire of the dam of BOURBON RUSSELL 2:30.

By STRATHMORE 408; sire of 31 in the 2:30 list; sire of 6 dams of 8 in the 2:30 list, and sire of 3 sires of 3 in 2:30 list.

1st dam ABBESS (dam of Solo 2:28, and Soprano, dam of C. F Clay 2:18, Eminence 2:27 and Strathbridge, 3 year old record 2:28½) by ALBION, sire of VANITY FAIR 2:24½, and of the dam of FAVORITE 2:25½.

2nd dam by MARSHALL NEY.

3rd dam by BERTRAND, a son of SIR ARCHY.

TERMS—$100 for the season.

CHARLES DERBY 4907

Brown Horse, Foaled 1885.

By STEINWAY 1808.

1st dam by the great ELECTIONEER, sire of SUNOL 3 year old record 2:10½, Palo Alto 2:12½, etc., etc.

2nd dam FANNY MALONE, by NIAGARA.

3rd dam FANNY WICKHAM, by HERALD.

4th dam by Imp. TRUSTEE.

TERMS—$100 for the season.

CRESCO 4908.

(BROTHER TO SPARTAN, 2,24.)

By STRATHMORE 408, sire of 31 in the 2:30 list, etc.

1st dam the dam of SPARTAN 2:24, by ALMONT 33; sire of 71 with performers in the 2:30 list

2nd dam the dam of HENDERSON 2:27, by BRIGNOLI 77, sire of the dam of KING WILKES 2:22.

3rd dam by CRIPPLE, a son of MEDOC.

4th dam by AMERICAN ECLIPSE.

TERMS—$50 for the season.

Pasturage $5 per month. Accidents and escapes at owner's risk. Mares consigned to the farm should be sent to Fashion Stables, Oakland; Geary & Grindle's Stable, Haywards; or to Bennett's Stable, Martinez; from and to which places they will be delivered free of charge. Address

COOK STOCK FARM,
Danville, Contra Costa, Co., Cal.

The Trotting Stallion

ARBITRATOR

Will make the Season of 1890 at NILES, Alameda County.

PEDIGREE.

ARBITRATOR
- Director 1989, 2:17 in a race, Sire of Direct, 4 yrs., 2:18½ in a race, Margaret S., 3 yrs., 2:19½ in a race, Guide, 4 yrs., 2:28½ in a race.
- Lady Earnest.
  - Speculation 918, sire of Oakland Maid, 2:22 in a race, Gracie S., 2:22 in a race, Crown Point, 2:24 in a race, He the sire of Valensin, 3 yrs., 2:23 in a race, Sire of Dam of Alfred G., 2:19½.
  - Lady Hibbard, dam of Lou Whipple, 2:26½ in a race.

Speculation's dam was Martha Washington, dam of Whipple's Hambletonian, sire of 15 in 2:30 and granddaughter of Burr's Napoleon, sire of Black Harry, who in 1850 won two miles in 5:14½. He sired Smith Burr, sire of Gen. Butler, 2:21, Wagon, 4:56½. He sired the dam of Fanny Mapes, dam of Jerome Eddy, 2:16½. He sired Telegraph, sire of dam of Rarus, 2:13¼.

DESCRIPTION.

ARBITRATOR was foaled 1885. He is of good size, fine conformation, and a beautiful seal brown.

TERMS.

Non-standard mares	$45
Standard mares by inheritance	35
Standard mares by performance or produce	25

For further particulars, address

H. A. MAYHEW, owner,
Niles, Alameda Co.

ST. NICHOLAS.

A Son of the World Renowned SIDNEY,

Will Make the Season of 1890, at the Oakland Trotting Park.

ST. NICHOLAS was bred by Mr. G. Valensin at the Arno Stock Farm, Sacramento Co., California, in 1885. He is a beautifully proportioned bright bay horse, 16.3 hands high; is well muscled, lengthy, and lots of bone, with splendid natural action and a phenomenal turn of speed. As a three-year-old he easily worked three heats on the Oakland Track in 2:32, 2:29 and 2:27¾. His breeding is just what one would expect from such a highly formed bloodlike horse. Sidney, his sire, is the most successful young stallion—whether for getting pacers or trotters—America has ever seen, and no wonder for his blood lines are exceptional fine and are all trotting lines, Santa Claus, Strathmore, Rysdyk's Hambletonian and Abdallah, while Sweetness again runs back through that great sire Volunteer, to Rysdyk's Hambletonian and also through her dam to Rysdyk's Hambletonian and Harry Clay 45, the sire of Electioneer's dam. St. Nicholas' dam is by Echo, an exceptionally prepotent son of Hambletonian thus giving St. Nicholas four Rysdyk's Hambletonian crosses and further back a Harry Clay cross which with his grand dam's thoroughbred cross should make him invaluable in the stud.

TERMS: Fifty dollars the season, which will commence on the 5th of February and close on the 1st of July. Due care will be taken of mares, but no responsibility for accidents or escapes.

Mares taken and kept as desired by the owners, and at reasonable rates.

JOHN ROWEN.
Oakland Trotting Park.

Season of 1890.

February 15 to June 15

LYNWOOD,

(STANDARD 3017.)

AT WOLF'S (RUSSELL'S) STABLES, STOCKTON, CAL.

TERMS.

$50 for the season, payable at the close of season. Pasturage at $3 per month. Accidents or escapes at owner's risk.

PEDIGREE.

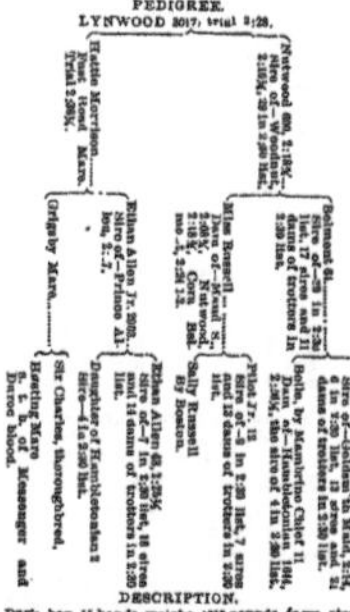

DESCRIPTION.

Dark bay, 15 hands, weighs 1050 pounds, form stout and elegant, gait pure and rapid. He was foaled July 15, 1880, has done but little work in the stud, but enough to demonstrate that he is one of the best foal getters in the State. Only one of his get has had any systematic handling, and that could have gone into the 2:30 list last year as a two-year-old, had the owner desired.

It will be observed from an examination of Lynwood's pedigree, that he is one of the best bred sons of the GREAT NUTWOOD, who commands a service fee of $500 for the season.

P. VISHER, Stockton.

The Thoroughbred Stallion

INTRUDER

Will make the Season of 1890 at Agricultural Park, SACRAMENTO.

Bay Horse, foaled 1871, bred by Sir L. Newman, England. Imported by D. D. Withers, Esq., New York.

By Crater, Son of Orlando and Vesuvienne by Gladiator.

1st dam Lady Bountiful by Rataplan (Rataplan is own brother to Stockwell, and winner of 42 races, including the Doncaster Cup and 19 Queen's Plates, and proved himself the most distinguished race horse of his day in England).

2d dam Plentiful by Don John (the winner of St. Leger and Doncaster Cup).

3d dam Plenty by Bay Middleton (winner of the Derby and Two Thousand Guinea Stakes).

4th dam Plenary, own sister of Plenipotentiary, by Emilius. (Both Emilius and Plenipotentiary were Derby winners).

5th dam Harriet, dam of the renowned Plenipotentiary by Pericles.

6th dam by Selim, winner of the One Thousand Guinea Stakes.

7th dam by Pypiline, by Sir Peter.

8th dam Rally, by Trumpeter.

9th dam Fancy, by Florizel. Fancy was full sister to Diomed, the first Derby winner in England, and after his importation into this country, sired the illustrious Sir Archy, etc. See English Stud Book.

Imported INTRUDER is a beautiful bay, standing fully 16 hands high, of great length and substance, and descends through close and strong currents from the most illustrious winners and winning lines of blood of which the English Stud Book bears record.

A careful review of the first six crosses of the pedigree of INTRUDER will show nine Derby winners, five St. Leger winners; two winners of The Oaks; two winners of the Two Thousand Guineas; two winners of the One Thousand Guineas; one Goodwood Cup winner; one Cesarwich Cup winner; one Cambridgeshire Stakes winner, and four Doncaster Cups, in addition to a great number of Steeplechases and other races of less import.

INTRUDER, at the great fair held at St. Louis, Mo., in 1876, was awarded the highest stallion honors—the blue ribbon and the $500 purse—in the sweepstakes ring for stallion of any age or blood. The list of competitors embraced the large number of thirty-three animals, and they represented England, Canada, Kentucky, Tennessee, and other states. He also took first premium in his class and in sweepstakes for the best stallion of any age or breed at the State Fair at Peoria, Ill., 1881. He is the sire of Tidal Wave, George Hakes, Bernice and April Fool.

INTRUDER is the sire of Interpose, who is the dam of Spokane, winner of the Kentucky Derby, in which he beat the great horse Proctor Knott and broke the record.

TERMS: $50 for the season. Mares not proving with foal can be returned the next season free of charge. Good pasturage at $4 per month. Mares cared for in any manner owners may desire, and fed on hay and grain, either or both, at reasonable rates. While every precaution will be taken, no responsibility will be assumed for escapes or accidents. Mares sent from a distance in care of the undersigned, will be met and taken to the park. For further particulars, address

T. J. KNIGHT.
Agricultural Park, Sacramento.

Shoes For Comfort, Elegance and Durability.

Having my own Factory, and giving my personal supervision to all work. I am in a position to warrant perfect satisfaction. Inspection invited.

AGENT for the VISCALIZED SHOES.

FACTORY—S W. cor. Battery and Jackson Sts.
SALESROOM—Pioneer Building, corner Stevenson and Fourth Streets.

A full line of Boots and Shoes constantly on hand, and rules for Self-Measurement by Mail.

JNO. T. SULLIVAN.

Second Grand Combination Sale of Kidd, Edmonson & Morse.

CHICAGO, ILL; MARCH 17 to 21, in Battery D, adjoining Exposition Building.

In addition to the following light horses we have catalogued consignments from the breeding establishments also named below:—

Judge Hayes 4436, by Robert McGregor 2:17½; dam Luna 2:29½, by Almont; second dam by Abdallah 15; third dam, dam of Lula 2:14¾.

Passenger Boy, 2.24½ (trial 2:18). A game race horse and campaigner.

Kentucky, by Prince [?]; dam Sister by Volunteer; second dam by American Star.

Flaxman, 10148, by Lexington Wilkes 4878; dam by Alexander's Abdallah 15; second dam Kate Crockett, dam of Lula 2:14¾.

Llewellen 3929, by Satellite 7800 dam by Volunteer 55; second dam by Seely's American Star 14

Waters Stock Farm, Genoa Junction, Wis., a lot of their best bred ones.

S. A. Brown & Co., Kalamazoo, Mich., a grand pick of their choicest.

W. D. Crockett, Waukegan, Ill., one of Robert McGregor's best sons: Lexington Wilkes 4878; Star Hambletonian 2:25½.

H. D. McKinney, Janesville, Wis., sons of Phallas 2:13¾.

Granger Smith, Waukegan, Ill., grandsons and daughters of Dictator.

Eben Remington, Fenton, Mich., stallions by Louis Napoleon 207.

M. L. Hare, Indianapolis, Ind., Hambrinos and a selection never excelled.

Rock River Stock Farm, Dixon, Ill., twenty-five head of choice ones.

Wildwood Stock Farm, Janesville, Wis., a picked consignment.

Chas. M. Smith, Earlville, Ill., some good ones.

L. U. Shippee, Stockton, Cal., a nice draft from his establishment, got by a son of Nutwood.

Ayers' Stock Farm, Burlington, Wis., Swigerts and other well bred ones.

P. C. Kidd, Lexington, Ky. No better lot ever sold.

R. C. Church, Frankfort, Ky., some fine ones.

Lewis Cook, Lexington, Ky., an extra good lot.

Albino Park Farm, Bozeman, Mont., sixty head mares, stallions, colts, geldings and fillies. They are by sons of Clark Chief, Administrator, Mambrino Chief and Belmont.

S. & H. Stock Farm Co., Deadwood, Dak., twenty head of Trotters, Thoroughbreds, Draft and Saddle horses. A choice collection.

In draft horses we have entries of Percherons, Shires and Clydes (imported, pure bred and grade) from the following well known parties:—

W. L. Ellwood, De Kalb, Ill., car load Percherons.

J. D. Beckett, Western Springs, Ill., Percherons and French Coachers.

Evans & Bluett, Oregon, twenty-five imported Percherons.

D. J. Nicely, Union City, Ind., imp. Clydesdales.

Rockdale Farm, Lake Forest, Ill., imported Shires; both sexes.

Havens Stock Farm, Alma, Neb., stallions, mares and geldings.

Marsh Black, Knoxville, Ia., stallions.

R. D. Lowell, Sharon, Wis., Clydesdale stallions and mares.

Degen Bros., Ottawa, Ill., imported Percherons and French Coachers.

Morse Stock Farm, Kewanna, Ind., imported Percherons.

Chicago is the great horse centre and the best place in the world to sell all kinds of horses. This sale will enjoy the largest and wealthiest audience that ever faced an auctioneer. **ENTRIES CLOSE FEBRUARY 20.** Address

KIDD, EDMONSON & MORSE, 806 West Madison Street, Chicago, Ill., or Lexington, Ky.

2:20 1-2 (Half Mile Track) at 4 Years. — Fastest Record (in a Race) of any Wilkes — 2:14 1-2 at 5 Years.

ROY WILKES, $2:12\frac{3}{4}$,

Seal brown; 15½ hands; foaled 1883; by Adrian Wilkes 6660, son of Geo. Wilkes; 1st dam by Blue Bull 75; 2d dam by grandson of American Eclipse; 3d and 4th dams thoroughbred.

THE GREATEST CAMPAIGNER OF 1889.

Handsome, Game, Pure Gaited. Level Headed.

Will make a season at the PLEASANTON STOCK FARM, PLEASANTON, CAL Service Fee $150. Money refunded if mare does not get with foal. Season ends April 1st, 1890

For full record of performances, extended pedigree, etc., address

L. A. DAVIES, Hotel Pleasanton,
SUTTER AND JONES STREETS, San Francisco, Cal.

MEMO.

The Best Son of SIDNEY

Will Make the Season of 1890 at the OAKLAND RACE TRACK

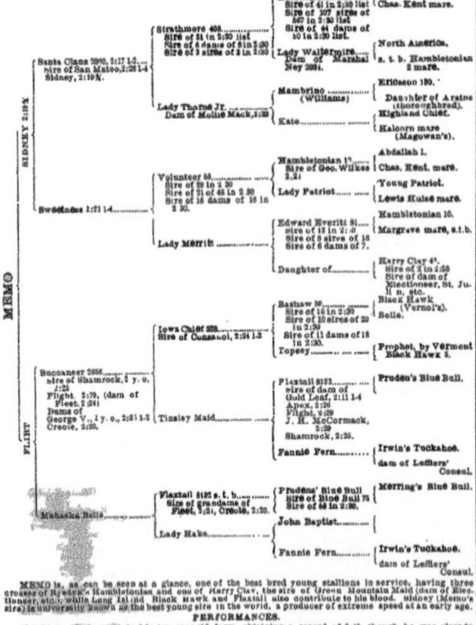

MEMO is, as can be seen at a glance, one of the best bred young stallions in service, having three crosses of Rysdyk's Hambletonian and one of Harry Clay, the sire of Green Mountain Maid (dam of Electioneer, etc.), while Long Island Black Hawk and Flaxtail also contribute to his blood. Sidney (Memo's sire) is universally known as the best young sire in the world, a producer of extreme speed at an early age.

PERFORMANCES.

MEMO trotted in public in his two year-old form, obtaining a record of 2:49, though he was close to Grandee in a race on the Bay District Track, the second heat of which was made in 2:31 1-2, the first in 2:3[?]. He exhibited phenomenal speed when three years old, and had it not been for a slight strain of his fore fetlock, there is little question that he would have shown in public very close to the best record. On the Oakland track he was timed a mile in 2:26 1-4, and frequently trotted quarters in from 32 1-2 to 34 seconds.

As a four-year-old Memo only started once—at Sacramento—when, although out of condition, he showed great speed, and improving as he went on, great hopes were entertained of his going well down in the 'teens at the P. C. T. H. B. A. meeting, but after showing several very fast miles his leg filled and he was laid up for the season. He is sixteen hands high, and of powerful build throughout. His color is a glossy black, with both fore-feet white. His disposition is all that could be desired, and his action superb. He is a sure foal getter, only one mare being reported not in foal during his last season.

TERMS, $100, with usual return privileges, for a limited number of mares. Season to close JUNE 15th, when he will be prepared for track purposes. Pasturage $5 per month. Have leased the cricket ground adjoining the track for pasturage, where there is fine feed. Reasonable charges if fed hay and grain. Best of care taken of mares in any manner owners may desire, but positively no responsibility assumed for accidents or escapes. For further particulars address

J. P. KERR, 313 Bush Street, San Francisco,
or, JOHN ROWEN, Race Track, Oakland, Cal.

Pleasanton Stock Farm Co.'s Stallions.

DIRECTOR, 2:17.

Director's book is open for 15 good mares more than already booked for the season of 1890, at [?] each.

This is the cheapest service fee ever charged for a stallion, taking into consideration his BREEDING and RACE RECORD and the RACE RECORDS OF HIS COLTS.

Season to Commence February 15th and Close August 1st.

PLEASANTON.

Sire Director 2:17. Dam May Day 2:30.

PLEASANTON is a light bay, 16 hands high, and is full brother to Margaret S, three year old record 2:19½.

His book is now open for 10 good mares at $100 for the season, which will commence March 1st and end June 1st.

Mares not proving with foal may be returned next season free of charge of service fees to the same stallion, if he is still in our possession; if not, to some other stallion equally as good, or money will be refunded at option of the company.

Pasturage $4 per month; hay and grain extra. Accidents and escapes at owner's risk.

Service fees due at time of service, and must be paid, together with pasturage, etc., before mares are taken away, or a good approved note given, payable August 1st, 1890, at which date all bills must be settled.

For further information call or address M. SALISBURY, 320 Sansome Street, Room 26 San Francisco, or

PLEASANTON STOCK FARM CO.;
Pleasanton, Alameda Co., Cal.

BAY STALLION

ECLECTIC

11,321

By Electioneer, dam Manette (full sister to Woodnut 2.16 1-2)

Manon 2:21 and Maple, dam of Hattie D. (three year-old record 2:36½) by Nutwood 2:18¾, etc., etc.

Terms $100 for the Season.

BROWN STALLION

MORTIMER

5,346

Four-year-old Record, 2:27

By ELECTIONEER, dam MARTI, by Whipple's Hambletonian (sire of 15 in 2:30, and of dams of eight in 2:30). Second dam Ida Martin by Rifleman (sire of Col. Lewis 2:18¾).

Terms $60 for the Season.

Horses shipped via San Francisco may be consigned to J. W. MORSHEAD, City Front Stables, who will attend to their forwarding.

Season closes JULY 1st, 1890. Usual return privileges.

For further particulars address owner,

WILFRED PAGE, Penns Grove,
Sonoma County, Cal.

The Trotting Stallion

Silver Bow

Will make the season of 1890 at the Oakland Race Track.

Pedigree.

SILVER BOW, 11708. 2 y. o. rec., 2:37.

- Robert McGregor 647, 2:17½, sire of Bonnie McGregor, 2:13½, Earl McGregor, 2:21¾, Mac D., 2:30, McGregor Boy, 2:29¾, Mark Time, 2:30, Roxie McGregor, 2:30½
  - Major Edsall, 2:11, 2:29
    - Alexander's Abdallah 15, sire of Goldsmith Maid, 2:14.
      - Hambletonian 10, sire of Dexter, 2:17¼
      - by Young Patriot
    - by Harris' Hambletonian 2.
      - Bishop's Hambletonian
      - The Munson Mare
  - Nancy Whitman, 2:30¼
    - American Star 14
      - Stockholm's American Star
      - Sally Slouch
    - Nance, Dam of Madeleine, 2:23½.
      - Durland's Young Messenger Duroc
      - untraced
- Sadie
  - Hambletonian 10, Sire of Geo. Wilkes, 2:22, (sire of Guy Wilkes, 2:15¼) also Electioneer, sire of Sunol, 3 y. o. record, 2:10½, and Palo Alto, 2:12¾.
    - Abdallah
      - Mambrino
      - Amazonia
    - Chas. Kent Mare
      - imp. Bellfounder
      - One Eye
  - Lady Wynne
    - Wm. Welch 341, sire of Jeremiah, 2:22½.
      - Hambletonian 10
      - the dam of Prince, 2:27
    - Eleanora Margrave
      - imp. Margrave 1455
      - Fanny Wright, thoroughbred

DESCRIPTION.

SILVER BOW is a handsome bay, no white; 15-2½ hands high; weighs 1075 pounds; of fine form, with the best of legs and a clean cut, intelligent head. Is remarkably level headed, seldom making a break; wears 7-ounce shoes in front. His record 2:37, is no mark of his speed; he can beat 30 easy, and with his gilt-edge breeding, he is just what he ought to be, a trotter sired by a trotter whose dam was herself a trotter and his grandam the dam of two trotters. His dam Sadie being by Hambletonian 10, shows him to be bred from the cream of the trotting blood.

TERMS: $100 for the season. Mares not proving in foal returnable for the season of 1891 free of charge. Good pasturage and first-class care taken of mares for $5 per month. No responsibility assumed for escapes or accidents. For further particulars, address

Limited to 15 approved mares.
Season to end June 1st, 1890.

P. J. WILLIAMS.
Care Race Track, Oakland, Cal.

Langtry Farms' Stud

Imp. FRIAR TUCK

By the Immortal HERMIT.

DAM ROMPING GIRL BY WILD DAYRELL,

AT $50 THE SEASON.

Mares not proving with foal may be returned the following season. Good care taken of mares, but no liabilities for accidents or escapes.

Good Pasturage at $5 per month.

Mares shipped to ST. HELENA, care CHARTES WILLIAM ABY, St. Helena Stables, will be cared for. For further particulars address,

CHAS. WILLIAM ABY,
Middletown, Lake County, Cal.

2:08 3-4 2:10 2:12

MAMBRINO WILKES, 6083.

SIRE OF

GUS WILKES, 2:22; ALPHEUS, 2:27; CLARA P, 2:29½; BALKAN, 2:29½ (3-year-old) and timed separately 2:22½ in 4-year-old Stake, Bay District Track, October 14, 1889.

DESCRIPTION.

Black; sixteen hands; weighs, in exercise, 1,260 lbs. For style, finish, symmetry and proportion, comparison is challenged with any trotting bred horse. His colts follow in size, style and beauty. Balkan, for instance, being "facile princeps" of trotters in these particulars.

PEDIGREE.

Sired by Geo. Wilkes, sire of Harry Wilkes, 2:13½, Guy Wilkes, 2:15¼, and 60 other trotters in the 2:30 list, in addition to 5 pacers, and of the sire of Axtell, 2:12 (three-year-old), beating all stallions of any age, and the sire of Regal Wilkes, 2:20¾, best two-year-old stallion record.

First dam Lady Chrisman by Mambrino (Todhunter's, son of Mambrino Chief 11; sire of Lady Thorn, 2:18¼; Woodford Mambrino, 2:21½, and four others in 2:30, and of the dams of Director, 2:17, Piedmont, 2:17¼, Onward, 2:25¼, etc.

Second dam by Pilot Jr. 12, sire of nine in the 2:30 list, and of the dams of Maud S., 2:08¾, Jay-Eye-See, 2:10, Nutwood, 2:18¾, Viking, 2:19¼, Pilot Boy, 2:20, Naiad Queen, 2:20¼, etc.

TERMS.

Mares from a distance will be received at the Dexter Stables, Oakland, or Livery Stable, Martinez, the owner notifying Smith Hill, Superintendent at the farm. Good pasture and plenty of water. For the purpose of placing the service of a Wilkes within reach of breeders, the same rate will be maintained as last year, to wit, $75 for the season. Although it is not admitted thereby that this horse is inferior as a producer to the horses whose fees are placed at from $150 to $500. Address

SMITH HILL,
San Miguel Stock Farm,
Walnut Creek, Contra Costa Co., Cal.

$2:12\frac{3}{4}$ $2:13\frac{1}{2}$ $2:15\frac{1}{4}$

$2:08\frac{3}{4}$ 2:10 2:12

BALKAN

By Mambrino Wilkes.

(See that Horse's Advertisement.)

DAM FANNY FERN BY JACK HAWKINS Son of Boston.

The grandam of Maud S. (2:08¾) was by Boston and the grandam of Jay-Eye-See (2:10) was by Lexington, son of Boston. So Balkan is the same remove from Boston that Maud is, and one remove nearer than Jay-Eye-See.

Fanny Fern has produced Molly Drew, Onyx, Fred Arnold, Molly Fern and Balkan, all by different sires.

Balkan's sire and dam both being producers, and he being a trotter himself with a record of 2:29 1-2 (three-year-old) and timed separately 2:22 1-4 in 4-year-old Stake, Bay District Track, October 14, 1889—it is but fair to presume that he will get trotters of the highest order.

DESCRIPTION.

He is seal brown, 16-1 hands high, in style rivalled by few, and excelled by none with as pure a gait as has yet been exhibited in public—bar none.

Balkan will be at Oakland Trotting Park for the season of 1890, and will be limited to ten mares, at 100 fee, in order to be put in training early, as it is morally certain that if given a reasonable opportunity he will be fast enough to compete with the best of his age. For further particulars address

A. L. HINDS,
Dexter Stables, Oakland.

$2:12\frac{3}{4}$ $2:13\frac{1}{2}$ $2:15\frac{1}{4}$

JESSE E. MARKS & CO.,

Wholesale and Retail Dealers of Choice Brands

Havana & Key West Cigars

922 MARKET ST., S. F.

2:19 NOONDAY $2:20\frac{1}{2}$

STANDARD No. 10,000.

This celebrated trotting bred stallion will make the season of 1890 at the stable of the undersigned at Sacramento, Cal., at $75 for the season and $100 to insure a mare in foal. Payable on or before July 1st, 1-90. Money will be refunded on mares bred by insurance as soon as the fact becomes known that they are not in foal.

NOONDAY.

- Wedgewood, 2:19, Sire of Favonia, 2:15, fastest 4th heat for any mare or gelding, and eight others in 2:27 or better.
  - Belmont, Sire of Wedgewood, 2:19, Nutwood, 2:18¾, Viking, 2:19¼, and 29 others in 2:30 list.
    - Alexander's Abdallah, sire of Goldsmith Maid, 2:14; Almont, with 35 horses in 2:30 list, etc.
    - Belle, dam of Hambletonian, 2:26½; Bicara, dam of Pancoast, 2:21¾, the sire of Patron, 2:14¼.
  - Woodbine, Dam of Wedgewood, 2:19, Woodford Mamb., 2:21½, the sire of Pancoast, 2:21¾, the sire of Patron, 2:14¼.
    - Woodford.
    - Singleton Mare.
- Noontide, 2:20½ (Trial, 2:13½).
  - Harold, Sire of Maud S., 2:08¾, and 26 others in 2:30 list.
    - Hambletonian (Rysdyk's), sire of George Wilkes, 2:22, the sire of Guy Wilkes, 2:15¼; Electioneer, the sire of Sunol, 2:10½, and scores of noted trotters and producers.
    - Enchantress, by Abdallah 1.
  - Midnight, Dam of Jay-Eye-See, 2:10, Noontide, 2:20½.
    - Pilot Jr., sire of dams of Maud S., 2:08¾, Jay-Eye-See, 2:10, Nutwood, 2:18¾, etc.
    - Twilight, by Lexington, sire of the dam of Ansel, 2:20.

NOODAY is a dark seal brown, foaled 1884, 15 hands 1½ inches high. Individually he is equal to his royal breeding. He is all that can be desired in conformation, intelligence, color and trotting action, and no stallion now in public service can show a pedigree with such fast records and royal game trotting blood as Noonday.

DON MARVIN,

Record 2:28 as a five-year-old. Standard by Breeding and Performance

Standard No. 7927.

Don Marvin 2:28.

Don Marvin is a beautiful seal brown, foaled 1881, bred by Hon. Leland Stanford, Palo Alto, Cal., standing 15 hands, and weighs, in ordinary condition, 1200 lbs. He is a fine individual, good style and form, combined with great substance, and good temper. Is very level headed: in his first race the past season he only made one break in five closely contested heats. He has great speed and endurance, with the pure, rapid Electioneer gait. He trots without toe weights, and wears only 8 oz. shoes in front. He gained his record the past season in the third heat, on a slow track, after making a season (serving over 60 mares), with scarcely any preparation. His record is no mark of his speed. He was a natural born trotter, and Mr. Charles Marvin considered him the fastest two year old at Palo Alto that season.

By FALLIS, 2:23, - - by Electioneer, sire of
Sire of Don Marvin, 2:28. — Sunol, three-year-old, 2:10 1-2, Palo Alto, 2:12¾, and 47 others in 2:30 list.

Dam CORA, by Don Victor by Belmont, sire of
Dam of Don Marvin, 2:28. — Ventura, 2:27¾, and sire of the dam of Bell Echo, 2:20, and six others in 2:30 list.

2d dam CLARABEL, - by Abdallah Star,
Dam of Clifton Bell, 2:24 1-2, and grandam of Rexford, three years, 2:24. — Sire of Hattie Maples, 2:33.

3d dam FAIRY, - - by Rysdyk's Hambletonian,
Sister of Sweepstakes, sire of 16 in 2:30 list. — Sire of Electioneer, George Wilkes, and many other noted sires and trotters.

4th dam EMMA MILLS, by Seely's American Star,
Dam of 4 horses that have 2:30 performers. — The great broodmare sire of the world.

The above pedigree should show every intelligent breeder that Don Marvin is "high" bred though very strong in trotting blood. All the comment it is deemed necessary to make as to the value of "thoroughbred blood" in the trotter is simply to refer to the very significant fact that the first and second dams of Maud S. 2:08¾, Jay-Eye-See 2:10, Sunol, three years 2:10 1-2, Palo Alto 2:12¾, Anteeo 2:16¼, Nutwood 2:18¾, Wedgewood 2:19, and many other successful sires and sensational trotters of the day are thoroughbred.

TERMS—Don Marvin will make the ensuing season from February 1st to July 1st, 1890, at $40 the season, with the usual privilege of returning the mare next season if not proving in foal. Mares from a distance met at the cars or boats on notification, and carefully handled, but no responsibility assumed for accidents or escapes.

Good alfalfa pasture furnished (free from barb wire fence) at $4 per month. For further particulars or complete circulars address

F. P. LOWELL,
1520 F Street, Sacramento, Cal.

The Produce of Eros Averaged $2,200 Each at New York Auction Sale in 1889.

THE ELECTIONEER TROTTING STALLI N,

5326 EROS 5326

Will make the season of 1890—February 1st to July 1st—at LA SIESTA RANCH, MENLO PARK, adjoining Palo Alto.

PEDIGREE.

EROS (5326)
Standard by his sire
" " dam
" " record
" " produce
" under all rules

EROS (5326)..

- Electioneer, Grandsire of Norlaine, 1 yr., 2:31 1-2, Sire of Sunol, 2 yrs., 2:18, Sunol, 3 yrs., 2:10 1-2, Hinda Rose, 4 yrs., 2:16, Palo Alto, 2:12¾.
  - Hambletonian 10, Sire of Dictator, George Wilkes, Happy Medium, and 40 others in 2:30 list, and grandsire of 728 in list.
    - Abdallah 1, Sire of the dams of Goldsmith Maid, 2:14, and 7 other producing dams.
    - Charles Kent mare By imp. Bellfounder.
  - Green Mountain Maid, Dam of Prospero, 2:20, Elaine, 2:20, Dame Trot, 2:22, Elista, 2:22¾, Storm, 2:26¾, Antonio, 2:28¾, Miranda, 2:31, Mansfield, 2:26.
    - Harry Clay, Sire of the dams of St. Julian, 2:11¾, Bodine, 2:19¼, and 17 more in 2:30 list
    - Shanghai Mary.
- Sontag Mohawk, Dam of Eros, 2:29 1-2, Sport, 2:22¾, Sallie Benton, 2:17¾, Conductor, trial, 2:26, Colma, 3-y-o trial, 2:24.
  - Mohawk Chief, Sire of the dams of Lot Slocum, 2:17¾, Sallie Benton, 4 yrs., 2:17¾, Pediar, 2 yrs., 2:27¾, Stanford, 4 yrs., 2:30, Eros, 6th heat, 2:29 1-2.
    - Hambletonian 10, Sire of the dams of Stamboul, 2:12¾, Wilton, 2:19¾, and 20 other trotters.
    - Lady Perrine
  - Sontag Nellie
    - Toronto Sontag, By Toronto Chief,
    - Nellie Gray, 5-mile record, 13:45.

Produce of Eros
Wanda, 4 yrs., 2:24.
Solita, 2 yrs., 2:41 1-2.
Meriquita, 3 yrs., 2:42.
Daylight, 2 yrs., 2:54.
Hiram B., trial, 2:28.

These are the only colts by him that have ever had a harness on except one in New York that went a trial last July in 2:26 1:2.

DESCRIPTION.

EROS is a rich seal brown stallion, bred by Hon. Leland Stanford at Palo Alto, and is the nearest living likeness of his celebrated sire, Electioneer. Stands 15.2 hands high, and weighs 1050 pounds

In breeding to Eros, the owners of mares will strictly follow the great rule of breeding, viz., breed to a stallion by a producer and out of a sure producer of great speed. Eros is by the stallion that has produced more 2:30 trotters that any living horse, and is also the sire of more 2:30 performers than any horse living or dead

EROS is out of the dam of Sally Benton, four years old, record 2:17¾, Sport 2:22¾, and Eros 2:29½ in the sixth heat, against a field of nine horses. He is from a family that is endowed with great natural speed, trot fast at an early age, train on, throw trotters from all classes of mares, are of good substance, bone, style and action, and breed solid colors.

TERMS.

$100 for the season, with the privilege of return next season should mares not be in foal and horse and mare still remain in the same hands.

Good pasturage can be obtained at $5 per month, but no responsibility for accidents or escapes. There are a large number of box stalls, and animals can be kept up and fed on hay and grain at reasonable rates if required. Mares already in foal can be sent to the ranch for foaling, and will receive all the attention bestowed upon our own mares. Mares left with Mr. Peter Pomyea, Broadway Street Stable, Oakland, or with Mr. F. H. Burke, 401 Montgomery Street, San Francisco, will be forwarded to the ranch free of charge. For further particulars apply to

W. H. VIOGET,
LA SIESTA RANCH, MENLO PARK, CAL.

EROS is the only stallion offered to the public on this Coast that has a dam that has three in the 2:30 list.

POPLAR GROVE

Breeding Farm

STALLIONS.

CLOVIS, 4909,

CLOVIS is a beautiful black, Eight Years Old, 16 1-2 Hands High, and weighs 1260 lbs.

He is a horse of beautiful symmetry and magnificent action.

PEDIGREE.

CLOVIS was sired by Sultan, 2:24, sire of Stamboul, 2:12 1-4, Ruby, 2:19¾, and fifteen others with records of 2:30 or better.

First dam Sweetbriar by Thorndale 2:22 1-2, sire of Edwin Thorne, 2:16 1-2, Daisy Dale, 2:19, and May Thorne, 2:24

Second dam Ulster Queen, dam of Volmer, 2:24¾, by Hambletonian 10. Sire of Dexter, 2:17¼, George Wilkes, 2:22.

Third dam by Thomas Jefferson, a son of Mambrino Paymaster, Jr.

Fourth dam by Mambrino Paymaster, sire of Mambrino Chief.

Sultan, by The Moor, sire of Beautiful Bells, dam of Hinda Rose, 2:19 1-2, and Sable, dam of Sable Wilkes, three year old record 2:18.

First dam of Sultan, Sultana, by Delmonico. Sire of Darby, 2:16 1-2, by Guy Miller, sire of Whipple's Hambletonian.

Second dam by Mambrino Chief.

Third dam by Downing's Bay Messenger.

Fourth dam Mrs. Caudle, dam of Ericsson, four year old record 2:30 1-2.

Clovis will make the season of 1890 at Poplar Grove Breeding Farm, near Wildflower, Fresno County, commencing February 1st and ending July 1st.

Terms, $75, due at time of service.

Mares cared for in any manner owners may desire; pasturage $2 per month. Every care exercised, but no liability for escapes or accidents. Mares not proving with foal can be returned next season, providing I still own this stallion.

APEX, 8935.

FOUR-YEAR-OLD RECORD, FOURTH HEAT, 2:26.

Will make the present season at the Poplar Grove Breeding Farm, near Wildflower, Fresno Co., season commencing Feb. 1st, and ending July 1, 1890. Terms, $50 the season, due at time of service. Apex is eight years old, a beautiful bay, 15 1-2 hands high, and weighs 1140 lbs. He is a horse of fine disposition, and his gait is faultless.

PEDIGREE.

Apex was sired by Promptor 2305, he by Blue Bull 75; first dam Mary by Flaxtail, he by Pruden's Blue Bull, Flaxtail being the sire of the dams of Buccaneer, five-year-old record, 2:24 1-2; Pride, yearling record, 2:44 1-2, and Shamrock, two-year old record, 2:26, third heat. Second dam by Bright Eyes, son of Boanarages. Promptor (sire of Apex, record 2:26, and Transit, 2:26 1-2), by Wilson's Blue Bull, by Pruden's Blue Bull, son of Merring's Blue Bull. Promptor's dam Prairie Bird, by Flaxtail; second dam by John the Baptist, son of Tally Ho Morgan, by Sherman Morgan; third dam Fannie Fern by Irwin's Tuckaho.

Apex made his appearance in the circuit as a two-year-old, and obtained a record of 2:42. As a three-year-old he reduced this in a race at Santa Rosa against Stamboul to 2:31, it taking six heats to decide the contest, which was won by Apex. As a four year-old he gained his present record of 2:26.

Mares cared for in any manner owners may desire. Pasturage $2 per month. Every care exercised, but no liabilities for escapes or accidents. Mares not proving with foal can be returned next season, providing I still own this stallion.

The Standard Stallion

JUNIO,

RECORD 2:22.

WILL MAKE THE PRESENT SEASON OF 1890 AT FRESNO FAIR GROUNDS.

Season Commencing Feb. 1st and ending July 1st.

TERMS—$100 the season, due at time of service.

JUNIO is eight years old, a handsome dark bay 16 hands high, and weighs 1250 pounds. He is the personification of the light harness horse, and his trotting action is superb. At the State Fair of 1886 he took first premium over forty of the finest trotters in the State.

PEDIGREE.

Junio, by Electioneer, premier stallion of Palo Alto (sire of Sunol 2:10 1-2, Palto Alto 2:12 1-4, and 47 others in the 2:30 list. Dam by Granger by imp. Hercules.

Granger, by imp. Hercules, dam Jenny Lind, by Stockbridge Chief, Jr., he by Stockbridge Chief, he by Vermont Black Hawk. Second dam by Kentucky Whip.

Imp. Hercules, by Kingston, first dam daughter of Tuscar, by Bay Middleton, second dam Malvina, by Oscar; 3rd dam Spotless by Walton; 4th dam by Trumpator (see Bruce's American Stud Book, Vol. 1, page 28). Hercules is the sire of the dam of Azmoor 2:20¾; also sire of dam of Menlo 2:21 1-2.

Mares not proving in foal may be returned next year free of charge, providing I still have the horse. Pasturage $3 per month. While every care will be taken of horses, no liability will be assumed for accidents or escapes.

For further particulars address

S. N. STRAUBE, Fresno, Cal.

Poplar Grove Breeding Farm.

2:10¾ 2:13¾ 2:10

DEXTER PRINCE.

This Royally-bred Stallion will make the Season of 1890 at the LIVE OAKS Breeding Farm, 2 miles from Lodi, San Joaquin County, Cal.

DESCRIPTION.

DEXTER PRINCE is a blood bay, 16 hands high, weighs over 1,100 pounds; has great power and substance, and the highest finish. When two years old, at Palo Alto, he was timed quarters by Gov. Stanford in 31½ seconds, and he was driven eighths by Mr. Marvin at a faster rate of speed than that. He is a sure foal-getter, and invariably sires foals of good size, of fine form and finish, and the highest rate of speed.

PEDIGREE.

By KENTUCKY PRINCE, the sire of Guy, 2:10¾, Spofford, 2:18¾, Company, 2:19¾, Bayonne Prince, 2:21 1-4, Fred Folger, 2:20¾, and a score more in the 2:30 list.

First dam LADY DEXTER, full sister of the greatest of trotters, Dexter, and the greatest of sires, Dictator, the sire of Director, 2:17, Phallas, 2:13¾, in a fourth heat, and Jay-Eye-See, 2:10.

Second dam Clara, the dam of Dexter, 2:17 1-4, Dictator, Astoria 2:29 1-4, and Alma, 2:29¾. Clara was by American Star, that has 34 daughters that have produced 2:30 or better trotters.

Third dam the McKinstry mare, the dam of Shark, 2:27¾. HAMBLETONIAN, the grandsire of DEXTER PRINCE, has 40 trotters in the 2:30 list, 44 daughters that have produced 2:30 trotters, and more than 100 sons that have sired 2:30 trotters.

CLARK CHIEF, the grandsire on the sire's side, was the sire of performing and producing sons and daughters.

DEXTER PRINCE has faster blood lines, on both sides, than any other stallion in the world—Guy, 2:10¾, and Jay-Eye-See, 2:10.

TERMS.

$100 for the season, with usual return privileges. Payable before mares are removed. Good pasture, and the best care furnished, but no responsibility assumed for accidents.

PREMIUM.

$200 will be given to the first of the produce of DEXTER PRINCE put in the 2:30 list, and $100 each after the first. Address

L. M. MORSE, Lodi, Cal.

A SON OF ALMONT 33.

Only $25 for the Season.

ASHLAND ALMONT 3481.

PEDIGREE.

ASHLAND ALMONT 3481

- Almont 33 — Sire of 34 in 2:30 or better, of 12 daughters and of 49 sires that have produce in 2:30 or better.
  - Abdallah 15 — Sire Goldsmith Maid, 2:14; 6 in 2:30 list; 13 sires and 25 dams of trotters in 2:30 list.
    - Hambletonian 10 — Sire of 41 in 2:30 list; sire of 107 sires of 567 in 2:30 list.
    - Katy Darling.
  - Sally Anderson
    - Mambrino Chief 11
    - Lady Thorn, 2:18½.
    - Kate, by Pilot Jr. 12.
- Pauline — Dam of Sapho.
  - Ashland Chief — Sire Black Cloud, 2:17¾.
    - Mambrino Chief 11
    - Lady Thorn, 2:18¼.
    - dau. of imp. Yorkshire, (thoroughbred).
  - Rosina — Dam Almonia, the dam of Sally Cossack, 2:29¾, dau. Mamb. Abdallah, sire Mam Prince, 2:3[illegible], and of Mamb. Bashaw, sire of Graham's Mambrino, 2:38.
    - Abdallah 15
    - Sire Goldsmith Maid, 2:14.
    - Prof. Smith's Sir William.

DESCRIPTION.

ASHLAND ALMONT 3481 is a handsome chestnut; stands 16 hands; was foaled 1883, and bred by Gen. Withers, of Lexington, Ky. He is of fine form, and remarkably intelligent, sweet-tempered and absolutely sound. His oldest foal may be seen with him, and while he has never served a standard mare or one that was a producer of speed, all of his colts are large, sound, fast and handsome.

TERMS: $25 for the season, with usual return privileges. The best of care taken of mares in any manner that the owner may desire, but no responsibility assumed for escapes or accidents. This horse will make the season at the corner of 8th and Brush Streets, Oakland. For further particulars, address

T. J. WHITEHEAD, Manager.

579 36th Street, bet. Telegraph Ave. and Grove St., Oakland, Cal.

or, W. H. ASHBY, Oakland, Cal.

THE BRUNSWICK BALKE COLLENDER COMPANY,

MANUFACTURERS OF

Standard Billiard and Pool Tables, Saloon and Bank Fixtures,

653--655 Market Street, San Francisco, Cal.

AXTELL'S PICTURE FREE.

Do not waste a minute, the supply will not last forever. These pictures are a genuine work of art. Good judges do not hesitate to say they are the finest likeness yet seen of the fastest stallion in the world. They are in size 18x25 inches, finished in nine colors, and in the highest style of the lithographer's art. The rich bay color of the horse is set off by the dark back ground of the box stall, around the walls of which are arranged in proper form and colors the boots, bits, muzzles, brushes, blankets, cloths, etc., usually found in the quarters of "crack trotters." The colored attendant stands near the horse, carelessly holding the blanket which has been removed to show AXTELL to an admiring group of ladies and gentlemen present.

These pictures will literally "knock your eye out." You want one for your house, office or stable. Send at once. They will go fast and you will regret not having secured one when they are all gone. Sent to any address upon receipt of 15 cents in stamps to pay postage and packing.

Send in your name and address at once to Jas. B. Campbell & Co., Chicago, Ill., and get by return mail AXTELL'S picture in nine colors 18x25, suitable for framing.

NOTICE: Stamps will be returned and orders refused from parties failing to mention the paper they saw the advertisement in.

THE "BLUE ROCK" TARGET.

Quotations furnished F. O. B. at Cleveland, Ohio, or San Francisco.

CLABROUGH, GOLCHER & CO.,

630 and 632 Montgomery Street, S. F., Cal.

SOLE AGENTS for the Pacific Coast.

The Park Training Stable.

CHAS. DAVID, PROPRIETOR.

Corner Grove and Baker Streets, near Entrance to Golden Gate Park.

EVERY FACILITY FOR TRAINING COLTS and taking care of Gentlemen's Roadsters.

Finely appointed stable with every convenience and sixteen roomy box stalls.

The best care given all horses by experienced help, under the personal superintendence of the proprietor.

Convenient to the Park Speed Drive, and Accessible to Six Lines of Cable Cars.

THE TRAINING OF COLTS AND ROADSTERS A SPECIALTY.

TROTTERS AND ROADSTERS FOR SALE.

HORSES SOLD ON COMMISSION.

The proprietor trained and brought out the following well known horses: "Sister, Huntress," "Peribelion," "Nona Y," and others.

GOLDEN EAGLE HOTEL

Corner SEVENTH and K STREETS, SACRAMENTO.

FIRST CLASS IN EVERY RESPECT.

The LARGEST and FINEST HOTEL in the City.

W. O. BOWERS, Proprietor.

Free 'Buss to and from the Hotel.

Telephone, Telegraph Office and Messenger Service at Hotel

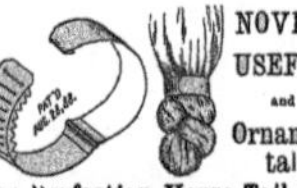

NOVEL, USEFUL and Ornamental.

The Perfection Horse Tail Tie,

Saves Time and the Tail.

Send 25 Cents for Sample,

BREEDER AND SPORTSMAN,

313 Bush Street, San Francisco.

or to BARNES & PARKER, Des Moines, Ia., Manufrs

Trade  Mark

Six Cases

S. ALLCOCK & CO.'S

Unequalled Fishing Tackle

Received direct by Steamer EXPLORER, from Liverpool, December 26, 1889.

E. T. ALLEN,

Sole Agent for Pacific Coast,

Fire Arms and Sporting Goods

416 Market St., S. F.

Singleton & Addington,

Bank Exchange,

2d and K Streets, Sacramento.

Superior Wines, Liquors and Cigars.

Old Hermitage Whiskies

"STEINER'S,"

No. 311 BUSH STREET,

San Francisco.

Under Breeder and Sportsman Office.

THE HICKS-JUDD CO.

Successors to HICKS & JUDD, Bookbinders, and Women's Co-operative Printing Office.

Printers, Bookbinders, Publishers,

23 First St., San Francisco.

BREEDERS' CATALOGUES A SPECIALTY.

KENNEL ADVERTISEMENT[illegible]

Thoroughbred Pugs, $40 each.

PEDIGREE.

PUPPIES
- Fido
  - imp. Jumbo — Marshall's / Lady Bess
  - Fanni — Rex / imp. Fly
- Budge
  - Senator Fair's Fritz
  - McCleery's Mamma Sweets — Sam / imp. Alice

Can be seen daily from 9 A. M. to 3 P. M. at 411 [illegible] Street, San Francisco.

J. F. B. McCLEER[illegible]

Irish Setters & Pointe[illegible]

In the Stud, winner of 16 first and special pr[illegible] CHAMPION MIKE T., 6435, A. K. S. B. [illegible] Setter puppies by Champion Mike T. 6435 A. K. S. B.—Champion Lady Elcho T. 6451 A. K. S. B., [illegible] sale. Two pointers, a year old, by Rush T. 10[illegible] K. S. B.—Champion Patti Croxteth T. 10138 A. K. S. B. for sale. Yard broken. Address.

A. B. TRUMAN,

1425 Steiner St., S. F., Ca[illegible]

CALIFORNIA SPANIEL KENNEL[illegible]

Oakland, Califor[illegible] H. P. RENNIE, Pr[illegible] Breeder and impor[illegible] of typical COCK[illegible] SPANIELS. Win[illegible] of first prizes at S[illegible] and Los Angeles, [illegible] also, Columbus, [illegible] New York, 1887. [illegible] the stud, solid Bl[illegible] Cockerdog, GIFF[illegible] won 1st and G[illegible] Medal at S. F., [illegible] Fee, $25. Puppies [illegible] grown dogs at reas[illegible] able prices. My d[illegible] can neither talk [illegible] climb a tree, but are fielders and prize winners.

Fiske's Vanes.

MADE OF COPPER And Gilded with PURE GOLD LEAF.

Manufacturer's Agent.

The HOWE SCALE C[illegible]

411 & 413 Market Street, S. F.

Scales for Weighing of

Live Stock

SEEDS, FEED, Etc.

Write for Catalogue.

PERRIER-JOU[illegible] & Co.

EPERNAY

CHAMPAGN[illegible]

W. B CHAPMA[illegible]

Sole Agent for Pacif[illegible] Coast.

For sale by all first-c[illegible] Wine Merchants and Grocer[illegible]

R. LIDDLE & SO[illegible]

538 Washington St., S. F.,

Wholesale and Retail Dealers in

Guns, Rifles and Pisto[illegible]

A Full Line of FISHING TACKLE and SPORTSMAN'S GOODS.

Orders by mail receive prompt attention.

Southern Pacific Co.

(PACIFIC SYSTEM.)

Trains leave and are due to arrive at San Francisco.

LEAVE (FOR)	FROM JANUARY 1, 1890.	ARRIVE (FROM)
7.30 A M	Haywards, Niles and San Jose ...	*12.45 P M
7.30 A M	Sacramento and Redding, via Davis	7.15 P M
7.30 A M	Sacramento, Auburn, Colfax	5.45 P M
8.00 A M	Martinez, Vallejo, Calistoga and Santa Rosa	6.15 P M
8.30 A M	Los Angeles Express, Fresno, Bakersfield Mojave and East and Los Angeles	11.15 A M
8.30 A M	Niles, San Jose, Stockton, Ione, Sacramento, Marysville, Oroville and Red Bluff	5.45 P M
10.30 A M	Haywards and Niles	2.15 P M
*12.00 M	Haywards, Niles and San Jose	* 3.45 P M
*1.00 P M	Sacramento River Steamers	**6.00 A M
3.00 P M	Haywards, Niles and San Jose	9.45 A M
3.30 P M	2d Class for Ogden and East	10.45 P M
4.00 P M	Stockton and Milton; Vallejo, Calistoga and Santa Rosa	9.45 A M
4.30 P M	Sacramento and Knight's Landing via Davis	10.45 A M
* 4.30 P M	Niles and Livermore	* 8.45 A M
* 4.30 P M	Niles and San Jose	‡ 4.15 P M
5.30 P M	Haywards and Niles	7.45 A M
6.00 P M	Sunset Route, Atlantic Express, Santa Barbara, Los Angeles, Deming, El Paso, New Orleans and East	8.45 P M
7.00 P M	Shasta Route Express, Sacramento, Marysville, Redding, Portland, Puget Sound and East	7.45 A M
8.00 P M	Central Atlantic Express, Ogden and East	9.45 A M

SANTA CRUZ DIVISION.

‡ 8.00 A M	Hunters train to San Jose	‡ 7.20 P M
8.15 A M	Newark, Centerville, San Jose, Felton, Boulder Creek and Santa Cruz	5.50 P M
* 2.15 P M	Centerville, San Jose, Almaden, Felton, Boulder Creek and Santa Cruz	*11.50 A M
4.15 P M	Centerville, San Jose, and Los Gatos	9.50 A M

Coast Division (Third and Townsend Sts.)

7.25 A M	San Jose, Almaden and Way Stations	2.30 P M
8.30 A M	San Jose, Gilroy, Tres Pinos; Pajaro, Santa Cruz; Monterey; Pacific Grove, Salinas, San Miguel, Paso Robles, Santa Margarita (San Luis Obispo) and principal Way Stations	6.12 P M
10.30 A M	San Jose and Way Stations	5.02 P M
12.01 P M	Cemetery, Menlo Park and Way Stations	3.38 P M
* 3.30 P M	San Jose, Tres Pinos, Santa Cruz, Salinas, Monterey Pacific Grove and principal Way Stations	*10.00 A M
4.20 P M	Menlo Park and Way Station	* 7.58 A M
5.20 P M	San Jose and Way Stations	9.03 A M
6.30 P M	Menlo Park and Way Stations	6.35 A M
†11.45 P M	Menlo Park and principal Way Stations	†7.28 P M

A M for Morning. P M for Afternoon.
*Sundays excepted †Saturdays only. ‡Sundays only.
**Mondays excepted. §Saturdays excepted.

OCEANIC STEAMSHIP CO.

Carrying United States, Hawaiian and Colonial Mails.

WILL LEAVE THE COMPANY'S WHARF, foot of Mission Street, No. 1,

For Honolulu, Auckland and Sydney,

WITHOUT CHANGE,

The Splendid New 3,000-ton Iron Steamer.
ZEALANDIA ..... Saturday, March 8, 1890, at 12 M.,
Or immediately on arrival of the English mails.

For Honolulu,

SS. AUSTRALIA (3,000 tons), February 28, 1890, at 12 M

☞ For freight or passage, apply at office, 327 Market Street. JOHN D. SPRECKELS & BROS.,
General Agents.

KILLIP & CO.,

LIVE STOCK AND GENERAL AUCTIONEERS,

22 Montgomery Street, San Francisco

SPECIAL ATTENTION PAID TO SALES OF

High-Bred Horses and Cattle.

At auction and private sale.

Will Sell in All Cities and Counties of the State.

REFERENCES.

HON. C. GREEN, Sacramento. — HON. J. D. CARR Salinas.
J. P. SARGENT, ESQ., Sargents. — HON. JOHN BOGGS Colusa.
HON. L. J. ROSE, Los Angeles. — HON. A. WALRATH Nevada.
J. B. HAGGIN, ESQ., San Francisco.

Represented at Sacramento by Edwin F. Smith Secretary State Agricultural Society.

At San Jose by Messrs. Montgomery & Rea, Real Estate Agents.

Being the oldest established firm in the live-stock business on this Coast, and having conducted the important auction sales in this line for the past fifteen years, amounting to one half a million of dollars, we feel justified in claiming unequaled facilities for disposing of live stock of every description, either at auction or private sale. Our list of correspondents embraces every breeder and dealer of prominence upon the Pacific Coast, thus enabling us to give full publicity to animals placed with us for sale. Private purchases and sales of live stock of all descriptions will be made on commission, and stock shipped with the utmost care. Purchases and sales made of land of every description. We are authorized to refer to the gentlemen whose names are appended.

KILLIP & CO., 22 Montgomery Street.

LAMBORN ROAD MACHINE

LIGHT DRAFT. MADE OF IRON. STRONG, SIMPLE, DURABLE. EASILY OPERATED.

TRUMAN HOOKER & CO.
SAN FRANCISCO, - - CALIFORNIA

San Francisco and North Pacific Railway.

THE DONAHUE BROAD-GAUGE ROUTE.

COMMENCING SUNDAY, MARCH 17, 1889, AND until further notice, boats and trains will leave from and arrive at the San Francisco Passenger Depot, Market-street Wharf, as follows:

Leave San Francisco. Week Days.	Leave San Francisco. Sundays.	Destination	Arrive San Francisco. Sundays.	Arrive San Francisco. Week Days.
7.40 A M 3.30 P M 5.00 P M	8.00 A M 5.00 P M	Petaluma and Santa Rosa	10.40 A M 6.10 P M	8.50 A M 10.30 A M 6.05 P M
7.40 A M 3.30 P M	8.00 A M	Fulton, Windsor, Healdsburg, Litton Springs, Cloverdale, and way stations.	6.10 P M	10.30 A M 6.05 P M
7.40 A M	8.00 A M	Hopland and Ukiah.	6.10 P M	6.05 P M
7.40 A M	8.00 A M	Guerneville	6.10 P M	6.05 P M
7.40 A M 5.00 P M	8.00 A M	Sonoma and Glen Ellen.	10.40 A M 6.10 P M	8.50 A M 6.05 P M

Stage connects at Santa Rosa for White Sulphur Springs, Sebastopol and Mark West Springs; at Geyserville for Skaggs Springs, and at Cloverdale for the Geysers; at Hopland for Highland Springs, Kelseyville, Soda Bay, Lakeport and Bartlett Springs, and at Ukiah for Vichy Springs, Saratoga Springs, Blue Lakes, Willits, Cahto, Calpella, Potter Valley, Sherwood Valley and Mendocino City.

EXCURSION TICKETS from Saturdays to Mondays, to Petaluma, $1.50; to Santa Rosa $2.25; to Healdsburg, $3.40; to Litton Springs, $3.60; to Cloverdale, $4.50; to Hopland, $5.70; to Ukiah, $6.75; to Guerneville, $3.75; to Sonoma, $1.50; to Glen Ellen, $1.80.

EXCURSION TICKETS, good for Sundays only, to Petaluma, $1; to Santa Rosa, $1.50; to Healdsburg, $2.25; to Litton Springs, $2.40; to Cloverdale, $3; to Guerneville, $2.50, to Sonoma, $1; to Glen Ellen, $1.20.

From San Francisco for Point Tiburon and San Rafael: Week Days—7.40, 9.20, 11.20, A. M.; 3.30, 5.00, 6.15 P. M. Sundays—8.00, 9.30, 11.00 A. M.; 1.30, 5.00, 6.20 P. M.

To San Francisco from San Rafael: Week Days—6.20, 7.55, 9.30 A. M.; 12.45, 3.40, 5.05 P. M. Sundays—8.10, 9.40 A. M.; 12.15, 3.40, 5.00 P. M.

To San Francisco from Point Tiburon: Week Days—6.50, 8.20, 9.55 A. M.; 1.10, 4.05, 5.30 P. M.; Sundays—8.40, 10.05 A. M.; 12.40, 4.05, 5.30 P. M.

On Saturdays an extra trip will be made from San Francisco to San Rafael, leaving at 1.40 P. M.

H. C. WHITING, General Manager.

PETER J. McGLYNN, Gen. Pass. & Tkt. Agt.

Ticket Offices at Ferry, 222 Montgomery Street and 2 New Montgomery Street.

CHICAGO, MILWAUKEE AND ST. PAUL RAILWAY.

Steam Heated and Electric Lighted Vestibuled Trains between Chicago, St. Paul and Minneapolis.

Electric Lighted and Steam Heated Vestibuled Trains between Chicago, Council Bluffs and Omaha.

Finest Dining Cars in the world.

Free Reclining Chair Cars between Chicago and Omaha.

Fast Mail Line between Chicago, Milwaukee, St. Paul and Minneapolis.

Transcontinental Route between Chicago, Council Bluffs and Omaha, or St. Paul.

Great National Route between Chicago, Kansas City and St. Joseph, Mo.

5,700 miles of road in Illinois, Wisconsin, Minnesota, Iowa, Missouri, South and North Dakota.

Everything First-Class.

First-Class People patronize First-Class Lines.

Ticket Agents everywhere sell Tickets over the Chicago, Milwaukee and St. Paul Railway.

W. T. ALLEN,
Pacific Coast Passenger Agent
Office, No 138 Montgomery St., San Francisco, Cal.
Under Occidental Hotel

6 DONTS

DON'T own a racehorse.
DON'T be a breeder.
DON'T be a trainer.
DON'T be a jockey.
DON'T bet on the races.
DON'T go to a race track.

WITHOUT

HAVING IN YOUR POCKET ONE OF

Goodwin's

ANNUAL

OFFICIAL TURF GUIDES.

Price, in cloth $5.00
Price, in half morocco 3.00
Price, in half calf 4.00
If sent by mail .... 10 cents extra

SUBSCRIBE TO IT FOR 1890.

It is published semi-monthly during the racing season, and is but **$10 per year.** Address

GOODWIN BROS.,
241 Broadway, New York City.

HEALD'S

Business College, 24 Post St.
—San Francisco.—
The most popular school on the Coast
E. P. HEALD, President. C. S. HALEY, Sec'y.
☞ Send for Circulars

RUB YOUR HORSES

In cases of **SWELLING** or **STIFFNESS** of **THE JOINTS**, with

DARBYS FLUID.

If you value your Horses, Dogs and Cattle always keep it on hand.

IT HAS NO EQUAL

For Cuts, Scratches, Bruises, Bites, Sores, Etc.

It gives immediate relief, and prevents Poison, Gangrene and Proud Flesh.

J. H. ZEILIN & CO., - Philadelphia, Pa

SOLD BY ALL DRUGGISTS.

DR. FISHERMAN'S

Carbolized Alkaline

LOTION

Cures after all other Remedies have Failed.

Sprains, Sores, Bruises, Galls, Swellings, Scratches, Thrush, Grease Heels, Curb, Rheumatism. Restoring Weak Knees and Ankles to their original condition. As a wash it insures glossy manes and tails. Valuable as an internal remedy for Coughs, Colic, Congestion or Fever. You really get Half a Gallon of Remedy for $1.00, or Two Gallons for $3.00, after being adulterated as directed.

This Liniment has received the endorsement of some of our best horsemen. Recommended by Jos. Cairn Simpson. See BREEDER AND SPORTSMAN of November 10th, 1888.

LYNDE & HOUGH, Proprietors.

116 California St., S. F.

Or ask your Druggist for it.

HORSE OWNERS! TRY GOMBAULT'S CAUSTIC BALSAM.

A Safe, Speedy and Positive Cure for Curb, Splint, Sweeny, Capped Hock, Strained Tendons, Founder, Wind Puffs, all Skin Diseases or Parasites, Thrush, Diphtheria, Pinkeye, all Lameness from Spavin, Ringbone or other Bony Tumors. Removes all Bunches or Blemishes from Horses and Cattle.

Supersedes all Cautery or Firing.

Impossible to Produce any Scar or Blemish.

Every bottle sold is warranted to give satisfaction. Price **$1.50** per bottle. Sold by druggists, or sent by express, charges paid, with full directions for its use. Send for descriptive circulars. Address
LAWRENCE, WILLIAMS & CO., Cleveland, O.

BROU'S INJECTION

A PERMANENT CURE

in from 3 to 6 days, of the most obstinate cases; guaranteed not to produce Stricture; no sickening doses; and no inconvenience or loss of time. Recommended by physicians and sold by all druggists. J. Ferré, (successor to Brou), Pharmacien, Paris.

For any Kind of a

SORE THROAT

USE

McCLELLAN'S

DIPHTHERIA REMEDY

An Unfailing Cure.

FOR SALE BY ALL DRUGGISTS

"DICKEY'S,"

SIXTH AVENUE AND D ST.

Near entrance to Bay District Track.

Choicest Brands of

WINES AND CIGARS.

A Delightful Resort.

Telephone 1485. J. R. DICKEY, Propr.

PHIL J. CRIMMINS. JOHN C. MORRISON.

"Silver Palace,"

36 Geary Street,

San Francisco, Cal.

VETERINARY.

Dr. Wm. H. Jones, M.R.C.V.S.

Veterinary Surgeon,
(OLYMPIC CLUB STABLES)
503 Sutter Street, San Francisco.
Telephone, No. 1404.

Consultations by letter, and cases of URGENT NECESSITY in the interior will receive prompt attention.

Dr. A. E. BUZARD,

VETERINARY SURGEON,

Member of the Royal College of Veterinary Surgeons, London, England. Graduated April 22d, 1870.

All Operations on the Horse Performed Skillfully.

Special attention given to the Diseases of Dogs. Calls to the country promptly attended to. Advice and prescriptions by mail $2. Office and Residence, No. 11 Seventh street, S. F. (opp. Odd Fellows Hall. Telephone No. 3 69.

W. H. WOODRUFF.

Veterinary Dentist,

AT FASHION STABLES,

221 Ellis Street, San Francisco

Improved Instruments, Humane Methods, First-Class Work.

H. E. CARPENTER,

Veterinary Surgeon,

Graduate of Ontario Veterinary College, Toronto, Canada.

RESIDENCE AND VETERINARY INFIRMARY
331 Golden Gate Ave., San Francisco.
Telephone 3069.

☞ OPEN DAY AND NIGHT. ☜

No risk in throwing Horses. Veterinary Operating Table on the premises.

DR. C. MASOERO,

Veterinary Surgeon,

Successor to **DR. A. DeTAVEL,**

GRADUATE OF ROYAL VETERINARY COLLEGE, TURIN.

OFFICE AND INFIRMARY,

No. 811 HOWARD STREET,

Between Fourth and Fifth. SAN FRANCISCO.

Telephone, No. 457.

R. WATKINS,

Veterinary Dentist,

Of twelve years practice, is now permanently located in San Francisco, and may be found at C. S. Crittendens' Golden Gate Livery and Riding Academy, **24 to 28 Golden Gate Avenue.**

Will treat ailments of the horse's mouth, and cure all such. Sidereín Pullers and Tongue Lollers etc. Satisfaction guaranteed. Orders by mail will receive prompt attention. Examination Free.

E. J. O'ROUKE.

I have the honor to announce to my old patrons and the general public that I may be found at my old stand, where, as heretofore, the

Shoeing of Horses,

whether for the Track, Drive, or for general work, will receive my personal attention.

Telephone 2011.

E. J. O'ROUKE,
209 Ellis Street

California Horse Shoe Co's

STEEL SHOE

Light, Strong and Perfect.

Superior to all others for Speed Horses.

ALSO

The Celebrated GOODENOUGH Pattern Shoe.

OFFICE:
202 Market St.,
San Francisco, Cal.

I have used in my business the Steel and Iron Shoes made by the above Company, and take great pleasure in saying they are the best I have ever used in twenty-two years' practice. I have never seen anything like the STEEL SHOE made by this Company. I can fully recommend them to every practical Horseshoer in the country. Yours respectfully,

No. 8 Everett Street. JOHN GRACE.

THE BOHANON SULKY!

OUR IMPROVED. ALL SIZES AND WEIGHTS. G.W. BOHANON.

BEST MADE.
Perfect Riding Buggies.
Breaking Carts.
Fine Repairing, Reasonable Prices.

Bohanon Carriage Co., 161-163 Ogden Ave., CHICAGO.

Send for Catalogue.

"STANDARD" SHOTGUN CARTRIDGES

SELBY STANDARD 0 THE BEST IS THE CHEAPEST

Everything for

Trotter or Runner,

At J. A. McKERRON'S,

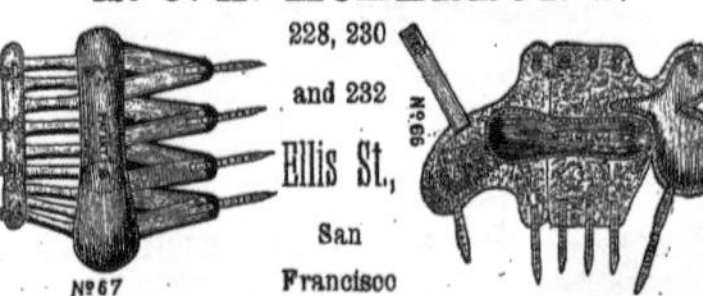

228, 230 and 232 Ellis St., San Francisco

The PARKER Hammerless Shot Gun.

At the Annual Tournament of 1889, held at Cannes, France, the grand prize, consisting of 2000 Francs and a Valuable Cup. was won by The Parker Hammerless.

The first Parker Hammerless Gun made won the championship of America at Decatur Illinois.

SEND FOR ILLUSTRATED CIRCULAR.

PARKER BROS., Makers,

New York Salesroom, 97 Chambers St., Meriden Conn.

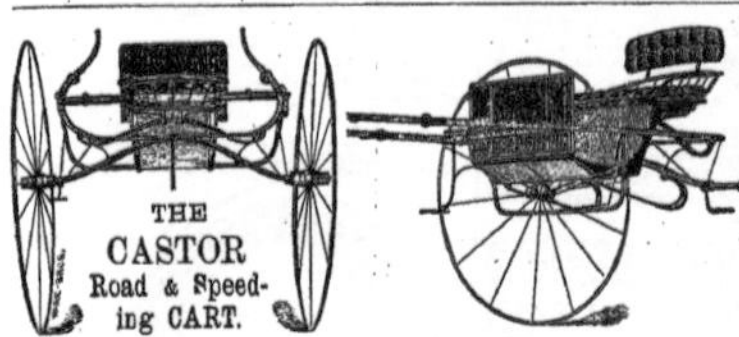

ALWAYS GIVES SATISFACTION.

Combining perfect riding qualities, proportions and balance, with genteel appearance.

No vehicle exhibits a horse to better advantage, and no Cart approaches them for speeding or training purposes.

A stylish vehicle for exercising or pleasure driving, at one-fourth the cost of a carriage. Have none of the horse jockey or objectionable features of other Road Carts.

They are the Leading Cart wherever introduced, and are in use by the most prominent breeders and pleasure drivers everywhere.

Elegant Shifting Top Carts.

Perfectly Balanced Stylish Pole Carts.

For Illustrated Catalogue, with Prices, address,

LEWIS F. CASTOR,
Frankford, Philadelphia, Pa.
JOHN SPLAN, General Agent.

Brothers of the Angle.

OUR NEW EIGHT-STRIP SPLIT BAMBOO is the "King" of all fishing-rods. Chubb's New Catalogue for 1890 is now ready. In addition to a complete list of anglers' supplies, it contains articles from the pens of Dr. James A. Henshall, Petronella, W. H. Murray, Geo. P. Goff, Norman, Brother Gardner, and others.

These papers are by the best writers on angling subjects, and are very interesting.

Send 25 cents, and receive Catalogue, post-paid. This amount will be deducted from first order (if accompanied with COUPON in book) for one dollar's worth or more of our goods. Address

THOS. H. CHUBB.
The Fishing-Rod Manufacturer,
POST MILLS, VT.

Please mention BREEDER AND SPORTSMAN.

MANHATTAN FOOD.

keeps horses healthy, promotes digestion, fattens horses, loosens the hide, assists the appetite, prevents leg swelling, strengthens the kidneys, regulates the bowels and destroys worms. **$7.50 per 100 lbs.** Ask your dealer for it or send to

MANHATTAN FOOD CO., 206 Clay St., S. F.

THE IMPROVED NOYES ROAD-CART.

PATENTED JULY 17, 1883, *AND JUNE* 8, 1886.

Some of the Advantages of the Noyes Cart Over All Others.

There is no bar for the rider to climb over in getting in or out. The horse can be hitched eighteen inches nearer than any other road-cart made. You can get in or out with perfect safety—no danger of being thrown into the wheel—a great advantage in breaking colts. THE EASIEST CART FOR ROAD OR TRACK. The only cart that a horse can be speeded to within one second as fast as to a sulky. All our carts are made of the very best materials and are warranted. Manufactured by the NOYES CART COMPANY, Kalamazoo, Mich.

They are indorsed by the following horsemen, all of whom are using them. Ask their opinion of the Noyes Cart: John Splan, who drove Guy a full mile in 2:17¼ and Chanter a half-mile in 1:05¾ to a Noyes Cart, says he would not take $250 for it if he could not get another; W. J. Gordon, Glenville, O.; W. B. Fasig, Cleveland, O.; Dave Muckel, Cleveland, O.; R. J. Moorehead, North East, Pa.; W. J. Chamberlain, Cleveland, O.; H. P. Malone, Bradford, Pa.; S. A. Brown & Co., Kalamazoo Stock Farm; Charles Marvin, Menlo Park, Cal.; W. H. Crawford, Lexington, Ky.; S. L. Caton, who gave Bell Boy a mark at Los Angeles, Cal., of 2:19¼, and drove Chanter a half mile in 1:05¾ and Lowland Girl a full mile in 2:22 to a Noyes Cart; Mike Bowerman, Lexington, Ky.; James Golden, Medford, Mass.; John E. Turner, Philadelphia, Pa.; T. L. Newton, Beaver Dam, Wis.; P. V. Johnston, Marshall, Mich.; W. H. McCarthy, Los Angeles, Cal.; A. W. Dennison, El Dorado, Kan.; P. O. Shank, Cleveland, O.; Charles Barnard, Boston, Mass.; Johnson Bros., Greenville, Mich.; John G. Avery, Buffalo, N. Y.; General R. L. Howard, Buffalo, N. Y.; Howard Conklin, Buffalo, N. Y.; W. D. Ham, Hennepin, Ill.; R. G. Henry, Waterbury, Conn; J. E. Hayer, Newburgh, O.; J. C. Hart, Jefferson, Tex.; A. W. Harbison, Rock Point, Pa.; Carl Hodges, Battle Creek, Mich.; Barney Treacy, Lexington, Ky.; George Forbes, Cleveland, O.; Gifford Dudley, Topeka, Kan.; William and J. L. Thompson Lamont, Pa.; C. P. Emery, Forest City Stock Farm, Cleveland, O.; H. F. Jones, Minneapolis, Minn.; John Forbes, Elyria, O.; D. J. Downs Battle Creek, Mich.; Frank Caton, Randall Station, O.; Arthur D. Sutton, Ind., Pa.; W. F. Neely, Grand Ridge, Ill.; Walter Clark, owner of Pilot Medium, Battle Creek, Mich.; H. R. Kingman, Battle Creek, Mich.; Dr. Sutton and H. C. Reed, Kalamazoo, Mich.; Budd Doble, Chicago, Ill.

SOLE MANUFACTURERS OF STONE'S PATENT SULKY CASE.

They will more than save their cost in one season, and horsemen campaigning trotters cannot afford to do without them. Would refer to Samuel A. Brown, Kalamazoo Stock Farm, S. L. Caton and W. H. McCarthy. Address

NOYES CART COMPANY, Kalamazoo, Mich.

Office and Factory, corner Rose and Eleanor streets. H. ARTHUR STONE, Manager.

OSSIDINE

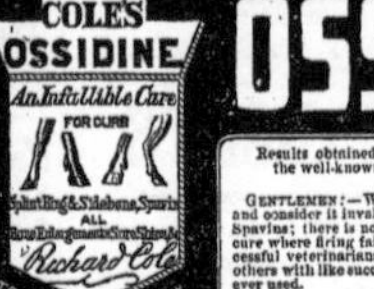

Results obtained at the well-known **KALAMAZOO FARM.**

KALAMAZOO, MICH., Sept. 15, 1888.

GENTLEMEN:—We have used **OSSIDINE** for the past two years and consider it invaluable for Sprung Tendons, Curbs, Ringbone, and Spavins; there is nothing equals it: and for us it effected a permanent cure where firing failed, although performed by one of the most successful veterinarians on the continent. We have recommended it to others with like success, and believe it has more merit than any blister ever used.

Very respectfully yours,
S. A. BROWNE & CO., Prop's.

This scientific preparation is an absolute cure for all bony or callous lumps on horses, and is a more powerful absorbent than "firing," without creating the slightest blemish.

Acknowledged by leading horsemen of the world to be the **ONLY** preparation that will remove a Bone Spavin after it has become ossified.

We have authority also to refer to
Mr. JEROME I. CASE, Mr. FRED. GEBHARD,
Mr. JOHN PORTER (Trainer to H.R.H. the Prince of Wales),
And hundreds of others from whom we have very flattering testimonials.

One Style Only. $3.00 per Bottle.

A. P. BUSH & CO.,
149 Pearl St.,
BOSTON, MASS.,
Sole Agents for United States and Canada.
Beware of Imitations.

SOLD BY C. N. Crittenton, A. R. Van Nest & Co., and C. M. Moseman & Bro., NEW YORK CITY. Morrisson, Plummer & Co., Peter Van Schaack & Sons, CHICAGO, ILL. John D. Park & Son, CINCINNATI, O.; Floyd & Foster, DETROIT, MICH.; F. S. Slosson, CLEVELAND, O.; Meyer Bros. Drug Co., ST. LOUIS, MO.; R. A. Robinson, LOUISVILLE, KY.; H. H. Moore & Sons, STOCKTON, Cal.

Nutwood 2:22¾, 2:21½, 2:18¾ } Sire

DAWN 6407

Dam Countess } DAM OF: Strathway (2-y-o) 2:26, " trial 2:21; Placida, Morna } Double team Trial 2:26

2:18¾; 2:20; 2:19½.

$100 Popular Price for season of 1890. $100

Not having a breeding farm, and being dependent on the public for patronage, I have set the above low price in order to be within the reach of any one desiring to breed. Good pasturage $3 per month.

For further particulars, address

A. L. WHITNEY, Petaluma.

TWENTY-FOUR PAGES.

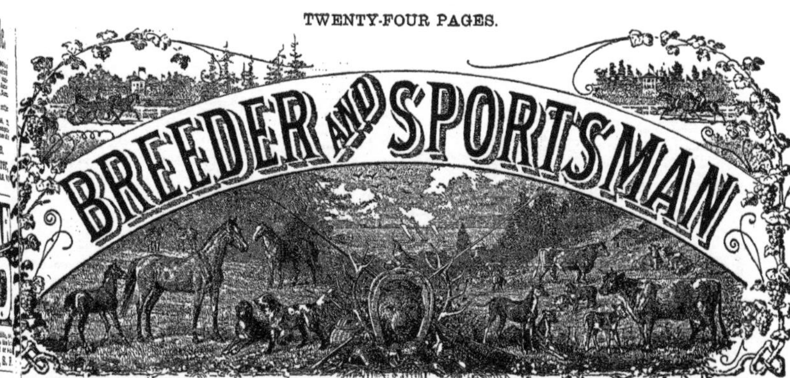

Vol. XVI, No. 9. No. 313 BUSH STREET. | SAN FRANCISCO, SATURDAY, MARCH 1, 1890. | SUBSCRIPTION FIVE DOLLARS A YEAR.

ALBERT W., 2:20.

By Electioneer, dam Sister. The property of J. B. Haggin, Esq., Rancho Del Paso, California.

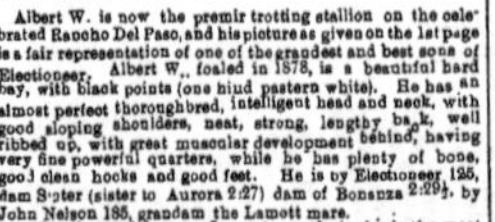

Albert W. is now the premir trotting stallion on the celebrated Rancho Del Paso, and his picture as given on the 1st page is a fair representation of one of the grandest and best sons of Electioneer. Albert W., foaled in 1878, is a beautiful hard bay, with black points (one hind pastern white). He has an almost perfect thoroughbred, intelligent head and neck, with good sloping shoulders, neat, strong, lengthy back, well ribbed up, with great muscular development behind, having very fine powerful quarters, while he has plenty of bone, good clean hocks and good feet. He is by Electioneer 125, dam Sister (sister to Aurora 2:27) dam of Bonanza 2:29½, by John Nelson 185, grandam the Lamott mare.

Of Electioneer it is superfluous to speak, for his is the most sought after blood in the world. Albert's dam, Sister, is also the dam of Bonanza, 2:29½—it is an open secret that Bonanza can trot in 2:24 or 2:25 any time—and she is a sister to Aurora 2:27, who gained her record in 1872, and was supposed to be the best mare of her day. Her sale to Governor Stanford was reported to be for $20,000, she is the dam of Arol 2:24.

John Nelson 187 was by imported Trustee out of the Redmond mare by Abdallah 1, and was the sire of Nerea 2:23½, Aurora 2:27, Governor Stanford 2:27½, and Nemo 2:30, and the dams of, among others, Albert W, 2:20, Bonanza 2:29½, Blanche 2:25½, and Valensin 2:23.

Although nothing was definitely known of the Lamott mare (Albert's granddam), she was, from her appearance, a high bred mare and has proved herself a grand broodmare through her daughters—Sister and Aurora. It will be seen that Albert has a double Abdallah cross, backed up by a thoroughbred cross through Trustee, one of our best imported sires.

Albert W. was bred by Mr. A. Waldstein, San Francisco, who purchased his dam, Sister, from Mr. E. Pond. He was foaled June 7, 1878, and was not broken to harness until late in March, 1880, while he received his first track work late in the season, consequently he did not have the benefit of an early education, yet as a race-horse he was a grand success. As a three-year-old he won three races out of four, and walked over for another. In 1882, Albert started out at Santa Rosa, and though he had not fairly recovered from an attack of "pink-eye," he beat Inca, Poscora Hayward and Blackmore after a hard struggle, Inca taking the first and third heats in 2:27, 2:27½, Albert W. the second in 2:27, the fourth was a dead heat with Poscora Hayward in 2:28½, and then Albert took the fifth and sixth in 2:29½ and 2:32. His second appearance was at Petaluma, where he defeated the same trio in straight heats: 2:27, 2:26½ and 2:24½. His third race was at Oakland, and was a phenomenal race for a four-year-old against veteran performers; Sweetness took the first two heats in 2:22, 2:24½, Nellie R. took the third in 2:23½, Albert the fourth in 2:28½, Nellie R. the fifth in 2:26½, distancing Sweetness. Albert then took the next two heats in 2:25 and 2:26½. Poscora Hayward, the other starter, broke down badly in the first heat.

Albert met his only defeat in 1882 at Sacramento, Sweetness winning in straight heats, with Albert on her wheel, in 2:24, 2:21½ and 2:22½. Albert then went to Stockton, and trotted the race of his life against Nellie R. and Sweetness.

Nellie R took the first two heats in 2:22½, 2:20; then in the third heat Albert, after trailing to the half began to close up, and with Sweetness breaking at the head of the stretch went in hot pursuit of Nellie R and collaring her at the draw gate beat her out by three lengths in 2:22. The race was now over as Albert took the fourth heat by three lengths from Sweetness in 2:22½, and the last heat he won in a jog by six lengths in 2:24.

Albert in the above race equalled the *stallion record of 2:22 made* by George Wilkes a few years prior and did it in the third heat, the fourth being only half a second slower while the fifth was in 2:24. Albert wound up the season of 1882 by easily winning a two mile race 5:04½ and 4:51, it being generally acknowledged that he could have beaten the two mile record if necessary.

In 1884, Albert reduced his record to 2:20½ and beat Manon at Petaluma, winning the 1st, 3rd and 5th heats in 2:22½, 2:22½ and 2:26. In 1885 Albert beat Sister at San Francisco, taking the 1st, 3rd and 5th heats in 2:23½, 2:24 and 2:26. In 1886 he took the first heat at Nevada City in 2:20. McConnell (Buster) who drove him when he made his record, 2:20, and also when he trotted in 2:20½, says he could easily have trotted in 2:15, the day he went in 2:20½, and he several times drove him in his work at Oakland in 2:17, while the day he went in 2:20 he was dead lame and only his sheer gameness carried him through. Orrin Hickok took Albert W. next season and only started him once when dead lame and he was beaten by Manon. Hickok says of him that his record of 2:20 is no estimate of his speed and gameness, and that he worked him a half in 1:07, and could assuredly have finished the mile in 2:15, which was an exceptional performance when one considers that at the time Albert was dead lame, but his courage was such that he never flinched until he was pulled up. He was then retired and was shortly afterwards purchased for Mr. Haggin. His colts are like the horse, wonderfully docile and intelligent. Only two of his get have been trained, the twin filly (Aurelia) and Little Albert; the latter at two years old showed a 2:28 gait, but never recovered from an attack of cerebro spinal meningintis and was not worked afterwards. Aurelia showed tremendous pace and would probably have trotted in 2:22 had she been persevered with, as she several times showed a 2:20 gait at Oakland.

All of Albert W.'s colts since Mr. Haggin purchased him will be offered for sale in New York on the 10th of March, and it is confidently expected that their average will be as good as any of the California sales, for a more even high-class lot of youngsters are rarely seen, it being remarked by everyone who has seen them that they were exceptionally clean limbed, sound and free from all blemishes, while their action is of the free, resolute style which characterized their sire.

Among the Albert youngsters are some treasures, a colt and a filly out of daughters of Echo and Mabel, sister to Beautiful Bells, dam of Bell Boy, etc., while there is also a filly by Albert W out of Mabel (sister to Beautiful Bells). Another well bred colt is a chestnut by Albert W out of Rosa Clay by Sayres' Henry Clay 45 out of Lady Winfield by Edward Everett 81, out of a daughter of Rattler, son of Abdallah.

The big handsome chestnut colt by Albert W, dam Hilda, by Nutwood, grandam Eudora by Volunteer 55, next dam by Seely's American Star, out of a Seagull-on (son of Duroc) mare, should fetch a big price, as he is a splendid trotter and has grand action, a good deal resembling Nutwood in style and make.

The colt by Albert W out of the Jones mare (dam of Senator 2:21½) by Winthrop Morrill should also sell well.

Among the other stallions on the ranch are Old Echo, who is cared for like a prince, as he deserves. Echo 462, record 2:37½; bay horse; foaled 1866. Bred by Jesse T. Seely, Warwick, Orange County, New York.

SIRE OF

Belle Echo	2:20	Lohengrin	2:27½
Senator	2:21½	Pasha	2:27½
Victor	2:2½	Elmople	2:29
Gibraltar	2:22½	Col. Hawkins	2:29½
Echora	2:23½	Annie Laurie	2:30
Tippie	2:25½	Economy	2:30

Sam Lewis, pacer, 2:25.

AND SIRE OF THE DAMS OF

Direct, 4 years old	2:18½	Pink	2:25

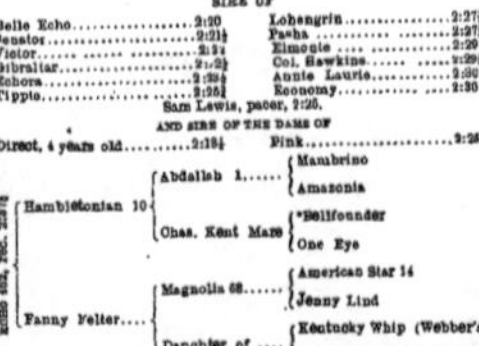

ECHO 462, REC. 2:37½

Hambletonian 10 — Abdallah 1 (Mambrino, Amazonia); Chas. Kent Mare (*Bellfounder, One Eye)

Fanny Felter — Magnolia 68 (American Star 14, Jenny Lind); Daughter of (Kentucky Whip (Webber's), Daughter of Shakespeare)

As will be seen from the pedigree above, Echo is royally bred. He is a son of Rysdyk's old horse, and through his dam he is a grandson of Magnolia, a son of Seely's American Star; the combination of the Star and Hambletonian blood being invaluable. Echo was a good performer himself, beating The Moor and Vaughn a two-mile heat race, and among the other performances of his daughter Echora, in 1875 when three years old, she distanced Beautiful Bells and Arabia, and was the only horse in California to beat *Director*, which she did in 1882 at Santa Rosa, never allowing the black horse to get a heat.

Among others of Echo's get, Victor is probably as game as most horses at present on the track, having proved his staunchness many a time as did Gibraltar, Belle Echo, and in fact all of his get that have been trained. Echo is also the sire of the dams of Direct, 2:18½, and Pink, 2:25.

Algona 11543 was foaled in 1876 at General W. T. Wither's celebrated Fairlawn Farm in Kentucky. He is by Almont 33, dam Emma Kincaid by Conscript, grandam Effie Deans by Mambrino Chief 11, great grandam by Powell's Bertrand. Almont was the sire of Fanny Witherspoon 2:16½ and 31 others better than 2:30; also Westmont pacer 2:13½ and grandsire of innumberable others. Algona is therefore a son of one of the best stallions in America and has a double infusion of the invaluable Mambrino Chief blood. Algona is a rich chestnut of grand style and build. Addie E, the only one of his get that has been trained, obtained a record of 2:22½ at Chico, taking the 1st, 4th, and 5th heats in 2:22½, 2:25 and 2:26½.

Cornelius 11,335 is a handsome bay horse, a Nutwood all over, and but for an accident would have had a low mark. He is one of the handsomest horses in California, and has a pure square gait, while his breeding of course is exceptional. He is by Nutwood 600, 2:18½, dam Jennie G., by Echo 462, grandam Jenny Noyes, 2:40 (dam of Gus 2:26½). Cornelius' colts are like himself, handsome and powerful, with good legs and feet and rapid action.

Western 11,334 is a full brother to Whippleton 1883, sire of Lilly Stanley 2:17½, Homestake 2;16½, etc. He is by Hambletonian Jr. 1882, dam Lady Livingston (dam of Lady Blanchard 2:26½) by General Taylor, son of the Morse Horse 6, grandam the Lou Mills mare.

Hambletonian Jr. is by Hambletonian 725, out of Aschat by Hambletonian 10, grandam by American Star 14, great grandam by Abdallah.

Western's breeding is wonderfully good, and Whippleton has proved that it reproduces itself, for he added two more to his list of 2:30 performers last season, and is now the sire of five in the 2:30 list.

Bob Lee is by Nutwood 600, first dam Blackbird (the Singletary mare) by Blackbird 482, out of a Morgan mare. Bob Lee is a grand looking, neat, short backed, powerful chestnut horse and is getting good stock useful as well as handsome.

Del Paso 11,807 is by Algona 11543, dam Nettie by Nutwood br a grand dam Sister to Voltaire 685 by Tattler 300 out of Young Portia etc.

With such an exceptionally well bred collection of stallions and with an equally high class lot of mares, including as they do Mabel, sister to Beautiful Bells, and four daughters—two by Echo and two by Algona, the dams of Pasha, 2:27½, Monarch, 2:28½, daughters of Lady Hamilton, the dam of Arab 2:15, sisters to Ben Ali 2:22 and Ha Ha 2:22½, the dam of Wells Fargo 2:18½, Nettie by Nutwood 2:18½, out of sister to Voltair 2:20½, Middletown mare by Middletown 152 out of sister to Voltair 2:20½, Hilda and Galena (sisters) by Nutwood, dam Eudora by Volunteer, second dam by Seely's American Star 14, third dam by Seagullson, son of Duroc.

Augusta by Gus 2:26½; 1st dam Mollie by Speculation, 2nd dam Asheat (dam of Ajax 2:29, etc.,) by Hambletonian 10, 3rd dam by Seely's American Star 14; 4th dam by Abdallah 1. Lady Berkey dam of Economy 2:30, Jones mare dam of Senator 2:21½. Lightfoot dam of El Monte 2:29½, the dam of Tippie 2:25½ and a host of others. It is no wonder that yearling trotting sales will take place annually in future.

Last Sunday the first consignment, consisting of six of Mr. Haggin's private cars and a load of hay left the ranch for New York. It was one of the most perfectly equipped trains that ever left the coast. Mr. John Mackey, the Superintendent, was in command, while veterinary attention was ensured by the presence of Dr. Thos. Bowhill, M. R. C. V. S. The cars individually were under the charge of such expert shippers as Ben Timmons, C. Kelly, Doc Ruggles, Henry Vaughan, etc. The cars for the yearlings were subdivided into four padded compartments, in each of which five youngsters were turned loose, while the older animals were loaded in the usual way.

The loading was done with marvellous celerity and safety, and about 4 o'clock, after Messrs. Salisbury and Shippee's four cars had arrived, the train pulled out in the wake of the Patti special, and despite a wait of several hours on the summit for a refractory freight train, passed safely through the scene of the recent blockade, and should arrive in New York to-day.

Additions and Corrections.

SACRAMENTO, Cal., Feb. 25, 1890.

EDITOR BREEDER AND SPORTSMAN:—After sending you the entries for the Sacramento Colt Stakes, I received the following additional ones from H. S. Hogoboom, of Rohnerville, Humboldt Co., Cal., for the yearling trot. Brown filly Why Not by Walstein, dam by Tom Benton.

Brown filly Remember Me by Walstein, dam Gertrude by The Moor.

I also wish to correct the entry of Fred Bean, of Vallejo, for his bay filly Blanche by Woodnut, dam by Eugene Casserly, which should have been in the yearling trot, instead of the two-year-old trotting stake. Yours,

F. P. LOWELL, Sec'y.

The Chris Green Handicap.

Secretary Smith, of the State Fair Association, announces the following weights for the Chris Green Handicap, a sweepstakes for all ages, of $50 each, half forfeit, or $10 if declared, with $500 added; second horse to receive $100 out of stakes. Weights announced March 1st; declarations due by 5 P. M. April 1st. A winner of any race after publication of weights, of one mile or upwards, to carry 3 lbs; of two races, 5 lbs.; of three or more, 7 lbs. This will not apply to horses handicapped at 125 lbs, or over. One and one-quarter miles.

	Age.	Entrance Weight.	Handicap.
Mikado	5	126	120
Daisy D	aged	120	118
Al Farrow	5	125	120
Ed McGinnis	5	126	115
Longshot	4	121	110
Picnic	4	116	110
Hotspur	4	121	113
Lurline	4	116	110
Odette	4	116	105
G. W.	4	121	110
Raindrop	3	1 1	95
Steve Stroud	3	106	90
Sabeau	5	126	95
Corona	5	120	95

How to Get Stock to the Souther Farm.

The Souther Farm is one and a half miles northeast of San Leandro and eight miles southeast of Oakland. The stables are about one mile east of the county road, which runs between Oakland and San Leandro. The place to turn off is at Stanley Road, where a large signboard of the farm is placed. Guide boards will be found at every cross road. In any ordinary weather the roads are very good, and they are fairly good after the unusually heavy rainfall of the past winter.

All stock sent from San Francisco may be brought over by Garcia's Express, No 3 Market street, San Francisco. They also have an order box outside of Hawley Bros.' Hardware house on the corner of Market and Beale streets. The express leaves San Francisco on the Creek route boat, which starts at 1:30, but all orders should be in the order box at Market and Beale streets by 10 o'clock, or at the office, No. 3 Market street, by 11 o'clock at the latest. In the case of very young or very valuable horses, the Souther Farm will send reliable men to lead or drive over any stock that will not lead behind a wagon. A small charge will be made in such cases to cover the extra expense incurred.

Horses are very easily taken from Oakland to the farm, and where it is inconvenient for owners to bring them or send them, the farm will send after anything that is to come. On horses that stay three months or over there is no charge for getting or delivering. Where a horse stays a short time the actual time and expense only is charged to him.

Horses can be shipped by rail from almost all parts of the State to San Leandro. Always notify the Farm several days before shipping anything, and then men will be on hand to receive stock on arrival. The railroad station is but two miles from the Southern Farm, and the agent invariably gives immediate notice of the arrival of any stock consigned to the above farm, but when word is sent to the farm in good season by letter or telegram, the animals sent are saved waiting a couple of hours in the car.

Passenger trains leave San Francisco (from the broad gauge ferry) and First & Broadway, Oakland at frequent intervals during the day. There are several trains from San Jose to San Leandro on both the broad and narrow guage railroads; the broad guage, by way of Niles, is much more convenient for getting to the farm. There are trains each day from Sacramento, Stockton, and Livermore to San Leandro. In ordinary weather it is a short and pleasant drive from Oakland to the Southern Farm or from San Francisco to the Farm by way of the Creek route ferry boat. Always notify the Southern Farm just when you will arrive at San Leandro, and some one will meet you at the station. If you do not recognize the farm conveyance ask the stage driver who will point it out. GILBERT TOMPKINS

Southern Farm,

P. O. Box 208. San Leandro, Cal.

The Salisbury Consignment.

Last Sunday Mr Salisbury and Andy McDowell left Pleasanton with two car loads of horses, which will be offered at public auction at P. C. Kellogg & Co.'s sale on March 7th. The lot are picked especially for the New York market, and many of the gems of the collection should bring long prices. Several of them we are sorry to lose from the coming circuit, and they will be sadly missed by those who love the sports of the turf. The list is:—

Goldleaf 2:11½, by Sidney, dam Fern Leaf, 5 years old.

Thistle, by Sidney, dam Fern Leaf, 3 years old.

Countess, by Sidney, dam Grey Dale, 2 years old (dam of Longworth 2:19); and her full sister, by Sidney, dam Grey Dale, 1 year old.

Saccharine, 2 years old, by Director, dam Sweetness 2:21½.

Alda H., 4 years old, by Director, dam by Priam; in foal to Guy Wilkes.

Erect, 2 years old, by Director, dam Echora 2:23½ (full brother to Direct 2:18½).

Miss J. I. C., 2 years old, by Director, dam by Blue Bull (Wilson's).

Highland Belle, 5 years old, by Director, dam by Nutwood; and her full brother, Jet, 4 years old.

Pleasanton, 2 years old, by Director, dam May Day (full brother to Margaret S 2:19½).

Lady Crittenden, 4 years old, by Director, dam Ellen Swigert.

Lady Patti, 5 years old, by Director, dam Lady Bayswater.

Diana, by Director, dam Roxana (half sister to Margaret S).

Filly, 1 year old, by Director, dam Nellie Gilmer, by Norfolk.

Lady Guy, 2 years old, by Guy Wilkes, dam by Nutwood.

Two 2-year old fillies sired by Guy Wilkes.

Maid of Oaks 2:23, in foal to Director.

Sister to Blue Belle 2:26½.

Young Lizzie, by Inca, dam sister to Little Brown Jug 2:11½; in foal to Thistle.

Navarro, 3 year old stallion, by Nutmont 2:28½, dam Nellie G. by Electioneer.

Lady Monroe, by Monroe Chief, dam by Carr's Mambrino.

Gertrude S, 2 years old, by Monroe Chief, dam by Overland.

Sister Gilmer, 3 years old, by Monroe Chief, dam by Norfolk; in foal to Thistle.

A challenge to shoot a team match at pigeons, four residents of San Joaquin County against four residents of San Francisco and Alameda Counties, fifty birds to the man, for a hundred dollars per entry is floating about. Either Mr. C. J. Haas of Stockton or Mr. C. B. Smith of this city may be consulted about the matter, and either will put up a forfeit. The match would be most interesting, and we hope may be arranged.

Grim's Gossip.

Massachusetts now has its *Breeder*, New York its *Sportsman*, but California has its BREEDER AND SPORTSMAN.

W. T. Bartlett of Suisuna reports that his mare Mollie by Eugene Casserly, who was bred last season to Coligny, is not in foal.

Those who desire to purchase a fine stylish horse should not overlook Rex Volo, which is advertised to be sold at a bargain.

S I. Allen of Santa Rosa, and A. L. Whitney of Petaluma, have been appointed by the Governor as Directors of the Sonoma and Marin Agricultural Society.

Col. Pepper is seemingly not satisfied with Norval's 2:17$\frac{1}{2}$, for the Kentucky papers informs us that the son of Electioneer will be sent this year for a very fast record.

I am pleased to think that L. J. Rose sent out a general denial of the rumor that Alcazar was sold. If it had been true the sale would not have been a success.

A match running race, $500 a side, mile heats, two in three, will take place July 4 at Silver Lake, Or., between J. B. Blair's Fred F. and G. W. Small's horse, Mackey M.

The counties of Sonoma, Marin, Napa, Solano, Mendocino, Lake, Yolo, Colusa and Contra Costo should make large quantities of entries to-day in the Petaluma colt stakes.

Memo, considered one of Sidney's best sons, will have a full book this year. Mr. Rowan reports mares coming in rapidly. Read the pedigree and see how you like him.

Governor Sanford authorized Col. Strader to buy from a half a dozen to a dozen thoroughbred mares in his discretion, to bred to Col. Strader's great Electioneer stallion Clay.

Numerous operations have been performed lately by English veterinaries to cure roaring by removing the arytenoid cartilage, but the result is now officially declared to be a failure.

The Harris sale of horses will take place at 11 o'clock this morning, at the Railroad Stables, corner Turk and Stiner St. This is a grand chance to secure a good roadster or saddle horse.

R. S. Strader, of Lexington, Ky., has sold to John E. Madden, the bay colt Delmar, three years old, by Electioneer, dam Sontag Dixie, by Toronto Sontag. The price is private but is in the thousands.

Part of the Haggin string of thoroughbreds in training, is wintering at Saratoga under the charge of George Ayers. Matt Byrnes takes an occasional up from New York, to see how the stock is getting on.

From Petaluma we learn that the progeny of Hernani are showing up in splendid shape this year. Steve Crandall is handling the young ones owned by J H. White of Lakeville, and a more promising lot it would be hard to find anywhere.

Many of the Eastern writers seem to think that Gorge has a "cinch" on the Brooklyn handicap. She is in at the modest impost of 110 pounds. From the way she run last year it would seem, that if she is fit, that nothing in the entry list can beat her.

J. F. Maguire has finally located at Suisun, where he is receiving deserved encouragement for his fine young stallion Fresno. Jim is also a good trainer and has already had several horses placed in his hands for educational purposes, and we know they will receive the best of care.

Mr. Baldwin has been asked to allow "Pike Barnes" his jockey to ride at New Orleans, until such time as he sends his stable East. "Lucky" has granted the request and the famous little rider will in all probability ride the remainder of the Spring season for the Avondale stable.

The brood mare Lou, whose fame rests upon the 2:12 record of her great son Axtell, last week foaled a filly by William L. The little one is a full sister to Axtell, a bay without marking, and is said to resemble its brother with the single exception that its hocks are straight and well formed.

J. A. Murray of Butte City, Montana, has purchased from J. S. Trask, Prescott, Wash, the two year old filly Zora, daughter of Vanderbilt, and Molly Duke by Marma Duke; 2d dam Victoria (dam of Roly Boly), by Vanderbilt; 3rd dam April Fool (dam of Kitty Van) by Waterloo. Price not stated.

Some of the visitors at the Fresno track are "a little gone" on Heylin, one of the Budd Doble string, although he has no record; 2:20 is about highest mark that anyone seems to place on him, while some are candid enough to fancy he can touch 2:15. Pretty good for a horse eligible to the three minute class.

Col. J. Mervin Donahue has sent four mares to be bred to Dawn 2:19$\frac{3}{4}$ From the present outlook this great son of Nutwood will have a very heavy stud season, and those who patronize him should not be disappointed as he has many a promising youngster that will be knocking for admission to the charmed circle before long.

The life of a breeder is not one entirely of roses; the Pierce Bros. owners of the Brookdale Stock Farm, informs me through their agent that "An Tricks," bred to Sidney last year, is not in foal; Mr. Ira Pierce's Poscora Belle, bred to Danger by Director, has missed, and Robert Bonner's "Lady Bonner" has slipped a foal to St. Nicholas.

H. S. Hogoboom of Rohnerville, is not far wrong when he says, "I have the best bred stallion to-day on earth, and there is no other bred like him. Sired by Director, record 2:17, dam Nelly W. (full sister to Albert W. record 2:20,) by Electioneer; 2d dam Sister by John Nelson; 3d dam the Lemont mare (dam of Aurora, record 2:27.")

Mr. Valensin, as is known, shipped his Eastern consignment for the Kellogg sale via the Central Pacific, but on account of the snow blockade it was found necessary to change the route, so the cars were sent from Sacramento via the Southern Pacific. At last accounts the horses were in good order and none of them the worse for the trip.

There are one hundred and fifteen entries in the Kentucky Derby for 1890. Up to February 3, 1890, fourteen have been declared, namely: Athlete Punster Jr, King Charlie, Pullman Watch Me, Glen Scot, Fatafan, Tigress, Flambeau, Virginia Mail Pouch, Randolph, Marlborough, Winston and Clean Heels. There will likely be a number of others declared by May 1, the last declaration day, at $20 each.

Old friends turn up occasionally, and it is with pleasure that we notice the advent once more, for public service, of Admiral 488. He is by Volunteer 55, dam Lady Pierson by Cassius M. Clay 20. Admiral is the sire of Sister, 2.19$\frac{1}{2}$, Nono Y, 2:25, Perihelion 2:25, and Huntress 2:27$\frac{1}{2}$. Mr. Drake, the owner, also has King David 2576 in the stud, terms, etc., being found in the proper column.

Electioneer has sired a horse with a record of 2:12$\frac{1}{2}$ from a thoroughbred mare. No other stallion has sired one with a record of 2:20 or better whose dam is thoroughbred. One of his sons sired a yearling that went a mile in 2:31$\frac{1}{2}$, the best record for that age. He has sired nine two year-olds with records from 2:18 to 2:30$\frac{1}{2}$. He has sired eight three-year-olds with records from 2:10$\frac{1}{2}$ to 2:27$\frac{1}{2}$.

The Fresno Turf says that 'Porter Ashe is a clever entertainer, and men prominent in the affairs of the church and State have at various times enjoyed his generous hospitality around the festive board and made the welkin ring with a joyous appreciation of the opportunity.' Good for Porter! but a little rough on the church. Perhaps our contemporary intended to say 'men prominent in the affairs of the circuit.'

Two sons of Electioneer, four and five year old, sold at Brasfield sale for $5 600 a peice. The only horse that brought a higher price ($9,500) in the first three days sale was the noted stallion Hinder Wilkes 7-year-old (by Red Wilkes,) who has a record of 2:20$\frac{1}{2}$ and has shown much faster time. One of the Electioneers was out of a Benton mare, the other out of a Don Victor (dam of F. P. Lowell's Don Marvin 2:28) neither had a record.

The sad news comes to hand of the demise of George G. Parker, a brother of Edward F. and Willie H. Parker of Stockton. George was well known as a careful, conscientious man among horses, and had worked for some time at Palo Alto, where he was highly esteemed. He had also handled trotters for Dr. Finlaw of Santa Rosa, and for Willis H. Parker of Stockton. Mr. Parker was 31 years of age.

My Red Bluff correspondent says that the new track there is well under way and that when finished it will equal anything in the State. This has long been needed, for there are many fine horses in that neighborhood that have not been worked simply because there has been no place to exercise them. Mr. Johnson who owns the standard stallion Fern has booked a large quantity of mares for his horse and the promise of a good season is assured.

Dr. C. W. Aby manager of the Guenoc Stock Farm, has just finished six box stalls 12x14 and a foaling box 20x20 with two new sheds 18x50. As soon as the stallion season fairly opens, which with St Savior and imp Greenback promises to be extremely large this year, a new mile track will be built, directly in front of the residential quarters, the porch of the main building taking the place of a grand stand. The ground is extremely level and but little grading will be necessary.

Some time ago many of the sporting papers throughout the country stated that Malcolm the sire of Marion had perished in a cellar in Chicago. The real facts of the case are that Malcolm was purchased in the winter or early spring of 1885 by Mr. A. Hankins, proprietor of Suburban Stock Farm, in Northern Indiana and by him bred to several of his mares He died the following summer at his place. His last days were spent in peace and plenty. Two of his get ran at West Side Park Chicago last year.

On Thursday next, the most important sale of horses and stock that has taken place in some time, will occur at Woodside Farm, Napa Co The proprietor, Mrs. Silas Skinner, has very large interests in Oregon which needs her personal attention and therefore every thing at the Napa place will be sold including the land. Many of the trotting horses are well known and for some of them there will be active competition. Messrs Killip & Co. will manage the sale and all particulars, including catalogues can be obtained from them at 22 Montgomery Street.

The Lawn View Farm have three stallions before the public this season, all of which are fine individuals and worthy of public patronage. Actor is by Prompter, dam Etelka, by Sultan; 2nd dam by Fireman, he by Langford. Young Elmo is a son of Elmo 2:27, dam by Woodburn, a cross that is fashionable among the believers in the thoroughbred theory. Douglasdale is a registered Clydesdale imported from Scotland, and is a grand representative of his class. The owners of Lawn View Farm are young and energetic, and will keep up with the more advanced ideas in breeding.

One of our correspondents pointed out over a year ago that there were already two circuits in this State, and that it would soon be necessary to have three. The time seems to be close at hand, as I note that Bakersfield promises to come into the field. A circuit commencing at San Diego and running through Los Angeles, Bakersfield, Fresno, Visalia, Merced and Stockton; a second one commencing at Salinas, thence to San Jose, Napa, Petaluma and Oakland, and third through Chico, Marysville, etc, all meeting at Sacramento, and adjourning thence to the Breeder's meeting at San Francisco, is not so far in the future as many may suppose.

About a score of the principal horsemen living in and about Petaluma have formed what is called the "Petaluma Stockbreeders Club." At the first meeting held a few days ago, W. P. Edwards was elected president; A. L Whitney, Vice-president; Dr. T. Macley, Secretary. The object of the Association as I understand it, is to have a place of meeting where all the books of authority may be found for the use of members, likewise all the principal Journals devoted to stock breeding, and at the same time to provide a place of resort where breeders may talk over their common interests The association is the first of the kind in California and is deserving of every success.

Apropos of names, the Petaluma breeders and horsemen have perfected their arrangements to secure Wallace's Trotting Register and Year Book, Chester, Bruce, etc, besides the leading weekly and monthly stock publications throughout the country. By referring thereto before naming their stallions and forwarding same for registry, they will frequently save themselves and the register much unnecessary correspondence and annoyance. Why would it not be a good idea for the smaller breeders and horsemen in other horse centers to do likewise? Judging from my own experience, I should say that a trotting horse breeder, without the Register, Year Book and Chester, would come pretty near being like a ship at sea without compass, rudder or sails.

Among the advertisements this week will be found one offering a fine mare for sale. She is called Lady Dexter, by Dexter Prince 11362, he by Kentucky Prince, (sire of Guy 2:10$\frac{3}{4}$), dam Kitty Thorn by Whipple's Hambletonian; 2nd dam by Geo. M. Patchen Jr. It is dollars to buttons that if the seller does not ask an exhorbitant price for her, that she will be sold before this day week.

Last Monday the horsemen of Los Angeles were given a little treat in the shape of a match between Adam, owned by C. A. Davis, and Kitty Van, owned by L. J. Ross. The race was an eighth of a mile in distance, for $25 a side, and the conditions were that Kitty Van at the outcome should have more than a length of daylight between her and Adam. David Bridgers was chosen as starter, while Ed. Ryan and Cy Mulkey were the judges. The horses were given a splendid start and ran head and head until near the wire, when Kitty drew slightly ahead, but could beat Adam by half a length only, and thus lost the money for her owner as daylight was not visible. Time, 12 seconds.

I have received a letter from St. Louis, which says;

The Western contingent of the Winters stable passed through Sunday night on the way to Nashville. Alf Estell is in charge. In the stable are: B c Rey del Rey, 2 (brother to Emperor of Norfolk, The Czar, El Rio Rey, etc.), by Norfolk—Marion; ch c San Juan, 2, by Norfolk—Ballinette; ch c Judge Post, 2, by Joe Hooker—Countess Zeika (and therefore brother to Don Jose); ch f Joanna, 2, by Joe Hooker—Addie O'Neal; ch f Otilia, 2, by Joe Hooker—Alice N; ch f Belle Spencer, 2, by Joe Hooker—Lou Spencer; b f Noretta, 3, by Norfolk—Ballinette; ch c Uno Grande, 2, by Joe Hooker—Jessie R, and two others—10 in all. Rey del Rey has been suffering with symptoms of pneumonia, but is now convalescing.

Funny is'nt it, that if you figure up the eight fastest trotters the world ever saw, three of them are California born and a fourth one came to his great speed in this state, when trained and driven by one who has called California his home, lo these many years. New York has produced two, Kentucky two, and Iowa one. The following is the list, and the time by quarters.

Maud S—32$\frac{1}{4}$, 32, 31, 33$\frac{1}{4}$—2:08$\frac{3}{4}$.
Jay-Eye-See—33$\frac{1}{2}$, 32$\frac{1}{2}$, 33, 31—2:10.
Sunol—32, 33, 32$\frac{1}{2}$, 33$\frac{1}{4}$—2:10$\frac{1}{2}$.
Guy—32$\frac{1}{4}$, 33$\frac{1}{4}$ 32$\frac{3}{4}$, 32$\frac{1}{4}$—2:10$\frac{3}{4}$.
St. Julien—32$\frac{3}{4}$, 32$\frac{1}{2}$, 33$\frac{1}{4}$, 33—2:11$\frac{1}{4}$.
Axtell—33, 32$\frac{1}{2}$, 32$\frac{1}{2}$, 34$\frac{1}{4}$—2:12.
Stamboul—33, 32$\frac{1}{2}$, 34$\frac{1}{2}$, 32$\frac{1}{4}$—2:12$\frac{1}{2}$.
Palo Alto—32$\frac{1}{2}$, 32$\frac{3}{4}$, 34, 33$\frac{1}{4}$—2:12$\frac{1}{4}$.

It has been suggested that next year in January or early in February, the P. C. T. H. B. A. should hold a grand horse and colt show at San Francisco and close the exhibition with an auction sale of such stock as the members may catalogue for the occasion. There is every reason to believe that it would prove a financial success and would go far towards educating the public in this city in regard to the financial benefits to themselves of encouraging the noble sports of the trotting turf We believe the Mechanic's Pavilion could be secured for the purpose, and an eighth-mile track of tan bark layed therein without injury to the building, and to the advantage of those who would exhibit their colts in harness. The exhibition and sale would undoubtedly draw large numbers of visitors from the East, who could there see specimens from all of our breeding farms without travelling all over the State. What say you, gentlemen breeders?

There is but one way in which a horse's lungs can be helped and that is by calling on the skin to do some of their work or more frequently by taking care that the skin does not leave its own work for the lungs to do. The skin and the lungs should both be at work purifying the same blood, and, roughly speaking, each usually takes about the same quantity of waste material out of the blood. Each breath that carries out its load of carbonic acid gas, water, and waste material, while the skin is silently carrying off almost the same, so that any failure on the part of the one puts more work on the other. When the lung cells are closing, and consequently dying, as in consumption, the skin trys to do double duty, as in the night sweats that mark that disease. When some of the pores of the skin have been closed, as they are in what we call a common cold, each breath of the lungs is overloaded with the moisture that the skin should have taken off.

The Board of Directors of the 17th District Agricultural Association, composed of the counties of Lake and Mendocino, met pursuant to call at Lakeport, Monday, February 24, 1890 Directors present: L. G. Simmons, C. W. Aby, M. Keating and D. Alexander. After effecting a temporary organization, the following officers were unanimously elected for the ensuing term: President, L. G. Simmons; Secretary, A. B McCutchen; Treasurer, Marshal Arnold. On motion, it was decided that the fair of the 12th District be held at Lakeport, September 23 to 27 inclusive, on the grounds of the Lakeport Park Association. The following committees and officers were appointed: Speed programme, L. G. Simmons, C. W. Aby; Revision premium list, M. Keating, D. Alexander, J. M. Mannon; superintendent park, C. W. Aby; superintendent pavilion, D Alexander. It was ordered that the pavilion be held in the tent belonging to the association. It was resolved that there should be no charge for entries in the pavilion, but that a fee would be exacted for entries at the park.

"Can you give me any good reason why Electioneers should bring high or higher prices, aside of course, from the fact that he is the greatest living speed producer?" was asked a few days ago of a breeder. 'Certainly and several' was the answer, 'there is *only one* Electioneer; he neither has nor can have full brothers or sisters; he is twenty two years old; he has not to date sired to exceed 350 colts, male and female, living or dead; at least 15 per cent. of them are dead and gone, or gelded; he has covered a great many mares, but has never got a *large* percentage of colts; he covered only 42 mares last year; the number of mares covered and his percentage of colts will probably grow less every year; he may and is liable to stop producing at any time even though he may live on. For the reasons I have stated, I am of the opinion that no high priced horses are as safe an investment to-day, as the sons and daughters of Electioneer.

Geo. Wilkes was similarly situated to Electioneer; he had neither brothers nor sisters; he was a great speed producer and see how his sires sell, even at this late day, when so many of the latter have proved themselves equal and superior producers to their sire at the same age. But George Wilkes, I believe, has sired at least two and a half colts to Electioneer's one, and by the time the latter dies or quits breeding he will scarcely have sired one to Wilkes' two.

TURF AND TRACK.

Freeman will ride for Dave Pulsifer this season.

Buffalo Girl 2:12½, will be bred to Red Wilkes this season,

It is said that Colonel R. G. Stoner has been offered $80,-000 for Baron Wilkes 2:18.

Capt. S. S. Brown's Garnet has foaled a brown colt by his favorite horse Troubadour.

Mr. Baldwin has given Barnes permission to ride at the New Orleans Spring meeting.

The Auburndale Stables' colt King Hasem is one of the fastest sprinters seen on the Winter tracks this year.

E. J. Baldwin has gone down to his Santa Anita Ranch to look over his racing prospects for the coming season.

The Walla Walla (Washington Territory) Fair Association has decided to give a series of trotting and running races in June.

Capt. Estill has been duly promoted, and is now Col. Alt Estill; he has fifteen head of the Winters stable under his charge at Nashville.

Armstrong, the jockey, was on the 19th of February ruled off the course at New Orleans for drunkenness and insubordination at the post and at the scales.

The general impression seems to be that Madge L, the Warwick-Altitude filly, lost the Early Blossom Stakes through Taylor attempting to draw the finish fine.

Wright Bros., Baldwinsville, N. Y. have sold to A. J. Peek Syracuse, N. Y. the stallion Kite Bird (full brother to Kitefoot 2:17½), by Landmark 3505, dam Pluck.

Rufus Murphy of Santa Rosa has one colt by Anteeo already on the scenes. Mr. Murphy is probably the only Californian who will have an Anteeo foal this season.

George Middleton, of Chicago, owner of Jack 2:15 has purchased from Walter Clark, of Battle Creek, Mich., the gray gelding Pilot H. (three-year-old record 2:29½) by Pilot Medium 1597.

At the Woodard sale on the 20th the five-year-old bay stallion Electrotype by Electioneer, out of Addie (dam of Manon 2:21, Maple—dam of Hattie D. 2:26½—and Woodnut 2:16½), by Hambletonian Chief, was sold to R. C. Church, Frankfort, Ky., for $7,100.

R. B. Milroy says his mare Adeline by Enquirer out of Analyne is heavy in foal to Mr. Cassatt's Stratford. Adeline was unfortunately cut down on the track prior to going East and had to be taken out in slings, and was never really strong enough to race again.

R. P. Ashe has sent two thoroughbred mares to Col. Thornton's imported Mariner (Oatcake). They are Minnet foaled 1883, by Norfolk out of Neapolitan by War Dance and Sinfire, foaled 1886, by imported Kyrle Daly out of Cousin Peggy (dam of Geraldine) by Woodburn.

The Valensin consignment to New York were unfortunate. They first of all went to Sacramento, then turned back and started on the Southern road, only to be stopped by a bridge down. Mike Kelly, in charge of Mr. Ashe's three two year olds, and Mr. Valensin were both on the train.

Elkhorn by Onward, dam by Long Island Patchen, was sold for a big figure a few weeks ago, provided his three-year-old record of 2:28½ was accepted by Wallace. As it was not accepted, he was put up at the Woodard sale on the 20th, and sold for $9,250 to W. Dolnan, Delphi, Ind.

Mr. J. K. Newton's imported Fleetwings by Lord of Lynn, having proved barren to St. Saviour, will be bred to imp Greenback. Of Mr. Newton's other imported mares, Zara by Marvellous has a fine Three Cheers colt foaled on Jan. 17th, while Mary Anderson by The Drummer is in foal to Cheviot.

Among the many foals already dropped at Rancho del Paso are a grand filly by Darebin out of that great race mare Lou Lanier and an exceptionally high class filly by Sir Modred out of Bonnie Kate, the dam of Bonnie Lizzie, etc. Maud Hampton and Explosion have not yet foaled. Both are stinted to Sir Modred.

Susie S., the six-year old mare who, last August, lowered her record to 2:15½, was sold at the late Woodard sale for $10,000. She is by Hylas 831, dam Lady Byron by Byron 84, and was handled in most of her fast work by Laird, who left Palo Alto (where he was second trainer) last spring to drive her again and succeeded admirably, as has been seen by her low mark.

The Santa Rosa Republican says: "There are such a number of horsemen and those interested in good stock in Santa Rosa and vicinity, and such a large number of good horses about here, that it is considered likely the race grounds will be purchased by them and maintained. Otherwise a county association will be formed to hold the grounds as originally intended, for agricultural purposes."

An Exchange says that while at the post for the last race at Clifton, one day last week, Father Bill Daly, who held a strong hand in the race, said to Willie Lamley, sotto voce, and winking to Willie as he did so: "Don't go out in front like that, Willie," looking over at Starter Caldwell as he said this. Query—"If Willie had not not gone out in front, how many sound bones would he have had after the race?"

The Hearst Stable this season should be a very strong one including as it does the older horses.

Gorgo, blk f, 5, by Isonomy—Flirt.
Philander, ch c, 4, by Wildidle—Precious.
Rhono, ch c, 4, by Ficod—imp. Rosetta.
King Thomas, b c, 3, by King Ban—Maud Hampton.
Ballarat, b c, by Sir Modred—Favorita.
Sir Lancelot, b c, 3, by Sir Modred—Faustina
Anaconda, b c, 3, by Spendthrift—Maid of Athol.
Gloaming, b f, 3, by Sir Modred—Twilight.
Everglade, blk f, 3, by Iroquois—Agenoria.
Golden Horn, b f, 3, by Spendthrift—Constantinople.
Miss Belle, b f, 3, by Prince Charlie—Linnet.

and among the two year olds are some royally bred ones, the $10,000 full sister to Dewdrop, the $5,100 colt by Warwick or Ban Fox out of Second Hand the dam of Exile, a filly by Hyder Ali out of Graciosa and five or six others.

The Rancho Del Paso consignment (6 car loads) for Messrs Easton's trotting sale in New York, left the ranch in beautiful weather on Sunday last on their special train, with Superintendent John Mackey in charge. On the same train were also two car loads each of the Pleasanton Stock Farm with Mr. Salisbury and Andy McDowell in charge, and of the Shippee trotters. The train is to run ahead of the overland all the way.

By comparison it will be found that the leading American two-year-olds start in double the number of races that the best of English two-year olds do. Last season the best colts of the year, El Rio Rey and St. Carlo were not over taxed, El Rio starting 7 times and St. Carlo 6. But what of the others Gregory started 19 times, Reclare 17, Chaos 10, Civil Service 48, Magnate 10, Padishah 13, Onaway 16, Cayuga 15, Burlington 12, Contrast this with the great English two year olds of last year. Le Nord started 6 times, Heaume 6, Signorina 9, Surefoot 4, Riviera 13, Semolina 15, Golden Gate 5, Garter 11, Dearest 2.

The thoroughbred yearlings at Rancho Del Paso will be most assuredly the best lot that have ever been offered at auction in any country. Even Kentuckians will be astonished at the magnificent proportions and racy appearance of the colts, particularly the Sir Modreds, which are out of such mares as Preciosa, Plaything, Carissima, Marian, etc., while Darebin's filly out of Altitude, the dam of Madge L., will not go begging. The two cracks are the chestnut St. Blaise—Maud Hampton colt, who might have had a better color, but is a race horse all over, while the brown filly by Falsetto out of Explosion is one of the best looking of that grand old mare's produce.

The Nashville American of last week says: Last night the 3-year-old stallion Bow Bells, by Electioneer, dam Beautiful Bells, and Moquette, a yearling filly by Wilton out of Alma Mater the property of the Hermitage Stud, arrived in this city on the Southern Pacific stock-car Grasmere, over the Northwestern road from Palo Alto, Senator Stanford's California stock farm. Bow Bells had four other traveling companions besides Moquette, two of which are the property of a Mr. Pearce, of Pennsylvania. The other two will be taken care of by the Hermitage Stud until the winter has completely broken. Bow Bells will make a short season in the stud and will then be trained.

Among our winter visitors none has been more popular —and deservedly so—than Major DuBois of Denver, his genial smile and pleasant trotting conversation being quite a feature at the racy re-unions, which take place among trotting men every evening. The Major will leave some few of his mares and colts for a few weeks longer, but the majority of his stock, including the well known stallions Superior 2:19½ (despite urgent requests to stand him here), and Magnet 2:28½, will leave to-day, or early next week, for Denver. Next winter, if the Major returns, as he says he probably will, he will be a welcome visitor in trotting circles, and the earlier he comes the better he will please every one.

No horse's temperature can be too sanguine or too fibrous, but it may be too nervous or too lymphatic. What is wanted in every horse is a large and good heart and lungs and well developed, strong enduring muscles; but a totally different degree of nervousness is wanted on the race horse to what would be tolerated in the dray horse. In the one you want a horse that will kill himself in two minutes, rather than be overtaken; in the other one you want a horse to contentedly strut about the streets of a city, with a glassy coat, a great load of beef, and allowing nothing to move him from the even tenor of his way. You cannot speak even of either of these extremes as good or bad. Both are good in their place.

A meeting of trainers and jockeys was held at the club house of the New York Jockey Club, Westchester, N. Y., February 16. Among the prominent horsemen present were: J. E. Brewster, D. L. Pulsifer, Walter Rollins, J. J. Dyer Henry Stu'l, J. J. Hyland, Jacob Pincus, James Lee, E. V. Snedeker, J. B Gray, F. T. Clarke, L. L. Lloyd, W. P. Ward, Charles O'Leary, J. W. Smith, James Rowe, Thomas Orgill, Snip Donovan, Jockeys Winchell, Freeman, and many others. A committee was appointed, consisting of Messrs. Pincus, Hyland, Lee and Dyer, who were requested to call a meeting of all trainers and jockeys to be held at the St. James Hotel, New York, Monday, March 3d, at 7:30 P. M., the purpose being to complete a permanent organization of the Trainers' and Jockeys' Mutual Benefit Association and elect officers.

THE WHIP.—The following are the conditions governing the contests for this historical trophy, one of England's most time honored races, which is now held by Mr. Warren De la Rue, his colt Traylee having received forfeit from the Duke Beaufort's Benburb at the last Newmarket Second October Meeting:—The whip may be challenged for twice in each year, viz., on the Tuesday after the July Meeting, when the acceptance must be signified or the Whip resigned on the Tuesday following, or challenged for on Tuesday in the Houghton Meeting, when the acceptance must be signified or the Whip resigned by the Tuesday following; if challenged for and accepted in July, to be run for on the Friday in the Second October Meeting following, and if in the Houghton on the Thursday in the First Spring Meeting following: weight 10st.; and to stake 200 sovs. each, play or pay; but in no case shall the Whip leave the United Kingdom. Beacon Course (4 miles 1 furlong 143 yards).

J. W. Rogers, the well known trainer of Capt S. S Brown's Stable was in Pittsburg a fortnight ago. He had just returned from Denver, where he had been for the past two months, and was in Pittsburg for the purpose of conferring with Capt. Sam Brown regarding the spring campaign.

"How do you like the way the handicappers treated you?" he was asked by a reporter.

"Well, I can't complain. Several are a good piece up and are classed with the good horses. What I mean by a good horse is Kingston, Firenzi or Troubadour. Senorita is a fair horse, but we haven't had a good one for several years. Senorita is never herself in the spring, so the weights given are a little heavy. Longstreet she gives 4 pounds according to the allowance. She beat him once on an off day. However, I guess we can't complain. Reporter is well placed in handicaps, but you can't put any confidence in him. I don't put much. He has the speed, but is an ugly brute, with a poor mouth, who gets mulish after a few pull ups at the post.

"Buddhist isn't badly placed, but there are a good many fair horses who can beat him. This will be a great year for racing, undoubtedly. It looks that way on all sides."

Hark Comstock says that George Wilkes and his get were not game horses, and enjoyed the reputation of not being able to go the route until he was crossed with the stout blood of Mambrino Patchen. Ever since then the Wilkeses have all been "bull dogs," even when out of Blue Bull mares, and without the speed sustaining blood of Mambrino Patchen. Perhaps there is something in a name, after all, and Blue Bull may have imparted from his what did not exist in the blood. We must look a little deeper into the mystery of the breeding problem.

The World says that C. H. Nelson, of Waterville, was in Lewiston on the 19th inst., and was interviewed relative to the recent suspension of himself and his famous stallion Nelson, from the tracks of the National Trotting Association, Mr. Nelson expressed the greatest confidence that he would be reinstated, and expects to trot his horse on the Grand Circuit next summer. He claims that the National Association has no jurisdiction over the case, because the Beacon track was not a member of the association at the time of the Nelson-Alcryon race. He says, however, that he is willing to have them investigate the race, and has no fear of the result. "The whole matter," said he, "is a personal affair between John Shepherd, a former member of the Board of Review of the National Association, and myself, and it dates back to the sale of Young Rolfe. I sold the horse to him upon the written agreement that he was to pay me an extra thousand dollars if Young Rolfe trotted a mile in 2:20. That season Young Rolfe made a mile in 2:19½, but was afterwards killed. Mr. Shepherd denied the agreement until I showed him his signature, and he has never paid it. Last year Mr. Shepherd failed of re-election to the Board of Review, and he failed again this year; that's the whole trouble." Mr. Nelson said further that he should drive his own horses next summer. He will trot Nelson this summer and keep Dictator Chief in the stud. In 1891 he will keep Nelson in the stud and trot Dictator Chief, and is confident that the latter will trot in from 2:16 to 2:14. Mr. Nelson received a day or two ago a request from a man in France for a catalogue of his Sunnyside Farm, showing that the great Maine breeding establishment has more than a national reputation.

The Breeders' Gazette gives a just comparison of Sunol and Axtell in its issue of the 19th. It says: Axtell, after a winter of rest at Terra Haute, has had his shoes put on and is being jogged every day by his groom, who naturally handles the $105,000 piece of horseflesh very carefully. Just what will be done in the way of trotting Axtell during the coming season is not known. Budd Doble slipped away to New York last week, presumably for the purpose of arranging for some trotters whose owners are desirous of having them in his stable this season, and when he returns it is understood that the syndicate which owns Axtell will have a conference on the subject of the great stallion's future. It is known that certain of those who put up the money for the purchase of the colt are of the opinion that he should not be handled at all for speed until well toward fall, they holding that by placing him in training at an earlier date there is nothing to be gained, especially in the case of a young stallion that has made a season of forty mares. There is no doubt that Palo Alto and Stamboul will try to lower the stallion record of 2:12 now held by Axtell, and the chances are all in favor of their succeeding. As to his finishing the season with the best four year old record, that will be a difficult feat to accomplish, as Sunol will come East with the Palo Alto horses, and she will no doubt try to go as good a mile as possible. She now has a record one and a half seconds faster than that of Axtell, and as between a filly and a stallion that has made a large season in the stud at four years of age the chances are considered by horsemen to be in favor of the filly. The plain truth of the matter is that Sunol has been faster than Axtell at all ages thus far. Her 2.18 as a two year old was far superior to his 2:23 at the same age, and her 2:10½ at three years is just as much, proportionately, in advance of his 2.12, so that according to the records of public performances she ought to beat him as a four year old. Williams, who trained and drove Axtell so successfully, has put himself on record as saying that he thought the 2:12 of Axtell at Terra Haute was as good as the 2:10½ of Sunol on a California track later in the season, but this estimate will hardly be concurred in by other horsemen. The chances are that Axtell will not do much trotting between now and next fall unless some special offer is made for him to go a good mile at one or two of the larger meetings.

The news that Capt. W. P. Ward has resigned his position as superintendent of the Westchester race track will occasion no little surprise among that gentleman's acquaintances. The Sporting World of the 18th says: He sent his resignation some days ago to Mr. J. A. Morris at New Orleans, and yesterday received an answer by telegraph stating his resignation had been accepted and his successor appointed. Capt. Ward, losing no time, will to-day leave the attractive little cottage at the entrance to the track on the Williamsbridge road.

Superintendant Ward did a lot of hard work on the Westchester track last year, and was rapidly becoming one of the best known and most popular men there are in his profession. All the trainers with whom he has come in contact, and, in point of fact, every one else, have admired and respected Capt. Ward, he being just one of those kind of liberal and gentlemanly fellows who are bound to attain popularity. He was a genial host and spared no pains, both in entertaining his visitors and furnishing any requisite information in his power.

Although the news is sudden, the trouble that leads to this culmination has been brewing for some time, the superintendent and the civil engineer of the estate, a Mr. Jackson, seeming not able to hitch together, and rather than be the cause of or subject to unpleasantness Mr. Ward adopted his course, which resulted as given above.

On Sunday last he performed his last official public duty in formally throwing open the trainers' club house, just by the Bradford gate, and afterward, as Mr. Morris' representative, entertaining those present at luncheon. A number of owners, trainers and jockeys were present, when the subject of a Trainers and Jockeys' Association was discussed and a determination arrived at to hold a meeting at the St. James Hotel on March 7th, when a permanent organization will be perfected, officers elected and machinery set in motion to attain the desired result.

In the telegram received from Mr. Morris, announcing his acceptance of Capt. Ward's resignation, he stated that a Southern gentleman had been appointed to the position, and the belief is that he will be a New Orleans resident, a Mr. Ezell, who has been racing horses at the New Orleans meeting, having been named as the probable successor.

Mr. Ward has strong racing inclinations, and has owned horses. Only a few months ago he disposed of a stable the better to perform his duties at Westchester. He will now blossom out as a full fledged owner.

Martin Bergen, the crack jockey, has returned from the Hot Springs, where he was sojourning for his health.

J. Shields and his friends made about the biggest winnings of the season on Little Jim's victory at Clifton last week.

Jimmy Shields' colt Gregory, who beat Reclare last year, is wintering well, and, barring accidents, will be one of the crack three-year-olds this season.

Jockey Freeman, it is said, has a good reputation as a rider, but he seems to be afraid to take the turns sharp enough, and has lost several races lately on account of this.

"Alfy" Lakeland was very much surprised when his filly Madge L. was beaten for the Early Blossom Stakes. He made no secret as to how good his filly was, and, as the saying goes, "he thought he had a mortgage on the race."

It is understood that three or four of the leading athletic clubs of New York have made application for the tenancy of the athletic grounds and grand stand at the Westchester track. No application has yet been granted for a permanency.

Mr. A. C. Dietz has sent Longworth 2:19, his well-known five-year-old Sidney pacer, to his Ferndale ranch in Ventura County. The trotting breeders in that section will have a chance to breed a few mares to the fashionable son of Sidney, who should—like his sire—get trotters and pacers with equal facility.

Austria is rapidly falling into line as a trotting country. The dates claimed for Vienna, for 1890 are as follows; Spring meeting—May 4, 6, 8, 11, 13, 15 and 18. Summer meeting—August 10, 13, 15 and 17. Autumn meeting—September 28 and Oct. 2, 5, 9 and 12.

The laws of the State of New Jersey provide a severe punishment for pool selling, while for bookmaking a nominal fine can only be imposed. The Monmouth Association might permit pools to be sold on its track on the same terms as Guttenberg and Clifton if its officers wished to do so.

A. A. Wetherill, of Salinas, has purchased the standard bred brood mare Clarissa. She is seven years old, and in foal to Elector, a son of Electioneer. Clarissa is by General McClellan, dam by Geo. M. Patchen Jr., 2d dam by Williamson's Belmont; 3rd dam by McCracken's Black Hawk, 4th dam Belle of the Lake, a thoroughbred.

Ex-Senator James G. Fair is making extensive preparations on his ranch near Grafton, Yolo county, for the reception of his race horses. A track for training and speeding colts has been laid out and is nearing completion. He is about to erect commodious stables and other necessary buildings. His trotters will be taken up to the ranch as soon as the barn is finished.

Captain S. S. Brown, after due deliberation, has definitely made up his mind to move his thoroughbreds from his farm at La Grange, Ky., to his Eastern possession in Pennsylvania. It is said to be the intention of this gentleman to locate some of his yearlings at Mobile. He will move the more fit and promising colts and fillies up to Westchester as two-year-olds from time to time.

B. C. Holly, Vallejo has sold to Thomas Lynch, Grand Rapids, Michigan, the bay colt 'Sheeny' foaled 1886 by Arthurton 366 out of Vixen by Nutwood 2:18¾, grand dam Sister (dam of Albert W 2:20 and Bonanza 2:29½) by John Nelson 187. Price $1000. Judging from his breeding and looks, The Sheeny should prove a bargain to his purchaser.

Mr. Morris is intending to provide an ambulance and all necessary medical appliances in case of accidents at Westchester, in doing which he follows the example of all racing associations who have already provided these very necessary accommodations, and who therefore have shown their sympathy with jockeys and other employes who may be injured during the races or otherwise.

At the election of officers for the new Memphis Jockey Club, President Arnold resigned, and S. R. Montgomery was unanimously elected in his place. The selection is a very happy one, for Mr. Montgomery was secretary under his father's (Colonel Montgomery) regime, and is in every way well adapted for the office. The secretary, Captain Rees, should prove an invaluable assistant to the Jockey Club.

At a meeting of the directors of Charter Oak Park, held on February 19th, it was voted to offer $7000 for the spring meeting to be held the last week in June; also $25,000 for stakes for the grand circuit meeting the last week in August; also $10,000 for foals of 1889 to be trotted in 1892.

The latter is the largest purse ever offered by any association for youngsters, and it will be trotted at the regular circuit meeting.

It has been decided to have dash races at Fleetwood for members' horses on every Saturday afternoon during the season. The track of the Gentleman's Driving Club of New York will probably be opened earlier this season than usual. The members of the Executive Committee visit the Morrisania grounds nearly every day to watch the improvements being made in stabling and other facilities, as well as to plan features for the spring and fall meetings.

The case of Nelson, owner of the famous stallion Nelson, against the Board of Review of the National Trotting Association has been discontinued by order of Judge Corbett, Nelson paying the costs. This brings the matter before the Board of Review in the same condition as when the congress convened, and the question now is whether the Alcryon-Nelson race in Boston was sold or not. The decision will be awaited with great interest among horsemen.

The Monmouth Park Racing Association has announced two new handicaps for its mid-summer meeting. They are called the Hackensack and Hollywood handicaps. The first is a sweepstakes for three-year-olds of $50 each, with $1,500 added money, and $250 to the second and $100 to the third. The distance is one mile. The Hollywood handicap is a sweepstakes for fillies two years old, of three-quarters of a mile, with $1,500 added, of which $500 goes to the second.

The question drivers and trainers of speedy roadsters are interested in now is whether the common law or turf law is pre-eminent on the trotting track. The decision on the appeals of Messrs. Nelson and Noble, the owners of the famous stallions Nelson and Alcryon, offers a solution. The National Trotting Association has disbarred both these owners for collusion when their horses met in the ten thousand dollar Balch stallion race last season. Will the law back up the trotting organization?

The executors of the estate of the late T. J. Megibben have decided not to dispose of his great breeding establishment, Edgewater, but will continue to carry on the business of breeding thoroughbreds, under the management of his son, T. Megibben, who is a young man thoroughly conversant with horses. It has not been decided yet whether or not the yearlings of this stud will be sold this spring, as it is highly probable they will be raced by young Megibben, who inherits all the love his father had for the turf.

Under Crit Davis' management, the track of the Harrodsburg Association, over which he trains, is being graded and every hollow filled, and the hills which obstructed the view removed. This has always been one of the slowest tracks in Kentucky, but the improvements now going on will make it equally as fast as the best. Great efforts will be made to have a fine meeting there next summer, it being the intention to largely increase the value of the purses, which will be so arranged as to accommodate all classes of trotters, from the three-minute horse down.

The celebrated broodmare Christine bears the name of Mrs. L. P. Tarleton's daughter, Miss Christine Hunt Reynolds, who is now the belle of Franklin County society and the queen of Kentucky's capital this season. The mare Christine deserves being named for such a beautiful and popular young lady, as she has given to the turf such shining lights as Bonnie Australian, Vice Regent, Montana Regent, Julia L. and Beth Broeck. These performers have won on the turf forty-four races and $31,095. Christine is owned by S. E. Larabie, a wealthy banker of Butte City, Mont.

Mr. Haggin's great mare, Firenzi, is treading close upon the heels of Miss Woodford, the largest winner of any mare ever on the American turf. Should she win $23,084 this year, which is quite likely, she would then be up with Miss Woodford, whose total winnings were $118,750. She won forty-five races during her turf career, while thus far Firenzi has secured thirty-eight victories and won $95,666. Miss Woodford is also owned by Mr. Haggin, but is unfortunately not in feel this year.

Lew P. Tarleton, Jr., Fleetwood Stud, is making arrangements for the importation of a highly bred English stallion to take the place made vacant by his stallion Whisper. It is his intention to buy a horse with a good racing record and a faultless pedigree. If he finds a horse to suit him he will not stand on price, and it will be his endeavor to secure him before the spring season is over. There being so many native bred mares at Fleetwood, Mr. Tarleton thinks it better to import an English than to buy a good American stallion.

At 5 o'clock on February 14th, the ten-year-old mare Lou, by Mambrino Royal, owned by the Ivy Stock Farm at Independence, foaled a full sister to Axtell, his only living full relative, having been sired by William L. The filly is brown, marked precisely like the dam, and is exceedingly strong and lively on its pins. Mr. Barnhart, her owner, is grievously disappointed in the sex. Though Mr. Barnhart is the exclusive owner of the mare Lou, C. W. Williams, former owner of Axtell, has a half interest in her produce by stipulation. She will be immediately shipped to Lexington and again bred to William L.

The first foal in the vicinity of New York was dropped on February 14th at the Brooklyn Jockey Club track, from Emma B., and sired by Pontiac. The mare and her foal are the property of Mr. Brush, the popular superintendent of the track. He was given his choice between Hanover and Pontiac for a sire when the mare was covered. Specially significant and picturesque is this fealing when it is remembered that Emma B. herself was an early foal, she having been dropped by Chickadee to her owner, Mr. L. C. Behman, early in 1885 at Sheepshead Bay track, only just across the way. Emma B. is by Sensation.

The walls of the new club house at Westchester are beginning to rise rapidly, and is busily and continuously carries on under the personal superintendence of the architect. Mr. Rogers, trainer for Capt. S. S. Brown, is expected back for good certainly by Saturday to-day. Capt. S. S. Brown made a flying visit to New York last week, but his business interests compelled his immediate return to Pittsburg. Matt Byrnes, the trainer for Mr. J. B. Haggin, visited the Westchester track on Monday in order to choose a site for the erection of a stable where a string of horses belonging to Mr. Haggin will in the future be quartered.

It is probable that Col. Jack Chinn, the well-known running turfman, will be offered and will accept the position of starter on the Kentucky trotting circuit this season, which will embrace meetings at upwards of a dozen places in the blue-grass State next summer, as well as on the Cincinnati (O.) and Rushville (Ind.) tracks, which two will probably join the Kentucky circuit. The old style of allowing the presiding judge to fill this position, whose only claim to the distinction is that he is a member of the association over whose track the trots take place, has become unsatisfactory to patrons of the trotting turf, and on this account a professional starter will be called into service. Col. Chinn has had considerable experience at the business, and would certainly give satisfaction.

I have often wondered why Three Cheers did not receive more patronage in the stud. This year he is making the season at Sacramento and should have some good brood mares sent to him, for surely breeders cannot afford to neglect to breed to a grandson of Newminster (whom he greatly resembles), and he is also a grandson of that grand old mare Fashion, who beat Boston in the celebrated four mile heat race. Three Cheers' breeding is the equal of any in the State, and what few of his get that have been trained have won races. Only a fortnight ago Mr. Winters refused $800 for a two-year old by him, and there are many other promising two year olds by him. The old horse is as spry and lively as a two year old, and shows no traces of his age, and should have many years before him.

In all diseases of the respiratory organs the horse refuses to lie down. This will always distinguish them from diseases of the digestive organs. In inflammation of the lungs the horse stands with his forelegs stiffly fixed and sloping outwards like the legs of a rough stool. He is unwilling to move, and though evdiently weak, determined not to be down. He stretches out his head and neck so as to keep his windpipe as straight as possible, and lets the head drop low enough to put the weight on the strong ligament or cord, called the pack wax, and relieve the muscles from any exertion in supporting the head. His nostrils open wide and their lining is a livid red, turning purple as the disease progresses. The breathing quick but not deep. As the blood cannot get through the gorged lungs the circulation is impeded, the heart is struggling on arteries that have no outlet, so that the pulse is felt, if felt at all as a mere feeble fruitless vibration. The ears and legs are very cold.

Sam Bryant, of Louisville, Ky., has purchased of B. J. Treacy of Lexington, the chestnut colt Charley Treacy, three years old, by imported Prince Charley, dam sister to Joe Daniels, by imported Australian, she out of Dolly Carter by imported Glencoe. Price, $2,500. The purchase of this colt and two other youngsters in Kentucky by Mr. Bryant, seems to set at rest the rumor that he would retire from the running turf, which was started by his buying a couple of fillies at the Brasfield sale.

Mrs. C. R. Noyes, of Boston, one of the best posted ladies in the world on trotting stock, has lately received two very handsome photographs of fillies in Maine. One is Greta, by Dictator Chief (2:21½), dam, Gretchen, the dam of Nelson (2:11¼) and others of note; the other is Crescent, by Dictator Chief; dam of Drew and Witherell stock. The latter is but a three-year-old, yet raised a filly foal by Nelson (2:14½), the past Summer that is a little trotting wonder. When but seven and a-half months old, Mrs. Noyes timed this little miss an eighth of a mile in thirty-seven and-a-half seconds, pulling a jumper. It was the fourth time the filly was ever harnessed. Mrs. Noyes has two choicely-bred fillies in Kentucky; one a three-year-old, by Director (2:17); dam, full sister to Pantalette, the dam of Epaulet (2.19' and Burglar (2.24½. This filly was booked to the renowned Bell Boy (2.19¼. Mrs. Noyes thinks of sending her to California and mating her with Guy Wilkes (2.15¼. She thinks of sending Greta to Nutwood (2.18¾) in 1891. Some time in the future all of Mrs. Noyes's trotting stock will be sent to Riverside Park Farm, Livermore, Me., and will prove a valuable acquisition to the horse stock of the Pine Tree State.

As there has been much discussion lately as to the best horse ever on the American turf, an old retired trainer of Lexington was asked his opinion as to the best horse now in training. Saith he: "I would rather possess El Rio Rey than any horse on the American turf. My reasons are that his great grandsire, Boston, was the best horse of his day, and, I think, the best that ever run in this country. Lexington, his grandsire, was the phenomenal performer of his day, and a record breaker; while his sire, Norfolk, retired to the stud without having once suffered defeat. I believe in the theory of like begetting like, and therefore in my opinion, El Rio Rey will of necessity be a great sire."

Major B. G. Thomas, the veteran breeder and proprietor of the Dixiana Stud, had the following to say on the same subject: "I have long since learned that every foal is simply a reproduction of some preceding horse or mare in the family to which it belongs, and my aim is now to use no more for raising race horses any save those which have no stains in their pedigrees, and can trace their lineage through good performers on the turf, back to an Oriental origin." Thus the Major and the old trainer agree (though the Major could not be referring to El Rio Rey) that like begets like. Prince Charlie's success in the stud is a proof of this fact. He was a high type of the race horse; his sire, Blair Athol, was a great turf performer, and sold for more money at action than any horse in the world—$62,500, while his grandsire, Stockwell, was not only a great race horse, but so successful in the stud that his fee was the highest ever known.

The following is a complete list of the horses taken to Memphis by Tom Kiley, and they constitute one portion of the Chicago Stable this season, the horses of which are jointly the property of George Hankins, Eugene Leigh and Tom Kiley. The other members of this stable, which number about twenty head, will be taken up in a few days and will be trained in Lexington by Eugene Leigh:

Little Minch, b h, aged, by Glenelg—Goldstone.
Terra Cotta, ch h, 6, by Harry O'Fallon—Laura B.
Jacobin, br g 6, by Jils Johnson—Agnes.
Wheeler T., br h, 5, by Speculation—Kitty.
Huntress, ch m, 5, by Springbok—Edith.
Santalene, ch g, 5, by St. Martin or Harry O'Fallon—Ollena.
Orderly, b g, 5, by Bramble—Tidy.
Fan King, ch g, 4, by King Ernest—Fan Fan.
Chilhowie, b g, 4, by King Ban—Locust Bloom.
Girondes, ch g, 4, by Jils Johnson—Agnes.
Wrestler, ch g, 3, by Bramble—Guildean.
Robespierre, br c, 3, by Rossiter—Maggie Hunt.
Ollie Benjamin, b g, 2, by Springbok—Minnie.
Bay colt, 3, by Pizarro—by Australian.
Wimmer, ch c, 3, by Rossiter—Maggie Hunt.

Of these fifteen head all save the Pizarro colt are winners. The purchase prices of these horses aggregate the neat sum of $62,180.

The Breeders' Gazette says that "the California papers, with that enthusiasm which is, perhaps, due to the climate, are already telling what an easy thing the trotters from the Pacific Slope are going to have next summer on the Eastern tracks. (I deny that any California paper has made such an assertion.—Ed. T. & T.) About the only Californian that made a trip East last year was the three-year-old filly Margaret S., she coming across the continent to go to Cleveland in the fall and win the Spirit of the Times stake for trotters of her age, doing the trick in straight heats and with no trouble (Have you forgotten Sensation, that trotted out Nelson in 2:15 at Buffalo?—Ed. T. & T.) At the close of the year Margaret S. had a record of 2:19½, and now the California papers are telling what havoc she is going to make next season in the stakes for four year-olds. It is true that in the richest event of the coming season for trotters of her age, the Horseman stake, which will be worth at least $7,000 to the winner, Margaret S. seems to have no formidable competitor, now that Axtell's lameness has been found to be of such a character that he will not appear on the turf in 1890, but for all this she may not have a walk over in that stake. But supposing this to be the case, she will find other good material in other stakes, and as she is certain to come East, it is only fair to presume that her owner will engage the filly as heavily as possible. That she will make a creditable showing in whatever company she starts no one who has seen the daughter of Director and May Day perform can doubt but that she will have a walk over next season is not so certain." On the same page of the Gazette there is another item evidently written by the same person. It is as follows, and shows how one can write both hot and cold: "That the foaling of a sister to Margaret S. is a matter upon which her owner is to be congratulated there is no doubt, for Margaret is about as speedy a miss as one often sees at her age, and in addition to this she is as steady as a clock in her races. During the early part of last season she was fairly outclassed by Sunol and Lillian Wilkes, both of whom she was obliged to meet in her early stake engagements. But later Margaret showed the metal of which she was made by doing a mile in 2:19½, and as it happens that neither Lillian Wilkes nor Sunol are in some of the big stakes for four-year-olds in which Margaret is engaged, it looks as though she would have an easy time winning them, as her other most dangerous competitor, Allerton, is laid up for the season with a bad leg.'

A Romance of Mexico in 1857.

[Written for the BREEDER AND SPORTSMAN.]

It was dusk in the old city of Mexico. From the holiday appearance of the streets, it had evidently been a *fete* day. The garb of the *caballeros* parading the thoroughfares was bestrewn with silver and tinsel, while the *senoritas* were attired in gaudy apparel, of which the gay silk scarfs were a prominent and fetching feature. The season was well advanced, the autumn being all but gone, yet the evening air was langourous and soft, a charkcteristic of that dreamy senuous clime.

Upon the *esplanada* merry groups were holding high carnival. Shouts of laughter broke the semi-stillness of the night, while the tinkling of guitars and mandolinatas echoed throughout the city. In the distance the spire of the cathedral shot heavenward, and through its decorated windows the wax tapers shone dimly. Toward this place of worship many persons were making their way, to take part in the evening services peculiar to the day. The archbishop himself and two *padres* had just entered the sacristy by a side door. Inside the edifice the worshipers were kneeling before the shrine of that particular saint they had come to invoke.

Meanwhile the moon had risen, and was bathing the haciendas and hovels in its soft effulgence. A block away from the cathedral a huge umbrella tree reared its dense top above the prominade. In its shadow, dense and forbidding looking in the moonlight, stood two men; one dressed in the wide trousers, short coat, sash and broad-brimmed sombrero of a Spanish *caballero* of that date. The other man was older than the first, and dressed in plainer attire. His face was clean-shaven, and its peculiar immobility, lit up occasionally by a pair of keen gray eyes, made him look not unlike a priest. Although the dusky skin, piercing black eyes and curling hair of the first betrayed his nationality at a glance (to say nothing of his costume) there was nothing in the appearance of the second man to betoken his race. He looked slightly like a Spaniard, yet his garb was American. He spoke the native dialect fluently, yet his English was flawless.

The first man was Don Ignacio Murrillo, and the second was known throughout the city of Mexico as "Doc" Leonard. The social and financial position of Don Ignacio was assured; that of "Doc" Leonard was unknown and, to say the least, problematical!

"Well, said Leonard, and he laughed softly, "the fair Selita is to marry our foreign friend, eh?"

"*Caramba!* not if I can help it, replied Don vehemently.

"But the means, Don; what can you do?" and the first speaker regarded the Spaniard quizzically.

"The way, the way, I know not; but we must find it. He must not wed the Senorita Selita, do you hear, Leonardus; he must not, even though he——"

"Well? Even though he——"

"Be put out the way!"

"Don! you rave! To your excited imagination anything is possible. 'Tis no easy matter to 'remove' men of prominence, even in this land of stilletos and stealth."

"*Perdita,*" exclaimed Don Ignacio, "listen to me. One year ago the Senorita Selita was promised to me by the Senora Mariana, her mother. The Baneres family are poor, Leonardus, and I was thought a brilliant match for their daughter, but she never took to me; *por Dias!* I know not why! Then came this American, with his white face and race horses, and he has stolen her from me. We met at her home—this Chester Parker, as he calls himself. We disliked each other from the first. The Senora Mariana told me of his wealth, his fine family, his horses—by the Virgin, I could have tweaked her ears, the garrulous crone! The Senorita Selita was captivated by the white stranger. He praised her singing, her guitar-playing—everything; he made compliments for her, and in many ways showed his admiration. I am no man to flatter, thus I saw Selita gradually lost to me. As I appreciated this thing, my blood ran hot. For days I knew not sleep, and my companions jeered me, saying: 'See, see, all for the love of Selita Baneres, whose father sells mescal on the alameda!' I thought his pretentions to wealth were perhaps like other Americans I have seen—and whose paper I still hold and always will—thought him an adventurer. I set on foot inquiries, only to find his statements true. Next meeting at her house, I ridiculed his race-horses; told him none could run with my horse Fulano. He quietly said that his racing was attended to by his manager. I could go to him, and could get any sort of wager. The next day I went. We placed five hundred *doblones*. The day afterward I bantered for five hundred more. They acquiesced. The next, five hundred more, and the next, the next, and the next, until I have bet all the money I have and can get. I pressed this thing, thinking Fulano could surely win, and I thought to ruin this American, but *Caramba!* his purse must be long. Now, Leonardus, do you understand? He has not only stolen the Senorita Selita from me, but should his horse beat Fulano, I am ruined!"

Leonard had been listening attentively, and when Don had finished his passionate outburst, he gazed abstractedly at the people entering and leaving the cathedral. Presently he inquired:

"Don Murrillo, what end would you achieve in putting this man out of the way? His horse is in his trainer's hands, he could win as well with his owner, dead or with him alive, for you know I caught a trial, as I told you, and his horse Isban can beat Fulano with ease. Again, you might not better your cause with the Senorita should Parker be "stilled". She thinks much of him I am told!"

"Ah! Leonardus, you are stupid for once! Should he disappear, the race would not take place, we would draw down our money, and my fortune would be saved. With him out of the way I would have a chance. Now I have none!"

"When is this race?"

"The day after to-morrow. Every body will be there. *Dios*, I could not withstand defeat!"

"Suppose we "fixed the Americans' horse. He could'nt race at all then, and as your race is pay or play, you would take all the stake money."

"*Bueno*, can you do it?" and the Don's eyes glittered excitedly.

"I think I can, I'm sure I can!"

"A thousand *pesos* for you if you succeed.

"Very good, Don, I will see you to-morrow. Till then, "*adios*", and "Doc" walked jauntily toward the cathedral, muttering to himself, "guess I'll go in and say a few lines to my own patron saint, I've neglected him long enough."

Don Ignacio Murrillo stood looking after his late companion, until his form passed through the arched entrance to the Cathedral, there, smiling sardonically he walked swiftly the other way.

As his footsteps grew faint in the distance, a singular thing occurred. A boy about fifteen years of age, ragged, and with a preternaturally old face, dropped softly to the ground from somewhere in the umbrella tree! Looking first one way, then the other, he ejaculated, "my eyes, them's a pair, they is sure! Nothin' they would'nt do, I reckon. Goin ter dose Isban? After ther white way his trainer done me? Well, they never will, er my name aint Shorty Briggs" and he darted away on a run.

II.

A slight breath of wind passed murmuring through the feathery crowns of the slender cocoa-palms, two great spears of light shot up the sky, somewhere a bird sang—the sun had risen.

Morning came as it always comes in a tropical country—all at once. It was the day of the much talked of race. The residents, from the Alcalde to the *ladrones*, had for weeks gossiped of nothing but the race between the unbeaten Fulano, belonging to Don Ignacio Murillo, of the hiacienda Caselabanca, and Isban, a stranger to them, owned by the American, Senor Parker. All thought Fulano should win, and came prepared to wager their all upon him, whether it should be a few *rials* or many *doblones*. * * * * *

In a narrow *paseo* near the outskirts of the city two men were earnestly talking, one speaking excitedly, the other impassively. The former looks around furtively and asks:—

"Are you sure, Leonadus, that he got the poison; sure?"

"Why, of course; I know the lay of the feed box. At three this morning I quietly bored a hole through the stall about three feet above the box, and pumped in enough with a syringe to finish four horses. The hungry brute, I could hear him lap it up like a hog does swill. Depend upon it if he is not dead he soon will be."

"At least, Leonadus, it will take from him some strength even should they discover him sick and promptly doctor him —and a slight falling away and Fulano wins."

"A slight falling away, indeed. Why, man, the horse is dead long ago. The dose I gave will kill in ten minutes. A slight falling away!" and Leonardus laughed hoarsely.

"But," persisted the Don, uneasily. "I met Senor Parker —may the Devil grasp his soul—this morning, an, having realized from some personal holdings, I dared him to bet more. He promptly accepted. Why should he do so if his horse was dead?"

The other seemed somewhat startled by this intelligence, and hastily inquired:—

"What time this morning, Don?"

"About 8.30, I presume."

"Oh, he had not been to the track yet this morning. Trust me, it's all right." And thus they parted.

* * * * * * *

Let us return to the boy that dropped like a Mazatlan monkey from the umbrella tree. Without slacking speed he ran to the race track, fully three-fourths of a mile away. Upon arriving he headed for the stalls where Chester Parker's horses were domiciled. He approached Mr. Campbell, the trainer, who was watching a stable boy leading a blanketed horse.

Shorty was out of breath, and as he stood before Campbell, puffing and blowing, his eyes very wide open, he reminded one of a puppy pulled by an invisible string. The trainer regarded him with some alarm and inquired:—

"Well, my boy, what ails you?"

"'Vited me ter eat wid ther boys tother day, didn't you?"

"Yes," responded Campbell; "believe I did."

"I never goes back on nobody as asks me ter eat," said Shorty, concisely.

"Well, what's the matter now? Hungry again?"

"Naw," answered the boy, contemptuously. "Old woman up town set me out nice lay—tomales, tortillas, goat's milk—fit for a king. I tells yer, but I've come ter do yer good, I have. Never forgit the old woman, either."

"How will you do one any good, sonny?"

"Know Spanish feller named Don Murrillo?"

"Yes, I know him."

"Got a race wid him day after to-morrow, ain't ye?"

"Yes."

"Know feller named Leonard—everybody calls him Doc?"

"Yes, he was here to-day."

"He's goin' to pizen yer governor's hoss what's goin' to run."

"What!" said Campbell, his abstracted manner taking flight instantly, "who's going to poison a horse?"

"Leonard, I told yer, him as wears the preacher-clothes and looks solemn as old Agubrre's Jack."

Without delay the trainer took the boy into one of the box-stalls, shutting the door, and there Shorty told him all he had overheard from his perch in the tree.

* * * * * * * * * *

Even before noon of the day of the race, crowds could be seen going to the track. By 1 o'clock the grand stand was full to overflowing, mostly women, the bright cloaks of the younger generation contrasting startlingly with the sombre garb of the older ladies. Upon the grounds, each side of the track, the men held forth. Some standing, some sitting in wagons and carts, some riding gayly caparisoned horses up and down in front of the stand, the chains on their heavy spurs clanking in unison to the horse's movements. At a distance was an ox harnessed to a primative cart, while the occupants, an old Mexican and his wife, were each deftly rolling a cigarette.

Among these men could be seen Campbell, the trainer. He was taking the bets of all comers. The stake holder for all was the Alcalde. For half an hour Campbell had been steadily covering bets offered him, some large, some small, all, however, being placed upon Don Murrillo's horse Fulano. When it appeared that nobody else among the Mexicans had any more money—for the true Mexican bets his last cent upon a horse race—Campbell went to the stables. As he left the grounds, a carriage drawn by a slashing pair of bays, drew up near the railing. In it was seated Mr. Parker and Senorita Selita Baneres. At 2:15, the judges ascended the steps leading to the stand. Five minutes later the horses came out, both looking very fit, and as they cantered by the stand, the presiding judge advanced and stated the conditions of the race, two miles and repeat.

Imagine the consternation of the Don and his ally, when when they saw the stall doors thrown open and Isban walked out.

"*Diablo*," hissed the Don, turning toward Leonard, while his hand moved toward his hip, "you play me false!"

"You lie," responded the other coolly, "I thought he must be dead. Don't see why he ain't! Must be like a cat!"

An ashy pallor crept over the Spaniard's dusky face, and a haunted look came into his eyes, as he muttered:

"I am lost"

"Yes," said Doc, flippantly, "our dog's dead."

The first heat showed the American's horse quite the superior of Fulano. The natives were appalled. They had been wont to think Fulano the fastest upon earth. They received the judge's decision after the first heat in silence. Only Parker and the lady with him evinced delight.

The second heat saw Fulano finish twenty lengths away.

"*Caramba*," said the crowd, "the white man's horse runs as the eagle flys," and they left the grounds much poorer than they entered, but saying never a word, for as a race they are born gamblers and accept the decrees of Dame Fortune nonchalantly.

Late that night two well-known residents accosted each other near the Cathedral. A Mexican boy approached their hastily and inquired of one.

"Are you the Senor Quito Kaytan?"

"I am."

"They want you at Sherber's, near the Post office, Don Murrillo is dead!"

"What exclaimed both men, simultaneously."

"Don Murrillo' killed himself a little while ago. Lost two much money on the race to-day, Senor Valde says,"

The man addressed as Kaytan hastened down the street, while the other crossed himself, and softly saying:

"May the Virgin rest his soul," hurried away to spread the news.

Two days afterward Don Ignocio Murrillo was burried from the Cathedral with much form and pomp, and masses were said for the repose for his soul, for many weeks. Conspicuous in the funeral procession was shorty Briggs, dressed in a new suit of clothes. HARVEY W. PECK.

Washington Park Club Declarations.

From the following letter it will be noticed that quite a number of Californian horses have been declared out of the stakes there:

CHICAGO, Feb. 15, 1890.

Please note the following Declarations out of Stakes of the Washington Park Club, Feb. 1, 1890.

The American Derby, at $20 each.—King Charlie, Tarceur, Warsaw, Transit, Armour, Pullman, Watterson, Virginia Mail Pouch, France, Ill Spent, Roseberry, Tacitus, Blackstone, Athlete, March Wind, Barrett, Chan Baskell, Miss Maud, Expense, Sequence, Sam Morse, Onerard, Ukraine. Shoemaker, Pasadena, Jasper, Frederick, Estelle, Miss Hattie, Davidson, Orange Leaf, Ocelita, Formosa, Magdalena, Jersey Pat, Lisimony, Vitality, Kanesville, Pandora, Dennis Dougherty and Dreamer. 41.

The Sheridan Stakes, at $10 each.—King Charlie, Armour, Pullman, Watterson, France, Ill-Spent, Roseberry, Tacitus, Blackstone, Gamarra, Athlete, Chan Haskell, Barrett, Expense, Sequence, Sam Morse, Onsrard, Pasadena, Jasper, Miss Hattie, Rhythm, Ocelita, Orange Leaf, St. Cecilia, Magdalena, Major Ban, Mabel F. Faisalara, Abdiel, Warsaw, Poison, Pandora, Dennis Dougherty and Dreamer. 34.

The Englewood Stakes, at $10 each.—Felipa, Madam Reel, Charlotte Cushman, Finella, Millie Williams, Pinkie T., Sally Ann, Ramoni, Edith Gray, Maud Moon, Hannah, Violante, La Ban, Scioto, Black Belle, Glidaga, Pasadena, Can Can, Minuet, Estelle, Lucretia Borgia, Miss Hattie, Rhythm, Princess Glen, Violetta, St. Cecilia, Orange Leaf, Ocelita, Magdalena, Elsie S., Faisalera, Whisban, Mirope, Pandora, Fortitude and Oriana. 36.

The Hyde Park Stakes, at $10 each.—John P. White, Black Bart, Caperton, Pelion, San Rafael, San Gabriel, Strathmeath and Cerberus. 8.

The Kenwood Stakes, at $10 each. Black Bart, Consternation, San Rafael and San Gabriel. 4.

The Lakeside Stakes, at $10 each.—Blizzard and Hettie Humphreys. 2.

The Drexel Stakes, at $10 each.—Princess Lexington, (formerly Josie C.,) Chan Haskell, Maduma and Major Ban. 4. J. E. BREWSTER, Sec'y.

THE FARM.

Thoroughbred Game Cocks.

How to Breed and Handle this Hardy Strain of Birds.

The law that "like produces like" is only true if the birds are of a pure and known blood, and this is the great secret in breeding. For color we chiefly look to the hen in game, and the cock for style and symmetry; but the most wonderful point is the suddenness with which any change of cocks in a run will change the blood and apparently reverse this rule. I have proved this by setting the fourth egg after change, having put a brown-red to black-red hens, taking away the same evening the black-red cock. The fourth egg produced a splendidly colored brown-red cockerel; and, wonderful to say, from one hen of pure black-red blood I thus obtained nine brown-reds and not one black-red Nevertheless, the rule will generally hold good of depending on the hen for color. The selfsame hen, two years before, when a pullet, was left without a mate after the first two eggs were laid, and every egg of the batch produced a good black-red. This is the mystery how soon the influence of one cock seems destroyed by the introduction of another in the run; and there is no way of proving this so well as breeding the different colors in game.

As an instance of how birds with any admixture of blood will retain it and "throw back," even after twenty years have passed, I may mention the following: A short, very hard feathered spangled cock having been put to a black red hen, a cockerel of this class, put to the mother, threw some of the finest black reds ever seen in England. A cockerel from this cross, put to the hens of the first cross, gave a second family, which were bred backward and forward as required, and kept the color well for twelve years. At the end of this time a cockerel and pullets being mated of the same hatch, produced a few spangles, which were shown and won the first prize in the Any Variety Class of game at Birmingham. Again nine years later, by putting together a cockerel and pullets from the same hatch, and from the same blood, I had a still greater number of Spangles come out. This retention of the cross being so remarkable, I thought it worth mentioning, especially as the difference in color being so great there was no mistaking it; and it shows how careful we ought to be after putting together different colors, to keep it from reappearing when not wanted.

One very mistaken notion is the idea of most breeders as to the few hens they think ought to be put to a cock. Just keep in mind how many prolific eggs you will get from a hen after the cock has been taken away, and consider in that time, even if twenty hens had been running with the cock, whether during the length of time she would have been in laying trim—say while she laid eleven eggs—the cock would not have paid attention to each of those twenty, and the eggs be far more likely to produce strong chickens? I have proof, and very strong proof, even in heavy birds, for the most successful year I ever had in Dorkings I ran seventeen hens with one cockerel, and never had I such heavy and strong constituted birds. Feed well and give a good run, and I should not be afraid to run twenty-five hens with one cock, though he must be a young, healthy bird; but even a two-year-old I should not fear to mate with eleven hens, and would expect to be successful.

Game hens, on the whole, are good average layers, and there are no better mothers for protecting the chickens. I have seen a game hen with chickens drive off all sorts of enemies, from a horse to a rat, and I have seen a game hen actually kill a rat, a rook, and even a hawk; nothing is so big or savage but that she will defend her brood from it. In general, I put eleven eggs under each hen. Unless a few hens hatch off the same day, we are obliged to set the coops far apart, or destruction would be the result. The best time to get game hatched is from the middle of March to the end of April. Get them to nice cottage runs as early as possible after they leave the hens; and, if this is not convenient, divide pullets and cockerels—it will save many a fight. Dub as you find walks for them.

A few hints as to rearing will not be out of place to those who may be about starting. Never put more than eleven eggs under a game hen. When hatched be in no hurry to take them from the nest, for they will want nothing for twenty-four hours, and very little then; and as you should feed the first two or three days with egg custard and a few dry crumbs of bread mixed with the custard, they will require no water; so put none near for them to dabble in. In a day or two take the hen away from where she has hatched to a dry shed facing the south, or a dry bank sheltered from north and east winds, and coop them on the ground. If too wet put some dry ashes under the coop, soft and free from lumps, and by no means put them on boards, for by this we get crooked toes; and rough cinders or gravel sometimes indent the small gristle of the breast, and if it gets the least askew while with the hen, it soon goes worse and worse. Some breeders say they have had them come straight, but this is doubtful. Let your coop remain four or five days at first, by merely drawing the hen's droppings out. When you do shift, do so at midday, and if damp or wet put more dry ashes or dry earth at night. You will find fussing about this dry lodging pay for the trouble, by seeing your chickens come out quite frisky in the morning, and it conduces greatly to health. Coop the hens for six or seven weeks with the chicks, feeding principally on egg custard, coarse oatmeal and bruised wheat until about five weeks old, when give well soaked whole wheat a few times daily, weaning them off to the common food by degrees. It is very useful, if there is no old hedge or low trees near by where your coops are placed, to drive four stakes in the ground standing about a foot high and place a hurdle on them, then lay a few loose boughs on it This serves as a playground in a cold morning, as they soon commence to fly up and down after one another; then again before the earth gets warm for their feet, they will cluster on the top of it when the sun comes out and preen themselves. It makes a nice break between the coops, and is a protection as well, for if there should be any large bird on the wing they are under in a moment. Do not let them roost until about three months old if you can help it, so that you have plenty of soft clean stuff to let them sleep on. They keep warmer in a heap and grow stronger, and it establishes a stronger constitution. Use sulphate of iron in water and your fowl will never have the gapes or roup. The egg custard is made as follows: Beat three eggs up in half a pint of new milk, put in a saucepan, and stir over a fire until it becomes a thick curd; then press the whey out by squeezing in a cloth. Give this custard every morning, and as they get older mix oatmeal and ground rice, which forms a very nutritious food, and they will grow and thrive on it wonderfully. The great effect of custard thus fed, to the chickens getting the rich and strengthening diet the first thing every morning, is, it is digested quicker than any other. If sulphate of iron is in the water, it is not requisite to change it so often as it would be if pure water.

Raising Calves.

At a recent meeting of the Elmira Farmers' Club, President McCann said he wanted to know how to raise a good calf without milk. In response, John Bridgman said: "I have raised calves on hay tea with a very little milk and a handful of wheat middlings or ground oats mixed with it. It will keep them growing, and make them strong, but not fleshy. I have also fed a porridge made of buckwheat flour. I think they need milk until a week or more old." G. W. Hoffman said "I would feed calves dry meal. I never had any trouble to get them to eat it. I would feed them milk for two weeks, and three is better; either skimmed or buttermilk is as good to raise calves on as new milk." D. Shappee said: "To raise calves I would feed them new milk until three or four weeks old, and if I was selling my milk I would go to the creamery and get skimmed or buttermilk to feed them, with cornmeal mixed with it. I would prefer buttermilk to skimmed milk."

Dehorning in England.

At a farmers' meeting not long ago in England the subject of dehorning cattle was considered. The majority of speakers were in favor of dehorning up to a certain point. One gentleman argued that the operation caused little or no pain, at least far less than castration. The same gentleman considered that with regard to older cattle, where the horn had grown large, half-horning was quite sufficient. At the conclusion the following resolution was carried by a unanimous vote: "That this meeting expresses its opinion strongly that young cattle should be dehorned close to the head, and older cattle not so near the head, in proportion to their age."

Feeding Horses.

An English veterinary surgeon recommends that those who have charge of horses, especially farm horses, should be taught that the stomach of a horse is not like the rumen of a cow, a mere receptable for food, but an essential organ of digestion of limited capacity, which does not need to be crammed in order to perform its proper functions, and that it cannot be so treated without danger to the animal; that the teeth of the horse are provided for the purpose of masticating the food, and that the food which does not required mastication should be sparingly, if ever used. He further recommends that no horse be put to work immediately after a full meal, and where a horse has done a heavy day's work it should be allowed to stand in the stable until it is cool and comfortable before being fed. A little water may be given and if a little good hay be put into the rack it will occupy his attention, and besides requiring proper mastication will further have the effect to slightly stimulate the stomach to secretion and prepare it for the reception of the feed which is to follow. Should a horse require more food than usual to supply the extra waste of tissues caused by hard work, give it by all means, but let it be excess in its albuminoids, and let the horse be fed oftener and not in increased quantities at a time.

New Mexico Sheep History.

Col. T. B. Mills, of Las Vegas furnishes the following interesting article in the Stock Grower.

Sheep were brought into the territory from the Southern Mexican States in the early settlement, and after the Indian rebellion in 1680, and the resettlement of the country sheep-raising became the leading industry. The breed which was probably originally merino from Spain, degenerated by inattention to a very inferior class as respects wool, making a good mutton, however. Previous to the annexation to the United States large herds were annually driven to the southern market from this territory, principally for mutton meat. The wool was of but little value and was almost solely used in the territory for the manufacture by the people of blankets, coarse cloth, and bed mattresses. Knives were used in shearing, and the first sheep shears were brought into the territory and used in 1854, by John L. Taylor, a native of Urbana County, Ohio. The first blooded merino sheep were brought in, driven across the plains in 1859, by George Giddings from Kentucky.

Sheep raising has been a prominent industry since the annexation, and the drives to the surrounding States and territories have been large and numerous.

"Drives into California began about the year 1852, 40,000 (some sold as high as $16 per head); sheep driven from New Mexico into California in 1853, 135,000 (sold from $9 to $12 per head); Colonel Chaves himself drove in 1854 (the total drives that year) 27,000; total sheep drive in 1855, 19,000; total sheep drive in 1856 200,000; total sheep drive in 1857, 130,000. (Sheep brought about $3 37 per head in these last years.) In 1858 and 1859 Indians troublesome, small number driven; in 1860 business ceased; total number of sheep driven from New Mexico into California from 1852 to 1860, inclusive, 551,000."

From Colonel Stoneroad and Colonel Chaves, both of New Mexico, we have the following records of sheep driven from California to New Mexico in more recent years:

In 1876 Colonel Stoneroad took from Merced county, California, to Puerto de Luna, New Mexico, 10,000. His route was up San Joaquin Valley to Bakersfield and along the railroad to Tehichipa Pass, in Sierra Nevada; thence to Cottonwood on the Mojave river, where the desert begins; thence down stream to a point much below sea-level. Here comes the real desert trail from the "Sinks" to Union Pass through the Blue Ridge Mountains of Arizona, about 150 miles, with very little water. The whole distance, about 1600 miles, consumed seven months and a half. Others (Pinkerton, Carpenter and Cosner Bros., who were robbed and murdered) drove 16,500.

In 1877 by same route, Stoneroad, Hugo, Zuber. Captain Clancy, McKeller, Robinson and Curtis took 12,500; other flocks say 5,000 in 1878. Booth and Clancy took 4,000.

All the above were grade merinos, such being very scarce in New Mexico. They cost $2 per head in California, and were worth in New Mexico $3 50.

It is estimated by men conversant with the subject that from 1876 to 1878 there were annually driven out of New Mexico to Wyoming, Kansas and Nebraska 350,000 head of sheep. This annual drive rather increased in number than otherwise until 1883 to 1885, when the number reached nearly 1,000,000 head per annum, driven principally to Texas. At that time cattle were considered the best investment and sheep raisers disposed of their herds in order to go into the cattle business. The average price realized for the sheep, which were all Mexican, was $1 50 per head.

Ram Fighting in Ceylon.

The natives of Ceylon, besides taking delight in cock fighting, are given to ram fighting as well, the rams, it is said, being specially imported by the Mohammedan settlers from the Indian coast. A law recently passed with regard to betting and lawful amusements appears to make no provision against that form of amusement, the Government being content to rely upon the general law against cruelty to animals. Ram fighting will, apparently, therefore, be lawful or unlawful in Ceylon according to circumstances. If the owners of combatant rams bet upon the battle, it will be a contravention of the gaming act; if they do not bet, but if they allow their rams to fight with sufficient energy to hurt themselves, then the law of cruelty comes in. If they neither bet nor allow the animals to hurt themselves, they are held to be honest sportsmen, against whom no one could complain, and the fight is supposed to be to the edification of all men.

Animal Food for Great Britain.

The complete statistics of British imports for the year 1889 have just been issued, and contain some figures in which Americans are highly interested. Great Britain imported in that year no less than 555,221 live cattle against 377,086 in the preceding year, and almost doubling the imports of two years ago. The total of sheep imported was 678,058, that of the preceding year being 956,210. This is the only point in which the imports show a decline. In swine and horses there was a very slight increase, and in fresh beef the total of 657,574 cwt. in 1887 was increased to 1,379,511 cwt. in 1889. These figures are highly significant to the countries which furnish Great Britain with its food supplies. Of the great increase in cattle the United States furnished the bulk, our exports of cattle last year being 294,423 head, against 143,495 head in 1888, and 94,858 head in 1887, the trade of the latter year having been about trebled in 1889. Of the fresh beef which Great Britain imports the United States furnishes about nine-tenths. If as many sagacious observers think our exportation of animal foods should show an increase in 1890, the total to report a year hence will be large indeed.—National Stockman.

Shorthorn Sales in England.

Our English exchanges give us some very interesting comparisons of the Shorthorn sales of the last year with those of previous years, as follows:

In 1889, there were forty sales at which 2,085 head were sold, at an average price of $167 per head. In 1888, the number of sales was thirty-nine, number of cattle sold 1594, average price $132. In 1887, 1353 cattle were sold at thirty-seven sales, at an average price of $131 50. In 1886 the average price was $176.

Shorthorn breeders in England certainly have no right to complain. They are not only realizing good prices, but the price is slowly advancing until it has almost reached the average of 1885. There can be no advance in Shorthorns or other improved cattle in America until beef cattle advance as they have done in England, nor can there be such a wide disparity between the prices in the two counties very long after congress metes out the proper punishment to the beef combine. It is not possible to name another article of commerce in which there is not a proper correspondence in prices between the old world and the new.—Homestead.

Lump Jaw in Cattle.

The following resolutions were passed by the Central Illinois Farmers' Institute:

Whereas, The Live-Stock Commissioners of Illinois have assumed the authority to condemn and destroy good, healthy, fat steers at the union stock yards when only affected with small lumps on their jaws under the pretense of preventing the spread of contagious disease, and

Whereas, We are informed by the address of Prof. D. McIntosh, veterinary surgeon of the Illinois university, delivered before this institute, that the disease called "lump jaw" in cattle is not contagious, and that the flesh of such cattle is not unwholesome for food so long as the animal is in a thriving condition, and fat and well, and

Whereas, Years of experience with cattle convinces us that his conclusions are correct.

Resolved, That we consider the action of the Live-Stock Commission in condemning such cattle and consigning them to the rendering tanks, a high-handed outrage, resulting in the robbery of farmers and producers, and enriching the Union Rendering Company of Chicago, and we respectfully request the governor of Illinois to make prompt investigation into the matter, and to take steps to stop this unjust and arbitrary exercise of power by the Live-Stock Commissioners.

Contagious Diseases Act.

The Breeders' Gazette says: We have shown that public sentiment in Great Britain is ripe for the pressing of this question upon the Imperial authorities, and the very latest English mail brings the subjoined report of a recent public expression upon this subject from Mr. Moreton Frewen—than whom no man is more familiar with the cattle trade of both Great Britain and America:

There was one point, he said, of which he had made a close study, and it was worth while to consider whether the legislation which was responsible for the present application of the Contagious Diseases (Animals) Act was entirely warranted by the circumstances of the time. The result of the rigid exclusion of lean stock from America had been to drive this country more and more into the dead and fat cattle meat trade. As long as the Contagious Diseases (Animals) Act precluded the importation of store cattle from the United States to this country, he did not think the conditions of agriculture would be quite healthy. The result of the enforcement of that act had been to prohibit English farmers from buying their store cattle in the one cheap market of the world. He was aware there was a breeders' side of the question. He had no cattle interests to preserve in America, but he was convinced that Ireland could carry one-third more cattle than she had now, and the only chance of her increasing her stock was to buy heifer stock from across the Atlantic and bring it in alive. On this side of the Atlantic there were advantages for fattening cattle which no other country enjoyed. If the cattle trade of which he was speaking was not subjected to the existing restrictions, and if the English farmers had their agents at Chicago who would forward 4,000 or 5,000 head of lean cattle a day, quite a new phase would be put on the agriculture of this country. As to the "bogey" of disease, he pointed out that in dealing with America there were conditions of security which were offered nowhere else. Five or six years ago there was pleuro-pneumonia, but there had never been a single outbreak of foot-and-mouth disease in the United States.

THE KENNEL.

Dog owners are requested to send for publication the earliest possible notices of whelps, sales, names claimed, presentations and deaths, in their kennels, in all instances writing plainly names of sire and dam and of grandparents, colors, dates and breed.

Regular Annual Meeting of the American Kennel Club, February 13, 1890.

PRESENT.

American Pet Dog Club, M. H. Cryer; American Spaniel Club, James Watson; Long Island Live Stock Fair Association, T. Prime; Maryland Kennel Club, H. Malcolm; New England Kennel Club, F. B. Fay; St Paul (Minn.) Kennel Club, A. D. Lewis; Southern Field Trial Club, A. C. Wilmerding; Massachusetts Kennel Club, R. Leslie; Hartford Kennel Club, A. C. Collins.

On motion, Mr. James L. Anthony was appointed chairman in the absence of the President and vice-President.

The minutes of the last annual meeting were read and approved.

The reading of the Treasurer's report was dispensed with, owing to its publication in the Gazette.

The report of the Stud-book Committee was then read and adopted, and is as follows:

To the American Kennel Club:

GENTLEMEN:—Your committee begs to report that during the year 1889, it acted upon the most important matters referred to it by the American Kennel Club, and reported its action at the regular meetings of the Executive Committee of said club, and by them approved. Several unimportant matters are still in abeyance, and your committee in such cases reports progress. The Stud-book received during the year 4,217 voluntary registrations made up from the following sources:

Cash entries	3,947
Less, returned as not eligible	35
	3,912
Associate entries	297
A. K. R. entries (under the rule)	8
Total	4,217

The rule allowing A. K. R. entries to be accepted (without charge) upon application of owners, was rescinded by the Advisory Committee April 15, 1889, and said action was ratified by the American Kennel Club May 28, 1889. The copy for Vol. VI. of the Stud-book was delivered to the printers February 1st, and the book will be ready for sale and distribution the first part of March next. The delay in publishing Vol. VI was caused by the great number of entries received during the month of December, amounting to 1,153, examination and compilation of which, together with the other business of the office, consumed the entire month of January, notwithstanding the employment of additional clerical force. The composition, proof-reading, examination by the Committee of the Specialty Clubs, and finally the binding of the volumes, will consume from four to six weeks, and as early in March as possible the Secretary will forward the book to each associate and subscriber.

Respectfully submitted,

THOS. H. TERRY } Committee.
A. D. LEWIS, }

The following are the Articles and Sections of the Constitution to be amended, and notice of the proposed changes is hereby given:

ARTICLE IV.

Sec. 1. Any person vouched for, in writing to the Secretary of the American Kennel Club, by not less than two members of any club, a member of this association, or by two associate members, shall, upon payment of five dollars annual dues and the endorsement of his application by the President of the American Kennel Club or of the associate members, become an associate member and be announced as such in the next issue of the Kennel Gazette.

Sec. 2. An associate member shall be entitled to the Kennel Gazette and Stud Book, and to two free registrations in the Stud Book during the current year, for which his dues are paid.

Sec. 3. The annual dues of five dollars shall be paid on the 1st of January of each year to the Secretary of the American Kennel Club, and any person whose dues are not paid on or before January 10th shall thereby forfeit his right to be included in the list of members eligible for election to office, and to vote for officers for the ensuing year; and if his dues shall remain unpaid at the next annual meeting of the associate members his name may be stricken from the roll, provided, however, that upon remitting the five dollars dues with an application for membership he shall be reinstated upon the endorsement of his application by the Presidents as hereinbefore provided.

Mr. Watson—I move that the American Kennel Club consider the recommendations of the associate members made in the report.

Seconded and carried.

The recommendations contained in said report were then taken up, read, and severally adopted.

The Article IV with proposed amendments was then read, and on motion the Secretary was instructed to publish them for thirty days in the ordinary form, to be acted upon at the next regular meeting of the American Kennel Club.

In answer to questions by Mr. Jas. Watson, Treasurer Vredenburgh specifically explained the financial statement of the club as it appeared in the Kennel Gazette, and clearly showed that the accounts were in proper form, and the club in a most satisfactory condition.

The Chairman stated that the Advisory Committee had instructed the Secretary to show the books to any person properly authorized to see them, or, in other words, any delegate, it not being necessary for a club even to instruct their delegates, but he wanted it distinctly understood that the books were not open for investigation by the general public, or those who have no personal interest in the affairs of the club.

The election of officers now being in order Mr. Watson nominated Mr. August Belmont, Jr., for President. Mr. Leslie nominated Mr. Thomas H. Terry for Vice President.

On motion the Secretary was instructed to cast a ballot for Messrs. Belmont and Terry, as President and Vice president respectively.

The Secretary proceeded to cast such a ballot, and Messrs. Belmont and Terry were elected to the offices named.

Mr. Leslie—I move that we now proceed to ballot for members of the Advisory Committee.

The Chair appointed Messrs. Wilmerding and Lewis as tellers, to receive and count the votes for the members of the Advisory Committee, who later announced such vote to be as follows: Total number of votes cast seventeen. For Mr. John S. Wise, 9; for Mr. J. L. Anthony, 7; and for James Watson, 1.

On motion of Mr. Watson the election of Messrs. Wise and Anthony was made unanimous.

Mr. Fay nominated Messrs. Thomas H. Terry, A. D. Lewis, and James Watson, as Stud Book Committee.

On motion the Secretary was instructed to cast a ballot for the three gentlemen named as such Stud Book Committee.

The Secretary cast the vote, and they were declared elected. Adjourned. A. P. VREDENBURGH, Secretary.

MEETING OF THE EXECUTIVE COMMITTEE.

American Pet Dog Club, M. H. Cryer; American Spaniel Club, James Waton; Long Island Live Stock Fair Assn., T. Price; Maryland Kennel Club, H. Malcolm; New England Kennel Club, F. B. Fay; St. Paul Minnesota Kennel Club; A. D. Lewis; Southern Field Trial Club, J. L Anthony: New Jersey Kennel Club, A C. Wilmerding; Massachusetts Kennel Club, R. Leslie; Hartford Kennel Club, A. C Collins; American English Beagle Club, H. F. Schellhass. Mr. James Watson, appointed Chairman.

The Secretary read his report as follows:

To the Delegates of the American Kennel Club—gentlemen, since my last report, I have received application in proper form, from the Duquesne Kennel Club of Pittsburgh, Pa; the Buffalo Kennel Club of Buffalo, N. Y., and the Kansas City Kennel Club, of Kansas City, Mo. These applicants are eligible to membership, and their admission is respectfully recommended.

The application of the California Kennel Club, which has been laid over since the September meeting, cannot yet be acted upon, as no official notice has yet been received of the expected amalgamation of that Club and the Pacific Kennel Club. The latest communicaton on the subject was written December 26th, 1889, and signed by Mr. J. B Martin, Committee of the California Club, in which he advises this Club that he will inform it immediately when the matter is taken up.

I have a communication from Mr. J. Otis Fellows, requesting that the awards made at the Elmira show, held in September 1889, be officially recognized by this club, that the entries were made with the understanding that the wins would count, and he respectfully asks for your favorable action. In this connection I would say that the Elmira show was held September 17, 18, 19 and 20, 1889, and it is stated in its catalogue that the judging will commence promptly at ten o'clock on the morning of the 17th. The club was elected to active membership in the American Kennel Club, September 19th, 1889, two days after the awards were made, and, while it has been stated in some of the weekly journals that the Elmira awards should have been published in the list of "recognized shows," I beg to submit that I had no authority so to do, and would quote from my report read at the September meeting as follows:

"Your Secretary begs to call your attention to the fact that some of the clubs whose applications for membership are "now before you, have held shows since filing such applications, and, if said clubs are admitted, he would respect-"fully recommend that some action should be taken at this meeting as to whether *this* Association will, or will not re-"cognize the awards made at such shows." There was no action taken on my request, and the wins at Elmira have not been recognized by the American Kennel Club.

At the meeting of the Advisory Committee of this Club, held September 19, 1889, it ordered the suspension of the Albany Kennel Club for the non-payment of its prizes at its show held March 6, 7 and 8, 1889, and passed a resolution that if said prizes were not paid within thirty days, that the penalty under Rule 28 should be enforced. The thirty days expired on the 19th day of December, 1889, and as no official notification of the payment of arrears of prizes has ever reached this office, president Belmont, Jr., suspended all the officers of said club under Rule 28, referring to the application of Rule 25. I only mailed notices to that effect to Doctor W. C. Hudson, President; Geo. B. Gallup, Secretary; and General Amasa J. Parker, Jr., and Robert C. Pruyn, members of the Bench Show Committee. This matter is now before you, and in accordance with the rules, "the "Executive Committee of the American Kennel Club must in every case of suspension, at their first meeting thereafter, either remove the same, or impose a penalty of disqualification for such period as they may decide upon."

At our last meeting Mr. Lorenzo Daniels preferred charges against Mr. Wm. Graham of Belfast, Ireland, but the same were ordered laid upon the table, on the ground that Daniels had not obeyed the orders of this club, and could not have his case considered until he had complied with the decision of the club rendered in July 1880. Under date of January 15th 1889, Mr. Daniels enclosed to your secretary a check, drawn to the order of the American Kennel Club for $50.10, being the amount awarded by the Advisory Committee, to Mr. Graham, and requested that his charges against said Graham be taken up by this this club, and acted upon. Your secretary promptly referred this matter to Pres. Belmont Jr., for instructions, and under date of January 20, 1890, he forwarded me the following communication: "I beg herewith to notify you that in view of the payment to you by Mr. Lorenzo Daniels oof $50.10 being amount due Mr. Graham under the decision of the American Kennel Club of July 1889, the suspension imposed upon Mr. Daniels by the American Kennel Club December 19th 1889, is removed pending final action of the American Kennel Club at its next quarterly meeting. You will be kind enough to hold the amount before paying the same to Mr. Graham until such action as referred to above is taken." A copy of the above notice from President Belmont Jr., was duly mailed to both Mr. Daniels and Mr. Graham, and the check was disposited in the bank, pending such directions regarding it, that you may deem proper to give at this meeting. Respectfully submitted,

A. P. VREDENBURGH Secretary.

The Treasurer's report was read and adopted, and is as follows:

Feby. 12, 1890.

To the Delegates of the American Kennel Club,—Gentlemen:—In accordance with the resolution adopted at the last meeting, I published my annual report in detail in the Gazette of January, which fully sets forth the financial condition of this Club, and I leave it in your hands without comment, for your action in the premises. Since January 1, 1890, I beg to submit the following:

Receipts from all sources to date	$2,974.72
Expenses for same period	294.38
Balance on hand	$2,680.30

The following clubs have failed to pay their annual dues for the year 1890—Albany Kennel Club, Chattahoochee Valley Exp. Co., Connecticut State Kennel Club, Elmira Poultry & Pet Stock Assn., Hartford Kennel Club, Montana Kennel Club Pacific Kennel Club, Southern Field Trial Club, Syracuse Kennel Club. Respectfully submitted,

A. P. VREDENBURGH, Treas.

Mr. Anthony—I move that the clubs whose names appear on that report be notified by the Secretary, that if their dues are not paid within thirty days their names will be dropped.

Laid over.

The matter of the charges of Lorenzo Daniels against Graham, referred to in the Secretary's report was on motion referred to the Advisory Committee.

In the matter of the request of the Elmira Kennel Club, Dr. Cryer moved that said request be granted.

Motion seconded and carried.

On motion of Mr. Lewis, the Secretary was instructed to notify W. C. Hudson, G. B. Gallup, A. J. Parker Jr., and Robert C. Pruyn, of the Albany Kennel Club, that they are disqualified until the awards given by that club are paid in full.

The following kennel clubs were admitted to membership: The Duquesne Kennel Club, the Buffalo Kennel Club and the Kansas City Kennel Club.

The request of the American Gordon Setter Club to change their name to "The Gordon Setter Club of America," was on motion granted.

Mr. Anthony's original motion that the delinquent clubs be notified that if their dues are not paid within thirty days they shall be dropped from the roll, was then put and carried.

Mr A. P. Vredenburgh was unanimously elected as Secretary-Treasurer of the American Kennel Club for the ensuing year.

Mr. Leslie—Before we adjourn I move that a vote of thanks be tendered to all the officers of this club for the satisfactory manner in which they have performed their duties for the past year.

Motion seconded and unanimously carried.

Adjourned. A. P. VREDENBURGH, Sec'y.

Names Claimed.

Mr. Geo. T. Allender claims the name of Edmund for lemon and white pointer pup whelped September 4, 1889, sire Roscoe (Don—Sal), dam California (Point—Blossom).

Visit.

Mr. A. B. Truman's (San Francisco) pointer Queen Croxteth (Rush T.—Patti Croxteth T.) to Baron J. H. F. von Schroder's Point (Vandevort's Don—Drab), Jan. 16th, 1890.

Mr. W. S. Kittle's cocker Spaniel Gift to Donald Campbell's Teddy, on February 10th, '90.

Mr. J. E. Lucas' English setter Bessie (Fred-Gypsie) to M. W. Stackpools, Whit, Whittler's Rock—Shorb's Nellie) on February 19th, '90.

Mr. J. B. Martin's fox terrier Beatrice (13830) by Champion Bacchanal to C. A. Sumner's Blemton Vesuvian (14290) by Champion Lucifer, on Feb. 4, '90.

Mr. L. L. Campbell (Benicia) bred his Irish setter, Belle C (Mike T—Lady Elcho T) to his Barrymore (Elcho Jr—Maid) on February 16th.

Echo Cocker Kennels (A. C. Davenport & Co., Stockton) dark orange cocker Spaniel bitch Senora by Robin A. K. C. S. B. 8535, dam Devon Beauty to same owners, solid black cocker Spaniel stud dog Bronta by Champion Brant, dam McDougald's Mollie, Feb. 17, 1890.

Woodstock Ada, blk cocker Spaniel bitch by Champion Obo II (4911), dam Woodstock Dinah to same owners liver and white and ticked stud dog Kute by Carlo, dam Beauty, Feb. 21, 1890.

C. W. Binsse, who attended the field trials, has come to San Rafael for a little stay and we hope will permit his sportsmen friends to see something of him.

It appears that a clay soil with decided slope would be the proper thing upon which to keep dogs through the winter. The rain could drain away quickly and no vapors or miasmatic poisons pass up through clay. The worst of all places is a sandy yard.

Several notable breeding items appear at the head of this department. California should have, and has as good dogs in certain breeds as are to be found anywhere, and prospective buyers should keep the fact in mind, thereby encouraging local breeders and building up the interest.

It seems probable that the three or four gentlemen who make the training of pointers and setters a specialty in California will soon all be located near San Francisco. George T. Allender was in the city on Monday and Tuesday to look at several places offered him. William DeMott is casting about for an abiding place. M. D. Walter has his eye on a Berkeley spot, and also on one near Haywards, L. L. Campbell is thinking of going into training, and if he does so will wish to be near town.

A little cross-firing is going on in one or two of our contemporaries about the comparative merit of setters and pointers. In so far as we have followed the controversy it seems that all of the writers are a little indefinite in their premises. If the proposition be that all setters are better than all pointers, conclusive disproofs might be adduced. If it be merely that the best English setter is better than the best pointer, then individual opinion may properly be permitted to each one interested. Given suitable conditions under which to work the best English setter and there can be no doubt that a brilliant exhibition will result, and a like remark might be made of the best pointer. Individual preference, however, may not be based upon the rare bits of work shown at rare intervals by types of rare species, but rather upon the average adaptability of the dog preferred to the work usually done.

We have known devoted sportsmen who would not own a setter because on the quail ground most accessible there were cockle burrs and other burry stuff which filled the long haired coats and necessitated sitting up for hours to clean the dog after an afternoon's sport. On the other hand, there are sportsmen equally devoted, who are able to go once a week or so to a clean ground for a few hours and who prefer a dashing, snappy setter dog for the little work to be done. To oppose either choice is to be absurd. A good dog is a good dog, and is rare enough at best.

From President H. T. Payne.

EDITOR BREEDER AND SPORTSMAN:—Some comment which I heard during my late visit to your city regarding the show given by the Southern California Kennel Club last June, impels me to ask the indulgence of your columns in order that the cause of our awards not being recognized by the American Kennel Club be fully explained and the blame placed where it properly belongs. Our club as you well know, was organized, and the show held within the short space of six weeks, and matters necessarily had to be pushed onward at a very lively rate. Immediately on the organization of the club, we wrote the Secretary of the A. K. C., asking for the rules of said club and the necessary steps to be taken in order to gain membership. We received a reply stating that we must forward a copy of our Constitution and $10 as entrance fee, but no rules were sent us. The Secretary also stated that the A. K. C. would hold a meeting on the May 19th, and that if our application was in, we would undoubtedly be admitted and our awards recognized. On the receipt of this letter a meeting of our club was called, the necessary action taken and our constitution and a draft on New York mailed to him the next day. But as the time was very short for the mail to reach there by the 19th, we telegraphed the Secretary that the constitution, draft, etc., was in the mail and on their way to the great metropolis, hoping that the A. K. C, would act on the statement of the telegram provided the letter failed to reach them by the date of their meeting. We soon discovered, however, by a letter from the Secretary, that our hopes were in vain, and that in the eyes of the A. K. C the gentlemen composing the Southern California Kennel Club were not good for the enormous sum of $10, coin of the realm, the Secretary stating that although he had received our telegram, the fact that our coin was not spread out before their eyes prevented action being taken on our admission, but to go ahead with the show and our awards would be recognized. But still he failed to send us a copy of the rules or make any suggestions to guide us. Another appeal for rules was made, for it was our desire to comply with all requirements, for we believed that the Southern California Kennel Club had come to stay.

At last when our catalogue was printed, we were forced to get our knowledge of the A. K. C. show rules from a few old copies of catalogues of such other shows as happened to be in our possession, and here was where we committed the crime which has debarred our awards. In one of these catalogues appeared a rule stating that "the entry must clearly identify the dog to be exhibited by name," etc., with a foot note stating that a dog registered in the American Kennel Register previous to January 1, 1888, may be registered free of charge in the American Kennel Club Stud book. Therefore, in order to fully identify four or five of our dogs that under this foot-note were entitled to free registration, their American Kennel Register numbers were published in our catalogue, we very naturally supposing, that as the American Kennel Club had purchased the Register, they had got through fighting what was now their property. But alas! how fallible is human judgment!

After our catalogue was printed, and the show had already been open two days, we received another letter from the A. K. C.'s secretary, giving us a little advice, but containing no copy of the rules yet, and later, when a copy of our catalogue had reached his hands, another letter stating that we had violated an imperative rule by publishing in our catalogue the A. K. R. numbers of a few dogs, and that he should therefore "advise that our awards be not recognized."

This was the head and front of our offense and nothing more, and for this our awards were rejected. Had the secretary of the A. K. C. performed his duties as he should, we would have had in our possession a copy of the show rules long before our catalogues were printed, and this most inexcusable error of showing that some of our exhibitors had been patrons of the A. K. R. when the stud book was lingering in that uncertain condition between life and death, would have been avoided. Now, when the matter of the rejection of our awards was brought before the A. K. C. for re-consideration, the plea was made that we had refused to register our entries.

But why and how? When the club refused us admittance simply because a draft on New York did not reach the Secretary's hands until the day after the meeting of the committee, we did not feel that we could demand registration of our exhibitors when we were not a member, but wrote the said Secretary stating that we would register at the expense of our club all dogs entered not already registered if our awards were recognized. To this we have never received any reply. The proposition was certainly fair and just. Why should we be expected to compel registration when we were not a member of the A. K. C, and not to receive the benefit of the recognition of our rewards?

When the attention of the Secretary of the A. K. C. was called to the causes which led to this technical violation —if it can be characterized by so mild a term—his reply was that he had cautioned us against making this error, viz: the publication of A. K. R. numbers. But unfortunately for the exhibitors at our show, his knowledge of the vast extent of that territory over which "old glory" floats, caused his "cautioning" letter to reach us just two days after our interesting show had opened its doors to an admiring and liberal public. While every one will concede the necessity of stringent rules for the government of all organizations of any magnitude, yet it is the general supposition that these national heads are formed for the purpose of encouraging and assisting the subordinate clubs in all manner possible to disseminate the principles or advance the interests of that special work for which the subordinate bodies have been formed, instead of picking technical flaws in work that is honestly intended for the general advancement and good of all.

It was my intention to let this whole matter drop with the last action of the A. K. C., and quietly abide by its decision, but the unfavorable comment growing out of a late publication of the reasons for its action compells me in justice to our young club to place the matter before the exhibitors of this coast in its proper light, hewing straight to the line of truth, letting the chips fall where they may.

H. T. PAYNE.
President S. Cal. Kennel Club.

The color standard adopted by the Irish Setter Club of the United States is as follows: "*Color and markings.*—The color should be a rich golden chestnut or mahogany red, with no trace whatever of black; white on chest, throat or toes, or a small star on the forehead, or a narrow streak, or blaze on the nose or face not to disqualify." Stonehenge says: "There is no doubt that the preponderance of white, so as to constitute what is called white and red, is met with in some good strains."

THE GUN.

Great Work.

The three live bird matches, arranged between Dr. G. F. Knapp of the Westminster Kennel Club of New York and Charles Macalester of the Riverton Gun Club of Philadelphia, at 500 pigeons, for a purse of $16,000, resulten in a victory for Macalester, who won all three matches by a total of 36 birds. The conditions were as follows: First day, 100 live birds, 30 yards rise, 50 yards boundary. The score in detail were as follows: Friday, Feb. 6th:—

C. Macalester	2 2 2 1 2 1 2 1 1 2 1 0 2 2 1 1 0 2 1 1 2 2 2 1 1	
	1 1 2 1 1 1 1 1 2 2 1 2 1 1 1 1 2 1 1 1 2 1 1 1 1	
	1 1 2 0 1 1 0 1 1 1 1 1 1 1 1 1 1 1 1 2 1 1 2 1 2 1	
	1 1 1 2 1 1 1 2 2 1 2 0 1 1 2 2 1 0 0 0 2 1 1 2	—92
Dr. Knapp	1 2 1 1 2 1 2 1 2 2 2 2 0 1 1 1 1 0 2 0 1 2 0 1 1	
	1 2 2 0 1 2 1 0 2 2 0 1 1 1 2 2 2 0 0 1 1 2 1 2 1	
	1 2 2 1 2 0 1 1 1 1 2 2 1 1 2 2 2 1 0 2 1 1 0 0 1	
	1 1 1 2 2 0 1 1 1 1 0 1 0 1 1 1 2 0 0 2 1 0 0 0 2 2	—79

Referee, Mr. Howard Jaffray. Scorer, Mr. Grant.

The conditions of the second match—200 live birds, 30 yards rise, 50 yards boundary. The scores in detail for the second day, Feb. 8th:—

C. Macalester,		Dr. Knapp.	
1 1 1 0 2 1 1 1 1 1 2 1 0		2 2 2 1 2 0 2 0 2 1 2 0 1	
2 1 2 2 0 1 2 1 0 2 1 1	—21	2 1 2 1 1 0 1 1 0 1 1 1	—20
2 0 1 2 2 2 2 0 2 1 1 2 1		2 2 1 2 2 0 0 2 1 0 1 2 2	
2 1 2 1 1 0 1 1 2 0 2 0	—20	0 0 0 0 2 0 2 2 0 1 0 2	—15
1 1 1 1 2 2 1 1 1 0 1 0 1		2 2 2 0 0 1 2 2 2 2 2 2 2	
1 0 0 0 2 1 1 1 2 1 1 1	—20	2 2 2 0 7 2 0 0 0 2 2 2	—19
2 0 0 1 1 1 1 1 1 0 1 1 1		1 1 0 1 2 2 2 2 2 2 1 0 1	
1 2 2 1 1 1 2 2 0 1 1 0	—21	2 0 1 2 1 2 0 2 2 2 0 1	—20
2 1 2 2 1 2 2 2 2 1 1 2 1		2 0 0 0 1 0 2 1 1 1 1 1 0	
1 0 1 1 2 1 1 1 1 0 1 1	—23	1 2 1 2 0 2 2 1 0 2 1 2	—18
2 1 1 2 1 0 1 2 2 1 0 1 1		2 2 2 1 2 0 2 2 2 2 1 1 2	
2 1 1 2 1 0 1 0 1 1 1 2	—21	0 2 1 0 2 2 2 1 2 1 1 1	—22
2 2 2 1 2 2 2 1 1 0 2 0 2		1 2 2 1 1 0 1 0 0 1 0 0 0	
2 1 2 0 1 1 1 2 2 0 2 1	—21	2 1 1 0 2 0 1 1 2 1 0 2	—16
0 1 0 2 1 1 1 1 0 1 1 2 0		1 0 2 0 0 0 2 1 1 1 2 0 1	
1 2 0 1 1 2 2 1 0 1 2 0	—18	1 2 0 1 0 0 2 2 2 0 1 2	—16
Total	165	Total	146

Referee for first hundred, Mr R. Lawrence of New York; for the second, Mr. M. Bayley of Philadelphia. Mr. Walter B. Smith handled the birds for Dr. Knapp, and Mr. Handy for Mr. Macalester.

3d Match—100 live birds, 30 yards' rise, 30 yards' boundary. The scores for the third day, Feb. 10th were:

C. Macalester—1st 100	2 2 1 2 1 2 0 2 2 1 1 1 0 1 2 2 2 1 1 0 0 1 1 2 1	
	1 1 0 2 2 2 1 1 1 1 2 2 0 2 0 1 2 1 2 1 1 1 2 1 2	
	1 0 2 1 1 0 1 1 2 2 1 1 1 1 1 2 2 2 1 1 0 2 2 1 0	
	1 1 2 1 1 2 0 0 2 2 1 2 2 1 1 1 2 0 2 1 0 2 1 1 0 1	—85
2nd 100	2 2 1 2 1 2 2 2 2 1 1 1 1 2 1 1 2 1 0 2 2 0 2 0 1 0 1 1 1 0 0 2 0 1	
	1 0 1 1 2 2 0 1 2 2 1 2 0 1 1 2 1 0 1 0 1 1 2 1 0 2 2 2 1 2 1 2 1 2 1	
	1 2 2 0 1 1 2 0 1 0 1 0 1 2 1 1 2 1 0 2 1 1 2 1 1 0 1 0 2	—166
Dr. Knapp—1st 100	2 1 1 2 2 2 2 1 1 1 1 2 2 2 2 1 2 0 2 2 2 2 0 1 1	
	2 2 2 1 1 0 2 2 1 2 2 0 2 1 0 1 2 1 0 2 1 0 0 2 0	
	1 2 1 0 2 0 2 1 2 1 2 2 1 2 2 1 2 1 0 0 1 0 2 2 2	
	0 1 2 1 1 0 2 2 2 2 0 2 1 2 2 2 2 2 2 0 2 0 2 2 1	—81
2nd 100	2 2 2 1 1 1 2 1 1 2 0 2 1 2 1 1 1 2 2 2 7 1 0 1 1 2 2 0 2 2 0 1 1 2 2 0 2 2 0 2 3	
	0 2 2 1 2 0 1 2 2 2 0 2 1 2 2 1 0 1 2 1 2 1 0 0 1 2 1 1 1 1 2 2 2 1 2 2	
	2 2 2 0 2 2 0 2 2 0 0 2 2 2 2 2 0 2 0 2 2 1 0 2	—162

Referee for the first 100 Mr. Oakleigh Thorne; for second 100, Mr. F. Sands. 2 denotes killed with second barrel.

The record of the three matches is as follows: C. Macalester, Feb 6th, 92; 8th, 82; 8th, 83; 10th, 85; 10th, 81; total, 423. Dr. Knapp, Feb. 6th, 79; 8th, 73; 8th, 73; 10th, 81; 10th, 81; total, 387.

California Against America.

The most brilliant match between teams of ten on a side that has ever been shot off at pigeons was that of Saturday afternoon last at the Haight street ball grounds in this city. The match was a peculiar one in several respects. It was instituted at short notice, to give eclat to the visit of the expert trap shots who are touring the country under management of Colonel C. W. Dimick, in the interest of the United States Cartridge Company. No opportunity was afforded the local men to practice, and none of them had shot over traps to any extent since October last, while the visitors were in perfect form. Several of the very best of Californian shots could not take part, such as Crittenden Robinson, A. W. Bruner, Frank J. Bassford, and others, but a good, safe team was selected, and the splendid scores made fully justified the wisdom of the choice. It was thought that one hundred and twenty-five kills would win, but in the outcome the home team rolled up one hundred and thirty, an average of thirteen out of fifteen, while the visiting wizards scored one hundred and thirty-seven, just under fourteen birds to the man. Such work cannot but arouse admiration and emulation. The Californians were beaten fairly and squarely, after a closely shot-out race, and took their beating in good spirit.

The visitors were evidently shooting up to their highest capacity, and they needed to do so.

The Californians were John K. Orr, Captain, whose first pigeon match in the State was shot in 1856, and who is always brilliant, quick and effective; Martinez Chick, of San Diego, a quick shot and reliable; Chas. J. Haas and Chas. A. Merrill, of Stockton, both in the first rank of any company at the traps; Henry A. Bassford, of Vacaville, a little slow, but a dead shot; Jos. Delmas, of San Jose, not particularly graceful in handling a gun, but as reliable as any man in the State; Dr. S. E. Knowles, of this city, who has reduced trap shooting to certainties, bar luck; Colonel S. I. Kellogg, not as experienced at live birds as the others, but a clean, fine shot; H. C. Golcher, a Hercules in frame and a master of the gun, and Edward Fay, whose race was as brilliant as any of the day. The team did not work together with sufficient care, and lost several birds which might have been scored dead with more watchfulness.

The ten visiting world-beaters were Harvey McMurchy, a model in style, judgment and skill; W. H. Wolstencroft, the quickest shot alive, and deadly withal; W. F. Quimby, a little slower, and not given to leading his birds quite enough; H. B. Whitney, trim, precise, sure as fate, and the equal of any man ever seen in the State as a shot; W. E. Perry, whose shooting actually seems automatic; C. W. Budd, clean-cut, masterly and perfect at the traps.

James R. Stice, a massive man, but lithe and speedy; Rolla O. Heikes, a first rate shot and first class in all other respects; S. A. Tucker, known and read of all our readers, and John A. Ruble, a little morose in manner and failing to center his birds, yet scoring them all dead.

All of the visitors were cracks, and their styles afforded most interesting matter for study and reflection. Mr. Wolstencroft in particular was a study. Such marvellous quickness was never before seen. His second barrel is fired almost simultaneously with the first.

Colonel C. W. Dimick was referee, Ramon E. Wilson and H. H. Briggs judges, Ed Hough and H. T. Payne scorers.

Bassford, of the California team, was the first to face the traps, and opened the contest suspiciously by dropping a black-tailer within three feet of the trap with the first barrel, the appreciative crowd in the grand stand applauding the performance with much patriotic enthusiasm.

Wolstencroft, the lightning marksman of the champion team, came next, and fairly discounted Bassford's clever performances by slaughtering his bird before he was six inches above the trap.

Kellogg of the local team then followed and knocked a fistful of feathers out of a powerful red left-quarterer that dashed wildly away toward the Cliff House the moment the trap was sprung. The second barrel of the Colonel's twelve-gauge stopped the fugitive, however, within twenty yards of the boundary, and the grand stand resounded again with local enthusiasm. Budd of the visiting team then killed a white-tailer in fine style, and the shooting kept on alternating, Golcher scoring with his second barrel, Murchy with his first, Knowles with his first, Stice with his first, Perry with his first, Fay with his second, Quimby with his second, Chick with his first, Heikes with his first, Merrill with his first, Ruble with his first, Delmas with his first and Whitney with his second.

Nine men of each team had killed their birds, only two of the Californians being compelled to use the second barrel, while five of the champions deemed it prudent to pull the second trigger and lose no chance. Haas was the last of the Californians to face the traps on the first round and he killed his bird in fine style. Tucker of the visiting team was the last of the champions, and the echo of his ten-gauge gun was dimmed by the shout in the grand stand, as the right quarter he aimed at defied his first barrel and carried the charge of shot from his second outside the fifty-yard boundary. This was the first miss of the day, and the Californians had won the initial round, having scored ten straight birds to the champion's nine.

On the next round, however, Bassford, Chick and Delmas missed, and the champions led by one bird, the score standing 18 to 17. The champions gained another bird on the third round, scoring 27 to the Californians' 25. The next round was a stand-off and the score stood 36 to 34. The Californians held the champions level in the next two rounds, and in the seventh killed ten straight birds, while Perry of the champions missed one, the score then standing 63 for the visitors to 62 for the Californians. Evener shooting is not often seen, but the champions shot with more method if less brilliancy than the local men. The visitors threw away no chance, and killed their birds almost on the traps, while the local men very often let the birds get a start that needed the hardest kind of shooting to stop.

At the end of the tenth round the score stood 93 for the visitors to 89 for the Californians, and then the home talent experienced a streak of bad luck that lost them the match. Bassford began the round by failing to stop a left-quarterer with both barrels, though the fugitive dropped dead at the fence. Golcher gave a swift black-tailor both barrels, but the load of shot only increased the fugitive's pace. Fay, who had a clear score of nine straight kills, gave a right-quarterer both barrels, but the bird struggled out of bounds and died there. Chick wasted two cartridges on a fleet-tailer. The climax for the Californians was capped when a left quarterer that was apparently dropped dead in bounds by Merrill fluttered across the field in front of the retreating pointer and got well outside of bounds before yielding up the ghost. Heikes was the only member of the visiting team who failed to score, as his bird, a strong red tailer, took both barrels and got to the fence before dropping. The score stood 102 for the champions to 95 for the Californians. On the next round the demoralized Californians dropped behind two more, and at the end of the thirteenth the score stood 121 for the visitors to 111 for the Californians.

On the fourteenth round the Californians shook themselves together once more, and Wolstencroft and Quimby missing easy birds, the visitors' lead was reduced to eight birds. On the final round Kellogg missed a strong left-quarterer that skimmed over the fence like a swallow. The other Californians all scored in fine style. Heikes, of the visiting team, missed a lively black-tailer that made a bee-line for Alameda the moment the trap was sprung, and Tucker, the last of the visitors to shoot, missed by the failure of his first cartridge to explode. He got a second chance, and missed his bird, and the match ended in favor of the visitors by the score of 137 to 130.

Budd, McMurchy, Ruble and Whitney of the champion team made clean scores. Of the Californians, Merrill was the only man who killed fifteen straight birds. Orr, Fay, Delmas and Haas came within one of clean scores, and but for bad luck would have equalled the visitors.

Colonel Dimick was the perfect referee, being alert, at home in the position, quick in applying the rules, and so affable as to make everything run smoothly. The local men were not familiar with the rules and lost two birds by the fact. The scores were:

At 15 live birds per man; for teams of 10 on a side, chosen from California and from the U. S. Cartridge Company's Aggregation; revised American Association Rules; for a trophy presented by Mr. E. T. Allen. Referee, Colonel C. W. Dimick; judges, Ramon E. Wilson and H. H. Briggs; Scorers, E. Hough and H. T. Payne.

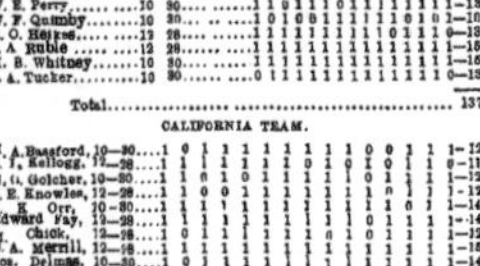

Name	Gauge	Yards	Score	Total
W. H. Wolstencroft	12	28	1 1 1 1 1 1 1 1 1 1 1 1 1 1 0 1	14
C. W. Budd	12	28	1 1 1 1 1 1 1 1 1 1 1 1 1 1 1	15
H. McMurchy	12	28	1 1 1 1 1 1 1 1 1 1 1 1 1 1 1	15
J. R. Stice	12	28	1 1 1 1 1 0 1 1 1 1 1 1 1 1 1	14
W. E. Perry	10	30	1 1 0 1 1 1 0 1 1 1 1 1 1 1 1	13
W. F. Quimby	10	30	1 0 1 0 0 1 1 1 1 1 1 0 1 0 1	10
R. O. Heikes	12	28	1 1 1 1 1 1 1 1 1 1 0 1 1 1 0	13
J. A. Ruble	12	28	1 1 1 1 1 1 1 1 1 1 1 1 1 1 1	15
H. B. Whitney	10	30	1 1 1 1 1 1 1 1 1 1 1 1 1 1 1	15
S. A. Tucker	10	30	0 1 1 1 1 1 1 1 1 1 1 1 1 1 0	13
Total				137

CALIFORNIA TEAM.

Name	Gauge—Yards	Score	Total
H. A. Bassford,	10—30	1 0 1 1 1 1 1 1 1 1 0 0 1 1 1	12
S. I. Kellogg,	12—28	1 1 1 1 1 1 1 0 1 0 1 0 1 1 0	11
H. C. Golcher,	10—30	1 1 0 1 0 1 1 1 1 1 0 1 1 1 1	12
S. E. Knowles,	12—28	1 1 0 0 1 1 1 1 1 1 1 0 1 1 1	12
J. K. Orr,	10—30	1 1 1 1 1 1 1 1 1 1 1 1 0 1 1	14
Edward Fay,	12—28	1 1 1 1 1 1 1 1 1 1 0 1 1 1 1	14
M. Chick,	12—28	1 0 1 1 1 1 1 1 0 1 0 1 1 1 1	12
C. A. Merrill,	12—28	1 1 1 1 1 1 1 1 1 1 1 1 1 1 1	15
Jos. Delmas,	10—30	1 0 1 1 1 1 1 1 1 1 1 1 1 1 1	14
C. J. Haas,	12—28	1 1 1 1 1 0 1 1 1 1 1 1 1 1 1	14
Total			130

The visiting sportsmen last week went away with many expressions of pleasure at the treatment received from the local lovers of the gun. Major Kellogg, Mr. E. T. Allen Mr. Golcher, Mr. Robert Liddle, Fred. P. Callundan and others gave much time to showing the friends about.

The Gun Club of this city, will hold its first meeting of the season at San Bruno this afternoon, going down from Third and Townsend streets by the 12 M. train. At a meeting of the Executive Committee held on Tuesday last it was resolved to use the revised rules of the American Shooting Association for the season of '90. The prizes for the season are:

First—A rifle.
Second—A fishing rod.
Third—A gentleman's travelling case.
Fourth—A shooting outfit.

Colonel Dimick's Aggregation at Sacramento.

The United States Cartridge Company's teams shot in Sacramento on Monday afternoon last, before a small audience, at Agricultural Park. The day was the coldest and most disagreeable experienced in that usually pleasant city during the present season. The match was, as usual, at thirty single Blue Rock targets and five pairs, American Shooting Association rules. The party was pleasantly received by local shots, and in return entertained their hosts at the special car, the Iolanthe, in their own peculiar, gorgeous, picturesque fashion. The Sacramentans did ample justice to the entertainment offered by Colonel Dimmick, and were as favorably impressed by that most cordial and delightful man as were those who have come to know him at other points along his route.

The scores bespeak the trying conditions under which the shooting was done, and were as follows:

EASTERN TEAM.

H. McMurchy	(singles)	1 1 1 1 1 1 0 1 1 1 1 1 1 1 1	
		1 0 1 1 1 1 1 1 1 1 1 1 1 1 1	
	(doubles)	11 11 11 11 11	28
W. H. Wolstencroft	(sing)	1 1 1 1 1 1 1 1 1 1 1 1 1 0 1	
		1 1 1 0 1 1 1 1 0 0 1 1 1 1 1	
	(doubles)	11 11 11 10 11	34
W. E. Perry	(singles)	1 1 1 0 1 0 0 1 1 1 1 1 0 1 1	
		1 1 1 1 0 0 0 1 1 1 1 1 1 1 1	
	(doubles)	10 11 00 11 10	29
W. B. Perry	(singles)	1 1 1 0 1 0 1 1 0 0 1 0 1 0 1	
		1 0 0 1 1 1 1 1 1 0 1 1 0 1 0	
	(doubles)	11 10 11 10 00	24
H. B. Whitney	(singles)	1 0 1 1 1 1 1 1 1 1 1 1 1 1 1	
		1 1 1 1 1 1 1 1 1 0 1 1 1 1 1	
	(doubles)	10 11 10 10 10	32
Total			158

WESTERN TEAM

C. W. Budd	(singles)	1 1 1 1 0 1 1 1 1 1 0 1 1 1 1	
		1 0 1 1 1 1 1 1 1 1 1 1 1 1 1	
	(doubles)	11 11 10 11 11	36
J. R. Stice	(singles)	1 1 1 1 1 1 1 1 1 1 1 1 1 1 1	
		1 1 1 1 1 1 1 1 1 1 1 1 1 1 1	
	(doubles)	10 11 01 01 11	37
R. O. Heikes	(singles)	1 1 1 1 0 0 1 1 1 1 1 1 1 1 1	
		1 1 0 1 1 1 1 1 1 1 1 1 1 0 11	
	(doubles)	10 11 10 10 11	33
C. E. Cahoon	(singles)	1 1 0 1 0 1 1 0 1 0 0 0 1 1 1	
		1 1 1 1 1 1 1 0 0 1 1 0 1 1 1	
	(doubles)	10 00 11 10 10	26
J. A. Ruble	(singles)	1 0 1 1 1 1 1 1 1 1 1 1 1 1 1	
		1 1 1 1 1 1 1 1 1 1 1 1 1 1 1	
	(doubles)	11 10 11 10 11	37
Total			169

The Blue Rock Club met last evening and arranged its schedule for the coming season.

Frank Russell, of Hanover, Me., while fox hunting, slipped on some icy ledges and would have slid over the precipice if the hammers of his gun had not cut into the crust. As it was he slid until one foot was over the edge. Here, at least, was a case where a hammer gun saved a life.

A match of 100 live birds for $500 a side is being arranged between Mr. Crittenden Robinson and Mr. Martinez Chick. The gentlemen have shot two similar matches, Mr. Robinson having been successful in both. The match to come off will be shot in or near this city. Mr. Robinon is ready and willing, and the making of the match depends upon Mr. Chick.

The finest elk now extant, an animal larger than the elk of the Rocky Mountain plateau, still roams in herds the country about Gray's harbor in the State of Washington, and the foot-hills of the Coast Range. His antlers are magnificent. When pursued by dogs he turns to fight them, and thus falls an easy prey to the hunter. When in fight he throws his nose high in the air. His immense widespread antlers fall upon each side of his back, and away he goes at a round trot, for he never gallops—crashing through the saplings and underbush as though a railroad train had broken loose.

They can tell pretty good hunting stories in Rhode Island. Here is one that is current: Jeremiah G. Dunbar, of Waterford, is not slow with a gun. He was out for a few hours on Monday, and came back with twenty birds. Two partridges got up together and he dropped one with each barrel of his gun. On another day he killed sixteen quails and three partridges, with but two misses that time; but his best work was the killing of twenty-three quails in twenty-four shots one day recently. The twenty-fourth shot was carelessly fired at a bird that was out of reach of the gunner.

Col. C. W. Dimick left California on Monday night last for Salt Lake City, Denver, Kansas City, St. Louis and the East. That his visit to this coast has been productive of much real benefit to the sport of trap shooting cannot be gainsaid. The personality of the man is most impressive, and all of the impressions work for the elevation of all interests which he touches. Of course the primary purpose of his visit was to popularize the shot shells made by the United States Cartridge Company, and he has undoubtedly done much in that behalf, but aside from that purpose he has shown the operation of the American Association Rules, as interpreted by a skilled referee, has coincided with every effort to push other sportsman's interests, and has left remembrances of his energy clear-headedness, grasp and suavity which will remain for many a day.

On Monday of last week Philip Scott Louis B. Woodard and George Barber, three conductors on the Southern Pacific, with Mr. Haley an attache of the same road went out into the country near Bakersfield for a drive and hunt. While returning homeward and within about three miles of town Scott and Woodard upon the back seat, the former saw a meadow lark upon his side of the road and called to Woodard to shoot it, and still looking at the game as the carriage was passing by threw up his arm to scare the bird, just as Woodard shot. The charge from the gun entered Mr Scott's left fore arm, so shattering it that amputation was deemed necessary. This was done late in the evening, Dr. Fergusson cutting off the injured member just below the elbow, assisted by Dr. Snook and Franz Backrens. Everything possible was done for the comfort of the wounded man, and as soon as they could come, his wife and his brother arrived. Phil Scott, as his many friends call him, is during well and has every chance of recovery.

Accidents of this kind are shocking because they come right right in the mist of pleasure. All accidents do that it is true, but it is hard, most especially for one who is the innocent cause when by the incident of accident, joy is converted into sorrow and particularly painful when the unwitting one who inflicts injury is one of such friendly, sunny nature as Mr. Woodard, who would at any time endure misfortune, to save a friend harmless.

ATHLETICS.

Athletic Sports and Other Pastimes.

EDITED BY ARCHIPPUS.

SUMMARY.

As we go to press the weather appears to have taken another turn, and the chances are about even that the rain is over at last.

Athletic sports were booming during the past week, several important events having been decided.

On Wednesday evening a handicap five mile run was given at the Olympic club rooms.

On Thursday evening the Alpine Amateur Athletic Club held its first indoor exhibition, and on the same date the California Club's regular monthly boxing exhibition took place.

On Friday evening a very important meeting of the Pacific Coast Amateur Athletic Association was held at the Olympic club rooms.

To-morrow afternoon the postponed out-door handicap games of the Alpine Club will be decided at Harbor View Park. The new out-door grounds of the Olympic Club are now ready for the use of the members, and the out-door season may be fairly said to have commenced.

RUNNERS, WALKERS, JUMPERS, ETC.

It is possible that the challenge recently issued by J. B. Buchanan, the Australian amateur athlete, will remain unanswered, at least as far as any of the Pacific Coast athletes are concerned. There are one or two amateurs in the East who might make a creditable showing against this young gladiator, but we doubt if there is one man in California strong or experienced enough to be compared with him.

The new track of the Olympic Club is perfection itself, and there is now no reason why the old records should not be all knocked on the head.

The P. C. A. A. A. should make an effort to hold the annual championship meeting on May 30th. By putting the meeting off until July 4th, the association will be doing an injustice to the Berkeley athletes, whose vacation will begin in the middle of June. The Olympic Club might easily arrange for the formal opening of their new grounds on some Saturday afternoon, in April or early in May, so as to allow the P C A A A a chance to hold their games on the usual date, Decoration Day.

The Alpine Club will hold its initial cross country run from Sausalito on Sunday, March 23d. Several of the members have promised to take part. After the race the boys will indulge in a salt water bath and then sit down to a toothsome lunch. Captain J. J. Larkey, under whose direction the run will take place, expects to bring out over twenty starters. He intends calling a run about twice a month during the season.

Captain George W. Jordan and Lieutenant S. V. Cassidy, of the Olympic Club, are already making preparations for their next cross country run. Judging from the success of the last run from Milbrae the next one promises to be the best given so far.

Carpenter, the high jumper and ex member of the Golden Gate Athletic Club, is now residing in Astoria, Oregon, where he is publishing a newspaper.

The twenty-fourth annual games of the Caledonian Club will be held at Badger's Park, on Saturday, May 31st. The P C A A A should ask the athletic committee to add several amateur events to their programme. The athletes will all be in tip top trim for Decoration Day and as the Caledonian games will be held the following day the idea suggested would surely be a good one.

The first regular foot ball game of the season will be played on the Berkeley campus this afternoon. The contesting teams will be the Universities and the Volunteers.

The Olympic and Alpine Clubs will probably place football teams in the field before long and then there will be some grand kicking.

C. A. Eldridge of the Alpine Club, while practicing the "clown act" in the gymnasium on Tuesday evening last, got a bad fall which cut and bruised his face severely.

The P. C. A. A. A. should have a benefit entertainment for the purpose of sending a couple of its best athletes back East this summer to represent it at the American championship meeting.

At a meeting of the Directors of the Alpine Amateur Athletic Club held last Monday evening, it was decided to hold the first out door games to-morrow afternoon. The track at Harbor View is in fine condition, and some very good performances may be expected. The track is 220 yards in circumference, or eight laps to the mile. There is a straight 120 yards stretch. The games will begin at one o'clock sharp and the spectators will be able to reach town in time for 5:30 o'clock dinner.

A. Cook, the champion walker of the Los Angeles Athletic Club, who recently joined the Alpines, will receive 20 seconds start of P. N. Gafney in the mile walk. He will also compete in the 220 yard run.

Cassidy, the scratch man in the run, is practicing hard at San Leandro. He will have no easy task overhauling some of the long start men.

The 440 yard run will be a very exciting race between Little, Luttrenger and Garrison.

J. J. McKinnon is liable to lower the record in the hammer throwing event.

George W. Armbruster will make the pace hot in the novice walk.

E. P. Moody should carry off the prize in the half mile.

THE WHEELMEN.

There will be a big race-meet on Decoration Day.

George P. Natmore of the Bay City Wheelmen will shortly resume pratice. His good showing last year is a clear proof that he will carry off a good many prizes this season.

There are some good wheelmen in Alpine Club and the Directors will offer them many inducements during the summer months.

Several local riders appeared on their wheels on Sunday last for the first time in weeks.

JOTTINGS FROM ALL OVER.

Our usual Eastern notes have failed to come to hand again this week owning to the delayed mails. After this week we hope the storms will not prevent us from publishing in full our "Jottings from all over."

The annual fireman's tournament for the counties of Napa, Sonoma, and Marin will be held at Healdsburg during the month of May. A great interest is taken in the tournament and it will not be surprising if a number of records are broken.

W. M. Meeker, who has long been regarded as the greatest road rider of California, has sold his ordinary and will ride a Psydio Safety.

R. M. Thompson, Chief Consul, will also have a safety this coming year, but he will still retain his ordinary.

Plummer, Hammer, Doane and Wetmore intend taking the first long ride of their season on Sunday. The trip will be for the purpose of finding out the condition of the roads after the prolonged storms.

The San Bruno road is impossible and will probably remain so far a couple of months.

It is to be hoped that the San Francisco Bicycle club will take an active part in getting up the Decoration Day race-meet. The Bay city wheelmen should not be left to work alone.

Captain George F. Drake of the Oakland Bicycle club has called the first run of the season for to-morrow. The members will assemble on the 8:30 A. M train from Oakland to San Francisco. The run will be through the Golden Gate Park. Dinner will be taken at the park.

AT THE OARS.

The majority of the local oarsmen took advantage of the fine weather on Sunday and indulged in practice spins on the bay.

Two crews from the Pioneer Club rowed to Hunters Point.

A couple of the Ariel crews took a spin around to Fort Point.

Two regular crews and two single scullers from the South End Club passed along the Water Front.

The canoe fleet of the Lurline Club took a spin around Goat Island.

At the next meeting of the Pacific Rowing Associatian arrangements will be made for the holding of the annual regatta. As several new clubs have lately joined the association, it is expected that this years regatta will be the most successful one ever held on the Pacific Coast.

The Dolphin Club will hold open house to-morrow. A fine programme of athletic and aquatic sports has been arranged and an enjoyable time is assured all who have been fortunate enough to receive invitations.

A special meeting of the Oakland Canoe Club will be held at 8 o'clock this evening, to adopt rules for the holiday cup races.

The recent wet weather has been a great drawback to Charley Long, and he has found it impossible to keep down in weight. Now that a fine spell has set in, he will be able to do some work, and his backers are confident that he will row up to the starting point in first-class shape. Whitehead and Co. will have the exclusive pool privileges both in the city and at the course.

Henry Henceman of Stockton will be down next week and will finish his training on the bay. He is in fine trim and will be heavily backed by his Stockton friends, who think that he will again easily defeat Long.

LAWN TENNIS.

The tournament of the California Tennis Club, which was held at the club grounds, on the corner of Bush and Scott streets, on Saturday and Sunday last, was well attended. The arrangements were admirably carried out under the supervision of the Board of Directors, consisting of Mrs. H. H. Sherwood, C. R. Yates, F. H. Beaver, E. N. Bee and B. Lindermann. The winners of the preliminary bouts on Saturday were Kilgariff and Beaver, and Yates and Harrison. Of the final sets the former had won two and the latter one. On the second day the play began at 2 o'clock, with the score at three games all in the fourth set.

Seventh game—Kilgariff won.

Eighth game—This was lost by Yates and Harrison through their weak returns.

Ninth game—Won by Yates and Harrison.

Tenth and last game—Beaver served well, playing his usual steady game, and, assisted by Kilgariff, succeeded in scoring the winning stroke by placing the ball back of Harrison. This decided the match, giving Kilgariff and Beaver three sets out of five to their opponents' one. The following couples will play this afternoon for second prize: Yates and Harrison, scratch; Haight brothers, 1 bisque; Taylor and Hoffman, owe 15; Magee brothers, ½ 30; Morris and Haslett 15.

The third annual open tournament for the championship of the Pacific Coast will be played on the Fourth of July, probably at San Rafael. The California Tennis Club will offer a handsome championship cup, value $300, to become the property of the first player winning it three times. The winner of the tournament will be given a $75 cup, subject to no conditions, but for the $300 championship cup he will be obliged to play W. H. Taylor, Jr., the present amateur champion of the State.

CLUB JOTTINGS.

The Pacific Coast Amateur Athletic Association held a meeting last evening, but as we had already gone to press a report of the proceedings must be held over until our next issue.

The regular monthly meeting of the California Athletic Club was largely attended on Thursday evening.

The Alameda Olympic Club held a "Ladies' night" exhibition on Thursday evening.

An account of the Alpine Athletic Club's exhibition, which was held at the club rooms, 706 Powell street, on Thursday evening, will appear next week.

The Directors of the Golden Gate Athletic Club have decided to raise the initiation fee to $10 for March. The dues will be $2.50. The following standing committee were appointed: On boxing, L. G. Flannigan, J. J. Jamison and W. L. Brown; on finance, C. H. Smith, Cress Unger and Henry Lunstedt; on improvements, A. Rudyear, Leon Dennery and George K. Liddle.

The Acme Club of Oakland expects to place a team in the field at the P. C. A. A. A. championship meeting.

A high jinks will be held by the Dolphin S. and B. Club at their handsome quarters, North Beach, to-morrow afternoon. The festivities will begin at two o'clock.

Several of the Olympic Club members are anxious that a social be given at the club rooms in the near future. It is quite a while since the lady friends of the club have had a chance to waltz over the smooth gymnasium floor.

The next regular meeting and exhibition of the Occidental Athletic Club will take place on Friday evening, March 14th, at 8 o'clock, at the rooms of the club, southwest corner of Grove and Laguna streets.

Cooley will be presented with a diamond locket, Collins will receive a diamond ring, and Espinosa a gold watch charm.

The five mile handicap run for members of the Olympic Club was decided in the gymnasium on Wednesday evening last. The race was close and exciting, and was witnessed by a large crowd of members and their friends. The following men toed the scratch and were started according to their handicaps: M. L. Espinosa, scratch; Frank L. Cooley, scratch; J. A. Code, 30 seconds; W. T. Haberly, 2 minutes; Newton L. Williams, 2 minutes 30 seconds; H. M. Collins, 2 minutes 30 seconds; Steve V. Cassidy, 2 minutes 30 seconds; J. J. Blake, 2 minutes 30 seconds; W. J. Moore, 3 minutes.

After the first mile had been finished it was easily to be seen that Cooley was in fine condition and stood an excellent chance of overhauling his men. Espinosa also ran in good style and looked like another winner. The race was won in good style by Cooley; Collins, who had a start of 2½ minutes, finishing a close second and Espinosa a good third. Williams retired after finishing 2¼ miles. Cassidy was taken with a stitch in his side after he had made 4 miles and was obliged to retire from the contest. The winner's time was 32 min. 5 secs., which will stand as the Pacific Coast record for five miles. Had Cooley been on the outside track of the club he would have done considerably under those figures. The following gentlemen acted as officials: Handicapper, Capt. George W. Jordan; Referee, D. W. Donnelly; Judges, J. H. Gilhulv and J. P. Kelly; Timers, Peter McIntyre, Walter A. Scott and G. W. Jordan; Scorers, J. F. Larkin, C. H. Stanyan, J. P, H. Wentworth, W. H. Mitchell and J. F. McDonald.

ROD.

A New Hatchery.

The Government has just established at Camp Gaston, in Hoopa Valley, Humboldt County, a fish hatchery. The plant was built by Captain Brice, a naval officer of the Government, now on detail duty as a fish commissioner.

The hatchery was established, and Mr. Morgan is still there in charge, but the business will soon be turned over to Captain Dougher y, commander of the post. The hatchery has a capacity to hatch out and put in the streams from two to three millions of young salmon yearly. Aside from the great benefit to resident whites and Indians of this great increase, the canneries will be benefited, and to supply their drain a hatchery is absolutely necessary; otherwise there will be no fish.

There have already been sent out from the East Penobscot salmon eggs, and the ova of the Eastern brook trout that are to be hatched at Camp Gaston and put into the streams. Gaston was selected on account of its proximity to the spawning beds of the salmon, also for its pure and abundant supply of clear water of the proper temperature. The eggs can only be taken from salmon in the vicinity of their spawning grounds, which are near the heads of the small streams flowing into the rivers, and fish hatcheries are always located with reference to the convenience of taking the fish when ready to spawn. By comparison, one thousand eggs are hatched out artificially to one hatched naturally, and of the fish put into streams still a greater per cent. live than those hatched naturally. The Government determined, some time ago, to establish sixteen hatcheries on military reservations, and the one at Gaston is one of the number.

Chief of Patrol F. P. Callundan is receiving many complaints of violation of the fish laws by prominent citizens of San Mateo and other counties near San Francisco.

Certain citizens of Sonoma County have petitioned the supervisors of that county to change the law regulating the size of meshes in salmon seines, so as to enable fishermen to catch what in their petition are styled a smaller variety or species of salmon known as the "steel heads." It is probable the petition was circulated by parties more interested in selling a few fish during the spawning season than in observing the law and regarding the rights of their fellow men. The supervisors very wisely deferred action on the petition, and we trust will refuse to grant the prayer.

Kennel Continued.

California Kennel Club.

The California Kennel Club held an adjourned meeting last Wednesday evening at 439 Montgomery street, J. B. Lewis presiding and W. F. Cue acting as secretary. The Conference Committee which was appointed to confer with the Pacific Kennel Club, made a report and stated the terms on which the Pacific Kennel Club desired to consolidate: that both clubs should unite under the name of the Pacific Kennel Club; that the present officers, constitution and by-laws of the Pacific Club, as they now are, should be accepted and govern the new club; that the California Kennel Club should assume half of the indebtedness of the Pacific Kennel Club, which is between $400 and $500 for unpaid prizes won at their last bench show in May, 1889.

On motion of James Sumner the report was received and the committee, consisting of J. B. Lewis, A. B. Truman, J. H. Martin and John M. Crane was discharged.

Thomas Higgs moved that the terms be not accepted and the motion was seconded by W. G. O'Hara. All of the members present were opposed to the terms offered by the Pacific Club and it appeared to be the unanimous opinion that the only terms which would be acceptable to the club were as follows: That the California Kennel Club should name First and Third Vice-Presidents; that the Executive Committee should consist of sixteen members, eight from each club; that they should not assume any indebtedness of the Pacific Club; that the funds now in the treasury of the California Kennel Club should be placed in the hands of a responsible person, and should be used for no purpose other than giving a bench show; that the name of the new club should be the "California Pacific Kennel Club," and that the constitution and by-laws be revised to conform with the constitution and by-laws of the American Kennel Club.

[It is to be regretted that the Committee of Conference from the California Club did not simply report progress and ask further time. It is admittedly desirable that the clubs should fuse, and the more conservative members of both organizations are willing to meet upon a plane of mutual consideration. If fusion does not result it will be because of thoughtless haste and inconsiderate demands. We think that the Conference Committees have not made a report, and are surprised that any one should undertake to report to the California Club the views of the Pacific Club men until they are formally drafted and in black and white.—KEN. ED.]

Trotters and Pacers of 1890.

We give below the list of trotters and pacers who have made records in the 2:30 list during the past season, and also those who have lowered former ones during 1890 in California. This is compiled from the advance list of the year book published by the Wallace registration company, published in the monthly for February. We noticed a mistake int he record of Fleet. It is given as 2:24½ made at Stockton, whereas she made a record of 2:24 at the Napa meeting prior to going to Stockton. It will be noticed that many of the names have stars in front of them, which indicates that the pedigree if fautly. If any of our readers can give further information regarding those so marked we will feel obliged if they will send the same to this office.

CALIFORNIA TABLE OF 2:30 TROTTERS FOR 1889.

*Acrobat (3 yrs.), b h, by Sterling, 6223—Madam Buckner, s t b, by Tom Hal, 3000, Salinas City, Cal., Oct. 11 ....(n) 2:29
Addie E., ch m, by Algona 11,543—dam by A. T. Stewart, Chico, Cal., Aug. 31 .... 2:22½
Albion, b h, by Gen. Benton, 1755—Amy, by Messenger Duroc, 106. Los Angeles, Cal., Jan. 10 .... 2:2[illegible]
Alfred G (4 yrs.), b h, by Anteeo, 7868—Josie B., by Speculation, 928. Napa, Cal., Nov. 16 ....(n) 2:19¾
*Alfred S., b g, by Elmo 891—dam not traced, Fresno, Cal., Oct. 4 .... 2:18
*Allorita, ch m, by Altoona, 8850—Marysville, Cal., Sept. 3 ..(n) 2:26½
*Almonta, b m, by Tilton Almont, 1583—dam not traced. Chico, Cal., Aug. 28 ....(n) 2:26
Arol, br m, by Electioneer, 125—Aurora, 2:27, by John Nelson 187. Stockton, Cal., Sept. 24 ....(n) 2:24
Atto Rex, b h, by Attorney, 1005—dam by Brougham, 800, Petaluma, Cal., Aug. 31 ....(n) 2:22½
*Belle A., blk m, by Tilton Almont, 1583—Flora, not traced. Sacramento, Cal., Sept. 19 ....(n) 2:29
Belle B, blk m, by Jim Hawkins—dam by Mormon Chief. Los Angeles, Cal., April 11 ....(n) 2:26½
Big Jim, b g, by Gen. Benton, 1755—Dame Winnie, by Planet. San Francisco Cal., Oct. 12 ....(n) 2:28½
Carlisle, ch h, by Piedmont, 904—Idabelle, by Hambletonian 10 San Francisco, Cal., July 6 ....(n) 2:26½
*Charley D., ch g—pedigree not traced. Los Angeles, Cal., April 8 ....(n) 2:28½
*Clara P., b m, by Mambrino Wilkes, 6083. Oakland, Cal., August 9 ....(n) 2:29½
*Danger, b g, by Oddfellow (?) Los Angeles, Cal., Oct. 31 ..(n) 2:26¾
Dawn, ch h, by Nutwood, 600—Countess, by Hambletonian, 725, Petaluma, Cal., Aug. 31 .... 2:18½
Del Mar (2 years), b h, by Electioneer, 125—Sontag Dixie, by Toronto Sontag, 397. Napa, Cal., Aug. 14 ....(n) 2:30
Direct (4 years), blk h, by Director, 1989—Echora, 2:23½, by Echo, 462. Sacramento, Cal., Sept. 19 .... 2:18½
Don Marvin, br h, by Fallis, 4781—Cora, by Don Victor. Nevada City, Cal., Aug. 22 ....(n) 2:28
*Ed, b g, by Erwin Davis, 5558—dam not traced. Fresno, Cal., April 19 .... 2:26
Emaline, b m, by Electioneer, 125—Emma Robson, by Woodburn. Sacramento, Cal, May 17 ....(n) 2:27½
Emma Temple, b m, by Jackson Temple—Lizzie R., by Emigrant. Stockton, Cal., Sept. 28 .... 2:21
Express, b g, by Electioneer, 125—Esther, by Express. Petaluma, Cal., Aug. 31 .... 2:21
Fleet, (2 yrs.) b m, by Sidney, 4770—Flight, 2:29, by Buccaneer 2656. Stockton, Cal, Sept. 24 ....(n) 2:24½
*Flora B, ch m, by Whippleton, 1883. Petaluma, Cal., Aug. 31 2:27
Flora Belle, blk m, by Alcona, 730—Fortuna, by Almont, 33. Napa, Cal., Aug. 13 ....(n) 2:26
George Washington (3 yrs.), b h, by Mambrino Chief Jr., 11,622—Fanny Rose, by Ethan Allen Jr., 2904. Petaluma, Cal, Aug. 30 ....(n) 2:30
Glendine (3 yrs.), ch h, by Judge Salisbury, 5872—Tempest, by Sultan, 1513. Los Angeles, Cal., April 15 ....(n) 2:30
*Gracie S., ch m, by Speculation, 928. San Francisco, Cal., Nov. 9 .... 2:22
Guide (4 yrs.), blk h, by Director, 1989—Imogene, by Norwood, 522. Napa, Cal, Aug. 16 ....(n) 2:29
Hazel Kirke, b m, by Brigadier, 797—Fancy, by Jim Brown. Petaluma, Cal., Aug. 29 .... 2:24
Hazel Wilkes (4 yrs.), ch m, by Guy Wilkes, 2867—Blanche, by Arthurton, 365. Stockton, Cal, September 28 ....(n) 2:20
*Idaho Patchen, b h. Rohnerville, Cal., Sept. 27 ....(n) 2:26½
Ira, b h, by Piedmont, 904—Irene, by Mohawk Chief. Rohnerville, Cal., Sept. 27 ....(n) 2:24½
*J. R. (3 yrs.), b g, by Elector, 2170—Topsy, s. t. b., by son of St. Lawrence. Stockton, Cal., Sept 26 ....(n) 2:24
*Kate Agnew, gr m Nevada City, Cal., Aug. 21 ....(n) 2:28½
*Kitty Almont, blk m, by Tilton Almont, 1583—dam not traced. San Francisco, Cal., Oct. 11 ....(n) 2:22¼
*Lillian Wilkes (3 yrs.), b m, by Guy Wilkes, 2867—Flora Langford, pacer, not traced. Petaluma, Cal, Aug. 29 ....(n) 2:17½
Lohengrin, b g, by Echo, 462—Vixen, by George M. Patchen Jr. 31. Nevada City, Cal., Aug. 21 ....(n) 2:27¼
*Lookout, b g, by Arab, 2:15, or Stanford, son of George M. Patchen Jr. 31. Napa, Cal., Aug. 13 ....(n) 2:26
Lord Byron (4 yrs.), b h, by Gen. Benton, 1755—May Day, by Wissahickon, 947. Sacramento, Cal, Sept. 14 .... 2:18
Lorena (2 yrs.), blk m, by Jim Mulvenna, 3881—Elmorene, by Elmo, 891. Petaluma, Cal., Aug. 28 ....(n) 2:30
Lorita, ch m, by Piedmont, 904—Lady Lowell, by St. Clair (Schultz's). Napa, Cal., Aug 16 ....(n) 2:22½
Margaret S. (3 yrs.), b m, by Director, 1989—May Day, 2:30, by C. M. Clay Jr. 54 Sacramento, Cal., Sept. 14 ....(n) 2:19½
Marion, b m, by Piedmont, 904—Lady Morgan, by Hambletonian 10. Napa, Cal., June 8 ....(n) 2:26½
Mary Lou, ch m, by Tom Benton, 2:32½—Brown Jenny, by Dave Hill Jr. Stockton, Cal., Sept. 24 ....(n) 2:25½
*Maud H., ch m, s. t. b., by Mambrino, 1789. Salinas City, Cal., Oct. 9 ....(n) 2:30
Melrose, br g, by Sultan, 1513—dam by California Ten Broeck. Oakland, Cal., Sept. 9 ....(n) 2:27
Mista (2 yrs.), b m, by Alcazar, 5102—Lady Day, by California Dexter. Petaluma, Cal., Aug. 29 ....(n) 2:29
Moro, blk m, by Pasha, 2039—Adele, by Messenger Duroc, 106. San Jose, Cal., Oct. 3 ....(n) 2:27
*Ned Lock, ch h, by Antelope (?). Santa Rosa, Cal., Aug. 24 (n) 2:28½
Nebuenta (4 yrs.), b m, by Stamboul, 5101—Neluska, 2:30½, by Sultan, 1513. Los Angeles, Cal., Jan. 10 ....(n) 2:30
Nina D. (4 yrs.), ch m, by Nutwood 600—Adelaide (2:19½), by Phil Sheridan 630. Napa, Cal., Aug. 16 .... 2.28½
Nona Y., b m, by Admiral, 488—Black Flora, by Black Prince. San Francisco, Cal., Nov 3 ....(n) 2.25
*Old Sport, dn g. San Francisco, Cal., Feb. 2 ....(n) 2:26½
Pedlar (2 yrs.) b h, by Electioneer 125—Penelope, by Mohawk Chief. Petaluma, Cal., Aug. 18 .... 2:27½
Palo Alto, b h, by Electioneer, 125—Dame Winnie, by Planet, Napa, Cal., Nov. 16 .... 2:12¾
Pasha, b h, by Echo, 462—Young Fashion, by Correct. Marysville, Cal, Sept. 7 ....(n) 2:27½
*Pond Lily, b m, by California Patchen (?). Los Angeles, Cal., April 11 ....(n) 2:29½
*Rabe, ch g, by Strader 673—Rose, s. t. b., by Bashaw 50 Chico, Cal, Aug. 30 ....(n) 2:24
Raymon (4 yrs.), b h, by Simmons, 2744—Lady Raymond, by Carlisle, 395. Los Angeles, Cal., Nov. 1 ....(n) 2:27¼
Redwood (4 yrs.), b h, by Anteeo, 7868—Lou Milton, by Milton Medium, 4782. Napa, Cal., Aug. 17 ....(n) 2:24½
Redwood, ch h, by Nutwood, 600—Alice R., by Naubuc, 504. Chico, Cal., Aug. 28 ....(n) 2:27
Regal Wilkes (2 yrs.), b h, by Guy Wilkes, 2867—Margaret, 2:26, by Sultan, 1513. San Francisco, Cal., Nov. 9 ....(n) 2:20½
*Richmond Jr., b g s. t. b., by A. W. Richmond, 1687. San Francisco, Cal, Oct 13 ....(n) 2:22½
Rose S., b h, by Nutwood, 600—dam by State of Maine, Marysville, Cal., Sept 6 .... 2.25
*Sargent, gr g, by Brown Jug, son of Nutwood, 600—Seven Oaks Mare, s t b., by Gen. Taylor. San Jose, Cal., Oct. 3 ....(n) 2:28
Simmocolon (4 yrs), ch h, by Simmons, 2744—Colon, by Strathmore, 408. San Francisco. Cal., Aug. 3 ....(n) 2:20½
Soudan, blk h, by Sultan, 1513—Lady Babcock, by Hambletonian, 725. Nevada City, Cal., Aug. 22 .... 2:27½
Sport, gr h, by Piedmont, 904—Sontag Mohawk, by Mohawk Chief. San Francisco, Cal., Nov. 9 ....(n) 2:22½
Stamboul, br h, by Sultan, 1513—Fleetwing, by Hambletonian 10. Napa, Cal., Nov. 15 .... 2:12½
Sunol (3 yrs.), b m, by Electioneer, 125—Waxana, by Gen. Benton, 1755. San Francisco, Cal., Nov. 9 .... 2:10½
Thapsin, blk g, by Berlin, 3514—Lady Hubbard, by Benecia Boy, San Francisco, Cal., Nov. 9 .... 2:21½
*Victor, b h, by Echo, 462. Santa Rosa, Cal., Aug. 20 .... 2:32
*Wanda, b m, by Fallis, 4781—Girofla, by Elmo, 891. Santa Rosa, Cal., Aug. 23 ....(n) 2:24
*What Ho, gr g, by A. W. Richmond, 1687. Los Angeles, Cal., April 8 ....(n) 2:28½

CALIFORNIA TABLE OF 2:30 PACERS FOR 1889.

*Adonis (4 yrs.), b g, by Sidney, 4770—Venus, s. t. b., by Captain Webster, 10,173. San Jose, Cal., Oct. 5 .... 2:14
Belle Button (4 yrs.), br m, by Alexander Button, 1997—Flora by St Clair (Dietz's). Napa, Cal., Aug. 17 ....(n) 2:20
Creole (4 yrs.), b h, by Prompter, 2305—Grace, by Buccaneer, 2656. Napa, Cal, Aug. 14 ....(n) 2:20
Edwin C., b g, by Electric, 10,830—Lady Coonie, by Venture 310. Sacramento, Cal., Sept. 21 ....(n) 2:15
Ellwood, ch m, by A. W. Richmond, 1687—Crichton's First, by Crichton. Los Angeles, Cal., Jan. 23 .... 2:20
Eugenia, (4 yrs.), blk m, by Alcantara, 729—Lady Conklin, by Strathmore, 408. Los Angeles, Cal., April 18 ....(n) 2:19½
*Frank, ch g, s. t. b., by Nutwood, 600, Oakland, Cal, Sept. 3 ....(n) 2:20
Gold Leaf (4 yrs.), ch m, by Sidney, 4770—Fern Leaf, by Flaxtail, 8132. Napa Cal., Aug. 17 .... 2:11½
Irma (4 yrs), b m, by Nutwood, 600—Maggie Medium, by Happy Medium, 400. Los Angeles, Cal., Jan. 10 .... 2:18½
*Johnny Skelton, gr g, s. t. b., by Milton Medium, 4782, Sacramento, Cal., May 16 ....(n) 2:29½
Little Dock, b g, by Little Johnnie—Jennie Wells, by Jack Hawkins. Fresno, Cal., April 18 .... 2:26
Longworth (4 yrs.), b h, by Sidney, 4770—Grey Dale, by American Boy Jr. Oakland, Cal., Sept. 3 ....(n) 2:19
*Mink, b g. Pedigree not traced. Stockton, Cal., Sept. 26 .... 2:24
Ned Winslow, blk g, by Tom Benton, 2:32½—Brown Jenny, by Dave Hill Jr. Stockton, Cal., Sept. 28 .... 2:17½
*Phil Freiler, ro g, by Copperbottom (?). Los Angeles, Cal., Nov. 2 ....(n) 2:28½
*Racquet, blk g, pedigree not traced. Napa, Cal., Aug. 14 .... 2:20½
St. Patrick, b h, by Volunteer, 55—Young Selene, by Guy Miller. Sacramento, Cal, Sept. 21 .... 2:19½
Silkwood, blk h, by Blackwood Mambrino—Lucy Woodruff, by Hiram Woodruff. Los Angeles, Cal., Nov. 2 ....(n) 2:25½
*Snicklefritz, b g, by Gladiator, 8338, Marysville, Cal, Sept. 7 ....(n) 2:29½
Thomas Ryder, b g, by Alexander Button, 1997—dam by Black Ralph, 10,678. Napa, Cal., Aug. 17 ....(n) 2:20½
*Wapple, ch g, by Brigadier, 797. Chico, Cal., Aug. 29 ....(n) 2:27
Yolo Maid (4 yrs.), ch m, by Alexander Button, 1997—Molly, by St. Clair (Dietz's). Sacramento, Cal, Sept. 19 .... 2:12½

VETERINARY.

Conducted by W. Henry Jones, M. R. C. V. S.

Subscribers to this paper can have advice through this column in all cases of sick or injured horses or cattle by sending an explicit description of the case. Applicants will send their name and address that they may be identified. Questions requiring answers by mail should be accompanied by two dollars, and addressed to W. Henry Jones, M. R. C. V. S., Olympic Stables, Sutter street, San Francisco.

Horses With Corns.

I have been asked several times of late, as to whether corns constitute unsoundness. There is but little doubt, that while they exist, the animal is unsound. Corns are caused in the majority of cases, from defective shoeing, also from heavy concussion on hard macadamized roads, and on cobble-paved streets. They are not as some persons imagine, hereditary. I do not know of any colt being foaled with corns, but I have seen dozens of youngsters dropped with spavins, curbs, ringbones, and other hereditary diseases. The best way to treat corns, is to study the shoeing. When an animal becomes lame and there is nothing to see, the majority of persons put it down for shoulder lameness.

If they take the trouble to move the shoes and carefully examine the feet, they will find that a large percentage of lameness arise from the feet. If the corns are likely to suppurate, poultice with flaxseed, for a few days, afterwards, have the animal shod with leathers for about two weeks, then remove the leathers. See that the shoes are properly fitted, and no undue pressure placed on the hind heel.

In some cases it would be advisable to use a three-quarter shoe and so do away with any pressure on the part of the foot affected. W. HENRY JONES, M. R. C. V. S.
Olympic Club Stables, Sutter Street, SAN FRANCISCO.

T. R. A.
I have got a bull bitch who had pups some three months ago. Since weaning the pups, a hard swelling has appeared on the teats. Please inform me what the swelling is, and what the best thing to do with it. Also what the probable cost would be to ensure a certain cure.

Answer.—Judging by your description of your bitch, I have no hesitation in pronouncing it a tumor on the mammary gland. I would recommend you to have the tumour removed by excision. With reference to cost, it would depend entirely how you make your arrangements with the veterinary surgeon you engage.

J. N. B. Healdsburgh.
I have a horse afflicted with the thrush in one of his fore feet. The frog seems to be decaying and exudes a foetid dark colored matter. No contraction of the heels as yet. What remedy would you advise?

Answer.—With reference to your enquiry about horse with diseased frog, should advise you to have the diseased portion of the frog removed carefully, then poultice with flax seed poultice until the discharge becomes less fetid. Afterwards apply calomel in small quantities to the cleft of the frog and keep the foot dry. When the discharge has stopped apply oil of Tar in some cotton wool or tow. I do not think you need fear contraction of the heels. If there is no improvement in a week after treatment be good enough to notify the BREEDER AND SPORTSMAN.

BILLIARDS.

John Roberts, Jr., of London, the noted billiardist, has challenged any American pool-player for a reasonable number of games, pyramid pool, £500 to £1,000 a side. It is Malone the American champion who will accept. Half the games to be played in England and half in America.

William Goldthwaite, the most formidable antagonist whom Dudley Cavanagh used to battle with for old-time four-ball carrom championship honors, died at Bellevue Hospital, New York, Feb. 8th. The chief and determining cause of death was colitis, which was contributed to by exhaustion. Funeral services were held from the warerooms of Patterson, Bevins & Plowright, 355 Fourth Avenue, at 2 o'clock, Feb. 13th. The interment was in Woodlawn. "Billy" was a grand player in his day, and was accounted by many the finest player in America. For some years he had been living from hand to mouth, his physical infirmities unfitting him for the long hours which are necessary to devote to a billiard room.

The highly nervous horse can never be mistaken. Every portion of the body and every motion will give some indication of that temperament. The skin will be thin and sensitive the bones small, the pulse quick, and easily affected by anything done to or near the horse. The thin lips will be highly compressed the prominent eye will catch everything that moves either far or near, and the small, thin, transparent ear will be in frequent quick motion. The walk will incline to a dance, and the gallop to a rapid succession of springs.

THE WEEKLY

Breeder and Sportsman.

JAMES P. KERR, PROPRIETOR.

The Turf and Sporting Authority of the Pacific Coast.

Office, No. 313 Bush St.
P. O. Box 2300.

TERMS—One Year, $5; Six Months, $3; Three Months, $1.50.
STRICTLY IN ADVANCE.

Money should be sent by postal order, draft or by registered letter, addressed to JAMES P. KERR, San Francisco, Cal.

Communications must be accompanied by the writer's name and address, not necessarily for publication, but as a private guarantee of good faith.

ALEX. P. WAUGH, - - - - - Editor.

Advertising Rates

Per Square (half inch)

One time	$1 50
Two times	2 50
Three times	3 25
Four times	4 00

And each subsequent insertion 75c. per square.

Advertisements running six months are entitled to 10 per cent. discount.

Those running twelve months are entitled to 20 per cent. discount.

Reading notices set in same type as body of paper, 50 cents per line each insertion.

To Subscribers.

The date printed on the wrapper of your paper indicates the time to which your subscription is paid.

Should the BREEDER AND SPORTSMAN be received by any subscriber who does not want it, write us direct to stop it. A postal card will suffice.

Special Notice to Correspondents.

Letters intended for publication should reach this office not later than Wednesday of each week, to secure a place in the issue of the following Saturday. Such letters to insure immediate attention should be addressed to the BREEDER AND SPORTSMAN, and not to any member of the staff.

San Francisco, Saturday, March 1, 1890.

Stallions Advertised
IN THE
BREEDER AND SPORTSMAN.

Thoroughbreds.

DOUGLASDALE—Thoroughbred Clydesdale....Lawn View Farm, Cal.
FRIAR TUCK, Hermit—Romping Girl..........C. W. Aby, Middletown.
GREENBACK, Dollar—Music....................C. W. Aby, Middletown.
INTRUDER, Crater—Lady Bountiful..........T. J. Knight, Sacramento.
REVEILLE, Shiloh—Norfolk......................B. C. Holly, Vallejo.
ST. SAVIOR, Eolus—War Song...............C. W. Aby, Middletown.
THREE CHEERS Imp. Harrah—Young Fashion.........E. S. Culver, San Francisco.

Trotters.

ADMIRAL, Volunteer—Lady Pierson........... Frank Drake, Vallejo.
ACTOR Prompter—Dam by Sultan ....Lawn View Farm, Cal.
ARBITRATOR, Director—Lady Earnest.........H. A. Mayhew, Niles.
ANTEEOP, Anteeo—Bessie G.........Guy E. Grosse, Santa Rosa.
ANTEEOP, Anteeo—Nance.........Guy E. Grosse, Santa Rosa.
ADMIRO, Admiral—dam by San Bruno........Smith & Sutherland, Pleasanton.
ASHLAND ALMONT, Almont—Pauline.........T. J. Whitehead, Oakland.
ALEXANDER BUTTON, Alexander—Lady Button.........Cache Creek Farm, Yolo.
APEX, Prompter—Mary.........Poplar Grove Breeding Farm, Wildflower.
ALOONA, Almont—Queen Mary........... Fred W. Loeber, St. Helena
BALKAN, Mambrino Wilkes—Fanny Fern.........A. L. Hinds, Oakland.
BONANZA, Artburton—Sister .... Richard Havey, Oakland
BAY ROSE, Sultan—Madam Baldwin..............W. W. Ayres, Oakland.
CLOVIS, Sultan—Sweetbriar.........Poplar Grove Breeding Farm, Wildflower.
CUPID, Sidney—Venus .... C. O. Thornquest, Oakland
CHRISMAN'S HAMBLETONIAN 10173, Whipple's Hambletonian—Flora Jesse Chrisman, San Jose
CANNON BALL, Simmons—Gurgle. ....Lockhaven Stock Farm, Burbank.
CHARLES DERBY, Steinway—by Electioneer. Cook Stock Farm, Contra Costa Co.
CRESCO, Strathmore—Spartan. .....Cook Stock Farm, Contra Costa Co
CALIFORNIA NUTWOOD, Nutwood—Fanny Patchen....Martin Carter, Alameda Co.
CORRECT R, Director—Brainey..................Pleasanton Stock Farm.
DECORATOR, Director—Chess.................Pleasanton Stock Farm
DEXTER PRINCE, Kentucky Prince—Lady Dexter.........L. M. Morse, Lodi.
DAWN, Nutwood—Countess ....A. L. Whitney, Petaluma
DIRECTOR, Dictator—Dolly.........Pleasanton Stock Farm, Pleasanton.
DON MARVIN, Fallis—Cora........................F. P. Lowell, Sacramento
DESIGNER, Director—May Queen.........................H. Scott, Oakland.
ELECTOR, Electioneer—Gilberta...........L. A. Richards, Grayson.
ELECTO, Antevolo, dam by Capt. Webster...G. W. Stimpson, Oakland
ELECTION, Electioneer—Lizzie H.....................B. C. Holly, Vallejo.
ELEGANCE ....G. W. Stimpson, Oakland
EL BENTON, Electioneer—Nellie Benton.........Souther Farm, San Leandro.
ECLECTIC, Electioneer—Manette.........Wilfred Page, Sonoma County
EROS, Electioneer—Sontag Mohawk..........W. H. Vioget, Menlo Park
FIGARO, Hambletonian—Emblem ....Souther Farm, San Leandro.
GROVER CLAY, Electioneer—Maggie Norfolk...........Denis Gannon, Oakland.
G. & M., Anteeo—Rosa B.....................George E. Guerne, Santa Rosa.
GUY WILKES, George Wilkes—Lady Bunker ....San Mateo Stock Farm, San Mateo.
GLEN FORTUNE, Electioneer—Glenna...........Souther Farm, San Leandro.
GEORGE WASHINGTON, Mambrino Chief—Fanny Rose.........Thos. Smith, Vallejo.
GUIDE, Director—Imogene..............Smith & Sutherland, Pleasanton.
GRANDISSIMO, LeGrande—Norma..........Fred W. Loeber, St Helena
ILLUSTRIOUS, Happy Medium—Abdalletta.........George A. Stone, Santa Rosa.
JESTER D, Almont—Hortense..................Souther Farm, San Leandro
JUNIO, Electioneer—by Granger........................S. N. Straube, Fresno.
KAFIR, Alcazar—Flower Girl ....B. C. Holly, Vallejo.
KING DAVID, Admiral—Black Flora ....Frank Drake, Vallejo.
LEO WILKES, Guy Wilkes—Sable.........San Mateo Stock Farm, San Mateo.
LYNWOOD, Nutwood—Hattie Morrison ....P. Visher, Stockton.
MEMO, Sidney—Flirt.......................Valensin Stock Farm, Pleasanton.
MOUNTAIN BOY, Kentucky Prince—Elsie..........B. C. Holly, Vallejo.
MAMBRINO WILKES, George Wilkes—Lady Chrisman.........San Miguel Stock Farm, Walnut Creek.
MART BOORHEM, Sidney—Towhead...............B. C. Holly, Vallejo.
MAMBRINO JR. 1789, Mambrino Patchen, dam by Mambrino Chief Geo. P. Bull, San Jose.
MAMBRINO CHIEF, McDonald Chief—Venus.........Thos. Smith, Vallejo.
MORTIMER, Electioneer—Marti ....Wilfred Page, Sonoma County
NOONDAY, Wedgewood—Noontide..............F. P. Lowell, Sacramento.
PASHA, Sultan—Madam Baldwin.. ....D. Bryson, Linden
PHILOSOPHER, Pilot Wilkes—Belle.......... George E. Guerne, Santa Rosa.
ROY WILKES, Adrian Wilkes—Flora .. ..Pleasanton Stock Farm Pleasanton.
REDWOOD, Anteeo—Lou Wilton ....A. McFayden, Oakland.
SILVER BOW, Robert McGregor—Sadie ....P. J. Williams, Oakland.
STEINWAY, Strathmore—Abbess ...Cook Stock Farm, Contra Costa Co
SUNSET, Anteeo—Bessie G.................................Guy E. Grosse, Santa Rosa.
SHAMROCK, Bucaneer—Fernleaf...... ...... G. W. Stimpson, Oakland
SIDNEY, Santa Claus—Sweetness.........Valensin Stock Farm, Pleasanton.
SIMMOCOLON, Simmons—Colon.........Valensin Stock Farm, Pleasanton.
SABLE WILKES, Guy Wilkes—Sable........San Mateo Stock Farm, San Mateo.
ST. NICHOLAS, Sidney—Towhead.........John Rowen, Oakland Trotting Park.
WOODNUT, Nutwood—Flora.... ....Jas. Weatherhead, San Jose
WHIPPLETON 1883, Hambletonian Jr.—Lady Livingston....Fred W. Loeber, St. Helena
WOODSIDE, Woodnut—Veronica........................B. C. Holly, Vallejo.
YOUNG ELMO, St. Elmo—Dam by Woodburn....Lawn View Farm Cal.

Dates Claimed.

FRESNO (Spring Meeting)	March 18th to 29th
SAN JOSE (Blood Horse Meeting)	April 4th, 7th and 9th
IONE	Aug 7th to 9th.
NAPA	Aug. 18th to 23rd
SAN JOSE (Fall Meeting)	Aug 25th to 30th inclusive
PETALUMA	Aug. 25th to 30th
OAKLAND (District No. 1)	Sept. 1st to Sept. 6th
CALIFORNIA STATE FAIR	Sept. 8th to 20th
FRESNO (Fall Meeting)	Sept. 29th to Oct. 4th

ENTRIES CLOSE TO-DAY FOR

P. C. T. H. B. A. Stakes.
Petaluma Colt Stakes.
Helena (Montana) Stakes.
The Stanford Stake.

TO CLOSE MARCH 5th.

P. C. Blood-Horse Association.
San Jose Blood-Horse Asso'n.

Pacific Coast Trotting Horse Breeders' Association.

A printed circular has been issued by this association which merits the attention of not only all upon this coast who are engaged in the breeding of trotters, but also of those who, as farmers, have the facilities to raise horses for their own use, or for occasional sale. It has become the settled condition of the farming class, who must have horses to perform much of the work upon their farms and for their drives to and from market, that is is practical economy to raise the better grades of horses for their purpose. The trotting horse is the most useful, as well as the most valuable horse for every purpose. He excels every other kind of horse for general use as farm horse, as horse of all work, as driving horse for every member of the family, as roadster, and as the horse for speed and lasting qualities in cases of urgency when dispatch and distance are chief considerations. Besides these material facts to the farmer to recommend to him the trotting horse, there remains the more material point with many—that of the market or selling value of the horse. Every breeder who breeds to supply the market and meet the growing demand for fast trotters for turf uses and for the stud, understand the prime quality in the breeding. He procures the very best blood and line, with less regard to cost, and uppermost care as to pedigree and performance and form, because in this case and study of selection and breeding, is involved the all-important matter of producing the trotter to excel in speed and staying quality, to lower the record, to command the topmost price, and to be of greatest value in the stud when the time of turf performance is past. The extraordinary prices which have been paid for trotters within the last thirty years have in great measure revolutionized the general sentiment in regard to horses, and largely instructed breeders to the advanced system of the present period.

It is the development of the reasoning faculty which instruct that it costs at the outset little more for the breeding of a horse that may be sold for thousands of dollars than it costs for the breeding of a horse that will never attain a value beyond the low hundreds, or, for that matter, that may never be worth one hundred dollars. All the while it is possible that the farmer who breeds intelligently and with discretion superior to the consideration of the first cost of breeding may be the breeder of the phenominal trotter to command a price even beyond any sum yet paid, and thus become not only famous for his greatly superior breeding, but rich besides. The great trotting sires of forty years ago, whose descendants have since astonished the world by their performances, and whose sons and daughters are the marvels of the turf and track, were of the stud, with values commensurate, were bred upon ordinary farms by common farmers who bred simply for the farm and not for the turf or stud. The champions of the trotting turf—the Hambletonians, the Wilkes and other great lines, now of highest valuation—were in such manner bred; but the farmers who bred them and thence became famous, had the sagacity and possessed the pride to breed to the superior blood of their period. Rysdick and Goldsmith were farmers of this class. Their systems have developed into the great and very profitable breeding farms of this period. Those engaged in them, such as the owners of Palo Alto, of San Mateo, of Rose Farm, of Rancho Del Paso, of Pleasanton and of other similar establishments, require no hint or comment on the subject. There are still, however, many farmers who are apparently careless, indifferent and unmindful in this important branch of farming, although better attention to it is more likely to profit and enrich them than any other of the branches of farming. It is to this class of farmers that the benefits set forth and made feasible by the opportunities which the Association offer are easiest attainable. Many of the farmers, and they are the most intelligent, as they are the most prosperous, have adopted the wise lessons derived from the valuable example of the most noted breeders, and similarly profit thereby.

The Pacific Coast Trotting Horse Breeders' Association, as its title indicates, is organized and established for the purpose of better developing the trotting horse breeding industry in California and in every one of the Pacific States. In the circular to which reference is made the situation is clearly and succinctly set forth, with sound reasoning and assuring examples.

The association proposes to supply the means to the better benefit of the farmer who breeds for his own farm and to sell the produce, whether of crops or horses. It enables the owners of horses to devote them to the better opportunities of the turf, particularly in respect to the youngsters who develop good speed, though not of the highest order. It is designed to encourage the better condition and improvement of the trotting turf in every manner. It will afford fair play and equal chance to all. It will greatly advance the trotting horse interests of the whole coast. In California these will be materially benefitted by the labors of the association, composed and governed as it is by practical men, breeders and turfmen who are actuated by the commendable spirit which seeks the best and pursues the right course to the ultimate highest results. An association of the kind has been much needed on this coast, especially in this State. This need is now supplied. It rests with those most interested to encourage and sustain the association. In view of the increasing demand for California bred stock at the East, even from the famous Blue Grass region of Kentucky, from the great breeding farms of the Northwest, and from the great turf counties of the Atlantic sea-board—as sales every year in these States and in the rich market of New York attest—the establishment of this association may be compared to an institution in which the highest preparatory training is guaranteed by most effective methods, and likewise will flow the most profitable outcome. The circular has been sent broadcast over the State and coast, for the common benefit of breeders and farmers and turfmen. It should be read and well considered by all.

Fresno Spring Meeting.

The Directors of the Fresno Fair Association, with energy characteristic of them, now make announcement that a spring meeting will be held in their thriving little city during the week commencing March 24th. Three races have been selected for each day, and there is variety enough in the distances to warrant good entries and excellent sport. In the way of money, the Directorate have, as usual, displayed a lavish hand, putting on the "added" with a generous spirit. Fresno is one of the favorite spots for horsemen to visit, the accommodations being of the best, and the management cannot be excelled. That old time horseman, Frank Baldwin, is the Superintendent, and realizes what horsemen require, so that there is nothing lacking, and everything to tempt the owner, trainer and jockey to make Fresno a visit.

The Balch Races.

For many years Welsey Balch, of Boston, has promoted sensational trotting races which have drawn the eyes of the trotting world toward the "Hub of the universe." His stallion race of last year has raised a stench that is now stinking in the nostrils of all honest men. The Alcryon and Nelson affair has been ventilated so freely through the press that it is not to be wondered at that outsiders believe in the axiom, "that there must be some fire when there is so much smoke." Mr. Balch has been in correspondence for some time with the owners of the most prominent stallions throughout the country, and now proposes to arrange a race for a purse of $20,000, and the Eastern newspapers state that at least twenty possessors of famous stallions will agree to enter. With an entrance of $2,000 the scheme is a good one from a financial stand point for Mr. Balch, but can the owners of these horses afford to have their animals trot under the management of a man who denies membership in either of the associations, and seems to feel agrieved that Mr. John Sheppard, of Boston, sent on the annual membership fee for the course over which the race took place. Mr. Balch evidently does not believe in keeping up the ethics of the turf, but believes solely in lining his pockets with the filthy lucre, to be made from arranging such races. It is a fact known of all men that the old sensational events did more to keep down racing than anything else could possibly, and the large purses given for four mile races on the Pacific Coast, gave the thoroughbreds such a black eye that its effect on the attendance is still felt.

Answers to Correspondents.

Answers for this department must be accompanied by the name and address of the sender, not necessarily for publication, but as proof of good faith. Write the questions distinctly, and on one side of the paper only. Positively no questions will be answered by mail or telegraph.

Another Query For Our Readers.

Do you know anything of the breeding and history of a horse brought to California some time in the '50s called Toronto Chief Jr. He was brought out (so I am informed) by J. Roff; was owned by J. Agnew, then in San Francisco; next by Sawyer, of San Antone, Contra Costa Co., then John Rogers, San Francisco; then Wm. Woods, Sulphur Springs Valley, near Vallejo. He was a pacing stallion, dark brown or chestnut, white strip in face, and three or four white feet. The Boston Cultivator, in an article about a year or more ago, about the early day trotters and pacers, speaks of a pacing stallion Toronto Chief Jr that went to California. It gives him a record to harness of about 2:34, and 2:32 to saddle. Maybe some of the readers of the BREEDER AND SPORTSMAN will known his history. F. W. L.

Who Can Answer.

Can any of your readers give the history and breeding of a brown mare called Capitola, at one time owned by J. B. Finney, Menlo Park. She is represented as being by Whipple's Hambletonian dam by Norfolk. She is a mare of considerable speed and looks like the Whipple Hambletonians in many respects. A SUBSCRIBER.

A Subscriber.

How fast in your opinion could Direct have trotted last season had he been driven for a record?

Answer.—2:16 or better.

S. H. DeWitt.

Will you be kind enough to send me the pedigree of Signal (Singletary's Rattler) and oblige.

Answer.—We do not mail answers. Signal 3327 by Bunday's Rob Roy, son of Bennett's Rob Roy, dam not traced.

F. K L.

1st.—What is General Knox's best record? and was he standard? Did any of his get have records of 2;30, or better? and how many?

2nd.—What is the breeding of L. A. Richards' Electric, by Elector? Has he a record, and is he standard? If so, what is his number?

Answer.—Gen. Knox 140, (record 2.31¼). He has 14 in the 2:30 list. We do not know the breeding of Electric, write to Mr. Richards. He is not in the 2:30 list.

A Constant Reader.

Will you please answer through the columns of your valuable paper what horse trotted the fastest heat in Montana last year in his races, who owns him and how bred. Please give the owner of the roan mare Wanita, her record, and how bred.

Answer.—Faust trotted the fastest heat in Montana last year, 2:18½. He is owned by A. C. Beckwith, Evanston, Wyoming Faust by Florida 482, dam Claire by Bayard 53, 2nd dam Lady Kittridge, said to be by Cassius M. Clay Jr. 20. Wanita is owned by the same party; her record is 2:20¼ She is by Aberdeen 27, dam Wyoming Belle by Lowe's Pilot, 2nd dam Juanita by Pilot Jr 12, etc.

San Jose Reader.

Does a mare become eligible to the standard under the following conditions? She was sired by a standard horse, has a son producer of two performers with records better that 2:30. She has herself a record better than 2:40.

Answer.—She is not eligible unless her record is 2:35 or better.

San Jose.

Will you inform me if Cosmo by Shiloh, dam the Rudolph mare by Rudolph etc, was the sire of Ten Broeck 1:39¾ running; also state the breeding of Ten Broeck 3 removes in sires and dams.

Answer.—You have the first question mixed. Cosmo, by Shiloh, dam Lady Edgerton is what the stud book says Ten Broeck's sire was imp Pheaton, dam Fanny Holton by Lexington; 2nd dam Nantura by Brawner's Eclipse; 3rd dam Quiz by Bertrand. Imp Phaeton by King Tom; 1st dam Merry Sunshine by Storm; 2nd dam by Falstaff; 3rd dam Sister to Pompey by Emilius.

Napa.

About 1878, a trotting bred stallion called Young Tippoo by Hambletonian Tippoo was in the stud at Petaluma. Is he or his sire registered? Can you give his breeding?

Answer.—He is not registered, neither is his sire. We do not know the breeding.

J. W. D.

Is 10 the registered number of Rysdyk's Hambletonian, if so, when did he die?

Answer.—(1) Yes. (2) March 27, 1876.

J. C.

Will you please answer at your earliest convenience and let me know the pedigree of Oregon Pathfinder.

Answer.—He was sired by French Morrill, son of the Tennison colt, by Young Bullrush, son of Bullrush by Justin Morgan; 1st dam unknown; second dam by the Farrington horse, son of Vance, by imp. Messenger.

G. B.

Can you tell me if Jenny Walker (thoroughbred) ever had a colt called Nameless.

Answer.—Mr. Williamson, former owner of Belmont, sends us the following letter:

SAN JOSE, Feb. 22, 1890.

EDITOR BREEDER AND SPORTSMAN:—Jenny Walker by Boston was never bred to Belmont. Nameless was bred by J. F. Walker, of Irvington, Alameda Co., and was by Belmont, dam by imp Monarch. Mr. Walker can gi you more information about the mare than I can, as he brought her to the country and I think bred her. Respectfully, etc,

W. M. WILLIAMSON.

A. B. C.

Can you give me the name of the breeder of Belmont Boy 2;15, and the pedigree of the horse?

Answer.—The following letter will answer this question:

SAN JOSE, Feb 24th.

EDITOR BREEDER AND SPORTSMAN:—Belmont Boy was bred by me, description and pedigree as follows: Chestnut gelding, near hind foot and pastern white, and white strip in face. Foaled April 7, 1879, sire Nutwood 600, 1st dam Lilly Vernon by Tom Vernon or Tarpey horse, 2nd dam Fanny Belmont by Williamson's Belmont, Tom Vernon by Hamilton Chief, Hamilton Chief son of Royal George.

Very truly yours, W. A. PARKHURST.

Martinez.

Will you please publish the breeding of Kate Agnew 2:28½.

Answer.—Her owner gives the following, by Chrisman's Hambletonion 10,165, he by Hambletion 725, dam by Oakland Boy, a son of Winthrop 505, second dam by Shakespeare (thoroughbred).

A Reader.

Will you kindly give me the breeding of Brigadier? Where and by whom owned, his record, age, and number of his get in the 30 list, with their names.

Answer.—Brigadier 797, bay horse, foaled 1873 by Happy Medium 400, dam Lady Turner by Frank Pierce Jr. 485, etc. Bred by R Penistan, Philadelphia, Pa. Now owned by J. B. McDonald, Marysville, Cal. Record 2;21¼. His get in the list is Hazel Kirke, 2:24

The Sacramento Programme.

We have received from Secretary Smith, of the State Agricultural Society, the following programme for their spring running meeting:

FIRST DAY—SATURDAY, APRIL 26th.

No. 1. Purse $400, for three-year-olds and upwards: $15 from starters to go to second horse. A winner this year, at this distance to carry three pounds extra. Maidens allowed, if three years old, five pounds; four or more, ten pounds. Three-quarters of a mile.

No. 2 Norfolk Stakes, for two-year-olds, closed Aug. 1st, with thirty-seven nominations. Five-eighths of a mile.

No. 2. Selling purse $400, of which $50 to second. For all ages; winners to be sold at auction. Horses entered to be sold at $1,500, to carry rule weight. One pound off for each $100 down to $500 Value placed on starters only, by 6 P. M. night before the race. One mile and a sixteenth.

No. 4. The California Oaks, for three year-old fillies. Closed in 1889 with seventeen nominations. One and one-eighth miles.

SECOND DAY.—TUESDAY, APRIL 29TH.

No. 5. The Matadero stakes, for two-year-olds. Closed in 1889, with nineteen nominations. Three-quarters of a mile.

No 6 The Chris. Green handicap. Closed February 1st, with fourteen nominations. One and one-quarter miles.

No. 7. Purse $400, for all ages, $10 from starters to go to second horse. Maiden allowances—If three years, five pounds; four and upward, ten pounds. Non-winners this year allowed five pounds. Allowances cumulative. One mile and a sixteenth.

No. 8: The Weinstock, Lubin & Co. stake. Closed in 1889, with thirty-two nominations. One mile.

THIRD DAY.—THURSDAY, MAY 1ST.

No. 9. The Spring Stakes —A sweepstakes for three year olds, (foals of 1887) that have not won a race previous to Jan'y 1, 1890; $50 entrance, h. f., or $15 if declared April 1, 1890; $400 added; second to receive $75 from stakes Maidens at time of starting, allowed 5 lbs. Closed Feb'y 1, 1890 with 12 nominations One mile.

No. 10 The Western Hotel Stakes, for two year old fillies. Closed in 1889 with twenty-seven nominations. Five-eighths of a mile.

No. 11. The Hall Luhrs & Co. Handicap. Closed in 1889 with twenty-nine nominations. One and one-quarter miles.

No. 12. Selling purse, $400; of which $50 to second; for all ages. Horses entered to be sald for $2,500 to carry rule weight. One pound off for each $100 down to $800. Value placed on starters only by 5 P. M. night before the race. One and one-eighth miles.

FOURTH DAY.—SATURDAY. MAY 3D.

No 13 The Golden Eagle Hotel Handicap for two year olds. Closed in 1889 with twenty-nine nominations Weights to be announced by 8 P. M. second day before race. Declarations by 4 P. M day before race. Three-quaters of a mile

No. 14 The Hopeful Handicap. A sweep stakes for all ages; of $25 each; $15 forfeit or $20 if declared, with $400 added; second to received $100. Weights announced by 10 P. M. day before race; declaration due by 5 P. M. same day. One and one-eighth miles.

No 15. The California Derby. Closed in 1889 with thirty-two nominations. One and one-half miles.

No. 16. Purse $400; for all ages. Ten dollars from starters to go to second horse. Non-winners this year at time of starting allowed, if three years old five pounds; four years; ten pounds; five and upwards, twelve pounds. Entries to close with clerk of course at 5 P. M. day before the race. Mile heats.

Kidd, Edmonson and Morse Sale.

LEXINGTON, KY, Feb. 17, 1890.

EDITOR BREEDER AND SPORTSMAN, SAN FRANCISCO, CAL.—DEAR SIR:—This is the last call for entries in the Kidd, Edmonson and Morse's great contest sale at Chicago, March 17th to 21st.

Those that have not sent their entries should do so at once, as the catalogue is now being prepared for the press.

Chicago is destined to have the largest horse sales of fine and valuable horses, of all breeds, in the world. No other city offers such advantages in location and population within a radius of 500 miles. The untold wealth and enterprise of her people, located in the heart of America. The center of the demand where people can go with ease and comfort, buy and sell their valuable horses, of all classes and breeds, to the best advantage by men that have given the sale business a life long study, and piloted the greatest sales to a success, that has ever been held on American soil. Entries have already been made by prominent breeders of Illinois, Iowa, Minnesota, Missouri, Kansas, Ohio, Indiana, Kentucky, Michigan, California, Dakota, Nebraska and Wisconsin. We hope this will be a united action of every breeder to pull of the sale. Bring your friends with you to Chicago to be fitted in any kind of a horse that may be needed. This alone will make a rousing attendance.

Mr. L U. Shippee of Stockton, Cal., in speaking of his consignment, says: "I have just gotten out the pedigrees of the colts, and have them in the stables. I think they are a choice lot; they are well bred, and are undoubtedly fine animals." Mr. Shippee is the third largest breeder of trotters on the Pacific Slope, and the California trotters at the present time are enjoying an unequal boom.

The horsemen will await with great interest the coming of his consignment, as much is expected both in breeding and quality.

Mr. Jackson I. Case, the owner of J. I. C. enters in the sale a number of good ones from his great breeding farm at Racine, Wis.

Parties having mares that are barren or irregular breeders would do well to consult Dr. G. W. Stimpson, V. S. Office and Hospital 19th Street, near San Pablo Avenue, Oakland, Cal. Best of references.

Foals of 1890.

February 3rd, a filly was foaled at the Valensin farm. She is bay, two hind ankles white; by Sidney 2:19¾, dam Mary by Buccaneer 2656, 2nd dam by Echo. This is a full sister to Mariana, sold last year in New York, to Mr. Robt Bonner for $3,000.

Names Claimed.

I hereby claim the name of Mambrino Blackhawk for my seal brown stallion, foaled 1887, by Grosvenor 1833, dam Alice Garrett 2:33½ (ninth heat), by Ruben, son of Vermont Black Hawk, 2nd dam by Cock of the Rock, etc.

PETER EINSFELD, San Jose.

The following characteristic letter has been received:

IRVINGTON, ALAMEDA COUNTY, Feb, 23, 1890.

EDITOR BREEDER AND SPORTSMAN:—The winner of the Futurity Stakes has arrived. She is a fine bay filly with star, by Director, 1st dam Lida W., record 2:26 pacing, by Nutwood, record 2:18¾, 2nd dam by George M. Patchen Jr., record 2:27, 3rd dam Rebel Daughter by Williamson's Belmont, sire of Venture, record 2:27¼. For her I claim the name Zeta Carter. She was foaled February 20, 1890. Also brown filly with right hind pasturn white to ankle, foaled February 20, 1890, by Noonday, 1st dam by Director, 2nd dam by Echo, full sister to Gibralter, record 2:22½. For her I claim the name Thursday, as she was foaled on that day. These two should make pretty hot stuff. Yours truly,

MARTIN CARTER.

Cyrus R. vs. Argent.

In reference to the letter from Mr. Walton, owner of Argent, that appeared in the BREEDER AND SPORTSMAN of last week, we have received the following note, which is self-explanatory:

EDITOR BREEDER AND SPORTSMAN:—I am ready to put up on or before the 1st of March $500, forfeit the amount put up by R. H. Walon, to trot my horse Cyrus R. against his horse Argent, and accept all the terms named by Mr. Walton, except that I still claim the right to name the balance to be put up July 1st, as it was the only right I claimed in my challenge through the BREEDER AND SPORTSMAN.

Yours truly, T. W. BARSTOW.

SAN JOSE, February 20, 1890.

Our Southern California Letter.

LOS ANGELES, Feby. 27th.

A comparison of the best turf records of Australia and America will be of special interest, inasmuch as it now is the popular fad to purchase the Colonial bred horse for a cross on the native bred animal. A newspaper friend of mine residing in Australia sent me the following table by the last steamer. I beleive that it will be found to be correct to the end of 1889.

AUSTRALIAN RECORDS.

3 furlongs, Inuendo. Argus Scandal—Report, run at Mooney Valley; age, 2 years; weight, 103 lbs: time, 37½ seconds.

4 furlongs. Sextan, Robinson Crusoe—Sunshine; run in New Zealand; age, 2 years; weight, 111 lbs.; time, 47¼ seconds

5 furlongs, Ned of The Hills, Pride of The Hills—Euterpe; run in South australia; age, 3 years; weight, 101 lbs.; time, 1 minute and 1 second.

6 furlongs, Volcano, Chester—Etna; run at Randwick; age, 2 years; weight, 114 lbs; time, 1 minute and 14 seconds.

7 furlongs, Phantom, Lecturer—Lancashire Witch; run at Flemington; aged; weight, 116 lbs.; time 1 minute 27¼ seconds.

One mile, Bolka, Glorious—Bridget; run at Flemington; age, 3 years; weight, 123 lbs.; time, 1 minute 40 seconds.

1¼ miles, Cerise & Blue, Wilberforce—Myrtle, run at Flemington; age, 4 years; weight, 101 lbs.; time, 1 minute 55½ seconds

1¼ miles, Abercorn. Chester—Cinnamon; run at Flemington; age, 5 years; weight, 130 lbs; time, 2 minutes 7 seconds.

1 mile 3 furlongs, All Gold, Infidel—Golden Locks; run at Randwick; age, 3 years; weight, 86 lbs.; time 2 minutes 22½ seconds.

1½ miles, Prince Imperial, Kelpie—Queen's Head; run at Hawkesbury; aged 4 years; weight, 96 lbs; time, 2 minutes 35½ seconds.

1¾ miles, Ensign, Grandmaster—Formosa; run at Randwick; age, 3 years; weight, 108 lbs; time, 3 minutes, 4 seconds

2 miles, Dunlop, Neckerrgat—Etta; run at Flemington; age, 5 years; weight, 118 lbs.; time, 3 minutes 28½ seconds.

2¼ miles, Nelson, King Cole—My Idea; run at Auckland, N. Z.; age, 5 years; weight, 105 lbs; time, 4 minutes.

3 miles, Trident, Robinson Crusoe—Cocoa Nut; run at Flemington; age, 3 years; weight, 101 lbs; time, 5 minutes 25¾ seconds.

It will be seen that the Australian records compare very favorably with the American records, and this, too, in spite of the fact that the races are run on turf in the Antipodes. They have no toboggan slide tracks in Australia, consequently Sextant's 47¼ seconds is probably as good as Geraldine's 46 seconds for a half mile.

The American record for a mile is just a quarter of a second better than the Australian record, but the latter record was obtained in a race, consequently Maori's 1:39 4-5 is the only American record better than Bolka made in a race. America has half a second the best of it at a mile and a quarter, but Abercorn's performance is as good if not better than Kingston's when it is taken in consideration that Abercorn packed 130 pounds in 2:07, while Kingston was only weighted at 122 pounds, when he made his record of 2:06½. At two miles Ten Broeck has a second the best of the Australian record and Drake Carter's celebrated three miles in 5:24 is a second and three-quarters faster than the best record of Australia.

QUARTER-STRETCH GOSSIP:

Cordova is the name of a race-horse by Balboa who is now being trained at Santa Anita. This horse was bred by Charley Thomas, of San Jacinto.

A feature of the next fair to be held in Los Angeles will be a two and three-year-old trotting stake.

Hancock Johnston expects to send two car-loads of trotters next month to either Lexington or New York to be sold under the hammer. They are principally by A. W. Richmond, Monroe Chief, Del Sur and Dashwood.

Dr. K. D. Wise is to establish a breeding farm near the Centenella Ranch on the Redondo Beach road. He has purchased 400 acres of land admirably adapted for breeding purposes. His stallions will be Emmin Bey by Guy Wilkes, dam Tempest by Sultan; Rajah by Sultan, dam Kitty Wilkes by George Wilkes, and Glendine by Saulsbury, dam Tempest by Sultan. The broodmares will be purchased from time to time whenever the opportunity presents itself.

Ellwood, a pacing mare with a record of 2:17¾, will shortly drop a foal by Alcazar 2:20½. Ellwood is a full sister to Arrow 2:13¼. The new comer should be speedy.

There is no breeding farm in the state more in need of new stables than Santa Anita. The present stables are in a hollow and are entirely unfit for winter quarters.

DAGWORTH.

It is an item worth knowing, that Dave Pulsifer has engaged the services of the crack little light weight Jockey Freeman for the season of 1890.

Breeders' Directory.

Advertisements under this heading 50c. per line per month.

HORSES AND CATTLE.

W. S. JACOBS, Sacramento, Cal.—Breeder of Thoroughbred Shorthorns and Berkshire Hogs.

J. H. WHITE, Lakeville, Sonoma County—Breeder of Registered Holstein Cattle.

EL ROBLAS RANCHO—Los Alamos, Cal., Francis T. Underhill, proprietor, importer and breeder of thoroughbred Hereford Cattle. Information by mail. C. F. Swan, manager.

PAGE BROTHERS.—Penn's Grove, Sonoma Co. Cal. Breeders of Short-Horn Cattle; Draft, Roadster and Standard Bred Horses.

SETH COOK, breeder of Cleveland Bay Horses, Devon, Durham, Polled Aberdeen-Angus and Galloway Cattle. Young stock of above breeds on hand for sale. Warranted to be pure bred, recorded and average breeders. Address, Geo. A. Wiley, Cook Farm, Danville, Contra Costa Co., Cal.

MAMBRINO WILKES COLTS and FILLIES, full brothers and sisters to Gus. Wilkes 2:22, and Balkan 2:29¾, for Sale. Address SMITH HILL, Walnut Creek, Contra Costa County, Cal.

B. F. RUSH, Suisun, Cal., Shorthorns, Thoroughbred and Grades. Young Bulls and Calves for Sale.

PETER SAXE & SON, Lick House, San Francisco, Cal.—Importers and Breeders for past 18 years of every variety of Cattle, Horses, Sheep and Hogs.

HOLSTEIN THOROUGHBREDS of all the noted strains. Registered Berkshire Swine. Catalogues. F. H. BURKE, 401 Montgomery St., S. F.

HENRY C. JUDSON, Wild Idle Farm.—Breeder of Thoroughbred Horses. The home of "Wild Idle." P. O. Santa Clara; Box 223.

FERGUSON & AUSTIN,
FRESNO, CAL.
Registered Polled Angus and Short-Horn Cattle.

Attention! Sportsmen!!

An exploring party will leave San Francisco about April 10th for the Alaska Coast, St. Matthews Island and Yukon River, stopping at numerous places on the way where Seal, Walrus, Sea Lions, Brown Bear, White Polar Bear and Deer are plentiful; also splendid fishing for Salmon, Halibut, Trout and Cod, offering to the hunter and fisherman a trip of five months' unparalleled for sport. A novel feature of this offer is that each one taking the trip becomes a stockholder in the Company.

For further information apply to
NORTHERN DEVELOPMENT CO.
No. 5 Market St., Room 5.

Oysters.

M. B. MORAGHAN

Is the only importer, planter and wholesale dealer in the CALIFORNIA MARKET, Stalls 68, 69 to 71 and 47, 48. All the choicest brands of Fresh Oysters constantly on hand. Prompt attention paid to hotel and country orders. Price List.

Large Eastern Oysters .... $1 00 per 100
Transplanted Eastern Oysters .... 1 80 per 100
California Oysters .... 2 00 " sack
Fresh Frozen Eastern Oysters at $7 00 per doz. Cans.

HORSES PURCHASED ON COMMISSION.

THOROUGHBREDS A SPECIALTY.

Will select and buy, or buy selected Animals for all desiring, for reasonable compensation.
KEEPS PROMISING YOUNGSTERS IN VIEW.
L. M. LASLEY, Stanford, Ky.

References:—J. W. Guest, Danville, Ky.
B. G. Bruce, Lexington, Ky.
S. H. Baughman, Stanford, Ky.
G. A. Lackey, Stanford, Ky.
Geo. McAlister, Stanford, Ky.
First National Bank, Stanford, Ky.

Trade Mark

Six Cases

S. ALLCOCK & CO.'S
Unequalled Fishing Tackle

Received direct by Steamer EXPLORER, from Liverpool, December 25, 1889.

E. T. ALLEN,
Sole Agent for Pacific Coast,
Fire Arms and Sporting Goods
416 Market St., S. F.

SAMUEL VALLEAU. JAS. R. BRODIE.

J. R. BRODIE & CO.,
Steam Printers,
—And Dealers in—
Poolseller's and Bookmaker's Supplies.
401—403 *Sansome Street, corner Sacramento, San Francisco.*

GRANDISSIMO,

Full Brother to GRANDEE, 3-year-old Record 2-23½.

GRANDISSIMO.

- Le Grande 2868 (trial, 2:24), Sire of Grandee, 3 y. o. r., 2:23½.
  - Almont 33. Sire of Westmont, 2:13¾, Puritan, 2:16, Fannie Wetherspoon, 2:16¾, Piedmont, 2:17¼, and 32 others in 2:30, and sire of 49 sons and 22 daughters that have produced 2:30 performers.
    - Abdallah 15. Sire of Goldsmith Maid, 2:14, and 8 others in 2:30, and sire of 13 sons and 21 dams, producers of 2:30 performers.
    - Sally Anderson, by Mambrino Chief.
  - Jessie Pepper. Dam of Iona, 2:17½, Alpha, 2:23½, and grandam of Montezuma, 2:29¼.
    - Mambrino Chief 11. Sire Lady Thorne, 2:18¼, and 5 others in 2:30 with 23 sires and 15 dams, producers of 2:30 performers.
    - Sidi Hamet (thoroughbred).
- Norma. Dam of Grandee, 3 y. o. r., 2:23½.
  - Arthurton 365. Sire Arab, 2:15, and 4 others in 2:30, and dams of Hidalgo, 2:27, Hazel Wilkes, 2:20, Reverie (yearling), 2:36½.
    - Hambletonian 10. Sire of Dexter, 2:17¼, and 40 others in 2:30.
    - Imogene. Dam of Arthurton, with 4 in 2:30; Leland, with 3 in 2:30.
  - Nourmahal, 2:39½. Full sister to A. W. Richmond 1687, sire of Arrow, 2:13½, Romero, 2:19¼, and 3 others in 2:30.
    - Blackbird 401. Sire of Blackbird, 2:22, A. W. Richmond, sire of 5 in 2:30, and dam of Anteeo, 2:16¼, Antevolo, 2:19½.
    - by Rattler (thoroughbred).

SAN DIEGO, 8776.

SAN DIEGO 8776

- Alcona Clay 2786.
  - Alcona 730. Sire of Flora Belle, 2:24, Clay Duke, 2:31½, etc.
    - Almont 33. Sire of Westmont, 2:13¾, Piedmont, 2:17¼, Puritan, 2:16, and 33 others in 2:30 list.
    - by Mambrino Chief 11. Sire of Lady Thorne, 2:18¼.
  - Madonna. Dam of Del Rey, trial 2:31, Alcona Jr., 2:41, sire of Silas Skinner, trial 2:23½.
    - Cassius M. Clay Jr. 22. Sire of Durango, 2:23¾, Harry Clay, 2:23½, and sire of dam of Happy Thought, 2:22¼, and others.
    - by Joe Downing 710. Sire of Abe Downing, 2:20¾, Dick Jamison, 2:26, and sire of dams of Kentucky Hambletonian, 2:27, Lorena, 2:15, and others.
- Fontana. Dam of Flora Belle, 2:24, Silas Skinner, trial 2:23½.
  - Almont 33. Sire of 36 in 2:30 list, 49 sons and 22 daughters that have produced 2:30 performers.
  - Fanny Williams. Dam of Bay Chieftain, 2:28½.
    - Abdallah 15. Sire of Goldsmith Maid, 2:14, Thorndale, 2:22¼, also Almont, Belmont, Jim Monroe, etc.
    - by Denmark (thoroughbred).

GRANDISSIMO is a blood bay, handsome-modelled colt, and a natural trotter. He is four years old, and trotted one quarter miles in 36 seconds, with very limited training, last Fall.

SAN DIEGO is dark seal brown, three years old, and trotted one-quarter miles in 40 seconds as a two-year old.

These are two grand young horses, and, barring accidents, will both make fast records next fall.

They will both be allowed a limited number of mares, at $50 for the season. Mares not proving in foal to be returned free 1891. Best of pasture for mares at $4 per month, but no liability for accidents or escapes.

They will make the season from February 1st to June 1st at Napa Fair Grounds. For further particulars, address or call on

H. B. STARR, Race Track, Napa, Cal.,
or FRED W. LOEBER, St. Helena

IMPORTANT
AUCTION SALE
—OF—
THOROUGHBRED
CLYDESDALE HORSES

At 12 O'clock M,
Tuesday, March 4, 1890,
AT
Bay District Track, S. F.

These horses comprise the importation of Messrs. J. Teefail, J. Burns and J. Scott. They consist of EIGHT STALLIONS and SEVEN MARES, all THOROUGHBRED CLYDES, specially selected for the California market by the above gentlemen, whose experience with former shipments enabled them to choose animals specially adapted for this State. These horses may be seen at the Bay District Track, and Villa adjoining, and parties desirous of purchasing are urged to call and critically examine them. Stockmen throughout the coast are assured this is the best lot of Clydes yet imported, and should avail themselves of the opportunity to secure first-class animals.

Terms at sale.

KILLIP & CO., Auctioneers,
22 Montgomery Street S. F., Cal.

John D. Gall. Jas. P. Dunne

"The Resort,"
No. 1 Stockton Street, cor. Ellis,
San Francisco.

BERGEZ'S
RESTAURANT.
FIRST-CLASS. Charges Reasonable.
Private Rooms for Families,
332—334 Pine St., below Montgomery St.
JOHN BERGEZ, Propr.

Sunny Side Breeding Farm.
Admiral 488.

Foaled 1867—Sired by Volunteer 55, Son of Rysdyk's Hambletonian 10.

First dam Lady Pierson by Cassius M. Clay (Neaves') 20; second dam by Diamond; third dam a running mare said to be thoroughbred. He is fitted in an eminent degree to produce colts that will in all respects justify his patrons in their expectations.

Admiral is the sire of Huntress, record 2:27¼, Sister, 2:19¼, Perhelion, 2:25, Nona Y., 2:25, and others equally as promising, but have not had the advantage of track work. He will serve a limited number of approved mares at $50 the season, with usual return privilege. Season ending August 1, 1890. No liability for accidents or escapes.

KING DAVID 2576.

Bay Stallion—Foaled 1883.

Sired by Admiral 488, dam Black Flora (the dam of Huntress, 2:27¼, Sister, 2:19¼, Perhelion, 2:25, Nona Y., 2:25) by Black Prince.

King David is one of the best gets of Admiral. He has a good disposition, kind to drive, smooth and even-gaited, and can speed fast. Barring accidents he will trot in the twenties this Fall. His colts are large, rangy, and well finished. Will serve a limited number of mares at $30 the season, to end July 1, 1890. Every precaution will be taken to prevent accidents and escapes, but no liability will be assumed. Pasturage $4 per month.

Sunny Side Farm is situated two miles east of Vallejo, on the Sulphur Spring road. For further particulars, address

FRANK DRAKE,
Vallejo, Cal.

HENRY J. COX W. S. JOHNSON

The "EDWIN C."
40 EDDY STREET.
Cor. of Mason, San Francisco.
(Private Entrance Mason Street.)

Singleton & Addington,
Bank Exchange,
2d and K Streets, Sacramento.
Superior Wines, Liquors and Cigars.

Solano and Napa Agricultural Society.

Trotting Colt Guarantee Stakes for 1890.

The Solano and Napa Agricultural Society have opened the following Colt Stakes for Trotters:

NO. 1. TWO YEAR OLDS—Free for all; $400 guaranteed. $50 entrance, payable as follows: $10 April 1st, when entries close; $10 May 1st, $10 June 1st $10 July 1st, $10 August 1st, when colts must be named. Nominations transferrable any time before colts are named. If the payments amount to more than the amounts guaranteed the additional amount to be added to the stake. All moneys divided as follows: 60, 30 and 10 per cent; in case of only two starting, 65 and 35 per cent; and in case of one horse walking over the whole amount to go to such horse. A failure to make any payment when due shall be considered a withdrawal and forfeiture of the amounts paid in. National or American Rules to govern, as the Society may elect. The right reserved to refund the first payment in case the stakes do not fill reasonably well.

No. 2. FOR THREE YEAR OLDS.—Free for all. $500 guaranteed. $100 entrance, payable as follows: $20 April 1st, when entries close; $20 May 1st, $20 June 1st, $20 July 1st, $20 August 1st, when colts must be named. Conditions same as in No. 1.

District Colt Stakes for districts comprising Counties of Solano, Napa, Sonoma, Marin, Lake, Colusa, Yolo, Mendocino and Butte.

No. 3. FOR YEARLINGS.—$250 guaranteed, District. $40 entrance, payable as follows: $10 April 1st, when entries close; $10 June 1st, $10 July 1st, $10 Aug. 1st, when colts must be named. Conditions same as in No. 1.

No. 4. FOR TWO YEAR OLDS.—$350 guaranteed, District. $50 entrance, payable as follows: $10 April 1st, when entries close; $10 May 1st, $10 June 1st, $10 July 1st, $10 August 1st when colts must be named. Conditions same as in No. 1.

No. 5. FOR THREE YEAR OLDS.—$400 guaranteed. District. $50 entrance, payable as follows: $10 April 1st when entries close; $10 May 1st, $10 June 1st, $10 July 1st, $10 August 1st, when colts must be named. Conditions same as in No. 1.

Yearling Stake. Single dash; one mile. Two Year Olds.—Mile heats, two in three. Three Year Olds.—Three in five, to harness. Parties entering colts will be notified by mail when payment becomes due.

The Society also offers the following stakes for Class horses.

TROTTING STAKES.—Free for all.
2:30 CLASS—Trotting; purse $1500.
2:24 CLASS—Trotting; purse $1500.
2:20 CLASS—Trotting; purse $1500.

Horses eligible January 1st, 1890. Entrance $150, payable as follows: $25 April 1st, when entries close; $25 May 1st, $25 June 1st, $25 July 1st, $50 August 1st, when horses must be named. Nominations transferable any time before August 1st. Right reserved to refund entrance fee in any of the stakes should they not fill reasonably well. Money divided, 50, 25, 15 and 10 per cent. National or American Association Rules to govern, as the Society shall elect. To be trotted at our regular summer meeting, upon days to be here after arranged.

Entries to close April 1st, 1890, with

A. H. CONKLING, Secretary,
Napa City, Cal.
L. L. JAMES, President.

LAWN VIEW BREEDING FARM STALLIONS.

ACTOR.

A beautiful bay horse foaled 1887 by Prompter 2305 sire of Apex (four-year-old record) 2:26, Transit 2:26¾, Creole 2:20, Blue Belle 2:27, Daisy (yearling record) 2:36¼, he by Blue Bull 75, 1st dam by Sultan 1513 2:24, sire of Stamboul 2:12 1-4, Ruby 2:19¾, Sweetheart 2:22¾, Alcazar 2:20¾, Eva 2:23¾, La Grange 2:23¾, and eleven others in 2:30 list, second dam by Fireman by Langford.

Actor, as his pedigree shows, is as purely bred a young stallion as ever made a season in the stud. Blue Bull stock is much sought after in the East, and Sultan, sire of his first dam will make the season in Kentucky this year at $100 per mare. Actor is a handsome bay colt 16 hands high, clean limbed and possesses all the points of a speedy trotter.

TERMS, $40 FOR THE SEASON, usual return privileges.

DOUGLASDALE 7650.

Thoroughbred Registered Clydesdale Stallion

Imported from Scotland, December, 1889, bay, three years old.

TERMS, $25 FOR THE SEASON.

YOUNG ELMO

Two years old sorrel stallion by St. Elmo 2:27, dam by Woodburn.

TERMS, $20 FOR THE SEASON.

For further particulars, address
MANAGER LAWN VIEW FARM, Auburn, Cal.

Fine Hats,

Latest Styles and Colors.
Meussdorffer & Hubner
8 Kearny Street, San Francisco,
Next to New Chronicle Building

For Sale.

THE HANDSOME SORREL FILLY

Lady Dexter,

By Dexter Prince, by Kentucky Prince, the sire of Guy 2:10 3-4. First dam full sister of the greatest of trotters, Dexter, and the greatest of sires, Dictator. Second dam Clara, by American Star. Third dam the McKinstry mare. Hambletonian, the grandsire of Dexter Prince, has 40 trotters in the 2:30 list, 44 daughters that have produced 2:30 trotters, and more than 100 sons that have sired 2:30 trotters.

LADY DEXTER'S dam was Kitty Thorn, by Whipple's Hambletonian, out of a daughter of Kimball's Jackson; granddam by George M. Patchen.

Kitty Thorn's record, four years old, 2:31, was made at Santa Rosa in the :30 class. She won the race against Judge Shafter's Rustic, Hancock, Gladstone and Dave. Kitty Thorn trotted the same season in 2:27 1-2, but has no record in the 2:30 list.

This filly is four years old, and has never been trained, but can easily show quarters at a 2:40 gait, and demonstrates that with a little systematic work she will prove very fast. She is stylish, of gentle disposition, intelligent and a square trotter. For further information address or apply to

H. QUIGG.
317 Fifth Street, San Francisco, Cal.

CALIFORNIA NUTWOOD

Will stand for mares the season of 1890, commencing February 15th, and ending July 15th, at the NUTWOOD STOCK FARM, one mile from Irvington.

DESCRIPTION AND PEDIGREE.

He is a dark chestnut, with star in forehead; foaled September 16th, 1881; is 16 hands 1½ inches high and weighs 1200 pounds. Has a beautiful flowing mane and tail, with remarkable style and lofty carriage, a bold, open movement like his sire, but has never been handled for speed. He moves and looks like his sire, except that he is a larger horse.

CALIFORNIA NUTWOOD by Nutwood, record 2:18¾, has 34 trotters and pacers with records from 2:15 to 2:30, and put 8 in the 2:30 list in 1889. He is the only horse that ever lived with a record under 2:20 that produced five under 2:20. He is now serving mares at Dubuque, Iowa, at $500 for the season, and his colts at yearlings sell from $2500 to $5000 each. He is out of the dam of Maud S., record 2:08¾.

Nutwood, by Alexander's Belmont, sire of 32 with records from 2:15½ to 2:30. Alexander's Belmont by Alexander's Abdallah, sire of Goldsmiths Maid, record 2:14, and 5 others in 2:30 list. Alexander's Abdallah, by Rysdyk's Hambletonian, sire of 41 with records from 2:17¼ to 2:30, and is the founder of the Hambletonian family.

FANNY PATCHEN, dam of California Nutwood, by George M. Patchen Jr., record 2:27, and sire of Wells Fargo, 2:18¾, Sam Purdy 2:20½, Ben Ali 2:20¾, and 7 others from 2:21 to 2:30. He has 7 sons who together produced 12 trotters in 2:30 list, and 5 daughters who together produced 6 trotters and 1 pacer in 2.30 or better. He sired Alexander 2:31½. Alexander sired Alex. Button 2:26½; Alex. Button sired Yolo Maid, pacing record 2:14 at 4 years old, the fastest on record; George M. Patchen Jr., by George M. Patchen 2:23½, is sire of Lucy 2:18¾, and 3 others in the 2:30 list; he has 12 sons who together produced 40 trotters from 2:14½ to 2:30, and 6 daughters who together produced 6 trotters in 2:30 list or better, he is grand sire of Hopeful 2:14¾, and best wagon record 2:16½, and sire of the granddam of Stamboul 2:12½.

George M. Patchen, by Cassius M. Clay, and he by Henry Clay, founder of the Clay family.

Laura, second dam of California Nutwood, was a fine large bay mare, a very fast roadster brought from Chicago by Wm. Wilson, of San Jose, and is said to have made a record of 2.35 in Chicago. Pedigree not traced.

TERMS.

$40 for the season, payable invariably before the animal is removed. Mares not proving in foal can be returned free next season. Pasturage $4 per month, but no liability for accidents or escapes.

For further particulars address the owner,

MARTIN CARTER,

Newark, Alameda Co., Cal., or Irvington, Alameda County Cal.

Sire of Yolo Maid, 2:12½

Alexander Button 1197,

FOUR YEAR-OLD RECORD, 2:26 1-2.

SIRE OF

YOLO MAID, 2:12½, BELLE BUTTON, 2:20,
TOM RIDER, 2:20½, ROSA MAC, 2:20¾,
J. H. (seperately timed in a race) 2:22½,
KEHOE, 2:34½, ALEX. BUTTON (3), 2:35¾,
BURBANK S. (2 y. o., ½-mile track), 2:53.

PEDIGREE.

Alex. Button was Sired by Alexander 490, Record, 2:31 1-4.

First dam Lady Button by Napa Rattler; 2d dam a pacing mare (S. T. B.) by a Copperbottom horse.

ALEXANDER (490), record, 2:31½.

Sire of Alex. Button, 2.26 1-2, Reliance, 2:22 1-2, Tommy Dodd, 2:26, Nelly Patchen, 2:27 1-4, by Geo. M. Patchen Jr. (31), record 2:27; first dam Lady Crum by Brown's Bellfounder.

GEO. M. PATCHEN JR. (31), rec., 2:27.

Sire of Wells Fargo, 2:18¾, Sam Purdy, 2:20 1-2, Vanderlynn, 2.21, Star King, 2 22, Ben Ali, 2:24, and five others in the 30 list, by Geo. M. Patchen (30), 2:23 1-2; first dam Bell by Top Bellfounder, son of imp. Bellfounder; 2d dam Hoot a Laddie mare.

GEO. M. PATCHEN (30). RECORD 2:23½.

Sire of Lucy, 2:18¾; Chas. E. Low, 2 25¾; Geo. M. Patchen, Jr., 2 27; Mary, 2:2-; by Cassius M. Clay (18), 1st dam by Head'em, son of imp. Trustee; 2nd dam Itaska, by American Eclipse.

CASSIUS M. CLAY (18).

Sire of Geo. M. Patchen, 2:23¼, etc.; by Henry Clay (8), 1st dam Jersey Kate, the dam of John Anderson.

HENRY CLAY (8).

Sire of Black Douglass, 2:30; Centerville (w), 2:33; by Andrew Jackson (4); 1st dam Surry.

ANDREW JACKSON (4).

By Young Bashaw; dam an Ohio mare of unknown blood.

YOUNG BASHAW.

By imp. Grand Bashaw; 1st dam Pearl, by First Consul; 2nd dam Fancy, by imp. Messenger; 3rd dam by imp. Rockingham.

NAPA RATTLER.

By Biggart's Rattler; 1st dam Poll, by imp. Consternation; 2nd dam Betsy Baker, by Mambrino.

BIGGART'S RATTLER.

Grandsire of Joe. Brown, 2:22; Lady Snell, 2:23¾; Mary Davis, 2:2¾; Nellie Webster, 2:28¾, by Sir Henry, son of the Garrett Horse, by imp. Leonidas; 1st dam by the Hyde Horse, son of Long's Magnum Bonum; 2nd dam of Messenger blood.

BROWN'S BELLFOUNDER.

By imp. Bellfounder; 1st dam Lady Allport, by Mambrino; 2nd dam by Tippo Saib, son of imp. Messenger; 3rd dam by imp. Messenger.

DESCRIPTION.

ALEXANDER BUTTON is a dark bay with fine flowing mane and tail; stands 15¾ hands high; weighs 1,200 pounds, and is of excellent disposition. He is a natural trotter, inherited through the speed-lines of his ancestors, and imparts his speed to his offspring with uniform certainty. His colts show him to be a wonderful producer—and with his breeding and terms of service, he is the cheapest and most wonderful horse in the State.

TERMS.

TERMS.—$100, payable at end of season. Mares not proving with foal may be returned next season free of charge. Good pasturage furnished at $4 per month, and due care taken to prevent accidents or escapes, but no liability whatever assumed.

Will stand at Cache Creek Farm, which is situated about one and one-half miles west of Yolo Station.

All mares sent to Yolo in my care will be forwarded free of charge.

G. W. WOODARD, Proprietor.

Yolo, Yolo Co., Cal.

SEASON 1890.

The Great Son of Buccaneer

SHAMROCK,

Two-Year Old Record of 2:25, beating the World's Record 4 1-2 Seconds when made.

SHAMROCK

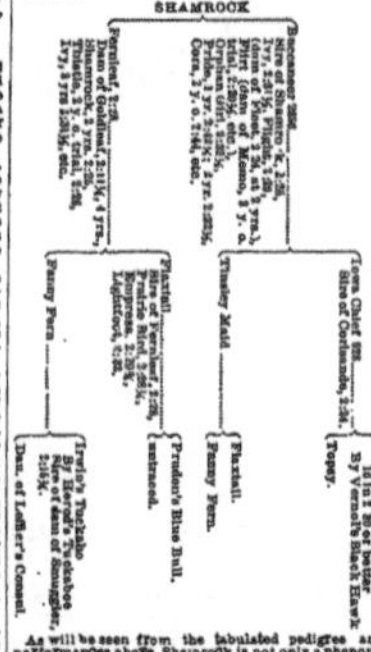

As will be seen from the tabulated pedigree and performances above, Shamrock is not only a phenomenal horse himself, but his ancestors on both sides have shown themselves to be uniformly producers of GREAT and PARTICULARLY early speed, and his record like many others of his family was made in a hotly contested race, instead of a trial against time.

HE IS NOW IN SPLENDID FORM, AND I TRULY BELIEVE WILL LOWER HIS RECORD TO 2:18 THIS YEAR.

TERMS, $100, with usual return privilege, for a limited number of CHOICE mares, season ending June 1st.

Electo.

By Antevolo 2:19¾ by Electioneer, dam Captain Webster 2:30, (sire of dam of Adonis 2:14), by Williamson's Belmont.

Electo, while but three years old this spring, is, as well as being grandly bred, a great individual.

TERMS, $50, with the usual return privilege, limited to 15 approved mares. Season to end June 1st.

Imported Cleveland bay stallion

Elegance.

(Registered in Cleveland Bay Stud Book No. 75.) Prize winner over twenty of his own breed in the GREAT YORKSHIRE SHOW OF ENGLAND.

The Cleveland Bays are the most prepotent coach horses in the world, and their get from ordinary mares makes the most stylish and serviceable horses for that purpose that can be raised. Rich bays with black points having the preference over ALL OTHERS.

TERMS, $25, with usual return privilege, season ending July 1st.

Care taken but no responsibility assumed for accidents or escapes. Pasturage, $5 per month. For further particulars call at or address me at my hospital, where horses will make the season.

G. W. STIMPSON, V. S.

Veterinary Hospital, 19th St., near San Pablo Ave, Oakland, Cal.

WOODNUT

(Weatherhead's) by Nutwood 600

Sire of Belmont Boy, 2:15, pacer, Woodnut, 2:16¾, Felix, 2 18¾, Dawn, 2:18¾, Maggie E., 2 19¾, Irma, 2 18¾, and 35 others in 2 30 or better; 1st dam Flora, 2:39¾, trial 2 26, dam of Chrisman's Hambletonian, sire of Steve Whipple, 2:22, Kate Agnew, 2:28¾, by Chieftain 721, sire of Defiance 2:17¾ pacing and 2 24 trotting, Cairo, 2:26, Onward, 2:34, pacer; second dam by Wilson's Leaman.

Woodnut is a beautiful bay with black points, 15¾ hands high, weighing 1,075 pounds. His Colts are all larger than himself, and sell readily for road and carriage purposes, being of good color and very docile, yet prompt to obey, and always ready.

Service fee, $25, with usual privileges. Colts and fillies from Tilton Almont, Patchen, Stockbridge Chief, and other desirable crosses, FOR SALE. For further particulars, pedigrees, or any communication in horse matters, address

JAS. WEATHERHEAD, Prop.

San Jose, Cal.

The Fast Trotting Stallion

REDWOOD.

Four-Year-Old Record 2:24 1-2

Will make the season of 1890—February 1st to July 1st—at the

OAKLAND RACE TRACK.

REDWOOD is a dark bay colt, 15.2¾ hands high, Weighs 1100 lbs. Foaled in 1885 by Anteeo, 2:16¾, sire of Alfred G., 2 19¾. Anteeo is by Electioneer. First dam Lou Milton, by Milton Medium; second dam Old Fly, a thoroughbred mare brought from the East in 1871 by W. C. Ralston, Esq.

Redwood's sire was out of Columbine by A. W. Richmond, the sire of the pacers Arrow 2:13¾, and Elwood 2:22, and the trotters Romero, 2:19¾, and Len Rose, 2:27. Redwood has shown a quarter in 33 seconds.

Terms $100

For the season. Mares not proving with foal may be returned next season free of charge, provided Redwood remains the property of the present owners. Good pasturage at $5 per month. No responsibility assumed for escapes or accidents. Service fees payable before removal of the mare. Limited to 30 approved mares. For further particulars address,

A. McFADYEN.

Race track, Oakland, Cal.

BAY ROSE

REGISTERED No. 9814

Record 2:20½, third Heat.

Will make the season of 1890 from March 1st to July 1st at the race track, Oakland

DESCRIPTION.

BAY ROSE is a dark bay or brown, with black points, 15 1-2 hands high and weighs 1150 pounds. He is remarkably intelligent, of good disposition and a pure gaited trotter. He was foaled in 1881. His Colts are large, stylish, rangy animals and inherit the qualities of speed and endurance.

PEDIGREE.

BAY ROSE 9814

- Sultan, 2:24, SIRE OF 19 in the 2:30 list.
  - The Moor, 870, SIRE OF Beautiful Bells, 2:29 1-2; Del Sur, 2:24 1-2; Inez, 2:3-; Sir Guy, 2:28 1-2; Sultan, 2:24; Tommy Gates, 2:24.
  - Sultana.
- Madam Baldwin.
  - The Moor, 870. Sire of 6 in the 2:30 list.
  - By Ben Lippincott by Williamson's Belmont.

TERMS: $100 FOR THE SEASON.

Good pasturage near the track, and first-class care taken of mares for $4 per month. No responsibility assumed for escapes or accidents.

For further particulars, address

W. W. AYRES,

Care of Jas. Corcoran, Race Track, Oakland, Cal.

THE MAMBRINO Patchen Stallion.

MAMBRINO JR., 1789 (formerly Carr's) Sire of Lady Ellen 2:28 (dam of Ella 2:29), Maud H. 2:30, Mambrino Boy (Carr's) 2:31 1 2.

Will stand at my farm, 2 1-2 miles north of San Jose, on the Milpitas road. Season to commence February 1st, 1890, at $40, with return privilege 1891. Fifteen mares of approved breeding, besides my own, will be given him. Parties owning good mares, performers or out of producing dams, will find an opportunity to breed them on shares, and the best of care taken of them till colt is weaned, if so desired.

PEDIGREE.

MAMBRINO JR., 1789, by Mambrino Patchen 58 [full brother of Lady Thorne 2:18 1-4] by Mambrino Chief 11. First dam by Mambrino Chief 11; 2nd dam by imp. Jordan [thoroughbred]; 3rd dam by Bertrand, son of Sir Archy; 4th dam by Chewkees, son of Sir Archy.

For further particulars address

GEO. P. BULL.

San Jose, Cal.

Box 1067.

The Trotting Stallion

CUPID,

Full Brother to Adonis 2:14,

—Sired by—

The Celebrated SIDNEY 2:19 3-4, and out of Venus.

Will make the season of 1890 at the OAKLAND TROTTING PARK.

PEDIGREE.

CUPID is by Sidney out of Venus by Capt. Webster 10173, record 2:30, and sire of Prestone 2:29. Second dam by Skenandoah 838, sire of Daisy Burns 2 29¾, Erwin Davis (sire of two in the 30 list) and dams of four in the 30 list.

DESCRIPTION.

Cupid is a handsome bright bay 15.3¾ hands high, weighs 1100 lbs.; was foaled in 1886. As a yearling, with very little work he showed quarters in 44 seconds, and at 2 years old, quarters in 36 seconds. As a three year old he has not been worked, but he shows the speed and endurance that must come from his excellent blood lines.

TERMS $50 for the season, with the usual return privileges. Good pasturage near the track at $4 per month. The best of care taken of mares in any way that owners may desire, but no responsibility assumed for accidents or escapes.

For further particulars address

C. O. THORNQUEST,

Oakland Trotting Park, or

C. BAAB, 972 Broadway, Oakland.

PASTURAGE AND FIRST-CLASS CARE

TAKEN OF

Gentlemen's Road Horses and Trotters.

Colts Broken and Trained to Harness or Saddle.

Twenty new Box Stalls. First-Class Pasturage, and the best of care given to all horses. **Terms, $4 per month.** Satisfaction Guaranteed.

Address,

K. O'GRADY,

Laural Creek Farm,

SAN MATEO, CAL.

Brushes.

BUCHANAN BROS.,

Brush Manufacturers,

609 Sacramento Street, two doors above Montgomery.

Horse Brushes of every description on hand and made to order. Bristle Body Brushes our Specialty

---

Vineland Stock Farm

Whippleton 1883,

Sire of

LILY STANLEY - - -	Record	2:17½
HOMESTAKE - -	"	2:16½
FLORA B. - - - - -	"	2:27
CORA C. - - - - -	"	2:31½
BLACK PRINCE - - - -	"	2:36½
RACHEL - - - - -	"	2:38
PRINCE W. - - -	"	2:40

WHIPPLETON is not only the sire of trotters, but he is the greatest sire of Carriage Horses on the Pacific Coast. Some of the best carriage and road teams in San Francisco are sired by Whippleton. A carriage team by Whippleton received First Premium at Napa, Petaluma, Oakland, Sacramento, Stockton and San Jose. Whippleton and his Colts have never been beaten in the show ring.

DESCRIPTION.

WHIPPLETON is black, tan muzzle and flanks, 17 hands, and weighs 1,400 lbs. Most of his colts are 16 hands or over, and with a few exceptions, bay, brown or black. He never sired a sorrel or white face colt. (If he does, I agree to refund service money.)

PEDIGREE.

WHIPPLETON, sired by Hambletonian Jr. (sire of Hancock 2.29), by Whipple's Hambletonian (sire of Graves, 2:19, Westfield, 2:20¾, Express, 2:24, and 12 others in the 2:30 list), dam Lady Livingston (dam of Lady Blanchard, 2 26¾, Bloomfield Maid, trial 2:22), by General Taylor (sire of the dams of Wells Fargo, 2:18¾, Nerea, 2:23¾, Bickford, 2:29¾, Lady Blanchard, 2:26¾, etc., and sire of grandam of Hazel Wilkes, 2:20) by the Morse Horse 6 sire of Norman 25 (sire of Lulu, 2:14¾, May Queen 2:20, etc.).

TERMS at $50, limited to 20 mares, for the season, usual return privileges. I would like to get about ten well bred mares with the proper combination of blood to breed to Whippleton on shares this season.

Alcona 730.

Sire of

FLORA BELLE - - -	Record	2:24
CLAY DUKE - - - - -	"	2:31½

ALCONA will be a great sire, but four of his colts have ever been trained, and all have shown full miles better than 2:30, and two of them as good as 2:20. Two of his first sons each sired a colt as a two-year-old, and last season one as a four-year-old trotted a full mile in 2:23¾, and the other, a three-year-old, a mile in 2:31. With opportunities, Alcona is destined to be one of Almont's best sons. Almont, for his opportunities, is beyond doubt the most prepotent sire of his age. He has 36 representatives in the 2:30 list; 40 sons and 22 daughters that have already produced 2:30 performers. Almont died five years ago at 20 years old. If he lived he would be but 25 years old.

PEDIGREE.

ALCONA sired by the great Almont (sire of Westmont 2:13¾, Fanny Witherspoon 2:16¾, Piedmont 2:17¾, and 31 others with records better than 2:30, and grandsire of Belle Hamlin 2 13¾, etc.); by Alexander's Abdallah (sire of Goldsmith Maid 2:14), he by Rysdyk's Hambletonian. Alcona's dam, Queen Mary, by Mambrino Chief (sire of Lady Thorne 2 18 1-4, and 5 others in the 2:30 list, and sire of the dams of Director 2:17, Piedmont 2:17¾, Onward 2:25 1-4, Red Wilkes Almont, Belmont and many other noted sires).

DESCRIPTION.

Alcona is a beautiful chestnut 16 3 1-2 hands high, and weighs 1300 lbs. His colts possess speed, style, finish and beauty, and if they don't trot they command the highest prices for carriage horses.

$40 for the season. Usual return privilege.

Season on Whippleton and Alcona ends July 1st, 1890.

Best kind of pasturage at $4 per month. Mares kept in any manner desired.

For further particulars send for circular or call at stables, one mile south of St. Helena.

FRED W. LOEBER.

St. Helena, Napa Co., Cal.

The Trotting Stallion

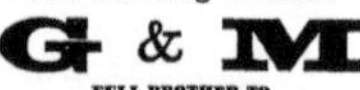

FULL BROTHER TO

ALFRED G, 2:19¾.

(Who has been taken to Kentucky to stand at $200)

Will make the season of 1890 from FEBRUARY 1st to JULY 1st, at

SANTA ROSA.

G. & M. is by Anteeo, 2:16¾; was foaled 1886; first dam Rosa R. by Speculation (son of Hambletonian 10); 2d dam Elizabeth by Alexander 490; 3d dam Nora by imp. Glencoe. Anteeo is by Electioneer, out of Columbine by A. W. Richmond 1687.

G. & M. is a handsome dark bay; stands 16-2 1-2 hands high, and weighs 1060 pounds. Gameness, stoutness, speed and stamina are indelibly impressed in every line of the pedigree of G. & M. Owners of broodmares in search of these qualities, will do well to patronize this promising colt.

PHILOSOPHER,

Foaled 1886 by Pilot Wilkes 2987; first dam Bella by George Wilkes 519; second dam by Bell Morgan 81.

Philosopher's sire, Pilot Wilkes 2987, is by George Wilkes 519, dam Grace (the dam of Alice Woodburn, etc.), by Pilot Jr. 12, grandam by Orphan Boy.

Will make the season of 1890, from FEBRUARY 1st to JULY 1st, at Santa Rosa.

TERMS for the season:

G. & M., $50,

PHILOSOPHER, $30,

with privilege of returning mares that do not prove in foal the next season free of charge, provided the horse bred to remains the property of the present owners. Good pasturage at $3 per month. No responsibility assumed for accidents or escapes. Service fees payable before removal of the mare. For further particulars, address

GEO. E. GUERNE,

Santa Rosa Cal.

Highland Farm,

LEXINGTON, KY.,

Home of Red Wilkes.

Standard-bred Trotting Stock

For Sale,

Sired by Red Wilkes, Wilton, 2:19¾; Allandorf and Sentinel Wilkes, out of highly bred Standard Mares of the most fashionable blood of the day.

W. C. FRANCE, Proprietor.

Race Track for Sale.

The One Mile Track & Grounds

—OF THE—

Sonoma County Agricul'l Park Association,

Situated at

SANTA ROSA, CALIFORNIA,

Consisting of 84 acres fine agricultural land, 700 Box and Cattle Stalls, a two story Pavilion 60x120, commodious grand stand, and many out-buildings, a lovely Park of 15 acres, rolling ground, ornamental, nut and native oak trees; a fine cypress "windbreak" hedge ¾ mile around the track, and abundant water facilities. This elegant property will be sold at a great bargain, and possession given immediately if required. Sealed bids for same will be received up to February 17th, 1890.

B. M. SPENCER, Secretary.
GUY E. GROSSE, President.

For Sale

A FIRST-CLASS

Napa County Farm

—OR—

STOCK RANCH,

800 Acres Improved,

SITUATED TWO AND A HALF MILES FROM NAPA CITY, with good roads leading thereto, a good hard finished house of nine rooms, with all modern improvements, streams running all summer, a great amount of live oak and black oak timber. It lies in a fruit belt, surrounded by fine vineyards and orchards growing upon the same quality of soil, and originally a part of this tract. About one-half hill, and one-half rolling land, but none of it is steep and all easily cultivated, splendidly situated for the breeding of fine horses. Price, $65 per acre. Further particulars given at this office.

BREEDER AND SPORTSMAN,
313 Bush St.

Stallion for Sale

AT A BARGAIN.

Full Brother to Fairmont.

By Piedmont, dam Queen by Garibaldi—see State Fair Edition of BREEDER AND SPORTSMAN, September 14, 1889, for description of Fairmont—three years old, solid bay. Can trot a 2:10 gait or better. Sound in every particular. Can be seen at Oakland Trotting Park, Oakland.

P. J. WILLIAMS.

Attention Stockmen!

FOR SALE

At Chowchilla Ranch,

Thoroughbred Durham Cattle

Three Hundred Young DAIRY COWS, 2000 graded SHE CATTLE, Yearlings and up; a fine lot of high grade Durham Bulls; also have Mares, Horses, Mules and Norman Colts.

For particulars, apply to

ISAAC BIRD, JR., Supt.,
Merced, California.

FOR SALE

AT

Vineland Stock Farm

STALLIONS, BROODMARES AND FILLIES

ONE STALLION FIVE YEARS OLD, SEAL-BROWN, by WHIPPLETON (sire of Lily Stanley, 2:17 1-2, Homestakes 2:16 1-2, etc.), dam Sally Gorham by Werner's Rattler. This horse is scarcely 15 1-2 hands high, but very compactly built. He breeds exceptionally large and well finished colts. Any one understanding the business could clear him in one season, or he would make a No. 1 road horse, as he can trot a 40 gait any time.

ONE THREE-YEAR-OLD, SEAL-BROWN, by WHIPPLETON (sire of Lily Stanley, 2:17 1-2, Homestakes 2:16 1-2, etc.), dam Sally Gorham, etc. This ought to make a great General Purpose sire, and with opportunities get trotters, as he is compact, strong-boned, and will measure when grown about 16 hands and weighs 1,200 lbs. With a little road work last fall he developed a wonderful burst of speed.

ONE THREE-YEAR-OLD, BLACK, by WHIPPLETON (sire of Lily Stanley, 2:17 1-2, etc.), dam by Naubuc (sire of the dam of Eva W., 2:23 1-2, etc.), full brother to Thomas Jefferson, 2:23. This horse will be fully 16 1-2 hands high. He is smooth rapid gaited and from size and conformation should breed, like his sire, large, rangy, finished colts.

ONE TWO-YEAR-OLD, BRIGHT CHESTNUT, sired by DAWN 2:18¾, dam Alida (dam of Directa, three-year-old record 2:31¼, trial 2:26) by Admiral (sire of sister 2:19 1-2, Nona Y 2:25, etc.). This colt is the making of an extraordinary horse. He is large boned and will be over sixteen hands high when grown; he is of the true Nutwood type, is clean gaited and can lead a piece as fast as any man's colt.

ONE TWO-YEAR-OLD, BLOOD BAY, (full brother to Alcona Jr. sire of Silas Skinner, trial 2:23) sired by ALCONA (sire of Flora Belle 2:24, etc.,) dam Madonna by Cassius M. Clay Jr. This colt will make a trotter and a great stock horse if developed; he has the combined blood of Almont, Mambrino Chief, Cassius M. Clay Jr. and Joe Downing.

These colts are all sound and promising. The only reason I offer them for sale is, that I have three aged stallions in use, and the surplus is growing on me. If I were starting a breeding business for profit, I should consider either of these colts a representative to commence with. Also brood mares and fillies for sale. Correspondence solicited.

FRED. W. LOESER, St. Helena.
Napa Co., Cal.

Woodside Farm

IMPORTANT SALE OF

Standard Trotting Mares Young Stallions and Fillies,

ROAD AND DRIVING HORSES
Farming Implements,
Etc.

By direction of MRS. SILAS SKINNER.

Mrs. Skinner having determined to retire permanently from the breeding of Fine Stock, has decided to offer at

PUBLIC AUCTION

Thursday, March 6, '90,

at 12 M., on the Premises.

THE WELL-KNOWN

WOODSIDE FARM,

Near Napa,

together with all the highly bred trotting stock thereon.

The brood mares at Woodside are among the choicest in the State. Among them are mares by Almont, dam by Alexander's Abdallah; by Cassius M. Clay Jr., dam by Joe Downing; by Cassius M. Clay Jr., dam by Richelieu son of Mambrino Chief; by Duke of Orange Jr., dam by Cassius M. Clay Jr.; by Almont Mambrino, dam by Blood's Black Hawk; by Alcona—dam Fontana, dam of Flora Belle, 2:24, and Silas Skinner, trial 2:20¼—by Almont; by Alcona Clay—dam Metamora, dam of Clay Duke, 2:31¼—by Duke of Orange Jr. These mares have been bred to Director, Noonday, Mountain Boy and Wildwood, and are with foal. The young stallions are by Sitka, son of Alaska, by Electioneer, Whippleton, sire of Lillie Stanley, 2:17¼, Alcona Clay, etc. About twenty head well-bred trotting and driving animals will be sold in addition to the standard bred horses.

Catalogues giving extended pedigrees and full information are being prepared, and will be forwarded upon application.

At the conclusion of sale of horses.

WOODSIDE FARM

will be sold.

WOODSIDE FARM is situated three and a half miles from Napa City, up the river, upon what is known as the middle or big ranch road. It contains 87 1-2 acres of the choicest quality of land for alfalfa or any kind of grain, 40 acres being now in alfalfa, over a foot high. The land produces from four to six tons of hay to the acre, of choice quality. Five of the fields are in pasture, four in alfalfa, one in timothy, the other kept in hay or grain necessary for stock, though well adapted for alfalfa. There is a nice orchard, small vineyard, and comfortable dwelling house of nine rooms. There is a good school house directly opposite, the best in the County. As to its adaptability as a stock ranch: There is living water in every field, and plenty of it, corrals and stock yards, stable room for forty horses, besides seven good box stalls, two good stables, granery, etc. It is within two miles of the Napa Agricultural Society's race track, the finest constructed in the State for years. Should there not be sufficient land, 52 acres adjoining can be purchased at reasonable figures.

There is no more eligible location in the State for a small stock farm, and this affords a rare opportunity, with the stock, to at once engage in this remunerative pursuit.

The sale will be positive. Upon all sales of Live Stock and personal property, one years' credit will be given on approved notes. Interest 10 per cent. per annum. Three per cent. discount for cash.

Upon Land, one-half cash; balance can remain upon mortgage for a term of years to suit purchasers. Interest eight per cent. per annum.

Vehicles will be in attendance at Napa Depot to convey parties to the farm. Lunch will be served upon the ground.

Mrs. Skinner having large interests in Oregon which will require her personal attention during the greater portion of the year, compels the sale of the Woodside Farm.

Parties are invited to visit the farm and look over the stock. The undersigned will be glad to give any information required, either as to stock or ranch.

KILLIP & CO.
Live Stock Auctioneers,
22 Montgomery St., S. F.

For Sale

A HALF BROTHER TO

ALMONT PATCHEN,

(2:15, trial 2:13 3-4).

JUANITO JR. is a beautiful bright bay, black points, with no white, foaled 1886. As a colt he has given much more promise than did Almont Patchen at the same age. Instead of being a pacer, he is a good square trotter, with every indication of great speed, and is so gentle and kind, that a lady can drive him. The owner's only reason for selling him is that business calls him away from this section of the State. He will be sold at a reasonable figure. This is a splendid opportunity for a gentleman to secure a first-class trotter at a very low figure.

The pedigree of Juanito Jr. is by Juanito (sire of Almont Patchen), dam Nettie Moore by Old Tom Moore. For further particulars, address

JUANITO JR.,
Santa Clara P. O., Cal.

Antevolo Colt

For Sale.

AVOLO REX, foaled February 22, 1888; dam Catchup by Rustic; grandam Huntress by Don Victor; g g dam Betty Denice by American Boy Jr. Is 15.1 hands high, well developed, muscular, and without a blemish. Has a very gentle disposition, and shows speed and a good gait. Apply

HOME FURNISHING CO.,
113 Fifth Street, S. F., Cal.

For Sale

A First-Class.

BREEDING FARM.

Of 800 Acres.

Four hours' ride from the City. Good roads to a first class track. Climate unexcelled. Plenty of wood and running water.

For further information apply to the office of the

BREEDER AND SPORTSMAN,
313 Bush Street. San Francisco.

First Special Auction Sale

—OF—

HORSES,

For account of CAPT. BEN. E. HARRIS,

On Saturday, March 1, '90

At the Cor. TURK and STEINER STS.,

WE WILL SELL AT

Public Auction

A CATALOGUE OF 25 HEAD OF SUPERIOR ROADSTERS AND SADDLE-HORSES OF ALL GAITS.

Also a few select colts, mares and fillies of royal breeding, most all of which have been bred, raised and broken by Captain Harris, whose reputation for the culture of swift roadsters and saddle horses to a high degree, is sufficient to warrant the public a rare opportunity for supplying their wants without the risk of disappointment. Among the lot there are several pairs of roadsters, one of which can trot in 2:30, besides a number of extra fine single flyers.

☞ The attention of ladies is particularly called to this sale, as many of the animals have been prepared especially for their use and safety.

This stock may be seen at the owner's stables, corner of Turk and Steiner Streets, from now until day of sale.

TERMS cash, or an equivalent in approved paper. Catalogues at our office.

KILLIP & CO.,
Live Stock Auctioneers.
22 Montgomery St., S. F.

For Sale.

14

Pure bred

PERCHERONS.

Stallions and Mares.

OF ALL AGES.

Part Imported, and all Registered Proof.

For further information, address

E. J. TURNER, Hollister, Cal.

Well bred Stallions

FOR SALE.

SATINWOOD

Is 3 years old, stands 16.1 hands high and weighs 1150 pounds; is a beautiful dark chestnut; was sired by Wormwood, a full brother to Eva W (2:25) and Redwood (2:27). First dam by John Nelson; second dam by Argyle; third dam Blackhawk Worm - ood by Nutwood 2:28 3-4, sire of Woodnut 2:16 1-4; dam the Cropey Mare by Naubuc, dam Gipsy Queen by George M. Patchen; second dam Capt. Roberts Mare. Nutwood 2:18 3-4, by Belmont, dam Miss Russell (dam of Maud S. 2:08 3-4. Belmont, by Abdallah (sire of Goldsmith Maid) dam Belle by Mambrino Chief. Miss Russell, by Pilot Jr. dam Sally Russell by Boston.

Full pedigree and all particulars on application.

J. A. C.

Sorrell stallion, foaled April 22nd, 1887. Bred by Wm. Jeffries of San Francisco, Cal. Sired by C. C. Bemis' Lancelot. First dam Bay Mare Nellie, sired by Ulster Chief he by Rysdyk's Hambletonian, her dam by Kentucky Hunter, noted for his speed and endurance (see Stud Book).

For further particulars apply to

J. A. CARLETON,
1302 Broadway, Oakland, Cal.

ARGONAUT HERD.

POLLED ABERDEEN—ANGUS CATTLE.

Thirty head choice pure bred and high grade (cross bred) HEIFERS and a few grand young BULLS for sale at reasonable prices. A fine opportunity for persons wishing to establish choice herds or change their bulls. Representatives from this herd were grand prize winners at the last California State Fair. Address

DR. G. M. DIXON,
Sacramento, Cal.

NOTICE.

C. BRUCE LOWE,

Pedigree Stock Agent,

19 Bligh Street,

SYDNEY, New South Wales.

Reference—J. B. HAGGIN, ESQ.

HOLLYWOOD BREEDING FARM.

MOUNTAIN BOY 4841.

Brs MOUNTAIN BOY, 4841, bred by Charles Backman, Orange County, New York, foaled 1882, sire Kentucky Prince 2470, dam Elise, sister to Elaine, by Messenger Duroc 106; grandam Green Mountain Maid, 3d dam, Shanghai Mary, will serve a limited number of mares at $100 the season.

ELECTION.

Bay stallion ELECTION, bred at Senator Stanford's Palo Alto Stock Farm, foaled 1884, sire Electioneer, dam Lizzie H. by Whipple's Hambletonian 725, grandam Lizzie Harris (by Comus son of Green's Bashaw 50), great grandam by Arnold Harris, thoroughbred.

Election is one of the handsomest bloodlike sons of Electioneer, and with his thoroughbred cross through Arnold Harris should prove invaluable as a sire. TERMS, $100 the season.

KAFIR.

B c KAFIR, bred by L. J. Rose, Los Angeles, foaled 1887, sire Alcazar, 2:20½, dam Flower Girl by Arthurton, sire of Arab, 2:15, grandam Flora by General McClellan, 144, sire of three in 2:30 list, great grand dam by Langford, he by Williamson's Belmont, will serve a limited number of mares at $60 the season.

WOODSIDE.

Ch c WOODSIDE, sire Woodnut, 2:16½; 1st dam Veronica by Alcona, 730; 2nd dam Fontana by Almont, 33; 3rd dam Fannie Williams by Alexander's Abdallah, 15. Book full.

MART BOORHEM.

B c MART BOORHEM, by Sydney, 2:19¾; 1st dam Towhead by Echo. This colt is a full brother to St. Nicholas who showed a mile in 2:27½ at three years old. TERMS, $25 the season.

REVEILLE.

The well known thoroughbred stallion REVEILLE, by Shiloh, dam by Norfolk. Reveille is a brother to John Treat and is the sire of Tycoon and Gladstone. TERMS, $25 the season.

Hollywood is nicely situated three miles from Vallejo on the Napa road. Good pasturage and every care will be taken of mares at reasonable rates. For further particulars, apply,

B. C. HOLLY, Vallejo.

CANNON BALL, 8820

BY SIMMONS 2744.

RECORD 2:28, (Full Brother to Rosa Wilkes, 2:18 1-4), Sire of Nine in 2:30 List at 10 Years Old.

First dam Gurgle, pacing record 2:20; trial of 2:15½ for W. H. Crawford; by Pocahontas Boy, sire of Buffalo Girl, 2:12½; Raven Boy, 2:15½, and ten others in the list.

Second dam Matlock by Grey Diomed.

Third dam by Tom Hal.

DESCRIPTION.

Brown bay, right hind foot and left inside hind heel white. Foaled May 20, 1887. Bred by W. M. Wilson, Abdallah Park, Cynthiana, Ky.

He is a grand individual, large boned, fine size and appearance. When fully matured will probably be 16 hands, and weigh 1200 lbs.

Is of speedy conformation and level headed. His blood lines are stout and fashionable, being the Wilkes and Mambrino Patchen on pacing and thoroughbred foundations, and from a family of producers on both sides.

Can be seen until February 1st at Agricultural Park, Los Angeles, in charge of C. A. Durfee, after which he will serve ten approved mares at $60 the season, with usual privilege of return in 1891, at Lockhaven Stock Farm, Burbank, Cal. Mares kept on grass $4 per month, and extra charge where grain and alfalfa are fed. For further particulars, address

O. H. LOCKHART, Proprietor,
Lockhaven Stock Farm,
Burbank, Cal.

Nine Miles from Los Angeles.

The Pure Trotting-bred Stallion

ILLUSTRIOUS

STANDARD No. 4178.

DESCRIPTION.

Dark bay, black points, 16 1-2 hands high, weight 1000 pounds, foaled May 30, 1885; bred by General W. T. Withers, Lexington, Ky.

PEDIGREE.

By Happy Medium, sire of Maxey Cobb 2:13¼ and 52 with records of 2:30 or better. First dam Abdallietta by Cassius M. Clay Jr., sire of Durango 2:23¾, Harry Clay 2:23¾ and sire of the dams of Minnehaha, Bertha 2:27¾, Charley West 2:28¾, Grandmont 2:25 1-4, Lottie K 2:26¾, Mambrino Diamond 2:28, Richwood 2:28 1-2, Topsy 2:29¾, Happy Thought 2:21 1-2, Pequot 2:23 1-2, Fairlawn Medium 2:27 1-4, Folley 2:27¾ and Mambrino Boy 2:26 1-2; second dam Laura Crockett by Almont, sire of Westmont 2:13¾, Puritan 2:16, Fanny Witherspoon 2:16¾, Piedmont 2:17¼, Aline 2:19½ and 37 with records better than 2:30; third dam Sally Tee by Alexander's Abdallah, sire of Goldsmith Maid 2:14; fourth dam Kate Crockett, the dam of Lulu 2:14¾, by imp Hooton.

Illustrious is a horse of extra fine finish, large clean bone, good feet, back short and strong, loins and quarters well muscled, and powerful. He has a kind disposition and splendid trotting action, and is as handsome and bloodlike in form and finish as any trotting stallion in the land.

He is pronounced by his breeder, General Withers, to be the best bred son of Happy Medium living, and is undoubtedly one of the very best bred trotting stallions in the State. He has had but six weeks' regular training, and a part of that time was sick with epizootic, but was trotted quarters in 39 1-4 seconds, and barring accidents will certainly trot better than 2:30 this season.

TERMS—$50 the season. Mares not proving with foal may be returned next year free.

Good pasturage at $3 per month.

Season to begin February 1st and end June 15th.

GEO. A. STONE,
Santa Rosa, Cal.

Guenoc Stud Farm, Lake Co., Cal.

Imp. GREENBACK

(Sire of the English winners Greenlight, Greenjacket, Greenshank, Greenwave and Greenhorn)

By Dollar, dam Music, by Stockwell. $100 the Season

ST. SAVIOR,

(FULL BROTHER TO EOLE)

By Eolus, dam War Song, by War Dance. $100 the Season.

PASTURAGE, $5 PER MONTH.

With right to return the following year if mare does not prove with foal. The best of care taken, but no liability for accidents or escapes. Mares shipped to C. W. ABY, care of ST. HELENA STABLES, St. Helena Napa County, will be taken in charge by competent men.

For further information write to

DR. C. W. ABY, Middletown, Lake County, Cal.

SOUTHER FARM

P. O. Box 208. San Leandro, Cal.

1½ miles northwest of San Leandro; 3 miles southeast of Oakland. Turn off County road between above places at "Stanley Road," ¾ mile north of San Leandro.

Horses boarded at all times in any manner desired. Best of care but no responsibility for accidents. Colts broken and handled for the road or track. Terms reasonable.

Glen Fortune,	Jester D,	El Benton,	Figaro,
By Electioneer.	By Almont.	By Electioneer.	Hambletonian 725
$50 for 1889.	$50 for 1890.	Limited to 5 mares.	Limited to 12 mares
		Book Full.	Book Full.

If horses are to last for a profitable time they must occasionally have a change from hard pavements, wooden floors, and dry, hard feed.

THE SOUTHER FARM

Has Green Feed the Year Round,

and feeds Hay in connection with the green feed; which a horse must have if he is to thrive. Every animal is given

A Dry, Warm Place to Sleep,

No matter how stormy the weather. All Stock under cover when it rains.

VISITORS WELCOME ANY DAY EXCEPT SUNDAY.

Write to the above address for references, circulars and price lists. Terms reasonable.

GILBERT TOMPKINS, Proprietor.

SAN MATEO STOCK FARM

HOME OF GUY WILKES,

Record, 2:15 1-4.

Guy Wilkes' Book is full for 1890 and 1891, and positively no more mares will be received.

Sable Wilkes, three-year-old record 2:18, will be allowed to serve 25 mares in addition to those already engaged at $250 the season of 1890. SABLE Wilkes, 15½ hands, black horse, by Guy Wilkes, first dam Sable by The Moor; second dam Gretchen by Mambrino Pilot; third dam Kitty Kirkman by Canada Chief; fourth dam by Fanning's Tobe; fifth dam by imp. Leviathan.

Leo Wilkes, brown horse, four years, 16 hands, full brother to Sable Wilkes, will be allowed to serve 30 mares at $100 the season

Mares not proving with foal may be returned the following season free of service fee. Parties engaging the services of any of the above horses must send a deposit of 10 per cent. of service money with engagement. Pasturage $6 per month, and when the condition of the animal requires it, hay or grain, or both, are fed, the charge will be $12 50 Per month. Good care will be taken of all mares sent to the Farm, but no liability will be assumed for accidents or escapes.

All bills are due at time of service, but must be paid by August 1st of each year. No stock will be allowed to leave the place until all bills are paid.

WILLIAM CORBITT.
San Mateo Stock Farm.

Poplar Grove Breeding FARM.

Standard-bred Trotters, Colts and Fillies.

The get of CLOVIS, 4909; PASHA, 2039; APEX, 8935.

For Sale.

Address S. N. STRAUBE, Poplar Grove Breeding Farm,

Fresno, Cal.

Inspection by intending purchasers invited, and information by mail.

1890 Three Anteeo Stallions 1890

SUNSET, 5 years old, by Anteeo
ANTEEOF, 4 years old, by Anteeo
ANTEEOP, 3 years old, by Anteeo

ANTEEO. Standard 786 Record, 2:16 1-4, by Stanford Electioneer, and dam Columbine.

DESCRIPTIONS, PEDIGREES AND CONDITIONS.

"SUNSET" is a rich, dark bay, small star on forehead, portion of hind left foot white; was foaled March 17, 1885; is by ANTEEO and the inbred HAMBLETONIAN mare, BESSIE G, she by KING PHILLIP, son of WHIPPLE'S HAMBLETONIAN. He is 16 1-2 hands high, and weighs 1,200 lbs. He is of perfect build and splendid action, cool headed and g es. speed for his size, having trotted a trial mile as a three-year-old in 2:34. He then e tered heavy in the stud and was matched against Whalebone at the Healdsburg races November 4, 1889, winning just as he pleased in three straight heats; time, 2:47, 2 46 1-2, 2:52 1-2. He was then matched for a race to come off last Thanksgiving Day at Petaluma but owing to the heavy rains the event did not take place. A few days previous to Thanksgiving Day Mr. Lawrence worked Sunset out and then he trotted three square miles and heats in 2:33¾, 2:34 and 2:37.

SUNSET will be bred to 40 mares only, at $60 each, no colt no pay.

"ANTEEOF" is a jet black, was foaled April 13, 1886, is 16¼ hands high, and weighs 1,200 lbs., has a very fine, heavy black mane and tail; is well proportioned, moves majestically, is of easy, lofty carriage; is symmetrical, in fact is a beautiful horse. He was sired by Anteeo and the O. A. Taylor mare "Nance," her dam was raised by Dr. Oliver Plummer, of Consumnes, Cal., and sired by "Napoleon"; Napoleon was foaled May 29, 1849, and raised by James Kyle of Butler County, Ohio. He was sired by Benj. Sweet's horse Bellfounder, and he by Old Bellfounder, his dam was sired by Doc. Daniel Mulligan's horse, Cadmus, G. G. sire the celebrated Eclipse; his G. dam was sired by Big Shakespeare, G. G., sires dam by Messenger and Expedition. ANTEEOF will be bred to 25 mares only, at $50 each. No colt, no pay.

"ANTEEOP" is a rich seal brown; was foaled March 7, 1887; by Anteeo and the inbred Hambletonian mare Bessie G., also dam of Sunset, his full brother and Midget his full sister; he is 15 1-2 hands high and weighs 950 lbs. and measures 22 inches around the arm, good head, fine neck, full, broad breast; withers and rump on nearly equal line, well proportioned bones, ankle shoulders, loins and hips; strong legs all around, with great muscular development and splendid sinews; wirey pasterns and sound, compact feet; the lines from hip to hoof show power and speed; stands square and has excellent action, has a superb lustrous coat of rich deep brown fur of seal color without defect; an even, honest trotter, and has gone the mile as a two-year-old in 3:12, the last quarter in 38 seconds; is intelligent and of high spirit, with much temper, but is not vicious, has very fine eyes, is a handsome, showy colt; attractive in harness.

ANTEEOP will be bred to 15 mares only, at $50. No colt, no pay.

SEASON to commence February 1st, ending July 1, 1890. Book now ready. Apply to John H. Lawrence, "Manager and Trainer," on my fruit and hop ranch, 1 mile east of Court House, on Sonoma road. Excellent pasture furnished with running water, also dry knolls with oak shelter, at $4 per month for mares. Two of the above stallions will be for sale after the expiration of the their stud season.

GUY E. GROSSE,
SANTA ROSA, SONOMA CO., CAL.

Valensin Stock Farm Stallions,

SIDNEY, 2:19 3-4.

At Eight Years of Age Sire of the following Fastest on Record:

FAUSTINO, yearling stallion, record of the world 2:35
FLEET, fastest yearling record in 1888 .... 2:36
FLEET, fastest two-year-old filly in 1889 .... 2:24
GOLD LEAF, fastest four-year-old Pacing record in the world 2:11½
ADONIS, fastest three-year-old Pacing Gelding in the world 2:14½
ADONIS, four-year-old Gelding Pacing record 2:14

—Also the Sire of—

LONGWORTH, four years old 2:19
SISTER V., four years old (trial 2:23) 2:27
SANTA RITA 2:39
MEMO, two-year-old (three-year-old trial 2:20½) 2:49

And many others.

SIDNEY is the sire of Faustino 2:35, and Fleet 2:36, the two fastest yearlings the world has ever known by one sire, and his slowest yearling is faster than the great Electioneer's fastest.

Terms, $250, with usual return privileges, for a limited number of approved mares. Book nearly full.

Only eight more mares can be taken for Season of '90.

Pasturage $5 per month. Reasonable charges if fed hay and grain. Best of care taken of mares, but positively no responsibility assumed for accidents or escapes. For further particulars address

G. VALENSIN, Pleasanton, Cal.

The Trotting Stallion

Guide 2:29

(At Four Years)

Will make the season of 1890 at the SANTA RITA RANCH, about one mile North of Pleasanton.

DESCRIPTION.

GUIDE is a handsome seal brown, five years old, stands 15¾ hands high, and weighs 1085 pounds. He is of fine form, level headed, intelligent, and comes from blood lines that are noted for the qualities of speed and gameness.

PEDIGREE.

GUIDE, 2:28½.

- Director, 2:17. Sire of Direct, 2 18¾. Margaret S., 2:19¾.
  - Dictator 113. Sire of 23 trotters and 3 pacers in 2:30.
    - Hambletonian 10.
    - Clara, by American Star 14.
  - Dolly. Dam of Onward, 2:25¾. Thorndale, 2:22¾.
    - Mambrino Chief 11.
    - Fannie, by Ben Franklin.
- Imogene.
  - Norwood 522. Sire of Tommy Norwood, 2:26¾.
    - Hambletonian 10.
    - Lady Fallis, by American Star 14.
  - daughter of
    - American Star 14.
    - daughter of Harry Clay 45.

The attention of breeders is especially called to the above pedigree as showing 3 crosses of American Star.

GUIDE trotted into the 2:30 list last season with little training, and he will trot into the 2:20 list the coming season barring accidents.

Guide's sire has a record of 2:17, made in a five heat race, and Guide is closely related to Phallas, who made a record of 2 13¾ in a fourth heat, and to Jay-Eye-See, record 2:10.

TWO HUNDRED AND FIFTY DOLLARS will be given to the owner of the first of the produce of Guide put in the 2:30 list, and $100 to each one after the first.

TERMS—$75 for the season, with the usual return privileges.

Admiro,

Sire Admiral; dam by San Bruno, by Easton's David Hill.

This magnificent horse is a handsome bay, eight years old; stands 17 1-2 hands high, and weighs 1400 pounds. He is very speedy for a large horse, and breeds fine large carriage horses. His produce possess every qualification of the Cleveland Bay, with the added qualities of speed and endurance resulting from his high trotting breeding.

TERMS—$35 for the season, with usual return privileges.

Will stand three days each week at Santa Rita Ranch, Pleasanton, and at A. T. Hatch's Ranch "Almono," Alamo, Contra Costa County, alternately. All mares sent care of SMITH & SUTHERLAND, Pleasanton will be taken in charge of on arrival, and will receive the best care and attention in any manner the owners may desire. Good pasturage at $4 per month. Only a limited number of approved mares will be served by this horse this season.

No responsibility assumed for escapes or accidents. For further particulars, address

SMITH & SUTHERLAND, Pleasanton,

or A. T. HATCH, care Palace Hotel, San Francisco.

J. O'KANE, Horse Boots, Clothing and Furnishings, For Track, Driving Training and Stable. Every requisite for Horsemen. Harness, Medicines, Etc

PASHA,

Registered No. 2039.

RECORD 2:36.

SIRE OF MORO 2:27.

Will make the present season at Linden, twelve miles east of STOCKTON,

Season commencing FEBRUARY 1st and ending JULY 1, 1890.

DESCRIPTION.

PASHA is a beautiful black; 16½ hands high, and weighs 1,240 pounds. He is a horse of beautiful symmetry and magnificent action.

PEDIGREE.

PASHA was sired by Sultan 1518, sire of Stamboul 2:12½, Ruby 2:18½, Alcazar 2:20½, Bay Rose 2:20½, and sixteen others with records below 2:30. First dam Madam Baldwin by The Moor 870; second dam Ben Lippincott by Belmont. Pasha is a full brother to Bay Rose, record 2:20½.

Sultan, by The Moor, sire of Beautiful Bells, dam of Hinda Rose, 2:19½, Bell Boy 2:19¼, and Sable, dam of Sable Wilkes, three-year-old record 2:18. First dam Sultana, by Delmonico, sire of Derby 2:16, by Guy Miller, sire of Whipple's Hambletonian. Second dam by Mambrino Chief. Third dam by Downing's Bay Messenger. Fourth dam Miss Caudle, dam of Ericsson, four-year-old recor 2:30½.

Terms for the season, $50.

With privilege of returning mares that do not prove in foal next season free of charge.

Good pasturage at $2 per month No responsibility will be assumed for accidents or escapes Service fee payable before the removal of the mare.

For further particulars, address

D. BRYSON,
Linden Cal.

DESIGNER, 11,157

Son of Director 2:17.

Sire of DIRECT, 2:18½, as a four-year-old, (lapping out PALO ALTO in 2:16½), and MARGARET S., 2:19¼, as a three-year-old, and GUIDE, 2:28½, as a three-year-old. DIRECTOR is brother to JAY-EYE-SEE, 2:10, and PHALLAS, 2:13¾.

At the State Fair of 1889, he received the Gold Medal as the best producer of averaged speed in colts of two, three and four years of age, beating Electioneer, Guy Wilkes, Sidney, Stamboul and others. He is the only trotting sire who has to his credit two performers in the 2:20 list, when his oldest colts were only four years old; his services are eagerly sought by breeders, with a fee of $300.

Designer's dam is May Queen, by Abbotsford, 2:19½, sire of Conde, 2:19¼; Abbotsford is brother to Pancoast, 2:21¾, sire of Patron, 2:14¼.

May Queen was never trained. When two years old was driven over the road three weeks, and trotted to a cart two miles in six minutes. A few days after she paced a quarter in 40 seconds bare-footed; after being shoed she trotted a quarter in 37 seconds.

Second dam by Elmo, 2:27¾ (half mile in 1:06), full sister in blood to Overman, 2:19 1-4, sister to the sire of L. C. Lee, 2:16, made when he defeated Arab in a match-race in three straight heats in 2:15, 2:17, 2:17¾. Only two of her produce were handled very little, one trotted as a three-year-old, with three weeks' work early in the spring, a mile in 2:35, last quarter in 35 seconds; the other trotted as a three-year-old, a mile in 2:37¾, quarters in 35 seconds, with seven weeks' work. If her produce had been given proper training, she would surely have had three in the 2:30 list.

Third dam by David Hill, sire of Geo. Treat, 2:25 1-4, and Black Swan, 2:28¾.

Fourth dam by Gen. Taylor, sire of the dam of Wells Fargo, 2:18¾.

Fifth dam by Williamson's Belmont.

Designer is a rich bay horse, 5 years old, 15¾ hands high, weighs 1,050 pounds, disposition the very best, has a perfect gait, and shows every indication of being very fast. He has never been trained, but will be given a low record, barring accidents. He is a horse of great substance and high finish; his family on both sides are producers of great speed, and he can not fail to make a great producer, as his colts inherit all these qualities—the same disposition and natural trotting action being large, and showing great breeding. He has but 14 colts in all (three two-year-olds); one of them has been broken, and last Fall trotted a quarter in 40¾ seconds, which proves that he produces early trotters. Those having colts from him are highly pleased with them, and all returned the mares to him the following season but two.

Breeders will see by carefully examining his pedigree, that his blood lines are invaluable for the production of high breeding and great speed. No stallion now in public service can show a pedigree with such fast records as enrich the blood of Designer. Considering his breeding, he is by far the cheapest horse in California. This is a rare opportunity to get the service of a good horse at a low price, as within a short period his price will be much higher.

Limited to 20 mares, at $50 for the season, commencing March 1st, ending June 15th. Mares can be returned next season if not with foal, provided mares or horse have not changed hands. Fee due at time of service, and must be paid before mares are removed. Pasturage $5 per month. All mares at owners' risk.

H. SCOTT.
Race Track, Oakland, Cal.

My present address is 1406 Grove Street, one block from entrance to Golden Gate Park, San Francisco.

The Hambletonian Stallion 10178.

Sire of Steve Whipple, 2:23, Kate Agnew, 2:28¾, etc.

- Whipple's Hambletonian, Sire of 14 trotters and 1 pacer from 2:19 to 2:30, and 7 sons with 8 performers from 2:21¾ to 2:30, and dams of 6 from 2:19¾ to 2:30.
  - Guy Miller, By Hambletonian 10.
  - Martha Washington, Dam of Speculation 928, Sire of Crown Pt., 2:24, Oakland Maid, 2:22, Gracie S., 2:28¾, and dam of Waterford, 2:27
- Flora, 2:30¾, trial, 2:26. Dam of Chrisman's Hambletonian, sire of Steve Whipple, 2:23, Kate Agnew, 2:28¾.
  - Chieftain 721, Sire of Defiance, 2:24 and 2:17¾, pacing; Cairo, 2:26, and Onward, 2:24, pacer.
  - daughter of Wilson's Learnon.

Stud season now on till the 1st of August, 1890, at $40 each mare, with return privilege in 1891, provided stallion and mare, or either, do not change owners. Good pasture at hand, and comfortable accommodation for good mares and colts. For further particulars, address

JESSE CHRISMAN, Proprietor.
San Jose, Cal.

GEO. WASHINGTON.

11,623.

RECORD 2:30.

Bay colt, bred by Thomas Smith of Vallejo, Cal. Foaled 1886 by Mambrino Chief, Jr., 11,622, record 2:34 1-2. 1st dam Fanny Rose by Vick's Ethan Allen Jr. 2,903, sire of Prince Allen 2:27. 2nd dam Jenny Lind, thoroughbred, dam of Prince Allen 2:27. Will serve a limited number of mares at $50 for the season. Mares not proving with foal may be returned next season free.

Mambrino Chief, Jr.

11,622.

RECORD 2:34 1 2.

Sire of George Washington, record 2:30 at three years old. Bay horse bred by Rufus Ingalls of Belvedere, Ill. By McDonald Chief 3583. First dam Venus by Mambrino Patchen 58. 2nd dam by Wardlow's Shakespeare. 3rd dam Lone Gold 4th dam by Silver Heels. Has not been in the stud before. He was 5 years old when he served a few mares, and his colts all show good style and form.

Terms for the season $50. For further particulars see or address

THOMAS SMITH,
Vallejo, Cal.

Elector 2170.

Sire of J. R.

Three-Year Old Record 2:24.

Sired by Electioneer 125, sire of Sunol, three-year-old, 2:10½, Palo Alto, 2:12¾, etc.; dam Gilberta by Fred Low 656, sire of Clay, 2:25½, etc.

Second dam Lady Gilbert (grandam of Lot Slocum, 2:17½) by General Knox 140 (sire of Lady Maud, 2:18¼, and many others).

TERMS.

$150 for the season. Book full for 1890.

L. A. RICHARDS,
Grayson, Stanislaus Co., Cal.

The Thoroughbred Stallion

Three Cheers

Will make the season of 1890 at

Sacramento.

PEDIGREE.

THREE CHEERS
- Imp. Hurrah
  - Newminster
    - Touchstone, by Camel
    - Beeswing, by Dr. Syntax
  - Jovial
    - Bay Middleton, by Sultan
    - Sister to Grey Momus, by Comus
- Young Fashion
  - imp. Monarch
    - imp. Priam, by Emilius
    - imp. Delphine, by Whisker
  - Fashion
    - imp. Trustee, by Catton
    - Bonnets o' Blue, by Sir Charles

Hurrah was imported by John Reber, of Lancaster, Ohio, a locality where there were but few breeders of thoroughbreds. Under these disadvantages he sired a long list of winners. His sire Newminster, won the St. Leger 1851, and his dam, Jovial by Bay Middleton, winner of the Derby 1836. Newminster by Touchstone, winner St. Ledger 1834. Dam Beeswing, winner of 54 races out of 64 starts, by Dr Syntax, winner of the Doncaster Cup, 1837—40—41—42, the only horse that ever accomplished that feat.

On the side of the dam Three Cheers is equally well related. Young Fashion was the dam of Surprise, Scotland (the only horse that ever beat Asteroid a heat), Liverpool, Columbia, and Bonnie Kate, the dam of Little Buttercup, and the flying Bonnie Lizzie. His grandam, Fashion was the greatest race mare of her day and beat Boston in that historical match at four mile heats, which is recorded as one of the greatest events in the annals of the turf.

Horsemen who are qualified to judge, pronounce Three Cheers to be the finest type of the Newminster line in America.

LOCATION.

THREE CHEERS will be located at the Arcade Training Stable, Rancho del Paso. This place has been selected for the reason that first class pasturage has been secured there for the exclusive use of these mares and the other facilities to be obtained there for the care of mares (especially mares in foal) are better than can be found elsewhere in the locality.

TERMS.

$50 for the season with the usual return privileges. Pasturage $5 per month. Mares cared for as owners may desire at bottom rates for grain and hay. All bills payable before the mare is removed.

Mares shipped care of WM. IRVINE, Pacific Stables, Sacramento, will be properly cared for and sent to the ranch without delay.

Three Cheers will be in charge of one of the most experienced and competent stud grooms in the State, who will exercise every care, but no reponsibility assumed for accidents or escapes.

For further particulars apply to Louis Criesler, at the ranch; Wm. Irvine, Pacific Stables, Second St., Sacramento; or to the owner,

E. S. CULVER,
318 Bush St., San Francisco.

GROVER CLAY.

Bay Stallion, Black Points, 15 3-4 hands high.

Bred by W. W. Traylor, San Francisco.

BY ELECTIONEER.

First dam Maggie Norfolk by Norfolk, son of Lexington, he by Boston. Second dam Tilda Quill by Billy Cheatham he by Cracker, and he by Boston. Third dam by Dorsey's Golddust.

TERMS.

Will make the season of 1890 at the Training Stables of Denis Gannon, near Oakland Trotting Park, at $50 the season, payable at time of service. Season to commence February 1st and ending July 1st. Proper care of mares will be taken, but no responsibility incurred for accidents or escapes. Address,

DENIS GANNON, Oakland, Cal.

COOK STOCK FARM.

Season of 1890.

STEINWAY 1808.

Three-Year-Old Record 2:25 3-4.

Sire of STRATHWAY, three year old record 2:26, and sire of the dam of BOURBON RUSSELL 2:30.

By STRATHMORE 408; sire of 31 in the 2:30 list; sire of 5 dams of 8 in the 2:30 list, and sire of 3 sires of 8 in 2:30 list.

1st dam ABBESS (dam of Solo 2:28, and Soprano, dam of C. F. Clay 2:18, Eminence 2:27 and Strathbridge, 3 year old record 2:28½) by ALBION, sire of VANITY FAIR 2:24½, and of the dam of FAVORITE 2:25½.

2nd dam by MARSHALL NEY.

3rd dam by BERTRAND, a son of SIR ARCHY.

TERMS—$100 for the season.

CHARLES DERBY 4907

Brown Horse, Foaled 1885.

By STEINWAY 1808.

1st dam by the great ELECTIONEER, sire of SUNOL 3 year old record 2:10½, Palo Alto 2:12¾, etc., etc.

2nd dam FANNY MALONE, by NIAGARA.

3rd dam FANNY WICKHAM, by HERALD.

4th dam by Imp. TRUSTEE.

TERMS—$100 for the season.

CRESCO 4908.

(BROTHER TO SPARTAN, 2,24.)

By STRATHMORE 408, sire of 31 in the 2:30 list, etc.

1st dam the dam of SPARTAN 2:24, by ALMONT 33; sire of 71 with performers in the 2:30 list.

2nd dam the dam of HENDERSON 2:27, by BRIGNOLI 77, sire of the dam of KING WILKES 2:22.

3rd dam by CRIPPLE, a son of MEDOC.

4th dam by AMERICAN ECLIPSE.

TERMS—$50 for the season.

Pasturage $5 per month. Accidents and escapes at owner's risk. Mares consigned to the farm should be sent to Fashion Stables, Oakland; Geary & Grindle's Stable, Haywards; or to Bennett's Stable, Martinez; from and to which places they will be delivered free of charge. Address

COOK STOCK FARM,
Danville, Contra Costa, Co., Cal.

The Trotting Stallion

ARBITRATOR

Will make the Season of 1890 at NILES, Alameda County.

PEDIGREE.

ARBITRATOR.
- Director 1989, 2:17 in a race, Sire of Direct, 4 yrs., 2:18½ in a race, Margaret S., 3 yrs., 2:19½ in a race, Guide, 4 yrs., 2:28½ in a race.
- Lady Earnest.
  - Speculation 928, sire of Oakland Maid, 2:22 in a race, Gracie S., 2:22 in a race, Crown Point, 2:24 in a race, He the sire of Valensin, 3 yrs., 2:23 in a race, Sire of Dam of Alfred G., 2:19½.
  - Lady Hibbard, dam of Lou Whipple, 2:26½ in a race.

Speculation's dam was Martha Washington, dam of Whipple's Hambletonian, sire of 15 in 2:30 and granddaughter of Burr's Napoleon, sire of Black Harry, who in 1850 won two miles in 5:14½. He sired Smith Burr, sire of Gen. Butler, 2:21, Wagon, 4:56½. He sired the dam of Fanny Mapes, dam of Jerome Eddy, 2:16½. He sired Telegraph, sire of dam of Barus, 2:13½.

DESCRIPTION.

ARBITRATOR was foaled 1885. He is of good size, fine conformation, and a beautiful seal brown.

TERMS.

Non-standard mares	$45
Standard mares by inheritance	35
Standard mares by performance or produce	25

For further particulars, address

H. A. MAYHEW, owner,
Niles, Alameda Co.

ST. NICHOLAS.

A Son of the World Renowned

SIDNEY,

Will Make the Season of 1890, at the Oakland Trotting Park.

ST. NICHOLAS was bred by Mr. G. Valensin at the Arno Stock Farm, Sacramento Co., California, in 1886. He is a beautifully proportioned bright bay horse, 15.3 hands high; is well muscled, lengthy, and lots of bone, with splendid natural action and a phenomenal turn of speed. As a three-year-old he easily worked three heats on the Oakland Track in 2:32, 2:29 and 2:27¾. His breeding is just what one would expect from such a highly formed bloodlike horse. Sidney, his sire, is the most successful young stallion—whether for getting pacers or trotters—America has ever seen, and no wonder for his blood lines are exceptional fine and are all trotting lines, Santa Claus, Strathmore, Rysdyk's Hambletonian and Abdallah, while Sweetness again runs back through that great sire Volunteer, to Rysdyk's Hambletonian and also through her dam to Rysdyk's Hambletonian and Harry Clay 45, the sire of Electioneer's dam. St. Nicholas' dam is by Echo, an exceptionally prepotent son of Hambletonian thus giving St. Nicholas four Rysdyk's Hambletonian crosses and further back a Harry Clay Cross which with his grand dam's thoroughbred Cross should make him invaluable in the stud.

TERMS: Fifty dollars the season, which will commence on the 5th of February and close on the 1st of July. Due care will be taken of mares, but no responsibility for accidents or escapes.

Mares taken and kept as desired by the owners, and at reasonable rates.

JOHN ROWEN.
Oakland Trotting Park.

Season of 1890.

February 15 to June 15

LYNWOOD,

(STANDARD 3017.)

AT WOLF'S (RUSSELL'S) STABLES, STOCKTON, CAL.

TERMS.

$50 for the season, payable at the close of season. Pasturage at $3 per month. Accidents or escapes at owner's risk.

PEDIGREE.

LYNWOOD 3017, trial 2:26.

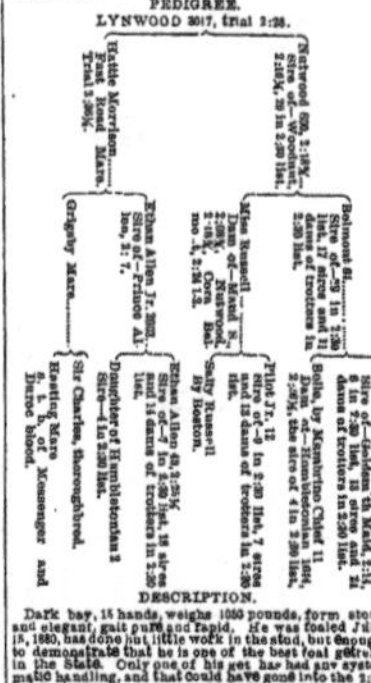

DESCRIPTION.

Dark bay, 15 hands, weighs 1050 pounds, form stout and elegant, gait pure and rapid. He was foaled July 15, 1880, has done but little work in the stud, but enough to demonstrate that he is one of the best foal getters in the State. Only one of his get has had any systematic handling, and that could have gone into the 2:30 list last year as a two-year-old, had the owner desired.

It will be observed from an examination of Lynwood's pedigree, that he is one of the best bred sons of the GREAT NUTWOOD, who commands a service fee of $500 for the season.

P. VISHER, Stockton.

The Thoroughbred Stallion

INTRUDER

Will make the Season of 1890 at Agricultural Park, SACRAMENTO.

Bay Horse, foaled 1871, bred by Sir L. Newman, England. Imported by D. D. Withers, Esq., New York.

By Crater, Son of Orlando and Vesuvienne by Gladiator.

1st dam Lady Bountiful by Rataplan (Rataplan is own brother to Stockwell, and winner of 42 races, including the Doncaster Cup and 19 Queen's Plates, and proved himself the most distinguished race horse of his day in England).

2d dam Plentiful by Don John (the winner of St. Leger and Doncaster Cup).

3d dam Plenty by Bay Middleton (winner of the Derby and Two Thousand Guinea Stakes).

4th dam Plenary, own sister of Plenipotentiary, by Emilius. (Both Emilius and Plenipotentiary were Derby winners).

5th dam Harriet, dam of the renowned Plenipotentiary by Pericles.

6th dam by Selim, winner of the One Thousand Guinea Stakes.

7th dam by Pypilina, by Sir Peter.

8th dam Rally, by Trumpeter.

9th dam Fancy, by Florizel. Fancy was full sister to Diomed, the first Derby winner in England, and after his importation into this country, sired the illustrious Sir Archy, etc. See English Stud Book.

Imported INTRUDER is a beautiful bay, standing fully 16 hands high, of great length and substance, and descends through close and strong currents from the most illustrious winners and winning lines of blood of which the English Stud Book bears record.

A careful review of the first six crosses of the pedigree of INTRUDER will show nine Derby winners; five St. Leger winners; two winners of The Oaks; two winners of the Two Thousand Guineas; two winners of the One Thousand Guineas; one Goodwood Cup winner; one Cesarwich Cup winner; one Cambridgeshire Stakes winner, and four Doncaster Cups, in addition to a great number of Steeplechases and other races of less import.

INTRUDER, at the great fair held at St. Louis, Mo., in 1876, was awarded the highest stallion honors—the blue ribbon and the $500 purse—in the sweepstakes ring for stallion of any age or blood. The list of competitors embraced the large number of thirty-three animals, and they represented England, Canada, Kentucky, Tennessee, and other states. He also took first premium in his class and in sweepstakes for the best stallion of any age or breed at the State Fair at Peoria, Ill., 1881. He is the sire of Tidal Wave, George Hakes, Bernice and April Fool.

INTRUDER is the sire of Interpose, who is the dam of Spokane, winner of the Kentucky Derby, in which he beat the great horse Proctor Knott and broke the record.

TERMS: $50 for the season. Mares not proving with foal can be returned the next season free of charge. Good pasturage at $4 per month. Mares cared for in any manner owners may desire, and fed on hay and grain, either or both, at reasonable rates. While every precaution will be taken, no responsibility will be assumed for escapes or accidents. Mares sent from a distance in care of the undersigned, will be met and taken to the park. For further particulars, address

T. J. KNIGHT.
Agricultural Park, Sacramento.

Shoes For Comfort, Elegance and Durability.

Having my own Factory, and giving my personal supervision to all work I am in a position to warrant perfect satisfaction. Inspection invited.

AGENT for the VISCALIZED SHOES.

FACTORY—S. W. cor. Battery and Jackson Sts.
SALESROOM—Pioneer Building, corner Stevenson and Fourth Streets.

A full line of Boots and Shoes constantly on hand, and rules for Self-Measurement by Mail.

JNO. T. SULLIVAN.

2:20 1-2 Half Mile Track) at 4 Years. | Fastest Record (in a Race) of any Wilkes | 2:14 1-2 at 5 Years

ROY WILKES, 2:12¾,

Seal brown; 15¾ hands; foaled 1883; by Adrian Wilkes 6560, son of Geo. Wilkes; 1st dam by Blue Bull 75; 2d dam by grandson of American Eclipse; 3d and 4th dams thoroughbred.

THE GREATEST CAMPAIGNER OF 1889.

Handsome, Game, Pure Gaited, Level Headed.

Will make a season at the PLEASANTON STOCK FARM, PLEASANTON, CAL Service Fee $150. Money refunded if mare does not get with foal. Season ends April 1st, 1890

For full record of performances, extended pedigree, etc., address

L. A. DAVIES, Hotel Pleasanton,
SUTTER AND JONES STREETS, San Francisco, Cal.

MEMO.

The Best Son of SIDNEY

Will Make the Season of 1890 at the OAKLAND RACE TRACK

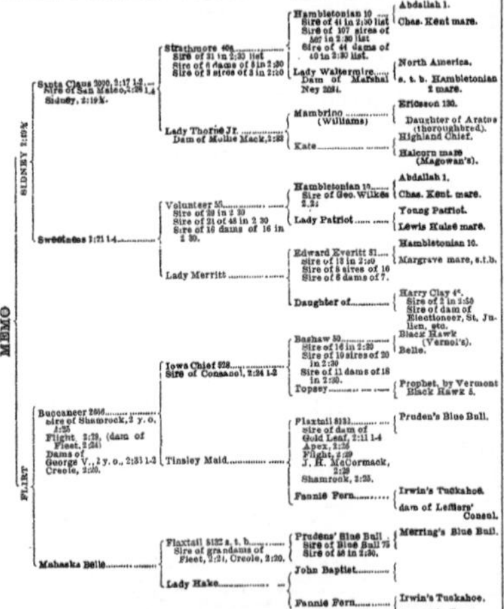

MEMO is, as can be seen at a glance, one of the best bred young stallions in service, having three crosses of Rysdyk's Hambletonian and one of Harry Clay, the sire of Green Mountain Maid (dam of Electioneer, etc.), while Long Island Black Hawk and Flaxtail also contribute to his blood. Sidney (Memo's sire) is universally known as the best young sire in the world, a producer of extreme speed at an early age.

PERFORMANCES.

MEMO trotted in public in his two year-old form, obtaining a record of 2:49, though he was close to Grandee in a race on the Bay District Track, the second heat of which was made in 2:31 1-2, the first in 2:37. He exhibited phenomenal speed when three years old, and had it not been for a slight strain of his fore fetlock, there is little quest on that he would have shown in public very close to the best record. On the Oakland track he was timed a mile in 2:30 1-2, and frequently trotted quarters in from 32 1-2 to 34 seconds.

As a four-year-old Memo only started once—at Sacramento—when, although out of condition, he showed great speed, and improving as he went on, great hopes were entertained of his going well down in the 'teens at the P. C. T. H. B. A. meeting, but after showing several very fast miles his leg filled and he was laid up for the season. He is sixteen hands high, and of powerful build throughout. His color is a glossy black, with both fore-feet white. His disposition is all that could be desired, and his action superb. He is a sure foal getter, only one mare being reported not in foal during his last season.

TERMS. $100, with usual return privileges, for a limited number of mares. Season to close JUNE 15th, when he will be prepared for track purposes. Pasturage $5 per month. Have leased the cricket ground adjoining the track for pasturage, where there is fine feed. Reasonable charges if fed hay and grain. Best of care taken of mares in any manner owners may desire, but positively no responsibility assumed for accidents or escapes. For further particulars address

J. P. KERR, 313 Bush Street, San Francisco,
or, JOHN ROWEN, Race Track, Oakland, Cal.

2:10¾ | 2:13¾ | 2:10

DEXTER PRINCE.

This Royally-bred Stallion will make the Season of 1890 at the LIVE OAKS Breeding Farm, 2 miles from Lodi, San Joaquin County, Cal.

DESCRIPTION.

DEXTER PRINCE is a blood bay, 16 hands high, weighs over 1 100 pounds; has great power and substance, and the highest finish. When two years old, at Palo Alto, he was timed quarters by Gov. Stanford in 33½ seconds, and he was driven eighths by Mr. Marvin at a faster rate of speed than that. He is a sure foal-getter, and invariably sires foals of good size, of fine form and finish, and the highest rate of speed.

PEDIGREE.

By KENTUCKY PRINCE, the sire of Guy, 2:10¾, Spofford, 2:18¾, Company, 2:19¾, Bayonne Prince, 2:21 1-4, Fred Folger, 2:20¾, and a score more in the 2:30 list.

First dam LADY DEXTER, full sister of the greatest of trotters, Dexter, and the greatest of sires, Dictator, the sire of Director, 2:17, Phallas, 2:13¾, in a fourth heat, and Jay-Eye-See, 2:10.

Second dam Clara, the dam of Dexter, 2:17 1-4, Dictator, Astoria 2:29 1-4, and Almah, 2:28¾. Clara was by American Star, that has 31 daughters that have produced 2:30 or better trotters.

Third dam the McKinstry mare, the dam of Shark, 2:27¾. HAMBLETONIAN, the grandsire of DEXTER PRINCE, has 40 trotters in the 2:30 list, 44 daughters that have produced 2:30 trotters, and more than 150 sons that have sired 2:30 trotters.

CLARK CHIEF, the grandsire on the sire's side, was the sire of performing and producing sons and daughters.

DEXTER PRINCE has faster blood lines, on both sides, than any other stallion in the world—Guy, 2:10¾, and Jay-Eye-See, 2:10.

TERMS.

$100 for the season, with usual return privileges. Payable before mares are removed. Good pasture, and the best care furnished, but no responsibility assumed for accidents.

PREMIUM.

$250 will be given to the first of the produce of DEXTER PRINCE put in the 2:30 list, and $100 each after the first. Address

L. M. MORSE, Lodi, Cal.

2:10 1-2 **ELECTIONEER** 2:12 1-4

BAY STALLION	BROWN STALLION
ECLECTIC	**MORTIMER**
11,321	5,346
By Electioneer, dam Manette (full sister to Woodnut 2.16 1-2 Manon 2:21 and Maple, dam of Hattie D., three-year-old record 2.26¾) by Nutwood 2:18¾, etc., etc.	Four-year-old Record 2:27 By ELECTIONEER, dam MARTI, by Whipple's Hambletonian (sire of 15 in 2:30, and of dams of eight in 2:30). Second dam Ida Martin by Rifleman (sire of Col. Lewis 2:18¾).
Terms $100 for the Season.	Terms $60 for the Season.

Horses shipped via San Francisco may be consigned to J. W. MORSHEAD, City Front Stables, who will attend to their forwarding.

Season closes JULY 1st, 1890. Usual return privileges.

For further particulars address owner,
WILFRED PAGE, Penns Grove,
Sonoma County, Cal

The Trotting Stallion

Silver Bow

Will make the season of 1890 at the Oakland Race Track.

Pedigree.

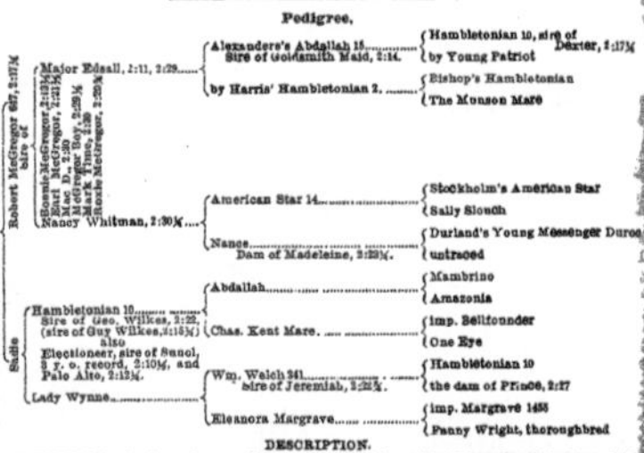

DESCRIPTION.

SILVER BOW is a handsome bay, no white; 15-3½ hands high; weighs 1075 pounds; of fine form, with the best of legs and a clean cut, intelligent head. Is remarkably level headed, seldom making a break; wears 7-ounce shoes in front. His record 2:37, is no mark of his speed; he can beat 30 easy, and with his gilt-edge breeding, he is just what he ought to be, a trotter sired by a trotter whose dam was herself a trotter and his grandam the dam of two trotters. His dam Sadie being by Hambletonian 10, shows him to be bred from the cream of the trotting blood.

TERMS: $100 for the season. Mares not proving in foal returnable for the season of 1891 free of charge. Good pasturage and first-class care taken of mares for $5 per month. No responsibility assumed for escapes or accidents. For further particulars, address

Limited to 15 approved mares.
Season to end June 1st, 1890.

P. J. WILLIAMS.
Care Race Track, Oakland, Cal.

Pleasanton Stock Farm Co.'s Stallions.

DIRECTOR, 2:17.

Director's book is open for 15 good mares more than already booked for the season of 1890, at $300 each.

This is the cheapest service fee ever charged for a stallion, taking into consideration his BREEDING and RACE RECORD and the RACE RECORDS OF HIS COLTS.

Season to commence February 15th and close August 1st.

CORRECTOR, Four Years Old.

Sire Director 2:17, dam Brainey, she by Echo. Echo sired by Rysdyk's Hambletonian, out of Magnolia, she by Seely's American Star. Brainey's dam Lady Dudley, she by Tom Dudley by Blacknose, a son of Medoc, he by American Eclipse. Lady Dudley's dam by Bertrand, Jr., a son of Bertrand.

CORRECTOR is a rich seal brown 15¾ hands high, and is the fastest young stallion in the world under the same conditions, never having been off the farm where raised and never been shod or driven for speed before last Christmas, and can trot quarters now in 35 seconds, a 2:20 gait

He will be allowed to serve ten good mares, at $100 each for the season, which closes June 1st.

DECORATOR, Four Years Old.

Sire Director 2:17, dam Chess, sired by Cardinal 2.37, trial 2:28, he by Gen. Gifford's Morgan, dam of Cardinal, sired by Joe Gales of Ohio, he by Marlborough out of the Duchess of Marlborough by Southern Eclipse; second dam old Duchess of Marlborough by Sir Archy; third dam by imp Eclipse. Decorator's second dam a Morgan and Messenger mare.

Decorator is a light bay 15½ hands high, and with but little handling for speed can show quarters in 37½ seconds, a 2:30 gait.

He will be allowed to serve ten good mares at $50 each for the season, which closes June 1st.

For further information call or address M. SALISBURY, 320 Sansome Street, Room 16, San Francisco, or

PLEASANTON STOCK FARM CO.;
Pleasanton, Alameda Co., Cal.

THE "BLUE ROCK" TARGET.

Quotations furnished F. O. B. at Cleveland, Ohio, or San Francisco.

CLABROUGH, GOLCHER & CO.,
630 and 632 Montgomery Street, S. F., Cal.
SOLE AGENTS for the Pacific Coast.

Langtry Farms' Stud

Imp. FRIAR TUCK

By the Immortal HERMIT

DAM ROMPING GIRL BY WILD DAYRELL,

AT $50 THE SEASON.

Mares not proving with foal may be returned the following season. Good care taken of mares, but no liabilities for accidents or escapes.

Good Pasturage at $5 per month.

Mares shipped to ST. HELENA, care CHARTES WILLIAM ABY, St. Helena Stables, will be cared for. For further particulars address,

CHAS. WILLIAM ABY,
Middletown, Lake County, Cal.

2:08 3-4 2:10 2:12

MAMBRINO WILKES, 6083.

SIRE OF

GUS WILKES, 2:22; ALPHEUS, 2:27; CLARA P, 2:29½; BALKAN, 2:29½ (3-year-old) and timed separately 2:22¼ in 4-year-old Stake, Bay District Track, October 14, 1889.

DESCRIPTION.

Black; sixteen hands; weighs, in exercise, 1,240 lbs. For style, finish, symmetry and proportion, comparison is challenged with any trotting bred horse. His colts follow in size, style and beauty. Balkan, for instance, being "facile princeps" of trotters in these particulars.

PEDIGREE.

Sired by Geo. Wilkes, sire of Harry Wilkes, 2:13½, Guy Wilkes, 2:15¼, and 60 other trotters in the 2:30 list, in addition to 8 pacers, and of the sire of Axtell, 2:12 (three-year-old), beating all stallions of any age, and the sire of Regal Wilkes, 2:20¾, best two-year-old stallion record.

First dam Lady Chrisman by Mambrino (Todhunter's), son of Mambrino Chief 11; sire of Lady Thorn, 2:18¼; Woodford Mambrino, 2:21½, and four others in 2:30, and of the dams of Director, 2:17, Piedmont, 2:17¼, Onward, 2:25¼, etc.

Second dam by Pilot Jr. 12, sire of nine in the 2:30 list, and of the dams of Maud S., 2:08¾, Jay-Eye-See, 2:10, Nutwood, 2:18¾, Viking, 2:19¾, Pilot Boy, 2:20, Naiad Queen, 2:20¾, etc.

TERMS.

Mares from a distance will be received at the Dexter Stables, Oakland, or Livery Stable, Martinez, the owner notifying Smith Hill, Superintendent at the farm. Good pasture and plenty of water. For the purpose of placing the service of a Wilkes within reach of breeders, the same rate will be maintained as last year, to wit, $75 for the season. Although it is not admitted thereby that this horse is inferior as a producer to the horses whose fees are placed at from $150 to $500. Address

SMITH HILL,
San Miguel Stock Farm,
Walnut Creek, Contra Costa Co., Cal.

2:12¾ 2:13½ 2:15¼

2:08¾ 2:10 2:12

BALKAN

By Mambrino Wilkes.

(See that Horse's Advertisement.)

DAM FANNY FERN BY JACK HAWKINS
Son of Boston.

The grandam of Maud S, (2:08¾) was by Boston and the grandam of Jay-Eye-See (2:10) was by Lexington, son of Boston. So Balkan is the same remove from Boston that Maud is, and one remove nearer than Jay-Eye-See.

Fanny Fern has produced Molly Drew, Onyx, Fred Arnold, Molly Fern and Balkan, all by different sires.

Balkan's sire and dam both being producers, and he being a trotter himself with a record of 2:29 1-2 (three-year-old) and timed separately 2:22 1-4 in 4-year-old Stake, Bay District Track, October 14, 1889—it is but fair to presume that he will get trotters of the highest order.

DESCRIPTION.

He is seal brown, 16-1 hands high, in style rivalled by few, and excelled by none with as pure a gait as has yet been exhibited in public—bar none.

Balkan will be at Oakland Trotting Park for the season of 1890, and will be limited to ten mares, at $100 fee, in order to be put in training early, as it is morally certain that if given a reasonable opportunity he will be fast enough to compete with the best of his age. For further particulars address

A. L. HINDS,
Dexter Stables, Oakland.

2:12¾ 2:13½ 2:15¼

JESSE E. MARKS & CO.,

Wholesale and Retail Dealers of Choice Brands

Havana & Key West Cigars

922 MARKET ST., S. F.

2:19 NOONDAY 2:20½

STANDARD No. 10,000.

This celebrated trotting bred stallion will make the season of 1890 at the stable of the undersigned at Sacramento, Cal., at $75 for the season and $100 to insure a mare in foal. Payable on or before July 1st, 1890. Money will be refunded on mares bred by insurance as soon as the fact becomes known that they are not in foal.

NOONDAY.
- Wedgewood, 2:19. Sire of Favonia, 2:15, fastest 4th heat for any mare or gelding, and eight others in 2:27 or better.
  - Belmont. Sire of Wedgewood, 2:19, Nutwood, 2:18¾, Viking, 2:19½, and 39 others in 2:30 list.
    - Alexander's Abdallah, sire of Goldsmith Maid, 2:14; Almont, with 35 horses in 2:30 list, etc.
    - Belle, dam of Hambletonian, 2:26½; Bicara, dam of Pancoast, 2:21¾, the sire of Patron, 2:14¼.
  - Woodbine. Dam of Wedgewood, 2:19, Woodford Mamb., 2:21½, the sire of Pancoast, 2:21¾, the sire of Patron, 2:14¼.
    - Woodford.
    - Singleton Mare.
- Noontide, 2:20½ (Trial, 2:13½).
  - Harold. Sire of Maud S., 2:08¾, and 26 others in 2:30 list.
    - Hambletonian (Rysdyk's), sire of George Wilkes, 2:22, the sire of Guy Wilkes, 2:15¼; Electioneer, the sire of Sunol, 2:10½, and scores of noted trotters and producers.
    - Enchantress, by Abdallah 1.
  - Midnight. Dam of Jay-Eye-See, 2:10, Noontide, 2:20½.
    - Pilot Jr., sire of dams of Maud S., 2:08¾, Jay-Eye-See, 2:10, Nutwood, 2:18¾, etc.
    - Twilight, by Lexington, sire of the dam of Ansel, 2:20.

NOODAY is a dark seal brown, foaled 1884, 15 hands 1¼ inches high. Individually he is equal to his royal breeding. He is all that can be desired in conformation, intelligence, color and trotting action, and no stallion now in public service can show a pedigree with such fast records and royal game trotting blood as Noonday.

DON MARVIN,

Record 2:28 as a five-year-old. Standard by Breeding and Performance

Standard No. 7927.

Don Marvin 2:28.

Don Marvin is a beautiful seal brown, foaled 1884, bred by Hon. Leland Stanford, Palo Alto, Cal., standing 16 hands, and weighs, in ordinary condition, 1200 lbs. He is a fine individual, good style and form, combined with great substance, and good temper. Is very level headed; in his first race the past season he only made one break in five closely contested heats. He has great speed and endurance, with the pure, rapid Electioneer gait. He trots without toe weights, and wears only 8 oz. shoes in front. He gained his record the past season in the third heat, on a slow track, after making a season (serving over 60 mares), with scarcely any preparation. His record is no mark of his speed. He was a natural born trotter, and Mr. Charles Marvin considered him the fastest two year old at Palo Alto that season.

By FALLIS, 2:23, - - by Electioneer, sire of
Sire of Don Marvin, 2:28. — Sunol, three-year-old, 2:10 1-2, Palo Alto, 2:12¾, and 47 others in 2:30 list.

Dam CORA, by Don Victor by Belmont, sire of
Dam of Don Marvin 2:28. — Ventura, 2:27¼, and sire of the dam of Bell Echo, 2:20, and six others in 2:30 list.

2d dam CLARABEL, - by Abdallah Star,
Dam of Clifton Bell, 2:24 1-2, and grandam of Rexford, three years, 2:24. — Sire of Hattie Maples, 2:33.

3d dam FAIRY, - - by Rysdyk's Hambletonian,
Sister of Sweepstakes, sire of 16 in 2:30 list. — Sire of Electioneer, George Wilkes, and many other noted sires and trotters.

4th dam EMMA MILLS, by Seely's American Star,
Dam of 4 horses that have 2:30 performers. — The great broodmare sire of the world.

The above pedigree should show every intelligent breeder that Don Marvin is "high" bred, though very strong in trotting blood. All the comment it is deemed necessary to make as to the value of "thoroughbred blood" in the trotter is simply to refer to the very significant fact that the first and second dams of Maud S, 2:08¾, Jay-Eye-See 2:10, Sunol, three years 2:10 1-2, Palo Alto 2:12¾, Anteeo 2:16¼, Nutwood 2:18¾, Wedgewood 2:19, and many other successful sires and sensational trotters of the day are thoroughbred.

TERMS—Don Marvin will make the ensuing season from February 1st to July 1st, 1890, at $40 the season, with the usual privilege of returning the mare next season if not proving in foal. Mares from a distance met at the cars or boats on notification, and carefully handled, but no responsibility assumed for accidents or escapes.

Good alfalfa pasture furnished (free from barb wire fence) at $4 per month. For further particulars or complete circulars address

F. P. LOWELL,
1520 F Street, Sacramento, Cal.

The Produce of Eros Averaged $2,200 Each at New York Auction Sale in 1889.

THE ELECTIONEER TROTTING STALLION,

5326 EROS 5326

Will make the season of 1890—February 1st to July 1st—at LA SIESTA RANCH, MENLO PARK, adjoining Palo Alto.

PEDIGREE.

EROS (5326)
Standard by his sire
" " dam
" " record
" " produce
" under all rules

EROS (5326)..
- Electioneer. Grandsire of Norlaine, 1 yr., 2:31 1-2, Sire of Sunol, 2 yrs., 2:18, Sunol, 3 yrs., 2:10 1-2, Hinda Rose, 4 yrs., 2:16, Palo Alto, 2:12¾.
  - Hambletonian 10. Sire of Dictator, George Wilkes, Happy Medium, and 40 others in 2:30 list, and grandsire of 728 in list.
    - Abdallah 10. Sire of the dams of Goldsmith Maid, 2:14, and 7 other producing dams.
    - Charles Kent mare. By imp. Bellfounder.
  - Green Mountain Maid. Dam of Prospero, 2:20, Elaine, 2:20, Dame Trot, 2:22, Elista, 2:22¼, Storm, 2:26¾, Antonio, 2:28¾, Miranda, 2:31, Mansfield, 2:26.
    - Harry Clay. Sire of the dams of St. Julian, 2:11¼, Bodine, 2:19¼, and 17 more in 2:30 list
    - Shanghai Mary.
- Sontag Mohawk. Dam of Eros, 2:29 1-2, Sport, 2:22¼, Sallie Benton, 2:17¾, Conductor, trial, 2:26, Colma, 3-y-o trial, 2:24.
  - Mohawk Chief. Sire of the dams of Lot Slocum, 2:17¼, Sallie Benton, 4 yrs., 2:17¾, Pedlar, 2 yrs., 2:27¾, Stanford, 4 yrs., 2:30, Eros, 6th heat, 2:29 1-2.
    - Hambletonian 10. Sire of the dams of Stamboul, 2:12¼, Wilton, 2:19¼, and 20 other trotters.
    - Lady Perrine
  - Sontag Nellie.
    - Toronto Sontag. By Toronto Chief,
    - Nellie Gray. 5-mile record, 13:45.

Produce of Eros
Wanda, 4 yrs., 2:24.
Solita, 2 yrs., 2:41 1-2.
Meriquita, 2yrs., 2:42.
Daylight, 2 yrs., 2:54.
Hiram B., trial, 2:28.

These are the only colts by him that have ever had a harness on except one in New York that went a trial last July in 2:26 1:2.

DESCRIPTION.

EROS is a rich seal brown stallion, bred by Hon. Leland Stanford at Palo Alto, and is the nearest living likeness of his celebrated sire, Electioneer. Stands 15.2 hands high, and weighs 1050 pounds

In breeding to Eros, the owners of mares will strictly follow the great rule of breeding, viz., breed to a stallion by a producer and out of a sure producer of great speed. Eros is by the stallion that has produced more 2:30 trotters that any living horse, and is also the sire of more 2:30 performers than any horse living or dead.

EROS is out of the dam of Sally Benton, four years old, record 2:17¾, Sport 2:22¼, and Eros 2:29½ in the sixth heat, against a field of nine horses. He is from a family that is endowed with great natural speed, trot fast at an early age, train on, throw trotters from all classes of mares, are of good substance, bone, style and action, and breed solid colors.

TERMS.

$100 for the season, with the privilege of return next season should mares not be in foal and horse and mare still remain in the same hands.

Good pasturage can be obtained at $5 per month, but no responsibility for accidents or escapes. There are a large number of box stalls, and animals can be kept up and fed on hay and grain at reasonable rates if required. Mares already in foal can be sent to the ranch for foaling, and will receive all the attention bestowed upon our own mares. Mares left with Mr. Peter Pomyea, Broadway Street Stable, Oakland, or with Mr. F. H. Burke, 401 Montgomery Street, San Francisco, will be forwarded to the ranch free of charge. For further particulars apply to

W. H. VIOGET.
LA SIESTA RANCH, MENLO PARK, CAL.

EROS is the only stallion offered to the public on this Coast that has a dam that has three in the 2:30 list.

POPLAR GROVE

Breeding Farm

STALLIONS.

CLOVIS, 4909,

CLOVIS is a beautiful black, Eight Years Old, 16 1-2 Hands High, and weighs 1260 lbs.

He is a horse of beautiful symmetry and magnificent action.

PEDIGREE.

CLOVIS was sired by Sultan, 2:24, sire of Stamboul, 2:12 1-4, Ruby, 2:19¾, and fifteen others with records of 2:30 or better.

First dam Sweetbriar by Thorndale 2:22 1-2, sire of Edwin Thorne, 2:16 1-2, Daisy Dale, 2:19, and May Thorne, 2:22

Second dam Ulster Queen, dam of Volmer, 2:24¾, by Hambletonian 10. Sire of Dexter, 2:17¼, George Wilkes, 2:22.

Third dam by Thomas Jefferson, a son of Mambrino Paymaster, Jr.

Fourth dam by Mambrino Paymaster, sire of Mambrino Chief.

Sultan, by The Moor, sire of Beautiful Bells, dam of Hinda Rose, 2:19 1-2, and Sable, dam of Sable Wilkes, three year old record 2:18.

First dam of Sultan, Sultana, by Delmonica. Sire of Darby, 2:16 1-2, by Guy Miller, sire of Whipple's Hambletonian.

Second dam by Mambrino Chief.

Third dam by Downing's Bay Messenger.

Fourth dam Mrs. Caudle, dam of Ericsson, four year old record 2:30 1-2.

Clovis will make the season of 1890 at Poplar Grove Breeding Farm, near Wildflower, Fresno County, commencing February 1st and ending July 1st.

Terms, $75, due at time of service.

Mares cared for in any manner owners may desire; pasturage $2 per month. Every care exercised, but no liability for escapes or accidents. Mares not proving with foal can be returned next season, providing I still own this stallion.

APEX, 8935.

FOUR-YEAR-OLD RECORD, FOURTH HEAT, 2:26.

Will make the present season at the Poplar Grove Breeding Farm, near Wildflower, Fresno Co., season commencing Feb. 1st, and ending July 1, 1890. Terms, $50 the season, due at time of service. Apex is eight years old, a beautiful bay, 15 1-2 hands high, and weighs 1100 lbs. He is a horse of fine disposition, and his gait is faultless.

PEDIGREE.

Apex was sired by Promptor 2305, he by Blue Bull 75; first dam Mary by Flaxtail, he by Pruden's Blue Bull. Flaxtail being the sire of the dams of Buccaneer, five-year-old record, 2:24 1-2; Pride, yearling record, 2:44 1-2, and Shamrock, two-year old record, 2:25, third heat. Second dam by Bright Eyes, son of Boanarges. Promptor (sire of Apex, record 2:26, and Transit, 2:26 1-2), by Wilson's Blue Bull, by Prudee's Blue Bull, son of Merring's Blue Bull. Promptor's dam Prairie Bird, by Flaxtail; second dam by John the Baptist, son of Tally Ho Morgan, by Sherman Morgan; third dam Fannie Fern by Irwin's Tuckaho.

Apex made his appearance in the circuit as a two-year-old, and obtained a record of 2:42. As a three-year-old he reduced this in a race at Santa Rosa against Stamboul to 2:31, it taking six heats to decide the contest, which was won by Apex. As a four year-old he gained his present record of 2:26.

Mares cared for in any manner owners may desire. Pasturage $2 per month. Every care exercised, but no liabilities for escapes or accidents. Mares not proving with foal can be returned next season, providing I still own this stallion.

The Standard Stallion

JUNIO,

RECORD 2:22.

WILL MAKE THE PRESENT SEASON OF 1890 AT FRESNO FAIR GROUNDS.

Season Commencing Feb. 1st and ending July 1st.

TERMS—$100 the season, due at time of service.

JUNIO is eight years old, a handsome dark bay 16 hands high, and weighs 1200 pounds. He is the personification of the light harness horse, and his trotting action is superb. At the State Fair of 1886 he took first premium over forty of the finest trotters in the State.

PEDIGREE.

Junio, by Electioneer, premier stallion of Palo Alto (sire of Sunol 2:10 1-2, Palo Alto 2:12 1-4, and 47 others in the 2:30 list). Dam by Granger by imp. Hercules.

Granger, by imp. Hercules, dam Jenny Lind, by Stockbridge Chief, Jr., he by Stockbridge Chief, he by Vermont Black Hawk. Second dam by Kentucky Whip.

Imp. Hercules, by Kingston, first dam daughter of Tuscar, by Bay Middleton, second dam Malvina, by Oscar; 3rd dam Spotless by Walton; 4th dam by Trumpator (see Bruce's American Stud Book, Vol. 1, page 28). Hercules is the sire of the dam of Azmoor 2:20¼; also sire of dam of Menlo 2:21 1-2.

Mares not proving in foal may be returned next year free of charge, providing I still have the horse. Pasturage $3 per month. While every care will be taken of horses, no liability will be assumed for accidents or escapes.

For further particulars address

S. N. STRAUBE, Fresno, Cal.
Poplar Grove Breeding Farm.

A SON OF ALMONT 33.

Only $25 for the Season.

ASHLAND ALMONT 3481.

PEDIGREE.

ASHLAND ALMONT 3481

Almont 33 — Sire of 34 in 2:30 or better of 21 daughters and of 49 sires that have produce in 2:30 or better.
- Abdallah 15 — Sire Goldsmith Maid, 2:14; 6 in 2:30 list; 15 sires and 25 dams of trotters in 2:30 list.
  - Hambletonian 10 — Sire of 41 in 2:30 list; sire of 107 sires of 567 in 2:30 list.
  - Katy Darling.
- Sally Anderson
  - Mambrino Chief 11
  - Lady Thorn, 2:18½.
  - Kate, by Pilot Jr. 12.

Pauline — Dam of Sapho.
- Ashland Chief — Sire Black Cloud, 2:17¼.
  - Mambrino Chief 11
  - Lady Thorn, 2:18¼.
  - dau. of imp. Yorkshire, (thoroughbred).
- Rosina — Dam Almonia, the dam of Sally Cossack, 2:22¼, dau. Mamb. Abdallah, sire Mam. Prince, 2:33, and of Mamb. Pashaw, sire of Graham's Mambrino, 2:38.
  - Abdallah 15 — Sire Goldsmith Maid, 2 14.
  - Prof. Smith's Sir William.

DESCRIPTION.

ASHLAND ALMONT 3481 is a handsome chestnut; stands 16 hands; was foaled 1888, and bred by Gen. Withers, of Lexington, Ky. He is of fine form, and remarkably intelligent, sweet-tempered and absolutely sound. His oldest foal may be seen with him, and while he has never served a standard mare or one that was a producer of speed, all of his colts are large, sound, fast and handsome.

TERMS: $25 for the season, with usual return privileges. The best of care taken of mares in any manner that the owner may desire, but no responsibility assumed for escapes or accidents.

For further particulars, address

T. J. WHITEHEAD, Manager

or, W. H. ASHBY, Oakland, Cal. — 579 36th Street, bet. Telegraph Ave. and Grove St., Oakland, Cal.

THE BRUNSWICK BALKE COLLENDER COMPANY,

MANUFACTURERS OF

Standard Billiard and Pool Tables, Saloon and Bank Fixtures,

653--655 Market Street, San Francisco, Cal.

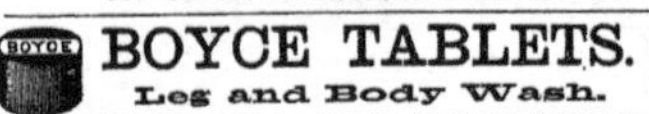

BOYCE TABLETS.

Leg and Body Wash.

THE BOYCE TABLETS are packed in a nicely decorated metal box with hinged lid—one hundred tablets in each box; directions for use plainly engraved upon the box; therefore, the convenience of the package—no liability to leakage and breakage—economy and ready solubility, together with the absolute certainty of their action, will at once commend the use of BOYCE'S TABLETS to the intelligent horsemen of the country. TABLETS sufficient to make one hundred pints of leg and body wash are conveniently carried in an inside coat pocket or in the hip-pocket of the trousers.

The BOYCE WASH can be applied ALL OVER THE BODY WITHOUT FEAR OF BLISTERING NOR DOES IT AFFECT THE KIDNEYS.

The BOYCE WASH will cure CRACKED HEELS, PUFFS, STOCKINGS, SCRATCHES, INFLAMED TENDONS and FEVERED LEGS.

Price per Box of One Hundred Tablets, $2, sent postpaid to any part of the United States; six boxes for $10. A sample of BOYCE'S TABLETS will be mailed to any address on application.

These TABLETS are warranted to keep in any climate. Address

BOYCE TABLET COMPANY,

600 Wabash Avenue, - - - Terre Haute, Indiana.

J. A. McKERRON, Pacific Coast Ag't,

228-230-232 Ellis Street, San Francisco, Cal.

ADVERTISE YOUR STALLIONS

—IN THE—

Breeder & Sportsman

For the Season---1890.

We are pleased to announce that we have the best facilities for furnishing

Stallion Pictures,

Stallion Cards,

Pedigrees, Folders.

Contracts, Bills, Etc.

We make a specialty of this department of our business, and have UNRIVALED FACILITIES FOR LOOKING UP PEDIGREES and doing accurate and handsome work.

Promptness, Good Work, Low Prices.

BREEDER AND SPORTSMAN,

313 Bush Street, S. F.

THE BUCKINGHAM.

OLD STRAIGHT WHISKIES.

141 Montgomery Street,

303 Bush Street, S. F.

M. J. BALFE, Proprietor.

"DICKEY'S,"

SIXTH AVENUE AND D ST.

Near entrance to Bay District Track.

Choicest Brands of

WINES AND CIGARS.

A Delightful Resort.

Telephone 1485. J. R. DICKEY, Propr.

PHIL J. CRIMMINS. JOHN C. MORRISON.

"Silver Palace,"

36 Geary Street,

San Francisco, Cal

ROME HARRIS. JOHN MERIGAN.

"Laurel Palace,"

N. W. corner Kearny and Bush Streets

SAN FRANCISCO.

The Park Training Stable.

CHAS. DAVID, PROPRIETOR.

Corner Grove and Baker Streets, near Entrance to Golden Gate Park.

EVERY FACILITY FOR TRAINING COLTS and taking care of Gentlemen's Roadsters.

Finely appointed stable with every convenience and sixteen roomy box stalls.

The best care given all horses by experienced help, under the personal superintendence of the proprietor

Convenient to the Park Speed Drive, and Accessible to Six Lines of Cable Cars.

THE TRAINING OF COLTS AND ROADSTERS A SPECIALTY.

TROTTERS AND ROADSTERS FOR SALE.

HORSES SOLD ON COMMISSION.

The proprietor trained and brought out the following well known horses: "Sister, Huntress," "Perihelion," "Nona Y," and others.

GOLDEN EAGLE HOTEL

Corner SEVENTH and K STREETS, SACRAMENTO.

FIRST CLASS IN EVERY RESPECT.

The LARGEST and FINEST HOTEL in the City.

W. O. BOWERS, Proprietor.

Free 'Buss to and from the Hotel.

Telephone, Telegraph Office and Messenger Service at Hotel

NOVEL, USEFUL and Ornamental.

The Perfection Horse Tail Tie,

Saves Time and the Tail.

Send 25 cents for Sample,

BREEDER AND SPORTSMAN,

313 Bush Street, San Francisco.

or to BARNES & PARKER, Des Moines, Ia., Manufrs

Old Hermitage Whiskies

"STEINER'S,"

No. 311 BUSH STREET,

San Francisco.

Under Breeder and Sportsman Office.

THE HICKS-JUDD CO.

Successors to

HICKS & JUDD, Bookbinders,

and Women's Co-operative Printing Office.

Printers, Bookbinders, Publishers,

23 First St., San Francisco.

BREEDERS' CATALOGUES A SPECIALTY.

By-Laws

—AND—

Rules and Regulations

—OF THE—

NATIONAL

Trotting Association

ALSO THE

AMERICAN

Trotting Association,

AND THE

PACIFIC COAST BLOOD-HORSE ASSOCIATION.

With Betting Rules.

For Sale at the Office of the

Breeder and Sportsman,

313 Bush St., S. F., Cal.

Price, 25c. each.

By Mail, Postage Paid, 30c. each.

KENNEL ADVERTISEMENTS

Thoroughbred Pugs,

$40 each.

PEDIGREE.

PUPPIES
- Fido
  - Imp. Jumbo — Marshall's Un[illegible], Lady Bess
  - Fanni — Rex, Imp. Fly
- Budge
  - Senator Fair's Fritz
  - McCleery's Mammy Snoots — Sam, Imp. Alice

Can be seen daily from 9 A. M. to 3 P. M. at 411 Ellis Street, San Francisco.

J. F. B. McCLEERY.

Irish Setters & Pointers

In the Stud, winner of 16 first and special prizes CHAMPION MIKE T., 6435, A. K. S. B. Irish Setter puppies by Champion Mike T. 6435 A. K. S. B.—Champion Lady Elcho T. 6451 A. K. S. B., for sale. Two pointers, a year old, by Rush T. 10[illegible] A. K. S. B.—Champion Patti Croxteth T. 10128 A. K. S. B. for sale. Yard broken. Address,

A. B. TRUMAN,

1426 Steiner St., S. F., Cal.

FOX TERRIERS--C. A. SUMNER, 7[illegible] Fort St., Los Angeles, Breeder of Fox Terriers. Blemton Vesuvian (14299), by Champion Lucifer, at stud.

CALIFORNIA SPANIEL KENNELS

Oakland, California. H. P. RENNIE, Prop. Breeder and importer of typical COCKER SPANIELS. Winner of first prizes at S. F. and Los Angeles, 188[illegible] also, Columbus, 188[illegible] New York, 1887. In the stud, solid Black Cocker dog, GIFFER, won 1st and Gold Medal at S. F., 18[illegible] Fee, $25. Puppies and grown dogs at reasonable prices. My dogs can neither talk nor climb a tree, but are fielders and prize winners.

Fiske's Vanes.

MADE OF COPPER And Gilded with PURE GOLD LEAF.

Manufacturer's Agent.

The HOWE SCALE CO

411 & 413 Market Street, S. F.

Scales for Weighing of

Live Stock

SEEDS, FEED, Etc.

Write for Catalogue.

PERRIER-JOUET & Co.

EPERNAY

CHAMPAGNE

W. B. CHAPMAN

Sole Agent for Pacific Coast.

For sale by all first-class Wine Merchants and Grocers.

R. LIDDLE & SON

538 Washington St., S. F.,

Wholesale and Retail Dealers in

Guns, Rifles and Pistols

A Full Line of FISHING TACKLE and SPORTSMAN'S GOODS.

Orders by mail receive prompt attention.

Southern Pacific Co.

(PACIFIC SYSTEM.)

Trains leave and are due to arrive at San Francisco.

LEAVE (FOR)	FROM JANUARY 1, 1890.	ARRIVE (FROM)
7.30 A M	Haywards, Niles and San Jose...	*12.45 P M
7.30 A M	Sacramento and Redding, via Davis...	7.15 P M
7.30 A M	Sacramento, Auburn, Colfax...	5.45 P M
8.00 A M	Martinez, Vallejo, Calistoga and Santa Rosa...	6.15 P M
8.00 A M	Los Angeles Express, Fresno, Bakersfield, Mojave and East and Los Angeles...	11.15 A M
8.30 A M	Niles, San Jose, Stockton, Ione, Sacramento, Marysville, Oroville and Red Bluff...	5.45 P M
10.30 A M	Haywards and Niles...	2.15 P M
12.00 M	Haywards, Niles and San Jose...	* 3.45 P M
*1.00 P M	Sacramento River Steamers...	**6.00 A M
3.00 P M	Haywards, Niles and San Jose...	9.45 A M
3.30 P M	2d Class for Ogden and East...	10.45 P M
4.00 P M	Stockton and Milton; Vallejo, Calistoga and Santa Rosa...	9.45 A M
4.30 P M	Sacramento and Knight's Landing via Davis...	10.45 A M
4.30 P M	Niles and Livermore...	* 8.45 A M
4.30 P M	Niles and San Jose...	‡ 4.15 P M
5.30 P M	Haywards and Niles...	7.45 A M
6.00 P M	Sunset Route, Atlantic Express, Santa Barbara, Los Angeles, Deming, El Paso, New Orleans and East...	8.45 P M
7.30 P M	Shasta Route Express, Sacramento, Marysville, Redding, Portland, Puget Sound and East...	7.45 A M
8.00 P M	Central Atlantic Express, Ogden and East...	9.45 A M
	SANTA CRUZ DIVISION.	
3.00 A M	Hunters train to San Jose...	‡ 7.20 P M
8.15 A M	Newark, Centerville, San Jose, Felton, Boulder Creek and Santa Cruz...	5.30 P M
*2.15 P M	Centerville, San Jose, Almaden, Felton, Boulder Creek and Santa Cruz...	*11.50 A M
4.15 P M	Centerville, San Jose, and Los Gatos...	9.50 A M
	Coast Division (Third and Townsend Sts.)	
7.25 A M	San Jose, Almaden and Way Stations...	2.30 P M
8.30 A M	San Jose, Gilroy, Tres Pinos; Pajaro, Santa Cruz; Monterey; Pacific Grove, Salinas, San Miguel, Paso Robles, Santa Margarita (San Luis Obispo) and principal Way Stations...	6.12 P M
10.30 A M	San Jose and Way Stations...	5.02 P M
12.01 P M	Cemetery, Menlo Park and Way Stations...	3.38 P M
*3.30 P M	San Jose, Tres Pinos, Santa Cruz, Salinas, Monterey, Pacific Grove and principal Way Stations...	*10.00 A M
*4.20 P M	Menlo Park and Way Station...	* 7.58 A M
5.20 P M	San Jose and Way Stations...	9.03 A M
6.30 P M	Menlo Park and Way Stations...	6.35 A M
†11.45 P M	Menlo Park and principal Way Stations...	†7.28 P M

A M for Morning. P M for Afternoon.
*Sundays excepted. †Saturdays only. ‡Sundays only.
**Mondays excepted. §Saturdays excepted.

OCEANIC STEAMSHIP CO.

Carrying United States, Hawaiian and Colonial Mails.

WILL LEAVE THE COMPANY'S WHARF, foot of Mission Street, No. 1,

For Honolulu, Auckland and Sydney,

WITHOUT CHANGE,

The Splendid New 3,000 ton Iron Steamer.

ZEALANDIA ..... Saturday, March 8, 1890, at 12 M., Or immediately on arrival of the English mails.

For Honolulu,

SS. AUSTRALIA (3,000 tons), February 28, 1890, at 12 M

For freight or passage, apply at office, 327 Market Street. JOHN D. SPRECKELS & BROS. General Agents.

KILLIP & CO.,

LIVE STOCK AND GENERAL AUCTIONEERS,

22 Montgomery Street, San Francisco

SPECIAL ATTENTION PAID TO SALES OF

High-Bred Horses and Cattle.

At auction and private sale.

Will Sell in All Cities and Counties of the State.

REFERENCES.

Hon. C. Green, Sacramento. — Hon. J. D. Carr, Salinas.
J. P. Sargent, Esq., Sargents. — Hon. John Boggs, Colusa.
Hon. L. J. Rose, Los Angeles. — Hon. A. Walrath, Nevada.
J. B. Haggin, Esq., San Francisco.

Represented at Sacramento by Edwin F. Smith, Secretary State Agricultural Society.

At San Jose by Messrs. Montgomery & Rea, Real Estate Agents.

Being the oldest established firm in the live-stock business on this Coast, and having conducted the important auction sales in this line for the past fifteen years, amounting to one half a million of dollars, we feel justified in claiming unequaled facilities for disposing of live stock of every description, either at auction or private sale. Our list of correspondents embraces every breeder and dealer of prominence upon the Pacific Coast, thus enabling us to give full publicity to animals placed with us for sale. Private purchases and sales of live stock of all descriptions will be made on commission, and stock shipped with the utmost care. Purchases and sales made of land of every description. We are authorized to refer to the gentlemen whose names are appended.

KILLIP & CO., 22 Montgomery Street

LAMBORN ROAD MACHINE

LIGHT DRAFT. MADE OF IRON. STRONG, SIMPLE, DURABLE. EASILY OPERATED.

TRUMAN HOOKER CO.

SAN FRANCISCO, - - CALIFORNIA

San Francisco and North Pacific Railway.

THE DONAHUE BROAD-GAUGE ROUTE.

COMMENCING SUNDAY, MARCH 17, 1889, AND until further notice, boats and trains will leave from and arrive at the San Francisco Passenger Depot, Market-street Wharf, as follows:

Leave San Francisco: Week Days.	Leave San Francisco: Sundays.	Destination	Arrive San Francisco: Sundays.	Arrive San Francisco: Week Days.
7.40 A M 3.30 P M 5.00 P M	8.00 A M 5.00 P M	Petaluma and Santa Rosa.	10.40 A M 6.10 P M	8.50 A M 10.31 A M 6.05 P M
7.40 A M 3.30 P M	8.00 A M	Fulton, Windsor, Healdsburg, Litton Springs, Cloverdale, and way stations.	6.10 P M	10.30 A M 6.05 P M
7.40 A M	8.00 A M	Hopland and Ukiah.	6.10 P M	6.05 P M
7.40 A M	8.00 A M	Guerneville	6.10 P M	6.05 P M
7.40 A M 5.00 P M	8.00 A M	Sonoma and Glen Ellen.	10.40 A M 6.10 P M	8.50 A M 6.05 P M
3.30 P M	5.00 P M	Sebastopol	10.40 A M	10.30 A M

Stage connects at Santa Rosa for White Sulphur Springs, and Mark West Springs; at Geyserville for Skaggs Springs, and at Cloverdale for the Geysers; at Hopland for Highland Springs, Kelseyville, Soda Bay, Lakeport and Bartlett Springs, and at Ukiah for Vichy Springs, Saratoga Springs, Blue Lakes, Willits, Cahto, Calpella, Potter Valley, Sherwood Valley and Mendocino City.

EXCURSION TICKETS from Saturdays to Mondays, to Petaluma, $1.50; to Santa Rosa, $2.25; to Healdsburg, $3.40; to Litton Springs, $3.60; to Cloverdale, $4.50; to Hopland, $5.70; to Ukiah, $6.75; to Guerneville, $3.75; to Sonoma, $1.50; to Glen Ellen, $1.80.

EXCURSION TICKETS, good for Sundays only, to Petaluma, $1; to Santa Rosa, $1.50; to Healdsburg, $2.25; to Litton Springs, $2.40; to Cloverdale, $3; to Guerneville, $2.50; to Sonoma, $1; to Glen Ellen, $1.20.

From San Francisco for Point Tiburon and San Rafael: Week Days—7.40, 9.20, 11.20, A. M.; 3.30, 5.00, 6.15 P. M. Sundays—8.00, 9.30, 11.00 A. M.; 1.30, 5.00, 6.20 P. M.

To San Francisco from San Rafael: Week Days—6.20, 7.55, 9.30 A. M.; 12.45, 3.40, 5.05 P. M. Sundays—8.10, 9.40 A. M.; 12.15, 3.40, 5.00 P. M.

To San Francisco from Point Tiburon: Week Days—6.50, 8.20, 9.55 A. M.; 1.10, 4.05, 5.30 P. M.; Sundays—8.40, 10.05 A. M.; 12.40, 4.05, 5.30 P. M.

On Saturdays an extra trip will be made from San Francisco to San Rafael, leaving at 1.40 P. M.

H. C. WHITING, General Manager.

PETER J. McGLYNN, Gen. Pass. & Tkt. Agt.

Ticket Offices at Ferry, 222 Montgomery Street and 2 New Montgomery Street.

CHICAGO, MILWAUKEE AND ST. PAUL RAILWAY.

Steam Heated and Electric Lighted Vestibuled Trains between Chicago, St. Paul and Minneapolis.

Electric Lighted and Steam Heated Vestibuled Trains between Chicago, Council Bluffs and Omaha.

Finest Dining Cars in the world.

Free Reclining Chair Cars between Chicago and Omaha.

Fast Mail Line between Chicago, Milwaukee, St. Paul and Minneapolis.

Transcontinental Route between Chicago, Council Bluffs and Omaha, or St. Paul.

Great National Route between Chicago, Kansas City and St. Joseph, Mo.

5,700 miles of road in Illinois, Wisconsin, Minnesota, Iowa, Missouri, South and North Dakota.

Everything First-Class.

First-Class People patronize First-Class Lines.

Ticket Agents everywhere sell Tickets over the Chicago, Milwaukee and St. Paul Railway.

W. T. ALLEN,
Pacific Coast Passenger Agent
Office, No. 138 Montgomery St., San Francisco, Cal.
Under Occidental Hotel

6 DONTS

DON'T own a racehorse.
DON'T be a breeder.
DON'T be a trainer.
DON'T be a jockey.
DON'T bet on the races.
DON'T go to a race track.

WITHOUT HAVING IN YOUR POCKET ONE OF

Goodwin's ANNUAL OFFICIAL TURF GUIDES.

Price, in cloth $5.00
Price, in half morocco 3.00
Price, in half calf 4.00
If sent by mail .... 10 cents extra

SUBSCRIBE TO IT FOR 1890.

It is published semi-monthly during the racing season, and is but **$10 per year.** Address

GOODWIN BROS.,
241 Broadway, New York City

HEALD'S

Business College, 24 Post St.

—San Francisco.—

The most popular school on the Coast

E. P. HEALD, President. C. S. HALEY, Sec'y.

Send for Circulars

FOR STOCK.

COLIC AND GRUBS.

I have used Simmons' Liver Regulator in Colic and Grubs with my mules and horses, giving them about half a bottle at a time, and have not lost one that I gave it to. You can recommend it to every one who has stock as the best medicine known for all complaints that horseflesh is heir to.

E. T. Taylor, Ag't for Grangers of Ga.

FOR CHICKENS.

In using Simmons' Liver Regulator (Powder) with my chickens for Cholera, I take and mix it with the dough and feed it to them once a day. By this treatment I have never lost a single chicken in the last five years from either Chicken Cholera or Gapes.

T. G. Bacon, Edgefield, S. C.

HOG CHOLERA.

A reliable gentleman who raises every year about one hundred head of hogs told me he never lost one from Cholera, although the disease had often appeared among his herd. His remedy is Simmons' Liver Regulator given in drenching—about double that given to a man. I give this information for the benefit of those whose hogs may be attacked with Cholera.—Prof. F. P. Hobgood, Oxford, N. C.

SIMMONS LIVER REGULATOR

is so conveniently given. The Powder mixed with the feed will be eaten by horses, cattle hogs, and chickens readily, while the Liquid (prepared) is easily given as a drench.

—ONLY GENUINE.—

Manufactured by J. H. ZEILIN & CO., Philadelphia, Pa. Price **$1.00.**

DR. FISHERMAN'S

Carbolized

Alkaline

LOTION

Cures after all other Remedies have Failed

Sprains, Sores, Bruises, Galls, Swellings, Scratches, Thrush, Grease Heels, Curb, Rheumatism. Restoring Weak Knees and Ankles to their original condition. As a wash it insures flossy manes and tails. Valuable as an internal remedy for Coughs, Colic, Congestion or Fever. You really get Half a Gallon of Remedy for $1.00, or Two Gallons for $3.00, after being adulterated as directed.

This Liniment has received the endorsement of some of our best horsemen. Recommended by Jos. Cairn Simpson. See BREEDER AND SPORTSMAN of November 10th, 1888.

LYNDE & HOUGH, Proprietors.

116 California St., S. F.

Or ask your Druggist for it.

HORSE OWNERS!

TRY GOMBAULT'S

CAUSTIC BALSAM.

A Safe, Speedy and Positive Cure for Curb, Splint, Sweeny, Capped Hock, Strained Tendons, Founder, Wind Puffs, all Skin Diseases or Parasites, Thrush, Diphtheria, Pinkeye, all Lameness from Spavin, Ringbone or other Bony Tumors. Removes all Bunches or Blemishes from Horses and Cattle.

Supersedes all Cautery or Firing. **Impossible to Produce any Scar or Blemish.**

Every bottle sold is warranted to give satisfaction. Price **$1.50** per bottle. Sold by druggists, or sent by express, charges paid, with full directions for its use. Send for descriptive circulars. Address LAWRENCE, WILLIAMS & CO., Cleveland, O.

BROU'S INJECTION

A PERMANENT CURE

in from 3 to 6 days, of the most obstinate cases; guaranteed not to produce Stricture; no sickening doses; and no inconvenience or loss of time. Recommended by physicians and sold by all druggists. J. Ferré, (successor to Brou), Pharmacien, Paris.

For any Kind of a

SORE THROAT

USE

McCLELLAN'S

DIPHTHERIA REMEDY

An Unfailing Cure.

FOR SALE BY ALL DRUGGISTS

OUR IMPROVED. ALL SIZES AND WEIGHTS. G. W. BOHANON. ESTAB. 1866.

THE BOHANON **SULKY!** BEST MADE.

Perfect Riding Buggies. Breaking Carts.

Fine Repairing, Reasonable Prices

Bohanon Carriage Co., 161-163 Ogden Ave., CHICAGO.

Send for Catalogue.

VETERINARY.

Dr. Wm. H. Jones, M.R.C.V.S.

Veterinary Surgeon,

(OLYMPIC CLUB STABLES)

503 Sutter Street, San Francisco.

Telephone, No 1404.

Consultations by letter, and cases of URGENT NECESSITY in the interior will receive prompt attention.

Dr. A. E. BUZARD,

VETERINARY SURGEON,

Member of the Royal College of Veterinary Surgeons, London, England. Graduated April 22d, 1870.

All Operations on the Horse Performed Skillfully.

Special attention given to the Diseases of Dogs. Calls to the country promptly attended to. Advice and prescriptions by mail $2. Office and Residence, No. 11 Seventh street, S. F. (opp. Odd Fellows Hall. Telephone No. 3 69.

W. H. WOODRUFF.

Veterinary Dentist,

AT FASHION STABLES,

221 Ellis Street, San Francisco

Improved Instruments, Humane Methods, First-Class Work.

H. E. CARPENTER,

Veterinary Surgeon,

Graduate of Ontario Veterinary College, Toronto, Canada.

RESIDENCE AND VETERINARY INFIRMARY

331 Golden Gate Ave., San Francisco.

Telephone 3069.

OPEN DAY AND NIGHT.

No risk in throwing Horses. Veterinary Operating Table on the premises.

DR. C. MASOERO,

Veterinary Surgeon,

Successor to **DR. A. DeTAVEL,**

GRADUATE OF ROYAL VETERINARY COLLEGE, TURIN.

OFFICE AND INFIRMARY,

No. 811 HOWARD STREET,

Between Fourth and Fifth. SAN FRANCISCO.

Telephone, No. 457.

R. WATKINS,

Veterinary Dentist,

Of twelve years practice, is now permanently located in San Francisco, and may be found at **C. S. Crittenden's** Golden Gate Livery and Riding Academy, **24 to 28 Golden Gate Avenue.**

Will treat ailments of the horse's mouth, and cure all such. Sidereim Pullers and Tongue Lollers etc. Satisfaction guaranteed. Orders by mail will receive prompt attention. Examination Free.

E. J. O'ROUKE.

I have the honor to announce to my old patrons and the general public that I may be found at my old stand, where, as heretofore, the

Shoeing of Horses,

whether for the Track, Drive, or for general work, will receive my personal attention.

Telephone 2011.

E. J. O'ROUKE,
209 Ellis Street

California Horse Shoe Co's

I have used in my business the Steel and Iron Shoes made by the above Company, and take great pleasure in saying they are the best I have ever used in twenty-two years' practice. I have never seen anything like the STEEL SHOE made by this Company. I can fully recommend them to every practical Horseshoer in the country. Yours respectfully,

No. 8 Everett Street. JOHN GRACE.

IF YOU WISH A GOOD REVOLVER PURCHASE ONE OF **SMITH & WESSON'S**

Finest small arms ever manufactured and the first choice of all experts. In calibres 32, 38 and 44-100. Single or double action, Safety Hammerless and Target models. **Best quality wrought steel,** carefully inspected for workmanship and stock. Unrivaled for **finish, durability and accuracy.** Do not be deceived by cheap *malleable iron imitations* often sold for the genuine article. They are unreliable and dangerous. The SMITH & WESSON REVOLVERS are stamped upon the barrels with firm's name, address and dates of patents, and are **guaranteed** perfect. Insist upon having them, and if your dealer cannot supply you, an order sent to address below will receive prompt attention. Descriptive catalogue and prices upon application.

SMITH & WESSON,
Springfield, Mass.

TWENTY-FOUR PAGES.

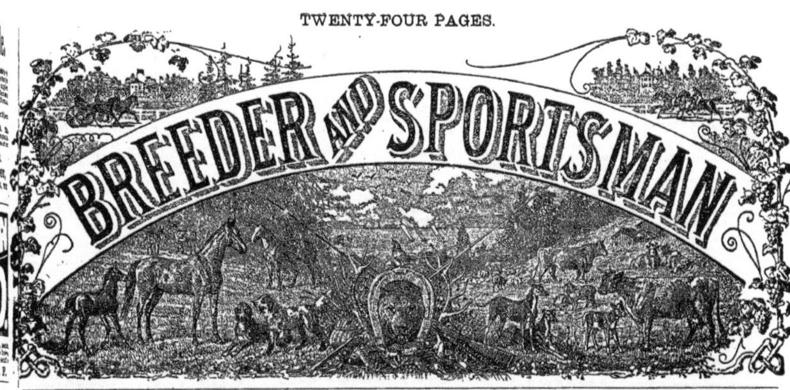

Vol. XVI. No. 10. No. 313 BUSH STREET. | SAN FRANCISCO. SATURDAY. MARCH 8, 1890. | SUBSCRIPTION FIVE DOLLARS A YEAR.

ANTEVOLO, JR.,

The property of Mr. L. Hewlett, Oakland, California.

The subject of our sketch this week, which has been produced in most inimitable style by the BREEDER AND SPORTSMAN's artist, Mr. Boyd, is Antevola Jr., the property of Mr. L. Hewlett, Oakland, Cal. The colt is three years old, and gives every promise of being as good as his notable sire when he fully matures. Antevolo Jr. is a dark bay, 16 hands high, well developed, with plenty of bone and muscle, and has extremely good feet. He is in stature, probably one of the tallest of the get of Mr. Simpson's horse, but he is so evenly turned that his height is carried off with his otherwise grand proportions. He has not been driven to exceed thirty times, but is well broken, and already shows a good gait, with a smooth, easy action that should ultimately cause him to become one of Californian's best stallions; taken all in all, he is a very handsome colt, as will be seen by his picture. The dam of Antevolo Jr. is Brownie H. by Priam, a son of Whipple's Hambletonian. Brownie H. is a large, fine mare, with star in forehead, one white hind ankle, and is a very speedy animal herself; she also stands 16 hands high, and weighs in the neighborhood of 1,250 pounds. Mr. Hewlett has frequently had her exhibited, and she invariably carries off the blue ribbons. Brownie H. was never trained, but can show a "twenty" gait almost any day. Although comparatively speaking a young mare, she has already had six foals, each and every one of whom have proved themselves to be very fast roadsters, and the elder ones would undoubtedly have proved themselves good track horses, but have never been trained; she herself was entered in a gentleman's race, for a set of harnesses at the Oakland track, and although receiving no special preparation, was enabled to win easily, her best mile being 2:36, and shortly afterwards she showed in private trial at the same place, 2:28 to a cart.

Brownie H. is the dam of Santa Rita Belle, by Echo Jr. Santa Rita Belle, with but six weeks' handling by Andy McDowell, showed a mile in 2:26, and two half miles, the first in 1:11 and the second in 1:12. Mr. Hewlett sold this good filly to Mr. Sturgis, but the latter gentleman was not willing to go to any more expense in training, and has had her bred to Director, by whom she should get an exceedingly fine foal.

Brownie H. is also the dam of Alda H., by Director, who is now three years old. This young filly so took the eye of Mr. Salisbury, that the owner of Director purchased her, and now he claims that she is the fastest filly he ever sat behind. With less than three months' handling, she was able to speed with Goldleaf, and was driven alongside of the noted pacer very frequently by Mr. Salisbury. She has been relegated to the broodmare division, having been bred to Guy Wilkes, and from the opinion that Mr. Salisbury has of her, we know it would take a very handsome sum to purchase Alda H.

Still another of the colts of Brownie H. is Greenwood by Lynwood, now two years old and weighs 1,000 pounds, and is 15.2 in height. Greenwood is owned by Geo. W. Russell, of East Oakland, and is considered one of the most stylish colts in Alameda County. Although but little exercised, Greenwood can show better than a 2:40 clip, and will undoubtedly prove himself as fast as any of Brownie H.'s foals.

Hulda H. also claims Brownie H. as her dam, she being by Director. This little lady is only a yearling, of very handsome conformation, and should prove herself one of the speedy lot. Mr. Hewlitt refused $1,000 for this filly when only three weeks old. One of the peculiarities of Brownie H. is that she invariably breeds after whatever horse she is bred to, and having produced such a very handsome foal by Director, Mr. Hewlett has bred her back once more to the premier stallion of the Pleasanton Stock Farm Company. Another peculiarity of Brownie H. is, she is both a natural pacer as well as a speedy trotter, and it makes no difference at which gait she is going, a spectator is apt to believe that she could not go at any other.

In speaking of the dam of Brownie H., Mr. Hewlitt said: "Her dam was Black Bess, also a fast pacer, who, before I bought her, some eighteen years ago, showed me a mile in better than 2:40 to a buggy, with two heavy men in it, on the old half-mile track, and although there was no pedigree to go with her, I became convinced she was one of the sort we needed here, and I paid for her what was then termed an insane price; notwithstanding the fun poked at me by my friends, I was offered more than one-half of my money back for the use of her to take part in a pacing race which was about to come off during the fair; however, I refused, as I did not purchase her for racing purposes, but only for my own amusement. I wanted to clean the road with her, and there are those still living who remember the extreme speed of my grand old mare, Black Bess. I bred her to Priam, a son of Whipple's Hambletonian, and the first year I got the mare Ila, which is the dam of Echo Jr. Ila, when three years old, pulled my buggy a mile in 2:50. I then bred Ila to Echo, and got Echo Jr.; at four years old I drove him a half mile during the stud season in 1:11 to a cart, showing that the family would breed on in speed during many generations. Mr. Simpson, in speaking of the death of Echo Jr., said he was the best colt of his age in California, and so I considered him. Echo Jr. died in June, 1884. After the birth of Echo Jr., Black Bess was bred once more to Priam, and got Brownie H., the dam of Antevola Jr., and every one of her colts as you will see have speed. Ila also has a Nutwood, a Monroe Chief, and a five-year-old stallion by Echo, none of which I have worked to amount to anything, but either of them can pull a cart any day in 2:40; they only require work to show how extremely fast they are."

Mr. Hewlett is a very busy man, and his time will not permit of his working his horses as he would desire, but there is no doubt if he should turn his young stock over to some reliable trainer, that there would be several additions to the 2:30 list during the year of 1890.

To show the peculiarities of families, and how their gaits will alternate, it might be as well to say here that Greenwood is a natural trotter, as was also Hulda H., on the contrary Alda H. paced as did also Santa Rita Belle; Antevolo Jr. is another of the trotters, and all of Ila's colts are trotters likewise.

Brownie H. is now twelve years old, and with her colts, make as fine a family for premium purposes as can be found on the coast. The extreme beauty of Antevolo Jr. is well known in Oakland and vicinity, so much so, in fact, that Mr. Hewlett has been urgently solicited by many of his friends to stand the horse for the season of 1890, and he has finally consented to accept fifteen mares for service. The youngster will not be trained this year, but his owner will in all probability turn him over to one of our crack drivers in 1891 to receive preparation for a campaign during that year.

Mr. Hewlett is the owner of a very nice ranch joining the Valensin Stock Farm, but for the present has it rented out; however, there is a prospect that in the near future he will begin the nucleus of another breeding establishment which will be a fitting neighbor for the many at present in Livermore valley.

To those who desire fast, young stock, we would advise them to call on Mr. Hewlett at his Oakland address, to see what grand individuals can be there purchased at a very moderate sum.

The following is the pedigree of Antevolo Jr.:

ANTEVOLO JR.

Sired by Antevolo 7648 (record 2:19½) by Electioneer 125.
First dam Brownie H. by Priam 1798.
Second dam Black Bess by Ladd's Kentucky Hunter.
Third dam a pacing mare, pedigree untraced.
ANTEVOLO BY ELECTIONEER 125 (sire of Sunol, 2:10½, Palo Alto, 2:12¾, etc.)
First dam Columbine by A. W. Richmond 1687 (sire of Romero, 2:19½, Arrow, 2:13¾, etc.)
Second dam by imp. Bonnie Scotland (sire of Scotland, 2:22½.)
Third dam Young Fashion by imp. Monarch. (See American Stud Book.)
PRIAM 1798 (sire of Honesty, 2:25½) by Hambletonian 725 (sire of 15 in the 2:30 list).
First dam Revere by imp. Glencoe.
Second dam by imp. Harkforward, etc.
HAMBLETONIAN 725, by Guy Miller (son of Hambletonian 10).
First dam Martha Washington by Washington 332.
Second dam by Abdallah 1.

Second Meeting of the Arlington Jockey Club.

Friday, the 28th of February was a perfect day. The track was in splendid condition and the crowd of people present to witness the races was joyous. It is seldom that you see so many people present at a postponed meeting. Santa Barbara surely has no equal. Only three or four days before the meeting the track was heavy, as it had rained for several days till 72 hours before the race, and yet Friday was a glorious spring day, and the track could not be better for runners. The first event of the afternoon was a one quarter mile dash, weight 160 lbs. In this race eleven horses were entered, so that the race was run in heats. In the first heat the following horses started:

Blue Rock, r g, entered by Bayard Thayer.
Butcher Boy, cr g, entered by A. A. Freeman.
McGinty, br g, entered by J. J. McKeel.
Billy, b g, entered by C. Carter.
Mark B., b g, entered by C. H. Gates.

This heat was soon over, as the starters, Thayer and Stow, caught the horses all in a bunch and sent them away to a splendid start. Butcher Boy was a disappointment. Mark B., ridden by P. Menchaca, won the heat handily, McGinty second; time, :26½. This left Mark B. and McGinty to run in the final heat. In the second heat the following horses started:

Blackfoot, r g, entered by H. I. V. Blake.
Killjoy, c g, entered by P. H. Duryea.
Bay Billy, b g, entered by H. T. Pendry.
Tom, b g, entered by Seth Loomis.
Charlie K., c g, entered by R. H. Kissell.
Modoc, blk g, entered by I. G. Waterman.

This heat was won, "hands down," by Tom, ridden by Frank Stoddard, Bay Billy second; time, 0:26.

This left the following four horses to run off for the purse: Mark B., Tom, McGinty and Bay Billy.

In the pools Mark B. sold for $5, Tom for $3 and the field for $2. Tom was unknown to the "boys," but they argued that Mark B. had so superior a rider that he should win the race. The starters gave the horses a good send off, and from the start to the finish the distance was contested by Tom and Mark B, Tom winning by half a length, Mark B second, Boy Billy third and McGiuty fourth; time, 0:26.

The second event of the day was the "Holiday Stakes," one-quarter mile handicap. Purse $45. The following horses started:

Blackfoot, r g, entered by H. J. V. Blake, ridden by Cordero.
Gladstone, b g, entered by E. R. Den, ridden by Menchaca.
Bob, br g, entered by C. Divers, ridden by Divers.
Jane, b m, entered by A. J. Boesgke, ridden by Boesche.

Although Gladstone is out of Lillian, she by Crighton and by Hardwood, still the talent played Bob, of unknown breeding, to win the race, and he did not disappoint his backers, for Bob won the race by a neck, and was never touched with the whip or spurs. This little brown gelding is a good horse. Bob won, Gladstone second, Jane third; time, 0:25½.

The half mile dash purse $100 was a sure thing for Grimbo. Lima Beans, the old stand by, was lame and sore, so that Grimbo was an easy winner. Very few pools were sold in this race. What few were sold were for second place, Lima Beans selling for $5, and the field for $3. The starters had much difficulty. The horses were half an hour fooling at the post, and after severe reprimands the horses were sent off to a fair start, Grimbo taking the lead and won easily. The following horses were entered:

Grimbo, s g, entered by Duryea and ridden by Duryea.
Pete, s g, entered by Mrs. Schawb, and ridden by Marquell.
Lima Beans, g g, entered by F. Stoddard, and ridden by Stoddard.
Domerio, s g, entered by C. H. Gates, and ridden by Romero.
Lightfoot, s g, entered by Duryea, and ridden by Menchaca.

Grimbo 1st, Pete 2nd, Lightfoot 3rd, Domerio fourth. Time, 0:56.

This ended the day's sport. In a few days the third event of the Arlington Jockey Club will be announced. Purses will be very liberal and thoroughbred horses will be eligible.

Santa Barbara will soon become famous in the equine world, for gentlemen of means are purchasing the best bred horses and mares that can be procured. E. R. Den and J. S. Bell have purchased from H. I. Thornton, thoroughbreds that will be shipped to Santa Barbara this week. J. W. Cooper's handsome two-year-old colt has been brought in from the country and will be put to work. He will be prepared for the races of this fall. The colt has developed wonfully. His muscular development is astonishing. He has the kindest disposition, and is very intelligent. He was being shod to-day and the colt appeared to realize the importance of the work. He stood it like one accustomed to it. The colt will make a record for himself this year. T. M.

Feb'y 28, 1890.

New York Jockey Club Declarations.

Great Eclipse Stakes, 223 entries. Spring meeting, 1890: Longitude colt, Lepanto, St. Omer, Jack of Diamonds, Semiramuis, La Cigale colt, Chesterton, Mon Droit, Mary Howard colt, Agenoria colt, Susan colt, Young George, Westchester (Dwyers), Manahatta filly, Mayonnaise filly, Wildwood, Etna colt, Morgan Girl colt, Scotia Riot, Rocket, Artic, Baritone, Penitent, Two Lips, Hands Off, Footlight, Chatham, Missive, Mountain Deer, Terrifier, Lita, All Hope, False, Arbutus, Glucose, Zulu, Putnam, Pandora, Portia, Morgheda, Varina, Janet colt, Bob Arthur, My Craft, Memnon. Total, 46.

Elms Stakes, 47 entries. Spring meeting, 1890: Her Highness, Abaca, Maudina filly, Kinosem, Equal Rights, Miss Rhodie, Grace Ely, Tigress, Frailty, Mamie Russell, Whisban, Fannie C. Total, 12.

Fleetwood Stakes, 74 entries. Spring meeting, 1890: Lord Dalmeny, Queen Toy, Australitz, Civil Service, Mucilage, Frailty, Windsor. Total, 7.

Hickory Stakes, 83 entries. Fall meeting, 1890: Abaca, Australitz, Minuet, Ralph Bayard. Total, 4.

Elms Stakes, 132 entries. Spring meeting, 1891: Bessie Payton filly, Pandora filly, Manahatta filly, Arbutus, False, Lita, All Hope Everywhere, Nimble, Pandora, Portia, Morgheda, Varina, Lady Mary, Aunt Betsy, Hazy, Virginia filly. Total, 17.

Fleetwood Stakes, 141 entries. Spring meeting, 1891: La Cigale colt, Agenoria colt, Susan colt, Beware, Young George, Footlight, Chatham, Terrifier, Citizen, Arbutus, Putnam, Lillian, Pandora, Bob Arthur, My Craft, Memnon. Total, 16.

Hickory Stakes, 218 entries. Fall meeting, 1891: La Cigale colt, Agenoria colt, Nonage filly, Beware, Young George, Lillie Babbitt colt, Mayonnaise filly, Footlight, Missive, Terrifier, Chatham, Arbutus, Putnam, Lillian, Adorer, Pandora, Portia, Morgheda, Bob Arthur, My Craft, Memnon, Tokay. Total, 22.

VETERINARY.

Conducted by W. Henry Jones, M. R. C. V. S.

Subscribers to this paper can have advice through this column in all cases of sick or injured horses or cattle by sending an explicit description of the case. Applicants will send their name and address that they may be identified. Questions requiring answers by mail should be accompanied by two dollars, and addressed to W. Henry Jones, M. R. C. V. S., Olympic Stables, Sutter Street, San Francisco.

FRESNO, Cal., Feb. 25, 1890.

VETERINARY EDITOR BREEDER AND SPORTSMAN:—I have a young horse which was cut by a barbed wire on the inside of the right fore leg, just above and touching the hoof. The cut seems to be deep and is circular in shape. The wound has been growing worse for a month and promises to leave an unsightly lump when it heals over. At first it caused scarcely any lameness, but now he can with difficulty use the foot. As the horse is at a ranch remote from a resident veterinary, will you kindly inform me through your query column what treatment to pursue to avoid leaving a blemish when the wound heals. Thanking you in advance, I am,

Yours very truly, A. D. FERGUSON.

Answer.—In answer to your enquiry on your young horse, I consider it a very bad case, and I do not think I can prescribe for the horse without seeing it. But in the meantime I would suggest, that you poultice the foot with flax seed, and apply carbolic acid two drams, Glycerine one ounce.

Laminitis or Founder in Horses.

Many enquiries having been made relative to the above disease, I think it advisable that the subscribers of the BREEDER AND SPORTSMAN should have some information on the subject.

There are several causes for this affection. Many cases arise from over driving and then giving the animal a quantity of cold water. It may arise from feeding on wheat or barley to a large extent, more especially in young horses.

The treatment to be pursued in any case is to remove the shoes at once, pare down the soles, administer a purgative, poultice the feet with flax seed, keep the animal on low diet, for instance, bran mashes and hay. On no account give any grain.

If the horse after a few days shows any indication of walking on his heels, it would be advisable to call in a veterinary surgeon.

W. HENRY JONES, M. R. C. V. S.

The Vital Force.

EDITOR BREEDER AND SPORTSMAN:—There have been a number of articles on "The Impregnation of Sire Strains" and the "Theory of Control of Sex" produced by different able writers, and their arguments in most cases have been self sustaining. I beg leave for admission of a few remarks on the subject, based on perhaps a different light than that which has been heretofore advanced.

I have always considered the universal force that governs the entire universe as the cause that controls everything created therein, either animate or inanimate; and for a reason that such a belief is applicable to our case, I give that the Creator has undoubtedly invented the most economical force to accomplish his purpose, and that everything that is created is subject to man, I hope all will admit.

This great force is electricity. By its action, the centre of which is our solar system, we are able to be, and without it evolution would cease. The subject as applied to the horse I shall endeavor to illustrate by taking for granted that electricity exists in all matter, and its presence is shown in all chemical actions. That there is chemical action in transforming or converting organic food into animal force or power will conclusively be granted, and while the living body appears an unvarying form, it is yet composed of infinitely small particles in a state of swift transition. The moment food is taken into the digestive organs the manufacture of force, which was in a dormant state, begins in a most industrious manner, selecting its respective ingredients for their proper destination. The hundreds of muscles that adorn the strong bony system, so framed as to admit free motion, are the instruments of action; its circulatory system is the foundation of force, and its nervous system binds all into a unit for effective efforts which alone are voluntary to the animal life, and which is controlled by the will, the seat of which, as in man, is found in the brain.

The office of the brain need not be explained further than to say it is the recipient of the dictates of man and any surrounding objects that may come within influential contact, and these dictates are transmitted in less time than is within the conception of man to grasp, and an idea is only formed by mathematical comparison with the transit of less speedy mediums.

As in fulfillment of his duty, the horse brings into action certain portions of his frame, nature demands a replacement of the exhausted power, and rotation progresses in proportion to the exertion or intensity. The parts that are called upon to act in the practice of certain gaits, the trot for instance, are consequently developed and the seat in the brain which is called instinct is also proportionately developed and eventually become a faculty which is adopted as a natural characteristic which in turn is transmittable to the progeny and in many cases for a series of generations, and if kept in agitation they become a fixed type which distinguishes different families.

This electrical force which is considered synonymous to nervous force, is no doubt possessed in different individuals in as many different degrees, yet it can be increased where it is scarce by abundance of food and exercise, the same as it can be reduced in high strung animals by severe work and insufficient diet. Scientific breeders have acquired this knowledge and stay by it.

The six hereditary rules will be adopted for generations to come, and the arguments are favorable to prove that they are governed by the universal force, and these hereditary qualities are as inherited from nature, plus that which is acquired by teaching and are transmittable to the progeny in proportion to the intensity it is possessed by the individual parents, either male or female.

The embryo in womb of dam is, in the same proportion, possessed of the characteristics of sire, yet subject to incidental changes the result of which are governed in a marked extent by the characteristics of the dam, her occupation, etc. That the sire should have such strong prepotency (vital force) as to stamp himself and maintain his control in the fœtus for the 49 or 50 weeks it is carried by the dam seems to me somewhat exaggerated by some, for this newly formed being which once was in the loins of sire and a part of him, is taken into a new world as it were, and if the habits or nature of dam are different to those of sire, they cease to be developed and remain in a dormant state until after birth when with the aid of man they can be awakened. These truths have been brought before your readers repeatedly, and several illustrations might be produced where horses of unknown breeding unexpectedly showed phenomenal bursts of speed and became famous turf performers and the investigation of their ancestary, breeders, etc. proved their descendants from prominent trotting families.

I hope that from the above there has been sufficient said to show that electricity is the medium which transmits to the progeny the characteristics of sire and dam in proportion to the intensity that it is possessed by the respective individuals, and subject to development both whilst in the embryo and after birth.

Now, in regard to the control of sex, our subject reaches a point which is really beyond the comprehension of the average man, but, nevertheless, I beg leave to state that this same electrical force is the sole controller, and that regardless of the physical condition of either male or female, but governed by the intensity of vigor of the generative organs at the time of copulation, when the one possessed of the greatest amorous intensity will control the sex. To illustrate, I shall produce a stallion to serve a mare, and both in full vigor, and at the highest stage of sexual heat the mare deposits her eggs into the generative organs, by the repulsive qualities it possesses, to be met by the germ therein placed by the male, and possessed with the opposite qualities which in turn are attractive as like electricities repel and unlike attract each other.

I consider that in the germ there are males and females, and in the eggs male and female eggs also, but in a reverse nature in each, so to make them have an affinity for each other, the male germ attracting the male egg and vice versa; and the control of sex will, according to this, be governed by the parent with the great intensity of sexual heat. In conclusion I would say, that man would have to know when this stage of sexual heat is in the required intensity to produce the sex sought for. There are some men that imagine that breeding as the mare comes in season, the produce will be one sex, and if at the time she is going out, the produce will be the other, and yet there have not been sufficient proofs come to my knowledge to make me convinced that the idea is practicable, and I doubt if it can ever be done more than to have it in our list of theories. Yet when these cease to be of sufficient strength to convince the student, he deems it necessary to surrender to the great and universal force.

These are my sentiments, and hope I have done my duty in expressing my views to the many readers of your valuable paper, and I will be attentive and studious to the arguments that may arise, endeavoring to discredit the same.

ELECTRIC.

Difficult Birth.

Time is very often the essence of the contract in affording relief, where delivery is difficult in the mare, cow, and ewe; consequently a few hints to breeders may enable them in some cases to give aid promptly, and thus avert the bad results to the mother of prolonged paining, and the great jeopardy to the unborn young from delayed birth, says Dr. C. F. Greenside in the Canadian Live Stock Journal. A little knowledge, confidence and judgment, are all that are necessary to enable one to rectify the majority of conditions that prevent delivery from taking place spontaneously.

Certainly experience is also valuable. The attendant upon animals that are about to bring forth should avoid being unnecessarily meddlesome, for while in this condition they should be disturbed as little as possible. An eye however, should be kept on them in order to observe if any progress is being made towards delivery after paining begins. This is particularly necessary in the mare, for a natural birth usually only occupies from fifteen to thirty minutes. If the period of delivery is prolonged beyond half an hour interference is justifiable, for the foal seldom survives more than an hour or two; three at the outside—but with the cow it is different, and there is not much danger in allowing her to go an hour or two, or even more, before affording relief.

As already stated, if progress is not noticeable, in due time an examination must be made. In doing this the hand and arm should be thoroughly cleansed and oiled in order to prevent the introduction of any foul matter, or the irritation of the maternal passage.

The introduction of the hand into the passage is not so easy until the first six inches have been passed, then the canal is larger. At from twelve to sixteen inches from the point of introduction the mouth of the womb is reached. This can be recognized as a ring-like ridge, which varies in prominence according to the extent to which it is dilated. If any portion of the foetus has passed through the mouth it will usually be found of considerable size, but in some instances it may not be large enough to admit the hand until it is pressed through gradually.

When the fœtus is reached it can then usually be ascertained why birth is being delayed, for in nine cases out of ten it is the result of some wrong position of the fœtus, which renders it a mechanical impossibility for it to pass through the passage, owing to its increased volume. Occasionally, and especially with the first young, and particularly the cow, even although the fœtus is in its proper position, the walls of the canal are not sufficiently dilatable to admit of birth by the unaided efforts of the mother, so that help has to be given. The natural position for the fœtus at the time of birth is to find the two fore feet with the head between them presented. It can readily be seen how favorable this presentation is for the gradual expansion of the passage. The front of the fœtus forms something of a cone-shaped mass, the point of the cone coming first, and gradually making room for the circular base. But as has been already stated, deviations from this natural presentation are usually the cause of difficult birth. One naturally inquires the cause of variations in position. The most reasonable explanation of the majority of wrong positions is that when the pains begin and the womb begins to press on the fœtus and force it towards the mouth of that organ, if the mouth is not sufficiently open to receive it, the pressure continuing, turns the presented position backwards, and a malposition is produced. However, this will not account for all cases, for in some instances there is undoubted evidence that the fœtus has been in an unnatural position for a length of time, as shown by the legs and neck being bent and stiffened.

Up to one month prior to birth the fœtus is not in the position naturally found at the time of delivery. A month before it is time for it to be born it alters its position to that found at birth, and doubtless it is then that some cases of malposition are brought about.

On making an examination if it is found that the mouth of the womb is not sufficiently dilated, the hand should be gradually forced through it until the fœtus is reached, when the fore legs and muzzle should be drawn into the narrow position and left there.

When paining recurs, the force being exerted on the fœtus, in the natural direction, the passage soon expands to a sufficient extent to allow the fœtus to pass. In a case in which the fœtus is large in proportion to the size of the passage it may be necessary to aid the mother in its expulsion by drawing on the presented parts. In applying traction to the fœtus some care should be exercised in order to prevent injury to the mother. The drawing efforts should be made simultaneously with the expulsive ones of the mother.

Between the pains only sufficient force should be exerted in order to prevent retraction. In drawing, the traction should be applied in a downward direction, as this is the natural one, and consequently less opposition is likely to result from following it. When great force is required in order to effect delivery, some advantage may be gained by drawing first to one side and then toward the other. From the slippery condition of the fœtus very little grip can be got with the hands, and it is consequently almost always necessary to use ropes with the ends looped over the presented parts. Ropes of the size of the ordinary plough lines are suitable. They should be applied as far back on the fœtus as possible in order to take advantage of all power. In order to make an examination of the position of the fœtus it is often necessary to tear the water bags. There should be no hesitation in doing so when necessary.

In some cases of prolonged birth, if the bags are ruptured early, and paining goes on, all the water is ejected and the walls of the passage become dry, which greatly adds to the difficulty of extracting the fœtus. In such cases some benefit may be derived from the pouring in or injecting of some lubricant such as oil or cream.

Protecting the Feet.

An ingenious little device has been patented in England for the protection of horses' feet, which is said to not only be much neater but much more effective than the boots or rings hitherto used for that purpose. It consists of a molded piece of rubber with a flange and a half round edge, tapering from the toe of the shoe to the heel, which is nailed through between the iron-shoe and the hoof. The rubber filled thus applied acts as a buffer, and prevents injury in the case of horses that are prone to cut one leg by the shoe of the other. It also does away with the necessity of rasping the feet or drawing in the shoes, which causes the feet to contract and often leads to lameness. It is a useful appliance for colts when broken into harness, as there is no danger of damaging their back sinews, as is now often done when the use of certain kinds of boots are resorted to. It is further claimed that it supplies a valuable addition in the racing stable for horses in training, as it prevents injury to the fetlock joint by treading or striking.

Declarations in the East.

Declarations from the spring handicaps were due February 20th. Considering the large number of entries very few are declared out. So far returns received at the jockey clubs show but few stars of the first magnitude. Dwyer Bros. declared Hanover and Kingston from all but the Brooklyn Handicap, the first of the great handicaps to be run. In the absence of the Dwyers, the reason is said to be too heavy an impost of weight. Kingston headed the Brooklyn Handicap at 128 pounds, and the Suburban at 136. Following are the declarations received as far as known.

The Brooklyn Handicap—Exile, Taragon, Belinda, Reclare, Ben Harrison, Sentiment and Glendale.

The Coney Island Jockey Club's Handicaps—The Suburban: Kingston and Hanover. The Sheepshead Bay Handicap: Kingston and Hanover. The Bay Ridge Handicap; Kingston, Hanover and Exile. The Volunteer Handicap; St. Carlo, Blackburn and Longford.

The New York Jockey Club's Handicaps—The Toboggan Slide Handicap: Kingston, Hanover, Salvator, Prince Royal, Firenzi, Come-to-taw, Magnate, Phoebe and Coots. The Bowling Brook Handicap: Padisha, Blackburn, June Day and Ralph Bayard.

The Standard.

[AS REVISED AND ADOPTED BY THE NATIONAL ASSOCIATION OF TROTTING-HORSE BREEDERS, DECEMBER 14, 1887.]

IN order to define what constitutes a trotting-bred horse and to establish a BREED of trotters on a more intelligent basis, the following rules are adopted to control admission to the records of pedigrees. When an animal meets the requirements of admission and is duly registered, it shall be accepted as a standard trotting-bred animal:—

FIRST.—Any stallion that has himself a record of two minutes and thirty seconds (2:30) or better, provided any of his get has a record of 2:35 or better, or provided his sire or his dam is already a standard animal.

SECOND.—Any mare or gelding that has a record of 2:30 or better.

THIRD.—Any horse that is the sire of two animals with a record of 2:30 or better.

FOURTH.—Any horse that is the sire of one animal with a record of 2:30 or better, provided he has either of the additional qualifications: (1) A record himself of 2:35 or better. (2) Is the sire of two other animals with a record of 2:35 or better. (3) Has a sire or dam that is already a standard animal.

FIFTH.—Any mare that has produced an animal with a record of 2:30 or better.

SIXTH.—The progeny of a standard horse when out of a standard mare.

SEVENTH.—The female progeny of a standard horse when out of a mare by a standard horse.

EIGHTH.—The female progeny of a standard horse when out of mare whose dam is a standard mare.

NINTH.—Any mare that has a record of 2:35 or better, and whose sire or dam is a standard animal.

Best Trotting Records.

1 mile—2:08¾, Maud S., against time, in harness, accompanied the distance by a running horse, Glenville, O., July 30, 1885 ......2:13¼, best time in a race between horses, Maud S., Chicago, Ills., July 24, 1880 ......2:12, Axtell, against time, accompanied by running horse—fastest stallion time, Terre Haute, Ind., Oct. 11, 1889 ......2:13¾, Phallas, fastest heat by a stallion against other horses, Chicago, July 14, 1884 ......2:12¾, Palo Alto, third heat in race at Stockton, Cal., Sept. 26, 1889 ......2:15¼, Jay-Eye-See, half-mile track, Lincoln, Neb., Sept. 14, 1887 ......2:15¼, Great Eastern, under saddle, third heat, Morrisania, N. Y., Sept. 22, 1877 ......2:10¾, Jay-Eye-See, against time, best five-year-old record, Providence, R. I., Sept. 15, 1883 ......2:16, Manzanita, third heat, best four-year-old record, Lexington, Ky., Sept. 3, 1876 ......2:16, Edgemark, four-year old stallion record, against time, Lexington, Ky., Oct. 16, 1889 ......2:10½, Sunol, in Stanford stake, accompanied by a runner, best three-year-old record, San Francisco, Nov. 9, 1889 ......2:18, Sunol 2 years, against time, San Francisco, Cal., Oct. 27, 1888 ......2:20½, Regal Wilkes, two-year-old stallion record, San Francisco, Nov. 9, 1889 ......2:31½, Norlaine, yearling, against time, San Francisco, Cal., Nov. 12, 1887 ......2:35, Faustino, yearling stallion record, San Francisco, Nov. 9, 1889.

2 miles—4:43 against time, Fanny Witherspoon, Chicago, Ill., Sept. 25, 1885.

3 miles—7:21¼, Huntress, harness, Brooklyn, L. I., Sept. 21, 1872.

4 miles—10:34½, Longfellow, Wagon, California, Dec. 31, 1869.

5 miles—13:00, Lady Mac, harness, San Francisco, Cal., April 2, 1874.

10 miles—27:23½, Controller, harness, San Francisco, Cal., Nov. 23, 1878.

20 miles—58:25, Captain McGowan, harness, half-mile track, Boston, Oct. 31, 1865.

Pacing Records at One Mile.

Johnston, harness, against time, Chicago, Ills., Oct. 9, 1884, 2:06¼.

Brown Hal, best stallion record, Cleveland, Ohio, July 31, 1889, 2:12½.

Westmont, July 10, 1884, Chicago, Ills., with running mate, 2:01¾.

Daisy, yearling, Sacramento, Dec. 31, 1885, 2:38½.

Ed Rosewater, two years old, Council Bluffs, Iowa, Nov. 3, 1888, 2:20¼.

Yolo Maid, 3 years old, San Francisco, Oct. 13, 1888, 2:14.

Gold Leaf, four years old, 2:11¼ on August 17, 1889, at Napa.

Arrow, five years old, 2:13¼, made at Cleveland, Ohio, August 1, 1888

Fastest Time on Record.

RUNNING.

Miles.		Time
¼	Jim Miller, 2, Deer Lodge (Mont.), Aug. 16, 1888 ...... †Sleepy Dick, a, Kiowa (Kan.), Nov. 24, 1888	0:21¼
⅜	Cyclone, a, 120 lbs., Helena (Mont.), Aug. 28, 1889	0:34¼
½	Geraldine, 4, 122 lbs., Westchester Course, Aug. 30, 1889 ...	0:46
⅝	Britannic, 5, 122 lbs, Westchester Course, Aug. 31, 1889 ...	0:59
⅝	Fordham, a, 115 lbs., Westchester Course, Oct. 4, 1889	0:59
¾	El Rio Rey, 2, 120 lbs. Westchester Course, Aug. 31, 1889.	1:11
¾	Tipstaff, 3, 107, Westchester Course, Oct. 4, 1889	1:11
⅞	Britannic, 5, 110 lbs., Sheepshead Bay, Sept. 5, 1889	1:25 2-5
	Ten Broeck, 5, 110 lbs., Louisville, May 24, 1877 ...... (against time)	1:39¾
1	Maori 4, 105 lbs, Chicago, July 12, 1889, (in a race)	1:39 1-5
1 1-16	Wheeler T., 3, 98 lbs., St. Louis, June 1, 1888	1:47¾
1 1-16	Evlton 4, 108, Chicago, Ill., June 28, 1889	1:47¾
1⅛	Terra Cotta, 4, 124 lbs., Sheepshead Bay, June 23, 1888	1:53
1 3-16	Joe Cotton, 5, 109½ lbs., Sheepshead Bay, Sept. 7, 1887	2:00¾
1¼	Kingston, 5, 122 lbs., Gravesend, Sept. 21, 1889	2:06¼
1 m	500 yds. Ben d'Or, 4, 115 lbs., Saratoga, July 25, 1882	2:10¼
1⅜	Triboulet, 4, 117 lbs, San Francisco, April 26, 1888 ...... Richmond, 6, 122 lbs., Sheepshead Bay, June 27, 1888	2:21¼
1½	Firenzi, 4, 113 lbs., Monmouth Park, Aug. 2, 1888 ...... Luke Blackburn, 3, 102 lbs., Monmouth Park, Aug. 17, '80 Jim Guest, 4, 98 lbs., Chicago (Washington Park), July 24 '88	2:34
1⅝	Hindoocraft, 3, 75 lbs, Westchester, Aug. 27, 1889	2:48
1¾	Glidelia, 5, 116 lbs, Saratoga, Aug. 5, 1882	3:01
1⅞	Enigma, 4, 90 lbs., Sheepshead Bay, Sept. 15, 1885	3:2[illegible]
2	Ten Broeck, 5, 110 lbs., Louisville, May 29, 1877	3:27½
2¼	Monitor, 4, 110 lbs., Baltimore, Oct. 20, 1880	3:41½
2½	Springbok, 5, 114 lbs., Preakness, a, 114 lbs., Saratoga, July 29, 1875	3:56¼
2⅝	Aristides, 4, 104 lbs., Lexington, May 13, 1876	4:27½
2¾	Ten Broeck, 4, 104 lbs., Lexington, Sept. 16, 1876	4:58½
2⅞	Hubbard, 4, 107 lbs., Saratoga, Aug. 9, 1873	4:[illegible]8¾
3	Drake Carter, 4, 115 lbs., Sheepshead Bay, Sept. 6, 1884	5:24
4	Ten Broeck, 4, 104 lbs., Louisville, Sept. 27, 1876	7:15¾

HEAT RACES.

Miles.		Time
¼	Sleepy Dick, a, Kiowa (Kan.), Nov. 24, 1888	0:21½—0:22½
½	Bogus, a, 118 lbs., Helena (Mont.), Aug. 21, 1888	0:48—0:48
⅝	Kittie Pease, 4, Dallas (Tex.), Nov. 2, 1887	1:00—1:00
	Sudie McNairy, 3, 95 lbs., Chicago, July 2, 1883	1:02¼—1:03
¾	Lizzie S., 5, 118 lbs, Louisville, Sept. 28, 1883	1:13½—1:13½
1	Bounce, 4, 90 lbs., Sheepshead Bay, Sept. 7, 1881	1:42—1:41½
1	3 in 5. L'Argentine, 6, 115 lbs., St. Louis, June 14, 1879	1:43—1:44—1:47½
1 1-16	Slipalong, 6, 115 lbs., Chicago (Wash. Park), Sept. 2, 1885	1:50¼—1:48
1⅛	Gabriel, 4, 112 lbs., Sheepshead Bay, Sept. 23, 1880	1:56—1:56
1¼	Glenmore, 5, 114 lbs., Sheepshead Bay, Sept. 25, 1880	2:10—2:14
1¼	Keno, 6, Toledo, Sept. 16, 1883 (1st and 3d heats)	2:10¼—2:15
2	Miss Woodford, 4, 107½ lbs., Sheepshead Bay, Sept. 20, 1884	3:33—3:31½
3	Norfolk, 4, 100 lbs., Sacramento, Sept. 23, 1865	5:27¼—5:29½
	Ferida, 4, 105 lbs., Sheepshead Bay, Sept. 18, 1880	7:23½—7:41

†Made in a heat race.

*Doubtful, and made in a heat race.

TURF AND TRACK.

J. H. McCormick's health does not improve.

Ed. Corrigan has been at Arkansas Hot Springs.

Alcryon heads the list of winning trotters with $21,500.

Surefoot stills heads the list of quotations for the English Derby.

The Belle Meade yearlings 64 head will be sold next month.

Exile was one of the first scratchings for the Bay Ridge handicap.

The total for the eight day's Woodward sale at Lexington of 485 horses was $379,620.

It is said West & Francis are about the only two straightforward riders at New Orleans.

Frank Whitney, the celebrated artist, is making an oil painting of the phenomenal Axtell, 1:12.

Starter Caldwell, on February 21st, reinstated all jockeys at Clifton and Guttenberg up to date.

The Law and Order League have been making things lively lately for the gamblers in Spokane.

Jou Jou after his Saturdays victory was sent down to San Jose to be kept in good trim for the spring races.

D. D. Withers sold Fitzroy and Laggard to W. C. Daly a while ago. Father Bill soon earned oats with the former.

The Old Guard Stakes and the Green Isle Selling Stake will be the features at Clifton on March 17 (St. Patrick's Day).

Four car loads of mares came down from Vina to Palo Alto last Wednesday. They will be bred and then shipped back again.

Little Monarch, a gray three-year-old gelding, by that game old sprinter Little Minch, is said to be a speedy five furlong customer.

The well-known race-horse Applause was sent down to San Jose last Monday, and will be trained in future by W. L. Appleby.

On February 17th B. C. Holly's Ninena foaled a bay colt, "Sidney," by Sid, dam Ninena by Jim Brown out of Nannie Hubbard.

Dr. L. Herr the veteran breeder of Lexington, Kentucky, will have a string of trotters on the circuit for the first time for several years.

The star of the Monmouth track is *Firenzi*, the Brooklyn track habitues worship Kingston, while the pride of Westchester is Tenny.

T. H. Williams Jr. will have a small stable on the circuit this season, including the two-year-old Glenlivet, a sister to Guenn and Geoffrey.

"McGinty Wilkes." Thank goodness! no thoroughbred owner has yet been imbecile enough to name a horse after the would be immortal.

It is said Arrow, 2:13½, the ex-California pacer, is looking exceptionally well, and is confidently expected to lower his record this season.

Firenzi and Salvator are both scratched for the Toboggan Slide Handicap. They were probably only entered out of compliment to Mr. Morris.

Col. J. W. Guest is said to have a slashing three-year-old Prince Charlie colt called Dr. Nave, who will probably be seen in the Louisville Derby.

Buffalo Girl 2:12½, dropped a bay filly at Lexington, Ky., recently, by Jerome Eddy, 2:16½. She was sent to Lexington to be bred to Red Wilkes.

John Fayler has left Santa Anita, presumably for Santa Anita's good, as two valuable broodmares and three colts have been lost through neglect.

Judson H. Clarke the purchaser of Wellington, brother to Sunol 2:19½ has changed his name to Lord Wellington as there was already a Wellington.

In fourteen years Dwyer Bros. have won $1,240,065. Last year their winnings were 168,717, and Longstreet headed the list with $38,809 and Kingston with $22,957 is second.

The Rosemeade sale is quite phenomenal, with Alcazar $25,800, and Voodoo (2 years old, by Stamboul 2:12½, dam Eva 2:23½) $24,100, and the broodmares selling in proportion.

Marie Stuart, the dam of Caliente, died at Santa Anita last week, heavy in foal to the Emperor. She had been kept up for several days, but was turned out one wet day and took cold.

A great opportunity is offered by the Short-horn breeders. On April 3rd they will offer to the public some registered Short-horns, and all stock raisers should then take the bull by the horns.

The Trainers and Jockeys' Association will meet March 3 in the large room of the Monmouth Park Association instead of at the St. James Hotel, which Capt. W. M. Conner offered for the purpose.

On February 19th B. C. Holly's Phyllis (by imp Admirable, dam Daphne by Whipple's Hambletonian, granddam Phœbe Cary by Chieftain 721, etc.) foaled a bay filly by McDonald Chief, he by Clark Chief.

Peter Johnston the well known trainer and driver of the Kalamazoo Stock Farm is safe home after his trip on the Pacific Coast, where everyone was delighted to see him come and loth to see him depart.

In the report of the Secretary of the Ormsby District Agricultural Association he reports the receipts of the last Fair at $22,801.53, and the expenses $23,110 07, leaving a deficiency of $308.54, which he states is covered by unpaid life memberships.

The Sacramento Race track has practically been useless for runners all through the winter. The extreme outside of the track only being usable while the inside track which is used by runners alone, has never been in good condition for horses to even canter on.

Mr. N. Finzer, the owner of Maori, last Monday engaged Barnes to ride the well known mare at 107 lbs. in the Suburban. The imported mare, who ran such a cracking mile at Washington Park last year, carrying 105 lbs., in 1:39 4 5, should render a good account of herself with the colored crack up, although it would seem almost a furlong too far.

Mr. N. Finzer of Louisville, Ky., has been taking a look through the State, and besides engaging Barnes to ride Maori, Mr. Finzer purchased Volante from Santa Anita; the old horse whose face is well known on almost every race course, will go immediately to Louisville, and will be installed at Mr. Finzer's farm, a few miles outside Louisville, as premier stallion. The price paid was $7,000.

Messrs. Miller & Sibley, Prospect Hill Stock Farm, Franklin, Pa., on February 28th, purchased from E. F. Coe, of New York, for $7,500, the three-year old stallion Conductor, by Electioneer, dam Sontag Mohawk. Sontag Mohawk is the dam of Sallie Benton, 2:17¾; Eros, 2:29½; Sport, 2:22¾. Conductor will after a short season in the stud be handled for a record.

One of the best known faces on the turf in Australia in Sam Cashmer, the blind bookmaker, who travels about arm in arm with a deaf and dumb man. During a race the deaf and dumb man holds Sam's hand, tells him what is going on, and so rapid is the signaling between them that Sam will often shout at the last turn that he will lay so-and-so, which horse the dumb man has communicated to him is already beaten.

A. G. Hunt, a Boston horseman, sent a trotter down to Bangor Me., one day last week, and would have gone down himself the next but he happened to step into Walker's, and when he went up the street he was leading a horse. That horse kept him in the Hub a week. He swapped eleven times, and got two harnesses, a buggy and three watches, and more money than the horse cost to boot, and then got him back, sent him to Walker's and sold him for more than he first gave. Then he started for Bangor, scolding about his luck, "couldn't get away."

The well-known sprinter Energy, brother to Enthusiast, died last month at M. E. Blanc's Stud Farm at St. Cloud, France. He has been replaced by Retreat, who, although well bred, by Hermit, out of Quick March by Rataplan out of Qui Vive (sister to Vedette) by Voltigeur out of Mrs. Ridgeway by Birdcatcher, has not proved a success, his winners at the stud in the last three seasons being only Fastness, Father O'Flynn, Ritualist, St. Serge, Archer, Alice and Hinnington—in all twelve races, value £1,890 14s. M. Menier has purchased Claymore for a stallion, and he has left for France.

Secretary McIntyre has announced the following stakes to be run at the Spring meeting at Elizabeth, which begins on April 14.

For two-year-olds—The Jersey Central and Pamrapo, at half a mile, and the Claremont and Roselle Stakes, at five furlongs.

For three-year-olds—The Luke Blackburn, at a mile, and the Bayonne Stakes, at a mile and a furlong.

For three-year-olds and upwards—The New Jersey Jockey Club Handicap, a double event. The first to be run at a mile and a furlong and the second at a mile and a quarter. The Oakwood Stakes, at six furlongs; the Seward, at six furlongs; the Great Long Island, at a mile and a quarter; and the Meadow Stakes, at six furlongs. The latter is for fillies.

The stakes will close March 20.

Truth says: The policy of increasing the value of the English Grand National (the Blue Riband of cross country sportsmen) to £2,000 appeared to practical people to be of very questionable prudence, and it is clear that the extra sum might as well have been thrown into the Mersey, as there are actually four entries less than last year, nor is there any compensation (indeed, were any possible) in point of quality. There are four previous winners in Voluptuary (1884), Roquefort (1885), Gamecock (1887), and Frigate, who won last year, after having been three times placed second or third. There are ten Irish horses, two from France (Fetiche and Content-Tout-de-Meme) and a German candidate in Parnais. The stable over which Mr. Arthur Yates presides has six representatives. There are all the old stagers, such as Hettie, Battle Royal, Ballot Box, Bellona, Why Not, Usna, Johnny Longtail, Come Away, and The Sikh. Among the new names the best known are Phil, Latania, and Grey Friar, to which may be added that of Touane, who is now twelve years old. The chances are that there will be a small field.

Firmness, kindness and patience are three of the essential elements in the make up of any one who is a success in handling horses. Without the first a man would naturally be a failure. The condition of a horse when under the subjection of man is unnatural, although no domestic animal submits to its surroundings more gracefully and carefully. To control him perfectly the one doing it must be master of the situation under all circumstances. A firm man will prevent disasters where a faint one would fail. When a horse is to be brought under subjection it must be done by conquering his will and not his strength. It would be a dismal failure if the reverse were true. As to the second element, kindness, the more of this the better. No horse was ever spoiled or injured by kind treatment. There is no animal upon the mind of which kindness will make a greater impression than upon that of a horse. Without the latter, patience, no man can hope for success in handling horses. The man who can patiently develop the good traits of an animal and discourage the vicious ones, has it within his power to change the horse of bad habits into one that will be valuable. These points are certainly apparent to every thinking man, and the "three graces" should be acquired, if not already possessed by all who have the management of horses to look after.—Canadian Agriculturalist.

Before the last race at Clifton on February 24th Jockey McCarthy received his final instructions fro[m] Owner Flynn as to how he should ride Young Duke i[n] the race about to be run. "Now, Andy, I know you like t[o] ride as suits you best, but I want you for once to do as I te[ll] you and you will win," handing the jockey as he said th[is] a ticket on Young Duke calling for $250.

"Now bear in mind from the first jump to lay with Autocrat. He is the horse you have to beat and the d——l tak[e] the others. Never mind where the leaders are, you mak[e] your race with him from the turn home."

A few minutes later, showed McCarthy racing helter ske[l]ter after Sundial and so taking it out of Young Duke that [he] failed to beat Autocrat by a small margin. What Flynn sa[id] afterwards won't bear repetition.

The famous old thoroughbred Aristides, winner of the fir[st] Kentucky Derby, and whose time of 4:27½ for two and on[e] half miles still stands as the best on record, has been sol[d] by Patton & Crosswhite. Aristides was foaled in 187[2] and in his three and four-year-old form disputed wit[h] Ten Broeck the claim to the title "King of the Turf." I[t] was as a four-year-old, on September 16, 1876, with 104 lbs up, that he made the record for two and a half mile[s]. Although he was supreme on the turf, he has been a failur[e] in the stud. It has been the experience of breeders of bot[h] trotters and runners, that the performance of a horse is n[ot] always a criterion of his value as a sire. Aristides was in Luc[as] Turner's Kinlock stud for years, and when the stud was di[s]posed of at auction 14 months ago, the old horse was bough[t] by Patton & Crosswhite, and put in the stud at their far[m] near Sturgeon, Mo. Aristides had several starters on th[e] turf last season, and the best of the lot was W. J. Widener['s] Aristi, br c, 5, who, as a three-year-old and four-year-ol[d] won a number of good races. Atticus, ch c, 3, and Artisti[c] b f, 2, failed to secure brackets. Mr. Patton said to a S[t.] Louis Republic reporter: 'We have sold Aristides, but w[e] are under pledge not to reveal the name of purchaser o[r] price. You can say that Aristides' new owner will probabl[y] sell him, and that he is now considering a good offer." M[r.] Patton was part owner of Favor, the first St. Louis Der[by] winner.

Affairs of the Linden Park Blood Horse Association see[m] to be in a decidedly unsettled condition, which is extremel[y] unfortunate, for the track's surroundings and its buildin[gs] are such as to make it a most attractive spot. The openin[g] meeting was a complete fiasco, because the track was n[ot] ready at that time. The trouble seemed to be that the original builder of the track constructed it on wrong principle[s]. Superintendent Frank Clark of the Coney Island Jock[ey] Club was called upon at the eleventh hour, and although h[e] did all he knew how, to remedy the trouble, it was impossib[le] to make the track anything but a peaty-like mass, ov[er] which it was unsafe to race. Lucien O. Appleby, the principal capitalist, interested in the scheme, did all he could [to] induce his associates to abandon the meeting of last Octobe[r]. But he was outvoted, and, as will be remembered, with diastrous results. Since that short meeting the track has bee[n] entirely rebuilt, and will be in good condition for racing [in] April, when, under arrangements made last fall, it was pr[o]posed to again try racing at the track on alternate days wi[th] the New Jersey Jockey Club. There is now more troub[le] among the owners of the property, caused, it is said, by [an] unwillingness on the part of some of them to advance an[y] more money. Whether there will be racing there in th[e] spring is as yet undecided, but there will be in all probab[il]ity, if the latest reports regarding the track be true. Th[e] report is that the Pennsylvania Railroad people, who ha[ve] been to considerable expense in constructing side track[s] propose to step into the breach and furnish whatever mon[ey] may be necessary to put the club on a good financial footi[ng] and enable it to have a spring meeting. It would surpr[ise] no one familiar with racing matters if this should be t[he] case. In fact, many expect to see the track eventually pa[ss] wholly into the hands of the railroad people, who know th[at] racing has proved very profitable to its backers in New Jersey.

Leslie Macleod, assistant editor of Wallace's Month[ly] wrote a long account of his Palo Alto visit in the New Y[ork] Tribune. Among other things he says:

"Charles Marvin, Senator Stanford's trainer, is a man [of] great resources in his profession, an indefatigable work[er] and a close student of the mental traits of the horses [he] trains. He is far and away the most successful trotti[ng] horse trainer of this age, and a man of even temper a[nd] superior intelligence. My visit to Palo Alto was for t[he] purpose of preparing for publication a work on traini[ng] written by Mr. Marvin, and necessarily I had to study t[he] Palo Alto methods closely. The usual course was follow[ed] with Sunol. The colt at Palo Alto is weaned at about f[ive] months old, and is then taught to lead by the halter. Af[ter] he becomes thoroughly accustomed to this, he is given [his] first preparation for his turf career. This is on the mi[nia]ture track, or, as I call it, the kindergarten, and mark y[ou] this innovation is one of the distinctive features of the s[ys]tem of training which Senator Stanford and Mr. Marvin p[er]fected. This is a covered track, about one-fifteenth o[f a] mile in circumference, and in fact, a counterpart in mi[nia]ture of the regulation mile track. This colt is led around until the novelty wears off, and is then turned loose, af[ter] being carefully booted with perfect fitting shin and quar[ter] boots. Of course the colt's first impulse is to gallop arou[nd] the track, but he soon settles into a trot, and is thereaf[ter] kept at it as much as possible, being controlled by the vo[ice] and the whips of the trainers, but he is never struck [or] treated with the slightest violence.

"The youngsters learn surprisingly fast what is wanted [of] them, and after a few months take the exercise with scar[cely] a mistake. Prominent among the good features of this tr[ain]ing equipment, it may be mentioned that it sifts the g[ood] from the bad, and enables the trainer to pick out those t[hat] are most promising. This is no small advantage at a pl[ace] of the extent of Palo Alto, where there are about 300 br[ood] mares in the stud, and from 70 to 100 horses and colts alw[ays] in training."

"How long does this training on the miniature track c[on]tinue?"

"Until the colt is about fourteen months old it is the o[nly] training. After that he is worked, both in harness and [on] the miniature track, until, say two years old, when he [is] the last of the kindergarten. At about fourteen month[s of] age the colt is broken to harness, and his work begins on [a] mile track. This work consists in short, sharp brushe[s to] develop high speed, and this 'brush system' is also a [Palo] Alto innovation. This, with the miniature track, has b[een] criticised by trainers of the old school, but their criticism [can]not have much weight against the fact that horses bred [and] trained at Palo Alto hold the fastest trotting record for y[ear]lings, two-year-olds, three-year-olds and four-year-old, [and] Sunol's three-year-old record is within one-half second [of] Jay-Eye-See's five-year-old record."

Oriflamme, the gray son of Flood and Frolic, is said to be in as good trim as he ever was in his life, and great things are expected from him this season.

Charlie Kerr, the sporting owner of Apache and other well-bred race-horses, has, with all due formalities, christened his ranch near Bakersfield, "The Antrim Stock Farm."

Mr. Ijams says that Axtell has grown during the winter and that he now stands 15.3½. He is higher forward than behind and he is jogged every day.

Mr. Corrigan's horses have left Guttenburg for Lexington in charge of the old foreman of the Chicago stable. From Lexington they will go to Memphis.

There were 4,792 races run in America in 1889, against 4,130 in 1888, and 3,548 in 1887. The added money in 1889 foots up $2,379,192 against $1,839,275 in 1888.

Mr. R. A. Swigert will probably send the yearling colt Carlsbad by Glenelg out of Lady Wayward, to England next fall. He is said to be exceptionally good looking while his breeding is gilt edged.

Matt Allen, Senator Hearst's trainer, has a challenge out to fight his ½ Jap against any bird of any feather in New York, New Jersey or Pennsylvania, for any sum up to $1,000 a side.

In conformity with the recent decision of the Supreme Court that the act legalizing the selling of pools on races run outside of the State was unconstitutional, the poolrooms in Memphis on the 24th closed by order of the Criminal Court.

The string of thoroughbreds belonging to Amos McCampbell has arrived at the Louisville track. They are Bonita, Joyful, Longsides, Rollin Hawley, Victorine, Eugenius, Laughter, Florence Shanks, Grayson and Flyaway.

The first mare served to Axtell this year was Myra by Electioneer, dam Addie Lee, by Culver's Black Hawk. Myra is a full sister to Adair 2:17¼, and Grace Lee 2:29½, owned by W. P. Ijams, one of the owners of the champion stallion.

The New Yorkers who wintered at Hot Springs, Arkansas, were so highly satisfied with the environs and possibilities of the place that C. W. Barton, of New York, leased the track, and also the one at Little Rock, and will have both put into good trim for racing next Fall.

It is said a big suit has been entered against John A. Morris, of Westchester fame, in connection with Louisiana Lottery stock, involving $2,000 000. Mr. Morris will be defended by ex-President Grover Cleveland, while R. Newcombe will look after the interests of the plaintiffs.

Of the Winters' string which left Reno, and are at present in Nashville, Rey Del Rey (brother to El Rio Rey), Noretta (a three-year-old sister to Alta), and Average (a two-year-old filly by Hooker, out of the dam of Laura Gardner), received especially favorable comments on their arrival.

A. F. Cridge, head of the bookmaking firm of that name, is enjoying a winter's rest in Florida, having journeyed there when the city rooms closed. He is at Oak Point, near New Smyrna, where also Mike Murray and M. F. Dwyer are located. Mr. Cridge will not return until business is resumed.

Pate's Stock Farm Company filed articles of incorporation last week. The capital stock is $150,000 in 1,500 shares. Mr. Pate owns 1,340, and the rest are owned by L. J. Howard, Fred Burgdorfer and W. H. Mayo. The farm will be devoted to the production and care of thoroughbred and trotting horses.

The sale of thoroughbred yearlings during 1889 shows a fall in the average. During the year 862 head offered brought $536,845, an average of $622 79. This is a falling off from 1888, when 778 head brought $520,238, an average of $667.-82. High water mark was reached in 1887, when 692 brought $465,395, an average of $672.54.

There are about 150 horses now in training at the Louisville track, and fifty or so at the Latonia course. The Memphis track will soon be swarming with thoroughbreds, and the Nashville contingent is quite a numerous one. The repairs and alterations on the Lexington course have served to banish a good many of the stables to other points.

The New Jersey Jockey Club Handicap is a double event affair, the first race at a mile and a furlong and the second at a mile and a quarter. If the same horse wins both the Messrs. Dwyer will present the owner with the historic Woodlawn Vase, which recalls reminiscences of the victories of Bramble and Miss Woodford.

John A. Morris purchased twenty six head of thoroughbred yearlings at public sales in 1889 for $44,259. Marcus Daly purchased nineteen head for $43,450. The Dwyer Brothers purchased eighteen head for $30,250. Pierre Lorillard for thirty-four head paid $24,625, while five yearlings cost Senator Hearst $19,000.

The two-year-olds sold at the Rancho del Paso sale last year, have already commenced to show up well. Madge L. (Darebin or Warwick—Altitude) won the Washington Stakes, $1,000 added, by half a length from Eclipse (Kyrie Daly—Billow); Florence (Warwick, out of Ysabel) also created a favorable impression in the same race.

Last year one hundred and eighteen dashes of a mile were run over the various tracks in this country in less time than 1:43. Five years ago 1:43 was beaten in only twenty four races. Of the fast mile records last year, seven were made at Washington Park and thirteen at West Side Park, Chicago. Maori's 1:39 4-5 at Washington Park, heads the list as the fastest mile ever made in a race.

The Lamasney Bros. have just made arrangements with Barnes, the famous colored knight of the pig skin, to ride for them during the early part of the coming season. Barnes has signed with "Lucky" Baldwin, but as Mr. Baldwin will not begin racing until the Washington Park meeting, he consented to Barnes riding for the Lamasneys until he needs him.

Allen Farm claims the distinction of having the first foal of the season in the North dropped on its place. The foal is a fine filly by Sable Wilkes out of Minnie Wilkes, a daughter of Sultan (sire of Stamboul 2:12½) and Kitty Wilkes (dam of Rajah 2:29½) by George Wilkes. Minnie Wilkes is own sister to Elizabeth that brought $6,100 in the recent Brasfield sale, the highest price paid for a brood mare in sale.

Rey Del Rey, brother to the Emperor and El Rio Rey had a severe attack of pneumonia on his outward journey, but rapidly recovered. It would have been very hard luck if Mr. Winters had lost him, as only last year The Czar, his (then three-year-old) brother, died on the way out and a few weeks ago the yearling half brother, by Hooker—Marian, died on the ranch.

The news of the resignation of Captain Ward from the superintendency of the New York Jockey Club track is still a matter of comment among turfmen, and all who knew him regret the necessity for such a step, as he was becoming very popular. It is said his wife has fallen heir to considerable money in England, and his unexpected luck to some extent indu d him to break the ties that bound him to the position.ce

---

While many horses quartered about Coney Island show great improvement on their form of last year, yet some few have become developed to such an extent that they will surprise racegoers when the season begins. The black racer Defense orginally Satan, will be likely to make the fur fly if he keeps clear of mishaps. He is looking grand and is high in flesh, while work improves him.

Major Du Bois, Denver, has purchased of Mr. A. Spreckles the chestnut mare Lucy Abbott, and last Saturday he shipped Magnet 2:28¾, Superior 2:19½, Lucy Abbott, Egberta, already bred to Magnet, and a Magnet mare already bred to Superior, back to Denver in a new baggage car admirably fitted up under the Major's supervision. In the car were Col. Streeter's two horses which have been under B. C. Holly's care this winter.

The dates for this season's running meetings in the West will be as follows: New Orleans, Feb. 15 to April 7th; Birmingham, April 9th to 15th; Memphis, April 12th to 23rd; Los Angeles, April 14th to 19th; Nashville, April 26th to May 3d; Lexington, May 6th to 13th; Louisville, May 14th to 23d; Latonia, May 24th fo June 7th; St. Louis, June 7th to 20th; Kansas City, June 10th to 19th; Chicago, June 21st to July 10th; Twin Cities, Minn , July 23d to Aug. 2nd.

Messrs. McMahon & Co. will sell at auction their entire stable in order to settle the interests of the individual members of the firm. There are some twenty horses to be disposed of, including Speedwell, Eolian, and others less well known. This sale is the outcome of the quarrel between Garrison and his father-in-law. Garrison too had to close out his interest in the stable because the Messrs. Dwyer, to whom he is engaged for next season, desire that he shall have no pecuniary interest in a racing stable while he is in their employ.

Now that it has been demonstrated that even low class platers can run three miles without difficulty, the Clifton management will give a long distance race, to be decided March 17th, for horses of a better grade. The conditions for the stake will be announced in a few days. Probably a race will be given at the Clifton track in about a week for horses to be ridden by their owners, W. and Alf Lakeland, W. Rollins, W. Olney, L. Lloyd and several others have consented to make entries and ride if such a race is given.

Bels, the winner of the Old Dominion at Clifton, is bred to go a distance, his dam being Weiland by Wanderer (a well known four miler), out of a Lexington mare, and she out of old Iodine by imp Sovereign. The time was fairly good considering the track was slow and a three-quarter track, too. The fractional time of the race was, quarter 28, half 55, three-quarters 1:23, mile 1:51½, mile and a quarter 2:21½, mile and a half 2:49½, mile and three quarters 3:18, two miles 3:46¾, two miles and a quarter 4:14, two miles and a half 4:42¾, two miles and three-quarters 5:11½, three miles 5:38½.

Dr. W. T. Monsarratt, the veterinary surgeon who was located in Danville, Ky., for a short time, but left to accept a position at Honolulu, Sandwich Islands, is now enjoying the emoluments of the very lucrative post of Government veterinarian. The Kentucky Advocate says: An idea of the perquisites he receives can be obtained from the statement that for every animal imported, he is paid the following fees: Horses, mules and bovines, $1 per head, and hogs and sheep, 10 cents per head. The veterinarian's income from this source is about $400 per month. He is also allowed the privilege of a private practice, and adds to his income from this source.

Congressman W. L. Scott's splendid winter quarters for his thoroughbreds at Cape Charles City, Va , are arranged on a magnificent scale, 2,700 acres of land being enclosed. The thoroughbred stables are simply superb. They might, without exaggeration be easily termed "horse parlors." One large house covers over fifty weather boarded and padded stalls. Immediately in front of the big stable is the track, one mile in circumference, always kept in prime condition and very fast, for exercising the horses and many frisky youngsters. On the north side of the track is that part of the farm used for trucking purposes, the principle truck being spinach and strawberries. On the west side and directly opposite the stables are the quarters for the men and boys employed in the stable. On the south side one has a good view of the Chesapeake. The quarters for the employees are fitted up in a very comfortable and homelike manner. With the exception of Chaos, all the horses have wintered well, and among the two-years are some slashing lookers.

The satisfactory result of the original cross with English horses, soon lead to a great deal of attention being given to the importation of the best Eastern horses. Oliver Cromwell for war, and King Charles II for sport, both sent emissaries from England to the East in search of good horses. The Barb seems to have been chiefly used, though often under the name of Turk or the Arabian. There is much confusion in the manner in which names were applied at this period, not in accordance with the strain of the horses, but after the name of the country from which they happen to have been imported. Some twenty Oriental horses are known to have been used in the formation of the thoroughbred between 1620 and 1750, but the pedigree of no English horse can be reliably traced back further than to Place's White Turk about 1655. Place was Cromwell's stud master, and like all Cromwell's officers no doubt understood his business. His horse, the White Turk, is known to have been the sire of several horses and mares to which some of our best stock is now traced. The right quantity of Oriental blood seems to have been infused in the English stock, and a new breed of a fixed character formed in little more than 100 years. No further infusion of Eastern blood has succeeded. All late experiments in that direction have entirely failed, but the superior speed and staying power of the English thoroughbred horse is now so undoubted, that no cross whatever can be adopted without deterioration.

One of the best looking Shetland ponies seen in the State was sent a fortnight ago by Baldy Hamilton as a present to his veteran friend Luke Du Bois now of Denver, Colorado. The Sheltie was a magnificent sturdy looking, stout built 7 year old stallion.

Secretary Brewster has been striving hard to get a National Jockey Club formed which shall have control of the racing rules on all tracks. It is time it was done and Mr. Withers, it is understood, has formulated a new set of racing rules based on the English racing law, supplemented by such innovations as a careful study of American racing for many years have taught him to be necessary in this country. It is even said among racing men that when the new Monmouth Park track is opened, Mr. Withers will ask owners to give his new code a practical trial. Perhaps this would be the very best way out of the present wholly unsatisfactory condition of affairs, which is especially annoying to owners who race both in the East and West, and who are at times unable to say under what rules, if any, they are racing. Mr. Withers' rules would certainly be welcome if they tend to secure uniformity in these matters throughout the country, and it is pretty certain that the Western clubs, in their anxiety to secure a truly American code, will come more than half way in an effort to adopt them.

The Supreme Court, on the 22nd, affirmed the verdict of the Davidson County Criminal Court in the poolroom cases, deciding that the making of books and the selling of pools on races run outside of the State (Tennessee) is in violation of law, and therefore indictable. These cases were against H. C. Brown for bookmaking and Palmer & Cartwright for selling pools. The opinion in the former cause was delivered by Justice Folkes and in the latter by Justice Lurton. Soon after the action of the Supreme Court became known, the four poolrooms in Nashville ceased business, and of course all other establishments of the kind in the State were likewise closed. An attempt was made at the session of the Legislature in 1887 to legalize bookmaking and poolselling, but the bill looking to that end was defeated. Two years later license clauses were interpolated in the general revenue bill, and a day or two after the measure had been signed by the Governor the poolrooms were opened.

Brown was indicted in a test case, tried and fined $50 for gambling by betting on a horse race in violation of law. The defendant appealed in error, relying on the clause in the revenue act, which fixed the license on bookmakers at $25 per annum. Defendant acted as a bookmaker, and made bets on a race run over a track not in this State.

Palmer & Cartwright were convicted of selling pools on a horserace also run outside of the State, and fined. They also appealed, with the result stated.

The New York World has been issuing reminiscences of the Old Guard, headed by Barnum, Exile, etc., and later on says:—

The oldest member of the Old Guard is Hickory Jim. No man knows his age. Years ago, when the present generation of trainers and jockeys were in their swaddling clothes, Hickory Jim was a veteran on the. The oldest turf guide printed, records, "Hickory Jim, aged." His life bridges the old and the new turf. He goes back to the days when the Bufords and the Blackburns and the Swigerts raced their horses for pleasure on their private tracks over the blue grass of Central Kentucky, and discussed pedigrees beneath the shade of their old oaks with the aromatic juleps near by.

Old Jim has no royal pedigree, nor were his ancestors from the priceless strains of Arabia. His sire was Geo. Dasher, a Western horse, and his dam is unknown. His owner, D. D. Davis, who has had him for eighteen years, bought him in the far West. They have seen many strange sights, old Davis and Hickory Jim, and they have been together so much that they have grown to resemble each other in a manner half ludicrous, half pathetic.

Davis, in a quaint, halting way, tells how for years he raced old Jim through the territories of the Northwest. Scores of times Jim ran against the best Indian horses, and on one memorable occasion, he beat the best horse of the Sioux, and every buck in the tribe was a bankrupt for a year.

The horse became so famous through all that region that Davis could get no odds against him, and he determined to change his name. After much consultation he thought Red Mike the proper title, and cunningly entered the horse by that name at the thriving mining town of Butte, where the miners had built a little track. As it happened, the miners were nearly all Irishmen, and the name, Red Mike, seemed to recall patriotic memories to them. One and all plunged on Red Mike and Davis could not get a bet. He left in disgust, and since then the old fellow has been Hickory Jim. After running him on every race track in the far West, Davis went South with him and raced him against the Mexicans and Indians of New Mexico and Arizona, and he was always successful. After years of this kind of running, Jim was taken to Galveston, New Orleans and Mobile, and at length struck the big tracks.

One day there appeared on the Lexington track a weather-beaten, ragged, angular old horse with hair all over him two inches long, and altogether the most extraordinary spectacle ever seen on that aristocratic track. As he galloped around the track with a weazened-faced little jockey on his back, such a roar of laughter went up as never greeted a horse before. Every one asked who the stranger was and where he came from. No one knew aught of him except that his name was Hickory Jim.

The old horse seemed to feel that he was not fit for such fine company, and when the prancing thoroughbreds came out one by one, many of them with ribbons knotted in their manes, the gloom on his scarred old face became deeper and deeper.

He got off badly, and as he passed the stand he was several yards behind the bunch and the crowd cheered him derisively. He paid no attention to their insult, but continued on his way with his head down, giving strict attention to business.

As they rounded the turn some one yelled:—

"Why, old Hickory Jim is winning!" And sure enough he was. With long, steady strides he closed up the gap, and one by one he had overtaken his rivals. He passed through the midst of them like a resistless machine, and never varying his long stride, as regular as a pendulum, he came under the wire winner by half a dozen open lengths.

The crowd gave him a great ovation, but old Jim, still wrapped in the deepest gloom, hung his head down mournfully and went off to his stable. His owner says Jim has run hundreds of races, and the records show that this is true. In purses and bets Davis won with old Jim half a million dollars. He has won creditable races at Monmouth and Sheepshead Bay, but for the last few years he has only run at the winter tracks, where now and then, by his superior sagacity, he slips in through a crowd of stupid youngsters who have not had the experience of wily old Jim.

The New York Jockey Club.

Printer's ink, when used judiciously, is one of the most important factors in the success of any business. That fact has been amply demonstrated to Secretary Kook of the New York Jockey Club, who inserted an advertisement in the BREEDER AND SPORTSMAN for entries for the Spring and Fall events of 1890. We have been forwarded a full list of the entries, but lack of space prevents us from giving them in their entirety, but, however, a list of the horses owned on the Pacific Coast will be of interest to our readers, so we subjoin them:

SPRING MEETING, 1890.

Larchmont Stakes, for two years old. A sweepstakes of $50 each, half forfeit or only $10 if declared by April 1st, with $1,500 added, of which $300 to second and $100 to third. Winner of a race of the value of $2,000 to carry 5 pounds extra; or of two such races, or one of $5,000, 7 pounds extra. Beaten maidens allowed 5 pounds. Six furlongs.

Aby, C. W.—ch c Rodman by Rutherford, dam Leveret.

Daly, Marcus—ch c Gold Dollar by imp. Sir Modred, dam Trade Dollar; ch f Leonora by imp. Sir Modred, dam Lizzie Lucas; b f Mistletoe by imp. Sir Modred, dam Letola; b c Montana by Ban Fox, dam imp. Queen; b f Namouna by imp. Sir Modred, dam La Favorita; b c Prince Charming by imp. Sir Modred, dam Carissima; ch c Silver King by imp. St. Blaise, dam Maud Hampton.

Hearst, Geo.—blk f Firework by Falsetto, dam Explosion; ch c Algernon by Joe Daniels, dam Faustina; ch c Atlas by Hyder Ali, dam Fidelity; b c Warpath by Ban Fox or Warwick, dam imp. Second Hand; ch c Snow Ball by Joe Hooker, dam Chestnut Bell; ch c Anarchist by Joe Hooker, dam Laura Winston; b c J. B. by Warwick, dam Maria F.; b c Yosemite by Hyder Ali, dam Nellie Collier.

Palo Alto Stock Farm—ch c Rinfax by Argyle, dam imp. Amelia; ch f Tearless by Wildidle, dam imp. Teardrop; ch f Rosebud by Wildidle, dam imp. Rosetta.

Rose, L. J.—b c Conrad by Flood, dam imp. Gouls.

Santa Anita Stable—b c Ensenada by Rutherford, dam Arritta; b f Ogarita by Longfellow, dam Mission Belle; b c San Joaquin by Longfellow, dam Santa Anita Belle; b f Esperanza by Grinstead, dam Hermosa; b f Cleopatra by Grinstead, dam Maggie Emerson; ch c El Carman by Gano, dam Grey Anne.

Gaillard Stakes, for two years old. A sweepstakes of $50 each, half forfeit, or only $10 if declared by April 1st, with $1,500 added, of which $300 to second and $200 to third. Half a mile.

Aby, C. W.—ch c Rodman by Rutherford, dam Leveret.

Daly, Marcus—ch c Gold Dollar by imp. Sir Modred, dam Trade Dollar; ch f Leonora by imp. Sir Modred, dam Lizzie Lucas; b f Mistletoe by imp. Sir Modred, dam Letola; b c Montana by Ban Fox, dam imp. Queen; b f Namouna by imp. Sir Modred, dam La Favorita; b c Prince Charming by imp. Sir Modred, dam Maud Hampton.

Hearst, Geo.—blk f Firework by Falsetto, dam Explosion; ch c Algernon by Joe Daniels, dam Faustina; ch f Babicora by Hyder Ali, dam Graciosa; b c War Path by Ban Fox or Warwick, dam imp. Second Hand; ch c Atlas by Hyder Ali, dam Fidelity; ch c Anarchist by Joe Hooker, dam Chestnut Bell; ch c Snow Ball by Joe Hooker, dam Laura Winston; ch c Primero by Powhattan, dam Speed; b c Yosemite by Hyder Ali, dam Nellie Collier.

Maltese Villa Stock Farm—br f Romeetta by imp. Woodlands, dam Dizzy Blonde.

Palo Alto Stock Farm—ch c Rinfax by Argyle, dam imp. Amelia; ch f Tearless by Wildidle, dam imp. Teardrop.

Rose, L. J.—br c Oscar by Wildidle, dam imp. Petroleuse.

Santa Anita Stable—ch c El Carman by Gano, dam Grey Anne; b c San Joaquin by Longfellow, dam Santa Anita Belle; b f Esparanza by Grinstead, dam Hermosa; ch c Silverado by Rutherford, dam Josie C.; b f Laciengs by Grinstead, dam Jennie D.; b f Cleopatra by Grinstead, dam Maggie Emerson.

Anticipation Stakes, for two years old. A sweepstakes of $100 each, half forfeit, or only $20 if declared by April 1st, with $2,100 added, of which $500 to second and $200 to third. Winner of a race of the value of $2,500 to carry 5 pounds extra; of two such races, 7 pounds; of three such races, 10 pounds. Beaten maidens allowed 5 pounds. Six furlongs.

Aby, C. W.—ch c Rodman by Rutherford, dam Leveret.

Daly, Marcus—ch c Gold Dollar by imp. Sir Modred, dam Trade Dollar; ch f Leonora by imp. Sir Modred, dam Lizzie Lucas; b f Mistletoe by imp. Sir Modred, dam Letola; b c Montana by Ban Fox, dam imp. Queen; b f Namouna by imp. Sir Modred, dam La Favorita; b c Prince Charming by imp. Sir Modred, dam Carissima; b c Silver King by imp. St. Blaise, dam Maud Hampton.

Hearst, Geo.—blk f Firework by Falsetto, dam Explosion; ch c Algernon by Joe Daniels, dam Faustina; ch c Atlas by Hyder Ali, dam Fidelity; b c Warpath by Ban Fox or Warwick, dam imp. Second Hand; b c El Verano by Hock-Hocking, dam Vixen; b c J. B. by Warwick, dam Maria F.; b c Yosemite by Hyder Ali, dam Nellie Collier.

Palo Alto Stock Farm—ch c Rinfax by Argyle, dam imp. Amelia; ch f Tearless by Wildidle, dam imp. Teardrop; ch f Rosebud by Wildidle, dam imp. Rosetta.

Rose, L. J.—b f Ban by Flood, dam Frolic.

Santa Anita Stable—b c Ensenada by Rutherford, dam Arritta; b c San Joaquin by Longfellow, dam Santa Anita Belle; b f Esperanza by Grinstead, dam Hermosa; b f Cleopatra by Grinstead, dam Maggie Emerson; b f Ogarita by Longfellow, dam Mission Belle; ch c Silverado by Rutherford, dam Josie C.; b f Laciengs by Grinstead, dam Jennie D.

Van Nest Stakes, for two years old. A sweepstake of $50 each, $15 forfeit, with $1,250 added, of which $250 to second and $100 to third. The winner to be sold at auction for $5,000. If entered by 4 P. M. on the day before the day appointed for the race, to be sold for $3,000, allowed 5 pounds; then 1 pound allowed for each $100 down to $2,000. Beaten horses not liable to be claimed. Five furlongs.

Aby, C. W.—ch c Rodman by Rutherford, dam Leveret.

Haggin, J. B.—Ch f Pearl Kinney, Geo. Kinney—Pearl; ch c Kil Kenny, Geo. Kenney—Bijou.

Hearst, Geo.—Ch c Anarchist, Joe Hooker—Chestnut Bell; ch c Snow Ball, Joe Hooker—Laura Winston; ch c Primero, Powhattan—Speed; b c J. B., Warwick—Maria F.; b c Yosemite, Hyder Ali—Nellie Collier.

Palo Alto Stock Farm.—Ch c Rinfax, Argyle—imp. Amelia.

Rose, L. J.—B c Mas Rico, Shannon—Fanny Lewis.

Santa Anita Stable.—Ch c El Carman, Gano—Grey Anne.

Debutante Stakes, for fillies two years old. A sweepstakes of $50 each, h. f., or only $10 if declared by April 1st, with $1,250 added, of which $250 to second and $100 to third. Winners excluded from starting, and not to pay forfeit. Five furlongs.

Daly, Marcus.—ch f Bonnie Lass, imp. Sir Modred—Bonnie Kate; ch f Leonora, imp. Sir Modred—Lizzie Lucas; b f Mistletoe, imp. Sir Modred—Letola; b f Namouna, imp. Sir Modred—La Favorita.

Hearst, Geo.—Blk f Firework, Falsetto—Explosion; ch f Babicora, Hyder Ali—Graciosa.

Maltese Villa Stock Farm.—Br f Rometta, imported Woodlands—Dizzy Blonde.

Palo Alto Stock Farm.—Ch f Tearless, Wildidle—imp. Teardrop; ch f Rosebud, Wildidle—imp. Rosetta.

Rose, L. J.—B f Flight, Flood—imp. Flirt.

Santa Anita Stable.—B f Esperanza, Grinstead—Hermosa; b f Cleopatra, Grinstead—Maggie Emerson; b f Ogaritta, Longfellow—Mission Belle; b f Laciengs, Grinstead—Jennie D.

Hearst, Geo.—Blk f Firework, Falsetto—Explosion; ch f Babicora, Hyder Ali—Graciosa.

Maltese Villa Stock Farm.—Br f Romeetta, imp. Woodlands—Dizzy Blonde.

Palo Alto Stock Farm.—Ch f Tearless, Wildidle—imp. Teardrop; ch f Rosebud, Wildidle—imp. Rosetta.

Rose, L. J.—B f Fury, Argyle—imp. Fairy Rose.

Santa Anita Stable.—B f Esperanza, Grinstead—Hermosa; b f Cleopatra, Grinstead—Maggie Emerson; b f Ogarita—Longfellow—Mission Belle; b f Laciengs, Grinstead—Jennie D.

Shippee, L. U.—B f May H., Falsetto—Glenuline; b f False Queen—Falsetto—Queen Victoria.

Trial Stakes. For three year olds. A sweepstakes of $100 each, h. f. or only $20 if declared by April 1st, with $3,000 added, of which $600 to second and $300 to third. Winners in 1890 of a race of $4,000, or of two of $2,000, to carry 15 lbs. extra. One mile and a quarter.

Hearst, Geo.—b c King Thomas, imp. King Ban—Maud Hampton; b c Tournament, imp. Sir Modred—Plaything; b c Anaconda, Spendthrift, imp. Maid of Athol; b c Ballarat, imp. Sir Modred—La Favorita; ch c Baggage, Warwick—Maria F.; b c Sacramento, Joe Hooker—Ada C.

Palo Alto Stock Farm.—ch c Flambeau, Wildidle—imp. Flirt.

Rose, L. J.—b g Rico, Shannon—Fannie Lewis.

Santa Anita Stable.—ch f Sinaloa, Grinstead—Maggie Emerson; ch c Honduras, Grinstead—Jennie D.; ch c Amigo, imp. Prince Charlie—Mission Belle; b c Clio, Grinstead—Glenita; b c Santiago, Grinstead—Clara D.

Baychester Stakes. For three years old which have not won a race of $1,000 in 1889. A sweepstakes of $50 each, $15 forfeit, with $1,250 added, of which $250 to second and $100 to third. Beaten maidens allowed 4 lbs. One mile.

Haggin, J. B.—blk c Fernwood, Falsetto—Quickstep; b c Hawkstone, Hindoo—imp. Queen Maud; ch f Rosette, Joe Hooker—Rosa B.

Hearst, Geo.—Anaconda, Spendthrift—imp. Maid of Athol; b c Sir Lancelot, imp. Sir Modred—Faustina; b f Golden Horn, Spendthrift—imp. Constantinople; br f Miss Belle, imp. Prince Charlie—Linnet; blk f Everglade, Iroquois—imp. Agenoria; b f Gloaming, imp. Sir Modred—Twilight.

Maltese Villa Stock Farm.—b c Abdell, Jocko—Cousin Peggy.

Santa Anita Stable.—b c Clio, Grinstead—Glenita; b f Magdalena, imp. Glenelg—Malta; ch c Amigo, imp. Prince Charlie—Mission Belle; b f Atalanta, Grinstead—Blossom.

Shippee, L. U.—Take Notice—imp. Prince Charlie—Nota Bene.

Throgg's Neck Stakes.—For three years old. A sweepstakes of $50 each, $15 forfeit, with $1,250 added, of which $250 to second and $100 to third. The winner to be sold at auction for $5,000. If entered by 4 P. M. on the day before the day appointed for the race, to be sold for $3,000, allowed 5 lbs.; then 1 lb. allowed for each $100 down to $2,000. Beaten horses not liable to be claimed. Seven furlongs.

Haggin, J. B.—blk c Fernwood, Falsetto—Quickstep; b c Hawkstone, Hindoo—imp. Queen Maud; ch f Rosette, Joe Hooker—Rosa B.

Rose, L. J.—b f Glenloch, Flood—Glenden.

Santa Anita Stable.—b c Clio, Grinstead—Glenita.

New York Jockey Club Handicap.—For all ages. A sweepstakes of $750 each, h. f., or only $25 if declared by 4 P. M. on the day before the day appointed for the race, with $5,000 added, of which $1,000 to second and $500 to third. Weights to be published on the second day before the race. One mile and a quarter.

Haggin, J. B.—b m Firenzi, 6, imp. Glenelg—Florida; br c Fitz James, 5, imp. Kyrle Daly—Electra; ch c Salvator, 4, imp. Prince Charlie—Salina.

Hearst, Geo.—ch c Rhono, 4, Flood—imp. Rosetta; blk m Gorgo, 5, Isonomy—imp. Flirt; b c King Thomas, 3, imp. King Ban—Maud Hampton; br c Tournament, 3, imp. Sir Modred—Plaything; b c Anaconda, 3, Spendthrift—imp. Maid of Athol; ch c imp. Del Mar, 4, Somnes—Maid of the Hills; b c Almont, 4, Three Cheers—Question.

Santa Anita Stable.—ch m Los Angeles, 5, imp. Glenelg—La Polka; b c Santiago, 3, Grinstead—Clara D.; ch c Honduras, 3, Grinstead—Jennie B.; ch c Amigo, 3, imp. Prince Charlie—Mission Belle; b c Clio, 3, Grinstead—Glenita.

West Chester Cup. For all ages. A sweepstakes of $100 each, h. f. or only $20 if declared by April 1st, with $3,000 added, of which $600 to second and $300 to third. Winner of a race in 1890 of $5,000, when carrying weight for age or more, to carry 5 lbs. extra. One mile and a half.

Haggin, J. B.—b m Firenzi, 6, by imp. Glenelg, dam Florida; ch c Salvator, 4, by imp. Prince Charlie, dam Salina.

Hearst, Geo.—ch c Baggage, 3, by imp. Warwick, dam Maria F.; b c Almont, 4, by Three Cheers, dam Question.

Rose, L. J.—ch c Rover, 3, by Wildidle, dam imp. Rosetta.

Santa Anita Stable—ch m Los Angeles, 5, by imp. Glenelg, dam La Polka; ch c Honduras, 3, by Grinstead, dam Jennie B.; b c Santiago, 3, by Grinstead, dam Clara D.

All Breeze Stakes, for all ages. A sweepstakes of $50 each, $15 forfeit, with $1,250 added, of which $250 to second and $100 to third. Winners in 1890 of $3,000 to carry 5 lbs. extra; horses which have never won $5,000 allowed 7 pounds; $2,500, 10 pounds; $1,000, 14 lbs. Seven furlongs.

Gebhard, F.—b g Volunteer, 6, by imp. Mortimer, dam Sly Boots.

Haggin, J. B.—br c Fitz James, 5, by imp. Kyrle Daly, dam Electra; blk c Fresno, 4, by Falsetto, dam Cachuca; blk c Fernwood, 3, by Falsetto, dam Quickstep; b c Hawkstone, 3, by Hindoo, dam imp. Queen Maud.

Hearst, Geo.—blk m Gorgo, 5, by Isonomy, dam imp. Flirt; b c Ballarat, 3, by imp. Sir Modred, dam La Favorita; br f Miss Belle, 3, by imp. Prince Charlie, dam Linnet; b f Gloaming, 3, by imp. Sir Modred, dam Twilight; b f Golden Horn, 3, by Spendthrift, dam imp. Constantinople; b c Sir Lancelot, 3, by imp. Sir Modred, dam Faustina; ch c imp. Del Mar, 4, by Somnes, dam Maid of the Hills; ch f imp. Gertrude, 4, by Somnes, dam Geraldine; ch f Cosette, 3, by Joe Hooker, dam Abbie W.

Rose, L. J.—b f Glenloch, 3, by Flood, dam Glendew.

Santa Anita Stable—ch m Los Angeles, 5, by imp. Glenelg, dam La Polka; b f Magdalena, 3, by imp. Glenelg, dam Malta; ch c Sinaloa, 3, by Grinstead, dam Maggie Emerson.

Fort Schuyler Stakes, for all ages. A sweepstakes of $50 each, $15 forfeit, with $1,250 added, of which $250 to second and $100 to third. The winner to be sold at auction for $5,000. If entered by 4 P. M. on the day before the day appointed for the race to be sold for $3,000, allowed 8 lbs.; then 1 lb. allowed for each $100 down to $2,000. One mile.

Haggin, J. B.—br c Fitz James, 5, by imp. Kyrle Daly, dam Electra; blk c Fernwood, 3, by Falsetto, dam Quickstep; b c Hawkstone, 3, by Hindoo, dam imp. Queen Maud.

Rose, L. J.—ch g Mikado, 6, by Shiloh, dam Margery.

Santa Anita Stable—b c Clio, 3, by Grinstead, dam Glenita.

FALL MEETING, 1890.

White Plains Handicap, for two years old. A sweepstakes of $100 each, half forfeit, or $25 if declared by 4 P. M. on the day before the day appointed for the race, or only $10 if declared by August 1, 1890. The club to guarantee the gross value of the stake to be $10,000, of which $2,000 to second and $1,000 to third. Weights to be published on the second day before the race. Six furlongs.

Aby, C. W.—ch c Rodman by Rutherford, dam Leveret.

Daly, Marcus—ch f Bonnie Lass by imp. Sir Modred, dam Bonnie Kate; ch c Gold Dollar by imp. Sir Modred, dam Trade Dollar; ch f Leonora by imp. Sir Modred, dam Lizzie Lucas; b f Mistletoe by imp. Sir Modred, dam Letola; b c Montana by Ban Fox, dam imp. Queen; b f Namouna by imp. Sir Modred, dam La Favorita; b c Prince Charming by imp. Sir Modred, dam Carissima; ch c Silver King by imp. St. Blaise, dam Maud Hampton.

Hearst, Geo.—blk f Firework by Falsetto, dam Explosion; ch c Algernon by Joe Daniels, dam Faustina; ch c Atlas by Hyder Ali, dam Fidelity; b c Warpath by Ban Fox or Warwick, dam imp. Second Hand; ch c Anarchist by Joe Hooker, dam Chestnut Bell; ch c Snowball by Joe Hooker, dam Laura Winston; ch c Primero by Powhattan, dam Speed; ch c Charley Brown by Jim Brown, dam Viola; b c J. B. by Warwick, dam Maria F.; b c Yosemite by Hyder Ali, dam Nellie Collier; b c El Verano by Hock-Hocking, dam Vixen.

Maltese Villa Stock Farm—br c King Alta by Alta, dam Cousin Peggy; ch c Judge Terry by Alta, dam Pet; br f Romeetta by imp. Woodlands, dam Dizzy Blonde.

Undine Stable—b c Homer by Shannon, dam Sallie Gardner; ch f Glenlivet by Flood, dam Glendew.

Palo Alto Stock Farm—ch c Rinfax by Argyle, dam imp. Amelia; ch f Tearless by Wildidle, dam imp. Teardrop; ch f Rosebud by Wildidle, dam imp. Rosetta.

Santa Anita Stable—b f Laciengs by Grinstead, dam Jennie D.; b c Ensenada by Rutherford, dam Arritta; ch c El Carman by Gano, dam Grey Anne; b c San Joaquin by Longfellow, dam Santa Anita Belle; b f Esperanza by Grinstead, dam Hermosa; b f Cleopatra by Grinstead, dam Maggie Emerson; b f Ogarita by Longfellow, dam Mission Belle; ch c Silverado by Rutherford, dam Josie C.

Shippee, L. U.—b c Lodowic by Longfellow, dam Carrie Phillips.

Winchell, C. E.—b c Senor by Bersan, dam Sister to Joe Daniels.

Winters, Theo.—b c Reydel Rey by Norfolk, dam Marian; ch c San Juan by Norfolk, dam Ballinette; ch c Judge Post by Joe Hooker, dam Countess Zeika; ch f Belle Songer by Joe Hooker, dam Lou Spencer.

Dunmow Stakes, for two years old. A sweepstakes of $100 each, half forfeit, or only $20 if declared by August 1st, with $5,000 added, of which $1,000 to second and $500 to third. Winners after August 1st of $3,000, when carrying weight for age or more, to carry 5 lbs. extra; of two such races or one of $5,000, 7 lbs. extra. Those not having won in 1890, $3,000, when carrying weight for age or more, allowed 5 lbs. Beaten maidens allowed 10 lbs. Six furlongs.

Aby, C. W.—ch c Rodman by Rutherford, dam Leveret.

Daly, Marcus—ch f Bonnie Lass by imp. Sir Modred, dam Bonnie Kate; ch c Gold Dollar by imp. Sir Modred, dam Trade Dollar; ch f Leonora by imp. Sir Modred, dam Lizzie Lucas; b f Mistletoe by imp. Sir Modred, dam Letola; b c Montana by Ban Fox, dam imp. Queen; b f Namouna by imp. Sir Modred, dam La Favorita; b c Prince Charming by imp. Sir Modred, dam Carissima; ch c Silver King by imp. St. Blaise, dam Maud Hampton.

Hearst, Geo.—blk f Firework by Falsetto, dam Explosion; ch c Algernon by Joe Daniels, dam Faustina; ch c Atlas by Hyder Ali, dam Fidelity; b c Warpath by Ban Fox or Warwick, dam imp. Second Hand; ch c Anarchist by Joe Hooker, dam Chestnut Bell; ch c Snow Ball by Joe Hooker, dam Laura Winston; b c J. B. by Warwick, dam Maria F.; b c Yosemite by Hyder Ali, dam Nellie Collier; b c El Verano by Hock-Hocking, dam Vixen; ch c Charley Brown by Jim Brown, dam Viola; ch c Primero by Powhattan, dam Speed.

Maltese Villa Stock Farm—br f Romeetta by imp. Woodlands, dam Dizzy Blonde.

Murry, W. M.—b c Ignacio by Three Cheers, dam Dairy Maid by Shannon; ch c Gold Pan by Panique, dam Nenetzia; b c Aristocrat by Flood, dam Cuba.

Undine Stable—b c Homer by Shannon, dam Sallie Gardner; ch f Glenlivet by Flood, dam Glendew.

Palo Alto Stock Farm—ch c Rinfax by Argyle, dam imp. Amelia; ch f Tearless by Wildidle, dam imp. Teardrop; ch f Rosebud by Wildidle, dam imp. Rosetta.

Santa Anita Stable—b c Ensenada by Rutherford, dam Arritta; b c San Joaquin by Longfellow, dam Santa Anita Belle; b f Esperanza by Grinstead, dam Hermosa; b f Cleopatra by Grinstead, dam Maggie Emerson; b f Ogarita by Longfellow, dam Mission Belle; ch c Silverado by Rutherford, dam Josie C.; b f Laciengs by Grinstead, dam Jennie D.

Shippee, L. U.—b c Lodowic by Longfellow, dam Carrie Phillips; b f May H. by Falsetto, dam Glenluine.

Winchell, C. E.—b c Senor, 3, Bersan—Sister to Joe Daniels.

Winters, Theo.—b c Rey Del Rey, 2, Norfolk—Marian; ch c San Juan, 2, Norfolk—Ballinette; ch c Uno Grande, 2, Joe Hooker—Jessie R.; ch c Overaga, 2, Joe Hooker—Avail.

Fashion Stakes.—For fillies two years old. A sweepstakes of $50 each. $15 forfeit, with $1,250 added, of which $250 to second and $100 to third. Winners of any race of $1,500 to carry 3 lbs. or of two such races, or one of $5,000, to carry 7 lbs. extra. Non-winners of $1,500 allowed 5 lbs.; of $1,000 7 lbs. Beaten maidens allowed 12 lbs. Six furlongs.

Daly, Marcus.—ch f Bonnie Lass, 2, imp. Sir Modred—Bonnie Kate; ch f Leonora, 2, imp. Sir Modred Lizzie Lucas; b f Mistletoe, 2, imp. Sir Modred—Letola; b f Namouna, 2, imp. Sir Modred—La Favorita.

Hearst, Geo.—ch f Babicora, 2, Hyder Ali—Graciosa; blk f Firework, 2, Falsetto—Explosion; b f El Vera, Jim Brown—Carrie C.

Maltese Villa Stack Farm.—br f Romeetta, imp. Woodlands—Dizzy Blonde.

Murry, W. M.—b f Lady Scoffin, Little Ruffin—Hiawasse.

Undine Stable.—ch f Glenlivet, Flood—Glenden.

Palo Alto Stock Farm.—ch f Tearless, Wildidle—imp. Teardrop; ch f Rosebud, Wildidle—imp. Rosetta.

Santa Anita Stable.—b f Esperanza, Grinstead—Hermosa; b f Cleopatra, Grinstead—Maggie Emerson; b f Ogarita, Longfellow—Mission Belle; b f Laciengs, Grinstead—Jennie D.

Shippee, L. U.—b f May H., Falsetto—Glenluine; b f False Queen, Falsetto—Queen Victoria.

Winters, Theo.—ch f Belle Songer, Joe Hooker—Lou Spencer; ch f Oletta, Joe Hooker—Alice N.; ch f Joanna—Joe Hooker—Addie O'Neil.

Farewell Stakes.—For two years old. A sweepstakes of $50 each, $15 forfeit, with $1,000 added, of which $200 to second and $100 to third. The winner to be sold at auction for $4,100; if entered by 4 P. M. on the day before the day appointed for the race, to be sold for $2,500, allowed 7 lbs; or, if for $1,000, 14 lbs. Beaten horses not liable to be claimed. Six furlongs.

Daly, Marcus.—ch f Bonnie Lass, imp. Sir Modred—Bonnie Kate; ch c Gold Dollar, imp. Sir Modred—Trade Dollar; ch f Leonora, imp. Sir Modred—Lizzie Lucas; br f Mistletoe, imp. Sir Modred—Letola; b c Montana, Ban Fox—imp. Queen; b f Namouna, imp. Sir Modred—La Favorita; b c Prince Charming, imp. Sir Modred—Carissima; ch c Silver King imp. St. Blaise—Maud Hampton.

Santa Anita Stock Farm.—ch c El Carmen, Gano—Grey Anne.

Winters, Theo.—b c Rey del Rey, Norfolk—Marian; ch c Judge Post, Joe Hooker—Countess Zeka; ch c Uno Grande, Joe Hooker—Jessie R.

Pelham Bay Handicap.—For three years old. A sweepstakes of $100 each, h. f., or $25 if declared by 4 P. M. on the day before the day appointed for the race, or only $10 if declared by August 1st. The club to guarantee the gross value of the stake to be $5,000, of which $1,000 to second and $100 to third. Weights to be published on the second day before the race. One mile and five furlongs.

Haggin, J. B.—ch f Rosette, Joe Hooker—Rosa B.

Hearst, Geo.—b c King Thomas, imp. King Ban—Maud Hampton; br c Tournament, imp. Sir Modred—Plaything; b c Anaconda, Spendthrift—imp. Maid of Athol; b f Golden Horn, Spendthrift—imp. Constantinople; blk f Everglade, Iroquois—imp. Agenoria; br f Miss Belle, imp. Prince Charlie—Linnet; b c Sacramento, Joe Hooker—Ada C; ch c Baggage, Warwick—Maria F.

Murry, W. M.—b c Lord of the Harem, Wildidle—Frolic.

Palo Alto Stock Farm.—ch c Flambeau, Wildidle—imp. Flirt.

Santa Anita Stable.—ch f Sinaloa, Grinstead—Maggie Emerson; ch c Honduras, Grinstead—Jennie B.; ch c Amigo, imp. Prince Charlie—Mission Belle; b c Clio, Grinstead—Glenita; b c Santiago, Grinstead—Clara D.

Winters, Theo.—ch c El Rio Rey, Norfolk—Marian; b f Noretto, Norfolk—Ballinette.

Protectory Stakes, for three years old. A sweepstakes of $50 each, $15 forfeit, with $1,250 added, of which $250 to second and $100 to third. Winners in 1890 of $2,000 to carry 5 lbs. extra; twice, 7 lbs.; thrice, 10 lbs. Non-winners in 1890 of $2,000 allowed 5 lbs.; or of $1,000, 10 lbs. Beaten maidens allowed 15 lbs. One mile.

Haggin, J. B.—blk c Fernwood, Falsetto—Quickstep; b c Hawkstone, Hindoo—imp. Queen Maud; ch f Rosette, Joe Hooker—Rosa B.

Hearst, Geo.—b c King Thomas by imp. King Ban, dam Maud Hampton; b c Sir Lancelot by imp. Sir Modred, dam Faustina; br c Tournament by imp. Sir Modred, dam Plaything; b c Anaconda by Spendthrift, dam imp. Maid of Athol; br f Miss Belle by imp. Prince Charlie, dam Linnet; b f Gloaming by imp. Sir Modred, dam Twilight; blk f Everglade by Iroquois, dam imp. Agenoria; b f Golden Horn by Spendthrift, dam imp. Constantinople; b c Ballarat by imp. Sir Modred, dam La Favorita; ch c Baggage by Warwick, dam Maria F.; ch f Cosette by Joe Hooker, dam Abbie W.

Palo Alto Stock Farm—b c Racine by Bishop, dam imp. Fairy Rose.

Santa Anita Stable—ch c Honduras by Grinstead, dam Jennie B.; b c Clio by Grinstead, dam Glenita; b c Santiago by Grinstead, dam Clara D.; b f Magdalena by imp. Glenelg, dam Malta; ch c Amigo by imp. Prince Charlie, dam Mission Belle.

Winters, Theo.—ch c El Rio Rey by Norfolk, dam Marian; ch f Florence A. by Joe Hooker, dam Atalanta.

Echo Stakes, for three years old. A sweepstakes of $50 each, $15 forfeit, with $1,000 added, of which $200 to second and $100 to third. The winner to be sold at auction for $5,000; if entered by 4 P. M. on the day before the day appointed for the race to be sold for $4,000, allowed 3 lbs.; if for $3,000, 7 lbs.; if for $2,000, 12 lbs.; if for $1,000, 20 lbs. Beaten horses not liable to be claimed. One mile and a sixteenth.

Haggin, J. B.—blk c Fernwood by Falsetto, dam Quickstep; b c Hawkstone by Hindoo, dam imp. Queen Maud; ch f Rosette by Joe Hooker, dam Rosa B.

Santa Anita Stable—b c Clio by Grinstead, dam Glenita; ch c Amigo by imp. Prince Charlie, dam Mission Belle.

Peytona Stakes, for fillies three years old. A sweepstakes of $50 each, $15 forfeit, with $1,250 added, of which $250 to second and $100 to third. Winners in 1890 of $2,000 to carry 3 lbs.; of two such races or one of $5,000, to carry 7 lbs. extra. Non-winners in 1890 of $1,500 allowed 5 lbs.; of $1,000, 7 lbs. Beaten maidens allowed 10 lbs. One mile and a furlong.

Haggin, J. B.—ch f Rosette by Joe Hooker, dam Rosa B.

Hearst, Geo.—b f Gloaming by imp. Sir Modred, dam Twilight; br f Miss Belle by imp. Prince Charlie, dam Linnet; blk f Everglade by Iroquois, dam imp. Agenoria; b f Golden Horn by Spendthrift, dam imp. Constantinople; ch f Cosette by Joe Hooker, dam Abbie W.

Palo Alto Stock Farm—ch f Muta by Wildidle, dam imp. Mutiny.

Santa Anita Stable—ch f Sinaloa by Grinstead, dam Maggie Emerson; b f Magdalena by imp. Glenelg, dam Malta; b f Atlanta by Grinstead, dam Blossom.

Winters, Theo.—b f Noretto by Norfolk, dam Ballinette; ch f Florence A. by Joe Hooker, dam Atalanta.

Country Club Handicap, for all ages. A sweepstakes of $100 each, half forfeit, or $25 if declared by 4 P. M. on the day before the day appointed for the race, or only $10 if declared by August 1st, with $2,000 added, of which $500 to second and $.00 to third. Weights to be published on the second day before the race. One mile and a furlong.

Gebhard, F.—b g Volunteer, 6, by imp. Mortemer, dam Sly Boots.

Haggin, J. B.—b m Firenzi, 6, by imp. Glenelg, dam Florida; br c Fitz James, 5, by imp. Kyrle Daly, dam Electra; blk c Fresno, 4, by Falsetto, dam Cachuca; b c Saracen, 4, by Longfellow, dam Salara; ch c Salvator, 4, by imp. Prince Charlie, dam Salina.

Hearst, Geo.—b c King Thomas, 3, by imp. King Ban, dam Maud Hampton; br c Tournament, 3, by imp. Sir Modred, dam Plaything; b c Anaconda, 3, by Spendthrift, dam imp. Maid of Athol.

Hearst, Geo.—b c Sir Lancelot, 3, imp. Sir Modred—Faustina; b c Ballarat, 3, imp. Sir Modred—La Favorita; blk m Gorgo, 5, Isonomy—imp. Flirt; ch c imp. Del Mar, 4, Somnes—Maid of the Hills; ch f imp. Gertrude, 4, Somnes—Geraldine.

Santa Anita Stable.—ch m Los Angeles, 5, imp. Glenelg—La Polka; ch c Honduras, 3, Grinstead—Jennie B.; b c Clio, 3, Grinstead—Glenita; ch c Amigo, 3, imp. Prince Charlie—Mission Belle; b c Santiago, 3, Grinstead—Clara D.

Winters, Theo.—ch c Don Jose, 4, Joe Hooker—Countess Zeika; ch c Joe Courtney, 4, Joe Hooker—Abbie W.

New Rochelle Stakes, for all ages. A sweepstakes of $100 each, h. f. or only $20 if declared by August 1st, with $2,500 added, of which $500 to second and $200 to third. Winners in 1890 of $3,000 to carry 3 lbs. extra; of two such races, or one of $5,000, 5 lbs. Non-winners in 1890 of $2,000 allowed 5 lbs.; of $1,000, 7 lbs. One mile and a quarter.

Gebhard, F.—b g Volunteer, 6, imp. Mortimer—Sly Boots.

Haggin, J. B.—b m Firenzi, 6, imp. Glenelg—Florida; br c Fitz James, 5, imp. Kyrle Daly—Electra; blk c Fresno, 4, Falsetto—Cachuca; b c Saracen, 4, Longfellow—Salara; ch c Salvator, 4, imp. Prince Charlie—Salina.

Hearst, Geo.—b c King Thomas, 3, imp. King Ban—Maud Hampton; br c Tournament, 3, imp. Sir Modred—Plaything; b c Anaconda, Spendthrift—imp. Maid of Athol; ch c Rono, 4, Flood—imp. Rosetta; blk m Gorgo, 5, Isonomy—imp. Flirt; blk f Everglade, 3, Iroquois—imp. Agenoria; b f Golden Horn, 3, Spendthrift—imp. Constantinople.

Murry, W. M.—b c Lord of the Harem, 3, Wildidle—Frolic.

Santa Anita Stable.—ch m Los Angeles, 5, imp. Glenelg—La Polka; ch f Sinaloa, 3, Grinstead—Maggie Emerson; b c Clio, 3, Grinstead—Glenita; ch c Amigo, 3, imp. Prince Charlie—Mission Belle; b c Santiago, 3, Grinstead—Clara D.; ch c Honduras, 3, Grinstead—Jennie B.

Winters, Theo.—ch c El Rio Rey, 3, Norfolk—Marian; ch c Don Jose, 4, Joe Hooker—Countess Zeika; ch c Joe Courtney, 4, Joe Hooker—Abbie W.

THE FARM.

Promoting Milk.

The London Live Stock Journal says: "A copious flow of milk, sustained through many months, is a quality which has been produced by art in domestication. Wild cattle rarely provide more than enough milk to rear their own offspring, and the flow of it is of comparatively short duration. Small in volume, the milk is rich in quality, but the lacteal organs soon dry off again. This, of course, is in harmony with the requirements of the young animals in a wild state, and is a correlation of the roving life and hap-hazard feeding of the dams. More milk than the calf requires under such conditions would be a waste of material energy which nature does not encourage. It would, moreover, be an encumbrance to the mother. Wild cattle are neither good milkers nor good fatteners, and in parts of England where calves are allowed to run with their domesticated dams generations after generations, the breed of such animals is not famous for milk-giving. Like that of the mare and ewe, the milk is smaller in quantity, rich in quality and of short duration. The desultory and irregular sucking of a calf or foal or lamb is not conducive to the development of a large flow of milk, and it distinctly tends to shorten the flow, Hand-milking of a sim lar character has the same effect. Young people are allowed to learn how to milk on cows who are going dry for calving, not on those who are still in full flow. New beginners soon dry up a cow's milk, and bad milkers do the same.

"Heavy milking properties, then, are artificial, in the sense that they have been developed under domestication, and by careful breeding, for a given end; yet, like many other qualities, which are a little more than mere germs of nature, they become hereditary by long usage. Few sorts of animals, if any, are more susceptible than cattle of being moulded into what we want; no physical quality is so easily trained and developed as that of giving milk. It is a function which constantly varying of itself can be dwarfed or extended at will. By means of careful training, kind treatment and intelligent breeding, it can be developed and made hereditary; an opposite system keeps it in a state of nature. The habits of a cow and the food she receives, have a great deal to do with her milking powers; quick and silent hand-milking does the rest. The practice of hand-milking cows has all along tended greatly to the development of the lacteal glands, and this development has become hereditary in some of our milking breeds. The ewes of the Larzac breed of sheep, from whose milk the famous Roquefort cheese is made in France, have been hand-milked for generations, so that their milking properties are now considerable and inherited. By repeatedly exciting the teats it is even possible to cause an animal that has never borne offspring to yield a small quantity of milk, and a cow sometimes remains barren several years after having had a calf, giving a profitable quantity of milk all the while."

A Pure Breed of Polled Durhams.

Our British contemporary. Farming World, under the heading of "A New Breed of Cattle," says:

"Our enterprising cousins on the other side of the Atlantic are ever hunting for improvements. There is no limit to their inventive genius. Not satisfied with the pure breeds of cattle which we send them from this country, they have now resolved to found a breed of their own. By mating Aberdeen-Angus sires with shorthorn cows, they have succeeded in forming a class or cross [bred?] without horns, but in regard to color and other cattle characteristics strongly resembling the shorthorns."

The Polled Durhams originated not by crossing Aberdeen-Angus or any other polls or shorthorns. They are of two sub-families. One from a sport in the herd of high grade shorthorns of Mr. A. G. Burleigh of Illinois, prepotent, and now fixed by careful selection for many years.

The other strain of Polled Durhams is from descendants of thoroughbred shorthorns, regularly registered in the American Shorthorn Hand-book, and the descendants registered and entitled thereto. Upon the authority of Hon. J. H. Pickrell, secretary of the American Shorthorn Association, which will not be questioned, and from an examination of the record, we find that the herd of Mr. W. S. Miller of Ohio, was established as follows:

This herd is descended from a naturally polled cow, not only of the purest shorthorn blood, but of a herd second to none now in the United States or England. We refer to the late herd of Hon. Wm. S. King of Minnesota, and noted for the superior breeding of its animals. The origin of the pure bred herd alluded to was originally from twin heifers of Mr. King's herd. These became the joint property of Mr. H. McNair and the estate of Hon. W. W. McNair, of Minneapolis, and all descended, either through dam or sire, from Oakwood Gwynne 4th (an imp. Medora, by Horatio), by Marquis of Geneva 10451.

Nellie Gwynne and Mollie Gwynne (twins of October, 1881). From this cow and the 7th Duke of Hilhurst 34221, her bull calf King of Kine (August 15, 1883), by Bright Eyes Duke 31894. Also Nellie Gwynne 2d, out of Nellie Gwynne, and by Favorite 48182; Mollie Gwynne 2d out of Mollie Gwynne, and by King of Kine; all entirely devoid of horns at birth. King of Kine, at the head of this herd, has in only one instance got a calf with horns, and these very small. Many of the animals descended from the Ohio importation of 1834 were noted for very small horns, and this importation certainly was not noted for under-bred cattle.)

To return, Mr. W. S. Miller, of Ohio, was so impressed with these cattle (the McNair sport) that he bought the whole herd, and has since been breeding them carefully. He had previously been breeding Red Polled Shorthorns—if the term may be admissible—starting, of course, with grades. Yet so potent are the Polled Durhams (the name now established) that Mr. Miller affirms that, no matter which parent is hornless, nine-tenths of the progeny are hornless. So far as the pure breeds are concerned, they come hornless, except in occasional instances, and then with imperfect horns.

Our contemporary will thus see that the now well established Polled Durhams are in neither case descended from a cross of Aberdeen-Angus are any other polled cattle; and in the case of the pure-bred stock they are not even indebted to the far away Galloway infusion of blood in some of the shorthorn sub-families, but are from as purely bred as possible. As originally stated by us, we believe that the "Polled Durhams" have come to stay; and, equally, with the three distinct origins of this breed; but we do not assert that the hornless are better than the magnificent horned variety, except that it is better to breed natural polls than to dehorn.—Prairie Farmer.

Prospects of Shorthorn Breeders.

Before we engage on our subject, it may be well to give, in a prominent way, an explanation of certain terms which must necessarily crop up time after time as we consider the prospects of breeders of Shorthorns.

DEFINITIONS.

SHORTHORNS	Cattle entered in or eligible for entry in Coates' Herd Book.
HIGHLY BRED SHORTHORNS.	Cattle bred either from "in and inbred" sires and dams of one strain or family, or cattle bred from one strain or family, and, without being "in-and in bred, that are termed "line bred Shorthorns."
WELL BRED SHORTHORNS.	Cattle good in themselves, either good butchers' cattle or good dairy cattle, or better butchers' and dairy cattle combined than the cattle of any other known breed.

We might supplement this by saying a good animal is necessarily a well bred one, and an inferior animal is a badly bred one, let its pedigree be what it may. And now to our subject. About twenty years ago a great change came over the Southern world. Prices went up, and all sorts of stock shared in the inflation which occurred in the first of the "seventies." Herds were started in new centers, and many took to breeding Shorthorns either as a hobby or because it was a fashionable occupation. Certain families of Shorthorns were termed "highly bred," and breeders vied with each other in obtaining representatives of these families. The trade of the country was good, farming was prospering, and hundreds and thousands were expended in the purchase of single animals. Men altogether unfitted for the pursuit embarked in Shorthorn breeding, and for a time judgment was of no account whatever. When a sale catalogue was published the whole business was reduced to such a simple certainty that one could tell almost to a trifle the number of hundreds or, as the case might be, thousands every animal would make. It mattered not whether the animal was "good, bad or indifferent," if its pedigree read right it was "highly bred" and worth so much money. This was very nice, and all was smooth sailing. We had "highly bred Shorthorns" spread over the country, and a large proportion of the breeders who owned "well bred Shorthorns" began to use bulls from "highly bred families. Men departed from lines they and their fathers had gone upon in building up those "well bred" herds. They knew certain strains of blood were worth so much money under the glass; they pored over pedigree, finding happy combinations here and flaws there, till they lost sight of the qualifications of the individuals that composed these pedigrees. Their great ambition was to get their herds as closely related to "highly bred Shorthorns" as possible. Everything for a time went off merrily as marriage bells. As we have said, it became a fashionable pastime with wealthy men to breed Shorthorns; and it was neither a question of meat nor milk with them so long as the pedigree read all right. "Well-bred Shorthorns," however, suffered after a time. Instead of sharing in the increased values they lost ground. They were neither fish nor flesh, they could show no straight line of descent; and although they were either good beef or milk cattle, or perhaps both good beef and milk cattle, they were of no account in the sale ring. They only brought tens when their aristocratic "highly bred," but comparatively poor blood relations made thousands.

Towards the close of the "seventies," corn growing, through bad seasons and foreign importations, became unprofitable. American and continental cattle and meat poured into our ports, trade of all sorts was in a bad state, and money got scarce, not only with the ordinary farmers but also with Shorthorns breeders. Prices began to fall off, even for "highly bred Shorthorns," and much as was then and has since been done, by one breeder buying from another to keep prices up whenever such cattle were put upon the market, values decreased enormously. Let us take any of the fashionable families and compare the prices of to day with what they at one time brought, and we are pretty near the truth when we say they are worth little more than a tenth of what they would at one time have realized.

Did these "highly bred Shorthorns" benefit the breed? I do not think they did. As we have seen, they were not bred to produce meat or milk; but beyond being a negative, they were a positive evil. Bred from paper, as we may be allowed to call it, they were produced weaklings. Mischief in the shape of hereditary diseases, through in-and-in breeding, became developed, and several herds lost constitution and flesh. There was no difficulty in making cattle bred in this way fat, but it was "beyond the power of man" to give them flesh and constitution.

Just as the early Shorthorn breeders bred for fat, we must to-day breed for flesh. Those excessively fat Shorthorns were required seventy years ago, when the ordinary stock of the country were full of flesh but wanting in fat, but they are no longer necessary. The ordinary farmers' cattle are changed, and what is now needed are strong constitutioned, thick-flesh Short-horns.

And now as to the prospects before breeders of Shorthorns. We hold that at no period of the breeder's history have they been brighter. We have quite got over the theoretical period —we have returned to the practical. Of all the breeds of cattle in the world we venture to say that under all circumstances, in all climates, and on all soils, there is no known breed that can compare with "well bred Shorthorns." If, perchance, Shorthorns have lost touch with the ordinary farmer, the butcher and the dairyman, it is not the breed that is to blame—it was the people who made a sport, a pastime, a play of them, and to-day we find those men at their wits' end to know what to do for a cross of blood that can bring life and living into their herds.

We have no doubt that many will sneer at much that we have written, but facts speak for themselves; and a good wide-chested, well-fleshed specimen of a "well-bred Shorthorn" is worth in the market to day five times as much as he was worth ten years ago, while, in point of fact, he is worth any number of "highly-bred Shorthorns," whose definition we gave at the opening of this paper.

Seeing, therefore, that Shorthorn breeding has made a fresh start, as it were, men's hands are free; and any-one with judgment can purchase and breed good cattle, assured that there are many keen buyers for every good animal he can rear. The best buyers will never ask if the animals for sale are fashionably bred; they will judge of their breeding by their looks, and if the breeder does not make a good price for good cattle it will only be because he does not ask enough and stick to his price. Really good cattle are not thickly sown over the country; the drain upon this class for foreign countries is great, and it requires little foresight to predict that "well-bred" Shorthorns have a great future before them.

On looking over what I have written it strikes me that I may be blamed for making light of pedigree. Let me in a single word say I believe in a good pedigree, but not in the too common interpretation of a good pedigree. I do not care however straight an animal may be bred if he is not good himself if "like begets like," which is a certainty, what good can come of breeding anything inferior? At the same time I value beyond measure a good animal from a stock of good ancestors, and I hold he has a good pedigree.—Robert Bruce, in London Live-Stock Journal Almanac.

The Boundary Changed.

The Drovers' Journal, of Chicago, learns from Col. Pearson, the Bureau of Animal Industry representative now at the stock yards, that the government authorities have decided upon a new quarantine line for splenic or Texas fever.

Last year's line started in Clayton county. Arkansas, just above the 35th parallel, ran northwesterly through the Cherokee nation to the center of the Osage reservation, then southwesterly in a straight line, crossing Indian territory diagonally to Wichita county, Texas, and continuing through the counties of Baylor, Haskell, Jones, Nolan, Tom Green and Crocket to the southern boundary of Pecos county, below the 30th parallel

The new line starts at the northest corner of Kansas, running due west along the Kansas southern boundary to "No Man's Land," then directly south to Cottle county, Texas, and due west on the 34th parellel to the center of Baily county, Texas. In other words, the new quarantine line places under the ban all of Indian territory all of Texas except the Panhandle portion lying north of the 30th parallel.

This move will please some, and it will dispose of the trouble heretofore encountered of driving cattle from below the line into Indian territory and shipping from there.

As it Should Be.

A representative of Nels Morris one of the "big four" in the Chicago cattle market, was in the office of Young & Kuhen inquiring after beef steers and trying to convince those who were there that Morris was one of the best friends the cattle. men ever had. so good in fact that he would go out on the market and buy cattle for more than the market price when he did not want them just to keep the market up.

"Well," said Col. Young, "I will look and see what I have got. Here it is I can let you have 900 head of two-year-old steers at $13, 700 head of threes at $16, or 750 head of fours and fives at $20."

Morris' man rubbed down his mustache a time or two and remarked:

"I guess I will wait until figures get more our way."

"All right," answered the colonel. "It is for us to say what we will take and what you will give. No hard feelings, you know. I said I would take $13 for the twos, but I would take $14 if you would offer it. You see, it is just this way. When we ship out cattle to Chicago we have to take just what you fellows offer us, if it is only $3 a head, but when we get you down here we have something to say about what we will take—that's the way of it."

The colonel was right, and if cattlemen would study his concluding remark they would find it pregnant with sound sense. Get the buyers here and you will have something to say about what you will sell your cattle for. "If the mountain will not go to Mahommed, Mahommed must go to the mountain." If cattle are not shipped to the "big four," the "big four," will have to go where cattle are if they want them. Every cock has an advantage on his own dunghill that he has not in his rival's territory, and is in better condition and has more heart to defend his interests.

It might be tough on the cattlemen in the start, and for some time afterwards to hold their cattle back, but if they could only starve a little while the feast would surely come to them in the end.—Ft. Worth Gazette.

Saltless Butter.

On many occasions we have told it as a fact that the best butter used in London and Paris is entirely free from salt. That information was gained many years ago from a visit we made to these cities. Mr. Basham, a skilled English dairyman who has just arrived in this country and made us a visit, tells us that to-day no butter sells at or near the top of the market in London that possesses a trace of salt in it.

The butter of the very highest class he thinks is made in England, but there is not much of it, representing the same position probably that our dollar-a-pound dairy butter does. The great bulk of fine butter he says comes from the northern part of France and is made by the French farmers, collected and worked together according to quality, has little color and no salt. That is the pat butter to be seen on the tables of the best hotels and restaurants of London. This French butter comes to England in two pound rolls and boxes containing twenty-four pounds and is exposed for sale in the stores in this shape. Fine cheese cloth is used for wrapping with pinked edges, but only covering about two-thirds of the top of the roll leaving a space open for testing. Danish butter, he says, is more salt and takes a rank below the Normandy or French rolls.

This evidence bears us out in the statement that the world is working toward butter sweet and entirely free from salt. Mr. Basham says this is insipid butter to those accustomed to sour milk butter freely salted, but he also says those who like the former eat two or three times as much of it as those do who prefer the salted sour milk article.

It may be said that New York is not the London and Paris market. but only the last year the reported talks of dairymen who supply the Boston market all gave evidence of the strong tendency of the market toward butter without salt, many of them furnishing it in that condition. It was only the other day when the writer took dinner with a friend at the Fifth Avenue Hotel, this city, which our country friends know is the swell hotel in the city, and we noted particularly the butter that it was nearly if not quite free from any taste of salt. Go into the highest class of restaurants in the city, and do you find "high flavored sour cream butter?" Not at all, everything in the establishment is of delicate flavor, butter and all.

The dairyman who has an eye to business will take a note of this fact and measure his actions accordingly.—American Dairyman.

THE GUN.

The Game and General Situation.

It is not necessary to the existing situation to recite the Game laws of the State concerning either fish, flesh or fowl. Unprecedented rains and snows have deluged and covered the State—the entire coast for that matter—to such a condition that as the quotation goes, as in the midst of war, between nations, the laws are silent, similarly amidst the war of the elements all of Nature's regulations in ordinary course are tumultuously over-ridden. The waters of the heavens have drenched the earth, and compelled the waters of the earth to rise in disastrous greeting to submerge the earth already oversoaked. The beautiful snow has made of itself the dreaded snow, and in a shroud of white has covered and wrapped the giants of hill and mountain which overlook the valleys and the plains, as in coverments which wax weary to all of human kind. These natural provinces of the tributary streams which feed the rivers and the oceans, and supply to the husbandmen the nourishment of prosperous tillage and to all in traffic the means to transportation and commerce, have this sad Winter become as the lodgements of the violent storms, and from these Vantage heights have plunged the avalanches which have made the gorges of the Sierras and of the Siskiyou to resemble the renowned valley of Chamonia where from the towering Alps the vast slides are precipitated.

Railroads, bridges, dams, and artificial works of every kind, have been as sacrifices to the extraordinary burst of the elements. What the high lands could not resist, the low lands are unable to withstand. To what man could not master or meet, every creature of the earth has had to succumb. Fin, flesh and wing are in the category. The burrowing rodents have not escaped. It is the gratifying fact—the gophers are drowned almost to extermination for the year. They will increase, but they will not formidably multiply for the year to come.

With every species of game, whether of land or of water, the trouble is apparent. The brutes which hibernate and are privileged to prey at all seasons are the only exception. No hunter has ever discovered the carcase of a bear snowed under. Bruin has his own special browse upon his paws, on which to tramp it in the open season and subsist during the close season. His claws are his clauses of exemption. The antlered species fare not so well.

Crops and vegetation useful to man and beast will be so much spared. It is a boon in view of the diminuition of production. Philosophers, who retort from every evil something of good, and the optimists who argue that every calamity is a blessing in disguise, have now their full swing of delighting and uplifting remarks to console the downhearted and cheer the despondent. Shakespeare's note, that "the toad, though ugly and venomous, yet wears a precious jewel in its head," is solacing. "Every cloud has a silver lining," is as a bow of promise in the heavens, still we suffering mortals, drenched and chilled, the snow bound and the deluged, pray fervently for the single glimpse of the white wing which may in season blush to the golden hue which is assurance of rich reward that every mortal strives for in the life that is, while he heeds not the life that is everlasting, nor can take with him thither the gold that would impart color or make weight. There is a sound lesson—"out of the nettle danger, pluck the flower safety.". The moral of it is, now that the elements have manifested their powers; the genius and ingenuity and study of California should be directed to the betterment of all antecedent methods to meet and overcome these elements. There was a deluge. It had its Noah and the Omnipotent design. Noah and all that he had saved, better peopled and occupied the earth. We have had more than the forty days and forty nights of rain—the biblical record has no account of snows, so that the fair inference is that these piling stores of heavy wet are as the heaping of the measure; and the indications are that tremendous interest has accumulated in all the ages which this generation is destined to liquidate, or be snowed under. Signal Service fails, and there are no assets. "Old Probabilities" has sunk his reputation to the condition below the shattering of the astrologers. Like the dreams of Rory O'More, his prognostications are safest when accepted by the rule of contraries. "All signs fail in fair weather." We pray for that order of weather which shall not convince us that "the rain it raineth every day," and in which the sign shall be of the old tavern style." entertainment for man and beast."

They are the beast we think of, make intercession for. The unsophisticated youthful girl pupil who gave us the answer to the question direct. "Tell me of beasts," that "all living creatures are beasts; brutes are imperfect beasts; man is the only perfect beast," taught her preceptor a new theory of instruction. As the little girl answered to the question of the reverend Father, "what is matrimony?" and had her mind set upon the answer as to purgatory—that it was "a middle state of suffering for soules"—so it is with the germs and species to be classed as beasts. Are fish to be so classed? Is a whale a fish? What shall be said of the whale which took in Jonah? Would any other than a beast or a bunko sharp have done that thing? Fishes swim in the vasty deep; sport in shallower waters. The whale comes up to blow or spout. How like the "perfect beast? He is the rising politician of the great salt sea. Sharks and other species attack him and devour him. The simile holds good. One touch of Nature makes all mankind kin." The harpoon of the "perfect beast" of the whaler signifies to the whole that also is the "perfect beast" of the blubber hunter in touch with him—even to going through his vitals.

There is a distinction, yet hardly a difference, between hunting offal and hunting office. It is the whale which blows and spouts. The sharks and others are direct on business. Business is the means to pleasure, and the longer is the enjoyment. Pleasure has its days; business keeps right on.

But all this is not of game quality. I am getting to it. Game itself is getting gamey this extraordinary season. As the Chinaman remarked, "No can catchee, how can haves." The game laws require no improvement. There are no offenders. Cause why, principally, they can't; lastly, as Dogheny put it, there isn't any game swimming, running or flying; and secondly, nothing of the kind will pan out or pay. It may be called the close open season, temporarily closed on account of the weather. Deer hide, every winged creature except the geese and ducks, don't obtrude; and the mute fish experience what it is to have a rush of waters and a flood of adversity. The Fish Commissioners are in the anomalous condition of being afloat as they are kept at home. Callundan and his deputies are housed and in the swim. What is the use? Mountain avalanches of snows sweeping away storages of spawn; swollen and roaring rivers surmounting their accustomed banks, and the ordinary means of travel impossible—what are any of them to do? To do nothing, and to do it gracefully and effectually is the best that is left them to do. The elements are their obstructionists, and between the elements and man the yielding place is with man. Senator Routier and his colleague, Hon. Mr. Harvey of the Fish Commission are unresignedly resigned to their compulsory inactivity to restive degree; Callundan and his assistants are as pike in pickle, and still the rivers rise and their tributaries roar as audiences delighted to encore and swell the volume as the rains pour and the snows, like Zaccheus, come down.

In the very ancient and mythical war of the Titans the giant gods threw rocks and smashed things generally. The railroads appear now to be the objects of the fury of the elements. Bravely do they withstand the terror of snow and rain Driving through avalanches, removing landslides, compelling floods and washouts to make way, the iron horse, harnessed to the cyclone steeds of the rail, hitched to the snow plow, and combatting every obstruction with steam and brain, with skill and pluck, with endurance and toil, wins the right of road, restores travel and communication, maintains the linking of the continent from the Pacific to the Atlantic, battles for the longitudinal line from California to Oregon, and contests with valley floods and mountain snows the whole way through from San Francisco to Puget Sound.

There is game all along the route—the game of the water and the land; the heroic game of men. This winter will tell the story. It will be of enduring record. The oldest native Californian recollects no equal to it. The youngest of the native born will probably never have experience of its parallel in the allotted age of man. It is phenomenal.

King Richard was premature in his "Now is the winter of our discontent." Shakespeare ought to have awaited events. Yet the glorious summer of the markets of New York and the increasing demands of the East for the fruits of this golden West will uplift and bring out shining prosperity at last. The wines of California will cheer, the superior horses of California will speed the greeting; the "glorious climate" of the State will yet entice, and the wild game of the coast will have its charm.

COLTON STATION, Feb. 27, 1890.

EDITOR BREEDER AND SPORTSMAN:—Enclosed I hand you a score of our shoot on February 22nd for the Selby Medal. Dr. M. E. Taber of our club was the lucky man. This makes the fourth time the Doctor has captured the medal and it now becomes his personal property. I also enclose a little live bird shooting done the same day. We shot at the same number, and under the same conditions our boys did against the Eastern cracks, and by the way, it almost makes me sick our boys did not get the cake. We never will have such a chance again, and had it been possible for me to have left my business I would have been on hand.

At 50 singles and 25 pairs Blue Rock targets, Chamberlin Rules.

Taber.........1 1 1 1 1 1 1 1 1 0 1 1 1 1 1 1 1 1 0 1 1 1 1 1 1 0 1 0—21
H. A. Smith..
19 and 10 yds 1 1 1 1 1 0 0 0 1 1 1 1 1 1 1 0 0 0 1 1 1 1 1 0 1 1 1—18
A. B. Black.... 01 11 01 10 11 10 01 11 11 10 11 11
11 11 10 11 10 21 01 00 10 11 11 10 00—35—74

Knight.........1 1 1 1 1 1 1 1 1 1 1 1 0 1 1 0 1 1 0 1 0 0 1 1 0 1 1 0—18
10 Parker....
19 and 17 yds 1 1 1 0 1 1 1 1 0 1 1 0 0 0 1 1 1 1 1 1 1 0 1 1 1—18
F F A 5 1½..... 11 01 10 10 10 11 10 11 10 10 11 10
00 00 11 10 10 10 11 10 10 10 11 11 01—31—67

Roberts........1 0 1 1 1 0 1 1 1 1 1 0 0 1 0 1 1 1 1 0 1 1 1 1 1—19
10 Smith.....
15 and 16 yds 1 1 1 1 0 1 0 1 1 1 1 1 0 1 0 1 0 0 1 1 1 0 0 1—17
A. B. Black..... 00 10 00 11 10 11 10 00 11 11 00 00
11 10 11 00 11 01 11 11 00 11 11 11 11—32—68

Bruner........1 1 1 1 1 1 1 0 1 1 1 1 1 1 1 1 1 1 1 1 1 1 0 1 1 1—22
12 Smith....
17 and 15 yds. 1 1 1 0 0 1 1 1 1 0 1 0 1 1 0 0 1 1 1 1 1 1 1 1 1—18
Wood 2½ 1½-5... 00 00 10 11 11 10 11 11 11 00 00 11
10 11 11 00 10 10 10 11 11 11 11 11 11—33—78

Unger.........1 1 1 1 1 1 1 1 1 1 1 1 1 0 1 0 0 1 1 1 0 1 0 0 1 1—19
12 Smith.....
16 and 14 yds 1 0 1 1 1 0 1 0 0 1 1 0 1 1 0 1 1 0 1 1 0 0 1 1—16
A. B. Schultz.. 10 11 11 11 10 01 10 01 11 11 10 11
11 11 10 01 10 10 11 11 00 10 10 01 11—35—70

The above score is the eighth contest for the Selby Challenge Medal for Southern California, Dr. M. E. Taber having won the medal three times. The boys was after him but the Dr. proved to be a little swift for the boys and captured the medal for the fourth time. It now becomes his personal property. The birds were thrown very low and swift.

At fifteen live birds, American Shooting Association Rules. $7.50 entrance.

Bruner........	12	28	1	1	1	1	2	1	1	1	1	1	2	1	1	1	1—15
Unger....	12	28	2	1	1	2	0	1	1	1	1	0	1	1	1	1	1—13
Taber.........	12	28	2	1	1	1	1	1	0	1	1	1	2	2	1	1	2—14
Roberts.......	10	30	2	0	2	2	0	2	2	1	1	1	0	w			
Robb..........	12	28	1	2	0	0	0	w									

A. W. B.

Student and Sportman's Club.

A special meeting of the club was held Wednesday evening of last week to listen to the report of the committee on conference with the proposed Athletic Club of Bakersfield. Its recommendations, clause by clause, were unanimously adopted. Then the names of Senator E. Wolcott of Colorado, Senator Leland Stanford, Hon. Charles N. Felton, Hon. John Sanford, Hon. Theodore Roosevelt, Gen. William Shaeffer and Gen. E. F. Beale were presented for membership. A communication from Truxton Beale was read, which stated that ex-Gov. Stanford had expressed himself very much interested in the club and its object and would see that the railroad company aid it by refusing to carry any kind of game, deerskins, etc., (out of season, of course) as freight and that it would gladly help in any other way that the club should suggest.

The letter stated further, that if the club felt so disposed, efforts would be made to have the government allow some of the buffalo now in the Yellowstone Park, to be located either upon the lands of Gen. Beale or upon Haggin & Carr's property, under the care of the club, as a blizzard or a hard winter might destroy them all where they now are. The matter was referred to a committee, which was given full power to act in the premises.

An interesting discussion followed, resulting in a very important step being taken by the club. Preservation of the timber in the high Sierras and upper watersheds of Kern river is a vital matter, and recently has been a subject of petition to the authorities at Washington. It was decided that if all of the country on the upper Kern, above a certain altitude to be hereafter determined upon, should be taken possession of by the government and declared a game preserve, the desired results would be accomplished. Messrs. H. A. Blodget, W. E. Houghton and H. C. Park were appointed a committee to consider the matter and urge upon the eastern and other influential non-resident members, concerted action to that end.

Editor Claude King, of substantial Sports Afield, in his current issue, says that the journal is prospering beyond its founder's most sanguine expectations, and we are glad to know it. We have followed Mr. King since his salutatory, and have found in each issue evidences of painstaking and clear title to general regard at the hands of sportsmen.

In Baja California.

"Wake up, Gus."

"All right; I'm with you."

And hearing him moving about the room I ran across to the stable, soon had Santa hooked up to the cart, and in a few minutes Gus and Sam came over clad in overcoats, hunting boots, etc., with De (Sam's pointer) frisking at their heels. It took us only a few seconds to get under way, and long before day broke we were well on our way towards old Mexico, fifteen miles south of National City, bound on a quail hunt, and determined to make this the hunt of the season, as the 1st of March was getting very close at hand, and we should have to drop field work after that date until next September.

Down across the Sweetwater Valley, through Chula Vista, past Otay, and daylight found us near the Mexican Custom House at the line, and after being overhauled by the Mexican guards stationed there, we were allowed to pass, and away we went up the first big canyon to the right, some five or six miles, until we came to a water hole in the middle of the valley, which was overhung by two or three huge sycamore trees, making as pretty a camp ground as one could wish for.

"Now, boys, here we are, and if we don't kill some birds to-day it's our own fault. Just look at that!" I said, as about one hundred birds got up with a whirr all around us as we pulled up under one of the trees. And as we were unhitching we could hear on all sides the clear notes of hundreds of California quails. The ground was simply superb, level as a floor, very little cactus (that bane of California quail shooting), and the cover consisted of tar weeds and brush not over three feet high.

We were in the centre of a valley about three miles wide, and it seemed as though the supply of quail was inexhaustible, to judge from the tracks we could see on every hand. The dogs could hardly be kept quiet while we were getting ourselves into hunting trim, and when we left camp about six o'clock with old Sol just commencing to disperse the night vapors, and with the knowledge that we had all day before us, accoutreed with an abundance of shells and with hundreds of quails calling on every side, three good dogs, wild to get to work, no wonder we felt our muscles swell and our blood bound along through our veins with a thrill that put every sense on the alert as we called to the dogs "Hie on, sir," and with a plunge away went De with Trix and Countess through the undergrowth, and we hadn't got fifty yards away from the camp until De "froze" solid as a rock, and before we could get close enough to get action on him, up jumped at least a hundred birds, and as they got up away went another covey on the right of as many more.

"Mark."

"All right."

"I'm on," we answer, and away went the dogs again, perfectly frantic, with their owners not much better.

"Look there, Ad," and sure enough, Trix was all out of shape, backed by the pointer Countess. "Steady, sir, steady, old fellow," and I walked slowly up until I was within eight or ten feet of the dogs, when out with a "cut, cut, cut" and a whirr, jumped a couple of quail, and as I pulled on the right hand bird I heard Sam away on my left turn loose with his old No 10 Parker, and wheeling I saw the air just full of birds, rising on all sides. *Bang!* went my left barrel, and breaking the gun, I slipped in two more shells and was just in time to make as clean a miss as any one very well could make on an old cock who went hurtling away from under my dog's nose, twisting like a veritable old "long bill" does under a stiff March wind. "Won't do, old man," says Gus, and as a bird gets up under his feet and starts off he swings his gun onto him, and before he can pull the trigger, *bur-r-r!* away go about a dozen birds from right under his gun, and Gus frantically tries to cover first one and then the other, until when he does shoot, the nearest quail is about seventy-five yards away, and just everlastingly making the air hum as he goes through it.

"Ha, ha! there, found that hole, did you?" I call out, and Gus, with a rather unpleasant remark about game birds in general, swings off towards Sam, who is just piling into the quail right and left.

"This won't do," I think, and I call Trix and Countess in and work along cautiously towards the right, where I had marked down at least a hundred birds. Trix is quartering finely when around comes his nose until the point of his tail and his nose are within an inch of each other. "*Who-a-p*, sir, *steady*, Countess," and as my bird gets up and I wait until I can be certain that I don't tear him all to pieces and then "let him go," what solid satisfaction one feels as he sees the bird double up and come down, and as your retriever fetches to hand and you bag your bird and throw your hammerless forward with a "Hie on," you wouldn't change places just then, with the greatest ruler on earth.

But away goes another bird, quartering away to the left, and I pile him up about forty yards away, and look over to see how the boys are getting on. I don't need to look to find out whether they are getting any shooting or not as the continued bang, bang, of their guns attests the fact that they are very busy.

The birds are lying finely now, and I don't go over twenty feet until both dogs are standing, and as two birds break away and are successively brought to *terra firma*, and the dogs start to retrieve, and *both* draw down again on two different quail, I mentally exclaim, 'Oh! that I could only put this on canvas!" I have shot quail all over Southern California, but this day's outing in old Mexico beats them all.

The supply of birds seem inexhaustible, and it is not long before I turn towards camp loaded down and out of shells (I left camp with sixty in my coat); there I find Sam bent on the same errand.

"Did you ever see any thing like this," he says, as he wipes off his manly brow, and old De hunts the shade of the sycamore.

"Grand indeed," I reply, and we commence to unload birds, fill up our pockets with shells, and after we have opened a bottle of Anheuser-Busch, we strike out again over the same ground.

"How is Gus making it?" I ask. "Why didn't he come in?"

"Well, you know this is his first season, and he don't shoot as fast as we do, but I saw him do some mighty good shooting over there, and was just enjoying himself hugely."

We walk along about a hundred yards further, coming near to an elderberry tree, and Sam says:

"Good Lord! Ad, look there!" and I wheel quickly around only to see, it seems to me, a thousand quail rise with a mighty whirr, only to settle down not over another hundred yards in front of us. I look at Sam, and Sam looks at me.

"I'm going back for the balance of my shells," Sam says. "I don't want to lose any time going back to camp after we get into them."

"Oh, come on!"

"No siree!" and away he goes, and I swing along until a bird gets up right in front of me, only to plunge downward again as the Parker 12 spits an ounce of No. 8's into him before he gets 30 yards away. I work along into a little depression in the ground, and there I find Gus seated under a wide spreading mesquite bush fanning himself with his straw hat. (Its too warm in Mexico to hunt with any other kind of head covering).

"Well Gussie, how is it?" I ask, as I join him.

"Well, I've got nearly two dozen birds, and as its nearly 11 o'clock, I'm going to camp and have a drink and a bite to eat before I get used up. I never saw so many quail in my life before, and I don't understand how it is that none of San Diego's market hunters have got in here before this."

"Probably they are not on," I reply; "but, Gus, you are shooting finely. By George! if you keep on, some of our local champions will have to look out. A man who has never shot a gun off a dozen times in his life until this season, that can take the field as you have to-day, and bag 24 quail by even noon, and kill every bird in the air, is not to be sneezed at." And Gus tries to blush as he starts towards camp, but as he is of rather a florid complexion, and his late exertions has rendered his face the color of a red, red beet, the attempts is a dismal failure.

About this time I see De come tearing through the brush ahead of Sam, and I pull myself together, knowing that I have about two hours hard work ahead of me.

"I knew you would want it,' he remarks, as he gently twisted the handle of his corkscrew after inserting the screw into a bottle of cool beer which he takes out of his inner pocket, "because I'm not going back to that wagon until I'm shot out, and you've got to stay with me too, old son, or I'll roast you when we get back to town. You have been giving it to me long enough, my boy. Now look out for yourself or I'll wipe your eye."

And he took out of a sack all the *loaded shells* I had left in camp and turned them over to me.

"We'll *cache* them, Ad, until we shoot our pockets empty, so we won't have to carry too many."

"Well, as you seem to have arranged it all yourself go ahead." I returned and away we went.

"Two to one on the gun on the first quail that flushes," says Sam, and as he has no takers, we work along silently for a minute or two, when a bird gets up so suddenly right under my gun, that ere I am aware of it I have pulled into him and literally torn him into fragments.

"What in thunder are you doing Ad," says Sam disgustedly, as the pieces of quail, feathers, etc., come down about a dozen feet away. "I don't see any use in acting the hog that way," he continues, as I laugh. "Sam you were too anxious to wipe my eye that time," and I don't get the words fairly out before whirr goes Mr. Quail up from under his feet, and I turn as his gun speaks, only to catch sight of a fluff in the air as Sam tears his bird all to pieces.

"What's the matter with you," I yell.

"Ad, I couldn't help it; I had to shoot!" he says, and we both laugh, and as we get into the birds, we gradually get further apart and now I find myself in the prettiest cover you ever saw, and as I don't travel over twenty yards between shots, it can be seen that I am having a regular picnic.

It is not long until I am loaded down and I turn back to our *cache* and unload some thirty quail and fill my pockets with shells, but after shooting half an hour or so longer I made up my mind to hunt camp and lay off for an hour as the sun is boiling down on me and it is just after noon and oh, so hot.

I find Gus in camp coolly taking his ease, and as the blue clouds of smoke float away over his head from his fragrant Havana, as he lies on his back in the shade, with his hands clasped under his head, he looks too comfortable for any thing.

"Used up?" he asks as I drop hunting coat and gun and throw myself on the ground beside him.

"No," I reply "but this is too nice a ground to use up in half a day, and as we don't want to start home until nearly dark, we have lots of time to get our work in this afternoon.

"Right you are" and we open another bottle of "choke bore" and silently enjoy a long, strong pull at it, and Gus continues "I wish Sam was here; it would be more sociable; I wonder what he is about; I have'nt heard him shoot for some time.

"Should'nt wonder if he was headed this way now," I remark and sure enough in a few minutes Sam shows up laughing.

"Thought you was going to use up your shells before —".

"Oh, you go to blazes" he breaks in, and Gus and I join in the laugh.

"Well boys, lets count up and see what we have done," says I, and I turn out 72 birds; Sam shows up as many more counting from his pockets and sack, and after Gus had added 22, Sam quitely drew one eyelid down, and pulled out a dozen extra from inside his shirt and sack.

"Got you on the hip, to-day," he says, and turns to me with a laugh.

"Wait till night, Sam, don't be in a hurry" I reply as we pile our 178 quail in three heaps and commence to draw them.

"All right, old boy" after our present job is completed we feed the dogs and refresh our inner selves with more lunch and loll around until we can feel the cool afternoon breeze come up the valley from the ocean making us feel like new men.

"Come, boys," and once more we don coats and grasp our guns and start a'resh more quail to slaughter.

a hundred shells left, and, (we left town with

the evening, where we sit down to an elegant supper ordered "afore hand," and over our roast joint and claret we recount the events of the day and kill over again some lusty old cock, as he gets up under our dog's nose away down in old Mexico.

SAN DIEGO, March 2, '90. TRIX.

Perplexity is ours, for the reason that an enthusiastic owner of an Irish setter by Mr. Truman's Rush T.—Lady Elcho T. sends to us a card inscribed "Arthur Allan Briggs, Sierra City, California, February 1st, 1890." We recall the existence of a brother in Sierra City; a Benedict; and not a bad fellow withal, and in the absence of any explanatory line conclude that the house of Briggs is waxing in the land.

Mr. J. S. Fanning of this city has gone North on a seal shooting trip with Captain Miner, on the sealing schooner Allie J. Alger, of Seattle, Wash. He made a similar trip last year that was quite successful, thanks to his superior marksmanship, and we hope he will return from his present venture loaded with pelts and profits in time to participate in the next meeting of the State Sportsman's Association.

There will be a grand pigeon shoot at Lathrop on Wednesday, March 12th. All matches will be governed by the American Association Shooting Rules of 1890. Prizes to be divided according to number of entries, viz: 5 entries or less two-thirds and one-third; 6 to 9 entries 50, 30 and 20 per cent; 10 or more entries 40, 30, 20 and 10 per cent.

First match—Six single live birds. Entrance, $2 50.

Second match—Five pairs double live birds. Entrance, $5 00.

Third match—Fifteen single live birds. Entrance, $7 50

Fourth match—Freeze out at live birds. Entrance, $2 50.

Fifth match—15 single and 5 pair double clay birds. Entrance $2 50.

Plenty of live and clay birds will be on hand and the public are assured of a good day's sport. Shooting to begin at 10 o'clock Scarlett and Howland will act as managers and the success of the meeting is consequently assured.

THE KENNEL.

Dog owners are requested to send for publication the earliest possible notices of whelps, sales, names claimed, presentations and deaths, in their kennels, in all instances writing plainly names of sire and dam and of grandparents, colors, dates and breed.

Visit.

Mr. Geo. W. Bassford's pointer Blossom (Glen R.—Josie Bow) to Baron J. H. F. von Schroder's Point (Don—Drab).

A. K. C. Stud Book Registration.

Mr. J. Lansing Lane, at Auburn, requests us to publish the regulations governing entries to the American Kennel Club Stud Book, and as there seem to be doubts in the minds of many in relation to the matter, we take pleasure in doing so. Entry blanks may be had from this office, or from Mr. A. P. Vredenburgh, Secretary A. K. C 44 Broadway, N. Y.

The Stud Book rules are these:

The American Kennel Club Stud Book, will be issued annually; will contain a full index and will publish bound in cloth. Numbers will be assigned upon the receipt of each entry, and will be published monthly in the American Kennel Gazette. Registry in the Stud Book can be made only under the following conditions:

Where sire and dam are already registered, or are directly descended from dogs already registered in said book.

Where dogs possess an authenticated pedigree extending back three generations.

Where dogs (not eligible under the provisions as above required) have won not less than two first prizes in the regular classes, at any show recognized by the American Kennel Club.

All entries for the Stud Book will be published in the issue of the American Kennel Gazette following the receipt of said entry, to enable inspection, and the correction of any error that may appear.

The fee for entry in the Stud Book will be one dollar for each entry.

All dogs shown at any show held by a member of the American Kennel Club, and not already registered in the Stud-Book must be registered in the American Kennel Gazette. The fee for such entry will be twenty five cents.

The American Kennel Gazette will be published on the last day of each and every month.

The Occidental Coursing Club meets at Newark to-day to run off a sixteen dog aged stake for eight dogs. The meeting offers great attractions and should be largely attended.

J. L. Miller of Bakersfield, was busy about this city all last week laying in goods for a store which he is about to open in [illegible] s he found time for a little

ROD.

The Board of Fish Commissioners.

The regular meeting of the Fish Commission, held on Tuesday afternoon last at 220 Sutter street, was very properly confined to consideration of such matters as were urgent, for the reason that the much regretted demise of Colonel J. Mervyn Donahue, a relative of Hon. J. Downey Harvey, indisposed that gentleman for more than rigid duty. The minutes of the preceding meeting were approved.

The demand for $150 for legal services from Mr. Henry Hogan in the matter of the State vs. the Sawyer Tanning Company of Napa was then audited and the Board resolved to stand in favor of paying Mr. Hogan $100.

The monthly report of Chief of Patrol F. P. Callundan was then read as follows:

The Honorable, the Board of Fish Commissioners:—

GENTLEMEN, In obedience to your order the monthly report of the Chief of Patrol for February is submitted.

Comparatively little has been done for the reason that the prevailing high waters have prevented successful fishing by Chinese and others who practice illegal methods.

Three Chinese have been arrested during the month, and are now in jail in this County pending a hearing, all of them for having the young of fish in possession.

The appeal cases of the Chinese recently convicted at Martinez remain in *statu quo*, but Assistant District Attorney Wells of Contra Costa County is about to move actively in the matter, and a speedy consummation is anticipated.

Your Deputy at Eureka, Humboldt County, has placed the officers of the gas company of that city under arrest for permitting tar and other deleterious substances to pass into waters of the State. Public sentiment is strongly with Deputy Smith, and he is quite sure of convicting his men.

Deputy Ennis has been very efficient in watching the city for doe and fawn skins, and reports that none have been received here during the month.

Since March 1st, upon which day the open season for quails closed, the San Francisco markets have been regularly inspected, and it is a gratifying evidence of the success attained by your Honorable Board to be able to report that no quails can now be had, and that the dealers generally offer positive assurances that they will refuse to receive or handle quails until September 10th next.

The Cold Storage Company of this city has no quails on storage and will receive none, so that that door to annoyance and legal complications is closed.

Three days of last week were passed in Marin County by three of your Deputies in the hope of finding some of the persons said to be taking salmon trout and other trout from the streams of that County. It was only with the utmost difficulty that the fishing grounds could be reached, and when they were reached no fishermen were found. There remain several creeks to be visited, and your Deputies will go to them at an early day. Deputy Herzog, at Bethany, reports high water and little fishing at that point.

During the month he found and took possession of two Chinese sturgeon lines—one with 216 hooks and the other with 400 hooks. Both lines were taken in Middle river.

Deputy Herzog desires your honorable Board to provide him with oil, to be used as fuel upon his steam launch. He states that the consumption, while in active service, is about 50 gallons in three days, and requests that 250 gallons be sent to him, or enough to keep him supplied for 15 days.

He also reports that he has located five gangs of Chinese of seven men to the gang, all working under one boss or superintendent. All of these men are located in the sloughs between Old river and Middle river; have their camps made, and are ready to fish as soon as the water falls sufficiently.

After consultation with Assistant District Attorney White of Stockton, Deputy Herzog states that he considers it advisable to take all persons arrested by him to Stockton for trial. The nearest justice is at Tracy, but it would be quite impossible to secure the presence of the District Attorney at a trial held there.

Deputy Thomas Tunstead is constantly on duty about the markets, and among the wharves and commission houses.

Respectfully submitted, F. P. CALLUNDAN,
Chief of Patrol.

The report was approved and filed as read. The Board upon suggestion of President Joseph Routier resolved to purchase two hundred dozens of quail and distribute them in Los Angeles, Santa Clara, San Mateo, Napa and Sacramento counties. Immediate applications for the birds were invited from persons controlling places where they could be protected for four or five years. A communication from Mr. C H. Eigenmann, the pisiculture of the coast, was received in which it was stated that two trouts, the salmo iridseus and the salmo gairdneri were found in the coast streams of California. After consideration of the regular monthly bills and the usual orders, the Commission adjourned to meet on the first Tuesday in April at the same place.

A Present of English Trout Eggs for America.

There is a desire on the part of our American cousins to get that fine game and table fish, the European trout, *S. fario*, or brown trout, acclimatised to stock trout streams from which the native brook trout, or *S. fontinalis* (which is a char), has disappeared, or is disappearing. Several consignments of eggs have been sent to America from England

The Rosemeade Sale.

From the published telegraphic reports, the sale of the Rosemeade trotters has been an unqualified success, the prices being particularly good. The following are the prices that each of the animals brought on the first day of the sale

The first animal led out was Alcazar. A bid of $15,000 was promptly made by John E. Madden of Kentucky. From that price bidding was by thousands until the $18,000 mark was reached, then it mounted to $18 100, when there was a lull. Mr. Rose then got up and said Alcazar was the greatest horse he had ever bred. Then the bidding proceeded, with Robert Steele of Philidelphia, E. A. Tipton (Secretary of Lexington track) and Uhlein Bros. (brewers of Milwaukee) as contending bidders. Mr. Steele was first to drop out at $21,500. Then Mr. Tipton quit at $22,500 and John Madden at $25,500. After a few moments of hesitation the Uhlein Brothers and F. Babst bid $25,800, at which price they secured him in partnership amid great applause.

Alcazar, b s, 7 years, by Sultan, dam Minnehaha by Stevens' Bald Chief, $25,800; bought by Uhlein Bros. and Fred Pabst, brewers, of Milwaukee.

Harvester, b s, 8 years, by Sultan, dam Harvest Queen by Rysdyk's Hambletonian, $3,000; bought by Wilson & Handy, of Lexington, Ky.

Thor, b c, 3 years, by Alcazar dam Lady Mackay by Silver Threads, $3,000; bought by C. M. Fogg, of Nashville, Tenn.

Voodoo, b c, 2 years, by Stamboul, dam Eva, 2:23 1-2, by Sultan, $24,200; bought by F. G. Babcock, of Hornellsville, N. Y.

Agnes Clark, b m, 15 years, by Almont, dam Nellie, $875; bought by Wilson & Handy, of Lexington, Ky.

Aimee, b m, 4 years, by Del Sur, dam Durferine, $1,400; bought by C. L. Cushman, of Auburn Me.

Alcyola, b f, 3 years, by Alcyone, dam Lady Bryan, $2,125; bought by Andrew J. Welch, of Hartford, Conn.

Blondet e, b m, 6 years, by Cadet (thoroughbred), dam Blonde $1,000; bought by George H. Bailey, of Portland, Me.

Majola, thoroughbred ch f, 3 years, by Hook Hocking, dam Monica by Grinstead, $400; bought by J. H. Shults of Parkville, N. Y.

Clara Wall, b m, 7 years, by Strathmore, dam Madame Bell by Pacing Abdallah, $1,700; bought by J. R. Means, of Scranton, Pa.

Carrollee, b m, 8 years, by Carr's Mambrino, dam by Elmo, $425; bought by C. S. Freud, of Connecticut.

Choice, b m, 8 years, by Dictator, dam Coral by Clark Chief, $3,000; bought by Wilson & Handy.

Del Fay, b m, 5 years, by Del Sur, dam Lady Fay by Modoc Chief, $1,75; bought by H. W. Burgett, of Brookline, Mass.

Dido, 2:22 1-4, b m, foaled in 1876 by Scott's Hiatoga, dam Columbia (dam of Abbotsford, 2:19 1-2), $1,000; bought by William E. Spier, of Glensfalls, N. Y.

Dimple, b m, 11 years, by Echo, dam Chromo by McCracken's Black Hawk, $300; H. L. Horn of Maine.

Ednah, blk m, 7 years, by Indianapolis, dam Verbena by Messenger Duroc, $1,7 3; bought by Rensselaer Stock Farm of Indiana.

Flora Graves, br m, foaled in 1 87 by Whipple's Hambletonian, dam Rose Mare by Bell Alta, $250; bought by W. Whitson, Long Island.

Flower Girl, ch m, 9 years, by Arthurton, dam Flora by General McClellan, $350; bought by Wilson & Handy.

Georgiana, br m, foaled 1874, dam of La Grange by Overland, dam Maggie Mitchell by Clay Pilot, $650; bought by Wilson & Handy.

Gracie, b m, 10 years, by Arthurton, dam Old Lady by David Hill, Jr., $550; bought by H. F. Pierce, Quebec, Canada.

Grace Andrews, ch m, 4 years, by Le Grande, dam by Arthurton out of Venturess, $900; bought by Robert Steele of Philadelphia.

Grecian Bend, b m, 4 years, by Director 2.17, dam Sweetness by Volunteer, $3,200; bought by A. J. Welch of Hartford, Conn.

Gulnare, b m, 10 years, by The Moor, dam Lulu Jackson by Jack Malone, $2,8.0; bought by J. H. Shults of New York.

Highland Maid, br m, 10 years, by Arthurton, dam Highland Mary by David Hill, Jr., $1,300; bought by F. C. Smith of Providence, R. I.

Helen, blk m, 8 years, by Kentucky Prince, dam Lady Irwin by George Wilkes, $2,100; bought by C. M. Fogg of Nashville.

Inez 2:0, b m, foaled 187 by The Moor, dam Katy Did by Fireman, $1,800; bought by James E. Clay of Paris, Ky.

San Mateo Maid, ch m, foaled 1868, by Whipple's Hambletonian, dam Abdullah mare, s t b, $230; bought by A. J. Welch.

Jennie, b f, 2 years, by Kentucky Prince, dam Saisun 2:31 1-2 at 2 years, by Electioneer, $4,000; Bought by A. J. Welch.

Lady Ferguson, br m, 10 years, by Inca, 2:27, dam Kate Craigue, $1000; bought by Edward Moore of Portland, Me.

Laura Corbitt, b m, 6 years, by Guy Wilkes, 2:15¼, dam Sallie Durbrow, by Arthurton, $8,000; bought by F. C. Smith of Providence.

Lady Mackay, br m, 15 years [dam of Lucy R, 2:30 at 3 years] by Silver Threads, dam Fleetwing by Hambletonian, $5,000; bought by Wilson & Handy.

Lady Graves, ch m, 15 years, by Nutwood, dam Lady Babcock by Whipple's Hambletonian, $2,00; bought by William Marks of Philadelphia.

Loka, ch m, 4 years by Le Grande, dam Sallie Durorow by Arthurton, $45 ; bought by E. A. Hambleton of Emporia, Kans.

Luna, br m, 5 years, by Simmons, dam Moonshine by Daniel Lambert, $4,100; bought by E. A. Hambleton of Emporia, Kans.

Lady Dey, br m, foaled 1878—dam of Mista, 2.39 at 2 years, and Dubec 2:25 at 4 years—by California Dexter dam Lady Mayberry, by Chieftain, $1,40 ; bought by Charles Robertson of New York.

Mista 2:29 at 3 years, by Alcazar, dam Lady Dey by California Dexter, $8200; bought by Fred Pabst of Milwaukee, Wis.

Altogether forty-three head were sold for a total of $138,330, or an average of $3,220.78.

ATHLETICS.

Athletic Sports and Other Pastimes.

EDITED BY ARPSIPPUS,

SUMMARY.

The first out-door games of the Alpine Club on Sunday last were a success. The athletes have commenced to train for the opening games of the Olympic Athletic Club. The Long-Henceman boat race is causing great excitement in rowing circles. Judging from the present out-look, several of the Pacific Coast records which we print below will need to be changed before the year is over.

RUNNERS, WALKERS, JUMPERS, ETS.

A tug of war for Married vs. Single members will be added to the O. C. programme for Decoration Day.

Walter Scott is thinking of donning his spikes again this season. He has been out of practice for a long time, and should not neglect to train before meeting Cooley, McArthur and H. C. Cassidy.

The Alpine runners say that if Captain George W. Jordan makes up his mind to raffle his stop watch they will gladly buy up all the chances.

John D. Garrison surprised the boys with his great show of speed on Sunday. Handicapper Jordan gave a knowing wink each time the Alpine sprinter breasted the tape.

The Olympic Club's Championship team are being mustered up already. The following men have promised to train faithfully: Scott, McArthur, Espinosa, Cooley, Coffin, Jarvis, Henderson, O'Kane, Casady, and McGee, Purcell and Scuifferstein may also help the Club out.

AT THE OARS.

The fine weather on Sunday morninging was highly appreciated by the oarsmen, and a good many crews were out for a practice spin.

The Dolphin Swimming and Boating Club held its high jinks on Sunday. The house was crowded all day long.

One week from to-morrow Charley Long and Henry Henceman will struggle for first place over the Alameda mole course. So far the betting has been light but a couple of days previous to the race there is no doubt but that several thousand dollars will be staked. Both men are in fine trim and the betting is about even.

LAWN TENNIS.

The second prize in the handicap tournament was finally won by the Magee brothers, after a hard battle with Harrison and Yates.

The directors of the California Club will try to get up a ladies championship tournament if enough players can be induced to enter.

There still seems to be a doubt about the championship tournament being held at San Rafael. The majority of the players favor San Rafael and the chances are the tournament be held there.

JOTTING FROM ALL OVER.

The annual handicap decided at Sheffield, Eng., on Feb., 17 and for which several American sprinters were entered was won by James Collins, the western flyer, whose defeat in the previous handicap in which he took part there was so great a surprise to his friends here.

A. G. Mills has resigned as a member of the Board of Governors of the New York Athletic Club, and also as a delegate from that organization to the Amateur Athletic Union.

John Rotherman has been elected president of the Scottish American Athletic Club, of Jersey, vice Henry Reagan, resigned.

The annual boxing tournament of the New York Athletic Club will begin this evening.

The competitions for the Western Amateur Athletic Association championship in boxing and wrestling, took place at St. Louis, Mo., on the night of Feb., 20. There was a large gathering of athletes and others, and the contests were watched with much interests some of the competitions being very exciting. The winners were: Boxing—130lb and under, Steve Mallory, Missouri Gymnasium; 130 to 140lb, Joseph E. Stewart, Missouri Gymnasium; 140 to 150lb, Harry Brown. P. A. C.; 150 to 160lb, John Victor; 160lb and over, John Victor, for Harry Morris. Wrestling—130lb and under Ed. Barth, Missouri Gymnasium; 130 to 130lb, B. A. McFadden, M. A. A. C.; 140 to 150lb, John C. Meyers, M. A. A. C. 150 to 160lb John Schran, Missouri Gymnasium; 160lb and over, George Baptiste, M. A. A. C.

UNIVERSITY JOTTINGS.

At a meeting of the Board of Directors of the Tennis Club, held on Wednesday afternoon, February 26th, the following action was taken in regard to the tournament voted by the club. The date was set for Saturday, March 8th. As there will be from eight to twelve entries, it is an assured fact that the entire afternoon will be consumed at the two courts. There will be some exciting sets, as all the players play about the same sort of game. Several visitors are expected over from San Francisco.

The Occident, the official organ of the University, in the last issue, makes some rather hard assertions regarding the Olympic Club. It stated that at a meeting of the associated students, held on the previous Wednesday, it was decided to withdraw from the P. C. A. A. A. in the event of the championship games being held later than May 30th. It can scarcely be considered the fault of the O. C. if the annual championship meeting is not held on the regular date, May 30th, and the associate clubs should bear in mind that the O. C established its new grounds for its own members, and not solely for the benefit of the P. C. A. A. A. The Olympic Club, if broached in the proper manner, might consider the matter in a favorable light, but we doubt if any good result will come from threatening. The Olympic athletes are not quite as fearful of the students as the Occident would have its readers believe, and if the University boys had the interest of their club at heart as much as the Olympic members have, then the fact that vacation had commenced should not prevent them from training. The kick, under the circumstance, appears to be a very unreasonable one, and the Berkeley champions should not be so uncivil towards their brethren on this side of the bay.

CLUB JOTTINGS.

The Garden City Athletic Club of San José, Cal., an organization founded through the exertions of Mr. Victor E Schifferstein of the Olympic Club of San Francisco, was admitted into the P. C. A. A. A. at the last meeting of that body.

On account of the new rules adopted by the P. C. A. A. A. the Golden Gate Athletic Club will not the represented at the next championship meeting.

There are now eight bona fide Amateur Athletic Clubs in the P. C. A. A. A. and keen competition may be expected in the future.

The new grounds of the Olympic Club will be entirely ready for the members' use in about four weeks. The track is now in condition but the club house and handball court are not quite finished.

The membership of the Alpine Amateur Athletic Club is rapidly increasing and there is a talk of limiting the membership after 250 names have been signed to the roll,

A meeting of the Pacific Coast Amateur Athletic Association was held in the parlor of the Olympic Club on Friday evening Feb. 28, Walter A. Scott occupied the chair.

Secretary J. J. Jamison requests that a temporary secretary be appointed in his place as he desires a chance to defend his club which was to be tried that evening for violating the rules of the association. E P. Moody one of the delegates from the Pacific Athletic Club was appointed secretary *pro tem.* Delegates from the following associate clubs were present; Olympic, Golden Gate, Acme, Alameda Olympic, Alpine, Pacific, Reliance and Pacific. The trial of the Golden Gate Athletic Club was begun. W. P. Lawlor of the O. C. questioned delegate Jamison at length and it was finally decided to lay the case over another week in order to allow the G. G. A. C. a chance to enter or withdraw from the association. Immediately after the adjournment of the regular meeting a special meeting was called for the purpose of taking action on the application of the San Jose, Cal. Garden City Athletic Club. After it was decided that the application was correctly made out the Garden City club was admitted to membership.

The first in-door exhibition of the Alpine Amateur Athletic Club was held at the club rooms, 706 Powell St., on Thursday evening, Feb. 27th. The club had only been in the building a couple of days previous to the exhibition and the committee in charge of the affair deserve credit for their quick work. The gymnasium, which was lit up by powerful electric lights, was packed and even standing room was at a premium. President M. C. Giry officiated as master of ceremonies. It was pleasing to observe that the usual ring was missing Amateurs can exhibit on the floor just as well without as with the ring.

The exhibition began about 8:30, with a parallel bar act by Messrs. Cherry, Barr and Edwards. The trio received unbounded applause for their fine work.

Next came boxing by Messrs. Kramer and Rochette. These young men gave an exceedingly clever exhibition, Rochette appearing to the best advantage. Smith and Cook boxed three rounds and their scientific bouts were loudly encored. Messrs, Barr, Edwards and Henry performed some hard feats on the rings and J R Collins and Otto Lunn sparred three lively rounds.

The champion bantam weight of the club, J McLaughlin, faced Turnbull, another amateur of some note and both men deserved the applause which they received for their quick, clean hitting and scientific ducking.

Mr. Dooly proved that he could swing clubs as well as any professional and he fell in for his share of hand clapping.

Messrs, Kennedy and McSweeney boxed three good rounds and raised themselves in the estimation of the audience. Messrs. Barr, Edwards and Henry exercised their muscle on the horizontal bar in great style and their act was well received. Charles Vultee, Charles Armbruster, E P Young and Hogan competed in a running high jump. Vultee cleared the bar at 5ft 2in, Hogan 5ft and Armbruster at 4ft 10in.

Vultee gave exhibitions of standing high, and hopping high jumps. With proper practice he should make a first rate jumper. The closing event of the evening was a four-round set to between J Sheehan and Ed Morrissey. This promised to be the most interesting item on the programme but unfortunately Sheehan sprained his wrist at the beginning of the third round. The first two rounds were hot; each man proving that he was not afraid of the other. The next in-door exhibition of the club will be given about the first week in April.

There will be a general meeting of the Alpine Club on Thursday evening, March 13th, at 8 o'clock.

THE WHEELMEN

The party of wheelmen who intended trying the roads on Sunday last were prevented on account of the gloomy state of the weather.

There will shortly be a meeting of the bicycle men to consider the ways and means of holding a race meeting on Decoration Day.

The next regular meeting of the Oakland Bicycle Club will be held at 1857 San Jose avenue, Alameda, Cal., on Tuesday evening, March 11, 1890, at 8 o'clock.

Alpine Field Day.

A Fine Programme of Sports at Harbor View.

The games of the Alpine Athletic Club, which, on account of the bad weather, had to be postponed from February 16th, were successfully decided at Harbor View Park on Sunday last. When the sports began at 2 30 P. M. at least 1,200 people, many of whom were ladies, were in the Park. The club members were not prepared for such a big rush, and the consequence was that the track was crowded all the afternoon with men and boys, which made it rather unpleasant for the competitors. There were nineteen events on the programme, and be it said to the club's credit, the last race was over before five o'clock. Out of about thirty five entries not more than twenty stripped, but the majority of the men who competed were in fine trim, and they made an excellent showing. Three prizes were to be awarded for each event, and three special medals were to be presented to the three members making the greatest number of points during the day. The points were to count as follows: Five for first place, three for second, one for third. John D. Garrison won the first special medal. His record was as follows: Five first prizes, one third. Total points 26. C. A. Eldridge won the second special medal, with the following score: Two first prizes, four second prizes, three third prizes. Total points 25 P. N. Gafney won the third special medal, with the following score: Three first prizes, two second prizes. Total points 21. Garrison, Eldridge, Cassidy, Sexsmith, Moody, Luttringer and Gafney showed up in fine condition, and had the track and field been in better condition their records would have been much better. The most notable performances of the day were the running of Garrison in the 440 and 880 yards run, the pole vaulting and standing jump of James Sexsmith, the walking and high jumping of P. N. Gafney, and the running of H. C. Cassidy in the mile race.

The handicapping was excellent, reports to the contary notwithstanding. The only circumstance to mar the pleasure of the day was the appearance of one or two professional athletes who took a great delight in expressing their opinions and in essaying to beat the records made by the amateurs. Such persons should not be allowed on the track. The following is a correct account of the different events with the names of the winners, their handicaps and records:—

100 yards run—final heat, R J Luttringer, 1 yard, 1st C A Eldridge, 2 yards, 2nd James Sexsmith, Scratch 3. Time 11 1-5 seconds.

880 yards run—J D Garrison, 30 yards, 1st E P Moody, 15 yards, 2nd H C Cassidy, 10 yards, 3d. Time 2 min. 9¼ sec.

1 mile walk—P N Gafney, Scratch, 1st C A Eldridge, 20 seconds, 2nd. Time 7 min. 36 seconds.

Pole Vault—J Sexsmith, Scratch, 1st C Myer, 1 foot, 2nd J Sheehan, 9 inches, 3d height 8ft 10½ inches.

Putting 16lb shot—C A Eldridge, 3 feet, 1st F M Howard, 4 feet, 2nd R J Luttringer, 2 feet, 3d. Distance 28 feet 2 inches.

440 yards run—J D Garrison, 5 yards, 1st, H C Cassidy, 10 yards, 2nd. Time 54 seconds.

Standing broad Jump—Charles Vultee, 1 foot, 1st. J Sexsmith, 6 in. 2nd, C Meyer, 1 foot 3d, distance 6 ft. 3 in.

Flinging 56 lb. weight—J Sexsmith, scratch 1st, P N Gafney, 1 foot, 2nd, J R Collins, 1 foot, 3d, distance 15 ft. 1 in.

220 yards run—J D Garrison, 2 yds ; 1st, C A Eldridge, 3 yards 2nd, H C Cassidy 4 yards 3d. Time 24¼ sec.

880 yards Novice Walk—H C Cassidy 1st, C Meyer 2nd. Time 3 min. 47 secs.

Running high Jump—P N Gafney scratch 1st, Charles Tulter, scratch, 2nd, J Sexsmith, scratch, 3d. Height 5 ft. 1½ in.

Throwing 12 lb hammer—C A Eldridge, 35 ft, 1st; P N Gafney, 30 ft, 2d; C Vultee, 35 ft, 3d. Distance, 66 ft 6 in. Gafney, 69 ft 1 in.

120-yards run—J D Garrison, 2 yds, 1st; E P Moody, 4 yds, 2d; C A Eldridge, 2 yds, 3d. Time, 12 3-5 sec.

Running broad jump—J D Garrison, 1½ ft, 1st; H. C. Cassidy, 1½ ft, 2d; C A Eldridge, 1½ ft, 3d. Distance, 16ft 4in.

Half-mile "Alpine" race—P N Gafney, 1st; C A Eldridge, 2d; J D Garrison, 3d. No time taken.

One-mile run—H C Cassidy, scratch, 1st; E P Moody, 50 yds, 2d; C A Eldridge, 75 yds, 3d. Time, 4m 58sec.

Charles Little, who had been placed at scratch in several events, was too ill to make any effort to win a prize. He had been confined to his bed for several days previous to the games. The following officers of the day had charge of the games:

Referee—J P Bean. Starter—H O Farrell. Judges—Dr C A Bonestell, Louis Thors, Sanford Plummer, S V Cassidy, O A C. Clerks of Course—J Muth, T J Quinlan. Timers—G W Jordan, O A C, C V W O'Brien, W. Farrell. Official Announcer, A C Rouard. Call Steward, J J Larkey. Judge of Walking—Horace Coffin, O A C. Marshals—T H McCarthy, W C Gifford. Reception Committee—J Nicholson, P J Sheedy, W C Bean, G H Brown, S Conlan. Athletic Committe—Charles Vultee, P N Gafney, J J Larkey, J J McKinnon, H O'Farrell.

Grim's Gossip.

Killip & Co. are arranging for a monster sale of trotting stock from Rancho Del Paso.

Peter V. Johnston of the Kalamazoo Stock Farm has returned East from his trip throughout the Pacific Coast.

A meeting of the directors of the P. C. T. H. B. A. will be held this (Saturday) afternoon at 1 o'clock at the office of the BREEDER AND SPORTSMAN.

Ned Winslow 2:17¼ is reported to be in fine condition at Sacramento and Mr. McCord has every confidence that Ned will reduce his record this year.

When horses eat their oats too greedily a few stones about the size of hens' eggs mixed with the oats may compel them to go slow in order not to bite the stones.

One of the papers published in the interior of the state, has a long article on horse breeding, in a recent issue and says "Abdallah and Glencoe stand at the head of the list of sires of famous trotters.

I. DeTurk of Santa Rosa has purchased of Wm. McGraw the black stallion "Silas Skinner," sire "Alcona Jr.," dam "Fontana" by "Almont," and will trot him through the circuit this fall. Boys, lookout for "Silas" when the bell rings.

Mr. Judson H. Clark has changed the name of Wellington (the brother to Sunol, recently purchased by him) to Lord Wellington, there being another horse already called Wellington. He has been placed in the stud, the service fee being $300.

Mr. W. P. Fine is naturally well pleased at the large list of entries in his colt stakes, but notes that a mistake was made in the published list, as Mr. Wisecarver's "Antelulu" should have placed under the yearlings, instead of among the three-year-olds.

The first of the get of Edgemark, four year old record 2:16 was foaled last week at Colonel Russell's farm Milton, Mass., and is a colt out of a mare by Smuggler, 2:15¼; 2nd dam Madam Powell (dam of Monroe Chief, 2:18¼), by Bay Chief, son of Mambrino Chief II.

Messrs. Sweeney & Co., of Carson, are going to have a great combination sale of trotters, thoroughbreds, Holstein cattle and jacks during April and as the stock is of the best, buyers should be plenty. We will give a description of some of the horses to be sold in our next issue.

The dam of Bismarck, owned by Mr. Marshall of Denver, Col., was a fine saddle mare, a single footer, and a daughter of the good horse Pat Clayborn of Missouri. Before being taken West she had once been matched against time to pace a mile in 2:40 trot a mile in 2:50 and run a mile in 1:50. She won all three events.

As Mr. Corbett of the San Mateo Stock Farm won the two year old stake last year at San Jose, with Regal Wilkes, be has been given the privilege of naming the three year old colt stake of this year. The gentleman has named it after the colt, so the stake, will, for 1890 be known as the "Regal Wilkes."

During the finish of a recent trotting race at the Bay District track four dogs were loose on the track, and at the gentlemans roadster race at the Oakland Park, a like number, dashed down the turn barking at the heels of the contestants. Track Superintendents should make it an imperative rule that "dogs will not be allowed on the track."

In answer to the question, What suggestions would you make as to the best methods of popularizing trotting races? A. J. Hook of Paris, Ky., writes to a contemporary: "To popularize trotting racing, give large purses, charge five per cent. to enter, five per cent. additional for starters. Conduct races strictly according to rules, and don't forget to use printer's ink."

The grandly bred horse Topic will be offered for sale at the Kellogg combination sale, March 19th. Topic was bred by A. J. Alexander, Woodburn Farm, Ky., and greatly resembles his sire, Belmont. He has trotted a trial in 2:31½, and quarters in 36 seconds, driven by Crit Davis. His speed is still undeveloped. Is a first-class horse to train or put in the stud, and is perfectly sound.

Among the many stallions standing for service in Oakland is one should commend himself to all fanciers of good blood. Ashland Almont is a son of the mighty Almont 33, dam Pauline by Ashland Chief: 2nd dam Rosina by Abdallah 15. He is a particularly good looker, has plenty of speed himself and transmits it to his progeny. The low price at which he is offered should warrant a full book for this finely bred stallion.

I have received a letter from Mr. L. A. Richards of Greyson, in which he informs me that he fully expects to place six or eight of the get of his stallion Elector in the 2:30 list this year. The success of J. R. last season, shows that all of the Electioneers breed on, and Mr. Richards is to be congratulated on the ownership of such a fine young horse.

When Col. R. S. Strader of Lexington, Ky., started East with a lot of California horses some weeks ago, one of the number was Hernani, owned by J. H. White of Lakeville, Sonoma Co., which was consigned to the great Woodard Sale. Hernani was sold on Thursday, Feby. 20th, and brought $3,250, Col. Strader becoming the purchaser.

Mr. W. H. Wilson of Abdallah Park, Cynthiana, Ky., has sold to Schmulbach, Hamilton & Park, Wheeling, W. Va., the two year-old bay filly Bonnie Bon by Director 2:17, dam Bonnie Wilkes 2:29½, dam of Bon Bon, 4 years, record 2:26, by George Wilkes, and to the same parties b f Antea Wilkes, 2 years, by Guy Wilkes 2:15¼, dam by Anteeo 2:16¼, 2nd dam by Alexander, record 2:31½, 3rd dam by Naubuc (brother to Thomas Jefferson), 4th dam Sacramento Maid. No price given, but the quality of the goods tells us it was a long one.

Elector! Election! Election! Elector! For heaven's (and all horsemen's) sake, gentlemen, please to use a little ingenuity and originality in naming your stallion colts! Hambletonian's was not a play upon the name of his sire; nor was Mambrino Chief's upon that of his; Electioneer and George Wilkes, sons of the same sire, and founders of great families, owe none of their success to their names, but to their individual merits. Imagine half a dozen Electors and as many Elections, founding great families! The next generation of pedigree experts would soon find itself fit for an insane asylum.

The Chicago Horseman is responsible for the following: Mrs. Langtry hopes to some day win one or more of the classic events in England with the youngsters raised on her stock farm in Lower California. Several yearlings from her ranch are now enroute East, and will be shipped from New York to England, where they will be trained and raced next year if they prove to be of any account.

We hope Mrs. Langtry may read the above for the entire item will be news for her. It may also surprise the lady to know that her Stock Farm is in Southern California.

On last Saturday a large assemblage of horsemen congregated at the Railroad Stables, corner of Turk and Steiner, to attend the sale of roadsters, saddle horses and trotters advertised to be sold by order of Captain B. E. Harris. Killip & Co. were the auctioneers, but notwithstanding the earnest efforts of Mr. Killip, those present would not pay what the horses were worth, the prices proving a disappointment to the owner. Quite a number that were catalogued did not find purchasers, as it was only cheap horses that were in demand.

Verily California is a great state and she excels in every thing. On Wednesday evening the fifteenth annual commencement of the New York Veterniary college was held at Chickering Hall on Fifth Avenue, there being two hundred and seven graduates to receive their diplomas. During the exercise Edward John Creely of San Francisco, was presented with a gold medal for having passed the best practical examination before a committee appointed by the Faculty from among the local veterinary experts. Mr. Creely will shortly locate in this city and will unquestionably be a valued member of the profession which he has adopted.

The two-year old trotter Sacramento Girl has been kept out of a lot of stakes for trotters of that age in California, she having shown so much speed last fall as a yearling trotting a mile in 2:56 on a slow track, that the owners of other two-year old trotter do not think their colts have any show of beating her. The owner of Sacramento Girl seems to be a very accommodating gentleman, for on learning that that the owners of other young trotters were discouraged at the prospect of starting against his filly, he very courteously informed them that she would not be entered in any of the events to which she was eligible—Breeders' Gazette.

For gracious sake, Dear Old Gazette, where do you manage to pick up such nonsensical items.

Some of the pedigrees found in the interior papers are very unique. The following are a few samples:

"Dictator, the sire of Jay-Eye-See (2:10), Phallas (2:13¾), Maxey Cobb (2:13¼), Director (2:17), Stamboul (2:14) and Electioneer, the great sire of colt trotters."

"The produce of Beautiful Bells, by Electioneer, have three crosses by Guy Wilkes."

"Is a son of Young Prince, the thoroughbred English race horse. And his dam, Nettie, is by Kentucky Hunter, also an imported English thoroughbred, her dam, Flora, was by Chieftain, a thoroughbred."

When at the Oakland track a few days ago I had the pleasure of taking a peep at Mr. Ayres young horses which have been taken up, preparatory to being put through their work. Of the lot I am rather prejudiced in favor of Kodiac a two year old by Mambrino Wilkes, dam Fancy by Bonner. He is a full brother to Gus Wilkes 2:22, and is a perfect beauty. There are many who think the best of the collection is Chaldean, by Mambrino Wilkes, dam Fredolia by Fred Arnold, but while the latter is a good one, still I will pin my faith to the former. Balkan is looking superb, and all traces of his illness has disappeared, giving him a much improved appearance. Mr. Ayres has a good string on hand and the fame of Mambrino Wilkes should ring throughout the State this year.

Last Sunday afternoon a match race took place at the Oakland track between C. Nathan's Encinal, C. Lapham's Tony and W. F. Schultz's Alameda Lily. Mr. Lapham drove his own horse, which is a pacer. C Thornquest handled Alameda Lily, another pacer, and Tallman sat behind Encinal, a trotter. Each of the interested parties selected a judge, and about 2 30 o'clock the fun began. Encinal showed a lack of work, and was really never in the race, the interest centering in Tony and Alameda Lily. The latter won with comparative ease in consecutive heats. Time 2:55, 2:44½ and 2:39½. Encinal was distanced in the second heat and Tony in the third, but the judges decided that Lapham was entitled to his money back, probably because he and his judge "kicked" so. When the flag fell Tony was fully five lengths outside.

A dispatch from Nashville says that the three-year-old stallion Bow Bells, by Electioneer, dam Beautiful Bells, and Moquette, a yearling filly, by Wilton, out of Alma Mater, the property of the Hermitage Stud, arrived in that city on the Southern Pacific stock-car Gasmere, over the Northwestern road, from Palo Alto in good condition. Bow Bells has four other traveling companions besides Moquette, two of which are the property of a Mr. Pearce, of Pennsylvania. The other two will be taken care of by the Hermitage Stud until the winter has completely broken. Bow Bells will make a short season at the stud and will then be trained. He has a two year-old record of 2:32½, but as he comes from the most illustrious trotting family in the world, on both sides, he is expected to make a great showing as a three-year-old.

Last Saturday afternoon was a typical Californian day and the announcement that there would be four races at the Bay District track should have drawn a large concourse of spectators, but notwithstanding the attractions only a very small number were present. The first race had as entries, the trotters Success and Lacoma and the pacer Creighton. The pacer was not troubled much in his efforts to win taking three successive heats very easily in 2:49, 2:45½ and 2:46.

The next event was a match race between James L and Mission Boy. The latter was the favorite in the few pools that were sold, but James L won the first, second and fourth heat handily in 2:33½, 2:36 and 2:38. Mission Boy taking the fourth heat in 2:35.

The runners now took possession of the track and three of them appeared for a half mile dash, they being Asa, Black Pilot and Jou Jou. Asa proved the Victor in 50¾ seconds.

A dash of five lengths of a mile brought out the same trio, and in the pools Black Pilot was a pronounced favorite, selling at $15 to $7 for the field, but in the outcome Jou Jou managed to win by a very short head. Owing to a couple of fouls being made, the Judges ordered the race run over again and admonished Bally, who rode Jou Jou, that if he did not win, a severe penalty would be inflicted. The second attempt was a very hollow affair, Jou Jou winning by twenty or more lengths in the excellent time of 1:03.

Send for a likeness of Axtell. These pictures are a genuine work of art. Good judges do not hesitate to say they are the finest likeness yet seen of the fastest stallion in the world. They are in size 18x25 inches, finished in nine colors, and in the highest style of the lithographer's art. The rich bay color of the horse is set off by the dark background of the box stall, around the walls of which are arranged in proper form and colors the boots, bits, muzzles, brushes, blankets, cloths, etc. usually found in the quarters of "crack trotters." The colored attendant stands near the horse, carelessly holding the blanket which has been removed to show Axtel to an admiring group of ladies and gentlemen present. These pictures will literally knock your eye out. You want one for your house, office or stable. Send at once! They will go fast and you will regret not having secured one when they are all. Sent to any address upon receipt of 15 cents in stamps to pay postage and packing. Send in your name and address at once to Jas B. Campbell & Co., Chicago, Ills., and mention the BREEDER AND SPORTSMAN and get by return mail Axtel's picture in nine colors, 18x25 suitable for framing. Notice: Stamps will be returned and orders refused from parties failing to mention the paper they saw the advertisement in, so don't fail to say BREEDER AND SPORTSMAN.

The following is from an Eastern sporting paper: "It appears that during the 'boom' in real estate throughout Southern California in '85, '86 and '87, a vast number of driving horses of excellent individual merit were shipped to the State from the East, notably from Kentucky. The men who purchased them were coining money hand over fist, and did not begrudge a thousand or twelve hundred dollars for a road horse possessing style, and capable of going a mile in 2:40, or thereabouts. At the present time, these self-same dealers in 'sunshine and climate'—for that was all there ever was to the California boom—find themselves loaded down with property which is valueless except for purposes of taxation, and are compelled to keep close within the shore. Their expenses have been cut to the very quick, and whereas they formerly lived on 'calves liver and bacon' and other toothsome viands, they are now glad to dine on cracker soup backed up with a small piece of sage brush mutton, and in order that they might exist at all, it is necessary to dispense with the quick stepping Kentucky roadster, the speedy native bred son or daughter of any of their famous stallions, and so cheap are these horses in Los Angeles, that you can purchase them at prices commonly paid in the East for street car stock. Then again, no one cares for the ten or twelve-year-old horse when fashionably bred youngsters can be purchased at the same price."

If there is any class of trotting horses needed by the breeders of this State it is fine brood mares.

Breeders will have a rare opportunity of supplying this need at the coming combination sale of Messrs. Killip & Co. which will occur about the 3rd of April next.

Among the offerings will be seven mares by Mambrino Wilkes—sire of four, "in the 30 list" including Gus Wilkes, and the "coming horse" Balkan, 2:29½, as a three year old. Each and every one is a choice individual, of fine size, style, and muscular developement, as will more fully appear in the published catalogue—

We can not refrain from mentioning Clara P., a most beautiful blood-like animal, deep bay with black points, just the right size, 15-2 with extra fine muscles, Standard (registered) and with a record of 2:29½. She is the beau ideal of a brood mare. Istar by the same sire Mambrino Wilkes, is but two years old but gives promise of being "a sure enough trotter." She is the perfection of form, of fine size, and gentle disposition, well broken to harness, and in admirable condition for track work. She is entered in the Occidental Stake and the last payment due has been made. Her dam Narka presents a royal line of breeding, viz., by Nephew 1220, dam Baby by Chieftain 721; second dam Fanny Hays (dam of Gold Note) by Jack Hays, thoroughbred; third dam s. t. b. by Imp Leviathan. Space forbids further allusion to the fine line of horses to be offered by the above named gentlemen. We await with impatience the forth coming of their catalogue, remarking that it is unnecessary to go out of this State to procure animals of the choicest breeding.

Foals of 1890.

George H. Bull of San Jose writes:—

I had for a valentine a brown filly by Mambrino Jr., 1789, and Bessie Baxter (dam of Dick Barry 244) by Primus 255; second dam by Cosmo (thoroughbred son of Shiloh). I will have her registered and named Albani.

EDITOR BREEDER AND SPORTSMAN:—The following are my foals for 1890 to date—

Lottie J., by Wildidle, dam Lizzie Brown, dropped Feb. 9th; a bay filly by Flood; star in forehead.

Monday, filly, by Monday, dam Mary Givens, dropped Feb. 1st. Bay Filly by Wildidle; star in forehead, white on hind feet.

Fedora, by Monday or Shannon, dam Lady Clare by Norfolk, dropped March 1st; a bay colt by Wildidle strip in face, three white feet.

HENRY S. JUDSON.

Santa Clara, March 4th.

Palo Alto Stock Farm, San Mateo Co., Cal.

B c by Electioneer—Dame Winnie by Planet.
B f by Azmoor—Emma Robson by Woodburn.
B f by Wildnut—Claremont by Arthurton.
B c by Nephew—Camma by Norway.
B c by Electioneer—Telie by General Benton.
Ch f by Ansel—American Girl by Toronto Sontag.
B c by Azmoor—Myrtha by Contractor.
Br f by St. Bel—Belle D. by Belmont.
Ch f by Palo Alto—Jennie Benton by General Benton.
B c by Azmoor—Mecca by Mohawk Chief.
B c by Azmoor—Clarabel by Abdallah Star.
B f by Electioneer—Nellie Benton by General Benton.
B c by Electioneer—Manette by Nutwood.

THOROUGHBREDS.

Ch c by Argyle—imp. Amalia by Salvator.
B c by imp. Cheviot—Precious by Lever.
B f by imp. Cyrus—Neva by Shannon.

TROTTERS.

Foaled at Vina Ranch, Tehama Co., Cal:

B f by Nephew—Miss Williamson by Ware's Bismarck.
B f by Alban—Miss Gift by Wildidle.
B c by Wildnut—Nina by Piedmont.
B f by Wildnut—Ivy by Don Victor.
B c by Alban—Lola by Alexander's Norman.
B c by Azmoor—Diana by Don Victor.
B c by Nephew—Mamie C. by imp. Hercules.
Ch c by Piedmont—Frou Frou by Asteroid.

THE WEEKLY

Breeder and Sportsman.

JAMES P. KERR, PROPRIETOR.

The Turf and Sporting Authority of the Pacific Coast.

Office, No. 313 Bush St.

P. O. Box 2300.

TERMS—*One Year, $5; Six Months, $3; Three Months, $1.50.*

STRICTLY IN ADVANCE.

Money should be sent by postal order, draft or by registered letter, addressed to JAMES P. KERR, San Francisco, Cal.

Communications must be accompanied by the writer's name and address, not necessarily for publication, but as a private guarantee of good faith.

NEW YORK OFFICE, Room 14, 181 Broadway.

ALEX. P. WAUGH, - - - Editor.

To Subscribers.

The date printed on the wrapper of your paper indicates the time to which your subscription is paid.

Should the BREEDER AND SPORTSMAN be received by any subscriber who does not want it, write us direct to stop it. A postal card will suffice.

Special Notice to Correspondents.

Letters intended for publication should reach this office not later than Wednesday of each week, to secure a place in the issue of the following Saturday. Such letters to insure immediate attention should be addressed to the BREEDER AND SPORTSMAN, and not to any member of the staff.

San Francisco, Saturday, March 8, 1890.

Dates Claimed.

FRESNO (Spring Meeting)....................March 26th to 29th
SAN JOSE (Blood Horse Meeting)....................April 5th, 7th and 9th
IONE....................Aug 5th to 8th.
LOS ANGELES (6th District)....................Aug. 11th to 16th
NAPA....................Aug. 18th to 23rd
GLENBROOK PARK, 17th District....................August 19th to 23d
SAN JOSE (Fall Meeting)....................Aug. 25th to 30th inclusive
PETALUMA....................Aug. 25th to 30th
OAKLAND (District No. 1)....................Sept. 1st to Sept. 6th
LAKEPORT, 12th District....................September 23d to 27th
CALIFORNIA STATE FAIR....................Sept 8th to 20th
FRESNO (Fall Meeting)....................Sept. 29th to Oct. 4th

Our New York Office.

The Eastern business of the BREEDER AND SPORTSMAN has improved so much of late that it has been found necessary to have an office in New York City. Mr. W. H. Gould, an experienced newspaper man, will be our representative there, and he will be pleased to meet all friends of the BREEDER AND SPORTSMAN at 181 Broadway.

Haggin's Sale Postponed.

A telegram was received Thursday morning at this office announcing that the J. B. Haggin sale of trotting horses announced to take place in New York city on March 10th, had been unavoidably postponed until Thursday and Friday, the 13th and 14th inst. The telegram does not state why the sale has been postponed, but it is probable that the combination sale which was announced to take place prior to that of Haggin's has been unavoidably drawn out, so that it will not be finished as soon as was expected. There are many first-class animals catalogued in the lot that will be disposed of by Mr. Easton for the Rancho del Paso, and we feel assured that the contest to secure possession of many of them will be just as eager and intense as has been displayed at the Rosemeade Sale.

Entries forthe P. C. T. H. B. A.

On another page we give a full list of the entries received for the P. C. T. H. B. A., and while there are some that have not been filled as well as might have been expected, still there is such a very large entry list that the members cannot help but feel a certain amount of self satisfaction at the grand result.

The Stanford Stake, which has been for many years a prominent event in California, received fifty six entries, which goes to show that it is just as popular as ever, for while in the past there may have been a larger number of entries, still the class of horses represented would not compare favorably with those that have just been entered. The other stakes and purses have also been well patronized, and with the additional purses which will shortly be offered by the Directors of the Association, should make a programme that will far surpass any that has ever been given in the past. Quite a number of new members have joined the Association, and there is an increased interest being displayed on all hands. California is now the recognized leading State in the country for the produce of trotting horses, and it is only fit and right that such an organization as is now in existence should receive the hearty support of all breeders of the light harness horses.

The Rosemeade Sale.

It is extremely gratifying to be able to publish this week the first installment of the Rose sale which commenced in New York City on Wednesday last. The prices obtained were of the very best, and it must be a source of great satisfaction to the owner of Rosemeade to feel that the Eastern public have such great confidence in his word, as to pay the large prices which have been given for his choice stock.

Rosemeade has for many years been one of the principal breeding farms of California, and it is to the indefatigable energy and perseverance of Mr. Rose, that much of California's reputation as a great speed producing State is due. By his very fortunate purchase of The Moor, a new trotting family has been established, and to-day the reputation of Stamboul, Alcazar and Sultan, have made this family celebrated from one end of the Union to the other; these three great horses are now scattered, one fortunately remaining in the State, while another has been for several seasons in Kentucky, adding both fame to his own name and financial success to his purchaser; the third has now been sold to go to Milwaukee, where he will undoubtedly prove a profitable venture for his new owner.

In next week's BREEDER AND SPORTSMAN, we will continue the list of the animals sold and the prices paid, as each animal sold is a direct encouragement to the many small breeders who are springing up on every hand. Time had demonstrated that the best pays best in the long run, and those who have elected to breed their mares to California's great stallions, will reap a profitable harvest before many years.

The Race Track Question.

The daily papers of San Francisco have for the past few weeks been trying to stir up a certain amount of excitement in regard to the demolition of the Bay District Track which is simply a question of time; and it has already been announced that the grounds will be cut up and sold for building lots sometime within the near future. The various articles that have been written all seem to point to one proposition, that action should be taken immediately toward procuring the necessary land before the breaking up of the Bay District Track; but there is one thing that has been overlooked in all the articles, and that is the fact that there are only two Associations in the State that feel interest enough to warrant them in talking about such matters, and neither of the organizations have any money wherewith to buy or lease land or even to put up the necessary buildings.

The Trotting Horse Breeders Association is an organization of such recent date that there has been no chance to accumulate a large fund, and the Blood Horse Association have always conducted their business, not as a matter of money making, but of pleasure alone, therefore as a consequence have not the many thousands on hand which will be necessary for the equipment of a new course.

The BREEDER AND SPORTSMAN has had a commissioner search the San Francisco peninsula over to find out where there were any eligible sites for a first class race track, and the gentleman reports that there are six places, all of which can be secured for that purpose and at a very reasonable outlay for the land, and in more than half of the cases the property can be leased at a very small rental; however, that is neither here nor there, when the two associations interested have not the wherewithall to commence operations there is only one feasible way by which a new race track can be secured for this city. If a number of wealthy gentlemen who are at present interested in breeding horses, will associate themselves together and build a track at their own expense, making it a close corporation, a very good interest can be realized on the money invested; in addition to which there are hundreds living in this city and State who would gladly become members of a first-class organization, if founded in the way before mentioned. The Washington Park Club, of Chicago, which is now one of the most influential turf and social organizations in the country, was started in this same manner. There is a proprietary interest among a few gentlemen who organized the institution, and they control the grounds, club houses, etc., while the members pay an initiation fee and annual dues, and are allowed all the privileges of the same during good behavior; it is by these means alone that a race track can be secured for San Francisco, and if they are not carried out very shortly there is every prospect of this western Metropolis being without a race track. Some of the prominent and influential breeders must take this matter in hand if it is deemed necessary to have a course on this peninsula, and when such a question is agitated the BREEDER AND SPORTSMAN will very gladly lay before such gentlemen all the data that we now have as to where eligible lands may be secured.

Appointments to Agricultural District Boards.

A few weeks ago Governor Waterman appointed Mr. I. De Turk of Santa Rosa as a Director of Agricultural District No. 4 (Sonoma and Marin). This was an excellent selection, and met with not only the approval of the acting Directors, but with that of all the people in the County of Sonoma, who take a deserved pride in their District, and who desire to see the lately existing jealousy between its northern and soutoern sections allayed, and its people all working together to support and build up the great district fair annually held at Petaluma.

Now, low and behold, it is discovered that Mr. De Turk is *not* and Mr. Sam I. Allen of Santa Rosa *is* one of the Directors.

Mr. De Turk, it appears, was in the East at the time his credentials were issued; either he knew nothing of it, or, even if he did, was, owing to his absence, unable to qualify within the time prescribed by law.

Without, so far as we learn, any enquiries being made as to Mr. De Turk's negligence or the cause of delay, and without consulting the people most interested in the efficiency and harmony of the District Board, a substitute was appointed and Mr. Allen now fills the vacancy.

Mr. Allen may, and it is hoped will, prove the next best man to Mr. De Turk for the place; but it would be interesting to know the why and wherefore of his selection.

His prominence in Republican political circles, his influence with "the boys," and his indefatigable working abilities and propensities are generally recognized, acknowledged, and, let us hope, appreciated—but what have politics to do with Agricultural Boards?

We are unable to say with what degree of justice, but

certain it is that when Mr. Allen was in the Legislature the people of the southern half of the County credited him with using his political influence to defeat the Agricultural District appropriations for the purpose of injuring the *District* Fair held at Petaluma, and placing on a fairer footing of competition the *County* Fair then being held at Santa Rosa. The people of the southern half still entertain suspicions of distrust against Mr. Allen's disinterestedness, and point to the fact that only last week and immediately almost after his appointment as a Director of the *District* Board, he made a motion at a meeting of the defunct Sonoma County Agricultural Park Association to the effect that the further consideration of selling that Association's property (located in Santa Rosa) be postponed until March 1st, to give the people an opportunity *to form an agricultural organisation.*

It must be admitted that this does not look very encouraging as regards the efficiency and co-operation of the new director in the *District* Board; his willingness and desire to rehabitate a rival institution certainly will not tend towards "harmonious" action in that Board.

These, however, so far as we are concerned, are little side issues, which we only desire to use to "point a moral." It is neither wrong nor unfair to Mr. Allen to commend these data and items to the attention of our worthy governor, in order that their oversight should not in the future jeopardise the usefulness of our Agricultural Boards—as it certainly will do if a man's qualifications thereto be gauged solely by his political prominence or influence. The agriculturists of the State cannot afford to have the ends and purposes of these institutions sacrificed to attain for the "powers that be" the political support of their appointee, the forthcoming conventions.

As hereinbefore intimated, there is no intention on our part to reflect in the slightest degree upon the character, ability or intentions of Mr. Allen. But the manner of his appointment, apparently neither solicited nor recommended, gives it the appearance of a "still hunt" after political support on the part of the administration.

The last three or four Governors have been guided more or less by the desires and advice of those members of the respective boards who were known to have the interests of the associations at heart, but Governor Waterman has, we trust, unwittingly established a precedent which, if persisted in, will certainly bring ruination to the Agricultural Societies—as the Sonoma County people say, he has thrown the first "political" firebrand into their lapful of agricultura products.

True, they may be mistaken; it may only prove a "tempest in a teapot," but the agricultural teapot, Governor, is very slim; it is sadly in need of "protection!" The annual fair is the agriculturist's best, and often his only advertisement; fair week is his one and only holiday. We trust its management is not to be relegated to politicians merely because they are politicians.

Answers to Correspondents.

Salinas.

1. Please give breeding of the sire of the second dam of Harry Agnew's pacer, Boswell Jr. 2. Was Belmont Boy's dam by a son of the same sire as Boswell Jr.'s second dam?

Answer.—Hamilton Chief, by Royal Chief Jr., dam full sister to the dam of Toronto Chief 85. Belmont Boy's dam was by Tom Vernon, a son of Hamilton Chief.

Reader.

The following letter has been received from H. D. Albright of San Luis Obispo.

In answer to "Reader" in your paper of Feb. 22nd, will say that "Magic" owned by C. W. Weeks now of this place is by Elmo dam by Whipples Hambletonian, 2nd dam by Algerine by Capt. Fisher etc.

Can any of our readers furnish the full pedigree of Warner's Hamlet.

T. Quinn.

Will you kindly give through the BREEDER AND SPORTSMAN the pedigree and record of Silkwood owned by Mr. Willetts Santa Ana, California.

Answer.—Silkwood (pacer) by Blackwood Mambrino, dam Lucy Woodruff by Hiram Woodruff. Record 2:25½.

Petaluma.

(1) Did Mr. Toddhunters horse Jim Lick ever trot a race? (2) Has he any record? (3) Do you know how fast he could trot?

Answer.—We have no record of his having ever trotted in a race. Do not know how fast he could trot.

U. H., San Diego.

Please give breeding of Queen; dam of Hector, he sired by Elector 2170, owned by R. Morrow. Also, is she a pacer or a trotter. Queen was said to be by Smuggler, and he by Gen. McClellan. Queen was said to be raised by M. V. Higgins of Sonoma County.

State Capitol.

Can you give me the breeding of Bois d'Arc, Rifleman and Jumbo?

Answer.—Bois d'Arc was by Norfolk, dam Liberty by Rifleman. Rifleman, by imp. Glencoe, dam Rodolph mare by Rodolph, etc. Jumbo by California, dam Big Gun (Kate George) by Old George (Big Gun was the dam of Jim Renwick).

Can any of our readers give the pedigree desired. (There is a mistake in the question as to Elector 2170. He was not owned by Mr. Morrow, but by Mr. Richards of Greyson, Stanislaus County. The Morrow Elector, 2:21½, is another horse.—ED.)

P. C. T. H. B. A. Entries.

THE STANFORD STAKES FOR 1892.

FOALS OF 1889—OPEN TO THE WORLD.

Mile heats, 3 in 5. Entrance $100, with $100 added for each starter over two and up to five head, and $25 for each additional starter up to ten head. Payments: $10 on March 1, 1890; $10 on January 2, 1891; $10 on January 2, 1892; $20 on May 1, 1892, and $50 on the fifth day preceding the first advertised day of the meeting at which the stakes shall be trotted.

Chino Ranch's b c Ira Woolsey by Woolsey, dam Lady Inca by Inca; b f Susie Crocker by Will Crocker, dam Eliza Craft by Kelly's Ethan Allen.

E. McLees' b f Lady Thorne by Thornhill, dam Lady Woodnut by Nutwood.

Jno. A. Goldsmith's blk c Milroy by Guy Wilkes, dam Manon by Nutwood.

San Mateo Stock Farm's b f Rubina Wilkes by Guy Wilkes, dam Ruby by Sultan; b c Legal Wilkes by Guy Wilkes, dam Margaret by Sultan; blk f Mabel Wilkes by Guy Wilkes, dam Sable by The Moor; b c Rey Wilkes by Guy Wilkes, dam Rosedale by Sultan; b c Vetce by Sable Wilkes, dam Vixen by Nutwood; blk c Macleay by Sable Wilkes, dam Mamie Comet by Nutwood; br f Thora by Sable Wilkes, dam Theo by Le Grande; b f Princess by Sable Wilkes, dam Minnie Princess by Nutwood.

Wilfred Page's b f Mortrica by Mortimer 5346, dam Reka Patchen by Alexander 490; b c Lorilad by Admont 5349, dam Lorilee by Glasgow 3348.

Souther Farm's ch c Puss in Boots by Figaro, dam Puss by Kentucky Hunter; b c Rooney by Figaro, dam Strawberry by Newland's Hambletonian; b f Fleeting by Figaro, dam by Fleetwood; b f San Leandro by Figaro, dam by Erwin Davis; b c Hawser by Jester D., dam Hawes mare; ch c Souther Farm by Jester D., dam Kitty Collier by Collier (Johnson's).

Gilbert Tompkin's br f Unnamed by Lancelot, dam by Whipple's Hambletonian.

Harris & Harris' blk c Acorn by Sevenoaks, dam Elmorene by Elmo; b c Sirocco by Tempest, dam Daisy by Gen. Taylor; b f Sidena by Sidney, dam Lena Bowles by Vick's Ethan Allen Jr.; br f Belle Abbot by Stanford, dam Rose Abbot by Abbotsford; b f Gleam by Dawn, dam Sweetwood by Nutwood.

Wilber Field Smith's b c Algiers by Alcazar, dam Yerba Santa by Santa Claus; blk f Remora by Guy Wilkes, dam Belle Blanche by The Moor.

Palo Alto Stock Farm's b f Bellflower by Electioneer, dam Beautiful Bells; b f Luta by Electioneer, dam Lula Wilkes by Geo. Wilkes; b f Helena by Electioneer, dam Lady Ellen by Carr's Mambrino; br f Starlight by Electioneer, dam Sallie Benton by Gen. Benton; b f Tiny by Electioneer, dam Telie by Gen. Benton; ch f Captive by Piedmont, dam Clariurso by Electioneer; b f Jet by Piedmont, dam Bess by Gen. Benton; b f Silvia by Piedmont, dam Ash by Electioneer; br f Elden by Nephew, dam Eleanor by Electioneer; b f Wildbud by Nephew, dam Wildflower by Electioneer; b f Laurel by Nephew, dam Laura C. by Electioneer; br f Leola by Nephew, dam Lilly by Electioneer.

L. H. Titus' blk f Clara N. by Director, dam Belle Echo by Echo.

J. J. Hallinan's b f (not named) by Director, dam Grindelia by Gen. Benton.

Jno. F. English's br f Rosetta by Tempest, dam Kitty Dubois.

Thos. Smith's br c Columbus by McDonald Chief 3583, dam Fanny Rose by Ethan Allen Jr. 2903.

A. McFayden's b f Alein by Anteeo, dam Lou Milton by Milton Medium.

Lafayette Funk's b f Helen Wood by Wedgewood 692, dam by Geo. Wilkes 519; b f Lola D. by Elector 2170, dam Lady McLoughlin by Duke McClellan 9080.

I. M. Proctor's rn f Vesper Bells by Dawn, dam Gypsy by Nameless.

Robert S. Brown's br f Rayannetta by Antcee, dam Debonair by Sultan; b c Sparrow Wilkes by Guy Wilkes, dam Birdie by Plimere.

Napa Stock Farm's b m Wood Nymph by Woodnut, dam Belle Irvington by Irvington.

A. T. Hatch's blk f Night by Guide, dam Mollie by Admar.

H. W. Crabb's br f Directess by Director, dam Wisp by Whippleton.

H. I. Thornton's blk c Clarion by James Madison, dam Lena by Berlin; blk c Reflector by Director, dam Oriole by Monroe Chief.

San Miguel Stock Farm's b h Sargon by Mambrino Wilkes, dam Contra by Electioneer.

YEARLINGS—FOALS OF 1889.

One mile dash, $50 entrance, payable $5 March 1, 1890, $10 July 1, 1890, and $25 on the fifth day preceding the first advertised day of the meeting.

La Siesta Ranch's b f Luck of Eros by Eros, dam Nettie Vanderlyn by Nutwood; b f Donzella by Eros, dam by Crisman's Hambletonian.

Wilfred Page's b f Mortrica by Mortimer 5346, dam Reka Patchen by Alexander 490.

San Mateo Stock Farm's br f Thora by Sable Wilkes, dam Theo by Le Grande; b f Princess by Sable Wilkes, dam Minnie Princess by Nutwood; b c Votce by Sable Wilkes, dam Vixen by Nutwood; blk c Macleay by Sable Wilkes, dam Minnie Comet by Nutwood.

Souther Farm's b f Fleeting by Figaro, dam by Fleetwood; b c Hawser by Jester D, dam Hawes Mare; gr f Myra by Jester D, dam Mary; br c Pinkerton by Figaro, dam Pinkie by Reliance.

Ben E. Harris' blk c Acorn by Sevenoaks, dam Elmorene by Elmo; b c Sirocco by Tempest, dam Daisy by Gen. Taylor; b f Sidena by Sidney, dam Lena Bowles by Vick's Ethan Allen Jr.

Wilber Field Smith's b c Algiers by Alcazar, dam Yerba Santa by Santa Claus.

H. S. Hogoboom's br f Remember Me by Waldstein, dam Gertrude by The Moor; br f Why Not by Waldstein, dam by Tommy Benton.

Jno. F. English's br f Rosetta by Tempest, dam Kitty Dubois.

Thos. Smith's br c Columbus by McDonald Chief 3583, dam Fannie Rose by Vick's Ethan Allen Jr. 2903.

Lafayette Funk's b f Lola D by Elector 2170, dam Lady McLoughlin by Duke McClellan 9080; br f. Helen Wood by Wedgewood 692, dam by Geo. Wilkes 519.

A. T. Hatch's blk f Night by Guide, dam Mollie by Admar; ch f Light by Sidney, dam Ida by Irvington.

H. I. Thornton's blk c Clarion by Jas. Madison, dam Lena by Berlin; blk c Reflector by Director, dam Oriole by Monroe Chief.

STAKE—TWO YEAR OLDS—FOALS OF 1888.

One mile and repeat. $75 entrance, $25 added, payable $10 on March 1st, 1890, $10 May 1, 1890, $15 July 1st, 1890, and $40 on the fifth day preceding the first advertised day of the meeting.

Souther Farm's b c El Benton by Electioneer, dam Nellie Benton by Gen. Benton; blk c Jim Linfoot by Figaro, dam Fannie Linfoot by Erwin Davis; b f Florence L by Figaro, dam Fan Collier; b g Meyer by Figaro, dam by Erwin Davis.

A. L. Whitney's b f Duchess by Sidney, dam Young Countess by Sam Patchen.

San Mateo Stock Farm's ch m Vida Wilkes by Guy Wilkes, dam Vixen by Nutwood; b m Tasso Wilkes by Guy Wilkes, Tabbie Rosenbaum by Nutwood; blk c Cognac by Guy Wilkes, dam Lottie by Belmont 64; b c Siris Wilkes by Guy Wilkes, dam Laura Drew by Arthurton.

Joseph Cairn Simpson's blk f Volo by Sanel, dam Avolo by Alhambra.

Ben E. Harris' ch f Starlight by Dawn, dam Lena Bowles by Vick's Ethan Allen Jr.

Palo Alto Stock Farm's br c Almoneer by Alban, dam America by Rysdyk's Hambletonian; b f Eleneer by Electioneer, dam Lady Ellen by Carr's Mambrino; br f Linnet by Electioneer, dam Lizzie Whips by Enquirer; b f Wild Bee by Piedmont, dam Wildflower by Electioneer.

H. S. Hogoboom's b f Sacramento Girl by Alcazar, dam Viola by Flax Tail.

H. I. Thornton's b c Chandelier by Jas. Madison, dam Betsy Trotwood by Abbotsford; b f Emma Nevada by Jas. Madison, dam Kate Dudley by St. Joe.

H. W. Crabb's s f Woodlane by Woodnut, dam Maud by Whippleton.

San Miguel Stock Farm's b h Kodiac by Mambrino Wilkes, dam Fancy by Bonner; b f Mylitta by Mambrino Wilkes, dam Mollie Fern by Capt. Kohl.

STAKE—THREE YEAR OLDS; FOALS OF 1887.

Mile heats, best three in five; entrance $100, with $300 added, payable $10 on March 1st, 1890, $10 on May 1st, 1890, $30 on July 1st, 1890, and $50 on the fifth day preceding the first advertised day of the meeting.

San Mateo Stock Farm's b c Regal Wilkes by Guy Wilkes, dam Margaret by Sultan.

Palo Alto Stock Farm's b f Wildmont by Piedmont, dam Wildflower by Electioneer; b c Pedlar by Electioneer, dam Penelope by Mohawk Chief; b c Hugo by Electioneer, dam Helpmate by Planet; br f Alzira by Ansel, dam American Girl by Toronto Sontag.

STAKE—FOUR YEAR OLDS, FOALS OF 1886.

Mile heats, best three in five; entrance $100, with $400 added, payable $10 on March 1st, 1890, $10 on May 1st, 1890, and, $30 on July 1st, 1890, and $50 on the fifth day preceding the first advertised day of the meeting.

San Mateo Stock Farm's br m Lillian Wilkes by Guy Wilkes, dam Flora Langford by Langford.

Souther Farm's b c Glen Fortune by Electioneer, dam Glenne by Messenger Duroc.

Palo Alto Stock Farm's gr f Colma by Electioneer, dam Sontag Mohawk by Mohawk Chief; blk f Ladywell by Electioneer, dam Lady Lowell by Shultz's St. Clair; b f Ariana by Ansel, dam Rebecca by Gen. Benton.

Pleasanton's Stock Farm Co.'s b m Margaret S by Director, dam May Day by Ballard's Cassius M. Clay; blk f Katie S by Director, dam Alpha Medium by Happy Medium.

THREE-YEAR-OLDS.—FOALS OF 1887.

Purse $500. Eligible to three-minute class. Mile heats, three in five. Entrance 10 per cent.; payable 2 per cent., March 1, 1890, 2 per cent. May 1, 1890, 2 per cent. July 1, 1890 and 4 per cent. on the fifth day preceding the first advertised day of the meeting.

Wilfred Page's b f Leoline by Clovis 4909, dam Leah by Woodford Mambrino 345.

Jos. Cairn Simpson's b c Antecello by Antevolo, dam Ruby by Winthrop.

San Mateo Stock Farm's b m Millie Wilkes by Guy Wilkes, dam Rosetta by The Moor.

B. C. Holly's b s Katir by Alcazar, dam Flower Girl by Arthurton.

Lafayette Funk's b f Lizzie F by Elector 2170, dam Lady McLoughlin by Duke McClellan 9080.

Wm. Murray's b s Mark E. by Elector 2170, dam Bell Robbins by Tarrascon.

FOUR-YEAR-OLDS. FOALS of 1886.

Purse $500. Eligible to 2:40 class. Mile heats, three in five. Entrance 10 per cent; payable 2 per cent. March 1, 1890, 2 per cent. May 1, 1890, 2 per cent. July 1, 1890 and 4 per cent. on the fifth day preceding the first advertised day of meeting.

Souther Farm's b c Glen Fortune by Electioneer, dam Glenne by Messenger Duroc.

San Mateo Stock Farm's b m Una Wilkes by Guy Wilkes, dam Blanche by Arthurton.

Geo. E. Guerne's b s G. & M. by Anteeo, dam Rosa B. by Speculation.

Geo. Hearst's ch c Clearmont by McGinnis, dam Creole by Scamperdown.

Theo. Lamoureaux's blk c Detect by Director, dam Kate Guenette by Billy Roberts.

TWO-YEAR-OLDS—FOALS OF 1888.

Open to the get of stallions with no representatives in the 2:30 list.

Purse, $500. Mile and repeat. Entrance 10 per cent; payable 2 per cent. March 1, 1890, 2 per cent. May 1, 1890 2 per cent. July 1, 1890, and 4 per cent. on the fifth day preceding the first advertised day of Meeting.

A. L. Whitney's s f Anna Belle by Dawn, dam Pacheco by Hubbard.

Joseph Cairn Simpson's b f Volita by Antevolo, dam Ruby by Winthrop.

Souther Farm's blk c Jim Linfoot by Figaro, dam Fannie Linfoot by Erwin Davis; gr c The Barber by Figaro, dam Roberta by Vernon Patchen; b g Kit Carson by Figaro, dam Kitty Collier by Collier (Johnson's); b g Meyer by Figaro, dam by Erwin Davis; b f Florence L by Figaro, dam Fan Collier; br f Freda by Fred Arnold, dam Bernarda.

Ben E. Harris' ch f Starlight by Dawn, dam Lena Bowles by Vick's Ethan Allen, Jr.

Palo Alto Stock Farm's b g Guide by Electricity, dam Gipsy by Paul's Abdallah; blk c Norman by Electricity, dam Norma by Alexander's Norman.

Chino Ranch's ch f Ellen by Albion, dam Easter by Billy Norfolk; b f Alcove by Albion, dam Nettie Norfolk by Billy Norfolk.

B. C. Holly's ch s Woodside by Woodnut, dam Veronica by Algona.

M. Kemper's b f Analisto by Antevolo, dam Allis by Admiral.

W. T. Bartlett's ch f Edrie by Coligny, dam Mollie by Eugene Casserly.

Robert S. Brown's s f Nellie K by Dawn, dam Nellie by Brown's McClellan.

Frank Drake's ch c not named by Woodnut, dam Topsy by Admiral.

H. I. Thornton's br c Chandelier by James Madison, dam Betsy Trotwood by Abbotsford; b f Emma Nevada by James Madison, dam Kate Dudley by St. Joe.

Chas. Greene's b f Ione by Junio, dam Queen by Sultan.

J. A. McCloud's b f Daisy Vernon by Mount Vernon, dam by McClellan.

A. T. Hatch's f Admira by Admiro, dam by Steinway.

David Young's b c Pilot Prince by Dexter Prince, dam Emma by Nutwood.

THREE-YEAR-OLDS—FOALS OF 1887.

Open to the get of stallions with no representatives in the 2:30 list.

Purse $500. Mile heats, three in five. Entrance 10 per cent; payable 2 per cent. March 1, 1890, 2 per cent. May 1, 1890, 2 per cent. July 1, 1890, and 4 per cent. on the fifth day preceding the first advertised day of the meeting.

Joseph Cairn Simpson's b f "A" by Antevolo, dam Lady del Sur by Del Sur.

Palo Alto Stock Farm's ch c Norris by Ansel, dam Norma by Alexander's Norman; br f Alzira by Ansel, dam American Girl by Toronto Sontag.

L. M. Morse's b f Maggie C by Dexter Prince, dam by Peerless.

Chino Ranch's b f Alice by Albion, dam Lady Inca by Inca; ch g Alice by Albion, dam Nettie Norfolk by Billy Norfolk.

W. T. Bartlett's b c Frank B by Coligny, dam Molly by Eugene Casserly.

U. S. Gregory's b f Lynette by Lynnwood, dam Lady Belle by Kentucky Hunter.

L. M. Morse's b f Ada by Dexter Prince, dam Ida by Abbottsford.

Lafayette Funk's b s Lottery Ticket by Dexter Prince, dam Emma by Nutwood.

A. Weske's s c Dictator by Prince Imperial, dam Flora Temple by Tecumseh.

G. W. Stimpson's b s Electro by Antevolo, dam by Capt. Webster.

FOUR-YEAR-OLDS.—FOALS OF 1886.

Open to the get of stallions with no representatives in the 2:30 list.

Purse $500. Mile heats, three in five. Entrance 10 per cent., payable 2 per cent. March 1, 1890, 2 per cent. May 1, 1890, 2 per cent. July 1, 1890, and 4 per cent. on the fifth day preceding the first advertised day of the meeting.

Jos. Cairn Simpson's br c Anthedon by Antevolo, dam Ruby by Winthrop.

Palo Alto Stock Farm's b f Ariana by Ansel, dam Rebecca by Gen. Benton; b g Navidad by Whips, dam Lady Thorne Jr. by William's Mambrino.

George Hearst's ch c Clearmont by McGinnis, dam Creole by Scamperdown.

L. M. Morse's blk f Chloe by Dexter Prince, dam by Hawthorne.

N. H. Ball's b g Lightfoot by Bob Mason dam Belinda by Inca.

STALLION PURSE, $1,000.

Open to stallions eligible to the 2:30 class.

Mile heats, three in five. Entrance 10 per cent.; payable 2 per cent. March 1, 1890, 2 per cent. May 1, 1890, 2 per cent. July 1, 1890, and 4 per cent. on the fifth day preceding the first advertised day of the meeting.

Wilfred Page's b h Eclectic 11321 by Electioneer 125, dam Manette by Nutwood 600.

Souther Farm's b s Glen Fortune by Electioneer, dam Glenne by Messenger Duroc; b s Figaro by Whipple's Hambletonian, dam Emblem by Tattler; ch s Jester D. by Almont, dam Hortense by Messenger Duroc.

Palo Alto Stock Farm's b c Amigo by Electioneer, dam Nadine by Wildidle; br s Electricity by Electioneer, dam Midnight by Pilot, Jr.

Pleasanton Stock Farm Co.'s b s Corrector by Director, dam Brainy by Echo.

H. S. Hogoboom's br h Waldstein by Director, dam Nellie W by Electioneer.

Thos. Smith's b s George Washington by Mambrino Chief Jr., dam Fannie Rose by Vick's Ethan Allen Jr. 2903.

Rose Dale Breeding Farm's b s Daly 5341 by Gen. Benton, 1755, dam Dolly by Electioneer 125.

Crabb & Loeber's b s Grandissimo by Le Grande, dam Norma by Arthurton.

Isaac De Turk's blk s Silas Skinner by Alcona Jr., dam Fontana by Almont.

San Miguel Stock Farm's br h Balkan by Mambrino Wilkes, dam Fanny Fern by Jack Hawkins.

A Match Race.

For some weeks past there has been a spirit of rivalry existing between the respective friends of T. W. Barstow owner of Cyrus R. and R. H. Walton owner of Argent 2:24½. On March 1st the two gentlemen met, and the following agreement was signed.

SAN JOSE, March 1st, 1890.

We the undersigned agree to trot our respective horses, viz., Cyrus R and Argent a match race, for the sum of five hundred dollars ($500) a side, said race to take place over the track of the Santa Clara Valley Agricultural Society; at San Jose Cal., on the 31st day of July 1890, the race to be mile heats three in five to harness, and under the rules of the American or National Trotting Association, that the said Society may adopt. A deposit of five hundred dollars ($500) each must be made with the BREEDER AND SPORTSMAN of San Francisco, Cal on or before March 5th 1890.

Mr. T. W. Barstow reserves the right to make the said stake five hundred dollars ($500) or one thousand dollars ($1000) more, on or before the 30th day of July 1890.

If the said day (July 31st) is unfavorable, the race may be postponed to the first fair day thereafter.

[Signed] T. W. BARSTOW, owner of Cyrus R.;
R. H. WALTON, owner of Argent.

[Witness] G. H. BRAGG.

(We have received five hundred dollars from each of the gentlemen which we will hold subject to the decision of the judges of the race.—Ed.

CORRESPONDENCE.

EDITOR BREEDER AND SPORTSMAN:—Your correspondent "Jerd" under the head of Yolo County correspondence, undertakes to give the readers of the BREEDER AND SPORTSMAN some idea of the fast horses of Yolo county, but makes the mistake of touching the horse element very lightly to give some gilt-edged taffy to a very few among our many owners of highly bred stock.

My complaint against him comes in when, after naming Yolo, Tom Rider, Belle Button and J. H., all by Alex Button, as among our prominent young flyers, he makes a fling at my training, by telling "what J. H. might have done if handled differently."

Now when I took J. H. he was a very badly spoiled colt, and utterly unfit to appear on a race track. After a few almost hopeless attempts I found that the colt was really amenable to discipline and I literally broke him anew, and he showed me such fast quarters, halves, and such good miles, that it was agreed among all interested that he should be put into the race at Napa, against Belle Button, Tom Rider and Cora C., without expectation of victory, but as a lesson in company.

That race gave Belle Button and Tom Rider their records, and J. H. would also have obtained a better record than his separately timed 2:22½, but for a combination.

I claim that I brought him to the post and handled him in a first class manner, considering his antecedent bad education, and that he will continue to improve until fit to stay in the best of company. I think that in his admiration for certain horse owners of this vicinity, "Jerd" has overlooked the fact that there are some other valuable strains in this section with produce which will be heard from in good time.

I wonder if he has ever heard of such horses as Langford, Owen Dale, St. Charles, Odd Fellow, Norfolk, Jim Douglas, all runners and sires of numerous descendants now mingling with such horses as Killarney (2:20½), Alex Button (2:26½) and others too many for mention now.

I may some day tell you about the difference between tin cup trophies and real victories, but for the present I shall be content to expect that the BREEDER AND SPORTSMAN will have occasion during the coming racing season to chronicle the doings of a few more Yolo horses and their enterprising owners. Our wealthy ranchers are beginning to realize that it pays to have colts of good stock developed.

THOMAS B. WHITE.

Breeders' Directory.

Advertisements under this heading 50c. per line per month.

HORSES AND CATTLE.

S. JACOBS, Sacramento, Cal.—Breeder of Thoroughbred Shorthorns and Berkshire Hogs.

H. WHITE, Lakeville, Sonoma County—Breeder of Registered Holstein Cattle.

EL ROBLAS RANCHO—Los Alamos, Cal., Francis T. Underhill, proprietor, importer and breeder of thoroughbred Hereford Cattle. Information by mail. C. F. Swan, manager.

PAGE BROTHERS.—Penn's Grove, Sonoma Co. Cal. Breeders of Short-Horn Cattle; Draft, Roadster and Standard Bred Horses.

SETH COOK, breeder of Cleveland Bay Horses, Devon, Durham, Polled Aberdeen-Angus and Galloway Cattle. Young stock of above breeds on hand for sale. Warranted to be pure bred, recorded and average breeders. Address, Geo. A. Wiley, Cook Farm, Danville, Contra Costa Co., Cal.

MAMBRINO WILKES COLTS and FILLIES, full brothers and sisters to Gus. Wilkes 2:22, and Balkan 2:29¾, for Sale. Address SMITH HILL, Walnut Creek, Contra Costa County, Cal.

J. F. RUSH, Suisun, Cal., Shorthorns, Thoroughbred and Grades. Young Bulls and Calves for Sale.

PETER SAXE & SON, Lick House, San Francisco, Cal.—Importers and Breeders for past 18 years of every variety of Cattle, Horses, Sheep and Hogs.

HOLSTEIN THOROUGHBREDS of all the noted strains. Registered Berkshire Swine. Catalogues. F. H. BURKE, 401 Montgomery St., S. F.

HENRY C. JUDSON, Wild Idle Farm.—Breeder of Thoroughbred Horses. The home of "Wildidle." P. O. Santa Clara; Box 223.

FERGUSON & AUSTIN,

FRESNO, CAL.

Registered Polled Angus and Short-Horn Cattle.

Attention! Sportsmen!!

An exploring party will leave San Francisco about April 10th for the Alaska Coast, St. Matthews Island and Yukon River, stopping at numerous places on the way where Seal, Walrus, Sea Lions, Brown Bear, White Polar Bear and Deer are plentiful; also splendid fishing for Salmon, Halibut, Trout and Cod, offering the hunter and fisherman a trip of five months' unparalleled for sport. A novel feature of this offer is that each one taking the trip becomes a stockholder in the Company.

For further information apply to

NORTHERN DEVELOPMENT CO.

No. 5 Market St., Room 5.

Oysters.

M. B. MORAGHAN

The only importer, planter and wholesale dealer in CALIFORNIA MARKET, Stalls 68, 69 to 71 and 77. All the choicest brands of Fresh Oysters constantly on hand. Prompt attention paid to hotel and country orders. Price List.

Large Eastern Oysters .... $2 00 per 100
Transplanted Eastern Oysters .... 1 50 per 100
California Oysters .... 2 00 " sack
Fresh Frozen Eastern Oysters at $7 50 per doz. cans.

John D. Gall. Jas. P. Dunne

"The Resort,"

No. 1 Stockton Street, cor. Ellis,

San Francisco.

The Hambletonian Stallion 10178.

Whipple's Hambletonian, Sire of 14 trotters and 1 pacer from 2:19 to 2:30, and 7 sons with 8 performers from 2:23¼ to 2:30, and dams of 6 from 2:19¼ to 2:30.
- Guy Miller, By Hambletonian 10.
- Martha Washington, Dam of Speculation 928, Sire of Crown Pt. 2:24, Oakland Maid, 2:22, Gracie S., 2:28½, and dam of Waterford, 2:27

Flora, 2:30½, trial, 2:26, Dam of Chrisman's Hambletonian, sire of Steve Whipple, 2:23, Kate Agnew, 2:28½.
- Chieftain 721, sire of Defiance, 2:24 and 2:17¾, pacing; Cairo, 2:26, and Onward, 2.24, pacer.
- daughter of Wilson's Leamon.

The season now on till the 1st of August, 1890, at $40 the mare, with return privilege in 1891, provided stallion and mare, or either, do not change owners. Good pasture at hand, and comfortable accommodation for mares and colts. For further particulars, address

JESSE CHRISMAN, Proprietor.
San Jose, Cal.

Well bred Stallions

FOR SALE.

SATINWOOD

Is 3 years old, stands 16.1 hands high and weighs 1150 lbs; is a beautiful dark chestnut; was sired by Nutwood, a full brother to Eva W (2:25) and Redwood (2:27). First dam by John Nelson; second dam by ..le; third dam Blackhawk Wormwood by Nutwood 2:18 3-4, sire of Woodnut 2:16 1-4; dam the Cropsey mare by Naubuc, dam Gipsy Queen by George M. Patchen; second dam Capt. Roberts Mare. Nutwood by Belmont, dam Miss Russell (dam of Maud S. 2:08 3-4). Belmont, by Abdallah (sire of Goldsmith Maid), dam Belle by Mambrino Chief. Miss Russell, by Pilot Jr., dam Sally Russell by Boston. Pedigree and all particulars on application.

J. A. C.

Bay stallion, foaled April 22nd, 1887. Bred by Wm ... of San Francisco, Cal., sired by C. C. Bemis' ... First dam Bay Mare Nellie, sired by ... Chief he by Rysdyk's Hambletonian, her dam Lucky Hunter, noted for his speed and endurance (Stud Book).

For further particulars apply to

J. A. CARLETON,
1802 Broadway, Oakland, Cal.

SPRING

Running Meeting

1890.

Fresno Fair Grounds

Agricultu'l Dist. No. 21

March 25, 26, 27, & 28,

With an Extra Day on SATURDAY.

$2,500 in Purses

Open to the World.

SPEED PROGRAMME.

ENTRIES CLOSE, MARCH 10, 1890.

Entrance Fee—10 per cent. in all races.

FIRST DAY.

1. Half-mile dash. Purse $150; $15 to second horse. For two-year-olds owned in Mariposa, Merced, Tulare, Kern and Fresno Counties.
2. One-and-one-eighth mile dash. Purse $250, $25 to second horse.
3. One-quarter mile and repeat. Purse $150; $15 to second horse.

SECOND DAY.

4. Five-eighths mile dash. Purse $200; $20 to second horse.
5. One mile and repeat. Purse $250; $25 to second horse.
6. Half-mile dash. Purse $150; $15 to second horse.

THIRD DAY.

7. One and-one-quarter mile dash. Handicap. Purse $250; $25 to second horse.
8. Five-eighths mile and repeat. Purse $200; $20 to second horse.
9. One quarter mile dash. Purse $100; $10 to second horse.

FOURTH DAY.

10. Three-eighths mile and repeat. Purse $200; $20 to second horse.
11. One and one-quarter mile dash. Owners' Handicap. Purse $250 $25 to second horse.
12. Three quarter mile dash. Handicap for beaten horses. Purse $250; $25 to second horse.

CONDITIONS FOR SPRING RACES.

Entrance ten per cent on amount of purse, to accompany nomination. Any horse distancing the field will only be entitled to first money.

American Association rules to govern all running races, but the Board reserve the right to run heats of any two classes alternately, or to run a special race between heats; also, to change the day or hour of any race if deemed necessary.

A horse making a walk-over shall be entitled to only entrance money paid in.

Entries not declared out by 6 P. M. of the day preceding the race will be required to start.

When there is more than one entry by one person, or in one interest, in heat races, the particular horse they are to start must be named by 6 P. M. of the day preceding the race.

If, in the opinion of the judges, any race cannot be finished on the closing day of the meeting, it may be continued or declared off at the option of the judges.

Non-starters in running races will be held for entrance under Rule 36.

Maidens allowed 7 pounds in all races.

Non-winners having run two races or more in 1889 allowed 5 pounds, but no maiden allowance.

Weights in the handicap races will be declared at 6 o'clock P. M. the day previous to the race. Owners must accept or declare out by 8 o'clock P. M. of the day previous to race, or will be required to start.

Racing Colors to be named on entries.

The last rule will be strictly enforced.

All races to be called at 2 P. M. sharp.

Entries to all the above races to close with the Secretary at 11 P. M. Monday, March 10th, 1890.

Hay and straw free.

LEWIS LEACH, President.

N. I. BALDWIN, Secretary.
P. O. Drawer "U," Fresno, Cal.

F. R. BALDWIN, Manager.

HOLLYWOOD BREEDING FARM.

MOUNTAIN BOY 4841.

Br s MOUNTAIN BOY, 4841, bred by Charles Backman, Orange County, New York, foaled 1882, sire Kentucky Prince 2470, dam Elise, sister to Elaine, by Messenger Duroc 106; grandam Green Mountain Maid, 3d dam, Shanghai Mary, will serve a limited number of mares at $100 the season.

ELECTION.

Bay stallion ELECTION, bred at Senator Stanford's Palo Alto Stock farm, foaled 1884, sire Electioneer, dam Lizzie H. by Whipple's Hambletonian 725, grandam Lizzie Harris (by Comus son of Green's Bashaw 50), great grandam by Arnold Harris, thoroughbred.

Election is one of the handsomest bloodlike sons of Electioneer, and with his thoroughbred cross through Arnold Harris should prove invaluable as a sire. TERMS, $100 the season.

KAFIR.

B c KAFIR, bred by L. J. Rose, Los Angeles, foaled 1887, sire Alcazar, 2:20½, dam Flower Girl by Arthurton, sire of Arab, 2:15, grandam Flora by General McClellan, 144, sire of three in 2:30 list, great grand dam by Langford, he by Williamson's Belmont, will serve a limited number of mares at $50 the season.

WOODSIDE.

Ch c WOODSIDE, sire Woodnut, 2:16½; 1st dam Veronica by Alcona, 730; 2nd dam Fontana by Almont, 33; 3rd dam Fannie Williams by Alexander's Abdallah, 15. Book full.

MART BOORHEM.

B c MART BOORHEM, by Sydney, 2:19¾; 1st dam Towhead by Echo. This colt is a full brother to St. Nicholas who showed a mile in 2:27½ at three years old. TERMS, $25 the season.

REVEILLE.

The well known thoroughbred stallion REVEILLE, by Shiloh, dam by Norfolk. Reveille is a brother to John Treat and is the sire of Tycoon and Gladstone. TERMS, $25 the season.

Hollywood is nicely situated three miles from Vallejo on the Napa road. Good pasturage and every care will be taken of mares at reasonable rates. For further particulars, apply,

B. C. HOLLY, Vallejo.

SAN JOSE

Colt Stakes,

TO BE TROTTED AT THE

FALL MEETING

OF 1890.

No. 1. REGAL WILKES TROTTING STAKES. For three year olds. $60 entrance, of which $10 must accompany nomination; $25 on June 1st, and $25 on August 1st; with $250 added. Mile heats, three in five.

No. 2. MOUNT HAMILTON TROTTING STAKES. For two year olds. $50 entrance, of which $10 must accompany nomination. $15 on June 1st and $25 on August 1st; with $200 added. Mile and repeat.

No. 3. SANTA CLARA COUNTY TROTTING STAKES.—For two year olds (for above county only). $30 entrance, of which $10 must accompany nomination. $10 on June 1st and $10 on August 1st, with $150 added. Mile and repeat.

Parties must have owned their colts prior to February 1st, 1890, to be eligible in this stake.

No. 4. INFANT TROTTING STAKES.—For the get of the following stallions: Jim L, Argent, Eros, Bismarck, J. Weatherhead's horses (2), Guy Davis, Nutwood Boy, Orion, King William, Tommy T., Stranger, John Sevenicks, Col. Benton, Wilmington, Dick Patchen, Baywood, Fleetwood, Sultan Jr., Billy Thornhill, Amphion, Magic, Chancellor, Monte, Chrisman's Hambletonian, Boxwood, Nutgrove, Prince Albert, Alex Graham, Designer, Cyrus R., Harry Almont, ...'s Nutwood, Poodle, Parnell, Robin Adair, Fred ..., Elect, Mambrino Jr., California Nutwood, ..., Jim Mulvenna, Brown Jug, Menlo, Almont Patchen, Antinous, Electric Light, May Boy, C. W. S. Henderson's Henry, ..., H. Emerson, Carr's Mambrino, Designer, Prince Warwick, Henry Burr, J. Dunn's horses (3). For yearling foals of 1889. $25 entrance, of which $5 must accompany nomination; $10 on June 1st, and $10 Aug. 1st, with $100 added. Mile dashes.

CONDITIONS.

Entries to close in the above stake Tuesday, April 1st, 1890. Stake and added money divided 60 per cent. to first, 30 per cent. to second, and 10 per cent. to third.

For a walkover the colt will take the whole stake, but no added money. If two colts start they must contest for entrance money only, divided two-thirds and one-third.

Declarations are void unless accompanied by the money.

Nominations not making payments when due forfeit previous payments.

WM. BUCKLY, President.

G. H. BRAGG, Secretary.

Solano and Napa Agricultural Society.

Trotting Colt Guarantee Stakes for 1890.

The Solano and Napa Agricultural Society have opened the following Colt Stakes for Trotters:

NO. 1. TWO YEAR OLDS.—Free for all; $100 guaranteed. $50 entrance, payable as follows: $10 April 1st, when entries close; $10 May 1st, $10 June 1st, $10 July 1st, $10 August 1st, when colts must be named. Nominations transferable any time before colts are named. If the payments amount to more than the amounts guaranteed the additional amount to be added to the stake. All moneys divided as follows: 60, 30 and 10 per cent; in case of only two starting, 60 and 40 per cent; and in case of one horse walking over the whole amount to go to such horse. A failure to make any payment when due shall be considered a withdrawal and forfeiture of the amounts paid in. National or American Rules to govern, as the Society may elect. The right reserved to refund the first payment in case the stakes do not fill reasonably well.

No. 2. FOR THREE YEAR OLDS.—Free for all. $600 guaranteed. $100 entrance, payable as follows: $20 April 1st, when entries close; $20 May 1st, $20 June 1st, $20 July 1st, $20 August 1st, when colts must be named. Conditions same as in No. 1.

District Colt Stakes for districts comprising Counties of Solano, Napa, Sonoma, Marin, Lake, Colusa, Yolo, Mendocino and Butte.

No. 3. FOR YEARLINGS.—$250 guaranteed. District. $40 entrance, payable as follows: $10 April 1st, when entries close; $10 June 1st, $10 July 1st, $10 August 1st, when colts must be named. Conditions same as in No. 1.

No. 4. FOR TWO YEAR OLDS.—$300 guaranteed. District. $50 entrance, payable as follows: $10 April 1st, when entries close; $10 May 1st, $10 June 1st, $10 July 1st, $10 August 1st when colts must be named. Conditions same as in No. 1.

No. 5. FOR THREE YEAR OLDS.—$400 guaranteed. District. $50 entrance, payable as follows: $10 April 1st when entries close; $10 May 1st, $10 June 1st, $10 July 1st, $10 August 1st, when colts must be named. Conditions same as in No. 1.

Yearling Stake. Single dash; one mile. Two Year Olds.—Mile heats, two in three. Three Year Olds—Three in five, to harness. Parties entering colts will be notified by mail when payment becomes due.

The Society also offers the following stakes for class horses.

TROTTING STAKES.—Free for all.

2:30 CLASS—Trotting; purse $1500.
2:24 CLASS—Trotting; purse $1500.
2:20 CLASS—Trotting; purse $1500.

Horses eligible January 1st, 1890. Entrance $150, payable as follows: $25 April 1st, when entries close; $25 May 1st, $25 June 1st, $25 July 1st, $50 August 1st, when horses must be named. Nominations transferable any time before August 1st. Right reserved to refund entrance fee in any of the stakes should they not fill reasonably well. Money divided 50, 25, 15 and 10 per cent. National or American Association Rules to govern, as the Society shall elect. To be trotted at our regular summer meeting, upon days to be hereafter arranged.

Entries to close April 1st, 1890, with

A. H. CONKLING, Secretary,
Napa City, Cal.

L. L. JAMES, President.

R. LIDDLE & SON

538 Washington St., S. F.,

Wholesale and Retail Dealers in

Guns, Rifles and Pistols.

A Full Line of FISHING TACKLE and SPORTSMAN'S GOODS.

Orders by mail receive prompt attention.

Speed Programme

—OF THE—

Twelfth District Ag'l Society

To be held at

LAKEPORT,

SEPTEMBER 23 to 27 INCLUSIVE.

First Day—Tuesday, Sept 23, 1890.

RACE NO. 1—TROTTING.

Yearling Stake; $200 guaranteed. Entrance $30, payable as follows: $5 May 1st, $10 July 1, $10 September 1st (when entry must be named), and $5 additional for starters. Entries to close May 1, 1890. See general conditions.

RACE NO. 2—RUNNING.

One-half mile dash. $100 added; $25 to second. Entrance $10, to close 6 P. M. day before race.

RACE NO. 3—TROTTING.

Three-minute Class. Mile heats 3 in 5. District. $150 added. Entrance $20; to close 6 P. M. day before race. 5 to enter, 3 to start. See general conditions.

Second Day—Wednesday, September 24th.

RACE NO. 4—RUNNING.

Three-quarter mile heats; 2 in 3. $200 added; $25 to second. Entrance $10, to close 6 P. M. day before race.

RACE NO. 5—TROTTING.

District Stallion. Mile heats 3 in 5. Purse $500. Entrance $50, to close 6 P. M. day before race; 5 to enter, 3 to start. See general conditions.

RACE NO. 6—TROTTING.

Three-year-old stake; $300 guaranteed. $50 entrance, payable as follows: May 1st, $10; July 1st, $10; September 1, $15 (when entry must be named), and $15 additional to start. Open to Napa, Solano, Sonoma, Marin, Lake, Colusa, Yolo, Mendocino and Humboldt Counties.

Third Day—Thursday, Sept. 25th.

RACE NO. 7—RUNNING.

Seven-eighths mile dash. $150 added; $25 to second. Entrance $10, to close 6 P. M. day before race.

RACE NO. 8—TROTTING.

Two-year-old stake; free for all. Mile heats, best 2 in 3. $300 guaranteed. Entrance $50, payable as follows: May 1st, $10; July 1st, $10; September 1st, $10, and $15 additional to start. See general conditions.

Fourth Day—Friday, Sept. 26th.

RACE NO. 9—TROTTING.

Mile heats, 3 in 5. For all described counties in race No. 6. $400 added. Entrance $60, payable as follows: May 1st, $10; July 1st, $20; September 1st, $20—when entries must be named—$10 additional to start. See general conditions.

RACE NO. 10—RUNNING.

Citizens' Handicap. $100 added. Five-eighths mile; heats, 2 in 3. Entrance $10, to close 6 P. M. day before race.

Fifth Day—Saturday, September 27th.

RACE NO. 11—RUNNING.

GENTLEMEN'S NOVELTY.—For non-professional jockeys. One mile dash. $10 added; $5 entrance. Purse divided as follows: First horse at each quarter to get $25; slowest average at all quarters to get Society medal.

NO. 12.—LADIES' TOURNAMENT

Free for all in District. Purse $80, divided as follows: $45 to first, $15 to second, $10 to third.

No. 13.—GENTLEMAN'S TROTTING.

Same conditions as gentlemen's Novelty. Mile heats, two in three. Entrance $5. Entrance money divided 60, 30 and 10 per cent.

GENERAN CONDITIONS.

Nominations in colt stakes transferrable any time before colts are named. If the payments in stake races amount to more than the sum guaranteed the additional amount to be divided 60, 30 and 10 per cent; in case of only two starting, 60 and 40 per cent.; and in case of one horse walking over, the whole amount to go to such horse.

A failure to make any payment when due shall be considered a withdrawal, and forfeiture of the amounts paid in. National Rules to govern all trotting races. The right reserved to refund the first payment in case the stake does not fill satisfactorily.

All running races, unless otherwise specified, governed by the Pacific Coast Blood Horse Association Rules.

The Directors reserve the right to change the hour and date of any race, and in case of a race being antedated the nominator will receive notice.

A horse distancing the field shall receive only first and third moneys.

L. G. SIMMONS, President.

A. B. McCUTCHEN, Secretary.

STATE AGRICUL'L SOCIETY

State Fair, 1890.

TROTTING COLT SWEEPSTAKES

TO CLOSE MARCH 15, 1890.

No. 1. For Two-Year-Olds.

$50 entrance, of which $10 must accompany nomination; $15 payable July 1st, and remaining $25 payable August 10th, 1890. $300 added by the Society.

No. 2. For Three Year-Olds.

$100 entrance, of which $25 must accompany nomination; $25 payable July 1st, and remaining $50 payable August 10th, 1890. $400 added by the Society.

No. 3. For Four-Year-Olds.

[Conditions same as for three year olds.]

In all stakes failure to make payments as they become due forfeits entry and money paid in. Five to enter; three or more to start. Money in each stake to be divided as follows: To winning colt all the stakes and 50 per cent of added money; second colt, 33⅓ per cent; third colt, 16⅔ per cent of added money.

Two year old stake, mile heats; three and four year olds, three in five, to harness. No added money for a walkover. If only two start, they must contest for the stakes paid in, and divide two-thirds and one-third. Otherwise National Rules to govern.

CHRISTOPHER GREEN, President.

EDWIN F SMITH, Secretary.

PASTURAGE

And Care of Horses

AT ALL SEASONS, A SPECIALTY,

—AT—

MURRAY'S RANCH. - - - Laurel Creek

SAN MATEO COUNTY.

Horses pastured, in the season, $4 per month.

Horses stabled and fed hay, per month $8 to $10.

Small pastures for fine stock at agreed rates. Yearly contracts at agreed rates. Best of attention given to all stock.

Stock can be delivered at the ranch or shipped to San Mateo.

Parties are requested to visit the ranch and satisfy themselves of its adaptation for the above purpose.

There are no barb wire fences on the farm.

Address

B. C. MURRAY,
San Mateo.

First Grand Annual Sale

—OF—

PURE BRED SHORTHORN CATTLE

Under the management of

The Pacific Coast Shorthorn Breeders' Asssociation.

Will be held at

AGRICULTURAL PARK, SACRAMENTO, April 3d, 1890.

(Sale to commence at 1 o'clock P. M.)

This society is composed of the best breeders of Short Horn Cattle on the Pacific Coast, and is organized upon a permanent basis.

Nothing but Pure Bred Registered Cattle Will be Offered at this Sale.

The stock offered at this sale come from the herds of the following well known breeders:—

F. A. BRIDGEFORD, Colusa, Colusa County.
PETER PETERSON, Sites, Colusa County.
A. HEILBRON & BRO., Sacramento.
F. S. CHILES, Davisville, Yolo County.
P. H. MURPHY, Perkins, Sacramento County.
E. S. DRIVER, Antelope, Sacramento County.
JOSEPH MARZEN, Lovelocks, Nevada.

Catalogues can be had by addressing

J. F. CHILES, Secretary, Davisville, Yolo County.

A Grand Combination Sale

—OF—

Standard-bred Trotters & Thoroughbreds

CLYDESDALES AND PERCHERONS,

Fine Roadsters, Work Horses, Etc.

—AND—

Registered and Graded Holstein CATTLE,

REGISTERED JACKS,

And other first-class Live Stock of all kinds, will be held at

CARSON CITY, NEV., April 15, 16 and 17, '90

BROOD MARES, COLTS AND FILLIES by the following well known Sires will be sold:

Standard Bred.
ECHO.
GIBRALTAR. (will be sold)
PROMPTER.
BUCCANEER.
ST. CLAIR.
SIGNAL.
BLUE BULL.
ST. LAWRENCE.

Thoroughbred.
NORFOLK.
HOOKER.
LODI.
BRECKENBRIDGE.
THREE CHEERS.
LANGFORD.
BOI DE ARC.
McMAHON.

And among the fine stock to be offered will be the grand HOLSTEIN BULL SARATOGA, and a number of fine calves and heifers by him and other well known thoroughbred Holsteins.

Over 100 entries were made up to March 1st, and a big sale is assured.

Send in your entries.

For further particulars address

JNO. P. SWEENY & CO., Carson City, Nev.

For Sale

A First-Class.

BREEDING FARM.

Of 800 Acres.

Four hours' ride from the city. Good roads to a first class track. Climate unexcelled. Plenty of wood and running water.

For further information apply to the office of the

BREEDER AND SPORTSMAN,

San Francisco.

313 Bush Street.

For Sale.

THE HANDSOME SORREL FILLY

Lady Dexter,

By Dexter Prince, by Kentucky Prince, the sire of Guy 2:10 3-4. First dam full sister of the greatest of trotters, Dexter, and the greatest of sires, Dictator. Second dam Clara, by American Star. Third dam the McKinstry mare. Hambletonian, the grandsire of Dexter Prince, has 40 trotters in the 2:30 list, 44 daughters that have produced 2:30 trotters, and more than 100 sons that have sired 2:30 trotters.

LADY DEXTER'S dam was Kitty Thorn, by Whipple's Hambletonian, out of a daughter of Kimball's Jackson; granddam by George M. Patchen.

Kitty Thorn's record, four years old, 2:31, was made at Santa Rosa in the :30 Class. She won the race against Judge Shafter's Rustic, Hancock, Gladstone and Lave. Kitty Thorn trotted the same season in 2:27 1-2, but has no record in the 2:30 list.

This filly is four years old, and has never been trained, but can easily show quarters at a 2:45 gait, and demonstrates that with a little systematic work she will prove very fast. She is stylish, of gentle disposition, intelligent, and a square trotter. For further information address or apply to

H. QUIGG.

217 Fifth Street, San Francisco, Cal.

For Sale

A FIRST-CLASS

Napa County Farm

—OR—

STOCK RANCH,

800 Acres Improved,

SITUATED TWO AND A HALF MILES FROM NAPA CITY, with good roads leading thereto, a good hard finished house of nine rooms, with all modern improvements, streams running all summer, a great amount of live oak and black oak timber. It lies in a fruit belt, surrounded by fine vineyards and orchards growing upon the same quality of soil, and originally a part of this tract. About one-half hill, and one-half rolling land, but none of it is steep and all easily cultivated, splendidly situated for the breeding of fine horses. Price, $65 per acre. Further particulars given at this office.

BREEDER AND SPORTSMAN,

313 Bush St.

For Sale

A HALF BROTHER TO

ALMONT PATCHEN,

(2:15, trial 2:13 3-4).

JUANITO JR. is a beautiful bright bay, black points, with no white, foaled 1886. As a colt he has given much more promise than did Almont Patchen at the same age. Instead of being a pacer, he is a good square trotter, with every indication of great speed, and is so gentle and kind, that a lady can drive him. The owner's only reason for selling him is that business calls him away from this section of the State. He will be sold at a reasonable figure. This is a splendid opportunity for a gentleman to secure a first-class trotter at a very low figure.

The pedigree of Juanito Jr. is by Juanito (sire of Almont Patchen), dam Nettie Moore by Old Tom Moore. For further particulars, address

JUANITO JR.,

Santa Clara P. O., Cal.

For Sale.

14

Pure bred

PERCHERONS.

Stallions and Mares.

OF ALL AGES.

Part Imported, and all Registered Proof

For further information, address

E. J. TURNER, Hollister, Cal.

Antevolo Colt

For Sale.

AVOLO REX, foaled February 22, 1888; dam Catchup by Rustic; grandam Huntress by Don Victor; g g dam Betty Denice by American Boy Jr. Is 15.1 hands high, well developed, muscular, and without a blemish. Has a very gentle disposition, and shows speed and a good gait. Apply

HOME FURNISHING CO,

113 Fifth Street, S. F., Cal.

Stallion for Sale

AT A BARGAIN.

Full Brother to Fairmont.

By Piedmont, dam Queen by Garibaldi—see State Fair Edition of BREEDER AND SPORTSMAN, September 14, 1889, for description of Fairmont—three years old, solid bay. Can trot a 2:40 gait or better. Sound in every particular. Can be seen at Oakland Trotting Park, Oakland.

P. J. WILLIAMS.

FOR SALE

AT

Vineland Stock Farm

STALLIONS, BROODMARES AND FILLIES

ONE STALLION FIVE YEARS OLD, SEAL-BROWN, by WHIPPLETON (sire of Lily Stanley, 2:17 1-2, Homestakes 2:16 1-2, etc.), dam Sally Gorham by Werner's Rattler. This horse is scarcely 15 1-2 hands high, but very compactly built. He breeds exceptionally large and well finished colts. Any one understanding the business could clear him in one season, or he would make a No. 1 road horse, as he can trot a 40 gait any time.

ONE THREE-YEAR-OLD, SEAL-BROWN, by WHIPPLETON (sire of Lily Stanley, 2:17 1-2, Homestakes 2:16 1-2, etc.), dam Sally Gorham, etc. This ought to make a great General Purpose sire, and with opportunities get trotters, as he is compact, strong-boned, and will measure when grown about 16 hands and weighs 1,200 lbs. With a little road work last fall he developed a wonderful burst of speed.

ONE THREE-YEAR-OLD, BLACK, by WHIPPLETON (sire of Lily Stanley, 2:17 1-2, etc.), dam by Naubuc (sire of the dam of Eva W., 2:23 1-2, etc.), full brother to Thomas Jefferson, 2:23. This horse will be fully 16 1-2 hands high. He is smooth, rapid gaited and from size and conformation should breed, like his sire, large, rangy, finished colts.

ONE TWO-YEAR-OLD, BRIGHT CHESTNUT, sired by DAWN 2:18¾, dam Alida (dam of Directa, three-year-old record 2:21¼, trial 2:26) by Admiral (sire of sister 2:19 1-2, Nona Y 2:25, etc). This colt is the making of an extraordinary horse. He is large boned and will be over sixteen hands high when grown; he is of the true Nutwood type, is clean gaited and can lead a piece as fast as any man's colt.

ONE TWO-YEAR-OLD, BLOOD BAY, (full brother to Alcona Jr. sire of Silas Skinner trial 2:20) sired by ALCONA (sire of Flora Belle 2:24, etc.,) dam Madonna by Cassius M. Clay Jr. This colt will make a trotter and a great stock horse if developed; he has the combined blood of Almont, Mambrino Chief, Cassius M. Clay Jr. and Joe Downing.

These colts are all sound and promising. The only reason I offer them for sale is, that I have three aged stallions in use, and the surplus is growing on me. If I were starting a breeding business for profit, I should consider either of these colts a representative to commence with. Also brood mares and fillies for sale. Correspondence solicited.

FRED. W. LOEBER, St. Helena,
Napa Co., Cal.

The Annual Combination Sale

—OF—

Road Mares, Harness Horses, Colts and Fillies,

WILL TAKE PLACE AT

Bay District Track, San Francisco

At 11 A. M. on

THURSDAY, APRIL 3, 1890.

The offering will consist of the get of ELECTIONEER, GUY WILKES, MAMBRINO WILKES, ARTHURTON, SIDNEY, ALEX. BUTTON, ANTEROS, and other noted stallions.

Catalogues will be ready March 11th, and will be furnished upon application.

KILLIP & CO., Auctioneers,

22 Montgomery Street, San Francisco

SOUTHER FARM

P. O. Box 208. San Leandro, Cal.

1¼ miles northwest of San Leandro; 8 miles southeast of Oakland. Turn off County road between above places at "Stanley Road," ¼ mile north of San Leandro.

Horses boarded at all times in any manner desired. Best of care but no responsibility for accidents. Colts broken and handled for road or track. Terms reasonable.

—:o:—

Glen Fortune,	Jester D,	El Benton,	Figaro,
By Electioneer.	By Almont.	By Electioneer.	Hambletonian
$50 for 1889.	$50 for 1890.	Limited to 5 mares.	Limited to 12 mares
		Book Full.	Book Full.

THE SOUTHER FARM

Has Green Feed the Year Round,

and feeds Hay in connection with the green feed, which a horse must have if he is to thrive. Every animal is given

A Dry, Warm Place to Sleep,

No matter how stormy the weather. All Stock under cover when it rains.

VISITORS WELCOME ANY DAY EXCEPT SUNDAY

How to Get Stock to the Souther Farm:

The Souther Farm is one and a half miles northeast of San Leandro and eight miles southeast of Oakland. The stables are about one mile east of the county road, which runs between Oakland and San Leandro. The place to turn off is at Stanley Road, where a large signboard of the farm is placed. Guide boards will be found at every cross road. In any ordinary weather the roads are very good, and they are fairly good after the unusually heavy rainfall of the past winter.

All stock sent from San Francisco may be brought over by Garcia's Express, No. 2 Market street, San Francisco. They also have an order box outside of Hawley Bros.' Hardware house on the corner of Market and Beale streets. The express leaves San Francisco on the Creek route boat, which starts at 1:30, but orders should be in the order box at Market and Beale streets by 10 o'clock, or at the office, No. 2 Market street, by 11 o'clock at the latest. In the case of very young or very valuable horses, the Souther Farm will send reliable men to lead or drive over any stock that will not lead behind a wagon. A small charge will be made in such cases, to cover the extra expense incurred.

Horses are very easily taken from Oakland to the farm, and where it is inconvenient for owners to bring them or send them, the farm will send after anything that is to come. On horses that stay three months or over there is no charge for getting or delivering. Where a horse stays a short time the actual time and expense only is charged to him.

Horses can be shipped by rail from almost all parts of the State to San Leandro. Always notify the Farm several days before shipping anything, and then men will be on hand to receive stock on arrival. The railroad station is but two miles from the Souther Farm, and the agent invariably gives immediate notice of the arrival of any stock consigned to the above farm, but when word is sent to the farm in good season by letter or telegram, the animals sent are saved waiting a couple of hours in the car.

Passenger trains leave San Francisco (from the broad gauge ferry) and First and Broadway, Oakland, at frequent intervals during the day. There are several trains from San Jose to San Leandro on both the broad and narrow gauge railroads; the broad gauge, by way of Niles, is much more convenient for getting to the farm. There are trains each day from Sacramento, Stockton and Livermore to San Leandro. In ordinary weather it is a short and pleasant drive from Oakland to the Souther Farm or from San Francisco to the Farm by way of the Creek route ferry boat. Always notify the Souther Farm just when you will arrive at San Leandro, and some one will meet you at the station. If you do not recognize the farm conveyance ask the stage driver, who will point it out.

Write to the above address for references, circulars and price lists. Terms reasonable.

GILBERT TOMPKINS, Proprietor.

CALIFORNIA NUTWOOD

Will stand for mares the season of 1890, commencing February 15th, and ending July 15th, at the NUTWOOD STOCK FARM, one mile from Irvington.

DESCRIPTION AND PEDIGREE.

He is a dark chestnut, with star in forehead; foaled September 16th, 1881; is 16 hands 1½ inches high and weighs 1250 pounds. Has a beautiful flowing mane and tail, with remarkable style and lofty carriage, a bold, open movement like his sire, but has never been handled for speed. He moves and looks like his sire, except that he is a larger horse.

CALIFORNIA NUTWOOD by Nutwood, record 2:18¾, has 32 trotters and pacers with records from 2:15 to 2:30, and put 8 in the 2:30 list in 1889. He is the only horse that ever lived with a record under 2:20 that produced five under 2:20. He is now serving mares at Dubuque, Iowa, at $500 for the season, and his colts at yearlings sell from $2500 to $5000 each. He is out of the dam of Maud S., record 2:08¾.

Nutwood, by Alexander's Belmont, sire of 32 with records from 2:15½ to 2:30. Alexander's Belmont by Alexander's Abdallah, sire of Goldsmiths Maid, record 2:14, and 5 others in 2:30 list. Alexander's Abdallah, by Rysdyk's Hambletonian, sire of 41 with records from 2:17¼ to 2:30, and is the founder of the Hambletonian family.

FANNY PATCHEN, dam of California Nutwood, by George M. Patchen Jr., record 2:27, and sire of Wells Fargo, 2:18¾, Sam Purdy 2:20½, Ben Ali 2:20¾, and 7 others from 2:21 to 2:30. He has 7 sons who together produced 12 trotters in 2:30 list, and 6 daughters who together produced 5 trotters and 1 pacer in 2:30 or better. He sired Alexander 2:31½. Alexander sired Alex. Button 2:26½; Alex. Button sired Yolo Maid, pacing record 2:14 at 4 years old, the fastest on record; George M. Patchen Jr., by George M. Patchen 2:23½, is sire of Lucy 2:18¼, and 3 others in the 2:30 list; he has 12 sons who together produced 40 trotters from 2:14½ to 2:30, and 6 daughters who together produced 6 trotters in 2:30 list or better, he is grand sire of Hopeful 2:14¾, and best wagon record 2:16½, and sire of the granddam of Stamboul 2:12½.

George M. Patchen, by Cassius M. Clay, and he by Henry Clay, founder of the Clay family.

Laura, second dam of California Nutwood, was a fine large bay mare, a very fast roadster brought from Chicago by Wm. Wilson, of San Jose, and is said to have made a record of 2.35 in Chicago. Pedigree not traced.

TERMS.

$40 for the season, payable invariably before the animal is removed. Mares not proving in foal can be returned free next season. Pasturage $3 per month, but no liability for accidents or escapes.

For further particulars address the owner,

MARTIN CARTER,

Newark, Alameda Co., Cal., or Irvington, Alameda County, Cal.

Sunny Side Breeding Farm.

Admiral 488.

Foaled 1867—Sired by Volunteer 55, Son of Rysdyk's Hambletonian 10.

First dam Lady Pierson by Cassius M. Clay (Neaves') 20; second dam by Diamond; third dam a running mare said to be thoroughbred. He is fitted in an eminent degree to produce colts that will in all respects justify his patrons in their expectations.

Admiral is the sire of Huntress, record 2:27½, Sister, 2:19½, Perhelion, 2:25, Nona Y., 2:25, and others equally as promising, but have not had the advantage of track work. He will serve a limited number of approved mares at $50 the season, with usual return privilege. Season ending August 1, 1890. No liability for accidents or escapes.

KING DAVID 2576.

Bay Stallion—Foaled 1883.

Sired by Admiral 488, dam Black Flora (the dam of Huntress, 2:27½, Sister, 2:19½, Perhelion, 2:25, Nona Y., 2:25), by Black Prince.

King David is one of the best gets of Admiral. He has a good disposition, kind to drive, smooth and even-gaited, and can speed fast. Barring accidents he will trot in the twenties this Fall. His colts are large, rangy, and well finished. Will serve a limited number of mares at $30 the season, to end July 1, 1890. Every precaution will be taken to prevent accidents and escapes, but no liability will be assumed. Pasturage $4 per month.

Sunny Side Farm is situated two miles east of Vallejo, on the Sulphur Spring road. For further particulars, address

FRANK DRAKE,

Vallejo, Cal.

The Fast Trotting Stallion

REDWOOD.

Four-Year-Old Record 2:24 1-2

Will make the season of 1890—February 1st to July 1st—at the

OAKLAND RACE TRACK.

REDWOOD is a dark bay colt, 15.2¾ hands high, weighs 1100 lbs. Foaled in 1885 by Anteeo, 2:16¼, sire of Alfred G., 2:19¾. Anteeo is by Electioneer. First dam Lou Milton, by Milton Medium; second dam Old Fly, a thoroughbred mare brought from the East in 1871 by W. C. Ralston, Esq.

Redwood's sire was out of Columbine by A. W. Richmond, the sire of the pacers Arrow 2:13¼, and Elwood 2:23, and the trotters Romero, 2:19¾, and Len Rose, 2:27. Redwood has shown a quarter in 33 seconds.

Terms $100

For the season. Mares not proving with foal may be returned next season free of charge, provided Redwood remains the property of the present owners. Good pasturage at $5 per month. No responsibility assumed for escapes or accidents. Service fees payable before removal of the mare. Limited to 40 approved mares. For further particulars address,

A. McFADYEN.

Race track, Oakland, Cal.

Singleton & Addington,

Bank Exchange,

2d and K Streets, Sacramento,

Superior Wines, Liquors and Cigars.

Valensin Stock Farm Stallions.

SIDNEY, 2:19 3-4.

At Eight Years of Age Sire of the following Fastest on Record:

FAUSTINO, yearling stallion, record of the world....2:35
FLEET, fastest yearling record in 1888....2:36
FLEET, fastest two-year-old filly in 1889....2:24
GOLD LEAF, fastest four-year-old Pacing record in the world....2:11¼
ADONIS, fastest three-year-old Pacing Gelding in the world....2:14¼
ADONIS, four-year-old Gelding Pacing record....2:14

—Also the Sire of—

LONGWORTH, four years old....2:19
SISTER V., four years old (trial 2:23)....2:27
SANTA RITA....2:39
MEMO, two-year-old (three-year-old trial 2:20½)....2:49

And many others.

SIDNEY is the sire of Faustino 2:35, and Fleet 2:36, the two fastest yearlings the world has ever known by one sire, and his slowest yearling is faster than the great Electioneer's fastest.

Terms, $250, with usual return privileges, for a limited number of approved mares. Book nearly full.

Only eight more mares can be taken for Season of '90.

Pasturage $5 per month. Reasonable charges if fed hay and grain. Best of care taken of mares, but positively no responsibility assumed for accidents or escapes. For further particulars address

G. VALENSIN, Pleasanton, Cal.

CANNON BALL, 8820

BY SIMMONS 2744.

RECORD 2:28, (Full Brother to Rosa Wilkes, 2:18 1-4), Sire of Nine in 2:30 List at 10 Years Old.

First dam Gurgle, pacing record 2:20; trial of 2:15¼ for W. H. Crawford; by Pocahontas Boy, sire of Buffalo Girl, 2:12¼; Raven Boy, 2:15¼, and ten others in the list.

Second dam Matlock by Grey Diomed.

Third dam by Tom Hal.

DESCRIPTION.

Brown bay, right hind foot and left inside hind heel white. Foaled May 30, 1887. Bred by W. H. Wilson Abdallah Park, Cynthiana, Ky.

He is a grand individual, large boned, fine size and appearance. When fully matured will probably be 16 hands, and weigh 1200 lbs.

Is of speedy conformation and level headed. His blood lines are stout and fashionable, being the Wilkes and Mambrino Patchen on pacing and thoroughbred foundations, and from a family of producers on both sides.

Can be seen until February 1st at Agricultural Park, Los Angeles, in charge of C. A. Durfee, after which he will serve ten approved mares at $60 the season, with usual privilege of return in 1891, at Lockhaven Stock Farm, Burbank, Cal. Mares kept on grass $3 per month, and extra charge where grain and alfalfa are fed. For further particulars, address

O. H. LOCKHART, Proprietor,

Lockhaven Stock Farm,

Burbank, Cal.

Nine Miles from Los Angeles.

The Pure Trotting-bred Stallion

ILLUSTRIOUS

STANDARD No. 4178.

DESCRIPTION.

Dark bay, black points, 15 1-2 hands high, weight 1000 pounds, foaled May 30, 1886; bred by General W. T. Withers, Lexington, Ky.

PEDIGREE.

By Happy Medium, sire of Maxey Cobb 2:13¼ and 82 with records of 2:30 or better. First dam Abdalletta by Cassius M. Clay Jr., sire of Durango 2:23¼, Harry Clay 2:23¼ and sire of the dams of Minnehaha, Bertha 2:27¼, Charley Wise 2:28¼, Grandmont 2:25 1-2, Lottie K 2:28¼, Mambrino Diamond 2:26, Richwood 2:28 1-2, Topsy 2:29¼, Happy Thought 2:22 1-2, Pequot 2:28 1-2, Fairlawn Medium 2:27 1-2, Polley 2:27¼ and Mambrino Boy 2:26 1-2; second dam Laura Crockett by Almont, sire of Westmont 2:13¼, Puritan 2:16, Fanny Witherspoon 2:16¼, Piedmont 2:17¼, Altine 2:19¼ and 37 with records better than 2:30; third dam Sally Tea by Alexander's Abdallah, sire of Goldsmith Maid 2:14; fourth dam Kate Crockett, the dam of Lulu 2:14¾, by imp Hooton.

Illustrious is a horse of extra fine finish, large clean bone, good feet, back short and strong, loins and quarters well muscled, and powerful. He has a kind disposition and splendid trotting action, and is as handsome and bloodlike in form and finish as any trotting stallion in the land.

He is pronounced by his breeder, General Withers, to be the best bred son of Happy Medium living, and is undoubtedly one of the very best bred trotting stallions in the State. He has had but six weeks' regular training, and a part of that time was sick with epizootic, but was trotted quarters in 39 1-4 seconds, and barring accidents will certainly trot better than 2:30 this season.

TERMS—$50 the season. Mares not proving with foal may be returned next year free.

Good pasturage at $3 per month.

Season to begin February 1st and end June 15th.

GEO. A. STONE,

Santa Rosa, Cal.

WOODNUT

(Weatherhead's) by Nutwood 600

Sire of Belmont Boy, 2:16, pacer, Woodnut, 2:16¼, Felix, 2:18¼, Dawn, 2:18¼, Maggie E., 2:19¼, Irma, 2:18¾, and 26 others in 2:30 or better; 1st dam Flora, 2:30¾, trial 2:26, dam of Chrisman's Hambletonian, sire of Steve Whipple, 2:22, Kate Agnew, 2:28¾, by Chieftain 721, sire of Defiance 2:17¼ pacing and 2:24 trotting, Cairo, 2:26, Onward, 2:24, pacer; second dam by Wilson's Leaman.

Woodnut is a beautiful bay with black points, 15.3 hands high, weighing 1,075 pounds. His colts are all larger than himself, and sell readily for road and carriage purposes, being of good color and very docile, yet prompt to obey, and always ready.

Service fee, $25, with usual privileges. Colts and fillies from Tilton Almont, Patchen, Stockbridge Chief, and other desirable crosses, FOR SALE. For further particulars, pedigrees, or any communication in horse matters, address

JAS. WEATHERHEAD, Prop.

San Jose, Cal.

BAY ROSE

REGISTERED No. 9814

Record 2:20½, third Heat.

Will make the season of 1890 from March 1st to July 1st at the race track, Oakland.

DESCRIPTION.

BAY ROSE is a dark bay or brown, with black points, 16 1-2 hands high and weighs 1150 pounds. He is remarkably intelligent, of good disposition and a pure gaited trotter. He was foaled in 1881. His colts are large, stylish, rangy animals and inherit the qualities of speed and endurance.

PEDIGREE.

BAY ROSE 9814
- Sultan, 2:24. Sire of 18 in the 2:30 list.
  - The Moor, 870. Sire of Beautiful Bells, 2:29 1-2; Del Sur, 2:24 1-2; Inez, 2:30; Sir Guy, 2:28 1-2; Sultan, 2:24; Tommy Gates, 2.24.
  - Sultana.
- Madam Baldwin
  - The Moor, 870. Sire of 6 in the 2:30 list.
  - By Ben Lippincott by Williamson's Belmont.

TERMS: $100 FOR THE SEASON.

Good pasturage near the track, and first-class care taken of mares for $5 per month. No responsibility assumed for escapes or accidents.

For further particulars, address

W. W. AYRES,

Care of Jas. Corcoran, Race Track, Oakland, Cal.

THE MAMBRINO Patchen Stallion.

MAMBRINO JR., 1789 (formerly Carr's) Sire of Lady Ellen 2:28 (dam of Ella 2:29), Maud H. 2:30, Mambrino Boy (Carr's) 2:31 1 2.

Will stand at my farm, 2 1-2 miles north of San Jose, on the Milpitas Road. Season to commence February 1st, 1890, at $40, with return privilege 1891. Fifteen mares of approved breeding, besides my own, will be given him. Parties owning good mares, performers or out of producing dams, will find an opportunity to breed them on shares, and the best of care taken of them till colt is weaned, if so desired.

PEDIGREE.

MAMBRINO JR. 1789, by Mambrino Patchen 58 (full brother of Lady Thorne 2:18 1-4) by Mambrino Chief 11. First dam by Mambrino Chief 11; 2nd dam by imp. Jordan [thoroughbred]; 3rd dam by Bertrand, son of Sir Archy; 4th dam by Chewkees, son of Sir Archy.

For further particulars address

GEO. P. BULL.

San Jose, Cal.

Box 1067.

The Trotting Stallion

CUPID,

Full Brother to Adonis 2:14,

—Sired by—

The Celebrated SIDNEY 2:19 3-4, and out of Venus.

Will make the season of 1890 at the OAKLAND TROTTING PARK.

PEDIGREE.

CUPID is by Sidney out of Venus by Capt. Webster 10173, record 2:30, and sire of Pyrestone 2:19. Second dam by Skenandoah 996, sire of Daisy Rufus 2:29¼, Erwin Davis (sire of two in the 30 list) and dams of four in the 30 list.

DESCRIPTION.

Cupid is a handsome bright bay 15.2¾ hands high, weighs 1100 lbs.; was foaled in 1886. As a yearling, with very little work he showed quarters in 42 seconds, and at 2 years old, quarters in 36 seconds. As a three year old he has not been worked, but he shows the speed and endurance that must come from his excellent blood lines.

TERMS $50 for the season, with the usual return privileges. Good pasturage near the track at $5 per month. The best of care taken of mares in any way that owners may desire, but no responsibility assumed for accidents or escapes.

For further particulars address

C. O. THORNQUEST,

Oakland Trotting Park, or

C. BAAB, 972 Broadway, Oakland.

Vineland Stock Farm

Whippleton 1883,

Sire of

LILY STANLEY - - - Record 2:17½
HOMESTAKE - - - " 2:16½
FLORA B. - - - " 2:27
CORA C. - - - " 2:31½
BLACK PRINCE - - - " 2:36½
RACHEL - - - " 2:38
PRINCE W. - - - " 2:40

WHIPPLETON is not only the sire of trotters, but he is the greatest sire of Carriage Horses on the Pacific Coast. Some of the best carriage and road teams in San Francisco are sired by Whippleton. A carriage team by Whippleton received First Premium at Napa, Petaluma, Oakland, Sacramento, Stockton and San Jose. Whippleton and his colts have never been beaten in the show ring.

DESCRIPTION.

WHIPPLETON is black, tan muzzle and flanks, 17 hands, and weighs 1,400 lbs. Most of his colts are 16 hands or over, and with a few exceptions, bay, brown or black. He never sired a sorrel or white face colt. (If he does, I agree to refund service money.)

PEDIGREE.

WHIPPLETON, sired by Hambletonian Jr. (sire of Hancock 2.29), by Whipple's Hambletonian (sire of Graves, 2:19, Westfield, 2:20¼, Express, 2:24, and 12 others in the 2:30 list), dam Lady Livingston (dam of Lady Blanchard, 2:26¼, Bloomfield Maid, trial 2:22), by General Taylor (sire of the dams of Wells Fargo, 2:18¾, Wenona, 2:23¼, Bickford, 2:19¾, Lady Blanchard, 2:26¼, etc., and sire of grandam of Hazel Wilkes, 2:20) by the Morse Horse 6 sire of Norman 25 (sire of Lulu, 2:14¾, May Queen 2:20, etc.).

TERMS at $40, limited to 20 mares, for the season, usual return privileges. I would like to get about ten well bred mares with the proper combination of blood to breed to Whippleton on shares this season.

Alcona 730.

Sire of

FLORA BELLE - - - Record 2:24
CLAY DUKE - - - " 2:31½

ALCONA will be a great sire, but four of his colts have ever been trained, and all have shown full miles better than 2:30, and two of them as good as 2:20. Two of his first sons each sired a colt as a two-year-old, and last season one as a four-year-old trotted a full mile in 2:23¼, and the other, a three-year-old, a mile in 2:31. With opportunities, Alcona is destined to be one of Almont's best sons. Almont, for his opportunities, is beyond doubt the most prepotent sire of his age. He has 36 representatives in the 2:30 list; 49 sons and 22 daughters that have already produced 2:30 performers. Almont died 6-8 years ago at 20 years old. If he lived he would be but 28 years old.

PEDIGREE.

ALCONA sired by the great Almont (sire of Westmont 2:13¼, Fanny Witherspoon 2:16¼, Piedmont 2:17¼, and 33 others with records better than 2:30, and grandsire of Belle Hamlin 2:13¾, etc.); by Alexander's Abdallah (sire of Goldsmith Maid 2:14), he by Rysdyk's Hambletonian. Alcona's dam, Queen Mary, by Mambrino Chief (sire of Lady Thorne 2:18 1-4, and 5 others in the 2:30 list, and sire of the dams of Director 2:17, Piedmont 2:17¼, Onward 2:25 1-4, Red Wilkes, Almont, Belmont and many other noted sires).

DESCRIPTION.

Alcona is a beautiful chestnut 16 3 1-2 hands high, and weighs 1300 lbs. His colts possess speed, style, finish and beauty, and if they don't trot they command the highest prices for carriage horses.

$40 for the season. Usual return privilege.

Season on Whippleton and Alcona ends July 1st, 1890.

Best kind of pasturage at $4 per month. Mares kept in any manner desired.

For further particulars send for circular or call at stables, one mile south of St. Helena.

FRED W. LOEBER.

St. Helena, Napa Co., Cal.

The Trotting Stallion

G & M

FULL BROTHER TO

ALFRED G, 2:19¾.

(Who has been taken to Kentucky to stand at $200)

Will make the season of 1890 from FEBRUARY 1st to JULY 1st, at

SANTA ROSA.

G. & M. is by Anteeo, 2:16¼; was foaled 1886; first dam Rosa B. by Speculation (son of Hambletonian 10); 2d dam Elizabeth by Alexander 497; 3d dam Nora by imp. Glencoe. Anteeo is by Electioneer, out of Columbine by A. W. Richmond 1687.

G. & M. is a handsome dark bay; stands 15-2 1-2 hands high, and weighs 1060 pounds. Gameness, stoutness, speed and stamina are indelibly impressed in every line of the pedigree of G. & M. Owners of brood-mares in search of these qualities, will do well to patronize this promising colt.

PHILOSOPHER,

Foaled 1886 by Pilot Wilkes 2967; first dam Bella by George Wilkes 519; second dam by Bell Morgan 6).

Philosopher's sire, Pilot Wilkes 2967, is by George Wilkes 519, dam Grace (the dam of Alice Woodburn, etc.), by Pilot Jr. 12, grandam by Orphan Boy.

Will make the season of 1890, from FEBRUARY 1st to JULY 1st, at Santa Rosa.

TERMS for the season:

G. & M., $50.

PHILOSOPHER, $30,

with privilege of returning mares that do not prove in foal the next season free of charge, provided the horse bred to remains the property of the present owners. Good pasturage at $3 per month. No responsibility assumed for accidents or escapes. Service fees payable before removal of the mare. For further particulars, address

GEO. E. GUERNE,

Santa Rosa Cal.

Highland Farm,

LEXINGTON, KY.,

Home of Red Wilkes.

Standard-bred Trotting Stock

For Sale,

Sired by Red Wilkes, Wilton, 2:19¼; Allandorf and Sentinel Wilkes, out of highly bred Standard Mares of the most fashionable blood of the day.

W. C. FRANCE, Proprietor,

Guenoc Stud Farm, Lake Co., Cal.

Imp. GREENBACK

(Sire of the English winners Greenlight, Greenjacket, Greensback, Greenwave and Greenhorn)

By Dollar, dam Music, by Stockwell. $100 the Season

ST. SAVIOR,

(FULL BROTHER TO EOLE)

By Eolus, dam War Song, by War Dance. $100 the Season.

PASTURAGE, $5 PER MONTH.

With right to return the following year if mare does not prove with foal. The best of care taken, but no liability for accidents or escapes. Mares shipped to C. W. ABY, care ST. HELENA STABLES, St. Helena Napa County, will be taken in charge by competent men.

For further information write to

DR. C. W. ABY, Middletown, Lake County, Cal.

1890 Three Anteeo Stallions 1890

SUNSET, 5 years old, by Anteeo
ANTEEOF, 4 years old, by Anteeo
ANTEEOP, 3 years old, by Anteeo

ANTEEO. Standard 7868. Record, 2:16 1-4, he by Stanford's Electioneer, and dam Columbine.

DESCRIPTIONS, PEDIGREES AND CONDITIONS.

"SUNSET" is a rich, dark bay, small star on forehead, portion of hind left foot white; was foaled March 11, 1885; is by ANTEEO and the inbred HAMBLETONIAN mare, BESSIE G, she by KING PHILLIP, son of WHIPPLE'S HAMBLETONIAN. He is 16 1-2 hands high, and weighs 1,200 lbs. He is of perfect build and splendid action cool headed and great speed for his size, having trotted a trial mile as a three-year-old in 2:38. He then entered heavy in the stud and was matched against Whalebone at the Healdsburg races November 2, 1888, winning just as he pleased in three straight heats; time, 2:47, 2:46 1-2, 2:52 1-2. He was then matched for a race to come off last Thanksgiving Day at Petaluma but owing to the heavy rains the event did not take place. A few days previous to Thanksgiving Day Mr. Lawrence worked Sunset out and then he trotted three square miles and heats in 2:33¾, 2:34 and 2:37.

SUNSET will be bred to 40 mares only, at $50 each, no colt no pay.

"ANTEEOF" is a jet black, was foaled April 13, 1886, is 15¾ hands high, and weighs 1,200 lbs., has a very fine, heavy black mane and tail; is well proportioned, moves majestically, is of easy, lofty carriage; is symmetrical, in fact is a beautiful horse. He was sired by Anteeo and the O. A. Taylor mare "Nance," her dam, was raised by Dr. Oliver Plummer, of Consumnes, Cal., and sired by "Napoleon"; Napoleon was foaled May 20, 1852, and raised by James Kyle of Butler County, Ohio. He was sired by Benj. Sweet's horse Bellfounder, and he by Old Bellfounder, his dam was sired by Doc. Daniel Mulligan's horse Cadmus, G. G. sire the celebrated Eclipse; his G. dam was sired by Big Shakespeare, G. G., sires dam by Messenger and Expedition.

ANTEEOF will be bred to 25 mares only, at $30 each. No Colt, no pay.

"ANTEEOP" is a rich seal brown; was foaled March 7, 1887; by Anteeo and the inbred Hambletonian mare Bessie G., also dam of Sunset, his full brother and Midget his full sister; he is 15 1-2 hands high and weighs 950 lbs. and measures 22 inches around the arm, good head, fine neck, full, broad breast; withers and rump on nearly equal line, well proportioned bones, ankle, shoulders, loins and hips; strong legs all around, with great muscular development and splendid sinews; wirey pasterns and sound, compact feet; the lines from hip to hock show power and speed; stands square and has excellent action, has a superb lustrous coat of rich deep brown fur of seal color without defect; an even, honest trotter, and has gone the mile as a two-year-old in 2:48, the last quarter in 38 seconds; is intelligent and of high spirit, with much temper, but is not vicious, has very fine eyes, is a handsome, showy colt; attractive in harness.

ANTEEOP will be bred to 15 mares only, at $50. No colt, no pay.

SEASON to commence February 1st, ending July 1, 1890. Book now ready. Apply to John H. Lawrence, "Manager and Trainer," on my fruit and hop ranch, 1 mile east of Court House, on Sonoma road. Excellent pasture furnished with running water, also dry knolls with oak shelter, at $4 per month for mares. Two of the above stallions will be for sale after the expiration of the their stud season.

GUY E. GROSSE,
SANTA ROSA, SONOMA CO., CAL.

The Trotting Stallion

Guide 2:29

(At Four Years)

Will make the season of 1890 at the SANTA RITA RANCH, about one mile North of Pleasanton.

DESCRIPTION.

GUIDE is a handsome seal brown, five years old, stands 15¾ hands high, and weighs 1085 pounds. He is of fine form, level headed, intelligent, and comes from blood lines that are noted for the qualities of speed and gameness.

PEDIGREE.

GUIDE, 2:28½
- Director, 2:17. Sire of Direct, 2:18¾, Margaret S., 2:19¾.
  - Dictator 113. Sire of 22 trotters and 3 pacers in 2:30.
    - Hambletonian 10.
    - Clara, by American Star 14.
  - Dolly. Dam of Onward, 2:25¾, Thorndale, 2:22¾.
    - Mambrino Chief 11.
    - Fannie, by Ben Franklin.
- Imogene.
  - Norwood 522. Sire of Tommy Norwood, 2:26¾.
    - Hambletonian 10.
    - Lady Fallis, by American Star 14.
  - daughter of
    - American Star 14.
    - daughter of Harry Clay 45.

The attention of breeders is especially called to the above pedigree as showing 3 crosses of American Star.

GUIDE trotted into the 2:30 list last season with little training, and he will trot into the 2:20 list the coming season barring accidents.

Guide's sire has a record of 2:17, made in a five heat race, and Guide is closely related to Phallas, who made a record of 2:13¾ in a fourth heat, and to Jay-Eye-See, record 2:10.

TWO HUNDRED AND FIFTY DOLLARS will be given to the owner of the first of the produce of Guide put in the 2:30 list, and $100 to each one after the first.

TERMS—$75 for the season, with the usual return privileges.

Admiro,

Sire Admiral; dam by San Bruno, by Easton's David Hill.

This magnificent horse is a handsome bay, eight years old; stands 17 1-2 hands high, and weighs 1400 pounds He is very speedy for a large horse, and breeds fine large carriage horses. His produce possess every qualification of the Cleveland Bay, with the added qualities of speed and endurance resulting from his high trotting breeding.

TERMS—$35 for the season, with usual return privileges.

Will stand three days each week at Santa Rita Ranch, Pleasanton, and at A. T. Hatch's Ranch "Almono," Alamo, Contra Costa County, alternately. All mares sent care of SMITH & SUTHERLAND, Pleasanton, will be taken in charge of on arrival, and will receive the best care and attention in any manner the owners may desire. Good pasturage at $4 per month. Only a limited number of approved mares will be served by this horse this season.

No responsibility assumed for escapes or accidents. For further particulars, address

SMITH & SUTHERLAND, Pleasanton,
or A. T. HATCH, care Palace Hotel, San Francisco.

THE BRUNSWICK BALKE COLLENDER COMPANY,

MANUFACTURERS OF

Standard Billiard and Pool Tables, Saloon and Bank Fixtures,
653-655 Market Street, San Francisco, Cal.

GRANDISSIMO,

Full Brother to GRANDEE, 3-year-old Record 2-23½.

GRANDISSIMO
- Le Grande 2868 (trial, 2:24). Sire of Grandee, 3 y. o. r., 2:23½.
  - Almont 33. Sire of Westmont, 2:13½, Puritan, 2:16, Fannie Wetherspoon, 2:16½, Piedmont, 2:17¼, and 32 others in 2:30, and sire of 49 sons and 22 daughters that have produced 2:30 performers.
    - Abdallah 15. Sire of Goldsmith Maid, 2:14, and 8 others in 2:30, and sire of 13 sons and 21 dams, producers of 2:30 performers.
    - Sally Anderson, by Mambrino Chief.
  - Jessie Pepper. Dam of Iona, 2:17½, Alpha, 2:23½, and grandam of Montezuma, 2:29½.
    - Mambrino Chief 11. Sire Lady Thorne, 2:18½, and 5 others in 2:30 with 28 sires and 15 dams, producers of 2:30 performers.
    - Sidi Hamet (thoroughbred).
- Norma. Dam of Grandee, 3 y. o. r., 2:23½
  - Arthurton 365. Sire Arab, 2:15, and 4 others in 2:30, and dams of Hidalgo, 2:27, Hazel Wilkes, 2:20, Reverie (yearling), 2:36½.
    - Hambletonian 10. Sire of Dexter, 2:17¼, and 40 others in 2:30.
    - Imogene. Dam of Arthurton, with 4 in 2:30; Leland, with 8 in 2:30.
  - Nourmahal, 2:39½. Full sister to A. W. Richmond 1687, sire of Arrow, 2:13½, Romero, 2:19½, and 3 others in 2:30.
    - Blackbird 401. Sire of Blackbird, 2:22, A. W. Richmond, sire of 6 in 2:30, and dam of Anteeo, 2:16¼, Antevolo, 2:19¼.
    - by Rattler (thoroughbred).

SAN DIEGO, 8776.

SAN DIEGO 8776
- Alcona Clay 2786.
  - Alcona 730. Sire of Flora Belle, 2:24, Clay Duke, 2:31½, etc.
    - Almont 33. Sire of Westmont, 2:13½, Piedmont, 2:17¼, Puritan, 2:16, and 33 others in 2:30 list.
    - by Mambrino Chief 11. Sire of Lady Thorne, 2:18½.
  - Madonna. Dam of Del Rey, trial 2:31, Alcona Jr., 2:41, sire of Silas Skinner, trial 2:23½.
    - Cassius M. Clay Jr. 22. Sire of Durango, 2:23½, Harry Clay, 2:29½, and sire of dam of Happy Thought, 2:22½, and others.
    - by Joe Downing 710. Sire of Abe Downing, 2:20½, Dick Jamison, 2:26, and sire of dams of Kentucky Hambletonian, 2:27, Lorena, 2:18, and others.
- Fontana. Dam of Flora Belle, 2:24, Silas Skinner, trial 2:29½.
  - Almont 33. Sire of 36 in 2:30 list, 49 sons and 22 daughters that have produced 2:30 performers.
  - Fancy Wilkins. Dam of Bay Chieftain, 2:28½.
    - Abdallah 15. Sire of Goldsmith Maid, 2:14, Thorndale, 2:21¼ also Almont, Belmont, Jim Monroe, etc.
    - by Denmark (thoroughbred).

GRANDISSIMO is a blood bay, handsome-modelled colt, and a natural trotter. He is four years old, and trotted one quarter miles in 36 seconds, with very limited training, last Fall.

SAN DIEGO is dark seal brown, three years old, and trotted one-quarter miles in 40 seconds as a two-year old.

These are two grand young horses, and, barring accidents, will both make fast records next fall.

They will both be allowed a limited number of mares, at $50 for the season. Mares not proving in foal to be returned free 1891. Best of pasture for mares at $4 per month, but no liability for accidents or escapes.

They will make the season from February 1st to June 1st at Napa Fair Grounds. For further particulars, address or call on

H. B. STARR, Race Track, Napa, Cal.,
or FRED W. LOEBER, St. Helena

A SON OF ALMONT 33.

Only $25 for the Season.

ASHLAND ALMONT 3481.

PEDIGREE.

ASHLAND ALMONT 3481
- Almont 33. Sire of 34 in 2:30 or better of 21 daughters and of 49 sires that have produce in 2:30 or better.
  - Abdallah 15. Sire Goldsmith Maid, 2:14; 6 in 2:30 list; 13 sires and 25 dams of trotters in 2:30 list.
    - Hambletonian 10. Sire of 41 in 2:30 list; sire of 107 sires of 567 in 2:30 list.
    - Katy Darling.
  - Sally Anderson.
    - Mambrino Chief 11. Lady Thorn, 2:18¾.
    - Kate, by Pilot Jr. 12.
- Pauline. Dam of Sapho.
  - Ashland Chief. Sire Black Cloud, 2:17¾.
    - Mambrino Chief 11. Lady Thorn, 2:18¾.
    - dau. of imp. Yorkshire, (thoroughbred).
  - Rosina. Dam Almonia, the dam of Sally Cossack, 2:22¾, dau. Mamb. Abdallah, sire Mam. Prince, 2:23, and of Mamb. Bashaw, sire of Graham's Mambrino, 2:38.
    - Abdallah 15. Sire Goldsmith Maid, 2:14.
    - Prof. Smith's Sir William.

DESCRIPTION.

ASHLAND ALMONT 3481 is a handsome chestnut; stands 16 hands; was foaled 1883, and bred by Gen. Withers, of Lexington, Ky. He is of fine form, and remarkably intelligent, sweet-tempered and absolutely sound. His oldest foal may be seen with him, and while he has never served a standard mare or one that was a producer of speed, all of his colts are large, sound, fast and handsome.

TERMS: $25 for the season, with usual return privileges. The best of care taken of mares in any manner that the owner may desire, but no responsibility assumed for escapes or accidents.

For further particulars, address

T. J. WHITEHEAD, Manager.
579 36th Street, bet. Telegraph Ave. and Grove St., Oakland, Cal.
or, W. H. ASHBY, Oakland, Cal.

2:10 1-2 ELECTIONEER 2:12 1-4

BAY STALLION	BROWN STALLION
ECLECTIC	**MORTIMER**
11,321	5,346
By Electioneer, dam Manette (full sister to Woodnut 2.16 1-2 Manon 2:21 and Maple, dam of Hattie D., three year-old record 2:26¾) by Nutwood 2:18¾, etc., etc.	Four-year-old Record 2:27. By ELECTIONEER, dam MARTI, by Whipple's Hambletonian (sire of 15 in 2:30, and of dams of eight in 2:30). Second dam Ida Martin by Rifleman (sire of Col. Lewis 2:18¾).
Terms $100 for the Season.	Terms $60 for the Season.

Horses shipped via San Francisco may be consigned to J. W. MORSHEAD, City Front Stables, who will attend to their forwarding.

Season Closes JULY 1st, 1890. Usual return privileges.

For further particulars address owner,

WILFRED PAGE, Penns Grove,
Sonoma County, Cal.

PASHA,

Registered No. 2039.

RECORD 2:36.

SIRE OF MORO 2:27.

Will make the present season at Linden, twelve miles east of STOCKTON.

Season commencing FEBRUARY 1st and ending JULY 1, 1890.

DESCRIPTION.

PASHA is a beautiful black; 16½ hands high, and weighs 1,240 pounds. He is a horse of beautiful symmetry and magnificent action.

PEDIGREE.

PASHA was sired by Sultan 1513, sire of Stamboul 2:12½, Ruby 2:19¼, Alcazar 2:20½, Bay Rose 2:20½, and sixteen others with records below 2:30. First dam Madam Baldwin by The Moor 870; second dam Ben Lippincott by Belmont. Pasha is a full brother to Bay Rose, record 2:20½.

Sultan, by The Moor, sire of Beautiful Bells, dam of Hinda Rose, 2:19½, Bell Boy 2:19¼, and Sable, dam of Sable Wilkes, three-year-old record 2:18. First dam Sultana, by Delmonica, sire of Derby 2:16, by Guy Miller, sire of Whipple's Hambletonian. Second dam by Mambrino Chief. Third dam by Downing's Bay Messenger. Fourth dam Miss Caudle, dam of Ericsson, four-year-old record 2:30½.

Terms for the season, $50.

With privilege of returning mares that do not prove in foal next season free of charge.

Good pasturage at $2 per month. No responsibility will be assumed for accidents or escapes. Service fee payable before the removal of the mare.

For further particulars, address

D. BRYSON,
Linden Cal.

DESIGNER, 11,157

Son of Director 2:17.

Sire of DIRECT, 2:18½, as a four-year-old, (lapping out PALO ALTO in 2:16½), and MARGARET S., 2:19½, as a three-year-old, and GUIDE, 2:28½, as a three-year-old. DIRECTOR is brother to JAY-EYE-SEE, 2:10, and PHALLAS, 2:13¾.

At the State Fair of 1889, he received the Gold Medal as the best producer of averaged speed in colts of two, three and four years of age, beating Electioneer, Guy Wilkes, Sidney, Stamboul and others. He is the only trotting sire who has to his credit two performers in the 2:20 list, when his oldest colts were only four years old; his services are eagerly sought by breeders, with a fee of $300.

Designer's dam is May Queen, by Abbotsford, 2:19¾, sire of Conde, 2:19¾; Abbotsford is brother to Pancoast, 2:21¾, sire of Patron, 2:14¾.

May Queen was never trained. When two years old was driven over the road three weeks, and trotted to a cart two miles in six minutes. A few days after she paced a quarter in 40 seconds bare-footed; after being shod she trotted a quarter in 37 seconds.

Second dam by Elmo, 2:27¾ (half mile in 1:06), full sister in blood to Overman, 2:19 1-4, sister to the sire of L. C. Lee, 2:15, made when he defeated Arab in a match-race in three straight heats in 2:16, 2:17, 2:17¾. Only two of her produce were handled very little, one trotted as a three-year-old, with three weeks' work early in the spring, a mile in 2:35, last quarter in 35 seconds; the other trotted as a three-year-old, a mile in 2:27¾, quarters in 33 seconds, with seven weeks' work. If her produce had been given proper training, she would surely have had three in the 2:30 list.

Third dam by David Hill, sire of Geo. Treat, 2:26 1-4, and Black Swan, 2:28¾.

Fourth dam by Geo. Taylor, sire of the dam of Wells Fargo, 2:18¾.

Fifth dam by Williamson's Belmont.

Designer is a rich bay horse, 5 years old, 15¾ hands high, weighs 1,000 pounds, disposition the very best, has a perfect gait, and shows every indication of being very fast. He has never been trained, but will be given a low record, barring accidents. He is a horse of great substance and high finish; his family on both sides are producers of great speed, and he can not fail to make a great producer, as his colts inherit all these qualities—the same disposition and natural trotting action being large, and showing great breeding. He has but 15 colts in all (three two-year-olds); one of them has been broken, and last Fall trotted a quarter in 40¾ seconds, which proves that he produces early trotters. Those having colts from him are highly pleased with them, and all returned the mares to him the following season but two.

Breeders will see by carefully examining his pedigree, that his blood lines are invaluable for the production of high breeding and great speed. No stallion now in public service can show a pedigree with such fast records as enrich the blood of Designer. Considering his breeding, he is by far the cheapest horse in California. This is a rare opportunity to get the service of a good horse at a low price, as within a short period his price will be much higher.

Limited to 20 mares, at $50 for the season, commencing March 1st, ending June 15th. Mares can be returned next season if not with foal, provided mares or horse have not changed hands. Fee due at time of service, and must be paid before mares are removed. Pasturage $5 per month. All mares at owners' risk.

H. SCOTT,
San Jose Race Track, Cal.

LAWN VIEW BREEDING FARM STALLIONS.

ACTOR.

A beautiful bay horse foaled 1887 by Prompter 2305 sire of Apex (four-year-old record) 2:26, Transit 2:28¾, Creole 2:20, Blue Belle 2:32, Daisy (yearling record) 2:56¾, he by Blue Bull 75, 1st dam by Sultan 1513 2:24, sire of Stamboul 2:12 1-4, Ruby 2:19¾. Sweetheart 2:22¾, Alcazar 2:20¾, Eva 2:23¾, La Grange 2:23¾, and eleven others in 2:30 list, second dam by Fireman by Langford.

Actor, as his pedigree shows, is as purely bred a young stallion as ever made a season in the stud. Blue Bull stock is much sought after in the East, and Sultan, sire of his first dam will make the season in Kentucky this year at $400 per mare. Actor is a handsome bay colt 16 hands high, clean limbed and possesses all the points of a speedy trotter.

TERMS, $40 FOR THE SEASON, usual return privileges.

DOUGLASDALE 7650.

Thoroughbred Registered Clydesdale Stallion

Imported from Scotland, December, 1889, bay, three years old.

TERMS, $35 FOR THE SEASON.

YOUNG ELMO

Two years old sorrel stallion by St. Elmo 2:27, dam by Woodburn.

TERMS, $30 FOR THE SEASON.

For further particulars, address
MANAGER LAWN VIEW FARM, Auburn, Cal.

GEO. WASHINGTON.

11,623.

RECORD 2:30.

Bay colt, bred by Thomas Smith of Vallejo, Cal. Foaled 1886 by Mambrino Chief, Jr., 11,622, record 2:34 1-4, 1st dam Fanny Rose by Vick's Ethan Allen Jr. 2,903, sire of Prince Allen 2:27, 2nd dam Jenny Lind, thoroughbred, dam of Prince Allen 2:27. Will serve a limited number of mares at $30 for the season. Mares not proving with foal may be returned next season free.

Mambrino Chief, Jr.

11,622.

RECORD 2:34 1 2.

Sire of George Washington, record 2:30 at three years old. Bay horse bred by Rufus Ingalls of Belvedere, Ill. By McDonald Chief 3'52. First dam Venus by Mambrino Patchen 58, 2nd dam by Wardlow's Shakespeare, 3rd dam Lone Gold 4th dam by Silver Heels. Has not been in the stud before. He was 5 years old when he served a few mares, and his colts all show good style and form.

Terms for the season $40. For further particulars see or address

THOMAS SMITH,
Vallejo, Cal.

Elector 2170.

Sire of J. R.

Three-Year Old Record 2:24.

Sired by Electioneer 125, sire of Sunol, three-year-old, 2:10½, Palo Alto, 2:12¼, etc.; dam Gilberta by Fred Low 656, sire of Clay, 2:25½, etc.

Second dam Lady Gilbert (grandam of Lot Slocum, 2:17½) by General Knox 140 (sire of Lady Maud, 2:18½, and many others).

TERMS.

$150 for the season. Book full for 1890.

L. A. RICHARDS,
Grayson, Stanislaus Co., Cal.

The Thoroughbred Stallion

Three Cheers

Will make the season of 1890 at

Sacramento.

PEDIGREE.

THREE CHEERS

- Imp. Hurrah
  - Newminster
    - Touchstone, by Camel
    - Beeswing, by Dr. Syntax
  - Jovial
    - Bay Middleton, by Sultan
    - Sister to Grey Momus, by Comus
- Young Fashion
  - imp. Monarch
    - imp. Priam, by Emilius
    - imp. Delphine, by Whisker
  - Fashion
    - imp. Trustee, by Catton
    - Bonnets o' Blue, by Sir Charles

Hurrah was imported by John Reber, of Lancaster, Ohio, a locality where there were but few breeders of thoroughbreds. Under these disadvantages he sired a long list of winners. His sire Newminster, won the St. Leger 1851, and his dam, Jovial by Bay Middleton, winner of the Derby 1836. Newminster by Touchstone, winner St. Ledger 1834. Dam Beeswing, winner of 64 races out of 64 starts, by Dr. Syntax, winner of the Doncaster Cup, 1837—40—41—42, the only horse that ever accomplished that feat.

On the side of the dam Three Cheers is equally well related. Young Fashion was the dam of Surprise, Scotland (the only horse that ever beat Asteroid a heat), Liverpool, Columbia, and Bonnie Kate, the dam of Little Buttercup, and the flying Bonnie Lizzie. His grandam, Fashion was the greatest race mare of her day and beat Boston in that historical match at four mile heats, which is recorded as one of the greatest events in the annals of the turf.

Horsemen who are qualified to judge, pronounce Three Cheers to be the finest type of the Newminster line in America.

LOCATION.

THREE CHEERS will be located at the Arcade Training Stable, Rancho del Paso. This place has been selected for the reason that first class pasturage has been secured there for the exclusive use of these mares, and the other facilities to be obtained there for the care of mares (especially mares in foal) are better than can be found elsewhere in the locality.

TERMS.

$60 for the season with the usual return privileges. Pasturage $5 per month. Mares cared for as owners may desire at bottom rates for grain and hay. All bills payable before the mare is removed.

Mares shipped care of WM. IRVINE, Pacific Stables, Sacramento, will be properly cared for and sent to the ranch without delay.

Three Cheers will be in charge of one of the most experienced and competent stud grooms in the State, who will exercise every care, but no reponsibility assumed for accidents or escapes.

For further particulars apply to Louis Criesler, at the ranch; Wm. Irvine, Pacific Stables, Second St., Sacramento; or to the owner,

E. S. CULVER,
315 Bush St., San Francisco.

GROVER CLAY.

Bay Stallion, Black Points, 15 3-4 hands high.

Bred by W. W. Traylor, San Francisco.

BY ELECTIONEER.

First dam Maggie Norfolk by Norfolk, son of Lexington, he by Boston. Second dam Tilda Quill by Billy Cheatham he by Cracken, and he by Boston. Third dam by Dorsey's Golddust.

TERMS.

Will make the season of 1890 at the Training Stables of Denis Gannon, near Oakland Trotting Park, at $50 the season, payable at time of service. Season to commence February 1st and ending July 1st. Proper care of mares will be taken, but no responsibility incurred for accidents or escapes. Address,

DENIS GANNON, Oakland, Cal.

COOK STOCK FARM.

Season of 1890.

STEINWAY 1808.

Three-Year-Old Record 2:25 3-4.

Sire of STRATHWAY, three year old record 2:26, and sire of the dam of BOURBON RUSSELL 2:30.

By STRATHMORE 408; sire of 31 in the 2:30 list; sire of 6 dams of 8 in the 2:30 list, and sire of 3 sires of 8 in 2:30 list.

1st dam ABBESS (dam of Solo 2:28, and Soprano, dam of C. F Clay 2:18, Eminence 2:27 and Strathbridge, 3 year old record 2:28½) by ALBION, sire of VANITY FAIR 2:24½, and of the dam of FAVORITE 2:26½.

2nd dam by MARSHALL NEY.

3rd dam by BERTRAND, a son of SIR ARCHY.

TERMS—$100 for the season.

CHARLES DERBY 4907

Brown Horse, Foaled 1885.

By STEINWAY 1808.

1st dam by the great ELECTIONEER, sire of SUNOL 3 year old record 2:10½, Palo Alto 2:12¼, etc., etc.

2nd dam FANNY MALONE, by NIAGARA.

3rd dam FANNY WICKHAM, by HERALD.

4th dam by Imp. TRUSTEE.

TERMS—$100 for the season.

CRESCO 4908.

(BROTHER TO SPARTAN, 2:24.)

By STRATHMORE 408, sire of 31 in the 2:30 list, etc.

1st dam the dam of SPARTAN 2:24, by ALMONT 33; sire of 71 with performers in the 2:30 list

2nd dam the dam of HENDERSON 2:27, by BRIGNOLI 77, sire of the dam of KING WILKES 2:22.

3rd dam by CRIPPLE, a son of MEDOC.

4th dam by AMERICAN ECLIPSE.

TERMS—$50 for the season.

Pasturage $5 per month. Accidents and escapes at owner's risk. Mares consigned to the farm should be sent to Fashion Stables, Oakland; Geary & Grindle's Stable, Haywards; or to Bennett's Stable, Martinez; from and to which places they will be delivered free of charge. Address

COOK STOCK FARM,
Danville, Contra Costa. Co., Cal.

The Trotting Stallion

ARBITRATOR

Will make the Season of 1890 at NILES, Alameda County.

PEDIGREE.

ARBITRATOR

- Director 1989, 2:17 in a race, sire of Direct, 4 yrs., 2:18½ in a race, Margaret S., 3 yrs., 2:19¼ in a race, Guide, 4 yrs., 2:28½ in a race.
- Lady Earnest.
  - Speculation 918, sire of Oakland Maid, 2:22 in a race, Gracie S., 2:22 in a race, Crown Point, 2:24 in a race, He the sire of Valensin, 4 yrs., 2:23 in a race, Sire of Dam of Alfred G., 2:19½.
  - Lady Hibbard, dam of Lou Whipple, 2:26½ in a race.

Speculation's dam was Martha Washington, dam of Whipple's Hambletonian, sire of 15 in 2:30 and granddaughter of Burr's Napoleon, sire of Black Harry, who in 1850 won two miles in 5:14½. He sired Smith Burr, sire of Gen. Butler, 2:21, Wagon, 4:56½. He sired the dam of Fanny Mapes, dam of Jerome Eddy, 2:16½. He sired Telegraph, sire of dam of Rarus, 2:13¼.

DESCRIPTION.

ARBITRATOR was foaled 1886. He is of good size, fine conformation, and a beautiful seal brown.

TERMS.

Non-standard mares	$45
Standard mares by inheritance	35
Standard mares by performance or produce	25

For further particulars, address

H. A. MAYHEW, owner,
Niles, Alameda Co.

ST. NICHOLAS.

A Son of the World Renowned SIDNEY,

Will Make the Season of 1890, at the Oakland Trotting Park.

ST. NICHOLAS was bred by Mr. G. Valensin at the Arno Stock Farm, Sacramento Co., California, in 1886. He is a beautifully proportioned bright bay horse, 15.3 hands high; is well muscled, lengthy, and lots of bone, with splendid natural action and a phenomenal turn of speed. As a three-year-old he easily worked three heats on the Oakland Track in 2:22, 2:23 and 2:17¾. His breeding is just what one would expect from such a highly formed bloodlike horse. Sidney, his sire, is the most successful young stallion—whether for getting pacers or trotters—America has ever seen, and no wonder for his blood lines are exceptional fine and are all trotting lines, Santa Claus, Strathmore, Rysdyk's Hambletonian and Abdallah, while Sweetness again runs back through that great sire Volunteer, to Rysdyk's Hambletonian and also through her dam to Rysdyk's Hambletonian and Harry Clay 45, the sire of Electioneer's dam. St. Nicholas' dam is by Echo, an exceptionally prepotent son of Hambletonian thus giving St. Nicholas four Rysdyk's Hambletonian crosses and further back a Harry Clay cross which with his grand dam's thoroughbred cross should make him invaluable in the stud.

TERMS: Fifty dollars the season, which will commence on the 5th of February and close on the 1st of July. Due care will be taken of mares, but no responsibility for accidents or escapes.

Mares taken and kept as desired by the owners, and at reasonable rates.

JOHN ROWEN.
Oakland Trotting Park.

Season of 1890.

February 15 to June 15

LYNWOOD,

(STANDARD 3017.)

AT WOLF'S (RUSSELL'S) STABLES, STOCKTON, CAL.

TERMS.

$50 for the season, payable at the close of season. Pasturage at $3 per month. Accidents or escapes at owner's risk.

PEDIGREE.

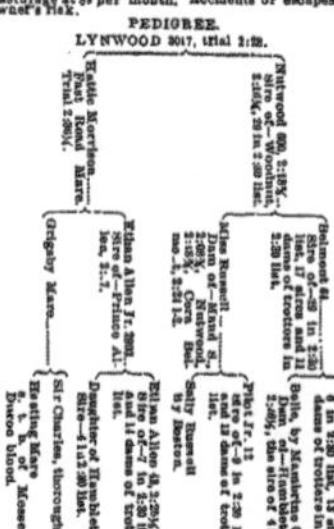

DESCRIPTION.

Dark bay, 16 hands, weighs 1050 pounds, form stout and elegant, gait pure and rapid. He was foaled July 15, 1880, has done but little work in the stud, but enough to demonstrate that he is one of the best foal getters in the State. Only one of his get has had any systematic handling, and that could have gone into the 2:30 list last year as a two-year-old, had the owner desired.

It will be observed from an examination of Lynwood's pedigree, that he is one of the best bred sons of the GREAT NUTWOOD, who commands a service fee of $500 for the season.

P. VISHER, Stockton.

The Thoroughbred Stallion

INTRUDER

Will make the Season of 1890 at Agricultural Park, SACRAMENTO.

Bay Horse, foaled 1871, bred by Sir L. Newman, England. Imported by D. D. Withers, Esq., New York.

By Crater, Son of Orlando and Vesuvienne by Gladiator.

1st dam Lady Bountiful by Rataplan (Rataplan is own brother to Stockwell, and winner of 41 races, including the Doncaster Cup and 16 Queen's Plates, and proved himself the most distinguished race horse of his day in England).

2d dam Plentiful by Don John (the winner of St. Leger and Doncaster Cup).

3d dam Plenty by Bay Middleton (winner of the Derby and Two Thousand Guinea Stakes).

4th dam Plenary, own sister of Plenipotentiary, by Emilius. (Both Emilius and Plenipotentiary were Derby winners).

5th dam Harriet, dam of the renowned Plenipotentiary by Pericles.

6th dam by Selim, winner of the One Thousand Guinea Stakes.

7th dam by Pypilina, by Sir Peter.

8th dam Rally, by Trumpeter.

9th dam Fancy, by Florizel. Fancy was full sister to Diomed, the first Derby winner in England, and after his importation into this country, sired the illustrious Sir Archy, etc. See English Stud Book.

Imported INTRUDER is a beautiful bay, standing fully 16 hands high, of great length and substance, and descends through close and strong currents from the most illustrious winners and winning lines of blood of which the English Stud Book bears record.

A careful review of the first six crosses of the pedigree of INTRUDER will show nine Derby winners; five St. Leger winners; two winners of The Oaks; two winners of the Two Thousand Guineas; two winners of the One Thousand Guineas; one Goodwood Cup winner; one Cesarwich Cup winner; one Cambridgeshire stakes winner, and four Doncaster Cups, in addition to a great number of Steeplechases and other races of less import.

INTRUDER, at the great fair held at St. Louis, Mo., in 1878, was awarded the highest stallion honors—the blue ribbon and the $500 purse—in the sweepstakes ring for stallion of any age or blood. The list of competitors embraced the large number of thirty-three animals, and they represented England, Canada, Kentucky, Tennessee, and other states. He also took first premium in his class and in sweepstakes for the best stallion of any age or breed at the State Fair at Peoria, Ill., 1882. He is the sire of Tidal Wave, George Makes, Bernice and April Fool.

INTRUDER is the sire of Interpose, who is the dam of Spokane, winner of the Kentucky Derby, in which he beat the great horse Proctor Knott and broke the record.

TERMS: $50 for the season. Mares not proving with foal can be returned the next season free of charge. Good pasturage at $4 per month. Mares cared for in any manner owners may desire, and fed on hay and grain, either or both, at reasonable rates. While every precaution will be taken, no responsibility will be assumed for escapes or accidents. Mares sent from a distance in care of the undersigned, will be met and taken to the park. For further particulars, address

T. J. KNIGHT.
Agricultural Park, Sacramento.

Shoes For Comfort, Elegance and Durability.

Having my own Factory, and giving my personal supervision to all work I am in a position to warrant perfect satisfaction. Inspection invited.

AGENT for the VISCALIZED SHOES.

FACTORY—S. W. cor. Battery and Jackson Sts.

SALESROOM—Pioneer Building, corner Stevenson and Fourth Streets.

A full line of Boots and Shoes constantly on hand, and rules for Self-Measurement by Mail.

JNO. T. SULLIVAN.

2:20 1-2 Half Mile Track) at 4 Years. Fastest Record (in a Race) of any Wilkes 2:14 1-2 at 5 Years

ROY WILKES, 2:12 3/4,

Seal brown; 15½ hands; foaled 1883; by Adrian Wilkes 6560, son of Geo. Wilkes; 1st dam by Blue Bull 75; 2d dam by grandson of American Eclipse; 3d and 4th dams thoroughbred.

THE GREATEST CAMPAIGNER OF 1889.

Handsome, Game, Pure Gaited. Level Headed.

Will make a season at the PLEASANTON STOCK FARM, PLEASANTON, CAL. Service Fee $150. Money refunded if mare does not get with foal. Season ends April 1st, 1890

For full record of performances, extended pedigree, etc., address

L. A. DAVIES, Hotel Pleasanton,
SUTTER AND JONES STREETS, San Francisco, Cal.

MEMO.

The Best Son of SIDNEY

Will Make the Season of 1890 at the OAKLAND RACE TRACK

MEMO

- SIDNEY 2:19¾
  - Santa Claus 2000, 2:17 1-2, sire of San Mateo, 2:28 1-4 Sidney, 2:19¾.
    - Strathmore 408, Sire of 31 in 2:30 list, Sire of 4 dams of 3 in 2:30, Sire of 2 sires of 3 in 2:30
      - Hambletonian 10, Sire of 41 in 2:30 list, Sire of 107 sires of 567 in 2:30 list, Sire of 44 dams of 50 in 2:30 list. { Abdallah 1. / Chas. Kent mare.
      - Lady Waltermire, Dam of Marshal Ney 2084. { North America. / s. t. b. Hambletonian 2-mare.
    - Lady Thorne Jr., Dam of Mollie Mack, 2:33
      - Mambrino (Williams) { Ericsson 130. / Daughter of Aratus (thoroughbred).
      - Kate { Highland Chief. / Halcorn mare (Magowan's).
  - Sweetness 2:21 1-4
    - Volunteer 55, Sire of 29 in 2:30, Sire of 21 of 48 in 2:30, Sire of 16 dams of 16 in 2:30.
      - Hambletonian 10, Sire of Geo. Wilkes 2:22 { Abdallah 1. / Chas. Kent mare.
      - Lady Patriot { Young Patriot. / Lewis Hulse mare.
    - Lady Merritt
      - Edward Everitt 81, sire of 13 in 2:30, Sire of 8 sires of 16, Sire of 6 dams of 7. { Hambletonian 10. / Margrave mare, s.t.b.
      - Daughter of { Harry Clay 45. Sire of 3 in 2:30, Sire of dam of Electioneer, St. Julien, etc.
- FLIRT
  - Buccaneer 2656, sire of Shamrock, 2 y. o., 2:25, Flight, 2:29, (dam of Fleet, 2:24) Dams of George V., 2 y. o., 2:31 1-2, Creole, 2:20.
    - Iowa Chief 528, Sire of Consacol, 2:24 1-2
      - Bashaw 50, Sire of 16 in 2:30, Sire of 10 sires of 20 in 2:30, Sire of 11 dams of 18 in 2:30. { Black Hawk (Vernol's). / Belle.
      - Topsey { Prophet, by Vermont Black Hawk 5.
    - Tinsley Maid
      - Flaxtail 8132, sire of dam of Gold Leaf, 2:11 1-4, Apex, 2:26, Flight, 2:29, J. R. McCormack, 2:29, Shamrock, 2:25. { Pruden's Blue Bull.
      - Fannie Fern { Irwin's Tuckahoe. / dam of Leffiers' Consul.
  - Mahaska Belle
    - Flaxtail 8132 s. t. b., sire of grandams of Fleet, 2:24, Creole, 2:20.
      - Prudens' Blue Bull, Sire of Blue Bull 75, Sire of 58 in 2:30. { Merring's Blue Bull.
    - Lady Hake
      - John Baptist
      - Fannie Fern { Irwin's Tuckahoe. / dam of Leffiers' Consul.

MEMO is, as can be seen at a glance, one of the best bred young stallions in service, having three crosses of Rysdyk's Hambletonian and one of Harry Clay, the sire of Green Mountain Maid (dam of Electioneer, etc.), while Long Island Black Hawk and Flaxtail also contribute to his blood. Sidney (Memo's sire) is universally known as the best young sire in the world, a producer of extreme speed at an early age.

PERFORMANCES.

MEMO trotted in public in his two year-old form, obtaining a record of 2:49, though he was close to Grandee in a race on the Bay District Track, the second heat of which was made in 2:31 1-2, the first in 2:37. He exhibited phenomenal speed when three years old, and had it not been for a slight strain of his fore fetlock, there is little question that he would have shown in public very close to the best record. On the Oakland track he was timed a mile in 2:20 1-2, and frequently trotted quarters in from 32 1-2 to 34 seconds.

As a four-year-old Memo only started once—at Sacramento—when, although out of condition, he showed great speed, and improving as he went on, great hopes were entertained of his going well down in the 'teens at the P. C. T. H. B. A. meeting, but after showing several very fast miles his leg filled and he was laid up for the season. He is sixteen hands high, and of powerful build throughout. His color is a glossy black, with both fore-feet white. His disposition is all that could be desired, and his action superb. He is a sure foal getter, only one mare being reported not in foal during his last season.

TERMS, $100, with usual return privileges, for a limited number of mares. Season to close JUNE 15th, when he will be prepared for track purposes. Pasturage $5 per month. Have leased the cricket ground adjoining the track for pasturage, where there is fine feed. Reasonable charges if fed hay and grain. Best of care taken of mares in any manner owners may desire, but positively no responsibility assumed for accidents or escapes. For further particulars address

J. P. KERR, 313 Bush Street, San Francisco,

or, JOHN ROWEN, Race Track, Oakland, Cal.

2:10¾ 2:18¾ 2:10

DEXTER PRINCE.

This Royally-bred Stallion will make the Season of 1890 at the LIVE OAKS Breeding Farm, 2 miles from Lodi, San Joaquin County, Cal.

DESCRIPTION.

DEXTER PRINCE is a blood bay, 16 hands high, weighs over 1 100 pounds; has great power and substance, and the highest finish. When two years old, at Palo Alto, he was timed quarters by Gov. Stanford in 33¼ seconds, and he was driven eights by Mr. Marvin at a faster rate of speed than that. He is a sure foal-getter, and invariably sires foals of good size, of fine form and finish, and the highest rate of speed.

PEDIGREE.

By KENTUCKY PRINCE, the sire of Guy, 2:10¾, Spofford, 2:18¾, Company, 2:19¾, Bayonne Prince, 2:21 1-4, Fred Folger, 2:20¾, and a score more in the 2:30 list.

First dam LADY DEXTER, full sister of the greatest of trotters, Dexter, and the greatest of sires, Dictator, the sire of Director, 2:17, Phallas, 2:13¾, in a fourth heat, and Jay-Eye-See, 2:10.

Second dam Clara, the dam of Dexter, 2:17 1-4, Dictator, Astoria 2:29 1-4, and Alma, 2:28¾. Clara was by American Star, that has 31 daughters that have produced 2:30 or better trotters.

Third dam the McKinstry mare, the dam of Shark, 2:27¾. HAMBLETONIAN, the grandsire of DEXTER PRINCE, has 40 trotters in the 2:30 list, 44 daughters that have produced 2:30 trotters, and more than 100 sons that have sired 2:30 trotters.

CLARK CHIEF, the grandsire on the sire's side, was the sire of performing and producing sons and daughters.

DEXTER PRINCE has faster blood lines, on both sides, than any other stallion in the world—Guy, 2:10¾, and Jay-Eye-See, 2:10.

TERMS.

$100 for the season, with usual return privileges. Payable before mares are removed. Good pasture, and the best care furnished, but no responsibility assumed for accidents.

PREMIUM.

$250 will be given to the first of the produce of DEXTER PRINCE put in the 2:30 list, and $100 each after the first. Address

L. M. MORSE, Lodi, Cal.

The Trotting Stallion

Silver Bow

W ll make the season of 1890 at the Oakland Race Track.

Pedigree.

SILVER BOW, 11708. 2 y. o. rec., 2:37.

- Robert McGregor 647, 2:17½, Sire of Bonnie McGregor 2:13½, Earl McGregor, 2:21¼, Mac D., 2:30, McGregor Boy, 2:29¾, Mark Time, 2:30, Roxie McGregor, 2:20¾
  - Major Edsall, 2:11, 2:29
    - Alexander's Abdallah 15, Sire of Goldsmith Maid, 2:14. { Hambletonian 10, sire of Dexter, 2:17¼ / by Young Patriot
    - by Harris' Hambletonian 2. { Bishop's Hambletonian / The Munson Mare
  - Nancy Whitman, 2:30¾
    - American Star 14 { Stockholm's American Star / Sally Slouch
    - Nance, Dam of Madeleine, 2:23½. { Durland's Young Messenger Duroc / untraced
- Sadie
  - Hambletonian 10, Sire of Geo. Wilkes, 2:22, (sire of Guy Wilkes, 2:15¼) also Electioneer, sire of Sunol, 3 y. o. record, 2:10½, and Palo Alto, 2:12¼.
    - Abdallah { Mambrino / Amazonia
    - Chas. Kent Mare. { imp. Bellfounder / One Eye
  - Lady Wynne
    - Wm. Welch 341, sire of Jeremiah, 2:22¾. { Hambletonian 10 / the dam of Prince, 2:27
    - Eleanora Margrave { imp. Margrave 1455 / Fanny Wright, thoroughbred

DESCRIPTION.

SILVER BOW is a handsome bay, no white; 15-2½ hands high; weighs 1075 pounds; of fine form, with the best of legs and a clean cut, intelligent head. Is remarkably level headed, seldom making a break; wears 7-ounce shoes in front. His record, 2:37, is no mark of his speed; he can beat 30 easy, and with his gilt-edge breeding, he is just what he ought to be, a trotter sired by a trotter whose dam was herself a trotter and his grandam the dam of two trotters. His dam Sadie being by Hambletonian 10, shows him to be bred from the cream of the trotting blood.

TERMS: $100 for the season. Mares not proving in foal returnable for the season of 1891 free of charge. Good pasturage and first-class care taken of mares for $5 per month. No responsibility assumed for escapes or accidents. For further particulars, address

Limited to 15 approved mares.
Season to end June 1st, 1890.

P. J. WILLIAMS.
Care Race Track, Oakland, Cal.

SANMATEO STOCKFARM

HOME OF GUY WILKES,

Record, 2:15 1-4.

Guy Wilkes' Book is full for 1890 and 1891, and positively no more mares will be received.

Sable Wilkes, three-year-old record 2:18, will be allowed to serve 25 mares in addition to those already engaged at $250 the season of 1890. SABLE Wilkes, 15½ hands, black horse, by Guy Wilkes, first dam Sable by The Moor; second dam Gretchen by Mambrino Pilot; third dam Kitty Kirkman by Canada Chief; fourth dam by Fanning's Tobe; fifth dam by imp. Leviathan.

Leo Wilkes, brown horse, four years, 16 hands, full brother to Sable Wilkes, will be allowed to serve 30 mares at $100 the season

Mares not proving with foal may be returned the following season free of service fee. Parties engaging the services of any of the above horses must send a deposit of 10 per cent. of service money with engagement. Pasturage $6 per month, and when the condition of the animal requires it, hay or grain, or both, are fed, the charge will be $12 50 per month. Good care will be taken of all mares sent to the Farm, but no liability will be assumed for accidents or escapes.

All bills are due at time of service, but must be paid by August 1st of each year. No stock will be allowed to leave the place until all bills are paid.

WILLIAM CORBITT.
San Mateo Stock Farm.

Pleasanton Stock Farm Co.'s Stallions,

DIRECTOR, 2:17.

Director's book is open for 15 good mares more than already booked for the season of 1890, at $300 each.

This is the cheapest service fee ever charged for a stallion, taking into consideration his BREEDING and RACE RECORD and the RACE RECORDS OF HIS COLTS.

Season to commence February 15th and close August 1st.

CORRECTOR, Four Years Old.

Sire Director 2:17, dam Brainey, she by Echo. Echo sired by Rysdyk's Hambletonian, out of Magnolia, she by Seely's American Star, Brainey's dam Lady Dudley, she by Tom Dudley by, Blacknose, a son of Medoc, he by American Eclipse. Lady Dudley's dam by Bertrand, Jr., a son of Bertrand.

CORRECTOR is a rich seal brown 15¾ hands high, and is the fastest young stallion in the world under the same conditions, never having been off the farm where raised and never been shod or driven for speed before last Christmas, and can trot quarters now in 35 seconds, a 2:20 gait

He will be allowed to serve ten good mares, at $100 each for the season, which closes June 1st.

DECORATOR, Four Years Old.

Sire Director 2:17, dam Chess, sired by Cardinal 2.37, trial 2:28, he by Gen. Gifford's Morgan, dam of Cardinal, sired by Joe Gales of Ohio, he by Marlborough out of the Duchess of Marlborough by Southern Eclipse; second dam old Duchess of Marlborough by Sir Archy; third dam by imp Eclipse. Decorator's second dam a Morgan and Messenger mare.

Decorator is a light bay 15½ hands high, and with but little handling for speed can show quarters in 37½ seconds, a 2:30 gait.

He will be allowed to serve ten good mares at $50 each for the season, which closes June 1st.

For further information call or address M. SALISBURY, 320 Sansome Street, Room 26, San Francisco, or

PLEASANTON STOCK FARM CO.;
Pleasanton, Alameda Co., Cal.

THE "BLUE ROCK" TARGET.

Quotations furnished F. O. B. at Cleveland, Ohio, or San Francisco.

CLABROUGH, GOLCHER & CO.,

630 and 632 Montgomery Street, S. F., Cal.

SOLE AGENTS for the Pacific Coast.

Langtry Farms' Stud

Imp. FRIAR TUCK

By the Immortal HERMIT

DAM ROMPING GIRL BY WILD DAYRELL,

AT $50 THE SEASON.

Mares not proving with foal may be returned the following season. Good care taken of mares, but no liabilities for accidents or escapes.

Good Pasturage at $5 per month.

Mares shipped to ST. HELENA, care CHARTES WILLIAM ABY, St. Helena Stables, will be cared for. For further particulars address,

CHAS. WILLIAM ABY,
Middletown, Lake County, Cal.

2:08 3-4 2:10 2:12

MAMBRINO WILKES, 6083.

SIRE OF

GUS WILKES, 2:22; ALPHEUS, 2:27; CLARA P, 2:29½; BALKAN, 2:29½ (3-year-old) and timed separately 2:22¼ in 4-year-old Stake, Bay District Track, October 14, 1889.

DESCRIPTION.

Black; sixteen hands; weighs, in exercise, 1,260 lbs. For style, finish, symmetry and proportion, comparison is challenged with any trotting bred horse. His colts follow in size, style and beauty. Balkan, for instance, being "facile princeps" of trotters in these particulars.

PEDIGREE.

Sired by Geo. Wilkes, sire of Harry Wilkes, 2:13½, Guy Wilkes, 2:15¼, and 80 other trotters in the 2:30 list, in addition to 8 pacers, and of the sire of Axtell, 2:12 (three-year-old), beating all stallions of any age, and the sire of Regal Wilkes, 2:20¾, best two-year-old stallion record.

First dam Lady Chrisman by Mambrino (Todhunter's), son of Mambrino Chief 11; sire of Lady Thorn, 2:18¼; Woodford Mambrino, 2:21½, and four others in 2:30, and of the dams of Director, 2:17, Piedmont, 2:17¼, Onward, 2:25¼, etc.

Second dam by Pilot Jr. 12, sire of nine in the 2:30 list, and of the dams of Maud S., 2:08¾, Jay-Eye-See, 2:10, Nutwood, 2:18¾, Viking, 2:19¼, Pilot Boy, 2:20, Naiad Queen, 2:20¼, etc.

TERMS.

Mares from a distance will be received at the Dexter Stables, Oakland, or Livery Stable, Martinez, the owner notifying Smith Hill, Superintendent at the farm. Good pasture and plenty of water. For the purpose of placing the service of a Wilkes within reach of breeders, the same rate will be maintained as last year, to wit, $75 for the season. Although it is not admitted thereby that this horse is inferior as a producer to the horses whose fees are placed at from $150 to $500. Address

SMITH HILL,
San Miguel Stock Farm,
Walnut Creek, Contra Costa Co., Cal.

2:12¾ 2:13½ 2:15¼

2:08¾ 2:10 2:12

BALKAN

By Mambrino Wilkes.

(See that Horse's Advertisement.)

DAM FANNY FERN BY JACK HAWKINS
Son of Boston.

The grandam of Maud S. (2:08¾) was by Boston and the grandam of Jay-Eye-See (2:10) was by Lexington, son of Boston. So Balkan is the same remove from Boston that Maud is, and one remove nearer than Jay-Eye-See.

Fanny Fern has produced Molly Drew, Onyx, Fred Arnold, Molly Fern and Balkan, all by different sires.

Balkan's sire and dam both being producers, and he being a trotter himself with a record of 2:29 1-2 (three-year-old) and timed separately 2:22 1-4 in 4-year-old Stake, Bay District Track, October 14, 1889—it is but fair to presume that he will get trotters of the highest order.

DESCRIPTION.

He is seal brown, 16 hands high, in style rivalled by few, and excelled by none with as pure a gait as has yet been exhibited in public—bar none.

Balkan will be at Oakland Trotting Park for the season of 1890, and will be limited to ten mares, at $100 fee, in order to be put in training early, as it is morally certain that if given a reasonable opportunity he will be fast enough to compete with the best of his age. For further particulars, address

A. L. HINDS,
Dexter Stables, Oakland

2:12¾ 2:13½ 2:15¼

JESSE E. MARKS & CO.,

Wholesale and Retail Dealers of Choice Brands

Havana & Key West Cigars

922 MARKET ST., S. F.

2:19 NOONDAY 2:20½

STANDARD No. 10,000.

This celebrated trotting bred stallion will make the season of 1890 at the stable of the undersigned at Sacramento, Cal., at $75 for the season and $100 to insure a mare in foal. Payable on or before July 1st, 1890. Money will be refunded on mares bred by insurance as soon as the fact becomes known that they are not in foal.

- NOONDAY.
  - Wedgewood, 2:19... Sire of Favonia, 2:15, fastest 4th heat for any mare or gelding, and eight others in 2:27 or better.
    - Belmont... Sire of Wedgewood, 2:19, Nutwood, 2:18¾, Viking, 2:19¼, and 29 others in 2:30 list.
      - Alexander's Abdallah, sire of Goldsmith Maid, 2.14; Almont, with 35 horses in 2:30 list, etc.
      - Belle, dam of Hambletonian, 2:26½: Bicara, dam of Pancoast, 2:21¾, the sire of Patron, 2:14½.
    - Woodbine... Dam of Wedgewood, 2:19, Woodford Mamb., 2:21½, the sire of Pancoast, 2:21¾, the sire of Patron, 2:14½.
      - Woodford.
      - Singleton Mare.
  - Noontide, 2:20½... (Trial, 2:13½).
    - Harold... Sire of Maud S., 2:08¾, and 26 others in 2:30 list.
      - Hambletonian (Rysdyk's), sire of George Wilkes, 2:22, the sire of Guy Wilkes, 2:15¼; Electioneer, the sire of Sunol, 2:10½, and scores of noted trotters and producers.
      - Enchantress, by Abdallah 1.
    - Midnight... Dam of Jay-Eye-See, 2:10, Noontide, 2:20½.
      - Pilot Jr., sire of dams of Maud S., 2:08¾, Jay-Eye-See, 2:10, Nutwood, 2:18¾, etc.
      - Twilight, by Lexington, sire of the dam of Ansel, 2:20.

NOODAY is a dark seal brown, foaled 1884, 15 hands 1½ inches high. Individually he is equal to his royal breeding. He is all that can be desired in conformation, intelligence, color and trotting action, and no stallion now in public service can show a pedigree with such fast records and royal game trotting blood as Noonday.

DON MARVIN,

Record 2:28 as a five-year-old. Standard by Breeding and Performance

Standard No. 7927.

Don Marvin 2:28.

Don Marvin is a beautiful seal brown, foaled 1884, bred by Hon. Leland Stanford, Palo Alto, Cal., standing 16 hands, and weighs, in ordinary condition, 1200 lbs. He is a fine individual, good style and form, combined with great substance, and good temper. Is very level headed; in his first race the past season he only made one break in five closely contested heats. He has great speed and endurance, with the pure, rapid Electioneer gait. He trots without toe weights, and wears only 8 oz. shoes in front. He gained his record the past season in the third heat, on a slow track, after making a season (serving over 30 mares), with scarcely any preparation. His record is no mark of his speed. He was a natural born trotter, and Mr. Charles Marvin considered him the fastest two year old at Palo Alto that season.

By FALLIS, 2:23, - - by Electioneer, sire of
Sire of Don Marvin, 2:28. — Sunol, three-year-old, 2:10 1-2, Palo Alto, 2:12¾, and 47 others in 2:30 list.

Dam CORA, by Don Victor by Belmont, sire of
Dam of Don Marvin, 2:28. — Ventura, 2:27¾, and sire of the dam of Bell Echo, 2:20, and six others in 2:30 list.

2d dam CLARABEL, - by Abdallah Star,
Dam of Clifton Bell, 2:24 1-2, and grandam of Rexford, three years, 2:24. — Sire of Hattie Maples, 2:33.

3d dam FAIRY, - - by Rysdyk's Hambletonian,
Sister of Sweepstakes, sire of 16 in 2:30 list. — Sire of Electioneer, George Wilkes, and many other noted sires and trotters.

4th dam EMMA MILLS, by Seely's American Star,
Dam of 4 horses that have 2:30 performers. — The great broodmare sire of the world.

The above pedigree should show every intelligent breeder that Don Marvin is "high" bred though very strong in trotting blood. All the comment it is deemed necessary to make as to the value of "thoroughbred blood" in the trotter is simply to refer to the very significant fact that the first and second dams of Maud S., 2:08¾, Jay-Eye-See 2:10, Sunol, three years 2:10 1-2, Palo Alto 2:12¾, Anteeo 2:16¼, Nutwood 2:18¾, Wedgewood 2:19, and many other successful sires and sensational trotters of the day are thoroughbred.

TERMS—Don Marvin will make the ensuing season from February 1st to July 1st, 1890, at $40 the season, with the usual privilege of returning the mare next season if not proving in foal. Mares from a distance met at the cars or boats on notification, and carefully handled, but no responsibility assumed for accidents or escapes.

Good alfalfa pasture furnished (free from barb wire fence) at $4 per month. For further particulars or complete circulars address

F. P. LOWELL,
1520 F Street, Sacramento, Cal.

The Produce of Eros Averaged $2,200 Each at New York Auction Sale in 1889.

THE ELECTIONEER TROTTING STALLION,

5326 EROS 5326

Will make the season of 1890—February 1st to July 1st—at LA SIESTA RANCH, MENLO PARK, adjoining Palo Alto.

PEDIGREE.

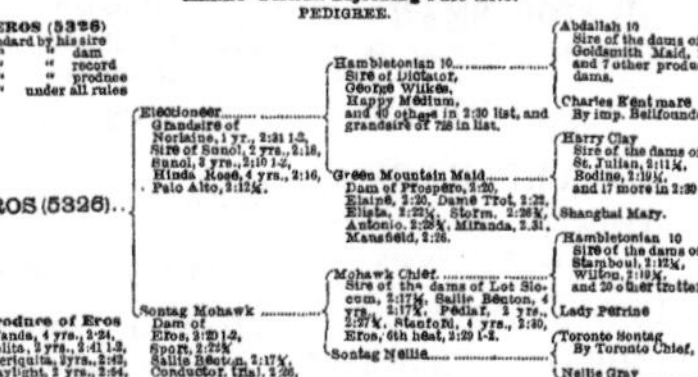

EROS (5326)
Standard by his sire
" " dam
" " record
" " produce
" under all rules

- EROS (5326)..
  - Electioneer... Grandsire of Norlaine, 1 yr., 2:31 1-2, Sire of Sunol, 2 yrs., 2:18, Sunol, 3 yrs., 2:10 1-2, Hinda Rose, 4 yrs., 2:16, Palo Alto, 2:12¾.
    - Hambletonian 10... Sire of Dictator, George Wilkes, Happy Medium, and 40 others in 2:30 list, and grandsire of 728 in list.
      - Abdallah 10. Sire of the dams of Goldsmith Maid, 2:14, and 7 other producing dams.
      - Charles Kent mare By imp. Bellfounder.
    - Green Mountain Maid... Dam of Prospero, 2:20, Elaine, 2:20, Dame Trot, 2:22, Elista, 2:22¾, Storm, 2:26¾, Antonio, 2:28¾, Miranda, 2.31, Mansfeld, 2:26.
      - Harry Clay. Sire of the dams of St. Julian, 2:11¾, Bodine, 2:19¼, and 17 more in 2:30 list
      - Shanghai Mary.
  - Sontag Mohawk... Dam of Eros, 2:29 1-2, Sport, 2:22¾, Sallie Benton, 2:17¾, Conductor, trial, 2:26, Colma, 2-y-o trial, 2:24.
    - Mohawk Chief... Sire of the dams of Lot Slocum, 2:17¾, Sallie Benton, 4 yrs., 2:17¾, Pedlar, 3 yrs., 2:27¾, Stanford, 4 yrs., 2:30, Eros, 6th heat, 2:29 1-2.
      - Hambletonian 10. Sire of the dams of Stamboul, 2:12¾, Wilton, 2:19¼, and 20 other trotters.
      - Lady Perrine
    - Sontag Nellie...
      - Toronto Sontag. By Toronto Chief,
      - Nellie Gray. 5-mile record, 13:45.

Produce of Eros
Wanda, 4 yrs., 2:24,
Solita, 2 yrs., 2:41 1-2,
Meriquita, 2 yrs., 2:42,
Daylight, 2 yrs., 2:44,
Hiram B., trial, 2:28.

These are the only colts by him that have ever had a harness on except one in New York that went a trial last July in 2:26 1-2.

DESCRIPTION.

EROS is a rich seal brown stallion, bred by Hon. Leland Stanford at Palo Alto, and is the nearest living likeness of his celebrated sire, Electioneer. Stands 15.2 hands high, and weighs 1050 pounds

In breeding to Eros, the owners of mares will strictly follow the great rule of breeding, viz., breed to a stallion by a producer and out of a sure producer of great speed. Eros is by the stallion that has produced more 2:30 trotters that any living horse, and is also the sire of more 2:30 performers than any horse living or dead.

EROS is out of the dam of Sally Benton, four years old, record 2:17¾, Sport 2:22¾, and Eros 2:29½ in the sixth heat, against a field of nine horses. He is from a family that is endowed with great natural speed, trot fast at an early age, train on, throw trotters from all classes of mares, are of good substance, bone, style and action, and breed solid colors.

TERMS.

$100 for the season, with the privilege of return next season should mares not be in foal and horse and mare still remain in the same hands.

Good pasturage can be obtained at $5 per month, but no responsibility for accidents or escapes. There are a large number of box stalls, and animals can be kept up and fed on hay and grain at reasonable rates if required. Mares already in foal can be sent to the ranch for foaling, and will receive all the attention bestowed upon our own mares. Mares left with Mr. Peter Pomyea, Broadway Street Stable, Oakland, or with Mr. F. H. Burke, 401 Montgomery Street, San Francisco, will be forwarded to the ranch free of charge. For further particulars apply to

W. H. VIOGET,
LA SIESTA RANCH, MENLO PARK, CAL.

EROS is the only stallion offered to the public on this Coast that has a dam that has three in the 2:30 list.

POPLAR GROVE Breeding Farm

STALLIONS.

CLOVIS, 4909,

CLOVIS is a beautiful black, Eight Years Old, 16 1-2 Hands High, and weighs 1260 lbs.

He is a horse of beautiful symmetry and magnificent action.

PEDIGREE.

CLOVIS was sired by Sultan, 2:24, sire of Stamboul, 2:12 1-4, Ruby, 2:19¾, and fifteen others with records of 2:30 or better.

First dam Sweetbriar by Thorndale 2:22 1-2, sire of Edwin Thorne, 2:16 1-2, Daisy Dale, 2.19, and May Thorne, 2:28

Second dam Ulster Queen, dam of Volmer, 2:24¾ by Hambletonian 10. Sire of Dexter, 2 17¼, George Wilkes, 2:22.

Third dam by Thomas Jefferson, a son of Mambrino Paymaster, Jr.

Fourth dam by Mambrino Paymaster, sire of Mambrino Chief.

Sultan, by The Moor, sire of Beautiful Bells, dam of Hinda Rose, 2:19 1-2, and Sable, dam of Sable Wilkes, three year old record 2:18.

First dam of Sultan, Sultana, by Delmonico. Sire of Darby, 2:16 1-2, by Guy Miller, sire of Whipple's Hambletonian.

Second dam by Mambrino Chief.

Third dam by Downing's Bay Messenger.

Fourth dam Mrs. Caudle, dam of Ericsson, four year old record 2.30 1-2.

Clovis will make the season of 1890 at Poplar Grove Breeding Farm, near Wildflower, Fresno County, commencing February 1st and ending July 1st.

Terms, $75, due at time of service.

Mares cared for in any manner owners may desire; pasturage $2 per month. Every care exercised, but no liability for escapes or accidents. Mares not proving with foal can be returned next season, providing I still own this stallion.

APEX, 8935.

FOUR-YEAR-OLD RECORD, FOURTH HEAT, 2:26.

Will make the present season at the Poplar Grove Breeding Farm, near Wildflower, Fresno Co., season commencing Feb. 1st, and ending July 1, 1890. Terms, $50 the season, due at time of service. Apex is eight years old, a beautiful bay, 15 1-2 hands high, and weighs 1140 lbs. He is a horse of fine disposition, and his gait is faultless.

PEDIGREE.

Apex was sired by Prompter 2305, he by Blue Bull 75; first dam Mary by Flaxtail, he by Pruden's Blue Bull, Flaxtail being the sire of the dams of Buccaneer, five-year-old record, 2:24 1-2; Pride, yearling record, 2:44 1-2, and Shamrock, two-year old record, 2:25, third heat. Second dam by Bright Eyes, son of Boanarages. Prompter (sire of Apex, record 2:26, and Transit, 2:26 1-2), by Wilson's Blue Bull, by Pruden's Blue Bull, son of Merring's Blue Bull. Prompter's dam Prairie Bird, by Flaxtail; second dam by John the Baptist, son of Tally Ho Morgan, by Sherman Morgan; third dam Fannie Fern by Irwin's Tuckaho.

Apex made his appearance in the circuit as a two-year-old, and obtained a record of 2:42. As a three-year-old he reduced this in a race at Santa Rosa against Stamboul to 2:31, it taking six heats to decide the contest, which was won by Apex. As a four year-old he gained his present record of 2:26.

Mares cared for in any manner owners may desire. Pasturage $2 per month. Every care exercised, but no liabilities for escapes or accidents. Mares not proving with foal can be returned next season, providing I still own this stallion.

The Standard Stallion

JUNIO,

RECORD 2:22.

WILL MAKE THE PRESENT SEASON OF [illegible]
AT FRESNO FAIR GROUNDS.

Season Commencing Feb. 1st an ending July 1st.

TERMS—$100 the season, due at time of service.

JUNIO is eight years old, a handsome dark bay 16 hands high, and weighs 1250 pounds. He is the personification of the light harness horse, and his trotting action is superb. At the State Fair of 1886 he took first premium over forty of the finest trotters in the State.

PEDIGREE.

Junio, by Electioneer, premier stallion of Palo Alto (sire of Sunol 2 10 1-2, Palo Alto 2:12 1-4, and 47 others in the 2 30 list.). Dam by Granger by imp. Hercules.

Granger, by imp. Hercules, dam Jenny Lind, by Stockbridge Chief, Jr., he by Stockbridge Chief, he by Vermont Black Hawk. Second dam by Kentucky Whip.

Imp. Hercules, by Kingston, first dam daughter of Tuscar, by Bay Middleton, second dam Malvina, by Oscar; 3rd dam Spotiless by Walton; 4th dam by Trumpator (see Bruce's American Stud Book, Vol. 1, page 28). Hercules is the sire of the dam of Azmoor 2:20¼; also sire of dam of Menlo 2:21 1-2.

Mares not proving in foal may be returned next year free of charge, providing I still have the horse. Pasturage $3 per month. While every care will be taken of horses, no liability will be assumed for accidents or escapes.

For further particulars address

S. N. STRAUBE, Fresno, Cal.
Poplar Grove Breeding Farm.

BOYCE TABLETS.

Leg and Body Wash.

THE BOYCE TABLETS are packed in a nicely decorated metal box with hinged lid—one hundred tablets in each box; directions for use plainly engraved upon the box; therefore, the convenience of the package—no liability to leakage and breakage—economy and ready solubility, together with the absolute certainty of their action, will at once commend the use of BOYCE'S TABLETS to the intelligent horsemen of the country. TABLETS sufficient to make one hundred pints of leg and body wash are conveniently carried in an inside coat pocket or in the hip-pocket of the trousers.

The BOYCE WASH can be applied ALL OVER THE BODY WITHOUT FEAR OF BLISTERING NOR DOES IT AFFECT THE KIDNEYS.

The BOYCE WASH will cure CRACKED HEELS, PUFFS, STOCKINGS, SCRATCHES, INFLAMED TENDONS and FEVERED LEGS.

Price per Box of One Hundred Tablets, $2, sent postpaid to any part of the United States; six boxes for $10. A sample of BOYCE'S TABLETS will be mailed to any address on application. These TABLETS are warranted to keep in any climate. Address

BOYCE TABLET COMPANY,
600 Wabash Avenue, - - - Terre Haute, Indiana.

J. A. McKERRON, Pacific Coast Ag't,
228-230-232 Ellis Street, San Francisco, Cal.

Poplar Grove Breeding FARM.

Standard-bred Trotters, Colts and Fillies.

The get of CLOVIS, 4909; PASHA, 2039; APEX, 2935,

For Sale.

Address S. N. STRAUBE, Poplar Grove Breeding Farm,

Fresno, Cal.

Inspection by intending purchasers invited, and information by mail.

J. O'KANE, Horse Boots, Clothing and Furnishings,
For Track, Driving Training and Stable.
Every requisite for Horsemen.
Harness, Medicines, Etc.

ADVERTISE YOUR STALLIONS

—IN THE—

Breeder & Sportsman

For the Season---1890.

We are pleased to announce that we have the best facilities for furnishing

Stallion Pictures,
Stallion Cards,
Pedigrees, Folders,
Contracts, Bills, Etc.

We make a specialty of this department of our business, and have UNRIVALED FACILITIES FOR LOOKING UP PEDIGREES and doing accurate and handsome work.

Promptness, Good Work, Low Prices.

BREEDER AND SPORTSMAN,
313 Bush Street, S. F.

THE BUCKINGHAM.
OLD STRAIGHT WHISKIES.
141 Montgomery Street.
303 Bush Street, S. F.
M. J. BALFE, Proprietor.

"DICKEY'S,"
SIXTH AVENUE AND D ST.
Near entrance to Bay District Track.
Choicest Brands of
WINES AND CIGARS.
A Delightful Resort.
Telephone 1485. J. R. DICKEY, Propr

PHIL J. CRIMMINS. JOHN C. MORRISON.
"Silver Palace,"
36 Geary Street,
San Francisco, Cal.

ROME HARRIS. JOHN MERIGAN.
"Laurel Palace,"
N. W. corner Kearny and Bush Streets
SAN FRANCISCO.

NOTICE.

C. BRUCE LOWE,
Pedigree Stock Agent,
19 Bligh Street,
SYDNEY, New South Wales.
Reference—J. B. HAGGIN, ESQ.

HORSES PURCHASED ON COMMISSION.
THOROUGHBREDS A SPECIALTY.
Will select and buy, or buy selected Animals for all desiring, for reasonable compensation.
KEEPS PROMISING YOUNGSTERS IN VIEW.
L. M. LASLEY, Stanford, Ky.
References:—J. W. Guest, Danville, Ky.
B. G. Bruce, Lexington, Ky.
S. H. Baughman, Stanford, Ky.
G. A. Lackey, Stanford, Ky.
Geo. McAlister, Stanford, Ky.
First National Bank, Stanford, Ky.

Fine Hats,
Latest Styles and Colors.
Meussdorffer & Hubner
8 Kearny Street, San Francisco,
Next to New Chronicle Building.

The Park Training Stable.

CHAS. DAVID, Proprietor.
Corner Grove and Baker Streets, near Entrance to Golden Gate Park.
EVERY FACILITY FOR TRAINING COLTS and taking care of Gentlemen's Roadsters.

Finely appointed stable with every convenience and sixteen roomy box stalls.
The best care given all horses by experienced help, under the personal superintendence of the proprietor.
Convenient to the Park Speed Drive, and Accessible to Six Lines of Cable Cars.
THE TRAINING OF COLTS AND ROADSTERS A SPECIALTY.
TROTTERS AND ROADSTERS FOR SALE.
HORSES SOLD ON COMMISSION.
The proprietor trained and brought out the following well known horses: "Sister, Huntress," "Perihelion," "Nona Y," and others.

GOLDEN EAGLE HOTEL

Corner SEVENTH and K STREETS,
SACRAMENTO.
FIRST CLASS IN EVERY RESPECT.
The LARGEST and FINEST HOTEL in the City.
W. O. BOWERS, Proprietor.
Free 'Buss to and from the Hotel.
Telephone, Telegraph Office and Messenger Service at Hotel

Trade  Mark

Six Cases
S. ALLCOCK & CO.'S
Unequalled Fishing Tackle
Received direct by Steamer EXPLORER, from Liverpool, December 26, 1889.
E. T. ALLEN,
Sole Agent for Pacific Coast,
Fire Arms and Sporting Goods
416 Market St., S. F.

THE HICKS-JUDD CO.

Successors to
HICKS & JUDD, Bookbinders,
and Women's Co-operative Printing Office.
Printers, Bookbinders, Publishers,
23 First St., San Francisco.
BREEDERS' CATALOGUES A SPECIALTY.

By-Laws
—AND—
Rules and Regulations
—OF THE—
NATIONAL
Trotting Association
ALSO THE
AMERICAN
Trotting Association,
AND THE
PACIFIC COAST BLOOD-HORSE ASSOCIATION.
With Betting Rules.
For Sale at the Office of the
Breeder and Sportsman,
313 Bush St., S. F., Cal.
Price, 25c. each.
By Mail, Postage Paid, 30c. each.

KENNEL ADVERTISEMENTS

Puppies for Sale

TWO GORDON SETTER BITCH PUPPIES, months old.
TWO YORKSHIRE TERRIER DOG PUPPIES, months old, by Sirlp's Mash, winner of first prize in last three Bench Shows.
SIX MASTIFF PUPPIES, by a son of Scott "Dick," winner of first prize in last two Bench Shows.
Apply to JAMES E. WATSON,
516 Sacramento street,
P. O. Box 1838. San Francisco

Thoroughbred Pugs, $40 each.

PEDIGREE.

PUPPIES: Fido — Imp. Jumbo (Marshall's Ut..., Lady Bess); Fanni (Rex, Imp. Fly). Budge — Senator Fair's Fritz; McCleery's Mamma Snoots (Sam, Imp. Alice).

Can be seen daily from 9 A. M. to 3 P. M. at 411 Bush Street, San Francisco.
J. F. B. McCLEERY.

Irish Setters & Pointers

In the Stud, winner of 16 first and special prizes, CHAMPION MIKE T., 6436, A. K. R. B. Irish Setter puppies by Champion Mike T. 6436 A. K. B.—Champion Lady Elcho T. 6451 A. K. S. B., for sale. Two pointers, a year old, by Rush T. 10,069 K. S. B.—Champion Patti Croxteth T. 10128 A. K. B. for sale. Yard broken. Address,
A. B. TRUMAN,
1425 Steiner St., S. F., Cal.

FOX TERRIERS—C. A. SUMNER, Fort St., Los Angeles, Breeder of Fox Terriers. Blemton Vesuvian (14290), by Champion Lucifer, at stud.

CALIFORNIA SPANIEL KENNELS

Oakland, California. H. P. RENNIE, Prop. Breeder and importer of typical COCKER SPANIELS. Winner of first prizes at S. F. and Los Angeles, also, Columbus, New York, 1887. In the stud, solid Black Cocker dog, GIFFIE, won 1st and Gold Medal at S. F. Fee, $25. Puppies and grown dogs at reasonable prices. My dogs can neither talk nor climb a tree, but are fielders and prize winners.

Fiske's Vanes.
MADE OF COPPER
And Gilded with PURE GOLD LEAF.
Manufacturer's Agent.
The HOWE SCALE CO
411 & 413 Market Street, S. F.
Scales for Weighing of
Live Stock
SEEDS, FEED, Etc.
Write for Catalogue.

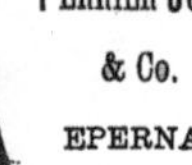

PERRIER-JOUET
& Co.
EPERNAY
CHAMPAGNE
W. B CHAPMAN,
Sole Agent for Pacific Coast.
For sale by all first-class Wine Merchants and Grocers.

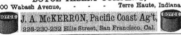

Southern Pacific Co.

(PACIFIC SYSTEM.)

Trains leave and are due to arrive at San Francisco.

LEAVE (FOR)	FROM JANUARY 1, 1890.	ARRIVE (FROM)
7.30 A M	Haywards, Niles and San Jose ...	*12.45 P M
7.30 A M	Sacramento and Redding, via Davis	7.15 P M
7.30 A M	Sacramento, Auburn, Colfax	5.45 P M
8.00 A M	Martinez, Vallejo, Calistoga and Santa Rosa	6.15 P M
8.30 A M	Los Angeles Express, Fresno, Bakersfield, Mojave and East and Los Angeles	11.15 A M
8.30 A M	Niles, San Jose, Stockton, Ione, Sacramento, Marysville, Oroville and Red Bluff	5.45 P M
10.30 A M	Haywards and Niles	2.15 P M
12.00 M	Haywards, Niles and San Jose	* 3.45 P M
1.00 P M	Sacramento River Steamers	**6.00 A M
3.00 P M	Haywards, Niles and San Jose	9.45 A M
3.30 P M	2d Class for Ogden and East	10.45 P M
4.00 P M	Stockton and Milton; Vallejo, Calistoga and Santa Rosa	9.45 A M
4.30 P M	Sacramento and Knight's Landing via Davis	10.45 A M
4.30 P M	Niles and Livermore	* 8.45 A M
4.30 P M	Niles and San Jose	‡ 4.15 P M
5.30 P M	Haywards and Niles	7.45 A M
6.00 P M	Sunset Route, Atlantic Express, Santa Barbara, Los Angeles, Deming, El Paso, New Orleans and East	8.45 P M
7.00 P M	Shasta Route Express, Sacramento, Marysville, Redding, Portland, Puget Sound and East	7.45 A M
9.00 P M	Central Atlantic Express, Ogden and East	9.45 A M

SANTA CRUZ DIVISION.

LEAVE		ARRIVE
7.00 A M	Hunters train to San Jose	‡ 7.20 P M
8.15 A M	Newark, Centerville, San Jose, Felton, Boulder Creek and Santa Cruz	8.50 P M
2.15 P M	Centerville, San Jose, Almaden, Felton, Boulder Creek and Santa Cruz	*11.50 A M
4.15 P M	Centerville, San Jose, and Los Gatos	9.50 A M

Coast Division (Third and Townsend Sts.)

LEAVE		ARRIVE
7.25 A M	San Jose, Almaden and Way Stations	2.30 P M
8.30 A M	San Jose, Gilroy, Tres Pinos; Pajaro, Santa Cruz; Monterey; Pacific Grove, Salinas, San Miguel, Paso Robles, Santa Margarita (San Luis Obispo) and principal Way Stations	6.12 P M
10.30 A M	San Jose and Way Stations	5.02 P M
12.01 P M	Cemetery, Menlo Park and Way Stations	3.38 P M
3.30 P M	San Jose, Tres Pinos, Santa Cruz, Salinas, Monterey Pacific Grove and principal Way Stations	*10.00 A M
4.20 P M	Menlo Park and Way Station	* 7.58 A M
5.20 P M	San Jose and Way Stations	9.03 A M
6.30 P M	Menlo Park and Way Stations	6.35 A M
11.45 P M	Menlo Park and principal Way Stations	†7.28 P M

A M for Morning. P M for Afternoon.
*Sundays excepted. †Saturdays only. ‡Sundays only.
**Mondays excepted. §Saturdays excepted.

OCEANIC STEAMSHIP CO.

Carrying United States, Hawaiian and Colonial Mails.

WILL LEAVE THE COMPANY'S WHARF, foot of Mission Street, No. 1,

For Honolulu, Auckland and Sydney,

WITHOUT CHANGE,

The Splendid New 3,000-ton Iron Steamer.

ZEALANDIA ..... Saturday, March 8, 1890, at 12 M., Or immediately on arrival of the English mails.

For Honolulu,

AUSTRALIA (3,000 tons), February 28, 1890, at 12 M

☞ For freight or passage, apply at office, 327 Market Street. JOHN D. SPRECKELS & BROS. General Agents.

KILLIP & CO.,

LIVE STOCK AND GENERAL AUCTIONEERS,

22 Montgomery Street, San Francisco

SPECIAL ATTENTION PAID TO SALES OF

High-Bred Horses and Cattle.

At auction and private sale.

Will Sell in All Cities and Counties of the State.

REFERENCES.

HON. C. GREEN, Sacramento.	HON. J. D. CARR Salinas.
J. P. SARGENT, ESQ., Sargents.	HON. JOHN BOGGS Colusa.
HON. L. J. ROSE, Los Angeles.	HON. A. WALRATH Nevada.

J. B. HAGGIN, ESQ., San Francisco.

Represented at Sacramento by Edwin F. Smith Secretary State Agricultural Society.

At San Jose by Messrs. Montgomery & Rea, Real Estate Agents.

Being the oldest established firm in the live-stock business on this Coast, and having conducted the important auction sales in this line for the past fifteen years, amounting to one half a million of dollars, we feel justified in claiming unequaled facilities for disposing of live stock of every description, either at auction or private sale. Our list of correspondents embraces every breeder and dealer of prominence upon the Pacific Coast, thus enabling us to give full publicity to animals placed with us for sale. Private purchases and sales of live stock of all descriptions will be made on commission, and stock shipped with the utmost care. Purchases and sales made of land of every description. We are authorized to refer to the gentlemen whose names are appended.

KILLIP & CO., 22 Montgomery Street.

TRUMAN HOOKER & CO.

SAN FRANCISCO. - - CALIFORNIA

San Francisco and North Pacific Railway.

THE DONAHUE BROAD-GAUGE ROUTE.

COMMENCING SUNDAY, MARCH 17, 1889, AND until further notice, boats and trains will leave from and arrive at the San Francisco Passenger Depot, Market-street Wharf, as follows:

Leave San Francisco. Week Days.	Leave San Francisco. Sundays.	DESTINATION	Arrive San Francisco. Sundays.	Arrive San Francisco. Week Days.
7.40 A M 3.30 P M 5.00 P M	8.00 A M 5.00 P M	Petaluma and Santa Rosa	10.40 A M 6.10 P M	8.50 A M 10.30 A M 6 05 P M
7.40 A M 3.30 P M	8.00 A M	Fulton, Windsor, Healdsburg, Litton Springs, Cloverdale, and way stations.	6.10 P M	10.30 A M 6.05 P M
7.40 A M	8.00 A M	Hopland and Ukiah.	6.10 P M	6.05 P M
7.40 A M	8.00 A M	Guerneville	6.10 P M	6.05 P M
7.40 A M 5.00 P M	8.00 A M	Sonoma and Glen Ellen.	10.40 A M 6.10 P M	8.50 A M 6.05 P M
3.30 P M	5.00 P M	Sebastopol	10.40 A M	10.30 A M

Stage connects at Santa Rosa for White Sulphur Springs, and Mark West Springs; at Geyserville for Skaggs Springs, and at Cloverdale for the Geysers; at Hopland for Highland Springs, Kelseyville, Soda Bay, Lakeport and Bartlett Springs, and at Ukiah for Vichy Springs, Saratoga Springs, Blue Lakes, Willits, Cahto, Calpella, Potter Valley, Sherwood Valley and Mendocino City.

EXCURSION TICKETS from Saturdays to Mondays, to Petaluma, $1.50; to Santa Rosa, $2.25; to Healdsburg, $3.40; to Litton Springs, $3.60; to Cloverdale, $4.50; to Hopland, $5.70; to Ukiah, $6.75; to Guerneville, $3.75; to Sonoma, $1.50; to Glen Ellen, $1.80.

EXCURSION TICKETS, good for Sundays only, to Petaluma, $1; to Santa Rosa, $1.50; to Healdsburg, $2.25; to Litton Springs, $2.40; to Cloverdale, $3; to Guerneville, $2.50, to Sonoma, $1; to Glen Ellen, $1.20.

From San Francisco for Point Tiburon and San Rafael: Week Days—7.40, 9.20, 11.20, A. M.; 3.30, 5.00, 6.15 P. M. Sundays—8.00, 9.30, 11.00 A. M.; 1.30, 5.00, 6.20 P. M.

To San Francisco from San Rafael: Week Days—6.20, 7.55, 9.30 A. M.; 12.45, 3.40, 5.05 P. M. Sundays—8.10, 9.40 A. M.; 12.15, 3.40, 5.00 P. M.

To San Francisco from Point Tiburon: Week Days—6.50, 8.20, 9.55 A. M.; 1.10, 4.05, 5.30 P. M.; Sundays—8.40, 10.05 A. M.; 12.40, 4.05, 5.30 P. M.

On Saturdays an extra trip will be made from San Francisco to San Rafael, leaving at 1.40 P. M.

H. C. WHITING, General Manager.

PETER J. McGLYNN, Gen. Pass. & Tkt. Agt.

Ticket Offices at Ferry, 222 Montgomery Street and 2 New Montgomery Street.

CHICAGO, MILWAUKEE AND ST. PAUL RAILWAY.

Steam Heated and Electric Lighted Vestibuled Trains between Chicago, St. Paul and Minneapolis.

Electric Lighted and Steam Heated Vestibuled Trains between Chicago, Council Bluffs and Omaha.

Finest Dining Cars in the world.

Free Reclining Chair Cars between Chicago and Omaha.

Fast Mail Line between Chicago, Milwaukee, St. Paul and Minneapolis.

Transcontinental Route between Chicago, Council Bluffs and Omaha, or St. Paul.

Great National Route between Chicago, Kansas City and St. Joseph, Mo.

5,700 miles of road in Illinois, Wisconsin, Minnesota, Iowa, Missouri, South and North Dakota.

Everything First-Class.

First-Class People patronize First-Class Lines.

Ticket Agents everywhere sell Tickets over the Chicago, Milwaukee and St. Paul Railway.

W. T. ALLEN,
Pacific Coast Passenger Agent
Office, No 138 Montgomery St., San Francisco, Cal.
Under Occidental Hotel

6 DONTS

DON'T own a racehorse.
DON'T be a breeder.
DON'T be a trainer.
DON'T be a jockey.
DON'T bet on the races.
DON'T go to a race track.

WITHOUT

HAVING IN YOUR POCKET ONE OF

Goodwin's

ANNUAL

OFFICIAL TURF GUIDES.

Price, in cloth	$2.00
Price, in half morocco	3.00
Price, in half calf	4.00
If sent by mail	10 cents extra

SUBSCRIBE TO IT FOR 1890.

It is published semi-monthly during the racing season, and is but **$10 per year.** Address

GOODWIN BROS.,
241 Broadway, New York City.

Business College, 24 Post St.

—San Francisco.—

The most popular school on the Coast

P. HEALD, President. C. S. HALEY, Sec'y.

☞ Send for Circulars

Unfailing Specific for Liver Disease.

It acts with extraordinary efficacy on the *LIVER, KIDNEYS and BOWELS.*

AN EFFECTUAL SPECIFIC FOR

Malaria, Bowel Complaints, Dyspepsia, Sick Headache, Constipation, Billiousness, Kidney Affections, Jaundice, Mental Depression, Colic.

If you are a miserable sufferer with Constipation, Dyspepsia, Billiousness or Kidney Affections, seek relief at once in Simmons Liver Regulator. It does not require continual dosing and costs but a trifle. It will cure you.

☞ ONLY GENUINE ☜

Has our Z stamp in red on front of Wrapper.

J. H. ZEILIN & CO., - Philadelphia, Pa., Sole Proprietors. Price, $1.00.

DR. FISHERMAN'S

Carbolized Alkaline

LOTION

Cures after all other Remedies have Failed.

Sprains, Sores, Bruises, Galls, Swellings, Scratches, Thrush, Grease Heels, Curb, Rheumatism. Restoring Weak Knees and Ankles to their original condition. As a wash it insures flossy manes and tails. Valuable as an internal remedy for Coughs, Colic, Congestion or Fever. You really get Half a Gallon of Remedy for $1.00, or Two Gallons for $3.00, after being adulterated as directed.

This Liniment has received the endorsement of some of our best horsemen. Recommended by Jos. Cairn Simpson. See BREEDER AND SPORTSMAN of November 10th, 1888.

LYNDE & HOUGH, Proprietors.

116 California St., S. F.

Or ask your Druggist for it.

HORSE OWNERS!

TRY GOMBAULT'S

CAUSTIC BALSAM.

A Safe, Speedy and Positive Cure for Curb, Splint, Sweeny, Capped Hock, Strained Tendons, Founder, Wind Puffs, all Skin Diseases or Parasites, Thrush, Diphtheria, Pinkeye, all Lameness from Spavin, Ringbone or other Bony Tumors. Removes all Bunches or Blemishes from Horses and Cattle.

Supersedes all Cautery or Firing. **Impossible to Produce any Scar or Blemish.**

Every bottle sold is warranted to give satisfaction. Price $1.50 per bottle. Sold by druggists, or sent by express, charges paid, with full directions for its use. Send for descriptive circulars. Address LAWRENCE, WILLIAMS & CO., Cleveland, O.

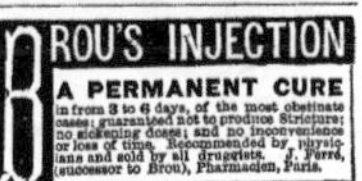

For any Kind of a

SORE THROAT

USE

McCLELLAN'S

DIPHTHERIA REMEDY

An Unfailing Cure.

FOR SALE BY ALL DRUGGISTS

OUR IMPROVED. ALL SIZES AND WEIGHTS. C.W. BOHANON.

THE BOHANON

SULKY!

BEST MADE.
Perfect Riding Buggies.
Breaking Carts.
Fine Repairing, Reasonable Prices.

Bohanon Carriage Co., 161-163 Ogden Ave., CHICAGO.

Send for Catalogue.

VETERINARY.

Dr. Wm. H. Jones, M.R.C.V.S.

Veterinary Surgeon,

(OLYMPIC CLUB STABLES)

503 Sutter Street, San Francisco.

Telephone, No. 1404.

Consultations by letter, and cases of URGENT NECESSITY in the interior will receive prompt attention.

Dr. A. E. BUZARD,

VETERINARY SURGEON,

Member of the Royal College of Veterinary Surgeons, London, England. Graduated April 22d, 1870.

All Operations on the Horse Performed Skillfully.

Special attention given to the Diseases of Dogs. Calls to the country promptly attended to. Advice and prescriptions by mail $2. Office and Residence, No. 11 Seventh street, S. F. (opp. Odd Fellows Hall. Telephone No. 3 69.

W. H. WOODRUFF.

Veterinary Dentist,

AT FASHION STABLES,

221 Ellis Street, San Francisco

Improved Instruments, Humane Methods, First-Class Work.

H. E. CARPENTER,

Veterinary Surgeon,

Graduate of Ontario Veterinary College, Toronto, Canada.

RESIDENCE AND VETERINARY INFIRMARY

331 Golden Gate Ave., San Francisco.

Telephone 3069.

☞ OPEN DAY AND NIGHT. ☜

No risk in throwing Horses. Veterinary Operating Table on the premises.

DR. C. MASOERO,

Veterinary Surgeon,

Successor to DR. A. DeTAVEL,

GRADUATE OF ROYAL VETERINARY COLLEGE, TURIN.

OFFICE AND INFIRMARY,

No. 811 HOWARD STREET,

Between Fourth and Fifth. SAN FRANCISCO.

Telephone, No. 457.

R. WATKINS,

Veterinary Dentist,

Of twelve years practice, is now permanently located in San Francisco, and may be found at C. S. Crittendens' Golden Gate Livery and Riding Academy, 24 to 28 Golden Gate Avenue.

Will treat ailments of the horse's mouth, and cure all such. Sidereln Pullers and Tongue Lollers, etc. Satisfaction guaranteed. Orders by mail will receive prompt attention. Examination Free.

E. J. O'ROUKE.

I have the honor to announce to my old patrons and the general public that I may be found at my old stand, where, as heretofore, the

Shoeing of Horses,

whether for the Track, Drive, or for general work, will receive my personal attention.

Telephone 2011.

E. J. O'ROUKE,
209 Ellis Street

California Horse Shoe Co's

I have used in my business the Steel and Iron Shoes made by the above Company, and take great pleasure in saying they are the best I have ever used in twenty-two years' practice. I have never seen anything like the STEEL SHOE made by this Company. I can fully recommend them to every practical Horseshoer in the country. Yours respectfully,

No. 8 Everett street. JOHN GRACE.

NOVEL, USEFUL and Ornamental.

The Perfection Horse Tail Tie,

Saves Time and the Tail.

Send 25 cents for Sample

BREEDER AND SPORTSMAN,
313 Bush Street, San Francisco.
or to BARNES & PARKER, Des Moines, Ia., Manufrs.

TWENTY-FOUR PAGES.

Vol. XVI. No. 11.
No. 313 BUSH STREET.

SAN FRANCISCO, SATURDAY, MARCH 15, 1890.

SUBSCRIPTION
FIVE DOLLARS A YEAR.

Our Tennessee Letter.

GALLATIN, TENN., March 5, 1890.

EDITOR BREEDER AND SPORTSMAN:—Until the past four days the winter in Tennessee has been marked by its extreme mildness, and breeders and trainers of horses could not have been more delighted than were they. The weather of the past four days has been most fickle, and at times very severe. A sudden change of temperature, accompanied by rain, which was followed by snow and sleet, means lots of mud and slush, and a let-up of training at Memphis and Nashville. While no wonderful trials are reported at either place, it is said that the older division at Memphis are going like chain lightning.

Memphis seems to have an extra good chance of again furnishing us with another Derby winner. There is some good Derby material wintering at Memphis, and, as a friend writes me "they will take a deal of beating." Ed Corrigan's Riley is the most prominent Derby candidate there, or at least he will receive a good deal of backing in the winter books. Then there are Blarneystone Jr., Milton, Blue Blazes, Kitty Cheathan and other lesser lights that will do to keep an eye on. On last year's form I should think Kitty Cheathan the best 3 year old in the West, but a year's time often works wonders in an animal losing or discovering unlooked for speed. Then, too, mares are uncertain creatures in the flowery months of spring, and very often have to succumb to horses not within ten pounds of them. The Kentucky Derby of 1890 seems to be a very open race and even those who have great predilictions for giving forecasts of future events, shake their heads when asked for their opinion.

The Winters string of horses have arrived at Nashville, including the *Eastern* and Western divisions. The Western division as is well-known have been in quarters at Nashville for several weeks, but the Eastern division have only been at the Park for a few days. Nashville turfmen were very much disappointed at the absence of El Rio Rey when the Eastern division arrived. Owing to a delay of 12 hours en route from Westchester, the big son of Norfolk and Marian tired badly, and it was thought best to leave him over at Louisville until he had recuperated sufficiently to again resume his southward journey. He was taken from Louisville to Nashville yesterday, and did not look any the worse for his trip. Many have fears that his illness at Westchester recently may yet result in something serious, and that he may turn "roarer", while others say he will be as good as last season, and even better than the Emperor of Norfolk was at the same age. He does not look as if he ever knew what sickness was, and it will take a great horse to ever give him a race.

The Supreme court of this State has closed all the pool rooms in operation, and none of them will be allowed to open until racing is resumed in this State, and then only as long as racing continues at Memphis and Nashville. An enterprising book-making firm has, or will, open a room across the river from Memphis and will charter a ferry boat, and will give all speculators free transportation over the river. There is no law in Arkansas to prohibit book making, and it can now be carried on to the convenience of Memphis sports, as well as if it were in that city.

The twenty-third annual sale at Belle Meade is looked upon as the coming event in turf circles in this State. At this sale every thoroughbred animal upon the place will be sold, including the stallions Bramble, Luke Blackburn, Iroquois, imp. Great Tom, and Enquirer, sixty-four yearlings and one hundred broodmares, together with the foals that will have been dropped by the date of the sale. Two days—April 24th and 25th—will be consumed in disposing of the entire stud. Capt. Phil Kidd will wield the gavel, and some long prices may be expected. This sale is for a division, Judge Howell E. Jackson wishing to retire. Gen. W. H. Jackson will be a bidder at the sale, and it is thought will be the purchaser of the stallions Iroquois and Luke Blackburn.

Upon the heels of this great sale, Messrs. C. H. Gillock, Lyle & Parmer will hold their inaugural sale of yearlings at Lyle & Parmer's Horse Exchange, near West Side Park. This is a new firm, composed of three gentlemen well known in turf circles. Mr. Gillock is the genial Secretary of West Side Park, while Messrs. Lyle & Parmer are known as the Southern Mule Kings, and as prominently connected with some good turf performers. About seventy head of yearlings will be sold by these gentlemen on April 26th. The colts to be sold are the produce of Richland, Lakewood, Peytonia and Clifflawn farms, and are by such sires as Luke Blackburn, imp. Saxon, imp. Glengary, Blazes, imp. Pickwick, Eequador, and Vanderbilt. It is said that Capt. Franklin of Kennesaw Stud may decide to sell his colts at the same sale. Catalogues have not yet been issued, and upon their appearance I hope to make further mention of some of the good ones numbered therein.

The proprietor of Kennesaw Stud is yet undecided as to where he will sell his yearlings. I would not be surprised if the Kennesaw colts were disposed of in New York City, together with the forty-nine colts at Fairview, owned by Charles Reed.

Rumor has it that the Hermitage Stud last week refused an offer of $20,000 for the three year old trotting colt Ponce de Leon, by Pancoast 2:21¼, dam Elvira, four year old record 2:18, by Cuyler. The offer was refused as the colt is not for sale. This was a pretty high figure for a three year old colt that had never made a mark. The Hermitage Stud people are gradually getting together some of the best horses that can be had, and in a few years it will stand second to no establishment of its kind, excepting *Palo Alto* Farm, the pride of the famed-golden State upon the Pacific. Bow Bells, who recently arrived from California, is looking exceptionally well after his long journey across the continent. We are glad to have him added to the list of the great horses in our State. What is Tennessee's gain is California's loss. The filly Moquette, by Wilton, that came through from California with Bow Bells, is said to have distemper, and is not doing so well at her new-home in Tennessee.

Dave Waldo has purchased the steeplechaser Brac-a-Ban by imp. King Ban, dam Little Fanny, and he is now at Memphis where he will remain during the winter.

St. Louis, Terre Haute, Lexington, and Nashville are trying to arrange a trotting circuit for 1890. If the different association can agree upon purses and classes the meetings will be held in the order named.

Col. G. M. Fogg, President of the West Side Park Association, and proprietor of "Melrose" Farm, intends purchasing a few thoroughbred mares which he will bred to Benton, 2:27¼, by Gen. Benton, Mr. Fogg, like Senator Stanford, has faith in the crossing of runners and trotters, and to the embrace of Benton his thoroughbred mares may drop a Sunol or Palo Alto.

KENNESAW.

Famous Horses

And the Prices at Which They Were Sold.

Mr. A. E. Whyland of New York has prepared a list of the prices for which horses have sold in America and England, and we publish it as a matter for reference.

TROTTERS.		RUNNERS.	
Axtell	$105,000	Kentucky	$40,000
Bell Boy	51,000	King Thomas	40,000
Stamboul	50,000	Dewdrop	29,500
Sunol	41,000	Brother of Bassett	25,000
Acolyte	40,000	Vigil	25,000
Maud S.	40,000	Duke of Magenta	20,000
Pocahontas	40,000	Ban Fox	20,000
Rarus	36,000	Iroquois	20,000
Antevolo	35,000	Foxhall	20,000
Dexter	33,000	Spendthrift	18,000
Goldsmith Maid	32,000	Falsetto	18,000
Smuggler	30,000	Pontiac	17,500
Anteeo	30,000	Drake Carter	17,500
Blackwood	30,000	Sir Dixon	17,500
Jay Gould	30,000	Proctor Knott	17,500
Lady Thorn	30,000	Terra Cotta	17,100
Prince Wilkes	30,000	Norfolk	15,001
Pancoast	28,000	Lexington	15,000
Gov. Sprague	27,500	Kingfisher	15,000
Patron	27,000	Hindoo	15,000
Mascot	26,000	Baden Baden	15,000
Fearnaught	25,000	Panique	14,000
Jerome Eddy	25,000	Rossington	12,500
Wedgewood	25,000	Vagrant	12,000
Geo. M. Patchen	25,000	Hindoocraft	11,000
Happy Medium	25,000	Come to Taw	10,500
Nutwood	22,000	Grey Planet	10,000
Sam Purdy	21,000	Glenelg	10,000
Startle	20,000	Barnes	10,000
Edward Everett	20,000	Egmont	10,000
Edward	20,000	Knight of Ellerslie	10,000
St. Julien	20,000	Runnymede	10,000
Lady Maud	20,000	George Kinney	10,000
Socrates	20,000	Finesse	10,000
Constantine	20,000	Ulrica	10,000
Rosalind	20,000	IN ENGLAND: Ormonde	75,000
Russia	18,000	Doncaster	70,000
Lucy	17,000	Kangaroo	70,000
Edgemark	16,000	Blair Athol	62,500
Edwin Forrest	16,000	Harvester	43,000
Prospect Maid	15,000	Gladiator	35,000
Alma Mater	15,000	Isonomy	30,000
Grafton	15,000	Spinaway	27,500
Electric Bell	12,500	Wheel of Fortune	25,000
Chimes	12,500	Janette	21,000
Electioneer	12,500	Cantiniere	20,500
Lancelot	12,500	Louisburg	20,000
	$1,282,000		$1,089,500

The above list shows that the Trotter is the most valuable type of horses in the world, and that the United States has not produced enough high-priced Runners to balance the same number of Trotters. While Electioneer sold for $12,500 some time ago, he has proven the most valuable horse on the list.

Notes From Sacramento.

EDITOR BREEDER AND SPORTSMAN:—Owing to the extremely bad winter, our track has been in a deplorable condition for several months. It is true that at times we have been favored with one or two good days, but taken all in all we have had a very hard time in working our horses. Those who have wintered at the Bay District Track have been fortunate inasmuch as they could at least walk their horses in the Park, but our roads and streets have been so bad that we have not been able to utilize them for that purpose; in fact, it would have been dangerous to the horses to do so. Within the last few days our worthy President and Secretary have issued a very sensible order to the Park Superintendent, showing him the danger in having trotters and runners working on the track at the same time, and now the thoroughbreds will have the advantage of morning work, while the trotters will occupy the course during the afternoon—providing it don't rain. There is no use in disguising the fact, there is not a horse here fit to run a mile in 1:50, and I hardly think we will be able to get them in first class condition by the time set for your Blood Horse Meeting.

Frank De Poyster's string looks about the best of the lot here, and it may just be possible that if the horses which have been wintered at other sections are in no better condition than ours, that those under Frank's charge may be found leading the van in April next.

Al Farrow and Longshot are about the best that Frank has in training. Guido also looks fairly well, and one of which I have great hopes is a Gano filly belonging to Mr. Paddock of San Francisco; she is a little beauty and will be heard from before long.

The old stand-by, Ab Stemler is looking after the Shippee stable; he has Fellow Charm which I may mention is the best of the lot; the two-year-old Longfellow has a very slick appearance, and the Prince Charlies may soon be fit for a race. The King Ban colt is a big, strapping fellow and if he stands the "grand prep," is liable to get to the front. Picnic has not grown much and is about the same as when you saw her here.

The well known Matt Storn has eight altogether in his stable, the more prominent of which are Lurline, Marigold, Kildare and Larghette, the latter he has lately bought from Charles Aby of the Langtry Stock Farm for quite a long figure so I am told. A three-year-old colt by Jils Johnson and out of that great old mare Leverett by Lever, he is rather a handsome looking colt and showed up fairly well until last summer when he had the misfortune to spring an ugly curb. However, all signs of that has now disappeared and he is likely to make a moderate good race horse.

Wm. M. Murry is looking after a number of youngsters but their names and breeding I have as yet failed to learn, with the exception of Kiro which is the best Hooker I have ever seen, and while all of Mr. Murry's horses are looking well, yet none of them are fit to be seen on a public course yet.

Col. Harry I. Thornton's stable is about on a par with the balance as far as the amount of work given them is concerned. However, I am satisfied that he has some good two-year-olds amongst them; the Carrie C. filly is very taking to the eye, and as our old friend Senator McCarthy would say "will race to a finish." The big Darebin colt out of Bavaria, and the John Happy youngster are a pair of good ones, and the Colonel also has a Hyder Ali filly which will tempt me to back her for a little the first time she starts; the old mare Abi if she has not lost her speed will be a very dangerous opponent for anything that may start against her this year.

I was going to say something about the Dennison Bros.'s stable, but there you know how slick they are; it is impossible to tell at the present writing whether "Lucky Dan" has a good thing up his sleeve or not. Will send you another letter in the course of a few days whenever the weather brightens up sufficiently to warrant the boys in giving the horses the necessary exercising gallops.

LOOKOUT.

Entries for Denver Spring Races.

Following is a full list of nominations to the racing stakes of the Overland Park Club Association, to be run at their spring meeting, May 30th to June 7, 1890, closed February 15, 1890.

THE PRAIRIE STAKES.

A sweepstakes for two-year-olds (foals of 1888), $10 entrance to accompany the nomination, $15 additional to start, with $500 added by the club, of which $100 to second horse, $50 to the third. Winners of any race of the value of $750 or more to carry three pounds extra, of two or more such races five pounds extra. Maidens (at the time of starting) allowed five pounds. Five furlongs. To be run on the second day of the meeting.

1 Carlile & Shields, Pueblo, ch f Sister Carrie by John W. Norton, dam Alletta.
2. Same, ch c Brookwood by King Alfonso, dam Spring Branch.
3. Denver Racing Association, Denver. b c Alamosa (formerly Alamo III) by Astral. dam Mollie Powers.
4 Same, ch c Vasistas (formerly Governor Martin) by Astral, dam Eureka.
5 Same, ch f Naomi (formerly Streak), by Faustus, dam Alma Lamar.
6 Same, b f Francesca (formerly Affie Prather) by Faustus, dam Emma Warner.
7 A. M. Prior, Beaver Creek, Colo, ch c A. S. Tooke by John W. Norton, dam Daisy Miller.
8 Lesher & Paff, Grand Junction, Colo., b c Playtime by Rufus, dam Mabel.
9 Same, b c Lucky by Owen Bowling, dam Kate.
10 M. M. Sage, Pueblo, Colo., b c Ben Carlile by Bruce, dam Gypsy.
11 Same, b c Tim McCarthy by Bruce, dam Mollie McCrary.
12 Same, b c Matches by Lucifer, dam Mary Williams.
13 Charles Feeney, Denver, ch f Celia (formerly Mirk) by Day Star, dam imported Miss McGregor.
14 O'Brien Brothers, Lexington, Ky., b f Minnie Elkins by Duke of Montrose, dam Badge.
15 John Winfield, Denver, b c John Winfield by John W. Norton, dam Retribute.
16 John A. Davis, Denver, ch c Cactus Blossom by Clifton Bell, dam Lucille.
17 Charles Johnson, Dolores, Colo., b c Lew Douglass by Jim Douglass, dam Mary S.
18 Orange Grove Stable, Los Angeles, Cala., ch c Bon Ton by Flood, dam May D.
19 Same. b c Joe Woolman by imported Cyrus, dam Ella Dow.
20 James Madsen, Wakefield, Neb., b f Clara G by Leveller, dam Sorrel Nell.
21 John Doherty, Mora, N. M., c Fandango by Jils Johnson, dam Ultimatum.
22. Kelly & Samuels, San Francisco, ch f Lizette by Hyder Ali, dam Katie Fletcher.

THE FAR WEST STAKES.

A sweepstakes for two-year-olds (foals of 1888), $10 entrance to accompany the nominations, $15 additional to start, with $500 added by the club, of which $100 to the second horse, $50 to the third. Colts and fillies bred, raised and owned in Colorado, Wyoming, New Mexico, Utah, Montana or Idaho allowed 5 pounds. The winner of the Prairie stakes to carry 7 pounds extra. Maidens (at time of starting) allowed 5 pounds. Half a mile. To be run on the fifth day of the meeting. The allowance to colts and fillies bred, raised and owned in states and territories named to be allowed in addition to the maiden allowance, if any, also in taking up penalties, if any.

1 Carlile & Shields, Pueblo, ch f Sister Carrie by John W. Norton, dam Alleta.
2 Same, ch c Brookwood by King Alfonso, dam Springbranch.
3 Denver Racing Association, Denver, b c Alamosa (formerly Alamo III.) by Astral, dam Mollie Powers.
4 Same, ch c Vasitas (formerly Governor Martin) by Astral, dam Eureka.
5 Same, ch f Naomi (formerly Streak) by Faustus, dam Alma Lamar.
6 Same, b f Francesca (formerly Affie Prater) by Faustus, dam Emma Warner.
7 A. M. Prior, Beaver Creek, Colo., ch c A. S. Tooke by John W. Norton, dam Daisy Miller.
8 Palmer & Keys, Beaver Creek, Colo., b c Ben Wood by Jack Hardwood, dam Venice.
9 Lesher & Paff, Grand Junction, Colo., b c Playtime by Rufus, dam Mabel.
10 Same, b c Lucky by Owen Bowling, dam Kate.
11 M. M. Sage, Pueblo, b c Ben Carlile by Bruce, dam Gypsy.
12 Charles Feeney, Denver, ch f Celia (formerly Mirk) by Day Star, dam imp. Miss McGregor.
13 O'Brien Brothers, Lexington, Ky., b f Minnie Elkins by Duke of Montrose, dam Badge.
14 John Winfield, Denver, b c John Winfield by John W. Norton, dam Retribute.
15 G. S. Carey, Byers, Colo., Conchets by Heythorpe, dam Starlight by Startle.
16 John A. Davis, Denver, ch c Cactus Blossom by Clifton Bell, dam Lucille.
17 Charles Johnson, Dolores, Colo., b f Netta Douglass by Jim Douglass, dam Red Girl.
18 Orange Grove Stable, Los Angeles, Cal, br c Jos. Woolman by imported Cyrus, dam Ella Dow.
19 Orange Grove Stable, Los Angeles, Cal., br c Bon Ton by Flood, dam May D.
20 John Doherty, Mora, N. M., c Fandango by Jils Johnson, dam Ultimatum.
21 Kelly & Samuels, San Francisco, ch f Lizette by Hyder Ali, dam Katie Fletcher.

THE COLORADO DERBY.

A sweepstakes for 3 year olds (foals of 1887) $10 for entrance to accompany the nomination, $15 additional start, with $600 added by the club, of which $100 to the second horse $50 to the third. Winners of any stake race to carry three pounds extra, of any 3 year old stakes, five pounds extra. Maidens on February 15 allowed five pounds—if maidens at time of starting, allowed seven pounds. One mile and a quarter. To be run on the first day of the meeting.

1 Carlile & Shields, Pueblo, b g Ollie Benjamin, by Springbok, dam Minnie.
2 Same, b c Governor Adams, by Nathan Oaks, dam Alleta.
3 Denver Racing association, Denver, br c Advent, by Astral, dam Bonnie May.
4 A. M. Pryor, Beaver Creek, Colo., ch g Henry Ward Beecher, by John W. Norton, dam Daisy Miller.
5 Same, ch c Bob Ingersoll, by John W. Norton, dam Nannie B.
6 L. Ogilvy, Greeley, Colo., br f Zafola, by Falsetto, dam Mintdrop.
7 M. M. Sage, ch c Chut, by Mexique, dam Mollie McCrary.
8 Charles Feeney, Denver, b g Blue Rock (formerly Pick), by imported Mr. Pickwick, dam Nettie's Last.
9 Edward Gaylord, Denver, b c Billy Duncan, by Fairplay, dam Lucille.
10 Same, br c Sir Launcelot, by Fairplay, dam Lady Tough.
11 G. C. Gray, Galt, Kan., b c Samaritan, by W. Martin, dam Cousin Judy.
12 Joseph S. Gilbreath, Denver, b c Orphan King, by International, dam May Flower.
13 John Winfield, Denver, b f Eva Rogers, by Nathan Oaks dam Retribute.
14 Charles Dutt, Denver, b f Egypt, by Quartermaster, dam Full Moon.
15 Same, b c Hualpa, by Quartermaster, dam Virago.
16 Golden Gate stable. San Francisco, b c, Snook, by Wildidle, dam Wath tah Wath.
17 Same, b c, Oscio, by Wildidle, dam Prosephine.
18 Same, b c Gascolia, by Wildidle, dam Nighthawk.
19 Kelly & Samuels, San Francisco, b g, Pliny, by Flood, dam Precious.
20 H. D. Miller of Fresno, California, brown colt Captain Al, by Kingston, dam Black Maria.
21 Joseph P. Woolman of Helena. Montana, bay filly Emma Nevada. 3 years old, by John A, dam May D.

THE MOUNTAIN STAKES.

A sweepstakes for 3-year-olds (foals of 1887), $10 entrance to accompany the nomination, $15 additional to start, with $500 added by the club, of which $100 to the second horse, $50 to the third. Non-winners of $1,000 in 2-year-old form allowed five pounds. Maidens on February 15th allowed seven pounds, if maidens at time of starting, allowed ten pounds. The winner of the Colorado Derby to carry five pounds extra. One mile. To be run on the fourth day of the meeting.

1 Carlisle & Shields, Pueblo, b c Governor Adams by Nathan Oaks, dam Alletta.
2 Same, br g Low Carlisle by Nathan Oaks, dam Tulolia.
3 Same, br f Bonnie Grace by Nathan Oaks, dam Natchitoches.
4 Same, b g, Ollie Benjamin by Springbok, dam Minnie.
5 Denver Racing Association, Denver, br c Advent by Astral, dam Bonnie May.
6 A. M. Pryor, Beaver Creek, Col., ch c Bob Ingersoll by John W. Norton, dam Nannie B.
7 L. Ogilvie, Greeley, Col., br f Zufola by Falsetto, dam Mintdrop.
8 M. M. Sage, Pueblo, ch c Chut by Mexique, dam Mollie McCrary.
9 Charles Feeney, Denver, b g Blue Rock (formerly Pick) by imported Mr. Pickwick, dam Nettie's Last.
10 J. M. Broadwell, Denver, b g Senator by Clifton Bell, dam Sparkle.
11 Edward Gaylord, Denver, b g Billy Duncan by Fairplay, dam Lucille.
12 Same, br c Sir Launcelot by Fairplay, dam Lady Tough.
13 G. C. Gray, Galt, Kan., b c Samaritan by St. Martin, dam Cousin Judy.
14 Same, ch f Silence by St. Martin, dam Miss Guest.
15 John Winfield, Denver, b f Eva Rogers by Nathan Oaks, dam Retribution.
16 Charles Dutt, Denver, b f Egypt by Quartermaster, dam Full Moon.
17 Same, b c Hualpa by Quartermaster, dam Virago.
18 Charles Johnson, Dolores, Col., b c King Faro Third by King Faro, dam Theodosia.
19 Orange Grove Stables, Los Angeles, Cal., b f Rosemeade by Wildidle, dam Duchess.
20 H. D. Miller, Fresno, Cal., br c Captain Al by Kingston, dam Black Maria.
21 Golden Gate Stable, San Francisco, b c Oscio by Wildidle, dam Prosephine.
22 Same, b c Gascolia by Wildidle, dam Night Hawk.
23 Kelly & Samuels, San Francisco, b g Pliny by Flood, dam Precious.
24 J. P. Woolman, Helena, Montana, b f Emma Nevada by John A, dam May D.

THE MERCHANTS' STAKE.

A sweepstakes for all ages; $10 entrance, to accompany the nomination: $15 additional to start, with $500 added by the club, of which $$100 to the second horse, $50 to the third. Winners of any race of the value of $1000 or more to carry 3 lbs. extra; of two or more such races, 5 lbs extra. Non-winners in 1890 allowed 3 lbs. Maidens on February 15th allowed 5 lbs. If maidens at time of starting, allowed 7 lbs. One mile amd a half. To be run on the third day of the meeting.

1 Carlile & Shield, Pueblo, ch g Justice (4) by Alarm, dam Equity.
2 Same, b g Olie Benjamin (3) by Springboe, dam Minnie.
3 Denver Racing Association, Denver, br c Advent (3) by Astral, dam Bonnie May.
4 Same, ch h Kismet (5) by St. Patrick, dam Fanny Platte.
5 L. Oglivie, Greeley, Col., b m Patricia (4) by Ten Broeck, dam La Platte.
6 Same, br c Receiver (4) by Regent, dam Minnie Holton.
7 M. M. Sage, Pueblo, ch c Chut (3) by Mexique, dam Mollie McCreary.
8 Edwin Gayford, Denver, b g Parnell (a) by Trump, dam Third Cousin.
9 Same, b c Sympathetic's Last (4) by Fairplay, dam Sympathetic.
10 E. V. S. Pomroy, Bronson, Neb., m g Hark (6) by Harkaway, dam Mollie Powers.
11 Clifton Bell, Denver, b h Beaconsfield (a) by Hock Hocking, dam Aileen Allanah.
12 John D. Morrisey, Denver, ch h Montana Regent (a) by Regent, dam Christine.
13 Orange Grove Stable, Los Angeles, Cal., b h Jack Brady (6) by Wildidle, dam Sour Grapes.
14 Golden Gate Stable, San Francisco, b c Oscio (3) by Wildidle, dam Prosephine.
15 Kelly & Samuels, San Francisco, b h Ed McGinnis (5) by Grinstead, dam Jennie G.

THE OVERLAND HANDICAP.

A handicap sweepstakes for all ages; $5 entrance, to accompany the nomination; $20 additional to start, with $500 added by the club, of which $100 to the second horse, $50 to the third. Weights to appear at 1 o'clock P. M. the first day of the meeting. Acceptances to be made through the entry box at the usual time of closing, the day before the race. Winners of a race after publication of weights to carry 3 lbs. additional, of two or more such races, 5 lbs additional. One mile and a quarter. To be run on the last day of the meeting.

1 Carlisle & Shields, Pueblo, ch g Justice (4) by Alarm, dam Equity.
2 Same, b g Ollie Benjamin (3) by Springbook, dam Minnie.
3 Same, b g Governor Adams (3) by Nathan Oaks, dam Alletta.
4 Denver Racing Association, Denver, br c Advent (3) by Astral, dam Bonnie May.
5 Same, ch h Kismet (5) by St. Patrick, dam Fanny Platte.
6 A. M. Pryor, Beaver Creek, Col., ch g Henry Ward Beecher (3) by John W. Norton, dam Daisy Miller.
7 L. Oglivie, Greeley, Col., b m Patricia (4) by Ten Broeck, dam La Platte.
8 Same, br c Receiver (4) by Regent, dam Fannie Holton.
9 Charles Feeney, Denver, b g Blue Rock (3), formerly Pick, by imported Mr. Pickwick, dam Nettie's Last.
10 S. M. Broadwell, Denver, b g Senator (3) by Clifton Bell, dam Sparkle.
11 Edwin Gaylord, Denver, b g Parnell (a) by Trump, dam Third Cousin.
12 Same, b c Sympathetic's Last (4) by Fairplay, dam Sympathetic.
13 J. J. Ross, Denver, b h Dan Meek (5) by Fairplay, dam Impudence.
13 E. N. S. Pomroy, Bronson, Neb., m g Hark (6) by Harkaway, dam Mollie Powers.
15 Joseph S. Gilbreath, Denver, b c Orphan King (3) by International, dam May Flower.
16 John Winfield, Denver, ch m Miss Happy Jack (4) by Fairplay, dam Miss Trump.
17 Clifton Bell, Denver, b h Beaconsfield (a) by Hock Hocking, Aileen Allanah.
18 Joseph Wurler, Denver, b g Mart Walden (a) by Clifton Bell, dam Lucille.
19 John D. Morrissey, Denver, ch h Montana Regent (a) by Regent, dam Christine.
20 Charles Dutt, Denver, ch c Chickasaw (5) by Quartermaster, dam Mary Wynne.
21 Same, b f Egypt (3) by Quartermaster, dam Full Moon.
22 Same, b c Hallpa (3) by Quartermaster, dam Virago.
23 Charles Johson, Dolores, Col., b h King Buck (5) by King Faro, dam Plannetta Second.
24 Orange Grove Stable, Los Angeles, Cal., b h Jack Brady, (6) by Wildidle, dam Sour Grapes.
55 Golden Gate Stable, San Francisco, b c Gascolia (3) by Wildidle, dam Night Hawk.
26 Same, b g Jubilee (4) by Kyrle Daly, dam Joy.
27 Same, blk g Black Pilot (a) by Echo, dam Madge Duke.
28 Kelly & Samuels, San Francisco, b h Ed McGinnis (5) by Grinstead, dam Precious.
29 H. D. Miller, Fresno, b m Daisy D (a) by Wheatley, dam Black Maria.
30 J. P. Woolman, Helena, Mon., b f Emma Nevada by John A, dam May D.

THE DENVER TROTTING STAKE.

For colts and fillies, three years old or under, that have never beaten 2:30; mile heats, best 3 in 5, in harness and to the rules and regulations of the American Trotting Association; $10 on Thursday, May 1st (when the entries for trotting purses will close) and $10 from those who declare to start at 8 o'clock the night before the race, with $500 added by the club. The stakes, forfeits and added money to be put together and divided—50 per cent. to first horse, 25 per cent. to second, 15 per cent. to third and 10 per cent. to fourth. In case of an entry distancing the field or any part thereof it shall be entitled to the stakes and forfeits, with 50 per cent. of the added money, and no more. A walkover shall be entitled to all the stakes and forfeits and 25 per cent. of the added money, Nominations are only liable for the first payment, but failure to make either of the subsequent payments when due shall be considered a forfeiture and debar the entry from competing in the race.

1 D. D. Streeter, of Denver, Colorado, b f Martha by Stamboul, dam Flaxtail.
2, DuBois Brothers, of Denver, Colorado, b f Dazzle by Slander, dam Daphne by Jay Gould.
3 DuBois Brothers, of Denver, Colorado, b f Elsiewood by Nutwood, dam Elsie by George Wilkes.
4 DuBois Brothers, of Denver, Colorado, b f Diadem by King Rene, dam Cauta by Dictation.
5 John Weese, of Longmont, Colorado, br f —— by Marshall's Logan, dam by Iowa Chief.
6 C. E. Westbrook, of Peabody, Kansas, blk c Le Roy by Joe Young.
7 Charles T. Limberg, of Leadville, Colorado, b c Testator by Spectator, dam May Fleet.
8 M. A. Foss, of Junction City, Kansas, f Mollie Russel by Alley Russell, dam Mollie Bawn by Netherland.
9 James O. Kinney, of Denver, Colorado, blk c Dutch Boy by Black Ranger, dam Dutch Girl.
10 Frank C. Graves, of Franktown, Colorado, b f Polly by Alarm, dam Kentucky Girl by Kentucky Clay.
11 Frank C, Graves, of Franktown, Colorado, ch c Captain Woodson (2 years) by Jarfeld, dam Galetta.
12 George W. Baldwin, of West Liberty, Iowa, br c Brown Cedar by Red Cedar, dam Polln Duck by Guide.
13 Millett Brothers, of Langley, Kansas, b f Effie Rene by Dictator, dam Musette.
14 Millett Brothers, of Langley, Kansas, b f Laura B by Prairie Star.
15 D. T. Sabin, of Beatrice, Nebraska, b c Sabin's Councellor by Councellor, dam Julia by Chickamauga.

Another Loss.

SACRAMENTO, March 3, 1890.

EDITOR BREEDER AND SPORTSMAN:—I have the misfortune to report to you the loss of Fanny by McCracken's Black Hawk, and her foal, that was entered in your Futurity Stake. She was the mother of Silvia, owned by A. L. Nichols of Chico, who has shown her ability to trot in 2:30. She and her mater took the first premium at the State Fair for the best road team. She was also the dam of Billy Mac, owned in Bieber, Lassen County, by James H. Hall; that is a pacer which will be sent for a record this season; also the dam of Carl, owned by James Bowers, now in training at Agricultural Park. She leaves two more fillies at Sunny Knoll, one that is quite speedy, the other a yearling that has not been tried. All her family are sired by Tom Benton. Yours truly,

J. L. McCORD.

The Blood Horse Entries.

All of the daily newspapers of last Saturday and Sunday had a list of the entries for the forthcoming meeting of the Pacific Coast Blood Horse Association, but all of them had so many omissions and mistakes that we have made the necessary corrections and publish the list in its entirety.

FIRST DAY, SATURDAY, APRIL 12, 1890.

No. 1.—Introduction Purse, $400, of which $50 to second, $25 to third. For three-year-olds and upward, beaten maidens of three years old allowed five pounds, if four years old or over, ten pounds. One mile and a sixteenth.

W. L. Appleby's b f, 3 years, Raindrop by Wildidle, dam Teardrop.
Kelly & Samuels' b g, 3, Pliny by Flood, dam Precious.
W. M. Murry's b f, 3, Lady Ali by Hyder Ali, dam Mollie Ward.
W. M. Murry's b g, 3, Leland by Flood, dam Amelia.
Owen Brothers' b m, 5, Carona by Norfolk, dam Sister to Lottery.
Palo Alto's b m, 4, Faustine by Flood, dam Flirt.
J. R. Ross' b g, a, Oro by Norfolk, dam Golden Gate.
W. H. E. Smith's b h, 5, Al Farrow by Connor, dam Della Walker.
H. I. Thornton's b m, a, Abi by Red Boy dam Abi.
George Hearst's ch c, 3, Baggage by Warwick, dam Maria F.
George Hearst's b h, 4, Almont by Three Cheers, dam Question.

No. 2—The California Stakes; for two-year-olds. Half a mile.

John Adams' ch g Havoc by Joe Hooker, dam Pearl.
J. B. Chase's b c Jubilee by Kinglight, dam Lady Clare.
J. B. Chase's b f Mystery by Three Cheers, dam Mistake.
S. F. Fulkerson's b f Centerella by Ironclad, dam Bayswater.
George Hearst's ch c Anarchist by Joe Hooker, dam Chestnut Belle.
George Hearst's ch c Snowball by Joe Hooker, dam Laura Winston.
George Hearst's b c Yosemite by Hyder Ali, dam Nelly Collier.
Kelly & Samuels' ch f Lizette by Hyder Ali, dam Kate Fletcher.
Kelly & Samuels' ch c Wild Air by Kyrle Daly, dam Zuina.
P. Herzog's ch c Joe Harding by Joe Hooker, dam Irene Harding.
G. H. Kennedy's b f Acclaim by Three Cheers, dam Rosette.
W. M. Murry's b c Parapet by Bulwer, dam Nettie Brady.
W. M. Murry's ch g Gold Pan by Panic, dam Neutilyn.
G. Pacheco's b c Ignacio by Three Cheers, dam Dairy Maid.
L. J. Rose's b f Fairy by Argyle, dam Fairy Rose.
L. J. Rose's b c Conrad by Flood, dam Gonala.
Palo Alto's c f Tearless by Wildidle, dam Teardrop.
Palo Alto's c c Rinfax by Argyle, dam Amelia.
L. J. Rose's b c Sinfax by Wildidle, dam Forestress.
L. U. Shippee's b f May H. by Falsetto, dam Glenluine.
L. U. Shippee's b f False Queen by Falsetto, dam Queen Victoria.
G. W. Trahern's c f Minnie B. by Prince of Norfolk, dam by Wildidle.
Undine Stable's b c Homer by Shannon, dam Sallie Gardner.
Theodore Winter's b c Rey del Rey by Norfolk, dam Marion.
Theodore Winters' c c San Juan by Norfolk, dam Ballinette.
Theodore Winters' blk c Black Bart by Three Cheers, dam Bonita.
Theodore Winters' ch c Una Grande by Joe Hooker, dam Jessie R.
Undine Stables' c f Glenlivette by Flood, dam Glendew.

No. 3.—Selling purse, $350; of which $50 to second; for three year olds and upwards. Horses entered to be sold for $1,200 to carry rule weights; 3 lbs. allowed for each $100 less down to $800, then 2 lbs. for each $100 down to $300 Horses entered not to be sold to carry 10 lbs. above the scale. Three-quarters of a mile.

J. J. Abbott's g, 3, Abbott Colt, by Billy Lee, dam Flight.
T. Bally's b g, a, Jou Jou, by Monday, dam Plaything.
Dennison Bros.' b m, 4, Sallie C. by Thornhill, dam by Wildidle.
Elmwood Stable's b g, 6, Vinco, by Bob Wooding, dam Mollie H.
C. Foster's b f, 3, Rosemead, by Wildidle, dam Duchess.
W. George's b g, a, Applause, by Three Cheers, dam Alice N.
J. G. Hill's b g, 3, Steve Stroud, by Billy Lee, dam by Woodburn.
J. Hilton's b g, 4, Albatross, by Pill Box, dam Della Walker.
G. Howson's g g, a, Johnnny Gray, by Shiloh, dam Margery.
Kelly & Samuels' ch g, 4, Rosebug, by Jim Brown, dam Rosemary.
S. Meninhall's ch m, 3, Maggie B, by Milner, dam Young Grecian Bend.
H. D. Miller's ch m, a, Ida Glenn, by Glen Elm, dam Queen.
C. Mulkey's ch g, a, Tom Daly, by Patsy Duffy, dam Sunshine.
W. M. Murry's b c, 3, Oakdale, by Partisan, dam Spector.
Charles Nickerson, b h, 5, Hernanda, by Wildidle, dam Viola Bey.
Owen Bros.' b m, 4, Emma by Joe Daniels, dam Jenny C.
Orange Grove Stable's ch g, 6, Adam, by Shiloh, dam Mollie Adams.
J. Reavey's b m, 4, Bessie Shannon, by Shandon, dam Betty Bishop.
P. Seibenthaler's ch c, 3, Sheridan, by Young Bazar, dam Lost Girl.
M. Storn's ch g, 5, Kildare, by Kyrle Daly, dam Mistake.
Undine Stable's b m, 5, Recess, by Kelpie, dam Belle Belmont.

No. 4.—Purse $350, of which $50 to second; for all ages. Weights 10 lbs. below the scale. Seven furlongs.

W. L. Appleby's ch m, 4, Odette, by Shiloh, dam Margery.
W. L. Appleby's ch m, 5, Carmen, by Wildidle, dam Nettie Brown.
Dennison Bros.' b g, a, Dave Douglas, by Leinster, dam Lilly Simpson.
Elmwood Stable's b m, 4, Installation, by Inauguration, dam Brown, Maria.
N. S. Hamlin, ch g, 4, Sir Reginald, by Joe Hooker, dam Dolly Varden.
Kelly & Samuel's br f, 3, Adelaide, by Grinstead, dam Victoria.
G. Lyman's b h, 5, Painkiller, by Joe Hooker, dam Patsy McGuire
J. T. McBride's ch h, 4, Longshot, by Duke of Norfolk, dam by Langford.
Miller & Owens' b m, a, Daisy D., by Wheatly, dam Black Maria.
Miller & Owen's blk c, 3, Captain Al, by Kingston, dam Black Maria.
W. M. Murry, ch c, 3, Kiro, by Joe Hooker, dam by Foster.
C. Nickerson's b m, 5, Fanny F, by Wildidle, dam Sally Hart.
P. Seibenthaler's ch c, 3, King Hooker, by Joe Hooker, dam Violet.
Undine Stable's ch f, 3, Bettie B., by Joe Hooker, dam Kate Carson.
George Hearst's ch f, 4, Gertrude, by Somnus, dam Geraldine.
George Hearst's ch c, 4, Del Mar, by Somnus, dam Maid of the Hills.
W. L. Whitmore's ch h, 5, Coloma, by Joe Hooker, dam Callie Smart.

No. 5—The Tidal Stakes; for three-year-olds. One mile and a quarter.

C. Halverson's ch f Fabiola by Warwick, dam Maggie S.
S. Stroud's b c King David by Kyrle Daly, dam Trophy.
P. Herzog's b c Herzog by Norfolk, dam Irene Harding.
George Hearst's b c Sacramento by Joe Hooker, dam Addie C.
Oak Grove Stables' ch c Morton by Leinster, dam Lilly H.
Oak Grove Stable's ch c Tippecanoe by Young Bazaar, dam Lillie P.
Oak Grove Stable's ch c Sheridan by Young Bazaar, dam Lost Girl.
Oak Grove Stable's ch c Oregon by Joe Hooker, dam Hattie Ball.
Oak Grove Stable's ch f Philena by Joe Hooker, dam Lena's First.
Kelly & Samuels' b f Adelaide by Grinstead, dam Victoria.
Palo Alto's ch c Flambeau by Wildidle, dam imp. Flirt.
Palo Alto's ch f Muta by Wildidle, dam imp. Mutiny.
Palo Alto's b c Racine by Bishop, dam imp. Fairy Rose.
W. M. Murry's b c Lord of the Harem by Wildidle, dam Florrie.
L. J. Rose's ch c Rover by Wildidle, dam imp. Rosetta.
L. J. Rose's b f Glenloch by Flood, dam Glendew.
Scoggin Bros.' b f Evelina by Flood, dam Evangeline.
L. U. Shippee's b c Fellowcharm by Longfellow, dam Trinket.
C. V. Tupper's blk c High Jack by Three Cheers, dam Regina.
W. H. Babb's ch c Guido by Double Cross, dam Aurora.
A. Wakeman's ch c Kiro by Joe Hooker, dam Foster.

SECOND DAY, TUESDAY, APRIL 15, 1890.

No. 6—Purse $400, of which $50 to second, $25 to third; for three-year-olds and upwards. Winner of No. 1 at this meeting to carry five pounds extra. Horses starting and not placed in that race allowed three pounds. One mile.

W. L. Appleby's b f, 3, Raindrop by Wildidle, dam Teardrop.
N. S. Hamlin's ch g, 4, Sir Reginald by Joe Hooker, dam Dolly Varden.
Kelly & Samuels' b g, 3, Pliny by Flood, dam Precious
J. T. McBride's ch h, 4, Longshot by Duke of Norfolk, dam by Langford.
Miller & Owens' b m, a, Daisy D. by Wheatley, dam Black Maria.
W. M. Murry's b f, 3, Lady Ali by Hyder Ali, dam Mollie Ward.
W. M. Murry's b g, 3, Leland by Flood, dam Amelia.
J. R. Ross' b m, 4, Kittie Van by Vanderbilt, dam April Fool.
W. H. E. Smith's b h, 5, Al Farrow by Connor, dam Della Walker.
P. Seibenthaler's ch c, 3, King Hooker by Joe Hooker, dam Violet.
H. I. Thornton's b m, a, Abi by Red Boy, dam Abi.
Undine Stable's ch f, 3, Bettie B. by Joe Hooker, dam Kate Carson.
George Hearst's b h, 4, Almont by Three Cheers, dam Question.
George Hearst's ch f, 4, Gertrude by Somnus, dam Geraldine.
W. L. Whitmore's ch h, 5, Coloma by Joe Hooker, dam Callie Smart.

No. 7—Free Handicap Sweepstakes, for two-year-olds; $10 each if not declared out, with $300 added. First horse to take the added money, second to receive 70 per cent, and the third 30 per cent. of the stakes. Weights announced Monday, April 14th, at 10 o'clock A. M. Declarations due at 5 o'clock P. M. the same day. Five furlongs.

R. B. Cockrill's b c Nero by Wildidle, dam Precious.
Elmwood Stables' b c Sir Walter by Nathan Coombs, dam Bessie.
William Fitzgerald's b f Miss Melbourne-Gano, dam Victoria.
Kelly & Samuels' ch f Lizette by Hyder Ali, dam Kate Fletcher.
Cy Mulkey's b c Sinfax by Wildidle, dam Forestress.
W. M. Murry's b c Joe Harding by Joe Hooker, dam Irene Harding.
W. M. Murry's b c Parapet by Bulwer, dam Nettie Grady.
W. M. Murry's blk c Power by Powhattan, dam Lawn Tennis.
W. M. Murry's ch c Gerald by Powhattan, dam Geneva.
Orange Grove Stable's br h Joe Woolman by imp. Sirus, dam Ella Doane.
Palo Alto's ch c Rinfax by Argyle, dam imp. Amelia.
Palo Alto's ch f Tearless by Wildidle, dam Teardrop.
H. I. Thornton's ch c Arcade by Milner, dam Nanny Hubbard.
H. I. Thornton's b c Cimeter by Hyder Ali, dam Sabrina.
H. I. Thornton's b f Madaline by John Happy, dam Jongleuse.
Undine Stable's ch f Glenlivet by Flood, dam Glendew.
Undine Stable's b c Homer by Shannon, dam Sallie Gardner.
George Hearst's ch c Primero by Powhattan, dam Speed.

No. 8—Selling Purse $350, of which $50 to second; for all ages. Horses entered to be sold for $1,500 to carry rule weights; three lbs. allowed for each $100 less down to $500. Horses entered not to be sold to carry eight pounds above the scale. One mile and a sixteenth.

W. L. Appleby's b g, 4, Wild Oats by Wildidle, dam Mary Givens.
T. Bally's b g, a, Jou Jou by Monday, dam Plaything.
Dennison Bros.'s b g, a, Dave Douglas by Leinster, dam Lilly Simpson.
Elmwood Stables' ch m, a, Nerva by Bob Wooding, dam Lizzie Marshal.
W. George's b g, a, Applause by Three Cheers, dam Alice N.
J. Hilton's b g, 4, Albatross by Pill Box, dam Della Walker.
H. D. Miller's ch m, a, Ida Glenn by Glen Elm, dam Queen.
Cy Mulkey's ch g, a, Tom Daly by Patsy Duffy, dam Sunshine.
C. Nickerson's b m, 5, Fanny F. by Wildidle, dam Sally Hart.
Orange Grove Stable's b h, a, Jack Brady by Wildidle, dam Sour Grapes.
J. Reavey's b m, 4, Bessie Shannon by Shannon, dam Bettie Bishop.
J. R. Ross' b m, 4, Kittie Van by Vanderbilt, dam April Fool.
P. Seibenthaler's ch c, 3, Sheridan by Young Bazar, dam Lost Girl.
M. Storn's ch g, 5, Kildare by Kyrle Daly, dam Mistake.

No. 9—The Pacific Derby; for three-year-olds. One mile and a half.

C. Halverson's ch f Fabiola by Warwick, dam Maggie S.
S. Stroud's b c King David by Kyrle Daly, dam Trophy.
P. Herzog's b c Mohawk by Norfolk, dam Irene Harding.
George Hearst's b c Sacramento by Joe Hooker, dam Addie C.
Oak Grove Stable's ch f Gypsy by Leinster, dam Aunt Jane.
Oak Grove Stable's ch c Morton by Leinster, dam Lily H.
Oak Grove Stable's ch c Tippecanoe by Young Bazaar, dam Lizzie P.
Oak Grove Stable's ch c Oregon by Joe Hooker, dam Hattie Ball.
Oak Grove Stable's ch c Sheridan by Young Bazaar, dam Lost Girl.
Kelly & Samuels' b f Adelaide by Grinstead, dam Victoria.
Palo Alto's ch c Flambeau by Wildidle, dam imp Flirt.
Palo Alto's b c Racine by Bishop, dam imp Fairy Rose.
W. M. Murry's b c Lord of the Harem by Wildidle, dam Florie.
L. U. Shippee's b c Fellowcharm by Longfellow, dam Trinket.
C. V. Tupper's blk c High Jack by Three Cheers dam Legena.
W. H. Babb's ch c Guido by Double Cross, dam Aurora.
A. Wakeman's ch c Kiro by Joe Hooker, dam by Foster

THIRD DAY, THURSDAY, APRIL 17, 1890.

No. 10—Selling purse, $350, of which $50 to second; for three-year-olds and upwards. Horses entered to be sold for $1,000 to carry rule weights; three pounds allowed for each $100 less down to $600, then two pounds for each $100 down to $300. Horses entered not to be sold to carry ten pounds above the scale. Fifteen sixteenths of a mile.

Dennison Bros.' b m, 4, Sallie C. by Thornhill, dam by Wildidle.
Elwood's Stable's ch m, a, Nerva by Bob Wooding, dam Lizzie Marshal.
W. George's b g, a, Applause by Three Cheers, dam Alice N.
N. S. Hamlin's ch g, 4, Sir Reginald by Joe Hooker, dam Dolly Varden.
G. Howson's g g, a, Johnny Gray by Shiloh, dam Margery.
Kelly & Samuels' ch g, 4, Rosebug by Jim Brown, dam Rosemary.
G. Lyman's b h, 5, Painkiller by Joe Hooker, dam Betsy McGuire.
H. D. Miller's ch m, a, Ida Glenn by Glen Elm, dam Queen.
Cy Mulkey's ch g, a, Tom Daly by Patsy Duffy, dam Sunshine.
W. M. Murry's br c, 3, Oakdale by Partisan, dam Spectator.
Charles Nickerson's b h, 5, Hernanda by Wildidle, dam Viola Bey.
Orange Grove Stable's b h, a, Jack Brady by Wildidle, dam Sour Grapes.
J. Reavey's b m, 4, Bessie Shannon by Shannon, dam Betty Bishop.
J. R. Ross' b g, a, Oro by Norfolk, dam Golden Gate.
P. Seibenthaler's ch c, 3, Sheridan by Young Bazar, dam Lost Girl.
M. Storn's ch g, 5, Kildare by Kyrle Daly, dam Mistake.
Undine Stable's b m, 5, Recess by Kelpie, dam Belle Belmont.

No. 11.—Racine Stakes; for two year olds. Three-quarters of a mile. Closed.

J. B. Chase's b c Jubilee, by Kinglight, dam Lady Clare.
S. F. Fulkerson's b f Cantella, by Ironclad, dam Bayswater.
George Hearst's ch c Snowball, by Joe Hooker, dam Laura Winston.
George Hearst's b c J. B., by Warwick, dam Maria F.
George Hearst's b c El Verano, by Hock Hocking, dam Vixen.
P. Herzog's ch c Joe Harding, by Joe Hooker, dam Irene Harding.
Kelly & Samuel's c f Lizette, by Hyder Ali, dam Kate Fletcher.
Kelly & Samuel's ch c Wild Air, by Kyrle Daly, dam Lima.
W. M. Murry's blk c Power, by Powhattan, dam Lawn Tennis.
W. M. Murry's b f Lady Scoggans, by Little Ruffian, dam Hiawassa.
Oak Grove Stable's b c Happy John, by John Happy, dam Little Flush.
Oak Grove Stable's ch c Frank, by Frank Rhoades, dam Aunt Jane.
G. Pacheco's b c Ignacio, by Three Cheers, dam Dairy Maid.
L. J. Rose's b f Fairy, by Argyle, dam Fairy Rose.
L. J. Rose's br c Conrad, by Flood, dam Goula.
Palo Alto's ch f Tearless, by Wildidle, dam Teardrop.
Palo Alto's ch c Rinfax, by Argyle, dam Amelia.
R. B. Cockrill's b c Nero, by Wildidle, dam Precious.
L. U. Shippee's b c Lodowic, by Longfellow, dam Carrie Phillips.
L. U. Shippee's b f May H., by Falsetto, dam Glenluine.
L. U. Shippee's b f False Queen, by Falsetto, dam Queen Victoria.
H. I. Thornton's br f Bessie Barnes, by Darebin, dam Carrie C.
H. I. Thornton's b f Madeline, by John Happy, dam Jongleuse.
G. W. Trahern's ch f Minnie B., by Prince of Norfolk, dam by Wildidle.
Undine Stable's b c Homer, by Shannon, dam Sallie Gardner.
Undine Stable's ch f Glenlivet, by Flood, dam Glendew.
Theo. Winter's b c Rey del Rey, by Norfolk, dam Marion.
Theo. Winter's ch c San Juan, by Norfolk, dam Ballinette.
Theo. Winter's blk c Black Bart, by Three Cheers, dam Bonita.
Theo. Winter's ch c Una Grande, by Joe Hooker, dam Jessie R.
Theo. Winter's ch c Judge Post, by Joe Hooker, dam Countess Zicka.

No. 12.—Purse $400; of which $50 to second, $25 to third; for all ages. Mile heats.

W. L. Appleby's ch m, 5, Carmen, by Wildidle, dam Nettie Brown.
Dennison Bros.' b g, a, Dave Douglas, by Leinster, dam Lilly Simpson.
J. T. McBride's ch f, 4, Longshot, by Duke of Norfolk, dam Langford.
Miller & Owen's b m, a, Daisy D., by Wheatly, dam Black Maria.
Orange Grove Stable's b h, a, Jack Brady, by Wildidle, dam Sour Grapes.
W. L. Whitmore's ch h, 5, Coloma, by Joe Hooker, dam Callie Smart.

No. 13—The Sequel Stakes, a handicap for all ages; $25 each, half forfeit, $5 if declared out, with $500 added; second horse to receive $75, third to save stake. Weights announced Wednesday, April 16th, at 10 o'clock A. M. Declarations at 5 P. M. the same day. One mile and three-eighths.

W. L. Appleby's b f, 3, Raindrop by Wildidle, dam Teardrop.
W. L. Appleby's ch m, 4, Odette by Shiloh, dam Margery.
Dennison Bros.' b h, 4, Hotspur by Joe Daniels, dam Sister to Jim Douglas.
Elmwood Stables' b g, a, Nabeau by Nathan Coombs, dam Beauty.
J. Hilton's b g, 4, Albatross by Pill Box, dam Della Walker.
Kelly & Samuel's b h, a, Ed McGinnis by Grinstead, dam Jenny G.
Kelly & Samuels' b g, 3, Pliny by Flood, dam Precious.
Owen Bros.' b m, 5, Carona by Norfolk, dam Sister to Lottery.
Orange Grove Stables' b h, a, Jack Brady by Wildidle, dam Sour Grapes.
Palo Alto's b m, 4, Faustine by Flood, dam Flight.
W. H. E. Smith's b h, 6, Al Farrow by Connor, dam Della Walker.
M. Storn's ch m, 4, Lurline by Longfield, dam Katy Pease.
H. I. Thornton's b m, a, Abi by Red Boy, dam Abi.
George Hearst's b h, 4, Almont by Three Cheers, dam Question.
W. L. Whitmore's ch h, 5, Coloma by Joe Hooker, dam Callie Smart.

FOURTH DAY, SATURDAY, APRIL 19, 1890.

No. 14—Purse $350, of which $50 to the second horse; a handicap for two-year-olds; entrance free for starters. Declarations $5 to go to the racing fund. Weights announced Friday, April 18th, at 10 o'clock A. M. Declarations due at 5 P. M., the same day. Eleven-sixteenths of a mile.

Elmwood Stables' br c Sir Walter by Nathan Coombs, dam Bessie.
William Fitzgerald's b f Miss Melbourne by Gano, dam Victoria.
Kelly & Samuels' ch f Lizette by Hyder Ali, dam Kate Fletcher.
Cy Mulkey's b c Sinfax by Wildidle, dam Fortress.
W. M. Murry's blk c Powder by Powhattan, dam Lawn Tennis.
W. M. Murry's ch g Gold Pan by Panique, dam Neunetzen.
Orange Grove Stables' br h Joe Woolman by imp. Cyrus, dam Ella Doane.
Palo Alto's ch c Rinfax by Argyle, dam imp. Amelia.
Palo Alto's ch f Tearless by Wildidle, dam Teardrop.
H. I. Thornton's ch c Arcade by Milner, dam Nanny Hubbard.
H. I. Thornton's b f Cimeter by Hyder Ali, dam Sabrina.
H. I. Thornton's b f Madeline by John Happy, dam Jongleuse.
Undine Stable's b c Homer by Shannon, dam Sallie Gardner.
Undine Stables' ch f Glenlivet by Flood, dam Glendew.
George Hearst's ch c Anarchist by Joe Hooker, dam Chestnut Belle.
George Hearst's b c Yosemite by Hyder Ali, dam Nellie Collier.

No. 15—Selling purse, $350; of which $50 to the second; for all ages. Horses entered to be sold for $1,000 to carry rule weights. Three pounds allowed for each $100 less. Three-quarters of a mile.

J. J. Abbott's g, 3, Abbott Colt by Billy Lee, dam Flight.
T. Bally's b g, a, Jou Jou by Monday, dam Plaything.
Dennison Bros' b m, 4, Sallie C. by Thornhill, dam by Wildidle.
Elmwood Stable's b g, 6, Vinco by Bob Wooding, dam Mollie H.
C. Foster's b f, 3, Rose Meade by Wildidle, dam Duchess.
W. George's b g, a, Applause by Three Cheers, dam Alice N.
N. S. Hamlin's ch g, 4, Sir Reginald by Joe Hooker, dam Dolly Varden.
J. G. Hill's b g, 3, Steve Stroud by Billy Lee, dam by Woodburn.
G. Howson's g g, a, Johnny Gray by Shiloh, dam Margery.
Kelly & Samuels' ch g, 4, Rosebug by Jim Brown, dam Rosemary.
S. Meninhall's ch m, 3, Maggie B by Milner, dam Young Grecian Bend.
H. D. Miller's ch m, a, Ida Glenn by Glen Elm, dam Queen.
Cy Mulkey's ch g, a, Tom Daly by Patsy Duffy, dam Sunshine.
W. M. Murry's b f 3, Lady Ali by Hyder Ali dam Mollie Ward.
C. Nickerson, b h, 5, Hernanda by Wildidle, dam Viola Bey.
Orange Grove Stable's ch g, a, Adam by Shiloh, dam Mollie Adams.
J. Reavey's b m, 4, Bessie Shannon by Shannon, dam Betty Bishop.
J. R. Ross' b m, 4, Kittie Van by Vanderbilt, dam April Fool.
M. Storn's ch g, 5, Kildare by Kyrle Daly, dam Mistake.
Undine Stable's b m, 5, Recess by Kelpie, dam Bell Belmont.

No. 16—Purse $400, of which $50 to second, $25 to third; for three-year-olds and upwards. Winners of any race at this distance or more at this meeting when carrying weight for age or more, to carry five pounds extra; of two such races eight pounds extra. Horses beaten at this distance this year once allowed three pounds, twice five pounds. One mile.

W. L. Appleby's b f, 3, Raindrop by Wildidle, dam Teardrop.
Kelly & Samuels' br f, 3, Adelaide by Grinstead, dam Victoria.
Miller & Owen's blk c, 3, Captain Al by Kingston, dam Black Maria.
W. M. Murry's ch c, 3, Kiro by Joe Hooker, dam by Foster.
C. Nickerson's b m, 5, Fanny F. by Wildidle, dam Sally Hart.
P. Seibenthaler's ch c, 3, Sheridan by Joe Hooker, dam Sally Hart.
P. Seibenthaler's ch c, 3, Sheridan by Joe Hooker dam Lost Girl.
George Hearst's ch h, 4, Del Mar by Somnus, dam Maid of the Hills.
W. L. Whitmore's ch h, 5, Coloma by Joe Hooker, dam Callie Smart.

No. 17—Purse $350; of which $50 to second horse, an owners' handicap for horses that have started and not won at this meeting. Weights to be given through the entry box at 5 o'clock P. M. the day before the race; ten pounds over weight allowed. Winners excused without penalty. One mile and a sixteenth.

W. L. Appleby's ch m, 5, Carmen by Wildidle, dam Nettie Brown.
W. L. Appleby's ch m, 4, Odette by Shiloh, dam Margery.
Elmwood Stable's ch m, a, Nerva by Bob Wooding, dam Lizzie Marshall.
Elmwood Stable's br m, 4, Installation by Inaugurasion, dam Brown Maria.
W. George's b g, a, Applause by Three Cheers, dam Alice N.
N. S. Hamlin's ch g, 4, Sir Reginald by Joe Hooker, dam Dolly Varden.
Kelly & Samuels' b g, 3, Pliney by Flood, dam Precious.
Miller & Owen's b m, a, Daisy D. by Wheatley, dam Amelia.
W. M. Murry's b c, 3, Leland by Flood, dam Amelia.
A. Wakeman's ch c, 3, Kiro by Joe Hooker, dam by Foster.
Owen Bros.'s b m, 5, Carona by Norfolk, dam Sister to Lottery.
Owen Bros.'s b m, 4, Emma by Joe Daniels, dam Jenny C.
J. Reavey, b m, 4, Bessie Shannon by Shannon, dam Betty Bishop.
W. H. E. Smith's b h, 5, Al Farrow by Connor, dam Della Walker.
M. Storn's ch g, 5, Kildare by Kyrle Daly, dam Mistake.
Undine Stable's ch f, 3, Bettie B by Joe Hooker, dam Kate Carson.
George Hearst's ch m, 4, Gertrude by Somnus, dam Geraldine.
George Hearst's ch c, 3, Baggage by Warwick, dam Maria F.

No. 18—The Ocean Handicap, a sweepstake for all ages; $50 entrance $10 forfeit; $5 declarations with $600 added, of which $75 to the second, third to save stake. Weights announced Thursday, April 17th, at 5 o'clock P. M. Declarations due Friday, April 18th, at 5 o'clock P. M. One mile and five-eighths.

W. L. Appleby's b f, 3, Raindrop by Wildidle, dam Teardrop.
Dennison Bros.' b h, 4, Hotspur by Joe Daniels, dam Sister to Jim Douglas.
Elmwood Stables's b g, a, Nabeau by Nathan Coombs, dam Beauty.
Kelly & Samuels' b h Ed McGinnis by Grinstead, dam Jenny G.
Palo Alto's b m, 4, Faustine by Flood, dam Flirt.
J. R. Ross' b g, a, Oro by Norfolk, dam Golden Gate.
George Hearst's b h, 4, Almont by Three Cheers, dam Question.
George Hearst's b h Sacramento by Joe Hooker, dam Ada C.
W. L. Whitmore's ch h, 5, Coloma by Joe Hooker, dam Callie Smart.

Foreign Demand for the American Trotter.

It is not at all unlikely that ere long the tables will be turned in the matter of trade in horses between the United States and foreign countries, and instead of importing hundreds of thousands of dollars' worth annually and exporting practically none, our exportations across the seas, before many years elapse, may become largely in excess of any importations that have been made in the past, says an exchange. While we do not look for any immediate falling off in the importation of first-class draft horses for breeding purposes, owing to the fact that our supply is still very much less than the demand, yet the eyes of the whole world are constantly being turned to this country on account of the wonderful excellence that has attached to our fast driving horses, or as they are generally called "roadsters." There has been an occasional demand upon our breeders for horses of this type from foreign countries for several years past, but this demand appears to be rapidly growing of late. In fact, within the past month we have been in receipt of inquiries from South America and from prominent dealers in two European countries making inquiries concerning the prices at which fast trotting and roadster horses can be purchased. The European papers especially have expressed the opinion that a very extensive and important trade might with very little effort be built up for horses of this type. It is a universally conceded fact among the horsemen the world over that for fast driving upon the road there is no horse bred anywhere that is equal to the American trotter. The nearest approach to it is doubtless the Orloff trotter of Russia; but these are unquestionably inferior to our horses in speed, and probably in powers of endurance as well. Our last inquiry comes from a European dealer who is engaged in furnishing horses in large numbers for the German market. This correspondent says: "Everybody in this country wants to drive fast now-a-days, and the Germans generally have come to understand that the place to get fast driving horses is in America." It is pleasant to note that while the business of cattle breeding may be suffering temporary depression, owing largely to over production and to the practical exclusion of our meats from a considerable portion of the markets of the world, yet there is every indication of continued prosperity to every branch of the horse breeding interests. Heavy draft horses sell readily and at good prices. High stepping, stylish carriage horses cannot be found in sufficient numbers to supply the demand, while our fastest roadsters and trotting horses bring almost fabulous prices. Of course the weeds, the culls, and the inferior ones of all types are a drug on the market, and this is as it should be, for it affords encouragement to the enterprising, intelligent breeder who values good blood, exercises sound judgment in the selection of his breeding stock, practices judicious methods of feeding, training and management and hence produces the very best.

TURF AND TRACK.

It is now said that Axtell has not gone lame.

David Waldo has purchased Brac a Ban, the chaser.

El Rio Rey is in Nashville, and is said to be as sound as a dollar.

It is said that at New Orleans overweight to any extent is allowed.

Bithers' salary at the Allen Stock Farm is reported as $4,500 per annum.

Mr. Bonner will have Russella the sister to Maud S. 2:08¾ trained this season.

Old Inspector B, is to have a rest, and will not be taken up and put into work until Fall.

Proctor Knott is said to be looking exceptionally well, but has had no work so far this season.

White Hat Dan McCarty's brother will probably go East as plating expert for the Santa Anita Stable.

Mr. Belmont has a yearling brother to St. Carlo who is as big and as well furnished as a three-year-old.

The New Orleans spring meeting will open on April 2nd and continue on the 3d, 5th. 7th, 8th and 9th.

There seems to be no doubt now that Terra Cotta will be raced this season if he stands the preparation.

Ira L. Harris who purchased Protection 2:19¼ at the Brasfield sale has since sold him realizing a big profit.

If Sir Dixon does not stand training, he will be relegated to the Clay and Woodford stud farm (Runnymede).

It is said that Elphin will be sent to England this fall to try his luck among the chasers in the mother country.

Mr. Jennings has purchased My Own and will breed her, Swift, Biggonet and Telie Doe to Superior this season.

The Electioneer—Sallie Benton youngster has been broken, and although having had no fast work, shows great promise.

Prodigal Son by Pat Molloy out of imported Homeward Bound, is the favorite of many speculators for the Kentucky Derby.

Hon. F. G. Babcock, owner of Rosa Wilkes, 2:18¼, has, after some persuasion, induced the owners of Axtell to breed her to the crack.

Ed Bither is due to start work at the Allen farm to-day. He will take ten of twelve head to Hartford early next month and commence training.

Marion Briggs, Jr., is building a new race track near Oroville. The track when completed is expected to be one of the fastest in the State.

Col. R. S. Strader has sold to S. A. Browne & Co. Kalamazoo, the bay yearling filly Nina by Clay 4779 dam Sallie Hamlet by Hamlet 160.

Messrs Wilson & Handy, owners of Sultan 1513, have given the Macey Bros., who suffered such a severe loss by fire, a service of Sultan free.

Horse thieves were busy in Los Angeles last week, Mr. Wilshire, of Fullerton, having a five-year old A. W. Richmond mare and a bay horse stolen.

Ben Benjamin the well known Southern sporting writer, is doing good work now as the Secretary of the Los Angeles, Sixth District Agricultural, Association.

California Writers originated the statement that Los Angeles can trot a mile in three minutes, yet it is singular no Californians believe that the mare can do it.

Brown Dick will have a strong stable this season, among the older ones under his care are Prodigal Son, Pearl Set, and Ruperta. Allen will ride for the stable again.

O. A. Hickok has been jogging his pacer Adonis for the last couple of weeks at Palo Alto. The Wilkes—Lucy pacer has also been taken up and put into jogging.

Ione Race Track has had a fair amount of patronage this fall, Rondo and several other sprinters being on the track, while a host of trotters have been jogging along.

Charles Marvin left for New York last Tuesday with 104 head of trotting stock, including Ansel, who will be delivered to Mr. Bonner. The remainder are to be sold in New York.

Frederick Vanderbilt is said to have been offered $25,000 for the offspring of Aldine and Early Rose if both are fillies, $30,000 if there is one of either sex, and $35,000 if both are colts.

Bayonne Prince 1939, record 2:21½, by Kentucky Prince 2470, dam Emily C. (dam of Marcus 2:29½), was sold on March 6th by R. Cadogan to A. Cordova and E. R. Brown. Price $25,000.

The Italian Trotting Derby for 1893 (for four year olds) has forty one entries, thirty-six of which are by American stallions. Amber has fourteen, Hambleton twelve, and Ellwood Medium ten.

On Thursday the 27th, at Easton's Hunt's Point paddocks, imp. Gruditz, by Kisber (winner of the Derby), dropped a filly foal by imp. Esher, son of Claremont, who was second in the Derby to Galopin in 1875.

It is said Mr. Chas. Reed has presented Capt. J. B. Howeson, of Gallatin, with two stallions, Highlander and Rossifer. Mr. Reed's stallions, Forrester, Mr. Pickwick, Miser and Long Taw, will serve no outside mares.

Mr. F. J. Baldwin, Managing Director of the Fresno Racetrack Association, has been in town for several days. He says their prospects are exceptionally good, and he expects to have a highly successful spring meeting.

Immediately the announcement appeared in the BREEDER AND SPORTSMAN last Saturday, that Barnes would ride Maori in the Suburban. The mare was cut to 80 to 1, and on Monday to 20 to 1, at which price she now stands.

The yearlings of Cliff Lawn, Richland, Kennesaw, Peytonia, Lakewood and other Tennessee stud farms, and those of Greener, Malone, Rutherford and others, about sixty in number, will be sold at West Side Park, Nashville, this season.

Among the McMahon, Garrison & Co.'s stock to be sold on April 7th are Eolian, Speedwell, sister to Kingston, Falcon, Pocatello, Banbridge, Sterling, 3 year old brother to Eurus, and a lot of other well known performers.

The Trainers and Jockeys' Protective and Benefit Organization was formed on March 3rd at the Monmouth Club rooms. The officers elected were Chas. Littlefield, president, Wm. Hayward, vice president: R. W. Walden, treasurer: Jacob Pincus, secretary.

Dan McCarty has purchased Bay Rose, price $10,000. Dan says he will breed about thirty mares of his own to him and trot him next fall. McCarty also traded a mare and cash for Designer, the five-year-old son of Director and May Queen by Abbotsford.

The horses owned by Messrs. Costello & Granner will be sold next month, when McMahon & Co.'s lot are disposed of. Lucy H, Satisfaction, Maid of Orleans, Bay Ridge and Lillie M are in the Stable. The stable effects will also be offered at the sale.

Mr. S. H. Baughman, Stanford, Ky., has purchased from William McCloy, Frankfort, Ky., the bay horse Powattan II, foaled 1881, by imp. Glenelg, dam Florence I (dam of Florio) by imp. Australian, her dam Charlotte Buford by Lexington, out of Kitty Clark by imp. Glencoe.

J. L. McCord, of Sacramento, was in town this week. He says Mary Lou, 2:25½, is in better trim than she ever was before, and that he is going to bring Ned Winslow, 2:17½, down to San Francisco next week to have a drive through the Park a few times.

Mabel (sister to Beautiful Bells) foaled a slashing bay filly by Albert W. 2:20. Among the thoroughbred mares Carissima has a big powerful chestnut colt by imp Sir Modred. Up to the 25th of February, there were fifty-four foals on Rancho Del Paso. How would that look in Kentucky?

The Duke of Portland should have a few good two year olds again this season, among them are Simon Magnus by St Simon out of Wheel of Fortune. The Wheel was probably the best race mare Lord Falmouth ever owned; and Koorali is a full sister to the flying Semolina.

Robert Bonner says: "If I desired to produce only the greatest possible number of 2:30 trotters, I should not use any thoroughbred blood but would stick to tested trotting families. If, however, extreme speed was the result I wished to obtain, I should want at least 25 per cent. of approved thoroughbred blood."

Mr. Charles Backman writes: The first foal here is a bay filly, foaled February 23d, got by Kentucky Prince, 1st dam Regina by Wood's Hambletonian; 2d dam Mary Ann by Magnolia; 3d dam by McConnell's Champion. I have added 102 acres to my farm, having purchased the Gavin Farm between my place and the station.

Mr. Theodore Winters says he has heard nothing of the reported offers that have been made for El Rio Rey. Nearly all his Hooker fillies which are in Nevada are already bred to Jumbo, by California out of Big Gun. The mares at Sacramento will be bred to Hooker, and all will be taken across the mountains shortly to Washoe Valley.

There should be quite lively bidding at the Belle Meade sale for Iroquois, sire of Cayuga, and Luke Blackburn, sire of Proctor Knott, both were high class racehorses in their day—Iroquois in England and Blackburn in America. Some of the Scotland mares too should provoke a good deal of spirited bidding, while the yearlings always sell well.

Jas. Lee, ex-trainer for Mr. Chas. Reed, will hold the starter's flag at the Washington meeting, beginning April 1st. Lee has already officiated with success as starter several times at the winter meetings, and should give every satisfaction at Washington. It seems a pity, though, that his long connection with Mr. Reed is severed.

Hon. C. M. Thomas has introduced the following in the Kentucky Legislature: "An act to prevent false timing at trotting contest in the common-wealth; making it unlawful for any party acting as official timers to announce a slower or faster time than that actually made, and fixing a Fine not to exceed $500 and imprisonment of six months.',

I received a letter, but too late for the public, last week, from New York, from which it seems that the veteran cross-country traveller John Mackey landed in New York with the Rancho del Paso trotters at 2 A. M. on the preceding Saturday, having been five days and ten hours on the cars. The horses all turned out in good shape after their journey.

The Shire horse trade in England seems very brisk, as I notice that, on the 5th, Mr. Clarke of the Moulton Chapel Stud, Spaolding, sold fifty-one animals for an average of 121 guineas, ($600) the highest price being 400 guineas for a two year old filly, the Prince of Wales, the Duke of Marlborough, Lord Ellesmere, and others being purchasers.

Little Teddy Martin, the precocious infant who was mixed up in the Aylesbury racing scandal, has returned from Buenos Ayres without very exalted ideas of the Buenos Ayrians. Martin, who was a very capable light weight, should have plenty of riding in England next season as he was practically exonerated on account of youth, etc., when the expose occured.

White hat Dan McCarty's stable in the East is not as large as usual. The Eastern papers say the stable of McCarthy, of California, is in good shape just now, although it contains but three racers. He has Pandora, three years old and two, two-year-olds, one a black filly by Joe Daniels—Test, the other, a bay filly by Bon d'Or—Lady Glasgow, also four trotters.

John Splan has returned from England. He says that the English people will pay a reasonable figure for a moderately fast stepping road horse that can go a distance. If American breeders will send that class of animal across, they will find it prove remunerative. The horses must be of good class, capable of going a distance at a good clip, have courage and be good lookers. Splan brought back with him an Orloff or Russian trotter, the gift of Mr. Winans of Brighton. He is a brown stallion, 15.3 hands, and Splan will breed him to mares here as an experiment.

Wm. Hendrickson who was (with Old Patchen) for years a feature on the California race tracks, has after carefully travelling around, bought a horse of Mr. John Gordon, San Jose. He is an eight year old chestnut, son of Nutwood 2:18¾, and out of a Patchen mare. Mr. Hendrickson's old friend John Williams will handle the horse for a while in Sacramento.

Mr. Lee, the owner of Robert McGregor, 2:17½, has farmed of A. A. Kitzmiller, Plane View Stud, to be bred to that horse, the fast four-year-old pacing mare, Lydia Wilkes by Red Wilkes, dam Aileen by Mambrino Boy, paying for her services this year $2,000. She has no record, but was timed a mile out in 2:20 in her race with Don Pizarro last summer, which was won by him in 2:15½.

The experience of Paris tramway companies with regard to the hardihood of horses is corroborated in New York, namely, that gray horses are the longest lived and give the greatest amount of service. The roan horse is equally good. Black and cream-colored horses lack staying power, especially in summer. Bays show an average. Black hoofed horses are the stronger and tougher.

Mr. H. P. Headley, administrator of the late Mr. B. F. Pettit, Lexington Ky. has sold to Milton Young, McGrathiana Stud Lexington, Mr. Pettit's half interest in the imported brown horse Pirate of Penzance, foaled 1882 by imp Prince Charlie, dam Plunder, by Buccaneer, her dam Sister to Aegis by Defence out of Soldier's Joy, by The Colonel. The Pirate, who was a fair racehorse in England will make the season at the McGrathiana Stud.

A road match for $250 a side came off last week at New York between the pacer Monkey Rolla, 2:15½, and the trotter Little Wonder, trial to road wagon. The course was from One Hundred and Thirty-third Street to One Hundred and Fifty third Street and Seventh Avenue, Monkey Rolla to pull two men weighing 300 pounds, and Little Wonder one man. The distance is about one mile, and the contest was to be best two in three. The pacer, driven by the veteran Pete Manee, won in two straight heats.

W. H. Madden, the clever light weight attached to W. M. Murry's stable, has in conjunction with with his parents signed a contract for two years to ride for Murry. Mr. Murry says the reason for having the contract drawn up so stringently was that one of our wealthy Western racing men had been making vigorous attempts to entice the boy away, but Mr. Murry has had too much experience in that line of business to be fooled with and soon put a stop to it.

Among the many new rules passed at the National Trotting Congress most of which are necessary there is one commends itself to all straight forward even minded men, viz.: "When two or more horses have each won two heats and there shall have occurred between them a dead heat in any part of the race, they alone shall start in the next heat." The effect of this is, it does not make any difference where the dead heat was trotted, if there be two heats won by each horse and a dead heat between them.

Maj. J. L. Hallett, Spring Hill Farm, Washington County, Or., has sold to Van B. DeLashmutt, Portland, the bay mare Almonette, record 2:29½, dam Favorite, by Post's Hambletonian; bay mare Mattie, full sister to Almonette; black mare Vita, by Altamont, dam Tecora; bay filly Tinto, by Altamont, dam by Bacon's Hambletonian; bay mare Lapento, by Altamont, dam Kitty Lynn; grey filly Olly, by Mambrino Duke, dam Dolly by Bellfounder. Price $5000.

The dispatch stating that Paterson, N. J. would offer a $10,000 purse for a match race between Sunol and Axtell was shown to Mr. Ijams, one of the owners of Axtell at Terra Haute on March 7th. He said: "I cannot tell what opinion the other gentlemen may have in the matter. It may be accepted, but I hardly think Axtell will be in shape for a test of speed. He now has over 40 engagements in the stud and will not be through until some time in July. Axtell is at Mr. Ijams' stock Farm at Terra Haute and is in fine condition.

Fleur de Champs died on February 28th at Mr. A. Belmont's Nursery Stud in Kentucky. She was one of the very few daughters of the mighty Newminster imported into America, and resembled the old horse uncommonly, having all his well known qualities and finish. By her side, when she was imported, was Nellie James, who afterwards won the Hopeful and other crack races, and is the dam of Jacobus, Jack of Hearts, St. James, etc. Woodbine was the best of Fleur de Champs' many good foals sweeping the deck in filly races, and since is the dam of Forester, etc.

The Melbourne Cup of the 4th was won by the three-year-old Dreadnaught two and a quarter miles in 3:59½. Dreadnaught is by Chester, dam imported Trafalgar by Blair Athol, grandam Mosquito, sister to Musket. The three-year-old ran the course in the best time ever made since its initiation race, in 1863, which was won by Barwon, three years old, 106 lbs, in 4:27. Among other winners of the cup is Lurline (dam of J. B. Haggin's imported Darebin) in 1875, when five years old with 113 pounds up in 4:25.

W. Field Smith made a very successful sale last week of his Wilkes stock, Mr. Miller of New York buying his three-year-old stallion Kalibar by Guy Wilkes 2:15¼, dam by Sultan, granddam Inez 2:30, by The Moor, and his two-year-old filly Felucca by Guy Wilkes out of Cora by Buccaneer. Wilbur will probably soon have the vacancies in his stable filled, as he is one of the most capable, reliable drivers and trainers in California, his word being better than most men's affidavits.

Prof. Fred Smith, of the Army Veterinary School at Aldershot, England, says that the compression to which the navicular bones of the fore limbs are exposed is something enormous. A horse weighing 1000 pounds throws 187½ pounds more weight on his forelegs than on the hind ones, and the total amount on his forelegs is 600 pounds, or 300 pounds on each leg. This shows how important it is to take especial notice of the forelegs, as well as the hind, in purchasing a horse.

Mr. W. E. Holloway has bought several thoroughbreds from Col. Jas. McNasser which he will ship to Messrs. Grant & Co., Valpariso, Chili, to be raced or trained as is deemed advisable. The horses are Lady Della, 3-year-old chestnut filly by Longfield out of Maud Turney, by Harry Bluff; Lillias, 4-years-old bay filly, by Norfolk, out of Madam Turney, by Harry Bluff; the trotting stallion Bambletonian King Jr., by Hambletonian King, dam Morosa by Autocrat, and the three-year-old colt San Victor, bred by W. L. Pritchard, by Young Bazaar out of Lizzie P. by Leinster.

At the Pleasanton Stock Farm sale in New York, Gold Leaf 2:11½, the crack Sidney pacer sold for $8,000; Thistle, full brother to Gold Leaf, brought $4,000, both being purchased by J. H. Schults; Erect, three-year-old brother to Direct 2:18½ fetched $5,000, the purchaser being H. Kirkendall, of Helena, Montana; Saccharine, two years old by Director 2:17, out of Sweetness 2:21¼ (dam of Sidney 2:19¾) was bought by E. J. Travis, Chicago, for $4,500.

The fact that in the English handicaps the fields are invariably larger than in this country shows that something is wrong in the American system, and the only plausible theory is that the low weight limit is responsible. Messrs. Lawrence and McIntyre, the leading Eastern handicappers, have caused the withdrawal of many cracks from the big events for this spring by asking for instance, one 3-year-old to run against others of the same age, at a difference of forty pounds, and by placing in all aged contests the same limit between top and bottom weights.

The high-bred horse is the animal nearest to man in intelligence. Horse-breeding has become a science. In France it has reached a wonderful degree of perfection. The French people are lovers of horses. This sentiment has been kept alive amid all the turmoils of France. The government has lent its interest to secure a valuable animal for army use. The government has its own stud horses selected with the greatest care. This fostering has resulted in wonderful progress. Over 12,000 have been recorded under the direction of the government. The most valuable horse in France is the French coach horse.

Better betting is to be had this year on the English spring handicaps than for several seasons past. The latest figures on the Lincolnshire Handicap show 100 to 8 against Nunthorpe (111), 100 to 7 each against Laureate (128), Sweet Briar (103), Clarabelle (106) and Danbydale (103), and from 20 to 33 to I against the others The four Suburban favorites are Pioneer (106), at 100 to 7; Amphion (121), 100 to 6; Laureate (119), 20 to 1, and Theophilus (110), 20 to 1. For the Derby Surefoot is a steady favorite, the price being 4 to 1. Le Nord, Heaume and Riviera are next in order, and long odds can be had against the other candidates.

Wilfred Blunt, a noted English breeder of Arab horses, gives it as his opinion that the Arab belongs to the original wild races of Africa rather than of Asia, and was introduced to Arabia by way of Abyssinia, whence it is historical that he spread northward. He was not known in Europe before the Mohammedan conquest, but since then his blood has spread through all lands visited by communication with Mecca through the pilgrimage. The Barb of North Africa, the Andalusian horses of Spain, the Turk, the Persian and the Turcoman have been all largely infused for centuries with Arab blood. The first Arab blood in England was probably brought through Spain and France, and the latter from Palestine by the Crusaders.

Last week owing to hurried work, I stated that Marion's yearling was dead. I should have said her foal to Hooker came dead. Mr. Winters has the yearling half sister to El Rio Rey, near Sacramento. She is a fine Hooker filly, a rich chestnut, with a little white on one hind fetlock and resembles the Czar more than any other of the family. Alice N., the dam of Applause, has a very racy looking brown colt by Hooker. Countess Zerika has a good looking Hooker foal. Mr. Winters was in the city this week and will take all his stock into Nevada, including Norfolk. The old horse is in such wonderfully good trim just now that it seems a pity to transplant him.

The City and Surburban, to be decided on April 23, at the Epsom Spring Meeting, closed with an entry of nearly 70. The old established Great Metropolitan Stakes (April 22), which is run under slightly different conditions this year, has been supported to double the extent it was last year, the entries numbering between 50 and 60. So far as class is concerned, the City and Surburban is well represented. Amongst the older horses nominated are Veracity, Sheen, Reve d'Or, The Baron, Ringmaster, Felix, etc. The four-year-olds include Vasistas (the winner of the Grand Prix) and Miguel, who was second to the Donovan for the Derby, whilst many good-class three-year.olds have also been entered.

There were on the Palo Alto special train eight head of horses, the property of Mr. Charles Miller of New York, who had purchased them in California. Three of them were bought from Wilber Field Smith, viz.: Calabar, bay three year old stallion by Guy Wilkes 2:15½, dam Rosedale by Sultan, granddam Inez 2:30 by The Moor; Felucca, two year old brown filly by Guy Wilkes 2:15½, dam Cora 2:44 at two years old, by Buccaneer 2656, granddam Pearl 2:32½, by Blue Bull and Neola, by Sidney 2:19¾, dam Mollie by Chieftain 721. Mr. Miller paid $6000 for the trio. The other five were a bay mare, sister to Adair 2:17½, by Electioneer, dam Addie Lee; bay mare Lona, by General Benton, dam Lady Hamilton; black mare Arabella by Berlin, dam Arabia; a yearling black colt by Norval 2:17½, dam Pansy 2:24¼ (sister to Thapsin 2:21¼) by Berlin, and a yearling brown filly by Norval, dam Thalia (sister to Thapsin 2:21¼ and Pansy 2:24¼).

Porterville is keeping up its racing proclivities. The Enterprise has a graphic account of a two days' meeting on Mr. Kelly's mile track. On the first day the stallion trot had three entries—Capt. Hayes bay stallion Judge Kyle, Mr. Hawkins' black stallion Black Dick, and Mr. Anderson's bay stallion Bey Wilkes. Black Dick won the first heat in 2:43¾. Judge Kyle the second in 2:48. Bey Wilkes wound up the race, taking the next three in 2:38½, 2:41 and 2:43.

On the second day the free-for-all pace had two entries—Mr. G. Nanny's bay mare Birdie and Mr. J. Jackson's bay horse Ed. Birdie took the first heat in 2:29½, the second in 2:33½. Ed took the third and fourth in 2:41 and 2:38. The fifth was declared no heat on account of several fouls, and as Mr. Jackson did not appear for the final, Birdie walked over in 2:34½.

A meeting of the prominent Kentucky breeders was held to fix dates for the spring yearling sales. John S. Clark took the chair, and B. G. Bruce acted as Secretary. Dates agreed on were:

Monday, May 5th—Clay & Woodford, John S. Clark and Mrs. W. Cassius Goodloe.

Tuesday, May 6th—H. C. Headley and other breeders.

Wednesday and Thursday, May 7th and 8th—Bruce & Kidd's combination sale, consisting of the Edgewater, Kingston and other well known yearlings.

Mr. Milton Young of the McGrathiana Stud was present at the meeting, but took no part. He will sell thirty-seven head of yearlings in New York this spring, and the remainder will be sold here next fall.

Neither the Woodburn nor Elmendorf Studs were represented.

J. H. Oglebay, treasurer of the Kansas City Jockey Club, who has been absent for some time, has succeeded in perfecting his big scheme. The Western circuit as now arranged takes in Chicago, Independence, Ia., St. Louis, Kansas, City Jockey Club, Topeka, Kansas City Exposition Driving park, Terre Haute, Lexington and Nashville. It will open up at Chicago on August 18-23. Then will follow Independence Ia., August 25-30; St. Louis September 1-6; Kansas City Jockey club September 7-13; Topeka, September; 14-20 Kansas City Exposition Driving park September 21-27, followed in October by Terre Haute, Lexington and Nashville in the order named,

The Kansas City Jockey club will open no stakes for the September meeting, but will hang up large purses, none less than $1,000.

Geo. Van Gorden, the Superintendent of Senator Hearst's San Simeon Ranch, was in town last week making entries for the Blood Horse and Breeders' Meeting. Despite the heavy rains, he says the stock are all in good order, several hundred head of cattle being fat and ready for killing, while the thoroughbred stock are doing very well. Twelve or thirteen thoroughbred foals have already been dropped on the ranch, Jim Brown's get being unfortunately all fillies this year. Mr. Van Gorden sent six mares to Sacramento last week to Cheviot, the rest of the mares are being bred to imported San Simeon (Peter Jr.), Jim Brown and the Australian stallions. Among the trotters, Mr. Van Gorden has great expectations of the four-year-old Claremont, by McGinnis, out of Maggie C., a thoroughbred daughter of Swamperdown. McGinnis is a bay pacing stallion by Algona 11543, out of Creole by The Moor 870, grandam Madam Gibson by Ten Broeck .(Cosmo—Fannie Howard by Illinois Medoc).

It is semi-officially stated that the St. Louis Jockey Club will race three days a week during spring and summer. The subject was discussed on March 1st at the meeting of the board of Directors and all seemed to be in favor of it. The plan is to begin in April the same as last season, and race three days a week until the spring meeting in June. After the meeting inducements are to be offered owners to keep their stables there and continue racing through the summer. The question of success depends largely on owners. It is a well known fact that the St. Louis track is not popular with owners, Many of the most prominent stables have not entered there at all. The minor string now in training are going to Nashville as fast as possible, Owners assert that stable room is offered free in the South, and that St. Louis puts a price on it. If owners could be induced to make their headquarters as the Fair Grounds successful racing could be given through the season, but the indications now are that there will be a lage vacancy in the stalls.

The annual meeting of the Directors of the Mt. Shasta Agricultural Society was held March 1st.

Directors present—James Vance, President J. V. Brown, J. T. Moxley, S. D. Prather, F. A. Autenrieth, J. M. Walbridge, J. E. Harmon. W. S. Stone proxy for J. T. Griffiths of Trinity County.

Reports of Secretary and Treasurer examined, found correct, and ordered to be placed on file.

Election of officers held, and James Vance re-elected President, C. S. Smith, Secretary, and Maurice Renner, Treasurer.

The following committees were then appointed:

On Collection of Subscriptions—J. T. Moxley.

On Track—J. E. Harmon, J. T. Moxley and W. S. Stone.

On Speed Programme—J. M. Walbridge, S. D. Prather and F. A. Autenrieth.

There being no further business, the Board adjourned to the call of the President.

When a Gaucho wishes to catch a wild horse, he mounts one that has been used to the sport, and gallops over the plain. As soon as he comes sufficiently near his prey, the lasso is thrown round the two hind legs, and as the Gaucho rides a little on one side the jerk pulls the entangled horse's feet laterally, so as to throw him on his side, without endangering his knees or his face. Before the horse can recover the shock the rider dismounts, and, snatching his poncho or cloak from his shoulders, wraps it around the prostrate animal's head. He then forces into his mouth one of the powerful bridles of the country, straps a saddle on his back, and bestriding him removes the poncho, upon which the astonished horse springs on his legs, and endeavors by a thousand vain efforts to disencumber himself of his new master, who sits quite composedly on his back, and by a discipline which never fails, reduces the horse to such complete obedience that he is soon trained to lend his whole speed and strength in the capture of his companions.

Interested parties are forming a stock company to lease the track and its equipments from the St. Louis Jockey Club, give races and guarantee the purses, none of which shall be under $250. This company is to have the track all the year except during the regular spring meeting and the regular trotting meeting. Agents of the company recently submitted the matter to President Green, and he said he would lease the track for $20,000 a year. The chief object of the company in securing the track is to provide for the anti-pool bill, which is expected to come up before the next Legislature. In case pooling is prohibited, except on race tracks, bookmakers can make books on the Eastern races at the St. Louis track. This is anticipating the Legislature, which body may not disturb the bookmakers, and if they do, a year's grace is usually given. Chicago is the only city in the West which holds races through the spring and summer, and the important factor in the success in the West Side Track is that the company which operates it is composed of horse owners.

One of the English papers some months ago, spoke very plainly about the Duke of Portland. It said a good deal of fulsome rubbish has been written and said about the sportsmanlike qualities of His Grace. If genuine sportsmanship on the turf consists in literally running horses off their legs, then it must be candidly admitted that His Grace is *facile princeps* of all the noble patrons of that branch of sport. Not content with breaking down Semolina, he succeeded in the Champion Stakes in finally closing Ayrshire's career, by starting the horse in a condition which made it apparent to the veriest tyro that defeat was inevitable. As a matter of fact, the suspensory ligament of the off foreleg gave way during the race. Even if the Duke were a poor man, it would be inexcusable to work his horses in the way he has done during the present season, but as he is the possessor of a princely income, his conduct appears suspiciously like callous, or is tinged with an inordinate greed for winning heavy stakes. That he has not yet succeeded in breaking down Donovan is a matter of pure luck. How often is it here we see a good horse run off his legs and then if a gelding?

The feature of the Shelburne Farm's Sale, held in the American Horse Exchange, was imported Siddartha, 10 years old, by Pero Gomez, out of The Pearl by Newminster, granddam Caller Ou by Stockwell out of Haricot by Mango or Lanercost, out of the famous Queen Mary. Siddartha is one of the highest bred horses ever imported. His sire Pero Gomez, was beaten a head for the Derby of '69 by Pretender, but easily turned the tables in the Leger. Pero Gomez is the sire of Pontiac, Hidalgo, Merry Thought, Gil Blas, Harbinger, Espada, Titania, etc. The Pearl is the dam of Selby, winner of the Great Yorkshire Handicap in 1886. Siddartha's granddam is Caller Ou, winner of thirty-four Queen's plates and stakes innumerable; and among other famous winners in his family are Blink Bonny, out of Queen Mary; Blair Athol, Sir Bevys, Blinkhoolie, Freeman, Good Hope, Thrift; etc. Siddartha is a dark brown stallion, imported by Pierre Lorillard, ten years old and 16 hands high. The bidding for him was not very lively, and he was knocked down to Dr. A. W. McAlester of Columbia, Mo., for $1,800.

Sam Bryant, the picturesque owner of Proctor Knott when he won the Futurity and the Junior Champion, was at one time, according to a new Western story, the superintendent of a small southern track, and owner of some two year olds, to one of which a horseman took a great fancy. The horseman said he would buy him if the colt could go half a mile inside fifty seconds. Bryant told him to come to the track early next morning and see for himself. The man came and the colt was sent from the half mile pole to the wire in forty-nine seconds. The delighted horseman paid his money and departed with the colt. Friends of Bryant who visited the track that afternoon say that Sam was busily engaged in digging up the half mile pole.

"What's the matter, Sam?" questioned one of the party.

"Oh, this half mile pole's well-nigh rotten, an' I thought I'd plant a new one," was the crafty Sam's reply.

People do say that the new pole when in position was 100 yards farther from the wire than that which marked the half mile pole when the trial was run that morning.

Which will turn out the crack two year old among the high priced ones is the problem of the day. Marcus Daly the Montana millionaire has among others Silver King by St. Blaise, dam Maud Hampton, bought as a yearling for $22,000; Montana, by Ban Fox, dam Queen $6000, Prince Charming, by Sir Modred, dam Carissima, $3,650; Mistletoe, Brown Fox and Bonnie Lass. Senator Hearst's expensive collection is as small as it is select. It is headed by Finework sister to Dewdrop, a brown filly by Falsetto, out of Explosion, secured at $10,000. Warpath, by Ban Fox, or Warwick, dam Secondhand, $5,100; Algernon, by Joe Daniels, dam Faustina, $2,500; Rubicon, by Hyder Ali, dam Graciosa, $1,000, and Atlas, by Hyder Ali, dam Fidelity, $500. The Morris stable has among its luxuries Key West, by Glenelg, dam Florida, $7,000; Westchester (half brother to Tremont), $6,700; Compassion, by Alarm, dam Sister of Mercy, $3,600; Arbutus (Miss Woodford's first foal), $2,550; Hands Off, by Luke Blackburn, $2,500; Hypatia, by Woodlands, $2,100, and Aspen, by Petrarch, $2,000. Dwyer Bros. have Blacklock (brother to Sir Dixon), $4,000; Baldwin (sister to Miss Ford), $3,500; Hannibal, by Billet—Mercedes, $3,200; Bushbolt, by Himyar-Booty, $2,200, and a big lot of other costly and promising colts and fillies. William Walker has Silver Prince, by Spendthrift, dam Phœbe Mayflower, at $3,025, and Sydney, by Spendthrift, dam Constantinople $1,800. D. T. Pulsifer, has Sir George, by Spendthrift, dam Piccadilly, paid $1,200; Kirkover, by Attila, dam The Squaw, $1,000. E. V. Snedecker paid $1,500 for a sister to Kingston and there are many others.

A good deal of interest was caused at the Haggin sale of yearling thoroughbreds last July by the announcement that six fillies, some choice lots of the sale, purchased by Mr. C. Reed, were for Mr. John H. Shults, a Brooklyn breeder of prominence. It was further added that Mr. Shults proposed to race them until they matured sufficiently for breeding purposes, and signs of interest in racing shown by such a man were hailed as renewed evidence of the growing popularity of thoroughbred contests. The Sporting World says: Mr. Shults, however, has changed his mind, if in reality he ever seriously contemplated racing the fillies. Being trained would be of great benefit to the fillies, and Mr. Shults' decision, therefore, will not meet with general approval, especially as, should any show signs of special ability, they would be great acquisitions to racing talent. Some of them are exceedingly promising, as Mr. Moser, superintendent of the farm, gave four out of the six, furlong gallops, with 110 pounds up, in 12½ seconds, they not previously having received any training other than that acquired by themselves in a natural way. The entire lot look remarkably well, and are as follows:

Bay filly by Arthur H.—Augusta E.
Chestnut filly by Warwick—Clarissa.
Bay filly by Warwick—Cordelia Planet.
Bay filly by Himyar—Alice.
Bay filly by Kyrle Daly—Alva.
Chestnut filly by Darebin or Kyrle Daly—Agnes.

It is the present intention of Mr. Shults to have them served, when they have sufficiently matured, by some promising thoroughbred stallion, and they may prove the nucleus of a breeding farm for thoroughbreds.

The Old Guard Stakes at a mile and a half on March 7th, was the most comical race ever seen on a winter course. The conditions were that only non-professional jockeys should ride at weights 60 pounds above the scale. There were eleven entries and all started, the weights ranging from 150 to 165 pounds. The wind was keen and piercing, but the track was muddy and sloppy. Most of the riders were old-timers who had outgrown their business. They were received with shouts of laughter. The gentleman jockey who caused the greatest outburst of merriment was Mr. W. Woodlands, owner of the imported horse Dochart. He rode his own horse at 156 pounds and the post betting was 15 to 1 against him. Woodlands is a very short man with a rotund body. He wore a bright orange jacket and a black cap was pulled down over his head almost to his shoulders. His nose resembled a beak. At the start it looked as though Dochart was carrying a prize pumpkin with a crow perched on top of it. The black horse Falcon strode away in the lead. There was nothing else in the race for nearly a mile. Then the orange-colored pumpkin loomed up in the front and was never headed, winning by half a length. The shouts of laughter and applause which greeted the winner were mild, compared with those which hailed him when he proceeded to the post. In the excitement of winning Mr. Woodlands forgot to salute the judges before dismounting. Major Wheeler, who presides with the dignity and solemnity of a Supreme Court justice, added to the fun by informing Mr. Woodlands that he must pay a fine of 75 cents for dismounting without permission. All wondered how the rotund jockey finished without tumbling out of the saddle. Several of the riders nearly came to grief, and all were covered with mud.

The San Jose Spring Entries.

Secretary Bragg of the San Jose Blood Horse Association, has forwarded us the following list of entries for their spring meeting.

INTRODUCTION STAKE.

A sweepstake for all ages: $25 entrance, $10 forfeit, with $200 added; $75 to second horse, $25 to third. Maidens, if 3 years old, allowed 5 pounds, 4 years old and upwards 7 pounds. Three-fourths of a mile.

Owner	Horse
G. Lyman	5—b g Pain Killer
J. B. Stults	a—s m Little Girl
W. L. Appleby	3—b f Raindrop
J. Beavey	4—b m Bessie Shannon
Alex. Graham	4—b m Mable H.
Miller & Owens	A—b m Daisy D.
Orvill Appleby	3—b f Juniata
T. Bally	a—b g Jou Jou
J. Dowd	A—b g Sunday
Chris Peterson	4—b g Jubilee
Kelly & Samuels	3—br f Adelaide
J. J. Abbot	3—b g Abbot Colt
J. B Ross	4—b f Kitty Van
Orange Grove Stable	A—ch g Adam
George Hearst	4—ch h Del Mar

VENDOME STAKE.

For 3-year-olds; $25 entrance; $10 forfeit, with $175 added; $50 to second horse, $25 to third. One mile.

Owner	Horse
Palo Alto Stock Farm	ch f Muta
Palo Alto Stock Farm	b c Racine
Miller & Owens	blk c Captain Al
Kelly & Samuels	b g Pliny
George Hearst	b c Sacramento
George Hearst	ch c Baggage

DEBUT STAKES.

For 2-year-olds: $25 entrance; $10 forfeit; with $150 added; $50 to second horse. Half mile.

Owner	Horse
W. L. Appleby	b c No Name
Palo Alto Stock Farm	ch f Tearless
Palo Alto Stock Farm	ch c Rinfax
R. B. Cockrell	b c Mero
Wm. Fitzgerald	b f Miss Melbourne
Kelly & Samuels	ch f Lizette
Orange Grove Stable	br c Joe Woolman
George Hearst	ch c Charlie Brown
George Hearst	ch c Primero

ST. JAMES HOTEL STAKE.

A sweepstakes for all ages; $25 entrance, $10 forfeit, with $175 added. Stake and money divided: 60 per cent. to first horse, 30 per cent. to second, and 10 per cent to third. One mile.

Owner	Horse
W. L. Appleby	4—ch f Odette
Palo Alto Stock Farm	4—b f Faustine
C. Nickerson	5—b m Fannie F
J. McM. Shafter	4—b m Louisa M
Elmwood Stable	7—ch m Nerva
Kelly & Samuels	3—b g Pliny
J R. Ross	4—b f Kitty Van
Orange Grove Stable	5—b s Jack Brady

SANTA CLARA STAKE.

A sweepstakes for all ages; $25 entrance, $10 forfeit, with $175 added; $50 to second horse. Winner of the Introduction Stakes to carry 5 lbs. above the scale weight. Seven furlongs.

Owner	Horse
G. Lyman	b b Pain Killer
W. L. Appleby	3—b f Raindrop
J. Beavey	4—b m Bessie Shannon
Miller & Owens	a—b m Daisy D
Chris Peterson	4—b g Jubilee
Elmwood Stable	a—ch m Norva
Kelly & Samuels	3—b g Pliny
J. R. Ross	a—b g Oro
Geo. Hearst	4—ch m Gertrude
Geo. Hearst	4—ch h Del Mar

LAURELWOOD FARM STAKE.

A sweepstake for all ages; $25 entrance, $10 forfeit, with $200 added; $75 to second horse. Weight 10 lbs. above scale. One and one-eighth miles.

Owner	Horse
W. L. Appleby	4—ch m Odette
Palo Alto Stock Farm	4—b f Faustine
Kelly & Samuels	5—br m Welcome
Orange Grove Stable	5—b s Jack Brady

LAMOLLE HOUSE STAKE.

For three-year-olds; $25 entrance, $10 forfeit, with $175 added; $50 to second, $25 to third. Winner of the Vendome stake to carry 10 pounds extra. One mile.

Owner	Horse
Palo Alto Stock Farm	ch f Minta
Palo Alto Stock Farm	b c Racine
Miller & Owens	blk m Captain Al
J. O. Woolman	b f Emma Nevada
Kelly & Samuels	b g Pliny
Geo. Hearst	ch c Baggage
Geo. Hearst	b c Sacramento

MILPATAS STAKE.

A sweepstakes for all ages; $25 entrance, $10 forfeit, with $175 added; $50 to second horse. Half mile heats.

Owner	Horse
G. Lyman	5—b b Pain Killer
D. F. Abel	ch g Rondo
W. L. Appleby	5—ch m Carmen
Miller & Owens	a—b m Daisy D
Orvill Appleby	4—br m Alfarata
T. Bally	9—b g Jou Jou
J. Dowd	a—b g Sunday
Kelly & Samuels	4—ch g Roseberg

AL FARROW STAKE.

A sweepstake for all ages (owner's handicap); $50 entrance, $25 forfeit or $10 if declared out by April 1st, with $250 added; $75 to second horse, $50 to third. Weights to be announced by 6 o'clock P. M, the evening before the race. Stake to be named after the winner if Al Farrow's time of 1:40 is beaten.

Owner	Horse
W. L. Appleby	5—ch m Carmen
Chas. Nickerson	5—b m Fannie F
Miller & Owens	A—b m Daisy D
Chris Peterson	4—b g Jubilee
Elmwood Stable	5—b g Nabean
J. B Ross	4—b f Kitty Van
J B. Ross	A—b g Oro
Orange Grove Stable	A—ch g Adam
Geo. Hearst	4—ch h Del Mar
Geo. Hearst	4—ch m Gertrude

LICK HOUSE STAKE.

For two-year-olds; $25 entrance; $10 forfeit, with $150 added, $50 to second horse. Winner of the Debut Stake to carry five pounds extra. Five furlongs.

Owner	Horse
Palo Alto Stock Farm	ch c Rinfax
Palo Alto Stock Farm	ch f Tearless
R. B. Cockrell	b c Mero
Wm. Fitzgerald	b f Miss Melbourne
Kelly & Samuels	ch f Lizette
Orange Grove Stable	br c Joe Woolman
Orange Grove Stable	ch c Bon Ton
Geo. Hearst	ch c Primero
Geo. Hearst	b c J. B.

HOBSON STAKE.

A sweepstake for all ages; $25 entrance, $10 forfeit with $175 added. $50 to second horse, $25 to third. Weight ten pounds below the scale. Winner of any race at this meeting to carry five pounds extra, of two races seven lbs. of three races ten pounds. Messrs. T. W. Hobson & Co. will present the winning jockey with a fine suit of clothes—made to order. One and one-quarter mile.

Owner	Horse
W. L Appleby	4—ch m Odette
Palo Alto Stock Farm	4—b f Faustine
Owens Bros	5—b m Carona
J. McM Shafter	4—b m Louisa M
Kelly & Samuels	5—b h Ed McGinnis
Kelly & Samuels	3—b g Pliny
J. R. Ross	a—b g Oro
George Hearst	3—b b Sacramento
Geo. Hearst	3—ch c Baggage

SPRINTER'S STAKE.

A sweepstake for all ages; $25 entrance, $10 forfeit, with $75 added, $50 to second horse. Quarter-mile heats.

Owner	Horse
D. F. Abel	ch g Rondo
Ed Williams	s g Jew
J. B. Stults	s m Little Girl
Wm. Walsh	s m Lilley Belle
Alex Ayers	m Oregon Annie
F. E. Randel	g Comet
J. Dowd	b g Sunday
Martin Duffy	s g Cyclone
Alex Graham	s g Jack the Ripper
Ed Fitzgerald	m Gypsy Girl

The Rose Sale.

This year Mr. Rose desired to clear out Rosemeade Stud, and hence he brought his gilt edged property to New York, says the Herald, the second time, and once more placed it into Mr. Kellogg's hands to dispose of. It was of the same sort that created such a sensation one year ago, only better, if possible. Great merit is claimed for it, and the great trotting judges of the country admit there is much in the claim. Mr. Rose is sure of the merit of the blood he has been propagating and he defies contradiction when he says that all in all there are no trotters superior to those he has been breeding and developing at his farm.

The eagerness of the breeders to obtain the first class stock is proof that they entertain a like feeling with Mr. Rose, and the fact goes to show that the trotting families not of the highest notch must fall into the utility classes in the future. There is a great number of wealthy gentlemen in the country interested in the production of trotters, and they are willing to pay big money to obtain the fashionable blood to work with. This was demonstrated yesterday at the sale of about one-half of Mr. Rose's consignment. Forty-three head were sold, and they brought the enormous sum of $140,270—an average of $3,262—which is the largest average for any number of horses that was ever made at any sale in this or any other country, either of trotters or racers.

The Rosemeade owner was naturally pleased, and once more he will go to his distant home satisfied that he has been on the right road in his breeding business.

The sale commenced with the seven-year-old bay stallion Alcazar by Sultan, dam Minnehaha. Mr. Kellogg referred to the merits of the horse and of his owner's judgment in his breeding interests. Then Mr. Rose had something to say about Alcazar being in his opinion a sire without an equal. The bidding commenced by Mr. John E. Madden, of Lexington, Ky., offering $15,000. The starter was only needed. Half a dozen took a hand in the bidding at once, and soon it was $20 000 offered. Here Madden quit. Then Mr. Robert Steel, of Philadelphia, seemed to hesitate, and at $21,500 he had gone far enough. Mr. Edward A. Tipton, of the firm of Messrs. W. R. Brasfield & Co., of Lexington, Ky., chimed in, and with Captain Fred Pabst, of Messrs. Uhlien Bros. of Milwaukee, Wis., and Mr F. C. Babcock, of Hornellsville, N. Y., made it merry and gave Mr. Kellogg all he could do to keep track of the offers. Tipton fell out of the ranks at $25,-300, and then Pabst and Babcock had it to themselves. The crowd was intensely interested. Cries of "Don't weaken!" were frequent. Babcock hesitatingly offered $25,600, and at the same time a friend shouted to him:—"Go in, Babcock. If you are too nervous to sign a check I'll sign one for you!" But Pabst wouldn't be denied. He boldly cried $25,800, and the building rang with cheers. Babcock was turned to, but he was silent, and the "going-going-gone" was soon heard giving the stallion to the Uhlien Bros., of Milwaukee, for $25,800. Mr. Kellogg smiled, so did Mr. Rose, and so did the crowd.

The start was a good one. There is nothing like it at an auction sale, and to the end the gilt edged stock brought marvellous prices.

The next offering to create big excitement was Voodoo, a bay colt, foaled June 2, 1888, by Stamboul, dam Eva, by Sultan. The crowd was at fever heat. The opening bid was $5,000, and soon Mr. John H. Shults, of Brooklyn, who has a breeding farm at Parkville, L. I., was an interested party. He sent the thousands flying upward with a freedom that seemed to say, "I'm in to stay!" But Mr. Babcock, who had been unsuccessful in his pursuit of Alcazar, had his courage doubly riveted and he "saw all of Mr. Shults' bids" and went a great deal better. With $24 000 Mr. Shults quit. Then "$24,100" from Mr. Babcock secured the promising youngster.

"Mr. Babcock," said Mr. Rose, looking thoroughly pleased, "won't you go to the best tailor in New York, get the best suit of clothes he can make and send me the bill?" Mr. Babcock smiled in return, and doubtless he will be in a nobby suit in a few days, even if he has placed many thousands at interest in a two year old trotting colt.

Thor, a two year old by Alcazar, brought $9,000, (the telegraphic account sent us stated the price at $4,000,—Ed.), Mr. Tipton, of Kentucky, buying him for Mr. G. M. Fogg, of Nashville. Harvester, an eight year old stallion, was sold for $3,600 and goes to the Blue Grass region of Kentucky. Choice a Dictator mare with a colt at foot, sold for $3.000 and follows Harvester to Kentuckey. Grecian Bend, another Director mare was purchased by "Andy" Welch, of Hartford a young gentleman who started a few years ago with nothing, but now whose bid is as good as anybody's at a horse sale. Henlen, a Kentucky Prince mare, joined Thor for $3,100 and will go to Tennessee.

Laura Corbett, a Guy Wilkes mare caused a bitter fight between several gentleman, among whom was Mr. Shults, but she was finally secured by Mr. F. C. Sayles and will go to Providence, R. I. Lady Mackey was considered worth $5,000 and will be heard from in Kentuckey. Mista by Alcazar, dam Lady Dey, by California Dexter, who took a two year old record of 2:29 in the second heat of a race, was secured by Mr. William Pabst, Jr., and will be found in Milwaukee in the future. She will attract attention anywhere. Mispah, sister to Mista, brought $4,600, and goes to Pennsylvania, and so the great work of rolling the dollars into Mr. Rose's treasury continued in fine style until forty three lots were sold and the day's catalogue was exhausted.

Then Mr. Rose lighted a cigarrette and leaving the side of Mr. Kellogg looked around among his friends and said something which everybody addressed understood. It sounded like this "There's plenty of wine, gentlemen."

Our Nashville Letter.

West Side Park, Nashville, Tenn., Mar. 1, 1890.

Editor Breeder and Sportsman:—The weather here has been exceedingly wet for the last few days, which has impeded the galloping somewhat, though some were sent along regardless of weather. The horses here are all healthy, and mostly in good condition. Reports from Memphis of work both strong and fast there reach here daily. There are about one hundred and fifty horses there, and one hundred and thirty here. Major Elliot has Bridge Light and Sam Doxey here, both in Eastern Stakes, and they are looking remarkably well and working along slowly and kindly. Mr. Winters' car arrived from New York this morning with Joe Courtney, Don Jose and others looking fresh and well, but El Rio Rey, who showed fatigue and uneasiness, was taken off at Louisville and left there to rest. The car was, through the negligence of that worst than all impostors, a railroad official, side tracked and left twelve hours at Cincinnati, notwithstanding it was coming by express. It is to be hoped that Mr. Winters will try them a heat through the courts, for their motto seems to be to take your money, promise everything and perform only as they like.

The catalogue of the twenty-third annual sale of the Belle Meade yearlings is just out, and contains sixty-four yearlings—the get of Enquirer, Iroquois, Luke Blackburn, Bramble and Great Tom. Many of them are from dams of winners, and some full brothers and sisters to winners. They are said, by competent judges, to be a superb lot of youngsters. In addition to the yearlings, the entire stud of mares, one hundred in number, and the five stallions will be sold, to dissolve the existing partnership. The sale will be made the 24th and 25th of April. Of the imported stallions since the days of Diomed, Glencoe, Bonnie Scotland and Leamington have proven of greatest worth to the American thoroughbred. Their sons and daughters have raced to the front, and have got and thrown winners of greatest worth. Many of the broodmares at Belle Meade are rich in the blood of the two former. Two sons of Old Queen Mary's son—Bramble and Luke Blackburn—are doing service there, and two of Leamington's sons—Enquirer, the good racehorse and sire, and Iroquois, probably the best son of Leamington, and likely to prove as famous in the stud as he was on the turf. His get will rank with the best America or England can produce.

The locality that secures this young sire will go to the front as a producing section. Who does not like the Leamingtons? They go all distances, carry all weights and win. They may be said to train themselves, for they win with any kind of handling, and in any kind of hands. Some of these youngsters that are to be sold, perhaps some of the cheap ones, will make great horses one or two years hence. Mr. Cherry has just shipped his pacer, Jesse James, to New York City, to make a race of half mile heats against a roadster of that city. A recent decision of the Supreme Court has closed all the pool rooms here; and hereafter, pools can only be sold and books made during races here. It is becoming popular these days for men who play stable-boys "tips" and invest two or three dollars on a loser to go straight away to the Legislature and introduce a bill to prohibit the demoralizing business of pool selling, then pose as benefactors. The contempt they have for everything connected with horses and racing, and for men who engage in it, is pompously paraded on all occasions, and their denunciation loud and severe, whilst they generally run their fingers into their vest pockets, as if the subject was suggestive of pick pockets, or perhaps reminded of the missing change before they turned moralists. They bear a strong likeness to each other in feature and manners. They generally drive to the stables and want to stop a rubber from his work to hold their Jade, while they light a "twofr" and quiz the boys for information; sometimes, not always, giving the boy who holds for them, a "nickle." It is hoped the pool room is the only place of wickedness known to them. Pity some of them ever figure in more degrading resorts. Only those who do, need be offended—the innocent are not herein, as aforesaid mentioned. The blood horse has made his presence known and valued here. The roadsters of the city and 'roundabout, are well bred, handsome, stylish, and with plenty of "go along" in them. An infusion of the thoroughbred can be recognized wherever seen, even in the commonest cob. Sheridan is engaged to do the starting here, and at Memphis. The weather is raw and cold at this writing.

Silence.

The American Trotting Association.

M. F. Tarpey, Esq., has received the following letter from the Secretary of the American Association, which may be of interest to the local associations which are unattached at present:

Dear Sir: The prospects of the American Trotting Association are very bright for 1890, and we especially desire to increase our membership in California and its contiguous states and territories. We have one hundred more members than the National Trotting Association, and by the change in our rules at the last Congress, give almost entire jurisdiction to all cases arising west of the continental divide, thereby virtually giving you control of your own cases and all the facilities of this office. It is tantamount to a Pacific Coast Association without the attendant large expense necessary for carrying on a central office.

I send you by mail to-day (in another inclosure) a lot of our circular letters setting forth a few of the many advantages of belonging to the American Trotting Association, which I hope you will be able to use to advantage. I would also thank you to send me the names of any and all parties to whom you think it would be advisable for me to write with a view to increasing our membership in your State. I believe that we have transacted our business to the entire satisfaction of every member we have in California—at least I have never received a single complaint.

Kindly give this matter your thought, and me your views, as to the best method to be pursued to increase our membership in California, and much oblige.

Yours truly,

J. H. Steiner, Secretary.

THE FARM.

Is It Best to Breed for Mutton and Let the Wool Take Care of Itself?

[A paper read by I. J. Williams, Muncie, Ind., at the Indiana Wool Growers' Meeting held at Indianapolis, Jan 21-22.]

The question whether sheep can be profitably bred for mutton alone has been one to which considerable thought has been given; and yet we find a diversity of opinion among men who it would seem are fairly able to judge. To the question I would venture to say no, and try to give reasons afterwards.

Now if we raise sheep for the mutton only why not abandon them and raise cattle? From my experience I have arrived at the conclusion that in raising sheep the wool will pay for the keeping, and we have that much more profit; and that when we breed for the mutton alone we necessarily decrease the wool product and proportionately decrease the profits arising therefrom, and therefore we must not breed for one thing only.

If the numerous flocks of this country were bred for mutton alone it would be but a short time until the entire wool business would be turned over to our Australian friends, who would supply the demand, which would have a tendency to increase the price of wool, which in turn would of necessity increase the price of common wearing apparel. Or if we would turn the whole wool business over to our Merino friends to supply us with fine wool, then we could not afford to wear such fine clothing. The Merino breeders don't raise very much mutton, as their sheep are nearly all wool, and after the fleece is clipped there is nothing left but a very small carcass. In order to gain a requisite amount of profit we must raise a sheep that will combine a growth of wool with a growth of mutton, and that will make the most mutton and a good grade of wool. The greatest number of pounds of mutton with the least feed is where we get our profit. Where we drop the wool interest we are losing that which we should have; for if the wool pays for the keeping then all we make on the lambs pays us well for our money invested.

For illustration suppose that we take $100 in the fall and start out and buy under favorable conditions. And in the handling of sheep, as of other farm animals, the best fed and yield the highest profit.

For bringing up lands, no farm animal is the superior of the sheep, and for bringing up quite poor lands, no other farm animal is its equal. This is because the sheep will utilize more of the growth of such lands than will any other stock, and while the composition and quantity of manure made by the sheep for certain food is not superior to the manure of other animals using the same food, the fine division and more general distribution of the manure of the sheep make it a superior animal for improving lands, particularly poor lands. The man with worn or thin lands to enrich, can use sheep to better advantage than he can any other animal.

For several reasons sheep commend themselves to the man with limited ready capital. For example, to stock land with sheep requires less money than to stock it with horses or cattle, and the sheep will make returns earlier and more frequently. Many men cannot afford to wait two or three years before getting a substantial return on their investment; but sheep will produce an income within a year, and will afford two sources of income every year—wool, and the increase for mutton.

It is not contended that every farmer should grow sheep extensively, or that every farmer should keep sheep; but it is submitted that a careful inquiry into the advantages of sheep husbandry, close figuring on costs and returns, will show that more farmers should have sheep, and that many flockmasters would do well to increase their flocks.—National Stockman.

Reciprocity.

The following is from a Canadian paper, the Free Press of London:—

"The attention of Parliament has been called to the largely increased import of fresh beef into Canada from the United States, and a recommendation comes from Mr. Joseph Marshall, the member from East Middlesex, to increase the duty, with a view to affording further protection to our own farmers. It is probable that some such course as this will be taken. In western Ontario the force of this competition is not felt, but in the Maritime Provinces several millions of pounds are annually brought in. It is said that the facilities for transportation are such that fresh beef can be laid down in the Lower Provinces at a very small cost; so small, indeed, as to be about the same as it would cost a farmer 150 miles away to deliver his beef. It is known that the industry in beef raising has grown to be such a large matter in the Western States that special means of carriage have been found. Refrigerator cars are now run in large numbers over the through routes, and at a cost most astonishingly low. In dealing with this matter it must be borne in mind that Canada aims to be a large cattle and beef producing country, and it would be an anomaly if we should send large numbers of live cattle across the Atlantic, while doing little to preserve the relatively more valuable home market. There need be no compunction on the part of the Canadian authorities in taking high protective grounds. No one can read the recent announcements of the Secretary of Agriculture at Washington and fail to see that the definite policy of the American Administration is to take every means within their power to protect their farmers. Considerations of self interest should dictate the propriety of our authorities being equally vigilant in the interests of our agriculturists. If large quantities of beef, either salted or fresh, are wanted in the Maritime Provinces, it will hardly do to have the Americans supply it, while we have abundance of the finest meat in our own country. This is a proposition which will commend itself to the judgment of Canadians generally.

Chester Whites.

At a discussion in the National Chester White Association of "Black spots in Chester Whites," it was decided that black spots and black hairs were an evidence of impurity of blood and were therefore objectionable; that the blue flecks in the skin, while not any evidence of impurity, were not desirable; and that the only method of suppressing these objectionable spots was to discard all pigs having them, or pigs from litters any of which were so spotted. Breed entirely from hogs which are pure white and whose ancestors were also pure white with pure white skins and the spots will soon disappear; was the general conclusion.

Montana Stockmens' Opinion.

The stockmen of Montana have nothing to fear from the present agitation in regard to taxing range privileges, which is now going on in the east. Certainly the government cannot exact a tax upon our cattle without giving some guarantee of furnishing a supply of feed; and if the scheme of renting its domain at a given price per acre were adopted, it would have to guarantee the exclusive right to use the same and allow it to be fenced, which would be contrary to its present attitude towards the unenclosed lands. It is only the poor man who is struggling to lay the foundation of a home, who is barely able to supply his family with the rudest necessaries of life that this scheme would discommode. The cattle owners would profit by this system, as it would enable him to control his range. We do not favor it because it would retard the progress of civilization. We have no fears as to its not meeting the approbation of a large number of stockmen, and we are rather inclined to think that it would be advantageous to the heavy grower. The feeling that prompts the agitation, though, is not calculated for the benefit of the weak, but is engenered through jealousy based upon assumptions which have no foundation in facts. Our stockmen have richly earned every privilege they enjoy, and there was a time when there was an advantage in free range. But the country is now so crowded with stock that there is no security whatever offered and there are few heavy owners who would not be willing to pay a fair price if they could have a given range for their own exclusive use. And, unless the agitators of the scheme are ready to assure this, it is idle to discuss the question; but, when they do this, they must remember that they raise a formidable barrier against further settlement.—Rocky Mountain Husbandman.

Acute Tympanitis or Hoven in Cattle.

This peculiar affection is known by a variety of terms hoven, hoose, blown, dewblown, grass-sickness, etc. It occurs very rarely among cattle grazed on the range country, but frequently in cattle permitted to graze on clover or alfalfa pastures; and especially in cattle that have been driven long distances and while very hungry turned into damp or dewy pastures, Almost any kind of food in excessive quantities may produce it.

The symptoms are a well marked enlargement and elevation of the left flank; sometimes the stomach becomes enormously distended and ruptures; the breathing is much impaired and there is dribbling of frothy saliva from the mouth and constant belching of gases; pain and suffering is manifested by moans and grunts, also general uneasiness and stamping the feet or striking the abdomen with the hind feet; the eyes look wild and the animal glances frequently at its sides. If not relieved in a short time, death may result from rupture of the stomach, blood poisoning due to absorption of gases, or suffocation due to pressure of the enlarged stomach against the diaphragm.

The treatment must be very prompt to save the life of the animal. In very severe cases the best and proper course is to clip the hair off a small spot on the most prominent point in the left flank, then plunge a small lance through the skin and push a trochar and cannula through the muscles and into the stomach, then withdraw the trochar and allow the cannula to remain in till all the gases escape. Push the trochar into the cannula whenever it becomes obstructed with escaping food. A small or medium knife blade may be used, cattle feeders often used a medium sized butcher knife on cattle in alfalfa pastures. In California the cattlemen always watch the stock carefully for a week or ten days after changing to a new location from range to alfalfa pastures.

The wound in the side ought to be treated with some healing lotion or carbolic acid ointment. The mild cases may be treated successfully without any operation in the side and stomach. Both the severe and mild cases ought to be treated with a half teacupful of bicarbonate of soda, or baking powder, a tablespoonful of black pepper, or a teaspoonful of red pepper, with a pint of water. Those remedies are generally at hand on every ranch, and may be repeated every two hours till the animal shows signs of recovery, then cease giving medicine and drive the animal several miles. A tablespoonful of powdered ginger and a pint of water makes a serviceable drench, or a tablespoonful of carbolic acid and a pint of linseed oil will answer very well when no other medicines are at hand.

It would be good policy for every ranch man to have a few good books on diseases of live stock, and devote some of those long winter evenings to study.

James A. Waugh, V. S., in Las Vegas Stock Grown.

Markings of Berkshire Hogs.

Editors Country Gentleman:—Mr. A. B. Allen, page 92, referring to the English breeders in confining the markings of Berkshire pigs to four white feet, white tip to the tail, and white on face, but white anywhere else objectional, says, "It seems a very foolish and hurtful thing to confine them to such narrow markings." Mr. Allen is certainly right if there were any difficulty in securing these marks, so that some of the best must be rejected, but the Berkshires have been so long and carefully bred that these marks are almost certain. Out of thirty-seven pigs dropped since January 7, 1890, not more than two would be ruled out. Pigs can be bred so easily that it would be folly to breed anything but the best, and to expect a fancy price for these is also folly.

In the same paper, same page, Mr. S. H. Todd says "the coming hog" must be large and light, with lean meat. "Large and light" means much bone and little meat. A large, leggy, thin carcass is certainly not the best for lean meat. A thick, fleshy, compact carcass, with heavy hams and shoulders, fine bone, superb back and loin, fine, short head, fine tail and a good coat of fine hair—these points of excellence are found in the Berkshire. Any pig with these qualities will be free fleshers, which can never be said of the large, light hog, of whatever breed. I do not know whether Mr. Todd's hog is an imaginary one, or whether he knows of such a breed. I can hardly understand how a hog with superb back and loin, splendid ham, medium shoulders and smooth, firm body can be the large, light hog described. The hog we are after is a small, heavy hog of early maturity and small offal, and such I find in the Berkshire. With skimmed milk, peameal and bran, our pigs will dress 200 lbs. at six months, with good, solid meat, not too fat for the market. If it is desired to have them leaner, feed slower by giving less meal and more milk—they must not be stinted in quantity. The breed that has more points of excellence than the Berkshire is yet "the coming hog," and when he does come he will not be some new breed, but some of the present breeds yet more perfected. We cannot afford to throw away the many points of excellence secured to us by the many years of careful study by skilled breeders. We must breed as well as feed for first quality meat, which means marbled, not lean, for although it has been proved that lean meat can be produced to a limited extent by forced feeding, yet if the natural assimilation is forced by a food over rich in albuminoids, it will be at a loss, and our aim in all operations is to avoid this.

Thomas B. Scott.

Ontario, Canada.

Cattle Statistics.

We are in receipt of a few additional statistics on the cattle interest of the United States from the Agricultural Department. The number of cattle exported during 1889 was 603,952 head, alive and dressed, as many in 1889, as in 1888 and 1887. The market value of British and foreign cattle in the market, taking the weekly quotations for the last half of 1889, and quoting the average of the markets for the last half of the year, was follows: British cattle second quality, fourteen; first quality, 5 6-10; foreign cattle, second quality, 11-65-100; first quality, thirteen. The above prices are the dressed weight. It will be noticed that as between British and foreign cattle there is about two cents on each quality, or, to be more exact, on second there is a difference of 2 4-10 cents and on first quality 3 6-16. Mr. P. D. Armour, in his statement to the committee of the United States Senate, said that his firm purchased in 1888 340,649 head of cattle: that the average dressed to live weight was 54.76 per cent., nearly fifty-five per cent. The export cattle are of a higher quality, and ought to dress sixty per cent. dressed to live weight. The shipping rate during 1889 has ruled higher than usual for the reason that the large shippers have undertaken to control the shipping room of the steamers. The low prices that have prevailed during 1889 at Chicago have been charged to over-production. As between the first and second quality of British cattle and the same classes of foreign cattle there is a difference of $2.60 per hundred. If American breeders and feeders will breed and feed for the top of the market they can cover $1.60 of this differene, which would give about $14 per 100 pounds for a dressed carcass or for a well bred and well fed 1500-pound steer there is $100 at Chicago.—American Cultivator.

Suggestions in Milk Setting.

1. To make the finest flavored and longest keeping butter the cream must undergo a ripening process by exposure to the oxygen of the air while it is sweet. This is best done while it is rising. The ripening is very tardy when the temperature is low.

2. After cream becomes sour, the more ripening the more it depreciates The sooner it is then skimmed and churned the better, but it should not be churned while too new. The best time for skimming and churning is just before acidity becomes apparent.

3 Cream makes better butter to rise in cold air than to rise in cold water, but it will rise sooner in cold water, and the milk will keep sweet longer.

4. The deeper milk is set the less airing the cream gets while rising.

5. The depth of setting should vary with the temperature; the lower it is the deeper milk may be set; the higher, the shallower it should be. Milk should never be set shallow in a low temperature nor deep in a high one. Setting deep in cold water economizes time, labor and space.

6. While milk is standing for cream to rise the purity of the cream and consequently the fine flavor and keeping of the butter, will be injured if the surface of the cream is exposed freely to air much warmer than the cream.

7. When the cream is colder than the surrounding air, it takes up moisture and impurities from the air.* When the air is colder than the cream, it takes up moisture and whatever escapes from the cream. In the former case the cream purifies the surrounding air; in the latter, the air helps to purify the cream. The selection of a creamer should hinge on what is most desired—highest quality, or greatest convenience and economy in time, space and labor.—Ex.

Shorthorn Sales.

The announcement that an auction sale of registered Shorthorn cattle will be held at Sacramento on April 3rd, is made in our advertising columns. Being held under the management of the Pacific Coast Short-horn Breeders' Association, is a guarantee that the animals will be exactly what they are advertised to be, and all breeders of cattle and ranch owners should attend the sales and not neglect such a grand opportunity to improve their herds.

Large Imports of Meat.

"Twelve steamers," says the North British Agriculturist of January 22nd, "arrived at Liverpool during last week from American and Canadian ports, bringing 2,435 cattle, 18,803 qrs. of beef and 69 carcasses of mutton. As compared with the arrivals of the preceding week, these show an increase of 1,312 cattle, 8,127 qrs. of beef, and 28 carcasses of mutton."

The Secretary of Agricultural is in receipt of advices from Senor Ernesto Bosch, Acting Charge d' Affairs of the Argentine Republic at Washington, to the effect that the date fixed for the presentation of applications by foreign exhibitors for space at the forthcoming Cattle Show and Exhibition at Buenos Ayres, opening April 20, 1890, has been extended until the first of January next.

The Nebraska Farmer says: "The demand for first-class Holstien-Friesian cattle is good, and while they are not selling at fancy figures they bring good prices. There is no grade cow that sell as readily as a grade of this breed, because most of them are large milkers and the demand for more milk is increasing as the dairy interest of our state developes. We have frequent inquiries for grade Holstein cows and heifers, but the demand is so great that those who are known to breed these grades find ready sales for them."

The success attending the new creameries in Hombolt has been so great that another has already been started there. The Ferndale Enterprise says:

Another creamery company was organized in Ferndale Monday, with a capable stock of $6000, at $12 per share each share to represent a cow, and none but dairymen allow in the company. The creamery is to be built on the Sam Fulmore place on the Island, and all the stock has been taken but $400. The stockholders are: James Niesin, Smith Fulmore, Jorgen Christiansen, Neils Hansen, Chris Knudsen Rasmus Mortensen, Mads Madsen, Jes N. Geisseman, Peter Silacci, Jacob Jacobsen and W. P. Capwell, and the directors for the first year are Jes Geisseman, James Nissen, W. D. Capwell J. Christiansen, Smith Fulmore, Mads Madsen and Niels Hansen.

THE GUN.

"Crack" loading.

The superb work done by the United States Cartridge Company teams during the recent visit has doubtless aroused in many minds a desire to know precisely what guns, of what weights and what methods of loading contributed to the remarkable scores of the invincibles.

Not forgetting that a bad gun and poor load in the hands of a good man are better than the finest weapon and Selby cartridges in the hands of a poke there yet seems interest enough in what may be considered the highest attainment in the art of shooting, by the men selected from All America as most skillful, to justify presentation of all attainable details tending to their success up to the moment the word "pull' 'is given.

As the oldest at the traps and with practice, perhaps as hard a man as any to down Mr. S. A. Tucker may be first mentioned. He uses a nine and one half pound Parker hammerless ten bore.

Three and three-quarter drams of American dead-shot powder, one card wad, two No. 9 pink-edge wads, and one and one-quarter ounces of soft 7's at live birds.

At artificial targets, the powder charge is three and one-half drams; otherwise the load is the same.

Mr. Harvey McMurchy, dividing with Tucker, popularity as a travelling gun representative, and also entitled to the highest honor as a trap shot, uses an L. C. Smith 12-bore gun weighing seven pounds twelve ounces; at live birds, three and one-half drams of American Wood powder, one card wad, two No. 11 black-edge wads, and one and one-eighth ounces of soft 8's in the right barrel; in the left, three and one-half drams of Laflin & Rand powder, otherwise the same load. At artificial targets he uses Laflin & Rand powder in both barrels, otherwise the same load.

Mr. J. R. Stice, six feet of good shot, uses a seven-pound fifteen-ounce Parker hammerless 12-bore. At both live birds and targets, uses three and one-half drams of American Wood powder, one card wad, three No. 11 black-edge wads, one and one-eighth ounces of Tatham's trap shot No. 7.

Mr. C. W. Budd, who divides with Stice the claim to the American championship at live birds, prefers and uses an L. C. Smith, of seven pounds twelve ounces in weight, and 12 bore, invariably uses American Wood powder, three and one-fourth drams, one card wad, three No. 11 black-edge wads, and at live birds, one and one-eighth ounces of chilled 7's; at targets he uses No. 8's instead of 7's.

Mr. W. H. Wolstencroft, thirty per cent. quicker than lightning, uses a W. W. Greener ejector, seven pounds four ounces, and twelve bore. Mr. Wolstencroft always uses Schultze powder and loads his own shells. He uses three drams of the powder by measure, just seating a card wad and two No 11 black edge wads on the powder, one and one-eighth ounces of chilled 8's in the right and the same quantity of chilled 7's in the left at live birds. At targets he uses chilled 8's in both barrels.

Mr. H. B. Whitney, the boy of the party, handles a nine and one-half pound ten gauge L. C. Smith, with four drams of Schultze, one card wad, two No. 9 pink edge and one No. 10 pink edge wads, and one and one-fourth ounces of Taltham's trap shot No. 8 in the right barrel at live birds. In the left he uses four and one-half drams of Laflin and Rands' powder F. F. G.; otherwise, the same load. At targets he uses three and three-quarter drams of Laflin and Rand's F. F. G. powder; otherwise the same load.

Mr. John A. Ruble uses a twelve bore Lefever weighing eight pounds. At live birds three and one-half drams of American wood powder, one card, three black edge wads, one and one-eighth ounces of Raymond Chicago shot No. 7 in both barrels. At targets three and one-fourth drams of Laflin and Rand powder F. F. G., one card, two black edge wads, and one and one-eighth ounces of Raymond Chicago shot No. 8's.

Mr. Rolla O. Heikes also uses a Lefever, twelve bore of eight pounds, Laflin & Rand powder, three and one-fourth drams; at targets, one card and two black-edge wads, with one and one-eighth ounces of No. 8 Tatham chilled shot. At live birds he uses No. 7's in both barrels, with three and one-fourth drams of Schultze, one card and three black-edge wads in the right barrel.

Parson W. F. Quimby misuses a 10-bore L. C. Smith weighing eight and three fourths pounds; four and one-fourth drams of American Wood powder, one card, three No. 9 black-edge wads, and one and one-fourth ounces of No. 7 Tatham's trap shot. At targets he uses No. 8's.

Mr. W. R. Perry shoots a ten-gauge Parker which weighs nine pounds three ounces, three and three-quarter drams of American Rifle Cartridge powder, three No. 9 black-edge wads and one and one-fourth ounces of No. 8 chilled Tatham's shot at live birds.

The other Perry, Mr. W. S., is also a Parker gun admirer, using a ten gauge that weighs nine pounds one ounce. At live birds he shoots four and one-quarter drams of American Dead Shot powder, one card, two black edge wads No. 9, one and one-fourth ounces of No. 8 Tatham soft shot. At targets he reduces his powder load to three and one-half drams; otherwise the same.

These suggestions are not offered in the belief that adoption of any one of the guns or loads will insure the making of a Stice or a Whitney or a Budd, but there must be something in the manner of loading or the men would not use any care, but shoot any cartridges at hand.

A Differentiation.

An angling reader of the Breeder and Sportsman in far away Prussia send this analysis of two words often misused. "The two words sportsman and sporting affect me very differently. I read the word sporting for instance and into my mind rushes the image of a tall, well-built, clean-shaven individual, jaunty of air and short of purse, who is surrounded by trotters, jockeys, boxing gloves, billiard tables, cards and dice. How different is the picture called out by the word sportsman! Mountains, green fields and quiet nooks of every sort for back ground; for fore ground a running stream in which stands a man tender of heart, clear of mind, faithful of thought and full of love for animals, out-of-door life and all things poetical and artistic."

Blue Rock Club.

San Francisco, March 13, 1890.

Editor Breeder and Sportsman:—The officers of the Blue Rock Club newly elected are: J. O. Cadman, President; Dr. S. E. Knowles, Vice-President; Chas. F. Stone, Secretary and Treasurer; Captain F. R. Noyes (resigned), Captain; S. L. Abbot, Jr., and Henry C. Golcher, Directors.

No election as yet to fill the place vacated by Mr. Noyes. The first match was to have been shot last Saturday, but owing to the bad condition of the grounds, traps, etc., nothing but an informal shoot took place. No scores were recorded. The future dates of matches have not yet been decided on. Mr. J. O. Cadman, 101 Sansome street, has the power to appoint the days of meeting.

Charles F. Stone, Sec'y.

New Trap Ground.

Editor Breeder and Sportsman:—The Gun Club and I believe all the other wing shooting clubs, will shoot this season at the Oakland race track. Arrangements have been completed with the lessee of the track, Mr. Hinchman, to put up a suitable and neatly built club house on the grounds with all the necessary conveniences for shooters. The location of traps, seats for spectators, etc., are all arranged, and Mr. Hinchman promises that gentlemen will find every convenience at his place, and with timely notice birds will always be on hand, trappers, etc. The track is just 35 minutes from town, and trains leave between 6 A. M. and 10 A. M. Every half hour between 10 A M and 3 m, every hour after 3, half hourly until 7 or 8 P M. I was at the track last week, and the grounds inside are in excellent condition being dry, even after this past severe winter. Altogether, I fancy that pigeon shooting men will be much pleased when they visit Mr. Hinchman's place.

Secretary.

A very crisp and pleasant monthly comes to us with the title Amateur Sportsman. Published in New York City, and well edited, it is a desirable visitor to any fireside.

The California Wing Shooting Club meets at Oakland Trotting Park to-morrow, at 10 o'clock A. M., via Berkeley train. A general invitation to sportsmen is always extended by the club.

A large and vigorous Rod and Gun Club has been formed at Santa Cruz of which Mr. E. C. Williams is secretary. The Club offers a reward of $25 for information that will lead to the conviction of any person violating the game or fish laws. We wish the utmost success to the new organization, and shall be very pleased to receive reports of its meetings regularly.

Mr. A. H. Woolery in sending his shooting programme at Traver on April 7th and 8th sends these words: We have some good shots in this part of the country. They do not bar anyone, and there is a chance for any one to come and shoot and if they can beat the home boys they will do well financially, as there will be some good sweepstakes."

Colonel C. W. Dimick telegraphed us on Wednesday last, from Kansas City: "We beat the Kansas City champions to-day at live birds ten birds a man ninety three eighty six, regards to all."

More tinware for the Menagerie! The Iolanthe will rival Hammersmith and Fields in brilliancy, if luck remains with the tourists.

Some of the Chinese quails distributed by the Fish Commission were sent to Colonel J. N. Bailhache near Healdsburgh. When the birds were set loose some ran into the brush, some flew into trees and the whole lot disappeared in short order. They will be strictly protected for five years. We invite others who have received the birds to send us notes about their behavior and progress.

In response to a request for the scores made by the Gun Club at San Bruno on March 1st, the Secretary, Mr. John K. Orr, writes: "I am not authorized to give the scores of the Gun Club to any one this season, as the members have determined not to have any scores published in *any* of the papers." Such a rule is extraordinary, to speak mildly, and hardly to be sustained.

County Clerk Hall of Tehama County informs us that hunters from the Coast Range mountains state that a great amount of wild game has been frozen to death in the mountains. Very often the carcass of a deer is found where it had died in seeking shelter under a tree; and quail and other birds are found frozen stiff upon limbs where they have perched. This is noticeable to a greater extent on the country above Hay Fork. It proves that the season, outside of human observation and knowledge, was something positively exceptional, because the instinct nature gives to the denizens of the mountains and forest would have prevented these fatal results if winter's such as we are just emerging from were recurrences from time to time.

Mr. W. L. Colville (the "Dick Swiveller" of Commerce) is in the city representing the Baker gun. He is pleasant and bright as ever, and about ten years younger than last year, because his sales are so encouraging. He goes hence to the North on Monday next, and is commended to the mercy of our Portland and Seattle friends.

The Northern Development company, whose office is at No. 5 Market street, Room 5, in this city, in another column calls the attention of sportsmen and anglers to a most inviting programme of travel and sport just projected. An exploring party will leave San Francisco about April 10th for the Alaska coast, St. Matthews Island and the Yukon River, stopping at numerous places on the way where game is abundant and the finest of fishing for salmon, trout, halibut and cod. The scheme embraces five months of travel and is to be a joint stock affair, thus reducing the cost to the sum actually and necessarily expended. A grander opportunity was never afforded those fond of the gun and rod, and the Development Company will undoubtedly soon have its roster filled.

A grand Shooting Tournament, will take place at Traver, on Monday and Tuesday, April 7 and 8, 1890.

Monday's Programme.—Grand Sweeptakes at 50 blue rocks, 12 pairs and 27 singles; $50 entrance; all entries to this shoot to close April 1st, 1890; 20 per cent of entrance money to accompany nominations. There are four bora fideentri s already made for this shoot. Also same day other Sweeptakes, both at live birds and blue rocks, to be made up on the grounds.

Tuesday's Programme.—Grand Live Bird Sweepstake, 12 birds each, $10 entrance, in one money. Ample provisions will be made to have plenty of birds on the ground to accommodate all shooters for any amount of sweepstake shooting. All shoots to be under revised trap shooting rules of the American Shooting Association, except in live bird shooting, where plunge traps will be used. Come all shooters; nobody barred.

Says a Pacific Beach, San Diego County, correspondent: "The close season has arrived for the little quail, but by the booming of guns on the hill back from the beach is good proof that the quail get no rest in this part of the country, there is a move among the leading sportsmen here to organizing a gun club and game protective association, but it seems to be up hill work as the inducements put out by some of our leading hotel men for game in close season is so tempting, some of our crack shots tumbled in and got fat. If we had a fearless game warden here he could make it quite warm for a few local sports in town."

Until San Diego Sportsmen arouse themselves and stamp out the pot-shots, there is little encouragement to the Fish Commission in planting game birds and fish in that section. Why do not the local officers place the hotel proprietors who serve quail out of season, under arrest?

ROD.

A Washington Commissioner.

Mr. George Ferguson of Artondale, Washington makes these suggestions to which we gladly give place and endorsement. Mr. Hume's standing in this community and his long time acquaintance with the needs of the fisheries fairly entitle him to such consideration.

Mr. Ferguson writes: All persons interested in the propagation and preservation of fish must be highly pleased with the action of the legislature of Washington in passing an act for the appointment of a fish commissioner. During a residence of ten years on Puget Sound I have seen salmon decrease in number year after year, until there is not now one-quarter of the number that there were when I first came here. I have often seen tons of herring and smelt drawn out on the beach and left there to rot by fisherman who cared nothing about the future supply of food fishes. These fishermen had long seines with very small meshes, and they would haul in their net and find in it half a dozen salmon and two or three tons of herring. The salmon they would put in their boat and the herring they would leave on the beach to rot. They cared not, though they were exterminating the food of the salmon. A majority of the fishermen around here are Italinas and Greeks, who care nothing about the future supply of fish, and who will require a man of nerve and energy to compel them to respect any laws relating to the preservation of our food fishes

The man who canddo this better than any other man on Puget Sound is Davi H. Hume, of Tacoma. He has been fishing or dealing in fish all his life. He has twenty year's experience on Puget Sound as fisherman and wholesale dealer in fish. For years past he has advocated legislation to prevent the extermination of our food fishes. His thorough knowledge of the "propagation, protection and preservation of food fishes and oysters," his practical experience of forty years among fish, and his business abilities make him the fittest man in Washington for the position of fish commissioner.

A truck load of great packing cases was being dumped before Mr. E. T. Allen's store at 416 Market street the other day, and curiosity prompted us to ask as to the contents. The reply was that a shipment of S. Allcock & Co's standard fishing tackle had just been received from Liverpool. There seemed to be enough to supply all the anglers in creation, but Mr. Allen blandly remarked that his orders then in hand would absorb most of the shipment, but that more tackle would be coming for some weeks.

Rod makers are fairly distancing gun builders in increasing the excellence of their products and reducing prices. Messrs. Clabrough, Golcher & Co., at 630 Montgomery, are displaying a fine line of specialties in the tackle way, particularly split bamboo rods. Such implements as they offer now for fifteen or twenty dollars could not have been purchased five years ago for thirty-five. In balance, material, jointing, play and finish, their light weight "Webber Lake Rod" is a marvel, and will become the standard for ordinary trouting uses in California.

THE KENNEL.

Dog owners are requested to send for publication the earliest possible notices of whelps, sales, names claimed, presentations and deaths, in their kennels, in all instances writing plainly names of sire and dam and of grandparents, colors, dates and breed.

Occidental Club's Spring Meeting.

A more unpropitious day than Saturday last could not have been selected by the Occidental Coursing Club for its Spring meeting for 1890. Washington's Birthday was originally selected, but constant rain storms made it advisable to choose another day.

Saturday opened drizzling, and at eight o'clock only Treasurer S. L. Abbot, Jr., Secretary J. F. Carroll and a lone reporter appeared at the South Pacific Coast Railroad depot. Very soon, however, others came along, and by 8:10, fifteen of the twenty-four dogs entered were on hand, together with a few spectators. Hurried consultation among the Directors of the club resulted in an order to proceed with the meeting, and with many misgivings, tickets for Newark were purchased. The intervening country was one great lake. Water, water, everywhere, except in the train, where a peculiar amber liquid seemed to be the only diluent. The hour's ride was short, because of lively chat.

Newark was reached in a driving storm, which made an umbrella more to be prized than a section of land. The coursers huddled in an old barn on the coursing grounds, peered out through sundry crevices, and exerted all their Mark Tapleyism in making the best of it. At 10:30 the Santa Clara County delegation arrived with the rest of the dogs, and as the rain had ceased for the time, the sport was inaugurated. Rubber boots were fitted to President Gregory and Secretary Carroll, while Slipper Wren was fitted out with top-boots. The dogs were all in good condition, except Dr. W. E. Wadam's Midnight, which had a broken toe, and Mr. J. F. Carroll's Dark Rustic, which was injured on Friday by a barbed wire fence. Midnight did well in the run-up, but could not work his hare because of his sore foot. Dark Rustic did not appear.

The All-Aged Stake was won by Mr. S. Milliken's brindle and white bitch Peasant Girl by Tribute—Tampete. Peasant Girl is a medium weight bitch of fine points, very speedy to her hares and when in possession very hard to displace, being exceedingly clever and a close worker. The runner-up, Mr. T J Cronin's black and white dog Dan B by Chicopee—Lily of Killarney, was a favorite for the stake and there was little to choose between him and the winner. He is a ru-her, goes a little wide on turns, but is very fast, true and clever.

In the Sapling Stake, Mr. T. Cooney named the white and black bitch Kathleen by Killarney—Culverine and won with her. Kathleen had the foot of any thing in the stake in the straight, was in fine condition and won with something to spare. Mr. Cooney also owned the runner-up Dandy Jim by Stranger—Jersey Lily, a very neat, white and blue dog, a bit largish, but very able. The names of those enthusiastic enough to brave the elements deserve record. They were Messrs. S. L. Abbot Jr., T. J. O'Keeffe, S. O. Gregory, J. F. Carroll, James E. Watson, Dr. W. E. Wadams, J. R. Dickson, J. Sennett, T. Gallagher, G. G. Taylor, James Wren, Thomas Shea, A. J. McCoy, M. Airtes, E. Portal, M. McCarthy, Pat Behan, T. J. Cronin, D. J. Flannery, L. H. Garrigus, C. C. Wilkinson, H. Boyd and J. McDonald.

The ground was soft, sloppy, under water in many places, and the hares only ordinary as a rule, with now and then a clinker which had managed to keep out of the wet. The judging of Mr. J. B. Dickson gave satisfaction, as did the work of the slipper, Mr. James Wren. The officers of the day were: Field Stewards, Col. S. O. Gregory, T. J. O'Keeffe and J. E. Watson; Slip Steward, J. F. Carroll; and Flag Steward, H. Boyd. All performed their duties admirably. Perfect order and the best of feeling prevailed throughout the day. Coursing began at 11 o'clock and ended at 2:35.

ALL-AGED STAKE.

WOODSIDE—TINNIE—A good slip and an even run up to a good hare, which turned, and another hare starting each dog took one and killed. Slipped again, Woodside led to the quarry, wrenched, again wrenched and placed Tinnie for a wrench, when Woodside killed and won.

MIDNIGHT—DAN B—The brace got a good hare, and from a long slip Midnight made a pretty burst, but Dan B scored a go—by. Then each had two wrenches, when Dan B killed and won.

SATURDAY NIGHT—LAURELWOOD—Slipped at fifty yards to a cliker. Laurelwood got the run up and turned, placing Saturday Night for a turn, when Laurelwood again took the hare for two wrenches and the kill. The race, from different standpoints, appeared to some to belong to Saturday Night, but the judge and those in the most favorable positions coincided in believing the course properly Laurelwood's.

MOLLIE BAWN—FREESTONE—The slip was a long one to a lively hare. Freestone had all the speed, scored the run-up—three wrenches and the kill, beating Mollie pointless.

CHICOPEE LASS, a bye, Dark Rustic not appearing by reason of severe injuries received the day before. Chicopee Lass ran a bye, which was a hard one.

HARRIET S—PEASANT GIRL—Peasant Girl broke from slips like a whirlwind, got first to the hare, held it for four wrenches, then turned to Harriet S, who killed. Peasant Girl won, hands down.

JUANITA—DAISY—After two short no—go's a fair hare was started. Juanita got the run up and turned, but Daisy when placed scored rapidly, three wrenches and the kill. The course was given to Juanita.

MOSQUITO—FAUGH A BALLAGH—The scut was an ordinary one. Mosquito cut out the work and scored all but the kill. which was made by Faugh a Ballagh, Mosquito winning.

FIRST TIES.

WOODSIDE—DAN B—The dogs ran a no course, then Dan B did some fast and close work one a good hare and shut Woodside out.

LAURELWOOD—FREESTONE—Freestone shut his competitor out brilliantly, did some quick work, staying close, killing and winning.

CHICOPEE LASS—PEASANT GIRL—The course was short, but the Girl was too clever, and won hands down against her good opponent.

JUANITA—MOSQUITO—Mosquito, not the favorite, won a short, sharp course, scoring the run up, two wrenches and the kill, against three wrenches for Juanita.

SECOND TIES.

DAN B.—FREESTONE—A close thing. Dan B speediest a little. Both exceedingly clever. Dan getting the kill and win.

PEASANT GIRL—MOSQUITO—The hare was a cracker, but Peasant Girl made a grand dash, turned it without placing Mosquito, wrenched several times and finally killed, shutting her competitor out pointless.

FINAL.

DAN B—PEASANT GIRL—After a short no-course the dogs were slipped to a fine hare, the Girl racing away from her fine brace-mate by superior speed, held her hare for two turns, three wrenches and the kill, a performance rarely equalled, when the quality of Dan B is considered.

SUMMARY.

Newark, March 8th, 1890. All aged stake for 16 greyhounds, at $5 each. Winner $40 and portrait of the dog. Runner-up $20. Two dogs, $10 each.

T. J. O'Keeffe's n s w f b Woodside	beat	John Grace's w br b Tinnie.
T. J. Cronin's blk w d Dan B	beat	W. E. Wadam's blk w d Midnight.
S Milliken's w br d Laurelwood,	beat	J. E. Watson's blk w d Saturday Night.
D. J. Healey's blk w d Freestone,	beat	J. E. Watson's w blk b Mollie Bawn.
T. J. Cronin's w blk b Chicopee Lass a bye.		
S Milliken's br w b Peasant Girl	beat	J. F. O'Connor's w br b Harriet S.
D. W. Swain's br w b Juanita,	beat	D. J. Healey's blk b Daisy.
M. Curtis' br b Mosquito,	beat	P. Gallagher's blk d Faugh a Ballagh.

I.

Dan B beat Woodside. Freestone beat Laurelwood.
Peasant Girl beat Chicopee Lass. Mosquito beat Juanita.

II.

Dan B beat Freestone. Peasant Girl beat Mosquito.

FINAL.

Peasant Girl beat Dan B and won.

SAPLING STAKE.

VOLUNTEER—SWEEP—The hare was a good one. In the run-up Sweep made a strong play, but Volunteer had the foot, turned without placing Sweep, wrenched and let Sweep in for a wrench, then resumed possession, killed and won.

KATHLEEN—AMERICAN BOY—The dogs were almost upon the hare when slipped. Kathleen, a rattler from slips, showed the way to the hare, turned it, placed the Boy for a wrench into Kathleen's mouth for the kill and win.

DANDY JIM—KILLARNEY BOY II.—Jim led to the best hare of the day, turned it and placed the Boy; resumed after a wrench and worked his quarry to the escape, winning easily.

PAULINE—BO PEEP—The slip was a bad one, Pauline having much the best of it, and improving her advantage by leading to the hare for a turn without letting Bo Peep in; held the scut for three wrenches, then placed Bo Peep for a wrench or two, the hare finally wrenching to Pauline for the kill and win.

FIRST TIES.

VOLUNTEER—KATHLEEN—Mr. Wren sighted the dogs on a good hare, but could not level them except to a long slip, which he gave Volunteer made a brilliant burst, but Kathleen was too fast and secured the run up and a turn, Volunteer using the hare for two wrenches, when Kathleen replaced herself, killed and won.

DANDY JIM—PAULINE—Jim led to a good hare, turned it, but another hare started, and the dogs took it to a lumber pile. A boy succeeded in dislodging it, the dogs scoring about equally, with Pauline perhaps a shade the best of it, until the hare again reached the pile of lumber. The judge called it an undecided course, and the dogs were again slipped to a fine hare. Dandy Jim had the pace, used his hare for a half dozen wrenches and the kill and win, shutting Pauline out pointless.

FINAL.

KATHLEEN—DANDY JIM—After a short no-course on a sick hare, Kathleen fairly flew to a lively hare, turned it, regained possession without letting Dandy Jim score, wrenched twice, killed and won the course and first money.

SUMMARY.

Newark, March 8, 1890—Sapling Stake; for eight dogs at $5 each; winner $25. Runner-up $15.

S. L. Abbot Jr.'s blk w d Volunteer,	beat	J. E. Watson's blk w d Sweep.
T. Cooney's ns w blk b Kathleen.	beat	H. E Deane's blk w d American Boy.
T. Cooney's w be d Dandy Jim,	beat	T. J. Cronin's bk w d Killarney Boy II.
S. O. Gregory's br w b Pauline,	beat	H. Boyd's w bk b Bo Peep.

I.

Kathleen beat Volunteer. Dandy Jim beat Pauline.

FINAL.

Kathleen beat Dandy Jim and won.

O. C. C. Annual Meeting.

The annual meeting of the Occidental Coursing Club was held last Tuesday evening at Mr. William Schreibers, No. 21 Kearney St., with fifteen members present. The Treasurer, Mr. S. L. Abbot Jr., reported the financial standing of the club satisfactory, there being a balance of six dollars after payment of all bills. It was proposed that an all-aged stake and puppy stake be held at Newark Park on the 30th of May. The election of officers for the ensuing year followed. Mr. S. O. Gregory was unanimously re-elected President; T. J. O'Keeffe, John Grace, S. Milliken and C. C. Wilkinson, vice-Presidents; S. L. Abbot Jr. re elected Treasurer and J. F. Carroll Secretary. The Executive Committee is composed of H. E. Dean, J. R. Dickson, H. Boyd, T. J. Cronin and W. S. Kittle. The club voted also to have an annual dinner in March of each year, the first one to be given during the present month. Messrs. H. E. Deane S. L. Abbott Jr. and T. J. O'Keeffe were appointed a committee to arrange the banquet, and they especially request members of the club to write whether they can and will be present at the banquet or not. Mr. Abott can be addressed at 228 Montgomery Street, City.

It is with field trials as with any other races, the best dog does not always come fittest to the post, and too often a dufferish beast is advanced in a stake more by luck than merit, while a really superior performer, because of the very keenness which makes him superior, is exposed to a thousand dangers which do not menace the more ordinary brute.

The pointer Sankey (Point—Blossom), which won second in the last field, is an example. In his preparatory work he was brilliant, but just when the critical time came he was sick. Since then he has regained his strength, and Mr. Joe Bassford writes of him:

"I had a good time with Mr. J. F. Hughes on the last day of the season. We worked his pointer Sankey for three days as hard as a dog was ever worked, we going out in a cart in the morning and back at night, making Sankey run the distance. And of all the dogs I ever shot over or ever saw work he is the best, surest and gamest, and for staying power, which is one of the best points in a dog he is the 'boss.' He was beat in the trials, but for a quail dog I would prefer him to any that run at the last trials or ever did run in California."

California Kennel Club.

The California Kennel Club met last Wednesday evening at 436 Montgomery street and elected officers for the ensuing year as follows: President, J. B. Lewis; First Vice-President, George Flournoy, Jr.; Second Vice-President, Thomas Higgs; Secretary, J. B. Martin; Treasurer, John de Vaull; Sergeant-at-Arms, W. G. Cue: Collector, H. A. Senfried. John D. Siebe Jr., D. C. Babin and Julius Deluc were elected members. A committee consisting of J. B. Martin, Joseph King and A. B. Truman, were appointed to draft a set of resolutions in respect to the memory of the late J. Mervyn Donahue, who was a lover of huting dogs. The Secretary was instructed to notify the Secretary of the Pacific Kennel Club that the members of the California Kennel Club positively refuses to assume any of the Pacific Kennel Club's debts, and a consolidation cannot be had until such terms as have been proposed by the California Kennel Club are accepted.

Any reader who chances to recall the pedigrees of the bull terriers Jerry and Buttons, owned in San Francisco, will confer a favor by sending them to us. Jerry we believe was at one time owned by Mr. Gillig.

Dr. A. C. Davenport sends from Stockton a nice photograph of his stud dog Kute. Kute is by Carle—Beauty, and is a very fine specimen of the breed. We hope Dr. Davenport will show Kute, Bronta and his other superb cockers at the Los Angeles dog show in May.

Mr. James E. Watson, at 516 Sacramento Street, city, offers for sale, through the advertising columns, two Gordon setter bitch puppies, two Yorkshire terrier dog puppies, and six mastiff puppies. Most reasonable prices are asked, and the animals are good ones.

A local journal devoted to poultry and pigeons intimates that the delay in paying some of the poultry prizes at the last bench show has deterred the California Poultry Association from giving its usual January show at San Jose. The conclusion argues either squalor among poultry fanciers or a lack of interest which should lead them to disband the "California Poultry Association."

The Southern California Kennel Club will give a bench show during the first week in May next. The club is now regularly a member of the American Kennel Club and will give its show under A. K. C. rules and wins there will count for championship honors. It is altogether improbable that a bench show will be given in San Francisco before next fall, and local owners will do well to condition their dogs and send them to Los Angeles, By clubbing together and selecting some careful man who knows how to care for a dog the expense can be reduced to a nominal figure. Most dogs will be in good coat on May 1st and can easily be fitted for the show. We hope many entries from the Northern part of the state will appear. Premium lists may be had from Mr. H. T. Payne, President of the Club, at Los Angeles or from E. K. Benchley, Secretary, or E. B. Tufts, both of Los Angeles.

BILLIARDS.

J. L. Malone, the pool expert, who has been laid up at the Laclede Hotel, St. Louis, Mo., for several weeks, was recently removed to the Mullanphy Hospital. Malone has had a severe attack of the "grip." He has been convalescent several times, but had relapses, and at last resolved to go to the hospital, where it is expected a final cure will be effected.

Schaefer & McCleery play during May for $4000 ($2000 a side) half forfeit. Each party has $1000 up as a forfeit with the "Examiner" the exact dates of the contest will be named, and all preliminaries settled on the night of May 1st at the Baldwin Hotel Billiard Room and the other $1000 each posted. The game is 3,000 points up to be played on three successive evenings.

We have a semi professional billiardist in the city at present who it is whispered intends to challenge McCleery. At any rate he practices daily at the Baldwin and knocks out 300 and 400 points very often. He should have no trouble if he wants a game, as Mc's ideas on that point are well known, and to play a match at any and all times is right into his hand.

Why don't some energetic man arrange to bring out the great players to this city, say, in May. Put up a good purse include McCleery and Sayler, thus having eight contestants—make it a handicap at 8 inch balkline making a weeks play. There is certainly a good lump of money in the venture and as Schaefer is coming to play McCleery and being on the heels of the great Chicago tournament the interest would be at fever heat.

Ladies and gentlemen who are fond of billiard playing can take instructions either at private residences or at Professor McCleery's Parlor, up stairs in the Baldwin Hotel.

Jim Chesley thinks well of having the players all come out. Jim Orndorff and he both say that if a season ticket be not more than $25, they certainly would have to have one each.

CLENDENYONE.

ATHLETICS.

Athletic Sports and Other Pastimes.

EDITED BY ARISTIPPUS,

SUMMARY.

The Secretary of the Students and Sportsman's Club of Bakersfield, Mr. S. N. Reed writes under date, March 5th as follows:

"In a few days we will begin the execution of a gymnasium bath rooms, etc in rear of our club room. All is progressing nicely and our club promises to be a phenomenal success.

The Willows Athletic Club went to Colusa on March 1st and gave an entertainment which was highly praised by the Willows Journal, says our valued exchange:

"Upon reaching Colusa about 200 citizens of Colusa were at the depot and bade the excursionists welcome to their fair city. From the depot all made a bee line for the Colusa House, where R. Poirer the proprietor, assigned about 100 Willow-ites to the rooms.

At 4 o'clock the Club formed in front of the Opera House, and with Silvey's Cornet Band at their head, paraded the principal streets of the town.

The exhibition by the Athletic Club was good, considering the time the members have been practicing. The house was crowded from the door to stage. Every seat was sold before 4 o'clock. The performance was highly appreciated by the citizens of Colusa. No people ever entertained a crowd better than the citizens of Colusa did those from Willows. Everyone who went to Colusa speak in the highest terms of Colusa's hospitality, and all unite in returning their heartfelt thanks for their royal reception."

At a meeting of the P C A A A held last Friday evening, the Golden Gate Athletic Club resigned as a member of that body. The annual championship athletic meeting will be held on Decoration Day at the new grounds of the Olympic Athletic Club, and it would appear that a hot battle will ensue between the teams from the different clubs for the champion flag. The falling through of the Long-Henceman sculling match has been a great dissappointment to the rowing men.

RUNNERS, WALKERS, JUMPERS, ETC.

P J Higgins, the Irish distance runner, has returned to the city from La Porte, Cal. He may possibly compete in the mile run on May 30th.

J B Buchanan, the Australian champion all round athlete, will leave for Chicago in a couple of weeks. He intended joining the Olympic Club but his business pursuits will compel him to take an early departure.

McDonald says he will train hard for the Novice hundred on May 30th.

The opening of the Olympic Grounds will be attended by the largest audience ever seen at an athletic meeting in San Francisco.

Frank L Cooley, the amateur champion five mile runner of the Pacific Coast, is willing to run any of the local amateurs a five mile race for a gold medal. Mr. Cooley does not desire to issue a challenge but he says if any one disputes his title he will be only too glad to settle the question.

John D Garrison, who has been on the path only a short time, is looked upon as a dangerous man in the quarter-mile run.

Like the majority of good athletes, Victor E Schefferstein finds it impossible to remain in retirement and he will be seen on the track again on May 30th.

There will be a grand gathering of athletes on Decoration Day, as all the old timers will be on hand to protect their records.

It is generally believed that the records in the following events will be broken at the championship meeting: 880 yards run, one and five-mile runs, one and three-mile walks, putting 16-lb. shot, running high jump, throwing 16-lb. hammer, 120 yards hurdle race and pole vault.

A young man named Rankin, who claims to be the champion ten-mile runner of America, will represent one of the clubs in the five-mile run at the championship meeting.

On Sunday last several of the Olympic Athletic Club's out-door men took a trip out to their new grounds and indulged in trial spins. McArthur jogged a mile in 5:36; Jarvis walked a mile at a moderate pace, covering the ground in 7:45, and several of the sprinters ran short trials. Walter Scott ran a couple of miles at an easy gait, and he did not appear to have lost any of his old-time staying powers. Jarvis, the walker, who has been on the best tracks in England and in the East, says that the new track will be equal to any track he has ever raced on. It will be at least three seconds faster in a mile than the old track at 14th and Center Streets, Oakland.

Charles Little, who, through illness, did not make a very good showing at the Alpine games, may surprise some of the boys in the half-mile run at the next games.

With proper training, James Sexsmith should vault 10 feet with the pole. He holds the coast record of 9ft 3½in.

J. J. McKinnon, the hammer thrower, will apply for reinstatement to the P C A A A.

A running hop, step and jump would be a very interesting event to add to the championship programme.

Messrs. Lichtenstein and Cherry, the well known amateur swordsmen, will give an exhibition of their skill at the 'Ladies' Night" entertainment of the Alpine Club next month.

J B Buchanan, the Australian Hercules, has also promised to be present on that evening, to show the fair sex what he can do with the heavy weights and clubs.

Some of the local amateur walkers would like to see John Elliott, of the Olympic Club, appointed judge of walking for the championship meeting. Mr. Elliott has been all over England and Ireland, and has an excellent idea of what "square" heel and toe means.

Fred D. Schultzer, the Financial Secretary of the Acme Athletic Club of Oakland, died last week and was buried on Sunday. The members of the club attended the funeral in a body. The deceased athlete was held high in the estimation of his fellow members.

Walter A. Beatty, the one mile runner of the University Athletic Club, suffered a painful experience at Tiburon on Sunday last. He was out sailing in the Corinthian Yacht Club's sloop, Lark, with a fellow lawyer named John F. Sullivan Jr., and when passing through the straits near Point Tiburon, Sullivan, who was forward, was thrown overboard by a sudden lurch of the vessel, and owing to the strong tide running, although being a good swimmer was drowned before the eyes of his companion, who was unable to offer any help. The sloop was carried beyond Sausalito and Beatty would have perished too had not some boats gone to his aid.

Secretary J. J. Jamison, of the Golden Gate Athletic Club, is very much worried on account of the club having to resign from the P. C. A. A. A. Mr. Jamison has been a delegate to the Association almost since its foundation, and his brother delegates are heartily sorry for his loss. Individually Mr. Jamison has always been a hard worker in the interests of amateur athletics, and he never failed to do all in his power to help the P. C. A. A. A. out at their annual out-door meetings.

Pacific Coast Amateur Athletic Records.

Some weeks ago Captain George W. Jordan was appointed a committee of one by the President of the P. C. A. A. A. to compile a correct list of the Pacific Coast Amateur Athletic records and the following table shows the result of his labor:

RUNNING.

75 yards—Joseph Masterson, Oakland, Cal, Nov. 30., 1883. 7 4 5 seconds.

100 yards—R. S. Haley, Sept. 23, 1882. 10 seconds.
Victor E. Schifferstein, Oakland, Cal., June 9, 1888. 10 seconds.

200 yards—R. S. Haley, San Francisco, Nov. 30, 1881. 20½ seconds.

220 yards—R. S. Haley, Oakland, Cal. Sept. 23, 1882 22 3-5 seconds.

250 yards—W. R. Stewart, Oakland, Cal., July 4, 1883. 28 seconds.

250 yards—(Flying start.) A. E. Verrinder, Oakland, Cal., Nov. 30, 1883. 27 4-5 seconds.

440 yards—John T. Belcher, Oct. 9, 1880. 50 3 5 seconds.

880 yards—Walter A. Scott, Oakland Cal. Feb. 22, 1886. 2 min. 8 secs.
J. G. Sutton, Oakland, Cal., May 30, 1889. 2 min. 6 2-5 seconds.

1, 000 yards—J. G. Sutton, Oakland, Cal., Sept. 9, 1887. 2 min. 30 sec.

1 mile—Peter McIntyre, Occident C. C. Feb. 22 1878. 4 min. 43 1 5 sec.
Walter A. Scott, Oakland, Cal., Sept. 9, 1884. 4 min. 46 seconds.

WALKING.

440 yards—D, Eiseman, San Francisco, Cal , Feb. 22, 1884. 1 min. 27½ secs.

880 yards—Horace Coffin, Oakland, Cal., August 6 1887. 3 min. 31 secs.

1 mile—Charles B. Hill, Oakland, Cal., Sept. 9, 1885. 7 min. 10½ secs.

2 miles—Philip N. Gafney, Oakland Cal., August 6, 1887. 16 min. 57 2-5 secs.

3 miles—Philip N. Gafney, Oakland Cal , August 6, 1887. 25 min. 51½ secs.

HURDLES.

120 yards—John Purcell, Oakland Cal., July 12 1888. 18 3 5 seconds.
H. C. Moffet, Oakland, Cal , May 30, 1889. 17 3-5 seconds.

JUMPING.

Running high Jump—A. H. Lean, Nov. 24, 1887. 5 ft. 8 in.
H. C. Moffett, May 30, 1889. 5 ft. 8½ in.

Standing high Jump—H. Powers, Nov. 17, 1883 4 ft. 2½in.

Running broad Jump—Victor E. Schifferstein, June 9, 1888. 23 ft. 2½ in.

THROWING HAMMER.

Throwing 12lb. hammer—J. Bouse May 25, 1889. 108 ft. 9in.

Throwing 16lb. hammer—W. H. Quinn, Sept. 6th 1887. 81 ft. 11½ in.

PUTTING SHOT.

Putting 16 lb. shot—John Purcell, July 28 1888. 38 ft. 7in.

KICKING FOOT BALL.

F. B. Peterson San Francisco, Feb 22 1883. 156½ feet.

CLUB JOTTINGS.

It has been decided that the annual championship games of the P. C. A. A. A. will be held on the grounds of the Olympic club on Friday May 30, (Decoration Day.) The track will be in fine condition, the prizes will be the most costly ever given on the Pacific Coast a fine band of music will perform during the day and everything possible will be done to please and make comfortable both the audience and the contestants. Should the weather be fine it is safe to calculate on 5,000 people being present to see the sport.

The first "Ladies Night" of the Alpine Amateur Athletic Club will be held at the club rooms, 706 Powell St., early in April. A first class programme will be given and the special medals and prizes won at the late field-day of the club will be distributed.

At a meeting of the P. C. A. A. A. held in the parlor of the Olympic Club on Friday evening March 7, the Golden Gate Athletic Club tendered its resignation as a member of the Association. The reason why the G. G. A. C. resigned was because the P. C. A. A. A. recently adopted rules which prevented any club that fosters professional sport from being a member.

A meeting of the P C A A A was held last evening, an account of which will appear next week. A committee has been appointed to formulate a programme for the annual championship out-door meeting which will be held May 30th. It is probable that the programme adopted by the American Athletic Union will be passed upon. This programme would add the following events to the usual list of games given by the P C A A A: 1—Five-mile run; 2—Three-mile walk; 3—220 yards hurdle; 4—Individual tug-of-war (unlimited weight); 5—Tug-of-war, four men on each side (unlimited weight); 6—Flinging 56-lb, weight; 7—Throwing 16-lb (formerly 12-lb) hammer. The committee would do well to replace the tug-of-war with a running, hop, step and jump.

AT THE OARS.

The Ariel Club members have repaired all their boats, and are ready to begin the summer season. The club had out four crews and five single scullers on Sunday.

E. Heenan of the Pioneer Club has commenced to train, expecting to row for the championship at the amateur regatta of the Columbia Club of Oakland which will be held on Decoration Day.

The Long-Henceman race has ultimately fallen through on account of Charley Long being obliged to give up training, though having contracted a severe cold which settled in his stomach. His managers asked for a two week's postponement, which he was entitled to but Henceman would not sanction the postponement, claiming that the race should be decided on the date already set. Knowing that Long would not be in proper condition to row to-morrow, his backers decided to forfeit the money deposited with the San Francisco Chronicle, on the grounds that it would be much better to forfeit the $250 than to have him run the risk of being defeated, when his friends would be all left in the lurch. Long says he is by no means scared by the Stockton oarsman's speed and he feels positive that he can defeat him under favorable conditions.

William Hanrahan and E. M. Coffey of last years champion Amateur crew who resigned from the Ariel club last January have made application to join the Pioneer club. They deserve high compliments for their devotion to the art of sculling.

The canoe fleet of the Lurline club was out in full force on Sunday. Captain A. C. Ronard was obliged to remain on shore on account of some evilly disposed person having cut several holes through the bottom of his canoe the "Ho-Bo."

James Cochran, President of the Ariel club has purchased the shell of Tom Brown and says if he makes a success he will keep his club mate, Billy Growney, hustling for first honors in the Ariel club.

The directors of the S. P. Co. will at their next meeting take action on the proposed building of a new boat house on the site of the old depot of the Narrow Gauge Rail Road. It would be a capital investment for the S. P. Co., as the different rowing clubs have already a membership of 978 and with the Olympic proposed rowing annex the improvement would net the Rail Road Company a handsome sum each month during the season. They will have the entire support of the Rowing Association comprised of the following clubs;—The Ariel, Dolphin, Alpine, Lurline, Pioneer, South End and the Union Club of Stockton.

UNIVERSITY JOTTINGS.

The field-team have made up their minds to be in good trim for May 30. Their motto is "Now or never." They feel confident of victory, and with the addition of a couple of good new men, last years team should certainly make it interesting for the athletes representing the Olympic and Alpine Clubs.

The game of foot-ball which was played on Saturday week was rather uninteresting. But very few spectators were present to watch the game which was won by the U. C. team with a score of 12 to 0. The University foot-ball team before essaying to play a good game needs lots of hard practice.

At last the heating apparatus has been placed in the gymnasium, and the athletes are able to enjoy a warm shower.

The Students are highly pleased to hear that the championship games will be held on May 30. They will now train with a good will.

Moffet will go in for the running high jump and hurdle race and should break the records in both events.

E. Coke Hill and J. G. Sutton will make a good show if in the middle and long distance runs and possibly both men may earn a new record.

All of last years team will compete.

ON THE WHEEL.

The roads are not sufficiently hard as yet for riding. A couple of weeks of warm weather will put them in fine condition.

The wheelmen should join hands and build a new track of their own.

Sanford Plummer will shortly take his departure from San Francisco.

On account of the Olympic Club track being so small the P. C. A. A. A. will probably omit the bicycle events on May 30.

JOTTINGS FROM ALL OVER.

A sculling match for the championship of the world has been arranged between Neil Matterson and Peter Kemp, to take place on the Parramatta course April 25th. William J. O'Connor, the American champion, who has arrived in Australia, will challenge the winner.

College athletes are getting into shape for the annual intercollegiate championships. Harvard is getting a lot of novices and expects to develop some good men at the different games. Princeton and Columbia will have a rare old tussle for first place, and if there is any upset it will be furnished by Yale, with Sherrill in the 100, 220 and 440. The meeting will be held in the vicinity of New York on the last Saturday in May, and the Berkeley Oval or Morris Park will be the venue.

T. P. Conniff, the well known distance runner of the Manhattan Athletic Club of New York City, has left the hospital, and is now convalescing at his residence, 347 West 41st street. He will enter athletic games as soon as he can do so with safety.

The initiation fee of the Manhattan Athletic Club of New York is to be raised from $50 to $100.

It is said that the Nautilus Boat Club of Brooklyn, N. Y., cleared nearly $900 by their joint games with Company H, Thirteenth Regiment, at New York, on February 5th.

There was great excitement over the election of a President for the New York Athletic Club. There were two candidates —Jennings S. Cox, a banker, and Walter G. Schuyler, a prominent man in athletic circles. The excitement during the contest on Tuesday evening last was something fearful. Schuyler was elected by a large majority.

The Board of Managers of the Amateur Athletic Union held a meeting at Wilmington, Del., March 1st, at which the following clubs were admitted to membership: Massachusetts Institute of Technology A. A.; Prospect Harriers of Brooklyn; Cathedral A. C., New York; Actors' A. A. A., New York; Bedford A. C., Brooklyn, and West End A. C., Newark, N. J. It was decided to hold the annual schedule meeting in New York City on March 19th, and the discussion regarding the employment of amateurs in a clerical capacity by athletic clubs led to the passage of the following resolution: "Any person receiving compensation for services performed in any athletic club, or in any capacity in connection with athletic games, will be ineligible and remain ineligible until his case has been passed upon by the Board of Managers." The Board, on this, very wisely decided that a rule would not be applicable to all cases, and each must be investigated and decided upon its individual merits. The large clubs of the present day call for the appointment of clerical help, which in no way interferes with the amateur status of the employee; but a rule permitting this is liable to be stretched to cover other employment of a questionable nature, and it was to avoid such a rule that the above resolution was adopted.

The progress of the M A C new building is being watched with interest by the members, and the exterior is nearing completion. The iron girders to support the roof of the garden at the top of the building are in place, and this will undoubtedly be completed in a few weeks, when work on the interior will be begun. It is authoritatively stated that the club will move into its new quarters on the first of May, though it is not expected that more than the first two floors will be ready for occupancy by that time.

Grim's Gossip.

The Directors of the Monterey Agricultural Association have claimed the dates from September 30th to October 4th for their annual fair and races.

"Andy" Welch, of Hartford, paid $4,600 for the Kentucky Prince mare Jeanne on Wednesday at Rose's sale and on Thursday turned her over to J. E. Madden of Lexington, Ky. for $5,000.

Mr. Rose says that the rumor that he has been offered $15,-000 for the yearling brother to Mascot, the buyer to take the risk of his recovery from his tempoorary illness, is without foundation.

I will esteem it a favor if my many readers will send to this office any stallion cards they may have containing pedigrees of horses. Not only for the present year: but also any old ones they may have on hand.

Wilson & Handy, Cynthiana, Ky., on Thursday of last sold to Stoner & Clay of Paris, that State, the Silver Threads mare Lady Mackey, bought by them on Wednesday at Rose's sale for $5,000 at an advance of $1,000.

E. C Archer of Linden sends me the bad news that his mare Nellie by Partizan is not in foal this year. Her produce was entered in the BREEDER AND SPORTSMAN Futurity Stake and her owner is sadly disappointed.

At a meeting of the Directors of the Napa Agricultural Society held last week, it was ordered that Humboldt County be added to the list of counties comprising the district from which entries an eligible for their district race.s

Several gentlemen have bonded a piece of land in San Mateo County for the purpose of building a race track, at least so it is stated. The land is situated near Colma on what is known as the Knowles ranch, and it is claimed to be a most excellent site for the purposes intended.

On Tuesday last Fontana by Almont, dam Fannie Williams by Abdallah 15, was sent to the ranch of W. S. Hobart, near San Mateo. She is one of the best broodmares in the State, and should prove an acceptable addition to the many choice matrons already at the home of Stamboul.

The good folks in and around Pleasanton are puzzled in selecting stallions for service, as there are so many rare ones to choose and select from. Among the number advertised are Director 2:17, Sidney 2:19¾, Roy Wilkes 2:12½, Guido 2:28½, Corrector, Decorator and Admiro. All royally bred and worthy of this great state.

Mr. Frank H. Burke has determined to send Eros for a record this year, and with that end in view will only serve him to a few mares. Competent judges assert that this son of Electioneer and Sontag Mohawk is as speedy as any stallion that ever left Palo Alto, and he should be, from his breeding.

After the forms had gone to press containing the entries to the Blood Horse meeting, a letter was received from W. H. Babb of Oregon, entering ch c Guido (3) by Double Cross dam Aurora by Thad Stevens, in races 1, 4, 6, 12, 16, and 17. Those who save the list on another page for reference should also bear this in mind.

Alfred De Cordova and E. R. Bowne, member of the New York Stock Exchange, last week bought the eleven-year-old black trotting stallion Bayonne Prince 2:21¼, from R. Cadougan of Bayonne, N. J., for $25,000. The stallion, which is a son of Kentucky Prince, was originally bought by Mr. Cadougan for $500 His earnings in the stud last year are said to have been $22,000.

Within the past few days ex-Senator Tim McCarthy has been carrying his hat on one side and putting on "a sight of frills," as one of his friends remarked, but he is justified in his assuming superior airs, as M. M. Sage, of Pueblo, Colorado, has named a well bred two year old "Tim McCarthy." If the colt is as much of a thoroughbred as the well known politician, no road will be too long for him.

I had a pleasant call a few days ago from Mr. F. D. Cottle, Superintendent of the Frankella Stock Farm, owned by J. J. Evans, Esq., of this city. The gentleman reports the young stock to be in good condition and the stallions Heraldic 8137 and Amberline in the pink of condition. Next year "Frankella" will be represented in the colt stakes and from the character of the brood mares that Mr. Evans has picked up from time to time, there should be a few of the "babies" that will bring him fame and profit.

A dispatch announcing that the Trotting Association at Paterson, N. J., would offer a $10,000 purse for a match race between Sunol and Axtell, the $105,000 stallion, was shown to Mr. Ijames, one of the owners of the latter. He said:

"I cannot say what the opinion of the gentlemen will be in the matter. It may be that it will be accepted, but I hardly think Axtell will be in shape for a test of speed. He now has over forty engagements in the stud, with which he will not be through until some time in July."

The Rochester Driving Park, will as usual this year, give their $10,000 purse for 2:30 performers. The "Flower City Stake" is now one of the regularly recognized events of their annual meeting, and as it is open to all comers has generally a large list of entries. This year should prove no exception to the rule and we confidently expect to find a number of Californian representatives in the list when it closes. If any of our readers contemplate taking horses East, the advertisement of the Association should be carefully read.

Secretary Kock, of the New York Jockey Club, writes me that on February 20th the following horses were declared out of the Toboggan Slide Handicap: Kingston, Hanover, Salvator, Prince Royal, Firenzi, Come to Taw, Chaos, Blackburn, Torso, Magnate, Tipstaff, Patrocles, Leighton, Bavarian, Paradox, Phœbe, Ban Chief, Good By, Martha, France, Coats, and Season. The following declarations were also received on the same day for the Bowling Brook Handicap: Torso, Padishah, Blackburn, June Day, Ralph Bayard, Paradox, Maximus and Franco.

Harry B. Starr paid the city a flying visit on Tuesday to deliver some of the mares that were sold at the Skinner sale last week. Harry informed me that the Napa track was in good condition, considering the frightful winter we have had. A drain has been placed parallel with the backstretch, which has relieved that portion of a great deal of the water which formerly lodged there, and now the track is fit to use on any fair day. By the first of May, a large number of horses will be there in training, stall-room being already engaged for almost fifty.

Ed. Bither will leave for Pittsfield, Mass, to take charge of the Allen trotters on the 15th of this month. "Ed" writes that he will have a good string to go on the grand circuit, and that he will in all probability train on the Hartford track.

John A. Goldsmith, Superintendent of the San Mateo Stock Farm, was in the city on Monday last, and promises the public a surprise or two during the coming season. Lillian Wilkes is running out, and has entirely recovered from her disability.

J. J. Evans of California Street, has two fine young colts for sale, and it will pay to take a look at them. One of them is by Abbotsford Jr. (son of Abbotsford 2:19½), dam Jane Cottle by Victor (son of Geo. M. Patchen Jr. 31); 2nd dam by Billy Cheatham; 3rd dam by Collier. The second one is by Cornelius 11335 (son of Nutwood 600) dam Young Grecian Bend by Shannon; 2nd dam Grecian Bend by Lodi; 3rd dam Fanny Johnson by St Louis. These fine youngsters can be bought cheap, as Mr. Evans has too many horse colts, and he will dispose of them at a bargain.

Theodore Winters has been in town several days this week, and he denies completely that he has had any offer for his great crack, El Rio Rey. The sensational reports which were telegraphed from the East relative to a syndicate who were willing to pay $100,000 for the son of Norfolk and Marion, evidently eminated from the brain of some reporter who dreamed what he wrote. At the present writing Mr. Winters has no intention of selling his horse, and he has yet to hear from the mythical syndicate.

Harry Cohen, formerly Secretary of the Eureka Jockey Club, is in San Francisco at present, and he gives the cheering information that W. S. Clarke, owner of the race track there, has built a neat two-story hotel in the grounds, and will spend at least a thousand dollars in improving the track. H. M. Devoy, President of the club, and W. Rideout, Secretary, are at present preparing a programme for the July races, and they promise to furnish a card that will draw horsemen from all quarters of the State. They had a good meeting last year, and I hope they may have a still better one this.

Mr. Salisbury's New York sale was a successful one and the following prices were obtained:—

Gold Leaf $8 000 J. H. Shults; Saccharine, $4500, E. J. Travis, Chicago; Navaro, $1900, F. C. Fowler, Connecticut; Alda H, $2600, Chas. Roberts, New York; Lady Guy, $2600, J. W. Daly, Mykisco, N. Y.; Sister Gilmer, $1200, E. J. Travers; Miss Jay-Eye-See, $1000, H. Kirkendall, Mont., Lady Monroe, $600 H. Kirkendall; Gertrude S, $675. S V. Lines, Rochester, N. Y.; No. 226, E J. Travis, Chicago; Young Lizzie, $1100 E. J. Travis; Thistle, $4000, J. H. Shults; Countess, $975, F. C. Fowler, Connecticut.

Black F, Sire Sydney, dam Grey Dale, $525, F. C. Fowler; Guys Sunol. $1,325, F. E. Fowler; Miss Guy, $525, E. J. Travis; Maid of Oaks, $1,440, C. D. Ely, Clyde, N. Y.

Erect, $5,000, H. Kirkendall, Mont.; Pleasanton, $2,500 E. J. Travis; Jet, $2,500 Marcus Munsell, Hartford, Conn.; Highland Belle, $1,050, H. S. Russell, Milton, Mass; Patti, $1,500, James McClenahan, New York; Lady Crittenden, $2,825, F. C. Fowler, Conn.; Diana, $2,600, H. Kirkendall; No. 242, foal of 1889, sire Director, $625.

The following are the prices obtained for the Mrs. Silas Skinner stock last Thursday week:—

Madonna, b m, foaled 1887, by Cassius M. Clay Jr, dam Joe Downing; Dr. J. P. Dunne, Berkeley ... $2,000

Pansy, br m, foaled 1877, by Cassius M. Clay Jr., dam Lady Richelieu by Richelieu; A. C. Henry, Oakland ... 1,125

Fontana, br m, foaled 1879, by Almont, dam Fannie Williams by Abdallah 15; Samuel Gamble, San Mateo ... 4,400

Metamora, b m, foaled 1879, by Duke of Orange Jr., dam Viella by Cassius M. Clay Jr.; A. C. Henry, Oakland ... 800

Namora, br m, foaled 1879, by Almont Mambrino, dam Lackey mare by Blood's Black Hawk; A. C. Henry, Oakland ... 575

Veronica, b m, foaled 1884, by Alcona, dam Fontana by Almont; Gilbert Tompkins, San Leandro ... 2,500

Lady Clay, b m, foaled 1886, by Alcona Clay, dam Metamora by Duke of Orange; A. C. Henry, Oakland ... 600

Bay colt, foaled 1887, by Sitka, dam Pride of the West by Alcona; G. W. Scott, Napa ... 680

J. A. J., b c, foaled 1888, by Alcona Clay dam Metamora by Duke of Orange; J. W. Martin, Woodland ... 310

Horatio, b c, foaled 1888, by Alcona, dam Namora by Almont Mambrino; Gilbert Tompkins, San Leandro ... 340

Black colt, foaled 1889, by Whippleton, dam Namora by Almont Mambrino; Gilbert Tompkins, San Leandro ... 320

Lula H., ch f, foaled 1889, by Alcona, dam Pansy by Cassius M. Clay; George E. Guerne, Santa Rosa ... 510

The sensational prices which were given at the Rose sale, did not keep up when the Valensin consignment was offered, but taken all in all, the prices were fairly good. Those which brought over $500 are as follows:

Lassie, bay filly, two years old, by Sidney, dam Highland Lass, $650; bought by H. T. Russell of Milton, Mass.

Thought, bay colt, three years old, by Sidney, dam Crown Point Maid, $600; bought by the Water Stock Farm of Chicago.

Tobasco, bay filly, three years old, by Sidney, dam Old Lady Hayes, $800; bought by H. T. Russell.

Muscadin, bay colt, two years old, by Valensin, dam Flirt, $1,000; bought by Scott Quinton of Trenton, N. J.

Valensin (2:23), chestnut stallion, seven-year-old, by Crown Point, dam Nellie Lambert, $3300; bought by Flo. Fowler of Connecticut.

Consolation, bay colt, yearling, by Sidney, dam Surprised, $800; bought by William Achriffe of Philadelphia.

Pleasanton Boy, chestnut colt, yearling, by Sidney, dam Oak Grove Belle, $875; bought by E. S. Cole of New York.

Elegance, chestnut colt, yearling, by Sidney, dam Dell Foster, $525; bought by Water Stock Farm, Genoa Junction, Wis.

Cassie, chestnut colt, yearling, by Sidney, dam Miss Casserly, $600; bought by Scott Quintin of Trenton N. J.

Moss Rose, bay filly, yearling, by Sidney, dam Rose Leaf, $1650; bought by M. Murphy of Pennsylvania.

Habibi, brown filly, two year old, by Valensin, dam Ivy (2:21½), $3300; bought by Jacob Rupert of Poughkeepsie.

Bouton d'Or, chestnut filly, four year old, by Sydney, dam Grey Dale, $2000; bought by I. T. Burden of New York.

Many of the old time drivers have issued books giving the benefit of their experience to the American public, and many of the publications have attained a large sale. The new work to be issued by Charles Marvin of Palo Alto will be ready to issue about April 15th, and we predict a larger sale for it than was ever attained by any similar work. It will be 12 mo., of convenient thickness, and will be bound in cloth, with gilt back and title. Frank Whitney will be responsible for the illustrations, which is sufficient guarantee that they will be of a high order. Mr. Marvin relates his experiences in a very readable way and also tells the reader the inside method of his training theory at Palo Alto. There will be chapters by other well known writers, and we have no hesitancy in recommending it to our readers. The price will be $3.50, and those who desire to subscribe for the book can leave orders at this office.

Entries for the Petaluma Colt Stakes.

The following stakes and purses open to the counties of Sonoma, Marin, Napa, Solano, Lake, Menducino, Yolo, Colusa, and Contra Costa.

YEARLING STAKE.

For foals of 1889 Mile dash. $30 entrance, of which $10 must accompany the nomination March 1st; $10 to be paid on May 1st, and $10 on July 1st. $100 added.

1—Ben E. Harris, San Francisco, b f Sidena by Sidney, dam Lena Bowles by Vick's Ethan Allen.
2—Wilfred Page, Penn's Grove, b f Mortrica by Mortimer 5346, dam Beka Patchen by Alexander 490.
3—Thomas Smith, Vallejo, br c Columbus by McDonald Chief 3583 dam Fanny Rose by Ethan Allen Jr., 2903.
4—E. McLees, Vallejo, f Lady Thorn by Thornhill.
5—P. J. Shafter, Olema, Rustic King by Rustic, dam Gazette by General McClellan 144.
6—I. M. Proctor, Petaluma, rn f Vesper Bells by Dawn 6407, dam Gipsy by Nameless.
7—Robert S Brown, Petaluma, br f Bayannetta by Anteeo, dam Debonair by Sultan
8—A. L. Whitney, Petaluma, br c by Dawn 6407, dam Jennie Offut by Gen. McClellan 144.
9—Jos. Wiercarver, Geyserville, blk f Antelcia by Anteeo, dam Nellie by Belle Alta Jr.
10—J. F. Mulgrew, Santa Rosa, br c Zouave by Daly, dam Zaga by Berlin.
11—B. C. Holly, Vallejo, b c Hollywood by Woodnut, dam Arvelia by Albert W.
12—Fred Been, Vallejo, b f Blanch by Woodnut, dam by Eugene Casserly.
13—Perry Sears, Sonoma, b f El Verano Maid by Dawn 6407.
14—A. T. Hatch, Suisun, blk f Night by Guide, dam Mollie by Admar.

TWO YEAR OLD STAKE.

For foals of 1888. Mile and repeat. $60 entrance, of which $10 must accompany the nomination March 1st: $20 to be paid on May 1st, and $20 on July 1st. $200 added.

1.—S K. Dougherty, Santa Rosa, s f Aurora, by Dawn 6407, dam Fan by Rustic.
2.—Ben E. Harris, San Francisco, ch f Starlight, by Dawn 6407, dam Lena Bowles by Vick's Ethan Allen
3.—Wilfred Page, Penn's Grove, blk c Gran Moro, by Le Grande 2869, dam Sunny Slope Belle, by The Moor 870.
4.—I. De Turk, Santa Rosa, br f Myrtle, by Anteeo, dam by Nutwood.
5.—E. McLees, Vallejo, Walnut, by Woodnut.
6.—Henry Bimsbatch, Petaluma, b f Allie H, by Alcona, dam Mollie by Edwin Booth.
7.—W. P. Fine, Petaluma, ch c Examiner, by Dawn 6407, dam Vasta by Chieftain.
8.—W. H. Warfield, Healdsburg, gr c Warde, by Capri, dam Minnie, by Belle Alta Jr.
9.—John Mc A. Brown, Petaluma, blk c Stammoor, by Stamboul, dam Moor Maid, by The Moor.
10.—Robert S. Brown, Petaluma, ch f Nelly K., by Dawn 6407, dam by Brown's McClellan.
11.—A L. Whitney, Petaluma, s f Annabelle, by Dawn 6407, dam Pacheco by Hubbard
12.—Thos. Donahue, Lytton Springs, b f Tamarack, by Carr's Mambrino, dam by Belle Alta Jr.
13.—San Miguel Stock Farm, Walnut Creek, b c Chaldean, by Mambrino Wilkes, by Fredolia dam by Fred Arnold.
14.—San Miguel Stock Farm, Walnut Creek, b f Mylitta, by Mambrino Wilkes, dam Molly Fern, by Capt. Kohl.
15.—H. W. Crabb, Oakville, s f Woodlene, by Woodnut, dam Maud, by Whippleton.
16.—W. B. Sanborn, Santa Rosa, s c Charlie Dodge, by Daly, dam Lady S., by Smuggler.
17.—Rufus Murphy, Santa Rosa, b f ———, by Anteeo, dam Daisy.
18.—W. L. Bartlett, Suisun, ch f Edrie, by Coligny, dam Molly, by Eugene Casserly.
19.—J. H. White, Lakeville, b f Tillie Almont, by Hernani, dam Kitty Almont, by Tilton Almont.
20.—Dan McGovern, Petaluma, b f Donis, by Dawn 6407, dam Kitty, by Don Juan.
21.—B. C. Holly, Vallejo, ch c Woodside, by Woodnut, dam Veronica, by Alcona.
22.—M. Kemfir, Vallejo, b f Analysis, by Antevolo, dam Allis, by Admiral.
23.—Gerry Sears, Sonoma, s c Cleveland, by Dawn 6407.
24.—F. W. Loeber, St. Helena, blk c Alcona 730, dam Fansey by Cassius M. Clay Jr., 22.

THREE-YEAR-OLD PURSE.

Three in five. Purse $300. Entrance fee 10 per cent. of the purse, of which five per cent. must accompany the nomination March 1st, and five per cent. paid on August 1st. Four colts to make the last payment.

1—Wilfred Page, Penns Grove, b f Leoline by Clovis 4909, dam Leah by Woodford Mambrino 345.
2—E. McLees, Vallejo, - f Berty.
3—P. J. Shafter, Olema, — Antevenio by Antevolo, dam Pastime by Rustic
4—A. L. Whitney, Petaluma, ch c Dor by Dawn 6407, dam Jennie Offut by Gen. McClellan.
5—Rufus Murphy, Santa Rosa, b f Maud Dee by Anteeo, dam Maud by Nutwood.
6—W. F. Bartlett, Suisun, dk b c Frank B. by Coligny, dam Mollie by Eugene Casserly.
7—J. H. White, Lakeville, b c Joe by Marco, dam Kate by Bellfounder.
8—Guy E. Grosse, Santa Rosa, br c Anteeop by Anteeo, dam Bessie G. by King Philip
9—B. C. Holly, Vallejo, b c Kafir by Alcazar, dam Flower Girl by Artherton.

FREE-FOR-ALL COLTS.

1st: For two-year-olds, foals of 1888; purse $400. Entrance 10 per cent. of the purse, of which 2½ per cent. must accompany the nomination, to be made on March 1st; 2½ per cent. to be paid on May 1st, and 5 per cent. on August 1st. Four colts to make the last payment, and three to start.

1—Ben E. Harris, San Francisco, ch f Starlight by Dawn 6407, dam Lena Bowles by Vick's Ethan Allen.
2—A. L. Whitney, Petaluma, b f Duchess by Sidney, dam Young Countess by Sam Patchen.
3—San Mateo Stock Farm, San Mateo, ch f Vida Wilkes by Guy Wilkes, dam Vixen by Nutwood.
4—Jos. Cairn Simpson, Oakland, b f Volita by Antevolo, dam Ruby by Winthrop
5—Palo Alto Stock Farm, Menlo Park, br c Almoneer by Alban, dam America by Rysdyk's Hambletonian.
6—Palo Alto Stock Farm, Menlo Park, b f Elloneer by Electioneer, dam Lady Ellen by Carr's Mambrino.
7—Palo Alto Stock Farm, Menlo Park, br f Linnet by Electioneer, dam Lizzie Whipe by Enquirer.
8—Palo Alto Stock Farm, Menlo Park, b f Wild Bee by Piedmont, dam Wildflower by Electioneer.

2d: For three-year-olds, foals of 1887. Purse $400. Entrance 10 per cent. of the purse, of which 2½ per cent. must accompany the nomination to be made on March 1st, 2½ per cent. to be paid on May 1st, and 5 per cent. on August 1st. Four colts to make the last payment, and three to start.

1—San Mateo Stock Farm, San Mateo, b c Regal Wilkes by Guy Wilkes, dam Margaret by Sultan.
2—Palo Alto Stock Farm, Menlo Park, b f Wildmont by Piedmont, dam Wildflower by Electioneer.
3—Palo Alto Stock Farm, Menlo Park, b c Pedlar by Electioneer, dam Penelope by Mohawk Chief.
4—Palo Alto Stock Farm, Menlo Park, b c Hugo by Electioneer, dam Helpmate by Planet.
5—Palo Alto Stock Farm, Menlo Park, br f Aizira by Ansel, dam American Girl by Toronto Sontag.

THE WEEKLY

Breeder and Sportsman.

JAMES P. KERR, PROPRIETOR.

The Turf and Sporting Authority of the Pacific Coast.

Office, No. 313 Bush St.

P. O. Box 2300.

TERMS—*One Year, $5; Six Months, $3; Three Months, $1.50.*
STRICTLY IN ADVANCE.

Money should be sent by postal order, draft or by registered letter, addressed to JAMES P. KERR, San Francisco, Cal.

Communications must be accompanied by the writer's name and address, not necessarily for publication, but as a private guarantee of good faith.

NEW YORK OFFICE, ROOM 15, 181 BROADWAY.

ALEX. P. WAUGH, - - - - Editor.

Advertising Rates

Per Square (half inch)

One time	$1 50
Two times	2 50
Three times	3 25
Four times	4 00

And each subsequent insertion 75c. per square.

Advertisements running six months are entitled to 10 per cent. discount.

Those running twelve months are entitled to 20 per cent. discount.

Reading notices set in same type as body of paper, 50 cents per line each insertion.

To Subscribers.

The date printed on the wrapper of your paper indicates the time to which your subscription is paid.

Should the BREEDER AND SPORTSMAN be received by any subscriber who does not want it, write us direct to stop it. A postal card will suffice.

Special Notice to Correspondents.

Letters intended for publication should reach this office not later than Wednesday of each week, to secure a place in the issue of the following Saturday. Such letters to insure immediate attention should be addressed to the BREEDER AND SPORTSMAN, and not to any member of the staff.

San Francisco, Saturday, March 15, 1890.

Dates Claimed.

SAN JOSE (Blood Horse Meeting)....April 5th, 7th and 9th
SACRAMENTO (Running Meeting)....April 26th, 29th, May 1st and 3d
IONE....Aug. 7th to 9th.
LOS ANGELES (6th District)....Aug. 11th to 16th
NAPA....Aug. 18th to 23rd
GLENBROOK PARK, 17th District....August 19th to 23d
SAN JOSE (Fall Meeting)....Aug. 25th to 30th inclusive
PETALUMA....Aug. 25th to 30th
OAKLAND (District No. 1)....Sept. 1st to Sept. 6th
LAKEPORT, 12th District....September 23d to 27th
CALIFORNIA STATE FAIR....Sept 8th to 20th
FRESNO (Fall Meeting)....Sept. 29th to Oct. 4th
MONTEREY, Salinas, Agricultural Society....Sept. 30th to Oct. 4th

Stallions Advertised

IN THE

BREEDER AND SPORTSMAN.

Thoroughbreds.

DOUGLASDALE—Thoroughbred Clydesdale....Lawn View Farm, Cal
FRIAR TUCK, Hermit—Romping Girl....C. W. Aby, Middletown.
GREENBACK, Dollar—Music....C. W. Aby, Middletown.
INTRUDER, Crater—Lady Bountiful....T. J. Knight, Sacramento.
REVEILLE, Shiloh—Norfolk....B. C. Holly, Vallejo.
ST. SAVIOR, Eolus—War Song....C. W. Aby, Middletown.
THREE CHEERS, Imp. Hurrah—Young Fashion....E. S. Culver, San Francisco.

Trotters.

ADMIRAL, Volunteer—Lady Pierson....Frank Drake, Vallejo.
ACTOR, Prompter—Dam by Sultan....Lawn View Farm, Cal.
ARBITRATOR, Director—Lady Earnest....H. A. Mayhew, Niles.
ANTEEOP, Anteeo—Bessie G....Guy E. Grosse, Santa Rosa
ANTEEOP, Anteeo—Nance....Guy E. Grosse, Santa Rosa.
ADMIRO, Admiral—dam by San Bruno....Smith & Sutherland, Pleasanton.
ASHLAND ALMONT, Almont—Pauline....T. J. Whitehead, Oakland.
ALEXANDER BUTTON, Alexander—Lady Button....Cache Creek Farm, Yolo.
APEX, Prompter—Mary....Poplar Grove Breeding Farm, Wildflower.
ALCONA, Almont—Queen Mary....Fred W. Loeber, St. Helena
BALKAN, Mambrino Wilkes—Fanny Fern....A. L. Hinds, Oakland.
BONANZA, Arthurton—Hester....Richard Havey, Oakland
BAY ROSE, Sultan—Madam Baldwin....W. W. Ayres, Oakland.
CLOVIS, Sultan—Sweetbriar....Poplar Grove Breeding Farm, Wildflower.
CUPID, Sidney—Venus....C. O. Thornquest, Oakland
CHRISMAN'S HAMBLETONIAN 10178, Whipple's Hambletonian—Flora....Jesse Chrisman, San Jose
CHARLES DERBY, Steinway—by Electioneer. Cook Stock Farm, Contra Costa Co.
CRESCO, Strathmore—Spartan....Cook Stock Farm, Contra Costa Co
CALIFORNIA NUTWOOD, Nutwood—Fanny Patchen....Martin Carter, Alameda Co.
CORRECTOR, Director—Brainey....Pleasanton Stock Farm.
DECORATOR, Director—Chess....Pleasanton Stock Farm.
DEXTER PRINCE, Kentucky Prince—Lady Dexter....L. M. Morse, Lodi.
DAWN, Nutwood—Countess....A. L. Whitney, Petaluma
DIRECTOR, Dictator—Dolly....Pleasanton Stock Farm, Pleasanton.
DON MARVIN, Fallis—Cora....F. P. Lowell, Sacramento
DESIGNER, Director—May Queen....H. Scott, Oakland.
ELECTOR, Electioneer—Gilberta....L. A. Richards, Grayson.
ELECTION, Electioneer—Lizzie H....B. C. Holly, Vallejo.
EL BENTON, Electioneer—Nellie Benton....Souther Farm, San Leandro.
ECLECTIC, Electioneer—Manette....Wilfred Page, Sonoma County
EROS, Electioneer—Sontag Mohawk....W. H. Vioget, Menlo Park
FIGARO, Hambletonian—Emblem....Souther Farm, San Leandro.
GROVER CLAY, Electioneer—Maggie Norfolk....Denis Gannon, Oakland.
G. & M., Anteeo—Rosa B....George E. Guerne, Santa Rosa.
GUY WILKES, George Wilkes—Lady Bunker....San Mateo Stock Farm, San Mateo.
GLEN FORTUNE, Electioneer—Glenna....Souther Farm, San Leandro.
GEORGE WASHINGTON, Mambrino Chief—Fanny Rose....Thos. Smith, Vallejo.
GUIDE, Director—Imogene....Smith & Sutherland, Pleasanton.
GRANDISSIMO, LeGrande—Norma....Fred W. Loeber, St Helena
ILLUSTRIOUS, Happy Medium—Abdalletta....George A. Stone, Santa Rosa.
JESTER D., Almont—Hortense....Souther Farm, San Leandro
JUNIO, Electioneer—by Granger....S. N. Straube, Fresno.
KAFIR, Alcazar—Flower Girl....B. C. Holly, Vallejo.
KING DAVID, Admiral—Black Flora....Frank Drake, Vallejo.
LEO WILKES, Guy Wilkes—Sable....San Mateo Stock Farm, San Mateo.
LYNWOOD, Nutwood—Hattie Morrison....P. Visher, Stockton.
MEMO, Sidney—Flirt....Valensin Stock Farm, Pleasanton.
MOUNTAIN BOY, Kentucky Prince—Elsie....B. C. Holly, Vallejo.
MAMBRINO WILKES, George Wilkes—Lady Chrisman....San Miguel Stock Farm, Walnut Creek.
MART BOORHEM, Sidney—Towhead....B. C. Holly, Vallejo.
MAMBRINO JR. 1789, Mambrino Patchen, dam by Mambrino Chief....Geo. P. Bull, San Jose.
MAMBRINO CHIEF, McDonald Chief—Venus....Thos. Smith, Vallejo.
MORTIMER, Electioneer—Marti....Wilfred Page, Sonoma County
NOONDAY, Wedgewood—Noontide....F. P. Lowell, Sacramento.
PASHA, Sultan—Madam Baldwin....D. Bryson, Linden
PHILOSOPHER, Pilot Wilkes—Belle....George E. Guerne, Santa Rosa.
ROY WILKES, Adrian Wilkes—Flora....Pleasanton Stock Farm Pleasanton.
REDWOOD, Anteeo—Lou Wilton....A. McFayden, Oakland.
STEINWAY, Strathmore—Abbess....Cook Stock Farm, Contra Costa Co
SUNSET, Anteeo—Bessie G....Guy E. Grosse, Santa Rosa.
SIDNEY, Santa Claus—Sweetness....Valensin Stock Farm, Pleasanton.
SIMMOCOLON, Simmons—Colon....Valensin Stock Farm, Pleasanton.
SABLE WILKES, Guy Wilkes—Sable....San Mateo Stock Farm, San Mateo.
ST. NICHOLAS, Sidney—Towhead....John Rowen, Oakland Trotting Park.
WOODNUT, Nutwood—Flora....Jas. Weatherhead, San Jose
WHIPPLETON 1883, Hambletonian Jr.—Lady Livingston....Fred W. Loeber, St. Helena
WOODSIDE, Woodnut—Veronica....B. C. Holly, Vallejo.
YOUNG ELMO, St. Elmo—Dam by Woodburn....Lawn View Farm Cal.

Spring Sales.

If there have ever been any doubts existing in the minds of the general public as to the desirability of selling first-class horses in this State, they must have been removed on Thursday of last week when the highly-bred brood mares of Mrs. Silas Skinner were sold at public auction at Woodside Farm. Notwithstanding the bad weather a large representative assemblage of prominent stock breeders met there, each and all desirous of securing some of the gilt-edged trotters offered by the proprietor of the place. It was understood that the sale was to be a clearance and without reserve. Mrs. Skinner having determined some time ago to move to Oregon for the purpose of looking after her very large interests in that State.

When Mr. Killip announced that the sale was about to proceed, the crowd that pressed closely around him showed that the stock which had been catalogued were being eagerly sought after. Samuel Gamble, manager for W. S. Hobart, was there to try and add to the numbers of the royally-bred matrons which are at present under his charge. B. C. Holly also wanted several of the animals to take with him to his well known Hollywood farm near Vallejo. Gilbert Tompkins had determined that the brood mare list of the Souther Farm should be increased and he secured one excellent individual. Fred W. Loeber, of the Vineland Stock Farm, was here, there and everywhere. The Hon. F. L. Coombs was also an interested spectator; Judge W. E. Greene, of Oakland, Geo. E. Guerne of Santa Rosa and Alfred G. fame, was there to see what could be picked up towards improving his stock, and Harry Agnew was there to see what he could get hold of, but was very unfortunate in his bids as there were those present who seemed to take a special delight in outbidding him. Fred Talbot, of San Francisco, wanted a few of the good ones but had to leave without purchasing. Charlie Scott, of Napa, was looking for bargains as were Dr. P. J. Dunne, C. C. Clay, C. M. Dougherty, A. C. Henry and many others.

The gem of the collection and for which there were many prospective buyers and liberal bidders was Fontana, the well known Almont mare, dam of Flora Belle 2:24, Silas Skinner trial 2:23½, San Diego and many other good ones; the bidding was lively and spirited and she finally changed hands, Mr. Gamble being the lucky purchaser at $4,400. Veronica, a six-year-old mare by Alcona 730, dam Fontana, was secured by the Souther Farm at an outlay of $2,500. Dr. Dunne, of Berkeley, was fortunate enough to secure Madonna by Cassius M. Clay, Jr., dam by Joe Downing, for $2,000.

All of the stock brought large prices and the lesson to be learned by the sale is, that where good stock is offered and when it is understood that there are no restrictions and no by-bidding, that the public will be tempted to give good fair prices for well-bred horses.

Mrs. Skinner is to be congratulated on the prices which were obtained for her stock, and the gentlemen who bought are to be congratulated also in becoming the possessors of animals which they need not feel ashamed to show anywhere.

Messrs. Killip & Co. worked up the sale in a truly masterly manner, and as we learn from the firm, it will only be a matter of a few weeks until they give the first of their spring combination sales, in which has already been entered many first-class representatives from some of our principal California breeding farms. It is to be presumed that their next sale will be equally as successful as the one just alluded to.

In conversation with Gilbert Tompkins, he informed us that at a near future day he will offer for sale some of the youngsters from the Souther Stock Farm; he has gone into the business methodically and with a system that is bound to pay in the long run. He proposes to have his stock go to the highest bidder, no matter what the prices may be. There will be no bidding in, and by these means the public will become convinced that whenever sales be advertised for and in behalf of the Souther Farm, horses will really go to the highest bidder and without any reservation.

Mr. Irvin Ayres has determined to follow in the same footsteps, and Mr. Wilfred Page of the Rancho Catote is inclined to follow suit. If the stock farms of California will keep up what has now been inaugurated, it will take but a very short time for the large Eastern buyers to come to California and attend our sales in this State without the necessity of our breeders having to send their stock to a far distant market.

The Belle Meade Sale.

When the annual advertisement for the Belle Meade sale came in during the week, it made our mind revert back to the many happy days spent in that great blue grass country in which is situated the Belle Meade Farm, one of the oldest of American nurseries. We have to trust to memory a great deal, but we can safely say that within the confines of the old farm, there were over 3,500 acres. The soil the finest to be found anywhere in the Western country, with plenty of timber, which is one of the best tests of fertility; the great meadows are well watered by the beautiful stream Richland Creek, and as the great grazing paddocks are well filled with the choicest youngsters to be found on any thoroughbred farm in the country, the sight as we saw it last was one beggaring description. The name itself, Belle Meade, means beautiful meadow, and it is aptly named. For over half a century it has had the reputation of being the nursery of race horses. The imported cracks, Priam, Eagle and Bluster, have been the veritable Alexander Selkirks of that remarkable region; they have ruled supreme in the Belle Meade harem, and although their bones are laid beneath the mighty oaks, and their dust mingles with the fertile soil of a foreign home, their spirit still lives in the fleet descendants of succeeding years, and brings more delight to the eye, and new fame to the race track of their remarkable sires. Vandal, Jack Malone, Sir Richard, Highlander and Child Harold, have all held court here, and these great kings were finally succeeded by that greatest of all imported sires, the mighty Bonny Scotland, who died full of years and honor in 1880; all these have passed away, and we find reigning in their stead Enquirer, Great Tom, Luke Blackburn, Bramble, and the great horse of whom all Americans feel justly proud for his great victories on the English turf, Iroquois.

The number of race horses that have been bred at Belle Meade are simply legion; here was foaled Gamma, the mighty grey mare who dominated the turf forty years ago; among those of more modern celebrities, those whose names are familiar to the present generation of the race going public we might mention Vandalite, Voltigeur, Bramble, Eland, Bazar, Euchre, Vidette, Ventilator, Sentinel, Planchette, Nellie Ransom, Camargo, Belle of the Meade, Bombast, Bushwhacker, Bancroft, Bootjack, Barnum, Barrett, General Harding, Balance All, Inspector B., Biggonet, Tyrant, Proctor Knott, Niagara, Bendigo, Bella B., Egmont, Reporter, Banner Bearer, Kee-vee-Nah, and a host of others whose names are still fresh in the public mind.

More convincing proof of the excellencies of this stud could not be given; the names alone are enough to stamp it as being one of the greatest breeding farms in the United States. From those who have seen the lot that will be sent to the auction block this year nothing but words of praise can be heard. One gentleman told us only a few weeks ago that next to Rancho Del Paso, Belle Meade was the grandest breeding farm in the country, and even then, said he, there are several individuals among their youngsters that I prefer to many on your great California farm.

The twenty-third annual sale will take place at Belle Meade, at public auction, on Thursday and Friday, April 24th and 25th, commencing promptly at 10 o'clock A. M. The well known live stock auctioneer, Capt. P. C. Kidd has been retained to sell this extremely choice lot, and we can safely recommend any of our readers who feel disposed to purchase any of the youngsters catalogued at the sale that they will receive good value for their money by sending on a commission to Capt. Kidd, whom we have known for many years.

A Great Combination Sale.

The State of Nevada has never had such a combination sale as will take place at Carson City, commencing April 15th, and continuing until all the stock is sold. Trotters, thoroughbreds and cattle of all descriptions will be catalogued, and as the sale is positive and without reserve bidders should be plenty. The stock represented will be by Echo, Gibraltar, Promptor, Buccaneer, St. Clair, Signal and Blue Bull in the trotting lines, while the runners will be the get of Norfolk, Hooker, Lodi, Breckenbridge, Three Cheers, Langford, Bois d'Arc and McMahon. Fine roadsters, work horses, Holstein cattle, registered jacks and other first-class live stock of all kinds, will tend to make a very attractive sale, which should draw the attention of dealers from all over the country. Many of the trotters are now in training and the most of them give promise of great speed. Read the advertisement and you will see what is to be sold.

Colors Claimed.

The Spokane Stable of Spokane claims for its racing colors white jacket, black sleeves and white cap.

State Agricultural Society Colt Stakes

The colt stakes that have already closed received earnest support from all sections, and it is only natural to suppose that those offered by the State Society, which close to-day, will also be equally well patronized. The events consist of two, three and four-year-old stakes, the added money being $1,100 in all. Owners of good colts should not overlook these important stakes.

The Rose Sale.

It was a smiling crowd at the American Institute Building yesterday morning, says the New York Herald.

Mr. L. J. Rose, whose California trotting stock, "good as gold," was being sold, walked in with a pink bud in his buttonhole, and, greeting his acquaintances, his face became radiant.

Auctioneer Peter C. Kellogg had ridden from one of the Jersey Oranges, and upon his bright countenance there were no traces of the fatigue felt the evening before at the close of the biggest sale of horseflesh that had ever taken place.

The buyers of the day before and the prospective purchasers of the occasion all felt happy, and even the horses whinnied as they were led under the hammer.

Forty-three head had been sold on Wednesday, and forty-four still remained. There was as much gilt edge about the latter as ornamented the former, and this was proven by the prices obtained.

Mr. Rose and his pink bud took a seat on the right of the persuasive Kellogg, and the sale continued. Nava, a Dictator mare, was the first lot that really rustled the breeders. She was wanted, and thousands answered the auctioneer's invitations, until $5,250 was had, when she became the property of Mr. W. S. Hobart, and will again journey across the continent, as her new owner lives in San Francisco.

Sensation the second followed immediately. Nelly May, an Electioneer mare, five years old, caused it. She is of very fashionable blood and will prove a gem for the nobbiest breeding farm in America. The first bid was $1,000, but it increased and rolled up bigger and bigger until $8100 was the notch, and the palms of Mr. Kellogg's hands meeting, that was her selling price.

And the buyer? Why Commodore J. Malcolm Forbes of Boston, whose yacht Puritan smothered Sir Richard Sutton's cutter Genesta when she wanted the America's Cup, and who is also owner of the "Flying Fisherman" from Mr. Burgess' hands—a yachtsman known the world over. a few years ago Commodore Forbes or his representative purchased liberally of high trotting stock in Kentucky, and the addition of Nellie May causes the impression that he may start a breeding farm somewhere near Boston. If he does and is as successful as he has been in his career as a yachtsman he will be among the first producers of trotting stock in the land.

And then another ripple, another sensation! Reverie, bay filly, foaled January 5, 1888, was brought in. As a yearling she took a record of 2:36, and trotted a public trial on September 15th last in 2:31½. She is by Alcazar, dam Sallie Durbrow by Arthurton. Mr. Rose considered her a gem. And no doubt somebody else, quite as good a judge, thought so. It was in December last that Mr. Robert Bonner and Mr. David Bonner were at Mr. Rose's farm at Los Angeles, and Reverie was one of the animals shown the New York gentlemen.

It may be shrewdly guessed that the owner of Maud S and Sunol made a note about Reverie, as he was among the early arrivals at the sale yesterday, and when Mr. Kellogg quietly talked of her royal lineage and of what she has done and is expected to do, Mr. Bonner was an attentive listener. And now how much for this great filly?

"Ten thousand dollars!"

"It's Bonner's bid, Bonner's bid!"

Chairs were mounted, heads stretched, and dozens ran around to the place where the bidder was standing.

It was Bonner's bid and the only one made.

"Ten thousand—thousand—thousand—any more?"

Mr. Rose laid his hand on Mr. Kellogg's arm with this remark: "Don't dwell on the filly. I want to take off my hat to Mr. Bonner!"

"Ten thousand dollars! Sold to Mr. Bonner!"

Mr. Rose raised his hat, Mr. Bonner lifted his, and the crowd cheered. Reverie will go to her new owner's farm at Tarrytown.

Broodmares of high quality are always as gold to the breeder, and the catalogue being rich with them there were frequent tilts for their possession. Chief among these was that for Zoraya, a Guy Wilkes mare, four years old. There was $5,000 sent at Mr. Kellogg at first, which increased until all bidders dropped out but Mr. H. L. Stout of Dubuque, and Colonel R. G. Stoner of Kentucky. Both were game and didn't yield an inch until Mr. Stout quit at $13,000, and with $13,100 Zoraya became the property of Stoner & Clay of Paris, Ky.

Zoraya had a foal at her foot, which was dropped as the train containing Mr. Rose's horses was crossing the mountains bound to New York.

The Stamboul and Alcazar youngsters also brought staggering prices. One colt, not yet a year old, pulled $6,100 from the pockets of Mr. George B. Easton of Peoria, Ill.

Mr. Ruppert considered a bay filly a year old the 19th of last month, by Alcazar, worth $3,000, and so the great work went on to the close of the lot.

And then Mr. Rose, smiling as he can, said to the assemblage, "You may be sure, gentlemen, I am greatly obliged to you!"

To me a minute later he remarked:—"It is a great sale—greater than I anticipated. I feel like treating the whole house to wine!"

Among the interested spectators toward the close of the sale were Governor Morgan G. Bulkeley, of Connecticut, and his friends, Mr. Burdett Loomis and Mr. Leverett Brainerd, of Hartford.

Forty-four head yesterday brought $95,725, an average of $2,175,57.

Add forty-three head sold on Wednesday for $140.270, and there is had eighty-seven head bringing $235,955, making a grand average of $2,712,59.

Beat it!"

The sales of yesterday in detail are as follows:—

Zoraya, blk m, 1886, by Guy Wilkes, 2:15½—Neluska, 2:30½, by Sultan; Col. R G Stoner and James E Clay, Paris, Ky.......$13,100

Reverie, 2:36, b f, January 5, 1888, by Alcazar, 2:20½—Sally Durbrow by Arthurton; Robert Bonner, New York.......10,000

Nellie May, b m, 1885, by Electioneer—Lady Ellen, 2:28, by Carr's Mambrino; J Malcolm Forbes, Boston, Mass.......8,100

Bay colt, April 11, 1889, by Stamboul, 2:12½—Lady Graves by Nutwood, 2:18¾; George B Easton, Peoria, Ill.......6,100

Nava, b m, 1884, by Dictator—Belle Brasfield by Viley's Cripple; W S Hobart, San Francisco.......5,250

Victoria, b m, 1883, by Electioneer—Victress by Baird's Hambletonian; W E Spiers, Glens Falls.......3,525

Bay colt, March 4, 1889, by Alcazar—Chino by Guy Wilkes; W E McMillan, Lobo, Kan.......3,125

Bay filly, February 19, 1889, by Alcazar—Laura Corbitt; Jacob Ruppert, New York.......3,000

Brown filly, 1889, by Stamboul—Minnie Corbitt by Guy Wilkes; M. Murphy, Downingtown, Chester county, Pa.......2,300

Unis, b m, 1881, by Electioneer—Barnes' Idol by Aker's Idol; G M Fogg, Nashville, Tenn.......2,150

Bay filly, March, 7, 1889, by Stamboul—Nellie Monroe by Inca; M. Murphy, Downingtown, Chester county, Pa.......2,100

Wiggle Waggle, b m, 1883, by Prompter—Posey by Flaxtail; Charles Robertson, New York.......2 050

Young Josie, ch m, 1879, by Sweepstakes—Josephine by Young Morrill; Young & Hathaway, Paw Paw, Mich.......2,050

Gumbo, b g, 1884, by Sultan—Georgiana by Overland; Theo. D. Palmer, Stonington, Conn.......1,900

Brown filly by Stamboul—dam by A W Richmond; C D Ely, Clyde, N Y.......1,750

Bay filly, April 11, 1889, by Stamboul—Dora by Gibraltar; G M Fogg, Nashville, Tenn.......1,725

Bay colt, 1889, by Stamboul—Mary Arnold by Arnold; Powell Bros., Springboro, Pa.......1,675

Bay filly, May 9, 1889, by Stamboul—Young Signal by Arthurton; H C Hamilton, Wilkesbarre, Pa.......1.650

Bay filly, April 28, 1888, by Alcazar—Uris by Electioneer; W L Field, Brocton, Mass.......1,650

Young Signal, b m, 1880, by Arthurton—Lady Signal by Signal; H C Hamilton, Wilkesbarre, Pa.......1,650

Bay colt, January 5, 1889, by Stamboul—Highland Maid by Arthurton; G A Deane, Copake, N Y.......1,600

Rosa C, b m, 1884, by Junius, 2.27½—Castila by Almont; Robert Steel, Philadelphia, Pa.......1,550

Bay filly, May 8, 1889 by Stamboul—Kate Barium by Wedridge Horse; T J Havemeyer, Westchester, N Y.......1,275

Bay filly, 1889, by Alcazar—San Mateo Maid by Whipple's Hambletonian; S V Lines, N Y.......1,150

Bay gelding, 1889, by Stamboul—Monte Lass by Chief of the Echoes; James Hanley, Providence, R I.......1,100

Zinfandel, b m, 1885, by Steinway—Dolly McMann; John H Gray, New York.......1,100

Nellie Monroe, b m, 1881, by Inca, dam by Crockett; J R Mears, Scranton, Pa.......1,050

Bay colt, April 25, 1889, by Alcazar—Dimple by Echo; E A Powell, Syracuse, N. Y.......1,025

Ruth Flint, ch m, 1882 by Nutwood, 2:18¾—dam by California Dexter; W O Seekregg, North East, Pa 1,025

Ophir, blk f, 1886, by Simmons—Miss Smalley by Indianapolis; Wilson & Handy, Cynthiana, Ky.......1,025

Bay filly, February 5, 1889, by Stamboul—Flora Graves by Whipple's Hambletonian; E Fitzgerald, Troy, N Y.......900

Bay filly, February 12, 1889, by Alcazar—Aimee by Del Sur; H A Moyer, Syracuse, N. Y.......900

Bay colt, May 18, 1889, by Stamboul—Dufferine by Echo; J W Page, White River Junction, Vt.......825

Bay filly, March 5, 1888 by Alcazar—Nellie by Inca; F C Fowler, Moodus, Conn.......800

Bay colt, February 20, 1889, by Harvester—Nelly by Rysdyk's Hambletonian; R H Plant, Macon, Ga.......800

Nona, blk f, 1886, by Byerly Abdallah—Mary Arnold by Arnold; W H Wilson, Cynthiana, Ky.......775

Bay colt, March 17, 1889, by Alcazar—Monte Lass by Chief of the Echoes; T J Havemeyer, Westchester, N Y.......750

Bay filly, 1888, by Stamboul—pedigree untraced; A J Welch, Hartford, Conn.......550

Bay gelding, 1887, by Stamboul—Lady Fay, by Modoc Chief; Martin Clark, Scranton, Pa.......500

Souvenir, b m, 1876, by The Moor—Lulu Jackson, by Jack Malone (thoroughbred); Count Valensin, Pleasanton, Cal.......500

Yerba Santa, b m, 1883, by Santa Claus—Pacific Maid, by Elmo; Mrs. M L Carhart, White Plains, N. Y., 450

Nana Shepherd, br m, 1884, by Nephew—Lena R. (thoroughbred), by Joe Daniels; George Thompson, New York.......450

Brown filly, May 12, 1887, by Harvester—The Mackay Mare, by a St. Lawrence horse; Wilson & Handy, Cynthiana, Ky.......430

Bay gelding, 1886, by Sultan—Gibson's Pacing Mare, by son of Ethan Allen; Wilson & Handy, Cynthiana, Ky.......320

Foals of 1890.

Property of Wilfred Page, Penn's Grove, Cal.:—

March 10, b f, by Eclectic 11321, dam Pattipatch, by Alexander 490.

March 10, b f, by Eclectic 11321, dam Minnie Allen, by Arthurton, 365; 2nd dam Lady Allen, by Geo. M. Patchen Jr. 31.

The property of W. J. Casey, Santa Clara, February 3, 1890, bay filly with black points, few white hairs in forehead, by Eros, dam Maud Center by imp. Hercules. Mr. Casey claims the name Elyria for the little lady.

I hereby notify you that the mare Molly Drew, entered in Breeder and Sportsman Futurity Stake, foaled on January 6th a bay colt, star and black points.

San Mateo Stock Farm, per John A. Goldsmith.

Names Claimed.

I hereby claim the following names:

Eurynome, for chestnut mare, foaled in 1882 by Nutwood, dam the Ben Holliday mare.

Aglaia, for brown filly, foaled in 1887 }
Thalia, for bay filly, foaled in 1888 } by Anteeo, dam by Nutwood.
Euphrosyne, for bay filly, foaled in 1889 }

Playmate, for sorrel filly, foaled in 1885 by Stanford, dam by Biggart's Rattler.

Antemina, for bay filly, foaled in 1884 by Anteeo, dam Amina by California Chief. M. F. Tarpey.

Alameda, March 1, 1890.

I claim the name of "Sidney" for the bay colt (star and left hind foot white), foaled February 17, 1890, by Sid, dam Ninena by Jim Brown. B. C. Holly.

Vallejo, March 5th.

VETERINARY.

Conducted by W. Henry Jones, M. R. C. V. S.

Subscribers to this paper can have advice through this column in all cases of sick or injured horses or cattle by sending an explicit description of the case. Applicants will send their name and address that they may be identified. Questions requiring answers by mail should be accompanied by two dollars, and addressed to W. Henry Jones, M. R. C. V. S., Olympic Stables, Sutter Street, San Francisco.

J. B. H.

I have an aged mare which suffers frequently from colic. I feed her on bran and oats, but the latter do not appear to be well masticated, the greater portion being passed in the fæces in a whole condition. Can you kindly give me an opinion how to treat her, and if anything can be done to assist her mastication

Answer.—In answer to your query with reference to your mare, I would advise you to feed on crushed oats instead of in the whole condition, also to have her teeth attended to, by a veterinary dentist, (see advertisements Breeder and Sportsman). If she should be attacked with Colic in future, administer spirit of nitric ether two ounces, spirit ammonia aromatic two ounces, tincture opium one and a half ounce in a pint of warm water. If no relief is derived, give another draught in two hours. A dose of cathartic medicine could be given with safety, on the first appearance of pain.

Wm. Henry Jones, M. R. C. V. S.,
Olympic Club Stables, Sutter St., S. F.

Answers to Correspondents.

Answers for this department must be accompanied by the name and address of the sender, not necessarily for publication, but as proof of good faith. Write the questions distinctly, and on one side of the paper only. Positively no questions will be answered by mail or telegraph.

Who Knows the Brand.

Some twelve or thirteen years ago, an estray mare was picked up in the neighborhood of San Luis Obispo, and it is important that her breeding should be established. She was branded ◯ If any of our readers know any gentleman who used ◯ that brand, we will esteem it a favor if his name is forwarded to this office.

Old Subscribers, Sacramento.

We own a bay stallion whose pedigree is as follows Bay colt foaled Feb. 7th, 1888, sired by Fallis, dam by Prompter, grand dam Spec. by Speculation, great grand dam Alicia Mandeville. Alicia was by Boston Boy, out of Peggy Magee, dam of Paddy Magee. Is he eligible to registration.

Answer.—He is eligible to registration, if the dam is registered, if not you can have her registered and then your colt is eligible.

T. C.

Please give breeding of Marco, brown stallion, owned by J. H. White of Lakeville, Sonoma County. Also give record, if he has made any.

Answer.—Marco by Elector 2:21¼, dam by Gen. McClellan; 2nd dam full sister to St. Helena, 2:27½. He is not in the 2:30 list.

R. B.

Will you be kind enough to give me the pedigree of Warwick and has he any colts that trotted in or below 2:30. He is owned by Bob Warden of Marin Co.

Answer.—We do not know his pedigree. He has no colts in the 2:30 list.

O. V. T.

Please give pedigree of br colt High Jack.

Answer.—High Jack by Double Cross or Three Cheers, dam Lugena by Thad Stevens; 2nd dam Kate Dudley by St. Joe; 3rd dam by Tom Dudley etc.

Ukiah.

Did Ed. Waverly trot a mile in 2:23½ on the Golden Gate Park, as published in the Oakland Tribune Oct. 8th 1889. The Ed. Waverly I wish to know about is a small bay stallion owned by A. W. Burbank and made the season of 1889, at Ukiah and Lakeport.

Answer.—We cannot learn of any such mile being trotted.

W. B. R.

I make the bet that Iroquois is the only living horse that has won the Grand Prix. The Derby and the St. Leger. Am I right or not.

Answer.—You are wrong, inasmuch that Iroquois did not win the Grand Prix. You possibly have confounded him with Foxhall, who won that event in the same year that Iroquois won the Derby and St. Leger.

J. M., Jr.

Please give me pedigree of Nene Sahib, Jim Crow and A. T. Stewart?

Answer—Nena Sahib, foaled 1857, by Horn of Chase, dam Independence's dam by Irish Birdcatcher; 2d dam The Cuckoo by Drone; 3d dam Stork by Oiseau; 4th dam Miss Stavely by Shuttle; 5th dam by Drone; 6th dam by Matchem, etc. Nena Sahib was imported in 1862 by John Batterby.

Which Jim Crow do you mean? there are three or four of them.

A. T. Stewart 1558 by Mambrino Patchen, dam the Harris mare by Mambrino Chief; 2d dam Young's Pilot Jr.

J. D. H.

Please give pedigree of Dashaway; also the history of Dragon, owned in Colusa or Yolo counties many years ago.

Answer—Dashaway by Belmont, dam Lady Davis by Red Bill; 2d dam Maria Collier by Collier; 3d dam by Gallatin. We do not know the history of Dragon.

J. W. G., Sacramento.

Which Lady Moscow do you mean? Nutwood Jr. is not in the 2:30 list. Primus had a record of 2:39½. John Nelson was by a son of imp. Trustee, dam Redmond mare by Abdallah 1. Which Young Bayswater is it you refer to?

F. N. S.

You do not require any blanks for registering thoroughbreds. Make out the full pedigree and forward to S. D. Bruce, 251 Broadway, New York City.

The horsemen of Ukiah are busy at present discussing the pedigree and performances of Ed. Waverley a horse owned by A. W. Burbank. We have received at least a dozen letters asking us about the horse, his record and his pedigree. Although we have written to those who should know whether he ever made a trial of 2:23½ at the Oakland track, the enquiries have failed to elicit a response. Probably Mr. Whitney of Petaluma, can give as much information about Ed. Waverly as any other one person, and he would be the proper party to apply to for any information desired. As to the reported trial, Mr. Burbank can surely give the names of those who saw his horse perform the feat.

Breeders' Directory.

Advertisements under this heading 50c. per line per month.

HORSES AND CATTLE.

W. S. JACOBS, Sacramento, Cal. — Breeder of Thoroughbred Shorthorns and Berkshire Hogs.

J. H. WHITE, Lakeville, Sonoma County—Breeder of Registered Holstein Cattle.

EL ROBLAS RANCHO—Los Alamos, Cal., Francis T. Underhill, proprietor, importer and breeder of thoroughbred Hereford Cattle. Information by mail. C. F. Swan, manager.

PAGE BROTHERS.—Penn's Grove, Sonoma Co. Cal. Breeders of Short-Horn Cattle; Draft, Roadster and Standard Bred Horses.

SETH COOK, breeder of Cleveland Bay Horses, Devon, Durham, Polled Aberdeen-Angus and Galloway Cattle. Young stock of above breeds on hand for sale. Warranted to be pure bred, recorded and average breeders. Address, Geo. A. Wiley, Cook Farm, Danville, Contra Costa Co., Cal.

MAMBRINO WILKES COLTS and FILLIES, full brothers and sisters to Gus. Wilkes 2:22, and Balkan 2:29¼, for Sale. Address SMITH HILL, Walnut Creek, Contra Costa County, Cal.

B. F. RUSH, Suisun, Cal., Shorthorns, Thoroughbred and Grades. Young Bulls and Calves for Sale.

PETER SAXE & SON, Lick House, San Francisco, Cal.—Importers and Breeders for past 18 years of every variety of Cattle, Horses, Sheep and Hogs.

HOLSTEIN THOROUGHBREDS of all the noted strains. Registered Berkshire Swine. Catalogues. F. H. BURKE, 401 Montgomery St., S. F.

HENRY C. JUDSON. Wild Idle Farm.—Breeder of Thoroughbred Horses. The home of "Wild Idle." P. O. Santa Clara; Box 223.

FERGUSON & AUSTIN,
FRESNO, CAL.
Registered Polled Angus and Short-Horn Cattle.

J. J. EVANS
—SELLS—
WALLACE'S YEAR BOOK,
WALLACE'S REGISTER No. 8,
STALLION SERVICE BOOKS,
For Office and Pocket.
—ALL KINDS—
PEDIGREE BLANKS.
J. J. Evans,
Stationer and Printer,
406 California Street, San Francisco, Cal.
Mail orders receive prompt attention.

Attention! Sportsmen!!

An exploring party will leave San Francisco about April 10th for the Alaska Coast, St. Matthews Island and Yukon River, stopping at numerous places on the way where Seal, Walrus, Sea Lions, Brown Bear, White Polar Bear and Deer are plentiful; also splendid fishing for Salmon, Halibut, Trout and Cod, offering to the hunter and fisherman a trip of five months' unparalleled for sport. A novel feature of this offer is that each one taking the trip becomes a stockholder in the Company.

For further information apply to
NORTHERN DEVELOPMENT CO.
No. 5 Market St., Room 5.

For Rent.

San Mateo.

Several acres on county road—Belle View Avenue Barn, two Cottages, Shed, completed. Location unsurpassed.

Apply to or address
R. TEN BROECK.
San Mateo, opposite Orphanage.

Oysters.

M. B. MORAGHAN

Is the only importer, planter and wholesale dealer in the CALIFORNIA MARKET, Stalls 68, 69 to 71 and 47, 48. All the choicest brands of Fresh Oysters constantly on hand. Prompt attention paid to hotel and country orders. Price List.

Large Eastern Oysters .... $1 00 per 100
Transplanted Eastern Oysters .... 1 50 per 100
California Oysters .... 2 00 " sack
Fresh frozen Eastern Oysters at $7 50 per doz. cans.

JOHN FORGIE,
Importing Tailor,
204 Montgomery Street,
N. E. corner Bush, SAN FRANCISCO.

The Poodle Dog
"Rotisserie,"
FIRST-CLASS IN EVERY RESPECT.
Elegant Family Dining Rooms.
S. E. cor. GRANT AVE. and BUSH STREET.
ANDRE POTENTINI, Proprietor.

PASTURAGE And Care of Horses

AT ALL SEASONS, A SPECIALTY,
—AT—
MURRAY'S RANCH, - - - Laurel Creek
SAN MATEO COUNTY.

Horses pastured, in the season, $1 per month.
Horses stabled and fed hay, per month $8 to $10.
Small pastures for fine stock at agreed rates. Yearly contracts at agreed rates. Best of attention given to all stock.
Stock can be delivered at the ranch or shipped to San Mateo.
Parties are requested to visit the ranch and satisfy themselves of its adaptation for the above purpose.
There are no barb wire fences on the farm.
Address
B. C. MURRAY,
San Mateo.

The Montana Circuit.

Thirty-one Days of Racing--Running, Trotting and Pacing.

$45,000 in Purses and Stakes.

Nominations to the Following Stakes close April 1st:

MISSOULA, July 14th to 19th Inclusive.

J. L. SLOANE, Secretary.

MISSOULA STAKES—Running. Six furlongs .... $250 added
For two-year-olds.
HOTEL STAKES—Running. One and one-half miles .... $400 added
For three-year-olds.
BITTER ROOT STAKES—Trotting .... $250 added
For three-year-olds bred and raised in Montana.

DEER LODGE, July 22d to 26th Inclusive.

JAS. B McMASTER, Secretary.

DEER LODGE STAKES—Running. Six furlongs .... $250 added
For two-year-olds.
HOTEL STAKES—Running. One and one-half miles .... $300 added
For three-year-olds.
MONTANA STAKES—Trotting .... $100 added
For two-year-olds bred and raised in Montana.
ORO FINO STAKES—Trotting .... $300 added
For three-year-olds. Free for all.
YOSPEL MONTAIN STAKES—Trotting .... $300 added
For two-year-olds. Free for all.
MERCHANTS' STAKES—Trotting .... $200 added
For three-year-olds bred and raised in Montana.

Anaconda, July 30th to August 9th Inclusive.

W. M. THORNTON, Secretary.

BANKERS' STAKES—Running. Five furlongs .... $400 added
For two-year-olds.
MONTANA SUBURBAN—Running. One and one-half miles .... $500 added
For three-year-olds.
BREEDERS' STAKES—Trotting .... $250 added
For two-year-olds bred and raised in Montana.
BREEDERS' STAKES—Trotting .... $250 added
For three-year-olds bred and raised in Montana
LOWER WORKS STAKES—Trotting .... $750 added; $250 more if 2:35 is beaten
For two-year-olds. Free for all.
UPPER WORKS STAKES—Trotting .... $340 added; $250 more if 2:25 is beaten
For three-year-olds. Free for all.

BUTTE, August 13th to 23rd Inclusive.

E. W. WYNNE, Secretary.

ANACONDA STAKES.—Running .... $400 added
For 2 year olds.
WEST SIDE DERBY.—Running .... $500 added
For 3 year olds.
MONTANA STAKES.—Trotting .... $250 added
For 2 year olds bred and raised in Montana.
MONTANA STAKES.—Trotting .... $250 added
For 3 year olds bred and raised in Montana.
MOULTON STAKES.—Trotting .... $250 added, $250 more if 2:36 is beaten
For 2 year olds. Free for all.
SILVER CITY STAKES.—Trotting .... $250 added, $250 more if 2:25 is beaten
For 3 year olds. Free for all.

In all of the above stakes each nomination must be accompanied with $10 and a full description of animal. A second payment of $15 must be made on or before the first day of June; the remaining $25 must be paid before six o'clock the evening before the race.

All stakes to be divided as follows: 70 per cent. to the first horse, 20 per cent, to second, and 10 per cent, to third.

For entry blanks, programmes, etc., address any of the Secretaries.

2:10¾ 2:13¾ 2:10

DEXTER PRINCE.

This Royally-bred Stallion will make the Season of 1890 at the LIVE OAKS Breeding Farm, 2 miles from Lodi, San Joaquin County, Cal.

DESCRIPTION.

DEXTER PRINCE is a blood bay, 16 hands high, weighs over 1 100 pounds; has great power and substance, and the highest finish. When two years old, at Palo Alto, he was timed quarters by Gov. Stanford in 34½ seconds, and he was driven eighths by Mr. Marvin at a faster rate of speed than that. He is a sure foal-getter, and invariably sires foals of good size, of fine form and finish, and the highest rate of speed.

PEDIGREE.

By KENTUCKY PRINCE, the sire of Guy, 2:10¾, Spofford, 2:18¾, Company, 2:19¾, Bayonne Prince, 2:21 1-4, Fred Folger, 2:20¾, and a score more in the 2:30 list.

First dam LADY DEXTER, full sister of the greatest of trotters, Dexter, and the greatest of sires, Dictator, the sire of Director, 2:17, Phallas, 2:13¾, in a fourth heat, and Jay-Eye-See, 2:10.

Second dam Clara, the dam of Dexter, 2:17 1-4, Dictator, Astoria 2:29 1-4, and Almah, 2:29¾. Clara was by American Star, that has 34 daughters that have produced 2:30 or better trotters.

Third dam the McKinstry mare, the dam of Shark, 2:27¾. HAMBLETONIAN, the grandsire of DEXTER PRINCE, has 40 trotters in the 2:30 list, 44 daughters that have produced 2:30 trotters, and more than 100 sons that have sired 2 30 trotters.

CLARK CHIEF, the grandsire on the sire's side, was the sire of performing and producing sons and daughters.

DEXTER PRINCE has faster blood lines, on both sides, than any other stallion in the world—Guy 2:10¾, and Jay-Eye-See, 2:10.

KENTUCKY PRINCE is one of the best bred and speediest stallions in the world. David Bonner, in the presence of Governor Stanford, timed him when he trotted a 2:16 gait. He is by Clark Chief, one of the great broodmare sires; his first dam is Kentucky Queen by Morgan Eagle, son of Hale's Green Mountain Morgan, 2nd dam by Blythe's Whip, 3rd dam by Martin's Brummier, 4th dam by Quicksilver 960, on through the strongest thoroughbred blood.

TERMS.

$100 for the season, with usual return privileges. Payable before mares are removed. Good pasture, and the best care furnished, but no responsibility assumed for accidents.

PREMIUM.

$250 will be given to the first of the produce of DEXTER PRINCE put in the 2:30 list, and $100 each after the first. Address

L M. MORSE, Lodi, Cal.

PHIL J. CRIMMINS. JOHN O. MORRISON.
"Silver Palace,"
36 Geary Street,
San Francisco, Cal

SAMUEL VALLEAU. JAS. R. BRODIE.
J. R. BRODIE & CO.,
Steam Printers,
—And Dealers in—
Poolseller's and Bookmaker's Supplies.
401—403 *Sansome Street, corner Sacramento, San Francisco.*

BERGEZ'S
RESTAURANT.
FIRST-CLASS. Charges Reasonable.
Private Rooms for Families.
332—334 Pine St., below Montgomery St.
JOHN BERGEZ, Propr.

HENRY J. COX JW. S. JOHNSON
The "EDWIN C."
40 EDDY STREET.
Cor. of Mason. San Francisco.
(Private Entrance Mason Street.)

FOR SALE
AT

Vineland Stock Farm

STALLIONS, BROODMARES AND FILLIES

ONE STALLION FIVE YEARS OLD, SEAL-BROWN, by WHIPPLETON (sire of Lily Stanley, 2:17 1-2 Homestakes 2:16 1-2, etc.), dam Sally Gorham by Werner's Rattler. This horse is scarcely 15 1-2 hands high, but very compactly built. He breeds exceptionally large and well finished colts. Any one understanding the business could clear him in one season, or he would make a No. 1 road horse, as he can trot a 40 gait any time.

ONE THREE-YEAR-OLD, SEAL-BROWN, by WHIPPLETON (sire of Lilly Stanley, 2:17 1 2, Homestakes 2:16 1-2, etc.) dam Sally Gorham, etc. This ought to make a great General Purpose sire, and with opportunities get trotters, as he is compact, strong-boned, and will measure when grown about 16 hands and weighs 1,200 lbs. With a little road work last fall he developed a wonderful burst of speed.

ONE THREE-YEAR-OLD, BLACK, by WHIPPLETON (sire of Lilly Stanley 2 17 1-2, etc.), dam by Naubuc (sire of the dam of Eva W., 2:23 1-2, etc.), full brother to Thomas Jefferson, 2 23. This horse will be fully 16 1-2 hands high. He is smooth, rapid gaited and from size and conformation should breed, like his sire, large, rangy, finished colts.

ONE TWO-YEAR-OLD, BRIGHT CHESTNUT, sired by DAWN 2:18¾, dam Alida (dam of Directa, three-year-old record 2:31¾, trial 2:26) by Admiral (sire of sister 2:19 1-2, Nona Y 2:25, etc). This colt is the making of an extraordinary horse. He is large boned and will be over sixteen hands high when grown; he is of the true Nutwood type, is clean gaited and can lead a piece as fast as any man's colt.

ONE TWO-YEAR-OLD, BLOOD BAY, (full brother to Alcona Jr. sire of Silas Skinner, trial 2:23) sired by ALCONA (sire of Flora Belle 2:24, etc.,) dam Madonna by Cassius M. Clay Jr. This colt will make a trotter and a great stock horse if developed; he has the combined blood of Almont, Mambrino Chief, Cassius M. Clay Jr. and Joe Downing.

These colts are all sound and promising. The only reason I offer them for sale is, that I have three aged stallions in use, and the surplus is growing on me. If I were starting a breeding business for profit, I should consider either of these colts a representative to commence with. Also brood mares and fillies for sale. Correspondence solicited.

FRED. W. LOEBER, St. Helena,
Napa Co., Cal.

Wellbred Stallions

FOR SALE.

SATINWOOD

Is 8 years old, stands 16.1 hands high and weighs 1150 pounds; is a beautiful dark chestnut; was sired by Wormwood, a full brother to Eva W (2:25) and Redwood (2:27). First dam by John Nelson; second dam by Argyle; third dam Blackhawk Worm—ood by Nutwood 2 28 1-4, sire of Woodnut 2:16 1-4; dam the Cropsy Mare by Naubuc, dam Gipsy Queen by George M. Patchen; second dam Capt. Roberts Mare. Nutwood 2:18 3-4, by Belmont, dam Miss Russell (dam of Maud S, 2:08 3-4. Belmont, by Abdallah (sire of Goldsmith Maid) dam Belle by Mambrino Chief. Miss Russell, by Pilot Jr, dam Sally Russell by Boston.

Full pedigree and all particulars on application.

J. A. C.

Sorrell stallion, foaled April 22nd, 1887. Bred by Wm' Jeffries of San Francisco, Cal. Sired by C. C. Bemis' Lancelot. First dam Bay Mare Nellie, sired by Ulster Chief he by Rysdyk's Hambletonian, her dam by Kentucky Hunter, noted for his speed and endurance (see Stud Book).

For further particulars apply to
J. A. CARLETON,
1302 Broadway, Oakland, Cal.

FOR SALE.

A Mohawk Chief BROODMARE
and a
Director Colt, 6 months old.

For particulars address or apply to ANCON HOTEL, 9 and 11 Pacific Street, San Francisco.

Antevolo Colt

For Sale.

AVOLO REX, foaled February 22, 1888; dam Catchup by Rustic; grandam Huntress by Don Victor; g g dam Betty Denice by American Boy Jr. Is 15.1 hands high, well developed, muscular, and without a blemish. Has a very gentle disposition, and shows speed and a good gait. Apply
HOME FURNISHING CO,
113 Fifth Street, S. F., Cal.

ARGONAUT HERD.
POLLED ABERDEEN-ANGUS CATTLE.

Thirty head choice pure bred and high grade (cross bred) HEIFERS and a few grand young BULLS for sale at reasonable prices A fine opportunity for persons wishing to establish choice herds or change their bulls. Representatives from this herd were grand prize winners at the last California State Fair.
Address DR. S. M. DIXON,
Sacramento, Cal.

For Sale

A First-Class.
BREEDING FARM.
Of 800 Acres.

Four hours' ride from the city. Good roads to a first class track. Climate unexcelled. Plenty of wood and running water.

For further information apply to the office of the
BREEDER AND SPORTSMAN,
San Francisco.
313 Bush Street.

Sire of Yolo Maid, 2:12½

Alexander Button 1197.

FOUR YEAR-OLD RECORD, 2:26 1-2.

SIRE OF

YOLO MAID, 2:12½, BELLE BUTTON, 2:20, TOM RIDER, 2:20½, ROSA MAC, 2:20½, J. H. (seperately timed in a race) 2:22½, KEHOE, 2:34½, ALEX. BUTTON (3), 2:35½, BURBANK S. (2 y. o., ½-mile track), 2:53.

PEDIGREE.

Alex. Button was Sired by Alexander 490. Record, 2:31 1-4.

First dam Lady Button by Napa Rattler; 2d dam a pacing mare (S. T. B.) by a Copperbottom horse.

ALEXANDER (490), record, 2:31½.

Sire of Alex. Button, 2:26 1-2, Reliance, 2:22 1-2 Tommy Dodd, 2:24, Nelly Patchen, 2:27 1-4, by Geo. M. Patchen Jr. (31), record 2:27; first dam Lady Crum by Brown's Bellfounder.

GEO. M. PATCHEN JR. (31), rec., 2:27.

Sire of Wells Fargo, 2:18¾, Sam Purdy, 2:20 1-2, Vanderlynn, 2:21, Star King, 2:22, Ben Ali, 2:24, and five others in the 30 list, by Geo. M. Patchen (30), 2:23 1-2; first dam Bell by Top Bellfounder, son of imp. Bellfounder; 2d dam Hoota Laddie mare.

GEO. M. PATCHEN (30). RECORD 2:23½.

Sire of Lucy, 2:18¼; Chas. E. Low, 2:25½; Geo. M. Patchen, Jr., 2:27; Mary, 2:2-; by Cassius M. Clay (18). 1st dam by Head'em, son of imp. Trustee; 2nd dam Itaska, by American Eclipse.

CASSIUS M. CLAY (18).

Sire of Geo. M. Patchen, 2:23½, etc.; by Henry Clay (8). 1st dam Jersey Kate, the dam of John Anderson.

HENRY CLAY (8).

Sire of Black Douglass, 2:30; Centerville (w), 2.32; by Andrew Jackson (4); 1st dam burry.

ANDREW JACKSON (4).

By Young Bashaw; dam an Ohio mare of unknown blood.

YOUNG BASHAW.

By imp. Grand Bashaw; 1st dam Pearl, by First Consul; 2nd dam Fancy, by imp. Messenger; 3rd dam by imp. Rockingham.

NAPA RATTLER.

By Biggart's Rattler; 1st dam Poll, by imp. Consternation; 2nd dam Betsy Baker, by Mambrino.

BIGGART'S RATTLER.

Grandsire of Joe. Brown, 2:22; Lady Snell, 2:23½; Mary Davis, 2:2¼; Nellie Webster, 2:23¼, by Sir Henry, son of the Garrett Horse, by imp. Leonidas; 1st dam by the Hyde Horse, son of Long's Magnum Bonum; 2nd dam of Messenger blood,

BROWN'S BELLFOUNDER.

By imp. Bellfounder; 1st dam Lady Allport, by Mambrino; 2nd dam by Tippo Saib, son of imp. Messenger; 3rd dam by imp. Messenger.

DESCRIPTION.

ALEXANDER BUTTON is a dark bay with fine flowing mane and tail; stands 15-3¼ hands high; weighs 1,200 pounds, and is of excellent disposition. He is a natural trotter, inherited through the speed-lines of his ancestors, and imparts his speed to his off-spring with uniform certainty. His colts show him to be a wonderful producer—and with his breeding and terms of service, he is the cheapest and most wonderful horse in the State.

TERMS.

TERMS.—$100, payable at end of season. Mares not proving with foal may be returned next season free of charge. Good pasturage furnished at $4 per month, and due care taken to prevent accidents or escapes, but no liability whatever assumed.

Will stand at Cache Creek Farm, which is situated about one and one-half miles west of Yolo Station.

All mares sent to Yolo in my care will be forwarded free of charge.

G. W. WOODARD, Proprietor.
Yolo, Yolo Co., Cal.

HOLLYWOOD BREEDING FARM.

MOUNTAIN BOY 4841.

Br s MOUNTAIN BOY, 4841, bred by Charles Backman, Orange County, New York, foaled 1882, sire Kentucky Prince 2470, dam Elise, sister to Elaine, by Messenger Duroc 106; grandam Green Mountain Maid, 3d dam, Shanghai Mary, will serve a limited number of mares at $100 the season.

ELECTION.

Bay stallion ELECTION, bred at Senator Stanford's Palo Alto Stock Farm, foaled 1884, sire Electioneer, dam Lizzie H. by Whipple's Hambletonian 725, grandam Lizzie Harris (by Comus son of Green's Bashaw 50), great grandam by Arnold Harris, thoroughbred.

Election is one of the handsomest bloodlike sons of Electioneer, and with his thoroughbred cross through Arnold Harris should prove invaluable as a sire. TERMS, $100 the season.

KAFIR.

B c KAFIR, bred by L. J. Rose, Los Angeles, foaled 1887, sire Alcazar, 2:20½, dam Flower Girl by Arthurton, sire of Arab, 2:15, grandam Flora by General McClellan, 144, sire of three in 2:30 list, great grand dam by Langford, he by Williamson's Belmont, will serve a limited number of mares at $50 the season.

WOODSIDE.

Ch c WOODSIDE, sire Woodnut, 2:16½; 1st dam Veronica by Alcona, 730; 2nd dam Fontana by Almont, 33; 3rd dam Fannie Williams by Alexander's Abdallah, 15. Book full.

MART BOORHEM.

B c MART BOORHEM, by Sydney, 2:19¾; 1st dam Towhead by Echo. This colt is a full brother to St. Nicholas who showed a mile in 2:27½ at three years old. TERMS, $25 the season.

REVEILLE.

The well known thoroughbred stallion REVEILLE, by Shiloh, dam by Norfolk. Reveille is a brother to John Treat and is the sire of Tycoon and Gladstone TERMS, $25 the season.

Hollywood is nicely situated three miles from Vallejo on the Napa road. Good pasturage and every care will be taken of mares at reasonable rates. For further particulars, apply,

B. C. HOLLY, Vallejo.

Speed Programme

—OF THE—

Twelfth District Ag'l Society

To be held at

LAKEPORT,

SEPTEMBER 23 to 27 INCLUSIVE.

First Day—Tuesday, Sept. 23, 1890.

RACE NO. 1—TROTTING.

Yearling Stake; $250 guaranteed. Entrance $30, payable as follows: $5 May 1st, $10 July 1, $10 September 1st (when entry must be named), and $5 additional for starters. Entries to close May 1, 1890. See general conditions.

RACE NO. 2—RUNNING.

One-half mile dash. $100 added; $25 to second. Entrance $10, to close 6 P. M. day before race.

RACE NO. 3—TROTTING.

Three-minute Class. Mile heats 3 in 5. District. $150 added. Entrance $30; to close 6 P. M. day before race. 5 to enter, 3 to start. See general conditions.

Second Day—Wednesday, September 24th

RACE NO. 4—RUNNING.

Three-quarter mile heats; 2 in 3. $200 added; $25 to second. Entrance $10, to close 6 P. M. day before race.

RACE NO. 5—TROTTING.

District Stallion. Mile heats 3 in 5. Purse $500. Entrance $50, to close 6 P. M. day before race; 5 to enter, 3 to start. See general conditions.

RACE NO. 6—TROTTING.

Three-year-old stake; $300 guaranteed. $50 entrance, payable as follows: May 1st, $10; July 1st, $10; September 1, $15 (when entry must be named), and $15 additional to start. Open to Napa, Solano, Sonoma, Marin, Lake, Colusa, Yolo, Mendocino and Humboldt Counties.

Third Day—Thursday, Sept. 25th.

RACE NO. 7—RUNNING.

Seven-eighths mile dash. $150 added; $25 to second. Entrance $10, to close 6 P. M. day before race.

RACE NO. 8—TROTTING.

Two-year-old stake; free for all. Mile heats, best 2 in 3, $3 0 guaranteed. Entrance $50, payable as follows: May 1st, $10; July 1st, $10; September 1st, $10, and $15 additional to start. See general conditions.

Fourth Day—Friday, Sept. 26th.

RACE NO. 9—TROTTING.

Mile heats, 3 in 5. For all described counties in race No. 6. $400 added. Entrance $60, payable as follows: May 1st, $10; July 1st, $20; September 1st, $20—when entries must be named—$10 additional to start. See general conditions.

RACE NO. 10—RUNNING.

Citizens' Handicap. $100 added. Five-eighths mile; heats, 2 in 3. Entrance $10, to close 6 P. M. day before race.

Fifth Day—Saturday, September 27th.

RACE NO. 11—RUNNING.

GENTLEMEN'S NOVELTY.—*For non-professional jockeys.* One mile dash. $10 added; $5 entrance. Purse divided as follows: First horse at each quarter to get $25; slowest average at all quarters to get Society medal.

NO. 12.—LADIES' TOURNAMENT.

Free for all in District. Purse $50, divided as follows: $25 to first, $15 to second, $10 to third.

No. 13.—GENTLEMAN'S TROTTING.

Same conditions as gentlemen's Novelty. Mile heats, two in three. Entrance $5. Entrance money divided 60, 30 and 10 per cent.

GENERAN CONDITIONS.

Nominations in colt stakes transferrable any time before colts are named. If the payments in stake races amount to more than the sum guaranteed the additional amount to be divided 60, 30 and 10 per cent; in case of only two starting, 60 and 40 per cent.; and in case of one horse walking over, the whole amount to go to such horse.

A failure to make any payment when due shall be considered a withdrawal, and forfeiture of the amounts paid in. National Rules to govern all trotting races. The right reserved to refund the first payment in case the stake does not fill satisfactorily.

All running races, unless otherwise specified, governed by the Pacific Coast Blood Horse Association Rules.

The Directors reserve the right to change the hour and date of any race, and in case of a race being antedated the nominator will receive notice.

A horse distancing the field shall receive only first and third moneys.

L. G. SIMMONS, President.

A. B. McCUTCHEN, Secretary.

Rochester Driving Park

ROCHESTER, N. Y.

FLOWER CITY

Guarantee Stakes.

$10,000,

OPEN TO ALL SUBSCRIBERS.

For Trotting Horses that never beat 2:30 prior to the closing of this Stake

To be Trotted on the Rochester Driving Park, during Circuit Meeting, Aug. 12th, 13th, 14th and 15th, date to be decided by the Association.

ENTRANCE, FIVE PER CENT. OF PURSE, TO BE PAID AS FOLLOWS:

$125 payable at the time of subscription, which is to close Tuesday, April 1, 1890. Each subscriber to give his residence and Post Office address with his subscription. $125 payable Thursday, May 15th. $125 payable Tuesday, July 1st. $125 payable Friday, August 1, 1890, when the horses are to be named.

No subscription received unless the first payment of $125 shall accompany the same.

Subscribers liable only for the amount they have actually paid in but all subscriptions paid in shall be forfeited to the Association for this stake. Subscribers may transfer their subscription. Horses eligible April 1, 1890, shall be eligible for the race.

The entire stake subscribed shall be devoted to this purse, and it is guaranteed by the Association not to be less than $10,000. In case the subscription should exceed the amount of $10,000, such excess if under $500, will be added to the amount of purse; but if such excess should amount to $500 or over, then the excess will be devoted to another purse to be given as a Consolation Purse, for horses starting and winning no part of the original purse. Purses to be divided into fifty, twenty-five, fifteen and ten per cent., for first, second, third and fourth horses.

Bear in mind that subscriptions close Tuesday, April 1st, and that the whole subscription is but five per cent. of the guaranteed amount of purse ($10,000). Subscriptions accompanied by the first payment ($125), must be addressed to the secretary.

Send for circulars for distribution.

A. COLLINS, Secretary,
Rochester, N. Y.

SAN JOSE

Colt Stakes,

TO BE TROTTED AT THE

FALL MEETING

OF 1890.

No. 1. REGAL WILKES TROTTING STAKES. For three year olds $60 entrance, of which $10 must accompany nomination; $25 on June 1st, and $25 on August 1st; with $250 added. Mile heats, three in five.

No. 2. MOUNT HAMILTON TROTTING STAKES. For two year olds. $50 entrance, of which $10 must accompany nomination. $15 on June 1st and $25 on August 1st; with $200 added. Mile and repeat.

No. 3. SANTA CLARA COUNTY TROTTING STAKES.—For two year olds (for above County only). $30 entrance, of which $10 must accompany nomination. $10 on June 1st and $10 on August 1st, with $150 added. Mile and repeat.

Parties must have owned their colts prior to February 1st, 1890, to be eligible in this stake.

No. 4. INFANT TROTTING STAKES.—For the get of the following stallions: Jim L, Argent, Eros, Bismarck, J. Weatherhead's horses (2), Guy Davis, Nutwood Boy, Orion, King William, Tommy T., Stranger, John Sevenicks, Col. Benton, Wilmington, Dick Patchen, Baywood, Fleetwood, Sultan Jr., Billy Thornhill, Amphaan, Magic, Chancellor, Monte, Chrisman's Hambletonian, Boxwood, Nutgrove, Prince Albert, Alex Graham, Designer, Cyrus R., Harry Almont, Rea's Nutwood, Boodle, Parnell, Robin Adair, Fred Grant, Elect, Mambrino Jr., California Nutwood, Soudan, Jim Mulvenna, Brown Jug, Menlo, Almont Patchen, Antinous, Electric Light, May Boy, C. W. S. Henderson's Henry, S. B. Emerson, Carr's Mambrino, Designer, Prince Warwick, Henry Buff, J. Dunn's horses (3). For yearling foals of 1889, $25 entrance, of which $5 must accompany nomination; $10 on June 1st, and $10 Aug. 1st, with $100 added. Mile dashes.

CONDITIONS.

Entries to close in the above stakes Tuesday, April 1st, 1890. Stake and added money divided 60 per cent. to first, 30 per cent. to second, and 10 per cent. to third.

For a walkover the colt will take the whole stake, but no added money. If two colts start they must contest for entrance money only, divided two-thirds and one-third.

Declarations are void unless accompanied by the money.

Nominations not making payments when due forfeit previous payments.

WM. BUCKLY, President.

G. H. BRAGG, Secretary.

Solano and Napa Agricultural Society.

Trotting Colt Guarantee Stakes for 1890.

The Solano and Napa Agricultural Society have opened the following Colt Stakes for Trotters:

NO. 1. TWO YEAR OLDS.—Free for all; $100 guaranteed. $50 entrance, payable as follows: $10 April 1st, when entries close; $10 May 1st, $10 June 1st, $10 July 1st, $10 August 1st, when colts must be named. Nominations transferrable any time before colts are named. If the payments amount to more than the amounts guaranteed the additional amount to be added to the stake. All moneys divided as follows: 60, 30 and 10 per cent; in case of only two starting, 60 and 40 per cent: and in case of one horse walking over the whole amount to go to such horse. A failure to make any payment when due shall be considered a withdrawal and forfeiture of the amounts paid in. National or American Rules to govern, as the Society may elect. The right reserved to refund the first payment in case the stakes do not fill reasonably well.

No. 2. FOR THREE YEAR OLDS.—Free for all $[illegible] guaranteed. $100 entrance, payable as follows: $20 April 1st, when entries close; $20 May 1st, $20 June 1st, $20 July 1st, $20 August 1st, when colts must be named. Conditions same as in No. 1.

District Colt Stakes for districts comprising Counties of Solano, Napa, Sonoma, Marin, Lake, Colusa, Yolo, Mendocino, Humboldt and Butte.

No. 3. FOR YEARLINGS.—$250 guaranteed. District. $40 entrance, payable as follows: $10 April 1st, when entries close; $10 June 1st, $10 July 1st, $10 Aug. 1st, when colts must be named. Conditions same as in No. 1.

No. 4. FOR TWO YEAR OLDS.—$300 guaranteed. District. $50 entrance, payable as follows: $10 April 1st, when entries close; $10 May 1st, $10 June 1st, $10 July 1st, $10 August 1st, when colts must be named. Conditions same as in No. 1.

No. 5. FOR THREE YEAR OLDS.—$400 guaranteed. District. $50 entrance, payable as follows: $10 April 1st when entries close; $10 May 1st, $10 June 1st, $10 July 1st, $10 August 1st, when colts must be named. Conditions same as in No. 1.

Yearling Stake. Single dash; one mile. Two Year Olds.—Mile heats, two in three. Three Year Olds—Three in five, to harness. Parties entering colts will be notified by mail when payment becomes due.

The Society also offers the following stakes for class horses.

TROTTING STAKES.—Free for all.

2:30 CLASS—Trotting; purse $1500.
2:24 CLASS—Trotting; purse $1500.
2:20 CLASS—Trotting; purse $1500.

Horses eligible January 1st, 1890. Entrance $150, payable as follows: $25 April 1st, when entries close; $25 May 1st, $25 June 1st, $25 July 1st, $50 August 1st, when horses must be named. Nominations transferable any time before August 1st. Right reserved to refund entrance fee in any of the stakes should they not fill reasonably well. Money divided, 50, 25, 15 and 10 per cent. National or American Association Rules to govern, as the Society shall elect. To be trotted at our regular summer meeting, upon days to be here after arranged.

Entries to close April 1st, 1890, with

A. H. CONKLING, Secretary,
Napa City, Cal.

L. L. JAMES, President.

R. LIDDLE & SON

538 Washington St., S. F.,

Wholesale and Retail Dealers in

Guns, Rifles and Pistols.

A Full Line of FISHING TACKLE and SPORTSMAN'S GOODS.

Orders by mail receive prompt attention.

State Agricultural Society's

SPRING

RACE MEETING

AT

SACRAMENTO, CAL.,

APRIL 26 to 29, and MAY 1 and 3, 1890

ENTRIES CLOSE APRIL 7, 1890.

PROGRAMME.

FIRST DAY—SATURDAY, APRIL 26.

NO. 1.

Purse $400, for three-year-olds and upwards; $15 from starters to go to second horse. A winner this year at this distance to carry 3 pounds extra. Maidens allowed, if three years old, 5 pounds; four or more, 10 pounds. Three-quarters of a mile.

NO. 2.

Norfolk Stakes, for two-year-olds. Closed with 37 nominations. Five-eighths of a mile.

NO. 3.

Selling purse $400, of which $50 to second; for all ages. Winner to be sold at auction. Horses entered to be sold for $1,500 to carry full weight. One pound off for each $100 down to $500. Value placed on starters only by 6 P. M. night before race. One mile and a sixteenth.

NO. 4.

The California Oaks, for three-year-old fillies. Closed in 1889 with 17 nominations. One and one-eighth miles.

SECOND DAY—TUESDAY, APRIL 29.

NO. 5.

The Matadero Stake, for two-year-olds. Closed in 1889 with 19 nominations. Three-quarters of a mile.

NO. 6.

The Chris. Green Handicap. Closed February 1st, with 14 nominations. One and one-quarter miles.

NO. 7.

Purse $400, for all ages; $40 from starters to go to second horse. Maiden allowances: if three years old, 5 pounds; four and upwards, 10 pounds. Non-winners this year allowed 5 pounds. Allowances cumulative. One mile and a sixteenth.

NO. 8.

The Weinstock, Lubin & Co. Stake. Closed in 1889, with thirty-two nominations. One mile.

THIRD DAY—THURSDAY, MAY 1.

NO. 9.

The Spring Stakes. A sweepstakes for three-year olds (foals of 1887) that have not won a race previous to January 1st, 1890. Closed February 1, 1890, with 12 nominations. One mile.

No. 10.

The Western Hotel Stakes for two-year-old fillies. Closed in 1889 with 27 nominations. Five-eighths of a mile.

NO. 11.

The Hall, Luhrs & Co. Handicap. Closed in 1889 with 29 nominations. One and one-quarter miles.

NO. 12.

Selling purse $400, of which $50 to second: for all ages. Horses entered to be sold for $2,000 to carry full weight. One pound off for each $100 down to $600. Value placed on starters only by 6 P. M. night before race. One and one-eighth miles.

FOURTH DAY—SATURDAY, MAY 3.

NO. 13.

The Golden Eagle Hotel Handicap, for two-year-olds. Closed in 1889 with 29 nominations. Weights to be announced before 8 P. M. second day before race. Declarations due by 4 P. M. day before race. Three-quarters of a mile.

NO. 14.

The Hopeful Handicap: a sweepstakes for all ages, of $50 each, $15 forfeit, or $10 if declared, with $400 added; second to receive $100. Weights announced by 10 P. M. day before race. Declarations due by 5 P. M. same day. One and one-eighth miles.

NO. 15.

The California Derby. Closed in 1889 with 32 nominations. One and one-half miles.

NO. 16.

Purse $400, for all ages; $40 from starters to go to second horse. Non-winners this year at time of starting allowed, if three years old, 5 pounds; four years old, 10 pounds; five and upwards, 12 pounds. Entries to close with clerk of course at 5 P. M. day before the race. Mile heats.

The State Agricultural Society's rules of 1889 to govern, except when conditions are otherwise.

Starters in stake races must be named through the entry box by 6 P. M. of the day before the race. The right of forfeit ceases at 10 o'clock A. M. day of race. Entries in purses not declared out by 6 P. M. day before race is run, must start.

Non starters in all purse races held for entrance under Rule 22.

The right to postpone races on account of the weather or other sufficient cause, is reserved. In event of postponement, handicaps stand, other declarations are off.

All declarations, either of starters, non-starters or non-acceptance of handicaps or otherwise, must be made in writing. Blanks will be furnished by the Secretary.

Declarations in handicaps must be accompanied by the money.

Entries in Nos. 1, 3, 7, 12 and 16 to close with the Secretary Monday, April 7, 1890.

CHRIS GREEN, President.

EDWIN F. SMITH, Secretary.

First Grand Annual Sale

—OF—

PURE BRED SHORTHORN CATTLE

Under the management of

The Pacific Coast Shorthorn Breeders' Asssociation.

Will be held at

AGRICULTURAL PARK, SACRAMENTO, April 3d, 1890.

(Sale to commence at 1 o'clock P. M.)

This society is composed of the best breeders of Short Horn cattle on the Pacific Coast, and is organized upon a permanent basis.

Nothing but Pure Bred Registered Cattle Will be Offered at this Sale.

The stock offered at this sale come from the herds of the following well known breeders:—

E. A. BRIDGFORD, Colusa, Colusa County.
PETER PETERSON, Sites, Colusa County.
A. HEILBRUN & BRO., Sacramento.
P. S. CHILES, Davisville, Yolo County.
P. H. MURPHY, Perkins, Sacramento County.
E. S. DRIVER, Antelope, Sacramento County.
JOSEPH MARZEN, Lovelocks, Nevada.

Catalogues can be had by addressing J. F. CHILES, Secretary, Davisville, Yolo County.

ANNUAL SPRING SALE

—OF—

Road & Harness Horses

Work and Draft Horses!

SHETLAND PONIES!

From Ranchos of J. B. Haggin, Esq.

WILL TAKE PLACE

Tuesday, May 6, 1890,

AT SAN FRANCISCO.

Location to be hereafter designated.
Catalogues are being prepared.

KILLIP & CO., Live Stock Auctioneers,
22 Montgomery Street, S. F.

A Grand Combination Sale

—OF—

Standard-bred Trotters & Thoroughbreds

CLYDESDALES AND PERCHERONS,

Fine Roadsters, Work Horses, Etc.

—AND—

Registered and Graded Holstein CATTLE,

REGISTERED JACKS,

And other first-class Live Stock of all kinds, will be held at

CARSON CITY, NEV., April 15, 16 and 17, '90.

BROOD MARES, COLTS AND FILLIES by the following well known Sires will be sold:

Standard Bred.	*Thoroughbred.*
ECHO.	NORFOLK.
GIBRALTAR. (will be sold)	HOOKER.
PROMPTER.	LODI.
BUCCANEER.	BRECKENBRIDGE.
ST. CLAIR.	THREE CHEERS.
SIGNAL.	LANGFORD.
BLUE BULL.	BOI DE ARC.
ST. LAWRENCE.	McMAHON.

And among the fine stock to be offered will be the grand HOLSTEIN BULL SARATOGA, and a number of fine calves and heifers by him and other well known thoroughbred Holsteins.

Over 50 entries were made up to March 1st, and a big sale is assured.

Send in your entries.

For further particulars address

JNO. P. SWEENY & CO., Carson City, Nev.

The Annual Combination Sale

—OF—

Road Mares, Harness Horses,

Colts and Fillies,

WILL TAKE PLACE AT

Bay District Track, San Francisco,

At 11 A. M. on

THURSDAY, APRIL 3, 1890.

The offering will consist of the get of ELECTIONEER, GUY WILKES, MAMBRINO WILKES, ARTHURTON, SIDNEY, ALEX. BUTTON, ANTEROS, and other noted stallions.

Catalogues will be ready March 11th, and will be furnished upon application.

KILLIP & CO., Auctioneers,
22 Montgomery Street, San Francisco.

Poplar Grove Breeding FARM.

Standard-bred Trotters, Colts and Fillies.

The get of CLOVIS, 4909; PASHA, 2039; APEX, 2935,

For Sale.

Address S. N. STRAUBE, Poplar Grove Breeding Farm,

Fresno, Cal.

Inspection by intending purchasers invited, and information by mail.

For Sale.

14

Pure bred

PERCHERONS.

Stallions and Mares.

OF ALL AGES.

Part Imported, and all Registered Proof.

For further information, address

E. J. TURNER, Hollister, Cal.

For Sale

A HALF BROTHER TO

ALMONT PATCHEN,

(2:15, trial 2:13 3-4).

JUANITO JR. is a beautiful bright bay, black points, with no white, foaled 1886. As a colt he has given much more promise than did Almont Patchen at the same age. Instead of being a pacer, he is a good square trotter, with every indication of great speed, and is so gentle and kind, that a lady can drive him. The owner's only reason for selling him is that business calls him away from this section of the State. He will be sold at a reasonable figure. This is a splendid opportunity for a gentleman to secure a first-class trotter at a very low figure.

The pedigree of Juanito Jr. is by Juanito (sire of Almont Patchen), dam Nettie Moore by Old Tom Moore. For further particulars, address

JUANITO JR.,
Santa Clara P. O., Cal.

Attention Stockmen!

FOR SALE

At Chowchilla Ranch,

Thoroughbred Durham Cattle

Three Hundred Young DAIRY COWS, 200 graded SHE CATTLE, Yearlings and up; a fine lot of high grade Durham Bulls; also have Mares, Horses, Mules and Norman Colts.

For particulars, apply to

ISAAC BIRD, Jr., Supt.,
Merced, California.

For Sale

A FIRST-CLASS

Napa County Farm

—OR—

STOCK RANCH,

800 Acres Improved,

SITUATED TWO AND A HALF MILES FROM NAPA CITY, with good roads leading thereto, a good hard finished house of nine rooms, with all modern improvements, streams running all summer, a great amount of live oak and black oak timber. It lies in a fruit belt, surrounded by fine vineyards and orchards growing upon the same quality of soil, and originally a part of this tract. About one-half hill and one-half rolling land, but none of it is steep and all easily cultivated, splendidly situated for the breeding of fine horses. Price, $65 per acre. Further particulars given at this office.

BREEDER AND SPORTSMAN,
313 Bush St.

Stallion for Sale

AT A BARGAIN.

Full Brother to Fairmont.

By Piedmont, dam Queen by Garibaldi—see State Fair Edition of BREEDER AND SPORTSMAN, September 14, 1889, for description of Fairmont—three years old, solid bay. Can trot a 2:40 gait or better. Sound in every particular. Can be seen at Oakland Trotting Park, Oakland.

P. J. WILLIAMS.

Twenty-Third Annual Sale!

169
THOROUGHBREDS

64
YEARLINGS,

100
BROODMARES,

5
GREAT STALLIONS

23d ANNUAL SALE OF

Belle Meade Stud,

Will take place at BELLE MEADE STUD, near Nashville, Tennessee, on

THURSDAY AND FRIDAY, APRIL 24 & 25

169 Head Thoroughbreds at Public Auction.

SOLD FOR DIVISION. | SOLD WITHOUT RESERVE

Five Great Stallions

To the Highest Bidder.

LUKE BLACKBURN
Imp GREAT TOM,
ENQUIRER,
BRAMBLE,
IROQUOIS.

FOR CATALOGUES ADDRESS THIS OFFICE. P. C. KIDD, Auctioneer.

For other information and Catalogues address JOHN J. CARTER, No. 9 Baxter Block, Nashville, Tenn.

CALIFORNIA

NUTWOOD

Will stand for mares the season of 1890, commencing February 15th, and ending July 15th, at the NUTWOOD STOCK FARM, one mile from Irvington.

DESCRIPTION AND PEDIGREE.

He is a dark chestnut, with star in forehead; foaled September 16th, 1881; is 16 hands 1½ inches high and weighs 1250 pounds. Has a beautiful flowing mane and tail, with remarkable style and lofty carriage, a bold, open movement like his sire, but has never been handled for speed. He moves and looks like his sire, except that he is a larger horse.

CALIFORNIA NUTWOOD by Nutwood, record 2:18¾, has 32 trotters and pacers with records from 2:15 to 2:30, and put 8 in the 2:30 list in 1889. He is the only horse that ever lived with a record under 2:20 that produced five under 2:20. He is now serving mares at Dubuque, Iowa, at $500 for the season, and his colts at yearlings sell from $2500 to $5000 each. He is out of the dam of Maud S., record 2:08¾.

Nutwood, by Alexander's Belmont, sire of 32 with records from 2:15½ to 2:30, Alexander's Belmont by Alexander's Abdallah, sire of Goldsmiths Maid, record 2:14, and 8 others in 2:30 list. Alexander's Abdallah, by Rysdyk's Hambletonian, sire of 41 with records from 2:17¼ to 2:30, and is the founder of the Hambletonian family.

FANNY PATCHEN, dam of California Nutwood, by George M. Patchen Jr., record 2:27, and sire of Wells Fargo, 2:18¼, Sam Purdy 2:20½, Ben Ali 2:20¾, and 7 others from 2:21 to 2:30. He has 7 sons who together produced 13 trotters in 2:30 list, and 5 daughters who together produced 5 trotters and 1 pacer in 2.30 or better. He sired Alexander 2:31¼. Alexander sired Alex. Button 2:26½; Alex. Button sired Yolo Maid, pacing record 2:14 at 4 years old, the fastest on record; George M. Patchen Jr., by George M. Patchen 2:23½, is sire of Lucy 2:18¼, and 3 others in the 2:30 list; he has 12 sons who together produced 40 trotters from 2:14¾ to 2:30, and 6 daughters who together produced 5 trotters in 2:30 list or better, he is grand sire of Hopeful 2:14¾, and best wagon record 2:16½, and sire of the granddam of Stamboul 2:12¼.

George M. Patchen, by Cassius M. Clay, and he by Henry Clay, founder of the Clay family.

Laura, second dam of California Nutwood, was a fine large bay mare, a very fast roadster brought from Chicago by Wm. Wilson, of San Jose, and is said to have made a record of 2.35 in Chicago. Pedigree not traced.

TERMS.

$40 for the season, payable invariably before the animal is removed. Mares not proving in foal can be returned free next season. Pasturage $4 per month, but no liability for accidents or escapes.

For further particulars address the owner,

MARTIN CARTER,

Newark, Alameda Co., Cal., or Irvington, Alameda County, Cal.

Sunny Side Breeding Farm.

Admiral 488.

Foaled 1867—Sired by Volunteer 55, Son of Rysdyk's Hambletonian 10.

First dam Lady Pierson by Cassius M. Clay (Neaves') 20; second dam by Diamond; third dam a running mare said to be thoroughbred. He is fitted in an eminent degree to produce colts that will in all respects justify his patrons in their expectations.

Admiral is the sire of Huntress, record 2:27¼, Sister, 2:19½, Perhelion, 2:25, Nona Y., 2:25, and others equally as promising, but have not had the advantage of track work. He will serve a limited number of approved mares at $50 the season, with usual return privilege. Season ending August 1, 1890. No liability for accidents or escapes.

KING DAVID 2576.

Bay Stallion—Foaled 1883.

Sired by Admiral 488, dam Black Flora (the dam of Huntress, 2:27¼, Sister, 2:19½, Perhelion, 2:25, Nona Y., 2:25), by Black Prince.

King David is one of the best gets of Admiral. He has a good disposition, kind to drive, smooth and even-gaited, and can speed fast. Barring accidents, he will trot in the twenties this Fall. His colts are large, rangy, and well finished. Will serve a limited number of mares at $30 the season, to end July 1, 1890. Every precaution will be taken to prevent accidents and escapes, but no liability will be assumed. Pasturage $4 per month.

Sunny Side Farm is situated two miles east of Vallejo, on the Sulphur Spring road. For further particulars, address

FRANK DRAKE,

Vallejo, Cal.

The Fast Trotting Stallion

REDWOOD.

Four-Year-Old Record 2:24 1-2

Will make the season of 1890—February 1st to July 1st—at the

OAKLAND RACE TRACK.

REDWOOD is a dark bay colt, 15.2¾ hands high, weighs 1100 lbs. Foaled in 1885 by Anteeo, 2:16¼, sire of Alfred G., 2:19¾. Anteeo is by Electioneer. First dam Lou Milton, by Milton Medium; second dam Old Fly, a thoroughbred mare brought from the East in 1871 by W. C. Ralston, Esq.

Redwood's sire was out of Columbine by A. W. Richmond, the sire of the pacers Arrow 2:13¾, and Elwood 2:23, and the trotters Romero, 2:19¾, and Len Rose, 2:27. Redwood has shown a quarter in 33 seconds.

Terms $100

For the season. Mares not proving with foal may be returned next season free of charge, provided Redwood remains the property of the present owners. Good pasturage at $5 per month. No responsibility assumed for escapes or accidents. Service fees payable before removal of the mare. Limited to 40 approved mares. For further particulars address;

A. McFADYEN.

Race track, Oakland, Cal.

Singleton & Addington,

Bank Exchange,

3d and K Streets, Sacramento.

Superior Wines, Liquors and Cigars.

The Pure Trotting-bred Stallion

ILLUSTRIOUS

STANDARD No. 4178.

DESCRIPTION.

Dark bay, black points, 15 1-2 hands high, weight 1000 pounds, foaled May 30, 1885; bred by General W. T. Withers, Lexington, Ky.

PEDIGREE.

By Happy Medium, sire of Maxey Cobb 2:13¼ and 64 with records of 2:30 or better.

First dam Abdalletta by Cassius M. Clay Jr., sire of Durango 2:23¾, Harry Clay 2:23½, and sire of the dams of Minnehaha, Bertha 2:27½, Charley West 2:28¼, Grandmont 2:25 1-4, Lottie K 2:26¾, Mambrino Diamond 2:26, Richwood 2:28 1-2, Tonsy 2:21¼, Happy Thought 2:21 1-2, Pequot 2:23 1-2, Fairlawn Medium 2:27 1-4, Folley 2:27¼, and Mambrino Boy 2:26 1-2.

Second dam Laura Crockett by Almont, sire of Westmont 2:13¾, Puritan 2:16, Fanny Witherspoon 2:16¼, Piedmont 2:17¼, Aldine 2:19¼, and 37 with records better than 2:30.

Third dam Sally Tee by Alexander's Abdallah, sire Goldsmith Maid 2:14.

Fourth dam Kate Crockett, the dam of Lulu 2:14¾, by imp Hooton.

Illustrious is a horse of extra fine finish, large clean bone, good feet, back short and strong, loins and quarters well muscled, and powerful. He has a kind disposition and splendid trotting action, and is as handsome and bloodlike in form and finish as any trotting stallion in the land.

He is pronounced by his breeder, General Withers, to be the best bred son of Happy Medium living, and is undoubtedly one of the very best bred trotting stallions in the State. He has had but six weeks' regular training, and a part of that time was sick with epizootic, but was trotted quarters in 39 1-4 seconds, and barring accidents will certainly trot better than 2:30 this season.

TERMS—$50 the season. Mares not proving with foal may be returned next year free.

Good pasturage at $3 per month.

Season to begin February 1st and end June 15th.

GEO. A. STONE,

Santa Rosa, Cal.

WOODNUT

(Weatherhead's) by Nutwood 600

Sire of Belmont Boy, 2:18, pacer, Woodnut, 2:16½, Felix, 2:18¾, Dawn, 2:18¾, Maggie E., 2:19¾, Irma, 2:18½, and 26 others in 2:30 or better; 1st dam Flora, 2:39¼, trial 2:26, dam of Chrisman's Hambletonian, sire of Steve Whipple, 2:23, Kate Agnew, 2:28¼, by Chieftain 721, sire of Defiance 2:17¼ pacing and 2:24 trotting Cairo, 2:26, Onward, 2:24, pacer; second dam by Wilson's Leamon.

Woodnut is a beautiful bay with black points, 15¾ hands high weighing 1,075 pounds. His colts are all larger than himself, and sell readily for road and carriage purposes, being of good color and very docile, yet prompt to obey, and always ready.

Service fee, $25, with usual privileges. Colts and fillies from Tilton Almont, Patchen, Stockbridge Chief, and other desirable crosses, FOR SALE. For further particulars, pedigrees, or any communication in horse matters, address

JAS. WEATHERHEAD, Prop.

San Jose, Cal.

The Trotting-Bred Stallion

RINGWOOD

THE FINEST SON OF THE NOTED SIDNEY,

Will make a Season at Oakland, commencing March 1, and ending June 1, 1890.

DESCRIPTION.

RINGWOOD is a dark, rich colored bay, black points, 15 1-2 hands, weight 1100 lbs., and a pure gaited trotter. Has shown great speed. He is now five years old. As a four year old he showed a trial in 2:19 1-2, and but for an accident would have received a record as a four year old of 2:18 or better.

PEDIGREE.

RINGWOOD is by Sidney, record 2:19 3-4, and a half brother to Gold Leaf 2:11 1-4, Adonis 2:14, Flee (two year old) 2:24, Longworth 2:19, Sister V. 2:27, Faustino, yearling, 2:35, Fleet, yearling, 2:35 Memo, three year old trial 2:20 1-2.

Sidney is by Santa Claus, record 2:17 1-2; he by Strathmore, sire of 31 in 2:30 list; he by Hambletonian 10, the greatest of all producers; he by Abdallah. Sidney's dam, Sweetness, record 2:21 1-4; she by Volunteer, the sire of St. Julien 2:11 1-4.

RINGWOOD'S dam Alma; she by Dashway, thoroughbred; he by Belmont, he by American Boy; he by Sea Gull; he by imported Expedition. Alma's 1st dam, Fanny Cobb, was a great road mare, pedigree untraced.

TERMS; $50 for the Season.

Payable June 1st, or sooner if mares are taken away. Address communications to

A. C. DIETZ,

Oakland, Cal.

The Hambletonian Stallion 10178.

CHRISMAN'S HAMBLETONIAN
Sire of Steve Whipple, 2:23, Kate Agnew, 2:28¼, etc.

Whipple's Hambletonian — Sire of 14 trotters and 1 pacer from 2:19 to 2:30, and 7 sons with 8 performers from 2:21¼ to 2:30, and dams of 6 from 2:19¾ to 2:30.
 - Guy Miller — By Hambletonian 10.
 - Martha Washington — Dam of Speculation 928 — Sire of Crown Pt. 2:24, Oakland Maid, 2:22, Gracie S., 2:28¼, and dam of Waterford, 2:27

Flora, 2:39¼, trial, 2:26 — Dam of Chrisman's Hambletonian, sire of Steve Whipple, 2:23, Kate Agnew, 2:28¼.
 - Chieftain 721 — Sire of Defiance, 2:24 and 2:17¼, pacing; Cairo, 2:26, and Onward, 2:24, pacer.
 - daughter of Wilson's Leamon.

Stud season now on till the 1st of August, 1890, at $40 each mare, with return privilege in 1891, provided stallion and mare, or either, do not change owners. Good pasture at hand, and comfortable accommodation for brood mares and colts. For further particulars, address

JESSE CHRISMAN, Proprietor.

San Jose, Cal.

Pedigrees Tabulated

IN THE MOST ARTISTIC MANNER.

Giving speed performers under sires and dams. Catalogues compiled. Stallion cards and circulars written up ready for the press. Pedigree blanks for sale. Prices reasonable. Horses bought and sold on commission. References furnished.

R. Y. HARDIN.

506 W. Madison St., Chicago, Ill.

BAY ROSE

REGISTERED No. 9814

Record 2:20½, third Heat.

Will make the season of 1890 from March 1st to July 1st at the race track, Oakland.

DESCRIPTION.

BAY ROSE is a dark bay or brown, with black points, 15 1-2 hands high and weighs 1150 pounds. He is remarkably intelligent, of good disposition and a pure gaited trotter. He was foaled in 1883. His colts are large, stylish, rangy animals and inherit the qualities of speed and endurance.

PEDIGREE.

BAY ROSE 9814

Sultan, 2:24 — SIRE OF 19 in the 2:30 list.
 - The Moor, 870 — SIRE OF Beautiful Bells, 2:29 1-2, Del Sur, 2:24 1-2, Inez, 2:33, Sir Guy, 2:28 1-2, Sultan, 2:24, Tommy Gates, 2:24.
 - Sultana.

Madam Baldwin
 - The Moor, 870 — Sire of 8 in the 2:30 list.
 - By Ben Lippincott by Williamson's Belmont.

TERMS: $100 FOR THE SEASON.

Good pasturage near the track, and first-class care taken of mares for $5 per month. No responsibility assumed for escapes or accidents.

For further particulars, address

W. W. AYRES,

Care of Jas. Corcoran, Race Track, Oakland, Cal.

THE MAMBRINO

Patchen Stallion.

MAMBRINO JR., 1789 (formerly Carr's) Sire of Lady Ellen 2:28 (dam of Ella 2:29), Maud H. 2:30, Mambrino Boy (Carr's) 2:31 1 2.

Will stand at my farm, 2 1-2 miles north of San Jose, on the Milpitas road. Season to commence February 1st, 1890, at $50, with return privilege 1891. Fifteen mares of approved breeding, besides my own, will be given him. Parties owning good mares, performers or out of producing dams, will find an opportunity to breed them on shares, and the best of care taken of them till colt is weaned, if so desired.

PEDIGREE.

MAMBRINO JR., 1789, by Mambrino Patchen 58 [full brother of Lady Thorne 2:18 1-4] by Mambrino Chief 11. First dam by Mambrino Chief 11; 2nd dam by imp. Jordan (thoroughbred); 3rd dam by Bertrand, son of Sir Archy; 4th dam by Chewkees, son of Sir Archy.

For further particulars address

GEO. P. BULL.

Box 1087. San Jose, Cal.

The Trotting Stallion

CUPID,

Full Brother to Adonis 2:14,

—Sired by—

The Celebrated SIDNEY 2:19 3-4, and out of Venus.

Will make the season of 1890 at the OAKLAND TROTTING PARK.

PEDIGREE.

CUPID is by Sidney out of Venus by Capt. Webster 10173, record 2:30, and sire of Prestone 2:19. Second dam by Skenandoah 936, sire of Daisy Burns 2:29¾, Erwin Davis (sire of two in the 30 list) and dams of four in the 30 list.

DESCRIPTION.

Cupid is a handsome bright bay 15.2¾ hands high, weighs 1100 lbs.; was foaled in 1886. As a yearling, with very little work he showed quarters in 42 seconds, and at 2 years old, quarters in 36 seconds. As a three year old he has not been worked, but he shows the speed and endurance that must come from his excellent blood lines.

TERMS $30 for the season, with the usual return privileges. Good pasturage near the track at $5 per month. The best of care taken of mares in any way that owners may desire, but no responsibility assumed for accidents or escapes.

For further particulars address

C. O. THORNQUEST,

Oakland Trotting Park, or

C. BAAB, 972 Broadway, Oakland.

The Trotting Stallion

BONANZA $2:29\frac{1}{2}$

Will make the season of 1890, from February 1st to July 1st, at the OAKLAND TROTTING PARK.

PEDIGREE.

BONANZA, 2:29½

Artherton 365 — Sire of Arab, 2:15, Joe Artherton 2:20¼, Lady Knout, 2:29½. Dams of Grandee, 2:23¼, Hidalgo, 2:27.
 - Hambletonian 10 — Sire of 41 in 2:30 list. Sires of 107 of the sires of 567 in 2:30 list.
 - Imogene, by Am. Star 14 — Dam of Leland 1330 — Sire of Clara, 2:21, Miss Leland, 2:25¼, Hades, 2:27¾.

Sister — Dam of Albert W., 2:20.
 - John Nelson 187 — Sire of Nerea, 2:21¾, Gov. Stanford, 2:27¾, Aurora, 2:27, Nemo, 2:30.
 - Lamott Mare — Dam of Aurora, 2:27; g d of Arol, 2:21¾.

DESCRIPTION.

BONANZA is a very handsome chestnut of commanding form and splendid proportions. He stands nearly 16 hands high, is remarkably intelligent, level headed and pure gaited. His record is no mark of his speed. He is a great foal getter, and his colts are handsome rangy animals.

TERMS, $40 for the season, with the usual return privileges. Excellent pasturage near the track at $5 per month. The best of care taken of mares, but no responsibility assumed for accidents or escapes.

For further particulars, address

RICHARD HAVEY,

Oakland Trotting Park, Oakland.

Vineland Stock Farm

Whippleton 1883,

Sire of

LILY STANLEY	Record 2:17½
HOMESTAKE	" 2:16½
FLORA B.	" 2:27
CORA C.	" 2:31¾
BLACK PRINCE	" 2:36½
RACHEL	" 2:38
PRINCE W.	" 2:40

WHIPPLETON is not only the sire of trotters, but he is the greatest sire of Carriage Horses on the Pacific Coast. Some of the best carriage and road teams in San Francisco are sired by Whippleton. A carriage team by Whippleton received First Premium at Napa, Petaluma, Oakland, Sacramento, Stockton and San Jose. Whippleton and his colts have never been beaten in the show ring.

DESCRIPTION.

WHIPPLETON is black, tan muzzle and flanks, 17 hands, and weighs 1,100 lbs. Most of his colts are 16 hands or over, and with a few exceptions, bay, brown or black. He never sired a sorrel or white face colt. (If he does, I agree to refund service money.)

PEDIGREE.

WHIPPLETON, sired by Hambletonian Jr. (sire of Hancock 2:29), by Whipple's Hambletonian (sire of Graves, 2:19, Westfield, 2:29¼, Express, 2:24, and 11 others in the 2:30 list), dam Lady Livingston (dam of Lady Blanchard, 2:26¼, Bloomfield Maid, trial 2:22), by General Taylor (sire of the dams of Wells Fargo, 2:18¼, Nerea, 2:21¾, Bickford, 2:29¼, Lady Blanchard, 2:26¼, etc., and sire of grandam of Hazel Wilkes, 2:2[illegible]) by the Morse Horse 6 sire of Norman 25 (sire of Lulu 2:14¾, May Queen 2:20, etc.).

TERMS at $40, limited to 20 mares, for the season, usual return privileges. I would like to get about ten well bred mares with the proper combination of blood to breed to Whippleton on shares this season.

Alcona 730.

Sire of

FLORA BELLE	Record 2:24
CLAY DUKE	" 2:31

ALCONA will be a great sire, but four of his colts have ever been trained, and all have shown full miles better than 2:3[illegible], and two of them as good as 2:20. Two of his first sons each sired a colt as a two-year-old and last season one as a four-year-old trotted a full mile in 2:23½, and the other, a three-year-old, a mile in 2:31. With opportunities, Alcona is destined to be one of Almont's best sons. Almont, for his opportunities, is beyond doubt the most prepotent sire of his age. He has 36 representatives in the 2:30 list; [illegible] sons and 22 daughters that have already produced 2:30 performers. Almont died five years ago at 20 years old. If he lived he would be but 28 years old.

PEDIGREE.

ALCONA sired by the great Almont (sire of Westmont 2:13¾, Fanny Witherspoon 2:16¼, Piedmont 2:17¼, and 3[illegible] others with records better than 2:30, and grandsire of Belle Hamlin 2:13¾, etc.); by Alexander's Abdallah (sire of Goldsmith Maid 2:14), he by Rysdyk's Hambletonian. Alcona's dam, Queen Mary by Mambrino Chief (sire of Lady Thorne 2:18 1-4, and 5 others in the 2:30 list, and sire of the dams of Director 2:17, Piedmont 2:17¼, Onward 2:25 1-4, Red Wilkes, Almont, Belmont and many other noted sires).

DESCRIPTION.

Alcona is a beautiful chestnut 16 3 1-2 hands high, and weighs 1300 lbs. His colts possess speed, style, finish and beauty, and if they don't trot they command the highest prices for carriage horses.

$40 for the season. Usual return privilege.

Season on Whippleton and Alcona ends July 1st, 1890.

Best kind of pasturage at $4 per month. Mares kept in any manner desired.

For further particulars send for circular or call at stables, one mile south of St. Helena.

FRED W. LOEBER.

St. Helena, Napa Co., Cal.

The Trotting Stallion

G & M

FULL BROTHER TO

ALFRED G, 2:19¾.

(Who has been taken to Kentucky to stand at $200)

Will make the season of 1890 from FEBRUARY 1st to JULY 1st, at

SANTA ROSA.

G. & M. is by Anteeo, 2:16¼; was foaled 1886; first dam Rosa B. by Speculation (son of Hambletonian 10); 2d dam Elizabeth by Alexander 490; 3d dam Nora by imp. Glencoe. Anteeo is by Electioneer, out of Columbine by A. W. Richmond 1687.

G. & M. is a handsome dark bay; stands 15-2 1/2 hands high, and weighs 1060 pounds. Gameness, stoutness, speed and stamina are indelibly impressed in every line of the pedigree of G. & M. Owners of brood mares in search of these qualities, will do well to patronize this promising colt.

PHILOSOPHER,

Foaled 1886 by Pilot Wilkes 2837; first dam Bella by George Wilkes 519; second dam by Bell Morgan 6.

Philosopher's sire, Pilot Wilkes 2837, is by George Wilkes 519, dam Grace (the dam of Alice Woodburn, etc.), by Pilot Jr. 12, grandam by Orphan Boy.

Will make the season of 1890, from FEBRUARY 1st to JULY 1st, at Santa Rosa.

TERMS for the season:

G. & M., $50,

PHILOSOPHER, $30,

with privilege of returning mares that do not prove in foal the next season free of charge, provided the horse bred to remains the property of the present owners. Good pasturage at $3 per month. No responsibility assumed for accidents or escapes. Service fees payable before removal of the mare. For further particulars, address

GEO. E. GUERNE,

Santa Rosa Cal.

Highland Farm,

LEXINGTON, KY.,

Home of Red Wilkes.

Standard-bred Trotting Stock

For Sale,

Sired by Red Wilkes, Wilton, 2:19¼; Allandorf and Sentinel Wilkes, out of highly bred Standard Mares of the most fashionable blood of the day.

W. C. FRANCE, Proprietor.

Guenoc Stud Farm, Lake Co., Cal.

Imp. GREENBACK

(Sire of the English winners Greenlight, Greenjacket, Greenshank, Greenwave and Greenhorn)

By Dollar, dam Music, by Stockwell. $100 the Season

ST. SAVIOR,

(FULL BROTHER TO EOLE)

By Eolus, dam War Song, by War Dance. $100 the Season.

PASTURAGE, $5 PER MONTH.

With right to return the following year if mare does not prove with foal. The best of care taken, but no liability for accidents or escapes. Mares shipped to C. W. ABY, care ST. HELENA STABLES, St. Helena Napa County, will be taken in charge by competent men.

For further information write to

DR. C. W. ABY, Middletown, Lake County, Cal.

1890 Three Anteeo Stallions 1890

SUNSET, 5 years old, by Anteeo
ANTEEOF, 4 years old, by Anteeo
ANTEEOP, 3 years old, by Anteeo

ANTEEO, Standard 7868. Record, 2:16 1-4. by Stanford's Electioneer, and dam Columbine.

DESCRIPTIONS, PEDIGREES AND CONDITIONS.

"SUNSET" is a rich, dark bay, small star on forehead, portion of hind left foot white; was foaled March 21, 1885; is by ANTEEO and the inbred HAMBLETONIAN mare, BESSIE G., she by KING PHILLIP, son of WHIPPLE'S HAMBLETONIAN. He is 16 1-2 hands high, and weighs 1,250 lbs. He is of perfect build and splendid action cool headed and great speed for his size, having trotted a trial mile as a three-year-old in 2:36. He then entered heavy in the stud and was matched against Whalebone at the Healdsburg races November 3, 1889, winning just as he pleased in three straight heats; time, 2:47, 2:48 1-2, 2:52 1-2. He was then matched for a race to come off last Thanksgiving Day at Petaluma but owing to the heavy rains the event did not take place. A few days previous to Thanksgiving Day Mr. Lawrence worked Sunset out and then he trotted three square miles and heats in 2:33¼, 2:34 and 2:37.

SUNSET will be bred to 40 mares only, at $50 each, no colt no pay.

"ANTEEOF" is a jet black, was foaled April 13, 1886, is 16¾ hands high, and weighs 1,280 lbs., has a very fine, heavy black mane and tail; is well proportioned, moves majestically, is of easy, lofty carriage; is symmetrical, in fact is a beautiful horse. He was sired by Anteeo and the O. A. Taylor mare "Nance," her dam, was raised by Dr. Oliver Plummer, of Consumnes, Cal., and sired by "Napoleon"; Napoleon was foaled May 23, 1852, and raised by James Kyle of Butler County, Ohio. He was sired by Benj. Sweet's horse Bellfounder, and he by Old Bellfounder, his dam was sired by Doc. Daniel Melligan's horse, Cadmus, G. G. sire the celebrated Eclipse; his G. dam was sired by Big Shakespeare. G. G. sires dam by Messenger and Expedition.

ANTEEOF will be bred to 25 mares only, at $50 each. No colt, no pay.

"ANTEEOP" is a rich seal brown; was foaled March 7, 1887; by Anteeo and the inbred Hambletonian mare Bessie G., also dam of Sunset, his full brother and Midget his full sister; he is 15 1-2 hands high and weighs [illegible] lbs, and measures 22 inches around the arm, good head, fine neck, full, broad breast; withers and rump on nearly equal line, well proportioned bones, ankle shoulders, loins and hips; strong legs all around, with great muscular development and splendid sinews; wiry pasterns and sound, compact feet; the lines from hip to hock show power and speed; stands square and has excellent action, has a superb lustrous coat of rich deep brown fur of seal color without a spot; an even, honest trotter, and has gone the mile as a two-year-old in 2:48, the last quarter in 38 seconds; is intelligent and of high spirit, with much temper, but is not vicious, has very fine eyes, is a handsome, showy colt; attractive in harness.

ANTEEOP will be bred to 15 mares only, at $35. No colt, no pay.

SEASON to commence February 1st, ending July 1, 1890. Book now ready. Apply to John H. Lawrence, "Manager and Trainer," on my fruit and hop ranch, 1 mile east of Court House, on Sonoma road. Excellent pasture furnished with running water, also dry knolls with oak shelter, at $4 per month for mares. Two of the above stallions will be for sale after the expiration of the their stud season.

GUY E. GROSSE,
SANTA ROSA, SONOMA CO., CAL.

The Trotting Stallion

Guide 2:29

(At Four Years)

Will make the season of 1890 at the SANTA RITA RANCH, about one mile North of Pleasanton.

DESCRIPTION.

GUIDE is a handsome seal brown, five years old, stands 15¾ hands high, and weighs 1085 pounds. He is of fine form, level headed, intelligent, and comes from blood lines that are noted for the qualities of speed and gameness.

PEDIGREE.

GUIDE, 2:28¼.
- Director, 2:17. Sire of Direct, 2:18¾. Margaret S., 2:19½.
  - Dictator 113. Sire of 22 trotters and 3 pacers in 2:30.
    - Hambletonian 10.
    - Clara, by American Star 14.
  - Dolly. Dam of Onward, 2:25¾. Thorndale, 2:22¾.
    - Mambrino Chief 11.
    - Fannie, by Ben Franklin.
- Imogene.
  - Norwood 522. Sire of Tommy Norwood, 2:26¾.
    - Hambletonian 10.
    - Lady Fallis, by American Star 14.
  - daughter of
    - American Star 14.
    - daughter of Harry Clay 45.

The attention of breeders is especially called to the above pedigree as showing 3 crosses of American Star.

GUIDE trotted into the 2:30 list last season with little training, and he will trot into the 2:20 list the coming season barring accidents.

Guide's sire has a record of 2:17, made in a five heat race, and Guide is closely related to Phallas, who made a record of 2 13¾ in a fourth heat, and to Jay-Eye-See, record 2:10.

TWO HUNDRED AND FIFTY DOLLARS will be given to the owner of the first of the produce of Guide put in the 2:30 list, and $100 to each one after the first.

TERMS—$75 for the season, with the usual return privileges.

Admiro,

Sire Admiral; dam by San Bruno, by Easton's David Hill.

This magnificent horse is a handsome bay, eight years old; stands 17 1-2 hands high, and weighs 1470 pounds. He is very speedy for a large horse, and breeds fine large carriage horses. His produce possess every qualification of the Cleveland Bay, with the added qualities of speed and endurance resulting from his high trotting breeding.

TERMS—$25 for the season, with usual return privileges.

Will stand three days each week at Santa Rita Ranch, Pleasanton, and at A. T. Hatch's Ranch "Almono," Alamo, Contra Costa County, alternately. All mares sent care of SMITH & SUTHERLAND, Pleasanton, will be taken in charge of on arrival, and will receive the best care and attention in any manner the owners may desire. Good pasturage at $4 per month. Only a limited number of approved mares will be served by this horse this season.

No responsibility assumed for escapes or accidents. For further particulars, address

SMITH & SUTHERLAND, Pleasanton,
or A. T. HATCH, care Palace Hotel, San Francisco.

GRANDISSIMO,

Full Brother to GRANDEE, 3-year-old Record 2-23½.

GRANDISSIMO
- Le Grande 2868 (trial), 2:24. Sire of Grandee, 3 y. o. r., 2:23½.
  - Almont 33. Sire of Westmont, 2:13¾, Puritan, 2:16, Fannie Wetherspoon, 2:16¼, Piedmont, 2:17¼, and 32 others in 2:30, and sire of 49 sons and 22 daughters that have produced 2:30 performers.
    - Abdallah 15. Sire of Goldsmith Maid, 2:14, and 5 others in 2:30, and sire of 13 sons and 21 dams, producers of 2:30 performers.
    - Sally Anderson, by Mambrino Chief.
  - Jessie Pepper. Dam of Iona, 2:17½, Alpha, 2:23½, and grandam of Montezuma, 2:29½.
    - Mambrino Chief 11. Sire Lady Thorne, 2:18¼, and 5 others in 2:30 with 28 sires and 15 dams, producers of 2:30 performers.
    - Sidi Hamet (thoroughbred).
- Norma. Dam of Grandee, 3 y. o. r., 2:23½.
  - Arthurton 365. Sire Arab, 2:15, and 4 others in 2:30, and dams of Hidalgo, 2:27, Hazel Wilkes, 2:20, Reverie (yearling), 2:36½.
    - Hambletonian 10. Sire of Dexter, 2:17¼, and 40 others in 2:30.
    - Imogene. Dam of Arthurton, with 4 in 2:30; Leland, with 3 in 2:30.
  - Nourmahal, 2:39½. Full sister to A. W. Richmond 1687, sire of Arrow, 2:13½, Romero, 2:19½, and 3 others in 2:30.
    - Blackbird 401. Sire of Blackbird, 2:22, A. W. Richmond, sire of 5 in 2:30, and dam of Anteeo, 2:16¼, Antevolo, 2:19½.
    - by Rattler (thoroughbred).

SAN DIEGO, 8776.

SAN DIEGO 8776
- Alcona Clay 2756.
  - Alcona 730. Sire of Flora Belle, 2:24, Clay Duke, 2:31½, etc.
    - Almont 33. Sire of Westmont, 2:13¾, Piedmont, 2:17¼, Puritan, 2:16, and 33 others in 2:30 list.
    - by Mambrino Chief 11. Sire of Lady Thorne, 2:18¼.
  - Madonna. Dam of Del Rey, trial 2:31, Alcona Jr., 2:41, sire of Silas Skinner, trial 2:23½.
    - Cassius M. Clay Jr. 22. Sire of Durango, 2:23½, Harry Clay, 2:23½, and sire of dam of Happy Thought, 2:22½, and others.
    - by Joe Downing 710. Sire of Abe Downing, 2:20½, Dick Jamison, 2:26, and sire of dams of Kentucky Hambletonian, 2:27, Lorena, 2:15, and others.
- Fontana. Dam of Flora Belle, 2:24, Silas Skinner, trial 2:23½.
  - Almont 33. Sire of 36 in 2:30 list, 49 sons and 22 daughters that have produced 2:30 performers.
  - Fanny Williams. Dam of Bay Chieftain, 2:28½.
    - Abdallah 15. Sire of Goldsmith Maid, 2:14, Thorndale, 2:21¼, also Almont, Belmont, Jim Monroe, etc.
    - by Denmark (thoroughbred).

GRANDISSIMO is a blood bay, handsome-modelled colt, and a natural trotter. He is four years old, and trotted one-quarter miles in 36 seconds, with very limited training, last Fall.

SAN DIEGO is dark seal brown, three years old, and trotted one-quarter miles in 40 seconds as a two-year old.

These are two grand young horses, and, barring accidents, will both make fast records next fall.

They will both be allowed a limited number of mares, at $50 for the season. Mares not proving in foal to be returned free 1891. Best of pasture for mares at $4 per month, but no liability for accidents or escapes.

They will make the season from February 1st to June 1st at Napa Fair Grounds. For further particulars, address or call on

H. B. STARR, Race Track, Napa, Cal.,
or FRED W. LOEBER, St. Helena.

A SON OF ALMONT 33.

Only $25 for the Season.

ASHLAND ALMONT 3481.

PEDIGREE.

ASHLAND ALMONT 3481
- Almont 33. Sire of 34 in 2:30 or better of 21 daughters and of 49 sires that have produce in 2:30 or better.
  - Abdallah 15. Sire Goldsmith Maid, 2:14; 6 in 2:30 list; 13 sires and 23 dams of trotters in 2:30 list.
    - Hambletonian 10. Sire of 41 in 2:30 list; sire of 107 sires of 587 in 2:30 list.
    - Katy Darling.
  - Sally Anderson.
    - Mambrino Chief 11. Lady Thorn, 2:18¾.
    - Kate, by Pilot Jr. 12.
- Pauline. Dam of Sapho.
  - Ashland Chief. Sire Black Cloud, 2:17¾.
    - Mambrino Chief 11. Lady Thorn, 2:18¾.
    - dau. of imp. Yorkshire, (thoroughbred).
  - Rosina. Dam Almonia, the dam of Sally Cossack, 2:22¾, dau. Mamb. Abdallah, sire Mam. Prince, 2:23, and of Mamb. Bashaw, sire of Graham's Mambrino, 2:38.
    - Abdallah 15. Sire Goldsmith Maid, 2:14.
    - Prof. Smith's Sir William.

DESCRIPTION.

ASHLAND ALMONT 3481 is a handsome chestnut; stands 16 hands; was foaled 1883, and bred by Gen. Withers, of Lexington, Ky. He is of fine form, and remarkably intelligent, sweet-tempered and absolutely sound. His oldest foal may be seen with him, and while he has never served a standard mare or one that was a producer of speed, all of his colts are large, sound, fast and handsome.

TERMS: $25 for the season, with usual return privileges. The best of care taken of mares in any manner that the owner may desire, but no responsibility assumed for escapes or accidents.

For further particulars, address

T. J. WHITEHEAD, Manager.
579 36th Street, bet. Telegraph Ave. and Grove St., Oakland, Cal.
or, W. H. ASHBY, Oakland, Cal.

2:10 1-2 ELECTIONEER 2:12 1-4

BAY STALLION	BROWN STALLION
ECLECTIC	**MORTIMER**
11,321	5,346
By Electioneer, dam Manette (full sister to Woodnut 2.16 1-2 Manon 2:21 and Maple, dam of Hattie D., three year-old record 2:28¾) by Nutwood 2:18¾, etc., etc.	Four-year-old Record 2:27. By ELECTIONEER, dam MARTI, by Whipple's Hambletonian (sire of 15 in 2:30, and of dams of eight in 2:30). Second dam Ida Martin by Rifleman (sire of Col. Lewis 2:18¾).
Terms $100 for the Season.	Terms $60 for the Season.

Horses shipped via San Francisco may be consigned to J. W. MORSHEAD, City Front Stables, who will attend to their forwarding.

Season Closes JULY 1st, 1890. Usual return privileges.

For urther particulars address owner,

WILFRED PAGE, Penns Grove,
Sonoma County, Cal.

PASHA,

Registered No. 2039.

RECORD 2:36.

SIRE OF MORO 2:27.

Will make the present season at Linden, twelve miles east of STOCKTON.

Season *commencing FEBRUARY 1st and ending JULY 1*, 1890.

DESCRIPTION.

PASHA is a beautiful black; 16½ hands high, and weighs 1,240 pounds. He is a horse of beautiful symmetry and magnificent action.

PEDIGREE.

PASHA was sired by Sultan 1513, sire of Stamboul 2:12½, Ruby 2:13½, Alcazar 2:20½, Bay Rose 2:20½, and sixteen others with records below 2:30. First dam Madam Baldwin by The Moor 870; second dam Ben Lippincott by Belmont. Pasha is a full brother to Bay Rose, record 2:20½.

Sultan, by The Moor, sire of Beautiful Bells, dam of Hinda Rose, 2:19½, Bell Boy 2:19½, and Sable, dam of Sable Wilkes, three-year-old record 2:18. First dam Sultana, by Delmonico, sire of Derby 2:16, by Guy Miller, sire of Whipple's Hambletonian. Second dam by Mambrino Chief. Third dam by Downing's Bay Messenger. Fourth dam Miss Caudle, dam of Ericsson, four-year-old recor 2:30½.

Terms for the season, $50.

With privilege of returning mares that do not prove in foal next season free of charge.

Good pasturage at $2 per month. No responsibility will be assumed for accidents or escapes. Service is payable before the removal of the mare.

For further particulars, address

D. BRYSON,
Linden Cal.

DESIGNER, 11,157

Son of Director 2:17.

Sire of DIRECT, 2:18½, as a four year-old, (lapping out PALO ALTO in 2:16½), and MARGARET S., 2:19½, as a three-year-old, and GUIDE, 2:28½, as a three-year-old. DIRECTOR is brother to JAY-EYE SEE, 2:10, and PHALLAS, 2:13½.

At the State Fair of 1889, he received the Gold Medal as the best producer of averaged speed in colts of two, three and four years of age, beating Electioneer, Guy Wilkes, Sidney, Stamboul and others. He is the only living sire who has to his credit two performers in the 2:20 list, when his oldest colts were only four years old; his services are eagerly sought by breeders, with a fee of $300.

Designer's dam is May Queen, by Abbotsford, 2:19¾, sire of Conde, 2:19¾; Abbotsford is brother to Sonoma, 2:21¾, sire of Patron, 2:14¾.

May Queen was never trained. When two years old she was driven over the road three weeks, and trotted to a cart two miles in six minutes. A few days after she trotted a quarter in 40 seconds bare-footed; after being shod she trotted a quarter in 37 seconds.

Second dam by Elmo, 2:27¾ (half mile in 1:06), full sister in blood to Overman, 2:19 1-4, sister to the sire of L. C. Lee, 2:15, made when he defeated Arab in a match-race in three straight heats in 2:15, 2:17, 2:17¾. Only two of her produce were handled very little, one trotted as a three-year-old, with three weeks' work early in the spring, a mile in 2:35, last quarter in 35 seconds; the other trotted as a three-year-old, a mile in 2:37¾, quarters in 33 seconds, with seven weeks' work. If her produce had been given proper training, she would surely have had three in the 2:30 list.

Third dam by David Hill, sire of Geo. Treat, 2:25 1-4, and Black Swan, 2:28¾.

Fourth dam by Gen. Taylor, sire of the dam of Wells Fargo, 2:18¾.

Fifth dam by Williamson's Belmont.

Designer is a rich bay horse, 5 years old, 15¾ hands high, weighs 1,050 pounds, disposition the very best, has a perfect gait, and shows every indication of being very fast. He has never been trained, but will be given a low record, barring accidents. He is a horse of great substance and high finish; his family on both sides are producers of great speed, and he can not fail to make a great producer, as his colts inherit all these qualities—the same disposition and natural trotting action being large, and showing great breeding. He has but 15 colts in all (three two-year-olds); one of them has been broken, and last Fall trotted a quarter in 40¾ seconds, which proves that he produces early trotters. Those having colts from him are highly pleased with them, and all returned the mares to him the following season but two.

Breeders will see by carefully examining his pedigree, that his blood lines are invaluable for the production of high breeding and great speed. No stallion now in public service can show a pedigree with such fast records as enrich the blood of Designer. Considering his breeding, he is by far the cheapest horse in California. This is a rare opportunity to get the service of a good horse at a low price, as within a short period his price will be much higher.

Limited to 20 mares, at $60 for the season, commencing March 1st, ending June 15th. Mares can be returned next season if not with foal, provided mares and horse have not changed hands. Fee due at time of service, and must be paid before mares are removed. Pasturage $5 per month. All mares at owner's risk.

H. SCOTT,
San José Race Track, Cal.

LAWN VIEW BREEDING FARM STALLIONS.

ACTOR.

A beautiful bay horse foaled 1887 by Promptor 2305 (sire of Apex (four-year-old record) 2:26, Transit 2:26¾, Flora 2:30, Blue Belle 2:31, Daisy (yearling record) 3:08¾, he by Blue Bull 75, 1st dam by Sultan 1513 2 24, sire of Stamboul 2:12 1-4, Ruby 2:19¾, Sweetheart 2:22¾, Alcazar 2:20¾, Eva 2:23¾, La Grange 2:23¾, and eleven others in 2:30 list, second dam by Fireman by Abbotsford.

Actor, as his pedigree shows, is as purely bred a young stallion as ever made a season in the stud. The Bull stock is much sought after in the East, and Sultan, sire of his first dam will make the season in Kentucky this year at $150 per mare. Actor is a handsome bay colt 16 hands high, clean limbed and possesses all the points of a speedy trotter.

TERMS, $40 FOR THE SEASON, usual return privileges.

DOUGLASDALE 7650.

Thoroughbred Registered Clydesdale Stallion

Imported from Scotland, December, 1889, bay, three years old.

TERMS, $35 FOR THE SEASON.

YOUNG ELMO

Six years old sorrel stallion by St. Elmo 2:37, dam by Woodburn.

TERMS, $20 FOR THE SEASON.

For further particulars, address

MANAGER LAWN VIEW FARM, Auburn, Cal.

GEO. WASHINGTON,

11,623.

RECORD 2:30.

Bay colt, bred by Thomas Smith of Vallejo, Cal. Foaled 1886 by Mambrino Chief, Jr., 11,622, record 2:34 1-2, 1st dam Fanny Rose by Vick's Ethan Allen Jr. 2,903, sire of Prince Allen 2:27, 2nd dam Jenny Lind, thoroughbred, dam of Prince Allen 2:27. Will serve a limited number of mares at $50 for the season. Mares not proving with foal may be returned next season free.

Mambrino Chief, Jr.

11,622.

RECORD 2:34 1 2.

Sire of George Washington, record 2 30 at three years old. Bay horse bred by Rufus Ingalls of Belvedere, Ill. By McDonald Chief 3,583. First dam Venus by Mambrino Patchen 58. 2nd dam by Wardlow's Shakespeare. 3rd dam Lone Gold 4th dam by Silver Heels. Has not been in the stud before. He was 8 years old when he served a few mares, and his colts all show good style and form.

Terms for the season $40. For further particulars see or address

THOMAS SMITH,
Vallejo, Cal.

Elector 2170.

Sire of J. R.

Three-Year Old Record 2:24.

Sired by Electioneer 125, sire of Sunol, three-year-old, 2:10½, Palo Alto, 2:12¾, etc.; dam Gilberta by Fred Low 656, sire of Clay, 2:25½, etc.

Second dam Lady Gilbert (grandam of Lot Slocum, 2:17½) by General Knox 140 (sire of Lady Maud, 2:18½, and many others)

TERMS.

$150 for the season. Book full for 1890.

L. A. RICHARDS,
Grayson, Stanislaus Co., Cal.

The Thoroughbred Stallion

Three Cheers

Will make the season of 1890 at

Sacramento.

PEDIGREE.

THREE CHEERS:
- imp. Hurrah
  - Newminster
    - Touchstone, by Camel
    - Beeswing, by Dr. Syntax
  - Jovial
    - Bay Middleton, by Sultan
    - Sister to Grey Momus, by Comus
- Young Fashion
  - imp. Monarch
    - imp. Priam, by Emilius
    - imp. Delphine, by Whisker
  - Fashion
    - imp. Trustee, by Catton
    - Bonnets o' Blue, by Sir Charles

Hurrah was imported by John Reber, of Lancaster, Ohio, a locality where there were but few breeders of thoroughbreds. Under these disadvantages he sired a long list of winners. His sire Newminster, won the St. Ledger 1851, and his dam, Jovial by Bay Middleton, winner of the Derby 1836. Newminster by Touchstone, winner St. Ledger 1834. Dam Beeswing, winner of 54 races out of 64 starts, by Dr Syntax, winner of the Doncaster Cup. 1837—40—41—42, the only horse that ever accomplished that feat.

On the side of the dam Three Cheers is equally well related. Young Fashion was the dam of Surprise, Scotland (the only horse that ever beat Asteroid a heat), Liverpool, Columbia, and Bonnie Kate, the dam of Little Buttercup, and the flying Bonnie Lizzie. His grandam, Fashion was the greatest race mare of her day and beat Boston in that historical match at four mile heats, which is recorded as one of the greatest events in the annals of the turf.

Horsemen who are qualified to judge, pronounce Three Cheers to be the finest type of the Newminster line in America.

LOCATION.

THREE CHEERS will be located at the Arcade Training Stable, Rancho del Paso. This place has been selected for the reason that first class pasturage has been secured there for the exclusive use of these mares and the other facilities to be obtained there for the care of mares (especially mares in foal) are better than can be found elsewhere in the locality.

TERMS.

$60 for the season with the usual return privileges. Pasturage $5 per month. Mares cared for as owners may desire at bottom rates for grain and hay. All bills payable before the mare is removed.

Mares shipped care of WM. IRVINE, Pacific Stables, Sacramento, will be properly cared for and sent to the ranch without delay.

Three Cheers will be in charge of one of the most experienced and competent stud grooms in the State, who will exercise every care, but no reponsibility assumed for accidents or escapes.

For further particulars apply to Louis Crissler, at the ranch; Wm. Irvine, Pacific Stables, Second St., Sacramento; or to the owner,

E. S. CULVER,
313 Bush St., San Francisco.

GROVER CLAY

Bay Stallion, Black Points,

15 3-4 hands high.

Bred by W. W. Traylor, San Francisco.

BY ELECTIONEER.

First dam Maggie Norfolk by Norfolk, son of Lexington, he by Boston. Second dam Tilda Quill by Billy Cheatham he by Cracken, and he by Boston. Third dam by Dorsey's Golddust.

TERMS.

Will make the season of 1890 at the Training Stables of Denis Gannon, near Oakland Trotting Park, at $50 the season, payable at time of service. Season to commence February 1st and ending July 1st. Proper care of mares will be taken, but no responsibility incurred for accidents or escapes. Address,

DENIS GANNON, Oakland, Cal.

COOK STOCK FARM,

Season of 1890.

STEINWAY 1808.

Three-Year-Old Record 2:25 3-4.

Sire of STRATHWAY, three year old record 2:26, and sire of the dam of BOURBON RUSSELL 2:30.

By STRATHMORE 408; sire of 31 in the 2:30 list; sire of 6 dams of 8 in the 2:30 list, and sire of 3 sires of 3 in 2:30 list.

1st dam ABBESS (dam of Solo 2:28, and Soprano, dam of C. F Clay 2:18, Eminence 2:27 and Strathbridge, 3 year old record 2:28½) by ALBION, sire of VANITY FAIR 2:24½, and of the dam of FAVORITE 2:25½.

2nd dam by MARSHALL NEY.

3rd dam by BERTRAND, a son of SIR ARCHY.

TERMS—$100 for the season.

CHARLES DERBY 4907

Brown Horse, Foaled 1885.

By STEINWAY 1808.

1st dam by the great ELECTIONEER, sire of SUNOL 3 year old record 2:10½, Palo Alto 2:12¾, etc., etc.

2nd dam FANNY MALONE, by NIAGARA.

3rd dam FANNY WICKHAM, by HERALD.

4th dam by Imp. TRUSTEE.

TERMS—$100 for the season.

CRESCO 4908.

(BROTHER TO SPARTAN, 2,24.)

By STRATHMORE 408, sire of 31 in the 2:30 list, etc.

1st dam the dam of SPARTAN 2:24, by ALMONT 33; sire of 71 with performers in the 2:30 list

2nd dam the dam of HENDERSON 2:27, by BRIGNOLI 77, sire of the dam of KING WILKES 2:22.

3rd dam by CRIPPLE, a son of MEDOC.

4th dam by AMERICAN ECLIPSE.

TERMS—$50 for the season.

Pasturage $5 per month. Accidents and escapes at owner's risk. Mares consigned to the farm should be sent to Fashion Stables, Oakland; Geary & Grindle's Stable, Haywards; or to Bennett's Stable, Martinez; from and to which places they will be delivered free of charge. Address

COOK STOCK FARM,
Danville, Contra Costa, Co., Cal.

The Trotting Stallion

ARBITRATOR

Will make the Season of 1890 at NILES, Alameda County.

PEDIGREE.

ARBITRATOR:
- Director 1989, 2:17 in a race, Sire of Direct, 4 yrs., 2:18½ in a race, Margaret S., 3 yrs., 2:19½ in a race, Guide, 4 yrs., 2:28½ in a race.
- Lady Earnest.
  - Speculation 928, sire of Oakland Maid, 2:22 in a race, Gracie S., 2:22 in a race, Crown Point, 2:24 in a race, He the sire of Valensin, 3 yrs., 2:23 in a race, Sire of Dam of Alfred G., 2:19½.
  - Lady Hibbard, dam of Lou Whipple, 2:26½ in a race.

Speculation's dam was Martha Washington, dam of Whipple's Hambletonian, sire of 15 in 2:30 and granddaughter of Burr's Napoleon, sire of Black Harry, who in 1850 won two miles in 5:14½. He sired Smith Burr, sire of Gen. Butler, 2:21, Wagon, 4:50½. He sired the dam of Fanny Mapes, dam of Jerome Eddy, 2:16½. He sired Telegraph, sire of dam of Barus, 2:13½.

DESCRIPTION.

ARBITRATOR was foaled 1885. He is of good size, fine conformation, and a beautiful seal brown.

TERMS.

Non-standard mares	$45
Standard mares by inheritance	35
Standard mares by performance or produce	25

For further particulars, address

H. A. MAYHEW, owner,
Niles, Alameda Co.

ST. NICHOLAS.

A Son of the World Renowned

SIDNEY,

Will Make the Season of 1890, at the Oakland Trotting Park.

ST. NICHOLAS was bred by Mr. G. Valensin at the Arno Stock Farm, Sacramento Co., California, in 1886. He is a beautifully proportioned bright bay horse, 15.3 hands high; is well muscled, lengthy, and lots of bone, with splendid natural action and a phenomenal turn of speed. As a three-year-old he easily worked three heats on the Oakland Track in 2:32, 2:29 and 2:27¾. His breeding is just what one would expect from such a highly formed bloodlike horse. Sidney, his sire is the most successful young stallion—whether for getting pacers or trotters—America has ever seen, and no wonder for his blood lines are exceptional fine and are all trotting lines, Santa Claus, Strathmore, Rysdyk's Hambletonian and Abdallah, while Sweetness again runs back through that great sire Volunteer, to Rysdyk's Hambletonian and also through her dam to Rysdyk's Hambletonian and Harry Clay 45, the sire of Electioneer's dam. St. Nicholas' dam is by Echo, an exceptionally prepotent son of Hambletonian thus giving St. Nicholas four Rysdyk's Hambletonian crosses and further back a Harry Clay cross which with his grand dam's thoroughbred cross should make him invaluable in the stud.

TERMS. Fifty dollars the season, which will commence on the 5th of February and close on the 1st of July. Due care will be taken of mares, but no responsibility for accidents or escapes.

Mares taken and kept as desired by the owners, and at reasonable rates.

JOHN ROWEN.
Oakland Trotting Park.

Season of 1890.

February 15 to June 15

LYNWOOD,

(STANDARD 8017.)

AT WOLF'S (RUSSELL'S) STABLES, STOCKTON, CAL.

TERMS.

$50 for the season, payable at the close of season. Pasturage at $3 per month. Accidents or escapes at owner's risk.

PEDIGREE.

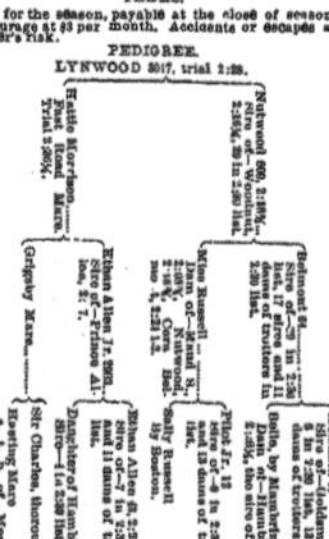

DESCRIPTION.

Dark bay, 15 hands, weighs 1050 pounds, form stout and elegant, gait pure and rapid. He was foaled July 15, 1880, has done but little work in the stud, but enough to demonstrate that he is one of the best foal getters in the State. Only one of his get has had any systematic handling, and that could have gone into the 2:30 list last year as a two-year-old, had the owner desired.

It will be observed from an examination of Lynwood's pedigree, that he is one of the best bred sons of the GREAT NUTWOOD, who commands a service fee of $500 for the season.

P. VISHER, Stockton.

The Thoroughbred Stallion

INTRUDER

Will make the Season of 1890 at Agricultural Park, SACRAMENTO.

Bay Horse, foaled 1871, bred by Sir L. Newman, England. Imported by D. D. Withers, Esq., New York.

By Crater, Son of Orlando and Vesuvienne by Gladiator.

1st dam Lady Bountiful by Rataplan (Rataplan is own brother to Stockwell, and winner of 42 races, including the Doncaster Cup and 16 Queen's Plates, and proved himself the most distinguished race horse of his day in England).

2d dam Plentiful by Don John (the winner of St. Leger and Doncaster Cup).

3d dam Plenty by Bay Middleton (winner of the Derby and Two Thousand Guinea Stakes).

4th dam Plenary, own sister of Plenipotentiary, by Emilius. (Both Emilius and Plenipotentiary were Derby winners).

5th dam Harriet, dam of the renowned Plenipotentiary by Pericles.

6th dam by Selim, winner of the One Thousand Guinea Stakes.

7th dam by Pypilina, by Sir Peter.

8th dam Rally, by Trumpeter.

9th dam Fancy, by Florizel. Fancy was full sister to Diomed, the first Derby winner in England, and after his importation into this country, sired the illustrious Sir Archy, etc. See English Stud Book.

Imported INTRUDER is a beautiful bay, standing fully 16 hands high, of great length and substance, and descends through close and strong currents from the most illustrious winners and winning lines of blood of which the English Stud Book bears record.

A careful review of the first six crosses of the pedigree of INTRUDER will show nine Derby winners; five St. Leger winners; two winners of The Oaks; two winners of the Two Thousand Guineas; two winners of the One Thousand Guineas; one Goodwood Cup winner; one Cesarwich Cup winner; one Cambridgeshire Stakes winner, and four Doncaster Cups, in addition to a great number of Steeplechases and other races of less import.

INTRUDER, at the great fair held at St. Louis, Mo., in 1876, was awarded the highest stallion honors—the blue ribbon and the $500 purse—in the sweepstakes ring for stallion of any age or blood. The list of competitors embraced the large number of thirty-three animals, and they represented England, Canada, Kentucky, Tennessee and other states. He also took first premium in his class and in sweepstakes for the best stallion of any age or breed at the State Fair at Peoria, Ill., 1882. He is the sire of Tidal Wave, George Hakes, Bernice and April Fool.

INTRUDER is the sire of Interpose, who is the dam of Spokane, winner of the Kentucky Derby, in which he beat the great horse Proctor Knott and broke the record.

TERMS: $50 for the season. Mares not proving with foal can be returned the next season free of charge. Good pasturage at $4 per month. Mares cared for in any manner owners may desire, and fed on hay and grain, either or both, at reasonable rates. While every precaution will be taken, no responsibility will be assumed for escapes or accidents. Mares sent from a distance in care of the undersigned, will be met and taken to the park. For further particulars, address

T. J. KNIGHT.
Agricultural Park, Sacramento.

Shoes For Comfort, Elegance and Durability.

Having my own Factory, and giving my personal supervision to all work I am in a position to warrant perfect satisfaction. Inspection invited.

AGENT for the VISCALIZED SHOES.

FACTORY - S W. cor. Battery and Jackson Sts.
SALESROOM - Pioneer Building, corner Stevenson and Fourth Streets.

A full line of Boots and Shoes constantly on hand, and rules for Self-Measurement by Mail.

JNO. T. SULLIVAN.

2:20 1-2 Half Mile Track) at 4 Years. — Fastest Record (in a Race) of any Wilkes — 2:14 1-2 at 5 Years.

ROY WILKES, 2:12 3/4,

eal brown; 15¾ hands; foaled 1883; by Adrian Wilkes 6560, son of Geo. Wilkes; 1st dam by Blue Bull 75; 2d dam by grandson of American Eclipse; 3d and 4th dams thoroughbred.

THE GREATEST CAMPAIGNER OF 1889.

Handsome, Game, Pure Gaited. Level Headed.

Will make a season at the PLEASANTON STOCK FARM, PLEASANTON, CAL. Service Fee $150. Money refunded if mare does not get with foal. Season ends April 10, 1890 Limited to 20 mares. For full record of performances, extended pedigree, etc., address

L. A. DAVIES, Hotel Pleasanton,
SUTTER AND JONES STREETS, San Francisco, Cal.

Valensin Stock Farm Stallions,

SIDNEY, 2:19 3-4.

At Eight Years of Age Sire of the following Fastest on Record:

FAUSTINO, yearling stallion, record of the world 2:35
FLEET, fastest yearling record in 1888 .... 2:36
FLEET, fastest two-year-old filly in 1889 .... 2:24
GOLD LEAF, fastest four-year-old Pacing record in the world 2:11¼
ADONIS, fastest three-year-old Pacing Gelding in the world 2:14¼
ADONIS, four-year-old Gelding Pacing record 2:14¾

—Also the Sire of—

LONGWORTH, four years old 2:19
SISTER V., four years old (trial 2:23) 2:27
SANTA RITA 2:39
MEMO, two-year-old (three-year-old trial 2:20½) 2:49

And many others.

SIDNEY is the sire of Faustino 2:35, and Fleet 2:36, the two fastest yearlings the world has ever known by one sire, and his slowest yearling is faster than the great Electioneer's fastest.

Terms, $250, with usual return privileges, for a limited number of approved mares. Book nearly full.

Only eight more mares can be taken for Season of '90.

Pasturage $5 per month. Reasonable charges if fed hay and grain. Best of care taken of mares, but positively no responsibility assumed for accidents or escapes. For further particulars address

G. VALENSIN, Pleasanton, Cal.

MEMO.

The Best Son of SIDNEY

Will Make the Season of 1890 at the OAKLAND RACE TRACK

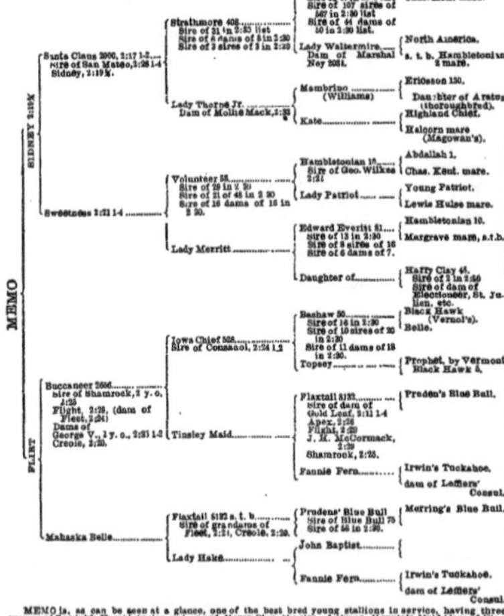

MEMO is, as can be seen at a glance, one of the best bred young stallions in service, having three crosses of Rysdyk's Hambletonian and one of Harry Clay, the sire of Green Mountain Maid (dam of Electioneer, etc.), while Long Island Black Hawk and Flaxtail also contribute to his blood. Sidney (Memo's sire) is universally known as the best young sire in the world, a producer of extreme speed at an early age.

PERFORMANCES.

MEMO trotted in public in his two year-old form, obtaining a record of 2:49, though he was close to Grandee in a race on the Bay District Track, the second heat of which was made in 2:31 1-2, the first in 2:32. He exhibited phenomenal speed when three years old, and had it not been for a slight strain of his fore fetlock, there is little question that he would have shown in public very close to the best record. On the Oakland track he was timed a mile in 2:20 1-2, and frequently trotted quarters in from 32 1-2 to 34 seconds.

As a four-year-old Memo only started once—at Sacramento—when, although out of condition, he showed great speed, and improving as he went on, great hopes were entertained of his going well down in the 'teens at the P. C. T. H. B. A. meeting, but after showing several very fast miles his leg filled and he was laid up for the season. He is sixteen hands high, and of powerful build throughout. His color is a glossy black, with both fore-feet white. His disposition is all that could be desired, and his action superb. He is a sure foal getter, only one mare being reported not in foal during his last season.

TERMS, $100, with usual return privileges, for a limited number of mares. Season to close JUNE 15th, when he will be prepared for track purposes. Pasturage $4 per month. Have leased the cricket ground adjoining the track for pasturage, where there is fine feed. Reasonable charges if fed hay and grain. Best of care taken of mares in any manner owners may desire, but positively no responsibility assumed for accidents or escapes. For further particulars address

J. P. KERR, 313 Bush Street, San Francisco,
or, JOHN ROWEN, Race Track, Oakland, Cal.

SAN MATEO STOCK FAR[M]

HOME OF GUY WILKES,
Record, 2:15 1-4.

Guy Wilkes' Book is full for 1890 and 1891, and positively no mares will be received.

Sable Wilkes, three-year-old record 2:18, will be allowed to ser[ve] mares in addition to those already engaged at $2[...] season of 1890. SABLE Wilkes, 15½ hands, black horse, by Guy Wilkes, first dam Sa[...] The Moor; second dam Gretchen by Mambrino Pilot; third dam Kitty Kirkman by C[...] Chief; fourth dam by Fanning's Tobe; fifth dam by imp. Leviathan.

Leo Wilkes, brown horse, four years, 16 hands, full brother to [...] Wilkes, will be allowed to serve 30 mares at $100 the[...]

Mares not proving with foal may be returned the following season free of service fee[...] ties engaging the services of any of the above horses must send a deposit of 10 per c[...] service money with engagement. Pasturage $6 per month, and when the condition [...] animal requires it, hay or grain, or both, are fed, the charge will be $12 50 per m[...] Good care will be taken of all mares sent to the Farm, but no liability will be assum[...] accidents or escapes.

All bills are due at time of service, but must be paid by August 1st of each year. No [...] will be allowed to leave the place until all bills are paid.

WILLIAM CORBITT.
San Mateo Stock Farm.

Pleasanton Stock Farm Co.'s Stallions,

DIRECTOR, 2:17.

Director's book is open for 15 good mares more than already booked for the season of 1890, [...] each.

This is the cheapest service fee ever charged for a stallion, taking into consideration his BRE[...] and RACE RECORD and the RACE RECORDS OF HIS COLTS.

Season to commence February 15th and close August 1st.

CORRECTOR, Four Years Old.

Sire Director 2:17, dam Brainey, she by Echo. Echo sired by Rysdyk's Hambletonian, out of Ma[...] she by Seely's American Star. Brainey's dam Lady Dudley, she by Tom Dudley by Blacknose, a[...] Medoc, he by American Eclipse. Lady Dudley's dam by Bertrand, Jr., a son of Bertrand.

CORRECTOR is a rich seal brown 15¾ hands high, and is the fastest young stallion in the world [...] the same conditions, never having been off the farm where raised and never been shod or driv[...] speed before last Christmas, and can trot quarters now in 35 seconds, a 2:20 gait

He will be allowed to serve ten good mares, at $100 each for the season, which closes June 1st.

DECORATOR, Four Years Old.

Sire Director 2:17, dam Chess, sired by Cardinal 2.37, trial 2:28, he by Gen. Gifford's Morgan, [...] Cardinal, sired by Joe Gales of Ohio, he by Marlborough out of the Duchess of Marlborough by So[...] Eclipse; second dam old Duchess of Marlborough by Sir Archy; third dam by imp Eclipse. Deco[...] second dam a Morgan and Messenger mare.

Decorator is a light bay 15¾ hands high, and with but little handling for speed has shown eig[...] 17½ seconds, a 2:20 gait.

He will be allowed to serve ten good mares at $50 each for the season, which closes June 1st.

Mares not proving with foal may be returned next season free of charge of service fees to the stallion, if he is still in our possession; if not, to some other stallion equally as good, or money [...] refunded at option of the company.

Pasturage $4 per month; hay and grain extra. Accidents and escapes at owner's risk.

Service fees due at time of service, and must be paid, together with pasturage, etc., before ma[res are] taken away, or a good approved note given, payable August 1st, 1890, at which date all bills m[ust be] settled.

For further information call or address M. SALISBURY, 320 Sansome Street, Room [...] San Francisco, or

PLEASANTON STOCK FARM CO.;
Pleasanton, Alameda Co., C[al.]

SOUTHER FARM

P. O. Box 208. San Leandro, [Cal.]

1½ miles northwest of San Leandro; 8 miles southeast of Oakland. Turn off county road between above places at "Stanley Road," ½ mile north of San Leandro.

Horses boarded at all times in any [...] desired. Best of care but no responsibi[lity for] accidents. Colts broken and handled [...] road or track. Terms reasonable.

Glen Fortune,	Jester D,	El Benton,	Figar[o]
By Electioneer.	By Almont.	By Electioneer.	Hambletonia[n]
$50 for 1889.	$50 for 1890.	Limited to 5 mares.	Limited to 12
		Book Full.	Book Fu[ll]

THE SOUTHER FARM

Has Green Feed the Year Rou[nd]

and feeds Hay in connection with the green feed, which a h[orse] must have if he is to thrive. Every animal is given

A Dry, Warm Place to Sleep,

No matter how stormy the weather. All Stock under cover when it rains.

VISITORS WELCOME ANY DAY EXCEPT SUND[AY]

How to Get Stock to the Souther Farm.

The Souther Farm is one and a half miles northeast of San Leandro and eight miles southeast [of Oak]land. The stables are about one mile east of the county road, which runs between Oakland and Sa[n Lean]dro. The place to turn off is at Stanley Road, where a large signboard of the farm is placed. Guide[boards] will be found at every cross road. In any ordinary weather the roads are very good, and they are fai[r] after the unusually heavy rainfall of the past winter.

All stock sent from San Francisco may be brought over by Gafola's Express, No. 3 Market str[eet, San] Francisco. They also have an order box outside of Hawley Bros.' Hardware house on the corner of [Market] and Beale streets. The express leaves San Francisco on the Creek route boat, which starts at 1:3[0] orders should be in the order box at Market and Beale streets by 10 o'clock, or at the office, No. 3 [Market] street, by 11 o'clock at the latest. In the case of very young or very valuable horses, the Souther Fa[rm will] send reliable men to lead or drive over any stock that will not lead behind a wagon. A small charge [is] made in such cases, to cover the extra expense incurred.

Horses are very easily taken from Oakland to the farm, and where it is inconvenient for ow[ners to] bring them or send them, the farm will send after anything that is to come. On horses that sta[y three] months or over there is no charge for getting or delivering. Where a horse stays a short time the [...] time and expense only is charged to him.

Horses can be shipped by rail from almost all parts of the State to San Leandro. Always no[tify the] Farm several days before shipping anything, and then men will be on hand to receive stock on arriv[al. The] railroad station is but two miles from the Souther Farm, and the agent invariably gives immediate [notice] of the arrival of any stock consigned to the above farm, but when word is sent to the farm in good [time] by letter or telegram, the animals sent are saved waiting a couple of hours in the car.

Passenger trains leave San Francisco (from the broad gauge ferry) and First and Broadway, O[akland] at frequent intervals during the day. There are several trains from San Jose to San Leandro on b[oth] broad and narrow gauge railroads; the broad gauge, by way of Niles, is much more convenient for g[etting to] the farm. There are trains each day from Sacramento, Stockton and Livermore to San Leandro. [In ordi]nary weather it is a short and pleasant drive from Oakland to the Souther Farm or from San Fran[cisco to] the Farm by way of the Creek route ferry boat. Always notify the Souther Farm just when you wi[ll arrive] at San Leandro, and some one will meet you at the station. If you do not recognize the farm conveya[nce ask] the stage driver, who will point it out.

Write to the above address for references, circulars and price lists. [...] reasonable.

GILBERT TOMPKINS, Proprie[tor]

Langtry Farms' Stud

Imp. FRIAR TUCK

By the Immortal HERMIT

DAM ROMPING GIRL BY WILD DAYRELL,

AT $50 THE SEASON.

Mares not proving with foal may be returned the following season. Good care taken of mares, but no liabilities for accidents or escapes.

Good Pasturage at $5 per month.

Mares shipped to ST. HELENA, care CHARTES WILLIAM ABY, St. Helena Stables, will be cared for. For further particulars address,

CHAS. WILLIAM ABY,
Middletown, Lake County, Cal.

2:08 3-4 2:10 2:12

MAMBRINO WILKES, 6083.

SIRE OF

GUS WILKES, 2:22; ALPHEUS, 2:27; CLARA P, 2:29½; BALKAN, 2:29½ (3-year-old) and timed separately 2:22¼ in 4-year-old Stake, Bay District Track, October 14, 1889.

DESCRIPTION.

Black; sixteen hands; weighs, in exercise, 1,260 lbs. For style, finish, symmetry and proportion, comparison is challenged with any trotting bred horse. His get to follow in size, style and beauty. Balkan, for instance, being "facile princeps" of trotters in these particulars.

PEDIGREE.

Sired by Geo. Wilkes, sire of Harry Wilkes, 2:13¼, Guy Wilkes, 2:15¼, and 60 other trotters in the 2:30 list, in addition to 6 pacers, and of the sire of Axtell, 2:12 (three-year-old), beating all stallions of any age, and the sire of Regal Wilkes, 2:20¾, best two-year-old stallion record.

First dam Lady Chrisman by Mambrino (Todhunter's, son of Mambrino Chief 11; sire of Lady Thorn, 2:18¼; Woodford Mambrino, 2:21½, and four others in the list, and of the dams of Director, 2:17, Piedmont, 2:17¼, Onward, 2:25¼, etc.

Second dam by Pilot Jr. 12, sire of nine in the 2:30 list, and of the dams of Maud S., 2:08¾, Jay-Eye-See, 2:10, Nutwood, 2:18¾, Viking, 2:19¼, Pilot Boy, 2:20, Bad Queen, 2:20¾, etc.

TERMS.

Mares from a distance will be received at the Dexter Stables, Oakland, or Livery Stable, Martinez, the owner notifying Smith Hill, Superintendent at the farm. Good pasture and plenty of water. For the purpose of placing the service of a Wilkes within reach of breeders, the same rate will be maintained as last year, to wit, $75 for the season. Although it is not admitted thereby that this horse is inferior as a producer to the horses whose fees are placed at from $150 to $500. Address

SMITH HILL,
San Miguel Stock Farm,
Walnut Creek, Contra Costa Co., Cal.

2:12¾ 2:13½ 2:15¼

2:08¾ 2:10 2:12

BALKAN

By Mambrino Wilkes.

(See that Horse's Advertisement.)

DAM FANNY FERN BY JACK HAWKINS
Son of Boston.

The grandam of Maud S, (2:08¾) was by Boston and the grandam of Jay-Eye-See (2:10) was by Lexington, son of Boston. So Balkan is the same remove from Boston that Maud is, and one remove nearer than Jay-Eye-See.

Fanny Fern has produced Molly Drew, Onyx, Fred Arnold, Molly Fern and Balkan, all by different sires. Balkan's sire and dam both being producers, and he being a trotter himself with a record of 2:29 1-2 (three-year-old) and timed separately 2:22 1-4 in 4-year-old Stake, Bay District Track, October 14, 1889—it is but fair to presume that he will get trotters of the high order.

DESCRIPTION.

He is seal brown, 16-1 hands high, in style rivalled by few, and excelled by none with as pure a gait as has yet been exhibited in public—bar none.

Balkan will be at Oakland Trotting Park for the season of 1890, and will be limited to ten mares, at $50 fee, in order to be put in training early, as it is morally certain that if given a reasonable opportunity he will be fast enough to compete with the best of his age. For further particulars, address

A. L. HINDS,
Dexter Stables, Oakland.

2:12¾ 2:13½ 2:15¼

JESSE E. MARKS & CO.,

Wholesale and Retail Dealers of Choice Brands

Havana & Key West Cigars

922 MARKET ST., S. F.

2:19 NOONDAY 2:20½

STANDARD No. 10,000.

This celebrated trotting bred stallion will make the season of 1890 at the stable of the undersigned at Sacramento, Cal., at $75 for the season and $100 to insure a mare in foal. Payable on or before July 1st, 1890. Money will be refunded on mares bred by insurance as soon as the fact becomes known that they are not in foal.

NOONDAY.
- Wedgewood, 2:19... Sire of Favonia, 2:15, fastest 4th heat for any mare or gelding, and eight others in 2:27 or better.
  - Belmont... Sire of Wedgewood, 2:19, Nutwood, 2:18¾, Viking, 2:19½, and 29 others in 2:30 list.
    - Alexander's Abdallah, sire of Goldsmith Maid, 2:14; Almont, with 36 horses in 2:30 list, etc.
    - Belle, dam of Hambletonian, 2:26½; B'cara, dam of Pancoast, 2:21¾, the sire of Patron, 2:14¼.
  - Woodbine... Dam of Wedgewood, 2:19, Woodford Mamb., 2:21½, the sire of Pancoast, 2:21¾, the sire of Patron, 2:14¼.
    - Woodford.
    - Singleton Mare.
- Noontide, 2:20½... (Trial, 2:13½).
  - Harold... Sire of Maud S., 2:08¾, and 26 others in 2:30 list.
    - Hambletonian (Rysdyk's), sire of George Wilkes, 2:22, the sire of Guy Wilkes, 2:15¼; Electioneer, the sire of Sunol, 2:10½, and scores of noted trotters and producers.
    - Enchantress, by Abdallah 1.
  - Midnight... Dam of Jay-Eye-See, 2:10, Noontide, 2:20½.
    - Pilot Jr., sire of dams of Maud S., 2:08¾, Jay-Eye-See, 2:10, Nutwood, 2:18¾, etc.
    - Twilight, by Lexington, sire of the dam of Ansel, 2:20.

NOODAY is a dark seal brown, foaled 1884, 15 hands 1¾ inches high. Individually he is equal to his royal breeding. He is all that can be desired in conformation, intelligence, color and trotting action, and no stallion now in public service can show a pedigree with such fast records and royal game trotting blood as Noonday.

DON MARVIN,

Record 2:28 as a five-year-old. Standard by Breeding and Performance

Standard No. 7927.

Don Marvin 2:28.

Don Marvin is a beautiful seal brown, foaled 1884, bred by Hon. Leland Stanford, Palo Alto, Cal., standing 16 hands, and weighs, in ordinary condition, 1200 lbs. He is a fine individual, good style and form, combined with great substance, and good temper. Is very level headed; in his first race the past season he only made one break in five closely contested heats. He has great speed and endurance, with the pure, rapid Electioneer gait. He trots without toe weights, and wears only 8 oz. shoes in front. He gained his record the past season in the third heat, on a slow track, after making a season (serving over 50 mares), with scarcely any preparation. His record is no mark of his speed. He was a natural born trotter, and Mr. Charles Marvin considered him the fastest two year old at Palo Alto that season.

By FALLIS, 2:23, - - by Electioneer, sire of
Sire of Don Marvin, 2:28. — Sunol, three-year-old, 2:10 1-2, Palo Alto, 2:12¾, and 47 others in 2:30 list.

Dam CORA, by Don Victor by Belmont, sire of
Dam of Don Marvin, 2:28. — Ventura, 2:27¾, and sire of the dam of Bell Echo, 2:20, and six others in 2:30 list.

2d dam CLARABEL, - by Abdallah Star,
Dam of Clifton Bell, 2:24 1-2, and grandam of Rexford, three years, 2:24. — Sire of Hattie Maples, 2:23.

3d dam FAIRY, - - by Rysdyk's Hambletonian,
Sister of Sweepstakes, sire of 16 in 2:30 list. — Sire of Electioneer, George Wilkes, and many other noted sires and trotters.

4th dam EMMA MILLS, by Seely's American Star,
Dam of 4 horses that have 2:30 performers. — The great broodmare sire of the world.

The above pedigree should show every intelligent breeder that Don Marvin is "high" bred though very strong in trotting blood. All the comment it is deemed necessary to make as to the value of "thoroughbred blood" in the trotter is simply to refer to the very significant fact that the first and second dams of Maud S., 2:08¾, Jay-Eye-See 2:10, Sunol, three years 2:10 1-2, Palo Alto 2:12¾, Anteeo 2:16¼, Nutwood 2:18¾, Wedgewood 2:19, and many other successful sires and sensational trotters of the day are thoroughbred.

TERMS—Don Marvin will make the ensuing season from February 1st to July 1st, 1890, at $40 the season, with the usual privilege of returning the mare next season if not proving in foal. Mares from a distance met at the cars or boats on notification, and carefully handled, but no responsibility assumed for accidents or escapes.

Good alfalfa pasture furnished (free from barb wire fence) at $4 per month. For further particulars or complete circulars address

F. P. LOWELL,
1520 F Street, Sacramento, Cal.

The Produce of Eros Averaged $2,200 Each at New York Auction Sale in 1889.

THE ELECTIONEER TROTTING STALLION,

5326 EROS 5326

Will make the season of 1890—February 1st to July 1st—at LA SIENTA RANCH, MENLO PARK, adjoining Palo Alto.

PEDIGREE.

EROS (5326)
Standard by his sire
" " dam
" " record
" " produce
" under all rules

EROS (5326)..
- Electioneer... Grandsire of Norlaine, 1 yr., 2:31 1-2, Sire of Sunol, 2 yrs., 2:18, Sunol, 3 yrs., 2:10 1-2, Hinda Rose, 4 yrs., 2:16, Palo Alto, 2:12¾.
  - Hambletonian 10... Sire of Dictator, George Wilkes, Happy Medium, and 40 others in 2:30 list, and grandsire of 728 in list.
    - Abdallah 10. Sire of the dams of Goldsmith Maid, 2:14, and 7 other producing dams.
    - Charles Kent mare By imp. Bellfounder.
  - Green Mountain Maid... Dam of Prospero, 2:20, Elaine, 2:20, Dame Trot, 2:22, Elista, 2:22¾, Storm, 2:26¾, Antonio, 2:28¾, Miranda, 2:31, Mansfield, 2:26.
    - Harry Clay. Sire of the dams of St. Julian, 2:11¾, Bodine, 2:19¼, and 17 more in 2:30 list
    - Shanghai Mary.
- Sontag Mohawk... Dam of Eros, 2:29 1-2, Sport, 2:22¾, Sallie Benton, 2:17¾, Conductor, trial, 2:28, Colma, 3-y-o trial, 2:24.
  - Mohawk Chief... Sire of the dams of Lot Slocum, 2:17¼, Sallie Benton, 4 yrs., 2:17¾, Pedlar, 2 yrs., 2:27¼, Stanford, 4 yrs., 2:30, Eros, 6th heat, 2:29 1-4.
    - Hambletonian 10. Sire of the dams of Stamboul, 2:12¼, Wilton, 2:19¼, and 20 other trotters.
    - Lady Perrine
  - Sontag Nellie...
    - Toronto Sontag By Toronto Chief,
    - Nellie Gray 5-mile record, 13:45.

Produce of Eros
Wanda, 4 yrs., 2:24.
Solita, 2 yrs., 2:41 1-2.
Meriquita, 2yrs., 2:42.
Daylight, 2 yrs., 2:54.
Hiram B., trial, 2:28.

These are the only colts by him that have ever had a harness on except one in New York that went a trial last July in 2:26 1:2.

DESCRIPTION.

EROS is a rich seal brown stallion, bred by Hon. Leland Stanford at Palo Alto, and is the nearest living likeness of his celebrated sire, Electioneer. Stands 15.2 hands high, and weighs 1050 pounds.

In breeding to Eros, the owners of mares will strictly follow the great rule of breeding, viz., breed to a stallion by a producer and out of a sure producer of great speed. Eros is by the stallion that has produced more 2:30 trotters that any living horse, and is also the sire of more 2:30 performers than any horse living or dead.

EROS is out of the dam of Sally Benton, four years old, record 2:17¾, Sport 2:22¾, and Eros 2:29¼ in the sixth heat, against a field of nine horses. He is from a family that is endowed with great natural speed, trot fast at an early age, train on, throw trotters from all classes of mares, are of good substance, bone, style and action, and breed solid colors.

TERMS.

$100 for the season, with the privilege of return next season should mares not be in foal and horse and mare still remain in the same hands.

Good pasturage can be obtained at $5 per month, but no responsibility for accidents or escapes. There are a large number of box stalls, and animals can be kept up and fed on hay and grain at reasonable rates if required. Mares already in foal can be sent to the ranch for foaling, and will receive all the attention bestowed upon our own mares. Mares left with Mr. Peter Pomyea, Broadway Street Stable, Oakland, or with Mr. F. H. Burke, 401 Montgomery Street, San Francisco, will be forwarded to the ranch free of charge. For further particulars apply to

W. H. VIOGET,
LA SIENTA RANCH, MENLO PARK, CAL.

EROS is the only stallion offered to the public on this Coast that has a dam that has three in the 2:30 list.

POPLAR GROVE

Breeding Farm

STALLIONS.

CLOVIS, 4909,

CLOVIS is a beautiful black, Eight Years Old, 16 1-2 Hands High, and weighs 1260 lbs.

He is a horse of beautiful symmetry and magnificent action.

PEDIGREE.

CLOVIS was sired by Sultan, 2:24, sire of Stamboul, 2:12 1-4, Ruby, 2:19¾, and fifteen others with records of 2:30 or better.

First dam Sweetbriar by Thorndale 2:22 1-2, sire of Edwin Thorne, 2:16 1-2, Daisy Dale, 2:19, and May Thorne, 2:24.

Second dam Ulster Queen, dam of Volmer, 2:24¾ by Hambletonian 10. Sire of Dexter, 2:17¼, George Wilkes, 2:22.

Third dam by Thomas Jefferson, a son of Mambrino Paymaster, Jr.

Fourth dam by Mambrino Paymaster, sire of Mambrino Chief.

Sultan, by The Moor, sire of Beautiful Bells, dam of Hinda Rose, 2:19 1-2, and Sable, dam of Sable Wilkes, three year old record 2:18.

First dam of Sultan, Sultana, by Delmonico. Sire of Darby, 2:16 1-2, by Guy Miller, sire of Whipple's Hambletonian.

Second dam by Mambrino Chief.

Third dam by Downing's Bay Messenger.

Fourth dam Mrs. Caudle, dam of Ericsson, four year old record 2:30 1-2.

Clovis will make the season of 1890 at Poplar Grove Breeding Farm, near Wildflower, Fresno County, Commencing February 1st and ending July 1st.

Terms, $75, due at time of service.

Mares cared for in any manner owners may desire; pasturage $2 per month. Every care exercised, but no liability for escapes or accidents. Mares not proving with foal can be returned next season, providing I still own this stallion.

APEX, 8935.

FOUR-YEAR-OLD RECORD, FOURTH HEAT, 2:26.

Will make the present season at the Poplar Grove Breeding Farm, near Wildflower, Fresno Co., season commencing Feb. 1st, and ending July 1, 1890. Terms, $50 the season, due at time of service. Apex is eight years old, a beautiful bay, 15 1-2 hands high, and weighs 1140 lbs. He is a horse of fine disposition, and his gait is faultless.

PEDIGREE.

Apex was sired by Promptor 2305, he by Blue Bull 75; first dam Mary by Flaxtail, he by Pruden's Blue Bull. Flaxtail being the sire of the dams of Buccaneer, five-year-old record, 2:24 1-2; Pride, yearling record, 2:44 1-2, and Shamrock, two-year old record, 2:25, third heat. Second dam by Bright Eyes, son of Boanarages. Promptor (sire of Apex, record 2:26, and Transit, 2:26 1-2), by Wilson's Blue Bull, by Pruden's Blue Bull, son of Merring's Blue Bull. Promptor's dam Prairie Bird, by Flaxtail; second dam by John the Baptist, son of Tally Ho Morgan, by Sherman Morgan; third dam Fannie Fern by Irwin's Tuckahoe.

Apex made his appearance in the circuit as a two-year-old, and obtained a record of 1:42. As a three-year-old he reduced this in a race at Santa Rosa against Stamboul to 2:31, it taking six heats to decide the contest, which was won by Apex. As a four year-old he gained his present record of 2:26.

Mares cared for in any manner owners may desire. Pasturage $2 per month. Every care exercised, but no liabilities for escapes or accidents. Mares not proving with foal can be returned next season, providing I still own this stallion.

The Standard Stallion

JUNIO,

RECORD 2:22.

WILL MAKE THE PRESENT SEASON OF AT FRESNO FAIR GROUNDS.

Season Commencing Feb. 1st an ending July 1st.

TERMS—$100 the season, due at time of service.

JUNIO is eight years old, a handsome dark bay 16 hands high, and weighs 1250 pounds. He is the personification of the light harness horse, and his trotting action is superb. At the State Fair of 1886 he took first premium over forty of the finest trotters in the State.

PEDIGREE.

Junio, by Electioneer, premier stallion of Palo Alto (sire of Sunol 2:10 1-2, Palo Alto 2:12 1-4, and 47 others in the 2:30 list,. Dam by Granger by imp. Hercules.

Granger, by imp. Hercules, dam Jenny Lind, by Stockbridge Chief, Jr., he by Stockbridge Chief, he by Vermont Black Hawk. Second dam by Kentucky Whip.

Imp. Hercules, by Kingston, first dam daughter of Tuscar, by Bay Middleton, second dam Malvina, by Oscar; 3rd dam Spotless by Walton; 4th dam by Trumpator (see Bruce's American Stud Book, Vol. 1, page 26). Hercules is the sire of the dam of Anmoor 2:24¾; also sire of dam of Menlo 2:21 1-2.

Mares not proving in foal may be returned next year free of charge, providing I still have the horse. Pasturage $3 per month. While every care will be taken of horses, no liability will be assumed for accidents or escapes.

For further particulars address

S. N. STRAUBE, Fresno, Cal.
Poplar Grove Breeding Farm.

Southern Pacific Co.

(PACIFIC SYSTEM.)

[T]rains leave and are due to arrive at San Francisco.

LEAVE (FOR)	FROM JANUARY 1, 1890.	ARRIVE (FROM)
7.30 A M	Haywards, Niles and San Jose	*12.45 P M
7.30 A M	Sacramento and Redding, via Davis	7.15 P M
7.30 A M	Sacramento, Auburn, Colfax	5.45 P M
8.00 A M	Martinez, Vallejo, Calistoga and Santa Rosa	6.15 P M
8.30 A M	Los Angeles Express, Fresno, Bakersfield, Mojave and East and Los Angeles	11.15 A M
8.30 A M	Niles, San Jose, Stockton, Ione, Sacramento, Marysville, Oroville and Red Bluff	5.45 P M
10.30 A M	Haywards and Niles	2.15 P M
12.00 M	Haywards, Niles and San Jose	*3.45 P M
1.00 P M	Sacramento River Steamers	**6.00 A M
3.00 P M	Haywards, Niles and San Jose	9.45 A M
3.30 P M	2d Class for Ogden and East	10.45 P M
4.00 P M	Stockton and *Milton; Vallejo, Calistoga and Santa Rosa	9.45 A M
4.30 P M	Sacramento and Knight's Landing via Davis	10.45 A M
4.30 P M	Niles and Livermore	*8.45 A M
4.30 P M	Niles and San Jose	‡4.15 P M
5.30 P M	Haywards and Niles	7.45 A M
6.00 P M	Sunset Route, Atlantic Express. Santa Barbara, Los Angeles, Deming, El Paso, New Orleans and East	8.45 P M
7.00 P M	Shasta Route Express, Sacramento, Marysville, Redding, Portland, Puget Sound and East	7.45 A M
8.00 P M	Central Atlantic Express, Ogden and East	9.45 A M

SANTA CRUZ DIVISION.

8.00 A M	Hunters train to San Jose	‡7.20 P M
8.15 A M	Newark, Centerville, San Jose, Felton, Boulder Creek and Santa Cruz	5.50 P M
2.15 P M	Centerville, San Jose, Almaden, Felton, Boulder Creek and Santa Cruz	*11.50 A M
4.15 P M	Centerville, San Jose, and Los Gatos	9.50 A M

[C]oast Division (Third and Townsend Sts.)

7.25 A M	San Jose, Almaden and Way Stations	2.30 P M
8.30 A M	San Jose, Gilroy, Tres Pinos; Pajaro, Santa Cruz; Monterey; Pacific Grove, Salinas, San Miguel, Paso Robles, Santa Margarita (San Luis Obispo) and principal Way Stations	6.12 P M
10.30 A M	San Jose and Way Stations	5.02 P M
12.01 P M	Cemetery, Menlo Park and Way Stations	3.36 P M
3.30 P M	San Jose, Tres Pinos, Santa Cruz, Salinas, Monterey, Pacific Grove and principal Way Stations	*10.00 A M
4.20 P M	Menlo Park and Way Station	*7.58 A M
5.30 P M	San Jose and Way Stations	9.03 A M
6.30 P M	Menlo Park and Way Stations	6.35 A M
11.45 P M	Menlo Park and principal Way Stations	†7.28 P M

A M for Morning. P M for Afternoon.
*Sundays excepted. †Saturdays only. ‡Sundays only.
**Mondays excepted. §Saturdays excepted.

OCEANIC STEAMSHIP CO.

[C]arrying United States, Hawaiian and Colonial Mails.

WILL LEAVE THE COMPANY'S WHARF, foot of Mission Street, No. 1,

For Honolulu, Auckland and Sydney,

WITHOUT CHANGE,

The Splendid New 3,000-ton Iron Steamer,
[A]LAMEDA ..... Saturday, April 5, 1890, at 12 M.,
Or immediately on arrival of the English mails.

For Honolulu,

[S]S. AUSTRALIA (3,000 tons), March 28, 1890, at 12 M

☞ For freight or passage, apply at office, 327 Market [S]treet. JOHN D. SPRECKELS & BROS. General Agents.

KILLIP & CO.,

LIVE STOCK AND GENERAL AUCTIONEERS,

22 Montgomery Street, San Francisco

SPECIAL ATTENTION PAID TO SALES OF

High-Bred Horses and Cattle.

At auction and private sale.

Will Sell in All Cities and Counties of the State.

REFERENCES.

HON. C. GREEN, Sacramento.	HON. J. D. CARR Salinas.
J. P. SARGENT, ESQ., Sargents.	HON. JOHN BOGGS Colusa.
HON. L. J. ROSE, Los Angeles.	HON. A. WALRATH Nevada,

J. B. HAGGIN, ESQ., San Francisco.

Represented at Sacramento by Edwin F. Smith Secretary State Agricultural Society.
At San Jose by Messrs. Montgomery & Rea, Real Estate Agents.

Being the oldest established firm in the live-stock business on this Coast, and having conducted the important auction sales in this line for the past fifteen years, amounting to one half a million of dollars, we feel justified in claiming unequaled facilities for disposing of live stock of every description, either at auction or private sale. Our list of correspondents embraces every breeder and dealer of prominence upon the Pacific Coast, thus enabling us to give full publicity to animals placed with us for sale. Private purchases and sales of live stock of all descriptions will be made on commission, and stock shipped with the utmost care. Purchases and sales made of land of every description. We are authorized to refer to the gentlemen whose names are appended.

KILLIP & CO., 22 Montgomery Street

NOTICE.

C. BRUCE LOWE,
Pedigree Stock Agent,
19 Bligh Street,
SYDNEY, New South Wales.

Reference—J. B. HAGGIN, ESQ.

San Francisco and North Pacific Railway.

THE DONAHUE BROAD-GAUGE ROUTE.

COMMENCING SUNDAY, MARCH 17, 1889, AND until further notice, boats and trains will leave from and arrive at the San Francisco Passenger Depot, Market-street Wharf, as follows:

Leave San Francisco. Week Days.	Leave San Francisco. Sundays.	Destination	Arrive San Francisco. Sundays.	Arrive San Francisco. Week Days.
7.40 A M, 3.30 P M, 5.00 P M	8.00 A M, 5.00 P M	Petaluma and Santa Rosa	10.40 A M, 6.10 P M	8.50 A M, 10.30 A M, 6.05 P M
7.40 A M, 3.30 P M	8.00 A M	Fulton, Windsor, Healdsburg, Litton Springs, Cloverdale, and way stations.	6.10 P M	10.30 A M, 6.05 P M
7.40 A M	8.00 A M	Hopland and Ukiah.	6.10 P M	6.05 P M
7.40 A M	8.00 A M	Guerneville	6.10 P M	6.05 P M
7.40 A M, 5.00 P M	8.00 A M	Sonoma and Glen Ellen.	10.40 A M, 6.10 P M	8.50 A M, 6.05 P M
3.30 P M	5.00 P M	Sebastopol	10.40 A M	10.30 A M

Stage connects at Santa Rosa for White Sulphur Springs, and Mark West Springs; at Geyserville for Skaggs Springs, and at Cloverdale for the Geysers; at Hopland for Highland Springs, Kelseyville, Soda Bay, Lakeport and Bartlett Springs, and at Ukiah for Vichy Springs, Saratoga Springs, Blue Lakes, Willits, Cahto, Calpella, Potter Valley, Sherwood Valley and Mendocino City.

EXCURSION TICKETS from Saturdays to Mondays, to Petaluma, $1.50; to Santa Rosa $2.25; to Healdsburg, $3.40; to Litton Springs, $3.60; to Cloverdale, $4.50; to Hopland, $5.70; to Ukiah, $6.75; to Guerneville, $3.75; to Sonoma, $1.50; to Glen Ellen, $1.80.

EXCURSION TICKETS, good for Sundays only, to Petaluma, $1; to Santa Rosa, $1.50; to Healdsburg, $2.25; to Litton Springs, $2.40; to Cloverdale, $3; to Guerneville, $2.50, to Sonoma, $1; to Glen Ellen, $1.20.

From San Francisco for Point Tiburon and San Rafael: Week Days—7.40, 9.20, 11.20, A. M.; 3.30, 5.00, 6.15 P. M. Sundays—8.00, 9.30, 11.00 A. M.; 1.30, 5.00, 6.20 P. M.

To San Francisco from San Rafael: Week Days—6.20, 7.55, 9.30 A. M.; 12.45, 3.40, 5.05 P. M. Sundays—8.10, 9.40 A. M.; 12.15, 3.40, 5.00 P. M.

To San Francisco from Point Tiburon: Week Days—6.50, 8.20, 9.55 A. M.; 1.10, 4.05, 5.30 P. M.; Sundays—8.40, 10.05 A. M.; 12.40, 4.05, 5.30 P. M.

On Saturdays an extra trip will be made from San Francisco to San Rafael, leaving at 1.40 P. M.

H. C. WHITING, General Manager.

PETER J. McGLYNN, Gen. Pass. & Tkt. Agt.

Ticket Offices at Ferry, 222 Montgomery Street and 2 New Montgomery Street.

CHICAGO, MILWAUKEE AND ST. PAUL RAILWAY.

Steam Heated and Electric Lighted Vestibuled Trains between Chicago, St. Paul and Minneapolis.
Electric Lighted and Steam Heated Vestibuled Trains between Chicago, Council Bluffs and Omaha.
Finest Dining Cars in the world.
Free Reclining Chair Cars between Chicago and Omaha.
Fast Mail Line between Chicago, Milwaukee, St. Paul and Minneapolis.
Transcontinental Route between Chicago, Council Bluffs and Omaha, or St. Paul.
Great National Route between Chicago, Kansas City and St. Joseph, Mo.
5,700 miles of road in Illinois, Wisconsin, Minnesota, Iowa, Missouri, South and North Dakota.
Everything First-Class.
First-Class People patronize First-Class Lines.
Ticket Agents everywhere sell Tickets over the Chicago, Milwaukee and St. Paul Railway.

W. T. ALLEN,
Pacific Coast Passenger Agent
Office, No. 138 Montgomery St., San Francisco, Cal.
Under Occidental Hotel

6 DONTS

DON'T own a racehorse.
DON'T be a breeder.
DON'T be a trainer.
DON'T be a jockey.
DON'T bet on the races.
DON'T go to a race track.

WITHOUT

HAVING IN YOUR POCKET ONE OF

Goodwin's
ANNUAL
OFFICIAL TURF GUIDES.

Price, in cloth $2.00
Price, in half morocco 3.00
Price, in half calf 4.00
If sent by mail .... 10 cents extra

SUBSCRIBE TO IT FOR 1890.

It is published semi-monthly during the racing season, and is but **$10 per year.** Address

GOODWIN BROS.,
241 Broadway, New York City

HEALDS

Business College, 24 Post St.
——San Francisco.——
The most popular school on the Coast
P. HEALD, President. C. S. HALEY, Sec'y.
☞ Send for Circulars

FOR STOCK.

COLIC AND GRUBS

I have used Simmons' Liver Regulator in Colic and Grubs with my mules and horses, giving them about half a bottle at a time, and have not lost one that I gave it to. You can recommend it to every one who has stock as the best medicine known for all complaints that horseflesh is heir to.

E. T. TAYLOR, Ag't for Grangers of Ga.

FOR CHICKENS.

In using Simmons' Liver Regulator (Powder) with my chickens for Cholera, I take and mix it with the dough and feed it to them once a day. By this treatment I have never lost a single chicken in the last five years from either Chicken Cholera or Gapes.

T. G. BACON, Edgefield, S. C.

HOG CHOLERA.

A reliable gentleman who raises every year about one hundred head of hogs told me he never lost one from Cholera, although the disease had often appeared among his herd. His remedy is Simmons' Liver Regulator given in drenching—about double that given to a man. I give this information for the benefit of those whose hogs may be attacked with Cholera.—PROF. F. P. HOPGOOD, OXFORD, N. C.

SIMMONS LIVER REGULATOR

is so conveniently given. The Powder mixed with the feed will be eaten by horses, cattle hogs, and chickens readily, while the Liquid (prepared) is easily given as a drench.

—ONLY GENUINE.—

Manufactured by J. H. ZEILIN & CO., Philadelphia, Pa. Price **$1.00.**

DR. FISHERMAN'S

Carbolized  Alkaline

LOTION

Cures after all other Remedies have Failed.

Sprains, Sores, Bruises, Galls, Swellings, Scratches, Thrush, Grease Heels, Curb, Rheumatism. Restoring Weak Knees and Ankles to their original condition. As a wash it insures glossy manes and tails. Valuable as an internal remedy for Coughs, Colic, Congestion or Fever. You really get Half a Gallon of Remedy for $1.00, or Two Gallons for $3.00, after being adulterated as directed.

This Liniment has received the endorsement of some of our best horsemen. Recommended by Jos. Cairn Simpson. See BREEDER AND SPORTSMAN of November 10th, 1888.

LYNDE & HOUGH, Proprietors.
116 California St., S. F.
Or ask your Druggist for it.

HORSE OWNERS!

TRY GOMBAULT'S

CAUSTIC BALSAM.

A Safe, Speedy and Positive Cure for Curb, Splint, Sweeny, Capped Hock, Strained Tendons, Founder, Wind Puffs, all Skin Diseases or Parasites, Thrush, Diphtheria, Pinkeye, all Lameness from Spavin, Ringbone or other Bony Tumors. Removes all Bunches or Blemishes from Horses and Cattle.

Supersedes all Cautery or Firing.
Impossible to Produce any Scar or Blemish.

Every bottle sold is warranted to give satisfaction. Price $1.50 per bottle. Sold by druggists, or sent by express, charges paid, with full directions for its use. Send for descriptive circulars. Address
LAWRENCE, WILLIAMS & CO., Cleveland, O.

BROU'S INJECTION

A PERMANENT CURE in from 3 to 6 days, of the most obstinate cases; guaranteed not to produce Stricture; no sickening doses; and no inconvenience or loss of time. Recommended by physicians and sold by all druggists. J. Ferré, (successor to Brou), Pharmacien, Paris.

For any Kind of a

SORE THROAT

USE

McCLELLAN'S
DIPHTHERIA REMEDY

An Unfailing Cure.
FOR SALE BY ALL DRUGGISTS

VETERINARY.

Dr. Wm. H. Jones, M.R.C.V.S.

Veterinary Surgeon,
(OLYMPIC CLUB STABLES)
503 Sutter Street, San Francisco.
Telephone, No 1404.
Consultations by letter, and cases of URGENT NECESSITY in the interior will receive prompt attention.

Dr. A. E. BUZARD,

VETERINARY SURGEON,
Member of the Royal College of Veterinary Surgeons, London, England. Graduated April 22d, 1870.
All Operations on the Horse Performed Skillfully.
Special attention given to the Diseases of Dogs. Calls to the country promptly attended to. Advice and prescriptions by mail $2. Office and Residence, No. 11 Seventh street, S. F. (opp. Odd Fellows Hall, Telephone No. 3 69.

W. H. WOODRUFF.

Veterinary Dentist,
AT FASHION STABLES,
221 Ellis Street, San Francisco
Improved Instruments, Humane Methods, First-Class Work.

H. E. CARPENTER,

Veterinary Surgeon,
Graduate of Ontario Veterinary College, Toronto, Canada.
RESIDENCE AND VETERINARY INFIRMARY
331 Golden Gate Ave., San Francisco.
Telephone 3069.
☞ OPEN DAY AND NIGHT. ☜
No risk in throwing Horses. Veterinary Operating Table on the premises.

DR. C. MASOERO,

Veterinary Surgeon,
Successor to DR. A. DeTAVEL,
GRADUATE OF ROYAL VETERINARY COLLEGE, TURIN.
OFFICE AND INFIRMARY,
No. 811 HOWARD STREET,
Between Fourth and Fifth. SAN FRANCISCO.
Telephone, No. 457,

R. WATKINS,

Veterinary Dentist,
Of twelve years practice, is now permanently located in San Francisco, and may be found at C. S. Crittendens' Golden Gate Livery and Riding Academy, 24 to 28 Golden Gate Avenue.
Will treat ailments of the horse's mouth, and cure all such. Sidereln Pullers and Tongue Lollers etc.
Satisfaction guaranteed. Orders by mail will receive prompt attention. Examination Free.

E. J. O'ROUKE.

I have the honor to announce to my old patrons and the general public that I may be found at my old stand, where, as heretofore, the

Shoeing of Horses,

whether for the Track, Drive, or for general work, will receive my personal attention.

Telephone 211.

E. J. O'ROUKE,
209 Ellis Street

California Horse Shoe Co's

I have used in my business the Steel and Iron Shoes made by the above Company, and take great pleasure in saying they are the best I have ever used in twenty-two years' practice. I have never seen anything like the STEEL SHOE made by this Company. I can fully recommend them to every practical Horseshoer in the country.
Yours respectfully,
No. 8 Everett Street. JOHN GRACE.

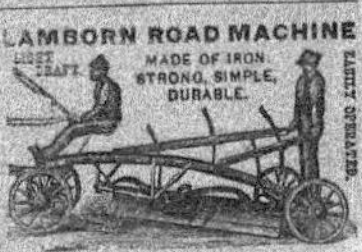

TRUMAN HOOKER & CO.
SAN FRANCISCO, - - CALIFORNIA

At J. A. McKERRON'S,

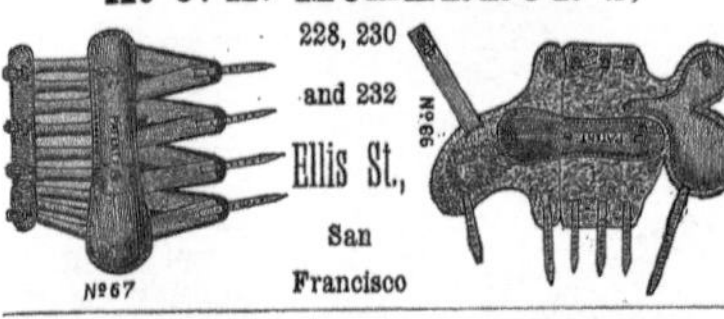

228, 230 and 232 Ellis St., San Francisco

Brothers of the Angle.

OUR NEW EIGHT-STRIP SPLIT BAMBOO is the "King" of all fishing-rods. Chubb's New Catalogue for 189[illegible] is now ready. In addition to a complete list of anglers' supplies, it contains articles from the pens of Dr. James A. Henshall, Petronelle, W. H. Murray, Geo. P. Goff, Norman, Brother Gardner, and others.

These papers are by the best writers on angling subjects, and are very interesting.

Send 25 cents, and receive Catalogue, post-paid. This amount will be deducted from first order (if accompanied with COUPON in book) for one dollar's worth or more of our goods. Address

THOS. H. CHUBB.

The Fishing-Rod Manufacturer,

POST MILLS, VT.

Please mention BREEDER AND SPORTSMAN.

keeps horses healthy, promotes digestion, fattens horses, loosens the hide, assists the appetite, prevents leg swelling, strengthens the kidneys, regulates the bowels and destroys worms. **$7.50 per 100 lbs.** Ask your dealer for it or send to

MANHATTAN FOOD CO., 206 Clay St., S. F.

The PARKER Hammerless Shot Gun.

At the Annual Tournament of 1889, held at Cannes, France, the grand prize, consisting of 2000 Francs and a Valuable Cup. was won by The Parker Hammerless.

The first Parker Hammerless Gun made won the championship of America at Decatur Illinois.

SEND FOR ILLUSTRATED CIRCULAR.

PARKER BROS., Makers,

New York Salesroom, 97 Chambers St., Meriden Conn.

THE IMPROVED NOYES ROAD-CART,

PATENTED JULY 17, 1883, *AND JUNE* 8, 1886.

Some of the Advantages of the Noyes Cart Over All Others.

There is no bar for the rider to climb over in getting in or out. The horse can be hitched eighteen inches nearer than any other road-cart made. You can get in or out with perfect safety—no danger of being thrown into the wheel—a great advantage in breaking colts. THE EASIEST CART FOR ROAD OR TRACK. The only cart that a horse can be speeded to within one second as fast as to a sulky. All our carts are made of the very best materials and are warranted. Manufactured by the NOYES CART COMPANY, Kalamazoo, Mich.

They are indorsed by the following horsemen, all of whom are using them. Ask their opinion of the Noyes Cart: John Splan, who drove Guy a full mile in 2:17¼ and Chanter a half-mile in 1:10¾ to a Noyes Cart, says he would not take $250 for it if he could not get another; W. J. Gordon, Glenville, O.; W. B. Fasig, Cleveland, O.; Dave Muckel, Cleveland, O.; R. J. Mourehead, North East, Pa.; W. J. Chamberlain, Cleveland, O.; H. P. Malone, Bradford, Pa.; S. A. Brown & Co., Kalamazoo Stock Farm; Charles Marvin, Menlo Park, Cal.; W. H. Crawford, Lexington, Ky.; S. L. Caton, who gave Bell Boy a mark at Los Angeles, Cal., of 2:19¼, and drove Chanter a half mile in 1:06¾ and Lowland Girl a full mile in 2:22 to a Noyes Cart; Mike Bowerman, Lexington, Ky.; James Golden, Medford, Mass.; John E. Turner, Philadelphia, Pa.; T. L. Newton, Beaver Dam, Wis.; P. V. Johnston, Marshall, Mich.; W. H. McCarthy, Los Angeles, Cal.; A. W. Dennison, El Dorado, Kan.; P. O. Shank, Cleveland, O.; Charles Barnard, Boston, Mass.; Johnson Bros., Greenville, Mich.; John G. Avery, Buffalo, N. Y.; General R. L. Howard, Buffalo, N. Y.; Howard Conklin, Buffalo, N. Y.; W. D. Ham, Hennepin, Ill.; R. G. Henry, Waterbury, Conn; J. E. Hayer, Newburgh, O.; J. C. Hart, Jefferson, Tex.; A. W. Harbison, Rock Point, Pa.; Carl Hodges, Battle Creek, Mich.; Barney Treacy, Lexington, Ky.; George Forbes, Cleveland, O.; Gifford Dudley, Topeka, Kan.; William and J. E. Thompson Lamont, Pa.; C. P. Emery, Forest City Stock Farm, Cleveland, O.; H. F. Jones, Minneapolis, Minn.; John Forbes, Elyria O.; D. J. Downs Battle Creek, Mich; Frank Caton, Randall Station, O.; Arthur D. Sutton, Ind., Pa.; W. F. Neely, Grand Ridge, Ill.; Walter Clark, owner of Pilot Medium, Battle Creek, Mich.; H. R. Kingman, Battle Creek, Mich.; Dr. Sutton and H. C. Reed, Kalamazoo, Mich.; Budd Doble, Chicago, Ill.

SOLE MANUFACTURERS OF STONE'S PATENT SULKY CASE.

They will more than save their cost in one season, and horsemen campaigning trotters cannot afford to do without them. Would refer to Samuel A. Brown, Kalamazoo Stock Farm, S. L. Caton and W. H. McCarthy. Address

NOYES CART COMPANY, Kalamazoo, Mich.

Office and Factory, Corner Rose and Eleanor streets. R. ARTHUR STONE, Manager.

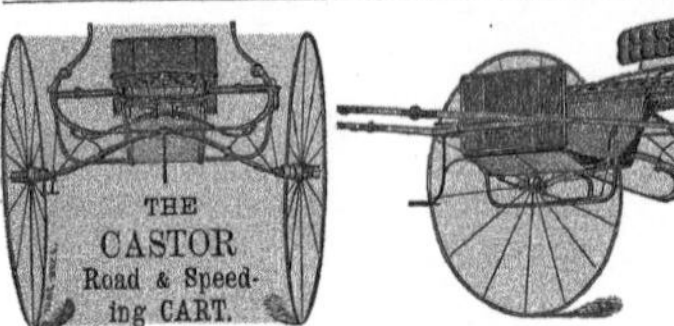

ALWAYS GIVES SATISFACTION.

Combining perfect riding qualities, proportions and balance, with genteel appearance.

No vehicle exhibits a horse to better advantage, and no Cart approaches them for speeding or training purposes.

A stylish vehicle for exercising or pleasure driving, at one-fourth the cost of a carriage. Have none of the horse jockey or objectionable features of other Road Carts.

They are the Leading Cart wherever introduced, and are in use by the most prominent breeders and pleasure drivers everywhere.

Elegant Shifting Top Carts.

Perfectly Balanced Stylish Pole Carts.

For Illustrated Catalogue, with Prices, address,

LEWIS F. CASTOR,

Frankford, Philadelphia, Pa.

JOHN SPLAN, General Agent.

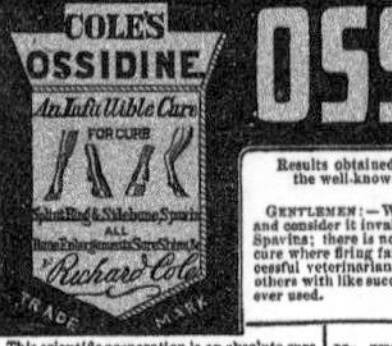

OSSIDINE

Results obtained at the well-known **KALAMAZOO FARM.**

KALAMAZOO, MICH., Sept. 15, 188[illegible].

GENTLEMEN:—We have used **OSSIDINE** for the past two years, and consider it invaluable for Sprung Tendons, Curbs, Ringbone, and Spavins; there is nothing equals it: and for us it effected a permanent cure where firing failed, although performed by one of the most successful veterinarians on the continent. We have recommended it to others with like success, and believe it has more merit than any blister ever used.

Very respectfully yours,

S. A. BROWNE & CO., Prop's.

This scientific preparation is an absolute cure for all bony or callous lumps on horses, and is a more powerful absorbent than "firing," without creating the slightest blemish.

Acknowledged by leading horsemen of the world to be the **ONLY** preparation that will remove a Bone Spavin after it has become ossified.

We have authority also to refer to Mr. JEROME I. CASE, Mr. FRED. GEBHARD, Mr. JOHN PORTER (Trainer to H.R.H. the Prince of Wales).

And hundreds of others from whom we have very flattering testimonials.

One Style Only. $3.00 per Bottle.

A. P. BUSH & CO., 149 Pearl St., BOSTON, MASS., Sole Agents for United States and Canada. *Beware of Imitations.*

SOLD BY C. N. Crittenton, A. R. Van Nest & Co., and C. N. Moseman & Bro., NEW YORK CITY. Morrisson, Plummer & Co., Peter Van Schaack & Sons, CHICAGO, ILL. John D. Park & Son, CINCINNATI, O.; Floyd & Foster, DETROIT, MICH.; F. S. Slosson, CLEVELAND, O.; Meyer Bros. Drug Co., ST. LOUIS, MO.; R. A. Robinson, LOUISVILLE, KY.; H. H. Moore & Sons, STOCKTON, CAL.

Nutwood [illegible] Sire

DAWN 6407

Dam Countess } DAM OF Strathway (2-y-o) 2:26, " trial 2:21; Placida } Morna } Double team Trial 2:2[illegible]

2:18¾; 2:20; 2:19½.

$100 Popular Price for season of 1890. $100

Not having a breeding farm, and being dependent on the public for patronage, I have set the above low price in order to be within the reach of any one desiring to breed.

Good pasturage $3 per month.

For further particulars, address

A. L. WHITNEY, Petaluma.

TWENTY-FOUR PAGES.

Vol. XVI. No. 12.
No. 313 BUSH STREET.

SAN FRANCISCO. SATURDAY, MARCH 22, 1890.

SUBSCRIPTION
FIVE DOLLARS A YEAR.

Santa Rosa Horses.

HARVEY W. PECK.

A friend and myself made a flying trip to Santa Rosa a short time since. Our time was limited, but a slight sketch of what we saw may be of interest to the readers of the BREEDER AND SPORTSMAN.

The first horseman to cross my line of vision was Mr. J. H. Lawrence, Captain Grosse's able trainer, driving the Anteeo stallion Sunset. This horse is 16½ hands high and will weigh 1200 pounds. He is a grand, big horse, smooth, well turned everywhere, full of style, a handy-gaited fellow, with speed enough to beat 2:30 this season. In fact his owner claims for him a trial at Petaluma in 2:33½. I know of no better big horse anywhere than Sunset.

As Mr. Lawrence drove away, Mr. Mart Rollins came up, and we repaired to the stable occupied by Mr. Rufus Murphy's horses, who are in charge of Mr. Rollins. The tidy appearance of the stable and the sleek coats of the horses showed that Mr. Rollins understands his business.

The only colt in the stable that is known to horsemen at large is the three-year-old filly Maud D. She participated in two races last year, winning second money at Santa Rosa and first money at Petaluma, getting a two-year-old record of 2.46½, if I remember correctly. Maud is by Anteeo, her dam being a good little mare by Nutwood. She is a low, long-bodied mare, and strikes the beholder as being "good goods" as soon as seen. She has a conformation built upon lasting principles, and as a "wear and tear" trotter should equal the best. She went a mile in 2:38½ as a two-year-old last fall, and considerable is expected of her the coming season.

Later on I met Mr. W. B. Sanborn, who, in answer to my inquiry, stated that Ned Lock, owned by himself and Rufus Murphy, had wintered nicely. Ned Lock is the first grandson of Nutwood in this State to beat 2:30. I make this statement from memory alone, as I can think of no other grandson of "the old horse" that has entered the list. I am sure there is none in the male line at least. Lock's sire was Antelope, a horse that was brought to Santa Rosa six years ago, and made one season. He was afterwards taken to Oregon, where he made a record this last season of 2:23½. While Antelope was in Santa Rosa, I went out to the track in company with his owner, Mr. Duncan, to see him. I greatly admired him, remarking to Mr. Duncan that I could see no reason why his horse should not be a trotter, with opportunity. He was a highly formed, solidly built horse, with grand muscular development for a young horse, while his disposition was perfect and his intelligence of high order.

Like many another good horse, he did not receive very much patronage. The great mass of people never find out the excellence of a highly bred horse until he is sold and taken away, or dies, and then they silently kick themselves. Antelope has a worthy son in Ned Lock.

We visited the farm of Dr. W. Finlaw next. This place is known as Rosedale, and is situated in the suburbs of Santa Rosa. The Doctor has some highly bred stock, both mares and stallions. The stallions are Daly (Gen. Benton—Electioneer), Laurel Dale (Anteeo—Don Juan), and Kingman (Anteeo—Gen. McClellan), while the best of the brood mares are two full sisters to Alexander Button, a couple of mares by Steinway, and others the breeding of which I do not recall, are worthy representative matrons.

Our next call was upon Mr. McGraw, who is in charge of Mr. De Turk's horses. Everybody knows Mac, a whole souled man and a competent and careful driver.

We looked at the brown stud by Anteeo out of the dam of Alexander Button. This is a good looking little horse and, Mac says, can go some. Mr. E. C. Spear, of St. Helena, Napa Co., has rented the horse of Mr. De Turk, and will make the coming season with him at St. Helena, where the horse should certainly do a good business. We next entered the box of Anti-Coolie. This stallion has always had the reputation of being bad tempered, and hard to manage. He developed no bad symptoms, however, as we entered, and Mac says he is gradually getting over his bad traits. It may be that he will be like his owner's wine—improve with age. Anti-Coolie has always had speed, but he never could be got to "rate" a mile, always wanting to rush off and trot over himself. As a three year old he had a high flight of speed, but his unreliability ruined his prospects. If he gets settled and becomes a good actor it will interest most any trotter of his age to beat him. Mac has confidence that he will make a low record the coming season.

A very handsome filly is the Anteeo—Nutwood. A seal brown, two years old, good size, finely finished, and is threatened with speed. She is entered, I believe, in a couple of stakes.

Several more were brought out until we finally wound up at the stall of the black stallion, Silas Skinner, formerly owned by Mr. McGraw, but now by Mac and Mr. I De Turk. This horse was sired by Alcona Jr. (son of Alcona by Almont) and his dam was Fontana by Strader's Cassius M. Clay. Fontana recently sold at Mrs. Skinner's sale for $4,400. She is the dam of Flora Belle also.

Few horses can outshow Skinner in style and beauty. He has a fine coat of hair, black as a raven's wing, and is a fine feeling and toppy horse. His good qualities are not confined to appearance alone, as men who know say he can go down the line a right merry clip.

From here we drove to the S. P. R. R. depot. Mr. George A. Stone, the agent for the Southern Pacific, is the owner of the horse Illustrious. This horse was bred by Wm. T. Withers, of Kentucky. He was sired by Happy Medium; his first dam by Strader's Clay, second dam by Almont, third dam by Alexander's Abdallah, fourth dam the dam of Lula 2:15. He is 15½ hands and weighs 1010 pounds. He is a very kind, gentle horse, and I liked his appearance very much. He is after the blocky order, and if breeding counts for much, will make a record that his owner will be proud of. I saw a little filly by him, running loose in a grass lot, and she can certainly move fast. Her dam, Mr. Stone informed me, was Irene, (the dam of Florence R. 2:26½) by Erwin Davis.

Our last call was upon Mr. Geo. Guerne, who is well known as a pleasant gentleman and hospitable host. Mr. Guerne has an elegant home in Santa Rosa and is always glad to see his friends.

In the stables the first horse viewed was the full brother to Alfred G. This colt is of a heavier mould than his noted brother, having wonderful substance everywhere. He is in the stud this season.

Mr. Guerne's bay mare Eva G. is a fine specimen of the well bred trotter. She is a long bodied, well turned, racy looking mare, with a splendid neck and head, while the expression of her eyes and the constant motion of the ears betoken a high degree of courage. She is by Anteeo, her dam being by Nutwood. If she fails to make a trotter she will have to meet with accident that will unfit her for training. Several colts were shown, and then the little brown horse Philosopher was brought out. This horse was foaled in 1886, stands about 15 hands high and weighs about 975 pounds. He was brought from Kentuckey by J. W. Knox about 18 months ago. He was bred by Mr. T. E. Simmons of Wilkes Lodge, Lexington, Ky. His pedigree is as follows: Sired by Pilot Wilkes (son of Geo. Wilkes and Grace by Pilot Jr.) dam Bella by Geo. Wilkes: 2nd dam by Bell Morgan, sire of Lady Tarpin 2:23. He is a horse of great length, considering his height. He is double gaited and can show lots of speed at a pace. As will be noticed he is very strongly inbred, and he represents very valuable strains of blood. He is a horse of singularly quiet disposition for a stallion; in truth, I have never seen his equal in that respect. I am compelled to say that many men in Sonoma county have attempted, without knowing anything whatever of the facts of the case, to do this little horse, his owner and the gentlemen who have had him in charge, an injustice. Several men have told me individually, that his breeding was not as represented. When I pinned them down to the facts, they knew less about heaven. Those kind of people remind me of a dog that comes bouncing out of a door yard and barks himself weak at the rushing railway trains. He really accomplishes nothing, but do you suppose you could convince his cannie brain that he was not a terror to the numerous trains at which he barks? Just so with some people; They look at things of which they know nothing, just as long as the Lord in his inscrutible providence prolongs their breath, and proudly imagine that the voice of their vantings accomplishes a purpose in the world. The fact that they display their ignorance whenever they open their mouths is not realized by them, and thus the fine edge of their wisdom is never dull. I append Mr. Simmons note, answering my own in which I give the pedigree given by Mr. Knox,

LEXINGTON, KY. Feby., 7th 1890.

DEAR SIR:—The breeding of Philosopher is as stated in your note. Yours truly, L. E. SIMMONS.

I regret that time would not permit me to see several other gentlemen who are interested in the horse business, but the train waits for no man. Redwood is in Oakland, and Alfred G. in Kentucky. Santa Rosa horsemen are proud of these young horses, and justly so, for if ever two young horses acquired fast records under more unfavorable circumstances than these stallions, I am unaware of the fact. That they both will lower their present records is beyond doubt.

The race track question is being discussed vigorously. It would seem a great pity to have the Santa Rosa Track close its gates. Even if no Fair was given, the track itself, as a training ground, is of great value to many of the residents, and of considerable value indirectly to the general public. I certainly hope that it may be reserved from utter oblivion.

Our Australian Letter.

EDITOR BREEDER AND SPORTSMAN:—It will be a matter of news to the many who have visited Australia from Yankee land to learn that the Hon. James White is about to retire from the track. He has been one of the most successful that has ever appeared on this great continent, as the well known colors "blue and white" have been carried to many a victory.

The announcement that his racing stable was to be sold in conjunction with a liberal draft of yearlings and two year olds from his mammouth breeding farm has caused a ripple to appear over the somewhat dull waters of the running turf here. During the many years that Mr. White has been connected with the turf he has placed to his credit 11 Derbies, 8 Legers, 3 Champions, 3 Maribyrnong Plates, 3 V. R. C. Oaks, 3 Australian Cups, 3 Metropolitans, 2 Melbourne Cups, 4 Ascot Vale Stakes, 1 Newmarket handicap and 1 Sydney cup; truly, a marvellous record for any one man, and something of which he may well feel proud. It was originally intended that Mr. White would leave for England so as to be present when the English Derby was run, he having, as your readers will know, two of his Australian bred colts entered for that classic event, but owing to bad health his trip has been postponed for the present, so he will not have the satisfaction of seeing his entries start.

His great sale will take place on Friday, April 11th, and it seems a pity that information had not been sent to the United States sooner, for beyond a doubt there are many of your large breeders who would have sent representatives or commissions here for the purpose of trying to get some of his royally bred horses. Of the entire lot which he has in training at present, but one will be reserved, and that is our great champion Abercorn. Some of the youngsters will include the get of Chester, Martini-Henry and Phil Athol. [Our Australian correspondent may be somewhat surprised when he finds the Hon. T. B. Merry on the grounds waiting to nod his head for any of those offered for sale that may suit his fancy.—Ed. Breeder and Sportsman.]

I am sorry to have to chronicle the death of one who is well known to all visiting Americans. I refer to Hon. Andrew Town, owner of the Hobartville stud. For some years his colors were prominent on the turf, but of late he has made a world wide reputation for himself in the Judge's box, he being always seen at our important race meetings, and to his credit be it said his decisions were never questioned. He was the owner of the well known American trotting stallion Childe Harold, whose get in the 1889 sales brought such large sums; although I am sorry to say that at the sales lately held the trotting stock brought but very low figures, averaging only a little more than $250. Although it was generally known that Mr. Town was laid up with illness at his private residence at Lady Robinson's Beach, it was a great surprise to hear of his demise, which occured on Monday, February 10th. Typhoid fever was the cause of his death. Mr. Towne was well known and highly respected throughout all the Australian colonies, and especially in Windsor, where he was best known.

It is only occasionally that we hear of a "welcher" in the colonies, but one Wm. Brown was recently brought before the magistrate at Williamstown, Victoria, being charged with having levanted after losing a wager on one of the local races there. On Brown's being asked to plead, he said guilty, and the Magistrate gave him three months with hard labor.

It seems to be the proper thing nowadays to send horses to England, owners probably being influenced by the success of Ringmaster in the old country. The latest of our local celebrities to leave is Chicago, a son of the Drummer and Corisande, who has proven himself a Caulfield Cup winner as well as being victor in other important races; while he can not be compared with Carbine and Abercorn, still he is a good all-round performer, and if his legs will only stand preparation he should make a name for himself on the other side; his underpinnings have already given his trainer considerable trouble, and it was only as late as last New Year's day when he pulled up lame after running in the Bagot Handicap. Should he stand conditioning, Mr. Saville, into whose hands he goes on arrival in England, will probably have a good bread-winner. The Hon. Mr. White will also very soon ship to England the colts Wentworth and Nepean as well as the filly Mons. Meg. As Mr. White has made up his mind to go to England, that is probably the reason why he has determined to rid himself of the horses already in training.

Mr. C. Bruce Lowe of Sydney has received a commission from one of your Californian breeders to procure for him a first-class stallion, and it goes without saying, if the animal required is not up to all the expectations Mr. Lowe will have nothing to do with him, he being one of the most conscientious agents we have in New South Wales. If there are any others in your State who wish to improve their stock by importing from our shores, they cannot do better than to leave their business in the hands of Mr. Lowe.

The weather here has been very warm for this season of the year, and the attendance at many of the smaller race meetings has suffered considerably in consequence.

Cheap English Horses.

Some very interesting particulars, anent prices paid for and doings of horses "in the past" appear in the Bird of Freedom. It states that Octavian was purchased for £10 as afoal, and afterwards won the St. Leger; he became the sire of Octavians, who, in turn, was the dam of the great Crucifix. Mother and daughter were purchased for £60, and after the latter's brief but brilliant career on the turf—winning twelve races in as many months—she bred Surplice, winner of a Derby and St. Leger. Venison was one of the nailing good horses of the "thirties," who, costing but £100, went, as a three-year-old, from one racecourse to another, and won eleven races between Epsom and Doncaster, at the latter place defeating Mundig, the Derby winner of the previous year. Miss Ellis cost £40, and won the Goodwood Stakes and Cup the same year (1845), landing for her owner, the famous Lord George Bentinck, a tolerable percentage on outlay. The Hero, winner of two Ascot Cups, a Doncaster Cup, a Goodwood Cup, and every kind of long-distance race, besides defeating all the best animals then running, and Sweetmeat, one of the best horses of his day, for whom 4,000 guineas was subsequently refused cost the first owner, with his dam, £30, the second £20! Van Tromp, at 300 guineas, and his stable-companion, the Flying Dutchman, at 1,000 guineas, won between them two St. Legers and a Derby (Van Tromp ought also to have won the Derby), besides an Ascot Cup each and all sorts of other races. Voltigeur was sent to Doncaster as a yearling, and no one would look at him, and he was refused by the late Mr. Jacques of Elsby Abbey at £100, only being purchased at last, after an extraordinary trial (three, in fact), by the late Lord Zetland for £1,500 and contingencies. He won the Derby and St. Leger, and his match with the Flying Dutchman is a historical event. He was a grandson of Blacklock, and sixth in descent from Eclipse; he is also the grandson of St. Simon. Stockwell won the St. Leger, but his fame rests upon his marvelous career at the stud. He was foaled at Mr. Theobald's paddocks at Stockwell and sold to Lord Exeter as a yearling for £180. Six of his get won the St. Leger, three the Derby, four the Two Thousand, and one the Oaks. Indeed he is one of the chief landmarks in the Stud-Book, the winnings of his stock in a single year having reached over £61,000, and without the colossal prizes which so assist the totals of our present racehorses and sires. Kettledrum and Musjid cost, as yearlings, 400 guineas each and Thormanby and Virago 350 each; the three colts all won the Derby, while the filly turned out simply the best mare the world has ever seen. Fisherman was one of the stoutest horses ever foaled, and he, Weathergage, and old Tom Parr, their owner, were a trio hard to beat, and such as are seldom now met with. Weathergage cost £63, sold, or rather given away, out of the Bedford Stable, by the order of that most prejudiced of men, the late Admiral Rous. The horse landed two coups, in the Goodwood Stakes and Cesarewitch, at the old "list" day prices, which meant a fortune, and was sold for a big sum afterwards. Our contemporary does not refer to horses purchased in recent years for a trifling sum. Bendigo, for instance, fetched £70 as a yearling, and afterwards had a brilliant career in England.

A young Western horse which had evidently been pampered up and dragged for sale was completely let down and suffering from much fever. Finding it necessary to employ an active purge, I, at the request of the owner, used Simmon's Liver Regulator, giving one pint doses twelve hours apart, and as soon as he could eat, giving it in powder form in bran. In one week he had fully recovered.—Geo. W. Rodfong. V. S. Germantown, Pa.

Our Tennessee Letter.

Gallatin, Tenn., March 12, 1890.

Editor Breeder and Sportsman:—The light snows of last week were followed by much warmer weather in Tennessee. The rapidly melting snow and ice caused an over abundancy of mud and slush and training has been considerably delayed in both this State and Kentucky. In Kentucky the bitter pangs of real winter have been more severely felt than in Tennessee, and the horses in training in that State are several weeks behind those wintered in Tennessee. After the snow, which was general throughout this State, came rain in torrents, with no indications of its stopping for several days yet. The owners of spring horses are getting a little chary over the prospects of being able to bring their horses to the post fit for their earlier engagements.

The horses in quarters at Memphis are much earlier than those at Nashville, and, with one exception, seem to far outclass the stake animals at the latter place. The two-year-olds at Memphis are, or have been doing, four furlongs near :50 and many of them are stepping quarters in :24, with weight up. The elder division are not so forward as the youngsters, and a mile in 1:48 is about the way the more advanced of them are going. The Memphians have pinned their faith to old Terra Cotta, and many of them believe him to have a cinch on the more prominent stake events in which he is engaged. George Hankin's faith in the hero of other years, seems to strengthen as the old horse grows older. He now has Jacobin, Little Minch and Terra Cotta at Memphis, and all are said to be in fine fettle These three horses deserve a rest, not only for a few months, but for the remainder of their days. We have seen Jacobin when he could do his miles in 1:41, and Little Minch and Terra Cotta have at times seemed invincible. The Hankins, Leigh and Kiley combination will probably be one of the strongest stables in the West this season, and before the curtains have been drawn over the racing drama of 1890, it should have a lion's share of the Western Stakes.

The Cassidy string at Memphis looks to be one of the most formidable stables of its size in the West, and a goodly number of races are likely to be captured by a representative of the cherry and black stripes of the St. Louis turfman. In the three-year-old division Kitty Cheatham and Blue Blazes look to be about the best, and are suggestive of good stake winners.

Long Fish, one of the grandest looking horses that ever wore plates, and Clara C, both of which have a "dickey" leg, will be the main reliances of the stable in the older classes. A pretty fair string of two-year-olds will doubtless make the stable successful the coming season. Other horses of the stable should pay for their winter oats, and render a considerable balance on the right side of the ledger. Sir Abner by imported Uhlan, dam Barbary, is the tip of the two-year-old lot, and it is said he has the making of a race horse in him, As a yearling Sir Abner was a very ordinay looking youngster, but, as an old turfman remarked to me a few days since, "They go in all shapes." The Cassidy string field of operation will be confined to the West.

The present bad weather has almost suspended training at Nashville, but now and then a fast two-year-old trial serves to break the monotony. In the younger division they say that the Wandering Jew by Kosciusko is the best one upon the course. The Wandering Jew is owned by J. G. Greener, and is in the charge of Major Buck Elliott of Billy Gilmore fame. His sire, Kosciusko, was sired by Kyrle Daly, out of Colossa, dam of Bella B, Inspector B and Getaway. As a 3-year-old Kosciusko was quite a good horse, and he ran that good mare Modesty to a head for the American Derby, after one of the most hotly contested and exciting finishes ever witnessed upon any course. After the Derby Kosciusko defeated Modesty very easily. In the Derby it took all of a great jockey's persuasive powers and great skill to land the mare a winner by a head in front of the blaze-faced son of the Irish Kyrle Daly.

Charles Reed, proprietor of Fair View Farm, is at home this week from the city of Gath. The Fairview Stable is in winter quarters at Westchester. The horses of the Fairview turfman were, we might say, a sore disappointment last season, and it cannot be said that Mr. Reed's return to racing was signalized by any great amount of success. Timothy, their crack two-year-old, only won one bracket during the season, and then only a small purse at the Nashville spring meeting. I believe he was troubled with a sore mouth all the season, and was never able to show how good a colt he was. Violante and Rebecca captured several purses for the stable, and Peterborough succeeded in winning the Good-Bye stakes at Coney Island, which was the only stake victory for the stable during the entire year. This season, however, the stable has quite a string of good-looking two-year-olds, and a more successful season for the Fairview Stable than was last may be expected.

Now it seems as if the Birmingham (Ala.) Jockey Club has again fallen through. The management has failed to arrange a programme, which does not look favorable towards a spring meeting. Last year they expected to give a meeting, but owing to a failure of the contractors in not having the stables, grand stand, etc. completed, the inaugural meeting was postponed until last fall. The Birmingham people do not take very kindly to horse racing, and their taste for such will have to be cultivated as was the trotting horse interest in Tennessee. A presiding judge at the meeting this last year tells me that thousands of the inhabitants of the Magic City knew nothing of the race meeting being held there until the meeting had been inaugurated for several days. This however, did not encourage the management to any great extent, and it is likely they had to go down in their pockets for enough funds to make both ends meet.

Addie Belle, 2:22½, pacing, who was campaigned last season by Frank Jenkins, has been returned to her owner at this place. I think this is one of the most remarkable mares Tennessee has yet produced and had she received the attention that is necessary to produce extreme speed, she would no doubt have been the equal of Mattie Hunter, and others of that class. When a 3-year-old I saw her pace over the Gallatin track in 2:24¼ in the second heat of a winning race, at that time the track was very slow, and had it been prepared for the race, she would have easily paced in 2:18. Until she was 3-years-old no one ever suspected that she had any speed, but she showed a remarkable gait while working to a wagon upon the farm. She is by Archie, an obscure saddle stallion that stood here many years ago, who also sired W. R. W. 2:22¼. Addie Belle has repeatedly paced halves in 1:05 with but little training. She has a head of her own, and if she can ever be induced to pace a few heats at her best, she will make the record tremble.

Bookmakers are generally a very sharp and shrewd set of people, but that bookmaker who thinks he can violate the law under the nose of Judge Riddley of Nashville only has to try it once to be convinced that the judge means business in regard to the recent amendment of the pool room law by the Tennessee Legislature. Johnny Payne, an enterprising and successful bookmaker of Louisville came down from that city to Nashville and established a branch agency of the Climax Pool Room of the former city. He would not lay the odds himself, but would telegraph all bets to his Louisville house, and they would telegraph results after each race. In this manner Payne hoped to avoid the strong arm of the law, but Judge Riddley instructed his grand jury to attend to the matter and to return indictments against all parties concerned. Some one gave Payne a friendly tip, and he vamoosed. The Nashville authorities seem determined to break up pool rooms in that city, and the actions of the last legislature are favored by all thorough horsemen.

Hickman Weakley, of Murfreesboro, Rutherford County, has purchased for $1,500 the stallion Cuthbert by Cuyler, dam Marcie S. He is a well bred horse and will prove a valuable addition to the rapidly increasing development of the harness horse in that country.

The Tennessee Pacing Horse Breeders' Association met in the Commercial Club rooms at Nashville Wednesday morning. Mr. Frank Buford, the president, presiding over the meeting, and in a few words explained that the meeting was the annual one and the most important business was the consideration of a standard, formulated by the Directors, who were appointed at the first meeting. In formulating the rules of registration the phraseology of the trotting horse register was closely followed, and in but few instances do they differ.

In Kentucky over a hundred broodmares have slipped their foals this spring. The cause of this cannot be accounted for unless it has been the mild winter up to March 1st, which caused the grass to be very forward and sappy for the early season of the year. At the Coldstream stud, imported Queen Maud died in foaling to Springbok, and The Niece by Alarm slipped a foal to Springbok. Kingston Stud's imported Underernst, by Brown Bread, slipped a foal to Longfellow, and many other breeding establishments have suffered by this strange freak of nature. Had Kentucky, Tennessee and California thoroughbred breeding farms shared the same fate together, the average prices of yearlings in 1891 would be considerably higher. There will be enough—even had one third as many more mares slipped their foals—to supply the demand to keep up racing until another crop could be produced.

Yours,

Kennesaw.

High Prices! High Averages! Happy Breeders!

Horses Whose Get Sell for Large Amounts.—Guy Wilkes First, Director Second, Sidney Third—Nearly Distanced.—Valensin Displeased.

Such I found to be the general topic of conversation upon my return home yesterday. Will you allow me to make a short statement in my own behalf, and a little longer one (based on figures) in behalf of Sidney? Yes? Thanks.

Well, I am satisfied. My good stock sold fairly well, my poor stock cheap, as it should have. Poor stock is worthless. Sidney's get were very much sought after, therefore I am pleased. Was it sought after, though? some will say who saw the average. Let us see. Yearlings sell lower than two year olds and upwards. As Sidney had ten of his in the sale, Guy Wilkes one, and Director two, it made my average lower. I shall discard the yearlings for all three of these horses, and then may be we can place them differently. Fair for one fair for all.

Director's Get.		Sidney's Get.	
Erect, 2 yrs	$5000 00	Goldleaf, 5 yrs	$8000 00
Saccharine, 2 yrs	4600 00	Thistle, 3 yrs	4000 00
Lady Chittenden	[illegible] 00	Fleet, 3 years	8000 00
Ada H., 4 yrs	2600 00	Countess, 2 yrs	975 00
Jet, 4 yrs	2550 00	Bonton D'or, 4 yrs	2000 00
Pleasanton, 2 yrs	2500 00	Tobasco, 3 yrs	800 00
Patti, 4 yrs	1800 10	Lassie, 2 yrs	650 00
Miss J. I. C., 2 yrs	1000 00	Thought	600 00
Highland Belle, 5 yrs	1050 00	Broken Shoulder filly	110 00
Grecian Bend, 4 yrs	3200 00		
Grand total	$26,725 00	Grand total	$25,135 00
Average	2672 50	Average	2,792 55

Fleet was sold just after the sale, providing the swelling in her ankle went down, and I have just received a telegram that it is all right.

Guy Wilkes' Get.

Laura Corbett, 5 yrs., being in foal by Stamboul	$6,050 00
Minnie Corbett, 4 yrs., being in foal by Stamboul	1,500 00
Zuraya, 4 yrs., with stallion colt at foot by Stamboul	13,100 00
Total	$20,650 00
Average	6,883 33⅓
Lady Guy, 3 yrs	$2,600 00
Guy's Sunol, 2 yrs	1,325 00
Miss Guy, 2 yrs	525 00
Total	$4,450 00
Average	1,483 33⅓

When it is taken into consideration that three of Guy Wilkes' daughters *heavy in foal to Stamboul* or with Stamboul colt, brought $20,650 or an average of $6,883.33, while three *not* bred brought $4,450 or an average of $1,483.33, it will be conceded that the buyer certainly gave as much for the prospective Stamboul colt, or the colt at the dam's foot, as they did for the dams themselves. None of Director's, nor of Sidney's daughters had been bred or had colts that I know of—certainly none of Sidney's. Should Guy Wilkes get all the credit for the high prices paid for three of his daughters when those not bred brought so much less? Should the average of the three stallions be looked at equally under such different circumstances?

Director, 10 head $26,725, an average of $2,672 50.

Sidney, 8 head $25,025, an average of $3,128.12½.

Guy Wilkes, 3 head in foal to Stamboul $20,650, an average of $6 883.33⅓.

Guy Wilkes, 3 head not in foal, $4,450, an average of $1,483 33⅓.

Let any fair-minded man decide.

I trust Messrs. Corbitt and Salisbury will not see anything personal in this statement. I have great admiration for their stock, but on account of the distorted reports of the sale I owed to mine a word of defense.

Yours very truly, G. Valensin.

Alterations and Additions to the Rules of the National Trotting Association, Passed at the Biennial Congress, Feb. 12, at Buffalo, N. Y.

Rule 1. After Section 1, two new sections will read as follows:

Sec. 2. All owners entering horses in any of the stake or purse races of any member of this association, and all drivers in such races shall be required to submit themselves to the jurisdiction of the National Trotting Association. Any such owner or driver who fails or refuses so to submit himself to said jurisdiction and abide by its judgment and rulings, or those of any member thereof, shall not be entitled to or receive the protection of this association, or of its rules, nor shall such owner or driver be permitted to start or drive any horse upon the track of any member. All members shall be required to enforce this rule under a penalty of not less than $100, or by suspension or expulsion.

Sec. 3. It shall be the duty of each member to report to this association all material violations of the rules that may come to its knowledge within one year after such violation occurred; and it shall be the duty of the Board of Review to investigate all material violations of the rules coming to its knowledge from any source, and to adjudge the punishment prescribed by the rules for such offense.

Rule 2. In Section 2, after the word "telegram" is added "as well as the written entry." The effect of this amendment is that the telegram and the written entry must be exact copies.

Rule 3. In Sec. 3, after the word "conditions" the section will now read as follows: "And any nominator who is allowed privileges not in accordance with the published conditions of the race, or which are in conflict with these rules, shall be debarred from winning any portion of the purse; and upon sufficient proof of the fact, he shall refund the amount, if any, awarded him, and it shall be awarded to the remaining horses entitled thereto. And the said nominator and the Secretary or other persons who allowed such privileges, shall be deemed to have been parties to a fraud, and be punished by fine, suspension or expulsion, according to the judgment of the Board of Review."

Rule 6. In Sec. 4, the word "may" is substituted for "shall" in the sentence which imposes a fine of $100. This makes the punishment optional with the Board.

Rule 7. In Sec. 3, after the word "identity" there has been added "and eligibility." In future, in case of protest, the identity of the horse must not only be proved; he must also be proved eligible. In the same section the date "twenty-one days allowed for identification" is altered to "thirty days." In Sec. 4 of the same rule, after the word "association" there is added the sentence "or any party competing in the race." This addition gives authority to such parties, as well as the officers of the association, to call for proofs of identity and eligibility.

Rule 8. In Section 1 a most important addition has been made, which reads as follows: "But nothing in this restriction shall be construed to prohibit a member from opening a stake or purse race with a condition that a nominator therein may start two or more of his entries." The old rule still remains that an owner can only start one horse in a race, but the above addition gives associations the privilege of opening special purses or stakes with wider conditions.

Rule 15. In Sec. 1 the opening sentence has been altered to read: "A reward of $50 may, in the discretion of the Board of Review, be paid," etc. The old section read "Will be paid." The giving of the reward is now optional with the Board.

In Sec. 3 of the same rule the word "conclusive" before evidence is altered to "satisfactory," and the time for returning the premium or for furnishing information to sustain a protest is altered from "three weeks" to "thirty days." In Secs. 7 and 8 the same alterations occur as to time.

Rule 18. In Sec. 1, after the word "meeting," these words are interpolated, "except as to an unfinished race." The effect of this amendment will enable a member to trot out an unfinished race on the week following its meeting.

Rule 26. A new section has been added, which reads as follows: Sec. 2. The judges shall have power to examine on oath all parties connected with a race, as to any wrong or complaint made bringing in question the conduct of the same.

Rule 28. In Sec. 5 after the word "improperly" there is now inserted "at any time during the conduct of a race." This does not really extend the meaning of the rule; it simply makes it more definite. At the end of this section the following important addition is made: "The judges may waive distance, except for fouls as to any horse for which they have substituted a rider or driver." A new section is also added to the rule, as follows: "Sec. 6. Any driver who is intoxicated or refuses to comply with the directions of the judges, or who is reckless in his conduct, and endangers the safety of horses or their drivers in the race, may be removed and another driver substituted at any time during the race, and the offending driver may be fined, suspended, or expelled; and the substitued driver shall be compensated as provided in Sec. 5 of this rule."

Rule 29.—In Section 6, with regard to dead heats, the sentence will now read: "When two or more horses shall make a dead heat the remaining horses shall start for the succeeding heat in the same positions with reference to the pole that they occupied at the finish of the dead heat. Those making a dead heat shall be placed for the succeeding heat by allotment by the judges."

In Section 10 that part of which once read "He shall not change from the right to the left, or from the inner to the outer side of the track," will now read "he shall not change either to the right or left." This refers to the leading horse. The following important addition is made to this section:—

"If in the opinion of the judges the horse coming to the wire first was enabled to do so because of the help rendered him by the offending horse, rider or driver, the judges may declare such heat 'no heat,' and have the heat trotted over (after the customary time between heats). In case the offence occurred during a deciding heat between the leading horse and the one interfered with, *and the horse interfered with finished second*, then only the first and second horses shall be started in the next heat, otherwise all shall be started except those disqualified under the rules. If in the opinion of the judges an arrangement or collusion existed between the drivers of the horses helping and the one helped, then both horses and drivers shall be punished as hereinafter provided in Section 11."

Rule 30. In Sec. 3 there is a vital addition, which very much simplifies a judge's duties. It reads thus: "A horse breaking four times in a heat shall be regarded as repeatedly breaking, but nothing herein shall be construed into permitting a horse to make four or less number of breaks without being liable to the penalties prescribed. If in the opinion of the judges a driver, allows his horse to make repeated breaks without being liable to the penalties prescribed. If in the opinion of the judges a driver allows his horse to make repeated breaks for the purpose of fraudulently losing a heat he shall be liable to the penalties elsewhere provided for frauds and fouls."

Rule 31. In Sec. 1 the latter part of the section, which reads as follows, is stricken out: "And where ten or more horses shall start in a race every horse not distanced shall have the right to compete until the race is completed—subject however, to all other penalties in these rules." This erasure will send all horses to the barn who have not won a heat in five, irrespective of the number which start.

Rule 32. Sec. 2 will now read: "When two or more horses have each won two heats, and there shall have occurred between them a dead heat in any part of the race, they alone shall start in the next heat."

Rule 42. Sec. 1 has been altered to read: "Any contest for purse, premium, stake or wager, or involving admission fee, on any course, and in the presence of judges appointed in accordance with Rule 25, shall constitute a public race." The alteration simply emphasizes the fact that the judges must be regularly appointed.

Rule 44. Sec. I has the following addition: "but time made to wagon shall be a record or bar, as the case may be, in races of every character.

Rule 49. Sec. I will now read: "All persons who shall have been fined under these rules, unless they pay the fines in full on the day when imposed, or when demanded, shall be suspended until they are so paid and deposited with the Treasurer of the National Trotting Association."

The new part of the Rule consists of the words "or when demanded."

Rule 62 is a new one and reads as follows:

Rule 62. Sec. I. Whenever reasonable grounds exist for a belief that any person can give material evidence that would aid in the detection or exposure of any fraud or wrong on the trotting turf, in a case under investigation, or pending before the Board of Review, or before any District Board, the President or Secretary may require such person to testify by deposition or affidavit, or in person before such Board, but without cost to the witness for necessary expenses. Any person required to testify as aforesaid, who shall fail or refuse to comply, may after due notice be suspended by the President until the requirement is complied with, or until relieved by the President or by the Board of Review."

Third Meeting of the Arlington Jockey Club.

The races of March 8th were postponed on account of the rain and run off Tuesday, March 11th. Tuesday was a most delightful day, and all who are fond of equine sports were present to witness the best races of the Arlington Jockey Club. The track was heavy, but in better condition than could be expected. There were many handsome turnouts on the track and much interest was manifested in the contests. The "short end" boys were jubilant, for they made money, and the talent lost heavily. The pool selling was very animated. In the first event the following horses started:

Montecito Stakes; three-eighths of a mile handicap; purse $30.

C. D. Diver entered br g Bob, and ridden by Diver; weight, 160 pounds.

Crawford entered b g Joe Dandy, and ridden by Brown; weight, 150 pounds.

J. Daniels entered ch g Ed. S, and ridden by Seth Loomis; weight, 160 pounds.

Duryea entered ch g Grimbo, and ridden by Duryea; weight, 160 pounds.

The pools in this event sold rapidly, Grimbo selling for $10, Bob $4 and the field $3. The four horses were given the word to go to a most excellent start. Grimbo took the lead immediately, closely followed by Ed. S. The latter horse made a good effort for the race, but Grimbo had too much speed. Grimbo won easily, Edward S. second, Bob third. Time, 0:40.

The second event was a surprise to all the knowing ones. The following horses started:—

Amateur Stakes, 28 class; one-fourth mile dash. Purse $30.

C. D. Diver entered f g McGinty; ridden by Diver.

J. Ballard entered g m Nellie Grey; ridden by F. Stoddard.

P. Lorillard; Jr., entered br m Dudu; ridden by Smith.

R. H. Stevens entered c m She; ridden by Menchaca.

A. Boeseke entered b m Mary; ridden by Boeseke.

Nellie Grey hails from Carpenteria in this county, and as she beat in Ventura three years ago the famous Dotty Dimple a half mile in :48½ the boys thought that Nellie Grey could not be downed. It was rumored that she could run a quarter in :24. In the pools Nellie Grey sold for $10, She for $3; and the field for $4. It was the liveliest betting race of the day. A great many outside bets were made. Two were that Nellie Grey would win the race. All the horses behaved so well at the start that they were soon dispatched to a splendid start. Nellie Grey was in the lead till she reached the eighth pole. She was then passed by McGinty and Mary. McGinty won as he pleased, Mary second, Nellie Grey third. Time :26. The boys who had bought the field were rich, and for the next race they "plunged."

In the third event were entered the following horses:—

Gaviota Stakes. One half mile handicap. Purse $40.

Mrs. Schaub entered s g Pete, ridden by McGuill, 150 lbs.

Duryea entered c g Lightfoot, ridden by Brown, 140 lbs.

Duryea entered c g Grimbo, ridden by Duryea, 175 lbs.

E. R. Den entered b g Mark B., ridden by Menchaca, 145 lbs.

S. Loomis entered br g Tom, ridden by Stoddard, 150 lbs.

J. Daniels entered c g Ed. S., ridden by Seth Loomis, 150 lbs.

Grimbo was a hot favorite at $10, Tom second choice at $4, and the field for $3. Many of the field buyers argued that Grimbo was fast, but that 175 lbs. was too much weight for him. Many pools were sold in this race, the admirers of Grimbo feeling certain of success. The horse gave trouble at the starting post, but all the spectators were so delighted by the beautiful afternoon that the time seemed short. When the horses were sent away they were all in a bunch. Grimbo immediately took the lead and ran easy for the first quarter, but at the eighth pole he was a beaten horse. His rider then let up on him. Mark B. won easily, Ed S. second, Pete third, and Grimbo fourth. Again the field boys made money. The time for the race was :54.

The fourth event was the drawing card of the afternoon. Free-for-all Stakes, purse $60, one-half mile, Free-for-all.

G. W. Leland entered g f Lucy, ridden by Clark.

J. S. Bell entered b g Sid Law, ridden by Pico.

A. Boeseke entered by ch m Maid, ridden by Appleton.

Sid Law and Maid are by Robbery Boy and Lucy by Accident. It was rumored in the track that Sid Law could run a half in :48¼. The pools sold: Sid Law $10, field $4. Mr. Leland had faith in the grey filly by his stallion Accident by Monday, dam Flora by Norfolk. The filly looked worn out by hard work. In the scoring she showed her chances, for the race were ten to one. She could not even break with the other two. When the word was given Sid Law and Maid were half a length ahead and both immediately ran away from her. She was never within four lengths of the leaders. Sid Law and Maid ran like a double team, and under the wire Sid Law showed off first, Maid a neck behind and Lucy away back. Time, 0:50¼.

W. L. Low, proprietor of the Commercial Hotel, was an interested witness of the races. He sat behind his handsome span of black geldings valued by him at $1,000. These horses were in superb condition Tuesday and Wednesday, but Thursday morning at 6, Mr. Low was called out to his stables and when he got there his groom was leading one of the black geldings, and Mr. Low had hardly time to ask what was up, as the horse dropped dead a few minutes later. They immediately suspicioned foul play. They examined the feed and found in the oats and barley enough "rough on rats" to poison all the horses in the county. An examination was made of the dead horses and it was found that the horses had been fed crushed barley about 4 A. M. that morning. The fiends who perpetrated the foul deed intended to poison the fine horses, but were frightened by some noise. In a closed box stall was Mr. Low's valuable stallion Royal George by Seely's Royal George, and next to the black geldings poisoned were two handsome mares. What will not the fiend do that did poison two handsome, kind and valuable horses? Mr. Low will not leave a stone unturned to find the wretch, and if he be found woe be to him, for these handsome geldings were looked upon by Mr. and Mrs. Low as almost members of the family.

A deed almost as brutal came to light on Friday. J. S. Bell had his valuable bred mare Carrie B., by A. W. Richmond, out at pasture. The mare has a most handsome yearling by Stamboul, 2:12½, and is in foal by Alcazar. Carrie B. has never been worked, and only driven a little to a light buggy. The man who has the Rincon ranch rented, was much in need of a working horse. He saw Carrie B. running on the ranch, so he took her up, harnessed her, and put her behind (with other horses) his plough. Carrie B. was seen by a *passer-by*, who noticed that the mare was in a critical condition. He brought her to town, and when J. S. Bell saw his favorite mare in a dying condition, he immediately went for a physician. The mare, it is thought, will die; at any rate, the colt that is due in April will surely come dead. Legal proceedings were immediately commenced against the farmer who took up a mare to work because he needed a horse so badly.

Saturday, 15th of March, at 11 A. M., there was a match race for $200 a side between Duryea's Fandango and Pierre Lorillard Jr.'s Baby. Both horses carried 160 pounds. The race was looked upon with much interest, as both horses are well known here. Both were raised in the county.

Duryea entered s g Fandango by Arrellane's horse; ridden by Duryea.

P. Lorillard Jr. entered s g Baby by Robbery Boy; ridden by P. Menchaca.

The starters were Mr. Thayer and Mr. Barnes. The judges, Chas. Fay and P. Duryea. Distance, half-mile dash. Both Fandango and Baby acted so well at the starting post, that they were sent off on the first attempt to a most even start, Fandango having a neck the best of it. Baby had the pole. The horses ran the first eight in 0:12¾. A blanket would have covered them both. They reached the quarter in 0:23¼, the three-eighths in 0:37¾. Fandango gave it up. Mr. Duryea saw it was useless to punish his horse, and pulled him up. Baby won the race very easily; time, 0:53½. Both horses are evenly matched as far as speed goes, but Fandango can not carry weight. Baby is a powerfully-built horse, six year old. He can run a quarter with 160 pounds almost any day in 0:23.

T. M.

March 17, 1890.

Communication.

Racine, Wis., March 10, 1890.

Editor Breeder and Sportsman, San Francisco, Cal.:—You stated in your paper a short time since that I had gone back on my contract, or had broken it with Mr. Valensin. I don't know who gave you such information, and it matters not whoever it was. I think it would have been only fair if they had stated both sides of the story, and not tried to advertise their stock at my expense. I will give you the facts, and I wish you would please correct your former statement. While I was in California Mr. Valensin made me a liberal offer to train and drive for him, and left it open until about January 1st or thereabouts. About that date I received a telegram from Mr. Valensin saying that he wished to know my decision as he wanted to make stake entries, etc. I wired him that I would accept his offer and had mailed a contract to him to sign.

Instead of Mr. Valensin signing my contract, he made out another one, which differed greatly from the one that I had mailed him. I have both contracts, and it is just as I have stated. There was nothing between Mr. Valensin and myself, only that we misunderstood each other as to the conditions of the contract. If he had signed my contract, I should have certainly gone to California and tried to please Mr. Valensin, which I think I could have done, notwithstanding all reports about him to the contrary. Hoping that you will give this a place in your columns, I am,

Yours truly, Edwin D. Bither.

Blue Bull 75.

At last the blood of the Hero of Flat Rock is beginning to be appreciated. At the recent Kellogg sales of California trotting stock in New York City several animals were offered having more or less of the blood of Blue Bull, and as but little of this blood has ever been offered in this section before, there was great speculation among our breeders as to what the public estimate would be as expressed by the crucial test of the auction ring.

The prices brought by these animals were as follows: Gold Leaf, ch f, $8000, J. H. Shults, Brooklyn, N. Y.; Thistle, blk f, $4000, J. H. Shults, Brooklyn, N. Y.; Habibi, br f, $3300, J. H. Rupert, New York City; Miss Jay Eye See, blk f, $1000, H. Kirkendall, Helena, Mont.; Muscadin, b c, $1000, Scott Quintin, Trenton, N. J.; Chestnut mare, $300, said to be by Blue Bull 75, but not eligible to registration.

But the most convincing argument of all was the price brought by the ch m Wiggle Waggle, $2050, she being an inbred Blue Bull and having no outcross to get the credit. Her breeding is as follows:

Wiggle Waggle, b m, 7 years, by Prompter, son of Blue Bull 75, dam Posey by Flertail, he by the Pruden Blue Bull.

"Tuxedo."

TURF AND TRACK.

Bourbon Belle, the dam of Hanover, is barren this year.

Mr. Gilman will again hold the flag at West Side, Chicago

Patsy Clinker, pacing record 2:20, has been sold for $1800.

Leonatus, since going to the stud at Runnymede has gone stone blind.

The Beverwyck stable has second claim on Bergen for the coming season.

In the central provinces of India there are a high class of trotting bullocks.

The Maltese Villa Stable has moved from Westchester to the Brooklyn track.

Col. Thornton will breed two mares to Dan McCarty's new purchase Bay Rose.

The erstwhile crack sprinter, Sam Harper, is said to have broken down for good.

Prodigal Son is a better favorite in New Orleans than Riley for the Kentucky Derby.

$13,000 is the price that Knap McCarthy is said to have refused for Geneva S 2:19¼.

The best looking youngster in the Belmont stable is to be the brother to St. Carlo.

Walla Walla will commence racing on Monday, Oct. 6th and continued for six days.

A Memphis firm of bookmakers are opening a new pool room in Little Rock, Arkansas.

Pittsburg Phil is back again from Europe, and is plunging again at the New Jersey tracks.

Billy Weeks did not find France the paradise he thought it would be, and returned with Splan.

St. C. Ditmas, who is said to be the Apollo Belvidere of the Eastern tracks, has filled all the books already in the East on Dunboyne for the Suburban.

The Dwyers have forty one horses in training at Gravesend, and to look after them fifty men and boys.

J. S. Campbell, one of the partners in the Beverwyck Stable, will make his home in New York hereafter.

Little Brown Jug, the king of pacers, is being driven on the road at Bangor, Maine, by his owner, Mr. E. J. Murch.

It is reported that the Spendthrift stud, including Spendthrift, will be removed from Kentucky to Virginia in the near future.

It is probable that the Sire Bros. will sell Harry Wilkes to purchasers in Germany, who are anxious to beat the unknown invincible Polly.

Pat Sheedy has suggested to the Washington Park Club that $25,000 be added to the American Derby in 1892, so that it will be worth $50,000 to the winner.

It is rumored that M. Walters, the owner of Al Farrow, will have several horses on the California Circuit this year, including a half brother to Al Farrow.

Jockey Stoval has been called upon by G. R. Tompkins to report for duty. Amos McCampbell also claims to have a contract with Stoval, and trouble may result.

Havillah, the four year old daughter of Longfellow and Miss Haverly, has been sent to Belle Meade by her owners, the Ireland Bros. She will be stinted to Luke Blackburn.

Orrin Hickok will handle Monterey, the four-year-old son of Electioneer and Minx, this season, for his new owner, Mr. Chas. Miller, of New York, who purchased him from Mr. Lathrop.

Wash. T. Smith who trained for the last two seasons for the Hon. C. M. Reed of Erie, Pa., has gone to Deer Lodge, Montana, he and his son having been engaged by Mr. S. E. Larabie.

Luke, who rode here for Mr. Belmont several seasons ago, and since his return to Europe has ridden successfully for Mr. M. Ephrussi, will again ride in France for the same gentleman this season.

Fresno should have a highly successful meeting next week. Ed McGinnis, Welcome, Pliny, Rosebud, Jack Brady, Kitty Van, Oro, and a host of others, are already in Fresno waiting for the flag to drop.

Col. R. S. Strader sold for John E. Madden, the brown mare Hattie Wilkes, eight years old by George Wilkes, dam by Edwin Forrest, grandam by Pilot, Jr.; price $5,800, in foal Robt. McGregor.

S. G Larimore, of Chicago, has gone to Mr. Marcus Daly's ranch in Bitter Root Valley to superintend the horse department, and will probably have some of the horses in the Montana and California circuit.

Taken all round the Rancho Del Paso sale was very successful, and when some of the Albert W's show up, as they are bound to (I know one now who can beat 2:25), the Rancho Del Paso sale will equal the Rosemeade.

Jockey Ray made a contract with Nick Finzer, the owner of Maori, to ride for his stable this season, but it must be held in abeyance for the present, pending the action of the Louisville Association regarding Ray's suspension.

Col. North, the Nitrate King, is said, on good authority, to pay Sherwood, the well known trainer, $25,000 a year as a retaining fee and $15 a week for each horse, and in addition ten per cent on all stakes won by Mr. North's horses.

Claude Thomas of Paris, Ky., has sold to J. Macolm Forbes of Boston the bay filly Edgeline, two years old, a sister to Edgemark, who holds the four-year-old stallion record 2:16. The price is not made public, but it is upward of $5000.

Jockey Martin Bergen has been endeavoring to buy several colts of the Brown stable, offering a good sum for the Longfellow-Insignia colt. Capt. Brown thinks Bergen is acting for another party, and does not intend to operate a stable of his own.

It seems that DanMcCarty has gone into partnership with Mr. Richards, the owner of the well known Elector by which Mr. Richards is a half owner in Bay Rose and ten of Dan's trotting mares which will be removed to Mr. Richard's ranch in San Joaquin.

The Shelby County Trotting Horse Breeder's Association has decided to hold a four days' meeting at Montgomery Park commencing May 20. Purses aggregating $2450 with $750 added money, will be offered. The association will join the American Association

At a meeting of the Directors of the Dixon Driving Park Association held last week, it was decided to postpone the proposed May Day races indefinitely, the reason given being that the Sacramento races have been extended over another week from the date first published.

Jeanne, the Kentucky Prince mare, purchased last week by John E. Madden, has been shipped to Terre Haute, Ind., where she will be bred to Axtell. Jeanne, who is now heavy in foal to Stamboul, is a daughter of Suisun, by Electioneer, and her foal by Axtell should prove to be a grand one.

The veteran trainer John Hannigan, who has handled many good ones, and who developed first for the Dwyer Bros. their crack Longstreet, has been quite ill at Milldale for some time, with something like pneumonia. He is now slowly recovering, and his physicians say he is out of danger.

Molly has been one of the largest trotting winners on the continent (France and Germany) the last two seasons she is owned by Mr. McDonald a Dublin man who claims she is Irish bred though it is said she is a ringer. She has beaten Zoe B 2:17½, Valkyr 2:19¾, and Misty Morning 2:21 with ease.

It is reported from Berlin that the Emperor William who like his brother-in-law, the Duke of Augustenberg and Prince Frederick Leopold, takes a great interest in the German turf, has just intimated his intention to give $15,000 out of his private purse to a stake for three year olds to be called the Prussian Derby to be run at Berlin.

Isaac Murphy will remain in Kentucky until after the spring meeting of the Kentucky Association, when he will go East with the Dwyer Bros.' string of horses, which he will take charge of. Murphy is in better health this spring than ever before. He weighs 133 pounds, but expects to reduce it to 112 pounds before the racing season begins.

The various tracks in the state have been so bad that it is probable some peculiar form will be shown at the coming running meetings. Sacramento, San Jose and Oakland and the Bay District track have practically been unfit to work on for the last two months, while Henry Walsh at Palo Alto has been in as bad a plight having to use the lane.

The larger pool rooms in the city have a struggle on hand to freeze out the smaller ones. The grievance is that the smaller rooms get the starters, odds, etc., from the larger rooms who have to pay a large sum monthly to the Telegraph Department for their lists. The probability is that the lesser rooms will stay as long as their wealthy rivals, unless they go broke some hard day.

Mr. M. Dwyer who recently passed through Memphis on his way from Hot Springs, Ark., visited the track, and among other things said to a reporter: "I took a look at Terra Cotta, and I never saw him when he appeared in better condition. There, I think, is one of the greatest horses in this country, and those people who think he will not yet win great races will be badly disappointed when he comes to start."

At the Sweeny Combination Sale in Carson City, Nevada, many promising youngsters will be sold. I have heard very flattering accounts of several of them, and hopes of seeing some of them on the California circuit. The grand stallion Gibraltar (Old Gib), with a record of 2:22½, and among others the conqueror of Echora, Abbotsford, and many other well-known performers, will also be offered at auction.

As a horse likely to run frequently this year J. M. Brown & Co's. Texas bred sprinter Creole is invested with interest. He is said to be half bred only, and was a noted quarter horse, but after Brown secured him he trained Creole as he did other horses in the string, and now the New Orleans touts swear he can go a mile with anybody's horse. In a six-furlong dash recently he won handily in 1:14¾ with a good weight up.

Santa Anita has already lost four broodmares: Too Hard, Maggie Emerson (dam of Lucky B), Fallen Leaf and Marie Stuart (dam of Caliente), all in foal to The Emperor. It is extremely doubtful whether Miss Ford will recover, while Grisette (in foal to the Emperor) is expected to be all right in a week or two. Cold, wet weather, bad stabling, and worse attendance, is said to be the reason for the unusual sickness at Santa Anita.

At the Kempton Park March meeting on March 8th the race for the champion hurdle handicap of 1000 sovereigns, subscription of five sovereigns each, two mile over eight flights of hurdles, fifty four subcribers, twenty five of whom paid five sovereigns each, was won by Capt. L. H. Jones' five-year old bay colt Theodolite. Mr. F. S. Gooch's four-year-old bay colt Papyrus was second and Mr. C. Hibbert's six-year old Castillian third.

A few days ago Ed Corrigan, the famous Western turfman, paid a flying visit to New Orleans, but was off again before his presence in the city had become generally known. It now transpires that Mr Corrigan visited New Orleans for the purpose of buying J. M. Brown & Co.'s three-year-old bay colt Red Light by Leonatus, dam Idalia by Red Dick, but his offer of $5,000 failed to tempt Mr. Brown to part with the promising youngster.

Clay & Woodford, Runnymede stud, shipped East 10 days ago a brother to Fordham two years old, which was purchased last Spring by The Dwyer brothers at the Woodburn yearling sale. He was not sent on with their other yearlings, owing to being hurt by an accident too bad to travel. His heel was bruised but it is now well, and from appearances he promises to tread in the footsteps of his speedy brother. He cost the Dwyer Brothers $1000 last spring.

The yearlings at Woodburn this season number nearly fifty head, and according to Mr. Brodhead's estimation are fully up to those of any other year. Prominent among the number are full brothers to Fordham, Troubadour and Penn P., and half brothers to Foxhall, Fresno and Gallifet. Since 1869, when yearling sales were first inaugurated at this establishment, twenty-one sales have been held and 782 colts and fillies disposed of for $542,404, an average of $693.

W. G. Bennett, Weston, West Virginia, has sold to John Alexander, Buckhannon, West Virginia, the chestnut filly Phœbe, foaled 1887, by Partnership (son of Asteroid and Katona, Tom Ochiltree's dam), dam Glimmer by Doswell (son of Planet and Deucalia by Deucalion), her dam Carlotta by imp. Australian, out of Hilarity by Lexington, and the brown colt Prince Albert, foaled 1887, by Partnership, dam Bubble by Leader, her dam Sparkle by Doswell, out of Carlotta, as above.

Jockey Anthony Hamilton, the famous middle-weight rider, was at Clifton yesterday. Hamilton has been several weeks with some relatives at St. Louis, and looks in good fettle. He said that he expects to report for duty to Trainer Rowe at Babylon L. I., about the last week in this month or the first of the next, and that he will be able to ride a pound or two lighter this season than last. With the material in the Belmont stable to handle, Hamilton has a good opportunity this year if he sticks to his business.

Although late in the season Mr. Dietz is out with his Ringwood cards. $50 the season seems no price for a son of Sydney 2:19¾—the greatest young speed producer at an early age in the world—with a thoroughbred cross to give stamina. Ringwood himself showed great promise as a four year old working a trial handily in 2:19½, and but for an unfortunate accident at Napa would undoubtedly have obtained a record of 2:18 or better. All Ringwood's colts show great promise and style, and he is a sure foal getter.

Ben Bruce is of the opinion that Riley, Protection and Prince Fonso, in the order named will end this year's Derby. In the East most of the trainers seem to favor the Prodigal Son. A well-known trainer said recently: "I think Prodigal Son will win the Kentucky Derby. He was pretty well up in most of his races, and met the best of the East. But he is one of the kind that improves, and will beat most of them who beat him last year. He is a beautiful colt. He looks like a Lexington, and I'm satisfied he'll improve.

Following if a list of the thoroughbred mares Clay & Woodford will breed this spring to Mambrino Russell (half brother to Maud S. 2:08¾): Dreamland by Billet—Delight; Retreat by Virgil—Return; Vellum by Bertram or Billet—Vassar; Meddle by Wanderer—Manhatta, Theckla by Billet—Glena; Waif by Wanderer—Ei; Bastante by Bramble—Melrose; Gramacita by John Morgan—Meteor· bay filly by King Alfonso—Benita and Fairy Girl by King Faro. If this experiment proves a success trotters will also be bred at Runnymede.

Despite the graphic accounts to the contrary, *it is not* Mr. Baldwin's habit to break all, or any of, his thoroughbreds to harness. As a matter of fact, Los Angeles, Volante, The Emperor, and the other Santa Anita cracks, never had harness on them, and there is only one instance where one of the Santa Anita racers has been hitched up (I think it was Carrientes), and that was a few months ago, and he kicked the harness into pieces, and did a good deal of damage to a barbed wire fence, dying from blood poisoning, the result of his attack on the barbed wire fence.

Among the many trotting stallions at Oakland Bonanza is attracting as much attention as any on account of his looks and his near relationship to so many game, speedy performers. Bonanza is by Arthurton, sire of Arab 2:15, Joe Arthurton 2:20½, etc.; his dam is Sister dam of Albert W 2:20 and she is by Trustee out of the Lamott mare dam of Aurora 2:27, who is the dam of Arol 2:24¼. Bonanza has a record of 2:29½, and has repeatedly shown miles better than 2:25, and with his Hambletonian, Star, and thoroughbred blood all close up should prove invaluable in the stud.

In a little stable near the winter track of Clifton an old horse stands all the day long and listens with head erect to the thunder of the hurrying hoofs when the races are being run. Shaggy and rough does the old horse look, and his once glossy sides are branded and marked by many a cruel whip and spur. In spite of his humble surroundings, however, there is an air of conscious pride and power about him, and at times he appears to be listening to the applause of the shouting thousands of the by-gone years; for as he stands he is the great captain of the old guard of the turf, the last and the mightiest of the illustrious line of Bonnie Scotland, grand old Barnum.

A great deal of unnecessary disease is, even now, contracted in some stables by the indiscriminate use of the same stable bucket, and frequently of clothing, says the Sporting World In glanders there is only one thing to be done, which is to destroy the infected animal and bury him deep with quick lime, everything, harness, blankets, etc., and all the things which come in contact with the body should be burned, and the stable, after scraping, thoroughly dosed with carbolized whitewash and then planked over, or, better still, the stable should not be used at all for some time for stock. There are literally no remedies to be given when once the disease has been developed. In its first stages, as farcy, it is in many cases amendable to remedies, but in its developed stage, as glanders, curative remedies are still entirely unknown.

The Supreme Court decided a few days ago that betting and bookmaking on races run outside of the State of Kentucky was illegal, and persons violating the law were liable to indictment. The sporting fraternity were determined not to be outdone, and the Climax Pool Room of Louisville, Ky., established a betting agency in Nashville, bets on races being transmitted by wire.

Judge Ridley, of the Criminal Court, learning of this move, summoned the grand jury before him on the 12th, and instructed them to make an investigation and indict every person connected in any way with the agency, or assisting in making bets. He said the betting was in violation of the law, the claim of agency being of no avail. The action of the grand jury is awaited with no little interest.

There have been many attempts at artificial starting. Mr. Finigan had his idea some seasons ago, but it was given up as a failure. Capt. Harris's was just as much of a failure, and so are all ways of starting except with a *born starter*. Mr. Hunt, an Australian gentleman, has a novel idea for starting, but the chances are it will not work well, and it, like all other contrivances of that kind, brings one back to the old standing start Mr. Hunt's invention consists of a pair of flexible steel gates, meeting on the centre of the course. On these is placed a red flag, the horses being drawn up in a line some 90 feet behind them. The starter pulls a string which causes the flag to fall, and releases the catch in the gate, which, being made of vulcanite and steel, and operated upon by a powerful spring, disappears into cylinders fixed on either side of the course.

The New York Spirit of the Times of March 8th, says: At the Hoffman House there was a notable little crowd of gentlemen from California devoted to the trotting horse comparing notes on Monday night, the evening preceding the initial day of the great Kellogg sales. Count Valensin, the owner of the wonderful sire Sidney, smiling and affable, discussed the breeding problem with Mr. Monroe Salisbury, the owner of that magnificent campaigner and sire, Director, 2:17, while the evergreen veteran from Kentucky, W. H. Wilson, put in an occasional sentence replete with wit and wisdom. Mr. Kerr, the proprietor of the Californian Breeder and Sportsman, a very genial and well informed horseman, who is here attending the sales, talked glowingly of the gigantic strides which California was making as a breeding State. The unanimous sentiment of the crowd was that the present prosperity of trotting horse interests was thoroughly healthy, and that good stock would always command high prices.

I had a very pleasant, chatty visit from Wilber Field Smith last Monday. Wilber says that although he sold several youngsters—the three I mentioned last week—he is still in the ring, and will soon have their places filled. Mr. Smith, after careful consideration, has decided to send three mares to Sidney, 2:19¾: His grey mare by The Moor, dam by Peck's Idol, granddam by Pilot Jr.; Pansy, 2:24½ (sister to Thapsin, 2:21½), by Berlin, dam Lady Hubbard by Benecia Boy, and a mare by Echo 462, the well known son of Rysdyk's Hambletonian, and sire of Belle Echo, 2:20, Senator, 2:21½, Victor, 2:22, Gibraltar, 2:22½, Echora, 2:23½, and eight others in the 2:30 list, and dams of Direct, four-year-old, 2:18¼, and Pink, 2:25. The mare's dam is a grandly bred thoroughbred mare, and all three should produce trotters by the crack producer of early speed at an early age.

Robert McGregor, 2:17½, one of the most famous of trotting sires, has been purchased by John E. Madden, of Lexington, Ky., from R. I. Lee, of Topeka, Kan., for a fancy price. The stallion is the sire of Bonnie McGregor, 2:13½; of Burns McGregor, 2:29 as a two year-old; Roxie McGregor, 2:20¾, and others in the list. Robert McGregor is nineteen years old, and combines in his breeding the blood of Alexander's Abdallah and Seely's American Star. He and his son, Bonnie McGregor, hold the fastest combined record for sire and son. He is a game horse, and his get develop early speed and stamina. His book, forty mares, is full for the season at $500, and breeders are anxious to secure his services. Mr. Madden, who is in New York, refuses to state what he paid for the stallion, but it is know that the price is upwards of $25 000. The horse will remain in Kentucky at Mr. Madden's farm.

The New York pool rooms have opened up again, and many were in full blast during the last two days of last week. Their managers profess to be doing only a "commission business" on the races at Clifton and Guttenberg. It was generally believed that they would remain closed until after the legislative committee had finished its investigation of the various city departments. A disagreement as to the terms for protection seems now to have been the reason for their closing. It is said that they paid some one $150 a month for protection and that this some one raised the price to $200. This the pool room men refused to pay, but the story now is that a compromise was effected at $175 a month. At one time there were forty-three rooms which contributed to this protection fund. How many contributors there are to the new fund is not known, except to the collector and his principals.

The bill to kill the winter race tracks in New Jersey by permitting racing for only thirty days in the year on any course came up for final passage in the House on March 12th, and created a spirited debate. Kalisch, the introducer of the measure, made a long and effective speech for it, denying that the act would in any way legalize gambling. Voorhees, of Union County, said the devil himself would be puzzled to give a good reason for the existence of the winter tracks. The frequenters of those courses were of the lowest type of humanity, he held, but laws prohibiting gambling upon them could not be enforced, owing to the grip that the associations had upon the officials of the counties in which they are located. The tracks were maintained in winter for the purpose of gambling, he declared. The sentiment of the State is against this kind of sport. At some of these tracks eighteen-year-old horses were run as often as two-year-olds, a form of cruelty that should be abolished without delay. The bill was passed by a vote of 34 to 10.

Peter Manee dropped into a reminiscent mood the other day, and there was a good lesson in shoeing brought out at the same time. The Horsemen says: He contends that in nine cases out of ten a trotter or pacer will go faster if shod all around, with very low toe and heel calks. It gives the horse surer foothold and less liability to make missteps and hit his legs or feet. On calling for proofs he said. "Well William H. Allen and Mary A. Whitney. I tried them both ways and they could go much faster with the calks. Mr. Bonner tried them on Pocahontas and Murphy drove her down to the half in 1:05¼. Then Mr. Bonner gave me $25 for the hint." Speaking of Mary A. Whitney, Peter says she could have had a much faster record, but he was saving her for the 2:30 class and the day she made her mark of 2:28 at Fleetwood, in W. H. VanCott's time it was given him, as there was a "grand kick" about calling slow time. He then made Daniel Mace drive Vanity Fair the next heat in 2;25 to win it. Peter will be on the war-path the coming season with Monkey Rolla.

Sunol and Axtell will not meet this season. All the recent talk about a match between these great trotters has not the slightest foundation. There did exist a hope of such a race, and it was caused by the offer of the managers of the new trotting track, Dundee Park, near Paterson, N. J., to give a purse of $10,000 for a race between these phenomenal trotters. The proposed race was to be best three in five, in harness, National Trotting Association rules to govern. Ijams, one of Axtell's five owners, in speaking of the proposed event, said that Axtell was stabled at the Terre Haute (Ind.) farm, and would earn $40,000 this year in the stud. This being the case, the horse would hardly be in shape for a great test of speed. Robert Bonner, the owner of Sunol, said the other day, that there was not the slightest probability of a race. "When I paid for Sunol," said Bonner, "it was with the agreement and understanding that I should let her remain at Gov. Stanford's farm until next October, to give him an opportunity of lowering her record. He therefore has charge of her racing record this year, and I have nothing to do with her. Gov. Stanford holds the mare at my risk, and should anything happen to her it is my loss."

The Board of Directors of the Sixth District Agricultural Association met last week, pursuant to the call of the President, at No. 7½ North Main street. President Lichtenberger was in the chair, and Directors Wright, Binds, Wise, Workman, Robinson and Newton present. The President reported that the sale had been consummated and the money paid for the lots at Agricultural Park owned by the association, to the Redondo Beach Railway Company. The lots were sold for $6,000. The President reported that there was $8,628 in the bank to the credit of the association. A discussion was had as to the next annual fair, and it was decided to claim the dates of August 11th to 16th inclusive. The Directors decided to meet in seven days at Agricultural Park and look over the race track with a view to deciding about the new grand stand, club houses, etc., which are to be erected at a cost of several thousand dollars.

The Secretary was instructed to advertise two and three-year-old trotting stakes for 1890 and 1891.

The sporting exhibition which opened on the 18th at the Grosvenor Gallery, London is one of the most interesting and remarkable collections of the present day. Amongst the exhibitors are her Her Majesty The Queen who sends with other great works Landseer's "Sanctuary," and two paintings by Carl Haag, which have a special value apart from their merits—viz., "The Royal Family at Rochnagar," with portrait of the Queen and Prince Consort and their children, and "Evening at Balmoral," in which the Duke of Saxe Coburg-Gotha and Lord Aberdeen are also represented. Emil Adams's 'Bend Or" and "Ormonde," and Stubbs's "Mambrino," the ancestor of every first-rate trotter in the United States, are amongst the canvases representing equine wonders. Among curiosities there are W. M. Turner's fishing-rod, the first racing prize ever given in England, a set of silver bells belonging to the Corporation of Carlisle, the portrait of old Mr. Tattersall and Tattersall's "as it was," and a complete series of English fowling-pieces, from the cross-bow down to the latest breechloader.

Protection, the junior champion winner, shows great signs of improvement. He has grown and spread out in a remarkable degree, and trainers at Latonia think highly of his chances for the Kentucky *Derby*. Dungarren, the brother to Catalpa, is a very handsome two-year-old, and Trainer Hannigan believes he has in him another Hanover. None of the horses at Latonia have as yet done any rapid work, but their preparation has been steadily going on, and from present prospects they will be ready to meet their Southern rivals when the bugle calls them to the post in May. The outside track was put in order last week, but its use was only available for a few days owing to the heavy rains. So soon as the weather again settles it will then be kept in first-class condition until spring. Among the stables in Central Kentucky that contemplate going shortly to Latonia is that of Frank Harper, which is one of the most formidable aggregations in the West. The programme book of the coming spring meeting at Latonia will be out in a few days, and its principal feature will be its large array of rich purses, which will be up to any series of like races ever offered by any Western association.

The first homebred mare the late Lord Falmouth ran was the celebrated Queen Bertha, who won the Oaks in 1863 In regard to his betting propensities, his only bet is always said to be as follows: In the autumn of 1861, Lord Falmouth, who then raced under the assumed name of Mr. T. Valentine, betted Mrs. John Scott, the wife of his then trainer, sixpence that Queen of Hearts beat Q. E. D. in a Criterion Course Sweepstakes for two-year-olds. His lordship lost. On the One Thousand Guineas day of 1862, he presented Mrs. John Scott with the sixpence, set in a handsome pin, and that very afternoon carried off the stake just mentioned with the Wild Dayrell filly Hurricane. An English sporting writer says this is not the only bet Lord Falmouth ever had. The other gamble was a new hat on the St. Leger of 1878, with Lord Alington, to the effect that Jannette, the bearer of the "magpie," beat Childeric, (both the property of the Lord of Mereworth) and this Lord Falmouth won. Lord Alington afterwards offered the late Lord Falmouth a sovereign in payment, to which his lordship good-humouredly replied: "Oh, no; our bet was a new hat; and mine cost 30s each!"

H. L Levy & Brother, manufacturers of boys' clothing, at No. 19 Mercer street, New York, failed, and their place of business has been closed by the Sheriff. They have been in business since December, 1883, when they succeeded Norris & Levy. Their stock was damaged by fire July 26, 1888, and it is said they received $6000 insurance and the damaged goods. Their statement January 19, 1889, claimed assets of $74,450, and liabilities $14,000, leaving a capital of $60,450. Both the partners, Herman L. and Aaron, are young men, and their failure is attributed to horse racing, in which they are currently reported to have lost $22,000. Herman Joseph, attorney for the judgment creditors, said that the boys tried to run horses and were heavy losers. They formerly had a stable of twelve horses, and were interested in a race track in New Jersey, but they made a failure at it, were attached there, and the horses were sold out. They also lost heavily in a Twenty-eighth street pool-room. Aaron Levy, when he was married a few years ago, received $10,000 from his father-in-law, Mr. Jacobs, who since then also lent him $5,000.

That well known horseman, Capt. W. A. Kerr, in a recent letter to the London Live Stock Journal, gives his reason for the importation of American remounts: The more I see of the manner in which our batteries are horsed and our cavalry mounted, the more am I confirmed in my opinion that never, within the memory of man, has the British army been so infamously underhorsed. The fault lies, not with the Inspector-General of Remounts, but with those who vote the sinews of war. By paying a better price, the French and Germans secure the pink of the market.

I have not heard that Major-General Ravenhill has expressed an opinion adverse to the Canadians; that officer's hurried canter through the Dominion would not, however, justify an opinion opposed to those of others equally entitled to rank high, and who have had wider and longer experience of the North American horse.

I never ventured to suggest that our island general-purpose breeds are to be improved by those importations, though I did recommend the getting back of some of the Margrave, Glencoe, Priam, Tranby and Leamington mares. Moreover, I have hazarded an opinion that Blue Grass is about the best of the premium stallions. Foxhall's performances, not to mention those of Iroquois, taught us how transatlantic horses gallop, and I question if we have many horses capable of lowering the record of Spokane, the winner of last year's Kentucky Derby, who covered the mile and a half in 2:34½.

The aristocrats of the English turf have always held aloof from the trotting element and such tales—probably correct—as the Col. Wood one are not calculated to create any respect for trotters. It seems according to the N. Y. Sun that apropos of Col. Wood, it has come to light that a clever bit of turf jugglery was performed in connection with his shipment abroad. The gelding was purchased by C. G. Frazier, formerly of Eagle Bridge, New York state, who had previously bought horses and taken them to England. Frazier acted for J. A. Prince Smith, of Vienna, and it was supposed that the horse would be taken direct to Austria. Shortly after Col Wood was shipped from this port, it was given out that he had been lost on the voyage. The horse, however, was quietly taken to London, where an important handicap trot was about to take place at Alexandra Park, and for which the contestants had already been named and bets made on the result.

One of the favorites had broken down in training, and as Col. Wood bore a strong resemblance to him he was substituted, and before the trick was discovered the race was captured by the fleet American, and a good sum, said to be about $100,000, went into the pockets of the principals in the job. The English managers of the race ruled the conspirators off their track when they learned the truth.

Soon after this Col Wood turned up in Vienna, where he was no longer masquerading. In his first race there he was distanced for running, though he was known over here as one of the handiest trotters on the turf. The European method is to divide the course into sections, marked by flags, and the rule requires that when a horse leaves his feet he must recover and be trotting when he reaches the next flag. Since then Col. Wood has retrieved his lost honors, and is now looked on as one of the cracks of the continent.

There is an almost prodigal liberality about everything done under the auspices of the New York Jockey Club, says Town Topics. Tiffany & Co. recently received the largest order for high class engraved stationery that was ever given out for private distribution. It consisted of an engraved announcement of the erection of the new club house and an invitation to become a member of the New York Jockey Club without payment of the initiation fee, at annual dues of $25.

The club house, it is stated, will be kept open all the year round. Thousands of these announcements with accompanying engraved blanks signifying a desire of the recipient to be listed were sent to men of the leading clubs throughout the country. The new club house will be the finest building of its kind in the world. The applications for membership are, I am informed, coming so fast that the limit will soon be reached. But the lavish expenditure upon the new clubhouse, and the quite irresistible inducements held out to insure a select membership has an ulterior purpose in elevating the social tone and fixing the standard far above the ordinary in racing associations. The many eligible men of the Union, Knickerbocker, New York, Manhattan and other clubs of this and smaller cities that have already joined the New York Jockey Club guarantees the excellence of its composition. That the fashionable clientele of Jerome Park which gave to that historical racing ground the especial stamp of social distinction, will transfer its fealty to the younger organization, is no longer a matter of doubt. The contiguity of the New York Jockey Club in this city, the location near at hand of several of the swell suburban and hunt clubs, combined with the opportunity of enjoying the privileges of the handsome clubhouse and grounds, will make a racing day scene with the gathering of drags, stately equipages and mounted men and women, strongly suggestive of the English Ascot. It is a deft hand and facile mind that may grasp the various details of the business management of so prodigious a turf enterprise, and at the same time manipulate with requisite finesse the social side of the project into enviable prominence. It is peculiarly fortunate for the New York Jockey Club that its Secretary, Mr. T. H. Kock, combines the business energy and *savoir faire* that have put the association in the front rank of racing organizations in this country. In the meed of praise accorded Secretary Kock the capable Assistant Secretary, W. H Powers, must not be forgotten. I am sure that his fair minded chief would be the first to desire that his efficient aid should have becoming recognition.

The Rosemeade sale seems to have either supplied every one or disgusted every one with any other class of horses. The Backman sale on the 11th was practically a failure, and the Rockefeller mares sold badly, considering their great performances and grand breeding. Prominent among them were:

Kate Sprague (2:18), br m. 15, by Gen Sprague, son of Rhode Island, dam Fan by Lance, son of Flying Morgan, second dam Queen by Gen. Gifford, third dam Fan by Chancellors was bought by Jacob Ruppert, of New York, for $1,-500.

Ethel Sprague, gr m. 6, by Independence, dam Kate Sprague by Gov. Sprague, bought by F. M. Lawrence, $800.

Mabel Sprague, 5, by Independence, dam Kate Sprague; S. W. McKeever, Brooklyn, $660.

Bay filly, 2, by Independence, dam Kate Sprague; W. H. Merritt, $460.

Roan colt, 1, by Independence, dam Kate Sprague; C. S. Upton, New York, $425.

Roan gelding, by Independence, dam Kate Sprague; Alexander McLean, $625.

Femme Sole (2:20), br m, 9, by Princeps, dam Duroc Maid by Messenger Duroc, second dam Lady Winfield by Edward Everett, third dam by Rattler, son of Abdallah 1, was bought by Jacob Ruppert for $5,100.

Wild Rake (2:22¾) b s, 7, by Hambletonian Mambrino, dam Merry by John Dillard, second dam Old Den, third dam Slumy: A J Welch, Hartford, Conn., $5,500.

Calamus (2:24½), b m, 8, by Swigert, dam Merrimac by Richard's Bellfounder; Frank K. Smith Goshen, N. Y., $450.

Nina, gr m, 6, by Independence, dam Calamus by Swigert; J. Wicks, $1,050.

Urbana Belle (2:20½), 12, by J. H. Welsh, dam Mary Belle by J. C. Breckinridge, thoroughbred, son of Lexington; S. L. McMillan, $1,400.

Bay filly, 1, by Independence, dam Urbana Belle by J. H. Welch; F. M. Lawrence, $510.

Bay gelding, 3, by Independence, dam Urbana Belle; J. P. Doyle, $410.

Bay filly by Independence, dam Kate Hall by Wilson's Blue Bull; O. D. Reid, Brooklyn, $625.

Magic (2:25¼), blk g, 16, by Jim Fisk, dam by Sam Slick; S. A. Walker, New York, $470.

Enchantress (2:29¾), b m, 16, by Happy Medium, dam Kitty Clover by Hero; Hugh Brien, $1,050.

Maggie Morrill (2:29¼), ch m, 14, by Charley B, dam unknown; F. H. Selleck, Huntington, N. J., $430

Bay filly, 2, by Independence, dam Maggie Morrill; J. S. Ferguson, New York, $420.

Grey stallion Independence, 9, by Gen Knox, dam Skip by Gideon, sold to Wm. Riley, Cos Cob, Conn., $900.

ATHLETICS.

Athletic Sports and Other Pastimes.

EDITED BY ARISTIPPUS,

SUMMARY.

Great preparations are being made for the coming championship games. The students at Berkeley are more determined than ever that the flag will cross the bay this time. The Field captains of the Olympic and Alpine Clubs are urging their men to train that the pennant may remain on this side. The athletes of the Olympic Club held a cross-country run from Sausalito on Sunday, and to-morrow the Alpine boys will hold their initial cross-country run from the same place.

RUNNERS, WALKERS, JUMPERS, ETC.

A glee club has been organized at the University by the following students: P. G. Somers, '92, and H. C. Baldwin, '91, first tenors; A. W. Gunnison, '91, and G. W. Howard, second tenors; Hugh Howard, '90, and C. H. Bentley, '91, first bass; and V. C Carroll, '93, and Walter Mayee, second bass. During the summer vacation the club will make a tour of the interior towns, the proceeds of their concerts to be applied toward the furtherance of athletics at the college.

The annual games of the St. Andrew Society will be held on Saturday, May 3rd.

Both Lean and Kolb are getting into good trim for their coming wrestling match, which will take place at the Olympic Club rooms April 29th. Lean has already reduced twenty pounds, and expects to be as hard as a board on the evening of the contest. Kolb is also getting rid of his fat, and there is no doubt but that the bouts will be long and hotly contested.

The date of the "Ladies' Night" exhibition of the Alpine Amateur Athletic Club has been set for Tuesday, April 8th. The next outdoor games of the club will be held probably at the Bay District Track on Sunday, May 4th. The programme will be given out in a few days, and will be published in these columns next Saturday. There will be ten events in all, four of which will be open to the members of clubs belonging to the Pacific Coast Amateur Association. The open events will possibly be: 100 yards handicap run, 880 yards handicap run, 5 mile handicap run, and seven mile walk handicap. Gold and silver medals or jewelry prizes will be awarded the winners.

The members of the University Athletic club are becoming quite proficient in the horizontal bar exercise under the able tention of Leader Magee. He is also instructing his pupils in the art of high jumping and expects to develope one or two new men in this branch of sport of May 30.

A couple of hundred people were drawn to the Bay District track on Sunday by the announcement that a Series of sword contests would be given on that day in which some of the crack swordsmen of the world would figure. Before the tournament had been brought to a close those present were satisfied that they had been duped and it was with weary hearts that they made their way to the cars which brought them to the city again.

In the issue of the Occident, (the University official organ) of March 14, a letter appeared over the *nom de plume* of "Athletic," the concluding portion of which ran as follows: "The U. C. has in its team all the men who won places for us last year and it has besides the best class athletically considered that ever entered the U. C. from which to draw men.

Dubbers, Hunt, McNear, Gates, Mays, Van Dyke and Whiting are all "phenoms" in their lines and they are not afraid to train. Put a little enthusiasm back of them and the Olympic Athletic club will have to import more than one all-round Irish athlete in order to carry off that game." We presume "athletic" is one of the college athletes, and we are really sorry to discover that the U. C. boys are so deeply embittered against the Olympians. Be it said to the credit of the O. A. C. athletes that while they are doing all in their power to encourage each other to train for the coming games they certainly are not publishing discourteous articles relative to their rivals across the bay; they believe in rivalry, good natured, manly rivalry, but they do not stoop so far as to incourage unfriendly emulation. The Olympic team will be even stronger than ever and with the Alpine Club to help it out it is very doubtful if the championship play of '90 will be carried across the bay.

The tenth cross country run of the Olympic Club was held at Sausalito on Sunday last. About twenty-five runners were present and enjoyed the journey. The air was cool and fresh and just suited for this kind of sport. The course was in fairly good condition and lay along side the sea shore. The run was to Lime Point and return, the headquarters being Dexter's Cottage. The first men home covered the distance in 55 minutes. The following athletes toed the scratch: Frank O'Kane, W H Woods, J A Christie, W M Phelps, P F McDonald, D B Crane, F F Plowden, G F Green, D J Barnett, H M Collins, F F Foster, H Egbert, W T Haberly, Frank L Cooley, C T Hess, A C Thornton, P Ward, J Kortick, C J Jellineak, A S Henderson, E S Martin, R G Cole, J H Davies E Gross and H S Allen. W A Scott, S V Cassidy and Capt. George W Jordan. In the afternoon the men sat down to a nice lunch which was prepared by Mrs. Rose Jackson.

Messrs. Lakeman (Chairman) and Townsend have been appointed senior representatives on the athletic committee of of the University Athletic Club.

F E Holland, the well known sprinter and jumper has joined the Alpine Club.

The new running track at the California Athletic club rooms is now used only by fat prize fighters who desire to reduce their avoirdupois. The amateurs have all turned their backs on the club and are now members of legitimate athletic clubs.

Walter Smith, formerly boxing instructor to the Lurline Club, has been engaged to instruct the members of the Alpine Club. He began his duties on Wednesday evening last, and those who took lessons from him regard him as a first-class teacher. His class-nights will be Monday, Wednesday and Friday, from eight to ten P. M.

The members of the Olympic Club are anxious for Professor Corbett's return from the East. His old class badly feels his loss.

Every afternoon and evening the out-door men of the O. A. C. practice on their new track. On account of their cross-country run on Sunday last, only a few athletes visited the grounds. Several of the championship team will sleep at the grounds for some weeks previous to the games, that they may better be able to get into good condition.

Peter McIntyre is proud of "his" track, and he says he will never give the boys a chance to grumble about its condition.

The initial cross-country run of the Alpine Amateur Athletic Club will take place to-morrow from Dexter's cottage, Sausalito. Over thirty of the members have already signified their intention of starting. Captain J. J. Larkey will act as the pace-maker. The course will be to the Lime Point Light-house and return. Lunch will be served after the run.

If earnest solicitation counts for anything, Captain E. Coke Hill, of the University Club, will have his field team in good trim for Decoration Day. Like Richmond, he goes from "tent to tent" urging his men to battle.

Up to date the field captain of the Alpine Athletic Club has selected the following men to form his team for the championship games: For the sprints, John D. Garrison, J. J. Larkey, R. J. Luttringer, F. E. Holland, C. A. Eldridge; for the half and mile runs, H. C. Cassidy, E. P. Moody, Charles Little; for the walks, P. N. Gafney, A. Cook and H. C. Philips; for the field events, Charles Vultee, Jas. Sexsmith, J. J. McKinnon, F. E Holland. This list does not include include the names of several prominent amateurs who have been proposed for membership, but who have not been yet elected. The team will probably be made up of about thirty men.

The report that McLaughlin of the Alpine Club had been matched to fight a member of the Acme Club of Oakland is not correct. The Directors of the Alpine Club know nothing whatever of the affair.

The new outdoor grounds of the Olympic Club will be turned over to the Athletic Committee early next week, when the athletes of the club will be enabled to commence regular training. The grounds and track are now entirely finished.

THE WHEELMEN.

The Oakland Bicycle club held its second run of the season on Sunday last. The run was to the Cliff House, through the Golden Gate Park and home by the Presidio.

The Bay City Wheelmen contemplate building a club house of their own.

Several wheelmen visited the Park on Sunday and enjoyed the musical programme.

The Alpine Athletic Club will include a bicycle race on its next out-door programme.

AT THE OARS.

An unusually large number of boats were out on Sunday. Several crews from Long Bridge rowed to Hunters Point, and to the Sugar Refinery. The North End Clubs sent out crews to Harbor View and along the water front.

The different boating clubs are beginning in earnest to make preparations for the coming season. Crews are being formed, boats are being overhauled and the club houses and slips are being repaired.

The Alameda Boat Club is gaining in membership and some of the local oarsmen will need to train hard in order to keep the prizes at this side of the bay during the summer months.

The Lurline Club intends purchasing several new racing shells in the near future.

The Ariel Club will sadly miss its last years champion crew at the coming regatta.

Charley Long has almost entirely recovered from the effects of a severe cold which he contracted while training.

CLUB JOTTINGS.

The regular monthly meeting of the Golden Gate Athletic Club will be held on Wednesday evening next, March 26th, at the club rooms, 190 Stevenson street. A fine programme of boxing bouts has been arranged.

It is only a matter of time until some of the so-called athletic clubs are broken up. The exhibition given a few evenings ago under the auspices of the Occidental Club was a sufficient proof that square, scientific boxing matches are on the wane, and that lovers of genuine sport will soon have to become members of our amateur clubs in order to witness first class exhibitions.

A meeting of the Pacific Coast Amateur Athletic Association was held in the club rooms of the Olympic Club on Friday evening last, Walter A. Scott presiding. E. P. Moody, of the Alpine Amateur Athletic Club, was elected Secretary of the Association vice J. J. Jamison of the Golden Gate Athletic Club, resigned. It was decided to hold the annual championship meeting on Decoration Day, May 30th, at the new grounds of the Olympic Athletic Club. A committee was appointed to act in conjunction with the O. C. A. in forming a suitable programme of events. The games will be held under the auspices of the O. A. C. In addition to the regular list of events there will be a couple of events added to the programme in which only members of the Olympic Athletic Club will be allowed to compete. Handsome souvenir programmes are to be gotten up for the occasion to commemorate the opening of the new grounds.

At a meeting of the Silver Gate Athletic club of San Diego last week, a board of seven directors was elected for the ensuing year. The directors elected were as follows: W. E. Hayden, T. J. Walcott, Frank Goodendorf, Thomas Gallagher, A. Whitmore and Fred Matheison.

The officers elected were W. E. Hayden, president; T. J. Walcott, vice president; Frank Goodendorf, financial secretary; A. Whitmore, treasurer.

The club has a membership of 70, each member paying dues of $1 per month, and it now has several hundred dollars in the treasury.

The ambition of the club is to have grounds and build club rooms of its own, as did the Turn Verein society a year or more ago.

JOTTINGS FROM ALL OVER.

The Cornell Foot-Ball Association is in debt $700. It cost $3,000 to run the eleven last season.

There are over fifty cross-country clubs in New York.

The annual championship meeting of the Canadian Amateur Athletic Association will be held on Sept. 27th, at Montreal.

The great eight-mile handicap cross-country run under the auspices of the National Cross Country Association was decided at New York on Saturday last. W H Day, the scratch man won easily.

The Racing Board of the League of American wheelman recently adopted the following rule: Any cycle club will be allowed under special sanction of this Board, to pay the entrance fees and reasonable traveling expenses of a member whom they may desire to represent them upon the path, but without this special sanction no competitor in amateur events shall accept from his own club, or from a club promoting sports at which he competes, any payment for his expenses, under penality of suspension from the track for a time at the discretion of the board. No rider will be allowed to have his entrance fees or any expenses whatever paid by an officer, member, committee or department of an athletic organization other than a cycling club.

At the annual meeting of the Intercollegiate Association of Amateur Athletics of America, it was decided to hold the annual championship games at the Berkeley Oval on May 31st. The following board of officers were elected: President, F C Miller, of Princeton, class of '90; Vice-President, F R Coates, of Lehigh, class of '90; Secretary, D C Babbitt, of Lafayette, class of '90; Treasurer, H H Sanger, of Cornell, class of '91. Executive Committee, E E Sturgis, of Harvard; F C Wolcott, of Yale; M Langthorn, of Columbia and J M Emley, of the College of the City of New York.

At a meeting of the National Cross Country Association held at the Grand Union Hotel, New York City, Feb. 13th, a resolution offered by C C Hughes, of Manhattan Athletic Club to amend the rule which prevents athletes who have not resided in this country one year from competing in championship runs, so as to allow such athletes to compete in individual runs, not for the championship, was adopted.

It is about time that the proprietors of the New York Spirit of the Times and of the Turf, Field and Farm put a stop to the personal controversy of their athletic editors. Each week the readers of both journals are compelled to digest column upon column of spiteful personal matter. These quarreling scribes should be made confine their notes to legitimate athletic news.

The largest canoe ever constructed in the United States is that now being built for the Rochester (N. Y.) Canoe Club by Capt. Ruggles. It is modeled after the Toronto Club's big canoe Huck-ta-hee, is 30 feet over all, 50 inches wide, and 22 inches deep amidships. It will be manned by sixteen paddles, although it can be easily handled by four men, and is intended to comfortably accommodate thirty-five persons.

The Union Armory in New Haven, Conn., was well filled with interested spectators on the evening of Saturday, March 8th, gathered to witness the annual joint meeting of the Yale Athletic Association and the Second Regiment. The meeting was open to all amateur athletes, and the clubs of New York and vicinity, together with Harvard University, were well represented in the different events. The entertainment afforded satisfaction to the lovers of athletics, although no specially good performances took place.

SUMMARY.

Forty yard run—A. H. Green, Manhattan Athletic Club and Harvard Athletic Association, 1ft., first, in 5⅗s.; W. C. Downs, New York Athletic Club and Harvard Athletic Association, 5ft., second.

Regimental fifty yard run—T. J. Lee, Company E, scratch, first, in 6½s.; P. Kennedy, Company K, 1ft., second.

Regimental one mile walk—A. C. Hunt, Company E, 30s., first, in 8m. 45s.; W. Schubert, Company D, 20s., second.

Two hundred and twenty yard hurdle race—E. Lentilhon, New York Athletic Club, 1yd., first, 31½s.; E. E. Barnes, New Jersey Athletic Club, 1yd., second.

Regimental one mile walk—H. M. Lee, Company C., 10yds., first, in 31s. 2-5; H. W. Embler, Company D, second.

One mile walk—C. H. Bardeen, Harvard, 25s., first, in 7m. 30s.; J. K. Punderfore, Yale, second.

Putting the Shot—W. P. Nugent, New Haven, Ill., first, 37ft. 7½in.; E. J. Giannini, New York Athletic Club, scratch second.

One mile run.—J. P. Lloyd, Yale '91 scratch first in 4m. 53 s.; W. S. French, New Jersey Athletic Clubs 35yds., second.

Quarter mile run.—C. H. Pierre, Harvard 22yds., first in 57 1-5s., J. McQueeney, New Haven 8yds, second.

Running high jump.—A. H. Green, Harvard scratch won 5ft. 8in.

Potato race.—W. S. French New Jersey Athletic Club, first F. C. Puffer, New Jersey Athletic Club, second.

The meeting of the National Cross Country Association Games Committee, held at the Grand Union Hotel, New York City, March 1st, was presided over by President B C Williams, who tendered a complimentary breakfast to his confreres, C C Hughes, J H Mellor and Will Frank. The preliminaries of the monster handicap run, to take place at Morris' Park at 3:30 P M March 15th, were decided upon. The committee will visit Morris' Park next Sunday, 9, to lay out the course, which will be done in such a manner as to have the entire race run in full view of the spectators in the grand stand. The obstacles in the shape of fences, hedges and water Jumps will be of the most approved kind. The committee is in receipt of valuable prizes from E W Kearney, N Y A C; A G Mills, N Y A C; W G Schuyler, N Y A C; J H Mellor, Prospect Harriers; J F Pedemen, M A C; the New York Jockey Club, New York Herald, and from five other patrons of cross country running. The winner of the race will receive a magnificent prize, the runner who finishes second will receive a handsome and valuable gold watch, and the next eight placed men will receive a fine trophy. The runner who makes the fastest time in the race will be awarded a handsome silver cup by the New York Herald. The cup will be a credit alike to the paper and the lucky winner, and the competition for it will be the feature of the great race. The New York Jockey Club will give a handsome trophy to the club having the first six men to finish. Each starter will receive a solid silver souvenir medal, to be stricken from one of the National Cross Country Association's standard dies. The Games Committee has received assurances from about every prominent club and college within 250 miles of New York City to the effect that entries will be sent to this gigantic run!

A proposition has been made by the League of American Wheelmen that a committee from that body and one from the Amateur Athletic Union meet and arrange a settlement of the differences now existing between them concerning the payment of travelling expenses and entrance fees of the racing men. It is hoped that the impending war may be averted by carrying out this proposition.

Tempest, 2:19, has not won a race in South America as yet, although she has been in the hands of that careful conditioner, Charlie Parker, who has also handled J. Q. A gentleman writing to an Eastern contemporary, says: A great many of the owners of trotters are dissatisfied with the judgment on the races this season. The facts are that they received their just dues. As they cannot win with a hop-skipping runner, they kick. Our rules are very strict in regard to running. A horse running twenty-five meters is distanced, and twenty-five meters is not far. The kick comes when they finish first, and are set back for running. People coming here with trotters should bear this in mind, as a good level-headed horse that can go the distance on a trot, if not a record-breaker, will prove a bread-winner, as there is plenty of racing.

THE FARM.

The Beef Outlook.

BY JOHN M. STAHL.

We all know that the price of cattle is too low. Eighty per cent. of the men that have fattened cattle during the past three or four years have fed at a loss. What are the reasons for this? Some put the blame on Armour and the other dressed meat men. I have no love for Armour, but I believe that if the dressed meat men are guilty the butchers are far more guilty. Whether or not there is a combination among dressed beef men to put the price of cattle down, no outsider knows; but it is significant that there is a widespread impression that such combination exists. It is certain that in some stock yards the buyers for the dressed meat men are in command of the situation; they fix prices; Further, cattle bid in by a dressed beef buyer in Kansas City cannot be sold for more in Chicago than was offered in Kansas City. This indicates pretty clearly that the dressed beef men have control of the market. It may be only an "understanding," not a combination. Does not this control of prices on certain grades also argue collusion on the part of stockyards companies?

But while Armour pays low prices for cattle, he pays a better price than do the local butchers, even considering quality, and the dressed beef men handle better cattle on an average than do the local butchers. Further, Armour sells to consumers for much less than do the local butchers. The local butchers sell to consumers now at the same prices they got when they paid from two to three times as much per pound for live cattle, except where dressed beef competition forced them to lower their prices. Good butchers' cattle sell in Quincy now for from two to two and one-quarter cents per pound; one-third of what the butchers buy cost them less than two cents per pound on the hoof. Yet steaks cost ten to twelve and one-half cents per pound. Isn't that a handsome margin? It is so big that butchers are making money, although the wide margin has attracted to the business twice as many men as are needed Every town now has butchers galore. And if the dressed beef men have combined to fix prices, so have local butchers; there is the same evidence in the one case that there is in the other. The dressed beef men make prices in the big markets and the butchers in the local markets. The farmer is helpless. He cannot raise a butcher's bid. He must take what is offered at home and he must take what is offered at Chicago. The butchers are just as hard on the farmer as is Armour, and they are much harder on the consumer. Armour has brought good beef within the every day reach of many that could rarely afford it when they were compelled to buy of local butchers. Thus he has increased the consumption of beef, which is at least an indirect good. People that have become accustomed to meat every day will continue to use it though the price has advanced somewhat. Armour has effected a permanent increase in meat consumption.

I believe that supply and demand is yet stronger than any combination or understanding among dressed beef men or butchers; and therefore I believe that better prices for beef cattle are ahead of us. The low prices that have prevailed during past years have discouraged cattle rearing and have latterly rushed cattle to market. At present we are not fully stocked with growing cattle. Two years from now a scarcity of ripe cattle will be apparent and prices will be better. The man that starts with young things now will come out all right. Low prices have increased beef consumption and, as already stated, this will be largely permanent. People will have beef and good prices will accompany a shorter supply. The man that is fattening good cattle will make a good profit. Where good stockers were bought in the fall for two cents per pound, they are being fed on twenty cent corn. Three cents per pound on the farm when they are ripe will make a profit and they will bring more than that.

It is important, as affecting the supply of cattle on the market and the disposition to sell, to understand correctly the figures given out from Chicago and Kansas City. Those figures are correct, but comparing the receipts at Chicago or Kansas City now with the receipts of ten years ago gives an erroneous idea of the growth of the cattle supply, for this season. On account of the development of the dressed and canned meat industry, a considerably larger proportion of cattle are now put on the large markets. A less per cent. are slaughtered on the farms and in villages. The cattle supply has not grown near so fast as the receipts at Chicago and Illinois.—Indiana Farmer.

Abandoning Beef.

The discouragements connected with the production of beef cattle in the last few years have been great—unparalleled, in fact, in the history of the country; and in consequence a very considerable percentage of farmers have turned away altogether from the business of cattle feeding to some other specialty which seemed for the time to promise better. This change is most natural under the circumstances, and is only history repeating itself. But there is a tendency to carry the matter beyond reason, and it strikes us that just here is room for a word of caution.

If the general industry of farming is to be carried on with good average results to the bulk of those engaged in it there must be a wide diversification of labor and products. The fact that each may grow what he pleases is the source of infinite variation in the relative qualities of the various food staples produced; and while it is one thing one season it may be entirely another thing another season which suffers in value from overproduction. In some things overproduction can be corrected in a single year, and in others—as in cattle—years are required for restoring a wholesome tone to the trade. In other words, a widespread abandonment of beef-growing does not at once show itself in a positive improvement in prices.

The original trouble with the cattle industry some years ago was overproduction. This has for some time been gradually correcting itself, until we believe that it is no longer the great diffiulty in the way of good cattle times. As an obstacle to improvement it has been so far eliminated that, in good to choice cattle at least, it is getting to be a problem as to where the markets are after a while to get their supplies. So decided are the proofs of the correctness of this position that we believe that if the dressed beef industry were not in the way good beef cattle would command today prices which would thoroughly satisfy producers. The signs of the times are that the power of beef monopoly to oppose and thus stand in the way of farm prosperity will one of these days in some way be curtailed. But whether efforts to compass this end are successful or not, there is reason to believe that the time is coming when, in spite of this hindrance, the market will assert itself again.

To the man who will sit down and carefully "size up" the situation it must appear that there is more danger of overproduction in some other things in the early future than in beef cattle. Take dairying, for instance. There is no lack of evidence that this may one of these days be overdone; not that more fine butter may be made than there is a market for, but that the average maker of decently good butter will find himself after a while in an overstocked market. We do not expect to ever see dairying so depressed as beef-making has been—for a good beef market affords an easy remedy; but we cannot believe with so many of the enthusiastic dairy writers of the day, that dairying will be periennially so much better than the other side of the cattle industry, or that it cannot be badly overdone.

In view of the signs of the times, we feel like remonstrating with those who act as though there were no future for the beef breeds of cattle. The craze for abandoning beef has well nigh driven the possibility of anything better to come out of the minds of many people. Those who would keep their business well in hand for taking advantage of probable developments should not fail to keep the beef idea in view in shaping up their farm stock. We must be largely beef producers if we are a nation of successful farmers; and both branches of the cattle industry will flourish best when neither is abandoned for the other.—Stockman and Farmer.

Cattle Trading in Ireland.

An aged Irish cattle dealer was at death's door, and surrounded by his family, was slowly and surely departing. Suddenly with a holy calm in his eyes, he said, "Boys listen to me; I've nothing much to lave yez, but"—and here his sons drew closer round his bed—"there's wan bit of advice I'd like yez to keep in moind." "Go on father dear," said one. The old man with a struggle seemed to gather his remaining strength, and with a gleam of light borrowed from other days, touching to behold, gasped out, "boys this that I've to tell will be useful to yez all the days of your loife. Whisper." Closer and closer drew the expectant sons, anxious to catch the faint tones of the dying man. "Boys when you're at markets or fairs, buying or selling, never—drink—whisky wid yer back to the fire." And conscious of a duty nobly done, the old man departed in peace."

Dehorning.

We devote this week a considerable portion of our space to a report of the interesting trial at Haddington, in which a cattle dealer named George Wilson was charged with cruelty to certain bullocks caused by dehorning them. Notwithstanding the mass of evidence—professional and otherwise—led by the Procurator Fiscal, the learned sheriff had no difficulty in arriving at a decision completely exonerating the defendant. We, as butchers, are deeply interested in cases of this kind, and our influence should be exerted in every possible way to induce breeders, feeders and dealers to practice dishorning in every case. The anomoly which makes the practice illegal only in England was the result of persistent prosecution by the Royal Society for the Prevention of Cruelty to Animals, and this Haddington case no doubt had its origin from the same quarter. The splendid work done by this Royal Society is freely admitted, but there are many who, like ourselves, consider the action of the Society in this particular matter as neither more nor less than meddlesome persecution.—London Meat Trades Journal.

Around El Paso.

George B. Loving, of El Paso, writing to the Fort Worth Journal, says:

There is but little doing in the cattle business through this section. Kansas feeders are picking up quite a number of three and four-year-old steers through southern New Mexico and Arizona, for which they are paying $15 to $17 per head. These cattle go to Kansas to assist in eating the over-supply of corn, and later on to help glut the market. Speaking of Kansas reminds me of a conversation I overheard a few weeks ago in a restaurant in Hutchinson, Kansas. A farmer came in and asked the price of a dinner; and when told that he could have a good square meal for 20 cents, replied that he was very hungry, but thought he had better fast until he could reach home, as he did not feel disposed to give two bushels of corn for one meal.

As stated in a former letter, some 30,000 to 40,000 cattle will be driven from that part of Texas lying between El Paso and the Pecos river. These cattle are now being gathered, and most all of them will be on the trail by the 15th of March. Quite a number of these cattle were intended for the Cherokee strip, but will now be ruled out of that section by the recent proclamation of the President. Suppose, however, that they will be able to find grazing grounds in the Chickasaw, Choctaw and other nations of the big Indian Territory.

C. B. Zeek, a well known cattle buyer through this section, who is connected with the well known live stock commission house of the James H. Campbell company, with headquarters at Kansas City, was in El Paso yesterday, and purchased of the International Investment agency 500 Arizona feeders, three and four years old, for which he paid $15 per head.

Care of Brood-Sows.

Those who are to have early litters of spring pigs must give the brood sows proper treatment during the winter months. The first requisite is good shelter and a clean, wholesome sleeping place. The next is a reasonable amount of liberty. It will not do to keep a brood sow shut up continuously in a small pen, even if it is kept reasonably clean. She will become sluggish and inert, with none of the vigor and muscular stamina needed to produce and rear healthy pigs. A certain amount of exercise every day is necessary. If she will not take her daily "constitutional" of her own accord, it is best to drive her out. Nothing is better during mild open weather than the run of a lot where she may root to her heart's content. Never put a ring in the nose of a brood sow.

The food should be abundant, but not of a fattening character. Milk, bran and middling, with a small modicum of oil-meal, varied frequently by boiled turnips, carrots, beets or other roots, clover-hay chopped short and mixed with the cooked ration, and in cold weather a small proportion of corn meal will keep the animal in good thrifty condition. It is well to remember that swine are omniverous, and an occasional morsel of animal food is always acceptable. The 'lights,' entrails and other waste material of a slaughter house when attainable are desirable additions to the animal's dietary. It is well to keep a mixture of salt, charcoal, and a little sulphur in a trough where the sow can help herself *ad libitum*. It is always best to keep brood sows separate from the rest of the herd. This is specially imperative as the time for farrowing approaches.—Colman's Rural World.

Crossbred Buffaloes.

Twenty-two years ago there was a buffalo half breed cow slaughtered in New York City, and the editor of an agricultural journal was invited to dinner to test some of the beef. He pronounced it tender and juicy, and averred that it possessed a slight but agreeable wild taste, and was superior to the beef of domestic animals. And now a breeder out West is engaged largely in producing a herd of crosses between buffalo bulls and Black Polled cows. Three-year-old crossbred steers weigh 2,500 to 3,000 pounds, and the cows 1,200 to 1,500. The steers make excellent oxen. They are strong, hardy and quick in their movements. The cows give less milk, but richer than domestic cows. The crossbreds are docile. It is believed that a crossbred bull mated with a Jersey cow will give to the progeny greater size and hardiness and equal milking qualities for butter when richness of milk is considered. The hair of the crossbred is glossy and silky, and a good-sized hide will sell for $50. It makes two large "buffalo robes." The crossbreds retain the characteristic of the buffalo in assembling together and facing storms instead of separately seeking the lee side of fences and buildings, as domestic animals do. A neighbor is negotiating for a bull buffalo for breeding purposes. While these animals are nearly extinct in America, "Buffalo Jones" possessing nearly all that remain, there are many thousands of them in Australia.

GALEN WILSON,

The Light Brahma.

The Light Brahma is justly termed the grandest fowl on earth. In disposition, quiet, loving and lovable; in carriage, majestic, dignified, the very king of all Asiastic breeds, he runs, for general utility, about an even race with America's national fowl the Plymouth Rock. Thoroughbred he is, if properly fed and cared for entirely free from the hackneyed objections urged against mongrel Asiatic stock; he is not lazy nor gluttonish, and does not run around for months in summer time without any clothes on. He thrives equally well in confined quarters or with free range, and in confinement he distances all competitors in the return given for his keeping. His flesh is toothsome as the ideal spring chicken at an early stage of his growth from the broiler size up until he is a year old, and a spring chicken that will weigh ten pounds is by no means to be sniffed at about Thanksgiving time.

The breed as we know it to-day is an American production, evolved from the old long-legged Shanghai, by eliminating its undesirable qualities and engrafting certain foreign features upon it. The poultry literature of the past twenty years contains more relating to this grand bird than to any other. Its economic qualities are of the highest order—witness the production of eggs at the most profitable season and the fine quantity and quality of its flesh. As a fancier's fowl it fills the bill; its particolored plumage furnishing an incentive to the most careful breeding, and the noble bearing of the best birds a sufficient reward for all the efforts required to secure it. Few who have bred the Light Brahma ever care to give it up entirely, its loving disposition endearing it to the true fanciers no less than the courage of the game fowl fascinates its admirers.

Now that the breed has a special association pledged to its advancement, which started with a generous support and is rapidly growing in membership, we may expect it to still further widen the circle of its influence in fancierdom.—Colman's Rural World.

Duck Raising in China.

Duck and goose-farming are great industries in South China. I saw duck boats at Canton upon some of which lived as many as two thousand birds. These birds were of all ages and sizes, from half to full grown, and I consider them one of the most wonderful things in the land of Celestials. The owners of the boats were big-hatted Chinamen in blue gowns and wide blue pantaloons, which flapped against their bare legs as they moved about watching their flocks. These duck herders row or scull the boats along the low banks of the rivers and creeks, and stop from time to time to let the ducks crawl out upon the marshy lands, where they are expected to get their living by digging in the mud with their bills for worms and snails. It is "root duck or die," and the duck roots to such an extent that he fattens very quickly and grows very fast. These feeders have such a control that the ducks will come back on the boat the moment they are called. They come with a rush, too, and I noted that the bird last on board always got a sharp slap from the bamboo rod of the herder. When the ducks are fat they are sold to the salting establishments or are peddled out to the market men.

The herder in the first instance gets his birds, when half grown, from the duck farmers, who buy them from the duck hatching establishments, a peculiar institution of China. These incubators hatch thousands of eggs at a time, and, rude as they are, they are managed so carefully by experienced hands that very few birds are lost. The eggs are placed in baskets filled with heated chaff, and are for the first twenty-four hours hung over charcoal fires in a close room kept at such a temperature that the egg will be just so warm, and no warmer. The experience of the semi-naked employees rather than the thermometer regulates the height of the temperature, and I am not able to give the degree Fahrenheit at which the rooms are heated. At the end of this time the eggs are carried in cloths to another room of a different temperature, and in order that they may be equally heated they are put in rattan baskets lined with coarse brown paper, and moved about from day to day. The eggs are in the upper part of the basket during the day, and are put in the lower part at night, and they are thus moved about for two weeks. At the end of this time they are taken to a third room and laid upon shelves, wrapped up in thick paper or warm cotton. This room is also heated and the temperature is so well regulated throughout that the eggs hatch out at the same time. During almost the same hour a thousand little bills pick their way through a thousand white shells and the little ducklings voice forth their first weak quack. The duck farmers of the vicinity know when each big hatching is to take place and are on hand to buy the fluffy little creatures. They carry them to their farms, which are located on the rivers or creeks, and they have as many rules for treating them as our stock breeders have for their Jersey cows and their blooded horses. They first let them have rice water to drink, and after this change them to a diet of boiled rice. They next give them bran mixed with chaff, and after a time allow them to go to the creek and forage for themselves. They are as careful of them during their babyhood as an American mother is of her child, and for five days after they are born they try to keep them away from all noise whatsoever. They pen them in a coop, the bottom of which is covered with grass, until they are two weeks old, and are very particular to see that they are provided with clear spring water to drink during the first two weeks.—F. Carpenter, in American Agriculturist.

THE GUN.

Trap at Lathrop.

EDITOR BREEDER AND SPORTSMAN:—Inclosed find scores of our tournament on March 12th. We had quite a nice representation from the central part of the State. Everything ran smoothly and the participants said many pleasant things of the management, for which myself and Mr. Howland desire to express the highest appreciation. Among the visiting sportsmen were O. M. Judy of Turlock; F Coykendall, G. Anderson and J. Delmas of San Jose; J. Kelly and D. McAvoy of San Francisco. The famous shots of the home team were present and found it necessary to do their best work. There was a large attendance of spectators, and the sport was enjoyed by everybody.

The first match was at six single live birds, Hurlingham style, entrance $2 50, with three prizes of 50, 30 and 20 per cent. Following is the score:—

Name	Score
C. J. Haas	1 0 1 1 2 1—5
J. Kelley	0 1 2 0 1 0-3
F. O. Scarlett	1 2 1 1 1 0—5
A. B Sperry	1 0 1 2 2 1-5
C. A. Merrill	1 1 1 1 2 1—6
O. M. Judy	1 1 1 1 1 0—5
D. MCAvoy	1 0 0 1 2 0—3

Merrill took the first prize; Haas, Scarlett and Perry shot for the second and third prizes in the fifteen bird match.

The next match was at five pairs of live birds, entrance $5 with prizes of 50, 30 and 20 per cent. The score:—

Name	Score
Merrill	10 11 11 11 01—8
Scarlett	11 10 10 10 11—7
Kelly	01 11 01 01 10—5
Haas	11 00 11 10 11—7
Coykendall	11 00 11 10 00—4
Anderson	00 00 11 00 11—4
Delmas	10 00 w
Judy	10 00 w
Sperry	00 10 10 w

Merrill took the first prize and Scarlett and Haas divided the other Prizes.

The next match was at fifteen single live birds, Hurlingham style, entrance $7.50, divided into four prizes of 40, 30, 20 and 10 per cent. The score:—

Name	Score
Merrill	1 0 0 1 2 1 1 1 1 1 0 1 1 1 1—13
Coykendall	1 2 1 2 2 1 0 2 1 0 2 1 1 1 2—12
Anderson	2 1 0 1 2 1 1 2 1 2 0 1 0 0 1—13
Haas	1 1 2 1 1 1 1 0 2 1 1 0 1 2 1—11
McAvoy	1 0 1 1 0 2 1 1 0 w
Delmas	0 1 0 1 1 0 0 w
Scarlett	2 1 1 0 1 1 0 1 1 2 1 1 1 2 1—13
Kelly	2 1 0 1 1 1 2 2 1 1 2 2 2 1 1-14
Sperry	2 2 1 0 1 0 2 1 1 0 1 2 2 0 1—11
Judy	2 0 1 1 1 1 1 2 1 1 1 1 1 2 2—14
Dr. Phillips	1 0 0 0 2 1 1 w

Kelly and Judy divided the first and second prizes $52.50; Judy also won the tie on the first match for $8 75. Coykendall, Haas and Scarlett agreed to shoot off for the third and fourth prizes in the next match.

The next match was at eight single birds. $5 entrance with three prizes of 50, 30 and 20 per cent. The score.

Name	Score
Scarlett	1 2 1 1 2 1 2 1—8
Coykendall	1 1 2 1 2 1 1 0—7
Sperry	2 2 2 0 0 1 1 1—6
Haas	1 1 1 1 1 1 1 1—8
Merrill	1 1 0 1 1 1 0 2—6
Judy	2 1 1 1 1 1 2 1—8
Kelly	1 2 1 1 1 1 1 1—8
Phillips	0 1 2 1 1 0 0 1—5
Cadwallader	1 2 1 2 2 0 2 w—6
Anderson	0 2 1 w
Delmas	1 1 0 w

Scarlett, Haas, Judy and Kelly divided the money, $55; Haas and Scarlett divided the former tie of $22.50.

The next was a freeze out at live birds, entrance $2.50. The score:

Name	Score
Coykendall	2 2 2 0
Scarlett	1 1 2 1 2
Delmas	2 1 1 1 1
Judy	1 1 1 1 1
Merrill	1 1 0
Kelly	2 2 0
Haas	1 0
Anderson	0
Sperry	0

Scarlett, Judy and Delmas agreed to shoot off for the prize in the next contest.

The next was a freeze out at live birds, use of one barrel only, at thirty yards, entrance $2 50. The score:

Name	Score
Coykendall	1 1 1 1
Delmas	1 1 1 1
Scarlett	1 1 1 0
Judy	1 1 1 1
Merrill	1 1 1 1
Haas	0

Coykendall, Delmas, Judy and Merrill divided the pot of $15; Delmas and Judy divided the tie of the last match, $22.50.

The following match was at fifteen singles and five pairs of doubles, clay birds, making a possible twenty-five; entrance, $2.50, divided into four prizes of 40, 30, 20 and 10 per cent. The score.

Sperry	0 1 1 0 1 1 1 1 1 1 1 1 0 1 1	00 11 00 10 00—14
Haas	1 0 1 1 0 1 1 1 1 1 0 1 0 0 1	10 11 01 11 11—16
Scarlett	1 1 1 1 1 1 1 1 1 0 0 1 0 0 1	11 10 10 10 01— 9
Phillips	0 0 1 1 1 1 1 1 1 0 1 0 0 1 1	10 10 10 00 01—14
Coykendall	0 1 1 1 1 1 1 1 1 1 1 1 1 1 1	11 10 10 10 10—19
Anderson	1 1 1 1 1 1 0 1 1 1 0 1 1 1 0	11 11 11 11 11—22
Kelly	0 1 1 1 0 1 1 0 1 1 1 1 1 1 1	11 10 01 11 11—20
Knight	0 1 0 0 0 0 0 1 1 1 1 0 0 1 1	10 10 10 01 11—13
Delmas	0 1 1 1 0 1 1 1 1 1 1 10 0 1	11 11 11 11 11—22
Cadwallader	1 1 1 1 1 1 1 1 1 1 1 1 1 1 1	11 01 11 10 11—22
Judy	1 0 1 1 1 1 1 1 1 1 1 0 1 0 1	11 11 11 01 01—20

Anderson and Cadwallader divided the first and second moneys; Delmas won the third; Kelly and Judy divided the fourth.

The last match was at six singles and three pairs of doubles, clay birds: entrance $2.50, with three moneys. The score:

Anderson	0 1 1 0 0 1	0 01 01— 6
Delmas	1 1 1 1 1 1	11 10 10—10
Coykendall	1 1 1 0 1 1	11 11 10—10
Cadwallader	1 1 1 1 0 0	10 10 11— 8
Judy	0 1 1 1 1 1	11 11 11—11
Scarlett	1 1 1 0 1 0	11 10 01— 7

Judy won the first money; Delmas and Coykendall divided the second and third moneys. F. O. SCARLETT.

LATHROP, March 13, '90.

California Homing Club.

The California Homing Club has announced the following as its schedule of races in its pigeon race tournament to commence on April 13th. First race, April 13th, from San Jose, distance 37½ miles; second race, May 4th, from Pajaro, distance 70 miles; third race, May 18th, from Soledad, distance 105½ miles; fourth race, June 1st, from San Lucas, distance 140 miles; fifth race, July 1st, from San Luis Obispo, distance 200 miles; sixth race, August 1st, from Santa Barbara, distance 282 miles; seventh race, August 22nd, from Los Angeles, distance 340 miles.

California Wing Shooting Club.

The days of San Bruno as a resort for trap shooters seem to have been numbered. The ground during the summer is undoubtedly the most suitable in the State and one of the best in the country because of the generally prevailing high winds which blow from the score to the traps and cause many twisting tailers which try the mettle of the most expert shots. But the ground is comparatively inaccessible, can be reached by but two trains daily, and people must wait until the late afternoon before being able to return. The attendance of spectators has fallen away until only very few visit the place. In place of San Bruno, however, a new ground has been fitted up that more nearly meets the needs of local experts than any place hitherto at command. The Oakland Trotting Park is reached by San Franciscans via the Berkeley train to Shell Mound Station, from whence a walk of three hundred yards brings one to the shooting ground.

Visitors from a distance can leave their trains at 16th street Station, Oakland, and then take the Berkeley train back to Shell Mound Station. The place is reached by half-hourly trains between 6 and 10 o'clock A. M. From 10 to three the trains run hourly. Between three and 8 half-hourly.

The proprietor is Mr. W. H. Hinchman, a very pleasant and popular young gentleman, whose whole energies are being given to the care of the trotting park. He has erected a convenient shooting house, gun racks, seating, etc., and is ready at any time to entertain those who care to do a little trap shooting.

That jolly and accommodating old time purveyor of live birds, Mr. Murphy, in the Center Market, has contracted to furnish the birds, which is sufficient guarantee that they will be lively ones.

Blue Rock targets will be supplied by Messrs. Clabrough and Golcher, together with the latest devices in the way of traps and appurtenances.

The park is level, nicely swarded, pretty as a picture, convenient, well suited for shooting.

A nicely conducted club house is at hand for luncheons and the like, and the movement is one that will conduce to the development of the shooting interest in a high degree

Last Sunday was one of the typical California spring days, clear, warm and delightful, and it was only fitting that the new ground should be opened formally by the oldest club in the State, the California Wing Shooting Club.

The birds were fairly good and the scores creditable. American Shooting Association Rules have been adopted by the California as well as all other clubs of any prominence, and in operation were pronounced very good. Messrs. Orr, Eidy, Cadman and Grimchen shot by invitation. Mr. Crittenden Robinson had the only clean score, and that he made with all his old-time sureness and brilliancy.

Messrs. Orr, H. C. Golcher, Thompson, Schroder and Fay scored eleven each, all of them losing birds dead out of bounds. Dr. Knowles lost a bird in the same way, and Mr. C. M. Osborn had the unusual bad luck to see both of the birds which he failed to score just wabble out of bounds and die. Will De Vaull was clear off, scoring only 7, an absurdly low record for him.

The club will meet at Oakland Trotting Park on the third Sunday in each month, beginning to shoot at 10 A. M. The first event of yesterday was the club match at 12 pigeons, American Shooting Association rules, for the regular club prizes, and the scores were:

Name	Score
Knowles	1 1 1 1 1 0 0 1 1 1 1 1—10
Osborn	1 1 0 1 1 1 1 1 0 1 1 1—10
Heath	0 1 1 1 1 1 0 1 1 1 1 1— 9
H. C. Golcher	1 1 1 1 1 1 1 1 1 1 1 0—11
A. Schwenn	1 1 1 1 1 0 1 1 0 1 1 1—10
Haas	1 1 0 1 1 1 1 1 1 1 1 0—10
Thompson	1 1 1 1 1 0 1 1 1 1 1 1—11
Lewis	0 0 1 1 0 0 1 0 1 0 0 0— 4
DeVaull	0 1 0 0 0 1 1 0 1 1 1 1— 7
Orr	1 1 1 1 0 1 1 1 1 1 1 1—11
A. Heath	1 0 1 0 1 1 0 0 1 0 0 0— 5
Grimchen	0 1 1 1 1 1 1 0 1 0 1 0— 8
Schroder	1 1 1 1 1 1 1 0 1 1 1 1—11
Fay	1 1 0 1 1 1 1 1 1 1 1 1—11
Eddy	1 1 1 1 0 1 1 1 1 0 1 1—10
Cadman	0 1 1 1 0 1 1 1 1 1 1 1—10
Robinson	1 1 1 1 1 1 1 1 1 1 1 1—12
Arnold	1 0 0 1 1 1 0 1 w

After the main match, a $5 pool at 7 birds was shot off, the score being:

Name	Score
Osborn	1 0 1 1 1 1 1—6
Robinson	1 1 1 1 1 0 1—6
Haas	1 1 1 1 1 1 1—7
Eddy	1 1 1 0 0 1 1—5
Slade	1 1 1 1 1 0 0—5
H. C. Golcher	1 1 1 1 1 1 1—7
F. E. Coykendall	0 1 1 0 1 0 1—4
Fay	1 1 1 0 0 w
Schroder	0 1 1 1 1 1 0—5
Curl	1 0 0 1 1 1 0—4

The pool was divided by Messrs. Haas and H. C. Golcher.

Captain Brewer in Australia.

Considerable interest was shown by knights of the trigger in the match between Captain Brewer of the United States, and Mr. Clarke, one of the crack shots of the Melbourne Gun Club, on January 22nd, on the ground of the Melbourne Club at North Brighton, says the Melbourne Sportsman. The attendance was large, and the match passed off in the most pleasant manner. The American at first desired that the contest should be carried out under London Gun Club Rules, but agreed to the shooting being under the Melbourne Gun Club rules. The difference in the rules of these bodies is this: The shootist under Melbourne rules, after sighting, is not allowed to keep the gun at his shoulder. He must at once remove it, and wait until the bird rises before he elevates the weapon. The London rules allow that the gun can be kept at the shoulder. Captain Brewer was not altogether comfortable as regards this, but he shot nevertheless with wonderful accuracy, and upheld his reputation. His opponent performed well too. The match was for $1000 a side, 100 birds each 30 yards rise. Mr Holske stood umpire for Captain Brewer, and Mr. W. Sayer, the well known Melbourne pigeon shot, for Mr. Clarke. Mr. P. Glenister was appointed referee. The American had a trial at half a dozen birds before the match, and at 1:45 o'clock the contest was commenced. Captain Brewer's first bird got away, although it had been hit. He essayed the task of gathering it, but the pigeon eluded him. Thus the opening shot was a miss. The next was beautifully grassed, but the third got away.

Mr. Clark started much better by killing his first brace. However, he missed the succeeding two. Matters were pushed on speedily, and when half the number of birds allowed each competitor had been set free, Captain Brewer's record was 42, and Mr. Clarke's 37. Truly, this was very fair shooting, but a great improvement was to come, and after shooting three more Captain Brewer killed 35 in succession, and out of 56 he only missed once. Mr. Clarke missed 5 out of 55. The outcome of the match was a win for Capt. Brewer with 91 to his credit. Mr. Clarke killed 82. The winner used a Cashmore gun, and Mr. Clarke a Pu[illegible] Both fired with Schultz powder. The following were scores:—

Name	Score
Captain Brewer (United States), 30 yds—	0 1 0 1 1 1 1 1 1 1 1 1 0 1 1 1 1 1 1 1 1 1 1 1 1 [illegible]
	1 1 1 1 1 1 1 1 0 0 1 0 1 1 1 1 1 1 0 1 1 0 1 1 1 1 [illegible]
	1 1 1 1 1 1 1 1 1 1 1 1 1 1 1 1 1 1 1 1 1 1 1 1 1 1 [illegible]
	1 1 1 1 0 1 1 1 1 1 1 1 1 1 1 1 1 1 1 1 1 1 1 1 1 1 [illegible]
Mr. L. Clark (Australia), 30 yds—	1 1 0 1 1 1 0 0 0 1 0 1 1 1 1 1 1 1 1 0 1 1 1 1 1 0 [illegible]
	0 1 1 1 1 1 1 1 1 0 1 0 1 1 1 1 1 1 1 1 0 1 0 1 1 1 [illegible]
	1 1 1 1 1 1 1 1 1 0 1 1 1 1 1 1 1 0 0 1 1 1 1 1 1 [illegible]
	1 1 1 1 1 1 1 1 1 0 1 1 1 1 1 1 1 0 1 1 1 1 1 1 1 [illegible]

Captain Brewer called at the Herald office the day follow[illegible] his match with Mr. Clarke. He freely acknowledged tha[illegible] had received far better treatment and had more courte[illegible] extended to him by the Melbourne Gun Club than he [illegible] had in any portion of Europe. Speaking of the match [illegible] said, "I found Mr Clarke a gentleman who only wis[illegible] fair play, and I am satisfied were any advantage offered [illegible] he and his father, in fact all his friends, would have shun[illegible] the offer, however advantageous it might have been. I h[illegible] travelled all over Europe and can candidly state that [illegible] Clarke is the best shot that I have thus far met. Of co[illegible] I believe we could produce say two better ones in Ame[illegible] Messrs. Crittenden, Robinson and Mitchell; but they ma[illegible] livelihood out of the game; consequently they should be [illegible] perior to a gentleman like Mr Clarke. who merely han[illegible] a gun for pure love of the sport, and devotes no great amo[illegible] of time to practice. He has the makings of a wonderful s[illegible] and when I hang up my implement and go on the retired [illegible] you may then remark that Mr. Clarke will be safe in di[illegible] ing the World's Championship and taking all comers. W[illegible] I came here I hardly expected to meet a man who could [illegible] over 80 birds in 100, and when Mr. Clarke disposed o[illegible] within the boundary line, and under Melbourne rules, [illegible] I became convinced that I had met a real good man. [illegible] should like to hear of him going into a match against [illegible] best shots of Europe. You may rest assured all I posses[illegible] would go on the Australian as a winner. I found the m[illegible] bers of the Gun Club here, as well as Sydney, to be thoro[illegible] gentlemen, and on my return I'll not hesitate to inform [illegible] the Americans that Australia is the best country—outs[illegible] the States, of course—for fair play and hospitality.

[Captain Brewer is in error in presuming that Mr. Critt[illegible] den Robinson makes a living out of the game of trap sho[illegible] ing. It is true that Mr. Robinson is ready to match hi[illegible] self against anyone for almost any amount, but in fact he [illegible] only rarely able to get a match, and is engaged in busin[illegible] in San Francisco, being Secretary of the State Mining [illegible] reau.—ED.]

He Surprised Them.

Clarence Jarvis, Ione's champion quail shot, who is at p[illegible] sent residing in San Francisco, gave some of the crack sh[illegible] of the City a lesson in fine shooting last Sunday. Clarence [illegible] tended a pigeon shooting match of one of the sportsmens cl[illegible] of the City and although he had never tried his hand at t[illegible] shooting before, he took part in the contest. He "paraly[illegible] them all," for he started in by making a clean score of ten [illegible] single birds and then followed up with a clean score at d[illegible] bles winnings the first prize of the match. It's a picnic [illegible] Clarence to shoot pigeons as they go from a trap, but if [illegible] had some of those city sportsmen up here hunting quail [illegible] the brush he'd make them think they couldn't shoot a lit[illegible] bit. "Tramp" Clarence's great quail dog, also took in [illegible] shoot and won much applause by bringing in every bird sh[illegible] by his master, while refusing to get any shot by others [illegible] matter how near they fell to him.—Ione Valley Echo.

[The shooting of "Clarence Jarvis" whose name is unfa[illegible] liar, is not half so surprising as his wonderful nerve in "[illegible] ing" his admirable home paper.—Ed.]

A Match Off.

It has been rumored that Mr. Martinez Chick of San [illegible] ego desired to shoot a match with Mr. Crittenden Robin[illegible] at 100 birds for $500 a side, but the following letter pla[illegible] the matter in another light. We hope another match betw[illegible] the two cracks may soon be brought about. Mr. Chick wr[illegible] to Mr. Robinson on March 10th as follows:

DEAR MR. ROBINSON:—Your letter came to hand, find [illegible] me not in the best of health, and my wife down with [illegible] Grippe. Well, I am anxious to burn some more pow[illegible] with you, but at present you will have to wait a while lon[illegible] as I am not prepared for business reasons to meet you [illegible] the amount, as in our previous matches, and when I [illegible] ready you will receive a formal challenge from your com[illegible] itor. Hoping when we do come together that I may g[illegible] you a three bird harder race, and hoping it may be soon.

SAN DIEGO, March 10, 1890. MARTINEZ CHICK

The tournament at Traver on April 7th and 8th is attr[illegible] ing much attention and will be generally attended.

Wildfowl are plenty about Tulare Lake now, probably [illegible] their northward flight. Sportsmen can reach the lake ei[illegible] from Tulare or Visalia.

The Alameda County Sportsmen's Club shoots this af[illegible] noon at Oakland Trotting Park. The park is reached by [illegible] Berkeley train to Shell Mound. On Saturday afternoon [illegible] the Gun Club will use the same ground.

L. L. Gaffney informs us that the town of Downievill[illegible] at present inhabited by quite a number of deer that w[illegible] captured during the storms the past two months. They w[illegible] around town and are as tame as cattle, some of them go [illegible] up to children on the street to eat food and delicacies gi[illegible] them. One band of fourteen were found near the banks of [illegible] river, above town. They were all bunched in the snow [illegible] left over night, The next day those who found them pic[illegible] out what they wanted and took them to town, where in a [illegible] days they became perfectly tame. Some are kept tied in [illegible] bles and some wander around town at will, returning to [illegible] barn when they have had their exercise. The town dogs [illegible] not disturb them when they are out.

Hector Williamson, when going to Washington on sn[illegible] shoes a short time since, saw two deer, a young and an old [illegible] He took after them and soon caught the old one, which c[illegible] near finishing him by making a lunge at him. He ca[illegible] the animal around the neck and held him until his comp[illegible] ions gave him a knife with which he dispatched the animal. [illegible] caught the young deer and took him home, where he is [illegible] tame and domesticated

A Query.

EDITOR BREEDER AND SPORTSMAN:—In a live bird match of 12 singles, A B C and D, shoot for 1st, 2nd and 3rd money. A and B each get 11 birds, C 10, and D 8. How are stakes to be divided. TUCSON.

Answer.—A and B tie for 1st and 2nd and most shoot off or divide. C takes 3rd.

The officers of the recently organized Santa Cruz Rod and Gun Club are: President, Dr. T. W. Drullard; Vice-President, John Severio; Secretary, E. C Williams; Treasurer, Le Baron Olive. F. L. Stevens, Ed. Abraham and Geo. Ready were appointed a committee to solicit membership.

A crate of Chinese quails was sent to Senator G. G. Goucher of Fresno a few days ago by the Fish Commission and distributed as follows:

W. L. Hedrick, Wildflower, 26; Barton's vineyard, 18; F. G. Parry's orange ranch, 15; J. N. Walker, San Joaquin river, 12; S. H. Williams, near Barton's vineyard, 12; Major Dennett, Wildflower, 12.

The Senator expects to receive in the near future a consignment of pheasants from Oregon and also quail from the East.

Judge Sloane's court room in San Diego was comfortably filled with local nimrods one night last week, called thither for the purpose of organizing a gun club. Mr Tel Grather was chosen as temporary chairman and D. H. Johnson temporary secretary. The matter of indiscriminate slaughter of game was thoroughly discussed, and it was the sense of the meeting that positive steps should be taken at once to put a stop to the unlawful practice. Reference was made to the act passed at the sitting of the last legislature wherein $2,000 was appropriated, not only for the importation of wild turkeys, Bob White quail, pheasants, prairie chickens and other wild birds, but for the lawful protection of the same. The act makes it a misdemeanor for any one to kill certain birds, so imported, until after the last day of the year 1895. It is the object of the sportsmen of San Diego city and county to form a club for the propagation and protection of game in Southern California, and at the same time to provide all lovers of the dog and gun with a vehicle of pleasure and sociability. The initiation fee was placed at $1, and the yearly dues at $1.

ROD.

Perversions.

We regret to note that the Evening Post of this city has been led into taking a wrong position with reference to the relations existing between the State Board of Fish Commissioners and that body of sportsmen known as the State Protective Association. With the association as a body, none but the most friendly relations exist. At a regular meeting of the association, a representative of the Fish Commission asked the club to suggest names of suitable persons to receive appointments as Deputy Fish Commissioners, and some six or more such names were taken and the men appointed.

We are informed by a leader and director in the State Protective Association, that the position taken by the Post is the result of misrepresentations made by a few members who dislike the Fish Commission because of the very qualities which commend the Board to all fair-minded, law-abiding and reputable sportsmen. The Fish Commission was compelled to withdraw the appointments as deputies of several members of the Protective Association, because they persistently violated the law and used their power as Deputy Fish Commissioners to shield themselves in doing so. These men have since desired the Protective Association to champion their cause, and have endeavored to arouse a feeling of enmity against the Fish Commission, but have only succeeded in securing the co-operation of a little handful of men, not of particular moment, and men of whom it is said that they have endeavored, and are now endeavoring, to give a political cast to the Protective Association. The better class of members, which includes a great majority, repudiates those schemers, and intends to hold the Protective Association to its legitimate aims, and to uphold the Fish Commission in its efforts to do its duty.

The association is a large one, and includes many men of wide reputation as sportsmen of the genuine sort. Such men cannot afford to be manipulated for base ends by a few wire-workers, and we hope they will stamp out the undesirable element at once, and that the Evening Post will set itself straight in the matter

All of the acts of the Fish Commission can be canvassed by any gentleman of the press, and such canvass will, we are persuaded, convince any one that the Commission is doing grand work, honest work and effective work, and is fairly entitled to unreserved support.

A visit to the streams along the North Pacific Coast Railway was made last Saturday by Chief of Patrol Callundan and deputies. Many men with fishing tackle were found, but not one of them did any actual fishing, some one having given warning.

In another column will be found the advertisement of Messrs. Clabrough, Golcher & Co., 630 and 632 Montgomery street, San Francisco, announcing that they are wholesale and retail dealers in the finest fishing tackle procurable in any of the markets of the world and agents for the leading tackle manufacturers of America and Europe. The firm has been noted among anglers, from fish and game warden Allen, of Bangor, Maine, to those in the South Sea Islands, for the invariable superiority of the goods handled; the finest things in gut, flies snelled or eyed and lines, while its specialities in reels and split bamboo rods have given it a commanding position among those given to the refinements of the gentle art. Trap shooters needs are also especially catered to, the firm being agents for Blue Rock targets and traps, and all of the leading gun manufacturers. The time is at hand when legitimate fishermen must begin to select their tackle and none should do so without consulting Clabrough, Golcher & Co.

The Supervisors of El Dorado county have under consideration an ordinance to protect the fish in the streams by preventing them from getting into the irrigating and mining ditches and destroyed in them. The proposed ordinance is as follows: "The proprietors of all water ditches and flumes drawing their supply from the waters of this county, shall place and keep in good repair at the heads of their respective ditches or flumes, through which the water from the stream or lake entering the ditch or flume shall pass, strips of wood or other material, the meshes between which shall not exceed one inch in width, for the prevention of the passage of fish from the stream or lake into the ditches or flumes. Any person taking water from any stream or lake in this county in violation of the provisions of this ordinance is guilty of a misdemeanor."

"Another feature of fish protection," says the Republican, "is to require ditch owners to leave at all times at least ten inches of water in the stream at the head of the ditch, so that fish can exist and get up and down the stream. The Board is also urged to adopt an ordinance for the protection of deer by making it a misdemeanor to kill any of these animals for the next two years. This measure is deemed necessary by some of our citizens, as these animals have died by hundreds in the mountains this winter on account of the unusually heavy snowfall, and have also been destroyed in large numbers by those who hunt them for their hides."

THE KENNEL.

Dog owners are requested to send for publication the earliest possible notices of whelps, sales, names claimed, presentations and deaths, in their kennels, in all instances writing plainly names of sire and dam and of grandparents, colors, dates and breed.

Visit.

Mr. R. M. Pogson's fox-terrier Jill (Tally—Clover Blossom) to C. A. Sumner's Blemton Vesuvian 15290 (Champion Lucifer—Blemton Vesta) March 12, 1890, Los Angeles

Whelps.

Mr. A. V. Steubenranch's skye-terrier Rowdy whelped, February 27th, five, four dogs, to Dick.

Occidental Coursing Club.

March 11, 1890.

It is the intention of the Occidental Coursing Club, to hold an annual dinner on Thursday evening, March 27, 1890, at Delmonico Restraurant, Nos. 8 to 14 O'Farrell street, at 6:30 o'clock

The attendance is voluntary, and cost of tickets for the dinner has been placed at three dollars each. Any member desiring to invite a friend, must send his name to the Committee on Arrangements, for approval.

It is absolutely necessary for the Committee to know by Monday noon, March 24th, how many to provide for. You are therefore urged to immediately notify any one of the Committee of your acceptance.

A failure to respond on or before above date will be considered as declining to attend the dinner.

Committee—Thos. J. O'Keeffe, 324 Montgomery street, H. E. Deane, care Murphy, Grant & Co., S. L. Abbot Jr., 228 Montgomery street.

Fred Taft a'sailing.

PACIFIC OCEAN, March 4, 1890.

Steamer City of Sidney, nearing Panama.

EDITOR BREEDER AND SPORTSMAN:—After leaving you on Saturday Feb. 15th, we had very rough weather until Monday. I was the only passenger out of about 30, but what was sea sick. There were not half a dozen that appeared at their meals on Sunday, and they disappeared in five minutes. I had a lonesome day of it. On Monday the sea settled down and we have had fine weather since. We stopped at seven ports in Mexico, Guatemala and San Salvador, remaining about a day at each. Another gentleman and myself fished at each, but caught nothing but catfish 5 to 12 inches long, and no good. They are like the fresh water fish, but lighter in color. We saw large numbers of red snappers (a fine fish) of five pounds and upwards, swimming near the surface, picking up scraps from the ship. Several at a time would rise and tear up pieces of floating bread. We tried them with the following baits, but could not get a bite. Raw and cooked beef, salt pork, catfish belly, dough and cotton mixed, bread, flies and spoons. Fished on the surface, and various depths of water. It was aggravating to see the big fellows skipping about. Perhaps you can suggest something that may be of benefit to some of your readers that may take the trip. There were some on board that took an interest in our fishing, encouraging us with bites, even if some didn't hook anything. For instance, I had a good one—soon another, which was that of a twenty-pounder.

On looking over the side, I found my line within reach of a dead light on the lower deck. The third time I caught him, and on threatening to shoot, they let up for the day. Another day we adjourned at 11 o'clock for a short time, leaving our lines out, tied to the rail. On our return we found short pieces of plank attached for floats. At another time, after a short absence, we couldn't pull our lines in, and upon examination found that they had been pulled through a hawser hole and made fast to a stanchion on lower deck. It all helped to pass away the time. I will finish on the other side of the isthmus.

Atlantic Ocean, March 10th, steamer Colon.

Arrived Panama 4th, left Colon 5th; am now half way to New York, where I shall mail this, as it will reach you sooner than from Panama. Still having fine weather—not as hot as on the Pacific. Last night was the first for two weeks that I had a sheet over me.

March 13th, 8 A. M.—Sandy Hook sighted; be in New York this noon. Had an elegant voyage. Yours,

FRED A. TAFT.

Mr. G. Howard Thompson has lost by death the famous old cocker spaniel Sport, the first really fine dog of the breed that was brought to California. Sport was a fine field dog, of good size, typical points, and a prepotent sire. He was imported by Mr. George S. Ladd, whose death a few months ago removed one of the truest of sportsmen. Poor old Sport was run down by an Ellis-street cable car on Thursday last.

The Waterloo Cup Win.

The third day (Friday), on which the Waterloo Cup was decided, was the most glorious of the whole meeting. The weather was delightful, and the Lydiate meadows had all the appearance of a far-advanced spring. The company was very large, and as there were only seventeen courses to run off, enough hares were to be found in a short beat.

Of course the *piece de resistance* of the meeting was when Mr. J. Trevor's nomination, Downpour, and Colonel North's Fullerton by Greentick—Bit o' Fashion came together says the London Stock-Keeper. So confident were the backers of the latter that they did not hesitate to lay six to one on the son of Greentick and Bit o' Fashion. Just as Wright, the slipper, had his dogs ready, the sun came out from behind the clouds with a glare, and everyone was on the tiptoe of excitement. Downpour was on the near side of the slips, and Fullerton was conspicuous by his splendid long and arched neck, and from the manner he stands in the slips. Wright delivered them to a good hare, when the crack shot away three or four lengths the better of the bitch up to the hare, and kept there, and of course won.

When the white flag went up the vast crowd burst into a wild cheer while pigeons were tossed here, there and everywhere. Signals were flashed by means of flags from one point to the other, and the winner was known at Formby Post Office in a couple of minutes after the course had been won, and doubtless the news was known in London a minute or so afterwards. All was over by 11:40 A. M. so that seventeen courses had been run off in less than one and a half hours.

When Fullerton was brought back through the crowd by his trainer Dent, both man and dog received quite an ovation, for many old coursers are of the opinion that Colonel North's highly-priced dog is quite on a par with the never-to-be-forgotten Master M'Grath. Fullerton shows such exceptional speed, devil, and cleverness on his game that he is undoubtedly one of the best long-tails ever delivered to a hare. The Nitrate King will now, we should say, be very partial to Liverpool, for has he not won a brace of Waterloo Cups, and the Liverpool Cup with his horse Philomel!

The advertisement of the Los Angeles dog show appears in another column, and should be read by all fanciers.

Doctor A. C. Davenport, the cocker spaniel breeder of Stockton, called at this office on Monday last, and dilated for an hour upon the excellences of cockers generally and his own superb animals in particular. He thinks of sending a team of dogs to Los Angeles in May if any others do so in company.

President H. T. Payne, of the Southern California Kennel Club, which is to hold a dog show at Los Angeles on May 6th, 7th, 8th and 9th next, writes: "Our premium lists will be out by the first of next week, when I will send you some for distribution. Tell Mr. P. D. Linville that Florine must be here without fail. If he can't come down himself, I will take personal care of her myself. Should like to have him send the pointer puppies also. Our committee has decided to return the entrance fee to all winners of firsts that come from a distance of over 200 miles. The feeling here is good, and the club-men are all enthusiastic. I think we will reach nearly 200 entries this time.

Mr. E. J. Roy, at Room 87, S. P. Company's building, Fourth and Townsend sts., City, is interesting himself in behalf of those who may wish to attend the Los Angeles dog show. If fifteen persons go down a very material reduction in fair can be obtained, as well as reduced rates for any dogs taken along. Mr. Roys kindness should be appreciated, and if those who intend visiting the show will write to him they will receive full information.

At a meeting of the Executive Committee of the Pacific Kennel Club held on Wednesday evening last, a communication from the California Kennel Club was read in which notice of the discharge of the C. K. C. Conference Committee on consolidation was given. The communication was to the effect that the C. K. C. could not meet the demand of the P. K. C. that the former should assume half of the indebtedness of the last show, should accept the P. K. C. constitution and name, and officers. A more absurd jumble of misunderstandings could not be imagined. At the meetings of the Conference Committees, the P. K. C. Committee was ready with membership list and full statements with reference to the condition of the club.

The other club could not be induced to present a candid statement of its condition. It professed to have $80 in its treasury which sum represented the accumulation of nearly four years from dues, initiations and all scources, with no outlays. Its dues are twenty-five cents per month, or three dollars per year, and a simple deduction will show that it has but seven members in good standing.

The Pacific Kennel Club asked but one thing, which was that the conjoined organization should retain the name Pacific, so that the continuity of the record might not be disturbed. All other matters the P. K. C. was willing to leave to the action of the amalgamated clubs, such as the election of officers, formation of Constitution etc:

It is patent to any fair mind that San Francisco does not present a field broad enough to sustain two Kennel Clubs, and since the Pacific Kennel Club is and always has been a member of the American Kennel Club, in good standing, it is hoped that the application of the California Kennel Club for membership in the A. K. C. will be closely scrutinized and not accepted without the consent of the P. K. C.

Success in an enterprise is not always double-barreled, and while the Continental Kennel Club's show in Denver last December was eminently successful so far as the public were concerned, there was still a deficit in the treasury of $428 91. At a meeting of the club on the 28th ult. to consider ways and means, it was decided that each member should be assessed for the sum of $20—this to be looked upon as a loan, to be repaid at such time as the club is in a position, financially, to reimburse them.

This is the statement:

Receipts, all sources	$2,152.62
Deficit	428.91
	$2,581 53
Expenses, all sources	2,581.53

I hear that the members are answering the call promptly, and all liabilities are paid. Let us hope that next winter's show will net a large enough amount to not only pay all expenses, but at the same time reimburse these public-spirited gentlemen.—DOGWHIP, in *Sports Afield*.

[We congratulate the Continental Kennel Club upon its emergence from the cloud of debt—that accursed shade which deprives all institutions of life and aggressiveness.—ED.]

Grim's Gossip.

A full brother to Sunol 2:10½ has been foaled at Palo Alto during the past week.

The sales of the Pleasanton Stock Farm in New York averaged $2,084, 60 per head, not bad.

Ed. Lafferty, trainer for Mr. Kirkendall of Helena, Montana has several of his horses at Pleasanton, wintering.

Lee Rose has returned from his trip East, and is now looking after his trotters in the southern part of the State.

Theodore Winters tells me that he will start East about the 20th of May, and will continue with the stable during the the balance of the season.

Quite a number of horsemen are going to leave the city Monday evening, to be on hand at the opening of the spring racing meeting at Fresno.

Hernani, the property of J. H. White, has been farmed out to Dr. J. R. Tilton, of Carlisle, Ky., who will stand him during the season at that place.

The match race between the horses owned by Messrs. Byington and Healy of Santa Rosa, will probably take place within a few days at Petaluma.

Every horseman and breeder who has tried the columns of the BREEDER AND SPORTSMAN as an advertising medium will tell you that it pays. Try it and see.

J. H. Neal, Secretary of the Pleasanton Stock Farm Co., sends word that four foals have been born at their Pleasanton place and that all of them are during well.

Antevolo 2:19½ has been taken to his new home near Detroit, and has been much admired by prominent horsemen who visited Clairview Farm to see the new comer.

If there are any persons who wish to send horses East between the 1st and 15th of April, they can hear of an oppertunity by addressing L. A. Davies, care of this office.

Those who have returned from the New York sales say that W. H. Wilson of Kentucky, made $4,000 by reselling some of his purchases before leaving the American Institute building.

A recent advice from Nashville tells me that El Rio Rey is being galloped daily on the track. Winchell pilots him, and he is usually accompained by Don Jose, ridden by trainer Joe Courtney.

Somebody asked Mr. Alf Estill which was the best thoroughbred stallion in California. Without any hesitancy he replied that Joe Hooker was the best stallion in California or any other State.

"There is but one intelligent opinion throughout the country," says the Turf, Field and Farm, "and that is that Noble, owner of Alcryon, should never be allowed to start another horse on a national track."

I wonder what truth there is in the rumor that W. H. Wilson of Cynthiana, Ky, has a strong notion of starting a breeding farm in California. If he should decide to come out and settle we can guarantee him a hearty welcome.

Mr. Salisbury has publicly announced in the East that he will send a string of trotters to the other side of the Rocky Mountains during the latter part of the present season. This will somewhat cripple the interest in our late meetings.

Harry J. Agnew of San Francisco, has purchased a brood mare from John F. Henrichs of this city. She is by Mohawk Chief, dam by Gen. Taylor, and she has a filly foal at her side by Director 2:17. The price given is not stated.

A trainer who has seen all the fastest and best colts that has come to the Oakland track, and who has no interest in the matter, declares that he thinks Mylitta, 2 years, by Mambrino Wilkes—is the best colt that he ever saw on the track.

As will be seen by glancing at the list of foals born lately at Palo Alto, the great brood mare Beautiful Bells has produced a brown filly by Electioneer. With ordinary luck there are three more of her get that should enter the 2:30 list, during 1890.

John Lawrence has taken a string of horses to Petaluma, where they will receive their work preparatory to the opening of the circuit. It is more than likely that the Petaluma track will be extensively patronized this year, owing to the closing of the one at Santa Rosa.

Among the advertisements this week, will be found one, calling attention to the fact that a son of Albert W. is for sale. He is reported to be fast and should be a good roadster for any of the gentleman who are now looking for animals to speed on the new Park road.

The Cook Stock Farm has sold the Standard Stallion Cresco 4908, by Strathmore 408, dam Alla by Almont 33, 2nd dam by Brignoli 77. Cresco has been purchased by the Wiley Bros. of Emporia, Kansas. The horse has already been shipped to his new home in the East.

Messrs. Stoddart & de Gomez are doing a "land office" business with their stallions at the new breeding farm near Auburn. In addition to horses, the firm will also deal largely in fine Holstein cattle and Berkshire pigs, in which there is plenty of money to those who understands the business.

Miller & Sibley, Prospect Hill Farm, Franklin, Pa., have purchased from E. E. Coe of New York, for $7,500 the three year old grey stallion Conductor by Electioneer, dam Sontag Mohawk (dam by Sallie Benton, four year old record 2:17¾, Sport 2:22½, and Eros 2:29½) by Mohawk Chief; second dam Nellie by Toronto Sontag.

Among the many promising young fillies which I have seen this spring, one of the best is Rosetta. She has a nice easy way of going that is particularly striking and if she is not heard from in the yearling stakes this fall, I will be considerably surprised. Rosetta is owned by Mr. English, who has secured a perfect gem in this little miss.

The usual frequenters of the Park roads were out in full force on Saturday afternoon and all seemed to enjoy the fine weather. Capt. White, "Billy" Waters, Hank Hunt, Nick Steiner, Capt. Harris, N. J. Killip, Mr. Crittenden, Major Denicke, E. A. Fargo, S. Seymour, and scores of others who are well known as frequenters of the track were seen.

F. C. Babcock, the purchaser of the Stamboul colt Voodoo, says: "I will send Voodoo to my farm and breed him this year to four or five mares, among them Rosa Wilkes, 2:18¼." Later on Thursday evening he received the following dispatch: "Rosa Wilkes has a colt, pure bay, very large, and is all right; looks like her. The colt is by Nutwood.

The old trotter Commodore 2:20, which lately astonished the attendants at a racing meeting in Queensland (Australia) was at one time driven on the ice at Newburg, N. Y., by Jack Edgar, and afterwards was owned by Harry Agnew of this city. The old horse is almost thirty years of age, but he managed to win his race notwithstanding his feeble legs and emaciated appearance.

The Victorian (Australia) Racing Club's programme on New Year's Day had a handicap with 197 lbs. as top weight. That enormous weight was allotted to the six year old Corythus in a hurdle race of two miles, and was accepted. Corythus finished second, a length and a half behind the four year old Parnell, 156 lbs., in 4:04½, and ten lengths ahead of Drildool, 173 lbs.

Death has again invaded the ranks of old-time, famous trotting owners, and William H. Humphrey, once known as the owner of Judge Fullerton 2:18, and other noted performers, has passed from the busy scenes of life Some years ago, when Dexter, 2:19½, Judge Fullerton, 2:18, Lady Thorne 2:18¼, and Lucy 2:18½, were the star performers, Mr. Humphrey was a familiar figure at all prominent trotting meetings.

Hon. C. M. Thomas, has introduced the following in the Kentucky House of Representatives: "An act to prevent false timing at trotting contests in the Commonwealth; making it unlawful for any party acting as official timer to announce a slower or faster time than that actually made, and fixing a fine not to exceed $500 and imprisonment for six months." Every State in the Union should have such a law.

If you do not know Hugh Kirkendall of Montana, there is a treat in store when you receive an introduction, for Hugh is one of the most enthusiastic horsemen in the business. At the Salisbury sale, he purchased a full brother to Direct, 2:18½, and at once offered to wager Mr. F. C. Babcock $5,000 that he could beat the $24,100 Voodoo any time during the Fall, but the banter only ended in words, as no match was made.

Many complaints were heard last year about the colors worn by drivers on the circuit, or rather I should say a lack of colors, as it was at times rather difficult to distingush one horse from another, especially by those who only visit a fair ground once a year. Directors of associations should make it obligatory on drivers to send in their colors, and then have the same entered on the programmes. It would increase the interest and lend an additional beauty to the scene.

Shippee is a lucky man," said many when he sold an Electioneer colt for a very long price some time ago to Mr. Campbell of Kan as, but Mr. Campbell was equally fortunate, as during last summer 'Campbell's Electioneer" made a mark of 2:22½. The colt was then driven by Thompson, who will this season march down the line with Mr. Shippee's string, while Dick Tilden, a well known reinsman from Nebraska, will handle the Campbell lot.

We notice that C. J. Hamlin appears with a chip on his shoulder and offers to match Chimes against any other son of Beautiful Bells. The Herald will go you one better. We will match Campbell's Electioneer against Chimes or any of the Beautiful Bells family. There is nothing small about us and we are willing to go outside of the beautiful family just to accommodate the gentleman. Come and see us Mr. Hamlin; we mean business. Our address is the Herald, Kiowa, Kans.—Kiowa Herald.

George W. Blial is the name of the young man who showed the Valensin stock at yesterday's sale of trotters says the N Y. Times. Next week he will take to Italy the four-year-old roan mare Wanita, 2:18, which is the property of Mr. Beckwith of Evanston, Mon. The mare is to be pitted against the best trotters in Italy, and her ultimate destination will probably be the breeding farm of the Italian Government, which already contains a number of American trotters.

A note from Secretary McCollum, of the California State Veterinary Association gives the information that the regular quarterly meeting of the society will take place at the Baldwin Hotel, on Wednesday, March 26th, at 7 o'clock P. M. It is a very strange fact that so few practicing "vets" have their names enrolled as members of the State Association, because most assuredly the public are ready to believe that those who are not members, really belong to the "quack brigade."

Among the rules of a New York livery stable where the animals of many wealthy men are kept, are the following: "No man will be employed who drinks intoxicating liquors. No man shall speak loud to any of the horses, or in the stable where they are. Horses of good blood are nervous, and loud excited conversation is felt by every horse who hears it, and keep them all nervous and uneasy. No man shall use profane language in the hearing of horses."

Mr. W. W. Ayres sends me word that he has disposed of Bay Rose 2:20½ to Dan McCarty for $10,000. During the week many rumors have been afloat about the buying of the stallion, but not a single person who claimed to know anything of the transaction put the price quite so high. It is also *on dit* that Dan has sold a half interest in all his brood mares and also a half interest in Bay Rose to Mr. L. A. Richards of Grayson, Stanislaus County. The price received from the latter has not transpired.

Charlie Andrews, of Milwaukee, formerly owner of the stallion Elmo, from whom Orrin A. Hickok bought him, sends me the following, from the Semi-Weekly Star of Boonville, Mo: "A mare owned by Frank Martin of Chotean Springs recently gave birth to twins—a mare mule colt and a horse colt. Stockmen say this is an unusual happening." Well I should say it was an unusual happening. However, Mr. Andrews does not vouch for the truth of the yarn, and the reporter who furnished the item to the paper will have to father the responsibility.

James Delaney of Salinas City has sold to C. C. Clay of San Francisco the grandly bred stallion Herodian 3337, by Belvidere (son of Belmont 64), dam Hattie Sparks by Sweepstakes 298, 2nd dam by Young Washington (son of Burr's Washington), 3rd dam by American Star 14. Herodian is a grand individual, and will be placed at the head of a breeding farm which Mr. Clay will shortly start near Livermore. The gentleman already has a choice lot of broodmares which will be added to from time to time as opportunity affords.

To get very fixed character, with undoubted power to transmit its qualities, it is necessary to often keep working the same strain of blood, but under general circumstances there is no use to keep to what are called very close relations. The more closely one blood is kept to, the more vigilance in necessary to avoid the defects to which that strain has the strongest tendency, and to shun the slightest symptom of disease.

It seems to be the proper thing now-a-days for the Californians to bet on something or another when they get to New York, and this season has proved no exception to the rule. During the sales lately held in the Empire City, Mr. Valensin and Andy McDowell got into an argument about the speed of Direct and it finally culminated in a wager being made, the "White Knight" of the sulky putting up $100, against $300, by Valensin that, Direct would trot this year in 2:15. It is a pretty low mark Andy, but I sincerely hope you may win the money.

The mails bring information that Valensin's lot of twenty, sold for $19,520, an average of $976, so that he has no reason for complaint. This average would have been greatly increased had Sydney's three-year old daughter Fleet been in such condition that she could be sold. But in some way she calked herself on the train when en route, and an ugly-looking cut on one coronet made her slightly lame and considerably sore. The injury however, told against her, and Mr Kellogg therefore allowed her to be withdrawn, as he could secure no bid of $8,000 or better for her, and he did not desire that Mr. Valensin should fail to obtain a fair value for his property because of the accident.

During the week I received a pleasant visit from C. H. Burton, who formerly worked for G. W. Woodard and C. H. Hoppin of Yolo County. Mr. Burton is now the manager of the new track which has lately been built at Tacoma, Washington Territory. Harry Morgan, of that lively burg, has expended a lot of money in clearing away a site situated between the old and new towns, and already two lines of street cars pass the front entrance. It is intended that the course and all its appointments shall surpass anything west of the Rocky Mountains, as money will not be spared to make it perfect in every particular. With tracks at Olympia, Seattle, Port Townsend and also at Victoria, a good circuit can be arranged, and if the purses are liberal no doubt many of the California horsemen would go up to "take chances" with the light harness brigade that make their headquarters on the Sound.

A letter from Cynthiana, Ky., says that "On the morning of the 11th inst., Wilson & Handy's car reached Cynthiana, Ky., laden with their purchases of last week at the New York sale. The 10 head cost $13,190. They were as follows: Harvester, b s, 8, by Sultan, dam Harvest Queen, 2:29½, by Hambletonian 10; 2d dam by American Star. Choice, b m by Dictator, dam Coral by Clark Chief 89; 2d dam of Caliban, 2:34½, with a b f by her side by Stamboul, 2:12½. Ophir, blk f by Simmons, 2:28, dam Miss Smalley by Indianapolis. Nona, blk f by Byerly Abdallah, dam by Arnold; 2d dam Lady Monroe, 2:26½. Agnes Clark, b m by Almont, dam by Clark Chief; 2d dam, dam of J. Q., 2:17½, in foal to Alcazar. Alcyola, b m, 3, by Alcyone, 2:27, dam the dam of Gossiper, 3, 2:29½, by Smuggler, 2:15½. Flower Girl, ch m by Arthurton, dam by Gen. McClellan; foal to Alcazar. Astonish, bay coach s by Mambrino King, dam Dictatrice. Bay yearling colt by Harvester. B g by Sultan.

Last Monday morning Mr. Valensin returned from New York extremely well pleased with his trip, and far from being the disgruntled person that the New York dailies would make him out to be. He says that there was only one animal that sold for less than she should have brought, and that was Lassie; but with all the others he is extremely well pleased. Out of the twenty which he took with him, five were of very poor breeding on the dam's side, and that lot of poor ones only aggregated $1,275. The balance were from good dams, and sold for an average of over $1,200 each, a good, fair price. Mr. Valensin has sold Fleet, conditionally. As I have already stated in another paragraph, the fleet daughter of Sidney hurt herself while on the cars, but Mr. Valensin is inclined to think that the injury is not a permanent one, so Mr. J. H. Shults, the wealthy Brooklyn baker, will take her if the swelling in her leg reduces in size. The price agreed on is $8,000, and the Californian fancies the sale as good as made.

In regard to the proposed match between Axtell and Sunol, Mr. Bonner says: "There is no probability of its occurring. I met Mr. Ijams, one of the five owners of Axtell, very recently, and he told me that the stallion was on his farm at Terre Hautte, Ind., and would earn $40,000 this year, so he would hardly be in shape for a great test of speed. As regards Sunol, when I paid for her it was with the agreement and understanding that I should let her remain with Governor Stanford until next October, to give him an opportunity of lowering her record. He therefore has charge of her racing record this year, and I have nothing to do with her. He holds her at my risk, and if anything happened to her it would be my loss. When I made the offer I told him I would take her just as she was for a certain sum that has never been named, but which was more than that paid for Maud S.—$40,000—and the highest price ever paid for any mare in the world. I always keep myself posted about her, and she is at present doing finely on Governor Stanford's farm in California."

Passing from one group to another and equally popular with each, says the N. Y. Spirit in speaking of the Rosemeade Sale, was Col. Conley, of Chicago, the hero of the syndicate which purchased the great Axtell for $105,000. In response to a direct inquiry by us with regard to Axtell trotting next Autumn he said: Three responsible associations have notified us that they will give large purses for a race between Sunol, 2:10½, and Axtell. One association offers a purse of $15,000, while Dundee Park, N. J., and another well known association offer $10,000 each with *free entrance*. If Axtell is fit and well and Senator Stanford will allow Sunol to compete we will accept these three offers and trot three races. The Senator controls her racing qualities until the bill of sale calls for her being handed over to Mr. Robert Bonner, and as the great Californian will in all probability send a stable East, it is to be hoped that he will allow the young trotting queen to meet in friendly rivalry the stallion king. This is very different from the many versions which the daily papers have published, but as it comes from an authentic source it looks more than probable that the great pair may meet. What will Senator Stanford say? is now the question. His well known courtesy will probably induce him to consult Mr. Bonner. It is to be hoped that the latter gentleman will not use his influence to prevent three of the greatest contests ever seen on the trotting turf.

CORRESPONDENCE.

An Agricultural District Matter.

EDITOR BREEDER AND SPORTSMAN:—An article in the BREEDER AND SPORTSMAN of March 8, relating to the appointment of Hon. S. I. Allen of Santa Rosa as Director of Agricultural District No 4, does much injustice to Mr. Allen, and unjustly reflects upon Governor Waterman, who made the appointment. The article is, evidently, not of editorial parentage, as its tone, temper, style and dragooning of italics manifest. The animus which inspired the article is apparent throughout, and it is to make it appear that the appointment of Mr Allen should not have been made. To this purpose it is intimated that the position was solicited by Mr. Allen himself· that he designs to use it to promote his own political interest; and that he has not reasonable claim to the place, except as a politician. In addition to these intimations are imputations to the effect that Mr. Allen is inimical to the interests of the Agricultural District to which he is appointed Director. It is alleged that while a member of the Legislature he endeavored to defeat the appropriation to the Agricultural District of which he is now Director—the District comprised of Sonoma and Marin Counties, which holds annual Fairs in Petaluma, and that he did so in the interest of the Sonoma County Agricultural Association, which held annual County Fairs in Santa Rosa.

The allegation is unfounded and not true. Mr. Allen voted for the appropriation to the District Association which has in charge the Fair at Petaluma. He made no effort to cripple that Fair, or to desert from it to the Santa Rosa Fair any portion of the appropriation voted to the Petaluma District. Another allegation is that Mr. Allen, about the time of his appointment as director of the District, at a meeting of the Sonoma Agricultural Park Association, in Santa Rosa, to consider the proposition to sell the property of the association, made a motion that the selling be postponed to a further day in order to give the people opportunity to form an Agricultural organization. Mr. Allen made no motion to such effect, his motion, as he stated his design was to postpone the sale to enable parties to obtain possession of the Association grounds for turf purposes and to so maintain the track and building and stables, to complete their arrangements.

The holding of annual fairs was not contemplated in the motion made by Mr. Allen, Santa Rosa had for years been assigned a good place in the great racing circuit of the State, and Mr. Allen, with many others of Santa Rosa and Sonoma county, desired to have this place continued in the yearly assignment of race meetings. His motion suggested the customary and friendly connection with Petaluma, in the racing circuit, and not competition, to impose or detract from the annual Fairs of the District Association.

As to the effort to make it appear that the appointment of Mr. Allen as Director was by himself sought and solicited, and that his own political interests are to be advanced by the office, it will suffice to state that Mr. Allen did not seek and did not solicit the appointment.

He was recommended for the position to Governor Waterman, by leading representative citizens of Santa Rosa. He will not trail the Directorship in political channels. The author of the offending article protests against the admission of politics into the Agricultural Board. He is himself the only offender in that direction. Mr. Allen has no intention to that design. He is President of the Santa Rosa Board of Trade, a member of the State Grange, and also of the Agricultural and Horticultural Associations. Personally, in ownership and business way, he is interested in farming, in viticulture and fruit growing, and in the breeding of cattle and of live stock generally. He is respected as a private citizen and honored in public life. Santa Rosa has been his home for many years, and throughout the country he is esteemed for his integrity, probity and fidelity to every trust and obligation. His popularity needs no aids through public position, and he would scorn to pervert any such to the promotion of partisan or personal ends. He will fulfill the duties of Director with ability, discretion and keen judgment. Governor Waterman has not made any mistake in the appointment of Mr. Allen to the Agricultural Board, and is to be commended for his action. The undeserved strictures of his unfriendly critics will not affect the good standing of Mr. Allen with any who know him. M.

SANTA ROSA, March 11, 1890.

[Our correspondent mistakes the intent of the article referred to, and has misinterpreted its language. We simply desired to call attention to the fact that as Mr. De Turk was not in the state to qualify, Mr. Allen's appointment was made without consulting the other members of the Board as to their wishes in the matter. No imputation was cast on Mr. Allen's integrity, nor was it even suggested that the gentleman used any influence to gain the honorable position.—EDITOR BREEDER AND SPORTSMAN.]

List of Entries for Trotting Sweepstakes, to Be Contested For at the State Fair This Year.

TWO-YEAR-OLD TROTTING STAKE.

San Mateo Stock Farm's blk c Cognac by Guy Wilkes, dam Lottie by Alexander Belmont; dk b c Sirio Wilkes by Guy Wilkes, dam Laura Drew by Arthurton; ch f Vida Wilkes by Guy Wilkes, dam Vixen by Nutwood.

J. A. McCloud's br f Daisy Vernon by Mount Vernon, dam by Berkeley, he by Ulster Chief.

Souther Stock Farm's b c El Benton by Electioneer, dam Nellie Benton by General Benton; blk c Jim Sinfoot by Figaro, dam Fanny Sinfoot by Erwin Davis; g c The Barber by Figaro, dam Roberta by Vernon Patchen.

N. B. Whittaker's b g Arnot.

Palo Alto Stock Farm's br c Almoneer by Alban, dam America by Hambletonian 10; b f Elleneer by Electioneer, dam Lady Ellen, b f [illegible]nnet by Electioneer, dam Lizzie Whips by Enquirer; b f Wild Bee by Piedmont, dam Wildflower by Electioneer.

S. E. Harris' ch f Starlight by Dawn, dam Lena Bowles by Ethan Allen.

THREE-YEAR-OLD STAKE.

San Mateo Stock Farm's b c Regal Wilkes by Guy Wilkes, dam Margaret by Sultan; b f Minnie Wilkes by Guy Wilkes, dam Rosetta by the Moor.

Palo Alto Stock Farm's b f Wildmont by Piedmont, dam Wildflower by Electioneer; b c Pedlar by Electioneer, dam Penelope by Mohawk Chief; b c Hugo by Electioneer, dam Helpmate by Planet; br f Elzira by Ansel, dam American Girl by Toronto Sontag.

FOUR-YEAR-OLD STAKE.

San Mateo Stock Farm's b m Lillian Wilkes by Guy Wilkes, dam Flora Langford by Langford.

Pleasanton Stock Farm's b m Margaret S by Director 2:17, dam May Day by Cassius M. Clay, Jr.; blk m Katie S by Director 2:17, dam Alpha Medium by Happy Medium.

Palo Alto Stock Farm's gr m Colma by Electioneer, dam Sontag Mohawk by Mohawk Chief; blk m Ladywell by Electioneer, dam Lady Ladywell by Shultz's St. Clair; b m Ariana by Ansel, dam Rebecca by General Benton.

The Standard.

[AS REVISED AND ADOPTED BY THE NATIONAL ASSOCIATION OF TROTTING-HORSE BREEDERS, DECEMBER 14, 1887.]

IN order to define what constitutes a trotting-bred horse and to establish a BREED of trotters on a more intelligent basis, the following rules are adopted to control admission to the records of pedigrees. When an animal meets the requirements of admission and is duly registered, it shall be accepted as a standard trotting-bred animal:—

FIRST.—Any stallion that has himself a record of two minutes and thirty seconds (2:30) or better, provided any of his get has a record of 2:35 or better, or provided his sire or his dam is already a standard animal.

SECOND.—Any mare or gelding that has a record of 2:30 or better.

THIRD.—Any horse that is the sire of two animals with a record of 2:30 or better.

FOURTH.—Any horse that is the sire of one animal with a record of 2:30 or better, provided he has either of the additional qualifications: (1) A record himself of 2:35 or better. (2) Is the sire of two other animals with a record of 2:35 or better. (3) Has a sire or dam that is already a standard animal.

FIFTH.—Any mare that has produced an animal with a record of 2:30 or better.

SIXTH.—The progeny of a standard horse when out of a standard mare.

SEVENTH.—The female progeny of a standard horse when out of a mare by a standard horse.

EIGHTH.—The female progeny of a standard horse when out of a mare whose dam is a standard mare.

NINTH.—Any mare that has a record of 2:35 or better, and whose sire or dam is a standard animal.

Best Trotting Records.

1 mile—2:08¾, Maud S., against time, in harness, accompanied the distance by a running horse, Glenville, O., July 30, 1885......2:13¾, best time in a race between horses, Maud S., Chicago, Ills., July 24, 1880......2:12, Axtell, against time, accompanied by running horse—fastest stallion time, Terre Haute, Ind., Oct. 11, 1889......2:13¾, Phallas, fastest heat by a stallion against other horses, Chicago, July 14, 1884......2:12¾, Palo Alto, third heat in race at Stockton, Cal., Sept. 26, 1889......2:15¼, Jay-Eye-See, half-mile track, Lincoln, Neb., Sept. 14, 1887......2:15¾, Great Eastern, under saddle, third heat, Morrisania, N. Y., Sept. 22, 1877......2:10¾, Jay-Eye-See, against time, best five-year-old record, Providence, R. I., Sept 15, 1883......2:16, Manzanita, third heat, best four-year-old record, Lexington, Ky., Sept. 3, 1876......2:16, Edgemark, four-year old stallion record, against time, Lexington, Ky., Oct. 18, 1889......2:16½, Sunol, in Stanford Stake, accompanied by a runner, best three-year-old record, San Francisco, Nov. 9, 1889..2:18, Sunol 2 years, against time, San Francisco, Cal., Oct. 27, 1888......2:20½, Regal Wilkes, two-year-old stallion record, San Francisco, Nov. 9, 1889......2:31½, Norlaine, yearling, against time, San Francisco, Cal., Nov. 12, 1887......2:35, Faustino, yearling stallion record, San Francisco, Nov. 9, 1889.

2 miles—4:43 against time, Fanny Witherspoon, Chicago, Ill., Sept. 25, 1885.

3 miles—7:21¼, Huntress, harness, Brooklyn, L. I., Sept. 21, 1872.

4 miles—10:34½, Longfellow, wagon, California, Dec 31, 1869.

5 miles—13:00, Lady Mac, harness, San Francisco, Cal., April 2, 1874.

10 miles—27:23¼, Controller, harness, San Francisco, Cal., Nov. 23, 1878.

20 miles—58:25, Captain McGowan, harness, half-mile track, Boston, Oct. 31, 1865.

Pacing Records at One Mile.

Johnston, harness, against time, Chicago, Ills., Oct 9, 1884, 2:06¼.

Brown Hal, best stallion record, Cleveland, Ohio, July 31, 1889, 2:12½.

Westmont, July 10, 1884, Chicago, Ills., with running mate, 2:01¾.

Daisy, yearling, Sacramento, Dec. 31, 1885, 2:38¾.

Ed Rosewater, two years old, Council Bluffs, Iowa, Nov. 3, 1888, 2:20½.

Yolo Maid, 3 years old, San Francisco, Oct. 13, 1888, 2:14.

Gold Leaf, four years old, 2:11¼ on August 17, 1889, at Napa.

Arrow, five years old, 2:13¾, made at Cleveland, Ohio, August 1, 1888.

Fastest Time on Record.

RUNNING.

Miles.		
¼	Jim Miller, 2, Deer Lodge (Mont.), Aug. 16, 1888 / †Sleepy Dick, a, Kiowa (Kan.), Nov. 24, 1888	0:21¼
⅜	Cyclone, a, 120 lbs., Helena (Mont.), Aug. 28, 1889	0:34¼
½	Geraldine, 4, 122 lbs., Westchester Course, Aug. 30, 1889	0:46
⅝	Britannic, 5, 122 lbs., Westchester Course, Aug. 31, 1889	0:59
⅝	Fordham, a, 115 lbs., Westchester Course, Oct. 4, 1889	0:59
¾	El Rio Rey, 2, 126 lbs., Westchester Course, Aug. 31, 1889	1:11
¾	Tipstaff, 3, 107, Westchester Course, Oct. 4, 1889	1:11
⅞	Britannic, 5, 110 lbs., Sheepshead Bay, Sept. 5, 1889	1:26 2-5
	Ten Broeck, 5, 110 lbs., Louisville, May 24, 1877 (against time)	1:39¾
1	Maori, 4, 105 lbs., Chicago, July 12, 1889, (in a race)	1:39 4-5
1 1-16	Wheeler T., 3, 98 lbs., St. Louis, June 1, 1888	1:47¼
1 1-16	Erlton, 4, 106, Chicago, Ill., June 28, 1889	1:47¼
1⅛	Terra Cotta, 4, 124 lbs., Sheepshead Bay, June 22, 1888	1:52
1 3-16	Joe Cotton, 5, 109½ lbs., Sheepshead Bay, Sept. 7, 1887	2:00¼
1¼	Kingston, 5, 122 lbs., Gravesend, Sept. 24, 1889	2:06¼
1 m 500 yds.	Bend'Or, 4, 115 lbs., Saratoga, July 25, 1882	2:10¼
1⅜	Triboulet, 4, 117 lbs., San Francisco, April 26, 1888 / Richmond, 6, 122 lbs., Sheepshead Bay, June 27, 1888	2:21¼
1½	Firenzi, 4, 113 lbs., Monmouth Park, Aug. 2, 1888 / Luke Blackburn, 3, 102 lbs., Monmouth Park, Aug. 17, '80 / Jim Guest, 4, 98 lbs., Chicago (Washington Park, July 24 '86)	2:34
1⅝	Hindoocraft, 3, 75 lbs., Westchester, Aug. 27, 1889	2:48
1¾	Glidelia, 5, 116 lbs., Saratoga, Aug. 5, 1882	3:01
1⅞	Enigma, 4, 90 lbs., Sheepshead Bay, Sept. 15, 1885	3:20
2	Ten Broeck, 5, 110 lbs., Louisville, May 29, 1877	3:27½
2¼	Monitor, 4, 110 lbs., Baltimore, Oct. 20, 1880	3:44½
2½	Springbok, 5, 114 lbs. / Preakness, a, 114 lbs., Saratoga, July 29, 1875	3:56¼
2⅝	Aristides, 4, 104 lbs., Lexington, May 13, 1876	4:27½
2¾	Ten Broeck, 4, 104 lbs., Lexington, Sept. 16, 1876	4:58½
2⅞	Hubbard, 4, 107 lbs., Saratoga, Aug. 9, 1873	4: 8¾
3	Drake Carter, 4, 115 lbs., Sheepshead Bay, Sept. 6, 1884	5:24
4	Ten Broeck, 4, 104 lbs., Louisville, Sept. 27, 1876	7:15¾

HEAT RACES.

Miles.		
¼	Sleepy Dick, a, Kiowa (Kan.), Nov. 24, 1888	0:21¼—0:22¼
½	Bogus, a, 118 lbs., Helena (Mont.), Aug. 24, 1888	0:48—0:48
⅝	Kittie Pease, 4, Dallas (Tex.), Nov. 2, 1887	1:00—1:00
⅝	Sudie McNairy, 3, 96 lbs., Chicago, July 2, 1883	1:02¼—1:03
¾	Lizzie S., 5, 118 lbs., Louisville, Sept. 28, 1883	1:13¼—1:13½
1	Bounce, 4, 90 lbs., Sheepshead Bay, Sept. 7, 1881	1:42—1:41½
1	3 in 5. L'Argentine, 6, 115 lbs., St. Louis, June 14, 1879	1:43—1:44—1:47¼
1 1-16	Slipalong, 5, 115 lbs., Chicago (Wash. Park), Sept. 2, 1885	1:50½—1:48
1⅛	Gabriel, 4, 112 lbs., Sheepshead Bay, Sept. 22, 1880	1:56—1:56
1¼	Glenmore, 5, 114 lbs., Sheepshead Bay, Sept. 25, 1880	2:10—2:14
1½	Keno, 4, Toledo, Sept. 16, 1887 (1st and 3d heats)	2:43½—2:45
2	Miss Woodford, 4, 107½ lbs., Sheepshead Bay, Sept. 20, 1884	3:33—3:31½
3	Norfolk, 4, 100 lbs., Sacramento, Sept. 23, 1865	5:27¼—5:29½
	Ferida, 4, 105 lbs., Sheepshead Bay, Sept. 18, 1880	7:23½—7:41

†Made in a heat race.
*Doubtful, and made in a heat race.

A peculiar illustration, says The Lexington Transcript, of the reward Providence bestows upon breeders who treat their customers in a liberal manner, is the following little story which has the merit of being true in every detail: Some years ago, Mr. Luke Brodhead, the manager of Woodburn Farm, sold a promising trotting colt to a Western gentleman for $2,000. In the shipment of the youngster he was injured, and for over thirteen months showed no signs of improvement. His owner wrote this fact to Mr. Brodhead, and having previously been a good buyer at Woodburn, the manager enclosed him a check for $2,000, at the same time requesting him to ship the horse back to Woodburn. He arrived in due time, in his general dilapidated condition, but strange to say, he had not been on the place a week before showing signs of improvement. In two months he was ready to enter training, and so nicely did he take to his work that last year he got a mark of 2:27. Being satisfied he had in him the making of a grand horse Mr. Brodhead took him out of training, it being his intention to give him a winter's rest and train him again this year. Another breeder, however, happened to inspect him a few days ago, and, after hearing his strange history, paid Mr. Brodhead $5,000 for the colt, which less than a year ago, was considered worthless. Further than saying the horse is located in Iowa, Mr. Brodhead is dumb as to the animal's identity."

Comparative Value of Trotters and Thoroughbreds as Purse Winners

While the trotter appears to be outselling the thoroughbred, the latter offsets this by the increased amount of money won by them. The ten largest winning trotting horses last season only won $540 more than Salvator alone earned on the running turf. The following table, giving the ten largest winning trotters and thoroughbreds for 1889, shows the latter are away ahead in the matter of winnings:

Trotters		Thoroughbreds	
Alcryon, eight races	$21,500	Salvator, seven races	$71,380
Nelson, four races	7,464	Chaos, three races	63 550
Reference, four races	7,020	El Rio Rey, seven races	47,535
Star Lily, four races	6,560	Longstreet, ten races	39,020
Jack, six races	6,175	Tenny, ten races	38,780
Gean Smith, twelve races	5,460	St. Carlo, two races	38,958
Sprague Goldddust, 5 races	5,450	Senorita, eight races	26,640
Henrdryx, five races	4,490	Protection, two races	26,225
Aubine, three races	3,865	Spokane, three races	25,420
Geneva S., four races	3,865	Raceland, eight races	25,790
Total	$71,930	Total	$392,248

This shows a balance in favor of the thoroughbred over the trotter of five races and $320,318 in money won.—J. K. S. in Kentucky Leader.

THE WEEKLY
Breeder and Sportsman.

JAMES P. KERR, PROPRIETOR.

The Turf and Sporting Authority of the Pacific Coast.

Office, No. 313 Bush St.
P. O. Box 2300.

TERMS—One Year, $5; Six Months, $3; Three Months, $1.50.
STRICTLY IN ADVANCE.

Money should be sent by postal order, draft or by registered letter, addressed to JAMES P. KERR, San Francisco, Cal.

Communications must be accompanied by the writer's name and address, not necessarily for publication, but as a private guarantee of good faith.

NEW YORK OFFICE, ROOM 15, 181 BROADWAY.

ALEX. P. WAUGH, - - - Editor.

Advertising Rates

Per Square (half inch)

One time	$1 50
Two times	2 50
Three times	3 25
Four times	4 00

And each subsequent insertion 75c. per square.

Advertisements running six months are entitled to 10 per cent. discount.

Those running twelve months are entitled to 20 per cent. discount.

Reading notices set in same type as body of paper, 50 cents per line each insertion.

To Subscribers.

The date printed on the wrapper of your paper indicates the time to which your subscription is paid.

Should the BREEDER AND SPORTSMAN be received by any subscriber who does not want it, write us direct to stop it. A postal card will suffice.

Special Notice to Correspondents.

Letters intended for publication should reach this office not later than Wednesday of each week, to secure a place in the issue of the following Saturday. Such letters to insure immediate attention should be addressed to the BREEDER AND SPORTSMAN, and not to any member of the staff.

San Francisco, Saturday, March 22, 1890.

Dates Claimed.

SAN JOSE (Blood Horse Meeting)	April 5th, 7th and 9th
SACRAMENTO (Running Meeting)	April 26th, 29th, May 1st and 3d
EUREKA JOCKEY CLUB	July 2d to 5th
IONE	Aug 7th to 9th.
LOS ANGELES (6th District)	Aug. 11th to 16th
NAPA	Aug. 18th to 23rd
GLENBROOK PARK, 17th District	August 19th to 23d
SAN JOSE (Fall Meeting)	Aug 25th to 30th inclusive
PETALUMA	Aug. 25th to 30th
OAKLAND (District No. 1)	Sept. 1st to Sept. 6th
LAKEPORT, 12th District	September 23d to 27th
CALIFORNIA STATE FAIR	Sept 8th to 20th
FRESNO (Fall Meeting)	Sept. 29th to Oct. 4th
MONTEREY, Salinas, Agricultural Society	Sept. 30th to Oct. 4th

Stallions Advertised
IN THE
BREEDER AND SPORTSMAN.

Thoroughbreds.

DOUGLASDALE—Thoroughbred Clydesdale......Lawn View Farm, Cal.
FRIAR TUCK, Hermit—Romping Girl......C. W. Aby, Middletown.
GREENBACK, Dollar—Music......C. W. Aby, Middletown.
INTRUDER, Crater—Lady Bountiful......T. J. Knight, Sacramento.
REVEILLE, Shiloh—Norfolk......B. C. Holly, Vallejo.
ST. SAVIOR, Eolus—War Song......C. W. Aby, Middletown.
THREE CHEERS, Imp. Hurrah—Young Fashion......E. S. Culver, San Francisco.

Trotters.

ADMIRAL, Volunteer—Lady Pierson......Frank Drake, Vallejo.
ACTOR, Prompter—Dam by Sultan......Lawn View Farm, Cal.
ARBITRATOR, Director—Lady Harnes......H. A. Mayhew, Niles.
ANTEEOP, Anteeo—Bessie G......Guy E. Grosse, Santa Rosa.
ANTEEOP, Anteeo—Nance......Guy E. Grosse, Santa Rosa.
ADMIRO, Admiral—dam by San Bruno......Smith & Sutherland, Pleasanton.
ASHLAND ALMONT, Almont—Pauline......T. J. Whitehead, Oakland.
ALEXANDER BUTTON, Alexander—Lady Button......Cache Creek Farm, Yolo.
APEX, Prompter—Mary......Poplar Grove Breeding Farm, Wildflower.
ALOONA, Almont—Queen Mary......Fred W. Loeber, St. Helena.
BALKAN, Mambrino Wilkes—Fanny Fern......A. L. Hinds, Oakland.
BONANZA, Arthurton—Sister......Richard Havey, Oakland.
BAY ROSE, Sultan—Madam Baldwin......W. W. Ayres, Oakland.
CLOVIS, Sultan—Sweetbriar......Poplar Grove Breeding Farm, Wildflower.
CUPID, Sidney—Venus......C. O. Thornquest, Oakland.
CHRISMAN'S HAMBLETONIAN 10178, Whipple's Hambletonian—Flora......Jesse Chrisman, San Jose.
CHARLES DERBY, Steinway—by Electioneer. Cook Stock Farm, Contra Costa Co.
CRESCO, Strathmore—Spartan......Cook Stock Farm, Contra Costa Co.
CALIFORNIA NUTWOOD, Nutwood—Fanny Patchen......Martin Carter, Alameda Co.
CORRECT R, Director—Brainey......Pleasanton Stock Farm.
DECORATOR, Director—Chess......Pleasanton Stock Farm.
DEXTER PRINCE, Kentucky Prince—Lady Dexter......L. M. Morse, Lodi.
DAWN, Nutwood—Countess......A. L. Whitney, Petaluma.
DIRECTOR, Dictator—Dolly......Pleasanton Stock Farm, Pleasanton.
DON MARVIN, Fallis—Cora......F. P. Lowell, Sacramento.
DESIGNER, Director—May Queen......H. Scott, Oakland.
ELECTOR, Electioneer—Gilberta......L. A. Richards, Grayson.
ELECTION, Electioneer—Lizzie H......B. C. Holly, Vallejo.
EL BENTON, Electioneer—Nellie Benton......Souther Farm, San Leandro.
ECLECTIC, Electioneer—Manette......Wilfred Page, Sonoma County.
EROS, Electioneer—Sontag Mohawk......W. H. Vioget, Menlo Park.
FIGARO, Hambletonian—Emblem......Souther Farm, San Leandro.
GROVER CLAY, Electioneer—Maggie Norfolk......Denis Gannon, Oakland.
G. & M., Anteeo—Rosa B......George E. Guerne, Santa Rosa.
GUY WILKES, George Wilkes—Lady Bunker......San Mateo Stock Farm, San Mateo.
GLEN FORTUNE, Electioneer—Glenna......Souther Farm, San Leandro.
GEORGE WASHINGTON, Mambrino Chief—Fanny Rose......Thos. Smith, Vallejo.
GUIDE, Director—Imogene......Smith & Sutherland, Pleasanton.
GRANDISSIMO, LeGrande—Norma......Fred W. Loeber, St. Helena.
ILLUSTRIOUS, Happy Medium—Abdalletta......George A. Stone, Santa Rosa.
JESTER D, Almont—Hortense......Souther Farm, San Leandro.
JUNIO, Electioneer—by Granger......S. N. Straube, Fresno.
KAFIR, Alcazar—Flower Girl......B. C. Holly, Vallejo.
KING DAVID, Admiral—Black Flora......Frank Drake, Vallejo.
LEO WILKES, Guy Wilkes—Sable......San Mateo Stock Farm, San Mateo.
LYNWOOD, Nutwood—Hattie Morrison......P. Visher, Stockton.
MEMO, Sidney—Flirt......Valensin Stock Farm, Pleasanton.
MOUNTAIN BOY, Kentucky Prince—Elsie......B. C. Holly, Vallejo.
MAMBRINO WILKES, George Wilkes—Lady Chrisman......San Miguel Stock Farm, Walnut Creek.
MART BOORHEM, Sidney—Towhead......B. C. Holly, Vallejo.
MAMBRINO JR. 1789, Mambrino Patchen, dam by Mambrino Chief......Geo. P. Bull, San Jose.
MAMBRINO CHIEF, McDonald Chief—Venus......Thos. Smith, Vallejo.
MORTIMER, Electioneer—Marti......Wilfred Page, Sonoma County.
NOONDAY, Wedgewood—Noontide......F. P. Lowell, Sacramento.
PASHA, Sultan—Madam Baldwin......D. Bryson, Linden.
PHILOSOPHER, Pilot Wilkes—Belle......George E. Guerne, Santa Rosa.
ROY WILKES, Adrian Wilkes—Flora......Pleasanton Stock Farm, Pleasanton.
REDWOOD, Anteeo—Lou Wilton......A. McFayden, Oakland.
STEINWAY, Strathmore—Abbess......Cook Stock Farm, Contra Costa Co.
SUNSET, Anteeo—Bessie G......Guy E. Grosse, Santa Rosa.
SIDNEY, Santa Claus—Sweetness......Valensin Stock Farm, Pleasanton.
SIMMOCOLON, Simmons—Colon......Valensin Stock Farm, Pleasanton.
SABLE WILKES, Guy Wilkes—Sable......San Mateo Stock Farm, San Mateo.
ST. NICHOLAS, Sidney—Towhead......John Rowen, Oakland Trotting Park.
VICTOR, Echo—Daughter of Woodburn......G. W. Hughes, Napa City.
WOODNUT, Nutwood—Flora......Jas. Weatherhead, San Jose.
WHIPPLETON 1883, Hambletonian Jr.—Lady Livingston......Fred W. Loeber, St. Helena.
WOODSIDE, Woodnut—Veronica......B. C. Holly, Vallejo.
YOUNG ELMO, St. Elmo—Dam by Woodburn......Lawn View Farm, Cal.

A Combination Sale.

Catalogues are out for a combination sale to be held at the Bay District Track on Thursday, April 3rd, at 11 o'clock A. M., under the direction of Killip & Co., live stock auctioneers of this city. The class of animals offered are such that there should be plenty of competition, as the breeders of California are constantly on the lookout to secure the best that money can buy. It is rarely that a catalogue is issued which contains such regally bred stock, the names of Guy Wilkes, Electioneer, Alexander Button, Sidney, Mambrino Wilkes, George M. Patchen Jr., and Arthurton figuring prominently throughout its pages. To show what a selection there is, it may not be out of place to give a short synopsis of what can be bought at the sale.

Flora W by Guy Wilkes 2:15½, dam Lyla A by Arthurton, 2nd dam Flora Langford, dam of Lillian Wilkes 2:17½, and Joe Arthurton 2:20½.

Laurel B by Sable Wilkes 2:18, dam Lyla A by Arthurton.

Lyla A by Arthurton (sire of Arab 2.15), dam Flora Langford by Langford.

Mambrino Wilkes is just commencing to be appreciated by the breeders, and his get should bring good prices. Mr. Irvin Ayres of the San Miguel Stock Farm has sent in several contributions, among which are:

Clara P 2:29½, by Mambrino Wilkes, dam Cora by Corsican, 2nd dam by Jack Hawkins.

Istar, by Mambrino Wilkes, dam Narka by Nephew, 1220, 2nd dam Baby by Chieftain 721, 3rd dam Fanny Hayes (dam of Gold Note 2:25) by Jack Hayes. Istar is entered in the Occident Stake and second payment made.

Veronica, by Mambrino Wilkes, dam by Winthrop 505, 2nd dam by Chieftain, 721, etc. This mare took first premium as a two year old standard trotter at the State Fair of 1886.

Nercha, by Bay Frank, dam by Mambrino Wilkes.

Maud, by Don Juan, dam by Young Niagara. Maud has a colt at her side by Mambrino Wilkes.

Paska, by Alpheus 2:27, dam Sister to Doty 2:21, by Challenge.

P. J. Williams is represented in the sale by a bay stallion sired by Piedmont 2:17¼, dam Queen by Garibaldi, 2nd dam Lady McClellan by Royal George. This young stallion should bring a fair price, as he is bred right and should prove acceptable to many of the small farmers who wish to purchase a good horse.

D. J. Murphy of San Jose sends in a number of richly bred ones, the first on the list being Lady Carter, by California Nutwood, dam Newark Belle by Nutwood 600. This four year old mare is an inbred Nutwood, and should be eagerly sought after by those who fancy "good goods." Mr. Murphy also has several of each by Rea's Nutwood, Jack Patchen and others which are entitled to the consideration of prospective purchasers.

Mr. D. E. Fortin of Oakland has four head catalogued, three fillies and a stallion colt, the latter by Orient, a son of Millimen's Bellfounder. Those of the opposite sex are by Geo. M. Patchen, Jr. and Anteros. One of the mares is heavy in foal to St. Nicholas, the produce being entered in the BREEDER AND SPORTSMAN Futurity Stake.

Capt. B. E. Harris has half a dozen good ones entered, Harry Mac, Starlight and Sidena being the bright gems in the collection. Harry Mac is by Alexander Button, dam Young Rosedale (the dam of Rosa Mac 2:20¾) by Sawyer's Messenger. This is a very racy looking gelding and can earn more than his oats on the track.

Starlight made a name for herself last season as a yearling, winning the colt stake at Napa in 3:12, she having been handled but six weeks prior to the race. Starlight is by Dawn, 2:18¾, dam Lena Bowles by Vick's Ethan Allen 2993, 2nd dam Shafer by Sidney 4770, dam Lena Bowles. This is a very promising filly and a perfect trotter.

Marvel, Hugo and Brentwood are all well bred and should find ready purchasers.

Some of the sires about which less is known than those already mentioned are Geo. C. Gorham, Norwood, Leland Stanford and Elmwood, all of which are represented in the sale by their progeny, and we have no hesitancy in assuring our readers that this is a *bona fide* auction, and that Messrs. Killip & Co. will see that these choicely bred animals are knocked down to the highest bidders.

The Late Sales.

The fact has been proven beyond a doubt that Easter[n] breeders will pay larger prices for California bred hors[es] than for those reared in any other section. The fiat ha[s] gone forth, and there is not a scintilla of evidence lack[ing] to convince the world that the Golden State occupi[es] the premier position in the eyes of those who desire [to] purchase the best trotting stock. Rosemeade, Valensi[n] Stock Farm, Pleasanton Stock Farm and Rancho d[el] Paso have each sent on consignments, the prices ob[tained] being such that no one could grumble at them. Following closely on the heels of the California produc[tions], Mr. Chas. Backman of Stony Ford, G. E. Reynolds of Utica, N. Y., the estate of B. E. Bates of Water[town], Mass., and a choice consignment from the grea[t] breeding farms of William Rockefeller, were offered fo[r] sale by Messrs. Kellogg & Co of New York, but take[n] in general average, they sold for nowhere near the me[dial] brought by the stock from this State, and yet M[r.] Backman and Mr. Rockefeller are reputed to have a[s] gilt-edged matrons as there are in the country. Th[e] climatic influences of California are such that the youn[g] foals are much more forward in growth, are hardie[r], better able to stand the wear and tear of training, an[d] develop sooner than do those reared in the Eastern State[s]. The native grasses of California are better adapted fo[r] young stock than any of those to be had in the East, an[d] as a consequence when offered for sale, our horses comman[d] top prices. Breeding Farms are springing up on ever[y] hand, and the day is not far distant when buyers will b[e] just as anxious to come here to purchase, as breeders ar[e] now to send their stock to New York.

The Golden Gate Association.

In the appropriate column will be found a new adver[tisement] from the officials of the Golden Gate Agricul[tural] District No. 1. They announce four new purse[s] which should receive the earnest consideration of every horse owner in the State, as the purses offered are larg[e] and the terms of payment for entrance, extremely liberal.

The first, or "New List" is a purse of $1,000, fo[r] three-year-olds whose sires up to January 1, 1890, hav[e] not produced an animal with a record of 2:30 or better the entrance fee is ten per cent. divided into four payments.

The second is a Guaranteed Purse of $1,200 for th[e] three-minute class, free-for-all, and an entrance fee o[f] ten per cent. which is also divided into four payments.

The third is a Guaranteed Purse of $1,200 for the 2:4[0] class, entrance ten per cent. also payable in four installments. Entrances for all the above close on May 1s[t] with the Secretary.

The fourth is called the Guaranteed Futurity Purs[e] for foals of 1890, and has been placed at the magnificen[t] figure of $4,000, and the Directors have seen fit to charg[e] only five per cent. entrance, payments to be paid in fiv[e] equal installments. This particular purse should receiv[e] a very large number of nominations; the enormous entry list secured for the BREEDER AND SPORTSMAN Futurit[y] Stakes being a guarantee that there are many now breeding first-class horses who are willing to subscribe to, an[d] support such stakes as those just instituted by the Oaklan[d] Association. The payments for this purse are as follow[s]: $40, August 1, 1890 at which time the entries close; $4[0] August 1, 1891; $40, January 1, 1892; $40, January [1], 1893, and the last and final payment is $40, August [1], 1893; the race to be trotted at the regular meeting of th[e] association in the fall of that year. The usual condition[s] can be seen in the advertisement, and it goes withou[t] saying that each of the purses will receive unqualifie[d] indorsement by the horse breeders of this State.

Imported Game Birds.

The Board of Fish Commissioners is actively engage[d] in importing and distributing Chinese quails. The[se] birds are protected by statute, but unless the good wi[ll] and high spirit of shooting men in the neighborhoo[d] where the birds have been planted can be enlisted th[e] birds will soon be destroyed, and the generosity of th[e] State set at naught. The birds are hardy, easily becom[e] acclimated, are prolific, are excellent table birds, and [in] every way desirable. When the sportsman chances up[on] a bevy of the brown little beauties the temptatio[n] will be strong to try a shot or two, but if the tempta[tion] be resisted for a few years there will be sport f[or] every one, and beside that consideration, there will [be] an increased self-respect in the sportsman, which alo[ne] will be ample reward for the forbearance exercise[d]. The localities in which the birds have been planted wi[ll] be published, and it is the hope of the Fish Commissio[n] that both sportsmen and citizens generally will make [it] a matter of pride to conserve the quails until 1895.

Catalogues.

It is now the correct thing for breeders to issue catalogues so that prospective purchasers may know what can be bought at the various stock farms throughout the country. During the past few weeks we have received the following catalogues which are valuable to an office such as this, in more senses than one.

The Highland Stock Farm, property of H. L. & F. D. Stout, Dubuque, Iowa, principal stallion Nutwood 600.

Property of W. F. Kendrick, Denver, Colorado, principal stallion Republic 4898.

Edgewood Farm, Terre Haute, property of W. R. McKeen, principal stallion Jersey Wilkes 2516.

Faustiana Stock Farm, Maryville, Missouri, property of J. B. Prather, principal stallion Faustus. (Thoroughbred.

Village Farm, East Aurora, Erie Co. N. Y., property of C. J. Hamlin, principal stallion Chimes 5348.

Mambrino Park, Des Moines, Iowa, the property of D. R. Mills, principal stallion Chestnut Wilkes 11410.

Chino Ranch, Chino, San Bernardino Co., property of Richard Gird; principal stallion Woolsey 5337.

Indian Hill, Louisville, Ky., property of R. S. Veech; principal stallion Princeps 532.

Kalamazoo Farm., Kalamazoo, Mich., the property of S. A. Browne & Co.; principal stallion Anteeo 7868.

Woodside Farm, Rushville, Indiana, the property of Campbell Bros.; principal stallion Haw Patch 1140.

Uihlein Bros.' Stock Farm, Truesdell, Wisconsin, property of Uihlein Bros.; principal stallion Alencon 9342. (Probably the next catalogue of this farm will have Alcazar as premier.)

Parkville Farm, Parkville, Long Island, N. Y., the property of John H. Shults; principal stallion Pancoast 1439.

Prospect Hill Stock Farm, Franklin, Venango County Pa. The property of Miller & Sibley; principal stallion St. Bel 5336.

Last, though not least, the mammouth catalogue of L. U. Shippee of Stockton has also been received, which is very complete in its way, and gives a good idea of what stock the millionaire banker has on his many ranches. Hawthorne 10,935 is the leading stallion among the trotters, while Fellowcharm by Longfellow has the post of honor among the thoroughbreds.

The Future of Trap Shooting.

The recent visit of the shooting aggregation piloted by the President of the American Shooting Association, Colonel C. W. Dimick, has exerted an influence upon the trap shooting interest of the State, which cannot as yet be accurately measured. One most desirable effect is already in operation, the adoption by all shooting clubs of the Association rules. The rules are in a degree faulty, as for instance, in allowing any position of the gun, but when gentlemen compete everywhere under the same rules a line as to the merit of trap work can be obtained, which is unattainable in any other way. Another noticeable effect of Colonel Dimick's visit is the general desire to become as finished in manipulation of the gun as the more skillful men of the visiting teams.

Among local shots some might be mentioned whose quickness and certainty stamp them as peers in the Shooting House of Lords, but it cannot be denied that a degree of laxity has been permitted at matches in California hitherto, which has made the scores rather uncertain guides to the actual excellence of the performances.

Fish Thieves.

A harsh sounding title, perhaps, but one justified not only by sportsmanly ethics, but also by that more stern interpreter, the common sense of the average citizen, when applied to those who persist in appropriating common property to their private uses, as is done by the men who fish out of season.

The day has gone by long since in which it was necessary to cite precedents at common law, to sustain the belief that the fowls of the air, the wild beasts of the field, and the fish of the waters were owned jointly by all citizens and were proper subjects for legislative consideration and conservation. As long ago as the times of the earliest records, game and fish were protected. At first by autocratic decrees, and later by statutes enacted by popular representative bodies. The invariable principle being that at certain seasons, when males were erotic or the females gravid, they were alike unfit for food and for sport.

It is left for these latter days, that the sun shall rise upon men willing to stand in the runways of deer blind to all but the instinctive promptings of nature and shoot them down; or stand over riffles and kill fish oblivious to any danger but one which seems to hinder completion of a necessary function.

Using words with moderation, the term "fish thief" may fitly be applied to one who goes upon spawning beds and kills salmon, salmon trout, trout, or any fish, the killing of which is prohibited by law, either the statutory or that higher unwritten law which should guide all above the grade of brutes.

Foals of 1890.

PALO ALTO, March 16, 1890.

Palo Alto Stock Farm, property of Leland Stanford:

Br f by Electioneer—Beautiful Bells by The Moor.
B f by Wildnut—Helpmate by Planet.
B f by Azmoor—Sonnet by Bentonian.
Br c by Azmoor—Lucy.
B c by Nephew—Lorinne by General Benton.
B c by Electioneer—Waxana by General Benton.
B c by Beverly—Floweret by Electioneer.
B f by Azmoor—Glenerva by Mohawk Chief.
Ch f by Palo Alto—Margia by General Benton.
B f by Stamboul—Manzanita by Electioneer.
Ch f by Piedmont—Della by Electioneer.
Br f by Ansel—Mattie by Rysdyk's Hambletonian.

At Vina Ranch:

B f by Benefit—Asthore by Kentucky Prince.
B f by Nephew—Barbara Ma'd by Richmond.
B c by Nephew—Bess by General Benton.
B f by Beverly—Cora by Don Victor.
B f by Benefit—Lady Kline by Mohawk Chief.

There were foaled at San Mignel Stock Farm on the 12th and 13th inst. respectively, black filly by Balkan, dam Amy by Mambrino Wilkes, 2nd dam by Pill Box; and bay colt by Mambrino Wilkes, dam Annie Laurie by Echo, 2nd dam Black Swan by Ten Broeck, thoroughbred son of Jack Hawkins.

Both Annie Laurie and Amy were entered in the BREEDER AND SPORTSMAN'S Futurity Stakes. The owner of these colts says: That stake has been won so often already that it is now too late for him to lay claim to it, but he ventures the prediction that either colt will stay in the race till it is finished, even if it should be prolonged for ten heats.

Answers to Correspondents.

Answers for this department must be accompanied by the name and address of the sender, not necessarily for publication, but as proof of good faith. Write the questions distinctly, and on one side of the paper only. Positively no questions will be answered by mail or telegraph.

A Subscriber.
Will you please inform me through the columns of your valuable paper, if the stallion called Monroe Chief Jr., bred by Henry Meyer of Oakland, Cal., is a standard bred horse. Also please give his breeding and oblige.

Answer.—He is not registered and we do not know his breeding.

W. W. S.
Please give me the breeding of Sur Del, bred by R H. Newton, Woodland, Cal., now the property of George Ellis, Ukiah.

Answer.—By Del Sur, dam by Black Ralph.

S. Lyons.
Neither of your stallions are standard bred. They cannot be registered.

P. G.
Can you give me any account of a race at San Jose in which Maggie E and Alfred S trotted?

Answer.—Alfred S beat Maggie E, Old Nick and Howard on August 16, 1887, in three straight heats. Time, 2:30, 2:25 and 2:23.

J. W. G.
The mare is not in the 2:30 list. We do not know her breeding. Drop a note to Mr. Ober and he can inform you.

L.
Please give full pedigree of Director Jr. and all the horses named on the enclosed slip.

Answer.—The pedigree given on the slip you enclosed is correct for Director Jr. His name has been changed to Corrector, and he is now at the Pleasanton Stock Farm. It would take at least a column to give the pedigrees you ask for, and we cannot spare the space.

Marco.
Last week by an oversight we made a mistake in the pedigree of Marco, and hasten to correct it. He is by Elector 2:21½, 1st dam Mesquite by Washington, 2nd dam Fanny (full sister to St. Helena 2:27½) by Gen. McClellan, 3rd dam Buttermilk Sal (dam of Gladiator 8336.

J. W. R.
Can you send me the pedigree of Capt. Webster?

Answer.—We do not send answers by mail. Capt. Webster by Belmont, dam not traced.

Playboy.
Please inform me as to the pedigree of Naubuc.

Answer.—Naubuc 504, by Toronto Chief 85, dam Gipsey Queen, believed to be by a son of Vermont Black Hawk 5. Gipsey Queen was the dam of Thomas Jefferson 2:23.

R. S.
Please give breeding of thoroughbred mare Queen Bess, we think by Hyder Ali; also breeding of Bess, owned by Davis & Hall of Keysers, W. Va, and raced by them; also whether they are good ones or not.

Answer.—Queen Bess by Hyder Ali, dam Interpose by Intruder. She is a full sister to Spokane, so you can judge as to what her merits should be. Bess is by Fadladeen, dam Betsy by Curles; 2d dam Red Eyes by Red Eye; 3d dam by Bailie Peyton; 4th dam by imp. Emancipation; 5th dam by Sir Charles, etc. We do not know whether she is good or not.

Fresno.
Can you give me the history of Sweet Briar, dam of Clovis?

Answer—Sweet Briar, the dam of Clovis 4909 was a brown mare 15 3 hands in height, and weighed about 1,050 pounds. She had received about three months training prior to the time she was bought from her former owner. Mr. Kitteridge, by Samuel Gambel, now Superintendent for W. S. Hobart of this city. Mr. Kitteridge lived in Peekskill, New York; he told Mr. Gamble that the mare had showed a mile in 2:47, but that she had received an injury which disabled her for any further development, and Mr. Gamble simply bought her as a broodmare and paid $400 for her, shipping her to a stable in 42nd street, New York. Mr. Gamble traveled around considerably and left her there, with instructions that she should be exercised as necessity required. On his return from one of his trips the well known Colonel Dickey who had driven the mare on the road, informed Mr. Gamble that Sweet Briar was going to prove a trotter. "Sam" could hardly believe it after what had been told him by Kitteridge, but was persuaded to go out and see her work on the following day. Mr. Gamble drove her himself the first mile in 2:42 and a repeat in 2:31¼. He then had her shipped along with Imogene (dam of Guide 2:28¼) and Priceless (dam of Ernest Maltravers 2:22) to Chicago. On arriving in the Western city some six weeks afterwards, Mr. Gamble was very much surprised to find the mares in a most horrible condition. Imogene was so stiff she appeared foundered, and Sweet Briar seemed all used up from long standing in the stable and high feeding, coupled with no exercise; however, the three were brought to this State and were very poor looking mares to prove trotters, but they were all turned into the matron list, the three proving themselves of a high order. This is the history of Sweet Briar as given us by Mr Gamble.

List of Fresno Entries—March 25th, 26th, 27th and 28th, 1890.

HALF-MILE DASH, FOR TWO-YEAR-OLDS IN THE DISTRICT.

Owner	Horse
Maltese Villa Stables, Merced	c c Judge Terry
J. H. Walker, Wildflower	b c Gilderoy
Sidney Ash, Merced	c c Garnet
W. B. Fudge, Visalia	b s Tulare Chief

ONE AND ONE-EIGHTH MILE DASH.

Owner	Horse
Owen Bros., Fresno	b m Corona
Dennison Bros, Sacramento	b s Hot Spur
Sidney Ashe, Merced	b c Willoughby
Kelly & Samuels, Los Angeles	b g Pliny
Golden Gate Stables, San Francisco	b m Louisa M.
Orange Grove Stable, Los Angeles	b g Jack Brady

ONE-QUARTER MILE AND REPEAT.

Owner	Horse
D. F. Able, Ione	c g Rondo
A. D. Hitchcock, Fresno	c g Cyclone
Wm Sherwood, Fresno	c s Billy Button
Ed Fitzgerald, Fresno	c m Gypsy Girl
T. F. Lynch, Sacramento	b g Sunday
F. Work, Visalia	b s Spring Water

FIVE-EIGHTHS OF A MILE DASH.

Owner	Horse
G. Lyman, Ione	b s Pain Killer
H. D. Miller, Fresno	ch m Ida Glenn
Maltese Villa Stables, Merced	c c Judge Terry
J. J. Abbott, Los Angeles	b g Abbott's Colt
T. F. Lynch, Sacramento	b g Sunday
J. R. Ross, Los Angeles	b g Kitty Van
T. Boyle, Sacramento	Morton
Golden Gate Stables, San Francisco	b g Jubilee
Orange Grove Stables, Los Angeles	c g Adam

ONE MILE AND REPEAT.

Owner	Horse
Miller & Owens, Fresno	b m Daisy D.
Golden Gate Stables, San Francisco	blk g Black Pilot
Orange Grove Stables, Los Angeles	br g Jack Brady

HALF-MILE DASH.

Owner	Horse
D. F. Able, Ione	c g Rondo
A. D. Hitchcock, Fresno	c g Little Dick
Ed Fitzgerald, Fresno	b s Claudroy
Maltese Villa Stables, Merced	c f Birnie
J. J. Abbott, Los Angeles	b g Abbott's Colt
T. F. Lynch, Sacramento	b g Sunday

MILE AND A QUARTER DASH—HANDICAP.

Owner	Horse
Owen Bros., Fresno	c m Carone
Dennison Bros., Sacramento	b s Hotspur
J. R. Ross, Los Angeles	b g Ora
Sydney Ash, Merced	b c Willoughby
Kelly and Samuels, Los Angeles	b g Pliny
Golden Gate Stables, San Francisco	b m Louisa M.
Orange Grove Stables, Los Angeles	br g Jack Brady

FIVE-EIGHTHS OF A MILE AND REPEAT.

Owner	Horse
G. Lyman, Ione	b s Painkiller
Miller & Owens, Fresno	b c Captain Al
J. J. Dolan, Modesto	Revolver
Maltese Villa Stables, Merced	c f Mirope
J. J. Abbott, Los Angeles	b g Abbott's Colt
Golden Gate Stables, San Francisco	c m Asa
Orange Grove Stables, Los Angeles	c g Adam
J. R. Ross, Los Angeles	b m Daisy D

ONE-QUARTER MILE DASH.

Owner	Horse
D F. Abel, Ione	c g Rondo
Wm. Sherwood, Fresno	c s Billy Button
A. D. Hitchcock, Fresno	c g Cyclone
A. D. Hitchcock, Fresno	bk g Funny
Ed. Fitzgerald, Fresno	c m Gypsy Girl
T. F. Lynch, Sacramento	b g Sunday
W. B. Fudge, Visalia	rn m Fair Maid

THREE-EIGHTHS MILE AND REPEAT.

Owner	Horse
D. F. Abel, Ione	c g Rondo
A. D. Hitchcock, Fresno	c g Cyclone
J. J. Dolan, Modesto	Laura K.
Maltese Villa Stable, Merced	c f Birnie
J. J. Abbott, Los Angeles	c g Abbott's Colt
T. F. Lynch, Sacramento	b g Sunday
F. Work, Visalia	br s Springwater
Ed. Williams, Winnemucca, Nev	s g The Jew

ONE AND ONE-QUARTER MILE DASH—OWENS' HANDICAP.

Owner	Horse
Miller & Owens, Fresno	b m Daisy D
J. R. Ross, Los Angeles	b g Ora
Kelly & Samuels, Los Angeles	b h Ed McGinnis
Golden Gate Stables, San Francisco	blk g Black Pilot
Golden Gate Stables, San Francisco	b m Louisa M.
Orange Grove Stables, Los Angeles	br g Jack Brady

VETERINARY.

Conducted by W. Henry Jones, M. R. C. V. S.

Subscribers to this paper can have advice through this column in all cases of sick or injured horses or cattle by sending an explicit description of the case. Applicants will send their name and address that they may be identified. Questions requiring answers by mail should be accompanied by two dollars, and addressed to W. Henry Jones, M. R. C. V. S., Olympic Stables, Sutter Street, San Francisco.

I. N. M.
I have a grey mare with a large, hard swelling on the off fore elbow. I have used warm fomentation, but without any good result. Can you tell me the cause, and what to do with it?

Answer.—The swelling arises from the horse lying on the inside heel of the shoe. I would advise you to have it excised by a veterinary surgeon.

Mrs. C.
I have a skye terrier which was stolen from me some three weeks ago. I got possession of him on Monday last. He has been dyed with a pink dye. Since recovery, he has nervous twitchings, which he did not have before. Could the dye have produced these effects?

Answer.—It is difficult to form an opinion of such a case without seeing the animal. The twitchings may arise from many causes. Aniline dyes contain a percentage of poison, and it is possible that the absorption of the same may have produced the symptoms in your dog. I would advise you to take him to a veterinary surgeon at once, and get his advice on the case.

Breeders' Directory.

Advertisements under this heading 50c. per line per month.

HORSES AND CATTLE.

W. S. JACOBS, Sacramento, Cal. — Breeder of Thoroughbred Shorthorns and Berkshire Hogs.

J. H. WHITE, Lakeville, Sonoma County—Breeder of Registered Holstein Cattle.

EL ROBLAS RANCHO—Los Alamos, Cal., Francis T. Underhill, proprietor, importer and breeder of thoroughbred Hereford Cattle. Information by mail. C. F. Swan, manager.

PAGE BROTHERS.—Penn's Grove, Sonoma Co. Cal. Breeders of Short-Horn Cattle; Draft, Roadster and Standard Bred Horses.

SETH COOK, breeder of Cleveland Bay Horses, Devon, Durham, Polled Aberdeen-Angus and Galloway Cattle. Young stock of above breeds on hand for sale. Warranted to be pure bred, recorded and average breeders. Address, Geo. A. Wiley, Cook Farm, Danville, Contra Costa Co., Cal.

MAMBRINO WILKES COLTS and FILLIES, full brothers and sisters to Gus. Wilkes 2:22, and Balkan 2:29¼, for Sale. Address SMITH HILL, Walnut Creek, Contra Costa County, Cal.

B. F. RUSH, Suisun, Cal., Shorthorns, Thoroughbred and Grades. Young Bulls and Calves for Sale.

PETER SAXE & SON, Lick House, San Francisco, Cal.—Importers and Breeders for past 18 years of every variety of Cattle, Horses, Sheep and Hogs.

HOLSTEIN THOROUGHBREDS of all the noted strains. Registered Berkshire Swine. Catalogues. F. H. BURKE, 401 Montgomery St., S. F.

HENRY C. JUDSON, Wild Idle Farm.—Breeder of Thoroughbred Horses. The home of "Wild Idle." P. O. Santa Clara; Box 223.

FERGUSON & AUSTIN,
FRESNO, CAL.
Registered Polled Angus and Short-Horn Cattle.

Solano and Napa Agricultural Society.

Trotting Colt Guarantee Stakes for 1890.

The Solano and Napa Agricultural Society have opened the following Colt Stakes for Trotters:

NO. 1. TWO YEAR OLDS.—Free for all; $500 guaranteed. $50 entrance, payable as follows: $10 April 1st, when entries close; $10 May 1st, $10 June 1st $10 July 1st, $10 August 1st, when colts must be named. Nominations transferable any time before colts are named. If the payments amount to more than the amounts guaranteed the additional amount to be added to the stake. All moneys divided as follows: 60, 30 and 10 per cent; in case of only two starting, 60 and 40 per cent; and in case of one horse walking over the whole amount to go to such horse. A failure to make any payment when due shall be considered a withdrawal and forfeiture of the amounts paid in. National or American Rules to govern, as the Society may elect. The right reserved to refund the first payment in case the stakes do not fill reasonably well.

No. 2. FOR THREE YEAR OLDS.—Free for all $500 guaranteed. $110 entrance, payable as follows: $20 April 1st, when entries close; $20 May 1st, $20 June 1st, $20 July 1st, $20 August 1st, when colts must be named. Conditions same as in No. 1.

District colt stakes for districts comprising Counties of Solano, Napa, Sonoma, Marin, Lake, Colusa, Yolo, Mendocino, Humboldt and Butte.

No. 3. FOR YEARLINGS.—$250 guaranteed. District. $40 entrance, payable as follows: $10 April 1st, when entries close; $10 June 1st, $10 July 1st, $10 August 1st, when colts must be named. Conditions same as in No. 1.

No. 4. FOR TWO YEAR OLDS.—$350 guaranteed. District. $50 entrance, payable as follows: $10 April 1st, when entries close; $10 May 1st, $10 June 1st, $10 July 1st, $10 August 1st when colts must be named. Conditions same as in No. 1.

No. 5. FOR THREE YEAR OLDS.—$400 guaranteed. District. $50 entrance, payable as follows: $10 April 1st when entries close; $10 May 1st, $10 June 1st, $10 July 1st, $10 August 1st, when colts must be named. Conditions same as in No. 1.

Yearling Stake. Single dash; one mile. Two Year Olds.—Mile heats, two in three. Three Year Olds—Three in five, to harness. Parties entering colts will be notified by mail when payment becomes due.

The Society also offers the following stakes for Class horses.

TROTTING STAKES.—Free for all.
2.30 CLASS—Trotting; purse $1500.
2:21 CLASS—Trotting; purse $1500.
2:20 CLASS—Trotting; purse $1500.

Horses eligible January 1st, 1890. Entrance $150, payable as follows: $25 April 1st, when entries close; $25 May 1st, $25 June 1st, $25 July 1st, $50 August 1st, when horses must be named. Nominations transferable any time before August 1st. Right reserved to refund entrance fee in any of the stakes should they not fill reasonably well. Money divided, 50, 25, 15 and 10 per cent. National or American Association Rules to govern, as the Society shall elect. To be trotted at our regular summer meeting, upon days to be hereafter arranged.

Entries to close April 1st, 1890, with

A. H. CONKLING, Secretary,
Napa City, Cal.
L. L. JAMES, President.

Second Annual Bench Show
OF THE
South'n California Kennel Club
AT THE
City of Los Angeles,
MAY 6, 7, 8 & 9 '90.

The SOUTHERN CALIFORNIA KENNEL CLUB was admitted a member of the AMERICAN KENNEL CLUB September 18, 1889. The coming show will therefore be held under the A. K. C. rules.

Entries will positively close May 1st.

A special committee will take personal charge of all dogs sent from a distance and insure their proper care. For premium lists and entry blanks address E. K. BENCHLEY, Secretary, 14 South Spring Street, Los Angeles; or H. H. BRIGGS, Breeder and Sportsman, San Francisco.

The Trotting Stallion
Silver Bow
Will make the season of 1890 at the Oakland Race Track

PEDIGREE.

SILVER BOW 11706, two-year-old record 2:37, is by Robert McGregor 647, 2:17½ (sire of Bonnie McGregor, 2:13½, Earl McGregor, 2:21½, Mac D., 2:30, McGregor Boy, 2:29½, Mark Time, 2:30, Roxie McGregor, 2:20½) by Major Edsall 2:1, 2:29, by Alexander's Abdallah 15—sire of Goldsmith Maid, 2:14—by Hambletonian 10—sire of Dexter, 2:17¼.

Robert McGregor's dam was Nancy Whitman by American Star 14, by Stockholm's American Star.

SILVER BOW's first dam is Sadie by Hambletonian 10, sire of Geo. Wilkes, 2:22—sire of Guy Wilkes, 2:15¼, also Electioneer, sire of Sunol, three-year-old record, 2:10½, and Palo Alto, 2:12¾; second dam Lady Wynne by Wm. Welch 341; third dam Elenora Margrave by imp. Margrave.

DESCRIPTION.

SILVER BOW is a handsome bay, no white; 15-3½ hands high; weighs 1075 pounds; of fine form, with the best of legs and a clean-cut, intelligent head. Is remarkably level-headed, seldom making a break; wears seven-ounce shoes in front. His record, 2:37, is no mark of his speed; he can beat 30 easy, and with his gilt-edge breeding, he is just what he ought to be, a trotter sired by a trotter whose dam was herself a trotter and his grandam the dam of two trotters. His dam Sadie being by Hambletonian 10, shows him to be bred from the cream of the trotting blood.

TERMS: $100 for the season. Mares not proving in foal refundable for the season of 1891 free of charge. Good pasturage and first-class care taken of mares for $5 per month. No responsibilities assumed for escapes or accidents. For further particulars, address

Limited to 15 approved mares.
Season to end June 1st, 1890.

P. J. WILLIAMS,
Care Race Track, Oakland, Cal.

The Trotting Stallion
VICTOR,
Record 2:22.

Will make the season of 1890 at NAPA CITY.

DESCRIPTION.

VICTOR is a handsome dark bay; 15-3 hands high; weighs about 1,100 pounds, and is remarkably intelligent, level-headed of kind disposition, and a magnificent animal in every respect. He is well boned and muscled, of splendid conformation, and possesses the qualities of speed and endurance to an eminent degree—qualities that he imparts to his progeny.

PEDIGREE.

VICTOR, record 2:22	Echo 462	Hambletonian 10. Sire of 42 in the 2:30 list.	Abdallah 1
			Chas. Kent mare
		Fanny Felter	Magnolia 68
			by Webber's Kentucky Whip
	Daughter of	Woodburn	Lexington
			Lulu Horton
		daughter of	Ashland
			thoroughbred

ECHO is the sire of Belle Echo, 2:20, Senator, 2:21½, Victor, 2:22, Gibraltar, 2:22½, Echora, 2:22½, Tippie, 2:25½, Lohengrin, 2:27½, Pasha, 2:27½, Elmonte, 2:29, Col. Hawkins, 2:29½, Annie Laurie, 2:30, Economy, 2:30, Sam Lewis, pacer, 2:21.

TERMS—$60 FOR THE SEASON.

Mares not proving with foal may be returned next season free of charge, provided the horse remains the property of the present proprietor, and stands at the same place, otherwise money will be refunded. The best of care taken of mares in any manner that owners may desire, but no responsibility assumed for accidents or escapes. For further particulars, apply to or address

G. W. HUGHES, Agent,
G. A. DOHERTY, Proprietor. Napa City.

J. J. EVANS
—SELLS—
WALLACE'S YEAR BOOK,
WALLACE'S REGISTER No. 8,
STALLION SERVICE BOOKS,
For Office and Pocket.
—ALL KINDS—
PEDIGREE BLANKS.

J. J. Evans,
Stationer and Printer,
406 California Street, San Francisco, Cal.
Mail orders receive prompt attention.

Attention! Sportsmen!!

An exploring party will leave San Francisco about April 10th for the Alaska Coast, St. Matthews Island and Yukon River, stopping at numerous places on the way where Seal, Walrus, Sea Lions, Brown Bear, White Polar Bear and Deer are plentiful; also splendid fishing for Salmon, Halibut, Trout and Cod, offering to the hunter and fisherman a trip of five months' unparalleled for sport. A novel feature of this offer is that each one taking the trip becomes a stockholder in the Company.

For further information apply to
NORTHERN DEVELOPMENT CO.
No. 5 Market St., Room 5.

JOHN FORGIE,
Importing Tailor,
204 Montgomery Street,
N. E. Corner Bush, SAN FRANCISCO.

The Poodle Dog
"Rotisserie,"
FIRST-CLASS IN EVERY RESPECT.
Elegant Family Dining Rooms.
S. E. cor. GRANT AVE. and BUSH STREET.
ANDRE POTENTINI, Proprietor.

PHIL J. CRIMMINS. JOHN C. MORRISON.
"Silver Palace,"
36 Geary Street,
San Francisco, Cal.

THE
GOLDEN GATE
Fair Association

Extra Attractions
To take place at the
Fall Meeting, 1890,
—AT—
Oakland.

The New List Purse $1,000.

For three year olds whose sires up to Jan. 1st, 1890, have not produced an animal with a record of 2:30 or better. Entrance 10 per cent., payable as follows: $25 May 1st, 1890, $25 June 1st, 1890, $25 July 1st, 1890, $25 August 1st, 1890. Entries close May 1st, 1890.

GUARANTEED PURSE $1,200.

For three minute class. Entrance 10 per cent., payable as follows: $30 May 1st, 1890, $30 June 1st, 1890, $30 July 1st, 1890, $30 August 1st, 1890. Entries close May 1st, 1890.

GUARANTEED PURSE $1,200.

For 2:40 class. Entrance 10 per cent., payable as follows: $30 May 1st, 1890, $30 June 1st, 1890, $30 July 1st, 1890, $30 August 1st, 1890. Entries close May 1st, 1890.

—ALSO A—
Guaranteed Futurity Purse $4,000.

To take place during the Fall Meeting of 1893.

For foals of 1890. Entrance 5 per cent. payable as follows:
$40, Aug. 1, 1890.
$40, Aug. 1, 1891.
$40, Jan. 1, 1892.
$40, Jan. 1, 1893.
$40, Aug. 1, 1893.
Entries close Aug. 1, 1890.

CONDITIONS.

Neglect to provide payments on the dates stipulated will incur forfeiture of all previous payments.

The Directors reserve the right to change the hour and day of any race except when it becomes necessary to antedate a race, in which instance the nominator will receive three days notice of change by mail to address of entry.

Entries not declared out by 6 P. M. the day preceding the race, shall be required to start.

Purses will be divided into four moneys viz., 50 per cent. to the winner, 25 per cent. to the second horse, 15 per cent. to the third horse, and 10 per cent. to the fourth horse.

A horse distancing the field shall only be entitled to first and third moneys.

Trotting and racing colors shall be named by six o'clock on the day preceding the race, and MUST be worn upon the track.

All purse races, mile heats, best three in five to harness. Five horses required to enter and three to start.

Otherwise than the above, National or American Trotting Association Rules—as this Association may select—will govern the races offered.

Entries to close with the Secretary.

R. T. CARROLL, President.
JOS. I. DIMOND, Sec'y, 326 Market St., S. F.

Antevolo Colt
For Sale.

AVOLO REX, foaled February 22, 1888; dam Catchup by Rustic; grandam Huntress by Don Victor; g g dam Betty Denice by American Boy Jr. Is 15.1 hands high, well developed, muscular, and without a blemish. Has a very gentle disposition, and shows speed and a good gait. Apply

HOME FURNISHING CO.,
119 Fifth Street, S. F., Cal.

ARGONAUT HERD.
POLLED ABERDEEN—ANGUS CATTLE.

Thirty head choice pure bred and high grade (Cross bred) HEIFERS and a few grand young BULLS for sale at reasonable prices. A fine opportunity for persons wishing to establish choice herds or change their bulls. Representatives from this herd were grand prize winners at the last California State Fair. Address DR. G. M. DIXON,
Sacramento, Cal.

AUCTION SALE
—OF—
Brood Mares,
Colts and Fillies,
Harness & Draft Horses

—The property of—
D. J. MURPHY, San Jose.
TO BE SOLD AT
Public Auction,
—AT 11 A. M., ON—
Wednesday, April 16, '90
—AT—
a ir Ground, San Jose,
KILLIP & CO., Auctioneers,
22 Montgomery Street S., F., Cal.
Catalogues may be had on application.

FOR SALE
AT
Vineland Stock Farm
STALLIONS, BROODMARES AND FILLIES

ONE STALLION FIVE YEARS OLD, SEAL-BROWN, by WHIPPLETON (sire of Lily Stanley, 2:17 1-2 Homestakes 2:16 1-2, etc.), dam Sally Gorham by Werner's Rattler. This horse is scarcely 16 1-2 hands high, but very compactly built. He breeds exceptionally large and well finished colts. Any one understanding the business could clear him in one season, or he would make a No. 1 road horse, as he can trot a 40 gait any time.

ONE THREE-YEAR-OLD, SEAL-BROWN, by WHIPPLETON (sire of Lilly Stanley, 2:17 1-2, Homestakes 2:16 1-2, etc.), dam Sally Gorham, etc. This ought to make a great General Purpose sire, and with opportunities get trotters, as he is compact, strong-boned, and will measure when grown about 16 hands and weighs 1,350 lbs. With a little road work last fall he developed a wonderful burst of speed.

ONE THREE-YEAR-OLD, BLACK, by WHIPPLETON (sire of Lilly Stanley, 2:17 1-2, etc.), dam by Naubuc (sire of the dam of Eva W., 2:23 1-2, etc.), full brother to Thomas Jefferson, 2:23. This horse will be fully 16 1-2 hands high. He is smooth, rapid gaited and from size and conformation should breed, like his sire, large, rangy, finished colts.

ONE TWO-YEAR-OLD, BRIGHT CHESTNUT, sired by DAWN 2:18¾, dam Alida (dam of Directa, three-year-old record 2:31½, trial 2:26) by Admiral (sire of sister 2:19 1-2, Nona Y 2:25, etc). This colt is the making of an extraordinary horse. He is large boned and will be over sixteen hands high when grown; he is of the true Nutwood type, is clean gaited and can lead a piece as fast as any man's colt.

ONE TWO-YEAR-OLD, BLOOD BAY, (full brother to Alcona Jr. sire of Silas Skinner, trial 2:22) sired by ALCONA (sire of Flora Belle 2:24, etc.,) dam Madonna by Cassius M. Clay Jr. This colt will make a trotter and a great stock horse if developed; he has the combined blood of Almont, Mambrino Chief, Cassius M. Clay Jr. and Joe Downing.

These colts are all sound and promising. The only reason I offer them for sale is, that I have three aged stallions in use, and the surplus is growing on me. If I were starting a breeding business for profit, I should consider either of these colts a representative to commence with. Also brood mares and fillies for sale. Correspondence solicited.

FRED. W. LOEBER, St. Helena,
Napa Co., Cal.

Well bred Stallions
FOR SALE.
SATINWOOD

Is 3 years old, stands 16.1 hands high and weighs 1150 pounds; is a beautiful dark chestnut; was sired by Wormwood, a full brother to Eva W (2:23) and Redwood (2:27. First dam by John Nelson; second dam by Argyle; third dam Blackhawk Wormwood by Nutwood 2:18 3-4, sire of Woodnut 2:16 1-4; dam the Cropsy Mare by Naubuc, dam Gipsy Queen by George M. Patchen; second dam Capt. Roberts Mare. Nutwood 2:18 3-4, by Belmont, dam Miss Russell (dam of Maud S, 2:08 3-4. Belmont, by Abdallah (sire of Goldsmith Maid) dam Belle by Mambrino Chief. Miss Russell, by Pilot Jr, dam Sally Russell by Boston.

Full pedigree and all particulars on application.

J. A. C.

Sorrell stallion, foaled April 22nd, 1887. Bred by Wm. Jeffries of San Francisco, Cal. Sired by C. C. Bemis' Lancelot. First dam Bay Mare Nellie, sired by Ulster Chief he by Rysdyk's Hambletonian, her dam by Kentucky Hunter, noted for his speed and endurance (see Stud Book).

For further particulars apply to
J. A. CARLETON,
1302 Broadway, Oakland, Cal.

For Sale
A First-Class.
BREEDING FARM.
Of 800 Acres.

Four hours' ride from the city. Good roads to a first class track. Climate unexcelled. Plenty of wood and running water.

For further information apply to the office of the
BREEDER AND SPORTSMAN,
San Francisco.
313 Bush Street.

First Grand Annual Sale

—OF—

PURE BRED SHORTHORN CATTLE

Under the management of

The Pacific Coast Shorthorn Breeders' Asssociation.

Will be held at

AGRICULTURAL PARK, SACRAMENTO, April 3d, 1890.

(Sale to commence at 1 o'clock P. M.)

This society is composed of the best breeders of Short Horn cattle on the Pacific Coast, and is organized upon a permanent basis.

Nothing but Pure Bred Registered Cattle Will be Offered at this Sale.

The stock offered at this sale come from the herds of the following well known breeders:—

E. A. BRIDGFORD, Colusa, Colusa County.
PETER PETERSON, Sites, Colusa County.
A. HEILBRUN & BRO., Sacramento.
P. S. CHILES, Davisville, Yolo County.
P. H. MURPHY, Perkins, Sacramento County.
E. S. DRIVER, Antelope, Sacramento County.
JOSEPH MARZEN, Lovelocks, Nevada.

Catalogues can be had by addressing

J. F. CHILES, Secretary, Davisville, Yolo County.

ANNUAL SPRING SALE

—OF—

Road & Harness Horses

Work and Draft Horses!

SHETLAND PONIES!

From Ranchos of J. B. Haggin, Esq.

WILL TAKE PLACE

Tuesday, May 6, 1890,

AT SAN FRANCISCO.

Location to be hereafter designated.

Catalogues are being prepared.

KILLIP & CO., Live Stock Auctioneers,

22 Montgomery Street, S. F.

A Grand Combination Sale

—OF—

Standard-bred Trotters & Thoroughbreds

CLYDESDALES AND PERCHERONS,

Fine Roadsters, Work Horses, Etc.

—AND—

Registered and Graded Holstein CATTLE,

REGISTERED JACKS,

And other first-class Live Stock of all kinds, will be held at

CARSON CITY, NEV., April 15, 16 and 17, '90.

BROOD MARES, COLTS AND FILLIES by the following well known Sires will be sold:

Standard Bred.	*Thoroughbred.*
ECHO.	NORFOLK.
GIBRALTAR. (will be sold)	HOOKER.
PROMPTER.	LODI.
BUCCANEER.	BRECKENBRIDGE.
ST. CLAIR.	THREE CHEERS.
SIGNAL.	LANGFORD.
BLUE BULL.	BOI DE ARC.
ST. LAWRENCE.	McMAHON.

And among the fine stock to be offered will be the grand HOLSTEIN BULL SARATOGA, and a number of fine calves and heifers by him and other well known thoroughbred Holsteins.

Over 1 0 entries were made up to March 1st, and a big sale is assured.

Send in your entries.

For further particulars address

JNO. P. SWEENY & CO., Carson City, Nev.

The Annual Combination Sale

—OF—

Road Mares, Harness Horses, Colts and Fillies,

WILL TAKE PLACE AT

Bay District Track, San Francisco,

At 11 A. M. on

THURSDAY, APRIL 3, 1890.

The offering will consist of the get of ELECTIONEER, GUY WILKES, MAMBRINO WILKES, ARTHURTON, SIDNEY, ALEX. BUTTON, ANTEROS, and other noted stallions.

Catalogues will be ready March 11th, and will be furnished upon application.

KILLIP & CO., Auctioneers,

24 Montgomery Street, San Francisco.

Poplar Grove Breeding FARM.

Standard-bred Trotters, Colts and Fillies.

The get of CLOVIS, 4909; PASHA, 2039; APEX, 2935,

For Sale.

Address S. N. STRAUBE, Poplar Grove Breeding Farm,

Fresno, Cal.

Inspection by intending purchasers invited, and information by mail.

For Sale.

14

Pure bred

PERCHERONS.

Stallions and Mares.

OF ALL AGES.

Part Imported, and all Registered Proof.

For further information, address

E. J. TURNER, Hollister, Cal.

For Sale

A HALF BROTHER TO

ALMONT PATCHEN,

(2:15, trial 2:13 3-4).

JUANITO JR. is a beautiful bright bay, black points, with no white, foaled 1886. As a colt he has given much more promise than did Almont Patchen at the same age. Instead of being a pacer, he is a good square trotter, with every indication of great speed, and is so gentle and kind, that a lady can drive him. The owner's only reason for selling him is that business calls him away from this section of the State. He will be sold at a reasonable figure. This is a splendid opportunity for a gentleman to secure a first-class trotter at a very low figure.

The pedigree of Juanito Jr. is by Juanito (sire of Almont Patchen), dam Nettie Moore by Old Tom Moore. For further particulars, address

JUANITO JR.,

Santa Clara P. O., Cal.

Attention Stockmen!

FOR SALE

At Chowchilla Ranch,

Thoroughbred Durham Cattle

Three Hundred Young DAISY COWS, 20 0 graded SHE CATTLE, Yearlings and up; a fine lot of high grade Durham Bulls; also have Mares, Horses, Mules and Norman Colts.

For particulars, apply to

ISAAC BIRD, Jr., Supt.,

Merced, California.

For Sale

A FIRST-CLASS

Napa County Farm

—OR—

STOCK RANCH,

800 Acres Improved,

SITUATED TWO AND A HALF MILES FROM NAPA CITY, with good roads leading thereto, a good hard finished house of nine rooms, with all modern improvements, streams running all summer, a great amount of live oak and black oak timber. It lies in a fruit belt, surrounded by fine vineyards and orchards growing upon the same quality of soil, and originally a part of this tract. About one-half hill, and one-half rolling land, but none of it is steep and all easily cultivated, splendidly situated for the breeding of fine horses. Price, $60 per acre. Further particulars given at this office.

BREEDER AND SPORTSMAN,

313 Bush St.

Twenty-Third Annual Sale!

169 THOROUGHBREDS

64 YEARLINGS,

100 BROODMARES,

5 GREAT STALLIONS

23d ANNUAL SALE OF

Belle Meade Stud,

Will take place at BELLE MEADE STUD, near Nashville, Tennessee on

THURSDAY AND FRIDAY, APRIL 24 & 25

169 Head Thoroughbreds at Public Auction.

SOLD FOR DIVISION. | SOLD WITHOUT RESERVE

Five Great Stallions

To the Highest Bidder.

LUKE BLACKBURN,
Imp GREAT TOM,
ENQUIRER,
BRAMBLE,
IROQUOIS.

FOR CATALOGUES ADDRESS THIS OFFICE.

P. C. KIDD, Auctioneer.

For other information and Catalogues address JOHN J. CARTER, No. 9 Baxter Block, Nashville, Tenn.

Stallion for Sale

AT A BARGAIN.

Full Brother to Fairmont.

By Piedmont, dam Queen by Garibaldi—see State Fair Edition of BREEDER AND SPORTSMAN, September 14, 1889, for description of Fairmont—three years old, solid bay. Can trot a 2:10 gait or better. Sound in every particular. Can be seen at Oakland Trotting Park, Oakland.

P. J. WILLIAMS.

Speed Programme

—OF THE—

Twelfth District Ag'l Society

To be held at

LAKEPORT,

SEPTEMBER 23 to 27 INCLUSIVE.

First Day—Tuesday, Sept. 23, 1890.

RACE NO. 1—TROTTING.

Yearling Stake; $200 guaranteed. Entrance $30, payable as follows: $5 May 1st, $10 July 1, $10 September 1st (when entry must be named), and $5 additional for starters. Entries to close May 1, 1890. See general Conditions.

RACE NO. 2—RUNNING.

One-half mile dash. $100 added; $25 to second. Entrance $10, to close 6 P. M. day before race.

RACE NO. 3—TROTTING.

Three-minute class. Mile heats 3 in 5. District. $150 added. Entrance $15; to close 6 P. M. day before race. 5 to enter, 3 to start. See general Conditions.

Second Day—Wednesday, September 24th

RACE NO. 4—RUNNING.

Three-quarter mile heats: 2 in 3. $200 added; $25 to second. Entrance $10, to close 6 P. M. day before race.

RACE NO. 5—TROTTING.

District Stallion. Mile heats 3 in 5. Purse $500. Entrance $50, to close 6 P. M. day before race; 5 to enter, 3 to start. See general Conditions.

RACE NO. 6—TROTTING.

Three-year-old stake; $300 guaranteed. $50 entrance, payable as follows: May 1st, $10; July 1st, $10; September 1, $15 (when entry must be named), and $15 additional to start. Open to Napa, Solano, Sonoma, Marin, Lake, Colusa, Yolo, Mendocino and Humboldt Counties.

Third Day—Thursday, Sept. 25th.

RACE NO. 7—RUNNING.

Seven-eighths mile dash. $150 added; $25 to second. Entrance $10, to close 6 P. M. day before race.

RACE NO. 8—TROTTING.

Two-year-old stake: free for all. Mile heats, best 2 in 3. $300 guaranteed. Entrance $50, payable as follows: May 1st, $10; July 1st, $10; September 1st, $15, and $15 additional to start. See general Conditions.

Fourth Day—Friday, Sept. 26th.

RACE NO. 9—TROTTING.

Mile heats, 3 in 5. For all described counties in race No. 6. $400 added. Entrance $60, payable as follows: May 1st, $10; July 1st, $20; September 1st, $20—when entries must be named—$10 additional to start. See general Conditions.

RACE NO. 10—RUNNING.

Citizens' Handicap. $100 added. Five-eighths mile; heats, 2 in 3. Entrance $10, to close 6 P. M. day before race.

Fifth Day—Saturday, September 27th.

RACE NO. 11—RUNNING.

GENTLEMEN'S NOVELTY.—For non-professional jockeys. One mile dash. $100 added; $5 entrance. Purse divided as follows: First horse at each quarter to get $25; slowest average at all quarters to get Society medal.

NO. 12.—LADIES' TOURNAMENT

Free for all in District. Purse $60, divided as follows: $35 to first, $15 to second, $10 to third.

No. 13.—GENTLEMAN'S TROTTING.

Same Conditions as gentlemen's Novelty. Mile heats, two in three. Entrance $5. Entrance money divided 60, 30 and 10 per cent.

GENERAN CONDITIONS.

Nominations in colt stakes transferrable any time before colts are named. If the payments in stake races amount to more than the sum guaranteed the additional amount to be divided 60, 30 and 10 per cent; in case of only two starting, 60 and 40 per cent.; and in case of one horse walking over, the whole amount to go to such horse.

A failure to make any payment when due shall be considered a withdrawal, and forfeiture of the amounts paid in. National Rules to govern all trotting races. The right reserved to refund the first payment in case the stake does not fill satisfactorily.

All running races, unless otherwise specified, governed by the Pacific Coast Blood Horse Association Rules.

The Directors reserve the right to change the hour and date of any race, and in case of a race being antedated the nominator will receive notice.

A horse distancing the field shall receive only first and third moneys.

L. G. SIMMONS, President.

A. B. McCUTCHEN, Secretary.

Rochester Driving Park

ROCHESTER, N. Y.

FLOWER CITY

Guarantee Stakes.

$10,000,

OPEN TO ALL SUBSCRIBERS.

For Trotting Horses that never beat 2:30 prior to the closing of this Stake

To be Trotted on the Rochester Driving Park, during Circuit Meeting Aug. 12th, 13th, 14th and 15th, date to be decided by the Association.

ENTRANCE, FIVE PER CENT. OF PURSE, TO BE PAID AS FOLLOWS:

$125 payable at the time of subscription, which is to close Tuesday, April 1, 1890. Each subscriber to give his residence and Post Office address with his subscription. $125 payable Thursday, May 15th. $125 payable Tuesday, July 1st. $125 payable Friday, August 1, 1890, when the horses are to be named.

No subscription received unless the first payment of $125 shall accompany the same.

Subscribers liable only for the amount they have actually paid in but all subscrip ions paid in shall be forfeited to the Association for this stake. Subscribers may transfer their subscription. Horses eligible April 1, 1890, shall be eligible for the race.

The entire stake subscribed shall be devoted to this purse, and it is guaranteed by the Association not to be less than $10,000. In case the subscription should exceed the amount of $10,000, such excess if under $500, will be added to the amount of purse; but if such excess should amount to $500 or over, then the excess will be devoted to another purse to be given as a Consolation Purse, for horses starting and winning no part of the original purse. Purses to be divided into fifty twenty-five, fifteen and ten per cent., for first, second, third and fourth horses.

Bear in mind that subscriptions close Tuesday, April 1st, and that the whole subscription is but five per cent. of the guaranteed amount of purse ($10,000).

Subscriptions accompanied by the first payment ($125), must be addressed to the Secretary.

Send for circulars for distribution.

A. COLLINS, Secretary,
Rochester, N. Y.

The Montana Circuit.

Thirty-one Days of Racing--Running, Trotting and Pacing.

$45,000 in Purses and Stakes.

Nominations to the Following Stakes close April 1st:

MISSOULA, July 14th to 19th Inclusive.

J. L. SLOANE, Secretary.

MISSOULA STAKES—Running. Six furlongs .... $250 added
For two-year-olds.

HOTEL STAKES—Running. One and one-half miles .... $400 added
For three-year-olds.

BITTER ROOT STAKES—Trotting .... $250 added
For three-year-olds bred and raised in Montana.

DEER LODGE, July 22d to 26th Inclusive.

JAS. B. McMASTER, Secretary.

DEER LODGE STAKES—Running. Six furlongs .... $250 added
For two-year-olds.

HOTEL STAKES—Running. One and one-half miles .... $300 added
For three-year-olds.

MONTANA STAKES—Trotting .... $100 added
For two-year-olds bred and raised in Montana.

ORO FINO STAKES—Trotting .... $300 added
For three-year-olds. Free for all.

YOSPEL MONTAIN STAKES—Trotting .... $200 added
For two-year-olds. Free for all.

MERCHANTS' STAKES—Trotting .... $200 added
For three-year-olds bred and raised in Montana.

Anaconda, July 30th to August 9th Inclusive.

W. M. THORNTON, Secretary.

BANKERS' STAKES—Running. Five furlongs .... $400 added
For two-year-olds.

MONTANA SUBURBAN—Running. One and one-half miles .... $600 added
For three-year-olds.

BREEDERS' STAKES—Trotting .... $250 added
For two-year-olds bred and raised in Montana.

BREEDERS' STAKES—Trotting .... $250 added
For three-year-olds bred and raised in Montana.

LOWER WORKS STAKES—Trotting .... $250 added; $250 more if 2:35 is beaten
For two-year-olds. Free for all.

UPPER WORKS STAKES—Trotting .... $240 added; $250 more if 2:25 is beaten
For three-year-olds. Free for all.

BUTTE, August 13th to 23rd Inclusive.

E. W. WYNNE, Secretary,

ANACONDA STAKES.—Running .... $400 added
For 2 year olds.

WEST SIDE DERBY.—Running .... $500 added
For 3 year olds.

MONTANA STAKES.—Trotting .... $250 added
For 2 year olds bred and raised in Montana.

MONTANA STAKES.—Trotting .... $250 added
For 3 year olds bred and raised in Montana.

MOULTON STAKES.—Trotting .... $250 added, $250 more if 2:35 is beaten
For 2 year olds. Free for all.

SILVER CITY STAKES.—Trotting .... $250 added, $250 more if 2:25 is beaten
For 3 year olds. Free for all.

In all of the above stakes each nomination must be accompanied with $10 and a full description of animal. A second payment of $15 must be made on or before the first day of June; the remaining $25 must be paid before six o'clock the evening before the race.

All stakes to be divided as follows: 70 per cent. to the first horse, 20 per cent. to second, and 10 per cent. to third.

For entry blanks, programmes, etc., address any of the Secretaries.

ST. NICHOLAS.

A Son of the World Renowned

SIDNEY,

Will Make the Season of 1890, at the Oakland Trotting Park.

ST. NICHOLAS was bred by Mr. G. Valensin at the Arno Stock Farm, Sacramento Co., California, in 1886. He is a beautifully proportioned bright bay horse, 15.3 hands high; is well muscled, lengthy, and lots of bone, with splendid natural action and a phenomenal turn of speed. As a three-year-old he easily worked three heats on the Oakland Track in 2:32, 2:29 and 2:27½. His breeding is just what one would expect from such a highly formed bloodlike horse. Sidney, his sire, is the most successful young stallion—whether for getting pacers or trotters—America has ever seen, and no wonder for his blood lines are exceptionally fine and are all trotting lines, Santa Claus, Strathmore, Rysdyk's Hambletonian and Abdallah, while Sweetness again runs back through that great sire Volunteer, to Rysdyk's Hambletonian and also through her dam to Rysdyk's Hambletonian and Harry Clay 45, the sire of Electioneer's dam. St. Nicholas' dam is by Echo, an exceptionally prepotent son of Hambletonian thus giving St. Nicholas four Rysdyk's Hambletonian crosses and further back a Harry Clay cross which with his grand dam's thoroughbred cross should make him invaluable in the stud.

TERMS: Fifty dollars the season, which will commence on the 5th of February and close on the 1st of July. Due care will be taken of mares, but no responsibility for accidents or escapes.

Mares taken and kept as desired by the owners, and at reasonable rates.

JOHN ROWEN.
Oakland Trotting Park.

PASTURAGE
And Care of Horses

AT ALL SEASONS, A SPECIALTY,

—AT—

MURRAY'S RANCH, - - - Laurel Creek
SAN MATEO COUNTY.

Horses pastured, in the season, $1 per month.
Horses stabled and fed hay, per month $8 to $10.
Small pastures for fine stock at agreed rates. Yearly contracts at agreed rates. Best of attention given to all stock.

Stock can be delivered at the ranch or shipped to San Mateo.

Parties are requested to visit the ranch and satisfy themselves of its adaptation for the above purpose.

There are no barb wire fences on the farm.

Address

B. C. MURRAY,
San Mateo.

SAN JOSE
Colt Stakes,

TO BE TROTTED AT THE

FALL MEETING
OF 1890.

No. 1. REGAL WILKES TROTTING STAKES.For three year olds. $60 entrance, of which $10 must accompany nomination; $25 on June 1st, and $25 on August 1st; with $250 added. Mile heats, three in five.

No. 2. MOUNT HAMILTON TROTTING STAKES. For two year olds. $50 entrance, of which $10 must accompany nomination. $15 on June 1st and $25 on August 1st; with $200 added. Mile and repeat.

No. 3. SANTA CLARA COUNTY TROTTING STAKES.—For two year olds (for above County only). $30 entrance, of which $10 must accompany nomination. $10 on June 1st and $10 on August 1st, with $150 added. Mile and repeat.

Parties must have owned their colts prior to February 1st, 1890, to be eligible in this stake.

No. 4. INFANT TROTTING STAKES.—For the get of the following stallions: Jim L., Argent, Eros, Bismarck, J. Weatherhead's horses (3), Guy Davis, Nutwood Boy, Orion, King William, Tommy T., Stranger, John Sevenicks, Col. Benton, Wilmington, Dick Patchen, Baywood, Fleetwood, Sultan Jr., Billy Thornhill, Amphion, Magic, Chancellor, Monte, Chrisman's, Hambletonian, Boxwood, Nutgrove, Prince Albert, Alex Graham, Designer, Cyrus R., Harry Almont, Hes's Nutwood, Poodle, Parnell, Robin Adair, Fred Grant, Elect, Mambrino Jr., California Nutwood, Soudan, Jim Mulvenna, Brown Jug, Menlo, Almont Patchen, Antinous, Electric Light, May Boy, C. W. S. Henderson's Henry, S. B. Emerson, Carr's Mambrino, Designer, Prince Warwick, Henry Burr, J. Dunn's horses (3). For yearling foals of 1889, $25 entrance, of which $5 must accompany nomination; $10 on June 1st, and $10 Aug. 1st, with $100 added. Mile dashes.

CONDITIONS.

Entries to close in the above stakes Tuesday, April 1st, 1890. Stake and added money divided 60 per cent. to first, 30 per cent. to second, and 10 per cent. to third.

For a walkover the colt will take the whole stake but no added money. If two colts start they must contest for entrance money only, divided two-thirds and one-third.

Declarations are void unless accompanied by the money.

Nominations not making payments when due forfeit previous payments.

WM. BUCKLY, President.

G. H. BRAGG, Secretary.

State Agricultural Society's

SPRING

RACE MEETING

AT

SACRAMENTO, CAL.,

APRIL 26 to 29, and MAY 1 and 3, 1890

ENTRIES CLOSE APRIL 7, 1890.

PROGRAMME.

FIRST DAY—SATURDAY, APRIL 26.

NO. 1.

Purse $400, for three-year-olds and upwards; $[illegible] from starters to go to second horse. A winner this year at this distance to carry 3 pounds extra. Maidens allowed, if three years old, 5 pounds; four or more, 10 pounds. Three-quarters of a mile.

NO. 2.

Norfolk Stakes, for two-year-olds. Closed with [illegible] nominations. Five-eighths of a mile.

NO. 3.

Selling purse $400, of which $50 to second; for all ages. Winner to be sold at auction. Horses entered to be sold for $1,500 to carry rule weight. One pound off for each $100 down to $500. Value placed on starters only by 6 P. M. night before race. One mile and a sixteenth.

NO. 4.

The California Oaks, for three-year-old fillies. Closed in 1889 with 17 nominations. One and one-eighth miles.

SECOND DAY—TUESDAY, APRIL 29.

NO. 5.

The Matadero Stake, for two-year-olds. Closed 1889 with 19 nominations. Three-quarters of a mile.

NO. 6.

The Chris. Green Handicap. Closed February 1st with 14 nominations. One and one-quarter miles.

NO. 7.

Purse $400, for all ages; $10 from starters to go to second horse. Maiden allowances: if three years old, 5 pounds; four and upwards, 10 pounds. Non-winners this year allowed 5 pounds. Allowances cumulative. One mile and a sixteenth.

NO. 8.

The Weinstock, Lubin & Co. Stake. Closed in 18[illegible] with thirty-two nominations. One mile.

THIRD DAY—THURSDAY, MAY 1.

NO. 9.

The Spring Stakes. A sweepstakes for three-year-olds (foals of 1887) that have not won a race previous to January 1st, 1890. Closed February 1, 1890, with [illegible] nominations. One mile.

No. 10.

The Western Hotel Stakes for two-year-old fillies. Closed in 1889 with 27 nominations. Five-eighths of a mile.

NO. 11.

The Hall, Lohrs & Co. Handicap. Closed in 1889 with 29 nominations. One and one-quarter miles.

NO. 12.

Selling purse $400, of which $50 to second; for all ages. Horses entered to be sold for $2,500 to carry [illegible] weight. One pound off for each $100 down to [illegible]. Value placed on starters only by 6 P. M. night before race. One and one-eighth miles.

FOURTH DAY—SATURDAY, MAY 3.

NO. 13.

The Golden Eagle Hotel Handicap, for two-year-olds. Closed in 1889 with 20 nominations. Weights to be announced before 5 P. M. second day before race. Declarations due by 4 P. M. day before race. Three-quarters of a mile.

NO. 14.

The Hopeful Handicap: a sweepstakes for all ages of $25 each, $15 forfeit, or $10 if declared, with $[illegible] added; second to receive $100. Weights announced 10 P. M. day before race. Declarations due by 5 P. M. same day. One and one-eighth miles.

NO. 15.

The California Derby. Closed in 1889 with 22 nominations. One and one-half miles.

NO. 16.

Purse $150, for all ages; $10 from starters to go to second horse. Non-winners this year at time of starting allowed, if three years old, 5 pounds; four years old, 10 pounds; five and upwards, 12 pounds. Entries to close with clerk of course at 5 P. M. day before race. Mile heats.

The State Agricultural Society's rules of 1889 to govern, except when conditions are otherwise.

Starters in stake races must be named through the entry box by 6 P. M. of the day before the race. The right of forfeit ceases at 10 o'clock A. M. day of race. Entries in purses not declared out by 6 P. M. day before race is run, must start.

Non starters in all purse races held for entrance under Rule 22.

The right to postpone races on account of bad weather or other sufficient cause, is reserved. In event of postponement, handicaps stand, other declarations are off.

All declarations, either of starters, non-starters, non-acceptance of handicaps or otherwise, must be made in writing. Blanks will be furnished by the Secretary.

Declarations in handicaps must be accompanied by the money.

Entries in Nos. 1, 3, 7, 12 and 14 to close with the Secretary Monday, April 7, 1890.

CHRIS GREEN, President.

EDWIN F. SMITH, Secretary.

CALIFORNIA
NUTWOOD

Will stand for mares the season of 1890, commencing February 15th, and ending July 15th, at the NUTWOOD STOCK FARM, one mile from Irvington.

DESCRIPTION AND PEDIGREE.

He is a dark chestnut, with star in forehead; foaled September 16th, 1881; is 16 bands 1½ inches high and weighs 1250 pounds. Has a beautiful flowing mane and tail, with remarkable style and lofty carriage, a bold, open movement like his sire, but has never been handled for speed. He moves and looks like his sire, except that he is a larger horse.

CALIFORNIA NUTWOOD by Nutwood, record 2:18¾, has 82 trotters and pacers with records from 2:15 to 2:30, and put 8 in the 2:30 list in 1889. He is the only horse that ever lived with a record under 2:20 that produced five under 2:20. He is now serving mares at Dubuque, Iowa, at $500 for the season, and his colts at yearlings sell from $2500 to $5000 each. He is out of the dam of Maud S., record 2:08¾.

Nutwood, by Alexander's Belmont, sire of 82 with records from 2:15½ to 2:30. Alexander's Belmont by Alexander's Abdallah, sire of Goldsmiths Maid, record 2:14, and 5 others in 2:30 list. Alexander's Abdallah, by Rysdyk's Hambletonian, sire of 41 with records from 2:17¼ to 2:30, and is the founder of the Hambletonian family.

FANNY PATCHEN, dam of California Nutwood, by George M. Patchen Jr., record 2:27, and sire of Wells Fargo, 2:18¾, Sam Purdy 2:20½, Ben Ali 2:20¾, and 7 others from 2:21 to 2:30. He has 7 sons who together produced 12 trotters in 2:30 list, and 6 daughters who together produced 5 trotters and 1 pacer in 2.30 or better. He sired Alexander 2:31½. Alexander sired Alex. Button 2:26½; Alex. Button sired Yolo Maid, pacing record 2:14 at 5 years old, the fastest on record; George M. Patchen Jr., by George M. Patchen 2:23½, is sire of Lucy 2:18¼, and 3 others in the 2:30 list; he has 12 sons who together produced 40 trotters from 2:14¾ to 2:30, and 6 daughters who together produced 6 trotters in 2:30 list or better, he is grand sire of Hopeful 2:14¾, and best wagon record 2:16½, and sire of the granddam of Stamboul 2:12½.

George M. Patchen, by Cassius M. Clay, and he by Henry Clay, founder of the Clay family.

Laura, second dam of California Nutwood, was a fine large bay mare, a very fast roadster brought from Chicago by Wm. Wilson, of San Jose, and is said to have made a record of 2.35 in Chicago. Pedigree not traced.

TERMS.

$40 for the season, payable invariably before the animal is removed. Mares not proving in foal can be returned free next season. Pasturage $3 per month, but no liability for accidents or escapes.

For further particulars address the owner,

MARTIN CARTER,

Newark, Alameda Co., Cal., or Irvington, Alameda County, Cal.

Sunny Side Breeding Farm.
Admiral 488.

Foaled 1867—Sired by Volunteer 55. Son of Rysdyk's Hambletonian 10.

First dam Lady Pierson by Cassius M. Clay (Neaves') 20; second dam by Diamond; third dam a running mare said to be thoroughbred. He is fitted in an eminent degree to produce colts that will in all respects justify his patrons in their expectations.

Admiral is the sire of Huntress, record 2:27½, Sister, 2:19½, Perhelion, 2:25, Nona Y., 2:25, and others equally as promising, but have not had the advantage of track work. He will serve a limited number of approved mares at $50 the season, with usual return privilege. Season ending August 1, 1890. No liability for accidents or escapes.

KING DAVID 2576.

Bay Stallion—Foaled 1883.

Sired by Admiral 488, dam Black Flora (the dam of Huntress, 2:27½, Sister, 2:19½, Perhelion, 2:25, Nona Y., 2:25), by Black Prince.

King David is one of the best gets of Admiral. He has a good disposition, kind to drive, smooth and even-gaited, and can speed fast. Barring accidents, he will trot in the twenties this Fall. His colts are large, rangy, and well finished. Will serve a limited number of mares at $30 the season, to end July 1, 1890. Every precaution will be taken to prevent accidents and escapes, but no liability will be assumed. Pasturage $4 per month.

Sunny Side Farm is situated two miles east of Vallejo, on the Sulphur Spring road. For further particulars, address

FRANK DRAKE,

Vallejo, Cal.

LAWN VIEW BREEDING FARM STALLIONS.
ACTOR.

A beautiful bay horse foaled 1887 by Promptor 2305 sire of Apex (four-year-old record) 2:26, Transit 2:26¼, Creole 2:25, Blue Belle 2:32, Daisy (yearling record) 2 36¼, he by Blue Bull 75, 1st dam by Sultan 1513 2 24, sire of Stamboul 2:12 1-4, Ruby 2:19¼, Sweetheart 2 22¼, Alcazar 2:20¼, Eva 2:23¼, La Grange 2:23¼, and eleven others in 2:30 list, second dam by Fireman by Langford.

Actor, as his pedigree shows, is as purely bred a young stallion as ever made a season in the stud. Blue Bull stock is much sought after in the East, and Sultan, sire of his first dam will make the season in Kentucky this year at $100 per mare. Actor is a handsome bay colt 16 hands high, clean limbed and possesses all the points of a speedy trotter.

TERMS, $40 FOR THE SEASON, usual return privileges.

DOUGLASDALE 7650.

Thoroughbred Registered Clydesdale Stallion

Imported from Scotland, December, 1889, bay, three years old.

TERMS, $35 FOR THE SEASON.

YOUNG ELMO

Two years old sorrel stallion by St. Elmo 2:27, dam by Woodburn.

TERMS, $20 FOR THE SEASON.

For further particulars, address MANAGER LAWN VIEW FARM, Auburn, Cal.

Singleton & Addington,
Bank Exchange,

3d and K Streets, Sacramento.

Superior Wines, Liquors and Cigars.

The Pure Trotting-bred Stallion

ILLUSTRIOUS

STANDARD No. 4178.

DESCRIPTION.

Dark bay, black points, 15 1-2 hands high, weight 1090 pounds, foaled May 20, 1885; bred by General W. T Withers, Lexington, Ky.

PEDIGREE.

By Happy Medium, sire of Maxey Cobb 2:13¼ and 82 with records of 2:30 or better.

First dam Abualletta by Cassius M. Clay Jr., sire of Durango 2:2¼, Harry Clay 2:23¼, and sire of the dams of Minnehaha, Bertha 2.27¼, Charley West 2:28¼, Grandmont 2:25 1-4, Lottie K 2:28¼, Mambrino Diamond 2:26, Richwood 2 28 1-2, Tobey 2 2¼, Happy Thought 2 21 1-2, Pequot 2:22 1-2, Fairlawn Medium 2 27 1-2, Polley 2:27¼, and Mambrino Boy 2:26 1-2.

Second dam Laura Crockett by Almont, sire of Westmont 2:13¼, Puritan 2 16, Fanny Witherspoon 2:16¼, Piedmont 2:17¼, Aldine 2.19¼, and 37 with records better than 2:30.

Third dam Sally Tee by Alexander's Abdallah, sire Goldsmith Maid 2:14.

Fourth dam Kate Crockett, the dam of Lulu 2:14¼, by imp Hooton.

Illustrious is a horse of extra fine finish, large clean bone, good feet, back short and strong, loins and quarters well muscled, and powerful. He has a kind disposition and splendid trotting action, and is as handsome and bloodlike in form and finish as any trotting stallion in the land.

He is pronounced by his breeder, General Withers, to be the best bred son of Happy Medium living, and is undoubtedly one of the very best bred trotting stallions in the State. He has had but six weeks' regular training, and a part of that time was sick with epizootic, but was trotted quarters in 39 1-4 seconds, and barring accidents will certainly trot better than 2:30 this season.

TERMS—$50 the season. Mares not proving with foal may be returned next year free.

Good pasturage at $3 per month.

Season to begin February 1st and end June 15th.

GEO. A. STONE,

Santa Rosa, Cal.

WOODNUT

(Weatherhead's) by Nutwood 600

Sire of Belmont Boy, 2:35, pacer, Woodnut, 2:16¼, Felix, 2:18¼, Dawn, 2:18¼, Maggie E., 2 19¼, Irma, 2:18¼, and 26 others in 2:30 or better; 1st dam Flora, 2:39¼, trial 2 26, dam of Chrisman's Hambletonian, sire of Steve Whipple, 2:23, Kate Agnew, 2:28¼, by Chieftain 721, sire of Defiance 2:17¼ pacing and 2 24 trotting, Cairo, 2:26, Onward, 2:24, pacer; second dam by Wilson's Leaman.

Woodnut is a beautiful bay with black points, 15¾ hands high, weighing 1,075 pounds. His colts are all larger than himself, and sell readily for road and carriage purposes, being of good color and very docile, yet prompt to obey, and always ready.

Service fee, $25, with usual privileges. Colts and fillies from Tilton Almont, Patchen, Stockbridge Chief, and other desirable crosses, FOR SALE. For further particulars, pedigrees, or any communication in horse matters, address

JAS. WEATHERHEAD, Prop.

San Jose, Cal.

The Trotting-Bred Stallion

RINGWOOD

THE FINEST SON OF THE NOTED SIDNEY;

Will make a Season at Oakland, commencing March 1, and ending June 1, 1890.

DESCRIPTION.

RINGWOOD is a dark, rich colored bay, black points, 15 1-2 hands, weight 1100 lbs., and a pure gaited trotter. Has shown great speed. He is now five years old. As a four year old he showed a trial in 2:19 1-2, and but for an accident would have received a record as a four year old of 2:18 or better.

PEDIGREE.

RINGWOOD is by Sidney, record 2:19 3-4, and 's half brother to Gold Leaf 2:11 1-4, Adonis 2:14, Flee (two year old) 2:24, Longworth 2:19, Sister V. 2:20, Faustino, yearling, 2:35, Fleet, yearling, 2:35 Memo, three year old trial 2:20 1-2.

Sidney is by Santa Claus, record 2:17 1-2; he by Strathmore, sire of 31 in 2:30 list; he by Hambletonian 10, the greatest of all producers; he by Abdallah. Sidney's dam, Sweetness, record 2:21 1-4; she by Volunteer, the sire of St. Julien 2:11 1-4.

RINGWOOD'S dam Alma; she by Dashway, thoroughbred; he by Belmont, he by American Boy; he by Sea Gull; he by imported Expedition. Alma's 1st dam, Fanny Cobb, was a great road mare, pedigree untraced.

TERMS: $50 for the Season.

Payable June 1st, or sooner if mares are taken away. Address communications to

A. C. DIETZ,

Oakland, Cal.

The Hambletonian Stallion 10178.

CHRISMAN'S HAMBLETONIAN, Sire of Steve Whipple, 2:23, Kate Agnew, 2:28¼, etc.

- Whipple's Hambletonian, Sire of 14 trotters and 1 pacer from 2:19 to 2:30, and 7 sons with 8 performers from 2:21¼ to 2:30, and dams of 6 from 2:19¼ to 2:30.
  - Guy Miller, By Hambletonian 10.
  - Martha Washington, Dam of Speculation 928, Sire of Crown Pt., 2 24, Oakland Maid, 2:22, Gracie S., 2:28¼, and dam of Waterford, 2:27
- Flora, 2:39¼, trial, 2:26, Dam of Chrisman's Hambletonian, sire of Steve Whipple, 2 23, Kate Agnew, 2:28¼.
  - Chieftain 721, sire of Defiance, 2:24 and 2 17¼, pacing; Cairo, 2:26, and Onward, 2.24, pacer.
  - daughter of Wilson's Leamon.

Stud season now on till the 1st of August, 1890, at $40 each mare, with return privilege in 1891, provided stallion and mare, or either, do not change owners. Good pasture at hand, and comfortable accommodation for brood mares and colts. For further particulars, address

JESSE CHRISMAN, Proprietor.

San Jose, Cal.

Pedigrees Tabulated

IN THE MOST ARTISTIC MANNER.

Giving speed performers under sires and dams. Catalogues compiled. Stallion cards and circulars written up ready for the press. Pedigree blanks for sale. Prices reasonable. Horses bought and sold on commission. References furnished.

R. Y. HARDIN.

806 W. Madison St., Chicago, Ill.

THE MAMBRINO Patchen Stallion.

MAMBRINO JR., 1789 (formerly Carr's) Sire of Lady Ellen 2:38 (dam of Ella 2:29), Maud H. 2:30, Mambrino Boy (Carr's) 2:31 1 2.

Will stand at my farm, 2 1-2 miles north of San Jose, on the Milpitas road. Season to commence February 1st, 1890, at $10, with return privilege 1891. Fifteen mares of approved breeding, besides my own, will be given him. Parties owning good mares, performers or out of producing dams, will find an opportunity to breed them on shares, and the best of care taken of them till colt is weaned, if so desired.

PEDIGREE.

MAMBRINO JR., 1789, by Mambrino Patchen 58 [full brother of Lady Thorne 2:1·1-4] by Mambrino Chief 11. First dam by Mambrino Chief 11; 2nd dam by imp. Jordan [thoroughbred]; 3rd dam by Bertrand, son of sir Archy; 4th dam by Chewkees, son of Sir Archy.

For further particulars address

GEO. P. BULL.

San Jose, Cal.

Box 1067.

The Trotting Stallion

CUPID,

Full Brother to Adonis 2:14,

—Sired by—

The Celebrated SIDNEY 2:19 3-4, and out of Venus.

Will make the season of 1890 at the OAKLAND TROTTING PARK.

PEDIGREE.

CUPID is by Sidney out of Venus by Capt. Webster 10173, record 2:30, and sire of Firestone 2:19. Second dam by Skenandoah 936, sire of Daisy Burns 2:29¼, Erwin Davis (sire of two in the 30 list) and dams of four in the 30 list.

DESCRIPTION.

Cupid is a handsome bright bay 15.2¼ hands high, weighs 1100 lbs.; was foaled in 1886. As a yearling, with very little work he showed quarters in 42 seconds, and at 2 years old, quarters in 35 seconds. As a three year old he has not been worked, but he shows the speed and endurance that must come from his excellent blood lines.

TERMS $30 for the season, with the usual return privileges. Good pasturage near the track at $4 per month. The best of care taken of mares in any way that owners may desire, but no responsibility assumed for accidents or escapes.

For further particulars address

C. O. THORNQUEST,

Oakland Trotting Park, or

C. BAAB, 972 Broadway, Oakland.

The Trotting Stallion

BONANZA $2{:}29\frac{1}{2}$

Will make the season of 1890, from February 1st to July 1st, at the OAKLAND TROTTING PARK.

PEDIGREE.

BONANZA, 1:29¼.

- Arthurton 365, Sire of Arab, 2:15, Joe Arthurton 2.20¼, Lady Escot, 2:26¼. Dams of Grandee, 2:23¼, Hidalgo, 2:27.
  - Hambletonian 10, Sire of 41 in 2:30 list, Sires of 107 of the sires of 867 in 2:30 list.
  - Imogene, by Am. Star 14, Dam of Leland 1300, Sire of Clara, 2:21, Miss Leland, 2:25¼, Hades, 2:27¼.
- Sister, Dam of Albert W., 2:20.
  - John Nelson 187, Sire of Nerea, 2:23¼, Gov. Stanford, 2:27¼, Aurora, 2:27, Nemo, 2:30.
  - Lamott Mare, Dam of Aurora, 2.27; g d of Arol, 2.24¼.

DESCRIPTION.

BONANZA is a very handsome chestnut of commanding form and splendid proportions. He stands nearly 16 hands high, is remarkably intelligent, level headed and pure gaited. His record is no mark of his speed. He is a great foal getter, and his colts are handsome rangy animals.

TERMS. $40 for the season, with the usual return privileges. Excellent pasturage near the track at $5 per month. The best of care taken of mares, but no responsibility assumed for accidents or escapes.

For further particulars, address

RICHARD HAVEY,

Oakland Trotting Park, Oakland.

The Fast Trotting Stallion

REDWOOD.

Four-Year-Old Record 2:24 1-2

Will make the season of 1890—February 1st to July 1st—at the

OAKLAND RACE TRACK.

REDWOOD is a dark bay colt, 15.2¼ hands high, weighs 1100 lbs. Foaled in 1885 by Anteeo, 2:16¼, sire of Alfred G., 2 19¾. Anteeo is by Electioneer. First dam Lou Milton, by Milton Medium; second dam Old Fly, a thoroughbred mare brought from the East in 1871 by W. C. Ralston, Esq.

Redwood's sire was out of Columbine by A. W. Richmond, the sire of the pacers Arrow 2:13¼, and Elwood 2:20, and the trotters Romero, 2:19¼, and Len Rose, 2:27. Redwood has shown a quarter in 33 seconds.

Terms $100

For the season. Mares not proving with foal may be returned next season free of charge, provided Redwood remains the property of the present owners. Good pasturage at $5 per month. No responsibility assumed for escapes or accidents. Service fees payable before removal of the mare. Limited to 10 approved mares. For further particulars address,

A. McFADYEN.

Race track, Oakland, Cal.

Vineland Stock Farm
Whippleton 1883,

Sire of

LILY STANLEY	Record	2:17½
HOMESTAKE	"	2:16½
FLORA B.	"	2:27
CORA C.	"	2:31½
BLACK PRINCE	"	2:36½
RACHEL	"	2:3
PRINCE W.	"	2:40

WHIPPLETON is not only the sire of trotters, but he is the greatest sire of Carriage Horses on the Pacific Coast. Some of the best carriage and road teams in San Francisco are sired by Whippleton. A Carriage team by Whippleton received First Premium at Napa, Petaluma, Oakland, Sacramento, Stockton and San Jose. Whippleton and his colts have never been beaten in the show ring.

DESCRIPTION.

WHIPPLETON is black, tan muzzle and flanks, 17 hands, and weighs 1,400 lbs. Most of his colts are 16 hands or over, and with a few exceptions, bay, brown or black. He never sired a sorrel or white face colt. (If he does, I agree to refund service money.)

PEDIGREE.

WHIPPLETON, sired by Hambletonian Jr. (sire Hancock 2.29), by Whipple's Hambletonian (sire of Graves, 2 19 Westfield, 2:20¼, Express, 2:24, and 12 others in the 2:30 list), dam Lady Livingston (dam of Lady Blanchard, 2 26¼, Bloomfield Maid, trial 2:22), by General Taylor (sire of the dams of Wells Fargo, 2:18¾, Nerea, 2:23¼, Bickford, 2:20¼, Lady Blanchard, 2:26¼, etc., and sire of grandam of Hazel Wilkes, 2:20) by the Morse Horse 6, sire of Norman 25 (sire of Lulu, 2:14¾, May Queen 2:20, etc.).

TERMS at $40, limited to 20 mares, for the season, usual return privileges. I would like to get about ten well bred mares with the proper combination of blood to breed to Whippleton on shares this season.

Alcona 730.

Sire of

FLORA BELLE	Record	2:24
CLAY DUKE	"	2:31½

ALCONA will be a great sire, but four of his colts have ever been trained, and all have shown full miles better than 2:30, and two of them as good as 2:30. Two of his first sons each sired a colt as a two-year-old, and last season one as a four-year-old trotted a full mile in 2:23¼, and the other, a three-year-old, a mile in 2:31. With opportunities, Alcona is destined to be one of Almont's best sons. Almont, for his opportunities, is beyond doubt the most prepotent sire of his age. He has 36 representatives in the 2:30 list; 49 sons and 22 daughters that have already produced 2:30 performers. Almont died five years ago at 20 years old. If he lived he would be but 25 years old.

PEDIGREE.

ALCONA sired by the great Almont (sire of Westmont 2:13¼, Fanny Witherspoon 2:16¼, Piedmont 2:17¼, and 31 others with records better than 2:30, and grandsire of Belle Hamlin 2:12¾, etc.); by Alexander's Abdallah (sire of Goldsmith Maid 2:14), he by Rysdyk's Hambletonian. Alcona's dam, Queen Mary, by Mambrino Chief (sire of Lady Thorne 2 18 1-4, and 5 others in the 2:30 list, and sire of the dams of Director 2:17, Piedmont 2:17¼, Onward 2:25 1-4, Red Wilkes Almont, Belmont and many other noted sires).

DESCRIPTION.

Alcona is a beautiful chestnut 16 3 1.2 hands high, and weighs 1200 lbs. His colts possess speed, style, finish and beauty, and if they don't trot they command the highest prices for carriage horses.

$40 for the season. Usual return privilege.

Season on Whippleton and Alcona ends July 1 1890.

Best kind of pasturage at $4 per month. Mare in any manner desired.

For further particulars send for circular or stables, one mile south of St. Helena.

FRED W. LOEBER.

St. Helena, Napa Co., Cal.

The Trotting Stallion

G & M

FULL BROTHER TO

ALFRED G, $2{:}19\frac{3}{4}$.

(Who has been taken to Kentucky to stand at $200)

Will make the season of 1890 from FEBRUARY 1st to JULY 1st, at

SANTA ROSA.

G. & M. is by Anteeo, 2:16¼; was foaled 1886; first dam Rosa B. by Speculation (son of Hambletonian 10); 2d dam Elizabeth by Alexander 490; 3d dam Nora by Imp. Glencoe. Anteeo is by Electioneer, out of Columbine by A. W. Richmond 1687.

G. & M. is a handsome dark bay; stands 15-2 1-2 hands high, and weighs 1080 pounds. Gameness, stoutness, speed and stamina are indelibly impressed in every line of the pedigree of G. & M. Owners of brood mares in search of these qualities, will do well to patronize this promising colt.

PHILOSOPHER,

Foaled 1886 by Pilot Wilkes 2387; first dam Bella by George Wilkes 519; second dam by Bell Morgan 61.

Philosopher's sire, Pilot Wilkes 2387, is by George Wilkes 519, dam Grace (the dam of Alice Woodburn, etc.), by Pilot Jr. 12, grandam by Orphan Boy.

Will make the season of 1890, from FEBRUARY 1st to JULY 1st, at Santa Rosa.

TERMS for the season:

G. & M., $50,

PHILOSOPHER, $30,

with privilege of returning mares that do not prove in foal the next season free of charge, provided the horse bred to remains the property of the present owners. Good pasturage at $3 per month. No responsibility assumed for accidents or escapes. Service fees payable before removal of the mare. For further particulars, address

GEO. E. GUERNE,

Santa Rosa Cal.

Highland Farm,

LEXINGTON, KY.,

Home of Red Wilkes.

Standard-bred Trotting Stock

For Sale,

Sired by Red Wilkes, Wilton, 2:19¼; Allandorf and Sentinel Wilkes, out of highly bred Standard Mares of the most fashionable blood of the day.

W. C. FRANCE, Proprietor.

Guenoc Stud Farm, Lake Co., Cal.

Imp. GREENBACK

(Sire of the English Winners Greenlight, Greenjacket, Greenshank, GreenWave and Greenhorn)

By Dollar, dam Music, by Stockwell. $100 the Season

ST. SAVIOR,

(FULL BROTHER TO EOLE)

By Eolus, dam War Song, by War Dance. $100 the Season.

PASTURAGE, $5 PER MONTH.

With right to return the following year if mare does not prove with foal. The best of care taken, but no liability for accidents or escapes. Mares shipped to C. W. ABY, care ST. HELENA STABLES, St. Helena Napa County, will be taken in charge by competent men.

For further information write to

DR. C. W. ABY, Middletown, Lake County, Cal.

1890 Three Anteeo Stallions 1890

SUNSET, 5 years old, by Anteeo
ANTEEOF, 4 years old, by Anteeo
ANTEEOP, 3 years old, by Anteeo

ANTEEO. Standard 7868. Record, 2:16 1-4, by Stanford's Electioneer, and dam Columbine.

DESCRIPTIONS, PEDIGREES AND CONDITIONS.

"SUNSET" is a rich, dark bay, small star on forehead, portion of hind left foot white; was foaled March 11, 1885; is by ANTEEO and the inbred HAMBLETONIAN mare, BESSIE G, she by KING PHILLIP, son of WHIPPLE'S HAMBLETONIAN. He is 16 1 2 hands high, and weighs 1,100 lbs. He is of perfect build and splendid action, cool headed and great speed for his size, having trotted a trial mile as a three-year-old in 2:30. He then entered heavy in the stud and was matched against Whalebone at the Healdsburg races November 2, 1889, winning just as he pleased in three straight heats; time, 2:47, 2:46 1-2, 2:52 1-2. He was then matched for a race to come off at Thanksgiving Day at Petaluma but owing to the heavy rains the event did not take place. A few days previous to Thanksgiving Day Mr. Lawrence worked Sunset out and then he trotted three square miles and heats in 2:33¼, 2:34 and 2:37.

SUNSET will be bred to 40 mares only, at $50 each, no Colt no pay.

"ANTEEOF" is a jet black, was foaled April 13, 1886, is 16¾ hands high, and weighs 1,200 lbs., has a very fine heavy black mane and tail; is well proportioned, moves majestically, is of easy, lofty carriage; is symmetrical, in fact is a beautiful horse. He was sired by Anteeo and the O. A. Taylor mare "Nance," her dam, was raised by Dr. Oliver Plummer, of Consumnes, Cal., and sired by "Napoleon"; Napoleon was foaled May 20, 1858, and raised by James Kyle of Butler County, Ohio. He was sired by Benj. Sweet's horse Bellfounder, and he by Old Bellfounder, his dam was sired by Doc. Daniel Mulligan's horse, Cadmus, G. G. sire the celebrated Eclipse; his G. dam was sired by Big Shakespeare, G. G., sires dam by Messenger and Expedition.

ANTEEOF will be bred to 25 mares only, at $50 each. No Colt, no pay.

"ANTEEOP" is a rich seal brown; was foaled March 7, 1887; by Anteeo and the inbred Hambletonian mare Bessie G., also dam of Sunset, his full brother and Midget his full sister; he is 15 1-2 hands high and weighs 950 lbs, and measures 22 inches around the arm, good head, fine neck, full, broad breast; withers and rump on nearly equal line, well proportioned bones, ankle, shoulders, loins and hips; strong legs all around, with great muscular development and splendid sinews; wiry pasterns and sound, compact feet; the lines from hip to hoof show power and speed; stands square and has excellent action, has a superb lustrous coat of rich, deep brown fur of seal color without defect; an even, honest trotter, and has gone the mile as a two-year-old in 2:45, the last quarter in 38 seconds; is intelligent and of high spirit, with much temper, but is not vicious, has very fine eyes, is a handsome, showy colt; attractive in harness.

ANTEEOP will be bred to 15 mares only, at $40. No colt, no pay.

SEASON to commence February 1st, ending July 1, 1890. Book now ready. Apply to John H. Lawrence, "Manager and Trainer," on my fruit and hop ranch, 1 mile east of Court House, on Sonoma road. Excellent pasture furnished with running water, also dry knolls with oak shelter, at $3 per month for mares. Two of the above stallions will be for sale after the expiration of the their stud season.

GUY E. GROSSE,
SANTA ROSA, SONOMA CO., CAL.

The Trotting Stallion

Guide 2:29

(At Four Years)

Will make the season of 1890 at the SANTA RITA RANCH, about one mile North of Pleasanton.

DESCRIPTION.

GUIDE is a handsome seal brown, five years old, stands 15¾ hands high, and weighs 1035 pounds. He is of fine form, level headed, intelligent, and comes from blood lines that are noted for the qualities of speed and gameness.

PEDIGREE.

GUIDE, 2:28½.

- Director, 2:17. Sire of Direct, 2:18¾. Margaret S., 2:19¼.
  - Dictator 113. Sire of 23 trotters and 3 pacers in 2:30.
    - Hambletonian 10.
    - Clara, by American Star 14.
  - Dolly. Dam of Onward, 2:25¼, Thorndale, 2:22¾.
    - Mambrino Chief 11.
    - Fannie, by Ben Franklin.
- Imogene.
  - Norwood 522. Sire of Tommy Norwood, 2:26¾.
    - Hambletonian 10.
    - Lady Fallis, by American Star 14.
  - daughter of
    - American Star 14.
    - daughter of Harry Clay 45.

The attention of breeders is especially called to the above pedigree as showing 3 crosses of American Star.

GUIDE trotted into the 2:30 list last season with little training, and he will trot into the 2:20 list the coming season barring accidents.

Guide's sire has a record of 2:17, made in a five heat race, and Guide is closely related to Phallas, who made a record of 2:13¾ in a fourth heat, and to Jay-Eye-See, record 2:10.

TWO HUNDRED AND FIFTY DOLLARS will be given to the owner of the first of the produce of Guide put in the 2:30 list, and $100 to each one after the first.

TERMS—$75 for the season, with the usual return privileges.

Admiro,

Sire Admiral; dam by San Bruno, by Easton's David Hill.

This magnificent horse is a handsome bay, eight years old; stands 17 1-2 hands high, and weighs 1400 pounds. He is very speedy for a large horse, and breeds fine large carriage horses. His produce possess every qualification of the Cleveland Bay, with the added qualities of speed and endurance resulting from his high trotting breeding.

TERMS—$50 for the season, with usual return privileges.

Will stand three days each week at Santa Rita Ranch, Pleasanton, and at A. T. Hatch's Ranch "Almono," Alamo, Contra Costa County, alternately. All mares sent care of SMITH & SUTHERLAND, Pleasanton, will be taken in charge of on arrival, and will receive the best care and attention in any manner the owners may desire. Good pasturage at $4 per month. Only a limited number of approved mares will be served by this horse this season.

No responsibility assumed for escapes or accidents. For further particulars, address

SMITH & SUTHERLAND, Pleasanton,
or A. T. HATCH, care Palace Hotel, San Francisco.

THE BRUNSWICK BALKE COLLENDER COMPANY,

MANUFACTURERS OF

Standard Billiard and Pool Tables, Saloon and Bank Fixtures,
653–655 Market Street, San Francisco, Cal.

GRANDISSIMO,

Full Brother to GRANDEE, 3-year-old Record 2-23½.

SAN DIEGO, 8776.

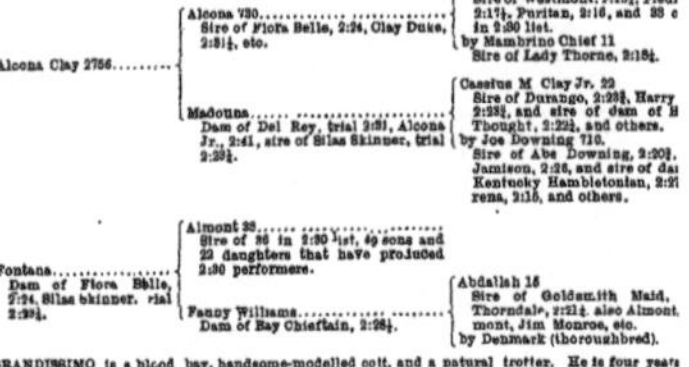

GRANDISSIMO is a blood bay, handsome-modelled colt, and a natural trotter. He is four years and trotted one quarter miles in 36 seconds, with very limited training, last Fall.

SAN DIEGO is dark seal brown, three years old, and trotted one-quarter miles in 40 seconds as a year old.

These are two grand young horses, and, barring accidents, will both make fast records next fall.

They will both be allowed a limited number of mares, at $50 for the season. Mares not provi foal to be returned free 1891. Best of pasture for mares at $4 per month, but no liability for acciden escapes.

They will make the season from February 1st to June 1st at Napa Fair Grounds. For further par lars, address or call on

H. B. STARR, Race Track, Napa, Cal.,
or FRED W. LOEBER, St. Helena

A SON OF ALMONT 33.

Only $25 for the Season.

ASHLAND ALMONT 348

PEDIGREE.

ASHLAND ALMONT 3481

- Almont 33. Sire of 34 in 2:30 or better of 21 daughters and of 49 sires that have produce in 2:30 or better.
  - Abdallah 15. Sire Goldsmith Maid, 2:14; 8 in 2:30 list; 13 sires and 25 dams of trotters in 2:30 list.
    - Hambletonian 10 sire of 41 in 2:30 list; sire of 107 si 147 in 2:30 list.
    - Katy Darling.
  - Sally Anderson.
    - Mambrino Chief 11 Lady Thorn, 2:18½.
    - Kate, by Pilot Jr. 12.
- Pauline. Dam of Sapho.
  - Ashland Chief. Sire Black Cloud, 2:17¾.
    - Mambrino Chief 11 Lady Thorn, 2:18¾.
    - dau. of imp. Yorkshire, (thoroughbr
  - Rosina. Dam Almonia, the dam of Sally Cossack, 2:22¾, dau. Mamb. Abdallah, sire Mam. Prince, 2:28, and of Mamb. Bashaw, sire of Graham's Mambrino, 2:35.
    - Abdallah 15 Sire Goldsmith Maid, 2:14.
    - Prof. Smith's Sir William.

DESCRIPTION.

ASHLAND ALMONT 3481 is a handsome chestnut; stands 16 hands; was foaled 1885, and bred b Withers, of Lexington, Ky. He is of fine form, and remarkably intelligent, sweet-tempered and abso sound. His oldest foal may be seen with him, and while he has never served a standard mare or o was a producer of speed, all of his colts are large, sound, fast and handsome.

TERMS: $25 for the season, with usual return privileges. The best of care taken of mares manner that the owner may desire, but no responsibility assumed for escapes or accidents.

For further particulars, address

T. J. WHITEHEAD, Manager.

or, W. H. ASHBY, Oakland, Cal.

579 38th Street, bet. Telegraph Ave. and Grove St Oakland, C

2:10 1-2 ELECTIONEER 2:12 1

BAY STALLION	BROWN STALLIO
ECLECTIC	**MORTIME**
11,321	5,346
By Electioneer, dam Manette (full sister to Woodnut 2.16 1-2 Manon 2:21 and Maple, dam of Hattie D., three-year-old record 2.26¾) by Nutwood 2:18¾, etc., etc.	Four-year-old Record 2:2 By ELECTIONEER, dam MARTI, by W Hambletonian (sire of 15 in 2:30, and of dams o in 2:30). Second dam Ida Martin by Rifleman of Col. Lewis 2:18¾).
Terms $100 for the Season.	Terms $60 for the Season.

Horses shipped via San Francisco may be consigned to J. W. MORSHEAD, City Front Stables, w attend to their forwarding.

Season closes JULY 1st, 1890. Usual return privileges.

For further particulars address owner,

WILFRED PAGE, Penns Grove,
Sonoma County,

GEO. WASHINGTON, 11,623.

RECORD 2:30.

Bay colt, bred by Thomas Smith of Vallejo, Cal. foaled 1886 by Mambrino Chief, Jr., 11,622, record 2:34 1-4, 1st dam Fanny Rose by Vick's Ethan Allen 2,903, sire of Prince Allen 2:27. 2nd dam Jenny Lind, thoroughbred, dam of Prince Allen 2:27. Will serve a limited number of mares at $50 for the season. Mares not proving with foal may be returned next season free.

Mambrino Chief, Jr. 11,622.

RECORD 2:34 1 2.

Sire of George Washington, record 2 30 at three years old. Bay horse bred by Rufus Ingalls of Belvedere, Ill. By McDonald Chief 3'83. First dam Venus by Mambrino Patchen 58. 2nd dam by Wardlow's Shakespeare. 3rd dam Lone Gold 4th dam by Silver Heels. Has not been in the stud b fore. He was 2 years old when he served a few mares, and his colts all show good style and form.

Terms for the season $40. For further particulars come or address

THOMAS SMITH,
Vallejo, Cal.

Elector 2170.

Sire of J. R.

Three-Year Old Record 2:24.

Sired by Electioneer 126, sire of Sunol, three-year-old, 2:10½, Palo Alto, 2:12¾, etc.; dam Gilberta by Fred Low 656, sire of Clay, 2:25½, etc.

Second dam Lady Gilbert (grandam of Lot Slocum, 2:17½) by General Knox 140 (sire of Lady Maud, 2:18¼, and many others).

TERMS.

$150 for the season. Book full for 1890.

L. A. RICHARDS,
Grayson, Stanislaus Co., Cal.

The Thoroughbred Stallion

Three Cheers

Will make the season of 1890 at

Sacramento.

PEDIGREE.

- imp. Hurrah
  - Newminster
    - Touchstone, by Camel
    - Beeswing, by Dr. Syntax
  - Jovial
    - Bay Middleton, by Sultan
    - Sister to Grey Momus, by Comus
- Young Fashion
  - imp. Monarch
    - imp. Priam, by Emilius
    - imp. Delphine, by Whisker
  - Fashion
    - imp. Trustee, by Catton
    - Bonnets o' Blue, by Sir Charles

Hurrah was imported by John Reber, of Lancaster, Ohio, a locality where there were but few breeders of thoroughbreds. Under these disadvantages he sired a long list of winners. His sire Newminster, won the St. Ledger 1851, and his dam, Jovial by Bay Middleton, winner of the Derby 1836. Newminster by Touchstone, winner St. Ledger 1834. Dam Beeswing, winner of 54 races out of 64 starts, by Dr. Syntax, winner of the Doncaster Cup, 1837—40—41—42, the only horse that ever accomplished that feat.

On the side of the dam Three Cheers is equally well bred. Young Fashion was the dam of Surprise, Ireland (the only horse that ever beat Asteroid a ...), Liverpool, Columbia, and Bonnie Kate, the dam of Little Buttercup, and the flying Bonnie Lizzie. His grandam, Fashion was the greatest race mare of her day and beat Boston in that historical match at four mile heats, which is recorded as one of the greatest events in the annals of the turf.

Horsemen who are qualified to judge, pronounce Three Cheers to be the finest type of the Newminster line in America.

LOCATION.

THREE CHEERS will be located at the Arcade Training Stable, Rancho del Paso. This place has been selected for the reason that first class pasturage has been secured there for the exclusive use of the mares, and the other facilities to be obtained there for the care of mares (especially mares in foal) are better than can be found elsewhere in the locality.

TERMS.

$... for the season with the usual return privileges. Pasturage $5 per month. Mares cared for as owners may desire at bottom rates for grain and hay. All bills payable before the mare is removed.

Mares shipped care of WM. IRVINE, Pacific Stables, Sacramento, will be properly cared for and sent to the ranch without delay.

Three Cheers will be in charge of one of the most experienced and competent stud grooms in the State, who will exercise every care, but no reponsibility assumed for accidents or escapes.

For further particulars apply to Louis Crissler, at ...ance; Wm. Irvine, Pacific Stables, Second St., Sacramento; or to the owner,

E. S. CULVER,
313 Bush St., San Francisco.

GROVER CLAY

Bay Stallion, Black Points,
15 3-4 hands high.

Bred by W. W. Traylor, San Francisco.

BY ELECTIONEER.

First dam Maggie Norfolk by Norfolk, son of Lexington, he by Boston. Second dam Tilda Quill by ... Cheatham he by Cracken, and he by Boston. Third dam by Dorsey's Golddust.

TERMS.

Will make the season of 1890 at the Training Stable of Denis Gannon, near Oakland Trotting Park, $... the season, payable at time of service. Season commence February 1st and ending July 1st. Proper care of mares will be taken, but no responsibility incurred for accidents or escapes. Address,

DENIS GANNON, Oakland, Cal.

2:10¾ 2:13¾ 2:10

DEXTER PRINCE.

This Royally-bred Stallion will make the Season of 1890 at the LIVE OAKS Breeding Farm, 2 miles from Lodi, San Joaquin County, Cal.

DESCRIPTION.

DEXTER PRINCE is a blood bay, 16 hands high, weighs over 1 100 pounds; has great power and substance, and the highest finish. When two years old, at Palo Alto, he was timed quarters by Gov. Stanford in 35½ seconds, and he was driven eighths by Mr. Marvin at a faster rate of speed than that. He is a sure foal-getter, and invariably sires foals of good size, of fine form and finish, and the highest rate of speed.

PEDIGREE.

By KENTUCKY PRINCE, the sire of Guy, 2:10¾, Spofford, 2:18¾, Company, 2:19¾, Bayoune Prince, 2:21 1-4, Fred Folger, 2:20¾, and a score more in the 2:30 list.

First dam LADY DEXTER, full sister of the greatest of trotters, Dexter, and the greatest of sires, Dictator, the sire of Director, 2:17, Phallas, 2:13¾, in a fourth heat, and Jay-Eye-See, 2:10.

Second dam Clara, the dam of Dexter, 2:17 1-4, Dicta or, Astoria 2:29 1-4, and Almah, 2:28¾. Clara was by American Star, that has 24 daughters that have produced 2:30 or better trotters.

Third dam the McKinstry mare, the dam of Shark, 2:27¾. HAMBLETONIAN, the grandsire of DEXTER PRINCE, has 40 trotters in the 2:30 list, 44 daughters that have produced 2:30 trotters, and more than 100 sons that have sired 2 30 trotters.

CLARK CHIEF, the grandsire on the sire's side, was the sire of performing and producing sons and daughters.

DEXTER PRINCE has faster blood lines, on both sides, than any other stallion in the world—Guy 2:10¾, and Jay-Eye-See, 2:10.

KENTUCKY PRINCE is one of the best bred and speediest stallions in the world. David Bonner, in the presence of Governor Stanford, timed him when he trotted a 2:10 gait. He is by Clark Chief, one of the great broodmare sires; his first dam is Kentucky Queen by Morgan Eagle, son of Hale's Green Mountain Morgan, 2nd dam by Blythe's Whip, 3rd dam by Martin's Brummier, 4th dam by Quicksilver 880, on through the strongest thoroughbred blood.

TERMS.

$100 for the season, with usual return privileges. Payable before mares are removed. Good pasture, and the best care furnished, but no responsibility assumed for accidents.

PREMIUM.

$250 will be given to the first of the produce of DEXTER PRINCE put in the 2:30 list, and $100 each after the first. Address

L M. MORSE, Lodi, Cal.

HOLLYWOOD BREEDING FARM.

MOUNTAIN BOY 4841.

Br s MOUNTAIN BOY, 4841, bred by Charles Bachman, Orange County, New York, foaled 1882, sire Kentucky Prince 2470, dam Elise, sister to Elaine, by Messenger Duroc 106; grandam Green Mountain Maid, 3d dam, Shanghai Mary, will serve a limited number of mares at $100 the season.

ELECTION.

Bay stallion ELECTION, bred at Senator Stanford's Palo Alto Stock farm, foaled 1884, sire Electioneer, dam Lizzie H. by Whipple's Hambletonian 726, grandam Lizzie Harris (by Comus son of Green's Bashaw 50), great grandam by Arnold Harris, thoroughbred.

Election is one of the handsomest bloodlike sons of Electioneer, and with his thoroughbred cross through Arnold Harris should prove invaluable as a sire. TERMS, $100 the season.

KAFIR.

B c KAFIR, bred by L. J. Rose, Los Angeles, foaled 1887, sire Alcazar, 2:20½, dam Flower Girl by Arthurton, sire of Arab, 2:15, grandam Flora by General McClellan, 144, sire of three in 2:30 list, great grand dam by Langford, he by Williamson's Belmont, will serve a limited number of mares at $50 the season.

WOODSIDE.

Ch c WOODSIDE, sire Woodnut, 2:16½; 1st dam Veronica by Alcona, 730; 2nd dam Fontana by Almont, 33; 3rd dam Fannie Williams by Alexander's Abdallah, 15. Book full.

MART BOORHEM.

B c MART BOORHEM, by Sydney, 2:19½; 1st dam Towhead by Echo. This colt is a full brother to St. Nicholas who showed a mile in 2:27½ at three years old. TERMS, $25 the season.

REVEILLE.

The well known thoroughbred stallion REVEILLE, by Shiloh, dam by Norfolk. Reveille is a brother to John Treat and is the sire of Tycoon and Gladstone TERMS, $25 the season.

Hollywood is nicely situated three miles from Vallejo on the Napa road. Good pasturage and every care will be taken of mares at reasonable rates. For further particulars, apply.

B. C. HOLLY, Vallejo.

PASHA,

Registered No. 2039.

RECORD 2:36.

SIRE OF MORO 2:27.

Will make the present season at Linden, twelve miles east of STOCKTON.

Season commencing FEBRUARY 1st and ending JULY 1, 1890.

DESCRIPTION.

PASHA is a beautiful black; 16½ hands high, and weighs 1,240 pounds. He is a horse of beautiful symmetry and magnificent action.

PEDIGREE.

PASHA was sired by Sultan 1513, sire of Stamboul 2:12½, Ruby 2:19¾, Alcazar 2:20½, Bay Rose 2:20½, and sixteen others with records below 2:30. First dam Madam Baldwin by The Moor 870; second dam Ben Lippincott by Belmont. Pasha is a full brother to Bay Rose, record 2:20½.

Sultan, by The Moor, sire of Beautiful Belle, dam of Hinda Rose, 2:19½, Bell Boy 2:19½, and Sable, dam of Sable Wilkes, three-year-old record 2:18. First dam Sultana, by Delmonica, sire of Derby 2:16, by Guy Miller, sire of Whipple's Hambletonian. Second dam by Mambrino Chief. Third dam by Downing's Bay Messenger. Fourth dam Miss Caudle, dam of Ericsson, four-year-old recor 2:30½.

Terms for the season, $50.

With privilege of returning mares that do not prove in foal next season free of charge.

Good pasturage at $2 per month No responsibility will be assumed for accidents or escapes Service fee payable before the removal of the mare.

For further particulars, address

D. BRYSON,
Linden Cal.

Cook STOCK FARM.

Season of 1890.

STEINWAY 1808.

Three-Year-Old Record 2:25 3-4.

Sire of STRATHWAY, three year old record 2:26, and sire of the dam of BOURBON RUSSELL 2:30.

By STRATHMORE 408; sire of 31 in the 2:30 list; sire of 6 dams of 8 in the 2:30 list, and sire of 3 sires of 3 in 2:30 list.

1st dam ABBESS (dam of Solo 2:28, and Soprano, dam of C. F Clay 2:18, Eminence 2:27 and Strathbridge, 3 year old record 2:29½) by ALBION, sire of VANITY FAIR 2:24½, and of the dam of FAVORITE 2:25½.

2nd dam by MARSHALL NEY.

3rd dam by BERTRAND, a son of SIR ARCHY.

TERMS—$100 for the season.

CHARLES DERBY 4907

Brown Horse, Foaled 1885.

By STEINWAY 1808.

1st dam by the great ELECTIONEER, sire of SUNOL 3 year old record 2:10½, Palo Alto 2:12¼, etc., etc.

2nd dam FANNY MALONE, by NIAGARA.

3rd dam FANNY WICKHAM, by HERALD.

4th dam by Imp. TRUSTEE.

TERMS—$100 for the season

Pasturage $5 per month. Accidents and escapes at owner's risk. Mares consigned to the farm should be sent to Fashion Stables, Oakland; Geary & Grindle's Stable, Haywards; or to Bennett's Stable, Martinez; from and to which places they will be delivered free of charge. Address

COOK STOCK FARM,
Danville, Contra Costa, Co., Cal.

The Trotting Stallion

ARBITRATOR

Will make the Season of 1890 at NILES, Alameda County.

PEDIGREE.

ARBITRATOR

- Director 1989, 2:17 in a race, Sire of
  - Direct, 4 yrs., 2:18½ in a race.
  - Margaret S., 3 yrs., 2:19½ in a race,
  - Guide, 4 yrs., 2:28½ in a race.
- Lady Earnest.
  - Speculation 918, sire of
    - Oakland Maid, 2:22 in a race,
    - Gracie S., 2:22 in a race,
    - Crown Point, 2:24 in a race, He the sire of Valensin, 4 yrs., 2:23 in a race, Sire of Dam of Alfred G., 2:19½.
  - Lady Hibbard, dam of Lou Whipple, 2:26½ in a race.

Speculation's dam was Martha Washington, dam of Whipple's Hambletonian, sire of 15 in 2:30 and granddaughter of Burr's Napoleon, sire of Black Harry, who in 1850 won two miles in 5:14½. He sired Smith Burr, sire of Gen. Butler, 2:21, Wagon, 4:56½. He sired the dam of Fanny Mapes, dam of Jerome Eddy, 2:16½. He sired Telegraph, sire of dam of Rarus, 2:13¼.

DESCRIPTION.

ARBITRATOR was foaled 1885. He is of good size, fine conformation, and a beautiful seal brown.

TERMS.

Non-standard mares	$45
Standard mares by inheritance	35
Standard mares by performance or produce	25

For further particulars, address

H. A. MAYBEW, owner,
Niles, Alameda Co.

THE BUCKINGHAM.
OLD STRAIGHT WHISKIES.

141 Montgomery Street.
303 Bush Street, S. F.
M. J. BALFE, Proprietor.

Season of 1890.

February 15 to June 15

LYNWOOD,

(STANDARD 3017.)

AT WOLF'S (RUSSELL'S) STABLES, STOCKTON, CAL.

TERMS.

$50 for the season, payable at the close of season. Pasturage at $3 per month. Accidents or escapes at owner's risk.

PEDIGREE.

LYNWOOD 3017, trial 2:28.

- Nutwood 600, 2:18¾, Sire of—Woodnut, 2:16½, 59 in 2:30 list.
  - Belmont 64, Sire of—38 in 2:30 list, 17 sires and 11 dams of trotters in 2:30 list.
    - Abdallah 15, sire of—Goldsmith Maid, 2:14, 8 in 2:30 list, 18 sires and 21 dams of trotters in 2:30 list.
    - Belle, by Mambrino Chief 11, Dam of—Hambletonian 1644, 2:29½, the sire of 4 in 2:30 list.
  - Miss Russell, Dam of—Maud S., 2:08¾, Nutwood, 2:18¾, Cora Bel. ... 2:28 1-2.
    - Pilot Jr. 12, sire of—8 in 2:30 list, 7 sires and 15 dams of trotters in 2:30 list.
    - Sally Russell by Boston.
- Hattie Morrison, Fast Road Mare, Trial 2:30¾.
  - Ethan Allen Jr. 2903, Sire of—Prince Allen, 2:27.
    - Ethan Allen 43, 2:25¾, sire of—7 in 2:30 list, 16 sires and 11 dams of trotters in 2:30 list.
    - Daughter of Hambletonian 2, sire—4 in 2:30 list.
  - Grigsby Mare.
    - Sir Charles, thoroughbred.
    - Hosting Mare s. t. b. of Messenger and Duroc blood.

DESCRIPTION.

Dark bay, 15 hands, weighs 1050 pounds, form stout and elegant, gait pure and rapid. He was foaled July 15, 1880, has done but little work in the stud, but enough to demonstrate that he is one of the best foal getters in the State. Only one of his get has had any systematic handling, and that could have gone into the 2:30 list last year as a two-year-old, had the owner desired.

It will be observed from an examination of Lynwood's pedigree, that he is one of the best bred sons of the GREAT NUTWOOD, who commands a service fee of $500 for the season.

P. VISHER, Stockton.

The Thoroughbred Stallion

INTRUDER

Will make the Season of 1890 at Agricultural Park, SACRAMENTO.

Bay Horse, foaled 1871, bred by Sir L. Newman, England. Imported by D. D. Withers, Esq., New York.

By Crater, Son of Orlando and Vesuvienne by Gladiator.

1st dam Lady Bountiful by Rataplan (Rataplan is own brother to Stockwell, and winner of 42 races, including the Doncaster Cup and 19 Queen's Plates, and proved himself the most distinguished race horse of his day in England).

2d dam Plentiful by Don John (the winner of St. Leger and Doncaster Cup).

3d dam Plenty by Bay Middleton (winner of the Derby and Two Thousand Guinea Stakes).

4th dam Plenary, own sister of Plenipotentiary, by Emilius. (Both Emilius and Plenipotentiary were Derby winners).

5th dam Harriet, dam of the renowned Plenipotentiary by Pericles.

6th dam by Selim, winner of the One Thousand Guinea stakes.

7th dam by Pypilina, by Sir Peter.

8th dam Rally, by Trumpeter,

9th dam Fancy, by Florizel. Fancy was full sister to Diomed, the first Derby winner in England, and after his importation into this country, sired the illustrious Sir Archy, etc. See English Stud Book.

Imported INTRUDER is a beautiful bay, standing fully 16 hands high, of great length and substance, and descends through close and strong currents from the most illustrious winners and winning lines of blood of which the English Stud Book bears record.

A careful review of the first six crosses of the pedigree of INTRUDER will show nine Derby winners; five St. Leger winners; two winners of The Oaks; two winners of the Two Thousand Guineas; two winners of the One Thousand Guineas; one Goodwood Cup Winner; one Cesarwich Cup winner; one Cambridgeshire Stakes winner, and four Doncaster Cups, in addition to a great number of Steeplechases and other races of less import.

INTRUDER, at the great fair held at St. Louis, Mo., in 1878, was awarded the highest stallion honors—the blue ribbon and the $500 purse—in the sweepstakes ring for stallion of any age or blood. The list of competitors embraced the large number of thirty-three animals, and they represented England, Canada, Kentucky, Tennessee, and other states. He also took first premium in his class and in sweepstakes for the best stallion of any age or breed at the State Fair at Peoria, Ill., 1882. He is the sire of Tidal Wave, George Hakes, Bernice and April Fool.

INTRUDER is the sire of Interpose, who is the dam of Spokane, winner of the Kentucky Derby, in which he beat the great horse Proctor Knott and broke the record.

TERMS: $50 for the season. Mares not proving with foal can be returned the next season free of charge. Good pasturage at $4 per month. Mares cared for in any manner owners may desire, and fed on hay and grain, either or both, at reasonable rates. While every precaution will be taken, no responsibility will be assumed for escapes or accidents. Mares sent from a distance in care of the undersigned, will be met and taken to the park. For further particulars, address

T. J. KNIGHT.
Agricultural Park, Sacramento.

Shoes For Comfort, Elegance and Durability.

Having my own factory, and giving my personal supervision to all work I am in a position to warrant perfect satisfaction. Inspection invited.

AGENT for the VISCALIZED SHOES.

FACTORY—S W. cor. Battery and Jackson Sts.
SALESROOM—Pioneer Building, corner Stevenson and Fourth Streets.

A full line of **Boots and Shoes** constantly on hand, and rules for Self-Measurement by Mail.

JNO. T. SULLIVAN.

2:20 1-2 (Half Mile Track) at 4 Years. | Fastest Record (in a Race) of any Wilkes | 2:14 1-2 at 5 Years.

ROY WILKES, $2{:}12\frac{3}{4}$,

Seal brown; 15¾ hands; foaled 1883; by Adrian Wilkes 6660, son of Geo. Wilkes; 1st dam by Blue Bull 75: 2d dam by grandson of American Eclipse; 3d and 4th dams thoroughbred.

THE GREATEST CAMPAIGNER OF 1889.

Handsome, Game, Pure Gaited. Level Headed.

Will make a season at the PLEASANTON STOCK FARM, PLEASANTON, CAL. Service Fee $150. Money refunded if mare does not get with foal. Season ends April 10, 1890 Limited to 20 mares. For full record of performances, extended pedigree, etc., address

L. A. DAVIES, Hotel Pleasanton,

BOOK FULL. SUTTER AND JONES STREETS, San Francisco, Cal.

Valensin Stock Farm Stallions,

SIDNEY, 2:19 3-4.

At Eight Years of Age Sire of the following Fastest on Record:

FAUSTINO, yearling stallion, record of the world.......2:35
FLEET, fastest yearling record in 1888.......2:36
FLEET, fastest two-year-old filly in 1889.......2:24
GOLD LEAF, fastest four-year-old Pacing record in the world.......2:11¼
ADONIS, fastest three-year-old Pacing Gelding in the world.......2:14¼
ADONIS, four-year-old Gelding Pacing record.......2:14

—Also the Sire of—

LONGWORTH, four years old.......2:19
SISTER V., four years old (trial 2:23).......2:27
SANTA RITA.......2:39
MEMO, two-year-old (three-year-old trial 2:20½).......2:49

And many others.

SIDNEY is the sire of Faustino 2:35, and Fleet 2:36, the two fastest yearlings the world has ever known by one sire, and his slowest yearling is faster than the great Electioneer's fastest.

Terms, $250, with usual return privileges, for a limited number of approved mares. Book nearly full.

Only eight more mares can be taken for Season of '90.

Pasturage $5 per month. Reasonable charges if fed hay and grain. Best of care taken of mares, but positively no responsibility assumed for accidents or escapes. For further particulars address

G. VALENSIN, Pleasanton, Cal.

MEMO.

The Best Son of SIDNEY

Will Make the Season of 1890 at the OAKLAND RACE TRACK

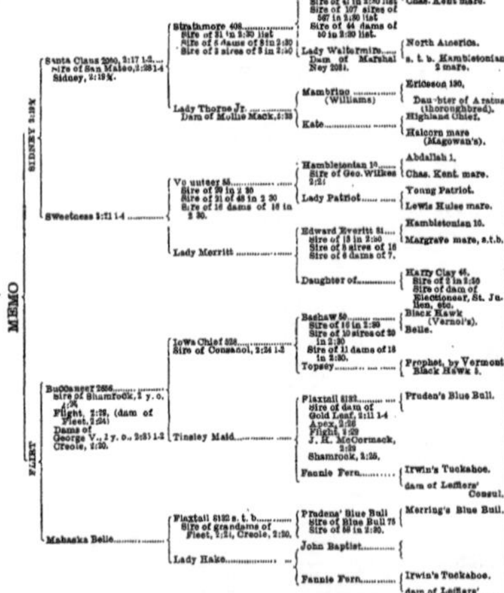

MEMO is, as can be seen at a glance, one of the best bred young stallions in service, having three crosses of Rysdyk's Hambletonian and one of Harry Clay, the sire of Green Mountain Maid (dam of Electioneer, etc.), while Long Island Black Hawk and Flaxtail also contribute to his blood. Sidney (Memo's sire) is universally known as the best young sire in the world, a producer of extreme speed at an early age.

PERFORMANCES.

MEMO trotted in public in his two year-old form, obtaining a record of 2:49, though he was close to Grandee in a race on the Bay District Track, the second heat of which was made in 2:31 1-2, the first in 2:3?. He exhibited phenomenal speed when three years old, and had it not been for a slight strain of his fore fetlock, there is little question that he would have shown in public very close to the best record. On the Oakland track he was timed a mile in 2:20 1-2, and frequently trotted quarters in from 33 1-2 to 34 seconds.

As a four-year-old Memo only started once—at Sacramento—when, although out of condition, he showed great speed, and improving as he went on, great hopes were entertained of his going well down in the 'teens at the P. C. T. H. B. A. meeting, but after showing several very fast miles his leg filled and he was laid up for the season. He is sixteen hands high, and of powerful build throughout. His color is a glossy black, with both fore-feet white. His disposition is all that could be desired, and his action superb. He is a sure foal getter, only one mare being reported not in foal during his last season.

TERMS, $100, with usual return privileges, for a limited number of mares. Season to close JUNE 15th, when he will be prepared for track purposes. Pasturage $5 per month. Have leased the Cricket ground adjoining the track for pasturage, where there is fine feed. Reasonable charges if fed hay and grain. Best of care taken of mares in any manner owners may desire, but positively no responsibility assumed for accidents or escapes. For further particulars address

J. P. KERR, 313 Bush Street, San Francisco,

or, JOHN ROWEN, Race Track, Oakland, Cal.

SANMATEO STOCKFAI

HOME OF GUY WILKES,

Record, 2:15 1-4.

Guy Wilkes' Book is full for 1890 and 1891, and positively mares will be received.

Sable Wilkes, three-year-old record 2:18, will be allowed to mares in addition to those already engaged at season of 1890. SABLE Wilkes, 15½ hands, black horse, by Guy Wilkes, first dam The Moor; second dam Gretchen by Mambrino Pilot; third dam Kitty Kirkman b Chief; fourth dam by Fanning's Tobe; fifth dam by imp. Leviathan.

Leo Wilkes, brown horse, four years, 16 hands, full brother Wilkes, will be allowed to serve 30 mares at $100 t

Mares not proving with foal may be returned the following season free of service ties engaging the services of any of the above horses must send a deposit of 10 pe service money with engagement. Pasturage $6 per month, and when the conditio animal requires it, hay or grain, or both, are fed, the charge will be $12 50 per Good care will be taken of all mares sent to the Farm, but no liability will be ass accidents or escapes.

All bills are due at time of service, but must be paid by August 1st of each year. will be allowed to leave the place until all bills are paid.

WILLIAM CORBITT.
San Mateo Stock Far

Pleasanton Stock Farm Co.'s Stallion

DIRECTOR, 2:17.

Director's book is open for 15 good mares more than already booked for the season of 18 each.

This is the cheapest service fee ever charged for a stallion, taking into consideration his B and RACE RECORD and the RACE RECORDS OF HIS COLTS.

Season to commence February 15th and close August 1st.

CORRECTOR, Four Years Old.

Sire Director 2:17, dam Brainey, she by Echo. Echo sired by Rysdyk's Hambletonian, out of she by Seely's American Star. Brainey's dam Lady Dudley, she by Tom Dudley by Blacknos Medoc, he by American Eclipse. Lady Dudley's dam by Bertrand, Jr., a son of Bertrand.

CORRECTOR is a rich seal brown 15¾ hands high, and is the fastest young stallion in the wo the same conditions, never having been off the farm where raised and never been shod or speed before last Christmas, and can trot quarters now in 35 seconds, a 2:20 gait

He will be allowed to serve ten good mares, at $100 each for the season, which closes June 1s

DECORATOR, Four Years Old.

Sire Director 2:17, dam Chess, sired by Cardinal 2.37, trial 2:28, he by Gen. Gifford's Morga Cardinal, sired by Joe Gales of Ohio, he by Marlborough out of the Duchess of Marlborough by Eclipse; second dam old Duchess of Marlborough by Sir Archy; third dam by imp Diomed, D second dam a Morgan and Messenger mare.

Decorator is a light bay 16 hands high, and with but little handling for speed has shown 17½ seconds, a 2:20 gait.

He will be allowed to serve ten good mares at $50 each for the season, which closes June 1

Mares not proving with foal may be returned next season free of charge of service fees to stallion, if he is still in our possession: if not, to some other stallion equally as good, or mon refunded at option of the company.

Pasturage $4 per month: hay and grain extra. Accidents and escapes at owner's risk.

Service fees due at time of service, and must be paid, together with pasturage, etc., before taken away, or a good approved note given, payable August 1st, 1890, at which date all bills settled.

For further information call or address M. SALISBURY, 320 Sansome Street, Ro San Francisco, or

PLEASANTON STOCK FARM CO.,
Pleasanton, Alameda Co.,

SOUTHER FARM

P. O. Box 208. San Leandro

1½ miles northwest of San Leandro; 8 miles southeast of Oakland. Turn off county road between above places at "Stanley Road," ¼ mile north of San Leandro.

Horses boarded at all times in ar desired. Best of care but no respon accidents. Colts broken and handl road or track. Terms reasonable.

Glen Fortune,	Jester D,	El Benton,	Fig
By Electioneer.	By Almont.	By Electioneer.	Hambleto
$50 for 1889.	$50 for 1890.	Limited to 5 mares.	Limited to
		Book Full.	Book

THE SOUTHER FARM

Has Green Feed the Year Rou

and feeds Hay in connection with the green feed, which a must have if he is to thrive. Every animal is given

A Dry, Warm Place to Sleep,

No matter how stormy the weather. All Stock under cover when it rains.

VISITORS WELCOME ANY DAY EXCEPT SUN

How to Get Stock to the Souther Farm.

The Souther Farm is one and a half miles northeast of San Leandro and eight miles southea land. The stables are about one mile east of the county road, which runs between Oakland an dro. The place to turn off is at Stanley Road, where a large signboard of the farm is placed. G will be found at every cross road. In any ordinary weather the roads are very good, and they are after the unusually heavy rainfall of the past winter.

All stock sent from San Francisco may be brought over by Garcia's Express, No. 3 Market Francisco. They also have an order box outside of Hawley Bros.' Hardware house on the corne and Beale streets. The express leaves San Francisco on the Creek route boat, which starts at orders should be in the order box at Market and Beale streets by 10 o'clock, or at the office, No street, by 11 o'clock at the latest. In the case of very young or very valuable horses, the Souther send reliable men to lead or drive over any stock that will not lead behind a wagon. A small c made in such cases, to cover the extra expense incurred.

Horses are very easily taken from Oakland to the farm, and where it is inconvenient for bring them or send them, the farm will send after anything that is to come. On horses that months or over there is no charge for getting or delivering. Where a horse stays a short time time and expense only is charged to him.

Horses can be shipped by rail from almost all parts of the State to San Leandro. Alway Farm several days before shipping anything, and then men will be on hand to receive stock on a railroad station is but two miles from the Souther Farm, and the agent invariably gives immed of the arrival of any stock consigned to the above farm, but when word is sent to the farm in g by letter or telegram, the animals sent are saved waiting a couple of hours in the car.

Passenger trains leave San Francisco (from the broad gauge ferry) and First and Broadway at frequent intervals during the day. There are several trains from San Jose to San Leandro broad and narrow gauge railroads; the broad gauge, by way of Niles, is much more convenient f the farm. There are trains each day from Sacramento, Stockton and Livermore to San Leand nary weather it is a short and pleasant drive from Oakland to the Souther Farm or from San the Farm by way of the Creek route ferry boat. Always notify the Souther Farm just when you at San Leandro, and some one will meet you at the station. If you do not recognize the farm conv the stage driver, who will point it out.

Write to the above address for references, circulars and price lists, reasonable.

GILBERT TOMPKINS, Prop

...ngtry Farms' Stud

...p. FRIAR TUCK

By the Immortal HERMIT

...ROMPING GIRL BY WILD DAYRELL,

AT $50 THE SEASON.

...es not proving with foal may be returned the ...ring season. Good care taken of mares, but no ...ties for accidents or escapes.

Good Pasturage at $5 per month.

...es shipped to ST. HELENA, care CHARLES ...LIAM ABY, St. Helena Stables, will be cared ... For further particulars address,

CHAS. WILLIAM ABY,
Middletown, Lake County, Cal.

...8 3-4 2:10 2:12

...MBRINO WILKES, 6083.

SIRE OF

...S WILKES, 2:22; ALPHEUS, 2:27; ...RA P, 2:29½; BALKAN, 2:29½ (3-year-...and timed separately 2:22½ in 4-year-old ...s, Bay District Track, October 14, 1889.

DESCRIPTION.

...k; sixteen hands; weighs, in exercise, 1,280 lbs. ...yle, finish, symmetry and proportion, compari... challenged with any trotting bred horse. His ...follow in size, style and beauty. Balkan, for ...ce, being "facile princeps" of trotters in these ...ulars.

PEDIGREE.

...d by Geo. Wilkes, sire of Harry Wilkes, 2:13½, ...Wilkes, 2:15¼, and 60 other trotters in the 2:30 ... addition to 6 pacers, and of the sire of Axtell, ...three-year-old), beating all stallions of any age, ...e sire of Regal Wilkes, 2:20¾, best two-year-old ...n record.

...t dam Lady Chrisman by Mambrino (Todhun... son of Mambrino Chief 11; sire of Lady Thorn, ... Woodford Mambrino, 2:21½, and four others in ...nd of the dams of Director, 2:17, Piedmont, ... Onward, 2:25¼, etc.

...nd dam by Pilot Jr. 12, sire of nine in the 2:30 ...d of the dams of Maud S., 2:08¾, Jay-Eye-See, ...Nutwood, 2:18¾, Viking, 2:19½, Pilot Boy, 2:20, ... Queen, 2:20¼, etc.

TERMS.

...es from a distance will be received at the Dexter ...s, Oakland, or Livery Stable, Martinez, the ... notifying Smith Hill, Superintendent at the ... Good pasture and plenty of water. For the ...se of placing the service of a Wilkes within ...of breeders, the same rate will be maintained as ...ar, to wit, $75 for the season. Although it is not ...ted thereby that this horse is inferior as a pro... to the horses whose fees are placed at from $150 ... Address

SMITH HILL,
San Miguel Stock Farm,
Walnut Creek, Contra Costa Co., Cal.

...2¾ 2:13½ 2:15¼

...08¾ 2:10 2:12

BALKAN

...y Mambrino Wilkes.

(See that Horse's Advertisement.)

...FANNY FERN BY JACK HAWKINS
Son of Boston.

...grandam of Maud S, (2:08¾) was by Boston and ...andam of Jay-Eye-See (2:10) was by Lexington, ... Boston. So Balkan is the same remove from ... that Maud is, and one remove nearer than ...e-See.

...y Fern has produced Molly Drew, Onyx, Fred ... Molly Fern and Balkan, all by different sires. ...an's sire and dam both being producers, and he ... trotter himself with a record of 2:29 1-2 (three-...d) and timed separately 2:22 1-4 in 4-year-old ... Bay District Track, October 14, 1889—it is but ... presume that he will get trotters of the high ...er.

DESCRIPTION.

... seal brown, 16-1 hands high, in style rivalled ..., and excelled by none with as pure a gait as ... been exhibited in public—bar none.

...n will be at Oakland Trotting Park for the ... of 1890, and will be limited to ten mares, at ..., in order to be put in training early, as it is ... certain that if given a reasonable opportun... will be fast enough to compete with the best of ... For further particulars address

A. L. HINDS,
Dexter Stables, Oakland

...2¾ 2:13½ 2:15¼

...SSE E. MARKS & CO.,

Wholesale and Retail Dealers of Choice Brands

...ana & Key West Cigars

922 MARKET ST., S. F.

2:19 NOONDAY 2:20½

STANDARD No. 10,000.

This celebrated trotting bred stallion will make the season of 1890 at the stable of the undersigned at Sacramento, Cal., at $75 for the season and $100 to insure a mare in foal. Payable on or before July 1st, 1-90. Money will be refunded on mares bred by insurance as soon as the fact becomes known that they are not in foal.

NOONDAY.

- Wedgewood, 2:19 .. Sire of Favonia, 2:15, fastest 4th heat for any mare or gelding, and eight others in 2:27 or better.
  - Belmont .... Sire of Wedgewood, 2:19, Nutwood, 2:18¾, Viking, 2:19½, and 29 others in 2:30 list.
    - Alexander's Abdallah, sire of Goldsmith Maid, 2:14; Almont, with 36 horses in 2:30 list, etc.
    - Belle, dam of Hambletonian, 2:26½; B'cara, dam of Pancoast, 2:21¾, the sire of Patron, 2:14½.
  - Woodbine .... Dam of Wedgewood, 2:19, Woodford Mamb., 2:21½, the sire of Pancoast, 2:21¾, the sire of Patron, 2:14½.
    - Woodford.
    - Singleton Mare.
- Noontide, 2:20½ .... (Trial, 2:18½).
  - Harold .... Sire of Maud S., 2:08¾, and 26 others in 2:30 list.
    - Hambletonian (Rysdyk's), sire of George Wilkes, 2:22, the sire of Guy Wilkes, 2:15¼; Electioneer, the sire of Sunol, 2:10½, and scores of noted trotters and producers.
    - Enchantress, by Abdallah 1.
  - Midnight .... Dam of Jay-Eye-See, 2:10, Noontide, 2:20½.
    - Pilot Jr., sire of dams of Maud S., 2:08¾, Jay-Eye-See, 2:10, Nutwood, 2:18¾, etc.
    - Twilight, by Lexington, sire of the dam of Ansel, 2:20.

NOODAY is a dark seal brown, foaled 1884, 16 hands 1¼ inches high. Individually he is equal to his royal breeding. He is all that can be desired in conformation, intelligence, color and trotting action, and no stallion now in public service can show a pedigree with such fast records and royal game trotting blood as Noonday.

DON MARVIN,

Record 2:28 as a five-year-old. Standard by Breeding and Performance

Standard No. 7927.

Don Marvin 2:28.

Don Marvin is a beautiful seal brown, foaled 1884, bred by Hon. Leland Stanford, Palo Alto, Cal., standing 16 hands, and weighs, in ordinary condition, 1200 lbs. He is a fine individual, good style and form, combined with great substance, and good temper. Is very level headed; in his first race the past season he only made one break in five closely contested heats. He has great speed and endurance, with the pure, rapid Electioneer gait. He trots without toe weights, and wears only 8 oz. shoes in front. He gained his record the past season in the third heat, on a slow track, after making a season (serving over 60 mares), with scarcely any preparation. His record is no mark of his speed. He was a natural born trotter, and Mr. Charles Marvin considered him the fastest two year old at Palo Alto that season.

By FALLIS, 2:23, - - **by Electioneer, sire of**
Sire of Don Marvin, 2:28. — Sunol, three-year-old, 2:10 1-2, Palo Alto, 2:12¾, and 47 others in 2:30 list.

Dam CORA, by Don Victor by Belmont, sire of
Dam of Don Marvin, 2:28. — Ventura, 2:27¼, and sire of the dam of Bell Echo, 2:20, and six others in 2:30 list.

2d dam CLARABEL, - **by Abdallah Star,**
Dam of Clifton Bell, 2:24 1-2, and grandam of Rexford, three years, 2:24. — Sire of Hattie Maples, 2:28.

3d dam FAIRY, - - **by Rysdyk's Hambletonian,**
Sister of Sweepstakes, sire of 16 in 2:30 list. — Sire of Electioneer, George Wilkes, and many other noted sires and trotters.

4th dam EMMA MILLS, by Seely's American Star,
Dam of 4 horses that have 2:30 performers. — The great broodmare sire of the world.

The above pedigree should show every intelligent breeder that Don Marvin is "high" bred, though very strong in trotting blood. All the comment it is deemed necessary to make as to the value of "thoroughbred blood" in the trotter is simply to refer to the very significant fact that the first and second dams of Maud S. 2:08¾, Jay-Eye-See 2:10, Sunol, three years 2:10 1-2, Palo Alto 2:12¾, Anteeo 2:16¼, Nutwood 2:18¾, Wedgewood 2:19, and many other successful sires and sensational trotters of the day are thoroughbred.

TERMS—Don Marvin will make the ensuing season from February 1st to July 1st, 1890, at $40 the season, with the usual privilege of returning the mare next season if not proving in foal. Mares from a distance met at the cars or boats on notification, and carefully handled, but no responsibility assumed for accidents or escapes.

Good alfalfa pasture furnished (free from barb wire fence) at $4 per month. For further particulars or complete circulars address

F. P. LOWELL,
1520 F Street, Sacramento, Cal.

The Produce of Eros Averaged $2,200 Each at New York Auction Sale in 1889.

THE ELECTIONEER TROTTING TALLION,

5326 EROS 5326

Will make the season of 1890—February 1st to July 1st—at LA SIESTA RANCH, MENLO PARK, adjoining Palo Alto.

PEDIGREE.

EROS (5326)
Standard by his sire
" " dam
" " record
" " produce
" under all rules

EROS (5326)..

- Electioneer .... Grandsire of Norlaine, 1 yr., 2:31 1-2, Sire of Sunol, 2 yrs., 2:18, Sunol, 3 yrs., 2:10 1-2, Hinda Rose, 1 yrs., 2:18, Palo Alto, 2:12¾.
  - Hambletonian 10 .... Sire of Dictator, George Wilkes, Happy Medium, and 40 others in 2:30 list, and grandsire of 728 in list.
    - Abdallah 10 — Sire of the dams of Goldsmith Maid, 2:14, and 7 other producing dams.
    - Charles Kent mare — By imp. Bellfounder.
  - Green Mountain Maid .... Dam of Prospero, 2:20, Elaine, 2:20, Dame Trot, 2:22, Elista, 2:22¼, Storm, 2:26¾, Antonio, 2:28½, Miranda, 2:31, Mansfield, 2:26.
    - Harry Clay — Sire of the dams of St. Julian, 2:11¼, Bodine, 2:19¼, and 17 more in 2:30 list
    - Shanghai Mary.
- Sontag Mohawk .... Dam of Eros, 2:29 1-2, Sport, 2:22¼, Sallie Benton, 2:17¾, Conductor, trial, 2:26, Colma, 3-y-o trial, 2:24.
  - Mohawk Chief .... Sire of the dams of Lot Slocum, 2:17½, Sallie Benton, 4 yrs., 2:17¾, Pedlar, 2 yrs., 2:27¾, Stanford, 4 yrs., 2:20, Eros, 6th heat, 2:29 1-2.
    - Hambletonian 10 — Sire of the dams of Stamboul, 2:12¾, Wilton, 2:19¼, and 20 other trotters.
    - Lady Perrine
  - Sontag Nellie ....
    - Toronto Sontag — By Toronto Chief,
    - Nellie Gray — 8-mile record, 13:45.

Produce of Eros
Wanda, 4 yrs., 2:24.
Solita, 2 yrs., 2:41 1-2.
Meriquita, 2yrs., 2:42.
Daylight, 2 yrs., 2:54.
Hiram B., trial, 2:28.

These are the only colts by him that have ever had a harness on except one in New York that went a trial last July in 2:26 1-2.

DESCRIPTION.

EROS is a rich seal brown stallion, bred by Hon. Leland Stanford at Palo Alto, and is the nearest living likeness of his celebrated sire, Electioneer. Stands 15.2 hands high, and weighs 1060 pounds

In breeding to Eros, the owners of mares will strictly follow the great rule of breeding, viz., breed to a stallion by a producer and out of a sure producer of great speed. Eros is by the stallion that has produced more 2:30 trotters that any living horse, and is also the sire of more 2:30 performers than any horse living or dead.

EROS is out of the dam of Sally Benton, four years old, record 2:17¾, Sport 2:22½, and Eros 2:29½ in the sixth heat, against a field of nine horses. He is from a family that is endowed with great natural speed, trot fast at an early age, train on, throw trotters from all classes of mares, are of good substance, bone, style and action, and breed solid colors.

TERMS.

$100 for the season, with the privilege of return next season should mare not be in foal and horse and mare still remain in the same hands.

Good pasturage can be obtained at $5 per month, but no responsibility for accidents or escapes. There are a large number of box stalls, and animals can be kept up and fed on hay and grain at reasonable rates if required. Mares already in foal can be sent to the ranch for foaling, and will receive all the attention bestowed upon our own mares. Mares left with Mr. Peter Pomyea, Broadway Street Stable, Oakland, or with Mr. F. H. Burke, 401 Montgomery Street, San Francisco, will be forwarded to the ranch free of charge. For further particulars apply to

W. H. VIOGET,
LA SIESTA RANCH, MENLO PARK, CAL.

EROS is the only stallion offered to the public on this Coast that has a dam that has three in the 2:30 list.

POPLAR GROVE

Breeding Farm

STALLIONS.

CLOVIS, 4909,

CLOVIS is a beautiful black, Eight Years Old, 16 1-2 Hands High, and weighs 1260 lbs.

He is a horse of beautiful symmetry and magnificent action.

PEDIGREE.

CLOVIS was sired by Sultan, 2:24, sire of Stamboul, 2:12 1-4, Ruby, 2:19¾, and fifteen others with records of 2.30 or better.

First dam Sweetbriar by Thorndale 2:22 1-2, sire of Edwin Thorne, 2:16 1-2, Daisy Dale, 2:19, and May Thorne, 2:24

Second dam Ulster Queen, dam of Volmer, 2:14¾, by Hambletonian 10. Sire of Dexter, 2:17¼, George Wilkes, 2:22.

Third dam by Thomas Jefferson, a son of Mambrino Paymaster, Jr.

Fourth dam by Mambrino Paymaster, sire of Mambrino Chief.

Sultan, by The Moor, sire of Beautiful Bells, dam of Hinda Rose, 2:19 1-2, and Sable, dam of Sable Wilkes, three year old record 2:18.

First dam of Sultan, Sultana, by Delmonico. Sire of Darby, 2:16 1-2, by Guy Miller, sire of Whipple's Hambletonian.

Second dam by Mambrino Chief.

Third dam by Downing's Bay Messenger.

Fourth dam Mrs. Caudle, dam of Ericsson, four year old record 2:30 1-2.

Clovis will make the season of 1890 at Poplar Grove Breeding Farm, near Wildflower, Fresno County, commencing February 1st and ending July 1st.

Terms, $75, due at time of service.

Mares cared for in any manner owners may desire; pasturage $2 per month. Every care exercised, but no liability for escapes or accidents. Mares not proving with foal can be returned next season, providing I still own this stallion.

APEX, 8935.

FOUR-YEAR-OLD RECORD, FOURTH HEAT, 2:26.

Will make the present season at the Poplar Grove Breeding Farm, near Wildflower, Fresno Co., season commencing Feb. 1st, and ending July 1, 1890. Terms, $50 the season, due at time of service. Apex is eight years old, a beautiful bay, 15 1-2 hands high, and weighs 1150 lbs. He is a horse of fine disposition, and his gait is faultless.

PEDIGREE.

Apex was sired by Promptor 2305, he by Blue Bull 75; first dam Mary by Flaxtail, he by Pruden's Blue Bull. Flaxtail being the sire of the dams of Buccaneer, five-year-old record, 2:24 1-2; Pride, yearling record, 2:44 1-2, and Shamrock, two-year old record, 2:25, third heat. Second dam by Bright Eyes, son of Boanarges. Prompter (sire of Apex, record 2:26, and Transit, 2:26 1-2), by Wilson's Blue Bull, by Pruden's Blue Bull, son of Merring's Blue Bull. Promptor's dam Prairie Bird, by Flaxtail; second dam by John the Baptist, son of Tally Ho Morgan, by Sherman Morgan; third dam Fannie Fern by Irwin's Tuckaho.

Apex made his appearance in the circuit as a two-year-old, and obtained a record of 2:42. As a three-year-old he reduced this in a race at Santa Rosa against Stamboul to 2:31, it taking six heats to decide the contest, which was won by Apex. As a four year-old he gained his present record of 2:26.

Mares cared for in any manner owners may desire. Pasturage $2 per month. Every care exercised, but no liabilities for escapes or accidents. Mares not proving with foal can be returned next season, providing I still own this stallion.

The Standard Stallion

JUNIO,

RECORD 2:22.

WILL MAKE THE PRESENT SEASON OF AT FRESNO FAIR GROUNDS.

Season Commencing Feb. 1st an ending July 1st.

TERMS—$100 the season, due at time of service.

JUNIO is eight years old, a handsome dark bay 16 hands high, and weighs 1250 pounds. He is the personification of the light harness horse, and his trotting action is superb. At the State Fair of 1886 he took first premium over forty of the finest trotters in the State.

PEDIGREE.

*Junio, by Electioneer, premier stallion of Palo Alto (sire of Sunol 2:10 1-2, Palto Alto 2:12 1-4, and 47 others in the 2:30 list,. Dam by Granger by imp. Hercules.

Granger, by imp. Hercules, dam Jenny Lind, by Stockbridge Chief, Jr., he by Stockbridge Chief, he by Vermont Black Hawk. Second dam by Kentucky Whip.

Imp. Hercules, by Wingston, first dam daughter of Tuscar, by Bay Middleton, second dam Malvina, by Oscar; 3rd dam Spotless by Walton; 4th dam by Trumpator (see Bruce's American Stud Book, Vol. 1, page 28). Hercules is the sire of the dam of Anmoor 2:20¾; also sire of dam of Menlo 2:21 1-2.

Mares not proving in foal may be returned next year free of charge, providing I still have the horse. Pasturage $2 per month. While every care will be taken of horses, no liability will be assumed for accidents or escapes.

For further particulars address

S. N. STRAUBE, Fresno, Cal.

Poplar Grove Breeding Farm.

WHOLESALE AND Retail Fishing Tackle

WHOLESALE AND Retail Fishing Tackle

Agents for all the principal Manufacturers of FISHING TACKLE in England and the United States.

Trap Shooters Supplies a Specialty.

CLABROUGH, GOLCHER & CO.,
630 and 632 Montgomery Street, S. F., Cal.

BOYCE TABLETS.

Leg and Body Wash.

THE BOYCE TABLETS are packed in a nicely decorated metal box with hinged lid—one hundred tablets in each box; directions for use plainly engraved upon the box; therefore, the convenience of the package—no liability to leakage and breakage—economy and ready solubility, together with the absolute certainty of their action, will at once commend the use of BOYCE'S TABLETS to the intelligent horsemen of the country. TABLETS sufficient to make one hundred pints of leg and body wash are conveniently carried in an inside coat pocket or in the hip-pocket of the trousers.

The BOYCE WASH can be applied ALL OVER THE BODY WITHOUT FEAR OF BLISTERING NOR DOES IT AFFECT THE KIDNEYS.

The BOYCE WASH will cure CRACKED HEELS, PUFFS, STOCKINGS, SCRATCHES, INFLAMED TENDONS and FEVERED LEGS.

Price per Box of One Hundred Tablets, $2, sent postpaid to any part of the United States; six boxes for $10. A sample of BOYCE'S TABLETS will be mailed to any address on application. These TABLETS are warranted to keep in any climate. Address

BOYCE TABLET COMPANY,
600 Wabash Avenue, - - - Terre Haute, Indiana.

J. A. McKERRON, Pacific Coast Ag't,
228-230-232 Ellis Street, San Francisco, Cal.

J. O'KANE, | Horse Boots, Clothing and Furnishings, For Track, Driving Training and Stable. Every requisite for Horsemen. Harness, Medicines, Etc.

ADVERTISE YOUR STALLIONS

—IN THE—

Breeder & Sportsman

For the Season---1890.

We are pleased to announce that we have the best facilities for furnishing

Stallion Pictures,

Stallion Cards,

Pedigrees, Folders,

Contracts, Bills, Etc.

We make a specialty of this department of our business, and have UNRIVALED FACILITIES FOR LOOKING UP PEDIGREES and doing accurate and handsome work.

Promptness, Good Work, Low Prices.

BREEDER AND SPORTSMAN,
313 Bush Street, S. F.

PASTURAGE

AND

FIRST-CLASS CARE

TAKEN OF

Gentlemen's Road Horses and Trotters.

Colts Broken and Trained to Harness or Saddle.

Twenty new Box Stalls. First-class Pasturage, and the best of care given to all horses. Terms, $4 per month. Satisfaction Guaranteed. Address,

K. O'GRADY,
Laural Creek Farm,
SAN MATEO, CAL.

"DICKEY'S,"

SIXTH AVENUE AND D ST.

Near entrance to Bay District Track.

Choicest Brands of

WINES AND CIGARS.

A Delightful Resort.

Telephone 1486. J. R. DICKEY, Propr.

HORSES PURCHASED ON COMMISSION.

THOROUGHBREDS A SPECIALTY.

Will select and buy, or buy selected Animals for all desiring, for reasonable compensation.

KEEPS PROMISING YOUNGSTERS IN VIEW.

L. M. LASLEY, Stanford, Ky.

References:—J. W. Guest, Danville, Ky.
B. G Bruce, Lexington Ky.
S. H. Baughman, Stanford, Ky.
G. A. Lackey, Stanford, Ky.
Geo. McAlister, Stanford, Ky.
First National Bank, Stanford, Ky.

Fine Hats,

Latest Styles and Colors.

Meussdorffer & Hubner

8 Kearny Street, San Francisco,
Next to New Chronicle Building

Brushes.

BUCHANAN BROS.,
Brush Manufacturers,

609 Sacramento Street, two doors above Montgomery.

Horse Brushes of every description on hand and made to order. Bristle Body Brushes our Specialty

The Park Training Stable.

CHAS. DAVID, PROPRIETOR.

Corner Grove and Baker Streets, near Entrance to Golden Gate Park.

EVERY FACILITY FOR TRAINING COLTS and taking care of Gentlemen's Roadsters.

Finely appointed stable with every convenience and sixteen roomy box stalls.

The best care given all horses by experienced help, under the personal superintendence of the proprietor

Convenient to the Park Speed Drive, and Accessible to Six Lines of Cable Cars.

THE TRAINING OF COLTS AND ROADSTERS A SPECIALTY.

TROTTERS AND ROADSTERS FOR SALE.

HORSES SOLD ON COMMISSION.

The proprietor trained and brought out the following well known horses: "Sister, Huntress," "Perihelion," "Nona Y," and others.

GOLDEN EAGLE HOTEL

Corner SEVENTH and K STREETS, SACRAMENTO.

FIRST CLASS IN EVERY RESPECT.

The LARGEST and FINEST HOTEL in the City.

W. O. BOWERS, Proprietor.

Free 'Buss to and from the Hotel.

Telephone, Telegraph Office and Messenger Service at Hotel

Trade Mark

Six Cases

S. ALLCOCK & CO.'S

Unequalled Fishing Tackle

Received direct by Steamer EXPLORER, from Liverpool, December 26, 1889.

E. T. ALLEN,
Sole Agent for Pacific Coast,

Fire Arms and Sporting Goods

416 Market St., S. F.

THE HICKS-JUDD CO.

Successors to
HICKS & JUDD, Bookbinders,
and Women's Co-operative Printing Office.

Printers, Bookbinders, Publishers,

23 First St., San Francisco.

BREEDERS' CATALOGUES A SPECIALTY.

By-Laws

—AND—

Rules and Regulations

—OF THE—

NATIONAL

Trotting Association

ALSO THE

AMERICAN

Trotting Association,

AND THE

PACIFIC COAST BLOOD-HORSE ASSOCIATION.

With Betting Rules.

For Sale at the Office of the

Breeder and Sportsman,
313 Bush St., S. F., Cal.

Price, 25c. each.
By Mail, Postage Paid, 30c. each.

KENNEL ADVERTISEME

FOR SALE.

Pointer Puppie

By Tom Pinch ex Galatea.

Tom Pinch has won at two field trials, a never beaten on the bench, winning first w. shown. At the recent Bench Show at Elmi York, Tom Pinch won first, Galatea second, a Pinch [Tom Pinch—Galatea] first in their re classes. For prices and particulars, address J. MARTIN BARNEY, Dutch Fl

Puppies for Sa

TWO GORDON SETTER BITCH PUP months old.

TWO YORKSHIRE TERRIER DOG PU 2 months old, by Sieff's Mash, winner of fir in last three Bench Shows.

SIX MASTIFF PUPPIES, by a son of "Dick," winner of first prize in last two Shows.

Apply to JAMES E. WATSO
516 Sacramento st
P. O. Box 1898. San Fran

DOGS---Pointer Pu

FOR SALE.

Sure Bench Show and Field Trial Winners, have more bench-show and field-trial blood than any that have ever been whelped on the Coast.

Sire, POINT, double field trial winner; he devoir's Don, great field trial and bench sh ner, out of Drab, field trial and bench show w

Dam, QUEEN CROXTETH by Rush T. show winner, out of Champion Patti Croxte trial and bench show winner. This is the be-t blood in the world. Breeding and health guar Address,

A. B. TRUMAN,
1425 Steiner St., near Ellis, S. F

FOX TERRIERS--C. A. SUMNE Fort St., Lo les, Breeder of Fox Terriers. Blemton V (14290), by Champion Lucifer, at stud.

CALIFORNIA SPANIEL KENN

Oakland, Cal
H. P. RENNIE
Breeder and in of typical CO SPANIELS, of first prizes and Los Angel also, Columbu New York, 18 the stud, solid Cocker dog, G won 1st and Medal at S. Fee, $25. Pupp grown dogs at able prices. can neither to climb a tree, but are fielders and prize winne

Fiske's Vanes.

MADE OF
COPPER
And Gilded with
PURE
GOLD LEAF.

Manufacturer's Agent.

The HOWE SCALE
411 & 413 Market Street, S.

Scales for Weighing o
Live Stoc
SEEDS, FEED, Etc.

Write for Catalogue.

PERRIER-J

& Co.

EPERNA

CHAMPA

W. B CHAP
Sole Agent for
Coast.

For sale by all Wine Merchants and

VETERINARY.

Everything for

Trotter or Runner,

At J. A. McKERRON'S,

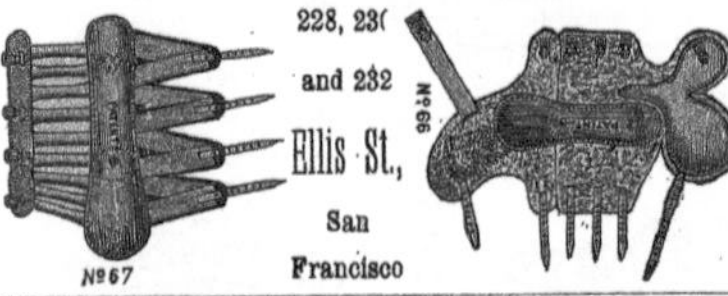

228, 230 and 232 Ellis St., San Francisco

The PARKER Hammerless Shot Gun.

At the Annual Tournament of 1889, held at Cannes, France, the grand prize, consisting of 2000 Francs and a Valuable Cup. was won by The Parker Hammerless.

The first Parker Hammerless Gun made won the championship of America at Decatur Illinois.

SEND FOR ILLUSTRATED CIRCULAR.

PARKER BROS., Makers,

New York Salesroom, 97 Chambers St.. Meriden Conn.

ALWAYS GIVES SATISFACTION.

Combining perfect riding qualities, proportions and balance, with genteel appearance.

No vehicle exhibits a horse to better advantage, and no Cart approaches them for speeding or training purposes.

A stylish vehicle for exercising or pleasure driving, at one-fourth the cost of a carriage. Have none of the horse jockey or objectionable features of other Road Carts.

They are the Leading Cart wherever introduced, and are in use by the most prominent breeders and pleasure drivers everywhere.

Elegant Shifting Top Carts. Perfectly Balanced Stylish Pole Carts.

For Illustrated Catalogue, with Prices, address,

LEWIS F. CASTOR,
Frankford, Philadelphia, Pa.

JOHN SPLAN, General Agent.

Brothers of the Angle,

OUR NEW EIGHT-STRIP SPLIT BAMBOO is the "King" of all fishing-rods. Chubb's New Catalogue for 1890 is now ready. In addition to a complete list of anglers' supplies, it contains articles from the pens of Dr. James A. Henshall, Petronella, W. H. Murray, Geo. P. Goff, Norman, Brother Gardner, and others.

These papers are by the best writers on angling subjects, and are very interesting.

Send 25 cents, and receive Catalogue, post-paid. This amount will be deducted from first order (if accompanied with COUPON in book) for one dollar's worth or more of our goods. Address

THOS. H. CHUBB.

The Fishing-Rod Manufacturer,
POST MILLS, VT.

Please mention BREEDER AND SPORTSMAN.

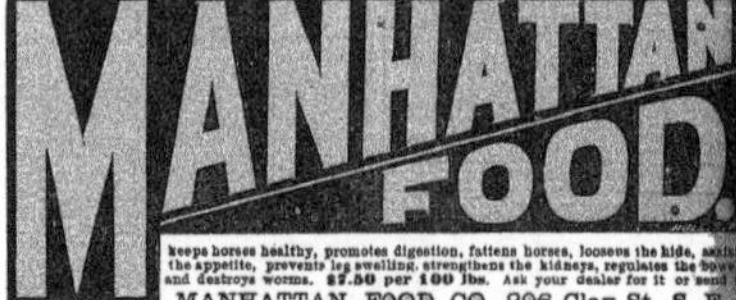

keeps horses healthy, promotes digestion, fattens horses, loosens the hide, assists the appetite, prevents leg swelling, strengthens the kidneys, regulates the bowels and destroys worms. $7.50 per 100 lbs. Ask your dealer for it or send to

MANHATTAN FOOD CO.. 206 Clay St., S. F.

THE IMPROVED NOYES ROAD - CART

PATENTED JULY 17, 1883, *AND JUNE* 8, 1886.

Some of the Advantages of the Noyes Cart Over All Others.

There is no bar for the rider to climb over in getting in or out. The horse can be hitched eighteen inches nearer than any other road-cart made. You can get in or out with perfect safety—no danger of being thrown into the wheel—a great advantage in breaking colts. THE EASIEST CART FOR ROAD OR TRACK. The only cart that a horse can be speeded to within one second as fast as to a sulky. All our carts are made of the very best materials and are warranted. Manufactured by the NOYES CART COMPANY, Kalamazoo, Mich.

They are indorsed by the following horsemen, all of whom are using them. Ask their opinion of the Noyes Cart: John Splan, who drove Guy a full mile in 2:17¾ and Chanter a half-mile in 1 10¾ to a Noyes Cart, says he would not take $250 for it if he could not get another; W. J. Gordon, Glenville, O.; W. B. Fasig, Cleveland, O.; Dave Muckel, Cleveland, O.; R. J. Moorehead, North East, Pa.; W. J. Chamberlain, Cleveland, O.; H. P. Malone, Bradford, Pa.; S. A. Brown & Co., Kalamazoo Stock Farm; Charles Marvin, Menlo Park, Cal.; W. H. Crawford, Lexington, Ky.; S. L. Caton, who gave Bell Boy a mark at Los Angeles, Cal., of 2:19¼, and drove Chanter a half mile in 1:06¾ and Lowland Girl a full mile in 2:12 to a Noyes Cart; Bib Bowerman, Lexington, Ky.; James Golden, Medford, Mass.; John E. Turner, Philadelphia, Pa.; T. L. Newton, Beaver Dam, Wis.; P. V. Johnston, Marshall, Mich.; W. H. McCarthy, Los Angeles, Cal.; A. W. Dennison, El Dorado, Kan.; P. O. Shank, Cleveland, O.; Charles Barnard, Boston, Mass.; Johnson Bros., Greenville, Mich.; John G. Avery, Buffalo, N. Y.; General R. L. Howard, Buffalo, N. Y.; Howard Conkling, Buffalo, N. Y.; W. D. Ham, Hennepin, Ill.; B. G. Henry, Waterbury, Conn; J. E. Hayer, Newburgh, O.; C. Hart, Jefferson, Tex.; A. W. Harbison, Rock Point, Pa.; Carl Hodges, Battle Creek, Mich.; Barnes Treacy, Lexington, Ky.; George Forbes, Cleveland, O.; Gifford Dudley, Topeka, Kan.; William and J. Thompson Lamont, Pa.; C. F. Emery, Forest City Stock Farm, Cleveland, O.; H. F. Jones, Minneapolis, Minn.; John Forbes, Elyria O.; D. J. Downs Battle Creek, Mich; Frank Caton, Randall Station, O.; Arthur D. Sutton, Ind., Pa.; W. F. Neely, Grand Ridge, Ill.; Walter Clark, owner of Pilot Medium, Battle Creek, Mich.; H. R. Kingman, Battle Creek, Mich.; Dr. Sutton and H. C. Reed, Kalamazoo, Mich.; Budd Doble, Chicago, Ill.

SOLE MANUFACTURERS OF STONE'S PATENT SULKY CASE.

They will more than save their cost in one season, and horsemen campaigning trotters cannot afford to be without them. Would refer to Samuel A. Brown, Kalamazoo Stock Farm, S. L. Caton and W. H. McCarthy. Address

NOYES CART COMPANY, Kalamazoo, Mich.

Office and Factory, Corner Rose and Eleanor streets. H. ARTHUR STONE, Manager.

OSSIDINE

Results obtained at the well-known KALAMAZOO FARM

KALAMAZOO, MICH., Sept. 15, 1889.

GENTLEMEN:—We have used OSSIDINE for the past two years and consider it invaluable for Sprung Tendons, Curbs, Ringbone, and Spavins; there is nothing equals it: and for us it effected a perfect cure where firing failed, although performed by one of the most successful veterinarians on the continent. We have recommended it to others with like success, and believe it has more merit than any blister ever used. Very respectfully yours,

S. A. BROWNE & CO., Prop's.

This scientific preparation is an absolute cure for all bony or callous lumps on horses, and is a more powerful absorbent than "firing," without creating the slightest blemish.

Acknowledged by leading horsemen of the world to be the ONLY preparation that will remove a Bone Spavin after it has become ossified.

We have authority also to refer to
Mr. JEROME I. CASE, Mr. FRED. GERHARD,
Mr. JOHN PORTER (Trainer to H.R.H. the Prince of Wales),
And hundreds of others from whom we have very flattering testimonials.

One Style Only. $3.00 per Bottle

A. P. BUSH & CO.,
149 Pearl St.,
BOSTON, MASS.,
Sole Agents for United States and Canada.
Beware of Imitations.

SOLD BY C. N. Crittenton, A. R. Van Nest & Co., and C. Moseman & Bro., NEW YORK CITY. Morrisson, Plummer & Co., Peter Van Schaack & Sons, CHICAGO, ILL. John D. Park & Son, CINCINNATI, O.; Floyd & Foster, DETROIT, MICH.; F. S. Slosson, CLEVELAND, O.; Meyer Bros. Drug Co., ST. LOUIS, MO.; R. A. Robinson, LOUISVILLE, KY.; H. H. Moore & Sons, STOCKTON, CAL.

Nutwood 2:22¾ 2:21¼ 2:18¾ } Sire

DAWN 6407

Dam Countess } DAM OF Strathway (2-y-o) trial; Placida; Morna } Double team Trial

2:18¾; 2:20; 2:19½.

$100 Popular Price for season of 1890. $100

Not having a breeding farm, and being dependent on the public for patronage, I have set the above low price in order to be within the reach of any one desiring to breed.

Good pasturage $3 per month.

For further particulars, address

A. L. WHITNEY, Petaluma.

Vol. XVI. No 13.
No. 313 BUSH STREET.

SAN FRANCISCO. SATURDAY, MARCH 29, 1890.

SUBSCRIPTION
FIVE DOLLARS A YEAR.

Our Tennessee Letter.

GALLATIN, TENN., March 19th.

EDITOR BREEDER AND SPORTSMAN:—It is only a little over three weeks from to-day until the Memphis spring meeting will have been inaugurated. The heavy winds of the last few days came when most needed, and have served materially in drying the tracks at Memphis and Nashville. The work of training has been resumed and the trainers and horses are at it in dead earnest. The horses at both Memphis and Nashville are not as far advanced at this time as was expected, but they are coming around now in great shape. At Memphis faster work has been reported than at Nashville, but with a continuance of this good weather the horses at Westside Park will be fit by the time of the Spring meeting. Last Sunday, at Memphis, Blarneystone Jr., a Kentucky Derby aspirant, worked a mile very easily in 1:50. Cataline, who is in Charley Doherty's string, was sent six furlongs in 1:22, while the two-year-old filly Sweet Alice covered the same distance in 1:26. Riley, Ed. Corrigan's Derby Candidate, was galloped a mile in 2:00. He has not been given any fast work as yet, but it is said that a mile and a half is his distance. Blue Blazes, under the watchful eye of George Muldoon, cantered seven furlongs in 1:43, and pulled up with plenty of wind. Blue Blazes has the making of a race horse in him, and if he does not play a prominent part in the three-year-old racing drama of 1890, I am badly mistaken. Thomas Mackin, a good-looking two-year-old colt by Old Blazes, in Ruddy Brothers' Stable, is said to be a corn-cracker. He is trained by Jim Cartes, and as yet has only been given moderate work. Little Minch, the hero of many battles for turf supremacy, has covered a half mile in :52, and not extended at that. He will be a sure winner at Memphis and Nashville if nothing ails him. Captain Widener has two two-year-olds at Memphis that are said to be about first-class, and they are being closely watched by the toots and race track habitues.

No sensational work has been done at Nashville unless it is being done between the setting and rising of the sun. Sam Doxey by Casino, and who is the much talked of three-year-old, has not improved much by his winter's rest. He has not been sent along very fast yet, and will hardly start at the Nashville meeting. The Wandering Jew, in the same stable, is a coltish looking youngster, and can not be got ready for the spring meetings. It is said that Buford, three-year-old, by Boulevard, is "fit to kill," and his party have great faith in his future success. El Rio Rey, and the rest of Mr. Winters' string have not been asked to do any fast work yet, but the whole stable seems to be in the pink of condition. El Rio Rey will be started at Nashville in the Link's Hotel and Kinney Handicap. It was given out that he would not see the red bandanna fall at Nashville, but Mr. Estell decided to have the big son of Marion start. Rey del Rey has been the cynosure of all eyes since his arrival, and when he starts Tennesseeans will back him to a man.

There will be something over 60 foals droppedat Fairview Farm this season. About twenty have already been foaled, and the rising of the mornings sun falls for the first time upon a new arrival nearly every day. The youngsters are by Imp. Pickwick, Forrester, Long Taw, Miser and Muscovy.

Our horsemen here have arranged to have some 2 year-old trotting races about April 15. Some speculation on the result has already begun. Billy Downing, the veteran knight of the sulky, and of Lady Mack, 2:19¾. fame, has quite a string of good looking youngsters. and he will get a lion's share of the purses.

Bow Bells, by Electioneer, is the most sought after stallion in the State, and his limit of ten outside mares at $300, has already been filled. With the high class mares that he will embrace at his new Tennessee home he should become one of the most famous of this great tribe of trotters.

Dr. Ed. N. Franklin of this city tells me he has decided to sell his 2 year old filly by Bomont(son of Belmont) dam Edgefield Girl, in one of the combination sales at Nashville next month. She will probably bring a long price as her dam is the dam of Annie W., record 2:20. In the fifth heat of a winning race when dead lame, Billy Downing, who is now handling her, tells me he thinks the young filly considerably faster than Annie W. at the same age.

Mr. Jno. R. Head, of Brownsville, Tenn., has sold to Grady & Co., of Kentucky, the mare Annie W., 2:20, to Gen. Thomas, for $5,000. Annie W. will be immediately put in training, and she will doubtless lower her record of 2:20 the coming season.

Mary M. (dam of McEwen, 2:18½, Annie W., 2:20, and Andante, 2:27¾), foaled at Maj. Campbell Brown's Ewell Farm on the 13th inst., a brown colt, with star and white hind ankles, by Almont Jr. This youngster is a full brother to Annie W., 2:20, and Andante, 2:27¾.

Frank Jenkins, who has been in winter quarters at Pensacola, Fla., with his string of trotters, has returned home. Frank had rather indifferent luck last season, and the campaign of 1890 was unsuccessful. This season he will have quite a large string of one and two-year-olds, mostly the get of Wedgewood and Nuthunter, and he may be expected to get his share of the "pie" in the southern circuit.

An unusual large number of horse sales will be held in Tennessee this season. The Tennessee Importing Company will hold a combination sale of trotting and saddle horses April 1st, 2d, 3d. A. P. McKimmin's 13th annual sale will take place at Nashville March 27th and 28th. Babcock and Buford will hold their sale of trotting, road and saddle horses at Columbia April 14th and 15th. The Belle Meade closing out sale will be held the 24th and 25th of April, and Messrs. Gillock, Lyle & Parmer will hold their sale April 26th, the first day of the spring meeting at Nashville.

Wilson Abeel, trainer for Mr. Van L. Kirkman at Oak Hall, near Nashville, came up to this city a few weeks ago, and was mixing with his friends. He tells me that he has seven or eight horses in training, all of which give promise of getting a good deal of first money the coming season. He thinks Bell Archer, two-year-old record 2:49½, by McCurdy's Hambletonian, will be a good one in her class, and says she will get a mark far below 2:30.

The programme of the Memphis meeting has just been published. The meeting will last ten days, and has five races each day. Of the fifty races on the programme, seven are at a half-mile, all of which are for two-year-olds; six are at five furlongs, most of which are for two-year olds; five are at six furlongs; five at seven furlongs; eight at one mile; seven at one and one-sixteenth miles; six at a mile and an eighth; two a mile and a fourth, and one two miles. There will also be two three-quarter mile heat races. Of the fifty races to be run, twenty-five are a mile and over, and two of the others are heat races. This is not a bad showing for Memphis, and while that club does not belong to the Turf Congress, it has, in but few instances, offered purses at a distance, not favored by the rules of the Congress. This is not a bad showing for the Memphis management, and the programme just printed is approved of by every lover of long distance and honest racing.

As the racing season of 1890 draws near we hear much about the coming three-year old champions, and the question of "What about King Thomas?" is frequently asked. Although he was a failure last season, his party think he will be one of the stars of the new racing season that is soon to be inaugurated. It is said that in his work lately he has shown great speed and powers. In America, as a general rule, the high priced yearlings have been a failure. After Luke Blackburn proved himself to be such a great three year old, the Dwyers paid $7,500 for Joe Blackburn, the brother to Luke. Joe Blackburn developed a vicious temper and was never a winner during the two years the Dwyers owned him. He had speed, and the Dwyers retained him until he was four years old, hoping he would run kindly, but he never did. He is now drawing a buggy on Long Island, after being sold for $150. Three years ago the Dwyers paid Capt. Franklin $6,500 for Kern, out of Kathleen, the dam of George Kinney. Kern was afterwards transfered to the Haggin's stable. and has been almost a complete failure, only winning once out of many starts, and then in poor company. Year before last the Dwyers paid $8,200 for Houston, the brother to Hanover, and he has failed to get a winning bracket. Senator Hearst paid $40,000 for King Thomas, and everyone knows what a great disappointment he has been. Upon the other hand we could mention hundreds that were sold for a mere song and afterwards were performers of the first light. Luke Blackburn, Aranza, Glidelia, Kennesaw, Diablo, Proctor Knott, Madstone, Lord Murphy, Reclare and many others of that ilk were lead away from the auctioneer's box for a mere song.

At the meeting of the Tennessee Pacing Horse Breeders' Association at Nashville a few days since, the following rules for registration of standard animals were adopted:—

Rule 1.—Any stallion that has himself a pacing record of 2:30 or better, provided any of his get have either a pacing or trotting record of 2:35 or better, or provided his sire or dam is a registered animal.

Rule 2.—Any mare or gelding that has a pacing record of 2:30 or better.

Rule 3.—Any horse that is the sire of two animals with pacing records of 2:30 or better.

Rule 4.—Any horse that is the sire of one animal with a pacing record of 2:30 or better, provided he has either of the following additional qualifications: 1st—A pacing record himself of 2:35 or better. 2nd—Is the sire of two other animals with pacing records of 2:35 or better. 3rd—Has a sire or dam that is already a standard animal.

Rule 5.—Any mare that has produced an animal with a pacing record of 2:30 or better.

Rule 6.—The progeny of a standard horse when out of a standard mare.

Rule 7.—The female progeny of a standard horse when out of a mare by a standard horse.

Rule 8. The female progeny of a standard horse when out of a mare whose dam is a standard mare.

Rule 9. Any mare that has a pacing record of 2:35 or better, and whose sire or dam is a standard animal.

Rule 10. Any horse that is the sire of two mares, each of which has produced a pacer with a record of 2:30 or better, provided he has either of the following additional qualifications: 1st—a pacing record of 2:30 or better. 2nd—Is the sire of one pacer with a record of 2:30 or better. 3rd—Has a sire or dam that is already a standard animal. 4th—Has two pacers with records of 2:35 or better.

Rule 11. Any horse that is the sire of one pacer and one trotter, or of two trotters with records of 2:30 or better, provided he is of recognized pacing blood.

The rules regarding the registration of non-standard animals are as follows:

Rule 1. Any horse that has sired one pacer with a record of 2:30 or better, or two pacers with records of 2:35 or better.

Rule 2. Any animal that has a pacing record of 2:35 or better.

Rule 3. Any animal that is by a sire or out of a dam of recognized pacing blood.

With the organization of the Tennessee Pacing Horse Breeders' Association, a long and much needed measure was inaugurated. Breeders of Kentucky, California and other States will most likely co-operate with the Tennessee Association, and in a few years the breeders of pacing horses may be able to ascertain, and establish the breeding of some of our best pacing horses whose breeding is now obscure.

KENNESAW.

Fresno Races.

The Fresno Association has since its formation spared neither money nor time in improving its track, beautifying the grounds and generally adding to the attractive appearance of the course, which can now be said to be the equal of any in the State. A grand stand superior to even Sacramento and Stockton provides for the comfort of the spectators, while the track proper has been re-clayed for the last two furlongs, and is in first class order, being one of the few tracks in the State on which any kind of work could be done during the exceptionally wet weather we have just had. The energetic manager, Mr. Baldwin, noticing the gradual but sure increase in the interest taken in running this year decided to hold a spring running meeting, and on my arrival on Tuesday I found the town thronged with racing men, prominent among whom were J. Woolman, the wealthy Montanan, D. Brown, the Petaluman, so well known to old time trotting horsemen, Percy Williams of Grand Island, H. D. Miller, the owner of Daisy D and other well known horses; Porter and Sidney Ashe—by the way, the latter sports his own colors, black and white stripes, white cap; Kelly & Samuels of McGinnis fame; N. S. Straube, the popular owner of Clovis and other promising trotters; B. C. Holly, equally at home among runners or trotters; Tim Lynch, looking lonely, for Jon Jon was at San Jose; J. R. Ross, the owner of the speedy Kitty Van, Oro and others; F. W. Wickersham, D. Brown, Jr., and among a host of other well known faces, last but not least, Dan Dennison, with a horse or two threatened with a great turn of speed.

The opening day had a small but sporting attendance and gave great promise of a good attendance later in the week.
The Judges were President Dr. Lewis Leach and Messrs: Straube and W. Helm. Starter, W. Hughes.

Three races were on the programme for the opening day, the first being noteworthy for the appearance of R. P. Ashe's Judge Terry, the first of Alta's get to face the starter, peculiarly in-bred, too, by Alta, a son of Norfolk and out of Pet, a Norfolk mare; he is a good looking bald faced chestnut colt, with both hind legs white to the hocks, and won like a race horse, though he had nothing to beat, Corrigan's representative being out of a $25 mustang, while Tulare Chief, though speedy, was too small to be in the hunt.

The second race was an exceptionally good one. The betting public seemed to think it a gift for Louise M., but after running well in front to the half-mile pole, she came back to her field, and a tight finish ensued between the three placed horses, Oro on his favorite ground (he always seems to run 7 pounds better here) just winning by a short head from Pliny, who ran like a race-horse, and with a stronger boy up, would probably have won. The last mile was run in 1:44.

The repeat race was really a gift for Cyclone, though the public pinned their faith on Gypsy Girl, who could never live with Cyclone, who won readily in straight heats.

SUMMARY.

Purse $150, of which $15 to second. For District two-year-olds. Half a mile.
Maltese Villa Stable's ch c Judge Terry, Alta—Pet, 118....H. Pierce 1
W. B. Fudge's b c Tulare Chief, Sleepy Dave—Fallen Leaf. L. Jones 2
J. H. Walker's b c Guilderoy, Ed Corrigan—unknown.....F. Barton 3
Time, 0:51.

There was very little betting, at $20 Judge Terry to $6 the field, and after a short delay a start was effected, Judge Terry being quickest on his legs, showed in front, but was taken back, and Tulare Chief cut out the pace to the head of the stretch, when Judge Terry closed up and won in a big gallop by five lengths. Guilderoy was never in the hunt.

SUMMARY.

Purse $250, of which $25 to second. One mile and a furlong.
J. R. Ross' b g Oro, 4, Norfolk—Golden Gate, 124.............Stewart 1
Kelly & Samuel's b g Pliny, 3, Flood—Precious, 106...... ....Ward 2
Dennison Bros.' b h Hotspur, 4, Joe Daniels—Sister to Jim Douglass, 120................................ ......Bustillos 3
Time, 1:57.

Louisa M., 115, Corona, 113, Willoughby, 99, Jack Brady, 124, also ran.

Louisa M. sold a big favorite at $20 to $6 for the field, and $5 each for Pliny and Hotspur. A start was readily effected, and Louise M. taking the rails, led Hotspur a neck past the stand, the rest close up, and increasing her lead, was four open lengths to the good at the quarter, with Corono third, close up to Hotspur; Oro and Pliny showing in front of the rear division. Up the backstretch Louisa came back to her field, and Hotspur, Pliny and Oro were at her heels round the turn, and the mare dying away, the trio ran a hard, punishing race home, Oro winning by a head from Pliny, who was a long neck in front of Hotspur; Louisa M. was three lengths back, and then came Brady, Corona and Willoughby last all the way.

SUMMARY.

Purse $150, of which $15 to second. Quarter mile and repeat.
A. D. Hitchcock's ch g Cyclone, a, Ironclad—Unknown, 118 ....Stewart 1 1
F. Work's b h Springwater, a, Hubbard—by Lommax, 118 ....Moore 2 2
E. Fitzgerald's ch m Gypsy Girl, 109................Hennessy 3 3
Time, 0:24½, 0:23½.

The talent made Gypsy Girl favorite at $20 to $20 for the other two. After several breakaways all three got well away and kept together to the drawgate, when, with Hennessy and Moore riding hard, Cyclone showed in front, winning cleverly by a neck.

Very few pools were sold after the first heat at $20 for Cyclone to $8 for the field.

The second heat was a repetition of the first except that Cyclone won easier, while Springwater beat Gypsy after a whipping finish by half a length for the place.

WENESDAY.

The second day opened out well, but owning probably to the wind which was rather troublesome, very few ladies graced the grand stand by their presence. The three races were run through in good style, Mr. Hughes, the starter, being very happy in his effort. In the first race, a five furlong sprint, Kitty Van was made favorite, only to be displaced by Jubilee who went to the post first choice. First thoughts would have been best, for Kitty Van won readily, though Jubilee might probably have made a closer race, as he got well away and ran head and head with the mare to the turn, when he was taken back and turned into the stretch last, finished strongly, was only beaten by half a length.

The mile and repeat was a gift for Daisy D who outclassed her two opponents and won easily in straight heats. The last race a half mile dash was a gift for Sunday, who won as he pleased.

Purse $200, for all ages, five furlongs.
J. R. Ross' b m Kitty Van, 4, Vanderbilt—April Fool, 118 lbs.. ....Hennessey 1
Golden Gate Stable's b g Jubilee, 4, Kyrle Daly—Ivy, 120 lbs..Hazlett 2
Orange Grove Stable's ch g Adam, a, Shiloh—Mollie Adams, 123 lbs ....Stewart 3
Time, 1:02½.

Painkiller 123, ran also.

After varying a good bit Jubilee settled down a pronounced favorite at $20 to Kitty Van $16, and the field $8.

After a few breakaways the flag fell with Kitty Van and Jubilee a length in front and both ran together to the turn, when Jubilee dropped back last. Adam taking second place two lengths behind the leader and one in front of Painkiller. When fairly in the stretch Jubilee passed Painkiller and went in pursuit of the leaders, and finishing strongly beat Adam a length for second place, only half a length behind Kitty Van who won cleverly. Time, 1:02½.

SUMMARY.

Purse $250, for all ages. One mile and repeat.
Miller & Owen's b m Daisy D., a, Wheatley—Black Maria, 114, ...Hennessy 1 1
Orange Grove Stable's b h Jack Brady, a, Wildidle—Sour Grapes, 119........................ .... Stewart 3 2
Golden Gate Stable's blk g Black Pilot, Echo—Madge Duke, 119 ....Hazlett 2 3
Time, 1:45½, 1:46½.

Very few pools were sold at $25 Daisy D. to $5 each Pilot and Brady. A start was soon effected, Daisy cutting out the pace, led Brady a length round the turn and past the half, with Pilot five lengths back. Pilot closed up a little round the turn, and passed Brady in the straight, hunting Daisy home, the mare winning easily by a length. No pools could be sold, and after a short delay, the flag fell. Brady jumped off in front, and, with the mare hard held, led a length round the first turn. Daisy closed up on the backstretch, and took the lead at the half, and Pilot, making up a good deal of ground, was level with Brady at the head of the stretch, with the favorite two open lengths in front, running easy; Daisy D. won by a length without being stretched, Brady beating Pilot a good half length for the place after a tight finish.

SUMMARY.

Purse $150, for all ages. Five furlongs.
T. F. Lynch's b g Sunday, a, Sundance—Norma, 123.... ......Davis 1
E. Fitzgerald's b h Clauderoy, 4, imp. Kelpie—Little John's dam, 118 ....Hennessy 2
J. J. Abbott's b g Abbott's colt, 3, Billie Lee—Flight, 107...O'Hearn 3
Time, 0:49½.

Birnie, 75 lbs., ran also.

A few pools were sold at $25 Sunday to $6 to the field, then, with Sunday barred, Clauderoy and Abbott's Colt sold for $10 each, while Birnie brought $6.

A good deal of time was consumed getting the quartette away, and when the flag dropped, Sunday and Clauderoy had two lengths the best of it and ran away from the other two, Sunday winning as he pleased by an open length. Birnie who started very slow chased up rapidly in the stretch, finishing close up to Abbott's colt, who was five lengths behind the leaders.

The Palo Alto Sales.

The following are the telegraphed results of the Palo Alto sales in New York:

Bay filly by Ansel, dam Addie, $900; bought by T. J. Nolan of New York.

Chestnut filly by Piedmont, dam Adele, $650; bought by Miller & Sibley of Franklin, Pa.

Bay mare by Electioneer, dam Alamêda Maid, $900; bought by Robert Steele of Philadelphia.

Bay colt by Alfred, dam Amlet, $190; bought by M. Flynn of Plainfield, N. J.

Bay filly by Whips, dam Amrah, $410; bought by Frank Clark of New Haven.

Bay filly by Electioneer, dam Aragon, $2800; bought by Jacob Rupert of New York.

Chestnut filly by Will Crocker, dam Ashland, $250, bought by A. R. Miller of Ohio.

Bay filly by Alfred, dam Barnes, $330; bought by T. J. Langford of Milton, Mass.

Brown filly by Electioneer, dam Barbara Maid, $2600; bought by Malcolm Forbes of Boston, Mass.

Bay filly by Alfred, dam Belle, $350; bought by Robert Steele of Philadelphia.

Bay filly by Ione, dam Belle, $300; bought by W. H. Lines of Rochester, N. Y.

Chestnut filly by Benton Frolic, dam Blooming, $222; bought by John Crane of Yonkers, N. Y.

Bay colt by Whips, dam Camola, $260; bought by Powell Bros. of Pennsylvania.

Bay colt by Whips, dam Cassie, $360; bought by W. E. Pruden of Newark, N. J.

Brown filly by Electioneer, dam Cecilia, $1700; bought by S. A. Brown & Co., of Kalamazoo, Mich.

Brown filly by Electioneer, dam Cecilia, $2350; bought by S. A. Brown & Co.

Bay colt by Eectioneer, dam Cecil, $5750; bought by Jacob Rupert of New York.

Bay filly by Electioneer, dam Cora, $3000; bought by H. S. Henry of Norristown, Penn.

Bay filly by Electioneer, dam Cora, $2500; bought by S. A. Brown & Co.

Bay colt by Alfred, dam Daisy C, $350; bought by Lawson Valentine of New York.

Bay filly by Nephew, dam Diana, $195; bought by W. J. Wheeler of Maine.

Bay filly by Electioneer, dam Dora, $2550; bought by S. A. Brown & Co.

Bay colt by Clay, dam Edith Carr, 2 years old, $1000; bought by L. J. Fitzgerald, Portland, N. Y.

Black filly by Electioneer, dam Ella, 4 years old, $3800; bought by J. Malcom Forbes.

Black colt, 2 years old, by Clay, dam Elite, $4500; bought by Russell & Hepburn of New York.

Chestnut colt, 2 years old, by Piedmont, dam Elsie, $1450; bought by J. J. Crawford of Massachusetts.

Chestnut filly, 2 years old, by Whips, dam Euticia, $300; bought by R. L. Pettebone of Wyoming, Pa.

Bay filly, 3 years old, by Clay, dam Fidelia, $850; bought by Robert Steele of Philadelphia.

Bay filly, 5 years old, by Clay, dam Florida, $320; bought by Alexander Brown of New York.

Bay filly, 2 years old, by Whips, dam Florida, $300; bought by C. F. Sheehan of Springfield, Mass.

Bay colt, 3 years old, by Piedmont, dam Flower Girl, $1135; bought by Smith, Powell & Lamb of Syracuse.

Bay colt, 2 years old, by Piedmont, dam Flower Girl, $2800; bought by Jacob Rupert.

Bay colt, 2 years old, by Electioneer, dam Frolic, $4100; bought by Charles Keiner of New York.

Chestnut mare, 5 years old, by Piedmont, dam Gazelle, $1300; bought by Robert Ele of Philadelphia.

Bay filly 3 years old, by Benton dam Frolic, $810; bought by John R. Richardson of New York.

Bay mare 5 years old, by General Benton, Dam Hattie C, $1000; bought by B. M. Babcock of Binghamton, N. Y.

Bay mare 6 years old, by Eros, dam Ida, $700; bought by Robert Steele.

Chestnut colt 3 years old, by Piedmont dam Irene, $1000; bought by Mr. Morgan of Long Island;

Bay filly by Electioneer dam Isma, 3 years old, $2250; bought by B. M. Babcock of Binghamton.

Bay filly by Electioneer dam Ivy, 2 years old, $1250; bought by R. J. Morehead of North Easton, Penn.

Isonomy, chestnut colt, 4 years old, by Piedmont, dam Ivy, $950; bought by S. H. Baird of Connecticut.

Gray filly by Will Crocker, dam Julia, 4 years old, $500; bought by E. D. Morgan.

Bay filly by Whips, dam Lady Rhodes, $420; bought by E. D. Keyes of Rutland, Vt.

Bay filly by Will Crocker, dam Lillian, $400; bought by G. Johnson, New York.

Chestnut colt by Piedmont, dam Lily, 2 years old, $780; bought by S. S. Vandruff; New York.

Brown filly by Electioneer, dam Lily B, 2 years old, $500; bought by Robert Steele of Philadelphia.

Bay colt by Electioneer, dam Lina K, 3 years old, $2550; bought by F. C. Fowler of Connecticut.

Lorna, bay colt by Electioneer, dam Lizzie, three years old, $3200; bought by F. C. Fowler.

Bay colt by Electioneer, dam Lizzie, 2 years old, $2000; bought by H. Roe of Meadville, Va.

Bay filly by Eros, dam Lizzie, 4 years old, $1100; bought by Edward Appel of Rochester, New York.

Chestnut filly by Piedmont, dam Lizzie H, 4 years old, $1050; bought by Robert Steele of Philadelphia.

Bay filly by Electioneer, dam Lora, 2 years old, $4000; bought by R. J. Moorehouse of Pennsylvania.

Monteith, bay stallion by Electioneer, dam Mamie C, 5 years old, $4600; bought by Robert Steele.

Bay colt by Electioneer, dam Maria, 4 years old, $4500; bought by R. Hoe.

Bay colt by Electioneer, dam Maria, 3 years old, $3100; bought by R. Hoe.

Bay colt by Whips, dam Martha by Mohawk Chief, 2 years old, $1200; bought by A. J. Welch of Hartford.

Bay colt by Eros, dam Marti, 2 years old, $620; bought by Thomas Richardson of New York.

Bay filly by Electioneer, dam May, 2 years old, $2800; bought by S. A. Brown & Co. of Kalamazoo.

Bay filly by Ione, dam Mayflower Hawk, 4 years old, $700; bought by F. B. Tracy of Brooklyn, N. Y.

Bay colt by Whips, dam Melissa, 2 years old, $725; bought by Russell & Hepburn of New York.

Brown filly by Ione, dam Melissa, 3 years old, $310; bought by G. S. Ferguson of Lynn, Mass.

Brown filly by Alfred, dam Minnie, 3 years old, $520; bought by A. Pardee of Philadelphia.

Bay filly by Electioneer, dam Minx, 5 years old, $4,500; bought by B. M. Babcock of Binghampton, N. Y.

Brown filly by Electioneer, dam Minx, 2 years old, $2,700; bought by William Marks of Philadelphia

Bay filly by Clay, dam Monte Belle, 3 years old, $450; bought by C. M. Waterbury of New York.

Chestnut filly by Will Crocker, dam Mozelle, 4 years old, $320; bought by R. Hoe of New York.

Bay colt by Whips, dam Nellie Walker, 2 years old, $300; bought by James Collins of New York.

Nemo, brown stallion by Clay, dam Nettie Benton, 6 years old, bought by R. Crippen of Scranton, Pa.

Nettie B., brown filly by Ansel, dam Nettie Benton, 3 years old, $1,650; bought by C. P. Huntington.

Bay mare by Eros, dam Nettie Walker, 5 years old, $3,250; bought by R. Hoe of New York.

Bay filly by Ione, dam Nettie Walker, 4 years old, $600; bought by W. A. Hutchinson or Long Island.

Brown mare by Bentonian, dam Patti, 5 years old $425; bought by Jabez Tarr of New York.

Bay filly by Electioneer, dam Patti, 5 years old, $2600; bought by J. W. Daly, Mount Kisko, N. Y.

Bay stallion by Electioneer, dam Pearl, 5 years old $3000; bought by A. J. Welch of Hartford.

Bay filly by Piedmont, dam Pearl, 4 years old, $500; bought by F. H. Wickwire of Cortland, N. Y.

Bay filly by Piedmont, dam Rachel by Electioneer; 2 years old, $1600; bought by Jacob Rupert, New York.

Bay filly by Electioneer, dam Rebecca, 2 years old, $525; bought by Miller & Sibley, of Franklin, Pa.

Rusenoll: bay filly by Electioneer, dam Rebecca, 2 years old, $1585; bought by G. H. Hicks of Boston.

Bay filly by Electioneer, dam Sarah 4 years old, $3000; bought by C. Eastman of New York.

Bay colt by Electioneer dam Sarah 2 years old $2000; bought by Miller & Sibley.

Bay mare by Piedmont, dam Sister of Irene 5 years old $750; bought by L. J. Fitzgerald of New York.

Brown colt by Whips, dam Sister of Irene, 2 years old, $398; bought by John Moore Portland Me.

Bay filly by Benton Frolic, dam Sultana, 4 years old $600; bought by Robinson of New York.

Bay filly by Alfred, dam Sultana, 2 years old $500 bought by Charles Robinson.

Bay filly by General Benton, dam Urania 4 years old; bought by Charles Robinson.

Brown colt by Electioneer dam Victoria, 3 years old $1500; bought by Miller & Sibley.

Bay filly by Piedmont dam Violet, 2 years old, $3300; bought by T. C. Eastman, New York.

Bay mare by General Benton dam Wilfred, 7 years old, $500; bought by Charles Robinson.

Bay filly by Ione dam Wildred, 4 years old, $500; bought by H. M. Cochran, New York.

Bay colt by Alfred, dam Wilmina, 2 years old, $530; bought by C. C. Wilbur of Smyrna, N. Y.

Bay filly by Electioneer dam Claribel, 4 years old, $3500; bought by Miller & Sibley.

Laws of Heredity.

Following are the six leading laws of heredity which we reprint by request:—

1. That from the male parent is mainly derived the external structure, configuration and outward characteristics, also the locomotive system of development.

2. From the female parent is derived the internal structure, the vital organs, and, in a much greater proportion than from the male, the constitution, temper and habits, in which endurance and bottom are included.

3. That the purer the race of the parent, the more certainty there is of its transmitting its qualities to the offspring; say if two animals are mated, if one is of purer descent than the other, he or she will exercise the influence in stamping the character of the progeny, particularly if the greater purity is on the side of the male.

4. That apart from certain disturbing influences or causes, the male, if of pure race and descended from a stock of uniform color, stamps the color of the offspring.

5. That the influence of the first male is not infrequently protracted beyond the birth of the offspring of which he is the parent and his mark is left upon subsequent progeny.

6. That the transmission of diseases of the vital organs is more certain if on the side of the female, and diseases of the joints if on the side of the male parent.

Saratoga Association Entries.

Nominations for Stakes Closed March 1st for Meetings of 1890.

FLASH STAKES FOR TWO YEAR-OLDS. HALF A MILE.

Beverwyck Stable's ch c Brocker; Empire Stable's ch f Landscape; Salamander Stable's b f Gold Step; Hough Brother's b c Leveller; Excelsior Stable's b c Sir David; A. C. Sohne & Co.'s blk c by Vanderbilt, ch c by Hyder Ali, ch c Fairview, ch g Forfeit; New York Stable's ch f Mauve, ch g Plato; Labold Brothers' br c Sir Martin, br c Monterey; Clover Stable's br f Marguerite; M. Hogan's br c F. D. Ward, ch f Maggie Ward; Wm. Hendries' ch f Orneo; Dwyer Brothers' b c Black, b c Baychester; Scoggan Brothers' b f Lady Washington, b c National; Oden Bowie's br c Mirthwood; Wm. Jenning's ch c Kilrue; Byron McClelland's ch f Sallie Moulelland; George H. Kernaghan's br f Dodo; Poll Stable's b c by imp Mr. Pickwick; W. H. Laudeman's ch c Palestine; George Hearst's ch f Babicora, b f by Mr. Pickwick; E. Sheppard's b f Alarming; Kentucky Stable's b c Ganges, b f Mary McGowan; Ed Brown's ch c Forerunner, b c King Solomon, ch f Falerna; H. Simon's b c Lee S; Jas. B. Clay's blk f Mon Droit; Joseph E. Seagram's blk c by Onondaga, b c by Bend'Or; J. G. Greener's ch f Eugenie; J. K. Megibben & Co.'s gr c Hippolite, ch c McKinley, b c Avalon, ch c Vallera; Maltese Villa Stock Farm's br c King Alta, br f Romeetta; Santa Anita Stable's b f La Cienega, b c Enseunda, ch c El Carmen, ch f Santa Ana, b f Esperanza, R. E. Campbell's b f Saxonette.

CALIFORNIA STAKES, ALL AGES, ONE MILE.

Beverwyck Stable's b h Cassius, 4 yrs; Empire Stables's br c Maastone, 4 yrs; Hough Bros.'s b c Drizzle, 3 yrs; A. C. Sohne & Co's b g Lintram, 4 yrs; Wm. Lovell's ch m Lady Pulsifer, 4 yrs; New York Stable's b c Austerlitz, 3 yrs; Labold Bros.' br m Retrieve, 4 yrs; Labold Bros.' ch c Isaac Lewis, 3 yrs; Labold Bros.' br c Experience, 3 yrs; Clover Stable's b h Hindoocraft, 4 yrs; Keystone Stable's b f Insight, 3 yr; Keystone Stable's b c Mr. Pelham, 3 yrs; A. J. Scott's b b Gunshot, 4 yrs; A. J. Scott's b c Blue Spring, 3 yrs.; A. J. Scott's br g Gun Rod, 4 yrs; J. H. McCormick's b m Belinda, 5 yrs; Dwyer Bros.' ch h Hanover, 6 yrs; Dwyer Bros.' br h Kingston, 6 yrs; b c Longstreet, 4 yrs; Rensselaer Stable's b f Barcarola, 4 yrs; A. Kraemer (Manager) br c Grammercy, 3 yrs; Scoggan Bros.' b c Ja Ja, 3 yrs; Scoggan Bros.' ch c Proctor Knott, 4 yrs; T. H. Stevens' ch f Mora, 3 yrs; Oden Bowie's ch m Belle D'Or, 5 yrs; J. W. Guest's b c Heron, 4 yrs; George Hearst's b c Sir Launcelot, 2 yrs; George Hearst's bl m Gorgo, 5 yrs; George Hearst's ch c Philander, 4 yrs; George Hearst's b c Ballarat, 3 yrs; Blenheim Stable's b m Annie Burge, 4 yrs; R. T. Holloway's ch c Bannerette, 4 yrs; James Murphy's b f Estelle, 3 yrs; Joseph E. Seagram's ch c, 3 yrs; John G. Greene's ch c Culprit, 4 yrs; Henry Boudy's ch g Ben Harrison, 4 yrs; H. S. Durham's ch f Daisy F, 3 yrs; H. P. Headley & Co's ch f Princess Bowling, 4 yrs; J. C. Tyman & Co's ch c Sportsman, 4 yrs; J. K. Megibben & Co's ch c Contender, 3 yrs; J. K. Megibben's br c Abalene, 3 yrs; Santa Anita Stable's ch m Los Angeles, 5 yrs; Santa Anita Stable's b c Santiago, 3 yrs; Santa Anita Stable's ch f Sinaloa, 3 yrs; Santa Anita Stable's b h Emperor of Norfolk.

ADIRONDACK HANDICAP, ONE MILE AND A FURLONG.

Beverwyck Stable's b m Brown Princess, 4 yrs; Hough Bros.' b c Drizzle, 3 yrs; Excelsior Stable's b m Gipsey Queen, 4 yrs; Excelsior Stable's ch g Sam D., 4 yrs; A. C. Shue & Co's b g Lintram, 4 yrs; New York Stable's b c Australitz, 3 yrs; Keystone Stable's b g Ten Booker, aged; Keystone Stable's b c Mr. Pelham, 3 yrs; Wm. Hendrie's b m Banjo, 5 yrs; J. H. McCormick's b m Belinda, 5 years; A. Kraemer (manager) br c Grammercy, 3 yrs; Scoggan Bros.' b f Dollikins, 3 yrs; Scoggan Bros' ch c Ban Chief, 3 years; T. H. Steven's b m Waxy, 6 yrs; M. Cole's ch f Queen of Trumps, 4 years; W. P. Burch's br h Prather, 5 years; Poll Stable's b c Pelham, 4 yrs; George Hearst's ch c Philander, 4 yrs; George Hearst's ch c Rhono, 4 yrs; George Hearst's br f Miss Bell, 3 yrs; Ed Brown's b f Charming, 3 yrs; Ed Brown's b f Ruperta, 3 yrs; Joseph E. Seagram's ch c, 3 yrs; H. B. Durham's ch f Daisy F, 3 yrs; H. P. Headley & Co's ch f Princess Bowling, 4 yrs; J. C. Lyman & Co's ch c Prince Fonso, 3 yrs; Santa Anita Stable's b m Los Angeles, 5 yrs; Santa Anita Stable's b c Clio, 3 yrs; Santa Anita Stable's b c Santiago, 3 yrs.

AMERICAN HOTEL STAKES, FOR TWO-YEAR-OLDS—ONE MILE.

Beverwyck Stable's ch f Cau Cau; Empire Stable's ch c Tormentor; T. H. Lore's b g Cortland; Wm. Lovell's b f Marie Lovell; New York Stable's b c Successor; New York Stable's b c Australitz; Labold Bros.' b f Ocypete; Labold Bros.' ch c Isaac Lewis; Labold Bros.' br c Experience; Keystone Stable's b f Insight; Keystone Stable's b c Mr. Pelham; A. J. Scott's b c Blue Spring; A. J. Scott's b g Gun Wad; Wm. Hendrie's br c Ravenhill; Dwyer Bros.' b c Flatbush; Dwyer Bros.' b c Sir John; A. Kraemer (manager) br c Grammercy; Scoggan Bros.' br c Hy-Dy; Scoggan Bros.'s ch c Goodbye; Scoggan Bros.' b c Ja-Ja; T. H. Stevens' ch f Mora; Oden Browie's b c Lordlike; Oden Bros.' b f Alarm Bell; Wm. Jennings' b g Mohican; Strauss & Lyne's ch f Origana; Gorman & Co.'s gr c Fellowship; W. P. Burch's b f Cornelia; R. T. Holloway's ch g Outright; Samuel Bryant's b c Uncle Bob; Samuel Bryant's ch f Charlotte Cushman; Ed Brown's b f Ruperta; Ed Brown's b f Charming; Ed Brown's b f Pearl Set; Joseph Seagram's ch c by Stonehenge; J. G. Greener's ch c Sam Doxey; H. B. Durham's ch f Daisy F.; J. C. Lyman & Co.'s ch c Prince Fonso; J. B. Megibben & Co.'s br c Abaline; J. K. Megibben & Co.'s ch c Contenda; Santa Anita Stable's b c Olio; Santa Anita Stable's ch c Amigo; Santa Anita Stable's ch f Sinaloa.

SPINAWAY STAKES, FILLIES, TWO YEARS. FIVE FURLONGS.

L. & J. E. Kittson's ch f Flozette; Beverwyck Stable's b f Lotty, Empire Stable's ch f Landscape; Salamander Stable's b f Gold Step; P. Mack's b f Mary Conroy; Hough Brothers' ch f Lithe, b f Queer Girl; A. C. Sohne & Co.'s ch f Miss Harris; New York Stable's ch f Mauve, ch f Mary Roberts; M. Hogan's ch f Maggie Ward; Wm. Hendrie's ch f Omeo, ch f Ayrshire; J. H. McCormick's b f Early Blossom; Dwyer Brothers' b or br f by Hindoo, blk or br f by Hindoo; Scoggan Bros.' b f Lady Washington, ch f Apex; Stevens & Moore's b f Fauna; Wm. Jennings' br f Marystone; Hurricanna Stock Farm's b f Ethelair, b f Elvira; Byron McClelland's ch f Sallie McClelland, br f by Billet; Geo H. Kernaghan's br f Dodo, b f by Duke of Montrose; Poll Stable's b f by Luke Blackburn, b f by Luke Blackburn; W. H. Laudeman's ch f Prettiwit; George Hearst's b f Fire Work, ch f Babicora, b f by Mr. Pickwick; E. Sheppard's b f Alarming; Samuel Bryant's ch f Nyola, b f Nettie Beatrice; Kentucky Stable's b f Mary McGowan, b f St. Bridget; Ed Brown's ch f Falerna; Jas. B. Clay's blk f Mon Droit; Joseph E. Seagram's b f by Stratford; John G. Greener's ch f Eugenie; J. K. Megibben & Co's ch f Flower Dellie, ch f Actress, ch f Birdella; Maltese Villa Stock Farm's br f Romeetta; Santa Anita Stable's b f Santa Ana, b f Esperanza, b f La Cienega, b f Cleopatra; R. E. Campbell's b f Saxonette.

EXCELSIOR STAKES, ALL AGES. ONE MILE AND A QUARTER.

Beverwyck Stable's b h Cassius, 4 yrs; James P. Dawes' b f Red Fellow, 4 yrs; P. Mack's ch c Penn P; Hough Bros.' b g Come-to-Taw, 4 yrs; New York Stable's b c Successor, 3 yrs; Labold Bros.' b h Montrose, 6 yrs, b h Retrieve, 4 yrs; Clover Stable's b h Hindoocraft, 4 yrs; Keystone Stable's b f Ten Booker, aged, b c Mr. Pelham, 3 yrs; J. H. McCormick's b m Belinda; Dwyer Brothers' ch h Hanover, 6 yrs, br h Kingston, 6 yrs, b c Longstreet, 4 yrs; Rensselaer Stable's b c Daniel formerly Daredevil, 4 yrs; A. Kraemer, Manager's br c Grammercy, 3 yrs; Scoggan Bros.' b c Ja-Ja, 3 yrs, ch c Ban Chief, 3 yrs; J. W. Guest's b c Heron, 4 yrs; R. T. Holloway's ch c Teuton, 4 yrs; Joseph E. Seagram's ch h Marauder, 5 yrs, ch c by Stonehenge, 3 yrs; H. Boudy's ch g Ben Harrison, 4 yrs; J. K. Megibben & Co.'s ch c Sportsman, 4 yrs, br c Eberlee, 3 yrs, br c W. G. Morris, 3 yrs; Santa Anita Stable's ch c Honduras, 3 yrs, ch f Sinaloa, 3 yrs, ch m Los Angeles, 5 yrs, b h Emperor of Norfolk.

VIRGINIA STAKES, TWO-YEAR-OLDS—FIVE FURLONGS.

Beverwyck Stable's ch c Brocker; Empire Stable's ch f Landscape; Salamander Stable's b f Gold Step; Excelsior Stable's br g by Bramble; Excelsior Stable's b c Sir David; Alesohme & Co.'s ch c Fairview; Alesohme & Co.'s ch f Miss Harris; New York Stable's ch g Plato; New York Stable's ch f Mauve; Labold Bros.' br c Sir Martin; Labold Bros.' b c Monterey; M. Hogan's br c S. D. Ward; M. Hogan's ch f Maggie Ward; Wm Hendrie's b c Chippewa; Wm. Hendrie's br g Calgary; Dwyer Bros.' b c Blacklock; Dwyer Bros.' b c Baychester; Scoggan Bros.' b g R. F. D.; Scoggan Bros.'s b g National; Basil Guest's ch c Carroll; Oden Brown's br c Mirthwood; Oden Brown's blk c Blackwood; Hurricanna Stock Farm's b f Ethelair; Hurricanna Stock Farm's b f Elvira; Geo. H. Kernaghan's br f Dodo; S. P. Knut's b c Tom Alma; W. P. Burch's ch c Simon Pure; C. Cornehlsen's b f Hydra; C. Cornehlsen's b f Coriolanus; Poll Stable's b c by imp. Mr Pickwick; W. H. Laudeman's ch c Palestine; James Murphy's br c Tarquin; Kentucky Stable's b c Ganges; Kentucky Stable's b f Mary McGowan; Ed Brown's ch c McCabe; Ed Brown's ch c Forerunner; Ed Brown's b c King Solomon; H. Simons' b c Lee S.; Joseph E. Seagram's blk c by Onondaga; Joseph E. Seagram's b c by Bend'Or; J. G. Greener's b c The Wandering Jew; J. K. Megibben & Co.'s ch f Flower Dellie; J. K. Megibben & Co.'s ch f Actress, J. K. Megibben & Co.'s b c Avalon; Maltese Villa Stock Farm's br c King Alta; Santa Anita Stable's b f Ogarita; Santa Anita Stable's b f La Cienega; Santa Anita Stable's ch c Silverado; Santa Anita Stable's b f Santa Ana.

KEARNEY STAKES—HANDICAP—1¼ MILES.

Beverwyck Stable's b h Cassius, 4 yrs.; James P. Dawes' b h Red Fellow, 4 yrs.; Empire Stable's ch c Tormentor, 3 yrs.; Excelsior Stable's ch g Sam D., 4yrs.; New York Stable's b c Successor, 3yrs.; Labold Bros.' b h Montrose, 6yrs.; Labold Bros.' b m Retrieve, 4yrs.; Clover Stable's b h Hindoocraft, 4yrs.; Keystone Stable's b g Ten Broker, aged; Keystone Stable's b c Mr. Pelham, 3yrs.; Wm. Hendrie's b m Pee Weep, 5yrs.; Rensselaer Stable's b c Daniel (formerly Daredevil), 4yrs; A. Kraemer (manager) br c Grammercy, 3yrs.; Scoggan Bros.' b f Dollikins, 3yrs; T. H. Stevens' b m Wary, 6yrs.; W. P. Burch's br h Prather, 5yrs.; Joseph E. Seagram's ch h Marauder, 5yrs; Maltese Villa Stock Farm's b c Flood Tide, 4yrs; Santa Anita Stable's ch m Los Angeles, 5yrs.; Santa Anita Stable's b h Emperor of Norfolk, 5yrs.

FOSTER MEMORIAL STAKES, THREE-YEAR-OLDS—ONE MILE AND HALF A FURLONG.

Beverwyck Stables ch f Cau Cau; Empire Stable's ch c Tormentor; H. Warnke & Son's br f Reclare; New York Stable's b c Australitz; Labold Bros.' ch c Isaac Lewis; Labold Bros.' b f Ocypete; Labold Bros.' br c Experience; Keystone Stable's b c Mr. Pelham; Keystone Stable's b f Insight; A. J. Scott's b g Gun Wad; A. J. Scott's b c Blue Spring; Wm. Hendrie's br c Ravenhill; Dwyer Bros.' b c Flatbush; Dwyer Bros.' b c Sir John; A. Kraemer (manager) br c Grammercy; Scoggan Bros.' ch c Ban Chief; Scoggan Bros.'s ch f English Lady; Oden Bowie's ch c Tennesseean; Wm. Jennings' b g Mohican; Gorman & Co.'s gr c Fellowship; W. P. Burch's b f Cornelia; E. Cornehlsen's ch c Onward; George Hearst's b c Sir Launcelot; George Hearst's b c Ballarat; George Hearst's b c Anaconda; George Hearst's b f Gloaming; George Hearst's b c King Thomas; Samuel Bryant's b c Uncle Bob; Samuel Bryant's ch f Charlotte Cushman; Ed Brown's b f Ruperta; Ed Brown's b f Charming; Ed Brown's b f Pearl Set; H. Simons' b f Annie Sharpe; Joseph E. Seagram's ch c by Stonehenge; John G. Greener's ch c Sam Doxey; H. B. Durham's ch f Daisy F.; J. C. Lyman & Co.'s ch c Prince Fonso; T. J. Megibben & Co.'s br c Abalene; T. J. Megibben & Co.'s c Contender; T. J. Megibben & Co.'s c Avondale; Santa Anita Stables' b c Santiago; Santa Anita Stable's ch f Sinaloa; Santa Anita Stable's ch c Amigo.

MERCHANTS' STAKES, ALL AGES. ONE MILE AND FIVE FURLONGS.

Beverwyck Stable's b m Lavinnia Belle, 5 yrs; Western Union Stable's b h Dunboyne; P. Mack's ch c Penn P., 3 yrs; New York Stable's b c Successor, 3 yrs; Labold Brothers b h Montrose, 6 yrs; Clover Stable's b h Hindocraft, 4 yrs; Keystone Stable's b g Ten Broker, aged; Keystone Stable's b c Mr. Pelham, 3 yrs; Wm. Hendrie's b m Pee Weep 5 yrs; A. C. Sohne & Co's b g Lintram, 4 yrs; Dwyer Bros' br h Kingston, 6 yrs; Dwyer Bros' b c Longstreet, 4 yrs.; Rensselaer Stable's b h Daniel, (formerly Dare Devil) 4 yrs; A. Kraemer (Manager) br c Grammercy, 3 yrs; Scoggan Bros' b c Ja Ja, 3 yrs; Scoggan Bros' b f Dollikins, 3 yrs; J. W. Guest's b c Heron, 4 yrs; George Hearst's b c Tournament, 3 yrs; George Hearst's b c King Thomas, 3 yrs; George Hearst's ch c Rhone, 4 yrs; George Hearst's bl m Gorgo, 5 yrs; George Hearst's b c Anaconda, 3 yrs; George Hearst's ch c Philander, 4 yrs; R. T. Holloway's ch f Dilemma, 3 yrs; Joseph E. Seagram's ch c Marauder, 5 yrs; J. H. Megibben & Co's ch g Avondale, 3 yrs; J. H. Megibben & Co's br c W. G. Morris, 3 yrs; J. H. Megibben & Co's br c Eberlee, 3 yrs; Maltese Villa Stock Farm's b c Floodtide, 4 yrs; Santa Anita Stable's b c Santiago, 3 yrs; Santa Anita Stables ch f Sinaloa, 3 yrs; Sante Anita Stable's ch m Los Angeles, 5 yrs.

UNITED STATES HOTEL STAKES, THREE YEARS OLD, ONE AND A HALF MILES.

Empire Stable's ch c Tormentor; Empire Stable's b c Favorite; P. Mack's ch c Penn P; New York Stable's b c Successor; Labold Bros' br c Experience; Labold Bros' ch c Isaac Lewis; Keystone Stable's b c Mr. Pelham; Keystone Stable's b f Insight; Madison Stable's b c Devotee, Dwyer Bros' b c Flatbush; Dwyer Bros b c Sir Johny; A. Kraemer's (manager) br c Grammercy; Scoggan Bros' ch c Ban Chief; T. H. Steven's ch f Mora; Gorman & Co's gr c Fellowship; George Walbaum's ch c Rancocas; P. M. West & Co's ch f Flyaway; P. M. West & Co's b c Grayson; Beverwyck Stable's ch f Can Can; Ed Brown's b c Prodigal Son, Joseph E. Seagram's ch c by Stonehenge; John G. Greener's ch c Sam Doxey; J. H. Megibben & Co's ch g Avondale; J. H Megibben & Co's br c W. G. Morris; J. H. Megibben & Co's br c Eberlee; Santa Anita Stables' b c Clio; Santa Anita Stable's ch c Honduras; Santa Anita Stable's ch f Sinaloa.

HOTEL BALMORAL STAKES, HANDICAP. ONE AND ONE-HALF MILE.

Beverwyck Stable's b m Lavinia Belle, 5 yrs; Hough Bros.' b c Drizzle, 3 yrs; Excelsior Stable's ch g Sam D, 4 yrs; New York Stable's b c Successor, 3 yrs; Labold Bros.' br c Experience, 3 yrs, ch c Isaac Lewis, 3 yrs, b h Montrose, 6 yrs; Clover Stable's b h Hindoocraft, 4 yrs, b f Bertelle, 3 yrs; Keystone Stable's b g Ten Booker, aged, b c Mr. Pelham, 3 yrs; Wm. Hendrie's ch h Gladiator, 6 yrs, b m Pee Weep, 5 yrs; O. O. West, Jr.'s b f Brandolette, 4 yrs; A. Kraemer's (Manager) br c Grammercy, 3 yrs; Scoggan Bros.' ch f English Lady, 3 yrs, b f Dollikins, 3 yrs, b c Ja Ja, 3 yrs; M. Cole's ch f Queen of Trumps, 4 yrs; George Walbaum's ch c Sorrento, 4 yrs; M. G. Thompson Jr.'s gr c Sunny Brook, 3 yrs; J. W. Guest's b c Heron, 4 yrs; Joseph E. Seagram's ch h Marauder, 5 yrs; J. K. Megibben & Co's ch g Avondale, 3 yrs, br c Eberlee, 3 yrs, br c W. G. Morris, 3 yrs, ch c Sportsman, 4 yrs; Maltese Villa Stock Farm's b c Flood Tide, 4 yrs; Santa Anita Stable's ch m Los Angeles, 5 yrs.

TENNESSEE STAKES FOR TWO-YEAR-OLDS. SIX FURLONGS.

Beverwyck Stable's b f Bertha Campbell; Empire Stable's b c Lyceum; P. Meany's b c Sam Corey; Hough Bros.' b c Stratagem; Excelsior Stable's br g Jule G, b c Sir David; A. C. Sohne & Co.'s blk c by Vanderbilt, ch c by Hyder Ali, ch c Fairview, ch g Forfeit; New York Stable's ch g Plato, ch f Mauve; Labold Bros.' br c Sir Martin, br c Monterey; M. Hogan's br c F. D. Ward, b c Alderman Mac; Wm Hendrie's b c Chippewa; Dwyer Bros.' b c Blacklock, b c Baychester; Scoggan Bros.' b g R. F. D., b c Eli Kindig; Stevens & Moore's b f Fauna; Basil Guest's ch c Carroll Reed; Oden Bowie's blk c Blackwood, ch f Stratrine; Byron McClelland's ch c Outcry; George H. Kernaghan's b f by Duke of Montrose; S. P. Kunt's b c Tom Alma; W. P. Burch's ch c Simon Pure; W. H. Laudeman's ch c Palestine; James Murphy's br c Tarquin; Kentucky Stable's b c Ganges, b c Oklahoma; Ed. Brown's ch c McCabe; H. Simon's b c Lee S; Joseph E. Seagram's b f by Stratford; J. G. Greener's b c The Wandering Jew; J. K. Megibben & Co's gr c Hippolite, ch c Vallera, ch c McKinley, ch c Tom Reed; Santa Anita Stable's b c Ensenada, b f Ogarita, b c San Joaquin, b f La Cienega.

THE CONGRESS HALL STAKES, ALL AGES, HEATS OF SIX FURLONGS.

Beverwyck Stable's b h Dashaway II., 4yrs.; Empire Stable's b g Express, 3yrs.; A. C. Sohne & Co.'s b g Sintrain, 4yrs.; Wm. Lovell's ch g Harbor Lights, 5yrs.; Labold Bros.'s b h Glitter, 5yrs.; Keystone Stable's b f Insight, 3yrs.; A. J. Scott's b h Gunshot, 4yrs.; Wm. Hendrie's ch m Minnie Palmer, 4yrs.; O. O. West Jr.'s b f Brandolette, 4yrs.; O. O. West Jr.'s b f Ballyhoo, 3yrs; A. Kraemer (manager) br c Grammercy, 3yrs.; Scoggan Bros.' b f Dollikins, 3yrs.; Scoggan Bros.' ch f English Lady, 3yrs.; Scoggan Bros.' ch g Proctor Knott, 4yrs.; T. H. Stevens' b m Wary, 6yrs.; P. J. Flinn's b g Young Duke; Geo. Walbaum's b c Kenwood, 3yrs.; J. W. Guest's b c Heron, 4yrs.; Blenheim Stable's ch c Portuguese, 3yrs.; P. M. West & Co.'s ch f Flyaway, 3yrs.; Ed Brown's b h Duke of the Highlands, 4yrs.; John G. Greener's ch c Culprit, 4yrs.; John G. Greener's br f Ophelia, 3yrs.; H. Boudy's ch g Ben Harrison, 4yrs.; E. C. Hopper's ch f Sweet Alice, 3yrs.; E. C. Hopper's ch g Harry Weldon, 3yrs.; J. K. Megibben & Co.'s ch c Sportsman, 4yrs.; J. K. Megibben & Co.'s br c Abalene, 3yrs.; Santa Anita Stable's ch m Los Angeles, 5yrs.; Santa Anita Stable's b c Santiago, 3yrs.

MISSES STAKES, FILLIES, TWO-YEAR-OLDS—SIX FURLONGS.

L. & J. E. KITTSON'S ch f by Woodlands; Beverwyck Stable's b f Bertha Campbell; James P. Dawes' b f Belle of Orange; Ed R. Cassidy's b f Festuna; Empire Stable's ch f Landscape; P. Mack's b f Mary Conroy; Hough Bros.' b f Queer Girl; A. C. Sohne & Co.'s ch f Miss Harris; New York Stable's ch f Mauve; New York Stable's ch f Mary Roberts; M. Hogan's ch f Maggie Ward; Wm. Hendrie's ch f Omeo; Wm. Hendrie's ch f Ayrshire Lass; James M. Cormick's b f Early Blossom; Harvest Stable's b f May Washington; Dwyer Bros.' b or br f by Hindoo; Dwyer Bros.' blk or br f by Hindoo; Scoggan Bros.' ch f Apex; Scoggan Bros.' b f Lady Washington; Scoggan Bros.' ch f Planchette; T. H. Stevens' b f Modjeska; Stevens & Moore's b f Fauna; Oden Bowie's ch f Stratrine; Wm. Jennings' b f Release; Hurricanna Stock Farm's b f Ethelair; Hurricanna Stock Farm's b f Elvira; Byron McClelland's ch f Sallie McClelland; Byron McClelland's br f by Billet; George H. Kernaghan's br f Dodo; George H. Kernaghan's b f by Duke of Montrose; George H. Kernaghan's b f by Lisbon; C. Cornehlsen's b f Hydra; Poll Stable's b f by Luke Blackburn; Poll Stable's b f by Luke Blackburn; W. H. Landeman's ch f Prettiwit; Samuel Bryant's b f Nettie Beatrice; Samuel Bryant's ch f Nydia; Samuel Bryant's br f Louisiana; Kentucky Stable's b f Mary McGowan; Kentucky Stable's b f St. Bridget; Ed Brown's ch f Falerna; Ed Brown's ch f Fossetta; Joseph E. Segram's b f by Spendthrift; Joseph E. Seagram's b f by Stratford; J. G. Greener's ch f Eugenie; J. K. Megibben & Co.'s ch f Birdella M.; J. K. Megibben & Co.'s ch f Flower Dellie; J. K. Megibben & Co.'s ch f Actress; Maltese Villa Stock Farm's br f Romeetta; Santa Anita Stable's b f Esperanza; Santa Anita Stable's b f Cleopatra; Santa Anita Stable's b f La Cienega; Santa Anita Stable's b f Ogarita; R. C. Campbell's b f Saxonette.

BEVERWYCK STAKES, ALL AGES. ONE MILE AND FIVE HUNDRED YARDS.

Beverwyck Stable's b h Cassius, 4 yrs; Beverwyck Stable's b m Lavinia Belle, 5 yrs, P. Mack's ch c Penn P., 3 yrs; Excelsior Stable's ch g Sam D., 4 yrs; Excelsior Stable's ch h Barrister, 5 yrs; Labold Bros.' b h Montrose, 6 yrs, Labold Bros.' br c Experience, 3 yrs; Keystone Stable's b g Ten Booker, aged; Keystone Stable's b c Mr. Pelham, 3 yrs; Wm. Hendrie's b m Pee Weep, 5 yrs; Dwyer Brothers' br h Kingston, 6 yrs; Dwyer Bros.' b c Longstreet, 4 yrs; Dwyer Bros' ch h Hanover, 6 yrs; Rensselaer Stable's b f Barcarola, 4 yrs; A. Kraemer's (manager) br c Grammercy 3 yrs; Scoggan Brothers' b c Ja Ja, 3 yrs; Scoggan Brothers' b f Dollikins, 3 yrs; Geo. Walbaum's ch c Sorrento, 4 yrs; M. G. Thompson Jr's gr c Sunny Brook, 3 yrs; J. W. Guest's b c Heron, 4 years; George Hearst's bl m Gorgo, 5 yrs; George Hearst's bl m King Thomas, 3 yrs; George Hearst's b c Anaconda, 3 yrs; George Hearst's b c Anaconda, 3 yrs; George Hearst's b f Golden Horn, 3 yrs; George Hearst's ch c Rhona, 4 yrs; George Hearst's ch c Philander, 4 yrs; Jos. E. Segram's ch h Marauder, 5 yrs; H. Boudy's ch g Ben Harrison, 4 yrs; Maltese Villa Stock Farm's b h Gannymede, 4 yrs; Santa Anita Stable's Stable's ch c Honduras, 3 yrs; Santa Anita Stable's ch f Sinaloa, 3 yrs; Santa Anita Stable's ch m Los Angeles, 5 yrs; Santa Anita Stable's b h Emperor of Norfolk, 5 yrs.

POCAHONTAS STAKES, FILLIES, THREE YEARS, ONE AND THREE-SIXTEENTHS MILES.

Beverwyck Stable's ch f Can Can; H. Warnke & Son's br f Reclare, P. Mack's b f Lizzie Fonso, Labold Brothers' b f Ocypete; Keystone Stable's b f Insight; Dwyer Bros.' b f Red Dress; Dwyer Bros.' b f Blue Dress; Dwyer Bros.' b f by Enquirer; Scoggan Bros.' ch f English Lady; Scoggan Bros' b f Dollikins; T. H. Stevens' ch f Mora by Bramble; Oden Brown's ch f by Vassal; Oden Brown's b f Alarm Bell; Strauss & Lyne's ch f Origana; W. P. Burch's b f Cornelia; George Hearst's b f Golden Horn; George Hearst's br f Miss Bell; George Hearst's b f Everglad; George Hearst's b f Gloaming; James Murphy's b f Kinceem, P. M. West & Co's ch f Flyaway; P. M. West & Co's ch f Eugenie; Samuel Bryant's ch f Cushman; Ed Brown's b f Ruperta; Ed Brown's b f Charming by Prince Charlie; H. Simons' b f Annie Sharp by Ten Broeck; E. C. Hopper's ch f Sweet Alice by Voltaruo; Santa Anita Stable's ch f Sinaloa by Grinstead.

EQUITY STAKES, TWO-YEAR-OLDS. SIX FURLONGS.

Beverwyck Stable's b c Craft; Edward R. Cassidy's ch c Freedom, b f Festina; Empire Stable's ch f Landscape, b c Lyceum, Salamander Stable's b f Gold Step; Hough Bros.' b c Leveller; Excelsior Stable's b c Sir David, br g by Bramble; A. C. Sohne & Co.'s blk c by Vanderbilt, ch c by Hyder Ali, ch c Fairview, ch g Forfeit; New York Stable's, ch g Plato, ch f Mauve; La Bold Bros.' blk c Sir Martin, br c Monterey; M. Hogan's br c F. D. Ward, b c Alderman Mac; Wm. Hendrie's b c Chippewa; J. H. McCormick's b f Early Blossom; Dwyer Bros.' b c Baychester, b c Blacklock; Scoggan Bros.' b c Eli Kindig, b c National; Basil Guest's ch c Carroll Reed; Oden Bowie's blk c Blackwood, ch f Stratrine; George Walbaum's ch f Josie W; C. Cornehlsen's b f Hydra, ch c Coriolanus; Poll Stable's b c by imp Mr. Pickwick; W. H. Landeman's ch c Palestine; Kentucky Stable's b c Ganges, b c Oklahoma; Ed. Brown's ch c McCabe, b c Oberlin, H. Simons's b c Lee S; Joseph E Seagram's b c by Bend'Or; J. G. Greener's b c The Wandering Jew; Maltese Villa Stock Farm's b f Romeetta, Santa Anita Stable's b c San Joaquin, b f Cleopatra, ch c Silverado, b f Ogarita.

MORRISSEY STAKES, HANDICAP ONE AND THREE-QUARTERS MILES.

Beverwyck Stable's b h Cassius, 4 yrs; Beverwyck Stable's b m Lavinia Belle, 5 years; Western Union Stable's b h Dunboyne, 4 yrs, Jas. P. Dawes' b h Red Fellow, 4 yrs; Hough Bros' b g Come-to-Taw, 4 yrs; Excelsior Stable's ch g Sam D., 4 yrs; Excelsior Stable's b m Gipsey Queen, 4 years; Labold Bros.' b h Montrose, 6 yrs; Clover Stable's b h Hindoocraft, 4 yrs; Clover Stable's b f Bertelle, 3 yrs, Keystone Stable's b g Ten Booker, aged; Keystone Stable's b c Mr. Pelham, 3 yrs; Wm Hendrie's b m Pee Weep, 5 yrs; O O West Jr's b f Brandolette, 4 yrs; A. Kraemer (manager) br c Grammercy, 3 yrs; Scoggan Bros.' b f Bettina, 4 yrs; T. H. Stevens' br m Florimon, 6 yrs; T. H. Steven's b m Wary, 6 yrs; Lewellyn Lloyd's ch g St. Luke, aged; Gorman & Co's ch f Sally O., 4 yrs; M. G. Thompson Jr's gr c Sunny Brook, 3 yrs; J. W. Guest's b c Heron, 4 yrs, Blenheim Stable's ch c Portuguese, 3 yrs, Louis Cook's b c Tenteen, 4 yrs; Joseph E. Seagram's ch h Marauder, 5 yrs; Maltese Villa Stock Farm's b c Flood Tide, 4 years; Santa Anita Stable's ch m Los Angeles, 5 yrs.

RELIEF STAKES, THREE YEAR OLDS, ONE MILE AND FIVE HUNDRED YARDS.

Beverwyck Stable's ch f Can Can; Empire Stable's ch c Tormentor; Empire Stable's b c Favorite; T. H. Love's b g Cortland; H. Warnke & Son's br f Reclare; P. Mack's b f Lizzie Fonso; New York Stable's b c Australitz; Keystone Stable's b c Mr. Pelham; Keystone Stable's b f Insight; Dwyer Brothers' b c Sir John; Dwyer Bros.' b c Flatbush; A. Kraemer (manager) br c Grammercy; Scoggan Bros' b c Ja Ja, Scoggan Bros.' ch c Ban Chief; T. H. Stevens' ch f Mora; Oden Bowie's ch f by Vassal; Strauss & Lyne's ch f Origina; James Murphy's b f Kincseem; P. M. West & Co's ch f Flyaway; P. M. West & Co's b c Grayson; Ed Brown's b f Ruperta; Ed Brown's b f Charming; Joseph E. Seagram's ch c by Stonehenge; J. G. Greener's ch c Sam Doxey; E. C. Hopper's ch f Sweet Alice; Santa Anita Stable's b c Clio; Santa Anita Stable's ch c Honduras; Santa Anita Stable's ch f Sinaloa.

Stud Horse Pedigrees.

Last week a correspondent who lives in Oregon, asked for the pedigree of Director Jr., and enclosed one which he wished to ascertain if it were correct. We answered that it was, but incidentally mentioned that the name of the horse had been changed to Corrector, and that he was now standing at the Pleasanton Stock Farm. On looking over the Portland Rural Spirit, we find the following, advertised by one John Pender of Salem, Oregon, who says the horse will stand there this season:

Director Jr. is a black horse, 15 hands 1½ inches high, foaled 1886; bred by F. S. Malone, of San Francisco.

Pedigree: Sired by Director 2:17, dam Brainy by Echo; 2nd dam Lady Dudley by Tom Dudley; (for extended pedigree see Bruce's American Stud Book, Vol. 1, page 604.)

Director by Dictator (sire of Jay-Eye See 2:10, Phallas, 2:13¾, etc.,) dam Dolly (dam of Thorndale, 2:22½; Onward, 2:25¼; Cezarina 2:27½), by Mambrino Chief.

Echo (sire of the dams of Direct, 4 years, 2:18½; Pink, 2:25, and twelve trotters and one pacer in the 2:30 list), is by Rysdyk's Hambletonian, dam Fanny Felter, by Magnolia 68, son of American Star, 14, sire of six stallions that have eleven trotters in the 2:30 list, and sire of thirty-five dams that produced forty three trotters and one pacer with records of 2:30 or better.

Director, sire of Director Jr. is also the sire of Direct, four-year-old record 2:18½: Margaret S, three-year-old record 2:19½; Guide, three-year-old record 2:28½. Margaret S. is claimed by noted horsemen to be the greatest and gamest three-year-old ever produced, considering age, as she was not foaled until August, 1886, as is also Direct one of the gamest colts that ever faced the starter. Director also has the honor of being the only stallion alive or dead that has sired two colts with records better than 2;20, with his oldest colts but 4 years old.

Now, if our readers will turn to the advertisement of the Pleasanton Stock Farm in the present issue of the BREEDER AND SPORTSMAN they will find the following:—

Corrector, four years old. Sire Director 2:17, dam Brainey, she by Echo, Echo sired by Rysdyk's Hambletonian, out of Magnolia, she by Seely's American Star. Brainey's dam Lady Dudely, she by Tom Dudley by Blacknose, a son of Medoc, he by American Eclipse. Lady Dudley's dam by Bertrand Jr., a son of Bertrand.

Corrector is a rich seal brown, 15½ hands high, and is the fastest young stallion in the world under the same conditions, never having been off the farm where raised, and never having been shod or driven for speed before last Christmas, and can trot quarters now in 35 seconds, a 2:20 gait.

He will be allowed to serve ten good mares, at $100 each for the season.

Now it would seem, after reading the two advertisements, that Brainey had two foals that year, or that Mr. Pender or Mr. Salisbury is claiming a wrong pedigree for his horse. Those who are acquainted with Mr. Salisbury know that he would not misrepresent anything. Mr. Pender we do not know, so cannot say whether he has been swindled in the pedigree that he presents to the public or whether he is willfully trying to impose on the owners of brood mares in Oregon. An explanation is in order.

TURF AND TRACK.

Proctor Knott may be seen in the Toboggan Slide Handicap.

Bonita. Mr. Baldwin's cast off a few years ago, is said to be rounding too again in great shape.

Dan Honig has purchased the bay colt Ripley, 3 yrs. old by Alarm, dam Lady's Maid by imp Leamington.

Mr. Peters has sent his speedy mare Lulu B, by Langford, to the Guenoc Stud Farm to be bred to St, Saviour.

Game old Inspector B. has been leased to the Kittson Bros, and will join Elkwood in the Erdenheim stud.

Frank Elliott has purchased the brown gelding Pericles, aged by imp Strachino, dam Grecian Maid by imp Glenelg.

Red and Blue, by Alarm out of Maggie B. B., dam of Iroquois, foaled a slashing chestnut colt by Hindoo at Runnymede.

Governor Waterman has appointed F. A. Antenreith, Siskiyou, Agricultural Director for District No. 10 and David Alexander for District No. 12 (Lake).

Washington Park, Chicago, has selected Major Joseph J. Burke of New York for presiding judge this season, the selection should prove a very happy one.

Messrs. Clay and Woodford (Runnymede) will after this season give up yearling sales and race their own colts on account of the big stakes which are being hung up.

It is rumored that Mr. Pierre Lorillard will attempt to repurchase Iroquois (who carried his colors so nobly in England) when the Belle Meade sale takes place.

A. Lakeland has sold to H. Harris the bay horse Troy, 6 years old by Lelaps, dam Reel Dance by War Dance, her dam Blanche Rousseau by imp Mickey Free.

Dan Honig has purchase from T. B. Doswell the chestnut filly Wild Cherry 4 yrs old by Wilful, dam Cerise by imp. Moccasin, her dam Lizzie Lucas by imp Australian.

M. Daly has named the two four-year old fillies he purchased from Mr. Withers. The Stonehenge—Ecola filly is called Rose and the Stonehenge—Maxim filly Ross.

There is a vague rumor gradually growing stronger that H. D. McIntyre, the popular Secretary of the Brooklyn and New Jersey Jockey Clubs will give up the turf for politics.

Matt Allen is getting still more anxious to match his Jap. He tried Green Morris for a while, but Green was too wily to be caught. Matt is now hunting Messrs. Blackburn & Co.

W. Lovell, New York City, lost recently at Guttenburg N. J., from the result of an accident the chestnut filly Nanine 3 yrs old by imp. Kantaka, dam Nannie King by Ringmaster.

W. B. Jennings, Washington, D. C. has purchased the chestnut mare My Own, 5 yrs old by Sensation, dam Queen's Own by imp Australian, her dam Queen Victoria by Lexington.

The San Simeon stable, with W. L. Donathan in charge, have arrived at San Jose, and are said to be looking exceptionally well. They will race at San Jose, the Blood Horse, and then go to Chicago.

The first of Edgemark's foals is out of a mare by Smuggler 2:15¼, granddam Madam Rowell, the dam of Monroe Chief 2:18¼. Edgemark last year got a record of 2:16, and the colt should have unlimited speed.

One of the most promising two year olds in Kentucky is Mount Joy, by Pontiac out of Accidenta, the dam of Mt. Lebanon, etc. Will McDaniel, who trains the colt, says he is one of the best he ever handled.

The Australian race horse Chicago has arrived safely in England. In his own country he was a fair performer, not really first-class, and should render a good account of himself in the mother country if well placed.

Ex-Senator James G. Fair has purchased the Adams Ranch —owned by John Adams—in the upper end of the Berryessa Valley for $35,000. The mortgage which was recently foreclosed on the ranch was for $28 000.

J. C. Kenkell, Harrisburg, Pa., has purchased from W. H. Laughlin, Woodstock, Pa., a mare well known to Californians, viz., Empress 2:24, foaled 1876 by Hambletonian 725, dam Katy Tricks (dam of Tricks 2:20) by Colonel.

The Scoggan stable has twenty one head of horses in training, most of them heavily engaged. Robin Hood, who was bought from W. M. Murry last year, has a leg, and as it is very doubtful whether he will stand training, he has not been heavily engaged for this season.

Homewood 3970, record 2:23½, foaled 1878, by Hambletonian Tranby 3969, dam Belle, has been sold by Mr. McCormick, Pittsburg, Pa., for $5.000 to the Sire Bros, who are acting for the German Market. Homeward will be shipped to the Fatherland at the earliest opportunity.

Mr. L. J. Rose has evidently decided to stay in the thoroughbred business, for immediately after his return from the East he visited Palo Alto, and last Saturday purchased seven yearling colts for $13 500 Among the lot which are, of course only halter broken is a full brother to Flambeau,

Dick Havey has had the misfortune to lose his well known stallion Bonanza 2:29½, who died last Saturday from inflammation of the lungs. It is a severe loss for Mr. Havey, as irrespective of his racing prospects, the horse had already twenty mares booked to him, and many more applications.

Mr. J. B. Ferguson, who acted as starter at the last meeting at Jerome Park and who is now acting in a like capacity says he has been engaged to act as starter at the meetings to be held at Lexington, St. Louis, Louisville, St. Paul, and at "one Eastern track." He was by no means a success at Jerome Park last season.

Dan McCarty, as I stated last week, took Mr. Richards into partnership with him in Bay Rose and ten mares. Dan put them on the cars to go to Grayson but Messrs. Allen Mayhew and Ira Pierce bought the horse for $20,000 and took him off the cars at 16th street, Oakland. Dan says Designer will fill his place at Grayson.

Imported Leopold by Doncaster, dam imp. Princess by King Tom has been bred to Accidenta (dam of Valparaiso, Liera and Mt. Lebanon) by Messrs. Talbott Bros, Paris. Ky. Prince Leopold was bought last fall by Messrs. Talbott Bros., but he will not be trained this season as was intended, owing to the great demand for his services as a stallion.

Old Norfolk (28) is as lively as can be and feeds well, but is practically impotent. Marion is quite youthful in appearence and is a typical looking brood mare, the only thing being that there are few of so high a type. It seems almost a shame and is anyhow a risky spec transplanting a lot of oldish mares from Sacramento's sunny plains to Nevada's chilly hills and dales.

Mr. Boots who lately purchased imported Brutus from Palo Alto will use him in the stud, but may possibly race him this fall. Brutus foaled 1885, is by Macgregor who won the Two Thousand Guineas in 1870, and went to the post for the Derby with Fordham up at 9 to 4 on, running unplaced to Kingcraft, Palmerston and Muster, his dam imp. Teardrop is by Scottish Chief,

The Linden Park Association announces $50,000 in added money for its first spring meeting, to begin at Linden, N. J., on April 22nd, and that the average will be $3,500 a day, which indicates a fourteen or fifteen days meeting. If fourteen or fifteen clear days can be had from April 22nd the meeting will probably pay. James R. English is announced as President and Richard Stockton as Secretary and Treasurer.

Prince Charlie's successor at Elmendorff is said to have got several flying two-year-olds, Heiress by Rotherhill out of Finance by Leamington being said to be the best filly in the Rancocas Stable, while Andrew Thompson has a slashing colt out of Pauline Sprague. It is to be hoped for Mr. Swigert's sake that imported Rotherhill will breed on and rival his gr predecessor, Prince Charlie, the Prince of the T. Y. C.eat

Harold was nine years old when he got Maud S., 2:08¾, while Electioneer was seventeen when he sired Sunol, 2:10½. Harry Wilkes the fastest of the Geo Wilkes breed was among the first of his sires get as was also Axtell, 2:12 among the first of the get of William L, In the same line brood mares follow stallions, some dropping their best foals early in life, while others only show up prominently when their days are nearly over.

H. L. & F. D. Street of Highland Farm, Dubuque, Iowa, have been offered and refused $10,000 for a weanling colt, by Nutwood, 2:18¾, out of Sohoxeo, 2:17¼. The offer was made by a Pennsylvania gentleman, who wishes his name kept secret. The colt is a beautiful solid bay. He is entered in the yearling stakes in Iowa this season. He has been named Ohen, and his owners think him the best yearling in the country.

The Duke of Westminster has now in his stable two yearlings by Ormonde, the first one a chestnut colt out of Angelica, and the other a bay colt, out of Shotover. Angelica is a near relative to St. Simon, the great sire of Signorina and Shotover is a daughter of Hermit, the well known Derby winner of 1882. The last named is therefore sired by a Derby winner, as well as being out of a dam that had also won the great blue ribbon, a feature of breeding that never happened in England before.

Unless a horse is known to be very quiet and unexcitable, he should never be whipped on the hind quarters, as it often tempts a horse to kick. Strike him on the shoulder or fore leg, and if he does not answer to it immediately, strike him harder. It will not hurt him so much as jerking his mouth with the reins, and you had better do it yourself than be obliged to sell him to some one that will drive him and whip him without measure or mercy. There is as little real kindness in spoiling a horse as there is in spoiling a child.

"Having given the breeding problem many years of study, all the time trying to "keep up with the procession," writes Editor Dunton in the Spirit of the Turf, it is our logical conclusion that the next move on this chess-board will be to look dispassionately through all branches of our great trotting and thoroughbred families for those horses which go over the ground with the least possible waste motion; easiest to themselves, with the lightest shoe that it is possible for a horse to wear, and with the greatest lung and will power.

We are strongly in favor of early breeding says the Agriculturist. If the mare is bred at two and has a colt at three years, she may be longer maturing, but she will be no smaller and will make a better broodmare. This is the experience of the draft horse breeders of France to early establish regular breeding. The mares are given full work upon the farm, and the most careful attention is given to breeding, to be sure of a colt the next year as the leading feature of the annual cash income.

"That one well bred mare is worth a field of scrubs was never better illustrated than at the Brasfield s sale," says the Terra Haute Express. "The late Col. Wm. Cassius Goodloe's stud, consisting of but three mares by Geo. Wilkes, and five fillies by such sires as Dictator, Mambrino Russell and Lord Russell brought $27,850 an average. of $3,351. The people all over the country are being educated to the fact that breeding horses of an inferior class is not a profitable business. Poor horses are not in demand at any price. There is always a demand for the best."

The American Turf Congress met on the 13th and Judge Perkins of the Latonia Jockey Club was unanimously elected President in the place of the late T. J. McGibben Esq., after highly eulogistic complimentary remarks which were certainly deserved by the late President. Col. L. Clark was elected vice-president, and B. G. Bruce secretary, without a single dissenting vote. It was tacitly understood when the meeting adjourned that another meeting would soon be held to come to a definite conclusion with regard to the wire reports to the various pool rooms.

A writer in a New York sporting paper makes an interesting comparison of the various modes of locomotion with the following results: A man can swim a mile in 26m. 52s., he can walk it in 6m. 23s. he can cover it on snow shoes in 5m. 39⅘. he can run the distance in 4m. 12¾s.; he can ride it on a tricycle in 2m. 12 3-5s. Behind a trotting horse he gains nearly four seconds by covering the distance in 2m. 8¾s.; while on a running horse he gallops the mile in 1m. 39¾.; and last and fastest he sits in a railroad train and flies over a mile of the steel rails in 50½s.

The Kentucky Derby at a rough estimate will be worth $5000 to the winner the following will probably include all the starters. Avondale, Bill Letcher, Corticelli, Eberlee, Ely Good-bye, Grayson, Honduras, Mount Lebanon, Outlook, Outright, Palisade, Phoenix, Prince Fonso, Prodigal Son, Protection, Portlaw Riley, Robespierre, Rosemount, Santiago, Sunnybrook and W, G. Morris.

After a good deal of dickering here and there the Santa Rosa Agricultural Park Association have sold the race track to Mr. Ira Pierce of this city for $17,500. Mr. Pierce who has a number of good horses himself hopes with the co-operation of the Santa Rosa horsemen to make the track as popular as any in the state, and judging from the admirable situation it should prove a successful venture.

A telegram from Los Angeles says that John H. Shults, the millionaire horse owner, is a guest at the Hollenbeck. Mr. Shults came here two years ago and purchased the celebrated pacer, Arrow, and the Brooklynite now owns probably the fastest team in the United States, having recently purchased Gold Leaf. Arrow and Gold Leaf have records faster than 2:14. Mr. Shults is a great admirer of California stock, and it was he who bid $24,000 for Voodoo. It is not improbable that he will make some purchases while in this part of the State. Next to Mr. Bonner, Mr. Shults has the choicest collection of trotters in New York.

H. B. Dickinson, Ocean Point, Long Island, New York, has imported from England the bay horse Helicon, foaled 1878, bred by Lord Durham, by Cardinal York (son of Newminster and License by Gameboy), dam Artemis by Thormanby, her dam The Nymph by The Flying Dutchman, 3d. dam by the Cure, 4th dam Elphine by Emilus, 5th dam Variation by Bustard, &c. Helicon won three times out of five starts at two years old, did not win at three years old out of seven starts, won once at five years old of eight starts, won three times out of five starts at six years old, at seven years old started seven times and won four races, and at eight years old won once out of five starts.

"My choice," says Samuel A. Browne in the Sportsman, "is in tried producing dams, no matter how bred, and the Kalamazoo Farm has adopted this as the only sure basis. Pedigree with me is of little consequence if there is no performing blood. This will ultimately be the only standard for trotters. I would not give anything for a standard-bred pedigree of five or six standard crosses, provided some of the dams of the animal had not produced speed, and the more of them that have, and the lower the records, coupled with campaigning ability, the more valuable they are to the breeder. Non-producing blood is only worth intrinsically what it will bring for hack or work horse purposes, no matter how many standard crosses it may have."

Prince Soltykoff's bay horse Tibthorpe, foaled 1864, by Voltiguer, out of Little Agnes by The Cure, her dam Miss Agnes by Birdcatcher, out of Agnes by Clarion, died at Newmarket, Friday, February 21, 1890, aged 26 years. Tibthorpe was a speedy horse, and though a frequent performer only one event of importance was won by him. That was the Steward's Cup at Goodwood. He sired several horses of fair class, some of whom could stay well, though he himself was deficient in stamina. Among them may be mentioned Althorp (winner of the Great Metropolitan, Ascot Stakes, Ascot Cup and Prix de Deauville), Lucetta (winner of the Cambridgeshire Stakes), Tip and Kingthorpe.

Ansel, George Rice and Fayette, who respectively trained Artistides, Lord Murphy and Buchanan, winners of the Kentucky Derby are dead. John McGinty, now Labold Bros.' trainer, is the only man that has prepared two Kentucky Derby winners. He sent Leonatus and Montrose to the post. Of the other victors in this great race, Vagrant was trained by Dudley Allen, Baden-Baden by Brown Dick. Day Star by Lee Paul, Fonso by Tice Hutsell, Hindoo by James Rowe, Appollo by Green Morris, Joe Cotton by Abe Perry, Ben Ali by James Murphy, Macbeth II by John S. Campbell, and Spokade by J. Rodegap. With the exception of Lord Murphy bred in Tennessee and Spokane, foaled in Montana, all the winners of the Derby were Kentucky bred and born.

At Independence, Ia., last week, Fischer and Borroughs of Allison served a writ of replevin on C. W. Williams for the recovery of Mambrino Boy, sire of the dams of Axtell and Allerton. They were met with locked doors and a refusal to deliver. About fourteen months ago the owners placed Mambrino Boy in the hands of Williams for a term of five years with the agreement that he should not be sold for one year and then for not less than $5000. Yesterday he was sold to John Graham of Biggsville, Ill., for $5500. Williams considers this a ruse to obtain possession and refused to deliver. He has also a claim against the horse which has not been settled. A delivery bond was executed, and the case will be tried at the next term of court, in about two weeks.

With moderate care and good usage a horse's life may be prolonged to 25, 35 or 40 years. An Englishman had three horses which severally died in his possession at the age of 35, 37 and 39 years. The oldest was in a carriage the very day he died, strong and vigorous, but was carried off by spasmodic colic to which he was subject. A horse in use in a riding school at Woolwich lived to be 40 years old. A gray horse bred and raised in Lockport, N. Y., and owned for 37 years by a Mr. Braun of that city, will be 44 years old next May. He worked daily in a pottery mill to grind clay up to last year, and now kicks and frisks about in a box stall History tells of a horse belonging to the Mersey & Irwell Navigation Company, London, that was declared to have been in his 62nd year when he died.

A horse can hardly be said to have passed his primary education until he has been taught all that is really necessary for an ordinary roadster to understand. He will have more to do than most other riding horses in the way of passing and meeting vehicles, and other objects on the road, and great care and patience should be exercised to teach him to do this pleasantly, without getting dangerously near them, or shying too far away from them. He should be taught to go a little faster when overtaking than when meeting an object. A good bold rider may allow him to select a soft path near the side of the road to save his feet, but when so indulged there is always more risk of a sudden swerve to one side, so that a less accomplished rider had better teach his nag to keep the best path he can find nearer the middle of the road. Cantering on hard mettled roads is an expensive luxury, especially with a heavy weight, as few horses stand it long without failing in the leading forefoot or leg, so that a young men who wants to save his horse from lameness had better be content to walk or trot. As in every other riding horse, a good, fast, easy walk is a valuable accomplishment.

Secretary Kock has been at work quietly but very effectively, and his efforts have been attended with most gratifying results. Within the past month the New York Jockey Club has received an accession of nearly 1,000 members to its rolls made up of club men from New York, as well as from other parts of the country. San Francisco, St. Louis, New Orleans Chicago, Buffalo, Washington, Baltimore, Cincinnati, Philadelphia and Albany have now many representative club men on the rolls of the club, and new applications for membership are being received daily. With the clubhouse completed and the attractions offered to both resident and non-resident members, it is not at all strange that the club's growth is so phenomenal. A social future as well as great racing future is clearly open to the new track.

W. L. Donathan has twelve head of the Hearst stable at San Jose. Owing to the incessant rains they have had little or no work on the ranch, but all look exceptionally well. Several of them are entered at San Jose and the Blood Horse, including the well known four year old Almont, by Three Cheers, out of Question; Del Mar and Gertrude, both four year olds imported from Australia, by Somnus; Baggage 3, Warwick—Maria F., is the hero of the sensational Chicago race in which Redlight and Protection were in front from start to finish, but the judges made a mistake—afterwards acknowledged—which gave Baggage the race; Sacramento is a three year old by Joe Hooker out of Ada C.; Primero 2, Powhattan—Speed, Anarchist 2, Joe Hooker—Chestnut Belle, and Yosemite 2, Hyder Ali—Nellie Collier; the last named shows exceptional promise.

The subscribers to the stock of the driving park and race course, met this morning at Maze & Abbott's office, says the Modesto News, and perfected a preliminary organization. The capital stock of the corporation is $30,000, of which $17,600 is already subscribed. The following Board of Directors were chosen: L. A. Richards and R. M. Wilson, of the West Side; J. J. Dolan of Turlock, and A. L. Cressey, J. W. Davison, L. B. Walthall and Thomas Wallace of Modesto. The name selected was the "Stanislaus County Agricultural Society." L. B. Walthall, the Secretary pro tem, was instructed to secure the articles of incorporation of different agricultural societies, after which a permanent organization will be perfected. The society have already negotiated for 100 acres of land near the railroad track, northwest of town. The next meeting will be held in about a month.

Owing to the severe storms in the Northern section of this state and Oregon, during the winter, many mares have died, the latest returnes, coming from the Jacksonville (Oregon) Times. It says: A heavy loss was sustained by Jas. McDonough of Willow Springs recently in the loss of three of his fine Morgan race stock, including "Mary," one of his best animals and also another choice mare the dam of the promising young trotter "George Woodthrope" which surprised the trotting fraternity here by trotting in 2:38 at the district fair last fall less than 4 months after being broken to harness It is a county calamity to lose such valuable stock in the prime of life. The cause of death in all three animals was the ulcerating distempter known as "the railroad disease," which has caused so many animals to die in various part of the state during the past year.

As intelligent a gentleman and good a critic as Mr. Robert Bonner was at Columbia, Tenn., last May, says Colman's Rural World, and claimed that he could invariably tell from the looks of a horse whether he was a pacer or trotter. This statement being challenged, he commenced to examine some of the horses there at the fair grounds. One of the first ones exhibited was the great pacer Duplex, record 2:17½. After looking him over and wisely examining his conformation, he pronounced him a pure gaited trotter. Duplex is not only a natural pacer, but has not a drop of trotting blood in him, and unlike most pacers, is not inclined to trot.

The fallacy of the contention that the pacing gait is controlled by the conformation is illustrated over and over again by the fact that nearly all the fast pacers are also fast trotters by the use of a little weight. Little Brown Jug 2:11¾, when three years old could trot faster than he could pace. Brown Hal, 2:12½ has a well authenticated trial trotting record of 2:21, and nearly always trots in a jog, while Bonesetter, with a trotting record of 2:19, was a natural pacer, and took many prizes in the saddle ring before he entered the trotting arena.

It is not often that a horse is ruled off after winning a race, but this is what occurred at New Orleans last week, says the Turf, Field and Farm, when the brown gelding Tom Karl, his owner, S. C. Hildreth, and the jockey, Bunn, were ruled off after Tom Karl had finished in front of his field, but it was not for winning this race but for losing one on the preceding Saturday, March 8th, that the punishment was inflicted. On that occasion the odds opened short against Karl, but steadily lengthened until a false price was quoted at the close of the betting. His jockey, Bunn, seemed not to try to get the horse off at the start, and when the flag fell, Lady Blackburn took the head and easily held it to the end. Bunn made some show of whipping Karl, but it was a weak effort. On the Monday following the two met again in a race of the same distance. Tom Karl had a little less weight up than on Saturday, but not enough to have made any material difference. Before the race Hildreth went to the post Tom Karl was at 1 to 4, and Lady Blackburn at 2 to 1. This time Bunn was alert at the post, and getting away well placed he soon had the lead, which his horse held to the end, winning the race in a big gallop under a strong pull. This was a little too much for the judges, and as Hildreth's explanation failed to satisfy them, all were ruled off.

A friend to the standard, looking to a higher rank for the trotter, based on merit, suggests the following, and invites the views of breeders from all parts of the country to ascertain whether higher standard is desirable. The proposed new rules are intended to cover the whole ground, but not retroactive. It is not intended to upset, or make any animal non-standard that is now recorded, but to cover the ground for the future. Some change appears necessary to get rid of weeds and establish merit. The following are the proposed rules, to which we invite attention, and would be pleased to hear the concised views of breeders upon them, and to have any suggestions looking to improvement:

1. Any stallion or mare that has a record of 2:20 or better, or that has produced a yearling with a record of 2:40 or better, or a two or three-year-old with a record of 2:30 or better, or four-year-old with a record of 2:25 or better, or has produce of any age, with a record of 2:20 or better.

2. The produce of any stallion or mare becoming standard under these rules, together with any animal making the foregoing record, shall be entitled to standard rank and entitled to registry.—Western Sportsman.

John Mackey returned from the East last Saturday bringing him ten head of horses, seven of which went to Mr. Salisbury's farm at Pleasanton while the other three stayed on the Rancho Del Paso. The most notable of Mr. Mackey's purchases was Roxaline, own sister, a year younger, to Marian dam of the Emperor of Norfolk. El Rio Roy, etc. She is the dam of Fred B Princess, Brait and other well known horses.

Spirit of the Times:—Decidedly one of the swell campaigners of the day was Rosa Wilkes 2:18¼, and as a grand individual daughter of one of the incomparable George Wilkes her value as a broodmare can hardly be estimated. The Hon. F. G. Babcock, owner of the Babcock Stock Farm, Hornellsville, N. Y., her owner, conceived the idea that he would like to send the fair Rosa to the embraces of the gallant Axtell 2:12, but unfortunately his book was full. In this dilemma the good offices of the editor of The Spirit was invoked, and, in answer to a letter from the office, Mr. William P. Ijams sent the following gracious reply: "Terra Haute, Ind., Feb. 26—Your favor of the 24th inst. at hand. Contents carefully noted. I have written to the Hon. F. G. Babcock, offering him a place for his mare instead of one of my own if it would be any accommodation to him. You know Axtell is young and we must keep him within the limits. I booked six of my own mares and will allow him one of these places. Thanking you for the interest you have taken in the matter, I am very sincerely, etc., W. P. Ijams." The little incident is a very pleasant one. It is an instance of the chivalrous courtesy which exists among our leading breeders although personally stangers to each other, and it is another instance of the universal popularity of the young stallion king.

We learn says the Kern County Californian that work has been commenced on the ninety-acre track, north of the railroad, which Mr. Haggin has determined to use for a race track and for Agricultural Fair grounds and the necessary sheds, stables, etc. The principal entrance to the grounds will be reached by way of Chester avenue, upon which a responsible company have a franchise for a street railway. The situation is probably as well adapted for the purpose as any that could be found. It is near to town, on the prolongation of one of the widest and best streets and convenient for visitors and stock that may come by the railroad. The nature of the soil is such that dust will not be troublesome, and is of fine texture and easy and elastic or springy for the feet of animals. When all is completed, it will be conspicuous and of considerable interest to passengers on the railroad. As no one knows better than Mr. Haggin, the importance this vicinity is rapidly attaining as an agricultural and stock-growing district, he is naturally impressed with the importance of making ready a suitable, convenient and prominent place for training and exhibition purposes as soon as possible. He evidently believes as all men of affairs do, that it is the true policy to be ready for a need by the time it comes, instead of incurring the delay, trouble and damage that comes by putting off action until afterward. As was stated last week, it is proposed, if an Agricultural Fair Association is formed and they desire these grounds, to give them the privilege of purchasing them on easy terms.

Another Tennessee driver that has done well with pacers is Bob Anderson. His face is also guiltless of hirsute adornment, and he has given the boys in the North several hard falls with the grey gelding Argyle, record 2:14¼, that could get himself distanced any time by merely making one break. Two years ago when Anderson and Argyle were at Detroit and taking part in a pacing race it struck Orrin Hickok, who was watching the contest from the grand stand, that, properly driven, Argyle could win the race, a feat that he was not by any means performing under the guidance of Anderson. So Hickok had a hurried consultation with Capt. John De Mass, who has been on the turf for forty years, and John Turner, the driver, the result being that the three formed a combine and leased the services of Argyle for the race, agreeing to pay Anderson first money whether the horse won it or not, the only stipulation being that Hickok should drive. He got up behind Argyle and won two heats easily, but in the third it was a close fit as to whether Argyle or another horse that had won two heats would get to the wire first. Anderson saw this, and as he had quietly bought a few tickets on his pet he wandered up to the head of the homestretch; to see how things were coming on. Soon after he reached that point Argyle and his competitor came tearing around the turn, and as they passed Anderson he saw that Argyle was going steady and strong and had a nose the best of it. Being well aware that once he was in the stretch where the road was a straight one Argyle would not break, Anderson sung out to Hickok in tones that could be heard for half a mile: "Hit him, Orrin! Hit that old hoss on the back!" Hickok followed instructions, Argyle won by a neck, and everybody but the losers were happy.—Breeder's Gazette.

A Sun correspondent interviewed Mr. Scoggan at Louisville last week, and this is what that gentleman had to say about Proctor Knott: "I do not intend that he shall at any time work faster than 0:53 outside of a race. That is fast enough to keep him on edge. I don't propose to let him waste his speed and strength in record-breaking trials. I'll save that for the actual race. He is certain to start in the Suburban if he has four good legs under him. I propose to race him when he is ready, whether that be at Nashville, or Coney Island, or elsewhere. We begin the season at Nashville, and from thence take in the entire Western circuit. If at the end of the Latonian meeting Proctor is good, I will send him and two others East. He won't start at Brooklyn, and probably not at Westchester. I don't quite like the idea of sending him down that hill. I've seen a number of good ones go wrong that tried it, and shall probably not take any risk. But here's one that will start in the Toboggan," referring to English Lady.

"Proctor Knott's weight in the Suburban wouldn't have suited me better, if I had fixed it myself. No, it won't be the weight that will keep Proctor Knott from winning the Suburban. And, if he's fit next June, it won't be Longstreet, Salvator nor Tenny that will keep him from winning, either. Murphy let Longstreet beat my horse in the Omnibus last summer by stupid riding, but there'll be no mistake of that kind committed this year. Proctor is a horse that will not submit to being pulled back in the rut, as Murphy did on that occasion. He likes to either cut out the pace or else keep well up with the leaders. If Murphy had followed our instructions to this effect, he couldn't have lost the race. Instead of that, he kept Proctor in the rear for almost a mile, then feeling his speed and letting him get into a good position alongside the leader, pulled him back again to last place. The consequence was that Longstreet had reached the stretch before Murphy began to make his run. Once given his head, Proctor came like a cannon ball, and while he passed them all save the leader, the distance was too short in which to catch the Dwyer horse. But I'll have another go at these Eastern chaps this summer, and if they beat me again I'll give up, but not before."

The following extract from a letter written by a well known turfman now in Nashville, Tenn., will be interesting, as it gives considerable information about Theodore Winters' stable: "Yesterday I was at the track and took a look at the Californians. El Rio Rey looks in splendid health, but is a little low in flesh. Rey Del Rey has a strong resemblance to the Emperor, but is a little larger. Don Jose, Joe Courtney and the other horses from the East look very well, except the first named had one of his fore legs dressed in a wet bandage. Judge Post, a brother to Don Jose, is a nice looking two-year-old, of fine size, and from his manner will train quickly and run fast. Average is a cat-like going fellow, and will carry their colors in the Trial Stake here. Noretta, three years old, a full sister to Alta, will be prepared for the Duncan Hotel Stake, and it is no secret that the stable expect to get the money with her.

The racing sensation in New Orleans last week, was the ruling off the turf of the well-known trainer S. C Hildreth, Bunn, the jockey who rides for him, and the brown gelding Tom Karl. On Saturday a fortnight ago, Lady Blackburn was made the favorite over Tom Karl in a race in which they met, whereas nearly every well posted man on the track knew that the latter was much the faster of the two. The odds opened up short enough against Karl, but a rumor got out that he was not to win, and they steadily went up against him until a false price was quoted at the close of the betting. Tom Karl's jockey, the boy Bunn, seemed not to try to get the horse off at the start, and when the flag fell Lady Blackburn took the lead, and easily held it to the end. Bunn made some show of whipping Karl, but it was a weak effort. On Monday the two met again in a race of the same distance. Tom Karl had a little less weight up than on Saturday, but not enough to have made any material difference. Before the race Hildreth went into the ring and backed his horse, and when they went to the post Tom Karl was at 1 to 4, and Lady Blackburn at 2 to 1 This time Bunn was alert at the post, and getting away well placed he soon had the lead, which his horse held to the end, winning the race in a big gallop under a strong pull. This was a little too much for the judges, and they called Hildreth into the stand and asked him to explain how it was that his horse had made such a wonderful improvement in two days' time. He claimed that the difference in weight was the cause, but with all the light furnished by the peculiar betting, this failed to satisfy the judges, and all were ruled off. Hildreth is said to be a capable trainer, but his horses have run in a very uncertain manner all winter.

Speaking of the different trotting horse breeders the Horseman says: Monroe Salisbury owner of Director, is tall, of athletic frame, gray hair and close-trimmed mustache, fair complexioned and blue eyed. He is good company and ever ready to defend the merits of Margaret S. and Direct. He hopes to land The Horseman's Great Expectation Stake with the former, which is, like her owner, a good traveler, and apparently looks forward to a trip across the continent with pleasure.

L. J. Rose, former owner of Stamboul, and proprietor of Rosemeade Stud, is a medium sized strongly built man, with a smooth face and dark, curling hair, tinged with gray. He is a most genial companion, a man of the world, and as an authority on breeding the trotter has no superior. Beginning with The Moor, Overland and Minnehaha he founded a stud which passed under the hammer recently for a sum hitherto unknown in auction records. Thousands were given for the representatives of the blood lines he blended at Sunny Slope, and later at Rosemeade. With Sultan's get he first achieved fame as a breeder, and the youngsters tracing to that horse have kept him in the swim since Sweetheart made her first bow to the public about ten years ago.

Leland Stanford, proprietor of Palo Alto Farm, is a tall, middle-aged, dark complexioned man, with gray hair and beard. He always dresses in black, with no jewelry or any other symbols of the great wealth he possesses. He is very dignified in his manner, but is of the nature that draws men to him. He has given the subject of breeding the trotter much study, and although many do not agree with his theories he is respected for having the courage to practically apply his convictions. With Electioneer and the mares purchased in the East, as well as a few selected in California, he has founded a family which by the records ranks as the fastest. To this sire belongs the honor of having four performers with records below 2:17, which is something never enjoyed by any trotting-breed stallion that has as yet been brought before the public. Palo Alto also developed a new era in colt-trotting, and its successes and methods have been instrumental in bringing many other families to the front early in life.

Wm. H. Mathews, well known as a superior care-taker of trotters, has just got back from South America, and among his first acts upon reaching his former home in Ticonderoga, N. Y., was to sit down and indite a letter to the Mirror and Farmer. The letter is a chatty one, and feeling sure that many of "Bill's" friends will be glad to hear from him again, we cull from it as follows: "I have just returned from Buenos Ayres, South America, and thought I would drop you a line to let you know that I have had a very fair season in the Spanish country. The horses that I took there have done well. I had on my staff Century, 2:25, Piano Boy 2:21½, and Little Walter, 2:29½. Among the other North American trotters there are Prince Wilkes, 2:14¾, Spofford, 2:18½, Gov. Hill, 2:18½, J. Q., 2:17½, Tempest, 2:19, Mambrino Archy, 2:24½, Pickwick, 2:26, Clara M., 2:29¾, Chasey Maid, 2:27¾, Endymion, 2:23½, Sir Roger, 2:22, and a few others. Prince Wilkes did not take kindly to the South American ways of racing; the standing starts didn't suit him at all; he won three races and went lame, and has been fired. Gov. Hill is by far the best there; he won nine races last season. Spofford comes next, with five winning brackets. J. Q. is also a failure in long races. Those people are the gamest set of men that ever attended a race meeting, and will bet more money than anybody, but it is more than a money matter to take a good horse there, as the risk is great. It takes about forty-five days to go from New York to Buenos Ayres, and there are few animals that it don't knock out. The boys here at Ti advertised a week's races, but the weather is so mild that they have declared them off. The horsemen here are all engaged in getting in ice for the New York market, and the colts are munching hay. There is no snow and the roads are very bad, not much like the weather last year, when we were looking over the stock. I saw John Splan in London, also Madam Marantanette and her manager, Mr. Harris, who all do their little tricks in Barnum's show. Splan has sold all the horses that he took to England, except Mambrino Sparkle, 2:17, and he will take her back. I leave here about the 14th with a carload for the Kellogg sale, belonging to the Baldwin estate, and after that I am ready to sign with any gentleman who wants the services of one of my calibre. Hoping to find you well, I remain, Yours truly,

W. H. Mathews.

THE FARM.

Cattle in the Torrid Zone.

The rearing of cattle in the torrid is neither so extensively nor so profitably carried on as in the temperate zones. The region within the tropics where cattle rearing is most successful, is on the elevated plains of South America; yet Brazil, fully as large as the United States, contains only about 20,000,000 cattle, while our country has over 50,000,000. The Brazilian cattle are long-horned, long-legged animals, of a yellow brown color resembling those of Mexico and Texas, and no improvement has taken place in this stock during the past 200 years. Butter, cheese and milk are almost unknown in Brazil, and what butter is used is imported from other countries. The milk consumed is the condensed product imported from the United States, while cheese is so rarely used as to cause but little demand for it. While cattle are numerous in Brazil, Rio Janeiro, the leading city, imports 54,000,000 pounds of dried beef from Uruguay and the Argentine Republic for the use of its people.

Many cattle are raised in the United States of Colombia, but there has been no attempt to improve the breed since they were introduced into South America by the Spaniards. Those raised upon the low plains when taken to the higher plateaus give to the grass through their saliva a poison known as "ranilla," which destroys many cattle of the cooler climate.

The grass has to be burned several times to kill this pest, which will often last a whole year before it can be got rid of. The hot country cattle, after being kept for some months on the higher plains, lose the power of poisoning the grass. Further losses are occasioned by tigers, as it is estimated that five per cent. of the cattle raised are killed by these animals. All cattle are pastured the whole year in the countries of South America, and receive no care during summer or winter, though twice a year the herds are rounded up to brand and mark the calves. In Peru no butter or cheese is made, and milk is seldom used. This country does not produce enough cattle for its own use, and many head are imported from Chili and the Argentine Republic.

In Venezuela, cattle roam at large during the whole year, no attention being paid to them except to brand the calves in the Spring and Fall. Many animals run wild, and are as unapproachable as deer or antelope. In Bolivia the guanac, the llama, alpaca and the iounha, take the place of cattle to a great extent. In the West Indies, owing to the heat of the climate, cattle do not thrive as well as in colder lands, and but few of them are raised.

In Honduras, while many cattle are reared, some peculiar customs prevail. The State law prohibits the slaughtering of cows; bulls are not castrated till three years of age, and are not killed for beef till six or seven years of age, so that Honduras has the poorest and toughest beef of any cattle country in the world. Instead of keeping their finest and best bulls to breed from, they select their strongest and largest for slaughtering, hence there is no improvement in the stock of that region.

Two causes interfere with cattle rearing in Honduras. The first is the presence of the puma or tiger, which is capable of killing a full grown bull, and annually destroys thousands of head; the second is a venomous spider which stings the animal just above the hoof, causing the foot to rot and drop off. Ownership in that country is indicated by branding, the same as in the western part of the United States.

In all Honduras there is not a butcher's block, saw or cleaver, but beef is torn from the bones with butcher knives, and is consumed in a few hours after the animal is slaughtered.

Cattle in Ceylon are of native stock, as the natural pasturage is so poor that European cattle will not thrive. The grass being of a coarse, wiry character, collects in a ball in the animal's stomach, and cannot be digested. The cattle must therefore be fed upon roots, grain, or other artificial food. The imported cattle cannot endure the humid climate of the sea coast, and must be kept on the elevated plains of the interior. The native cattle are the small, humpbacked, Singhalese breed which are difficult to improve, for when they are crossed with other breeds they do not produce a hardy and vigorous stock. While they improve in milking qualities, they lose in other points. These native cattle are only four feet high, and weigh when alive but 350 pounds. The cows give only two quarts of milk a day, and unless they are fed upon roots, grain, cotton-seed cake or poonac, they will give but half of this small amount. The milking season only lasts during six months of the year. These cattle are tough and hardy little animals, used as beasts of burden, and are driven in carts, often at the rate of six miles an hour.

Siam and Malaysia are not cattle breeding countries, and the cows are the lop-eared hump-backed kind, with a thin covering of hair. Milk and butter are almost unknown, and the cow is generally used as a beast of burden. For hundreds of years there has been no attempt to improve this class of animals. In Zanzibar the cattle are few in numbers and of little value. On the Philipine Islands the cattle are like most of those in hot countries, kept as beasts of burden rather than for dairy purposes.

In southern China, buffalos are more common than ordinary cattle. These animals, like those in parts of India and tropical Africa, are well adapted to the low marshy regions and hot climate of those countries. The buffalos are larger and more powerful, and can haul a greater load than the ordinary ox; they bear the heat better, and are not so subject to disease. In many parts of Asia and Africa they are packed like horses, but the loads they carry must be such that the water will not injure them, for the buffalo is almost certain to lie down in every stream he crosses. He prefers the rough, coarse herbage found in the marshy districts, and will wallow for hours in the water and mud till he is completely covered with a coat of the latter. These animals are extensively used in India, parts of China, the islands along the coast of Asia, in Egypt, Italy and Hungary.

The flesh of the buffalo is greatly inferior to that of the ox, but the buffalo cow gives a large quantity of milk, and it is from this milk that Ghee or the semi-fluid butter of India is made.

Cattle of Sierra Leone are of the scrub kind, and quite small. The beef is dry and tasteless, no butter is made, and what is used comes from goats. The Balonda negroes of Africa raise cattle, but they are wild, and have to be shot down like deer. Among the Demara tribes cattle are common, but milk is rarely used. The Kaffirs, on the other hand, milk their cows take good care of their stock. A hole is made through the nostrils of the animal, and through this a stick is inserted, so that if the cow does not stand still, the stick can be twisted, giving great pain to the animal and obliging her to remain quiet. Among the Kaffir tribes the yard where the cows are kept is called the Isi-Baya, and into this the women are never allowed to come on pain of death. Wives are bought and paid for with cows, each wife costing from eight to fourteen cows.

The Latooka tribes keep large numbers of cattle, and to prevent any being stolen. they are driven at night into large stockades, passing through a narrow gate-way just wide enough to admit one animal. Over this is hung a bell in such a manner that each one rings it in passing in or out. Cattle in the tropical parts of Australia are not so successful as in the temperate parts, and during the past ten years there has been a decrease there of almost 2,000,000 head. A little further south or in New Zealand, some of the finest cattle in the world are produced, and all the breeds are reared in great perfection.

In no part of the world are there such vast numbers of cattle and such splendid breeds as in the United States and Western Europe, nor is it probable that any part of the Torrid Zone will ever compete with the region just named in the rearing of fine cattle, though there is a good market for pure bred cattle, which will keep increasing. It is in our own country and those of Europe that cows are raised for dairy purposes, while in the tropical regions they become only beasts of burden or are killed for their hides and tallow.

G. S. Boynton, Oroville.

The Management of Boars.

One of the easiest things possible is to be able to find fault with the writings and mode of action of other people. Just to prove the truth of this to a slight extent, I will suggest that the communications of "A Farmer's Son" would have been read with more pleasure and profit had he given his name, as your readers would then have been able to estimate the value which ought to be placed on the opinions expressed by his communications which appeared in the Journal of the 3rd and 17th ult.

The system recommended in his first letter is not such a one as I adopt—this may simply prove that in this there are two ways of arriving a tthe same end—and to me it also appears as though the thirst for learning exhibited by "A Beginner" in the letter given in your issue of the 10th ult., will not be completely assuaged by the reply of "A Farmer's Son," which you gave last week. It struck me that "A Beginner" gave such valid reasons for his disagreement with the advice given that he was deserving of a somewhat more specific reply than was furnished by "A Farmer's Son" who seemed more anxious to show fight, to deal in generalities, and to credit "A Beginner" with opinions not expressed, than to really grasp the question and to give reasons for his actions and definite proof for his statements. If we closely analyze or boil down his reply it may prove to be very good; but it is no answer to, "A Beginner," nor does it furnish us with much of fact or instruction; of statement the reply is liberal, and here comes in the great necessity of your readers being furnished with the name of the person who gives his opinions and practices, as unsigned statements are nowadays looked upon with a certain amount of doubt. Besides this, if the public were only aware of the large and successful experience of "A Farmer's Son" how much more valuable for argumentative and practical purposes his writings might become.

Being myself, as I take "A Farmer's Son" to be of a retiring disposition. I too should like to air my opinions over a synonym, but I fear you might not allow me to do so after my remarks on anonymous writers. I must therefore keep my notions to myself and give you only my system of managing my boars and the sows at certain times.

As some few of your readers may be aware, I have for nearly thirty years, humored my fancy for pigs, and during that period I have tried well nigh every variety, some of them on a tolerably large scale. One of my greatest difficulties has been to obtain a really good boar, which will not only please the eye or win prizes, but a boar which will beget pigs true to type and well formed, and with no variety have I had greater difficulty than with Large Whites. I have not hesitated to give long prices. I have bought boars from the greatest prize winning herds, and the result has been much the same, the produce would come black and white, as did some of those by a noted Royal winner; of the little pigs from one litter would furnish small, middle or large whites, as did some litters begotten by a boar from one herd. This annoyance has caused me to try to do without purchasing many stock boars, and to effect this I am obliged to keep a somewhat larger number of boars of my own breeding to cross with the sows of the other distinct families or strains. This would strike some persons as an expensive system; so it is, but to it I attribute much of my success in pig breeding. In this opinion I am partially supported by a remark I heard made some years since by Mr. G. M. Sexton, whose success with his Small Blacks was almost phenomal. It was to the effect that he found himself well repaid by keeping a boar solely to mate with one particular sow which produced to this boar such good pigs. I have now eleven boars which are used more or less; ten of these were bred by myself. Four of the oldest of these—Holywell Giant 15th 699, Holywell Joseph (Vol. VI.) Holywell Jackie 989, and Holywell Judge 993—are located in an old shed divided off with rails, so that at all times the boars can see and smell each other, and, when they choose, can have a little talk with each other over the tops of the division rails. As these boars are all over two years old, they require little or no exercise beyond that which they give themselves when a sow is taken to be mated with one or other of them; there is then a little excitement amongst the disappointed ones, but this does not last long. As the sow is only allowed one service, she is then taken away at once, the uproar soon subsides, and a stranger going to look at the boars a few minutes afterwards would notice nothing unusual, although he might be surprised that boars so situated should be so quiet, all the boars coming to the gates in their turn to have their usual share of notice.

It is the greatest possible mistake to suppose that boars are naturally savage, they simply require to be well, but firmly treated, never give them an opportunity to prove that they are stronger than their attendants or feeders: I have had hundreds of boars, and only one has been really savage; this was Sampson VI, 123, a boar which won for me a number of prizes, including two at the Royal, and which I afterwards sold into the North, where he continued his showyard successes, and also sired a number of splendid pigs. This boar was made savage solely through the harsh treatment and nervousness of the old man who attended to him for a time. A change of feeder had some effect, but the bad habits were never wholly lost. None of his stock inherited the weakness, so we may infer that it was not hereditary. All young stock boars should be walked out for a few minutes occasionally, the attendant having a stick or a whip, keeping close to the quarters of the boar, and not allowing him to stop and to commence pawing and champing; the trouble begins when, if at any time, the boar faces the driver, and is thus better prepared for an attack, which, if serious and determined, is likely to be in favor of the quadruped. Many young boars of about a year old will champ and fume when first let out of their stye, especially if another boar has just been exercised on the same ground, but if he is kept on the move he soon quiets down, and walks off "like a Christian," as an old pig man of mine used to say.

Before we have got as far as this we have to select the young boar, and this ought, if possible, to be done almost as soon as the little pigs are farrowed. This can be done then just as easily, and with greater certainty, than when the pigs are weaned. The thickest, best shaped and most robust at two days will, barring accidents, be the best of the litter at maturity, whereas the best and fattest pig at weaning time often owes its apparent superiority to the position of the teat at which it has sucked, and sometimes to the decease of its neighbor, so that it has had two teats to suck instead of one. This or any other advantage cannot be obtained by any of the litter before birth. They then share alike, and the one best developed when farrowed is constitutionally stronger, or is by nature better formed than its brothers and sisters. This is no theory or assertion, but approved fact.

One of the chief requirements in the successful growth of a young boar, whether he be intended solely for breeding or exhibition purposes or for the two combined, is plenty of exercise from the age of two to at least six months. You may appear to sacrifice flesh, and even at times growth, but you secure health, muscle and sound joints. Numbers of boars are rendered useless at an early age by being kept shut up in a small stye and highly fed when they are young in order to bring them early to maturity and to improve their appearance, the owner entirely forgetting that in a state of nature the young boar is of a most roaming disposition, and that by the repeated selection of the most sleepy and the most prone to lay on fat, we have made the boar still more dependent upon a certain amount of liberty to secure a healthy development of the chief organs.

Many young boars are also rendered infertile at an early age through being used as soon as they show any desire, from being too frequently used when young or being turned amongst a considerable number of yelts or sows. In the latter case the boar will often completely exhaust himself in his frequent attentions to an old sow which will persist in remaining in a state of heat for three or four days. If this be often repeated the boar loses muscle and appetite and soon becomes sterile, whilst the number of pigs in each litter will be small, and the pigs often weakly and sometimes ruptured. I have more than once proved that by too frequent use of a boar, the number of pigs which he will beget from the sow put to him at the latter period, are neither so numerous nor so good. It is also a great mistake to have the boars' house within hearing of the place where the sows are located; the boar becomes restless and iritated, and he acquires bad habits if the sows at certain times are allowed to be within sight, scent, or hearing. The young boar should be at least seven or eight months old before he is mated with a young sow, and if properly managed a boar of really good constitution will often remain fertile until he be seven or eight years old.—Sanders Spencer, in London Live Stock Journal.

Shipment of Holsteins to South America.

By the steamer "City of New York", sailing on the 22nd of March, 1890, there was shipped from Mr. F. H. Burke's ranch at Menlo Park, two bulls and four females, thoroughbred Holstein—Friesians, to Valparaiso. These were shipped to fill an order, and were the first ever sent to South America, although Mr. Burke has sent cattle to British Columbia, the Sandwich Islands and Mexico, but has never before sent them south of the equator.

The largest bull sent was "El Cuervo Netherland", one of the best bulls ever seen in a California show ring and for him an extra large stall had to be built, being ten inches longer than any other ever put upon a mail steamer on this coast. He is a winner of the following prizes:

First prize in Oakland in 1888 as the best two year old Holstein bull; at the Sacramento State Fair in the same year, first prize as a two year old, at Stockton Fair the same year he took the first prize and also stood at the head of the herd winning first prize, and won the sweepstakes himself.

In 1889, first prize in Napa as the best bull of any age, head of the winning herd in Napa, first prize in Petaluma the same year, head of the herd there and sweepstakes. At the Sacramento State Fair in 1889 he was awarded the first prize as the best Holstein bull of any age, showing against the largest number of Holsteins ever entered for prizes in California. Also stood at the head of the sweepstake herd at the State Fair, and as an individual winning the sweepstakes for Holsteins.

The other bull is a youngster by El Cuervo Netherland. In the consignment goes the show cow "Edna of Troy" who was in the herd winning the first prize in Stockton in 1886, and was also awarded (the same year and at the same fair) first prize as the best yearling cow; also first prize in San Jose as the best yearling and was one of the herd winning there in 1887. She was awarded the first prize in Oakland as a two year old, and also at Stockton and San Jose the same year.

The other animals are as yet untried heifers These animals have been brought by large ranch owners in South America to experiment with the breed.

Imports and Exports.

In 1889 the United States imported sheep for food purposes to the value of $1,130,281, against $1,206,328 the year before. Of sheep for breeding purposes we imported $95,11[illegible] worth, against $74,034 worth the year before. Our imports of wool in the same time were worth $18,696,277, against $14,547,244, in 1888: manufactures of wool to the value of $54,080,159 against $49,984,298 in 1888. The total importations of sheep, wool and manufactures of wool last year then amounted in value to $74,001,835 against $65,806,90[illegible] in 1888.

In the same time we exported sheep to the value of $393,[illegible]185 against $243,483 in 1884; mutton, $30,642, against $16,[illegible]955; wool, $43,433, against $5,228; manufactures of wool $397,235, against $396,757. Our total exports of this kind would then foot up $864,495 against $662,483 in 1888. That is to say, in 1888 our imports of flock products were worth over 85½ times as much as our exports.

Horses, Cattle and Chickens.

For colic and grubs, for lung fever, cough or hide-bound I give Simmons Liver Regulator (liquid) in one ounce doses or, one teaspoonful of the powder in a mash twice a day. You can recommend it to every one having stock as the best medicine known for the above complaints. In using it with my chickens, for cholera and gapes, I mix it with the dough and feed it to them once a day. By this treatment I have lost none where the Regulator was given promptly and regularly.—E. T. Taylor, Agt. for Grangers of Ga.

ATHLETICS.

Athletic Sports and Other Pastimes.

EDITED BY ARPHIPPUS.

SUMMARY.

The first cross country run of the Alpine Amateur Athletic Club which took place at Sausalito on Sunday last was a great success. Below will be found the programmes of two very important out-door athletic meetings which will come off in this city within two months. Several notes of interest to the athletes will be found in these columns under their particular headings.

RUNNERS, WALKERS, JUMPERS, ETC.

The report that James Jarvis the English walker was about to leave the city is not true. Mr. Jarvis has no intention of departing from San Francisco at present and he will represent the Olympic Club in the one and three mile walks at the championship meeting on May 30.

Messrs Cherry and Lichtenstein of the Alpine Club are practicing daily with the rapiers and will give an exhibition of their skill at the coming "Ladies Night" exhibition.

Frank L. Cooley the well known amateur runner is interesting himself in the study of Hamlet. It is his intention to appear in the role of an amateur actor in the near future.

It would appear that the members of the recently organized Garden City Athletic Club of San Jose are intent on making a great show at the championship games. Strange that so many good men spring up all at once. From the accounts published during the past week in the daily papers the San Jose athletes are all capable of winning championships. The morning of May 30 may see a good many disappointed athletes rise from their couches after having spent a weary night.

The annual games of the San Francisco Athletic Club will be held at Glen Ellen, Sonoma Co. Cal. on Sunday, April 20.

Judging from the success of the two cross country runs lately held at Sausalito a championship cross country run under the auspices of the P. C. A. A. A. may possibly be given during the summer.

The Atheneum Athletic Club has gone out of existence. Some of its members have retired entirely from the athletic world whilst others have connected themselves with other clubs.

It is claimed that the Pacific Athletic Club is still in existence, but we would like to know where the members meet. Action has already been taken in regard to the Standing of the club by the P. C. A. A. A. and in a short while it will be decided whether the club is a dead letter or not.

According to the New York Clipper of March 22. Horace Coffin is credited with holding the Pacific Coast Amateur half mile running record of 3min. 31sec. The eastern folks must think the runners out this way awful slow. Mr. Coffin's record is for a walk and not a run, hence the error. The same paper in its list of coming events announces that on May 30 the O. C. will will hold its spring games and on July 4 the P. C. A. A. A. will hold its annual championship games. These announcements are certainly new to the athletes here for it has already been decided that the grounds of the O. C. will be opened on May 30 with the championship games of the P. C. A. A. A.

A league has been formed to play for the amateur baseball championship of the Pacific Coast. The following clubs have already entered teams: The University of California, Berkeley, the Reliance of Oakland, and the Olympic and E & O. E.'s of San Francisco. A pennant will be played for, and each club will play two games with each of the others. The games are to take place at the new Oakland grounds which are being fitted up.

The University Lawn Tennis Club is in a very flourishing condition. The members pay their dues regularly, and one and all seem to take an active interest in the game.

The members of the Alpine Amateur Athletic Club held their initial cross-country run from the Dexter Cottage at Sausalito on Sunday last. Thirty-three members went over from this side on the 10 A. M. boat. Both Mr. and Mrs. Ross Jackson, of the Dexter Cottage, received the athletes with open arms, and the best rooms in the house were turned over to the runners to be used as dressing rooms. At 11:17, H. O. Farrell, the treasurer of the club, started the following men on their long tramp over to the Fog station at Lime Point and return: C. W. Meyer, C. Vultee, W. Frank, P. N. Gafney, E. P. Moody, J. D. Garrison, E. P. Levy, A. M. King, F. E Holland, C. Larkey, R. J Luttringer, E. Goodman, Harry Lechtenstein, M. Landeker, Sol Choynski, W. C. Clark, A. Cooke, S. Herzog, George W. Armbruster, Chas. Armbruster, C. Little, F. S. Ralph, H. C. Casidy, W. F. Vollmer, J. J Larkey, F. M. Howard, K. L. Martin, George Williamson, T. V. Kennedy, T. S. Brown, T. L. Carroll and E. Lewis.

The contestants were arrayed in different colored costumes, and they formed a very pleasing and interesting sight as they sped on their way towards the hills. The run to the Fog station, 3 miles, was made in 19 minutes. After resting a few minutes the pack started for home, but after going a short distance, the boys divided into two teams; one team under the guidance of John D. Garrison continuing on the old trial, the other team preferring to climb over a high hill which loomed up in the distance. The Garrison team arrived home in 39 minutes, the leader arriving at the finishing point some 2 minutes ahead of his men. The Cassidy team, on account of having covered more ground, did not get back until 4 minutes later.

The day was exceptionally fine, and the boys enjoyed the run immensely, the pace being very moderate. After bathing and cooling off, the hungry athletes assembled in the dining-room of the Dexter Cottage, where a fine lunch was served. H. O. Farrell acted as toast master. A vote of thanks was given to Mr. and Mrs. Jackson for the very hospitable manner in which they treated the Alpine boys. The participants all returned to the city on the boat which left Sausalito at 4:15.

The University cinder path is in a very bad condition, and should be fixed at once, so that the students may be able to train properly for the coming games.

The University athletes who intend competing in the distance races at the championship games are training on the road in front of the new Chemistry Department, the cinder path being in too bad a state to allow of training on it.

The second Field Day of the Alpine Amateur Athletic Club will be held, possibly at the Bay District track, on Sunday, May 4th, commencing at 1.30 P. M. sharp. The programme, which consists of seven closed events and four open, is as follows, for members of the club only:—

1. 100 yards run, novice.
2. 120 yards run, handicap.
3. 210 yards hurdle, handicap, 2ft. 6in.
4. 880 yards run, handicap.
5. Seven eighths mile steeplechase, handicap.
6. 1 mile run, handicap.
7. Running high jump, handicap.

The open events are:—

8. 3 mile walk, handicap.
9. 3 mile run, handicap.
10. 100 yards run, handicap.
11. 440 yards run, handicap.

Two prizes will be given for each event, and the winners may select either medals or prizes, according to their tastes. An entrance fee of fifty cents will be charged for each event. Entries may be made to the Secretary of the Alpine Athletic Club, 706 Powell street, San Francisco, or to the Secretaries of the different clubs belonging to the Pacific Coast Amateur Athletic Association.

We are in receipt of the following communication from Mr. F. L. Cooley, the champion amateur long distance runner of the Pacific Coast, and a member of the Olympic Club:

Editor Breeder and Sportsman:—

DEAR SIR, In one of the daily papers of Monday last appeared a challenge from Mr. Rankin of the Alpine Athletic Club, in which he offers to run any amateur in America. If Mr. Rankin will place a deposit in the hands of the BREEDER AND SPORTSMAN, I will immediately cover the same and arrange a five mile race with him to take place on the Olympic Club grounds five weeks after signing articles. The agreement must be drawn up in strict accordance with the amateur rules. Yours truly,

F. L. COOLEY,
Olympic Club, San Francisco, Cal.

March 26th, 1890.

The following is a list of the championship events which will be decided on Decoration Day at the new grounds of the Olympic Club:—

1. 100 yards run.
2. 220 yards run.
3. 440 yards run.
4. 880 yards run.
5. 1 mile run.
6. 3 mile run.
7. 1 mile walk.
8. 3 mile walk.
9. Running high jump.
10. Running long jump.
11. Pole vault.
12. Throwing 16 lb hammer.
13. Putting 16 lb. shot.
14. Flinging 56 lb. weight.
15. 120 yards hurdle, 2ft. 6in.
16. 220 yards hurdle, 2ft. 6in.

In addition three events will be added which will be open only to members of the Olympic Club.

The regular championship events will be all scratch, the Olympic events will be handicap. An entrance fee of $1 will be charged, fifty cents to be returned to starters. Three costly medals will be awarded for each event, and the club winning the most points will be presented with a handsome pennant emblematic of the championship for 1890. The entries will close on May 20, 1890.

Hereafter associate clubs of the P C A A A giving open games must comply with the rules of the American Athletic Union. All open handicap events must be handicapped by the official handicapper of the P C A A A. This official has not yet been elected but the probabilities are that Captain Jordan, of the O C, will be selected. In the past he has proven himself to be a competent handicapper, and it would be hard to find a man with more experience or better able to fill the position.

It is proposed to hold a wrestling tournament at the Olympic Club rooms sometime in May.

Two or three members of the Lurline Club who are good runners are anxious that the club make application for membership in the P C A A A.

THE WHEELMEN.

The rules of the League of American Wheelmen forbid racing on Sunday, and the Alpine Athletic Club will not add a bicycle race to its next outdoor programme on this account.

The Oakland Bicycle Club of 1889, will take an active interest in racing this year. The club will be strongly represented at the coming tournament.

The California Division, League of American Wheelmen, has decided to hold its next annual meeting on April 19th. At this meeting arrangements will be made for the Fourth of July tournament. The divisions of Napa, San Jose, Stockton and Sacramento are taking an active interest in the coming tournament and a number of good races are looked for. A road book will be issued to members giving the available country roads and the distances from this city.

There will be a picnic run of the Bay City Wheelmen tomorrow to Lake Honda. The start will take place from the corner of Van Ness and Market streets. Captain Richardson will start the men at 10 A. M. sharp, and all the wheelmen are requested to be on time.

According to the rules of the A A U, a two-mile bicycle race should be added to the championship programme of the P C A A A, but as the new track of the Olympic Club is so small the chances are that that event will be dropped from the list.

AT THE OARS.

Sunday was all that could be desired by the oarsmen, and several knights of the oars made their appearance on the bay.

The Lurline Club will hold its second high jinks next month. Jimmie Carroll has consented to spar four rounds with some other prominent middle weight. A good programme will be given.

John Muirhead, the amateur single sculler of the Ariel Club will send East and get a Ruddock boat as he seriously thinks of entering the regatta this year.

The Ariel Club has expended the sum of $100 in repairing the float in front of their house and underpinning the house itself, and the club will probably remain in its present quarters for some time to come.

James Cochran has at last began his career as a single sculler. Last Sunday, while taking the first trial in a shell, he received a sudden introduction to Neptune, and after getting back into his boat again he continued rowing for an hour without taking his second plunge. He is a very promising student in the art of sculling.

The Pioneer Club shows the most activity at present. All the club boats were out on Sunday. Hanrahan and Coffey, Espy and Larson will no doubt form the amateur crew from this club.

Referring to the challenge recently issued by Henry Petersen offering Henry Henceman of Stockton fifteen seconds' start in a three mile race, we do not see how the former can afford to be so liberal. From the tone of a letter which we received from a friend residing in Stockton, it would seem that Henceman can row just as fast as Petersen has ever done during his many trials. Henceman has rowed a trial this spring inside of 21 minutes while training for his race with Charley Long.

Messrs. Ronard (Captain) O'Brien, Berkeley and Murphy, with Dunn as coxswain, have been rowing to Harbor View during the pleasant evenings of the present week.

The Dolphin Club had out two barge crews, and their pleasure barge with several lady friends went to Hunters Point for dinner. After enjoying the sparkling wit of Brother Dwyer the ladies voted the sail a decided success.

The South End Club have at last awoke from their long slumber and sent out three crews on Sunday. The members indulged in several impromptu races around Mission Rock and back to the boat house.

H. O. Farrell, the Secretary of the Pacific Rowing Association, writes that the next meeting of the Association will be held at the rooms of the Alpine Club, 706 Powell street, on Monday evening, April 7th. The reconstruction of the amateur rules relating to the Pacific Rowing Association will be taken up, and the rules and amendments passed at the last meeting will be adopted.

CLUB JOTTINGS.

A general meeting of the Alpine Amateur Athletic Club will be held on Thursday evening next.

The regular monthly exhibition of the Golden Gate Athletic Club was successfully held last Wednesday evening at the club rooms on Stevenson street.

An athletic club is being formed at San Mateo. Messrs. T. Coleman C. Hatch, W. Price, Dr. Baldwin and P. Maloney are the Committee on Organization.

The Garden City Wheelman of San Jose, Cal., will try to shut out the Alpine Athletic Club at the coming championship games. There are some old and experienced athletes in the Alpine Club and the San Jose tyros will have their hands full in trying to defeat them.

The new out door grounds of the Olympic club are now in full possession of the athletic committee and the athletes may begin to use them whenever they desire.

A meeting of the P. C. A. A. A. was held at the Olympic Club rooms on Friday evening last. Walter A. Scott presiding. A programme of the events for the championship games was adopted and it was decided that the rules of the American Athletic Union will in future be adopted by the Association as far as the holding of games is concerned. The meeting adjourned to last evening.

A few of the Olympic Club members are kicking because the Directors agreed to allow a club of ladies to use the gymnasium two mornings each week. As only a handful of members are incommoded by this agreement it is probable the kick will amount to nothing. Perhaps if ten young men who are doing the kicking were allowed to watch the fair ones they would forget their objections and hold their tongues. The class began practice on Monday morning under the guidance of Professors Smyth and Trouchet and the headway made by the young ladies in the course of a couple of hours was most wonderful. When the class grows larger the fair ones may rent club rooms of their own where they will be enabled to practice muscular development without fear of being seen by the "horrid men."

The Inter-Collegiate Athletic Association has declined to join the Amateur Athletic Union.

J. M. Crowie, the ex-amateur champion sprinter of England, will run for the Manhattans this year.

Luther Cary, of Chicago, is running in grand form. He will represent the Manhattans at the championships the coming season.

At the last meeting of the Directors of the Western Association, it was decided to hold the boxing and wrestling championship at St. Louis, on March 28th and 29th, instead of at Chicago.

Eastern men are anxious to have the Western Association clubs go into the Union. It is likely that a meeting of representatives of both bodies will be held before long.

The Pennsylvania Bicycle Club of Philadelphia has twelve lady members.

The report of Secretary Bassett L. A. W., showed that income from membership had been $16,701. Of the sum collected, $10,342.50 had been distributed to 30 state divisions and the balance retained by the organization. The secretary said that of the 1558 members who joined the first year, but 95 now remain on the rolls. The membership of the league at present is 12,500. New York stands first in membership, Massachusetts second, and Pennsylvania third. Treasurer Brewster's report shows a balance of $1,887.

JOTTINGS FROM ALL OVER.

The indoor championship meeting for this year will be held at Mechanic's Building, Boston, Mass., on Saturday evening, April 12th. This is the second of these supplementary championships. The events are such as are, of course, not included in the outdoor programme, and the walks and runs are at intermediate distances. The standard A A U championship medals are given—gold to first, silver to second, bronze to third. The events are as follows: Seventy-five yard run, 150-yard run, 300-yard run, 600 yard run, 1000-yard run, two mile run, three-quarter mile walk, four-mile walk, standing broad jump, standing high jump, three standing broad jumps, running hop, step and jump; pole vault for distance, throwing 56 lb weight for height, putting 24-lb shot, 200-yard hurdle, 10 flights, 3ft 6in high; 300-yard hurdle, 10 flights, 2ft 6in high. An entrance fee of $2 will be charged for each event, and must be made before April 5th to James E. Sullivan, P. O. Box 611, New York City.

The following dispatch was received on Wednesday last:

LONDON, March 26th—The Oxford-Cambridge boat race was rowed to-day in the presence of an immense crowd of people. The Oxfords were strong favorites in the betting and the dark blue was the popular decoration.

The start was made promptly.

At Hammersmith Bridge Cambridge was leading by about half a length. But Oxford steadily forged to the front, and at Barnes Bridge was half a length ahead and won easily.

The time of the race was 22 minutes 3 seconds.

Thomas Cahill has brought suit against the Pastime Athletic Club of St. Louis, Mo., for $500 damages. He was expelled from the club on charges of bribery connected with a football game.

THE GUN.

The L. C. Smith Gun.

We would respectfully call your attention to some of the principal shooting events of 1887 and 1888, which we trust you will accept as substantial proof that the Smith Guns are far in the lead in handling and shooting qualities, which has led to its general adoption by expert trap shooters, who want the best shooting and handling guns obtainable.

At the Chamberlin Cartridge Co.'s Tournament, held at Cleveland, O., from September 13th to 16th inclusive, for the year 1887, the "Smith" gun won first money in every class. It also won nearly two-thirds of the entire amount ($3,000) of cash prizes, and championship Diamond Trophy which was awarded with first money in the 90 class. In the 90 class it won the 1st, 2d and 4th moneys; in the 80 class it took the 1st, 3d, 4th and 5th; in the 70 class it took 1st and 2d, with the 1st and 6th in the 60 class, making a total winning nearly four times greater than any other gun, of either foreign or home manufacture.

At the Chamberlin Cartridge Co.'s Tournament, held at Cleveland, O., September 12th to 14th inclusive, for the year 1888, the "Smith" gun won first money in the 90, 80 and 60 classes. It also won the Diamond Trophy, which was awarded to the winner of first money in 90 class, and nearly two-thirds of the entire amount (3,000) of cash prizes.

At the Keystone Manufacturing Co.'s Tournament, held at Corry, Pa., September 18, 19, 20, and 21, 1888, the "Smith" gun won all of the trophies, and out of the $1,351 50 in cash prizes in this tournament, it won $901.04. Considering that eight other makes of guns were used in this tournament, you will see what remarkable winners the "L. C. Smith" guns are.

Below we give the scores of the prize winners of above shoots as it appears upon the score-books. .... denotes guns of other manufacture.

HUNTER ARMS CO.

WINNERS IN CHAMBERLIN CARTRIDGE COMPANY'S TOURNAMENT IN 1887—AT 100 SINGLE BLUE ROCKS.

C. W. Budd	Score 95	1st Prize	$ 50.00 Trophy. / 300.00	Smith Gun.
H. McMurchy	Score 89	2d Prize	225.00	Smith Gun.
J. H. Stice	Score 88	3d Prize	150.00	....
R. E. Sheldon	Score 86	4th Prize	75.00	Smith Gun.
80 Class.				
H. W. Eager	Score 95	1st Prize	$250.00	Smith Gun
Al. Bandle	Score 93	2d Prize	200.00	....
L. S. Carter	Score 92	3d Prize	125.00	Smith Gun
R. Valentine	Score 91	4th Prize	75.00	Smith Gun
J. G. Parsons	Score 89	5th Prize	50 00	Smith Gun
70 Class.				
J. L. Winston	Score 96	1st Prize	$200 00	Smith Gun
John Sayle	Score 87	2d Prize	150.00	Smith Gun
T. A. Peacock	Score 86	3d Prize	125.10	....
S. A. Tucker	Score 85	4th Prize	75.00	....
A. W. Ball	Score 84	5th Prize	50.00	....
60 Class.				
T. D. Kelsey	Score 94	1st Prize	$200 00	Smith Gun
E. E. Sample	Score 93	2d Prize	175.00	....
C. W. Hart	Score 91	3d Prize	150.00	....
E. D. Keeney	Score 90	4th Prize	125.00	....
George Schatlete	Score 89	5th Prize	100 00	Smith Gun
S. Gay, Jr.	Score 88	6th Prize	75.(0	....
A. O. Tehrman	Score 87	7th Prize	50.00	....
A. O. Dick	Score 85	8th Prize	25 10	....

WINNERS IN CHAMBERLIN CARTRIDGE COMPANY'S TOURNAMENT IN 1888. AT 100 SINGLE BLUE ROCKS.

99 Class				
H. McMurchy	Score 94	1st prize	$5 00 Trophy. / $200.00	Smith Gun
C. W. Hart	Score 93	2nd Prize	150.00	....
L. S. Carter	Score 92	3rd Prize	100.00	Smith Gun
Al. Bandle	Score 91	4th Prize	90.00	Smith Gun
W. R. Huntington	Score 90	5th Prize	80.00	....
C. W. Budd	Score 89	6th Prize	60.00	Smith Gun
C. M. Roof	Score 88	7th Prize	40.00	....
D. C. Powers	Score 87	8th Prize	30.00	Smith Gun
80 Class.				
H. B. Whitney	Score 96	1st Prize	$150.00	Smith Gun
A. Burnison	Score 94	2nd Prize	125.00	Smith Gun
R. G. Heikes	Score 93	3rd Prize	100.00	....
George Osborne	Score 92	4th Prize	90.00	Smith Gun
O. Regadanz	Score 89	5th Prize	70.00	....
J. N. Whiteside	Score 88	6th Prize	60.00	Smith Gun
J. S. Acklin	Score 87	7th Prize	50.00	Smith Gun
E. H. Smith	Score 86	8th Prize	30.00	Smith Gun
J. A. Buble	Score 84	9th Prize	25.00	....
70 Class.				
Wm. Stegler	Score 94	1st Prize	$150.00	....
Paul North	Score 93	2nd Prize	125.00	....
Chas. Wagner	Score 88	3rd Prize	100.00	Smith Gun
A. B. Chandler	Score 87	4th Prize	90.00	Smith Gun
"R. Beiers"	Score 86	5th Prize	70 00	....
F. F. Cummings	Score 85	6th Prize	60.00	....
R. J. Martin	Score 84	7th Prize	50.00	....
A. C. Krueger	Score 83	8th Prize	30.00	Smith Gun
W. McCormack	Score 82	9th Prize	25.00	Smith Gun
60 Class.				
E. D. Miller	Score 94	1st Prize	$150.00	Smith Gun
Walter Keenan	Score 93	2nd Prize	125 00	....
H. G. Wheeler	Score 92	3rd Prize	100.00	Smith Gun
A. Baker	Score 91	4th Prize	90 00	Smith Gun
Vincent	Score 90	5th Prize	75.00	....
J. M. Girton	Score 89	6th Prize	60.00	....
C. W. McFee	Score 88	7th Prize	50.10	Smith Gun
T. A. Close	Score 87	8th Prize	40.00	....
S. D. West	Score 86	9th Prize	35.00	Smith Gun
D. S. Allen	Score 85	10th Prize	30.00	....
A. B. Jones	Score 84	11th Prize	25.00	....
J. Wayper	Score 83	12th Prize	2*.f0	....

WINNERS OF THE TROPHIES AT THE KEYSTONE MANUFACTURING CO'S TOURNAMENT AT CORRY, PA, 1888.

All of the trophies at this tournament were won with L. C. Smith Guns, with the following scores:

Keystone Trophy, Solid Silver Tankard, value $950, was won by J. E. Miller, Smith Gun, with a score of 49 out of 50, Keystone Targets.

L. C. Smith Trophy, L. C. Smith Cup, was won by Chas. Wagener, Smith Gun, with a score of 49 out of 50, Keystone Targets.

Peters Cartridge Co. Trophy. Silver pitcher, was won by E. D. Miller, Smith Gun, with a score of 50 straight, Keystone Targets.

Individual Championship Contest of America. Diamond Ring, by Keystone Manufacturing Co., won by C. W. Budd, Smith Gun, with a score of 98 out of 100, Keystone Targets.

Out of the $1,351 50 in cash prizes in this tournament the Smith Gun won $901.04.

The officers of the recently organized San Diego Game and Fish Protective Association are: T. J. Monahan, President; Martinez Chick, vice-President; F. S. Ecker, Secretary and Treasurer. An Executive Committe was formed as follows: T. J. Monahan, Percy Goodwin, M. Chick, F. S. Ecker and E. T. Grether. This committee is to act in connection with J. M. Bailhache, who has been appointed Fish and Game Commissioner of San Diego county. The intention is to secure a rigid enforcement of the game and fish laws, and the club will take measures for the prosecution of all persons found unlawfully killing, buying, selling or offering for sale, transporting or having in their possession.

Alameda County Club.

The first meeting of the season was held at Oakland Trotting Park on Saturday last. All conditions were most favorable, and the poor scores are only to be accounted for by the fact that the birds were all quick drivers, the best shot at for many a day.

Mr. C. M. Osborn carried away first prize. He was in great form and shot beautifully, getting but one incomer, But two others of the eighteen got into double figures, Messrs. J. O. Cadman and H. Schroeder.

The prizes for the year are a match box of gold and silver, fashioned into a shot cartridge, with a fine diamond for a primer; a medal and a gold dog whistle.

The scores were:

S. E. Knowles	0	1	2	0	2	2	1	2	0	0	0	1—7
J. O. Cadman	2	1	2	2	1	1	1	1	0	1	0	1—10
W. W. Haskell	0	2	1	2	0	0	0	1	0	1	1	1—7
A. H. Higgins	0	0	0	0	1	1	2	0	0	0	0	0—3
F. B. Norton	2	0	1	0	1	0	0	1	2	1	1	2—8
O. T. Boardman	0	1	2	0	0	1	2	0	2	2	0	0—6
J. O. Morrison	1	2	2	2	0	0	0	2	1	1	0	1—8
H. Schroeder	2	0	1	1	1	2	2	1	0	2	2	1—10
S. I. Kellogg	2	1	2	2	1	2	0	0	0	1	2	0—8
G. E. Plummer	0	0	1	0	0	1	1	0	0	0	0	0—3
C. M. Osborn	1	2	0	1	2	1	2	1	1	1	1	2—11
A. F. Adams	0	1	1	0	0	2	2	2	0	1	0	1—7
W. E. Mayhew	1	1	0	0	1	0	0	1	2	0	1	0—6
R. E. Bell	1	1	1	2	0	2	1	2	0	2	0	2—9
C. B. Smith	1	1	0	1	2	1	1	0	2	0	1	2—9
Charles Lainer	0	2	1	2	0	1	1	0	1	0	1	1—8
H. B. Houghton	2	0	0	1	2	1	2	1	2	1	0	0—8
J. H. Mangels	1	1	0	2	0	2	0	1	1	0	2	0—7

Pheasants.

The common English pheasant, *Phasianus colchicus*, has been so long naturalised in that country, we are apt to forget that it was originally introduced there. Its native haunts are supposed to be on the banks of the river Phasis, which runs through ancient Colchis in Asia Minor, and perhaps the earliest record of its presence in England is given by Bishop Stubbs, who shows by the regulations of Harold, 1059, *unus phasianus* is presented as alternative to two partridges or other birds as rations for the canons of Waltham Abbey.

The pheasant loves the shelter of the wood or copse, the thick bushy underwood composed of stunted shrubs, bramble bushes, and other wild plants, where it remains quietly resting most of the day, preferring the evening and early morning as the time for visiting its feeding ground in the adjacent fields. During the autumn and winter months it perches at night in the larch or other fir trees, where its conspicuous appearance on a moonlight night renders it an easy prey to the nocturnal poacher. In the winter the males usually keep by themselves, "and in spring again choose a domain of their own, strutting, crowing, and clapping their wings to the admiration of the females." The pheasant (as need not be said for the information of sportsmen), is liable to sport in its plumage, some being found pied, and occasionally white specimens have been met with, but the most common variety, which is now so numerous as to be almost considered distinct, has a white ring round its neck, and is in other parts slightly paler in color than the true specimens.

Some Shooting Men.

These are days of change in sport as in everything else. The very nature of shooting is altered. The cause has been assigned to the change in our agricultural system, or to the artificial rearing now in vogue, rendered necessary by the ever increasing number of shooting men, says an old English hand. Now and again one meets with a sportsman of the old school, who sneers at modern improvements, but as a rule they too have marched with the times, and have adapted themselves to modern ideas. Take for instance the case of the Major, who is to be met with at most shooting parties; that red-faced, jovial creature, the remains of a good shot and better billiard player. He has been a sportsman more or less all his life. He was in India at the time of the Mutiny, which he calls being "all through it, sir!" the difference dwindling during dinner and disappearing after it. The only remnant of old ideas in his case is that he always shoots black powder out of the second barrel; otherwise he moves with his age, and although not rich, spends his money like a prince, and his winters at Monte Carlo. A much more conservative individual is Jones, the senior partner in the city firm of that name. Precise business men are as a rule bad shots. They have mostly started sport comparatively late in life, and even then do not get any useful practice. It is confined to the barn-door sort of shooting which they get on their own or their friends' places, all, as the land agents have it, conveniently situated at so many minutes' run by fast train from the city. For obvious reasons they prefer shooting partridges out of standing corn, or pheasants out of hedgerows, to anything more ambitions, and if by chance a tall bird is put over them, they are quite at sea; indeed, if they manage to get their gun off at all at it, they are quite pleased. And so it is that from choice or necessity they are greatly behind the times, unless it be in the matter of guns, of which they have as a rule a fine selection, often buying a pair of chokebores before they know how to use one which has not the ghost of a "pinch" in it.

It is impossible to go out shooting much without meeting the most dangerous gun of all, a man about town. He comes out, not because he cares for the sport, but to display his gorgeous shooting attire, and to be able to have something to yarn about at the club afterwards. He is the sort of man that one hears of as going to have lessons on shooting, and who cannot understand why it is that he can make good practice with turnips thrown over his head to resemble pheasants, and yet that when face to face with the real article finds a distinct falling off. But it is the old story of the cabbages and the senators, with an eyeglass and perpetual cigarettes thrown in. A pseudo sportsman in every sense, his experience is derived solely from the none too trustworthy correspondence which fills some of our sporting papers, from which he has evolved sundry new doctrines, such as firing off both barrels at once at more than usually distant birds. He should be watched very narrowly at corners, else he will shoot your pheasants on the ground and the beaters in the legs.

Heaven forbid that it should ever be your bad fortune out shooting to meet a sporting parson who has brought his dog with him. Both master and dog may be quiet enough at home before the library fire, but as soon as they have seen a rabbit or two, and heard some shots fired, they both go raving mad. The parson shoots at birds flying low along the line, and swears at missing them. The dog catches the infection and darts into the covert after the next rabbit that hops across the ride. Yap, yap! away he goes up and down the wood, until at last he emerges from the corner where the last rise was to have taken place, amid a cloud of pheasants and a storm of oa——. No, that is just the worst of it, the presence of the holy man, albeit the cause of all the evil, is a check to such a free use of Her Majesty's English as might do justice to the occasion.

Very soon after a day's shooting begins, especially if the birds are flying well or the wind is high, the guns will find their real level. A really first class shot is rarely met with, the more's the pity; but each least bad shot among a lot of duffers will think himself to be one, and his friends will flatter the delusion. A man may be from some cause or another off color and shooting badly, but it is quite easy to see, from the way he handles his weapon and takes his birds, if he knows what he is about. Another man may, on the contrary, on the particular day make a fairly good average of kills out of the cartridges fired, but then if you watch him, you will see that he refuses all difficult chances, tailors a good many very fair shots, and if you ask him about his bag he will exaggerate, if not deliberately lie to you.

The San Diego Fish and Game Protective Association offers a reward of $25 to any person causing the arrest and conviction of anyone guilty of violating the game and fish laws. The club starts under good officers and fair auspices and should do good work.

There is no doubt but that the Indians in the mountains are wastefully killing deer. The snows have driven the game down, and Mr. Lo, who claims immunity from the game laws, has gone to slaughtering them for their hides. This course will soon exterminate the deer, for they do not even respect spotted fawns.—Kern Co, Californian.

[Indians have no rights superior to or other than those enjoyed by whites, and the Knights of the Trigger should prosecute them.—ED.]

THE KENNEL.

Dog owners are requested to send for publication the earliest possible notices of whelps, sales, names claimed, presentations and deaths, in their kennels, in all instances writing plainly names of sire and dam and of grandparents, colors, dates and breed.

Whelps.

J. B. Lewis' black and white pointer bitch, Gypsy Queen by Joseph King's liver and white pointer, King Croxteth. (Rush T—Champion Patti Croxteth,) five dogs and six bitches. Alive, five dogs, four white and liver and one white and lemon, whelped March 21, 1890

Visit.

Mr. C. W. Wilson's English setter Jennie (Dick—Belle) to W. S. Kittle's Luke (Carl R—Bessie) on Jan. 29, '90.

Mr. G. Waring's fox terrier Oxford Milley by Rattler III, ex-Norma to C. A. Sumner's Blemton Vesuvian (14290) by Champion Lucifer by Blemton Vesta, at Los Angeles, March 23, 1890.

Don—Croxteth Blood.

EDITOR BREEDER AND SPORTSMAN:—My kennel has recently been increased by the addition of fourteen pointers, seven dogs and seven bitches, all of one litter by Point (Vandevorts Don—Drab) out of Queen Croxteth (Rush T—Champion Patti Croxteth T.) The litter is unusual in number, although not quite equal to the fifteen presented to my friend Mr. George W. Bassford, whose Blossom littered fifteen to Point. I have destroyed all but five of the dog puppies and four of the bitches. Those remaining are sound, lively, well sized, nicely marked animals, and I expect every one of them to prove a bench and field trial winner. They have more bench and field trial winning blood in them than any pointers ever before whelped on the Pacific Coast. I must acknowledge the courtesy of Baron J. H. F. von Schroeder of this city in permitting the use of his grand dog Point. Point is undoubtedly one of the best field dogs of the day, both in his merit as a performer, and in his breeding which in tabular form is given.

POINT	Don	Price's Bang	Coham's Bang
			Price's Vesta
		Peg	Garth's Drake
			Smith's Sal
	Drab	Dan	Sensation
			Sleaford's Maid
		Arrow	Bow
			Sleaford's Maid

If that breeding is not an insurance of worth on the side of the sire, where can one be found?

Vandevort's Don is said to have been the best pointer that ever lived, in the field, where he ran with the best English setters and Irish setters and never failed to do brilliantly, at one time dividing honors with that wonderful dog Gath.

The dam of the litter I bred, and a little pride in her clean, trim form, high quality, and promising style and field attributes may be pardoned.

The breeding of Queen Croxteth is as follows:

Q'n Croxteth	Rush T.	Sensation	Jim
			Nell
		Seph G.	Dart
			Seney
	Patti Croxteth T.	Croxteth	Young Bang
			Jane
		Patti M.	Donald
			Devonshire Lass

Not perhaps quite so brilliant as the pedigree of Point, but yet a clean standard lineage that has produced a score of field trial winners. All of the dogs in both pedigrees are either bench or field trial winners and most of them both. I offered to match Rush T., sire of Queen Croxteth against any dog on the Pacific Coast for $200 a side in the field without an acceptance.

The maternal grand sire of Queen Croxteth was Mr. Godeffroy's Croxteth, sire of Godeffroy's Drake (Croxteth — Lass), winner of third prize in the Eastern field trials Derby at High Point in November, '83, and of first in the All Age Pointer Stake of the same club in November, '89 Croxteth also sired D. G. Elliott's Scout (Croxteth—Belle), which divided second with Mainspring in the Eastern Field trials All Age Pointer Stake in November, '84.

Also of Wm. Fitterington's Trinket's Bang (Croxteth—Trinket) winner of the 1st at the Western Field Trials, Abeline, Kansas, in November, 1885, and which divided 3rd with Bob Gates at the National Field Trials at Grand Junction in the All Age Stakes in '86.

Also of the Highland Kennel's splendid Robert le Diable (Croxteth—Spinaway), winner of 1st in the All Age Pointer Stake of the Eastern Field Trial Club at High Point in November '86.

Also of Paul Franke's Trinket's Countess (Croxteth—Trinket) which divided 3rd in the Western Field Trials Derby at Carthage, Mo., in November '87, with Molly Jr. and Belle of Kansas City.

Also of P. T. Madison's Ossian (Croxteth—Amine) which divided 3rd with Waterford in the Eastern Field Trial's Derby at High Point in November '87; won 3rd in the All Age Pointer Stake of the same club in November '88; won 2nd in the Southern Field Trials at Amory, Miss., in December '88.

Croxteth grandsired the Devonshire Kennel's Cherrystone (Trinket's Bang—Pearlstone) which won 1st at Bicknell, Ind. in the Indiana Field Trials Derby in November '87.

Truly a brilliant showing for old Croxteth, and one that few sires can equal. I recently suggested to Mr. E. K. Benchley of Los Angeles, owner of a litter brother to Queen Croxteth that he cross his dog upon a litter sister to Point, owned by Mr. R. T. Vanderwort at Pasadenia, and I understand the cross has been made. If so, another lot of youngsters of precisely the blood outlined in this letter will soon be coming along in that paradise, the Los Angeles region.

If any of your readers can show up more excellent and substantial breeding, I hope they will send to your very valuable journal and let us know where we stand in the matter of pointer strains.

A. B. TRUMAN.

Elcho Kennels, March 26th, 1890.

The Dimick Crowd.

Mr. Ed. Hough, the Forest and Stream representative travelling with the United States Cartridge Company's teams, has placed himself high up among keen, faithful reporters by the accounts of the trip furnished to his journal. While in these parts Mr. Hough made many warm friends, who learned to value him for his ability, earnestness and exceeding refinement. His work stamps him a fluent, elegant writer, a close observer and withal a breezy disseminator of "English as she is wrote." We shall expect a volume of rare interest from Mr. Hough after he shall have rested and digested the material obtained in his circum-continental journey.

In his latest report Mr. Hough presents these interesting data about the members of the teams.

"Up to March 11th the averages were as follows:

1.	Wolstencroft,	average	92½	per cent
2.	Stice	"	92	" "
3.	Whitney	"	90 25-38	" "
4.	McMurchy	"	90 5-12	" "
5.	Heikes	"	88½	" "
6.	Budd	"	88	" "
7.	W. E. Perry	"	86½	" "
8.	Ruble	"	89½	" "
9.	Cahoon	"	74 30-38	" "
10.	W. S. Perry	"	72 9-38	" "

Wolstencroft is only five birds ahead of Stice. Stice is top man on the doubles. Heikes is only one bird ahead of Budd.

It may be interesting to note that in two live bird races, California and Kansas City, nine men, namely Budd, McMurchy, Wolstencroft, Stice, W. E. Perry, Heikes, Ruble, Whitney and Tucker, have only lost 13 birds out of 125 they shot at. That is very strong team shooting indeed.

A trifle further in the way of statistics has developed the following acts as to the age and weight of the different members of this party, and the appended table may be of interest to the curious:—

Eastern Team.	Age, years.	Weight, pounds.	Western Team.	Age, years.	Weight, pounds.
McMurchy	38	183	Budd	36	187
Wolstencroft	27	159	Stice	37	209
W E Perry	36	188	Heikes	33	190
W S Perry	40	155	Cahoon	41	180
Whitney	21	150	Ruble	30	220
Quimby	38	178	Tucker	42	209
	202	1010		219	1195

Thus it will be seen that the Western team is older and heavier than the Eastern. It may be seen also that Mr. Dimick is carrying along 2,205 pounds—more than a ton—of live stock on this trip. Mr. Dimick himself is 31 years old, and weighs 200 pounds ordinarily. Since yesterday he weighs a little over 1,300.

Further statistics show us that the man with the largest foot is either Tucker or Jim Stice. The hungriest man is either Ruble or Mitchell, the property man. The wisest man (or the one that knows the most) is either Tucker, W. S. Perry or Mitchell. The fattest man is Tucker, and the leanest W. S. Perry. The crossest man didn't come along, and the best-natured man is everybody, as near as can be determined.

Elsewhere the breeding of Mr. C. W. Wilson's Jennie to Mr. Kittle's Luke is noted. Luke is a superb specimen of the English setter, and as Jennie is about equally good, the produce should be rarely beautiful as well as good in the field.

Another litter from Mountain Boy and Beautiful Queen may be expected, and we hope more will live than of the last lot. The cross seems a nick beyond question.

In another column Mr. J. Martin Barney of Dutch Flat, offers for sale pointer puppies by Tom Pinch—Galatea. Both sire and dam are animals of exquisite finish, and the very highest quality. Tom, especially, is probably the handsomest pointer living. Both Tom and Galatea have won on the bench, and Tom is also a field trial winner. The puppies should be fine as silk and pretty as possible.

Mr. Joe Bassford Jr. writes to Mr. William Schreiber, as follows, about his pointer puppy Queen's Last (Mountain Boy—Beautiful Queen). "On the last day of the season I had the pleasure of seeing my puppy do some extraordinarily fine work. Her nose is number one. On point she is perfectly petrified. No tail waggle there. She is a perfect backer and one of the greatest workers of her age that was ever turned loose. In fact she is to-day capable of doing a good hard days work, although only seven or eight months old, and doing it well. She is in fine condition, growing fast and filling out handsomely all over."

Never aim at display when driving. It will tell against you. Try no close shaving. Give especially plenty of room to lady drivers, to old men or to young, timid horses. Stop rather than drive anyone into a mess. Get out of the way of pedestrians if you can, rather than drive them into the dirt. Leave the most level part of the road to high, top heavy loads whether they are entitled to it or not. Do as you would be done by with everybody and everything, and don't foolishly get out of temper because other persons may not treat you the same, or do not even know their business. You may gain much by such conduct, and will never gain anything by the reverse.

ROD.

Fishing Out of Season.

EDITOR BREEDER AND SPORTSMAN:—I have seen for two weeks past, different persons fishing for trout in the San Antonio Creek, south-west of Petaluma, almost every day. On Sunday, the 23d, there were four well-known parties from Petaluma trying their luck with hook and line. I think it is a shame, and the practice should be stopped at once. What is the use of a fish law if people are not made to live up to it? It is just so with quail and deer. There is always some pot-hunter going around who will shoot the first living thing his eyes discover. The honest sportsman who waits for the opening of the season, as every man should do, is left without game to shoot or fish to rise at his flies on opening day. This way that certain "thieves" have of fishing and shooting during close time is played out, and I hope the people generally will sustain our excellent Board of Fish Commissioners in its efforts to make convictions, and administer the full penalties to all guilty persons.

PETALUMA, March 26, 1800. A SUBSCRIBER.

[The plaintive letter is like many which come to this office. The writer would feel better if he caused the arrest and prosecution of a few of the poachers. The law-abiding citizen has as many rights as anyone, and should maintain them. —ED.]

It is said that several beds of quohoag clams have been found near Moss Landing.

History of Lady Vernon.

Mr. Joseph Battell, of Middlebury, Vt., is writing a history of the "Morgan Horse," and has sent to California for all that could be found out about Lady Vernon. The gentleman to whom the letter was sent, has kindly permitted us to copy his answer, which may be of interest to our readers:

Mr. Sessions tells me that Lady Vernon was probably seven or eight years of age when she came to California, and that when she died, if his surmise is correct, she must have been in her twenty-eighth year or thereabouts. You must understand that some years after he bought Lady Vernon, Mr. Sessions visited New York, and was there introduced by Somerindyke to the man from whom Somerindyke bought her, and Mr. Sessions gives us the story as he got it from the hog dealer who sold Somerindyke the mare. I will now try to give the story as near as possible in his own words:

A party of Indiana horse dealers bought a lot of animals to sell in the New York market, and while passing through a small town in New Jersey, stopped at a hotel which was some distance from the railroad station; the hotel-keeper was in the habit of carrying the mail from this small town (the name of which Mr. Sessions cannot remember) to the railroad station, and required an extra horse to perform some of the work. The horse dealers sold the hotel-keeper the filly, which they considered would not bring a reasonable price in New York. When she started carrying the mail, it was found that she was very fleet of foot, and she was such a square trotter that she attracted the attention of the hog dealer, who bought her from the hotel-keeper. This hog dealer is the one who persuaded Mr. Somerindyke to buy a one-half interest in the filly for $900. Mr. Somerindyke, it seems, drove her on the road, giving her many brushing races with men who were in the habit of driving their own roadsters, and Somerindyke became so infatuated with her, that he bought the other half interest from the hog dealer, paying him another $900. Somerindyke sold the mare to Pat Hunt, who brought her to California, where he raced her, Mr. Sessions thinks, about six or seven times, securing for her a record of 2:31 (according to Chester, although there are people here who think she trotted in 2:28½). Pat Hunt had taken in with him a partner by the name of Edward Fulton, who finally secured entire possession of the mare.

In the course of time Mr. Fulton wanted to return to New Orleans, and asked Josiah Sessions to loan him $1,200, and Mr. Sessions mentioned the matter to Chas. Lux, and told Mr. Lux that if Mr. Fulton did not return the $1,200, that he (Sessions) would take the mare and pay the money. When Mr. Lux advanced the money, the mare was in foal to Easton's David Hill, and a short time afterwards gave birth to a filly foal.

At about this time Mr. Lux called upon Mr. Sessions and seemed somewhat afraid that if the mare died he would be out considerable money. Mr. Sessions took the mare and filly, paying Mr. Lux his $1200. Fancying that she would prove a good broodmare, he gave a one-half interest in her to Stephen Whipple, afterwards owner of Whipple's "Hambletonian" 725. Mr. Sessions tells me that after she had her colt by "David Hill," that notwithstanding the fact that her legs were badly fired and blistered, she having been repeatedly under veterinaries' care, she showed him a half mile in 1:09. After the first foal was born she was again mated to David Hill and produced Master Vernon, a horse colt. Her third foal was by Werner's Rattler and was called Rattler Vernon. Her fourth foal was by Vermont and did not have a name (so far as Mr. Sessions remembers) it was a horse colt. Her fifth foal was by George M. Patchen, Jr., and was called Billy Patchen. Her sixth foal was also by George M. Patchen Jr., and was called Patchen Vernon. Her seventh foal was by Hamilton Chief; this foal was called California Chief. The eighth foal was also by Hamilton Chief and was subsequently called Tom Vernon. Her ninth foal was Oakland Maid 2:22, by Speculation. Her tenth foal was again by Hamilton Chief; this colt was never named as he was poisoned. The eleventh foal was by Irwin Davis and was called Ned Vernon. Her twelfth foal was by Pine Knot (a son of Hamilton Chief and out of Trifle, a very fast road mare which was here in California in early days). Mr. Sessions tells me that while the mare was still carrying Patchen Vernon he got into a dispute with Mr. Whipple as to how the mare should be bred in future, and he finally bought out the one-half interest which he had originally given to Mr. Whipple, for $1600, which included Billy Patchen (the young colt) and her prospective progeny, the one which afterwards proved to be Patchen Vernon; from this time out he owned her altogether, and consequently all the following colts were his.

The first foal, which was called Young Vernon, proved very fast, and Mr. Sessions paid Mr. Whipple $775 for Whipple's half interest in the foal because as he had given one-half of the mare to Whipple, Whipple owned one-half of each of her foals; before the misunderstanding spoken of above occurred they had divided, Mr. Sessions taking Rattler Vernon and Mr. Whipple Master Vernon; the Vermont foal Mr. Sessions cannot remember what became of it.

Death of Ulster Chief.

In 1874 Josiah Sessions, of Oakland, brought to California the stallion Ulster Chief, which has served many mares since then, and the pedigree appears in many of the present California tabulations. On Saturday, March 1st, the horse died from old age. If he had lived to the 3d of May, he would have been 27 years old. The following is his geneological lines:

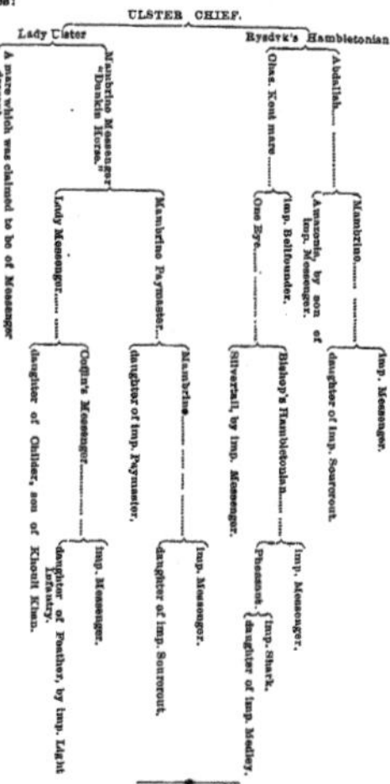

Our Southern California Letter.

There has been a dearth of live horse news in these parts for the past fortnight. The successful sale of L. J. Rose at New York has been a fruitful topic for conversation and the breeding industry in this section has been given a wonderful impetus in consequence. Mr. Rose has sold ten trotters off his ranch during the past fifteen months, the average of which exceeds $20,000, a showing I believe no other breeder in the country can equal.

The owners of fashionably bred stallions report good business notwithstanding the complaint of dull times and the fact that they have not yet learned the benefits accruing from the judicious use of printers ink.

A sensational and exaggerated report was sent out of this city over the Associated wires about the loss of broodmares at Santa Anita. The fine broodmares that died are: Fallen Leaf, Grisette, Maggie Emerson, Marie Stewart and Too Hard. They were all heavy in foal to Emperor of Norfolk. Maggie Emerson was the dam of Lucky B. The less said about the partial cause which led to their death the better.

The San Diego Union of March 23rd, contains a column about the trotters imported to San Diego by Captain Seaman, of Bell Boy fame. The genial captain owns H. B. Banning by Abdallah Mambrino, sire of Geneva S. 2:19, dam Queen by Clark Chief by Mambrino Chief, Thomas Rydyk by Rydsyk, dam Largesse 2:26 by Scott's Thomas; Josiah A, by Clingstone II, dam Miss Wilkes and Acquaintance by Stranger, dam by Mambrino Star.

It will therefore be seen that San Diego County is looming up as the home of the fashionable bred trotter.

QUARTER STRETCH GOSSIP.

Jockey Barnes started for New Orleans last week.

Los Angeles will be unusually well represented on the grand circuit this year.

The Woolsey youngsters at Chino are highly spoken of.

The Rose string of runners is doing finely at the track. They will be taken north for the Blood Horse Meeting.

The Sixth District Association have arranged for two and three-year old trotting stakes for 1890 and 1891. The conditions will shortly be advertised in the BREEDER AND SPORTSMAN.

A number of improvements are in contemplation for the Agricultural Park track in the very near future.

President Riffenburg of the Pacific Beach track was a recent visitor in Los Angeles. He reports that a meeting will shortly be announced for San Diego.

The entries for the spring meeting of the Sixth District Agricultural Association close with the Secretary, B. Benjamin, at 7½ North Main street, on Tuesday, April 1st.

Kelly & Samuels expect to take their string as far East as St. Paul this season. They expect to take in the Denver meeting en route.

Dr. K. D. Wise has sent Semi Tropic to the Corbett Ranch to be bred to Guy Wilkes.

The grand circuit of 1890 begins at Los Angeles. The Directors will shortly announce a tempting programme in the expectation of getting a big entry list from the Northern part of the State.

In the near future I will let the readers of the BREEDER AND SPORTSMAN know what the breeders of Orange County are doing in the way of raising runners and trotters.

DAGWORTH.

Grim's Gossip.

We will have a full history of Idaho Patchen in next week's BREEDER AND SPORTSMAN.

George Doherty of Indian Valley, owner of Victor 2:22, has purchased the Hedrick Ranch, and added it to his Indian Valley Stock Farm.

Mrs. B. C. Holly and Miss Lena Holly intend making a visit to the Eastern States before long, and it is within the possibilites that a European trip may be made as well.

A fine brood mare by Whipple's Hambletonian 725, dam by Jerseyman (son of Geo. M. Patchen Jr. 31), 2nd dam Whisky Jane (dam of Sam Purdy 2:20½) is advertised for sale this week.

The Pacific Coast Blood Horse Association have had exceedingly fine programmes for their spring meeting issued, which are being distributed to those interested in the sport of kings.

Among the pacing celebrities the produce of Roy Wilkes, 2:12½, and Jenny Lind, 2:17, is the representative of the fastest pair which have been coupled. The foal is a natural trotter.

Mr. J. H. Strobridge of Haywards has a fine Antevolo colt of whom great things are promised. He has been named Centella, and we wish his owner luck with his well bred youngster.

A veterinary dentist is advertising himself in the northern portion of the State by driving a stallion through the streets of whatever town he may be in, without bridle or lines, hitched to a cart.

Mr. A. B. Rodman, than whom there is no better posted horseman in Lake County, has been in town during the past few days. He reports Advocate in splendid condition, and his brood mares doing well.

George H. Morgan, who has contributed much of interest and value to the Horseman over the *nom de plume* of "Diomed," has cast his fortunes with the Chicago weekly Horse Review, and is now its editor.

No person can be a really accomplished driver, who does not know a good deal about the natural disposition of a horse —why he obeys and when he will be liable to disobey; how to educate him, and how to take advantage of that education.

Capt. C. M. Bellaire, the efficient Secretary of the St. Louis Jockey club, writes me that declarations must be made on April 1st, for the Derby, Oaks and Chas. Green stakes. Those who have entries and wish to declare should remember this.

Mrs. Wolfskill has sent the two thoroughbred mares, Heliotrope and Edelweiss to Santa Anita Ranch when they will be bred to Volante. Two foals by the gallant son of Grinstead, from two such game mares should prove the very Acme of breeding.

To show what trotters will bring in open market, when bred in the East, we quote from the New York World, which, in speaking of the Kellogg sale of March 18th, says: "A score or more of registered youngsters went for less than $100. Some were sold as low as $70."

A match race had been arranged to take place at Phoenix, A. T. on the 11th of this month, but one of the parties paid forfeit. My correspondent says that the match was for $500 a side between J. L. Ward's "Smokey" and the Casa Grande Suva mare, trotting, three in five, but that the Casa Grande people paid forfeit.

M. Sanders, now located at Fleetwood Park New York expresses great confidence of doing well in his new home. He says Guy 2:10¾ is one of the very greatest horses in training and that he has offered Mr. Gordon to take his horse for ninety days and free from expense, providing he does not succeed in driving him in 2:08¾ or better.

The fast trotting gelding Thapsin 2:21½, was shot on March 5th, at the Bay District Track. Ever since his last race on November 9th, 1889, the poor horse has been suffering, and E. H. Miller Jr, his owner, ordered him to be destroyed. All of the veterinaries who had examined Thapsin, pronounced him past aid, and his destruction was simply an act of mercy.

The Rohnerville Herald says: "Our friend Heity Fogoboom has two colts that are wonderful performers for their age. One is Why Not, and the other is Remember Me. Both were sired by Waldstein. One day last week Heity was exercising them on the track, and we are told by parties who saw them trot that they made wonderful fast time in a quarter-mile spurt. We might tell the time those little ones went that quarter in, but our readers would not believe us."

It may easily be determined whether advertising in the BREEDER AND SPORTSMAN pays, by asking any one who uses the columns for stallion announcements. From all quarters we hear the glad tidings that books are filling rapidly, and never before have farmers paid so much attention to the improvement of their stock. It cannot be presumed that poorly bred horses will receive the same amount of mares that are sent to the better bred ones, but those who bring their horses prominently before the public, are all doing good business.

The Moor blood seems to rule the trotting horse market at the present time, and mares or stallions by that now celebrated horse, or his progeny, command the top prices. Col. Harry I. Thornton, recognizing the wants of the public, has purchased the magnificent stallion Grand Moor 2374, by The Moor 870, dam Vashti by Mambrino Patchen 58; 2d dam Kate Taber by Mambrino Messenger (son of Mambrino Paymaster); 3d dam a mare of Messenger decent. Next week Rancho Rosaca will have an advertisement announcing where the horse will stand for the season of 1890.

Victor, 2:22; the name is hardly ever mentioned, but what one reverts to the summer of 1888, when "Hayseed" swept down on the trotters and made a clean-up that astonished the talent. To this day there is no telling what Victor can do in the way of speed, but there is one thing sure, he "trains on." Mr. Doherty, his owner, has decided to stand him this year at Santa Rosa, and there is no question but what he will receive plenty of patronage. Victor is by Echo, dam by Woodburn; 2d dam by Ashland. The advertisement in another column gives all necessary particulars.

During our fall meeting six pacers secured records from 2:13 to 2:19½. Can any other track equal this showing? Terra Haute Express.

That is right, Mr. Express; show what can be done in *six days* on your track; but just compare the time made on the San Francisco track, Saturday, Nov. 16th, 1890, with what has been done on any other track in the world for *any one day*. Sunol, 3 years old, 2:10½; Palo Alto, 2:12½; Stamboul, 2:13½; Regal Wilkes, two year old stallion, 2:20¾, and Faustino, yearling stallion, 2:35, and, remember, all trotters at that.

The owners of Axtell have publicly refused to allow, says the Cleveland Pain-Dealer, the great stallion to enter in a race with Mr. Robert Bonner's Sunol for the purse of $10,000 which has been offered. Another race can be made for Sunol which would be fully as interesting should it take place. Henry Sanders, trainer of Mr. W. J. Gordon's horses, said last evening that if it could be arranged, Mr. Gordon's great trotter Guy would go into a race with Sunol for a purse.

Such a race would be of national importance and interest, and efforts will without doubt be made to bring Sunol and Guy together.

Of course it will please all our readers to learn that Major Du Bois of Denver, arrived home safe and sound with his car load of trotters. A correspondent writes to say that the Major is delighted with his treatment on the Pacific Coast, and that he will probably return to buy a breeding farm in California. While here he made several entries in the BREEDER AND SPORTSMAN Futurity Stake, and we learn that one of the matrons whose produce was named, has had a foal and the owners confidently predict that they have the winner. The mare alluded to is Mandilene by Magnet, and her foal is by Superior.

Two weeks ago I requested that all persons having stallion cards, whether for the present season or for years gone by, should send them to this office, but I did not give my reasons for wishing them. We are trying to secure a list of all the horses that have ever stood in California, as many of the pedigrees are very faulty, simply because no one has ever been willing to spare the time to collect the necessary evidence. It can readily be seen that old stallion cards and catalogues of sales, will assist us materially in our efforts, and we trust that readers of the BREEDER AND SPORTSMAN will render whatever assistance they can. Remember this is for the benefit of every breeder in the State, and pedigrees of all horses, both trotters and thoroughbreds, are required.

One of the cutest horsemen in California is John Mackey, superintendent of the Rancho *Del Paso*, and he rarely allows himself to be outdone by others. While back East lately with the Haggin consignment he cast his eyes around and finally selected another trotting stallion to grace the realms of the great stock owner, his choice being George H. Lowe, a son of Florida 482, dam Mary Hunter by Guy Wilkes (sire of Whipple's Hambletonian); 2nd dam by Friday, a son of imp. Trustee. George H. Lowe is a producer of speed, being the sire of Eva 2:23½, etc., and also of Lowell Chief, the sire of Morris H. 2:22½, so that it can be seen that his stock breeds on. Mr. Mackey is entitled to congratulations for his happy selection.

A well-known minister in this country, says the Lexington correspondent of the N. Y. Spirit, and an owner and breeder of some excellent trotting stock, being desirous of giving to others the benefits of his experience, stated to a number of breeders recently, that a night or so previously he had found a fine filly suffering terribly from colic. As he had no tried remedy at hand, he gave her a tablespoonful of kerosene, and in ten minutes she was entirely relieved. Judge Johnson, who was present, said that the night before one of his colts was suffering the direst agony from the same complaint, he gave the colt nothing, and in five minutes the colt was free from pain, and apparently as well as ever. Difference in favor of letting nature alone, five minutes.

Andy McDowell returned last Monday from his Eastern trip and reports Mr. Salisbury as well satisfied with the New York sale. Andy had five days of sickness, in the "Big City", but claims that the Californians stuck to him like leeches and would not let him die. "There is but one Rose, and that is L. J." says the Pleasanton driver, "he knows every horseman in the country, and every one is his friend. How the buyers did bid on his stock! it was one of the most marvelous things I ever saw." In answer to the question, "will you win the bet you have made with Valensin," Andy answered with an emphatic "yes, I can beat any stallion, with possibly one exception, that draws breath, and I will make a mark for Direct this year that will put the young horse at the top of the heap."

"An auction sale of horses these days is different from what it was fifteen years ago," remarked Peter C. Kellogg the other day. Then no confidence existed in auction sales of horses. Buyers thought that unless a horse was too worthless to sell privately he was never sold at auction. That view is all changed now. If conducted in conformity with rules and regulations that secure and sustain the confidence of buyers they soon come to be respected. Most buyers who can afford it are willing to pay pretty well up toward the market price of a horse. If he sees others willing to pay more than the limit he first held in mind, he will often go on with the feeling that if another man can afford to pay more he can. In this way buyers often 'mark up' their bidding limits to conform to the evident market. But just let a bidder mistrust that the owner is getting in opposing bids and you will see him quit bidding on an animal at far below the mark he intended to go."

As is well known, the Santa Rosa track has been in the market for some time, the gentleman who owned the controlling interest wishing to dispose of the property. The Pierce Brothers of Oakland have purchased the land and all the appointments, giving them a training place to go on with at once. It is the intention to put the track in first-class order and make it second to none in the State. Trainers who wish to use the track will be allowed to do so, and a charge will be made for the use thereof, but only enough to keep the track always in the best of shape. The new owners have also purchased from D. J. McCarty the stallion Bay Rose 2:20½, by Sultan 2:24, dam Madam Baldwin by The Moor. The price paid was $15,000. They have bought in addition from Mr. McCarty ten head of trotters, all mares, which he brought out from the East with him. These are the mares which it was reported last week he had sold to L. A. Richards of Grayson. The Pierce Brothers have been interested for years in horses, but they will now branch out and go into the business in a thoroughly systematic manner.

Mr. A. J. Ross of Spokane Falls, has purchased from Charles Havens Esq., of San Francisco the black gelding Racquet 2:20½, the price paid being $1,500. Mr. Ross has secured a good campaigner and should be able to win him out in the northern circuit.

Harry Agnew keeps buying brood mares when they are of the right sort and has purchased since our last issue the following:

Nettie Nutwood, bred and raised by John Barry, of San Jose, Cal., nine years old, sired by Nutwood, 1st dam by Ethan Allen Jr. (Vicks), 2nd dam by Williamson's Belmont, 3rd dam by a. t. b Bertrand mare. In foal to Antinous, a son of Electioneer.

Baby Mine, record 2:27, nine years old, by Nephew; 1st dam Lady Burns by Black Boy, he by McCracken's Black Hawk, 2nd dam Kentucky mare imported by Gov. Low. In foal to Guy Wilkes.

Laska, 5 years old, bred by J. B. Haggin, sired by Alaska, son of Electioneer; 1st dam Sarah Kinny by Alexander 490, 2nd dam Lancaster, son of Owen Dale; 3rd dam Little Blossom by Billy Blossom. 1st, 2nd and 3rd dams raised by Hiram Kinney now employed at Rancho del Paso. Laska is in foal to Boodle.

When the Salisbury stock car arrived at Sacramento last Saturday, three head were taken off, they being the property of J. B. Haggin. Those which continued on to Pleasanton were four mares owned by Mr. Salisbury, two of which will be relegated to the Matrons division. They are both by Echo 462, and were purchased at the Haggin sale along with a yearling filly by Albert W. The fourth one is a chestnut mare, with a rattling turn of speed that will be seen on the circuit this year. The car also contained four head, bought by Mr. Hugh Kirkendall, of Montana, who forwarded them on to his trainer, Mr. Lafferty, who is at present domiciled at Pleasanton. One of the Kirkendall lot is Erect, a full brother to Direct 2:18½, that was purchased at the Salisbury sale for $5,000. Another is the black Director filly, Miss J. I. C., dam by Blue Bull, who is very promising. The third one is a Director filly, dam Roxana by Gibralter 2:22½. The other is a filly by Monroe Chief, dam by Carr's Mambrino. Still another that was on the car was the royally bred Mation Nava by Dictator, dam Belle Brasfield 2:20, which was purchased at the Rose sale for Mr. W. S. Hobart, of this city. The last one of the car load was the mare bought by Mr. Valensin.

Notwithstanding we sent on to one of our Eastern correspondents for an account of the sales at Peoria, as yet we have failed to get a list of prices for which the Shippee consignment was sold for at that point; however, from Chicago the news comes that the Stockton horses were sold as follows:

Bay filly, 3, by Hawthorne—Mary by Chieftain; George Wilds, Chicago, $375.

Bay filly, 2, by Abbey, dam by Hawthorne; W. D. Manchester, Newark, Ill, $300.

Black filly, 2, by Hawthorne—Nellie F by Daniel Lambert; S. J. Look, Louisville, Ky., $260.

Chestnut filly, 2, by Hawthorne—Right Motion by Motion, $340.

Tilton Thorne, br c, 2, by Hawthorne—Ella Boggs by Tilton Almont; G. H. Hammond, Detroit, Mich., $250.

Bay colt, 3, by Long Island—Trusswood by Nutwood; T. J. Kilpatrick, Wisconsin, $355.

Chestnutwood, ch c, 3, by Hawthorne—Mocking Bird by Priam; W. Dyer, Lancaster Wis., $1,010.

Major Thorne, blk c, 4, by Hawthorne—Old Tempest by Morgan Rattler; O. B. Hildreth, Newton, Kan., $625.

The regular quarterly meeting of the California State Veterinary Medical Association was held in the Baldwin Hotel on the evening of March 26th.

President Maclay of Petaluma occupied the chair, and the following members of the profession were present: Drs. Orvis, of Stockton; Spencer, of San Jose; Wadams, of Santa Clara; Egan, Masoero, Jones, Nief, Browns and Woodruff of San Francisco.

Mr. Hume Spencer of San Jose, student of the Chicago Veterinary College and Dr. Alex Rankin assistant to Dr. McCollum, Sacramento were among the visitors.

Letters of regret, at being unable to attend, were read from Dr. McCollum of Sacramento and several of the Southern members.

After the minutes had been read and approved the members present gave the benefit of their experience in interesting cases that had come under their observations during the last quarter. Dr. Maclay made a strong appeal to the members regarding the necessity of preparing a proper bill to present before the next legislature, regulating the veterinary practice, and for the benefit of the members who were unable to attend the quarterly meeting held at Los Angeles, told what had been done there, and the happy manner in which the members living in the southern portion of the state had entertained the visitors. At the next meeting Dr. Maclay will deliver an essay on Bog Spavin, and Dr. Jones will read an article on Tetanus,—Lockjaw.

One of the most unkind and uncalled for paragraphs that was ever penned, appears in last week's Mirror and Farmer. The clipping is as follows:

There has been considerable talk about the $5,000 wager between L. J. Rose and W. H. Crawford dependent on Stamboul's getting a record of 2:12 or better, which Mr. Rose lost by a scant quarter of a second. Hickok and Crawford have been fast friends for years, and the gossips do not hesitate to say that the famous California reinsman would not drive out Crawford's money. One critic remarks: "You will remember that Stamboul did not show any speed till late in the season and Hickok worked him in heavy shoes all the time. Then he turned him over to another trainer, who put on lighter shoes, and he soon went a mile in about 2:15. Less than a week after this was announced Crawford was registered at the Palace Hotel, San Francisco, and he remained out there for some time. To my mind that is conclusive evidence that Hickok did not try very hard to win Mr. Rose's money." Another wiseacre claims that Crawford got the bet declared off, and then Hickok sent Stamboul to his limit.

Orrin A. Hickok has been called the "Tallyrand of the Turf," on account of his great diplomacy, and he is justly entitled to the pseudonym, but the fifteen hundred persons who saw him drive Stamboul at Napa, will each and every one testify that man never drove before as did Orrin on that day. I was the clerk of the course, and occupied a position in the judges' stand from whence every foot of the journey was carefully noted, and the assertion is unqualifiedly made that Hickok never drove such a heat in his life nor tried harder to win. When he came up to be weighed it was all he could do to stand, the exertion and excitement having completely unnerved him for the moment, and his remarks made before the judges would convince the most skeptical that Hickok drove to make Crawford lose his bet.

The Pacer.

The wonderful speed of the pacer and the readiness with which he can be developed, his smooth, frictionless way of going that enables him to repeat mile after mile within the fractional part of a second of his best time, has at last won the respect and challenged the admiration of the turf-loving people of America, and the question naturally arises, will he be given an equal showing and an equal division of purse money with the trotter?

There is and always has been—less now than ever before—a strong prejudice against pacers for turf purposes. The gait, it is claimed, is not fashionable; but divest this feeling of fashion and there is not a single reason left—if this can be called a reason—why the pacer should not take precedence of the trotter in every respect.

Speed is the great attraction that draws the crowd to a race course, and there is no longer any doubt but that the pace is a much faster gait than a trot. In this respect, then, the pacer is unquestionable the superior of the trotter. It is equally true that a pacing sire will transmit his gait to his offspring with much greater uniformity than a trotting stallion. To those who have an opportunity of observing this strong prepotency in the pacer, a statement like the above may sound unreasonable; but whenever the two strains of blood have been placed side by side in breeding, it has as a rule proved true. But just at this time, when trotting is so fashionable, the strongest claim the pacer has upon lovers of the trotting horse is the value of his blood in producing the trotter. I have yet to hear of a single instance where the blood of a trotter added anything to the speed of a pacer. Westmont is not a pacing-bred horse, but it requires the plebeian blood of the side-wheeler to be united with the aristocratic blood of the trotter to produce a Maud S. or a Jay-Eye See.

Were I to summarize, I would say the pace was faster than the trot because it has been proved on the turf that it is an easier gait than a trot, because three of the fastest heats in a race in harness were made at pacing; that pacing blood is most valuable to produce speed in harness because it increases the speed of the trot, but gains nothing from it; that this gait is transmitted with more certainty and greater force than the trot; as witnessed by the great number of brilliant pacing performers, as compared with the number of trotters on the turf, that have come from unknown and obscure origin.

The question of fashion was decided by circumstances, except such part as we ape from our English cousins. It is claimed that the American trotter is purely a Yankee invention, and considering our best class of trotters he is; but after all we borrow the original idea from England, for horses were trotted against time and for money there long before Messenger ever came across the water. On the other hand, pacers are strictly and purely American, and it is safe to say there is not a horse in all Europe to-day that can pace a mile in 4:00, unless he was bred in America, or by an American bred horse. As this country became more thickly settled better roads were made, and the saddle was gradually abandoned for buggies and carriages. The trot was substituted for the pace, and has been assiduously cultivated ever since. Trotting races had their origin in these older sections of the country; hence the trot is fashionable there. More than a century has passed since then, and the marvels of time of 2:08¾ has been marked as the speed attained by the American trotter, and yet the despised pacer has beat it by two and a half seconds.

We are, as a people, quick to appreciate merit in anything, and now that our pacers have shown such speed, we may confidently expect a fair division of the spoils, as well as the honors of the trotting and pacing turf. Liberal purses were given at the principal trotting associations in the country the past season for pacers, and the disposition and indications are that they will gradually increase until we have as many classes for pacers as we now have for trotters. Especially in the South and West, when this is the case and more attention is given to breeding the pacer, you may look for some side-wheeler to cross the score in less than 2:00, and what State is more apt to produce him than Tennessee?—R. A. in Spirit of Farm.

Advertiser's Notes.

Mr. French calls the attention of horsemen this week to his fine young stallion Arlington, by Abbotsford, dam the Gillespie mare, by Blue Bull. The terms of service are only $50, and he should receive plenty of mares at that figure.

There are many of the California horsemen who will visit Carson City next month to attend the great combination sale which begins there April 15th. The stock is all of the best, and many of the animals are in training, so that they will be seen in the height of condition. Old "Gib," the hero of many battles, will pass under the hammer, and for him competition will be keen.

Mr. E. S. Culver, Secretary of the Blood Horse Association, has some choice fillies and a colt for sale that should tempt those who are looking for high class trotting stock. A son of Guy Wilkes is rarely offered for sale, and Mr. Culver should receive many answers to the advertisement which appears elsewhere.

Anteeo Button, as the name indicates, is a grand combination of two of California's blood lines, and should prove a drawing card to his owner. Terms, etc., will be found elsewhere.

THE WEEKLY

Breeder and Sportsman.

JAMES P. KERR, PROPRIETOR.

The Turf and Sporting Authority of the Pacific Coast.

Office, No. 313 Bush St.

P. O. Box 2300.

TERMS—One Year, $5; Six Months, $3; Three Months, $1.50. STRICTLY IN ADVANCE.

Money should be sent by postal order, draft or by registered letter, addressed to JAMES P. KERR, San Francisco, Cal.

Communications must be accompanied by the writer's name and address, not necessarily for publication, but as a private guarantee of good faith.

NEW YORK OFFICE, Room 15, 181 Broadway.

ALEX. P. WAUGH, - - - - Editor.

To Subscribers.

The date printed on the wrapper of your paper indicates the time to which your subscription is paid.

Should the BREEDER AND SPORTSMAN be received by any subscriber who does not want it, write us direct to stop it. A postal card will suffice.

Special Notice to Correspondents.

Letters intended for publication should reach this office not later than Wednesday of each week, to secure a place in the issue of the following Saturday. Such letters to insure immediate attention should be addressed to the BREEDER AND SPORTSMAN, and not to any member of the staff.

San Francisco, Saturday, March 29, 1890.

Dates Claimed.

SAN JOSE (Blood Horse Meeting)....April 5th, 7th and 9th
SACRAMENTO (Running Meeting)....April 28th, 29th, May 1st and 3d
EUREKA JOCKEY CLUB....July 7d to 5th
IONE....Aug 7th to 9th.
LOS ANGELES (6th District)....Aug. 11th to 16th
NAPA....Aug. 19th to 23rd
GLENBROOK PARK, 17th District....August 19th to 23d
SAN JOSE (Fall Meeting)....Aug 25th to 30th inclusive
PETALUMA....Aug. 25th to 30th
OAKLAND (District No. 1)....Sept. 1st to Sept. 6th
LAKEPORT, 12th District....September 22d to 27th
CALIFORNIA STATE FAIR....Sept 8th to 20th
FRESNO (Fall Meeting)....Sept. 29th to Oct. 4th
MONTEREY, Salinas, Agricultural Society....Sept. 30th to Oct. 4th

Stallions Advertised

IN THE

BREEDER AND SPORTSMAN.

Thoroughbreds.

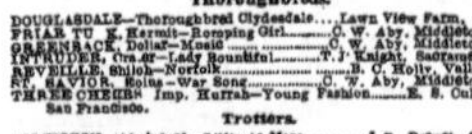

DOUGLASDALE—Thoroughbred Clydesdale....Lawn View Farm, Cal.
FRIAR TUCK, Hermit—Romping Girl....C. W. Aby, Middletown.
GREENBACK, Dollar—Music....C. W. Aby, Middletown.
INTRUDER, Crater—Lady Bountiful....T. J. Knight, Sacramento.
REVEILLE, Shiloh—Norfolk....B. C. Holly, Vallejo.
ST. SAVIOR, Eolus—War Song....C. W. Aby, Middletown.
THREE CHEERS Imp. Hurrah—Young Fashion....E. S. Culver, San Francisco.

Trotters.

ARLINGTON, Abbotsford—Gillispie Mare....J. R. French, S. F.
ANTEEO BUTTON, Anteeo—Dam of Alexander Button....E. C. Spear, St. Helena.
ADMIRAL, Volunteer—Lady Pierson....Frank Drake, Vallejo.
ACTOR Prompter—Dam by Sultan....Lawn View Farm, Cal.
ARBITRATOR, Director—Lady Earnest....H. A. Mayhew, Niles.
ANTEEOP, Antero—Bessie G....Guy E. Grosse, Santa Rosa.
ANTEEOP, Anteeo—Nance....Guy E. Grosse, Santa Rosa.
ADMIRO, Admiral—dam by San Bruno....Smith & Sutherland, Pleasanton.
ASHLAND ALMONT, Almont—Pauline....T. J. Whitehead, Oakland.
ALEXANDER BUTTON, Alexander—Lady Button....Cache Creek Farm, Yolo.
APEX, Prompter—Mary....Poplar Grove Breeding Farm, Wildflower.
ALCONA, Almont—Queen Mary....Fred W. Loeber, St. Helena
BALKAN Mambrino Wilkes—Fanny Fern....A. L. Hinds, Oakland.
CLOVIS, Sultan—Sweetbriar....Poplar Grove Breeding Farm, Wildflower.
CUPID, Sidney—Venus....C. O. Thornquest, Oakland
CHRISMAN'S HAMBLETONIAN 10178, Whipple's Hambletonian—Flora Jesse Chrisman, San Jose
CHARLES DERBY, Steinway—by Electioneer, Cook Stock Farm, Contra Costa Co.
CALIFORNIA NUTWOOD, Nutwood—Fanny Patchen....Martin Carter, Alameda Co.
CORRECT R, Director—Brainey....Pleasanton Stock Farm.
DECORATOR, Director—Chess....Pleasanton Stock Farm.
DEXTER PRINCE, Kentucky Prince—Lady Dexter....L. M. Morse, Lodi.
DAWN, Nutwood—Countess....A. L. Whitney, Petaluma
DIRECTOR, Dictator—Dolly....Pleasanton Stock Farm, Pleasanton.
DON MARVIN, Fallis—Cora....F. P. Lowell, Sacramento
DESIGNER, Director—May Queen....H. Scott, Oakland.
ELECTOR, Electioneer—Gilberta....L. A. Richards, Grayson.
ELECTION, Electioneer—Lizzie H....B. C. Holly, Vallejo.
EL BENTON, Electioneer—Nellie Benton....Souther Farm, San Leandro.
ECLECTIC, Electioneer—Manette....Wilfred Page, Sonoma County
EROS, Electioneer—Sontag Mohawk....W. H. Vioget, Menlo Park
FIGARO, Hambletonian—Emblem....Souther Farm, San Leandro.
GROVER CLAY, Electioneer—Maggie Norfolk....Denis Gannon, Oakland.
G. & M., Anteeo—Rosa B....George E. Guerne, Santa Rosa.
GUY WILKES, George Wilkes—Lady Bunker....San Mateo Stock Farm, San Mateo.
GLEN FORTUNE, Electioneer—Glenna....Souther Farm, San Leandro.
GEORGE WASHINGTON, Mambrino Chief—Fanny Rose....Thos. Smith, Vallejo.
GUIDE, Director—Imogene....Smith & Sutherland, Pleasanton.
GRANDISSIMO, LeGrande—Norma....Fred W. Loeber, St Helena
ILLUSTRIOUS, Happy Medium—Abdalletta....George A. Stone, Santa Rosa.
JESTER D, Almont—Hortense....Souther Farm, San Leandro
JUNIO, Electioneer—by Granger....S. N. Straube, Fresno.
KAFIR, Alcazar—Flower Girl....B. C. Holly, Vallejo.
KING DAVID, Admiral—Black Flora....Frank Drake, Vallejo.
LEO WILKES, Guy Wilkes—Sable....San Mateo Stock Farm, San Mateo.
LYNWOOD, Nutwood—Hattie Morrison....P. Visher, Stockton.
MEMO, Sidney—Flirt....John Rowen, Oakland
MOUNTAIN BOY, Kentucky Prince—Elsie....B. C. Holly, Vallejo.
MAMBRINO WILKES, George Wilkes—Lady Chrisman....San Miguel Stock Farm, Walnut Creek.
MART BOORHEM, Sidney—Towhead....B. C. Holly, Vallejo.
MAMBRINO JR. 1789, Mambrino Patchen, dam by Mambrino Chief Geo. P. Bull, San Jose.
MAMBRINO CHIEF, McDonald Chief—Venus....Thos. Smith, Vallejo.
MORTIMER, Electioneer—Marti....Wilfred Page, Sonoma County
NOONDAY, Weddgewood—Noontide....F. P. Lowell, Sacramento.
PASHA, Sultan—Madam Baldwin....D. Bryson, Linden
PHILOSOPHER, Pilot Wilkes—Belle....George E. Guerne, Santa Rosa.
ROY WILKES, Adrian Wilkes—Flora....Pleasanton Stock Farm Pleasanton.
REDWOOD, Anteeo—Lou Wilton....A. McFayden, Oakland.
STEINWAY, Strathmore—Abbess....Cook Stock Farm, Contra Costa Co
SUNSET, Anteeo—Bessie G....Guy E. Grosse, Santa Rosa.
SIDNEY, Santa Claus—Sweetness....Valensin Stock Farm, Pleasanton.
SABLE WILKES, Guy Wilkes—Sable....San Mateo Stock Farm, San Mateo.
ST. NICHOLAS, Sidney—Towhead....John Rowen, Oakland Trotting Park.
VICTOR, Echo—Daughter of Woodburn....G. W. Hughes, Napa City
WOODNUT, Nutwood—Flora....Jas. Weatherhead, San Jose
WHIPPLETON 1883, Hambletonian Jr.—Lady Livingston....Fred W. Loeber, St. Helena
WOODSIDE, Woodnut—Veronica....B. C. Holly, Vallejo.
YOUNG ELMO, St. Elmo—Dam by Woodburn....Lawn View Farm Cal.

There Are More Ways Than One to Kill a Cat.

The great success attained by breeders of trotting horses, and the enormous prices paid for fashionable strains of blood, is mainly due to the vigorous efforts put forward by the two associations that have looked so faithfully after the best interests of the sport for several years back, and to the "National," and "American" all credit is due. When the $10,000 National Stallion race, gotten up by and held under the auspices of Wesley P. Balch of Boston, was trotted last September, a hue and cry was immediately raised that the best horse had not won. A correspondent of the BREEDER AND SPORTSMAN who was present informed our readers about the ugly rumors that were in circulation, and his story was substantially corroborated by the turf journalists of the country. The matter got to be such an open secret that evidently the man who claims to be the owner of Alcryon did not hesitate to talk about the disgraceful affair, as he had a conversation with G. W. Archer, Esq., (the presiding Judge in the stand, on the day of the race), and the following affidavit has been prepared and entered as evidence in the Superior Court of Erie County, State of New York, in the case of Charles H. Nelson vs. The National Trotting Association:

George W. Archer, being duly sworn, deposes and says that he resides in the city of Rochester, N. Y., and is President of the Rochester Driving Park, and is, and during all the time hereinafter mentioned, was a member of the Board of Review and Board of Appeals of this defendant. That he was the presiding judge of what was called the Balch $10 000 stallion race trotted at Beacon Park on the 22nd day of September, 1889, in which the horses Alcryon and Nelson competed. That during the trotting of said race deponent and the other judges thereof, thinking that the horse Alcryon was not being driven to win the race, called the driver, Mr Robens, into the judges' stand and ordered him to drive said horse to win or a penalty would be imposed upon him. The next heat was the third and last; said horse Alcryon did not win the same, and the race was won by the horse Nelson.

That on or about October 4th, 1889, after said race, deponent met Frank L. Noble at the Murray Hill Hotel in New York City; said Noble is one of the plaintiffs in this action, and as deponent understands, had the control and management of the horse Alcryon during the season of 1889 and at said race. That deponent stated to Noble that it was fortunate for him that Alcryon threw his toe weights in the last heat; that Noble replied, "That made no difference; that he had had the horse shod a few days before so that no driver could drive him to win the race, and that if they had taken off Robens the horse would have lost just the same." Noble further stated "that before the race began he had agreed to let Nelson win the race, and had Nelson's check for $5,000 before the race started: that he (Noble) had won second money, and had got $7.500 out of the race."

That deponent replied to him, "Don't you think you are taking pretty desperate chances?" and Noble said, "I don't know; what could you have done about it if you had discovered the fraud at the time?" . Deponent replied that if they had known of the fraud at the time the judges would have declared the pools and the race off.

That as deponent understands and believes, large numbers of pools were sold and large amounts of money staked by the public on the horse Alcryon winning the race; that on the 11th day of November, 1889, he reported the said facts to the National Trotting Association, and upon such reports, as he understands, the charge of fraud was made against the plaintiffs; that deponent knows from conversation with other men connected with the turf that said Noble has made the statement to many others, and that many men interested in turf matters and members of the Congress, at *Buffalo*, believe that said Noble is unworthy of privileges on the association courses. Deponent further says that the public standing of the National Trotting Association and of its associated courses would, in his opinion, be degraded if men who publicly acknowledge their own participation in a fraud were permitted to take any part in the public exhibitions on the associated courses.

GEO. W. ARCHER.

Now the standing of Mr. Archer is such that every horseman in the United States will believe what he here states in his affidavit, but the thieves and blacklegs who follow the racing circuits of the country, will denominate him "an old crank" for meddling with something that does not concern him. Mr. Archer is to be commended for calling the attention of the "National" to the language of Noble, and it is to be sincerely hoped that an example will be made of every one concerned in the dirty business. As is well known, an injunction was served on the Board of Review, preventing them from investigating the charges of fraud, and the officers of the association have been called upon to show cause why they should not be punished for passing a resolution suspending Nelson, Noble and Robins until such time as the Board of Review can act on the case. A preliminary hearing of the case has been heard, and twenty days given attorneys to prepare briefs for the court. Now if the court should prevent a hearing of the testimony, it becomes the duty of every member of both associations to bar defendants and their horses from all races that may be advertised in future. We mention horses advis edly, as if only the men are barred the horses can t sold, or ostensibly so, and the present owners woul suffer no loss, but if the horses are also put under a bat then the defendants suffer a pecuniary loss, inasmuch their animals are only fit for private use and stud pu poses.

Then there is another way in which the Nation Association may reach at least two of the accused. Or of them was taken out of a sulky at the Lexington mee ing, because the judges thought he was pulling Ro Wilkes, the pacer, and was fined $500 for his style driving. Now would it not be a good plan to call u the case which is now on appeal of L. A. Davis vs. tl Kentucky Trotting Horse Breeders' Association, an have Robens testify in whose interests he acted as l did? Also have Mr. Noble as a witness, and find o how much money he played in *on Roy Wilkes, as his ow driver was up behind the pacing stallion.* But be sure an have the pool-sellers also as witnesses, so that the trut of the matter may be arrived at. Then it may not l necessary to try the Balch case at all, except in so far Nelson is concerned.

The trotting associations of America cannot afford have anything to do with such men on the track, an the sooner they are eliminated from the sport, the bett it will be for all concerned.

Short Horn Breeders' Association.

At the last annual meeting of the Pacific Coast Sho Horn Breeders' Association it was determined to hold a nual sales under the auspices of the Board of Director and certain rules were devised for the guidance of tl officials. Heretofore breeders have had individual sale some of which were successful, while others did not gi the satisfaction they might have done, owing, no doub to the apathy of the public to believe that the pedigre as given in the published catalogues were correct. Ho ever, that excuse can no longer deter would be purcha ers from attending and bidding at the sales to be co ducted by this Association, as the rules laid down a imperative, and only pedigreed animals will be accept for vendue. It behooves every breeder of Short Hor to join the Association which has been started, to aid a assist them in improving the breed, and by their suppo encourage the officers and members in the good wo which they have undertaken. The sale will take pla at the State Fair Grounds, Sacramento, April 3r commencing at one o'clock P. M., and it is only fair assume that purchasers will be present from all over tl State. The rules under which the sale takes place a as follows.—

All members of the Association who desire to offer c tle for sale at any public sale held under the auspices the Association shall, at least forty days prior to t time of such sale, send to the Secretary a complete list all such cattle, together with extended pedigree there which pedigree must be made satisfactory to the Boa of Directors by certificate from the Secretary of t National Short Horn Herd Book Association, or oth wise.

All sales shall be properly advertised by the Direct of the Association by the usual means—through ca logues and newspapers.

The Board of Directors shall employ a competent a tioneer, paying him such compensation as shall agreed upon by said Directors and auctioneer.

No stock advertised for sale can be withdrawn exc by order of consent of Board of Directors, but must sold at the time advertised, unless such sale be postpo until some future day by order of the Board of Directo

All expenses connected with the advertisement conduct of any sale shall be computed and, except hereinafter mentioned, be divided and charged per cap to the cattle connected therewith.

The Association shall charge and deduct from the p ceeds of all sales not to exceed 5 per cent. of the gr receipts as commission, which shall become the fund the Association, and shall be used for the purpose of p ing the auctioneer; the balance, if any, after paying s auctioneer, shall go into the general fund of the Ass ation.

In addition to the charges and expenses hereinbef provided for, there shall be charged on account of cattle connected with any sale the sum of one dollar head, as incidental fees, which shall become the fund the Association.

The Directors shall have the management and con of all sales conducted by the Association.

Any member willfully refusing to obey any of rules governing sales may be fined not to exceed f dollars, or excluded from participating in any presen future sale in the discretion of the Board of Direct but only after an opportunity for an explanation hearing has been afforded the person offending.

All moneys due the Association on account of any sale either as expenses or charges, shall be deducted from the receipts of such sale and the balance paid over to the owner of the cattle sold, as they are respectively entitled.

The Solano and Napa Stakes.

On April 1st entries are due for this wide awake young association's stakes, and as the fame of the Napa track is well known it is presumed that the entry list will be a large one. As will be seen by reference to the advertisement in the appropriate column, the stakes are of a diversified character, with easy payments in all cases. The first two are for two and three year olds respectively, entrance free for all, while the next three are for one, two and three year olds, for colts owned in the district. And then there are three nomination stakes for the 2:20 horses, the 2:24 class, and for those eligible to the 2:20 class. Fifteen hundred dollars is the amount offered for each of the last named, and the entrance is $150 in each class, payments divided as follows: $25 April 1st; $25 May 1st; $25 June 1st; $25 July 1st; and $50 August 1st, when horses must be named. Nominations are transferrable any time before August 1st. Remember April 1st is the date of closing.

The Pacing Standard.

Our Tennessee correspondent, "Kennesaw," gives to our readers this week the full list of rules which were adopted by the Tennessee Pacing Horse Breeders' Association March 12th, governing the standard of registration of pacers. They will naturally be the subject of much comment, as the trotting horse fraternity seem lothe to recognize the sidewheelers and owners of pacing animals have been forced to organize for their own protection. With but trivial alteration the rules of the National Trotting Horse Breeders' Association have been adopted by the Tennesseeans, taking 2:30 as the basis for entry into the standard list. We think this is a mistake, as they should have lowered the time mark to such a point that in time those who rule the destinies of the trotting division, might recognize the pacing association and their rules, but from the spirit displayed at the late meeting of the Directors of the National Breeders' Association, it would seem that they were unwilling at present to make even 2:25 the standard. However, a start has been effected, and we will watch with interest what revisions they will make at their next annual meeting.

Trouting Prospects.

The trouting season of 1890 bids fair to be one to be remembered, and it is altogether probable that for two or three years to come the beneficent effects, from an angler's standpoint, of the unprecedented floods which have swollen every little brook into a mad torrent, will be felt. Except for the few bait fishers, there is little encouragement to visit the streams. In all of them the whole contour of the beds has been changed. New pools, and deep, have been cut. Familiar ripples have disappeared. Snug resting places for big fish have been turned into bare gravel beds, and wading is impossible in all of the brooks from which reports have come. Meantime thousands of small salmon trout are passing up from the salt lagoons and fattening upon bottom feed and growing into the nice pan fish which will fill many baskets during June and July.

Letter from Saratoga.

March 21, 1890.

EDITOR BREEDER AND SPORTSMAN:—The following nominations received on the same day and duly recorded, were not added, (as intended,) to the lists which had been previously hektographed, and which were sent to the papers for publication. Please correct this blunder, and oblige,

Yours Respectfully, E. WHEATLY, Sec.

THE CALIFORNIA STAKES.

S. T. Hayden's b h Bridgelight, 5 yrs, by Brigadier—Romping Girl.

ADIRONDACK HANDICAP.

James T. Williams' b c Newcastle, 4 yrs, by King Alfonso—Lerna.

James T. Williams' b or br c Glockner, 4 yrs, by Duke of Montrose—Mrs. Chubbs.

S. T. Hayden's b h Bridgelight, 5 yrs, by Brigadier—Romping Girl.

EXCELSIOR STAKES.

S. T. Hayden's b h Bridgelight, 5 years, by Brigadier—Romping Girl.

MERCHANT'S STAKES.

James T. William's ch h Bob Miles, aged, by Pat Malloy—Dolly Morgan.

HOTEL BALMORAL.

James T. William's ch h Bob Miles, aged, by Pat Molloy—Dolly Morgan.

TENNESSEE STAKES.

James T. William's ch c Jugartha, by Bob Miles—Tuberose.

CONGRESS HALL STAKES.

Jas. T. Williams' b or br c Glockner, 4yrs., by Duke of Montrose—Mrs. Chubbs.

Jas. T. Williams' br h Tom Hood, 6yrs., by Virgil—La Belle Helene.

S. T. Hayden's b h Bridgelight, 5yrs., by Brigadier—Romping Girl.

MORRISSEY STAKES.

Jas. T. Williams' ch h Bob Miles, a, by Pat Malloy—Dolly Morgan.

SARATOGA ASSOCIATION.

The complete lists of nominations for stakes closed March 1st, 1889 and 1890, number as follows:

	1889	1890
Flash Stakes	70	62
California Stakes	24	47
Adirondack Handicap	27	32
Spinaway Stakes	66	50
American Hotel Stakes (new)	—	42
Excelsior Stakes	22	21
Virginia Stakes	61	49
Kearney Stakes Handicap	20	20
Foster Memorial	28	41
Merchants' Stakes	21	12
U. S. Hotel Stakes	30	28
Hotel Balmoral (new)	—	30
Grand Prize (discontinued)	20	—
Tennessee Stakes	65	46
Congress Hall Stakes	28	34
Misses Stakes	6	54
Beverwyck Stakes	22	54
Pocahontas Stakes	26	28
Equity Stakes	64	45
Morrissey Stakes (handicap)	19	28
Relief Stakes	21	29
	727	754

Foals of 1890.

The property of Thomas Smith, Vallejo.

March 15th, black or dark chestnut filly, off hind foot white, by Geo. Washington 11623, dam by Admiral; 2d dam by Bassford's Abdallah; 3d dam by Bassford's Abdallah. This foal is entered in the BREEDER AND SPORTSMAN'S Futurity Stakes.

Property of Hon. Leland Stanford, Palo Alto:

B f by Nephew, dam Guess by Electioneer.
B f by Piedmont, dam Thalia by Electioneer.
Br f by Liberty, dam Regina by Shannon.
B c by Electioneer, dam Lady Ellen by Carr's Mambrino.
B c by Electioneer, dam Sallie Benton by General Benton.
Br f by Ansel, dam Cecilia by Del Sur.
B f by Clay, dam Piney Lewis by Longfellow.
B f by Electioneer, dam Esther by Express.
B f by Beverly, dam Nadine by Wildidle.
B c by Ansel, dam Gretchen by Yorktown.

THOROUGHBREDS.

Br c by imp. Cyrus, dam Marcella by Grinstead.
B f by imp Cyrus, dam Mazelle by Monday.
B f by imp Cheviot, dam Aurelia by Wildidle.
B c by Ansel, dam imp. Music by Prince Charlie.
Foals at Vina Ranch, Tehama Co, Cal.
B f by Clay, dam Mollie Shelton by Rifleman.
B c by Clay, dam Minnie Norris by Leinster.
B c by Clay, dam Fiŝne by Norfolk.
B f by Benefit, dam Lady Beecher by Reserve.
B c by Clay, dam Eugenia by Norway.
B c by Liberty, dam Cassie V by Don Victor.
B f by Beverly, dam Cuba by imp Australian.
B f by Benefit, dam Signa by Bentonian.
B c by Benefit, dam Melissa by Mohawk Chief.
B f by Benefit dam Mayflower Mohawk by Mohawk Chief.
B c by Nephew, dam Elmira by Fallis.

The following are the standard bred arrivals at the Cook Stock Farm so far this year.

Bay colt by Chas. Derby 4907, dam by Administrator 357.
Brown filly by Chas. Derby 4907, dam by Antevo 7868.
Chestnut filly by Steinway 1808, dam by Guy Wilkes 2867.
Bay colt by Chas. Derby 4907, dam by Indianapolis 517.

The last named being one of our nominations for the BREEDER AND SPORTSMAN Futurity Stakes

GEO. A. WILEY.

The property of Mrs. M. Wolfskill:

Heliotrope by Joe Hooker—Yolone, dropped a filly foal on the 10th inst. by Wildidle. Bay with star and right hind foot white.

What Bither will Handle.

E. D. Bithers has arrived at the Allen Stock Farm and selections have been made already from the long list of promising trotters, and he will commence on the following:

Jet Wilkes, 4 yr. blk filly, by Guy Wilkes, 2:15¼; dam Sable by The Moor, etc.

Syene, 3yr., brn filly, full sister to Jet Wilkes and Sable Wilkes 3 yr. record. 2 18.

Atlanta Wilkes, black filly, by Guy Wilkes, 2:15¼, dam Atlanta, (sister to Beautiful Bells) by The Moor

Experta, 2 yr., b. f. (sister to Express 2:21) by Electioneer, 125; dam Esther, thoroughbred mare by Express.

Mica, 3 yr. b. f. by Chicester 2 25½; dam Mary Belle (sister to Dick Moore 2:22½) by Belmont.

Rubra, 3 yr. b. f. by Lord Russell (brother of Maud S.) dam Primrose, by Abdallah 15.

Salve, 2 yr. gr. f. by Lord Russell, dam Noonday, half sister to Jay Eye See, 2:10.

Venezuela, 3 yr. brn f. by Chicester 2:25½; dam Vassar, by Belmont etc.

Mr. Bither will also drive Elista, 2:23½ and Miss Majolica (sister of Majolica 2:15) now at Fleetwood also Maudlen 2:25¾, now in California, will be placed in Mr. Bither's hands later on.

For the past fifteen years Ed Bither has been in the employ of J. I. Case, of Racine, Wis., and has driven the following horses to the front and given them records as stated: Jay Eye See, 2:10, Phallas, 2:13¾, Brown, four years, 2:18¾, Edge Hill, 2:25¼, Richard R., 2:29½, Edwin B., 2:27, Don Pedro, 2:27, Dixie Sprague, 2:25¼, Linda Sprague, 2:21¼, Gurgle, 2.20, Monte Cristo, 2:29½, James G, 2:20 and Victoria Wilkes 2:25 at four years,

Mr. Bither left Racine last week, and on the eve of his departure his many friends gathered in force and tendered him a banquet; and in reply to the different toasts many flattering expressions of esteem were made. The toast "An Honest Horseman was responded to by A. P. Dutton as follows:

When our friend Bither is about to leave us, I could not if I would, and I would not if I could refrain from saying a few words.

Mr. Bither has been among us for many years. While I have not all times agreed with him I have looked the ground all over and have weighed him in the scale of mankind, and on the whole I find him much above the average of men who have followed his vocation.

He has been a true and faithful man for his employers. He would under no consideration deceive or betray them. Such men are valuable when such trusts, as he has held, and even larger trusts I assume, are to be placed in his hands.

I do not hesitate to say to the men where he is to go that they can rest in all confidence that Mr, Bither will be a faithful man and that he will not betray their confidence. He will never pretend to be a man's friend and then in the hour of darkness wound his heart with either a weapon or a pen.'

Ed. Bither is a native of Maine and his first driving was done for F. S. Palmer of Bangor. We hope he may prove successful with the Allen Farm trotters as he has been in the past with those of his former employer.

VETERINARY.

Conducted by W. Henry Jones, M. R. C. V. S.

Subscribers to this paper can have advice through this column in all cases of sick or injured horses or cattle by sending an explicit description of the case. Applicants will send their name and address that they may be identified. Questions requiring answers by mail should be accompanied by two dollars, and addressed to W. Henry Jones, M R. C. V. S., Olympic Stables, Sutter Street, San Francisco.

A Subscriber.

I have a yearling colt which was cut directly over the ball of the eye some time ago. I cured the cut through the eyelid, which had proud-flesh in it, by the use of carbolic acid. There is a red substance in the corner of the eye which I judge is the inflamed and swollen membrane of the eye. It is possible that it is proud flesh in the eye, but does not look like it. Can you kindly suggest through the columns of the BREEDER AND SPORTSMAN the best method to restore the eye to its normal condition?

Answer.—In answer to your inquiry, re., your colt, I think, judging from your description, that the malady lies more with the membrana nictitans than with the membrane covering the eye-ball. I would suggest the constant application of cold water; to do so, make a swab of two pieces of linen, and between the folds place a thick piece of lint or cotton wool.

To the red substance, apply twice daily a lotion containing nitrate of silver, ten grains, two ounces of distilled water. If no improvement in two weeks, send communication to BREEDER AND SPORTSMAN, and we will endeavor to assist you further.

Answers to Correspondents.

Answers for this department must be accompanied by the name and address of the sender, not necessarily for publication, but as proof of good faith. Write the questions distinctly, and on one side of the paper only. Positively no questions will be answered by mail or telegraph.

Who Can Answer.

Please give breeding of Young Pacific, said to be by Pacific; Bay horse about 16 hands high, one front and one hind foot white; if alive would be about 18 years old. He was brought to Felton, Santa Cruz Co., by a Mr. George Fritz, where he made a season or two about the year '77. He was then sold at sheriff's sale. The gentleman that Mr. Fritz got him from brought suit to recover the horse, claiming the horse as his, but did not get him. I am told he was raised at Petaluma. If you can not give breeding please ask your readers, as it is important that his breeding be established.

P. F.

Please give pedigree of Victor, called also Victor Patchen?

Answer.—Victor Patchen 1607 by Geo. M. Patchen Jr. 31, dam Victress (the dam of Monarch, 2:28½) by Williamson's Belmont.

Frank Grant.

Please give the breeding of the dam of John Nelson Jr.; also the breeding of Tecumseh, sire of Pat Hunt?

Answer.—Which John Nelson Jr. do you mean? Tecumseh's breeding is unknown.

Subscriber.

Can you give me pedigree of San Jose Damsel? San Jose Damsel was formerly owned by Mr. Edgar or D. O. Mills, and I think was driven some years ago by Mr. Edger Mills.

Answer—We do not know the breeding. Probably one of our readers may be able to answer.

John Early.

Some one has imposed on you. Eagless never had a filly called Clara A., consequently the pedigree is wrong. We do not know of a horse called Sheleyman.

W. M. G.

1. Tell me through your paper if Superior imported from France in 1875 was registered in the Percheron Stnd Book; also if Duke of Morris is? 2. What horse has paced the fastest mile? and what is meant by the term "running mate?"

Answer.—We have not got a set of the Percheron Stud books so cannot answer your first question. Johnson 2:06¼ without running mate, and Westmont 2:01¾ with running mate. The running mate is hitched to the shaft of the sulky in which the horse making the record is harnessed.

A Constant Reader.

Is Tom Vernon standard and has he a record. Also let me know if Werner's Rattler is registered, and has he a record?

Answer.—Tom Vernon is not standard, and is not in the 2:30 list. Werner's Rattler is registered, 262 is his number, his record is 2:35.

J. A. A. R.

Flambeau is not a maiden. The records you send are correct.

J. C. C. Merced.

Send us the printed pedigree of the horse you mention and we will try to oblige you.

Inyo.

Please tell me what year Mr. Aiken had Anteros, and can I get a book for keeping the pedigrees of mares and their get.

Answer.—Mr. Aiken had Anteros until the spring of 1886. The book you require can be procured from J. J. Evans 406 California Street San Francisco.

An Inquiry.

Can any of our readers inform us where Prussian Boy is at the present time and also where San Diego was sent to when B. C. Holly sold him.

San Jose.

Can you inform me of what breeding "Peacock" was?

Answer.—By Whipple's Hambletonian 725, dam Jane McLane, (dam of Jim Mulvenna 2:27½) by Budd Doble 3764.

Names Claimed.

I claim the following names for foals:
Daphne, for filly by Wildidle—Yolona.
Edelwild, for filly by Wildidle—Edelweiss.
Heliodora, for filly by Wildidle—Heliotrope.

SANTA MONICA, March 23, '90. M. WOLFSKILL.

Breeders' Directory.

Advertisements under this heading 50c. per line per month.

HORSES AND CATTLE.

W. S. JACOBS, Sacramento, Cal. — Breeder of Thoroughbred Shorthorns and Berkshire Hogs.

J. H. WHITE, Lakeville, Sonoma County—Breeder of Registered Holstein Cattle.

EL ROBLAS RANCHO—Los Alamos, Cal , Francis T. Underhill, proprietor, importer and breeder of thoroughbred Hereford Cattle. Information by mail. C. F. Swan, manager.

PAGE BROTHERS.—Penn's Grove, Sonoma Co. Cal. Breeders of Short-Horn Cattle; Draft, Roadster and Standard Bred Horses.

SETH COOK, breeder of Cleveland Bay Horses, Devon, Durham, Polled Aberdeen-Angus and Galloway Cattle. Young stock of above breeds on hand for sale. Warranted to be pure bred, recorded and average breeders. Address, Geo. A. Wiley, Cook Farm, Danville, Contra Costa Co., Cal.

MAMBRINO WILKES COLTS and FILLIES, full brothers and sisters to Gus. Wilkes 2:22, and Balkan 2:29¾, for sale. Address SMITH HILL, Walnut Creek, Contra Costa County, Cal.

B. F. RUSH, Suisun, Cal., Shorthorns, Thoroughbred and Grades. Young Bulls and Calves for Sale.

PETER SAXE & SON. Lick House, San Francisco, Cal.—Importers and Breeders for past 18 years of every variety of Cattle, Horses, Sheep and Hogs.

HOLSTEIN THOROUGHBREDS of all the noted strains. Registered Berkshire Swine. Catalogues. F. H. BURKE, 401 Montgomery St., S. F.

HENRY C. JUDSON. Wild Idle Farm.—Breeder of Thoroughbred Horses. The home of "Wild Idle." P. O. Santa Clara; Box 223.

FERGUSON & AUSTIN,
FRESNO, CAL.
Registered Polled Angus and Short-Horn Cattle.

Solano and Napa Agricultural Society.

Trotting Colt Guarantee Stakes for 1890.

The Solano and Napa Agricultural Society have opened the following Colt Stakes for Trotters:

NO. 1. TWO YEAR OLDS.—Free for all; $100 guaranteed. $50 entrance, payable as follows: $10 April 1st, when entries close; $10 May 1st, $10 June 1st, $10 July 1st, $10 August 1st, when colts must be named. Nominations transferrable any time before colts are named. If the payments amount to more than the amounts guaranteed the additional amount to be added to the stake. All moneys divided as follows: 60, 30 and 10 per cent; in case of only two starting, 60 and 40 per cent: and in case of one horse walking over the whole amount to go to such horse. A failure to make any payment when due shall be considered a withdrawal and forfeiture of the amounts paid in. National or American Rules to govern, as the Society may elect. The right reserved to refund the first payment in case the stakes do not fill reasonably well.

No. 2. FOR THREE YEAR OLDS.—Free for all $500 guaranteed. $100 entrance, payable as follows: $20 April 1st, when entries close; $20 May 1st, $20 June 1st, $20 July 1st, $20 August 1st, when colts must be named. Conditions same as in No. 1.

District Colt Stakes for districts comprising Counties of Solano, Napa, Sonoma, Marin, Lake, Colusa, Yolo, Mendocino, Humboldt and Butte.

No. 3. FOR YEARLINGS.—$250 guaranteed. District. $40 entrance, payable as follows: $10 April 1st, when entries close; $10 June 1st, $10 July 1st, $10 August 1st, when colts must be named. Conditions same as in No. 1.

No. 4. FOR TWO YEAR OLDS.—$350 guaranteed. District. $50 entrance, payable as follows: $10 April 1st, when entries close; $10 May 1st, $10 June 1st, $10 July 1st, $10 August 1st when colts must be named. Conditions same as in No. 1.

No. 5. FOR THREE YEAR OLDS.—$400 guaranteed. District. $50 entrance, payable as follows: $10 April 1st when entries close; $10 May 1st, $10 June 1st, $10 July 1st, $10 August 1st, when colts must be named. Conditions same as in No. 1.

Yearling Stake. Single dash; one mile. Two Year Olds.—Mile heats, two in three. Three Year Olds—Three in five, to harness. Parties entering Colts will be notified by mail when payment becomes due.

The Society also offers the following stakes for Class horses.

TROTTING STAKES.—Free for all.
2:30 CLASS—Trotting; purse $1500.
2:21 CLASS—Trotting; purse $1500.
2:20 CLASS—Trotting; purse $1500.

Horses eligible January 1st, 1890. Entrance $150, payable as follows: $25 April 1st, when entries close; $25 May 1st, $25 June 1st, $25 July 1st $50 August 1st, when horses must be named. Nominations transferable any time before August 1st. Right reserved to refund entrance fee in any of the stakes should they not fill reasonably well. Money divided, 50, 25, 15 and 10 per cent. National or American Association Rules to govern, as the Society shall elect. To be trotted at our regular summer meeting, upon days to be hereafter arranged.

Entries to close April 1st, 1890, with

A. H. CONKLING, Secretary,
Napa City, Cal.
L. L. JAMES, President.

Second Annual Bench Show
OF THE
South'n California Kennel Club
AT THE
City of Los Angeles,
MAY 6, 7, 8 & 9 '90.

The SOUTHERN CALIFORNIA KENNEL CLUB was admitted a member of the AMERICAN KENNEL CLUB September 18, 1889. The coming show will therefore be held under the A. K. C. rules.

Entries will positively close May 1st.

A special committee will take personal charge of all dogs sent from a distance and insure their proper care. For premium lists and entry blanks address E. K. BENCHLEY, Secretary, 14 South Spring Street, Los Angeles; or H. H. BRIGGS, Breeder and Sportsman, San Francisco.

The Trotting Stallion

Silver Bow

Will make the season of 1890 at the Oakland Race Track.

PEDIGREE.

SILVER BOW 11706, two-year-old record 2:37, is by Robert McGregor 647, 2:17¼ (sire of Bonnie McGregor, 2:13½, Earl McGregor, 2:21½, Mac D., 2:30, McGregor Boy, 3:29¼, Mark Time, 2:30, Roxie McGregor, 2:30¼) by Major Edsall 2:1, 2:29, by Alexander's Abdallah 15—sire of Goldsmith Maid, 2:14—by Hambletonian 10—sire of Dexter, 2:17¼.

Robert McGregor's dam was Nancy Whitman by American Star 14, by Stockholm's American Star.

SILVER BOW'S first dam is Sadie by Hambletonian 10, sire of Geo. Wilkes, 2:22—sire of Guy Wilkes, 2:15¼ also Electioneer, sire of Sunol, three-year-old record, 2:10½, and Palo Alto, 2:12¾; second dam Lady Wynne by Wm. Welch 341; third dam Elenora Margrave by imp. Margrave.

DESCRIPTION.

SILVER BOW is a handsome bay, no white; 15-7¾ hands high; weighs 1075 pounds; of fine form, with the best of legs and a clean-cut, intelligent head. Is remarkably level-headed, seldom making a break; wears seven-ounce shoes in front. His record, 2:37, is no mark of his speed; he can beat 30 easy, and with his gilt-edge breeding, he is just what he ought to be, a trotter sired by a trotter whose dam was herself a trotter and his grandam the dam of two trotters. His dam Sadie being by Hambletonian 10, shows him to be bred from the cream of the trotting blood.

TERMS: $100 for the season. Mares not proving in foal returnable for the season of 1891 free of charge. Good pasturage and first-class care taken of mares for $5 per month. No responsibilities assumed for escapes or accidents. For further particulars, address

Limited to 15 approved mares.
Season to end June 1st, 1890.

P. J. WILLIAMS,
Care Race Track, Oakland, Cal.

Sire of Yolo Maid, 2:12½
Alexander Button 1197,

FOUR YEAR-OLD RECORD, 2:26 1-2.

SIRE OF

YOLO MAID, 2:12½, BELLE BUTTON, 2:20,
TOM RIDER, 2:20½. ROSA MAC, 2:20½.
J. H. (seperately timed in a race) 2:22½,
KEHOE, 2:34½, ALEX. BUTTON (3), 2:35½,
BURBANK S. (2 y. o., ½-mile track), 2:53.

PEDIGREE.

Alex. Button was sired by Alexander 490. Record, 2:31 1-4.

First dam Lady Button by Napa Rattler; 2d dam a pacing mare (S. T. B.) by a Copperbottom horse.

ALEXANDER (490), record, 2:31½.

Sire of Alex. Button, 2:26 1-2, Reliance, 2:22 1-2 Tommy Dodd, 2:24, Nelly Patchen, 2:27 1-4, by Geo. M. Patchen Jr. (31), record 2:27; first dam Lady Crum by Brown's Bellfounder.

GEO. M. PATCHEN JR. (31), rec., 2:27.

Sire of Wells Fargo, 2:18¼, Sam Purdy, 2:20 1-2, Vanderlynn, 2:21, Star King, 2:22, Ben Ali, 2:24, and five others in the 30 list, by Geo. M. Patchen (30), 2:23 1-2; first dam Bell by Top Bellfounder, son of imp. Bellfounder; 2d dam Hoot a Laddie mare.

GEO. M. PATCHEN (30). RECORD 2:23½.

Sire of Lady, 2:18¾; Chas. R. Low, 2:25¾; Geo. M. Patchen, Jr., 2:27; Mary, 2:2–; by Cassius M. Clay (18). 1st dam by Head'em, son of imp. Trustee; 2nd dam Itaska, by American Eclipse.

CASSIUS M. CLAY (18).

Sire of Geo. M. Patchen, 2:23¾, etc.; by Henry Clay (8). 1st dam Jersey Kate, the dam of John Anderson.

HENRY CLAY (8).

Sire of Black Douglass, 2:30; Centerville (w), 2.32; by Andrew Jackson (4); 1st dam surry.

ANDREW JACKSON (4).

By Young Bashaw; dam an Ohio mare of unknown blood.

YOUNG BASHAW.

By imp. Grand Bashaw; 1st dam Pearl, by First Consul; 2nd dam Fancy, by imp. Messenger; 3rd dam by imp. Rockingham.

NAPA RATTLER.

By Biggart's Rattler; 1st dam Poll, by imp. Consternation; 2nd dam Betsy Baker, by Mambrino.

BIGGART'S RATTLER.

Grandsire of Joe. Brown, 2:22; Lady Snell, 2:23¾; Mary Davis, 2:2¾; Nellie Webster, 2:28¾, by Sir Henry, son of the Garrett Horse, by imp. Leonidas; 1st dam by the Hyde Horse, son of Long's Magnum Bonum; 2nd dam of Messenger blood.

BROWN'S BELLFOUNDER.

By imp. Bellfounder; 1st dam Lady Alleport, by Mambrino; 2nd dam by Tippo Saib, son of imp. Messenger; 3rd dam by imp. Messenger.

DESCRIPTION.

ALEXANDER BUTTON is a dark bay with fine flowing mane and tail; stands 15-3¾ hands high; weighs 1,200 pounds, and is of excellent disposition. He is a natural trotter, inherited through the speed lines of his ancestors, and imparts his speed to his offspring with uniform certainty. His colts show him to be a wonderful producer—and with his breeding and terms of service, he is the cheapest and most wonderful horse in the State.

TERMS.

Terms.—$100, payable at end of season. Mares not proving with foal may be returned next season free of charge. Good pasturage furnished at $1 per month, and due care taken to prevent accidents or escapes, but no liability whatever assumed.

Will stand at Cache Creek Farm, which is situated about one and one-half miles west of Yolo Station.

All mares sent to Yolo in my care will be forwarded free of charge.

G. W. WOODARD, Proprietor.
Yolo, Yolo Co., Cal.

PHIL J. CRIMMINS. JOHN C. MORRISON.

"Silver Palace,"

36 Geary Street,
San Francisco, Cal

Old Hermitage Whiskies
"STEINER'S,"
No. 311 BUSH STREET,
San Francisco.
Under Breeder and Sportsman Office.

THE
GOLDEN GATE
Fair Association

Extra Attractions

To take place at the

Fall Meeting, 1890,

—AT—

Oakland.

The New List Purse $1,000.

For three year olds whose sires up to Jan. 1st. 1890, have not produced an animal with a record of 2:30 or better. Entrance 10 per cent., payable as follows: $25 May 1st, 1890, $25 June 1st, 1890, $25 July 1st, 1890, $25 August 1st, 1890. Entries close May 1st, 1890.

GUARANTEED PURSE $1,200.

For three minute class. Entrance 10 per cent., payable as follows: $30 May 1st, 1890, $30 June 1st, 1890, $30 July 1st, 1890, $30 August 1st, 1890. Entries close May 1st, 1890.

GUARANTEED PURSE $1,200.

For 2:40 class. Entrance 10 per cent., payable as follows: $30 May 1st, 1890, $30 June 1st, 1890, $30 July 1st, 1890, $30 August 1st, 1890. Entries close May 1st, 1890.

—ALSO A—

Guaranteed Futurity Purse $4,000.

To take place during the Fall Meeting of 1893.

For foals of 1890. Entrance 5 per cent. payable as follows:
$40, Aug. 1, 1890,
$40, Aug. 1, 1891,
$40, Jan 1, 1892,
$40, Jan. 1, 1893,
$40, Aug. 1, 1893.
Entries close Aug. 1, 1890.

CONDITIONS.

Neglect to provide payments on the dates stipulated will incur forfeiture of all previous payments.

The Directors reserve the right to change the hour and day of any race except when it becomes necessary to ante-date a race, in which instance the nominator will receive three days notice of change by mail to address of entry.

Entries not declared out by 6 P. M. the day preceding the race, shall be required to start.

Purses will be divided into four moneys viz., 50 per cent. to the winner, 25 per cent. to the second horse, 15 per cent. to the third horse, and 10 per cent. to the fourth horse.

A horse distancing the field shall only be entitled to first and third moneys.

Trotting and racing colors shall be named by six o'clock on the day preceding the race, and MUST be worn upon the track.

All purse races, mile heats, best three in five to harness. Five horses required to enter and three to start.

Otherwise than the above, National or American Trotting Association Rules—as this Association may select—will govern the races offered.

Entries to close with the Secretary.

R. T. CARROLL, President.
JOS. I. DIMOND, Sec'y, 306 Market St., S. F.

Antevolo Colt
For Sale.

AVOLO REX, foaled February 22, 1888; dam Catchup by Rustic; grandam Huntress by Don Victor; g g dam Betty Denice by American Boy Jr. Is 15.1 hands high, well developed, muscular, and without a blemish. Has a very gentle disposition, and shows speed and a good gait. Apply

HOME FURNISHING CO.,
113 Fifth Street, S. F., Cal.

ARGONAUT HERD.
POLLED ABERDEEN—ANGUS CATTLE.

Thirty head choice pure bred and high grade (cross bred) HEIFERS and a few grand young BULLS for sale at reasonable prices. A fine opportunity for persons wishing to establish choice herds or change their bulls. Representatives from this herd were grand prize winners at the last California State Fair.

Address DR. G. M. DIXON,
Sacramento, Cal.

AUCTION SALE
—OF—
Brood Mares,
Colts and Fillies,
Harness & Draft Horses

—The property of—
D. J. MURPHY, San Jose.
TO BE SOLD AT

Public Auction,

—AT 11 A. M., ON—

Wednesday, April 16, '90

—AT—

Fair Ground, San Jose,

KILLIP & CO., Auctioneers,
22 Montgomery Street S., F., Cal,

Catalogues may be had on application.

FOR SALE
AT
Vineland Stock Farm
STALLIONS, BROODMARES AND FILLIES

ONE STALLION FIVE YEARS OLD, SEAL-BROWN, by WHIPPLETON (sire of Lily Stanley, 2:17 1-2, Homestakes 2:16 1-2, etc.), dam Sally Gorham by Werner's Rattler. This horse is scarcely 15 1-2 hands high, but very compactly built. He breeds exceptionally large and well finished colts. Any one understanding the business could clear him in one season, or he would make a No. 1 road horse, as he can trot a 40 gait any time.

ONE THREE-YEAR-OLD, SEAL-BROWN, by WHIPPLETON (sire of Lily Stanley, 2:17 1-2, Homestakes 2:16 1-2, etc.) dam Sally Gorham, etc. This ought to make a great General Purpose sire, and with opportunities get trotters, as he is compact, strong-boned, and will measure when grown about 16 hands and weighs 1,200 lbs. With a little road work last fall he developed a wonderful burst of speed.

ONE THREE-YEAR-OLD, BLACK, by WHIPPLETON (sire of Lilly Stanley, 2:17 1-2, etc.), dam by Naubuc (sire of the dam of Eva W., 2:23 1-2, etc.), full brother to Thomas Jefferson, 2.23. This horse will be fully 16 1-2 hands high. He is smooth, rapid gaited and from size and conformation should breed, like his sire, large, rangy, finished colts.

ONE TWO-YEAR-OLD, BRIGHT CHESTNUT, sired by DAWN 2:18¾, dam Alida (dam of Directa, three-year-old record 2:31¼, trial 2:26) by Admiral (sire of sister 2:19 1-2, Nona Y 2:25, etc). This colt is the making of an extraordinary horse. He is large boned and will be over sixteen hands high when grown; he is of the true Nutwood type, is clean gaited and can lead a piece as fast as any man's colt.

ONE TWO-YEAR-OLD, BLOOD BAY, (full brother to Alcona Jr. sire of Silas Skinner, trial 2:23) sired by ALCONA (sire of Flora Belle 2:24, etc.,) dam Madonna by Cassius M. Clay Jr. This colt will make a trotter and a great stock horse if developed; he has the combined blood of Almont, Mambrino Chief, Cassius M. Clay Jr. and Joe Downing.

These colts are all sound and promising. The only reason I offer them for sale is, that I have three aged stallions in use, and the surplus is growing on me. If I were starting a breeding business for profit, I should consider either of these colts a representative to commence with. Also brood mares and fillies for sale. Correspondence solicited.

FRED. W. LOEBER, St. Helena,
Napa Co., Cal.

Well bred Stallions
FOR SALE.
SATINWOOD

Is 3 years old, stands 16.1 hands high and weighs 11[illegible] pounds; is a beautiful dark chestnut; was sired by Wormwood, a full brother to Eva W (2:25) and Redwood (2:27. First dam by John Nelson; second dam by Argyle; third dam Blackhawk Worm[illegible] ood by Nutwood 2 23 3-4, sire of Woonut 2:18 1-4; dam the Cropsy Mare by Naubuc, dam Gipsy Queen by George M. Patchen; second dam Capt. Roberts Mare. Nutwood 2:18 3-4, by Belmont, dam Miss Russell (dam of Maud S, 2:08 3-4. Belmont, by Abdallah (sire of Goldsmith Maid) dam Belle by Mambrino Chief. Miss Russell by Pilot Jr, dam Sally Russell by Boston.

Full pedigree and all particulars on application.

J. A. C.

Sorrell stallion, foaled April 22nd, 1887. Bred by Wm. Jeffries of San Francisco, Cal. Sired by C. C. Bemis' Lancelot. First dam Bay Mare Nellie, sired by Ulster Chief he by Rysdyk's Hambletonian, her dam by Kentucky Hunter, noted for his speed and endurance (see Stud Book).

For further particulars apply to
J. A. CARLETON,
1202 Broadway, Oakland, Cal.

For Sale

A First-Class.

BREEDING FARM.

Of 800 Acres.

Four hours' ride from the city. Good roads to first-class track. Climate unexcelled. Plenty wood and running water.

For further information apply to the office of the

BREEDER AND SPORTSMAN,
San Francisco
313 Bush Street.

First Grand Annual Sale

—OF—

PURE BRED SHORTHORN CATTLE

Under the management of

The Pacific Coast Shorthorn Breeders' Asssociation.

Will be held at

AGRICULTURAL PARK, SACRAMENTO, April 3d, 1890.

(Sale to commence at 1 o'clock P. M.)

This society is composed of the best breeders of Short Horn cattle on the Pacific Coast, and is organized upon a permanent basis.

Nothing but Pure Bred Registered Cattle Will be Offered at this Sale.

The stock offered at this sale come from the herds of the following well known breeders:—

E. A. BRIDGFORD, Colusa, Colusa County.
PETER PETERSON, Sites, Colusa County.
A. HEILBRUN & BRO., Sacramento.
F. S. CHILES, Davisville, Yolo County.
P. H. MURPHY, Perkins, Sacramento County.
E. S. DRIVER, Antelope. Sacramento County.
JOSEPH MARZEN, Lovelocks, Nevada.

Catalogues can be had by addressing

J. F. CHILES, Secretary, Davisville, Yolo County.

ANNUAL SPRING SALE

—OF—

Road & Harness Horses

Work and Draft Horses!

SHETLAND PONIES!

From Ranchos of J. B. Haggin, Esq.

WILL TAKE PLACE

Tuesday, May 6, 1890,

AT SAN FRANCISCO.

Location to be hereafter designated.
Catalogues are being prepared.

KILLIP & CO., Live Stock Auctioneers,
22 Montgomery Street, S. F.

A Grand Combination Sale

—OF—

Standard-bred Trotters & Thoroughbreds

CLYDESDALES AND PERCHERONS,

Fine Roadsters, Work Horses, Etc.

—AND—

Registered and Graded Holstein CATTLE,

REGISTERED JACKS,

And other first-class Live Stock of all kinds, will be held at

CARSON CITY, NEV., April 15, 16 and 17, '90.

BROOD MARES, COLTS AND FILLIES by the following well known Sires will be sold:

Standard Bred.	*Thoroughbred.*
ECHO.	NORFOLK.
GIBRALTAR. (will be sold)	HOOKER.
PROMPTER.	LODI.
BUCCANEER.	BRECKENBRIDGE.
ST. CLAIR.	THREE CHEERS.
SIGNAL.	LANGFORD.
BLUE BULL.	BOI DE ARC.
ST. LAWRENCE.	McMAHON.

And among the fine stock to be offered will be the grand HOLSTEIN BULL SARATOGA, and a number of fine calves and heifers by him and other well known thoroughbred Holsteins.
Over 100 entries were made up to March 1st, and a big sale is assured.
Send in your entries.
For further particulars address

JNO. P. SWEENY & CO., Carson City, Nev.

The Annual Combination Sale

—OF—

Road Mares, Harness Horses, Colts and Fillies,

WILL TAKE PLACE AT

Bay District Track, San Francisco,

At 11 A. M. on

THURSDAY, APRIL 3, 1890.

The offering will consist of the get of ELECTIONEER, GUY WILKES, MAMBRINO WILKES, ARTHURTON, SIDNEY, ALEX. BUTTON, ANTEROS, and other noted stallions.

Catalogues will be ready March 11th, and will be furnished upon application.

KILLIP & CO., Auctioneers,
22 Montgomery Street, San Francisco.

Poplar Grove Breeding FARM.

Standard-bred Trotters, Colts and Fillies.

The get of CLOVIS, 4909; PASHA, 2039; APEX, 2935,

For Sale.

Address S. N. STRAUBE, Poplar Grove Breeding Farm,

Fresno, Cal.

Inspection by intending purchasers invited, and information by mail.

For Sale.

14

Pure bred

PERCHERONS.

Stallions and Mares.

OF ALL AGES.

Part Imported, and all Registered Proof.

For further information, address

E. J. TURNER, Hollister, Cal.

For Sale

A HALF BROTHER TO

ALMONT PATCHEN,

(2:15, trial 2:13 3-4).

JUANITO JR. is a beautiful bright bay, black points, with no white, foaled 1886. As a colt he has given much more promise than did Almont Patchen at the same age. Instead of being a pacer, he is a good square trotter, with every indication of great speed, and is so gentle and kind, that a lady can drive him. The owner's only reason for selling him is that business calls him away from this section of the State. He will be sold at a reasonable figure. This is a splendid opportunity for a gentleman to secure a first-class trotter at a very low figure.

The pedigree of Juanito Jr. is by Juanito (sire of Almont Patchen), dam Nettie Moore by Old Tom Moore. For further particulars, address

JUANITO JR.,
Santa Clara P. O., Cal.

Attention Stockmen!

FOR SALE

At Chowchilla Ranch,

Thoroughbred Durham Cattle

Three Hundred Young DAIRY COWS, 20.0 graded SHE CATTLE, Yearlings and up; a fine lot of high grade Durham Bulls; also have Mares, Horses, Mules and Norman Colts.

For particulars, apply to

ISAAC BIRD, Jr., Supt.,
Merced, California.

For Sale

A FIRST-CLASS

Napa County Farm

—OR—

STOCK RANCH,

800 Acres Improved,

SITUATED TWO AND A HALF MILES FROM NAPA CITY, with good roads leading thereto, a good hard finished house of nine rooms, with all modern improvements, streams running all summer, a great amount of live oak and black oak timber. It lies in a fruit belt, surrounded by fine vineyards and orchards growing upon the same quality of soil, and originally a part of this tract. About one-half hill, and one-half rolling land, but none of it is steep and all easily cultivated, splendidly situated for the breeding of fine horses. Price, $65 per acre. Further particulars given at this office.

BREEDER AND SPORTSMAN,
313 Bush St.

Twenty-Third Annual Sale!

169 THOROUGHBREDS

64 YEARLINGS,

100 BROODMARES,

5 GREAT STALLIONS

23d ANNUAL SALE OF

Belle Meade Stud,

Will take place at BELLE MEADE STUD, near Nashville, Tennessee, on

THURSDAY AND FRIDAY, APRIL 24 & 25

169 Head Thoroughbreds at Public Auction.

SOLD FOR DIVISION. | SOLD WITHOUT RESERVE

Five Great Stallions

To the Highest Bidder.

LUKE BLACKBURN
Imp GREAT TOM,
ENQUIRER,
BRAMBLE,
IROQUOIS.

FOR CATALOGUES ADDRESS THIS OFFICE. P. C. KIDD, Auctioneer.

For other information and Catalogues address JOHN J. CARTER, No. 9 Baxter Block, Nashville, Tenn.

Stallion for Sale

AT A BARGAIN.

Full Brother to Fairmont.

By Piedmont, dam Queen by Garibaldi—see State Fair Edition of BREEDER AND SPORTSMAN, September 14, 1889, for description of Fairmont—three years old, solid bay. Can trot a 2:40 gait or better. Sound in every particular. Can be seen at Oakland Trotting Park, Oakland.

P. J. WILLIAMS.

Speed Programme

—OF THE—

Twelfth District Ag'l Society

To be held at

LAKEPORT,

SEPTEMBER 23 to 27 INCLUSIVE.

First Day—Tuesday, Sept 23, 1890.

RACE NO. 1—TROTTING.

Yearling Stake; $200 guaranteed. Entrance $30, payable as follows: $5 May 1st, $10 July 1, $10 September 1st (when entry must be named), and $5 additional for starters. Entries to close May 1, 1890. See general conditions.

RACE NO. 2—RUNNING.

One-half mile dash. $100 added; $25 to second. Entrance $10, to close 6 P. M. day before race.

RACE NO. 3—TROTTING.

Three-minute class. Mile heats 3 in 5. District. $150 added. Entrance $30; to close 6 P. M. day before race. 5 to enter, 3 to start. See general conditions.

Second Day—Wednesday, September 24th

RACE NO. 4—RUNNING.

Three-quarter mile heats; 2 in 3. $200 added; $25 to second. Entrance $10, to close 6 P. M. day before race.

RACE NO. 5—TROTTING.

District Stallion. Mile heats 3 in 5. Purse $500. Entrance $50, to close 6 P. M. day before race; 5 to enter, 3 to start. See general conditions.

RACE NO. 6—TROTTING.

Three-year-old stake; $300 guaranteed. $50 entrance payable as follows: May 1st, $10; July 1st, $10; September 1, $15 (when entry must be named), and $15 additional to start. Open to Napa, Solano, Sonoma, Marin, Lake, Colusa, Yolo, Mendocino and Humboldt Counties.

Third Day—Thursday, Sept. 25th.

RACE NO. 7—RUNNING.

Seven-eighths mile dash. $150 added; $25 to second. Entrance $10, to close 6 P. M. day before race.

RACE NO. 8—TROTTING.

Two-year-old stake; free for all. Mile heats, best 2 in 3, $300 guaranteed. Entrance $50, payable as follows: May 1st, $10; July 1st, $10; September 1st, $15, and $15 additional to start. See general conditions.

Fourth Day—Friday, Sept. 26th.

RACE NO. 9—TROTTING.

Mile heats, 3 in 5. For all described counties in race No. 6. $400 added. Entrance $50, payable as follows: May 1st, $10; July 1st, $10; September 1st, $20—when entries must be named—$10 additional to start. See general conditions.

RACE NO. 10—RUNNING.

Citizens' Handicap. $100 added. Five-eighths mile; heats, 2 in 3. Entrance $10, to close 6 P. M. day before race.

Fifth Day—Saturday, September 27th.

RACE NO. 11—RUNNING.

GENTLEMEN'S NOVELTY.—For non-professional jockeys. One mile dash. $100 added; $5 entrance. Purse divided as follows: First horse at each quarter to get $25; slowest average at all quarters to get Society medal.

NO. 12.—LADIES' TOURNAMENT

Free for all in District. Purse $50, divided as follows: $25 to first, $15 to second, $10 to third.

No. 13.—GENTLEMAN'S TROTTING.

Same conditions as gentlemen's Novelty. Mile heats, two in three. Entrance $5. Entrance money divided 50, 30 and 10 per cent.

GENERAN CONDITIONS.

Nominations in colt stakes transferrable any time before colts are named. If the payments in stake races amount to more than the sum guaranteed the additional amount to be divided 60, 30 and 10 per cent; in case of only two starting, 60 and 40 per cent.; and in case of one horse walking over, the whole amount to go to such horse.

A failure to make any payment when due shall be considered a withdrawal, and forfeiture of the amounts paid in. National Rules to govern all trotting races. The right reserved to refund the first payment in case the stake does not fill satisfactorily.

All running races, unless otherwise specified, governed by the Pacific Coast Blood Horse Association Rules.

The Directors reserve the right to change the hour and date of any race, and in case of a race being antedated the nominator will receive notice.

A horse distancing the field shall receive only first and third moneys.

L. G. SIMMONS, President.

A. B. McCUTCHEN, Secretary.

Rochester Driving Park

ROCHESTER, N. Y.

FLOWER CITY

Guarantee Stakes.

$10,000,

OPEN TO ALL SUBSCRIBERS.

For Trotting Horses that never beat 2:30 prior to the closing of this Stake

To be Trotted on the Rochester Driving Park, during Circuit Meeting, Aug. 12th, 13th, 14th and 15th, date to be decided by the Association.

ENTRANCE, FIVE PER CENT. OF PURSE, TO BE PAID AS FOLLOWS:

$125 payable at the time of subscription, which is to close Tuesday, April 1, 1890. Each subscriber to give his residence and Post Office address with his subscription. $125 payable Thursday, May 15th. $125 payable Tuesday, July 1st. $125 payable Friday, August 1, 1890, when the horses are to be named.

No subscription received unless the first payment of $125 shall accompany the same.

Subscribers liable only for the amount they have actually paid in but all subscriptions paid in shall be forfeited to the Association for this stake. Subscribers may transfer their subscription. Horses eligible April 1, 1890, shall be eligible for the race.

The entire stake subscribed shall be devoted to this purse, and it is guaranteed by the Association not to be less than $10,000. In case the subscription should exceed the amount of $10,000, such excess if under $500, will be added to the amount of purse; but if such excess should amount to $500 or over, then the excess will be devoted to another purse to be given as a Consolation Purse, for horses starting and winning no part of the original purse. Purses to be divided into fifty, twenty-five, fifteen and ten per cent., for first, second, third and fourth horses.

Bear in mind that subscriptions close Tuesday, April 1st, and that the whole subscription is but five per cent. of the guaranteed amount of purse ($10,000).

Subscriptions, accompanied by the first payment ($125), must be addressed to the Secretary.

Send for circulars for distribution.

A. COLLINS, Secretary,
Rochester, N. Y.

The Montana Circuit.

Thirty-one Days of Racing—Running, Trotting and Pacing.

$45,000 in Purses and Stakes.

Nominations to the Following Stakes close April 1st:

MISSOULA, July 14th to 19th Inclusive.

J. L. SLOANE, Secretary.

MISSOULA STAKES—Running. Six furlongs .... $250 added
For two-year-olds.

HOTEL STAKES—Running. One and one-half miles .... $400 added
For three-year-olds.

BITTER ROOT STAKES—Trotting .... $250 added
For three-year-olds bred and raised in Montana.

DEER LODGE, July 22d to 26th Inclusive.

JAS. B. McMASTER, Secretary.

DEER LODGE STAKES—Running. Six furlongs .... $250 added
For two-year-olds.

HOTEL STAKES—Running. One and one-half miles .... $300 added
For three-year-olds.

MONTANA STAKES—Trotting .... $100 added
For two-year-olds bred and raised in Montana.

ORO FINO STAKES—Trotting .... $700 added
For three-year-olds. Free for all.

YOSPEL MONTAIN STAKES—Trotting .... $200 added
For two-year-olds. Free for all.

MERCHANTS' STAKES—Trotting .... $200 added
For three-year-olds bred and raised in Montana.

Anaconda, July 30th to August 9th Inclusive.

W. M. THORNTON, Secretary.

BANKERS' STAKES—Running. Five furlongs .... $400 added
For two-year-olds.

MONTANA SUBURBAN—Running. One and one-half miles .... $500 added
For three-year-olds.

BREEDERS' STAKES—Trotting .... $250 added
For two-year-olds bred and raised in Montana.

BREEDERS' STAKES—Trotting .... $250 added
For three-year-olds bred and raised in Montana

LOWER WORKS STAKES—Trotting .... $250 added; $250 more if 2:35 is beaten
For two-year-olds. Free for all.

UPPER WORKS STAKES—Trotting .... $250 added; $250 more if 2:25 is beaten
For three-year-olds. Free for all.

BUTTE, August 13th to 23rd Inclusive.

S. W. WYNNE, Secretary,

ANACONDA STAKES.—Running .... $400 added
For 2 year olds.

WEST SIDE DERBY.—Running .... $500 added
For 3 year olds,

MONTANA STAKES.—Trotting .... $250 added
For 2 year olds bred and raised in Montana.

MONTANA STAKES.—Trotting .... $250 added
For 3 year olds bred and raised in Montana.

MOULTON STAKES.—Trotting .... $250 added, $250 more if 2:35 is beaten
For 2 year olds. Free for all.

SILVER CITY STAKES.—Trotting .... $250 added, $250 more if 2:25 is beaten
For 3 year olds. Free for all.

In all of the above stakes each nomination must be accompanied with $10 and a full description of animal. A second payment of $15 must be made on or before the first day of June; the remaining $25 must be paid before six o'clock the evening before the race

All stakes to be divided as follows: 70 per cent. to the first horse, 20 per cent, to second, and 10 per cent. to third.

For entry blanks, programmes, etc., address any of the Secretaries.

ST. NICHOLAS.

A Son of the World Renowned

SIDNEY,

Will Make the Season of 1890, at the Oakland Trotting Park.

ST. NICHOLAS was bred by Mr. G. Valensin at the Arno Stock Farm, Sacramento Co., California, in 1885. He is a beautifully proportioned bright bay horse, 15.3 hands high; is well muscled, lengthy, and lots of bone, with splendid natural action and a phenomenal turn of speed. As a three-year-old he easily worked three heats on the Oakland Track in 2:32, 2:29 and 2:27½. His breeding is just what one would expect from such a highly formed bloodlike horse. Sidney, his sire, is the most successful young stallion—whether for getting pacers or trotters—America has ever seen, and no wonder for his blood lines are exceptional fine and are all trotting lines, Santa Claus, Strathmore, Rysdyk's Hambletonian and Abdallah, while Sweetness again runs back through that great sire Volunteer, to Rysdyk's Hambletonian and also through her dam to Rysdyk's Hambletonian and Harry Clay 45, the sire of Electioneer's dam. St. Nicholas' dam is by Echo, an exceptionally prepotent son of Hambletonian thus giving St. Nicholas four Rysdyk's Hambletonian crosses and further back a Harry Clay cross which with his grand dam's thoroughbred cross should make him invaluable in the stud.

TERMS: Fifty dollars the season, which will commence on the 5th of February and close on the 1st of July. Due care will be taken of mares, but no responsibility for accidents or escapes.

Mares taken and kept as desired by the owners, and at reasonable rates.

JOHN ROWEN.

Oakland Trotting Park.

PASTURAGE

And Care of Horses

AT ALL SEASONS, A SPECIALTY,

—AT—

MURRAY'S RANCH. - - - Laurel Creek

SAN MATEO COUNTY.

Horses pastured, in the season, $4 per month.

Horses stabled and fed hay, per month $8 to $10.

Small pastures for fine stock at agreed rates. Yearly contracts at agreed rates. Best of attention given to all stock.

Stock can be delivered at the ranch or shipped to San Mateo.

Parties are requested to visit the ranch and satisfy themselves of its adaptation for the above purpose.

There are no barb wire fences on the farm.

Address

B. C. MURRAY,
San Mateo.

SAN JOSE

Colt Stakes,

TO BE TROTTED AT THE

FALL MEETING

OF 1890.

No. 1. REGAL WILKES TROTTING STAKES. For three year olds. $60 entrance, of which $10 must accompany nomination; $25 on June 1st, and $25 on August 1st; with $250 added. Mile heats, three in five.

No 2. MOUNT HAMILTON TROTTING STAKES. For two year olds. $50 entrance, of which $10 must accompany nomination, $15 on June 1st and $25 on August 1st; with $200 added. Mile and repeat.

No. 3. SANTA CLARA COUNTY TROTTING STAKES.—For two year olds (for above County only). $30 entrance, of which $10 must accompany nomination, $10 on June 1st and $10 on August 1st, with $150 added. Mile and repeat.

Parties must have owned their colts prior to February 1st, 1890, to be eligible in this stake.

No 4. INFANT TROTTING STAKES.—For the get of the following stallions: Jim L, Argent, Eros, Bismarck, J. Weatherhead's horses (2), Guy Davis, Nutwood Boy, Orion, King William, Tommy T., Stranger, John Sevenoaks, Col. Benton, Wilmington, Dick Patchen, Sarwood, Fleetwood, Sultan Jr., Billy Thornhill, Amphion, Magic, Chancellor, Monte, Christman's, Hambletonian, Boxwood, Nutgrove, Prince Albert, Alex Graham, Designer, Cyrus R., Harry Almont, Rea's Nutwood, Foodie, Parnell, Robin Adair, Fred Grant, Elect, Mambrino Jr., California Nutwood, Soudan, Jim Mulvenna, Brown Jug, Menlo, Almont Patchen, Antinous, Electric Light, May Boy, C. W. S. Henderson's Henry, S. B. Emerson, Carr's Mambrino, Designer, Prince Warwick, Henry Buff, J. Dunn's horses (2). For yearling foals of 1889. $25 entrance, of which $5 must accompany nomination; $10 on June 1st, and $10 Aug. 1st, with $100 added. Mile dash.

CONDITIONS.

Entries to close in the above stakes Tuesday, April 1st, 1890. Stake and added money divided 60 per cent. to first, 30 per cent. to second, and 10 per cent. to third.

For a walkover the colt will take the whole stake but no added money. If two colts start they must contest for entrance money only, divided two-thirds and one-third.

Declarations are void unless accompanied by the money.

Nominations not making payments when due forfeit previous payments.

WM. BUCKLY, President.

G. H. BRAGG, Secretary.

State Agricultural Society's

SPRING

RACE MEETING

AT

SACRAMENTO, CAL.,

APRIL 26 to 29, and MAY 1 and 3, 1890

ENTRIES CLOSE APRIL 7, 1890.

PROGRAMME.

FIRST DAY—SATURDAY, APRIL 26.

NO. 1.

Purse $400, for three-year-olds and upwards; $50 from starters to go to second horse. A winner this year at this distance to carry 3 pounds extra. Maidens allowed, if three years old, 5 pounds; four or more, 10 pounds. Three-quarters of a mile.

NO. 2.

Norfolk Stakes, for two-year-olds. Closed with 37 nominations. Five-eighths of a mile.

NO. 3.

Selling purse $400, of which $50 to second; for all ages. Winner to be sold at auction. Horses entered to be sold for $1,500 to carry rule weight. One pound off for each $100 down to $500. Value placed on starters only by 6 P. M. night before race. One mile and a sixteenth.

NO. 4.

The California Oaks, for three-year-old fillies. Closed in 1889 with 17 nominations. One and one-eighth miles.

SECOND DAY—TUESDAY, APRIL 29.

NO. 5.

The Matadero Stake, for two-year-olds. Closed in 1889 with 18 nominations. Three-quarters of a mile.

NO. 6.

The Chris. Green Handicap. Closed February 1st with 14 nominations. One and one-quarter miles.

NO. 7.

Purse $400, for all ages; $50 from starters to go to second horse. Maiden allowances: if three years old 5 pounds; four and upwards, 10 pounds. Non-winners this year allowed 5 pounds. Allowances cumulative. One mile and a sixteenth.

NO. 8.

The Weinstock, Lubin & Co. Stake. Closed in 1889 with thirty-two nominations. One mile.

THIRD DAY—THURSDAY, MAY 1.

NO. 9.

The Spring Stakes. A sweepstakes for three-year olds (foals of 1887) that have not won a race previous to January 1st, 1890. Closed February 1, 1890, with [illegible] nominations. One mile.

No. 10.

The Western Hotel Stakes for two-year-old fillies. Closed in 1889 with 27 nominations. Five-eighths of a mile.

NO. 11.

The Hall, Luhrs & Co. Handicap. Closed in 1889 with 29 nominations. One and one quarter miles.

NO. 12.

Selling purse $400, of which $50 to second; for all ages. Horses entered to be sold for $2,500 to carry rule weight. One pound off for each $100 down to $500. Value placed on starters only by 6 P. M. night before race. One and one-eighth miles.

FOURTH DAY—SATURDAY, MAY 3.

NO. 13.

The Golden Eagle Hotel Handicap, for two-year-olds. Closed in 1889 with 29 nominations. Weights to be announced before 3 P. M. second day before race. Declarations due by 4 P. M. day before race. Three-quarters of a mile.

NO. 14.

The Hopeful Handicap; a sweepstakes for all ages of $25 each, $15 forfeit, or $10 if declared, with $[illegible] added; second to receive $100. Weights announced [illegible] 10 P. M. day before race. Declarations due by 6 P. M. same day. One and one-eighth miles.

NO. 15.

The California Derby. Closed in 1889 with 32 nominations. One and one-half miles.

NO. 16.

Purse $400, for all ages; $50 from starters to go to second horse. Non-winners this year at time of starting allowed, if three years old, 5 pounds; four years old, 10 pounds; five and upwards, 14 pounds. Entries to close with clerk of course at 6 P. M. day before the race. Mile heats.

The State Agricultural Society's rules of 1889 to govern, except when conditions are otherwise.

Starters in stake races must be named through the entry box by 6 P. M. of the day before the race. The right of forfeit ceases at 10 o'clock A. M. day of race. Entries in purses not declared out by 6 P. M. day before race is run, must start.

Non starters in all purse races held for entrance under Rule 22.

The right to postpone races on account of the weather or other sufficient cause, is reserved. In event of postponement, handicaps stand, other declarations are off.

All declarations, either of starters, non-starters, non acceptance of handicaps or otherwise, must be made in writing. Blanks will be furnished by the Secretary.

Declarations in handicaps must be accompanied by the money.

Entries in Nos. 1, 3, 7, 12 and 16 to close with the Secretary Monday, April 7, 1890.

CHRIS GREEN, President.

EDWIN F. SMITH, Secretary.

CALIFORNIA
NUTWOOD

Will stand for mares the season of 1890, commencing February 15th, and ending July 15th, at the NUTWOOD STOCK FARM, one mile from Irvington.

DESCRIPTION AND PEDIGREE.

He is a dark chestnut, with star in forehead; foaled September 16th, 1881; is 16 hands 1½ inches high and weighs 1250 pounds. Has a beautiful flowing mane and tail, with remarkable style and lofty carriage, a bold, open movement like his sire, but has never been handled for speed. He moves and looks like his sire, except that he is a larger horse.

CALIFORNIA NUTWOOD by Nutwood, record 2:18¾, has 32 trotters and pacers with records from 2:15 to 2:30, and put 8 in the 2:30 list in 1889. He is the only horse that ever lived with a record under 2:20 that produced five under 2:20. He is now serving mares at Dubuque, Iowa, at $600 for the season, and his colts at yearlings sell from $2500 to $6000 each. He is out of the dam of Maud S., record 2:08¾.

Nutwood, by Alexander's Belmont, sire of 32 with records from 2:15½ to 2:30. Alexander's Belmont by Alexander's Abdallah, sire of Goldsmiths Maid, record 2:14, and 5 others in 2:30 list. Alexander's Abdallah, by Rysdyk's Hambletonian, sire of 41 with records from 2:17¼ to 2:30, and is the founder of the Hambletonian family.

FANNY PATCHEN, dam of California Nutwood, by George M. Patchen Jr., record 2:27, and sire of Wells Fargo, 2:18¼, Sam Purdy 2:20½, Ben Ali 2:20¾, and 7 others from 2:21 to 2:30. He has 7 sons who together produced 12 trotters in 2:30 list, and 5 daughters who together produced 5 trotters and 1 pacer in 2.30 or better. He sired Alexander 2:31½. Alexander sired Alex. Button 2:26½; Alex. Button sired Yolo Maid, pacing record 2:14 at 4 years old, the fastest on record; George M. Patchen Jr., by George M. Patchen 2:23½, is sire of Lucy 2:18¼, and 3 others in the 2:30 list; he has 12 sons who together produced 40 trotters from 2:14¾ to 2.30, and 6 daughters who together produced 6 trotters in 2:30 list or better, he is grand sire of Hopeful 2:14¾, and best wagon record 2:16½, and sire of the granddam of Stamboul 2:12½.

George M. Patchen, by Cassius M. Clay, and he by Henry Clay, founder of the Clay family.

Laura, second dam of California Nutwood, was a fine large bay mare, a very fast roadster brought from Chicago by Wm. Wilson, of San Jose, and is said to have made a record of 2.35 in Chicago. Pedigree not traced.

TERMS.

$40 for the season, payable invariably before the animal is removed. Mares not proving in foal can be returned free next season. Pasturage $3 per month, but no liability for accidents or escapes.

For further particulars address the owner,

MARTIN CARTER,

Newark, Alameda Co., Cal., or Irvington, Alameda County, Cal.

Sunny Side Breeding Farm.
Admiral 488.

Foaled 1867—Sired by Volunteer 55, Son of Rysdyk's Hambletonian 10.

First dam Lady Pierson by Cassius M. Clay (Neaves')); second dam by Diamond; third dam a running mare said to be thoroughbred. He is fitted in an eminent degree to produce colts that will in all respects justify his patrons in their expectations.

Admiral is the sire of Huntress, record 2:27½, Sister, 2:19¼, Perhelion, 2:25, Nona Y., 2:28, and others equally as promising, but have not had the advantage of track work. He will serve a limited number of approved mares at $60 the season, with usual return privilege. Season ending August 1, 1890. No liability for accidents or escapes.

KING DAVID 2576.

Bay Stallion—Foaled 1883.

Sired by Admiral 488, dam Black Flora (the dam of Huntress, 2:27½, Sister, 2:19¼, Perhelion, 2:25, Nona Y., 2:28), by Black Prince.

King David is one of the best gets of Admiral. He has a good disposition, kind to drive, smooth and even-gaited, and can speed fast. Barring accidents, he will trot in the twenties this Fall. His colts are large, rangy, and well finished. Will serve a limited number of mares at $30 the season, to end July 1890. Every precaution will be taken to prevent accidents and escapes, but no liability will be assumed. Pasturage $4 per month.

Sunny Side Farm is situated two miles east of Vallejo, on the Sulphur Spring road. For further particulars, address

FRANK DRAKE,

Vallejo, Cal.

Finely Bred Trotting Stallion
ARLINGTON.

$50 $50

Trial 2:26 1-2; by

ABBOTSFORD.

DESCRIPTION.

ARLINGTON is a handsome rich rosewood bay, 16 hands high and weighs 1100 lbs. He is of beautiful conformation, well boned, and great muscular development and greatly resembles his famous sire in every particular.

PEDIGREE.

ARLINGTON was sired by Abbotsford, dam the maple mare by Blue Bull. Abbotsford is by Woodford Mambrino, dam Columbia by Young Columbus, by Columbus, Woodford Mambrino's dam Woodbine by Woodford, a thoroughbred son of Kosciusko. Woodford Mambrino is recognized as the best son of Mambrino Chief. His own record is 2:21½, that of his son Abbotsford, the sire of Arlington 2:19½ and his son Prince 2:21, and he has also a large number in the 2:30 list. He is also the sire of Princeps the sire of Trinket, record of 2:14. Abbotsford, for the short time he has been in the stud, has proven himself a sire worthy of merit, his daughter Jassemine having won the Embryo Stakes of 1884, and every one who was put in training has shown good speed. The dam of Arlington was a beautiful bay mare, 15¾ hands high, sired by Blue Bull, dam Lexington mare raised by Ezra Champion of White Hall, New York, thus showing that in Arlington are combined most of the purest blood in America.

TERMS: $50 the season, with usual return privilege. The best of attention will be given mares, but no liability assumed for escapes or accidents, good pasturage, $3 per month. Call on or address,

J. B. FRENCH,

905, 907 and 909 Golden Gate Ave, S. F.

The Pure Trotting-bred Stallion
ILLUSTRIOUS

STANDARD No. 4178.

DESCRIPTION.

Dark bay, black points, 15 1-2 hands high, weight 1000 pounds, foaled May 20, 1886; bred by General W. T. Withers, Lexington, Ky.

PEDIGREE.

By Happy Medium, sire of Maxey Cobb 2:13¼ and 82 with records of 2:30 or better.

First dam Abdalletta by Cassius M. Clay Jr., sire of Durango 2:23¼, Harry Clay 2:23¼, and sire of the dams of Minnehaha, Bertha 2:27¼, Charley West 2:28¼, Grandmont 2:25 1-4, Lottie K 2:26¼, Mambrino Diamond 2:25, Richwood 2:26 1-2, Topsy 2:24¼, Happy Thought 2:21 1-2, Pequot 2:22 1-2, Fairlawn Medium 2:27 1-2, Folley 2:27¼, and Mambrino Boy 2:26 1-2.

Second dam Laura Crockett by Almont, sire of Westmont 2:13¼, Puritan 2:16, Fanny Witherspoon 2:16¼, Piedmont 2:17¼, Aldine 2:19¼, and 37 with records better than 2:30.

Third dam Sally Tee by Alexander's Abdallah, sire Goldsmith Maid 2:14.

Fourth dam Kate Crockett, the dam of Lulu 2:14¼, by imp Hooton.

Illustrious is a horse of extra fine finish, large clean bone, good feet, back short and strong, loins and quarters well muscled, and powerful. He has a kind disposition and splendid trotting action, and is as handsome and bloodlike in form and finish as any trotting stallion in the land.

He is pronounced by his breeder, General Withers, to be the best bred son of Happy Medium living, and is undoubtedly one of the very best bred trotting stallions in the State. He has had but six weeks' regular training, and a part of that time was sick with epizootic, but was trotted quarters in 38 1-4 seconds, and barring accidents will certainly trot better than 2:30 this season.

TERMS—$50 the season. Mares not proving with foal may be returned next year free.

Good pasturage at $3 per month.

Season to begin February 1st and end June 15th.

GEO. A. STONE,

Santa Rosa, Cal.

WOODNUT

(Weatherhead's) by Nutwood 600

Sire of Belmont Boy, 2:16, pacer, Woodnut, 2:16¼, Felix, 2:19¼, Dawn, 2:18¼, Maggie E., 2:19¼, Irma, 2:18¼, and 26 others in 2:30 or better; 1st dam Flora, 2:30¼, trial 2:26, dam of Chrisman's Hambletonian, sire of Steve Whipple, 2:23, Kate Agnew, 2:28¼, by Chieftain 721, sire of Defiance 2:17¼ pacing and 2:24 trotting, Cairo, 2:26, Onward, 2:24, pacer; second dam by Wilson's Leaman.

Woodnut is a beautiful bay with black points, 15¾ hands high, weighing 1,076 pounds. His colts are all larger than himself, and sell readily for road and carriage purposes, being of good color and very docile, yet prompt to obey, and always ready.

Service fee, $25, with usual privileges. Colts and fillies from Tilton Almont, Patchen, Stockbridge Chief, and other desirable crosses, FOR SALE. For further particulars, pedigrees, or any communication in horse matters, address

JAS. WEATHERHEAD, Prop.

San José, Cal.

The Trotting-Bred Stallion
RINGWOOD

THE FINEST SON OF THE NOTED SIDNEY,

Will make a Season at Oakland, commencing March 1, and ending June 1, 1890.

DESCRIPTION.

RINGWOOD is a dark, rich colored bay, black points, 15 1-2 hands, weight 1100 lbs., and a pure gaited trotter. Has shown great speed. He is now five years old. As a four year old he showed a trial in 2:19 1-2, and but for an accident would have received a record as a four year old of 2:18 or better.

PEDIGREE.

RINGWOOD is by Sidney, record 2:19 3-4, and is half brother to Gold Leaf 2:11 1-4, Adonis 2:14, Flee' (two year old) 2:24, Longworth 2.19, Sister V. 2:21, Faustino, yearling, 2:35, Fleet, yearling, 2:35. Memo, three year old trial 2:20 1-2.

Sidney is by Santa Claus, record 2:17 1-2; he by Strathmore, sire of 31 in 2:30 list; he by Hambletonian 10, the greatest of all producers; he by Abdallah. Sidney's dam, Sweetness, record 2:21 1-4; she by Volunteer, the sire of St. Julien 2:11 1-4.

RINGWOOD'S dam Alma; she by Dashway, thoroughbred; he by Belmont, he by American Boy; he by Sea Gull; he by imported Expedition. Alma's 1st dam, Fanny Cobb, was a great road mare, pedigree untraced.

TERMS: $50 for the Season.

Payable June 1st, or sooner if mares are taken away. Address communications to

A. C. DIETZ,

Oakland, Cal.

The Fast Trotting Stallion
REDWOOD.

Four-Year-Old Record 2:24 1-2

Will make the season of 1890—February 1st to July 1st—at the

OAKLAND RACE TRACK.

REDWOOD is a dark bay colt, 15.2¼ hands high, weighs 1100 lbs. Foaled in 1885 by Anteeo, 2:16¼, sire of Alfred G., 2:19¾. Anteeo is by Electioneer. First dam Lou Milton, by Milton Medium; second dam Old Fly, a thoroughbred mare brought from the East in 1871 by W. C. Ralston, Esq.

Redwood's sire was out of Columbine by A. W. Richmond, the sire of the pacers Arrow 2:13¼, and Elwood 2:23, and the trotters Romero, 2:19¼, and Len Rose, 2:27. Redwood has shown a quarter in 33 seconds.

Terms $100

For the season. Mares not proving with foal may be returned next season free of charge, provided Redwood remains the property of the present owners. Good pasturage at $5 per month. No responsibility assumed for escapes or accidents. Service fees payable before removal of the mare. Limited to 30 approved mares. For further particulars address,

A. McFADYEN.

Race track, Oakland, Cal.

Pedigrees Tabulated

IN THE MOST ARTISTIC MANNER.

Giving speed performers under sires and dams. Catalogues compiled. Stallion cards and circulars written up ready for the press. Pedigree blanks for sale. Prices reasonable. Horses bought and sold on commission. References furnished.

R. Y. HARDIN.

806 W. Madison St., Chicago, Ill.

THE MAMBRINO
Patchen Stallion.

MAMBRINO JR., 1789 (formerly Carr's) Sire of Lady Ellen 2:38 (dam of Ella 2:29), Maud H. 2:30, Mambrino Boy (Carr's) 2:31 1 2.

Will stand at my farm, 2 1-2 miles north of San José, on the Milpitas road. Season to commence February 1st, 1890, at $50, with return privilege 1891. Fifteen mares of approved breeding, besides my own, will be given him. Parties owning good mares, performers or out of producing dams, will find an opportunity to breed them on shares, and the best of care taken of them till colt is weaned, if so desired.

PEDIGREE.

MAMBRINO JR., 1789, by Mambrino Patchen 58 (full brother of Lady Thorne 2:18 1-4) by Mambrino Chief 11. First dam by Mambrino Chief 11; 2nd dam by imp. Jordan (thoroughbred); 3rd dam by Bertrand, son of Sir Archy; 4th dam by Chewkees, son of Sir Archy.

For further particulars address

GEO. P. BULL.

Box 1067. San José, Cal.

The Trotting Stallion
CUPID,

Full Brother to Adonis 2:14,

—Sired by—

The Celebrated SIDNEY 2:19 3-4, and out of Venus.

Will make the season of 1890 at the OAKLAND TROTTING PARK.

PEDIGREE.

CUPID is by Sidney out of Venus by Capt. Webster 10173, record 2:30, and sire of Firestone 2:19. Second dam by Skenandoah 936, sire of Daisy Burns 2:29¼, Erwin Davis (sire of two in the 30 list) and dams of four in the 30 list.

DESCRIPTION.

Cupid is a handsome bright bay 15.2¼ hands high, weighs 1100 lbs.; was foaled in 1886. As a yearling, with very little work he showed quarters in 42 seconds, and at 2 years old, quarters in 36 seconds. As a three year old he has not been worked, but he shows the speed and endurance that must come from his excellent blood lines.

TERMS $50 for the season, with the usual return privileges. Good pasturage near the track at $5 per month. The best of care taken of mares in any way that owners may desire, but no responsibility assumed for accidents or escapes.

For further particulars address

C. O. THORNQUEST,

Oakland Trotting Park, or

C. BAAB, 972 Broadway, Oakland.

The Trotting Stallion
VICTOR,

Record 2:22.

Will make the season of 1890 at NAPA CITY.

DESCRIPTION.

VICTOR is a handsome dark bay; 15.3 hands high; weighs about 1,100 pounds, and is remarkably intelligent, level-headed, of kind disposition, and a magnificent animal in every respect. He is well boned and muscled, of splendid conformation, and possesses the qualities of speed and endurance to an eminent degree—qualities that he imparts to his progeny.

PEDIGREE.

VICTOR, record 2:22:
- Echo 462
  - Hambletonian 10, Sire of 42 in the 2:30 list.
    - Abdallah 1
    - Chas. Kent mare
  - Fanny Felter
    - Magnolia 68
    - by Webber's Kentucky Whip
- Daughter of
  - Woodburn
    - Lexington
    - Lulu Horton
  - daughter of
    - Ashland
    - thoroughbred

ECHO is the sire of Belle Echo, 2:20, Senator, 2:21¼, Victor, 2:22, Gibraltar, 2:22¼, Echora, 2:23¼, Tippie, 2:25¼, Lohengrin, 2:27¼, Pasha, 2:27¼, Elmonte, 2:29, Col. Hawkins, 2:29¼, Annie Laurie, 2.30, Economy, 2:30, Sam Lewis, pacer, 2:24.

TERMS—$60 FOR THE SEASON.

Mares not proving with foal may be returned next season free of charge, provided the horse remains the property of the present proprietor, and stands at the same place, otherwise money will be refunded. The best of care taken of mares in any manner that owners may desire, but no responsibility assumed for accidents or escapes. For further particulars, apply to or address

G. W. HUGHES, Agent,

G. A. DOHERTY, Proprietor. Napa City.

The Hambletonian Stallion 10178.

CHRISMAN'S HAMBLETONIAN, Sire of Steve Whipple, 2:23, Kate Agnew, 2:28¼, etc.:
- Whipple's Hambletonian, Sire of 14 trotters and 1 pacer from 2:19 to 2:30, and 7 sons with 8 performers from 2:21¼ to 2:30, and dams of 6 from 2:10¼ to 2:30.
  - Guy Miller, By Hambletonian 10.
  - Martha Washington, Dam of Speculation 928, Sire of Crown Pt., 2:24, Oakland Maid, 2:22, Gracie S., 2:28¼, and dam of Waterford, 2:27
- Flora, 2:30¼, trial, 2:26. Dam of Chrisman's Hambletonian, sire of Steve Whipple, 2:23, Kate Agnew, 2:28¼.
  - Chieftain 721, sire of Defiance, 2:24 and 2:17¼, pacing; Cairo, 2:26, and Onward, 2:24, pacer.
  - daughter of Wilson's Leamon

Stud season now on till the 1st of August, 1890, at $40 each mare, with return privilege in 1891, provided stallion and mare, or either, do not change owners. Good pasture at hand, and comfortable accommodation for brood mares and colts. For further particulars, address

JESSE CHRISMAN, Proprietor.

San Jose, Cal.

Vineland Stock Farm

Whippleton 1883,

Sire of

LILY STANLEY	Record	2:17½
HOMESTAKE	"	2:16½
FLORA B.	"	2:27
CORA C.	"	2:31½
BLACK PRINCE	"	2:36½
RACHEL	"	2:3
PRINCE W.	"	2:40

WHIPPLETON is not only the sire of trotters, but he is the greatest sire of Carriage Horses on the Pacific Coast. Some of the best carriage and road teams in San Francisco are sired by Whippleton. A carriage team by Whippleton received First Premium at Napa, Petaluma, Oakland, Sacramento, Stockton and San Jose. Whippleton and his colts have never been beaten in the show ring.

DESCRIPTION.

WHIPPLETON is black, tan muzzle and flanks, 17 hands, and weighs 1,100 lbs. Most of his colts are 16 hands or over, and with a few exceptions, bay, brown or black. He never sired a sorrel or white face colt. (If he does, I agree to refund service money.)

PEDIGREE.

WHIPPLETON, sired by Hambletonian Jr. (sire Hancock 2.29), by Whipple's Hambletonian (sire of Graves, 2:19 Westfield, 2:20¼, Express, 2:24, and 12 others in the 2:30 list), dam Lady Livingston (dam of Lady Blanchard, 2:26¼, Bloomfield Maid, trial 2:22), by General Taylor (sire of the dams of Wells Fargo, 2:18¼, Nerea, 2:23¼, Bickford, 2:29¼, Lady Blanchard, 2:26¼, etc., and sire of grandam of Hazel Wilkes, 2:20) by the Morse Horse 6, sire of Norman 25 (sire of Lulu, 2:14¼, May Queen 2:20, etc.).

TERMS at $50, limited to 20 mares, for the season, usual return privileges. I would like to get about ten well bred mares with the proper combination of blood to breed to Whippleton on shares this season.

Alcona 730.

Sire of

FLORA BELLE	Record	2:24
CLAY DUKE	"	2:31½

ALCONA will be a great sire, but four of his colts have ever been trained, and all have shown full miles better than 2:30, and two of them as good as 2:20. Two of his first sons each sired a colt as a two-year-old, and last season one as a four-year-old trotted a full mile in 2:22¼, and the other, a three-year-old, a mile in 2:31. With opportunities, Alcona is destined to be one of Almont's best sons. Almont, for his opportunities, is beyond doubt the most prepotent sire of his age. He has 36 representatives in the 2:30 list; 49 sons and 22 daughters that have already produced 2:30 performers. Almont died five years ago at 20 years old. If he lived he would be but 25 years old.

PEDIGREE.

ALCONA sired by the great Almont (sire of Westmont 2:13¼, Fanny Witherspoon 2:16¼, Piedmont 2:17¼, and 33 others with records better than 2:30, and grandsire of Belle Hamlin 2:13¼, etc.); by Alexander's Abdallah (sire of Goldsmith Maid 2:14), he by Rysdyk's Hambletonian. Alcona's dam, Queen Mary, by Mambrino Chief (sire of Lady Thorne 2:18 1-4, and 5 others in the 2:30 list, and sire of the dams of Director 2:17, Piedmont 2:17¼, Onward 2:25 1-4, Red Wilkes Almont, Belmont and many other noted sires).

DESCRIPTION.

Alcona is a beautiful chestnut 16 2 1-2 hands high, and weighs 1300 lbs. His colts possess speed, style, finish and beauty, and if they don't trot they command the highest prices for carriage horses.

$40 for the season. Usual return privilege.

Season on Whippleton and Alcona ends July 1st, 1890.

Best kind of pasturage at $4 per month. Mares kept in any manner desired.

For further particulars send for circular or call at stables, one mile south of St. Helena.

FRED W. LOEBER.

St. Helena, Napa Co., Cal.

The Trotting Stallion
G & M

FULL BROTHER TO

ALFRED G, 2:19¾.

(Who has been taken to Kentucky to stand at $200)

Will make the season of 1890 from FEBRUARY 1st to JULY 1st, at

SANTA ROSA.

G. & M. is by Anteeo, 2:16¼; was foaled 1886; first dam Rosa B. by Speculation (son of Hambletonian 10); 2d dam Elizabeth by Alexander 490; 3d dam Nora by imp. Glencoe. Anteeo is by Electioneer, out of Columbine by A. W. Richmond 1687.

G. & M. is a handsome dark bay; stands 15-2 1-2 hands high, and weighs 1060 pounds. Gameness, stoutness, speed and stamina are indelibly impressed in every line of the pedigree of G. & M. Owners of brood-mares in search of these qualities, will do well to patronize this promising colt.

PHILOSOPHER,

Foaled 1886 by Pilot Wilkes 2987; first dam Bella by George Wilkes 519; second dam by Bell Morgan 61.

Philosopher's sire, Pilot Wilkes 2987, is by George Wilkes 519, dam Grace (the dam of Alice Woodburn, etc.), by Pilot Jr. 12, grandam by Orphan Boy.

Will make the season of 1890, from FEBRUARY 1st to JULY 1st, at Santa Rosa.

TERMS for the season:

G. & M., $50,

PHILOSOPHER, $30,

with privilege of returning mares that do not prove in foal the next season free of charge, provided the horse bred to remains the property of the present owners. Good pasturage at $3 per month. No responsibility assumed for accidents or escapes. Service fees payable before removal of the mare. For further particulars, address

GEO. E. GUERNE,

Santa Rosa Cal.

Highland Farm,

LEXINGTON, KY.,

Home of Red Wilkes.

Standard-bred Trotting Stock

For Sale,

Sired by Red Wilkes, Wilton, 2:19¼; Allandorf and Sentinel Wilkes, out of highly bred Standard Mares of the most fashionable blood of the day.

W. C. FRANCE, Proprietor.

Guenoc Stud Farm, Lake Co., Cal.

Imp. GREENBACK

(Sire of the English winners Greenlight, Greenjacket, Greenshank, Greenwave and Greenborn)

By Dollar, dam Music, by Stockwell. $100 the Season

ST. SAVIOR,

(FULL BROTHER TO EOLE)

By Eolus, dam War Song, by War Dance. $100 the Season.

PASTURAGE, $5 PER MONTH.

With right to return the following year if mare does not prove with foal. The best of care taken, but no liability for accidents or escapes. Mares shipped to C. W. ABY, care ST. HELENA STABLES, St. Helena Napa County, will be taken in charge by competent men.

For further information write to

DR. C. W. ABY, Middletown, Lake County, Cal.

1890 Three Anteeo Stallions 1890

SUNSET, 5 years old, by Anteeo
ANTEEOF, 4 years old, by Anteeo
ANTEEOP, 3 years old, by Anteeo

ANTEEO. Standard 7868. Record, 2:16 1-4, ne by Stanford's Electioneer, and dam Columbine.

DESCRIPTIONS, PEDIGREES AND CONDITIONS.

"SUNSET" is a rich, dark bay, small star on forehead, portion of hind left foot white; was foaled March 11, 1885; is by ANTEEO and the inbred HAMBLETONIAN mare, BESSIE G., she by KING PHILLIP, son of WHIPPLE'S HAMBLETONIAN. He is 16 1-2 hands high, and weighs 1,200 lbs. He is of perfect build and splendid action cool headed and great speed for his size, having trotted a trial mile as a three-year-old in 2:34. He then entered heavy in the stud and was matched against Whalebone at the Healdsburg races November 1, 1889, winning just as he pleased in three straight heats; time, 2:47, 2:46 1-2, 2:52 1-2. He was then matched for a race to come off last Thanksgiving Day at Petaluma but owing to the heavy rains the event did not take place. A few days previous to Thanksgiving Day Mr. Lawrence worked Sunset out and then he trotted three square miles and heats in 2:33¼, 2:34 and 2:37.

SUNSET will be bred to 40 mares only, at $50 each, no colt no pay.

"ANTEEOF" is a jet black, was foaled April 13, 1886, is 16¾ hands high, and weighs 1,290 lbs., has a very fine, heavy black mane and tail; is well proportioned, moves majestically, is of easy, lofty carriage; is symmetrical, in fact is a beautiful horse. He was sired by Anteeo and the C. A. Taylor mare "Nance," her dam, was raised by Dr. Oliver Plummer, of Consumnes, Cal., and sired by "Napoleon"; Napoleon was foaled May 29, 1868, and raised by James Kyle of Butler County, Ohio. He was sired by Benj. Sweet's horse Bellfounder, and he by Old Bellfounder, his dam was sired by Doc. Daniel Mulligan's horse, Cadmus, G. G. sire the celebrated Eclipse; his G. dam was sired by Big Shakespeare. G. G., sires dam by Messenger and Expedition.

ANTEEOF will be bred to 25 mares only, at $50 each. No colt, no pay.

"ANTEEOP" is a rich seal brown; was foaled March 7, 1887; by Anteeo and the inbred Hambletonian mare Bessie G., also dam of Sunset, his full brother and Midget his full sister; he is 15 1-2 hands high and weighs 950 lbs, and measures 22 inches around the arm, good head, fine neck, full, broad breast; withers and rump on nearly equal line, well proportioned bones, ankle, shoulders, loins and hips; strong legs all around, with great muscular development and splendid sinews; wirey pasterns and sound, compact feet; the lines from hip to hoof show power and speed; stands square and has excellent action, has a superb lustrous coat of rich, deep brown fur of seal color without defect; an even, honest trotter, and has gone the mile as a two-year-old in 2:58, the last quarter in 38 seconds; is intelligent and of high spirit, with much temper, but is not vicious, has very fine eyes, is a handsome, showy colt; attractive in harness.

ANTEEOP will be bred to 15 mares only, at $50. No colt, no pay.

SEASON to commence February 1st, ending July 1, 1890. Book now ready. Apply to John R. Lawrence, "Manager and Trainer," on my fruit and hop ranch, 1 mile east of Court House, on Sonoma road. Excellent pasture furnished with running water, also dry knolls with oak shelter, at $3 per month for mares. Two of the above stallions will be for sale after the expiration of the their stud season.

GUY E. GROSSE,
SANTA ROSA, SONOMA CO., CAL.

The Trotting Stallion

Guide 2:29

(At Four Years)

Will make the season of 1890 at the SANTA RITA RANCH, about one mile North of Pleasanton.

DESCRIPTION.

GUIDE is a handsome seal brown, five years old, stands 15¾ hands high, and weighs 1035 pounds. He is of fine form, level headed, intelligent, and comes from blood lines that are noted for the qualities of speed and gameness.

PEDIGREE.

GUIDE, 2:28½

- Director, 2:17. Sire of Direct, 2:18¼, Margaret S., 2:19¼.
  - Dictator 113. Sire of 23 trotters and 3 pacers in 2:30.
    - Hambletonian 10.
    - Clara, by American Star 14.
  - Dolly. Dam of Onward, 2:25¼, Thorndale, 2:22¼.
    - Mambrino Chief 11.
    - Fannie, by Ben Franklin.
- Imogene.
  - Norwood 522. Sire of Tommy Norwood, 2:26¼.
    - Hambletonian 10.
    - Lady Fallis, by American Star 14.
  - daughter of
    - American Star 14.
    - daughter of Harry Clay 45.

The attention of breeders is especially called to the above pedigree as showing 3 crosses of American Star.

GUIDE trotted into the 2:30 list last season with little training, and he will trot into the 2:20 list the coming season barring accidents.

Guide's sire has a record of 2:17, made in a five heat race, and Guide is closely related to Phallas, who made a record of 2:13¾ in a fourth heat, and to Jay-Eye-See, record 2:10.

TWO HUNDRED AND FIFTY DOLLARS will be given to the owner of the first of the produce of Guide put in the 2:30 list, and $100 to each one after the first.

TERMS—$75 for the season, with the usual return privileges.

Admiro,

Sire Admiral; dam by San Bruno, by Easton's David Hill.

This magnificent horse is a handsome bay, eight years old; stands 17 1-2 hands high, and weighs 1450 pounds He is very speedy for a large horse, and breeds fine large carriage horses. His produce possess every qualification of the Cleveland Bay, with the added qualities of speed and endurance resulting from his high trotting breeding.

TERMS—$40 for the season, with usual return privileges.

Will stand three days each week at Santa Rita Ranch, Pleasanton, and at A. T. Hatch's Ranch "Almono," Alamo, Contra Costa County, alternately. All mares sent care of SMITH & SUTHERLAND, Pleasanton, will be taken in charge of on arrival, and will receive the best care and attention in any manner the owners may desire. Good pasturage at $4 per month. Only a limited number of approved mares will be served by this horse this season.

No responsibility assumed for escapes or accidents. For further particulars, address

SMITH & SUTHERLAND, Pleasanton,
or A. T. HATCH, care Palace Hotel, San Francisco.

GRANDISSIMO,

Full Brother to GRANDEE, 3-year-old Record 2-23½.

GRANDISSIMO

- Le Grande 2868 (trial, 2:24). Sire of Grandee, 3 y. o. r., 2:23½.
  - Almont 33. Sire of Westmont, 2:13¾, Puritan, 2:16, Fannie Wetherspoon, 2:16½, Piedmont, 2:17¼, and 32 others in 2:30, and sire of 49 sons and 22 daughters that have produced 2:30 performers.
    - Abdallah 15. Sire of Goldsmith Maid, 2:14, and 8 others in 2:30, and sire of 13 sons and 21 dams, producers of 2:30 performers.
    - Sally Anderson, by Mambrino Chief.
  - Jessie Pepper. Dam of Iona, 2:17½, Alpha, 2:23½, and grandam of Montezuma, 2:29½.
    - Mambrino Chief 11. Sire Lady Thorne, 2:18¼, and 5 others in 2:30 with 23 sires and 15 dams, producers of 2:30 performers.
    - Sidi Hamet (thoroughbred).
- Norma. Dam of Grandee, 3 y. o. r., 2:23½.
  - Arthurton 365. Sire Arab, 2:15, and 4 others in 2:30, and dams of Hidalgo, 2:27, Hazel Wilkes, 2:20, Reverie (yearling), 2:36½.
    - Hambletonian 10. Sire of Dexter, 2:17¼, and 40 others in 2:30.
    - Imogene. Dam of Arthurton, with 4 in 2:30; Leland, with 3 in 2:30.
  - Nourmahal, 2:39½. Full sister to A. W. Richmond 1687, sire of Arrow, 2:13½, Romero, 2:19½, and 3 others in 2:30.
    - Blackbird 401. Sire of Blackbird, 2:22, A. W. Richmond, sire of 5 in 2:30, and dam of Anteeo, 2:16¼, Anteeolo, 2:19¼.
    - by Rattler (thoroughbred).

SAN DIEGO, 8776.

SAN DIEGO 86

- Alcona Clay 2756.
  - Alcona 730. Sire of Flora Belle, 2:24, Clay Duke, 2:31½, etc.
    - Almont 33. Sire of Westmont, 2:13¾, Piedmont, 2:17¼, Puritan, 2:16, and 33 others in 2:30 list.
    - by Mambrino Chief 11. Sire of Lady Thorne, 2:18¼.
  - Madonna. Dam of Del Rey, trial 2:31, Alcona Jr., 2:41, sire of Silas Skinner, trial 2:23½.
    - Cassius M. Clay Jr. 22. Sire of Durango, 2:23½, Harry Clay, 2:23½, and sire of dam of Happy Thought, 2:22½, and others.
    - by Joe Downing 710. Sire of Abe Downing, 2:20¾, Dick Jamison, 2:26, and sire of dams of Kentucky Hambletonian, 2:27, Lorena, 2:15, and others.
- Fontana. Dam of Flora Belle, 2:24. Silas Skinner, trial 2:23½.
  - Almont 33. Sire of 36 in 2:30 list, 49 sons and 22 daughters that have produced 2:30 performers.
  - Fanny Williams. Dam of Bay Chieftain, 2:28½.
    - Abdallah 15. Sire of Goldsmith Maid, 2:14, Thorndale, 2:21¼, also Almont, Belmont, Jim Monroe, etc.
    - by Denmark (thoroughbred).

GRANDISSIMO is a blood bay, handsome-modelled colt, and a natural trotter. He is four years old, and trotted one quarter miles in 36 seconds, with very limited training, last Fall.

SAN DIEGO is dark seal brown, three years old, and trotted one-quarter miles in 40 seconds as a two-year old.

These are two grand young horses, and, barring accidents, will both make fast records next fall.

They will both be allowed a limited number of mares, at $60 for the season. Mares not proving in foal to be returned free 1891. Best of pasture for mares at $4 per month, but no liability for accidents or escapes.

They will make the season from February 1st to June 1st at Napa Fair Grounds. For further particulars, address or call on

H. B. STARR, Race Track, Napa, Cal.,
or FRED W. LOEBER, St. Helena

A SON OF ALMONT 33.

Only $25 for the Season.

ASHLAND ALMONT 3481.

PEDIGREE.

ASHLAND ALMONT 3481

- Almont 33. Sire of 34 in 2:30 or better, of 21 daughters and of 49 sires that have produce in 2:30 or better.
  - Abdallah 15. Sire Goldsmith Maid, 2:14; 6 in 2:30 list; 13 sires and 25 dams of trotters in 2:30 list.
    - Hambletonian 10. Sire of 41 in 2:30 list; sire of 107 sires of 567 in 2:30 list.
    - Katy Darling.
  - Sally Anderson.
    - Mambrino Chief 11. Lady Thorn, 2:18½.
    - Kate, by Pilot Jr. 12.
- Pauline. Dam of Sapho.
  - Ashland Chief. Sire Black Cloud, 2:17¼.
    - Mambrino Chief 11. Lady Thorn, 2:18½.
    - dau. of imp. Yorkshire, (thoroughbred).
  - Rosina. Dam Almonia the dam of Sally Cossack, 2:22¼, dau. Mamb. Abdallah, sire Mam. Prince, 2:28, and of Mamb. Bashaw, sire of Graham's Mambrino, 2:28.
    - Abdallah 15. Sire Goldsmith Maid, 2:14.
    - Prof. Smith's Sir William.

DESCRIPTION.

ASHLAND ALMONT 3481 is a handsome chestnut; stands 16 hands; was foaled 1883, and bred by Geo. Withers, of Lexington, Ky. He is of fine form, and remarkably intelligent, sweet-tempered and absolutely sound. His oldest foal may be seen with him, and while he has never served a standard mare or one that was a producer of speed, all of his colts are large, sound, fast and handsome.

TERMS: $25 for the season, with usual return privileges. The best of care taken of mares in any manner that the owner may desire, but no responsibility assumed for escapes or accidents.

For further particulars, address

T. J. WHITEHEAD, Manager.
579 36th Street, bet. Telegraph Ave. and Grove St., Oakland, Cal.
or, W. H. ASHBY, Oakland, Cal.

2:10 1-2 ELECTIONEER 2:12 1-4

BAY STALLION	BROWN STALLION
ECLECTIC	**MORTIMER**
11,321	5,346
By Electioneer, dam Manette (full sister to Woodnut 2.16 1-2 Manon 2:21 and Maple, dam of Hattie D., three-year-old record 2.26¾) by Nutwood 2:18¾, etc., etc.	Four-year-old Record 2:27. By ELECTIONEER, dam MARTI, by Whipple's Hambletonian (sire of 15 in 2:30, and of dams of eight in 2:30). Second dam Ida Martin by Rifleman (sire of Col. Lewis 2:18¾).
Terms $100 for the Season.	Terms $60 for the Season.

Horses shipped via San Francisco may be consigned to J. W. MORSHEAD, City Front Stables, who will attend to their forwarding.

Season closes JULY 1st, 1890. Usual return privileges.

For urther particulars address owner,

WILFRED PAGE, Penns Grove,
Sonoma County, Cal.

GEO. WASHINGTON,

11,623.

RECORD 2:30.

Bay colt, bred by Thomas Smith of Vallejo, Cal. Foaled 1886 by Mambrino Chief, Jr., 11,622, record 2:34 1-4, 1st dam Fanny Rose by Vick's Ethan Allen Jr. 2,903, sire of Prince Allen 2:27. 2nd dam Jenny Lind, thoroughbred, dam of Prince Allen 2:27. Will serve a limited number of mares at $50 for the season. Mares not proving with foal may be returned next season free.

Mambrino Chief, Jr.

11,622.

RECORD 2:34 1 2.

Sire of George Washington, record 2 30 at three years old. Bay horse bred by Rufus Ingalls of Belvedere, Ill. By McDonald Chief 3'83. First dam Venus by Mambrino Patchen 58. 2nd dam by Wardlow's Shakespeare. 3rd dam Lone Gold 4th dam by Silver Heels. Has not been in the stud b fore. He was 5 years old when he served a few mares, and his colts all show good style and form.

Terms for the season $40. For further particulars see or address

THOMAS SMITH,
Vallejo, Cal.

Elector 2170.

Sire of J. R.

Three-Year Old Record 2:24.

Sired by Electioneer 125, sire of Sunol, three-year-old, 2:10½, Palo Alto, 2:12¼, etc.; dam Gilberta by Fred Low 656, sire of Clay, 2:25½, etc.

Second dam Lady Gilbert (grandam of Lot Slocum, 2:17½) by General Knox 140 (sire of Lady Maud, 2:18¼, and many others).

TERMS.

$150 for the season. Book full for 1890.

L. A. RICHARDS,
Grayson, Stanislaus Co., Cal.

The Thoroughbred Stallion

Three Cheers

Will make the season of 1890 at

Sacramento.

PEDIGREE.

THREE CHEERS
- imp. Hurrah
  - Newminster
    - Touchstone, by Camel
    - Beeswing, by Dr. Syntax
  - Jovial
    - Bay Middleton, by Sultan
    - Sister to Grey Momus, by Comus
- Young Fashion
  - imp. Monarch
    - imp. Priam, by Emilius
    - imp. Delphine, by Whisker
  - Fashion
    - imp. Trustee, by Catton
    - Bonnets o' Blue, by Sir Charles

Hurrah was imported by John Reber, of Lancaster, Ohio, a locality where there were but few breeders of thoroughbreds. Under these disadvantages he sired a long list of winners. His sire Newminster, won the St. Ledger 1851, and his dam, Jovial by Bay Middleton, winner of the Derby 1836. Newminister by Touchstone, winner St. Ledger 1834. Dam Beeswing, winner of 54 races out of 64 starts, by Dr. Syntax, winner of the Doncaster Cup, 1837—40—41—42, the only horse that ever accomplished that feat.

On the side of the dam Three Cheers is equally well related. Young Fashion was the dam of Surprise, Scotland (the only horse that ever beat Asteroid a heat), Liverpool. Columbia, and Bonnie Kate, the dam of Little Buttercup, and the flying Bonnie Lizzie. His grandam, Fashion was the greatest race mare of her day and beat Boston in that historical match at four mile heats, which is recorded as one of the greatest events in the annals of the turf.

Horsemen who are qualified to judge, pronounce Three Cheers to be the finest type of the Newminster line in America.

LOCATION.

THREE CHEERS will be located at the Arcade Training Stable, Rancho del Paso. This place has been selected for the reason that first class pasturage has been secured there for the exclusive use of these mares, and the other facilities to be obtained there for the care of mares (especially mares in foal) are better than can be found elsewhere in the locality.

TERMS.

$60 for the season with the usual return privileges. Pasturage $5 per month. Mares cared for as owners may desire at bottom rates for grain and hay. All bills payable before the mare is removed.

Mares shipped care of WM. IRVINE, Pacific Stables, Sacramento, will be properly cared for and sent to the ranch without delay.

Three Cheers will be in charge of one of the most experienced and competent stud grooms in the State, who will exercise every care, but no reponsibility assumed for accidents or escapes.

For further particulars apply to Louis Criesler, at the rance; Wm. Irvine, Pacific Stables, Second St., Sacramento; or to the owner,

E. S. CULVER,
313 Bush St., San Francisco.

GROVER CLAY

Bay Stallion, Black Points,

15 3-4 hands high.

Bred by W. W. Traylor, San Francisco.

BY ELECTIONEER.

First dam Maggie Norfolk by Norfolk, son of Lexington, he by Boston. Second dam Tilda Quill by Billy Cheatham he by Cracken, and he by Boston. Third dam by Dorsey's Golddust.

TERMS.

Will make the season of 1890 at the Training Stables of Denis Gannon, near Oakland Trotting Park, at $50 the season, payable at time of service. Season to commence February 1st and ending July 1st. Proper care of mares will be taken, but no responsibility incurred for accidents or escapes. Address,

DENIS GANNON, Oakland, Cal.

2:10¾ 2:13¾ 2:10

DEXTER PRINCE.

This Royally-bred Stallion will make the Season of 1890 at the LIVE OAKS Breeding Farm, 2 miles from Lodi, San Joaquin County, Cal.

DESCRIPTION.

DEXTER PRINCE is a blood bay, 16 hands high, weighs over 1 100 pounds; has great power and substance, and the highest finish. When two years old, at Palo Alto, he was timed quarters by Gov. Stanford in 32¾ seconds, and he was driven eighths by Mr. Marvin at a faster rate of speed than that. He is a sure foal-getter, and invariably sires foals of good size, of fine form and finish, and the highest rate of speed.

PEDIGREE.

By KENTUCKY PRINCE, the sire of Guy, 2:10¾, Spofford, 2:18¾, Company, 2:19¾, Bayonne Prince, 2:21 1-4, Fred Folger, 2:20¾, and a score more in the 2:30 list.

First dam LADY DEXTER, full sister of the greatest of trotters, Dexter, and the greatest of sires, Dictator, the sire of Director, 2:17, Phallas, 2:13¾, in a fourth heat, and Jay-Eye-See, 2:10.

Second dam Clara, the dam of Dexter, 2:17 1-4, Dicta or, Astoria, 2:29 1-4, and Almah, 2:29¾. Clara was by American Star, that has 34 daughters that have produced 2:30 or better trotters.

Third dam the McKinstry mare, the dam of Shark, 2:27¾. HAMBLETONIAN, the grandsire of DEXTER PRINCE, has 40 trotters in the 2:30 list, 44 daughters that have produced 2:30 trotters, and more than 100 sons that have sired 2 30 trotters.

CLARK CHIEF, the grandsire on the sire's side, was the sire of performing and producing sons and daughters.

DEXTER PRINCE has faster blood lines, on both sides, than any other stallion in the world—Guy 2:10¾, and Jay-Eye-See, 2:10.

KENTUCKY PRINCE is one of the best bred and speediest stallions in the world. David Bonner, in the presence of Governor Stanford, timed him when he trotted a 2:1[illegible] gait. He is by Clark Chief, one of The great broodmare sires; his first dam is Kentucky Queen by Morgan Eagle, son of Hale's Green Mountain Morgan, 2nd dam by Blythe's Whip. 3rd dam by Martin's Brummler, 4th dam by Quicksilver 860, on through the strongest thoroughbred blood.

TERMS.

$100 for the season, with usual return privileges. Payable before mares are removed. Good pasture, and the best care furnished, but no responsibility assumed for accidents.

PREMIUM.

$250 will be given to the first of the produce of DEXTER PRINCE put in the 2:30 list, and $100 each after the first. Address

L M. MORSE, Lodi, Cal.

HOLLYWOOD BREEDING FARM,

MOUNTAIN BOY 4841.

Br s MOUNTAIN BOY, 4841, bred by Charles Backman, Orange County, New York, foaled 1882, sire Kentucky Prince 2470, dam Elise, sister to Elaine, by Messenger Duroc 106; grandam Green Mountain Maid, 3d dam, Shanghai Mary, will serve a limited number of mares at $100 the season.

ELECTION.

Bay stallion ELECTION, bred at Senator Stanford's Palo Alto Stock Farm, foaled 1884, sire Electioneer, dam Lizzie H. by Whipple's Hambletonian 725, grandam Lizzie Harris (by Comus son of Green's Bashaw 50), great grandam by Arnold Harris, thoroughbred.

Election is one of the handsomest bloodlike sons of Electioneer, and with his thoroughbred cross through Arnold Harris should prove invaluable as a sire. TERMS, $100 the season.

KAFIR.

B c KAFIR, bred by L. J. Rose, Los Angeles, foaled 1887, sire Alcazar, 2:20½, dam Flower Girl by Arthurton, sire of Amb, 2:16, grandam Flora by General McClellan, 144, sire of three in 2:30 list, great grand dam by Langford, he by Williamson's Belmont, will serve a limited number of mares at $50 the season.

WOODSIDE.

Ch c WOODSIDE, sire Woodnut, 2:16½; 1st dam Veronica by Alcona, 730; 2nd dam Fontana by Almont 33; 3rd dam Fannie Williams by Alexander's Abdallah, 15. Book full.

MART BOORHEM.

B c MART BOORHEM, by Sydney, 2:19¾; 1st dam Towhead by Echo. This colt is a full brother to St. Nicholas who showed a mile in 2:27¼ at three years old. TERMS, $25 the season.

REVEILLE.

The well known thoroughbred stallion REVEILLE, by Shiloh, dam by Norfolk. Reveille is a brother to John Treat and is the sire of Tycoon and Gladstone TERMS, $25 the season.

Hollywood is nicely situated three miles from Vallejo on the Napa road. Good pasturage and every care will be taken of mares at reasonable rates. For further particulars, apply,

B. C. HOLLY, Vallejo.

PASHA,

Registered No. 2039.

RECORD 2:36.

SIRE OF MORO 2:27.

Will make the present season at Linden, twelve miles east of STOCKTON.

Season commencing FEBRUARY 1st and ending JULY 1, 1890.

DESCRIPTION.

PASHA is a beautiful black; 16½ hands high, and weighs 1,240 pounds. He is a horse of beautiful symmetry and magnificent action.

PEDIGREE.

PASHA was sired by Sultan 1513, sire of Stamboul 2:12½, Ruby 2:19½, Alcazar 2:20½. Bay Rose 2:20½, and sixteen others with records below 2:30. First dam Madam Baldwin by The Moor 870; second dam Ben Lippincott by Belmont. Pasha is a full brother to Bay Rose, record 2:20½.

Sultan, by The Moor, sire of Beautiful Belle, dam of Hinda Rose, 2:19½, Bell Boy 2:19¼, and Sable, dam of Sable Wilkes, three-year-old record 2:18. First dam Sultana, by Delmonico, sire of Derby 2:16, by Guy Miller, sire of Whipple's Hambletonian. Second dam by Mambrino Chief. Third dam by Downing's Bay Messenger. Fourth dam Miss Caudle, dam of Ericsson, four-year-old recor 2:30½.

Terms for the season, $50.

With privilege of returning mares that do not prove in foal next season free of charge.

Good pasturage at $2 per month No responsibility will be assumed for accidents or escapes Service fee payable before the removal of the mare.

For further particulars, address

D. BRYSON,
Linden Cal.

Cook STOCK FARM,

Season of 1890.

STEINWAY 1808.

Three-Year-Old Record 2:25 3-4.

Sire of STRATHWAY, three year old record 2:26, and sire of the dam of BOURBON RUSSELL 2:30.

By STRATHMORE 408; sire of 31 in the 2:30 list; sire of 6 dams of 8 in the 2:30 list, and sire of 3 sires of 3 in 2:30 list.

1st dam ABBESS (dam of Solo 2:28, and Soprano, dam of C. F Clay 2:18, Eminence 2:27 and Strathbridge, 3 year old record 2:28½) by ALBION, sire of VANITY FAIR 2:24½, and of the dam of FAVORITE 2:25½.

2nd dam by MARSHALL NEY.

3rd dam by BERTRAND, a son of SIR ARCHY.

TERMS—$100 for the season.

CHARLES DERBY 4907

Brown Horse, Foaled 1885.

By STEINWAY 1808.

1st dam by the great ELECTIONEER, sire of SUNOL 3 year old record 2:10½, Palo Alto 2:12¼, etc., etc.

2nd dam FANNY MALONE, by NIAGARA.

3rd dam FANNY WICKHAM, by HERALD.

4th dam by Imp. TRUSTEE.

TERMS—$100 for the season.

Pasturage $5 per month. Accidents and escapes at owner's risk. Mares consigned to the farm should be sent to Fashion Stables, Oakland; Geary & Grindle's Stable, Haywards; or to Bennett's Stable, Martinez; from and to which places they will be delivered free of charge. Address

COOK STOCK FARM,
Danville, Contra Costa, Co., Cal.

The Trotting Stallion

ARBITRATOR

Will make the Season of 1890 at NILES, Alameda County.

PEDIGREE.

ARBITRATOR.
- Director 1989, 2:17 in a race, Sire of Direct, 4 yrs., 2:18½ in a race, Margaret S., 3 yrs., 2:19½ in a race, Guide, 4 yrs., 2:28½ in a race.
- Lady Earnest.
  - Speculation 918, sire of Oakland Maid, 2:22 in a race, Gracie S., 2:22 in a race, Crown Point, 2:24 in a race, He the sire of Valensin, 3 yrs., 2:23 in a race, Sire of Dam of Alfred G., 2:19½.
  - Lady Hibbard, dam of Lou Whipple, 2:26½ in a race.

Speculation's dam was Martha Washington, dam of Whipple's Hambletonian, sire of 15 in 2:30 and granddaughter of Burr's Napoleon, sire of Black Harry, who in 1860 won two miles in 5:14½. He sired Smith Burr, sire of Gen. Butler, 2:21, Wagon, 4:56½. He sired the dam of Fanny Mapes, dam of Jerome Eddy, 2:16½. He sired Telegraph, sire of dam of Barus, 2:18¼.

DESCRIPTION.

ARBITRATOR was foaled 1886. He is of good size, fine conformation, and a beautiful seal brown.

TERMS.

Non-standard mares	$45
Standard mares by inheritance	35
Standard mares by performance or produce	25

For further particulars, address

H. A. MAYHEW, owner,
Niles, Alameda Co.

Season of 1890.

February 15 to June 15

LYNWOOD,

(STANDARD 3017.)

AT WOLF'S (RUSSELL'S) STABLES, STOCKTON, CAL.

TERMS.

$50 for the season, payable at the close of season. Pasturage at $3 per month. Accidents or escapes at owner's risk.

PEDIGREE.

LYNWOOD 3017, trial 2:28.
- Nutwood 600, 2:18¾. Sire of—Woodnut, 2:16½, 29 in 2:30 list.
  - Belmont 64. Sire of—39 in 2:30 list, 17 sires and 11 dams of trotters in 2:30 list.
    - Abdallah 15. Sire of—Goldsmith Maid, 2:14, 8 in 2:30 list, 12 sires and 21 dams of trotters in 2:30 list.
    - Belle, by Mambrino Chief 11. Dam of—Hambletonian 1684, 2:26¾, the sire of [illegible] 2:30 list.
  - Miss Russell. Dam of—Maud S., 2:08¾, Nutwood, 2:18¾, Cora Belmont, 2:24 1-2.
    - Pilot Jr. 12. Sire of—8 in 2:30 list, 7 sires and 13 dams of trotters in 2:30 list.
    - Sally Russell by Boston.
- Hattie Morrison. Fast Road Mare. Trial 2:26¾.
  - Ethan Allen Jr. 2903. Sire of—Prince Allen, 2:27.
    - Ethan Allen 43, 2:25¾. Sire of—7 in 2:30 list, 16 sires and 14 dams of trotters in 2:30 list.
    - Daughter of Hambletonian 2 Sire—4 in 2:30 list.
  - Grigsby Mare.
    - Sir Charles, thoroughbred.
    - Hasting Mare s. t. b. of Messenger and Duroc blood.

DESCRIPTION.

Dark bay, 15 hands, weighs 1050 pounds, form stout and elegant, gait pure and rapid. He was foaled July 15, 1880, has done but little work in the stud, but enough to demonstrate that he is one of the best foal getters in the State. Only one of his get has had any systematic handling, and that could have gone into the 2:30 list last year as a two-year-old, had the owner desired.

It will be observed from an examination of Lynwood's pedigree, that he is one of the best bred sons of the GREAT NUTWOOD, who commands a service fee of $500 for the season.

P. VISHER, Stockton.

The Thoroughbred Stallion

INTRUDER

Will make the Season of 1890 at Agricultural Park, SACRAMENTO.

Bay Horse, foaled 1871, bred by Sir L. Newman, England. Imported by D. D. Withers, Esq., New York.

By Crater, Son of Orlando and Vesuvienne by Gladiator.

1st dam Lady Bountiful by Rataplan (Rataplan is own brother to Stockwell, and winner of 42 races, including the Doncaster Cup and 10 Queen's Plates, and proved himself the most distinguished race horse of his day in England).

2d dam Plentiful by Don John (the winner of St. Leger and Doncaster Cup).

3d dam Plenty by Bay Middleton (winner of the Derby and Two Thousand Guinea Stakes).

4th dam Plenary, own sister of Plenipotentiary, by Emilius. (Both Emilius and Plenipotentiary were Derby winners).

5th dam Harriet, dam of the renowned Plenipotentiary by Pericles.

6th dam by Selim, winner of the One Thousand Guinea stakes.

7th dam by Pypilina, by Sir Peter.

8th dam Rally, by Trumpeter.

9th dam Fancy, by Florizel. Fancy was full sister to Diomed, the first Derby winner in England, and after his importation into this country, sired the illustrious Sir Archy, etc. See English Stud Book.

Imported INTRUDER is a beautiful bay, standing fully 16 hands high, of great length and substance, and descends through close and strong currents from the most illustrious winners and winning lines of blood of which the English Stud Book bears record.

A careful review of the first six crosses of the pedigree of INTRUDER will show nine Derby winners; five St. Leger winners; two winners of The Oaks; two winners of the Two Thousand Guineas; two winners of the One Thousand Guineas; one Goodwood Cup winner; one Cæsarwich Cup winner; one Cambridgeshire Stakes winner, and four Doncaster Cups, in addition to a great number of Steeplechases and other races of less import.

INTRUDER, at the great fair held at St. Louis, Mo., in 1876, was awarded the highest stallion honors—the blue ribbon and the $600 purse—in the sweepstakes ring for stallion of any age or blood. The list of competitors embraced the large number of thirty-three animals, and they represented England, Canada, Kentucky, Tennessee, and other states. He also took first premium in his class and in sweepstakes for the best stallion of any age or breed at the State Fair at Peoria, Ill., 1884. He is the sire of Tidal Wave, George Hakes, Bernice and April Fool.

INTRUDER is the sire of Interpose, who is the dam of Spokane, winner of the Kentucky Derby, in which he beat the great horse Proctor Knott and broke the record.

TERMS: $50 for the season. Mares not proving with foal can be returned the next season free of charge. Good pasturage at $4 per month. Mares cared for in any manner owners may desire, and fed on hay and grain, either or both, at reasonable rates. While every precaution will be taken, no responsibility will be assumed for escapes or accidents. Mares sent from a distance in care of the undersigned, will be met and taken to the park. For further particulars, address

T. J. KNIGHT,
Agricultural Park, Sacramento.

Langtry Farms' Stud

Imp. FRIAR TUCK

By the Immortal HERMIT

DAM ROMPING GIRL BY WILD DAYRELL,

AT $50 THE SEASON.

Mares not proving with foal may be returned the following season. Good care taken of mares, but no liabilities for accidents or escapes.

Good Pasturage at $5 per month.

Mares shipped to ST. HELENA, care CHARTES WILLIAM ABY, St. Helena Stables, will be cared for. For further particulars address,

CHAS. WILLIAM ABY,
Middletown, Lake County, Cal.

2:08 3-4 2:10 2:12

MAMBRINO WILKES, 6083.

SIRE OF

GUS WILKES, 2:22; ALPHEUS, 2:27; CLARA P, 2:29½; BALKAN, 2:29½ (3-year-old) and timed separately 2:22½ in 4-year-old Stake, Bay District Track, October 14, 1889.

DESCRIPTION.

Black; sixteen hands; weighs, in exercise, 1,260 lbs. For style, finish, symmetry and proportion, comparison is challenged with any trotting bred horse. His colts follow in size, style and beauty. Balkan, for instance, being "facile princeps" of trotters in these particulars.

PEDIGREE.

Sired by Geo. Wilkes, sire of Harry Wilkes, 2:13½, Guy Wilkes, 2:15¼, and 60 other trotters in the 2:30 list, in addition to 5 pacers, and of the sire of Axtell, 2:12 (three-year-old), beating all stallions of any age, and the sire of Regal Wilkes, 2:20¾, best two-year-old stallion record.

First dam Lady Chrisman by Mambrino (Todhunter's, son of Mambrino Chief 11; sire of Lady Thorn, 2:18¼; Woodford Mambrino, 2:21½, and four others in 2:30, and of the dams of Director, 2:17, Piedmont, 2:17¼, Onward, 2:25¼, etc.

Second dam by Pilot Jr. 12, sire of nine in the 2:30 list, and of the dams of Maud S., 2:08¾, Jay-Eye-See, 2:10, Nutwood, 2:18¾, Viking, 2:19¼, Pilot Boy, 2:20, Naiad Queen, 2:20¼, etc.

TERMS.

Mares from a distance will be received at the Dexter Stables, Oakland, or Livery Stable, Martinez, the owner notifying Smith Hill, Superintendent at the farm. Good pasture and plenty of water. For the purpose of placing the service of a Wilkes within reach of breeders, the same rate will be maintained as last year, to wit, $75 for the season. Although it is not admitted thereby that this horse is inferior as a producer to the horses whose fees are placed at from $150 to $500. Address

SMITH HILL,
San Miguel Stock Farm,
Walnut Creek, Contra Costa Co., Cal.

$2:12\frac{3}{4}$ $2:13\frac{1}{2}$ $2:15\frac{1}{4}$

$2:08\frac{3}{4}$ 2:10 2:12

BALKAN

By Mambrino Wilkes.

(See that Horse's Advertisement.)

DAM FANNY FERN BY JACK HAWKINS
Son of Boston.

The grandam of Maud S. (2:08¾) was by Boston and the grandam of Jay-Eye-See (2:10) was by Lexington, son of Boston. So Balkan is the same remove from Boston that Maud is, and one remove nearer than Jay-Eye-See.

Fanny Fern has produced Molly Drew, Onyx, Fred Arnold, Molly Fern and Balkan, all by different sires.

Balkan's sire and dam both being producers, and he being a trotter himself with a record of 2:29 1-2 (three-year-old) and timed separately 2:22 1-4 in 4-year-old Stake, Bay District Track, October 14, 1889—it is but fair to presume that he will get trotters of the highest order.

DESCRIPTION.

He is seal brown, 16 1 hands high, in style rivalled by few, and excelled by none with as pure a gait as has yet been exhibited in public—bar none.

Balkan will be at Oakland Trotting Park for the season of 1890, and will be limited to ten mares, at $100 fee, in order to be put in training early, as it is morally certain that if given a reasonable opportunity he will be fast enough to compete with the best of his age. For further particulars, address

A. L. HINDS,
Dexter Stables, Oakland

$2:12\frac{3}{4}$ $2:13\frac{1}{2}$ $2:15\frac{1}{4}$

2:19 NOONDAY $2:20\frac{1}{2}$

STANDARD No. 10,000.

This celebrated trotting bred stallion will make the season of 1890 at the stable of the undersigned at Sacramento, Cal., at $75 for the season and $100 to insure a mare in foal. Payable on or before July 1st, 1-90. Money will be refunded on mares bred by insurance as soon as the fact becomes known that they are not in foal.

NOONDAY.
- Wedgewood, 2:19. Sire of Favonia, 2:15, fastest 4th heat for any mare or gelding, and eight others in 2:23 or better.
  - Belmont. Sire of Wedgewood, 2:19, Nutwood, 2:18¾, Viking, 2:19½, and 29 others in 2:30 list.
    - Alexander's Abdallah, sire of Goldsmith Maid, 2:14; Almont, with 35 horses in 2:30 list, etc.
    - Belle, dam of Hambletonian, 2:26½; B'cara, dam of Pancoast, 2:21¾, the sire of Patron, 2:14½.
  - Woodbine. Dam of Wedgewood, 2:19, Woodford Mamb., 2:21½, the sire of Pancoast, 2:21¾, the sire of Patron, 2:14½.
    - Woodford.
    - Singleton Mare.
- Noontide, 2:20½ (Trial, 2:13¼).
  - Harold. Sire of Maud S., 2:08¾, and 26 others in 2:30 list.
    - Hambletonian (Rysdyk's), sire of George Wilkes, 2:22, the sire of Guy Wilkes, 2:15¼; Electioneer, the sire of Sunol, 2:10½, and scores of noted trotters and producers.
    - Enchantress, by Abdallah 1.
  - Midnight. Dam of Jay-Eye-See, 2:10, Noontide, 2:20½.
    - Pilot Jr., sire of dams of Maud S., 2:08¾, Jay-Eye-See, 2:10, Nutwood, 2:18¾, etc.
    - Twilight, by Lexington, sire of the dam of Ansel, 2:20.

NOONDAY is a dark seal brown, foaled 1884, 15 hands 1¾ inches high. Individually he is equal to his royal breeding. He is all that can be desired in conformation, intelligence, color and trotting action, and no stallion now in public service can show a pedigree with such fast records and royal game trotting blood as Noonday.

DON MARVIN,

Record 2:28 as a five-year-old. Standard by Breeding and Performance

Standard No. 7927.

Don Marvin 2:28.

Don Marvin is a beautiful seal brown, foaled 1884, bred by Hon. Leland Stanford, Palo Alto, Cal., standing 16 hands, and weighs, in ordinary condition, 12 0 lbs. He is a fine individual, good style and form, combined with great substance, and good temper. Is very level headed; in his first race the past season he only made one break in five closely contested heats. He has great speed and endurance, with the pure, rapid Electioneer gait. He trots without toe weights, and wears only 8 oz. shoes in front. He gained his record the past season in the third heat, on a slow track, after making a season (serving over 60 mares), with scarcely any preparation. His record is no mark of his speed. He was a natural born trotter, and Mr. Charles Marvin considered him the fastest two year old at Palo Alto that season.

By FALLIS, 2:23, - - by Electioneer, sire of
Sire of Don Marvin, 2:28. — Sunol, three-year-old, 2:10 1-2, Palo Alto, 2:12¾, and 47 others in 2:30 list.

Dam CORA, by Don Victor by Belmont, sire of
Dam of Don Marvin, 2:28. — Ventura, 2:27¼, and sire of the dam of Bell Echo, 2:20, and six others in 2:30 list.

2d dam CLARABEL, - by Abdallah Star,
Dam of Clifton Bell, 2:24 1-2, and grandam of Rexford, three years, 2:34. — Sire of Hattie Maples, 2:33.

3d dam FAIRY, - - by Rysdyk's Hambletonian,
Sister of Sweepstakes, sire of 16 in 2:30 list. — Sire of Electioneer, George Wilkes, and many other noted sires and trotters.

4th dam EMMA MILLS, by Seely's American Star,
Dam of 4 horses that have 2:30 performers. — The great broodmare sire of the world.

The above pedigree should show every intelligent breeder that Don Marvin is "high" bred though very strong in trotting blood. All the comment it is deemed necessary to make as to the value of "thoroughbred blood" in the trotter is simply to refer to the very significant fact that the first and second dams of Maud S., 2:08¾, Jay-Eye-See 2:10, Sunol, three years 2:10 1-2, Palo Alto 2:12¾, Anteeo 2:16¼, Nutwood 2:18¾, Wedgewood 2:19, and many other successful sires and sensational trotters of the day are thoroughbred.

TERMS—Don Marvin will make the ensuing season from February 1st to July 1st, 1890, at $40 the season, with the usual privilege of returning the mare next season if not proving in foal. Mares from a distance met at the cars or boats on notification, and carefully handled, but no responsibility assumed for accidents or escapes.

Good alfalfa pasture furnished (free from barb wire fence) at $4 per month. For further particulars or complete circulars address

F. P. LOWELL,
1520 F Street, Sacramento, Cal.

The Produce of Eros Averaged $2,200 Each at New York Auction Sale in 1889.

THE ELECTIONEER TROTTING TALLION,

5326 EROS 5326

Will make the season of 1890—February 1st to July 1st—at LA SIESTA RANCH, MENLO PARK, adjoining Palo Alto.

PEDIGREE.

EROS (5326)
Standard by his sire
" " dam
" " record
" " produce
" under all rules

EROS (5326).
- Electioneer. Grandsire of Norlaine, 1 yr., 2:31 1-2, Sire of Sunol, 2 yrs., 2:18, Sunol, 3 yrs., 2:10 1-2, Hinda Rose, 4 yrs., 2:16, Palo Alto, 2:12¾.
  - Hambletonian 10. Sire of Dictator, George Wilkes, Happy Medium, and 40 others in 2:30 list, and grandsire of 738 in list.
    - Abdallah 10. Sire of the dams of Goldsmith Maid, 2:14, and 7 other producing dams.
    - Charles Kent mare. By imp. Bellfounder.
  - Green Mountain Maid. Dam of Prospero, 2:20, Elaine, 2:20, Dame Trot, 2:22, Elista, 2:22½, Storm, 2:28¾, Antonio, 2:28¾, Miranda, 2:31, Mansfield, 2:26.
    - Harry Clay. Sire of the dams of St. Julian, 2:11¾, Bodine, 2:19¼, and 17 more in 2:30 list.
    - Shanghai Mary.
- Sontag Mohawk. Dam of Eros, 2:29 1-2, Sport, 2:22¾, Sallie Benton, 2:17¾, Conductor, trial, 2:26, Colma, 3-y-o trial, 2:24.
  - Mohawk Chief. Sire of the dams of Lot Slocum, 2:17¾, Sallie Benton, 4 yrs., 2:17¾, Pedlar, 2 yrs., 2:27¼, Stanford, 4 yrs., 2:30, Eros, 6th heat, 2:29 1-2.
    - Hambletonian 10. Sire of the dams of Stamboul, 2:12¾, Wilton, 2:19¼, and 20 other trotters.
    - Lady Perrine.
  - Sontag Nellie.
    - Toronto Sontag. By Toronto Chief.
    - Nellie Gray. 3-mile record, 12:46.

Produce of Eros
Wanda, 4 yrs., 2:21.
Solita, 2 yrs., 2:41 1-2.
Meriquita, 2yrs., 2:12.
Daylight, 2 yrs., 2:54.
Hiram B., trial, 2:28.

These are the only colts by him that have ever had a harness on except one in New York that went a trial last July in 2:26 1-2.

DESCRIPTION.

EROS is a rich seal brown stallion, bred by Hon. Leland Stanford at Palo Alto, and is the nearest living likeness of his celebrated sire, Electioneer. Stands 15.2 hands high, and weighs 1050 pounds.

In breeding to Eros, the owners of mares will strictly follow the great rule of breeding, viz., breed to a stallion by a producer and out of a sure producer of great speed. Eros is by the stallion that has produced more 2:30 trotters that any living horse, and is also the sire of more 2:20 performers than any horse living or dead.

EROS is out of the dam of Sally Benton, four years old, record 2:17¾, Sport 2:22¾, and Eros 2:29½ in the sixth heat, against a field of nine horses. He is from a family that is endowed with great natural speed, trot fast at an early age, train on, throw trotters from all classes of mares, are of good substance, bone, style and action, and breed solid colors.

TERMS.

$100 for the season, with the privilege of return next season should mares not be in foal and horse and mare still remain in the same hands.

Good pasturage can be obtained at $5 per month, but no responsibility for accidents or escapes. There are a large number of box stalls, and animals can be kept up and fed on hay and grain at reasonable rates if required. Mares already in foal can be sent to the ranch for foaling, and will receive all the attention bestowed upon our own mares. Mares left with Mr. Peter Pomyea, Broadway Street Stable, Oakland, or with Mr. F. H. Burke, 401 Montgomery Street, San Francisco, will be forwarded to the ranch free of charge. For further particulars apply to

W. H. VIOGET,
LA SIESTA RANCH, MENLO PARK, CAL.

EROS is the only stallion offered to the public on this Coast that has a dam that has three in the 2:30 list.

POPLAR GROVE

Breeding Farm

STALLIONS.

CLOVIS, 4909,

CLOVIS is a beautiful black, Eight Years Old, 16 1-2 Hands High, and weighs 1260 lbs.

He is a horse of beautiful symmetry and magnificent action.

PEDIGREE.

CLOVIS was sired by Sultan, 2:24, sire of Stamboul, 2:12 1-4, Ruby, 2:19¾, and fifteen others with records of 2:30 or better.

First dam Sweetbriar by Thorndale 2:22 1-2, sire of Edwin Thorne, 2:16 1-2, Daisy Dale, 2:19, and May Thorne, 2:24.

Second dam Ulster Queen, dam of Volmer, 2:24¼, by Hambletonian 10. Sire of Dexter, 2:17¼, George Wilkes, 2:22.

Third dam by Thomas Jefferson, a son of Mambrino Paymaster, Jr.

Fourth dam by Mambrino Paymaster, sire of Mambrino Chief.

Sultan, by The Moor, sire of Beautiful Bells, dam of Hinda Rose, 2:19 1-2, and Sable, dam of Sable Wilkes, three year old record 2:18.

First dam of Sultan, Sultana, by Delmonico. Sire of Darby, 2:16 1-2, by Guy Miller, sire of Whipple's Hambletonian.

Second dam by Mambrino Chief.

Third dam by Downing's Bay Messenger.

Fourth dam Mrs. Candle, dam of Ericsson, four year old record 2:30 1-2.

Clovis will make the season of 1890 at Poplar Grove Breeding Farm, near Wildflower, Fresno County, commencing February 1st and ending July 1st.

Terms, $75, due at time of service.

Mares cared for in any manner owners may desire; pasturage $2 per month. Every care exercised, but no liability for escapes or accidents. Mares not proving with foal can be returned next season, providing I still own this stallion.

APEX, 8935.

FOUR - YEAR - OLD RECORD. FOURTH HEAT. 2:26.

Will make the present season at the Poplar Grove Breeding Farm, near Wildflower, Fresno Co., season commencing Feb. 1st, and ending July 1, 1890. Terms, $50 the season, due at time of service. Apex is eight years old, a beautiful bay, 15 1-2 hands high, and weighs 1140 lbs. He is a horse of fine disposition, and his gait is faultless.

PEDIGREE.

Apex was sired by Promptor 2305, he by Blue Bull 75; first dam Mary by Flaxtail, he by Pruden's Blue Bull, Flaxtail being the sire of the dams of Buccaneer, five-year-old record, 2:24 1-2; Pride, yearling record, 2:44 1-2, and Shamrock, two-year old record, 2:25, third heat. Second dam by Bright Eyes, son of Boanarges. Prompter (sire of Apex, record 2:26, and Transit, 2:26 1-2), by Wilson's Blue Bull, by Pruden's Blue Bull, son of Merring's Blue Bull. Promptor's dam Prairie Bird, by Flaxtail; second dam by John the Baptist, son of Tally Ho Morgan, by Sherman Morgan; third dam Fannie Fern by Irwin's Tuckaho.

Apex made his appearance in the circuit as a two-year-old, and obtained a record of 2:42. As a three-year-old he reduced this in a race at Santa Rosa against Stamboul to 2:31, it taking six heats to decide the contest, which was won by Apex. As a four year-old he gained his present record of 2:26.

Mares cared for in any manner owners may desire. Pasturage $2 per month. Every care exercised, but no liabilities for escapes or accidents. Mares not proving with foal can be returned next season, providing I still own this stallion.

The Standard Stallion

JUNIO,

RECORD 2:22.

WILL MAKE THE PRESENT SEASON OF AT FRESNO FAIR GROUNDS.

Season Commencing Feb. 1st an ending July 1st.

TERMS—$100 the season, due at time of service.

JUNIO is eight years old, a handsome dark bay 16 hands high, and weighs 1200 pounds. He is the personification of the light harness horse, and his trotting action is superb. At the State Fair of 1886 he took first premium over forty of the finest trotters in the State.

PEDIGREE.

*Junio, by Electioneer, premier stallion of Palo Alto (sire of Sunol 2:10 1-2, Palto Alto 2:12 1-4, and 47 others in the 2:30 list,. Dam by Granger by imp. Hercules.

Granger, by imp. Hercules, dam Jenny Lind, by Stockbridge Chief, Jr., he by Stockbridge Chief, he by Vermont Black Hawk. Second dam by Kentucky Whip.

Imp. Hercules, by Wingston, first dam daughter of Tuscar, by Bay Middleton, second dam Malvina, by Oscar; 3rd dam Spotless by Walton; 4th dam by Trumpator (see Bruce's American Stud Book, Vol. 1, page 29). Hercules is the sire of the dam of Atmoor 2:24½; also sire of dam of Menlo 2:21 1-2.

Mares not proving in foal may be returned next year free of charge, providing I still have the horse. Pasturage $3 per month. While every care will be taken of horses, no liability will be assumed for accidents or escapes.

For further particulars address

S. N. STRAUBE, Fresno, Cal.

Poplar Grove Breeding Farm.

Call and See the Telescopic Steel

FISHING RODS.

Line Runs Inside of the Rod.

9½ FEET TELESCOPES TO 32 INCHES, AND 10 FEET TO 37 INCHES.

Three and Four Joint Steel Fly and Bait Rods.

E. T. Allen, SOLE AGENT PACIFIC COAST,

Direct Imp rter of S. ALLCOCK & CO.'S Fine Tackle

416 Market Street, - - - - - - - San Francisco

THE IMPROVED NOYES ROAD - CART,

PATENTED JULY 17, 1883, *AND JUNE* 8, 1886.

Some of the Advantages of the Noyes Cart Over All Others.

There is no bar for the rider to climb over in getting in or out. The horse can be hitched eighteen inches nearer than any other road-cart made. You can get in or out with perfect safety—no danger of being thrown into the wheel—a great advantage in breaking colts. THE EASIEST CART FOR ROAD OR TRACK. The only cart that a horse can be speeded to within one second as fast as to a sulky. All our carts are made of the very best materials and are warranted. Manufactured by the NOYES CART COMPANY, Kalamazoo, Mich.

They are indorsed by the following horsemen, all of whom are using them. Ask their opinion of the Noyes Cart: John Splan, who drove Guy a full mile in 2:17¾ and Chanter a half-mile in 1:10¼ to a Noyes Cart, says he would not take $350 for it if he could not get another; W. J. Gordon, Glenville, O.; W. B. Fasig, Cleveland, O.; Dave Muckel, Cleveland, O.; R. J. Moorehead, North East, Pa.; W. J. Chamberlain, Cleveland, O.; H. F. Malone, Bradford, Pa.; S. A. Brown & Co., Kalamazoo Stock Farm; Charles Marvin, Menlo Park, Cal.; W. H. Crawford, Lexington, Ky.; S. L. Caton, who gave Bell Boy a mark at Los Angeles, Cal., of 2:19¼, and drove Chanter a half mile in 1:09¾ and Lowland Girl a full mile in 2:12 to a Noyes Cart; Mike Bowerman, Lexington, Ky.; James Golden, Medford, Mass.; John E. Turner, Philadelphia, Pa.; T. L. Newton, Beaver Dam, Wis.; P. V. Johnston, Marshall, Mich.; W. H. McCarthy, Los Angeles, Cal.; A. W. Dennison, El Dorado, Kan.; P. O. Shank, Cleveland, O.; Charles Barnard, Boston, Mass.; Johnson Bros., Greenville, Mich.; John G. Avery, Buffalo, N. Y.; General R. L. Howard, Buffalo, N. Y.; Howard Conklin, Buffalo, N. Y.; W. D. Ham, Hennepin, Ill.; R. G. Henry, Waterbury, Conn.; J. E. Hayer, Newburgh, O.; J. C. Hart, Jefferson, Tex.; A. W. Harbison, Rock Point, Pa.; Carl Hodges, Battle Creek, Mich.; Barney Treacy, Lexington, Ky.; George Forbes, Cleveland, O.; Gifford Dudley, Topeka, Kan.; William and J. L. Thompson Lamont, Pa.; C. F. Emery, Forest City Stock Farm, Cleveland, O.; R. F. Jones, Minneapolis, Minn.; John Forbes, Elyria O.; D. J. Downs Battle Creek, Mich.; Frank Caton, Randall Station, O.; Arthur D. Sutton, Ind., Pa.; W. F. Neely, Grand Ridge, Ill.; Walter Clark, owner of Pilot Medium, Battle Creek, Mich.; H. R. Kingman, Battle Creek, Mich.; Dr. Sutton and H. C. Reed, Kalamazoo, Mich.; Budd Doble Chicago, Ill.

SOLE MANUFACTURERS OF STONE'S PATENT SULKY CASE.

They will more than save their cost in one season, and horsemen campaigning trotters cannot afford to do without them. Would refer to Samuel A. Brown, Kalamazoo Stock Farm, S. L. Caton and W. H. McCarthy. Address

NOYES CART COMPANY, Kalamazoo, Mich.

Office and Factory, corner Rose and Eleanor streets. R. ARTHUR STONE, Manager.

ADVERTISE YOUR STALLIONS

—IN THE—

Breeder & Sportsman

For the Season---1890.

We are pleased to announce that we have the best facilities for furnishing

Stallion Pictures,

Stallion Cards,

Pedigrees, Folders,

Contracts, Bills, Etc.

We make a specialty of this department of our business, and have UNRIVALED FACILITIES FOR LOOKING UP PEDIGREES and doing accurate and handsome work.

Promptness, Good Work, Low Prices.

BREEDER AND SPORTSMAN,
313 Bush Street, S. F.

SAMUEL VALLEAU. JAS. R. BRODIE.

J. R. BRODIE & CO.,

Steam Printers,

—And Dealers in—

Poolseller's and Bookmaker's Supplies.

401—403 *Sansome Street, corner Sacramento, San Francisco.*

BERGEZ'S

RESTAURANT.

FIRST-CLASS. Charges Reasonable.

Private Rooms for Families,

332—334 Pine St., below Montgomery St.

JOHN BERGEZ, Propr.

"DICKEY'S,"

SIXTH AVENUE AND D ST.

Near entrance to Bay District Track.

Choicest Brands of

WINES AND CIGARS.

A Delightful Resort.

Telephone 1485. J. R. DICKEY, Propr.

The Poodle Dog

"Rotisserie,"

FIRST-CLASS IN EVERY RESPECT.

Elegant Family Dining Rooms.

S. E. cor. GRANT AVE. and BUSH STREET.

ANDRE POTENTINI, Proprietor.

The Park Training Stable.

CHAS. DAVID, PROPRIETOR.

Corner Grove and Baker Streets, near Entrance to Golden Gate Park.

EVERY FACILITY FOR TRAINING COLTS and taking care of Gentlemen's Roadsters.

Finely appointed stable with every convenience and sixteen roomy box stalls.

The best care given all horses by experienced help, under the personal superintendence of the proprietor

Convenient to the Park Speed Drive, and Accessible to Six Lines of Cable Cars.

THE TRAINING OF COLTS AND ROADSTERS A SPECIALTY.

TROTTERS AND ROADSTERS FOR SALE.

HORSES SOLD ON COMMISSION.

The proprietor trained and brought out the following well known horses: "Sister, Huntress," "Peribelion," "Nona Y," and others.

NEW BOOKS.

HORSE BREEDING

Seventh Edition, with Appendix,

By J. H. SANDERS,

In which the GENERAL LAWS OF HEREDITY are exhaustively discussed and applied to the PRACTICAL BUSINESS OF BREEDING HORSES, especially with reference to the Selection of breeding Stock and the Management of Stallions, Brood Mares, Young Foals, and Diseases Peculiar to Breeding Stock.

Price, Post Paid, $2.

The Theory and Practice

—OF—

CATTLE BREEDING

By WM. WARFIELD.

This great work is by common consent the most valuable treatise on cattle breeding ever published in America—valuable because pre-eminently practical—and will stand for years as the highest authority in the field it so admirably covers.

400 Pages. Price only $2, Post Paid.

The Breeds of Live Stock

By J. H. SANDERS,

It contains an exhaustive treatise on the general principles of breeding with descriptions of all the breeds of horses, cattle, sheep and swine known in this country Illustrated with 40 engravings. It is a work that cannot fail to interest and instruct any person who takes the slightest interest in the subject.

Four hundred and eighty large octavo pages printed on the very finest plate paper, strongly bound, in Cloth, $3; half morocco, marbled edges, $4; full morocco, gilt edges, $5.

FEEDING ANIMALS, by Prof. E. W. Stewart. A practical work upon the laws of animal growth, specially applied to the rearing and feeding of horses, cattle, dairy cows, sheep and swine. Fourth edition; illustrated; 560 pages. Price $2.

THE FARMERS' VETERINARY ADVISER, by Prof. James Law, Cornell University, Ithaca, N. Y. A guide to the prevention and treatment of diseases in domestic animals. Unquestionably the best work of its kind in existence. Eighth edition, with numerous illustrations; 600 pages. Sent by mail, post paid, on receipt of $3.

THE TROTTING HORSE OF AMERICA, by Hiram Woodruff. As interesting to horsemen as a romance, and the best book out upon training and driving trotting horses. 475 pages. Price $2.50 post paid.

LIFE WITH THE TROTTERS, by John Splan. All about Rarus, the pacer Johnston, Mattie Hunter, Wedgewood, Wilson, Charlie Ford Kansas Chief, King Wilkes, Fanny Witherspoon, Minnie R., Guy, Clingstone, Mambrino Sparkle, and many other famous ones Splan has driven. A handsome book of 500 pages. Tells how to condition a horse for any kind of race; how to handle colts; and all the secrets of the trainer's art. A chapter from material furnished by Budd Doble, showing how Goldsmith Maid and Dexter were trained. Price $3.

Any of the above books will be sent on receipt of price named.

BREEDER AND SPORTSMAN,
San Francisco, Cal.
313 Bush Street.

THE HICKS-JUDD CO.

Successors to

HICKS & JUDD, Bookbinders,

and Women's Co-operative Printing Office.

Printers, Bookbinders, Publishers,

23 First St., San Francisco.

BREEDERS' CATALOGUES A SPECIALTY.

Fine Hats,

Latest Styles and Colors.

Meussdorffer & Hubner

8 Kearny Street, San Francisco.

Next to New Chronicle Building

JOHN FORGIE,

Importing Tailor,

204 Montgomery Street,

N. E. corner Bush. SAN FRANCISCO.

KENNEL ADVERTISEMENTS.

FOR SALE.

Pointer Puppies

By Tom Pinch ex Galatea.

Tom Pinch has won at two field trials, and was never beaten on the bench, winning first whenever shown. At the recent Bench Show at Elmira, New York, Tom Pinch won first, Galatea second, and Lady Pinch (Tom Pinch—Galatea) first in their respective classes. For prices and particulars, address

J. MARTIN BARNEY, Dutch Flat, Cal.

Puppies for Sale.

TWO GORDON SETTER BITCH PUPPIES, 6 months old.

ONE YORKSHIRE TERRIER DOG PUP, two months old, by Sleep's Mash, winner of first prize in last three Bench Shows.

FIVE MASTIFF PUPPIES, by a son of Scott's "Dick," winner of first prize in last two Bench Shows. Also a litter of GREYHOUND PUPPIES, Saturday Night—Brunette.

Apply to JAMES E. WATSON,
516 Sacramento street,
P. O. Box 1038. San Francisco.

DOGS---Pointer Pups

FOR SALE.

Sure Bench Show and Field Trial Winners, as they have more bench-show and field-trial blood in them than any that have ever been whelped on the Pacific Coast.

Sire, POINT, double field trial winner; he by Vandevort's Don, great field trial and bench show winner, out of Drab, field trial and bench show winner.

Dam, QUEEN CROXTETH by Bush T., bench show winner, out of Champion Patti Croxteth, field trial and bench show winner. This is the best pointer blood in the world. Breeding and health guaranteed. Address,

A. B. TRUMAN,
1425 Steiner St., near Ellis, S. F., Cal.

FOX TERRIERS--C. A. SUMNER, 7 S. Fort St., Los Angeles, Breeder of Fox Terriers. Blemton Vesuvian (14290), by Champion Lucifer, at stud.

CALIFORNIA SPANIEL KENNELS, Oakland, California, H. P. RENNIE, Prop. Breeder and importer of typical COCKER SPANIELS. Winner of first prizes at S. F. and Los Angeles, 1889, also, Columbus, 1889, New York, 1887. In the stud, solid Black Cocker dog, GIFFEE, won 1st and Gold Medal at S. F., 1889. Fee, $25. Puppies and grown dogs at reasonable prices. My dogs can neither talk nor climb a tree, but are fielders and prize winners.

Fiske's Vanes.

MADE OF

COPPER

And Gilded with

PURE

GOLD LEAF.

Manufacturer's Agent.

The HOWE SCALE CO.

411 & 413 Market Street, S. F.

Scales for Weighing of

Live Stock

SEEDS, FEED, Etc.

Write for Catalogue.

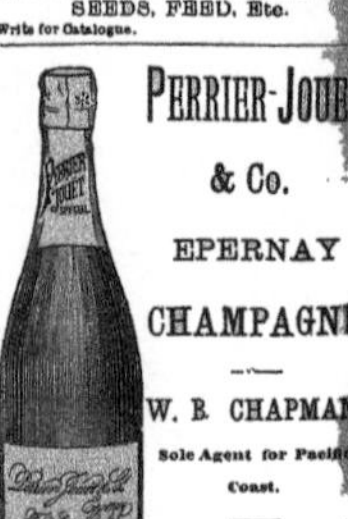

PERRIER-JOUET & Co.

EPERNAY

CHAMPAGNE

W. B. CHAPMAN,

Sole Agent for Pacific Coast.

For sale by all first-class Wine Merchants and Grocers.

Southern Pacific Co.

(PACIFIC SYSTEM.)

Trains leave and are due to arrive at San Francisco.

LEAVE (FOR)	FROM JANUARY 1, 1890.	ARRIVE (FROM)
7.30 A M	Haywards, Niles and San Jose	*12.45 P M
7.30 A M	Sacramento and Redding, via Davis	7.15 P M
7.30 A M	Sacramento, Auburn, Colfax	5.45 P M
8.00 A M	Martinez, Vallejo, Calistoga and Santa Rosa	6.15 P M
8.30 A M	Los Angeles Express, Fresno, Bakersfield, Mojave and East and Los Angeles	11.15 A M
8.30 A M	Niles, San Jose, Stockton, Ione, Sacramento, Marysville, Oroville and Red Bluff	5.45 P M
10.30 A M	Haywards and Niles	2.15 P M
*12.00 M	Haywards, Niles and San Jose	* 3.45 P M
*1.00 P M	Sacramento River Steamers	**6.00 A M
3.00 P M	Haywards, Niles and San Jose	9.45 A M
3.30 P M	2d Class for Ogden and East	10.45 P M
4.00 P M	Stockton and ‡Milton; Vallejo, Calistoga and Santa Rosa	9.45 A M
4.30 P M	Sacramento and Knight's Landing via Davis	10.45 A M
* 4.30 P M	Niles and Livermore	* 8.45 A M
* 4.30 P M	Niles and San Jose	‡ 4.15 P M
5.30 P M	Haywards and Niles	7.45 A M
6.00 P M	Sunset Route, Atlantic Express Santa Barbara, Los Angeles, Deming, El Paso, New Orleans and East	8.45 P M
7.00 P M	Shasta Route Express, Sacramento, Marysville, Redding, Portland, Puget Sound and East	7.45 A M
8.00 P M	Central Atlantic Express, Ogden and East	9.45 A M
SANTA CRUZ DIVISION.		
‡ 3.00 A M	Hunters train to San Jose	‡ 7.20 P M
8.15 A M	Newark, Centerville, San Jose, Felton, Boulder Creek and Santa Cruz	5.50 P M
* 2.15 P M	Centerville, San Jose, Almaden, Felton, Boulder Creek and Santa Cruz	*11.50 A M
4.15 P M	Centerville, San Jose, and Los Gatos	9.50 A M
Coast Division (Third and Townsend Sts.)		
7.25 A M	San Jose, Almaden and Way Stations	2.30 P M
8.30 A M	San Jose, Gilroy, Tres Pinos; Pajaro, Santa Cruz; Monterey; Pacific Grove, Salinas, San Miguel, Paso Robles, Santa Margarita (San Luis Obispo) and principal Way Stations	6.12 P M
10.30 A M	San Jose and Way Stations	5.02 P M
12.01 P M	Cemetery, Menlo Park and Way Stations	3.38 P M
* 3.30 P M	San Jose, Tres Pinos, Santa Cruz, Salinas, Monterey Pacific Grove and principal Way Stations	*10.00 A M
* 4.30 P M	Menlo Park and Way Station	* 7.58 A M
5.20 P M	San Jose and Way Stations	9.03 A M
6.30 P M	Menlo Park and Way Stations	6.35 A M
†11.45 P M	Menlo Park and principal Way Stations	†7.28 P M

A M for Morning. P M for Afternoon.
*Sundays excepted. †Saturdays only. ‡Sundays only.
**Mondays excepted. §Saturdays excepted.

OCEANIC STEAMSHIP CO.

Carrying United States, Hawaiian and Colonial Mails.

WILL LEAVE THE COMPANY'S WHARF, foot of Mission Street, No. 1,

For Honolulu, Auckland and Sydney,

WITHOUT CHANGE,

The Splendid New 3,000-ton Iron Steamer,
ALAMEDA ..... Saturday, April 5, 1890, at 12 M.,
Or immediately on arrival of the English mails.

For Honolulu,

SS. AUSTRALIA (3,000 tons), March 28, 1890, at 12 M

For freight or passage, apply at office, 327 Market Street. JOHN D. SPRECKELS & BROS.
General Agents.

KILLIP & CO.,

LIVE STOCK AND GENERAL AUCTIONEERS,

22 Montgomery Street, San Francisco

SPECIAL ATTENTION PAID TO SALES OF

High-Bred Horses and Cattle.

At auction and private sale.

Will Sell in All Cities and Counties of the State.

REFERENCES.

HON. C. GREEN, Sacramento. — HON. J. D. CARR, Salinas.
J. P. SARGENT, ESQ., Sargents. — HON. JOHN BOGGS, Colusa.
HON. L. J. ROSE, Los Angeles. — HON. A. WALRATH, Nevada.
J. B. HAGGIN, ESQ., San Francisco.

Represented at Sacramento by Edwin F. Smith Secretary State Agricultural Society.
At San Jose by Messrs. Montgomery & Rea, Real Estate Agents.

Being the oldest established firm in the live-stock business on this Coast, and having conducted the important auction sales in this line for the past fifteen years, amounting to one half a million of dollars, we feel justified in claiming unequaled facilities for disposing of live stock of every description, either at auction or private sale. Our list of correspondents embraces every breeder and dealer of prominence upon the Pacific Coast, thus enabling us to give full publicity to animals placed with us for sale. Private purchases and sales of live stock of all descriptions will be made on commission, and stock shipped with the utmost care. Purchases and sales made of land of every description. We are authorized to refer to the gentlemen whose names are appended.

KILLIP & CO., 22 Montgomery Street.

HEALD'S
Business College, 24 Post St.

—San Francisco.—

The most popular school on the Coast

P. HEALD, President. C. S. HALEY, Sec'y.
Send for Circulars

San Francisco and North Pacific Railway.

THE DONAHUE BROAD-GAUGE ROUTE.

COMMENCING SUNDAY, MARCH 17, 1889, AND until further notice, boats and trains will leave from and arrive at the San Francisco Passenger Depot, Market-street Wharf, as follows:

Leave San Francisco.		DESTINATION	Arrive San Francisco.	
WEEK DAYS.	SUNDAYS.		SUNDAYS.	WEEK DAYS.
7.40 A M 3.30 P M 5.00 P M	8.00 A M 5.00 P M	Petaluma and Santa Rosa	10.40 A M 6.10 P M	8.50 A M 10.30 A M 6.05 P M
7.40 A M 3.30 P M	8.00 A M	Fulton, Windsor, Healdsburg, Litton Springs, Cloverdale, and way stations.	6.10 P M	10.30 A M 6.05 P M
7.40 A M	8.00 A M	Hopland and Ukiah.	6.10 P M	6.05 P M
7.40 A M	8.00 A M	Guerneville	6.10 P M	6.05 P M
7.40 A M 5.00 P M	8.00 A M	Sonoma and Glen Ellen.	10.40 A M 6.10 P M	8.50 A M 6.05 P M
3.30 P M	5.00 P M	Sebastopol	10.40 A M	10.30 A M

Stage connects at Santa Rosa for White Sulphur Springs, and Mark West Springs; at Geyserville for Skaggs Springs, and at Cloverdale for the Geysers; at Hopland for Highland Springs, Kelseyville, Soda Bay, Lakeport and Bartlett Springs, and at Ukiah for Vichy Springs, Saratoga Springs, Blue Lakes, Willits, Cahto, Calpella, Potter Valley, Sherwood Valley and Mendocino City.

EXCURSION TICKETS from Saturdays to Mondays, to Petaluma, $1.50; to Santa Rosa, $2.25; to Healdsburg, $3.40; to Litton Springs, $3.60; to Cloverdale, $4.50; to Hopland, $5.70; to Ukiah, $6.75; to Guerneville, $3.75; to Sonoma, $1.50; to Glen Ellen, $1.80.

EXCURSION TICKETS, good for Sundays only, to Petaluma, $1; to Santa Rosa, $1.50; to Healdsburg, $2.25; to Litton Springs, $2.40; to Cloverdale, $3; to Guerneville, $2.50, to Sonoma, $1; to Glen Ellen, $1.20.

From San Francisco for Point Tiburon and San Rafael: Week Days—7.40, 9.20, 11.20, A. M.; 3.30, 5.00, 6.15 P. M. Sundays—8.00, 9.30, 11.00 A. M; 1.30, 5.00, 6.20 P. M.

To San Francisco from San Rafael: Week Days—6.20, 7.55, 9.30 A. M.; 12.45, 3.40, 5.05 P. M. Sundays—8.10, 9.40 A. M.; 12.15, 3.40, 5.00 P. M.

To San Francisco from Point Tiburon: Week Days—6.50, 8.20, 9.55 A. M.; 1.10, 4.05, 5.30 P. M.; Sundays—8.40, 10.05 A. M.; 12.40, 4.05, 5.30 P. M.

On Saturdays an extra trip will be made from San Francisco to San Rafael, leaving at 1.40 P. M.

H. C. WHITING, General Manager.

PETER J. McGLYNN, Gen. Pass. & Tkt. Agt.

Ticket Offices at Ferry, 222 Montgomery Street and 2 New Montgomery Street.

CHICAGO, MILWAUKEE AN ST. PAUL RAILWAY.

Steam Heated and Electric Lighted Vestibuled Trains between Chicago, St. Paul and Minneapolis.
Electric Lighted and Steam Heated Vestibuled Trains between Chicago, Council Bluffs and Omaha.
Finest Dining Cars in the world.
Free Reclining Chair Cars between Chicago and Omaha.
Fast Mail Line between Chicago, Milwaukee, St. Paul and Minneapolis.
Transcontinental Route between Chicago, Council Bluffs and Omaha, or St. Paul.
Great National Route between Chicago, Kansas City and St. Joseph, Mo.
5,700 miles of road in Illinois, Wisconsin, Minnesota, Iowa, Missouri, South and North Dakota.
Everything First-Class.
First-Class People patronize First-Class Lines.
Ticket Agents everywhere sell Tickets over the Chicago, Milwaukee and St. Paul Railway.

W. T. ALLEN,
Pacific Coast Passenger Agent
Office, No 138 Montgomery St., San Francisco, Cal.
Under Occidental Hotel

6 DONTS

DON'T own a racehorse.
DON'T be a breeder.
DON'T be a trainer.
DON'T be a jockey.
DON'T bet on the races.
DON'T go to a race track.

WITHOUT
HAVING IN YOUR POCKET ONE OF

Goodwin's
ANNUAL
OFFICIAL TURF GUIDES.

Price, in cloth $2.00
Price, in half morocco 3.00
Price, in half calf 4.00
If sent by mail .... 10 cents extra

SUBSCRIBE TO IT FOR 1890.

It is published semi-monthly during the racing season, and is but **$10 per year.** Address

GOODWIN BROS.,
241 Broadway, New York City.

OUR IMPROVED.
ALL SIZES AND WEIGHTS
G.W. BOHANON.

THE BOHANON
SULKY!
BEST MADE.
Perfect Riding Buggies.
Breaking Carts.
Fine Repairing. Reasonable Prices
Bohanon Carriage Co., 161-163 Ogden Ave., CHICAGO.
Send for Catalogue.

TAKE SIMMONS LIVER REGULATOR

It is really surprising how people will suffer month after month and year after year with

CONSTIPATION,

when a regular habit of body can be secured without changing the diet or disorganizing the system, if they will only

A Simple but Effective Vegetable Compound.

"I have used Simmons Liver Regulator for Constipation, and always with decided benefit."—HIRAM WARNER, Late Chief Justice of Ga.

—Prepared by—
J. H. ZEILIN & CO., Philadelphia, Pa.

HORSE OWNERS!

TRY GOMBAULT'S

CAUSTIC BALSAM.

A Safe, Speedy and Positive Cure for Curb, Splint, Sweeny, Capped Hock, Strained Tendons, Founder, Wind Puffs, all Skin Diseases or Parasites, Thrush, Diphtheria, Pinkeye, all Lameness from Spavin, Ringbone or other Bony Tumors. Removes all Bunches or Blemishes from Horses and Cattle.

Supersedes all Cautery or Firing.
Impossible to Produce any Scar or Blemish.

Every bottle sold is warranted to give satisfaction. Price $1.50 per bottle. Sold by druggists, or sent by express, charges paid, with full directions for its use. Send for descriptive circulars. Address
LAWRENCE, WILLIAMS & CO., Cleveland, O.

BROU'S INJECTION

A PERMANENT CURE in from 3 to 6 days, of the most obstinate cases; guaranteed not to produce Stricture; no sickening doses; and no inconvenience or loss of time. Recommended by physicians and sold by all druggists. J. Ferré, (successor to Brou), Pharmacien, Paris.

For any Kind of a

SORE THROAT

USE
McCLELLAN'S
DIPHTHERIA REMEDY

An Unfailing Cure.
FOR SALE BY ALL DRUGGISTS

R. LIDDLE & SON

538 Washington St., S. F.,
Wholesale and Retail Dealers in

Guns, Rifles and Pistols.

A Full Line of FISHING TACKLE and SPORTSMAN'S GOODS.

Orders by mail receive prompt attention.

SELBY STANDARD THE BEST IS THE CHEAPEST "STANDARD" SHOTGUN CARTRIDGES

By-Laws

—AND—
Rules and Regulations
—OF THE—
NATIONAL
Trotting Association
ALSO THE
AMERICAN
Trotting Association,
AND THE
PACIFIC COAST BLOOD-HORSE ASSOCIATION.
With Betting Rules.

For Sale at the Office of the
Breeder and Sportsman,
313 Bush St., S. F., Cal.
Price, 25c. each.
By Mail, Postage Paid, 30c. each.

VETERINARY.

Dr. Wm. H. Jones, M.R.C.V.S.

Veterinary Surgeon,
(OLYMPIC CLUB STABLES)
503 Sutter Street, San Francisco.
Telephone, No. 1404.

Consultations by letter, and cases of URGENT NECESSITY in the interior will receive prompt attention.

Dr. A. E. BUZARD,

VETERINARY SURGEON,
Member of the Royal College of Veterinary Surgeons, London, England. Graduated April 22d, 1870.

All Operations on the Horse Performed Skillfully.

Special attention given to the Diseases of Dogs. Calls to the country promptly attended to. Advice and prescriptions by mail $2. Office and Residence, No. 11 Seventh street, S. F. (opp. Odd Fellows Hall. Telephone No. 3 69.

W. H. WOODRUFF.

Veterinary Dentist,
AT FASHION STABLES,
221 Ellis Street, San Francisco
Improved Instruments, Humane Methods, First-Class Work.

H. E. CARPENTER,

Veterinary Surgeon,
Graduate of Ontario Veterinary College, Toronto Canada.
RESIDENCE AND VETERINARY INFIRMARY
331 Golden Gate Ave., San Francisco.
Telephone 3069.
OPEN DAY AND NIGHT.
No risk in throwing Horses. Veterinary Operating Table on the premises.

DR. C. MASOERO,

Veterinary Surgeon,
Successor to DR. A. DeTAVEL,
GRADUATE OF ROYAL VETERINARY COLLEGE, TURIN.
OFFICE AND INFIRMARY
No. 811 HOWARD STREET,
Between Fourth and Fifth. SAN FRANCISCO
Telephone, No. 457.

R. WATKINS,

Veterinary Dentist,
Of twelve years practice, is now permanently located in San Francisco, and may be found at C. S. Crittendens' Golden Gate Livery and Riding Academy, 24 to 28 Golden Gate Avenue.
Will treat ailments of the horse's mouth, and cure all such. Sidesein Pullers and Tongue Lollers etc. Satisfaction guaranteed. Orders by mail will receive prompt attention. Examination Free.

E. J. O'ROUKE.

I have the honor to announce to my old patrons and the general public that I may be found at my old stand, where, as heretofore, the
Shoeing of Horses,
whether for the Track, Drive, or for general work, will receive my personal attention.
Telephone 2011.
E. J. O'ROUKE,
209 Ellis Street

California Horse Shoe Co's

STEEL SHOE
Light, Strong and Perfect.
Superior to all others for Speed Horses.
ALSO
The Celebrated
GOODENOUGH
Pattern Shoe.
OFFICE:
202 Market St.,
San Francisco, Cal.

I have used in my business the Steel and Iron Shoes made by the above Company, and take great pleasure in saying they are the best I have ever used in twenty-two years' practice. I have never seen anything like the STEEL SHOE made by this Company. I can fully recommend them to every practical Horseshoer in the country. Yours respectfully,
No. 8 Everett Street. JOHN GRACE.

LAMBORN ROAD MACHINE

LIGHT DRAFT. MADE OF IRON. STRONG, SIMPLE, DURABLE. EASILY OPERATED.

TRUMAN HOOKER & CO.
SAN FRANCISCO. - - CALIFORNIA

TWENTY-FOUR PAGES.

BREEDER AND SPORTSMAN

Vol. XVI. No. 14.
No. 313 BUSH STREET.

SAN FRANCISCO, SATURDAY, APRIL 5, 1890.

SUBSCRIPTION
FIVE DOLLARS A YEAR.

BAY ROSE, 2:20 1-2.

The property of Henry and Ira Pierce, Santa Rosa Stock Farm.

The gallery of the notable horses of California would not be compete if a picture of Bay Rose, 2:20½, were omitted from our columns, and it can be truly said that Mr. Boyd, the artist, has given our readers an exceedingly good picture of the celebrated stallion that has changed hands so often within a few months. The subject of our sketch has been a consistant performer for several years, the first mention that we find of him being when his initial appearance was made at Fresno in 1884, the other entries being Elite and Lulu F. The black stallion Elite managed to win first money, with Bay Rose a close second in each heat. The colt was bred by the Hon. L. J. Rose, but had been sold to Mr. E. Giddings of Lemoore, Tulare county, in whose name he trotted for the first two seasons. In 1885 he made a second appearance at Fresno on October 9th, his opponents being Waterford and Legal Tender. Again he won second money, capturing the third heat and gaining a record of 2:41½.

Before the racing season of 1886 began, Bay Rose was purchased by J. N. Ayer of Visalia, who started him five times that year, the first being at the Bay District track, where he received third money, his half brother Hidalgo and Gus Wilkes beating him for higher honors. At Stockton, Mount Vernon, 2:21, and Adrian, 2:26½, beat him in the district stallion race; and in the 2:40 class he was also defeated, Lottie M. proving victor, but she had to trot one heat in 2:24 to win.

On December 14th of the same year, he met at Visalia Barbero, Milton R. and Waterford in the stallion stake, and won the first, fourth and fifth heats, reducing his record to 2:33. On the 17th of the same month he was entered in the free-for-all race, and again he won, getting the second, fourth and sixth heats to his credit, and entered the 2:30 list, winning the last heat in 2:29, the time of the different heats being 2:29, 2:29¾, 2:29, 2:32, 2:37 and 2:29.

The following season was a very unfortunate one for the son of Sultan, he only starting at the State Fair, but the prevailing epizootic had got such a hold on the stallion, that it was deemed expedient to cancel his entries, and therefore he did not start again until the following season.

Fresno was the starting point in the campaign of Bay Rose in 1888, he being pitted against his old opponents Barbero and Waterford, and he was fast enough to win in straight heats the time being 2:26½, 2:31 and 2:31. At the same meeting he started in the free for all, and secured second money from such good ones as, Don Tomas, Hidalgo and Emma Temple, Valentine proving the winning horse. Bay Rose won the first heat in 2:24, but lost the subsequent ones in 2:23, 2:22 and 2:28. We next find the stallion entered in a match race at the Bay District Track on October 18th, which as it required six heats to decide is well worthy of a recapitulation. The story of the contest was admirably told in these columns at the time of the occurance and is herewith reprinted.

A match race for a purse of $500 between Los Angeles stables's blk. g. Don Tomas and J. N. Ayer's b. s. Bay Rose was the next thing on the card. The first was driven by his owner, C. A. Durfee, the latter by J. A. Goldsmith. Though neither horse is what turfmen call fast the race was very close, and decidedly interesting. Before the first heat Bay Rose was the favorite at $40 to $25. They were sent off to a neck and neck start, Tomas going to the front on the turn. The bay hung on to his wheel down the backstretch around the turn, where he collared him and came into the straight half a length leader. Just then Tomas went up, but caught quickly, and they came down home for a hot finish, Bay Rose was leading slightly, when he went up for some unaccountable reason, and before he recovered Don Thomas was under the wire in 2:21.

After this heat the pools were about even. They were sent off with a good start, and Don Tomas, taking the lead, reached the quarter in 36 seconds, the half in 1:10, and the three-quarter pole in 1:45. Just at the head of the stretch Bay Rose, who had been from a half to a full length in the rear, came up even, and the horses came into the straight neck and neck. Bay Rose led a little way, then the black gelding got a slight advantage. Nearing the wire Tomas broke, and Bay Rose also went up, and both horses plunged under the wire together, making a dead heat in 2:21 After this heat. Don Tomas was $50 in the pools to $27 on Bay Rose.

The third heat was another hard one. Tomas took the lead. At the quarter the bay was at his wheel and stayed there down the back stretch. At the half Tomas broke and ran some distance, and Bay Rose led him into the upper turn. After he got down again Tomas began trotting fast and caught Bay Rose at the middle of the turn. They went around to the three quarters neck and neck. Down the straight there was not a perceptible difference in them, and it seemed as if there would be another dead heat, but right at the post Goldsmith lifted his horse and fairly shoved him in, winning with Don Tomas at the bay's throatlatch. The time was pretty fast for a third heat of that class—2:20½.

After this heat Bay Rose was the favorite at $70 to $43 for Don Tomas. To a good start Bay Rose took the lead at the first turn and was three lengths in advance at the half. At the three quarters Don Tomas was doing nicely, and only a length of daylight was between him and the leader as the stretch was fairly entered. Don Tomas made a grand trot coming home, and only those persons stationed right under the wire could see that he had lost by a nose. Time 2:27½.

Pool selling was brisk before the fifth heat, Bay Rose bringing $100 to $50.

The fifth heat was the most exciting of them all, and it was anybody's heat to about half way down the stretch, when Bay Rose broke and Don Tomas came on and won the heat easily in 2:23.

On account of darkness the deciding heat was postsoned until Saturday.

SATURDAY.

The finish of the postponed match race was next called for, and Bay Rose and Don Tomas promptly appeared.

Don Tomas is a big, rangy gelding by Del Sur. He has a high, bold action, and although not handsome, being too lightly built for his height, he has shown well this year and horsemen think well of him. There is too much daylight under him and he is too ragged in finish over the hips to please the critical observer.

Bay Rose is a dark brown stallion, tan muzzle, and flank like his sire Sultan. In common with many Sultans, he is very large—indeed, he is far above the average height of the Sultans, being 1?-3. He weighs 1,250 pounds, is well proportioned, beautifully finished. A "bay rose" is something of which no florist has ever heard, but his beautiful color and the name of his breeder has furnished the horse with a cognomen which at least has merit of oddity, and merit it surely is, in these days of multiplying initials and confusing foreign names.

On the third score a good start was given, and at the turn Don Tomas was slightly leading. He increased this lead to over a length as they neared the three-eighths, traveling well within himself, but when near the half he broke, coming almost to a standstill. He ran for half a furlong, Bay Rose gaining by the same. On the last turn the pace was faster, the black still in the lead on the stretch. Bay Rose was going better, but Don Tomas came under the wire an easy winner. Time, 2:22.

SUMMARY.

Match race, purse $500.

Los Angeles Stables' blk g Don Tomas by Del Sur, dam by Mambrino Patchen.................Durfee	1	0	2	2	1	1
J. N Ayers' b s Bay Rose by Sultan, dam Madam Baldwin by The Moor...........Goldsmith	2	0	1	1	2	2

Time, 2.21, 2:21, 2:20½, 2:27½, 2:23, 2:22.

On the 28th of the same month we find Bay Rose pitted against Lilly Stanley, Don Tomas, Valentine, Franklin, Mount Vernon and Gus Wilkes, a strong field to combat against, but even with the big odds, the Sultan stallion won the first heat in the creditable time of 2:20¾, Don Tomas winning the next two in 2:?0 and 2:22½, while the Whippleton wonder managed to secure the next three in 2:20½, 2:19½ and 2:21½. We next find Bay Rose at Sacramento, where he easily defeated Allo and Junio in 2:24½, 2:25¼ and 2:25.

This finished up his season for 1888 which brings us down to the opening of the circuit last year, when we find the gallant stallion in the hands of Mr. Hickok, who had prepared him for the arduous work of another campaign. Santa Rosa was the place selected to start the horse, and he met Victor, Don Tomas and Jim L., an array of talent that was hard to down, but he captured the first heat in 2:21, although he had to succumb later on, as the epizootic had taken a firm hold of him. At Petaluma he was again started, but this time in addition to a large field of horses, there was the "whirlwind of the Coast," Palo Alto to contend against and to the credit of Bay Rose be it said *he is the only horse that won a heat from Palo Alto in* 1889. The representative of Senator Stanford won the first, third and fourth heats. Bay Rose taking the second in 2:20½. At Oakland he was again pitted against a large field in the 2.20 class, but Palo Alto won in straight heats, Bay Rose being well up in each heat, the last of which was trotted in 2:20. At Sacramento he won second money in the 2:21 stallion purse, Direct 2:18½, getting first. At Stockton Bay Rose was third in each of the heats for the Pacific Coast Trotting Stallion Stake, the time of each heat being 2:16½, 2:17¾ and 2:13½. At San Jose he won second money to Direct, time 2:21½, 2:20½ and 2:19. Shortly after the San Jose race Bay Rose was sold by J. N. Ayres to W. W. Ayres of San Francisco, and the next appearance of the stallion was on November 2nd, when the trotting matinee was given for the benefit of the Speed Drive Fund, but his long retirement had unfitted him for hard work and he only secured third place. His last performance for the year was at the justly celebrated meeting of the Breeder's Association at the Bay District track, on November 9th, the occasion which is now known as "Record Day" for the California horses of last year. When the horses were called up to score Junio sold for $120, Thapsin $75 and Bay Rose $25. Thapsin won the first heat in 2:21½, but Bay Rose had no trouble in capturing the next three in 2:21½, 2:23 and 2:22¾.

Bay Rose was placed in service this year at Oakland by Mr. Ayres, but before there had been a chance to book a large number of mares to him, the indefatigable Dan McCarty purchased the horse, paying $10,000 for him, but before there was a chance to ship him to Stanislaus County, where Mr McCarty proposed sending him, the Pierce Brothers of Oakland bought the bay horse, paying a large increase on what Dan had paid for him. There is not a horseman in the State but what feels that the new buyers have made a wonderfully good purchase, and with the first-class mares now owned by the Santa Rosa Stock Farm Company, the near future should produce a crop of foals that will be a credit alike to the company and to the State.

There is not a driver that has handled Bay Rose for the past two seasons but what knows perfectly well that his present mark of 2:20½ can be lowered materially, and provided there be no further sickness to prevent his training on, a very low record should be gained for him this season. Bay Rose is by Sultan 2:24, one of the best sons of The Moor 870, the horse that laid the foundation stone for all the greatness attained by the Hon. L J. Rose in the horse world. The Moor is the sire of Beautiful Bells 2:29½, (dam of Bell Boy, three-year-old record 2:19¼, Hinda Rose, three-year-old record, 2:19½, St. Bel 2:24¼ and Palo Alto Belle, three-year-old record 2:22½) Del Sur 2:24¾, (sire of Don Tomas 2:20.) Inez 2:30, Sir Guy 2:28½, Sultan 2:24 and Tommy Gates 2:24.

Sultan 1513 by The Moor has an even twenty in "the list," three new ones having been added this year. They are as follows: Stamboul 2:12½, Alcazar 2:20½, Bay Rose, 2:20½, Big Frank 2:30, Center 2:29½, Contractor 2:24¾, Dubec 2:28, Eva 2:23¾ Hidalgo 2:27, Kismet 2:25½, La Grange 2:23½, Margaret 2:28 (dam of Regal Wilkes, two-year-old record 2:20¾), Rajah 2:29½, Ruby 2:19¾, Soudan 2:27¾, Sweetheart 2:22½, Sunny Slope 2:29¼, Melrose 2:27, Lucy R. 2:30 and San Gabriel 2:27¾. Every one of the sons of Sultan that have colts old enough to trot, shows that the great speed producing power of "The Moor" goes on in the family from generation to generation, and it requires no spirit of prophecy to foretell that Bay Rose will be equally successful with his other half brothers. A full brother of Bay Rose, Pasha 2039, had only one representative on the track this year, as far as memory serves us, and that was Moro that got a record of 2:27 at San Jose.

The dam of Bay Rose is Ma'am Baldwin, a mare highly valued by Mr. Rose, she having produced, not only the subject of our sketch, but Pasha 2:36, lately owned by S. N. Straube, of Fresno, who has a number of foals by that horse that are ready to knock for admission to the 2:30 list. Madam Baldwin was by The Moor, her dam being by Ben Lippencott a son of Belmont (Williamson's) who although a thoroughbred, was sire of Venture 2:27¼, and sire of the dams of Belle Echo 2:20, Flora Sheppard 2:30, Monarch 2:28½, Nelly Patchen 2:27½ and Prince 2:23½, showing that "Old" Belmont was able to impart his trotting instinct to his children and grandchildren.

The large prices paid by Eastern buyers for two of Mr. Rose's stock, Alcazar, $25,800, and Voodoo, $24,100, show in what appreciation the blood of The Moor is held by those who make breeding a study, and Messrs. Henry and Ira Pierce can be congratulated that they have added such a fast and game son of Sultan to their new stock farm. As is well known, they have lately purchased the Santa Rosa Race Track, and hereafter it will be called the Santa Rosa Stock Farm, and we can confidently predict that Bay Rose will prove equally as successful in the stud as he has been on the track.

Our Southern California Letter.

I notice that Protection is greatly fancied for the Kentucky Derby. I have it from the best of authority that the junior champion winner will not sport silk in that race. This will be a piece of news for the Eastern turf papers. My informant is none other than the lucky owner of the son of Prince Charley. In a conversation with your correspondent, Bob Campbell stated that Protection would be reserved for some of the big three-year-old events later in the season.

L. J. Rose was in an especially good humor when the BREEDER AND SPORTSMAN representative called at his mansion the other evening. The owner of Rosemeade is a good reader, and the accumulation of turf literature on his table while absent from the city a week or two, reminds one of a newspaper office. "They've got a sensational two-year-old at Santa Anita," opened up the newspaper man. "I have got two or three good ones myself," replied the former owner of Stamboul, "and I will back one of mine against anything in the State."

Do I think that Rico will win the Brooklyn Handicap? The race has never been won by a three-year-old, was the evasive answer, but Rico is a great horse, and he will be in the hunt.

Mr. Rose is more than satisfied with his Palo Alto purchases. The horses are showing up splendidly in their work, and it will be surprising if he does not capture some of the big Eastern stakes, especially for two-year-olds. The following is a list of the yearlings at Palo Alto recently purchased by Mr. Rose:

B c by Argyle—imported Amalia by Salvator.
B c by Wildidle—imported Amelia by Lowland.
B c by Flood—imported Cornelia by Isonomy.
Br c by Wildidle—imported Flirt by Hermit.
B c by Argyle—Jennie C by Norfolk.
Br c by Argyle—imported Patilla by Pero Gomez.
B c by Argyle—imported Rosetta by Stranan.
Br f by Flood imported Mutiny by Adventurer
B f by Flood—imported Goula by Exminster.

Governor Stanford refused to sell any fillies, consequently Mr. Rose was only able to secure the racing qualities of the two fillies given on the above list.

It took $5000 to secure the Wildidle—Flirt colt, but the youngster will be worth every dollar paid for him if he takes after his brother Flambeau.

The youngster whose dam is Cornelia should be hot property if breeding is any criterion. Cornelia is by Isonomy, and was purchased in England at a cost of three thousand dollars.

The impression prevails that Captain Merry has been instructed to purchase ten broodmares for L. J. Rose in Australia. This is partially incorrect. Captain Merry has been given a good round sum of money and has carte blanche to use his own judgment in expending the amount for broodmares and fillies. I am not at liberty to state the sum Captain Merry took to the Antipodes, but it should be enough to buy at least a couple of dozen broodmares and fillies.

I received word too late for my last letter of the death at Santa Anita, of the brood mare Freda. Freda will be remembered by old time race goers. She was quite speedy in her day and is credited with several good performances, a notable one being her two-mile race at the Bay District, when as a three year-old she packed 116 pounds in 3:32½. She was by Wild Idle out of Frolic.

QUARTER STRETCH GOSSIP.

Joe Narvice will in all probability go East with the Rose stable.

W. J. Robinson is highly pleased with Al West, his new trainer and driver. There are two new comers at Edgemont. A Stamboul colt out of Jessie Ballard 2:25 and a Red Wilkes colt out of Lady Coats by Dictator. Two well bred youngsters, to say the least.

Charley Durfee will make the circuit this year with Gossiper, McKinney and a green pacer.

Jack Felton has a string of trotters in training at Santa Ana, including the game gelding Danger 2:26½. He expects to take in the grand circuit this year.

Sam Caton, who has been wintering here with a string of trotters, expects to leave on Saturday for the East.

Cy Mulkey will be represented at the Blood Horse Meeting with Tom Daly and Sinfax. The latter colt Cy has been leased from L. J. Rose to take through the Montana Circuit.

The Rose string will probably leave here on Monday for San Francisco.

Mr. Reed has purchased from W. K. Robinson, Othello, the Sultan stallion. The dam of Othello is Atlanta, a full sister of Beautiful Bells. Mr. Reed will in all probability, take Othello to Ohio, where he will make the season.

DAGWORTH.

The Horse Interest of Inyo Co.

Up to three years ago, there was very little interest taken in the horse business here except by a few, among whom were Henry Giles, who had a horse by Budd Doble, Mike Muldoon who brought a roadster by Bismarck from Kern Co., and William Rowan, of Bishop, who brought several Normans from M. W. Dunhan, Ill. He also brought two Cleveland Bays into the valley a year ago. Three years ago, W. S. Enos Independence brought in the standard bred horse Albenton 4023, also a few well bred mares in foal by such horses as Fallis 4781, Sterling 6223, and Prompter 2345. The next horse brought was by Burns Peeler of Bishop, and was the thoroughbred horse Bronco by Jo Hooker. Last fall Holbert & Smith brought Pickpocket by Joe Daniels and Antare by Anteros, he by Electioneer 125. This winter, the Conklin Bros. purchased another good one from Mr. Saxe. It was Mount Vernon Prince by Mount Vernon, dam Libby B. by Winthrop, 2nd dam Fanny Fern by Jack Hawkins.

R. C Spears, of Lone Pine, has just purchased a fine young roadster Flash by Prompter 2305; 1st dam Lady Nelson by John Nelson, he by imp Trustee, 2nd dam Oregon Nell. This young stallion was raised in Inyo county, by Enos & McSweeny.

The cattle business has always been the principal stock industry of this section, but now that so great an interest is being taken in the raising of good horses, I predict that Inyo horses in a few years will become noted for their endurance as road and farm stock.

INYO.

Fresno Races.

THURSDAY.

There was a considerable improvement in the attendance at the race track on the third day. Three races were on the programme, the first of which was conceded a good thing for Pliny and he justified the confidence reposed in him by winning readily in 2:08¾. The second race, a five furlong repeat, was expected to be a certainty for Kitty Van, who sold for $20 to the field $8 in a few pools, after which she was barred and Painkiller brought $20, to the field $13.

The tactics used in the race combined with bad luck at the start beat the mare. Painkiller and Adam had two lengths the best of the start in the first heat and the mare had to go round both. A singular accident occurred to two of the horses. The Abbott colt fell and Revolver fell over him, both riders being on the ground together. Luckily neither was seriously injured, though Davis, who rode Revolver, had his foot and neck badly bruised.

In the second heat, exactly the same tactics were pursued, the result being that Kitty Van stopped at the finish a little and was beaten cleverly by Painkiller, who won the deciding heat easily, the mare being pumped out.

In the last race of the day, a quarter mile dash, Hazlitt rode Sunday, who did not seem to make a great effort to get away, and was easily beaten by Cyclone.

SUMMARY.

Purse $250. Handicap for all ages, one mile and a quarter.
Kelly & Samuel's b g Pliny, 3, Flood—Precious, 103............Ward 1
Dennison Bros' b h Hotspur, 4 Joe Daniels—Sister to Douglass, 115 ....Bustillos 2
Orange Grove Stable's br h Jack Brady, a, Wildidle—Sour Grapes, 112............Hennessy 3
Time, 2:08¾
Also ran Willoughby 70 lbs, and Louise M. 103.

Pliny sold a red hot favorite at $15 to $7 for Hotspur, and $6 for the field. After two breakaways Hotspur cut out the pace and hard ridden, was half a length in front of Pliny past the stand with Louise M a length back third. Louise went to the front round the turn and had about a length the best of Pliny and Hotspur up the backstretch. The two latter went passed her on the upper turn, and despite Bustillo's hard finish on Hotspur, Pliny won cleverly by a length, with Brady six lengths back third and Louise M fourth.

SUMMARY.

Purse $200. Five furlongs and repeat.
G. Lyman's b h Painkiller, a, Joe Hooker—Betsy Maguire 118............Hazlitt 2 1 1
J. B. Ross' b m Kitty Van, 4, Vanderbilt—April Fool, 109 ....Hennessey 1 2 2
Orange Grove Stable's ch g Adam, a, Shiloh—Molly Adams, 118............Stewart 3 3
Time, 1:01½, 1:02¼, 1:08.
Also ran Revolver, Mirope and Abbott's colt.

First Heat—Kitty Van sold for $20 to the field $8. With Kitty Van barred, Painkiller brought $20 to the field $13. A start was soon effected. Painkiller and Adam having two lengths the best of it set the race at a merry rate round the turn. When in the straight Kitty Van came very fast, and passing both, won the heat cleverly by half a length from Painkiller with Adam third and Mirope fourth. The Abbott colt and Revolver both fell on the upper turn, but the judges did not distance them and Abbott started in the next heat. Time, 1:01½.

Second Heat—A little betting was done at $20 for Kitty Van to $5 for the field. After a few breakaways Adam and Painkiller again were a couple of lengths in front of Kitty Van, and though Kitty Van came fast in the stretch, she never caught Painkiller, who won easily by a length and a half in 1:02¼.

Third Heat—Painkiller was a strong favorite at $20 to $7 for Kitty Van. Both got away well Painkiller, running easy, was half a length in front all the way, winning readily by that distance from the mare, who tired badly.

SUMMARY.

Purse $100. Quarter-mile dash.
A. D. Hitchcock's ch g Cyclone, a, Ironclad—unknown, 128. Stewart 1
E. Fitzgerald's ch m Gypsy Girl, 114............Smith 2
T. F. Lynch's b g Sunday, a, Sundance—Norma, 128............Hazlitt 3
Time, 0:23½.
Billy Button, 116, ran also.

Cyclone sold a big favorite at $20 to $5 for Sunday and $3 for the field. The flag was soon dropped, and Cyclone going right out, had a two lengths lead of Gypsy Girl, with Sunday well in the rear. Cyclone won easily by two lengths from Gypsy Girl, who just beat Sunday for the place, Hazlitt, on the latter, riding hard the last hundred yards. Time, 0:23½.

FRIDAY.

The chance of witnessing a good race between Daisy D. and McGinnis brought a better attendance to the track, and the public were certainly satisfied with the grand race given them, and the phenomenal time made, 2:07¾, is an exceptionally fast race for the time of year, and the winner, McGinnis had a little in reserve.

The first race, a three furlong repeat, was won readily by Sunday. The last race of the day, a handicap for beaten horses, was a mixed up affair. Jubilee, the favorite, won pretty handily, but Brown, who rode Revolver, and Hennessy, Clauderoy's pilot, both said they were fouled, and the judges, being of the opinion that all the riders had ridden foully except Ward, ordered the race to be run over again, when Mirope, after running slowly for the first quarter, went round the other trio, and won handily by a length from Jubilee.

SUMMARY.

Purse $200. Three furlongs and repeat.
T. F. Lynch's b g Sunday, a, Sundance—Norma, 118......Hazlett 1 1
A. D. Hitchcock's ch g Cyclone, a, Ironclad—unknown, 118 Stewart............ 2 2
Time, 0:35½, 0:35½.
Birnie, 63, The Jew, 118, Springwater, 118, ran also.

First Heat—Sunday sold for $20 to Cyclone $10 and the field $10. A very good start was made, with Springwater, Sunday and Birnie a shade in front, but the filly dropped back, and Sunday stayed in front all the way, winning by three-quarters of a length from Cyclone. Time, 0:35½.

Second Heat—There was no betting after the first heat. Springwater led to the straight, when Sunday and Cyclone passed him, and the former won by a longish head. Time, 0:35½.

Purse of $250. Owner's Handicap. One mile and a quarter.
Kelly & Samuel's b h Ed McGinnis, 5, Grinstead—Jennie G. 83 ....Ward 1
Miller & Owen's b m Daisy D., a, Wheatly—Black Maria, 100 ....Henney 2
Golden Gate Stable's blk Black Pilot, a, Echo—Madge Duke 85.... ....Lawler 3
Time—2:07¾.

The betting settled down $20 for McGinnis and $8 for the field. $100 to $60 was several times bet on the track that McGinnis would win. When the flag fell Daisy cut out the work at a lively rate, and Ward being instructed to make the pace on McGinnis, had to squeeze the bay horse to keep up with her down the stretch. Passing the stand Daisy had her head pulled round and was leading the horse half a length, but rounding the turn he closed up, at the quarter was about level, and both straightening out ran together to the half, when the horse began to show his head in front and gradually wearing Daisy down passed the starting post half a length in front, the mile being run in 1:41½. McGinnis drew away down the stretch and won handily by an open length. Pilot never was in the hunt. Time 2:07¾.

SUMMARY.

Purse $200, handicap for beaten horses, six furlongs.
Maltese Villa Stable's ch f Mirope, 3, Joe Hooker—Constellation, 80 ....Ward 1
Golden Gate Stable's b g Jubilee, 4, Kyrle Daly—Joy, 119,... Hazlitt 2
J. Delano's b c Revolver, 3, Joe Daniels—Ly Partisan, 90 lbs. Brown 3
Time, 1:15¾.
Also ran Clanderoy.

Jubilee was such a hot favorite that only $9 could be obtained against $35, and pools were sold with him barred Mirope bringing $20, Clanderoy $13, and Revolver $3.

When the flag fell Clanderoy jumped off in front and had a two lengths lead of Revolver and Jubilee, at the half pole. Jubilee then closed up the gap and passing Clanderoy on the turn won pretty easily by two open lengths while Mirope was last, half a length back. Time, 1.15¾.

After a good deal of arguing among the jockeys all of whom claimed fouls on each other except Mirope's rider, the race was ordered to be run again and the horses went to the post again after an interval of about half an hour. A start was soon effected Clanderoy and Revolver breaking away well led Mirope and Jubilee two lengths up the backstretch, and round the turn when Mirope moved up and passed the leaders, closely followed by Jubilee whom she beat out, a good length in exactly the same time as the first heat 1:15¾.

SATURDAY.

As no one was in a hurry to leave, the Directors gave an extra day on Saturday, and though the horses were not quite first class the betting was as good as, if not better, than any of the previous days. Of the three races on the programme, the second was very interesting, as the Maltese Villa colt, Terry, who had won easily earlier in the week, was expected by the stable to win again, but the colt had the worst of the weights with Captain Al, and really never could get alongside him.

The last race was a complete upset, as Funny, who had no friends, won cleverly. The Manager, Mr. Baldwin, held the starter's flag, and got the horses off in good time in all three races.

SUMMARY.

Purse $200. For named horses. One mile.
Orange Grove Stable's b h Jack Brady, a, Wildidle—Sour Grapes, 124............Hennessy 1
Kelly & Samuels' br m Adelaide, 3, Grinstead, Victoria, 103... Ward 2
S. Ashe's b g Willoughby, 3, Jocko—Fannie D., 101, O. Hearn...... 3
Time—1:46½.

Betting started out with Brady selling for $10 to the field's $8, but veered round, and the field sold for $10 to $8 for Brady. When the flag fell to an even start, Adelaide was sent to the front leading Willoughby half a length round the turn with Brady five lengths back. Willoughby hung on to the mare until the half was passed, and then retired while Brady closed up, being only half a length behind at the head of the stretch, and finishing strongly, beat Adelaide easily by a length, with Willoughby seven lengths back.

SUMMARY.

Purse $150 for named horses. Five furlongs.
Miller & Owen's b c Captain Al, 3, Kingston—Black Maria, 107 ....Hennessey 1
Maltese Villa Stable's ch c Judge Terry, 2, Alta—Pet, 100...... Ward 2
J. L. Abbott's b g Abbott's colt, 3, Billie Lee—Plight 107 ....Newell 3
Time, 1 03½.

After a few pools had been sold with Terry favorite, Captain Al deposed him and sold readily at $30 to $16 for the field. A start was soon effected, the Abbott colt breaking away well led Captain Al and Judge Terry two lengths at the end of the first quarter, but having shot his bolt, was passed by Captain Al, who turned into the straight a length in front, and striding on, won easily by a length and a half from Judge Terry. Time, 1:03½.

SUMMARY.

Purse $100, for named horses. 300 yards.
A. D. Hitchcock's b g Funny, 122............Stewart 1
F. Works' b h Springwater, 123............Knight 2
Orange Grove Stable's ch g Adam, 123 ....Hennessy 3
Time, 0:32½.
April Fool, 79, also ran.

Adam was made favorite at $10 to Springwater $7 and the field $6, but changing, Springwater sold choice for $10 to $6 each for the field and Adam.

The four were soon sent off, Funny leading Springwater half a length into the stretch, with Adam last. The two leaders had a tight race, Funny winning by a short head from Springwater, with Adam a bad third.

The Fresno Fair Grounds Association are certainly to be congratulated on the splendid order of their track which is probably the fastest and best appointed in the State, and reflects great credit on the efficient management headed by President Dr. Lewis Leach and Vice-President S. N. Straube, Esq., for despite the heavy rains all through the winter the natural condition of the soil and track are such that it readily dried out. A good many skeptical people doubted the phenomenal time made by Ed. McGinnis, but it was perfectly absurd for the timers were R. Porter Ashe, G. Starr, the well known trotting driver and R. B. Terry, all of whom should be qualified timers. Anyway, McGinnis has often shown his ability to run so fast, as when one allows for the difference in weight it must be a peculiar idea of how weight tells on a horse which will not allow three-quarters of a second for 44 pounds. Ed McGinnis carried 127 pounds at Ione early last August, and was beaten a head in 2:08½, being then four years old, and last week, as a five year old, carried 83 pounds. With regard to the other times, at short distances, probably the crack sprinters in the West were at Fresno, Sunday, Kitty Van and Cyclone being fast, among fast horses, and it was to be expected that something phenomenal would be done.

Imported Greenback.

A Magnificent Specimen of Blood Horse.

It is now a little more than two years ago that imported Greenback was brought to America, in company with some of the best animals ever sent over from England. At the time, "Vigilante," the well known authority on matters pertaining to the turf, wrote as follows in the New York Spirit of the Times:

"Greenback, the stallion, was out in the stallion paddock when we arrived, with Mr. Easton and Mr. Charles Reed viewing his capers as he lunged and trotted under the exhilarating influence of the keen bright air. Greenback is, bar Rayon d'Or, the most magnificent specimen of a blood horse that we have seen among the imported horses of the past fifteen years. He is thirteen years old, a whole colored brown, with broad, flat legs, great length and liberty, a fine spread of hips and every evidence of great constitution and animal vigor. About the head and neck he is much of the type of Stockwell, but bodily he is different, having more of that trim quality of the Leamingtons, only more substantial, straining probably to his grandsire, The Fying Dutchman. He is like an eel as he moves about with a quick, sinuous glide. He is a superbly coated horse, reflecting a purple sheen, which blazes in the sunlight, and no one would dream that he had so recently left the ship Greenback's blood is as high as his conformation. He is a son of the French horse Dollar, who was by Flying Dutchman, dam Payment, by Slave. Dollar's dam was the dam of Florin, the sire of Florintin, winner of the French Derby in 1866, and of Mantilla, the champion French two-year-old of 1878. Dollar's merit as a sire is famous, as he got Salvator, St. Cyr, Peris, Almanza, Nathan, Fontainebleau, Salvanos, Torrent and Androclee. One of his daughters, Nellie James, produced Jack of Hearts, Jacobus, etc., in Mr. Belmont's stud. Salvator won the Grand Prix de Paris and French Derby in 1875, and Salvanos won the Cesarewitch in 1872. On the side of his dam Greenback is glorious. His dam was the Duke of Hamilton's great mare Music, the best broodmare in Europe. She has foaled Ossian, Fiddler, Song, Songstress, Nina, Poetry, etc., Nina being one of the best two-year-olds of 1887, winning the Clearwell, Bretby and Homebred. As for Ossian, she won the St. Leger, while Fiddler beat Foxhall for the Alexandria Plate. Music is a daughter of Stockwell, from the invincible One Act by Annandale; 3d dam Extravaganza by Voltaire, etc., gives Greenback an infusion of Blacklock blood. Greenback was a really good race horse, winning the Stretchworth Stakes, at Newmarket, as a two-year-old, and the Earl Spencer Plate, at Northampton, as a three-year-old. The Peel Handicap, the Queen's Plate, at Ayr, and the Caledonian Cup, at the same place, also fell to his share. He has got several winners, having sired Greenlight, Greenjacket, Greenshank, Greenwave, Greenhorn, etc. He is the only direct representative of Bay Middleton's male line in America, and will be a grand outcross for our native mares.

More About Lady Vernon.

The readers of the BREEDER AND SPORTSMAN will be pleased to read the following letter, which tells more about the history of Lady Vernon. We are much obliged to Mr. Bement for his kindness, and would be pleased to receive letters from any of the "old timers" about the horses and races of "Auld Lang Syne":

MAPLE GROVE FARM, OAKLAND, March 30, 1890.

EDITOR BREEDER AND SPORTSMAN:—I have just been reading your article about Lady Vernon, and thinking perhaps you would like to know what little I remember about her, send you the following memorandum of her races and progeny. I saw her trot all her races in San Francisco and remember them perfectly. The first one was for a purse of $1,000, with an inside stake of $1000 each, against the pacer Lady Mac, and took place on the Pioneer course in April, 1854, and was won by Lady Vernon in one heat, distancing Lady Mac in 2:28½, but as she made several very long breaks, was set back four seconds for running, and the time was announced 2:32½. I remember the circumstance distinctly.

The next race was also in April, 1854, and was for a purse of $500, over the Union Course, Lady Mac to saddle and Lady Vernon to harness, and was won by Lady Mac in four heats, Lady Vernon winning the second. Time, 2:32, 2:34, 2:34 and 2:37.

She then trotted against Daniel Webster and Lady Mac, both pacers, over the Pioneer Course in May, and won in three straight heats. Time, 2:37, 2:33 and 2:35.

She also trotted at Sacramento a match for $1,000 aside, with Lady Jane, withdrawn, after the second heat. Time, 2:31 and 2:37.

In July, 1855, she trotted a match race with New York for $1,000, over the Pioneer Course, two mile heats, Lady Vernon to wagon and New York to harness, which was won by New York in straight heats, time 5:16 and 5:15, and I think these are the only races she ever trotted in California.

Young Vernon, Master Vernon and the Vermont Colt were afterwards owned by Mr. A. Hayward. The Rattler Colt by Erwin Davis: The first Patchen colt he sold to William Woodward, who trotted him in the colt Stake at Shell Mound Park under the name of Billy Vernon, and who dropped dead in a two mile race on the Ocean House track. California Chief ran away and broke his neck. Tom Vernon went to Watsonville and Oakland Maid he sold to W. S. Hobart. The other four I never saw. Yours truly,

GEO. BENNETT.

Salt For Animals.

Why do animals need salt? Because animals is an epitome of mineral and vegetable matters, and salt is a medium between them—a compound of these compounds in certain definite proportions, and grass and grain do not supply a sufficient proportion to complete the compound, and are not therefore complete nutrients. Horses fed on an excess of grain, in disproportion to most fibrous plants, will eat the ground with acidity when they can get at it, and it supplies in a measure a corrector of vegetable acidity. Salt being a chloride of sodium furnishes both chlorine and soda, the latter being a neutralizer of excessive acidity, especially derived from grasses, pampered horses should be provided with the following ball, always in easy reach: First, make a strong brine of rock salt with a tenth of saltpetre in it, then get a spit of pure clay and half a gallon of fresh wood ashes, and of these make a mixture with sufficient water, and roll into a ball and dry. Keep this in a till of the manger, clean and always in reach of the pet animal, just as are the grass and ground in his native wood. As I have said the horse is an epitome of all that he will eat in health, and this is why they nourish and build up each function.—S. F. Larkin, in Horse World.

TURF AND TRACK.

Isaac Murphy will probably ride Riley in the Kentucky Derby.

Mr. Samuels says he shall breed Welcome this spring, probably to Tyrant.

General Turner has among his string for the big circuit Fred Folger, 2:20½.

Dan McCarty and L. R. Richards (owner of Elector) were spectators at the Fresno races.

In Germany there were only 274 thoroughbred foals last year, of which nineteen died.

W. H. E. Smith has purchased from Mr. Walters a two-year-old half brother to Al Farrow.

B. C. Holly has sent Reveille, the sire of Gladstone and Tycoon up to the Reavis ranch at Chico.

The pool rooms in Baltimore are all closed now by the bill passed abolishing all pool rooms in Maryland.

Imp King Gallop has met with much favor in Kentucky as a stallion, although he is practically untried there.

Street railway companies say that gray horses or mules are the longest lived, and give the greatest amount of service.

H. D. Miller will put Corona, by Joe Hooker, out of Sister to Lottery, in the stud. She will be bred in a short while.

The useful mare Unite has been returned to F. B. Harper by Ed. Corrigan and will join the brood mares at Nantura.

There is a bill pending in the Kentucky Legislature to make the running of pool rooms a felony, but it will hardly pass.

R. P. Ashe's Mirope (the winner of the third race at Fresno on Friday), by Hooker out of Constellation, was bred this spring to Alta.

Jim Guest's old mare Mrs. Grigsby foaled 1861 is dead. She was the dam of Harry Gilmore, Buchanan and Jim Guest (Supervisor).

The only Splan, says Cleveland, will be his headquarters, and he has hopes of having Guy, 2:15½, in his string among the other flyers.

Al Leach sold pools at the Fresno races in his well-known style. This time he was acting for the association, who did not let the selling.

Little Ward, the Kelly & Samuels' light weight, can ride about 73 pounds, and it is said that he carries about 1 pound dead weight in his mouth.

W. Ayres, the one time owner of Trade Dollar and other good racehorses, is in town again, having come down on a visit from Portland, Or.

Cook, the jockey, is still out East, but Messrs. Kelly & Samuels expect him back in time for the Blood Horse meeting, or possibly San Jose.

Dan McCarty tried to get Kelly and Samuels to put a price on Ed McGinnis and Pliny. $20,000 was eventually the price, and Dan offered $5,000.

Rosa Wilkes 2:18¼ has a pretty foal by Nutwood 2:18¾. The average is 2:18½, but one should have good reason to hope for an improvement on both parents records.

Lady Stevens, full sister to Minnehaha, dam of Alcazar 2:20½, Mascot and Beautiful Bells, will be offered for sale at Woodard's sale in Lexington this month.

Percy Williams has, among other promising horses on the Island, a particular taking two-year-old stallion by Antevolo, 2:19½, dam by Sultan, grandam Ella Lewis, 2:27.

The trotting stock belonging to the estate of the late T. J. Megibben will be sold at auction in Lexington, Ky., this month. Some gilt-edged mares are among the number.

Rosebug, four year old chestnut gelding by Jim Brown out of Rosemary, was put up for sale at Fresno by Messrs. Kelly & Samuels, but was bought in, no one raising on $230.

The Dwyers' two-year-old colt Baldwin is said to be pleasing every one at Gravesend by his taking style. He is by Enquirer out of Bribery, and therefore a brother to Miss Ford.

At the request of Jockey Palmer "Father Bill" Daly has purchased for $500 the lad's apprenticeship deeds from Mr. Wm. McMahon. This will admit of Palmer riding for Daly for two years.

Dan McCarty, while in Fresno, bought from F. B. Baldwin a bay gelding by George M. Patchen Jr, out of an Echo mare, paying $950. McCarty also bought a yearling filly by Bay Rose, dam by Algona.

Miss Egbert 2:29¾, by Egbert, dam Miss Patchen, by Mambrino Patchen, will be bred for the first time this season. She will be stinted to Re-Election by Electioneer, dam Lady Russell (sister to Maud S, 2:08¾).

In the six furlong race on Friday at Fresno, with four starters, Porter Ashe's boy was the only one not accused of foul riding. He was always too far back, yet in the second heat Mirope outstayed the lot and won cleverly.

The first foal of the season dropped at F. B. Harper's Nantura Stud, is a bay colt by Longfellow, dam Lenora Morris (sister to Drake Carter). It came the other day, and the little fellow very much resembles Drake Carter.

Victor Von Bismarck (sire of Edgemark 2:16 as a four-year-old), will not be a public stallion from now on. G. G. White his owner, will keep him to serve his own mares at the Gilt-Edged Stock Farm in Bourbon County, Ky.

There are forty-six yearlings this Spring, twenty-four colts and 22 fillies, at McGrathiana Stud. They are the get of Harry O'Fallon, Strathmore, Duke of Montrose, Onondaga, imp. Rapture, imp St. Blaise, Aristides and Spendthrift.

It is stated by an authority that 75 per cent. of the trotting and thoroughbred broodmares in Kentucky are barren or have slipped their foals this season. The loss is not only large, but will cause a shortage of yearlings next spring.

In Kentucky only one thoroughbred stallion, Longfellow stands at $500. Four trotting stallions, Robert McGregor, Baron Wilkes, William L. and Red Wilkes, are advertised to stand at that price, all of them being in and near Lexington.

Mr. Kittson has sent imported Clara, the dam of Cartoon and Reclare, to Mr. Cassatt's Stratford. Cartoon and Reclare are both by Reform, a son of Leamington, Stratford should therefore nick with the mare, as he of course is a Leamington.

Pat Malloy, the renowned thoroughbred stallion, will not serve any mares this season, Mr. Brodhead, the manager of the Woodburn Farm, being of the opinion that a year's rest will help to reinvigorate the old horse, who was foaled in 1865.

Mr. W. E. Spier a year ago purchased from Palo Alto for for $8000 the bay stallion May King, foaled 1886, by Electioneer out of May Queen 2:20. Last week May King was sold to Messrs. Sibley and Miller, Frankfort, Pa., for about $20,000.

Last week in Turf and Track, I mentioned that Mr. Mackey, the Rancho del Paso superintendent, brought back Roxaline, sister to Marion, the dam of the Emperor of Norfolk, El Rio Rey, etc. I should have said Easter, a daughter of Roxaline, by Vicksburg.

The Duke of Malborough, despite a strong aristocratic backing after putting up his name for "The Turf," which is the crack sporting club in England, decided to withdraw his name and not be blackballed, as he was informed he most assuredly would be.

Magolica 2:15 only elicited one bid at auction, the Sire Bros. getting him for $1,000. Prior to the sale they offered $2,000 for the fourteen-year-old gelding, whose poor condition prevented any bidding for him. He will be sent to Europe with several other trotters.

Mr. William Thomas, of Chico, in a very characteristic, chatty letter to our Field editor, says he has a very useful looking colt by Signal Wilkes, a son of Guy Wilkes, 2:15¼, out of a mare by Arrow, grandam by Blackbird 402, record 2:22, great granddam by Lancet.

J. K. Megibben & Co.'s string of thoroughbreds consists of eighteen horses, among them being the Kentucky Derby candidates Eberlee, W. G. Morris and Avondale. James Rodegap, who prepared Spokane for his Derby and other victories last year, is training them.

Among the many well bred mares stinted to the Duke of Norfolk are Laura Gardner, Ida Glenn, the big Adams' mare and Mr. Winters' Ballinette, the dam of Alta; Dan Dennison says his colts are great lookers, and one or two he knows are more than threatened with a turn of speed—they have it.

Starter Caldwell has bought the horse Laggard, seven years old by Uncas out of imported Dawdle from M. Daly. This once famous racer who in 1887, won eight races and in the Raritan Stakes beat Hanover, who up to then had won fourteen straight races that season, will be retired to the stud.

Mr. Salisbury is back again from his eastern trip with which he was highly satisfied. He says as 2:12 is the fashionable mark to shoot at, Direct will receive no mares this year, but will be specially prepared for a low mark. Margaret S. is in grand trim, and will make a big race for the cup.

Clifton Bell, the well-known racing man has been in the city for several days, after spending the winter in Los Angeles. I am sorry to say Mr. Bell and his wife are both in very indifferent health. He says the mare Los Angeles has wintered exceptionally well and never looked so well in her life.

The McGinnis-Daisy D. race at Fresno last week, a mile and a quarter in 2:07¾, was a scorcher for the time of year. The first mile in 1:41½, took the kink out of the mare's neck; in fact, the horse beat her at the end of the six furlongs. It is noteworthy that McGinnis' dam, Jennie G, is a full sister to Daisy D.

The Fresno Association is making a great and meritorious effort to have on their track for their meetings all the best horses in the West and there is every indication that Mr. Baldwin will have the track extensively patronized next fall by Eastern stables who will send the pick of their strings to winter in Fresno.

One of the most successful and prolific broodmares ever owned by Col. R. P. Pepper, Frankfort, Ky., was Cropp. She was by Pilot Jr., out of a Canadian mare. Col. Pepper paid $100 for her at an executor's sale, and before she died he sold over $20 000 worth of her colts and fillies. Her ears were frozen off when a colt, hence the name.

Ed. Bither has arrived at Allen Farm, Pittsfield, Mass., and among the horses that will be campaigned are several which will be bred this spring, viz., Jet Wilkes to Yataghan; Eliets 2:22¼, to Electrite (brother to Sphinx 2:23½); Miss Majolica to Launcelot; Mentaka to America; Maudlen 2:25¾, to Electioneer (by courtesy of Senator Stanford).

The Belle Meade Stud, Nashville, Tenn., has lost the brown mare Hiawasse, foaled 1879, by imported Saxon, dam Vandalite, by Vandal, out of Vesperlight, by Childe Harold. She cost Belle Meade $2,000 at the Lorillard sale, but has been sick ever since, and had no produce. She was a superior racer, winner of the Mermaid Stakes, Monmouth Oaks and other races. Hiawasse was in fold to Enquirer.

That great race mare Freda and Griesette (in foal to the Emperor), died last week at Santa Anita. If the present rate of deaths continue, Mr. Baldwin will have nothing to breed to the Australian stallion—when he comes. Miss Ford is recovering rapidly and it is hoped is out of danger. She is believed not to be in foal, but as she was bred late in June (to Verano), there is a chance that she prove in foal yet.

Mr. Shippee is very unfortunate in his racing this year. He declared all his three year olds out of all engagements at the Blood Horse Meeting, except Fellowcharm, by Longfellow, out of Trinket, and a fortnight ago the colt partially broke down and was let up on with the expectation that he would be all right again, but unfortunately his first good gallop exposed the fallacy and his turf career is ended.

R. Porter Ashe was particularly pleased with Judge Terry's run last week at Fresno. He expects Alta to prove himself one of the crack stallions in another season or two, as his colts are an exceptionally fine lot, and all that have been worked are very speedy. A few weeks ago, he sold to Mr. James Davis, for $500, a yearling by Alta, out of Termagant. The colt will stay on the ranch until next Fall or Spring.

Mr. Salisbury says Mr. Case is delighted with the sister to Direct which Echora foaled on the 17th. She will be bred to Phallas this season.

Clifton closed two new stakes, the Passaic County Stakes, to be run April 11th, for three year olds; seven furlongs and a half, with $1,000 added. The Clifton Stakes, to be run April 14th, for all ages. $10 accompanied the entrance, and $1,200 is added; welter weights, and selling allowances. Distance four miles.

A number of mares which went to Ormonde during his first season proved to be barren, and he had only eight foals last year, of which one (colt out of Freia) died. The Duke of Westminster has colts by Ormonde out of Shotover and out of Angelica, dam of Blue Green. Lord Arlington has a colt out of Thistle, Lord Gerard a filly out of Bryonia, and Mr. J. S. Harrison a colt out of Crucible.

H. G. Scoggan says: "Yes, Proctor Knott has had something the matter with one of his forelegs, but I do not think that amounts to anything. I can hardly tell you what it was, but it will not affect his running. People who think so will be undeceived in a few days. He is not in anything like racing form, and I don't know how soon he will be, and for tha reason I am not certain when and where I will start him."

J. Dwyer is training a public stable of horses at Fresno, among them being an exceptionally good looking, rangy mare, two years old, by Clovis, out of Ida Davis by Del Nor, a son of Strathmore, the property of Mr. S. N. Straube, who also has a yearling in Dwyer's care. Mr. Straube has several other horses at the track, with his own trainer in charge, including Junio, 2:22, who is in splendid condition, and being extensively patronized. Clovis and Apex, 2:26, are on the ranch.

George Starr will probably leave for the East the middle of this month; it depends on the weather the other side of the Rockies when he will depart. Mr. Starr's horses are looking exceptionally well; Johnston, Little Ed. Annan, the gray horse Jack, Marie Jansen, Reina and the others under his care having been jogged for some time have lately had a few workouts. The Waters Stock Farm's Faustino has wintered well and has grown into an exceptionally fine looking two-year-old.

Wilber Field Smith wrote me on Monday that his thoroughbred mare Annie Laurie, entered in the great Matron Stakes was not in foal. He also said: "I have a foal for the BREEDER AND SPORTSMAN Futurity Stake, a chestnut colt foaled March 19th, sired by Albert W. 2:20, dam Belle Blanche by The Moor; 2nd dam Belle View Maid by Peck's Idol; 3rd dam Sue Monday by Pilot Jr; 4th dam Kate Taber by Mambrino Messenger, etc. He ought to stand the drilling and go the route.

The following authorative statement has been sent out by the Kentucky Association: The report that the Kentucky Association will have no racing this spring is utterly untrue. Our track is now in good condition; in a few days both inside and outside tracks will be equal to any in America. We have 150 horses on the grounds doing well, and have stables engaged for 60 more horses to arrive next week. We have completed sixty new stalls, and our club houses and betting shed will be complete for the races, May 6th. We expect an unprecedented meeting.

Shoes were used in very early ages; as a matter of fact, the feet of horses were protected by leather boots to keep the hoof from splitting and chipping while on long journeys, and by the wealthy people, as early as the times of Aristotle and Pliny. These boots were sometimes shod with metal. The mules of Nero were said to be shod with silver. Homer mentions "brazen-footed steeds." Iron shoes nailed to the hoof were first mentioned in the works of the Emperor Leo in the 9th century, and were introduced into England by William 1st, about 1688.

John Goldsmith tells me that Nina D., 2:26½, by Nutwood, 2:18¾, foaled a slashing bay colt on the San Mateo Ranch by Sable Wilkes, 2:18 Nina D. was sent out here last spring by her owner, Dan De Noyelles, to be bred to Sable Wilkes, and at the same time Mr. De Noyelles suggested to Goldsmith that if he could give her a record, he would be pleased. Goldsmith not only gave her a record but won several races with her. The colt should be a wonder, for the speed lines are astonishing: his dam is Nina D, 2:26½, dam Adelaide, 2:19¾, by Phil Sheridan, 2:26½, while his sire is Sable Wilkes, 2:18 at three years old, by Guy Wilkes, 2:15¼, a son of George Wilkes, 2:22.

The St. Louis Republic of the 26th says: Dr. A. C. Bernays' four-year-old mare Kidnap, by Luke Blackburn—Castilla, was killed at the Fair Grounds track yesterday. She was stone blind, and was out exercising with an 85-lb. boy named Sherman on her back. When opposite the betting stand she threw the boy and galloped around to the back stretch, where she ran into the track machine. Her fore leg was caught and wrenched completely off the trunk. She jumped around on three legs until J. G. Gibbons arrived, when he mercifully shot her. Kidnap was by Luke Blackburn out of Castilla, and was bought in a selling race for $475, during the last meeting.

Truth says the Paris correspondent of one of the morning papers made the absurd statement last week that the date of the Grand Prix has not been changed because many of the animals engaged have engagements at Ascot, whereas a change to the Sunday week after that meeting (June 29) would have enabled their animals to fulfil their engagements at Ascot, which they certainly cannot do under the present very inconvenient and idiotic arrangement. If the Grand Prix had been postponed until June 29, the race would undoubtedly have been benefited, as there would have been a larger field of English horses, and the alteration would have also been most beneficial for Ascot.

St. Gatien who ran a dead heat for the Derby in 1884, with Harvester, and whose stock will begin to run this season, had seventeen foals last year, of which one (colt out of Polaris) died. They include a colt out of Macaria (dam of Laureate) and a filly out of Florence, both owned by Mr. Hammond; Mr. Corlett has a filly out of his grandly bred mare Pretty Dance; and there are colts out of Lucy Glitters, Quilt and Balmoral; and fillies out Eira, Maxima and Peevish. Among St. Gatien's two year olds of this season will be the Duke of Portland's colt out of Modwena (sister to Donovan), Mr. Hammond's colts out of Electric and out of Decoration, and his filly out of Macaria who is said at Newmarket to be very smart; Mr. Gosling's colt out of Winifred, which was sold at Doncaster for 530 guineas, and M. Dawson's filly out of Galvanic.

During the recent Kellogg sales "Counselor" Crawford, C. H. Nelson and other noted horsemen got into quite a warm discussion over the merits of trotting stallions. Mr. Crawford offered to wager that Nelson 2:14¼, would not beat 2:12 this year, and in reply Mr. Nelson said: "Time is a funny thing; it is always on an edge, and is a hard thing to beat sometimes. It is different with a horse; he has his off days, and if I make any matches it will be horse against horse. Now, I will tell you what I will do. I will match Nelson against Axtell, Stamboul or Palo Alto for $5,000 a side, and trot the race this season.' The "Counselor" said he did not control either of the horses, and, therefore, could not make the match.

Col. R. S. Strader, who spent most of last fall and winter here and took away with him a high class list of trotters, shipped several mares to California from Kentucky. Among them were to Mr. W. S. Hobart Nancy Lee (the dam of Nancy Hanks) by Dictator out of Sophy by Alexander's Edwin Forest; Nola, a four-year-old mare by Nutwood out of Belle Bowman by Clark Chief and Valdosta, a five-year-old mare by Nutwood out of Emma Arteburn by Mambrino Patchen. To the San Mateo Farm, Bon Bon, a three-year-old filly by Baron Wilkes out of Mary Whitney; Little Odd, a three year old brown filly by Baron Wilkes out of Odd Stocking by Happy Medium and a Mambrino Russel filly. The last three will be bred to Guy Wilkes and are the property of Mr. John A. Skamnell, Shreldeport, La.

The Anaconda Review says: Through the courtesy of Mr. Ed S. Maxwell, who has just returned from a visit to Madison County, to the farm of Noah Armstrong, we are able to give the readers of the Review the names of the horses now in Mr. Armstrong's Eastern stable.

Spokane, ch b, 4, by Hyder Ali—Interpose.
Remini, b m, 4, by Red Boy—Bolus.
Mickey B, ch m, 4, by Red Boy—Bessie Douglass.
Polemus, b c, 3, by Red Boy—Lady Prewitt.
Crawsab, ch c, 3, by Rayon d'Or—Brienda.
Tacoma, b f, 3, by Tom Bowling—Annie Louisa.
Reinier, ch c, 2, by Pizarro—Electrical.
Orcas, br f, 3, by Patrick—Bessie Belle.

We also learn that it is very doubtful whether Spokane will be seen in public before the Suburban at Coney Island. The colt was never himself after the American Derby at Chicago last year, and Mr. Armstrong thinks that he can beat any horse in the land at a mile and a quarter or a mile and a half if he is in good condition.

Oats should be clean, dry, sound, plump, full of flour and rattle like dried peas. Good oats have no smell, except in fresh samples, when they savor slightly of earth. Before being fed to the horse they should be cleaned and winnowed to get all the dust out of them. They should never be used when kiln dried, which is sometimes done to preserve and whiten them. These are less nourishing and cause diabetes. To horses that bolt their food and do not masticate it thoroughly, chaff, or hay cut up fine, may be given in each feed, a good handful at a time. Clover hay treated in the same manner answers the same purpose and is an agreeable change. Light feeding horses will often eat their oats the better for it. The same may be said of carrots finely chopped, about half a pound to a feed, or even less as a relish. Horses are exceedingly fond of carrots, and will frequently be tempted by a feed so flavored when they would not finish a plain one. Nevertheless, in large quantities they are not recommended, being apt to produce eruptive blotches on the skin, difficult to eradicate and indicating that much of this food is injurious.

The Stewards of the French Jockey Club have just made some most important alterations in their rules, which will be much appreciated by owners of racehorses, whom they are particularly designed to benefit. London Truth says: Sweepstakes made up of entrance fees and forfeits are abolished, and the amount of the entrance fee to a race is never to exceed five per cent. of the added money. In future, moreover, managers of meetings must show that all the profits (except a certain and moderate percentage) are devoted to bona fide racing purposes, and there are to be a fixed proportionate number of handicaps, weight-for-age stakes, selling races, and two year old stakes every day. No meeting held within twenty-five miles of Paris is to give less than £720 added money every day, and there are never to be more than six races per day. It is a great pity that such rules cannot be passed by our Jockey Club, although they would not meet with the approval of "enterprising managers" and other turf cormorants, whose cupidity is notoriously insatiable.

For some weeks negotiations have been pending between the Sire Bros., of New York, and Hermann Dix, of Berlin, for the famous trotting campaigner Harry Wilkes, and it was common talk that the fastest son of old George Wilkes would soon bid adieu to his native land and make the ocean voyage to Germany, where his name and fame would insure him speedy recognition on the European turf. The deal has fallen through, however, and the swift-footed gelding will probably remain in this country for another season at least.

Mr. Sire was seen at his office on Broadway last week in relation to the matter. He said:

"We have heard from Mr. Dix, who had held an option on Harry for some time, with a proviso that he could have two other trotters, owned by us, if he did not decide to take him. He cables us that he will buy the two stallions, Red Star and George Peacemaker, and Harry Wilkes will no doubt be ready for the campaign this season and take part in whatever engagements are made for him."

In a paper read the other day before the London Royal Institution, Professor Flower, F. R. S. stated that the evolution of the horse is a subject almost equal in interest to that of the descent of man. This is largely because American fossil remains have thrown so much light on the matter that it seems likely to become as Professor Huxley remarks, a test case of the value of the Darwinian theory. Owen has shown that the hoofed vertebrates—which are further distinguished from animals with claws by having herbivorous teeth instead of carnivorous—are naturally divided into even-toed and odd toed. The odd-toed have a curious geological history, and may be traced by ample evidence back to a common ancestor, the fossil phenacodus There is proof that both the odd-toed and the even-toed swarmed in early Eocene time, though now the even-toed—oxen, sheep, deer, camels, pigs and hippopotamus—are kept going chiefly by the influence of man, while the odd-toed, there are only the tapir and rhinoceros, besides the horse. Concerning the phenacodus much has been learned within a year or two. More remains have been discovered, one skeleton being almost perfect, and these have the peculiarities of the horse and show that there has been but little change except in the long-boned tail. The size of the lower jaw, the teeth, the limbs, and, in short, every detail of structure regarded as important, are the same. The size of the animal varied from that of a terrier to that of a sheep.

Last year there were no fewer than 413 thoroughbred foals in the Austro-Hungarian Imperial studs, 216 colts, and 197 fillies, of which thirty-seven died. Doncaster, by Stockwell, the sire of Bend Or, was brought a few years ago from the Duke of Westminster, takes the first place, with thirty-one foals; Craig Millar, by Blair Athol, who won the Leger of 1875 for the late Mr. Stirling Crawfurd, had fourteen; and Kisber, by Buccaneer, had eight.

The top bone in the structure of the front supports of the horse is the scapula, blade bone, shoulder blade, or upper shoulder bone. Unlike the topmost bones in the hinder supports, it does not touch the spine, though it reaches above the spinal column, and it is not attached to it, except by the muscles that are attached to both. It is strongly imbedded in large muscles, and reaches from the point in the shoulder to nearly the top of the wither. Its height, its length, and above all the angle at which it slopes back as it rises, are all important features in considering the value of a horse. The more it slopes back the more advantageously it will be connected, both with the assisting muscles of the back and loins, and with the resisting weight that it has to sustain and move through the lower shoulder bone, so that with sufficient slope, the fore legs will be lifted farther and more easily, the saddle will be carried further back, and the fore legs will be set on further forward. Its back slope thus contributes in several different ways to the ease and safety of the rider, and to the moving power and endurance of the horse.

The New York Herald contained a communication from Newburg, N. Y., concerning the pedigree and history of Lady Dunn, the grandam of the great three year old trotter Axtell 2:12, which will prove of interest. It says: "Lady Dunn was bred in Newburg by Captain Samuel Roberts, then a resident here, and who is remembered as one of the contractors who, with George Law, built the Croton Aqueduct. While Captain Roberts was engaged on that work he bought from a Long Island breeder a fast road mare of imported Messenger blood. After using the mare for his own private driving in New York he brought her here and bred her to Seely's American Star, then standing at Goshen. The get was a gray filly, which he named Lady Dunn. She was purchased by John McQuoid, a well known horseman of Newburg, who broke her to harness and then sold her to Jesse Hulse, a neighbor. She began to develop remarkable speed and promise, and attracted the attention of Jack Nodine, then a noted New York horseman, who bought her of Mr. Hulse for another horse and $275 in cash. The subsequent history of the mare in connection with her removal to Kentucky and the performances of her progeny are well known."

Running away is a term applied to an uncontrollable gallop, which may proceed from very different causes and present very different degrees of danger. There is the self-willed gallop of the hard mouthed horse, who chooses to go his own pace, and in his own direction. There is the uncontrollable gallop, excited by emulation in company, or the determination not to be left behind, and there is the far more dangerous panic flight of the terrified horse. The panic stricken horse running away in terror under the impression that some frightful animal has got on his back, or is following on his heels, is a pitiable sight and one full of danger. His exertions are so desperate and exhausting, and the speed so terrific, that either a fall or a collision is sure to be something very serious, and the horse loses his senses so completely that he is far more likely to run into, than to avoid the most evident danger. It rarely if ever occurs with the well educated horse, but sometimes attacks a half educated horse. Such badly broken horses are always liable to catch a sight or sound of something thet they have not been reconciled to, and to gallop off in frantic terror, especially if ridden by young and timid boys who do not know how to manage them.

Mr. Briggs gave an interesting account of his experience with The Seer. It will be remembered that this colt, a very ordinary looking yearling, having a spike tail and crooked legs, was bought at the first Palo Alto sale in New York by Dr. Garcelon of Lewiston, Me., for a little over $200. He is by Electioneer, dam Queen by Young Consternation, son of imported Consternation. In the summer of 1888, as a three-year-old, Mr. Briggs took him in hand and found he was a mixed-gaited, shuffling sort of a foxy fellow, and that a radical change was necessary to straighten him out. So the teacher experimented with shoes until he hit the right combination of shoe and toe-weight, and then sent the colt along a big road gait on the highways and byways until an even stride was fixed in his head and heels. The next move was to take him to the track, where he was put through his paces by strong jogging and sharp brushes. Presently The Seer found he was a trotter and was anxious to show it. Then Mr. Biggs brought him out and gave him a record of 2:29 as a three-year-old on the half mile track at Lewiston, Me. Last season The Seer was put in shape by John F. Haynes of Biddeford, Me., and lowered his record to 2:22¾ on the mile track at Mystic Park. He is essentially a toe-weight trotter, and, strange to say, stands straighter on his fore legs when shod sufficiently heavy to make him go square, than if allowed to go bare-footed or with common shoes.

Some time ago the Licensed Victualler's Gazette gave the following reminiscences: Many a man has been ruined by a mistake; few, as in the following instances, have made lucky hits thereby. In 1856, Mr. J. M. Stanley deputed old Fred. Swindell, of Burton Brewery fame, to back Porta Rica for the Two Thousand Guineas. One day, while on the race course, Swindell received a telegram to back a certain number he would find in a little book on coming racing events, at that time published by Wright. Upon consulting this work he thought the instructions were intended to apply to Lord Stanley's colt Canezou, by Orlando, which was entered immediately after Mr. Stanley's horse, and he sent off at once to his commissioner Robinson, to put £500, at 25 and 30 to 1, on the former. After obeying instructions, it struck Robinson that there must be some mistake, as the colt had not been mentioned in the betting quotations and never yet run in public, so away he went to his principal. The error was now quickly observed, and the money considered as good as gone. Shortly afterwards, however, Lord Stanley's colt won a first-rate trial, and ultimately, under the name of Fazzoletto, the Two Thousand Guineas, when our friends had the satisfaction of pocketing several thousand pounds by a mistake. A very similar thing happened to the Marquis of Hastings. Mr. Edward Brayley had two horses in the Metropolitan Stakes, and, one day, while conversing upon the merits of the two competitors, his lordship, who was rather deaf, mixed up the names, and stood to win, on what was supposed to be the worse of the two £7,000. The horse carried off the stakes. But for the blunder the Marquis would have been a heavy loser.

A friend of mine, who is a greenhorn in the matter of horseflesh, was anxious to purchase a horse, but was afraid of being taken in, says The Pall Mall Gazette. He tried to persuade an acquaintance experienced in such matters to accompany him to inspect an animal on sale at a horsedealer's establishment. "There's no occasion," said the latter, for me to accompany you. All you have to do is to seem knowing. When you get to the place put your hands in your pockets and your stick under your arm, and in an off handed manner say: 'Groom, run him down. Now, then, pull him up and let him walk;' then in a knowing and doubtful tone: 'Open his mouth. What did you say his age was? I think he's a little long in the tooth. Seven years did you say he was? I should call him 10 or 11 years old. Oh, he's a very cobby little chap, but I think you're asking out of the way." My friend found the above an excellent formula.

St. Stephen's Review, the well known London paper, some weeks ago published the following questions and on March 15th says.

"Interesting and instructive answers keep coming to the following questions:

"1. What, in your experience, is the cost of breeding and rearing a yearling up to the July sales, or to the Doncaster ones?

"2. What is the best way to feed a foal and yearling so as to insure the fullest developments without undue fattening?

3. "What strains of blood on the sire's side are the surest to produce good results and command high prices; and from what blood would you select mares with a view to breeding winners?

"4. Do you advocate inbreeding; and, if so, to what extent, and to what strains—if you have any preference?

"5. Do you consider British blood stock better or worse than it used to be; and how, in your opinion, can it most readily be improved?

"6. What is the best old sire of the day: and which is the most promising young one, bar St. Simon?

Answers by John Porter, Kingsclere:

"1. £150; this amount will cover keep of yearling and mare, but not stallion fee or traveling expenses.

"2. Good old oats, beans, peas, with linseed mash and carrots occasionally, meadow hay and grass; and not less than four to six hours' paddock exercise daily.

"3. Hermit, Hampton, Galopin, St. Simon, Sterling and Isonomy: mares descended from Stockwell or Voltigeur to Hermit and Hampton; mares descended from Newminster and Macaroni to Galopin, St. Simon, Sterling and Isonomy.

"4. I do not object to moderate relationship. Stallion and mare removed from common ancestor four or five degrees would not be too much inbred, but I would go no nearer than that.

"5. Worse. We have fewer good stayers than formerly, with more roarers and unsound horses. You try to get your foal in January, February and March, the three coldest and worst months in the year, therefore you must house both mare and foal most of the time; if turned out you see the foal shivering by the side of its dam, it then sows the seed of roaring and many other diseases from which it never thoroughly recovers. Whereas if foaled in April or May, the mare gets natural food in the shape of Spring grass, which produces a better quality of milk than any artificial food you give her can produce. With this and warmth and sunshine the foal thrives, and in all probability goes right ahead without the many checks that early foals are subject to. I should therefore suggest that to improve the breed of thoroughbred horses you should be careful to select thoroughly sound mares and stallions of good running blood, have your foal if possible in April or May, run them later and less often at two years old, with more races of a mile and upwards for older horses.

"6. Ayrshire."

The most picturesqe man on the turf is old Burton the bookmaker. The New York World says: Long and loose-jointed, and lank of figure is old Burton. He has a quizzical look in his eyes, and a perfect flood of quaint words and queer expressions flows from him all day long. Everybody will be sorry to hear that the old man has lost a great deal of money during the past winter, and that he will be unable in, all probability, to make a book the coming season. The cause of Burton's misfortune may be traced to "contz" or "craps," a game with dice, which was played solely by the negroes in the South until the past winter, when an inexplicable craze seized the people of Louisville and Nashville, and men, women and children began playing "contz." The mania became so violent that the Legislature of Kentucky passed a bill a few months ago making "contz" playing a felony; but the law was not passed until hundreds of men had been ruined. Among those whose money was lost was old Burton. He is said to have lost $16,000 in one night at Nashville.

Burton's favorite method is to pick out a horse and plunge on him, and then when the race comes off run behind the grand stand, turn his back to the track and put his fingers in his ears. In this way he hears nothing and sees nothing. He thinks it is bad luck to watch a race. When he is making a book he lays extravagant odds against certain horses that he doesn't like, and his prejudices against horses are as bitter as men's hatred of their deadly enemies. When he happens to lose he will jump down from his box, and taking off his hat begin thumping his head.

"Burton, you ole fool," he cries in his broad Southern accent, "who tole you to bet on horses? Burton, you long-legged, pigeon-headed ole jay bird, what right you got to bet (banging his head vigorously meanwhile)? You ought to be drownded. Burton, you mis'able,good for nothing jack ass." All this in the midst of 10,000 people, to whom he pays not the slightest attention. After he has delivered his lecture to himself he gets back on his box and begins taking in bets.

Burton always walks with his hands behind him, talking enegetically to himself. This habit saved him $1,500 a year or so ago in New York. He was going down Broadway in his long, shambling way, swearing at himself vigorously. One of Inspector Byrne's men happened to be beside him.

"Burton, you ole fool, what you let them people rob you? Ain't you got no sense, Burton? About time you learned somethin'. Better go off and drown yourself, Burton, if you let yourself be robbed that way." The detective asked the old bookmaker what it was all about, and Burton told him very reluctantly how he had been "badgered" out of $1,500. The detective got the money back, although Burton was willing to let the badgers have it, as he wanted the matter hushed up. He was thought by the public to be a very rich man, as his books generally offered unusually liberal odds; but it is now said that Burton was only the representative of half a dozen others, and that he owned only a small share of his book. In spite of his whimsicalities and peculiarities he was a shrewd bookmaker, and every season found him a winner. Everyone likes the queer old fellow, and his misfortune will be universally regretted.

THE FARM.

Selection, Care and Management of the Breeding Bull.

Paper Read Before the Wisconsin Farmers' Convention at Madison, Feb. 5th, by John B. Kiser, Oregon.

In selecting a breeding bull obtain the very best animal that can be secured at a reasonable price. Do not call a price unreasonable if you are called upon to pay a little more for an excellent animal than the price of an "ornery" one. By all means secure a well bred animal. Let him be a true type of the breed whose name he bears. Let individual merit be the first point to be considered. Back this up with a strong, vigorous constitution and a well established lineage of meritorious animals. He should be uniform in quality, not strong in one point and weak in another, as his progeny is just as liable to inherit the weak points as the strong ones. With uniformity you can expect uniform results. The class of cows in a herd should to a certain extent govern the choice of bulls. If your cows are loose, rangy, over-grown animals, choose a bull of more compact build—an earlier maturing animal. If your cows are close built and undersized, choose a bull larger and more rangy. If your cows are of proper form and size, choose a bull of similar form and size. While early maturing, quick feeding cattle are desirable, I do not advocate the continuous mating of close built, compact animals, as observation and experience convince me that such a course will result in deterioration of size. As an old and reliable breeder once said to me, "It is an established fact that where such a course is pursued it is necessary to resort to a coarser and more growthy cross once in a while in order to retain size." * * *

While Short-horns stand to-day at the head of all breeds as beef animals yet they possess dairy strains to an extent with which no other beef breeds can begin to compare. These strains should be fostered and developed; therefore do not lose sight of the value of dairy strains in the breeding bull. * * * My model of a Short-horn bull would be one that weighs at maturity not less than 2,000 lbs. nor more than 2,300 lbs.; red or roan in color. His nose nut brown or copper colored; his eye clear and bright; his head well proportioned, broad and full between the eyes; his horns of medium length, strong and well set, curving in and down rather than upward; the neck in proportion to his body—not too long nor too short; it should be a little full midway between the horns and top of shoulder, and clean-cut and slightly arched from the throat to the breast. His front broad, deep, and full; his shoulders set smoothly on his body, his arm strong and well developed; his fore legs wide apart, yet set well under his body; straight, clean-cut, and fine from the knee to the hoof; from the top of his shoulder to the root of his tail straight and broad; well filled behind the shoulders and from point of hip to root of tail, and strong across the loins. His body good length and depth; his ribs well sprung and closely coupled to the hip; his lower line almost parallel with his upper line; his hind quarters broad and well developed, tied low down; his hind legs straight and strong. He should stand square on his feet. His tail set on a level with his back, small and tapering; his hide loose and mellow; his hair fine, thick and good length. Animals of pronounced dairy strains are usually of rougher build than those of a beef type. * * *

We should aim to keep the bull in good, healthy, thriving condition, not overfat. In order to do this he should be fed regularly and at proper intervals with good, substantial food, such as hay or grass or corn-fodder, with sufficient grain, such as corn, oats and bran, to keep him in proper condition. We have two bulls in service at present. One has reached maturity. His feed consists of all the timothy and clover mixed that he will eat, with three quarts of ground corn and oats and bran, equal parts, twice a day. The other is still growing and is fed the same as the first, except he is grained a little heavier, receiving five quarts twice a day. When kept in a good, cool box-stall in the summer time this is sufficient, but if kept in close hot quarters, or exposed to the sun in summer time he should be watered at least three times a day. He should be provided with proper shelter to protect him from summer's heat and winter's cold. A box-stall is best, as it gives him more freedom and is safer for an attendant, as he can feed and care for him without placing himself in such a position as to take chances of getting hurt. * * * His hind hoofs, when too closely confined in a stable, are apt to grow and become unshapely—not wearing off at all, but turning up in front and preventing the animal from walking squarely on his feet. When the hoof gets in this condition it should be shaped properly by means of saw, hammer and chisel. * * * He should have regular exercise. The best way to exercise an animal is to have a small lot or pasture in which he can be turned for exercise. * * *

Select the right kind of a bull to start with. Keep him in good, healthy, thriving condition. To accomplish this feed him well. Give him plenty of pure water, pure air and exercise. Provide him with good, clean, well-bedded quarters. Handle him kindly and quietly. Do not overtax his strength by excessive services. Then instead of being a nuisance and a disgrace he will be an object of admiration and a credit to his owner.—Breeders' Gazette.

The Feeding, Care and Management of Pigs.

After the sow has had her young she should be given food that she can easily digest. At first it is best to feed her lightly, and then gradually increase the amount of food she gets as the strain becomes greater on her. Sickness should be carefully guarded against both in the mother and her young, and the best protection against disease is pure air and sunshine. They should have a warm pen, with a yard attached. The young pigs should be taught to feed themselves as soon as possible. Their trough should be a shallow, flat-bottomed one, so arranged that the sow cannot get to it. The food of the young pigs should consist first of milk, then of middlings, oats or barley meal mixed with warm milk. They may be weaned gradually at the end of six or eight weeks, and a little oil-meal and also corn and pea meal may be added to their food. Their growth should now be pushed along as fast as possible, and they should be fed regularly, say about five times a day, but given only as much as they will eat up clean each time. A little salt may at times be added. Care should be taken that they are fed regularly as much as they will eat. Green corn pulled by the roots is a good form of green food for them, as is also green clover, and it is well to have a pasture, field or yard provided for the pigs to run it. They should not be fed on food too fattening in their nature, such as corn when growing, as a young pig will not grow well if too fat; but they should be given green food principally, as this will supply material for the building of bone and growing of muscle. To finish them off in the fall for the market, they should have corn, soaked peas, or pea-meal; the latter is said to make the meat solid. A very good mixture of food consists of barley, peas and oats chopped together. Some prefer cooked roots and pumpkins mixed with pea or barley meal to begin fattening on.

Prize essay in Canadian Farmer.

Light and Heavy Cows.

Some years ago, G. S. Smith made a carefully conducted experiment to see how light and heavy cows produced. He experimented on Holsteins and Ayrshires. He stated that the Holstein gave in a year over seven and three-fourths times her weight in milk, the Ayrshire gave eight and a half times her weight. He also compared the Holsteins with the natives, feeding them precisely alike, the natives being of average excellence. The Holstein gave about twelve pounds of milk more per day than the common cow and produced a pound of milk for one-fifth less feed consumed than the native cow did. Professor Rhode, of the Royal Agricultural Academy, in Eldena, Pomerania, in feeding, fattening and milching cows; also in making butter and cheese; and a precise account was kept with every cow, with results as follows:

1st. Four Tondern cows yielded on an average of 2,917 quarts per cow—highest yield 2,931 quarts; lowest, 2,525 qts. 2nd. Two Breitenburger cows yielded on an average 3,580 quarts—highest yield, 3,682 quarts; lowest, 3,525 quarts per cow. 3d. Ayrshire cow averaged 2 247 quarts per cow—highest, 2,811 quarts per cow—highest, 2,811 quarts; lowest, 1,769 quarts. 4th. Twenty-two Holstein cows yielded on an average 4,437 quarts per cow; highest, 5,677 quarts; lowest, 3,157 quarts.

These cows were fed during the winter ten pounds of cut straw, two and a half pounds of wheat and oat chaff, twenty-five pounds of turnips, ten pounds of hay, eight pounds refuse from the brewery, three pounds of rye bran, containing, said the chemist, three and 28 100ths pounds nitrogenous matter, and fourteen and 30-100ths of non-nitrogenous compounds, equivalent to forty-two and 90-100ths pounds of good hay. During the summer they were fed green clover and clover and vetches three times a day, each ration containing eight pounds of hay, equivalent in nutritive value to five and 70-100ths pounds of nitrogenous, and fourteen and 91-100ths pounds of non-nitrogenous compounds, equivalent to forty-five pounds of hay.

Professor Rhode was asked if the Holstein cows, severally, did eat much more feed than the smaller Tondern cows, and he said there were nine Holstein cows on the right, and ten of the smaller breed on the left. The same weight of feed is put into every trough or manger, and that before the smaller cows' feed is first consumed, the proportions being as nine to ten, i. e., the smaller breed consumed forty-five pounds per cow, and the larger fifty pounds. If desirable to know whether it requires more feed to make a quart of milk in the Holstein cows than in the other breeds, all the elements for the computation being at hand, show the following results:

1st. The Holstein eats five pounds of hay for every quart of milk produced.

2d. The Brettenburger eats six and one-quarter pounds of hay for a quart of milk.

3d. The Tondern seven pounds of hay for a quart of milk.

4th. The Ayrshire nine pounds of hay for a quart of milk.

Baron Oekel, in Frankfield experimented with Ayrshires and Holsteins with the following results: The average weight of the Ayrshires was 806 pounds, and of the Holsteins 1,016. The experiments showed that the Ayrshires eat three and three-tenths pounds of hay for every 100 pounds of live weight, while the Holsteins consume two and eight-tenths. Of the amount of feed consumed, one-sixtieth of their live weight only was required to keep the Holsteins in their normal condition, while it required one-fiftieth of the live weight to keep the Ayrshires in their normal condition. He then took four Holstein cows, the two heaviest of which weighed 2,112 pounds on June 14th, and the lighter two weighed 1,537 pounds. He put them in two groups, the heavier in one and the lighter in the other, and continued the experiment for sixteen days, the feed being weighed as fed to each group, and if not all eaten, what was left was weighed and deducted from which it formed a part—their live weights remaining unchanged during the time, with the following result:

	Lucern eaten by Cows. Pounds.	Milk yielded by Cows. Quarts.	Milk per 100 lbs of live weight. Pounds.
Heavy cows,	4,921	340	14.6
Light cows,	3,859	240	160.

This experiment shows that the heavier cows of the same breed, with the same treatment, consume, relatively, less feed than the lighter, and at the same time yield a greater relative return of milk from it.

Baron Weckerlin, for many years the leading "cattle man" in the Hohenheim Agricultural University, after having made many experiments with a great variety of breeds of cattle, came to the conclusion that a cow weighing 700 lbs. requires one-sixtieth of her live weight in hay equivalents to maintain her normal weight, and yield from four to five times her weight in milk, according to the breed or race, quantity, quality and manner in feeding.

In 1852 a series of experiments were made at eleven different localities in the kingdom of Saxony, by order of the Royal Agricultural Society, during a period of five years, the cows selected being some of the best "Scrubs," Allgauers, Oldenburgers and Holsteins, the latter two being only the same breeds, as reported, the only difference being traceable to different care and different localities. The results per annum for five years were reported as follows:—

With common feed and common care:—

The scrub cows averaged	1,437	quarts per annum
The Allgauers "	2,334	" " "
The Oldenburgers "	2,290	" " "
The Holsteins "	2,062	" " "

With the best feed and good care:—

The scrub cows averaged	2,3?6	quarts per annum
The Allgauers "	3,000	" " "
The Oldenburgers "	3,712	" " "
The Holsteins "	2,2?2	" " "

Our dairy of Holsteins, of 190 cows, averaged 4,076 quarts a cow her annum.

In regard to the size of cows, Professor Caspari made eighteen experiments in feeding milch cows with a view of ascertaining how many pounds of hay, or its equivalent, it required to make one hundred pounds of milk. He found that in Prussia one hundred pounds of hay fed to Holstein cows made twenty-five and one-half quarts of milk; and the same in the Allgauers made thirty and ninety-eight one-hundredths quarts of milk. At eleven dairies in Saxony, the value of one hundred pounds of hay produced in

Oldenburgers	25.40	quarts
Holsteins	26 10	"
Allgauers	30.06	"
Scrubs	28.65	"

Villeroy's experiments resulted as follows:—

Holsteins	28.92	quarts per 100 pounds hay
Yorkshires	27.45	" " " " "
Devons	19.13	" " " " "
Herefords	15.97	" " " " "
Jerseys	26.39	" " " " "
Allgauers	27.61	" " " " "

What Good Cattle Should Dress.

Some one desiring to know what weight good beef cattle should dress, The National Stockman and Farmer said: There is much variation in this, just as there is in the amount of butter a good cow is expected to furnish. Sixty pounds to the hundred weight is a very good outcome, and good cattle may go a pound or two less. Strictly choice beeves, though, should exceed sixty per cent., rather than go below it. There are many cases where this yield is increased several pounds to the hundred weight and in the Chicago Fat Stock Shows figures ranging from sixty seven to seventy pounds have been secured. In his late testimony before the Senate Committee, Armour stated that the average dressed weight of his beef was about 54½ per cent. of gross weight. Good feeders should of course do better than this average of cattle of so many kinds and grades.

Live Stock Numbers and Values.

The recently issued report of the Statistician of the Department of Agriculture, on "the Numbers and Values of Farm Animals," is full of suggestion and food for comment. A few of the salient points which will strike the reader on a first perusal of it may be epitomized just here advantage.

There are more horses in this country now than ever before, the present number being 14,213,837, an increase of 550,543 over last year. The current valuation is $68 84 per head, against $71.89 last year $71.82 two years ago, and an average of $72·58 for the past six years. As the report remarks, "this indicates a full supply," and mildly points to a possible tendency to over-production and lower prices, furnishing a point which horsmen will do well to study.

The number of milch cows shows a gain of 654,258 head, the total now being 15,952,883 head, worth $22 14 per head —$1.80 less than last year. The price now reached is the lowest in ten years. Other cattle number 36,849,024 head, an increase of 1,816,607. The decline in prices is even greater than in cows, the figure being $15.21, against $17.05 a year ago. Notwithstanding the growth in numbers there is an aggregate decrease in value of a little over five per cent. No other commentary is needed on the worse cattle year the country has ever known.

Sheep show an increase in numbers for the first time since 1884—1,736,993 of a gain—making the present total 44,336,072 head. This increase in number is accompanied, too, by an increase of over 6½ per cent in per capita value, or a change from $2 13 to $2.27 per head. Sheep are higher now than in any year since 1884, the average value for the five intervening years being about $2.05 per head. Considering the adverse conditions affecting the wool market the sheep industry has done at least as well as could have been expected, and it shows at the present time an excellent tone.

The country has 1,301,188 more swine than a year ago, the present aggregate being 51,602 780 head. Hogs show a sharp decline in value, the current $4.72 per head being $1.07 lower than a year ago. Notwithstanding this decline there is nothing especially discouraging in the outlook for swine. The average value for ten years has been $5 22, and it has been an unusually good ten years in swine prices.

Taking the live stock of the country in the aggregate we find nothing except mules and sheep which have increased in total value within the last year. All kinds of stock taken into the count, the valuation is placed at $2,418,766,028—a fall-off of 3½ per cent. from the valuation of January, 1889. Estimating the population of the United States at 65,000,000, and 44 per cent. of this as rural, there would be an average of about $8.45 worth of live stock for each individual living on a farm. It is not often that the per capita distribution of live stock would show as low a figure, and we question whether it will again for a number of years.—National Stockman and Farmer.

Thoroughbred Sires.

Mr. George Paris of North Dakota writes to Hoard's Dairyman an argument in favor of breeding to full-blooded sires that may give some new ideas to many farmers. Mr. Paris' theory is that during pregnancy the female of any animal is to a greater or less extent affected by the intermixing of her own blood with that of the fœtus, and that thus the characteristics of the male are impressed in part upon the dam. By breeding some native cows to a Jersey bull, he believes he has increased the milk and butter-producing capacity, not merely of the offspring, but of the cows themselves. Some of these are aged cows past their prime, but on the usual feed they are giving one-quarter more milk than before they were bred to pure sires. The natural corollary to this idea we believe to be also true, that is, the cows bred to bulls of inferior milk and butter strains are deteriorated in quality. It is not, therefore, a matter of no importance what bull is bred to if the calf is not to be raised. The milking capacity of a herd of cows may thus be unconsciously deteriorated without any suspicion by the owner of the cause. It is said in localities where mules are raised that a mare which has once borne a mule will ever thereafter be liable to impress some characteristic of the mule on her colts, though she is afterwards bred to a finely formed stallion.

Canning Milk.

One of the new ideas about the milk supply is the canning of sterilized milk. The milk is first brought to the boiling point, to destroy all the bacteria and other microbes, then put into cans and sealed while at the boiling temperature. Of course it must be nicely done, and the cans made perfectly air-tight, as is the case with condensed milk. A correspondent of the New York Tribune says that he put up milk in this way for family use, while milk was plenty, that he might have a supply on hand when milk was scarce. He was using out of cans "put up some weeks ago," and the ladies said it was "just lovely," while the correspondent says it is so nice that he wonders it was not long since brought into general use, as it is much more desirable than condensed milk, having a more natural flavor. For infants, it is much better, more fresh-like, than condensed milk, and must certainly be preferable to the watered and doctored stuff generally peddled in cities.

ATHLETICS.

Athletic Sports and Other Pastimes.

EDITED BY ARYSIPPUS,

SUMMARY.

Several prominent young athletes have recently set up in business for themselves. Ed A. Kolb who is to wrestle A. H. Lean in the O C, is the head of the firm of Kolb & Denhard. at 422 Montgomery street, and Mr. Ike Deutch has recently established an elegant business house at No. 8 Eddy street. We offer congratulations and wishes for great prosperity.

The out door men have settled down to strict training for the coming athletic meetings and the new track of the Olympic Club is being well held down by the club's runners and walkers. The wheelmen and oarsmen are also making extra preparations for the opening of the season, and the swimmers and anglers will be ready in a couple of weeks to begin work for 1890. Taking everything into consideration a busy season in all kinds of sports may be anticipated.

RUNNERS, WALKERS, JUMPERS, ETC.

A crowd of the Olympic and Alpine athletes enjoyed the moonlight nights of the past week. The former at their own grounds, the latter at the Bay District track.

Coffin, Cooley, McArthur, Jarvis, Espinosa, O'Kane, Henderson, Winslow, Cassidy, Williams, McDonald and Scott of the Olympic team, have made up their minds to train faithfully for Decoration Day and with such a good representation the O C should stand an excellent chance of walking off with the pennant.

It is now almost a certainty that J. Barr Buchanan, the champion all round athlete, will not be in the city when the championships will be decided. Were it possible for Mr. Buchanan to remain here and represent the O C, the other clubs would stand but a small chance of coming out ahead.

Garrison, Gafney, Goodman, Eldridge, Larkey, Little, Luttringer, Jefferey, Cooke, Holland and Armbruster, of the Alpine Club, began training at the Bay District track on Monday last. They take exercise every evening in the moonlight.

McGee is undecided whether to run or not in the "quarter" on May 30th. His friends are trying to force him to commence training.

Some individual without authority recently stated through the sporting columns of one of the daily papers that Rankin, of the Alpine Amateur Athletic Club, was willing to run any amateur in America five miles. Frank L Cooley, of the Olympic Club, called at this office the day after the challenge was issued and informed us that he would run Mr. Rankin for a valuable medal. It now appears that Rankin is a well known professional runner, he having on several occasions competed against professional runners for money prizes. The Directors of the Alpine Club are highly incensed over the matter and have asked us to state that Mr. Rankin is not and never was a member of this club. The supposition is that some scheming person had the challenge put in with the intention of making a little stake.

Capt. George W. Jordan, of the Olympic Club, has been elected official handicapper of the P. C. A. A. A. He will handicap the games of the different associate clubs in future. The open events in the Alpine games will form his initial task.

The Alpine Club has secured the Bay District track for Sunday, May 4th, and will hold their next out-door games there on that date. The track will be put in splendid condition, so that the athletes will have a chance to make fast time.

The coast records for three miles running and for two and three miles walking are very poor, and there is no doubt but that these records will be improved on May 4th. The three-mile run will be a very exciting contest between H. C. Cassidy and F. L. Cooley, as both men are evenly matched. Jarvis, Coffin and Gafney will possibly compete in the three-mile walk on the same day, and a fine race may be expected. Jarvis should certainly knock a couple of minutes off the two and three-mile records.

To-morrow afternoon there will be a series of professional handicap sprint races at the Central Park grounds, corner 8th and Market streets. Some of the fastest men in America will compete. The sum of $160 will be given for prizes. During the coming season it is the intention of the managers of the park to hold a series of long and short distance races there, when several thousand dollars will be paid out as prize money.

The athletic editor of a local weekly sporting paper, last week asserted that Charles Little, of the Alpine Club, was no other than the well-known Boston professional runner of the same name. Mr. Little desires us to contradict this statement, and informs us that his home is in Grand Junction, Colorado. Mr. Little has been successful in several amateur races, and has made very fast time, and he feels much put out to think that he is accused of being a professional. He will represent the Alpine Club in the quarter and half-mile races at the championship games on Decoration Day, and if the directors of the club had the least idea that Mr. Little was anything but a *bona fide* amateur, his name would at once be stricken off the membership roll, for the club does not admit professional athletes into its ranks.

We are in receipt of a communication from Frank C. Philips of Healdsburg, in which he informs us that he and several other amateurs of that town, are about to organize a new athletic club. Mr. Philips says that the people of Healdsburg take a very great interest in athletic sports, and that the proposed club will no doubt be a success. The club will apply for admission into the P. C. A. A. A.

The following schedule of games has been arranged for the amateur baseball championship of the Pacific Coast. All but the first game are to be played at the new grounds, which are situated at Emery station, on the Berkeley line. The first game will take place this afternoon between the U. C. and the E. and O. E. teams on the campus at Berkeley. All games will be called at 3:15 P. M. sharp, except the game which is scheduled for May 30th, which is to be called at 2 P M. The Olympic Club team has dropped out, and has been replaced by the Anglo-Nevada Assurance Corporation team. All communications should be addressed either to the president of the league, W. H. Chickering, or to the secretary, Richard Belcher. The schedule is as follows:

April 19th—E. and O. E. vs. A. N. A. C.
April 26th—Reliance vs. O. and E. O.
May 3d—U. C. vs. A. N. A. C.
May 10th—U C. vs. Reliance.
May 17th—U. C. vs. E. and O. E.
May 24th—U. C. vs. A. N. A. C.
May 30th—Reliance vs. E. and O. E.
May 31st—U. C. vs. Reliance.
June 7th—E. and O. E. vs A. N. A. C.
June 14th—Reliance vs. A. N. A. C.

With careful practice the U. C. team should carry off the pennant.

The U. C. tennis courts are constantly filled with those who are training for the class doubles which occur next Wednesday. Twenty-five lockers are to be built for the members in the dressing room by the cinder track.

President Davis of the U. C. has offered $100 for a trophy for the winners of the relay races on field days. Messrs. Lakeman, Stoney and Townsend of '90 and Ainsworth and Allen of '91 will form a committee to select the design. The trophy is to be given first to the team that won last field day.

The first "Ladies' Night" exhibition of the Alpine Amateur Athletic Club will be held at the club rooms, 706 Powell street, on Tuesday evening next, April 8th, commencing at 8 o'clock. The following is the programme for the occasion:

1. Horizontal bar—Prof. G. C. Rouse (Club Instructor), E. Barr, Russ and Eckbardt.
2. Boxing—W. F. Kennedy and W. H. Dooley, Hall Turnbull and Len Hueston.
3. Fencing (foils)—Professor Henry Ansot and Ashton R. Fry (pupil).
4. Club swinging—Prof. G. C. Rouse.
5. Swinging rings—E. Barr and W. Henry.
6. Boxing—M. Gallagher and Partner, Otto Luhn and J. Hore.
7. Distribution of prizes won at the late Field Day.
8. Feats of strength—J. Barr Buchanan, champion amateur all round athlete of the world.
9. Fencing (broad swords)—Professor Henry Ansot and Ashton R. Fry (pupil).
10. Parallel bars—Prof. G. C. Rouse, E. Barr and Will Henry.
11. Club swinging—Frank Hart, champion club swinger of the Pacific Coast.
13. Boxing—Prof. W. Smith (pupil of Eddy Graney) and W. Cook (Prof. Smith's pupil), Frank L. Cooley and J. L Lafferty.

Flinging the 56lb. weight and the individual tug of war have been dropped from the P C A A A programme for May 30th. The individual tug of war is never a very interesting event and was properly dropped. The team tug of war, in which four men of unlimited weight will be allowed to compete on each side, will prove exciting. This is a good chance for the different clubs to put forward their big men.

THE WHEELMEN

The members of the San Francisco Bicycle Club do not appear to be taking a very active interest in racing matters just now. The Bay City Wheelmen, as usual, are in the van, and they are doing their best to arouse the other clubs to action.

The Oakland Bicycle Club is making rapid strides. Several prominent wheelmen from across the Bay intend joining this young organization in the near future. Captain Drake is very busy at present mapping out a list of runs to come off during the summer months.

G. P. Wetmore and several other members of the B C W recently made a successful run to Livermore and return. They report the roads in fair condition.

The B. C. W. are on the lookout for a suitable lot upon which to build a club house. The club is now in a flourishing condition having a membership of over one hundred, and the members are of the opinion that the club should own its own club house.

The following card has been addressed to the members of the California Division, League of American Wheelmen:—

San Francisco, March 25th. 1890.

The annual business meeting of the California Division, League of American Wheelmen, will be held in Sachem Hall, Red Men's Building, 320 Post Street, on the evening of Saturday, April 19th, 1890.

This meeting will consider the reports of officers and select the date and place for holding the annual meet of the Division.

Any member may be represented by proxy, but no member shall vote more than ten.
Walter D. Sheldon,
Secretary and Treasurer.

At odd intervals during the past few years there has been mention made of the formation of a separate and distinct association of Pacific Coast wheelmen—separate from the L. A W., of which the Pacific Coast now forms a division. This project was at one time taken up somewhat enthusiastically by several prominent riders of this city on account of the unfair manner in which the League treated this division. The agitation, which they promised to bring forth good fruits, was, however, allowed to die. But latterly the respect for the L. A. W. has been gradually declining on this Coast on account of the neglect with which the National officers have treated the Pacific Division, and there is quite a strong though quiet feeling in favor of the formation of a distinct wheeling association.

Captain F. J. H. Manning of the San Franciscos is planning an active system of runs. While the roads are as yet impassable in the country, owing to the mud, the very first date that they are fit to be travelled over a short run will be called to Haywards or some near point. The first big run of the season will take place, if the roads are in condition, about April 5th, to Mount Hamilton, when the moon will be full. The trip will be so arranged as to permit those taking it to arrive at the summit of Mount Hamilton in time to have a look through the great *Lick* telescope.

Another two day's run on which a number of men have promised to go is through Napa and Sonoma Counties. Captain Manning was over the roads last year, and pronounces the journey one of the most delightful that can be taken awheel.

Still another will be called through the Santa Cruz Mountains. The start will be made early some Saturday after noon and San Jose reached by dinner time. After dinner the party will go to Los Gatos, remaining there all night, and make an early start for Santa Cruz on the next morning. The return will be made on the evening train to this city.

Bolinas and Pescadero are objective points for prospective runs. Both are splendid trips, though requiring good staying powers in those taking them. Besides all these, there will be moonlight runs to San Jose, Sunday morning's jaunts to the Cliff House for breakfast, and other enjoyable excursions to near by points.

AT THE OARS.

The Pacific Rowing Association will meet on Monday evening at 706 Powell Street.

The season will open on Sunday April 20 with the High Jinks of the Lurline Club.

The amateur crew will commence their coaching and training to-morrow.

Champion Henry Peterson has been the victor in a series of eight contests during the past week at the "Henley Regatta."

We are awaiting returns from the party having the management of the Victoria B. C. Regatta to be held on the Queen's Birthday.

CLUB JOTTINGS.

The next cross country run of the Alpine Athletic Club will take place from Dexter Cottage, Sausalito, on Sunday, April 13th.

The Alameda Olympic Club will give a party at its club rooms on Lincoln Avenue, on the 18th of April.

The Olympic Club will give one of its enjoyable "Ladies Night" exhibitions at the end of the present month.

A general meeting of the Alpine Athletic Club was held on Thursday evening. Final preparations were made for the coming "Ladies Night." Several new members were elected and E. P. Moody was elected a delegate to the P C A A A, vice M. C. Giry, resigned. It was decided to engage Prof. G. C. Rouse as gymnastic instructor to the club. His class nights will be Monday, Wednesday and Friday of each week.

A meeting of the P C A A A was held at the Olympic Club rooms on Friday evening, March 24th. J. J. McKinnon applied for reinstatement as an amateur. The case was put off until the next meeting, which was held last evening. Captain G. W. Jordan was appointed Official Handicapper. Several new rules connected with the A A U were adopted.

IN THE SURF.

In a couple of weeks the season will have fairly opened, although for some time past many persons have been indulging in daily dips in the open sea.

The Lurline boys will do much towards booming this past time during the summer months. The club will offer many valuable prizes for competition.

The Alpine Club will also hold races at its Harbor View Grounds.

The Terrace Swimming Club has disbanded and will be reorganized under the name of the Pacific Swimming Club. The membership will be limited probably to fifteen and only first class swimmers will be admitted to membership.

JOTTINGS FROM ALL OVER.

Jake Gaudaur is willing to row Hanlan any time before July 1st for any amount up to $5,000.

The following records of the present holders of the various lawn tennis championships will be of interest to all tennis players:—

England—Champion, W. Renshaw; lady champion, Mrs. Hillyard; double champions, E. Renshaw and W. Renshaw; ladies' doubles champions, Miss M. Steedman and Miss B. Steedman; ladies' and gentlemens' doubles champions, Miss L. Dodd and J. C. Kay; covered court champion E. W. Lewis.

Ireland—Champion, W. J. Hamilton; lady champion Miss Martin; doubles champions, E. W. Lewis and G. W. Hillyard; ladies' doubles champions, Miss Martin and Miss Stanuell; ladies' and gentlemen's doubles champions, Miss Rice and W. J. Hamilton.

America—Champion, H. W. Slocum. Jr., lady champion, Miss Bertha Townsend; doubles champions, H. W. Slocum, Jr., and H. A. Taylor; ladies' doubles champions, Miss. B. L. Townsend and Miss M. L. Ballard.

Australia—Champion, A. G. Colquhoun; doubles champions, C. W. Cropper and D. Webb.

Canada—C. S. Hyman.

Southern India—Champion, H. Grove.

Wales—Champion, W. J. Hamilton; lady champion, Miss Pope.

The Board of Managers of the Amateur Athletic Union held a meeting on Sunday evening, March 15th, at the Astor House, New York City. The application for reinstatement to the amateur ranks of A. E. Mansfield of Worcester, Mass.; of McNolan Watteawau of N. J., and Fremont Swain, of New York City, were rejected, and that of Charles F. Huck of the Syracuse Athletic Club was granted. The following clubs were elected to membership: Yonkers Athletic Club, St. George A C., Sixty-ninth Regiment A. C., and New Haven A. C It was decided that the next championship field meeting should be held at Washington, D. C., and that the Union should pay the expenses of the baseball teams of the East and West in travelling to play the games necessary to decide the amateur championship of 1890.

The proposed international match between Thomas Pettitt, professional court tennis champion of the world, and Charles Saunders, the English expert, who seeks to wrest from the Bostonian the laurels he has won, may now be considered as good as made. Pettitt has forwarded a draft for $250 to the editor of the London Sportsman, to bind the match, and has engaged passage on the Cunarder Umbria, which leaves New York on April 12th. He will be accompanied by Fisk Warren, of the Boston Athletic Club, members of which organization are finding the $2,500 constituting Pettitt's share of the stake to be contended for. The Britisher seems thoroughly in earnest in his desire for a meeting with the champion, and it is unlikely that he will hereafter interpose any obstacle to the ratification of articles to the match, which will create great interest among players of the game on both sides of the Atlantic.

The following is a list of the men who finished first in the great handicap cross-country run which took place at New York City, March 15th:

W. D. Day, N J A C, scratch, 53m 34s; F. Kuhlke, P H, 6m 30s—60m 30s; C. B. Gardiner, N J A C, 6m 45s—61m 12s Sidney Thomas, M A C, 30s—55m 47 2-5s; Edward Edwards, Acorn A C, 4m 15s—59m 47s; E. Hjertsberg, N J A C, 1m 45s—57m 40 4-5s; F. Dolan, P H, 1m 40s—57m 47 2-5s; S. T. Freeth, P H, 1m 15s—57m 36s; J. Rumpf, N J A C, 4m 45s—61m 14s; W S French, N J A C, 5m—62m 4s; A. S. McGregor, P H, 3m 40s—60m 45s; M. E. Healey, Acorn A C, 5m—62m 15s; J. Reid, American A C, 3m 30s—60m 57s; T. F. Conboy, W S A C, 5m 30s—63m 1s; J. D. Lloyd, P H, 50s—58m 24s; W. J. Rogers, Acorn A C, 5m—62m 38s; J. McCreery, St. G A C, 4m 30s—62m 23s; W. F. Lee, P A C, 5m 30s;—63m 7s; A. D. Tompkins, R A C, 5m 30s—63m 53s; H. Gray, N J A C, 2m 45s—61m 11s; J. Nolan, Acorn A C, 4m 25s—62m 58s; M. P Bailey, P H, 6m 30s—65m 10s; G. W. Conklin, P H, 5m 20s—64m 11s; Mike Bent, U A C 4m 50s 63m 47s.

Day won the first prize, an elegant solid silver bowl, together with the magnificent cup offered by The New York Herald to the runner making the best time, and there were nine other handsome and costly individual prizes. The valuable silver cup presented by the New York Jockey Club as a team prize was taken by the New Jersey Athletic Club, the first six representing that organization finishing as follows: Day, 1; Gardner, 3; E. Hjertsberg, 6; J. Rumpf, 9; M. S. French, 10; H. Gray, 19. Total, 48 points. The Prospect Harriers were second, with 64 points.

THE GUN.

The Gun Club.

The first meeting of the Gun Club was held at San Bruno on March 1st, at which time the scores were:—

At 12 birds, A. S. A. Rules.

Swett	8
W. J. Golcher	5
Jellett	12
Orr	8
W. Leviston	8
Butler	9
Black	11
G. Leviston	9
"Edwards'	6
Stone	8
Chapin	8

The second meeting was on Saturday afternoon last at Mr. Hinchman's elegant grounds, the Oakland Trotting Park. The day was good, and the birds more than usually so. The scores, however, were much below Gun Club form. Mr. J. H. Jellett shot superbly, using his second barrel but twice for a clean score. Messrs. Stone, Orr and Woodward came in for nine each of the ten shot at.

A feature of the day was Mr. Ed. Donahoe's shooting with a 6½lb. gun. It seemed quite as effective as the heavier weights.

Mr. J. M. Kilgarif did some "in and out" work. Several of his first barrel kills were perfectly made, but a fault of his work was that he was too anxious to get in the second barrel. Mr. Will Golcher, shooting a superb new ejecting Clabrough hammerless, lost a bird dead outside.

Messrs. Fred Webster and J D. Redding were outclassed by their chaffing competitor, Mr. Harvey, who made seven neat kills against six scored by the others.

Mr. "Frederick" under which name Mr. Fred L. Wooster will shoot hereafter, had the same sort of luck which followed him on Friday, losing several hard hit birds dead out of bounds.

The scores were:

At 10 birds. A. S. A. rules.

Name	Yds.											Total
Jellett	30	1	1	1	1	1	2	1	1	2	1	10
Chapin	28	2	0	0	1	1	1	1	0	1	2	7
Butler	28	1	1	0	1	1	1	1	0	0	1	7
Harvey	30	0	2	0	0	2	1	2	1	1	1	7
Redding	28	0	1	1	1	2	0	0	1	2	0	6
Alex. Hamilton	28	1	0	0	0	0	0	0	0	2	0	2
G. Leviston	30	1	2	2	1	2	1	2	1	0	0	8
Ed Donahoe	28	1	1	0	0	0	2	0	2	1	1	6
Black	30	0	1	1	1	1	1	0	1	1	2	8
F. K. Webster	28	0	0	1	2	2	0	0	1	1	1	6
W. Leviston	26	1	1	0	1	0	1	0	1	0	0	5
Riordan	26	0	0	1	0	0	0	0	0	w	d	1
Swett	30	2	0	2	0	1	1	1	0	0	0	5
Stone	28	1	2	1	1	2	1	2	1	2	0	9
Sanborn	28	1	0	1	2	1	1	0	1	1	1	8
Golcher	28	1	0	1	1	1	2	1	0	2	1	8
Kilgarif	30	1	2	0	0	0	1	1	0	0	1	5
"Edwards"	30	0	0	2	1	2	0	1	0	0	0	4
"Frederick"	30	0	1	2	1	0	0	1	1	1	0	6
Orr	30	0	1	1	2	1	1	1	1	1	1	9
Woodward	30	2	1	0	1	2	1	2	1	1	1	9

Distributing Brown Quails.

EDITOR BREEDER AND SPORTSMAN:—I have just returned from a little duck shoot and find your letter asking for a description of the ground on which I turned out the brown quails sent by the Board of Fish Commissioners.

I met the birds at the depot, fed and watered them, and forwarded them by the same train to Hon. Richard Gird's ranch, which is located just over the line between this and San Bernardino counties.

I had previously arranged with Mr. Gird for their care, and he turned them out in pairs placing from 8 to 12 in a place in the most favorable parts of the ranch. Mr. Girds domain consists of about 44,000 acres all fenced. A large portion of it is low meadow land with an abundance of water, besides this a large part of it is cultivated to grain, alfalfa, vines and fruit trees. There is also considerable upland, covered with low brush, affording the best of cover. In fact it is the very ideal country for the propagation of either quail or prairie chickens. I know of no ground in the state so well adapted to these varieties of game. Besides these qualifications of country Mr. Gird is par excellence the man to care for them. He allows no shooting of any kind on his vast premises. He is an enthusiastic game protectionist and a great admirer of the feathered tribe. He is a man of large heart and generous impulses, always feeling well repaid for the small modicum of fruits and grain that his feathered friends destroy, by the pleasure he experiences in knowing that he is adding to their enjoyment and preventing their ruthless destruction.

My object in placing all the birds on this one ranch is that their protection will be perfect, and that the place is so well adapted to their wants. It will therefore always be a preserve for their breeding, from which in future years when their number has increased, they can be trapped and distributed over other parts of this or other sections of the State.

I am sorry that the Commissioners did not succeed in getting Eastern quail and chickens for this season, as this same ranch would afford an excellent place for them.

[Eastern birds have been contracted for and will soon be here.—ED]

I shall try and make arrangements with the owners of Catalina Island for its use for the propagation of wild turkeys. They could be reared there in large numbers and then distributed on the main land.

Let us here whisper in your ear that the BREEDER AND SPORTSMAN is just a little slow in not prodding up our Honorable Fish Commissioners to more active work in procuring game for the State. The truth is they have let more than a whole year go by and might have accomplished more. I know that they think that I kick too much, but the only way to make a success of anything is to take hold of it and do it at once.

How are the dog men feeling about our coming show? Are they going to come down in force and give us a boom? We want to make the Los Angeles show a fixture and I believe that we can do it if we follow the course that we have adopted and keep within lines on the question of expenses.

H. T. PAYNE.

J. N. Bailhache reports the brown quails recently liberated on his place south of Healdsburgh as doing well. They were liberated near the spring back of his residence instead of Litton Springs. The Commissioners and Mr. Bailhache join in requesting that the birds be not disturbed and especially that parties will not thoughtlessly or carelessly shoot them.

From Chico.

EDITOR BREEDER AND SPORTSMAN:—I don't know enough of sporting news to fill a postal card from our town as Chico is not possessed of one thoroughbred sportsman. It has rained entirely too much for the farmers in the Sacramento Valley this year, (over 48 inches already and still raining) so times are dull and consequently no sport of any kind.

Game was scarce the past season except in the foot hills where it was driven down by the snow in the mountains.

There is a talk of having a pigeon shooting match in Chico this spring but I suppose it will be nothing but a local match.

I would have liked very much to have been with you when those Eastern sportsmen visited your city as I like to see good shooting, and they must have been world-beaters indeed.

CHICO.

CHICO, March 28th.

The Country Club.

The Pacific-Union Club, beside being the moving spirit in all prominent social events, is also an institution thoroughly en rapport with aquatics, athletics and field sports of all other legitimate sorts. Those members of the club who fancy trap shooting, recently organized what is styled the Country Club. The club meets once or twice in each week at the Oakland Trotting Park, and shoots a few pigeons, in a friendly way. It does not especially care for a large attendance of spectators, and is in other respects quite exclusive, but its meetings are most delightful, because of the abandon of the men, and the constant cross-fire of chaff. The shooting done is usually good, and some of the members are quite the equals of the best experts in the other shooting clubs of the city. The revised rules of the American Shooting Association are followed with the utmost strictness.

On Friday afternoon of last week an informal meeting was held, sides being chosen and a match shot for the evening's dinner. The best work of the day was done by Mr. W. B. Tubbs, whose twenty-one out of twenty-four hard birds were grassed in neat style, the second barrel being used but little. Mr. R. B. Woodward made the only clean score. Mr. Ramon E. Wilson, Mr. A. C. Tubbs and Mr. Worden ran up seven out of eight.

Mr. A. S. Tubbs was the eleventh man, and was chosen by one team, and four birds allowed the other team, for him, in each match.

Hon. J. Downey Harvey, in intervals between jokes, did some handsome shooting, and the same remark is applicable to Mr. J. D. Redding, although the work of the latter was uneven. Some of his kills indicated unusual ability, and some of the birds which escaped him suggested carelessness, Mr. John M. Adams shot in bad luck, as did Mr. "Fredericks," both losing many birds dead out of bounds. Mr. Fred Webster was very handy with his gun, but got some birds too strong for anyone to stop.

Mr. A. S. Tubbs, the new man at the game, did some of the best work, particularly with the second barrel. The scores were:—

TEAM NO. 1.

At 24 birds, A. S. A. Rules:—

"Frederick"	0 1 1 1 0 1 1 0 1 0 1 1 1 1 0 1 0 1 0 0 0 1 0 0	13
Wilson	1 1 1 1 0 1 1 1 1 1 0 1 1 1 0 0 1 0 1 1 1 1 1 0	18
A. E. Tubbs	1 0 0 1 1 1 1 1 1 0 1 0 1 1 1 1 1 1 0 1 1 1 1 0 1	18
J. B. Redding	0 0 0 1 1 1 1 0 1 1 0 1 1 1 0 0 1 0 1 1 1 1 1 1	16
W. B. Tubbs	0 1 1 1 1 1 1 1 1 1 1 0 1 1 1 0 1 1 0 0 1 1 1 1 1	18
A. S. Tubbs	1 1 1 0 0 0 0	4
Total		88
R. Woodward	1 1 1 0 0 1 0 1 1 1 1 1 1 1 1 1 1 0 0 1 1 1 1 1 0	18
J. D. Redding	1 0 0 1 1 1 1 1 1 1 0 1 1 1 1 1 1 0 0 1 1 1 0 1 1 0	17
Fred Webster	0 1 1 1 1 1 1 1 0 1 1 0 6 0 0 1 1 1 1 1 1 1 1 1 1 0	17
Worden	1 1 1 1 0 1 1 1 1 1 1 1 0 0 1 1 0 1 0 1 1 0 0 1 0	16
Adams	0 0 0 0 0 1 0 1 0 1 1 1 1 1 1 0 1 1 1 1 1 0 1 0 0 1	13
A. S. Tubbs	1 1 1 1 1 0 0 0 1 0 1 1 1 0 0 0 0	8
Total		89

Instructions About Transporting Pheasants, Quails, Etc.

The present general interest taken in stocking California with pheasants, brown quails and other desirable birds makes any information about care in transporting them valuable. The most exhaustive and sensible suggestions yet noted are these, which we transcribe from our valued exchange Shooting and Fishing:

1. For exportation, birds bred or reared in captivity should, if possible, be procured; but, if this cannot be done, the following rules should be attended to as regards wild-caught birds:—

2. As soon as the birds are captured, the feathers of one wing and of the tail should be cut off tolerably close to their bases. The birds should be placed in a room lighted only from a skylight above, and having the floor sprinkled with gravel or sand, mixed with tufts of grass and roots and a little earth. Among these the food should be thrown. A tame bird placed with the wild ones is a great advantage, because this bird will induce the new captives to feed. The birds should be kept in this way until they have become tame and are fit to be transferred to the packing-cases.

3. The food should consist of grain and seeds of various kinds, berries, fruit, insects, green food (such as cabbage, lettuce, etc.), bread or soaked biscuit, chopped meat, boiled eggs, etc.

4. Travelling-cages are most conveniently made of an oblong shape, divided into compartments about eighteen inches square, and not higher than just sufficient to allow the birds to stand upright in them. They should be boarded all around except in front, where strong wire netting may be employed; although, if the birds are at all wild, wooden bars, close enough to prevent the inmates from escaping between them, are preferable.

5. Every compartment should have the top on the inside padded with canvas, as, if this is not done, the birds are very liable to injure their heads by jumping upward.

6. A movable feeding-trough should be fixed along the front of each compartment; one-third of this should be lined with tin, pitch, or otherwise made to hold water; the remaining two-thirds will hold the food.

7. Coarse sand or gravel should be kept strewn on the bottom of the cages, and a supply of this should be sent along with the birds, as it is necessary to them for the healthy digestion of their food.

8. The front of the cage should have a piece of coarse canvas to let down as a blind to keep the birds quiet; and, in order to give them air, round holes should be bored at the back of the box in the upper part.

9. The box should be cleaned out when the birds are fed, through the opening in front made by removing the feeding-trough, care being taken that this opening is not wide enough to let the birds escape.

10. In order to supply the birds with green food during the voyage, a few small trays (the same as are used to hold the sand and gravel, may be sown with seeds, such as rape, mustard, or any quick-growing vegetable. The green food thus produced should be cut for them from time to time, and the sand and roots afterward thrown in the cages.

Smokeless Powders.

The most recent experiments with smokeless powders have been made at instance of the English government by Sir Frederick Abel, an authority in such matters, and his conclusions may profitably be studied. Four years ago smokeless powder of extraordinary power was said to have been introduced with the Lebel rifle in France. It has since transpired, however, that several successive experimental compositions were tried with this rifle. Guncotton pure and simple was tried by Sir F. Able for small arm cartridges for some years with marked but not uniform success. Great advances were made, however, on Von Lenk's achievements with guncotton, and the adoption of guncotton as an explosive was then achieved by Sir F. Abel, and, though not as a military propellant, it has been used with great success in sporting cartridges. Colonel Schultze of the Prussian Artillery, has brought in the sporting powder identified with his name, consisting of wood converted into nitro-cellulose. In its best form this closely resembles a granulated nitro-cotton powder made at Stowmarket. Absolute smokelessness was not, however, attained, nor a high degree of accuracy. The smokeless powder of Messrs. Johnson & Borland, and of the Smokeless Powder Company, are well established compounds in England. Camphor has been used with success to harden the surface and close the pores of the powder granules now used. In French and German smokeless powders, acetic acid and acetone have been used, not merely to harden the tablets or granules, but to convert them into horn-like material. The first powder used with the Lebel rifle took the form of yellowish brown tablets as thin as stout note paper. The composition was made a mystery of, but apparently it contained picric acid—the basis of melinite. The powerful and much vaunted French explosive employed in shells has for its basis picric acid, which was first used by Designolle about twenty years ago.

The earliest smokeless French powder undoubtedly failed in the quality of stability, and has been superseded by a simpler compound. German powder of great promise, elaborated at the Rothwell powder works, failed from the same defect of instability. Guncotton of slow explosive power has, by the use of solvents, been converted into horn-like material, and pressed into the shape of rods, tubes, sheets, and other forms, which may be cut up into tablets or strips of any required shape. Mr. Alfred Nobel, the inventor of dynamite and other powerful blasting agents depending on nitroglycerine for their basis, also made smokeless powder based on guncotton in the above form, bearing considerable resemblance to his blasting gelatine. Col. Hess, in Austria, rendered this substance less susceptible to accidental explosion by the incorporation of camphor previously used in the manufacture of the curious substitute for ivory, horn, etc, known as xylonite. Mr. Nobel has had some success in Italy with his smokeless powder, with which Krupp is also said to b experimenting. The government committee on explosive have used Nobel's powder and others in the form of wire and rods in bundles in small arms with excellent results The most promising of them, besides fulfilling the condition of smokelessness and stability, has developed much greate energy in small-bore arms.

Considerable erosive action is produced, and the arm i heated, while but little fouling is produced. Success wit small arms seems on the eve of attainment with smokeles powder, and its application to larger barrels of from 1.85 ir to 6 in. in caliber is attended with less difficulty. Probabl the form of the gun will need modification, the pressure i the chamber being less and in the bore greater than wit black powder. In our service the need of resisting climati action of all kinds involves unusually great difficulties, an modifications in our system of magazines may be necessary.

As to the effect on operations of war, much license has bee given to the imagination as to results arising from the us of powder from which noise as well as smoke has been elin inated. This has no foundation, the noise of smokeless pow der differing only from that of black powder by being rath sharper and of shorter duration. German field guns an our own experimental pieces are fired with powder generatin a very slight smoke, like the puff of a cigar, which is instan ly dissipated. Independent rifle firing is not visible at 3 meters distance. The main effect in battle will be to increas the elements of calculation, leaving less to chance.

A match at blue rocks between the clubs of Healdsbur and Windsor in Sonoma County is imminent. A meetin was held at Healdsburgh last Friday evening to reorgani the gun club of that city.

The Blue Rock Club meets this afternoon at Bird's Poin which place is reached by the 1:15 P. M. boat on the Sou Pacific Coast Railroad system. Both the March and Ap scores will be shot off, at 15 single Blue Rock targets and pairs.

The first match for the Selby medal representing the Bl Rock championship of Central California for 1890, will shot at Oakland Trotting Park on some day in the prese month, probably the last Saturday. The match this ye will be at 30 single and 10 pairs of Blue Rock targets, Ame can Shooting Association rules; entrance $2.50.

Leon Meyn, better known as Leon Martin, the champi rifle shot of Hoboken, would like to make a match with a man in the world for any amount from $200 to $1,000 a sid rifle and pistol shooting. A Sun reporter talked with Me yesterday at a rifle range in Hoboken. Just to show h good he could shoot, Meyn pinned a small card on the 1 yard target, and in twenty shots he cut out a hole in t shape of a heart in the centre of the card. With a pistol cut the bullseye out of the long-distance target in ten sho without a miss. Meyn can get all the backing he wants N. Y. Sun.

ROD.

Piscivorous Cows.

Last year's was the largest salmon pack in British Columbia, and the run was one of the largest ever known to have occurred. Cayoosh creek is a small stream dropping into the Fraser about 200 miles from its mouth. For over three miles the salmon in trying to ascend the stream were so thickly crowded together that one might kill any number by pushing a pitchfork into the water. Old Indians say they never saw such a steady run of salmon night and day as went up that stream for those three months, nor such a mass of dead ones floating down. So thick were they, that when the water receded, the shores were lined with the dead. About two miles up the river is a lake, and at the foot of it the salmon were piled a foot deep. The wind blowing up the lake dashed the water and the salmon up on the shore, mangling them into a confused mass, which afterward putrified, causing the death of the other kinds of fish. The wonderful part of the story is that along Cayoosh creek the cattle have developed a taste for salmon. Some cows have been known to eat bacon, but in Lillooet they eat salmon with apparent relish, preferring them to bunch grass, and thrive upon them. So plentiful was the supply, that the animals became choice in their use of this strange viand. The salmon on the shores were too dry for them. The cows have been seen to walk into the stream where it is shallow, catch live salmon and eat them with relish, the latter wriggling their tails lustily as they go down to—the bottom of the cow's belly. Several visitors to the creek have seen the occurrence, but not wishing to secure the fame of being the boss fish liars, have refrained from relating the story. But the foregoing was given us by a reliable resident of the vicinity, who vouches for its correctness in every particular, and invites any doubters to visit the creek and investigate for himself. It is stated, too, that the lacteal fluid is quite sweet, and does not taste a bit Siwashy. —Vancouver World.

[There's nothing more to guess until some Siwash who does not fear the future, writes about salmon which eat cows.—Ed.]

Keen Sport.

The Pacific Coast offers some sea fishing that is calculated to test, alike the courage and the strength of the fisherman, such as trolling for bonita. barracouta, and jew-fish, but it is probable that no such grand fighter as the tarpon is to be hooked in local waters. Much has been written of tarpon fishing, but perhaps the most graphic tale is one contributed to The Werks Sport, by one of its talented staff who says "The Tarpon is the Monarch, and when a fisherman strikes him he catches a veritable Tartar, besides whom even the shark is mild and gentle. I had heard so much of the prowess and savagery of this fish from the Florida fisherman that I was extremely desirous to tackle one; so I hired a native, who furnished boat, tackle, and a life-long experience. Just at the spot where the swell and sweep of the billows came heaviest, the native checked the boat and told me to get ready. The line was of the best hemp, about half an inch in diameter. One end was tied to a steel chain some two feet long, to prevent the cord being cut by the scales on each side of the creature's jaw. A shark hook was attached to this chain; the barb was baited with a live mullet. I dropped the line and the heavy sinker carried it many fathoms deep. I asked the native, in my innocence, if he wasn't going to fish, too. He grinned and laughed until the boat quivered from stern to stern. When he got his breath he said: "Jes you wait until a jew strikes."

Well, I had not long to wait. The line was resting idle and inert one moment. The next, Great Cæsar! it seemed as if a sub-marine comet had hooked on to the lower end and was going at the rate of a million miles a minute. I dropped it as quick as I would a red-hot poker. I would have as soon seized a line attached to a whale bound on a special express for the North Pole. The only thing I held was my breath. The cord which was coiled in the bottom of the boat was whizzing out the stern with frightful rapidity. Suddenly it became slack. He's got loose, I said to the native. It must have been a man-eater shark, a devil fish or an earthquake. The fisherman never moved from the tiller. Have you got any gloves? he said. No, I answered. Here, take this, and he jerked his old slouch hat from his head; make a turn in that line and hang on like all creation. I'll help you as soon as I find whar that air Jew is heading. I twisted the hat in a double knot in the rope, and waited all eyes to see what would turn up next. All at once I perceived a silvery glittering body jump at least six feet in the air, describing a beautiful parabolic curve before it struck water. Then there came a jerk that almost pulled my arms out of the sockets. then another spring of the maddened fish in the air, and still another splash that sent up a shower of spray, as if an ærolite had fallen in the water. A second pull of the rope, so powerful that I would have been dragged headlong out of the boat had not the Floridian grasped the line and bracing his feet against the seat swung on for dear life. The boat sprung forward as if it had a propelling screw in its stern. And this is called fishing, I thought, and memory flew back to the one-pound trout I had been bragging of hooking. Had I got the fish, or had the fish got me? It was like the song of the old darkey that was drowned by a huge drum fish:

> "And the people who found them could never tell,
> With all their thinking and figuring,
> Whether the nigger a fishing went, or the fish that
> Went a niggering."

Certainly, I felt as small as a dog tied to the tail-board of a four-horse wagon. Like the man who swung on to a mad bull's tail, I gripped tight, because I was afraid to let go, but, unlike him, I was not worrying over whether the tail would hold or not. The boat careened fearfully. My hat blew off, and my hair seemed as if it was going to keep it company. I gave a hasty glance backward; the native was stretched right, his eyes towards the sky, as if he had bidden farewell to earthly things, but I saw his jaws moving as he coolly chewed his quid, and that gave me courage. I thought if that three hundred pounds of steel, whalebone and deviltry that had the other end of the line in his mouth and was dragging the boat oceanward could not prevent that native from leisurely turning with his tongue a piece of tobacco from one cheek to another—then he was not such a "terror" after all. It braced me up. Still, I thought, if we go on as this rate speed we will soon double Cape Horn or strike the Straits of Magellan. I shut my eyes tighter and clutched the cord all I knew how. This scaly imp of Satan carried the boat through the heaving swells as straight as an arrow, and several times it seemed as if the overhanging crests would swamp it. I almost gave up the fight and hope too, and made some good resolutions for the future, one among them that I would never lie about the length of a fish—and the best proof is that I had this fish measured in the presence of three witnesses and sworn to, and his length was exactly six feet four inches. Again the line relaxed, and I devoutly hoped that the infernal fish had gotten loose. But the native shouted to me to gather up the slack and be certain not to let go. A succession of lugs and wrenches of the line showed that the tarpon was savagely shaking the fastened chain like a terrier does a rat. Now followed an ominous stillness. Pull up the slack again, ordered the fishermen, and I reeled it in hand over hand. About forty yards distant I could see plainly the silvery sheen of the fish but a few inches below the surface of the water. A torrent of foam, and the raging, furious Jew darted straight for the boat. Nothing but the coolness of the native saved us from the shock. He seized the rudder and gave it a twist. The boat was still forging ahead, and the craft sheered off several feet. The tarpon struck the water from a flying leap exactly where the boat had been, and made a report like a pile of bricks dumped in the sea, and lashed around like an incarnate demon. Now the native's knowledge came out strong. He pulled the fish by might and main close to the boat and told me to lean on the gunwale of the opposite side. In a second he had the gaff in its gills, and he held on and let the fish fight himself to death. In about a half an hour's frantic hammering the vanquished fish turned belly upward."

Webber Lake will be opened for anglers about June 1st, and it is probable that the fishing will be good.

We shall be very glad to receive and publish notes of sport by any angling readers who are making excursions during these early days of the season.

Mr. Clarence A. Haight, Secretary of the Pacific Kennel Club, is to spend May upon a ranch back of San Mateo, toward Spanishtown, driving, fishing and building up generally. We suspect he will have many visitors.

The best possible advice to offer those who desire to go fishing for trout is to "go as you please." There is no choice in streams; all are bank-full, muddy and unwadeable, except at the headwaters, and there brush prevents good, comfortable sport. There too, no flies are "up" and no number of fish can repay one for smearing himself with bait.

A much needed adjunct to the attractions at Point Tiburon has been added by Mr. B. F. Naphthaly, the well known angler and sportsman of this city. Mr. Napthaly has made his home at Tiburon for some time, and in a friendly way has entertained scores of friends who happened that way to fish. Now he has opened the Corinthian Cafe and Restaurant, where meals will be served to order at all hours and lunches prepared for fishidg parties. The Corinthian will be headquarters for yachting and fishing parties.

Deputy Fish Commissioner and Chief of Patrol F. P. Callundan visited San Jose, Los Gatos and Srnta Cruz last week in performance of his duties. Deputy Innis accompanied him. The gentlemen were received with the utmost cordiality. In San Jose Mr. Pirndiville, Mr. Joseph Delmas, Mr. Frank E. Coykendall and Mr. F. Schilling assisted materially in giving the Deputies information and showing them about. At Santa Cruz, Mr. E. C. Williams, Secretary of the Rod and Gun Club, was most courteous, and extended the privileges of the Club's rooms, beside devoting his time to the entertainment and instruction of the visitors. Dr. Plant, Dr. Bailey and other prominent citizens were called upon, and much good done in the way of arousing proper interest in the work of the Board of Fish Commissioners.

About May 1st the rock-cod season will be in full blast. The indications of good fishing are already very pronounced, as the fish appear to be more plentiful in the bay this year than for many seasons past.

The interior creeks are affording excellent trout fishing. Some of the creeks that have been fruitless for years are fairly swarming with speckled beauties. Many anglers who have lately been up in the vicinity of Pescadera, report good sport and lots of fish.

THE KENNEL.

Dog owners are requested to send for publication the earliest possible notices of whelps, sales, names claimed, presentations and deaths, in their kennels, in all instances writing plainly names of sire and dam and of grandparents, colors, dates and breed.

Names Claimed.

P. D. Linville claims the names Susie Post and El Rio Rey for white and lemon pointers, whelped June 7, 1889, by Climax (Bang Bang—Bellona) out of Roberta (Wise's Tom—Young Beulah).

Visits.

Echo Cocker Kennel, A. C. Davenport, Prop., Stockton, Cal.

Cocker spaniel bitch Pet H. (liver and white) to owners solid black cocker stud dog Bronta (Brant—Mollie) February 21, 1890.

Same kennels, cocker bitch Cluny (liver), A. K. C. S. B. 13056, to same stud dog, February 24, 1890.

Mr. J. M. Bassford Jr.'s pointer, Beautiful Queen (Ranger—Queen) to Mr. Wm. Schleiber, Mountain Boy (Grouse—Rinnie) April 1st and 2nd.

Plurality of Sires.

Editor Breeder and Sportsman:—Is it possible for a slut to give birth to a litter of pups, by a plurality of sires. For instance.—A setter slut is stiuted to a bull, a cur, and a pointer. Will the pups be a mixture of all the above breeds; or will they be a cross between one of the above named dogs and the sleet. A Subscriber.

Answer.—It is possible, and not uncommon, particularly among street curs. The ovum which is fructified by a zoosperm from the bull dog will be half setter and half bull, that impregnated by the pointer will be a dropper.

Mr. M. D. Walter writes from Galt that only the bad weather has prevented his renewing his search for a suitable kennel location near San Francisco. His grandly bred English setter puppies by Rodney—Phyllis II., are growing into beauties and are already showing lots of quality.

On "Dad" Wilson.

Editor Breeder and Sportsman:—No doubt many of your readers have heard of Mr. B. F. Wilson of Pittsburgh Pa., formerly President of the Eastern Field Trial Club; and Mr. George T. Leach a worthy member of the same club—two gentlemen whom its a pleasure to call sportsmen. Here is an amusing story about them, which was told the writer by Mr. Leach while being pleasantly entertained by him in New York several years ago. I was at High Point N. C. in November 1884, while contending for first honors of the members stake. The contest had narrowed down between the two dogs owned and handled by Mr. Wilson and Mr. Leach. The owners had agreed that the loser should pay for a bottle of extra dry, and a gentleman of color followed them with the refreshing beverage in a silver ice cooler. The understanding being that the winner was to be toasted upon the field soon as the heat was decided. The dogs were about equal in points and backs one more point would cause the cork to be pulled. A bevy was flushed, Leach being the younger, with eyesight more clear, marked them down correctly. His dog the Irish setter Brock, had been broken to point at command. As they neared the bevy Leach called his dog to heel, then ordered him on, when he thought he had gotten near enough to the birds Leach called out "Brock what are you doing, steady my boy," when Brock well understanding his owners wishes, drew himself up on a nice point. The claim was made' the birds to order were flushed, the dogs taken up, and the race and cup awarded to Brook and his owner. The ice cooler was brought forward, the bottle opened, and the throats of the Judges and owners were refreshed at Mr. Wilson's expense. C. M. Munhall.

Cleveland, Ohio.

Our exchange, the Fanciers Journal, strongly urges the consolidation of the Pacific Kennel Club and the California Kennel Club.

Working Scotch Collies are advertised in another column by Mr. W. A. Wickham of Tipton, Cedar County, Ia. Fashionable blood strains are utilized.

Those who own setter or pointer puppies whelped on or after January 1, 1889, should enter them in the Pacific Coast Field Trials Club Derby. Entries close on May 1st next; $5 forfeit; and the names, colors and descriptions of the dogs should be sent before that date to the secretary of the club, at 313 Bush street, San Francisco.

Mr. E. H. Husher recently showed us an English setter bitch procured from Mr. Hatch of Gold Hill, Nev. The bitch is well formed, beautifully marked, and of great quality. In breeding it is closely related to the noted Bohemian Girl, being by Duke (Count Noble—Mollie Belton) out of Countess Mollie (Dan—Mollie Belton). The field qualities of the bitch have not been fully developed, but are promising.

The Pacific Kennel Club will meet on Wednesday evening next at the office of the President, Mr. Ramon E. Wilson, at 419 California street, third floor. Those members of the club who have neglected it and remained away from meetings, will do well to attend, or they are likely to hear something drop. The few men whose time, energy and money have sustained bench show interests in San Francisco, are about ready to reorganize the Pacific Kennel Club, and cut off the drones, whose only activity is manifested at bench show times. A club of two workers is better than one of fifty pretenders.

A bit of good news for all who favor square sport at the field trials is that Mr. Robert T. Vandevort returned to California on Tuesday last. For four months he has been in Peru and Chili looking up manganese ore to be used in the manufacture of Bessmer steel by the Carnegie plant at Pittsburgh. Mr. Vandevort was accompanied by Mr. R. L. Hurst a mining expert, and the pair tell very funny stories about that singular region where Colonel North the "Nitrate King" is practically the autocrat. A land of rocks along the coast, with rich valleys inland, which only need water to make them equal to any land in productiveness; cultivated in a neglectful way by a population which is satisfied, if only it can keep the vital spark glowing. The country is not one to attract warm regard, except from those who chance to be able to handle at a profit the mining and fertilizing interests.

Mr. Vandevort saw and studied the "Chili partridge," which the Fish Commissioners at one time fancied for introduction to this State. The bird is about as large as the mountain quail; is brown in color, frequents grassland near grain farms in bevies of five or seven; lies well to the dog, and is a good table bird. In Chili it is not abundant, and in the markets costs the equivalent of fifty cents per bird. Mr. Vandervort does not consider it a desirable addition to the fauna of the State.

Two months of life maintained by the national dishes, "cazuela," a hotchpotch, and "charquican," a stew, brought the distinguished pointer man down to fighting form. Not an ounce of superfluous flesh, but Mr. Vandervort is still the same keen, likeable little man whose absence was so much regretted at the last field trials.

A few days ago an incident occurred in a village near Thirsk of a cur dog having been sold at so much per lb. live weight. One of the inhabitants had taken a great fancy to a neighbouring farmer's cur dog, and as the animal was an excellent worker amongst stock he was greatly valued by his master. The parties could not agree upon any definite price, and at last the villager offered to give the farmer 5s. per lb. for his dog live weight. The farmer accepted the offer, but begged that he should be allowed to keep the dog a week before he delivered him. This was agreed to, and on the farmer getting his dog home he laid him off work and set about feeding him up. On the delivery of the dog it is needless to say the purchaser was somewhat astonished at the weight of "Laddie," he having put on a considerable amount of flesh with his seven day's holiday.

Grim's Gossip.

Palo Alto Stock Farm has made a large number of entries for the Terre Haute Trotting Meeting, which begins October 7th, 1890.

It will be seen by the letter from our Los Angeles correspondent that Protection will not start for the Kentucky Derby.

Mr. Boucher of Woodland, Yolo Co., has a brother in blood to Yolo Maid for sale, and as he is a fast pacer there should be no trouble in finding a purchaser.

A climax has been reached in naming colts: H. A. Moyer of Syracuse N. Y., has named a youngster "William L. Sultan." He is by Sultan 2:24 dam Susie C. C., by William L. sire of Axtell 2:12.

Geo. A. Vignolo writes me that he fully expects to trot his horse "What Ho" in 2:20 or better this summer, and as he is eligible to the "30" class he will be a warm customer for some of the green horses to meet.

That good old brood mare Mineral, by Spendthrift, slipped a foal by St. Savior on March 17th, and Una, by Daniel Boone, had a bay filly by imp Greenback on March 23d. Dr. Aby reports the stallions in good fettle, and grass plenty.

A letter from Lexington, informs me that Alfred G. arrived in first class order, and that he has been much admired by the many who have paid "Woodlawn" a visit during the past week or two. The well known Anteeo is also at the same farm.

Mr. Corbitt of the San Mateo Stock Farm, has added to his brood mare list by purchasing from A. L. Whitney of Petaluma, a two year old filly, by Dawn, dam by Anteeo, the price paid being $1,000. Crossed with Guy Wilkes, the progeny should be as fast as the wind.

W. H. Wilson of Cynthiana, Ky., must have foreseen the great run there was going to be on the Moor blood when he purchased Sultan, in 1886 from Mr. Rose. At any rate he is fast accumulating a lot of youngsters by that noted sire that will add fame to Abdallah Park.

The Lakeport people are determind to make the fair of 1890 a big success. An exceedingly good speed programme has been arranged and generous purses are offered. Mr. McCutchen has sent a number of entry blanks to this office, where they may be had on application.

A. C. Henry of Oakland, has purchased from A. J. McGovern of the same city, a brown mare by Wissahicken 647, dam by Winthrop 505, 2nd dam by Chieftain 721; 3rd dam by Billy Wallace, etc. The mare has a foal at her side by Director, but the colt does not go with the purchase.

Atalanta Wilkes (always a favorite of mine) has been speeded on the snow at Pittsfield, Mass., and proved herself fit to travel with the best of the Eastern horses. I shall be sadly disappointed if Ed Bither fails to make a low mark with the daughter of Guy Wilkes and Atalanta this season.

My readers should remember that if a letter be sent to Dr. Jones, the veterinary editor, for advice, that a fee of two dollars should accompany the note. When letters are sent direct to this office, then the answers are published through our columns, so that all may be benefited thereby.

Jas. McNasear, of Sacramento, has sold to W. E. Holloway, the colt San Victor, 3 yrs. old, by Young Bazar, dam Lizzie P. by Leinster; Lady Della, 3 yrs. old, by Longfield, dam Maud Turney by Harry Bluff; Lillias, bay filly 4 yrs. old, by Norfolk dam Madam Turney by Harry Bluff; and they have been shipped to Valpariso, Chili, South America.

We would warn our Montana and Oregon friends to look out for a bay gelding 15½ hands high, star in forehead, good mane and tail, carries his head rather high when trotting, is a very bad scorer, but fast when once started. It is just possible that he may be seen in California before the season ends. The horse is Pawnee 2:21½, lately sold by his owner to suspicious parties.

Col. Harry I. Thornton has been fortunate enough to have his fine brood mare Adina drop a filly foal to Director 2:17. Adina is by Electioneer, dam Addie Lee (dam of Grace Lee 2:29½), by Culver's Black Hawk, grandam Old Nancy, said to be by Morrill 850. As will be seen, Adina is full sister to Adair 2:17¼, and if the lately foaled filly is not a trotter, pedigrees and fast time go for nothing.

After all the amount of talk there has been between the rival pacer owners, the following squib from the Terre Haute Express seems somewhat strange: "Mr. L. A. Davis, owner of Roy Wilkes, 2:12½, has written from California engaging fifteen boxes. He will ship his string to Terre Haute with Orin Hickok about the middle of April." We are inclined to doubt the statement that the two great pacers will travel in the same car.

The principal question asked by breeders throughout the State at present is: "Will Hickok go back East this year?" All are anxious to secure the services of the noted reinsman if he is going to stay, but it looks at present as though Orrin would journey toward the rising sun, and that with a really good stable. He has not stated positively as yet whether he will go or not, but appearances point strongly toward a journey.

Last week attention was called to the fact that two horses were standing for service, one in Oregon and the other in this State, the same age being claimed for both, and also a like pedigree. It now transpires that the horses are full brothers, the one in Oregon being a four year old, while the one standing at Pleasanton is a year older, the advertisement from the latter place containing a clerical error, which is corrected in this issue.

In the Gossip column last week there occurred a funny blunder in speaking of the stallion lately purchased by John Mackey for J. B. Haggin, Esq. The sire of Mary Hunter was given as being by Guy Wilkes when it should have been by Guy Miller. Mistakes will occur at times, but we are pleased to be able to say that fewer errors creep into the columns of the BREEDER AND SPORTSMAN than into any sporting paper in the United States.

The yearling filly Moquette that was purchased by the Hermitage Stud and taken across the continent in company with the celebrated Bow Bells, is not doing as well in her new Tennessee home as could be desired. She contracted a cold, it is said, which has caused distemper. This filly is by Wilton, the great son of the renowned George Wilkes, dam Alma Mater, and was foaled at Mr. Hobart's farm, the mare being in foal when he purchased her.

California is once more to the front. On Monday evening April 1st, at 10.30 P. M., Trinket 2:14 gave birth to a handsome bay filly, small star, both hind ankles white, by Stamboul 2:12½. Sam Gamble writes me that Trinket had a hard time, as the foal was turned (head inwards) and left fore leg turned under. It seemed for a time that she could not be saved, but at last accounts mother and daughter are doing well. This filly is the fastest combination of speed that has ever been foaled.

As was noticed last week, Col. Thornton has purchased Grand Moor 2374, by The Moor 870, dam Vashti by Mambrino Patchen 58; 2d dam Kate Taber by Mambrino Messenger, son of Mambrino Paymaster. Since his arrival at Oakland, he has been visited by many of the prominent breeders of the State, all of whom speak of the horse in eloquent terms, and many have booked mares to him. As this seems to be the great fashionable blood of the present day, it goes without saying that the book of Grand Moor will fill almost immediately.

Mr. Charles L. Fair, son of ex-Senator Fair, has joined the P. C. T. H. B. A., and will endeavor to breed trotters equal to any. The gentleman has lately purchased Oakland Maid, 2:22, by Speculation 928, dam Lady Vernon. Queen, by Garibaldi (son of Rysdyk's Hambletonian), dam by Royal George, he by Royal George 9. This mare, over whom there has been much controversy, was bred by Wells Veily, Pleasant Valley, Duchess County, N. Y. Mr. Fair has also bought a two-year-old filly by Woolsey (full brother to Sunol) dam Oakland Maid. Queen is in foal to Eros. The purchases were all made from James L. Flood. The price given is not stated.

The Directors of the Monterey Agricultural Association held a meeting on March 24th, a full board being present. It was determined to hold the fair of 1890 from Sept. 30th to Oct. 4th inclusive. $1500 was appropriated to enlarge the pavilion and a committee appointed with full power to act. The race track has been plowed and harrowed, and it was determined to have the track resurveyed, as it is claimed that the course is considerably over one mile. A committee was selected to prepare the speed programme, consisting of M. Lynn, B. V. Sargent and H. S. Ball. The outlook for the fair being a great success could not be better, and the residents of Salinas can rest assured that the exposition of 1890 will surpass any ever before held.

With a very free horse it is desirable to cautiously accustom him to the sound and feel of the whip lightly drawn across him so as not to hurt him at all. This will prevent him from rushing whenever you take the whip in hand, and make it possible to touch up a slug by his side. A slow, easy going horse on the other hand, should never feel the whip upon him except to hurt him. Ladies and tender hearted drivers often do great mischief to such horses by constantly flicking at them until the horse cares no more for the whip than he does for his own tail. With such horses a pretty heavy whip should be used, and used not often but so that they will feel it and know what it means. A horse that will not move, and move quickly to the whip, is neither pleasant nor safe.

On March 17th, Echora 2:23½, by Echo 462, foaled at the Glenview Stock Farm, Louisville, Ky., a large, strong, handsome black filly by Director, 2:17. This aristocratic young maiden is a full sister to Direct, three year record 2:23, four year record, 2:18½, and is the property of Hickory Grove Farm, Racine, Wis., by whom Echora was purchased at the Kidd, Edmonson & Morse Chicago sale last fall for $6150. Echora has been bred to Phallas, 2:13¾, blood brother to Director, 2:17, and Mr. Case is confident that this union will prove eminently successful on the turf. He reports having at Hickory Grove Farm a number of Phallas two and three year olds which, under the care and handling of their new trainer, Mr. R. E. Curry, will surely place the name of Phallas on the list of sires of 2:30 colt performers.

Last Saturday the four well known mares Julia P by Wheatley out of Mercedes; Dairymaid by Shannon out of Mercedes; Comanche by Leinster out of Vivian and Sophie by Bazar out of Sophie Jennison were shipped to Sacramento to be bred to E. S. Culver's Three Cheers. The grandson of the mighty Newminster is slowly but surely proving himself a sire among sires and why should he not be? He is a son of imported Hurrah a highly successful sire, he by Newminster whose fame will never die, out of Jovial by Bay Middleton, as speedy and as great a progenitor of speed as any horse in England. Three Cheer's dam is Young Fashion (the dam of Hock Hocking, Liverpool and other well known horses) by imported Monarch out of Old Fashion the great four mile heat mare. With such speed and stamina on both sides of his pedigree Three Cheers fillies should be priceless.

Two weeks ago the gossip column contained an item, sent me by Charles Andrews of Milwaukee, telling of a mare that had given birth to twins, one a mule colt and the other a horse colt. I rather doubted the statement, but am afraid that I will have to back down in face of the following letter from D. G. Hawkins of Vacaville.

"I see by my last paper that you seem to doubt a reporters word about a mare having a mule and horse colt. I can tell you about another case here which will bear out the Eastern reporter. My brother had a mare last spring that had twins, one a mule and the other a horse colt; he bred her to my Jack and brought her back on the ninth day as she was still in season, but I refused to breed her, so he left in a huff and bred her to a neighbors horse, and the result is as above stated. If you would like to have this substantiated, I can furnish all the proof necessary."

Peter Woods, a new comer to San Francisco, but of a quarter of a century's experience, east of the Rocky Mountains, has located at the Bay District Track, and is prepared to take horses for training purposes. "Pete" comes highly recommended from Chicago, and those who have already entrusted him with trotters, speak in the highest terms of his capability. Mr. E. Topham, of Milpitas, has sent up a Grosvenor colt, which is spoken of as a very speedy youngster, and which will be heard from in the slower classes this season. The Rancho Del Bosque is represented in the Wood's stable by a mare called La Belle by Gibralter 1186, dam Eleanor G by Billy Walker. She has a nice easy action, and promises well. Signa is a grey filly by Billy Lyle, son of Elector 2:21½, dam Tilly by Fairy (son of Joe Dake) owned by A. P. Waugh that Woods is also handling. A gelding by Altamont, who put five in the 2:30 list last year, is one that the betting fraternity should watch as he gives every indication of being as fast as a ghost. Mr. Woods should do well, as he is thoroughly competent and a skillful driver.

It is rarely that a firm of the standing of Acker, Merrill & Condit will give such an unqualified endorsement as they do in the BREEDER AND SPORTSMAN this week for Peruvian Bitters, a tonic that from merit alone has a good reputation on the coast. Wilmerding & Co. are the sole agents for the Pacific States, and those who are troubled with malaria, or a disordered stomach, can not do better than try this excellent remedy.

The mare will generally receive the horse some time between the seventh and twelfth day after foaling, and it is important to attend to that, as she does not remain in season long when suckling, and is more safe to conceive at that period than at any other time. While suckling the mare should do no hard work, and if she is taken off her pasture at all she should be well fed at very short intervals, and the foal fed with her and allowed to suck very often. The mare has no large retentive udder like the cow, no capacious stomach to hold a day's supply of food, no power at any time to go long without food safely, so that when she has to eat and digest for two, all her wants should be very liberally and very frequently supplied. It is in every way better to leave her for the first few months in a good pasture to attend to her own requirements. The foal can be weaned at four months old, but it will tell against its growth and size, so that unless it is a pony that you want to keep small, it is better not weaned until six months old.

The Horseman gives the following pen pictures of two well known trotting horse breeders which will prove interesting:

G. Valensin, owner of Sidney, is a short, slender man, dark-complexioned, and wears a slight mustache. He is a neat dresser, very gentlemanly, is fond of a good dinner, and very sociable. As a breeder of trotters and pacers of the first rank, no man has been more successful, considering the years Count Valensin has given to the pursuit. At the New York spring sales, the product of his farm has brought remarkable prices, a state of affairs that were warranted by the successes of Adonis, Gold Leaf, Faustino and Longworth.

Van B. de Lashmutt, Mayor of Portland, Ore., and proprietor of Witch-Hazel Farm, is medium-sized, dark-complexioned, and wears a full beard. He dresses in plain black, is the architect of his own fortune, a shrewd business man, will in time attain the highest political honors of his State, and is one of Oregon's most progressive trotting-horse breeders. He owns the stallions Hambletonian Mambrino and Pilot Champion, and has in his brood mare list six with records better than 2:30.

Killip & Co's Combination Sale at the Bay District Track.

Last Thursday, Messrs. Killip and Co. held their annual spring sale which was attended by all the prominent breeders and trotting men at present on the coast. Among the spectators and buyers were J. H. Shults, the well known New York trotting fancier, G. Valensin, of Sidney fame, B. C. Holly, the late owner of Woodnut, F. H. Burke the owner of Eros, G. Hancock, Sacramento; Wilfred Page, Penn's Grove; F. W. Loeber, the owner of the well known stallion Whippleton, who died last week, Sam Gamble—Mr. Hobart's manager, the versatile Dan McCarty with hat and diamonds, Harry Agnew owner of Emma Temple and other well known horses, L. E. Clawson who owned Palo Alto's half brother Big Jim 2:23½, Pete Williams the Montanan, W. Vioget from La Siesta Ranch, Dr Lathem, W. H. E. Smith, Humboldt Co, the owner of Al Farrow and Poscora Hayward, Charles Scott, Napa, R. T. Carroll, C. Havens, Drs. Carpenter and Jones and many others. The first three offered for sale were the property of the estate of John Keogh, and were the three which have lately been in litigation.

The first of the three was Flora W, bay filly foaled 1887 by Guy Wilkes 2:15¼, dam Lyla A, sister to Joe Arthurton 2:20½, by Arthurton 365, second dam Flora Langford, dam of Lillian Wilkes, three years, 2:17¾ by Langford. The mare who is a natural rapid trotter but unfortunately was devoid of hair on mane and tail, was sold to Dan McCarty for $1,000.

Laurel B. bay filly foaled 1889 by Sable Wilkes 2:18 at 3 years old dam Lyla A, sister to Joe Arthurton 2:20½ by Arthurton 365 sire of Arab 2:15 grand dam Flora Langford, dam of Lillian Wilkes 2:17¾ at three years old, by Langford. Such breeding is rarely seen. Look at the speed lines and breeding, sire Sable Wilkes 2:18 at three years old he by Guy Wilkes 2:15¼ he by George Wilkes 2:22. Sable Wilkes dam is Sable, full sister to Del Sur 2:24½ by the Moor 870 the sire of the celebrated brood mare Beautiful Bells 2:29½, Sultan 2:24—sire of Stamboul 2:12½, etc. Lyla A the filly's dam is a sister to Joe Arthurton 2:20½ by Arthurton, sire of Arab 2:15 out of Flora Langford by Langford a son of Belmont. It was no wonder therefore that bidding was rapid for such an astonishingly well bred filly and after determined opposition from Messrs Shults and Agnew, B. C. Holly secured her for $2600.

Lyla A., the dam of the two previous ones, a seven-year-old chestnut mare, was then put up, and after some spirited bidding, H. J. Agnew bought her for $2,050.

Ten head, the property of Irving Ayres, Esq., were then offered without reserve, the first being Clara P., 2:29½, bay mare, foaled 1883, by Mambrino Wilkes 6083, dam Cora by Corsican, grandam by Jack Hawkins; H. J. Agnew secured her, after a little opposition, for $1,050.

Istar, bay filly, foaled 1888, by Mambrino Wilkes 6083, dam Narka by Nephew, etc.; $350, H. J. Agnew.

Pashka, four-year-old gelding by Alphaeus 8847, dam Sister to Doty, 2:21, by Challenge 1698; $305, C. Havens.

Veronica, four-year-old brown mare by Mambrino Wilkes, dam by Winthrop; $200, H. J. Agnew.

Grace, black mare, eight years old, by Mambrino Wilkes, dam untraced; $225, F. W. Loeber.

Hope, black mare, eight years old, by Mambrino Wilkes, dam untraced; $305, F. H. Burke.

The other four were bought by D. J. McCarty, who paid $475 for them.

D. J. Murphy sold ten head, among them being Dick Patchen, a bay stallion by Tom Patchen, dam Lady Fisher by Captain Fisher, sire of Simcoe 2:26; granddam by St George; great granddam by American Eclipse; sold to W. H. Smith for $520, to take to Humbolt; the average of the whole ten was $189

Mr. D. E. Fortin put up four head, three of which were sold. Mr. W. H. Smith bought a very good looking three year old filly, Anterose, by Anteros, brother to Anteeo and Antevolo, dam May Hubbard by George M. Patchen Jr. 31, 2nd dam by Gen. McClellan. She was cheap at $435.

May Hubbard, nine years old, the dam of the previous mare, sold to W. H. Hammond for $240. The other mare, a nine-year-old bay, by George M. Patchen, Jr., dam by Rifleman, $175, to G. McCarty.

Our Tennessee Letter.

GALLATIN, Tenn., Mar. 26th.

EDITOR BREEDER AND SPORTSMAN:—The bangtails on the Tennessee and Kentucky tracks are being sent along at a merry clip these spring-like mornings. Many horses at Memphis are going at a winning clip for a short distance, but they are not advanced enough to go the entire circle. Yesterday at Memphis, Blarneystone Jr., a derby candidate, was sent a mile in 1:50. He turned the half in 55 seconds, and came home the remainner of the distance with his head pulled over his shoulders. Blarneystone is a handsome animal, a very dark brown, and from his racing form in the back end of last season, he has the making of a race horse. The filly Helter Skelter was given a spin of a mile in 1:47¾; she carried 123 pounds, and did the mile in that time very easily. Last spring she was considered as one of the best two-year-olds in the West, but she went amiss early in the season and did not regain her form. Blue Blazes and Doherty's Tom Stevens were given a mile together in 1:49½. Both horses finished strong, and Tom Stevens could have chipped several seconds off the time had Mat Monahan given him his head. The Chicago Stable including Jacobin, Huntress, Terra Cotta, Wrestler and Little Minch were out for an airing, but they were only speeded a short distance. Terra Cotta and Jacobin are yet high in flesh, and both seem to be better horses than at this time last season, or when we saw them at Nashville. Riley, Jake Saunders, Ten Times, Irish Pat, Brookwood and Shoshone in Ed. Corrigan's string did some clever work. Jake Saunders and Riley are Corrigan's Derby horses, and both are receiving a special preparation for that event.

Argenta, Stoney Montgomery, Artistic, Bonnie Tan, Oklahoma, Big Three, Bertha and a host of two-year-olds were also given strong work, and any of which will be thoroughly fit by the time the drum taps. It is only about two weeks unthe Memphis meeting begins, which marks the opening of the racing season on this side of the Rockies.

At West Side Park, Nashville every thing is push and bustle. Trainers and horses are working early and late. Daylight catches many of the trainers and horses upon the track, and the track is black with horses throughout the entire day. The horses in the winter's string have only been given short gallops, and I doubt if any of the string will be fit by the time the Nashville meeting begins. El Rio Rey is the picture of good health,—no ill effects from his sickness at Westchester being perceptible. They do say that Buford, by Boulevard, is going to cut a prominent figure in the Kentucky Derby. He is a stayer and the Derby distance will just suit him. It is said that Ophelia, by imp Glengarry, dam Venezuia, is the best 3-year-old at Nashville, barring El Rio Rey. She is moving like great guns, and she should get winning brackets at the spring meeting. Old Bridgelight, a pretty fair horse, last season, never looked better than he does now. An offer of $7000 was recently refused for the brown son of Brigadier. He is now in John Greene's stable, and will doubtless prove a good bread winner for the Nashville turfman's stable.

An authority who is in a position to know says that at least 75 per cent. of the brood mares in Kentucky, both trotting and thoroughbred, are either barren or have lost their foals this spring. The breeders attribute this great loss of foals to the mares eating too much of the rank grass the open winter caused to grow so luxuriantly. This belief is partially substantiated by the fact that mares that were barn fed are with few exceptions safe in foal. In Tennessee breeders have suffered but little of this strange freak of misfortune, at all the different breeding establishments mares have been foaling since early in January, and so far I can learn of but few instances where mares slipped their foals.

The Scoggan string of horses are expected to arrive at Nashville any day. The stable of horses were announced to be shipped from Louisville Sunday, but a severe spell of weather caused their departure from the Falls City to be delayed. The horses are Proctor Knott (that name makes a Tennesseean go into epileptic fits), English Luck, Betting, Good Bye, Ban Chief, Dollikins, National, Martha Washington, Apex, G. W., and several other lesser lights. Proctor Knott is said to be as sound as a dollar, and as good as he ever was. A report gained currency that Knott "had a leg," and that he had entirely broken down. The blaze-faced son of Luke Blackburn has not been given any strong work this Spring, and as he is such a big, muscular fellow, I doubt if he can be prepared for his earlier engagements. Tennesseeans will back him to a man in the Suburban Handicap at 15 to 1. I hardly think he will face the starter in the Brooklyn Handicap, or at least one of the Scoggan brothers recently said that he would not be taken East for that race. Mr. Scoggan also says that Knott will not start for the Toboggan Slide Handicap, which is run down the hill at Westchester. If Knott is himself Suburban day, there is no horse living that can give him a race at the distance with the weight he carries. Tennessee sports backed Knott in every race he started for last season, and unless he pulls off the Suburban, this State will "go broke."

Of all the newspaper comment about the probable winners of the next Kentucky Derby, we have heard but very little of that good colt Phœnix, in Billy Lakeland's stable at Westchester. Phœnix is by imp. Mr. Pickwick, and is an unbeaten horse. He started twice last year, and as many times he won first brackets. He started at Lexington during the spring meeting in a purse race, which he easily captured from a good field. His next and last start was at Latonia, where he won the Harold Stakes after a hard finish. Phœnix was bred at Fairview, and was purchased by Mr. Barnes of the Melbourne stable. On Mr. Barne's retirement from racing, Phœnix was sold at Lexington, together with The Lioness, Gallifet, and other horses of that stable. He was purchased by the ex-colored jockey Walker, who occupied the seat in the pig-skin on Ten Broeck in his most noted performances. Mr. A. J. Cassatt afterwards purchased the colt from Walker for $5,000, and upon Mr. Cassatt's retirement, Billy Lakeland's bid of $4,600 bought him. He is a rather small colt, but just the kind that improves, and if Billy Lakeland happens to come West with him, I expect to see him take the trick. As is well known, Lakeland's field of operation is entirely in the East, but the Kentucky Derby of this year will be worth coming after if he has a formidable candidate. Another Derby entry, seemingly unnoticed, that looks to have a chance is Honduras, a pretty fair colt. He showed to be about as good last season as did others that are well spoken of, and he should not be overlooked. Santiago, in the same stable, suggests some consideration. The Kentucky Derby has always been an uncertain race, and from the present outlook, we are compelled to believe that a dark horse may slip in and surprise us on Derby day.

The owner of Penn P., that good Powhattan colt, has been giving him a special preparation for the Derby, thinking his colt was eligible to start. He was surprised to learn a few days since that his entry was void, and that he had been rushing his colt for no purpose.

"How about the Suburban?" is the oft repeated sentence from every turfite's lips. The daily papers are full of "Handicap Gossip." Tennessee, of course, has pinned her faith to Proctor Knott, and California has a worthy representative in Senator Hearst's Gorgo. Kentucky feels sure of victory with Salvator, Kingston, Raceland and a few others. Tennessee's representative, Knott, has repeatedly walked over Kentucky's champion, Salvator—and he is reputed as the equal to Kingston and better than Raceland—and if both horses start, providing they are in condition, and considering weight, it looks very much like Knott and Gorgo at the finish with a verdict for the former.

KENNESAW.

An Auction Sale.

Messrs. Killip & Co. of 22 Montgomery St. will sell at public auction, at the Fair grounds, San Jose on Wednesday, April 16th a lot of brood mares, trotting and draught horses, the property of D. J. Murphy, Esq. of Santa Clara Co. Mr. Murphy has a great deal more stock than he has room for and therefore is compelled to sell, and the chances are that those who go, looking for bargains, may be able to pick up some real good ones at the sale. Among those we notice in the catalogues are Pinafore by George M. Patchen, Jr. 31, dam Prairie Flower by Williamson's Belmont, 2nd dam by McClellan. Pianafore is a nice driving horse with good style and conformation and her pedigree should recommend her to any breeder; she is in foal to Sondan (son of Sultan) 2:27¼.

Elsie has been driven single and to the pole and should make a fine mare for a gentleman's roadster, she is by Rea's Nutwood, dam Violet by Jack Patchen, 2nd dam, dam of Quinn's Patchen.

Emma should make a good brood mare for all who believe in the proper kind of a thoroughbred cross, she being by imp. Hercules. Emma is now in foal to Dick Patchen; drives single and double and is a good serviceable mare.

Hattie has also been broken single and double and is a nice kind driver, she is by Tom Patchen, dam Queen by Joseph (thoroughbred).

Hagar is a half sister to Hattie and has the same nervy, high strung way of going, she is by Dick Patchen, out of Queen.

Eva is a five-year-old and is a very speedy mare, showe gameness and bottom, travels well single or double and no road is too long for her, she has also been bred to Dick Patchen and is due to foal about the time of the sale. Eva is by Red Line, son of Wm. Welch, he by Rysdyk's Hambletonian, first dam Fanny McDonald by Castor, 2nd dam Pera by Sultan. (See Bruce's stud book).

Oneida is another fine driving mare and would make a splendid animal for ladies' driving; she can trot close to three minutes. Oneida is by Lame Deer, a son of Joe Daniels, dam Lady Fisher by Capt. Fisher, 2nd dam by St. George, 3rd dam by American Eclipse, etc.

There are a number of trotting colts, mares and geldings in the catalogues by such sires as Dick Patchen, Rea's Nutwood, Grosvenor 1833, Billy Mathews, Harold Cossack 4402 and Billy Thornhill 8707. Many of these colts are richly bred and will amply repay anyone who may be fortunate enough to purchase one of the well bred youngsters. There is also a large consignment of draught stallions, mares and geldings; one particularly that deserves mention, he being Prince Albert, Jr. by imp. Prince Albert, (Clydesdale) dam by imp. Clydesdale stallion, Pollock. Prince Albert Jr. has taken first prizes at the San Mateo and Santa Clara Fairs, and never fails to carry away a prize whenever exhibited, and his colts have taken first prizes in every class they were entered in; all of his colts show good action, and kind disposition; as to size and weight they are all that could be desired, several of his colts running in the pasture until they were three years old, weighing over 1600 lbs. one weighing over 1700 lbs., these were not awkard or overgrown, but compact, well formed horses.

Catalogues of the sale may be had by application to either Messrs. Killip & Co. or D. J. Murphy, San Jose.

News From Santa Barbara.

The thoroughbred colts from Colonel H. I. Thornton's Ranco Ressaca have arrived. The two colts were purchased by John S. Bell and E. R. Den. The smaller colt of the two is a bay foaled on March 16th, 1888. He is by imp. Partisan, dam Catalina by Wheatly. Catalina is as fashionally bred as any mare. Her dam, Carrie C., has produced Sobrante, that won the Gano Stakes in 1887, and Sonoma, that won the same stakes in 1888. This colt is named Sugar Plum. The other colt will make a large gelding; he is also a bay, but with a white forehead. He is by imported Partisan, dam Esmeralda. The pedigrees of imported Partisan, Catalina and Esmeralda are too well known to repeat here. Suffice it to say that in the pedigree of imported Partisan appears Pocahontas, England's greatest producing dam, Harmony, King Lorn, Sweetment, Mincemeat. Sweetmeat sired Mincemeat and Mince Pie, winners of the Oaks, and Macaronie, winner of the Derby and 2,000 guineas. If the pedigree assures running qualities, these colts will make a name for themselves. They look like racers and will surely run fast and strong.

The jockey Leu Rainey died at Santa Maria in this county March 15th, 1890. Leu was a good rider and a young man of judgment. His face will be missed at all the meetings in Southern California.

T. M.

On account of his feeble condition, the great sire, Pat Malloy, will not be allowed to serve any mares this season. Mr Brodhead thinks that a year's rest, should he live that long, will fit him for limited stud duties in 1891. This great horse's days, however, are numbered, and it is exceedingly doubtful if he lives to see another winter. He has had to be fed on mashes and other soft food, as he has not a tooth in his head. He will live in turf history as one of the most successful stallions that sprung from the loins of the great Lexington. Among his get are such noted turf lights as Ozark, Blue Grass, Irish Pat, Gen. Harney and Favor. Pat Malloy is 25 years old.

The Washington Park Club.

Weights for Handicaps.

THE OAKWOOD HANDICAP.

A Sweepstakes for all ages, $50 each, half forfeit, or only $10 if declared out on or before May 1, 1890; $1,000 added; the second to receive $300, and the third $100 out of the stakes. Weights to be announced April 1 1890. A winner of any race after the publication of weights, of the value of $1,000 to carry 5 pounds extra. Eighty six nominations. One mile and a furlong.

	Age.	Lbs.		Age.	Lbs.
Elyton	5	116	Somerset	6	108
Monita Hardy	4	113	Le Premier	4	112
Red Light	3	104	Sportsman	4	115
Argenta	4	104	Abilene	3	97
Guido	3	100	Lady Scoggan	2	80
Blair	4	100	Kiro	3	96
Nevada	5	112	Pantalette	4	101
Mary Malloy	3	97	Wamsutta	4	100
Carnot	6	98	Kate Malone	4	107
Labrador	3	98	Princess Bowling	4	114
Cole Miller	5	105	Pilgrim	3	98
Miss Leon	3	100	Big Three	a	106
Frank Shaw	3	96	Los Angeles	5	122
Cashier	6	102	Honduras	3	100
King Regent	4	98	Santiago	3	98
Outbound	4	107	Hypocrite	5	110
Maori	5	113	Getalong	5	[illegible]
Heron	4	110	Proctor Knott	4	121
Gilford	6	108	English Lady	3	101
Terra Cotta	6	128	Dollikins	3	101
Santalene	5	123	Good-Bye	3	96
Wheeler T.	5	112	Sis O'Lee	3	100
Kaloolah	a	114	Miss Longford	2	90
Macbeth II	5	118	Wary	a	114
Little Minch	a	120	Mora	3	95
Brandolette	4	110	Gunshot	4	100
Bridgelight	5	109	Gunwad	3	99
Silver Tip	4	106	Business	5	96
Romaine	3	95	Catalpa	5	112
Teuton	4	108	Prince Fonso	3	108
Bannerette	4	112	Lewis Clark	a	105
Gertrude	4	105	Jed	3	95
Del Mar	4	101	Blarneystone, Jr	3	103
Ireland	4	117	Cynthia	4	100
Carus	5	105	Woodcraft	5	109
Climax	a	107	Joe Courtney	4	116
Cruiser	5	112	Florence A	3	97
Tudor	5	100	Alphonse	4	105
St. Albans	5	101	Ballyhoo	3	101
Lucy Johnson	6	108	Newcastle	4	106
Spokane	4	124	Glockner	a	108
Dousman	a	104	May O.	4	104
Daisy D.	a	107	Emma Nevada	3	90

THE GREAT WESTERN HANDICAP.

A sweepstakes for all ages, $50 each, half forfeit, or only $10 if declared out on or before May 1st, 1890; $1,500 added; the second to receive $400, and the third $200 out of the stakes. Weights to be announced April 1st, 1890. A winner of any race after the publication of weights, of the value of $1,000, to carry 5 lbs.; of $1,500, 7 lbs. extra. 56 nominations. One mile and a half.

	Age.	Lbs.		Age.	Lbs.
Elyton	5	124	Lucy Johnson	5	107
Nevada	5	110	Climax	a	106
Cameo	3	98	Cruiser	5	110
Blair	4	97	Lord of the Harem	3	101
Monita Hardy	4	111	Royal Bess	4	119
Red Light	3	101	Sportsman	4	113
Carnot	6	97	W. G. Morris	3	103
Cole Miller	5	103	Hockey	3	95
Kitty Cheatham	3	109	Spokane	4	124
Stoney Montgomery	5	103	Ten Like	5	103
Enterprise	4	96	Pilgrim	3	98
Longevity	3	97	Wary	a	113
Harry Kuhl	3	98	Bettina	4	107
Del Norte	6	105	Ja Ja	2	94
King Regent	4	97	Dollikins	3	101
Outbound	4	105	Los Angeles	5	121
Maori	5	112	Santiago	3	99
Heron	4	109	Clio	2	94
Brandolette	4	106	Hypocrite	5	109
Dick Pryor	4	98	Business	5	95
Outright	3	90	Jed	3	96
Wheeler T.	5	110	Don Jose	4	115
Macbeth II	5	108	Norretto	3	98
Kaloolah	a	113	Cynthia	4	100
Huntress	5	119	Woodcraft	5	108
Baggage	3	98	Longside	4	105
Almont	4	106	Bonita	a	112
Ed. McGinnis	5	108	Blarneystone Jr.	3	103

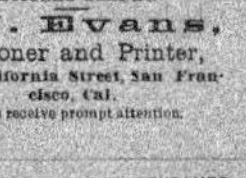

A Nashville friend tells me rather a good story of Uncle Bob," the famous old Belle Meade stud groom. It appears that recently Col. Estill and Mr. Courtney of the California Stable journeyed out to Gen. Jackson's place to see the yearlings.

"Why, Uncle Bob, all your colts hold their heads pretty high," said Mr. Courtney.

"Yes, sah," responded the oracle of BelleMeade—"dey knew de Californians was comin' to-day."

It would have put many a polished courtier to his wits end to have paid a more appropriate compliment.

Mr. C. W. Aby's colt Rodman, two years by Rutherford, dam Leverette, which was sent on recently to Pincus, has been transferred to Hyland's Stable, at Jerome Park, as Pincus had no room in his stable for more.

THE WEEKLY

Breeder and Sportsman.

JAMES P. KERR, PROPRIETOR.

The Turf and Sporting Authority of the Pacific Coast.

Office, No. 313 Bush St.

P. O. Box 2300.

TERMS—*One Year, $5; Six Months, $3; Three Months, $1.50.*
STRICTLY IN ADVANCE.

Money should be sent by postal order, draft or by registered letter, addressed to JAMES P. KERR, San Francisco, Cal.

Communications must be accompanied by the writer's name and address, not necessarily for publication, but as a private guarantee of good faith.

NEW YORK OFFICE, Room 15, 181 BROADWAY.

ALEX. P. WAUGH, ... - Editor.

To Subscribers.

The date printed on the wrapper of your paper indicates the time to which your subscription is paid.

Should the BREEDER AND SPORTSMAN be received by any subscriber who does not want it, write us direct to stop it. A postal card will suffice.

Special Notice to Correspondents.

Letters intended for publication should reach this office not later than Wednesday of each week, to secure a place in the issue of the following Saturday. Such letters to insure immediate attention should be addressed to the BREEDER AND SPORTSMAN, and not to any member of the staff.

San Francisco, Saturday, April 5, 1890.

Dates Claimed.

SACRAMENTO (Running Meeting)......April 26th, 29th, May 1st and 3d
EUREKA JOCKEY CLUB......July 2d to 5th
IONE......Aug 5th to 9th.
LOS ANGELES (6th District)......Aug. 11th to 16th
NAPA......Aug. 18th to 23rd
GLENBROOK PARK, 17th District......August 19th to 23d
PETALUMA......Aug. 25th to 30th
OAKLAND (District No. 1)......Sept. 1st to Sept. 6th
LAKEPORT, 12th District......September 23d to 27th
CALIFORNIA STATE FAIR......Sept 8th to 20th
STOCKTON......Sept. 23rd to 27th.
FRESNO (Fall Meeting)......Sept. 29th to Oct. 4th

Stallions Advertised

IN THE

BREEDER AND SPORTSMAN.

Thoroughbreds.

DOUGLASDALE—Thoroughbred Clydesdale......Lawn View Farm, Cal.
FRIAR TUCK, Hermit—Romping Girl......C. W. Aby, Middletown.
GREENBACK, Dollar—Music......C. W. Aby, Middletown.
INTRUDER, Crater—Lady Bountiful......T. J. Knight, Sacramento.
REVEILLE, Shiloh—Norfolk......B. C. Holly, Vallejo.
ST. SAVIOR, Eolus—War Song......C. W. Aby, Middletown.
THREE CHEERS Imp. Hurrah—Young Fashion......E. S. Culver, San Francisco.

Trotters.

ARLINGTON, Abbotsford—Gillispie Mare......J. R. French, S. F.
ANTEEO BUTTON, Anteeo—Dam of Alexander Button......E. C. Spear, St. Helena.
ADMIRAL, Volunteer—Lady Pierson......Frank Drake, Vallejo.
ACTOR Prompter—Dam by Sultan......Lawn View Farm, Cal.
ARBITRATOR, Director—Lady Earnest......H. A. Mayhew, Niles.
ANTEROP, Anteeo—Bessie G......Guy E. Grosse, Santa Rosa.
ANTEROP, Anteeo—Nance......Guy E. Grosse, Santa Rosa.
ADMIRO, Admiral—dam by San Bruno......Smith & Sutherland, Pleasanton.
ASHLAND ALMONT, Almont—Pauline......T. J. Whitehead, Oakland.
ALEXANDER BUTTON, Alexander—Lady Button......Cache Creek Farm, Yolo.
APEX, Prompter—Mary......Poplar Grove Breeding Farm, Wildflower.
ALCONA, Almont—Queen Mary......Fred W. Loeber, St. Helena
BAY ROSE Sultan—Madam Baldwin......Thos. Bonner, Santa Rosa
BALKAN Mambrino Wilkes—Fanny Fern......A. L. Hinds, Oakland.
CLOVIS, Sultan—Sweetbriar......Poplar Grove Breeding Farm, Wildflower.
CUPID, Sidney—Venus......C. O. Thornquest, Oakland
CHRISMAN'S HAMBLETONIAN 10178, Whipple's Hambletonian—Flora Jesse Chrisman, San José
CHARLES DERBY, Steinway—by Electioneer. Cook Stock Farm, Contra Costa Co.
CALIFORNIA NUTWOOD, Nutwood—Fanny Patchen......Martin Carter, Alameda Co.
CORRECT R, Director—Brainey......Pleasanton Stock Farm.
DECORATOR, Director—Chess......Pleasanton Stock Farm.
DEXTER PRINCE, Kentucky Prince—Lady Dexter......L. M. Morse, Lodi.
DAWN, Nutwood—Countess......A. L. Whitney, Petaluma
DIRECTOR, Dictator—Dolly......Pleasanton Stock Farm, Pleasanton.
DON MARVIN, Fallis—Cora......F. P. Lowell, Sacramento
DESIGNER, Director—May Queen......H. Scott, Oakland.
ELECTOR, Electioneer—Gilberta......L. A. Richards, Grayson.
ELECTION, Electioneer—Lizzie H......B. C. Holly, Vallejo.
EL BENTON, Electioneer—Nellie Benton......Souther Farm, San Leandro.
ECLECTIC, Electioneer—Manette......Wilfred Page, Sonoma County
EROS, Electioneer—Sontag Mohawk......W. H. Vioget, Menlo Park
FIGARO, Hambletonian—Emblem......Souther Farm, San Leandro.
GROVER CLAY, Electioneer—Maggie Norfolk......Denis Gannon. Oakland.
GRAND MOOR 2374, Moor 870—Vashti......H. I. Thornton, S. F.
G. & M., Anteeo—Rosa B......George E. Guerne, Santa Rosa.
GUY WILKES, George Wilkes—Lady Bunker......San Mateo Stock Farm, San Mateo.
GLEN FORTUNE, Electioneer—Glenna......Souther Farm, San Leandro.
GEORGE WASHINGTON, Mambrino Chief—Fanny Rose......Thos. Smith, Vallejo.
GUIDE, Director—Imogene......Smith & Sutherland, Pleasanton.
GRANDISSIMO, LeGrande—Norma......Fred W. Loeber, St Helena
ILLUSTRIOUS, Happy Medium—Abdalletta......George A. Stone, Santa Rosa.
JESTER D, Almont Hortense......Souther Farm, San Leandro
JUNIO, Electioneer—by Granger......S. N. Straube, Fresno.
KAFIR, Alcazar—Flower Girl......B. C. Holly, Vallejo.
KING DAVID, Admiral—Black Flora......Frank Drake, Vallejo.
LEO WILKES, Guy Wilkes Sable......San Mateo Stock Farm, San Mateo.
MEMO, Sidney—Flirt......John Rowen, Oakland
MOUNTAIN BOY, Kentucky Prince Elsie......B. C. Holly, Vallejo.
MAMBRINO WILKES, George Wilkes—Lady Chrisman......San Miguel Stock Farm, Walnut Creek.
MART BOORHEM, Sidney—Towhead......B. C. Holly, Vallejo.
MAMBRINO JR. 1789, Mambrino Patchen, dam by Mambrino Chief Geo. P. Bull, San Jose.
MAMBRINO CHIEF, McDonald Chief—Venus......Thos. Smith, Vallejo.
MORTIMER, Electioneer—Marti......Wilfred Page, Sonoma County
NOONDAY, Wedgewood—Noontide......F. P. Lowell, Sacramento.
PASHA, Sultan—Madam Baldwin......D. Bryson, Linden
PHILOSOPHER, Pilot Wilkes—Belle......George E. Guerne, Santa Rosa.
REDWOOD, Anteeo—Lou Wilton......A. McFayden, Oakland.
STAINWAY, Strathmore—Abbess......Cook Stock Farm, Contra Costa Co
SUNSET, Anteeo Bessie G......Guy E. Grosse, Santa Rosa.
SIDNEY, Santa Claus—Sweetness......Valensin Stock Farm, Pleasanton.
SABLE WILKES, Guy Wilkes—Sable......San Mateo Stock Farm, San Mateo.
VICTOR, Echo—Daughter of Woodburn......G. W. Hughes, Napa City
WOODNUT, Nutwood—Flora......Jas. Weatherhead, San José
WHIPPLETON 1883, Hambletonian Jr.—Lady Livingston......Fred W. Loeber, St. Helena
WOODSIDE, Woodnut—Veronica......B. C. Holly, Vallejo.
YOUNG ELMO, St. Elmo—Dam by Woodburn......Lawn View Farm Cal.

The Oakland Programme.

It will be seen by looking over the advertising columns that the Directors of the Golden Gate Agricultural Association have seen fit to change their programme very materially in regard to the Purses and Stakes which have been already advertised. In looking over both advertisements it seems to us that a very wise change has been made, one decidedly for the better. They now announce three nomination purses in which entries may close in the name of owners or trainers on May 15th. All nominations are transferable, and nominators are held only for the amounts already paid in; horses must be named five days before the first advertised day of the meeting.

The first, called the New List Purse, is for three-year-olds whose sires up to January 1, 1890, have not produced an animal with a record of 2:30 or better, at three years of age or under. The entrance, as usual, is 10 per cent., payable in installments as follows: $25 on May 15th, entries as already stated, close in the name of owners or trainers; $25 on June 15th; $25 July 15th, and the last and final payment of $25 five days before the first advertised day of the meeting, at which time horses must be named.

The second purse on the programme is a guaranteed one of $1200, for the three-minute class, entrance also 10 per cent., payable as follows. $30 on May 15th, when entries close, $30 on June 15th, $30 on July $15th and $30 five days before the first advertised day of the meeting, at which time horses must be named.

The third of the purses is also a guaranteed one of $1200 for the 2:40. class, entrance 10 per cent., $30 of which must be paid on May 15th, when the entries close, $30 June 15th, $30 July 15th, and $30 five days before the first advertised day of the meeting, at which time horses must be named.

Their guaranteed Futurity Purse of $4000, which we have had occasion to mention before, has had the entrance money considerably lowered, the Association now only asking 3 per cent. of the purse from those who wish to enter, the payment being also on the installment plan, so that those who wish to enter may do so at a very small outlay. The purse is for foals of 1890, entries to close on May 15, 1890, when $10 must accompany the nomination; the entries to close in the names of foals or of their dam and sire; $10 is due January 15, 1891; $15 June 15, 1891; $15 January 15, 1892; $15 June 15, 1892; $15 January 15, 1893; $20 June 15' 1893; and $20 five days before the first advertised day of the race.

If the last payment is made on twelve or more entries the horses shall be started in trial races, in which not more than eleven or less than six shall be allotted to start. The trial races shall be mile heats, three in five, for a purse of $1000, given by the Association for each race. If two trial races are trotted, the first four horses shall only be entitled to start in the final race. If three such trial races are trotted, only the first three horses in each trial race shall start in the final; and if four or more trial races are necessary, only the first two horses in each trial race shall start in the final race.

These trial races must be started not less than five nor more than ten days previous to the day set for the final race; and if possible all trial races will be trotted on the same day.

Alcona 730 and Grandissimo.

Owing to the death of Whippleton, Mr. F. W. Loeber, of the Vineland Stock Farm, has altered his arrangements for the season, and instead of Grandissimo standing at Napa, he will be taken to Mr. Loeber's place near St. Helena. This will make no difference to those who have already sent mares to Napa, as the matrons will be taken, free of charge, to Vineland and the best of care given them. In fact, the alteration should be beneficial, as the pasturage at the latter place cannot be surpassed in the State, and the mares will probably be benefitted by the change. Alcona will make a heavy season at Vineland, as it is an open secret that there are several of his colts that will make a very low mark this year, one especially, of whom it is claimed that he can put three heats inside of 2.20. Mr. Loeber is fortunate in having two such stallions, and his neighbors should take advantage of such a favorable opportunity to breed good mares to them at their present low figure. The change in the advertisement came in too late to correct this week, but will receive due attention in our next issue.

San Joaquin Valley Agricultural Association Colt Stakes.

In the appropriate column, and under the usual heading, will be found this week the advertisement of the above association for their colt stakes, the decision of which will take place as usual at their annual fair in September. The entrance for each has been placed at the same figures, viz., $50, of which $10 must accompany the nomination, $15 to be paid July 1st and $25 on Monday, September 1st. They are divided in sets of four each, the first of which are called the Pacific Coast Stakes, open to all, whereas the San Joaquin Valley Stakes, another set of four, are restricted to youngsters owned in the San Joaquin Valley only. In the first, or Pacific Coast Stakes, the events are for two-year-olds, best two in three; for three-year-olds, best three in five; for four-year-olds, best three in five, and a pacing race for two-year-olds, best two in three. To each of the above races the society adds $200. The four other events which are open to colts owned in the valley only, $150 is added to each race, for two-year-olds, best two in three; three-year-olds, best three in five; four-year-olds, best three in five, and a pacing race for two-year-olds, best two in three. Five or more full paid up entries are required to fill, with three or more colts to start. The money will be divided into 50, 25, 15 and 10 per cent.; however, if only two colts start, they may compete for the stakes paid in only, divided into two-thirds and one-third, otherwise the usual conditions of the San Joaquin Association for 1889 to govern the above races. The entries will close on Thursday, May 1st, with Mr. La Rue, the Secretary, P. O. box 188, Stockton, Cal.

The Breeder's Association.

The Directors of the P. C. T. H. B. A. held an important meeting last Friday afternoon at the editorial rooms of the BREEDER AND SPORTSMAN, on which occasion a large number of additional races were added to the programme for the fall meeting. There are some in the racing fraternity who have seen fit to characterize the Directors as tinged with a spirit of meanness, in offering what they term small amounts of added money to the stakes already advertised, but it seems by the amount of the purses offered in our columns this week, that the Directors have gone to still the other extreme, for generosity is strongly marked on the face of each and every event announced; the various classes are so diversified that it becomes necessary to enumerate each in turn and show what the Association offers to the breeders of the State for competition among the owners of the light harness horses.

The first race is for three year olds eligible to the 2.40 class, mile heats, best three in five, entrance $50, with $300 added; the entrance money is payable $10 on May 1st, $15 on July 1st, and $25 on the fifth day preceding the first advertised day of the meeting.

The next is for four year olds eligible to the 2,30 class, mile heats, best three in five, entrance $50, with $100 added; entrance money payable $10 on May 1st, $15 on July 1st, and $25 on the fifth day preceding the first advertised day of the meeting. The two events mentioned above are both stakes.

We now come to five nomination trotting purses, the first of which is a $2000 Purse, for stallions eligible to the 2:18 class, mile heats, best three in five, entrance 10 per cent., payable $40 on May 1st, $40 July 1st, $40 August 1st, and $80 on the tenth day preceding the first advertised day of the meeting.

The next is a $2000 Purse, free for all, mile heats, best three in five; entrance 10 per cent., payable $40 May 1st, $40 July 1st, $40 August 1st, and $80 the tenth day preceding the first advertised day of the meeting.

$1500 is also offered for five-year-olds, mile heats, best three in five, 10 per cent. entrance, payable $30 on May 1st, $30 July 1st, $30 August 1st, and $60 on the tenth day preceding the first advertised day of the meeting.

The 2:22 class has $1500 offered for them, mile heats, best three in five; entrance 10 per cent, payable $30 on May 1st, $30 July 1st, $30 August 1st, and $60 on the tenth day preceding the first advertised day of the meeting.

The 2:27 class has also a Purse of $1500, mile heats, best three in five; entrance 10 per cent., payable $30 on May 1st, $30 July 1st, $30 August 1st, and $60 on the tenth day preceding the first advertised day of the meeting.

The pacers have not been forgotten, and two purses are offered for them, the first of which is $1,500, free for all, mile heats, best three in five, entrance 10 per cent., payable $30 on May 1st, $30 July 1st, $30 August 1st and $60 on the tenth day preceding the first advertised day of the meeting.

One of the heaviest betting races of last year was the 2:25 class for pacers, and this year the association offers to them $1,000 for mile heats, best three in five, entrance

10 per cent., payable $20 on May 1st, $20 July 1st, $20 August 1st, and $40 on the tenth day preceding the first advertised day of the meeting.

In all of the above purses, both trotting and pacing, horses have to be named at the time the last payment is made. Any of our readers who are desirous of making entries in the above purses and stakes, and who have not as yet joined the association, should make application for membership to the secretary, and remit the sum of $25 to cover membership fee, prior to May 1st next. The advertisement should be read carefully, as there are many conditions which should be thoroughly understood by all who propose making entries in the stakes and purses.

Time Records.

The subject of "tin cup" records, or trials against the watch, has for sometime been the subject of much controversy among prominent breeders throughout the United States, so much so in fact, that at a meeting of the Executive Committee of the National Association of Trotting Horse Breeders held at Fifth Ave. Hotel, New York City, on Tuesday of last week, the subject was argued pro and con for some considerable time. There were those on the Board who favored records made in races only, while others were inclined to give the "beater of the watch" a chance to show what he could do when specially prepared for single heats. At the meeting there were present H. W. T. Mali, President of the Association, J. C. Sibley, J. W. Gay, W. E. Dickerman, S. H. Rundle, I. V. Baker Jr. and L. D. Packer, the Secretary.

After a great deal of discussion it was finally moved and seconded that a committee from the Association be selected, to meet like committees from the American and National Associations, to see whether the following scheme could be adopted by all of the Associations. The plan as formulated is as follows: A purse must be hung up, for which there may be any number of entries and the horse winning the first heat shall step down and out; at the expiration of the second heat, the horse winning said heat shall also be ineligible to start again, and so on with the third, fourth and successive heats, each winner going to the stable after each heat; the horse winning the fastest heat, to take the first money, the horse winning the second fastest heat, second money, etc., but if all of the horses fail to win in better than 2:30, the purse to revert to the Association offering it.

It is to be hoped that some means can be devised which will be found equitable for all concerned, so that there may be a spirit of harmony among all breeders as to what constitutes a perfect record.

Death of Whippleton.

We are extremely sorry to have to announce the death of Whippleton 1883, which occurred on Friday of last week; a stallion which has done much for the trotting and pacing interests of Napa County, and whose absence will be sadly missed by the owners of good brood mares in that neighborhood.

Whippleton, of late years, has been owned by Mr. F. W. Loeber of Vineland Stock Farm, St. Helena, Napa County, by whom he was thought a great deal of, and whose death caused a very serious loss to his owner. Whippleton first came into prominence when the phenominal speed of Lilly Stanley began to show, and there are many who still think that her record of 2:17½ is not near so low as it might have been. In addition to this good game mare, Whippleton was also the sire of the pacer Homestake 2:16½; Flora B. 2:27; Cora C. 2:31¼; Black Prince 2:36½; Rachel 2.38, and Prince W. 2:40, with at least a half dozen more that we know of, which, if given a show this year, should surely enter the charmed circle.

Whippleton was of great individuality, of perfect conformation and excellent disposition; in height he was 17 hands, and weighed when in condition almost 1400 lbs.; a great many of his progeny are 16 hands or over, and he had the remarkable faculty of stamping all his get either bay, brown or black. Mr. Loeber, his late owner, informs us that he never sired a sorrel or a white-faced colt; in fact, he has been so marked in this respect that of late years the advertisement about the horse has always contained the paragraph: "If he sires a sorrel or a white faced colt the service fee will be refunded."

Whippleton was sired by Hambletonian, Jr. (sire of Hancock 2:29), he by Whipple's Hambletonian 725, dam Lady Livingston (dam of Lady Blanchard 2:26½, and Bloomfield Maid, trial 2·22), by General Taylor, he by the Morse horse. There is no doubt but what if Whippleton had been spared for one or two more seasons, his fame as a producer of speed becoming so well known, his services would have been eagerly sought by breeders from all over the State.

We extend our sympathy to Mr. Loeber in his great loss, and sincerely trust that the day may not be far distant when he will have an equally as promising a producer of speed in either of his young horses, Alcona 30, or Grandissimo.

The Sacramento Spring Programme.

From the present outlook, the first spring meeting for thoroughbreds held under the auspices of the State Agricultural Society at Sacramento, beginning April 26th, will be one of the most successful affairs ever instituted in the State. The Stakes already closed, had large entry lists, and as there are a great many green horses in the field it is to be expected that the surprises will be many. The programme is a large and varied one, taking in all distances from five-eighths of a mile to one mile and a half. Five of the purses will close on April 7th, and those who have horses in training should read over the advertisement carefully, which is in this issue, and see wherein they can place their runners to advantage.

The first is a Purse of $400, for three-year-olds and upwards, $15 from starters, to go to second horse. A winner this year of three-quarters of a mile to carry three pounds extra, maidens allowed, if three years old, five pounds; four years old or more, ten lbs.

The next is a Selling Purse of $400, of which $50 goes to the second horse, for all ages, winner to be sold at auction, horses entered to be sold for $1,500 to carry rule weight with one pound off for each hundred dollars down to five hundred dollars. The value to be placed on starter at 6 o'clock P. M., the night before the race; the distance is one mile and one-sixteenth.

A Purse of $400, for all ages, next claims attention. $10 required from starters which will go to second horse; maiden allowances; if three years old five pounds; four and upwards, 10 lbs; non winners this year allowed five pounds, allowances cumulative, one mile and one-sixteenth.

Another Selling Purse of $400, of which $50 goes to second horse, is the fourth race which will close on Monday, for all ages; horses to be sold for $2,500 to carry rule weight with one pound off for each hundred dollars down to five hundred dollars. Value to be placed on starter by 6 o,clock P. M. the night before the race; the distance being one mile and one-eighth.

The last of the events to close on Monday is the Hopeful Handicap, a Sweepstakes for all ages, $25 each, $15 forfeit, and $10 if declared, with $400 added, the second to receive $100. Weights in this handicap will be announced by 10 o'clock P. M. the day before the race. Declarations are due at 5 o'clock P. M. same day; the distance in this race is one-eighth of a mile.

The programme is published in its entirety with the days in which each race will take place, and those which are still open are called on the programme, races No. 1, 3, 7, 12 and 14. As before stated they will close with the Secretary, Edwin F. Smith, at Sacramento, on Monday, April 7th.

Pedigree of Idaho Patchen.

The pedigree of Idaho Patchen has been in a measure lost, as Mr. Knight, who now owns him, could get but little track of how the horse was really bred from those from whom he purchased him. In a conversation some time ago with Mr. Knight, we talked the matter over, and it has finally resulted in the pedigree of the Humboldt horse, being explained to the satisfaction of everybody concerned.

Idaho Patchen is a mahogany bay, with black flowing mane and tail, star in forehead, 16 hands high, weighs about 1,130 pounds; he is very compact in form, of splendid disposition, and has been a prize winner on several occasions. Only last Fall he took the blue ribbon over such noted horses as Poscora Hayward, Grand Moor and Ira, as a roadster, at the District Fair held at Rohnerville last September. A few days after the fair, he was trotted a half mile in 1:09 with several watches on him; he has also worked out a fourth heat in 2:25 4-5, and pulled out around a harrow, which is considered about as good as 2:23. Those who know the horse best consider that his present record of 2:26½ is really nothing near the mark that he is liable to make when in first-class condition.

It was originally known that the horse was brought from Idaho, but it has taken a great deal of correspondence to place his pedigree with certainty; however, it is now cleared up with the necessary certificates and letters to show that he was by H. B. Patchen, who was taken to Idaho by Mr. Thos. Frood, who bought the horse in the East. The dam of Idaho Patchen is Kate Walling by Lusby (son of Ericsson 130, sire of six in the 2:30 list). Lusby's first dam was by Hooton; 2d dam by Grey Eagle; 3d dam by Artus, and it is well known that Ericsson was by Mambrino Chief 11; the dam of Kate Walling was a mare taken from Oregon to Idaho, and while she looked very much like a thoroughbred, it has been impossible to find her breeding. As there have been many doubts cast on Idaho Patchin as to whether he has any pedigree or not, this should satisfy all who have any colts by that good horse, for he undoubtedly will leave a great name behind him in Humboldt County.

VETERINARY.

Conducted by W. Henry Jones, M. R. C. V. S.

Subscribers to this paper can have advice through this column in all cases of sick or injured horses or cattle by sending an explicit description of the case. Applicants will send their name and address that they may be identified. Questions requiring answers by mail should be accompanied by two dollars, and addressed to W. Henry Jones, M. R. C. V. S., Olympic Stables, Butler Street, San Francisco.

M. H. N.

Please inform me, through your valuable paper, the necessary steps to take, that I may prevent injury to a mare after her foal has been taken from her. She gives a large quantity of milk, and her bag has been spoiled.

Answer.—With reference to your letter dated March 29th, I beg to inform you that I consider your communication very ambiguous. The udder of the mare may have been injured either before or after feeling: or the mare have been neglected. Under the circumstances I would advise you to take the milk from her twice daily. Keep her on a low diet, and apply a solution of alcohol to the udder daily—alcohol two ounces, water three ounces. If you have any pasture available turn her out in the day time. Write again if there is no improvement,

W. Henry Jones, M. R. C. V. S.

Answers to Correspondents.

Answers for this department must be accompanied by the name and address of the sender, not necessarily for publication, but as proof of good faith. Write the questions distinctly, and on one side of the paper only. Positively no questions will be answered by mail or telegraph.

Not a Subscriber, Ukiah.

We have no space to spare to ventilate your spite against a rival stallion owner.

Subscriber.

Please let me know the pedigree of Fearnaught, owned in San Francisco but now making the season in Ventura Co. Has he any record, or any colts in the 2:30 list.

Answer.—He was originally known as Baker's Fearnaught; sire Old Fearnaught; (record 2:23¼) by Young Morrill by Old Morrill, etc; 1st dam Haidee by Old Columbus, grandam by Harris Hambletonian by Hambletonian, by Imported Messenger. He is known here as Flaherty's Fearnaught. He was a very fast horse but has no record. He is the sire of Dick Flaherty 2:30.

Reno.

The pedigree of the stallion as printed, contains too much "pedigree" as the breeding of Lady Vernon is absolutely unknown.

Old Subscriber.

Would you kindly publish in your valuable paper, the pedigree of Skenandoah, both on the sire and dam's side, as far as it is known?

Answer.—Skenandoah, foaled 1854, by Broken-legged Kentucky Hunter, son of Old Kentucky Hunter; dam Sikes Mare by Hardin's Kentucky Hunter, son of Sorrel Kentucky Hunter.

Petaluma.

Can you let me know the pedigree of a brood mare named Kate, owned by J. H. White, of Lakeville, Sonoma County.

Answer.—Kate, by Milliman's Bellfounder, dam by Blodgett's Waterloo, a son of Biggart's Rattler; 2d dam by Crisp's Jim, by Leviathan. Kate was bred by Elisha Bidwell, North Yamhill, Oregon.

C. A. M.

Can you let me know the breeding of What Ho 2:29½?

Answer.—A letter sent to the owner has elicited the following reply:

Editor Breeder and Sportsman:—Yours of the 27th to hand and hasten to reply. My horse What Ho was sired by A. W. Richmond, and his dam was sired by Overland, formerly the property of L. J. Rose. Richmond's pedigree you have, therefore it is of no use in me giving it to you. Any information you want I will be glad to give you as far as my knowledge goes.

Geo. A. Vignolo.

Names Claimed.

Editor Breeder and Sportsman:—We claim the name of Umatilla for bay filly, star, black points, foaled March 23rd, 1890, by Leon, dam Repetta by Alarm or Reform.

Duffy Villard for sorrel colt, stripe, left hind foot white; foaled March 20th 1890, by Villard, dam Lady Duffy, by Patsy Duffy.

Heppner, Oregon. Matlock Bros.

Editor Breeder and Sportsman:—I enclose the names and descriptions of the following youngsters entered in the Breeder and Sportsman Futurity Stake.

Stoneway for the bay colt with star foaled Feb. 10th, 1890, by Strathway, dam Elizabeth Basler by Bill Arp (Pacer).

Homeway for the bay colt foaled March 9, 90, by Strathway, dam Ida May by Grosvenor No. 1833.

Richway for the brown or gray filly with star, foaled March 23rd, 90, by Strathway, dam Richmoor by Pasha, No. 2039.

Yours, R. O. Newman.

Visalia, Cal.

Foals of 1890.

At Santa Clara, the property of H. C. Judson.

Turban, by Longfield, dam Belle S. by Bazar, March 28th, dropped chestnut filly by Wildidle; stripe in face, both hind feet white, measures 40 inches in height.

Lockhart Stock Farm. Property O. H. Lockhart, Burbank, Cal.

March 22d, bay colt, small star, no other white, by Gossiper, 2:22½, out of Flora Dell by Del Sur, 2:24; 2d dam by Arthurton; 3d dam by Niagara; 4th to 10th dams thoroughbred.

I claim the name Gospel for above foal.

Buena Vista Ranch, property of W. H. Taylor.

Bay filly by Elberg's A. T. Stewart, dam Annie Sprague 2:27, March 5, 1890.

Brown filly by Monroe Chief 875, dam Nellie by Sir Garnet Woolsey, 2nd dam by imported Hercules, 3rd dam by Owen Dale, March 25, 1890.

Property of Dr. C. E. Farnum, S. F., March 8th.

B c by imported Friar Tuck, dam "Sister to Ruth Ryan" by Lodi.

March 23rd: B c by imported Greenback, dam Ela by Hock-Hocking. (The name Greenhock is claimed for this colt).

Breeders' Directory.

Advertisements under this heading 50c. per line per month.

HORSES AND CATTLE.

W. S. JACOBS, Sacramento, Cal. — Breeder of Thoroughbred Shorthorns and Berkshire Hogs.

J. H. WHITE, Lakeville, Sonoma County—Breeder of Registered Holstein Cattle.

EL ROBLAS RANCHO—Los Alamos, Cal., Francis T. Underhill, proprietor, importer and breeder of thoroughbred Hereford Cattle. Information by mail. C. F. Swan, manager.

PAGE BROTHERS.—Penn's Grove, Sonoma Co. Cal. Breeders of Short-Horn Cattle; Draft, Roadster and Standard Bred Horses.

SETH COOK, breeder of Cleveland Bay Horses, Devon, Durham, Polled Aberdeen-Angus and Galloway Cattle. Young stock of above breeds on hand for sale. Warranted to be pure bred, recorded and average breeders. Address, Geo. A. Wiley, Cook Farm, Danville, Contra Costa Co., Cal.

MAMBRINO WILKES COLTS and FILLIES, full brothers and sisters to Gus. Wilkes 2:22, and Balkan 2:29½, for sale. Address SMITH HILL, Walnut Creek, Contra Costa County, Cal

S. F. RUSH, Suisun, Cal., Shorthorns, Thoroughbred and Grades. Young Bulls and Calves for Sale.

PETER SAXE & SON Lick House, San Francisco, Cal.—Importers and Breeders for past 18 years of every variety of Cattle, Horses, Sheep and Hogs.

HOLSTEIN THOROUGHBREDS of all the noted strains. Registered Berkshire Swine. Catalogues. F. H. BURKE, 401 Montgomery St., S. F.

FERGUSON & AUSTIN,
FRESNO, CAL.
Registered Polled Angus and Short-Horn Cattle.

JESSE E. MARKS & CO.,
Wholesale and Retail Dealers of Choice Brands
Havana & Key West Cigars
922 MARKET ST., S. F.

K STREET.
SECOND ST.
Singleton & Addington
BANK EXCHANGE,
SACRAMENTO.
Wines, Liquors & Cigars.

PHIL J. CRIMMINS. JOHN C. MORRISON.
"Silver Palace,"
36 Geary Street,
San Francisco, Cal

Old Hermitage Whiskies
"STEINER'S,"
No. 311 BUSH STREET,
San Francisco.
Under Breeder and Sportsman Office.

John D. Gall. Jas. P. Dunne
"The Resort,"
No. 1 Stockton Street, cor. Ellis,
San Francisco.

HENRY J. COX W. S. JOHNSON
The "EDWIN C."
40 EDDY STREET.
Cor. of Mason, San Francisco.
(Private Entrance Mason Street.)

ROME HARRIS. JOHN MERIGAN.
"Laurel Palace,"
N. W. corner Kearny and Bush Streets
FRANCISCO.

THE CORINTHIAN
Cafe and Restaurant,
Point Tiburon.
MEALS SERVED TO ORDER AT ALL HOURS.
COLD LUNCHES
FOR FISHING AND PICNIC PARTIES.
Headquarters for Yachtsmen and Fishing Parties.
B. F. NAPTHALY, Manager.

Brushes.

BUCHANAN BROS.,
Brush Manufacturers,
609 Sacramento Street, two doors above Montgomery.
Horse Brushes of every description on hand and made to order. Bristle Body Brushes our Specialty

GRAND MOOR, 2374.

Grand Moor 2374.
- Moor 870
  - Clay Pilot 99, Sire of 2 in 2:30 list.
  - Belle of Wabash.
  - Sire of Beautiful Bells 2:29½
  - Sire of Sable (dam of Sable Wilkes) 2:18
  - Sire of Sultan 2:24
  - Sire of Tommy Gates 2:24
  - Sire of Del Sur 2:24½
  - Sire of Sir Guy 2:28½
  - Beautiful Bells is the dam of Hinda Rose, 2:19½ as a 3-year-old, Rosemeade, Chimes, St. Bell, Bell Boy (3 years) 2:19½, sold at auction for $51,000, etc.
  - Sultan, sire of Stamboul, 2:12½, sold for $50,000, has 19 in 2:30 list, and is now standing in Kentucky at $400 for the season.
- Vashti
  - Mambrino Patchen 58, Sire of 14 in 2:30 list, Sire of the dam of Guy Wilkes, 2:15¼; also sire of 20 stallions and 18 mares with get in 2:30 list.
  - Kate Taber, By Mambrino Messenger.
  - Dam of Don Tomas, who got a record of 2:20 in 1889.

Foaled 1876. Black. Sixteen hands high. Bred by L. J. Rose

A horse of highest form and quality; of great excellence in every point; a type of his celebrated family; of marked individuality, spirit and endurance; never properly trained or raced, but shows the possession of great speed; perfectly manageable in the stable and on the road and track.

As he is sired by The Moor 870, a son of CLAY PILOT, out of Vashti by MAMBRINO PATCHEN, he is a most valuable cross for mares of other families. THE MOOR sired Beautiful Bells and the dams of Sable Wilkes and Margaret 2:28 (dam of Regal Wilkes, 2-year-old record 2:20½).

MAMBRINO PATCHEN is regarded as the unsurpassed sire of broodmares, having, among many others, sired the dam of Guy Wilkes and of Wm. L (the sire of Axtell), and a son of his sired the dam of Axtell. The public sales this year have demonstrated with renewed emphasis the value of The Moor and Mambrino Patchen strains of blood. For combining particularly with the Hambletonians it may be called "the ready money cross."

GRAND MOOR will make the season of 1890 for a time at the Oakland Race Track and afterwards at my Ranch, fifteen miles from Oakland. Mares can be delivered at the race track to the groom in charge. Pasture at $5 per month. For other food, if requested, an additional charge will be made.

TERMS, $150 for the season, with privileges of return if the horse does not change hands. Every care exercised, but no liability for escapes or accidents.

H. I. THORNTON, 504 Kearny Street.

SHAW CARTS and SULKIES

For light road or track use, manufactured from the best selected material. Combines lightness with elegance and ease to riders. Weights 70 to 100 lbs. Used by the best horsemen on this coast. Inspection invited.

ONE CAFFREY SULKY FOR SALE AT A BARGAIN.

CARRIAGES & Light VEHICLES
Manufactured to Order.
W. E. SHAW,
1621 MARKET STREET, SAN FRANCISCO, CAL.
REPAIRING DONE—ALL WORK WARRANTED.

AN UNQUALIFIED ENDORSEMENT.

Peruvian Bitters are made of the purest ingredients and compounded as carefully as any prescription.

Peruvian Bark, one of its principal ingredients, was introduced into Spain by the Countess, wife of Count CINCHON, Spanish Viceroy to Peru in 1630, who was cured of a fever by its use, since which time, no better remedy for Malaria and for Restoring the Natural Tone of the Stomach has been discovered.

On the Atlantic Coast they are used in the principal Hotels, Clubs and Restaurants, and sold by all Grocers and Druggists. We have sold them for the past three years WITHOUT ANY ADVERTISING and sales have constantly increased UPON MERIT ALONE, and we unqualifiedly recommend them to our friends and customers.

ACKER, MERRALL & CONDIT.
New York, Feb. 1st, 1890.

WILMERDING & CO., Agents for Pacific Coast,
216 FRONT ST., SAN FRANCISCO, CAL.

FOR SALE.
Full Brother in Blood to Yolo Maid, 2:12 1-2.
A very fast pacer. No record. Also a RUNNING MARE. Can run a half in 49 or better.
Apply to
G. W. BOUCHER,
Woodlands, Cal.

ARGONAUT HERD.
POLLED ABERDEEN—ANGUS CATTLE.
Thirty head choice pure bred and high grade (cross bred) HEIFERS and a few grand young BULLS for sale at reasonable prices. A fine opportunity for persons wishing to establish choice herds or change their bulls. Representatives from this herd were grand prize winners at the last California State Fair.
Address DR. G. M. DIXON,
Sacramento, Cal.

Second Annual Bench Show
OF THE
South'n California Kennel Club
AT THE
City of Los Angeles,
MAY 6, 7, 8 & 9, '90.

The SOUTHERN CALIFORNIA KENNEL CLUB was admitted a member of the AMERICAN KENNEL CLUB September 18, 1889. The coming show will therefore be held under the A. K. C. rules.

Entries will positively close May 1st.

A special committee will take personal charge of all dogs sent from a distance and insure their proper care. For premium lists and entry blanks address E. K. BENCHLEY, Secretary, 14 South Spring Street, Los Angeles; or H. H. BRIGGS, Breeder and Sportsman, San Francisco.

Solano and Napa Agricultural Society.

Trotting Colt Guarantee Stakes for 1890.

The Solano and Napa Agricultural Society have opened the following Colt Stakes for Trotters:

NO. 1. TWO YEAR OLDS.—Free for all; $400 guaranteed. $50 entrance, payable as follows: $10 April 1st, when entries close; $10 May 1st, $10 June 1st, $10 July 1st, $10 August 1st, when colts must be named. Nominations transferrable any time before colts are named. If the payments amount to more than the amounts guaranteed the additional amount to be added to the stake. All moneys divided as follows: 60, 30 and 10 per cent; in case of only two starting, 60 and 40 per cent; and in case of one horse walking over the whole amount to go to such horse. A failure to make any payment when due shall be considered a withdrawal and forfeiture of the amounts paid in. National or American Rules to govern, as the Society may elect. The right reserved to refund the first payment in case the stakes do not fill reasonably well.

No. 2. FOR THREE YEAR OLDS.—Free for all, $500 guaranteed. $100 entrance, payable as follows: $20 April 1st, when entries close; $20 May 1st, $20 June 1st, $20 July 1st, $20 August 1st, when colts must be named. Conditions same as in No. 1.

District Colt Stakes for districts comprising Counties of Solano, Napa, Sonoma, Marin, Lake, Colusa, Yolo, Mendocino, Humboldt and Butte.

No. 3. FOR YEARLINGS.—$250 guaranteed. District. $40 entrance, payable as follows: $10 April 1st, when entries close; $10 June 1st, $10 July 1st, $10 Aug. 1st, when colts must be named. Conditions same as in No. 1.

No. 4. FOR TWO YEAR OLDS.—$370 guaranteed. District. $50 entrance, payable as follows: $10 April 1st, when entries close; $10 May 1st, $10 June 1st, $10 July 1st, $10 August 1st, when colts must be named. Conditions same as in No. 1.

No. 5. FOR THREE YEAR OLDS.—$400 guaranteed. District. $50 entrance, payable as follows: $10 April 1st when entries close; $10 May 1st, $10 June 1st, $10 July 1st, $10 August 1st, when colts must be named. Conditions same as in No. 1.

Yearling Stake. Single dash; one mile. Two Year Olds.—Mile heats, two in three. Three Year Olds—Three in five, to harness. Parties entering colts will be notified by mail when payment becomes due.

The Society also offers the following stakes for class horses.

TROTTING STAKES.—Free for all.
2:30 CLASS—Trotting; purse $1500.
2:24 CLASS—Trotting; purse $1500.
2:20 CLASS—Trotting; purse $1500.

Horses eligible January 1st, 1890. Entrance $150, payable as follows: $25 April 1st, when entries close; $25 May 1st, $25 June 1st, $25 July 1st, $50 August 1st, when horses must be named. Nominations transferable any time before August 1st. Right reserved to refund entrance fee in any of the stakes should they not fill reasonably well. Money divided, 50, 25, 15 and 10 per cent. National or American Association Rules to govern, as the Society shall elect. To be trotted at our regular summer meeting, upon days to be hereafter arranged.

Entries to close April 1st, 1890, with

A. H. CONKLING, Secretary,
Napa City, Cal.
L. L. JAMES, President.

Antevolo Colt
FOR SALE.

REX VOLO, foaled February 22nd 1888, dam Catchup by Rustler; granddam Huntess by Don Victor; great granddam Bettie Denice by American Boy Jr. Is 15.1 hands high, well developed, muscular and without a blemish. Has a very gentle disposition, and shows speed and a good gait.

HOME FURNISHING CO.,
125 Fifth Street, S. F. Cal.

FOR SALE.
A Mohawk Chief BROODMARE
and a
Director Colt, 6 months old.
For particulars address or apply to ANCON HOTEL, 9 and 11 Pacific Street, San Francisco.

For Sale
A HALF BROTHER TO
ALMONT PATCHEN,
(2:15, trial 2:13 3-4).

JUANITO JR. is a beautiful bright bay, black points, with no white, foaled 1886. As a colt he has given much more promise than did Almont Patchen at the same age. Instead of being a pacer, he is a good square trotter, with every indication of great speed, and is so gentle and kind, that a lady can drive him. The owner's only reason for selling him is that business calls him away from this section of the State. He will be sold at a reasonable figure. This is a splendid opportunity for a gentleman to secure a first-class trotter at a very low figure.

The pedigree of Juanito Jr. is by Juanito (sire of Almont Patchen), dam Nettie Moore by Old Tom Moore. For further particulars, address

JUANITO JR.,
Santa Clara P. O., Cal.

For Sale.
14
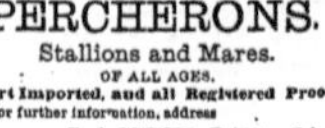
Pure bred
PERCHERONS.
Stallions and Mares.
OF ALL AGES.
Part Imported, and all Registered Proof
For further information, address
E. J. TURNER, Hollister, Cal.

Twenty-Third Annual Sale!

169 THOROUGHBREDS

64 YEARLINGS,
100 BROODMARES,
5 GREAT STALLIONS

23d ANNUAL SALE OF

Belle Meade Stud,

Will take place at BELLE MEADE STUD, near Nashville, Tennessee on

THURSDAY AND FRIDAY, APRIL 24 & 25

169 Head Thoroughbreds at Public Auction.

SOLD FOR DIVISION. | SOLD WITHOUT RESERVE

Five Great Stallions
To the Highest Bidder.

LUKE BLACKBURN
Imp GREAT TOM,
ENQUIRER,
BRAMBLE,
IROQUOIS.

FOR CATALOGUES ADDRESS THIS OFFICE.

P. C. KIDD, Auctioneer.

For other information and Catalogues address JOHN J. CARTER, No. 9 Baxter Block, Nashville, Tenn.

For Sale

A FIRST-CLASS

Napa County Farm

—OR—

STOCK RANCH,

800 Acres Improved,

SITUATED TWO AND A HALF MILES FROM NAPA CITY, with good roads leading thereto, a good hard finished house of nine rooms, with all modern improvements, streams running all summer, a great amount of live oak and black oak timber. It lies in a fruit belt, surrounded by fine vineyards and orchards growing upon the same quality of soil, and originally a part of this tract. About one-half hill, and one-half rolling land, but none of it is steep and all easily cultivated, splendidly situated for the breeding of fine horses. Price, $65 per acre. Further particulars given at this office.

BREEDER AND SPORTSMAN,
313 Bush St.

A Grand Combination Sale

—OF—

Standard-bred Trotters & Thoroughbreds
CLYDESDALES AND PERCHERONS,
Fine Roadsters, Work Horses, Etc.

—AND—

Registered and Graded Holstein CATTLE,
REGISTERED JACKS,

And other first-class Live Stock of all kinds, will be held at

CARSON CITY, NEV., April 15, 16 and 17, '90.

BROOD MARES, COLTS AND FILLIES by the following well known Sires will be sold:

Standard Bred.	*Thoroughbred.*
ECHO.	NORFOLK.
GIBRALTAR. (will be sold)	HOOKER.
PROMPTER.	LODI.
BUCCANEER.	BRECKENBRIDGE.
ST. CLAIR.	THREE CHEERS.
SIGNAL.	LANGFORD.
BLUE BULL.	BOI DE ARC.
ST. LAWRENCE.	McMAHON.

And among the fine stock to be offered will be the grand HOLSTEIN BULL SARATOGA, and a number of fine calves and heifers by him and other well known thoroughbred Holsteins.
Over 100 entries were made up to March 1st, and a big sale is assured.
Send in your entries.
For further particulars address

JNO. P. SWEENY & CO., Carson City, Nev.

ANNUAL SPRING SALE

—OF—

Road & Harness Horses

Work and Draft Horses!

SHETLAND PONIES!

From Ranchos of J. B. Haggin, Esq.

WILL TAKE PLACE

Tuesday, May 6, 1890,

AT SAN FRANCISCO.

Location to be hereafter designated.
Catalogues are being prepared.

KILLIP & CO., Live Stock Auctioneers,
22 Montgomery Street, S. F.

Important Closing Out SALE

—OF—

Trotting - Bred Stock,

COMPRISING THE ENTIRE STUD OF

JOHN G. HILL, Esq., of Ventura, California.

—TO BE HELD IN—

San Francisco,

Thursday. - - - May 15th, 1890.

It will embrace about 80 head of well bred Stallions, Mares and Geldings, principally the get of that celebrated standard bred sire

A. W. RICHMOND, 1687,

out of thoroughbred mares mostly from that noted horse, Woodburn, sire of Monarch 2:28¼, and the dam of Victor 2.22, and others.

This will no doubt be the last opportunity at public auction to obtain the blood of this great sire, that, in part, has made ANTEEO, ANTEVOLO, ARROW, ROMERO, RICHMOND JR., and others famous in the trotting history of our State.

The sale is positive and without reserve, as Mr. Hill will engage in other business.

☞ Catalogues now being prepared.

KILLIP & CO., Auctioneers,
22 Montgomery Street, San Francisco, Cal.

Poplar Grove Breeding FARM.

Standard-bred Trotters, Colts and Fillies.

The get of CLOVIS, 4909; PASHA, 2039; APEX, 2935.

For Sale.

Address S. N. STRAUBE, Poplar Grove Breeding Farm,
Fresno, Cal.

Inspection by intending purchasers invited, and information by mail.

AUCTION SALE

—OF—

Brood Mares,
Colts and Fillies,
Harness & Draft Horses

—The property of—

D. J. MURPHY, San Jose.

TO BE SOLD AT

Public Auction,

—AT 11 A. M., ON—

Wednesday, April 16, '90

—AT—

Fair Ground, San Jose,

KILLIP & CO., Auctioneers,
22 Montgomery Street S., F., Cal.

Catalogues may be had on application.

FOR SALE

AT

Vineland Stock Farm

STALLIONS, BROODMARES AND FILLIES

ONE STALLION FIVE YEARS OLD, SEAL-BROWN, by WHIPPLETON (sire of Lilly Stanley, 2:17 1-2, Homestakes 2:16 1-2, etc.), dam Sally Gorham by Werner's Rattler. This horse is scarcely 16 1-2 hands high, but very compactly built. He breeds exceptionally large and well finished colts. Any one understanding the business could clear him in one season, or he would make a No. 1 road horse, as he can trot a 40 gait any time.

ONE THREE-YEAR-OLD, SEAL-BROWN, by WHIPPLETON (sire of Lilly Stanley, 2:17 1-2, Homestakes 2:16 1-2, etc.), dam Sally Gorham, etc. This ought to make a great General Purpose sire, and with opportunities get trotters, as he is compact, strong-boned, and will measure when grown about 16 hands and weighs 1,200 lbs. With a little road work last fall he developed a wonderful burst of speed.

ONE THREE-YEAR-OLD, BLACK, by WHIPPLETON (sire of Lilly Stanley, 2:17 1-2, etc.), dam by Naubuc (sire of the dam of Eva W., 2:22 1-2, etc.), full brother to Thomas Jefferson, 2:23. This horse will be fully 16 1-2 hands high. He is smooth, rapid gaited and from size and conformation should breed, like his sire, large, rangy, finished colts.

ONE TWO-YEAR-OLD, BRIGHT CHESTNUT, sired by DAWN 2:18¾, dam Alida (dam of Direota, three-year-old record 2:31¾, trial 2:26) by Admiral (sire of sister 2:19 1-2, Nona Y 2:25, etc). This colt is the making of an extraordinary horse. He is large boned and will be over sixteen hands high when grown; he is of the true Nutwood type, is clean gaited and can lead a piece as fast as any man's colt.

ONE TWO-YEAR-OLD, BLOOD BAY, (full brother to Alcona Jr. sire of Silas Skinner, trial 2:23) sired by ALCONA (sire of Flora Belle 2:24, etc.,) dam Madonna by Cassius M. Clay Jr. This colt will make a trotter and a great stock horse if developed; he has the combined blood of Almont, Mambrino Chief, Cassius M. Clay Jr. and Joe Downing.

These colts are all sound and promising. The only reason I offer them for sale is, that I have three aged stallions in use, and the surplus is growing on me. If I were starting a breeding business for profit, I should consider either of these colts a representative to commence with. Also brood mares and fillies for sale. Correspondence solicited.

FRED. W. LOESER, St. Helena,
Napa Co., Cal.

Highland Farm,

LEXINGTON, KY.,

Home of Red Wilkes.

Standard-bred Trotting Stock

For Sale,

Sired by Red Wilkes, Wilton, 2:19¼; Allandorf and Sentinel Wilkes, out of highly bred Standard Mares of the most fashionable blood of the day.

W. C. FRANCE, Proprietor.

FOR SALE.

A DARK BAY TROTTING STALLION

Sired by ALBERT W. by Stanford's Electioneer; dam, a Patchen mare. This stallion was foaled in 1884, stands 16¼ hands, and weighs 1000 lbs. Is a handsome dark bay with black points, and has shown a trial mile in 2:38. For further particulars apply at

1228 HOWARD ST., S. F.

Stallion for Sale

AT A BARGAIN.

Full Brother to Fairmont.

By Piedmont, dam Queen by Garibaldi—see State Fair Edition of BREEDER AND SPORTSMAN, September 14, 1889, for description of Fairmont—three years old, solid bay. Can trot a 2:10 gait or better. Sound in every particular. Can be seen at Oakland Trotting Park, Oakland.

P. J. WILLIAMS.

Pure Bred Clydesdale Mares

TWO MARES (Full Sisters) Five and Six Years Old, Weighing About 1,900 lbs. Each.

Sire imp. BEN. LOMOND.
Dam's sire imp. GLANCER.

For particulars apply to

M. A. MAYHEW,
Niles, Alameda County.

BROOD MARE for SALE

DOT,

By WHIPPLE'S HAMBLETONIAN 725, dam, Victoria by Jerseyman (son of Geo. M. Patchen Jr., 31), 2nd dam Whiskey Jane (dam of Sam Purdy 2.20½). This mare will be sold at a reasonable figure. For further particulars apply AT THIS OFFICE.

Speed Programme

—OF THE—

Twelfth District Ag'l Society

To be held at

LAKEPORT,

SEPTEMBER 23 to 27 INCLUSIVE.

First Day—Tuesday, Sept. 23, 1890.

RACE NO. 1—TROTTING.

Yearling Stake; $250 guaranteed. Entrance $30, payable as follows: $5 May 1st, $10 July 1, $10 September 1st (when entry must be named), and $5 additional for starters. Entries to close May 1, 1890. See general conditions.

RACE NO. 2—RUNNING.

One-half mile dash. $100 added; $25 to second. Entrance $10, to close 6 P. M. day before race.

RACE NO. 3—TROTTING.

Three-minute Class. Mile heats 3 in 5. District. $150 added. Entrance $30; to close 6 P. M. day before race. 5 to enter, 3 to start. See general conditions.

Second Day—Wednesday, September 24th

RACE NO. 4—RUNNING.

Three-quarter mile heats; 2 in 3. $200 added; $25 to second. Entrance $10, to close 6 P. M. day before race.

RACE NO. 5—TROTTING.

District Stallion. Mile heats 3 in 5. Purse $500. Entrance $50, to close 6 P. M. day before race; 5 to enter, 3 to start. See general conditions.

RACE NO. 6—TROTTING.

Three-year-old stake; $300 guaranteed. $50 entrance, payable as follows: May 1st, $10; July 1st, $10; September 1, $15 (when entry must be named), and $15 additional to start. Open to Napa, Solano, Sonoma, Marin, Lake, Colusa, Yolo, Mendocino and Humboldt Counties.

Third Day—Thursday, Sept. 25th.

RACE NO. 7—RUNNING.

Seven-eighths mile dash. $150 added; $25 to second. Entrance $10, to close 6 P. M. day before race.

RACE NO. 8—TROTTING.

Two-year-old stake; free for all. Mile heats, best 2 in 3, $300 guaranteed. Entrance $50, payable as follows: May 1st, $10; July 1st, $10; September 1st, $15, and $15 additional to start. See general conditions.

Fourth Day—Friday, Sept. 26th.

RACE NO. 9—TROTTING.

Mile heats, 3 in 5. For all described counties in race No. 6. $400 added. Entrance $50, payable as follows: May 1st, $10; July 1st, $20; September 1st, $20—when entries must be named—$10 additional to start. See general conditions.

RACE NO. 10—RUNNING.

Citizens' Handicap. $100 added. Five-eighths mile; heats, 2 in 3. Entrance $10, to close 6 P. M. day before race.

Fifth Day—Saturday, September 27th.

RACE NO. 11—RUNNING.

GENTLEMEN'S NOVELTY.—*For non-professional jockeys.* One mile dash. $30 added; $5 entrance. Purse divided as follows: First horse at each quarter to get $25; slowest average at all quarters to get Society medal.

NO. 12.—LADIES' TOURNAMENT

Free for all in District. Purse $40, divided as follows: $25 to first, $15 to second, $10 to third.

No. 13.—GENTLEMAN'S TROTTING.

Same conditions as gentlemen's Novelty. Mile heats, two in three. Entrance $5. Entrance money divided 50, 30 and 10 per cent.

GENERAN CONDITIONS.

Nominations in colt stakes transferrable any time before colts are named. If the payments in stake races amount to more than the sum guaranteed the additional amount to be divided 60, 30 and 10 per cent; in case of only two starting, 60 and 40 per cent.; and in case of one horse walking over, the whole amount to go to such horse.

A failure to make any payment when due shall be considered a withdrawal, and forfeiture of the amounts paid in. National Rules to govern all trotting races. The right reserved to refund the first payment in case the stake does not fill satisfactorily.

All running races, unless otherwise specified, governed by the *Pacific Coast Blood Horse Association* Rules.

The Directors reserve the right to change the hour and date of any race, and in case of a race being antedated the nominator will receive notice.

A horse distancing the field shall receive only first and third moneys.

L. G. SIMMONS, President.

A. B. McCUTCHEN, Secretary.

San Joaquin Valley

AGRICULTURAL ASSOCIATION.

Stockton Fair, 1890,

September 23 to 27 inclusive.

TROTTING COLT STAKES.

$50 each, of which $10 must accompany nomination, $15 to be paid July 1st, and $25 on Monday, September 1, 1890.

Failure to make payments as above forfeits previous payments.

PACIFIC COAST STAKES.

For 2-year-olds	2 in 3	$200 added to each.
3 " "	3 in 5	
4 " "	3 in 5	
2 " "	Pacing 2 in 3	

SAN JOAQUIN VALLEY STAKES.

Open to all San Joaquin Valley counties for colts owned in the valley, February 1, 1890.

For 2-year-olds	2 in 3	$150 added to each.
3 " "	3 in 5	
4 " "	3 in 5	
2 " "	Pacing 2 in 3	

Five or more full paid up entries required to fill; three or more colts to start. Four moneys: 50, 25, 15 and 10 per cent. In case of only two colts starting, they may compete for the stakes paid in only, two-thirds and one-third, otherwise full conditions of this Association for 1889, to govern.

Entries close Thursday, May 1, 1890, with the Secretary,

J. M. LARUE, P. O. box 188,

L. U. SHIPPEE, President. Stockton, Cal.

Pacific Coast

Trotting-Horse

Breeders' Ass'n.

ADDITIONAL

Stakes & Installment Purses

FOR 1890.

Entries to close May 1, 1890.

Trotting Stakes.

THREE YEAR OLDS—FOALS OF 1*87.

Eligible to 2:40 class. Mile heats, best three in five. Entrance $50, with $200 added. Entrance payable, $10 May 1st, 1890, $15 July 1st, 1890, and $25 on the fifth day preceding the first advertised day of the meeting.

FOUR YEAR OLDS—FOALS 1886.

Eligible to 2:30 class. Mile heats, best three in five. Entrance $50, with $200 added. Entrance payable, $10 on May 1st, 1890, $15 on July 1st, 1890 and $25 on the fifth day preceding the first advertised day of the meeting.

Nomination Trotting Purses.

$2,000, Stallion Purse.

Open to stallions eligible to the 2:18 class. Mile heats best three in five. Entrance $200 payable $40 May 1st, 1890, $40 July 1st, 1890, $40 August 1st 1890, and $80 on the tenth day preceding the first advertised day of the meeting. Horses to be named at time of last payment.

$2,000, Free For All.

Mile heats, best three in five. Entrance $200, payable $40 May 1st 1890, $40 July 1st 1890, $40 August 1st 1890, and $80 on the tenth day preceding the first advertised day of the meeting. Horses to be named at time of last payment.

$1,500. Five-Year-Olds, Foals 1885.

Mile heats best three in five. Entrance $150, payable $30 May 1, 1890, $30 July 1, 1890, $30 August 1, 1890, and $60 on the tenth day preceding the first advertised day of the meeting. Horses to be named at the time of the last payment.

$1,500. 2:22 Class.

Mile heats, best three in five. Entrance $150. Payable $30 May 1, 1890, $30 July 1, 1890, $30 August 1, 1890, and $60 on the tenth day preceding the first advertised day of the meeting. Horses to be named at the time of the last payment.

$1,500. 2:27 Class.

Mile heats, best three in five. Entrance $150. Payable $30 May 1, 1890, $30 July 1, 1890, $30 August 1, 1890, and $60 on the tenth day preceding the first advertised day of the meeting. Horses to be named at time of last payment.

Nomination Pacing Purses.

$1,500. Free For All.

Mile heats, best three in five. Entrance $150. Payable $30 May 1, 1890, $30 July 1, 1890, $30 August 1, 1890, and $60 on the tenth day preceding the first advertised day of the meeting. Horses to be named at time of last payment.

$1,000. 2:25 Class.

Mile heats, best three in five. Entrance $100. Payable $20 May 1, 1890, $20 July 1, 1890, $20 August 1, 1890, and $40 on the tenth day preceding the first advertised day of the meeting. Horses to be named at time of last payment.

Conditions.

First payment, whether for purses payable in installments or for stakes, MUST ACCOMPANY NOMINATIONS, or they will not be considered.

Neglect to make payments on the dates stipulated will incur forfeiture of all previous payments.

No horses and colts owned on the Pacific Coast by others than members of the P. C. T. H. B. A. are eligible to the above purses and stakes, but horses and colts OWNED outside of the Pacific Coast are eligible thereto regardless of membership.

All States and Territories lying in whole or in part west of the Rocky Mountains are held to be part of the Pacific Coast.

The Directors reserve the right to change the hour and day of any race except when it becomes necessary to ante-date a race, in which instance the nominator will receive three days notice of change by mail to address of entry.

Entries not declared out by 6 P. M. of the day preceding the race, shall be required to start.

When there is more than one entry to stakes by one person or in one interest, the horse to be started must be named by 6 P. M. of the day preceding the race.

Purses and stakes will be divided into four moneys, viz., 50 per cent. to the winner, 25 per cent. to the second horse, 15 per cent. to the third horse, and 10 per cent. to the fourth horse.

No added money will be paid for a walk-over. If only three horses start in a stake race, only first, second and third money shall be paid—if but two start, the Directors reserve the right to call it a walk-over, and divide the stake money paid in, two-thirds to the winner and one-third to the second horse. In case of a walk-over, only the money received from entries to said stake will be paid.

A horse distancing the field shall only be entitled to first and third moneys.

The Board of Directors reserve the right to declare any purse or stake filled or not filled without binding itself to any specified number of entries.

In all nomination purses, eight entries will be required to fill, and four to make the last payment.

Trotting and racing colors shall be named by six o'clock on the day preceding the race, and MUST be worn upon the track.

Horses eligible in class races on records standing at time of entry.

Otherwise than the above National or American Trotting Association Rules—as this Association may select—will govern the stake and purse races offered.

Persons desirous of making entries in the above purses and stakes, and who have not as yet joined the P. C. T. H. B. A., should make application for membership to the secretary, and remit the sum of $25 to cover membership fee before May 1, 1890.

J. H. WHITE, President.

JAS. P. KERR, Secretary,
313 Bush Street, S. F.

ENTIRE CHANGE

—OF—

PROGRAMME

—OF THE—

Extra Attractions

To take place at the

Oakland.

Fall Meeting, 1890,

UNDER THE MANAGEMENT OF THE

GOLDEN GATE

Fair Association

NOMINATION PURSES.

In which entries close in the name of owners or trainers on May 15th. All nominations transferable and nominators held only for amounts paid in. Horses must be named five days before first advertised day of the meeting. Eight nominations required to fill, four of which must make last payments.

THE NEW LIST PURSE $1000.

For three-year-olds whose sires up to January 1, 1890, have not produced an animal with a record of 2:30 or better, at three years of age or under. Entrance 10 per cent. payable as follows:

$25 May 15th, when entries close in the names of owners or trainers.
$25 June 15th.
$25 July 15th.
$25 five days before first advertised day of meeting, when horses must be named.

GUARANTEED PURSE $1200.

For three-minute class, entrance 10 per cent, payable as follows:

$30 May 15th, when entries close in names of owners or trainers.
$30 June 15th.
$30 July 15th.
$30 five days before first advertised day of meeting, when horse must be named.

GUARANTEED PURSE $1200.

For 2:40 Class, entrance 10 per cent, payable as follows:

$30 May 15th, when entries close in names of owners or trainers.
$30 June 15th.
$30 July 15th.
$30 five days before first advertised day of meeting, when horses must be named.

—ALSO A—

Guaranteed Futurity Purse $4,000.

To take place during the Fall Meeting of 1893.

For foals of 1890. Entrance 5 per cent. payable as follows:

$10 May 15, 1890, when entries close in name of foals or of dams and sires.

$10 Jan. 15, 1891.
$15 June 15, 1891.
$15 Jan. 15, 1892.
$15 June 15, 1892.
$15 Jan. 15, 1893.
$20 June 15, 1893.

$30 fifteen days before advertised day of the race.

If the last payment is made on twelve or more entries the horses shall be started in trial races, in which not more than eleven or less than six shall be allotted to start. The trial races shall be mile heats, three in five, for a purse of $1,000, given by the Association for each race. If two trial races are trotted, the first four horses shall only be entitled to start in the final race. If three such trial races are trotted, only the first three horses in each trial race shall start in the final; and if four or more trial races are necessary, only the first two horses in each trial race shall start in the final race.

These trial races must be started not less than five nor more than ten days previous to the day set for the final race; and if possible all trial races will be trotted on the same day.

CONDITIONS.

Neglect to provide payments on the dates stipulated will incur forfeiture of all previous payments.

The Directors reserve the right to change the hour and day of any race except when it becomes necessary to ante-date a race, in which instance the nominator will receive three days notice of change by mail to address of entry.

Entries not declared out by 6 P. M. the day preceding the race, shall be required to start.

Purses will be divided into four moneys, viz., 50 per cent. to the winner, 25 per cent. to the second horse, 15 per cent. to the third horse, and 10 per cent. to the fourth horse.

A horse distancing the field shall only be entitled to first and third moneys.

Trotting and racing colors shall be named by six o'clock on the day preceding the race, and MUST be worn upon the track.

All purse races, mile heats, best three in five to harness.

Otherwise than the above, National or American Trotting Association Rules—as this Association may select—will govern the races offered.

Entries to close with the Secretary.

R. T. CARROLL, President.

JOS. I. DIMOND, Sec'y, 306 Market St., S. F.

Attention! Sportsmen!!

An exploring party will leave San Francisco about April 10th for the Alaska Coast, St. Matthews Island and Yukon River, stopping at numerous places on the way where Seal, Walrus, Sea Lions, Brown Bear, White Polar Bear and Deer are plentiful; also splendid fishing for Salmon, Halibut, Trout and Cod, offering to the hunter and fisherman a trip of five months' unparalleled for sport. A novel feature of this offer is that each one taking the trip becomes a stockholder in the Company.

For further information apply to

NORTHERN DEVELOPMENT CO.

No. 5 Market St., Room 5.

State Agricultural Society's

SPRING

RACE MEETING

AT

SACRAMENTO, CAL.,

APRIL 26 to 29, and MAY 1 and 3, 1890

ENTRIES CLOSE APRIL 7, 1890.

PROGRAMME.

FIRST DAY—SATURDAY, APRIL 26.

NO. 1.

Purse $400, for three-year-olds and upwards; $15 from starters to go to second horse. A winner this year at this distance to carry 3 pounds extra. Maidens allowed, if three years old, 5 pounds; four or more, 10 pounds. Three-quarters of a mile.

NO. 2.

Norfolk Stakes, for two-year-olds. Closed with 27 nominations. Five-eighths of a mile.

NO. 3.

Selling purse $400, of which $50 to second; for all ages. Winner to be sold at auction. Horses entered to be sold for $1,500 to carry rule weight. One pound off for each $100 down to $500. Value placed on starters only by 6 P. M. night before race. One mile and a sixteenth.

NO. 4.

The California Oaks, for three-year-old fillies. Closed in 1889 with 17 nominations. One and one-eighth miles.

SECOND DAY—TUESDAY, APRIL 29.

NO. 5.

The Matadero Stake, for two-year-olds. Closed in 1889 with 19 nominations. Three-quarters of a mile.

NO. 6.

The Chris. Green Handicap. Closed February 1st, with 14 nominations. One and one-quarter miles.

NO. 7.

Purse $400, for all ages; $10 from starters to go to second horse. Maiden allowances: if three years old, 5 pounds; four and upwards, 10 pounds. Non-winners this year allowed 5 pounds. Allowances cumulative. One mile and a sixteenth.

NO. 8.

The Weinstock, Lubin & Co. Stake. Closed in 1889 with thirty-two nominations. One mile.

THIRD DAY—THURSDAY, MAY 1.

NO. 9.

The Spring Stakes. A sweepstakes for three-year olds (foals of 1887) that have not won a race previous to January 1st, 1890. Closed February 1, 1890, with 12 nominations. One mile.

No. 10.

The Western Hotel Stakes, for two-year-old fillies. Closed in 1889 with 27 nominations. Five-eighths of a mile.

NO. 11.

The Hall, Luhrs & Co. Handicap. Closed in 1889 with 29 nominations. One and one-quarter miles.

NO. 12.

Selling purse $400, of which $50 to second; for all ages. Horses entered to be sold for $2,500 to carry rule weight. One pound off for each $100 down to $500. Value placed on starters only by 6 P. M. night before race. One and one-eighth miles.

FOURTH DAY—SATURDAY, MAY 3.

NO. 13.

The Golden Eagle Hotel Handicap, for two-year-olds. Closed in 1889 with 19 nominations. Weights to be announced before 6 P. M. second day before race. Declarations due by 4 P. M. day before race. Three-quarters of a mile.

NO. 14.

The Hopeful Handicap; a sweepstakes for all ages of $25 each, $15 forfeit, or $10 if declared, with $400 added; second to receive $100. Weights announced by 10 P. M. day before race. Declarations due by 5 P. M. same day. One and one-eighth miles.

NO. 15.

The California Derby. Closed in 1889 with 32 nominations. One and one-half miles.

NO. 16.

Purse $400, for all ages; $10 from starters to go to second horse. Non-winners this year at time of starting allowed, if three years old, 5 pounds; four years old, 10 pounds; five and upwards, 12 pounds. Entries to close with clerk of course at 6 P. M. day before the race. Mile heats.

The State Agricultural Society's rules of 1889 to govern, except when conditions are otherwise.

Starters in stake races must be named through the entry box by 6 P. M. of the day before the race. The right of forfeit ceases at 10 o'clock A. M. day of race. Entries in purses not declared out by 6 P. M. day before race is run, must start.

Non starters in all purse races held for entrance under Rule 22.

The right to postpone races on account of the weather or other sufficient cause, is reserved. In event of postponement, handicaps stand, other declarations are off.

All declarations, either of starters, non-starters or non acceptance of handicaps or otherwise, must be made in writing. Blanks will be furnished by the Secretary.

Declarations in handicaps must be accompanied by the money.

Entries in Nos. 1, 3, 7, 12 and 14 to close with the Secretary Monday, April 7, 1890.

CHRIS GREEN, President.

EDWIN F. SMITH, Secretary.

CALIFORNIA

NUTWOOD

Will stand for mares the season of 1890, commencing February 15th, and ending July 15th, at the NUTWOOD STOCK FARM, one mile from Irvington.

DESCRIPTION AND PEDIGREE.

He is a dark chestnut, with star in forehead; foaled September 16th, 1881; is 16 hands 1½ inches high and weighs 1250 pounds. Has a beautiful flowing mane and tail, with remarkable style and lofty carriage, a bold, open movement like his sire, but has never been handled for speed. He moves and looks like his sire, except that he is a larger horse.

CALIFORNIA NUTWOOD by Nutwood, record 2:18¾, has 32 trotters and pacers with records from 2:15 to 2:30, and put 8 in the 2:30 list in 1889. He is the only horse that ever lived with a record under 2:20 that produced five under 2:20. He is now serving mares at Dubuque, Iowa, at $500 for the season, and his colts at yearlings sell from $2500 to $5000 each. He is out of the dam of Maud S., record 2:08¾.

Nutwood, by Alexander's Belmont, sire of 52 with records from 2:15½ to 2:30. Alexander's Belmont by Alexander's Abdallah, sire of Goldsmiths Maid, record 2:14, and 5 others in 2:30 list. Alexander's Abdallah, by Rysdyk's Hambletonian, sire of 41 with records from 2:17¼ to 2:30, and is the founder of the Hambletonian family.

FANNY PATCHEN, dam of California Nutwood, by George M. Patchen Jr., record 2:27, and sire of Wells Fargo, 2:18½, Sam Purdy 2:20½, Ben Ali 2:29¾, and 7 others from 2:21 to 2:30. He has 7 sons who together produced 12 trotters in 2:30 list, and 6 daughters who together produced 5 trotters and 1 pacer in 2:30 or better. He sired Alexander 2:31½. Alexander sired Alex. Button 2:26½; Alex. Button sired Yolo Maid, pacing record 2:14 at 4 years old, the fastest on record; George M. Patchen Jr., by George M. Patchen 2:23½, is sire of Lucy 2:18¼, and 3 others in the 2:30 list; he has 12 sons who together produced 40 trotters from 2:14¾ to 2.30, and 6 daughters who together produced 6 trotters in 2:30 list or better, he is grand sire of Hopeful 2:14¾, and best wagon record 2:16½, and sire of the granddam of Stamboul 2:12½.

George M. Patchen, by Cassius M. Clay, and he by Henry Clay, founder of the Clay family.

Laura, second dam of California Nutwood, was a fine large bay mare, a very fast roadster brought from Chicago by Wm. Wilson, of San Jose, and is said to have made a record of 2.35 in Chicago. Pedigree not traced.

TERMS.

$40 for the season, payable invariably before the animal is removed. Mares not proving in foal can be returned free next season. Pasturage $3 per month, but no liability for accidents or escapes.

For further particulars address the owner,

MARTIN CARTER,

Newark, Alameda Co., Cal., or Irvington, Alameda County, Cal.

Bay Rose.

REGISTERED No. 9814.

Record 2:20 1-2 Third Heat.

Will make the season of 1890, ending July 1st, at the SANTA ROSA STOCK FARM, (formerly Santa Rosa Race Track), SANTA ROSA.

DESCRIPTION.

BAY ROSE is a dark bay or brown, with black points, 15¾ hands high, and weighs 1150 pounds. He is remarkably intelligent, of good disposition, and a pure-gaited trotter. He was foaled in 1881. His colts are large, stylish, rangy animals, and inherit the qualities of speed and endurance.

PEDIGREE.

BAY ROSE 9814
- Sultan, 2:24 — Sire of 19 in the 2:30 list.
  - The Moor 870, sire of Beautiful Bells ... 2:29½; Del Sur ... 2:24½; Ines ... 2:30; Sir Guy ... 2:28½; Sultan ... 2:24; Tommy Gates ... 2:24
  - Sultana.
- Madam Baldwin ......
  - The Moor 870 — Sire of 6 in the 2:30 list.
  - by Ben Lippincott, by Williamson's Belmont.

TERMS: $200 FOR THE SEASON.

Good pasturage $3 per month. First-class care taken of mares in any manner that owners may desire, but no responsibility assumed for escapes or accidents.

Limited to a few approved mares.

For further particulars, address

THOS. BONNER,

Santa Rosa Stock Farm, Santa Rosa.

Or apply to

IRA PIERCE,

728 Montgomery Street, S. F., Cal.

Sunny Side Breeding Farm.

Admiral 488.

Foaled 1867—Sired by Volunteer 55, Son of Rysdyk's Hambletonian 10.

First dam Lady Pierson by Cassius M. Clay (Neaves') 20; second dam by Diamond; third dam a running mare said to be thoroughbred. He is fitted in an eminent degree to produce colts that will in all respects justify his patrons in their expectations.

Admiral is the sire of Huntress, record 2:27¼, Sister, 2:19½, Perhelion, 2:25, Nona Y., 2:26, and others equally as promising, but have not had the advantage of track work. He will serve a limited number of approved mares at $50 the season, with usual return privilege. Season ending August 1, 1890. No liability for accidents or escapes.

KING DAVID 2576.

Bay Stallion—Foaled 1883.

Sired by Admiral 488, dam Black Flora (the dam of Huntress, 2:27¼, Sister, 2:19½, Perhelion, 2:25, Nona Y., 2:25), by Black Prince.

King David is one of the best gets of Admiral. He has a good disposition, kind to drive, smooth and even-gaited, and can speed fast. Barring accidents, he will trot in the twenties this Fall. His colts are large, rangy, and well finished. Will serve a limited number of mares at $30 the season, to end July 1, 1890. Every precaution will be taken to prevent accidents and escapes, but no liability will be assumed. Pasturage $4 per month.

Sunny Side Farm is situated two miles east of Vallejo, on the Sulphur Spring road. For further particulars, address

FRANK DRAKE,

Vallejo, Cal.

The Pure Trotting-bred Stallion

ILLUSTRIOUS

STANDARD No. 4178.

DESCRIPTION.

Dark bay, black points, 15 1-2 hands high, weight 1090 pounds, foaled May 30, 1883; bred by General W. T. Withers, Lexington, Ky.

PEDIGREE.

By Happy Medium, sire of Maxey Cobb 2:13¼ and 82 with records of 2:30 or better.

First dam Abdalletta by Cassius M. Clay Jr., sire of Durango 2:23¼, Harry Clay 2:23¼, and sire of the dams of Minnehaha, Bertha 2:27¼, Charley West 2:28¼, Grandmont 2:25 1-4, Lottie K 2:26¼, Mambrino Diamond 2:26, Richwood 2:28 1-2, Topsy 2:24¼, Happy Thought 2:21 1-2, Pequot 2:22 1-2, Fairlawn Medium 2.27 1-2, Folley 2:27¼, and Mambrino Boy 2:26 1-2.

Second dam Laura Crockett by Almont, sire of Westmont 2:13¼, Puritan 2:16, Fanny Witherspoon 2:16¼, Piedmont 2:17¼, Aldine 2.19¼, and 37 with records better than 2:30.

Third dam Sally Tee by Alexander's Abdallah, sire Goldsmith Maid 2:14.

Fourth dam Kate Crockett, the dam of Lulu 2:14¼, by imp Hooton.

Illustrious is a horse of extra fine finish, large clean bone, good feet, back short and strong, loins and quarters well muscled, and powerful. He has a kind disposition and splendid trotting action, and is as handsome and bloodlike in form and finish as any trotting stallion in the land.

He is pronounced by his breeder, General Withers, to be the best bred son of Happy Medium living, and is undoubtedly one of the very best bred trotting stallions in the State. He has had but six weeks' regular training, and a part of that time was sick with epizootic, but was trotted quarters in 39 1-4 seconds, and barring accidents will certainly trot better than 2:30 this season.

TERMS—$50 the season. Mares not proving with foal may be returned next year free.

Good pasturage at $3 per month.

Season to begin February 1st and end June 15th.

GEO. A. STONE,

Santa Rosa, Cal.

LAWN VIEW BREEDING FARM STALLIONS.

ACTOR.

A beautiful bay horse foaled 1887 by Promptor 2305 sire of Apex (four-year-old record) 2:26, Transit 2:26¼, Creole 2:20, Blue Belle 2:22, Daisy (yearling record) 2:38¼, he by Blue Bull 75, 1st dam by Sultan 1513 2:24, sire of Stamboul 2:12 1-4, Ruby 2:19¼, Sweetheart 2:22¼, Alcazar 2:20¼, Eva 2:23¼, La Grange 2:23¼, and eleven others in 2:30 list, second dam by Fireman by Langford.

Actor, as his pedigree shows, is as purely bred a young stallion as ever made a season in the stud. Blue Bull stock is much sought after in the East, and Sultan, sire of his first dam will make the season in Kentucky this year at $100 per mare. Actor is a handsome bay colt 16 hands high, clean limbed and possesses all the points of a speedy trotter.

TERMS, $40 FOR THE SEASON, usual return privileges.

DOUGLASDALE 7650.

Thoroughbred Registered Clydesdale Stallion

Imported from Scotland, December, 1889, bay, three years old.

TERMS, $35 FOR THE SEASON.

YOUNG ELMO.

Two years old sorrel stallion by St. Elmo 2:27, dam by Woodburn.

TERMS, $20 FOR THE SEASON.

For further particulars, address

MANAGER LAWN VIEW FARM, Auburn, Cal.

The Trotting-Bred Stallion

RINGWOOD

THE FINEST SON OF THE NOTED SIDNEY,

Will make a Season at Oakland, commencing March 1, and ending June 1, 1890.

DESCRIPTION.

RINGWOOD is a dark, rich colored bay, black points, 15 1-2 hands, weight 1100 lbs., and a pure gaited trotter. Has shown great speed. He is now five years old. As a four year old he showed a trial in 2:19 1-2, and but for an accident would have received a record as a four year old of 2:18 or better.

PEDIGREE.

RINGWOOD is by Sidney, record 2:19 3-4, and is half brother to Gold Leaf 2:11 1-4, Adonis 2:11, Fleet (two year old) 2:24, Longworth 2:19, Sister V. 2:27, Faustino, yearling, 2:35, Fleet, yearling, 2:35. Memo, three year old trial 2:20 1-2.

Sidney is by Santa Claus, record 2:17 1-2; he by Strathmore, sire of 31 in 2:30 list; he by Hambletonian 10, the greatest of all producers; he by Abdallah. Sidney's dam, Sweetness, record 2:21 1-4; she by Volunteer, the sire of St. Julien 2:11 1-4.

RINGWOOD'S dam Alma; she by Dashway, thoroughbred; he by Belmont, he by American Boy; he by Sea Gull; he by imported Expedition. Alma's 1st dam, Fanny Cobb, was a great road mare, pedigree untraced.

TERMS; $50 for the Season

Payable June 1st, or sooner if mares are taken away

Address communications to

A. C. DIETZ,

Oakland, Cal.

The Fast Trotting Stallion

REDWOOD.

Four-Year-Old Record 2:24 1-2

Will make the season of 1890—February 1st to July 1st—at the

OAKLAND RACE TRACK.

REDWOOD is a dark bay colt, 15.2¾ hands high, weighs 1100 lbs. Foaled in 1885 by Anteeo, 2:16¼, sire of Alfred G., 2:19¾. Anteeo is by Electioneer. First dam Lou Milton, by Milton Medium; second dam Old Fly, a thoroughbred mare brought from the East in 1871 by W. C. Ralston, Esq.

Redwood's sire was out of Columbine by A. W. Richmond, the sire of the pacers Arrow 2:13¾, and Elwood 2:28, and the trotters Romero, 2:19¾, and Len Rose, 2:27. Redwood has shown a quarter in 33 seconds.

Terms $100

For the season. Mares not proving with foal may be returned next season free of charge, provided Redwood remains the property of the present owners. Good pasturage at $5 per month. No responsibility assumed for escapes or accidents. Service fees payable before removal of the mare. Limited to 40 approved mares. For further particulars address

A. McFADYEN.

Race track, Oakland, Cal.

THE MAMBRINO Patchen Stallion.

MAMBRINO JR., 1789 (formerly Carr's) Sire of Lady Ellen 2:28 (dam of Ella 2:29), Maud H. 2:30, Mambrino Boy (Carr's) 2:31 1 2.

Will stand at my farm, 2 1-2 miles north of San Jose, on the Milpitas road. Season to commence February 1st, 1890, at $40, with return privilege 1891. Fifteen mares of approved breeding, besides my own, will be given him. Parties owning good mares, performers or out of producing dams, will find an opportunity to breed them on shares, and the best of care taken of them till colt is weaned, if so desired.

PEDIGREE.

MAMBRINO JR., 1789, by Mambrino Patchen 58 [full brother of Lady Thorne 2:18 1-4] by Mambrino Chief 11. First dam by Mambrino Chief 11; 2nd dam by imp. Jordan [thoroughbred]; 3rd dam by Bertrand, son of Sir Archy; 4th dam by Chewkees, son of Sir Archy.

For further particulars address

GEO. P. BULL.

Box 1067. San Jose, Cal

The Trotting Stallion

CUPID,

Full Brother to Adonis 2:14,

—Sired by—

The Celebrated SIDNEY 2:19 3-4, and out of Venus.

Will make the season of 1890 at the OAKLAND TROTTING PARK.

PEDIGREE.

CUPID is by Sidney out of Venus by Capt. Webster 10173, record 2:30, and sire of Freestone 2:19. Second dam by Shenandoah 936, sire of Daisy Burns 2:29¼, Erwin Davis (sire of two in the 30 list) and dams of four in the 30 list.

DESCRIPTION.

Cupid is a handsome bright bay 15.2¾ hands high, weighs 1100 lbs.; was foaled in 1886. As a yearling, with very little work, he showed quarters in 42 seconds, and at 2 years old, quarters in 36 seconds. As a three year old he has not been worked, but he shows the speed and endurance that must come from his excellent blood lines.

TERMS $50 for the season, with the usual return privileges. Good pasturage near the track at $4 per month. The best of care taken of mares in any way that owners may desire, but no responsibility assumed for accidents or escapes.

For further particulars address

C. O. THORNQUEST,

Oakland Trotting Park, or

C. BAAB, 972 Broadway, Oakland.

The Trotting Stallion

VICTOR,

Record 2:22.

Will make the season of 1890 at NAPA CITY.

DESCRIPTION.

VICTOR is a handsome dark bay; 15-3 hands high; weighs about 1,100 pounds, and is remarkably intelligent, level-headed, of kind disposition, and a magnificent animal in every respect. He is well boned and muscled, of splendid conformation, and possesses the qualities of speed and endurance to an eminent degree—qualities that he imparts to his progeny.

PEDIGREE.

VICTOR, record 2:22
- Echo 462
  - Hambletonian 10 — Sire of 42 in the 2:30 list.
    - Abdallah 1
    - Chas. Kent mare
  - Fanny Felter ....
    - Magnolia 68
    - by Webber's Kentucky Whip
- Daughter of
  - Woodburn ....
    - Lexington
    - Lulu Horton
  - daughter of........
    - Ashland
    - thoroughbred

ECHO is the sire of Belle Echo, 2:20, Senator, 2:21¼, Victor, 2:22, Gibraltar, 2:22¼, Echora, 2:23¼, Tippie, 2:25¼, Lohengrin, 2:27¼, Pasha, 2:27¼, Elmonte, 2:29, Col. Hawkins, 2:29¼, Annie Laurie, 2:30, Economy, 2:30, Sam Lewis, pacer, 2:24.

TERMS—$60 FOR THE SEASON.

Mares not proving with foal may be returned next season free of charge, provided the horse remains the property of the present proprietor, and stands at the same place, otherwise money will be refunded. The best of care taken of mares in any manner that owners may desire, but no responsibility assumed for accidents or escapes. For further particulars, apply to or address

G. W. HUGHES, Agent.

G. A. DOHERTY, Proprietor. Napa City.

The Hambletonian Stallion 10178.

CHRISMAN'S HAMBLETONIAN, Sire of Steve Whipple, 2:23, Kate Agnew, 2:28¼, etc.
- Whipple's Hambleto'n — Sire of 14 trotters and 1 pacer from 2:19 to 2:30, and 7 sons with 8 performers from 2:21¼ to 2:30, and dams of 6 from 2:19¼ to 2:30.
  - Guy Miller — By Hambletonian 10.
  - Martha Washington — Dam of Speculation 928 Sire of Crown Pt. 2:24 Oakland Maid, 2:22, Gracie S., 2:28¼, and dam of Waterford, 2:27
- Flora, 2:29¼, trial, 2:26. Dam of Chrisman's Hambletonian, sire of Steve Whipple, 2:23 Kate Agnew, 2:28¼.
  - Chieftain 721 — Sire of Defiance, 2:24 and 2:17¼, pacing; Califo, 2:18, and Onward, 2:24, pacer.
  - daughter of Wilson's Leamon

Stud season now on till the 1st of August, 1890, at $40 each mare, with return privilege in 1891, provided stallion and mare, or either, do not change owners. Good pasture at hand, and comfortable accommodation for brood mares and colts. For further particulars, address

JESSE CHRISMAN, Proprietor.

San Jose, Cal.

Vineland Stock Farm

Whippleton 1883,

Sire of

LILY STANLEY	Record	2:17½
HOMESTAKE	"	2:16½
FLORA B.	"	2:27
CORA C.	"	2:31½
BLACK PRINCE	"	2:36½
RACHEL	"	2:3
PRINCE W.	"	2:40

WHIPPLETON is not only the sire of trotters, but he is the greatest sire of Carriage Horses on the Pacific Coast. Some of the best carriage and road teams in San Francisco are sired by Whippleton. A carriage team by Whippleton received First Premium at Napa, Petaluma, Oakland, Sacramento, Stockton and San Jose. Whippleton and his colts have never been beaten in the show ring.

DESCRIPTION.

WHIPPLETON is black, tan muzzle and flanks, 17 hands, and weighs 1,100 lbs. Most of his colts are 16 hands or over, and with a few exceptions, bay, brown or black. He never sired a sorrel or white face colt. (If he does, I agree to refund service money.)

PEDIGREE.

WHIPPLETON, sired by Hambletonian Jr. (sire Hancock 2.29), by Whipple's Hambletonian (sire of Graves, 2:19, Westfield, 2:20¼, Express, 2:24, and 12 others in the 2:30 list), dam Lady Livingston (dam of Lady Blanchard, 2:26¼, Bloomfield Maid, trial 2:22), by General Taylor (sire of the dams of Wells Fargo, 2:18¾, Nerea, 2:23¼, Bickford, 2:29¼, Lady Blanchard, 2:26¼, etc., and sire of grandam of Hazel Wilkes, 2:20) by the Morse Horse 6, sire of Norman 25 (sire of Lulu, 2:14¾, May Queen 2:20, etc.).

TERMS at $50, limited to 30 mares, for the season, usual return privileges. I would like to get about ten well bred mares with the proper combination of blood to breed to Whippleton on shares this season.

Alcona 730.

Sire of

FLORA BELLE	Record	2:24
CLAY DUKE	"	2:31½

ALCONA will be a great sire, but four of his colts have ever been trained, and all have shown full miles better than 2:30, and two of them as good as 2:20. Two of his first sons each sired a colt as a two-year-old, and last season one as a four-year-old trotted a full mile in 2:23¼, and the other, a three-year-old, a mile in 2:31. With opportunities, Alcona is destined to be one of Almont's best sons. Almont, for his opportunities, is beyond doubt the most prepotent sire of his age. He has 36 representatives in the 2:30 list; 49 sons and 22 daughters that have already produced 2:30 performers. Almont died five years ago at 20 years old. If he lived he would be but 25 years old.

PEDIGREE.

ALCONA sired by the great Almont (sire of Westmont 2:13¼, Fanny Witherspoon 2:16¼, Piedmont 2:17¼, and 34 others with records better than 2:30, and grandsire of Belle Hamlin 2:12¾, etc.); by Alexander's Abdallah (sire of Goldsmith Maid 2:14), he by Rysdyk's Hambletonian. Alcona's dam, Queen Mary, by Mambrino Chief (sire of Lady Thorne 2:18 1-4, and 5 others in the 2:30 list, and sire of the dams of Director 2:17, Piedmont 2:17¼, Onward 2:25 1-4, Red Wilkes Almont, Belmont and many other noted sires).

DESCRIPTION.

Alcona is a beautiful chestnut 16 3 1-2 hands high, and weighs 1200 lbs. His colts possess speed, style, finish and beauty, and if they don't trot they command the highest prices for carriage horses.

$40 for the season. Usual return privilege.

Season on Whippleton and Alcona ends July 1st, 1890.

Best kind of pasturage at $4 per month. Mares kept in any manner desired.

For further particulars send for circular or call at stables, one mile south of St. Helena.

FRED W. LOEBER.

St. Helena, Napa Co., Cal.

The Trotting Stallion

G & M

FULL BROTHER TO

ALFRED G, 2:19¾.

(Who has been taken to Kentucky to stand at $200)

Will make the season of 1890 from FEBRUARY 1st to JULY 1st, at

SANTA ROSA.

G. & M. is by Anteeo, 2:16¼; was foaled 1886; first dam Rosa B. by Speculation (son of Hambletonian 10); 2d dam Elizabeth by Alexander 490; 3d dam Nora by imp. Glencoe. Anteeo is by Electioneer, out of Columbine by A. W. Richmond 1687.

G. & M. is a handsome dark bay; stands 16-3 1-2 hands high, and weighs 1060 pounds. Gameness, stoutness, speed and stamina are indelibly impressed in every line of the pedigree of G. & M. Owners of brood-mares in search of these qualities, will do well to patronize this promising colt.

PHILOSOPHER,

Foaled 1886 by Pilot Wilkes 2887; first dam Bella by George Wilkes 519; second dam by Bell Morgan 61.

Philosopher's sire, Pilot Wilkes 2887, is by George Wilkes 519, dam Grace (the dam of Alice Woodburn, etc.), by Pilot Jr. 12, grandam by Orphan Boy.

Will make the season of 1890, from FEBRUARY 1st to JULY 1st, at Santa Rosa.

TERMS for the season:

G. & M., $50,

PHILOSOPHER, $30,

with privilege of returning mares that do not prove in foal the next season free of charge, provided the horse bred to remains the property of the present owners. Good pasturage at $3 per month. No responsibility assumed for accidents or escapes. Service fees payable before removal of the mare. For further particulars, address

GEO. E. GUERNE,

Santa Rosa Cal.

ANTEEO BUTTON,

By Anteeo, 2:16 1-4.

And out of the dam of Alexander Button, four year old 2:26 1-2; Trial 2:16.

Will make the season of 1890 at ST. HELENA

DESCRIPTION.

ANTEEO BUTTON is five years old, a handsome dark bay, 15 1-2 hands high, and weighs 1[illegible] lbs. This horse has had but little or no systematic work, but he can trot fast and if there is anything in looks or breeding, he should produce trotters.

TERMS, $40 FOR THE SEASON, which closes July 1st. Best of alfalfa pasture on the premises at $4 per month. Mares cared for in any way that their owners may desire, but no responsibility assumed. For further particulars, address

E. C. SPEAR,

St. Helena, Cal.

Guenoc Stud Farm, Lake Co., Cal.

Imp. GREENBACK

(Sire of the English winners Greenlight, Greenjacket, Greenshank, Greenwave and Greenhorn)

By Dollar, dam Music, by Stockwell. $100 the Season

ST. SAVIOR,

(FULL BROTHER TO EOLE)

By Eolus, dam War Song, by War Dance. $100 the Season.

PASTURAGE, $5 PER MONTH.

With right to return the following year if mare does not prove with foal. The best of care taken, but no liability for accidents or escapes. Mares shipped to C. W. ABY, care ST. HELENA STABLES, St. Helena Napa County, will be taken in charge by competent men.

For further information write to

DR. C. W. ABY, Middletown, Lake County, Cal.

1890 Three Anteeo Stallions 1890

SUNSET, 5 years old. by Anteeo
ANTEEOF, 4 years old, by Anteeo
ANTEEOP, 3 years old, by Anteeo

ANTEEO. Standard 7868. Record, 2:16 1-4, he by Stanford's Electioneer, and dam Columbine.

DESCRIPTIONS, PEDIGREES AND CONDITIONS.

"SUNSET" is a rich, dark bay, small star on forehead, portion of hind left foot white; was foaled March 11, 1885; is by ANTEEO and the inbred HAMBLETONIAN mare, BESSIE G, she by KING PHILIP, son of WHIPPLE'S HAMBLETONIAN. He is 16 1-2 hands high, and weighs 1,310 lbs. He is of perfect build and splendid action cool headed and great speed for his size, having trotted a trial mile as a three-year-old in 2:38. He then entered heavy in the stud and was matched against Whalebone at the Healdsburg races November 1, 1889, winning just as he pleased in three straight heats; time, 2:47, 2:48 1-2, 2:52 1-2. He was then matched for a race to come off last Thanksgiving Day at Petaluma but owing to the heavy rains the event did not take place. A few days previous to Thanksgiving Day Mr. Lawrence worked Sunset out and then he trotted three square miles and beats in 2:32½, 2:34 and 2:37.

SUNSET will be bred to 40 mares only, at $50 each, no colt no pay.

"ANTEEOF" is a jet black, was foaled April 13, 1886, is 16¾ hands high, and weighs 1,200 lbs., has a very fine, heavy black mane and tail; is well proportioned, moves majestically, is of easy, lofty carriage; is symmetrical, in fact is a beautiful horse. He was sired by Anteeo and the C. A. Taylor mare "Nance," her dam, was raised by Dr. Oliver Plummer, of Cosumnes, Cal., and sired by "Napoleon"; Napoleon was foaled May 29, 1853, and raised by James Kyle of Butler County, Ohio. He was sired by Benj. Sweet's horse Bellfounder, and he by Old Bellfounder, his dam was sired by Doc. Daniel Mulligan's horse, Cadmus, G. G. sire the celebrated Eclipse; his G. dam was sired by Big Shakespeare, G. G., sires dam by Messenger and Expedition.

ANTEEOF will be bred to 25 mares only, at $50 each. No colt, no pay.

"ANTEEOP" is a rich seal brown; was foaled March 7, 1887; by Anteeo and the inbred Hambletonian mare Bessie G., also dam of Sunset, his full brother and Midget his full sister; he is 16 1-2 hands high and weighs 950 lbs, and measures 22 inches around the arm, good head, fine neck, full, broad breast; withers and rump on nearly equal line, well proportioned bones, ankle, shoulders, loins and hips; strong legs all around, with great muscular development and splendid sinews; wirey pasterns and sound, compact feet; the lines from hip to hock show power and speed; stands square and has excellent action, has a superb lustrous coat of rich, deep brown fur of seal color without defects; an even, honest trotter, and has gone the mile as a two-year-old in 2:48, the last quarter in 38 seconds; is intelligent and of high spirit, with much temper, but is not vicious, has very fine eyes, is a handsome, showy colt; attractive in harness.

ANTEEOP will be bred to 15 mares only, at $50. No colt, no pay.

SEASON to commence February 1st, ending July 1, 1890. Book now ready. Apply to John H. Lawrence, "Manager and Trainer," on my fruit and hop ranch, 1 mile east of Court House, on Sonoma road. Excellent pasture furnished with running water, also dry knolls with oak shelter, at $3 per month for mares. Two of the above stallions will be for sale after the expiration of the their stud season.

GUY E. GROSSE,
SANTA ROSA, SONOMA CO., CAL.

The Trotting Stallion

Guide 2:29

(At Four Years)

Will make the season of 1890 at the SANTA RITA RANCH, about one mile North of Pleasanton.

DESCRIPTION.

GUIDE is a handsome seal brown, five years old, stands 15¾ hands high, and weighs 1035 pounds. He is of fine form, level headed, intelligent, and comes from blood lines that are noted for the qualities of speed and gameness.

PEDIGREE.

GUIDE, 2:28¼

- Director, 2:17. Sire of Direct, 2:18¼, Margaret S., 2:19¼.
  - Dictator 113. Sire of 23 trotters and 3 pacers in 2:30.
    - Hambletonian 10.
    - Clara, by American Star 14.
  - Dolly. Dam of Onward, 2:25¼, Thorndale, 2:22¼.
    - Mambrino Chief 11.
    - Fannie, by Ben Franklin.
- Imogene.
  - Norwood 522. Sire of Tommy Norwood, 2:26¼.
    - Hambletonian 10.
    - Lady Fallis, by American Star 14.
  - daughter of
    - American Star 14.
    - daughter of Harry Clay 45.

The attention of breeders is especially called to the above pedigree as showing 3 crosses of American Star.

GUIDE trotted into the 2:30 list last season with little training, and he will trot into the 2:20 list the coming season barring accidents.

Guide's sire has a record of 2:17, made in a five heat race, and Guide is closely related to Phallas, who made a record of 2:13¾ in a fourth heat, and to Jay-Eye-See, record 2:10.

TWO HUNDRED AND FIFTY DOLLARS will be given to the owner of the first of the produce of Guide put in the 2:30 list, and $100 to each one after the first.

TERMS—$75 for the season, with the usual return privileges.

Admiro,

Sire Admiral; dam by San Bruno, by Easton's David Hill.

This magnificent horse is a handsome bay, eight years old; stands 17 1-2 hands high, and weighs 1400 pounds He is very speedy for a large horse, and breeds fine large carriage horses. His produce possess every qualification of the Cleveland Bay, with the added qualities of speed and endurance resulting from his high trotting breeding.

TERMS—$35 for the season, with usual return privileges.

Will stand three days each week at Santa Rita Ranch, Pleasanton, and at A. T. Hatch's Ranch "Almono," Alamo, Contra Costa County, alternately. All mares sent care of SMITH & SUTHERLAND, Pleasanton, will be taken in charge of on arrival, and will receive the best care and attention in any manner the owners may desire. Good pasturage at $4 per month. Only a limited number of approved mares will be served by this horse this season.

No responsibility assumed for escapes or accidents. For further particulars, address

SMITH & SUTHERLAND, Pleasanton,

or A. T. HATCH, care Palace Hotel, San Francisco.

For Rent.
San Mateo.

Several acres on county road—Belle View Avenue Barn, two Cottages, 8 ed, completed. House now building and will be completed in one month. Location unsurpassed.

Apply to or address

R. TEN BROECK.

San Mateo, opposite Orphanage.

Pedigrees Tabulated

IN THE MOST ARTISTIC MANNER.

Giving speed performers under sires and dams. Catalogues compiled. Stallion cards and circulars written up ready for the press. Pedigree blanks for sale. Prices reasonable. Horses bought and sold on commission. References furnished.

R. Y. HARDIN.

806 W. Madison St., Chicago, Ill.

SAN DIEGO, 8776.

SAN DIEGO 8776

- Alcona Clay 2756.
  - Alcona 730. Sire of Flora Belle, 2:24, Clay Duke, 2:31½, etc.
    - Almont 33. Sire of Westmont, 2:15½, Piedmont 2:17½, Puritan, 2:16, and 33 others in 2:30 list.
    - by Mambrino Chief 11. Sire of Lady Thorne, 2:18¼.
  - Madonna. Dam of Del Rey, trial 2:31, Alcona Jr., 2:41, sire of Silas Skinner, trial 2:23¼.
    - Cassius M. Clay Jr. 22. Sire of Durango, 2:23½, Harry Clay 2:29½, and sire of dam of Happy Thought, 2:22¼, and others.
    - by Joe Downing 710. Sire of Abe Downing, 2:20½, Dr. Jamison, 2:26, and sire of dams Kentucky Hambletonian, 2:27, Aurena, 2:19, and others.
- Fontana. Dam of Flora Belle, 2:24, Silas Skinner, trial 2:23¼.
  - Almont 33. Sire of 36 in 2:30 list, 49 sons and 22 daughters that have produced 2:30 performers.
  - Fanny Williams. Dam of Bay Chieftain, 2:28¼.
    - Abdallah 15. Sire of Goldsmith Maid, 2:14, Thorndale, 2:21¼, also Almont, Belmont, Jim Monroe, etc.
    - by Denmark (thoroughbred).

GRANDISSIMO is a blood bay, handsome-modelled colt, and a natural trotter. He is four years old and trotted one quarter miles in 36 seconds, with very limited training, last Fall.

SAN DIEGO is dark seal brown, three years old, and trotted one-quarter miles in 40 seconds as a two year old.

These are two grand young horses, and, barring accidents, will both make fast records next fall.

They will both be allowed a limited number of mares, at $50 for the season. Mares not proving foal to be returned free 1891. Best of pasture for mares at $4 per month, but no liability for accidents or escapes.

They will make the season from February 1st to June 1st at Napa Fair Grounds. For further particulars, address or call on

H. B. STARR, Race Track, Napa, Cal.,

or FRED W. LOEBER, St. Helena

A SON OF ALMONT 33.

Only $25 for the Season.

ASHLAND ALMONT 3481

PEDIGREE.

ASHLAND ALMONT 3481

- Almont 33. Sire of 34 in 2:30 or better of 23 daughters and of 49 sires that have produce in 2:30 or better.
  - Abdallah 15. Sire Goldsmith Maid, 2:14; 6 in 2:30 list; 13 sires and 25 dams of trotters in 2:30 list.
    - Hambletonian 10. sire of 41 in 2:30 list; sire of 107 sires 567 in 2:30 list.
    - Katy Darling.
  - Sally Anderson.
    - Mambrino Chief 11. Lady Thorn, 2:18¼.
    - Kate, by Pilot Jr. 12.
- Pauline. Dam of Sapho.
  - Ashland Chief. Sire Black Cloud, 2:17¼.
    - Mambrino Chief 11. Lady Thorn, 2:18¼.
    - dau. of imp. Yorkshire, (thoroughbred).
  - Rosina. Dam Almonia, the dam of Sally Cossack, 2:22¼, dau. Mamb. Abdallah, sire Mam. Prince, 2:28, and of Mamb. Bashaw, sire of Graham's Mambrino, 2:38.
    - Abdallah 15. Sire Goldsmith Maid, 2:14.
    - Prof. Smith's Sir William.

DESCRIPTION.

ASHLAND ALMONT 3481 is a handsome chestnut; stands 16 hands; was foaled 1883, and bred by Geo. Withers, of Lexington, Ky. He is of fine form, and remarkably intelligent, sweet-tempered and absolutely sound. His oldest foal may be seen with him, and while he has never served a standard mare or one that was a producer of speed, all of his colts are large, sound, fast and handsome.

TERMS: $25 for the season, with usual return privileges. The best of care taken of mares in any manner that the owner may desire, but no responsibility assumed for escapes or accidents.

For further particulars, address

T. J. WHITEHEAD, Manager.

579 36th Street, bet. Telegraph Ave. and Grove St., Oakland, Cal.

or, W. H. ASHBY, Oakland, Cal.

2:10 1-2 ELECTIONEER 2:12 1-4

BAY STALLION	BROWN STALLION
ECLECTIC	**MORTIMER**
11,321	5,346
By Electioneer, dam Manette (full sister to Woodnut 2.16 1-2 Manon 2:21 and Maple, dam of Hattie D., three year-old record 2:28½) by Nutwood 2:18¾, etc., etc.	Four-year-old Record 2:27. By ELECTIONEER, dam MARTI, by Whipple's Hambletonian (sire of 15 in 2:30, and of dams of [illegible] in 2:30). Second dam Ida Martin by Rifleman (sire of Col. Lewis 2:18¾).
Terms $100 for the Season.	Terms $60 for the Season.

Horses shipped via San Francisco may be consigned to J. W. MORSHEAD, City Front Stables, who will attend to their forwarding.

Season closes JULY 1st, 1890. Usual return privileges.

For further particulars address owner,

WILFRED PAGE, Penns Grove, Sonoma County, Cal.

Langtry Farms' Stud

Imp. FRIAR TUCK

By the Immortal HERMIT.

DAM ROMPING GIRL BY WILD DAYRELL,

AT $50 THE SEASON.

Mares not proving with foal may be returned the following season. Good care taken of mares, but no liabilities for accidents or escapes.

Good Pasturage at $5 per month.

Mares shipped to ST. HELENA, care CHARLES WILLIAM ABY, St. Helena Stables, will be cared for. For further particulars address,

CHAS. WILLIAM ABY,

Middletown, Lake County, Cal.

THE CEDARS

BANNER MARK, 9424.

Foaled in 1886; by Victor von Bismarck (sire Edgemark, four year old record 2:16; Von Wilkes yearling record 2:35¼, etc.); dam Moonlight by Almont one (sire of Alcryon 2:15 1-4, etc.); second dam Twilight (dam of Skylight Pilot 2:19) by Mambrino Pilot (sire of Hannis 2:17¾); third dam by Pilot Jr. (sire of the dam of Maud S. 2:08¾); fourth dam nearly or quite thoroughbred.

In his four double crosses he combines more of popular blood than any colt of his age. He is a double Hambletonian, double Clay through Bismarck and George Wilkes, double Mambrino and Pilot through Mambrino Pilot, Pilot Jr., and Mambrino Patchen. There is no other colt living bred like him. If you want Hambletonian, Clay, Mambrino or Pilot Jr., here you have it all combined in one grand colt. He has much of the finish of the thoroughbred.

Insurance $300. Limited to Seven Approved Mares.

Book full for 1890 and open for 1891 for fifteen approved mares. Address

T. E. MOORE,

The Cedars, Shawhan, Ky.

SUBSCRIBE FOR THE

Breeder and Sportsman

GEO. WASHINGTON, 11,623.

RECORD 2:30.

Bay colt, bred by Thomas Smith of Vallejo, Cal. Foaled 1886 by Mambrino Chief, Jr., 11,622, record 2:34 1-4. 1st dam Fanny Rose by Vick's Ethan Allen Jr. 2,903, sire of Prince Allen 2:27. 2nd dam Jenny Lind, thoroughbred, dam of Prince Allen 2:27. Will serve a limited number of mares at $50 for the season. Mares not proving with foal may be returned next season free.

Mambrino Chief, Jr. 11,622.

RECORD 2:34 1 2.

Sire of George Washington, record 2 30 at three years old. Bay horse bred by Rufus Ingalls of Belvedere, Ill. By McDonald Chief 3 St. First dam Venus by Mambrino Patchen 58. 2nd dam by Wardlow's Shakespeare. 3rd dam Lone Gold 4th dam by Silver Heels. Has not been in the stud b fore. He was 8 years old when he served a few mares, and his colts all show good style and form.

Terms for the season $40. For further particulars see or address

THOMAS SMITH,
Vallejo, Cal.

Elector 2170.

Sire of J. R.

Three-Year Old Record 2:24.

Sired by Electioneer 125, sire of Sunol, three-year-old, 2:10½, Palo Alto, 2:12¼, etc.; dam Gilberta by Fred Low 656, sire of Clay, 2:25½, etc.

Second dam Lady Gilbert (grandam of Lot Slocum, 2:17½) by General Knox 140 (sire of Lady Maud, 2:18¼, and many others).

TERMS.

$150 for the season. Book full for 1890.

L. A. RICHARDS,
Grayson, Stanislaus Co., Cal.

The Thoroughbred Stallion

Three Cheers

Will make the season of 1890 at

Sacramento.

PEDIGREE.

- imp. Hurrah....
  - Newminster
    - Touchstone, by Camel
    - Beeswing, by Dr. Syntax
  - Jovial
    - Bay Middleton, by Sultan
    - Sister to Grey Momus, by Comus
- Young Fashion
  - imp. Monarch
    - imp. Priam, by Emilius
    - imp. Delphine, by Whisker
  - Fashion
    - imp. Trustee, by Catton
    - Bonnets o' Blue, by Sir Charles

Hurrah was imported by John Reber, of Lancaster, Ohio, a locality where there were but few breeders of thoroughbreds. Under these disadvantages he sired a long list of winners. His sire Newminster, won the St. Ledger 1851, and his dam, Jovial by Bay Middleton, winner of the Derby 1836. Newminster by Touchstone, winner St. Ledger 1834. Dam Beeswing, winner of 54 races out of 64 starts, by Dr. Syntax, winner of the Doncaster Cup, 1837—40—41—42, the only horse that ever accomplished that feat.

On the side of the dam Three Cheers is equally well related. Young Fashion was the dam of Surprise, Scotland (the only horse that ever beat Asteroid a heat), Liverpool, Columbia, and Bonnie Kate, the dam of Little Buttercup, and the flying Bonnie Lizzie. His grandam, Fashion was the greatest race mare of her day and beat Boston in that historical match at four mile heats, which is recorded as one of the greatest events in the annals of the turf.

Horsemen who are qualified to judge, pronounce Three Cheers to be the finest type of the Newminster line in America.

LOCATION.

THREE CHEERS will be located at the Arcade Training Stable, Rancho del Paso. This place has been selected for the reason that first class pasturage has been secured there for the exclusive use of these mares and the other facilities to be obtained there for the care of mares (especially mares in foal) are better than can be found elsewhere in the locality.

TERMS.

$50 for the season with the usual return privileges. Pasturage $5 per month. Mares cared for as owners may desire at bottom rates for grain and hay. All bills payable before the mare is removed.

Mares shipped care of WM. IRVINE, Pacific Stables, Sacramento, will be properly cared for and sent to the ranch without delay.

Three Cheers will be in charge of one of the most experienced and competent stud grooms in the State, who will exercise every care, but no reponsibility assumed for accidents or escapes.

For further particulars apply to Louis Crissler, at Entrance; Wm. Irvine, Pacific Stables, Second St., Sacramento; or to the owner,

E. S. CULVER,
313 Bush St., San Francisco.

GROVER CLAY

Bay Stallion, Black Points,

15 3-4 hands high.

Bred by W. W. Traylor, San Francisco.

BY ELECTIONEER.

First dam Maggie Norfolk by Norfolk, son of Lexington, he by Boston. Second dam Tilda Quill by Billy Cheatham he by Cracken, and he by Boston. Third dam by Dorsey's Golddust.

TERMS.

Will make the season of 1890 at the Training Stable of Denis Gannon, near Oakland Trotting Park, $50 the season, payable at time of service. Season to commence February 1st and ending July 1st. Proper care of mares will be taken, but no responsibility incurred for accidents or escapes. Address,

DENIS GANNON, Oakland, Cal.

2:10¾ 2:13¾ 2:10

DEXTER PRINCE.

This Royally-bred Stallion will make the Season of 1890 at the LIVE OAKS Breeding Farm, 2 miles from Lodi, San Joaquin County, Cal.

DESCRIPTION.

DEXTER PRINCE is a blood bay, 16 hands high, weighs over 1,100 pounds; has great power and substance, and the highest finish. When two years old, at Palo Alto, he was timed quarters by Gov. Stanford in 33½ seconds, and he was driven eights by Mr. Marvin at a faster rate of speed than that. He is a sure foal-getter, and invariably sires foals of good size, of fine form and finish, and the highest rate of speed.

PEDIGREE.

By KENTUCKY PRINCE, the sire of Guy, 2:10¾, Spofford, 2:18¾, Company, 2:19¾, Bayonne Prince, 2:21 1-4, Fred Folger, 2:20¾, and a score more in the 2:30 list.

First dam LADY DEXTER, full sister of the greatest of trotters, Dexter, and the greatest of sires, Dictator, the sire of Director, 2:17, Phallas, 2:13¾, in a fourth heat, and Jay-Eye-See, 2:10.

Second dam Clara, the dam of Dexter, 2:17 1-4, Dictator, Astoria 2:29 1-4 and Almah, 2:29¾. Clara was by American Star, that has 34 daughters that have produced 2:30 or better trotters.

Third dam the McKinstry mare, the dam of Shark, 2:27¾. HAMBLETONIAN, the grandsire of DEXTER PRINCE, has 40 trotters in the 2:30 list, 44 daughters that have produced 2:30 trotters, and more than 100 sons that have sired 2:30 trotters.

CLARK CHIEF, the grandsire on the sire's side, was the sire of performing and producing sons and daughters.

DEXTER PRINCE has faster blood lines, on both sides, than any other stallion in the world—Guy 2:10¾, and Jay-Eye-See, 2:10.

KENTUCKY PRINCE is one of the best bred and speediest stallions in the world. David Bonner, in the presence of Governor Stanford, timed him when he trotted a 2:10 gait. He is by Clark Chief, one of the great broodmare sires; his first dam is Kentucky Queen by Morgan Eagle, son of Hale's Green Mountain Morgan, 2nd dam by Blythe's Whip, 3rd dam by Martin's Brummier, 4th dam by Quicksilver 560, on through the strongest thoroughbred blood.

TERMS.

$100 for the season, with usual return privileges. Payable before mares are removed. Good pasture, and the best care furnished, but no responsibility assumed for accidents.

PREMIUM.

$250 will be given to the first of the produce of DEXTER PRINCE put in the 2:30 list, and $100 each after the first. Address

L M. MORSE, Lodi, Cal.

The Trotting Stallion

Silver Bow

Will make the season of 1890 at the Oakland Race Track.

PEDIGREE.

SILVER BOW 11708, two-year-old record 2:37, is by Robert McGregor 647, 2:17¾ (sire of Bonnie McGregor, 2:13¾, Earl McGregor, 2:31¾, Mac D., 2:30, McGregor Boy, 2:29¾, Mark Time, 2:30, Roxie McGregor, 2:20¾) by Major Edsall 2:1, 2:29, by Alexander's Abdallah 15—sire of Goldsmith Maid, 2:14—by Hambletonian 10—sire of Dexter, 2:17¾.

Robert McGregor's dam was Nancy Whitman by American Star 14, by Stockholm's American Star.

SILVER BOW'S first dam is Sadie by Hambletonian 10, sire of Geo. Wilkes, 2:22—sire of Guy Wilkes, 2:15¾—also Electioneer, sire of Sunol, three-year-old record, 2:10¾, and Palo Alto, 2:12¾; second dam Lady Wynne by Wm. Welch 341; third dam Elenora Margrave by imp. Margrave.

DESCRIPTION.

SILVER BOW is a handsome bay, no white; 15-2¾ hands high; weighs 1075 pounds; of fine form, with the best of legs and a clean-cut, intelligent head. Is remarkably level-headed, seldom making a break; wears seven-ounce shoes in front. His record, 2:37, is no mark of his speed; he can beat 30 easy, and with his gilt-edge breeding, he is just what he ought to be, a trotter sired by a trotter whose dam was herself a trotter and his grandam the dam of two trotters. His dam Sadie being by Hambletonian 10, shows him to be bred from the cream of the trotting blood.

TERMS: $100 for the season. Mares not proving in foal returnable for the season of 1891 free of charge. Good pasturage and first-class care taken of mares for $5 per month. No responsibilities assumed for escapes or accidents. For further particulars, address

Limited to 15 approved mares.
Season to end June 1st, 1890.

P. J. WILLIAMS,
Care Race Track, Oakland, Cal.

HOLLYWOOD BREEDING FARM.

MOUNTAIN BOY 4841.

Br s MOUNTAIN BOY, 4841, bred by Charles Backman, Orange County, New York, foaled 1882, sire Kentucky Prince 2470, dam Elise, sister to Elaine, by Messenger Duroc 106; grandam Green Mountain Maid, 3d dam, Shanghai Mary, will serve a limited number of mares at $100 the season.

ELECTION.

Bay stallion ELECTION, bred at Senator Stanford's Palo Alto Stock Farm, foaled 1884, sire Electioneer, dam Lizzie H. by Whipple's Hambletonian 725, grandam Lizzie Harris (by Comus son of Green's Bashaw 50), great grandam by Arnold Harris, thoroughbred.

Election is one of the handsomest bloodlike sons of Electioneer, and with his thoroughbred cross through Arnold Harris should prove invaluable as a sire. TERMS, $100 the season.

KAFIR.

B c KAFIR, bred by L. J. Rose, Los Angeles, foaled 1887, sire Alcazar, 2:20½, dam Flower Girl by Arthurton, sire of Arab, 2:15, grandam Flora by General McClellan, 144, sire of three in 2:30 list, great grand dam by Langford, he by Williamson's Belmont, will serve a limited number of mares at $50 the season.

WOODSIDE.

Ch c WOODSIDE, sire Woodnut, 2:16½; 1st dam Veronica by Alcona, 730; 2nd dam Fontana by Almont 33; 3rd dam Fannie Williams by Alexander's Abdallah, 15. Book full.

MART BOORHEM.

B c MART BOORHEM, by Sydney, 2:19½; 1st dam Towhead by Echo. This colt is a full brother to St. Nicholas who showed a mile in 2:27½ at three years old. TERMS, $25 the season.

REVEILLE.

The well known thoroughbred stallion REVEILLE by Shiloh, dam by Norfolk. Reveille is a brother to John Treat and is the sire of Tycoon and Gladstone TERMS, $25 the season.

Hollywood is nicely situated three miles from Vallejo on the Napa road. Good pasturage and every care will be taken of mares at reasonable rates. For further particulars, apply,

B. C. HOLLY, Vallejo.

HORSES PURCHASED ON COMMISSION.

THOROUGHBREDS A SPECIALTY.

Will select and buy, or buy selected Animals for all desiring, for reasonable compensation

KEEPS PROMISING YOUNGSTERS IN VIEW.

L. M. LASLEY, Stanford, Ky.

References:—J. W. Guest, Danville, Ky.
B. G. Bruce, Lexington Ky.
S. H. Baughman, Stanford, Ky.
G. A. Lackey, Stanford, Ky.
Geo. McAlister, Stanford, Ky.
First National Bank, Stanford, Ky.

The Thoroughbred Stallion

INTRUDER

Will make the Season of 1890 at Agricultural Park, SACRAMENTO.

Bay Horse, foaled 1871, bred by Sir L. Newman, England. Imported by D. D. Withers, Esq., New York.

By Crater, Son of Orlando and Vesuvienne by Gladiator.

1st dam Lady Bountiful by Rataplan (Rataplan is own brother to Stockwell, and winner of 42 races, including the Doncaster Cup and 19 Queen's Plates, and proved himself the most distinguished race horse of his day in England).

2d dam Plentiful by Don John (the winner of St. Leger and Doncaster Cup).

3d dam Plenty by Bay Middleton (winner of the Derby and Two Thousand Guinea Stakes).

4th dam Plenary, own sister of Plenipotentiary, by Emilius. (Both Emilius and Plenipotentiary were Derby winners).

5th dam Harriet, dam of the renowned Plenipotentiary by Pericles.

6th dam by Selim, winner of the One Thousand Guinea Stakes.

7th dam by Pypilina, by Sir Peter.

8th dam Rally, by Trumpeter.

9th dam Fancy, by Florizel. Fancy was full sister to Diomed, the first Derby winner in England, and after his importation into this country, sired the illustrious Sir Archy, etc. See English Stud Book.

Imported INTRUDER is a beautiful bay, standing fully 16 hands high, of great length and substance, and descends through close and strong currents from the most illustrious winners and winning lines of blood of which the English Stud Book bears record.

A careful review of the first six crosses of the pedigree of INTRUDER will show nine Derby winners; five St. Leger winners; two winners of The Oaks; two winners of the Two Thousand Guineas; two winners of the One Thousand Guineas; one Goodwood Cup winner; one Cesarwich Cup winner; one Cambridgeshire Stakes winner, and four Doncaster Cups, in addition to a great number of steeplechases and other races of less import.

INTRUDER, at the great fair held at St. Louis, Mo., in 1876, was awarded the highest stallion honors—the blue ribbon and the $500 purse—in the sweepstakes ring for stallion of any age or blood. The list of competitors embraced the large number of thirty-three animals, and they represented England, Canada, Kentucky, Tennessee, and other states. He also took first premium in his class and in sweepstakes for the best stallion of any age or breed at the State Fair at Peoria, Ill., 1882. He is the sire of Tidal Wave, George Hakes, Bernice and April Fool.

INTRUDER is the sire of Interpose, who is the dam of Spokane, winner of the Kentucky Derby, in which he beat the great horse Proctor Knott and broke the record.

TERMS: $50 for the season. Mares not proving with foal can be returned the next season free of charge. Good pasturage at $4 per month. Mares cared for in any manner owners may desire, and fed on hay and grain, either or both, at reasonable rates. While every precaution will be taken, no responsibility will be assumed for escapes or accidents. Mares sent from a distance in care of the undersigned, will be met and taken to the park. For further particulars, address

T. J. KNIGHT.
Agricultural Park, Sacramento.

THE BUCKINGHAM.

OLD STRAIGHT WHISKIES.

141 Montgomery Street.
308 Bush Street, S. F.

M. J. BALFE, Proprietor.

Cook STOCK FARM,

Season of 1890.

STEINWAY 1808.

Three-Year-Old Record 2:25 3-4.

Sire of STRATHWAY, three year old record 2:26, and sire of the dam of BOURBON RUSSELL 2:30.

By STRATHMORE 408; sire of 31 in the 2:30 list; sire of 6 dams of 8 in the 2:30 list, and sire of 3 sires of 3 in 2:30 list.

1st dam ABBESS (dam of Solo 2:28, and Soprano, dam of C. F. Clay 2:18, Eminence 2:27 and Strathbridge, 3 year old record 2:28½) by ALBION, sire of VANITY FAIR 2:24½, and of the dam of FAVORITE 2:25½.

2nd dam by MARSHALL NEY.

3rd dam by BERTRAND, a son of SIR ARCHY.

TERMS—$100 for the season.

CHARLES DERBY 4907

Brown Horse, Foaled 1885.

By STEINWAY 1808.

1st dam by the great ELECTIONEER, sire of SUNOL, 3 year old record 2:10½, Palo Alto 2:12¼, etc., etc.

2nd dam FANNY MALONE, by NIAGARA.

3rd dam FANNY WICKHAM, by HERALD.

4th dam by Imp. TRUSTEE.

TERMS—$100 for the season

Pasturage $5 per month. Accidents and escapes at owner's risk. Mares consigned to the farm should be sent to Fashion Stables, Oakland; Geary & Grindle's Stable, Haywards; or to Bennett's Stable, Martinez; from and to which places they will be delivered free of charge. Address

COOK STOCK FARM,
Danville, Contra Costa, Co., Cal.

The Trotting Stallion

ARBITRATOR

Will make the Season of 1890 at NILES, Alameda County.

PEDIGREE.

ARBITRATOR.

- Director 1989, 2:17 in a race,
  - Sire of
    - Direct, 4 yrs., 2:18½ in a race,
    - Margaret S., 3 yrs., 2:19½ in a race,
    - Guide, 4 yrs., 2:28½ in a race.
- Lady Earnest.
  - Speculation 918, sire of
    - Oakland Maid, 2:22 in a race,
    - Gracie S., 2:22 in a race,
    - Crown Point, 2:24 in a race,
    - He the sire of Valensin, 3 yrs., 2:23 in a race,
    - Sire of Dam of Alfred G., 2:19½.
  - Lady Hibbard, dam of Lou Whipple, 2:26½ in a race.

Speculation's dam was Martha Washington, dam of Whipple's Hambletonian, sire of 15 in 2:30 and granddaughter of Burr's Napoleon, sire of Black Harry, who in 1859 won two miles in 5:14½. He sired Smith Burr, sire of Gen. Butler, 2:21, Wagon, 4:56½. He sired the dam of Fanny Mapes, dam of Jerome Eddy, 2:16½. He sired Telegraph, sire of dam of Rarus, 2:13¼.

DESCRIPTION.

ARBITRATOR was foaled 1886. He is of good size, fine conformation, and a beautiful seal brown.

TERMS.

Non-standard mares	$45
Standard mares by inheritance	35
Standard mares by performance or produce	25

For further particulars, address

H. A. MAYHEW, owner,
Niles, Alameda Co.

PASHA,

Registered No. 2039.

RECORD 2:36.

SIRE OF MORO 2:27.

Will make the present season at Linden, twelve miles east of STOCKTON,

Season commencing FEBRUARY 1st and ending JULY 1, 1890.

DESCRIPTION.

PASHA is a beautiful black; 16½ hands high, and weighs 1,240 pounds. He is a horse of beautiful symmetry and magnificent action.

PEDIGREE.

PASHA was sired by Sultan 1513, sire of Stamboul 2:12½, Ruby 2:19½, Alcazar 2:20½, Bay Rose 2:20½, and sixteen others with records below 2:30. First dam Madam Baldwin by The Moor 870; second dam Ben Lippincott by Belmont. Pasha is a full brother to Bay Rose, record 2:20½.

Sultan, by The Moor, sire of Beautiful Bells, dam of Hinda Rose, 2:19½, Bell Boy 2:19½, and Sable, dam of Sable Wilkes, three-year-old record 2:18. First dam Sultana, by Delmonico, sire of Derby 2:16, by Guy Miller, sire of Whipple's Hambletonian. Second dam by Mambrino Chief. Third dam by Downing's Bay Messenger. Fourth dam Miss Caudle, dam of Ericsson, four-year-old record 2:30½.

Terms for the season, $50.

With privilege of returning mares that do not prove in foal next season free of charge.

Good pasturage at $2 per month. No responsibility will be assumed for accidents or escapes. Service fee payable before the removal of the mare.

For further particulars, address

D. BRYSON,
Linden Cal.

Valensin Stock Farm Stallion.

SIDNEY, 2:19 3-4.

At Eight Years of Age Sire of the following Fastest on Record:

FAUSTINO, yearling stallion, record of the world....2:35
FLEET, fastest yearling record in 1888....2:36
FLEET, fastest two-year-old filly in 1889....2:24
GOLD LEAF, fastest four-year-old Pacing record in the world....2:11¼
ADONIS, fastest three-year-old Pacing Gelding in the world....2:14¼
ADONIS, four-year-old Gelding Pacing record....2:14¾

—Also the Sire of—

LONGWORTH, four years old....2:19
SISTER V., four years old (trial 2:23)....2:27
SANTA RITA....2:39
MEMO, two-year-old (three-year-old trial 2:20½)....2:49

And many others.

SIDNEY is the sire of Faustino 2:35, and Fleet 2:36, the two fastest yearlings the world has ever known by one sire, and his slowest yearling is faster than the great Electioneer's fastest.

Terms, $250, with usual return privileges, for a limited number of approved mares. Book nearly full.

Only eight more mares can be taken for Season of '90.

Pasturage $5 per month. Reasonable charges if fed hay and grain. Best of care taken of mares, but positively no responsibility assumed for accidents or escapes. For further particulars address

G. VALENSIN, Pleasanton, Cal.

MEMO.

The Best Son of SIDNEY

Will Make the Season of 1890 at the OAKLAND RACE TRACK

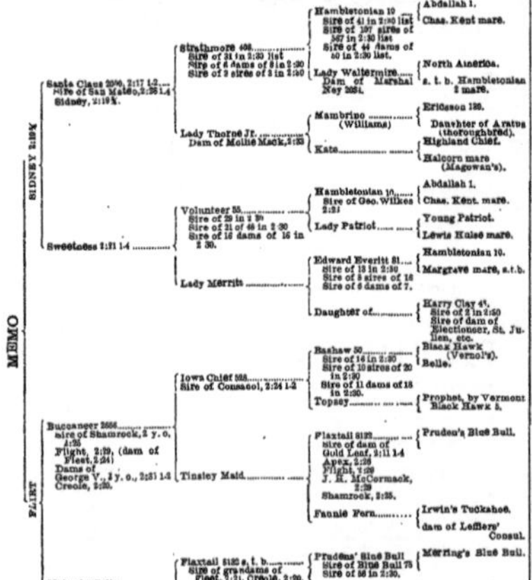

MEMO is, as can be seen at a glance, one of the best bred young stallions in service, having three crosses of Rysdyk's Hambletonian and one of *Harry Clay*, the sire of Green Mountain Maid (dam of Electioneer, etc.), while Long Island Black Hawk and Flaxtail also contribute to his blood. Sidney (Memo's sire) is universally known as the best young sire in the world, a producer of extreme speed at an early age.

PERFORMANCES.

MEMO trotted in public in his two year-old form, obtaining a record of 2:49, though he was close to Grandee in a race on the Bay District Track, the second heat of which was made in 2:31 1-2, the first in 2:32. He exhibited phenomenal speed when three years old, and had it not been for a slight strain of his fore fetlock, there is little question that he would have shown in public very close to the best record. On the Oakland track he was timed a mile in 2:20 1-2, and frequently trotted quarters in from 32 1-2 to 34 seconds.

As a four-year-old Memo only started once—at Sacramento—when, although out of condition, he showed great speed, and improving as he went on, great hopes were entertained of his going well down in the 'teens at the P. C. T. H. B. A. meeting, but after showing several very fast miles his leg filled and he was laid up for the season. He is sixteen hands high, and of powerful build throughout. His color is a glossy black, with both fore-feet white. His disposition is all that could be desired, and his action superb. He is a sure foal getter, only one mare being reported not in foal during his last season.

TERMS, $100, with usual return privileges, for a limited number of mares. Season to close JUNE 15th, when he will be prepared for track purposes. Pasturage $5 per month. Have leased the cricket ground adjoining the track for pasturage, where there is fine feed. Reasonable charges if fed hay and grain. Best of care taken of mares in any manner owners may desire, but positively no responsibility assumed for accidents or escapes. For further particulars address

J. P. KERR, 313 Bush Street, San Francisco,

or, JOHN ROWEN, Race Track, Oakland, Cal.

WOODNUT

(Weatherhead's) by Nutwood 600

Sire of Belmont Boy, 2:15, pacer, Woodnut, 2:16½, Felix, 2:18¾, Dawn, 2:18¾, Maggie E., 2:19¾, Irma, 2:18¾, and 26 others in 2:30 or better; 1st dam Flora, 2:30½, trial 2:26, dam of Chrisman's Hambletonian, sire of Steve Whipple, 2:22, Kate Agnew, 2:28½, by Chieftain 721, sire of Defiance 2:17¾ pacing and 2:24 trotting, Cairo, 2:28, Onward, 2:24, pacer; second dam by Wilson's Leaman.

Woodnut is a beautiful bay with black points, 15¾ hands high weighing 1,075 pounds. His colts are all larger than himself, and sell readily for road and carriage purposes, being of good color and very docile, yet prompt to obey, and always ready.

Service fee, $25, with usual privileges. Colts and fillies from Tilton Almont, Patchen, Stockbridge Chief, and other desirable crosses, FOR SALE. For further particulars, pedigrees, or any communication in horse matters, address

JAS. WEATHERHEAD, Prop.
San Jose, Cal.

PASTURAGE

AND

FIRST-CLASS CARE

TAKEN OF

Gentlemen's Road Horses and Trotters.

Colts Broken and Trained to Harness or Saddle.

Twenty new Box Stalls. First-class Pasturage, and the best of care given to all horses. **Terms, $4 per month.** Satisfaction Guaranteed.

Address,

K. O'GRADY,
Laurel Creek Farm,
SAN MATEO, CAL.

SAN MATEO STOCK FARM

HOME OF GUY WILKES,

Record, 2:15 1-4.

Guy Wilkes' Book is full for 1890 and 1891, and positively no more mares will be received.

Sable Wilkes, three-year-old record 2:18, will be allowed to serve 25 mares in addition to those already engaged at $250 the season of 1890. SABLE Wilkes, 15½ hands, black horse, by Guy Wilkes, first dam Sable by The Moor; second dam Gretchen by Mambrino Pilot; third dam Kitty Kirkman by Canada Chief; fourth dam by Fanning's Tobe; fifth dam by imp. Leviathan.

Leo Wilkes, brown horse, four years, 16 hands, full brother to Sable Wilkes, will be allowed to serve 30 mares at $100 the season.

Mares not proving with foal may be returned the following season free of service fee. Parties engaging the services of any of the above horses must send a deposit of 10 per cent. of service money with engagement. Pasturage $6 per month, and when the condition of the animal requires it, hay or grain, or both, are fed, the charge will be $12 50 per month. Good care will be taken of all mares sent to the Farm, but no liability will be assumed for accidents or escapes.

All bills are due at time of service, but must be paid by August 1st of each year. No stock will be allowed to leave the place until all bills are paid.

WILLIAM CORBITT.
San Mateo Stock Farm.

Pleasanton Stock Farm Co.'s Stallions.

DIRECTOR, 2:17.

Director's book is open for 15 good mares more than already booked for the season of 1890, at $300 each.

This is the cheapest service fee ever charged for a stallion, taking into consideration his BREEDING and RACE RECORD and the RACE RECORDS OF HIS COLTS.

Season to commence February 15th and close August 1st.

CORRECTOR, Four Years Old.

Sire Director 2:17, dam Brainey, she by Echo. Echo sired by Rysdyk's Hambletonian, out of Magnolia, she by Seely's American Star, Brainey's dam Lady Dudley, she by Tom Dudley by Blacknose, a son of Medoc, he by American Eclipse. Lady Dudley's dam by Bertrand, Jr., a son of Bertrand.

CORRECTOR is a rich seal brown 15¾ hands high, and is the fastest young stallion in the world under the same conditions, never having been off the farm where raised and never been shod or driven for speed before last Christmas, and can trot quarters now in 35 seconds, a 2:20 gait.

He will be allowed to serve ten good mares, at $100 each for the season, which closes June 1st.

DECORATOR, Four Years Old.

Sire Director 2:17, dam Chess, sired by Cardinal 2.37, trial 2:28, he by Gen. Gifford's Morgan, dam of Cardinal, sired by Joe Gales of Ohio, he by Marlborough out of the Duchess of Marlborough by Southern Eclipse; second dam old Duchess of Marlborough by Sir Archy; third dam by imp Diomed. Decorator's second dam a Morgan and Messenger mare.

Decorator is a light bay 16 hands high, and with but little handling for speed has shown eighths in 17½ seconds, a 2:20 gait.

He will be allowed to serve ten good mares at $50 each for the season, which closes June 1st.

Mares not proving with foal may be returned next season free of charge of service fees to the same stallion, if he is still in our possession; however, the company reserves the right to return the fee instead of giving service.

Pasturage $4 per month; hay and grain extra. Accidents and escapes at owner's risk.

Service fees due at time of service, and must be paid, together with pasturage, etc., before mares are taken away, or a good approved note given, payable August 1st, 1890, at which date all bills must be settled.

For further information call or address **M. SALISBURY, 320 Sansome Street, Room 96 San Francisco, or**

PLEASANTON STOCK FARM CO.,
Pleasanton, Alameda Co., Cal.

SOUTHER FARM

P. O. Box 208. San Leandro, Cal.

1¼ miles northwest of San Leandro; 8 miles southeast of Oakland. Turn off county road between above places at "Stanley Road," ¼ mile north of San Leandro.

Horses boarded at all times in any manner desired. Best of care but no responsibility for accidents. Colts broken and handled for road or track. Terms reasonable.

Glen Fortune,	Jester D,	El Benton,	Figaro,
By Electioneer.	By Almont.	By Electioneer.	Hambletonian 72[illegible]
$50 for 1889.	$50 for 1890.	Limited to 5 mares.	Limited to 12 mares
		Book Full.	Book Full.

THE SOUTHER FARM

Has Green Feed the Year Round

and feeds Hay in connection with the green feed, which a horse must have if he is to thrive. Every animal is given

A Dry, Warm Place to Sleep;

No matter how stormy the weather. All Stock under cover when it rains.

VISITORS WELCOME ANY DAY EXCEPT SUNDAY.

How to Get Stock to the Souther Farm.

The Souther Farm is one and a half miles northeast of San Leandro and eight miles southeast of Oakland. The stables are about one mile east of the county road, which runs between Oakland and San Leandro. The place to turn off is at Stanley Road, where a large signboard of the farm is placed. Guide boards will be found at every cross road. In any ordinary weather the roads are very good, and they are fairly good after the unusually heavy rainfall of the past winter.

All stock sent from San Francisco may be brought over by Garcia's Express, No. 3 Market street, San Francisco. They also have an order box outside of Hawley Bros.' Hardware house on the corner of Market and Beale streets. The express leaves San Francisco on the Creek route boat, which starts at 1:30, but orders should be in the order box at Market and Beale streets by 10 o'clock, or at the office, No. 3 Market street, by 11 o'clock at the latest. In the case of very young or very valuable horses, the Souther Farm will send reliable men to lead or drive over any stock that will not lead behind a wagon. A small charge will be made in such cases, to cover the extra expense incurred.

Horses are very easily taken from Oakland to the farm, and where it is inconvenient for owners to bring them or send them, the farm will send after anything that is to come. On horses that stay three months or over there is no charge for getting or delivering. Where a horse stays a short time the actual time and expense only is charged to him.

Horses can be shipped by rail from almost all parts of the State to San Leandro. Always notify the Farm several days before shipping anything, and then men will be on hand to receive stock on arrival. The railroad station is but two miles from the Souther Farm, and the agent invariably gives immediate notice of the arrival of any stock consigned to the above farm, but when word is sent to the farm in good season by letter or telegram, the animals sent are saved waiting a couple of hours in the car.

Passenger trains leave San Francisco (from the broad gauge ferry) and First and Broadway, Oakland, at frequent intervals during the day. There are several trains from San Jose to San Leandro on both broad and narrow gauge railroads; the broad gauge, by way of Niles, is much more convenient for getting to the farm. There are trains each day from Sacramento, Stockton and Livermore to San Leandro. In ordinary weather it is a short and pleasant drive from Oakland to the Souther Farm or from San Francisco to the Farm by way of the Creek route ferry boat. Always notify the Souther Farm just when you will arrive at San Leandro, and some one will meet you at the station. If you do not recognize the farm conveyance ask the stage driver, who will point it out.

Write to the above address for references, circulars and price lists. Terms reasonable.

GILBERT TOMPKINS, Proprietor

2:08 3-4 2:10 2:12

MAMBRINO WILKES, 6083.

SIRE OF

GUS WILKES, 2:22; ALPHEUS, 2:27; CLARA P, 2:29½; BALKAN, 2:29½ (3-year-old) and timed separately 2:22½ in 4-year-old Stake, Bay District Track, October 14, 1889.

DESCRIPTION.

Black; sixteen hands; weighs, in exercise, 1,280 lbs. For style, finish, symmetry and proportion, comparison is challenged with any trotting bred horse. His colts follow in size, style and beauty. Balkan, for instance, being "facile princeps" of trotters in these particulars.

PEDIGREE.

Sired by Geo. Wilkes, sire of Harry Wilkes, 2:13¼, Guy Wilkes, 2:15¼, and 60 other trotters in the 2:30 list, in addition to 6 pacers, and of the sire of Axtell, 2:12 (three-year-old), beating all stallions of any age, and the sire of Regal Wilkes, 2:20¾, best two-year-old stallion record.

First dam Lady Chrisman by Mambrino (Todhunter's), son of Mambrino Chief 11; sire of Lady Thorn, 2:18¼; Woodford Mambrino, 2:21½, and four others in 2:30, and of the dams of Director, 2:17, Piedmont, 2:17¼, Onward, 2:25¼, etc.

Second dam by Pilot Jr. 12, sire of nine in the 2:30 list, and of the dams of Maud S., 2:08¾, Jay-Eye-See, 2:10, Nutwood, 2:18¾, Viking, 2:19¼, Pilot Boy, 2:20, Naiad Queen, 2:20¼, etc.

TERMS.

Mares from a distance will be received at the Dexter Stables, Oakland, or Livery Stable, Martinez, the owner notifying Smith Hill, Superintendent at the farm. Good pasture and plenty of water. For the purpose of placing the service of a Wilkes within reach of breeders, the same rate will be maintained as last year, to wit, $75 for the season. Although it is not admitted thereby that this horse is inferior as a producer to the horses whose fees are placed at from $150 to $500. Address

SMITH HILL,
San Miguel Stock Farm,
Walnut Creek, Contra Costa Co., Cal.

2:12¾ 2:13½ 2:15¼

Finely Bred Trotting Stallion

ARLINGTON.

$50 $50

Trial 2:26 1-2; by

ABBOTSFORD.

DESCRIPTION.

ARLINGTON is a handsome rich rosewood bay, 15¾ hands high and weighs 1 00 lbs. He is of beautiful conformation, well boned, and great muscular development and greatly resembles his famous sire in every particular.

PEDIGREE.

ARLINGTON was sired by Abbottsford, dam the Gillespie mare by Blue Bull. Abbotsford is by Woodford Mambrino, dam Columbia by Young Columbus, he by Columbus. Woodford Mambrino's dam Woodbine by Woodford, a thoroughbred son of Kosciusko. Woodford Mambrino is recognized as the best son of Mambrino Chief. His own record is 2:21½, that of his son Abbotsford, the sire of Arlington 2:19½ and his son Conde 2:20, and he has also a large number in the 2:30 list. He is also the sire of Princeps the sire of Trinket, record of 2:14. Abbotsford, for the short time he has been in the stud, has proven himself a sire worthy of merit, his daughter Jassemine having won the Embryo Stakes of 1881, and every one who was put in training has shown good speed. The dam of Arlington was a beautiful bay mare, 15¾ hands high, sired by Blue Bull, dam Lexington mare raised by Ezra Champion of White Hall, New York, thus showing that in Arlington are combined most of the purest blood in America.

TERMS: $50 the season, with usual return privileges. The best of attention will be given mares, but no liability assumed for escapes or accidents, good pasturage, $2 per month. Call on or address,

J. B. FRENCH,
905, 907 and 909 Golden Gate Ave, S. F.

2:08¾ 2:10 2:12

BALKAN

By Mambrino Wilkes.

(See that Horse's Advertisement.)

DAM FANNY FERN BY JACK HAWKINS
Son of Boston.

The grandam of Maud S. (2:08¾) was by Boston and the grandam of Jay-Eye-See (2:10) was by Lexington, son of Boston. So Balkan is the same remove from Boston that Maud is, and one remove nearer than Jay-Eye-See.

Fanny Fern has produced Molly Drew, Onyx, Fred Arnold, Molly Fern and Balkan, all by different sires.

Balkan's sire and dam both being producers, and he being a trotter himself with a record of 2:29 1-2 (three-year-old) and timed separately 2:22 1-4 in 4-year-old Stake, Bay District Track, October 14, 1889—it is but fair to presume that he will get trotters of the highest order.

DESCRIPTION.

He is seal brown, 16-1 hands high, in style rivalled by few, and excelled by none with as pure a gait as has yet been exhibited in public—bar none.

Balkan will be at Oakland Trotting Park for the season of 1890, and will be limited to ten mares, at $100 fee, in order to be put in training early, as it is morally certain that if given a reasonable opportunity he will be fast enough to compete with the best of his age. For further particulars, address

A. L. HINDS,
Dexter Stables, Oakland.

2:12¾ 2:13½ 2:15¼

2:19 **NOONDAY** 2:20½

STANDARD No. 10,000.

This celebrated trotting bred stallion will make the season of 1890 at the stable of the undersigned at Sacramento, Cal., at $75 for the season and $100 to insure a mare in foal. Payable on or before July 1st, 1890. Money will be refunded on mares bred by insurance as soon as the fact becomes known that they are not in foal.

NOONDAY.
- Wedgewood, 2:19... Sire of Favonia, 2:15, fastest 4th heat for any mare or gelding, and eight others in 2:27 or better.
  - Belmont... Sire of Wedgewood, 2:19, Nutwood, 2:18¾, Viking, 2:19½, and 29 others in 2:30 list.
    - Alexander's Abdallah, sire of Goldsmith Maid, 2:14; Almont, with 35 horses in 2:30 list, etc.
    - Belle, dam of Hambletonian, 2:26½; B'cara, dam of Pancoast, 2:21½, the sire of Patron, 2:14½.
  - Woodbine... Dam of Wedgewood, 2:19, Woodford Mamb., 2:21½, the sire of Pancoast, 2:21½, the sire of Patron, 2:14½.
    - Woodford.
    - Singleton Mare.
- Noontide, 2:20½.... (Trial, 2:13½).
  - Harold... Sire of Maud S., 2:08¾, and 26 others in 2:30 list.
    - Hambletonian (Rysdyk's), sire of George Wilkes, 2:22, the sire of Guy Wilkes, 2:15¼; Electioneer, the sire of Sunol, 2:10½, and scores of noted trotters and producers.
    - Enchantress, by Abdallah 1.
  - Midnight... Dam of Jay-Eye-See, 2:10, Noontide, 2:20½.
    - Pilot Jr., sire of dams of Maud S., 2:08¾, Jay-Eye-See, 2:10, Nutwood, 2:18¾, etc.
    - Twilight, by Lexington, sire of the dam of Ansel, 2:20.

NOODAY is a dark seal brown, foaled 1884, 15 hands 1¼ inches high. Individually he is equal to his royal breeding. He is all that can be desired in conformation, intelligence, color and trotting action, and no stallion now in public service can show a pedigree with such fast records and royal game trotting blood as Noonday.

DON MARVIN,

Record 2:28 as a five-year-old. Standard by Breeding and Performance

Standard No. 7927.

Don Marvin 2:28.

Don Marvin is a beautiful seal brown, foaled 1884, bred by Hon. Leland Stanford, Palo Alto, Cal., standing 16 hands, and weighs, in ordinary condition, 12 0 lbs. He is a fine individual, good style and form, combined with great substance, and good temper. Is very level headed; in his first race the past season he only made one break in five closely contested heats. He has great speed and endurance, with the pure, rapid Electioneer gait. He trots without toe weights, and wears only 5 oz. shoes in front. He gained his record the past season in the third heat, on a slow track, after making a season (serving over 60 mares), with scarcely any preparation. His record is no mark of his speed. He was a natural born trotter, and Mr. Charles Marvin considered him the fastest two year old at Palo Alto that season.

By FALLIS, 2:23, - - by Electioneer, sire of
Sire of Don Marvin, 2:28. — Sunol, three-year-old, 2:10 1-2, Palo Alto, 2:12¼, and 47 others in 2:30 list.

Dam CORA, by Don Victor by Belmont, sire of
Dam of Don Marvin, 2:28. — Ventura, 2:27¼, and sire of the dam of Bell Echo, 2:20, and six others in 2:30 list.

2d dam CLARABEL, - by Abdallah Star,
Dam of Clifton Bell, 2:24 1-2, and grandam of Rexford, three years, 2:24. — Sire of Hattie Maples, 2:23.

3d dam FAIRY, - - by Rysdyk's Hambletonian,
Sister of Sweepstakes, sire of 16 in 2:30 list. — Sire of Electioneer, George Wilkes, and many other noted sires and trotters.

4th dam EMMA MILLS, by Seely's American Star,
Dam of 4 horses that have 2:30 performers. — The great broodmare sire of the world.

The above pedigree should show every intelligent breeder that Don Marvin is "high" bred though very strong in trotting blood. All the comment it is deemed necessary to make as to the value of "thoroughbred blood" in the trotter is simply to refer to the very significant fact that the first and second dams of Maud S. 2:08¾, Jay-Eye-See 2:10, Sunol, three years 2:10 1-2, Palo Alto 2:12¼, Anteeo 2:16¼, Nutwood 2:18¾, Wedgewood 2:19, and many other successful sires and sensational trotters of the day are thoroughbred.

TERMS—Don Marvin will make the ensuing season from February 1st to July 1st, 1890, at $40 the season, with the usual privilege of returning the mare next season if not proving in foal. Mares from a distance met at the cars or boats on notification, and carefully handled, but no responsibility assumed for accidents or escapes.

Good alfalfa pasture furnished (free from barb wire fence) at $4 per month. For further particulars or complete circulars address

F. P. LOWELL,
1520 F Street, Sacramento, Cal.

The Produce of Eros Averaged $2,200 Each at New York Auction Sale in 1889.

THE ELECTIONEER TROTTING STALLION,

5326 **EROS** 5326

Will make the season of 1890—February 1st to July 1st—at LA SIESTA RANCH, MENLO PARK, adjoining Palo Alto.

PEDIGREE.

EROS (5326)
Standard by his sire
" " dam
" " record
" " produce
" under all rules

EROS (5326)..
- Electioneer... Grandsire of Norlaine, 1 yr., 2:31 1-2, Sire of Sunol, 2 yrs., 2:18, Sunol, 3 yrs., 2:10 1-2, Hinda Rose, 4 yrs., 2:16, Palo Alto, 2:12¼.
  - Hambletonian 10... Sire of Dictator, George Wilkes, Happy Medium, and 40 others in 2:30 list, and grandsire of 728 in list.
    - Abdallah 10 Sire of the dams of Goldsmith Maid, 2:14, and 7 other producing dams.
    - Charles Kent mare By imp. Bellfounder.
  - Green Mountain Maid... Dam of Prospero, 2:20, Elaine, 2:20, Dame Trot, 2:22, Elista, 2:22¼, Storm, 2:26¼, Antonio, 2:28¼, Miranda, 2:31, Mansfield, 2:26.
    - Harry Clay Sire of the dams of St. Julian, 2:11¼, Bodine, 2:19¼, and 17 more in 2:30 list
    - Shanghai Mary.
- Sontag Mohawk... Dam of Eros, 2:29 1-2, Sport, 2:22¼, Sallie Benton, 2:17¾, Conductor, trial, 2:26, Colma, 3-y-o trial, 2:24.
  - Mohawk Chief... Sire of the dams of Lot Slocum, 2:17¼, Sallie Benton, 4 yrs., 2:17¾, Pediar, 2 yrs., 2:27¼, Stanford, 4 yrs., 2:30, Eros, 6th heat, 2:29 1-2.
    - Hambletonian 10 Sire of the dams of Stamboul, 2:12¼, Wilton, 2:19¼, and 20 other trotters.
    - Lady Perrine
  - Sontag Nellie...
    - Toronto Sontag By Toronto Chief,
    - Nellie Gray 5-mile record, 13:45.

Produce of Eros
Wanda, 4 yrs., 2:24,
Solita, 2 yrs., 2:41 1-2,
Meriquita, 2 yrs., 2:42,
Daylight, 2 yrs., 2:54,
Hiram B., trial, 2:26.

These are the only colts by him that have ever had a harness on except one in New York that went a trial last July in 2:26 1:2.

DESCRIPTION.

EROS is a rich seal brown stallion, bred by Hon. Leland Stanford at Palo Alto, and is the nearest living likeness of his celebrated sire, Electioneer. Stands 15.2 hands high, and weighs 1050 pounds

In breeding to Eros, the owners of mares will strictly follow the great rule of breeding, viz., breed to a stallion by a producer and out of a sure producer of great speed. Eros is by the stallion that has produced more 2:30 trotters that any living horse, and is also the sire of more 2:20 performers than any horse living or dead.

EROS is out of the dam of Sally Benton, four years old, record 2:17¾, Sport 2:22¼, and Eros 2:29½ in the sixth heat, against a field of nine horses. He is from a family that is endowed with great natural speed, trot fast at an early age, train on, throw trotters from all classes of mares, are of good substance, bone, style and action, and breed solid colors.

TERMS.

$100 for the season, with the privilege of return next season should mares not be in foal and horse and mare still remain in the same hands.

Good pasturage can be obtained at $5 per month, but no responsibility for accidents or escapes. There are a large number of box stalls, and animals can be kept up and fed on hay and grain at reasonable rates if required. Mares already in foal can be sent to the ranch for foaling, and will receive all the attention bestowed upon our own mares. Mares left with Mr. Peter Pomyea, Broadway Street Stable, Oakland, or with Mr. F. H. Burke, 401 Montgomery Street, San Francisco, will be forwarded to the ranch free of charge. For further particulars apply to

W. H. VIOGET,
LA SIESTA RANCH, MENLO PARK, CAL.

EROS is the only stallion offered to the public on this Coast that has a dam that has three in the 2:30 list.

POPLAR GROVE

Breeding Farm

STALLIONS.

CLOVIS, 4909,

CLOVIS is a beautiful black, Eight Years Old, 16 1-2 Hands High, and weighs 1260 lbs.

He is a horse of beautiful symmetry and magnificent action.

PEDIGREE.

CLOVIS was sired by Sultan, 2:24, sire of Stamboul, 2:12 1-4, Ruby, 2:19¼, and fifteen others with records of 2:30 or better.

First dam Sweetbriar by Thorndale 2:22 1-2, sire of Edwin Thorne, 2:16 1-2, Daisy Dale, 2:19, and May Thorne, 2:24

Second dam Ulster Queen, dam of Volmer, 2:24¼, by Hambletonian 10, sire of Dexter, 2:17¼, George Wilkes, 2:22.

Third dam by Thomas Jefferson, a son of Mambrino Paymaster, Jr.

Fourth dam by Mambrino Paymaster, sire of Mambrino Chief.

Sultan, by The Moor, sire of Beautiful Bells, dam of Hinda Rose, 2:19 1-2, and Sable, dam of Sable Wilkes, three year old record 2:18.

First dam of Sultan, Sultana, by Delmonico, sire of Darby, 2:16 1-2, by Guy Miller, sire of Whipple's Hambletonian.

Second dam by Mambrino Chief.

Third dam by Downing's Bay Messenger.

Fourth dam Mrs. Caudle, dam of Ericsson, four year old record 2:30 1-2.

Clovis will make the season of 1890 at Poplar Grove Breeding Farm, near Wildflower, Fresno County, commencing February 1st and ending July 1st.

Terms, $75, due at time of service.

Mares cared for in any manner owners may desire; pasturage $2 per month. Every care exercised, but no liability for escapes or accidents. Mares not proving with foal can be returned next season, providing I still own this stallion.

APEX, 8935.

FOUR-YEAR-OLD RECORD, FOURTH HEAT, 2:26.

Will make the present season at the Poplar Grove Breeding Farm, near Wildflower, Fresno Co., season commencing Feb. 1st, and ending July 1, 1890. Terms, $50 the season, due at time of service. Apex is eight years old, a beautiful bay, 15 1-4 hands high, and weighs 1140 lbs. He is a horse of fine disposition, and his gait is faultless.

PEDIGREE.

Apex was sired by Prompter 2305, he by Blue Bull 75; first dam Mary by Flaxtail, he by Pruden's Blue Bull. Flaxtail being the sire of the dams of Buccaneer, five-year-old record 2:24 1-4; Pride, yearling record, 2:44 1-2, and Shamrock, two-year old record, 2:25, third heat. Second dam by Bright Eyes, son of Boanarages. Prompter (sire of Apex, record 2:26, and Transit, 2:28 1-4), by Wilson's Blue Bull, by Pruden's Blue Bull son of Merring's Blue Bull. Prompter's dam Prairie Bird, by Flaxtail; second dam by John the Baptist, son of Tally Ho Morgan, by Sherman Morgan; third dam Fannie Fern by Irwin's Tuckahoe.

Apex made his appearance in the circuit as a two-year-old, and obtained a record of 2:42. As a three-year-old he reduced this in a race at Santa Rosa against Stamboul to 2:36, it taking six heats to decide the contest, which was won by Apex. As a four year-old he gained his present record of 2:26.

Mares cared for in any manner owners may desire. Pasturage $2 per month. Every care exercised, but no liabilities for escapes or accidents. Mares not proving with foal can be returned next season, providing I still own this stallion.

The Standard Stallion

JUNIO,

RECORD 2:22.

WILL MAKE THE PRESENT SEASON OF AT FRESNO FAIR GROUNDS.

Season Commencing Feb. 1st and ending July 1st.

TERMS—$100 the season, due at time of service.

JUNIO is eight years old, a handsome dark bay 16 hands high, and weighs 1250 pounds. He is the personification of the light harness horse, and his trotting action is superb. At the State Fair of 1886 he took first premium over forty of the finest trotters in the State.

PEDIGREE.

*Junio, by Electioneer, premier stallion of Palo Alto (sire of Sunol 2:10 1-2, Palo Alto 2:12 1-4, and 47 others in the 2:30 list). Dam by Granger by imp. Hercules.

Granger, by imp. Hercules, dam Jenny Lind, by Stockbridge Chief, Jr., he by Stockbridge Chief, he by Vermont Black Hawk. Second dam by Kentucky Whip.

Imp. Hercules, by Wingston, first dam daughter of Tuscar, by Bay Middleton, second dam Malvina, by Oscar; 3rd dam Spotless by Walton; 4th dam by Trumpator (see Bruce's American Stud Book, Vol. 1, page 28). Hercules is the sire of the dam of Azmoor 2:20¼; also sire of dam of Menlo 2:21 1-2.

Mares not proving in foal may be returned next year free of charge, providing I still have the horse. Pasturage $3 per month. While every care will be taken of horses, no liability will be assumed for accidents or escapes.

For further particulars address

S. N. STRAUBE, Fresno, Cal.

Poplar Grove Breeding Farm.

BOYCE TABLETS.

Leg and Body Wash.

THE BOYCE TABLETS are packed in a nicely decorated metal box with hinged lid—one hundred tablets in each box; directions for use plainly engraved upon the box; therefore, the convenience of the package—no liability to leakage and breakage—economy and ready solubility, together with the absolute certainty of their action, will at once commend the use of BOYCE'S TABLETS to the intelligent horsemen of the country. TABLETS sufficient to make one hundred pints of leg and body wash are conveniently carried in an inside coat pocket or in the hip-pocket of the trousers.

The BOYCE WASH can be applied ALL OVER THE BODY WITHOUT FEAR OF BLISTERING NOR DOES IT AFFECT THE KIDNEYS.

The BOYCE WASH will cure CRACKED HEELS, PUFFS, STOCKINGS, SCRATCHES, INFLAMED TENDONS and FEVERED LEGS.

Price per Box of One Hundred Tablets, $2, sent postpaid to any part of the United States; **six boxes for $10**. A sample of BOYCE'S TABLETS will be mailed to any address on application.

These TABLETS are warranted to keep in any climate. Address

BOYCE TABLET COMPANY,

600 Wabash Avenue, - - - Terre Haute, Indiana.

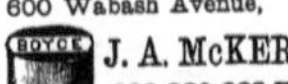

J. A. McKERRON, Pacific Coast Ag't,

228-230-232 Ellis Street, San Francisco, Cal.

keeps horses healthy, promotes digestion, fattens horses, loosens the hide, assists the appetite, prevents leg swelling, strengthens the kidneys, regulates the bowels and destroys worms. **$7.50 per 100 lbs.** Ask your dealer for it or send to

MANHATTAN FOOD CO., 206 Clay St., S. F.

THE IMPROVED NOYES ROAD-CART.

PATENTED JULY 17, 1883, *AND JUNE* 8, 1886.

Some of the Advantages of the Noyes Cart Over All Others.

There is no bar for the rider to climb over in getting in or out. The horse can be hitched eighteen inches nearer than any other road-cart made. You can get in or out with perfect safety—no danger of being thrown into the wheel—a great advantage in breaking colts. THE EASIEST CART FOR ROAD OR TRACK. The only cart that a horse can be speeded to within one second as fast as to a sulky. All our carts are made of the very best materials and are warranted. Manufactured by the NOYES CART COMPANY, Kalamazoo, Mich.

They are indorsed by the following horsemen, all of whom are using them. Ask their opinion of the Noyes Cart: John Splan, who drove Guy a full mile in 2:17¾ and Chanter a half-mile in 1:10¾ to a Noyes Cart, says he would not take $250 for it if he could not get another; W. J. Gordon, Glenville, O.; W. B. Fasig, Cleveland, O.; Dave Muckel, Cleveland, O.; R. J. Moorehead, North East, Pa.; W. J. Chamberlain, Cleveland, O.; H. P. Malone, Bradford, Pa.; S. A. Brown & Co., Kalamazoo Stock Farm; Charles Marvin, Menlo Park, Cal.; W. H. Crawford, Lexington, Ky.; S. L. Caton, who gave Bell Boy a mark at Los Angeles, Cal., of 2:19¾, and drove Chanter a half mile in 1:08¾ and Lowland Girl a full mile in 2:22 to a Noyes Cart; Mike Bowerman, Lexington, Ky.; James Golden, Medford, Mass.; John E. Turner, Philadelphia, Pa.; T. L. Newton, Beaver Dam, Wis.; P. V. Johnston, Marshall, Mich.; W. H. McCarthy, Los Angeles, Cal.; A. W. Dennison, El Dorado, Kan.; P. O. Shank, Cleveland, O.; Charles Barnard, Boston, Mass.; Johnson Bros., Greenville, Mich.; John G. Avery, Buffalo, N. Y.; General R. L. Howard, Buffalo, N. Y.; Howard Conklin, Buffalo, N. Y.; W. D. Ham, Hennepin, Ill.; R. G. Henry, Waterbury, Conn; J. E. Hayer, Newburgh, O.; J. C. Hart, Jefferson, Tex.; A. W. Harbison, Rock Point, Pa.; Carl Hodges, Battle Creek, Mich.; Barney Treacy, Lexington, Ky.; George Forbes, Cleveland, O.; Gifford Dudley, Topeka, Kan.; William and J. L. Thompson, Lamont, Pa.; C. P. Emery, Forest City Stock Farm, Cleveland, O.; R. F. Jones, Minneapolis, Minn.; John Forbes, Elyria, O.; D. J. Downs, Battle Creek, Mich.; Frank Caton, Randall Station, O.; Arthur D. Sutton, Ind., Pa.; W. F. Neely, Grand Ridge, Ill.; Walter Clark, owner of Pilot Medium, Battle Creek, Mich.; H. R. Kingman, Battle Creek, Mich.; Dr. Sutton and H. C. Reed, Kalamazoo, Mich.; Budd Doble, Chicago, Ill.

SOLE MANUFACTURERS OF STONE'S PATENT SULKY CASE.

They will more than save their cost in one season, and horsemen campaigning trotters cannot afford to do without them. Would refer to Samuel A. Brown, Kalamazoo Stock Farm, S. L. Caton and W. H. McCarthy. Address

NOYES CART COMPANY, Kalamazoo, Mich.

Office and Factory, Corner Rose and Eleanor streets. R. ARTHUR STONE, Manager.

ADVERTISE YOUR STALLIONS

—IN THE—

Breeder & Sportsman

For the Season---1890.

We are pleased to announce that we have the best facilities for furnishing

Stallion Pictures,

Stallion Cards,

Pedigrees, Folders,

Contracts, Bills, Etc.

We make a specialty of this department of our business, and have UNRIVALED FACILITIES FOR LOOKING UP PEDIGREES and doing accurate and handsome work.

Promptness, Good Work, Low Prices.

BREEDER AND SPORTSMAN,

313 Bush Street, S. F.

SAMUEL VALLEAU. JAS. R. BRODIE.

J. R. BRODIE & CO.,

Steam Printers,

—And Dealers in—

Poolseller's and Bookmaker's Supplies.

401—403 *Sansome Street, corner Sacramento, San Francisco.*

"DICKEY'S,"

SIXTH AVENUE AND D ST.

Near entrance to Bay District Track.

Choicest Brands of

WINES AND CIGARS.

A Delightful Resort.

Telephone 1485. J. R. DICKEY, Propr.

The Park Training Stable.

CHAS. DAVID, PROPRIETOR.

Corner Grove and Baker Streets, near Entrance to Golden Gate Park.

EVERY FACILITY FOR TRAINING COLTS and taking care of Gentlemen's Roadsters.

Finely appointed stable with every convenience and sixteen roomy box stalls.

The best care given all horses by experienced help, under the personal superintendence of the proprietor.

Convenient to the Park Speed Drive, and Accessible to Six Lines of Cable Cars.

THE TRAINING OF COLTS AND ROADSTERS A SPECIALTY.

TROTTERS AND ROADSTERS FOR SALE.

HORSES SOLD ON COMMISSION.

The proprietor trained and brought out the following well known horses: "Sister, Huntress," "Peribelion," "Nona Y," and others.

NEW BOOK.

HORSE BREEDING

Seventh Edition, with Appendix,

By J. H. SANDERS,

In which the GFNABAL LAWS OF HEREDITY are exhaustively discussed and applied to the PRACTICAL BUSINESS OF BREEDING HORSES, especially with reference to the Selection of Breeding Stock and the Management of Stallions, Brood Mares, Young Foals, and Diseases Peculiar to Breeding Stock.

Price, Post Paid, $3,

BREEDER AND SPORTSMAN,

313 Bush Street. San Francisco, Cal.

THE HICKS-JUDD CO.

Successors to

HICKS & JUDD, Bookbinders,

and Women's Co-operative Printing Office.

Printers, Bookbinders, Publishers,

23 First St., San Francisco.

BREEDERS' CATALOGUES A SPECIALTY.

GOLDEN EAGLE HOTEL

Corner SEVENTH and K STREETS, SACRAMENTO.

FIRST CLASS IN EVERY RESPECT.

The LARGEST and FINEST HOTEL in the City.

W. O. BOWERS, Proprietor.

Free 'Buss to and from the Hotel.

Telephone, Telegraph Office and Messenger Service at Hotel

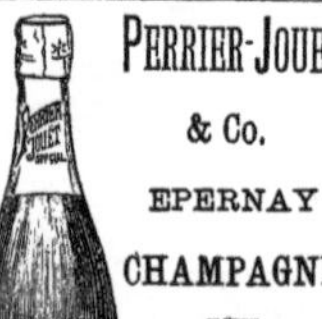

PERRIER-JOUET & Co.

EPERNAY

CHAMPAGNE

W. B. CHAPMAN,

Sole Agent for Pacific Coast.

For sale by all first-class Wine Merchants and Grocers.

BERGEZ'S

RESTAURANT.

FIRST-CLASS. Charges Reasonable.

Private Rooms for Families.

332—334 Pine St., below Montgomery St.

JOHN BERGEZ, Propr.

KENNEL ADVERTISEMENTS.

FOR SALE.

Pointer Puppies

By Tom Pinch ex Galatea.

Tom Pinch has won at two field trials, and was never beaten on the bench, winning first whenever shown. At the recent Bench Show at Elmira, New York, Tom Pinch won first, Galatea second, and Lady Pinch [Tom Pinch—Galatea] first in their respective classes. For prices and particulars, address

J. MARTIN BARNEY, Dutch Flat, Cal.

Puppies for Sale.

TWO GORDON SETTER BITCH PUPPIES, 4 months old.

ONE YORKSHIRE TERRIER DOG PUP, two months old, by Sierp's Mash, winner of first prize in last three Bench Shows.

FIVE MASTIFF PUPPIES, by a son of Scott's "Dick," winner of first prize in last two Bench Shows. Also a litter of GREYHOUND PUPPIES, Saturday Night—Brunette.

Apply to JAMES E. WATSON,

516 Sacramento street, San Francisco.

P. O. Box 1886.

DOGS---Pointer Pups

FOR SALE.

Sure Bench Show and Field Trial Winners, as they have more bench-show and field-trial blood in them than any that have ever been whelped on the Pacific Coast.

Sire, POINT, double field trial winner; he by Vandevort's Don, great field trial and bench show winner, out of Drab, field trial and bench show winner.

Dam, QUEEN CROXTETH by Rush T., bench show winner, out of Champion Patti Croxteth, field trial and bench show winner. This is the best pointer blood in the world. Breeding and health guaranteed. Address,

A. B. TRUMAN,

1428 Steiner St., near Ellis, S. F., Cal.

FOX TERRIERS--C. A. SUMNER, 7 S. Fort St., Los Angeles, Breeder of Fox Terriers. Blemton Vesuvian (14290), by Champion Lncifer, at stud.

SCOTCH COLLIE SHEPHERD DOGS. Pups all ages. Send stamp for descriptive circular. W. A. WICKHAM, Tipton, Ia.

CALIFORNIA SPANIEL KENNELS,

Oakland, California, H. P. RENNIE, Prop; Breeder and importer of typical COCKER SPANIELS. Winner of first prizes at S. F. and Los Angeles, 1889; also, Columbus, 1888, New York, 1887. In the stud, solid Black Cocker dog, GIFFER, won 1st and Gold Medal at S. F., 1888. Fee, $25. Puppies and grown dogs at reasonable prices. My dogs can neither talk nor climb a tree, but are fielders and prize winners.

Fiske's Vanes.

MADE OF COPPER

And Gilded with PURE GOLD LEAF.

Manufacturer's Agent.

The HOWE SCALE CO.

411 & 413 Market Street, S. F.

Scales for Weighing of

Live Stock

SEEDS, FEED, Etc.

Write for Catalogue.

Fine Hats,

Latest Styles and Colors.

Meussdorffer & Hubner

8 Kearny Street, San Francisco,

Next to New Chronicle Building

JOHN FORGIE,

Importing Tailor,

204 Montgomery Street,

N. E. corner Bush, SAN FRANCISCO.

The Poodle Dog

"Rotisserie,"

FIRST-CLASS IN EVERY RESPECT.

Elegant Family Dining Rooms.

S. E. cor. GRANT AVE. and BUSH STREET.

ANDRE POTENTINI, Proprietor.

Southern Pacific Co.

(PACIFIC SYSTEM.)

Trains leave and are due to arrive at San Francisco.

LEAVE (FOR)	FROM MARCH 30, 1890.	ARRIVE (FROM)
7.30 A M	Haywards, Niles and San Jose ...	*12.45 P M
7.30 A M	Sacramento and Redding, via Davis	7.15 P M
7.30 A M	Sacramento, Auburn, Colfax	4.45 P M
8.00 A M	Martinez, Vallejo, Calistoga and Santa Rosa	6.15 P M
8.30 A M	Los Angeles Express, Fresno, Bakersfield, Mojave and East and Los Angeles	11.15 A M
8.30 A M	Niles, San Jose, Stockton, Ione, Sacramento, Marysville, Oroville and Red Bluff	4.45 P M
10.30 A M	Haywards and Niles	3.45 P M
12.00 M	Haywards, Niles and Livermore.	*8.45 P M
*1.00 P M	Sacramento River Steamers	**6.00 A M
3.00 P M	Haywards, Niles and San Jose	9.45 A M
3.30 P M	2d Class for Ogden and East	10.45 P M
4.00 P M	Stockton and ‡Milton; Vallejo, Calistoga and Santa Rosa	9.45 A M
*4.30 P M	Niles and Livermore.	*8.45 A M
*4.30 P M	Niles and San Jose	‡6.15 P M
6.00 P M	Shasta Route Express, Sacramento, Marysville, Redding, Portland, Puget Sound, East and Knight's Landing via Davis	10.45 A M
6.00 P M	Haywards and Niles	7.45 A M
7.00 P M	Sunset Route, Atlantic Express Santa Barbara, Los Angeles, Deming, El Paso, New Orleans and East	8.45 P M
8.00 P M	Central Atlantic Express, Ogden and East	9.45 A M
	SANTA CRUZ DIVISION.	
‡ 8.00 A M	Hunters train to San Jose	‡ 7.20 P M
8.15 A M	Newark, Centerville, San Jose, Felton, Boulder Creek and Santa Cruz	5.50 P M
* 2.15 P M	Centerville, San Jose, Almaden, Felton, Boulder Creek and Santa Cruz	*11.50 A M
4.15 P M	Centerville, San Jose, and Los Gatos	9.50 A M
	Coast Division (Third and Townsend Sts.)	
7.25 A M	San Jose, Almaden and Way Stations	2.30 P M
8.30 A M	San Jose, Gilroy, Tres Pinos; Pajaro, Santa Cruz; Monterey; Pacific Grove, Salinas, San Miguel, Paso Robles, Santa Margarita (San Luis Obispo) and principal Way Stations	6.12 P M
10.30 A M	San Jose and Way Stations	5.02 P M
12.01 P M	Cemetery, Menlo Park and Way Stations	3.38 P M
* 3.30 P M	San Jose, Tres Pinos, Santa Cruz, Salinas, Monterey Pacific Grove and principal Way Stations	*10.00 A M
* 4.20 P M	Menlo Park and Way station	* 7.58 A M
5.20 P M	San Jose and Way Stations	9.03 A M
6.30 P M	Menlo Park and Way stations	6.35 A M
†11.45 P M	Menlo Park and principal Way Stations	†7.38 P M

A M for Morning. P M for Afternoon.
*Sundays excepted. †Saturdays only. ‡Sundays only.
**Mondays excepted. §Saturdays excepted.

OCEANIC STEAMSHIP CO.

Carrying United States, Hawaiian and Colonial Mails.

WILL LEAVE THE COMPANY'S WHARF, foot of Mission street, No. 1,

For Honolulu, Auckland and Sydney,

WITHOUT CHANGE,

The Splendid New 3,000-ton Iron Steamer.

ALAMEDA ..... Saturday, April 5, 1890, at 12 M.,
Or immediately on arrival of the English mails.

For Honolulu,

S. AUSTRALIA (3,000 tons), April 25, 1890, at 12 M

☞ For freight or passage, apply at office, 327 Market Street. JOHN D. SPRECKELS & BROS.
General Agents.

KILLIP & CO.,

LIVE STOCK AND GENERAL AUCTIONEERS,

22 Montgomery Street, San Francisco

SPECIAL ATTENTION PAID TO SALES OF

High-Bred Horses and Cattle.

At auction and private sale.

Will Sell in All Cities and Counties of the State.

REFERENCES.

HON. C. GREEN, Sacramento.	HON. J. D. CARR Salinas.
J. P. SARGENT, ESQ., Sargents.	HON. JOHN BOGGS Colusa.
HON. L. J. ROSE, Los Angeles.	HON. A. WALRATH Nevada.

J. B. HAGGIN, ESQ., San Francisco.

Represented at Sacramento by Edwin F. Smith Secretary State Agricultural Society.

At San Jose by Messrs. Montgomery & Rea, Real Estate Agents.

Being the oldest established firm in the live-stock business on this Coast, and having conducted the important auction sales in this line for the past fifteen years, amounting to one half a million of dollars, we feel justified in claiming unequaled facilities for disposing of live stock of every description, either at auction or private sale. Our list of correspondents embraces every breeder and dealer of prominence upon the Pacific Coast, thus enabling us to give full publicity to animals placed with us for sale. Private purchases and sales of live stock of all descriptions will be made on commission, and stock shipped with the utmost care. Purchases and sales made of land of every description. We are authorized to refer to the gentlemen whose names are appended.

KILLIP & CO., 22 Montgomery Street.

HEALD'S

Business College, 24 Post St.

——San Francisco.——

The most popular school on the Coast

E. P. HEALD, President. C. S. HALEY, Sec'y.

☞ Send for Circulars

San Francisco and North Pacific Railway.

THE DONAHUE BROAD-GAUGE ROUTE.

COMMENCING SUNDAY, MARCH 17, 1889, AND until further notice, boats and trains will leave from and arrive at the San Francisco Passenger Depot, Market-street Wharf, as follows:

Leave San Francisco. Week Days.	Leave San Francisco. Sundays.	Destination	Arrive San Francisco. Sundays.	Arrive San Francisco. Week Days.
7.40 A M 3.30 P M 5.00 P M	8.00 A M 5.00 P M	Petaluma and Santa Rosa	10.40 A M 6.10 P M	8.50 A M 10.30 A M 6.05 P M
7.40 A M 3.30 P M	8.00 A M	Fulton, Windsor, Healdsburg, Litton Springs, Cloverdale, and way stations.	6.10 P M	10.30 A M 6.05 P M
7.40 A M	8.00 A M	Hopland and Ukiah.	6.10 P M	6.05 P M
7.40 A M	8.00 A M	Guerneville	6.10 P M	6.05 P M
7.40 A M 5.00 P M	8.00 A M	Sonoma and Glen Ellen.	10.40 A M 6.10 P M	8.50 A M 6.05 P M
3.30 P M	5.00 P M	Sebastopol	10.40 A M	10.30 A M

Stage connects at Santa Rosa for White Sulphur Springs, and Mark West Springs; at Geyserville for Skaggs Springs, and at Cloverdale for the Geysers; at Hopland for Highland Springs, Kelseyville, Soda Bay, Lakeport and Bartlett Springs, and at Ukiah for Vichy Springs, Saratoga Springs, Blue Lakes, Willits, Cahto, Calpella, Potter Valley, Sherwood Valley and Mendocino City.

EXCURSION TICKETS from Saturdays to Mondays, to Petaluma, $1.50; to Santa Rosa $2.25; to Healdsburg, $3.40; to Litton Springs, $3.60; to Cloverdale, $4.50; to Hopland, $5.70; to Ukiah, $6.75; to Guerneville, $3.75; to Sonoma, $1.50; to Glen Ellen, $1.80.

EXCURSION TICKETS, good for Sundays only, to Petaluma, $1; to Santa Rosa, $1.50; to Healdsburg, $2.25; to Litton Springs, $2.40; to Cloverdale, $3; to Guerneville, $2.50, to Sonoma, $1; to Glen Ellen, $1.20.

From San Francisco for Point Tiburon and San Rafael: Week Days—7.40, 9.20, 11.20, A. M.; 3.30, 5.00, 6.15 P. M. Sundays—8.00, 9.30, 11.00 A. M.; 1.30, 5.00, 6.20 P. M.

To San Francisco from San Rafael: Week Days—6.20, 7.55, 9.30 A. M.; 12.45, 3.40, 5.05 P. M. Sundays—8.10, 9.40 A. M.; 12.15, 3.40, 5.00 P. M.

To San Francisco from Point Tiburon: Week Days—6.50, 8.20, 9.55 A. M.; 1.10, 4.05, 5.30 P. M.; Sundays—8.40, 10.05 A. M.; 12.40, 4.05, 5.30 P. M.

On Saturdays an extra trip will be made from San Francisco to San Rafael, leaving at 1.40 P. M.

H. C. WHITING, General Manager.

PETER J. McGLYNN, Gen. Pass. & Tkt. Agt.

Ticket Offices at Ferry, 222 Montgomery Street and 2 New Montgomery Street.

CHICAGO, MILWAUKEE AN ST. PAUL RAILWAY,

Steam Heated and Electric Lighted Vestibuled Trains between Chicago, St. Paul and Minneapolis.

Electric Lighted and Steam Heated Vestibuled Trains between Chicago, Council Bluffs and Omaha.

Finest Dining Cars in the world.

Free Reclining Chair Cars between Chicago and Omaha.

Fast Mail Line between Chicago, Milwaukee, St. Paul and Minneapolis.

Transcontinental Route between Chicago, Council Bluffs and Omaha, or St. Paul.

Great National Route between Chicago, Kansas City and St. Joseph, Mo.

5,700 miles of road in Illinois, Wisconsin, Minnesota, Iowa, Missouri, South and North Dakota.

Everything First-Class.

First-Class People patronize First-Class Lines.

Ticket Agents everywhere sell Tickets over the Chicago, Milwaukee and St. Paul Railway.

W. T. ALLEN,
Pacific Coast Passenger Agent
Office, No 138 Montgomery St., San Francisco, Cal.
Under Occidental Hotel

6 DONTS

DON'T own a racehorse.
DON'T be a breeder.
DON'T be a trainer.
DON'T be a jockey.
DON'T bet on the races.
DON'T go to a race track.

WITHOUT

HAVING IN YOUR POCKET ONE OF

Goodwin's

ANNUAL

OFFICIAL TURF GUIDES.

Price, in cloth $2.00
Price, in half morocco 3.00
Price, in half calf 4.00
If sent by mail .... 10 cents extra

SUBSCRIBE TO IT FOR 1890.

It is published semi-monthly during the racing season, and is but $10 per year. Address

GOODWIN BROS.,
241 Broadway, New York City.

OUR IMPROVED. ALL SIZES AND WEIGHTS. G. W. BOHANON.

THE BOHANON SULKY!

BEST MADE.

Perfect Riding Buggies.

Breaking Carts.

Fine Repairing. Reasonable Prices

Bohanon Carriage Co., 161-163 Ogden Ave., CHICAGO.

Send for Catalogue.

RUB YOUR HORSES

In cases of SWELLING or STIFFNESS OF THE JOINTS, with

DARBYS FLUID.

If you value your Horses, Dogs and Cattle always keep it on hand.

IT HAS NO EQUAL

For Cuts, Scratches, Bruises, Bites, Sores, Etc.

It gives immediate relief, and prevents Poison, Gangrene and Proud Flesh.

J. H. ZEILIN & CO., - Philadelphia, Pa

SOLD BY ALL DRUGGISTS.

HORSE OWNERS!

TRY GOMBAULT'S

CAUSTIC BALSAM.

A Safe, Speedy and Positive Cure for Curb, Splint, Sweeny, Capped Hock, Strained Tendons, Founder, Wind Puffs, all Skin Diseases or Parasites, Thrush, Diphtheria, Pinkeye, all Lameness from Spavin, Ringbone or other Bony Tumors. Removes all Bunches or Blemishes from Horses and Cattle.

Supersedes all Cautery or Firing. Impossible to Produce any Scar or Blemish.

Every bottle sold is warranted to give satisfaction. Price $1.50 per bottle. Sold by druggists, or sent by express, charges paid, with full directions for its use. Send for descriptive circulars. Address LAWRENCE, WILLIAMS & CO., Cleveland, O.

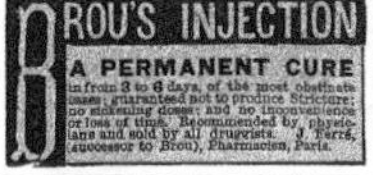

For any Kind of a

SORE THROAT

USE

McCLELLAN'S

DIPHTHERIA REMEDY

An Unfailing Cure..

FOR SALE BY ALL DRUGGISTS

R. LIDDLE & SON

538 Washington St., S. F.,

Wholesale and Retail Dealers in

Guns, Rifles and Pistols.

A Full Line of FISHING TACKLE and SPORTSMAN'S GOODS.

Orders by mail receive prompt attention.

"STANDARD" THE BEST IS THE CHEAPEST SHOTGUN CARTRIDGES

By-Laws

—AND—

Rules and Regulations

—OF THE—

NATIONAL

Trotting Association

ALSO THE

AMERICAN

Trotting Association,

AND THE

PACIFIC COAST BLOOD-HORSE ASSOCIATION.

With Betting Rules.

For Sale at the Office of the

Breeder and Sportsman,

313 Bush St., S. F., Cal.

Price, 25c. each.

By Mail, Postage Paid, 30c. each.

VETERINARY.

Dr. Wm. H. Jones, M.R.C.V.S.

Veterinary Surgeon,

(OLYMPIC CLUB STABLES)

503 Sutter Street, San Francisco.

Telephone, No. 1404.

Consultations by letter, and cases of URGENT NECESSITY in the interior will receive prompt attention.

Dr. A. E. BUZARD,

VETERINARY SURGEON,

Member of the Royal College of Veterinary Surgeons, London, England. Graduated April 22d, 1870.

All Operations on the Horse Performed Skillfully.

Special attention given to the Diseases of Dogs. Calls to the country promptly attended to. Advice and prescriptions by mail $2. Office and Residence, No. 11 Seventh street, S. F. (opp. Odd Fellows Hall. Telephone No. 3 85.

W. H. WOODRUFF.

Veterinary Dentist,

AT FASHION STABLES,

221 Ellis Street, San Francisco

Improved Instruments, Humane Methods, First-Class Work.

H. E. CARPENTER,

Veterinary Surgeon,

Graduate of Ontario Veterinary College, Toronto Canada.

RESIDENCE AND VETERINARY INFIRMARY

331 Golden Gate Ave., San Francisco.

Telephone 3069.

☞ OPEN DAY AND NIGHT. ☜

No risk in throwing Horses. Veterinary Operating Table on the premises.

DR. C. MASOERO,

Veterinary Surgeon,

Successor to DR. A. DeTAVEL,

GRADUATE OF ROYAL VETERINARY COLLEGE, TURIN.

OFFICE AND INFIRMARY

No. 811 HOWARD STREET,

Between Fourth and Fifth. SAN FRANCISCO

Telephone, No. 457.

R. WATKINS,

Veterinary Dentist,

Of twelve years practice, is now permanently located in San Francisco, and may be found at C. S. Crittendens' Golden Gate Livery and Riding Academy, 24 to 28 Golden Gate Avenue.

Will treat ailments of the horse's mouth, and cure all such. Sidecin Pullers and Tongue Lollers, etc. Satisfaction guaranteed. Orders by mail will receive prompt attention. Examination Free.

E. J. O'ROUKE.

I have the honor to announce to my old patrons and the general public that I may be found at my old stand, where, as heretofore, the

Shoeing of Horses,

whether for the Track, Drive, or for general work, will receive my personal attention.

Telephone 2011.

E. J. O'ROUKE,
209 Ellis Street

California Horse Shoe Co's

I have used in my business the Steel and Iron Shoes made by the above Company, and take great pleasure in saying they are the best I have ever used in twenty-two years practice. I have never seen anything like the STEEL SHOE made by this Company. I can fully recommend them to every practical Horseshoer in the country. Yours respectfully,

No. 8 Everett street. JOHN GRACE.

LAMBORN ROAD MACHINE

TRUMAN HOOKER & CO.

SAN FRANCISCO. - - CALIFORNIA

TWENTY-FOUR PAGES.

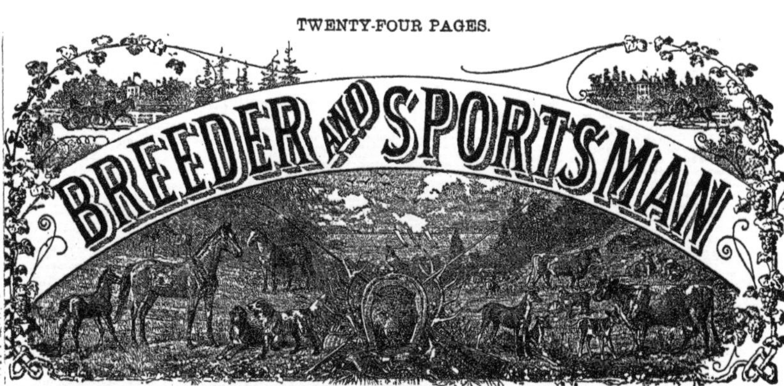

Vol XVI. No 15.
No. 313 BUSH STREET. SAN FRANCISCO, SATURDAY, APRIL 12, 1890. SUBSCRIPTION FIVE DOLLARS A YEAR.

SAN JOSE BLOOD-HORSE MEETING.

SATURDAY, APRIL 5TH.

The San Jose Blood Horse Association is gradually but surely working its way to the front. This year it had a great influx of new members, and all round an increased interest was taken in the management of the association and general working thereof, and it is now the expressed opinion of the racing public that it is only a matter of time, at the present rate of progress, when San Jose races will be the peer of any in the State. Since last Fall a club house—nearly completed—has been erected, and the exterior portion of it was used by the members. The initial day last Saturday showed a marked change in comparison to the previous San Jose meetings, when San Francisco and outsiders have been the principal patrons. Last Saturday a good attendance—for a first day—was almost entirely local, and the interest they took in the proceedings was equal to that shown on any track in the State.

For some days—weeks in some cases—before the races, horses had been congregating on the track, and Saturday found upwards of seventy horses located at the track, including as they did the best horses in the State. Palo Alto, with the veteran Henry Walsh in charge, had Geoffrey (4), the winner of three races out of five last year; Faustine (4), the winner of the Fame Stakes last year; Racine (3), the winner of the Gano—now Racine Stakes—in 1:14½, and ten other races last year; by the way, I have made a mistake, the Gano Stakes was changed to So-So the year previous, when Sonoma won in 1:14¾, and was disqualified; Flambeau, the acknowledged crack three-year-old of the stable, who ran second to his stable companion Racine last year in most of his races, and won three himself, including the California Annual Stakes in 1:43; Muta, a three-year-old filly who started three times last year, running second to Santa Anita's Atalanta in her first essay, winning the Ladies' Stakes in her second, and running third to her two stable companions Racine and Flambeau, in her third. The two-year-olds include Rinfax, by Argyle, out of imp. Amelia; (Undine Stables) Glenlivet (a sister to Gueen and Geoffrey) by Flood—Glendew; Tearless, a chestnut filly (sister to Raindrop and half-sister to imp. Brutus and imp. Cyrus) by Wildidle, out of imp. Teardrop, and several others.

Senator Hearst, with Geo. Van Gorden managing and W. L. Donathan training, had twelve representatives, two were imported from Australia, viz., Gertrude and Del Mar, both being by Somnus, and rank as four-year-olds here; Almont, the speedy four-year-old son of Three Cheers, as a two-year-old won six races, beating Don Jose and Picnic for the California Annual Stake in 1:42¾, and in the Night Hawk Stakes, also a mile, for all ages, he beat, among others, such horses as Daisy D., Al Farrow, Edelweiss, Welcome and Idalene Cotton in 1:42¼; last year he was taken sick on the way East, and nearly died, and though looking exceptionally well, is said to be thick in his wind; Baggage, the lucky horse in the sensational race at Chicago, won by Redlight and given to Baggage, and afterward paid to both horses, and Sacramento, by Joe Hooker, out of Ada C., represent the three-year-old division, while among the two-year-olds were Anarchist (a brother to Dynamite) by Joe Hooker, out of Chestnut Belle; Snowball (a brother to Snowdrop) by Joe Hooker, out of Laura Winston; Yosemite, by Hyder Ali, out of Nellie Collier; Primero, by Powhattan, out of Speed; Charley Brown, by Jim Brown, out of Viola. The horses in the Hearst stable all looked exceptionally well, but a little short of work, as they undoubtedly are, and they should keep improving on their form.

Kelly & Samuels had their old favorite McGinnis and Welcome, five-year-olds, Rosebug (4), Pliny and Adelaide (3), and Lizette, two years old.

W. L. Appleby had in his stable, among others, the well known horses Applause (a), Carmen (5), Odette (4), Wild Oats (4), Steve Stroud and Raindrop (3), and Wild Rose (2). The Elmwood Stable had their well known string Nerva, Nabean, Vinco, Index, Installation, and three three-year-old fillies and two two-year-olds. Miller & Owens had Daisy D. Corona and Capt. Al. Hazlitt had Louise M., Jubilee and Pilot, while among other well-known horses were Sunday, Kitty Van, Oro, Bessie Shannon, Alfaretta, Jack Brady, Painkiller and Jou-Jou.

With such a brilliant gathering of horses, it is no wonder that good racing was expected, and the four races on the card were run off in good shape, W. H. Coombs being very successful as starter. The first race was quite a surprise, as the unbacked Australian, after running three or four lengths behind the leaders, came fast up the stretch, and just got up in time, winning by a head from Daisy D., with Kitty Van a neck behind. The winner, who was very short of work, ran a slashing race, but was lucky in having an opening left, as the leaders made the turn into the stretch very wide, while he hugged the rails and came up on the inside. Racine was never half extended, and was galloped an extra quarter at the end of the mile (1:42½) without materially slowing up. The two-year-old race was won all the way by Rinfax, and the last race was won by Palo Alto's Faustine. The stable thus started in three races, and won all of them. Pliny and Faustine made one of the prettiest races ever seen, the mare on the inside leading a head all the way to the stretch, when it almost looked as though Pliny would win, but the 75-pound boy could not hold his lead up, and he was beaten about a length.

The officials for the day were: Judges, T. S. Montgomery, President of the Association, William Buckley, and Charles T. Boots. Timers, W. A. Parkhurst, G. H. Jefferson, T. F. Barnes, Secretary C. H. Bragg and Starter W. H. Coombs.

First race six furlongs. Punctually on time the horses were called out for the first race, a six furlong dash for all ages, which had fifteen entries, five of whom came to the post, viz., Daisy D., Kitty Van, Del Mar, Adam and Raindrop. The pools settled down to Daisy D. $20, Raindrop $4 and the field $5. A start was soon affected, Kitty Van, breaking away like a quarter horse, had two lengths the best of it, Daisy being a shade in front of Del Mar and Adam, with Raindrop last. When all were fairly straightened out Kitty Van was two lengths in front of Daisy, with Del Mar three back and a length in front of Adam, who was two open lengths ahead of Raindrop. The two leaders kept the same distance round the turn, while Raindrop drew up almost level with Del Mar. Turning into the straight Kitty Van, and Daisy, who was closing up a little, ran very wide and looked to have the race to themselves, but at the drawgate Kitty began to stop and Daisy caught her and both boys rode hard, but Morton on Del Mar, who hugged the rails all the way round, came with a clatter, and won on the post by a short head, Kitty a neck back third, Adam a moderate fourth.

Paris mutuals, Field against Daisy D., paid $14.10.

SUMMARY.

Introduction Stake a sweepstake for all ages: $25 entrance, $10 forfeit. with $200 added. $75 to second horse, $25 to third. Fifteen entries. Three-fourths of a mile.

G. Hearst's ch h imp. Del Mar, 4, Somnus—Maid of the Hills, 110 .... Morton 1
Miller & Owen's b m Daisy D, a, Wheatley—Black Maria, 115 .... Hennessy 2
J. B. Ross' b m Kitty Van, 4, Vanderbilt—April Fool, 113.. Narvice 3
Also ran Adam 117; Raindrop 101.
Time—1:14¼.

The Vendome Stakes for 3year olds brought out four starters but was productive of little or no betting, Racine selling for $20 to the field's $4.

The flag was soon dropped, Racine going to the front, being a length in front of Baggage and Capt. Al, with Muta two lengths in the rear.

Racine, running easy, increased his lead to two open lengths in the first quarter, where Baggage and Captain Al were level three lengths in front of Muta. The order was not changed until the head of the stretch, when Muta closed up to the two second horses. Racine was pulled back a little to the other three on whom whips were cracking, but at the drawgate Narvice gave him his head again and he shot out like a rocket, passing under the wire four open lengths in the lead and was worked another quarter without showing any signs of slackening up or tiring. After a hard finish for the place, Baggage got it by three-quarters of a length from Muta, with Captain Al a length back.

Paris Mutuals, Racine v Field, paid $5:80.

SUMMARY.

Vendome Stake. For three-year-olds. $25 entrance, $10 forfeit with $175 added. $50 to second horse $25 to third. One mile.

Palo Alto's b c Racine, Bishop—imp Fairy Rose, 118...... Narvice 1
Geo. Hearst's ch c Baggage, Warwick—Maria F, 118 .... Morton 2
Palo Alto's ch f Muta, Wildidle—imp Mutiny, 113........ Harrison 3
Time, 1:42½.
Also ran Captain Al, 118.

The Debut Stakes for two-year-olds, with three starters, was considered a certainty for the much vaunted Argyle colt—Rinfax, and pools sold Rinfax $20 to the field $12. A little—very little—delay was caused by the fractiousness of the youngsters, and when the flag fell Rinfax drew out and led Woolman a length and a half to the turn with Wild Rose a length behind. Wild Rose drew level with Woolman as they turned into the straight and was at one time two lengths in front of him, but both hard ridden for the last furlong, made a dead heat for second place, three lengths behind Rinfax, who won cleverly.

Paris mutuals paid, Rinfax v Field $7:70.

SUMMARY.

Debut Stake. For two-year-olds; $25 entrance, $10 forfeit, with $150 added, $50 to second horse. Four entries Half mile.

Palo Alto's ch c Rinfax, Argyle—imp Amelia, 110 .... Narvice 1
W. L. Appleby's b c Wild Rose. Wildidle—Rosetland, 110.. .. Murphy 2*
Orange Grove Stable's br c Joe Woolman, imp Cyrus—Ella Doane, 110 .... Cooper 2*
Time, 0:50½.
* dead heat.

The St. James Hotol Stakes one mile, for all ages, brought 3 horses to the post and was much the best betting race of the day, Pliny, who was sold from Palo Alto last spring being well backed on account of his good form at Fresno. Pools sold rapidly at $40 for Faustine to $32 the field. A good start was effected, Faustine (on the inside) and Pliny cutting out the pace at a merry clip ran locked together for six furlongs with Fannie F., outpaced all the way, Faustine and Pliny were level in the stretch and it looked anybody's race, but Narvice rode the mare brilliantly and drawing away inside the drawgate won by a length. Had Ward, who had twenty lbs. of lead, been strong enough to hold Pliny together, he would probably have won. Fanny F. was six lengths back. Mutuals (Faustine v the field) paid $8.80.

SUMMARY.

St. James Hotel Stake—A sweepstake for all ages; $25 entrance, $10 forfeit, with $150 added. Stake and added money divided, 60 per cent, to first, 30 per cent. to second, 10 per cent. to third. One mile.

Palo Alto's b m Faustine, 4, by Flood, dam imp Flirt, 113.... Narvice 1
Kelly & Samuel's b g Pliny, 3, by Flood, dam Precious, 99 .. Ward 2
C. Nickerson's b m Fannie F, 5, by Wildidle, dam Sally Hart, 116... Fergusson 3
Time, 1:42¼.

MONDAY.

The weather was almost perfection in the afternoon but the local race goers did not turn out as they should have done, and the consequence was a great decrease in the number of people who passed the gate. The officials for the day were: Judges T. S. Montgomery, W. Buckley and Jesse D. Carr. The times were Messrs. Jefferson, Parkhurst and Barnes; Secretary, C. A. Bragg, and starter, W. H. Coombs. The four races on the programme provided excellent sport. In the first Daisy D who was a big favorite won readily as did Palo Alto's Faustine in the second. The third race was the best betting race of the week; Muta was made favorite with Baggage selling well up and Pliny a fair third, but the line through

Saturdays running did not prove true, as under Monohan's handling Pliny carried his weight nicely and after trailing behind for almost six furlongs he came through and won easily. The repeat race was supposed to be a gift for Sunday but Carmen made a dead heat with him in the first heat, although it looked as though Hazlitt could easily have won the heat had he made an effort. In the second Newell was taken down, it being said he was not trying to win and Narvice rode Painkiller who got well away and won easily, Sunday being hard held all the way. The Judges ordered Morton to ride Sunday but when he had got ready, Hazlitt had persuaded them to leave him in the saddle. Painkiller and Sunday got well away and the former just won by a short neck.

The first race, the Santa Clara Stake, a seven-furlong sweepstakes for all ages, had four starters. Daisy D. sold a big favorite at $20 to Oro $5 and the field $9. Jubilee was very fractious, and delayed the start for some time, eventually the bag was dropped to a fairly successful start, Daisy being a little behind the rest, Raindrop was rushed to the front, leading past the six furlong pole by a length, Oro second, half a length in front of Jubilee, with the favorite close up, last. Down the backstretch Raindrop slightly increased her lead, Jubilee and Daisy passing Oro, followed her to the turn, when Daisy went up to the leader, and going on, turned into the stretch a length in front of Raindrop and Jubilee who were about level, two lengths in front of Oro. Daisy D. romped home an easy winner by a length and a half from Jubilee, who, hard ridden, was three lengths in front of Oro. Paris Mutuals paid $8.60.

SUMMARY.

Santa Clara Stake—A sweepstake for all ages: $25 entrance, $10 forfeit, with $175 added, $50 to second horse. Winner of the Introduction Stake to carry 5 lbs. above the scale weight; eight entries. Seven furlongs.

Miller & Owen's b m Daisy D., a, Wheatley—Black Maria, 115..........Hennessy 1
C. Peterson's b g Jubilee, 4, Kyrle Daly—Joy, 114..........Hazlitt 2
J. R. Ross' b g Oro, a, Norfolk—Golden Gate, 117..........Monohan 3
Time, 1:29¼.

Raindrop, 101, ran also.

The second race, one mile and a furlong, for all ages, had three starters, Faustine selling for $25, the other two as a field bringing $6 Welcome, acting in her well known style, sulked for half an hour and delayed the start. At last, however, the trio got away on good terms, passing the stand all level, Faustine gradually drew away, being half a length in front of Brady at the quarter, Welcome close up. Faustine, striding on, increased her lead to two lengths at the half, the other two being level. Brady was hard ridden round the turn, keeping within two lengths of the leader, who stayed in front to the finish, winning handily by an open length, Welcome came fast in the stretch, and looked like getting second place, but stopped again, and was beaten a length by Brady. Paris Mutuals paid $6.

SUMMARY.

Laurelwood Farm Stake. A sweepstake for all ages; $25 entrance, $10 forfeit, with $200 added, $75 to second horse. Weight 10 lbs. above the scale. One and one-eighth miles.

Palo Alto's b m Faustine, 4, Flood—imp. Flirt, 122..........Narvice 1
Orange Grove Stable's b h Jack Brady, a, Wildidle—Sour Grapes, 131..........Monohan 2
Kelly & Samuel's br m Welcome, 5, Wildidle—Æolia, 126....Morton 3
Time—1:59.

The mile for three year olds had only three starters. Betting was very rapid, Muta selling for $40, Baggage $26, and Pliny $17. A beautiful start was effected almost at once. Muta on the inside, with Baggage lapped on her, made the running neck and neck round the turn and down the back stretch, Pliny being pulled in behind, three lengths back. Baggage was ridden hard round the turn to keep his place, and turned into the stretch level with Muta, Pliny two lengths back. Monohan brought Pliny up on the outside and Baggage dropped back beaten. Despite Narvice's efforts, Muta could not stay with Pliny, who, admirably ridden by Monohan, won with a little in hand by a length. Baggage was six lengths back pulling up pumped out.

Paris Mutuals paid $9.

SUMMARY.

Lamolle House Stake.—For three year olds: $10 forfeit, with $175 added, $60 to second horse, $25 to third. Winner of the Vendome Stake to carry 10 lbs. extra. Four entries. One mile.

Kelly & Samuel's b g Pliny, Flood—Precious, 115..........Monohan 1
Palo Alto's ch f Muta, Wildidle—Mutiny, 113..........Narvice 2
G. Hearst's ch c Baggage, 3, Warwick—Maria F., 118..........Morton 3
Time—1:43½.

The last race was half mile heats for all ages.

First Heat. Sunday sold for $40, to Carmen and Painkiller as a field $15. Very little delay occured at the post. Carmen and Sunday had a shade the best of the start and cut out the work, Painkiller dropping in behind; Carmen, who was on the inside, ran level with Sunday round the turn. Murphy rode Carmen all the way up the stretch, making a dead heat with Sunday, Hazlitt seeming not to make a big effort—or possibly he drew it too fine. Painkiller finished three lengths back, running easy.

Paris Mutuals paid $7 on the field and $3 50 on Sunday. Time, 0:48½.

Second Heat—Narvice rode Painkiller. Pools sold, Field $20 to Sunday $11. There was quite a long delay at the post and when the flag fell Painkiller had a good two lengths the best of it, and ridden hard increased to it four before the turn was reached. Sunday closed the gap a little round the turn and finished with his head pulled round two lengths behind Painkiller. Carmen just saved her distance, getting badly away and laying up the heat. Time, 0:49.

Third Heat—Pools now changed entirely, Painkiller selling for $20 to $8 for the field. After a slight delay at the post Sunday being unwilling to face the starter, the flag was dropped with Painkiller and Sunday two lengths in front of Carmen. The two leaders ran head and head round the turn, Painkiller on the inside having about a neck the best of it inside the stretch and answering gamely to Narvice's efforts, won a hard finish by a neck, Sunday two lengths in front of Carmen. Paris Mutuals paid $6.95. Time, 0:49.

SUMMARY.

Milpitas Stake,—A sweepstake for all ages; $25 entrance, $10 forfeit, with $175 added, $50 to second horse. Six entries. Half mile heats.

G. Lyman's b h Painkiller, 5, by Joe Hooker, dam Betsy Maguire, 115..........Narvice 3 1 1
J. Dowd's b g Sunday, a, by Sundance, dam Norma, 112....Hazlitt *0 2 2
W. L. Appleby's ch m Carmen, 5, by Wildidle, dam Nettie Brown, 110..........Murphy *0 3 3
Time, 0:48½, 0:49, 0:49.

*Dead heat - for first place.

WEDNESDAY.

The third and last days racing of the San Jose Blood Horse Association was of the same style as the preceding two days. The fields were again small, Palo Alto having removed their horses to the Bay District Track. The first race of the day, an owners handicap at a mile, was a surprise to the talent as no one expected that Kitty Van could run a mile if turned loose, with Daisy D. It looked to me as though different tactics should have been pursued with Daisy, had she carried Kitty Van the first six furlongs in 1:15 or better she might have had made her stop at the end of the seven furlongs, as it was she allowed the crack sprinter to run the first six furlongs easy, and consequently she stayed the journey and won easily, admirably ridden by little Ward at 77lbs. The two year old race only had three starters, two of them from the Orange Grove Stables, and the other from the Hearst Stables. The latter was a useful looking chestnut by Powhattan, but unfortunately his eye was injured while at exercise in the morning and besides being unable to see out of it, it made him very nervous and frightened and he was never really in the race.

The third race was practically a walk-over for McGinnis, who is in pretty good form just now. Monohan rode the winner, and consequently received the order for a suit of clothes presented by Messrs. T. V. Hobson & Co. The special race did not fill, and a quarter mile and repeat wound up the meeting, and did not add much lustre to the proceedings. All short races of late have been productive of unseemly rows, and this was no exception; the sooner they are done away with the better, and I understand that the association, which is striving hard to please the public and thus make a success of their meetings, will have no more short races.

Christopher Green, Esq., President State Fair Association, presided in the judges' stand, assisted by Jesse D. Carr, Esq., Salinas, and T. S. Montgomery, Esq., President San Jose Blood Horse Association. W. H. Coombs, starter.

First race, Al Farrow Stakes, one mile, four horses turned out. Daisy D., with 102 pounds, was made a hot favorite in the pools, being backed as though the race were over, at $20 to Kitty Van $6 and the field $3. A very good start was made, all four being well under way when the flag fell, with nothing to choose between them. Kitty Van, pulling hard, rushed to the front, and went round the turn, hugging the rails, two lengths in front of Carmen, with the other two a length further back. Kitty Van ran easy down the backstretch two open lengths in the lead, Daisy D. second, a length in front of Carmen, who was the same distance in front of Fannie F. Kitty still had her lead when the stretch was reached, and though Hennessy made a vain attempt, he could never get up to her, and she won cleverly by two open lengths from Daisy D., Fannie F., five lengths back, just beat Carmen for third place. Time, 1:41. Paris mutuals, Field vs. Daisy D., paid $13.90.

SUMMARY.

Al Farrow Stake—A sweepstake for all ages (owner's handicap): $50 entrance, $25 forfeit, with $250 added; $75 to second, $50 to third horse. Stake to be named after winner if Al Farrow's time (1:40) is beaten. One mile.

J. R. Ross' b m Kitty Van, 4, Vanderbilt—April Fool, 77..........Ward 1
Miller & Owen's b m Daisy D., a, Wheatley—Black Maria, 102 lbs..........Hennessy 2
C. Nickerson's b m Fannie F., 5, Wildidle—Sally Hart, 95...Narvice 3
Time, 1:41.

Carmen, 85, ran also.

The Lick House Stakes, for two-year olds, had three starters, and all three were sold out in the auctions. Primero and Joe Woolman were favorites, first one and then the other, Woolman finally going to the post a decided favorite at $20 to $13 Primero and $5 Bon Ton.

A long delay occurred at the post caused by Bon Ton who refused to join the other two. The flag was eventually dropped with Bon Ton and Woolman two lengths the best of Primero. Woolman made the running a length in front of Bon Ton to the turn when he increased it to two. Primero, hard ridden, closed up, being almost level with Bon Ton, but dropped back again in the stretch after making his effort. Woolman won handily by two lengths from Bon Ton, Primero pulling up last.

Paris Mutuals, Woolman v. Field paid $7 85.

SUMMARY.

Lick House Stake.—For two-year olds, $25 entrance; $10 forfeit, with $150 added; $50 to second horse. Winner of Debut Stake to carry five pounds extra. Five furlongs.

Orange Grove Stable's br c Joe Woolman by imp Cyrus, dam Ella Doane, 110..........Narvice 1
Orange Grove Stable's ch c Bon Ton by Flood, dam May D. 110½..........Cooper 2
G. Hearst's ch c Primero by Powhattan, dam Speed, 110.....Morton 3
Time, 1:04½.

The Hobson Stake for all ages, at a mile and a quarter, only brought out three horses, McGinnis being in such good form that only three or four dollars could be got against $20 in the auctions and with McGinnis barred it was the same thing, Oro $20, Sacramento $4. Mr Coombs effected a beautiful start, all three being level and in motion. Sacramento on the rails and Oro next fighting for his head and pulling hard made the running, passing the stand level, McGinnis two lengths behind taking it easy. McGinnis running easy still, joined the two leaders at the quarter and stayed with them to the head of the stretch, when Monohan gave him his head and he romped home three lengths in front of Oro, who beat Sacramento a length and a half for the place. Paris Mutuals, McGinnis v. Field paid $6 75.

Hobson Stake. A sweepstake for all ages. $25 entrance, $10 forfeit. $175 added. Four entries. One and one-fourth miles.

Kelly & Samuel's b h Ed McGinnis, 5, Grinstead—Jennie G, 111..........Monohan 1
J. R. Ross' b g Oro, a, Norfolk—Golden Gate, 111..........Narvice 2
G. Hearst's b c Sacramento, 3, Joe Hooker—Ada C, 92..........Cota 3
Time—2:12.

The sprinters' stake, a quarter mile and repeat, had five starters, and after starting out with Sunday $20 to the field's $6, Comet was taken out of the field and pools sold, Sunday $20, Comet $11, and the field $9. Comet a big, powerful Oregon horse, ran a quarter some time ago at Yreka in 21 seconds, but it turned out the track was forty yards short.

First Heat—A long, wearying delay occurred at the post, there never being more than two horses ready to break away at once. The flag was, after three-quarters of an hour's wait, dropped with Jack the Ripper standing still. Sunday, who was on the extreme outside of the track, crossed to the others on the rails, and after a tight finish was beaten a head by Comet, The Jew half a length back and a length in front of Little Girl. Time :24.

Paris Mutuals—Field vs. Sunday, paid $9.75.

Second Heat—Sunday sold a still stronger favorite, bringing $20 to the field's $11. Almost as long a delay occurred again, and when the flag fell Comet had the worst of the send off and Sunday won the heat easily by three lengths. The Jew second, Little Girl third, and Comet last, should have been distanced, had the distance department handled their flags correctly.

Paris Mutuals—Sunday vs. field paid $7.20. Time :24.

Third Heat—A few pools were sold, Sunday $20 to Comet $5. No time was wasted on the start, which was affected at almost the first attempt. Sunday, running easy all the way, won by three lengths. Time :24.

Sprinter Stakes. A sweepstake for all ages. $25 entrance, $10 forfeit, with $75 added. One-fourth mile heats.

J. Dowd's b g Sunday, a, Sun Dance—Norma, 112..........Davis 2 1 1
E. E. Randal's b h Comet, a, Club Foot—by Jeff Davis, 115..........Fitten 1 4 2
E. Williams' br g The Jew, a, 112..........Hennessy 3 2
E. B. Stuit's ch m Little Girl, a, 112..........Malone 4 3
Alex Graham's ch g Jack the Ripper, a, 112..........Morton dis
Time—:24, :24, :24.

History of the Mohawk Horses.

EDITOR BREEDER AND SPORTSMAN:—Since Elmo 2:27, has been one of the greatest producers of extreme speed in California, no doubt your many readers would be interested in reading a history of the Mohawks. Old Mohawk was a dark chestnut, 16½ hands high, and would have weighed in fair flesh 1200 lbs. He had three white ankles, two behind and one in front, had a star and snip. For style, beauty, strength and great endurance he could not have had many equals, for he never was trained two months for speed, always was in the stud, and was fat and in no condition to trot races. I have known him to serve mares right up to the 4th of July and start on the 4th in a free-for-all stallion race, and win it, defeating as good trotting stallions as could be found in our State, or brought from other States. He was a good scorer and a great finisher. He was a nice big coach or carriage horse; his neck was very long and nicely arched; he had a nice neat head, powerful shoulders and loins, and was dead game—could trot all day. Mr Leek Yorks of Long Island, New York, bred and raised him. His sire was Long Island Black Hawk, his dam a daughter of Mambrino Chief. Mr. Yorks sold him to Geo Alley of New York City, Mr. Alley sold him to John J. Wise of 24th street, New York. He sold him to Joseph W. Hall of Knox County, Ohio. Jos. W. Hall purchased and brought him to Knox County, Ohio, in April, 1860. He made three seasons in Knox County, Ohio, siring Elmo 2:27, Clark's Mohawk Jr., 2:25, at 4 years old, Hall's Mohawk Jr. 2:26, and a score of others that could beat 2:40. Our mares were what are called common stock. Rysdyk's Hambletonian was at that time having a boom Mr. Hall took a carload of horses and money enough to buy Rysdyk's Hambletonian and went to Orange County for the purpose of bringing Hambletonian home with him. Mr. Rysdyk asked him $14,000 for him. While in New York selling his horses, he saw Mohawk and liked him much better than Hambletonian to cross with our mares It is believed by many good trotting horsemen that had he purchased old Hambletonian and brought him to this county, he would not have produced as well as Mohawk did. *Great opportunities make great producers* If old Mohawk had had access to standard mares, his roll of honor would rate with the best of them. We all know that Electioneer is one of the greatest sires on earth, but I will venture to state that there are many breeders in California that honestly believe that if Mr. Stanford had placed Elmo 2:27 where he placed Electioneer that Elmo would to-day rate where Electioneer rates.

I will give a short history of how Elmo came to exist. In the year 1862 an old Englishman by the name of Robinson, and his son Robert came from England and purchased a small farm near Fredericktown, Knox County, Ohio. I think the farm cost them twenty-five hundred dollars They had $1500 to pay on it, and gave a mortgage on the land for the balance ($1000). They moved on the farm in April, and about the 1st of May they came to our place to see the stock. The old gentleman bragged of his bay, Sir Richard's Mare, he was driving. My father said to him he thought old Mohawk and his mare would produce a valuable colt. The old man said he could not afford to pay $25 for a colt, for he had a mortgage on his farm for $1000 and had to be careful or he could not lift it. Father said to him that he thought a colt from Mohawk and his mare might help him to pay off the mortgage. The old man took with the idea and bred her, the produce being Elmo 2:27. When he was two years old he was broken to harness and driven once or twice a week on the road. He had plenty of natural speed the first time he was hooked up.

About three weeks before our county fair a local trainer took him to the track and trotted him, at the fair winning the three-year-old race in a jog in 2:52. This race gave him the name of being a great colt. Mr. Van Giesen, of Chicago, heard of him, and in the spring of 1866 he sent Mr. Sargent to buy Elmo. Mr. Sargent was afraid Mr. Robinson would back out when he would take him up, so took a friend to have hold of the strap when he purchased him. Mr. Robinson priced him at $2,000—a price at that time for a three-year old colt looked exorbitant. Mr. Sargent purchased him at $2 000, getting his sulky and harness. The old gentleman was not long in coming to see us, and was delighted in telling that the mortgage was lifted and had $1,000 left to improve his farm with. Elmo's career after he went to Chicago, is known by many of your readers. Clark's Mohawk Jr., 2:25, by Old Mohawk, was a great race horse. He met with an accident at five years old which caused his death. He would have been a grand stallion if he had lived. He was the sire of Fashion, 2:23, and Yellow Dock, with running mate, 2:11.

Hall's Mohawk Jr., 2:26, was foaled in 1862. He was 16 hands, dark bay, with four white ankles, star and snip. He got a record over a poor half-mile track of 2:26. He sired Belle Ogle, 2:21½; she trotted quarters in 0:29½ seconds. He also sired Mohawk Gift, 2:21½, McFadden (pacer) 2:24, Mohawk Kate, 2:26, and Mohawk Chief, 2:30. All the above-named horses are from now standard mares. Hall's Mohawk Jr. has over thirty of his get in this locality that can beat 2:45, from common mares, and used only as road horses. I know of a three-year old stallion by Hall's Mohawk Jr. that I saw trot quarters in 37 seconds with a three-ounce tip on. He is a fine, big, rangy fellow, and will beat 2:25 this season if trained. He is Senator Stanford's kind—trots with light tips. If Mr. Stanford had him, I am confident he would soon make a great stallion out of him, and one that would produce as well as Electioneer, for he is so much like Electioneer in every respect.

The Electioneers and Mohawks are almost 1st cousins as the Clays and Mohawks both originated from Andrew Jackson. Harry Clay was sired by Andrew Jackson dam unknown. Andrew Jackson sired Long Island Black Hawk, dam Sallie Miller record 2:33 by Tippo Saib by Messenger. We combine the Mohawks and Electioneers and then look out for great speed.

If any of your readers desire any information in regard to the Mohawk Horses, I will be glad to write them what I know about them. Yours, GEO. S. HALL.

FREDERICKTOWN, KNOX CO., OHIO.

Helena Colt Stakes.

Notwithstanding that the balance of the Montana Associations have left Helena out in the cold in making up the circuit for this year, the entry lists to their colt stakes have filled exceedingly well. Secretary Pope furnishes the following so that the Californians can see what there is pitted against them.

THE PIONEER STAKES.

A sweepstake for two-year old, (foals of 1888) of $50 each; $500 added; guaranteed value of stake $1,000. Winner of a race of the value of $610 to carry five pounds extra; of two such races seven pounds. Maidens allowed five pounds. Six furlongs.

Hundley & Preuitt's b c Datrus by Red Boy, dam Bolls.
Hundley & Preuitt's ch c Hamilt.e by Red Boy, dam Bessie Douglass.
W. C. Lewis' b c Leonidas by Red Boy, dam Pilgrim by Sargent.
J. R. Crawford's ch c Bonnieville by Sun Dance, dam Norma.
H. R. Baker's ch f Bessie by Regent, dam Nannie Holton.
John Bellenberg's ch c Malcolm by Regent, dam Lady Langtry.
Wm. D. Thornton's b c Butte by Aristices, dam Sallie Edwards.
Wm. D. Thornton's b f Bonnie Eloise by imp Athlete, dam Lady Wentworth.
Wm. D. Thornton's ch c Xenophan by Aristides, dam imp Crash.
Wm. D. Thornton's b c Needmore by Frogtown, dam Glorietta.
Wm. D. Thornton's ch c Boland by Tom Bowling, dam Lucy
W. J. Stafford's b f Lady Sapphire by Inaugural, dam Mollie.
Jas. A. Murray's b f Zora by Vanderbilt, dam Mollie Duke.
Hancock & Phelps' b c Vice Royal by Regent, dam Missadie.
Thos. P. O'Hara's b f Rosewater by Renown, dam Maud Lee.
Cy. Mulkey's b c Sinfax by Wild Idle, dam Foatress.

THE DERBY STAKES.

A sweepstake for three-year-olds, (foals of 1887) of $50 each; $500 added; guaranteed value of stake $1,000. Winner of any race this season of the value of $500 to carry five pounds extra; of two such races seven pounds. Maid ns allowed five pounds. One mile and a half.

J. P. Woolman's ch f Emma Nevada by John A., dam May D.
The Montana Draft Horse Co's b c Ladago by Spinning, dam Etta.
H. R. Baker's ch f Carrie Lee by Regent, dam Nannie Holton.
H. R. Baker's gr f Katie Putnam by George Wilkes, dam Jewell.
Frank C. Alexander's b c Joe Murphy by Lyrist, dam Belle Keith.
The Spokane Stables' ch f Miss Chariton by Chariton, dam Nannie Harris.
Robt. Milligan's b c Montana by Story, dam Vega.
John Hardwick's ch g Birdie H by Red Boy, dam Aus'raoid.
John Hardwick's ch g Skucum by Red Boy, dam Bessie Douglas.
Thos. P. O'Hara's ch f Teddy Venture by Bannack Lath, dam Adventure.
Fred F. Thurston's blk f Annie F. by Glen Elm, dam unknown.
Cy. Mulkey's gr f Miss Stoor by Reveille, dam by Valcien.
Golden Gate Stables' b c Gascia by Wildidle, dam Nighthawk.
Golden Gate Stables' b c Snook by Wildidle, dam Wah ta Wah.
Golden Gate Stables' b c Tom Hazlett by Wildidle, dam Lizzie Brown.
W. H. Babb's ch c Guido by Double Cross, dam Aurora.

THE LAST CHANCE HANDICAP.

A handicap sweepstakes for all ages of $50 each; $500 added, $10 to accompany the nomination, $40 additional to start, weights to appear two days before the race, starters to be named in the usual manner through the entry box the evening preceding the race. One mile and a quarter.

J. P. Woolman's b f (3) Emma Nevada by John A, dam May D.
John Duffy's b g (a) Olympia by Luke Blackburn, dam Belladonna.
H. R. Baker's ch m (5) Nevada by Regent, dam Miss Ella.
H. R. Baker's b g (5) Warpeake by Chesapeake, dam Ordnance.
Al Harrison's ch h (4) Millionaire by Milner, dam Mollie Simpson.
Wm. D. Thornton's ch m (4) Kee-vee-na by Enquirer, dam Blithsome.
C. M. Tate's ch h (4) Fandango by Billy Lee, dam by Rifleman.
N. D. Wood's br m (5) Dainty by Rocko dam Belle Keith.
The Spokane Stable's b m (5) Carrie M by Hyder Ali, dam Vivien.
John Hardwick's ch g (3) Birdie H by Red Boy, dam Austraoid.
Thos. P. O'Hara's br g (4) Mackenzie by Hyder Ali, dam Sunshine.
Thos. P. O'Hara's ch f (3) Teddy Venture by Bannack Lath, dam Adventure.
Golden Gate Stable's b c (3) Gascia by Wild Idle, dam Nighthawk.
Golden Gate Stable's b c (3) Snook by Wild Idle, dam Wah ta Wah.
W. H. Babb's ch c (3) Guido by Double Cross, dam Aurora.

THE NURSERY TROTTING STAKES.

A stake for two year olds bred and raised in Montana, of $50 each; $500 added, two in three.

Noah Armstrong's br c Grimanda. by Doncaster, dam Edna by Ed Woods.
Noah Armstrong's b c Ghilan. by Montana Wilkes, dam Celestia by Doncaster.
Noah Armstrong's blk f Geneva, by Montana Wilkes, dam Celia by Doncaster.
Noah Armstrong's br f Gyara, by Doncaster, dam Tweedle Dum by Golddust.
George Breck's blk f Genoro, by Montana Wilkes, dam Bessie, by Doncaster.
Wm. Long's blk c Genoa, by Montana Wilkes, dam Alberta by Doncaster.
A. L. Barber's br f Liberty, by Kentucky Volunteer, dam Brilliant by Mam. Diamond.
J. H. French's b f Nettie E., by Border King, dam Susie by Bill Smith.
Hugh Kirkendall's b f Lo Lo, by Tempest, dam Geraldine by Com. Belmont.
John Gleason & Co.'s br f Rosebud, by Ben Lomond, Jr., dam Tiny Tim by Victor Von Bismarck.
Sam Scott's b c Montana, by Ranchero, dam Nutmeg Maid, by Thos. Jefferson.
Robert Milligan's b c Clay Jr., by Superior Clay, dam by Mambrino Pilot Jr.
E. J. Patch's ch f Gipsy, by Superior Clay, dam unknown.
Huntley & Clarke's b c Volcano by Maxim, dam Becky Bishop by Bishop.
Huntley & Clarke's br c McGlinn, by Bishop, dam R. Dean by Aberdeen.
Huntley & Clarke's b f Mountain Maid, by Ky. Volunteer, dam Dolores by Bishop.
Huntley & Clarke's ch c Luminous, by Ky. Volunteer, dam Aurora by Ben Lomond Jr.
S. E. Larabie's ch g ——, by Frank Morgan, dam Favorite by Com. Belmont.
S. E. Laribe's b g Morgan Boy, by Frank Morgan, dam by Harrison Chief.
S. E. Larabie's b f ——, by Bishop, dam Ethel by Contractor.
D. H. Churchill's b f Lady Flash, by Red, Oak, dam May Be So, by Sun Dance.
D. H. Churchill's b f Belle Oaks, by Red Oak, dam Sallie Bett by Consul.
W. H. Raymond's b f Leapyear, by Tempest, dam Eulogy by Com. Belmont.
W. H. Raymond's ch g Locust, by Com. Belmont, dam Gracie H. by Fancy Golddust.
W. H. Raymond's b f Lucille, by Tempest, dam Golddrop by Com. Belmont.
Lee Mantle's ch f Clare by Com. Belmont, dam Dutch Girl, by Live Oak.

THE JUVENILE TROTTING STAKES.

A stake for three-year-olds, bred and raised in Montana, of $50 each, $500 added, three in five.

C. D. Jeffries' ch c Frankfort by Doncaster, dam Edna by Ed Wood.
Breck & Long's blk f Florida by Montana Wilkes, dam Alberta by Doncaster.
D. W Beech's b c Mountain Boy by Sir Rocco, dam Little May by Consul.
C. H. Bartruff's b f Pereda by Doncaster, dam Julia Adams by Indian Chief.
John E. O'Conner's ch f Axtella by Doncaster, dam Minnetta by Young Jim.
C. K. Hodges' b c Maxie Wagner by Maxim, dam Angie by Mam. Diamond.
H. Kirkendall's br g Seven H L by Ky. Volunteer, dam untraced.
Sam Scott's b c (2) Montana by Ranchero, dam Nutmeg Maid by Thos. Jefferson.
Robt. Milligan's b f Mary Clay by Superior Clay, dam by Mam. Pilot Jr.
Huntley & Clarke's br c Deacon by Bishop, dam Lady Greaves by Smuggler.
Huntley & Clarke's br f Go West by Ky. Volunteer, dam Ethel West by Abdallah West.
Huntley & Clarke's b f Little Nell by Maxim, dam Ethel by Contractor.
Barbour & Green's b f Fannie Fern by Montana Wilkes, dam Almieda by Doncaster.
S. E. Larabie's b f Divah by Fieldmont, dam Prima Donna.
S. E. Larabie's gr f Terah by Fieldmont, dam Crop Ear by Pilot Duroc.
D. H. Churchill's ch f Elite by Clarke Chief Jr., dam Nettie Lord by Consul.
W. H. Raymond's b g Kedee by Tempest, dam Fanny by Com. Belmont.
W. H. Raymond's ch g (2) Locust by Com. Belmont, dam Gracie H. by Fanny Golddust.
Lee Mantle's br f La Tosca by Com. Belmont, dam Charm by Crittenden.
P. Wagener's b f Mountain Girl by Doncaster, dam Daffodil by Com. Belmont.

FURTHER CONDITIONS.—A second payment of $15 on each nomination is due on or before June 1st, the third payment for starters, of $25, must be paid as in other races, through the entry box before six o'clock, P. M., of the day preceding that upon which the race is to take place. A failure to make the payments as above specified declares the nomination out of the stake.

The Home of Director.

The desire is always strong within us to pay visits to the various stock farms and keep the readers of the BREEDER AND SPORTSMAN posted as to what is going on, but there are so many calls on the time allotted to work, that from "sun up to sun down" is a long time to be away from the office. However, it is imperative that the many rumors prevalent in spring time, should be verified, or the minds of the public disabused, about the wonderful form shown at the various breeding farms, so on Saturday last the first of a long list of contemplated visits was made to the thrifty little town of Pleasanton, to take a peep at the sons and daughters of the "Iron Horse," a name given to Director years ago, when he was the brightest particular stallion star of the great galaxy that swept through the Septuple circuit.

A few hours give but little opportunity to carefully examine the many good ones that are always to be found at the Pleasanton Stock Farm, so that this initial call was more simply a visit of introduction to the little masters and fair maidens that are liable to make themselves celebrated on the fields of contest during the circuit season of "Ninety."

An early rise brought us in due season to the foot of Market street, where we found the "white knight" Andy McDowell and L. A. Davis, of Roy Wilkes fame, also in waiting to take the 8:30 train, each bound for the same destination. Just before the boat starts, Mr. Salisbury and his bonny little daughter Margaret (after whom the winner of the Spirit Futurity Stake of last year is named), make their appearance, and the party is complete. The principal owner of the now renowned breeding establishment at Pleasanton, is a pleasant gentleman, who always had a predeliction for fast horses, and it is not so many years ago that we remember him in Washington driving behind such good ones as Sweetners, 2:21½, Bateman, 2:22, and a few others equally well known. It was a subject of wonder then, where "the old fellow from California" picked up such good ones, but as he always managed to pass everything on the road, no matter what was turned against him, it finally came to be understood that "Salisbury's luck" was too much to battle against.

With indomitable courage and perseverance he kept on purchasing stallions until finally he secured the game and speedy Director, having had also Admiral, Romero, Monroe Chief, and a few others with which to give the boys a taste of his horse knowledge, but it was in the purchase of the little black that his name became famous, as the trotters that have eminated from the loins of Director are all noted for their speed and staying qualities; the great desideratum to those who are trying to purchase the best. That the day is not far distant when Director, as a sire, will stand as the peer of any stallion in the land, must be evident to any one who visits the Pleasanton Farm, that is, provided any bias already formed be laid to one side. Arriving at the stables, no time was lost and in a few minutes Andy was warming up Direct 2:18½. Mr. Salisbury was soon in a sulky himself, he moving the young stallion Corrector in a masterly manner. It will take one or two more calls to determine what there is in this big bay, as he has not had work enough to show what he is capable of doing. While Direct was being given a breathing spell, a black-grey filly was brought out which should astonish the natives this year. She is by Director, dam by Paddy McGee, and her mode of locomotion is nearly perfect; a little hitching is her only fault, a fault easy of correction. It should be within her province to make a mark close to 2:20 this year, and it will not be surprising if she even beats that.

Direct was brought out the second time and Andy drove him one or two very fast quarters, the little black showing that he had lost none of his former speed, and it is just possible that there are good grounds for McDowal's belief that his favorite can touch the 2:12 notch this year; it will be remembered that when in the East lately he made a bet with Mr. Valensin that Direct would trot during the season of 1889 in 2:12 or better: when we spoke at the time of the bet being made, we said it was rather doubtful as to whether he could get down so low, but from the manner in which he is moving there is a possibility that Andy may win his bet.

Katy S. another Director filly, was formerly owned by Col. H. I. Thornton, but was sold sometime ago to Mr. Salisbury, and she is another of the rare good ones that may astonish the turf patrons this season, smooth, easy and frictionless in gait, her prospects are good for adding fresh laurels to the brow of her sire. Those working on the farm place reliance on the speed of this animal, and many seem to think that Direct is the only one of the progeny of Director that will have a lower mark than she this year.

Margaret S. has filled out wonderfully and to those who have only seen the filly once or twice she would be hardly known again; she has only been worked a very little, but Mr. Salisbury fancies that if the four-year-old event in which she is entered back East is won by any other horse, at least 2:14 will have to be beaten. Having carried the colors of California so well in the Spirit Futurity Stake last year, all breeders in this State will bid her a hearty "God speed" when she goes back this year to contest with the crack ones of the Eastern Circuit.

We did not see Mr. J. H. White's Contention move, but we are told that he will be another of the astonishers in the California Circuit this year. McDowal thinks very well of him and there is no one who will begrudge his owner a low mark for the Director colt.

The time was so short that there was no opportunity to go to the field and take a look at the brood mares with the exception of a couple which were seen at a distance.

May Day by Ballard's Cassius M. Clay has a foal at her side by Director. This little Miss being a full sister to Margaret S., there is no reason in the world to doubt that she will be equal in speed to her illustrious sister, and barring accidents, good reports in the future should be heard from her.

We also saw the dam of Ranchero, who has a colt at her side by Montana Wilkes, he a son of Red Wilkes. This is another of the promising kind and Mr. Salisbury may well be congratulated upon having obtained possession of such a grand old brood mare.

When the season is a little farther advanced we will pay the Pleasanton Farm another visit, so that our readers may keep posted as to the speed shown by the sons and daughters of the great Director.

Chapter on Smuggler.

Taken from the Advance Sheets of Marvin's New Book.

In his work, "Training the Trotting Horse," now in press, it is not surprising that Mervin tells fully the brilliant career of Smuggler. We have seen some of the advance sheets of Marvin's work, and the story of how Marvin converted Smuggler from the pace to the trot is one of the most interesting things we have seen in any horse book. He says:—

"Mr. Morgan wished me to train him (Smuggler) as a pacer and take a half interest in him, which I promptly and emphatically refused, telling him that pacers were of no account, and he would have to allow me to train him to trot or I would not train him at all. This he refused, and came to see me almost every other day for two months, endeavoring to prevail upon me to meet his proposition. Morgan was a very erratic man, and had a peculiar old gray soldier-coat which he wore winter and summer. He, in copious and highly-seasoned language, would ridicule the idea of trying to make Smuggler trot. 'Why,' he exclaimed, 'if you knocked him down with a club he'd get up pacing.' It amuses me now to recall how, after Smuggler became famous as a trotter, Morgan would loudly tell how he bred him for a trotter, and how he knew from the first that he would be a great trotter. And I am bound to add that once after, when Smuggler was defeated, Mr. Morgan wrote Colonel Russell that if he would 'buy Marvin a pair of rubber reins he would always have a winner.' I trust I have outlived the astute Mr. Morgan's suspicion."

"Finally, finding it futile to urge me to train Smuggler as a pacer, Morgan compromised by giving him to me to train to trot, on condition that if I failed I was to make him pace as fast as he could when he came into my hands, which was not a very heavy contract to assume. Thus it was that Smuggler, obscure and unknown, came into my hands on August 15, 1872, the day he was six years old. I found him a good looking bay horse, 15 3 in front, and 16 hands high behind, and a white rear heel, and a star and snip. He was a well made horse all over, with excellent legs and grand feet. His head was well shaped, and his broad forehead and rich hazel eyes gave him an expression of great intelligence.

"I tried every known method of conversion with Smuggler, and at times I despaired of ever learning him to trot. He was a pacer through and through. First I shod him with an ordinary shoe, but had to increase this again and again until he finally wore two pounds on each front foot, his hind shoes being ordinary five ounce ones. It has been contended, I believe, that Smuggler was injured by carrying excessive weight, and that is possibly true. He had the best of feet, joints, cannons and tendons, and had it been otherwise, he might not have stood what seemed necessary to be done. If the reader will follow me after I have done with my story-telling into the discussions on shoeing and weighting, he will discover that I am on principle opposed to heavy shoes, and 'dead against' weights. But all cases cannot be treated alike: exceptional cases require exceptional treatment, and the case of Smuggler certainly was an exceptional one. It should be remembered that he was not the only horse that carried such weight. Nettie, 2:18, carried 10 ounces more than Smuggler ever did; and so did the little mares Lulu, 2:15, and May Queen, 2:20. None of these could compare with Smuggler in muscular development, and another thing greatly in his favor was that he was a mature horse before the task was asked of him. In many cases the end justifies the means, and those who criticise the methods pursued with Smuggler have in 2:15¼ a stubborn obstacle to brush away.

"As I have said, I tried every known method of conversion with this horse. Different methods of converting pacers will be treated later on, but here I may say that I tried the cross-straps by which it is made impossible for a horse to pace; I tried the plan of placing rails on the ground at such intervals as would compel the horse to put his feet down in the diagonal order; tried weighting in every way, and all availed nothing. Finally by a sort of inspiration, I struck on a plan which perhaps found its first growth in the knowledge that a horse cannot turn short at the pace. I would start him up slowly and rather suddenly throw him off to one side at a pretty sharp angle, compelling him to change his gait; and the new gait he would keep for a few steps. As soon as he came back to the pace I would swing him on sideways again. Of course this was virtually driving around in a small circle, until he began to go a considerable distance trotting. At each time he would remain at the trot a little longer, and after the long, tedious and discouraging experimenting, the reader may well understand how glad and encouraged I was when one day, after going around in a circle for eleven times, Smuggler struck a trot and kept it up for a quarter of a mile. Before this I had unsuccessfully worked him for 28 days. The third day after this evidence of a change of heart he went a full mile, trotting in 4:20, and two days later did a little better, trotting the mile in 4:00. The seventh day after showing his first inclination to trot he showed a mile in 2:59, and the rapidity of his improvement is shown by the fact that on the 13th day he trotted the mile in 2:41½; the 21st day he worked three heats in 2:48¼, 2:38¾ and 2:32, and the 28th day miles in 2:32¼, 2:30½. This ended the work for that season and during the winter Smuggler suffered from an attack of epizootic. He was jogged easily during March, 1873, and in April we began working him again. On May 1st, he was good enough to trot a mile in 2:27, and do it in a way that was full of promise of improvement. The second week in May he trotted a mile in 2:25, and three days afterwards in 2:23. Then Benjamin Akers offered $10,000 for him, but we declined the offer. He kept right on gathering speed and improving in form every day, and a week after Akers offered $10,000 for him he went a mile in 2:22; the next week he trotted three miles in 2:26, 2:21¼, 2.20, and the following week I worked him two miles in 2:19¾ and 2:20¼. He was then sold to Capt. W. S. Tough, of Leavenworth, Kansas, and shipped to New York in my charge."

The story of Smuggler's campaign is written vividly by his old driver in his great book. Those who desire Marvin's book can send orders to this office. Price, $3 50.

TURF AND TRACK.

Anteeo's book for 1890 is full.

Whitecloud, Appleby's crack sprinter is still turned out.

Matt Storn has bred Larlioe to imported Cheviot. She will be raced later in the season.

Wild Oats bas been added to the list since last fall having been gelded to improve his temper, etc.

Cook returned from the East last Monday, arriving in San Jose just too late to ride Pliny to victory in the Lamolle Stakes.

Faustine, the Palo Alto four-year-old mare, winner of the Fame Stakes last year, and two races at Fresno this Spring meeting, has already been bred to Argyle.

John Splan will locate at Cleveland, and it is said that Mr. Gordon will turn over to him the "black whirlwind" Guy, 2:10¾, to be prepared for an effort against his record.

Dwyer Bros. have leased their well known Inspector B. to the Kittson Bros., thus taking a favorite with the public from the public near the tracks near New York to those of Pennsylvania.

Major H. C. McDowell has refused an offer of $700 per acre for Ashland, near Lexington, Ky. Ashland as a stock farm was founded by Henry Clay, and has remained in the family ever since.

One of the seventeen mares Mr. R. S. Veech will breed to Axtell is Imogene 2:29½, at four years old (full sister to Geneva 2:19½) by Princeps, dam Ozone by Hambletonian 10, 2d dam by Magnolia, son of American Star.

The black mare Queen by Mambrino Boy, dam Fanny Lawton, property of T. F. Curtis, dropped a filly by Axtell early on the morning of April 2nd. This is the first and only produce by the great young stallion in existance.

The Charter Oak Driving Park, Hartford, Conn., will give a purse of $10,000 for trotting foals of 1889, to be trotted during its grand circuit meeting in 1892. Entries will close May 5th, when $10 must accompany each nomination.

Wigfall O'Hair of Paris, Ill., has sold Guy G. Crouse of New York State a bay pacing mare by the Watson Horse, for $1,000. She will be sent to the Argentine Republic. She showed a half mile over an Eastern track last summer in 1:09.

Oro, the well known son of Norfolk and Golden Gate, who has many a time and oft shown his long tail to a field of horses at the finish of a race, has been *altered*. He has, besides joining the list of geldings, had his tail squared, and looks every inch a race-horse.

Mr. Marvin's great book on developing trotters will soon be ready for delivery, and we predict for it a great sale. He is the greatest colt developer in the world, and if he tells all he knows, as we certainly believe he will, this will be the most valuable book ever published on the subject.

The license for standing stallions in Bourbon county, Ky., amounts to more than $3,500. It looks a little hard to charge one for improving the stock of his county, but as, ad vantages such as liens on colts for services, etc., are thereby secured, they more than make up for the outlay.

Harry Agnew, who purchased Lyla A. for $2,050, by Arthurton 365, out of Flora Langford, dam of Lillian Wilkes, three-year-old record 2:17¾, and Joe Arthurton, 2:20½, at the late Killip & Co.'s combination sale, has sent her to San Mateo Stock Farm to be bred back to Sable Wilkes, 2:18.

The 9 years-old Princeps mare Femme Sole, 2:20, who secured her record against time in '86 and was recently purchased at the Rockfeller sale by the Hudson river stock farm, Poughkeepsie, N. Y., will be campaigned, it is said. This will make another "bang-up" contestant for the rich 2:20 class.

It is reported that Count Potocki, an Austrian nobleman, who was lately on a visit to Calcutta, has purchased the Maharajah of Durbhunga's well-known Arab "Euclid" for £700 for breeding purposes on his estate in Austria, where he has a large stud farm, but it may be as well to add that the report requires confirmation.

Virginia Evans, 2:24 at four years old, by Kentucky Wilkes, will be handled this season by Ed Geers, and in whose hands she, no doubt, will perform with credit to her game and fast little sire. As a four-year-old she was badly handicapped with a driver afflicted with a "strong arm," which would everlastingly contract as soon as the turn for home was made.

Trotting horses that are compelled to carry extra toe weight to balance them and keep them square in their gait are less appreciated every season. Prince Wilkes and other fast toe weight trotters have not been successful in foreign countries, but have been repeatedly beaten by horses of less speed than can trot without extra weight. A material point in a trotting horse's favor is that he trots without weight.

The 15-year old mare Cleora, 2:18¾, by Menelaus, son of Rysdyks Hambletonian, dam Thornleaf, by Mambrino Patchen, was sold at the recent Kellogg sale for $585 to W. S. Spier, Glen Falls, N. Y. She was a sensational performer in 1882, never meeting defeat. After her purchase by Mr. Rockefeller she was driven on the road and in 1883 to pole carried the grey stallion, Independence, 2:21¼, a mile in 2:17.

It is reported upon good authority that a German musician of note has had an eye on Harry Wilkes (2:13½), but has decided to buy the trotters Red Star and George Peacemaker instead. The former is a gray stallion by A. W. Richmond, son of Simpson's Blackbird, and has a two mile record of 5:13. The latter is a full brother to Dauntless, sire of Gene Smith (2:15) and other fast ones. His record is 2:34½.

An exchange says that Messrs. Look & Smith of the Kentucky Live Stock Agency, Louisville, Ky., have sold the six-year-old stallion Auctioneer to Mr. Seth B. Rubert of Howell, Mich. The pedigree of this horse is one of the choicest found in the stud book, being by Alcantara, record 2:23; first dam Susie, dam of De Barry, 2:19½, by Happy Medium; second dam the dam of Nettie 2:18, by American Star. The sire of Auctioneer is one of the leading Wilkes stallions, having twelve to his credit in the 2:30 list, and both the first and second dams of the horse sold have produced a trotter with a record below 2:20.

You should put the wind power of any horse you intend buying to a severe test, if he is in good hard working condition, so as to bear it without injury. Trot him two miles or more and finish with a smart gallop up hill. Then get down and watch him, and you will estimate the wind power of the horse by the quietness of his flanks. A fat, soft fed horse will not bear so much driving however sound he may be, and must not be expected to breathe as quietly after exertion as a horse in working condition, but his breathing must be regular.

Verbal warranties or promises to warrant are worthless, and the most legally worded written warranties, even from the most respectable men, are best avoided. The interpretation that may be put on them in a court of law is very uncertain, and the amount of evidence that may be brought against you still more so. The amount of successful swearing that some witnesses can accomplish in such cases is truly astonishing. No sensible man with his eyes open will go into any transaction that may take him into a court of law, especially in a horse case.

The failure of so many in breeding may with assurance be charged to a want of daily exercise; owners of brood mares have the right to demand that the horse they patronize receive this work. It means everything to them, for the whole year's results rest here. Work the stallions. Give less attention to fancy points and more to the underlying principles. Build up strong, healthy muscles before the season of breeding opens, so that the per cent. of mares returned will be as low as possible and the character of colts assured. Work the stallions.

The owner of Thornless is anxious, so he says, to trot his horse in a sweepstake race against Belle Hamlin, Harry Wilkes, Jack and Gene Smith, for $500 a side, and added money to be offered by some association, or will trot a match race against any other horse under like conditions. Thornless must have improved wonderfully in that game leg of his. We have often heard it stated by good horsemen that they regard Thornless as a faster horse than Gene Smith, if his legs would stand the necessary fitting.—Horse Breeder.

Among the Boots' string are two useful two year-olds, one of whom looks more than useful, a fair-sized bay colt with black legs, by Duke of Norfolk out of Gipsy, by imp. Hercules, out of Miami by Belmont. He is a good looking colt with plenty of muscular power, rather cobby looking, but speedy. The chances are he will be sold to go East, as he is entered in the Futurity. The other is by Nathan Coombs, out of Bessie, and will run at the coming Blood Horse meeting. The stable have great faith in a three-year-old longish-backed light bay filly by Inauguration out of Mamie Hall.

At the late Kellogg sale the loquacious Splan, while "jollying" a crowd, was asked why he had not deserted the trotters like Rogers, Knap McCarthy, Johnny Campbell and other reinsmen and taken to the running turf, in which there appeared to be more money. "I never went in for runners but once," replied Span, "and that day I made more of the long green than I ever did on any given day in the sulky." Being quizzed for an explanation, Splan resumed: "I got three tips on as many different horses; bet $10 on each one. They all lost. Was struck for loans aggregating $2,000, which I didn't lend. Taking my $30 loss from $2,000, you have my winnings, $1,970."

For some time past a wealthy Tennessee horse fancier has been trying to get a proposition from our fellow-townsman, George W. Morrison, for the purchase of his great stallion Anteros.

Thus far Mr. Morrison has named no price and even refused to consider the matter, but the persistency of the fellow makes it look like he was determined, and he may offer so fabulous a price that Mr. Morrison could not afford to hold on.

It would be a great calamity to Eastern Indiana to lose this splendid animal, and we sincerely hope that the trade may be declared off.—Connersville News.

"What" asks a correspondent, "is the difference, if any, between a "pacing horse" and a "racking horse?" and is a racking horse a species of pacer? The difference between the pacing gait and that of racking is so slight that the two are considered identical, says an exchange. "Pacers when in motion extend the right hind and left fore feet at the same time. Both feet leave the ground at the same instant, throwing the body forward, and after being extended are brought to the earth again at the same instant. In racking the animal moves both feet on the same side at the same time, but the hind foot strikes the earth an instant before the forward one, so that two distinct strokes are heard, while in the pace the ear can detect but one. The rack is simply a fast amble.

One of our Kentucky exchanges contains the following account of remarkable precocity in a filly: "E. A. Robinson, of Lagrange, Ind., sends us a statement in regard to a very remarkable mare in Lagrange county.' Mr. Robinson says she is not five years old and has four foals. Her name is Moll Latta, and she is by Haw Patch 1140. She was foaled October 1, 1885. Her first foal (a filly) was dropped May 17, 1887; her second (a colt), May 8, 1888; her third (a filly), April 11, 1889; her fourth (a colt), March 19, 1890. She was less than twenty months old when she dropped her first foal and was four years, five months and eighteen days when she was delivered of her fourth. She was but nine months old when she first got with foal. She is the property of A. G. Hostetter, Lagrange, Ind. Mr. Robinson challenges the world to produce a parallel case."

It is said that the two coarsest mares at Palo Alto are a pair by Almont, their dam being the famous Mambrino Chief mare Dolly, that also produced Director, 2:19, Thorndale, 2:22½, Onward, 2:24½, and Czarina, 2:17½, the last named going into the list this year. It may be, as the editor of an Eastern paper, in which the above information regarding the two mares at Palo Alto appears, says: That the produce of old Dolly are coarse, but they are certainly first-class in other respects. Onward is a great sire; Thorndale has sired two with records better than 2:20, and Director has two in the 2:20 list before his stud career has fairly begun. As to Czarina, it is true that she is a big mare, and not a particularly fine one in appearance, but she is a trotter, as was evidenced by her work last fall. McHenry, who gave Czarina her record, says that she will trot close to 2:20 with another season's handling, and he is a man who does not overestimate his horses. To have produced Director, 2:17, by George Wilkes; Onward, 2:25½, by George Wilkes; Thorndale, 2:22½, by Alexander's Abdallah, and Czarina, 2:27½, by Egbert, would stamp Dolly as one of the greatest mares that ever lived, even if all three of her sons were not sires of 2:20 and better speed. —Ex.

An exchange says: The Memphis turf scribes are wildly touting Blarney Stone as a dangerous factor in the Kentucky Derby. He is covering miles in 1:45 and "running away from Riley" in all of his trials, etc. All of which would be interesting were it not for one single fact—Blarney Stone is not in the Derby. Amos McCampbell is trying to engage Isaac Murphy to ride Grayson in the Derby. Should he succeed this will be the fifth horse which Murphy, according to rumor, has agreed to ride in Kentucky's classic event.

Mr. Rody Patterson of Lexington, Ky., has been secured as successor to Captain W. H. Boyce as superintendent and trainer for Edgewood Farm. Mr. Patterson, although young in years, has won his way to the front rank of educators of the light harness horse. Among the many results of his teachings the most prominent is Bessimer, that he drove to a four year old record of 2:16 over the Cleveland track on his 21st birthday, and further reduced the pacer's record last year to 2:13½. Coupled with his skill in the sulky, he brings to Edgewood a manly and refined character. The scions of trotting nobility that roam Edgewood's pastures will be in charge of a master hand, who, ere the summer sun is high, will guide them to many a victory. Mr. Patterson will take charge about April 15th.

A great deal of unnecessary disease is, even now, contracted in some stables by the indiscriminate use of the same stable bucket, and frequently of clothing, says the Sporting World. In glanders there is only one thing to be done, which is to destroy the infected animal and bury him deep with quick lime. Everything, harness, blankets, etc., and all the things which come in contact with the body should be burned, and the stable, after scraping, thoroughly do ed with carbolized whitewash and then planked over, or, better still, the stable should not be used at all for some time for stock. There are literally no remedies to be given when once the disease has been developed. In its first stages, as farcy, it is in many cases amendable to remedies, but in its developed stage, as glanders, curative remedies are still entirely unknown.

Simeon B. Hoagland, the veteran jockey, driver and trainer, and all round sportsman whom every one knows, has recently lost by death his favorite roadster, old Privateer, which he bred and named after, perhaps, his greatest friend during life in turf ranks, the late Mr. Charles J. Foster. The horse died at Mr. Hoagland's homestead in Gravesend on March 17th, and has been buried back of the Brooklyn Jockey Club track hard by Green Morris' new house and stable. Mr. Hoagland, now a veteran of 73 never tires of sounding the praises, either of his great horse, or the wonderful turf writer whose nom de plume he bore. Anecdotes about the great little man he has by the score, and it is a source of pride to the old man to tell how many of "Privateer's stories were penned under Uncle Sim's roof. As to the horse he is famous if only for the fact that he sired *Lady Blanche*, the dam of the trotter Alcryon, whose case gained such notoriety last season, and it is still under review by the trotting authorities.

The introduction into Paris of horseflesh as an article of food was due to M. Decroix, former President of the Society for protection to animals, who brought it into public notice in 1866. He practiced what he preached, and partook largely of the viand that he recommended so highly, declaring that it possessed all the nutritive properties of the best beef. The statistics concerning the consumption of horseflesh as an article of food in Paris have just been published. No less than 17,000 horses were slaughtered for the market in 1888, to say nothing of 241 asses and 43 mules. Only one-third of the meat thus obtained was eaten in the form of steaks and roasts; the rest was worked up into sausages, and, in fact, the equine race furnishes by far the largest part of the material used by the sausage markets of Paris. Horseflesh is said to exhale a peculiar odor when uncooked, and can readily be detected by a practice inspector in that way. But when well cooked it is impossible for the daintiest palate to discover the difference between it and the very best beef.

Of the many things managers of trotting associations are required to do in order to secure and retain the confidence and good will of the horsemen who attend their meetings, says Dunton's Spirit, the securing of a competent starter is one of the most important. Not only is this true, in regard to horsemen who start their horses, but a stupid starter in the judges' stand will do more to cut down the gate receipts, than almost anything else. What is wanted is a man with a clear head, cool temperament and courageous enough to enforce the rules to the letter. No timed, nervous individual should be allowed in the judges' stand at all. What is more disgusting than to watch the tedious scoring of a field of horses, manipulated by drivers who have no respect for the "stand?" or, on the other hand, perhaps the starter has too much respect for some of the horses in the race. Above and beyond all, honest men should be secured for judges—men who would keep a close watch on the pool box, not from a speculative stand point as is commonly the case now adays, but so as to be the better able to thwart any attempt at fraud, for in nine cases out of ten, all fraud in trotting races originate at the betting boothe. Not only managers of trotting associations, but all interested in the trotting horse of America should exert their influence in every way to bring about honest turf contests, for in no way can the business be more substantially advanced.

The best English trotting records are far below the American marks, as will be seen by the following from the English racing calender:

One mile, Goodwin, March 13, 1882, Alexandra Park. Time, 2:35.

One mile and a half, Van Buren Girl, July 13, 1886, Alexandra Park. Time, 3:44.

Two miles, Steel Gray, May 1, 1876, Manchester. Time, 5:25.

Three miles, Leybournes, Aug 2, 1872, Aintree, Liverpool. Time, 8:15.

Four miles, Steel Grey, July 10, 1875, Lillie Bridge. Time, 11:27.

Five mile, Steel Grey, July 10, 2876, Lillie Bridge. Time, 14:14.

Ten miles, Steel Grey, March 9, 1875, Manchester. Time, 29:45.

OTHER NOTABLE PERFORMANCES.

Childe Harold trotted one mile, with running mate, at Alexandra Park in 2:47½, on Aug. 24, '80.

Juggler trotted five miles at Blackpool in 14:19½, on July 25, '87.

Jackey trotted ten miles to harness over grass at Aintree, Liverpool, in 29:53, on September 23, 1852.

Steel Grey trotted ten miles on the road at Leeming Lane, Yorkshire, in 27:36½ on April 13, 1875, in a match against Peeping Tom for £400.

Mr. Knock the secretary of the New York Jockey Club has revolutionized the management of race-tracks in the East says the World. He is a quiet, unpretentious gentleman who has few confidants and who believes that intelligent effort can accomplish everything. Mr. Koch was born in New Orleans and educated abroad. He was for years connected with the Morgan line, and Wells, Fargo & Co., and although he had a thorough business training when Mr. Morris put him in charge of his new race-track, he had never seen a horse-race and had to ask a friend what a filly was.

When Mr. Koch came to this city the newspapers laughed at him. He was called the "railroad man from Texas." Everybody predicted failure. No one anticipated success. It would be difficult to imagine a man having more things to contend against. Even the railroads opposed him, and he found that they had not signed a solitary contract to move the crowds, and that he was absolutely at their mercy. That Mr. Koch made a success, and a great success, in the face of all this is simply astounding.

"The easiest thing in the world to manage," said he the other day, "is a race-track. All you have to do is to apply business methods."

He worked for months from 6 in the morning till 2 or 3 at night. He thought it best to know the pedigrees of the horses, so he had a list of all the horses running in the world made out and learned them off by heart. He learned the great races in the same way. To-day he can give the trainers information.

Aradee in Independence Progress: The tabulation of pedigrees and extensions of blood lines that cross and recross in warp and woof of the breeders' equine fabric, has become a profession that requires the hand of an expert to disentangle the mass of fiction and imaginary stuff that hangs about the "manufactured pedigrees" of some of the "equine wonders" hauling wood wagons and dragging the plow in the West. If a man possesses the strength of a Sampson on other topics he is certain to display a weakness on the breeding of his horse when he sets up a claim of "Hambletonian on one side and Diomed on the other," the very antipodes of horse history. The records and standard registry of numbers serve a good purpose in forcing some men to tell the truth. To illustrate, a few days since a letter of inquiry of a mare that had been shipped far West with a colt by Governor Wilkes, claiming the mare to be Orange Girl, 2:20. As such mares and records as "twenty" do not, to use a popular phrase, "lay around loose," and particularly by Hambletonian, "gathered to his fathers" these many years, had the individual the least knowledge of trotting history he must have known such a fraud would be exposed. About the fastest mare that has a colt by Gov. Wilkes in Missouri is Bronze, 2:21¼, and she is in her owner's stable at Kansas City. Another fast mare, Lillian 2:23, dam by Almont 33, had a colt and was sold to J. I. Case, of Racine, Wis., and died at seven years old. These are the only two low record mares on Governor's books. The practice of misrepresentation in such high matters should be made subject to State law as well as turf law; it is a clear case of obtaining money under false pretense.

During the last years of his life Dan Mace drove horses occasionally, not for what there was to be made by it as much as for the sake of taking his mind off his bodily troubles. The last regular meeting in which he was an active participant was held in October, 1880, at West Side Park, Jersey City. Dan entered the bay mare Western Girl, and drove her in the 2:34 class against six others, standing good for his entrance money up to the fifth heat. Billy Button and Breeze Medium were the contending horses, and carried the clip too fast for Mace, who was shut out at the fifth round. Nothing daunted, Dan drove the mare the next day in the 2:38 class and got fourth money. Dan was in great glee. He was as full of fun as a school boy entering on his vacation. The West Side track at Jersey City was built on a salt meadow, where the high tide at times surrounded it. Thick planks were first laid down and clay placed on top, the surface of the track being about two feet above extreme high-water mark. On the day of Dan's second race there was an unusually high tide, and to make matters worse, a tremendous rain storm set in. All hands decided to start, and twelve horses scored down the narrow homestretch for the word. The tide water worked under the planking, and combining with the rain water on top, converted the half-mile ring into a perfect sea of mud. In fact, in places a scow could have floated. As the horses went in a bunch to the turn the spectators could see the track "pompey" like an ice pond, while the rush and weight of the contestants forced the water from beneath the track in fountains. Mud flew in showers, and it was impossible to distinguish the horses. Mace's laugh rang high above the din, while he drove as artistically as he ever did in his life. They put up five bang-up heats, ranging from 2:37 to 2:43. Western Girl was a close second in the first heat and finished fourth in the fifth. Each driver carried about five pounds of mud overweight, and, as Dan declared, had a hundred dollars' worth of fun.

The new Board of Directors of the Pacific Coast Blood Horse Association are going about matters in the right way. They have had cards printed and served on all the trainers and owners, notifying them that the following rules will be lived up to strictly:

TO OWNERS, TRAINERS AND JOCKEYS.

The following rules will be rigidly enforced by the officers of the Pacific Coast Blood Horse Association during the pending Spring Meeting:

1. Owners whose colors have not been registered will be required to file with the Secretary a written description of their colors by 5 o'clock P. M. of the day preceding the race in which they propose to start a horse.

2. Jockeys will be required to ride in the colors so registered. No substitution or change will be allowed.

3. The Secretary will be in attendance at the scale room from and after 12 o'clock noon of each racing day. Jockeys will be required to show their weight at least ten minutes before the advertised starting time of the race.

4. A bugler will be in attendance at the paddocks, and will sound three calls. The first will be to prepare the horses; the second to mount the riders and parade the horses in front of the judges' stand; the third for horses to go to the post, and no more than three minutes will be allowed after the post-call for horses to go to the starting post.

5. Owners, trainers and jockeys must understand that the horses are entirely under the charge of the starter immediately on going to the post. Any disobedience on the part of any of the said parties will result in a fine or other penalty. The Directors will uphold the authority of the starter.

Failure to comply with the above rules, will result in fines to either owner, trainer or jockey, or all of them. Infraction of rule 2 may disqualify a horse from starting.

Special attention is directed to the change in declaration hour to 5 o'clock P. M.

Albermarle, in the New York Sportsman, says: "We see strange things in the breeding world, remarked a man of observation, the other day. I, for one, would never have bred a thoroughbred mare to Gen. Benton to get the dam of a trotting wonder; yet Governor Stanford did it, and produced the fast filly Sunol, 2:10½. I never would have bred a mare of little or no developed speed, to William L., neither fast himself by record, nor the sire of fast ones. Yet a young man did it, and got the king of stallions, Axtell, 2:12. Nor would I have taken a mare by old Vermont Hero, and bred her to Dauntless, at that time considered a rather inferior stallion, and expected a race horse! Yet another man did it, and the result was Gean Smith, one of the greatest of all-round campaigners, a horse that last year started twelve times and won nine first moneys, and carries the record in the fifth heat, 2:16. Nor would I have thought that the mingling up of the blood of Happy Medium with that of a little Morgan mare would produce such a stayer and genuine race horse as Jack, 2:15. As a matter of fact, Gean Smith and Jack were the two best geldings seen in the circuit last year. Neither are fashionably bred, no Star cross, no Mambrino Patchen cross, no thoroughbred cross—just a couple of trotting-bred horses that happened to trot, and had the good luck to be driven by Goldsmith and Doble. These two horses show that breeding a race horse of the first water is still a mystery."

Dave Pulsifer, formerly of Chicago, who owns the great little four-year-old Tenny, said the other day: "I am not obliged to start Tenny in either the Brooklyn or Suburban, and persons who back him for either do so at their own risk. He is entered pretty well in all age stakes, and will have an abundance of racing before the season closes. I still think he is fast for his inches, and nothing would afford me more pleasure than to put him in a little sweepstakes with Salvator, Longstreet, Spokane and Proctor Knott for company, $2,500 or $5,000 each, some reputable racing association to add a few hundreds or thousands by way of increasing the value of the same. Such a race at, say, a mile and a quarter, weight for age, would draw all New York and Brooklyn to see it. I would not ask for an especially prepared track with only my jockey posted as to its peculiarities, nor would I seek to prevent good jockeys from betting in the race. Neither would I expect the judges to award the race if some other horse beat me a neck. A little sweepstakes like the one I suggest could be run over the new Monmouth track at the midsummer meeting without proving hurtful to fall engagements. The owners of the record breakers I have indicated may consider the matter favorably and a big race be the result. Little Tenny has not taken on much flesh and he is still sway-backed, but from the manner in which he kicks stalls into smithereens and seeks to climb out through the roof I infer that he is game enough for another campaign."

B. C. Holly says that his mares are foaling in good shape. Jennie H., (sister to El Monte 2:29) by Echo 462, sire of Belle Echo 2:20, Senator 2:21¼, Victor 2:22, Gibraltar 2:22½, Echora 2:23½, Tippie 2:25½, Lohengrin 2:27½, Pasha 2:27½, Elmonte 2:29, Col. Hawkins 2:29½. Annie Laurie 2:30, Economy 2:30, Sam Lewis (pacer) 2:25, and of the dams of Direct, four years old, 2:18½, and Pink 2:25. 1st dam Lightfoot by Hubbard, 2nd dam Brunette by Rifleman, sire of Col. Lewis 2:18½, 3rd dam Fannie Frazier by Bertrand, foaled a bay colt by Montana Boy 4841, he by Kentucky Prince 2470, sire of Guy, 2:10¾, Spofford 2:18¾, Company 2:19½, Fred Folger 2:20½, Bayonne Prince 2:21½, Cyprus 2:22, Sweepstakes 2:24½, Problem 2:24½, Compeer 2:24½, Jersey Prince 2:27½, Stevie 2:29½, and others, out of Elise, full sister to Prospero 2:20, Dame Trot 2:22, Mansfield 2:26, Antonio 2:28½, Miranda 2:31½, Elaine 2:20, and dam of Norlaine (at one year) 2:31½, by Messenger Duroc 106, out of Green Mountain Maid, dam of the renowned Electioneer, etc. Such a conglomeration of speed and high class breeding is astounding in a colt, and he should be a trotter sure. Violette by G. M. Patchen Jr. 31, out of Viola by Echo 462, out of Woodbine, sister to Monarch 2:28½, foaled a black filly by Happy Prince 10,546. Lady Patchen by Geo. M. Patchen Jr. foaled a chestnut filly with a white face by Happy Prince 10,546, by Bayonne Prince 2939, 2:21½, dam Belle Medium, sister to Mott Medium 2:29½, by Happy Medium, sire of Maxey Cobb 2:13¾, etc. by General Mott, etc., etc. Aurelia by Albert W, 2:20, out of Pacific Maid by Elmo 2:27, second dam by David Hill, third dam by General Taylor, fourth dam by Williamson's Belmont, foaled a bay colt (entered in the BREEDER AND SPORTSMAN Futurity Stake) by Happy Prince. The colt was given to Carrie Whippleton, and Aurelia will be trained this season. Carrie Whippleton by Whippleton, foaled a bay filly by Happy Prince, but stepped on it during the night and it had to be destroyed, Aurelia's colt being put on to the mare instead.

The Australiasian, in speaking of Chicago, the horse lately sent from the Antipodes to England, says: "In Australia we consider Chicago a bigger, and, perhaps, a better horse than Ringmaster, but he may not prove so in England, for big horses are apt to turn roarers in the old country. He ran a good horse on New Year's Day, but he pulled up rather lame. I don't think, however, that it was anything serious, and, if all goes well with him, he ought to win a race or two in England before the close of the season. There is a rule in the English Jockey Club Code which should not apply to horses hailing from any portion of the British Empire. It is this: 'No horse is eligible to be handicapped for any public race unless he shall have been habitually trained in the United Kingdom, or have twice run there during the six preceding months of the racing season.' Formerly only horses trained in England and Scotland were excepted. This was certainly 'another injustice to Ireland,' and, despite strong adverse criticism, it was retained for some time, and when a repeal was first mooted, it met with strong opposition from some members of the Jockey Club. The rule was introduced to provide against French horses sweeping the board, but it had little effect, for the wily Gaul—or rather, an English trainer, brought over Tenebreuse, ran her two byes, got into the Cesarewitch at a nice weight, and won the race and a tremendous amount of money in bets, all of which went over to France, the Britishers refusing to believe in her. By running Chicago twice in weight for-age races, he will be eligible to be handicapped, but he must necessarily be out of condition, and the handicapper, consequently, cannot form any thing like a true estimate of his capabilities. Chicago will go to Mr. J. E. Savill, who thoroughly understands the business of training horses in the Australian style. He is not too proud to admit that he learned much by watching such men as Mr. John Tait and Mr. James Wilson, and it will be remembered that he trained The Assyrian when he won the Melbourne Cup, and also won many races with other horses. I should like to see Mr. James White give him a chance with Rudolph and Sinecure. They are not much to look at, and would be laughed at in England, but our kinsmen would find them 'rum 'uns to go.'"

We take the following from the anecdote column of the Licensed Victuallers Gazette. Horses have curious fancies, likes and dislikes, and are at times as unreasonable as women. Squire Osbaldeston had a horse, called Grimaldi, who for some reason would not face running water, in consequence of which caprice he lost the Squire two races; but he had a third on hand, against Colonel Charritus's Napoleon for 500 guineas. The course was over the Dunchurch country; so Osbaldeston went to the famous rough-rider, Old Dick Christian, and consulted with this equine oracle as to what was to be done to get Grimaldi over a stiffish brook that lay in the line of country. Dick had a wonderful power over horses, his great secret being coaxing and kindness; he agreed to meet the Squire and his horse on the following morning at Brixworth, and there, having allowed Grimaldi to smell at a small stream, and patted and coaxed him, at last induced him to cross quite easily. He was then led to the brook. "He'll never cross this, Dick," said the Squire. "I'll bet you a guinea he will, Squire," answered Christian. Dick then waded into the stream, and finding a place where he could stand, he arranged with Osbaldeston that he would be in that place when the match took place. "I'll be here," he said, "with my hat on the top of a stick; gallop right for me and keep him going." The Squire carried out these instructions to the letter, and Grimaldi leapt clean over Christian, hat and all, cleared the brook, and won the match for his owner, because he had confidence in the man who coaxed him.

There should be some one to enlighten the amateur horsemen, says the Horse, in the proper use of check-rein, from the fact of there being a number that have tendency to imitate their neighbors. When any of these people see a horse hitched they go home and try the same plan, frequently checking a colt up as high as they can, and start in to break him. The result is that nine out of ten are partially spoiled and develop a dislike for the check, and it is years before they are cured of the habit of tossing their head. If the beginner would use a little forethought and check a colt up gradually, he would soon find the natural position and avoid future trouble. Under such treatment the colt will soon learn to drive pleasantly and speed without pulling. One colt likes an overdraw, another a side check, and so on, therefore the driver should endeavor to get a kind that will suit. It is never safe to check a colt up untill such a point is reached, as he will do his work easier and with more determination. This is especially true of the trotter and road horse. Get him where he trots steady and easy, after his feet are balanced, and do not try to drive him in 2:20 the first week. Wait patiently and find where he likes his head and what kind of check or bit makes him feel comfortable. In nearly every town an observing man sees horses speeded up the streets, over cross-walks with their heads stuck up in the air as if they were taking astronomical lessons. Such a method is not the best way to make a good track horse or even a safe roadster, as he has not liberty enough to see his way or what is going on around him. Give the horse a little freedom in harness, treat him kindly and speak to him when he is doing his work. It does not cost anything and it wins his confidence.

The New York Tribune says: While the wretched weather is keeping back training for the spring races, let us consider the subject of jockeys and their repute. It is an important one, and by continual hammering we may induce racing officials and racing associations to take some interest in it. Now "pulling" a horse is a figure of speech in nine cases out of ten. It means riding him to lose where he can win, but it by no means implies that there has been any direct use of the bridle to hold him back from winning. The writer has seen horses actually and literally "pulled," but perhaps not one of the 200 that go out for airings require such strong measures to prevent him from getting his head home first. A horse can be effectually "stopped" by other and more covert processes. A jockey can lie too far out of his ground; take a turn too wide; court a cross or collision in the stretch. Any one such occurrence may happen to him against his will when he really desires to win; it is high art to obtain them when he wants to lose. Again, when it comes to the actual finish, when jockeys "sit down" to "ride" their horses home, art also comes in. The orthodox rider should be feeling his horse's mouth with even reins and a light hand; his body should play to the stride of the animal, his hips being braced and his shoulders also. A bad rider who sits with slack hips and loins and windmill arms (like W. Donohue), and "grinds coffee" (like Soden), causes his center of gravity to wobble and so balks the stride of his horse; and if one rein is slackened the horse is not held together, nor his head balanced to his line of progress, and all this tends to shorten his stride. Without displaying wind mill action of arms or "grinding coffee" an artistically dishonest jockey can ride badly enough, and at the same time deceive the eyes of even good Judges—unless they happen not only to know his real powers, but also to be so posted at the moment as to have the clearest view of his action when he sweeps past them and happen to be fixing their eyes on him.

The Nashville authorities have set a good example in publicly declaring their special rules. They are as follows:

"36. No person whatever, whether he be an officer on the course or not, shall be permitted to remain in the judges' stand, during the pendency of a race, except the presiding judge, two assistants and the Secretary.

"37. If the presiding judge be unable to decide any question, he may call for the opinion of his assistants, and the decision of the majority shall rule.

"38. If in any case the judges have sufficient reason to believe that a fraud has been committed, they may exercise extraordinary powers for the administration of justice; may declare all pools and bets off, and if the winner of the race is implicated, declare the race void, return the added money to the association and the entrance money to the nominators; expel jockey, owner, trainer, horse or horses, and all other persons concerned.

"39. The executive committee may appoint patrol judges, whose duty it shall be, from places designated, to observe the running of the horses. If foul riding or any other irregularity comes under their observation, to report to the judges immediately after the race.

"40. The timer's stand is for persons appointed by the Secretary, who shall mark on the timing board the time of each race, which shall be official."

Of the rules above named No. 38 causes most discussion. As a general thing bets should not be declared off under any circumstances. The officials, under this rule, are given extraordinary power, but they cannot use it, only on certain special occasions. Louis P. Ezekiel will act as clerk of the scales during the meeting, and he will fill the same position at nearly every meeting in this section during the coming season. The executive committee include the following named gentlemen: John P. White, Gen. W. H. Jackson, A. H. Robinson, Dr. R. Doughlas and C. H. Gillock.

THE FARM.

Sheep-Feeding Experiment.

The fattening of coarse-wooled sheep for the market has received a new impulse of late and all facts throwing light upon the most economical methods of feeding are of interest. The science or art is an old one in England; accurate data are less common in this country. But it is not my purpose to treat of mutton sheep at this time, but to narrate a simple experiment in feeding the Spanish Merino sheep in Vermont, and no where else is the Spanish Merino so scientifically bred and cared for. The following is a small experiment, but it was carefully and accurately conducted with a view of ascertaining the normal growth and development of this breed of sheep when moderately fed and properly attended.

Twenty ewe lambs, small, oily, wrinkly, wooly specimens, were selected. Their average weight on January 2nd was only 52 3-20 pounds. They were confined to a comfortable shed, in which was running water, and were regularly fed with hay three times each day, while the grain ration, given at noon and night, consisting of oats, bran and a little cracked corn, weighed only one-third of a pound to each sheep per day. At the end of thirty days, or on February 1st, the lambs were re-weighed (at the same time of day as before) and showed an average gain of 5 3-5 pounds each in weight. This is apparently nothing extraordinary, but it is in reality an increase of over ten per cent on their original weight in thirty days. The grain ration, it will be observed, was very small indeed, and designed for a healthful growth, and not for fattening purposes. Mutton sheep are fed at least four or five times as much grain, and that of a more carbonaceous nature, when they are being fitted for the market. But a lot of ram lambs fed and treated in a similar way did even better. They made an average gain of exactly seven pounds each, or nearly 11 per cent. on their original weight. One lamb—a small one weighing but 54½ pounds—made the phenomenal growth of ten pounds, or an increase of over 18 per cent in the thirty days.

Does my high esteem for the constitutional vigor and power of assimilation of food in the Spanish Merino sheep mislead me in believing that the instances are rare where, with so small a grain ration, any breed of mutton sheep has made so creditable a feed record? The grain fed to each sheep cost less than one-third of a cent per day. It is claimed that the manurial value of bran is $13 a ton, and that the larger part of this value remains in the manure. The latter statement would apply to the feeding of oats, but not so fully to corn, which, however, is not a good or safe feed for sheep, as a rule, and may well be dispensed with. It was used in this experiment only to "strengthen" the oats which were light. I believe the cheapest way to purchase chemical fertilizers is to feed wheat bran largely. It would, however, be stating the truth but partially not to add that the lambs were fed the best hay possible for sheep. This consisted of rowen, Alsike Clover, a few daisies and some mixed grasses, all nicely cured and in every way palatable. Their feed, as a whole, both of grain and hay quite nitrogenous. Not only this experiment, but repeated observations in caring for sheep, induce me to believe that sheep demand for their best development both in carcass and wool a close feed ration.—L. W. Peet in Coleman's Rural World.

Cotswolds.

Stephen Lyle, in The Stockman of February 27, thinks I make unreasonable statements in regard to Cotswolds. However, he makes one assertion that I will not attempt to dispute when he says that Merino ewes will not give milk enough to raise their lambs when bred to a Cotswold ram.

He says that to claim the Cotswold is the best for wool and mutton is too much, and any one who is a judge of sheep knows that the Merino is better for wool and as good for mutton. But we will consult the figures and see who is in the dark: I sheared 20 Cotswold yearling ewes last May that sheared 20 pounds per head. This wool was sold in June, and brought 25cts. per pound, which made $5 per fleece. On the day I sold my wool a Merino breeder sold his wool to the same dealer for 16 cts. per pound, and his fleeces weighed 6 pounds on an average, which brought him 96 cts. per fleece. He was well satisfied with the sale, and said they made a fair average. This leaves a difference of $4.04 each in favor of the Cotswolds.

Now as to carcass, an ordinary bunch of Cotswold ewes should weigh in breeding order at least 200 pounds each, while I am told by a Merino breeder who breeds the Vermont Merinos that 90 pounds would be a good average for his flock. Taking any market quotations we find the Cotswold selling around $6 00 per cwt., while the little Merino must go at less than $4 00 per cwt., which would bring something like $3.50 each—a big difference in favor of the Cotswold. Even this is unfair for the Cotswold, for our shippers say a load of good Cotswolds would spring the market 50c. per cwt.

It may be that in portions of our country where there is no demand for mutton, and where the qualities of the pastures are such as to require a small, nimble, sure-footed sheep the Merino may prove more profitable. But of their fleeces from forty to seventy per cent is yolk, grease and dirt.

I have been a breeder of Cotswold sheep for a number of years, and I have yet to see the first Cotswold affected with scab, hoof-rot, paper-skin, or walking on sled-runner feet (while I have seen Merino sheep affected with all four of these complaints), and if all this does not constitute superior hardiness I am at a loss to know just what does.—Leonard Bryan in Stockman and Farmer.

Breeding Black Sheep.

It has always been a debateable point, says the Leader, whether it is possible to breed a flock of black sheep. All sheep breeders are aware that, by a freak of nature, black lambs are found in their flock every year, although the sires and dams of these have been pure white as far back as their pedigrees can be traced. The lambs come black, and no satisfactory explanation can be offered as to why they are so. Following up the breeding, however, it is found that the theory of like producing like does not hold good where black sheep are concerned. The progeny from a black sire and dam will in about seven cases out of ten, throw back to the previous generation. Mr. P. McFarlane, of Barooga, one of the most experienced and observant sheep breeders in Australia, is of the opinion that the type and color of black sheep can be fixed, and he is now devoting his attention to the carrying out of this theory. All the black lambs of Barooga are collected and sent to Malonga, a station in the Lachlan district. He finds that by careful selection and the rejection of all lambs having a trace of white about them, the color can, with a considerable degree of certainty, be depended on in the third generation. He intends persevering with the experiment.—Australasian.

Price of Mutton, and Great Demand For It.

Mutton has been higher for some time past than beef in the United States and Canada, and it is likely to continue so, as the taste for it when good is rapidly increasing. It does not cost so much to produce mutton as beef, and the return from its sale is one or two years sooner, thus not requiring half the capital to grow it. This is the same in England, it being now said there that "sheep farming is in fact by far the most promising of all farming, and of all flocks none are so much in request as the choicest of Downs." These have been my views for some years past, and I have repeatedly so stated them in various agricultural papers.

Our flockmasters ought to choose Down sheep in preference to any others in breed, as their mutton is of the best quality, the most tender, juicy and lean, and commands the highest price in the market. The sheep are hardy, fruitful and mature early, farrowing generally, since more improved, at an average of one year old when properly reared. They ought to be imported by the thousand, which is most cheaply done by attending the sheep fairs in Great Britain in the summer season, where they may be found numbering from five to forty thousand head, and held there at moderate prices. Companies of our stock raisers ought to be made up for the purpose of importation, and they should bring shepherds and dogs with the sheep for the purpose of rearing them. These would take such excellent care of the sheep that neither strange dogs nor animals of any kind would attack or destroy them. For the pastures they could select cheap lands, and it would be better that these were not in a latitude above 38 degrees north, and then the sheep would require little shelter from winter storms; and a little more south of this, pasture generally continues the year round.

The flockmasters should select large tracts of land near by each other, and then they would be less lonely in situation, and of material help to each other in their business.—A. B. Allen, in the Stockman and Farmer.

The Shire Horse at Home.

Shire horse breeders have never assembled under more more propitious circumstances than they will do this week. The most sanguine of them could hardly have expected such a rapid and signal development of the draft-horse trade as has latterly taken place. Within the past twelve months the wonderful progress has been made, as may be gathered from the fact that some 200 or more horses have to find accommodation within the Agricultural Hall to-morrow than were entered last year. What may be expected of the future, with Shire horse breeding still in its infancy?

The Agricultural Hall will this week contain the largest collection of Shire horses ever seen at any one meeting. Some two-thirds of their number will have to take "gallery seats" for the first time. Provision has been made for their ascent and descent by means of a tan-covered gradient—this erection passing over the heads of a number of the animals below. How to dispose of the enormous accessions to the entries has been a sort of Chinese puzzle to the accomplished Secretary and his associates. While the first floor affords sufficient relief, however, for the excessive entries good and well, but how is next year's increase to be stowed away?

As we have already hinted, Shire horse breeding is but in the spring time of its existence. This has been demonstrated beyond the faintest doubt. Of this the events of the past few months furnished sufficient proof. The Blagdon Stud Farm sale brought together an excellent company, and but for unfortunate weather the some sixty head of horses sold would have undoubtedly made a considerably higher average than 71 gs. Yet that figure is not to be despised; though it is somewhat annoying for the disposer to hear, as Mr. Clement Keevil did, that some of the horses afterward almost doubled the price he obtained for them.

The Earl of Ellesmere's sale gave an impression of great success, with an average of £122 for fifty-nine head of stock. His lordship's stud was noted for its show-yard achievements, and was bred and cared for as few stud owners can afford to do. Yet the prices realized at the Moulton Estate sale a few weeks later eclipsed the Worsley Hall results. In this instance fifty one horses made no less than an average of £127. When it is remembered that both in the case of the Earl of Ellesmere's sales and that of Mr. Clark's a considerable proportion of the stock sold were young these results must be regarded as very significant indeed.

If further proof were needed of the still infantile proportion of the Shire horse breeding industry we should direct attention to the organizations being formed in different parts of the country with a view to fostering the cause of the breed where it has never been espoused before. The work which these associations are calculated to do in the interests of the Shire is great and cannot fail to materially aid in swelling the entries at both the "local" and "open" exhibitions of the future. What of the readiness with which the best horses have been let for stud purposes? The entire agricultural community would almost seem bent on the attainment of one and the same object, viz., the improvement of the draft horses of the country generally. If union is strength, surely there is strength enough in this pursuit; and we have every reason to expect a very marked extension of operations in future in the department of pedigree horse breeding.

Foreign demands are obviously on the increase. Our good friends beyond the water do not conceal the fact that there is an unlimited market for draft horses in the United States. The few thousands of stallions that have crossed the "herring-pond" are positively buried in the vastness of the republican territory. An English visitor might roam over boundless tracts of that great country and never see an English bred horse, and yet we are told that her great and growing cities, her lumber trade and quarrymen are waiting to be supplied with short-legged, short-backed, thickly-built, powerful draft horses, varying in weight from 1,300 to 1,700 lbs.—London Farmer & Breeder.

The English Meat Trades Journal says: Purveyors of beef-tea and other "meaty" drinks and compounds do not seem to be in any hurry to take up the question of the played-out horses that our shipped from this country to Antwerp. Seeing what a success they are having with their new productions, we think they are unwise to let the question drift. "How do you think it will affect your sale of this kind of wholesome drink?" a newspaper representative asked a barkeeper. "Seriously," was his prompt reply; "several customers have referred to the subject this very day." It is true that one great company advertises a forfeit of £1,000 if it can be shown that they use anything but the best beef. For our own part we believe the popular meat beverages are genuine, and for that reason we think it is a pity there should be any question about it. The report of the Society for the Prevention of Cruelty to Animals touching Antwerp's "horse beef" can hardly be said to cover the latest English dealings in horse-flesh.

American Clydesdale Association.

The subjoined resolution have been adopted by the Clydesdale Association:

Whereas, The prime object of the American Clydesdale Association is to preserve accurate records of the pedigrees of well-bred Clydesdale horses, as well as to encourage the improvement in quality and breeding of the same, and

Whereas, There is every probability that the World's Fair of 1892 will be held at Chicago, conceded to be the most accessible point for the great majority of the prominent breeders of Clydesdale horses to exhibit their stock, and

Whereas, An exhibition of Clydesdale horses held in connection with the World's Fair of 1892 will enable breeders to widely advertise the superiority of this breed of draft horses, and

Whereas, The members of this association have resolved to make the exhibition of Clydesdale horses to be held in connection with the World's Fair of 1892, both in extent and superior quality of the display, most creditable to the breed, and of the greatest possible benefit to all interested in the same; therefore be it

Resolved, That it is the sense of the Executive Committee of the American Clydesdale Association that five thousand dollars in cash prizes be offered by this organization in addition to the premiums offered the breed by the general managers of the World's Fair of 1892, said five thousand dollars to be awarded to members of this association exhibiting at said show the best specimens of Clydesdale horses of their own breeding.

Resolved, That a committee of three be appointed to devise and report to this association at the next annual meeting the classification of prizes, the conditions that should govern the awards of this association and other matters in connection with the Clydesdale exhibit at the World's Fair of 1892.

Resolved, That the Secretary of this association be and is hereby instructed to transmit a copy of the foregoing resolutions to each member of this organization, with a request for such suggestions as will tend to make the proposed exhibition of the greatest possible benefit to the Clydesdale interest in America.

Valuable Cows.

Some years ago the writer hereof made an accurate computation as to the actual cash value of the descendants of the Bates Duchess Short-horn cow, 10th Duchess of Airdrie, from which it appeared than no less than $300,000 had to be placed to the credit of that grand old matron before her death. This case, exceptional as it is, may serve to illustrate the possibilities of the business of pedigreed cattle-breeding; but when contrasted with the marvelous aggregate wealth contributed to the general cattle stock of America by that other roan cow, imp. Young Mary by Jupiter, even the brilliant record of the Airdrie Duchess pales into comparative insignificance. It would require the staatical genius of an Atkinson to present in proper terms the full measure of the donation of this one cow to the cattle stocks of this continent. No matter what the bulls used—so they were of reasonable quality—the descendants of this cow retain even to this day a useful, work-a-day character which all unprejudiced persons freely concede. The record, too, of such cows as Rose of Sharon, Josephine, and Young Phyllis must furnish fresh inspiration for those who regard the breeding of pedigreed cattle as a calling worthy of the best attention of the most intelligent men. To breed such well-producing cows is an honor to which the most ambitious may properly aspire. Let the younger members of "the profession" imbibe new courage from these achievements of the older masters of the art. The production of an "epoch-making" bull or a famous family of cows has never yet failed to bring honor and gold to the intelligent manipulator of herd-book blood. Good cattle are an absolute necessity to the successful prosecution of American agricultural operations in general, and "in the long run" yield suitable rewards to all who give personal attention to their work.—Breeder's Gazette.

Shorthorn Breeders' Association.

EDITOR BREEDER AND SPORTSMAN:—Considering the long and severe winter our sale was a success, although high prices did not prevail, the sellers were satisfied. Many purchasers expressed themselves as well pleased with the manner of conducting the sale and felt assured in bidding that there was no by bidding, the rules being very strict in that regard and many promised to attend the Association's next sale to be held in Sacramento during the State Fair. The following are some of the prices:

Maunga Duke bought by P. Peterson, $225
Viscount bought by F. Stauffer, $325.
Hualpha bought by H. Gaupe, $120.
California Chief bought by John Bidwell, $150.
Scottish King bought by P. S Chilis, $140.
Humboldt Duke bought by John Bidwell, $150.
Red Prince bought by C. T. Elliot, $110.
The average for the cattle sold was over $100.

It is the intention of the Association to give annual sales, and every opportunity will be given purchasers to obtain choice cattle from the best herds in California.

Very Resp'y J. F. CHILIS.

Sale of Ayrshire Cattle.

Messrs. George Bement and Son of Maple Grove Farm, shipped last week on the steamer City of Pekin five head of Ayrshire cattle, purchased by Mr. A. B. Fay for parties in Japan, being the second shipment of that breed by the above named gentleman to that country. The herd consisted of the following named animals: Two-year-old bull Express 4503, sire Archie 3432, dam Elaine 7401; four-year-old cow Ethelberta 9579, sire Melancton 3435, dam Ethel Brown 4504; three year-old heifer Lavina 9522, sire Archie 3432, dam Lurline 7810; two-year-old heifer Frou Frou 9864, sire Archie 3432, dam Lady Faxon 7551, and two-year-old heifer Leoline 9865, sire Ethelbert 4313, dam Lurline 7810.

Sheep are now sheared by electricity in Australia, Frederick Wolseley, a brother of Lord Wolseley, having invented a machine for the purpose. The method of using the shears is very simple the operator having merely to throw a friction wheel into adjustment by means of a handle, and then push the comb into the wool, pressing it continuously forward and keeping it as close as possible to the body of the animal being operated upon. From one to one hundred shears can be operated at one time. By this mode the shearing is done more mecifully than when done by hand shears.

ATHLETICS.

Athletic Sports and Other Pastimes.

EDITED BY ARSHIPPUS.

SUMMARY.

The Ladies' Night exhibition at the Alpine Athletic Club rooms on Tuesday evening was a complete success. The swimmers opened their season on Wednesday. The athletes are getting down fine for the coming field days. The wheelmen are making active preparations for the 4th of July tournament. The meeting of the Pacific Rowing Association which was held on Monday evening last was largely attended and the delegates who were in attendance were of the opinion that the coming season will be the most successful one California has ever seen.

RUNNERS, WALKERS, JUMPERS, ETC.

The weather at the present time is all that an athlete can desire, and the men who intend competing in the games of the Alpine Club on May 4th and at the annual championship meeting of the P. C. A. A. A. on May 30th are hard at work preparing themselves for the different contests.

The Lurline Club will probably be a member of the P. C. A. A. A. before many weeks, and it is said that a couple of the Lurline boys who intend entering the games on May 30th will make the pace exceedingly hot in the sprint events for the other crack runners. The Lurline Club will make no bid for the pennant this year, and the club members will be fully satisfied if their athletes can get away with a couple of the gold medals.

A large number of the Olympic Club boys visited the club's new grounds on Sunday and took exercise.

Eugene Kelly, under the guidance of Jim Jarvis, is training for the championship one mile walk. On Sunday last this promising young heel and toe artist walked a mile considerably under nine minutes.

Cooley ran two miles against time within the past week, and judging from the showing which he made he should well be able to lower the long distance records at the coming athletic meetings.

The members of the Garden City Athletic Club of San Jose, Cal., are training hard, and it is more than probable that a good many points will go to this club on May 30th. The Scotch amateur champion 220 yards runner has become a member of the club, and will represent it at the championship meeting.

The fight for the flag will of course lay between the Olympic and University Clubs, but there will be considerable skirmishing done by the representatives of the Alpine, Garden City, Acme and Alameda Olympic Clubs. The Alpine Club stands a good show for that place. All the clubs named are determined to put strong teams in the field.

J. J. Moriarty, the well known distance runner, was recently appointed a member of the police force.

The annual Spring games of the University Athletic Club, will be held on Saturday, May 24th. The cinder path, which at the present time is in very bad condition, will be put in first class order for the occasion. The programme has not yet been made out, and it is to be hoped that some of the events will be left open. The out-door men will be in good condition about this time, and the students would do well to give the outside clubs a chance to compete.

Some prominent members of the Caledonian Club are about to try and establish new rules for the governing of the outdoor sports held under the auspices of the club. Their intention is chiefly to do away with money prizes.

The members of the Alpine Club, who intend taking part in the cross-country run to-morrow, are requested to meet on the 10 A. M. Sausalito boat. Over forty names have been signed to the entry list.

On Friday evening of last week, DeWitt C. Davis, of the Olympic Club, and Young Mertes, of the California Athletic Club, by mutual agreement met in the gymnasium of the Olympic Club and settled the question as to which was the better man at wrestling. There had been keen rivalry between the men for a long time, and it was thought that Mertes could easily defeat Davis, as the former considered himself good enough to meet Ungerman or Kolb The match was refereed by George Meihling; Oscar Tolle officiating as time-keeper. Mertes weighed 154 pounds, while Davis was 18 pounds lighter. The agreement was that one fall was to decide the match. After a hard struggle, which lasted 20 minutes and 30 seconds, the Olympian downed the California Club member, and received quite an ovation for his plucky and clever work. The contest was for glory, no prize having been agreed upon. For a small man, Davis has proven himself a wonder. He first came into prominence as a wrestler about five years ago, when he was a member of the Pythian Athletic Club.

The chief event at the coming "Ladies' Night" exhibition of the Olympic Club, will be the tug-of-war contest between members of the club. Several of the strongest men in the club are in training for the contest, which promises to be very interesting.

The entries for the Alpine Amateur Athletic Club games, which will come off at the Bay District track on Sunday, May 4th, will close at the club rooms, 706 Powell street, on Saturday evening, April 26th, at 10 o'clock. An entrance fee of fifty cents will be charged for each event. The programme consists of twelve events, four of which are open to all the amateur clubs. Good prizes will be awarded, and everything possible will be done to make the meeting a success.

Some of the lady admirers of E. P. Moody, the genial corresponding secretary of the Alpine Club, played a good joke on that athlete a couple of days ago. Mr. Moody was to have appeared in an exhibition high jumping contest at the recent "Ladies' Night" exhibition, and as the moths had somewhat disfigured his knee tights, Mr. Moody politely requested a young lady friend of his to sew up the holes which the moths had eaten through his pants. When they were returned by a committee of two females, Mr. Moody, of course, was profuse in his thanks for the supposed good work which had been performed. The package was laid aside for a couple of days, and on "Ladies' Night," Phil was about to step before the vast assemblage of ladies and gentlemen arrayed in his newly mended tights, when by chance one of his friends discovered to him the fact that his fair friends had been more than kind to him. They had embroidered the emblem of the club as well as the initials of his name on that portion of the tights which would show best when a person's back is turned to the audience. It was a narrow escape, and the corresponding secretary will be more careful in future when donning his exhibition costume.

The flowers and shrubs which were planted some time ago at the new Olympic grounds, are beginning to spring up, and by the 30th of May the place will present a very pretty sight.

The Directors of the Alpine Amateur Athletic Club have requested us to state that M. C. Giry is no longer connected with the club, his resignation having been requested by the Directors. The members of the club are very much incensed over the unmanly conduct of Giry in some of his actions towards the club. From what we have been given to understand Giry has left himself liable to arrest for trying to take property out of the club rooms.

THE WHEELMEN.

There will be a picnic run of the Bay City Wheelmen to Lake Merced to-morrow. The start will be from the corner of Van Ness and Market Sts, at 10 A. M.

The roads are now in good order and several of the local men ride far into the country on Sundays.

A large crowd of wheelmen were noticed in the park on Sunday last. A good many club riders rode out to the Cliff House during the moonlight nights.

We would be glad to print notes of interest from the wheelmen in these columns.

IN THE SURF.

The bath houses did a rushing business during the week on account of the unusually warm weather.

The Lurline boys are getting into trim for coming events.

The Terrace Baths at Alamada have changed hands.

The members of the Civil Service Swimming Club opened their season on Wednesday afternoon. The club's headquarters are at the Shelter Cove Baths, foot of Mason street. H O. Farrell, Henry McGowan, P J Fay and a couple of other members entered the water for the first time this year.

AT THE OARS.

Despite the bad weather on last Sunday a good many of the different crews were out. Now that the season will soon open, the oarsmen are trying hard to get into trim and a little rain does not seem to bother them in the least.

Julien, the Australian oarsman, Ed Finley and Douber, of the Ariel Club, were out for a practice spin.

Whitkopt, Phelan, Nunan, Willie Adams and Manheim of the same club, were out for a row.

H. A. Pless and Henry Tauk took the club's whitehall boat and rowed to Washington street wharf.

W. C Ellis made his debut as a single scull artist. He was made fully aware of the fact that he was no better than the average novice when he took his initial dump overboard. He is a big, strapping young fellow and promises to make an A 1 oarsmen.

The South End Club appears to be standing on very weak legs just at present. The membership is very small indeed, and the prospects are that the club will soon disband.

A very important meeting of the Pacific Rowing Association was held at 706 Powell street on Monday evening last. Delegates from all the associate clubs were present. Messrs. E J. Colvin, E Flanders, Al Rothkop, W. E. Ellis and H. O. Farrell were appointed a Picnic and Regatta Committee, with full power to act. The picnic will probably be held at Harbor View Park. Robert Christie applied for reinstatement. His case was referred to the Investigation Committee.

CLUB JOTTINGS.

The P C A A A held its regular weekly meeting last evening. There was to have been considerable business transacted, but owing to our going to press so early in the week we are unable to report the proceedings in the present issue. Next week full particulars will be given.

The Golden Gate Athletic Club does not appear to have been hurt any by the fact of its having been compelled to withdraw from the P C A A A, The members take just as great an interest in the club as ever, and every afternoon and evening the gymnasium is filled with young athletes who desire to improve their science and muscle. Young men can join the amateur annex by paying a small initiation fee. The monthly dues of the annex members are one dollar.

The ladies' athletic class at the Olympic Club rooms does not appear to be as big a success as was anticipated. The fair ones are now satisfied to allow the "horrid men" to take *all* the "gentle" exercise.

Ladies Night.

The Alpine Athletes entertain their Lady Friends.

On Tuesday evening last the large gymnasium of the Alpine Amateur Athletic Club at 706 Powell St., was filled by an audience of about 600 ladies and gentlemen who had assembled there at the invitation of the members of the Club to witness their initial "Ladies Night" exhibition. The people present were of the most respectable class which put to flight at once the slighest doubt as to the social standing of the club. The Alpine Club is the only club outside of the Olympic that has dared to hold a "ladies night" and the Alpine members being somewhat new in the business were anxious to discover if the ladies were "with them." They were, and the club is now an assured success. The hall was well lit with electric and gas lights, and all the arrangements especially the seating accommodations were perfect. The full programme was run off smoothly and there were none of the long waits generally found at similar exhibitions. I P. Bean made a first class Master of Ceremonies and during the evening he made some very appropriate remarks in the interest of the club. The exhibition began at 8.30 with boxing by W. H. Dooley. Both men are clever and the bouts which were very spirited elicited considerable applause from the audience.

Prof. Henry Ansot and one of his pupils, Ashton R. Fry next made their appearance in a fencing with foils contest. Prof. Ansot it will be remembered is the swordsman who fought the duel with Prof. Trochet at the Grand Opera House a couple of years ago.

Mr. Fry made an excellent showing against his more experienced teacher, and the ladies especially applauded their act.

The third event was a fine exhibition of club swinging by Prof. G. C. Rouse, the club instructor.

E Barr and W. Henry, two members of the club, next performed on the swinging rings and their very fine work was well received.

Event No. 5 was boxing by M. Gallagher and Partner, Otto Luhn and J. Horl. Each couple did clever work.

The next event was the presentation of the all round medals won at the late field day of the club. J D. Garrison was presented with the gold championship medal, having earned 26 points in the sports. C. A. Eldridge, for winning 25 points, received the second, silver, all round championship medal and P. N. Gafney, with a record of 21 points, took the third silver all round medal. After his medal was pinned on Gafney made a short speech, in which he said that he felt assured that the Alpine Amateur Athletic Club was now an assured success. He remarked that although the club just at the present time could not expect to have its rooms furnished with twenty dollars a yard carpets, or with oil paintings by the old masters, still it could expect in the near future to be able to furnish its gymnasium and club rooms in a comfortable manner. In conclusion he said that there was one thing the club could be sure of, and that was athletic talent. The club has on its membership list at the present time the names of several prominent athletes whose performances in the near future would build up the club to a level with any other club on the Pacific Coast.

When Mr. Gafney finished his remarks the members passed around ice-cold lemonade to their lady friends, and then the lion of the evening made his appearance in the shape of J. Barr Buchanan, the all round amateur champion. Mr. Buchanan, who is an exceedingly handsome and well proportioned man, was warmly received, and his fine appearance and great muscular development made a great impression on the ladies present. He gave a splendid exhibition of heavy club swinging, heavy weight lifting and weight lifting with his teeth. At the conclusion of his task Mr. Buchanan was presented with a handsome floral piece from the club. The floral tribute was gotten up by Lean Brothers, florists. The letter "B" was arranged in the centre of the piece.

Prof. Ansot and Ashton R. Fry appeared for the second time in a fencing act. This time broadswords were used. As before their work was a success and the pupil again proved himself to be quite an adept in the fencing line.

Parallel Bars were next performed on by Messrs. Rouse, Barr and Henry. Professor Rouse's work was very superior, he doing some very hard acts with perfect ease. Messrs. Barr and Henry also showed up to advantage, but of course their work was not quite as finished as that of the Professors, who has been in the business for over 15 years. The well known club swinger, Frank Hart, appeared next and his scientific performances with all kind of clubs drew forth rounds of applause. Every one present agreed that he was well entitled to the championship which he holds.

The closing event was a set to between Prof. W. Smith, the club instructor, and his pupil W. Cook. This proved to be the best boxing exhibition of the whole evening and Prof. Smith, who, by the way, is an old pupil of Eddy Graney's ducked and dodged and swung and countered in a manner that caused even the ladies to applaud continually. Cook made a fine standing against the Professor and proved himself to be a credit to his instructor. The entertainment was over at 10:30, and the large crowd left the rooms in good humor after having witnessed one of the best athletic exhibitions given in San Francisco for a long while. These "Ladies Nights" will be given about every three months and it is probable that advance will finish the next one.

JOTTINGS FROM ALL OVER.

We have taken the following interesting items from the report of the Treasurer of the New York Athletic Club:

Assets: New York City club house and contents, $279,249; Travers Island property, $132,550 72; merchandise, $483 02; book accounts, $6 356.86; sinking fund, $36,283.33; cash, $1,234.07; total, $456,157 00

Liabilities: Mortgage, $180,000.00; loan, $15,000.00; bonds $99,400.00; bank account, $12,498.13; total, $306,898 13. Excess of assets over liabilities, $149,258 87.

Among the receipts of the year ending February 28, 1890, were: Life members, $3,000. Initiation fees: Resident members, $12,000; non-resident members, $1,300; Dues: Resident members, $81,100; non-resident members, $3,010; junior members, $174; steward's privileges, 10 months, $5,433.63; rent of barber shop, cab stand, etc., $567.75; rent of private dining room, $105; sale of letter boxes, $300; receipts from billiard room, 10 months, $5,811.50; receipts from bowling alley, 6 months, $543 30; rent of club house lockers, $2,040; rent of boat house lockers, $227; sale of programmes Spring and Fall games, $800; entrance fees to Spring and Fall games, $111: miscellaneous sundries competition account, $235.94; Travers Island rooms during season, $2,556; Travers Island private dining room $3: Travers Island steward's privileges, $1,009 91: Travers Island insurance on Hunter house, $8,100. Travers Island insurance on furniture, $2,923 22: Travers Island billiards, $670.70: Travers Island bar, $2,077.12; Travers Island restaurant, $1,838.29; Travers Island Stables, $482 50; Travers Island trap shooting, $32.18. Receipts Turkish and swimming baths, $3,108.14. Boxing entertainments, $676. Total, $140,236.18.

Among the expenditures were: New York House: Furnishings, $6 083 98; improvements, $5,129 51; repairs, $53 05; repairs to furniture, $58 50. Sinking fund. $500. New boats, oars and fixings, $939.48; boat house expenses, $2,421.55; gymnasium expenses, $2,975.17; competition expenses, $9,100.63; track, ball field and tennis courts, $1,607.90. Baths: Washing, salaries and materials, $3,305 07. Entertainments: Boxing, ladies' days, annual games, etc. $1,858 70. Bowling alleys, $663 65; billiard room, New York, $1,696.66; postage, $852 25; kitchen, $87.52; interest on bonds, mortgages and loans, $15,386.11; taxes, New York property, $1,739,13 house and kitchen fuel, $176 65; reading room, $301 94; stationery and printing, both houses, $1777 93; suspense, $457,15; general expenses, $3247.70; house expenses, $7454 26; office expenses, $8611.50; engineer's department, $3750 37, private letter boxes $360; board or employees, $2528 50; water for the year, $911.30; gas account, 13 months, $964 88; electric lights, $1489 40; $1489.40; fuel for engine room, $4336 15; Travers Island: New club house, $17 791.66; furniture, carpets, shades, stages, etc., $13,494 14; improvements to grounds, stables, etc., $8,028.59; bar, $2049.45; restaurant, $1916 79; billiard room, $105.80; stables, $1462 89. general expenses, $4474.54; house expenses, $4413.04; board of employees, $555; shortage on stage tickets, $92 32; unsold tickets, N. Y., N. H. & H. R R Co, $33 25; trap shooting, $31 60; bank accounts, $7,198 83. Total, $155,453.49.

A rough summing up of the accounts shows that the ordinary receipts of the club for the year were about $129,000, and the ordinary expenses about $116,000, showing a profit of $13,000, and that this surplus, with $17,000 more, was expended in improving and beautifying the club's summer paradise at Traver's Island.

William O'Connor, the American champion sculler, has, challenged the winner of the coming race on the Paramatta River, in Australia, to row for the championship and $2500 a side, and the cable informs us that both Peter Kemp and Neil Matterson have signified their willingness to accommodate him with such a race. It is doubtful, however, if either will be willing to row at the time designated by the Canadian —not later than May 31, with the Queen's birthday, May 24th, for choice. O'Connor has created a favorable impression among the sporting men at the Antipodes, and his work during his spins on the river is favorably commented upon.

THE KENNEL.

Dog owners are requested to send for publication the earliest possible notices of whelps, sales, names claimed, presentations and deaths, in their kennels, in all instances writing plainly names of sire and dam and of grandparents, colors, dates and breed.

Visits.

Mr. E. Cawston's fox terrier Lassie by Laddie ex Oxford Mitley to C. A. Sumner's Blemton Vesuvian (14,290) by Champion Lucifer, ex Blemton Vesta, at Los Angeles, March 31, 1890.

A. B. Truman's (Elcho Kennel) Irish Red Setter Champion Lady Elcho T. to owner's Champion Mike T. on April 8th, 1890.

Whelps.

Mr. C. W. Wilson's English setter Jennie whelped six dogs and one bitch to Mr. W. S. Kittle's Luke on April 2, 1890.

J. B. Martin's, San Francisco, Cal., Beatrice (Champion Bacchanal—Arrow) Foxterrier whelped April 3, 1890, six—three dogs—by Blemton Vesuvian (Champion Lucifer—Blemton Vesta.

Field Trial Derby.

EDITOR BREEDER AND SPORTSMAN:—As the time is drawing near when the entries for the Derby for 1891 will close, it behooves the sportsmen to see that their young dogs are entered and placed in the different breakers hands to be prepared for the race. That the coming trials can be made the best yet run in the State, and to equal the great Eastern Trials there is no doubt, if the sportsmen will only take the interest that they should, for with the fine blooded dogs that are now being bred by the different breeders there should be not less than fifteen starters in the Derby, and fully that many in the Aged Stakes. Sportsmen who have no Derby entries can easily purchase them and by communicating with such breeders as A. B. Truman, the Bassfords and other noted breeders can find winners and dogs that when broken would gladden the hearts of the most ardent fancier.

Do not think because you have failed to win before that it is only folly to try again, but see that the puppies are entered. Some of the best dogs the writer has had were not Derby entries and to run them in the aged stakes was unfair because they were too heavily handicapped on account of lack of age and experience

So now brother sportsmen send in your entries and your dogs to the breakers and my word for it we will show you one of the best trials and some of the best work that the followers of the California Field trials ever saw.

GALT, April 6th, '90. M. D. WALTER.

A California Dog Appreciated.

843 EUCLID AVENUE, Cleveland, O.

A. B. TRUMAN, Esq., San Francisco, Cal.

Dear Sir:—Permit me to congratulate you on your success with Patti Croxteth, the bitch I sold to you in '88. I have often since then regretted parting with her, and my object in writing you now is to say that if she is in perfect health, etc., that I will give you $250 for her delivered at express office. My friend, Mr. Munhall, informed me that while in your city last summer, he offered you $200 for Patti, and as it was refused, I know you value her highly. However, if you do not wish to sell, I would like to make you a proposal. I think you will agree with me when I say that there are no dogs in California, or vicinity, worthy of her quality, when you think of breeding, and also that it is a pity *not* to breed such a bitch.

I presume Patti will be in season very shortly now, and if you will ship her to me (*at my expense*), I will breed her to Molton Baron. I mention this dog, as I consider him the most desirable dog in America to-day to breed to. He is of the same type as Patti; his breeding is superb, while as a sire I would say that my uncle bred a litter from him last Fall which exceeded in beauty any litter I ever saw. Only two are now living, and they will certainly be heard from before long. However, as regards his stud record, I presume you are fully posted. But to return. If you will send her on I will breed her to him at my expense, keep her until she has weaned the litter, return her to you free of charge, and when the puppies are three or four months old, send you half of them, also at my expense.

Let me say here, that I am going abroad the last of this month, to be gone until the last of May, but if you trust Patti to me, you can be sure she will not be neglected, as I will place her at our country place, twenty miles from this city, where she will be in charge of a thoroughly trustworthy and experienced man, who will give her the best of care and attention. As regards myself, I would refer you to Mr. Munhall or any other sportsman of this city, as of course you are not personally acquainted with me, and would want to be pretty sure as to whom you would send such a dog as Patti. I hope, if you do not desire to sell, that you will favorably consider my proposition, as I consider it a fair one, and am also sure that the cross I mention would produce something ahead of anything in the "doggy" line yet produced in this country. As soon as you receive this, please wire me what you think of my two offers.

If you will send Patti to me to breed I will immediately send you the amount of the express charges here and you can send her on at once. I will also mail you a receipt for the bitch and a contract, stating what I have agreed to do. Be sure and write me, as in case you send her I want to make all arrangements for breeding her, etc., before sailing. Again expressing the hope that you will favorably consider one of my offers and thus give Patti an opportunity to distinguish herself in a more substantial manner than heretofore, I am,

Yours most truly, WORTHINGTON HOYT.

March 5, 1890.

P S.—Should you prefer, I will, during my absence, place Patti in charge of R. B. Morgan, Akron, O., instead of at our country place. He has trained and handled for me and is a good man, and has a splendid place for dogs at Akron, see my description of his kennels in the Am. Field, of June 8th, (about) last. In either case as before stated, I will pay all expenses of express charges, stud fee, keeping, etc. W. H.

Dog owners should not forget that the Pacific Coast Field Trial Club's Derby for setters and pointers whelped on or after January 1, 1889, closes on May 1, next. Entry blanks can be had from the Secretary, 313 Bush street, San Francisco. When dogs are entered the names, date of whelping, sex, color, and names of sire and dam should be sent.

Mr. Allender's New Kennel.

EDITOR BREEDER AND SPORTSMAN:—I thought it might be of interest to the owners of the dogs, now in my charge, to learn something of my new quarters. I have leased a place of twenty acres, one mile from Vega Station, and five miles from Watsonville.

Visitors can stop off at Vega, and be at my place in fifteen minutes, and see their dogs on birds within an hour after leaving the station. I have some promising puppies, for the Derby. Mr. Norman Rideouts' (of Marysville) "Lord Chumley", Mr. Ramon E. Wilsons "Ned", and several others are to be entered. By the way, it is about time you should commence to mention the Derby, and stir up the "slow ones." I also have several all aged starters. GEO. T. ALLENDER.

WATSONVILLE, April 8, 1890.

F. A. Taft at Home.

EDITOR BREEDER AND SPORTSMAN.—The sixth Annual bench show of the New England Club opened on the 1st with a benching of our 700 dogs. I send you a catalogue, also a Boston paper, with a list of the awards. It is the finest exhibition that I have ever attended. There were but few poor dogs in any of the classes. The pointers, setters, mastiffs, St. Bernards and Great Danes were particularly fine, making it very difficult in many instances for the judges to make their decisions. You will notice that in the Challenge Class for Gordons that Little Boy wins over Beaumont. This is the 4th time that they have met, and they now stand even as to winnings. Messrs. Watson and Davidson were there, and inquired after their many California friends.

There was an interesting scene yesterday when over twenty blind girls and boys (from ten to twenty years old) from the institution for the blind were led by their attendants into the judging ring to see the dogs, which they did with their hands in a thorough manner, enjoying it muchly. A number of dogs of different varieties from the largest to the smallest, were introduced for their inspection. They would feel of every portion of their bodies, commenting among themselves. They were very much amused at the head of an enormous bull dog. The attendance has been good so far, and the weather fine. Yours,

FRED A. TAFT.

April 5th, 1890.

An advertiser wishes a St. Bernard dog about a year old. Address A. P. S. this office.

We are pleased to learn that Mr. A. B. Truman will visit Los Angeles during May, and exhibit his dogs in the dog show. His red setters Lady Elcho T. and Mike T., and his pointers Patti Croxteth T. and Queen Croxteth, will be taken down.

The letter to Mr. A. B. Truman from Mr. Worthington Hoyt about Patti Croxteth T., which is printed elsewhere, is an indication that interest in dogs owned in these regions is not confined to local circles. The offer is a most flattering one, and reflects credit upon the maker. We hope the cross may be made.

Mr. Kittle's Luke (Carl B—Bessie) should be a fashionable sire among English setter fanciers. His beauty, breeding and field excellence all entitle him to pre-eminence. The litter by him, noted elsewhere, is of the very highest quality, and as fine in every respect as dogs of the breed ever are. Mr. Wilson is to be congratulated upon the fact that so many dog puppies were in it. He will reserve those which please him best and the others may be had on application to him at 21 Kearny street, city.

The owner of the Mount Washington Kennels at Pittsburgh, Pa., Mr. S. L. Boggs, has been in San Francisco for a week, as nearly every body knows. Mr. Boggs beside owning Paul Gladstone (Gladstone—Lavalette) has a way of acquiring a sort of proprietary interest in everybody he becomes acquainted with and the consequence is that his friends in this city may already be numbered by hundreds. For ways that are peculiar and for aggressive likeableness that is unique there is but one Boggs.

Entry blanks and premium lists of the Southern California Kennel Club's bench show, listed for May 6th, 7th, 8th and 9th next, may be had on application to this office, a supply having been received on Monday last. The show will probably be as large as any hitherto held in California. Mr. B. F. Naphthaly, of this city, is going down with a string of dogs, and others will attend. If Mr. Geo. T. Allender, of Watsonville, Mr. M. D. Walter, of Galt, or Mr. Wm. De Mott would agree to go down, owners could send their dogs in confidence that the animals would be well cared for and well shown. The Los Angeles Club is showing sound judgment in keeping its expenses down to a point at which the receipts will undoubtedly equal them. Los Angeles and its environs are well worth visiting, even if no dog show, with its myriad attractions, was at hand.

There is no more effective way of teaching a dog to carry his head well up than over the wet meadows, or more pleasing opportunity to watch his work than in the open, where English snipe are always found. Being in the open is one of the chief attractions about snipe shooting. You constantly have your dogs before you, and you can observe their intelligent working in locating the birds, says an exchange. There is always good, clean, open, shooting, no branches or trees to interfere or to be avoided, and the bird is in sight from the time he flushes with his sharp skeap skeap, until he falls to your aim or goes twisting away from view over the green meadows. True, the walking is often difficult over the moist ground, with frequent wading of pools and rivulets, but then, one cannot have everything when hunting. Out, too, on the broad low lands, with the horizon far away on all sides, and the fresh breeze blowing in your face, a feeling of freedom and solitude is felt not experienced in the wood. Every shot, too, is a puzzle, as the snipe twists away, first this way, then that, in his zigzag flight, and more than a usual source of satisfaction is felt as you see him, with lifeless wings, pitching down to be retrieved. And what a delicious dish they make for supper when broiled with a tiny piece of bacon pinned to their little fat bodies, and served hot on soft brown toast, with a glass of dry sherry alongside. An Epicurean could not do better. May ye little wayfarers long flit over our country in your migratory flights.

ROD.

The Fish Commission.

The April meeting held on Tuesday afternoon last at 220 Sutter street, was not attended by a large number of persons, because of a misunderstanding as to the date of the meeting. The Board of Fish Commissioners usually meets on the first Tuesday of each month, but for sufficient reasons, the date for April was changed to the second Tuesday.

After presentation and approval of the minutes, the report of the Chief of Patrol, Mr. F. P. Callundan, was read and ordered on file. The report was as follows:

THE HONORABLE THE BOARD OF FISH COMMISSIONERS—GENTLEMEN:—Since the last report made by the Chief of Patrol very much has been accomplished by the deputies in the matter of stopping the taking of small fish by Chinese and other fishermen.

Frequent raids upon the fishing settlements along the shore of the bay in South San Francisco have been made and on several occasions men were arrested either in the act of fishing illegitimately or with evidence of having done so in their possession.

The raids were made in common row boats, and only with difficulty could the Chinese junks be overhauled. If it was possible to procure a steam launch from time to time a great portion of the fishing grounds could be visited in a few hours with certainty of being able to run down any depredators discovered. Your deputies have also endeavored to put a stop to trout fishing during March, and it is believed that some good has been done in that direction. The difficulties lying in the way of one who attempts to patrol a trout stream are such that under the present law it is next to impossible to detect violators of the law in the very act of killing trout, as is necessary to insure conviction. The sport is one necessarily pursued in quiet, and those who do most of the fishing out of season are always on the alert to detect the approach of possible officers. The usual rigid inspection of the markets and commission houses has been maintained during the month, and but one arrest made, in which case deer hides, from which evidence of sex had been removed, were traced to the possession of a glove manufacturer of this city.

During the two weeks last passed the markets of San Francisco have been offering striped bass varying in size from a half pound to two and a half pounds. The presence of the fish in such numbers has excited remark, and it has been intimated that your Honorable Board should prohibit their being taken until they have grown to much greater size. In the absence of specific instructions, your deputies have not interfered in the matter of striped bass.

The first week of March was spent in pushing the prosecution of the twenty-one Chinese jailed at Martinez for taking small fish. Twelve of them paid fines of $60 each, the money being apportioned according to law. The nine remaining were convicted, but moved for a new trial. The motion was denied by the court, and it is probable they will now pay their fines.

On March 15th, in company with Deputy Innis, the Paper Mill Creek was visited, and a search made for trout fishers. A number of men were on the creek, but none were detected.

On March 25th, with Deputy Curley, South San Francisco was visited, but the day was so stormy and the bay so rough, that nothing could be accomplished.

The 27th was also passed at South San Francisco, and five Chinese arrested with bag nets and small fish in possession. The case is now pending in the Police Court of this city before Judge Lawler. On the same day, Deputy Tunstead placed the firm of Conkling & Co. under arrest for having in possession deer-skins from which evidence of sex had been removed. The case was tried on April 1st, and Judge Joachimsen, of the Police Court in this city, dismissed the case, remarking in doing so, that the evidence seemed conclusive, but as it was a first offence, he would dismiss the matter.

April 4th, 5th and 6th were spent in San Jose and Santa Cruz. In both cities, strong sportsman's clubs exist, whose officers and members are actively in sympathy with the work of your Honorable Board. In Santa Cruz, particularly the Secretary of the Rod and Gun Club, Mr. E. C. Williams, and Deputy Fish Commissioners Barlow and Googin, are pushing the work of stopping unseasonable fishing and shooting. The club offers a reward for convictions, and the poaching has ceased practically in that vicinity.

For the coming month the collection of licenses and the prevention of the taking of small fish, will engage the deputies. Respectfully submitted, F. P. CALLUNDAN,

SAN FRANCISCO, April 8, 1890. Chief of Patrol.

Some of the suggestions made in the report were discussed by the Commissioners, Hon. Joseph Routier, Hon. J. Downey Harvey and Mr. Ramon E. Wilson. With reference to striped bass, no action was taken further than to request Mr. Wilson to draft a suitable ordinance, which will be presented to the Board of Supervisors of this city, limiting the size of the fish which may be offered for sale. A batch of bills from the State Hatchery, the deputies and other sources were then examined and audited, and after some general remarks by members and others, the Board adjourned.

Judge Joe E. Carney, the great fly fisherman of Sierra City, descended upon San Francisco on Sunday last for his first visit since 1854. He found the city somewhat changed in several respects. His favorite swimming hole in '52 at what is now Battery and Commercial, is now, much to his discomfiture, a half mile up town. The excellent cotton-tail shooting which in those early days he used to enjoy, where the Palace Hotel now stands, is no longer available for the reason that for five miles beyond that point the closely built city extends.

Judge Carney has been so long a denizen of the pathless woods in rugged Sierra that upon reaching San Francisco he purchased a tack hammer, and as he wanders about blazes his way by knocking chips from corner buildings chipping paint from the Lotta Fountain, and in general acting like the genuine free-spirited old mountaineer that he is. He must be a good fisherman because in all the three decades during which he has lived beside the Yuba nearly all the trout he has caught have averaged about four pounds in weight.

The opening of the trout season at Spokane, Washington, was highly appreciated by the admirers of the fascinating sport of fly fishing. The rods and reels which have been stored away were taken down, and the speckled beauties came to grief. Spokane boasts of a number of experts, and there are numbers of others who are learning the art rapidly, and who may soon be classed with the experts. The sport is unlimited in Eastern Washington, and the fish run large and are game as possible.

THE GUN.

Blue Rock Club.

The club met on Saturday afternoon last at Birds' Point and shot up its scores for both March and April, the March meeting having been omitted because of inclement weather. The day was not pleasant, being cloudy and at times misty, and the scores were somewhat affected by the unfavorable weather. The scores were:—

At 15 singles and 5 pairs of Blue Rock targets, American Association Rules.

MARCH SCORE.

	Singles.	Pairs.
A. F. Adams	1 1 1 1 1 1 0 1 1 1 0 1 0 1—11	01 10 10 10 10—5
H. C. Golcher	0 1 0 1 1 1 1 1 1 0 1 0 0 0 1 1—9	11 01 10 01 10—6
W. J. Fox	0 0 1 1 1 1 1 1 0 0 0 1 1 0—8	10 10 10 10 00—4
R. A. Eddy	0 1 1 1 0 0 1 0 0 1 0 1 0 1—7	01 11 11 11 10—8
F. G. Sanborn	0 1 1 0 0 0 1 0 0 1 0 0 0 1 1—6	01 00 11 00 00—3
S. L. Abbot	1 0 0 0 0 1 1 0 0 0 0 0 1 1—5	11 10 11 11 01—8
M. H. Cadwallader	0 1 0 1 1 0 0 1 1 0 0 1 1 1 1—9	11 10 11 11 10—8
S. E. Knowles	1 1 1 1 0 1 1 1 1 1 1 0 1 1 0—11	01 11 11 11 11—9
W. E. Mayhew	0 0 1 1 0 1 0 1 0 1 0 0 0 1—6	01 10 01 10 10—5
C. F. Stone	1 0 0 0 1 0 0 1 0 0 1 0 1 0 1—5	00 11 10 01 10—5
R. E. Bell	0 0 1 0 1 1 1 1 0 0 0 1 1 1 0—8	

APRIL SCORE.

	Singles.	Pairs.
Adams	0 0 1 0 0 1 1 1 1 1 1 1 1 0 1—10	00 00 00 10 01—2
Golcher	1 0 1 1 1 1 1 1 1 0 1 0 0 —*	00 10 10 01 10—3
Fox	1 0 0 1 1 1 1 1 1 0 1 1 0 1 1 1—11	11 00 10 11 11—7
Eddy	1 0 1 0 1 1 1 1 1 1 1 1 0 1 1—12	00 00 01 00 00—1
Sanborn	1 0 1 1 1 1 1 0 1 0 1 1 1 1 1—12	00 10 10 11 10—5
Abbot	0 1 0 0 0 1 1 0 1 0 1 0 0 0 1—6	11 11 10 10 10—7
Cadwallader	1 0 0 1 1 1 1 1 1 1 1 1 1 1 1—13	10 10 01 01 10—5
Knowles	1 1 1 1 1 1 1 0 1 1 1 0 0 1—12	11 10 10 00 10—5
Mayhew	1 0 1 1 0 1 1 1 1 1 1 1 1—12	10 10 00 11 01—5
Stone	1 1 0 0 0 0 0 0 0 1 1 1 0 0 0—5	10 11 11 10 10—
Bell	0 0 0 0 0 0 1 1 0 1 0 1 0 1 1—5	

Country Club.

A few members visited the Oakland Trotting Park on Wednesday afternoon last for practice. The club scores will not be published hereafter, because of an especial request by members.

Those made on Wednesday were at live birds, American Shooting Association rules, and are appended.

Woodward	2 1 1 1 2 2 2 0 0 1 1 0—9
Wilson	1 1 1 2 2 1 1 1 0 0 2 0—9
Webster	2 0 0 0 1 2 2 2 0 2 0 2—7
Adams	0 0 1 1 0 2 0 1 1 1 2 0—7
Total	32
"Fredericks"	2 1 1 0 2 0 2 1 2 2 1 2—10
W. B. Tubbs	0 2 1 2 1 1 1 0 1 1 2 0—9
W. Bourn	1 1 0 1 2 1 1 0 0 2 0 0—7
A. C. Tubbs	1 1 2 2 0 2 2 1 0 0 1 2—9
Total	35

In the second shoot, which was under the same conditions except the men shot as individuals. The score was:

Woodward	1 2 1 0 2 0 1 1 1 2 0 1—9
Wilson	2 2 2 1 1 0 1 1 1 0 0 2—9
Webster	2 0 0 2 0 2 1 1 2 1 1 1—9
Adams	0 2 1 0 1 0 0 2 0 1 1 1—7

A third shoot at two birds was then held, and resulted as follows:

Woodward	2 1—2	"Fredericks"	0 1—1
Webster	2 0—1	W. B. Tubbs	1 1—2
Woodward	1 2—2	Bourn	1 0—1
Adams	1 1—2	A. C. Tubbs	2 1—2
Total for team	7	Total for team	6

In the final shoot at one bird, the score was:

"Frederick"	2—1	R. Woodward	1—1
W. B. Tubbs	2—1	Wilson	2—1
Bourn	2—1	F. Webster	0—0
A. C. Tubbs	1—1	Adams	1—1
Total for team	4	Total for team	3

In the four-bird shoot, which was very interesting, the following scores were made:

Woodward	2 1 1 0—3	"Fredericks"	2 1 1 0—3
Webster	0 0 1 2—2	W. B. Tubbs	0 1 1 1—3
*Woodward	1 2 1 1—4	Bourn	0 1 1 0—2
Adams	0 2 2 0—2	A. C. Tubbs	0 2 0 1—2
Total of team	11	Total of team	10

*Woodward shot in place of Wilson.

The Nests and Eggs of Townsend's Junco (*Junco Townsendi*) and San Pedro Partridge (*Oreortyx pictus confinis*).

BY A. W. ANTHONY.

In the latter part of April and first of May, 1889, this junco was found by Mr. Charles H. Townsend and the writer to be very abundent throughout all of the San Pedro Martir region, above 7,000 feet elevation, and many nests could doubtless have been taken had the time at our disposal permitted of our making a more extensive search. But three sets were taken and these vary to such an extent that a description and comparison is of interest.

Set No. 178, collected by A. W. Anthony, from San Pedro Martir, Lower California, taken May 6th, 1889, at an elevation of 9,000 feet. Nest composed of soft, dry grasses and lined with finer grass stems and hair of the mule deer. Is unusually thick, but soft. It was very artfully concealed behind a thick bunch of grass and under the overhanging edge of a large granite boulder. The eggs were three in number and slightly incubated. The shell is pure white in two specimens, while the third shows a slight greenish wash. This specimen is also the most strongly marked of the set, being heavily blotched with pale lilac, chiefly on the larger end, but extending in small flecks over nearly the entire shell. The other two are marked with small spots of pale fawn color with a few small spots and lines of burnt umber collected about the large end. They measure in millimetres 19x15, 19x15, 19x14. The nest measures externally 130 mm. in width, by 60 mm. in height; inside diameter 57 mm. by 30 mm. in depth.

Set No. 177 was taken in the same locality May 5th. The nest was sunken to the level of the ground, apparently in a cow-track, and well hidden in the tall grass on the edge of a running stream. Owing to its location the walls are very thin, and the nest much smaller than the first mentioned; measuring inside 70 mm. in width by 40 mm. in depth. The material used in its construction is the same as that in set No. 178, with the addition in the lining of a little cow hair. The eggs of this set are alike in color and markings, and appear at first glance more like eggs of *Sialia mexicana* than those of any junco with which I am familiar. They are uniformly bluish-white, with a few of the faintest minute specks of burnt umber, on the large end, which are not at first noticeable. Incubation was well advanced. Measurements, 20x15; 19x15; 20x15 mm.

Set No. 179, May 1, presents features different from either of the others in their profuse markings, they being, I think, the heaviest I have seen in this genus. The ground color is faint bluish-white; one is heavily marked with large spots of raw umber and lilac, chiefly collected about the larger end, but covering the entire shell to a great extent; another has a heavy ring of raw umber encircling the large end, mixing with finer spots of lilac, a few fine markings straying over the entire egg. The third has similar markings, but collected about the small end, though it is hardly proper to call either end small in this case, the specimen being unique in having ends almost equal in diameter.

Unfortunately the nest was not saved with the set. The eggs measure 20x15; 19x15; 18x15 mm.

The single nest of the San Pedro partridge that I have seen was discovered near the base of the San Pedro Martir range March 29, 1889. It contained but a single egg, while the female, which was secured as she left the nest, furnished a second, which she was about to deposit. These specimens are of the usual pyriform shape common to the genus, and not distinguishable from eggs of *O. pictus* in my collection from Oregon.

In color, creamy white; measuring in millimetres, 37x27; 36x28.

The nest was a mere hollow under a manzanita bush, filled with dry leaves from the manzanita and lilac.

A Sacramento man claims to have foisted a young hare upon a cat with kittens, and states that the old cat thinks more of the foundling than of its own progeny.

A number of pheasants were imported to Vancouver recently and placed in the Park aviaries, where they will remain for a few days and then be turned loose at suitable spots.

Wells, Fargo & Co.'s Express has consented to take dogs to the Los Angeles show for half rates, a material reduction.

The premium list now at hand presents seventy six classes covering pretty much all breeds Forty-one nice special prizes had been offered when the list was printed and more have since been added.

Our Tennessee Letter.

GALLATIN, TENN., April 2, 1890.

EDITOR BREEDER AND SPORTSMAN:—Last Sunday morning I took a run down to West Side Park to see the horses take their work, and to hear the usual race track gossip that is always to be heard at the track. Only a high wind served to make the trip a disagreeable one, but as it takes cyclones and tornados to keep me away from the horses when an opportunity is presented, I boarded the South bound train, and in less than two hours found myself sitting on the outer rails of the track at West Side Park. Watch in hand, I anxiously awaited to see something "move," and after El Rio Rey had taken a preliminary gallop, I had sufficient cause to start the "ticker," for the big colt was going to work a quarter. The younger brother, Rey del Rey, was to accompany him, and they seemed to skim over the ground very easy and without any exertions. I once thought they would gallop past in about 0:30, but, nevertheless, they were going, and when I stopped my watch, it registered 0:26, many others made it 0:25½. They both finished strong, and looked like they could have gone in 0:24. I saw Don Jose and several of the two-year-olds out, but they did not try for fast time.

Major Elliott gave Bridgelight, Sam Doxey and The Wandering Jew an airing, but I don't think they were sent their best. Old Bridgelight never looked better than he does now, and that is saying a good deal. He was a pretty constant performer last season, and when he starts he will bear watching.

Jones Kleiser cut Osborne loose for six furlongs, and he surprised the knowing ones by finishing the distance in 1:18¾.

Tom Seyers had Miss Maud and Rhyme out on the track, but they did not show any fast work. They are both looking, and, Seyers says, are doing well. Blantyre was given a mile in 1:49, carrying 133 pounds. He finished the last quarter in 25 seconds, and he did not seem at all distressed. Blantyre was almost a failure last season, but he looks now as if he would take a good deal of beating.

The greatest mile at Nashville so far was made by Idle Girl, a sister to Kidnap. She worked a mile last Wednesday on a heavy track in 1:46½. She carried 142 pounds in this trial, and if she does not get stale, she ought to be dangerous when she first comes to the post. She was recently purchased by Ed Gorman, who will take her to Toronto, Canada. She will make the Canadians stretch their neck at any distance from a mile down to a half.

Secretary Gillock received a letter this week from P. M. West, whose stable is now at Louisville, asking that stable room be reserved for ten head of his horses. In West's string is the good colt Grayson, whose chances to capture the Kentucky Derby are pretty good, Longsides, Bonita and that speedy daughter of Geo. Kinney, Flyaway. The West stable has been expected at Nashville all the week, but there is some delay at Louisville.

Many say that Jonas Kleiser has another Big Three in the colt Osborne. He is certainly a good looking youngster, and just why he should not win is hard to account for. Uncle Jonas has always got a "good thing" in his stable, and he may surprise the talent with Osborne, as he did with Big Three last season, when the bookies were laying odds of a hundred to one against the colt.

At this writing the Scoggan Stable is still in Louisville, and contrary to all reports, the horses will be taken direct from Louisville to Memphis, where they will begin the campaign. On this side of the Rockies we hear but little horse talk, but what we hear is Knott's name frequently mentioned. He and Spokane will meet at Nashville for the first time this season, and if Spokane's leg is O. K. we may see a race. Tennesseeans must have backed Knott heavily in the Suburban, as I note that his price has fallen from 40 to 1 to 12 to 1. All this was done inside of a few days, and when he faces the flag on the Suburban day, there will be a mint of winter money hanging over the gelding.

Then there is Rico, the Californian. His price in the Suburban has been considerably lowered. Report has it that Mr. Rose has been backing him, and this alone gives the speculators food for thought. Well, we Tennesseeans have again pinned our hopes and purses to Proctor Knott, and if he fails this State will be more noted for "soup" than as the home of the blooded horse.

Latest news from Memphis is to the effect that everything will be ready for the spring meeting which begins in ten days. Last Sunday Blue Blazes and Tom Stevens were given a trial mile in 1:47. They worked together, and the latter was the stronger at the finish. Helter Skelter, the imported three year-old filly by Pell Mell has reeled off the fastest mile at Memphis—1:46—carrying loads of weight. She ought to win the first races she starts for.

Quite a stir was created in turf circles here a few days ago upon the announcement that Kitty Cheatham had gone lame at Memphis, and would not be trained any more this season. The report was without foundation, and lacks confirmation, as the namesake of the Tennessee actress is now taking her work at Memphis, and is said to be the best of her age there.

The programme of the Washington meeting is out, and is a very attractive one. Secretary Gillock has left no stone unturned in trying to make the coming meeting a success, and he has prepared a programme that is not to be excelled by any on this side of the Mississippi. The "card" for the seven days is one fit for historic Jerome Park or classic Monmouth. All in all, it is the best programme the West Side Park management has ever offered.

Mr. Shafer tells me that Kate Fisher, dam of Kitty Cheatham, Long Fish, Col. Clark, etc., has foaled a chestnut colt by Blazes. Kate Fisher is one of Tennessee's famous broodmares, as everything she has produced that has been trained has been a winner. There have been but five foals at Peytona this season, all of which are by Blazes. The Paytona yearling are said to be the finest lot of youngsters ever bred in Tennessee, and that is saying a good deal.

There are now thirty-five foals at Fairview. There will probably be as many more to come this season. The Fairview people have great faith in the ability of imp. Mr. Pickwick to sire good ones, and I believe he is the premier stallion of the harem. He was well represented last season by Picnic, Phœnix and Reelesborough—all stake winners.

The Memphis "talent" has selected the filly Helter Skelter to win the Tennessee Derby, run at Memphis the first day of the coming meeting. She worked a mile there last Sunday in 1:46 carrying 132 pounds, and on a heavy track at that. She will have to do some running to beat Riley, Jake Saunders and Blarneystone Jr., while there is a filly or two in the same race that can run a little.

The Memphis management has arranged a programme for two day's matinee racing. The matinee races heretofore held at Memphis have been a success, and with the hold that racing has upon Memphis people, I wonder why they do not hold a Fall meeting each year after the close of the Nashville meeting. A week of good racing in the late Fall would create considerable interest in the sport, and would assist in making the spring meetings a success.

KENNESAW.

Our Southern California Letter.

The Rose string of runners will have reached the Metropolis before this letter appears in print. The horses have wintered well and there are some flyers among them. Of all the Brooklyn Handicap candidates, Rico is probably in better condition than any of them with the possible exception of Los Angeles. The three year old has been especially prepared for this event, and will be dangerous with a good jockey in the pigskin. Mr. Rose has played him to win to some extent. Rico has shown a half in 48½ in his work, but has not gone over the Brooklyn distance faster than 2:13½. All the two year olds have been worked five-eighths in 1:04. They are a most promising lot of youngsters. Conrad, Fairy and Oscar are regarded as the best. The fastest one of this trio will be sent out to capture the great American Stake, and it will take a sensational youngster to catch the judge's eye ahead of the California bred youngster. The string that will make the Eastern trip is as follows: Mikado, Tycoon, Rico, Rover, Conrad, Oscar, Masrico, Fairy, Flight, Bianca and Pearl.

The Directors of the Sixth District Agricultural Association have declared the May meeting off. There were several reasons for this action. The running events did not fill very well and the Directors thinking that they could not present a good programme worthy of the patronage of the public, deemed it expedient to call the meeting off. This was a disappointment to many of the local horsemen who had been to some expense in training horses for the meeting. Another unfortunate feature was the fact that a letter containing a number of entries did not reach the Secretary until 2 o'clock, on April 6th, although they were mailed at the University Post Office, on April 1st. The letter took just six days to travel three miles. Isn't that another record for Los Angeles?

Your correspondent had quite a pleasant chat with Jake Gries, of Compton, the other day. Mr. Gries is an enthusiastic running horse man, and is the owner of the great stallion Bachelor. By the way, some of the Bachelor colts will make their debut this season. Bachelor was a great race horse, and with the proper opportunities should make his mark in the stud.

I want to put myself on record for Proctor Knott in the Suburban with Prince Royal as a second choice. If the great son of Luke Blackburn faces the starter in good trim, I don't see anything in the race to get away with him. I am not Proctor Knott crank by any means. I expected him to win the American Derby to be sure, but it is a matter of record that the horse was lamentably out of condition, although this fact was not known out here until after the race.

QUARTER STRETCH GOSSIP.

George Vignolo has a yearling by Alcazar out of a mare by Mohawk Chief. The colt was one year old on April 5th, and on that day he was sixteen hands, one inch high. How is that for a colt?

There is a distinguished new comer at Rosemeade. It is a Stamboul-Minnehaha colt. Who wants this aristocratic youngster for $15,000.

Len Rose will take Richmond Jr. East.

Nick Covarrubias has quite a string of trotters and runners in training. He owns a two-year-old brother to Gambo who should be speedy.

It is very doubtful whether Atto Rex will be seen on the circuit this year.

This is the time of year to hear about sensational trials. The latest is wafted in from Rosemeade, where Walter Maben is handling Dr. Wise's Glendine. No two agree on the time, but an average would make it about 2:21.

Cy Mulkey has taken his string north for the Blood Horse meeting.

The Agricultural Park is to be enclosed by a new fence, and many other improvements are under consideration.

DAGWORTH.

Grim's Gossip.

Edwin C. will go back East to his new owner, with Roy Wilkes.

Ed Newlands, of Oakland, has a half dozen trotters in exercise at the track across the bay.

Joe Courtney states in a letter that he paid Belle Meade a visit and that the best of the stallions there is Luke Blackburn.

Over a million and a half dollars has been paid for trotting horses at auction during the last two months. How is that for healthy boom.

It is claimed that "the black and gray check" of Budd Doble will be behind Houri, 2:17, as she goes down the circuit this season.

Allerton 2:18¼, the great three year old and former stable companion of Axtell, is being jogged every day and is showing no effects of his injury.

Captain Ed. Hackett of Oakland has an Anteeo gelding 6 years old that promises to enter the 2:30 list and earn a $100 bill from the owner of Anteeo.

Abdol, a son of Grand Moor, is moving in fine shape at the Oakland Trotting Park and it is probable that he will be entered on the trotting circuit this fall.

P. W. Bellingall has a fine two-year-old Antevolo colt that has shown good quarters, and there are many who fancy that with ordinary luck he will be as fast in time as his sire.

Mr. Burrell, who trained for J. H. White, of Sonoma County last season, will start for Maine about the 1st of June where he will resume the training of trotting horses.

The full list of the entries to the Sacramento Spring Meeting will be published in the next issue of the BREEDER AND SPORTSMAN. Lack of space prevents the publication in this issue.

Mr. Sutherland, who has charge of Guide 2:28¼ and other good ones near Pleasanton, is working on a race track at his place and will have it ready for exercising purposes within a few days.

The Austrian Government has imposed a tax on betting, the result being that the Vienna Jockey Club has withdrawn all the prizes offered. This action will stop eighty-two race meetings.

Ex-Sheriff Boggs, of Lakeport, has sent a mare over to breed to Director, and has also sent along his stallion Keepsake, which will receive his preliminary education at the hands of Andy McDowell.

Mr. Fred Gebhard of New York is paying the Pacific Coast a visit for the purpose of looking after his large interests in Lake County. The gentleman will probably remain in California for a month or so.

Dr. W. C. Aby was going to be one of the starters at the Blood Horse Meeting, but as Mr. Gebhard will start for the Guenoc Stock Farm on Monday, the Doctor will accompany him up to Lake County.

On Sunday Orrin A. Hickok removed all his stock from the Bay City Track to Oakland, from whence in the course of a week or two he will start East with the California horses that he intends to send for first money on the Eastern Circuit.

The Grand Moor is now located at the Oakland Track and has attracted much attention. Many gentlemen interested in the breeding problem has examined this fine son of The Moor, and already many mares have been booked to him.

Mr. Whitney of Petaluma is convinced that he has traced out the pedigree of Countess, dam of Dawn 2:18¾, and Strathway 2:26. When the matter is definately settled, the BREEDER AND SPORTSMAN will publish all about the investigation and its result.

James Corcoran who trained at Petaluma, last year and lately had charge of Bay Rose, has located at the Lakeport race track, where he has secured several trotters to handle. Jim is a good careful man and will give satisfaction to those who employ him.

On Tuesday next Mr Smith, who has been in charge of the Du Bois horses at Oakland, will start for Denver with the balance of the trotters that the Major left behind him. They have wintered in good shape, and will be ready to face the wire in short order.

V. C Cromwell, Lexington, Ky., has lost by death the five-year-old California-bred bay trotting stallion Glen Dower, by Guy Wilkes, 2:15¼, dam Woodford Queen, by Almont; second dam Virginia, by Billy Townes. Glen Dower's book for the season was full at $100.

I had a pleasant visit on Tuesday last, from H. G. Comstock Correspondent of the New York Spirit of the Times. He will devote his time for the present to the bangtail division, taking in both the Blood Horse Meeting here and the State Agricultural Society's meeting at Sacramento.

Mr. J. Sutherland, Hatch Farm, Pleasanton, has in training two fillies owned by N. J. Stone, one the daughter of Hazel Kirke 2:24, one by the same sire, dam a thoroughbred. He thinks well of them both, and especially of the Hazel Kirke filly. He says she can be put in the 2:30 list this season.

A practical horseman says that when the time for the mare to foal approaches, and she shows no signs of having milk, to give her a half gallon of sweet milk, mixed with enough bran to make a mash; salt slightly and feed once a day as long as they think necessary. A mare will eat it greedily, and it seems to be just what they want.

Some weeks ago, a match race occurred at the Oakland Track between Encinal, Tony Lee and Alameda Lilly, but the owner of Lee was dissatisfied, as he was beaten, and there is some talk of a return match between the grey pacer and Alameda Lily. Encinal has been sent away for stallion service, so he cannot contest with the others.

James D. McMann, who in his day was the peer of any man in the art and mystery of training and driving a trotter, having given to the three fastest mares of their time—Flora Temple, 2:19¾, Lady Thorne, 2:18¼, and the pacer Pocahontas, 2:17¼—their best records, is still alive and hearty, although well on toward eighty years of age.

Judge W. E. Greene, of Oakland, is the happy owner of a Director colt, dam Aldane by Wissahickon. The youngster is a deep seal brown, star in forehead and white heels behind. The Judge thinks most people will see those white heels as they drive under the wire behind his colt. He thinks 2:10 would be an appropriate name for him.

Sam Caton, who has wintered at Los Angeles, started for New York on Thursday of last week. Before leaving he bought Cousin Joe, a pacer by Del Sur; a full sister to Contractor, and the br. f Amber, 2 years old, by Stamboul. In addition to these he took back those he brought out to California, thirteen head belonging to Mr. Simpson of Cuba, N. Y.

F. L. Duncan, of Chico, had a very narrow escape from death a few days ago. He was driving a young horse on the road, and the colt becoming frightened at something turned suddenly and upset the cart, throwing Duncan out, the unfortunate driver sustaining a fracture of the left shoulder. However, he is doing as well as can be expected under the circumstances.

Mr. O H. Lockhart of Burbank, near Los Angeles, has purchased from J. B. Mason the b. m. Pond Lilly 2:29¼ by George M. Patchen Jr. dam unknown. The price paid was $1,000. Shortly after the purchase, the mare gave birth to a filly foal, by Alcazar 2:20½. Mr. Lockhart has named the newcomer Alcazette, as she looks as much like the sire as the name is.

Pete Williams is working a few trotters at the Oakland Track and I can assure readers of the gossip that Silver Bow will prove a wonder this season for he is moving in fine shape and can show well within 2:30 now. Pete is also moving Maud Singleton, John Henry and the Lamereaux string consisting of Detect, (a Director colt) T. O. by Anteeo and an Antevolo colt.

The little sister of Axtell has been known to the world under the name of Can't Tell, but it appears that this name is not acceptable to the owners. Mrs. Barnhart states: "It has never been recorded, and we may see fit to change the name,' and Williams, the joint owner, is of the same opinion. He says "that no colt can be expected to trot hampered with such a name."

Last week John Taylor took the three year old colt Lord Wilkes, by Guy Wilkes 2:15¼, dam Minnie Wilkes, by Sultan 2:24, to Fresno and delivered him over to George Starr, who will take the colt back East, for J. B. Houaker & Co. of Penick, Ky. This is the right cross for speedy animals and we expect to hear good reports from Lord Wilkes when his progeny are old enough to trot.

Last Saturday a match race took place at Petaluma between two Santa Rosa horses owned by W. Byington and W. E. Healy. The race was for $200 a side, and was won handily by Dandy, the horse owned by Healy, he taking the first, second and fourth heats in 3:08, 3:08, and 3:09½. Prince took the third heat in 3:13. About two hundred persons were in attendance, many of whom came over from Santa Rosa.

W. S. Johnson, owner of Edwin C, pacing record 2:15. has sold his fast horse to a party calling himself John Thomas, of Findley, Ohio. Edwin C. is by Elector 2:21½. dam Lady Cooney by Venture 2:27¼. The price paid was $5000. Although a great deal of Mr Johnson's time is taken up with his sportsman headquarters, corner of Mason and Eddy streets, he will be on the circuit this season with one or two fast ones.

J. H. Shults, Esq., of Brooklyn, N. Y., started East on Monday last, having made a careful examination of many of the California Stock Farms. It goes without saying that the gentleman was pleased with what he saw, and he got figures on several promising colts that struck his fancy. Mr. Shults is a pleasant affable gentleman, and made many friends during his short stay on the Pacific Coast.

Many of the authorities quote Sidney's age as nine, but in conversation with Mr. Salisbury a few days ago he stated that the well known horse was named after his little son Sidney, who was born the same year that the horse was. Now, Sidney Salisbury is only eight years old and necessarily Sidney the horse must be the same. Mr. Valensin should have Wallace make the correction at once as the mistake may lead to difficulty in after years.

A horse only requires opportunity to show what he can do in the stud, and Mambrino Wilkes, although his opportunities have been restricted, has shown his great power to produce speed he having four in the 2:30 list. Last week Mr. Ashby, of Oakland, sent to the harem of Mambrino Wilkes the standard mare By-By got by Nutwood 600, dam Rapidan by Dictator, 2nd dam by Edwin Forrest 851, 3rd dam by Mambrino Chief 11. If the progeny of this union is not a grand performer I will be greatly mistaken.

I see by the exchanges that Sunol, 2:10½, and Axtell, 2:12, are barred from the Hartford Capital Stakes for foals of 1886. Now, my fellow paragraphers, I have studied well the consequences of the following assertion, and am prepared to have you all assail my truthfulness, but I can prove what I say. There is a three-year-old stallion in California to-day, that at this early time of the year, trots faster than either Axtell or Sunol ever did during their three-year-old form; therefore, do not be surprised if Axtell's 2:12 is beaten in 1890 by a California bred colt, and I shall not be astonished if even Sunol's 2:10½ is wiped out.

The telegraph informed us that Chas. Marvin started back immediately on the conclusion of the Stanford sale, but instead of taking the train to San Francisco, he paid a visit to Prospect Hill Stock Farm, owned by Miller & Sibley at Franklin, Pa. The proprietors showed up all their young stock, and were especially proud of some young St. Bel's which have all the phenomenal speed of old Electioneer. One although not a year old until the 23rd of May, was driven by Marvin at a 2:40 gait. His dam is Nubia by Harold. Mr. Marvin was highly pleased with his visit and has an exalted opinion of the Miller & Sibley youngsters.

In a short time Charles David will take up a string of horses to the Napa Course, where he will prepare them for a summer campaign. Nona Y. will be the principal one and Charlie is satisfied that she is better than ever she was in her life. Gold Medal, the pacer, will be a candidate for the free for all class and there is every indication that he will be able to hold his own against the best of them. A two year old colt by Whippleton, dam Nona Y. will be exercised. He is a big fine lusty fellow and looks every inch a trotter. Several other good ones will be taken along and Mr. David has a bright out look for trotting honors.

The Board of Directors of the P. C. B. H. A. have secured the services of two veterinaries, one of whom will be in attendance constantly during the races.

You pay your money and can take your choice.

"Nashville, April 1.—It is reported here that El Rio Rey is suffering from lung fever at West Side Park track, and reliable turfmen have stated that El Rio Rey was blowing hard after work on Saturday and was wrapped up in neck clothes. The colt was led to the stable and treated for throat troubles."

Nashville, April 2nd.—El Rio Rey is perfectly sound and takes his work in a kindly manner. He is stout and lusty, showing up in good form, and it can confidently be said that he will surpass his efforts of last year.

An Eastern contemporary, in giving pen pictures of prominent horsemen, says that J. Beach, owner of Altamont, is slightly built, of medium height, fair complexion, and wears a blond moustache. Mr. Beach is one of the most progressive breeders on the North Pacific Coast. Late in the seventies he took Altamont to Oregon, and in a few years this son of Almont produced a marked influence on the horse stock of that State. In 1889 five of his get entered the 2:30 list, a number exceeded only by one other son of Almont in a single season. Mr. Beach owns a number of well bred mares, and from them bred the performers Wallula 2:29½, Almonette 2:29½, and Oneco 2:29¾.

Harry J. Agnew has made another ten strike by purchasing from A. L. Whitney the noted stallion Dawn 2:18¾. As the horse has been extensively advertised to stand at Petaluma this season, it was deemed expedient that Mr. Whitney should carry out his contracts, so Mr. Agnew will not gain possession of Dawn until the first day of August, by which time he will have all the arrang ments completed about his breeding farm. The price given for the horse was $15,000, and at the figure he is one of the cheapest horses in the State. Mr. Agnew is on the right road to success, and with his knowledge of what Eastern buyers want, the day is not far distant when the Agnew Farm will be one of the celebrated ones of California.

R. S. Strader, son of Col. Strader of Lexington, Ky., departed for home the beginning of the week. He brought with him two mares for Mr. Hobart, one of them Nancy Lee (dam of Nancy Hanks, 2:24½) by Dictator; the other was Nola by Nutwood, dam by Bowman's Clark Chief, he by Clark Chief. Col. Strader sent out the mare Valdosta by Nutwood, dam by Mambrino Patchen, to breed to Stamboul. In the same car was Bon Bon by Baron Wilkes, dam Odd Stocking by Happy Medium; Baroness by Baron Wilkes, dam Mary A. Whitney, 2:28, and a filly by Lord Russell. Bon Bon will be bred to Stamboul, and the other two to Guy Wilkes. The three last mentioned belong to Mr. Scannell of Tennessee.

The only representative of the noted Von Wilkes, yearling race record 2:38½ (Von Wilkes was lost by fire last May) is Lady Von Wilkes, bay filly, both hind legs white, foaled March 4, 1890, by Von Wilkes, yearling record 2:38¼; 1st dam Lutie S, by Victor Von Bismarck; second dam Mattie Sentinel, by Almont Sentinel; third dam Kate by Yankee Boy Jr.; 4th dam by Woodpecker, etc.

This being the only representative of the phenomenal Von Wilkes, and being so strongly inbred to Hambletonian 10, she is prized as a keepsake. She traces five time to Hambletonian 10, through Bismarck, Wilkes, Sentinel and Almont, twice to Clay, three times to Mambrino Chief, once to Pilot Jr., and then on thoroughbred. She ought to be able to do honor to her sire and kindred.—Paris Kentuckian-Citizen.

Mr. C. J. Hamlin is nothing if not original, and, according to a Sunday paper issued in Philadelphia, one page of which is devoted to original horse matter, Mr. Hamlin is preparing to convert Belle Hamlin into a runner, and according to the same authority, Senator Stanford, relying probably upon the influence of the thoroughbred dam of Palo Alto, desires to start the celebrated stallion in a running race against Belle.

This would certainly make a novel contest, and would undoubtedly draw more dollars into the treasury of the Buffalo Driving Park than did the Harry Wilkes—Belle Hamlin battle of last year. Here is what the Philadelphia Item states:

"Pa Hamlin says he will run Belle Hamlin a race against Palo Alto or any of the flyers during the circuit. Senator Stanford would like to start Palo Alto against Belle Hamlin or any other horse. With such expressions flying around loose there should be no trouble in arranging a match."

A correspondent writes from Farmington: It may be of interest to your readers to know that the Funk Bros. of this place have secured the services of John McConnell (Buster) as trainer and driver for the coming season, and that he will have full charge of the three quarter mile track at their place. As understood at present he will not be restricted in his work but will be allowed the privilege of handling any outside horses that may be sent to him to train. The Funks have quite a number of good trotters on hand and it is confidently expected that he will be ready with them to open up at the first meeting on the circuit. 'Buster" has already done well in the sulky having given records to Albert W. 2:20, Sidney 2:19¾, Tom Rider 2:20½, Fleet 2:24, Lorena 2:30, Simmocolon 2:29½, and many others which I cannot think of for the moment. Mr. Drais will have one or two to train and others in the neighborhood are going to take this opportunity of preparing their stock for track purposes. The track will be put in excellent repair and no money will be spared to make it the equal of any training grounds in the state.

Col. Harry I. Thornton has been well and favorably known on all the running tracks of the State for many years, he having owned in his time many famous thoroughbreds. This year will see his colors also in the sulky, as on May 1st he will send to Sacramento for training purposes, the bay stallion James Madison by Anteeo, dam Lucy Patchen by George M. Patchen Jr., 31. This grandson of Electioneer has already shown that he is possessed of speed, and it will be no trick for him to make a mark low down in the "twenties." Five youngsters will also be sent along, the first being the bay filly Emma Nevada, two years old, by James Madison, dam Kate Dudley by St. Joe. The next is a brown colt called Chandelier by James Madison, dam Betsey Trotwood by Abbotsford. Still another is a two year-old bay filly by James Madison, dam Lady Elmo by Elmo. The fourth one is a yearling by James Madison, dam Zeana by Berlin. The last of the lot is the black colt Reflector by Director, dam Oriole by Monroe Chief. With this selection, Mr. Swan, manager for Col. Thornton, should be enabled to land several first monies.

"California" Abdallah.

Many times we have been asked as to the breeding of Bassford's Abdallah, Ham's Abdallah, Paul's Abdallah, Bryant's Abdallah and the California Abdallah. The following letter received from Jos. M. Bassford, Sr., now of Solano County gives us the following history of the horse:—

I left San Francisco on the 26th day of August, 1857, on the steamship, Sonora, Capt. Richard Whiting, with the intention of buying two good horses and three good mares as a starter for a breeding farm, having for some time determined in my own mind that an enterprise of the sort would pay in California. I already had a fairly good ranch and therefore only needed the proper kind of stock. We arrived in Panama all right, but on the other side we connected with the Central America, on which we had a very rough time, which ultimately resulted in the ship's going down, and I arrived in New York in my stocking-feet, with a handkerchief tied around my head for a hat. My fond horse calculations were knocked in the head, and consequently I will make this letter to you as short as was my stay in New York.

I bought Abdallah from Henry Chanfrau, brother to the well known actor, paying him for the horse $1000. Chanfrau had acted in New York as an agent for Steve Whipple, and I therefore had every confidence in him. I left New York in March, 1858, on the ship Northern Light, Captain Tinkelpaugh; laid over one trip on the Isthmus, there being a perfect flood of passengers. Among others who staid over with me were Frank Jones, who had in his possession Princess (dam of Happy Medium), a mare that afterwards become well known on account of being taken from California by Eoff to trot against Flora Temple; another horse that remained over for the trip was Stockbridge Chief, Jr., who was in charge of P. Vibard. We all arrived in San Francisco safe and sound, and I considered that I had the very best horse that up to that time had ever been brought to this State. The pedigree as I received it at the time, and which has since been verified, is as follows: Abdallah, by Rysdyk's Hambletonian, he by Abdallah 1; the dam of my Abdallah was by imp. Roebuck, the 2nd dam being by Henry, who was the competitor of Eclipse in the great races East. I sold the horse to E. L. D. Bryant of Benecia in 1860, after serving ten mares with him in 1859, as I thought he was too young in that year for service, he being then only four years of age In 1860 Bryant had him served to sixty mares at $50 each, which was a handsome price at that time.

Bryant sold him to Ben Fish of Santa Clara County. Fish sold him to Capt. Paul of Mayfield; Paul afterwards sold him to Capt. Ham, in whose hands he died at twenty-one years of age, killed, I am satisfied, through kindness, as he was grain fed constantly, and was given little or no exercise. God bless the old horse; he was a good friend to me when I needed friends.

Yours sincerely,

Jos. M. Bassford.

The Last Meet of the Arlington Jockey Club.

The races were a great success! Although the wind blew disagreeably there was a good crowd to witness the interesting contests. The crowd was a most jolly one and they seemed to enjoy the sport amazingly. The track was in good condition and the time made in each race was fast, fast even for thoroughbred horses. There were six races on the programme and each one was closely contested.

SUMMARY.

Purse $30, Consolation Stakes, one quarter of a mile.
C. E. Sherman's br g Capitan—Menchaca.
W W. Hollister's g g Semito—Romero.
C. E. Gates' s g Domino—Duryea.
Updegrof's br m Kitty—Divers.
P. Freeman's cr g Butcher Boy—Freeman
Penry's b g Billy—Bolseke.
Time, :24¾.

Capitan won, Leralto 2nd, Domino 3rd. Time, :24¾.

A great many watches made the time 0:24. Considering the weight, and the class of horses and the time of the year, the time was excellent. Capitan, the winner, is a most handsome saddle horse. He is a dark brown, sixteen hands high and his style of travelling is very graceful and easy. C. E. Sherman is justly proud of this handsome fellow. In the pools Capitan sold for $5, Semito for $2, and the field for $3.

SUMMARY.

Purse $100, Match Race, one-quarter mile.
Pierre Lorillard Jr's b m Dudu, 160 lbs; Menchaca.
H. B. Duryea's s g Lightfoot, 160 lbs; Duryea.
Time, 0:26.

Pierre Lorillard Jr., the great New York sporting man, has been picking up horses and been winning most of his races. He is a good judge of horse flesh and when he pronounces a horse as a good runner you can safely bet on his judgment. In this race his mare Dudu won most handily and in splendid style. In the pools she sold favorite for $5 and Lightfoot for $2. She ran under a strong pull in :26. Lightfoot made a good effort to win the race; Duryea got out of him all the run there was in him, but the little sorrel gelding could not get there.

SUMMARY.

Purse $35. One-half mile, handicap.
Daniels' s g Ed S., 140, Appleton.
Menchaca's b g Mark B., 163, Menchaca.
Pierre Lorillard Jr.'s b m Miranda, 160, Brown.
W W. Hollister's blk g Laro, 128, Romero.
C. E. Sherman's br g Capitan, 128, Pico.
Time—:51½.

This race was a most interesting one. The talent were so certain that Mark B. would win, that the pool sellers could not get out the tickets fast enough. Mark B $10, Ed. S. $3, and the field $4.

The starters had little trouble to get the horses off. When the flag dropped all the horses were bunched, but soon after the start Ed. S., Mark B., and Capitan took the lead. At the three eighths pole Miranda came up like a race mare. She passed Mark B. and Capitan, and ran close up to Ed. S., who was punished severely, but the gelding took the punishment well, and she won the race by half a length, Miranda 2nd, Mark B 3rd, Capitan 4th, in excellent time, :51½.

SUMMARY.

Purse $100. Match race. Three-eighths mile.
Bayard Thayer's b g Blue Rock, 180, Thayer.
A. B. Duryea's s g Killjoy, 160, Duryea.
Time—:42.

No pools were sold in this race. Blue Rock won the race handily.

SUMMARY.

Purse $45. Five-eighths mile, handicap.
Pierre Lorillard's s g Baby, 160, Manchaca.
J. Clancy's s g Fandango, 140, Pico.
A. Ring's b s Gen. Logan, 160, Appleton.
Time—1:05½.

The talent sagely bought Baby for $10 and the field for $5. The crowd watched this race with great interest. After two false starts the horses were sent off to a good start. Baby and Gen. Logan ran like a double team, Fandango trailing behind. At the three-quarter pole Baby was two lengths ahead of Gen Logan. Fandango was three lengths behind Baby when the horses struck the home stretch. Baby quit, and so did Gen. Logan. Fandango ran strong, and won by two lengths, Baby 2nd.

SUMMARY.

Purse $60. One half mile. Free for all.
J. S. Bell's b g Sid Law, 125 lbs.; Pico.
A. Rinz's m Maid, 115 lbs.; Appleton.
Boeseke's b m Rowena, 120 lbs.; Boeseke.
Time, :49½.

The horses in this race were in superb condition. The betting was lively—Sid Law $20, the field $10. A great deal of money was bet on this race at these odds. The horses behaved well at the starting point, so that the starters had no trouble to send them off at a most even start. Sid Law immediately took the lead, and Maid ran a length behind. Sid Law won the race most handily. Many of the sports with their watches caught the time :49. Sid Law is a handsome bay gelding by Robbery Boy and out of Lillian by Crighton. He is very speedy; it is said that he ran a trial one half mile dash three days before the race in :48. This race ended the afternoon's racing. The Stewards of the Arlington Club deserve credit for the manner in which they have conducted their meetings. Their special care has been to give satisfaction, to treat all impartially and justly. They have done a great deal towards entertaining the numerous visitors from the East, and we all earnestly hope that they will return next winter. H. B. Duryea, the President of the club, has worked indefatigably for the success of each meeting. His efforts are thoroughly appreciated. Charles Fay, Secretary, has always been most accommodating, and althoug his handicaps have at times seemed too heavy, still he has always considered the interest of the club and has handicapped the horses according to their speed and capacity to carry weight. The starters, Bayard Thayer and L. P. Stone have given pronounced satisfaction. Pierre Lorillard, as weigher-in, was always accommodating, and he understands it perfectly. P. Duryea & Kissell were appreciated.

T. M.

THE WEEKLY

Breeder and Sportsman.

JAMES P. KERR, PROPRIETOR.

The Turf and Sporting Authority of the Pacific Coast.

Office, No. 313 Bush St.

P. O. Box 2300.

TERMS—*One Year, $5; Six Months, $3; Three Months, $1.50.*

STRICTLY IN ADVANCE.

Money should be sent by postal order, draft or by registered letter, addressed to JAMES P. KERR, San Francisco, Cal.

Communications must be accompanied by the writer's name and address, not necessarily for publication, but as a private guarantee of good faith.

NEW YORK OFFICE, ROOM 15, 181 BROADWAY.

ALEX. P. WAUGH, - - - - Editor.

Advertising Rates

Per Square (half inch)

One time	$1 50
Two times	2 50
Three times	3 25
Four times	4 00

And each subsequent insertion 75c. per square.

Advertisements running six months are entitled to 10 per cent. discount.

Those running twelve months are entitled to 20 per cent. discount.

Reading notices set in same type as body of paper, 50 cents per line each insertion.

To Subscribers.

The date printed on the wrapper of your paper indicates the time to which your subscription is paid.

Should the BREEDER AND SPORTSMAN be received by any subscriber who does not want it, write us direct to stop it. A postal card will suffice.

Special Notice to Correspondents.

Letters intended for publication should reach this office not later than Wednesday of each week, to secure a place in the issue of the following Saturday. Such letters to insure immediate attention should be addressed to the BREEDER AND SPORTSMAN, and not to any member of the staff.

San Francisco, Saturday, April 12, 1890.

Dates Claimed.

SACRAMENTO (Running Meeting)......April 26th, 29th, May 1st and 3d
EUREKA JOCKEY CLUB......July 2d to 5th
IONE......Aug. 7th to 9th.
LOS ANGELES (6th District)......Aug. 11th to 16th
NAPA......Aug. 18th to 23rd
GLENBROOK PARK, 17th District......August 19th to 23d
PETALUMA......Aug. 26th to 30th
OAKLAND (District No. 1)......Sept. 1st to Sept. 6th
LAKEPORT, 12th District......September 23d to 27th
CALIFORNIA STATE FAIR......Sept 8th to 20th
STOCKTON......Sept. 23rd to 27th.
FRESNO (Fall Meeting)......Sept. 29th to Oct. 4th

Stallions Advertised

IN THE

BREEDER AND SPORTSMAN.

Thoroughbreds.

DOUGLASDALE—Thoroughbred Clydesdale......Lawn View Farm, Cal.
FRIAR TUCK, Hermit—Romping Girl......C. W. Aby, Middletown.
GREENBACK, Dollar—Music......C. W. Aby, Middletown.
INTRUDER, Crater—Lady Bountiful......T. J. Knight, Sacramento.
REVEILLE, Shiloh—Norfolk......B. C. Holly, Vallejo.
ST. SAVIOR, Eolus—War Song......C. W. Aby, Middletown.
THREE CHEERS, Imp. Hurrah—Young Fashion......E. S. Culver, San Francisco.

Trotters.

ARLINGTON, Abbotsford—Gillispie Mare......J. R. French, S. F.
ANTEEO BUTTON, Anteeo—Dam of Alexander Button......E. O. Spear, St. Helena.
ADMIRAL, Volunteer—Lady Pierson......Frank Drake, Vallejo.
ACTOR Prompter—Dam by Sultan......Lawn View Farm, Cal.
ARBITRATOR, Director—Lady Earnest......H. A. Mayhew, Niles.
ANTEEOP, Anteeo—Bessie G......Guy E. Grosse, Santa Rosa.
ANTEEOP, Anteeo—Nance......Guy E. Grosse, Santa Rosa.
ADMIRO, Admiral—dam by San Bruno......Smith & Sutherland, Pleasanton.
ASHLAND ALMONT, Almont—Pauline......T. J. Whitehead, Oakland.
ALEXANDER BUTTON, Alexander—Lady Button......Cache Creek Farm, Yolo.
APEX, Prompter—Mary......Poplar Grove Breeding Farm, Wildflower.
ALCONA, Almont—Queen Mary......Fred W. Loeber, St. Helena
BAY ROSE Sultan—Madam Baldwin......Thos. Bonner, Santa Rosa
BALKAN Mambrino Wilkes—Fanny Fern......A. L. Hinds, Oakland.
CLOVIS, Sultan—Sweetbriar......Poplar Grove Breeding Farm, Wildflower.
CUPID, Sidney—Venus......C. O. Thornquest, Oakland
CHRISMAN'S HAMBLETONIAN 10178, Whipple's Hambletonian—Flora Jesse Cliffeman, San Jose
CHARLES DERBY, Steinway—by Electioneer. Cook Stock Farm, Contra Costa Co.
CALIFORNIA NUTWOOD, Nutwood—Fanny Patchen......Martin Carter, Alameda Co.
CORRECT R, Director—Brainey......Pleasanton Stock Farm.
DECORATOR, Director—Chess......Pleasanton Stock Farm.
DEXTER PRINCE, Kentucky Prince—Lady Dexter......L. M. Morse, Lodi.
DAWN, Nutwood—Countess......A. L. Whitney, Petaluma
DIRECTOR, Dictator—Dolly......Pleasanton Stock Farm, Pleasanton.
DON MARVIN, Fallis—Cora......F. P. Lowell, Sacramento
DESIGNER, Director—May Queen......H. Scott, Oakland.
ELECTOR, Electioneer—Gilberta......L. A. Richards, Grayson.
ELECTION, Electioneer—Lizzie H......B. C. Holly, Vallejo.
EL BENTON, Electioneer—Nellie Benton......Souther Farm, San Leandro.
ECLECTIC, Electioneer—Manette......Wilfred Page, Sonoma County
EROS, Electioneer—Sontag Mohawk......W. H. Vioget, Menlo Park
FIGARO, Hambletonian—Emblem......Souther Farm, San Leandro.
GROVER CLAY, Electioneer—Maggie Norfolk......Denis Gannon, Oakland.
GRAND MOOR 2374, Moor 870—Vashti......H. I. Thornton, S. F.
G. A. M., Anteeo—Rosa B......George E. Guerne, Santa Rosa.
GUY WILKES, George Wilkes—Lady Bunker......San Mateo Stock Farm, San Mateo.
GLEN FORTUNE, Electioneer—Glenna......Souther Farm, San Leandro.
GEORGE WASHINGTON, Mambrino Chief—Fanny Rose......Thos. Smith, Vallejo.
GUIDE, Director—Imogene......Smith & Sutherland, Pleasanton.
GRANDISSIMO, LeGrande—Norma......Fred W. Loeber, St Helena
ILLUSTRIOUS, Happy Medium—Abdalletta......George A. Stone, Santa Rosa.
JESTER D, Almont—Hortense......Souther Farm, San Leandro
JUNIO, Electioneer—by Granger......S. N. Straube, Fresno.
KAFIR, Alcazar—Flower Girl......B. C. Holly, Vallejo.
KING DAVID, Admiral—Black Flora......Frank Drake, Vallejo.
LEO WILKES, Guy Wilkes Sable......San Mateo Stock Farm, San Mateo.
MEMO, Sidney—Flirt......John Rowen, Oakland
MOUNTAIN BOY, Kentucky Prince Elsie......B. C. Holly, Vallejo.
MAMBRINO WILKES, George Wilkes—Lady Chrisman......San Miguel Stock Farm, Walnut Creek.
MART BOORHEM, Sidney—Towhead......B. C. Holly, Vallejo.
MAMBRINO JR. 1789, Mambrino Patchen, dam by Mambrino Chief Geo. P. Bull, San Jose.
MAMBRINO CHIEF, McDonald Chief—Venus......Thos. Smith, Vallejo.
MORTIMER, Electioneer—Marti......Wilfred Page, Sonoma County
NOONDAY, Wedgewood—Noontide......F. P. Lowell, Sacramento.
PASHA, Sultan—Madam Baldwin......D. Bryson, Linden
PHILOSOPHER, Pilot Wilkes—Belle......George E. Guerne, Santa Rosa.
REDWOOD, Anteeo—Lou Wilton......A. McFadyen, Oakland.
STEINWAY, Strathmore—Abbess......Cook Stock Farm, Contra Costa Co
SUNSET, Anteeo—Bessie G......Guy E. Grosse, Santa Rosa.
SIDNEY, Santa Claus—Sweetness......Valensin Stock Farm, Pleasanton.
SABLE WILKES, Guy Wilkes—Sable......San Mateo Stock Farm, San Mateo.
VICTOR, Echo—Daughter of Woodburn......G. W. Hughes, Napa City
WOODNUT, Nutwood—Flora......Jas. Weatherhead, San Jose
WHIPPLETON 1883, Hambletonian Jr.—Lady Livingston......Fred W. Loeber, St. Helena
WOODSIDE, Woodnut—Veronica......B. C. Holly, Vallejo.
YOUNG ELMO, St. Elmo—Dam by Woodburn......Lawn View Farm Cal.

The Judges' Stand.

It has been published and claimed to be true that John Splan once said.—

"I can do better when I am honest, and when I see men in the stand who are impartial and who will punish me when wrong and protect me when right, I will drive an honest race; but when I look up into that stand and see there a man whom I can steal out of his clothes, and he won't know until next morning he has been stolen, I am out for the stuff."

Have we any such men in California? There is not a track in the State but what the public feel that they have, at some time or other, been victimized by the sharp practise of drivers, and one of the main objects of each Board of Directors should be to see that thoroughly reliable men are in the judges' stand. There is no absolute necessity for the judges being members of the Association in whose stand they serve, so that gentlemen should be selected who are well up in the rules, able to distinguish when "funny business" is going on, and with backbone enough to apply the strict letter of the law in regard to penalties. Make the drivers understand they must be honest, or that they will have to change their business, and then we will have the best horses win irrespective of how the money is on in the pool box. Several of the Associations secure the services of Mr. La Rue each year, because it is a well known fact that the would be crooked ones are afraid of having him deal out justice to them, and consequently they try to win. We need many more such judges, and they can be found if the Directors will only take the matter in hand early enough, and we would advise a liberal payment to such. Do not ask good, capable men to give up their business for pleasure alone, but make it an object for them to do so. Let the year 1890 mark the beginning of a new era, in which satisfaction to the public will be the first thing considered, and combinations among the horsemen entirely broken up.

The Detroit Driving Club.

The announcement is made in the proper columns of the BREEDER AND SPORTSMAN this week that the Merchants' and Manufacturers' Stake, guaranteed to be worth $10,000, is offered by the Detroit Driving Club for their annual blue ribbon meeting. This Association has held for many years the premier place among the Associations on the grand circuit, and this year will be no exception to the general rule, as the Directors have determined to surpass anything ever accomplished before.

The guaranteed stake alluded to will be trotted on one of the days of the meeting which occurs July 22, 23, 24 and 25. Ample time will be given to each of the nominators so that the exact date will be known. The stake is an open one, free to all horses eligible to the 2:24 class on April 15th, 1890.

The entrance fee is only $500, and is payable as follows: $125 at time of subscription, which is to close Tuesday, April 15th, 1890, each subscriber to give his residence and post office address at the time of making the nomination; the second payment of $125 is due Thursday, May 15th; the third payment of a like amount is due Monday, June 16th; and the final payment of $125 must be paid on Monday, July 7th, at which time horses are to be named. No subscription will be accepted unless the first payment shall accompany same, as subscribers are liable only for the amount actually paid in. As in the case of all like stakes, a failure to make subsequent payments shall be construed to be a surrender of the subscription to the Association. Subscribers also may at any time transfer their subscriptions. The entrance money received shall be devoted to the purse, and it is guaranteed by the Association to be not less than $10,000; however, in case the entrance money should exceed that amount by less than $500 that will be also divided. but if the excess should be over $500, then the extra money will be devoted to a consolation purse for horses starting and winning no part of the original purse. The purse or purses will be divided into 50, 25, 15 and 10 per cent for first, second, third and fourth horses. As there are quite a number of horses going on from California, it is more than likely that this very liberal guaranteed purse will find full favor among those going from this State, and it is only necessary to advise our readers that nominations can be made to Mr. Campbell, Secretary of the Detroit Driving Club, Detroit, Michigan.

Goodwin's Official Turf Guide.

Some few weeks ago we received a letter from a tur man in New Jersey, asking if Bolero had ever won a ra in California, giving as his reasons for the inquiry th a protest had been entered against Bolero, the hor having been named in a maiden's race at one of the Ne Jersey tracks.

Goodwin's Guide shows that on Saturday, Sept. 10t 1887, Bolero won a race at Oakland, but from the files the BREEDER AND SPORTSMAN we learn that Lau Gardner won the race, with Bolero second. The Goodwi Bros. wrote a letter to this office, stating that they ha received official notice of the result from the Secreta of the Golden Gate Association, and that his letter stat that Bolero was the winner. The Secretary says h cannot remember to have sent any official notification the office of the Guide, and that if he did so, it must hav been copied from the books exactly as they are. N deeming it of very great importance we did not publis the letter sent from the Goodwin Bros., and have re ceived another, which is herewith appended.—

NEW YORK, April 3rd, 1890.

EDITOR BREEDER AND SPORTSMAN;—

In Re Bolero.

On March 4th last we mailed you a letter regarding th above named subject, and are somewhat surprised to fin that you have not displayed the same readiness to publis our reply that you did the article which tended to give th impression that our Guide was wrong. Will you please ex plain to us why you suppress our reply, and oblige you truly,

GOODWIN BROS.

Having mislaid or destroyed their former letter, it impossible to publish it, but can simply say that no sligh was intended, and it is surprising that so few mistake appear in the Guide, and the one alluded to is probabl a typographical displacement.

The Carson Combination Sale.

We wish to call the attention of our readers once mor to the grand combination sale of standard-bred trotter thoroughbreds, Clydesdales, Percherons, fine roadster work horses, registered and grand Holstein cattle an registered jacks, to be sold by John P. Sweeney & Co. of Carson City, Nevada, commencing Tuesday, Apri 15th, and continuing until the entire catalogue is dis posed of. Among the trotters are many of the get o Echo, Gibraltar, Prompter, Buccaneer, Blue Bull, Sig nal, etc. Many of these are already in training, notabl among which is Alpha, 2:40 (trial 2:25½), by Privatee son of Buccaneer, dam Fawn 2:30½ (trial 2:22), b Marion, son of Mambrino Chief.

Triumph, by Prompter, he by Wilson's Blue Bull dam Lady Brighton by St. Clair; Gibber, three year ol record 2:47, and a ninth heat at that; Ernest Harris, very promising young colt, by Gibraltar, Sam Lewi 2:24½, by Echo, and many others that should be wort lots of money to those who expect to have horses on th circuit.

Old Gibraltar, that good old game horse, will also b sold, and we have been creditably informed that he faster to-day than ever he was in his life, and that he in perfect condition.

Among the thoroughbreds, there will be the get of Jo Hooker, Norfolk, Lodi, Breckenbridge, Three Cheer Langford and others.

There is also catalogued the celebrated Holstein bul Saratoga, and a number of fine calves and heifers b him, together with other well known thoroughbred Hol steins. The sale will be positive and without reserve, s that those who attend may feel sure that there will be n bidding in or by bidding.

The Runnymede, Coldstream and Loudo Sale.

In the advertising columns will be found the annua announcement of the yearling sales, of Runnymede Coldstream and Loudon Stock Farms. The sale wil take place near Paris, Kentucky, on May 5th and is un der the supervision of Messrs. Baxter & Stringfield, o Lexington, Kentucky. These yearlings are the get o such sires as Hindoo, Billet, Leonatus, Onondaga, Fon so, Alarm, Springbok, Sensation, King Alfonso an Bend, Or. They include full brother to Hanover, Ji Gore, Bedford and The Lioness, Ballston, Perkins, Mado lin, Burton, Millie and Miss Motley. Sisters to Runny mede, Barnes, Meriden, Servia, Cameo, Heathen Hindo Rose, Lillian Lindsay, and Sunbeam. Half brothers t Pure Rye, Ocean, Middlestone, Catalpa, Miss Thoma Winslow and Stoney Montgomery, and Longshore, an half sisters to Alarm Bell, Warren Lewis, Shelby Barne Florence E., Brussels and Kilkenny.

To those of the California breeders who are intereste in thoroughbreds, the sale is of great importance as th choice youngsters to be disposed of can hardly b equalled in the country.

On application, catalogues will be sent from thi office.

The Belle Meade Sale.

Attention has already been called in these columns to the public auction, April 24th and 25th, of all the stallions and thoroughbred brood mares at Belle Meade Farm. This will be the greatest sale ever held in the United States, with possibly the exception of the one held by Mr. Lorillard in October, 1886, that was a truly marvelous sale, but we confidently predict that the Belle Meade one will surpass it, as the great Iroquois, Luke Blackburn, and other noted sires will be sold; the brood mares are the peers of any to be found in any country, and when it is considered for a moment that seventeen daughters of imp. Bonny Scotland will pass under the hammer, it will readily be seen that there are good grounds for our belief that this sale will surpass the Lorillard one. There are also sixteen mares by imp. Great Tom, and as his progeny have nearly all proved producers, it is fair to presume that they will also be eagerly sought after.

The catalogues have been sent to all prominent breeders, and we expect that there will be a number of California breeders represented at the sale.

The Blood Horse Meeting.

It has been usual to speak of any meeting of the Blood Horse Association as the "Mud Horse Meet" owing to the rainy weather which have so frequently fallen to their lot on the dates claimed, but from present appearances it would seem that beautiful weather is in store for the society. The race going public of San Francisco have always given approval to well conducted race meetings and for years have recognized the fact that the representative organization of the Pacific Coast is well worthy of every support that can be given it.

On looking over the list of those who have entered horses, we find Senator Stanford, Senator Hearst, Col. H. I. Thornton, Hon. L J. Rose and Hon. L. U. Shippee, names that are a sufficient guarantee to the public at large that the horses will be run on their merits and the contests be of an exciting nature. The Directors have left no stone unturned toward making a successful meeting, and it is impossible to give any reason why the Spring gathering should not prove a financial success.

Another Auction Sale.

Messrs. Killip & Co announces this week that they will offer at public auction on May 2d, by order of S. C. Tryon, Esq., the well-known pacing mare Pocahontas, 2:22½, who is heavy in foal to Dexter Prince. The grey gelding El Monte, 2:29½, will also pass under the hammer, together with the brown pacer Castello, 2.31½, and the three-year-old trotter Majester, two-year-old record, 2:49½. Some twenty others will be sold, all of which will be fully described in the catalogues, which will be out in a few days.

Roy Wilkes.

Taking advantage of a visit paid to the Pleasanton Stock Farm we took a look at the young pacing stallion Roy Wilkes, which has wintered in California, and improved wonderfully thereby, at least Mr. Davies, his owner, says the horse was never in such fine condition in his life. He is a seal brown in color, 15¾ hands in height and weighs in the neighborhood of 1,000 pounds. In bodily conformation he is apt to remind the spectator of old George Wilkes, being very much like his grandsire. He has a massive neck, built on the Patchen line, but there is the breast, barrel, shoulders, back and legs of Wilkes. His legs cannot be improved upon, the hocks being simply perfection, and he has excellent feet. He has a fine intelligent head, and seems to know at all times what is wanted of him. Of a kindly disposition he takes to his work in a good natured manner, and although he has been in active stud service for some time, his owner drove him at a 2:20 gait pacing and at word of command had the beautiful horse strike a trot, doing better than a "thirty clip." Mr. Davies seems to feel confident that he can beat all stallion records with Roy Wilkes, and proposes to fit him especially for exhibition miles. It is probable that the coming season will be his last as a pacer, as Mr. Davies has made up his mind to only start him in trotting races after this year. Roy Wilkes taken all in all, is one of the handsomest horses we have ever seen, and he should be a valuable animal for the head of a breeding farm. There never was a gamer horse ever seen on a track and he should stamp the same characteristics on all of his get.

Sales.

J. B. McDonald, of Marysville, sends word as follows:—

I have made the following sales: To James Linden of Sacramento (for other parties) the mare Fedora, record 2:30½, by Brigadier, dam American Maid. Price $2500.

Bay mare Patch Work, by Brigadier, dam by Signal. Price $1500.

To C. W. Godard, of Sacramento, chestnut mare Beckey Magee, by Brigadier, dam Magee mare, Price $500.

A Use for Skim Milk.

The well known turf writer "Aurelius" contributes an article to the Horse and Stable, part of which is herewith copied, as it is well worthy of perusal.

Several years ago I became acquainted with a gentleman well known to New England breeders as a prize winner against the severest competition. I refer to L. M. Payne, of Hinsdale, Mass. He has been a regular prize winner for a great many years back, not only at the American Horse Show in New York City, but also in the great New England Fair at Worcester, Mass., and at the Boston State Fair. I know of no person who has met with more success, considering the size of his stud, which is a small one, and the number of his exhibits. His premiums were won with William Tell, son of Knickerbocker, a magnificent young horse and also with his progeny for the most part. That Wm Tell should always prove a winner in the show ring against such competition as New England could muster, and that his progeny should meet with such uniform success as it has, is due primarilly to individual merit. Still, a large degree of praise should be given to the skill with which Mr. Payne prepared his stock for exhibition, and to the materials he used in their development. I say development, for I think the expression "forcing process" should be abolished from the language of breeders.

There is no such thing as a "forcing process" either with children or colts. If the child or colt is healthy, its appetite will be insatiable, and it is simply anew ring the call of nature to give it what it can eat. Neither can it be said that it is advisable to give colts or children food rich in fattening elements.

Charles Marvin was at Rochester several years ago, and in conversation with him he pointed out a colt saying, "There is a yearling that gets 15 quarts of oats daily, besides plenty of grass and hay, and he eats his oats clean; I can drive him a quarter in 35 seconds, and a half in 1:11 or better." This was Chimes, now owned by Mr. Hamlin.

The testimony of Mr. Williams as to the amount of food that Axtell was given and consumed daily, in his two-year form, far surpasses that consumed by Chimes.

Dr. J. W. Day, Dr. Thomas S. Flood and other successful colt handlers are unanimous in their testimony that there is no such thing as "forcing" colts. Their first condition is to give them all they will eat, and with it exercise sufficient to keep their digestive appatatus in order, and make them long for their work, as a healthy boy or girl does for a romp. Your steady going, meditative sort of a boy, girl or colt is not healthy, or else he doesn't get sufficient proper food.

To returned to Mr. Payne. No one can deny his success as a developer of colts for the show ring. His list of prizes tells its own story A prominent feature of his regimen for colts was the liberal use of skim milk, Polycrap says "he would as soon think of forcing a colt on wheat straw, as of forcing an abnormal growth on skim milk." Whilst there is no talk here of forcing an abnormal growth, but on the contrary, of assisting nature to its normal state of healthy growth I may say that in my brief experience I have learned to value wheat as well as skim milk. If wheat straw be cut when the berry is ripe, but before it is old and dry, before the sap and green has left the stalk and the straw has become woody, I may say that the grain will not only make better flour, but the stalks or straw will make excellent feed, nutritious and healthy, which the stock will eat readily. It would be better than half the hay which is fed to the city horses, gathered after it has been wet, and which is productive of heaves. With such wheat straw, and with skim milk and ground oats and bran, with carrots every day, I would run my risk of getting a colt into condition to exhibit any where.

I have conversed with several successful cattle breeders, who were also breeders of horses, about this very subject of feeding skim milk. Among these was Dudley Miller of Oswego, well known all over the United States as a breeder of Holstein cattle, and also as an interesting and judicious writer on the horse. Another was Mr. Powell, of the well-known firm of Smith, Powell & Lamb of Syracuse, N. Y. Both of these gentlemen agree that it would pay horse breeders to keep cattle for the sake of the skim milk, even if they threw the cream away. Mr. Powell was especially an enthusiast on the subject of feeding skim milk to calves and to colts. I know of no firm in the United States that receives as large prices for their bulls and heifers as does this firm, and their constant practice of feeding skim milk shows that it must have merit, as measured by that most infallible rule, public approbation. Messrs. Smith, Powell & Lamb have a centrifugal separator, and the milk is put into it as it comes from the cow, separated and fed to the calves and colts still warm.

It is worthy of note that the cream alone, from such a system, would well pay for the trouble and give a margin on the investment. Separate the cream whilst fresh, bottle it up and sell it to city customers, in pint or quart bottles, and I am sure that customer would rush to patronize such a dairy. I give the experience of others in preference to that of my own, for the gentlemen mentioned are well known experts, and I am sure would gladly give such information as lay in their power.

My own experience has been emphatically in favor of feeding skim milk. I bought Troublesome, 2:25½ last spring with a colt by her side by Sherman. I bought her low, and after a conversation with Gen. Tracey I found that he, too, sold her because he said, "She was a poor nurse." It is true that she is not not such a milker as I could desire, though I think at the present time was not properly handled. She was fat and sleek when I bought her, but her colt was poor and thin. It had all the fat producing elements which the mother could give. I shortly afterward bought the colt, when a good healthy man could put him under his arm and carry him off without difficulty. His hair was turned toward his head and a generally sorrowful look always haunted his countenance. I weaned him, and commenced to feed him 12 quarts of skim milk daily, besides oats ground with bran. After a month the improvment commenced, and he grew rapidly, until at the present time, as a yearling, he is far larger than the other two of Troublesome's progeny: Oracle 2:23½, trial 2:28 at three years, and Hildegrade (dam of Cheltenham, 2:28). As I believe Troublesome to be one of the best broodmares in this country, it was with no little satisfaction that I saw that I could give her colts all the growth that nature intended they should have. I have constantly fed skim milk for some years back, to backward colts and fillies, and I believe that a good herd of cows should prove a most valuable adjunct to any stock farm.

At the request of Horace Brown, C. J. Hamlin supplied a number of cows, and the results Mr. Brown tells me are most satisfactory. It is my own practice to set the milk in a Cooley creamery and feed in the morning what was milked at night and *vice versa*, the milk being warmed to take the chill off. I think Polycarp's experiments must have failed, if they did at all, for some other reason than that of the unfitness of such food in its condition without the cream. He says "he is satisfied it is a fairly good food to make bone and muscle." I think if he will write to Smith, Powell & Lamb of Syracuse, N. Y., he will be convinced that one first-class firm of dealers in Holstein stock, at least, believes in milk, skim milk and not milk with the cream, as a proper food for young stock.

It is by comparing notes that we will all learn, and I am very much indebted to the gentlemen who have, as named, made a practice of feeding skim milk, for the benefit of their experience. It has been a scource of profit to me, and I feel persuaded that it will be to every breeder who gives it a fair trial.

AURELIUS.

Answers to Correspondents.

Answers for this department MUST be accompanied by the name and address of the sender, not necessarily for publication, but as proof of good faith. Write the questions distinctly, and on one side of the paper only. Positively no questions will be answered by mail or telegraph.

F. P. L.

Please answer through the "BREEDER" what year John Nelson died, and the breeding of "State of Maine."

Answer.—Wallace says that Nelson died in 1871, but we know postively that he was alive in 1876. Inquiry has been started and we will be able to determine the matter in the course of a few days. State of Maine by Simpson's Messenger, son of Winthrop Messenger, dam said to be decended from the same stock.

J. J. H.

Will you please inform a subscriber to your paper if it has ever been known that a mare has carried a foal fourteen (14) months?

Answer.—We have never heard of such a case.

A constant reader.

Please answer the following questions and oblige: (1) Give pedigree of dam of Plumas 1699. (2) Give pedigree of Werner's Rattler. (3) Is dam of Ashley standard under rule 5.

Answer.—(1) Rose Thompson pedigree untraced. (2) Werner's Rattler, by Biggarts Rattler, dam by Mars, granddam by Defiance. (3) Yes.

H E. Chesebro.

No vertification of the pedigree has been made from this office during the time you mention. The horse can not be registered, unless you can get a record for him of 2.30 or better.

Subscriber.

Will you please publish the pedigree of "Adrian Almont," bred by Gen Withers, Lexington, Kentucky. Is he standard?

Answer.—He is not registered.

San Francisco, Cal.—Can you give me, through the Monthly, any information as to the breeding of a stallion named Jim Lick.

Answer.—We cannot place him.

We copy the above from Wallace's Monthly and as some of our readers may wish to know the pedigree, here with append it. James Lick, by Homer, he by Rysdyk's Hambletonian; dam Springer mare, by Harker's Buster, son of imp. Buster.

J. B. Palin.

Please give the breeding of old Gen. Taylor and his record?

Answer.—Gen Taylor by the Morse horse; record 2:41½ to saddle and 2:44 to harness.

Santa Rosa.

Can you let me know the breeding of Capt. Harris' Adventure?

Answer:—Adventure, by Venture 2.27¼, he by Belmont; 1st dam Young Rosedale (dam of Rosa Mac 2:20¾) by Sawyer's Messenger; 2nd dam Rosedale.

J. P. Cuddeback.

Can you let me know the make, color and description of a horse called Alexander Jr., bred in Sonoma County?

Answer—Write to Thomas Maclay, M. R. C. V. S., Petaluma, California.

Foals of 1890.

At San Luis Obispo; property of Brown and Taylor.

Black filly with white star, by Monroe S. he by Monroe Chief 875, dam Flora D. by Director 1989.

At Guenoc Stock Farm. Property of F. Gebhard.

Bay colt by St. Savior, dam Glen Queen by King Ban; foaled March 31st.

At Guenoc Stock Farm. Property of Hon. J. McM. Shafter.

Brown or bay colt by St. Savior, dam Night Hawk by imp. Haddington.

At Palo Alto, property of Hon. Leland Stanford;—

B c by Clay, dam Sallie Hamlet by Hamlet.
B c by Clay, dam Morgianna by General Benton.
B f by Electioneer, dam Elise by Mohawk Chief.
B f by Nephew, dam Gem by General Benton.
Br c by Beverly, dam Lulaneer, by Electioneer.
B f by Clay, dam Miss Walker by General Benton.
B c by Palo Alto, dam Wicket by General Benton.
B c by Clay, dam Tippera by Tipperary.
B c by Stamboul, dam Viola by General Benton.
B f by Electioneer, dam Niece by Nephew.
B f by Piedmont, dam Miss Knox by Knox.
B c by Azmoor, dam Ahwaga by General Benton.
B f by Electioneer, dam Flossy by General Benton.
B c by Electioneer, dam Eliza Dolph by Wildidle.
B f by Clay, dam Theressa by Don Victor.
Ch f by Palo Alto, dam Astoria by General Benton.

At Vina Ranch, Tehama County, Cal.;—

Ch c by Benefit, dam Miss Lancaster by Don Victor.
Br f by Clay, dam Nettie Walker by Mohawk Chief.
B c by Liberty, dam Enticia by Robert E Lee.
B c by Benefit, dam Cassie by Mohawk Chief.
B c by Piedmont, dam Kathleen by Shannon.
b f by Benefit, dam Electa by Electioneer.
B c by Benefit, dam Diva by Piedmont.
Grey c by Clay, dam Julia by Fred Low.
B c by Clay, dam Soprano by General Benton.
B f by Benefit, dam Gazelle Jr. by Primus.

Yours truly,

S. FERGUSON, Clerk.

Dr. Ross has arrived from Sacramento, and will be in attendance at the Blood Horse Association meeting.

Breeders' Directory.

Advertisements under this heading 50c. per line per month.

HORSES AND CATTLE.

W. S. JACOBS, Sacramento, Cal. — Breeder of Thoroughbred Shorthorns and Berkshire Hogs.

J. H. WHITE, Lakeville, Sonoma County—Breeder of Registered Holstein Cattle.

EL ROBLAS RANCHO—Los Alamos, Cal., Francis T. Underhill, proprietor, importer and breeder of thoroughbred Hereford Cattle. Information by mail. C. F. Swan, manager.

PAGE BROTHERS.—Penn's Grove, Sonoma Co. Cal. Breeders of Short-Horn Cattle; Draft, Roadster and Standard Bred Horses.

SETH COOK, breeder of Cleveland Bay Horses, Devon, Durham, Polled Aberdeen-Angus and Galloway Cattle. Young stock of above breeds on hand for sale. Warranted to be pure bred, recorded and average breeders. Address, Geo. A. Wiley, Cook Farm, Danville, Contra Costa Co., Cal.

MAMBRINO WILKES COLTS and FILLIES, full brothers and sisters to Gus. Wilkes, 2:22, and Balkan 2:29¼, for sale. Address SMITH HILL, Walnut Creek, Contra Costa County, Cal.

B. F. RUSH, Suisun, Cal., Shorthorns, Thoroughbred and Grades. Young Bulls and Calves for Sale.

PETER SAXE & SON, Lick House, San Francisco, Cal.—Importers and Breeders for past 18 years of every variety of Cattle, Horses, Sheep and Hogs.

HOLSTEIN THOROUGHBREDS of all the noted strains. Registered Berkshire Swine. Catalogues. F. H. BURKE, 401 Montgomery St., S. F.

Wanted.

A Saint Bernard Dog

ABOUT A YEAR OLD.

State price and where the Dog can be seen. Address A. P. S., care of Breeder and Sportsman Office.

FERGUSON & AUSTIN,

FRESNO, CAL.

Registered Polled Angus and Short-Horn Cattle.

JESSE E. MARKS & CO.,

Wholesale and Retail Dealers of Choice Brands

Havana & Key West Cigars

922 MARKET ST., S. F.

K STREET.

SECOND ST.

Singleton & Addington

BANK EXCHANGE,

SACRAMENTO.

Wines, Liquors & Cigars.

C. C. LINIMENT.

The Great Pain Conqueror for Man and Beast.

For Horsemen and Stockmen this Liniment is Invaluable

OWNERS OF FINE STOCK CANNOT AFFORD TO BE WITHOUT IT.

A remedy for every home, giving instant relief in pain and PERFORMING PERMANENT CURES.

To get the full benefit of the C. C. Liniment in chronic cases, in connection with C. C. Liniment use Compound Sulphur Powder, the "Great Blood Purifier," put up ONLY by The W. H. Bone Co., 17 Bush St., San Francisco. For Habitual Constipation, Indigestion, Piles, etc., it is the greatest remedy known to medical science.

If your druggist does not keep it, we will send direct, post paid, on receipt of price. COMPOUND SULPHUR POWDER is $1 per bottle, 6 for $5. Small bottles, 25c.

The C. C. Liniment Co

17 BUSH STREET, S. F.

W. H. BONE, - - General Manager.

FOR SALE BY ALL DRUGGISTS.

SHAW CARTS and SULKIES

For light road or track use, manufactured from the best selected material. Combines lightness with elegance and ease to riders. Weights 70 to 150 lbs. Used by the best horsemen on this coast. Inspection invited. ONE CAFFREY SULKY FOR SALE AT A BARGAIN.

CARRIAGES & Light VEHICLES

Manufactured to Order.

W. E. SHAW,

1621 MARKET STREET, SAN FRANCISCO, CAL.

REPAIRING DONE—ALL WORK WARRANTED.

AN UNQUALIFIED ENDORSEMENT.

Peruvian Bitters are made of the purest ingredients and compounded as carefully as any prescription.

Peruvian Bark, one of its principal ingredients, was introduced into Spain by the Countess, wife of Count CINCHON, Spanish Viceroy to Peru in 1630, who was cured of a fever by its use, since which time, no better remedy for Malaria and for Restoring the Natural Tone of the Stomach has been discovered.

On the Atlantic Coast they are used in the principal Hotels, Clubs and Restaurants, and sold by all Grocers and Druggists. We have sold them for the past three years WITHOUT ANY ADVERTISING and sales have constantly increased UPON MERIT ALONE, and we unqualifiedly recommend them to our friends and customers.

ACKER, MERRALL & CONDIT.

New York, Feb. 1st, 1890.

WILMERDING & CO., Agents for Pacific Coast,

216 FRONT ST., SAN FRANCISCO, CAL.

AUCTION SALE OF

Standard-Bred Trotters and ROADSTERS,

—AT—

AGRICULTURAL PARK, SACRAMENTO,

FRIDAY, - - May 2d, 1890,

At 1 o'clock P. M.

BY ORDER OF MR. S. E. TRYON

This sale will include the well known pacing mare POCAHONTAS, 2:22½. Heavy in foal to DEXTER PRINCE; g g EL MONTE 2:29½, brown pacer CASTELLO, 2:31½, and MAJESTER (3) at 2 years old 2:49¼, sired by Sterling 6223, dam Madam Baldwin (dam of Bay Rose 2:20½) by the Moor 870.

And twenty others, comprising broodmares, colts, fillies and geldings.

SALE POSITIVE.

Catalogues now being prepared.

KILLIP & CO., Auctioneers,

22 Montgomery Street, San Francisco.

FOR SALE.

A DARK BAY TROTTING STALLION

Sired by ALBERT W., by Stanford's Electioneer, dam, a Patchen mare. This stallion was foaled in 1884, stands 15¾ hands, and weighs 1000 lbs. Is a handsome dark bay with black points, and has shown a trial mile in 2:38. For further particulars apply at

2228 HOWARD ST., S. F.

FOR SALE.

Full Brother in Blood to Yolo Maid, 2:12 1-2.

A very fast pacer. No Record. Also a RUNNING MARE. Can run a half in 49 or better.

Apply to

G. W. BOUCHER,

Woodlands, Cal.

The Poodle Dog

"Rotisserie,"

FIRST-CLASS IN EVERY RESPECT.

Elegant Family Dining Rooms.

S. E. cor. GRANT AVE. and BUSH STREET.

ANDRE POTENTINI, Proprietor.

Pure Bred Clydesdale Mares

TWO MARES (Full Sisters) Five and Six Years Old, Weighing About 1,900 lbs. Each.

Sire imp. BEN. LOMOND.

Dam's sire imp. GLANCER.

For particulars apply to

H. A. MAYHEW,

Niles, Alameda County.

Brushes.

BUCHANAN BROS.,

Brush Manufacturers,

609 Sacramento Street, two doors above Montgomery.

Horse Brushes of every description on hand and made to order. Bristle Body Brushes our Specialty

McMaster Camping Car.

DRAWN BY TWO HORSES.

For the Tourist, Sportsman, Artist, Surveyor, Army Officer, Ranchman, Etc. Greatest invention of the age for Comfort. Send for Circular to

McMASTER MFG. CO., LOCKPORT, N. Y.

Sire of Yolo Maid, 2:12

Alexander Button 119

FOUR YEAR-OLD RECORD, 2:26 1-2

SIRE OF

YOLO MAID, 2:12½, BELLE BUTTON, 2:

TOM RIDER, 2:20½, ROSA MAC, 2:

J. H. (seperately timed in a race) 2:22½,

KEHOE, 2:34½, ALEX. BUTTON (3), 2:

BURBANK S. (2 y. o., ½-mile track), 2:53.

PEDIGREE.

Alex. Button was Sired by Alexander 4 Record, 2:31 1-4.

First dam Lady Button by Napa Rattler; 2d dam pacing mare (S. T. B.) by a Copperbottom horse.

ALEXANDER (490), record, 2:31½.

Sire of Alex. Button, 2:26 1-2, Reliance, 2:2 Tommy Dodd, 2:24, Nelly Patchen, 2:27 1-4, by Geo. Patchen Jr. (31), record 2:27; first dam Lady Crum Brown's Bellfounder.

GEO. M. PATCHEN JR (31), rec., 2:

Sire of Wells Fargo, 2:18¾, Sam Purdy, 2:20 1-2, derlynn, 2:21, Star King, 2:22, Ben Ali, 2:24, and others in the 2:1 list, by Geo. M. Patchen (30), 2:2 first dam Bell by Top Bellfounder, son of imp. founder; 2d dam Hoota Laddie mare.

GEO. M. PATCHEN (30). RECORD 2:

Sire of Lucy, 2:18¾; Chas. E. Low, 2:25¾; Geo. Patchen, Jr., 2:27; Mary, 2:2-; by Cassius M. Clay 1st dam by Head'em, son of imp. Trustee; 2nd Itaska, by American Eclipse.

CASSIUS M. CLAY (18).

Sire of Geo. M. Patchen, 2:23¼, etc.; by Henry (8). 1st dam Jersey Kate, the dam of John Ande

HENRY CLAY (8).

Sire of Black Douglass, 2:30; Centerville (w), by Andrew Jackson (4); 1st dam burry.

ANDREW JACKSON (4).

By Young Bashaw; dam an Ohio mare of unk blood.

YOUNG BASHAW.

By imp. Grand Bashaw; 1st dam Pearl, by Consul; 2nd dam Fancy, by imp. Messenger; 3rd by imp. Rockingham.

NAPA RATTLER.

By Biggart's Rattler; 1st dam Poll, by imp. Con nation; 2nd dam Betsy Baker, by Mambrino.

BIGGART'S RATTLER.

Grandsire of Joe. Brown, 2:22; Lady Snell, 2 Mary Davis, 2:2¾; Nellie Webster, 2:28¾, b Henry, son of the Garrett Horse, by imp. Leon 1st dam by the Hyde Horse, son of Long's Ma Bonum; 2nd dam of Messenger blood,

BROWN'S BELLFOUNDER.

By imp. Bellfounder; 1st dam Lady Allpor Mambrino; 2nd dam by Tippo Saib, son of imp. senger; 3rd dam by imp. Messenger.

DESCRIPTION.

ALEXANDER BUTTON is a dark bay with flowing mane and tail; stands 15-3¾ hands weighs 1,200 pounds, and is of excellent dispos He is a natural trotter, inherited through the lines of his ancestors, and imparts his speed to hi spring with uniform certainty. His colts show to be a wonderful producer—and with his bre and terms of service, he is the cheapest and wonderful horse in the State.

TERMS.

TERMS.—$100, payable at end of season. Mar proving with foal may be returned next season f charge. Good pasturage furnished at $1 per m and due care taken to prevent accidents or esc but no liability whatever assumed.

Will stand at Cache Creek Farm, which is sit about one and one-half miles west of Yolo Statio

All mares sent to Yolo in my care will be forw free of charge.

G. W. WOODARD, Proprietor.

Yolo, Yolo Co., C

HENRY J. COX W. S. JOH

The "EDWIN C

40 EDDY STREET,

Cor. of Mason, San Franc

(Private Entrance Mason Street.)

ROME HARRIS. JOHN MERI

"Laurel Palace

N. W. corner Kearny and Bush St

FRANCISCO

Stallion for Sal

AT A BARGAIN.

Full Brother to Fairmo

By Piedmont, dam Queen by Garibaldi—see Fair Edition of BREEDER AND SPORTS September 14, 1889, for description of Fairmont years old; solid bay. Can trot a 2:40 gait or b Sound in every particular. Can be seen at Oa Trotting Park, Oakland.

P. J. WILLIA

Highland Farn

LEXINGTON, KY.,

Home of Red Wilkes.

Standard-bred Trotting St

For Sale,

Sired by Red Wilkes, Wilton, 2:19¾; Allandorf Sentinel Wilkes, out of highly bred Standard of the most fashionable blood of the day.

W. C. FRANCE, Propri

Twenty-Third Annual Sale!

169
THOROUGHBREDS

64
YEARLINGS,
100
BROODMARES,
5
GREAT STALLIONS

23d ANNUAL SALE OF

Belle Meade Stud,

Will take place at BELLE MEADE STUD, near Nashville, Tennessee on

THURSDAY AND FRIDAY, APRIL 24 & 25

169 Head Thoroughbreds at Public Auction.

SOLD FOR DIVISION. | SOLD WITHOUT RESERVE

Five Great Stallions
To the Highest Bidder.

LUKE BLACKBURN
Imp GREAT TOM,
ENQUIRER,
BRAMBLE,
IROQUOIS.

FOR CATALOGUES ADDRESS THIS OFFICE.

P. C. KIDD, Auctioneer.

For other information and Catalogues address JOHN J. CARTER, No. 9 Baxter Block, Nashville, Tenn.

For Sale

A FIRST-CLASS

Napa County Farm

—OR—

STOCK RANCH,

800 Acres Improved,

SITUATED TWO AND A HALF MILES FROM NAPA CITY, with good roads leading thereto, a good hard finished house of nine rooms, with all modern improvements, streams running all summer, a great amount of live oak and black oak timber. It lies in a fruit belt, surrounded by fine vineyards and orchards growing upon the same quality of soil and originally a part of this tract. About one-half hill, and one-half rolling land, but none of it is steep and all easily cultivated, splendidly situated for the breeding of fine horses. Price, $65 per acre. Further particulars given at this office.

BREEDER AND SPORTSMAN,
313 Bush St.

A Grand Combination Sale

—OF—

Standard-bred Trotters & Thoroughbreds
CLYDESDALES AND PERCHERONS,
Fine Roadsters, Work Horses, Etc.

—AND—

Registered and Graded Holstein CATTLE,
REGISTERED JACKS,
And other first-class Live Stock of all kinds, will be held at
CARSON CITY, NEV., April 15, 16 and 17, '90.

BROOD MARES, COLTS AND FILLIES by the following well known Sires will be sold:

Standard Bred.
ECHO,
GIBRALTAR, (will be sold)
PROMPTER,
BUCCANEER,
ST. CLAIR,
SIGNAL,
BLUE BULL,
ST. LAWRENCE,

Thoroughbred.
NORFOLK,
HOOKER,
LODI,
BRECKENBRIDGE,
THREE CHEERS,
LANGFORD,
BOI DE ARC,
McMAHON.

And among the fine stock to be offered will be the grand HOLSTEIN BULL SARATOGA, and a number of calves and heifers by him and other well known thoroughbred Holsteins.
Over 1?0 entries were made up to March 1st, and a big sale is assured.
Send in your entries.
For further particulars address

JNO. P. SWEENY & CO., Carson City, Nev.

Important Closing Out SALE

—OF—

Trotting-Bred Stock,

COMPRISING THE ENTIRE STUD OF
JOHN G. HILL, Esq., of Ventura, California.

—TO BE HELD IN—

San Francisco,
Thursday. - - - May 15th, 1890.

It will embrace about 80 head of well bred Stallions, Mares and Geldings, principally the get of that celebrated standard bred sire

A. W. RICHMOND, 1687,

out of thoroughbred mares mostly from that noted horse, Woodburn, sire of Monarch 2:28½, and the dam of Victor 2:22, and others.

This will no doubt be the last opportunity at public auction to obtain the blood of this great sire, that, in part, has made ANTEEO, ANTEVOLO, ARROW, ROMERO, RICHMOND Jr., and others famous in the trotting history of our State.

The sale is positive and without reserve, as Mr. Hill will engage in other business.

☞ Catalogues now being prepared.

KILLIP & CO., Auctioneers,
22 Montgomery Street, San Francisco, Cal.

RUNNYMEDE, COLDSTREAM & LOUDOUN

-Thoroughbred Yearlings-

Will be sold at Auction
On Monday, May 5th, 1890,
—AT—
LACELAND, - - - - near Paris, Ky., at 12 M.

These yearlings are the get of Hindoo, imp. Billet, Leonatus, Onondaga, Fonso, Alarm, Springbok, [illegible]ession, King Alfonso and Ben d'Or. They include full brothers to Hanover, Jim Gore, Bedford and [illegible] Lioness, Saltston, Perkins, Modolin, Burton and Millie, and Miss Molley; sisters to Runnymede, [illegible]nes, Meriden, Sarvis, Cameo, Heathen, Hindoo Rose and Lillian Lindsay and Sunbeam; half-brothers [illegible] Pure Rye, Ocean Middleaton, Catalpa, Miss Thomas, Winslow and Stoney Montgomery and Longshore, [and] half-sisters to Alarm Bell, Warren Lewis, Shelby Barnes, Florence E., and Brussells and Kilkenney.

☞ THE LARGEST WINNING HORSE AND LARGEST WINNING MARE ON THE AMERICAN TURF WERE BOTH BRED AT RUNNYMEDE.

For catalogues, apply to

BAXTER & STRINGFIELD,
Box 35. Room 1, Reed Building, Lexington, Ky.

ANNUAL SPRING SALE

—OF—

200 HEAD

Road & Harness Horses

AND

Work and Draft Horses
AND SHETLAND PONIES!
From the Ranches of J. B. Haggin, Esq.

WILL TAKE PLACE AT

RAILROAD STABLES,
Corner Turk and Steiner Streets, San Francisco,
AT 10 A. M., ON

Tuesday, May 6, 1890,

Catalogues will be issued immediately.

KILLIP & CO., Live Stock Auctioneers,
22 Montgomery Street, S. F.

Poplar Grove Breeding FARM.

Standard-bred Trotters, Colts and Fillies.

The get of CLOVIS, 4909; PASHA, 2039; APEX, 2935.

For Sale.

Address S. N. STRAUBE, Poplar Grove Breeding Farm,
Fresno, Cal.

Inspection by intending purchasers invited, and information by mail.

AUCTION SALE

—OF—

Brood Mares,
Colts and Fillies,
Harness & Draft Horses

—The property of—

D. J. MURPHY, San Jose.

TO BE SOLD AT

Public Auction,

—AT 11 A. M., ON—

Wednesday, April 16, '90

—AT—

Fair Ground, San Jose,

KILLIP & CO., Auctioneers,
22 Montgomery Street S., F., Cal.

Catalogues may be had on application.

BROOD MARE for SALE

DOT,

By WHIPPLE'S HAMBLETONIAN 725, dam, Victoria by Jerseyman (son of Geo. M. Patchen Jr., 31), 2nd dam Whiskey Jane (dam of Sam Purdy 2:20½). This mare will be sold at a reasonable figure. For further particulars apply AT THIS OFFICE.

FOR SALE

AT

Vineland Stock Farm

STALLIONS, BROODMARES AND FILLIES

ONE STALLION FIVE YEARS OLD, SEAL-BROWN, by WHIPPLETON (sire of Lilly Stanley, 2:17 1-2 Homestakes 2:16 1-2, etc.), dam Sally Gorham by Werner's Rattler. This horse is scarcely 15 1-2 hands high, but very compactly built. He breeds exceptionally large and well finished colts. Any one understanding the business could clear him in one season, or he would make a No. 1 road horse, as he can trot a 40 gait any time.

ONE THREE-YEAR-OLD, SEAL-BROWN, by WHIPPLETON (sire of Lilly Stanley, 2:17 1-2, Homestakes 2:16 1-2, etc.) dam Sally Gorham, etc. This ought to make a great General Purpose sire, and with opportunities get trotters, as he is compact, strong-boned, and will measure when grown about 16 hands and weighs 1,?00 lbs. With a little road work last fall he developed a wonderful burst of speed.

ONE THREE-YEAR-OLD, BLACK, by WHIPPLETON (sire of Lilly Stanley, 2:17 1-2, etc.), dam by Nanbuc (sire of the dam of Eva W. 2:23 1-2, etc.), full brother to Thomas Jefferson, 2:23. This horse will be fully 16 1-2 hands high. He is smooth rapid gaited and from size and conformation should breed, like his sire, large, rangy, finished colts.

ONE TWO-YEAR-OLD, BRIGHT CHESTNUT, sired by DAWN 2:18¾, dam Alida (dam of Directa, three-year-old record 2:31½, trial 2:20) by Admiral (sire of sister 2:10 1-2, Nona Y 2:25, etc). This colt is the making of an extraordinary horse. He is large boned and will be over sixteen hands high when grown; he is of the true Nutwood type, is clean gaited and can lead a piece as fast as any man's colt.

ONE TWO-YEAR-OLD, BLOOD BAY, (full brother to Alcona Jr. sire of Silas Skinner trial 2:23) sired by ALCONA (sire of Flora Belle 2:24, etc.) dam Madonna by Cassius M. Clay Jr. This colt will make a trotter and a great stock horse if developed; he has the combined blood of Almont, Mambrino Chief, Cassius M. Clay Jr. and Joe Downing.

These colts are all sound and promising. The only reason I offer them for sale is, that I have three aged stallions in use, and the surplus is growing on me. If I were starting a breeding business for profit, I should consider either of these colts a representative to commence with. Also brood mares and fillies for sale. Correspondence solicited.

FRED. W. LOEBER, St. Helena,
Napa Co., Cal.

Speed Programme

—OF THE—

Twelfth District Ag'l Society

To be held at

LAKEPORT,

SEPTEMBER 23 to 27 INCLUSIVE.

First Day—Tuesday, Sept. 23, 1890.

RACE NO. 1—TROTTING.

Yearling stake; $150 guaranteed. Entrance $30, payable as follows: $5 May 1st, $10 July 1, $10 September 1st (when entry must be named), and $5 additional for starters. Entries to close May 1, 1890. See general conditions.

RACE NO. 2—RUNNING.

One-half mile dash. $100 added; $25 to second. Entrance $10, to close 6 P. M. day before race.

RACE NO. 3—TROTTING.

Three-minute class. Mile heats 3 in 5. District. $150 added. Entrance $20; to close 6 P. M. day before race. 5 to enter, 3 to start. See general conditions.

Second Day—Wednesday, September 24th

RACE NO. 4—RUNNING.

Three-quarter mile heats; 2 in 3. $200 added; $25 to second. Entrance $10, to close 6 P. M. day before race.

RACE NO. 5—TROTTING.

District Stallion. Mile heats 3 in 5. Purse $350. Entrance $30, to close 6 P. M. day before race. 5 to enter, 3 to start. See general conditions.

RACE NO. 6—TROTTING.

Three-year-old stake; $300 guaranteed. $30 entrance, payable as follows: May 1st, $10; July 1st, $10; September 1, $10 (when entry must be named), and $15 additional to start. Open to Napa, Solano, Sonoma, Marin, Lake, Colusa, Yolo, Mendocino and Humboldt Counties.

Third Day—Thursday, Sept. 25th.

RACE NO. 7—RUNNING.

Seven-eighths mile dash. $150 added; $25 to second. Entrance $10, to close 6 P. M. day before race.

RACE NO. 8—TROTTING.

Two-year-old stake; free for all. Mile heats; best 2 in 3. $200 guaranteed. Entrance $30, payable as follows: May 1st, $10; July 1st, $10; September 1st, $10, and $15 additional to start. See general conditions.

Fourth Day—Friday, Sept. 26th.

RACE NO. 9—TROTTING.

Mile heats, 3 in 5. For all described counties in race No. 6. $400 added. Entrance $50, payable as follows: May 1st, $10; July 1st, $20; September 1st, $20—when entries must be named—$10 additional to start. See general conditions.

RACE NO. 10—RUNNING.

Citizens' Handicap. $100 added. Five-eighths mile; heats, 2 in 3. Entrance $10, to close 6 P. M. day before race.

Fifth Day—Saturday, September 27th.

RACE NO. 11—RUNNING.

GENTLEMEN'S NOVELTY.—For non-professional jockeys. One mile dash. $10 added; $5 entrance. Purse divided as follows: First horse at each quarter to get $5; slowest average at all quarters to get Society medal.

NO. 12—LADIES' TOURNAMENT.

Free for all, in District. Purse $50, divided as follows: $25 to first, $15 to second, $10 to third.

No. 13.—GENTLEMAN'S TROTTING.

Same conditions as gentlemen's Novelty. Mile heats, two in three. Entrance $5. Entrance money divided 50, 30 and 10 per cent.

GENERAL CONDITIONS.

Nominations in colt stakes transferrable any time before colts are named. If the payments in stake races amount to more than the sum guaranteed the additional amount to be divided 60, 30 and 10 per cent; in case of only two starting, 60 and 40 per cent.; and in case of one horse walking over, the whole amount to go to such horse.

A failure to make any payment when due shall be considered a withdrawal, and forfeiture of the amounts paid in. National Rules to govern all trotting races. The right reserved to refund the first payment in case the stake does not fill satisfactorily.

All running races, unless otherwise specified, governed by the Pacific Coast Blood Horse Association Rules.

The Directors reserve the right to change the hour and date of any race, and in case of a race being antedated the nominator will receive notice.

A horse distancing the field shall receive only first and third moneys.

L. G. SIMMONS, President.

A. B. McCUTCHEN, Secretary.

San Joaquin Valley

AGRICULTURAL ASSOCIATION.

Stockton Fair, 1890,

September 23 to 27 inclusive.

TROTTING COLT STAKES.

$50 each, of which $10 must accompany nomination, $15 to be paid July 1st, and $25 on Monday, September 1, 1890.

Failure to make payments as above forfeits previous payments.

PACIFIC COAST STAKES.

For 2-year-olds..........2 in 3 } $200
3 " " ....3 in 5 } added to
4 " " ....3 in 5 } each.
2 " " ....Pacing 2 in 3 }

SAN JOAQUIN VALLEY STAKES.

Open to all San Joaquin Valley counties for colts owned in the valley, February 1, 1890.

For 2-year-olds..........2 in 3 } $150
3 " " ....3 in 5 } added to
4 " " ....3 in 5 } each.
2 " " ....Pacing 2 in 3 }

Five or more full paid up entries required to fill; three or more colts to start. Four moneys: 50, 25, 15 and 10 per cent. In case of only two colts starting, they may compete for the stakes paid in only, two-thirds and one-third, otherwise full conditions of this Association for 1889, to govern.

Entries close Thursday, May 1, 1890, with the Secretary,

J. M. LARUE, P. O. box 188, Stockton, Cal.

L. U. SHIPPEE, President.

Pacific Coast

Trotting-Horse

Breeders' Ass'n.

ADDITIONAL

Stakes & Installment Purses

FOR 1890.

Entries to close May 1, 1890.

Trotting Stakes.

THREE YEAR OLDS—FOALS OF 1887.

Eligible to 2:40 class. Mile heats, best three in five. Entrance $50, with $300 added. Entrance payable, $10 May 1st, 1890, $15 July 1st, 1890, and $25 on the fifth day preceding the first advertised day of the meeting.

FOUR YEAR OLDS—FOALS 1886.

Eligible to 2:30 class. Mile heats, best three in five. Entrance $50, with $400 added. Entrance payable, $10 on May 1st, 1890, $15 on July 1st, 1890 and $25 on the fifth day preceding the first advertised day of the meeting.

Nomination Trotting Purses.

$2,000. Stallion Purse.

Open to stallions eligible to the 2:18 class. Mile heats best three in five. Entrance $200 payable $40 May 1st, 1890, $40 July 1st, 1890, $40 August 1st 1890, and $80 on the tenth day preceding the first advertised day of the meeting. Horses to be named at time of last payment.

$2,000, Free For All.

Mile heats, best three in five. Entrance $200, payable $40 May 1st 1890, $40 July 1st 1890, $40 August 1st 1890, and $80 on the tenth day preceding the first advertised day of the meeting. Horses to be named at time of last payment.

$1,500. Five-Year-Olds, Foals 1885.

Mile heats best three in five. Entrance $150, payable $30 May 1, 1890, $30 July 1, 1890, $30 August 1, 1890, and $60 on the tenth day preceding the first advertised day of the meeting. Horses to be named at the time of the last payment.

$1,500. 2:22 Class.

Mile heats, best three in five. Entrance $150. Payable $30 May 1, 1890, $30 July 1, 1890, $30 August 1, 1890, and $60 on the tenth day preceding the first advertised day of the meeting. Horses to be named at the time of the last payment.

$1,500. 2:27 Class.

Mile heats, best three in five. Entrance $150. Payable $30 May 1, 1890, $30 July 1, 1890, $30 August 1, 1890, and $60 on the tenth day preceding the first advertised day of the meeting. Horses to be named at time of last payment.

Nomination Pacing Purses.

$1,500. Free For All.

Mile heats, best three in five. Entrance $150. Payable $30 May 1, 1890, $30 July 1, 1890, $30 August 1, 1890, and $60 on the tenth day preceding the first advertised day of the meeting. Horses to be named at time of last payment.

$1,000. 2:25 Class.

Mile heats, best three in five. Entrance $100. Payable $20 May 1, 1890, $20 July 1, 1890, $20 August 1, 1890, and $40 on the tenth day preceding the first advertised day of the meeting. Horses to be named at time of last payment.

Conditions.

First payment, whether for purses payable in installments or for stakes, MUST ACCOMPANY NOMINATIONS, or they will not be considered.

Neglect to make payments on the dates stipulated will incur forfeiture of all previous payments.

No horses and colts owned on the Pacific Coast by others than members of the P. C. T. H. B. A. are eligible to the above purses and stakes, but horses and colts OWNED outside of the Pacific Coast are eligible thereto regardless of membership.

All States and Territories lying in whole or in part west of the Rocky Mountains are held to be part of the Pacific Coast.

The Directors reserve the right to change the hour and day of any race except when it becomes necessary to antedate a race, in which instance the nominator will receive three days notice of change by mail to address of entry.

Entries not declared out by 6 P. M. of the day preceding the race, shall be required to start.

When there is more than one entry to stakes by one person or in one interest, the horse to be started must be named by 6 P. M. of the day preceding the race.

Purses and stakes will be divided into four moneys, viz., 50 per cent. to the winner, 25 per cent. to the second horse, 15 per cent. to the third horse, and 10 per cent. to the fourth horse.

No added money will be paid for a walk-over. If only three horses start in a stake race, only first, second and third money shall be paid—if but two start, the Directors reserve the right to call it a walk-over, and divide the stake money paid in, two-thirds to the winner and one-third to the second horse. In case of a walk-over, only the money received from entries to said stake will be paid.

A horse distancing the field shall only be entitled to first and third moneys.

The Board of Directors reserve the right to declare any purse or stake filled or not filled without binding itself to any specified number of entries.

In all nomination purses, eight entries will be required to fill, and four to make the last payment.

Trotting and racing colors shall be named by six o'clock on the day preceding the race, and MUST be worn upon the track.

Horses eligible in class races on records standing at time of entry.

Otherwise than the above National or American Trotting Association Rules—as this Association may select—will govern the stake and purse races offered.

Persons desirous of making entries in the above purses and stakes, and who have not as yet joined the P. C. T. H. B. A., should make application for membership to the Secretary, and remit the sum of $25 to cover membership fee before May 1, 1890.

J. H. WHITE, President.

JAS. P. KERR, Secretary, 13 Bush Street, S. F.

ENTIRE CHANGE

—OF—

PROGRAMME

—OF THE—

Extra Attractions

To take place at the

Oakland.

Fall Meeting, 1890,

UNDER THE MANAGEMENT OF THE

GOLDEN GATE

Fair Association

NOMINATION PURSES.

In which entries close in the name of owners or trainers on May 15th. All nominations transferable and nominators held only for amounts paid in. Horses must be named five days before first advertised day of the meeting. Eight nominations required to fill, four of which must make last payments.

THE NEW LIST PURSE $1000.

For three-year-olds whose sires up to January 1, 1890, have not produced an animal with a record of 2:30 or better at three years of age or under. Entrance 10 per cent. payable as follows:

$25 May 15th, when entries close in the names of owners or trainers.

$25 June 15th.

$25 July 15th.

$25 five days before first advertised day of meeting, when horses must be named.

GUARANTEED PURSE $1200.

For three-minute class, entrance 10 per cent, payable as follows:

$30 May 15th, when entries close in names of owners or trainers.

$30 June 15th.

$30 July 15th.

$30 five days before first advertised day of meeting, when horse must be named.

GUARANTEED PURSE $1200.

For 2:40 class, entrance 10 per cent. payable as follows:

$30 May 15th, when entries close in names of owners or trainers.

$30 June 15th.

$30 July 15th.

$30 five days before first advertised day of meeting, when horses must be named.

—ALSO A—

Guaranteed Futurity Purse $4,000.

To take place during the Fall Meeting of 1893.

For foals of 1890. Entrance 5 per cent. payable as follows:

$10 May 15, 1890, when entries close in name of foals or of dams and sires.

$10 Jan. 15, 1891.
$15 June 15, 1891.
$15 Jan. 15, 1892.
$15 June 15, 1892.
$25 Jan. 15, 1893.
$30 June 15, 1893.

$60 fifteen days before advertised day of the race.

If the last payment is made on twelve or more entries the horses shall be started in trial races, in which not more than eleven or less than six shall be allotted to start. The trial races shall be mile heats, three in five, for a purse of $1,000, given by the Association for each race. If two trial races are trotted, the first four horses shall only be entitled to start in the final race. If three such trial races are trotted, only the first three horses in each trial race shall start in the final; and if four or more trial races are necessary, only the first two horses in each trial race shall start in the final race.

These trial races must be started not less than five nor more than ten days previous to the day set for the final race; and if possible all trial races will be trotted on the same day.

CONDITIONS.

Neglect to provide payments on the dates stipulated will incur forfeiture of all previous payments.

The Directors reserve the right to change the hour and day of any race except when it becomes necessary to antedate a race, in which instance the nominator will receive three days notice of change by mail to address of entry.

Entries not declared out by 6 P. M. the day preceding the race shall be required to start.

Purses will be divided into four moneys viz., 50 per cent. to the winner, 25 per cent. to the second horse, 15 per cent. to the third horse, and 10 per cent. to the fourth horse.

A horse distancing the field shall only be entitled to first and third moneys.

Trotting and racing colors shall be named by six o'clock on the day preceding the race, and MUST be worn upon the track.

All purse races, mile heats, best three in five to harness.

Otherwise than the above, National or American Trotting Association Rules—as this Association may select—will govern the races offered.

Entries to close with the Secretary.

R. T. CARROLL, President.

JOS. I. DIMOND, Sec'y, 806 Market St., S. F.

HORSES PURCHASED ON COMMISSION.

THOROUGHBREDS A SPECIALTY.

Will select and buy, or buy selected Animals for all desiring, for reasonable compensation

KEEPS PROMISING YOUNGSTERS IN VIEW.

L. M. LASLEY, Stanford, Ky.

References:—J. W. Guest, Danville, Ky.
B. G. Bruce, Lexington, Ky.
S. H. Baughman, Stanford, Ky.
G. A. Lackey, Stanford, Ky.
Geo. McAlister, Stanford, Ky.
First National Bank, Stanford, Ky.

Solano and Napa Agricultural Society.

Trotting Colt Guarantee Stake[s] for 1890.

The Solano and Napa Agricultural Societ[y] have opened the following Colt Stakes fo[r] Trotters:

NO. 1. TWO YEAR OLDS.—Free for all; $100 guaranteed. $50 entrance, payable as follows: $10 April 1st, when entries close; $10 May 1st, $10 June 1st, $10 July 1st, $10 August 1st, when colts must be named. Nominations transferrable any time before colts are named. If the payments amount to more than the amounts guaranteed the additional amount to be added to the stake. All moneys divided as follows: 60, 30 and 10 per cent; in case of only two starting, 60 and 40 per cent; and in case of one horse walking over the whole amount to go to such horse. A failure to make any payment when due shall be considered a withdrawal and forfeiture of the amounts paid in. National or American Rules to govern, as the Society may elect. The right reserved to refund the first payment in case the stakes do not fill reasonably well.

No. 2. FOR THREE YEAR OLDS.—Free for all; $500 guaranteed. $100 entrance, payable as follows: $20 April 1st, when entries close; $20 May 1st, $20 June 1st, $20 July 1st, $20 August 1st, when colts must be named. Conditions same as in No. 1.

District colt stakes for districts comprising Counties of Solano, Napa, Sonoma, Marin, Lake, Colusa, Yolo, Mendocino, Humboldt and Butte.

No. 3. FOR YEARLINGS.—$250 guaranteed. District. $40 entrance, payable as follows: $10 April 1st, when entries close; $10 June 1st, $10 July 1st, $10 August 1st, when colts must be named. Conditions same as in No. 1.

No. 4. FOR TWO YEAR OLDS.—$350 guaranteed. District. $50 entrance, payable as follows: $10 April 1st, when entries close; $10 May 1st, $10 June 1st, $10 July 1st, $10 August 1st when colts must be named. Conditions same as in No. 1.

No. 5. FOR THREE YEAR OLDS.—$500 guaranteed. District. $60 entrance, payable as follows: $10 April 1st when entries close; $10 May 1st, $10 June 1st, $10 July 1st, $10 August 1st, when colts must be named. Conditions same as in No. 1.

Yearling Stake. Single dash; one mile. Two Year Olds.—Mile heats, two in three. Three Year Olds. Three in five, to harness. Parties entering colts will be notified by mail when payment becomes due.

The Society also offers the following stakes for old horses.

TROTTING STAKES.—Free for all.

2:30 CLASS Trotting; purse $1500.
2:24 CLASS—Trotting; purse $1500.
2:20 CLASS—Trotting; purse $1500.

Horses eligible January 1st, 1890. Entrance $[illegible] payable as follows: $25 April 1st, when entries close; $25 May 1st, $25 June 1st, $25 July 1st $50 August 1st when horses must be named. Nominations transferable any time before August 1st. Right reserved to refund entrance fee in any of the stakes should they not fill reasonably well. Money divided, 50, 25, 15 and 10 per cent. National or American Association Rules to govern, as the Society shall elect. To be trotted at our regular summer meeting, upon days to be hereafter arranged.

Entries to close April 1st, 1890, with

A. H. CONKLING, Secretary, Napa City, Ca[l].

L. L. JAMES, President.

Second Annual Bench Sho[w]

OF THE

South'n Californi[a]

Kennel Club

AT THE

City of Los Angele[s]

MAY 6, 7, 8 & 9 '90.

The SOUTHERN CALIFORNIA KENNEL CL[UB] was admitted a member of the AMERICAN KENN[EL] CLUB September 18, 1889. The coming show [will] therefore be held under the A. K. C. rules.

Entries will positively close May 1st.

A special committee will take personal charge [of] all dogs sent from a distance and insure their pro[per] care. For premium lists and entry blanks address K. BENCHLEY, Secretary, 14 South Spring Str[eet], Los Angeles; or H. H. BRIGGS, Breeder and Spo[rts]man, San Francisco.

Antevolo Colt

FOR SALE.

REX VOLO, foaled February 22nd 1888, [illegible] Catchup by Rustler; granddam Huntess by Don [illegible] tor; great granddam Bettie Denice by American [illegible] Jr. Is 15.1 hands high, well developed, musc[ular] and without a blemish. Has a very gentle disp[osi]tion, and shows speed and a good gait.

HOME FURNISHING CO., 126 Fifth Street, S. F. Ca[l].

ARGONAUT HERD.

POLLED ABERDEEN—ANGUS CATTL[E]

Thirty head choice pure bred and high grade (c[ross] bred) HEIFERS and a few grand young BULLS [for] sale at reasonable prices. A fine opportunity for [per]sons wishing to establish choice herds or cha[nge] their bulls. Representatives from this herd w[ere] grand prize winners at the last California State F[air]. Address DR. G. M. DIXON, Sacramento, Ca[l].

For Sale.

14

Pure bred

PERCHERONS

Stallions and Mares.

OF ALL AGES.

Part Imported, and all Registered Pr[...]

For further information, address

E. J. TURNER, Hollister, Ca[l].

CALIFORNIA

NUTWOOD

Will stand for mares the season of 1890, commencing February 15th, and ending July 15th, at the NUTWOOD STOCK FARM, one mile from Irvington.

DESCRIPTION AND PEDIGREE.

He is a dark chestnut, with star in forehead; foaled September 16th, 1881; is 16 hands 1½ inches high and weighs 1250 pounds. Has a beautiful flowing mane and tail, with remarkable style and lofty carriage, a bold, open movement like his sire, but has never been handled for speed. He moves and looks like his sire, except that he is a larger horse.

CALIFORNIA NUTWOOD by Nutwood, record 2:18¾, has 32 trotters and pacers with records from 2:15 to 2:30, and put 8 in the 2:30 list in 1889. He is the only horse that ever lived with a record under 2:20 that produced five under 2:20. He is now serving mares at Dubuque, Iowa, at $500 for the season, and his colts at yearlings sell from $2500 to $5000 each. He is out of the dam of Maud S., record 2:08¾.

Nutwood, by Alexander's Belmont, sire of 52 with records from 2:15½ to 2:30. Alexander's Belmont by Alexander's Abdallah, sire of Goldsmiths Maid, record 2:14, and 5 others in 2:30 list. Alexander's Abdallah, by Rysdyk's Hambletonian, sire of 41 with records from 2:17¼ to 2:30, and is the founder of the Hambletonian family.

FANNY PATCHEN, dam of California Nutwood, by George M. Patchen Jr., record 2:27, and sire of Wells Fargo, 2:18¼, Sam Purdy 2:20½, Ben Ali 2:20½, and 7 others from 2:21 to 2:30. He has 7 sons who together produced 12 trotters in 2:30 list, and 5 daughters who together produced 5 trotters and 1 pacer in 2:30 or better. He sired Alexander 2:31½. Alexander sired Alex. Button 2:26½; Alex. Button sired Yolo Maid, pacing record 2:14 at 4 years old, the fastest on record; George M. Patchen Jr., by George M. Patchen 2:23½, is sire of Lucy 2:18¼, and 3 others in the 2:30 list; he has 12 sons who together produced 40 trotters from 2:14¾ to 2:30, and 6 daughters who together produced 6 trotters in 2:30 list or better, he is grand sire of Hopeful 2:14¾, and best wagon record 2:16½, and sire of the granddam of Stamboul 2:12½.

George M. Patchen, by Cassius M. Clay, and he by Henry Clay, founder of the Clay family.

Laura, second dam of California Nutwood, was a large bay mare, a very fast roadster brought from Chicago by Wm. Wilson, of San Jose, and is said to have made a record of 2.35 in Chicago. Pedigree not traced.

TERMS.

$40 for the season, payable invariably before the animal is removed. Mares not proving in foal can be returned free next season. Pasturage $3 per month, but no liability for accidents or escapes.

For further particulars address the owner,

MARTIN CARTER,

Newark, Alameda Co., Cal., or Irvington, Alameda County, Cal.

Bay Rose.

REGISTERED No. 9814.

Record 2:20 1-2 Third Heat.

Will make the season of 1890, ending July 1st, at the SANTA ROSA STOCK FARM, (formerly Santa Rosa Race Track), SANTA ROSA.

DESCRIPTION.

BAY ROSE is a dark bay or brown, with black points, 16¼ hands high, and weighs 1150 pounds. He is remarkably intelligent, of good disposition, and a pure-gaited trotter. He was foaled in 1881. His colts are large, stylish, rangy animals, and inherit the qualities of speed and endurance.

PEDIGREE.

Sultan, 2:24, Sire of 19 in the 2:30 list.
- The Moor 870, sire of Beautiful Bells 2:29½, Del Sur 2:24½, Inez 2:30, Sir Guy 2:28½, Sultan 2:24, Tommy Gates 2:24
- Sultana.

Madam Baldwin
- The Moor 870, Sire of 6 in the 2:30 list.
- by Ben Lippincott, by Williamson's Belmont.

TERMS: $200 FOR THE SEASON.

Good pasturage $3 per month. First-class care taken of mares in any manner that owners may desire, but no responsibility assumed for escapes or accidents. Limited to a few approved mares.

For further particulars, address

THOS. BONNER,

Santa Rosa Stock Farm, Santa Rosa.

Apply to

IRA PIERCE,

728 Montgomery Street, S. F., Cal.

Sunny Side Breeding Farm.

Admiral 488.

Foaled 1867—Sired by Volunteer 55, Son of Rysdyk's Hambletonian 10.

First dam Lady Pierson by Cassius M. Clay (Neaves') second dam by Diamond; third dam a running mare said to be thoroughbred. He is fitted in an eminent degree to produce colts that will in all respects justify his patrons in their expectations.

Admiral is the sire of Huntress, record 2:27¼, Sister, 2:19½, Perhelion, 2:25, Nona Y., 2:25, and others equally as promising, but have not had the advantage of track work. He will serve a limited number of approved mares at $50 the season, with usual return privilege. Season ending August 1, 1890. No liability for accidents or escapes.

KING DAVID 2576.

Bay Stallion—Foaled 1883.

Sired by Admiral 488, dam Black Flora (the dam of Huntress, 2:27¼, Sister, 2:19½, Perhelion, 2:25, Nona Y. 25), by Black Prince.

King David is one of the best gets of Admiral, has a good disposition, kind to drive, smooth and pure-gaited, and can speed fast. Barring accidents, will trot in the twenties this Fall. His colts are large, rangy, and well finished. Will serve a limited number of mares at $30 the season, to end July 1, 1890. Every precaution will be taken to prevent accidents and escapes, but no liability will be assumed. Pasturage $4 per month.

Sunny Side Farm is situated two miles east of Vallejo on the Sulphur Spring road. For further particulars, address

FRANK DRAKE,

Vallejo, Cal.

The Pure Trotting-bred Stallion

ILLUSTRIOUS

STANDARD No. 4178.

DESCRIPTION.

Dark bay, black points, 15 1-2 hands high, weight 1000 pounds, foaled May 30, 1885; bred by General W. T. Withers, Lexington, Ky.

PEDIGREE.

By Happy Medium, sire of Maxey Cobb 2:13¼ and 52 with records of 2:30 or better.

First dam Abdalletta by Cassius M. Clay Jr., sire of Durango 2:23½, Harry Clay 2:23½, and sire of the dams of Minnehaha, Bertha 2:27½, Charley West 2:28½, Grandmont 2:25 1-4, Lottie K 2:26½, Mambrino Diamond 2:26, Richwood 2:26 1-2, Topsy 2:26½, Happy Thought 2:21 1-2, Pequot 2:28 1-2, Fairlawn Medium 2:27 1-2, Folley 2:27½, and Mambrino Boy 2:26 1-2.

Second dam Laura Crockett by Almont, sire of Westmont 2:13¾, Puritan 2:16, Fanny Witherspoon 2:16¼, Piedmont 2:17¼, Aldine 2:19½, and 37 with records better than 2:30.

Third dam Sally Tee by Alexander's Abdallah, sire Goldsmith Maid 2:14.

Fourth dam Kate Crockett, the dam of Lulu 2:14¾, by imp Hooton.

Illustrious is a horse of extra fine finish, large clean bone, good feet, back short and strong, loins and quarters well muscled, and powerful. He has a kind disposition and splendid trotting action, and is as handsome and bloodlike in form and finish as any trotting stallion in the land.

He is pronounced by his breeder, General Withers, to be the best bred son of Happy Medium living, and is undoubtedly one of the very best bred trotting stallions in the State. He has had but six weeks' regular training, and a part of that time was sick with epizootic, but was trotted quarters in 39 1-4 seconds, and barring accidents will certainly trot better than 2:30 this season.

TERMS—$50 the season. Mares not proving with foal may be returned next year free.

Good pasturage at $8 per month.

Season to begin February 1st and end June 15th.

GEO. A. STONE,

Santa Rosa, Cal.

LAWN VIEW BREEDING FARM STALLIONS.

ACTOR.

A beautiful bay horse foaled 1887 by Prompter 2305 sire of Apex (four-year-old record) 2:26, Transit 2:28½, Creole 2:20, Blue Belle 2:22, Daisy (yearling record) 2:36½, he by Blue Bull 75, 1st dam by Sultan 1513 2:24, sire of Stamboul 2:12 1-4, Ruby 2:19¾, Sweetheart 2:22½, Alcazar 2:20½, Eva 2:22½, La Grange 2:23½, and eleven others in 2:30 list, second dam by Fireman by Langford.

Actor, as his pedigree shows, is as purely bred a young stallion as ever made a season in the stud. Blue Bull stock is much sought after in the East, and Sultan, sire of his first dam will make the season in Kentucky this year at $400 per mare. Actor is a handsome bay colt 16 hands high, clean limbed and possesses all the points of a speedy trotter.

TERMS, $40 FOR THE SEASON, usual return privileges.

DOUGLASDALE 7650.

Thoroughbred Registered Clydesdale Stallion

Imported from Scotland, December, 1889, ba , three years old.

TERMS, $35 FOR THE SEASON.

YOUNG ELMO

Two years old sorrel stallion by St. Elmo 2:27, dam by Woodburn.

TERMS, $20 FOR THE SEASON.

For further particulars, address

MANAGER LAWN VIEW FARM, Auburn, Cal.

The Trotting-Bred Stallion

RINGWOOD

THE FINEST SON OF THE NOTED SIDNEY,

Will make a Season at Oakland, commencing March 1, and ending June 1, 1890.

DESCRIPTION.

RINGWOOD is a dark, rich colored bay, black points, 15 1-2 hands, weight 1100 lbs., and a pure gaited trotter. Has shown great speed. He is now five years old. As a four year old he showed a trial in 2:19 1-2, and but for an accident would have received a record as a four year old of 2:18 or better.

PEDIGREE.

RINGWOOD is by Sidney, record 2:19 3-4, and is half brother to Gold Leaf 2:11 1-4, Adonis 2:14, Fleet (two year old) 2:24, Longworth 2:19, Sister V. 2:27, Faustino, yearling, 2:35, Fleet, yearling, 2:35, Memo, three year old trial 2:20 1-2.

Sidney is by Santa Claus, record 2:17 1-2; he by Strathmore, sire of 31 in 2:30 list; he by Hambletonian 10, the greatest of all producers; he by Abdallah. Sidney's dam, Sweetness, record 2:21 1-4; she by Volunteer, the sire of St. Julien 2:11 1-4.

RINGWOOD'S dam Alma; she by Dashway, thoroughbred; he by Belmont, he by American Boy; he by Sea Gull; he by imported Expedition. Alma's 1st dam, Fanny Cobb, was a great road mare, pedigree untraced.

TERMS: $50 for the Season.

Payable June 1st, or sooner if mares are taken away

Address communications to

A. C. DIETZ,

Oakland, Cal.

The Fast Trotting Stallion

REDWOOD.

Four-Year-Old Record 2:24 1-2

Will make the season of 1890—February 1st to July 1st—at the

OAKLAND RACE TRACK.

REDWOOD is a dark bay colt, 15.2¼ hands high, weighs 1100 lbs. Foaled in 1885 by Anteeo, 2:16¼, sire of Alfred G., 2:19¾. Anteeo is by Electioneer. First dam Lou Milton, by Milton Medium; second dam Old Fly, a thoroughbred mare brought from the East in 1871 by W. C. Ralston, Esq.

Redwood's sire was out of Columbine by A. W. Richmond, the sire of the pacers Arrow 2:13¾, and Elwood 2:23, and the trotters Romero, 2:19½, and Len Rose, 2:27. Redwood has shown a quarter in 33 seconds.

Terms $100

For the season. Mares not proving with foal may be returned next season free of charge, provided Redwood remains the property of the present owners. Good pasturage at $5 per month. No responsibility assumed for escapes or accidents. Service fees payable before removal of the mare. Limited to 30 approved mares. For further particulars address,

A. McFADYEN.

Race track, Oakland, Cal.

Langtry Farms' Stud

Imp. FRIAR TUCK

By the Immortal HERMIT.

DAM ROMPING GIRL BY WILD DAYRELL.

AT $50 THE SEASON.

Mares not proving with foal may be returned the following season. Good care taken of mares, but no liabilities for accidents or escapes.

Good Pasturage at $5 per month.

Mares shipped to ST. HELENA, care CHARLES WILLIAM ABY, St. Helena Stables, will be cared for. For further particulars address,

CHAS. WILLIAM ABY,

Middletown, Lake County, Cal.

The Trotting Stallion

CUPID,

Full Brother to Adonis 2:14,

—Sired by—

The Celebrated SIDNEY 2:19 3-4, and out of Venus.

Will make the season of 1890 at the OAKLAND TROTTING PARK.

PEDIGREE.

CUPID is by Sidney out of Venus by Capt. Webster 10173, record 2:30, and sire of Freestone 2:19. Second dam by Skenandoah 336, sire of Daisy Burns 2:29½, Erwin Davis (sire of two in the 30 list) and dams of four in the 30 list.

DESCRIPTION.

Cupid is a handsome bright bay 15.2½ hands high, weighs 1100 lbs.; was foaled in 1886. As a yearling, with very little work he showed quarters in 42 seconds, and at 2 years old, quarters in 36 seconds. As a three year old he has not been worked, but he shows the speed and endurance that must come from his excellent blood lines.

TERMS $50 for the season, with the usual return privileges. Good pasturage near the track at $5 per month. The best of care taken of mares in any way that owners may desire, but no responsibility assumed for accidents or escapes.

For further particulars address

C. O. THORNQUEST,

Oakland Trotting Park, or

C. BAAB, 972 Broadway, Oakland.

The Trotting Stallion

VICTOR,

Record 2:22.

Will make the season of 1890 at NAPA CITY.

DESCRIPTION.

VICTOR is a handsome dark bay; 15-3 hands high; weighs about 1,100 pounds, and is remarkably intelligent, level-headed, of kind disposition, and a magnificent animal in every respect. He is well boned and muscled, of splendid conformation, and possesses the qualities of speed and endurance to an eminent degree—qualities that he imparts to his progeny.

PEDIGREE.

VICTOR, record 2:22
- Echo 462
  - Hambletonian 10, Sire of 42 in the 2:30 list.
    - Abdallah 1
    - Chas. Kent mare
  - Fanny Felter
    - Magnolia 68
    - by Webber's Kentucky Whip
- Daughter of
  - Woodburn
    - Lexington
    - Lulu Horton
  - daughter of
    - Ashland
    - thoroughbred

ECHO is the sire of Belle Echo, 2:20, Senator, 2:21¼, Victor, 2:22, Gibraltar, 2:22½, Kebora, 2:23½, Tippie, 2:25½, Lohengrin, 2:27½, Pasha, 2:27½, Elmonte, 2:29, Col. Hawkins, 2:29½, Annie Laurie, 2:30, Economy, 2:30, Sam Lewis, pacer, 2:21.

TERMS—$60 FOR THE SEASON.

Mares not proving with foal may be returned next season free of charge, provided the horse remains the property of the present proprietor, and stands at the same place, otherwise money will be refunded. The best of care taken of mares in any manner that owners may desire, but no responsibility assumed for accidents or escapes. For further particulars, apply to or address

G. W. HUGHES, Agent,

G. A. DOHERTY, Proprietor. Napa City.

THE CEDARS

BANNER MARK, 9424.

Foaled in 1888; by Victor von Bismarck (sire of Edgemark, four year old record 2:16; Von Wilkes, yearling record 2:38½, etc.); dam Moonlight by Alcyone (sire of Alcryon 2:15 1-4, etc.); second dam Twilight (dam of Skylight Pilot 2:19) by Mambrino Pilot (sire of Hannis 2:17¾); third dam by Pilot Jr. (sire of the dam of Maud S. 2:08¾); fourth dam nearly or quite thoroughbred.

In his four double crosses he combines more of the popular blood than any colt of his age. He is a double Hambletonian, double Clay through Bismarck and George Wilkes, double Mambrino and Pilot Jr., through Mambrino Pilot, Pilot Jr., and Mambrino Patchen. There is no other colt living bred like him. If you want Hambletonian, Clay, Mambrino or Pilot Jr., here you have it all combined in one grand colt. He has much of the finish of the thoroughbred.

Insurance $300. Limited to Seven Approved Mares.

Book full for 1890 and open for 1891 for fifteen approved mares. Address

T. E. MOORE,

The Cedars, Shawhan, Ky.

Vineland Stock Farm

Alcona 730.

Sire of

FLORA BELLE - - - - Record 2:24

CLAY DUKE - - - - - " 2:31½

ALCONA will be a great sire, but four of his colts have ever been trained, and all have shown full miles better than 2:37, and two of them as good as 2:20. Two of his first sons each sired a colt as a two-year-old, and last season one as a four-year-old trotted a full mile in 2:22½, and the other, a three-year-old, a mile in 2:31. With opportunities, Alcona is destined to be one of Almont's best sons. Almont, for his opportunities, is beyond doubt the most prepotent sire of his age. He has 36 representatives in the 2:30 list; 49 sons and 22 daughters that have already produced 2:30 performers. Almont died five years ago at 20 years old. If he lived he would be but 25 years old.

PEDIGREE.

ALCONA sired by the great Almont (sire of Westmont 2:13¾, Fanny Witherspoon 2:16¼, Piedmont 2:17¼, and 35 others with records better than 2:30, and grandsire of Belle Hamlin 2:12¾, etc.); by Alexander's Abdallah (sire of Goldsmith Maid 2:14), he by Rysdyk's Hambletonian. Alcona's dam, Queen Mary, by Mambrino Chief (sire of Lady Thorne 2:18 1-4, and 5 others in the 2:30 list, and sire of the dams of Director 2:17, Piedmont 2:17¼, Onward 2:25 1-4, Red Wilkes Almont, Belmont and many other noted sires).

DESCRIPTION.

Alcona is a beautiful chestnut 16 3 1-2 hands high, and weighs 1300 lbs. His colts possess speed, style, finish and beauty, and if they don't trot they command the highest prices for carriage horses.

$40 for the season. Usual return privilege.

Season of Alcona and Grandissimo ends July 1st, 1890.

Grandissimo,

Full Brother to GRANDEE, 3-year old record 2:23 1-2.

Sired by La Grande (son of Almont, and out of Jessie Pepper by Mambrino Chief; Jessie Pepper is the dam of Iona 2:17 1-2, Alpha 2:23 1-2, Sterling Wilkes 2:31½, and others) dam Norma, by Arthurton (sire of Arab 2:15, Joe Arthurton 2:20 1-2, etc.)

Grandam Nourmahal, (full sister to A. W. Richmond, sire of Arrow 2:13¾, Romero 2:19, and sire of Columbine, dam of Anteeo 2:16¼, and Antevolo 2:19¼ at four years old).

DESCRIPTION.

Grandissimo is four years old, will make a sixteen hand horse; he is a rich mahogany bay in color and perfect in style and action. $30 for the season. Usual return privileges.

"Grandissimo" with limited training last fall as a three-year-old, trotted quarters in 38 seconds and miles in 2:40.

I feel confident that he will trot fast this season, and will be a great sire as his colts this season are all grand youngsters.

The best of pasturage $4 per month; Mares taken care of in any manner that owners may desire, but no responsibility assumed for escapes or accidents.

For further particulars send for circular or call at stables, one mile south of St. Helena.

FRED W. LOEBER Prop'r.

The Trotting Stallion

G & M

FULL BROTHER TO

ALFRED G, 2:19¾.

(Who has been taken to Kentucky to stand at $200)

Will make the season of 1890 from FEBRUARY 1st to JULY 1st, at

SANTA ROSA.

G. & M. is by Anteeo, 2:16¼; was foaled 1886; first dam Rosa B. by Speculation (son of Hambletonian 10); 2d dam Elizabeth by Alexander 490; 3d dam Nora by imp. Glencoe. Anteeo is by Electioneer, out of Columbine by A. W. Richmond 1687.

G. & M. is a handsome dark bay; stands 15-2 1-2 hands high, and weighs 1050 pounds. Gameness, stoutness, speed and stamina are indelibly impressed in every line of the pedigree of G. & M. Owners of broodmares in search of these qualities, will do well to patronize this promising colt.

PHILOSOPHER,

Foaled 1886 by Pilot Wilkes 2987; first dam Bella by George Wilkes 519; second dam by Bell Morgan 61.

Philosopher's sire, Pilot Wilkes 2987, is by George Wilkes 519, dam Grace (the dam of Alice Woodburn etc.), by Pilot Jr. 12; grandam by Orphan Boy.

Will make the season of 1890, from FEBRUARY 1 to JULY 1st, at Santa Rosa.

TERMS for the season:

G. & M., $50.

PHILOSOPHER, $30,

with privilege of returning mares that do not prove in foal the next season free of charge, provided the horse bred to remains the property of the present owners. Good pasturage at $3 per month. No responsibility assumed for accidents or escapes. Service fees payable before removal of the mare. For further particulars, address

GEO. E. GUERNE,

Santa Rosa Cal.

ANTEEO BUTTON,

By Anteeo, 2:16 1-4.

And out of the dam of Alexander Button, four year old 2:26 1-2; Trial 2:16.

Will make the season of 1890 at ST. HELENA

DESCRIPTION.

ANTEEO BUTTON is five years old, a handsome dark bay, 15 1-2 hands high, and weighs 1-2? lbs. This horse has had but little or no systematic work, but he can trot fast and if there is anything in looks or breeding, he should produce trotters.

TERMS, $40 FOR THE SEASON, which closes July 1st. Best of alfalfa pasture on the premises at $4 per month. Mares cared for in any way that their owners may desire, but no responsibility assumed. For further particulars, address

E. C. SPEAR,

St. Helena, Cal.

THE CORINTHIAN

Cafe and Restaurant,

Point Tiburon.

MEALS SERVED TO ORDER AT ALL HOURS.

COLD LUNCHES

FOR FISHING AND PICNIC PARTIES.

Headquarters for Yachtsmen and Fishing Parties.

B. F. NAPTHALY, Manager.

Guenoc Stud Farm, Lake Co., Cal.

Imp. GREENBACK

(Sire of the English winners Greenlight, Greenjacket, Greenshank, Greenwave and Greenhorn)

By Dollar, dam Music, by Stockwell. $100 the Season

ST. SAVIOR,

(FULL BROTHER TO EOLE)

By Eolus, dam War Song, by War Dance. $100 the Season.

PASTURAGE, $5 PER MONTH.

with right to return the following year if mare does not prove with foal. The best of care taken, but no liability for accidents or escapes. Mares shipped to C. W. ABY, care ST. HELENA STABLES, St. Helena Napa County, will be taken in charge by competent men.

For further information write to

DR. C. W. ABY, Middletown, Lake County, Cal.

1890 Three Anteeo Stallions 1890

SUNSET, 5 years old, by Anteeo
ANTEEOF, 4 years old, by Anteeo
ANTEEOP, 3 years old, by Anteeo

ANTEEO. Standard 7868. Record, 2:16 1-4, by Stanford's Electioneer, and dam Columbine.

DESCRIPTIONS, PEDIGREES AND CONDITIONS.

"SUNSET" is a rich, dark bay, small star on forehead, portion of hind left foot white; was foaled March 11, 1885; is by ANTEEO and the inbred HAMBLETONIAN mare, BESSIE G, she by KING PHILLIP, son of WHIPPLE'S HAMBLETONIAN. He is 16 1 2 hands high, and weighs 1,200 lbs. He is of perfect build and splendid action cool headed and great speed for his size, having trotted a trial mile as a three-year-old in 2:38. He then entered heavy in the stud and was matched against Whalebone at the Healdsburg Races November 1, 1889, winning just as he pleased in three straight heats; time, 2:47, 2 46 1-2, 2:52 1-2. He was then matched for a race to come off last Thanksgiving Day at Petaluma but owing to the heavy rains the event did not take place. A few days previous to Thanksgiving Day Mr. Lawrence worked Sunset out and then he trotted three square miles and heats in 2:33¼, 2:34 and 2:37.

SUNSET will be bred to 40 mares only, at $50 each, no colt no pay.

"ANTEEOF" is a jet black, was foaled April 12, 1886, is 16¼ hands high, and weighs 1,200 lbs., has a very fine, heavy black mane and tail; is well proportioned, moves majestically, is of easy, lofty carriage; is symmetrical, in fact is a beautiful horse. He was sired by Anteeo and the C. A. Taylor mare "Nance," her dam, was raised by Dr. Oliver Plummer, of Consumnes, Cal., and sired by "Napoleon"; Napoleon was foaled May 20, 1853, and raised by James Kyle of Butler County, Ohio. He was sired by Benj. Sweet's horse Bellfounder, and he by Old Bellfounder, his dam was sired by Doc. Daniel Mulligan's horse, Cadmus, G. G. sire the celebrated Eclipse; his G. dam was sired by Big Shakespeare, G. G., sires dam by Messenger and Expedition.

ANTEEOF will be bred to 25 mares only, at $50 each. No Colt, no pay.

"ANTEEOP" is a rich seal brown; was foaled March 7, 1887; by Anteeo and the inbred Hambletonian mare Bessie G., also dam of Sunset, his full brother and Midget his full sister; he is 15 1-2 hands high and weighs 951 lbs, and measures 22 inches around the arm, good head, fine neck, full, broad breast; withers and rump on nearly equal line, well proportioned bones, ankle, shoulders, loins and hips; strong legs all around, with great muscular development and splendid sinews; wirey pasterns and sound, compact feet; the lines from hip to hoof show power and speed; stands square and has excellent action, has a superb lustrous coat of rich, deep brown fur of seal color without defect; an even, honest trotter, and has gone the mile as a two-year-old in 1:48, the last quarter in 28 seconds; is intelligent and of high spirit, with much temper, but is not vicious, has very fine eyes, is a handsome, showy colt; attractive in harness.

ANTEEOP will be bred to 15 mares only, at $35. No Colt, no pay.

SEASON to commence February 1st, ending July 1, 1890. Book now ready. Apply to John H. Lawrence, "Manager and Trainer," on my fruit and hop ranch, 1 mile e st of Court House, on Sonoma road, excellent pasture furnished with running water, also dry knolls with oak shelter, at $4 per month for mares. Two of the above stallions will be for sale after the expiration of the their stud season.

GUY E. GROSSE,
SANTA ROSA, SONOMA CO., CAL.

The Trotting Stallion

Guide 2:29

(At Four Years)

Will make the season of 1890 at the SANTA RITA RANCH, about one mile North of Pleasanton.

DESCRIPTION.

GUIDE is a handsome seal brown, five years old, stands 15¾ hands high, and weighs 1025 pounds. He is of fine form, level headed, intelligent, and comes from blood lines that are noted for the qualities of speed and gameness.

PEDIGREE.

GUIDE, 2:28½

- Director, 2:17 — Sire of Direct, 2:18¾, Margaret S., 2:19¾.
  - Dictator 113 — Sire of 23 trotters and 3 pacers in 2:30.
    - Hambletonian 10.
    - Clara, by American Star 14.
  - Dolly — Dam of Onward, 2:25¾, Thorndale, 2:22¾.
    - Mambrino Chief 11.
    - Fannie, by Ben Franklin.
- Imogene
  - Norwood 522 — Sire of Tommy Norwood, 2:26¾.
    - Hambletonian 10.
    - Lady Fallis, by American Star 14.
  - daughter of
    - American Star 14.
    - daughter of Harry Clay 45.

The attention of breeders is especially called to the above pedigree as showing 3 crosses of American Star.

GUIDE trotted into the 2:30 list last season with little training, and he will trot into the 2:20 list the coming season barring accidents.

Guide's sire has a record of 2:17, made in a five heat race, and Guide is closely related to Phallas, who made a record of 2:13¾ in a fourth heat, and to Jay-Eye-See, record 2:10.

TWO HUNDRED AND FIFTY DOLLARS will be given to the owner of the first of the produce of Guide put in the 2:30 list, and $100 to each one after the first.

TERMS—$75 for the season, with the usual return privileges.

Admiro,

Sire Admiral; dam by San Bruno, by Easton's David Hill.

This magnificent horse is a handsome bay, eight years old; stands 17 1-2 hands high and weighs 1470 pounds. He is very speedy for a large horse, and breeds fine large carriage horses. His produce possess every qualification of the Cleveland Bay, with the added qualities of speed and endurance resulting from his high trotting breeding.

TERMS—$50 for the season, with usual return privileges.

Will stand three days each week at Santa Rita Ranch, Pleasanton, and at A. T. Hatch's Ranch "Almonte," Alamo, Contra Costa County, alternately. All mares sent care of SMITH & SUTHERLAND, Pleasanton, will be taken in charge of on arrival, and will receive the best care and attention in any manner the owners may desire. Good pasturage at $4 per month. Only a limited number of approved mares will be served by this horse this season.

No responsibility assumed for escapes or accidents. For further particulars, address

SMITH & SUTHERLAND, Pleasanton.

or A. T. HATCH, care Palace Hotel, San Francisco.

FOR SALE.

A Mohawk Chief BROODMARE
and a
Director Colt, 6 months old.

For particulars address or apply to ANCON HOTEL, 9 and 11 Pacific Street, San Francisco.

Pedigrees Tabulated

IN THE MOST ARTISTIC MANNER.

Giving speed performers under sires and dams. Catalogues compiled. Stallion cards and circulars written up ready for the press. Pedigree blanks for sale. Prices reasonable. Horses bought and sold on commission. References furnished.

R. T. HARDIN.
806 W. Madison St., Chicago, Ill.

SAN DIEGO, 8776.

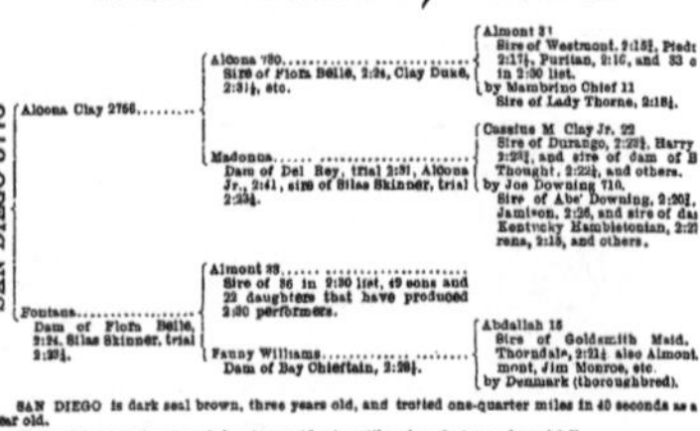

SAN DIEGO is dark seal brown, three years old, and trotted one-quarter miles in 40 seconds as a year old.

This grand young horse, and, barring accidents, will make a fast record next fall.

He will be allowed a limited number of mares, at $50 for the season. Mares not provi[ng with] foal to be returned free 1891. Best of pasture for mares at $4 per month, but no liability for acciden[ts or] escapes.

He will make the season from February 1st to June 1st at Napa Fair Grounds. For further par[ticu]lars, address or call on

H. B. STARR, Race Track, Napa, Cal.,
or FRED W. LOEBER, St. Helena

A SON OF ALMONT 33.

Only $25 for the Season.

ASHLAND ALMONT 348[1]

PEDIGREE.

ASHLAND ALMONT 3481

- Almont 33 — Sire of 34 in 2:30 or better of 21 daughters and of 49 sires that have produce in 2:30 or better.
  - Abdallah 15 — Sire Goldsmith Maid, 2:14; 8 in 2:30 list; 13 sires and 25 dams of trotters in 2:30 list.
    - Hambletonian 10 — Sire of 41 in 2:30 list; sire of 107 sire[s of] 587 in 2:30 list.
    - Katy Darling.
  - Sally Anderson
    - Mambrino Chief 11
    - Lady Thorn, 2:18¼.
    - Kate, by Pilot Jr. 12.
- Pauline — Dam of Sapho.
  - Ashland Chief — Sire Black Cloud, 2:17¼.
    - Mambrino Chief 11
    - Lady Thorn, 2:18¼.
    - dau. of imp. Yorkshire, (thoroughbred)
  - Rosina — Dam Almonia, the dam of Sally Cossack, 1:22¾. dau. Mamb. Abdallah, sire Mam. Prince, 2:23, and of Mamb. Bashaw, sire of Graham's Mambrino, 2:28.
    - Abdallah 15 — Sire Goldsmith Maid, 2:14.
    - Prof. Smith's Sir William.

DESCRIPTION.

ASHLAND ALMONT 3481 is a handsome chestnut; stands 16 hands; was foaled 1882, and bred by Withers, of Lexington, Ky. He is of fine form, and remarkably intelligent, sweet-tempered and absol[utely] sound. His oldest foal may be seen with him, and while he has never served a standard mare or one was a producer of speed, all of his colts are large, sound, fast and handsome.

TERMS: $25 for the season, with usual return privileges. The best of care taken of mares i[n any] manner that the owner may desire, but no responsibility assumed for escapes or accidents.

For further particulars, address

T. J. WHITEHEAD, Manager.
579 36th Street, bet. Telegraph Ave. and Grove St., Oakland, C[al.]

or, W. H. ASHBY, Oakland, Cal.

The Thoroughbred Stallion

INTRUDER

Will make the Season of 1890 at Agricultural Park, SACRAMENTO.

Bay Horse, foaled 1871, bred by Sir L. Newman, England. Imported by D. D. Withers, Esq., New York.

By Crater, Son of Orlando and Vesuvienne by Gladiator.

1st dam Lady Bountiful by Rataplan (Rataplan is own brother to Stockwell, and winner of 42 races, including the Doncaster Cup and 19 Queen's Plates, and proved himself the most distinguished race horse of his day in England).

2d dam Plentiful by Don John (the winner of St. Leger and Doncaster Cup).

3d dam Plenty by Bay Middleton (winner of the Derby and Two Thousand Guinea Stakes).

4th dam Plenary, own sister of Plenipotentiary, by Emiline. (Both Emilius and Plenipotentiary were Derby winners).

5th dam Harriet, dam of the renowned Plenipotentiary by Pericles.

6th dam by Selim, winner of the One Thousand Guinea Stakes.

7th dam by Pypilina, by Sir Peter.

8th dam Rally, by Trumpeter.

9th dam Fancy, by Florizel. Fancy was full sister to Diomed, the first Derby winner in England, and after his importation into this country, sired the illustrious Sir Archy, etc. See English Stud Book.

Imported INTRUDER is a beautiful bay, standing fully 16 hands high, of great length and substance, and descends through close and strong currents from the most illustrious winners and winning lines of blood of which the English Stud Book bears record.

A careful review of the first six crosses of the pedigree of INTRUDER will show nine Derby winners; five St. Leger winners; two winners of The Oaks; two winners of the Two Thousand Guineas; two winners of the One Thousand Guineas; one Goodwood Cup winner; one Cesarwich Cup winner; one Cambridgeshire Stakes winner, and four Doncaster Cups, in addition to a great number of Steeplechases and other races of less import.

INTRUDER, at the great fair held at St. Louis, Mo., in 1876, was awarded the highest stallion honors—the blue ribbon and the $500 purse—in the sweepstakes ring for stallion of any age or blood. The list of competitors embraced the large number of thirty-three animals, and they represented England, Canada, Kentucky, Tennessee, and other states. He also took first premium in his class and in sweepstakes for the best stallion of any age or breed at the State Fair at Peoria, Ill., 1881. He is the sire of Tidal Wave, George Hakes, Bernice and April Fool.

INTRUDER is the sire of Interpose, who is the dam of Spokane, winner of the Kentucky Derby, in which he beat the great horse Proctor Knott and broke the record.

TERMS: $50 for the season. Mares not proving with foal can be returned the next season free of charge. Good pasturage at $4 per month. Mares cared for in any manner owners may desire, and fed on hay and grain, either or both, at reasonable rates. While every precaution will be taken, no responsibility will be assumed for escapes or accidents. Mares sent from a distance in care of the undersigned, will be met and taken to the park. For further particulars, address

T. J. KNIGHT.
Agricultural Park, Sacramento.

HOLLYWOOD BREEDING FA[RM]

MOUNTAIN BOY 4841

Bra MOUNTAIN BOY, 4841, bred by Charles [illegible]man, Orange County, New York, foaled 18[illegible] Kentucky Prince 2470, dam Elise, sister to Elair[illegible] Messenger Duroc 106; grandam Green Mou[ntain] Maid, 3d dam, Shanghai Mary, will serve a li[mited] number of mares at $100 the season.

ELECTION.

Bay stallion ELECTION, bred at Senator [Stan]ford's Palo Alto Stock Farm, foaled 1884, sire [Elec]tioneer, dam Lizzie H. by Whipple's Hambl[etonian] 725, grandam Lizzie Harris (by Comus son of G[rand] Bashaw 60), great grandam by Arnold Harris, [thor]oughbred.

Election is one of the handsomest blood li[ke] of Electioneer and with his thoroughbred through Arnold Harris should prove invaluab[le] sire. TERMS, $100 the season.

KAFIR.

B c KAFIR, bred by L. J. Rose, Los Angeles, 1887, sire Alcazar, 2:20½, dam Flower Girl by A[illegible]ton, sire of Arab, 2:15, grandam Flora by G[eo.] McClellan, 144, sire of three in 2:30 list, great dam by Langford, he by Williamson's Belmon[t] serve a limited number of mares at $50 the se[ason].

WOODSIDE.

Ch c WOODSIDE, sire Woodnut, 2:16½; 1s[t dam] Veronica by Alcona, 730; 2nd dam Fontana [by Al]mont, 33; 3rd dam Fannie Williams by Alex[ander's] Abdallah, 15. Book full.

MART BOORHEM

B c MART BOORHEM, by Sydney, 2:19¾; 1s[t dam] Towhead by Echo, This colt is a full brothe[r to] Nicholas who showed a mile in 2:27½ at thre[e years] old. TERMS, $25 the season.

REVEILLE.

The well known thoroughbred stallion REV[EILLE] by Shiloh, dam by Norfolk. Reveille is a br[other to] John Treat and is the sire of Tycoon and Gla[illegible] TERMS, $75 the season.

Hollywood is nicely situated three mile[s from] Vallejo on the Napa road. Good pasturage an[d] care will be taken of mares at reasonable rate[s. For] further particulars, apply,

B. C. HOLLY, Val[lejo].

THE BUCKINGHA[M]
OLD STRAIGHT WHISK[Y]

141 Montgomery Street.
308 Bush Street, S.[F.]

M. J. BALFE, Proprietor.

GEO. WASHINGTON,

11,623.

RECORD 2:30.

Bay colt, bred by Thomas Smith of Vallejo, Cal. Foaled 1885 by Mambrino Chief, Jr., 11,622, record 2:34 1-2, 1st dam Fanny Rose by Vick's Ethan Allen Jr. 2,903, sire of Prince Allen 2:27. 2nd dam Jenny Lind, thoroughbred, dam of Prince Allen 2:27. Will serve a limited number of mares at $50 for the season. Mares not proving with foal may be returned next season free.

Mambrino Chief, Jr.

11,622.

RECORD 2:34 1 2.

Sire of George Washington, record 2 30 at three years old. Bay horse bred by Rufus Ingalls of Belvedere, Ill. By McDonald Chief 3'83. First dam Venus by Mambrino Patchen 58. 2nd dam by Wardlow's Shakespeare. 3rd dam Lone Gold 4th dam by Silver Heels. Has not been in the stud b fo e. He was 5 years old when he served a few mares, and his colts all show good style and form.

Terms for the season $40. For further particulars see or address

THOMAS SMITH, Vallejo, Cal.

Elector 2170.

Sire of J. R.

Three-Year Old Record 2:24.

Sired by Electioneer 125, sire of Sunol, three-year-old, 2:10½, Palo Alto, 2:12¾, etc.; dam Gilberta by Fred Low 886, sire of Clay, 2:25½, etc.

Second dam Lady Gilbert (grandam of Lot Slocum, 2:17½) by General Knox 140 (sire of Lady Maud, 2:18¼, and many others).

TERMS.

$150 for the season. Book full for 1890.

L. A. RICHARDS, Grayson, Stanislaus Co., Cal.

The Thoroughbred Stallion

Three Cheers

Will make the season of 1890 at

Sacramento.

PEDIGREE.

- imp. Hurrah
  - Newminster
    - Touchstone, by Camel
    - Beeswing, by Dr. Syntax
  - Jovial
    - Bay Middleton, by Sultan
    - Sister to Grey Momus, by Comus
- Young Fashion
  - imp. Monarch
    - imp. Priam, by Emilius
    - imp. Delphine, by Whisker
  - Fashion
    - imp. Trustee, by Catton
    - Bonnets o' Blue, by Sir Charles

Hurrah was imported by John Reber, of Lancaster, Ohio, a locality where there were but few breeders of thoroughbreds. Under these disadvantages he sired a long list of winners. His sire Newminster, won the St. Ledger 1851, and his dam, Jovial by Bay Middleton, winner of the Derby 1836. Newminister by Touchstone, winner St. Ledger 1834. Dam Beeswing, winner of 54 races out of 64 starts, by Dr. Syntax, winner of the Doncaster Cup, 1837—40—41—42, the only horse that ever accomplished that feat.

On the side of the dam Three Cheers is equally well related. Young Fashion was the dam of Surprise, Scotland (the only horse that ever beat Asteroid a heat), Liverpool, Columbia, and Bonnie Kate, the dam of Little Buttercup, and the flying Bonnie Liza. His grandam, Fashion was the greatest race mare of her day and beat Boston in that historical match at four mile heats, which is recorded as one of the greatest events in the annals of the turf.

Horsemen who are qualified to judge, pronounce Three Cheers to be the finest type of the Newminster line in America.

LOCATION.

THREE CHEERS will be located at the Arcade Training Stable, Rancho del Paso. This place has been selected for the reason that first class pasturage has been secured there for the exclusive use of these mares, and the other facilities to be obtained are for the care of mares (especially mares in foal) are better than can be found elsewhere in the locality.

TERMS.

$50 for the season with the usual return privileges. Pasturage $5 per month. Mares cared for as owners may desire at bottom rates for grain and hay. All bills payable before the mare is removed.

Mares shipped care of WM. IRVINE, Pacific Stables, Sacramento, will be properly cared for and sent to the ranch without delay.

Three Cheers will be in charge of one of the most experienced and competent stud grooms in the State, who will exercise every care, but no reponsibility assumed for accidents or escapes.

For further particulars apply to Louis Criesler, at the rance; Wm. Irvine, Pacific Stables, Second St., Sacramento; or to the owner,

E. S. CULVER, 318 Bush St., San Francisco.

GROVER CLAY

Bay Stallion, Black Points, 15 3-4 hands high.

Bred by W. W. Traylor, San Francisco.

BY ELECTIONEER.

First dam Maggie Norfolk by Norfolk, son of Lexington, he by Boston. Second dam Tilde Quill by Billy Cheatham he by Cracken, and he by Boston. Third dam by Dorsey's Golddust.

TERMS.

Will make the season of 1890 at the Training Stables of Denis Gannon, near Oakland Trotting Park, $50 the season, payable at time of service. Season commence February 1st and ending July 1st. Proper care of mares will be taken, but no responsibility incurred for accidents or escapes. Address,

DENIS GANNON, Oakland, Cal.

2:10¾ 2:13¾ 2:10

DEXTER PRINCE.

This Royally-bred Stallion will make the Season of 1890 at the LIVE OAKS Breeding Farm, 2 miles from Lodi, San Joaquin County, Cal.

DESCRIPTION.

DEXTER PRINCE is a blood bay, 16 hands high, weighs over 1,100 pounds; has great power and substance, and the highest finish. When two years old, at Palo Alto, he was timed quarters by Gov. Stanford in 32¼ seconds, and he was driven eighths by Mr. Marvin at a faster rate of speed than that. He is a sure foal-getter, and invariably sires foals of good size, of fine form and finish, and the highest rate of speed.

PEDIGREE.

By KENTUCKY PRINCE, the sire of Guy, 2:10¾, Spofford, 2:18¾, Company, 2:19¾, Bayonne Prince, 2:21 1-4, Fred Folger, 2:20¾, and a score more in the 2:30 list.

First dam LADY DEXTER, full sister of the greatest of trotters, Dexter, and the greatest of sires, Dictator, the sire of Director, 2:17, Phallas, 2:13¾, in a fourth heat, and Jay-Eye-See, 2:10.

Second dam Clara, the dam of Dexter, 2:17 1-4, Dieta or, Astoria, 2:29 1-4, and Almah, 2:28¾. Clara was by American Star, that has 24 daughters that have produced 2:30 or better trotters.

Third dam the McKinstry mare, the dam of Shark, 2:27¾. HAMBLETONIAN, the grandsire of DEXTER PRINCE, has 40 trotters in the 2:30 list, 44 daughters that have produced 2:30 trotters, and more than 100 sons that have sired 2:30 trotters.

CLARK CHIEF, the grandsire on the sire's side, was the sire of performing and producing sons and daughters

DEXTER PRINCE has faster blood lines, on both sides, than any other stallion in the world—Guy 2:10¾, and Jay-Eye-See. 2:10.

KENTUCKY PRINCE is one of the best bred and speediest stallions in the world. David Bonner, in the presence of Governor Stanford, timed him when he trotted a 2:1[illegible] gait. He is by Clark Chief, one of the great broodmare sires; his first dam is Kentucky Queen by Morgan Eagle, son of Hale's Green Mountain Morgan, 2nd dam by Blythe's Whip. 3rd dam by Martin's Brummier, 4th dam by Quicksilver 880, on through the strongest thoroughbred blood.

TERMS.

$100 for the season, with usual return privileges. Payable before mares are removed. Good pasture, and the best care furnished, but no responsibility assumed for accidents.

PREMIUM.

$250 will be given to the first of the produce of DEXTER PRINCE put in the 2:30 list, and $100 each after the first. Address

L. M. MORSE, Lodi, Cal.

2:10 1-2 ELECTIONEER 2:12 1-4

BAY STALLION	BROWN STALLION
ECLECTIC	**MORTIMER**
11,321	5,346
By Electioneer, dam Manette (full sister to Woodnut 2.16 1-2 Manon 2:21 and Maple, dam of Hattie D., three-year-old record 2:28¾) by Nutwood 2:18¾, etc., etc.	Four-year-old Record 2:27. By ELECTIONEER, dam MARTI, by Whipple's Hambletonian (sire of 18 in 2:30, and of dams of eight in 2:30). Second dam Ida Martin by Rideman (sire of Col. Lewis 2:18¾).
Terms $100 for the Season.	**Terms $60 for the Season.**

Horses shipped via San Francisco may be consigned to J. W. MORSHEAD, City Front Stables, who will attend to their forwarding.

Season closes JULY 1st, 1890. Usual return privileges.

For further particulars address owner,

WILFRED PAGE, Penns Grove, Sonoma County, Cal

The Trotting Stallion

Silver Bow

Will make the season of 1890 at the Oakland Race Track

PEDIGREE.

SILVER BOW 11708, two-year-old record 2:37, is by Robert McGregor 647, 2:17¼ (sire of Bonnie McGregor, 2:13¼, Earl McGregor, 2:21¼, Mac D., 2:30, McGregor Boy, 2:29¼, Mark Time, 2:30, Roxie McGregor, 2:20¼) by Major Edsall 2'1, 2:29, by Alexander's Abdallah 15—sire of Goldsmith Maid, 2:14—by Hambletonian 10—sire of Dexter, 2:17¼.

Robert McGregor's dam was Nancy Whitman by American Star 14, by Stockholm's American Star.

SILVER BOW'S first dam is Sadie by Hambletonian 10, sire of Geo. Wilkes, 2:22—sire of Guy Wilkes, 2:15¼—also Electioneer, sire of Sunol, three-year-old record, 2:10½, and Palo Alto, 2:12¾; second dam Lady Wynne by Wm. Welch 341; third dam Elenora Margrave by imp. Margrave.

DESCRIPTION.

SILVER BOW is a handsome bay, no white; 15-2¼ hands high; weighs 1075 pounds; of fine form, with the best of legs and a clean-cut, intelligent head. Is remarkably level-headed, seldom making a break; Wears seven-ounce shoes in front. His record, 2:37, is no mark of his speed; he can beat 30 easy, and with his gilt-edge breeding, he is just what he ought to be, a trotter sired by a trotter whose dam was herself a trotter and his grandam the dam of two trotters. His dam Sadie being by Hambletonian 10, shows him to be bred from the cream of the trotting blood.

TERMS: $100 for the season. Mares not proving in foal returnable for the season of 1891 free of charge. Good pasturage and first-class care taken of mares for $5 per month. No responsibilities assumed for escapes or accidents. For further particulars, address

Limited to 15 approved mares. Season to end June 1st, 1890.

P. J. WILLIAMS, Care Race Track, Oakland, Cal.

GRAND MOOR, 2374.

Grand Moor 2374.
- Moor 870
  - Sire of Beautiful Bells 2:29½
  - Sire of Sable (dam of Sable Wilkes) 2:18
  - Sire of Sultan 2:24
  - Sire of Tommy Gates 2:24
  - Sire of Del Sur 2:24½
  - Sire of Sir Guy 2:28½
  - Beautiful Bells is the dam of Hinda Rose, 2:19½ as a 3-year-old, Rosemeade, Chimes, St. Bell, Bell Boy (3 years) 2:19½, sold at auction for $51,000, etc.
  - Sultan, sire of Stamboul, 2:12½, sold for $50,000, has 19 in 2:30 list, and is now standing in Kentucky at $400 for the season.
  - Clay Pilot 92 — Sire of 2 in 2:30 list.
  - Belle of Wabash.
- Vashti
  - Dam of Don Tomas, who got a record of 2:20 in 1889.
  - Mambrino Patchen 58 — Sire of 14 in 2:30 list. Sire of the dam of Guy Wilkes, 2:15¼; also sire of 20 stallions and 18 mares with get in 2:30 list.
  - Kate Taber — By Mambrino Messenger.

Foaled 1876. Black. Sixteen hands high. Bred by L. J. Rose

A horse of highest form and quality; of great excellence in every point; a type of his celebrated family; of marked individuality, spirit and endurance; never properly trained or raced, but shows the possession of great speed; Perfectly manageable in the stable and on the road and track.

As he is sired by The Moor 870, a son of CLAY PILOT, out of Vashti by MAMBRINO PATCHEN, he is a most valuable cross for mares of other families. THE MOOR sired Beautiful Bells and the dams of Sable Wilkes and Margaret 2:26 (dam of Regal Wilkes, 2-year-old record 2:20½).

MAMBRINO PATCHEN is regarded as the unsurpassed sire of broodmares, having, among many others, sired the dam of Guy Wilkes and of Wm. L (the sire of Axtell), and a son of his sired the dam of Axtell. The public sales this year have demonstrated with renewed emphasis the value of The Moor and Mambrino Patchen strains of blood. For combining particularly with the Hambletonians it may be called "the ready money cross."

GRAND MOOR will make the season of 1890 for a time at the Oakland Race Track and afterwards at my Ranch, fifteen miles from Oakland. Mares can be delivered at the race track to the groom in charge. Pasture at $5 per month. For other food, if requested, an additional charge will be made.

TERMS, $150 for the season, with privileges of return if the horse does not change hands.

Every care exercised, but no liability for escapes or accidents.

H. I. THORNTON, 504 Kearny Street.

Cook STOCK FARM,

Season of 1890.

STEINWAY 1808.

Three-Year-Old Record 2:25 3-4.

Sire of STRATHWAY, three year old record 2:26, and sire of the dam of BOURBON RUSSELL 2:30.

By STRATHMORE 408; sire of 31 in the 2:30 list; sire of 6 dams of 8 in the 2:30 list, and sire of 3 sires of 3 in 2:30 list.

1st dam ABBESS (dam of Solo 2:28, and Soprano, dam of C. F Clay 2:18, Eminence 2:27 and Strathbridge, 3 year old record 2:28½) by ALBION, sire of VANITY FAIR 2:24½, and of the dam of FAVORITE 2:25½.

2nd dam by MARSHALL NEY.

3rd dam by BERTRAND, a son of SIR ARCHY.

TERMS—$100 for the season.

CHARLES DERBY 4907

Brown Horse, Foaled 1885.

By STEINWAY 1808.

1st dam by the great ELECTIONEER, sire of SUNOL 3 year old record 2:10½, Palo Alto 2:12¾, etc., etc.

2nd dam FANNY MALONE, by NIAGARA.

3rd dam FANNY WICKHAM, by HERALD.

4th dam by Imp. TRUSTEE.

TERMS—$100 for the season

Pasturage $5 per month. Accidents and escapes at owner's risk. Mares consigned to the farm should be sent to Fashion Stables, Oakland; Geary & Grindle's Stable, Haywards; or to Bennett's Stable, Martinez; from and to which places they will be delivered free of charge. Address

COOK STOCK FARM, Danville, Contra Costa, Co., Cal.

The Trotting Stallion

ARBITRATOR

Will make the Season of 1890 at NILES, Alameda County.

PEDIGREE.

ARBITRATOR.
- Director 1989, 2:17 in a race, Sire of
  - Direct, 4 yrs., 2:18½ in a race,
  - Margaret S., 3 yrs., 2:19½ in a race,
  - Guide, 4 yrs., 2:28½ in a race.
- Lady Earnest.
  - Speculation 918, sire of
    - Oakland Maid, 2:22 in a race,
    - Gracie S., 2:22 in a race,
    - Crown Point, 2:24 in a race, He the sire of Valensin, 4 yrs., 2:23 in a race,
    - Sire of Dam of Alfred G., 2:19½.
  - Lady Hibbard, dam of Lou Whipple, 2:26½ in a race.

Speculation's dam was Martha Washington, dam of Whipple's Hambletonian, sire of 15 in 2:30 and granddaughter of Burr's Napoleon, sire of Black Harry, who in 1850 won two miles in 5:14½. He sired Smith Burr, sire of Gen. Butler, 2:21, Wagon, 4:56½. He sired the dam of Fanny Mapes, dam of Jerome Eddy, 2:16½. He sired Telegraph, sire of dam of Rarus, 2:13½.

DESCRIPTION.

ARBITRATOR was foaled 1885. He is of good size, fine conformation, and a beautiful seal brown.

TERMS.

Non-standard mares	$45
Standard mares by inheritance	35
Standard mares by performance or produce	25

For further particulars, address

H. A. MAYBEW, owner, Niles, Alameda Co.

PASHA,

Registered No. 2039.

RECORD 2:36.

SIRE OF MORO 2:27.

Will make the present season at Linden, twelve miles east of STOCKTON.

Season commencing FEBRUARY 1st and ending JULY 1, 1890.

DESCRIPTION.

PASHA is a beautiful black; 16½ hands high, and weighs 1,240 pounds. He is a horse of beautiful symmetry and magnificent action.

PEDIGREE.

PASHA was sired by Sultan 1513, sire of Stamboul 2:12½, Ruby 2:19½, Alcazar 2:20½, Bay Rose 2:20½, and sixteen others with records below 2:30. First dam Madam Baldwin by The Moor 870; second dam Ben Lippincott by Belmont. Pasha is a full brother to Bay Rose, record 2:20½.

Sultan, by The Moor, sire of Beautiful Bells, dam of Hinda Rose, 2:19½, Bell Boy 2:19½, and Sable, dam of Sable Wilkes, three-year-old record 2:18. First dam Sultana, by Delmonica, sire of Derby 2:16, by Guy Miller, sire of Whipple's Hambletonian. Second dam by Mambrino Chief. Third dam by Downing's Bay Messenger. Fourth dam Miss Caudle, dam of Ericsson, four-year-old recor 2:30½.

Terms for the season, $50.

With privilege of returning mares that do not prove in foal next season free of charge.

Good pasturage at $2 per month No responsibility will be assumed for accidents or escapes Service fee payable before the removal of the mare.

For further particulars, address

D. BRYSON, Linden Cal.

2:8 3-4 2:10 2:12

MBRINO WILKES, 6083.

SIRE OF

...OS WILKES, 2:22; ALPHEUS, 2:27; ...RA P, 2:29½; BALKAN, 2:29½ (3-year-... ...nd timed separately 2:22½ in 4-year-old ..., Bay District Track, October 14, 1889.

DESCRIPTION.

...k; sixteen hands; weighs, in exercise, 1,260 lbs. ...yle, finish, symmetry and proportion, compari... ...challenged with any trotting bred horse. His ...follow in size, style and beauty. Balkan, for ..., being "facile princeps" of trotters in these ...ulars.

PEDIGREE.

...d by Geo. Wilkes, sire of Harry Wilkes, 2:13¼, ...Wilkes, 2:15¼, and 80 other trotters in the 2:30 ... addition to 8 pacers, and of the sire of Axtell, ...hree-year-old), beating all stallions of any age, ...e sire of Regal Wilkes, 2:20¾, best two-year-old ...n record.

...t dam Lady Chrisman by Mambrino (Todhun-...son of Mambrino Chief 11; sire of Lady Thorn, ... Woodford Mambrino, 2:21½, and four others in ...od of the dams of Director, 2:17, Piedmont, ...Onward, 2:25¼, etc.

...nd dam by Pilot Jr. 12, sire of nine in the 2:30 ...d of the dams of Maud S., 2:08¾, Jay-Eye-See, ...Nutwood, 2:18¾, Viking, 2:19¾, Pilot Boy, 2:20, ...Queen, 2:20¾, etc.

TERMS.

...s from a distance will be received at the Dexter ...s, Oakland, or Livery Stable, Martinez, the ... notifying Smith Hill, Superintendent at the ... Good pasture and plenty of water. For the ...e of placing the service of a Wilkes within ...of breeders, the same rate will be maintained as ...ar, to wit, $75 for the season. Although it is not ...ed thereby that this horse is inferior as a pro-... to the horses whose fees are placed at from $150 ... Address

SMITH HILL,
San Miguel Stock Farm,
Walnut Creek, Contra Costa Co., Cal.

2:23/4 2:13½ 2:15¼

...ly Bred Trotting Stallion

ARLINGTON.

...0 $50

Trial 2:26 1-2; by

ABBOTSFORD.

DESCRIPTION.

...INGTON is a handsome rich rosewood bay, ...as high and weighs 1:00 lbs. He is of beauti-... ...formation, well boned, and great muscular de-...ent and greatly resembles his famous sire in ...particular.

PEDIGREE.

...INGTON was sired by Abbottsford, dam the ...is mare by Blue Bull. Abbotsford is by Wood-... ...ambrino, dam Columbia by Young Columbus, ...olumbus Woodford Mambrino's dam Woodbine ...dford, a thoroughbred son of Kocious ko. Wood-... ...ambrino is recognized as the best son of Mam-... ...Chief. His own record is 2:21½, that of his son ...ford, the sire of Arlington 2:19½ and his son ...2:20, and he has also a large number in the 2:30 ...le is also the sire of Princeps the sire of Trink-... ...rd of 2:14. Abbotsford, for the short time he ...n in the stud, has proven himself a sire worthy ...it, his daughter Jassemine having won the Em-... ...akes of 1881, and every one who was put in ...g has shown good speed. The dam of Arling-... ...a beautiful bay mare, 15¾ hands high, sired ... Bull, dam Lexington mare raised by Ezra ...ion of White Hall, New York, thus showing ... Arlington are combined most of the pur-... ...d in America.

...MS: $50 the season, with usual return priv. ... The best of attention will be given mares, but ...ility assumed for escapes or accidents, good ...age, $2 per month. Call on or address,

J. B. FRENCH,
905, 907 and 909 Golden Gate Ave, S. F.

2:8 3/4 2:10 2:12

BALKAN

... Mambrino Wilkes.

(See that Horse's Advertisement.)

...FANNY FERN BY JACK HAWKINS

Son of Boston.

...randam of Maud S. (2:08¾) was by Boston and ...dam of Jay-Eye-See (2:10) was by Lexington, ...Boston. So Balkan is the same remove from ...that Maud is, and one remove nearer than ...-See.

... Fern has produced Molly Drew, Onyx, Fred ... Molly Fern and Balkan, all by different sires. ...n's sire and dam both being producers, and he ...trotter himself with a record of 2:29 1-2 (three-... ...) and timed separately 2:22 1-4 in 4-year-old ...ay District Track, October 14, 1889—it is but ...resume that he will get trotters of the high ...r.

DESCRIPTION.

...seal brown, 15 1-4 hands high, in style rivalled ...and excelled by none with as pure a gait as ... been exhibited in public—bar none. ...n will be at Oakland Trotting Park for the ...of 1890, and will be limited to ten mares, at ... in order to be put in training early, as it is ...certain that if given a reasonable opportun-... ...ill be fast enough to compete with the best of ... For further particulars, address

A. L. HINDS,
Dexter Stables, Oakland.

2 3/4 2:13½ 2:15¼

2:19 NOONDAY $2:20\frac{1}{2}$

STANDARD No. 10,000.

This celebrated trotting bred stallion will make the season of 1890 at the stable of the undersigned at Sacramento, Cal., at $75 for the season and $100 to insure a mare in foal. Payable on or before July 1st, 1890. Money will be refunded on mares bred by insurance as soon as the fact becomes known that they are not in foal.

NOONDAY.

- Wedgewood, 2:19 .. Sire of Favonia, 2:15, fastest 4th heat for any mare or gelding, and eight others in 2:27 or better.
  - Belmont.................... Sire of Wedgewood, 2:19, Nutwood, 2:18¾, Viking, 2:19½, and 29 others in 2:30 list.
    - Alexander's Abdallah, sire of Goldsmith Maid, 2:14; Almont, with 35 horses in 2:30 list, etc.
    - Belle, dam of Hambletonian, 2:26½; B'cars, dam of Pancoast, 2:21¾, the sire of Patron, 2:14½.
  - Woodbine.................... Dam of Wedgewood, 2:19, Woodford Mamb., 2:21½, the sire of Pancoast, 2:21¾, the sire of Patron, 2:14½.
    - Woodford.
    - Singleton Mare.
- Noontide, 2:20½.... (Trial, 2:18¼).
  - Harold .... Sire of Maud S., 2:08¾, and 26 others in 2:30 list.
    - Hambletonian (Rysdyk's), sire of George Wilkes, 2:22, the sire of Guy Wilkes, 2:15¼; Electioneer, the sire of Sunol, 2:10½, and scores of noted trotters and producers.
    - Enchantress, by Abdallah 1.
  - Midnight .... Dam of Jay-Eye-See, 2:10, Noontide, 2:20½.
    - Pilot Jr., sire of dams of Maud S., 2:08¾, Jay-Eye-See, 2:10, Nutwood, 2:18¾, etc.
    - Twilight, by Lexington, sire of the dam of Ansel, 2:20.

NOODAY is a dark seal brown, foaled 1884, 15 hands 1½ inches high. Individually he is equal to his royal breeding. He is all that can be desired in conformat on, intelligence, color and trotting action, and no s al-lion now in public service can show a pedigree with such fast records and royal game trotting blood as Noonday.

DON MARVIN,

Record 2:28 as a five-year-old. Standard by Breeding and Performance

Standard No. 7927.

Don Marvin 2:28.

Don Marvin is a beautiful seal brown, foaled 1884, bred by Hon. Leland Stanford, Palo Alto, Cal., standing 16 hands, and weighs, in ordinary condition, 1200 lbs. He is a fine individual, good style and form, combined with great substance, and good temper. Is very level headed: in his first race the past season he only made one break in five closely contested heats. He has great speed and endurance, with the pure, rapid Electioneer gait. He trots without toe weights, and wears only 8 oz. shoes in front. He gained his record the past season in the third heat, on a slow track, after making a season (serving over 60 mares), with scarcely any preparation. His record is no mark of his speed. He was a natural born trotter, and Mr. Charles Marvin considered him the fastest two year old at Palo Alto that season.

By FALLIS, 2:23, - - by Electioneer, sire of
Sire of Don Marvin, 2:28. — Sunol, three-year-old, 2:10 1-2, Palo Alto, 2:12¾, and 47 others in 2:30 list.

Dam CORA, by Don Victor by Belmont, sire of
Dam of Don Marvin, 2:28. — Ventura, 2:27¾, and sire of the dam of Bell Echo, 2:20, and six others in 2:30 list.

2d dam CLARABEL, - by Abdallah Star,
Dam of Clifton Bell, 2:24 1-2, and grandam of Rexford, three years, 2:24. — Sire of Hattie Maples, 2:28.

3d dam FAIRY, - - by Rysdyk's Hambletonian,
Sister of Sweepstakes, sire of 18 in 2:30 list. — Sire of Electioneer, George Wilkes, and many other noted sires and trotters.

4th dam EMMA MILLS, by Seely's American Star,
Dam of 4 horses that have 2:30 performers. — The great broodmare sire of the world.

The above pedigree should show every intelligent breeder that Don Marvin is "high" bred, though very strong in trotting blood. All the comment it is deemed necessary to make as to the value of "thoroughbred blood" in the trotter is simply to refer to the very significant fact that the first and second dams of Maud S. 2:08¾, Jay-Eye-See 2:10, Sunol, three years 2:10 1-2, Palo Alto 2:12¾, Anteeo 2:16¾, Nutwood 2:18¾, Wedgewood 2:19, and many other successful sires and sensational trotters of the day are thoroughbred.

TERMS—Don Marvin will make the ensuing season from February 1st to July 1st, 1890, at $40 the season, with the usual privilege of returning the mare next season if not proving in foal. Mares from a distance met at the cars or boats on notification, and carefully handled, but no responsibility assumed for accidents or escapes.

Good alfalfa pasture furnished (free from barb wire fence) at $4 per month. For further particulars or complete circulars address

F. P. LOWELL,
1520 F Street, Sacramento, Cal.

The Produce of Eros Averaged $2,200 Each at New York Auction Sale in 1889.

THE ELECTIONEER TROTTING STALLION,

5326 EROS 5326

Will make the season of 1890—February 1st to July 1st—at LA SIESTA RANCH, MENLO PARK, adjoining Palo Alto.

PEDIGREE.

EROS (5326)
Standard by his sire
" " dam
" " record
" " produce
" under all rules

EROS (5326)

- Electioneer.................. Grandsire of Norlaine, 1 yr., 2:31 1-2, Sire of Sunol, 2 yrs., 2:18, Sunol, 3 yrs., 2:10 1-2, Hinda Rose, 4 yrs., 2:16, Palo Alto, 2:12¾.
  - Hambletonian 10................ Sire of Dictator, George Wilkes, Happy Medium, and 40 others in 2:30 list, and grandsire of 728 in list.
    - Abdallah 10 Sire of the dams of Goldsmith Maid, 2:14, and 7 other producing dams.
    - Charles Kent mare By imp. Bellfounder.
  - Green Mountain Maid.............. Dam of Prospero, 2:20, Elaine, 2:20, Dame Trot, 2:22, Elista, 2:22¼, Storm, 2:26¾, Antonio, 2:28¾, Miranda, 2:31, Mansfield, 2:26.
    - Harry Clay Sire of the dams of St. Julian, 2:11¾, Bodine, 2:19¾, and 17 more in 2:30 list
    - Shanghai Mary.
- Sontag Mohawk .... Dam of Eros, 2:29 1-2, Sport, 2:22¾, Sallie Benton, 2:17¾, Conductor, trial, 2:28, Colma, 2-y-o trial, 2:24.
  - Mohawk Chief.................. Sire of the dams of Lot Slocum, 2:17¾, Sallie Benton, 4 yrs., 2:17¾, Pedlar, 2 yrs., 2:27¾, Stanford, 4 yrs., 2:30, Eros, 6th heat, 2:29 1-2.
    - Hambletonian 10 Sire of the dams of Stamboul, 2:12¼, Wilton, 2:19¾, and 20 other trotters.
    - Lady Perrine
  - Sontag Nellie.....................
    - Toronto Sontag By Toronto Chief,
    - Nellie Gray 5-mile record, 13:46.

Produce of Eros
Wanda, 4 yrs., 2:24,
Solita, 2 yrs., 2:41 1-2,
Mariquita, 2 yrs., 2:42,
Daylight, 2 yrs., 2:34,
Hiram B., trial, 2:28.

These are the only colts by him that have ever had a harness on except one in New York that went a trial last July in 2:26 1:2.

DESCRIPTION.

EROS is a rich seal brown stallion, bred by Hon. Leland Stanford at Palo Alto, and is the nearest living likeness of his celebrated sire, Electioneer. Stands 15.2 hands high, and weighs 1050 pounds

In breeding to Eros, the owners of mares will strictly follow the great rule of breeding, viz., breed to a stallion by a producer and out of a sure producer of great speed. Eros is by the stallion that has produced more 2:30 trotters that any living horse, and is also the sire of more 2:30 performers than any horse living or dead.

EROS is out of the dam of Sally Benton, four years old, record 2:17¾, Sport 2:22¾, and Eros 2:29½ in the sixth heat, against a field of nine horses. He is from a family that is endowed with great natural speed, trot fast at an early age, train on, throw trotters from all classes of mares, are of good substance, bone, style and action, and breed solid colors.

TERMS.

$100 for the season, with the privilege of return next season should mares not be in foal and horse and mare still remain in the same hands.

Good pasturage can be obtained at $5 per month, but no responsibility for accidents or escapes. There are a large number of box stalls, and animals can be kept up and fed on hay and grain at reasonable rates if required. Mares already in foal can be sent to the ranch for foaling, and will receive all the attention bestowed upon our own mares. Mares left with Mr. Peter Pomyea, Broadway Street Stable, Oakland, or with Mr. F. H. Burke, 401 Montgomery Street, San Francisco, will be forwarded to the ranch free of charge. For further particulars apply to

W. H. VIOGET,
LA SIESTA RANCH, MENLO PARK, CAL.

EROS is the only stallion offered to the public on this Coast that has a dam that has three in the 2:30 list.

POPLAR GROVE

Breeding Farm

STALLIONS.

CLOVIS, 4909,

CLOVIS is a beautiful black, Eight Years Old, 16 1-2 Hands High, and weighs 1260 lbs.

He is a horse of beautiful symmetry and magnificent action.

PEDIGREE.

CLOVIS was sired by Sultan, 2:24, sire of Stamboul, 2:12 1-4, Ruby, 2:19¾, and fifteen others with records of 2:30 or better.

First dam Sweetbrier by Thorndale 2:22 1-2, sire of Edwin Thorne, 2:16 1-2, Daisy Dale, 2:19, and May Thorne, 2:22

Second dam Ulster Queen, dam of Volmer, 2:24¾, by Hambletonian 10. Sire of Dexter, 2:17¼, George Wilkes, 2:22.

Third dam by Thomas Jefferson, a son of Mambrino Paymaster, Jr.

Fourth dam by Mambrino Paymaster, sire of Mambrino Chief.

Sultan, by The Moor, sire of Beautiful Bells, dam of Hinda Rose, 2:19 1-2, and Sable, dam of Sable Wilkes, three year old record 2:18.

First dam of Sultan, Sultana, by Delmonico. Sire of Darby, 2:16 1-2, by Guy Miller, sire of Whipple's Hambletonian.

Second dam by Mambrino Chief.

Third dam by Downing's Bay Messenger.

Fourth dam Mrs. Caudle, dam of Ericsson, four year old record 2:30 1-2.

Clovis will make the season of 1890 at Poplar Grove Breeding Farm, near Wildflower, Fresno County, commencing February 1st and ending July 1st.

Terms, $75, due at time of service.

Mares cared for in any manner owners may desire; pasturage $2 per month. Every care exercised, but no liability for escapes or accidents. Mares not proving with foal can be returned next season, providing I still own this stallion.

APEX, 8935.

FOUR - YEAR - OLD RECORD, FOURTH HEAT, 2:26.

Will make the present season at the Poplar Grove Breeding Farm, near Wildflower, Fresno Co., season commencing Feb. 1st, and ending July 1, 1890. Terms $50 the season, due at time of service. Apex is eight years old, a beautiful bay, 15 1-2 hands high, and weighs 1140 lbs. He is a horse of fine disposition, and his gait is faultless.

PEDIGREE.

Apex was sired by Promptor 2305, he by Blue Bull 75; first dam Mary by Flaxtail, he by Pruden's Blue Bull. Flaxtail being the sire of the dams of Buccaneer, five-year-old record, 2:24 1-2; Pride, yearling record, 2:44 1-2, and Shamrock, two-year-old record, 2:35, third heat. Second dam by Bright Eyes, son of Bonaparte. Prompter (sire of Apex, record 2:26, and Transit, 2:28 1-2), by Wilson's Blue Bull, by Pruden's Blue Bull son of Merring's Blue Bull. Promptor's dam Prairie Bird, by Flaxtail; second dam by John the Baptist, son of Tally Ho Morgan, by Sherman Morgan; third dam Fannie Fern by Irwin's Tuckaho

Apex made his appearance in the circuit as a two-year-old, and obtained a record of 2:42. As a three-year-old he reduced this in a race at Santa Rosa against Stamboul to 2:31, it taking six heats to decide the contest, which was won by Apex. As a four year-old he gained his present record of 2:26.

Mares cared for in any manner owners may desire. Pasturage $2 per month. Every care exercised, but no liabilities for escapes or accidents. Mares not proving with foal can be returned next season, providing I still own this stallion.

The Standard Stallion

JUNIO,

RECORD 2:22.

WILL MAKE THE PRESENT SEASON OF ... AT FRESNO FAIR GROUNDS,

Season Commencing Feb. 1st and ending July 1st.

TERMS—$100 the season, due at time of service.

JUNIO is eight years old, a handsome dark bay 16 hands high, and weighs 1250 pounds. He is the personification of the light harness horse, and his trotting action is superb. At the State Fair of 1886 he took first premium over forty of the finest trotters in the State.

PEDIGREE.

Junio, by Electioneer, premier stallion of Palo Alto (sire of Sunol 2:10 1-2, Palo Alto 2:12 1-4, and 47 others in the 2:30 list. Dam by Granger by imp. Hercules.

Granger, by imp. Hercules, dam Jenny Lind, by Stockbridge Chief, Jr., he by Stockbridge Chief, he by Vermont Black Hawk. Second dam by Kentucky Whip.

Imp. Hercules, by Kingston, first dam daughter of Tuscar, by Bay Middleton, second dam Malvina, by Oscar; 3rd dam Spotless by Walton; 4th dam by Trumpator (see Bruce's American Stud Book, Vol. 1, page 28). Hercules is the sire of the dam of Ansmoor 2:21¾; also sire of dam of Menlo 2:21 1-2.

Mares not proving in foal may be returned next year free of charge, providing I still have the horse. Pasturage $3 per month. While every care will be taken of horses, no liability will be assumed for accidents or escapes.

For further particulars address

S. N. STRAUBE, Fresno, Cal.

Poplar Grove Breeding Farm.

By-Laws

—AND—

Rules and Regulations

—OF THE—

NATIONAL

Trotting Association

ALSO THE

AMERICAN

Trotting Association,

AND THE

PACIFIC COAST BLOOD-HORSE ASSOCIATION.

With Betting Rules.

For Sale at the Office of the

Breeder and Sportsman,

313 Bush St., S. F., Cal.

Price, 25c. each.

By Mail, Postage Paid, 30c. each.

Everything for Trotter or Runner,

At J. A. McKERRON'S,

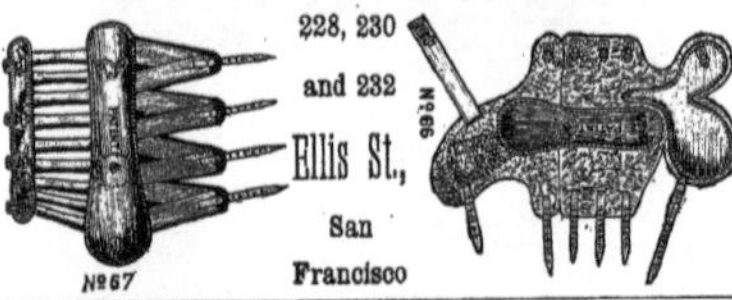

228, 230 and 232 Ellis St., San Francisco

The PARKER Hammerless Shot Gun.

At the Annual Tournament of 1889, held at Cannes, France, the grand prize, consisting of 2000 Francs and a Valuable Cup. was won by The Parker Hammerless.

The first Parker Hammerless Gun made won the championship of America at Decatur Illinois.

SEND FOR ILLUSTRATED CIRCULAR.

PARKER BROS.. Makers,

New York Salesroom, 97 Chambers St.. Meriden Conn.

ALWAYS GIVES SATISFACTION.

Combining perfect riding qualities, proportions and balance, with genteel appearance.

No vehicle exhibits a horse to better advantage, and no Cart approaches them for speeding or training purposes.

A stylish vehicle for exercising or pleasure driving, at one-fourth the cost of a carriage. Have none of the horse jockey or objectionable features of other Road Carts.

They are the Leading Cart wherever introduced, and are in use by the most prominent breeders and pleasure drivers everywhere.

Elegant Shifting Top Carts.

Perfectly Balanced Stylish Pole Carts.

For Illustrated Catalogue, with Prices, address,

LEWIS F. CASTOR,
Frankford, Philadelphia, Pa.

JOHN SPLAN, General Agent.

Brothers of the Angle.

Chubb The Fishing-Rod Manufacturer

OUR NEW EIGHT-STRIP SPLIT BAMBOO is th "King" of all fishing-rods. Chubb's New Catalogue for 18 is now ready. In addition to a complete list of angler supplies, it contains articles from the pens of Dr. James A Henshall, Petronella, W. H. Murray, Geo. P. Goff, Norma Brother Gardner, and others.

These papers are by the best writers on angling subject and are very interesting

Send 25 cents, and receive Catalogue, post-paid. Th amount will be deducted from first order (if accompanie with Coupon in book) for one dollar's worth or more of ou goods. Address

THOS. H. CHUBB.
The Fishing-Rod Manufacturer,
POST MILLS, VT.

Please mention BREEDER AND SPORTSMAN.

WHOLESALE AND Retail FishingTackle — WHOLESALI AND Retail FishingTackl

Agents for all the principal Manufacturers of FISHIN TACKLE in England and the United States.

Trap Shooters Supplies a Specialty

CLABROUGH, GOLCHER & CO.
630 and 632 Montgomery Street, S. F., Cal.

ABALONE PATENT SPOON.

PATENT APPLIED FOR.

These Spoons are made of Abalone Shells, which, on account of their iridescence, are more attract to fish than any other substance. To make them secure, we have patented a German Silver Bar runni the entire length of the Shell; the hook is fastened in one end of the bar, the swivel in the other.

These spoons have been tried on all kinds of game fish, *and are wonderfully sure kille* Sample by mail, Trout sizes, $.50, Salmon sizes, $1 00.

E. T. ALLEN,
Importer of Fire Arms, Fishing Tackle and Sporting Good
416 Market Street, - - San Francisco.

Studebaker Bros. Manufact'g Co.

Sole Agents for
FRAZIER
(OR CHICAGO)
Carts
AND
Sulkies,
201--203 Market Stree
SAN FRANCISCO, CAL.

J. O'KANE, Horse Boots, Clothing and Furnishing For Track, Driving Training and Stable. Every requisite for Horsemen. Harness, Medicines, Bit

THE BRUNSWICK BALKE COLLENDER COMPANY,
MANUFACTURERS OF
Standard Billiard and Pool Tables, Saloon and Bank Fixture
653--655 Market Street, San Francisco, Cal.

Nutwood 2:22¾, 2:21, 2:18¾ Sire — **DAWN 6407** — Dam Countess — DAM OF Strathway (2-y-o) ... trial ... Placida, Morna ... Double team Trial ...

2:18¾; 2:20; 2:19½.

$100 Popular Price for season of 1890. $100

Not having a breeding farm, and being dependent on the public for patronage, I have set the above low price in order to be within the reach of any one desiring to breed. Good pasturage $3 per month.

For further particulars, address

A. L. WHITNEY, Petaluma.

TWENTY-FOUR PAGES.

Vol XVI, No 16.
No. 313 BUSH STREET.

SAN FRANCISCO, SATURDAY, APRIL 19, 1890.

SUBSCRIPTION
FIVE DOLLARS A YEAR.

SPRING MEETING

Pacific Coast Blood Horse Association.

The initial day of the annual spring meeting of the Pacific Coast Blood Horse Association was as one especially selected, being a typical California day, one worthy of a trip from the East, to enjoy at this particular time of the year, perfect overhead and all that could be desired under foot. It is true the ocean winds tended to sharpen up the air, but only enough so that the term "bracing" could be aptly applied. "Little Jack Edgar" had been selected as the Superintendent of the grounds, and he filled the bill exactly. The club house had been cleaned as it should be, there being forms and chairs in plenty to accommodate the active supporters of the organization. The members part of the grand stand was filled with new chairs and even the reporters' stand had not been neglected. The pencilling fraternity were present in force, seven of them calling the odds to those who were disposed to patronize the books, while Messrs. Killip and Whitehead attended to those who were inclined to put their money in the auction pools. Combinations are also a favorite form of betting and one of the boxes was set apart for those who wanted to tempt Dame Fortune in that way, while the mutual cards could also be had by investing a "fiver." The wheel of fortune had a plentiful supply of the *Genius Sucker* hanging around, and the small change of spectators rolled in liberally to fill the pockets of the peanut vender. The attendance was good, their being probably between 1500 and 1800 persons present. The five events on the card were well filled and the contests exciting, with the exception of the last one, in which Palo Alto only had one competitor, and he was thoroughly outclassed. A pleasing innovation was the "bugle call," which for the first time was used instead of the old time bell. The carriage enclosure was well filled, some very handsome turnouts being noticable. As the time approached for the sport to begin, the judges of the day mounted the stand, the selected ones being Col. Caleb Dorsey, of Stanislaus, C. T. Boots, of the Elmwood Stable and Ariel Lathrop, President of the association. When Palo Alto had entries in any of the races, Mr. Lathrop would step out and Col. H. I. Thornton take his place. Dr. W. G. Ross was also used as an alternate when Mr. Boots had an entry, and there is no better judge of flat racing in America. The timers were Edwin F. Smith, Secretary of the State Agricultural Society, William Sullivan, Manager of the Rancho Del Paso, and R. T. Carroll, who represented the Directors of the Association. For the first race the bookmakers were well patronized, the auction pools doing little business. Abi was a strong favorite, her success last fall being still fresh in the minds of the public, but to the judge in such matters, it was plainly seen when her blanket was removed that she had been drawn too fine. The supporters of Pliny were rather jubilant when they saw the condition of Abi, but they overlooked Al Farrow, who never looked better in his life. And right here a word of compliment is due the old trainer, Frank De Poyster, who had all of his string in superb condition, notwithstanding the bad weather of the past winter. Farrow was in the pink of condition and by his performance he stamped himself a race horse equal to the best, for although he conceeded every horse that started from four to twenty-four pounds, he won easily considering his impost. Prior to his suspension last spring he was a general fav rite, and his win on Saturday was very popular. His new owner, Mr. W. H. E. Smith, of Humboldt County, was naturally jubilant over the victory and gave Hill, the jockey, two fifty dollar bills for his services.

Classified as on the programme, the Introduction purse was the opening race, in which there were seven starters, the eighth name on the programme, Oro, being scratched. Henry Walsh, of Palo Alto, was the starter, and the flag fell to a good send off, Al Farrow, taking the inside running, almost immediately. Before the horses reached the wire, Guido stumbled and fell, throwing his rider quite a distance, but fortunately neither horse nor jockey were injured. Al Farrow was the first past the stand, with Pliny and Baggage fighting for place honors, and the three leaders remained in the same position until the outcome. Coming down the homestretch, Pliny was sent for the leader, but the big bay had too much in reserve, and he landed the money for his stable by a length, and it could have been by several if necessary.

The time is wonderful when the season of the year is considered, and the weight carried taken into consideration. Eylton only carried 106 pounds when he made his mark of 1:47½, and that in June, so that the difference stamps Al Farrow's performance as a much better record. The following is the

SUMMARY.

Introduction purse, $400, of which $50 to second, $25 to third. For three-year-olds and upwards; beaten maidens of three years old allowed five pounds; if four years old or over, ten pounds. One mile and a sixteenth.

W. H. E. Smith's b h Al Farrow, 5, Connor—Della Walker, 121..Hill 1
Kelly & Samuels' b c Pliny, 3, Flood Precious, 99..........Narvaez 2
George Hearst's ch c Baggage, 3, Warwick—Maria F., 103..Sullivan 3

Time, 1:48½.

Raindrop, 3, 97 (Murphy,) Guido, 3, 102 (Spooner), Almont, 4, 117 (Morton), Abi, a, 116 (Casey) also ran.

Book betting straight: Al Farrow, 4 to 1; Pliny, 2½ to 1; Baggage, 15 to 1; Abi, 8 to 5; Almont, 12 to 1; Guido, 15 to 1; Raindrop, 40 to 1.

Place betting: Al Farrow, 6 to 5; Pliny, 4 to 5; Baggage, 5 to 1; Abi, 3 to 5; Almont, 4 to 1; Guido, 5 to 1; Raindrop, 15 to 1.

Auction pools—Abi $25, Pliny $17, Al Farrow $12, field $10.

The California Stakes, for two-year-olds, brought out nine promising youngsters to face the starter, who in this race was C. T. Boots, Mr. Walsh having Rinfax in the race. This race was of more than passing moment, as it reintroduced to the public, the colors of ex-Senator L. J. Rose of Los Angeles, who quit the running turf many years ago to take up the trotters, and it goes without saying that his victory in this event was the source of much gratification to his friends, who congratulated him warmly on his success. The old gentleman was heartily pleased, and we trust that his initial win is only the fore-runner of many more. At the third call from the bugle, they all started for the half-mile pole, and it was only with considerable difficulty that Mr. Boots could get them off in something like decent shape. When the flag finally fell, Fairy and Homer made fight for the leadership, with the latter a head to the good; Minnie B. led the balance, there being a length of daylight between her and the ruck.

In the upper turn Conrad and Anarchist made play for a few moments, but their chances had been lessened by the numerous false starts. When the head of the stretch was reached, it could easily be seen that Monahan had Fairy well in hand, Narvaez plying the whip on Homer, and although he made a gallant fight for supremacy, Fairy won handily by a length in the really good time of 49 seconds. Minnie B. and Conrad made excellent time in the straight, and both of them will bear watching, for they are liable to turn up winners at almost any time. Glenlivet must not be despised, for she is well put up, and shows racing qualities of no mean order.

SUMMARY.

The California Stakes—For two-year-olds (foals of 1888), $50 each $25 forfeit, or $10 if declared out on or before January 1, 1890. All declarations void unless accompanied by the money; with $500 added, second horse to receive $100, third to save stake. Half a mile.

L. J. Rose's b f Fairy, Argyle—imp Fairy Rose, 107......Monahan.. 1
Undine Stable's b c Homer, Shannon—Sallie Gardner, 110..Narvaez 2
G. W. Trahern's ch f Minnie B., Prince of Norfolk, by Wildidle, 107 ....Hazlett 3

Time, 0:49.

Anarchist, 110 (Ross); Yosemite, 110 (Morton); Parapet, 110 (Madden); Rinfax, 110 (Pierce); Conrad, 110 (Roach), and Glenlivet, 107 (Cook) also ran.

Book betting, straight—Fairy, 8 to 5; Homer, 4 to 1; Minnie B., 8 to 1; Conrad, 6 to 1; Rinfax, 6 to 1; Glenlivet, 10 to 1; Anarchist, 12 to 1; Yosemite, 12 to 1; Parapet, 25 to 1.

Place betting—Fairy, 3 to 5; Homer, 6 to 5; Minnie B., 3 to 1; Conrad, 1 to 5; Rinfax, 2 to 1; Glenlivet, 5 to 1; Anarchist, 4 to 1; Yosemite, 4 to 1; Parapet, 8 to 1.

Auction pools: Rose Stable (Fairy Rose and Conrad), $100; Hearst's pair (Yosemite and Anarchist), $32; Undine Stable (Homer and Glenlivet) $20; field, $40.

The California Stake is the first two-year-old event of the year in this State, and has been the means of introducing to the public many noted race horses, the following being the winners since its inception:

WINNERS OF THE CALIFORNIA STAKES.

Year.	Winner.	Sire.	Subs.	Str.	Time.	Second.
'79	Martin's Tillie C	Wildidle	7	3	:49½	Euchre.
'80	Pritchard's Frank Rhoads	Leinster	12	5	:51½	(F by Waterford Lilly Simpson.
'81	Baldwin's Anita	Rutherford	13	6	:51½	Albert C.
'82	Baldwin's Gano	Grinstead	30	12	:51	Panama.
'83	Winters' Prince of Norfolk	Norfolk	32	8	:52½	Callie Smart
'84	Winters' Estill	Norfolk	21	4	:53	Alta.
'85	Haggin's Billow	Longfield	16	4	:50	C by Norfolk—Jessie R.
'86	Haggin's Graciosa	imp Glengarry	37	9	:53	Robson.
'87	Todhunter's Pocatello	Joe Hooker	40	14	:49	Geraldine
'78	Haggin's Trade Mark	Kyrle Daly	84	14	:51	Faustine.
'89	Palo Alto's Racine	Bishop	76	8	:48½	Guido.
'90	Rose's Fairy	Argyle	42	9	:49	Homer.

The weights in 1879 were 88 lbs. for fillies; in 1880 they were raised to 100 lbs. for colts and 97 lbs. for fillies; in 1881 they were raised to 110 lbs for colts and 107 lbs. for fillies. Anita is said to be by Rutherford or Grinstead.

The winner is a handsome bay, bought as a yearling at Palo Alto, by Mr. Rose; his sire, Argyle is by Monday, dam Cuba by imp Australian. The dam of Fairy is imp Fairy Rose by Kisber, 2nd dam Hippolyta by King Tom, 3d dam Daughter of the Star by Kremlin, 4th dam Evening Star by Touchstone, 5th dam Bertha by Rubens, 6th dam Boadicea by Alexander, etc.

Selling races gives the poorer class of horses a chance to show their running qualities, and it seemed on the opening day as though every owner for miles around wanted to demonstrate the ability of his racing steed. Fifteen starters sported silk, and Henry Walsh had the sympathies of the audience as he took his place to send off the field. They were an unruly lot, and the jockeys were likewise unmanageable; so after numerous attempts to get them away in something like decent shape, Mr. Welch cautioned them that he would start them without further parley, and true to his word the flag was seen to fall to a very uneven start, Ida Glenn and Applause being first away in full flight before the others had caught their stride. The start absolutely left the fight between the two leaders for the next nearest horse was fully fifteen lengths behind when the half mile pole was reached. At this point Ida Glenn was a head to the good with Applause hanging on like grim death. As the three-quarter pole was being neared by the two leaders, Kildare was brought out from the stragglers, and made a desperate finish, Pierce working the son of Kyrle Daly for all there was in him, but without beneficial results as the others were too far in the van.

When the decision was given the judges announced a dead heat, between Ida Glenn and Applause, but from the reporters stand, it was clearly Ida Glenn's race by a head. After consultation between the owners of the two horses, it was decided to run it off, so after the last event on the card, the two were again started, Narvaez piloting Applause to a creditable victory, in the fast time of 1:13½, the first time this year that 1:14 has been beaten. Kildare was in rare condition to run and it was evident that if he had got an equal start with the others that he would have had a good chance for first money. Too much praise cannot be given the trainers of the other pair, for the outcome showed plainly that they were fit to race for a man's life.

SUMMARY.

Selling Purse $250 of which $50 to second, for three-year-old and upward. Horses entered to be sold for $1200, to carry rule weights; three pounds allowed for each $100 down to $800, then two pounds for each $100 less down to $300. Horses entered not to be sold to carry ten pounds above the scale. Three-quarters of a mile.

W. George's Applause, b g, a, by Three Cheers, dam Alice N., 105 ....Narvaez 0 1
H. D. Miller's Ida Glenn, ch m, a, by Glen Elm, dam Queen, 98 ....Ward 0 2
M. Storn's Kildare, ch g, 5, by Kyrle Daly, dam Mistake, 104 ....Pierce 3

Time, 1:15, 1:13½.

First heat, dead heat.

Sallie C., 4, 101, Bustellos up; Vinco, 4, 121, Cole; Rosemrade, 5, 11[illegible] Cooper; Steve Stroud, 3, 113, Baily; Rosebug, 4, 84, Brown; Maggie B., 5, 95, Lawless; Tom Daly, 3, 1[illegible]5, Morton; Bernanda, 6, 120, Ferguson; Emma, 4, 112, McIntosh; Adam, 6, 105, Casey; Sheridan, 3, 1[illegible]6, Williams; Recess, 5, 97, Francis, also ran.

Book betting—Applause, 2-1, 1-2; Ida Glenn, 12-1, 4-1; Kildare, 4-1, 7-5; Tom Daly, 10-1, 4-1; Steve Stroud, 10-1, 4-1; Sheridan, 3-1, 1-1; Roseburg, 12-1, 4-1; Sallie C., 10-1, 4-1; Maggie B., 50-1, 15-1; Vinco, 30-1 10-1; Rosemeade, 50-1, 15-1; Hernanda, 40-1, 20-1; Emma, 20-1, 8-1; Ida Adam, 30-1, 10-1; Recess, 20-1, 8-1. On the run off, Applause, 1-3; Ida Glenn, 2-1.

Auction pools—Field $20, Kildare $8, Tom Daly $2.

A purse of $350, was the next event on the programme, and was the means of bringing out half a score of starters, many of whom were old performers, Sir Reginald, belonging to N. S. Hamlin, being the only one that was a newcomer to a San Francisco audience. Owing to his many victories in the past, Longshot was a slight favorite, followed closely for choice by Mr. Whitmore's Coloma. For such a large field an excellent start was effected, Kiro and Carmen cutting out the pace, with Fanny F well up, the balance being bunched two lengths in the rear. The same order was maintained to the upper turn where Fanny F fell back beaten, Captain Al taking her place and making play for the leaders, but although he kept up his speed, he could not win, Longshot coming with a rush that soon settled all doubts, he passing under the wire winner by a length, Captain Al second and Coloma third. Kiro and Carmen having fallen back, in the run down the home stretch.

SUMMARY.

Purse $350, of which $50 to second, for all ages. Weights ten pounds below the scale. Seven furlongs.

J. T. McBride's ch h (4) Longshot by Duke of Norfolk—by Langford 107 .... Spooner 1
Miller & Owens's br c (3) Captain Al by Kingston—Black Maria, 98 .... McIntosh 2
W. L. Whitmore's ch h Coloma (5) by Joe Hooker—Callie Smart, 110 .... Hill 3

Time, 1:28½.

Carmen, 5, 105, Murphy up; Dave Douglas, a. 107, Bustellos up; Adelaide, 3, 91, Ward; Kiro, 3, 96, Madden; Fanny F, 105, Morton; Rettie B., 3, 91, Narvaez, ran unplaced.

Book betting—Longshot 2½ to 1, 4 to 5; Captain Al 20 to 1, 8 to 1; Coloma, 2½ to 1, 4 to 5; Kiro, 3 to 1, 1 to 1; Rettie B, 3 to 1, 1 to 1; Carmen, 5 to 1, 3 to 1; Fanny F, 20 to 1, 8 to 1; Dave Douglas, 20 to 1, 10 to 1; Adelaide, 30 to 1, 10 to 1.

The fifth and last race on the card was the annual renewal of the Tidal Stakes for three-year olds, which is usually attended with much interest as it gives the public a line on the Derby candidates, but the smallness of the field robbed the contest of much of its attractiveness, Mr. Rose being the only one that would venture a "go" against the two cracks from the Palo Alto Stable. Mr. Boots had no trouble in getting them away at the first time of asking. The race requires no description, for after passing the stand Flambeau took the lead by a length and kept it to the wire, Racine simply acting as an attendant, the big colt not being pushed to make the mile and a quarter better than 2:09. Rover was whipped all the way down the stretch, but could not get within half a dozen lengths of the second horse.

SUMMARY.

Tidal Stakes, for three year olds (foals of 1887), $100 each, half forfeit, or $10 if declared out on January 1st, 1889, or $20 if declared out August 1st, 1889, or $30 if declared out January 1st, 1890. All declarations void unless accompanied by the money; with $500 added; the second to receive $200; third to save stake. One mile and a quarter.

Palo Alto's ch c Flambeau, Wildidle—imp. Flirt, 118 .... Narvaez 1
Palo Alto's b c Racine, Bishop—imp. Fairy Rose, 118 .... Harris 2
L. J. Rose's ch c Rover, Wildidle—imp. Rosetta, 118 .... Monahan 3

Time—2:09.

Book betting—Racine, 4—1; Rover, 40—1, 3—4.

SECOND DAY.

Judges—Messrs. Ross, Tarpey and Thornton.

Timers—Messrs. Dustin, Ramsdell and Baldwin.

The second day of the Pacific Coast Blood Horse Meeting was all that could be desired, with the exception that the wind was a little too high for extreme speed. The crowd was large, almost equaling that of the opening day, and it was a pity that the starting was of such a nature as to cause great dissatisfaction, not that it changed the result of the races, but that it prevented close contests except in one instance. The bookmakers were kept busy, and the auction pools were largely patronized, the betting being a great deal heavier than it was on Saturday.

For the first race the talent seemed to have selected Al Farrow as the sure winner, but there was quite a tip out on Almont, the Three Cheers colt having showed up very well in his work at San Jose and also here. Daisy D. was exceedingly well backed, but she disappointed her supporters, although she did get second place.

When the last bugle call was sounded nine horses faced the starter. Al Farrow's superb condition gave his backers a fancied security which was not borne out by his running in the race. Daisy D. also looked extremely well, as did Almont and Gertrude; King Hooker was very nervous and fidgety, as was also Rettie B., and it was owing to the bad conduct of the two latter that the start was delayed fully thirty minutes. When the flag fell Mr. Walsh started them with Rettie B. two lengths to the good, with Coloma and the Three Cheers representative in second place, Daisy D. was a good fourth with Al Farrow and the balance in the ruck. Rettie B. cut out the pace going around the turn with a good advantage, Coloma falling a little behind and Almont taking second place. At the quarter the Undine Stable representative was still a length ahead with Almont second, Daisy D. a length and a half behind him and Coloma at the mare's flank. Al Farrow was not running up to his usual form, the heavy weight which the handicapper had given him making him show up very poorly. Going down the backstretch there was no change of positions except that Daisy D. was gradually crawling up on Almont and when they were fairly into the turn Rettie B., Almont and Daisy D. were all head and head; as they straightened into the stretch Rettie B. fell back beaten, leaving the fight between Almont and Daisy D. It was here noticed that Spooner, the jockey on Al Farrow was doing all he possibly could in the way of persistent urging, but the big horse could not respond and at the drawgate the fight lay between Almont and Daisy D. The mare was severely punished, but she could not get any better than Almont's flank, he winning in the exceedingly good time of 1:41½. The following is the

SUMMARY.

Purse $400, of which $50 to second, $25 to third. For three year olds and upwards. Winner of race 1 at this meeting to carry 5 lbs. extra. Horses starting and not placed in that race allowed three pounds. One mile.

George Hearst's b h Almont, 4, by Three Cheers—Question, 114 .... Morton 1
Miller & Owen's b m Daisy D, a, by Wheatley—Black Maria, 116 .... Hennessey 2
W. L. Whitmore's ch c Coloma, 5, by Joe Hooker—Callie Smart, 121 .... Hill 3

Time—1:41 1-2

Gertrude, 4, 112, Ross up; Lady All, 3, 97, Madden; Leland, 3, 97, Jones; Al Farrow, 5, 1..., Spooner; King Hooker, 3, 1.., Williams; Rettie B., 3, 97, Narvaez, ran unplaced.

Book betting—Almont, 6-1, 2-1; Daisy D, 8-5, 2-5; Al Farrow, 10-7; Gertrude, 20-1, 8-1; Lady All, 20-1, 8-1; Leland, 20-1, 10-1; Coloma, 15-1, 5-1; King Hooker, 30-1, 10-1; Rettie B, 20-1, 8-1.

The second race was a free handicap sweepstake for two year olds, the Association adding $300, the distance five furlongs. Eight names had been placed on the programme to start, but Rinfax, the Palo Alto colt, was scratched, leaving seven of the youngsters to contest for supremacy. Homer was represented on the card as belonging to the Undine Stables, a new name to the race goers of this coast, and it might not be out of place to state that the owners thereof are Ira Ramsdell and Thos. H. Williams, and fancying that they had a good thing, although their horse carried the top weight of 115 lbs., almost $5000 was placed with the bookmakers on Homer's chances; as Homer is trained in the stable of Henry Walsh for the present, he did not act as starter in this race, the unthankful position falling to the lot of Charles T. Boots. Unfortunately for those who had money on the other horses, Charlie dropped the flag with Homer a good three lengths in advance and at his full stride, while the others straggled along behind, wholly unprepared for the signal. The start finished the race. Homer was never headed, winning as he pleased by fully six lengths, with Parapet second and Joe Woolman third. Narvaez, on Homer, took no chances whatever, and carried the colt at his highest rate of speed, landing the owners of the colt many thousand dollars winner. As was only natural, a great deal of grumbling was expressed at the miserable start, but all felt assured that the best horse had won, the time, 1:01¼, at this season of the year and with the weights carried proving to all conclusively that Homer was the best horse in the race. The following is the

SUMMARY.

Free Handicap Sweepstakes—For two year olds. $10 each if not declared out, with $300 added; first horse to take the added money, second to receive 70 per cent and the third 30 per cent. of the stakes. Weights announced Monday, April 14th at 10 o'clock A. M. Declarations due at 5 o'clock P. M. the same day. Five furlongs.

Undine Stable's b c Homer, by Shannon—Sallie Gardner, 115.. Narvaez 1
W. M. Murray's b c Parapet, by Bulwark—Nettie Brady, 100... Madden 2
Orange Grove Stable's br c Joe Woolman, by imp. Cyrus—Ella Doane 100 .... Murphy 3

Time—1:01 1-4.

Miss Melbourne, 100, Ward; Sinfax, 103, Creedman; Arcade, 103 Casey; Cimeter, 103, Pierce, ran unplaced.

Book betting—Homer, 3-5, no place; Parapet, 20-1, 10-1; Joe Woolman, 8-1, 2-1; Arcade, 6-1, 8-5; Cimeter, 30-1, 10-1; Sinfax, 6-1, 2-1; Miss Melbourne, 30-1, 10-1.

Owing to the magnificent run made by Kildare in the selling race of Saturday last, the talent to a man selected him as the winner, and from the weights up it looked almost "a moral." Tom Daly was scratched, leaving eight starters, of which Applause was a good second choice, but again the knowing ones were doomed to disappointment, and Phil Siebenthaler's chestnut colt Sheridan was the first to catch the judges' eye, notwithstanding the fact that there were many who contended that Kildare had made a dead heat with him. After the race there were any quantity of claims of foul, but the judges listened to the bickerings of the jockeys, and the result as above stated was finally given in favor of Sheridan

When the flag fell, Dave Douglas had a slight advantage, with Kildare close on his flank, and as they swung into the lower turn, Douglas was still leading, Kildare and Applause fighting for second place, with Sheridan sticking to them like a plaster. Fanny F., Wild Oats, Nerva and Jack Brady strung out. As they swept down the back stretch, Kildare closed up with Dave Douglas, and Applause and Wild Oats close at hand. On the turn Dave Douglas, Kildare and Applause were almost together, with Sheridan trailing fully two or three lengths behind them. When they settled into the homestretch, Williams began his run on Sheridan, and right royally did he run for first honors, so much so, in fact, that as they passed under the wire, it was impossible to tell in whose favor would be the verdict, as it seemed to almost all spectators that the heat was a dead one. Applause seemingly was let up with on the straight, and did not run nearly as well as he did on Saturday, when he beat Ida Glenn. After consultation the judges decided Sheridan the winner, the following being the

SUMMARY.

Selling purse, $350, of which $50 to second; for all ages. Horses entered to be sold for $1,500 to carry rule weights; three pounds allowed for each $100 less down to $1,000, then one pound for each $100 less down to $400. Horses entered not to be sold to carry eight pounds above the scale. One mile and a sixteenth.

P. Siebenthaler's ch c Sheridan, 3, Young Bazaar—Lost Girl, 102 .... Williams 1
M. Storn's ch g Kildare, 5, Kyrle Daly—Mistake, 102 .... Pierce 2
W. George's b g Applause, 5, Three Cheers—Alice N., 101 .... Murphy 3

Time, 1:49¾.

Wild Oats, 4, 91, Baxter; Dave Douglas, a, 98, Dennison; Nerva, a, 101, Coty; Fanny F., 5, 101, Leer; Jack Brady, a, 101, Narvaez, ran unplaced.

Book betting: Sheridan 5—1, 8—5; Kildare 7—5, 2—5; Applause 2—1, 4—5; Jack Brady 5—1, 2—1; Wild Oats 5—1, 2—1; Fanny F. 15—1, 5—1; Nerva 15—1, 5—1; Dave Douglas 20—1, 8—1.

The Pacific Derby is supposed to be one of the most exciting and determined races of the spring meeting, but owing to the extreme high form shown by Flambeau, the race lost much of its interest as it seemed to be generally conceded that nothing could beat the chestnut colt, his running of last Saturday stamping him as being one of the speediest horses in the State. Henry Walsh gave the boys instructions as to how he wanted the race run, and they obeyed his orders to the letter.

There are many who to-day consider that Racine could have beaten Flambeau on Tuesday, but those who talk and think that way could have paid but little attention to the easy manner in which Flambeau came under the wire, for while he was only at a common canter Racine was at the top of his speed, and the boy necessarily had to pull him to prevent him from beating Flambeau at the wire. Mr. Walsh had determined to win with Flambeau, and consequently according to all racing rules, he was justified in instructing his jockies exactly as he did.

Five horses started in this race, and when the flag fell Lord of the Harem set out to make the run with Racine second, Sacramento third, Flambeau forth and Mohawk last. The first half mile was run in this order, all going in a very easy manner, but on the lower turn the Hearst Stable's colors were seen in front, and it was at this point that the Palo Alto colts were turned loose; going up the backstretch they found little or no trouble in getting on even terms with the leader, but it was simply a question of sufferance in allowing Sacramento an even position with them, as they could have run away from him at any time had the jockeys so desired. When they came into the homestretch Racine was leading by a half length, but Harris pulled him back, allowing Flambeau to take the lead, which the colt did very easily, and from this to the wire it was only a romp.

SUMMARY.

The Pacific Derby—For three-year-olds (foals of 1887); $100 each, half forfeit, or $10 if declared out January 1, 1889, or $20 if declared out August 1, 1889; or $30 if declared out January 1, 1890; all declarations void unless accompanied by the money; with $750 added; second to receive $200, third to save stake. One mile and a half.

Palo Alto's ch c Flambeau by Wild Idle—Flirt, 118 .... Narvaez 1
Palo Alto's b c Racine by Bishop—imp Fairy Rose, 118 .... Harris 2
George Hearst's b c Sacramento by Joe Hooker—Ada C, 118 .... Morton 3

Time, 2:41.

Mohawk, 118, Dennison, and Lord of the Harem, 118, Leonard, ran unplaced.

Book betting—Flambeau, 1 to 15, no place; Racine, 8 to 1, no place; Sacramento, 50 to 1, 8 to 1; Mohawk, 50 to 1, 10 to 1; Lord of the Harem, 60 to 1, 10 to 1.

Continued on page 347.

Our Southern California Letter.

The Santa Anita string selected to uphold the prestige of the famous breeding farm founded by Lucky Baldwin, left Monday night on the overland, bound for Brooklyn. The entire stable started out in fine form. Los Angeles never looked better, and should be able to run the race of her life during the approaching season. The Glenelg mare will carry the Maltese cross colors in the Brooklyn Handicap and given a muddy track, it is not five to one that she will not capture the classic event. It is rumored that Ciio is the stable reliance for the American Derby. Everybody connected with the Santa Anita establishment is very close mouthed, but I labor under the impression that there is very little difference between any of the three year olds and that the racing season will be far advanced before it is determined which is the best one. The two year olds are a racy looking lot. I fancy Esperanza the most. She looks speedy and if appearances are not deceptive, the daughter of Grinstead and Hermosa should make a record for herself.

The string which Bob Campbell took East is as follows:

Los Angeles' 5—Glenelg—La Polka.
Gannymede, 4—Grinstead—Jennie B.
Ciio, 3—Grinstead—Glenita.
Amigo, 3—Prince Charley.
Santiago, 3—Grinstead—Clara D.
Honduras, 3—Grinstead—Jennie B.
Sinaloa, 3—Grinstead—Maggie Emerson.
Esperanza, 2—Grinstead—Hermosa.
Ogrita, 2—Longfellow—Mission Belle.
Cleopatra, 2—Grinstead Maggie Emerson.
El Carmen, 2—Gano—Gray Anne.
Silverado, 2—Rutherford—Josie C.
Ensenada, 2—Rutherford—Arrita.

It is also intended to send a second string East sometime in June. Emperor of Norfolk will be included in the second consignment. Volante the hero of the second American Derby ever run, was also taken East to be turned over to his new owner. In discussing the Santa Anita three year olds I forgot to say a good word for Honduras. He is a slashing looking colt and his Equity win at Saratoga should not be overlooked. He packed 118 pounds and finished the ¾ mile in 1:15½, which is more than an ordinary performance over the Saratoga track.

E. B. Gifford was a visitor in Los Angeles during the past week. "We are to have a bang up meeting at San Diego in July," said the owner of Atto Rex, "and we are going to hang up some big purses. Mr Babcock, of Hotel Coronado fame, is sparing no expense in making the track at Coronado second to none in the State."

"Will Atto Rex make the circuit this year?" broke in the BREEDER AND SPORTSMAN representative

That is a matter of doubt, but I have still hopes that Rex will stand the necessary preparation"

The Directors of the Sixth District Agricultural Association held a meeting last Saturday evening, and decided to change the date of holding the Fair to Aug 4th to the 10th inclusive. This is one week earlier than originally announced. The change was made at the solicitation of severa[l] horse owners who desire to take in this meeting as well a[s] the one held at Napa. They claimed that the one day inter[-] vening was not sufficient time to make the journey.

QUARTER STRETCH GOSSIP.

Bob Campbell says that the Volante sucklings are the fin[-] est ever seen at Santa Anita. Lucky B. now regrets sellin[g] the great little horse.

George Baylis has a fast A. W. Richmond in training a[t] the Agricultural Park track, if current rumor can be relie[d] upon.

Ed Ryan, the lessee of the Agricultural Park, is taking i[n] the Blood Horse races at San Francisco.

Dr. Wise, J. W. Robinson, J C. Newton and George Hind[s] have been appointed a committee to arrange a programm[e] for the next fair. They were to meet on Wednesday.

Doc Burke and Vaughn both have a string of trotters i[n] training at Coronado. The latter has Jim Leach in hi[s] string.

Two of Atto Rex colts will make their debut this season.

Twenty-eight Will Crocker foals have made their appear[-] ance at Chino this year.

E. Duprey's mare by Inca has a foal by Radical.

Several of the local sports won on Fairy on Saturday.

The programme for the next fair is to be a tempting one. It should be ready for publication in the next issue of th[e] BREEDER AND SPORTSMAN.

Dr. Reese, of Los Angeles, is the latest addition to th[e] ranks of the breeders of California. The doctor has pur[-] chased a ranch near Riverside and starts up with several ex[-] cellent brood mares.

DAGWORTH.

New York Club Declarations.

GREAT ECLIPSE.—223 entries: (46 declared Jan. 1, 1890 spring meeting, 1890. St. Crescent, Oreda Colt St. Patrick Potomac, Flavina, Elknoa, Janet Morton Colt, Blacklock Beware, Headlight. Hannibal, Baldwin, Bourbon Belle Filly Borealis, Kate Clark Colt, Coupon Colt, Kinnet Colt, Al[...] Filly, Atlas, Babicora, Chimes, Flora McDonald Colt. Bonit[a] Heel Taps, Fresco, Compassion, Fugitive, Seashore, May[-] wood, Millrace, Snow Ball, Charley Brown. Total 37.

GALLIARD.—138 entries. (Spring meeting, 1890.) Drus[...] St. Patrick, Come and go, Gildeaway, Mistletoe, Montana Keyser, Grafton, Gaiety, Clover, Sinaloa Colt, Harpy, Vale[-] rian Filly, Penitent, Bonita, Rinfax, Tearless, John Lack[-] land, San Joaquin, Pestilence, Rushlight, Seashore, Sno[w] Ball. Total, 23.

LARCHMONT—110 entries. (Spring meeting, 1890) S[t.] Crescent, St. Patrick, Mistletoe, Montana, Grafton, Sequence Colt, Atlas, Rinfax, Tearless, Rosebud, John Lackland, Sa[n] Joaquin, Maywood, Cutalong. Total, 14.

ANTICIPATION—110 entries. (Spring meeting, 1890.) S[t.] Patrick, Flavia, Adair, Mistletoe, Montana, Keyser, Grafto[n] Atlas, Annapolis, Postmaster, Rinfax, Tearless, Rosebu[d] San Joaquin, Fugitive, El Verano. Total 16.

DEBUTANTE.—117 entries. (Spring meeting 1890.) Com[e] and Go, Sarah Hall, Mistletoe, Clover, Harpy, Valerian Fill[y] Miss Williams, Penitent, Bonita, Tearless, Rosebud, Ma[y-] wood, Cutalong. Fugitive, Seashore, May H, False Quee[n] Total 17.

CASANOVA.—92 entries. (Spring meeting, 1890.) Ma[r-] gherita, Sarah Hall, Corine Buckingham, Mistletoe, Eun[...] Gaiety, Calypso, Harpy, Valerian Filly, Miss Williams, In[...] False Queen, Miss Winkle. Total, 18.

TRIAL—35 entries. (Spring meeting, 1890.) Clarendo[n] Sacramento.

WESTCHESTER CUP—34 entries. (Spring meeting, 1890) Cortez, Buddhist, Baggage.

T. H. KOCK, Sec'y.

Sacramento Spring Meeting.

The following is the complete list of entries for the Sacramento Spring meeting:—

FIRST DAY—SATURDAY, APRIL, 26TH.

No. 1.—Purse $400; for three year olds and upwards; $15 from starters to go to second horse. A winner this year at this distance to carry three pounds extra. Maidens allowed, if three years old, five lbs.; four or more, ten pounds. Three-quarters of a mile.

J. McM. Shafter's b g, 4, Beowulf, by Kyrle Daly, dam Proserpine
Golden Gate Stable's b g, 4, Jubilee by Kyrle Daly, dam Joy.
Maltese Villa Stock Farm's ch f, 3, Mirope, by Joe Hooker, dam Constellation.
H. I. Thornton's br m, aged, Abi, by Red Boy, dam Abi by Woodburn.
W. S. Whitmore's ch h, 5, Coloma, by Joe Hooker, dam Callie Smart.
Dennison Bros.' b g, 4, G. W., by Kyrle Daly, dam Elizabeth.
W. H. E. Smith's b h, 5, Al. Farrow, by Conner, dam Della Walker
J. T. McBride's ch h, 4, Longshot, by Duke of Norfolk, dam by Langford.
Harry Howard's b h Jackson, by Luke Blackburn, dam Ivy Leaf.
L. U. Shippee's br m, 4, Picnic, by imp. Mr. Pickwick, dam imp. Countess.
J. J. Dolan's b c, 3, Revolver, by Joe Daniels, dam by Partisan.
Miller & Owen's b m, a, Daisy D., by Wheatley, dam Black Maria.
W. L. Appleby's ch m, 5, Carmen, by Wildidle, dam Nettie Brown.
W. L. Appleby's b f, 3, Raindrop, by Wildidle, dam Teardrop.
J. R. Ross' b m, 4, Kitty Van, by Vanderbilt, dam April Fool.

No. 2. Norfolk Stake—A sweepstakes for two-year-olds (foals of 1888) of $50 each, half forfeit, or only $10 if declared by January 1st, or $15 by March 1, 1890; with $500 added, of which $100 to second. Winners of any stake to carry three pounds; of two or more, five pounds penalty. Beaten maidens allowed, if once, three pounds; if twice, five pounds. Five-eighths of a mile.

P. Herzog's ch c Joe Harding by Joe Hooker, dam Irene Harding by Jack Malone.
Dennison Bros.' ch f Minnie B. by Prince of Norfolk, dam by Wildidle.
W. M. Murry's blk c Power by Powhattan, dam Lawn Tennis by Ten Broeck.
W. M. Murry's ch c Gerald by Powhattan, dam Geneva by Lexington.
W. M. Murry's b f Lady Scoggan by Little Ruffin, dam Hiawasse by War Dance.
C. Halverson's ch c Daniel S by Joe Daniels, dam Maggie S. by Bayonet.
L. J. Rose's b f Fairy by Argyle, dam imp Fairy Rose by Kisber.
Palo Alto Stock Farm's ch c Rinfax by Argyle, dam imp Amelia by Lowlander.
Palo Alto Stock Farm's ch f Tearless by Wildidle, dam imp. Teardrop by Scottish Chief.
T. H. Williams Jr's ch f Glenlevit by Flood, dam Glendew by imp. Glengarry.
John Adams' ch c Havor by Uncle Billy, dam Pearl.
L. U. Shippee's b c The Drake by Leonatus, dam The Teal by Hindoo.
L. U. Shippee's b f May H by Falsetto, dam Glenluine by Glenelg.
L. U. Shippee's b f False Queen by Falsetto, dam Queen Victoria by Lexington.
L. U. Shippee's b c Lodowic by Longfellow, dam Carrie Phillips by Malloy.
J. E. Smith's ch c Bon Ton by Flood, dam May D. by Wildidle.
Fashion Stable's b f Cheerful by Three Cheers, dam Queen Emma by Woodburn.
G. H. Kennedy's b f Acclaim by Three Cheers, dam Rosette by Beatty.
E. S. Paddock's b f Miss Melbourne by Gano, dam Victoria by Wildidle.
H. I. Thornton's ch c Arcade by Milner, dam Nannie Hubbard by Hubbard.
H. I. Thornton's b c Peralta by John Happy, dam Bertha W. by Wilmington.
Oak Grove Stable's b c Happy John by John Happy, dam Little Flush by Leinster.
Oak Grove Stable's ch c Frank by Frank Rhoads, dam Aunt Jane by Bazaar.

No. 3. Selling Purse, $400, of which $50 to second; for all ages. Winners to be sold at auction. Horses entered to be sold for $1,500 to carry rule weight. One pound off for each $100 down to $500. Value placed on starters only by 6 P. M. night before race; one mile and a sixteenth.

Wesley George's b g, aged, Applause by Three Cheers, dam Alice N. by Norfolk.
Dennison Bros.' b g, aged, Dave Douglas by Leinster, dam Lilly Simpson.
P. Siebenthaler's ch c, 3, Sheridan by Young Bazaar, dam Lost Girl.
J. Hilton's b g, 4, Albatross by Pill Box, dam Delia Walker.
Matt Storn's ch g, 5, Kildare by Kyrle Daly, dam Mistake.
Golden Gate Stable's blk g, aged, Black Pilot by Echo, dam Madge Duke.
G. Hill's b g, 3, Steve Stroud by Billy Lee, dam by Woodburn.
Kelly & Samuels' br m, 5, Welcome by Warwick, dam Aeolia.
J. R. Ross' b g, aged, Oro by Norfolk, dam Golden Gate
L. Menenhall's ch m (5) Maggie B. by Milner, dam Young Grecian Bend.
M. H. Smith's b g (a) Jou Jou by Monday, dam Plaything.
Orange Grove Stable's b h (6, Jack Brady by Wildidle, dam Sour Grapes.

No. 4. The California Oaks—A sweepstakes for three-year-old fillies (foals of 1887) of $50 each, $15 forfeit, with $600 added; $100 to second, $50 to third, out of stakes. Winners in 1890 to carry five pounds extra. Beaten maidens allowed five pounds. One mile and an eighth.

Dennison Bros.'s br f Eda by Powhattan, dam Haidee by King Alfonso.
G. W. Trahern's ch f Retta B. by Joe Hooker, dam Kate Carson by Joe Daniels.
J. P. Woolman's b f Emma Nevada by John A., dam May D. by Wildidle.
C. Halverson's ch f Fabiola by Warwick, dam Maggie S. by Bayonet.
Palo Alto Stock Farm's ch f Muta by Wildidle, dam imp. Mutiny by Adventurer.
W. L. Appleby's b f Raindrop by Wildidle, dam imp. Teardrop by Scottish Chief.
L. U. Shippee's b f Mabel F. by Longfellow, dam Carrie Phillips by Pat Malloy.
J. B. Chase's ch f Marigold by Milner, dam Katy Pease by Planet.
Kelly & Samuels' b f Adelaide by Grinstead, dam Victoria by Wildidle.
H. I. Thornton's ch f Reata by Milner, dam Marin by Thad Stevens.
Oak Grove Stable's ch f Philena by Joe Hooker, dam Lena's First by Bazaar.

SECOND DAY—TUESDAY, APRIL 29TH.

No. 5. The Matadero Stake—A sweepstakes for two-year-olds (foals of 1888), of $100 each, half forfeit, or only $10 if declared by January 1st or $25 March 1, 1890, with $500 added, $100 to second, $50 to third. Winners of any event of the value of $800 to carry three pounds; of $1000, five pounds; of two of any value, seven pounds extra. Beaten maidens allowed five pounds. Three-quarters of a mile.

P. Herzog's ch c Joe Harding by Joe Hooker, dam Irene Harding by Jack Malone.
Dennison Bros.' ch f Minnie B. by Prince of Norfolk dam by Wildidle.
W. M. Murry's blk c Power by Powhattan, dam Lawn Tennis by Ten Broeck.
W. M. Murry's b f Lady Scoggan by Little Ruffin, dam Hiawasse by War Dance.
Palo Alto Stock Farm's ch c Rinfax by Argyle, dam by imp. Amelia by Lowlander.
L. J. Rose's br c Conrad by Flood, dam imp. Gonia by Exminster.
R. B. Cockrill's b c Mero by Wildidle, dam Precious by Lever.
L. J. Rose' b f Fairy by Argyle, dam imp Fairy Rose by Kisber.
L. U. Shippee's b f May H. by Falsetto, dam Glenluine by Glenelg.
L. U. Shippee's b f False Queen by Falsetto, dam Queen Victoria by Lexington.
L. U. Shippee's b c Lodowic by Longfellow, dam Carrie Phillips by Pat Malloy.
L. U. Shippee's b c The Drake by Leonatus, dam The Teal by Hindoo.
J. E. Smith's ch c Bon Ton by Flood, dam May D. by Wildidle.

No. 6. The Chris Green Handicap.—A sweepstakes for all ages of $25 each, h f, or $10 if declared; with $500 added; second horse to receive $100 out of stakes. Weights announced March 1st. Declarations due by 6 P. M. April 1st. A winner of any race, after publication of weights, of one mile or upwards, to carry 3 lbs, extra; of two races 5 lbs; of three or more, 7 lbs. This will not apply to horses handicapped at 125 lbs. or over. One and one-quarter miles.

G. Hill's b g, 3, Steve Stroud 90, by Billy Lee, dam by Woodburn.
W. L. Appleby's b f, 3, Raindrop 95, by Wildidle, dam. imp. Teardrop.
W. L. Appleby's ch f, 4, Odette 105, by Shiloh, dam Margery by Error.
L. J. Rose's b g, aged, Mikado 120, by Shiloh, dam Margery by Error.
Dennison Bros.' b h, 4, Hotspur 113, by Joe Daniels, dam sister to Jim Douglas.
Dennison Bros.' b g, 4, G. W., 110, by Kyrle Daly, dam Elizabeth.
Kelly & Samuels' b h, 5, Ed. McGinnis 115, by Grinstead, dam Jennie G.
W. H. E. Smith's b h, 5, Al Farrow 120, by Conner, dam Della Walker.
J. T. McBride's ch m, 4, Longshot 110, by Duke of Norfolk, dam by Langford.
L. U. Shippee's br m, 4, Picnic 110, by imp. Mr. Picwick, dam imp. Countess.
Elmwood Stable's b g, 5, Nabean 95, by Nathan Coomb's, dam Beauty.
H. D. Miller's b m, aged, Daisy D 116, by Wheatley, dam Black Maria.

No. 7. Purse $400, for all ages; $10 from starters to go to second horse. Maiden allowances: if 3 years, 5 lbs; four and upwards, 10 lbs. Non winners this year allowed 6 lbs. Allowances cumulative. One and one sixteenth miles.

Wesley George's b g, aged, Applause, by Three Cheers, dam Alice N.
T. H. William's s f, 3, Retta B, by Norfolk, dam Kate Carson.
H. I. Thornton's br m, aged, Abi, by Red Boy, dam Abi.
W. L. Whitmore's ch h, 5, Coloma, by Joe Hooker, dam Callie Smart.
Dennison Bros.' b m Sallie C., by Thornhill, dam by Wildidle.
W. H. E. Smith's b h, 5, Al. Farrow, by Connor, dam Della Walker.
L. U. Shippee's br m, 4, Picnic, by imp. Picwick, dam imp. Countess.
Matt Storn's ch c, 3, Larghetta, by Jils Johnson, dam Leveret.
Miller & Owen's blk c Capt. Al, by Kingston, dam Black Maria.
W. L. Appleby's ch m Carmen, by Wildidle, dam Nettie Brown.
W. L. Appleby's b m Raindrop, by Wildidle, dam imp. Teardrop.

No. 8. The Weinstock, Lubin & Co. Stake.—A sweepstake for three year olds (foals of 1887), of $50 each, half forfeit, or only $15 each if declared January 1st, 1890, with $600 added, of which $100 to second, $50 to third. Winners in 1890 of any three year old event, when carrying weight for age or more, of the value of $500, to carry three pounds; of $1,000, or two of any value, 5 lbs. extra. Non-winners allowed 5 lbs. One mile.

P. Herzog's b c Mohawk by Norfolk, dam Irene Harding.
Dennison Bros.' br f Eda by Powhattan, dam Haidee by King Alfonzo.
G. W. Trahern's ch f Retta B. by Joe Hooker, dam Kate Carson by Joe Daniels.
Dennison Bros.' ch c Prince's First by Prince of Norfolk, dam by Wildidle.
J. P. Woolman's b f Emma Nevada by John A., dam May D. by Wildidle.
W. M. Murry's b f Lady Ali by Hyder Ali, dam Mollie Ward by imp. Intruder.
W. M. Murry's b g Leland by Flood, dam imp. Amelia by Lowlander.
W. M. Murry's ch c Kiro by Joe Hooker, dam by Foster.
C. Halverson's ch f Fabiola by Warwick, dam Maggie S. by Bayonet.
Palo Alto Stock Farm's b c Racine by Bishop, dam imp. Fairy Rose by Kisber.
Palo Alto Stock Farm's ch c Flambeau by Wildidle, dam imp. Flirt by The Hermit.
L. J. Rose's br g Rico by Shannon, dam Fanny Lewis by imp. Buckden.
P. Siebenthaler's ch c King Hooker by Joe Hooker, dam Violet by Leinster.
P. Siebenthaler's ch c Sheridan by Young Bazaar, dam Lost Girl by Leinster.
Thomas H. Boyle's ch c Morton by Leinster, dam Lilly H. by Newry.
L. U. Shippee's ch c Major Ban by King Ban, dam Hearsay by imp. Australian.
L. U. Shippee's b c Take Notice by Prince Charlie, dam Nota Bene by Glenelg.
L. U. Shippee's b c Fellowcharm by Longfellow, dam Trinket by Great Tom.
J. B. Chase's ch f Marigold by Milner, dam Katy Pease by Planet.
Kelly & Samuels' b g Pliny by Flood, dam Precious by Lever
Kelly & Samuels' b f Adelaide by Grinstead, dam Daisy D.
J. W. Donathan's ch c Hubert Earl by John A., dam Lottie J. by Wildidle.
H. D. Miller's br c Captain Al by Kingston, dam Black Maria by Belmont.
H. I. Thornton's ch c El Rayo by Grinstead, dam Sunlit by Monday.
H. I. Thornton's ch f Reata by Milner, dam Marin by Thad Stevens.
Oak Grove Stable's ch f Philena by Joe Hooker, dam Lena's First by Bazaar.
Oak Grove Stable's ch f May Dunbar by Leinster, dam Lizzie Dunbar by Bazaar.
Oak Grove Stable's ch c Tippecanoe by Bazaar, dam Lizzie P. by Leinster.
Golden Gate Stable's b c Tom Hazlett by Wildidle, dam Lizzie Brown by Rifleman.

THIRD DAY—THURSDAY, MAY 1ST.

No. 9. The Spring Stakes—A sweepstakes for three-year-olds (foals of 1887) that have not won a race previous to January 1, 1890; $50 entrance, half forfeit, or $15 if declared April 1, 1890; $400 added; second to receive $75 from stakes. Maidens at time of starting allowed five pounds. One mile.

L. J. Rose's s h Rover by Wildidle, dam imp. Rosetta.
L. J. Rose's b f Glenloch by Flood, dam Glendew.
Matt Storn's ch f Marigold by Milner, dam Katy Pease.
H. Howard's br f Mayetta by Joe Daniels, dam Amanda L.
W. M. Murry's ch h Kiro by Joe Hooker, dam by Foster.
W. M. Murry's b g Leland by Flood, dam Amelia.
P. Herzog's b h Mohawk by Norfolk, dam Irene Harding.
Dennison Bros.' ch h Prince's First by Prince of Norfolk, dam Lizzie Idle.
P. Siebenthaler's ch c King Hooker by Joe Hooker, dam Violet.
L. U. Shippee's b c Take Notice by Prince Charlie, dam Nota Bene.
L. U. Shippee's b f Mabel F. by Longfellow, dam Carrie Phillips.
L. Menenhall's ch m Maggie B. by Milner, dam Young Grecian Bend.

No. 10. The Western Hotel Stakes—A sweepstakes for two-year-old fillies (foals of 1888), of $50 each; $15 forfeit; with $500 added; of which $100 to second; winners to carry five pounds extra. Beaten maidens allowed five pounds. Five-eighths of a mile.

Maltese Villa Stock Farm's blk f Onti Ora by Alta, dam Thetis by Ten Broeck.
Maltese Villa Stock Farm's br f Itomeet'a by imp Woodlands, dam Dizzy Blonde.
Maltese Villa Stock Farm's ch f Zingarella by Ed Corrigan, dam Minuet by Norfolk.
Dennison Bros.' ch f Minnie B by Prince of Norfolk, dam by Wildidle.
W. M. Murry's b f Lady Scoggan by Little Ruffin, dam Hiawasse.
T. H. Williams' ch f Glenlivet by Flood, dam Glendew.
L. J. Rose's blk f Peri by Flood, dam Frolic.
L. J. Rose's b f Fairy by Argyle, dam imp Fairy Rose.
Palo Alto Stock Farm's ch f Tearless by Wildidle, dam imp Teardrop.
L. U. Shippee's b f False Queen by Falsetto, dam Queen Victoria.
L. U. Shippee's b f May H by Falsetto, dam Glenluine.
Ben Timmons' ch f Lisette by Hyder Ali, dam Kate Fletcher.
Fashion Stable's ch f Cheerful by Three Cheers, dam Queen Emma.
G. H. Kennedy's b f Acclaim by Three Cheers, dam Rosette.
E. S. Paddock's b f Miss Melbourne by Gano, dam Victoria.
H. I. Thornton's b f Madeline by John Happy, dam Jongleuse.
H. I. Thornton's b f Cimeter by Hyder Ali, dam Sabrina
Oak Grove Stable's ch f Alice C. by Joe Hooker, dam Hattie Ball.

No. 11. The Hall, Luhrs & Co. Handicap—A sweepstakes for three-year-olds (foals of 1887), of $50 each, half forfeit, or or only $10 if declared January 1, 1890, or $15 if by 4 P. M. day before the race; with $750 added, of which $100 to second, $50 to third. Weights to be announced by 8 P. M. second day before the race. One mile and a quarter.

P. Herzog's b c Herzog by Norfolk, dam Irene Harding.
Dennison's Bros.' br f Eda by Powhattan, dam Haidee.
Dennison Bros.' ch c Prince's First by Prince of Norfolk, dam by Wildidle.
J. P. Woolman's b f Emma Nevada by John A., dam May D.
C. Halverson's ch f Fabiola by Warwick, dam Maggie S.
Palo Alto Stock Farm's b c Racine by Bishop, dam imp Fairy Rose by Kisber
Palo Alto Stock Farm's ch c Flambeau by Wildidle, dam imp Flirt.
L. J. Rose's br g Rico by Shannon, dam Fanny Lewis.
Palo Alto Stock Farm's ch f Muta by Wildidle, dam imp Mutiny.
P. Siebenthaler's ch c King Hooker by Joe Hooker, dam Violet.
P. Siebenthaler's ch c Sheridan by Young Bazaar, dam Lost Girl.
Thos. H. Boyle's ch c Morton by Leinster, dam Lilly H.
L. U. Shippee's b c Fellowcharm by Longfellow, dam Trinket.
L. U. Shippee's b c Take Notice by Prince Charlie, dam Nota Bene.
L. U. Shippee's ch c Major Ban by King Ban, dam Hearsay.
L. U. Shippee's b f Mabel F. by Longfellow, dam Carrie Phillips.
Matt Storn's ch c Larghetta by Jils Johnson, dam Leveret.
Kelly & Samuels' b g Pliny by Flood, dam Precious.
Kelly & Samuels' b f Adelaide by Grinstead, dam Victoria.
J. W. Donathan's ch c Hubert Earl by John A. dam Lottie J.
H. D. Miller's br c Captain Al by Kingston, dam Black Maria.
H. I. Thornton's ch c El Rayo by Grinstead, dam Sunlit.
Oak Grove Stable's ch f May Dunbar by Leinster, dam Lizzie Dunbar.
Oak Grove Stable's ch f Gypsy by Leinster, dam Aunt Jane.
Oak Grove Stable's ch c Tippecanoe by Bazaar, dam Lizzie P.
Golden Gate Stable's b c Tom Hazlitt by Wild Idle, dam Lizzie Brown.

No. 12. Selling purse, $400, of which $50 to second; for all ages. Horses entered to be sold for $1500 to carry rule weight. One pound off for each $100 down to $400. Value placed on starters only by 6 P. M. night before race. One and one eighth miles.

Golden Gate Stable's blk g Black Pilot by Echo, dam Madge Duke.
Wesley George's b g Applause by Three Cheers, dam Alice N.
Dennison Bros.' b g Dave Douglas by Leinster, dam Lilly Simpson.
J. T. McBride's ch h Longshot by Duke of Norfolk, dam by Langford.
J. Hilton's b g Albatross by Pill Box, dam Delia Walker.
Matt Storn's ch g Kildare by Kyrle Daly, dam Mistake.
W. L. Appleby's b g Steve Stroud by Billy Lee, dam by Woodburn.
Kelly & Samuels' br m Welcome by Warwick, dam Aeola.
J. R. Ross' b g Oro by Norfolk, dam April Fool.
M. H. Smith's b g Jou Jou by Monday, dam Plaything.
Orange Grove Stable's b h Jack Brady by Wild Idle, dam Sour Grapes.

FOURTH DAY—SATURDAY, MAY 3D.

No. 13. Golden Eagle Hotel Handicap—A sweepstakes for two-year-olds (foals of 1888), of $100 each, half forfeit, or only $10 if declared January 1, 1890, or $25 if by 4 P. M. day before the race; with $600 added; of which $150 to second. Weights to be announced by 8 o'clock P. M. second day before the race. Three-quarters of a mile.

P. Herzog's ch c Joe Harding by Joe Hooker, dam Irene Harding.
Dennison Bros.' ch f Minnie B by Prince of Norfolk, dam by Wild Idle.
J. E. Smith's ch c Bon Ton by Flood, dam May D.
W. M. Murry's blk c Power by Powhattan, dam Lawn Tennis.
W. M. Murry's b f Lady Scoggan by Little Ruffin, dam Hiawasse.
C. Halverson's ch c Daniel S by Joe Daniels, dam Maggie S.
Palo Alto Stock Farm's ch c Rinfax by Argyle, dam imp Amelia.
R. B. Cockrill's b c Mero by Wild Idle, dam Precious.
L. J. Rose's br c Conrad by Flood, dam imp Gonia.
L. J. Rose's blk f Peri by Flood, dam Frolic.
L. U. Shippee's b f May H by Falsetto, dam Glenluine.
L. U. Shippee's b f False Queen by Falsetto, dam Queen Victoria by Lexington
L. U. Shippee's b c Lodowic by Longfellow, dam Carrie Phillips.
L. U. Shippee's b c The Drake by Leonatus, dam The Teal.
H. I. Thornton's ch c Arcade by Milner, dam Nannie Hubbard.
H. I. Thornton's b c Peralta by John Happy, dam Bertha W.
Oak Grove Stable's ch c Frank by Frank Rhoads, dam Aunt Jane.
Oak Grove Stable's b c Happy John by John Happy, dam Little Flush.

No. 14. The Hopeful Handicap—A sweepstakes for all ages of $25 each, $15 forfeit, or $10 if declared, with $400 added, second to receive $100. Weights announced at 10 P. M. day before race; declarations due by 5 P. M. same day. One and one-eighth miles.

J. McM. Shafter's b m (4) Louisa M by Kyrle Daly, dam Nighthawk.
Golden Gate Stable's b g (4) Jubilee by Kyrle Daly, dam Joy.
T. H. Williams' s f (3) Retta B by Norfolk, dam Kate Carson.
Palo Alto Stock Farm's b c (4) Geoffrey by Flood, dam Glendew.
Palo Alto Stock Farm's b f (4) Faustine by Flood, dam imp Flirt.
Maltese Villa Stock Farm's ch f (3) Mirope by Joe Hooker, dam Constellation.
H. I. Thornton's br m (aged) Abi by Red Boy, dam Abi.
W. L. Whitmore's ch h (5) Coloma by Joe Hooker, dam Callie Smart.
Wesley George's b g (aged) Applause by Three Cheers, dam Alice N.
P. Siebenthaler's ch c (3) Sheridan by Young Bazaar, dam Lost Girl.
W. H. E. Smith's b h (5) Al Farrow by Conner, dam Della Walker.
J. T. McBride's ch h, (4) Longshot by Duke of Norfolk, dam by Langford.
L. U. Shippee's br m (4) Picnic by imp Mr. Pickwick, dam imp Countess.
J. J. Dolan's b c (3) Revolver by Joe Daniels, dam by Partisan.
W. L. Appleby's ch m (5) Carmen by Wild Idle, dam Nettie Brown.
W. L. Appleby's b m (3) Raindrop by Wild Idle, dam imp Teardrop.
Kelly & Samuels' b g (3) Pliny by Flood, dam Precious.
Kelly & Samuels' b h (5) Ed McGinnies by Grinstead, dam Jennie G.
J. R. Ross' b g (aged) Oro by Norfolk, dam Golden Gate.

No. 15. The California Derby—A sweepstakes for three-year-olds (foals of 1887) of $100 each, half forfeit, or only $10 if declared January 1st, or $25 March 1, 1890; with $1000 added; of which $150 to second and $100 to third. A winner in 1890 of any three-year old event, when carrying weight for age or more, of the value of $500, to carry three pounds; of $1000, or two races of any value, five pounds extra. Non-winners of a sweepstakes allowed five pounds; maidens allowed seven pounds. One mile and a half.

P. Herzog's b c Mohawk by Norfolk, dam Irene Harding.
Dennison Brothers' b f Edna by Powhattan, dam Haidee.
Dennison Brothers' ch c Prince's First by Prince of Norfolk, dam by Wild Idle.
A. G. Todd's b c Floren by Wild Idle, dam Frolic.
J. P. Woolman's b f Emma Nevada by John A., dam May D.
W. M. Murry's b f Lady Ali by Hyder Ali, dam Molly Ward.
W. M. Murry's b g Leland by Flood, dam imp Amelia.
W. M. Murry's ch c Kiro by Joe Hooker, dam by Foster.
Palo Alto Stock Farm's ch f Muta by Wild Idle, dam imported Mutiny.
Palo Alto Stock Farm's ch c Flambeau by Wild Idle, dam imp Flirt.
Palo Alto Stock Farm's b c Racine by Bishop, dam Fairy Rose.
L. J. Rose's br g Rico by Shannon, dam Fanny Lewis.
P. Siebenthaler's ch c King Hooker by Joe Hooker, dam Violet.
P. Siebenthaler's ch c Sheridan by Young Bazaar, dam Lost Girl.
T. H. Boyle's ch c Morton by Leinster, dam Lily H.
L. U. Shippee's b c Take Notice by Prince Charlie, dam Nota Bene.
Matt Storn's ch c Larghetta by Jils Johnson, dam Leveret.
Kelly & Samuels' b g Pliny by Flood, dam Precious.
J. W. Donathan's ch c Hubert Earl by John A. dam Lottie J.
H. I. Thornton's ch c El Rayo by Grinstead, dam Sunlit.
Oak Grove Stable's ch c Gypsy by Leinster, dam Aunt Jane.
Oak Grove Stable's ch f May Dunbar by Leinster, dam Lizzie Dunbar.
Golden Gate Stable's b c Tom Halett by Wild Idle, dam Lizzie Brown.

No. 16. Purse $400, for all ages; $10 from starters to go to second horse. Non-winners this year at the time of starting allowed, if three years old, five pounds; four years, ten pounds; five and upwards, twelve pounds. Entries close with Clerk of Course at 5 P. M. day before the race. Mile heats.

San Jose Colt Stakes.

Secretary Bragg of the Santa Clara Valley Agricultural Society sends us the following list of entries for the two year olds and yearlings to be trotted at San Jose during the fall meeting:—

Santa Clara County Trotting Stakes.—*For two year olds* (for the County only) $30 entrance, $10 of which must accompany the nomination, $10 on June 1st, and $10 on Aug. 1st, with $150 added. Mile and repeat. Parties must have owned colts prior to Feb. 1st, 1890, to be eligible for this stake.

James W. Rea, San Jose, s f Johnie B., Abbottsford—Baby Mine
James W. Rea, San Jose, Bonnie Piedmont, Piedmont—Bonnie.
John Charleston, Mountain View, b c Riley, Sultan Jr—by Hercules.
William F Domesky, San Jose, b c Patchwood, Nutwood—by Geo. M. Patchen Jr.
H. Kralenburg, San Jose, b f Lady Bismarck, Bismarck—by Venture.
Boyd & Cox, San Jose, br f Foster, Boxwood—by Queen.
A. O. Hooker, San Jose ch f Nelly Goldford, Abbottsford—Nelly Allen.
T. S. Montgomery, San Jose, s g Coronado, Menlo—by Hambletonian George.
T. S. Montgomery, San Jose, blk f Cora R., Antinous—by Wilson's Patchen.
N. W. Stockton, San Jose, s f Queen Annie, King William—by Chrisman's Hambletonian.
W. H. Vioget Santa Clara, br f Clovewood, Clovis—Olita.

Infant Trotting Stakes.—The get of horses named for yearling foals of 1889; $25 entrance, $5 of which must accompany the nomination, $10 on June 1st, and $10 on Aug. 1st, with $100 added. Mile dash.

Ben E. Harris, San Francisco, blk c Acorn, John Sevenoakes—Elmorene.
H. C. Cox, San Jose, b c George Hill, Billy Thornhill—Pauline.
R. H. Walton, San Jose, b c Arctic, Argent—not given.
Ed. McLees, Vallejo, b f Lady Thornhill, Billy Thornhill—Lady Nutwood.
James Weatherhead, San Jose, b c Zound Herold, Royal George—by John Nelson.
James Weatherhead, San Jose, b f Lady Dashwood, Woodnut—Lumont.
M. Scott, Santa Clara, b c No Name, Designer—Winnie.
T. S Montgomery, San Jose, b c Alviso, Brown Jug—Big Liza.
Boyce & Topham, Milpitas, b f Winnie B. Billy Thornhill—by Electioneer.
La Siesta Ranch, Menlo Park, b f Dongella, Eros—by Chrisman's Hambletonian.
La Siesta Ranch, Menlo Park, b f Luck, Eros—by Nutwood.
T. S. Montgomery, San Jose, Alvina, Eros—by Nellie Nutwood

TURF AND TRACK.

D. D. Withers has engaged Reagan and Clayton to ride for him for the season.

Trainers at Memphis think the Chicago stable is the strongest string in the South.

Russia 2:28½ sister to Maud S. 2:08¾ has teen sent by the Woodburn Farm to Axtell.

M. J. Daly is now the owner of Salisbury, who was purchased from D. D. Withers.

H. S. Veech, Louisville, has built a straight covered track, a furlong in length on his farm.

That good but erratic mare Connemara has been sent to Kentucky to be bred to imp Verger a son of Cathedral.

Poor old Jim McGowan, the celebrated chaser, had to be killed on account of aggravating sores on his forelegs.

Jimmie Rowe says Harry Bassett was the best horse he ever rode, and was as good as any he ever saw saddled.

Col. R. S. Strader who recently made an eastern trip says that the best horse he saw was Woodnut—By Holly's old favorite.

It seems that all the third-class selling platers that can't win at any placeelse in the country are going to the St. Louis matinees.

Sorrento, once Dan McCarty's pet, now the property of G. Walbaum won his first race under the new colors last Saturday.

Tom Riley, owner of Rapine and others, died rather suddenly last week, having been sick but a few days. He was buried on Sunday.

Pantaloon, the chestnut stallion by imp. Leamington, has been brought to Kentucky from Illinois, and he will remain in the former state.

Joe Courtney, the Winters' four year old, who showed such speed last year, has been lame, but was expected to be all right in a few days.

James Galway, the master of the Preakness' Stable, has completely recovered his health and will not sell the stable as he had intended to.

Fresno was well represented in town and on the track last week by R. B. Terry, the Berrys, J. M. Reuck, F. N. Baldwin and other prominent men.

The best two-year-olds in the string of the late T. J. Megibben are the brother to Avondale and the sister to Abilene. They are known as Avalon and Actress.

Hanover's brother, Houston, is the "tip" at Gravesend for the Volunteer Handicap. It is said that Houston will be the big surprise party of the spring season.

Jimmy McLaughlin had a narrow escape a fortnight ago, being thrown from his buggy. Luckily he was not seriously injured, escaping without any broken bones.

The double-gaited turf performer Jewett (trotting record, 2:20; pacing, 2:11), has been placed in the hands of Jim Pettit, and will be campaigned by him this season.

It is said that the fast filly Flyaway worked a half-mile at Louisville the other day in 52 seconds, with weight up and pulled double. She is considered the best filly there.

Aristides Welch, the well known breeder, one owner of the mighty Leamington, and erstwhile proprietor of Erdenheim, died at Philadelphia last week in his seventy ninth year.

Senator Hose is now the owner of the thoroughbred stallion Argyle, six years old by Monday, out of Cuba, by imp. Australian etc. $5000 was the price paid the Palo Alto Stock Farm for him.

G. G. White of the Gilt Edge Stock Farm, sold to John Madden of Lexington, the black stallion Clay Wilkes, by George Wilkes, dam Madam Adams, by American Clay Price $20,000.

Ferryman is among the most promising two-year-olds at New Orleans. He is a slashing big bay colt by Vanderbilt—Eva S. Within a week he went a half mile in :50½ without being ridden out.

Old Hickory Jim is said to be in better trim than he has been for several seasons. Uncle Joe Elliot always declared that the old horse must have been a son of Glenelg, he resembled him so much.

Macuncas the winner of the Molyneux Stakes, worth £1240 to the winner for two year olds at Manchester, England, was purchased for £150 last Spring at the Neasham Annual yearling sale by Mr. Abington.

The San Jose Fair Association have changed their dates to Aug. 6th and following days so it will now immediately precede the Napa Fair. As the pavilion exhibit cannot be got ready by then, it will take place later.

Signor Francisco Alfarada of the City of Mexico has bought the chestnut three year old Auburndale by Harry O.Fallon out of Little Nell by King Lear of L. B. Fields of Lexington, Kentucky. Auburndale will be raced in Mexico.

W. H. Crawford has built a fire-proof stable for Wilton and Empire Wilkes. He says he doesn't want any Bell Boy accidents, and intends to use every precaution to keep his two stallions from meeting the fate of Electioneer's high-priced son.

John E. Madden is said to have the best stable of trotters in training at Lexington. They are bred in the purple and at least three of them can show a mile better than 2:20. Madden is also campaigning a select stable of thoroughbreds.

Mr. Pulsifer made a round sum by backing Tenny in the winter books on the Volunteer Handicap a year ago, and he evidently thinks that he now has a good chance of carrying off the rich Suburban honors, with a big barrel of the hard dollars of commerce to boot.

John Reavey has sold Bessie Shannon (sister to Bishop, sire of Racine) by Shannon, out of Bettie Bishop, to Mr. Vanini, Franktown, Washoe County. Bessie was a fair race mare herself, and with the strains of blood she has, should be invaluable as a broodmare.

M. F. Tarpey has traded Sour Grapes (the dam of Jack Brady) to Percy Williams, receiving in exchange a three-year-old filly by Nephew, dam by Nutwood, grandam thoroughbred. The filly has been sent to Director. Sour Grapes is heavy in foal to the Prince of Norfolk.

Senator Stanford is using as stallions on his Vina Ranch Benton Frolic, by General Benton 1756, out of Frolic, a thoroughbred mare; Azmoor 2:24½, by Electioneer 125, out of Mamie C., by imp. Hercules, and Liberty by Piedmont 2:17¼, out of American Girl by Toronto Sontag 307.

A club-house is in process of erection at the Kentucky Association course. A new grand stand will be built this summer, and great improvements have also been made on the track. It has been widened, and the hill which obstructed the view of the first quarter has been cut down.

The Sacramento talent did not score on the opening day at the Blood Horse meeting, although they won a race with Al Farrow and another with Longshot. Al Farrow was not backed much by them, while all backed Coloma and when he could not win Longshot in the same stable had to.

The success of a training stable does not altogether depend upon the skill, knowledge, etc., of the managing chief, but very materially upon detail, the faithfulness of subordinates, and their good judgment relative to the care, kindness, and the proper handling of the horses under their charge.

The Minnesota Driving Club will give a four days' racing meeting from July 1st to 4th. The amount hung up for stakes and purses is $20,000. The special race for July 4th is a free-for all pace, with Johnston barred, for a purse of $2000. There will be twelve races during the meeting.

Among the entries for the Helena Pioneer stakes, a six furlong two year old race, are Bonnieville, a full brother to Sunday the crack sprinter. Bessie a two year old sister to Hamlet formerly the property of B. C. Holly and Sinfax, a Palo Alto bred colt by Wildidle out of Fostress, the dam of Question.

John G. Kreyer has sold to Charles Boyle the five-year-old bay horse Longitude, by Longfellow, dam Indemnity. The horse will likely be sent to Canada for use as a stallion. As he was a fair racer, he might sport silk the other side of the border, and show his heels to many of the horses there before he is retired.

One of the principal features of Morris Park, when all the plans have been completed, will be the club house. This building will be of brick and wood, 120 feet long and 120 feet deep, with a tower 30 feet square and 130 feet high, which dimensions, however, give an inadequate idea of what the building will be.

It will hardly be credited what some of our big bookmakers lose over bad debts, says the London Sunday Times. One of the leviathans told me recently that his losses under this head during the last ten years, have amounted to over £150,000, but he cannot afford to press for the money for fear of losing custom.

J. Malcolm Forbes, of Boston, has purchased from George H. Hicks the two year old filly Rusenole by Electioneer, dam Rebecca (dam of Rexford 2:24), by Gen. Benton; second dam Clarabel (dam of Clifton Belle 2:24½), by Abdallah Star. This is the filly that Mr. Hicks bought at the recent New York sale for $1575, and declined an advance of $1000.

The track at the Bay District was this year in good shape for the horses to work on when they arrived, having been cut up and worked into good order, and great credit is due the Superintendent, J. F. Edgar, who was out early and late displaying an extraordinary amount of activity and vim, which was appreciated by every one who had horses to work or race on the track.

William Day, the veteran trainer who handled Foxhall in England, is about fifty years behind in some of his views. He would do away with ready-money betting, but it would in my opinion prevent heavy gambling if all our plungers were compelled to put up the stakes as they make their bets. Speculating on the nod is the cause of there being so many "brokers."

Among the many visitors to San Francisco for the Blood Horse races, there was no one more enthusiastic and better posted than R. B. Terry the brilliant Fresno lawyer. His knowledge of racing pedigrees and racing itself is astounding when one considers that he is so tied to his profession that he has very little leisure to devote to the sport of Kings. T'is ever true 'breeding will tell.'

The "Racing Calender" of March 27th states that a meeting of the Jockey Club will be held at Newmarket on Wednesday in the Craven meeting, when the following motion will be moved by Lord Durham:—"That in future a shorthand writer be present at all meetings of the Jockey Club, and that a full report of the proceedings be published in the next available "Racing Calender."

The farmers for miles around are complaining about Smith's bell at Guttenberg, which rings when the horses start. The farmers declare their hands are eating them out of house and home, as every time they hear the bell they think, for an instant, it is the dinner gong, and with their minds running so continually on food, they return with the appetite of a horse, and eat gigantic suppers.

Mr. Russell Manning, M. D., V S., said in 1881: "The day is passed for bleeding and purging for every ill that even horseflesh is heir to." Dr. Dixon says: "Nature is ever busy by the silent operation of her forces in curing disease. Her medicines are air, warmth, food, water and sleep. Their use is directed by instinct, and that man is most worthy the name of physician who most reveres her example."

The Tidal Stakes, 1¼ miles, brought out the Palo Alto cracks in grand style. The general opinion after the race was that at 1¼ miles there was very little to choose between the colts. Had Flambeau's saddle not slipped the race would have been run much faster. Luckily the horse had a martingale on which helped to keep the saddle in position, or possibly the plunger would have lost his $1000 on Flambeau.

The Hearst stable has shown up in good form this sp[...] with Del Mar a winner at San Jose and Almont at the B[...] Horse. The handsome son of Three Cheers ran a grand [...] on Tuesday, and had it not been for his severe illne[...] Fort Worth, would have been fit for any company.

Sam Caton, who wintered in Los Angeles, has left for [...] York State with sixteen head, including three purchase[...] California this winter, viz., Cousin Jo, pacer, by Del S[...] bay mare, sister to Contractor, by Sultan; and a two year [...] filly by Stamboul out of Soncie Lass. Mr. Caton was hi[...] pleased with the California climate and facilities for win[...]ing, and leaves many new friends behind him.

J. M. Reuck, the enterprising proprietor of the Fr[...] Turf, a rapidly improving monthly turf journal publishe[...] the raisin city, came up to town for the races. Just be[...] leaving home Mr. Reuck's mare Rose R., by Pasha [...] granddam by Hock Hocking, foaled a handsome fil[...] Apex 2:26. With the Hock Hocking blood to brace up [...] speedy trotting lines in the youngster, she should go d[...] the line.

The two-year-old filly Belligerent, by Fiddlesticks ou[...] Bellona, who was bred by August Belmont, died in Mc[...]mick's stable late Monday night. She was worked on Fr[...] and Saturday, and on Sunday morning was given mode[...] exercise. When she was returned to her stable she was [...]en with pneumonia and died within twenty-four ho[...] McCormick remained up all Sunday night attending the [...] but medical aid was useless.

Who's to be the champion English jockey of 1890? [...] English contemporary says. I think either T. Loates or [...] Barrett. The first named is tied to Golding's and Pe[...] stables, and he will have to ride their bad horses as wel[...] their good ones. On the other hand, Barrett will be free [...] pick some good outside mounts, as he will not be alw[...] wanted by Porter, and I think he stands a real good cha[...] of heading the winning list.

The news from Washington is that James Lee, the trai[...] whom Mr. Reed discharged because he showed his horse[...] a correspondent, has done good work. It is a curious [...] that good starters are so scarce. No position on the turf [...] better (in the East). Mr. Caldwell is now earning $100 a [...] and since his engagements at the Winter track, he has h[...] practically uninterrupted season from year's end to ye[...] end. More than one secretary in New York has been watch[...] Lee's work carefully, and he may be seen on one of the [...] tracks before the season is over.

It is currently reported and generally believed that G[...]son, who has been somewhat humbled by misfortune, [...] ride for the Dwyers this season, says the New York Trib[...] This young man, now friendless, could restore himsel[...] public favor in a week if he would set about it in the r[...] way. A few successful mounts would lift him out of [...] mire and bring back to his side the entire flock of fawn[...] flatterers that deserted him when he began to lose his [...] He loves flattery so much that that alone should be a suf[...]ent inducement for him to try to recover his prestige.

A row of frame buildings adjoining the Kentucky Ra[...] Association's grounds took fire on the 8th. The wind bl[...] gale, carrying the sparks to the stables of the Associa[...] setting them on fire. They were full of horses but by [...] heroic work of the stable hands all the horses were sa[...] Late at night the fire was still fiercely raging and owing t[...] absence of water two or three other stables might have [...] lost. Ten frame houses and two stables were consumed. [...] greatest confusion prevailed; Horses worth fortunes were [...]ing through the streets or jumping high fences in their flight across country.

There are two things that will cure fistula. One is c[...]sive sublimate liniment, to be used in the first stages o[...] disease, and the other is the May apple root liniments. [...] it until you obtain a thick syrup. Do not burn it. [...] still boiling, add a quarter as much lard as you have sy[...] stirring it all the time you are adding the lard. It is [...] ready for use. Spread this on the fistula every morning [...] night wash over with warm water and castile soap. [...] spread on some grease. When pus begins to ooze out f[...] spread on more thickly, and let it remain for twenty [...] hours, then wash off and grease as before. Do not [...] remain on longer than twenty-four hours at a time. I[...] cure.

The following letter, which is self-explanatory, was h[...] to Starter Ferguson on the 10th before he left New Or[...]

OFFICE OF THE NEW LOUISIANA JOCKEY CLU[B]
NEW ORLEANS, April 10. 1890.

J. B. FERGUSON, ESQ NEW ORLEANS—DEAR SIR:—It [...] me much pleasure to convey to you the sincere than[...] the officers and members of the New Louisiana Jockey [...] for your efficient and impartial services as starter duri[...] winter and spring races of 1890.

Fully appreciating your valuable assistance, please [...] our heartfelt good wishes for the future. Yours respec[...]

C. W. MILTENBERGER, Secret[...]

There is hardly a man in the world who can claim t[...] been so successful in breeding racehorses as the lat[...] Falmouth. His leading principles were: 1. To bree[...] from mares which had won first class stakes. 2. To [...] only from such mares as had not raced after their fou[...] old form. 3. To breed each mare to a different stallio[...] year or each alternate year. He changed the stalli[...] which he bred his mares nearly every season. He ke[...]eral stallions himself, but to get a change he never he[...] to send his mares to stallions owned elsewhere. H[...] three winners of the Derby, five of the Oaks, three [...] Two Thousand, five of the One Thousand, and three [...] St. Leger, besides running one-two in 1878 for the St. L[...]

Food that passes the bowels pleasantly and gives [...] nourishment freely is essentially necessary for the race[...] All corn for him must be perfectly sweet, but never [...] as to squeeze into balls rather than pulverize; it must [...]fectly dry, but must never have been kiln dried, as kil[...] oats frequently disorder the kidneys. Hay must be fr[...] injurious herbs, have been well made, quite sweet, and [...] on good strong land. The latter is important, as no [...] how sweet and good hay may appear, if it is grown on [...]ly light land it is not fit for the race horse. Many [...] trainers never change the ground for their hay, but co[...]ly procure it from ground they have found to be s[...] All agree that the best hay for the purpose is grown [...] dried clay.

By winning the Grand National Steeplechase at Aintree, lex credited Mr. G. Masterman with £1,680, as the value of the stakes. The race this year was more valuable than that of twelve months ago, as when Frigate won, the event was only worth £1,235. 15s., and in 1888, when Mr. E. W. Baird's Playfair was successful, the value was £1,175 5s. Some previous amounts follow:—1877, Mr. Jay's Gamecock, £1,206 15s.; 1886, Mr. Douglas's Old Joe, £1,380; 1885, Mr. A. Cooper's Roquefort, £1,035; 1884, Mr Boyd's Voluptuary, £1,035; 1883, Count Kinsky's Zoedone, £925; and 1882, Lord Manners's Seaman, £1,000.

Last Sunday Col. Thornton, Ariel Lathrop, Esq., and myself, visited the Oakland race track at the Colonel's invitation, to see his new purchase, The Grand Moor 2374 by The Moor 870, out of Vashti, dam of Don Tomas, 2:20, by Mambrino Patchen 58, etc. We were all highly pleased with the magnificent proportions, grand back and shoulders, a true Moor head (slightly disfigured by ill usage), with a beautiful neck, and legs like iron. His disposition was exceptionally good, being as docile as any stallion in the State, and he certainly is bred on the most fashionable lines. While there, we went down the track to see the broodmares, among them being Odina, a neat looking sister to Adair, 2:17½, with a very trim Director filly at foot, a bay Abbottsford mare who is very speedy looking, and several others.

One of Canada's most successful thoroughbred sires died at Galt, Canada, on April 1st, when Terror breathed his last. He was a brown horse, foaled in 1866, being by Ruric out of imp Maritana by Flatcatcher (son of Touchstone, a St. Leger winner. Ruric (Terror's sire) was by imp Sovereign (son of Emilius, a Derby winner), out of Levity by imp Trustee. Terror was bred by John White, at Bronte, and proved a good racehorse. He has done much for the stock in Canada, and had he a larger field he would doubtless have proved one of the greatest stallions in America. He sired more Queen's Plate winners than any other horse. Among the best of his get to be mentioned are Disturbance, Fanny Wiser, Will Jones, Chancellor, Marquis and Vice Chancellor. Among the half-breds he sired were such good ones as Gilt Edge, Alarm, and Silver King. At the time of his death Terror was owned by James Anderson.

It is said of Mr. Kock the Westchester secretary that his great weakness is art. He loves pictures and statuary. He would walk miles to see a drawing or an etching. Mr. Withers drops into his office frequently to have a chat with him, and the other night he happened to meet some old friends there. At once the conversation turned to horses. Mr. Withers grew eloquent on the subject of the blood of the great Lexington.

"What do you think?" he said at length, after a long speech about Lexington mares, turning to Mr. Kock. That gentleman had been carefully studying an etching in front of him. As Mr. Withers spoke he lifted his eyes rapturously and exclaimed: "Did you ever see anything more perfect than the curve of that neck?" "Why, confound the man," said Mr. Withers, "I don't believe he heard a word I said." With all his love of art, Mr Kock has taught the racing men of the East some invaluable lessons. If he lives he will teach them many more.

There is on the Memphis track a very remarkable horse, the property of W. L. Cassidy of St. Louis. Blue Blazes is by Blazes, out of Emma Howison, a three-year old raised by H. C. Shafer of Gallatin, and is a trim, dark grey, a little over fifteen hands high, with good, clean limbs, ample depth of chest, good driving power and a fine head. The prevailing dark grey is irregularly splashed with lighter marks. In the left ear of the horse is a well defined protuberance which cannot better be described than as a perfect claw of some bird of prey. In fact it is nearer like the claw of a hawk than any other bird. The claw, or semi-horny substance, grows from the membrane of the horse's ear to the length of two inches.

Mr George Muldrow, Mr. Cassidy's representative, says that he had had great expectations of Blue Blazes this year, but the horse had some unpleasant experience in wintering which has weakened him. One of these experiences was being on a car with some other stock and crowded where he could not be properly attended.

The New York World says: There are three great horses in the vicinity of New York which are entered in the big handicaps that are in superb condition for this season. One is Tenny. He is still a trifle high in flesh, but began his work this week, and although he has not been pushed he gives promise of developing into what may prove a world beater. He has not become any handsomer and his bowed back is as unsightly as ever; but his coat is as fine as spun silk, his eyes are full of fire and he fights for his head from the moment the boy mounts him at the stable door till he is back again.

The second one is the Faverdale colt. His new trainer "Knapsack" McCarthy, has adopted trotting-horse methods with his feet, and a veterinary surgeon who had occasion last week to look at them says they are sound and good. He has not been given any fast work, but he looks strong and well. If he stands training, and there is now every chance he will, the horse that can look him in the eye coming under the wire will be a good one.

That grand little mare Firenzi is the third one. Every report that comes from Monmouth is laden with her praises. She is taking her work well and her appearance is wonderfully good. There is a strong belief that she will face the flag on Suburban day, and it is a belief born of her present superb condition.

An exchange says Billy Donohue, the jockey, was in Chicago a few hours last week, direct from San Francisco, and left in the evening for New York. While on the Coast he had a glimpse of some of the racing cracks, and some of them heartily pleased him. "I went out to the Rose farm," (he meant Palo Alto, Ed.) "and saw Flambeau and ...s. Flambeau is one of the proudest racers I ever saw; in fact, both animals would make their mark when they come East. I am sorry they will not be seen East this season. I also paid a visit to Baldwin's farm. Los Angeles has thickened wonderfully, and is in better condition than ever. He will be given a thorough preparation for the Brooklyn handicap, and the others had better look out.

"Did you see the Emperor of Norfolk?"

"Yes, and he is doing some strong work, with no semblance of lameness. I examined his bad leg very carefully. I can't say whether he will train or not. The tendon is bowed, and when they commence to wind him up he may crack. I didn't like Baldwin's two-year-olds. He will ship his stable out pretty well, and not bring probably more than twenty horses East with him. The stable will start for Brooklyn in a few days."

Practical experience has taught owners of large breeding establishments that stallions in use must have regular exercise. Some managers of farms, however, have peculiar notions about such matters, and they rarely give their stallions work, as they are, as a rule, afraid that they may get injured. The most successful sire ever used in this country was no doubt the great Leamington. He sired Parole, Iroquois, Sensation, Spinaway, and hundreds of first class performers. While he stood at Chestnut Hill, near Philadelphia, and was owned by Mr. Aristides Welch, the horse was ridden at the very least twenty miles every day. This exercise was given the famous sire regardless of the state of the weather or the season of the year.

Some stallions are often considered too valuable to be put to hard work. This is an erroneous idea of some owners, and one which costs them considerable money each year. A good, sound stallion, and no other kind should be kept, might pay for his keep each year by the work he performs. The horse's health will be all the better for it, and his breeding qualities will be greatly improved by the exercise he thus gets. Owners of large breeding farms and importers of draught stallions generally, understand the importance of working their horses, and it is nothing unusual to see a team of two horses, the value of which represents as much money as a good sized farm, doing the hauling and general work. To be sure foal getters a certain amount of exercise is absolutely necessary. If this exercise can be given in the way of profitable work it is all the better, and an economy worth considering. This work should be regular and not of too severe a nature.

Pendragon says in the London Referee: Ah, if we only knew half as much about the coming season as we do about the past one! I am thinking what a beautiful horse Acme looked last Lincoln Handicap day, and how unlikely it then seemed he would in a few months die a cruel and torturing death owing to foul play on the torrid sands of Buenos Ayres. Also of the Juggins who was reported to have still sixty or seventy thousand left for daws to peck at, and who is now bankrupt as well as in correctional imprisonment. The list of stewards of the Hawthorne Hill Steeplechases has to do without E. Benzon's name this season. As some turfites have gone down others have gone up; there are men now described as gentlemen (by the reporters)—and "famous" gentlemen, too—who on last saddling-bell day by the side of the &c, were still members of the dangerous classes; and the only people who seem to object to the assumption of gentility and fame on their part are those who had only a year or so's start of the new-comers on the same road from the goal and the padding ken to the delights and privileges of noble sportsmanship. Change begets change, and reform comes fast and thick when once it has started—shall we yet live to see the gentlemen who picked my pocket at the Lincoln of '88 and the other gentleman whom I saw being kicked and punched as a welsher in '89 members of the renovated and enlarged Jockey Club that we are promised, if not in '90, in '91 at the very latest?

The Referee (London, Eng.) says:—In case I am right in thinking that I have not seen any where among our English sporting papers announcements of Mr. James White's plan of attack on our Derby, I may mention that a good friend of mine in Melbourne has been kind enough to write telling me that Mr. White has arranged to tackle us for three years straight away. No matter whether Narellan and Kirkham have good or bad luck the Australian sportsman will hope to be represented at Epsom and for other rich three-year old prizes up to 1892. The news is welcome if only because it removes the impression that the keen eyed veteran intends to cut horseracing altogether, as might be inferred from his disposing of his stud at home—I mean to say, in the colonies. Last year I committed myself to the opinion that if the Antipodeans will send their best goods here we simply cannot handicap them out of middle and long distance races—provided, that is, we treat them at all reasonably. Their gees are taught and trained to run over long courses from end to end. Of course, it is a matter of murdering each other, but they do stay long at the game. In a way, I hope that the bold spirits who are sending thoroughbreds to the old country will not be disappointed. I should be in a warm corner if the handicap horses intended for the 1890 campaign disappointed their proprietors, because I am informed that the speculation is due to remarks made on the subject in these sporting notions last summer. No doubt my interview with the gentlemen concerned, of whose advent I am forewarned by mutual friends in Melbourne, will be pleasant enough. What sort of a time shall we have together next back end if the experiment, not too put too fine a point on it, comes off crabs?

The Garrison—McMahon sale was a highly successful one, Garrison bought in Speedwell, the sister to Kingston for $2,500. The prices paid and purchasers were:

Eolian, brown horse, 7, by Eolus, dam Calash by imp Phaeton; Easton & Co, $3 400.

Kempland, ch c, 3, by Milner, dam Glorianne by Joe Daniels; Matt Corbett, $3,200.

Falcon, blk h, 5, by Falsetto, dam Molly Wood by Lexington; J. O'Farrell, $2,450.

Speedwell, full sister to Kingston by Spendthrift, dam Kapanga by Victorious; Ed Garrison, $2,500.

John Atwood, ch c, 3, by imp Rayon d'Or, dam Viola by imp Billet; J. Shields, $1,625.

Prince Edward, late Victor Sass, br c, 4 by Spendthrift, dam imp Piccadily by Pell Mell; W F. Clemens, $1,200.

Vera, full sister to Cyclops, ch f, 3, by imp Mortimer, dam Lizzie Lucas by imp Australian; W. F. Clemens, $1,500.

Garrison, br c, 3, by Attila, dam The Squaw by imp Leamington; W. F. Clemens, $2,000.

Emma J., ch f, 2, by Stratford, dam Roulette by Baden-Baden; J. H. McCormick $900.

Middleton, b c, 3, by imp Billet, dam Betty Lewis by Uncle Vic; W. F. Clemens, $775.

Sterling, late Euroclydon by Eolus, dam Majestic by Lexington; W. F. Clemens, $500.

Lillie M., late Litty M., b f, 3, by imp King Ernest, dam Nina by Kentucky; J. N. Kipson, $650.

Osman Digna, b c, 2, by Hyder Ali, dam Vanoni by imp Kyrle Daly; F. Costello, $525.

Ban Bridge, b h, 6, by imp King Ban, dam Dixie's War Flag by War Dance; W. L. Shepherd, $250.

Long Jack, b c, 4, by Virgil, dam Heliotrope by imp Knight of St George; J O'Farrell, $200.

Property of Jas. McAvoy; Ranette, late Maggie Ahrens, b m, 5, by imp Woodlands, dam Ranee by Reform; Melbourne Stud, $200.

Property of P. Nolan: Florita, b f, 3, by Telemachus, out of Floretta by Alarm; Melbourne Stud, $475.

Bay gelding, 2, by Ben d'Or, dam Inverkip by imp Hartington; A. Garson, $225.

The bay yearling filly by Victor Von Bismarck, dam Mattie Wilkes, by Colonel Wilkes, died lately at the home of her owner, George G. White, in Bourbon county, Kentucky. She was a very reliable youngster, being an own sister to Victor Wilkes, 2:29½, and Von Wilkes, yearling record, 2:38½. Her dam is one of the most remarkable and at the same time unfortunate mares in the stud in Kentucky. Her first foal was Victor Wilkes. Her next was Bismarck Wilkes, who was injured; then came Twilight Wilkes, who died before he could prove his powers. After him came the sensational Von Wilkes, who got a yearling stallion mark of 2:38½, the best on record at the time, but the fall that witnessed this triumph saw him roasted to death when Capt. Moore's barn burned. And now her next and last foal is dead. It was a most promising filly. Had not these misfortunes overtaken the produce of Mattie Wilkes, she would have entered a high rank in the list of famous producing dams. As it is, her record is noteworthy.

The value of the race horse in determining the improvement in breeding, is oftentimes underestimated. There must be docility enough to make a horse controllable under the utmost excitement; there must be toughness enough to stand the racket of the most trying pace and the wear and tear of severe training; there must be digestive organs good enough to supply the best possible blood; there must be animal brain and motor nerves of high quality, and, above all, there must be heart and lungs good enough to completely oxygenize a large supply of blood in the least possible time. Now, all these are qualities that add to the value of any horse, and many of them are qualities that the eye of the best judge could never estimate with the certainty with which they are proved on the race course. Men could judge something of the bones, sinews, muscles and form of the horse, and in so doing often expected to select with certainty the best, but experience proved that they could not do so. The brain, the nerves, the heart and the lungs were always out of sight, and the best judges were always at fault. The Godolphin Arabian was condemned to a shop keeper's cart, and not used as a sire until ten years old, when Lath, his then only son out of a good mare, proved on the race course that his father had latent qualities which fitted him, as they had destined him to be, the progenitor of the most successful animals that have since figured in the British Stud Book. Eclipse was never trained until five years old, and qualities which enabled him to enrich more than one owner, and to distance all competitors, were only discovered by trial and competition.

A special from Memphis says: While there are a dozen horses here right now capable of doing a mile in 1:42 or even better, the fastest work done yet was a mile in 1:46, accomplished by Santalene and Robespierre, both of the Chicago Stables. In this connection it is well enough to mention that all the horses belonging to this great organization are in the best of fettle. Trainer Kiley seems to have found out the humor of each horse and his likes and dislikes, and as a result they all bear the appearance of being ready to go to the string when the bugle calls. Little Minch and Terra Cotta are still both high in flesh, but the former, especially, runs better when in this condition. Jacobin pulls up lame after every strong gallop, but it is thought this will not keep him from winning several good races this year. The work done by Robespierre makes that horse loom up as a dangerous quantity in the Derby, while as to Huntress and Santalene, they look and act more as if they could run one, two, in any race in which they go to the post. From every standpoint it looks as though this stable this year will make even a better showing than in 1888, when, under the skillful handling of John Campbell, it was a terror to other stables all down the line. Coming on the track as if he had seen turf battles and participated in them for several years, with the tread of a king, came Riley, Corrigan's crack colt, the favorite in all quarters for the Kentucky Derby. Several trainers were at once asked how he was doing, and all with one accord professed utter ignorance, save to say that he had grown, spread out and improved in every way, which any observer who knew him last year could readily tell. He resembles the type of a Longfellow, being very much on the order of Linden and Freeland, although he moves with the daisy-cutting stride of Thora and The Bard.

The Nashville American tells a very pretty tale of seeing double in the judges' stand:—

"Were you ever at Swampsboro, Arkansas?" asked a drummer at the Duncan yesterday, as he joined a group of fellow travellers. None of the crowd had been there.

"I'm just from there," continued the speaker, as he passed the cigars and took a seat in the circle, "and while there I went to Mosquito Park, the new race course. There was a good deal of excitement and much betting, the contesting horses being an aged claybank and an old flea-bitten gray—only two entries. The regular judges were part owners of the horses entered, and it was deemed prudent to call in an unbiased and disinterested party to judge the races. So Col. Blood of Bear Ridge was requested to accept that important office. With the assistance of several members of the association the Colonel and his jug mounted the stand. After several false starts the flyers got off fairly well, and the race was closely contested as far as the home stretch, but at that point the gray horse, in passing through a swamp that had not been properly drained, mired up to his knees in mud. The claybank was a little more fortunate, being on the inside track) where she struck firmer dirt, and won easily, coming in at the finish probably 300 yards ahead.

"The claybank's backers were, of course, wild with delight, and they picked him up bodily and carried him around on their shoulders. Their joy was only momentary, however, for Col. Blood, standing up on a soap box and flourishing a pair of silver mounted derringers said:—

"'Gentlemen of the Swampsborough Blood Horse Association and fellow countrymen, all bets on the race what hev just been run air declared off.'

"Now was the time for the old gray's backers to yell, and you bet they never lost the opportunity. For fully ten minutes the shouts were deafening. In the meantime three men died unnatural deaths and two others were disabled for life.

"I don't mind getting my chitlings cut out,' said a wounded man who leaned against the judges' stand and held his hat over his abdomen; 'an' I ken manage to git along with only one eye, but Colonel, I'm a son of a wolf if I ken see how in the nation you can declar' the bets off when the gray wuz beat 300 yards!'

"'Gentlemen," roared the Colonel, as he finished reloading his derringer and took another pull at the jug, 'gentlemen, my decision war prompted by the rules and regulations of all first class race tracks, and that high sense of honah characteristic of a Kentucky bred gentleman. Sirs, I am not ignorant of the fact that the grays were left 300 yards behind in yonder neighboring swamp, but my decision wuz based on the fact that them two yellers run a dead heat, an' I am here to defend my judgment an' my honah.'"

THE FARM.

A Colony of Bees.

A colony of bees, in a normal condition, consists of about 80,000 workers, or female bees, several thousand drones and a queen. The queen is the mother of the entire colony, and lives from two to four years, generally being at her best during the second season, although some very good queens, bred from prolific mothers, continue to render good service until they are four years old, when they become unprolific, and if not then substituted by the aspirant will be superseded by the bees. A queen is easily distinguished from the worker bees by being longer, yellower and majestic in her carriage. Her wings are short, being only about two-thirds the length of her body, her abdomen tapering to a point. Every apiarist should become familiar with the appearance of the queen in order that she may be distinguished at a glance when examining the frames. The queen is of paramount importance, as everything depends upon her; hence the bee-keeper should know all about her, and always keep her safety in mind. She leaves the hide only once, except when a swarm issues, and then to be fecundated by the drone. She goes out to meet the drone when she is five days old, and in about five days thereafter she commences to lay, the eggs producing perfect bees in twenty-one days. The rule is thus applied to the product of the queen, viz: Three and a half days in the egg, three and a half days in the worm, and fourteen days sealed over. The apiarist should commit this to memory, as he will often have occasion to apply it all through his experience.

The queen lays from 2500 to 3000 eggs daily, beginning in early Spring and continuing at this rate until Fall, and then she ceases for the Winter. The ovaries of the queen occupy a large portion of her body, in consequence of which she should never be handled except by the wings, and never touched at all if it can be avoided. Many bee keepers do not handle her at all, but cage her by placing a cage over her and letting her run into it, and clipping her wings while she is travelling over the combs. It is said that the ovaries of the queen contain not less than 20,000,000 seminal filaments, to exhaust which would require twenty years, provided she laid 2000 eggs every day in the year. A fertile or fecundated queen lays drone or worker eggs at will, while an unfertile queen can deposit only drone eggs. The drones hatch in twenty-four days, and a perfect queen in sixteen days from the time the egg was laid. It is also worthy of mention here that the same egg that would have produced a worker does by different treatment by the bees produce a queen. If an egg is selected to produce a queen, the bees build a large wax cell over it, feed the egg with "royal pabulum," and in sixteen days from the egg the queen emerges. Until the bees are fourteen days old they are workers inside the hive; after that they become field foragers.

Wax is produced by the bees eating honey, and then hanging in clusters in the hives as lazily as possible. The wax appears on their backs. Other bees take it off and manipulate it into combs. Pollen or bee bread is the dust collected from flowers, which the bees roll into honey and then pack away, with which to feed their young. Propolis or bee glue is also collected by the bees from resinous plants and trees. They also bring and deposit water in the combs. The propolis is used to fasten combs, etc.

To further classify the inhabitants of a hive, it may be added that the workers do all the labor, the queens lay all the eggs, and the drones are fit only for one purpose (one of them only), to fecundate a newly hatched queen. When a queen once meets a drone, she becomes fertile for life. She begins to lay in five days thereafter, and never ceases during life, except as herein stated.

To become successful, every person who undertakes bee culture should carefully study all these things, and become familiar with all that pertains to these industrious creatures. —Republic.

How to Raise Turkeys.

Turkeys are considered by many farmers very delicate and hard to raise, and for this reason they are not found on many farms. If farmers understood their nature better, turkeys would soon become more common. Every poultry man or farmer that has ten acres of land or more can easily raise turkeys to advantage, and if the conditions are favorable they are one of the most profitable kinds of poultry to raise. Get a pure breed, either for market or home use. Such are cheaper in the long run, and do not let size be the only qualification, a flock of good medium sized, square bodied, well matured birds at Thanksgiving time, is what you want. Two plump, ten-pound turkeys will bring more money at that time than one lean, lank fellow that weighs twenty pounds. I do not strive to get great size in my breeders, either male or female. We do this for the reason that the eggs of the largest hens are not as a rule as large as those from fair to good sized birds and it is pretty generally conceded that for active vitality and sure breeding the male must not be too large.

It is mostly a question of feed as relates to size and heavy weights. I have taken the common turkey and made them weigh twenty-pounds at two years. With pure breeds of turkeys a good weight can be made with ordinary care and a small amount of feed. Here lies the superiority of the thoroughbred over the scrub. In picking out hens do not let great weight influence you. Good form, fine stout legs, square bodies and breasts, are what is wanted. Much the same will be proper with the male in buying. He should not be related to the females. One male is sufficient for one dozen females, all things considered. I have found the White Holland turkey the most profitable for the farmer to raise, as they are hardy, mature early, are docile in disposition, not inclined to stray off and fall victims to hawks and skunks. Like the wilder varieties in quality of flesh, they are par excellence as a table fowl and prolific layers of good sized eggs.

Desiring to raise as many as possible to the number of hens kept for breeding purposes, I set the first laying of eggs the turkey hens lay, under the chicken hens. When they hatch I examine to see if they have any vermin on them; if so, I dust them with insect powder and keeped them cooped closely for three or four days, until they get used to the call of the hen. If allowed to run out they are likely to stray after any hen that comes along. I feed often, and very sparingly the first week, with hard boiled eggs, and corn bread crumbs, mixed fine and dampened with a little milk. After the first week I give more bread crumbs, with a little barley meal, onion tops, and lettuce chopped fine. Milk should be given them as a drink, as it keeps them in a healthy condition. Corn meal dough should not be given them, as they are liable to diarrhœa, and it increases the tendency. Their food should be strictly fresh. Keep cooped in the morning until the dew is off the grass, until they are six weeks old, for cold spring rains and dew are fatal to young turkeys. The second laying of eggs I let the turkey hen sit on and raise the brood. I do not pay much attention to them except to feed a little each evening to get them accustomed to come up at night, and keep them growing. They will pick up most of their living in their rambles. Productiveness depends on the care. If you breed thoroughbreds, breed only from the best, and if you succeed in raising good birds let it be known by exhibiting and advertising. The owner of really good, high-scoring stock usually gets for them all conscience will allow him to ask.—J. Eflars in Ploughman and Farmer.

Capons.

There is probably no flesh more eagerly sought after than the large, tender, rich capon. They are always scarce in the market, and command high prices, and it is impossible to find one except in our largest city markets. Not one American in ten thousand ever tasted a piece of capon meat, and the farmers who have raised fowls for years hardly know what a capon is, when they might have been supplying their own tables with them all their lives. What is the reason for all this? Simply this. The common farmer and poultry raiser has never given the subject any attention. Each one could just as well have capons in their poultry-houses and around their doors as so many tough, strong and bony cockerels, that when dressed only weigh four or five pounds.

A capon is a cockerel that has been castrated, that is all. He may be of any breed in the wide world but if castrated successfully, he becomes then a capon. Farmers castrate their lambs, calves, colts, pigs, etc., but when it comes to a cockerel, the easiest of them all to do, they draw the line? Why? Because the fact has never struck them point blank that it was desirable to do so, or that they could do it themselves. Well, let me say right now to one and all of you, that you can perform the operation just as successfully as you can dress a chicken, and furthermore, let me say that you can increase the weight of your cockerel very much more in proportion than any animal you ever had castrated. In many cases, if the right breed of fowls is used, you can double their natural weight. Can this be done with any other animal? But you not only do that, but you double his market value per pound, and if you consume him yourself, you greatly improve the quality of his flesh, as you will find when you sit down to a good roast capon. The operation can be performed in four minutes, and the bird recovers from it in three days, and commences at once to grow and lay on flesh. All that is required is a good set of instruments, which cost but little now, and a box to lay the fowl on with two straps, to hold his legs and wings. In another article I will describe how to make a cheap table to perform the operation on. Cockerels may be caponized at any time of the year, and at any weight, but the best time is when the chicks weigh one pound and one-half—Geo. Q. Dow, in Ploughman and Farmer.

Annual Records and Net Profits.

I want to shake hands, figuratively, with F. C. Murphy for his article in the Dairyman of February 21st. As he says there is too much claiming of "the earth," by breeders of, not Holsteins alone, but some other varieties as well. Every breed of cows has its peculiar adherents, but there is no need of truth-stretching to give any breed popularity. If a breed has worth, it will be recognised fully as quickly by the better class of farmers and dairymen by sticking to the truth. That Holstein breeders have been enlarging on the merits of that breed as much as the average animal will bear, is self evident.

While private tests may be all right there is always an offensive odor attached, and public tests keep folks honest. At the New England fair of 1887, in the public butter test were 4 Holsteins giving from 45 to 53 lbs. milk, a Jersey with a record of 30 lbs. private test, two or three Ayrshires and a little old family cow, the only one the man had. The Holsteins made from 4 oz. to 9 oz. of butter from one day's milk, the little old cow tied the 30 lb. Jersey for first with 16 oz. to her credit. At the New England fair for 1889, public butter test for herds of five cows each, no alarming record was made. Two herds of Holsteim with immense butter records were recorded, but their owners after looking at the buttery-looking Jerseys, Guernseys and grades decided to stay out. Comparisons are odious. The manufacturer is always on the look-out and eagerly seizes upon any article or machine which returns him a larger dividend for the money invested than what he already has. So with the farmer and dairyman, they want the cow that at the end of the year will return them the largest net earnings. Therefore all tests of animals whether from Holsteins with a good sized balloon full of lacteal fluid attached, or from the smaller sized Jerseys with their miniature cream pots, should contain a full and tabulated amount of grain fed, how many kinds, who mixed, how much per diem from the cow, and how much said grain cost and what the butter was worth. Then can we, and perhaps some other poor worshipper of honest butter records and groper after an honest living, see which is best for our respective farms. A 1,500 lb. cow devouring $5 worth of feed to make $16 worth of butter or milk; or an 800 lb. cow that takes $8 worth of feed to make $10 worth of butter.

The cow irrespective of breed which will at the end of, not 7 days, but 362½ days returns us the largest amount net in dollars and cents is the cow we are after.—Down Easter in Hoard's Dairyman.

Jerseys, Guernseys and Alderneys.

Jersey, Guernsey and Alderney are the names of three islands situated in the English Channel near the French coast, and which, with a few smaller ones, form the group known as the Channel islands. The cattle of these islands are similar in most respects, and have been known by the general appellation of Channel Islands cattle, although when first introduced into this country they were all called Alderneys. They were all more or less distinguished for their dairy product. But while this is a common and general characteristic of the cattle of the Channel Islands, those of each of the islands named are kept distinct, and no crossing is permitted; neither are live cattle from any other country permitted to be brought into any of these islands other than for immediate slaughter for beef. The cattle of the Island of Jersey and those of Alderney resemble each other more closely, perhaps, than those of Jersey and Guernsey, but the points of difference between the cattle of all these islands are so slight that they might with some propriety all be classed as a single breed. The Guernseys will average more than the Jerseys, and the Jerseys will average larger than the Alderneys. There is no special distinction between the cattle of these several islands in the matter of color. Fawn color, squirrel grey, light and dark brown, all, with or without white markings, are very common. The Guernseys and Alderneys perhaps have a larger proportion of the light fawn and yellowish shades than the Jerseys.

Sheep and Cattle.

Can mutton be more cheaply produced than beef?
bearing upon this subject Stewart calls attention to the
that the sheep is a source of double income—meat and w
He refers, too, to the experiments of Sir J. B. Lawes, in re
ence to the percentage of food utilized or stored up by dif
ent animals, and these experiments presented the sheep i
very favorable light. Of the dry food consumed, he fo
that sheep stored up increased weight twelve per cent. w
cattle only laid up in increased weight eight per cent; that
eight and one-half pounds of dry food increased the
weight of cattle.

So that, relying upon these experiments, sheep must
considered as excellent utilizers of food, as producing
many pounds of mutton, besides the wool, from a given qu
tity of food, as can be produced of beef; and as the best m
ton brings as high a price as the beef, it would appear on
basis, the sheep would give the fleece as extra profit o
cattle. If this is not too favorable a view, the sheep on s
able lands must be considered among the most profitable
farm stock. It is true the dairy cows brings her profits
flow of milk to offset that of wool; but the dairy cow d
not lay on flesh while producing milk, as does the sh
while producing wool. A fleece of five pounds of wool, gro
in a year, requires only a daily growth of one-fifth of
ounce, which can take but a small portion of food to prod
The mineral matter taken from the soil by the fleece is o
1.6 ounces per year; and if six half-mutton sheep represe
cow, the whole mineral constituents taken by the six fle
would only be 9 6 ounces, and about 1.9 pounds of nitrog
whilst the ordinary cow, yielding 4 000 pounds of milk, wo
take twenty-six pounds of mineral matter or ash, and twe
five of nitrogen, or forty-three times as much mineral mat
and thirteen times as much nitrogen as the fleeces of the sh

Sheep Breeding.

The most difficult stock to breed is the sheep. There
many things to be taken into consideration in buying sh
About the first thing a purchaser will look at is the size
the sheep, and the next is the length of the wool it has
its back; and to the average man that is about all that c
stitutes a sheep. But is that all? Now what does it tak
constitute a typical sheep? First, it takes size. Wha
size? Is it a sheep that is stuck up in the air on a pai
legs two feet long? No, it is a sheep that has short legs
a heavy body of good length and properly shaped; is squ
on the shoulders, with a round rib, good, straight back,
rounded hams, heavy brisket, two or three rolls around
neck. The next point is the constitution. You don't w
to breed to a ram that is like two slabs laid together w
pins driven in for legs. How will we tell when a sheep
a good constitution? He will stand with his head erect,
tucked down; and a sheep with a good constitution
keep in good condition under favorable circumstan
What else should a typical sheep possess? Wool coveri
Does this mean wool three to five inches long on the b
and none on the legs and belly? "Nay, verily;" the m
sheep has a good length of wool on the back and sides,
the most important of all is to have good length on the b
and legs. Don't buy a ram unless he has a good lengt
wool on his belly and legs—wool down to the hoof.
about the head? It must be well wooled down the face
low the eyes and up the throat well along the chops.
wool should be white with dark points, throwing out ple
of oil. Some may say that a greasy sheep is not fit to br
as it cannot stand the cold. There is a difference betwee
oily sheep and a gummy one. A sheep that has yellow
in his wool can't stand anything, but a sheep that has w
oil will come through all right and will be fat and nic
Rarely, in Farmer & Stockman.

The New Schedule.

The Denver News contains the following, which will b
interest to all stock shippers:

The Fort Worth and Union Pacific issued yesterday a
joint tariff on range cattle in train loads, effective at o
It covers all points on the Panhandle and Union Pa
points in Wyoming. Local cattlemen seemed to be ple
with the rates quoted. Under this schedule the rate o
standard length car of cattle from Fort Worth to Chey
is $77.50; to Wendover, $85; Rawlins, $90; Rock Spr
$100.60; Granger, $105.20. Ten per cent additional to
above rates will be charged for shipments loaded in p
or stable cars. Cow ponies used in herding may be shi
with cattle under this schedule. Horses will be $12.50
car higher than the rate on cattle. Under the new tariff
rate from Clayton, N. M., to Cheyenne will be $42.50.
road also issued circular D 200 covering the admissio
southern cattle into New Mexico, Colorado, Wyoming,
tana and Nebraska.

Devon Cattle.

The Transfer of Pure Bred Devon Cattle during the
three months indicate that the hardy red breed are co
into great favor. J. Buckingham the Secretary of the A
ican Devon Club courteously furnished us with an adv
of the transfers among which we notice Lackawana
Boston's Pride 6564, Bride of Delaware 6565, Aviline
wood 6563, sold by M. W. Oliver to J. R. Rose, Lake
Cal.

Look 3677, Lactea 7835 sold by C. Rasown & Son to
Rose, Lakeville, Cal.

The Illinois State Board of Agriculture has issued it
report under the amended law for the protection of bre
of animals against damage from sires with bogus or fr
lent pedigrees. The report is a volume of 135 pages, co
invaluable information to stock men. It gives the pedi
of 381 sires that have been certified under the law i
State, with other hints, rules and suggestions for t
advantage of the protection afforded by the law.

The Argentine Republic has for some time been
especial encouragement to its export trade in beef and
ton, by paying a bounty to those engaged in the bus
This must have proved satisfactory in some degree at
as a bill has been passed by the proper legislative body
anteeing five per cent. profit on all capital invested in
panies whose business shall be the exportation of meat.
such a stimulus as this, it is certain that competition
that quarter will not soon diminish. The primary cau
bounty being offered was that the business did not pay
it is not likely that this condition has yet materially ch

ATHLETICS.

Athletic Sports and Other Pastimes.

EDITED BY ARISTIPPUS,

The athletic season is now fairly opened and the athletes both old and young, fat and thin, are working hard trying to prepare themselves for the great battles which will be decided within the next six weeks. The fine cinder path at the new grounds of the Olympic Club is attracting an unusually large number of runners and walkers, and some "dark horses" may soon make their appearance.

RUNNERS, WALKERS, JUMPERS, ETC

We predict a victory for young McDonald in the novice sprint for O C. members on May 30th.

Some of the University Club athletes have not yet commenced training, and they should remember that only six weeks are now left them in which to prepare themselves for battle with the cracks who represent clubs on this side of the bay.

The Olympic Club's "Ladies' Night" programme has been completed, and a good exhibition may be looked forward to.

On Tuesday evening, while engaged in a practice bout with Al. Lean at the Olympic Club rooms, Ungermann, the well known wrestler, was unfortunate enough to break one of his fingers.

Apropos of Lean, we understand that he had some trouble with the bosses of the California Athletic Club, and the result was that he handed in his resignation. It has been very evident from the start that the Directors of the New Montgomery street Club were never very fond of their amateurs, otherwise they would not have acted as they did towards some of the young athletes whom from time to time they have disgusted away from their ranks.

A. Cook, the English walker, is in strict training, and it is reported that he recently made a mile under 7:30 with only two days' training.

The old proverb, "A dying man will clutch at a straw," is very applicable to the case of M. C. Giry, the ex-President of the Alpine Amateur Athletic Club. We have before us a high pile of communications which refer to Giry's conduct in connection with the club mentioned, but as we do not wish to turn our columns into a literary battle field, we must refuse to publish them. In substance, however, the complaints state that Giry was one of the chief organizers of the Alpine Club. After the club had been running a couple of months Giry proposed certain things to which the balance of the Directors would not agree, and the consequence was that he, seeing that he was not the ruling power of the organization, began to circulate false stories, which he intended should undermine the good standing of the club and topple it over. His stories, however, were not sufficiently steeled with argument to have any effect, and the battering rams which he used against the stronghold of the club were suddenly turned on himself. In short, he was politely requested to hand in his resignation as President of the club, which he very speedily did. And now comes the grand climax of his meanness. He has announced his intention of reorganizing the defunct Pacific Athletic Club and placing a team of athletes (?) under its auspices in the field on Decoration Day. Had Mr. Giry silently retired after having resigned from the Alpine Club, his previous conduct might have been forgotten in time, but now that he shows fight his case is a hopele s one It is safe to presume that no athletes of sound caliber or entertaining any respect for himself will suffer himself to be guided or ruled by such a man as M. C. Giry. It is even questionable if the members of a club presided over by Giry would be permitted to compete in the championship games.

James McLaughlin has been expelled from the Alpine Club for aiding M. C. Giry in removing property from the club rooms.

J. Barr Buchanan, the amateur champion all-round athlete of the world, left this city for Chicago on Thursday last. The many friends which he left behind regret that he could not remain until after the championship meeting, for he would easily have broken some of the Pacific Coast records. Before leaving Mr. Buchanan presented the following letter to Mr. W. E. Holloway, the secretary of the Olympic Club:

"W. E. HOLLOWAY, Esq.,

Hon. Secretary O. A C—

Dear Sir: As I am about to leave your city for Chicago, I cannot help writing you these few lines expressing my sincere thanks for the great kindness bestowed on me by your club during my seven months' residence in San Francisco. Regarding your club in general, permit me to state that I have inspected the very finest gymnasiums and athletic clubs throughout the Australasian colonies, but never have I come across a club as handsomely and completely arranged, so well instructed or composed of a more manly and gentlemanly set of fellows than the Olympic Athletic Club of San Francisco. In conclusion, I again express my thanks, and hand the club herewith a life-size photograph of

Yours faithfully,

THOS. BARR BUCHANAN,

Champion Amateur Athlete of the World.

H. M. Johnson, the professional runner, every afternoon and evening instructs the runners of the O. C in the art of starting. Should Mr. Johnson decide to remain in San Francisco, he will probably be offered a permanent position by the club as trainer and athletic instructor.

The next meeting of the California Foot-racing Association will take place at Central Park, corner 8th and Market Streets, on Sunday, May 4th. There will be a large field of competitors, and nearly all the leading runners of America will take part. It is also proposed to hold race-meetings by electric light in the evenings. In a month or so, when the warm weather sets in, this should be a very profitable undertaking.

The amateur athletes should bear in mind that the entry list of the Alpine Club games will close at the club rooms, 706 Powell Street, on Saturday evening next at 10 o'clock. The open events are, 1—100 yards handicap run. 2—440 yards handicap run. 3—3 miles run, handicap. 4—3 mile walk, handicap. Valuable prizes or medals will be given for each event. The club will spare no expense to make this their first open field day a grand success. A fine brass band of 12 pieces has been engaged to perform at the Bay District track during the progress of the games. The University, Olympic and Garden City athletes should do all in their power to help the hard-working and well-meaning Alpine boys out by sending in their names to be entered for the open events.

The Bay District track is in good condition for training purposes, and every evening crowds of ambitious runners and walkers may be witnessed exercising on it. Immediately after the Blood Horse races, it will be put into good order for the Alpine sports, which will come off on Sunday, May 4th.

An "athlete" forwards us his views as to the results of the coming championship meeting which will take place at the Olympic Club's new grounds on May 30. Here is his speculation: 100 yards and 220 yards run Victor E. Schifferstein, O. C., 440 yards run, McGee, O C, Henderson, O C and Garrison A A A C. 880 yards run, Sutton, U C, Little, A A A C; 1 mile run, Cooley, O C, Hill, U C, Cassidy, A A A C; 5 mile run, Cooley, O C, Cassidy, A A A C; 1 mile walk, Jarvis, U A C, Gafney, A A A C, Coffin, O A C; 3 mile walk, Jarvis O C, Gafney A A A C, Caffin, O C. Running high jump, Moffet, U C, Schifferstein, O C; running broad jump, Schifferstein, O O, McGee, U C, Moffet, U C; hurdle races, Moffet U C. Putting 16 lb. shot, McKinnon, A A A C, Purcell, O C, Sheedy, A A A C; Throwing 17 lb. hammer, McKinnon A A A C; pole vault, Sexsmith, A A A C. Tug-of-war, O C team.

Before competing in picnic races Amateur Athletes should read the rules of the P. C. A. A. A. on the point.

IN THE SURF.

The season has already opened at Santa Cruz and at Camp Capitola. The prospects of a busy season at both places are very bright.

The swimmers are already beginning to desert the tank baths for the open sea. The Terrace Baths at Alameda and the Sheltered Cove Baths at the foot of Mason Street were well patronized during the past week.

Work has already begun on the new bathing establishment about to be put up at the corner of Sutter and Stockton Sts., on the site of the old Vienna Gardens.

ON THE WHEEL.

The local wheelmen are getting into condition for coming events. Every evening parties of bicycle men may be seen exercising in and around the Park.

The pastime appears to be gaining favor with the fair sex. Quite a number of ladies take their daily spins through the Park.

W. M. Meeber is still working on his road book and expects to have it issued in conjunction with the consul's hand book, which is to contain the names of all League hotels, Consuls, etc.

The Bay City Wheelmen are making great efforts to have a track built for the use of the wheelmen. The track will probably be a half mile one and will be located in a sheltered valley in the Golden Gate Park, just north of the new grounds of the Olympic Club.

Great performances are expected from some of the Oakland Bicycle Club boys this season. Many of them are in good condition at the present time.

It is also thought that the Alameda Scorchers will come to the front once more before the year is over. Clift, Ireland and other good men should not remain in oblivion.

AT THE OARS.

The Triton barge crew visited Sausalito on Sunday.

About twenty members of the Dolphin Club took a trip in the pleasure barge, Whieland, on Sunday. They went over to Sausalito and witnessed the cross country run of the Alpine Club.

To-morrow the Alpine Amateur crew will contest with a crew of the Lurline Club at their opening exercises The Alpine crew will consist of J J Larkey, stroke, A M King, 2, H Tank, 1, H O Farrell, Bow.

The Ariel Club will have several impromptu races in the near future between the members in order to pick out their regular amateur crew. There is an increased activity in club affairs, and probably a little jealously may arise from the selection.

J. Cochran takes regular exercise since his debut in single sculling.

The Lurline Club has made great preparations for its opening to-morrow, Several races are on the tapis. Single sculling, canoe and barge races together with a first class in-door athletic exhibition will form the programme. Refreshments will be served all day.

Harry Smith, the Captain of the Oakland Club, has begun training for the championship at the club regatta which will be held on May 30th, at the Estuary.

CLUB JOTTINGS.

There was no meeting of the P C A A A last Friday eve. Cause, want of a quorum. We think if the meetings were held every other week instead of weekly as at present the attendance of delegates would be much larger. From now until after the championship it would be a good idea to fine any delegate who was absent from two successive meetings.

The members of the Alpine Amateur Club held their second cross country run from Ross Villa, Sausalito, on Sunday. About thirty-four athletes started. The run was to the Fog Station at Lime Point and return, distance about 5½ miles. The distance out was made in about 16 minutes. After the spin the boys were treated to a fine chicken luncheon by Mrs. Ross Jackson, who, by the way, has become very popular with the young athletes. The next run of the club will be held about the second Sunday in May.

There will probably be an immense crowd of people at the opening of the new Olympic grounds on Decoration Day.

JOTTINGS FROM ALL OVER.

We would suggest that one of the Eastern athletic clubs put up a purse for a finish fight between the athletic editors of the New York Spirit of the Times and of the Turf, Field and Farm. The two writers in question for many weeks past have been engaging in a wordy war at their readers' expense, and it is high time a stop was put to their folly Let them meet in private and settle the question once and for all, and thus save their readers from a lingering death.

Sidney Meyer, a member of the Blackheath Harriers of England, has joined the Manhattan Athletic Club of New York City. He will prove a valuable addition to the "cherry diamond" list of athletes.

The joint athletic meeting of the Prospect Harriers and Company F, Thirteenth Regiment, N. G. S. N Y., which were held at the armory of the regiment in Brooklyn, N. Y., on Saturday evening, April 5th, were well attended, although there was not such a large turnout of the fair friends of the militiamen as usual on such occasions, probably due to the fact that boxing competitions formed a considerable proportion of the programme. The events were well contested, and a couple of them furnished surprises in the defeat of warm favorites. A summary follows:

Fifty yards run—Final heat: W. P. Belknap, Lawrenceville, Pa., 9ft start, first, in 5 3-5s; H. Thompson, Robertson's Gymnasium, 10ft, second; E. Rascover, New Jersey Athletic Club, 8ft, third.

Three hundred yards run—Final heat: S. B. Weirs, Ætna Athletic Club, 14yds start, first, in 35 3-5s; H. W. Beckle, Pastime Athletic Club, 14yds, second; G. S. Jackson, Acorn Athletic Club, 18yds, third.

One thousand yards run—Final heat: James Reed, American Athletic Club, 28yds start, first, in 2m 25 4-5s; F C. Clark, B. R. and A. A., 30yds, second; E. Hjertberg, New Jersey Athletic Club, scratch, third.

One mile and a half walk—C. E. Nicoll, Prospect Harriers, 25s start, first, in 11m 45 1-5s; T. W. Allen, National Athletic Club, 55s, second; E. D. Lange, Manhattan Athletic Club, penalized 10s, third, his actual time being 11m 50 4-5s.

One and a half mile run—W T. Young, Manhattan Athletic Club, 50yds start, first in 7m 3 2-5s; Willie D. Day, New Jersey Athletic Club, scratch, second, his time being 7m 6s; M. E. Healey, Acorn Athletic Club, 165yds, third. The men ran a lap short, through error of the scorers.

A half mile foot handicap was recently run in heats at Sheffield, Eng., and was participated in by a number of the fastest professionals over there. The final heat resulted as follows: A Perkins, London, 50 yards start, in one minute 57 3-5 seconds; J. Virtue, Newcastle, 45 yards, second, by a foot; W. Williams, Newcastle, 30 yards, third, by the same distance; F. Smith, Worksop, 30 yards, fourth. The winner fell in a dead faint at the finish, while both Virtue and Williams had to be carried off the track, showing what a punishing race it was. The purse was $500.

At a meeting of the indoor championship committee of the Amateur Athletic Union, held in New York City on the evening of April 7th the entries of Malcolm W. Ford of the Brooklyn Heights A. C., and F. H Bailey of the Sydenham Club of Providence, R. I, for the Boston games on Saturday evening were rejected.

The various teams of cross country runners in the East are busy preparing for the annual race for the championship, which this year is of more importance and interest than heretofore, for the reason that a junior contest is added to that of former years. Full details of the meeting were arranged at a meeting of the games committee held on April 1st, at which the following circular letter was adopted:

The annual team championships of America (senior and (junior) will be held at Morris Park, Westchester, N. Y. (New York Jockey Club), on Saturday, April 26th, at 3 P. M. Positively no postponement. The junior team championship will be open to all club teams under the following conditions: The junior cross country team championship of the United States shall be open to teams of not more than twelve, nor less than six, men from any recognized amateur athletic or cross country organization, providing such juniors shall never have competed in the cross country championship of the United States, nor in any cross country championship, either divisional or national, in any other country. Prizes for the junior team race will be awarded as follows: The members of the winning team will each receive a gold medal. The members of the second team will each receive a silver medal, and bronze medals will be given to each man in the third team, providing six teams start. In addition, a prize will be given to the first man in not a member of the winning team. The winning team of the junior championship race will be awarded a silver cup. The junior championship team race will be started at 3 o'clock precisely. The following clubs have entered teams for the senior championship race: New Jersey Athletic Club, American Athletic Club, Pastime Athletic Club, Prospect Harriers, St. George Athletic Club and Manhattan Athletic Club. Prizes for the senior team race will be awarded as follows: The members of the winning team will each receive a gold medal. The members of the second team will each receive a silver medal, and bronze medals will be given to each man in the third team, providing six teams start. The actual winner of the race will receive a silver cup, emblematic of the individual championship of America. This cup will be presented by the New York Jockey Club. In addition, a prize will be given to the first man in not a member of the winning team. The winning team of the senior championship will be presented with the New York Jockey Club cup.

The senior championship race will be started at half past 4 o'clock precisely. At the conclusion of the team races, the places of the first six men of each competing club shall be added together, and the club having the lowest aggregate in each race shall be declared the winner. All competing clubs will be required to wear distinguishing sashes, which will be furnished by the association. The following color schedule will be observed in senior championship race, for which event entries have already closed: Team No. 1, Prospect Harries, gold; Team No 2, New Jersey Athletic Club, maroon; Team No. 3, Manhattan Athletic Club, cherry; Team No. 4, American Athletic Club, red, white and blue; Team No 5, Pastime Athletic Club, blue; Team No. 6, St. George Athletic Club, black. The juniors will also wear colors to distinguish their teams, which colors will be assigned when the entries close April 19th. Club teams are requested, in addition to distinguishing sashes, to wear their club uniforms. Entrance fee to clubs belonging to the National Association $5 per team, and to clubs not members of the Association $10 per team.

The Board of Managers of the Amateur Athletic Union held a meeting at the Grand Union Hotel, New York City, on Friday evening, April 4th, at which considerable business was transacted. W. B. Curtis was appointed a committee of one to make necessary alterations in the rules for lacrosse, football, bicycling, lawn tennis and swimming, for the Union Handbook, and J. E. Sullivan and F. Gerow were appointed a committee to amend the rules for boxing, wrestling and fencing. The following clubs were elected to membership: Company D, Forty-seventh Regiment N. G. S., N Y.; Wayne Athletic Club, Jersey City, N. J.; Corinthian Athletic Club, Staten Island. The applications of Willie Haas and I Fraser for reinstatement were referred to the committee on investigation, and Walter Cantello was reinstated. On motion of Walton Storm it was resolved that when an athlete who is a member of a college and of an athletic club in the Union shall compete at championship meetings, the points made by him shall count for the A. A. U. Club, of which he is a member, in computing points for the Bailey, Banks & Biddle Plaque. A request was read from the Columbia Athletic Club, of Washington, D C., that the date of the championship meeting be changed to later in the season, for the reason that many of the residents of Washington will not be at home till after October 1st. Action was deferred.

ROD.

Great Sport.

EDITOR BREEDER AND SPORTSMAN:—The article in your issue of April 5th, concerning tarpon fishing in Florida waters brings to my mind the magnificent fishing we have had in San Diego Bay during the past ten years, but which now, I am afraid, is a thing of the past. Halibut trolling from our wharves was a year or two ago one of the most delightful pastimes imaginable. Blessed with the finest climate in the world, a magnificent sheet of perfectly calm, beautiful clear sea water, fourteen miles long by two wide, filled with an abundance of finny denizens from the two inch minnow to jew fish weighing 200 pounds, and plenty of time to allure them in, who would not enjoy life in San Diego, where one could hie himself to the wharves any day in the year armed with the necessary tackle, and rely on the assurance of returning home with his creel well filled with finny beauties. Pompano, mackerel, smelt, rock cod, bass, croakers, sea trout, halibut, flounder, perch, yellow fins and herring litterally swarmed in the waters of our beautiful bay.

During the fishing season I have counted 67 set lines for halibut alone on the P. C. S. S. Co.'s wharf in one afternoon, besides at least a hundred persons engaged with rod and reel, fishing for smelt, mackerel and pompano.

During the sea trout season (i. e., summer months) one could see dozens of these beautiful fish ranging from one foot in length to three, being brought off the wharf from a day's fishing.

Halibut weighing from two to fifty pounds have been caught with live bait by trolling along the wharf, and the man who has ever struck one of the game fish with a light rod and tackle that did not realize the fact that he had bit off a very large slice indeed don't exist.

During the spring of 1885 D. B. Hinman of this place, struck and successfully landed a halibut measuring 48 inches in length and weighing 42 lbs., from off the steamship wharf, using a 20 ounce Chubb rod and 55 feet of linen line Mr Hinman fought his fish up and down the entire length of the wharf several times (575 yards), and althoug several times Mr. Halibut sneaked around a pile under the wharf, at the expiration of about forty minutes from the time of the strike Mr. Hinman had beached his fish and had him weighed.

The old gentleman has cast his line in fishing waters from New York to the Pacific, but he has often said that that afternoon's work was the best he ever done, and he never expects to equal it again.

About the time the run of halibut ceases the king of them all, the sea trout, shows up. This is called sometimes the blue fish, but I believe erroneously, as far as the blue fish of the Eastern coast is concerned. Imagine yourself armed with a light joint rod, not heavier than 15 or 20 ounces, with a good click reel holding about 100 feet of hard braided linen line, at the end of which is a leader three or four feet long attached to a Carlisle hook, which is inserted into a live smelt, standing on the wharf in San Diego Bay with me today, your minno— (no, I won't say minnow, but I'll use the old familiar word so dear to all fishermen—*minny*) playing out in the water about thirty feet from you, just in sight through the clear water—"What was that? Look out there!" Bur-r-r-r goes your reel. There, you've lost him. You struck too quick, my boy. Keep cool, he'll be back. Now reel in your line, examine your minny. He's all right, still alive, but you had better change bait and give that one a chance to rest. Pull up your bait can in which repose about a dozen live bait, and gently drop that one in; now secure that smallest one, that one about five inches long; careful how you hook him; insert the point of the hook about two inches from his head, a little to one side of the dorsal fin; let the point of the hook come out towards the head; don't get it in too deep. Now cast him out gently; don't let him strike the water too hard, you'll stun him. Never mind your bait pail; I'll lower it again. Now look out. Ha the tide has turned; it carries your bait under the wharf. Never mind that; the piles are far apart; there's very little danger of your losing your fish if you do as I tell you. Look out there; let him have it, steady—steady, now, give it to him. What did I tell you?

He's a buster, ain't he? All right, reel him in; he'll go the other way in a second. There he goes. Bur-r-r-r; how he takes the line. Don't look so white around the gills! he's all right; but you have to cut him open to get your hook loose—he had that hook clear in his maw before he felt it. All right, bring him in. Moses! what a beauty! that fellow will go five pounds if an ounce. Now look out; where's your gaff. Aha! there he goes down; never mind, old boy, he is awfully tired; he'd never lay over on his side that way if he wasn't. Now steady; you can be cutting your hook loose in two minutes more if you will just let me get the point of this gaff right—in—under——there you are! Now what do you think of sea trout fishing? Just look at that fellow, will you! Isn't he the perfect picture of a salmon if he had the spots. Oh! I told you what you would have to do. Now open his mouth, run your knife blade down; that's it. See! he had that hook clean swallowed. There you are. Now wait, get out your scales; that's right. What's that? 5½ lbs.? good enough, my boy. Now put him in this basket, and I'll cover him with a wet sack; don't hang him down in the water. "Why?" Too many sharks and turtles around. "Turtles?" Oh, yes! I've seen as many as five and six come up at once off this wharf. Billy Littlefair caught one weighing nearly a hundred pounds here last summer while fishing for shark, and landed him, too. "Edible?" Why of course! same as they get on the lower coast and ship to 'Frisco. I've heard that they come in here to lay their eggs, and that on the bay side of Coronado Heights, the Chinese fishermen have often found their eggs. It may be only rumor, but I do know that during certain months, San Diego bay is full of turtles.

But this ain't fishing. Oh, you've got your line out? that's right, never mind my talk. Aha! got him again! By the Lord, Harry, that's no trout! that fellow means business. Look out there! now he's around that pile; never mind, don't give him an inch, unless he has your line fast in the oysters on the pile he'll come out. Ah-ha! told you so. Now bring him to the surface. Ho-ho! I thought so; a sea bass—a fine one, too. Now I've got him. We'll put him right alongside of your trout. No, not as long as the other, but will weigh nearly as much. You see, he's a whole lot thicker, and got much the larger head and mouth.

Well we wer'nt after bass, but they are here all the season and we catch them all the year around. You see they frequent the piles and as your line is under the wharf you happened to get into him. Oh, yes, they grow larger than that. I was trolling for halibut one day but about fifty yards from the wharf, and got a strike, and to my surprise I found I had hooked a bass. "Land him." You bet, weighed nearly thirteen pounds, I believe the largest ever caught in the bay, although the fishermen outside the heads occasionally bring one in weighing over a hundred lbs. There, you've got a rise. All right. Now watch out, I see you are on. That's right good, you are doing fine; only been here about an hour and you have about fifteen pounds of as fine fish as you can get in the world. Put him with the others. What! going to quit? 'Tired,' well I don't blame you, but I am going up to the hotel, so we will walk together.

"Yes,' our trout fishing is good, but the mackerel, smelt and small fishing in San Diego Bay is a thing of the past. 'Why?' well I'll tell you—for about three or four years past our bay has been afflicted with that curse of the Pacific Coast, the Chinese fisherman. With no respect at all for the laws of the country which supports him, he can be found wherever the fish are, plying his calling by day or night; armed with seines with meshes so small that he captures fish as small as three inches long. He can be seen at all hours of the day and night rowing from point to point until his boat has captured, say in 12 hours at least a half million of these minnows. Loaded down, he hies himself to Chinatown or La playa, unloads, and while he snatches a few hours rest, another crew take his boat and return for more fish while more of him spread the minnows out on boards to dry, after which they are shipped all over the country to other Chinamen.

Now this sort of thing has been going on here for, as I said before, about four years, and you can see what the result has been. Three years ago, I have stood on the wharf and seen the surface of the water so covered with minnows that you couldn't put your hand between them, *and schools of them covering two or three acres*. Fact, I can bring proof of it, and now—well you can see for yourself. 'Why don't the Fish Commissioners do anything?' Echo answers Why? I don't know of any arrest for violating game or fish law in this country for at least eight years past, and yet both the fish and game laws are being violated right along I hope something will be done, though, about it.' Well, here we are "See you to morrow.' Of course, I'm at the wharf whenever I am not busy, now that the quail season is closed and the ducks have left us. "Well, so long." TRIX.

SAN DIEGO, April 9, 1890.

Mr. J. M. Bassford Jr. left Vacaville on Sunday last for the forks of Butte Creek, above Chico, to examine into the edibility of the trout of that stream. We hope luck may attend him, and appetite as well.

Mr. E. T. Allen, of 416 Market Street, San Francisco, in another column advertises what he styles the "Abalone Spoon" for trout and salmon. The spoons are beautifully finished, strong and good spinners. We have not tried them, but in other hands they have proved most effective, being iridescent, and looking like nothing so much as a bright minnow.

THE GUN.

Standard Challenge Medal for 1890.

The conditions of competition for the Selby Smelting and Lead Co.'s Standard Challenge Medal for 1890, representing the individual championship of Central California at artificial birds, are as follows:—

The Selby Smelting and Lead Co., of San Francisco, donates for competition at the trap a medal emblematic of the championship of Central California, at artificial birds, under the following conditions:—

1. This competition is open to any bona fide resident of the counties north of San Luis Obispo, Ventura, Kern, San Bernardino, Santa Barbara, Los Angeles and San Diego.

2. All matches for the above medal shall be shot under the revised trap shooting rules of the American Shooting Association, and shall be at thirty single and ten pair artificial birds. Three traps shall be used, and should the number of entries be so large in any match as to require it, the Keystone System for squad shooting may be adopted.

3. The cartridges used in these matches shall be any of the Standard Shotgun Cartridges loaded by the Selby Smelting and Lead Co., which shall be taken to the score in original packages, the unbroken seals or labels of which shall be cut by the referee or judge, or in his presence by the contestants.

4. Each time a competitor wins the Standard Medal, 1890, he shall be set back one yard in the next match in which he may compete for the same. Mr. H. A. Bassford of Vacaville, the winner of the Standard Medal 1889, shall be additionally handicapped by being placed back five yards from the distance he would otherwise occupy.

5 All matches shall take place under the auspices of some regularly organized Gun Club, located where the matches occur.

6. Full and accurate scores of all matches shall be sent to the Selby Smelting and Lead Co., with complete details of guns and cartridges used. This condition is imperative.

7. Any competitor violating or attempting to violate any of the conditions and rules provided for these competitions (especially Rule 3), shall forfeit all claim to either the Medal or any cash prize.

8. All challenges shall be made in writing to the Selby Smelting and Lead Co.

9. First match, for the above medal, shall be shot at the Oakland Race Track, Oakland, under the auspices of the Blue Rock Club, on Saturday, April 26th, 1890, commencing at 1 P. M. The entrance fee to which will be $5, birds extra.

10. Fifty per cent. of the entrance fees in this initial match shall be forwarded to, and will be held by the Selby Smelting and Lead Co., and awarded to the competitor who shall first win the Standard Medal, 1890, four times, which shall, however, be done inside of one year from date of first match, failing which the donors reserve the right to otherwise dispose of the medal and entrance fees received from the first match.

11. In the first match, the Standard medal, 1890, shall be the first prize; 30 per cent. of the entrance fees shall be the second prize, and 20 per cent. the third prize.

12. The competitor winning the first match shall hold the medal subject to challenge against all comers of Central California, one week's time being given him upon being challenged to name time and place for next match, which shall take place inside of one month from date of challenge, failing which the donors will name time and place for next match.

13. Subsequent matches. All matches after the first one, shall be open to all comers (as per paragraph No. 1 of these conditions), the entrance fee to which shall be $2.50, and the total amount of which shall be divided as follows: 1st prize, Standard medal (40 per cent. of entrance fees shall be given to holder of medal on surrendering it to judge at each match); 2d prize, 30 per cent; 3d prize, 20 per cent., and 4th prize, 10 per cent. of entrance fees.

14. In the final match, 1st prize will be the medal; 2d prize, 40 per cent. of the entrance fees; 3d prize, 30 per cent.; 4th prize, 20 per cent.; 5th prize, 10 per cent.

15. The final winner of the Standard medal, 1890, may claim the championship of Central California for 1890, at artificial birds.

16. All points that may hereafter arise, not covered by the above conditions, will be decided by the Selby Smelting and Lead Company.

Fraud at Traver.

The tournament held at Traver, Tulare, County, week before last terminated most disadvantageously to the manager and one or two of the local participants. It is believed that fraud of the most flagrant and unjustifiable sort was deliberately planned and executed upon the gentlemen invited from a distance to the shoot. It was announced that live birds in plenty had been secured, but when the shooters reached the town and ground but about twenty-five or thirty dozens were on hand, which were shot off on the first day.

It was then stated that more were cooped in the town and would be on hand the next day, but in the morning none were to be had, and the only explanation offered was that the birds had escaped during the night. On the second day a match at 50 Blue Rock targets, $50 entrance, was shot, and it was in this match that the fraud mentioned is believed to have been practiced.

The manager of the tournament sold pools on the match which was participated in by Martinez Chick, H. T. Hopper, "Crane," Shiell and Bare. Chick was a strong favorite, and the money of visiting shots went on him at long odds as against either of the others individually or as a field. The scores by all but one of the local men Bare, were ludicrously small, but at the time no deceit was suspected and the stakes and pool money were paid. In discussing the match it was suggested that the visiting shots were either clear off, or that some trick had been practiced.

The next day when shooting began, some of the targets trapped for the visitors were secured and also some of those trapped for the local man Bare.

A marked dissimularity was noted. The visitors being given a target, just like the blue rocks but of a different and practically unbreakable material, while the local men were given the real blue rock target. Much indignation was felt and expressed by the citizens of Traver.

Bare was compelled to refund the money won by him, but the pool money was not repaid.

The target furnished the visiting shots is a patent fraud, and the scheme seems to have been one of the most rascally kind, as to which no condemnation is too severe.

In order to present a full statement of the case, we wrote to some of those present, inviting them to send their opinions for publication, and have received the following letters. Mr. Woolery was the promoter and manager of the tournament. Mr. Bare and Mr. Shiell are residents of Traver. Mr. Shiell writes:

FROM MR. SHIELL.

TRAVER, CAL., April 15, 1890.

EDITOR BREEDER AND SPORTSMAN—DEAR SIR:—In regard to yours of the 11th inst., I will try to give you as correct a statement as possible. I don't suppose there is a man that ever shot a clay pigeon or ever had anything to do with them but what will say those birds as you have seen were made for fraudulent purposes; but in what way were they meant as a fraud?

It does not look reasonable to say they were rung in by some of the contestant shooters, as everybody interested in the shoot had plenty of money to my personal knowledge; also, they had every opportunity to bet their money at odds. Why did they not bet it if they knew those birds were rung in in their favor? If so, they knew they had a sure thing as we thoroughly tested those birds after the discovery and found they could not be broke by shot of any size. Also, there were part of the time three trap tenders and never less than two, one of them being a young innocent boy that never loaded traps before. The boy has been pumped by his mother and many others, declares he was instructed in no way whatever concerning loading the traps with any different birds. Also when the discovery was made we found just as many of those frauds in his pile as either of the other two, and there were just as many in the field which had come from his trap as either of the other two traps; therefore it is a mystery to me how those birds came there and what they were put there for.

Concerning the discovery, I am not able to say who first made the discovery, as I had made such poor scores I had concluded I could not shoot a little bit, in fact had got disgusted and quit and was not paying much attention to the shoot at that time. But, hearing some loud talk, my attention was attracted, when I saw Martinez Chick have a bird in his hands which looked very peculiar to me; it looked as though it had been struck with 12 or 15 shot and was not broken, each shot leaving a blue spot; some of them had gone through, while others glanced off.

We found another of the same denomination and shot at it twelve times, hitting it with something like 70 shot; evidently the bird would have stood 70 more and have been a good bird after all.

I think they were put in by some malicious person for a damage to the Cleveland Target Company, or otherwise to damage the character of the Traver shooters. If any further discovery is made I will let you know at first chance.

Yours truly, J. W. SHIELL.

Mr. O. M. Judy, who shot as Crain, writes:

FROM MR. JUDY.

TURLOCK, CAL., April 15, 1890.

EDITOR BREEDER AND SPORTSMAN:—Replying to yours of the 11th inst., regarding the fraud practiced at the Traver Tournament, I will say there is no question whatever that the birds thrown for visiting shooters were a fraud of the vilest kind, and were used successfully in the way they were intended, viz.: To be shot at but not broken. As it proved to be an impossibility to break them at eighteen yards' rise, which I fully demonstrated by trapping one bird and shooting it twelve times and finally retrieved it from a stone pile and carried it home with me as a "trophy" of the shoot, the bird showing forty-one shot marks, including quite a number of holes through it just the size of the shot used, there being also shot buried in the bird which every shooter knows is an impossibility with any "breakable" target on the market. I am at a loss to know what the counterfeit is made of. It is the same in shape as the Blue Rock, only much thicker. The material is of a "doughy" texture and a bluish tint painted or dipped in black, and the top painted yellow, the same as the genuine. The bird is one that is calculated to deceive any one unless they take and examine it closely. To further try the breaking qualities of the bird I hung one up top to me, at a distance of about twenty-five yards, and fixed two charges of No. 8 and the same of No. 4

shot. Result, bird punctured full of holes and still in shape to be trapped. I agree with you in believing that the matter should be thoroughly sifted and the guilt placed where it belongs that other shooters may not be similarly imposed upon. The management claimed to have purchased the birds from Golcher & Co. (I think), Agents for the Pacific Coast, but it is hard to believe that the Blue Rock Co. or its agents would place a spurious article on the market and ruin the trade of the Blue Rock, which it would surely and speedily do. Being desirous of aiding, if possible, in ferreting out the perpetrators of the fraud, and showing them up in their true light, I add my mite by merely giving you a few of the facts, trusting that they may aid you in commenting on the matter, which I hope you will handle without gloves.

Yours truly, O. M. Judy.

FROM MARTINEZ CHICK.

San Diego, Cal., April 14th, 1890.

Editor Breeder and Sportsman:—Yours of April 11th at hand and contents duly noted, and in reply to your request will state the following: I arrived at Traver, Tulare County, April 6th, 1890, being one of the five competitors in the Blue Rock Sweepstakes, $50 entrance, being at 26 single and 12 pair Blue Rocks. On arriving at Traver was met by a Mr. A. H. Woolery, who kindly escorted me to the hotel, seemingly to be a perfect gentleman. After arranging all necessaries, had dinner, and was then invited to have a paactice shoot to spend the afternoon, in which there were four of us participated in sweepstakes. I, being lucky, could smash as many Blue Rocks as I wished to. Mr. A. H. Woolery remarked that I was hot stuff, after which we awaited the San Francisco train, which contained several sportsmen to join in the to-morrow's sport. Well, we all, after greeting each other, found our way to the hotel, had a nice time telling old tales, etc. Well, we one by one retired for the night to only find us up and on the ground by 8 o'clock the following morning. As the crowd thickened, pool selling commenced by Mr. Woolery, the manager. I then suggested a small sweepstake, as one of the contestants was absent, a Mr. Shiells. As soon as our sweepstake got under headway, being at six singles and three pair Blue Rocks, I still retained my good luck in smashing the Blue Rocks, scoring 11 out of the possible 12, winning first money. The pools were selling very good, first one and then another selling for first choice, so on arrival of Mr. Shiells the preliminaries were soon arranged so as to begin the race of the big sweepstake, in which I felt sure of being near the top man, but must confess that I was very much disappointed by scoring the enormous figure of 28 out of a possible 50. I murmured over my bad luck, as it had never heretofore happened, but contented myself, as I had company of the same nature. The scores resulted as follows: Chick 28, Hopper 25, Crain 28, Shields 31, Beare 42. Beare was declared the winner and the money delivered to him, after which we all joined to try our luck at live birds. Had a good time; but for the lack of birds could have had a better time.

Mr. Woolery said that he had plenty of birds in his barn, and would catch them all to-night ready for the morning shoot, but alas! on arising in the morning it was learned that all of the birds had made their escape, so consequently no live bird shooting to be had for that day; so there was nothing else to do but to try my hand at the Blue Rocks. Well, we started off in good shape, and as my luck seemed to be good I could handle things as I choose, until I had won first in several sweeps. My friend Mr. Beare, the "Traver champion," or "Jack Rabbit Hunter," as they termed it, approached me with a double eagle, stating that for its equal his score would beat mine, being at 20 single Blue Rocks. I, being there for my health, immediately accepted, and the result showed a score of 11 to 15 in favor Mr. Beare. Well, I must say that I knew my aim was true, and that by finding that the birds were too tough for my 10 gauge L. C. Smith, and with a good solid load of Selby & Co.'s best, aroused my suspicion in regard to the birds, which were dusted and could not break. Nevertheless, I ventured to try my luck again with "Mr. Beare" in the next match, similar to the one just shot. He accepted, placing the wager in my hands. I at once proceeded to the field to investigate the dusted birds, and did not have any trouble in finding the article, as the field was full of them; so I brought one in to my competitor, asking him if those were the kind of birds he was winning my money with, and as he did not seem to wish to face the music, told him that I would not give up the stakes which I held, as I did not come here to be robbed, and also told him that I wished him to refund the money in the $50 sweepstake the day previous. He seemed to look guilty, so I asked Mr. Woolery regarding the matter, in which he stated his innocence. As soon as I started the racket the boys, that is, the contestants in said shoot, became "red headed" at once over the matter, so as there were a party of the shooters made up to have a duck hunt, including Mr. Beare and myself, I left the grounds in hot water, or in an unpeaceful condition.

I said nothing more until I was out on the grounds for duck shooting, after which I made it my business to be in company with Mr. Beare, so when alone with him started the conversation regarding the thievery and asking him to refund the money, which after a long talk came to my desire. Of course I knew when we arrived at Traver in the evening the other shooters would be after him as he had the money, but what went on at Traver with Mr. Woolery and others do not know, while we were out duck shooting. On our arrival at the hotel in the evening things were still red hot. Mr. Beare was asked by several to refund the money for the big shoot. After considering the situation and feeling of his fellow competitors, and the style upon which the match was conducted, thought it best to satisfy all and return the money, which he did. I am satisfied in my own mind that this job of thievery was planned, cut and dried to rob us out of our money, which they would have done if they had not been so hoggish, and also am satisfied that Mr. Woolery, Mr. Beare and also the trapper were well aware of the plot. They stated that the birds came packed in the barrel with the others, which I do not believe. I hope that the exposure of this fraud will put all sportsmen on their guard against like attempts at robbery, and truly hope that I am not to be caught shooting against such odds, and also such men. If the Blue Rock Company does not manufacture the composition the they will be able to solve the matter. I can say for myself that I will not take part in any tournament that either of these rascals have anything to do with.

Yours most respectfully, Martinez Chick.

Mr. C. J. Haas, widely known as a rare shot, says:

FROM MR. HAAS.

Stockton, Cal., April 14th, 1890.

Editor Breeder and Sportsman:—In regard to the Traver shoot I was only there the first day and they had not found out about the putty Blue Rocks until the second day, so do not know anything about it, only from hear say.

Yours truly, Chas J. Haas.

The manager of the meeting. Mr. Woolery, has this to say:

FROM MR. WOOLERY.

Traver, Cal., April 12th, 1890.

Editor Breeder and Sportsman:—I herewith enclose you the scores made at shoot on 6th Inst, very poor scores. The fraud you mentioned is a kind of mystery; something never heard of before. I am endeavoring to get at the bottom of it. Until I do I cannot write you anything much concerning it. One thing sure they could not break them. Will be in the city in a few days and will explain all.

Yours, etc., A. H. Woolery.

Mr. Bare, the man suspected by some of connivance in the fraud, writes:

FROM MR. BARE.

Traver Cal., April 14th, 1890.

Editor Breeder and Sportsman:—Yours of the 11th just to hand. In reply will say that there was a fraud perpetrated there is do doubt. But to whom or where to lay it I do not know, and until the matter is settled where it belongs, I do not consider it prudent to give the matter too much publicity.

Hoping you may agree with me in the matter I am most respectfully, J. W. Bare.

In addition to the written statements, Messrs. R. M. Eddy and Crittenden Robinson of this city, in conversation, have expressed the opinion that a deliberate fraud was practiced by one or more of those interested in the tournament.

That the "fake" targets were on hand is to our notion conclusive proof of vicious intentions. Messrs. Clabrough, Golcher & Co., Pacific Coast Agents for Blue Rocks, disclaim all knowledge of the fraudulent target. The disclaimer was not necessary. The standing of the firm and its business interest in increasing the sale of the legitimate targets alike forbid any attempt at fraud. The use of the fraudulent targets could not have been accidental for the reason that the local man Beare had none of them, while the others had many.

It seems that explanation of the villainous scheme must rest between the Director of the shoot, Mr. Woolery, and the man who profited by taking the stake money, Mr. Bare.

It rests with the two mentioned to clear the matter if possible.

In the match in which fraud was detected, which was at 26 singles and 12 pairs of Blue Rock targets, $50 entrance, the scores were Martinez Chick, 28; S. H. "Crain," 28; H. T. Hopper, 25; J. Shiell, 31; J. W. Bare, 42.

Such scores are absurd for all but Bare, and in themselves suggest irregularity of some sort.

We hope next week to be able to present letters from others who were present at Traver.

The citizens of that town have as much interest in ferreting out the guilty ones as any others can.

Alameda Gun Club.

The Alameda County Sportsman's Club met at Oakland Trotting Park on Saturday afternoon last, and shot the regular club match at 12 live birds per man, American Shooting Association rules. The day was fair and the birds good. Colonel S. I. Kellogg led the procession, with 11 kills, followed by Messrs. C. M. Osborn, Morrison and Mayhew, with 10. The score were:

S. E. Knowles	1	2	1	2	0	1	1	0	1	0	2	1	9
W. W. Haskell	1	1	2	0	1	1	0	1	0	1	1	2	9
F. B. Norton	0	1	0	1	1	0	0	1	1	2	1	1	8
S. I. Kellogg	1	1	2	0	2	1	2	1	2	2	1	1	11
C. F. Morrison	2	0	2	1	1	2	2	0	2	2	1	1	10
C. E. Smith	1	2	1	1	0	1	2	1	0	1	0	1	9
W. E. Mayhew	1	1	1	1	1	1	1	0	1	1	1	0	10
Charles Larner	0	1	2	2	0	0	1	1	2	1	2	2	9
Osborn	1	1	1	0	2	1	1	1	2	1	1	0	10
G. E. Plummer	1	1	1	0	2	0	0	0	1	1	0	1	7
H. Schroeder	1	1	2	0	2	0	0	0	1	1	2	0	6
A. T. Boardman	0	1	0	0	0	0	1	0	0	0	2	0	3
H. B. Houghton	2	2	0	0	0	0	2	1	1	1	1	0	7
R. E. Bell	1	1	1	2	0	0	1	0	2	1	2	1	9

In a pool-shoot freeze-out, $2.50 entrance money, live birds, at 30 yards rise, the score was:

Eddy	1	1	1	1	1	5
Smith	1	1	1	1	1	5
Bironals	1	1	1	1	0	4
Larner	1	1	1	1	1	5
Brown	1	1	1	0	w	3
Boardman	1	1	0	w		2
Golcher	1	1	1	1	0	4
Schroeder	1	1	1	1	1	5
Bell	1	0	w			1

Do Deer Shad Every Year.

Editor Breeder and Sportsman:—Please inform several constant readers if a deer sheds its horns every year or not. Some contend that they do not shed their horns unless they are broken off or injured. Respectfully, J. S. W.

Tulare, Cal.

[Deer shed their horns every year. It is said that when bucks are enucleated, they grow "moose horns," and do not shed them, but such instances are not common.—Ed.]

The Parker Gun.

Editor Breeder and Sportsman:—The expert trap shots of the country making the tour of the U. S. in the interest of the U. S. Cartridge Co., finished in Boston, Mass., April 2d, a series of 32 matches between the Eastern and Western teams, 40 birds to a man, 30 singles and 5 pairs. J. R. Stice, Jacksonville, Ill., being one of the Western team, shooting a 12-bore Hammerless Parker Gun, was high man of the 10 contesting, making the wonderful average of 93 per cent. of birds shot at in all kinds of weather from Massachusetts to California. Parker Bros.

Meriden, Conn.

The California Wing Shooting Club meets at Oakland Trotting Park to-morrow morning. Visitors should take the 9 a. m. boat for Berkeley and alight at Shell Mound Station, near which the shooting ground is situated.

Mr. E. C. Williams, Secretary of the Rod and Gun Club of Santa Cruz, is proving himself an extremely effective officer. He is keeping his club stirred up to the necessity of observance of the game and fish laws, and Santa Cruz County will be anything but a happpy hunting ground for poachers hereafter.

Mr. William Schreiber at 21 Kearney Street has on exhibition two fine cock pheasants, one the Mongolian bird so common in Oregon, the other the Copper pheasant of Japan. The Board of Fish Commissioners is about to introduce both birds. The Japanese pheasant is to our notion the better looking bird, being heavier, of richer plumage and more game by report.

A most singular report of a trap match was sent us the other day from Carson City by Mr. Harry A. Weaver. That gentleman happened to be on the ground, and having no score book, just whittled a piece of soft wood smooth, checked the scores on it and mailed it to this office.

The match was between Hon. J. M. Dormer, Secretary of the State of Nevada, his Deputy, Pratt, and Mr. John Furlong, at seven birds per man. They killed six each, one of Mr. Dormer's falling dead out of bounds. Poor Mr. Weaver lost fifty cents on the only bird clean missed by Dormer, and must consequently wait until the snow melts and walking is good before he leaves Carson for his home in Stockton.

THE KENNEL.

Dog owners are requested to send for publication the earliest possible notices of whelps, sales, names claimed, presentations and deaths, in their kennels, in all instances writing plainly names of sire and dam and of grandparents, colors, dates and breed.

Visits.

Dr. M. E. Taber's (San Bernardino) Babbetta (Mainspring E. 13375—Dell, A. K. R. 1522) to Geo. Blake's Valentine Boy (Bang Ranger 41035—Bell Farris 9403) on March 31.

Mr. Wm. Schreiber's (San Francisco) pointer Sall (Bragg IV. 11282, E.—Forest Queen II. 18451, E.) to Mr. R. T. Vandevort's Billy (Vandevort's Don—Drab) on April 7th.

Names Claimed.

Mr. W. D. Howe (San Francisco) claims the name Flockfinder for liver and white pointer bitch by Professor—Gracie Bow.

Mr. C. M. Osborn (San Francisco) claims the name Student for liver and white flecked pointer dog, whelped August 26, 1889, by Professor—Gracie Bow.

Whelps.

Mr. H. W. M. Sandbach's beagle Nellie whelped, April 11th, four, two dogs, to Bobby.

Mr. W. S. Kittles' cocker spaniel Gift (Capt. Stubbs—Fern) whelped, April 11th, seven, four dogs, to Donald Campell's Teddy.

Pacific Coast Field Trials.

The time for closure of entries to the Pacific Coast Field Trials Derby has been extended to June 1st, 1890. May 1st has heretofore been the date, but for the present year it was deemed advisable by the Executive Committee to extend the time.

There is no reason why the Derby should not be the best yet run in California. Very many fine pointer litters have been noted during the two years last passed and some setter litters of more than ordinary excellence, which should have representations in the trials.

The Executive Committee ordered that the rule, that five dollars forfeit should accompany each Derby entry be strictly enforced, and no entry will be received unless the money is received by June 1st.

The general condition of the club was discussed by President J. E. Edwards, Treasurer J. M. Kilgarif, Directors William Schreiber and J. S. Dunham and Mr. P. S. Linville.

Inspection of the books showed that there was $410 due the Club from members, and $61.05 due from the Secretary. The liabilities are $176. The Treasurer was instructed to make a vigorous attempt to collect the dues and arrearages now owing.

Mr. P. D Linville suggested a vote in recognition of the extraordinary manner in which the secretary had performed his duties at the last field trial, but the suggestion did not seem to arouse enthusiasm.

The club has 52 members of whom probably thirty will square up and retain active relationship to the institution. A combined effort should be made to thoroughly rehabilitate the organization, secure new members and make the trials first rate in every respect.

From Inyo.

Editor Breeder and Sportsman:—I wish I were able to send you some dog news, but I believe I have the only thoroughbred dog with authenticated pedigree within fifty miles. She is named Fanny B; bred by G. W. Bassford, Suisun Valley. Her sire is Victor 2d, he by Glen R.—Josie Bow, etc.; her dam is Gracie Bow by King Bow—Grace, etc. Color, liver and white. Whelped November 27, 1886. There is but one other pointer in Owens River Valley, viz., Money, brought from the East to Arizona by U. S. A. officer; from there here by under-Sheriff W. P. Taney. Pedigree unknown; sire and dam s. t. b., imported from England. There are three or four good field dogs of the setter type at Bishop Creek, but I do not know their pedigree; will try and find out. I do not know of any other dogs in the valley except curs, which are too plenty.

I would be glad to furnish sporting items if they were to be had. Quail are very plenty in this valley, also ducks. Owens Lake would be a duck-hunters paradise. Some geese in winter, and once in awhile swans. Curlew and snipe are found along Black Rock and Fish Spring Sloughs. In the mountains may be found grouse, mountain-quail and some deer. Once in a while bear and mountain sheep may be met with. I have been along the Coast Range from Humboldt to San Diego, but have never seen a place where more or larger trout can be caught than in the streams leading into the Owens Valley from the Sierras, and along the headwaters of Kern and other streams opposite the valley. If you can use anything I have written, you are at liberty to cut it up to suit yourself, as I am unused to writing for publication. Will H. Graham.

Independence, Inyo Co.

Mr. W. D. Howe, 2922 Pine Street, San Francisco, informs us that he has a nice young pointer by Professor—Gracie Bow, for which he has no room, and he would be glad to place it in good hands.

Grim's Gossip.

Tom Hazlett and Kelly & Samuels will start for Denver with their horses immediately on the conclusion of the Sacramento meeting.

Griffin has a new name for the practice of burying great horses in the solitudes of non-racing stud farms: He calls it "Bonnerizing" them.

As is only natural, the race track has had any quantity of visitors during the early morning runs, and the touts have not failed to get on to one or two good things.

S. A. Eddy, of Hanford, is handling his three-year-old colt George J. by Pasha, 2:36, and he shows a great deal of speed. The Pasha colts are sure to come to the front before long.

Frank Baldwin, the manager of the Fresno track, has been in town during the week, shaking hands with old friends and making many new ones. It is a pity that there are not more such managers knocking around.

The pacer Westmont 2:13¾ that has wintered at Ed Smith's club house, Chicago, is in sound shape, and will start against time and with running mate in the Southeastern circuit, beginning April 29th at Washington, D. C.

It is of the highest importance that the rule requiring pedigrees of horses to be given with all entries be enforced by managers of trotting associations, and papers reporting trotting races should always pedigree their summaries.

S. N. Straube of Fresno has sold to G. H. Bernard the two fillies, Mattie Vickers and Matilda. They are both by Pasha 2:36 (sire of Moro 2:27) and out of a mare by Hock-hocking. The mares are both in foal to Apex 2:26.

Our old-time friend "Billy" Ayres, of Portland, Oregon, is in the city taking a look at the flyers now at the Bay District track. It is only a few years ago that Mr. Ayres was largely interested in "bang tails," and many times has his colors been seen past the wire first.

There is no probability that there will be any extra racing given by the Directors of the Blood Horse Association, as many of the gentlemen are opposed to the scheme. This will enable the runners to have a rest for a few days, prior to starting in at Sacramento.

A few minutes' thought of what the world would be without the horse, leads us to a true estimate of his value, and enables us to realize what our lives would lose of pleasure, power, profit and picturesqueness without the animal that brings such great, yet such controllable, powers to our aid.—Exchange.

The thousands which have assembled at the Bay District track since our last issue, have not been composed entirely of followers of the thoroughbred, for many prominent owners of trotting horses can daily be seen watching the runners in their work, and they seem to enjoy the sport just as much as they do the trotting meetings.

It is the general impression that the bookmakers' stands should be further apart in the betting enclosure. As at present situated, there is not room for persons to pass the large crowd that at all times stand around the "layers of the odds," and it is almost impossible for one to go to the upper stand. This should be remedied in future.

Ab Stemler is at present in San Francisco, and he states that he will start the Shippee string at Chicago and the Twin City races. Before Fellowcharm wrenched himself, the intention was to take in the extreme Eastern circuit, but from present appearances, only the two meetings mentioned will see the colors of the Stockton stable.

The Hon. L. J. Rose evidently knew what a choice bit of horse flesh he had in Fairy, the winner of the California Stakes, for on the day previous to the one on which the stake was run for; that gentleman bought from the Palo Alto Stock Farm the sire of Fairy; Argyle is by Monday, dam Cuba by imp. Australian; 2d dam Bettie Ward by Lexington, etc. Price paid, $5,000.

Pat Farrell is very anxious to find out the breeding of the dam of Coquette, and I have no doubt but what some of our readers can inform the old time horseman of the pedigree desired. It seems as though Mr. Prather, of Yolo County, or Frank Malone of this city, might be able to give some clue, by which the breeding could be obtained.

Woodnut 2:16½ has been promoted to the premier position at Cedar Farm, the California stallion being considered one of the best now standing for public service in the East. Col. R. S. Strader of Lexington, Ky., who lately visited many of the large establishments on the Atlantic Coast, says he is the best looking horse he saw on his entire trip.

The Kentucky Stock Farm, speaking about George Wilkes very seriously suggests, that Electioneer should be mated to a few Mambrino Patchen mares, or to the daughters of some of Patchen's best sons and says, "reasoning from analogy this should be Electioneer's best nick." Please Mr. Stock Farm what Patchen mare can produce another Sunol or Palo Alto.

One of the race animals that the public miss from the track this spring is Bessie Shannon, formerly owned by John Reavey. Meeting John on the track, he was asked where the mare was, and he answered that she had been sold to Charles Vanina of Washo County, Nevada and was shipped to her new home on Friday of last week. She is a good, useful mare, and will no doubt be heard from over there.

There is always a lot of knowing ones who fancy that simple assertions are enough to make facts. It has been common talk that Dan Miller especially prepared Ida Glenn for the Selling race on Saturday last, and that she was to be a big surprise to the bookmakers. Now the truth of the matter is the mare was taken from the stud and given two short trials, one of three-eighths and the other of half a mile, and then turned loose in the race; still in the run-off she made Applause go the three-quarters in 1:13½.

One of the prominent breeders of California has received a cablegram from T. B. Merry, asking if he wishes to purchase Dunlop for $5,000. If the price stated is correct, the horse is very cheap, and as his performances were of the best, he should prove a desirable animal for the stud on any of the breeding farms of America. He was prominently engaged as a two, three, four and five-year-old, winning at all distances, his greatest effort being the win for the Melbourne Cup, which he negotiated in the good time of 3:28½, the distance being two miles

Capt. Matthews has been adding to his stable by purchasing from Mr. Sargent, of Gilroy, the six-year-old black stallion John Gordon by Brown Jug, dam Maggie by Budd Doble 3764, 2nd dam Lady Clinton. The Captain's new purchase is a magnificent specimen of the trotting horse and already gives promise of proving very fast on the road. Several gentlemen owing fast horses have tackled the black, but he has so far beaten them all.

Whenever you hear the owner of a stallion going about denouncing the stallions owned by his neighbors,—trying to cast suspicions upon their pedigrees, and back-biting their owners, while he is profuse in his praises of his own horse, and unblushingly seeks to impress his listeners with his own superior horse knowledge and experience—look out for him, ten to one he is a fraud, and his horse a dung hill.

For years the Cockrill brothers of Soledad, have had horses on the running turf, but owing to their selling Daisy D. and Captain Al, last year Bruce Cockrill was left with only Mero b. c., by Wildidle, dam Precious, by Lever. Mero was entered at the spring meeting of the Blood Horse Association and made such a fine appearance that the Owens Bros. of Fresno, bought the colt before he was seen by the public. The price paid was $1,500.

It is stated that the weather is perfect at Memphis, and but for the prevalence of buffalo gnats the horsemen at Montgomery Park would be happy. The track is in the pink of condition, and the flyers are getting into shape rapidly. Proctor Knott has a cough. He and others of Scoggan's string caught cold while en route, and the great gelding is not at home to visitors. His trainer is giving him quinine.

During the present week there have been many gentlemen from the Eastern States present at the Bay District track to witness the races of the Blood Horse Association, and it has been the generally expressed opinion that the class of horses present were superior to those usually seen on an Eastern track. The two and three-year-olds are away above the average, and as several of them will be seen on the "big" tracks this season, the race goers on the Atlantic Coast will be able to judge what California can produce.

It will be remembered that not long ago I spoke of Mr. Merry's good luck in being in Australia when the Hon. James White's horses were to be sold. If rumor is correct, "Tom" will not benefit much by being on the ground, as the sale will in all probability be declared, off, as it is said that the entire stable has been sold to a young gentleman living in Sydney. Mr. Merry's knowledge of the Australian horses is such, however, that I confidently expect the next steamer to bring over a choice lot selected by him.

Attention has been called in this paper quite a number of times to the conflict in dates claimed by the various associations. I have received word from the Santa Clara Valley Agricultural Association that the date for the San Jose meeting has been changed from that originally claimed to the week preceding the Napa Meeting. According to this, San Jose will have the pride of opening the circuit this season. The Secretary of the Sixth District Agricultural Association also sends me word that Los Angeles will hold their meeting on the week beginning August 4th. It is to be presumed at the next meeting of the Board of Directors of the Breeders' Association that they will finally select the week they are going to have, so that all horsemen may know exactly how to arrange their circuit.

The knee of the horse is no common joint. It is, in fact, not one joint but three. As it is the only joint in the body in which one bone receives the weight of the body from another bone, in a perpendicular direction, it is furnished with the most extraordinary precautions to prevent any injurious concussion. Between the lower end of the arm bone and the upper ends of the shank bone and its two small bony attachments, six small flat bones are interposed in two layers, each bone being deeply covered with elastic cartilages. These are connected together by very strong ligaments, so contrived as to hold between each layer of polished elastic cartilage a supply of oil, sufficient not only to lubricate, but also to soften in the most effectual manner any otherwise injurious concussion.

Two months or better ago, James A. Dustin, better known as "Jim," went down to Palo Alto to take charge of the trotters during the absence of Mr. Marvin in the East with the horses that were lately sold at auction. As Marvin has returned, Mr. Dustin has turned over the stables once more, and now is looking for a stable to train on the circuit. He will work at the Bay District track, beginning operations immediately on the conclusion of the Blood Horse meeting. Jim is a careful trainer, and now that he is thoroughly posted on the Palo Alto methods, he should have a full stable in no time. Good drivers are going to be scarce on the coast this year, so that Dustin's entry into the field of competition, will add to the pleasures of the circuit this Fall. Owners caring to secure his services, can address him care of this office.

In his work entitled "Training the Trotting Horse," Marvin says: The Moor founded one of the greatest California families—horses noted for good, clean, sound legs and feet, solid colors and excellent form. The Moors are uniformly trotters, and as a rule are game, resolute horses. They are generally built on the greyhound order, the most objectionable feature being their heads, which are often large, and nearly always of the Roman order. Many of them are strong-willed and rattle-headed. The most noted descendants of the Moor are his daughter Beautiful Bells, his grandson Stamboul, and Sable Wilkes, whose dam was a daughter of The Moor. The blood of The Moor is a grand, speedy, fashionable strain in a pedigree, and one that is now widely appreciated. He died young, leaving few foals, but had in him the elements of greatness.

The following mares have been bred to Axtell 2:12:—

Missile, by Director 2:17, dam Lorette by Rysdyk's Hambletonian; second dam Lady Walkill, by C. M. Clay; third dam by Rockingham.

Maroon, by Director 2:17, dam Calumet by Volunteer; second dam Flight by Woodburn; third dam Silvertail (dam of Driver 2:19½) by American Star; fourth dam by Wildair.

Mignon, by Director 2:17, dam Caprice by Volunteer; second dam Change by Woburn; third dam Lady Sears (dam of Huntress, 2:20¼, Trio 2:23½, and Sister 2:30¼), by American Star; fourth dam by Abdallah 1.

Minuet, by Director 2:17, dam Pearl by Rysdyk's Hambletonian; second dam Star Queen by Seeley's American Star; third dam by Emancipation.

The above are the property of R. S. Veach, Indian Hill Farm, Ky.

Property of C. R. Noyes, Boston, Mass.: Mannette, by Director 2:17, dam Pantalette, as given above. This filly was sold by Indian Hill as a yearling for $4,000.

F. D. Myers, a prominent real estate broker of Oakland, has gone into the breeding business quite extensively, having purchased, in addition to what he already owns, several fine mares in the East. The gentleman started last Wednesday morning for Lexington to bring on the mares, and he will have room in his car for several more than his own. If there are any of our readers who wish to have animals brought out from Lexington or Dubuque, Mr. Myers can accommodate them. A letter will reach him if sent in care of the Kentucky Stock Farm, Lexington, Ky.

When I saw the Tidal Stakes run for on Saturday last, the conclusion was forced on me that Flambeau was the greatest colt ever seen, not even barring El Rio Rey. His run was made so easy that it looked better than even money that he could beat the record whenever called on. These thoughts passed through the mind with no nearer inspection than the reporters' stand afforded, but on Tuesday a close look was taken when he was stripped for the Pacific Derby, and my mind changed at once. I do not like the look of his hocks, and one of his forelegs seems in a very dickey condition. He may possibly pull through a light campaign in the East, but if he is given hard work, he will be another of the likely ones fit only for the stud. No doubt the racing reporter will say something about him in the account of the race, but the only inference I can draw from his looks is that he will be a failure in the East. Racine had a splint last fall, which has entirely disappeared and he looks as clean as a whistle, with plenty of run in him to make a mark for himself anywhere.

A note from Farmington informs me that Mr. C. E. Needham, of Bellota, has had exceedingly good luck this year with his foals, and as many of them are by his great horse Steve Whipple, 2:23 (trial 2:17½), and out of first class mares, it should not be long before we have many of the trotters from Mr. Needham's stock farm enrolled in the 2:30 list. Among those who have bought colts from him are W. T. Smith of Farmington; the colt has been given the name of Select, he being by Voter, he by Elect, a son of Electioneer. Select's first dam is Polly by Alexander's Belmont 64, he by Abdallah 15; 2d dam by Young Hambletonian by Bishop's Hambletonian; 3d dam represented as being a Messenger and Eclipse mare. Voter's 1st dam Twist (dam of Steve Whipple) by Hambletonian 725; 2d dam Jenny Lind by Vermont Black Hawk 5; 3d dam Old Stub by Young Telescope; 4th dam by Justin Morgan. Elect's dam Inez by Nordale; 2d dam Lizzie by Williamson's Belmont. Select, it will be noticed, is a great grandson of Electioneer, and shows three direct lines to Rysdyk's Hambletonian 10, each lines of the most approved breeding.

An old friend writes and asks, What treatment is necessary for mares and foals. Now it is many years since I had to personally attend to such matters and I feel that my memory is a bit treacherous, but for the sake of "old times" will say that mares should be carefully watched when about to foal, as many youngsters are lost, owing to lack of attention at the time of birth. When it is found that respiration is not as it should be, blowing into the mouth of the foal is considered necessary, and another good plan is to rub the body quite sharply with a handful of straw or hay. Brandy and water (about evenly divided) is also beneficial, a few teaspoonfuls given after the first respirations will tend to quicken the action of the vital forces. As soon as possible the mare should be allowed to show her maternal instinct by nursing the foal, which she will do by licking and caressing the colt; however, at times the mother will not do this; then it is necessary to dry the little one with flannel and assist it to the teat. Mares are at times ill natured and will not be sucked, but in that case the foal must be guarded to prevent the mother from hurting her offspring. When once the mare allows the colt to milk, there is little or no further danger, but if the mare absolutely refuses to nurse the colt it must be carefully watched over and brought up by hand. A case like this is rare, still it is necessary at times.

The large prices which have ruled in the East for California bred trotters have incited quite a number of gentlemen to purchase good young stallions, hoping that the day may not be far distant when they will be able to realize largely by the sale of well bred young stock.

It is with pleasure I note that Mr. S H. Hoy of Winters, Yolo County, has purchased from Fred W. Loeber of the Vineland Breeding Farm, St. Helena, Cal., the choice two-year-old colt Dawnlight by Dawn 2:18¾, dam Alida (dam of Directa, three year old record 2:31¼) by Admiral (sire of Sister 2:19½, Nona Y 2:25, Perihelion 2:25, Huntress 2:28, etc), son of Goldsmith's Volunteer, 2nd dam Mag Drake (granddam of Bud 2:33) by Mohawk, 3d dam Fanny Bassford. Mr. Hoy paid $1500 for the colt, and Mr. Loeber informs me that he considers him the most promising two-year-old he ever raised. There can be no doubt from the breeding here shown that Dawnlight should not only make a good record for himself, but that he should materially improve the stock in the vicinity of Winters, where he will stand for the future.

Mr Hoy is an energetic and well posted young breeder, who has had some experience already, and I have no doubt that he will find his new purchase a very profitable one.

Mr. Charles Marvin spent three hours with Mr. Robert Bonner on Tuesday of last week, before starting back for California, says the Turf, Field and Farm. The owner of Sunol has no anxiety about his great filly so long as she is controlled by Senator Stanford, and is trained and driven by Marvin. Sunol will be brought East in May, and if she keeps right, will not shrink from a meeting with Axtell or any other four year old. Marvin examined Maud S. with the greatest care, and he expressed astonishment at finding the Queen with such good legs after doing what she has done. Great as is his confidence in Sunol, he is in doubt as to what the result would be should Maud S. be put in shape and started on the same track and day in the month of August against the time effort of the daughter of Electioneer.

The improvement which Mr. Bonner has made in a few week's time in Reverie, purchased at the Rose sale for $10,000, also astonished Marvin. The filly now stands firmly on her feet, plainly showing what practical knowledge of balancing will do. Ansel was jogged up and down the stable floor, and his action was so elastic that Marvin ventured the opinion that he would stand training again. He added that the stallion had speed enough to trot in 2:15, if he could be kept at work. The change which has taken place in the horse under scientific shoeing is marvellous. Mr. Marvin remarked to us that the knowledge which he had derived from Mr. Bonner would prove of the greatest value to him in educating trotters at Palo Alto. He sees how he can avoid in shoeing many of the mistakes of the past. He left for the Pacific Coast strong in the faith that he would be able to keep Sunol so perfectly balanced that she would lower this season her record of 2:10½.

Pacific Coast Blood Horse Association.

Continued from Page 338.

THIRD DAY.

Notwithstanding the overcast sky on Thursday, a fairly good crowd assembled at the track to see the four events on the programme run off, and they were well repaid for their trouble, as the contests were highly interesting, and exciting enough to satisfy the most exacting. The selling race was, as usual, a guessing one, and considerable money went into the box, as each of the starters had more or less backing, the strong favorite being Kildare, although Sheridan, Applause and Ida Glenn had supporters by the score. On general appearances, the latter named was in the best condition, with Applause a good second choice. For the Racine Stakes, for two year olds, only four of the youngsters made an appearance, Murry's Power being scratched. The Los Angeles filly was not as shifty as on Saturday and Homer had no trouble in proving superiority, much to the delight of those who had pinned their faith to the Shannon colt. The mile heats, upset the calculations of the talent, for the race was generally conceded to Daisy D, although many of the owners who have watched the horses closely in their work seemed inclined to fancy Coloma. "There is many a slip 'twixt the cup and the lip" and as Dan Dennison expressed it "Dave knew he would have to walk home if he lost the race, so he used a little exertion." Many of the stable boys had a field ticket so the shouts of the lads when Douglas won, was something to be remembered. The Sequel Stakes brought forth another surprise, inasmuch as close observers have generally been willing to admit that Al Farrow could not go over a mile and an eighth, and many believed he was faint hearted. But the result must have caused such believers to change their minds for he proved himself a horse of courage, endurance, and more than all, a weight carrier. As a days sport, the like is rarely seen especially as the starting was much better than it was on the two previous days, and general satisfaction was expressed by all who went for sport alone, the only grumblers being those who lost their money.

The Judges of the day were Col. H. I. Thorton, M. F. Tarpey and Mr. Guntz, while the timers seats were filled by R. T. Carroll, James A. Dustin and Edwin F. Smith.

At the third bugle call, William Coombs, of Napa, took the flag, and although the gentleman has had a great deal of experience in the past, he was almost an hour in getting them in something like good shape before he could send them on their journey. Sallie C. and Nerva were particularly bad natured, and both gave signs of being in season. Many breakaways were made, and at last the welcome shout was raised "they're off." True enough; the flag descended, and Kildare was a length in the lead, but in a stride or two Sheridan was at his shoulder, he lapped by Ida Glenn. As they shot around the turn, Applause and Oakdale worked up on the leaders, the balance being strung out behind. On the backstretch, Kildare, Glenn and Sheridan were on even terms, and as Applause was given his head, the son of Three Cheers was soon on an equality with the others. At the half, the four were having a determined battle, with the nose of Sheridan showing in front for a moment or two, but he was quickly displaced by Kildare. On the upper turn Ida Glenn was taken back, but as the leaders swept into the homestretch, she was given her head, and a battle royal ensued between the mare, Applause and Kildare. At the draw gate the race was virtually over, as Glenn had the speed of the party, and went under the wire winner by a neck, Kildare second, and Applause on Kildare's flank. Of course it would not be a selling race if there had not been "a kick," so on dismounting, the jockeys on Kildare and Applause both claimed foul against the rider of Ida Glenn, and after a long conference, the judges placed Ida behind, and decided as follows:

SUMMARY.

Selling purse, $350; of which $50 to second; for three-year-olds and upwards. Horses entered to be sold for $1,500 to carry rule weights; three pounds allowed for each $100 less down to $500, then two pounds for each $100 down to $300. Horses entered not to be sold to carry ten pounds above the scale. Fifteen sixteenths of a mile.

M. Storn's ch g Kildare, a, Kyrle Daly—Mistake, 105............Pierce 1
W. George's ch g Applause, a, Three Cheers—Alice N., 104....Narvaez 2
P. Siebenthaler's ch c Sheridan, 3, Young Bazaar—Lost Girl, 105 ....Williams 3

Time, 1:37¾.

Ida Glenn, a, 98, Brown; Sallie C., 4, 93, Dennison; Nerva, a, 106, Casey; Rosebug, 4, 95, Stewart; Oakdale, 3, 91, Leonard; Hernanda, 5, 108, Ferguson, ran unplaced.

Bookbetting—Kildare 8—5, 1—2; Applause 1, 8—5; Sheridan 3—1, 1—1; Ida Glenn 5—1, 8—5; Nerva 12—1, 4—1 Rosebug; 30—1, 12 1; Sallie C. 15—1, 5—1; Oakdale 20—1; 8—1; Hernanda 30—1, 12—1.

Auction pools Kildare $35, Sheridan $12, Ida Glenn $11; field $9.

The second race on the card was the Racine Stakes, named after the winner last year, he having covered the distance in 1:14½. Whenever that time is beaten the stake will be renamed after the winner. Four two-year-olds sported silk, the favorite being Mr. Rose's Fairy, the filly which showed to such advantage in the California Stakes. Many prominent bettors fancied Homer, and several large amounts were booked anent the representative of the Undine Stable, his easy win on Tuesday gaining him many friends. When the starter got them away, it was with Homer in the lead, but he was quickly caught up to by Fairy, the two making a pretty race from the half mile pole around the turn and into the homestretch. As the castigation commenced, the filly wanted to quit, but kept up well to the drawgate, where she showed plainly that she had had enough, and Homer was allowed to win as he pleased by at least two open lengths, with Conrad three lengths behind Fairy. And now comes the

SUMMARY.

The Racine Stakes—For two-year-olds (foals of 1888); $50 each; $25 forfeit, or $10 if declared out on or before January 1, 1890. All declarations void unless accompanied by the money; with $500 added, second horse to receive $100; third to save stake. Stake to be named after the winner if Racine's time (1:14½) is beaten. Three-quarters of a mile.

Undine Stable's b c Homer by Shannon—Sallie Gardner, 110 ....Narvaez 1
L. J. Rose's b f Fairy by Argyle—imp Fairy Rose, 107............Monohan 2
L. J. Rose's b c Conrad by Flood—imp Gonia, 110............Stewart 3

Time, 1:15¾.

Snowball (110) ran unplaced.

Book betting—Homer, 2 to 1, no place; Fairy, 2 to 5, no place; Conrad, 18 to 1, 2 to 1; Sacramento, 10 to 1, 3 to 1.

Auction Pools Rose Stable (Fairy and Conrad) $25; field, $10.

The betting race of the day was the one of mile heats in which the starters were Daisy D., Coloma, Dave Douglas and Jack Brady. The mare was a great favorite and money poured in in handfuls on her both in the auctions and to the bookmakers. After a little delay Mr. Coombs trailed the flag and away they went, Douglas a length in advance, the others bunched. As the turn was reached, Coloma showed in front, Douglass having fallen behind, the leader being hard pressed by Jack Brady and the favorite. Down the backstretch and into the upper turn the positions were still the same, but when nearing the three-quarter pole, Brady was pulled back and the two leaders made a hot finish which resulted in Coloma winning by half a length, Daisy D. second, Brady, third.

Daisy still retained the position of favorite, with Coloma well up for second choice, pools selling until the flag again fell. This time Douglas was again away in the lead and by long odds he looked the freshest one of the quartette. Young Dennison took him back gradually, and as they rounded the turn and prepared for a run up the backstretch, they were paired, Coloma and Daisy leading, with Douglas and Brady at their heels. No change occurred until the middle of the upper turn was reached when Brady was sent up to join the leaders, the three turning into the straight together. Down the homestretch the four came, Douglas gaining at every stride on the others and at the head of the upper stand he was leading and won handily by almost two lengths, Brady coming in second, Daisy third and Coloma last.

Three hundred to eighty were now about the way the pools sold on the two remaining in the race, Douglas finishing so strongly that it was dollars to beans he would win the deciding heat. There was no misplaced confidence in this, as he won in a common canter, Coloma showing signs of distress.

SUMMARY.

Purse, $400, of which $50 to second, $25 to third; for all ages; mile heats.

Dennison Bros.' Dave Douglass, b g, a, by Leinster, dam Lillie Simpson 113............C. Dennison 4 1 1
W. L. Whitmore's Coloma, ch h, 5, by Joe Hooker, dam Callie Smart, 116............Hill 1 4 2
Miller & Owens' Daisy D., b m, a, by Wheatley, dam Maria, 111 ....Hennessey 2 3 3
Orange Grove Stables' Jack Brady, ch a, by Wildidle, dam Sour Grapes, 116............Monohan 3 2 0

Time, 1:43, 1:43¾, 1:43¾.

Bookbetting—First heat—Daisy D. 2 to 5, no place; Coloma, 2 to 1, 2 to 5; Jack Brady, 10 to 1, 2 to 1; Dave Douglas 20 to 1, 4 to 1. Second heat—Daisy D 3 to 5, no place; Coloma 7 to 5, no place; Dave Douglas, 30 to 1, 8 to 1; Jack Brady, 20 to 1, 4 to 1. Third heat—Dave Douglas, 2 to 5; Coloma 7 to 5.

Auction pools—First heat—Daisy D $70; Coloma $25; Field $12. Second heat—Daisy $75; Coloma $60, Field $12. Third heat—Douglas $300, Coloma $87.

For the last event of the day the Sequel Stakes, one and three-eighths miles, another surprise was sprung on the shrewd ones. If one would listen to horsemen's tales the Directory was giving everything in sight to Palo Alta. "Was not Faustine in at 114 pounds, who could beat her at the weight?" Still a few thought Pliny, with 110 pounds, might do the trick, and backed him accordingly, while Al Farrow had a slight support from those who back the "big horse" every time he starts. The horses scored several times before the flag fell, but at last they got an even start, with Raindrop showing in front first, Farrow and Abi in the second division, and the balance well bunched. As they passed the wire for the first time it was Raindrop, Farrow and Abi, the second horse being held well in hand by his rider. In the turn Raindrop was in the lead by four open lengths, Farrow second still under a pull, and "the long tailed mare" still third.

Down the backstretch the same relative positions were maintained, Raindrop making all the running, much to the discomfiture of field buyers, who fancied that she should not have been sent at such a cracking pace, and in the turn she proved the correctness of the theory by falling back to the field, having run herself out. Before the three quarters was reached, Abi was in the lead, but the pride of position was only on sufferance, as Al Farrow was let out at the head of the homestretch and quickly passed the mare never being again headed, he winning in a romp by two lengths, Abi second, McGinnis third. The following is the

SUMMARY.

The Sequel Stakes—A handicap for all ages; $25 each, half forfeit; $5 if declared out, with $750 added; second horse to receive $75, third to save stake. Weights announced Wednesday, April 16th, at 10 o'clock A. M. Declarations at 5 P. M. the same day. One mile and three-eighths.

W. E. H. Smith's b h Al Farrow, 5, Connor—Della Walker, 121...Hill 1
H. I. Thornton's br m Abi, a, Red Boy—Abi, 110............Casey 2
Kelly & Samuels' ch h Ed McGinnis, a, Grinstead—Jenny C., 125, Cook 3

Time, 2:23.

Faustine, 4, 114, Narvaez; Pliny, 3, 110, Monohan; Hotspur, 4, 117, Dennison; Raindrop, 3, 95, Morton, ran unplaced.

Bookbetting—Al Farrow 4—1, 7—5; Ed McGinnis 2½—1, 4—5; Abi 6—1, 2—1; Faustine 8—5, 1—2; Pliny 4—1, 7—5; Hotspur 12—1, 4—1; Raindrop 30—1, 12—1.

Mutuals Pools—Faustine $30, Kelly & Samuels' Stable (McGinnis and Pliny) $60, field $30.

Imported Greenback.

A Magnificent Specimen of Blood Horse.

It is now a little more than two years ago that imported Greenback was brought to America, in company with some of the best animals ever sent over from England. At the time, "Vigilante," the well known authority on matters pertaining to the turf, wrote as follows in the New York Spirit of the Times:

"Greenback, the stallion, was out in the stallion paddock when we arrived, with Mr. Easton and Mr. Charles Reed viewing his capers as he lunged and trotted under the exhilarating influence of the keen bright air. Greenback is, bar Rayon d'Or, the most magnificent specimen of a blood horse that we have seen among the imported horses of the past fifteen years. He is thirteen years old, a whole colored brown, with broad, flat legs, great length and liberty, a fine spread of hips and every evidence of great constitution and animal vigor. About the head and neck he is much of the type of Stockwell, but bodily he is different, having more of that trim quality of the Leamingtons, only more substantial, straining probably to his grandsire, The Fying Dutchman. He is like an eel as he moves about with a quick, sinuous glide. He is a superbly coated horse, reflecting a purple sheen, which blazes in the sunlight, and no one would dream that he had so recently left the ship. Greenback's blood is as high as his conformation. He is a son of the French horse Dollar, who was by Flying Dutchman, dam Payment, by Slave. Dollar's dam was the dam of Florin, the sire of Florintin, winner of the French Derby in 1866, and of Mantilla, the champion French two-year-old of 1878. Dollar's merit as a sire is famous, as he got Salvator, St. Cyr, Paris, Almanza, Nathan, Fontainebleau, Salvanos, Torrent and Androcles. One of his daughters, Nellie James, produced Jack of Hearts, Jacobus, etc., in Mr. Belmont's stud. Salvator won the Grand Prix de Paris and French Derby in 1875, and Salvanos won the Cesarewitch in 1872. On the side of his dam Greenback is glorious. His dam was the Duke of Hamilton's great mare Music, the best broodmare in Europe. She has foaled Ossian, Fiddler, Song, Songstress, Nina, Poetry, etc., Nina being one of the best two-year-olds of 1857, winning the Clearwell, Bretby and Homebred. As for Ossian, she won the St. Leger, while Fiddler beat Foxhall for the Alexandria Plate. Music is a daughter of Stockwell, from the invincible One Act by Annandale; 3d dam Extravaganza by Voltaire, etc., gives Greenback an infusion of Blacklock blood. Greenback was a really good race horse, winning the Stretchworth Stakes, at Newmarket, as a two-year-old, and the Earl Spencer Plate, at Northampton, as a three-year-old. The Peel Handicap, the Queen's Plate, at Ayr, and the Caledonian Cup, at the same place, also fell to his share. He has got several winners, having sired Greenlight, Greenjacket, Greenshank, Greenwave, Greenboro, etc. He is the only direct representative of Bay Middleton's male line in America, and will be a grand outcross for our native mares.

BILLIARDS.

McCleery has begun practice for his coming contest with Schaefer—which will be played here about the 20th of May. Jake has demonstrated that he is the champion of the world and McCleery says "if anyone can discount me and win it certainly is Schaefer."

There has been a great revival in the interest of the "gentlemens game" here of late, and the hope of many is to see the "big six" players enter for a tournament (handicap) here as played in Chicago (making it 8 inch balk line and add Ben Saylor & McCleery) for an $8,000 purse—giving a weeks play—financially it certainly would be a success.

The Local tournament at the Cafe Royal is drawing to a close. Prof. McCleery, manager of the Baldwin Rooms will arrange an amateur tourney to begin about May 1st.

There are two or more Pin Pool players lately arrived from the East. Query—if they want Pin Pool why don't they tackle McCleery instead of drawing in people who profess to play only for amusement.

The W. P. Fine Colt Stakes.

The interest in colt stables is increasing from year to year and 1890 will be far in advance of past seasons in the number of youngsters trained. Gen Fine, lessee of the Petaluma Track instituted a series of colt stakes some time ago and the following gentlemen have made the second payments on their entries.

YEARLING STAKES.

B. C. Holly, Vallejo; Perry Sears, El Verano; R. S. Brown, Marin county; H. G. Comstock, Petaluma; Wm. Fitch, Petaluma; W. J. Frost, Petaluma; I. M. Proctor, Petaluma; P. J. Shafter, Olema, and J. S. Wisecarver of Geyserville.

TWO-YEAR-OLD STAKE.

D. McGovern, W. P. Fine, A. L. Whitney, Edwards & Hinkle and R. Crane of Petaluma; Wilfred Page, Penns Grove; W. B. Sanborn, Santa Rosa; R. H. Warfield, Healdsburg; Isaac DeTurk, Santa Rosa; Perry Sears, Sonoma; T. J. Beggs, two, San Rafael; F. W. Lober, St. Helena; J. Mc. Brown, Marin county, Mrs. Silas Skinner, Napa, J. H. White, Lakeville; R. S. Brown, Marin county.

THREE-YEAR-OLD STAKE.

R. Murphy, Santa Rosa; George E. Guerne, Santa Rosa; J. H. Lawrence, Santa Rosa; J. H. White, Lakeville; Dr. G. M. Saul, Petaluma; B. C. Holly, Vallejo; P. J. Shafter, Olema, Marin county.

Best Trotting Records.

1 mile—2:08¾, Maud S., against time, in harness, accompanied the distance by a running horse, Glenville, O., July 30, 1885 .... 2:13¼, best time in a race between horses, Maud S., Chicago, Ills., July 24, 1880...... 2:12, Axtell, against time, accompanied by running horse—fastest stallion time, Terre Haute, Ind., Oct. 11, 1889...... 2:13¾, Phallas, fastest heat by a stallion against other horses, Chicago, July 14, 1884...... 2:12¾, Palo Alto, third heat in race at Stockton, Cal., Sept. 26, 1889...... 2:15½, Jay-Eye-See, half-mile track, Lincoln, Neb., Sept. 14, 1887 ...... 2:15¾, Great Eastern, under saddle, third heat, Morrisania, N. Y., Sept. 22, 1877 ...... 2:10¾, Jay-Eye-See, against time, best five-year-old record, Providence, R. I., Sept. 15, 1883...... 2:16, Manzanita, third heat, best four-year-old record, Lexington, Ky., Sept. 3, 1876 .... 2:16, Edgemark, four-year-old stallion record, against time, Lexington, Ky., Oct. 18, 1889...... 2:10½, Sunol, in Stanford Stake, accompanied by a runner, best three-year-old record, San Francisco, Nov. 9, 1889.. 2:18, Sunol 2 years, against time, San Francisco, Cal., Oct. 27, 1888...... 2:20¾, Regal Wilkes, two-year-old stallion record, San Francisco, Nov. 9, 1889 ...... 2:31½, Norlaine, yearling, against time, San Francisco, Cal., Nov. 12, 1887...... 2:38, Faustino, yearling stallion record, San Francisco, Nov. 9, 1889.

2 miles—4:43 against time, Fanny Witherspoon, Chicago, Ill., Sept. 25, 1885.

3 miles—7:21¼, Huntress, harness, Brooklyn, L. I., Sept. 21, 1872.

4 miles—10:34½, Longfellow, wagon, California, Dec. 31, 1869.

5 miles—13:00, Lady Mac, harness, San Francisco, Cal., April 2, 1874.

10 miles—27:23½, Controller, harness, San Francisco, Cal., Nov. 23 1878.

20 miles—58:25, Captain McGowan, harness, half-mile track, Boston, Oct. 31, 1865.

Pacing Records at One Mile.

Johnston, harness, against time, Chicago, Ills., Oct. 9, 1884, 2:06¼.

Brown Hal, best stallion record, Cleveland, Ohio, July 31, 1889, 2:12½.

Westmont, July 10, 1884, Chicago, Ills., with running mate, 2:01¾.

Daisy, yearling, Sacramento, Dec. 31, 1885, 2:38¼.

Ed Rosewater, two years old, Council Bluffs, Iowa, Nov. 8, 1888, 2:20½.

Yolo Maid, 3 years old, San Francisco, Oct. 13, 1888, 2:14.

Gold Leaf, four years old, 2:11¼ on August 17, 1889, at Napa.

Arrow, five years old, 2:13½, made at Cleveland, Ohio, August 1, 1888

Fastest Time on Record.

RUNNING.

Miles.		
¼	Jim Miller, 2, Deer Lodge (Mont.), Aug. 15, 1888 / †Sleepy Dick, a, Kiowa (Kan.), Nov. 24, 1888	0:21¼
⅜	Cyclone, a, 120 lbs., Helena (Mont.), Aug. 28, 1889	0:34¼
½	Geraldine, 4, 122 lbs., Westchester Course, Aug. 30, 1889	0:46
⅝	Britannic, 5, 122 lbs., Westchester Course, Aug. 31, 1889	0:59
⅝	Fordham, a, 115 lbs., Westchester Course, Oct. 4, 1889	0:59
¾	El Rio Rey, 2, 126 lbs., Westchester Course, Aug. 31, 1889	1:11
¾	Tipstaff, 3, 107, Westchester Course, Oct. 4, 1889	1:11
⅞	Britannic, 5, 119 lbs., Sheepshead Bay, Sept. 5, 1889	1:26 2-5
	Ten Broeck, 5, 110 lbs., Louisville, May 24, 1877 (against time)	1:39¾
1	Maori, 4, 105 lbs., Chicago, July 12, 1889, (in a race)	1:39 4-5
1 1-16	Wheeler T., 3, 98 lbs., St. Louis, June 1, 1888	1:47¾
1 1-16	Erlton, 4, 106, Chicago, Ill., June 24, 1889	1:47¼
1⅛	Terra Cotta, 4, 124 lbs., Sheepshead Bay, June 23, 1888	1:53
1 3-16	Joe Cotton, 5, 109½ lbs., Sheepshead Bay, Sept. 7, 1887	2:00¾
1¼	Kingston, 5, 122 lbs., Gravesend, Sept. 24, 1889	2:06¾
1 m 500 yds.	Ben d'Or, 4, 115 lbs., Saratoga, July 30, 1882	2:10¾
1⅜	Triboulet, 4, 117 lbs., San Francisco, April 26, 1888 / Richmond, 6, 122 lbs., Sheepshead Bay, June 27, 1888	2:21¾
1½	Firenzi, 4, 113 lbs., Monmouth Park, Aug. 7, 1888 / Luke Blackburn, 3, 102 lbs., Monmouth Park, Aug. 17, '80 / Jim Guest, 4, 98 lbs., Chicago (Washington Park), July 24 '88	2:34
1⅝	Hindoocraft, 3, 75 lbs., Westchester, Aug. 27, 1889	2:48
1¾	Glidelia, 5, 116 lbs., Saratoga, Aug. 5, 1882	3:01
1⅞	Enigma, 4, 90 lbs., Sheepshead Bay, Sept. 15, 1885	3:20
2	Ten Broeck, 5, 110 lbs., Louisville, May 29, 1877	3:27½
2¼	Monitor, 4, 110 lbs., Baltimore, Oct. 23, 1880	3:44½
2½	Springbok, 5, 114 lbs. / Preakness, a, 114 lbs. Saratoga, July 29, 1875	3:56¼
2⅝	Aristides, 4, 104 lbs., Lexington, May 13, 1876	4:27½
2¾	Ten Broeck, 4, 104 lbs., Lexington, Sept. 16, 1876	4:58½
2⅞	Hubbard, 4, 107 lbs., Saratoga, Aug. 9, 1873	4:[illegible]
3	Drake Carter, 4, 115 lbs., Sheepshead Bay, Sept. 6, 1884	5:24
4	Ten Broeck, 4, 104 lbs., Louisville, Sept. 27, 1876	7:15¾

HEAT RACES.

Miles.		
¼	Sleepy Dick, a, Kiowa (Kan.), Nov. 24, 1888	0:21¼—0:22¼
½	Bogus, a, 118 lbs., Helena (Mont.), Aug. 2?, 1888	0:48—0:48
⅝	Kittie Pease, 4, Dallas (Tex.), Nov. 2, 1887 / Sadie McNairy, 3, 9? lbs., Chicago, July 2, 1883	1:00—1:00 / 1:02¾—1:03
¾	Lizzie S., 5, 115 lbs., Louisville, Sept. 28, 1883	1:13½—1:13¾
1	Bounce, 4, 90 lbs., Sheepshead Bay, Sept. 7, 1881	1:42—1:41¼
1	3 in 5. L'Argentine, 6, 115 lbs., St. Louis, June 14, 1879	1:43—1:44—1:47½
1 1-16	Slipalong, 5, 115 lbs., Chicago (Wash. Park), Sept. 2, 1885	1:49¾—1:48
1⅛	Gabriel, 4, 112 lbs., Sheepshead Bay, Sept. 23, 1880	1:56—1:56
1¼	Glenmore, 5, 114 lbs., Sheepshead Bay, Sept. 25, 1880	2:10—2:14
1⅝	Reno, 5, Toledo, Sept. 18, 1883 (1st and 3d heats)	2:43¼—2:42
2	Miss Woodford, 4, 107½ lbs., Sheepshead Bay, Sept. 20, 1881	3:31—3:31¼
3	Norfolk, 4, 100 lbs., Sacramento, Sept. 23, 1865	5:27¼—5:29¼
	Ferida, 4, 105 lbs., Sheepshead Bay, Sept. 15, 1880	7:23½—7:41

†Made in a heat race.
*Doubtful, and made in a heat race.

THE WEEKLY

Breeder and Sportsman.

JAMES P. KERR, PROPRIETOR.

The Turf and Sporting Authority of the Pacific Coast.

Office, No. 313 Bush St.
P. O. Box 2300.

TERMS—One Year, $5; Six Months, $3; Three Months, $1.50.
STRICTLY IN ADVANCE.

Money should be sent by postal order, draft or by registered letter, addressed to JAMES P. KERR, San Francisco, Cal.

Communications must be accompanied by the writer's name and address, not necessarily for publication, but as a private guarantee of good faith.

NEW YORK OFFICE, Room 15, 181 Broadway.

ALEX. P. WAUGH, - - - - - Editor.

Advertising Rates

Per Square (half inch)

One time	$1 50
Two times	2 50
Three times	3 25
Four times	4 00

And each subsequent insertion 75c. per square.

Advertisements running six months are entitled to 10 per cent. discount.

Those running twelve months are entitled to 20 per cent. discount.

Reading notices set in same type as body of paper, 50 cents per line each insertion.

To Subscribers.

The date printed on the wrapper of your paper indicates the time to which your subscription is paid.

Should the BREEDER AND SPORTSMAN be received by any subscriber who does not want it, write us direct to stop it. A postal card will suffice.

Special Notice to Correspondents.

Letters intended for publication should reach this office not later than Wednesday of each week, to secure a place in the issue of the following Saturday. Such letters to insure immediate attention should be addressed to the BREEDER AND SPORTSMAN, and not to any member of the staff.

San Francisco, Saturday, April 19, 1890.

Dates Claimed.

SACRAMENTO (Running Meeting)......April 26th, 29th, May 1st and 3d
EUREKA JOCKEY CLUB......July 2d to 5th
IONE......Aug 7th to 9th.
LOS ANGELES [6th District]......Aug. 4th to 9th
SAN JOSE......Aug. 11th to 16th
NAPA......Aug. 18th to 23rd
GLENBROOK PARK, 17th District......August 19th to 23d
PETALUMA......Aug. 25th to 30th
OAKLAND (District No. 1)......Sept. 1st to Sept. 6th
LAKEPORT, 12th District......September 23d to 27th
CALIFORNIA STATE FAIR......Sept 8th to 20th
STOCKTON......Sept. 23rd to 27th.
FRESNO (Fall Meeting)......Sept. 29th to Oct. 4th
VISALIA......Oct. 7th to 11th

Stallions Advertised
IN THE
BREEDER AND SPORTSMAN.

Thoroughbreds.

DOUGLASDALE—Thoroughbred Clydesdale....Lawn View Farm, Cal.
FRIAR TUCK, Hermit—Romping Girl......C. W. Aby, Middletown.
GREENBACK, Dollar—Music......C. W. Aby, Middletown.
INTRUDER, Crater—Lady Beautiful......T. J. Knight, Sacramento.
REVEILLE, Shiloh—Norfolk......B. C. Holly, Vallejo.
ST. SAVIOR, Eolus—War Song......C. W. Aby, Middletown.
THREE CHEERS, Imp. Hurrah—Young Fashion......E. S. Culver, San Francisco.

Trotters.

ARLINGTON, Abbotsford—Gillispie Mare......J. R. French, S. F.
ANTEEO BUTTON, Anteeo—Dam of Alexander Button......E. C. Spear, St. Helena.
ADMIRAL, Volunteer—Lady Pierson......Frank Drake, Vallejo.
ACTOR, Prompter—Dam by Sultan......Lawn View Farm, Cal.
ARBITRATOR, Director—Lady Earnest......H. A. Mayhew, Niles.
ANTEEOP, Anteeo—Bessie G......Guy E. Grosse, Santa Rosa.
ANTEEOF, Anteeo—Nance......Guy E. Grosse, Santa Rosa.
ADMIRO, Admiral—dam by San Bruno......Smith & Sutherland, Pleasanton.
ALEXANDER BUTTON, Alexander—Lady Button......Cache Creek Farm, Yolo.
APEX, Prompter—Mary......Poplar Grove Breeding Farm, Wildflower.
ALCONA, Almont—Queen Mary......Fred W. Loeber, St. Helena
BAY ROSE, Sultan—Madam Baldwin......Thos. Bonner, Santa Rosa
BALKAN, Mambrino Wilkes—Fanny Fern......A. L. Hinds, Oakland.
CLOVIS, Sultan—Sweetbriar......Poplar Grove Breeding Farm, Wildflower.
CUPID, Sidney—Venus......C. O. Thornquest, Oakland
CHARLES DERBY, Steinway—by Electioneer..Cook Stock Farm, Contra Costa Co.
CALIFORNIA NUTWOOD, Nutwood—Fanny Patchen....Martin Carter, Alameda Co.
CORRECTOR, Director—Brainey......Pleasanton Stock Farm.
DECORATOR, Director—Chess......Pleasanton Stock Farm.
DEXTER PRINCE, Kentucky Prince—Lady Dexter......L. M. Morse, Lodi.
DAWN, Nutwood—Countess......A. L. Whitney, Petaluma
DIRECTOR, Dictator—Dolly......Pleasanton Stock Farm, Pleasanton.
DON MARVIN, Fallis—Cora......F. P. Lowell, Sacramento
DESIGNER, Director—May Queen......H. Scott, Oakland.
ELECTOR, Electioneer—Gilberta......L. A. Richards, Grayson.
ELECTION, Electioneer—Lizzie H......B. C. Holly, Vallejo.
EL BENTON, Electioneer—Nellie Benton......Souther Farm, San Leandro.
ECLECTIC, Electioneer—Manette......Wilfred Page, Sonoma County
EROS, Electioneer—Sontag Mohawk......W. H. Vioget, Menlo Park
FIGARO, Hambletonian—Emblem......Souther Farm, San Leandro.
GROVER CLAY, Electioneer—Maggie Norfolk......Denis Gannon, Oakland.
GRAND MOOR 2374, Moor 870—Vashti......H. I. Thornton, S. F.
G. & M., Anteeo—Rosa B......George E. Guerne, Santa Rosa.
GUY WILKES, George Wilkes—Lady Bunker......San Mateo Stock Farm, San Mateo.
GLEN FORTUNE, Electioneer—Glenna......Souther Farm, San Leandro.
GEORGE WASHINGTON, Mambrino Chief—Fanny Rose......Thos. Smith, Vallejo.
GUIDE, Director—Imogene......Smith & Sutherland, Pleasanton.
GRANDISSIMO, LeGrande—Norma......Fred W. Loeber, St Helena
ILLUSTRIOUS, Happy Medium—Abdalletta......George A. Stone, Santa Rosa.
JESTER D, Almont—Hortense......Souther Farm, San Leandro
JUNIO, Electioneer—by Granger......S. N. Straube, Fresno.
KAFIR, Alcazar—Flower Girl......R. C. Holly, Vallejo.
KING DAVID, Admiral—Black Flora......Frank Drake, Vallejo.
LEO WILKES, Guy Wilkes—Sable......San Mateo Stock Farm, San Mateo.
MEMO, Sidney—Flirt......John Rowen, Oakland
MOUNTAIN BOY, Kentucky Prince—Elsie......B. C. Holly, Vallejo.
MAMBRINO WILKES, George Wilkes—Lady Chrisman......San Miguel Stock Farm, Walnut Creek.
MART BOORHEM, Sidney—Towhead......B. C. Holly, Vallejo.
MAMBRINO CHIEF, McDonald Chief—Venus......Thos. Smith, Vallejo.
MORTIMER, Electioneer—Marti......Wilfred Page, Sonoma County
NOONDAY, Wedgewood—Noontide......F. P. Lowell, Sacramento.
PASHA, Sultan—Madam Baldwin......D. Bryson, Linden
PHILOSOPHER, Pilot Wilkes—Belle......George E. Guerne, Santa Rosa.
REDWOOD, Anteeo—Lou Wilton......A. McFayden, Oakland.
STEINWAY, Strathmore—Abbess....Cook Stock Farm, Contra Costa Co
SUNSET, Anteeo—Bessie G......Guy E. Grosse, Santa Rosa.
SIDNEY, Santa Claus—Sweetness......Valensin Stock Farm, Pleasanton.
SABLE WILKES, Guy Wilkes—Sable......San Mateo Stock Farm, San Mateo.
VICTOR, Echo—Daughter of Woodburn......G. W. Hughes, Napa City
WHIPPLETON 1883, Hambletonian Jr.—Lady Livingston....Fred W. Loeber, St. Helena
WOODSIDE, Woodnut—Veronica......B. C. Holly, Vallejo.
YOUNG ELMO, St. Elmo—Dam by Woodburn....Lawn View Farm Cal.

Leland Stanford and Palo Alto.

It is not the design of the BREEDER AND SPORTSMAN to interfere in any manner whatever in matters which have political trend, or in affairs which are of personal significance. It is eminently fitting at this time, however, that the chief paper of the State and coast, devoted to the interests of the turf, and the breeding of thoroughbreds and trotters, should present suitable tribute to Leland Stanford, as the foremost patron of the breeding industry on the whole Pacific coast, if not in the entire country.

California owes gratitude to Leland Stanford for his invaluable and munificent services in this respect, in the establisment of the great breeding farm at Palo Alto, which is famous for its grandeur of area and magnificence of system, yet more for its peerless product, in quality and performance, of the trotters that great farm has produced. This debt of gratitude is freely acknowledged throughout California, without disparagement or omission to any other of the ranking breeders.

Great wealth was required to engage in the undertaking. The vast area essential to the enterprise was of itself a matter of very large cost, and this was much exceeded in the purchase of the best lines of blood, and of highest type, with which to stock the Palo Alto farm. Superior judgment, studious care in the selection, and fine discrimination in the purchase, were prerequisites, and the ability as well as the disposition to overlook cost in the determination to secure these highest types of horses were indispensable qualities. Leland Stanford is endowed with these dominating natural faculties, and his years of experience have wrought their brightening influence. He devoted time to the quest, and from the noted breeding farms of Kentucky and Pennsylvania, and other portions of the East, he chose with singular intelligence the founders of his unrivalled stud at Palo Alto.

It was not for his own enjoyment only that he devoted his time and care, and disbursed his wealth; nor with the purpose to make Palo Alto farm a source of profit, that he embarked in this. His better motive, and loftier object were to the establishment of a system which would greatly improve the breeding interests of California and the Pacific coast, ultimately to produce the highest in type and choicest in commanding qualities of any quarter of the entire country. It has been to the greater renown and substantial benefit of California that the Palo Alto breeding farm has put forth so many celebrities of the turf and stud. Electioneer is at the head of the list of famous sires for speed and quality. Among his sons and daughters, the names and extraordinary performance are familiar, of Bell Boy, Manzanita, Sunol, Palo Alto, Anteeo, Antevolo. There are many more, but the mention of these will suffice.

The annual sales in New York are further in testimony of the advanced rank of California horses at the East. It is largely due to the sagacious founding of Palo Alto farm by Leland Stanford. The broader effect of his grand plan in breeding is every year better developed in the quality of the horses for daily use in every capacity —as the well-trained, spirited, yet gentle and safe horse for pleasure driving, the horse for city work, the farm horse, and, superior to all others, for roadsters and display.

Leland Stanford has, besides, visited England, and from the famous lines of thoroughbreds he has secured colts and sires of greatest celebrity in racing, to make Palo Alto Farm complete in its equipment. His example has encouraged other of the men of millions and disposed to stock breeding to engage in the enterprise on grand scales. These great farms will eventually work such improvement as to animate the farmers of California to the better system of breeding, which shall make the horse and other domestic animals of this State the boast and pride of owners, and the observation of all.

There are other great and noble works of Leland Stanford in California, aside from his railroad connection and apart from political concern, which have impressed the people with the deep sense of respect and honor they bear toward him. His crowning magnificent benificence, the Leland Stanford Jr. University, will endure as the splendid monument to educate the youths of California and to the enlightenment of all and the memory of its founder's most munificent gift to the equal benefit of every class and every grade, will be honored and revered inseparable from the great institution, in every Age. But within the sphere of the BREEDER AND SPORTSMAN, the reference is confined to the work of Leland Stanford in the establishment of Palo Alto Breeding Farm. Th highest praise is his in this connection. It is impulsivel awarded and popularly expressed. The great wealth h has accumulated in California is being returned to th better account of the people of the State by the mos advantageous and most useful methods, to the materia benefit and enduring good of all. His work and bount reaches beyond the present, and will be of greater wort and broader benefit as generations succeed. It is with out equal example in the history of the world, and ha no parallel in the vast measure of the endowment. I brings to California an enviable fame—alike in th grandeur of the work and the possession of a citize inspired to such nobleness of soul. The name and char acter and honor of Leland Stanford hold warm place i the hearts and memories of California, and these senti ments and emotions are not wisely to be disturbed.

Wanda, 2:24.

There is probably no one thing that will make a breeder feel so very much annoyed as the crediting of a animal with a record to a wrong horse. Last year w had occasion to call the attention of our readers to th fact that Wanda, 2:24, was by Eros, 2:29½, and not b Fallis, 2:23, as was then claimed. To substantiate ou statement, F. H. Burke, Esq., of this city, the owner o Eros, produced affidavits enough so that we were enable to positively state that Wanda should be accredited t Eros and not to Fallis. Owing to an oversight prob ably, the Wallace Registering Company, in publishin the year book for 1889, states that Wanda is by Fallis and her dam is given as Girofle by Elmo 891. In Wal lace's Monthly an advertisement of Fallis appears, an therein it is also stated that Wanda is by Fallis. Mr Burke has forwarded the necessary affidavits and certifi cates to the office of the Wallace Company, and in th last number of the Monthly we find the following edi torial:

"In the Year-Book, the bay mare Wanda, four-year-ol record 2:24, is credited to Fallis, 2:23, son of Electioneer, an her dam is given as Girofle, by Elmo 891.

Some time since we were made aware that this pedigre was disputed on behalf of Eros, 2:29½, another noted son o Electioneer. The evidence we had when the Year-Book wen to press seemed conclusive enough that Fallis was the sire o Wanda; but now, after some investigation and the filing o fuller evidence, we are convinced that Eros was the sire o Wanda, and that her dam was Accident, by Elmo.

In 1884, the late Mr. Henry W. Seales, of Mayfield, th neighboring town to Menlo Park, Cal., bred Girofle, by Elmo to Fallis, 2:23, and bred Accident, by Elmo, to Eros, 2:29½— both horses being in the stud at Palo Alto. Both mares ha foals, Accident, a bay filly, and Girofle, a bay colt. O November 17, 1886, Mr. Seales' horses were sold by auction at Mayfield, by Killip & Co., the live-stock auctioneers o San Francisco, and the bay filly was sold, being No. 36 in th catalogue, as by Fallis, out of Girofle. We have affidavit from the man in charge of Mr. Searles' broodmares and foal and from the men employed under him, in which they swea that the intention was to sell the bay gelding by Fallis, out o Girofle, and that it was he that was catalogued, but that i separating those that were to be sold from those that were t be kept, "those babies got mixed up," and the bay filly wa turned into the sale in place of the bay gelding.

The auctioneer swears further that after the sale Mr Seales told him the filly was sold by mistake, that she wa not bred as stated, and desired him to see at what figure sh could be repurchased from Mr. Burke. He also makes affi davit that Killip & Co. sold at auction, in San Francisco February 28, 1889, the bay gelding Samoa, by Fallis, out o Girofle, four years old—the same age as Wanda. As Mr Seales' foreman swears that Girofle never had twins, it i clear that she could not have produced both the geldin Samoa and the filly Wanda in one year. So, unless addi tional evidence reveals something new, we must credit Wand to Eros, dam Accident, by Elmo."

The Turf Guide.

It is now a number of years since the Goodwin Bros of New York issued their first volume of the Turf Guide which was a worthy successor to the annual books issue by "Krik." There was not an editor in the country bu felt sorry when the sporting editor of the New Yor World had to announce to the public that the support h received was insufficient to warrant him in continuin the publication of his guide, but the Goodwin Bros stepped at once into the breach and filled what woul have been a serious break in the turf records of thi country. From the date of their first issue they hav published a very serviceable work, one in fact which n association can afford to be without, and the supporter of the racing turf cannot expect to follow the form show by horses unless they constantly study the guide as it i now issued. The publishers have notified us that the will issue the first volume for this year on the 15th o the present month, and it is presumable that the book are now on their way here. There will be several ne features introduced, as for instance, the names of stable under which horses run, together with the individua name or names of owners of such stables. In the sum mary of the races they have also included the names o the owners of winning horses, and it goes without say ing that all the old prominent features will be retaine in the Guide for 1890.

Sale of Thoroughbreds.

At the annual spring sales of the yearling thoroughbreds in Kentucky or in New York there is always great competition for those which represent the produce of speedy families, and it may be therefore concluded that at the sale of the Edgewater and Kingston Stud yearlings, comprising thirty-five head, there will be a great deal of competition among the purchasers. The catalogue shows that the colts and fillies are by Springbok, Audrain, Onondago, imp. Silvermine and imp. Deceiver, the above being the stallions in service at Edgewater.

In the Kingston catalogue we find the get of Longfellow, imp. Zorilla, imp. The Ill Used, Jils Johnson and Duke of Montrose; we find yearling brothers to Audrain, Guano, Ascalon, Ascoli and Sierra Nevada; also half brothers to Weasel, Orlando, School Master, Warrior and Sonnet, a full sister to Lela May, and also a full sister to East Lynn.

Among the Kingston lot we find half brothers to Helter Skelter, Biscuit and Prodigal Son, together with half sisters to Winning Ways and Rollin Hawley, and a full sister to that great horse Kenney. On the day following the above sale there will also be sold at the same place fifty-two head of yearlings, two year olds and three year olds, brood mares, stallions and horses in training; the yearlings number twenty-nine and are the get of King Alfonso, Jils Johnson, Longfellow, Himyar, Duke of Montrose, imp. Rossington, Onondaga, Virginius, Falsetto, Col. Clark, Gov. Bowie, Harry O'Fallon, Berean, imp. Rapture, Melbourne (formerly Elias Lawrence), Turco or Melbourne, Volturno, imp. Stylites and Jim Gore. Among them is a full brother to Brandolette, half brothers and sisters to We Wa, Teuton, Yorick, Asceola, Marguerite, Autocrat, Monocrat and Jack Rose, and out of mares by Longfellow, imp. Gen. Athol, Pat Malloy, Reverberation, Lisbon, Knighthood, Lightning, King Ban, Thunder, Virgil, Bertram, King Alfonso, Lever, Eolus, War Dance, Tobe Drum, Charlton, Tom Bowling, Revolver, Hurrah, Wanderer, Wildidle, Jerome, Edgar, Gen. Shields, Aramis, and Ballinkeol, all from racing families.

Among the broomares are a full sister to Eolian, half-sisters to Jennie June and Explosion (Dew Drop's dam), by such sires as Eolus, Lisbon, Ten Broeck and Ringmaster.

Among the two year olds are full sisters to Burlington and Spendwest, by such well known sires as Powhattan, Harry O'Fallon, Spendthrift and Ten Broeck. The older horses are by Germantown, King Ban, Forester, Rossifer, Duke of Montrose, Allan Pinkerton, Ten Broeck and Kyrle Daly, from racing and producing families.

These sales will be held at Treacy & Wilson's stable, Lexington, Ky., beginning each day at 9 A. M. For catalogues address this office, or Bruce and Kidd, the auctioneers, who will execute any commissions that may be sent to them. We can vouch for the reliability of the firm, and know them to be thoroughly trustworthy.

Utah Driving Park Association.

At the opening of the racing season Salt Lake City has usually been in the van with its advertisement, announcing to owners of trotters and thoroughbreds that they would give an early meeting so that those who felt inclined to patronize the track at the Mormon City could do so before branching out for the Montana Circuit, and this year proves no exception to the rule. In the appropriate column will be found the announcement of $7,000 to be given in purses. The authorities state that the meeting is arranged to accommodate horsemen in their way to the great racing circuit of Montana, and as the meeting at Denver closes on June 7th and does not begin in Montana until July 14th, it gives ample time for resting at Salt Lake. At the present time the city is enjoying an era of prosperity which justifies the anticipation of the best meeting ever held. They extend a cordial invitation to all horsemen to visit their meeting, and as their programme is a long and varied one, almost all horse owners can find some purse in which they may enter their horses. Trotting, pacing and running, are equally distributed, and as there are five days in all with liberal disbursements of money, the meeting should receive a large number of entries from the Californians who will take their stables East immediately after the Sacramento meeting. The advertisement gives full particulars, amount of purses, and states that May 30th is the day for entries closing.

"Good Luck."

Mr. Rose will start East, on the conclusion of the Sacramento meeting, with a dozen of his well-bred thoroughbreds. He has every prospect of a successful season, and all his California friends wish him "good luck."

VETERINARY.

Conducted by W. Henry Jones, M. R. C. V. S.

Subscribers to this paper can have advice through this column in all cases of sick or injured horses or cattle by sending an explicit description of the case. Applicants will send their name and address that they may be identified. Questions requiring answers by mail should be accompanied by two dollars, and addressed to W. Henry Jones, M. R. C. V. S., Olympic Stables, Sutter Street, San Francisco.

W. J. D.

I have a large grey mare that has been lame for some time in the near hind leg. My friends tell me she has got a thorough-pin. The swelling has been there for some time, and does not increase or decrease. I have blistered her twice, but without any good result. Can you suggest any treatment that might be of service?

Answer.—I would suggest that you have the mare examined by some competent veterinary surgeon, but if there is not one in your neighborhood, send to Mr. McKerron, Ellis Street, San Francisco, for one of his patent thorough pin trusses. They possess many advantages, as the horse can be constantly worked with it, and also lie down. I have every reason to think that one would be beneficial on your animal.

I. M. C.

A chestnut mare of mine recently struck her knee against the manger while being dressed; the result is a large swelling on the joint. It is very hot and painful. Will you kindly suggest some treatment.

Answer.—Foment the leg with hot water, and apply a mixture of soup liniment four ounces, tinct of opium two ounces, twice daily. Give a purgative consisting of Aloes, six drams; common mass, half ounce. Keep the mare on a low diet, such as bran mashes and little hay. Give no exercise for a few days.

Testimonial.

We are pleased to again place the advertisement of Gombault's Caustic Balsam before our readers, as we know it to be a staple remedy for the many cases for which it is recommended. As a blister to be used in cases of enlargement, sprains, diphtheria, etc., it has no equal, being powerful, effective and perfectly safe for anyone to use, and with no danger of leaving any scar or blemish, as is the case with so many of the blisters used to-day. The importers, Lawrence, Williams & Co, of Cleveland, Ohio, are reliable, and our readers requiring anything of the kind, can afford to write them for circulars, and for any special information desired. *

Foals of 1890.

PLEASANTON, April 10, 1890.

EDITOR BREEDER AND SPORTSMAN:—On April 8th, Ometta gave birth to a fine chestnut colt by Sidney. Ometta is by Aberdeen 27, (sire of Hattie Woodward 2:15½, etc.) dam Kentucky Central, 4 years, record 2;31, by Balsora, (sire of Kentuckian 2;27½, and of the dam of Balsora Wilkes 2:17½); second dam None Such (dam of Lady Turpin 2;23 and Kentuckian 2;27½) by Brignoli 2;29¼. Balsora by Abdallah 1, dam Neva by Vincent Nolte by American Eclipse, second dam Mavis (dam of Dollie Carter 2;29) by Wagner. Brignoli 2;29¼ by Mambrino Chief, dam Sallie Woodford by Woodford. We claim for her the name of Omena. She will represent Sidney and Ometta in the BREEDER AND SPORTSMAN Stake. This morning, April 10th, Simmocolon's first offspring saw the light. Lightfoot gave birth to a beautiful black filly, who will also try for first money in the BREEDER AND SPORTSMAN Futurity Stake. She is pretty well bred too, her dam being full sister to Fernleaf, dam of Goldleaf 2;11¼. Shamrock 2;25 at two years, Ivy 2.31½ at three years, trial 2;26, etc, etc. Lightfoot is the dam of Pride 2;44½ as a yearling, 2;33¼ at two years, and Pearl 2;32½, and is sired by Flaxtail 8132, out of Fanny Fern by Irwin's Tuckahoe. Simmocolon 2;29¼ at four years by Simmons 2774, (sire of Bon Bon, 4 years, 2:26, Raymon 4 years, 2;27, Black Storm 3 years, 2;27½, and six others with records better than 2;30) dam Colon, (dam of Patchmore 2:32½) by Strathmore (sire of 27 in 2:30 list, of six dams of eight in 2:30, and of three sires of three in 2.30); second dam Coral, trial at two years 2;30, (dam of Coralloid 2;29½) by Clark Chief 89 (sire of six in 2;30). Simmons by George Wilkes 519. G. VALENSIN.

At Valensin Stock Farm, the property of G. Valensin.

Chestnut filly foaled April 12th, 1890, by Sidney; 1st dam Belle Grande by Legrand; 2nd dam Oak Grove Belle, by Arthurton; 3rd dam Henrietta (trial 2:21), by Belle Alta; 4th dam by Peacock, thoroughbred.

Brown colt, foaled April 13th, 1890, by Sidney; 1st dam by Red Wilkes; 2nd dam by Curtis' Hambletonian; 3rd dam by Pilot Jr.

Bay colt by Sidney; 1st dam by Dictator; 2nd dam by Mambrino Patchen; 3rd dam by Imp. Sovereign, etc., etc.

At Oakdale, property of L. L. Huntley:—

On April 10th, black filly by Sidney, dam Idellette, by Silverthreads. (This foal is entered in the BREEDER AND SPORTSMAN Futurity Stake.) Mr. Huntley claims the name SIDLETTE for the filly.

At Fresno, April 13th. Property of J. M. Reuck:—

Bright bay filly by Apex 2:26, dam Rose by Pasha 2:36. The name of Corinne R. is claimed for this filly.

Cynthiana, Ky., W. H. Wilson proprietor:—

March 5th, blk colt by Simmons 2:28, dam Ebony by Indianapolis; 2nd dam the dam of Indigo 2.23½, by Corbeau 98.

March 13th, bay colt by Simmons, dam Marie Roze by Smuggler 2:15¼; 2nd dam by Shelby Chief.

March 17th, bay or br colt by Ottoman two year old record 2:46, dam Mollie F. (dam of France 2:26), by George Wilkes; 2nd dam by Mambrino Chief 11.

March 29th, bay filly by Noonday 10,000 (a son of Wedgewood 2:19 and Noontide 2:20½), dam Linda Wilkes by Guy Wilkes 2:15¼; second dam Atalanta (sister to Beautiful Bells 2:29½, dam of four in the 2:30 list), by The Moor; 2nd dam Minnehaha, dam of 5 in the 2:30 list, by Bald Chief.

March 30th, blk colt by Simmons 2:22, dam Lady McDowell by Sultan 2:24; 2nd dam Lady Mayberry, dam of Dubec 2:28, and Mista 2:29.

April 5th, ch colt, by Ottoman (son of Sultan and Montana Maid, by George Wilkes), dam Almater 2:29½, by Bambrino 2:21½; 2nd dam Alma Mata (dam of four in 2·30 list), by Mambrino Patchen 58.

April 8th, bay or br colt by Simmons 2:28, dam Lottie Thorne, record 2:23¾ (trial 2;19½), by Mambrino Patchen 58; 2nd dam Lady Agnes, by Redmon's Abdallah; 3rd dam, dam of Don Carlos 2:23 and Granville 2:26, by Alex's Abdallah.

Answers to Correspondents.

Answers for this department must be accompanied by the name and address of the sender, not necessarily for publication, but as proof of good faith. Write the questions distinctly, and on one side of the paper only. Positively no questions will be answered by mail or telegraph.

W. M. G.

Is there a horse by the name of Copper Bottom, if so please trace him as far as you can, as I have a mare with some of his blood.

Answer —There have been scores of horses called Copperbottom. If you can tell which Copperbottom you have reference to, we may be able to assist you.

Subscriber.

Please give pedigree of Owen Dale and Belmont.

Answer.—Owen Dale, by Belmont, dam Maria Downing, by American Eclipse; 2nd dam, Brownlock by Tiger; 3rd dam, by imp. Speculator; 4th dam, by imp. Dare Devil; etc. Belmont by American Boy, dam imp. Prunella by Comus; 2nd dam by Partisan; 3rd dam Pawn by Trumpetor; 4th dam, Prunella by Highflyer, etc.

San Jose.

Can you let me know the pedigree of San Jose Damsel?

Answer.—San Jose Damsel, by Easton's Black Hawk, dam by Red Bill, son of Medoc.

Ukiah.

Give me the pedigree of Ed Waverley.

Answer.—We have received certificates from both Mr. Whitney and Mr. Burbank, and the proof is positive that Ed Waverley is by Ideal, he by Abbotsford, 2:19½, dam Mortality.

G. P. A.

Please give me the extended pedigree of Dan Voorhies 2nd, brown stallion foaled April '85, bred at McLaughlin's Ranch, Bantas Station, and oblige.

Answer.—We have not got the pedigree of Dan Voorhies 2nd on our books. Can any of our readers give the information desired.

Spokane Falls.

Can you tell me when colors were first worn by jockeys?

Answer—The first mention of an owner having distinctive colors is to be found in the first volume of Cluny's Racing Calendar, 1727, entered in this style: "The Duke of Somerset's b m Brown Betty, rid in yellow." But these were left entirely to the choice of the owner, for in seven entries two are "rid in white," two in yellow and three in red, so that the colors were of very little use in distinguishing a horse when running. Nor does there seem to have been any hard and fast line drawn until 1762.

R. N. C.

Will you please publish or give through the columns of your valuable paper, the pedigree of Sherman's Black Hawk? Also state if any of his get became in any way noted by performance. I think Sherman's Black Hawk was formerly owned in Stockton, Cal.

Answer.—You evidently refer to McCracken's Black Hawk, foaled 1857, got by Vermont Black Hawk 5, dam not traced. Bred near Utica, N. Y., and sold by a widow lady to Mr. McCracken, who took him to California in 1860. Black Hawk died in 1869, the property of Dr. Grattan, Stockton, Cal. He is the sire of Sisson Girl, 2:28½, and the sire of the dams of Ha-Ha, 2:22½, and Overman, 2:19½.

C. M. Visalia.

Can you let me know, to decide a bet, how and when Alexander's Abdallah died. Did he ever have another name?

Answer.—Abdallah 15, was taken from Woodburn Farm in February 1865 by confederate soldiers and along with Bay Chief was driven across the Kentucky river, where a company of Union soldiers came upon the camp of the southern soldiers. In the conflict which ensued Bay Chief was wounded and Abdallah was recaptured, he being found in a stable where he had been left by his first captors. Mr. Alexander claimed the stallion but the man who had him in possession refused to give him up, and the men from Woodburn followed the Union soldiers some fifty miles. Here Abdallah was turned loose by the troops and the Woodburn people caught the horse and took him back to Lawrenceburg where he was taken with pneumonia and after a few days died in his thirteenth year. He was called at one time Joe Love, when Joel F. Love, and James Miller owned him at Cynthiana, Ky.

Names Claimed.

I claim the name Expectation for bay colt by Prince of Norfolk, out of Jennie Belshaw by Wildidle, grandam Susie Williamson by imp. Hercules; great grandam Vixen by Belmont. M. F. TARPEY.

I hereby claim the following names:

WILL RICE, for bay colt, hind ankles white, foaled May 30, 1888, by Corsair (son of Privateer), dam Innocent by Prompter; 2d dam Rachel by Wayland Forrest.

THUJA (entered in Occident Stake, 92), for bay filly, narrow white strip in face, hind ankles white, foaled March 22, 1889, by Sterling, dam Olive by Prompter; 2d dam Mag by Old St. Clair.

CEPAR, for bay filly, broad white strip in face, near hind ankle white, foaled April 18, 1889, by Sterling, dam Rill by Prompter; 2d dam Lillian by Romulus.

LADY MARVIN, for black filly, small white spot on tip of nose, foaled March 20, 1890, by Don Marvin, dam Innocent by Prompter; 2d dam Rachel by Wayland Forrest.

ADDIE T. P., for light bay filly, small white spot in forehead, foaled February 15, 1890 (this is my Futurity winner), by Sterling, dam Crescent by Prompter; 2d dam Starlight by Wayland Forrest. CHAS. E. PINKHAM, M. D.

SACRAMENTO, April 11, 1890.

Washington Park Club.

CHICAGO, April 1, 1890.

EDITOR BREEDER AND SPORTSMAN:—The following are the declarations out of stakes of the Washington Park Club, due April 1st, received to date:

The American Derby—Herzog, Major Ban, Elsie S, Falsalara, Fellowcharm, G. W., Jim Oglesby, Corticelli, Abdiel, Jim Wasson and Guadeloup (11).

The Sheridan Stakes—Herzog, G. W., Corticelli, Fellowcharm and Jim Wasson (5).

The Englewood Stakes—Brigerta and Ten Per Cent (2).

The Hyde Park Stakes—Glen Rosh, Grand Duke Michael and San Joaquin (3).

The Kenwood Stakes—Altair, Snow Ball and El Verano (3).

The Lakeside Stakes—Ribbon, Maid of the Mist and El Vera (3).

The Drexel Stakes—Fellowcharm and Sacramento (2).

Very respectfully, J. E. BREWSTER, Secretary.

California Mares in the Great Table.

Answers to Correspondents are usually of such a nature that many items of information may be given in the column devote for that purpose. However, P. A. asks for a list of the brood mares that have been owned, or are now owned in California, which have put two in the 2:30 list, or put one, and sired a sire or dam. After a lot of sorting out, the following list is given, taken from the Year Book. It may not be absolutely correct but is very nearly so.

ADDIE, 2:39, by Hambletonian Chief, dam Manon, pedigree not traced.
Manon, b m by Nutwood, 600—1884 .... 2:21
Woodnut, ch h by Nutwood, 600—1888 .... 2:16½
Dam of—Hattie D. (3 yrs.), 2:26½.

ADDIE LEE, 2:36½, by Black Hawk (Culver's), dam old Nancy, pedigree not traced.
Adair, b g by Electioneer, 125—1886 .... 2:17½
Adalia, br m by St. Clair, 656—1889 .... 2:27
Grace Lee (3 yrs.), b m by Electioneer, 125—1888 .... 2:29½
Sire—Berlin, 8.

ALICE R. by Naubuc, 504, dam Nelly by George M. Patchen Jr., 31.
Eva W., ch m by Nutwood, 600—1889 .... 2:28½
Redwood, ch h by Nutwood, 600—1889 .... 2:27

ALMA MATER, by Mambrino Patchen, 58; dam Estella by imp. Australia.
Alcanatra (4 yrs.), b h by George Wilkes, 519—1880 .... 2:23
Alcyone, br h by George Wilkes, 519—1883 .... 2:27
Almater, ch m by Mambrino, 820—1889 .... 2:29½
Arbiter, bl h by Administrator, 357—1887 .... 2:30
Sires—Alcantara, 9, 3 p; Alcyone, 9, 1 p.

AMERICA, by Hambletonian, 10; dam Fanny Star by American Star, 14.
Benton, (4 yrs.), b h by Gen. Benton, 1755—1889 .... 2:27½
Bonnie (4 yrs.), br m by Gen. Benton, 1755—1889 .... 2:.8

AMY by Messenger Duroc, 106; dam Amanda by Hambletonian, 10
Albion, br h by Gen. Benton, 1755—1889 .... 2:26½
Arbutus, bl g by Electioneer, 125—1889 .... 2:26½

ASHCAT by Hambletonian, 10, dam by Black Hawk, 24.
Ajax, b h by Hambletonian, 725—1872 .... 2:29
Sire—Hambletonian Jr, 1881, 1.

BEAUTIFUL BELLS, 2:29½, by The Moor, 870, dam Minnehaha by Bald Chief (Stevens').
Bell Boy (3 yrs.), br h by Electioneer, 125—1888 .... 2:19½
Hinda Rose (3 yrs.), b m by Electioneer, 125—1883 .... 2:19½
St. Bel (4 yrs.), blk h by Electioneer, 125—1886 .... 2:24½
Palo Alto Belle (3 yrs.), b m by Electioneer, 125—1889 .... 2:22½

BLACK FLORA by Black Prince, dam Sprague; pedigree not traced.
Huntress, ch m by Admiral, 488—1883 .... 2:28
Perihelion, b h by Admiral, 488—1888 .... 2:25
Sister, ch m by Admiral, 488—1887 .... 2:19½
Nona Y., b m by Admiral 488—1889 .... 2:26

BROWN JENNY by Dave Hill Jr.
Mary Lou, ch m by Tom Benton; 2:32½—1889 .... 2:25½
Ned Winslow, bl g by Tom Benton, 2:32½—1889 .... 2:17½

CLARABEL by Abdallah Star, dam Fairy by Hambletonian, 10.
Clifton Bell, b h by Electioneer, 125—1887 .... 2:24½
Dams of—Don Marvin, 2:29; Rexford, 2:24

COLUMBINE by A. W Richmond, 1687, dam Columbia by imp Bonnie Scotland.
Anteeo, b h by Electioneer, 125—1883 .... 2:16½
Antevolo (4 yrs.), b h by Electioneer, 125—1886 .... 2:19½
Sire—Anteeo, 2.

COUNTESS by Hambletonian, 725, dam Fly, pedigree not traced.
Dawn, ch h by Nutwood, 600—1889 .... 2:18½
Strathway, ch h by Steinway, 1808—1889 .... 2:20

DAME WINNIE by Planet, dam Liz Mardie by imp Glencoe, running-bred.
Big Jim, b g by Gen. Benton 1755—1889 .... 2:23½
Gertrude Russell, b m by Electioneer, 125—1888 .... 2:23½
Palo Alto, b h by Electioneer, 125—1889 .... 2:12¾

FANNY FERN by Jack Hawkins, son of Boston, dam not traced.
Balkan (3 yrs), b h by Mambrino Wilkes, 6083—1888 .... 2:29½
Molly Drew, ch m by Winthrop, 506—1880 .... 2:27

FERN LEAF by Flaxtail, 8132, dam Fanny Fern by Tuckahoe (Irwin's).
Shamrock, br h by Buccaneer, 2656—1886 .... 2:25
Goldleaf (4 yrs.), ch m by Sidney, 4770—1889 .... 2:11½

FISHER MARE, pedigree unknown.
Dan Voorhees, ch h by Gen McClellan, 144—1876 .... 2:23½
Sires—Dan Voorhees 1; Duke McClellan, 1.

FLEETWING by Hambletonian 10, dam Patchen Maid by George M. Patchen, 0
Ruby, b m by Sultan, 1513—1886 .... 2:19¾
Stamboul, br h by Sultan, 1513—1889 .... 2:14½
Dam of—Lucy R., 2:30.

FLORA LANGFORD, a fast pacing mare, pedigree not traced.
Joe Arthurton, b g by Arthurton, 365—1887 .... 2:20½
Lillian Wilkes (3 yrs.), br m by Guy Wilkes, 2867—1889 .... 2:17½

GRETCHEN by Mambrino Pilot, 29, dam Kitty Kirkman by Canada Chief.
Del Sur, b h by The Moor, 870—1881 .... 2:24
Inca, br h by Woodford Mambrino, 345—1882 .... 2:27
Romero, gr h by A. W. Richmond, 1687—1881 .... 2:19½
Sires—Del Sur, 1; Inca, 2.
Dams of—Sable Wilkes (3 yrs.), 2:18; Nehushta (4 yrs.), 2:20.

IRENE by Mohawk Chief, son of Hambletonian 10, dam Laura Keene by Hambletonian 10.
Ira, b h by Piedmont, 904—1889 .... 2:24½
Stanford, b h by Piedmont, 904—1889 .... 2:30

JANE McLANE by Budd Doble, 3764, dam Lady Clinton, pacer.
Jim Mulvenna, gr h by Nutwood, 600—1884 .... 2:27½
Sires—Jim Mulvenna, 1; Peacock, 1.

JENNY LIND pedigree not traced.
Prince Allen, b g by Ethan Allen Jr., 2909—1876 .... 2:27
Dam of—George Washington, 2:30.

JENNY SHEPHARD by Belmont (Williamson's); dam not traced.
Flora Shepherd, ch m by Gen. McClellan, 144—1875 .... 2:30
Nelly Patchen, b m by Alexander, 490—1876 .... 2:27½

KATY TRICKS by Colonel, dam not traced.
Conde, ch g by Abbottsford, 707—1887 .... 2:20
Empress, ch m by Hambletonian, 725—1881 .... 2:24

LADY BABCOCK by Hambletonian, 725, dam Dubois Mare, said to be by a son of Exton Horse 132.
Elector, b h by Electioneer, 125—1888 .... 2:21½
Soudan, bl h by Sultan, 1513—1889 .... 2:27½

LADY DEY by California Dexter, son of Hambletonian, 725.
Dubec, b g by Sultan, 1513—1888 .... 2:28
Mista (2 yrs.), b m by Alcazar, 5102—1889 .... 2:39

LADY HUBBARD by Benicia Boy, dam not traced.
Pansy (4 yrs.), bl m by Berlin, 3514—1888 .... 2:24½
Thapsin, bl g by Berlin, 3514—1889 .... 2:21½

LADY LIVINGSTONE by Gen. Taylor, son of Morse Horse, 6, dam Lou Mills Mare, pedigree not traced.
Lady Blanchard, gr m by Hambletonian, 725—1872 .... 2:26½
Sire—Whippleton, 2 1 p.

LADY MORGAN by Hambletonian, 10, dam Fanny by Exton Eclipse.
Alban, b h by Gen. Benton, 1755—1887 .... 2:24
Marion, b m by Piedmont, 904—1889 .... 2:26½
Merriment, ch m by Happy Thoughts, 2436—1889 .... 2:19½
Sire—Victor Mohawk, 2.

LADY SUFFOLK by Harry Belmont, dam not traced.
Norman, gr g by Hambletonian, 725—1885 .... 2:28½
Rustic, gr h by Hambletonian, 725—1877 .... 2:30
Sire—Rustic, 1.

LADY WASHINGTON by American Boy Jr., dam not traced.
Ewing, b g by Primus, 255—1882 .... 2:21½
Kate Ewing, bl m by Berlin, 3514—1887 .... 2:21½

LAMOTT MARE, pedigree unknown.
Aurora, ch m by John Nelson, 187—1872 .... 2:27
Dams of—Arol, 2:24½; Albert W., 2:20; and Bonanza, 2:29½.

LUCY WOODRUFF by Hiram Woodruff, dam Lucy, pedigree not traced.
Baywood, b h by Blackwood Mambrino—1889 .... 2:20½
Grace W., b m by Blackwood Mambrino—1889 .... 2:25½
Silkwood, bl h by Blackwood Mambrino—1889 .... 2:25½

MAID OF CLAY, by Henry Clay, 8, dam by Messenger (Dey's).
Capt Smith, br g by Locomotive—1880 .... 2:20
Carrie C., br m by Electioneer, 124—1885 .... 2:24
Clay, bl g by St. Clair, 656—1881 .... 2:25½
Clay, br h by Electioneer, 125—1889 .... 2:25

MARY by Flaxtail, 813., dam by Bright Eyes.
Apex, b h by Prompter, 2305—1886 .... 2:26
Sire—Sterling, 6223, 1.
Dam of Creole, 2:20.

MAUD by Mambrino Rattler, dam by Green Mountain Morgan.
Magdallah, ch m by Primus, 255—1886 .... 2:23½
Reliance, b h by Alexander, 490—1882 .... 2:22½
Sire—Reliance, 2.

MAYFLOWER, 2:30½, by St. Clair, dam not traced.
Manzanita (4 yrs.), b m by Electioneer, 125—1886 .... 2:16
Wildflower (2 yrs.), b m by Electioneer, 125—1881 .... 2:21
Dam of—Maralia, 2:24½.

MIDNIGHT by Pilot Jr., 12, dam Twilight by Lexington.
Jay-Eye-See, bl g by Dictator, 113—1884 .... 2.10
Noontide, gr m by Harold, 413—1880 .... 2:20½

MINNEHAHA, by Bald Chief (Stevens'), dam Nettie Clay by Cassius M. Clay Jr., 22.
Alcazar, b h by Sultan, 1513—1888 .... 2:20½
Beautiful Bells, bl m by The Moor, 870—1878 .... 2:29½
Eva, b m by Sultan, 1513—1885 .... 2:23½
San Gabriel, b h by Sultan, 1513—1889 .... 2.29½
Sweetheart (3 yrs.), b m by Sultan, 1513—1881 .... 2:22½
Sire—Alcazar, 1.
Dams of—Hinda Rose (3 yrs.) 2:19½, St. Bell, 2:24½, Bell Boy (3 yrs.), 2:19½ and Palo Alto Belle (3 yrs.), 2:22½, Johnny Hayward, 2:28

OLD TEMPEST by Morgan Rattler, dam Page Mare by Jim Crow.
John C. Shelly, b h by Hawthorne, 10,935—1888 .... 2:29½
Dam of—Tempest, 2:19.

PRAIRIE BIRD 2:28½ by Flaxtail, 8132, dam not traced. Pacer.
Flight, br m by Buccaneer, 2656—1883 .... 2:29
Sire—Prompter, 2, 1 p.
Dam of—Fleet (2 yrs.), 2:24.

PRICELESS by Volunteer, 55, dam Silvertail by American Star, 14.
Ernest Maltravers, b g by Happy Medium, 400—1888 .... 2:22½
Dam of—Clarence, 2:30.

SISTER by John Nelson, 187, dam Lamott Mare, pedigree not traced.
Albert W., b h by Electioneer, 125—1886 .... 2:20
Bonanza, ch h by Arthurton, 365—1888 .... 2:29½

SONTAG DIXIE by Toronto Sontag, 307, dam Dixie by Billy Townes.
Del Mar (3 yrs.), b h by Electioneer, 125—1889 .... 2:30
Sonnet, b m by Bentonian, 5474—1888 .... 2:24½

SONTAG MOHAWK by Mohawk Chief, dam Sontag Nelly by Toronto Sontag, 307.
Rros, br h by Electioneer, 125—1887 .... 2:29½
Sally Benton (4 yrs.), gr m by Gen. Benton 1755—1884 .... 2:17¾
Sport, gr h by Piedmont, 904—1889 .... 2:22½

SPRITE by Belmont, 64, dam Waterwitch by Pilot Jr. 12.
Egotist (4 yrs.), b h by Electioneer, 125—1889 .... 2:29
Sphinx (4 yrs.), b h by Electioneer, 125—1887 .... 2:23
Spry (4 yrs.), b h by Gen. Benton, 1755—1886 .... 2:28½

VICTRESS by Belmont, dam Watson Mare, pedigree unknown.
Monarch, b g by Woodburn—1878 .... 2:28½
Dam of—Lohengrin, 2:27½.

Our Australian Letter.

SYDNEY, NEW SOUTH WALES, March 19, 1890.

EDITOR BREEDER AND SPORTSMAN:—There should be some big changes shortly in connection with Colonial racing by reason of the sales advertised by the Hon. James White: the Hobartville Stud, recently presided over by the late Andrew Town, and the New Zealand Stud Company. Mr. White is parting with everything, barring his stud stock and his pet, Abercorn. The yearlings—so it is reported—have been purchased by a syndicate of eleven persons, who have thrown in £500 pounds each for the eleven youngsters, eight colts and three fillies, a couple of the males being full brothers to Dreadnought and Titan. In the event of cups being won in the future to prevent discord amongst the owners as to proprietorship, it has been decided to hand them over to Mr. White. Amongst the adults to come under the hammer will be Dreadnought, Titan, Singapore, Sinecure, Rudolph, Lava and many others of tip-top quality. The Hobartville Stud will come before the public on the 29th of May, when the sires Trenton, Segenhoe, Gloucester, Cheviot, Sardonyx and Monmouth will in all probability change hands. The New Zealand Stud Company, at which the defunct and world-renowned Musket reigned as Lord of the Harem, will also put some first water animals on the market, and the three sales combined should prove of sufficient importance to draw the attention of buyers all the world over. The fact of Carbine and Maxim, two New Zealanders, heading the list in the handicap for the Australian Cup, may tend to show the respect with which the Moarilander is held in Australia. Maxim has never come over to Australia, but he is a magnificent animal, and, as I have before stated in a letter to your paper, is just the sort your studmasters should not let price stand in the way of obtaining.

A novelty in the way of racing has been introduced by the Rosehill Race Club, a proprietory institution, with its race course situated a few miles out of Sydney. It is called the Tontine Stakes for now yearlings to be run during the season of '90—'91. The winner of the three events, half mile to be run in August, 1890, six furlongs in April, 1891, and mile in July, 1891, secures the stake of £1000 added by the club, in addition to payments made by owners, but one horse failing to win the three, the stake goes on increasing year by year until it may assume big proportions. The winner of each event receives £100 from the fund. Australia received quite a shock a few weeks back when it became known that its idol Abercorn had severely injured himself whilst doing a gallop, and would in all probability never show again on a race course. However, "Abby" has continued on the improving list up to date, and although he will be unable to start at the coming A. J. C. autumn meeting, he is expected to sport silk later on.

The Victorian Racing Club autumn meeting, held at Flemington, near Melbourne, commenced on the 1st of March. The card opened with the Hopeful Stakes, for which the Hon James White's Marco, an untried son of Martini—Henry and Melanie were backed on the strength of his breeding and stable as first favorite, and he duly justified the confidence placed in him by winning from a moderate field. The St Leger, usually an uninteresting race, proved an exception to the rule, as only the Hon. James White's pair, Dreadnought and Singapore faced the music and the pair finished in the order named. For the Newmarket Handicap, six furlongs, all the flyers of repute put in an appearance, but aristocratic lineage and wonderful trials went for naught, as the winner turned up in the rank outsider Churchill, a 33 to 1 chance, who won from Boz, whilst Sir Modred's son, Sir William, filled third place. The Hon. White again scored with the gelding Titan by Chester—Tempe, which won the Ascot Vale Stakes. The hero Carbine annexed the Essenden Stakes, one mile 2½ furlongs, from Singapore, whilst Melos filled third position, and Titan secured another win for his popular owner in the Sires Produce Stakes. The Australian Cup, 2¼ miles, brought out the cracks again, when they finished in the order of Dreadnought, Melos and Sir William, in the great time of 3 minutes 59½ seconds. The Hon. James followed up his success by winning the Nursery Handicap with Prelude, a filly by Martini, Henry and Phillina. New Zealand was to the fore in the Autumn Handicap, one mile five furlongs, which was won by Scots Grey with 7st. 11lb. by the immortal Musket from the Maid of Athol. Singapore and Sir William started with 8st. 10lb. and 8st. 5lb. respectively, but were unable to run into a place. The champion Stakes, three miles, weight for age, brought out Melos, Dreadnought, Carbine and Rudolph, the betting being even on Dreadnought. Approaching home it looked like a duel between Dreadnought and Carbine, but Melos fairly electrified the onlookers by passing the pair and winning by a length all out. Melos is a four-year-old, which makes the win all the more meritorious, as a glance at the records will show that the three-year-old has all the best of the weight-for-age scale in a three mile race. Since Fishhook won in 1867, no less than sixteen three-year-olds have won the Champion race as against five other ages. £2500 has since been offered for Melos and refused. Titan won the Special Juvenile Stakes which is for geldings only, and Carbine added another winning bracket to his name in the All-aged Stakes. The Place Handicap, one and one-half mile, was won by Tantallon, Bonnie Spec second, and Sir William third. Carbine again showed his consistency by winning the Loch Plate, the test of beating Singapore and Fishwife proving only play for him. The meeting was a most successful one, the Hon. James White, as per usual, securing the largest portion of the stakes —£5547, 4, 0.

Moorebank the sensation horse of the Caulfield Cup, about whom I told you such a pot of money had been lost, was recently cast in his box, and received such injuries that it was found necessary to destroy him. An autopsy was held by a veterinarian, when it was found that his hind quarters were quite decayed, and it is now surmised that the horse was poisoned prior to the running for the Cup, which accounted for the poor show he made on the course after doing such wonderful things on the training track. "THE JUNGLE."

AUCTION SALE OF
Standard-Bred Trotters and ROADSTERS,

—AT—

AGRICULTURAL PARK, SACRAMENTO,

FRIDAY, - - May 2d, 1890,

At 1 o'clock P. M.

BY ORDER OF MR. S. E. TRYON

This sale will include the well known pacing mare POCAHONTAS 2:22½. Heavy in foal to DEXTER PRINCE; g g EL MONTE 2:29½, brown pacer CASTELLO, 2:31½, and MAJESTER (3) at 2 years old 2:49½, sired by Sterling 6223, dam Madam Baldwin (dam of Bay Rose 2:20½) by the Moor 870.

And twenty others, comprising broodmares, colts, fillies and geldings.

SALE POSITIVE.

Catalogues now being prepared.

KILLIP & CO., Auctioneers,
22 Montgomery Street, San Francisco.

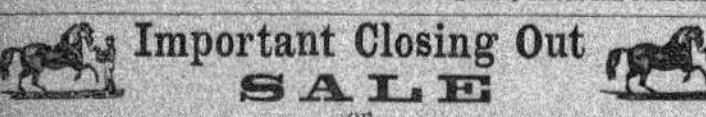

Important Closing Out SALE
—OF—
Trotting - bred Stock,

COMPRISING THE ENTIRE STUD OF

JOHN G. HILL, Esq., of Ventura, California.

—TO BE HELD IN—

San Francisco,

Thursday. - - - May 15th, 1890.

It will embrace about 80 head of well bred Stallions, Mares and Geldings, principally the get of that celebrated standard bred sire

A. W. RICHMOND, 1687,

out of thoroughbred mares mostly from that noted horse, Woodburn, sire of Monarch 2:28½, and the dam of Victor 2 22, and others.

This will no doubt be the last opportunity at public auction to obtain the blood of this great sire, that, in part, has made ANTEEO, ANTEVOLO, ARROW, ROMERO, RICHMOND JR., and others famous in the trotting history of our State.

The sale is positive and without reserve, as Mr. Hill will engage in other business.

☞ Catalogues now being prepared.

KILLIP & CO., Auctioneers,
22 Montgomery Street, San Francisco, Cal.

RUNNYMEDE, COLDSTREAM & LOUDOUN
-Thoroughbred Yearlings-

Will be sold at Auction

On Monday, May 5th, 1890,

—AT—

RACELAND, - - - - near Paris, Ky., at 12 M,

These yearlings are the get of Hindoo, imp. Billet, Leonatus, Onondaga, Fonso, Alarm, Springbok, Sensation, King Alfonso and Ben d'Or. They include full brothers to Hanover, Jim Gore, Bedford and The Lioness, Ballston, Perkins, Modolin, Burton and Millie, and Miss Motley; sisters to Runnymede, Barnes, Meriden, Servis, Cameo, Heathen, Hindoo Rose and Lillian Lindsay and Sunbeam; half-brothers to Pure Rye, Ocean Middlestone, Catalpa, Miss Thomas, Winslow and Stoney Montgomery and Longshore, and half-sisters to Alarm Bell, Warren Lewis, Shelby Barnes, Florence E., and Brussells and Kilkenney.

☞ THE LARGEST WINNING HORSE AND LARGEST WINNING MARE ON THE AMERICAN TURF WERE BOTH BRED AT RUNNYMEDE.

For catalogues, apply to

BAXTER & STRINGFIELD,
Box 35. Room 1, Reed Building, Lexington, Ky.

Poplar Grove Breeding FARM.

Standard-bred Trotters, Colts and Fillies.

The get of CLOVIS, 4909; PASHA, 2039; APEX, 2935.

For Sale.

Address S. N. STRAUBE, Poplar Grove Breeding Farm,

Fresno, Cal.

Inspection by intending purchasers invited, and information by mail.

Pure Bred Clydesdale Mares

TWO MARES (Full Sisters) Five and Six Years Old, Weighing About 1,900 lbs. Each.

Sire imp. BEN. LOMOND.
Dam's sire imp. GLANCER.

For particulars apply to

H. A. MAYHEW,
Niles, Alameda County.

Stallion for Sale

AT A BARGAIN.

Full Brother to Fairmont.

By Piedmont, dam Queen by Garibaldi—see State Fair Edition of BREEDER AND SPORTSMAN, September 14, 1889, for description of Fairmont—three years old, solid bay. Can trot a 2:40 gait or better. Sound in every particular. Can be seen at Oakland Trotting Park, Oakland.

P. J. WILLIAMS.

ANNUAL SPRING SALE

—OF—

200 HEAD
Road & Harness Horses

AND

Work and Draft Horses

AND SHETLAND PONIES!

From the Ranchos of J. B. Haggin, Esq.

WILL TAKE PLACE AT

RAILROAD STABLES,

Corner Turk and Steiner Streets, San Francisco,

Tuesday, May 6, 1890,

HORSES MAY BE SEEN AT STABLES ON AND AFTER MAY 3d.

Catalogues now ready, and may be had on application.

KILLIP & CO., Live Stock Auctioneers,
22 Montgomery Street, S. F.

B. G. BRUCE & P. C. KIDD'S
Spring Sales of
THOROUGHBREDS!

MAY 7—The Entire Produce of the EDGEWATER and KINGSTON STUD YEARLINGS, Comprising Thirty-five Head

In the Edgewater Stud are the get of Springbok, Audrain, Onondaga, imp. Silvermine and imp. Deceiver. In the Kingston Stud the get of Longfellow, imp. Zorilla, imp. The Ill Used, Jils Johnson and Duke of Montrose. Among the Edgewater Yearlings are full brothers to Audrain, Gosno, Ascalon Ascoli and Sierra Nevada. Half brothers to Wenzel Orlando, Schoolmaster, Warrior and Sonnet. Full sisters to Lela May and East Lynne. Half sisters to Zulu, Abilene, Tripple Cross, Irish Dan and Valisia.

In the Kingston Stud lot are half brothers to Helter Skelter, Biscuit and Prodigal Son. Half sisters to Winning Ways and Rollin Hawley, and a full sister to that fast horse Kenney.

On MAY 8 a Grand Combination Sale of Fifty-two Head of Yearlings, Two and Three Year Olds, Broodmares, Stallions and Horses in Training.

The Yearlings number 29, and are the get of King Alfonso, Jils Johnson Longfellow, Himyar, Duke of Montrose, imp Rossington, Onondaga, Virgilius, Falsetto, Col. Clark, Gov. Bowie, Harry O'Fallon, Persan, imp. Rapture, Melbourne (formerly Elias Lawrence), Turco or Melbourne, Volturno, imp. Stylites and Jim Gore. Among them is a full brother to Branpolette, half-brothers and sisters to We Wa, Teuton, Yorick, Asceola, Marguerite, Autocrat, Monocrat and Jack Rose, and out of mares by Longfellow, imp. Glen Athol, Pat Malloy, Reverberation, Lisbon, Knighthood, Lightning, King Ban, Thunder, Virgil, Bertram, King Alfonso, Lever, Eolus, War Dance, Tobe Dram, Chariton, Tom Bowling, Revolver, Hurrah, Wanderer, Wildidle, Jerome Edger, Gen. Shields, Aramis and Ballinkeel, from racing families.

Among the broodmares are a full sister to Eolian, half sisters to Jennie June and Explosion (Dew Drop's dam) by such sires as Eolus, Lisbon, Ten Broeck and Ringmaster.

Among the two-year-olds are full sisters to Burlington and Spendwest, by such well-known sires as Powhattan, Harry O'Fallon, Spendthrift, and Ten Broeck. The older horses are by Germantown, King Ban, Forester, Russifer, Duke of Montrose, Allan Pinkerton, Ten Broeck and Kyrle Daly, from racing and producing families.

These sales will be held at Treacy & Wilson's Stable, Lexington, Ky., beginning each day at 9 A. M. For catalogues address this office or

BRUCE & KIDD, Lexington, Ky.

FOR SALE.
Full Brother in Blood to Yolo Maid, 2:12 1-2.

A very fast pacer. No record. Also a RUNNING MARE. Can run a half in 49 or better.

Apply to

G. W. BOUCHER,
Woodlands, Cal.

For Sale.

14

Pure bred

PERCHERONS.

Stallions and Mares.

OF ALL AGES.

Part imported, and all Registered Proof.

For further information, address

E. J. TURNER, Hollister, Cal.

Antevolo Colt
FOR SALE.

REX VOLO, foaled February 22nd 1888, dam Catchup by Rustler; granddam Huntess by Don Victor; great granddam Bettie Denice by American Boy Jr. Is 15.1 hands high, well developed, muscular and without a blemish. Has a very gentle disposition, and shows speed and a good gait.

HOME FURNISHING CO.,
125 Fifth Street, S. F. Cal.

ARGONAUT HERD.
POLLED ABERDEEN—ANGUS CATTLE.

Thirty head choice pure bred and high grade (cross bred) HEIFERS and a few grand young BULLS for sale at reasonable prices. A fine opportunity for persons wishing to establish choice herds or change their bulls. Representatives from this herd were grand prize winners at the last California State Fair.

Address DR. G. M. DIXON,
Sacramento, Cal.

For Sale

A FIRST-CLASS

Napa County Farm

—OR—

STOCK RANCH,

800 Acres Improved,

SITUATED TWO AND A HALF MILES FROM NAPA CITY, with good roads leading thereto, a good hard finished house of nine rooms, with all modern improvements, streams running all summer, a great amount of live oak and black oak timber. It lies in a fruit belt, surrounded by fine vineyards and orchards growing upon the same quality of soil and originally a part of this tract. About one-half hill, and one half rolling land, but none of it is steep and all easily cultivated, splendidly situated for the breeding of fine horses. Price, $65 per acre. Further particulars given at this office.

BREEDER AND SPORTSMAN,
313 Bush St.

BROOD MARE for SALE
DOT,

By WHIPPLE'S HAMBLETONIAN 725, dam, Victoria by Jerseyman (son of Geo. M. Patchen Jr., 31), 2nd dam Whiskey Jane (dam of Sam Purdy 2:20½). This mare will be sold at a reasonable figure. For further particulars apply AT THIS OFFICE.

For Sale

A HALF BROTHER TO

ALMONT PATCHEN,

(2:15, trial 2:13 3-4).

JUANITO JR. is a beautiful bright bay, black points, with no white, foaled 1886. As a colt he has given much more promise than did Almont Patchen at the same age. Instead of being a pacer, he is a good square trotter, with every indication of great speed, and is so gentle and kind, that a lady can drive him. The owner's only reason for selling him is that business calls him away from this section of the State. He will be sold at a reasonable figure. This is a splendid opportunity for a gentleman to secure a first-class trotter at a very low figure.

The pedigree of Juanito Jr. is by Juanito (sire of Almont Patchen), dam Nettie Moore by Old Tom Moore. For further particulars, address

JUANITO JR.,
Santa Clara P. O., Cal.

Speed Programme

—OF THE—

Twelfth District Ag'l Society

To be held at

LAKEPORT,

SEPTEMBER 23 to 27 INCLUSIVE.

First Day—Tuesday, Sept. 23, 1890.

RACE NO. 1—TROTTING.

Yearling Stake; $250 guaranteed. Entrance $30, payable as follows: $5 May 1st, $10 July 1, $10 September 1st (when entry must be named), and $5 additional for starters. Entries to close May 1, 1890. See general conditions.

RACE NO. 2—RUNNING.

One-half mile dash. $100 added; $25 to second. Entrance $10, to close 6 P. M. day before race.

RACE NO. 3—TROTTING.

Three-minute class. Mile heats 3 in 5. District. $150 added. Entrance $30; to close 6 P. M. day before race. 5 to enter, 3 to start. See general conditions.

Second Day—Wednesday, September 24th

RACE NO. 4—RUNNING.

Three-quarter mile heats; 2 in 3. $200 added; $25 to second. Entrance $10, to close 6 P. M. day before race.

RACE NO. 5—TROTTING.

District Stallion. Mile heats 3 in 5. Purse $500. Entrance $50 to close 6 P. M. day before race; 5 to enter, 3 to start. See general conditions.

RACE NO. 6—TROTTING.

Three-year-old stake; $300 guaranteed. $50 entrance payable as follows: May 1st, $10; July 1st, $10; September 1, $15 (when entry must be named), and $15 additional to start. Open to Napa, Solano, Sonoma, Marin, Lake, Colusa, Yolo, Mendocino and Humboldt Counties.

Third Day—Thursday, Sept. 25th.

RACE NO. 7—RUNNING.

Seven-eighths mile dash. $150 added; $25 to second. Entrance $10, to close 6 P. M. day before race.

RACE NO. 8—TROTTING.

Two-year-old stake; free for all. Mile heats, best 2 in 3, $200 guaranteed. Entrance $50, payable as follows: May 1st, $10; July 1st, $10; September 1st, $15, and $15 additional to start. See general Conditions.

Fourth Day—Friday, Sept. 26th.

RACE NO. 9—TROTTING.

Mile heats, 3 in 5. For all described Counties in race No. 6. $400 added. Entrance $60, payable as follows: May 1st, $10; July 1st, $20; September 1st, $20—When entries must be named—$10 additional to start. See general Conditions.

RACE NO. 10—RUNNING.

Citizens' Handicap. $100 added. Five-eighths mile; heats, 2 in 3. Entrance $10, to close 6 P. M. day before race.

Fifth Day—Saturday, September 27th.

RACE NO. 11—RUNNING.

GENTLEMEN'S NOVELTY.—*For non-professional jockeys.* One mile dash. $10 added; $5 entrance. Purse divided as follows: First horse at each quarter to get $25; slowest average at all quarters to get Society medal.

NO. 12.—LADIES' TOURNAMENT

Free for all in District. Purse $40, divided as follows: $25 to first, $15 to second, $10 to third.

No. 13.—GENTLEMAN'S TROTTING.

Same Conditions as gentlemen's Novelty. Mile heats, two in three. Entrance $5. Entrance money divided 50, 30 and 10 per cent.

GENERAN CONDITIONS.

Nominations in colt stakes transferable any time before colts are named. If the payments in stake races amount to more than the sum guaranteed the additional amount to be divided 60, 30 and 10 per cent; in case of only two starting, 60 and 40 per cent.; and in case of one horse walking over, the whole amount to go to such horse.

A failure to make any payment when due shall be considered a withdrawal, and forfeiture of the amounts paid in. National Rules to govern all trotting races. The right reserved to refund the first payment in case the stake does not fill satisfactorily.

All running races, unless otherwise specified, governed by the Pacific Coast Blood Horse Association Rules.

The Directors reserve the right to change the hour and date of any race, and in case of a race being antedated the nominator will receive notice.

A horse distancing the field shall receive only first and third moneys.

L. G. SIMMONS, President.

A. B. McCUTCHEN, Secretary.

San Joaquin Valley

AGRICULTURAL ASSOCIATION.

Stockton Fair, 1890,

September 23 to 27 inclusive.

TROTTING COLT STAKES.

$50 each, of which $10 must accompany nomination, $15 to be paid July 1st, and $25 on Monday, September 1, 1890.

Failure to make payments as above forfeits previous payments.

PACIFIC COAST STAKES.

For 2-year-olds .... 2 in 3 } $200
3 " " .... 3 in 5 } added to
4 " " .... 3 in 5 } each.
2 " " .... Pacing 2 in 3 }

SAN JOAQUIN VALLEY STAKES.

Open to all San Joaquin Valley counties for colts owned in the valley, February 1, 1890.

For 2-year-olds .... 2 in 3 } $150
3 " " .... 3 in 5 } added to
4 " " .... 3 in 5 } each.
2 " " .... Pacing 2 in 3 }

Five or more full paid up entries required to fill; three or more colts to start. Four moneys: 50, 25, 15 and 10 per cent. In case of only two colts starting, they may compete for the stakes paid in only, two-thirds and one-third, otherwise full conditions of this Association for 1889, to govern.

Entries close Thursday, May 1, 1890, with the Secretary,

J. M. LaRUE, P. O. box 188,

L. U. SHIPPEE, President. Stockton, Cal.

Pacific Coast

Trotting-Horse

Breeders' Ass'n.

ADDITIONAL

Stakes & Installment Purses

FOR 1890.

Entries to close May 1, 1890.

Trotting Stakes.

THREE YEAR OLDS—FOALS OF 1887.

Eligible to 2:40 Class. Mile heats, best three in five. Entrance $50, with $300 added. Entrance payable, $10 May 1st, 1890, $15 July 1st, 1890, and $25 on the fifth day preceding the first advertised day of the meeting.

FOUR YEAR OLDS—FOALS 1886.

Eligible to 2:30 class. Mile heats, best three in five. Entrance $50, with $400 added. Entrance payable, $10 on May 1st, 1890, $15 on July 1st, 1890 and $25 on the fifth day preceding the first advertised day of the meeting.

Nomination Trotting Purses.

$2,000, Stallion Purse.

Open to stallions eligible to the 2:18 Class. Mile heats best three in five. Entrance $200 payable $40 May 1st, 1890, $40 July 1st, 1890, $40 August 1st 1890, and $80 on the tenth day preceding the first advertised day of the meeting. Horses to be named at time of last payment.

$2,000, Free For All.

Mile heats, best three in five. Entrance $200, payable $40 May 1st 1890, $40 July 1st 1890, $40 August 1st 1890, and $80 on the tenth day preceding the first advertised day of the meeting. Horses to be named at time of last payment.

$1,500. Five-Year-Olds, Foals 1885.

Mile heats best three in five. Entrance $150, payable $30 May 1, 1890, $30 July 1, 1890, $30 August 1, 1890, and $60 on the tenth day preceding the first advertised day of the meeting. Horses to be named at the time of the last payment.

$1,500. 2:22 Class.

Mile heats, best three in five. Entrance $150. Payable $30 May 1, 1890, $30 July 1, 1890, $30 August 1, 1890, and $60 on the tenth day preceding the first advertised day of the meeting. Horses to be named at the time of the last payment.

$1,500. 2:27 Class.

Mile heats, best three in five. Entrance $150. Payable $30 May 1, 1890, $30 July 1, 1890, $30 August 1, 1890, and $60 on the tenth day preceding the first advertised day of the meeting. Horses to be named at time of last payment.

Nomination Pacing Purses.

$1,500. Free For All.

Mile heats, best three in five. Entrance $150. Payable $30 May 1, 1890, $30 July 1, 1890, $30 August 1, 1890, and $60 on the tenth day preceding the first advertised day of the meeting. Horses to be named at time of last payment.

$1,000. 2:25 Class.

Mile heats, best three in five. Entrance $100. Payable $20 May 1, 1890, $20 July 1, 1890, $20 August 1, 1890, and $40 on the tenth day preceding the first advertised day of the meeting. Horses to be named at time of last payment.

Conditions.

First payment, whether for purses payable in installments or for stakes, MUST ACCOMPANY NOMINATIONS, or they will not be considered.

Neglect to make payments on the dates stipulated will incur forfeiture of all previous payments.

No horses and colts owned on the Pacific Coast by others than members of the P. C. T. H. B. A. are eligible to the above purses and stakes, but horses and colts OWNED outside of the Pacific Coast are eligible thereto regardless of membership.

All States and Territories lying in whole or in part west of the Rocky Mountains are held to be part of the Pacific Coast.

The Directors reserve the right to change the hour and day of any race except when it becomes necessary to ante-date a race, in which instance the nominator will receive three days notice of change by mail to address of entry.

Entries not declared out by 6 P. M. of the day preceding the race, shall be required to start.

When there is more than one entry to stakes by one person or in one interest, the horse to be started must be named by 6 P. M. of the day preceding the race.

Purses and stakes will be divided into four moneys, viz., 50 per cent. to the winner, 25 per cent. to the second horse, 15 per cent. to the third horse, and 10 per cent. to the fourth horse.

No added money will be paid for a walk-over. If only three horses start in a stake race, only first, second and third money shall be paid—if but two start, the Directors reserve the right to call it a walk-over, and divide the stake money paid in, two-thirds to the winner and one-third to the second horse. In case of a walk-over, only the money received from entries to said stake will be paid.

A horse distancing the field shall only be entitled to first and third moneys.

The Board of Directors reserve the right to declare any purse or stake filled or not filled without binding itself to any specified number of entries.

In all nomination purses, eight entries will be required to fill, and four to make the last payment.

Trotting and racing colors shall be named by six o'clock on the day preceding the race, and MUST be worn upon the track.

Horses eligible in class races on records standing at time of entry.

Otherwise than the above National or American Trotting Association Rules—as this Association may select—will govern the stake and purse races offered.

Persons desirous of making entries in the above purses and stakes, and who have not as yet joined the P. C. T. H. B. A., should make application for membership to the secretary, and remit the sum of $25 to cover membership fee before May 1, 1890.

J. H. WHITE, President.

JAS. P. KERR, Secretary,

13 Bush Street, S. F.

ENTIRE CHANGE

—OF—

PROGRAMME

—OF THE—

Extra Attractions

To take place at the

Oakland.

Fall Meeting, 1890,

UNDER THE MANAGEMENT OF THE

GOLDEN GATE

Fair Association

NOMINATION PURSES.

In which entries close in the name of owners or trainers on May 15th. All nominations transferable and nominators held only for amounts paid in. Horses must be named five days before first advertised day of the meeting. Eight nominations required to fill, four of which must make last payments.

THE NEW LIST PURSE $1000.

For three-year-olds whose sires up to January 1, 1890, have not produced an animal with a record of 2:30 or better at three years of age or under. Entrance 10 per cent. payable as follows:

$25 May 15th, when entries close in the names of owners or trainers.
$25 June 15th.
$25 July 15th.
$25 five days before first advertised day of meeting, when horses must be named.

GUARANTEED PURSE $1200.

For three-minute class, entrance 10 per cent, payable as follows:

$30 May 15th, when entries close in names of owners or trainers.
$30 June 15th.
$30 July 15th.
$30 five days before first advertised day of meeting, when horse must be named.

GUARANTEED PURSE $1200.

For 2:40 class, entrance 10 per cent, payable as follows:

$30 May 15th, when entries close in names of owners or trainers.
$30 June 15th.
$30 July 15th.
$30 five days before first advertised day of meeting, when horses must be named.

—ALSO A—

Guaranteed Futurity Purse $4.000.

To take place during the Fall Meeting of 1893.

For foals of 1890. Entrance 5 per cent. payable as follows:

$10 May 15, 1890, when entries close in name of foals or of dams and sires.

$10 Jan. 15, 1891.
$15, June 15, 1891.
$15, Jan. 15, 1892.
$15 June 15, 1892.
$15 Jan. 15, 1893.
$20 June 15, 1893.

$50 fifteen days before advertised day of the race.

If the last payment is made on twelve or more entries the horses shall be started in trial races, in which not more than eleven or less than six shall be allotted to start. The trial races shall be mile heats, three in five, for a purse of $1,000, given by the Association for each race. If two trial races are trotted, the first four horses shall only be entitled to start in the final race. If three such trial races are trotted, only the first three horses in each trial race shall start in the final; and if four or more trial races are necessary, only the first two horses in each trial race shall start in the final race.

These trial races must be started not less than five nor more than ten days previous to the day set for the final race; and if possible all trial races will be trotted on the same day.

CONDITIONS.

Neglect to provide payments on the dates stipulated will incur forfeiture of all previous payments.

The Directors reserve the right to change the hour and day of any race except when it becomes necessary to ante-date a race, in which instance the nominator will receive three days notice of change by mail to address of entry.

Entries not declared out by 6 P. M. the day preceding the race, shall be required to start.

Purses will be divided into four moneys viz., 50 per cent. to the winner, 25 per cent. to the second horse, 15 per cent. to the third horse, and 10 per cent. to the fourth horse.

A horse distancing the field shall only be entitled to first and third moneys.

Trotting and racing colors shall be named by six o'clock on the day preceding the race, and MUST be worn upon the track.

All purse races, mile heats, best three in five to harness.

Otherwise than the above, National or American Trotting Association Rules—as this Association may select—will govern the races offered.

Entries to close with the Secretary.

R. T. CARROLL, President.

JOS. I. DIMOND, Sec'y, 306 Market St., S. F.

HORSES PURCHASED ON COMMISSION.

THOROUGHBREDS A SPECIALTY.

Will select and buy, or buy selected Animals for all desiring, for reasonable compensation

KEEPS PROMISING YOUNGSTERS IN VIEW.

L. M. LASLEY, Stanford, Ky.

References:—J. W. Guest, Danville, Ky.
B. G. Bruce, Lexington, Ky.
S. H. Baughman, Stanford, Ky.
G. A. Lackey, Stanford, Ky.
Geo. McAlister, Stanford, Ky.
First National Bank, Stanford, Ky.

UTAH

Driving Park

ASSOCIATION,

1890.

JUNE 16 to 20, Inclusive

—AT—

SALT LAKE CITY.

Purses - $7,000

TROTTING, RUNNING & PACING,

Entries for all Races to close May 30, 1890.

This meeting is arranged to accommodate horsemen on way to the Great Racing Circuit of Montana, their purses aggregating $46,000. The meeting at Denver closes June 7th, and our meeting begins June 16th and closes June 20th inclusive, and the Montana meetings commence July 14th, thus giving ample time to rest up here. We expect to give a genuine first-class meeting, and will see that all horsemen have a "square deal." Our city is at present enjoying an era of prosperity never before seen, which justifies our hope for the best meeting ever given in Utah. A cordial invitation is extended to all horsemen to come. The Great Salt Lake bathing season is then on, thus affording all visitors a rare treat and pleasant time.

PROGRAMME

—OF—

Utah Driving Park Spring Race Meeting,

Salt Lake City, Utah.

Spring Racing and Trotting Meeting for Five Days, from June 16 to June 20, inclusive.

PURSES, $7000.

FIRST DAY—MONDAY, JUNE 16.

No. 1—Trotting, 2:27 class $500
No. 2—Pacing, 2:35 class 400
No. 3—Running, ¾ mile heats, all ages 300
No. 4—Running, ½ mile heats, all ages 300

SECOND DAY—TUESDAY, JUNE 17.

No. 5—Pacing, 2:24 class $500
No. 6—Trotting, 2:30 class 400
No. 7—Running, ¾ mile dash, three-year-olds 300
No. 8—Running, ½ mile heats, all ages 300

THIRD DAY—WEDNESDAY, JUNE 18.

No. 9—Trotting, 2:36 class $500
No. 10—Trotting, three-year-olds (added money) for Colorado, Wyoming, Montana, and Utah horses 300
No. 11—Running, ⅝ mile heats, all ages 300

FOURTH DAY—THURSDAY, JUNE 19.

No. 12—Pacing, free for all pacers $600
No. 13—Trotting, 2:34 class 400
No. 14—Running, 1¼ mile dash, all ages 300

FIFTH DAY—FRIDAY, JUNE 20.

No. 15—Trotting, free for all $600
No. 16—Trotting, 2:30 class 450
No. 17—Running, ½ mile heats, for horses that have run and not won a race this meeting 250
No. 18—Running, 1 mile heats, all ages 300

F. H. DYER, Secretary,

J. K. GILLESPIE, Manager. Salt Lake City.

Second Annual Bench Show

OF THE

South'n California Kennel Club

AT THE

City of Los Angeles,

MAY 6, 7, 8 & 9 '90.

The SOUTHERN CALIFORNIA KENNEL CLUB was admitted a member of the AMERICAN KENNEL CLUB September 18, 1889. The coming show will therefore be held under the A. K. C. rules.

Entries will positively close May 1st.

A special committee will take personal charge of all dogs sent from a distance and insure their proper care. For premium lists and entry blanks address E. K. BENCHLEY, Secretary, 14 South Spring Street, Los Angeles; or H. H. BRIGGS, Breeder and Sportsman, San Francisco.

JESSE E. MARKS. IKE DEUTCH

Yosemite Billiard Parlors,

ST. ANN'S BUILDING,

No. 8 Eddy Street, S. F.

The Poodle Dog

"Rotisserie,"

FIRST-CLASS IN EVERY RESPECT.

Elegant Family Dining Rooms.

S. E. cor. GRANT AVE. and BUSH STREET.

ANDRE POTENTINI, Proprietor.

Old Hermitage Whiskies

"STEINER'S,"

No. 311 BUSH STREET,

San Francisco.

Under Breeder and Sportsman Office.

Langtry Farms' Stud

Imp. FRIAR TUCK

By the Immortal HERMIT.

DAM ROMPING GIRL BY WILD DAYRELL,

AT $50 THE SEASON.

Mares not proving with foal may be returned the following season. Good care taken of mares, but no liabilities for accidents or escapes.

Good Pasturage at $5 per month.

Mares shipped to ST. HELENA, care CHARTES WILLIAM ABY, St. Helena Stables, will be cared for. For further particulars address,

CHAS. WILLIAM ABY,
Middletown, Lake County, Cal.

THE CEDARS

BANNER MARK, 9424.

Foaled in 1888; by Victor von Bismarck (sire of Edgemark, four year old record 2:16; Von Wilkes, yearling record 2:38¼, etc.); dam Moonlight by Alcyone (sire of Alcyon 2.15 1-4, etc.); second dam Twilight (dam of Skylight Pilot 2:19) by Mambrino Pilot (sire of Hannis 2:17¾); third dam by Pilot Jr. (sire of the dam of Maud S. 2:08¾); fourth dam nearly or quite thoroughbred.

In his four double crosses he combines more of the popular blood than any colt of his age. He is a double Hambletonian, double Clay through Bismarck and George Wilkes, double Mambrino and Pilot Jr., through Mambrino Pilot, Pilot Jr., and Mambrino Patchen. There is no other colt living bred like him. If you want Hambletonian, Clay, Mambrino or Pilot Jr., here you have it all combined in one grand colt. He has much of the finish of the thoroughbred.

Insurance $300. Limited to Seven Approved Mares.

Book full for 1890 and open for 1891 for fifteen approved mares. Address

T. E. MOORE,
The Cedars, Shawhan, Ky.

PASTURAGE

AND

FIRST-CLASS CARE

TAKEN OF

Gentlemen's Road Horses and Trotters.

Colts Broken and Trained to Harness or Saddle.

Twenty new Box Stalls. First-class Pasturage, and the best of care given to all horses. **Terms, $4 per month.** Satisfaction Guaranteed.

Address,

K. O'GRADY,
Laurel Creek Farm,
SAN MATEO, CAL.

Highland Farm,

LEXINGTON, KY.,

Home of Red Wilkes.

Standard-bred Trotting Stock For Sale,

Sired by Red Wilkes, Wilton, 2:19¼; Allandorf and Sentinel Wilkes, out of highly bred Standard Mares of the most fashionable blood of the day.

W. C. FRANCE, Proprietor.

The CLARKE POND

Anti-Side Pulling Bit

A positive and absolute cure for the worst case on earth. Looks like an ordinary bit, does not injure the mouth, is simple, and does not interfere with the using of an over-check bit or with the horse drinking.

It brings the horse's head square in front, putting him into line, and making a pleasant driver of the most confirmed side puller.

This bit is either straight or joint made of the best steel, hand forged, nicely proportioned, and nickel-plated.

In ordering above bit, please state which side the horse carries his head. Also state whether a straight or jointed bit is wanted.

We send single bits, prepaid, for $3 each, or two for $5. Discount to the trade.

Will sell State and County rights. Big thing for agents.

CLARKE POND & CO,
Olena, Huron County, Ohio.

Brushes.

BUCHANAN BROS.,
Brush Manufacturers,

199 Sacramento Street, two doors above Montgomery.

Horse Brushes of every description on hand and made to order. Bristle Body Brushes our Specialty

---

The Pure Trotting-bred Stallion

ILLUSTRIOUS

STANDARD No. 4178.

DESCRIPTION.

Dark bay, black points, 15 1-2 hands high, weight 1000 pounds, foaled May 20, 1885; bred by General W. T. Withers, Lexington, Ky.

PEDIGREE.

By Happy Medium, sire of Maxey Cobb 2:13¼ and 52 with records of 2:30 or better.

First dam Abdallietta by Cassius M. Clay Jr., sire of Durango 2:23¾, Harry Clay 2:23½, and sire of the dams of Minnehaha, Bertha 2:27¼, Charley West 2:28¼, Grandmont 2:25 1-4, Lottie K 2:26¾, Mambrino Diamond 2:26, Richwood 2:28 1-2, Topsy 2:2-¼, Happy Thought 2:21 1-2, Pequot 2:23 1-2, Fairlawn Medium 2:27 1-2, Folley 2:27¼, and Mambrino Boy 2:26 1-2.

Second dam Laura Crockett by Almont, sire of Westmont 2:13¾, Puritan 2:16, Fanny Witherspoon 2:16¼, Piedmont 2:17¼, Aldine 2:19¼, and 37 with records better than 2:30.

Third dam Sally Tee by Alexander's Abdallah, sire Goldsmith Maid 2:14.

Fourth dam Kate Crockett, the dam of Lulu 2:14¾, by imp Hooton.

Illustrious is a horse of extra fine finish, large clean bone, good feet, back short and strong, loins and quarters well muscled, and powerful. He has a kind disposition and splendid trotting action, and is as handsome and bloodlike in form and finish as any trotting stallion in the land.

He is pronounced by his breeder, General Withers, to be the best bred son of Happy Medium living, and is undoubtedly one of the very best bred trotting stallions in the State. He has had but six weeks' regular training, and a part of that time was sick with epizootic, but was trotted quarters in 39 1-4 seconds, and barring accidents will certainly trot better than 2:30 this season.

TERMS—$50 the season. Mares not proving with foal may be returned next year free.

Good pasturage at $4 per month.

Season to begin February 1st and end June 15th.

GEO. A. STONE,
Santa Rosa, Cal.

LAWN VIEW BREEDING FARM STALLIONS.

ACTOR.

A beautiful bay horse foaled 1887 by Prompter 2305 sire of Apex (four-year-old record) 2:26, Transit 2:26¾, Creole 2:20, Blue Belle 2:31, Daisy (yearling record) 2:36¾, he by Blue Bull 75, 1st dam by Sultan 1513 2:24, sire of Stamboul 2:12 1-4, Ruby 2:19¾, Sweetheart 2:22½, Alcazar 2:20¾, Eva 2:23¾, La Grange 2:23¾, and eleven others in 2:30 list, second dam by Fireman by Langford.

Actor, as his pedigree shows, is as purely bred a young stallion as ever made a season in the stud. Blue Bull stock is much sought after in the East, and Sultan, sire of his first dam will make the season in Kentucky this year at $100 per mare. Actor is a handsome bay colt 16 hands high, clean limbed and possesses all the points of a speedy trotter.

TERMS, $40 FOR THE SEASON, usual return privileges.

DOUGLASDALE 7650.

Thoroughbred Registered Clydesdale Stallion

Imported from Scotland, December, 1889, ba, three years old.

TERMS, $35 FOR THE SEASON.

YOUNG ELMO

Two years old sorrel stallion by St. Elmo 2:27, dam by Woodburn.

TERMS, $20 FOR THE SEASON.

For further particulars, address

MANAGER LAWN VIEW FARM, Auburn, Cal.

The Trotting-Bred Stallion

RINGWOOD

THE FINEST SON OF THE NOTED SIDNEY,

Will make a Season at Oakland commencing March 1, and ending June 1, 1890.

DESCRIPTION.

RINGWOOD is a dark, rich colored bay, black points, 15 1-2 hands, weight 1100 lbs., and a pure gaited trotter. Has shown great speed. He is now five years old. As a four year old he showed a trial in 2:19 1-2, and but for an accident would have received a record as a four year old of 2:18 or better.

PEDIGREE.

RINGWOOD is by Sidney, record 2:19 3-4, and a half brother to Gold Leaf 2:11 1-4, Adonis 2:11, Flee (two year old) 2:24, Longworth 2:19, Sister V. 2:27, Faustino, yearling 2:35, Fleet, yearling, 2:35, Memo, three year old trial 2:20 1-2.

Sidney is by Santa Claus, record 2:17 1-2; he by Strathmore, sire of 31 in 2:30 list; he by Hambletonian 10, the greatest of all producers; he by Abdallah. Sidney's dam, Sweetness, record 2:21 1-4; she by Volunteer, the sire of St. Julien 2:11 1-4.

RINGWOOD'S dam Alma; she by Dashway, thoroughbred; he by Belmont, he by American Boy; he by Sea Gull; he by imported Expedition. Alma's 1st dam, Fanny Cobb, was a great road mare, pedigree untraced.

TERMS; $50 for the Season

Payable June 1st, or sooner if mares are taken away

Address communications to

A. C. DIETZ,
Oakland, Cal.

The Fast Trotting Stallion

REDWOOD.

Four-Year-Old Record 2:24 1-2

Will make the season of 1890—February 1st to July 1st—at the

OAKLAND RACE TRACK.

REDWOOD is a dark bay colt, 15.2¼ hands high, weighs 1100 lbs. Foaled in 1885 by Anteeo, 2:16¼, sire of Alfred G., 2:19¾. Anteeo is by Electioneer. First dam Lou Milton, by Milton Medium; second dam Old Fly, a thoroughbred mare brought from the East in 1871 by W. C. Ralston, Esq.

Redwood's sire was out of Columbine by A. W. Richmond, the sire of the pacers Arrow 2:13¾, and Elwood 2:28, and the trotters Romero, 2:19¾, and Len Rose, 2:27. Redwood has shown a quarter in 33 seconds.

Terms $100

For the season. Mares not proving with foal may be returned next season free of charge, provided Redwood remains the property of the present owners. Good pasturage at $5 per month. No responsibility assumed for escapes or accidents. Service fees payable before removal of the mare. Limited to 40 approved mares. For further particulars address,

A. McFADYEN.
Race track, Oakland, Cal.

CALIFORNIA

NUTWOOD

Will stand for mares the season of 1890, commencing February 15th, and ending July 15th, at the NUTWOOD STOCK FARM, one mile from Irvington.

DESCRIPTION AND PEDIGREE.

He is a dark chestnut, with star in forehead; foaled September 16th, 1881; is 16 hands 1½ inches high and weighs 1700 pounds. Has a beautiful flowing mane and tail, with remarkable style and lofty carriage, a bold, open movement like his sire, but has never been handled for speed. He moves and looks like his sire, except that he is a larger horse.

CALIFORNIA NUTWOOD by Nutwood, record 2:18¾, has 32 trotters and pacers with records from 2:15 to 2:30, and put 8 in the 2:30 list in 1889. He is the only horse that ever lived with a record under 2:20 that produced five under 2:20. He is now serving mares at Dubuque, Iowa, at $500 for the season, and his colts at yearlings sell from $2500 to $5000 each. He is out of the dam of Maud S., record 2:08¾.

Nutwood, by Alexander's Belmont, sire of 32 with records from 2:15½ to 2:30. Alexander's Belmont by Alexander's Abdallah, sire of Goldsmiths Maid, record 2:14, and 8 others in 2:30 list. Alexander's Abdallah, by Rysdyk's Hambletonian, sire of 41 with records from 2:1¾ to 2:30, and is the founder of the Hambletonian family.

FANNY PATCHEN, dam of California Nutwood, by George M. Patchen Jr., record 2:27, and sire of Wells Fargo, 2:18½, Sam Purdy 2:20½, Ben Ali 2:2¾, and 7 others from 2:21 to 2:30. He has 7 sons who together produced 12 trotters in 2:30 list, and 8 daughters who together produced 5 trotters and 1 pacer in 2.30 or better. He sired Alexander 2:31½. Alexander sired Alex. Button 2:26½; Alex. Button sired Yolo Maid, pacing record 2:14 at 4 years old, the fastest on record; George M. Patchen Jr., by George M. Patchen 2:23½, is sire of Lucy 2:18½, and 3 others in the 2:30 list; he has 12 sons who together produced 40 trotters from 2:14½ to 2:30, and 6 daughters who together produced 6 trotters in 2:30 list or better, he is grand sire of Hopeful 2:14¾, and best wagon record 2:16½, and sire of the granddam of Stamboul 2:12½.

George M. Patchen, by Cassius M. Clay, and he by Henry Clay, founder of the Clay family.

Laura, second dam of California Nutwood, was a fine large bay mare, a very fast roadster brought from Chicago by Wm. Wilson, of San Jose, and is said to have made a record of 2.36 in Chicago. Pedigree not traced.

TERMS.

$40 for the season, payable invariably before the animal is removed. Mares not proving in foal can be returned free next season. Pasturage $3 per month, but no liability for accidents or escapes.

For further particulars address the owner,

MARTIN CARTER,
Newark, Alameda Co., Cal., or Irvington, Alameda County, Cal.

The Trotting Stallion

CUPID,

Full Brother to Adonis 2:14,

—Sired by—

The Celebrated SIDNEY 2:19 3-4, and out of Venus.

Will make the season of 1890 at the OAKLAND TROTTING PARK.

PEDIGREE.

CUPID is by Sidney out of Venus by Capt. Webster 10173, record 2:38, and sire of Firestone 2:29. Second dam by Skenandoah 836, sire of Daisy Burns 2:29¾, Erwin Davis (sire of two in the 30 list) and dams of four in the 30 list.

DESCRIPTION.

Cupid is a handsome bright bay 15.2¼ hands high, weighs 1100 lbs.; was foaled in 1886. As a yearling, with very little work he showed quarters in 42 seconds, and at 2 years old, quarters in 36 seconds. As a three year old he has not been worked, but he shows the speed and endurance that must come from his excellent blood lines.

TERMS $40 for the season, with the usual return privileges. Good pasturage near the track at $5 per month. The best of care taken of mares in any way that owners may desire, but no responsibility assumed for accidents or escapes.

For further particulars address

C. O. THORNQUEST,
Oakland Trotting Park, or
C. BAAB, 972 Broadway, Oakland.

The Trotting Stallion

VICTOR,

Record 2:22.

Will make the season of 1890 at NAPA CITY.

DESCRIPTION.

VICTOR is a handsome dark bay; 15-3 hands high; weighs about 1,170 pounds, and is remarkably intelligent, level-headed, of kind disposition, and a magnificent animal in every respect. He is well boned and muscled, of splendid conformation, and possesses the qualities of speed and endurance to an eminent degree—qualities that he imparts to his progeny.

PEDIGREE.

VICTOR, record 2:22
- Echo 462
  - Hambletonian 10, Sire of 42 in the 2:30 list.
    - Abdallah 1
    - Chas. Kent mare
  - Fanny Felter
    - Magnolia 68
    - by Webber's Kentucky Whip
- Daughter of
  - Woodburn
    - Lexington
    - Lulu Horton
  - daughter of
    - Ashland
    - thoroughbred

ECHO is the sire of Belle Echo, 2:20, Senator, 2:21¼, Victor, 2:22, Gibraltar, 2:22¼, Echora, 2:23¼, Tippie, 2:28¾, Lohengrin, 2:17¼, Pasha, 2:27¾, Fimonte, 2:29, Col. Hawkins 2:29¼, Annie Laurie, 2:30, Economy, 2:30, Sam Lewis, pacer, 2:21.

TERMS—$60 FOR THE SEASON.

Mares not proving with foal may be returned next season free of charge provided the horse remains the property of the present proprietor, and stands at the same place, otherwise money will be refunded. The best of care taken of mares in any manner that owners may desire, but no responsibility assumed for accidents or escapes. For further particulars, apply to or address

G. W. HUGHES, Agent,
G. A. DOHERTY, Proprietor. Napa City.

Vineland Stock Farm

Alcona 730.

Sire of

FLORA BELLE - - - - Record 2:24
CLAY DUKE - - - - - " 2:31½

ALCONA will be a great sire, but four of his colts have ever been trained, and all have shown full miles better than 2:30, and two of them as good as 2:20. Two of his first sons each sired a colt as a two-year-old, and last season one as a four-year-old trotted a full mile in 2:22¼, and the other, a three-year-old, a mile in 2:31. With opportunities, Alcona is destined to be one of Almont's best sons. Almont, for his opportunities, is beyond doubt the most prepotent sire of his age. He has 35 representatives in the 2:30 list; 49 sons and 22 daughters that have already produced 2:30 performers. Almont died five years ago at 20 years old. If he lived he would be but 25 years old.

PEDIGREE.

ALCONA sired by the great Almont (sire of Westmont 2:13¾, Fanny Witherspoon 2:16¼, Piedmont 2:17¼, and 30 others with records better than 2:30, and grandsire of Belle Hamlin 2:12¾, etc.); by Alexander's Abdallah (sire of Goldsmith Maid 2:14), he by Rysdyk's Hambletonian. Alcona's dam, Queen Mary, by Mambrino Chief (sire of Lady Thorne 2:18 1-4, and 5 others in the 2:30 list, and sire of the dams of Director 2:17, Piedmont 2:17¼, Onward 2:25 1-4, Red Wilkes Almont, Belmont and many other noted sires).

DESCRIPTION.

Alcona is a beautiful chestnut 16 3 1-2 hands high, and weighs 1300 lbs. His colts possess speed, style, finish and beauty, and if they don't trot they command the highest prices for carriage horses.

$40 for the season. Usual return privilege.

Season of Alcona and Grandissimo ends July 1st, 1890.

Grandissimo,

Full Brother to GRANDEE, 3-year old record 2:23 1-2.

Sired by La Grande (son of Almont, and out of Jessie Pepper by Mambrino Chief; Jessie Pepper is the dam of Iona 2:17 1-2, Alpha 2:23 1-2, Sterling Wilkes 2:31¾, and others) dam Norma, by Arthurton (sire of Arab 2:15, Joe Arthurton 2:20 1.2, etc.)

Grandam Nourmahal, (full sister to A. W. Richmond, sire of Arrow 2:13¾, Romero 2:19, and sire of Columbine, dam of Anteeo 2:16¼, and Anteeolo 2:19¼ at four years old).

DESCRIPTION.

Grandissimo is four years old, will make a sixteen hand horse; he is a rich mahogany bay in color and perfect in style and action. $30 for the season. Usual return privileges.

"Grandissimo" with limited training last fall as a three-year-old, trotted quarters in 36 seconds and miles in 2:40.

I feel confident that he will trot fast this season, and will be a great sire as his colts this season are all grand youngsters.

The best of pasturage $4 per month. Mares taken care of in any manner that owners may desire, but no responsibility assumed for escapes or accidents.

For further particulars send for circular or call at stables, one mile south of St. Helena.

FRED W. LOEBER Prop'r.

2:08¾ 2:10 2:12

BALKAN

By Mambrino Wilkes.

(See that Horse's Advertisement.)

DAM FANNY FERN BY JACK HAWKINS Son of Boston.

The grandam of Maud S, (2:08¾) was by Boston and the grandam of Jay-Eye-See (2:10) was by Lexington, son of Boston. So Balkan is the same remove from Boston that Maud is, and one remove nearer than Jay-Eye-See.

Fanny Fern has produced Molly Drew, Onyx, Fred Arnold Molly Fern and Balkan, all by different sires.

Balkan's sire and dam both being producers, and he being a trotter himself with a record of 2:29 1-2 (three-year-old) and timed separately 2:22 1-4 in 4-year-old Stake, Bay District Track, October 14, 1889—it is but fair to presume that he will get trotters of the highest order.

DESCRIPTION.

He is seal brown, 16-1 hands high, in style rivalled by few, and excelled by none with as pure a gait as has yet been exhibited in public—bar none.

Balkan will be at Oakland Trotting Park for the season of 1890, and will be limited to ten mares, at $100 fee, in order to be put in training early, as it is morally certain that if given a reasonable opportunity he will be fast enough to compete with the best of his age. For further particulars, address

A. L. HINDS,
Dexter Stables, Oakland.

2:12¾ 2:13½ 2:15¼

The Trotting Stallion

G & M

FULL BROTHER TO

ALFRED G, 2:19¾.

(Who has been taken to Kentucky to stand at $200)

Will make the season of 1890 from FEBRUARY 1st to JULY 1st, at

SANTA ROSA.

G. & M. is by Anteeo, 2:16¼; was foaled 1886; first dam Rosa B. by Speculation (son of Hambletonian 10); 2d dam Elizabeth by Alexander 490; 3d dam Nora by imp. Glencoe. Anteeo is by Electioneer, out of Columbine by A. W. Richmond 1687.

G. & M. is a handsome dark bay; stands 15.3 1-2 hands high, and weighs 1060 pounds. Gameness, stoutness, speed and stamina are indelibly impressed in every line of the pedigree of G. & M. Owners of broodmares in search of these qualities, will do well to patronize this promising colt.

PHILOSOPHER,

Foaled 1886 by Pilot Wilkes 2987; first dam Bella by George Wilkes 519; second dam by Bell Morgan 61.

Philosopher's sire, Pilot Wilkes 2987, is by George Wilkes 519, dam Grace (the dam of Alice Woodburn etc.), by Pilot Jr. 12, grandam by Orphan Boy.

Will make the season of 1890, from FEBRUARY 1st to JULY 1st, at Santa Rosa.

TERMS for the season:

G. & M., $50.

PHILOSOPHER, $30,

with privilege of returning mares that do not prove in foal the next season free of charge, provided the horse bred to remains the property of the present owners. Good pasturage at $3 per month. No responsibility assumed for accidents or escapes. Service fees payable before removal of the mare. For further particulars, address

GEO. E. GUERNE,
Santa Rosa Cal.

Guenoc Stud Farm, Lake Co., Cal.

Imp. GREENBACK

(Sire of the English winners Greenlight, Greenjacket, Greenshank, Greenwave and Greenhorn)

By Dollar, dam Music, by Stockwell. $100 the Season

ST. SAVIOR,

(FULL BROTHER TO EOLE)

By Eolus, dam War Song, by War Dance. $100 the Season.

PASTURAGE, $5 PER MONTH.

With right to return the following year if mare does not prove with foal. The best of care taken, but no liability for accidents or escapes. Mares shipped to C. W. ABY, care ST. HELENA STABLES, St. Helena Napa County, will be taken in charge by competent men.

For further information write to

DR. C. W. ABY, Middletown, Lake County, Cal.

1890 Three Anteeo Stallions 1890

SUNSET, 5 years old, by Anteeo
ANTEEOF, 4 years old, by Anteeo
ANTEEOP, 3 years old, by Anteeo

ANTEEO. Standard 7868. Record, 2:16 1-4, by Stanford's Electioneer, and dam Columbine.

DESCRIPTIONS, PEDIGREES AND CONDITIONS.

"SUNSET" is a rich, dark bay, small star on forehead, portion of hind left foot white; was foaled March 11, 1 85; is by ANTEEO and the inbred HAMBLETONIAN mare, BESSIE G, she by KING PHILLIP, son of WHIPPLE'S HAMBLETONIAN. He is 16 1 2 hands high, and weighs 1,1 0 lbs. He is of perfect build and splendid action cool headed and great speed for his size, having trotted a trial mile as a three-year-old in 2:4. He then entered heavy in the stud and was matched against Whalebone at the Healdsburg races November 3, 188 , winning just as he pleased in three straight heats; time, 2:47, 2 46 1-2, 2:52 1-2. He was then matched for a race to come off last Thanksgiving Day at Petaluma but owing to the heavy rains the event did not take place. A few days previous to Thanksgiving Day Mr. Lawrence worked Sunset out and then he trotted three square miles and heats in 2:33¼, 2:34 and 2:37.

SUNSET will be bred to 40 mares only, at $50 each, no colt no pay.

"ANTEEOF" is a jet black, was foaled April 13, 1886, is 16¼ hands high, and weighs 1,200 lbs., has a very fine, heavy black mane and tail; is well proportioned, moves majestically, is of easy, lofty carriage; is symmetrical, in fact is a beautiful horse. He was sired by Anteeo and the O. A. Taylor mare "Nance," her dam, was raised by Dr. Oliver Plummer, of Consumnes, Cal., and sired by "Napoleon"; Napoleon was foaled May 29, 1 56, and raised by James Kyle of Butler County, Ohio. He was sired by Benj. Sweet's horse Bellfounder, and he by Old Bellfounder, his dam was sired by Doc. Daniel Mulligan's horse, Cadmus, G. G. sire the celebrated Eclipse; his G. dam was sired by Big Shakespeare, G. G., sires dam by Messenger and Expedition.

ANTEEOF will be bred to 25 mares only, at $50 each. No Colt, no pay.

"ANTEEOP" is a rich seal brown; was foaled March 7, 1887; by Anteeo and the inbred Hambletonian mare Bessie G., also dam of Sunset, his full brother and Midget his full sister; he is 15 1-2 hands high and weighs 95 lbs, and measures 26 inches around the arm, good head, fine neck, full, broad breast; withers and rump on nearly equal line, well proportioned bones, ankle, shoulders, loins and hips; strong legs all around, with great muscular development and splendid sinews; wirey pasterns and sound, compact feet; the lines from hip to hoof show power and speed; stands square and has excellent action, has a superb lustrous coat of rich deep brown fur of seal color without defect; an even, honest trotter, and has gone the mile as a two-year-old in 2:42, the last quarter in 38 seconds; is intelligent and of high spirit, with much temper, but is not vicious, has very fine eyes, is a handsome, showy colt; attractive in harness.

ANTEEOP will be bred to 15 mares only, at $25. No Colt, no pay.

SEASON to commence February 1st, ending July 1, 1890. Book now ready. Apply to John H. Lawrence, "Manager and Trainer," on my fruit and hop ranch, 1 mile east of Court House, on Sonoma road. Excellent pasture furnished with running water, also dry knolls with oak shelter, at $3 per month for mares. Two of the above stallions will be for sale after the expiration of the their stud season.

GUY E. GROSSE,

SANTA ROSA, SONOMA CO., CAL.

The Trotting Stallion

Guide 2:29

(At Four Years)

Will make the season of 1890 at the SANTA RITA RANCH, about one mile North of Pleasanton.

DESCRIPTION.

GUIDE is a handsome seal brown, five years old, stands 15¼ hands high, and weighs 1035 pounds. He is of fine form, level headed, intelligent, and comes from blood lines that are noted for the qualities of speed and gameness.

PEDIGREE.

GUIDE 2:28¼

Director, 2:17 — Sire of Direct, 2 18¼. Margaret S., 2:19¼.
- Dictator 113 — Sire of 23 trotters and 8 pacers in 2:30.
  - Hambletonian 10.
  - Clara, by American Star 14.
- Dolly — Dam of Onward, 2:25¼, Thorndale, 2:22¼.
  - Mambrino Chief 11.
  - Fannie, by Ben Franklin.

Imogene
- Norwood 522 — Sire of Tommy Norwood, 2:26½.
  - Hambletonian 10.
  - Lady Fallis, by American Star 14.
- daughter of
  - American Star 14.
  - daughter of Harry Clay 45.

The attention of breeders is especially called to the above pedigree as showing 3 crosses of American Star.

GUIDE trotted into the 2 30 list last season with little training, and he will trot into the 2:20 list the coming season, barring accidents.

Guide's sire has a record of 2:17, made in a five heat race, and Guide is closely related to Phallas, who made a record of 2 13¾ in a fourth heat, and to Jay-Eye-See, record 2:10.

TWO HUNDRED AND FIFTY DOLLARS will be given to the owner of the first of the produce of Guide put in the 2:30 list, and $100 to each one after the first.

TERMS—$75 for the season, with the usual return privileges.

Admiro,

Sire Admiral; dam by San Bruno, by Easton's David Hill.

This magnificent horse is a handsome bay, eight years old; stands 17 1-2 hands high, and weighs 1450 pounds He is very speedy for a large horse, and breeds fine large carriage horses. His produce possess every qualification of the Cleveland Bay, with the added qualities of speed and endurance resulting from his high trotting breeding.

TERMS—$35 for the season, with usual return privileges.

Will stand three days each week at Santa Rita Ranch, Pleasanton, and at A. T. Hatch's Ranch "Alnono," Alamo, Contra Costa County, alternately. All mares sent care of SMITH & SUTHERLAND, Pleasanton, will be taken in charge of on arrival, and will receive the best care and attention in any manner the owners may desire. Good pasturage at $4 per month. Only a limited number of approved mares will be served by this horse this season.

No responsibility assumed for escapes or accidents. For further particulars, address

SMITH & SUTHERLAND, Pleasanton,

or A. T. HATCH, care Palace Hotel, San Francisco.

FOR SALE.

A Mohawk Chief BROODMARE

and a

Director Colt, 6 months old.

For particulars address or apply to ANCON HOTEL, 9 and 11 Pacific Street, San Francisco.

Pedigrees Tabulated

IN THE MOST ARTISTIC MANNER.

Giving speed performers under sires and dams. Catalogues compiled. Stallion cards and circulars written up ready for the press. Pedigree blanks for sale. Prices reasonable. Horses bought and sold on commission. References furnished.

R. Y. HARDIN.

306 W. Madison St., Chicago, Ill.

SAN DIEGO, 8776.

SAN DIEGO 8776

Alcona Clay 2756
- Alcona 730 — Sire of Flora Belle, 2:24, Clay Duke, 2:31½, etc.
  - Almont 33 — Sire of Westmont, 2:15¾, Piedmont, 2:17¼, Puritan, 2:16, and 33 others in 2:30 list.
  - by Mambrino Chief 11 — Sire of Lady Thorne, 2:18¼.
- Madonna — Dam of Del Rey, trial 2:31, Alcona Jr., 2:41, sire of Silas Skinner, trial 2:23¼.
  - Cassius M. Clay Jr. 22 — Sire of Durango, 2:23¾, Harry Clay, 2:29¾, and sire of dam of Happy Thought, 2:22¾, and others.
  - by Joe Downing 710. — Sire of Abe Downing, 2:20¾, D. Jamison, 2:28, and sire of dams of Kentucky Hambletonian, 2:27, ... rena, 2:15, and others.

Fontana — Dam of Flora Belle, 2:24, Silas Skinner, trial 2:23¼.
- Almont 33 — Sire of 36 in 2:30 list, 49 sons and 22 daughters that have produced 2:30 performers.
- Fanny Williams — Dam of Bay Chieftain, 2:28¼.
  - Abdallah 15 — Sire of Goldsmith Maid, 2:14, Thorndale, 2:21¼ also Almont, Belmont, Jim Monroe, etc.
  - by Denmark (thoroughbred).

SAN DIEGO is dark seal brown, three years old, and trotted one-quarter miles in 40 seconds as a two year old.

This grand young horse, and, barring accidents, will make a fast record next fall.

He will be allowed a limited number of mares, at $50 for the season. Mares not proving with foal to be returned free 1891. Best of pasture for mares at $4 per month, but no liability for accidents or escapes.

He will make the season from February 1st to June 1st at Napa Fair Grounds. For further particulars, address or call on

H. B. STARR, Race Track, Napa, Cal.,

or FRED W. LOEBER, St. Helena

The Thoroughbred Stallion

INTRUDER

Will make the Season of 1890 at Agricultural Park, SACRAMENTO.

Bay Horse, foaled 1871, bred by Sir L. Newman, England. Imported by D. D. Withers, Esq., New York.

By Crater, Son of Orlando and Vesuvienne by Gladiator.

1st dam Lady Bountiful by Rataplan (Rataplan is own brother to Stockwell, and winner of 42 races, including the Doncaster Cup and 19 Queen's Plates, and proved himself the most distinguished race horse of his day in England).

2d dam Plentiful by Don John (the winner of St. Leger and Doncaster Cup).

3d dam Plenty by Bay Middleton (winner of the Derby and Two Thousand Guinea Stakes).

4th dam Plenary, own sister of Plenipotentiary, by Emilius. (Both Emilius and Plenipotentiary were Derby winners).

5th dam Harriet, dam of the renowned Plenipotentiary by Pericles.

6th dam by Selim, winner of the One Thousand Guinea stakes.

7th dam by Pypilina, by Sir Peter.

8th dam Rally, by Trumpeter.

9th dam Fancy, by Florizel. Fancy was full sister to Diomed, the first Derby winner in England, and after his importation into this country, sired the illustrious Sir Archy, etc. See English Stud Book.

Imported INTRUDER is a beautiful bay, standing fully 16 hands high, of great length and substance, and descends through close and strong currents from the most illustrious winners and winning lines of blood of which the English Stud Book bears record.

A careful review of the first six crosses of the pedigree of INTRUDER will show nine Derby winners; five St. Leger winners; two winners of The Oaks; two winners of the Two Thousand Guineas; two winners of the One Thousand Guineas; one Goodwood Cup winner; one Cesarwich Cup winner; one Cambridgeshire Stakes winner, and four Doncaster Cups, in addition to a great number of Steeplechases and other races of less import.

INTRUDER, at the great fair held at St. Louis, Mo., in 1875, was awarded the highest stallion honors—the blue ribbon and the $500 purse—in the sweepstakes ring for stallion of any age or blood. The list of competitors embraced the large number of thirty-three animals, and they represented England, Canada, Kentucky, Tennessee, and other states. He also took first premium in his class and in sweepstakes for the best stallion of any age or breed at the State Fair at Peoria, Ill., 1882. He is the sire of Tidal Wave, George Hakes, Bernice and April Fool.

INTRUDER is the sire of Interpose, who is the dam of Spokane, winner of the Kentucky Derby, in which he beat the great horse Proctor Knott and broke the record.

TERMS: $50 for the season. Mares not proving with foal can be returned the next season free of charge. Good pasturage at $4 per month. Mares cared for in any manner owners may desire, and fed on hay and grain, either or both, at reasonable rates. While every precaution will be taken, no responsibility will be assumed for escapes or accidents. Mares sent from a distance in care of the undersigned, will be met and taken to the park. For further particulars, address

T. J. KNIGHT.

Agricultural Park, Sacramento.

Sunny Side Breeding Farm.

Admiral 488.

Foaled 1862—Sired by Volunteer 55, Son of Rysdyk's Hambletonian 10.

First dam Lady Pierson by Cassius M. Clay (Neaves') 20; second dam by Diamond; third dam a running mare said to be thoroughbred. He is fitted in an eminent degree to produce colts that will in all respects justify his patrons in their expectations.

Admiral is the sire of Huntress, record 2:27¼, Sister, 2:19¼, Perhelion, 2:25, Nona Y., 2:26, and others equally as promising, but have not had the advantage of track work. He will serve a limited number of approved mares at $50 the season, with usual return privilege. Season ending August 1, 1890. No liability for accidents or escapes.

KING DAVID 2576.

Bay Stallion—Foaled 1883.

Sired by Admiral 488, dam Black Flora (the dam of Huntress, 2:27¼, Sister, 2:19¼, Perhelion, 2:25, Nona Y., 2:26), by Black Prince.

King David is one of the best gets of Admiral. He has a good disposition, kind to drive, smooth and even-gaited, and can speed fast. Barring accidents, he will trot in the twenties this Fall. His colts are large, rangy, and well finished. Will serve a limited number of mares at $30 the season, to end July 1, 1890 Every precaution will be taken to prevent accidents and escapes, but no liability will be assumed. Pasturage $4 per month.

Sunny Side Farm is situated two miles east of Vallejo, on the Sulphur Spring road. For further particulars, address

FRANK DRAKE,

Vallejo. Cal.

HOLLYWOOD BREEDING FARM

MOUNTAIN BOY 4841.

Br s MOUNTAIN BOY, 4841, bred by Charles Backman, Orange County, New York, foaled 1882, sire Kentucky Prince 2470, dam Elise, sister to Elaine, by Messenger Duroc 106; grandam Green Mountain Maid, 3d dam, Shanghai Mary, will serve a limited number of mares at $100 the season.

ELECTION.

Bay stallion ELECTION, bred at Senator Stanford's Palo Alto Stock Farm, foaled 1884, sire Electioneer, dam Lizzie H. by Whipple's Hambletonian 725, grandam Lizzie Harris (by Comus son of Green Bashaw 50), great grandam by Arnold Harris, thoroughbred.

Election is one of the handsomest bloodlike sons of Electioneer and with his thoroughbred cross through Arnold Harris should prove invaluable as a sire. TERMS, $100 the season.

KAFIR.

B c KAFIR, bred by L. J. Rose, Los Angeles, foaled 1887, sire Alcazar, 2 20½, dam Flower Girl by Arthurton, sire of Arab, 2:15, grandam Flora by General McClellan, 144, sire of three in 2:30 list, great grandam by Langford, he by Williamson's Belmont, will serve a limited number of mares at $50 the season.

WOODSIDE.

Ch c WOODSIDE, sire Woodnut, 2:16½; 1st dam Veronica by Alcona, 730; 2nd dam Fontana by Almont, 33; 3rd dam Fannie Williams by Alexander's Abdallah, 15. Book full.

MART BOORHEM.

B c MART BOORHEM, by Sydney, 2:19¾; 1st dam Towhead by Echo, This colt is a full brother to Nicholas who showed a mile in 2:27½ at three years old. TERMS, $25 the season.

REVEILLE.

The well known thoroughbred stallion REVEILLE by Shiloh, dam by Norfolk. Reveille is a brother to John Treat and is the sire of Tycoon and Gladstone. TERMS, $25 the season.

Hollywood is nicely situated three miles from Vallejo on the Napa road. Good pasturage and every care will be taken of mares at reasonable rates. For further particulars, apply,

B. C. HOLLY, Vallejo.

Bay Rose

REGISTERED No. 9814.

Record 2:20 1-2 Third Heat

Will make the season of 1890, ending July 1st, at the SANTA ROSA STOCK FARM, (formerly Santa Rosa Race Track), SANTA ROSA.

DESCRIPTION.

BAY ROSE is a dark bay or brown, with black points, 16¼ hands high, and weighs 1150 pounds. He is remarkably intelligent, of good disposition, and a pure-gaited trotter. He was foaled in 1881. His colts are large, stylish, rangy animals, and inherit the qualities of speed and endurance.

PEDIGREE.

BAY ROSE 9814

Sultan, 2:24 — Sire of 10 in the 2:30 list.
- The Moor 870 — SIRE OF Beautiful Bells ... 2:; Del Sur ... 2:; Inez ... 2:; Sir Guy ... 2:; Sultan ... 2:; Tommy Gates ... 2:
- Sultana.

Madam Baldwin
- The Moor 870 — Sire of 8 in the 2:30 list
- by Ben Lippincott, by Williamson's Belmont.

TERMS: $100 FOR THE SEASON.

Good pasturage $3 per month. First-class care is taken of mares in any manner that owners may desire, but no responsibility assumed for escapes or accidents. Limited to a few approved mares.

For further particulars, address

THOS. BONNER,

Santa Rosa Stock Farm, Santa Rosa.

Or apply to

IRA PIERCE,

728 Montgomery Street, S. F., Cal.

THE BUCKINGHAM.

OLD STRAIGHT WHISKIES.

141 Montgomery Street.

308 Bush Street, S. F.

M. J. BALFE, Proprietor.

11,623.

RECORD 2:30.

Colt, bred by Thomas Smith of Vallejo, Cal. 1886 by Mambrino Chief, Jr., 11,622, record 1st dam Fanny Rose by Vick's Ethan Allen 6, sire of Prince Allen 2:27. 2nd dam Jenny thoroughbred, dam of Prince Allen 2:27. Will a limited number of mares at $50 for the season. Mares not proving with foal may be returned season free.

ambrino Chief, Jr.

11,622.

RECORD 2:34 1 2.

of George Washington, record 2:30 at three old. Bay horse bred by Rufus Ingalls of Belvedere. By McDonald Chief 3:53. First dam Venus by Mambrino Patchen 58. 2nd dam by Wardlow's Shakespeare. 3rd dam Lone Gold. 4th dam by Silver Heels. Not been in the stud b fore. He was 4 years old he served a few mares, and his colts all show style an' form.

... for the season $40. For further particulars address

THOMAS SMITH,
Vallejo, Cal.

lector 2170.

Sire of J. R.

Three-Year Old Record 2:24.

...ed by Electioneer 125, sire of Sunol, three-year 2:10½, Palo Alto, 2:12¼, etc.; dam Gilberta by Low 686, sire of Clay, 2:25½, etc.

Second dam Lady Gilbert (grandam of Lot Slo... 2:17½) by General Knox 140 (sire of Lady Maud, ..., and many others).

TERMS.

$0 for the season. Book full for 1890.

L. A. RICHARDS,
Grayson, Stanislaus Co., Cal.

The Thoroughbred Stallion

Three Cheers

Will make the season of 1890 at

Sacramento.

PEDIGREE.

Imp. Hurrah.... Newminster. Touchstone, by Camel; Beeswing, by Dr. Syntax
Jovial .... Bay Middleton, by Sultan; Sister to Grey Momus, by Comus
Young Fashion. Imp. Monarch. Imp. Priam, by Emilius; imp. Delphine, by Whisker
Fashion....... Imp. Trustee, by Catton; Bonnets o' Blue, by Sir Charles

Hurrah was imported by John Reber, of Lancaster, Ohio, a locality where there were but few breeders of thoroughbreds. Under these disadvantages he sired a long list of winners. His sire Newminster, won the St. Ledger 1851, and his dam, Jovial by Bay Middleton, winner of the Derby 1836. Newminister by Touchstone, winner St. Ledger 1834. Dam Beeswing, winner of 54 races out of 64 starts, by Dr. Syntax, winner of the Doncaster Cup, 1837—40—41—42, the only horse that ever accomplished that feat.

On the side of the dam Three Cheers is equally well related. Young Fashion was the dam of Surprise, Scotland (the only horse that ever beat Asteroid a mat), Liverpool, Columbia, and Bonnie Kate, the dam of Little Buttercup, and the flying Bonnie Lizzie. His grandam, Fashion was the greatest race mare of her day and beat Boston in that historical match at four mile heats, which is recorded as one of the greatest events in the annals of the turf.

Horsemen who are qualified to judge, pronounce Three Cheers to be the finest type of the Newminster line in America.

LOCATION.

THREE CHEERS will be located at the Arcade Training Stable, Rancho del Paso. This place has been selected for the reason that first class pasturage has been secured there for the exclusive use of these mares, and the other facilities to be obtained there for the care of mares (especially mares in foal) are better than can be found elsewhere in the locality.

TERMS.

$60 for the season with the usual return privileges. Pasturage $5 per month. Mares cared for as owners may desire at bottom rates for grain and hay. All bills payable before the mare is removed.

Mares shipped care of WM. IRVINE, Pacific Stables, Sacramento, will be properly cared for and sent to the ranch without delay.

Three Cheers will be in charge of one of the most experienced and competent stud grooms in the State, who will exercise every care, but no reponsibility assumed for accidents or escapes.

For further particulars apply to Louis Crissler, at the ranch; Wm. Irvine, Pacific Stables, Second St., Sacramento; or to the owner,

E. S. CULVER,
318 Bush St., San Francisco.

GROVER CLAY

Bay Stallion, Black Points,

15 3-4 hands high.

Bred by W. W. Traylor, San Francisco.

BY ELECTIONEER.

First dam Maggie Norfolk by Norfolk, son of Lexington, he by Boston. Second dam Tilda Quill by Billy Cheatham he by Cracken, and he by Boston. Third dam by Dorsey's Golddust.

TERMS.

Will make the season of 1890 at the Training Stables of Denis Gannon, near Oakland Trotting Park, at $60 the season, payable at time of service. Season to commence February 1st and ending July 1st. Proper care of mares will be taken, but no responsibility incurred for accidents or escapes. Address,

DENIS GANNON, Oakland, Cal.

DEXTER PRINCE.

This Royally-bred Stallion will make the Season of 1890 at the LIVE OAKS Breeding Farm, 2 miles from Lodi, San Joaquin County, Cal.

DESCRIPTION.

DEXTER PRINCE is a blood bay, 16 hands high, weighs over 1,100 pounds; has great power and substance, and the highest finish. When two years old, at Palo Alto, he was timed quarters by Gov. Stanford in 37½ seconds and he was driven eighths by Mr. Marvin at a faster rate of speed than that. He is a sure foal getter, and invariably sires foals of good size, of fine form and finish, and the highest rate of speed.

PEDIGREE.

By KENTUCKY PRINCE, the sire of Guy, 2:10¾, Spofford, 2:18¾, Company, 2:19¾, Bayonne Prince, 2:21 1-4, Fred Folger, 2:20¾, and a score more in the 2:30 list.

First dam LADY DEXTER, full sister of the greatest of trotters, Dexter, and the greatest of sires, Dictator, the sire of Director, 2:17, Phallas, 2:13¾, in a fourth heat, and Jay-Eye-See, 2:10.

Second dam Clara, the dam of Dexter, 2:17 1-4, Dictator, Astoria 2:29 1-4, and Alma, 2:28¾. Clara was by American Star, that has 24 daughters that have produced 2:30 or better trotters.

Third dam the McKinstry mare, the dam of Shark, 2:27¾. HAMBLETONIAN, the grandsire of DEXTER PRINCE, has 40 trotters in the 2:30 list, 44 daughters that have produced 2:30 trotters, and more than 100 sons that have sired 2:30 trotters.

CLARK CHIEF, the grandsire on the sire's side, was the sire of performing and producing sons and daughters.

DEXTER PRINCE has faster blood lines, on both sides, than any other stallion in the world—Guy 2:10¾ and Jay-Eye-See, 2:10.

KENTUCKY PRINCE is one of the best bred and speediest stallions in the world. David Bonner, in the presence of Governor Stanford, timed him when he trotted a 2:10 gait. He is by Clark Chief, one of the great broodmare sires; his first dam is Kentucky Queen by Morgan Eagle, son of Hale's Green Mountain Morgan, 2nd dam by Blythe's Whip, 3rd dam by Martin's Brummier, 4th dam by Quicksilver 860, on through the strongest thoroughbred blood.

TERMS.

$100 for the season, with usual return privileges. Payable before mares are removed. Good pasture, and the best care furnished, but no responsibility assumed for accidents.

PREMIUM.

$250 will be given to the first of the produce of DEXTER PRINCE put in the 2:30 list, and $100 each after the first. Address

L. M. MORSE, Lodi, Cal.

2:10 1-2 ELECTIONEER 2:12 1-4

BAY STALLION	BROWN STALLION
ECLECTIC	**MORTIMER**
11,321	5,346
By Electioneer, dam Manette (full sister to Woodnut 2.16 1-2 Manon 2:21 and Maple, dam of Hattie D., three-year-old record 2 28¾) by Nutwood 2:18¾, etc., etc.	Four-year-old Record 2:27. By ELECTIONEER, dam MARTI, by Whipple's Hambletonian (sire of 15 in 2:30, and of dams of eight in 2:30). Second dam Ida Martin by Rifleman (sire of Col. Lewis 2:18¾).
Terms $100 for the Season.	**Terms $60 for the Season.**

Horses shipped via San Francisco may be consigned to J. W. MORSHEAD, City Front Stables, who will attend to their forwarding.

Season closes JULY 1st, 1890. Usual return privileges.

For urther particulars address owner,

WILFRED PAGE, Penns Grove,
Sonoma County, Cal

The Trotting Stallion

Silver Bow

Will make the season of 1890 at the Oakland Race Track

PEDIGREE.

SILVER BOW 11706, two-year-old record 2:37, is by Robert McGregor 647, 2:17¾ (sire of Bonnie McGregor, 2:13½, Earl McGregor, 2:21¾, Mac D., 2:30, McGregor Boy, 2:29½, Mark Time, 2:30, Roxie McGregor, 2:30¾) by Major Edsall 2:29, by Alexander's Abdallah 15—sire of Goldsmith Maid, 2:14—by Hambletonian 10—sire of Dexter, 2:17¾.

Robert McGregor's dam was Nancy Whitman by American Star 14, by Stockholm's American Star.

SILVER BOW'S first dam is Sadie by Hambletonian 10, sire of Geo. Wilkes, 2:22—sire of Guy Wilkes, 2:15¼—also Electioneer, sire of Sunol, three-year-old record, 2:10½, and Palo Alto, 2:12¾; second dam Lady Wynne by Wm. Welch 341; third dam Elenora Margrave by imp. Margrave.

DESCRIPTION.

SILVER BOW is a handsome bay, no white; 15-2¼ hands high; weighs 1075 pounds; of fine form, with the best of legs and a clean-cut, intelligent head. Is remarkably level-headed, seldom making a break; wears seven-ounce shoes in front. His record, 2:37, is no mark of his speed; he can beat 30 easy, and with his gilt-edge breeding, he is just what he ought to be, a trotter sired by a trotter whose dam was herself a trotter and his grandam the dam of two trotters. His dam Sadie being by Hambletonian 10, shows him to be bred from the cream of the trotting blood.

TERMS: $50 for the season. Mares not proving in foal returnable for the season of 1891 free of charge. Good pasturage and first-class care taken of mares for $5 per month. No responsibilities assumed for escapes or accidents. For further particulars, address

Limited to 15 approved mares.
Season to end June 1st, 1890.

P. J. WILLIAMS,
Care Race Track, Oakland, Cal.

GRAND MOOR, 2374.

Grand Moor 2374.
- Moor 870.
  - Clay Pilot 93. Sire of 2 in 2:30 list.
  - Belle of Wabash.
  - Sire of Beautiful Bells ... 2:29¼
  - Sire of Sable (dam of Sable Wilkes) ... 2:18
  - Sire of Sultan ... 2:24
  - Sire of Tommy Gates ... 2:24
  - Sire of Del Sur ... 2:24¼
  - Sire of Sir Guy ... 2:28¼
  - Beautiful Bells is the dam of Hinda Rose, 2:19½ as a 3-year-old, Palo Alto Belle, 2:22¼, Chimes, St. Bell, 2:24¼, Bell Boy (3 years) 2:19¼.
  - Sultan, 2:24 (sire of Stamboul 2:12¼) has 19 in 2:30 list.
- Vashti.
  - Dam of Don Tomas, who got a record of 2:30 in 1889.
  - Mambrino Patchen 58. Sire of 14 in 2:30 list. Sire of the dam of Guy Wilkes, 2:15¼; also sire of 20 stallions and 18 mares with get in 2:30 list.
  - Kate Taber. By Mambrino Messenger, he by Mambrino Paymaster.

Foaled 1876. Black. Sixteen hands high. Bred by L. J. Rose

A horse of highest form and quality; of great excellence in every point; a type of his celebrated family; of marked individuality, spirit and endurance; never properly trained or raced, but shows the possession of great speed; perfectly manageable in the stable and on the road and track.

As he is sired by The Moor 870, a son of CLAY PILOT, out of Vashti by MAMBRINO PATCHEN, he is a most valuable cross for mares of other families. THE MOOR sired Beautiful Bells and the dams of Sable Wilkes and Margaret 2:28 (dam of Regal Wilkes, 2-year-old record 2:20½).

MAMBRINO PATCHEN is regarded as the unsurpassed sire of broodmares, having, among many others, sired the dam of Guy Wilkes and of Wm. L. (the sire of Axtell), and a son of his sired the dam of Axtell. The public sales this year have demonstrated with renewed emphasis the value of The Moor and Mambrino Patchen strains of blood. For combining particularly with the Hambletonians it may be called "the ready money cross."

GRAND MOOR will make the season of 1890 for a time at the Oakland Race Track and afterwards at my Ranch, fifteen miles from Oakland. Mares can be delivered at the race track to the groom in charge. Pasture at $5 per month. For other food, if requested, an additional charge will be made.

TERMS, $150 for the season, with privileges of return if the horse does not change hands. Every care exercised, but no liability for escapes or accidents.

H. I. THORNTON, 504 Kearny Street.

STOCK FARM.

Season of 1890.

STEINWAY 1808.

Three-Year-Old Record 2:25 3-4.

Sire of STRATHWAY, three year old record 2:26, and sire of the dam of BOURBON RUSSELL 2:30.

By STRATHMORE 408; sire of 31 in the 2:30 list; sire of 6 dams of 8 in the 2:30 list, and sire of 3 sires of 3 in 2:30 list.

1st dam ABBESS (dam of Solo 2:28, and Soprano, dam of C. F. Clay 2:18, Eminence 2:27 and Strathbridge, 3 year old record 2:28½) by ALBION, sire of VANITY FAIR 2:24½, and of the dam of FAVORITE 2:25½.

2nd dam by MARSHALL NEY.

3rd dam by BERTRAND, a son of SIR ARCHY.

TERMS—$100 for the season.

CHARLES DERBY 4907

Brown Horse, Foaled 1885.

By STEINWAY 1808.

1st dam by the great ELECTIONEER, sire of SUNOL 3 year old record 2:10½, Palo Alto 2:12¼, etc., etc.

2nd dam FANNY MALONE, by NIAGARA.

3rd dam FANNY WICKHAM, by HERALD.

4th dam by Imp. TRUSTEE.

TERMS—$100 for the season

Pasturage $5 per month. Accidents and escapes at owner's risk. Mares consigned to the farm should be sent to Fashion Stables, Oakland; Geary & Grindle's Stable, Haywards; or to Bennett's Stable, Martinez; from and to which places they will be delivered free of charge. Address

COOK STOCK FARM,
Danville, Contra Costa, Co., Cal.

The Trotting Stallion

ARBITRATOR

Will make the Season of 1890 at NILES, Alameda County.

PEDIGREE.

ARBITRATOR.
- Director 1989, 2:17 in a race, Sire of Direct, 4 yrs., 2:18½ in a race, Margaret S., 3 yrs., 2:19½ in a race, Guide, 4 yrs., 2:28½ in a race.
- Lady Earnest.
  - Speculation 928, sire of Oakland Maid, 2:22 in a race, Gracie S., 2:22 in a race, Crown Point, 2:24 in a race, He the sire of Valensin, 3 yrs., 2:23 in a race, Sire of Dam of Alfred G., 2:19½.
  - Lady Hibbard, dam of Lou Whipple, 2:26½ in a race.

Speculation's dam was Martha Washington, dam of Whipple's Hambletonian, sire of 15 in 2:30 and granddaughter of Burr's Napoleon, sire of Black Harry, who in 1850 won two miles in 5:14½. He sired Smith Burr, sire of Gen. Butler, 2:21, Wagon, 4:56½. He sired the dam of Fanny Mapes, dam of Jerome Eddy, 2:16½. He sired Telegraph, sire of dam of Rarus, 2:13¼.

DESCRIPTION.

ARBITRATOR was foaled 1885. He is of good size, fine conformation, and a beautiful seal brown.

TERMS.

Non-standard mares	$45
Standard mares by inheritance	35
Standard mares by performance or produce	25

For further particulars, address

H. A. MAYHEW, owner,
Niles, Alameda Co.

PASHA,

Registered No. 2039.

RECORD 2:36.

SIRE OF MORO 2:27.

Will make the present season at Linden, twelve miles east of STOCKTON.

Season commencing FEBRUARY 1st and ending JULY 1, 1890.

DESCRIPTION.

PASHA is a beautiful black; 16½ hands high, and weighs 1,240 pounds. He is a horse of beautiful symmetry and magnificent action.

PEDIGREE.

PASHA was sired by Sultan 1513, sire of Stamboul 2:12½, Ruby 2:19½, Alcazar 2:20½, Bay Rose 2:20½, and sixteen others with records below 2:30. First dam Madam Baldwin by The Moor 870; second dam Ben Lippincott by Belmont. Pasha is a full brother to Bay Rose, record 2:20½.

Sultan, by The Moor, sire of Beautiful Bells, dam of Hinda Rose, 2:19½, Bell Boy 2:19½, and Sable, dam of Sable Wilkes, three-year-old record 2:18. First dam Sultana, by Delmonico, sire of Derby 2:16, by Guy Miller, sire of Whipple's Hambletonian. Second dam by Mambrino Chief. Third dam by Downing's Bay Messenger. Fourth dam Miss Caudle, dam of Ericsson, four-year-old recor 2:30½.

Terms for the season, $50.

With privilege of returning mares that do not prove in foal next season free of charge.

Good pasturage at $2 per month. No responsibility will be assumed for accidents or escapes. Service fee payable before the removal of the mare.

For further particulars, address

D. BRYSON,
Linden C...

Valensin Stock Farm Stallion.

SIDNEY, 2:19 3-4.

At Eight Years of Age Sire of the following Fastest on Record:

FAUSTINO, yearling stallion, record of the world....2:35
FLEET, fastest yearling record in 1888....2:36
FLEET, fastest two-year-old filly in 1889....2:24
GOLD LEAF, fastest four-year-old Pacing record in the world....2:11½
ADONIS, fastest three-year-old Pacing Gelding in the world....2:14¾
ADONIS, four-year-old Gelding Pacing record....2:14

—Also the Sire of—

LONGWORTH, four years old....2:19
SISTER V., four years old (trial 2:23)....2:27
SANTA RITA....2:39
MEMO, two-year-old (three-year-old trial 2:20½)....2:49

And many others.

SIDNEY is the sire of Faustino 2:35, and Fleet 2:36, the two fastest yearlings the world has ever known by one sire, and his slowest yearling is faster than the great Electioneer's fastest.

Terms, $250, with usual return privileges, for a limited number of approved mares. Book nearly full.

Only eight more mares can be taken for Season of '90.

Pasturage $5 per month. Reasonable charges if fed hay and grain. Best of care taken of mares, but positively no responsibility assumed for accidents or escapes. For further particulars address

G. VALENSIN, Pleasanton, Cal.

MEMO.

The Best Son of SIDNEY

Will Make the Season of 1890 at the OAKLAND RACE TRACK

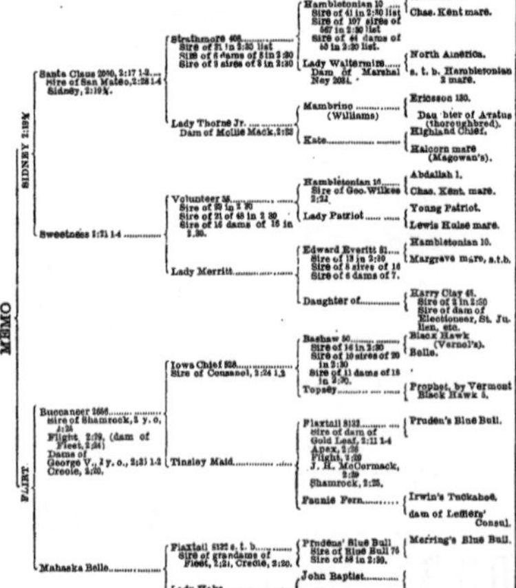

MEMO is, as can be seen at a glance, one of the best bred young stallions in service, having three crosses of Rysdyk's Hambletonian and one of Harry Clay, the sire of Green Mountain Maid (dam of Electioneer, etc.), while Long Island Black Hawk and Flaxtail also contribute to his blood. Sidney (Memo's sire) is universally known as the best young sire in the world, a producer of extreme speed at an early age.

PERFORMANCES.

MEMO trotted in public in his two year-old form, obtaining a record of 2:49, though he was close to Grandee in a race on the Bay District Track, the second heat of which was made in 2:31 1-2, the first in 2:32. He exhibited phenomenal speed when three years old, and had it not been for a slight strain of his fore fetlock, there is little question that he would have shown in public very close to the best record. On the Oakland track he was timed a mile in 2:20 1-2, and frequently trotted quarters in from 32 1-2 to 34 seconds.

As a four-year-old Memo only started once—at Sacramento—when, although out of condition, he showed great speed, and improving as he went on, great hopes were entertained of his going well down in the 'teens at the P. C. T. H. B. A. meeting, but after showing several very fast miles his leg filled and he was laid up for the season. He is sixteen hands high, and of powerful build throughout. His color is a glossy black, with both fore-feet white. His disposition is all that could be desired, and his action superb. He is a sure foal getter, only one mare being reported not in foal during his last season.

TERMS, $100, with usual return privileges, for a limited number of mares. Season to close JUNE 15th, when he will be prepared for track purposes. Pasturage $5 per month. Have leased the cricket ground adjoining the track for pasturage, where there is fine feed. Reasonable charges if fed hay and grain. Best of care taken of mares in any manner owners may desire, but positively no responsibility assumed for accidents or escapes. For further particulars address

J. P. KERR, 313 Bush Street, San Francisco,
or, JOHN ROWEN, Race Track, Oakland, Cal.

SHAW CARTS and SULKIES

For light road or track use, manufactured from the best selected material. Combines lightness with elegance and ease to riders. Weighs 70 to 100 lbs. Used by the best horsemen on this coast. Inspection invited.

ONE CAFFREY SULKY FOR SALE AT A BARGAIN.

CARRIAGES & Light VEHICLES

Manufactured to Order.

W. E. SHAW,
1621 MARKET STREET, SAN FRANCISCO, CAL.

REPAIRING DONE—ALL WORK WARRANTED.

Pleasanton Stock Farm Co.'s Stallions.

DIRECTOR, 2:17.

Director's book is open for 15 good mares more than already booked for the season of 1890, at $300 each.

This is the cheapest service fee ever charged for a stallion, taking into consideration his BREEDING and RACE RECORD and the RACE RECORDS OF HIS COLTS.

Season to commence February 15th and close August 1st.

CORRECTOR, Five Years Old.

Sire Director 2:17, dam Brainey, she by Echo. Echo sired by Rysdyk's Hambletonian out of Fanny Felter, by Magnolia he by Seely's American Star. Brainey's dam Lady Dudley, she by Tom Dudley by Blacknose, a son of Medoc, he by American Eclipse. Lady Dudley's dam by Bertrand, Jr., a son of Bertrand.

CORRECTOR is a rich seal brown 15¾ hands high, and is the fastest young stallion in the world under the same conditions, never having been off the farm where raised and never been shod or driven for speed before last Christmas, and can trot quarters now in 35 seconds, a 2:20 gait.

He will be allowed to serve ten good mares, at $100 each for the season, which closes June 1st.

DECORATOR, Four Years Old.

Sire Director 2:17, dam Chess, sired by Cardinal 2.37, trial 2:28, he by Gen. Gifford's Morgan, dam of Cardinal, sired by Joe Gales of Ohio, he by Marlborough out of the Duchess of Marlborough by Southern Eclipse; second dam old Duchess of Marlborough by Sir Archy; third dam by imp Diomed. Decorator's second dam a Morgan and Messenger mare.

Decorator is a light bay 16 hands high, and with but little handling for speed has shown eighths in 17½ seconds, a 2:20 gait.

He will be allowed to serve ten good mares at $50 each for the season, which closes June 1st.

Mares not proving with foal may be returned next season free of charge of service fees to the same stallion, if he is still in our possession; however, the company reserves the right to return the fee instead of giving service.

Pasturage $4 per month; hay and grain extra. Accidents and escapes at owner's risk.

Service fees due at time of service, and must be paid, together with pasturage, etc., before mares are taken away, or a good approved note given, payable August 1st, 1890, at which date all bills must be settled.

For further information call or address **M. SALISBURY, 320 Sansome Street, Room 26, San Francisco, or**

PLEASANTON STOCK FARM CO.,
Pleasanton, Alameda Co., Cal.

SOUTHER FARM

P. O. Box 208. San Leandro, Cal.

1½ miles northwest of San Leandro; 8 miles southeast of Oakland. Turn off county road between above places at "Stanley Road," ¾ mile north of San Leandro.

Horses boarded at all times in any manner desired. Best of care but no responsibility for accidents. Colts broken and handled for the road or track. Terms reasonable.

Glen Fortune,	Jester D,	El Benton,	Figaro,
By Electioneer.	By Almont.	By Electioneer.	Hambletonian 725
$50 for 1889.	$50 for 1890.	Limited to 5 mares.	Limited to 12 mares
		Book Full.	Book Full.

THE SOUTHER FARM

Has Green Feed the Year Round,

and feeds Hay in connection with the green feed, which a horse must have if he is to thrive. Every animal is given

A Dry, Warm Place to Sleep,

No matter how stormy the weather. All Stock under cover when it rains.

VISITORS WELCOME ANY DAY EXCEPT SUNDAY.

How to Get Stock to the Souther Farm.

The Souther Farm is one and a half miles northeast of San Leandro and eight miles southeast of Oakland. The stables are about one mile east of the county road, which runs between Oakland and San Leandro. The place to turn off is at Stanley Road, where a large signboard of the farm is placed. Guide boards will be found at every cross road. In any ordinary weather the roads are very good, and they are fairly good after the unusually heavy rainfall of the past winter.

All stock sent from San Francisco may be brought over by Garcia's Express, No. 3 Market street, San Francisco. They also have an order box outside of Hawley Bros.' Hardware house on the corner of Market and Beale streets. The express leaves San Francisco on the Creek route boat, which starts at 1:30, but all orders should be in the order box at Market and Beale streets by 10 o'clock, or at the office, No. 3 Market street, by 11 o'clock at the latest. In the case of very young or very valuable horses, the Souther Farm will send reliable men to lead or drive over any stock that will not lead behind a wagon. A small charge will be made in such cases, to cover the extra expense incurred.

Horses are very easily taken from Oakland to the farm, and where it is inconvenient for owners to bring them or send them, the farm will send after anything that is to come. On horses that stay three months or over there is no charge for getting or delivering. Where a horse stays a short time the actual time and expense only is charged to him.

Horses can be shipped by rail from almost all parts of the State to San Leandro. Always notify the Farm several days before shipping anything, and then men will be on hand to receive stock on arrival. The railroad station is but two miles from the Souther Farm, and the agent invariably gives immediate notice of the arrival of any stock consigned to the above farm, but when word is sent to the farm in good season by letter or telegram, the animals sent are saved waiting a couple of hours in the car.

Passenger trains leave San Francisco (from the broad gauge ferry) and First and Broadway, Oakland, at frequent intervals during the day. There are several trains from San José to San Leandro on both the broad and narrow gauge railroads; the broad gauge, by way of Niles, is much more convenient for getting to the farm. There are trains each day from Sacramento, Stockton and Livermore to San Leandro. In ordinary weather it is a short and pleasant drive from Oakland to the Souther Farm or from San Francisco to the Farm by way of the Creek route ferry boat. Always notify the Souther Farm just when you will arrive at San Leandro, and some one will meet you at the station. If you do not recognize the farm conveyance ask the stage driver, who will point it out.

Write to the above address for references, circulars and price lists. Terms reasonable.

GILBERT TOMPKINS, Proprietor.

SANMATEO STOCKFARM

HOME OF GUY WILKES,

Record, 2:15 1-4.

Guy Wilkes' Book is full for 1890 and 1891, and positively no more mares will be received.

Sable Wilkes, three-year-old record 2:18, will be allowed to serve 25 mares in addition to those already engaged at $250 the season of 1890. SABLE Wilkes, 15½ hands, black horse, by Guy Wilkes, first dam Sable by The Moor; second dam Gretchen by Mambrino Pilot; third dam Kitty Kirkman by Canada Chief; fourth dam by Fanning's Tobe; fifth dam by imp. Leviathan.

Leo Wilkes, brown horse, four years, 16 hands, full brother to Sable Wilkes, will be allowed to serve 30 mares at $100 the season.

Mares not proving with foal may be returned the following season free of service fee. Parties engaging the services of any of the above horses must send a deposit of 10 per cent. of service money with engagement. Pasturage $6 per month, and when the condition of the animal requires it, hay or grain, or both, are fed, the charge will be $12 50 per month. Good care will be taken of all mares sent to the Farm, but no liability will be assumed for accidents or escapes.

All bills are due at time of service, but must be paid by August 1st of each year. No stock will be allowed to leave the place until all bills are paid.

WILLIAM CORBITT.
San Mateo Stock Farm.

2:08 3-4 2:10 2:12

MAMBRINO WILKES, 6083.

SIRE OF

GUS WILKES, 2:22; ALPHEUS, 2:27; CLARA P, 2:29½; BALKAN, 2:29½ (3-year-old) and timed separately 2:22½ in 4-year-old Stake, Bay District Track, October 14, 1889.

DESCRIPTION.

Black; sixteen hands; weighs, in exercise, 1,290 lbs. For style, finish, symmetry and proportion, comparison is challenged with any trotting bred horse. His colts follow in size, style and beauty. Balkan, for instance, being "facile princeps" of trotters in these particulars.

PEDIGREE.

Sired by Geo. Wilkes, sire of Harry Wilkes, 2:13¼, Guy Wilkes, 2:15¼, and 90 other trotters in the 2:30 list, in addition to 8 pacers, and of the sire of Axtell, 2:12 (three-year-old) beating all stallions of any age, and the sire of Regal Wilkes, 2:20¾, best two-year-old stallion record.

First dam Lady Chrisman by Mambrino (Todhunter's), son of Mambrino Chief 11; sire of Lady Thorn, 2:18¼; Woodford Mambrino, 2:21½, and four others in 2:30, and of the dams of Director, 2:17, Piedmont, 2:17¼, Onward, 2:25¼, etc.

Second dam by Pilot Jr. 12, sire of nine in the 2:30 list, and of the dams of Maud S., 2:08¾, Jay-Eye-See, 2:10, Nutwood, 2:18¾, Viking, 2:19¾, Pilot Boy, 2:20, Naiad Queen, 2:20¼, etc.

TERMS.

Mares from a distance will be received at the Dexter Stables, Oakland, or Livery Stable, Martinez, the owner notifying Smith Hill, Superintendent at the farm. Good pasture and plenty of water. For the purpose of placing the service of a Wilkes within reach of breeders, the same rate will be maintained as last year, to wit, $75 for the season. Although it is not admitted thereby that this horse is inferior as a producer to the horses whose fees are placed at from $150 to $500. Address

SMITH HILL,
San Miguel Stock Farm,
Walnut Creek, Contra Costa Co., Cal.

2:12¾ 2:13½ 2:15¼

Finely Bred Trotting Stallion

ARLINGTON.

$50 $50

Trial 2:26 1-2; by

ABBOTSFORD.

DESCRIPTION.

ARLINGTON is a handsome rich rosewood bay, 15¾ hands high and weighs 1,100 lbs. He is of beautiful conformation, well boned, and great muscular development and greatly resembles his famous sire in every particular.

PEDIGREE.

ARLINGTON was sired by Abbotsford, dam the Gillespie mare by Blue Bull. Abbotsford is by Woodford Mambrino, dam Columbia by Young Columbus, he by Columbus. Woodford Mambrino's dam Woodbine by Woodford, a thoroughbred son of Kosciusko. Woodford Mambrino is recognized as the best son of Mambrino Chief. His own record is 2:21½, that of his son Abbotsford, the sire of Arlington 2:19½ and his son Conde 2:20, and he has also a large number in the 2:30 list. He is also the sire of Princeps the sire of Trinket, record of 2:14. Abbotsford, for the short time he has been in the stud, has proven himself a sire worthy of merit, his daughter Jassemine having won the Embryo Stakes of 1881, and every one who was put in training has shown good speed. The dam of Arlington was a beautiful bay mare, 15¾ hands high, sired by Blue Bull, dam Lexington mare raised by Ezra Champion of White Hall, New York, thus showing that in Arlington are combined most of the purest blood in America.

TERMS: $50 the season, with usual return privileges. The best of attention will be given mares, but no liability assumed for escapes or accidents, good pasturage, $2 per month. Call on or address,

J. B. FRENCH,
905, 907 and 909 Golden Gate Ave, S. F.

ANTEEO BUTTON,

By Anteeo, 2:16 1-4.

And out of the dam of Alexander Button, four year old 2:26 1-2; Trial 2:16.

Will make the season of 1890 at ST. HELENA

DESCRIPTION.

ANTEEO BUTTON is five years old, a handsome dark bay, 15 1-2 hands high, and weighs 1,125 lbs. This horse has had but little or no systematic work, but he can trot fast and if there is anything in looks or breeding, he should produce trotters.

TERMS, $40 FOR THE SEASON, which closes July 1st. Best of alfalfa pasture on the premises at $4 per month. Mares cared for in any way that their owners may desire, but no responsibility assumed. For further particulars, address

E. C. SPEAR,
St. Helena, Cal.

THE CORINTHIAN
Cafe and Restaurant,
Point Tiburon.

MEALS SERVED TO ORDER AT ALL HOURS
COLD LUNCHES
FOR FISHING AND PICNIC PARTIES.
Headquarters for Yachtsmen and Fishing Parties.
B. F. NAPTHALY, Manager.

2:19 NOONDAY $2:20\frac{1}{2}$

STANDARD No. 10,000.

This celebrated trotting bred stallion will make the season of 1890 at the stable of the undersigned at Sacramento, Cal., at $75 for the season and $100 to insure a mare in foal. Payable on or before July 1st, 1890. Money will be refunded on mares bred by insurance as soon as the fact becomes known that they are not in foal.

NOONDAY.
- Wedgewood, 2:19 — Sire of Favonia, 2:15, fastest 4th heat for any mare or gelding, and eight others in 2:27 or better.
  - Belmont — Sire of Wedgewood, 2:19, Nutwood, 2:18¾, Viking, 2:19½, and 29 others in 2:30 list.
    - Alexander's Abdallah, sire of Goldsmith Maid, 2:14; Almont, with 35 horses in 2:30 list, etc.
    - Belle, dam of Hambletonian, 2:26½; Bicara, dam of Pancoast, 2:21¾, the sire of Patron, 2:14¼.
  - Woodbine — Dam of Wedgewood, 2:19, Woodford Mamb., 2:21½, the sire of Pancoast, 2:21¾, the sire of Patron, 2:14¼.
    - Woodford.
    - Singleton Mare.
- Noontide, 2:20½ (Trial, 2:13½).
  - Harold — Sire of Maud S., 2:08¾, and 26 others in 2:30 list.
    - Hambletonian (Rysdyk's), sire of George Wilkes, 2:22, the sire of Guy Wilkes, 2:15¼; Electioneer, the sire of Sunol, 2:10½, and scores of noted trotters and producers.
    - Enchantress, by Abdallah 1.
  - Midnight — Dam of Jay-Eye-See, 2:10, Noontide, 2:20½.
    - Pilot Jr., sire of dams of Maud S., 2:08¾, Jay-Eye-See, 2:10, Nutwood, 2:18¾, etc.
    - Twilight, by Lexington, sire of the dam of Ansel, 2:20.

NOONDAY is a dark seal brown, foaled 1884, 15 hands 1¾ inches high. Individually he is equal to his royal breeding. He is all that can be desired in conformation, intelligence, color and trotting action, and no stallion now in public service can show a pedigree with such fast records and royal game trotting blood as Noonday.

DON MARVIN,

Record 2:28 as a five-year-old. Standard by Breeding and Performance

Standard No. 7927.

Don Marvin 2:28.

Don Marvin is a beautiful seal brown, foaled 1884, bred by Hon. Leland Stanford, Palo Alto, Cal., standing 16 hands, and weighs, in ordinary condition, 1250 lbs. He is a fine individual, good style and form, combined with great substance, and good temper. Is very level headed; in his first race the past season he only made one break in five closely contested heats. He has great speed and endurance, with the pure, rapid Electioneer gait. He trots without toe weights, and wears only 8 oz. shoes in front. He gained his record the past season in the third heat, on a slow track, after making a season (serving over 40 mares), with scarcely any preparation. His record is no mark of his speed. He was a natural born trotter, and Mr. Charles Marvin considered him the fastest two year old at Palo Alto that season.

By FALLIS, 2:23, - - by Electioneer, sire of
Sire of Don Marvin, 2:28. — Sunol, three-year-old, 2:10 1-2, Palo Alto, 2:12¾, and 47 others in 2:30 list.

Dam CORA, by Don Victor by Belmont, sire of
Dam of Don Marvin, 2:28. — Ventura, 2:27¼, and sire of the dam of Bell Echo, 2:20, and six others in 2:30 list.

2d dam CLARABEL, - by Abdallah Star,
Dam of Clifton Bell, 2:24 1-2, and grandam of Rexford, three years, 2:24. — Sire of Hattie Maples, 2:33.

3d dam FAIRY, - - by Rysdyk's Hambletonian,
Sister of Sweepstakes, sire of 16 in 2:30 list. — Sire of Electioneer, George Wilkes, and many other noted sires and trotters.

4th dam EMMA MILLS, by Seely's American Star,
Dam of 4 horses that have 2:30 performers. — The great broodmare sire of the world.

The above pedigree should show every intelligent breeder that Don Marvin is "high" bred though very strong in trotting blood. All the comment it is deemed necessary to make as to the value of "thoroughbred blood" in the trotter is simply to refer to the very significant fact that the first and second dams of Maud S, 2:08¾, Jay-Eye-See 2:10, Sunol, three years 2:10 1-2, Palo Alto 2:12¾, Anteeo 2:16¼, Nutwood 2:18¾, Wedgewood 2:19, and many other successful sires and sensational trotters of the day are thoroughbred.

TERMS—Don Marvin will make the ensuing season from February 1st to July 1st, 1890, at $40 the season, with the usual privilege of returning the mare next season if not proving in foal. Mares from a distance met at the cars or boats on notification, and carefully handled, but no responsibility assumed for accidents or escapes.

Good alfalfa pasture furnished (free from barb wire fence) at $4 per month. For further particulars or complete circulars address

F. P. LOWELL,
1520 F Street, Sacramento, Cal.

The Produce of Eros Averaged $2,200 Each at New York Auction Sale in 1889.

THE ELECTIONEER TROTTING STALLION,

5326 EROS 5326

Will make the season of 1890—February 1st to July 1st—at LA SIESTA RANCH, MENLO PARK, adjoining Palo Alto.

PEDIGREE.

EROS (5326)
Standard by his sire
" " dam
" " record
" " produce
" under all rules

EROS (5326).
- Electioneer — Grandsire of Norlaine, 1 yr., 2:31 1-2, Sire of Sunol, 2 yrs., 2:18, Sunol, 3 yrs., 2:10 1-2, Hinda Rose, 4 yrs., 2:16, Palo Alto, 2:12¾.
  - Hambletonian 10 — Sire of Dictator, George Wilkes, Happy Medium, and 40 others in 2:30 list, and grandsire of 728 in list.
    - Abdallah 10 — Sire of the dams of Goldsmith Maid, 2:14, and 7 other producing dams.
    - Charles Kent mare — By imp. Bellfounder.
  - Green Mountain Maid — Dam of Prospero, 2:20, Elaine, 2:20, Dame Trot, 2:22, Elista, 2:22¼, Storm, 2:28¼, Antonio, 2:28¾, Miranda, 2:31, Mansfield, 2:26.
    - Harry Clay — Sire of the dams of St. Julien, 2:11¼, Bodine, 2:19¼, and 17 more in 2:30 list
    - Shanghai Mary.
- Sontag Mohawk — Dam of Eros, 2:29 1-2, Sport, 2:22¾, Sallie Benton, 2:17¾, Conductor, trial, 2:28, Colma, 3-y-o trial, 2:24.
  - Mohawk Chief — Sire of the dams of Lot Slocum, 2:17¾, Sallie Benton, 4 yrs., 2:17¾, Pedlar, 2 yrs., 2:27¼, Stanford, 4 yrs., 2:30, Eros, 6th heat, 2:29 1-2.
    - Hambletonian 10 — Sire of the dams of Stamboul, 2:12¾, Wilton, 2:19¼, and 20 other trotters.
    - Lady Perrine
  - Sontag Nellie
    - Toronto Sontag — By Toronto Chief,
    - Nellie Gray — 9-mile record, 13:45.

Produce of Eros
Wanda, 4 yrs., 2:21,
Solita, 2 yrs., 2:41 1-2,
Meriquita, 2 yrs., 2:42,
Daylight, 2 yrs., 2:54,
Hiram B., trial, 2:28.

These are the only colts by him that have ever had a harness on except one in New York that went a trial last July in 2:26 1:2.

DESCRIPTION.

EROS is a rich seal brown stallion, bred by Hon. Leland Stanford at Palo Alto, and is the nearest living likeness of his celebrated sire, Electioneer. Stands 15.2 hands high, and weighs 1050 pounds.

In breeding to Eros, the owners of mares will strictly follow the great rule of breeding, viz., breed to a stallion by a producer and out of a sure producer of great speed. Eros is by the stallion that has produced more 2:30 trotters that any living horse, and is also the sire of more 2:20 performers than any horse living or dead.

EROS is out of the dam of Sally Benton, four years old, record 2:17¾, Sport 2:22¾, and Eros 2:29½ in the sixth heat, against a field of nine horses. He is from a family that is endowed with great natural speed, trot fast at an early age, train on, throw trotters from all classes of mares, are of good substance, bone, style and action, and breed solid colors.

TERMS.

$100 for the season, with the privilege of return next season should mares not be in foal and horse and mare still remain in the same hands.

Good pasturage can be obtained at $5 per month, but no responsibility for accidents or escapes. There are a large number of box stalls, and animals can be kept up and fed on hay and grain at reasonable rates if required. Mares already in foal can be sent to the ranch for foaling, and will receive all the attention bestowed upon our own mares. Mares left with Mr. Peter Pomyea, Broadway Street Stable, Oakland, or with Mr. F. H. Burke, 401 Montgomery Street, San Francisco, will be forwarded to the ranch free of charge. For further particulars apply to

W. H. VIOGET,
LA SIESTA RANCH, MENLO PARK, CAL.

EROS is the only stallion offered to the public on this Coast that has a dam that has three in the 2:30 list.

POPLAR GROVE

Breeding Farm

STALLIONS.

CLOVIS, 4909,

CLOVIS is a beautiful black, Eight Years Old, 16 1-2 Hands High, and weighs 1260 lbs.

He is a horse of beautiful symmetry and magnificent action.

PEDIGREE.

CLOVIS was sired by Sultan, 2:24, sire of Stamboul, 2:12 1-4, Ruby, 2:19¾, and fifteen others with records of 2:30 or better.

First dam Sweetbriar by Thorndale 2:22 1-2, sire of Edwin Thorne, 2:16 1-2, Daisy Dale, 2:19, and May Thorne, 2:22.

Second dam Ulster Queen, dam of Volmer, 2:24¾, by Hambletonian 10. Sire of Dexter, 2:17¼, George Wilkes, 2:22.

Third dam by Thomas Jefferson, a son of Mambrino Paymaster, Jr.

Fourth dam by Mambrino Paymaster, sire of Mambrino Chief.

Sultan, by The Moor, sire of Beautiful Bells, dam of Hinda Rose, 2:19 1-2, and Sable, dam of Sable Wilkes, three year old record 2:18.

First dam of Sultan, Sultana, by Delmonico. Sire of Darby, 2:16 1-2, by Guy Miller, sire of Whipple's Hambletonian.

Second dam by Mambrino Chief.

Third dam by Downing's Bay Messenger.

Fourth dam Mrs. Caudle, dam of Ericsson, four year old record 2:30 1-2.

Clovis will make the season of 1890 at Poplar Grove Breeding Farm, near Wildflower, Fresno County, commencing February 1st and ending July 1st.

Terms, $75, due at time of service.

Mares cared for in any manner owners may desire; pasturage $2 per month. Every care exercised, but no liability for escapes or accidents. Mares not proving with foal can be returned next season, providing I still own this stallion.

APEX, 8935.

FOUR - YEAR - OLD RECORD, FOURTH HEAT, 2:26.

Will make the present season at the Poplar Grove Breeding Farm, near Wildflower, Fresno Co., season commencing Feb. 1st, and ending July 1, 1890. Terms $50 the season, due at time of service. Apex is eight years old, a beautiful bay, 15 1-2 hands high, and weighs 1150 lbs. He is a horse of fine disposition, and his gait is faultless.

PEDIGREE.

Apex was sired by Promptor 2305, he by Blue Bull 75; first dam Mary by Flaxtail, he by Pruden's Blue Bull, Flaxtail being the sire of the dams of Buccaneer, five-year-old record, 2:24 1-2; Pride, yearling record, 2:44 1-2, and Shamrock, two-year old record, 2:25, third heat. Second dam by Bright Eyes, son of Boanarages. Prompter (sire of Apex, record 2:26, and Transit, 2:28 1-4), by Wilson's Blue Bull, by Pruden's Blue Bull, son of Merring's Blue Bull. Prompter's dam Prairie Bird, by Flaxtail; second dam by John the Baptist, son of Tally Ho Morgan, by Sherman Morgan; third dam Fannie Fern by Irwin's Tuckaho.

Apex made his appearance in the circuit as a two-year-old, and obtained a record of 2:42. As a three-year-old he reduced this in a race at Santa Rosa against Stamboul to 2:31, it taking six heats to decide the contest, which was won by Apex. As a four year-old he gained his present record of 2:26.

Mares cared for in any manner owners may desire. Pasturage $2 per month. Every care exercised, but no liabilities for escapes or accidents. Mares not proving with foal can be returned next season, providing I still own this stallion.

The Standard Stallion

JUNIO,

RECORD 2:22.

WILL MAKE THE PRESENT SEASON OF AT FRESNO FAIR GROUNDS.

Season Commencing Feb. 1st and ending July 1st.

TERMS—$100 the season, due at time of service.

JUNIO is eight years old, a handsome dark bay 16 hands high, and weighs 1250 pounds. He is the personification of the light harness horse, and his trotting action is superb. At the State Fair of 1886 he took first premium over forty of the finest trotters in the State.

PEDIGREE.

"Junio, by Electioneer, premier stallion of Palo Alto (sire of Sunol 2:10 1-2, Palo Alto 2:12 1-4, and 47 others in the 2:30 list.). Dam by Granger by imp. Hercules.

Granger, by imp. Hercules, dam Jenny Lind, by Stockbridge Chief, Jr., he by Stockbridge Chief, he by Vermont Black Hawk. Second dam by Kentucky Whip.

Imp. Hercules, by Kingston, first dam daughter of Tlacar, by Bay Middleton, second dam Malvina, by Oscar; 3rd dam Spotless by Walton; 4th dam by Trumpator (see Bruce's American Stud Book, Vol. 1, page 26). Hercules is the sire of the dam of Arnmoor 2:7¼; also sire of dam of Menlo 2:21 1-2.

Mares not proving in foal may be returned next year free of charge, providing I still have the horse. Pasturage $3 per month. While every care will be taken of horses, no liability will be assumed for accidents or escapes.

For further particulars address

S. N. STRAUBE, Fresno, Cal.

Poplar Grove Breeding Farm.

Southern Pacific Co.

(PACIFIC SYSTEM.)

Trains leave and are due to arrive at San Francisco.

LEAVE (FOR)	FROM APRIL 13, 1890.	ARRIVE (FROM)
7.30 A M	Haywards, Niles and San Jose ...	*12.45 P M
7.30 A M	Sacramento and Redding, via Davis ...	7.15 P M
7.30 A M	Sacramento, Auburn, Colfax ...	4.45 P M
8.00 A M	Martinez, Vallejo, Calistoga and Santa Rosa ...	6.15 P M
8.30 A M	Los Angeles Express, Fresno, Bakersfield, Mojave and East and Los Angeles ...	11.15 A M
8.30 A M	Niles, San Jose, Stockton, Ione, Sacramento, Marysville, Oroville and Red Bluff ...	4.45 P M
10.30 A M	Haywards and Niles ...	3.45 P M
12.00 M	Haywards, Niles and Livermore	8.45 P M
*1.00 P M	Sacramento River Steamers ...	**6.00 A M
3.00 P M	Haywards, Niles and San Jose ...	9.45 A M
3.30 P M	2d Class for Ogden and East ...	10.45 P M
4.00 P M	Stockton and Milton; Vallejo, Calistoga and Santa Rosa ...	9.45 A M
*4.30 P M	Niles and Livermore ...	*8.45 A M
*4.30 P M	Niles and San Jose ...	‡6.15 P M
6.00 P M	Shasta Route Express, Sacramento, Marysville, Redding, Portland, Puget Sound, East and Knight's Landing via Davis	10.45 A M
6.00 P M	Haywards and Niles ...	7.45 A M
7.00 P M	Sunset Route, Atlantic Express Santa Barbara, Los Angeles, Deming, El Paso, New Orleans and East ...	8.45 P M
8.00 P M	Central Atlantic Express, Ogden and East ...	9.45 A M

SANTA CRUZ DIVISION.

LEAVE		ARRIVE
‡7.45 A M	Excursion train to Santa Cruz ...	‡8.05 P M
8.15 A M	Newark, Centerville, San Jose, Felton, Boulder Creek and Santa Cruz ...	6.20 P M
*2.45 P M	Centerville, San Jose, Almaden, Felton, Boulder Creek and Santa Cruz ...	*11.20 A M
4.45 P M	Centerville, San Jose, and Los Gatos, and Saturday and Sunday to Santa Cruz ...	9.50 A M

Coast Division (Third and Townsend Sts.)

LEAVE		ARRIVE
7.25 A M	San Jose, Almaden and Way Stations ...	2.30 P M
8.30 A M	San Jose, Gilroy, Tres Pinos; Pajaro, Santa Cruz; Monterey; Pacific Grove, Salinas, San Miguel, Paso Robles, Santa Margarita (San Luis Obispo) and principal Way Stations ...	6.12 P M
10.30 A M	San Jose and Way Stations ...	5.02 P M
12.01 P M	Cemetery, Menlo Park and Way Stations ...	3.38 P M
*3.30 P M	San Jose, Tres Pinos, Santa Cruz, Salinas, Monterey, Pacific Grove and principal Way Stations ...	10.00 A M
*4.20 P M	Menlo Park and Way Station	7.58 A M
5.20 P M	San Jose and Way Stations ...	9.03 A M
6.30 P M	Menlo Park and Way stations ...	6.35 A M
†11.45 P M	Menlo Park and principal Way Stations ...	†7.28 P M

A M for Morning. P M for Afternoon.
*Sundays excepted. †Saturdays only. ‡Sundays only.
**Mondays excepted. §Saturdays excepted.

OCEANIC STEAMSHIP CO.

Carrying United States, Hawaiian and Colonial Mails.

WILL LEAVE THE COMPANY'S WHARF, foot of Mission street, No. 1,

For Honolulu, Auckland and Sydney,

WITHOUT CHANGE,

The Splendid New 3,000-ton Iron Steamer.
MARIPOSA ... Saturday, May 3d, 1890, at 12 M.,
Or immediately on arrival of the English mails.

For Honolulu,

SS. AUSTRALIA (3,000 tons), April 25, 1890, at 12 M

For freight or passage, apply at office, 327 Market Street. JOHN D. SPRECKELS & BROS. General Agents.

KILLIP & CO.,

LIVE STOCK AND GENERAL AUCTIONEERS,

22 Montgomery Street, San Francisco

SPECIAL ATTENTION PAID TO SALES OF

High-Bred Horses and Cattle.

At auction and private sale.

Will Sell in All Cities and Counties of the State.

REFERENCES.

HON. C. GREEN, Sacramento. — HON. J. D. CARR Salinas.
J. P. SARGENT, ESQ., Sargents. — HON. JOHN BOGGS Colusa.
HON. L. J. ROSE, Los Angeles. — HON. A. WALRATH Nevada.
J. B. HAGGIN, ESQ., San Francisco.

Represented at Sacramento by Edwin F. Smith Secretary State Agricultural Society.
At San Jose by Messrs. Montgomery & Rea, Real Estate Agents.

Being the oldest established firm in the live-stock business on this Coast, and having conducted the important auction sales in this line for the past fifteen years, amounting to one half a million of dollars, we feel justified in claiming unequaled facilities for disposing of live stock of every description, either at auction or private sale. Our list of correspondents embraces every breeder and dealer of prominence upon the Pacific Coast, thus enabling us to give full publicity to animals placed with us for sale. Private purchases and sales of live stock of all descriptions will be made on commission, and stock shipped with the utmost care. Purchases and sales made of land of every description. We are authorized to refer to the gentlemen whose names are appended.

KILLIP & CO., 22 Montgomery Street.

HEALD'S

Business College, 24 Post St.

—San Francisco.—

The most popular school on the Coast

E. P. HEALD, President. C. S. HALEY, Sec'y.

Send for Circulars

San Francisco and North Pacific Railway.

THE DONAHUE BROAD-GAUGE ROUTE.

COMMENCING SUNDAY, MARCH 17, 1889, AND until further notice, boats and trains will leave from and arrive at the San Francisco Passenger Depot, Market-street Wharf, as follows:

Leave San Francisco. WEEK DAYS.	Leave San Francisco. SUNDAYS.	DESTINATION	Arrive San Francisco. SUNDAYS.	Arrive San Francisco. WEEK DAYS.
7.40 A M 3.30 P M 5.00 P M	8.00 A M 5.00 P M	Petaluma and Santa Rosa	10.40 A M 6.10 P M	8.50 A M 10.30 A M 6.05 P M
7.40 A M 3.30 P M	8.00 A M	Fulton, Windsor, Healdsburg, Litton Springs, Cloverdale, and way stations.	6.10 P M	10.30 A M 6.05 P M
7.40 A M	8.00 A M	Hopland and Ukiah.	6.10 P M	6.05 P M
7.40 A M	8.00 A M	Guerneville	6.10 P M	6.05 P M
7.40 A M 5.00 P M	8.00 A M	Sonoma and Glen Ellen.	10.40 A M 6.10 P M	8.50 A M 6.05 P M
3.30 P M	5.00 P M	Sebastopol	10.40 A M	10.30 A M

Stage connects at Santa Rosa for White Sulphur Springs, and Mark West Springs; at Geyserville for Skaggs Springs, and at Cloverdale for the Geysers; at Hopland for Highland Springs, Kelseyville, Soda Bay, Lakeport and Bartlett Springs, and at Ukiah for Vichy Springs, Saratoga Springs, Blue Lakes, Willits, Cahto, Calpella, Potter Valley, Sherwood Valley and Mendocino City.

EXCURSION TICKETS from Saturdays to Mondays, to Petaluma, $1.50; to Santa Rosa, $2.25; to Healdsburg, $3.40; to Litton Springs, $3.60; to Cloverdale, $4.50; to Hopland, $5.70; to Ukiah, $6.75; to Guerneville, $3.75; to Sonoma, $1.50; to Glen Ellen, $1.80.

EXCURSION TICKETS, good for Sundays only, to Petaluma, $1; to Santa Rosa, $1.50; to Healdsburg, $2.25; to Litton Springs, $2.40; to Cloverdale, $3; to Guerneville, $2.50, to Sonoma, $1; to Glen Ellen, $1.20.

From San Francisco for Point Tiburon and San Rafael: Week Days—7.40, 9.20, 11.20, A. M.; 3.30, 5.00, 6.15 P. M. Sundays—8.00, 9.30, 11.00 A. M.; 1.30, 5.00, 6.20 P. M.

To San Francisco from San Rafael: Week Days—6.20, 7.55, 9.30 A. M.; 12.45, 3.40, 5.05 P. M. Sundays—8.10, 9.40 A. M.; 12.15, 3.40, 5.00 P. M.

To San Francisco from Point Tiburon: Week Days—6.50, 8.20, 9.55 A. M.; 1.10, 4.05, 5.30 P. M.; Sundays—8.40, 10.05 A. M.; 12.40, 4.05, 5.30 P. M.

On Saturdays an extra trip will be made from San Francisco to San Rafael, leaving at 1.40 P. M.

H. C. WHITING, General Manager.

PETER J. McGLYNN, Gen. Pass. & Tkt. Agt.

Ticket Offices at Ferry, 222 Montgomery Street and 2 New Montgomery Street.

CHICAGO, MILWAUKEE AND ST. PAUL RAILWAY.

Steam Heated and Electric Lighted Vestibuled Trains between Chicago, St. Paul and Minneapolis.
Electric Lighted and Steam Heated Vestibuled Trains between Chicago, Council Bluffs and Omaha.
Finest Dining Cars in the world.
Free Reclining Chair Cars between Chicago and Omaha.
Fast Mail Line between Chicago, Milwaukee, St. Paul and Minneapolis.
Transcontinental Route between Chicago, Council Bluffs and Omaha, or St. Paul.
Great National Route between Chicago, Kansas City and St. Joseph, Mo.
5,700 miles of road in Illinois, Wisconsin, Minnesota, Iowa, Missouri, South and North Dakota.
Everything First-Class.
First-Class People patronize First-Class Lines.
Ticket Agents everywhere sell Tickets over the Chicago, Milwaukee and St. Paul Railway.

W. T. ALLEN,
Pacific Coast Passenger Agent
Office, No 138 Montgomery St., San Francisco, Cal.
Under Occidental Hotel

6 DONTS

DON'T own a racehorse.
DON'T be a breeder.
DON'T be a trainer.
DON'T be a jockey.
DON'T bet on the races.
DON'T go to a race track.

WITHOUT

HAVING IN YOUR POCKET ONE OF

Goodwin's ANNUAL OFFICIAL TURF GUIDES.

Price, in cloth ... $2.00
Price, in half morocco ... 3.00
Price, in half calf ... 4.00
If sent by mail ... 10 cents extra

SUBSCRIBE TO IT FOR 1890.

It is published semi-monthly during the racing season, and is but **$10 per year.** Address

GOODWIN BROS.,
241 Broadway, New York City.

THE BOHANON SULKY!

BEST MADE.
Perfect Riding Buggies.
Breaking Carts.
Fine Repairing. Reasonable Prices.

Bohanon Carriage Co., 161-163 Ogden Ave., CHICAGO.
Send for Catalogue.

FOR HORSES, DOGS AND CATTLE.

Simmons Liver Regulator, a strictly vegetable compound and general Condition Powder, is

A SAFE AND SURE REMEDY FOR

COLIC,
GRUBS,
LUNG FEVER,
HIDE-BOUND.

No Stable or Kennel should be without it: it gives new life to a lazy or drooping horse, and is a positive preventive and cure for **Distemper** or **Mange** in Dogs.

J. H. ZEILIN & CO.,
Proprietors, Philadelphia, Pa

HORSE OWNERS!
TRY GOMBAULT'S

CAUSTIC BALSAM.

A Safe, Speedy and Positive Cure for Curb, Splint, Sweeny, Capped Hock, Strained Tendons, Founder, Wind Puffs, all Skin Diseases or Parasites, Thrush, Diphtheria, Pinkeye, all Lameness from Spavin, Ringbone or other Bony Tumors. Removes all Bunches or Blemishes from Horses and Cattle.
Supersedes all Cautery or Firing.
Impossible to Produce any Scar or Blemish.

Every bottle sold is warranted to give satisfaction. Price $1.50 per bottle. Sold by druggists, or sent by express, charges paid, with full directions for its use. Send for descriptive circulars. Address
LAWRENCE, WILLIAMS & CO., Cleveland, O.

BROU'S INJECTION

A PERMANENT CURE

in from 3 to 6 days, of the most obstinate cases; guaranteed not to produce Stricture; no sickening doses; and no inconvenience or loss of time. Recommended by physicians and sold by all druggists. J. Ferré, (successor to Brou), Pharmacien, Paris.

For any Kind of a

SORE THROAT

USE

McCLELLAN'S

DIPHTHERIA REMEDY

An Unfailing Cure.
FOR SALE BY ALL DRUGGISTS

R. LIDDLE & SON

538 Washington St., S. F.,
Wholesale and Retail Dealers in

Guns, Rifles and Pistols.

A Full Line of FISHING TACKLE and SPORTSMAN'S GOODS.

Orders by mail receive prompt attention.

By-Laws

—AND—

Rules and Regulations

—OF THE—

NATIONAL Trotting Association

ALSO THE

AMERICAN Trotting Association,

AND THE

PACIFIC COAST BLOOD-HORSE ASSOCIATION.

With Betting Rules.

For Sale at the Office of the

Breeder and Sportsman,

313 Bush St., S. F., Cal.

Price. 25c. each.
By Mail, Postage Paid, 30c. each.

VETERINARY.

Dr. Wm. H. Jones, M.R.C.V.S.

Veterinary Surgeon,
(OLYMPIC CLUB STABLES)
503 Sutter Street, San Francisco.
Telephone, No. 1404.

Consultations by letter, and Cases of URGENT NECESSITY in the interior will receive prompt attention.

Dr. A. E. BUZARD,

VETERINARY SURGEON,

Member of the Royal College of Veterinary Surgeons, London, England. Graduated April 22d, 1870.

All Operations on the Horse Performed Skillfully.

Special attention given to the Diseases of Dogs. Calls to the country promptly attended to. Advice and prescriptions by mail $2. Office and Residence, No. 11 Seventh street, S. F. (opp. Odd Fellows Hall. Telephone No. 3 69.

W. H. WOODRUFF.

Veterinary Dentist,

AT FASHION STABLES,

221 Ellis Street, San Francisco

Improved Instruments, Humane Methods, First-Class Work.

H. E. CARPENTER,

Veterinary Surgeon,

Graduate of Ontario Veterinary College, Toronto Canada.

RESIDENCE AND VETERINARY INFIRMARY
331 Golden Gate Ave., San Francisco.
Telephone 3069.

OPEN DAY AND NIGHT.

No risk in throwing Horses. Veterinary Operating Table on the premises.

DR. C. MASOERO.

Veterinary Surgeon,

Successor to **DR. A. DeTAVEL,**

GRADUATE OF ROYAL VETERINARY COLLEGE, TURIN.

OFFICE AND INFIRMARY
No. 811 HOWARD STREET,
Between Fourth and Fifth. SAN FRANCISCO
Telephone, No. 457.

R. WATKINS,

Veterinary Dentist,

Of twelve years practice, is now permanently located in San Francisco, and may be found at C. S. Crittendens' Golden Gate Livery and Riding Academy, **24 to 28 Golden Gate Avenue.**

Will treat ailments of the horse's mouth, and cure all such. Siderein Pullers and Tongue Lollers, etc. Satisfaction guaranteed. Orders by mail will receive prompt attention. Examination Free.

E. J. O'ROUKE.

I have the honor to announce to my old patrons and the general public that I may be found at my old stand, where, as heretofore, the

Shoeing of Horses,

whether for the Track, Drive, or for general work, will receive my personal attention.

Telephone 2011.

E. J. O'ROUKE,
209 Ellis Street

California Horse Shoe Co's

I have used in my business the Steel and Iron Shoes made by the above Company, and take great pleasure in saying they are the best I have ever used in twenty-two years' practice. I have never seen anything like the STEEL SHOE made by this Company. I can fully recommend them to every practical Horseshoer in the country. Yours respectfully,

No. 8 Everett Street. JOHN GRACE.

TRUMAN HOOKER & CO.
SAN FRANCISCO, - - CALIFORNIA

Everything for Trotter or Runner,

At J. A. McKERRON'S,

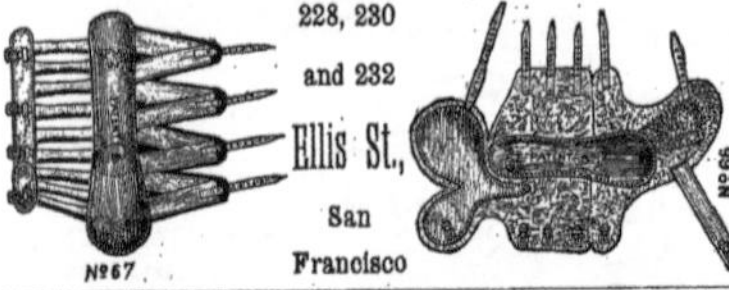

228, 230 and 232 Ellis St., San Francisco

The PARKER Hammerless Shot Gun.

At the Annual Tournament of 1889, held at Cannes, France, the grand prize, consisting of 2000 Francs and a Valuable Cup, was won by The Parker Hammerless.

The first Parker Hammerless Gun made won the championship of America at Decatur, Illinois.

SEND FOR ILLUSTRATED CIRCULAR.

PARKER BROS., Makers,

New York Salesroom, 97 Chambers St. Meriden Conn.

THE CASTOR Road & Speeding CART.

ALWAYS GIVES SATISFACTION.

Combining perfect riding qualities, proportions and balance, with genteel appearance.

No vehicle exhibits a horse to better advantage, and no Cart approaches them for speeding or training purposes.

A stylish vehicle for exercising or pleasure driving, at one-fourth the cost of a carriage. Have none of the horse jockey or objectionable features of other Road Carts.

They are the Leading Cart wherever introduced, and are in use by the most prominent breeders and pleasure drivers everywhere.

Elegant Shifting Top Carts.

Perfectly Balanced Stylish Pole Carts.

For Illustrated Catalogue, with Prices, address,

LEWIS F. CASTOR,
Frankford, Philadelphia, Pa.

JOHN SPLAN, General Agent.

Brothers of the Angle.

OUR NEW EIGHT-STRIP SPLIT BAMBOO is "King" of all fishing-rods. Chubb's New Catalogue for 1 is now ready. In addition to a complete list of angle supplies, it contains articles from the pens of Dr. James Henshall, Petronella, W. H. Murray, Geo. P. Goff, Norm Brother Gardner, and others.

These papers are by the best writers on angling subje and are very interesting

Send 25 cents, and receive Catalogue, post-paid. T amount will be deducted from first order (if accompan with Coupon in book) for one dollar's worth or more of goods. Address

THOS. H. CHUBB.

The Fishing-Rod Manufacturer,

POST MILLS, VT

Please mention BREEDER AND SPORTSMAN.

ABALONE PATENT SPOON.

PATENT APPLIED FOR.

These Spoons are made of Abalone Shells, which, on account of their iridescence, are more attract to fish than any other substance. To make them secure, we have patented a German Silver Bar runn the entire length of the Shell; the hook is fastened in one end of the bar, the swivel in the other.

These spoons have been tried on all kinds of game fish, *and are wonderfully sure kille*

Sample by mail, Trout sizes, $.50, Salmon sizes, $1.00.

E. T. ALLEN,

Importer of Fire Arms, Fishing Tackle and Sporting Good

416 Market Street, - - San Francisco.

Studebaker Bros. Manufact'g Co

Sole Agents for

FRAZIER

(OR CHICAGO)

Carts

AND

Sulkies,

201--203 Market Stree

SAN FRANCISCO, CAL.

J. O'KANE, Horse Boots, Clothing and Furnishing

For Track, Driving Training and Stable.

Every requisite for Horsemen.

Harness, Medicines, E

THE BRUNSWICK BALKE COLLENDER COMPANY,

MANUFACTURERS OF

Standard Billiard and Pool Tables, Saloon and Bank Fixture

653--655 Market Street, San Francisco, Cal.

keeps horses healthy, promotes digestion, fattens horses, loosens the hide, as the appetite, prevents leg swelling, strengthens the kidneys, regulates the bo and destroys worms. $7.50 per 100 lbs. Ask your dealer for it or sen

MANHATTAN FOOD CO., 206 Clay St., S. F

Nutwood } Sire

DAWN 6407

Dam Countess { DAM OF Strathway (2-y-o) trial; Placida, Morna } Double te Trial

2:18¾; 2:20; 2:19½.

$100 Popular Price for season of 1890. $10

Not having a breeding farm, and being dependent on the public for patronage, I have set the above low price in order to be within the reach of any one desiring to breed. Good pasturage $3 per month.

For further particulars, address

A. L. WHITNEY, Petaluma.

TWENTY-FOUR PAGES.

BREEDER AND SPORTSMAN

Vol. XVI. No. 17.
No. 313 BUSH STREET. SAN FRANCISCO, SATURDAY, APRIL 26, 1890. SUBSCRIPTION FIVE DOLLARS A YEAR.

Petaluma Horses.

BY HARVEY W. PECK.

For many years past Petaluma has been noted as one of the horse centers of California. When many of the counties now famous as homes of celebrated trotters were in an embryotic state as regards the rearing and training of race-horses and trotters, Petaluma enjoyed the reputation of being a "horsey" town. Long before Santa Clara Valley, San Mateo County, Contra Costa County and the Pleasanton country were widely known as the home of the trotter, Petaluma was pegging away at a few trotters of more or less speed on the old half mile track. While other sections have "gone by" the town in rearing horses of extreme speed, she has progressed slowly but surely and without doubt there glows within her aspiring bosom sweet dreams of the two-minute trotter.

During a recent visit to Petaluma I was taken under the protecting wing of General Fine, and shown every horse and colt to be found. General Fine is a hustler as well as a thorough horseman. He is in charge of the grounds and Club House of the Sonoma and Marin Association, and the excellence of the track at this time of year is the best evidence of the fact that he is the right man in the right place. Upon his invitation I took lunch at the Club House with him, in which we were shortly joined by Mr. Shaner and his charming wife. Lunch over, we started to inspect the horses.

The first string were those under Mr. Shaner's supervision. Mr. Shaner's popularity as a driver is well attested, when I mention that he has some 25 or 26 horses and colts in training. The consequence is that he rides many miles in a day, which every horseman knows is not as funny as it looks. I looked at so many horses and colts that only a limited description of them can be given.

Annabelle, chestnut filly, light mane and tail, by Dawn, dam a thoroughbred mare by Hubbard, bred by Mr. Pacheco, owned by Arthur Whitney. Fine looking filly; is now two years old. Made yearling record of 3:06. Went an easy mile the other day in 2:58. Can go quarters fast.

Black colt, one-year old, by Dawn, dam Jennie Offut by Gen. McClellan. Good looking colt. I am assured is a very promising colt. Owned by Arthur Whitney.

Oaknut, ch s, by Dawn, dam Miss Brown, by Volunteer son of Gen. Dana. This horse is a larger pattern of his sire, having great substance everywhere. He is 15.3 hands high and weighs 1180 pounds. He is five years old. Last year he went a mile in 2:32, and quarters in 35¼ seconds. Barring accident, he will be heard from this year. He is the property of W. R. Overholser.

Emma Temple 2:21 was the next one we saw. She is looking well. As all horsemen are aware, she is the property of Harry Agnew and is an enduring and good race mare.

Chestnut stud, owned by Harry Agnew, sired by son of Almont (could not find what one), dam Maud, pacer, 2:20. This horse is a pacer, 15.3 hands high, strong all over, and can pace a good clip. His dam, Maud, it will be remembered, went through the circuit two or three seasons ago. He was bred in the Sandwich Islands. (The sire of the horse here mentioned is Bosworth.—ED. BREEDER AND SPORTSMAN.)

Light bay filly by Sidney, dam Young Countess, by Sam Patchen; second dam Countess, the dam of Dawn and Strathway. This is a good looking filly, not large, but of considerable finish, and is claimed to have plenty of speed. She is entered in the two-year-old stakes. Owned by A. L. Whitney.

Stammoor, black colt, 15 hands high, small strip in face, foaled 1888, owned by Robert Brown, Petaluma. As his name indicates, he is a son of Stamboul, dam Moor Maid by the Moor. He is a fashionably bred youngster, and should he prove as good as his pedigree, he should make a race horse. He is a smooth looking, kindly dispositioned fellow. He is entered in the District and Fine stakes for two year olds.

Tamarack bay filly, two years old, sired by Mambrino Jr., dam by Belle Alta. This filly was purchased from her breeder, Mr. Jas. Wisecarver, of Geyserville, by Mr. Thomas Donohue, of Litton Springs. She is entered in the Fine Stake, I believe.

Light bay filly sired by Anteeo, dam by Nutwood. Owned by Lot Slocum, of San Francisco. A good looking and racy appearing youngster, now three years old.

Two year old filly by Junio 2:22, dam by Sultan. If she does not belie her breeding, she will trot some.

Yearling colt by Dawn, dam by Geo. Booth. A very good colt.

In the next stall was Mr. Shaner's two-year-old colt by Sidney. This is a small unprepossessing looking chap, but he makes up in speed what he lacks in appearance. He is a pacer and was very fast as a yearling. In truth, I was going to give away the fact that this colt as a yearling could make Lot Slocum brush a couple of hundred yards at his best rate, but I won't tell it without consulting Mr. Shaner.

Mr. Shaner has a yearling filly by Sidney, dam by Vick's Ethan Allen, that is speedy and good looking.

Clara Z., grey mare, foaled 1885, sired by Capri, dam by A. W. Richmond. This mare was bred by Mr. Zane, of Healdsburg, and recently sold by him to Mr. Shaner. She is a good looking mare, has been one of the improving kind, going a mile as a yearling in 3:05, and having sufficient speed last year to beat 2:30.

Two-year-old filly Donis by Dawn, dam by Don Juan, second dam by Roadhouse's St. Lawrence. This is a grand looking colt, fine size, speedy conformation, good disposition and will make a trotter. In my estimation she is among the best of the Dawn's. She is entered in the Fine Stake.

Warde, g c, two years, sired by Capri, dam by Belle Alta Jr. This is a good looking, good going colt, with considerable speed for his opportunities. He is entered in the Fine Stake.

Mr. J. B. Hinkle has a good looking colt in Whaler by Whalebone, dam by Gen. McClellan. This colt I understand is jointly owned by Mr. Hinkle and Mr. Edwards, of Penn's Grove. He is entered in the two-year old stake.

Mr. Hinkle has a running mare he thinks well of. She was sired by Boots, dam Dixie Maid by Woodburn, second dam Dixie by Kentucky Whip. She is five years old; will weigh about 1000 pounds; is a mare of good appearance, with lots of driving power. Mr. Hinkle says she can go a quarter fast enough to satisfy anybody for a "short horse," while she can maintain a high rate over a distance. Here is a chance for some one desiring a sure thing to campaign through "the bushes," and she can be bought at a reasonable figure.

The following are in charge of Mr. Burrell: Roan filly, one year old, sired by Dawn, dam by Nameless. Just broken. Belongs to Dr. Proctor.

Chestnut mare, seven years, sired by Elector 2:21½, dam by Venture 2:27. This is a grand looking mare, large, well shaped, fine coat of hair, combined with good disposition and level head in her work. She has been driven on the road by her owner, Mr. Asa Higgins, until recently. She can trot quarters better than a 2:40 gait with short work.

Bay mare, sired by Auctioneer Johnny (may the devil fly away with the man who evolved that name) a son of Geo. M. Patchen Jr., dam by Williamson's Belmont. This is a promising mare, with a lot of speed for the chance she has had. Owned by Mr. Burrill.

Yearling colt by Anteeo, dam by Alexander. This youngster is black and as large as any ordinary two-year-old. He has just been broken. He belongs to Robert Crane of Petaluma.

Yearling filly, black, small, sired by Abbotsford, dam by Rustic, grandam by Novato Chief. She is owned by Senator F. C. De Long, of Novato. Her education has just begun.

I next visited Mr. Fine's stable, containing Poco Tempo, Captor, Capri, and Examiner.

Poco Tempo is a brown stud sired by Anteeo, dam by Joe Daniels, grandam by The Moor. He is 15½ hands high, and will weigh I judge something over 1000 pounds. He went a mile last year in 2:40½, and that with being "worked out" but four times. His best previous performance was 2:56. Gen Fine thinks that *poco tempo* he will beat 2:30 and I think he will.

Capri is a grey stallion, sired by Jim Lick, dam by Williamson's Belmont. He is about 15½ hands, and weighs I believe 1050 pounds. He is the sire of Clara Z. two-year-old record 2:45 and Captor, three-year-old record 2:34. He is owned by Mr. Zane and is making the season at Petaluma in charge of Gen. Fine.

Captor, grey colt, four years old, sired by Capri, dam by A. W. Richmond. As stated above this colt acquired a three-year-old record of 2:34. He belongs to Mr. Zane and is in he hands of Gen. Fine for the coming season.

Examiner, chestnut colt, sired by Dawn, dam Vashti, 2:32½ by Chieftan. This colt, although undersized as a yearling, has developed into a good-sized, nice looking two-year-old. He is considered a very promising colt by those acquainted with his merits. He is owned by Gen. Fine and is entered in two stakes.

There are a couple of bay geldings quartered at the track, sired by Alexander. One belongs to Mr. Higgins, while I could not ascertain the owner of the other. They both have some speed.

In company with Gen. Fine, I drove to the stables in town.

The first place we stopped was at the barn occupied by Mr. J. R. Rose's horses that are under the supervision of W. J. Frost. The string contains the following:

Rosie R., brown mare, foaled 1887, 15½ hands high, weighs about 975 pounds—perhaps a little more; sired by Gen. McClellan Jr., dam Susie Rose by Sam McClellan. As the above pedigree shows, she is full sister to Nellie R., 2:17½. Rosie is a nicely turned mare; has just been broken, and shows a nice way of going.

Minnie R., brown mare, 15½ hands high, weighs 1,100; sired by Gen. McClellan Jr., dam by Ulster Chief, son of Rysdyk's Hambletonian. This is a fine appearing mare, resembling Rosie very closely in color and conformation. She trotted a mile last year in 2:33½, and quarters in 35½ seconds. She will be worked this year, and Mr. Frost thinks well of her.

Hernanci, light roan filly, foaled 1886, 15.2½ hands high, weighs about 1050 pounds; sired by Hernani, son of Electioneer, dam by Gen. McClellan; 2d dam Fan (dam of Sweetbrier, pacing, 2:26½). This mare Sweetbrier, it is said, acquired a record of 2:23½ in the East, while doing the circuit under the name of Lamplighter. I can find neither of these performances, but the roan filly is quite a trotter nevertheless. Considerable is expected of her the coming season by Mr. Frost.

Black colt, foaled 1888, sired by Alcona Jr., dam Kittie D. by Alexander; 2d dam Shoo Fly by Gen. McClellan. This colt was sick for a long time, but is now rounding to, and I do not think will disgrace his sire when he gets ready to start.

From Mr. Frost's stable we drove to Mr. O'Reilly's, near the depot. Mr. O'Reilly is a lover of a good horse. Away back in the dim and dusty past, he raised or purchased, I have forgotten which, a mare called Emma Taylor, sired by Alexander. From this mare Mr. O'Reilly has a string of young horses that any man would like to own.

He first bred the mare to Anteeo and got Annetto, a bay mare weighing about 975. She was foaled in 1885 I think, and got a record of 2:39½, in a matinee race. Could have gone quite a little faster.

He returned the mare to Anteeo and raised Alto, a dark brown horse, about 15½ hands, that would weigh in the neighborhood of 1,000 pounds. Alto is a fine looker, and has plenty of speed. His trainer told me that he drove Alto, when a yearling, a quarter in 40 seconds. He is now in the stud.

Mr. O'Reilly's next venture was to breed his mare to Antevolo, the result being a bay filly, with a strip in her face. She has received no particular attention.

Emma Taylor was next bred to Dawn, and in 1888 produced a colt by him. This colt is now a sort of dapple brown, fine size, well made, and with a chance should make a trotter. He is simply broken to drive.

In 1889 the mare had a colt by Secretary. I did not see it, but it is a good colt I am told.

This present season the mare has been again bred to Dawn.

From Mr. O'Reilly's we again drove up town. Mr. Mizner showed us a stallion in his charge. This horse is called Dauntless. He is a bright bay, 15.3½, and would weigh about 1050 pounds. He differs materially in appearance and make up from the majority of his sire produce. This must be accounted for by the influence of his dam, Miss Spiers, (dam of Mattie P. 2:31), by Tom Hyer, Jr. He is a good looking, well disposed stud, and although receiving as yet very little training, Dan thinks well of his future.

Dawn we found stabled at Mr. Whitney's place in town. Any extended description of him by me is unnecessary as every well informed horseman knows that he is a highly bred courageous racehorse, with speed beyond his record. Barring unusual accident, Dawn will have some representatives in the 2:30 list this year.

I took a flying glance at A. P. Patchen, a big son of Alexander and Gazelle by General McClellan, second dam Jenny Shepherd (dam of Flora Shepherd 2:30 and Nellie Patchen 2:27½) by Belmont (Williamson's). This horse is a light bay, 16 3, and weighs 1300 pounds. He is a stylish going horse, with good mane and tail.

Mr. Fraiser's horse Secretary is kept at his ranch in Chelanay Valley. He is now 16 hands high and will weigh about 1100 pounds. He is a large sized representative of his sire. He differs from him in some respects, to be sure, yet the resemblance is very strong. Secretary was sired by Director, dam by Volunteer (Goldsmith's). It is my humble conviction that a better colt than Secretary never heard the bell ring. He trotted as a yearling at Petaluma, and at the finish he and George V. by Sidney were the contesting colts, Secretary having thirty yards the best of it when close to the wire. He made a bad break and before he recovered George V. went by and beat him under the wire. As a two-year-old Secretary was taken to the Pleasanton track, and there received too many quarters in 34 and 34½ seconds. Mr. Fraieser says he is right now and expects to train him this coming season. If he stands work he will go down to a low mark, as he naturally is very speedy.

I looked in on Jackson Temple, sire of Emma Temple 2:21 and Mattie P. 2:31. Temple is a dark bay horse, weighing about 1150. He is a son of George M. Patchen Jr., and has a record of 2.38½. His daughter Emma is certainly about as conscientious and clever a race mare, up to her speed, as ever looked through a bridle.

Inside the track, busily at work on the rich grass, was Lot Slocum, 2:17½ and Chapman, the pacer, 2:22. They are looking rugged and strong. As the horses and colts went by they would raise their heads and look intently at them, and then suddenly drop them again, evidently thinking what an amount of drilling the youngsters would have to go through before their speed equaled their own. Chapman is said to be able to time a horse a quarter, with great accuracy. I hardly believe this although Geo. Fine vouches for it.

After a handshake with Dr. Maclay and several other horsemen, I entered the 'bus for the train, thoroughly impressed with the good fellowship of Petaluma horsemen and the conviction that Petaluma streets are the most devilish upon earth.

Fallibility of Trainers.

Noah Armstrong, owner of Spokane, tells a story illustrating the fallibility of trainers as authorities on racing form which we find in the Horseman: Said he: "I once had a trainer whose hindsight was a blank sight better than his foresight. One day at Latonia my horse Gray Cloud was to run for a stake against Mona, Kaloolah, Ed Corrigan and King Robin. I asked my trainer in the morning what he thought of our chances, and he said; 'Mr. Armstrong, we ain't in it; we won't be first, second or third. Mona will win it and Kaloolah will run second. Don't bet counterfeit money on our horse.' I went down to the betting ring when they began to sell the auction pools, and found fellows falling over each other to buy Mona and Kaloolah. Each sold for about $150, and King Robin had plenty of backers at $100, but nobody wanted to buy pools on Ed Corrigan or my horse, Gray Cloud; so when the auctioneer put the two together in the field, and the boys began to chaff me about Montana's bringing up the rear, I bought the field, paying $30 for the two horses against about $400 on the other three. I bought the field in every pool but one that was sold on the race, and then took a stroll around the ring and backed Gray Cloud for a place. He won it—won it easy, and Ed Corrigan came second. Right after the race my trainer came up and said: 'Did you put a crimp in the bookmakers, Mr. Armstrong?' 'Oh, no,' I said, 'I only bet a few soiled and torn small bills.' 'That's too bad,' said he, 'you should have won a fortune on that race. I don't see how you missed it. You didn't suppose those skates could beat our horse, did you?"

Suspensions and Expulsions.

We have received from M. M. Morse, Secretary of the National Trotting Association, the "Blue Book" compiled to and including January 1, 1890. The work contains a full list of all persons under suspension, or those who have been expelled, and remain penalized to the date mentioned. The list has been sent to the various secretaries of all tracks who have membership in the association, and it is to be presumed that those whose names are in the "Blue Book" will not be allowed to start unless the penalties are rescinded. The American Association recognizes the suspensions and expulsions of the National, so that the black-listed ones stand little show to trot horses unless the matter is arranged before the season opens. The list of Californian names is rather an extended one, and is here given in full, so that the parties interested may take the necessary steps to restore themselves to "good standing:"

Name.	Residence.	Penalty.
Adams, J. D.	Maxwell, Cal	Suspended Sept. 9, 1889
Agnew, J. B.	Visalia, Cal	Suspended Oct. 14, 1889 Suspended Oct. 21, 1889
Alexander, W. S.	Stockton, Cal	Suspended Oct. 17, 1881
Allen, M. M.	San Francisco Cal	Suspended Oct. 4, 1883
Allen, R. K.	Sacramento, Cal	Suspended Sept. 30, 1878
Anderson, Frank	Santa Rosa, Cal	Suspended Oct. 16, 1888
Bailey, G. O.	Portland, Ore	Suspended Oct. 3, 1889
Bambrick, Chas	San Francisco, Cal	Suspended Oct. 21, 1889
Barstow, T. W.	San Jose, Cal	Suspended Sept. 14, 1886
Beardsley, P. F.	San Francisco, Cal	Suspended Oct. 1, 1879
Blackmore, William	San Jose, Cal	Suspended Nov. 22, 1878
Boardman, William	Oakland, Cal	Suspended Oct. 27, 1881
Boucher, A.	Woodland, Cal	Suspended Oct. 7, 1889
Boyden, C. D.	Lincoln, Cal	Suspended Sept. 17, 1885 Suspended Oct. 23, 1886
Bozeman, H. B.	Visalia, Cal	Suspended Sept. 10 1889
Brown, J. H.	Fresno, Cal	Suspended Oct. 9, 1888
Bunch, C. T.	Ione, Cal	Suspended Sept. 7, 1888 Suspended Oct. 9, 1888
Cade, W. H.	Oakland, Cal	Suspended Oct. 11, 1881 Suspended Oct. 17, 1881 Suspended Oct. 27, 1881
Carroll, Col. R. W.	Sacramento, Cal	Suspended Dec. 7, 1870
Charles, Frank	San Francisco, Cal	Suspended Oct. 7, 1879 Suspended Oct. 15, 1879
Cockrill, B. B.	Santa Rosa, Cal	Suspended Oct. 16, 1888
Cocoran, J.	Petaluma, Cal	Suspended Oct. 21, 1880
Corbin, S. E.	Auburn, Cal	Suspended Sept. 2, 1889 Suspended Sept. 24, 1889
Corbin & Anderson	Auburn, Cal	Suspended Sept. 10, 1889 Suspended Oct. 12, 1889
Creighton, B. H.	San Francisco, Cal	Suspended Oct. 20, 1884
Cropsey, George	Pleasanton, Cal	Suspended Oct. 21, 1889
Daniels, S L	Chico, Cal	Suspended Oct. 16, 1877
De Groot, Harry	Watsonville, or Santa Cruz, Cal	Suspended June 20, 1881 Expelled Nov. 10, 1881
Dowell, J. W.	Marysville, Cal	Suspended Oct. 16, 1889
Duncan, Louis	Santa Clara, Cal	Suspended Oct. 14, 1884
Dyson, Joe	Summit, Cal	Suspended Oct. 11, 1889
Eddy, Chas. W.	Marysville, Cal	Suspended Sept. 2, 1889
Eddy, Stanley A.	Nevada City, Cal	Suspended Sept. 10, 1889
Ellis, George	Lakeport, Cal	Suspended Aug. 25, 1884
Emerson, S. B.	Oakland, Cal	Suspended Oct. 7, 1889
Fink, Henry	Chico, Cal	Suspended Sept. 25, 1884
Fisher, Charles	Sierra Valley, Cal	Suspended Oct. 14, 1886
Fitzgerald, W. J.	San Francisco, Cal	Suspended July 8, 1885
Gillespie, R. H.	San Francisco, Cal	Suspended Sept. 4, 1877
Gilmore, W. J.	Oakland, Cal	Suspended Oct. 27, 1881
Goldman, M.	Merced, Cal	Suspended Oct. 27, 1881
Guerrow, A.	Half Moon Bay, Cal	Suspended Nov. 22, 1878
Hart, Thomas	San Francisco, Cal	Suspended Oct. 3, 1878 Suspended Nov 22, 1878
Henry, James	Chico, Cal	Suspended Oct. 16, 1883
Henry, William	Oakland, Cal	Suspended Oct. 6, 1886 Suspended Oct. 18, 1886
Hicks, J. L.	San Francisco, Cal	Suspended Oct. 11, 1881 Suspended Oct. 17, 1881
Hill, Ben F.	Lakeside, Cal	Suspended Sept. 10, 1889
Hitchcock, H.	Petaluma, Cal	Suspended Oct. 18, 1887
Hodson, J. B.	Sacramento, Cal	Suspended Sept. 2, 1889 Suspended Sept. 24, 1889 Suspended Oct. 7, 1889 Suspended Oct. 12, 1889
Holland & Snyder	Hayden Hill, Cal	Suspended Oct. 12, 1887
Hooper, S.	Nevada City, Cal	Suspended Sept. 14, 1886
Hunt, D. R.	Oakland, Cal Oakland, Cal Napa, Cal Napa, Cal	Suspended Nov. 30, 1878 Suspended Oct. 20, 1880 Suspended Oct. 23, 1880 Suspended Jan. 24, 1881
Johnson, William M.	Oakland, Cal	Suspended Sept. 25, 1884 Suspended Sept. 25, 1884 Suspended Oct. 14, 1884
Jones, J. R.	Fresno, Cal	Suspended Sept. 10, 1889 Suspended Sept. 24, 1889
Jones, W. H.	San Francisco, Cal	Suspended Oct. 16, 1877
Kennedy, Tim	San Jose, Cal	Suspended Nov. 22, 1878
Killip, J N	San Francisco, Cal	Suspended Oct 25, 1881
Kingsbury, H M	Quincy, Cal	Suspended Nov. 18, 1882
Knight, John	San Francisco, Cal	Suspended Oct. 3, 1878 Suspended Oct. 8, 1878 Suspended Nov. 22, 1878
Lane, Tim	San Francisco, Cal	Suspended Oct. 8, 1878
Lightner, Al	Sierra Valley, Cal	Suspended Oct. 14, 1886
Lloyd, William	Susanville, Cal	Suspended Oct. 22, 1887
Macy & Co	San Francisco, Cal San Francisco, Cal San Francisco, Cal	Suspended Oct. 4, 1877 Suspended Oct. 16, 1877 Suspended Oct. 25, 1877
Maddox, James	Santa Rosa, Cal	Suspended Sept. 19, 1887
Marks, S.	San Francisco, Cal	Suspended Oct. 25, 1879
McCarty or McCarthy, John M.	San Francisco, Cal	Suspended Sept. 30, 1878 Suspended Oct. 3, 1878 Suspended Oct. 8, 1878 Suspended Nov. 22, 1878
McClellan, Thomas	— Cal	Suspended Oct. 1, 1879 Expelled Oct. 1, 1879
McFayden, A.	Santa Rosa, Cal	Suspended Oct. 7, 1889
McGovern, Dan	Petaluma, Cal	Suspended Nov. 3, 1887
McGuire, William	Oakland, Cal	Suspended Oct. 17, 1881
McHugh, H.	Fresno, Cal	Suspended Sept. 24, 1889
Mooney, M.	San Francisco, Cal	Suspended Oct. 1, 1879 Suspended Oct. 25, 1879
Moore, W. W.	Oakland, Cal	Suspended Oct. 20, 1880
Noonon, P. W.	San Francisco, Cal	Suspended Oct. 25, 1879 Suspended Nov. 5, 1879
Ober, Worth	Sacramento, Cal	Suspended Oct. 12, 1889
O'Dell, T H., M. D.	Woodbridge, Cal	Suspended Oct. 17, 1881
O'Rourke, John	San Francisco, Cal	Suspended Oct. 4, 1884 Suspended Oct. 14, 1884 Suspended Oct. 20, 1884
Patterson, Andrew	Pleasanton, Cal	Suspended Sept. 30, 1885 Suspended Oct 14, 1885
Patterson, John	Linden, Cal Stockton, Cal	Suspended Oct. 14, 1889 Suspended Oct. 14, 1889
Pinney, A. A. or H. H.	Grass Valley, Cal	Suspended Oct. 20, 1884
Price, W. Z.	San Mateo, Cal	Suspended Oct. 17, 1882
Ramsey, J. B.	Marysville, Cal	Suspended Sept. 14, 1886
Rix, Edward	San Francisco, Cal San Leandro, Cal	Suspended Oct. 8, 1878 Suspended Nov. 22, 1878
Rogers, G	Ione, Cal	Suspended Sept. 10, 1889
Sayer, D. J.	Petaluma, Cal	Suspended Oct. 18, 1887
Shear, Charles H.	Sacramento, Cal	Expelled May 31, 1884
Shear, W. H.	Sacramento, Cal	Suspended Dec. 2, 1876
Smith, A. F.	Sacramento, Cal	Suspended Sept. 30, 1878
Smith, M. H.	San Francisco, Cal	Expelled Nov. 28, 1887
Smith, W. H. B.	Oakland Cal	Suspended Sept. 25, 1884 Suspended Sept. 25, 1884 Suspended Oct. 14 1884
Spencer, E. V.	Susanville, Cal	Suspended Oct. 1, 1888 Suspended Oct. 16, 1888
Stagg, Cornelius	San Francisco, Cal	Suspended Dec 20, 1877
Tapp, R. H.	Long Valley, Cal	Suspended Nov. 18, 1882
Taylor, A. C.	Gridley, Cal	Suspended Oct. 22, 1887
Taylor, Frank	Sacramento, Cal	Suspended Sept. 24, 1889
Taylor, J. J.	Santa Rosa, Cal	Suspended Oct. 16, 1888
Tetreau, Frank J	Chico, Cal	Suspended Nov. 3, 1887
Thomas, Charles H	Oak Grove, Cal	Suspended Oct. 14, 1884 Suspended Oct. 20, 1884
Thomas, George	Benicia, Cal	Suspended Sept. 30, 1878 Suspended Oct. 3, 1878
Todhunter, George	Long Valley, Cal	Suspended Nov. 18, 1882
Todhunter, W. P	Sacramento Cal	Suspended Oct. 22, 1887
Touhey, James	Sacramento, Cal	Suspended June 1, 1889
Treanor, Grant	El Cajon, Cal	Suspended May 18, 1888
Waldstein, A.	San Francisco, Cal	Suspended Oct. 20, 1884
Warburton, John	Santa Clara, Cal	Suspended Oct. 12, 1887 Suspended Oct. 20, 1887
Welch, P. B.	Longville, Cal	Suspended Oct. 16, 1888
West, A. D.	Grass Valley, Cal	Suspended Sept 19, 1887
West, S. F.	Stockton, Cal	Suspended Aug. 6, 1885 Suspended Aug. 8, 1886
Williams, P J	San Jose, Cal	Suspended Nov. 20, 1878
Withrom, Capt	Sacramento, Cal	Suspended Oct. 25, 1881

The Edgewater and Kingston Stud Yearlings.

It is seldom our pleasure to notice a grander lot of yearlings than the Edgewater and Kingston stud youngsters, to be sold at Lexington, Ky., Wednesday, May 7, 1890, by Messrs. Bruce & Kidd. On Friday last, April 11th, we visited both farms and inspected the youngsters, and shall attempt to give your readers an idea of how each look, devoting a short notice to each, taking them as they appear in the catalogue. The Edgewater yearlings run from one to twenty.

No. 1. A chestnut colt, own brother to Audrain, Almera and Alameda, by Springbok, dam Alme by Planet.

No. 2. A large, splendid, and highly-formed chestnut colt, own brother to Goano, by Springbok, dam Genera by Planet.

No. 3. Chestnut colt, own brother to Ascalon and Ascoli, by Springbok, dam Astora by Asteroid.

No. 4. Chestnut colt, half brother to Weasel, Orlando and Kirklin, by Audrain, dam Aeolia by imp. Australian.

No. 5. A bay colt by Audrain, dam Mademoiselle (dam of War Lass, Rebok, Mandamus II) by Red Eye.

No 6. A chestnut colt by Onondaga, dam Electrical (dam of Schoolmaster, Warrior, etc.) by Springbok.

No. 7. Chestnut colt by Springbok, dam Jennie V. by Waverley.

No. 8. A large, big-boned bay colt, of great length, by imp. Silvermine, dam Olathe by Springbok.

No. 9. A chestnut colt by Audrain, dam War Lass (dam of Sonnet, Miss Charmer, Winona) by War Call.

No. 10. A chestnut colt by Springbok, dam Mayflower by Bob Woolley.

No. 11. A chestnut colt by Springbok, dam Fanny Hall by Norfolk.

No 12. A chestnut colt by imp. Silvermine, dam Minnarette by Springbok.

No. 13. Chestnut filly, sister to Lela May, by Springbok, dam Zulite by Lisbon.

No. 14. Chestnut filly, sister to East Lynne, Plunger, etc., by Springbok, dam Easter Planet by Planet.

No. 15. A chestnut filly, half sister to Zulu, Abilene, etc., by Onondaga, dam Zingarelli by Springbok.

No. 16. Chestnut filly, half sister to Irish Dan, by Springbok, dam imp. Grey Gown by Grey Palmer.

No. 17 Chestnut filly, half sister to Vallesia, Nimblefoot, Major Picket, etc., by Audrain, dam Mollie Cad by Lexington.

No. 18. A chestnut filly by Onondaga, dam Sister Monica by Springbok.

No. 19. A bay filly by imp. Deceiver, dam Bonairette by Springbok.

No. 20. A bay filly by Springbok, dam Minnie by Minwaukee.

The Kingston yearlings are fourteen in number, and the first on the list is

No. 21. Bay colt by Longfellow, dam imp. Encore (dam of Helter Skelter) by Cymbal.

No 22. Bay colt by Longfellow, dam Trophy by Alarm.

No 23. A bay colt, half brother to Biscuit, by imp. Zorilla, dam imp. Undercrust by Brown Bread.

No. 24. Brown or black colt, half brother to Prodigal Son, by Longfellow, dam imp. Homeward Bound by Coltness.

No. 25. A dark bay colt by imp. Zorilla, dam imp. Press Onward by Ethne.

No 26. A bay colt by imp. Zorilla, dam Fraulein by Wanderer.

No. 27. A beautiful chestnut colt by imp. The Ill Used, dam Attractive (dam of Winning Ways) by Kentucky.

No. 28. A brown filly by Longfellow, dam Fan Fare (dam St. Clair (Oscar) and Rollin Hawley) by imp. King Ernest.

No. 29. A bay filly by Longfellow, dam imp. Manzanita by Kaiser.

No 30. A bay filly by imp. Zorilla, dam Palmetto by Virgil.

No. 31. A chestnut filly by Jils Johnson, dam Ada by Kingfisher.

No. 32. A bay or brown filly by imp. Zorilla, dam Little Hopes (sister to Once Again and Ocean Wave) by Onondaga.

No. 33. A brown filly (sister to Kenny) by Duke of Montrose), dam (dam of Kenney and Startle) by imp. Leamington.

No. 34. A bay filly by imp. Zorilla, dam Mollie Reed (dam of Forest Black Knight, etc) by Reed's Yorkshire.

We can assure our readers that this is, taken as a whole, a grand lot of yearlings, some of them extra fine, and there will be few offerings this year that will exceed them in quality and merit. Catalogues may be obtained at this office, or by addressing Bruce & Kidd, Lexington, Ky. NIAGARA.

Flower City Stake.

The entries to the Flower City Stake were received too late for publication in our last issue, but are given below. It will be seen that Mr. Hickok wants to have a chance for first money, as he has made a nomination:

C. E. Mosher, Lawrence, Mass.
O. A. Hickok, San Francisco, Cal.
J. W. Quimby, Scranton, Pa.
Allen Farm, per N. R. Allen, Pittsfield, Mass.
A. R. Armstrong, Romeo, Mich.
A. C. Redfield, Galesburg, Knox Co., Ill.
Rensselaer Stock Farm, Rensselaer, Ind.
Glenville Stock Farm, per Shockancy, Louisville, Ky.
L. W. Russell, Canton, N. Y.
D. B. Harrington, Poughkeepsie, N. Y.
C. Nolan, Philadelphia, Pa.
Village Farm, C. J. Hamlin, proprietor, East Aurora, N. Y
B. Doble, Chicago, Ill.
Patchen Farm, Waterloo, N. Y., J. W. Day, proprietor.
Elm City Stock Farm, New Haven, Conn.
D. S. Hammond, New York City, N. Y.
H. G. Smith, New York City, N. Y.
J. E. Turner, Ambler, Pa.
G. W. Archer, Rochester, N. Y.
G. W. Eckstein, Philadelphia, Pa.

Last Day of the P. C. B. H. A. Spring Meeting.

Last Saturday was ushered in by heavy clouds and from all indications rain would surely spoil the afternoon's sport. However, on the evening previous the Directors, at a meeting, decided to have the programme run off, rain or shine, so the regular race goers turned their faces trackwards, immediately after luncheon. About noontime the clouds dispersed and the beautiful day tempted many to visit the Bay District, who would have stayed away, if the weather had still looked threatening. The Association had prepared an excellent card, there being five events to decide, all of which were well filled, and the promise of good sport seemed excellent. The carriage paddock presented a handsome appearance, the turn outs being numerous and pleasing to the eye, while the ladies' stand was nicely filled, the spring dresses, with their variegated hues, lending a charm to the scene that can only be appreciated by those who were present. The betting was fully up to what had been done on other days, and now that the racing is all over, it may not be out of place to tell the public that the bookmakers lost heavily. It seems to be the usual custom for all reporters, especially on the daily press, to state that "the bookmakers won on the day," but at the late meeting, we can safely say that the fraternity were all on the wrong side of the ledger when the racing terminated.

The first race of the day was for two-year-olds, the sensational Homer and the grand young filly Fairy, not being among those to start, caused the betting public to fancy the chances of the Palo Alto representative, Rinfax, the second choice being Col. Harry I. Thornton's pair, Arcade and Cimeter, while the field consisted of Sir Walter, who carried the colors of the Elmwood Stable, and Sinfax one of Mr. Rose's castoffs, that gentlemen having leased the running qualities of the colt to Cy Mulkey. There used to be an old saying "a Vandal for the mud," but from the outcome of Saturday's work, Californians are apt to change the quotation to "a Wildidle for the mud," as three of the events were won by the get of that game son of imp Australian, while for the fourth event on the card, another Wildidle was beaten only a very short length. The track was a muddy one in the strict sense of the word, the backstretch being more like a duck pond than a race course As on the previous day Mr. Wm. Coombs occupied the position of starter and upheld his previous high reputation in that respect. The judges of the day were Messrs. Ramsdell, Guntz and Anderson, and the time made was recorded by Messrs. Carroll, Smith and Sullivan. The youngsters made several ineffectual attempts to get away, the rider of the favorite, having determined that his mount should be in stride before the horses got off and he was successful as he accomplished his object.

The flag fell to a very even start, the nose of Rinfax showing first in front, Sinfax second, and as they got squared away Sir Walter was third, Cimeter fourth, and the chestnut colt Arcade a bad last. The contest quickly resolved itself into a duel between the two "faxes," the Palo Alto representative cutting out the pace, but Sinfax would not be shaken off, Dennison on the Mulkey entry keeping shoulder to shoulder with Rinfax. Coming into the homestretch Dennison tried to keep to the extreme outside of the track, but Narvaez was possessed of the same desire, fouling Sinfax quite perceptibly. Dennison stuck to his work, and by the sheer gameness of his horse won a grand race by three-quarters of a length. Time, 1:13¾. Considering the state of the track, the time made was excellent, and the finish by both colts was of the highest order and thoroughly enjoyed by the spectators.

SUMMARY.

Purse $350, of which $50 to the second horse, a handicap for two-year-olds; entrance free for starters. Declarations $5 to go to the racing fund. Eleven-sixteenths of a mile.

Mulkey's b c Sinfax by Wildidle—Fostress, 105 ......C. Dennison 1
Palo Alto's ch c Rinfax, by Argyle — Imp Amelia, 112, ...Narvaez 2
H. I. Thornton's ch c Arcade by Milner—Fanny Hubbard, 100 ......Casey 3

Time, 1:13¾.

Sir Walter, 107, Ross; Cimeter, 95, Madden, ran unplaced.

Book Betting—Sinfax, 5 to 1, 8 to 5; Rinfax, 7 to 10, no place; Arcade 6 to 1, 8 to 5; Cimeter, 5 to 1, 7 to 5; Sir Walter, 10 to 1, 3 to 1.

Auction Pools—Rinfax, $25; Thornton's Stable (Arcade and Cimeter), $13; Field, $8

The "Shortenders" were naturally jubilant over the result of the first race, and did not hesitate to invest liberally on the selling race which was next in order on the programme. There was plenty of time to get in all the money necessary, as two of the horses acted very unruly at the post and delayed the start for a long time, Steve Stroud being particularly stubborn and ill natured. The jockeys were also inclined to do as they pleased, so much so in fact that Starter Coombs set eleven of them down for fifteen days each, the only one to escape punishment being Casey, the rider of Tom Daly. This is unfortunate for many of the lads, as the time covers the Sacramento meeting. At last the field was sent away to a straggling start, Kildare, Tom Daly and Rose Meade showing first to the front. Ladi Ali came with a good burst of speed, and at the half was leading by two lengths, with the other three bunched and the field strung out, Adam bringing up the rear. On the turn Kildare fell back beaten, Ali being taken away on the outside, while Rosebug was kept next to the rails where the going was the heaviest. Maggie B. at the three-quarters came up gamely, but she also quit in the stretch when near the drawgate. Tom Daly was taken to the outside together with Kildare, Ida Glenn coming down the middle of the track. The mud told on Glenn and her chance was gone at the upper end of the Grand Stand.

At the draw gate Rosemeade was still in the heavy going and perfectly fresh, he finishing as he pleased in 1:22, Tom Daly second by a head from Kildare, the remainder strung out for a distance of fifty yards or more.

SUMMARY.

Selling purse $350, of which $50 to second; for all ages. Horses entered to be sold for $1000 to carry rule weights. Three pounds allowed for each $100 less. Three-quarters of a mile.

C. Foster's b f Rosemeade 3, Wildidle—Duchess, 80..........Ward 1
Cy Mulky's ch g Tom Daly a. by Patsy Duffy—Sunshine, 96...Casey 2
M. Storn's ch g Kildare, 6, by Kyrle Daly—Mistake, 105......Pierce 3

Time—1:22.

Sallie C, 4, 91, Dennison; Vinco, 5, 105, Ross; Steve Stroud, 3, 103, Williams; Rosebug, 4, 99, McIntosh; Ida Glenn, a, 97, Brown; Lady Ali, 3, 86, Madden; Hernanda, 5, 108, Ferguson; Adam, a, 96, Murphy; Maggie B, 5, 108, Roach, ran unplaced.

Book betting—Rosemeade, 10-1, 4-1; Tom Daly 4-1 7-5; Kildare 3-1, 1-1; Ida Glenn, 3-1, 1-1; Steve Stroud, 15-1, 5-1; Adam, 20-1, 8-1; Sallie C, 15-1, 5-1; Vinco, 20-1, 6-1; Rosebug, 15-1, 5-1; Hernanda, 20-1, 8-1; Lady Ali, 3-1, 1-1.

Auction pools—Kildare $25, Ida Glenn $14, Lady Ali $12, field $25.

Again were the field purchasers happy, but by this time those who allow no point to escape had noticed that two Wildidles had won, therefore there was a little rush to back Raindrop and Fannie F for the next race. There are those, however, that want stable tips, and play no other, and royally were this class cinched on the third race, as according to all the rubbers and stable boys, Captain Al would win in a walk, "there was nothing else in it." To the close observer, Raindrop was in the best of condition, and so was also Captain Al, but the Wildidle blood was there to back up the exquisite form, and money went in very freely on "Billy" Appleby's neatly turned filly. The Sacramento division had a fancy for Sheridan, so Phil Siebenthaler's Joe Hooker colt also carried a small pot of money, his running in the races of the previous days fully warranting the strong belief that he could beat the field he had to contend against. There was not much time wasted in breakaways, and the flag soon fell to a good start, the favorite, Captain Al, showing in front, as the seven passed the stand. Madden on Kiro at once set sail for the leader, and as they rounded into the first turn was flanking Captain Al. At this point Fannie F stumbled and fell, throwing her rider, Ross, the boy afterwards claiming that he was fouled. The balance kept on their journey. Kiro and Captain Al fighting every inch from the quarter pole to the upper turn, the others evidently waiting for them to tire themselves out; At the three quarters Captain Al fell back beaten, the running now being taken up by Coloma and Raindrop, the latter soon passing Kiro and winning in a handsome gallop by at least three lengths, Coloma gaining second place by a length from Kiro.

SUMMARY.

Purse $400, of which $50 to second, $25 to third; for three-year-olds and upwards. Winners of any race at this distance or more at this meeting when carrying weight for age or more, to carry five pounds extra; of two such races, eight pounds extra. Horses beaten at this distance this year once allowed three pounds, twice, five pounds. One mile.

W. L. Appleby's ch f Raindrop, 3, Wildidle—imp. Teardrop, 92 ......Murphy 1
W. L. Whitmore's ch h Coloma, 5, Joe Hooker—Callie Smart, 116 ......Hill 2
W. M. Murry's ch c Kiro, 3, Joe Hooker—by Foster, 102,....Madden 3

Time, 1:47½.

Adelaide, 3, 97, Ward; Captain Al, 3, 99, Narvaez; Fanny F., 5, 116, Ross; Sheridan, 3, 102, Williams, ran unplaced.

Book betting—Raindrop, 6—1, 2—1; Coloma 3—1, 1—1; Kiro 6—1, 2—1, Captain Al 8—5, 1—2; Sheridan, 4—1, 7—5; Fanny F. 20—1, 8—1; Adelaide, 10—1, 4—1.

Auction pools—Captain Al $25; Coloma $14, field $40.

An owner's handicap is at the best but a poor guessing affair, no one being able to draw a line on the runners, and more especially when the mud has also to be made one of the quantities in calculating the probable result. Light weights rule, and even stables are nonplussed at times, how to lay the money when there are more than one starter carrying the same colors. This was aptly illustrated on Saturday, the Hearst contingent feeling positive that Gertrude could beat Baggage with the light weight, and they played the Australian mare accordingly, but Baggage proved the victor after a peculiar run race. Eight horses sported silk, the distance being a mile and a sixteenth; Pliny, from the Kelly & Samuels' stable, owing to his light weight, was selected by the talent to win, but he was not in the hunt. The Hearst stable was second choice, with Carmen a close third, in fact before the flag fell, Pliny receded to third choice in the books. When Starter Coombs got them away, Pliny and Leland started out to make the pace, with Gertrude as a fast competitor. On reaching the backstretch, the three were making a show of the field, but gradually the Australian fell back, and in the turn Pliny turned faint-hearted, allowing Carmen to pass him. Coming down the stretch, Leland threw up his tail and quit, and a cracking race ensued between Carmen and Baggage, the latter coming down from the head of the straight with a great burst of speed, and he finally won by half a length from the mare, Pliny a fairly good third.

SUMMARY.

Purse $350, of which $50 to second horse; an owners' handicap for horses that have started and not won at this meeting; ten pounds over weight allowed; winners excused without penalty; one mile and a sixteenth.

George Hearst's Baggage, ch c, 3, by Warwick, dam Maria F., 74 ......Sullivan 1
W. L. Appleby's Carmen, ch m, 5, by Wildidle, dam Nettie Brown, 95......Murphy 2
Kelly & Samuels' Pliny, b c, by Flood, dam Precious, 80 lbs ......Ward 3

Time, 1:56½.

Gertrude, 4, 95, Madden; Leland, 3, 85, Jones; Emma, 4, 90, Brown; Bettie B., 8, 97, Narvaez, ran unplaced.

Bookbetting—Baggage, 2½ to 1, 4 to 5; Carmen, 8 to 1, 1 to 1; Pliny, 4 to 1, 1 to 1; Gertrude, 3 to 1, 1 to 1; Bettie B., 8 to 1, 3 to 1; Leland, 15 to 1, 5 to 1; Emma, 15 to 1, 5 to 1.

Auction pools—Pliny $25, Hearst's Stable (Baggage and Gertrude) $15, Field $15.

The final event was the longest race of the meeting, the distance being a mile and five-eighths, and the ones to face the flag were Sacramento, Ed McGinnis, Hotspur and Faustino. The bookmakers made this race "an air tight" for although there were four starters the highest odds on any one, was 3 to 1. Sacramento, the Hearst entry, was tipped as the sure winner, but what it was on gracious only knows, for he made a most miserable exhibition of himself calling down on his head the curses of his ardent supporters. The McGinnis backers were rather dubious as to the result of the heavy weight, causing them to fear a defeat. Of the four, Hotspur looked the most fitting for a hard race, and on his appearance was backed quite extensively for place, he justifying the fond hopes of his admirers. There is but little description required of the race. Hotspur was first away, with the Palo Alto mare second, McGinnis third and the favorite last. From the start the race was virtually between Hotspur and the "Irishman," the former leading to the middle of the homestretch where McGinnis came away and won as he pleased in 3:04, Faustine third, and Sacramento away off.

SUMMARY.

The Ocean Handicap—A sweepstakes for all ages; $20 entrance; $10 forfeit; $5 declaration with $500 added, of which $75 to the second, third to save stake. One mile and five-eighths.

Kelly & Samuels' Ed McGinnis, b h, 4, by Grinstead, dam Jenny G., 122......Cook 1
Dennison Bros.' Hotspur, b h, 4, by Joe Daniels, dam sister to Jim Douglas, 110......C. Dennison
Palo Alto's Faustine, b f, 4, by Flood, dam Flirt, 110........Narvaez

Time, 3:04.

Sacramento, 3, 100, Madden, ran unplaced.

Bookbetting—Ed McGinnis, 2½ to 1, 7 to 10; Hotspur, 2½ to 1, 7 to 10; Faustino, 3 to 1, 1 to 1; Sacramento, 2 to 1, 7 to 10.

Our Lakeport Letter.

EDITOR BREEDER AND SPORTSMAN:—With the return of pleasant weather, horses and horsemen are shaking off the lethargy of winter and are preparing, like the nimble bee, for immediate action.

Our horse breeders are becoming more and more alive to the imperative necessity of good blood. For blood is what counts. Auctioneers want it, racing interests demand it, breeders will have it, and the general public won't do without it. Blood it is that trots, runs, endures and wins. Blood is speed, beauty, intelligence. You can raise it easier, keep it cheaper, and sell it higher than the ordinary common sort, and so it pays. In short, blood is the all essential requisite for the successful breeding of good horses for any purpose. It is true that the raising of exceptionally fast horses is a lottery, but the chances against you are greatly diminished by judicious and careful breeding. Therefore, the motto of every horse breeder should be "Get the Best."

Bert Rodman, owner of Advocate (by Attorney, he by Harold) has bred his mare "Nellie Turner" a near relative of Geo. Washington 2:30 to Starrs Anteeo colt, dam Countess.

J. W. Boggs, bay stallion Daniel Deronda by Black Ralph, dam Bessie B by Milton Medium is in the stud, and deserves a liberal patronage.

Hildebrande & Kelling, proprietors of Alwood Stock Farm, have secured the services of Mr. Tracy as trainer for the ensuing season. Their horse Alwood is a well bred youngster, and will be sent for a record this year. In addition they have several promising colts that are to compete for stakes this fall.

"Jim" Corcoran has come to make his home with us, and will train for Hon. R. J. Hudson, ex-Sheriff Boggs and others. We extend to him a hearty welcome, and feel assured of his success.

Judge Hudson has an Anteeo filly, which, as a 2-year-old, trotted in 3:14 on a half mile track at Ukiah, without a murmur. The same gentleman also has a yearling by Anteeo, out of a Milton Medium mare, which should be a "hummer."

"Lil" Boggs claims the champion high jumping colt. He has a yearling by Advocate which cleared a fence 6 feet 2 inches high, with 6 inches to spare. How is that for a sky-scraper?

We stopped in this week to see the stallion colt Anti-C by Anteeo 2:16½, dam Countess (dam of Dawn 2:18¾, Strathway, 3-year-old, 2:26, etc). He is a beautiful bay, verging into black on the legs, of superb conformation, having a well turned barrel, strong loin, well set shoulders, sound feet and legs and the typical Electioneer head. He is undoubtedly a good one, and Mr. Starr is to be congratulated in being his fortunate possessor. "X."

Bad Shoeing Responsible.

Nine times out of ten faulty shoeing is responsible for lameness. Colts are born with perfect feet. Nature intended them to run on the ground constantly, and if they did their hoofs would wear away evenly, but instead they are kept indoors five months of the year, the hoofs become long and break off in pieces from time to time. If a considerable piece breaks off at the side the foot runs over, like an old boot, and the colt acquires the habit of walking partially on one side of the foot, which is very difficult to remedy. Sometimes both sides break off, leaving the toe unnaturally long, thus throwing more weight on the heels, causing them to wear away faster than they should. This produces flat feet. The uneven breaking off of the hoofs before the animal matures causes most of the imperfections in the feet of the horse, with resultant ringbones spavins, curbs and other ailments.

When a horse with a bad foot comes to be shod, it runs over at the side, it should be leveled up gradually at several succeeding shoeings by making the shoe thicker at one side and parting down the hoof a little the more on the opposite side. If the feet are flat the heels should be let alone and the toes cut as far back as it will answer at every shoeing. The shoe should never bear on the sole of the foot, but on the wall alone. If the sole is low down and presents a convex surface, as is often the case, the shoe should be made either concave, to match, or very narrow to fit only on the horny shell. If the animal has contracted feet the heels should be cut away all it will do, as well as the horn, on the bottom of the foot, and the shoes should be beveled out from the quarters back, that the feet may have a tendency to spread. If the animal has ringbone or any stiffness in the joints the toes should be cut back. This rule applies to cases of spavin, thoroughpin, curbs, etc. Bad feet in horses are generally traceable to inattention of men.

The feet of colts should be attended to once in three months, from the time they are first stabled in the fall, until they reach maturity, and then permanently good feet will be assured. If agricultural societies would employ a skillful man to shoe horses at their fairs and give illustrative lectures, they would accomplish more good than they do now by some of their transactions.

TURF AND TRACK.

If Racine goes East this year it will be in the Undine Stable.

Several of the mares in the Montana Stable have been stinted to Spokane.

Peter V. Johnson will beat Terre Haute with S. A. Browne's stable.

Snapper Garrison is having a frightful time getting down to his weight.

Casey Winchell, will, it is said, ride Burford in the Kentucky Derby.

Young Phil Dwyer is said to be exercising the Dwyer Brothers' horses,

W. H. E. Smith will send Al Farrow to Chicago after the Sacramento meeting.

The Sire Bros. have sent Harry Wilkes, Rosalind Wilkes and Jos. J. to J. E. Turner.

Mr. Belmont's celebrated mare Sultana has foaled a bay filly, sister to Padishah by St. Blaise.

R. Porter Ashe's string of racers has been removed from the Westchester to the Gravesend track.

Barnes signalized his return to New Orleans from California by piloting Semaphore to victory in his first race.

The San Diegan says the Coronado Beach Company report that the new race course will be opened in June.

L. C. Lee is said to be sound again and pacing fast; he will be sent East after the Overland Park meeting at Denver.

The sporting verdict in the East, after ex-trainer James Lee handled the flag at Washington, is that he is the coming man.

Rosa Wilkes 2:18¼ will be bred to Voodoo the sensational two year old colt purchased at the Rose sale by her owner G. Babcock.

The New Jersey State Breeders Association refuse to allow pool selling or any kind of gambling at their next trotting meeting.

Seventy-four bookmakers drew lots for the location of their stands at Elizabeth on the first day, and paid, cash down, $75 for the privilege.

Storm 2:26½, the first foal of Green Mountain Maid died recently. She was seventeen years old when she made her record, having been used on the road.

This year the Directors of the State Fair Association have let bookmaking privileges, and three books will be on the track each day at the spring meeting.

W. H. Mendenhall will send East with O. A. Hickok a six year old bay daughter of Brigadier. Mr. Mendenhall expects her to show up well on the circuit.

Messrs. Gamble and Clawson's entry in the BREEDER AND SPORTSMAN Futurity Stake is void as the mare Ellie C (by Cresco) slipped her foal, a filly by Noonday.

L J. Davies, the owner of Roy Wilkes, returned from Monterey last Tuesday night, and left on Wednesday morning for Chicago via Los Angeles and San Diego.

The latest fashion among the gentler sex who visit Eastern race tracks, is to take the last novel to read while escorts are finding the sure thing and investing the money.

The Senate at Albany on the 15th passed Mr. Deane's bill, which extends the Ives poll tax of 5 per cent. to the gross receipts and membership dues of racing associations.

The Pleasanton horses are shaping up in fine style. Only a few days ago Direct was worked an easy mile in 2:20, while Margaret S. was given a quarter in thirty-five seconds.

The Flower City Stake of $10,000 for the 2:30 class, closed on April 1st with twenty subscribers, among the subscribers being Orrin A. Hickok, Budd Doble and John E. Turner.

Eolian, the speedy son of Eolus and Calash, is for sale. If not purchased immediately Mr. Easton, who secured him at the Garrison McMahon sale, will relegate him to the stud.

A brother to Kingston by Spendthrift-Kapanga, was foaled at the Hazelwood Farm, Lexington, Ky., on the last day of March. The youngster is a chestnut, with a star; both hind feet white.

Dan McCarty is having a catalogue compiled of all his live stock. They are scattered about from the Atlantic to the Pacific, and Dan says he is not quite sure where some of them are.

The Emperor of Norfolk, who was left at Santa Anita in order to breed to several mares, will be sent East shortly in company with the speedy Laredo and several other Santa Anita horses.

Gertie McCarty, by imp. Hurrah or Duke of Magenta, out of La Gloria, foaled a grand-looking filly by C. H. Todd or imp. Oatcake. Dan says there is no doubt it is a Todd, and calls it Todd's Only.

The reports thus far from Kentucky and Tennessee make no mention of any damage to valuable throughbreds or trotters, and it is to be hoped that the race tracks and stock farms escaped the cyclone.

Jess Armstrong a three year old by imp. Glengarry out of Myrtle has been reeling off halves at astonishing rate in his work at Memphis and his owners think they have another Stuyvesant in him.

Secretary Crickmore writes that Mr. Withers is busy on the new code of rules for Monmouth Park, and he hopes to have them finished within the next week, or in time for the opening of the regular racing season.

P. J. Donahue Esq., is having his race track at Laurelwood, Santa Clara, put into working order again, after lying idle two years. W. L. Appleby will take up his quarters on the track and train there in future.

John McCarty did not go East with the Santa Anita Stable, as the shoeing-smith, having received an offer from Palo Alto, and White Hat's brother is now displaying his skill on Senator Stanford's well equipped ranch.

Sinfax, the Wildidle—Fostress two year old, who beat Rinfax in the handicap for two-year-olds last Saturday, is the property of L. J. Rose who had leased him to Cy. Mulkey. The colt is entered in several races in Oregon.

After the success of the Wildidles in the slippery going last Saturday, Mr. Van Gorden decided to send imported Gertrude to Wildidle instead of taking her East. The mare is exceptionally racy looking and should pick up a race this fall.

W. H. E. Smith hopes to make arrangements to take Longshot East with Al Farrow, and will probably purchase Mr. Boots' two year old Duke of Milpitas by Duke of Norfolk out of Gipsy by imported Hercules. The Duke has several valuable engagements in the East.

I am told that one of the best stables in England this year will be John Porter's. His horses are backward just now, but they are an even lot, and it is expected the master of Kingsclere will pick up some good prizes before the Manchester November Handicap is once more decided.

It is becoming quite fashionable to breed mares in the spring and race them until well into the fall. Already Faustine has been stinted to Argyle, Ida Glenn to Prince of Norfolk, Lurline to imported Cheviot, while Welcome will be sent to the Prince of Norfolk when in Sacramento.

An English exchange says: Our race-course officials are far too honorable to delay any event in the interests of Tattersell's ring: but if we get many more petty delays, there will be found no end of people ready to hint that these were caused so that more time for betting might accrue.

We understand that Major H. C. McDowell has refused an offer of $700 an acre for Ashland, says the Lexington Daily Press. He not only declined this offer, but refused to name a price at which he will sell. Mr. A. Smith McCann was offered $25,000 bonus on his purchase of Fairlawn.

Judge A. S. Green's Linwood mare Linda has proved barren to Sidney, and therefore her entry is void in the BREEDER AND SPORTSMAN Futurity Stake. The Judge still has an entry, though. which should prove dangerous. viz., Bessie Howard by Whipple's Hambletonian, in foal to Simmocolon.

Burns McGregor, a promising young trotter, with a record of 2:29 as a two year old, and the most promising of the get of Robert McGregor, is dead from an attack of pneumonia. He was three years old, and his dam was Birdie J., by Young Jim. He was owned by E. S. Muirs of Lexington, Ky., and could readily have been sold for $10,000.

Horse nomenclature seems to be falling away, and it is very seldom one sees an aptly named colt, but I notice that on the 16th, at Elizabeth, in a two-year-old race, the Messrs. Morris' Terrifier beat Pestilence and others in a two year old scramble. Terrifier is by Alarm out of Bonella, while Pestilence is by Wanderer out of Quarantine.

Col. H. I. Thornton received one of John Mackey's expressive telegrams on Wednesday evening. It read: Brown colt all right; and meant that the Colonel's favorite mare Carrie C had foaled a brown colt by imported Darebin. As Carrie C has already thrown two good racehorses in Sobrante and Sonoma, this colt should be a clinker.

Orrin Hickok will leave for Terre Haute on the first day of May with Adonis 2:14, the Wilkes—Lucy pacer, Monterey a four-year-old stallion by Electioneer—Minx and Prince Warwick a stallion by Alcona. Possibly Arol 2:24½, and several of the Palo Alto horses will go east to be campaigned by Hickok. Edwin C 2:15, and Roy Wilkes will go on the same car.

Sam Bryant thinks more attention should be paid to breeding jockies He says the cross should be sire Irish, dam English, grandam Jew, and explains it by saying Irish for pluck to go through, English to stay, and Jew for cunning. All the dare devil riders are Irish, the English are bull dogs for hanging on and Providence favors the Jews.

English bettors are getting tired of following the military, and an exchange says: Many officers fancy because they can sit a charger on parade they are, therefore, good jockeys. but the form displayed in race riding by some of them is simply ludicrous. They often lose their seats and more often their heads, the result being tantalizing in the extreme to poor backers.

Louis Whiting has a good claim to the championship as the veteran Judges' stand attendant. For 35 years he has been round the circuit and at the various meetings. At the State Fair, he has held his position for 27 years without any interruption which speaks volumes for his integrity and uprightness. This year he was in his old position at San Jose, The Blood Horse and Sacramento.

Rico, who is L. J. Rose's entry for the Brooklyn and Suburban got out of his stable at the Bay District track last Friday night (a week ago yesterday) and was found the next morning several miles away, tied to a lamp post. It had been raining all night and besides that the colt had badly skinned his legs, fortunately he was not seriously injured. Mr. Rose will probably in future employ a night watchman.

A prominent San Franciscan has received an intimation from The Thompson brothers, the wealthy Australian bookmakers, that they will take $100,000 of stock, if the rest of the money can be raised to build a track on the best possible lines. The intention is to have a lawn for the ladies to promenade on and every other accomodation and luxury that is to be found at Saratoga, Ascot, or the Australian tracks.

The last of old Maggie B. B.'s (dam of Iroquois, Harold, Panique, Pera, Francesca, Jaconet and Homeopathy) will be offered for sale among the Erdenheim yearlings on May 17th. He is a slashing chestnut colt by imported Woodlands, sire of Cracksman and other speedy horses and should run as well as half brothers and sisters, the most celebrated of whom was Iroquois, the winner of the English Derby and St. Leger in 1881.

Edwin F. Smith the popular secretary of the State Fair Association occupied a seat in the timers stand at the Blood Horse meeting. His young son was in the members enclosure, the youngster seemed to take great interest in racing. His pride at present is that he was the first to throw a leg over the now celebrated Emperor of Norfolk, being put on his back by Mr. Winters when the bay wonder was only a yearling.

Mr. William Hamlin, acting for a syndicate, purchased at public auction on Friday, April 11th, the property of the Buffalo International Fair Association, paying for it $267,-522.12. The Fair Association will now be reorganized, and the August races will be given as heretofore. The chances are against a fair being held this fall, but next year an exhibition can be given which will command the attention of the whole country.

A stockholders' meeting of the Philadelphia Driving Park Association was held at the club house on the Point Breeze track on the 15th. The meeting was called for the purpose of allotting the private box stalls for the coming season, and there was a large attendance of members. The bidding for the choice stalls was spirited, and the total amount realized from them was $1,326.50—about 25 per cent. more than they sold for last year.

Robert A. Pinkerton, the famous, shrewd and efficient detective of the Pinkerton Detective Agency, returned to New York from Hot Springs on April 10th, looking in the best of health. He will have charge of the secret police at the Westchester, Brooklyn, New Jersey and the Coney Island Jockey Club race tracks during the approaching racing season, and will look after the interest of the Association and the public in his usual watchful way.

Little Charlie Dennison received a round of applause from the fielders when he landed game old Dave Douglas, an easy winner in the repeat and on the last day when with Sinfax he beat Palo Alto's crack Rinfax by half a length, after a bumping finish he was again vociferously cheered. Old Dan is bringing his boys up in good shape. They are quiet, civil and neat, good riders and have a brilliant future before them, if Dan does not overfeed them.

At Woodsburg, L. I., a few weeks ago, several parties were brought before the court on a charge of docking ponies tails. The principal defendant pleaded guilty of performing the operation on twenty ponies, which were intended for polo purposes, and claimed ignorance of the law. The judge took a different view of it, and fined the operator $50 or twenty days, and each of his assistants $40 each. This was the first case of the kind in that section under the new law.

Scott Quinton, who handled the crack pacer Yolo Maid and the rest of Mr. Daly's string last year, is getting together a stable of horses at his home, Trenton, New Jersey. Among his purchases are a chestnut colt (brother to Silverone), two years, by Alcyone, dam Silver Lock by Mambrino Time: a bay colt, three years old, by Red Wilkes, dam by Mambrino Pet, and the bay colt, yearling, by Red Wilkes, dam by Nutwood. The three were bought of John E. Madden, Lexington, Ky.

One of the bargains at the recent Palo Alto sale in New York was the five year-old bay stallion Pomona, which was bought by A J. Welch of Hartford, Conn., for $3,000. He has since sold him at a good advance to Charles F. Forbes. of New York, who will have him trained for a fast record. Pomona is by Electioneer, dam Pearl by George Lancaster; second dam Mellnche (dam of Fred Crocker 2:25½, at two years of age) by St. Clair, sire of the dams of Wildflower 2:21, Manzanita 2:16 and Bonita 2:18½.

Eugene Leigh, the well known trainer of race horses, has broken the good performers Lucy Johnson and Florence E. to work in harness, and they can make a buggy spin on the road. It is his intention to train the last named filly, but if she does not show up well she will be bred to Electioneer if he can get a season to the big horse. Lucy Johnson will also be bred to a trotting stallion. As both mares have won many races on the running turf, their career as trotting matrons will be watched with interest.

Mr. Van Gorden, the Superintendent of the San Simeon Ranch, informed me last Monday that W. L. Donathan would start for New York with the Hearst stable the latter part of this week with eight head of horses, viz., Baggage, Almont and Del Mar, four year olds, all winners this spring; Primero, Anarchist, J. B., Snowball and Yosemite, two year olds. They will make their debut on the Eastern tracks at Brooklyn, and on the conclusion of the Brooklyn meeting will go to Washington Park, Chicago. Mr. Van Gorden will be unable to go East at present.

The Prince—not the Duke of Norfolk—was the horse referred to a couple of weeks ago as having some very promising colts. One of them Minnie B with the worst of the start ran an exceptionally good race in the California Stakes. The Prince has a chance second to none in the state this year as he already has booked to him among others Laura Gardner, Ida Glenn. The Adams' mare, Ballinette—the dam of Alta, Welcome. Della Walker—Al Farrow's dam, Lizzie Idle—the dam of Minnie B, Frankie Devine, Fusilades' Last and Why Not (Three Cheers—Nellie Collier.)

A meeting of the Board of Directors of the Nevada State Board of Agriculture was held last week, President Gould presiding, and Directors Martin, Flint, Mulcahy, Bailey and Powning being present. The premium list for this year was submitted and approved. Directors Winters and Powning and Secretary Stoddard were appointed to prepare the speed programme. President Gould said he would give a special premium of $50 for the best exhibit of horses at the fair of 1890. Director Martin stated that he would give a special premium of $50 for the best exhibit of cattle at the fair of 1890.

The Austrians are taking a great deal of interest just now in the trotting horse of America. Lewis Schopper, secretary of the Vienna Trotting Association, says the trotting interest in that country is growing very rapidly, and there is some talk of making purchases of a large number of high priced horses in America, both stallions and brood mares, for the purpose of starting an immense breeding establishment, He is of the opinion that the love for the trotter evinced by the Austrians is not just a fancy that will pass away in a short time, but he thinks it will grow into an industry, as it has in Kentucky.

Messrs. Look & Smith, Louisville, Ky., have bought for Dr. William Morrow, of Nashville, Tenn., from the owners, Messrs. Oliver Posey & Son, of Rushville, Ind., the two year old colt Guy Corbitt 11726, sired by Guy Wilkes, 2867, record 2:15¼; dam Minnie Wilkes, by Sultan 1530, record 2:24; 2nd dam Kitty Wilkes (dam of Rajah 2:20½), by George Wilkes 519, record 2:22; 3rd dam Snipnose (dam of Garnet 2:19), by American Clay 34; 4th dam by Downing's Bay Messenger. This is one of the most richly bred colts in the country, and should prove a great acquisition to the Tennessee breeders. Price private, but a long one.

The thoroughbred stallion imported Prince Leopold was sold by Bruce & Kidd in Lexington last December to Talbott Brothers of Paris, Ky. He was the property of August Belmont of New York. Last week, Talbot Brothers brought suit against Mr. Belmont for $1,950, the purchase price, with interest on the same from the day of the sale. The plaintiffs claim that the horse is unsound, and that he has been so ever since he came into their hands. The case will not come up for trial until next November. Prince Leopold is royally bred, being by Doncaster, out of Princess by King Tom.

The will of Aristides Welch, the famous breeder, was admitted to probate last week. His estate, which was estimated at $100,000 and upward, was bequeathed in trust to the Pennsylvania Company for Insurance on Lives for the benefit of his three sons, Robert A. Welch, William A. Welch and James Welch, until December 14, 1900, when it shall be equally divided among them. His personal effects, which were defined to be his diamond jewelry, plate, pictures, clothing, etc., and not moneys, bonds, stocks or securities, was also directed to be divided equally between the sons. He provided for an annuity for his sister.

To what enormous proportions Winter racing has grown is shown by the record of the Hudson and County Jockey Club, whose new track at Guttenberg was opened last December. The records of Secretary Whitehead show that during the sixty days of the meeting 361 races were run. The club distributed among horse owners $152,380, of which amount $129,250 was added money, the balance of the sum distributed, $23,130, being money paid for entrance fees, all of which went to horses running second or third. Of the owners who won $1,000 or upward during the meeting there were thirty-four, G. Walbaum being the highest winner with $11,833.

Injudicious feeding of a horse often produces far more baneful results than does overwork. When a horse is constantly kept upon food as concentrated as he can bear, there is necessarily a tendency to inflammation and consequent lameness, but lameness is more certainly produced with sudden changes from bulky to concentrated food, and that on the day when his feet are to be most severely tried by concussion on a hard road. It would be safer to abuse his digestive organs one day and his feet another than to abuse them both at the same time. Grass feeding horses can be lamed at any time, without any extra work, by simply giving them more corn and less chaff.

The sporting world says: Lon Myers was telling the tribulations he experienced with his stable boys. Everybody who knows him can testify to his generous, sunny disposition. Sometimes he discharges all hands, finds them around the stable next day, and hires them back. Recently he was dissatisfied with the condition of one of his help, and said: "Here, you'll have to go, I don't want you any more." Much to his surprise, the lad refused point blank to vacate the premises. "What's the use," argued Myers, "of my having you around, you're drunk all the time." "Well," responded the help, "what do you give me so much money for; you must expect me to get drunk!" He remains in Lon Myers' employ.

The Sportsman says: Knap McCarthy turned Salisbury over to Mike Daly in such magnificent shape, that the opponents of the employment of trotting methods with running horses had never a word to say. They were wont to say that a trotting trainer could keep the veriest cripple on his feet for any desired number of ages, but that his skill—like a certain late lamented gentleman's clock—stopped short right here. Their little tin horns will now have to toot a different air. Salisbury was fit to run for his own—or for Mike Daly's—life on Saturday last. He just galloped Fitzroy and Bradford half to death in that first half in 48 seconds. Everybody was anxious to know just what sort of a graveyard could afford to peddle such a ghost.

Perhaps no animal ever stood so entirely on his own merits as the English thoroughbred horse. His performances have shown the fallacy of a thousand theories, have put down a thousand prejudices, and have commanded the practical admiration of the world. For nearly two hundred years after the English racehorse was admitted to be the fastest horse in the world for the short distances run on an English race course, doubts were from time to time raised in various quarters as to whether he would prove the fastest in a very long distance. The most cruel distances were often proposed, but seldom accepted, but whenever they have been accepted the distance has only exhibited the superiority of the thoroughbred in a stronger light.

Mr. C. J. Hamlin recently remarked that he began breeding horses twenty years ago, in a small way, that he had kept an accurate account of all expenses, and that he had made twenty-five thousand dollars, and had three hundred of the best horses he ever bred left, "and," said he, "where can you find a better business than that? It pays to buy and breed only the best." He further said that he once sold ninety-six head, and put all the money into sixteen, for breeding purposes. He takes his best broodmares and gets two or three fillies from them, and when they are sixteen years of age, or thereabouts, he disposes of them and uses the best fillies, on the theory that a good mare should from a superior stallion bring a better foal than the mother.

A list of the high priced thoroughbreds in England and America has been published in almost every sporting paper. The American horses, 35 of which are given, run down to 10,000, while with the English, twelve of which are given, 20,000 is the lowest price. Several others might have been added including Busybody, 3, by Petrarch, out of Spinaway who was sold at the famous sale of Lord Falmouth in 1884 for $44,000; at the same sale Louisburg, 2, sold for $20,000, while Maximilian was—when sold—the highest priced yearling sold in England, being knocked down for $20,500, and Captain Machell paid $20,000 for Blue Blood, a brother to Doncaster. The two latter were not worth a twentieth of the price paid, but Busybody won the One Thousand and Oaks.

As some discussion has arisen lately regarding the identity of the famous racehorse Lecompte, the history of his ownership as told by Mr. M. Hertzog and Mr. J. Alphonse Prudhomme (son-in-law of the late Mr. Lecompte) becomes a matter of some interest. It is as follows:

Mr. Lecompte, while travelling through Kentucky, saw the great racehorse sire Boston, and determined, if possible, to secure a colt from him. Not having in his possession a mare suitable for breeding to such a famous sire as Boston, he bargained for the use of the grand old broodmare Reel by Glencoe, and the result of the union was the great Louisiana bred racehorse Lecompte. Mr. Lecompte and Mr. Wells were such intimate friends that the colt always remained in the hands of Mr. Wells, but all their friends at the time perfectly understood that Mr. Lecompte was the real owner of the horse.

Where weight, material, or lifting power has to be economized, a mechanic will always make his levers light at their fast moving end, and strong at their slow or powerful end. Each of the four supports of the horse's body is a lever, so arranged as to give speed to his feet at the expense of power, so that in judging of the horse's power or speed, we must estimate it, not by the small end of the lever at the shanks, but by the quantity and quality of the muscles, arranged on the loins, the haunches and the shoulders. The direction of each bone in these complicated supports, and the angle at which they lie to each other, is a matter of much consequence in estimating the cabilities and the pleasantness of the horse, but to go fully into this subject would require a very long chapter on anatomy, which we wish to avoid, as we know that such chapters are not often read.

The desk of Secretary Kuck of the New York Jockey Club, is now ornamented with a massive and handsome inkstand of black marble with silver trimmings, which is both admired and envied by all horsemen who have seen it. Above the ink well are arranged so as to make a clever pen rack one of the plates worn by the famous El Rio Rey when he made his record of 1:11 at the track of the New York Jockey Club in the White Plains Handicap on Saturday, Aug. 31, 1889. The nails which fastened the plate to the hoof of the flyer form rests for the pen holders, and the plate is supported at the back by one of the spurs which Winchell wore on that day. All these are heavily plated with Silver and held in place by a framework of the same material. On this work is the inscription "Presented to T. H. Kuck, Secretary of the N. Y. C., by Alf Estell." A smaller plate bears these words: "El Rio Rey, 1:11." The whole affair is in Tiffany's best style, and the donor, Mr. Estell, is the manager of the Theodore Winters' stable, to which El Rio Rey belongs.

The well-bred and game pacing mare Net dropped a very large and perfect filly foal on April 20th by Almont Patchen, 2:15, one of the greatest performers of the present day. The foal resembles the sire strongly; is of the same dark, handsome color, without white marks. Net, the dam, will be remembered as the large chestnut who, in 1888, beat a field of five, including Keogh, and was handled by Jack Nichol. At that time she had only been off pasture six weeks, had not been prepared for a race, and was eight months gone with foal; she won the stubbornly contested race—eight heats—the last in 2:34½. Three days afterward showed a mile in 2:27; it was the general opinion that 2:20 would not be a low mark for her with proper conditioning. Net was sired by Magic, he by Elmo out of Lady Whipple, she by Whipple's Hambletonian. Her filly should certainly be heard from some day if gameness and level-headedness are transmitted from sire and dam to their offspring. Mrs. Emily D. Knott, of Searsville, San Mateo Co., who is the fortunate owner of the mare and her filly, had an offer of $1,000 for the produce in the event of its proving to be a stallion. The filly should be as valuable.

The St. Louis Republic says: Mr. J. R. Farrington, Vice-President Newport News and Mississippi Valley Railroad, Lexington, Ky., accompanied by a party of friends, visited Franklin on the 19th, and purchased from Miller & Sibley the following gilt-edge trotting stock:

Brown colt, 2 years, by St Bel, dam Nubia by Harold.

Roan filly, Maltese, 2 years, by St. Bel, dam Mabel May by Raymond.

Bay filly, Kalleta, 2 years, by Whips, 2:27, dam by Gen. Benton.

Roan mare, Mabel May, record 2:33, by Raymond, dam Flora Pease, sister to Mink, 2:29.

Each one of the two-year-olds showed speed enough on the track to satisfy the Lexington parties that all were capable of beating 2:30 in their two-year-old form. The prices paid were private, but horsemen think it was more than was ever paid in Pennsylvania for three of like age. Trainer Williams of Lexington, who was of the party, states that he saw more speed in colts here than he had ever seen at this season of the year on any stock farm in America. Kentucky coming to Pennsylvania for trotters encourages breeders in this section, and indicated that they realize that trotters can be bred in the North as well as in Kentucky.

The Chicago Horseman of the 17th, in its pen-pictures of prominent breeders, says of Dr. Hicks of Sacramento: "M. W. Hicks, owner of the stallions Prompter, Sterling and Privateer, is a short, wiry man, wearing a grayish beard. He has a quick, nervous manner, is a man of learning, a logical reasoner, and has a wonderful fund of horse lore stored away in his vigorous brain. Dr. Hicks has been very successful as a breeder. Some years ago he took Buccaneer and Flaxtail to California. He bred his producing daughters Mary, Prairie Bird, Fern Leaf, Lucy (dam of J. H. McCormack, 2:29) and Flight. From Mary he bred Apex, 2:26, by Prompter, a sire also of his breeding. From Prairie Bird bred Flight, 2:29, by Buccaneer, and Flight produced Fleet, 2:24 at two years, bred by another party. Fern Leaf produced the pacer Gold Leaf, 2:11½, and Shamrock, 2:25 at two years. He is an admirer of the Blue Bull strain, and has ably maintained his opinion with his pen." And later on, in the same issue, By Holly is described: "B. C. Holly, of Holly wood Breeding Farm, bears a strong resemblance to John Splan. He is spare built, dark complexioned, and his hair and mustache are sprinkled with gray. Mr. Holly has at his California farm the stallions Election, Mountain Boy, Kafir, Woodside, Mart Boorhem and the thoroughbred Reveille, by Shiloh. The noted stallion Woodnut, 2:16½, was once his property, and was sold by him to Robert Steel for a long price."

There seems to be quite a difference of opinion among horsemen, says the Pennsylvania Farmer, as to the value of corn fodder as food for horses. A leading farm paper recently cautioned its readers against feeding horses on corn-stalks, stating that they would make the horses' coats rough. Mr. C. W. Williams, the breeder and trainer of Axtell, says that his wonderful colt had little besides corn-stalks for rough fodder during nearly two winters. He says he considers corn-stalks the best rough fodder he can get for colts. The writer once worked for a farmer who never cut any hay. His cattle and horses never had any fodder but cured corn-stalks. The animals always looked well, and the horses did their full share of work. The writer now has two that have very little to do and are not heavily fed.

One of them prefers corn-stalks to hay, while the other runs down if fed on stalks without hay. It is an old horse and cannot handle the stalks as well as a younger horse would. We find that this prejudice against corn-stalks for horses is quite common among a class of farmers. Except in the case of old horses with poor teeth we do not think the prejudice is just. In fact it seems reasonable that a moderate supply of well cured stalks will prove beneficial to a horse in winter, and even with old horses if the stalks could be cut and moistened.

The reason why race horses do not last as long in active service as trotters do, or one reason, at least, according to Mr. Huggins, Mr. A. J. Cassatt's trainer last season, is the tremendous strain under which they work. Take a racer moving through the air at the rate of fifty feet a second, which is not far from the actual speed, and the pressure the atmosphere exerts against him is tremendous. Say he weighs 1,000 pounds, and the atmospheric pressure on each square inch of his body is enormous. It strains every joint and muscle and finds out every tendon. Now, in addition, remember that every running horse is pounding along on the ground all the while, bringing each hoof down with a pressure of 10,000 or more, and is it any wonder racers go amiss?

Mr. W. C. Parker, of Newton, came dangerously near losing all of his trotting stock by fire on Saturday night, the 5th inst. Mr. Parker and his trainer, Mr. Ricker, drove over to Rose Hill Farm in the evening, leaving his stable in charge of a man employed for that purpose. When in sight of the stable upon their return, they noticed that a fire had started in that part of the stable in which the carriages were kept, and was making rapid progress. There were nineteen head of horse stock confined in the stables, including a very promising son of Alcyone (2:27), a magnificent filly by Woodbine (2:25¼), several youngsters by Gold Beater, and a number of broodmares. Seeing that it was impossible to arrest the flames, Mr. Parker ordered the doors leading from the carriage-room to the stable closed, and at once sprang to the rescue of the valuable animals, all excepting three of which were turned loose and saved. Two of those which perished were turned loose, but rushed back into a box-stall. The most valuable animals were rescued. Two broodmares and one young stallion were burned. The latter was by Gold Beater, dam by Daniel Lambert; second dam Bessie Snow by Garibaldi, son of the Bennett Horse. Great credit is due Mr. Parker and Mr. Ricker for the rare good judgment displayed under such trying circumstances. The fire probably resulted from the explosion of a kerosene lamp or lantern which the man in charge of the stable left burning when he went to bed. This man was found asleep, and would doubtless have perished, but for the timely arrival of the proprietor. This should be a lesson to those who are employed for the purpose of guarding valuable property.

Racing at Linden began last Tuesday under very favorable conditions. Linden Park is now certainly one of the most delightfully-located and picturesque race tracks in America. It was opened last fall under discouraging circumstances. The shortcomings that were then apparent have all been remedied. Something like $60,000 has been expended in necessary work, and now the track is pronounced by trainers and owners to be as good as any thereabout. The old clayey track has all been removed, and in its place has been substituted one of loam and sand, which slopes gently from the centre to each side, thus insuring complete drainage. To make this drainage perfect, ditches have been built on either side, these feeding into drains, which are laid under the track, so that all rain that falls is not only carried from the track but from the grounds and outside of the inclosure. The stables and paddock sheds unfinished at the time of the original opening have been completed, and are now as nearly perfect as possible. Fresh paint and the scrubbing brushes of the cleaners have made everything look in shipshape, and the clubhouse and members' stand are furnished as comfortably as the most exacting could wish for. Under its reorganization James R. English of Linden, a prominent lawyer and one of the counsel of the Pennsylvania Railroad Company, is President, Capt. William M. Conner Vice President, and Richard Stockton, of the well-known New Jersey family of that name, Secretary and Treasurer. C. T. Rowe, who has had years of experience, is the clerk of the course, and altogether the club seems thoroughly well equipped for what may really be considered its inaugural meeting.

It looks as though there were grave doubts about Hamilton's ability as a driver, for the New York Sportsman says:—

Mr. Belmont's $10,000 a year colored jockey, Anthony Hamilton, was in Judge Lachman's court recently as defendant in a suit in which his skill as a driver was seriously called in question. O'Halloran Brothers, livery stable keepers at No. 127 West Seventeenth street, were the plaintiffs. They wanted $55 for the damages they charged Hamilton with having inflicted upon an octagon-fronted brougham.

On a Sunday afternoon in the latter part of November one of the O'Hallorans was driving a lady down Fifth Avenue. The avenue was crowded with vehicles. At Forty-sixth street, O'Halloran said, in conformity with the unwritten code of the knights of the ribbons, he flourished his whip to indicate to the driver behind him that he was going to slow up. Almost instantly there was a crash, and turning he found a horse entangled with a hind wheel of the octagon-fronted brougham. The wheel had to be removed to release the horse. In the meantime the $55 worth of damage had been done.

The sleepy-looking little jockey was a thing of beauty as he took his mount on the witness stand. His attire was of the finest. An immense horseshoe blazed upon his red satin scarf, every nail a diamond, and a soltaire as big as a hickory nut sparkled upon a finger of his left hand. He languidly explained to Lawyer Tolman that he had ridden for Senator Hearst of California, and had carried such well known flyers as Exile, Tattler and others to victory. The turnout he was driving on that Sunday afternoon was his own. The horse was a trotter that he had paid $1,000 for. He had been taking his usual constitutional drive up the road with a friend. Had he drank anything? Yes; they had had a small bottle of wine, but he was not drunk—had never been drunk in his life.

"Now, wasn't it a quart bottle that you drank?" he was asked.

"No," with languid indignation. "You don't suppose I could get away with a quart bottle, do you?"

His horse has never known the touch of a whip, he said, and O'Halloran's flourish was so vigorous that the lash of the whip caught his trotter on the neck. He reared, the octagon-fronted brougham came almost to a stop, and although Hamilton managed to get the trotter partly to one side, he came down upon the hind wheel in such a manner that his hind leg could not be extricated. O'Halloran started to drive ahead, and the horse was badly hurt before Hamilton jumped out of his buggy and grabbed O'Halloran's team by the head. He remarked to the liveryman's complaint:—

"What have you got to growl about? My horse is worth a —— sight more than your old coach."

The horse was still lame, and Hamilton had been compelled ever since November to hire another trotter at $5 a day. There was some comment upon his ignorance as to the alleged signal to stop, and Hamilton remarked:—

"Well, I ain't a coachman. I drive just like any gentleman does, and I can drive as well as any of them."

Judge Lachman took the papers.

THE FARM.

Breeds of Cattle.

We are asked by a correspondent to give a sketch of the origin and history of several breeds of cattle which he names. It is a large task that he lays out for us, and we will not be able to fully satisfy him in the space we have to spare, but something can be done, and in doing it we can draw freely from the best sources at hand.

The Short-horns are the most widely distributed of any breed of beef cattle. We believe that it is fair to say that they are the standard cattle, though as young as any of the fixed breeds. In all its peculiar types it may fairly be called a modern breed.

The breed was greatly improved, and its types fixed by the Collings Brothers, Bates and Booth. The Bates and Booth blood is now the most fashionable Shorthorn blood. Shorthorns were imported to this country the beginning of the present century, but those imported before a herd book was established in England and known popularly as "Seventeens," while no doubt of pure blood and among the best for beef, are not "fashionable," and do not command as high prices as breeders of "fashionable" cattle. For the farmer who is raising only for beef they are just as good and much cheaper.

The Galloways are one of the oldest breeds. In fact history does not go back to their origin. They have been kept in Southern Scotland and Northern England from time immemorial. They are hardy as might be expected from their origin, black and hornless, and for rustling on the prairies they may be more valuable than Shorthorns. They are not deep milkers, but give rich milk. Their meat ranks high in the market. A steer at three years old should weigh about 1600 pounds and dress about 1000. They are prepotent, and a Galloway bull crossed with horned cattle will produce ninety per cent. of hornless calves.

The Polled Angus are a very old race and were probably introduced into Scotland from Norway. Black is the fashionable color for them, but they were originally red, yellow or brindled as well as black, and these colors sometimes show now, though they are regarded as a bad mark. Their Scottish home is in Aberdeenshire, from which they take their name of Aberdeen, in connection with Angus. There was no herd book of Polled Angus till 1862, and since that time the breed has been greatly improved, becoming noted for the character of the meat and for easy fattening. They are not deep milkers, but are prominently a beef breed.

There are several breeds of hornless cattle, all of which are beef cattle except the Red Polled. These are good milkers, and their admirers claim that they are more nearly the "general purpose" cattle that the average farmer wants more than any other. The polled cattle are all from northern counties, and as a rule are more hardy than any other breeds, standing cold weather better than their neighbors from more southern sections.

The Holsteins are a Dutch cattle, though there are no cattle in Holland called Holsteins. They are large, fatten fairly easily, but are a milking breed. They stand above any other breed in the quantity of milk given, and their admirers will also claim for them prominence in butter production.

The Jersey is no doubt the butter cow. They originated on the little Island of Jersey in the English channel, and with the Alderney and Guernsey are called Channel cattle. All of these breeds are superior milk and butter producers, but the Jersey has held the front rank for so long that it will not easily be dispossessed of it.

Our correspondent asks which of these breeds is best for the farmer. The question can't be answered as it stands. There are too many differing circumstances to answer it. If he wishes to raise beef he must, to be successful, get a beef breed, and even then the question of which one cannot be answered off hand. Circumstances must decide. If he wishes to make butter he must select a butter breed, and not beef stock, and which breed will still be a question for him to decide.

Our correspondent has by no means exhausted the list of cattle that are claimed to have peculiar excellencies as beef or dairy cattle. A list of a hundred names would not exhaust the breeds for which some special excellencies are claimed, though but few of them are found in this country. Among the easily obtained breeds that he does not mention are the Herefords and Sussex for beef, and the Ayrshire, Guernsey, Alderney and Red Polled for milk, butter and cheese. There is among them no breed that is absolutely the best, each having points or combinations of points in which it is superior to others, and it is in the adaptation of these points to the circumstances of the farmer that the best for him is found.—Western Plowman.

Disease Conveyed by Meat.

The question of tuberculosis has recently been much discussed in this country, and is, we understand, exciting a great deal of attention in Great Britain: The London Live Stock Journal says:

"The subject was discussed at some length before the Leeds Corporation on Monday, Dr. Cameron, the medical officer of health for the borough, has caused the carcasses of two beasts to be seized and destroyed, on the ground that the animals when killed were suffering from tuberculosis. A number of Leeds butchers took up the matter, and sent to the committee a numerous and influential deputation to urge that the condemned meat was perfectly sound and fit for human food. The deputation having put forward their case, Dr. Cameron explained his reasons for believing that the carcasses were not fit to eat. The medical officer also called Mr. Jessop and another medical gentleman, who concurred in the view he entertained. A full committee having debated the question at great length, it was resolved to seek the opinion of an expert. A joint is to be taken from each of three different beasts—one certified to be perfectly sound, another 'suffering partly from tuberculosis,' and a third that is beyond doubt not fit for human food. The expert is to be asked to distinguish between the three portions of meat, both before and after they are cooked, and to say to what extent a taint will remain after cooking."

The Farmers' Review appreciates fully the anxiety of the gentlemen mentioned to arrive at correct conclusions as to the character of the meat of tuberculous cattle, but it must express astonishment at the manner in which they intend to go about the business. We do not hesitate for a moment to predict that the butchers will come off victorious when the so-called expert renders his verdict. He is to say whether the meat of the three animals is fit for human use by merely depending upon his senses of taste, smell and sight. By such means he can not possibly tell anything as to whether the meat is safe food for human beings, and we are surprised that our excellent contemporary has not, apparently, recognized this fact.

Meat may appear perfectly sound, may taste all right, may show no taint, and yet be dangerous, and of this class is in all probability the meat of a tuberculous animal. We must go beyond the power of our vision, our taste or our smell to decide whether it is dangerous or not; for the bacillus of tuberculosis is not to be detected easily. Even by using a most powerful microscope to examine the blood or juice of the beef, ten chances to one not a trace of the bacillus will be found, and yet such meat may be most dangerous.

The proper way to decide regarding the meat in question would be to take some of the blood and some of the juice expressed from the muscles and therewith inoculate rabbits or guinea pigs and note the result. If the meat is unfit for human use the juice or blood injected into the live animals mentioned will probably kill them, and thus tell us the true story, which otherwise could not be ascertained.

The butchers could not have asked a better test, so far as their interests are concerned, than this opinion of an expert regarding the appearance, taste and smell of the meat of the animals in question, but the consumers should not allow themselves to be humbugged in this way. Let inoculation render the verdict instead of the expert, and the public health will be protected.

Shorthorns as Improvers.

The Shorthorn sire as an improver of all other beef breeds, as well as the native or scrub, has no equal. Some of the other beef breeds make a remarkably good first cross, but afterward the improvement is less marked than in the Shorthorn. Take a Hereford sire and cross on the native or scrub cow, and your first produce will most likely be a white-faced calf. Then take the cow calf and then, at the proper age, breed her to a pure-bred Hereford, and the produce is more likely to be a speckled or roan than it is to have a white face. For several years of my life I was connected with a ranchman who was the owner of ten thousand cattle, and I thoroughly believe one of the best informed men on breeding I have ever met—a man who had experimented and carefully studied, and amassed a fortune of nearly one million dollars, and has it yet. He tried nearly all the beef breeds, and finally discarded all but the Shorthorn. I have known him to take bulls worth to sell four hundred dollars each and turn them out on the ranch to breed his cows to, but he was careful to take them up when breeding season was over and feed and care for them until time to turn out again. He always claimed that where his cattle were located (Wyoming) they were better rustlers and made more improvement than any other breed, not only in the first cross, but in each cross afterwards.

AS MOTHERS.

The Shorthorn cow makes one of the finest mothers, always ready to protect her calf, although so mild and apparently intelligent when properly handled. I have heard that there are Shorthorn cows that will not give milk enough to raise their own calves, but in an experience of over twenty years I have never seen one of that kind. We have at present a pure bred cow only three years old and weighing over 1900 lbs., and has had her second calf, that is giving twenty quarts or milk a day. She is not fed high, nor in any way to make her give much milk. She was one of our show heifers for two years, In fact, I have seen hundreds of Shorthorn cows, and pure bred ones, too, that would give two twelve-quart pailfuls a day when in full flow of milk. If a farmer can raise that kind of a cow, one that is a good milker, and when he is through breeding her he can turn her off for beef, at a great weight, what more does he want? I think he should feel satisfied with her.

WHY USE SCRUB SIRES?

Does it not seem strange that there are not more pure bred sires used? They are certainly cheap and plentiful enough. It is either ignorance or indifference that makes men use a scrub sire of any kind or breed of stock. They will not pay the small amount asked by the publishers of agricultural or live stock papers to read and inform themselves, and have no ambition to learn, believing in their own narrow minds that they know it all now. So they continue in the old ruts. Scrubs are good enough for them; they are scrub men.

BUY SOME GOOD CATTLE.

A short time ago we concluded to have more stock to eat up our surplus feed, rather than sell it off the farm, as we need all the manure that we can get. Not knowing where we could get three or four car loads of high grade steers in Wisconsin, we concluded to go to Chicago. We went into the Exchange building, to the office of our commission man, and made our wants known. "Well," he said, "of course you want well bred ones. You will see very few coming from Wisconsin." It was really surprising to see the small number of good cattle there were among the twelve thousand on sale that day. Any farmer who will go to Chicago and see the difference in price between well bred steers and scrubs or natives, and not go home and sell the scrubs and buy some good cattle, does not deserve to ever be able to own any. I would like to know what better investment any farmer can make than to buy a Shorthorn cow or two, give to a growing up son, and then advise with him as to the proper manner of breeding for improvement. Buy books to read about pure bred stock: take all the agricultural and live stock papers within reach for him to read. How much better he would be employed than in reading a novel, or hanging around the village store, and how much better you would feel to see the mind of your boy trained in that direction.—P. Waken, in Wisconsin Farmer's Institute.

Controlling the Sex.

There have been many theories advanced in regard to controlling the sex; some of them were perfect until put into practice, but the one that, to me, seemed to be the most successful in practice was the "alternate heat" theory; that is, if a cow were bred and the result was a bull calf, if she had not been bred till the next heat, she would have had a heifer calf; every other heat giving a calf of the same sex. I have read of several breeders who have been successful in breeding according to this theory, and last year I tried it with two of my best cows from which I wanted to get heifer calves; the result was they both had heifer calves. I have just bred them again as a second trial, and if they will have heifer calves this time, I will have more faith in the theory.

The only trouble is to keep a record of every time the cow is in heat from the time she drops her calf till it is tim to have her served. If she does not get in calf at that service, you must wait six weeks—skipping one heat—before having her served again. This will interfere somewhat in our efforts to have our cows come in at a certain time, as it just doubles the time of waiting for the next service, and two misses of service will make a delay of twelve weeks.—The Stockman.

Colorado Against Texas Cattle.

A special telegram to the Gazette from Denver, Colorado, dated April 1st, says that a strong effort is being put forth by the cattlemen in the southern portion of the State to prevent the movement of Texas cattle by trail across their ranges to Wyoming and the north. Some years ago this was a favorite practice of drovers, and it was only discontinued when the local owners banded together, for a vigorous opposition to the use of their ranges for common trails and bed grounds for these through herds. The obstructive watch of the local cattlemen has been relaxed for the last few years, as the movement was inconsiderable, but the conduct of those who drove last year in getting range cattle into their herds, driving them long distances from home, as well as in stopping their herds whenever the fancy seized them, has aroused the Colorado man's ire, and he is again banding with his fellow suffers for protection. Petitions signed by every stock owner of the border counties are about to be filed with the quarantine board, urging the latter to enforce the regulations to the letter. The effect of such enforcement will be to tie up the trail cattle on the State line for a period of ninety days. The local owners are not wholly dependent upon the quarantine officials. The latter will act only in so far as disease may be threatened through the introduction. In the matter of the protection of their ranges, they propose to use the local courts and proceed by injunction, using every legal method available to carry out their policy of obstruction, and thus make the blockade effectual and permanent. Appearances now indicate that the lot of the Texas drover after he strikes the Colorado line, will be decidedly unpleasant. No objection will be offered to the movement of these cattle by rail. —Stock Grower.

Keeping Cold-Blooded Stallions.

The Stockman and Farmer justly says: The temptation to retain fine looking colts for stallions is often great, and many farmers fall in love with good, growthy young stallions and keep them for breeding purposes regardless of their breeding. It is a great mistake to do this, for several reasons. Where the farm horses are all, or nearly all, reared on the place where they are kept, there is danger of inbreeding or intermingling too much cold blood to produce the ordinary results expected from stallions of even ordinary blood. Again, a stallion may be, as an individual, all right himself, but any one with experience knows that a product of inferior parentage, although of good individuality, is liable, or almost certain, to "breed back," and the result of breeding such a horse is one of great uncertainty. It is certainly economy to make valuable work horses out of these promising colts instead of worthless stallions. There are too many well bred horses within the reach of all to encourage the keeping of stallions that cannot raise the quality of the horses of your district.

Classes of Fowls.

No one can obtain a clear understanding of the various breeds and varieties of fowls who does not understand the purposes for which they are kept. Classification becomes indispensable in this as in every other branch of human knowledge.

Fowls may be broadly separated into two classes—ornamental and useful. Such a principle of division, however, is far from satisfactory, for all useful fowls are more or less useful. Still there are some breeds which are kept primarily for ornament, and therefore this division is not without some value. To the ornamental class may be referred the whole lists of Bantams, the Exhibition Games, and, perhaps, the Hamburgs and Polish, although the latter breeds are very useful fowls. To the other class may be referred all other breeds.

The useful fowls are divisible into three pretty well defined classes—table fowls, general purpose fowls and laying fowls. Such division is extremely valuable. A table fowl is one bred primarily for the amount and quality of the flesh it will produce. It must lay some, enough to have eggs for hatching to produce table fowls. Among poultry it ranks where the Shorthorn and Hereford does among cattle, or the Southdown and Oxforddown among sheep. The laying fowls are those whose chief recommendation is the number of eggs which they will produce in a year. They are the Jerseys, Guernseys, Ayrshires and Holsteins of the poultry yard. Their value consists in what they produce while alive, not in what their carcass will bring when dead. Between these two classes, partaking of the quality of both, is the general purpose fowl. It must be a good layer, it must be a good table fowl; yet it is, after all, but a compromise between the table and the laying fowl, inferior to each in its speciality, superior to each in what it does not profess to be. The best table fowls are better for the table and not so good layers as the general purpose fowl; the best layers surpass it in laying, but are inferior to it in table qualities. Some general purpose fowls, as might naturally be expected, approach quite nearly to one class, some to the other.

The American breeds are prized because they are general purpose fowls. For a long time, and that time has perhaps not wholly passed, poultrymen expected to combine in one fowl all the excellencies to be found in the various breeds. The abundance and quality of the flesh which characterize the table fowl was to be united to the wonderful prolificacy which marks the great layers. The expectation had not been realized; it never will be. Antagonistic qualities can be combined only by robbing them of their antagonism. The great layer and the great table fowl are differently constituted, with different dispositions, and convert their food into different products. It is probable that general purpose fowls may be improved, that the nicest balance between their qualities has not been found, but the ideal general purpose fowl will never exist outside the imagination of its admirers.

There is need of all three classes of fowls. The man who raises poultry for market requires the table fowl; the one who produces eggs for general consumption needs the great layer, and hundreds and thousands of families, which keep fowls to produce eggs and poultry, demand the general purpose fowl. The general purpose is unquestionably the most popular fowl in the country, but the other two classes are steadily growing in favor, and as the number of those who make a business of keeping fowls increases the popularity of these classes will increase. Fowls for specific rather than general purpose will be more and more demanded as the people learn that there is more profit in having the highest development of a single quality than in having a moderate development of two or more qualities, but this demand will never wholly displace the general purpose fowl. In the future as in the past, all three classes of fowls will be required to meet the varied wants of the people.

H. S. Babcock, in Stockman.

ATHLETICS.

Athletic Sports and Other Pastimes.

EDITED BY ARPHIPPUS,

SUMMARY.

As the date of the championship games approaches, the interest in amateur athletics increases. The sport-loving public are looking forward to what promises to be one of the grandest athletic tournaments that San Francisco has so far witnessed. The Olympic Club's "Ladies' Night" exhibition was a great success. The Alpine athletes are making extra preparations for their first open athletic meeting. The wheelmen and oarsmen are taking advantage of the splendid weather, and are getting themselves into fine form for their coming races. The Lean-Kolb wrestling match is absorbing all the attention of the indoor athletes.

RUNNERS, WALKERS, JUMPERS, ETC.

It seems as if every amateur on the Pacific Coast is in training. At the new grounds of the Olympic Club, as well as at the Bay District track, runners, walkers, jumpers and weight performers by the score are practicing daily, and already in private trials many of the old coast records have been knocked on the head. May 30th is bound to be a red-letter day in the history of amateur athletics on the Pacific Coast. This year the athletes have had many good inducements offered them to go into strict training. In the first place, the splendid cinder path recently built by the Olympic Club, has helped to induce many of the old timers to go into harness once more, and then the organizing of the Alpine Amateur Athletic Club has considerably helped to boom athletics. The old time amateurs found it too hard a task to lay back in the shade while younger blown struggled tooth and nail to improve the existing records. The old saying is indeed true: "Once an athlete always an athlete." There appears to be some strange fascination connected with athletics. Men have retired again and again, and have fully made up their minds to give up training, but when they watch others train, and think of the cheers that have often rewarded their own exertions in the past, that settles it. They cannot stand idly by and see new men strive to break their records, the making of which cost them so much time and hard work. And then the spectators always receive the performances of the old-timers more warmly than they do those of the tyro. It is a happiness indeed, to be pointed out as one of the old-time athletes, and feeling this way, it becomes a rather hard task to place ones self on a level with the commonplace spectators by watching others gallop round the track in quest of glory and prizes, whilst you are simply looking on while you might also be earning fresh honor.

The next event of importance will be the Lean-Kolb wrestling match, which will take place in the gymnasium of the Olympic Club on Tuesday evening next. Both men are in fine condition, having trained faithfully for some weeks past. A couple of evenings ago Kolb strained his side while practicing with McLeod, but by the date of the match he will be all right again. On the evening of the contest, both men must weigh under 154 pounds. Lean has found it very difficult to reduce his weight on account of his hard muscles, but from his extensive knowledge of training, it is very safe to anticipate that he will weigh in all right. The prize will be worth $200, and the winner will be champion of the Pacific Coast.

The Field Captains of the Olympic and Alpine Clubs are at present making arrangements for a grand competitive cross-country run between their respective teams. The run will probably not take place until after the championship games on May 30th. The idea is indeed a capital one as such competitions will naturally tend to higher interest in athletics.

The sporting editor of the Examiner is evidently not thoroughly posted on athletic records. A couple of days since a small article appeared in that paper, stating that James Jervis of the Olympic Club had broken the world's record for a half mile walk the day before, making the distance in 3:24 against 3:31. Now it happens that the American record held by Frank P. Murray of New York City is 3 minutes 2 2 5 seconds, or about 21 seconds less than the record made by Mr. Jarvis. The 3.31 record broken was the Pacific Coast record held by Horace Coffin. It was said that Jarvis walked the first half of the mile in last year's championship in less than 3:15.

The entries for the Alpine games close at the rooms, 706 Powell street, to-night at 10 o'clock. Up to the hour of going to press several well known athletes had signified their intention of competing in the games, and when the handicapper takes down the list this evening it is probable that it will contain over fifty prominent names. Much interest will be taken in these competitions as, the championship meeting being so close at hand, they will help to give the public a chance to speculate on the performances that may be expected on May 30th.

A very large number of entries have already been received for the Central Park foot races which will take place on May 4th. Some of the runners are put out because the meeting was not postponed until Sunday, May 11th. They claim that the track will not be in good shape on the 4th on account of the Wild West Show which is at present exhibiting in the Park

A grand wrestling tournament for Olympic Club members only will be held on May 13th.

There is every likelihood of a boom in cricket this summer. There are players from Australia and England in the city at present, and efforts will be made to organize one or two good clubs in the near future.

The report that V. P. White, the well known amateur wrestler, was about to turn professional is incorrect.

W. J. Kenealey, a prominent member of the Olympic Club, has forfeited his standing as an amateur by competing in a race for professionals at the Lumbermen's picnic. We understand that one or two other well known amateur athletes are liable to be disqualified by the Pacific Coast Amateur Athletic Association for taking part in picnic races. The laws of the P C A A A forbids any amateur from competing in games not held under its auspices.

J. J. McKinnon, the well known hammer thrower, has been reinstated by the P C A A A, and is now training with the intention of breaking the coast record on May 30th. The Field Captain of the University Club thinks he has a man in his team who can beat McKinnon.

If Mr. C. Giry, the backer of J. McLaughlin, who aspires to the bantam championship of the Pacific Coast, really desires to match his man against Espinosa of the Olympic Club, he should back his talk by putting up a deposit in the hands of some prominent sporting editor or club man. Espinosa is very willing to arrange a match with McLaughlin, and if McLaughlin or his backer will come forward and plank down their coin, more than one bantam weight will be ready to cover it, provided McLaughlin would be willing to fight for a trophy.

The Lurline Club does not appear to be very anxious to gain admission into the P. C. A. A. A.

The students at Berkeley, under the guidance of E. Coke Hill, have at last settled down to steady training. The cinder track is now in fair condition and the runners are taking advantage of the fact. A new walker has turned up amongst the students, and if reports be correct he will take a place in the walks on May 30th.

Victor E. Schifferstein is in fine trim at present, and with proper care he should improve on some of his past performances at the championship meetings. Many are of the opinion that he will run the hundred under ten seconds, and clear over 24 feet in the long jump. He has also improved in the high jump, and is likely to give Moffet a hard rub for first place.

Within the past week the Bay District track has been placed in tip top condition for foot racing. The Alpine Athletic Club's team are training on it, and a good many of the boys will show up in great shape on May 4th. Garrison, Moods, Little, Luttringer. Eldridge, King, Goodman, Hudy, George and Charles Armbruster, Dodd, Jeffery, Steinway. Coleman, Whelan and O'Connor are training for the running events, while Phillips, Cooke, Gafney and Gallagher are confining themselves to walking. McKinnon, Hancock, Hart, White and a few others are practicing jumping and hammer throwing.

H. C. Cassidy is training for the runs at San Leandro and expects to be in good form for the games.

At the Olympic Club's new grounds every day and evening may be seen Scott, McArthur, O'Kane, Williams, McDonald, Henderson, Cooley, Espinosa, Schillinghyde, Winslow, Schifferstein, Jellineak, Foster and Hare representing the runners, with Jervis, Coffin and Kelly in the walks. Peter McIntyre is happy to see such interest taken in the sport, and says when he looks at the many old faces spinning round the track, it makes him feel like a boy again.

The following gentlemen have been selected as the officers of the day for the Alpine Club games which will take place at the Bay District track on Sunday, May 4th, commencing at 1:30 P. M. sharp: Master of Ceremonies—T J Cunningham, A A A C; Referee—E Coke Hill, U C; Starter—F M Howard, A A A C; Judges of track events—J P Bean, A A A C. Dr. C A Bonnestell, A A A C, George W Jordan, O A C; Timers—John T Sullivan, P B C, R McArthur, O A C; John Purcell, O A C; Judges of Walking—C B Hill, R B Jones, E Steinway, A A A C, Charles Vultee, A A A C; Clerks of Course—J H Donohoe, A A C, T J Gallagher, A A A C; Call Stewards—F J Ralph, A A A C, W C Bean, A A A C; Marshalls—A M King, A A A C, Henry Tank, A A A C, W C Gifford, A A A C J R Collins, A A A C. The full list of entries and handicaps will be published next week.

The struggle between the tug-of-war teams of the Olympic and Alpine Clubs at the championship games will be worth seeing. The latter team is training at the club rooms under the direction of Captain P. J. Sheedy.

A ladies annex will shortly be organized in connection with the Alameda Olympic Club. The class will meet in the gymnasium once a week.

Lean and Mertes have been "fired" out of the California Club. Lean is now up for membership in the Olympic Club. These are not the first men that have been fired from this amateur-hating club and the fact of an athlete being expelled from the California Club should be a sufficient recommendation that he is eligible for membership in any of the first class clubs. The California Club Directors prefer to see opium fiends laying around their quarters rather than healthy amateur athletes.

ON THE WHEEL.

Sydney R. Church is proposed for membership in the Bay City Wheelmen.

Doane, Plummer, Hammer and Wetmore, of the B C W, went to Haywards on Sunday and from there started for Niles. On account of the bad condition of the road they were compelled to turn back. They returned to the city had dinner, and spent the afternoon in the Golden Gate Park.

The fourth run of the Oakland Bicycle Club will be held to-morrow. The members are requested to assemble at the corner of 12th and Broadway streets, at 8:30 A. M. The run will be to San Leandro, when breakfast will be taken, after which the team will be dismissed.

C. N. Langton and companion started for Mount Tamalpais on Sunday, but owing to the muddy condition of the roads had to abandon the trip.

A largely attended meeting of the California division L A W was held in Red Men's Hall, Post St., on Saturday evening last. Chief Consul Thompson presiding. Reports were made by the different committees. It was decided to hold the League Meet at San Jose, Cal., on July 4th and 5th. The San Jose members promised to have a four lap track built in time if possible, otherwise the track at the park would be put into good condition for the meet. The following were appointed a committee to arrange for the tournament: Al, Col. Wagner, (Local Consul of San Jose) Dr. T L Hill, — McKenna and G. Drake. Should the winner of the League District race make good time he will probably be sent East to compete at the National Championship meeting.

AT THE OARS.

The water was exceedingly rough on Sunday, and in consequence but few of the local crews were out.

It is possible that the Alpine Club will purchase a new boat for its amateur crew before the date of the annual regatta.

The Lurline Club gave a very pleasant athletic entertainment at its quarters on Bay street last Sunday. About 5000 people were present. Refreshments were served all day, and the Committee of Arrangements deserve credit for the excellent manner in which they manage things. The aquatic programme could not be carried out owing to the roughness of the bay, but the indoor exhibition was good and fully satisfied those who were invited to attend. The programme consisted of several boxing bouts by some of the best talent on the Pacific Coast, wrestling, musical specialties, etc. The final boxing bout was between Messrs. Cook and Smith, and the result was a clean knock out. Cook apparently tapped Smith a little harder than was really necessary in an exhibition, and the latter retaliated by knocking his opponent under the ropes in the fourth round, where he lay until after the ten seconds had expired. The club will hold its first picnic at Wildwood Glen, Sausalito, to-morrow afternoon. All the boat and athletic clubs are cordially invited to attend.

Great preparations are being made for the annual picnic of the Pacific Rowing Association.

The members of the Oakland, Cal., Canoe Club have received an invitation from the Corinthian Yacht Club to attend their opening day, Saturday, April 26th, at Tiburon.

CLUB JOTTINGS.

The regular monthly exhibition of the Golden Gate Athletic Club was held last evening and was largely attended by the members of the club.

On exhibition nights President Fulda of the California Club tries to make the members think that they have no right to speak. Last Tuesday evening Mr. Fulda addressed the member at large and asked them if they were willing to have the club put up a purse of $20,000 for a battle between John L. Sullivan and Pete Jackson. Some of the members who were present suggested that $1,500 or $2,000 would be enough, and that such a sum as $20,000 was entirely too much to throw away in a prize fight. Now these members were quickly told to shut up, and made to feel that they ought to be thankful for being allowed the privilege of paying their dues every month. In brief, Fulda tried to impress all present with the fact that he was the power and the say of the club. It ill behooves the President of any club to try and bluff the members over which he presides, and the members of the California Club should strike boldly out and demand that their voices should be heard and their opinions respected. The humblest member in the club has just as much right to talk as Mr. Fulda, the President. A change in the officers might tend to make things more pleasant for the members at large, especially since some of the officers have declared that they do not want amateurs in the club.

A general meeting of the Alpine Amateur Athletic Club will be held on Thursday evening next, May 1st, at the club rooms, 706 Powell street, near Pine. Nominations of officers for the ensuing term will be made, and final arrangements will be completed for the coming games.

At a meeting of the P. C. A. A. A. held at the Olympic Club rooms on Friday evening, April 18th. Several new rules were adopted, J. J. McKennon, of the Alpine Club was reinstated into the amateur ranks, and the officers to manage the coming champ onship games were selected.

We understand that the Garden City Athletic Club of San Jose is fast gaining in membership, and that the team which is to represent it on May 30th is a strong one and liable to take away a good many points from the local clubs.

LADIES' NIGHT.

The Olympic Athletes Entertain Their Lady Friends in First-Class Style.

A Successful Tug of-War Contest.

Seats were at a premium in the spacious gymnasium of the Olympic Athletic Club on Wednesday evening last. It was Ladies' Night," and the place was packed with members and their fair friends. The committee of arrangements deserve much credit for the excellent manner in which every number on the programme was carried out. The pyramids and groupings by members of the Juvenile class, was loudly applauded by the ladies. The boxing was scientific and not too rough, and the fencing reflected credit on the instructors. The trapeze and horizontal bar acts were unusually good, and the performers showed the results of careful training. The club swinging act of Prof. Smyth was worthy of that gentleman. The tug-of-war contest on cleats was exciting, and both teams were loudly applauded for their fine work. This contest was the most exciting one of the whole evening, and with the fair sex in particular, it took well. The young athletes who took part in it, were without a single exception splendid specimens of athletic manhood.

The members of the Juvenile class who took part in the exhibition were exceptionally well drilled in their different parts, which fact proves that the instructors employed by the club are all first class men, and attentive to their duties. The following is a correct copy of the programme as given:

1. Pyramids and groupings—By juveniles of the Olympic Club, assisted by Prof. William Smyth and Assistant P. P. Bernhardt, Henry S. Russ, Otto Hesslinger, Eddie Winterburn, Harry Kennedy, Willie Smith, Warrie Shufeldt, James H. McCullough, Walter N. Hogg, Tom Pike.

Brother act—W and A Ensbury.

2. Double trapeze—Joseph G Mansfield and Arthur Arnold.

3. Horizontal bar—By juveniles of the Olympic Club: Henry S Russ, David Goldberg, Otto Hasslinger, George Bosworth, Tom Pike, Eddie Lyons, Eddie H Winterburn, E Wolf, Albert McCarthy.

4. Indian club swing—Prof. William Smyth.

5. Fencing—Broadsword, F A Chapuis and Prof. L. Tronchet; foils, Leonard M Waterman and Alvin L Liebes of the Olympic Club Juvenile Class; Gordon Blanding and Prof. L Tronchet.

6.—Tug of war—By juveniles of the Olympic Club. Invincibles (light blue ribbon), expectant champions; Eddie H Winterburn, coacher. 1 Nelson Eckhart. 2 Emery Smith. 3 Alex Ensbury. 4 Willie D Leahy. 5 Albert McCarthy. 6 Eddie A Diggins. 7 Walter D Schranz. 8 Fred S Knight, anchor. Nonpareils (cherry ribbon), now hold championship of the Juvenile Class; coacher, Tom Pike 1 Walter N Hogg. 2 James Woolrich. 3 Willie Smith. 4 James H McCullough. 5 Henry Newmark. 6 Herbert S Meyer. 7 Willie Ensbury. 8 Harry Kennedy, anchor.

7. Double horizontal bars—Joseph G Mansfield, Arthur Arnold, and the renowned Ben Bogner as clown.

8. Walter N Hogg and Jules Kullman, Sylvan Strauss and Joy Webster of the Olympic Club Juvenile Class; M L Espinosa and Philip Boulo, F L Cooley and J L Lafferty.

9. Tug of war (on cleats, against time)—Captain, E B Braden; 2, J S Helmer; 3. A G D Kerrell; anchor, D W Donnelly; substitute, R Y Cole. Captain, E N Winslow: 2 E A Kolb; 3, H Denhard; anchor, W T Heberly; substitute. R Belau.

The above style is adopted by the Amateur Athletic Union of America, and this is its first introduction on this coast.

A first class string orchestra added much to the enjoyment of the evening.

JOTTINGS FROM ALL OVER.

The fourth annual team championship of the National Cross Country Association will be held this afternoon at New York City.

At a meeting of the Executive Committee of the National Association of Amateur Oarsmen held at the Gilsey House, New York City, recently, it was resolved: That Erastus Rogers, Albany Rowing Club; William Caffrey, Crescent Boat Club, Boston· E J. Mahony, Bradford Boat Club, Boston; E J. Kearney, Institutes, Newark; H. F. Corcoran, Central Boat Club, Boston; and E N. Atherton Metropolitan Boat Club, New York, be and hereby are reinstated as amateur oarsmen.

THE GUN.

Blue Rock Shooting.

The contest at blue rock shooting, at Windsor, Sunday, April 16th, between the Healdsburgh and Windsor Gun Clubs, was won by the latter, as shown by the score below. Ewing of the Healdsburghs displayed considerable skill in bringing down tail-enders. McCutchen, "J. B.," deserves especial mention for having made a clean score and for bringing twenty-two straight to the ground at an exhibition shoot. Following is the score:

HEALDSBURG.

Dr. Swisher	1	0	0	0	0	0—1
H. Laymance	0	1	1	1	1	1—5
J. Ewing	0	0	1	1	1	1—4
Dr. Wilcox	0	0	0	1	0	0—1
Ben Lowry	1	0	1	1	1	0—4
Total						15

WINDSOR.

Wm. Lowry	1	1	0	1	1	1—5
Robt. Shane	0	1	0	1	1	1—4
McCutchen	1	1	1	1	1	1—6
Frank Hall	1	0	0	0	1	0—2
C. Macey	1	1	1	1	0	0—4
Total						21

Gun Club.

A very charming day and delightful trap meeting was that of the Gun Club at Oakland Trotting Park on Saturday afternoon last. The birds were almost without exception clinkers, and as many of them were white and flew directly toward the newly painted white fence, it was impossible to see them. The unusual quickness of the birds accounts in a measure for the low average scores, although several of the members had bad luck in having birds fall dead out of bounds, among them being Mr. Will J. Golcher, Mr. Fred Webster and Mr. H. W. Woodward. The only clean score was Mr. Orr's. He shot in superb form and fully maintained his position as a premier with the gun.

Messrs. R. B. Woodard, Fred Wooster and R. A. Eddy alone of the others got into double figures and that only by some of the cleanest and sharpest shooting that has been seen in local circles for a long time.

Mr. Ed Donohue, using his 6¾ lb. ejector, scored nine, a very fine performance for a novice.

Mr. Jellett, who seemed likely to make none but clean scores this season, dropped to eight.

The match was at twelve birds, American Shooting Association rules, and the scores were:

F. S. Butler	2	0	1	1	0	0	1	1	1	1	2	1—9
R. B. Woodward	2	2	1	2	1	1	1	0	0	1	1	1—10
Charles F. Stone	2	2	2	1	0	1	1	2	0	0	1	2—9
F. H. Swett	2	1	2	2	0	0	1	0	2	0	2	0—7
F. O. Sanborn	0	2	0	0	0	1	1	0	2	2	1	2—7
E. F. Tichenor	0	0	1	0	2	2	0	2	1	1	0	0—6
George Leviston	1	0	0	1	2	0	0	0	1	1	0	0—5
William Leviston	2	0	1	0	0	1	0	0	1	1	1	1—7
F. W. Chapin	0	1	2	2	0	2	1	0	1	2	0	2—8
Fred Wooster	2	1	1	1	1	1	1	2	0	1	2	1—10
Fred Webster	1	2	1	2	1	0	2	0	1	0	2	0—8
J. D. Harvey	2	1	0	1	1	0	2	2	1	2	2	0—9
John K. Orr	1	1	1	1	1	1	1	1	2	1	1	2—12
J. H. Jellett	2	0	2	0	1	2	2	0	2	1	2	0—8
H. W. Woodward	0	2	0	0	0	2	0	0	1	0	0	0—3
W. J. Golcher	2	0	0	1	0	2	1	1	2	1	2	0—8
Ed Donohue	1	0	2	1	1	1	0	1	1	0	1	2—9
R. A. Eddy	2	1	2	2	2	2	1	1	0	1	0	2—10

At the March meeting not enough birds were provided to enable the full twelve to be shot by each man and but ten rounds were shot. To complete the score each man on Saturday last shot at two birds with the following results:

F. S. Butler	1	1—2	Fred Wooster	2	2—2
R. B. Woodward	2	0—1	Fred Webster	1	1—2
Charles F. Stone	1	0—1	J. T. Harvey	0	0—0
F. H. Swett	1	1—2	John K. Orr	1	2—2
F. G. Sanborn	0	1—1	J. H. Jellett	1	0—1
E. F. Tichenor	1	1—2	H. W. Woodward	0	0—0
George Leviston	0	2—1	W. J. Golcher	0	2—1
William Leviston	2	0—1	Ed Donohue	1	1—2
E. W. Chapin	1	1—2	R. A. Eddy	1	2—2

After this followed a special shoot between Orr and Eddy as captains, of six men each, for two rounds, the stakes $30, and the losing side to pay for the birds. The names and scores of those who shot in this contest are:

John K. Orr	1	1—2	R. A. Eddy	0	1—1
Ed Donohoe	1	1—2	R. B. Woodward	1	0—1
E. S. Butler	2	1—2	J. D. Harvey	0	0—0
W. J. Golcher	1	1—2	S. I. Kellogg	1	2—2
Fred Webster	1	0—1	Fred Wooster	2	1—2
H. W. Woodward	1	0—1	E. F. Tichenor	1	1—2

The club's next match will be held on May 30th, at Ross Station, as it has been the custom every year to have a picnic and shoot on that day. The shooting will begin in the morning, and several side matches will be shot in addition to the stated shoot.

Lincoln Gun Club.

The Lincoln Gun Club held a shoot last Sunday afternoon on its new grounds recently laid out at Alameda Point. All the members were in attendance, but this being the first shoot of the season and on new grounds, with a heavy wind blowing, the scores were not up to championship form.

The first event on the programme was the medal contest for two classes—first and second.

In the first class Holmes won, breaking twelve birds out of a possible twenty.

In the second class Venker won with seven birds. The scores of the others were as follows, all being made at clay pigeons.

First class—Scovern 5, Holmes 12, Campbell 7, Mellish 8, Bruns 5, Potter 11, Parks 8, Ford 10, Kearney 10, Allen 4, Mallert 3, Framzen 9, Fisher 2, Wenzel 4, Cate 8, Fanning 5, White 9.

Second class—Quinten 5, Venker 7, Cohen 1, Brown 6.

The next contest was a free-for-all pool-shoot, in which twenty-two members entered, subscribing $2.50 each, the winner to take the entire purse. This was won by Parks, who brought down eight out of a possible twenty. Following was the score:

Ford 5, Cate 2, Brown 1, Holmes 1, Parks 8, Wenzel 3, Venker 3, Campbell 5, Frazer 4, Thorn 2, Potter 2, Mellish 5, Kearney 7, Cohen 2, Bruns 7, Fisher 4, Hughes 1, Briggs 1, Scovern 1, White 1, Foster 4, Quinten 2.

Two other pool contests were shot—the first by eleven members, in which Cohen won by breaking ten "birds," and the second, a double-bird shot, with thirteen entries, was won by Parks, who broke seven birds.

Mr. "Nick" White, of Sacramento, writes: "There are some snipe about here, and I managed to get a few one day last week in a fifteen-mile tramp. As many as fifty to the gun have there been killed in some localities, per day."

California Wing Shooting Club.

Oakland Trotting Park was enlivened on Sunday last by the pigeon-popping of the California Club. The birds were more than ordinarily good, and the shooting very fair. Mr. "Randall" won the first medal on a toss-up in the club match, killing eleven lively birds cleanly with his little 12-bore. Mr. Crittenden Robinson did what he rarely does, i. e. scored but eight. Second medal went to Mr. Chase, also with eleven. Captain Eddy, with the same score, took third medal, both places being allotted on a toss-up. The scores were made at 12 live birds, American Shooting Association rules:

Robinson	0	1	1	1	1	0	1	1	1	1	0	0—8
Randall	0	1	1	1	1	1	1	1	1	1	1	1—11
Haas	1	1	0	1	0	1	1	1	1	1	1	1—10
Liddle	1	1	1	0	0	1	0	1	1	0	0	0—6
Schwerin	0	1	1	1	1	1	1	1	1	1	1	0—10
Golcher	1	1	1	0	1	1	1	0	1	1	1	1—10
Thompson	1	1	0	0	0	1	1	1	1	0	1	1—8
Schroder	0	1	1	1	0	0	1	0	1	0	0	0—5
Hearst	0	0	0	0	1	0	0	1	1	0	0	0—3
DeVaull	0	0	0	1	1	1	1	1	1	1	1	1—9
West	1	1	1	1	1	1	0	1	1	1	0	1—10
Sharp	0	0	0	1	1	0	0	0	1	1	1	1—6
Clohns	1	1	1	1	1	1	1	0	1	1	1	1—11
Chase	1	0	1	1	1	1	1	1	1	1	1	1—11
Fay	1	1	0	1	0	0	1	0	1	1	1	1—8
Eddy	1	0	1	1	1	1	1	1	1	1	1	1—11

At six birds, $1 entrance. C. J. Haas first; Robinson, Randall and Eddy tied for second, Mr. Robinson winning on the shoot off.

Haas	1	1	1	1	1	1—6
Robinson	1	1	1	0	1	1—5
Randall	1	1	0	1	1	1—5
Fay	1	1	0	1	1	0—4
Terry	0	0	1	w		
Eddy	1	1	0	1	1	1—5
Golcher	1	0	1	1	1	0—4
Francis	0	1	1	0	1	w
Schroeder	0	1	0	w		

Freeze out, $2.50 entrance. Divided by Messrs. Haas and Fay.

Haas	1	1	1	1	1	1
Robinson	0					
Eddy	0					
Terry	1	1	1	1	1	0
Randall	0					
Fay	1	1	1	1	1	1

At 12 birds, $5.00 entrance, C. J. Haas, first. Messrs. Francis, Eddy and Maskey divided second and third.

Robinson	1	1	1	1	0	1	1	1	1	1	0	w—
Fay	1	0	1	0	1	1	1	1	1	1	1	1—10
Haas	1	1	2	1	1	1	1	1	1	1	1	1—12
Maskey	1	2	1	1	1	1	1	1	1	1	0	1—11
Golcher	1	2	2	1	1	0	1	1	0	0	w	
Schwerin	1	0	2	0	0	w						
Schroeder	1	1	1	0	0	1	1	1	1	1	0	1—9
Francis	1	2	1	1	1	1	1	1	0	1	1	1—11
Eddy	1	1	1	1	1	1	1	1	0	1	1	1—11
Chase	1	1	1	1	0	1	1	1	0	0	0	1—8
Randall	1	1	1	0	1	0	w					

Interesting Statistics.

Mr. E. Hough, chronicler of the doings of Col. C. W. Dimick's peripatetic pigeon pulverizers, in closing his annals of the memorable journey, recites some valuable and interesting details as to the trip:

The Iolanthe traveled rather more than 10,000 miles without any accident beyond one broken spring. The rent of the car was understood to be $45 per day. The total outlay of the trip must have been between $15,000 and $20,000. Shoots were held in 32 towns. The original schedule included about 42 towns. The count of towns actually shot in is as above. The public will not be interested in the fact that Dayton shoot was counted out, but will very naturally include that in the series, as it should be. The individual averages were made up with Dayton shoot included. On the above basis the Eastern term won 16 matches, the Western 18. There were three ties—Austin, Texas; Toledo, O., and New York.

Total number of birds broken by Eastern team, 5,346; total by Western team, 5,440. The West thus led in the totals by 93 birds. The number of birds shot at by each team was 6,400. Each man who shot in every race shot at 1,280 birds in all. Following are the individual totals and averages:

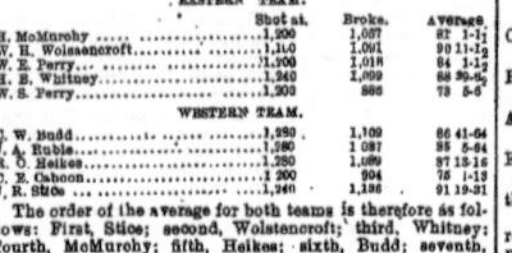

EASTERN TEAM.

	Shot at.	Broke.	Average.
H. McMurchy	1,200	1,057	87 1-11
W. H. Wolstencroft	1,160	1,091	90 11-12
W. E. Perry	1,200	1,018	84 1-12
H. B. Whitney	1,240	1,099	88 29-31
W. S. Perry	1,200	886	73 5-6

WESTERN TEAM.

	Shot at.	Broke.	Average.
C. W. Budd	1,280	1,109	86 41-64
J. A. Ruble	1,280	1 087	85 5-64
R. O. Heikes	1,280	1,089	87 13-16
C. E. Cahoon	1 200	904	75 1-13
J. R. Stice	1,240	1,136	91 19-31

The order of the average for both teams is therefore as follows: First, Stice; second, Wolstencroft; third, Whitney; fourth, McMurchy; fifth, Heikes; sixth, Budd; seventh, Ruble; eighth, W. E. Perry; ninth, Cahoon; tenth, W. S. Perry.

There were absent from matches at different times through physical debility, on the Eastern team, McMurchy twice, W. E. Perry twice, Whitney once; on the Western team, no absentees from that cause.

The Eastern team won the series. The Western team won greatest total and first average. It may be asked whether the matches were hippodromes, since the West came in suspiciously strong at the close. The answer is emphatically no. The boys shot their best throughout.

There is no special significance in the victory of the Eastern team. They just won races enough to win the series, that is all. Their victory is not due to any special condition of guns, loads or members. The teams were about alike in main regards.

The loss of the Western team is due to no special cause. Cahoon has received blame for shooting below his old average and so for losing the race. Yet we should observe that Cahoon beat his running mate 18 birds. Cahoon beat W. S. Perry in 14 races, and was beaten by him in 9 races, the others being ties. How shall we then saddle the blame upon this member of the Western team? The truth is, that the victories of the East were usually won in the doubles, and by a margin of two or three birds or the like. The East never did give the West such tremendous beatings as it received from the West. As therefore, it was first one Western man and then another that dropped a little and lost a day, it is only fair to say that any other man of the Western team might by picking up a little have won the series for his team. There were three men on the Eastern team who shot very regularly, and four who shot fairly together. On the Western team there was but one very regular shooter, the rest being more spasmodic.

The Western team made the highest score, 191, at Denver. The two teams tied on the lowest score, 132, at Claremont, N. J.

There were seven 40 straights made; Wolstencroft 2, Whitney 2, Heikes 2, Stice 1. On several occasions Budd, Wolstencroft and others made 39, losing the last bird.

A study of the scores will show that there is not any special significance in the winning of the first average, although the conditions of the two main contestants therefore were different. Wolstencroft shot a Greener gun and Schultze powder; Stice shot a Parker gun and American wood powder. Wolstencroft won in the greatest number of races where he met Stice. The latter never headed Wolstencroft from Dayton to Philadelphia. Wolstencroft left Cleveland 6 birds ahead of Stice, and skipped two shoots, going on to Philadelphia. It is doubtful whether he intended then to go on East of Philadelphia, but his friends insisted upon his doing so. Meantime, for some unknown reason, the Pittsburg race was shot at Harrisburg. The conditions were good, and Stice put up two 38 scores while Wolstencroft was absent. At Philadelphia, under the same conditions, Stice beat Wolstencroft so much as to lead him one bird. At New York the weather being so extremely unfavorable, that out of twenty of the best trap shots in the country only two, and one of them Wolstencroft, made so high a score as 30 out of 40, Stice announced his intention of not shooting, as he had already shot two races more than Wolstencroft. He therefore started for New Haven, and was back again in the evening by the time the boys had returned from the shoot. Had he shot in the high wind of Claremont day, it is fair to suppose that he would have been close around 30, one side or the other.

At New Haven, where Stice changed his mind and shot, Wolstencroft beat him three birds. At Boston Stice came out ahead one bird. Supposing Stice had shot at Claremont, as every one wished him to do, and had tied Wolstencroft's score, the public may then see how very close would have been the averages, and what a pretty contest of skill, man against man, it would have been right up to the end. It was no question of guns. Stice shot too good a gun to need fear to shoot it at Claremont or anywhere else. The public was interested in the contest, and would have been gladder had each man skipped no shoot at all, but had done his sportsmanlike best, win or lose. That was all the fun there was in it, and all the significance there was to it. The public likes good shooting immensely more than good figuring, but it is duty that the public, close watcher as it is of both the shooting and the figuring, should be in possession of all the facts, so that it may be fair in its judgment. It may be said that Stice had a right to shoot only as many races as Wolstencroft. Let the public study about that and decide. It may be said that Stice could have won anyhow. That is it. He robbed himself and his gun of an absolute privilege when he failed to shoot at Claremont, win or lose, when his opponent was on the ground ready to meet him. He robbed himself and his gun of the chance for the glory of an unreserved and unqualified victory. That was a mistake. It will not please the public so much as if he had won cleanly, clearly, fearlessly, shooting his best, win or lose. That was the only way to do in a race like this, and to point out what excuses or justifications there were for doing otherwise adds no significance to the winning in the eyes of the sportsmen of America, who best of all like good and plucky shooting. The facts have now been given.

The styles of Stice and Wolstencroft at the trap are very different. Stice is deliberate, steady, cool, erect, graceful and strong looking as he scores. He extends his left arm well and has not far to go to find his bird, but shoots deliberately. Wolstencroft is erect, nervy-looking, and quick as a cat. He shoots his birds yards and yards closer in than Stice, and it is indeed simply marvelous how he can get on to them so quickly. He needs steady, regular pulling, for he hardly calls "pull" before he shoots. There is no shooter in America who compares with him in quickness and brilliancy. His race is so risky and difficult that it almost puts one in suspense to see him shoot, and the relief nearly always comes in the form of involuntary applause.

Whitney, the gritty and good natured "boy wonder," shot the biggest gun of the party. He shoots his birds just before the top of the flight, and is a good one. For Harvey, Roll, Charlie, there is no need to say anything. All the boys know these boys.

WINNINGS OF THE TEAMS.

At Dayton, O., $25 in gold by the Heikes Hand Protector Co. by the West.

At Cincinnati, 5 silver cups, by Bandle Arms Co. and L. & R. Powder Co.; by the East.

At St. Louis, 5 silver shaving mugs, by the E. C. Meacham Arms Co; by the West.

At Memphis, 5 silver match safes, by Mr. Dimick; by the East.

At New Orleans, 5 silver match safes, by Mr. Dimick; by the West.

At San Francisco, the beautiful Clabrough & Golcher bluerock tankard trophy; by the East; won individually by Whitney.

At San Francisco, 6 elegant gold key-rings, by the Selby Smelting & Lead Co.; by the East.

At San Francisco, the grand E. T. Allen live bird trophy, California vs. the World; by the joint teams; presented by them to Mr. Dimick at Boston banquet.

At Kansas City, the J. F. Schmelzer live bird prize, Kansas City vs. United States, by the joint teams; presented by them to Mr. Dimick.

At Chicago, one dozen fine pocket knives, by the Jenney & Graham Gun Club, Chicago vs. United States; by the joint teams.

At Philadelphia, $25 in gold, by Wm. H. Wolstencroft & Sons; by the West.

At New Haven, $25 in gold, by Forest and Stream; tie from Claremont; won by the West.

At Boston, the magnificent silver team championship trophy offered by the United States Cartridge Company, and earlier described. Won on the series by the East. This great trophy will for a time be exhibited in the leading cities of the counry.

At Boston, the beautiful Wellington silver pitcher, for the West, won by Stice.

A correspondent anticipates part of this report by asking details as to traps, loads, etc. To repeat: The traps were three, unscreened, order determined by lot; a broken piece not shot, not to give the shooter the same trap again. The race was shot one man down, alternating teams, three birds per man, rapid firing system not used, angles all known, but traps unknown. The birds were thrown low and hard.

Two weeks ago we used an article about the "Townsends Junco" which originally appeared in "Zoe" a scientific journal recently established in this city and edited by Mr. Frank H. Vaslit. It was our intention to notice "Zoe" in an especial paragraph, but through inadvertence it was not done, and credit for the copied article was consequently omitted. We regret the fact.

THE KENNEL.

Dog owners are requested to send for publication the earliest possible notices of whelps, sales, names claimed, presentations and deaths, in their kennels, in all instances writing plainly names of sire and dam and of grandparents, colors, dates and breed.

Visits.

Ben O. Bush, Kalamazoo, Mich., pointer Lady Wallace 12768 (Champion Lad of Bow 7880 ex Lady Belle) to Jack of Naso 7044 (Champion Naso of Kippen ex Nympher 4420), March 21st.

Henry Waruf, Kalamazoo, Mich., English setter bitch Fly Noble to Toledo Blade, March 17th.

Geo. T. Allender's pointer bitch California (Point T.—Blossom) to Mr. William Schreiber's Nestor (Gladsome—Forest Queen II) on April 20, 1890.

Mr. Dan Mac Farland's fox-terrier Clochette to Mr. C. A. Sumner's Blemton Vesuvian (14290) by Champion Lucifer, April 22d, at Los Angeles, Cal.

Sales.

G. W. Bassford, Vallejo, has sold pointers by Scout Croxteth (6277)—Blossom (10,085), whelped August 8, 1889:

Dog, lemon and white, to T. G. Pinder, Santa Rosa.
Dog, lemon and white, to G. W. Hazzelett, San Bernardino.
Dog, lemon and white, to C. E. Fout, Los Angeles.
Dog, lemon and white, to H. Kahn, Portland, Oregon.
Dog, lemon and white, to J. M. Bassford, Jr., Vacaville.
Bitch, liver and white, to George Hood, Santa Rosa.
Lemon and white bitch reserved.

By Professor—Gracie Bow, whelped August 20, 1887.
Liver and white dog to C. M. Osborn, San Francisco.
Liver and white bitch to D. Leonard, Bakersfield.
Liver and white bitch to W. D. Howe, San Francisco.

Beagles by Duffer—Della:
B white and tan dog to F. Townsend, Napa.
B white and tan dog to F. Townsend, Napa.

By Bannerman, Jr.—Daisy:
B white and tan bitch to H. Boyce, Vacaville.
B white and tan dog to H. Boyce, Vacaville.

"California Belle" Dead.

Mr. E. M. Arthur writes from Portland, Or., that his noted red setter bitch California Belle died last week, the cause being some poisonous material picked from a barrel of refuse. Mr. Arthur adds: "Though past her usefulness for hunting, I was much attached to her, and regret her death." Her late owner is not without sympathy. Old Belle had a various and rather singular life. Whelped in this city on December 12, 1879, she was originally owned by Mr. Geo. A. Story, who turned her over to Mr. John B. Maynard, at that time shooting ducks for market on Sherman Island. Mr. Maynard kept the frowzy little red lump of fat with him for many months, until sufficient growth had been made to determine the fact that the form of the setter was to be excellent, and her courage and hunting instinct unusually good. Then, in '81 or '82, being about to enter other business in which he could not well care for the dog, he turned her over to the writer, who broke her and won with her in the Gilroy Field Trials, and those of the Pacific Coast Field Trials Club. After her last win, in '84 or '85, she was sent to Mr. Arthur, who has hunted her on grouse, quail, snipe and ducks ever since.

Belle littered sixty-five puppies to various sires, her best being those sired by Kaeding's Duke. Many of the puppies developed into good dogs, and some of them show very good quality. For nose, staying power, indomitable courage, excellence as a retriever, and general comfort as a shooting companion, Belle had few equals. She could not be kept down in flesh, being a greedy eater, but despite her grossness, would trundle along all day in upland shooting, and never flinch at the longest and coldest day on the marsh. We hope Mr. Arthur has some of her progeny as good as their dam.

A New Breeding Kennel, the Renton.

Editor Breeder and Sportsman:—Inclosed find card of the Renton Kennels, which Mr. Hiram Mott (my dog trainer) and myself have recently started. The breeding farm and part of kennels are located about one mile out of Bolinas, where Mr. Mott has about 160 acres of land, and birds are quite abundant. We also have a city office, where can always be found some of our dogs (situated at 2922 Pine St.). You note our specialty on the card, which we desire to call the attention of the readers of the Breeder and Sportsman to. We also take dogs to board and train at very reasonable figures. We have just about completed our kennel, that is, erecting new houses and fencing the dog quarters off, and shall be ready to invite those who are desirous of seeing and inspecting the kennels on or about the first of May. The writer extends a private invitation to you to accompany him at any time to visit the place. We have at present quite a number of promising pups on hand for sale, also a well broken water spaniel out of Senator Pinder's stock. Hoping you will bear us in mind, I remain

W. D. Howe.

San Francisco, April 21st, 1890.

Mr. George W. Bassford had two fine beagles accidentally poisoned a few days ago. They were Duffer (Bannerman Jr.—Daisy 2d) and Dolly (Drive—Countess).

A subscriber wishes a "Newfoundland pup, or a dog of some large species." Any reader who may have what is wished, will favor both himself and this office by letting the fact be known.

A noteworthy project in a peculiar way is the establishment at Bolinas of a pointer breeding plant. Pointers will be the specialty of the kennel, but other dogs will be bred and dogs will also be taken to board.

San Francisco exhibitors in the Los Angeles Dog Show, should remember that the entries close on the 1st of May, and cannot be received later. Also that the express company transports dogs at half rates.

Mr. George W. Bassford sends a handsome photograph of his pointer bitch Blossom by Glen R.—Josie Bow. Blossom is one of the best formed dogs of the breed ever shown in the State and is besides a fine field performer.

Mr. A. B. Truman (Elcho Kennels, San Francisco) has sold to Captain A. B. Anderson, San Gabriel Cal., two pointer puppies a dog and a bitch, whelped March 17, 1890, by Point (Vandevorts Don—Drab) ex Queen Croxteth (Rush T—Patti Croxteth T.)

Mr. W. P. Lawlor, of the Olympic Club, is going in for Scotch terriers, having already secured a fine specimen, and applied for admission to the Pacific Kennel Club. He has a fine site for a kennel at his country residence near Tamalpais Station, Marin County.

Mr. Richard Foote, of the histrionic profession in San Francisco, is the owner of a rarely good mastiff of pure breeding and great quality. His dog has been bred to Mr. E. F. Preston's superb Actress, winner at both Pacific Kennel Club shows. The puppies will be in demand.

Every one of the cross country runners of the Olympic and Alpine Athletic Clubs should own a finely bred fox-terrier, or one of the rough-haired terriers, and take his companion with him on the country jaunts. A deal of excitement and sport would result when the dogs chanced to take the trail of a wild cat, racooon or fox, and the runs would be sustained at better pace, for the interest incident to watching the freaks of the four-footed athletes.

An unusually large and fine Harlequin Great Dane has recently been brought to the city by Mr. Joseph D. Calegaris. The dog must stand thirty-two and one-half or thirty-three inches, and weigh near one hundred and eighty pounds. He is in the stud, but has not been much used heretofore.

Mr. McNabb, Assistant-manager of the Occidental Hotel of this city, has recently received from Southern California a very fine twelve months-old mastiff puppy. The dog weighs one hundred and twenty-seven pounds, is an upstanding, well-formed, well coated, well-masked and able animal.

Entries to the Southern California Kennel Club Show at Los Angeles, on May 6th, 7th, 8th and 9th, are coming in in gratifying numbers. About two hundred dogs will be benched, among them many rare good ones. Several San Francisco kennels will send down dogs, which can be done at half the usual express rates.

Mr. Richard P. Burr of Sacramento has been in San Francisco during the week, partly on business and partly to look about among the owners of large dogs with a view to buying something. The short-sightedness of local breeders in not advertising their kennels made it difficult to find them, but some great Danes, mastiffs and Leonbergs were seen.

We are told by Mr. T. J. Watson, of this city, that a New Yorker, who also has business interests here, Mr. George J. Harley has purchased and intends to bring to the coast the English setter Dan Gladstone by Gladstone—Sue. We know Dan very well, and while not perhaps the best Gladstone pup alive, he is yet a dog of great quality, and will be a most desirable sire.

Mr. H. T. Payne, President of the Southern California Kennel Club, together with Mr. F. H. Heald, of Elsinore, called at this office on Thursday last. Mr. Payne, as is usual with him in behalf of any enterprise into which he goes, is full of enthusiasm about the coming dog show at Los Angeles. He is anxious to have a good number of visitors and exhibitors from the northern portion of the State and we hope he may be gratified.

In sending notices of visits in Kalamazoo, Mich., Mr. Ben O. Bush, of that city, adds:

"I look over your columns devoted to the dog and gun with interest each week and notice that you have many good dogs and fine shots in California. I presume my old friend John O. Cadman, President of the Blue Rock Club, shoots in his snap, bang, happy go lucky style as of old, when he and I tramped the fields together."

Captain A. B. Anderson whose place, The Grange, near San Gabriel, Los Angeles County, is well known, has been in San Francisco for ten days purchasing the best dogs of various breeds that he could find. He has secured some pointers from Mr. A. B. Truman, some fox terriers from Mr. J. B. Martin, a sable collie from Mr. McFadden, some great Danes from Mr. Nahl, and is examining other dogs with a view to purchasing. He buys with excellent judgment and has the nucleus of a very fine dog breeding kennel. All of his dogs will be shown at Los Angeles in May.

Major J. M. Taylor, Manager of the American Shooting Association has recently been in correspondence with local trap shots, with a view to organizing a great tournament under the rules and auspices of the Association, sometime during the coming Fall.

A dog fancier who chanced to learn of the Major's possible presence here, suggested that a dog show be organized for about the same time and that he be invited to judge the dogs. The suggestion was conveyed to Major Taylor who replies, "It would give me great pleasure to be on the Coast during the Bench show, and if it was the pleasure of the Society, to judge for them."

Requests for entry blanks for the next field trial derby, which closes on June 1st, are coming in such numbers as to indicate considerable interest. Mr. Albert Peri, of Marysville, will make two entries. Mr. J. W. Harper of Suisun has a good one. Mr. A. B. Truman has two. Mr. F. B. Dexter of Fresno will enter Annie Rooney and Beautiful Language. After the last trials Mr. Geo. W. Bassford expressed himself rather discouraged and displeased with certain peculiarities of the stakes run in this State during the three or four years last passed, but we hope he will pull himself together and make some entries. Mr. P. D. Linville states that he has an entry. Mr. Ramon E. Wilson has one, and the list might be lengthened. Those making entries should bear in mind the fact that not one will be received, under any circumstances, unless accompanied by a forfeit of $5.

One day last week was passed at Santa Clara, by invitation of Mr. C. W. Wilson, of this city. Mr. James Sanderson was also of the party. The prime object of the visit was to look at the litter by Kittie's Luke (Carl R.—Bessie) ex-Wilson's Jennie (Dick—Belle). The pups, six dogs and a bitch, were whelped on April 2d, and are so notable in blood as to justify even a hard trip to see them. As it was, a two hours ride to Santa Clara, through green fields, budding orchards, and flowery meads, seemed to occupy but a few minutes. Then a home-breakfast prepared in most deft fashion, and with unequalled skill, by the lady of the house. Finally a chance to see the puppies. All of them of good size, fat, sturdy and clean; all but one nicely marked in black, white and tan. In so far as such young dogs can show beauty and quality, the litter is one than which no better has been bred within our observation. One of the pups is marked much like the Memphis and Avent Kennel's famous Chance, being black on one side of the head and muzzle and white on the other. The youngsters will go into the hands of trainers as soon as they are old enough, and will be heard from, barring accident, in the field trials.

In response to a query as to what fox-terriers were now in his kennel, Mr. J. B. Martin, of this city, writes:

"I have one bitch nine months old, all white, by Clover Turk (Mixture—Spite), out of Beatrice (Champion Bacchanal—Blemton Arrow) No. 13830 A. K. C. S. B. Clover Turk won first prize puppy 1886, New York. Beatrice is dam of Clover Patch, winner first at Los Angeles and other good ones. This white bitch Golden Lilly is a beauty, and probably the best bitch here at present. She has killed two rats. I have also six pups, three bitches and three dogs, two all white, the balance marked very nicely with black and tan markings. These pups are out of Beatrice (see above) and by Blemton Vesuvian (Champion Lucifer—Blemton Vesta by Resolute—Belgrave Viola by Belgrave Joe). Resolute by Champion Result—Champion Diadem. This is the best fox-terrier blood, coming from the best winning dogs of the day, and these pups should turn out to be something extra. I have been to a great deal of bother and trouble breeding to Vesuvian. Both Beatrice and Clover Turk, also Vesuvian, are good ratters, and I have seen Beatrice go to ground and hunt for hours. Vesuvian is also a nailing good terrier, being handsome and a useful dog.

ROD.

Fishing Notes.

Trout fishing has been fairly good this season considering the large amount of water in the different streams. Some good catches have been made in San Antonio, Adobe, Olema and Paper Mill creeks. Ed Hedges and Will Harris hooked a couple of baskets full in the latter stream one day last week.

Fred Ellsworth returned to this city Sunday evening after a couple of day's fishing in Mark West creek. Fred says he caught 80 or 800, he was not sure which, and a dog-face salmon.

Joe Bernhard is one of the most enthusiastic followers of Isaac Walton in our city. One day recently, armed with his trusty split-bamboo, a bent pin, and two fish-worms, he spent several hours in luring the cunning trout from the dark recesses of its watery home. The result of his day's sport was one water-dog and two bites that he did not catch on account of having on high rubber boots. At least that is what "Doc" says and he wouldn't lie about it.

Sam Hopkins and Captain Gould leave to-morrow for a couple of day's fishing in Olema creek.

Joe Bernhard says that Harry Maynard caught 280 trout the other day in the B-street sewer.

McGinty was caught for a sucker on April fool's day.

The two Jims and Joe were out after a mess of the speckled beauties the other day. Big Jim carried the bait and snake medicine, and his two companions were to do the fishing. They soon located a turtle's trail, and had followed it up a distance when Joe imagined he had been bit by a snake, and he turned to take a dose of the preventive, but Jim was missing. The two fishers bold then did some dry fishing for a couple of hours and finally caught Jim asleep under a pepper-wood tree. But sad to relate the medicine bottle was empty.—Petaluma Imprint.

The fish markets of San Francisco during these days are not uninteresting. Halibut in any desired numbers, and in weight from eight to thirty-five pounds. Clean, fat salmon of any size. Green cod eighteen inches long, and from that to three feet, freshly caught, and as sweet as any fish that swims are in plenty. Splendid shad at nominal prices. Red rock cod, black rock cod, craw fish, flounders, soles, smelts, anchovies, sardines, perch, striped bass, shrimps, crabs, oysters, clams of several sorts, trout, salmon trout, king fish, pin fish, pompano, sturgeon, hard mouths, eels, black bass, skates, and other sorts, might be found in one or another of the markets by any early riser who strolls through them. The bass, trout, pin fish, and others of the more rare and choice kinds, disappear from the stalls soon after being exposed for sale, the purchasers being the clubs and the high-priced restaurants, but at any hour, all but the most fastidious tastes may be gratified at a small outlay.

Grim's Gossip.

When Flambeau won the Pacific Derby, the result was telegraphed to the Eastern press, but with their usual perspicacity, the papers we have seen, show, Racine first, Flambeau second.

Mr. Eddy's colt, of which mention was made last week, is not by Pasha 2:36. but by Pasha 2:27½. he by Echo 462. The mistake was made owing to there being two stallions of the same name.

George Starr has taken the Budd Doble string from Fresno and if not already at Terre Haute is nearly there. The horses have all wintered well and left the Southern city in the best of condition.

Mervin will start during the first week in next month for the East, and Hickok will also make a move in the same direction on about the same time. Terre Haute is the objective point of both drivers.

The well known "Dagworth" will represent the BREEDER AND SPORTSMAN at the Sacramento races and our readers may rely on a bright newsy account of the spring meeting at the Capital City, in the next issue.

Although Mr. Rose has disposed of the running qualities of Sinfax, it is generally understood that he did not forget to back the Wildidle colt in the mud race, and made a very handsome profit for the money invested.

Marcus Daly, who has spent most of the winter in the East, returned to Anaconda a few days ago, and there is a strong probability that another trainer and driver will be secured for the trotting horses which have wintered at the Bitter Root Ranch.

The question will soon be asked, "What horse will win the Charter Oak $10,000 stake in 1890?" Heretofore it was won by Director 2:17, Harry Wilkes 2:13½, Joe Davis 2:17¾, Oliver K 2:16½, Patron 2:14¼, Spofford 2;18¾, and Alcryon 2:15¼. What horse will win it this year?

We have received the first number of Goodwin's Turf Guide for the current year and as usual it is full of useful information to the frequenters of the track. It contains all the summaries of races run from January 1st to April 12th and is very complete in other respects.

It may not be generally known that Mrs. Walsh names nearly all the thoroughbreds on the Palo Alto Stock Farm, but such is the case, and it is to that lady is due the pretty names that grace so many of the fast runners that Henry Walsh brings yearly before the public.

On Wednesday evening Alfred S. threw up his his head in the stall which he occupies, and striking against one of the rafters, scalped his head, tearing a large piece of skin from the poll. The injury is not a serious one, but will discommode the fast gelding for some few days.

E. F. Nash, of Deer Lodge, who has been driving the horses of S E. Larabie, has hired out to C. X. Larrabee, and will remain in Montana another year. Nash has driven quite a number into the 2:30 list, and is sure to increase his score with the material now at his command.

"Cap" Matthews was credited last week with having purchased a stallion from Mr. Sargent of Gilroy, it should have been a black gelding from J P. Sargent of Sargents Station. Gilroy or Sargents, it makes no difference to the speed of the horse, for he is a fast one on the road.

There is no reason to doubt, but that the new section of the Hearst stable which starts East next week, will be very successful, as there is good material to work on, and Donathan will see that the horses come to the post in good condition. The stable will be under the management of George Van Gordon.

Jockey Barnes will have to report to the Santa Anita Stable at once, he having received orders to that effect from E. J. Baldwin. "Pikey" has been riding for the Avondale stable at New Orleans and Memphis, and expected to stay with them for some weeks longer, but Mr. Baldwin has spoiled the plans of the demon jock.

L. A. Davies, owner of Roy Wilkes, started on Monday for Monterey to take a look at the marvelous beauty of that garden spot, preparatory to continuing his journey toward the rising sun. The great pacing stallion will be taken in the Hickok car when that gentleman starts East, probably about the first week in May.

It is now in order for Mr. J. I. Case, to promise a reduction in the records of Phallis and Brown. Last November I saw Phallis do two "workouts" and must confess that I think there is a lot of speed still left in the old stallion. He would make a good antagonist for Palo Alto and Bonnie McGregor, providing Axtell does not start.

Some strange pedigrees come to this office at times, and among them is the following which is given Verbatum:

St. Louis' dam Kentucky Eclipse, dam sired by Belmont and Glencoe, sired by St Louis, dam by Pet and sired by Modoc Chief, Modoc Chief sired by Spector, Spector by Donerel, Donerel by Lexington.

Although a little out of the line of horse news, it may not be out of place to notify my readers that A. L. Whitney of Petaluma sustained a severe loss last week by the sinking of a large schooner, that was consigned to A. L. Whitney & Co., loaded with barley. The schooner was partly owned by Mr. Whitney, and was not insured.

Cy Mulkey will not race at Sacramento during the meeting there, but will take his horses to Portland in time to take part in the meeting there. From Portland, Cy will wend his way Eastward to Montana, where he will participate in the circuit. There are several good horses in the Mulkey string, and they will all take a deal of beating.

At the Agricultural Park, Petaluma, this afternoon, there will be a trotting race between five local horses for a set of harness, offered as a premium by a firm in the town. The starters will be, A. N. Burrell's b m Daisy S, Louis Hoppy's s m Annie Laurie, A. J. Robinson's b h Fat Boy, B. Boman's g g Chapo and W. P. Fine's b g Wizard.

C. E. Needham, one of the Directors of the Stockton Fair, paid me a visit a few days ago, and reports the young stock at Belotta in superb condition. Mr. Needham also says that he will have Steve Whipple 2:23, sent for a fast record this year and I am glad to hear it, for every horseman in the State knows the stallion is capable of beating 2:16.

During the late meeting I had a chance to see several Prince of Norfolk colts, and a more racy lot were never looked at. This same impression evidently has become a settled conviction in the minds of many horsemen, for many first class mares have been booked to the son of Norfolk during the past few weeks. Among others, Ida Glenn, the fast sprinter has already received his embraces.

Major E. Hunter of Denver has started homeward from Fresno, taking with him his late purchase, Antevideo by Antevolo, dam Linden Belle by Mambrino Wilkes 6083, 2nd dam by Chieftain 721, etc. The colt was bred by S N. Straube, by whom he was sold to the Major. This colt from his breeding should be able to show plenty of trot, and it is to be hoped that he will be given a chance to.

Genial "Knap" McCarthy has finally sold his fleet footed trotting mare Geneva S. for a sum said to be $15,000. The Edgewood Stock Farm, of Terre Haute, Indiana, are the purchasers and a right good bargain they have made. The mare has only a record of 2:19½, but the number of times she could have beaten 2:16 last season, would almost prove that each of the 2:20 purses and stakes are at her mercy.

On the most successful breeding farms it is found profitable to employ a specialist to make an occasional thorough examination of the mouths of all the animals on the place. The high bred stock at Palo Alto and the San Mateo Stock Farm has recently received such attention from Dr Watkins, the well known veterinary dentist, who treated professionally 140 head at the former and 27 head at the latter place.

Tom Murray, who for several years has been in the employ of Orrin A. Hickok, will branch out for himself this season, and will be located at Petaluma, where he will train a stable of horses, quite a number of gentlemen having signified a desire to have Tom train and drive for them. Hickok is a first class mentor, so that the new comer should bring a lot of practical experience into the field where he proposes starting.

Quite a number of persons have asked the question, who will drive Stamboul, 2:12½, if Hickok goes East, seemingly thinking that Orrin will remain away too long to condition the great stallion. But the old driver will be back in plenty time to hand Mr Hobart's horse, as Rochester is the last meeting that he will attend east of the Rockies, and then he will hasten back to assist in lowering the record of the fleet son of Sultan.

W. E. Campbell purchased the stallion now known as Campbell's Electioneer from L. U Shippee of Stockton, for a comparatively small price, but he thinks so much of the young horse, that a few days ago he refused the munificent offer of $30,000 for him, the offer coming from some European parties. This goes to show that even across the broad Atlantic, the merits of California stock is now recognized, and therefore a new market opens up for our breeders.

Last year Richmond Jr., the gelding owned by Lee Rose, made additional reputation for his sire, A. W. Richmond, by trotting to a record of 2:22¾. When the thoroughbreds of the Rosemeade Stable start East, after the Sacramento meeting, Richmond Jr. will accompany them, where he goes to receive the handling of Jimmy Goldsmith, who will take him through the "big" circuit this season. Richmond Jr, in the hands of such a driver, should lower his mark to 2:17 or better.

I had a long chat a few days ago with John B. McCormick, who for many years has been known to the readers of sporting journals by his writings, which he always signs "Macon." Bro. McCormick is an able and instructive writer on all matters of a sporting nature, and while in California he will visit Palo Alto, San Mateo, Pleasanton and many other sections, to try and gain a lesson or two on the science of breeding. We bespeak a cordial reception on all the farms for "Mac," and tender him the hospitality of our sanctum.

W. H. E Smith of Rohnerville has purchased the ch. h. Longshot, four years old, by Duke of Norfolk, dam by Langford, from J. T. McBride of Sacramento, price $2,500. This is another valuable addition to the Smith stable which now includes Al Farrow, Susie S, and Longshot, with a chance of one or two youngsters being bought before long. After the Sacramento meeting. St. Louis, Kansas City, and Chicago will be visited and as Frank Du Poyster will be in charge, the horses will be fit to run when sent to the post.

The Twin City Jockey Club has followed Secretary Brewster's lead and engaged J. J. Burke as presiding judge at their meeting, which will follow that of the Washington Park Club. Judge Burke is also considering a call from the Overland Park Club, and may possibly appear in the stand at Kansas City. With an experience dating back to the early seventies, when the late Charles Foster wielded the most powerful pen in the school of turf journalism, Judge Burke has a spotless record, and enjoys the confidence of the public.

Unless Senator Stanford can secure the services of a first class driver and trainer, there is small chance of the Palo Alto colors being seen on California tracks this season. It was confidently expected that Dustin would drive their trotters, but as he has left Palo Alto, and Marvin is going East, there is no one to take charge of the stock on the local circuit. Mr. Ariel Lathrop thinks that Marvin can secure the services of such a person as is needed when he goes to Terre Haute, and if he can, Palo Alto will not hesitate to employ him.

A Brooklyn horse lately suffered an injury to one of his feet, and for some time traveled on three legs. Finally the wound was perfectly healed, but still the animal refused to put that hoof on the ground. A veterinary surgeon was called in, who made an examination and then pronounced it simply a case of nervousness. "Strap up the other hind foot and you'll see," he said. This was done, and the injured foot was thus forced into use. It did not take a block's travel to show the horse that his nervous fears were groundless, and when the strap was removed he trotted off squarely on four feet.

Mr. L. A. Richards has started an innovation which is well worthy of imitation by the trotting horse breeders in other sections of the State. Wishing to show what speed his young colts have, a general invitation was extended to all who wished to visit the home of Elector, and on the afternoon of the day selected a large company assembled and witnessed what the stock could do. Many trotters were driven and excellent time shown. The affair was a great success, and those who were present speak in the highest manner of the way in which they were treated by Mr. Richards.

Mr. William Boyd, the well-known horse-shoer has removed from San Francisco, and is now located in Stockton.

Deer Lodge *New North-West:* A most exciting horse race has been arranged between W. I. Higgins and M. S. Parker, to come off on the 19th of April. The bet of Mr. Higgins is that Deer Lodge Girl will beat the dark gray horse belonging to Mr. Parker, a race starting at the stable of Ward, Lodge & Co., on Main street, in Deer Lodge, and ending at the residence of James O'Donnell, on the road to Champion, a distance of twelve miles. The race will be up hill all the way. The horses go to buggies, each buggy to contain two persons. The judge of Higgins sits with Mr. Parker and the judge of Parker sits with Higgins. The race will start promptly at 10 o'clock. Mr. Higgins bets 3000 shares of American Ruby against the bay mare "Belle," belonging to Mr. Parker, and these are also the forfeits in case either refuses to make the race.

The reading public are all more or less tinged with curiosity and many are anxious to know how much was won by each of the different stables, during the Blood Horse Meeting. The amounts given are probably in excess of what each party received, as forfeits have to be deducted out, but horses in the various stables have won as follows: Palo Alto Stable, $4,-340; L. J. Rose, $1,600; Undine Stable, $1,590; W. H. E. Smith $940; George Hearst, $750; Kelly & Samuels $585; W. L. Appleby, $450; Dennison Stable, $450; P. Siebenthaler, $400; Cy Mulkey, $360; M. Storn, $350; W. George, $350; C. Foster, $300; J. T. McBridge, $300; Orange Grove Stable, $290; P. Herzog, $175; W. L. Whitmore, $140; Owen Bros., $100; H. I. Thornton, $75; W. M. Murry, $74; H. D. Miller, $50; Elmwood Stable $35.

The stockholders of the Stanislaus County Stock Breeders' Association met Saturday afternoon at Maze & Abbott's office and perfected a permanent organization, says the Modesto News. The following members were elected Directors: A. L. Cressey, Thos. Wallace, J. J. Dolan, L. A. Richards, J. W. Davison, R. M. Wilson and L. B. Walthall. The Board organized by electing A. L Cressey, President; L. B. Walthall, Secretary, and F. A. Cressey, Treasurer. By-laws were adopted, and an order made for the payment of twenty per cent. of the stock subscribed on or before May 7th, at 3 o'clock P. M., to the Treasurer at the Modesto Bank. The President and Secretary were instructed to procure the services of a surveyor and secure estimates for a mile track eighty feet wide, and report at a meeting to be held next Monday at 1 o'clock P. M.

Some difficulty has been experienced between 'The Circuit tracks and the Helena Directors, in Montana, about the time each should have, and bitter war has been carried on, which finally resulted in Helena being left out in the cold as regards dates. From the Anaconda Review we learn that the Secretary of the Helena Association last week wrote to E. W. Wynne, Secretary of the Butte Association, asking if some arrangements cannot be made to avoid the conflict of dates for the fall meeting. Mr. Wynne replied that the matter is one which concerns the whole circuit and therefore suggested a meeting of the Secretaries of the various associations at Anaconda, for last Saturday, for the amicable arrangement of the difficulty. It is probable that the Anaconda, Butte and Helena meeting will be cut to eight days, which arrangements will allow ample time for admitting Helena to the regular circuit. When the mail arrives we will have full particulars as to how the meeting resulted.

Harry J. Agnew has at last secured a breeding farm, which he is confident will fill the bill. The place is situated five miles from San Jose on the Monterey road, and was formerly called the Senter Ranch. It contains in the neighborhood of two hundred acres, of which fifty acres will be put in alfalfa, Mr. Agnew being a believer in the fattening qualities of that succulent grass. Already twenty broodmares have been secured, many of them choice individuals, and all of them rich in producing trotting blood. Here it is that Dawn, 2:18¼, will be taken on his retirement from Mr. Whitney's stud, and from his young get, it is natural to assume that he will have every opportunity afforded him to make a name for himself as a great producing sire. Mr. Agnew took possession of the farm yesterday morning, and will at once begin many alterations, which are deemed necessary, to place the ranch on an equality with the already prosperous ones of which there are so many in California.

In view of the large number of additions to the 2:30 list each year, it is a very common thing to hear the remark that a 2:30 horse is not of much account any more, and that unless a horse can beat 2:20 at least three times it is not worth while to start out with him says the Indiana Horseman. We admit that there is a great deal of significance and quite a good deal of truth in these remarks, and yet when we come to take individual sires and see the very small number of contributions they make to the 2:30 list in proportion to the whole number of colts sired by them, and, on the other hand when we come to count up the number of 2:30 horses that have been raised by breeders of our own immediate acquaintance, we are forced to believe that after all it is no very small matter to produce even 2:30 performers. Again, when we talk so glibly about 2:20 horses being the only ones worthy of our attention, we seem to forget that although the 2:20 list is each year growing, there are just nineteen horses living and dead that have ever contributed three or more trotters to that list. We were forcibly struck with a remark recently made to us by Mr. Brodhead, of the Woodburn Farm. He said: "A man does not know how hard it is to raise even a 2:30 trotter until he has tried it."

C. C. Seaman of San Diego, has received an interesting letter from W. J. Gordon of Gordon Glens, near Cleveland, Ohio, says the San Diegan. It will be remembered that some time ago Mr. Seaman bought two colts from Mr. Gordon, the colts being Thomas Rysdyk by Rysdyk, the sire of Clingstone 2:14, and Josiah A, by Clingstone II, a full brother to Clingstone.

In regard to Clingstone II., Mr. Gordon says he has been given regular work this winter, and has developed into a grand horse. Saunders, the trainer, claims a 2.20 gait for him, and is confident that he can be made to go a mile this season in 2:25. "If I was ten or fifteen years younger," says Mr. Gordon, I would put Clingstone II. at the head of a stock farm, and be disappointed if great results did not follow."

Mr. Gordon has been driving Guy 2:10 and Clingstone 2:14 as a team, and says they are the most perfect fast team he ever rode after, and intimates that they may be sent to beat the record this season. Individually they have the speed to do it.

E. B. Gifford, the owner of Atto Rex, will have quite a stable on the coast circuit this season. Besides Rex he will have two colts by A. W. Richmond and a mare by Echo. He expects to put Rex in training at Coronado Beach in the course of a week.

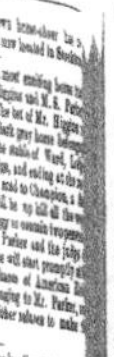

Foals of 1890.

The following speaks for itself:—

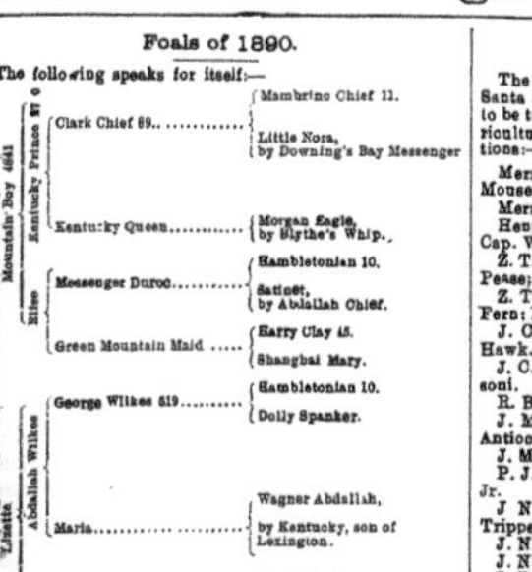

The above is the property of B. C. Holly, Vallejo.

At Vallejo, April 19th, property of A. McFadyen:—

B f by Mountain Boy 4841, dam Lou Medium (dam of Redwood 2:24½), by Milton Medium 4782.

At Livermore, property of W. W. Mendenhall.

B c by Grand Moor, Jr., dam Alice H. by Nutwood 600. Entered in the BREEDER AND SPORTSMAN Futurity Stake.

At Palo Alto. Property of Hon. Leland Stanford.

B f by Electioneer—Lilly B. by Homer.
B c by Azmoor—Miss Blooming by Benefit.
B f by Clay—Sallie G. by Flood.
B c by Ansel—Gabilan Maid by Carr's Mambrino.
Br c by Nephew—Lina K. by Don Victor.
B c by Azmoor—Sprite by Alexander's Belmont.
Ch c by Wildnut—Julia Benton by General Benton.
B c by Piedmont—Celia by Fallis.
B c by Beverly—Sarah by Shannon.
B f by Wild Boy—Monique by Fallis.
Ch c by Piedmont—Satinet by Shannon.
B c by Alban—Woodflower by Ansel.
B f by Piedmont—Lola by General Benton.
B c by Clay—Flora Anderson by Shannon.
Ch c by Electioneer—Mano by Piedmont.

Foals at Vina, Tehama Co., Cal.

B c by Clay—Abbie by Almont.
B c by Mac Benton—Monona by Don Victor.
B f by Liberty—Adele by General Benton.
B f by Benefit—Contention by Mohawk Chief.
Br f by Liberty—Hermana by General Benton.
B f by Liberty—Camiola by General Benton.

At Santa Clara, April 10th. Property of Henry C. Judson.

Chestnut filly, strip in face, left hind feet white, by Monday Final, dam May D. by Wildidle.

The Belle Meade Sale.

By telegraph we learn that the following thoroughbreds were sold on Thursday at the dis persal sale at Belle Meade, only those for which $1,000 or more was obtained is here given.

B. c. (brother to Egmont), by Enquirer, dam Melita, Dwyer Bros., $1500.

B. c. by Great Tom, dam Duchess, Tucker & Cherry, $1200.

B. c. (brother to Getaway, Belle B and Inspector B), by Enquirer, dam Colossa, Dwyer Bros., $3000.

Br. c. by Iroquois, dam Nubia, J. J. Grant, Reno, Nev., $2000.

B. c. (a brother to Miss Ford, Zulika and Boodle), by Enquirer, dam Bribery, Jake Johnson of Fort Worth, Tex., $2,000.

Br. c. by Iroquois, dam Toplight, J. J. Grant, Reno Nev., $1600.

Ch c (brother to Gralie) by Great Tom, dam Alaska, J. M. Brown, Fort Worth, Texas, $1,000.

B c (brother to Uncle Bob) by Luke Blackburn, dam Vintage, Sam Bryant, Louisville, $1,600.

Br c by Iroquois, dam Variola, Tom Kiley, $1,500.

Ch c by Great Tom, dam Janet Norton, C. A. Bradley, Nashville, $1,250.

Br c by Bramble, dam Toilet, Tom Kiley, $1,100

Br c by Iroquois, dam Bandana, R. W. Hall, N. Y., $3,000.

B c by Luke Blackburn, dam Sallie Mac, Tucker & Cherry, $1 100.

B c by Iroquois, dam Tamborine, Jake Johnson, $1,100.

B c by Iroquois, dam Tamborine, Jake Johnson, Fort Worth, Texas, $1,800.

Ch c by Iroquois, dam Willahoma, R W. Hall, N Y. $2,500.

Br c by Iroquois, dam Silver Maid, John Daly, New York, $1,500.

The fillies were twenty-nine in number and averaged $971. Those that brought $1000 and over were as follows:

Ch f, full sister to Blackburn, by Luke Blackburn, dam Tomboy; R. W. Hall, New York, $1700.

B f by Iroquois, dam Bric-a-brac; Tucker & Cherry, $1400.

B f, sister to Hands Off, by Luke Blackburn, dam Touch-Me-Not; Marcus Daly, Montana, $3600

B f by Iroquois, dam Tarantula; Sam Bryant, Louisville, $1500.

Ch f by Great Tom, dam Bonneta; Richard Johnson, Fort Worth, Tex., $1000.

B f by Enquirer, dam Oganta; Tucker & Cherry, Nashville, $1650.

Br f by Iroquois, dam Tallulah; J. S. Brown, Tennessee, $1025.

Br f by Iroquois, dam Babee; J. S. Brown. $1700.

B f by Luke Blackburn, dam Highland Bell; J. A. Johnson, $1350.

B f by Inquirer was sold to Bob Campbell, trainer for E. J. Baldwin, the price being $850.

Our Santa Barbara Letter.

The Breeders' stakes for trotting foals of 1889 open to Santa Barbara, Ventura and San Luis Obispo Counties, and to be trotted this fall at the meeting of the Santa Barbara Agricultural Association, closed with the following nominations:—

Merritt & Murray's blk f Fillet, by Electro, dam Brown Mouse, Electro by Electioneer.

Merritt & Murray's br f Louisa by Electro, dam One Eye.

Henry Delaney's b c Lottery by Electro dam Patti by Cap. Webster.

Z. T. Rucker's b c White Cloud by Bashaw, dam Kate Pease; Bashaw by Wapsie.

Z. T. Rucker's s f Miss Gifford by Rucker, dam Fanny Fern; Rucker is by Bashaw.

J. C. McReynolds' b c Bashaw Jr., by Bashaw, dam Black Hawk.

J. C. McReynold's s c Excelsior by Bashaw, dam Andersoni.

R. Bennett's b c W. H., by Bashaw, dam Warwick.

J. M Rochin's s f Ramonsita by Antioch, dam Angela; Antioch by A. W. Richmond.

J. M. Rochin's b c A. B. C. by Antioch, dam La Coyota.

P. J. Doyle's blk c Rysdick by Electro, dam by Shiloah Jr.

J N. Johnson's b f Juniata by Cashmer, dam Sussy Tripper; Cashmer by Sultan.

J. N Johnson's b f Orphan Girl by Cashmer, dam Queen.

J. N. Johnson's s f Cash Girl by Cashmer, dam Kitty.

I. K. Fisher's b c Don F by Don Patricio, dam Fanny; Don Patricio by A. W. Richmond.

I. K. Fisher's b f Santa Barbara by Don Patricio, dam Fanny.

E R Den's b c Harry Stamboul by Stamboul 2:17½, dam Carry B. by A W. Richmond.

The Breeders' Futurity Stake for mares covered in 1889, same counties as above admitted, closed with the following nominations:—

Merritt & Murray's sire Electro, dam May Queen by Enchanter.

Merritt & Murry, sire Electro, dam Altonita by Altona.
H. W. Fabing, sire Bashaw, dam Blossom by Hesperion.
H. W. Fabing, sire Bashaw, dam Nellie by B. H. Comount.
Z. T. Rucker, sire Bashaw, dam Kate Pease.
J. C. McReynolds, sire Bashaw, dam R. Lady.
Chas. W. Short, sire Bashaw, dam Two Dollars.
J. M. Rochin, sire Antioch, dam Angela.
I. K. Fisher, sire Don Patricio, dam Flora by Old Judge by Whipple's Hambletonian.
I. K Fisher, sire Don Patricio, dam Fanny.
J. N. Johnson, sire Cashmer, dam Kitty.
J. N. Johnson, sire Cashmer, dam Flora by Dick Joy.
Low & Wilson, sire Royal George, dam Maud.
A. J. McNam, sire Royal George, dam Lady.

Many of the colts for this fall's racing are being driven, and they all look well and act like trotters. Harry Stamboul looks as much like his sire as a yearling can look, and he is the proudest and purest gaited colt I have ever seen. News comes from Lompoc that the Bashaw colts are wonders, and Mr. Rucker writes that his yearling by Rucker is a marvel, and that he has a first mortgage on the race.

J. M. Rochin, who has been in the horse business for twenty years, is certain that his colts will carry the purse to Los Alamos, and Santa Maria says that the Electro colts can not be outtrotted. It is to be regretted that no colt by Glenwood by Nutwood has been entered.

At the Agricultural Meeting this fall there will be a grand running race of five-eighths of a mile for two-year-olds. At least ten colts will start in the race. The favorites here for the race are, J. Cooper's Solano, E. R. Den's Sugar Plum, the Arrellanes colt and G. Sherman's black gelding.

Races and a grand barbaque at Los Alamos on the 1st of May; but they have barred all horses from our city. Why so selfish?

T. M.

SANTA BARBARA, April 19, 1890.

Flaxtail 8122.

We do not know personally anything about the horse mentioned below. but as the Flaxtail blood plays a prominent part in many Californian pedigrees, we republish the following, taken from an Eastern exchange:

H. H. P. Oscaloosa, Iowa.—Can you tell me anything about a horse called Bull Pup, owned at one time by Jesse A. Mitchell of Bedford, Ind.? What did Mr. Mitchell do with the horse? I think he is the same horse that came here in 1863 or 1864. He is registered as Flaxtail 8122. This horse was brought here by Mr. Mitchell, who had a lame arm. and he called the horse Bull Pup. We have written to Mitchell, and he refuses to answer. This horse's history before coming here was always kept dark. Give us all the light you can, and oblige many of your readers.

ANSWER—The Bull Pup owned by Jesse Mitchell of Bedford, Ind., was the old or original owner of that name, son of old Racing Pilot. Mr. Mitchell bought him as a five-year-old, from his breeder, a few miles from Louisville, Ky. The Bull Pup that went to Iowa was bred by Newton Wiseman of Salem, Ind., and sired by old Bull Pup (Jesse Mitchell's), dam a small, fast, pacing, bay mare of unknown breeding. In 1864 a brother of Newton Wiseman, who was half owner of the sorrel Bull Pup, sold him to Joseph Mitchell of Salem, and he took him to Iowa. When the Wilson horse, known generally as Blue Bull 75 (but whose legitimate name was simply "Sam") was in the zenith of his glory as a sire; the story was started that the Iowa Bull Pup horse was got by Pruden's Blue Bull, the falsely reputed sire of the Wilson horse, and the then owner of Bull Pup Jr changed his name to "Flaxtail." This you can rely upon as the true history and pedigree of the horse now registered under the name of Flaxtail, which name together with the pedigree attached to it was manufactured out of whole cloth some time after he was sold to Iowa.

Pacing Records at One Mile.

Johnston, harness, against time, Chicago, Ills., Oct 3, 1884, 2:06¼.
Brown Hal, best stallion record, Cleveland, Ohio, July 31, 1889, 2.12½.
Westmont, July 10, 1884, Chicago, Ills., with running mate, 2:01¾.
Daisy, yearling, Sacramento, Dec. 31, 1886, 2:36½.
Ed Rosewater, two years old, Council Bluffs, Iowa, Nov. 3, 1888, 2:20½.
Yolo Maid, 3 years old, San Francisco, Oct. 13, 1888, 2:14.
Gold Leaf, four years old, 2:11½ on August 17, 1889, at Napa.
Arrow, five years old, 2:13¼, made at Cleveland, Ohio, August 1, 1888

VETERINARY.

Conducted by W. Henry Jones, M. R. C. V. S.

Subscribers to this paper can have advice through this column in all cases of sick or injured horses or cattle by sending an explicit description of the case. Applicants will send their name and address that they may be identified. Questions requiring answers by mail should be accompanied by two dollars, and addressed to W. Henry Jones, M. R. C. V. S., Olympic Stables, Butler Street, San Francisco.

W. I. D.

Some time ago a filly of mine, which I value very much, showed a slight swelling at the back of the near hock. The filly has never worked, and always had the best of care. Her dam was badly affected with curbs. Will you inform me if curbs are heriditary? Also inform me what is the best treatment to adopt.

Answer.—Your filly is no doubt developing a curb. Apply a blister, consisting of Biniodide of Mercury, two drams, to one ounce of lard. Curbs are not heriditary, but colts may be foaled with hocks of a curby formation, and will readily strain the ligament and soon become lame from the same.

I. I. R.

I have an old grey mare that has discharged from the nose for about six weeks. People say it is glanders. Myself, I do not think so What is best to be done?

Answer.—Your best plan would be to take her to a veterinary surgeon; he will tell you whether it is glanders or otherwise. Personally, I have not seen a case of glanders in this city, although I believe horses have been destroyed for that disease.

The Standard.

[AS REVISED AND ADOPTED BY THE NATIONAL ASSOCIATION OF TROTTING-HORSE BREEDERS, DECEMBER 14, 1887.]

IN order to define what constitutes a trotting-bred horse and to establish a BREED of trotters on a more intelligent basis, the following rules are adopted to control admission to the records of pedigrees. When an animal meets the requirements of admission and is duly registered, it shall be accepted as a standard trotting-bred animal:—

FIRST.—Any stallion that has himself a record of two minutes and thirty seconds (2:30) or better, provided any of his get has a record of 2:35 or better, or provided his sire or his dam is already a standard animal.

SECOND.—Any mare or gelding that has a record of 2:30 or better.

THIRD.—Any horse that is the sire of two animals with a record of 2:30 or better.

FOURTH.—Any horse that is the sire of one animal with a record of 2:30 or better, provided he has either of the additional qualifications: (1) A record himself of 2:35 or better. (2) Is the sire of two other animals with a record of 2:35 or better. (3) Has a sire or dam that is already a standard animal.

FIFTH.—Any mare that has produced an animal with a record of 2:30 or better.

SIXTH.—The progeny of a standard horse when out of a standard mare.

SEVENTH.—The female progeny of a standard horse when out of a mare by a standard horse.

EIGHTH.—The female progeny of a standard horse when out of mare whose dam is a standard mare.

NINTH.—Any mare that has a record of 2:35 or better, and whos sire or dam is a standard animal.

Best Trotting Records.

1 mile—2:08¾, Maud S., against time, in harness, accompanied the distance by a running horse, Glenville, O., July 30, 1885......2:13¾, best time in a race between horses, Maud S., Chicago, Ills., July 24, 1880......2:12, Axtell, against time, accompanied by running horse—fastest stallion time, Terre Haute, Ind., Oct. 11, 1889......2:13¾, Phallas, fastest heat by a stallion against other horses, Chicago, July 14, 1884......2:13¾, Palo Alto, third heat in race at Stockton, Cal., Sept. 26, 1889......2:15¼, Jay-Eye-See, half-mile track, Lincoln, Neb., Sept. 14, 1887......2:15¾, Great Eastern, under saddle, third heat, Morrisania, N. Y., Sept. 22, 1877......2:10¾, Jay-Eye-See, against time, best five-year-old record, Providence, R. I., Sept. 15, 1883......2:16, Manzanita, third heat, best four-year-old record, Lexington, Ky., Sept. 3, 1876 .... 2:16, Edgemark, four-year-old stallion record, against time, Lexington, Ky., Oct. 18, 1889......2:16½, Sunol, in Stanford stake, accompanied by a runner, best three-year-old record, San Francisco, Nov. 9, 1889..2:18, Sunol, 2 years, against time, San Francisco, Cal., Oct. 27, 1888......2:20½, Regal Wilkes, two-year-old stallion record, San Francisco, Nov. 9, 1889......2:31½, Norlaine, yearling, against time, San Francisco, Cal., Nov. 12, 1887......2:35, Faustino, yearling stallion record, San Francisco, Nov. 9, 1889.

2 miles—4:43 against time, Fanny Witherspoon, Chicago, Ill., Sept. 26, 1885.

3 miles—7:21¼, Huntress, harness, Brooklyn, L. I., Sept. 21, 1872.

4 miles—10:34½, Longfellow, wagon, California, Dec 31, 1869.

5 miles—13:00, Lady Mac, harness, San Francisco, Cal., April 2, 1874.

10 miles—27:23¼, Controller, harness, San Francisco, Cal., Nov. 23, 1878.

20 miles—58:25, Captain McGowan, harness, half-mile track, Boston, Oct. 31, 1865.

Fastest Time on Record.

RUNNING.

MILES.		Time
¼	Jim Miller, 2, Deer Lodge (Mont.), Aug. 16, 1888 / †Sleepy Dick, a, Kiowa (Kan.), Nov. 24, 1888	0:21½
⅜	Cyclone, a, 120 lbs., Helena (Mont.), Aug. 28, 1889	0:34½
½	Geraldine, 4, 122 lbs., Westchester Course, Aug. 30, 1889	0:46
⅝	Britannic, 5, 122 lbs., Westchester Course, Aug. 31, 1889	0:59
⅝	Fordham, a, 115 lbs., Westchester Course, Oct. 4, 1889	0:59
¾	El Rio Rey, 2, 126 lbs., Westchester Course, Aug. 31, 1889	1:11
¾	Tipstaff, 3, 107, Westchester Course, Oct. 4, 1889	1:11
⅞	Britannic, 5, 110 lbs., Sheepshead Bay, Sept. 5, 1888	1:26 2-5
1	Ten Broeck, 5, 110 lbs., Louisville, May 24, 1877 (against time)	1:39¾
1	Maori 4, 105 lbs., Chicago, July 12, 1889, (in a race)	1:39 4-5
1 1-16	Wheeler T., 3, 98 lbs., St. Louis, June 1, 1888	1:47¼
1 1-16	Eylton 4, 108, Chicago, Ill., June 28, 1889	1:47¼
1⅛	Terra Cotta, 4, 124 lbs., Sheepshead Bay, June 22, 1888	1:53
1 3-16	Joe Cotton, 5, 109½ lbs., Sheepshead Bay, Sept. 7, 1887	2:00½
1¼	Kingston, 5, 122 lbs., Gravesend, Sept. 24, 1889	2:06¼
1 m 500 yds.	Ben d'Or, 4, 115 lbs., Saratoga, July 25, 1882	2:10¼
1⅜	Triboulet, 4, 117 lbs., San Francisco, April 26, 1888 / Richmond, 6, 122 lbs., Sheepshead Bay, June 27, 1889	2:21¾
1½	Firenzi, 4, 113 lbs., Monmouth Park, Aug. 2, 1888 / Luke Blackburn, 3, 102 lbs., Monmouth Park, Aug. 17, '80 / Jim Guest, 4, 98 lbs., Chicago, (Washington Park, July 24 '86)	2:34
1⅝	Hindoocraft, 3, 73 lbs., Westchester, Aug. 27, 1889	2:48
1¾	Gildelia, 5, 116 lbs., Saratoga, Aug. 5, 1882	3:01
1⅞	Enigma, 4, 90 lbs., Sheepshead Bay, Sept. 15, 1885	3:2[illegible]
2	Ten Broeck, 5, 110 lbs., Louisville, May 29, 1877	3:27½
2⅛	Monitor, 4, 110 lbs., Baltimore, Oct. 20, 1880	3:44½
2¼	Springbok, 5, 114 lbs. / Preakness, a, 114 lbs., Saratoga, July 29, 1875	3:56¼
2½	Aristides, 4, 104 lbs., Lexington, May 13, 1876	4:27½
2⅝	Ten Broeck, 4, 104 lbs., Lexington, Sept. 16, 1876	4:58½
2¾	Hubbard, 4, 107 lbs., Saratoga, Aug. 9, 1873	4:58¾
3	Drake Carter 4 115 lbs., Sheepshead Bay, Sept. 6, 1884	5:24
4	Ten Broeck, 4, 104 lbs., Louisville, Sept. 27, 1876	7:15¾

HEAT RACES.

MILES.		Time
¼	Sleepy Dick, a, Kiowa (Kan.), Nov. 24, 1888	0:21½—0:22½
½	Bogus, a, 113 lbs., Helena (Mont.), Aug. 24, 1888	0:48—0:48
⅝	Kittie Pease, 4, Dallas (Tex.), Nov. 2, 1887	1:00—1:00
⅝	Sadie McNairy, 3, 98 lbs., Chicago, July 2, 1882	1:02¼—1:03
¾	Lizzie S., 5, 118 lbs., Louisville, Sept. 28, 1883	1:13¾—1:13¾
1	Bounce, 4, 90 lbs., Sheepshead Bay, Sept. 7, 1881	1:42—1:41¾
1	3 in 5. L'Argentine, 6, 115 lbs., St. Louis, June 14, 1879	1:43—1:44—1:47¾
1 1-16	Slipalong, 6, 115 lbs., Chicago (Wash. Park), Sept. 2, 1885	1:50½—1:48
1⅛	Gabriel, 4, 112 lbs., Sheepshead Bay, Sept. 28, 1889	1:56—1:56
1¼	Glenmore, 5, 114 lbs., Sheepshead Bay, Sept. 25, 1880	2:10—2:14
1½	Keno, 5, Toledo, Sept. 16, 1889 (1st and 2d heats)	2:43½—2:44
2	Miss Woodford, 4, 107½ lbs., Sheepshead Bay, Sept. 20, 1884	4:23—3:31¼
3	Norfolk, 4, 100 lbs., Sacramento, Sept. 23, 1865	5:27½—5:29½
4	Ferida, 4, 105 lbs., Sheepshead Bay, Sept. 18, 1880	7:23½—7:41

†Made in a heat race.
*Doubtful, and made in a heat race.

THE WEEKLY

Breeder and Sportsman.

JAMES P. KERR, PROPRIETOR.

The Turf and Sporting Authority of the Pacific Coast.

Office, No. 313 Bush St.

P. O. Box 2300.

T"RMS—*One Year, $5; Six Months, $3; Three Months, $1.50.*

STRICTLY IN ADVANCE.

Money should be sent by postal order, draft or by registered letter, addressed to JAMES P. KERR, San Francisco, Cal.

Communications must be accompanied by the writer's name and address, not necessarily for publication, but as a private guarantee of good faith.

NEW YORK OFFICE, Room 14, 181 Broadway.

ALEX. P. WAUGH, - - - - Editor.

Advertising Rates

Per Square (half inch)

One time	$1 50
Two times	2 50
Three times	3 25
Four times	4 00

And each subsequent insertion 75c. per square.

Advertisements running six months are entitled to 10 per cent. discount.

Those running twelve months are entitled to 20 per cent. discount.

Reading notices set in same type as body of paper, 50 cents per line each insertion.

To Subscribers.

The date printed on the wrapper of your paper indicates the time to which your subscription is paid.

Should the Breeder and Sportsman be received by any subscriber who does not want it, write us direct to stop it. A postal card will suffice.

Special Notice to Correspondents.

Letters intended for publication should reach this office not later than Wednesday of each week, to secure a place in the issue of the following Saturday. Such letters to insure immediate attention should be addressed to the Breeder and Sportsman, and not to any member of the staff.

San Francisco, Saturday, April 26, 1890.

Dates Claimed.

SACRAMENTO (Running Meeting)	April 26th, 29th, May 1st and 3d
EUREKA JOCKEY CLUB	July 2d to 5th
IONE	Aug 1th to 5th.
LOS ANGELES [6th District]	Aug. 4th to 9th
SAN JOSE	Aug. 11th to 16th
NAPA	Aug. 18th to 23rd
GLENBROOK PARK, 17th District	August 19th to 23d
PETALUMA	Aug. 25th to 30th
OAKLAND (District No. 1)	Sept. 1st to Sept. 6th
LAKEPORT, 12th District	September 23d to 27th
CALIFORNIA STATE FAIR	Sept 8th to 20th
STOCKTON	Sept. 23rd to 27th.
FRESNO (Fall Meeting)	Sept. 29th to Oct. 4th
VISALIA	Oct. 7th to 11th

Stallions Advertised

IN THE

BREEDER AND SPORTSMAN.

Thoroughbreds.

DOUGLASDALE—Thoroughbred Clydesdale....Lawn View Farm, Cal.
FRIAR TUCK, Hermit—Romping Girl....C. W. Aby, Middletown.
GREENBACK, Dollar—Music....C. W. Aby, Middletown.
REVEILLE, Shiloh—Norfolk....B. C. Holly, Vallejo.
ST. SAVIOR, Eolus—War Song....C. W. Aby, Middletown.
THREE CHEERS, Imp. Hurrah—Young Fashion....E. S. Colver, San Francisco.

Trotters.

ADMIRAL, Volunteer—Lady Pierson....Frank Drake, Vallejo
ACTOR, Prompter—Dam by Sultan....Lawn View Farm, Cal.
ANTEEOP, Antero—Bessie G....Guy E. Grosse, Santa Rosa.
ANTEEOP, Anteeo—Nance....Guy E. Grosse, Santa Rosa.
ADMIRO, Admiral—dam by San Bruno....Smith & Sutherland, Pleasanton.
APEX, Prompter—Mary....Poplar Grove Breeding Farm, Wildflower.
ALCONA, Almont—Queen Mary....Fred W. Loeber, St. Helena
BAY ROSE, Sultan—Madam Baldwin....Thos. Bonner, Santa Rosa
CLOVIS, Sultan—Sweetbriar....Poplar Grove Breeding Farm, Wildflower.
CUPID, Sidney—Venus....C. O. Thornquest, Oakland
CHARLES DERBY, Steinway—by Electioneer. Cook Stock Farm, Contra Costa Co.
CALIFORNIA NUTWOOD, Nutwood—Fanny Patchen....Martin Carter, Alameda Co.
CORRECTOR, Director—Brainey....Pleasanton Stock Farm.
DECORATOR, Director—Chess....Pleasanton Stock Farm.
DEXTER PRINCE, Kentucky Prince—Lady Dexter....L. M. Morse, Lodi.
DAWN, Nutwood—Countess....A. L. Whitney, Petaluma
DIRECTOR, Dictator—Dolly....Pleasanton Stock Farm, Pleasanton.
DON MARVIN, Fallis—Cora....F. P. Lowell, Sacramento
DESIGNER, Director—May Queen....H. Scott, Oakland.
ELECTOR, Electioneer—Gilberta....L. A. Richards, Grayson.
EL BENTON, Electioneer—Nellie Benton....Souther Farm, San Leandro.
ELECTION, Electioneer—Lizzie H....B. C. Holly, Vallejo.
ECLECTIC, Electioneer—Manette....Wilfred Page, Sonoma County
EROS, Electioneer—Sontag Mohawk....W. H. Vioget, Menlo Park
FIGARO, Hambletonian—Emblem....Souther Farm, San Leandro.
GROVER CLAY, Electioneer—Maggie Norfolk....Denis Gannon, Oakland.
GRAND MOOR 2374, Moor 870—Vashti....H. I. Thornton, S. F.
G. A. M., Anteeo—Rosa B....George E. Guerne, Santa Rosa.
GUY WILKES, George Wilkes—Lady Bunker....San Mateo Stock Farm, San Mateo.
GLEN FORTUNE, Electioneer—Glenna....Souther Farm, San Leandro.
GEORGE WASHINGTON, Mambrino Chief—Fanny Rose....Thos. Smith, Vallejo.
GUIDE, Director—Imogene....Smith & Sutherland, Pleasanton.
GRANDISSIMO, LeGrande—Norma....Fred W. Loeber, St Helena
JESTER D, Almont—Hortense....Souther Farm, San Leandro
JUNIO, Electioneer—by Granger....S. N. Straube, Fresno,
KAFIR, Alcazar—Flower Girl....B. C. Holly, Vallejo.
KING DAVID, Admiral—Black Flora....Frank Drake, Vallejo.
LEO WILKES, Guy Wilkes—Sable....San Mateo Stock Farm, San Mateo.
MEMO, Sidney—Flirt....John Rowen, Oakland
MOUNTAIN BOY, Kentucky Prince—Elsie....B. C. Holly, Vallejo.
MAMBRINO WILKES, George Wilkes—Lady Chrisman....San Miguel Stock Farm, Walnut Creek.
MART ROORHEM, Sidney—Towhead....B. C. Holly, Vallejo.
MAMBRINO CHIEF, McDonald Chief—Venus....Thos. Smith, Vallejo.
MORTIMER, Electioneer—Marti....Wilfred Page, Sonoma County
NOONDAY, Wedgewood—Noontide....F. P. Lowell, Sacramento.
PASHA, Sultan—Madam Baldwin....D. Bryson, Linden
PHILOSOPHER, Pilot Wilkes—Belle....George E. Guerne, Santa Rosa.
REDWOOD, Anteeo—Lou Wilton....A. McFayden, Oakland.
STEINWAY, Strathmore—Abbess....Cook Stock Farm, Contra Costa Co
SUNSET, Anteeo—Bessie G....Guy E. Grosse, Santa Rosa.
SABLE WILKES, Guy Wilkes—Sable....San Mateo Stock Farm, San Mateo.
VICTOR, Echo—Daughter of Woodburn....G. W. Hughes, Napa City
WHIPPLETON 1883, Hambletonian Jr.—Lady Livingston....Fred W. Loeber, St. Helena
WOODSIDE, Woodnut—Veronica....B. C. Holly, Vallejo.
YOUNG ELMO, St. Elmo—Dam by Woodburn....Lawn View Farm Cal.

The Haggin Annual Auction Sale.

The Superintendent of Mr. Haggin's breeding Farm has engaged the services of Messrs. Killup & Co., live stock auctioneers, to dispose of at public auction on Tuesday, May 6, 1890, at the Railroad Stables, corner of Steiner and Turk streets, San Francisco, an exceedingly choice selection of road and harness mares and geldings; work and draught horses, together with a superb lot of Shetland ponies. It has usually been the custom of Mr. Haggin to dispose of the stock as three-year-olds, and this is the first venture at placing four-year-olds on this market. It was considered by the gentleman injudicious to place harness and work animals at public auction so young, there being many exceptions taken by would-be purchasers, who would rather have older animals, those ready to put to work at once.

The entire consignment are of average size, good color and desirable in many particulars. The catalogue contains two hundred and three lots by such stallions as Norwood, George M. Patchen Jr., 31, Bismarck, Western, Kentucky, Dana, Charles Dickens, Muldoon, Victor and Zulu Chief.

Messrs. Killup & Co. have had very neat catalogues issued, and those desirous of receiving them can obtain them by addressing the auctioneers at 22 Montgomery street, San Francisco.

Hickory Grove Stock Farm.

We have received from J. I. Case, of Racine, Wisconsin, his new catalogue for 1890, which from the illustrations and typographical neatness, makes it one of the finest we have received this season. Comparing it with the catalogue of 1889 we find many additions and as is only natural, quite a number of eliminations.

In a private letter Mr. Case expresses himself as being confident that he will have quite a number of young horses go in the 2:30 list during the present year. In addition to Phallas 2:13¾ Brown 2:18¾, and Harold Wilkes we find that one of the stallions is Lexington Wilkes, another of extreme speed and which for beauty of form and finish is one of the best ever sired by George Wilkes. He stands 15 hands and 3½inches in height and weighs 1150 pounds, a quality lacking in many of the Wilkes family. As a sire of speed, the few colts he has, promise to make his name familiar to the race going public.

Quite a number of mares have been added to the new catalogue, some of which are very choice. We find among them our old favorite Echora 2:23½, dam of Direct 2.18¾; she is also the dam of Erect who trotted as a yearling several trial quarters in forty seconds, and was sold at the Kellogg sale to Mr. Hugh Kirkendall, of Montana, for $5,000. As we stated two weeks ago, Echora foaled on March 17th, a beautiful black filly, full sister to Direct, and has since then been bred to Phallas brother in blood and race horse fame to Director 2:17, the sire of all her fillies previous to this date.

Next in order of rank we should probably name Elizabeth, sister to the dam of Rajah, four-year-old record 2:29½ by George Wilkes out of Snip Nose, the dam of Garnet 2;19 by American Clay. Elizabeth had been bred to Phallas, and will probably be handled for speed this year.

Highwine is another of the likely mares, three years old by Nutwood 2:18¾, dam Alta 2:23¼ by Almont 33; 2nd dam Lady by Bourbon Chief; 3rd dam strictly thoroughbred.

Brilliantine is another of the good ones, her record of 2:32¾ being made last season; she is by Nutwood, dam Crepon by Princeps; second dam Crape Lisse by George Wilkes; this young mare is also in training and will be given a record, barring accidents. Brilliantine has been bred to Brown.

Maud Thomas, another of the additions is a black mare of great individual excellence by Voltaire 2:20¾, dam Tullahoma (the dam of J. R. Richardson 2:17½) by Almont; she is in foal to Almont Wilkes, and will be bred, later on, to Phallas.

Constance is peculiarly and intensely inbred to Mambrino Patchen, and Mr. Case assures us that if inbreeding produces such as she, he feels sorry that he has not commenced the theory of inbreeding much sooner than he has. Her sire is Ellerslie Wilkes by George Wilkes; the dam of Ellerslie Wilkes is Aileen by Mambrino Boy, son of Mambrino Patchen. The dam of Constance is Kincora by Mambrino Patchen; Kincora's dam is Kitty Tranby by Mambrino Tranby. Constance is in foal to Red Wilkes and is booked for 1890 to the great Wilton 2:19¼, through whom we get the double Hambletonian infusion, through his best son George Wilkes and one of his greatest dams Alley.

Mr. Case also has in training some seven or eight aged horses, and twenty-five or thirty, two and three-year-olds, all of whom are under the supervision of the new trainer, Mr. R. E. Curry, who has taken the place of Ed Bither. Mr. Curry is no stranger to the trotting tracks of America, and bringing as he does, his many years of experience to Hickory Grove Farm, it can be confidently asserted that this year there will be many first class trotters emanate from Mr. Case's establishment.

Since the catalogue was published Mr. Case has purchased the dark chestnut horse Philander by Pendennis 2:34, full brother to Calamos 2:34½ and Geanette trial 2:27, dam Victoria (the dam of Victoria Wilkes 2:25½). And now Mr. Case has on his farm all of this mare's produce, it would seem from the fact that he has purchased them all, that he is striving to make her family one of national reputation.

The Rosemeade Stud.

A few mornings ago we had the pleasure of a visit from the Hon. L. J. Rose, whose fame as a breeder of trotters is world-wide. In the course of conversation the gentleman informed us that he would not hang on very long to the thoroughbred division if he received many defeats; in fact as he put it himself, "I cannot stand many beatings; my disposition will not allow of it." Mr. Rose is generally supposed to have disposed of all the trotters in his possession, but this is a mistake, as he informs us that he has seventeen yearlings by Stamboul and Alcazar, and also two very good sons of Bob Mason (he by Echo) out of Almeh, she a daughter of Minnehaha. These two stallions Mr. Rose values quite highly, although they are both non-standard, still, as he says himself, if he finds it necessary to sell out the thoroughbreds, he has a much better nucleus to start with now than when he originally commenced. As is well known, Mr. Rose is an ardent believer in inbreeding, and his wonderful success in that line has been the means of making many converts; in fact not very long ago, when Harry Agnew, who has just bought Dawn, asked the question of a well known horseman, "What will be the best mares to breed to Dawn?" the answer was, "Nutwood mares by all means." Mr. Rose is so fully convinced that his theory is correct that he wants to breed Stamboul fillies to Alcazar colts and vice versa, and in such a cross he seems to feel assured that the acme of perfection can be obtained in the trotter. He is also satisfied that with proper handling Stamboul can beat his present record of 2:12½, and, like many others, is confident that the stallion will improve best with hard work; he seems to be satisfied in his own mind that if Stamboul had received more work last season that 2:12 would have been beaten beyond a doubt.

In addition to the yearlings that Mr. Rose has, there are also ten broodmares remaining, his reason for not selling them being, in the first place, that eight of them were not as highly bred as those he disposed of, the ninth Minnehaha, he will not sell under any consideration, and the tenth, Almeh, a daughter of Minnehaha, was not in condition to sell at the time when his consignment was sent East.

An Important Sale.

Jno. G. Hill, Esq., of Ventura, California, will hold a very important sale on Tuesday, May 15th, in this city. It will consist of about eighty head of well bred stallions, mares and geldings, principally the get of the celebrated standard bred sire, A. W. Richmond 1687, out of thoroughbred mares mostly from that noted horse Woodburn, sire of Monarch 2:28¾ and the dam of Victor 2;22 and others. Mr. Hill has determined to close out all his trotting bred stock and he owns at present nearly all of the mares in the State that contain Richmond blood. There should be great competion among the breeders of this State to secure those that will be offered at the sale.

A. W. Richmond has stamped himself as a prepotent sire, his speed lines being of the best and his get have all proven fast trotters or pacers. Richmond Jr. only last year came out as a green horse and trotted to a record of 2:22¾. Romero was as game a horse as ever stood on iron, he gaining a record of 2:19½; What Ho 2:29½, we are credibly informed, can trot in 2.20 or better. Arrow, the celebrated pacer, is another of Richmond's get whose record of 2:13½ is known of all turfmen in America. Ellwood 2:17¾ was another of Richmond's fast get, and the old horse should have also received credit for Len. Rose, he having trotted a mile in Australia in 2:27. In addition to the above A. W. Richmond's name has become famous by being the sire of the dam of Anteeo 2.16½ and Antevolo (four years) 2,19½. We are confident that the day is not far distant when if Richmond's mares are given favorable chances that they will prove themselves equal to any brood mares in the country. This is not an individual opinion but is largely shared by every breeder throughout the State, and we fully expect to find every breeding farm throughout California represensed at Mr. Hill's sale.

P. C. T. H. B. A.

Among the many events to close on May 1st are two trotting stake races, five nomination trotting purses, and two nomination pacing purses which should receive the attention of all horsemen throughout the State. The purses are liberal, the payments are easy, and it becomes the duty of every breeder in the State to support the efforts now being put forward by this association to forward the trotting-horse interests of California. The conditions are many, but lack of space will not permit us to give them entire; those interested can find the advertisement of the association in our advertising department. It must be born in mind that persons desirous of making entries in the purses and stakes must become members of the association, and those who desire to join, can send in their application for membership to the Secretary, care of this office. All of the other races filled so well, that these are sure to receive a likewise liberal support from the members.

The Lakeport Stakes.

By reference to the advertisement of the 12th District Agricultural Society it will be seen that four of their trotting stakes close on May 1st, and it would be well for those who contemplate entering at Lakeport to read the advertisement over, as there are other races which do not close until later on. Those to which we wish to call attention to at present are the yearling trotting stakes with $200, guaranteed; entrance $30, payable as follows: $5 May 1st, $10 July 1st and $10 September 1st, when entry must be named, and $5 additional for starters.

The second, is a two year-old stake, mile heats, best two in three, $300 guaranteed; entrance $50, payable $10 on May 1st, $10 July 1st, $15 September 1st and $15 additional to start.

The third, is a three-year old stake, $300 guaranteed with $50 entrance, payable $10 May 1st, $10 July 1st, $15 September 1st when entry must be named, and $15 additional to start. This race is open to Napa, Solano, Sonoma, Marin, Lake, Colusa, Yolo, Mendocino and Humboldt Counties.

The fourth race which closes on the 1st is a trotting race, mile heats, three in five, free for all horses owned in the counties described in the three year old stake, with $400 added; entrance fee $60, payable $10 on May 1st, $20 July 1st, $20 September 1st, when the entries must be named and $10 additional to start.

The same conditions apply to these races that applies to all nomination stakes, the subscription being transferable any time before the colts are named.

If the payments in the races amounts to more than the sum guaranteed the additional amount will be divided in 60, 30 and 10 per cent., and in case of only two horses starting, 60 and 40 per cent. and in case of only one horse walking over, the whole amount to go to such horse: A failure so make any payment when due shall be considered a withdrawal and all amounts already paid in shall be forfeited.

The Directors have determined to made this the most successful meeting ever held in the 12th District, and we feel assured that the entries will be liberal.

The Tryon Sale.

During the spring meeting of the State Agricultural Society at Sacramento, Messrs. Killip & Co. will dispose of, at public auction, a very fine lot of standard-bred trotters, pacers and roadsters, the property of Mr. S. C. Tryon, a gentleman well and favorably known to many of the track frequenters of this State. It has become necessary for Mr. Tryon to sell the animals offered in the catalogue, and from their breeding and ability to go fast, we feel assured that the sale will be a very successful one.

A catalogue has been sent to this office, from which we glean that among others to be offered for sale will be Castello, 2:31½, a black stallion seven years old, by Echo 462, sire of half a score or more in the 2:30 list. Castello's dam being Bessie Turner by Fred Low; 2d dam Benicia Maid by John Nelson. This is a very promising green pacer, and can show a 2:20 gait; he should make a grand stock-horse for those who desire good breeding.

Magister 8152 has a record of 2:49½, made as a two-year-old; he is a brown colt, foaled May 9, 1887, and was bred by M. W. Hicks of Sacramento. Magister is by Sterling 6223, dam Madam Baldwin (dam of Bay Rose, 2:20) by The Moor. This exceedingly fine colt is almost 16 hands high, and will weigh nearly 1,100 pounds; he is a beautiful mottled brown, and shows in every movement the blood he bears; he is reputed to be a level-headed, square-gaited horse, and should make a very fast trotter.

Pocahontas, 2:22½, is so well known that it is superfluous almost to tell what she is. Pocahontas is well known to the breeders of this State, who are well aware of her staying qualities, as she got her record in a sixth heat at Stockton, in 1886 defeating such good ones as Fred Ackerman, Shaker, Peacock and Mink; she is heavy in foal to Dexter Prince, and is about due to foal. She should make a grand broodmare, and is fit to grace any harem in California.

We also find in the catalogue colts, fillies and geldings by such well-known sires as Echo 462, Fallis 4781, Nutwood Jr., Berlin 3514, Alcantara Jr. 3703, Jack Nelson, Fred Low, Buccaneer, Chieftain 721, Apex, Castello, and others. The catalogue is well worthy the attention of every breeder in the State, as there are many choice lots to be disposed of.

San Joaquin Valley Agricultural Association.

The usual colt stakes advertised by the various societies throughout California have not been overlooked by the San Joaquin Valley Directors, and they announce in this issue that on May 1st eight stake races will close, four of which are free for all, while four other stakes are eligible for colts owned in the San Joaquin Valley only.

In the free-for-all $200 is added by the Society to each of the races, while in the restricted class $150 is added by the Society to each.

Stockton has always been noted for its successful Fairs, and it can be readily understood that this year will be no exception to the general rule. There are many first-class stallions owned in the San Joaquin Valley counties, and it is only fair to assume that those who own good colts will have a desire to participate in these colt stakes. Those open for the free-for-all classes should have ample entries, as from the present indications, 1890 will see more colts trotting in this State than any year previous. Those who have colts to enter should read the conditions as the stakes include both trotting and pacing events, and the payments are due on the installment plan. Entries, as usual, will close with Mr. La Rue, the Secretary at Stockton, California.

Horses in Training for Sale.

Mr. W. M. Murray has determined to cut down the size of his racing stable before starting for the East, and will offer for sale at public auction at Sacramento on May 2nd, eight thoroughbreds, six of which are in training at present. They are all useful animals and will be eagerly sought after by those who fancy the runners. As there will be a large representation of sportsmen from all sections of the State at Sacramento during the spring meeting, Mr. Murray has taken advantage of a favorable opportunity to dispose of these grandly bred horses. Several of them have already been seen by the public, and each of the starters has proved himself possessed of more than ordinary merit. That the sale will be a success there can be no doubt, as colts and fillies bred as those advertised for sale cannot help but bring good prices.

Messrs. Killup & Co, will have charge of the sale, and those who wish any further information than what is already given in the advertisement can receive it by addressing those gentlemen at 22 Montgomery street, San Francisco.

Thoroughbred Yearlings.

This will be the last chance for us to call the attention of our readers to the thoroughbred yearlings which will be offered for sale at Raceland, near Paris, Kentucky, on Monday, May 5th of this year. Messrs. Baxter & Stringfield of Lexington will on that day offer for sale all the youngsters from Runnymead, Coldstream and Loudon Stock Farms. These yearlings are the get of Hindoo, imp. Billet, Leonatus, Onondago, Fonso, Alarm, Springbok, Sensation, King Alfonso, and Ben d'Or. Such a rich array of blood should surely tempt some of the California buyers to send a commission to Raceland, as in all probability many very good bargains may be picked up there.

Names Claimed.

J. B. C. for dark seal brown stallion foaled March 16, 1887, by Antevolo, dam Nellie by Signal Chief, he by Signal 3327, out of a mare by Williamson's Belmont; also,

Antionette for bay filly foaled April 17, 1888, she a full sister to J. B. C. J. B. Cole, San Francisco.

Disector for black colt, few white hairs in forehead, foaled May, 1889, by Director Jr. (full brother to Corrector), dam Cesanola by Altamont, 2nd dam by Mike.

John Pender, Salem, Or.

Indirect for colt, foaled 1885, by Director 2:17, dam Dixie by Echo. Geo. Van Gordon, San Simeon Rancho.

Todd's Only for ch f, foaled April 3, 1890, by C. H. Todd, dam Gerty McCarty by Duke of Magenta or Hurrah. This colt is a perfect picture of Todd. D. J. McCarty.

Fi Fine. I hereby claim this name for my bay filly foaled April 12th, by Noonday 10000, dam Lady Prompter, by Prompter 2305; 2nd dam Flash by Egmont; 3rd dam Lightfoot by Flaxtail.

M. H. Murdock.

Answers to Correspondents.

Answers for this department must be accompanied by the name and address of the sender, not necessarily for publication, but as proof of good faith. Write the questions distinctly, and on one side of the paper only. Positively no questions will be answered by mail or telegraph.

G. F. G.

Please give pedigree of stallion Comet, which stood at or near Sacramento in 1888.

Answer.—We do not know his pedigree.

Reader.

Please give the breeding of Granger (by Hambletonian 725) bred by Scott near Sacramento, and oblige.

Answer.—We do not know the horse, but perhaps some of our readers may be able to give the information.

Sam Houstan.

Can any of our readers give the pedigree of a stallion that was engaged in running races at Sacramento during the early sixties called Sam Houstan? He was owned at one time by James Martin of Ione.

W. H. T.

Please give me the pedigree of Easton's Black Hawk, if you can in your next paper, and very much oblige yours, etc.

Answer.—The horse was bought in the East by B Fish, Esq., of Santa Clara County, from whom you will be able to get the information desired. There are so many David Hills and Black Hawks mixed up in California pedigrees that it seems almost impossible to straighten them out.

J. E. E.

Please state in your next paper where Whips is at present, record 2:27½, sired by Electioneer. He stood at Vina three or four years ago.

Answer—He is in service at Senator Stanford's Vina Ranch at present.

T. H. V, Tustin City, Orange Co., Cal.

Will you please tell me through the columns of your valuable paper whether Silkwood and Satinwood or either are standard bred horses? Owned by a Mr. Willets of Santa Ana, Cal. If so, will you give their pedigrees. Also tell me the rules for sending in names claimed.

Answer.—Satinwood is not standard, but Silkwood can be made standard if his breeder has not already registered him. Satinwood is by Blackwood Mambrino, dam Uarda by Buckeye Chief, a son of Provincial Chief 684. Silkwood is by Blackwood Mambrino, dam Lady Woodruff, by Hiram Woodruff. When claiming names, write name, color and markings, when foaled, names of sire, dam and sire of dam, and as much of the pedigree as possible.

Subscriber.

Will you inform through your valuable paper whether Electioneer was ever trained, and if he ever had a bad leg.

Answer.—Electioneer has not been prepared for participation in races, but he has frequently been driven a quarter in 35 seconds at Palo Alto. The leg that is generally spoken of as "bad" was hurt by a knock, but he was never troubled by weak legs, bad tendons, etc.

H. W. S.

Will you be kind enough to inform me if this horse is eligible to registery. By Abbotsford, dam Annie Nutwood, by Nutwood, 2nd dam by Hercules, 3rd dam by Greens Bashaw.

Answer.—If horse colt no, if filly yes.

Sherman Black Hawk.

Last week a correspondent asked for the pedigree of Sherman Black Hawk, but from the manner in which the question was put, it seemed as though he wanted the pedigree of McCrackens Black Hawk. We have received since then the pedigree of a horse called Young Sherman Black Hawk, which stood at Knights Ferry during the season of 1871, and also give his pedigree as that may be what was wanted. Young Sherman Black Hawk, bred at Bridport, Addison County, Vermont by Wm Braisted Esq.; was sired by Sherman Black Hawk, he by old Black Hawk, he by Sherman, he by Justin Morgan; 1st dam by Sir Jed, he by Cock of the Rock, he by Duroc, he by imp Diomed.

Los Angeles Notes.

It is reported here that the colors of the Santa Anita millionaire will be seen on the California Circuit this year. I don't know how much truth there is in the story, but the presumption is that half a dozen of the most likely bread winners at the ranch will be selected to carry the familiar Maltese cross. Rumor also has it that Mr. Harold, a son-in-law of "Lucky" Baldwin, will have charge of the string. The speedy Laredo is now in training at Santa Anita, but I rather think he is to be sent East some time next month.

In glancing over the weights for the Great Western Handicap to be run at Washington Park, Chicago, I notice that Ed McGinnis is weighted at 108 pounds. There are a number of crackerjacks in the race, but it appears to me that the great little son of Grinstead should be in the hunt at the finish if he starts in good condition. A mile and a half would not be too far for Ed McGinnis with only 108 pounds to pack.

I ran across the following squib in the Queenslander, published at Brisbane, Australia, which is of more than passing interest:

"It is reported that an offer of £2500 has been made for the racehorse Melos on behalf of an American gentleman. Melos, who performed very creditably in the last Melbourne Cup, and distinguished himself last week by winning the V. R. C. Champion Stakes from Dreadnought and Carbine, is a very stoutly bred horse, being by Goldsbrough from Melody, by The Barb from Mermaid, by Fisherman from Sweetheart (imp). For stud purposes he should be good value for the £3000 required for him by his owner, Mr. Gannon."

It would not prove surprising if Melos should be purchased for the owner of Santa Anita. Two other stallions for sale in Australia are Carlyon and Cranbrook. Both have performed well in the Antipodes. The sire of both is Chester.

I desire to register a good sized kick. Why is it that the Directors of many associations included in the California Circuit pay so little attention to the bangtail division? The runners never fail to draw out the crowd, yet few of the associations cater to the running horse men. The trotting men get much the biggest slice of the pie. In fact they get seven-eighths of the pie. This is the reason why so many running owners in California do not patronize the home circuit. I take as much interest in trotters as runners, but a glance at the programmes of 1889 convinces me that something will have to be done in the very near future. I am also aware of the fact that nearly all Directors of associations in this glorious State are trotting horse men, but isn't it poor policy ot neglect the running brigade? Dagworth.

BASE BALL.

The Game Last Saturday.

The Senators Badly Beaten by the Colonels.

SCORE 13 TO 15.

There was a fair-sized audience at Haight Street last Saturday to witness the Oakland-Sacramento game, and while the score was very much one-sided, the game abounded in many fine and brilliant plays. The river team was in poor condition to try issues with the aggregation of Colonels —through Roberts, Stapleton and Bowman being on the sick list, and their places were filled in by Buckley, Kavanaugh and McHale respectively—still, notwithstanding that the odds were greatly against them, the Senators fairly captured the fielding honors of the game. Reitz and Godar were "in it" for their lives, and their pretty stopping of base hits, wonderful pickups and clever throwing, stamp them as players of great ability. Goodenough played a marvellous game in the field, one of his catches being the finest ever seen on the grounds. The battery work of Harper and McHale was only fair, Harper sending six men to bases on balls, and was hit freely at opportune moments.

Cobb's pitching, Dungan's hitting and McDonald's second base play were the features for the Oaklands. The Sacramentos started off well. With two out and Daly at first, Buckley sent a beautiful drive to centre for two bases, scoring Daly, Buckley crossing the plate a moment after on Reitz's single. The Oaklands made three in the first inning on O'Neill's hit, base on balls, Dungan's hit to right a wild pitch and an error by McHale.

The second inning also resulted in the Oaklands increasing their score by four runs, taking a lead which the Sacramentos were never able to reach throughout the remainder of the game.

Following is the score:—

OAKLANDS	AB.	R.	BH.	SB.	PO.	A	E
C. O'Neill, l f	5	2	1	2	1	0	1
Stickney, s s	5	2	0	0	1	2	1
Dungan, c f	4	3	2	1	2	0	0
N. O'Neill, 3rd b	5	3	2	0	1	3	0
McDonald, 2nd b	4	2	1	1	2	4	1
Lohman, c	5	0	1	0	4	1	1
Hill, c f	5	0	0	0	1	0	0
Isaacson, 1st b	4	1	2	3	12	1	1
Cobb, p	4	1	1	1	3	3	0
Totals	37	13	9	8	27	14	5

SACRAMENTOS.	AB.	R.	BH.	SB.	PO.	A.	E.
Goodenough, c f	4	1	0	0	3	0	0
Daly, s s	4	2	2	0	0	3	1
Godar, 3rd b	5	0	0	0	4	3	0
Buckley, l f	4	1	1	0	1	0	1
Reitz, 2nd b	4	1	2	1	2	5	0
Kavanaugh, 1st b	3	0	0	1	7	0	3
Zeigler, r f	4	0	1	0	0	1	0
McHale, c	4	0	0	0	7	1	1
Harper, p	4	0	1	0	0	0	0
Totals	36	5	7	9	24	13	6

SCORE BY INNINGS.

	1	2	3	4	5	6	7	8	7
Oakland	3	4	1	0	0	0	1	4	1—13
Sacramento	2	0	1	1	0	0	1	0	0— 5

Earned runs—Sacramento, 2; Oakland 3. Two base hits—Buckley, Dungan. Daly, Reitz, Lohman. Sacrifice hits—Godar (2), Buckley. First base on errors—Sacramento 3; Oakland 6. Left on bases—Sacramento 6; Oakland 5. Struck out—By Harper 7; by Cobb 4. Hit by pitcher—Daly, Isaacson. Double plays—Godar (alone), Stickney, McDonald and Isaacson. Passed balls—McHale 1, Lohman 1. Wild pitches—Harper 2, Cobb 2. Umpire—Sheridan.

Sunday's Game.

BORCHERS IN GREAT SHAPE.

Which Resulted in the Defeat of the Oaklands 8 to 5.

Last Sunday there was a decided falling off in the attendance at the Haight St. Grounds, but nevertheless a fine quality of ball was "put up" and those who were absent missed it. It was a great day for Stockton though and the way Captain Fogarty's boys played ball made the 'Frisco contingent yell with delight. To use the phrase of the day the "Oaklands weren't in it" after the third inning. Borchers was in perfect form and pitched winning ball from the "go." His support was excellent with the exception of Fairhurst who was a little weak, not having fully recovered from his sore arm yet. Fudger covered himself with glory at the bat and Wilson's reappearance at third was the signal for hearty applause. The Oaklands played well too, the fielders having plenty to do. Meegan being hit out hard and freely. C. O. Neill had eight nice chances in left all of which he gracefully accepted and McDonald played an almost faultless game at second. The noisy Pooh-Bah of the team saved himself a lot of guying by merely playing on the bench. Farrell taking his place at third, and although he had little to do, that little was done well. The Stocktons crept ahead in the fourth inning and augmented their score in the eight inning by three runs maintaining a lead which the Oaklands could not overcome.

The following is the complete score:

STOCKTONS.	A. B.	R.	B.H.	S.B.	P.O.	A.	E.
Swan, r f	5	2	3	0	0	0	0
Cahill, l f	4	0	1	1	1	0	0
Holliday, c f	5	1	1	1	1	0	0
Fudger, s s	5	1	3	0	0	2	0
Fogarty, 2 b	4	2	2	1	4	2	1
Selna, 1 b	3	2	2	3	11	0	1
Wilson, 3 b	4	0	1	0	2	1	0
Borchers, p	4	0	1	0	0	4	0
Fairhurst, c	5	0	0	0	8	4	0
Totals	38	8	14	6	27	18	2

OAKLANDS.	A. B.	R.	B.H.	S.B.	P.O.	A.	E.
C. O'Neill, l f	3	1	2	3	7	1	0
Stickney, s s	5	0	0	0	1	2	0
Dungan, c f	4	0	0	0	2	0	1
Farrell, 3 b	5	0	0	0	1	1	0
McDonald, 2 b	3	1	2	1	3	5	1
Lohman, c	4	0	1	0	1	0	0
Hill, r f	0	2	0	5	1	0	0
Isaacson, 1 b	4	1	1	0	8	0	0
Meegan, p	3	0	0	1	0	1	0
Totals	31	5	6	10	24	10	2

SCORE BY INNINGS.

CLUBS.	1	2	3	4	5	6	7	8	9
Stocktons	0	1	2	1	0	0	3	1	*—8
Oaklands	0	2	1	0	0	1	0	0	1—5

SUMMARY.

At San Francisco, April 20, 1890—Stocktons 8, Oaklands 5. Earned runs—Oaklands 1, Stocktons 5. Three base hits—Fogarty. Two-base hits—Swan, McDonald 2, Isaacson, Fudger. Sacrifice hits—Dungan, Farrell, Lohman, Isaacson, Selna, Wilson 2, Borchers, Fairhurst. First base on errors—Oaklands 1. First base on called balls Oaklands 7, Stocktons 8. Left on bases—Oaklands 6, Stocktons 8. Struck out By Borchers 10, by Meegan 1. Hit by Pitcher—C. O'Neil, Hill. Double plays—C. O'Neil to McDonald, Fogarty to Selna, Passed balls—Fairhurst 3, Lohman 1.

Umpire—John Sheridan.
Scorer—J. W. Stapleton.
Time of game—Two hours.
Attendance—5,000

Amateur notes and scores and news from the interior will appear in the next issue of this paper.

PROFESSIONAL GROUNDERS.

Buchan is weak on fly balls.

Speed is throwing well to bases.

Billy Farrell is still open for engagements.

A chair in the Assessors office is graced by Senator Gagus.

Charley O'Neill of the Colonel's is putting up a great fielding game.

The Friscos are sadly in need of rigorous team practice.

Great things are expected from Harry O'Day by the Minneapolis management.

Comiskey will take a Brotherhood team to Mexico next Winter.

Phil Knell made a great showing in his initial game for the Pittsburg Players team.

It has been stated that Jimmy Fogarty's salary is a fraction over $700 monthly.

The Colonels in their mourning costume present a very sober appearance.

The Sporting Life is authority for the statements that as a coacher Tom Powers rivals Arlie Latham.

The BREEDER AND SPORTSMAN will be the most complete Base Ball paper ever issued on this Coast.

Abe Cahalin, at one time a leading player with the G. & M's is now playing in the field with Fresno.

Levy is still the reigning favorite with the Kindergarten. The Kids don't take kindly to any other of the fielders except probably Roberts.

The Jevne who will be remembered as the clever left fielder of the Pioneer of '88 is now taking care of the center garden for Spokane.

The Stocktons are badly in need of another catcher. Why don't they give young Stanley who last year caught Borchers in Merced, a chance?

The News says Comiskey is the big dog with the brass collar with the Chicago baseball public at present. Anson is not on the map.

The sympathy of the majority of the Eastern ball patrons is with the Brotherhood, as is evidenced by the vast superiority in numbers attending their games.

The Sacramentos were much handicapped in last Saturday's game. With Stapleton, Roberts and Bowman on the sick list their team is in a very crippled condition.

Jim McDonald never showed up in better form than he has this season. His second base play is of the finest quality and he is hitting the ball pretty regularly also.

The absence of Noisy O'Neill's ludicrous chestnutty and at times insulting remarks on the coaching lines, was a pleasing feature of last Sunday's game.

Tom Powers has fairly captivated the Baltimore cranks. His brilliant coaching, fine discretion, clever fielding and scientific hitting and base running have made him a big favorite in the Oriole City.

Godar, of the Sacramentos, will undoubtedly lead the third baseman of the League. His fielding of ground hits is magnificent and his throwing accurate and strong.

The League managers should lose no time in having the grass in the out field of the home grounds mowed down. It now presents more the appearance of a cow pasture than a ball field and greatly interferes with the fielding of fly and ground hits.

Jack Wilson was warmly applauded last Saturday when he made his reappearance at third with the Stocktons. Jack has always been a favorite and deservedly so, as he is a most conscientious, gentlemanly and able player.

Manager Zeigler could very materially strengthen the Sacramentos by securing the services of Tom Buckley and playing him permanently in right. His outfield would then be second to none in the League, and besides Buckley would be a valuable acquisition on account of his batting.

The Eastern pape s seem to be completely "at sea" when stating that Goldie now with Peoria lead the base stealing record of the California League. The fact of the matter is Goldie never played with any team in the California League. We remember him as a fairly clever and tricky second base man of the Los Angeles team and also with the Santa Cruz team of '86 of the California State League, but as no official scores were ever kept by this League the title to being champion base runner of even the State Leaguers is evidently self assumed.

Cooney, Hayes and Thompson intend going north to join the Northwestern League. Here are three excellent players who were overlooked by the local managers, and who would lend great strength to any team. Cooney, who played with the Stocktons and Pioneers is a very heavy hitter, speedy base runner, good outfielder and strong thrower. Daddy Hayes has always been a most popular player on this coast, and in all departments of the game can keep well up with the procession and genial John Thompson. Aside from being a good hard hitter he is a most promising back stop and infielder. The Northern League teams would do well to secure these players immediately, for as far as good playing is concerned, it would be a case of "satisfaction guaranteed,

Symptoms of Spavin.

Spavin is not always shown by an enlargement at the hock joint. It is sometimes "occult," or hidden, and occurs with in the joint where one bone works upon the other. Any tenderness there is very painful, and the animal is lame without any external sign as to the locality. The disease is characterized by an objection to put the heel to the ground and by frequent stumbling or knuckling under of the lower joint, also by stepping on the toe when running, causing the undue wearing at the toe of the shoe. A blister is the best remedy.—N. Y. Times.

It is announced that the National Trotting Association has decided to publish at the end of every season a book giving the official record of the year, with the full breeding of the horses making them, says the Indiana Horseman. The American Association should do the same. The National Association of Trotting Horse Breeders should co-operate with them and thus avoid much confusion and many disputes as to the authenticity of records.

How to Make Horses Win.

One of the sensational features at the winter tracks durin the season that closed yesterday was the administering t horses who "sulk" in races of a hypodermic injection of a se dative claimed to at once quiet their sulks and arouse, fo the time being at least, their courage, says the Sportin World. For a long time before it was fairly known that th same was a chimera or a reality, it used to be rumored aroun before a race that So and So's horse "had an injection."

Inquiry revealed that "the injection" was not a chimera but a reality, a young Missourian, P. B. Ring by name, formerly well known on the Western trotting circuit as the trainer and driver of Magoozler, was finally located as the origina tor of "the injection."

Since Mr. Ring left the trotting turf to become identifie with the bang tails, he has been more or less well known and always favorably known as interested in several rac horses in this vicinity, Free Lance being the last to carr his colors.

Lately, but particularly at the commencement of the season just closed, Mr. Ring became convinced that a hypoder mic injection, at once harmless, sedative and stimulating would be of benefit to horses who are found to sulk in races in other words, "soft hearted" racers.

The idea no sooner originated than it was at once put int application. What the fluid used is composed of is Mr. Ring' secret. His charges have been nominal for the same, and h rightly enough from the first has made the stipulation of "N success, no cost to the owner of the horse." Whatever it is it has shown itself to be of no bad or deleterious effects, fo the reason that horses who have experienced the treatmen have not only not been dependent on it, but have won race after its discontinuance.

One of the first to be treated was the mare Connemara, las August at Worcester. The mare had been a notorious "sulker," and before the mile and five furlong dash, won by Hin doocraft, Mr. Ring tried his hand, or rather hypodermi needle on her. The mare on that day led the party for near ly a mile and a half at such a stout pace that the merits o the treatment were manifest, although she did not win.

Later in the season Mr. Ring began operations at Clifton and Guttenberg. Adonis and Specialty at Clifton were among the first he treated, and both ran good races at long shots under the influence of the injection. The last named mare won twice on successive race days, and later Lancaster three times in succession. Bonanza, Adonis, Specialty, Barrister, Gendarme, Lottery, Top Sawyer, Cupid, Raveller and many others won under its at once sedative and stimulating effects.

It has been claimed by some that any hypodermic injection must necessarily be injurious in its after effects, as well as leaving the animal dependent on it at all times. Nothing can be more true, but as yet it has not shown ill effects in this instance. The cases of the racers Specialty and Top Sawyer, who have received this treatment the most frequently, are to the point. Both have so far not become dependent on the treatment, but appear to have improved on it, as their last two wins show, Top Sawyer at a mile in 1:43¼ at Guttenberg being the best race he has ever run. Therefore "the injection" may be noted as not deleterious, while it seems to have been demonstrated to be most useful in cases of a "sulky" animal. Yet it is not possible that it will ever be used on any horse of value.

Breeders' Directory.

Advertisements under this heading 50c. per line per month.

HORSES AND CATTLE.

W. S. JACOBS, Sacramento, Cal. — Breeder of Thoroughbred Shorthorns and Berkshire Hogs.

J. H. WHITE, Lakeville, Sonoma County—Breeder of Registered Holstein Cattle.

EL ROBLAS RANCHO—Los Alamos, Cal., Francis T. Underhill, proprietor, importer and breeder of thoroughbred Hereford Cattle. Information by mail. C. F. Swan, manager.

PAGE BROTHERS.—Penn's Grove, Sonoma Co. Cal. Breeders of Short-Horn Cattle; Draft, Roadster and Standard Bred Horses.

SETH COOK, breeder of Cleveland Bay Horses, Devon, Durham, Polled Aberdeen-Angus and Galloway Cattle. Young stock of above breeds on hand for sale. Warranted to be pure bred, recorded and average breeders. Address, Geo. A. Wiley, Cook Farm, Danville, Contra Costa Co., Cal.

MAMBRINO WILKES COLTS and FILLIES, full brothers and sisters to Gus. Wilkes 2:22, and Balkan 2:29¼, for Sale. Address SMITH HILL, Walnut Creek, Contra Costa County, Cal.

B. F. RUSH, Suisun, Cal., Shorthorns, Thoroughbred and Grades. Young Bulls and Calves for Sale.

PETER SAXE & SON, Lick House, San Francisco, Cal.—Importers and Breeders for past 18 years of every variety of Cattle, Horses, Sheep and Hogs.

HOLSTEIN THOROUGHBREDS of all the noted strains. Registered Berkshire Swine. Catalogues. F. H. BURKE, 401 Montgomery St., S. F.

FERGUSON & AUSTIN,
FRESNO, CAL.
Registered Polled Angus and Short-Horn Cattle.

THE CORINTHIAN
Cafe and Restaurant,
Point Tiburon.
MEALS SERVED TO ORDER AT ALL HOURS
COLD LUNCHES
FOR FISHING AND PICNIC PARTIES.
Headquarters for Yachtsmen and Fishing Parties
B. F. NAPTHALY, Manager.

Races, Races,

JULY WEEK.

AT

South Park Race Track

Eureka, Cal.

GIVEN BY THE

EUREKA JOCKEY CLUB.

FIRST DAY, JULY 2, 1890.

No. 1. Novelty Running Race. Free for all. Dash of one mile. Purse $250. First quarter, $40. Half, $50. Third quarter, $70. Mile, $90.

No. 2. Running Race. Purse $150. Five-eighths dash, for two-year-olds. $125 to first horse; $25 to second horse.

No. 3. Running. Purse $150. Three-quarters and repeat. $125 to first; $25 to second.

SECOND DAY, JULY 3, 1890.

No. 4. Trotting. Purse $200. Three minute Class. $150 to first; $50 to second. (Covey barred.)

No. 5. Running Stake. Five-eighths of a mile. For Humboldt raised two year-olds. $30 entrance, half forfeit. $15 added. First to receive 60 per cent.; second, 30 per cent., third, 10 per cent.

No. 6. Running Stake. Purse $200. Mile Dash. $150 to first horse; $50 to second horse.

THIRD DAY, JULY 4, 1890.

No. 7. Trotting Stake. 2:40 Class. Purse $250. $200 to first horse; $50 to second horse.

No. 8. Running Stake, 1¼ miles. Free-for-all. $40 entrance, ¼ forfeit, $200 added; second horse $75, third horse to save stake.

No. 9. Running Stake. Purse $150; 1-2 mile and repeat; $125 to first; $25 to second.

FOURTH DAY, JULY 5, 1890.

No. 10. Running Stake, 1-2 mile and repeat; for Humboldt horses owned prior to Jan 1, 1890. $125 to first, $25 to second.

No. 11. Running Stake. Purse $200; 7-8 mile and repeat. $150 to first, $50 to second.

CONDITIONS AND REMARKS.

All trotting races are best three in five, unless otherwise specified. Four to enter and three to start, but the Board reserves the right to hold a less number than four to fill by the withdrawal of a proportionate amount of the purse. Entrance fee, 10 per cent. of purse, to accompany nominations. In all trotting races the rules of the American Trotting Association, and all running races the rules of the Pacific Coast Blood Horse Association to govern, but the Board reserves the right to trot heats of any two classes alternately, if necessary, to finish any day's racing. In all entries not declared out by 6 P. M. of the day preceding the race, shall be required to start.

No added money paid for a walk over. In all races, four or more paid up entries required to fill, and three or more horses to start. Racing colors to be named in entries. In trotting races drivers will be required to wear caps of distinct colors to be named in entries. Entries in all races to close with the Secretary, Thursday, June 20, 1890. Entry blanks will be furnished upon application to the Secretary.

All trotting races for horses owned and in Humboldt County prior to June 1, 1890.

H. M. DEVOY, President.
J. P. MONROE, Secretary.

SHAW CARTS and SULKIES

For light road or track use, manufactured from the best selected material. Combines lightness with elegance and ease to riders. Weights 70 to 100 lbs. Used by the best horsemen on this coast. Inspection invited.
ONE CAFFREY SULKY FOR SALE AT A BARGAIN.

CARRIAGES & Light VEHICLES
Manufactured to Order.
W. E. SHAW,
1621 MARKET STREET, SAN FRANCISCO, CAL.
REPAIRING DONE—ALL WORK WARRANTED.

ADVERTISE YOUR STALLIONS

—IN THE—

Breeder & Sportsman

For the Season---1890.

We are pleased to announce that we have the best facilities for furnishing

Stallion Pictures,

Stallion Cards,

Pedigrees, Folders,

Contracts, Bills, Etc.

We make a specialty of this department of our business, and have UNRIVALED FACILITIES FOR LOOKING UP PEDIGREES and doing accurate and handsome work.

Promptness, Good Work, Low Prices.

BREEDER AND SPORTSMAN,
313 Bush Street, S. F.

The Trotting Stallion

CUPID,

Full Brother to Adonis 2:14,

—Sired by—

The Celebrated SIDNEY 2:19 3-4, and out of Venus.

Will make the season of 1890 at the OAKLAND TROTTING PARK.

PEDIGREE.

CUPID is by Sidney out of Venus by Capt. Webster 10178, record 2:30, and sire of Freestone 2:19. Second dam by Skenandoah 936, sire of Daisy Rufus 2:29¼, Erwin Davis (sire of two in the 30 list) and dams of four in the 30 list.

DESCRIPTION.

Cupid is a handsome bright bay 15.2¼ hands high, weighs 1100 lbs.; was foaled in 1886. As a yearling, with very little work he showed quarters in 41 seconds, and at 2 years old, quarters in 36 seconds. As a three year old he has not been worked, but he shows the speed and endurance that must come from his excellent blood lines.

TERMS $50 for the season, with the usual return privileges. Good pasturage near the track at $5 per month. The best of care taken of mares in any way that owners may desire, but no responsibility assumed for accidents or escapes.

For further particulars address

C. O. THORNQUEST,
Oakland Trotting Park, or
C. BAAR, 972 Broadway, Oakland.

PHIL J. CRIMMINS. JOHN C. MORRISON.

"Silver Palace,"

36 Geary Street,
San Francisco, Cal.

Highland Farm,

LEXINGTON, KY.,

Home of Red Wilkes.

Standard-bred Trotting Stock

For Sale,

Sired by Red Wilkes, Wilton, 2:19¼; Allandorf and Sentinel Wilkes, out of highly bred Standard Mares of the most fashionable blood of the day.

W. C. FRANCE, Proprietor.

K STREET.

SECOND ST

Singleton & Addington
BANK EXCHANGE,
SACRAMENTO.
Wines, Liquors & Cigars.

"DICKEY'S,"

SIXTH AVENUE AND D ST.
Near entrance to Bay District Track.
Choicest Brands of
WINES AND CIGARS.
A Delightful Resort.
Telephone 1485. J. R. DICKEY, Propr.

JOHN FORGIE,

Importing Tailor,

204 Montgomery Street,
N. E. corner Bush, SAN FRANCISCO.

HENRY J. COX W. S. JOHNSON

The "EDWIN C."

40 EDDY STREET,
Cor. of Mason, San Francisco.
(Private Entrance Mason Street.)

PASTURAGE
AND
FIRST-CLASS CARE
TAKEN OF
Gentlemen's Road Horses and Trotters.

Colts Broken and Trained to Harness or Saddle.

Twenty new Box Stalls. First-class Pasturage, and the best of care given to all horses. Terms, $4 per month. Satisfaction Guaranteed.

Address,
K. O'GRADY,
Laurel Creek Farm,
SAN MATEO, CAL.

C. C. LINIMENT.

For Catarrh, C. C. LINIMENT has no Peer. Try It.

Prescribed by San Francisco's Leading Physicians. Indorsed by the Medical Faculty.

C.C.LINIMENT.

The Great Pain Conqueror for Man and Beast.

For Horsemen and Stockmen this Liniment is Invaluable

OWNERS OF FINE STOCK CANNOT AFFORD TO BE WITHOUT IT.

A remedy for every home, giving instant relief in pain and PERFORMING PERMANENT CURES.

To get the full benefit of the C. C. Liniment in Chronic Cases, in connection with C. C. Liniment use Compound Sulphur Powder, the "Great Blood Purifier," put up ONLY by The W. H. Bone Co., 12 Bush St., San Francisco. For Habitual Constipation, Indigestion, Piles, etc., it is the greatest remedy known to medical science.

If your druggist does not keep it, we will send direct, post paid, on receipt of price. COMPOUND SULPHUR POWDER is $1 per bottle, 6 for $5. Small bottles, 25c.

The C. C. Liniment Co

12 BUSH STREET, S. F.
W. H. BONE, - - General Manager.
FOR SALE BY ALL DRUGGISTS.

CALIFORNIA

NUTWOOD

Will stand for mares the season of 1890, commencing February 15th, and ending July 15th, at the NUTWOOD STOCK FARM, one mile from Irvington.

DESCRIPTION AND PEDIGREE.

He is a dark chestnut, with star in forehead; foaled September 16th, 1881; is 16 hands 1½ inches high and weighs 1250 pounds. Has a beautiful flowing mane and tail, with remarkable style and lofty carriage, a bold, open movement like his sire, but has never been handled for speed. He moves and looks like his sire, except that he is a larger horse.

CALIFORNIA NUTWOOD by Nutwood, record 2:18¾, has 82 trotters and pacers with records from 2:15 to 2:30, and put 8 in the 2:30 list in 1889. He is the only horse that ever lived with a record under 2:20 that produced five under 2:20. He is now serving mares at Dubuque, Iowa, at $500 for the season, and his colts at yearlings sell from $2500 to $5000 each. He is out of the dam of Maud S., record 2:08¾.

Nutwood, by Alexander's Belmont, sire of 52 with records from 2:15½ to 2:30. Alexander's Belmont by Alexander's Abdallah, sire of Goldsmiths Maid, record 2:14, and 6 others in 2:20 list. Alexander's Abdallah, by Rysdyk's Hambletonian, sire of 41 with records from 2:17¼ to 2:30, and is the founder of the Hambletonian family.

FANNY PATCHEN, dam of California Nutwood, by George M. Patchen Jr., record 2:27, and sire of Wells Fargo, 2:18¾, Sam Purdy 2:20½, Ben Ali 2:30½, and 7 others from 2:21 to 2:30. He has 7 sons who together produced 12 trotters in 2:30 list, and 5 daughters who together produced 5 trotters and 1 pacer in 2.30 or better. He sired Alexander 2:31½. Alexander sired Alex. Button 2:26½; Alex. Button sired Yolo Maid, pacing record 2:14 at 4 years old, the fastest on record; George M. Patchen Jr., by George M. Patchen 2:23½, is sire of Lucy 2:18¼, and 3 others in the 2:30 list; he has 12 sons who together produced 40 trotters from 2:14¾ to 2.30, and 6 daughters who together produced 6 trotters in 2:30 list or better, he is grand sire of Hopeful 2:14¾, and best wagon record 2:16½, and sire of the granddam of Stamboul 2:12½.

George M. Patchen, by Cassius M. Clay, and he by Henry Clay, founder of the Clay family.

Laura, second dam of California Nutwood, was a fine large bay mare, a very fast roadster brought from Chicago by Wm. Wilson, of San Jose, and is said to have made a record of 2.35 in Chicago. Pedigree not traced.

TERMS.

$40 for the season, payable invariably before the animal is removed. Mares not proving in foal can be returned free next season. Pasturage $5 per month, but no liability for accidents or escapes.

For further particulars address the owner,

MARTIN CARTER,
Newark, Alameda Co., Cal., or Irvington, Alameda County, Cal.

Pedigrees Tabulated

IN THE MOST ARTISTIC MANNER.

Giving speed performers under sires and dams. Catalogues compiled. Stallion cards and circulars written up ready for the press. Pedigree blanks for sale. Prices reasonable. Horses bought and sold on Commission. References furnished.

R. Y. HARDIN.
806 W. Madison St., Chicago, Ill.

ANNUAL SPRING SALE

—OF—

200 HEAD

Road & Harness Horses

AND

Work and Draft Horses

AND SHETLAND PONIES!

From the Ranchos of J. B. Haggin, Esq.

WILL TAKE PLACE AT

RAILROAD STABLES,

Corner Turk and Steiner Streets, San Francisco,

Tuesday, May 6, 1890,

HORSES MAY BE SEEN AT STABLES ON AND AFTER MAY 3d.

Catalogues now ready, and may be had on application.

KILLIP & CO., Live Stock Auctioneers,
22 Montgomery Street, S. F.

AUCTION SALE OF

Standard-Bred Trotters and

ROADSTERS,

—AT—

AGRICULTURAL PARK, SACRAMENTO,

FRIDAY, - - May 2d, 1890,

At 1 o'clock P. M.

BY ORDER OF MR. S. E. TRYON

This sale will include the well known pacing mare POCAHONTAS, 2:22½. Heavy in foal to DEXTER PRINCE; g g EL MONTE 2:29½, brown pacer CASTELLO, 2:31½, and MAJESTER (3) at 2 years old 2:49½, sired by Sterling 6223, dam Madam Baldwin (dam of Bay Rose 2:20½) by the Moor 870.

And twenty others, comprising broodmares, colts, fillies and geldings.

SALE POSITIVE.

Catalogues now being prepared.

KILLIP & CO., Auctioneers,
22 Montgomery Street, San Francisco.

RUNNYMEDE, COLDSTREAM & LOUDOUN

-Thoroughbred Yearlings-

Will be sold at Auction

On Monday, May 5th, 1890,

—AT—

RACELAND, - - - - near Paris, Ky., at 12 M,

These yearlings are the get of Hindoo, imp. Billet, Leonatus, Onondaga, Fonso, Alarm, Springbok, Sensation, King Alfonso and Ben d'Or. They include full brothers to Hanover, Jim Gore, Bedford and The Lioness, Ralston, Perkins, Modolin, Burton and Millie, and Miss Motley; sisters to Runnymede, Barnes, Meriden, Servia, Cameo, Heathen, Hindoo Rose and Lillian Lindsay and Sunbeam; half-brothers to Pure Rye, Ocean Middleston, Catalpa, Miss Thomas, Winslow and Stoney Montgomery and Longshore, and half-sisters to Alarm Bell, Warren Lewis, Shelby Barnes, Florence E., and Brusselle and Kilkenney.

☞ THE LARGEST WINNING HORSE AND LARGEST WINNING MARE ON THE AMERICAN TURF WERE BOTH BRED AT RUNNYMEDE.

For catalogues, apply to

BAXTER & STRINGFIELD,
Box 35. Room 1, Reed Building, Lexington, Ky.

B. G. BRUCE & P. C. KIDD'S

Spring Sales of

THOROUGHBREDS!

MAY 7—The Entire Produce of the EDGEWATER and KINGSTON STUD YEARLINGS, Comprising Thirty-four Head.

In the Edgewater Stud are the get of Springbok, Audrain, Onondaga, imp. Silvermine and imp. Deceiver. In the Kingston Stud the get of Longfellow, imp. Zorilla, imp. The Ill Used, Jils Johnson and Duke of Montrose. Among the Edgewater Yearlings are full brothers to Audrain, Gosno, Ascalon, Ascoli and Sierra Nevada. Half brothers to Weasel, Orlando, Schoolmaster, Warrior and Sonnet. Full sisters to Lela May and East Lynne. Half sisters to Zulu, Abilene, Tripple Cross, Irish Dan and Vallisia.

In the Kingston Stud lot are half brothers to Helter Skelter, Biscuit and Prodigal Son. Half sisters to Winning Ways and Rollin Hawley, and a full sister to that fast horse Kenney.

On MAY 8 a Grand Combination Sale of Sixty Head of Yearlings, Two and Three Year Olds, Broodmares, Stallions and Horses in Training.

The Yearlings number 32, and are the get of King Alfonso, Jils Johnson, Longfellow, Himyar, Duke of Montrose, imp. Rossington, Onondaga, Virginius, Falsetto, Col. Clark, Gov. Bowie, Harry O'Fallon, Persan, imp. Rapture, Melbourne (formerly Elias Lawrence), Turco or Melbourne, Voltarno, imp. Stylites, Leonatus, Lord Clifden and Jim Gore.

Among them is a full brother to Brandolette, half-brothers and sisters to Wa Wa, Teuton, Yorick, Ascoola, Marguerite, Autocrat, Monocrat and Jack Rose, and out of mares by Longfellow, imp. Glen Athol, Pat Malloy, Reverberation, Lisbon, Knighthood, Lightning, King Ban, Thunder, Virgil, Bertram, King Alfonso, Lever, Eolus, War Dance, Tom-Tom, Drum, Charlton, Tom Bowling, Revolver, Hurrah, Wanderer, Wildidle, Jerome Edgar, Gen. [illegible], Aramis and Ballinkeel, from racing families.

Among the broodmares are a full sister to Eolian, half sisters to Jennie June and Explosion (Dew Drop's dam) by such sires as Eolus, Lisbon, Ten Broeck and Ringmaster.

Among the two-year-olds are full sisters to Burlington and Spendwell, by such well-known sires as Powhattan, Harry O'Fallon, Spendthrift, and Ten Broeck. The older horses are by Germantown, King Ban, Forester, Rossiter, Duke of Montrose, Allan Pinkerton, Ten Broeck and Kyrle Daly, from racing and producing families.

These sales will be held at Tracy & Wilson's Stable, Lexington, Ky., beginning each day at 9 A. M. For catalogues address this office or

BRUCE & KIDD, Lexington, Ky.

Important Closing Out Sale

—OF—

Trotting bred STOCK,

Comprising the Entire Stud of

JOHN G. HILL, of Ventura, Cal

To be held at 10 A. M., at

RAILROAD STABLES,

Corner STEINER and TURK STS., San Francisco.

Take McAllister or Turk Street Cars.

Thursday, May 15, 1890

It will embrace about 80 head of well bred Stallions, Mares and Geldings, principally the get of that celebrated standard-bred sire

A. W. RICHMOND, 1687,

out of thoroughbred mares mostly from that noted horse, Woodburn, sire of Monarch 2:28¼ and the dam of Victor 2:22, and others.

This will no doubt be the last opportunity to obtain at public auction the blood of this great sire, that, in part, has made ANTEEO, ANTEVOLO, ARROW, ROMERO, RICHMOND JR., and others famous in the trotting history of our State.

The sale is positive and without reserve, as Mr. Hill will engage in other business.

☞ Catalogues now ready.

KILLIP & CO., Auctioneers,
22 Montgomery Street, San Francisco, Cal.

AUCTION SALE

—OF—

THOROUGHBREDS

AT

SACRAMENTO,

May 2d, 1890,

By order of W. M. MURRY, ESQ.

Bay mare LADY ALI (3), by Hyder Ali, dam Mattie Ward by imp. Intruder (sire of dam of Spokane).
Br c OAKDALE (3), by imp. Partisan, dam by Spectre.
Blk colt POWER (2), by Powhattan, dam by Ten Broeck.
Bay colt PARAPET (2), by Bulwer, dam Nettie Brady by Jack Malone.
Bay colt JOE HARDING (2), by Joe Hooker, dam Irene Harding by Jack Malone.
Sorrel colt GERALD (2), by Powhattan, dam Geneva by Lexington.
Ch f (1) by Prince of Norfolk, dam Irene Harding.
Ch f (1) by Joe Hooker, dam Marguerita.
To be sold with engagements.

KILLIP & CO., Auctioneers.

Poplar Grove Breeding FARM.

Standard-bred Trotters, Colts and Fillies.

The get of CLOVIS, 4909; PASHA, 2039; APEX, 2935,

For Sale.

Address S. N. STRAUBE, Poplar Grove Breeding Farm,

Fresno, Cal.

Inspection by intending purchasers invited, and information by mail.

Stallion for Sale

AT A BARGAIN.

Full Brother to Fairmont.

By Piedmont, dam Queen by Garibaldi—see State Fair Edition of BREEDER AND SPORTSMAN, September 14, 1889, for description of Fairmont—three years old, solid bay. Can trot a 2:40 gait or better. Sound in every particular. Can be seen at Oakland Trotting Park, Oakland.

P. J. WILLIAMS.

Pure Bred Clydesdale Mares

TWO MARES (Full Sisters) Five and Six Years Old, Weighing About 1,900 lbs. Each.

Sire imp. BEN. LOMOND.
Dam's sire imp. GLANCER.

For particulars apply to

H. A. MAYHEW,
Niles, Alameda County.

FOR SALE.

Full Brother in Blood to Yolo Maid, 2:12 1-2.

A very fast pacer. No record. Also a RUNNING MARE. Can run a half in 49 or better.

Apply to

G. W. BOUCHER,
Woodland, Cal.

For Sale

A FIRST-CLASS

Napa County Farm

—OR—

STOCK RANCH,

800 Acres Improved,

SITUATED TWO AND A HALF MILES FROM NAPA CITY, with good roads leading thereto, good hard finished house of nine rooms, with all modern improvements, streams running all summer, great amount of live oak and black oak timber. It lies in a fruit belt, surrounded by fine vineyards and orchards growing upon the same quality of soil and originally a part of this tract. About one-half hill and one-half rolling land, but none of it is steep and all easily cultivated, splendidly situated for the breeding of fine horses. Price, $65 per acre. Further particulars given at this office.

BREEDER AND SPORTSMAN,
313 Bush St.

Antevolo Colt

FOR SALE.

REX VOLO, foaled February 22nd 1888, dam Catchup by Rustler; granddam Huntess by Don Victor; great granddam Bettie Denice by American Boy Jr. Is 15.1 hands high, well developed, muscular and without a blemish. Has a very gentle disposition, and shows speed and a good gait.

HOME FURNISHING CO.,
126 Fifth Street, S. F. Cal.

Speed Programme

—OF THE—

Twelfth District Ag'l Society

To be held at

LAKEPORT,

SEPTEMBER 23 to 27 INCLUSIVE.

First Day—Tuesday, Sept. 23, 1890.

RACE NO. 1—TROTTING.

Yearling Stake; $2 0 guaranteed. Entrance $30, payable as follows: $5 May 1st, $10 July 1, $10 September 1st (when entry must be named), and $5 additional for starters. Entries to close May 1, 1890. See general conditions.

RACE NO. 2—RUNNING.

One-half mile dash. $100 added; $25 to second. Entrance $10, to close 6 P. M. day before race.

RACE NO. 3—TROTTING.

Three-minute class. Mile heats 3 in 5. District. $150 added. Entrance $30; to close 6 P. M. day before race. 5 to enter, 3 to start. See general conditions.

Second Day—Wednesday, September 24th

RACE NO. 4—RUNNING.

Three-quarter mile heats; 2 in 3. $200 added; $25 to second. Entrance $10, to close 6 P. M. day before race.

RACE NO. 5—TROTTING.

District Stallion. Mile heats 3 in 5. Purse $500. Entrance $50, to close 6 P. M. day before race; 5 to enter, 3 to start. See general conditions.

RACE NO. 6—TROTTING.

Three-year-old stake; $300 guaranteed. $50 entrance, payable as follows: May 1st, $10; July 1st, $10; September 1, $15 (when entry must be named), and $15 additional to start. Open to Napa, Solano, Sonoma, Marin, Lake, Colusa, Yolo, Mendocino and Humboldt Counties.

Third Day—Thursday, Sept. 25th.

RACE NO. 7—RUNNING.

Seven-eighths mile dash. $150 added; $25 to second. Entrance $10, to close 6 P. M. day before race.

RACE NO. 8—TROTTING.

Two-year-old stake; free for all. Mile heats, best 2 in 3, $300 guaranteed. Entrance $50, payable as follows: May 1st, $10; July 1st, $10; September 1st, $15, and $15 additional to start. See general conditions.

Fourth Day—Friday, Sept. 26th.

RACE NO. 9—TROTTING.

Mile heats, 3 in 5. For all described counties in race No. 6. $400 added. Entrance $60, payable as follows: May 1st, $10; July 1st, $20; September 1st, $20—when entries must be named—$10 additional to start. See general conditions.

RACE NO. 10—RUNNING.

Citizens' Handicap. $100 added. Five-eighths mile; heats, 2 in 3. Entrance $10, to close 6 P. M. day before race.

Fifth Day—Saturday, September 27th.

RACE NO. 11—RUNNING.

GENTLEMEN'S NOVELTY.—For non-professional jockeys. One mile dash. $10 added; $5 entrance; purse divided as follows: First horse at each quarter to get $25; slowest average at all quarters to get society medal.

NO. 12.—LADIES' TOURNAMENT

Free for all in District. Purse $50, divided as follows: $25 to first, $15 to second, $10 to third.

No. 13.—GENTLEMAN'S TROTTING.

Same conditions as gentlemen's Novelty. Mile heats, two in three. Entrance $5. Entrance money divided 60, 30 and 10 per cent.

GENERAL CONDITIONS.

Nominations in colt stakes transferrable any time before colts are named. If the payments in stakes exceed amount to more than the sum guaranteed the additional amount to be divided 60, 30 and 10 per cent; in case of only two starting, 60 and 40 per cent.; and in case of one horse walking over, the whole amount to go to such horse.

A failure to make any payment when due shall be considered a withdrawal, and forfeiture of the amounts paid in. National Rules to govern all trotting races. The right reserved to refund the first payment in case the stake does not fill satisfactorily.

All running races, unless otherwise specified, governed by the Pacific Coast Blood Horse Association rules.

The Directors reserve the right to change the hour and date of any race, and in case of a race being antedated the nominator will receive notice.

A horse distancing the field shall receive only first and third moneys.

L. G. SIMMONS, President.

L. B. McCUTCHEN, Secretary.

San Joaquin Valley

AGRICULTURAL ASSOCIATION.

Stockton Fair, 1890,

September 23 to 27 inclusive.

TROTTING COLT STAKES.

$50 each, of which $10 must accompany nomination, $15 to be paid July 1st, and $25 on Monday, September 1, 1890.

Failure to make payments as above forfeits previous payments.

PACIFIC COAST STAKES.

For 2-year-olds..........2 in 3 ⎫ $200
" " ....3 in 5 ⎬ added to
" " ....3 in 5 ⎪ each.
" " ....Pacing 2 in 3 ⎭

SAN JOAQUIN VALLEY STAKES.

Open to all San Joaquin Valley counties for colts foaled in the valley, February 1, 1890.

For 2-year-olds..........2 in 3 ⎫ $150
" " ....3 in 5 ⎬ added to
" " ....3 in 5 ⎪ each.
" " ....Pacing 2 in 3 ⎭

Five or more full paid up entries required to fill; three or more colts to start. Four moneys: 50, 25, 15 and 10 per cent. In case of only two colts starting, they may compete for the stakes paid in only, two-thirds and one-third, otherwise full conditions of Association for 1889, to govern.

Entries close Thursday, May 1, 1890, with the Secretary.

J. M. LaRUE, P. O. box 188,

U. SHIPPEE, President. Stockton, Cal.

Pacific Coast

Trotting-Horse

Breeders' Ass'n,

ADDITIONAL

Stakes & Installment Purses

FOR 1890.

Entries to close May 1, 1890.

Trotting Stakes.

THREE YEAR OLDS—FOALS OF 1887.

Eligible to 2:40 class. Mile heats, best three in five. Entrance $50, with $300 added. Entrance payable, $10 May 1st, 1890, $15 July 1st, 1890, and $25 on the fifth day preceding the first advertised day of the meeting.

FOUR YEAR OLDS—FOALS 1886.

Eligible to 2:30 class. Mile heats, best three in five. Entrance $50, with $400 added. Entrance payable, $10 on May 1st, 1890, $15 on July 1st, 1890 and $25 on the fifth day preceding the first advertised day of the meeting.

Nomination Trotting Purses.

$2,000. Stallion Purse.

Open to stallions eligible to the 2:18 Class. Mile heats best three in five. Entrance $200 payable $40 May 1st, 1890, $40 July 1st, 1890, $40 August 1st 1890, and $80 on the tenth day preceding the first advertised day of the meeting. Horses to be named at time of last payment.

$2,000, Free For All.

Mile heats, best three in five. Entrance $200, payable $40 May 1st 1890, $40 July 1st 1890, $40 August 1st 1890, and $80 on the tenth day preceding the first advertised day of the meeting. Horses to be named at time of last payment.

$1,500. Five-Year-Olds, Foals 1885.

Mile heats best three in five. Entrance $150, payable $30 May 1, 1890, $30 July 1, 1890, $30 August 1, 1890, and $60 on the tenth day preceding the first advertised day of the meeting. Horses to be named at the time of the last payment.

$1,500. 2:32 Class.

Mile heats, best three in five. Entrance $150. Payable $30 May 1, 1890, $30 July 1, 1890, $30 August 1, 1890, and $60 on the tenth day preceding the first advertised day of the meeting. Horses to be named at the time of the last payment.

$1,500. 2:27 Class.

Mile heats, best three in five. Entrance $150. Payable $30 May 1, 1890, $30 July 1, 1890, $30 August 1, 1890, and $60 on the tenth day preceding the first advertised day of the meeting. Horses to be named at time of last payment.

Nomination Pacing Purses.

$1,500. Free For All.

Mile heats, best three in five. Entrance $150. Payable $30 May 1, 1890, $30 July 1, 1890, $30 August 1, 1890, and $60 on the tenth day preceding the first advertised day of the meeting. Horses to be named at time of last payment.

$1,000. 2:25 Class.

Mile heats, best three in five. Entrance $100. Payable $20 May 1, 1890, $20 July 1, 1890, $20 August 1, 1890, and $40 on the tenth day preceding the first advertised day of the meeting. Horses to be named at time of last payment.

Conditions.

First payment, whether for purses payable in installments or for stakes, MUST ACCOMPANY NOMINATIONS, or they will not be considered.

Neglect to make payments on the dates stipulated will incur forfeiture of all previous payments.

No horses and colts owned on the Pacific Coast by others than members of the P. C. T. H. B. A. are eligible to the above purses and stakes, but horses and colts OWNED outside of the Pacific Coast are eligible thereto regardless of membership.

All States and Territories lying in whole or in part west of the Rocky Mountains are held to be part of the Pacific Coast.

The Directors reserve the right to change the hour and day of any race except when it becomes necessary to ante-date a race, in which instance the nominator will receive three days notice of change by mail to address of entry.

Entries not declared out by 6 P. M. of the day preceding the race, shall be required to start.

When there is more than one entry to stakes by one person or in one interest, the horse to be started must be named by 6 P. M. of the day preceding the race.

Purses and stakes will be divided into four moneys, viz., 50 per cent. to the winner, 25 per cent. to the second horse, 15 per cent. to the third horse, and 10 per cent. to the fourth horse.

No added money will be paid for a walk-over. If only three horses start in a stake race, only first, second and third money shall be paid—if but two start, the Directors reserve the right to call it a walk-over, and divide the stake money paid in, two-thirds to the winner and one-third to the second horse. In case of a walk-over, only the money received from entries to said stake will be paid.

A horse distancing the field shall only be entitled to first and third moneys.

The Board of Directors reserve the right to declare any purse or stake filled or not filled without binding itself to any specified number of entries.

In all nomination purses, eight entries will be required to fill, and four to make the last payment.

Trotting and racing colors shall be named by six o'clock on the day preceding the race, and MUST be worn upon the track.

Horses eligible in class races on records standing at time of entry.

Otherwise than the above National or American Trotting Association Rules—as this Association may select—will govern the stake and purse races offered.

Persons desirous of making entries in the above purses and stakes, and who have not as yet joined the P. C. T. H. B. A., should make application for membership to the Secretary, and remit the sum of $25 to cover membership fee before May 1, 1890.

J. H. WHITE, President.

JAS. P. KERR, Secretary,
12 Bush Street, S. F.

ENTIRE CHANGE

—OF—

PROGRAMME

—OF THE—

Extra Attractions

To take place at the

Oakland.

Fall Meeting, 1890,

UNDER THE MANAGEMENT OF THE

GOLDEN GATE

Fair Association

NOMINATION PURSES.

In which entries close in the name of owners or trainers on May 15th. All nominations transferable and nominators held only for amounts paid in. Horses must be named five days before first advertised day of the meeting. Eight nominations required to fill, four of which must make last payments.

THE NEW LIST PURSE $1000.

For three-year-olds whose sires up to January 1, 1890, have not produced an animal with a record of 2:30 or better at three years of age or under. Entrance 10 per cent. payable as follows:

$25 May 15th, when entries close in the names of owners or trainers.
$25 June 15th.
$25 July 15th.
$25 five days before first advertised day of meeting, when horses must be named.

GUARANTEED PURSE $1200.

For three-minute class, entrance 10 per cent, payable as follows:

$30 May 15th, when entries close in names of owners or trainers.
$30 June 15th.
$30 July 15th.
$30 five days before first advertised day of meeting, when horse must be named.

GUARANTEED PURSE $1200.

For 2:40 class, entrance 10 per cent, payable as follows:

$30 May 15th, when entries close in names of owners or trainers.
$30 June 15th.
$30 July 15th.
$30 five days before first advertised day of meeting, when horses must be named.

—ALSO A—

Guaranteed Futurity Purse $4,000.

To take place during the Fall Meeting of 1893.

For foals of 1890. Entrance 2 per cent. payable as follows:

$10 May 15, 1890, when entries close in name of foals or of dams and sires.

$10 Jan. 15, 1891.
$15 June 15, 1891.
$15 Jan. 15, 1892.
$15 June 15, 1892.
$15 Jan. 15, 1893.
$20 June 15, 1893.

$20 fifteen days before advertised day of the race.

If the last payment is made on twelve or more entries the horses shall be started in trial races, in which not more than eleven or less than six shall be allotted to start. The trial races shall be mile heats, three in five, for a purse of $1,000, given by the Association for each race. If two trial races are trotted, the first four horses shall only be entitled to start in the final race. If three such trial races are trotted, only the first three horses in each trial race shall start in the final; and if four or more trial races are necessary, only the first two horses in each trial race shall start in the final race.

These trial races must be started not less than five nor more than ten days previous to the day set for the final race; and if possible all trial races will be trotted on the same day.

CONDITIONS.

Neglect to provide payments on the dates stipulated will incur forfeiture of all previous payments.

The Directors reserve the right to change the hour and day of any race except when it becomes necessary to ante-date a race, in which instance the nominator will receive three days notice of change by mail to address of entry.

Entries not declared out by 6 P. M. the day preceding the race, shall be required to start.

Purses will be divided into four moneys viz., 50 per cent. to the winner, 25 per cent. to the second horse, 15 per cent. to the third horse, and 10 per cent. to the fourth horse.

A horse distancing the field shall only be entitled to first and third moneys.

Trotting and racing colors shall be named by six o'clock on the day preceding the race, and MUST be worn upon the track.

All purse races, mile heats, best three in five to harness.

Otherwise than the above, National or American Trotting Association Rules—as this Association may select—will govern the races offered.

Entries to close with the Secretary.

R. T. CARROLL, President.

JOS. I. DIMOND, Sec'y, 306 Market St., S. F.

HORSES PURCHASED ON COMMISSION.

THOROUGHBREDS A SPECIALTY.

Will select and buy, or buy selected Animals for all desiring, for reasonable compensation

KEEPS PROMISING YOUNGSTERS IN VIEW.

L. M. LASLEY, Stanford, Ky.

References:—J. W. Guest, Danville, Ky.
B. G. Bruce, Lexington Ky.
S. H. Baughman, Stanford, Ky.
G. A. Lackey, Stanford, Ky.
Geo. McAlister, Stanford, Ky.
First National Bank, Stanford, Ky.

UTAH

Driving Park

ASSOCIATION,

1890.

JUNE 16 to 20, Inclusive

—AT—

SALT LAKE CITY.

Purses - $7,000

TROTTING, RUNNING & PACING,

Entries for all Races to close May 30, 1890.

This meeting is arranged to accommodate horsemen on way to the Great Racing Circuit of Montana, their purses aggregating $45,000. The meeting at Denver closes June 7th, and our meeting begins June 16th and closes June 20th inclusive, and the Montana meetings commence July 14th, thus giving ample time to rest up here. We expect to give a genuine first-class meeting, and will see that all horsemen have a "square deal." Our city is at present enjoying an era of prosperity never before seen, which justifies our hope for the best meeting ever given in Utah. A cordial invitation is extended to all horsemen to come. The Great Salt Lake bathing season is then on, thus affording all visitors a rare treat and pleasant time.

PROGRAMME

—OF—

Utah Driving Park Spring Race Meeting,

Salt Lake City, Utah.

Spring Racing and Trotting Meeting for Five Days, from June 16 to June 20, inclusive.

PURSES, $7000.

FIRST DAY—MONDAY, JUNE 16.

No. 1—Trotting, 2:27 class..........$500
No. 2—Pacing, 2:35 class..........400
No. 3—Running, ¾ mile heats, all ages..........300
No. 4—Running, ½ mile heats, all ages..........300

SECOND DAY—TUESDAY, JUNE 17.

No. 5—Pacing, 2:24 class..........$500
No. 6—Trotting, 2:50 class..........4 0
No. 7—Running, ¾ mile dash, three-year-olds..........300
No. 8—Running, ¾ mile heats, all ages..........300

THIRD DAY—WEDNESDAY, JUNE 18.

No. 9—Trotting, 2:26 class..........$500
No. 10—Trotting, three-year-olds (added money) for Colorado, Wyoming, Montana, and Utah horses..........200
No. 11—Running, ½ mile heats, all ages..........300

FOURTH DAY—THURSDAY, JUNE 19.

No. 12—Pacing, free for all pacers..........$600
No. 13—Trotting, 2:34 class..........400
No. 14—Running, 1¼ mile dash, all ages..........300

FIFTH DAY—FRIDAY, JUNE 20.

No. 15—Trotting, free for all..........$600
No. 16—Trotting, 2:30 class..........450
No. 17—Running, ½ mile heats, for horses that have run and not won a race this meeting..........250
No. 18—Running, 1 mile heats, all ages..........300

F. H. DYER, Secretary.

J. K. GILLESPIE, Manager. Salt Lake City.

Second Annual Bench Show

OF THE

South'n California Kennel Club

AT THE

City of Los Angeles,

MAY 6, 7, 8 & 9 '90.

The SOUTHERN CALIFORNIA KENNEL CLUB was admitted a member of the AMERICAN KENNEL CLUB September 18, 1889. The coming show will therefore be held under the A. K. C. rules.

Entries will positively close May 1st.

A special committee will take personal charge of all dogs sent from a distance and insure their proper care. For premium lists and entry blanks address E. K. BENCHLEY, Secretary, 14 South Spring Street, Los Angeles; or H. H. BRIGGS, Breeder and Sportsman, San Francisco.

JESSE E. MARKS. IKE DEUTCH

Yosemite Billiard Parlors,

ST. ANN'S BUILDING,

No. 8 Eddy Street, S. F.

The Poodle Dog

"Rotisserie,"

FIRST-CLASS IN EVERY RESPECT.

Elegant Family Dining Rooms.

S. E. cor. GRANT AVE. and BUSH STREET.

ANDRE POTENTINI, Proprietor.

Old Hermitage Whiskies

"STEINER'S,"

No. 311 BUSH STREET,

San Francisco.

Under Breeder and Sportsman Office.

SAN DIEGO, 8776.

SAN DIEGO is dark seal brown, three years old, and trotted one-quarter miles in 40 seconds as a two-year old.

This grand young horse, and, barring accidents, will make a fast record next fall.

He will be allowed a limited number of mares, at $50 for the season. Mares not proving in foal to be returned free 1891. Best of pasture for mares at $4 per month, but no liability for accidents or escapes.

He will make the season from February 1st to June 1st at Napa Fair Grounds. For further particulars, address or call on

H. B. STARR, Race Track, Napa, Cal.,

or FRED W. LOEBER, St. Helena

1890 Three Anteeo Stallions 1890

SUNSET, 5 years old, by Anteeo
ANTEEOF, 4 years old, by Anteeo
ANTEEOP, 3 years old, by Anteeo

ANTEEO. Standard 7868. Record, 2:16 1-4. He by Stanford's Electioneer, and dam Columbine.

DESCRIPTIONS, PEDIGREES AND CONDITIONS.

"SUNSET" is a rich, dark bay, small star on forehead, portion of hind left foot white; was foaled March 11, 1885, is by ANTEEO and the inbred HAMBLETONIAN mare, BESSIE G., she by KING PHILLIP, son of WHIPPLE'S HAMBLETONIAN. He is 16 1 2 hands high, and weighs 1,300 lbs. He is of perfect build and splendid action cool headed and great speed for his size, having trotted a trial mile as a three-year-old in 2:38. He then entered heavy in the stud and was matched against Whalebone at the Healdsburg races November 1, 1888, winning just as he pleased in three straight heats; time, 2:47, 2:46 1-2, 2:52 1-2. He was then matched for a race to come off last Thanksgiving Day at Petaluma but owing to the heavy rains the event did not take place. A few days previous to Thanksgiving Day Mr. Lawrence worked Sunset out and then he trotted three square miles and heats in 2:33½, 2:34 and 2:37.

SUNSET will be bred to 40 mares only, at $50 each, no colt no pay.

"ANTEEOF" is a jet black, was foaled April 15, 1886, is 16¼ hands high, and weighs 1,200 lbs., has a very fine, heavy black mane and tail; is well proportioned, moves majestically, is of easy, lofty carriage; is symmetrical, in fact is a beautiful horse. He was sired by Anteeo and the O. A. Taylor mare "Nance," her dam, was raised by Dr. Oliver Plummer, of Cosumnes, Cal., and sired by "Napoleon"; Napoleon was foaled May 29, 1853, and raised by James Kyle of Butler County, Ohio. He was sired by Benj. Sweet's horse Bellfounder, and he by Old Bellfounder, his dam was sired by Doc. Daniel Mulligan's horse, Cadmus, G. G. sire the celebrated Eclipse; his G. dam was sired by Big Shakespeare, G. G. sire dam by Messenger and Expedition.
ANTEEOF will be bred to 25 mares only, at $50 each. No colt, no pay.

"ANTEEOP" is a rich seal brown; was foaled March 7, 1887; by Anteeo and the inbred Hambletonian mare Bessie G., also dam of Sunset, his full brother and Midget his full sister; he is 15 1-2 hands high and weighs 950 lbs, and measures 21 inches around the arm, good head, fine neck, full, broad breast; withers and rump on nearly equal line, well proportioned bones, ankle, shoulders, loins and hips; strong legs all around, with great muscular development and splendid sinews; wirey pasterns and sound, compact feet; the lines from hip to hock show power and speed; stands square and has excellent action, has a superb lustrous coat of rich deep brown fur of seal color without defect; an even, honest trotter, and has gone the mile as a two-year-old in 3:43, the last quarter in 38 seconds; is intelligent and of high spirit, with much temper, but is not vicious, has very fine eyes, is a handsome, showy colt; attractive in harness.
ANTEEOP will be bred to 15 mares only, at $50. No colt, no pay.
SEASON to commence February 1st, ending July 1, 1890. Book now ready. Apply to John H. Lawrence, "Manager and Trainer," on my fruit and hop ranch, 1 mile east of Court House, on Sonoma road. Excellent pasture furnished with running water, also dry knolls with oak shelter, at $3 per month for mares. Two of the above stallions will be for sale after the expiration of the their stud season.

GUY E. GROSSE,

SANTA ROSA, SONOMA CO., CAL.

The Trotting Stallion

Guide 2:29

(At Four Years)

Will make the season of 1890 at the SANTA RITA RANCH, about one mile North of Pleasanton.

DESCRIPTION.

GUIDE is a handsome seal brown, five years old, stands 15¾ hands high, and weighs 1035 pounds. He is of fine form, level headed, intelligent, and comes from blood lines that are noted for the qualities of speed and gameness.

PEDIGREE.

GUIDE, 2:28½
Director, 2:17. Sire of Direct, 2:18¾, Margaret S., 2:19¾.
Dictator 113. Sire of 23 trotters and 3 pacers in 2:30. — Hambletonian 10. / Clara, by American Star 14.
Dolly. Dam of Onward, 2:25¼, Thorndale, 2:22¾. — Mambrino Chief 11. / Fannie, by Ben Franklin.
Imogene.
Norwood 522. Sire of Tommy Norwood, 2:28¼. — Hambletonian 10. / Lady Fallis, by American Star 14.
daughter of — American Star 14. / daughter of Harry Clay 45.

The attention of breeders is especially called to the above pedigree as showing 3 crosses of American Star.
GUIDE trotted into the 2:30 list last season with little training, and he will trot into the 2:20 list the coming season barring accidents.
Guide's sire has a record of 2:17, made in a five heat race, and Guide is closely related to Phallas, who made a record of 2:13¾ in a fourth heat, and to Jay-Eye-See, record 2:10.
TWO HUNDRED AND FIFTY DOLLARS will be given to the owner of the first of the produce of Guide put in the 2:30 list, and $100 to each one after the first.
TERMS—$75 for the season, with the usual return privileges.

Admiro,

Sire Admiral; dam by San Bruno, by Easton's David Hill.

This magnificent horse is a handsome bay, eight years old; stands 17 1-2 hands high, and weighs 1400 pounds He is very speedy for a large horse, and breeds fine large carriage horses. His produce possess every qualification of the Cleveland Bay, with the added qualities of speed and endurance resulting from his high trotting breeding.
TERMS—$35 for the season, with usual return privileges.
Will stand three days each week at Santa Rita Ranch, Pleasanton, and at A. T. Hatch's Ranch "Almono," Alamo, Contra Costa County, alternately. All mares sent care of SMITH & SUTHERLAND, Pleasanton, will be taken in charge of on arrival, and will receive the best care and attention in any manner the owners may desire. Good pasturage at $4 per month. Only a limited number of approved mares will be served by this horse this season.
No responsibility assumed for escapes or accidents. For further particulars, address

SMITH & SUTHERLAND, Pleasanton,

or A. T. HATCH, care Palace Hotel, San Francisco.

Guenoc Stud Farm, Lake Co., Cal

Imp. GREENBACK

(Sire of the English winners Greenlight, Greenjacket, Greenshank, Greenwave and Greenhorn)

By Dollar, dam Music, by Stockwell. $100 the Season

ST. SAVIOR,

(FULL BROTHER TO EOLE)

By Eolus, dam War Song, by War Dance. $100 the Season

PASTURAGE, $5 PER MONTH.

with right to return the following year if mare does not prove with foal. The best of care taken, but no liability for accidents or escapes. Mares shipped to C. W. ABY, care ST. HELENA STABLES, St. Helena, Napa County, will be taken in charge by competent men.
For further information write to

DR. C. W. ABY, Middletown, Lake County, Cal.

LAWN VIEW BREEDING FARM STALLIONS.

ACTOR.

A beautiful bay horse foaled 1887 by Promotor 2804 sire of Apex (four-year-old record) 2:26, Transit 2:28¾, Creole 2:20, Blue Belle 2:32, Daisy (yearling record) 2:38¾, he by Blue Bull 75, 1st dam by Sultan 1513 2:24, sire of Stamboul 2:12 1-4, Ruby 2:19¾, Sweetheart 2:22¾, Alcazar 2:20¾, Eva 2:23¾, La Grange 2:25¾, and eleven others in 2:30 list, second dam by Fireman by Langford.
Actor, as his pedigree shows, is as purely bred a young stallion as ever made a season in the stud. Blue Bull stock is much sought after in the East, and Sultan, sire of his first dam will make the season in Kentucky this year at $100 per mare. Actor is a handsome bay colt 16 hands high, clean limbed and possesses all the points of a speedy trotter.
TERMS, $40 FOR THE SEASON, usual return privileges.

DOUGLASDALE 7650.

Thoroughbred Registered Clydesdale Stallion

Imported from Scotland, December, 1889, bay, three years old.

TERMS, $50 FOR THE SEASON.

YOUNG ELMO

Two years old sorrel stallion by St. Elmo 2:27, dam by Woodburn.

TERMS, $30 FOR THE SEASON.

For further particulars, address
MANAGER LAWN VIEW FARM, Auburn, Cal.

Sunny Side Breeding Farm.

Admiral 488.

Foaled 1867—Sired by Volunteer 55, Son of Rysdyk's Hambletonian 10.

First dam Lady Pierson by Cassius M. Clay (Neave's) 20; second dam by Diamond; third dam a running mare said to be thoroughbred. He is fitted in an eminent degree to produce colts that will in all respects justify his patrons in their expectations.
Admiral is the sire of Huntress, record 2:27¼, Sister, 2:19¼, Perhelion, 2:25, Nona Y., 2:25, and others equally as promising, but have not had the advantage of track work. He will serve a limited number of approved mares at $50 the season, with usual return privilege. Season ending August 1, 1890. No liability for accidents or escapes.

KING DAVID 2576.

Bay Stallion—Foaled 1883.

Sired by Admiral 488, dam Black Flora (the dam of Huntress, 2:27¼, Sister, 2:19¼, Perhelion, 2:25, Nona Y., 2:25), by Black Prince.
King David is one of the best gets of Admiral. He has a good disposition, kind to drive, smooth and even-gaited, and can speed fast. Barring accidents, he will trot in the twenties this Fall. His colts are large, rangy, and well finished. Will serve a limited number of mares at $30 the season, to end July 1, 1890. Every precaution will be taken to prevent accidents and escapes, but no liability will be assumed. Pasturage $4 per month.
Sunny Side Farm is situated two miles east of Vallejo, on the Sulphur Spring road. For further particulars, address

FRANK DRAKE,
Vallejo, Cal.

The Trotting-Bred Stallion

RINGWOOD

THE FINEST SON OF THE NOTED SIDNEY,

Will make a Season at Oakland, commencing March 1, and ending June 1, 1890.

DESCRIPTION.

RINGWOOD is a dark, rich colored bay, black points, 15 1-2 hands, weight 1100 lbs., and a pure gaited trotter. Has shown great speed. He is now five years old. As a four year old he showed a trial in 2:19 1-2, and but for an accident would have received a record as a four year old of 2:18 or better.

PEDIGREE.

RINGWOOD is by Sidney, record 2:19 3-4, and is half brother to Gold Leaf 2:11 1-4, Adonis 2:14, Flee (two year old) 2:21, Longworth 2:19, Sister V. 2:27, Faustino, yearling, 2:35, Fleet, yearling, 2:35 Memo, three year old trial 2:23 1 2.
Sidney is by Santa Claus, record 2:17 1-2; he by Strathmore, sire of 34 in 2:30 list; he by Hambletonian 10, the greatest of all producers; he by Abdallah. Sidney's dam, Sweetness, record 2:21 1-4; she by Volunteer, the sire of St. Julien 2:11 1 4.
RINGWOOD'S dam Alma; she by Dashway, thoroughbred; he by Belmont, he by American Boy; he by Sea Gull; he by imported Expedition. Alma's 1st d m, Fanny Cobb, was a great road mare, pedigree untraced.

TERMS: $50 for the Season.

Payable June 1st, or sooner if mares are taken away Address communications to

A. C. DIETZ,
Oakland, Cal.

Vineland Stock Farm

Alcona 730.

Sire of

FLORA BELLE - - - - Record 2:24
CLAY DUKE - - - - - " 2:31

ALCONA will be a great sire, but four of his colts have ever been trained, and all have shown full mile better than 2:30, and two of them as good as 2:20. Two of his first sons each sired a colt as a two-year-old and last season one as a four-year-old trotted a full mile in 2:23¼, and the other, a three-year-old, a mile in 2:31. With opportunities, Alcona is destined to be one of Almont's best sons. Almont, for his opportunities, is beyond doubt the most prepotent sire of his age. He has 36 representatives in the 2:30 list; 49 sons and 22 daughters that have already produced 2:30 performers. Almont died five years ago at 20 years old. If he lived he would be but 25 years old.

PEDIGREE.

ALCONA sired by the great Almont (sire of Westmont 2:13¾, Fanny Witherspoon 2:16¾, Piedmont 2:17¼, and 31 others with records better than 2:30, and grandsire of Belle Hamlin 2:13¾, etc.); by Alexander's Abdallah (sire of Goldsmith Maid 2:14), he by Rysdyk's Hambletonian. Alcona's dam, Queen Mary by Mambrino Chief (sire of Lady Thorne 2:18 1-4, and 5 others in the 2:30 list, and sire of the dams of Director 2:17, Piedmont 2:17¼, Onward 2:25 1-4, Red Wilkes, Almont, Belmont and many other noted sires).

DESCRIPTION.

Alcona is a beautiful chestnut 16 3 1-2 hands high, and weighs 1300 lbs. His colts possess speed, style, finish and beauty, and if they don't trot they command the highest prices for carriage horses.
$40 for the season. Usual return privilege.
Season of Alcona and Grandissimo ends July 1st, 1890.

Grandissimo,

(Full Brother to GRANDEE, 3-year old record 2:23 1-2.

Sired by La Grande (son of Almont, and out of Jessie Pepper by Mambrino Chief; Jessie Pepper is the dam of Ione 2:17 1-2, Alpha 2:23 1-2, Sterling Wilkes 2:31¾, and others) dam Norma, by Arthurton (sire of Arab 2:15, Joe Arthurton 2:20 1-2, etc.)
Grandam Nourmahal, (full sister to A. W. Richmond, sire of Arrow 2:13¾, Romero 2:19, and sire of Columbine, dam of Anteeo 2:16¼, and Antevolo 2:19½ at four years old).

DESCRIPTION.

Grandissimo is four years old, will make a sixteen hand horse; he is a rich mahogany bay in color and perfect in style and action. $30 for the season. Usual return privileges.
"Grandissimo" with limited training last fall as three-year-old, trotted quarters in 36 seconds and miles in 2:40.
I feel confident that he will trot fast this season and will be a great sire as his colts this season are all grand youngsters.
The best of pasturage $4 per month. Mares taken care of in any manner that owners may desire, but no responsibility assumed for escapes or accidents.
For further particulars send for circular or call at stables, one mile south of St. Helena.

FRED W. LOEBER Prop'r.

Bay Rose

REGISTERED No. 9814.

Record 2:20 1-2 Third Heat.

Will make the season of 1890, ending July 1st, at the SANTA ROSA STOCK FARM, (formerly the Santa Rosa Race Track), SANTA ROSA.

DESCRIPTION.

BAY ROSE is a dark bay or brown, with black points, 16¼ hands high, and weighs 1150 pounds. He is remarkably intelligent, of good disposition, and a pure-gaited trotter. He was foaled in 1881. His colts are large, stylish, rangy animals, and inherit the qualities of speed and endurance.

PEDIGREE.

BAY ROSE 9814
Sultan, 2:24. Sire of 19 in the 2:30 list.
The Moor 870. Sire of Beautiful Bells, Del Sur, Inez, Sir Guy, Sultan, Tommy Gates.
Sultana.
Madam Baldwin.
The Moor 870. Sire of 6 in the 2:30 list.
by Ben Lippincott, by Williamson's Belmont.

TERMS: $200 FOR THE SEASON.

Good pasturage $3 per month. First-class care taken of mares in any manner that owners may desire, but no responsibility assumed for escapes or accidents. Limited to a few approved mares.
For further particulars, address

THOS. BONNER,
Santa Rosa Stock Farm, Santa Rosa

Or apply to
IRA PIERCE.
728 Montgomery Street, S. F., Cal.

SUBSCRIBE FOR THE

Breeder and Sportsman

The Thoroughbred Stallion

Three Cheers

Will make the season of 1890 at

Sacramento.

PEDIGREE.

THREE CHEERS
- imp. Hurrah
  - Newminster
    - Touchstone, by Camel
    - Beeswing, by Dr. Syntax
  - Jovial
    - Bay Middleton, by Sultan
    - Sister to Grey Momus, by Comus
- Young Fashion
  - imp. Monarch
    - imp. Priam, by Emilius
    - imp. Delphine, by Whisker
  - Fashion
    - imp. Trustee, by Catton
    - Bonnets o' Blue, by Sir Charles

Hurrah was imported by John Reber, of Lancaster, Ohio, a locality where there were but few breeders of thoroughbreds. Under these disadvantages he sired a long list of winners. His sire Newminster, won the St. Ledger 1851, and his dam, Jovial by Bay Middleton, winner of the Derby 1836. Newminister by Touchstone, winner St. Ledger 1834. Dam Beeswing, winner of 54 races out of 64 starts, by Dr Syntax, winner of the Doncaster Cup, 1837—40—41—42, the only horse that ever accomplished that feat.

On the side of the dam Three Cheers is equally well related. Young Fashion was the dam of Surprise, Scotland (the only horse that ever beat Asteroid a heat), Liverpool, Columbia, and Bonnie Kate, the dam of Little Buttercup, and the flying Bonnie Lizzie. His grandam, Fashion was the greatest race mare of her day and beat Boston in that historical match at four mile heats, which is recorded as one of the greatest events in the annals of the turf.

Horsemen who are qualified to judge, pronounce Three Cheers to be the finest type of the Newminster line in America.

LOCATION.

THREE CHEERS will be located at the Arcade Training Stable, Rancho del Paso. This place has been selected for the reason that first class pasturage has been secured there for the exclusive use of these mares and the other facilities to be obtained there for the care of mares (especially mares in foal) are better than can be found elsewhere in the locality.

TERMS.

$60 for the season with the usual return privileges. Pasturage $6 per month. Mares cared for as owners may desire at bottom rates for grain and hay. All bills payable before the mare is removed.

Mares shipped care of WM. IRVINE, Pacific Stables, Sacramento, will be properly cared for and sent to the ranch without delay.

Three Cheers will be in charge of one of the most experienced and competent s ud grooms in the State, who will exercise every care, but no reponsibility assumed for accidents or escapes.

For further particulars apply to Louis Crissler, at the rance; Wm. Irvine, Pacific Stables, Second St., Sacramento; or to the owner,

E. S. CULVER,
313 Bush St., San Francisco.

Elector 2170.

Sire of J. R.

Three-Year Old Record 2:24.

Sired by Electioneer 125, sire of Sunol, three-year-old, 2:10½, Palo Alto, 2:12¼, etc.; dam Gilberta by Fred Low 656, sire of Clay, 2:25½, etc.

Second dam Lady Gilbert (grandam of Lot Slocum, 2:17½) by General Knox 140 (sire of Lady Maud, 2:18¼, and many others).

TERMS.

$150 for the season. Book full for 1890.

L. A. RICHARDS,
Grayson, Stanislaus Co., Cal.

GEO. WASHINGTON.

11,623.

RECORD 2:30.

Bay colt, bred by Thomas Smith of Vallejo, Cal. Foaled 1883 by Mambrino Chief, Jr., 11,622, record 2:34 1-4, 1st dam Fanny Rose by Vick's Ethan Allen Jr. 2,903, sire of Prince Allen 2:27, 2nd dam Jenny Lind, thoroughbred, dam of Prince Allen 2:27. Will serve a limited number of mares at $50 for the season. Mares not proving with foal may be returned next season free.

Mambrino Chief, Jr.

11,622.

RECORD 2:34 1 2.

Sire of George Washington, record 2 30 at three years old. Bay horse bred by Rufus Ingalls of Belvedere, Ill. By McDonald Chief 3783. First dam Venus by Mambrino Patchen 58, 2nd dam by Wardlow's Shakespeare, 3rd dam Lone Gold, 4th dam by Silver Heels. Has not been in the stud before. He was 5 years old when he served a few mares, and his colts all show good style and form.

Terms for the season $40. For further particulars see or address

THOMAS SMITH,
Vallejo, Cal.

GROVER CLAY

Bay Stallion, Black Points,
15 3-4 hands high.

Bred by W. W. Traylor, San Francisco.

BY ELECTIONEER.

First dam Maggie Norfolk by Norfolk, son of Lexington, he by Boston. Second dam Tilda Quill by Billy Cheatham he by Cracken, and he by Boston. Third dam by Dorsey's Golddust.

TERMS.

Will make the season of 1890 at the Training Stables of Denis Gannon, near Oakland Trotting Park, at $50 the season, payable at time of service. Season to commence February 1st and ending July 1st. Proper care of mares will be taken, but no responsibility incurred for accidents or escapes. Address,

DENIS GANNON, Oakland, Cal.

2:10¾ 2:13¼ 2:10

DEXTER PRINCE.

This Royally-bred Stallion will make the Season of 1890 at the LIVE OAKS Breeding Farm, 2 miles from Lodi, San Joaquin County, Cal.

DESCRIPTION.

DEXTER PRINCE is a blood bay, 16 hands high, weighs over 1 100 pounds; has great power and substance, and the highest finish. When two years old, at Palo Alto, he was timed quarters by Gov. Stanford in 37¼ seconds, and he was driven eighths by Mr. Marvin at a faster rate of speed than that. He is a sure foal-getter, and invariably sires foals of good size, of fine form and finish, and the highest rate of speed.

PEDIGREE.

By KENTUCKY PRINCE, the sire of Guy, 2:10¾, Spofford, 2:18¾, Company, 2:19¾, Bayonne Prince, 2:21 1-4, Fred Folger, 2:20¾, and a score more in the 2:30 list.

First dam LADY DEXTER, full sister of the greatest of trotters, Dexter, and the greatest of sires, Dictator, the sire of Director, 2:17, Phallas, 2:13¾, in a fourth heat, and Jay-Eye-See, 2:10.

Second dam Clara, the dam of Dexter, 2:17 1-4, Dictator, Astoria, 2:29 1-4, and Almah, 2:29¾. Clara was by American Star, that has 24 daughters that have produced 2:30 or better trotters.

Third dam the McKinstry mare, the dam of Shark, 2:27¾. HAMBLETONIAN, the grandsire of DEXTER PRINCE, has 40 trotters in the 2:30 list, 44 daughters that have produced 2:30 trotters, and more than 100 sons that have sired 2 30 trotters.

CLARK CHIEF, the grandsire on the sire's side, was the sire of performing and producing sons and daughters.

DEXTER PRINCE has faster blood lines, on both sides, than any other stallion in the world—Guy 2:10¾, and Jay-Eye-See, 2:10.

KENTUCKY PRINCE is one of the best bred and speediest stallions in the world. David Bonner, in the presence of Governor Stanford, timed him when he trotted a 2:10 gait. He is by Clark Chief, one of the great broodmare sires; his first dam is Kentucky Queen by Morgan Eagle, son of Hale's Green Mountain Morgan, 2nd dam by Blythe's Whip, 3rd dam by Martin's Brummier, 4th dam by Quicksilver 880, on through the strongest thoroughbred blood.

TERMS.

$100 for the season, with usual return privileges. Payable before mares are removed. Good pasture, and the best care furnished, but no responsibility assumed for accidents.

PREMIUM.

$250 will be given to the first of the produce of DEXTER PRINCE put in the 2:30 list, and $100 each after the first. Address

L M. MORSE, Lodi, Cal.

2:10 1-2 ELECTIONEER 2:12 1-4

BAY STALLION	BROWN STALLION
ECLECTIC	**MORTIMER**
11,321	5,346
By Electioneer, dam Manette (full sister to Woodnut 2.16 1-2 Manon 2:21 and Maple, dam of Hattie D., three year-old record 2:26¾) by Nutwood 2:18¾, etc., etc.	Four-year-old Record 2:27. By ELECTIONEER, dam MARTI, by Whipple's Hambletonian (sire of 15 in 2:30, and of dams of eight in 2:30). Second dam Ida Martin by Rifleman (sire of Col. Lewis 2:18¾).
Terms $100 for the Season.	**Terms $60 for the Season.**

Horses shipped via San Francisco may be consigned to J. W. MORSHEAD, City Front Stables, who will attend to their forwarding.

Season closes JULY 1st, 1890. Usual return privileges.

For urther particulars address owner,

WILFRED PAGE, Penns Grove,
Sonoma County, Cal

The Trotting Stallion

Silver Bow

Will make the season of 1890 at the Oakland Race Track.

PEDIGREE.

SILVER BOW 11706, two-year-old record 2:37, is by Robert McGregor 647, 2:17¾ (sire of Bonnie McGregor, 2:13¾, Earl McGregor, 2:21¾, Mac D., 2:20, McGregor Boy, 2:29¾, Mark Time, 2:30, Roxie McGregor, 2:20¾) by Major Edsall 2:11, 2:29, by Alexander's Abdallah 15—sire of Goldsmith Maid, 2:14—by Hambletonian 10—sire of Dexter, 2:17¾.

Robert McGregor's dam was Nancy Whitman by American Star 14, by Stockholm's American Star.

SILVER BOW'S first dam is Sadie by Hambletonian 10, sire of Geo. Wilkes, 2:22—sire of Guy Wilkes, 2:15¾—also Electioneer, sire of Sunol, three-year-old record, 2:10½, and Palo Alto, 2:12¾; second dam Lady Wynne by Wm. Welch 341; third dam Elenora Margrave by imp. Margrave.

DESCRIPTION.

SILVER BOW is a handsome bay, no white; 15-3¼ hands high; weighs 1075 pounds; of fine form, with the best of legs and a clean-cut, intelligent head. Is remarkably level-headed, seldom making a break; wears seven-ounce shoes in front. His record, 2:37, is no mark of his speed; he can beat 30 easy, and with his gilt-edge breeding, he is just what he ought to be, a trotter sired by a trotter whose dam was herself a trotter and his grandam the dam of two trotters. His dam Sadie being by Hambletonian 10, shows him to be bred from the cream of the trotting blood.

TERMS: $100 for the season. Mares not proving in foal returnable for the season of 1891 free of charge. Good pasturage and first-class care taken of mares for $5 per month. No responsibilities assumed for escapes or accidents. For further particulars, address

Limited to 15 approved mares.
Season to end June 1st, 1890.

P. J. WILLIAMS,
Care Race Track, Oakland, Cal.

GRAND MOOR, 2374.

Grand Moor 2374.
- Moor 870
  - Sire of Beautiful Bells 2:29½
  - Sire of Sable (dam of Sable Wilkes), 2:18
  - Sire of Sultan 2:24
  - Sire of Tommy Gates 2:24
  - Sire of Del Sur 2:24¾
  - Sire of Sir Guy 2:28¾
  - Beautiful Bells is the dam of Hinda Rose, 2:19½ as a 3-year-old, Palo Alto Belle, 2:22¾, Chimes, St. Bell, 2:24¾, Bell Boy (3 years) 2:19¾.
  - Sultan, 2:24 (sire of Stamboul 2:12½) has 10 in 2:30 list.
  - Clay Pilot 92 — Sire of 2 in 2:30 list.
  - Belle of Wabash.
- Vashti
  - Dam of Don Tomas, who got a record of 2:30 in 1889.
  - Mambrino Patchen 58 — Sire of 14 in 2:30 list. Sire of the dam of Guy Wilkes, 2:15¾; also sire of 20 stallions and 18 mares with get in 2:30 list.
  - Kate Tuber — By Mambrino Messenger, he by Mambrino Paymaster.

Foaled 1876. Black. Sixteen hands high. Bred by L. J. Rose

A horse of highest form and quality; of great excellence in every point; a type of his celebrated family; of marked individuality, spirit and endurance; never properly trained or raced, but shows the possession of great speed; perfectly manageable in the stable and on the road and track.

As he is sired by The Moor 870, a son of CLAY PILOT, out of Vashti by MAMBRINO PATCHEN, he is a most valuable cross for mares of other families. THE MOOR sired Beautiful Bells and the dams of Sable Wilkes and Margaret 2:26 (dam of Regal Wilkes, 2-year-old record 2:20½).

MAMBRINO PATCHEN is regarded as the unsurpassed sire of broodmares, having, among many others, sired the dam of Guy Wilkes and of Wm. L. (the sire of Axtell), and a son of his sired the dam of Axtell. The public sales this year have demonstrated with renewed emphasis the value of The Moor and Mambrino Patchen strains of blood. For combining particularly with the Hambletonians it may be called "the ready money cross."

GRAND MOOR will make the season of 1890 for a time at the Oakland Race Track and afterwards at my Ranch, fifteen miles from Oakland. Mares can be delivered at the race track to the groom in charge. Pasture at $5 per month. For other food, if requested, an additional charge will be made.

TERMS, $150 for the season. With privileges of return if the horse does not change hands.

Every care exercised, but no liability for escapes or accidents.

H. I. THORNTON, 504 Kearny Street.

Cook STOCK FARM.

Season of 1890.

STEINWAY 1808.

Three-Year-Old Record 2:25 3-4.

Sire of STRATHWAY, three year old record 2:26, and sire of the dam of BOURBON RUSSELL 2:30.

By STRATHMORE 408; sire of 31 in the 2:30 list; sire of 6 dams of 8 in the 2:30 list, and sire of 3 sires of 3 in 2:30 list.

1st dam ABBESS (dam of Solo 2:28, and Soprano, dam of C. F Clay 2:18, Eminence 2:27 and Strathbridge, 3 year old record 2:28½) by ALBION, sire of VANITY FAIR 2:24½, and of the dam of FAVORITE 2:25½.

2nd dam by MARSHALL NEY.

3rd dam by BERTRAND, a son of SIR ARCHY.

TERMS—$100 for the season.

CHARLES DERBY 4907

Brown Horse, Foaled 1885.

By STEINWAY 1808.

1st dam by the great ELECTIONEER, sire of SUNOL 3 year old record 2:10½, Palo Alto 2:12¼, etc., etc.

2nd dam FANNY MALONE, by NIAGARA.

3rd dam FANNY WICKHAM, by HERALD.

4th dam by Imp. TRUSTEE.

TERMS—$100 for the season.

Pasturage $5 per month. Accidents and escapes at owner's risk. Mares consigned to the farm should be sent to Fashion Stables, Oakland; Geary & Grindle's Stable, Haywards; or to Bennett's Stable, Martinez; from and to which places they will be delivered free of charge. Address

COOK STOCK FARM,
Danville, Contra Costa, Co., Cal.

The Trotting Stallion

G & M

FULL BROTHER TO

ALFRED G, 2:19¾.

(Who has been taken to Kentucky to stand at $300)

Will make the season of 1890 from FEBRUARY 1st to JULY 1st, at

SANTA ROSA.

G. & M. is by Anteeo, 2:16¼; was foaled 1886; first dam Rosa B. by Speculation (son of Hambletonian 10); 2d dam Elizabeth by Alexander 490; 3d dam Nora by imp. Glencoe. Anteeo is by Electioneer, out of Columbine by A. W. Richmond 1687.

G. & M. is a handsome dark bay; stands 15-3 1-2 hands high, and weighs 1060 pounds. Gameness, stoutness, speed and stamina are indelibly impressed in every line of the pedigree of G. & M. Owners of brood-mares in search of these qualities, will do well to patronize this promising colt.

PHILOSOPHER,

Foaled 1886 by Pilot Wilkes 2967; first dam Bella by George Wilkes 519; second dam by Bell Morgan 61.

Philosopher's sire, Pilot Wilkes 2967, is by George Wilkes 519, dam Grace (the dam of Alice Woodburn etc.), by Pilot Jr. 12, grandam by Orphan Boy.

Will make the season of 1890, from FEBRUARY 1st to JULY 1st, at Santa Rosa.

TERMS for the season:

G. & M., $50,

PHILOSOPHER, $30,

with privilege of returning mares that do not prove in foal the next season free of charge, provided the horse bred to remains the property of the present owners. Good pasturage at $5 per month. No responsibility assumed for accidents or escapes. Service fees payable before removal of the mare. For further particulars, address

GEO. E. GUERNE,
Santa Rosa Cal.

PASHA,

Registered No. 2039.

RECORD 2:36.

SIRE OF MORO 2:27.

Will make the present season at Linden, twelve miles east of STOCKTON.

Season commencing FEBRUARY 1st and ending JULY 1, 1890.

DESCRIPTION.

PASHA is a beautiful black; 16½ hands high, and weighs 1,240 pounds. He is a horse of beautiful symmetry and magnificent action.

PEDIGREE.

PASHA was sired by Sultan 1513, sire of Stamboul 2:12½, Ruby 2:19½, Alcazar 2:20½, Bay Rose 2:20½, and sixteen others with records below 2:30. First dam Madam Baldwin by The Moor 870; second dam Ben Lippincott by Belmont. Pasha is a full brother to Bay Rose, record 2:20½.

Sultan, by The Moor, sire of Beautiful Bells, dam of Hinda Rose, 2:19½, Bell Boy 2:19¼, and Sable, dam of Sable Wilkes, three-year-old record 2:18. First dam Sultana, by Delmonico, sire of Derby 2:16, by Guy Miller, sire of Whipple's Hambletonian. Second dam by Mambrino Chief. Third dam by Downing's Bay Messenger. Fourth dam Miss Caudle, dam of Ericsson, four-year-old recor 2:30½.

Terms for the season, $50

With privilege of returning mares that do not prove in foal next season free of charge.

Good pasturage at $2 per month. No responsibility will be assumed for accidents or escapes. Service fee payable before the removal of the mare.

For further particulars, address

D. BRYSON,
Linden Cal

MEMO.

The Best Son of SIDNEY

Will Make the Season of 1890 at the OAKLAND RACE TRACK

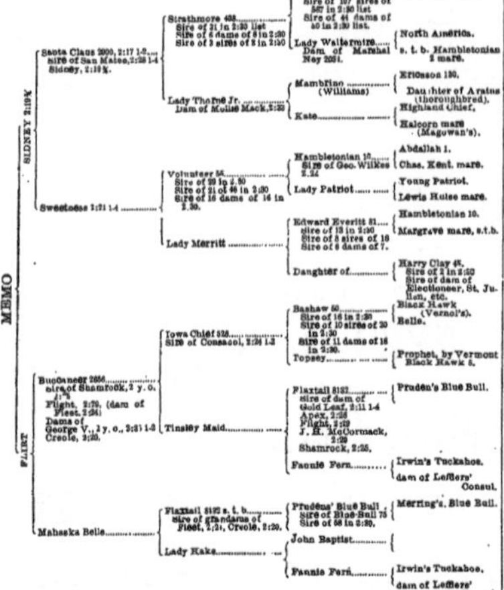

MEMO is, as can be seen at a glance, one of the best bred young stallions in service, having three crosses of Rysdyk's Hambletonian and one of Harry Clay, the sire of Green Mountain Maid (dam of Electioneer, etc.), while Long Island Black Hawk and Flaxtail also contribute to his blood. Sidney (Memo's sire) is universally known as the best young sire in the world, a producer of extreme speed at an early age.

PERFORMANCES.

MEMO trotted in public in his two-year-old form, obtaining a record of 2:46, though he was close to Grandee in a race on the Bay District Track, the second heat of which was made in 2:31 1-2, the first in 2 3[illegible]. He exhibited phenomenal speed when three years old, and had it not been for a slight strain of his fore fetlock, there is little question, he would have shown in public very close to the best record. On the Oakland track he was timed a mile in 2:20 1-2, and frequently trotted quarters in from 32 1-2 to 31 seconds.

As a four-year-old Memo only started once—at Sacramento—when, although out of condition, he showed great speed, and improving as he went on, great hopes were entertained of his going well down in the 'teens at the P. C. T. H. B. A. meeting, but after showing several very fast miles his leg filled and he was laid up for the season. He is sixteen hands high, and of powerful build throughout. His color is a glossy black, with both fore-feet white. His disposition is all that could be desired, and his action superb. He is a sure foal getter, only one mare being reported not in foal during his last season.

TERMS, $100, with usual return privileges, for a limited number of mares. Season to close JUNE 15th, when he will be prepared for track purposes. Pasturage $4 per month. Have leased the cricket ground adjoining the track for pasturage, where there is fine feed. Reasonable charges if fed hay and grain. Best of care taken of mares in any manner owners may desire, but positively no responsibility assumed for accidents or escapes. For further particulars address

J. P. KERR, 313 Bush Street, San Francisco,

or, JOHN BOWEN, Race Track, Oakland, Cal.

HOLLYWOOD BREEDING FARM.

MOUNTAIN BOY 4841.

Bro MOUNTAIN BOY, 4841, bred by Charles Backman, Orange County, New York, foaled 1882, sire Kentucky Prince 2470, dam Elise, sister to Elaine, by Messenger Duroc 106; grandam Green Mountain Maid, 3d dam, Shanghai Mary, will serve a limited number of mares at $100 the season.

ELECTION.

Bay stallion ELECTION, bred at Senator Stanford's Palo Alto Stock Farm, foaled 1884, sire Electioneer, dam Lizzie H. by Whipple's Hambletonian 725, grandam Lizzie Harris (by Comus son of Green's Bashaw 50), great grandam by Arnold Harris, thoroughbred.

Election is one of the handsomest bloodlike sons of Electioneer, and with his thoroughbred cross through Arnold Harris should prove invaluable as a sire. TERMS, $100 the season.

KAFIR.

B c KAFIR, bred by L. J. Rose, Los Angeles, foaled 1887, sire Alcazar, 2:20½, dam Flower Girl by Arthurton, sire of Arab, 2:15, grandam Flora by General McClellan, 144, sire of three in 2:30 list, great grand dam by Langford, he by Williamson's Belmont, will serve a limited number of mares at $50 the season.

WOODSIDE.

Ch c WOODSIDE, sire Woodnut, 2:16½; 1st dam Veronica by Alcona, 730; 2nd dam Fontana by Almont, 33; 3rd dam Fannie Williams by Alexander's Abdallah, 15. Book full.

MART BOORHEM.

B c MART BOORHEM, by Sydney, 2:19¾; 1st dam Towhead by Echo. This colt is a full brother to St. Nicholas who showed a mile in 2:27½ at three years old. TERMS, $25 the season.

REVEILLE.

The well known thoroughbred stallion REVEILLE, by Shiloh, dam by Norfolk. Reveille is a brother to John Treat and is the sire of Tycoon and Gladstone. TERMS, $25 the season.

Hollywood is nicely situated three miles from Vallejo on the Napa road. Good pasturage and every care will be taken of mares at reasonable rates. For further particulars, apply,

B. C. HOLLY, Vallejo.

Langtry Farms' Stud

Imp. FRIAR TUCK

By the Immortal HERMIT

DAM ROMPING GIRL BY WILD DAYRELL.

AT $50 THE SEASON.

Mares not proving with foal may be returned the following season. Good care taken of mares, but no liabilities for accidents or escapes.

Good Pasturage at $5 per month.

Mares shipped to ST. HELENA, care CHARLES WILLIAM ABY, St. Helena Stables, will be cared for. For further particulars address,

CHAS. WILLIAM ABY,

Middletown, Lake County, Cal.

THE CEDARS

BANNER MARK, 9424.

Foaled in 1888; by Victor von Bismarck (sire of Edgemark, four year old record 2:16; Von Wilkes, yearling record 2 38¼, etc.); dam Moonlight by Alcyone (sire of Alcryon 2:15 1-4, etc.); second dam Twilight (dam of Skylight Pilot 2:19) by Mambrino Pilot (sire of Mannie 2:17¼); third dam by Pilot Jr. (sire of the dam of Maud S. 2:08¾); fourth dam nearly or quite thoroughbred.

In his four double crosses he combines more of the popular blood than any colt of his age. He is a double Hambletonian, double Clay through Bismarck and George Wilkes, double Mambrino and Pilot Jr., through Mambrino Pilot, Pilot Jr., and Mambrino Patchen. There is no other colt living bred like him. If you want Hambletonian, Clay, Mambrino or Pilot Jr., here you have it all combined in one grand colt. He has much of the finish of the thoroughbred.

Insurance $300. Limited to Seven Approved Mares.

Book full for 1890 and open for 1891 for fifteen approved mares. Address

T. E. MOORE,

The Cedars, Shawhan, Ky.

Pleasanton Stock Farm Co.'s Stallions;

DIRECTOR, 2:17.

Director's book is open for 15 good mares more than already booked for the season of 1890, at $300 each.

This is the cheapest service fee ever charged for a stallion, taking into consideration his BREEDING and RACE RECORD and the RACE RECORDS OF HIS COLTS.

Season to commence February 15th and close August 1st.

CORRECTOR, Five Years Old.

Sire Director 2:17, dam Brainey, she by Echo. Echo sired by Rysdyk's Hambletonian, out of Fanny Felter, by Magnolia, he by Seely's American Star. Brainey's dam Lady Dudley, she by Tom Dudley by Blacknose, a son of Medoc, he by American Eclipse. Lady Dudley's dam by Bertrand, Jr., a son of Bertrand.

CORRECTOR is a rich seal brown 15¾ hands high, and is the fastest young stallion in the world under the same conditions, never having been off the farm where raised and never been shod or driven for speed before last Christmas, and can trot quarters now in 36 seconds, a 2:20 gait.

He will be allowed to serve ten good mares, at $100 each for the season, which closes June 1st.

DECORATOR, Four Years Old.

Sire Director 2:17, dam Chess, sired by Cardinal 2.37, trial 2:28, he by Gen. Gifford's Morgan, dam of Cardinal, sired by Joe Gales of Ohio, he by Marlborough out of the Duchess of Marlborough by Southern Eclipse; second dam old Duchess of Marlborough by Sir Archy; third dam by imp Diomed. Decorator's second dam a Morgan and Messenger mare.

Decorator is a light bay 16 hands high, and with but little handling for speed has shown eighths in 17½ seconds, a 2:20 gait.

He will be allowed to serve ten good mares at $50 each for the season, which closes June 1st.

Mares not proving with foal may be returned next season free of charge of service fees to the same stallion, if he is still in our possession; however, the company reserves the right to return the fee instead of giving service.

Pasturage $4 per month; hay and grain extra. Accidents and escapes at owner's risk.

Service fees due at time of service, and must be paid, together with pasturage, etc., before mares are taken away, or a good approved note given, payable August 1st, 1890, at which date all bills must be settled.

For further information call or address **M. SALISBURY, 320 Sansome Street, Room 96, San Francisco, or**

PLEASANTON STOCK FARM CO.,

Pleasanton, Alameda Co., Cal.

SOUTHER FARM

P. O. Box 208. San Leandro, Cal.

1½ miles northwest of San Leandro; 3 miles southeast of Oakland. Turn off County road between above places at "Stanley Road," ½ mile north of San Leandro.

Horses boarded at all times in any manner desired. Best of care but no responsibility for accidents. Colts broken and handled for the road or track. Terms reasonable.

Glen Fortune,	Jester D,	El Benton,	Figaro,
By Electioneer.	By Almont.	By Electioneer.	Hambletonian 725
$50 for 1889.	$50 for 1890.	Limited to 5 mares.	Limited to 12 mares
		Book Full.	Book Full.

THE SOUTHER FARM

Has Green Feed the Year Round,

and feeds Hay in connection with the green feed, which a horse must have if he is to thrive. Every animal is given

A Dry, Warm Place to Sleep,

No matter how stormy the weather. All Stock under cover when it rains.

VISITORS WELCOME ANY DAY EXCEPT SUNDAY.

How to Get Stock to the Souther Farm.

The Souther Farm is one and a half miles northeast of San Leandro and eight miles southeast of Oakland. The stables are about one mile east of the county road, which runs between Oakland and San Leandro. The place to turn off is at Stanley Road, where a large signboard of the farm is placed. Guide boards will be found at every cross road. In any ordinary weather the roads are very good, and they are fairly good after the unusually heavy rainfall of the past winter.

All stock sent from San Francisco may be brought over by Garcia's Express, No. 3 Market street, San Francisco. They also have an order box outside of Hawley Bros.' Hardware house on the corner of Market and Beale streets. The express leaves San Francisco on the Creek route boat, which starts at 1:3[illegible], but all orders should be in the order box at Market and Beale streets by 10 o'clock, or at the office, No. 3 Market street, by 11 o'clock at the latest. In the case of very young or very valuable horses, the Souther Farm will send reliable men to lead or drive over any stock that will not lead behind a wagon. A small charge will be made in such cases, to cover the extra expense incurred.

Horses are very easily taken from Oakland to the farm, and where it is inconvenient for owners to bring them or send them, the farm will send after anything that is to come. On horses that stay three months or over there is no charge for getting or delivering. Where a horse stays a short time the actual time and expense only is charged to him.

Horses can be shipped by rail from almost all parts of the State to San Leandro. Always notify the Farm several days before shipping anything, and then men will be on hand to receive stock on arrival. The railroad station is but two miles from the Souther Farm, and the agent invariably gives immediate notice of the arrival of any stock consigned to the above farm, but when word is sent to the farm in good season by letter or telegram, the animals sent are saved waiting a couple of hours in the car.

Passenger trains leave San Francisco (from the broad gauge ferry) and First and Broadway, Oakland, at frequent intervals during the day. There are several trains from San Jose to San Leandro on both the broad and narrow gauge railroads; the broad gauge, by way of Niles, is much more convenient for getting to the farm. There are trains each day from Sacramento, Stockton and Livermore to San Leandro. In ordinary weather it is a short and pleasant drive from Oakland to the Souther Farm or from San Francisco to the Farm by way of the Creek route ferry boat. Always notify the Souther Farm just when you will arrive at San Leandro, and some one will meet you at the station. If you do not recognize the farm conveyance ask the stage driver, who will point it out.

Write to the above address for references, circulars and price lists. Terms reasonable.

GILBERT TOMPKINS, Proprietor.

SAN MATEO STOCK FARM

HOME OF GUY WILKES,

Record, 2:15 1-4.

Guy Wilkes' Book is full for 1890 and 1891, and positively no more mares will be received.

Sable Wilkes, three-year-old record 2:18, will be allowed to serve 25 mares in addition to those already engaged at $250 the season of 1890. SABLE Wilkes, 15½ hands, black horse, by Guy Wilkes, first dam Sable by The Moor; second dam Gretchen by Mambrino Pilot; third dam Kitty Kirkman by Canada Chief; fourth dam by Fanning's Tobe; fifth dam by imp. Leviathan.

Leo Wilkes, brown horse, four years, 16 hands, full brother to Sable Wilkes, will be allowed to serve 30 mares at $100 the season

Mares not proving with foal may be returned the following season free of service fee. Parties engaging the services of any of the above horses must send a deposit of 10 per cent. of service money with engagement. Pasturage $6 per month, and when the condition of the animal requires it, hay or grain, or both, are fed, the charge will be $12 50 per month. Good care will be taken of all mares sent to the Farm, but no liability will be assumed for accidents or escapes.

All bills are due at time of service, but must be paid by August 1st of each year. No stock will be allowed to leave the place until all bills are paid.

WILLIAM CORBITT.

San Mateo Stock Farm.

2:08 3-4 2:10 2:12

MAMBRINO WILKES, 6083.

SIRE OF

GUS WILKES, 2:22; ALPHEUS, 2:27; CLARA P, 2:29½; BALKAN, 2:29½ (3-year-old) and timed separately 2:22½ in 4-year-old Stake, Bay District Track, October 14, 1889.

DESCRIPTION.

Black; sixteen hands; weighs, in exercise, 1,260 lbs. For style, finish, symmetry and proportion, comparison is challenged with any trotting bred horse. His colts follow in size, style and beauty. Balkan, for instance, being "facile princeps" of trotters in these particulars.

PEDIGREE.

Sired by Geo. Wilkes, sire of Harry Wilkes, 2:13¼, Guy Wilkes, 2:15¼, and 60 other trotters in the 2:30 list, in addition to 6 pacers, and of the sire of Axtell, 2:12 (three-year-old) beating all stallions of any age, and the sire of Regal Wilkes, 2:20¾, best two-year-old stallion record.

First dam Lady Chrisman by Mambrino (Todhunter's), son of Mambrino Chief 11; sire of Lady Thorn, 2:18¼; Woodford Mambrino, 2:21¼, and four others in 2:30, and of the dams of Director, 2:17, Piedmont, 2:17¼, Onward, 2:25¼, etc.

Second dam by Pilot Jr. 12, sire of nine in the 2:30 list, and of the dams of Maud S., 2:08¾, Jay-Eye-See, 2:10, Nutwood, 2:18¾, Viking, 2:19¾, Pilot Boy, 2:20, Naiad Queen, 2:20¾, etc.

TERMS.

Mares from a distance will be received at the Dexter Stables, Oakland, or Livery Stable, Martinez, the owner notifying Smith Hill, Superintendent at the farm. Good pasture and plenty of water. For the purpose of placing the service of a Wilkes within reach of breeders, the same rate will be maintained as last year, to wit, $75 for the season. Although it is not admitted thereby that this horse is inferior as a producer to the horses whose fees are placed at from $150 to $500. Address

SMITH HILL,
San Miguel Stock Farm,
Walnut Creek, Contra Costa Co., Cal.

2:12¾ 2:13½ 2:15¼

The Trotting Stallion

VICTOR,

Record 2:22.

Will make the season of 1890 at NAPA CITY.

DESCRIPTION.

VICTOR is a handsome dark bay; 15-3 hands high; weighs about 1,1[illegible] pounds, and is remarkably intelligent, level-headed of kind disposition, and a magnificent animal in every respect. He is well boned and muscled, of splendid conformation, and possesses the qualities of speed and endurance to an eminent degree—qualities that he imparts to his progeny.

PEDIGREE.

VICTOR, record 2:22
- Echo 462
  - Hambletonian 10, Sire of 42 in the 2:30 list.
    - Abdallah 1
    - Chas. Kent mare
  - Fanny Felter
    - Magnolia 68
    - by Webber's Kentucky Whip
- Daughter of
  - Woodburn
    - Lexington
    - Lulu Horton
  - daughter of
    - Ashland
    - thoroughbred

ECHO is the sire of Belle Echo, 2:20, Senator, 2:21¼, Victor, 2:22, Gibraltar, 2:22¼, Kebora, 2:23¼, Tippie, 2:25¾, Lohengrin, 2:27¼, Pasha, 2:27¾, Flinonte, 2:28, Col. Hawkins, 2:29¼, Annie Laurie, 2:30, Economy, 2:30, Sam Lewis, pacer, 2:23.

TERMS—$60 FOR THE SEASON.

Mares not proving with foal may be returned next season free of charge provided the horse remains the property of the present proprietor, and stands at the same place, otherwise money will be refunded. The best of care taken of mares in any manner that owners may desire, but no responsibility assumed for accidents or escapes. For further particulars, apply to or address

G. W. HUGHES, Agent,
G. A. DOHERTY, Proprietor. Napa City.

The Fast Trotting Stallion

REDWOOD.

Four-Year-Old Record 2:24 1-2

Will make the season of 1890—February 1st to July 1st—at the

OAKLAND RACE TRACK.

REDWOOD is a dark bay colt, 15.2¾ hands high, weighs 1[illegible] lbs. Foaled in 1885 by Anteeo, 2:16¼, sire of Alfred G., 2:19¾. Anteeo is by Electioneer. First dam Lou Milton, by Milton Medium; second dam Old Sly, a thoroughbred mare brought from the East in 1871 by W. C. Ralston, Esq.

Redwood's sire was out of Columbine by A. W. Richmond, the sire of the pacers Arrow 2:13¾, and Elwood 2:23, and the trotters Romero, 2:19¾, and Len Rose, 2:27. Redwood has shown a quarter in 33 seconds.

Terms $100

for the season. Mares not proving with foal may be returned next season free of charge, provided Redwood remains the property of the present owners. Good pasturage at $5 per month. No responsibility assumed for escapes or accidents. Service fees payable before removal of the mare. Limited to 40 approved mares. For further particulars address

A. McFADYEN.
Race track, Oakland, Cal.

2:19 **NOONDAY** 2:20½

STANDARD No. 10,000.

This celebrated trotting bred stallion will make the season of 1890 at the stable of the undersigned at Sacramento, Cal., at $75 for the season and $100 to insure a mare in foal. Payable on or before July 1st, 1890. Money will be refunded on mares bred by insurance as soon as the fact becomes known that they are not in foal.

NOONDAY.
- Wedgewood, 2:19, Sire of Favonia, 2:15, fastest 4th heat for any mare or gelding, and eight others in 2:27 or better.
  - Belmont, Sire of Wedgewood, 2:19, Nutwood, 2:18¾, Viking, 2:19½, and 29 others in 2:30 list.
    - Alexander's Abdallah, sire of Goldsmith Maid, 2:14; Almont, with 36 horses in 2:30 list, etc.
    - Belle, dam of Hambletonian, 2:26½; B'cara, dam of Pancoast, 2:21¾, the sire of Patron, 2:14½.
  - Woodbine, Dam of Wedgewood, 2:19, Woodford Mamb., 2:21½, the sire of Pancoast, 2:21¾, the sire of Patron, 2:14½.
    - Woodford.
    - Singleton Mare.
- Noontide, 2:20½ (Trial, 2:13½).
  - Harold, Sire of Maud S., 2:08¾, and 26 others in 2:30 list.
    - Hambletonian (Rysdyk's), sire of George Wilkes, 2:22, the sire of Guy Wilkes, 2:15¼; Electioneer, the sire of Sunol, 2:10½, and scores of noted trotters and producers.
    - Enchantress, by Abdallah 1.
  - Midnight, Dam of Jay-Eye-See, 2:10, Noontide, 2:20½.
    - Pilot Jr., sire of dams of Maud S., 2:08¾, Jay-Eye-See, 2:10, Nutwood, 2:18¾, etc.
    - Twilight, by Lexington, sire of the dam of Ansel, 2:20.

NOODAY is a dark seal brown, foaled 1884, 16 hands 1¼ inches high. Individually he is equal to his royal breeding. He is all that can be desired in conformation, intelligence, color and trotting action and no stallion now in public service can show a pedigree with such fast records and royal game trotting blood as Noonday.

DON MARVIN,

Record 2:28 as a five-year-old. Standard by Breeding and Performance

Standard No. 7927.

Don Marvin 2:28.

Don Marvin is a beautiful seal brown, foaled 1884, bred by Hon. Leland Stanford, Palo Alto, Cal., standing 16 hands, and weighs, in ordinary condition, 1200 lbs. He is a fine individual, good style and form, combined with great substance, and good temper. Is very level headed: in his first race the past season he only made one break in five closely contested heats. He has great speed and endurance, with the pure, rapid Electioneer gait. He trots without toe weights, and wears only 8 oz. shoes in front. He gained his record the past season in the third heat, on a slow track, after making a season (serving over 40 mares), with scarcely any preparation. His record is no mark of his speed. He was a natural born trotter, and Mr. Charles Marvin considered him the fastest two year old at Palo Alto that season.

By FALLIS, 2:23, - - by Electioneer, sire of
Sire of Don Marvin, 2:28. — Sunol, three-year-old, 2:10 1-2, Palo Alto, 2:12¾, and 47 others in 2:30 list.

Dam CORA, by Don Victor by Belmont, sire of
Dam of Don Marvin, 2:28. — Ventura, 2:27¾, and sire of the dam of Bell Echo, 2:20, and six others in 2:30 list.

2d dam CLARABEL, - by Abdallah Star,
Dam of Clifton Bell, 2:24 1-2, and grandam of Rexford, three years, 2:24. — Sire of Hattie Maples, 2:33.

3d dam FAIRY, - - by Rysdyk's Hambletonian,
Sister of Sweepstakes, sire of 16 in 2:30 list. — Sire of Electioneer, George Wilkes, and many other noted sires and trotters.

4th dam EMMA MILLS, by Seely's American Star,
Dam of 4 horses that have 2:30 performers. — The great broodmare sire of the world.

The above pedigree should show every intelligent breeder that Don Marvin is "high" bred, though very strong in trotting blood. All the comment it is deemed necessary to make as to the value of "thoroughbred blood" in the trotter is simply to refer to the very significant fact that the first and second dams of Maud S., 2:08¾, Jay-Eye-See 2:10, Sunol, three years 2:10 1-2, Palo Alto 2:12¾, Anteeo 2:16¼, Nutwood 2:18¾, Wedgewood 2:19, and many other successful sires and sensational trotters of the day are thoroughbred.

TERMS—Don Marvin will make the ensuing season from February 1st to July 1st, 1890, at $40 the season, with the usual privilege of returning the mare next season if not proving in foal. Mares from a distance met at the cars or boats on notification, and carefully handled, but no responsibility assumed for accidents or escapes.

Good alfalfa pasture furnished (free from barb wire fence) at $4 per month. For further particulars or complete circulars address

F. P. LOWELL,
1520 F Street, Sacramento, Cal.

The Produce of Eros Averaged $2,200 Each at New York Auction Sale in 1889.

THE ELECTIONEER TROTTING STALLION,

5326 **EROS** 5326

Will make the season of 1890—February 1st to July 1st—at LA SIESTA RANCH, MENLO PARK, adjoining Palo Alto.

PEDIGREE.

EROS (5326)
Standard by his sire
" " dam
" " record
" " produce
" under all rules

EROS (5326)
- Electioneer, Grandsire of Norlaine, 1 yr., 2:31 1-2, Sire of Sunol, 2 yrs., 2:18, Sunol, 3 yrs., 2:10 1-2, Hinda Rose, 4 yrs., 2:16, Palo Alto, 2:12¾.
  - Hambletonian 10, Sire of Dictator, George Wilkes, Happy Medium, and 40 others in 2:30 list, and grandsire of 728 in list.
    - Abdallah 10, Sire of the dams of Goldsmith Maid, 2:14, and 7 other producing dams.
    - Charles Kent mare By imp. Bellfounder.
  - Green Mountain Maid, Dam of Prospero, 2:20, Elaine, 2:20, Dame Trot, 2:22, Elista, 2:22¾, Storm, 2:28¾, Antonio, 2:28¾, Miranda, 2:31, Mansfield, 2:26.
    - Harry Clay, Sire of the dams of St. Julian, 2:11¾, Bodine, 2:19¾, and 17 more in 2:30 list
    - Shanghai Mary.
- Sontag Mohawk, Dam of Eros, 2:29 1-2, Sport, 2:22¾, Sallie Benton, 2:17¾, Conductor, trial, 2:26, Colma, 3-y-o trial, 2:24.
  - Mohawk Chief, Sire of the dams of Lot Slocum, 2:17¾, Sallie Benton, 4 yrs., 2:17¾, Pedlar, 2 yrs., 2:[illegible]¾, Stanford, 4 yrs., 2:30, Eros, 6th heat, 2:29 1-2.
    - Hambletonian 10, Sire of the dams of Stamboul, 2:12¾, Wilton, 2:19¾, and 20 other trotters.
    - Lady Perrine
  - Sontag Nellie
    - Toronto Sontag By Toronto Chief,
    - Nellie Gray 5-mile record, 13:46.

Produce of Eros
Wanda, 4 yrs., 2:24,
Solita, 3 yrs., 2:41 1-2,
Meriquita, 2 yrs., 2:42,
Daylight, 2 yrs., 2:54,
Hiram B., trial, 2:28.

These are the only colts by him that have ever had a harness on except one in New York that went a trial last July in 2:36 1-2.

DESCRIPTION.

EROS is a rich seal brown stallion, bred by Hon. Leland Stanford at Palo Alto, and is the nearest living likeness of his celebrated sire, Electioneer. Stands 15.2 hands high, and weighs 1060 pounds

In breeding to Eros, the owners of mares will strictly follow the great rule of breeding, viz., breed to a stallion by a producer and out of a sure producer of great speed. Eros is by the stallion that has produced more 2:30 trotters than any living horse, and is also the sire of more 2:20 performers than any horse living or dead.

EROS is out of the dam of Sally Benton, four years old, record 2:17¾, Sport 2:22¼, and Eros 2:29½ in the sixth heat, against a field of nine horses. He is from a family that is endowed with great natural speed, trot fast at an early age, train on, throw trotters from all classes of mares, are of good substance, bone, style and action, and breed solid colors.

TERMS.

$100 for the season, with the privilege of return next season should mares not be in foal and horse and mare still remain in the same hands.

Good pasturage can be obtained at $5 per month, but no responsibility for accidents or escapes. There are a large number of box stalls, and animals can be kept up and fed on hay and grain at reasonable rates if required. Mares already in foal can be sent to the ranch for foaling, and will receive all the attention bestowed upon our own mares. Mares left with Mr. Peter Pomyea, Broadway Street Stable, Oakland, or with Mr. F. H. Burke, 401 Montgomery Street, San Francisco, will be forwarded to the ranch free of charge. For further particulars apply to

W. H. VIOGET.
LA SIESTA RANCH, MENLO PARK, CAL.

EROS is the only stallion offered to the public on this Coast that has a dam that has three in the 2:30 list.

POPLAR GROVE

Breeding Farm

STALLIONS.

CLOVIS, 4909,

CLOVIS is a beautiful black, Eight Years Old, 16 1-2 Hands High, and weighs 1260 lbs.

He is a horse of beautiful symmetry and magnificent action.

PEDIGREE.

CLOVIS was sired by Sultan, 2:24, sire of Stamboul, 2:12 1-4, Ruby, 2:19¾, and fifteen others with records of 2:30 or better.

First dam Sweetbriar by Thorndale 2:22 1-2, sire of Edwin Thorne, 2:16 1-2, Daisy Dale, 2:19, and May Thorne, 2:22.

Second dam Ulster Queen, dam of Volmer, 2:24¾, by Hambletonian 10. Sire of Dexter, 2:17¼, George Wilkes, 2:22.

Third dam by Thomas Jefferson, a son of Mambrino Paymaster, Jr.

Fourth dam by Mambrino Paymaster, sire of Mambrino Chief.

Sultan, by The Moor, sire of Beautiful Bells, dam of Hinda Rose, 2:19 1-2, and Sable, dam of Sable Wilkes, three year old record 2:18.

First dam of Sultan, Sultana, by Delmonico. Sire of Darby, 2:16 1-2, by Guy Miller, sire of Whipple's Hambletonian.

Second dam by Mambrino Chief.

Third dam by Downing's Bay Messenger.

Fourth dam Mrs. Caudle, dam of Ericsson, four year old record 2:30 1-2.

Clovis will make the season of 1890 at Poplar Grove Breeding Farm, near Wildflower, Fresno County, commencing February 1st and ending July 1st.

Terms, $75, due at time of service.

Mares cared for in any manner owners may desire; pasturage $2 per month. Every care exercised, but no liability for escapes or accidents. Mares not proving with foal can be returned next season, providing I still own this stallion.

APEX, 8935.

FOUR-YEAR-OLD RECORD, FOURTH HEAT, 2:26.

Will make the present season at the Poplar Grove Breeding Farm, near Wildflower, Fresno Co., season commencing Feb. 1st, and ending July 1, 1890. Terms $50 the season, due at time of service. Apex is eight years old, a beautiful bay, 15 1-2 hands high, and weighs 1140 lbs. He is a horse of fine disposition, and his gait is faultless.

PEDIGREE.

Apex was sired by Prompter 2305, he by Blue Bull 75; first dam Mary by Flaxtail, he by Pruden's Blue Bull. Flaxtail being the sire of the dams of Buccaneer, five-year-old record, 2:24 1-4; Pride, yearling record, 2:44 1-2, and Shamrock, two-year old record, 2:25, third heat. Second dam by Bright Eyes, son of Hoamaragen. Prompter (sire of Apex, record 2:26, and Transit, 2:26 1-2), by Wilson's Blue Bull, by Pruden's Blue Bull son of Merring's Blue Bull. Prompter's dam Prairie Bird, by Flaxtail; second dam by John the Baptist, son of Tally Ho Morgan, by Sherman Morgan; third dam Fannie Fern by Irwin's Tuckahoe.

Apex made his appearance in the circuit as a two-year-old, and obtained a record of 2:42. As a three-year-old he reduced this in a race at Santa Rosa against Stamboul to 2:31, it taking six heats to decide the contest, which was won by Apex. As a four year-old he gained his present record of 2:26.

Mares cared for in any manner owners may desire. Pasturage $2 per month. Every care exercised, but no liabilities for escapes or accidents. Mares not proving with foal can be returned next season, providing I still own this stallion.

The Standard Stallion

JUNIO,

RECORD 2:22.

WILL MAKE THE PRESENT SEASON OF AT FRESNO FAIR GROUNDS.

Season Commencing Feb. 1st and ending July 1st.

TERMS—$100 the season, due at time of service.

JUNIO is eight years old, a handsome dark bay 16 hands high, and weighs 1250 pounds. He is the personification of the light harness horse, and his trotting action is superb. At the State Fair of 1886 he took first premium over forty of the finest trotters in the State.

PEDIGREE.

Junio, by Electioneer, premier stallion of Palo Alto (sire of Sunol 2:10 1-2, Palo Alto 2:12 1-4, and 47 others in the 2:30 list.). Dam by Granger by imp. Hercules.

Granger, by imp. Hercules, dam Jenny Lind, by Stockbridge Chief, Jr., he by Stockbridge Chief, he by Vermont Black Hawk. Second dam by Kentucky Whip.

Imp. Hercules, by Kingston, first dam daughter of Tuscar, by Bay Middleton, second dam Malvina, by Oscar; 3rd dam Spotless by Walton; 4th dam by Trumpator (see Bruce's American Stud Book Vol. I, page 26). Hercules is the sire of the dam of Azmoor 2:20¼; also sire of dam of Menlo 2:21 1-2.

Mares not proving in foal may be returned next year free of charge, providing I still have the horse. Pasturage $2 per month. While every care will be taken of horses, no liability will be assumed for accidents or escapes.

For further particulars address

S. N. STRAUBE, Fresno, Cal

Poplar Grove Breeding Farm.

FISHING TACKLE,

WHOLESALE AND RETAIL.

CLABROUGH, GOLCHER & CO.,

630 and 632 Montgomery St.

BOYCE TABLETS.

Leg and Body Wash.

THE BOYCE TABLETS are packed in a nicely decorated metal box with hinged lid—one hundred tablets in each box; directions for use plainly engraved upon the box; therefore, the convenience of the package—no liability to leakage and breakage—economy and ready solubility, together with the absolute certainty of their action, will at once commend the use of BOYCE'S TABLETS to the intelligent horsemen of the country. TABLETS sufficient to make one hundred pints of leg and body wash are conveniently carried in an inside coat pocket or in the hip-pocket of the trousers.

The BOYCE WASH can be applied ALL OVER THE BODY WITHOUT FEAR OF BLISTERING NOR DOES IT AFFECT THE KIDNEYS.

The BOYCE WASH will cure CRACKED HEELS, PUFFS, STOCKINGS, SCRATCHES, INFLAMED TENDONS and FEVERED LEGS.

Price per Box of One Hundred tablets, $2, sent postpaid to any part of the United States; six boxes for $10. A sample of BOYCE'S TABLETS will be mailed to any address on application. These TABLETS are warranted to keep in any climate. Address

BOYCE TABLET COMPANY,

600 Wabash Avenue, - - - Terre Haute, Indiana.

J. A. McKERRON, Pacific Coast Ag't,

228-230-232 Ellis Street, San Francisco, Cal.

THE IMPROVED NOYES ROAD-CART,

PATENTED JULY 17, 1883, AND JUNE 8, 1886.

Some of the Advantages of the Noyes Cart Over All Others.

There is no bar for the rider to climb over in getting in or out. The horse can be hitched eighteen inches nearer than any other road-cart made. You can get in or out with perfect safety—no danger of being thrown into the wheel—a great advantage in breaking colts. THE EASIEST CART FOR ROAD OR TRACK. The only cart that a horse can be speeded to within one second as fast as to a sulky. All our carts are made of the very best materials and are warranted. Manufactured by the NOYES CART COMPANY, Kalamazoo, Mich.

They are indorsed by the following horsemen, all of whom are using them. Ask their opinion of the Noyes Cart: John Splan, who drove Guy a full mile in 2:17¾ and Chapter a half-mile in 1:10¾ to a Noyes Cart, says he would not take $250 for it if he could not get another; W. J. Gordon, Glenville, O.; W. B. Fasig, Cleveland, O.; Dave Muckel, Cleveland, O.; R. J. Mourehead, North East, Pa.; W. J. Chamberlain, Cleveland, O.; M. P. Malone, Bradford, Pa.; S. A. Brown & Co., Kalamazoo Stock Farm; Charles Marvin, Menlo Park, Cal.; W. H. Crawford, Lexington, Ky.; S. L. Caton, who gave Bell Boy a mark at Los Angeles, Cal., of 2:19¼, and drove Chanter a half mile in 1:05¾ and Lowland Girl a full mile in 2:12 to a Noyes Cart; Mike Bowerman, Lexington, Ky.; James Golden, Medford, Mass.; John E. Turner, Philadelphia, Pa.; T. L. Newton, Beaver Dam, Wis.; P. V. Johnston, Marshall, Mich.; W. H. McCarthy, Los Angeles, Cal.; A. W. Dennison, El Dorado, Kan.; P. O. Shank, Cleveland, O.; Charles Barnard, Horton, Mass.; Johnson Bros., Greenville, Mich.; John G. Avery, Buffalo, N. Y.; General R. L. Howard, Buffalo, N. Y.; Howard Conklin, Buffalo, N. Y.; W. D. Ham, Hennepin, Ill.; R. G. Henry, Waterbury, Conn.; J. E. Hayer, Newburgh, O.; J. C. Hart, Jefferson, Tex.; A. W. Harbison, Rock Point, Pa.; Carl Hodges, Battle Creek, Mich.; Barney Treacy, Lexington, Ky.; George Forbes, Cleveland, O.; Gifford Dudley, Topeka, Kan.; William and J. L. Thompson Lamont, Pa.; C. P. Emery, Forest City Stock Farm, Cleveland, O.; H. F. Jones, Minneapolis, Minn.; John Forbes, Elyria O.; D. J. Downs Battle Creek, Mich.; Frank Caton, Randall Station, O.; Arthur D. Sutton, Ind., Pa.; W. F. Neely, Grand Ridge, Ill.; Walter Clark, owner of Pilot Medium, Battle Creek, Mich.; H. R. Kingman, Battle Creek, Mich.; Dr. Sutton and H. C. Reed, Kalamazoo, Mich.; Budd Doble, Chicago, Ill.

SOLE MANUFACTURERS OF STONE'S PATENT SULKY CASE.

They will more than save their cost in one season, and horsemen campaigning trotters cannot afford to do without them. Would refer to Samuel A. Brown, Kalamazoo Stock Farm, S. L. Caton and W. H McCarthy. Address

NOYES CART COMPANY, Kalamazoo, Mich.

Office and Factory, corner Rose and Eleanor streets. H. ARTHUR STONE, Manager.

AN UNQUALIFIED ENDORSEMENT.

Peruvian Bitters are made of the purest ingredients and compounded as carefully as any prescription.

Peruvian Bark, one of its principal ingredients, was introduced into Spain by the Countess, wife of Count CINCHON, Spanish Viceroy to Peru in 1630, who was cured of a fever by its use, since which time, no better remedy for Malaria and for Restoring the Natural Tone of the Stomach has been discovered.

On the Atlantic Coast they are used in the principal Hotels, Clubs and Restaurants, and sold by all Grocers and Druggists. We have sold them for the past three years WITHOUT ANY ADVERTISING and sales have constantly increased UPON MERIT ALONE, and we unqualifiedly recommend them to our friends and customers.

ACKER, MERRALL & CONDIT.

New York, Feb. 1st, 1890.

WILMERDING & CO., Agents for Pacific Coast,

216 FRONT ST., SAN FRANCISCO, CAL.

SAMUEL VALLEAU. JAS. R. BRODIE.

J. R. BRODIE & CO.,

Steam Printers,

—And Dealers in—

Poolseller's and Bookmaker's Supplies.

401—403 *Sansome Street, corner Sacramento, San Francisco.*

ROME HARRIS. JOHN MERIGAN.

"Laurel Palace,"

N. W. corner Kearny and Bush Streets

FRANCISCO.

The Park Training Stable.

CHAS. DAVID, PROPRIETOR.

Corner Grove and Baker Streets, near Entrance to Golden Gate Park.

EVERY FACILITY FOR TRAINING COLTS and taking care of Gentlemen's Roadsters.

Finely appointed stable with every convenience and sixteen roomy box stalls.

The best care given all horses by experienced help, under the personal superintendence of the proprietor

Convenient to the Park Speed Drive, and Accessible to Six Lines of Cable Cars.

THE TRAINING OF COLTS AND ROADSTERS A SPECIALTY.

TROTTERS AND ROADSTERS FOR SALE.

HORSES SOLD ON COMMISSION.

The proprietor trained and brought out the following well known horses: "Sister, Huntress," "Perihelion," "Nona Y," and others.

NEW BOOK.

HORSE BREEDING

Seventh Edition, with Appendix,

By J. H. SANDERS,

In which the GENERAL LAWS OF HEREDITY are exhaustively discussed and applied to the PRACTICAL BUSINESS OF BREEDING HORSES, especially with reference to the Selection of Breeding Stock and the Management of Stallions, Brood Mares, Young Foals, and Diseases Peculiar to Breeding Stock.

Price, Post Paid, $2.

BREEDER AND SPORTSMAN,

313 Bush street. San Francisco, Cal.

THE HICKS-JUDD CO.

Successors to

HICKS & JUDD, Bookbinders,

and Women's Co-operative Printing Office.

Printers, Bookbinders, Publishers,

23 First St., San Francisco.

BREEDERS' CATALOGUES A SPECIALTY.

GOLDEN EAGLE HOTEL

Corner SEVENTH and K STREETS, SACRAMENTO.

FIRST CLASS IN EVERY RESPECT.

The LARGEST and FINEST HOTEL in the City.

W. O. BOWERS, Proprietor.

Free 'Buss to and from the Hotel.

Telephone, Telegraph Office and Messenger Service at Hotel

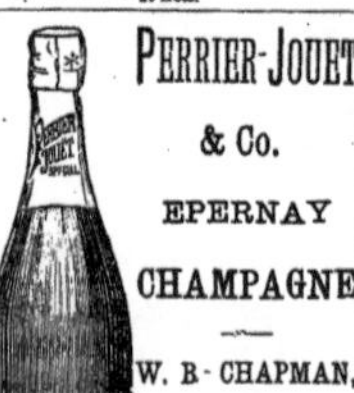

PERRIER-JOUET & Co.

EPERNAY

CHAMPAGNE

W. B. CHAPMAN,

Sole Agent for Pacific Coast.

For sale by all first-class Wine Merchants and Grocers.

BERGEZ'S

RESTAURANT.

FIRST-CLASS. Charges Reasonable.

Private Rooms for Families,

332—334 Pine St., below Montgomery St.

JOHN BERGEZ, Propr

KENNEL ADVERTISEMENTS.

RENTON KENNELS,

SAN FRANCISCO OFFICE, 2922 Pine St.

Kennels located at Bolinas, Cal.

Dogs taken to board and broken at reasonable rates.

POINTER PUPPIES FOR SALE.

By Professor—Gracie Bow; Professor—Belle H.; Climax—Drab; Don—Diana.

Thoroughly broken water spaniel, Bock, out of the Prinder stock. Address

W. D. HOWE,

2922 Pine Street, San Francisco.

Puppies for Sale.

TWO MASTIFFS (Dog and Bitch, 2 months). Sired by a son of Scott's Dick, No. 10,449.

EIGHT MASTIFFS (7 Dogs), Lyon—Nellie, whelped April 1 1890.

ONE GREYHOUND DOG, 14 months, Saturday Night—Brunette.

ONE GREYHOUND DOG, 14 months, breeding unknown.

NINE GREYHOUNDS (4 Dogs), whelped March 18, 1890, Saturday Night—Brunette.

ONE BLACK AND TAN POINTER, 19 months, and broken; Old Black Joe—Black Bess.

ONE GORDON BITCH, 12 months.

ONE GORDON BITCH, 5 months.

TWO FOX TERRIER BITCHES, 12 months.

TWO FOX TERRIER BITCHES, 5 weeks.

ONE YORKSHIRE TERRIER DOG, 3½ months, by Sierp's Mash.

Apply to JAMES E. WATSON,

516 Sacramento street, San Francisco.

P. O. Box 1838.

DOGS---Pointer Pups FOR SALE.

Sure Bench Show and Field Trial Winners, as they have more bench-show and field-trial blood in them than any that have ever been whelped on the Pacific Coast.

Sire, POINT, double field trial winner; he by Vandevort's Don, great field trial and bench show winner, out of Drab, field trial and bench show winner.

Dam, QUEEN CROXTETH by Rush T., bench show winner, out of Champion Patti Croxteth, field trial and bench show winner. This is the best pointer blood in the world. Breeding and health guaranteed. Address,

A. B. TRUMAN,

1425 Steiner St., near Ellis, S. F., Cal.

FOX TERRIERS—C. A. SUMNER, 7 S. Fort St., Los Angeles, Breeder of Fox Terriers. Blemton Vesuvian (14290), by Champion Lucifer, at stud.

SCOTCH COLLIE SHEPHERD DOGS. Pups all ages. Send stamp for descriptive circular. W. A. WICKHAM, Tipton, Ia.

Llewellyn Setter Bitch

GYPSY QUEEN,

Black, White and Tan. Whelped July 24, 1888.

By Hamlet W. 5098—Miss Alice 3763.

Winner First Prize in San Francisco in 1889. Call on or address

SAM. A. WATTSON,

844—854 Harrison Street, City.

CALIFORNIA SPANIEL KENNELS,

Oakland, California, H. P. RENNIE, Prop. Breeder and importer of typical COCKER SPANIELS. Winner of first prizes at S. F. and Los Angeles, 1889; also, Columbus, 1889, New York, 1887. In the stud, solid Black Cocker dog, GIFFEE, won 1st and Gold Medal at S. F., 1889, Fee, $25. Puppies and grown dogs at reasonable prices. My dogs can neither talk nor climb a tree, but are fielders and prize winners.

Fiske's Vanes.

MADE OF COPPER And Gilded with PURE GOLD LEAF.

Manufacturer's Agent.

The HOWE SCALE CO.

411 & 413 Market Street, S. F.

Scales for Weighing of

Live Stock

SEEDS, FEED, Etc.

Write for Catalogue.

Fine Hats,

Latest Styles and Colors.

Meussdorffer & Hubner

8 Kearny Street, San Francisco,

Next to New Chronicle Building.

Everything for Trotter or Runner,

At J. A. McKERRON'S,

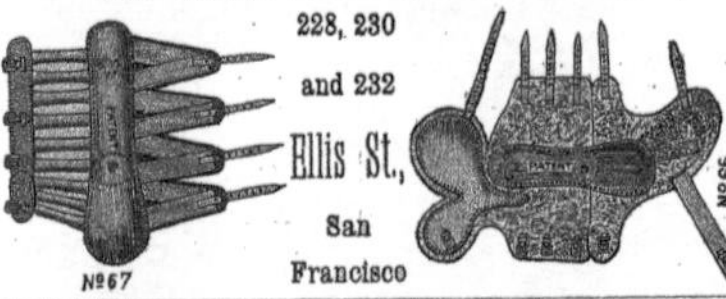

228, 230 and 232 Ellis St., San Francisco

The PARKER Hammerless Shot Gun.

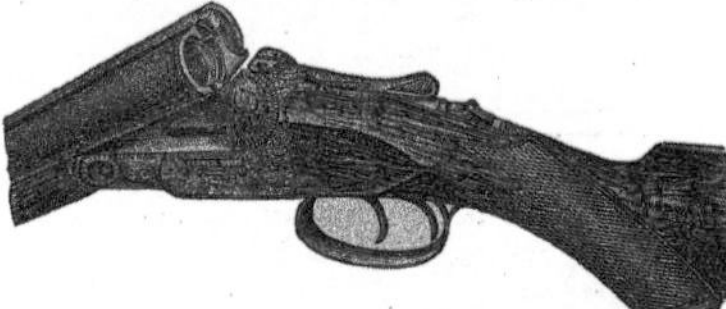

At the Annual Tournament of 1889, held at Cannes, France, the grand prize, consisting of 2000 Francs and a Valuable Cup was won by The Parker Hammerless.

The first Parker Hammerless Gun made won the championship of America at Decatur Illinois.

SEND FOR ILLUSTRATED CIRCULAR.

PARKER BROS., Makers,

New York Salesroom, 97 Chambers St., Meriden Conn.

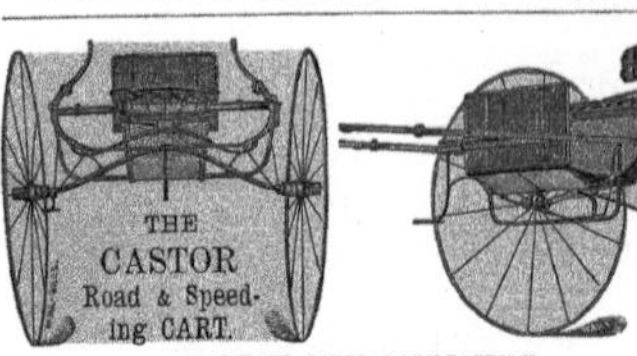

ALWAYS GIVES SATISFACTION.

Combining perfect riding qualities, proportions and balance, with genteel appearance.

No vehicle exhibits a horse to better advantage, and no Cart approaches them for speeding or training purposes.

A stylish vehicle for exercising or pleasure driving, at one-fourth the cost of a carriage. Have none of the horse jockey or objectionable features of other Road Carts.

They are the Leading Cart wherever introduced, and are in use by the most prominent breeders and pleasure drivers everywhere.

Elegant Shifting Top Carts.

Perfectly Balanced Stylish Pole Carts.

For Illustrated Catalogue, with Prices, address,

LEWIS F. CASTOR,
Frankford, Philadelphia, Pa.

JOHN SPLAN, General Agent.

The Brunswick Balke Collender Co.

MANUFACTURERS OF

Standard Billiard and Pool Tables, Saloon and Bank Fixtures

653--655 Market Street, San Francisco, Cal.

Brothers of the Angle

Our NEW EIGHT-STRIP SPLIT BAMBOO is the "King" of all fishing-rods. Chubb's New Catalogue for 1890 is now ready. In addition to a complete list of anglers' supplies, contains articles from the pens of Dr. James Henshall, Petronelis, W. H. Murray, Geo. Goff, Norman, Brother Gardner, and others.

These papers are by the best writers on angling subjects, and are very interesting.

Send 25 cents, and receive Catalogue, post paid. This amount will be deducted from first order (if accompanied with Coupon in book) for one dollar's worth or more of our goods.

Address

THOS. H. CHUBB.
Fishing-Rod Manufacturer
POST MILLS, VT.

Please mention BREEDER AND SPORTSMAN.

ABALONE PATENT SPOON.

PATENT APPLIED FOR.

These Spoons are made of Abalone Shells, which, on account of their iridescence, are more attractive to fish than any other substance. To make them secure, we have patented a German Silver Bar running the entire length of the Shell; the hook is fastened in one end of the bar, the swivel in the other.

These spoons have been tried on all kinds of game fish, *and are wonderfully sure killers.* Sample by mail, Trout sizes, $.50, Salmon sizes, $1.00.

E. T. ALLEN,

Importer of Fire Arms, Fishing Tackle and Sporting Goods

416 Market Street, - - San Francisco.

Studebaker Bros. Manufact'g Co

Sole Agents for

FRAZIER (OF CHICAGO) Carts AND Sulkies,

201--203 Market Street

SAN FRANCISCO, CAL

J. O'KANE, Horse Boots, Clothing and Furnishings For Track, Driving Training and Stable. Every requisite for Horsemen. Harness, Medicines, Etc.

keeps horses healthy, promotes digestion, fattens horses, loosens the hide, and the appetite, prevents leg swelling, strengthens the kidneys, regulates the bowels and destroys worms. $7.50 per 100 lbs. Ask your dealer for it or send

MANHATTAN FOOD CO., 206 Clay St., S. F.

Nutwood 2:18¾ Sire — **DAWN 6407** — Dam Countess, Dam of Strathway (2-y-o), Trial; Placida, Morna, Double team Trial

2:18¾; 2:20; 2:19½.

$100 Popular Price for season of 1890. $100

Not having a breeding farm, and being dependent on the public for patronage, I have set the above low price in order to be within the reach of any one desiring to breed. Good pasturage $3 per month.

For further particulars, address

A. L. WHITNEY, Petaluma.

TWENTY-FOUR PAGES.

Vol. XVI. No 18.
No. 313 BUSH STREET.

SAN FRANCISCO. SATURDAY, MAY 3, 1890.

SUBSCRIPTION
FIVE DOLLARS A YEAR.

Electioneer and George Wilkes.

EDITOR BREEDER AND SPORTSMAN:—I have lately received from Kentucky a breeder's printed circular of four pages with the significant heading, "By their acts ye shall know them" —"George Wilkes vs. Electioneer—Which produced the most speed?" There is no word or line to indicate its source; it is simply a circular containing certain records of performances of the Wilkes family—Harry Wilkes, Guy Wilkes, Rosa Wilkes, Wilson, Wilton, Baron Wilkes, J. B. Richardson, Joe Bunker, and Tom Rogers; also, performances of the Electioneers—Sunol, Palo Alto, Norval, Manzanita, Hinds Rose, Lot Slocum, Bell Boy, Bonita, Adair, Anteeo, Antevolo, Ansel and Albert W. More than three pages are devoted to the Wilkes family; to the Electioneers is allowed less than one page. The intention of the circular is readily apparent. It is to detract from the just merits of Electioneer and to make it appear that to George Wilkes, as the greatest of producers, is the palm of superiority to be awarded. To this purpose it is misleading to ordinary readers; but practical breeders, experienced turfmen and informed patrons of the turf will easily detect the peculiar and studied method employed in presenting the facts. It is set forth that Electioneer has thirteen sons and daughters that have publicly trotted in 2.20 or better in sixty-eight heats; and that George Wilkes has ten sons and daughters that have publicly trotted in 2·20 in one hundred and sixty-seven heats—showing a difference in favor of the Wilkeses of ninety-nine heats in 2:20 or better. Note is made that George Wilkes has been dead eight years, while Electioneer still lives and is doing service.

It is remarkable that in stating the records no mention is made in the circular of the ages at which any of the performances were made. Everything is omitted except the bare record of heats without remark whatever. Next follows a statement of the one hundred and forty-eight heats trotted by Harry Wilkes in from 2:13½ to 2:20, in which the average in one hundred and seven heats is better than 2:18, and the average in forty-one heats is better than 2:16. The records of the Electioneers of 2:20 and better are then given, to the effect that all the noted sons and daughters of Electioneer trotted only fourteen heats in 2:17 and better against the forty-one heats made by Harry Wilkes, showing to the credit of Wilkes twenty-seven heats more than was trotted by all the Electioneers. Further, that against the one hundred and seven heats by Harry Wilkes in 2:20 and better, all the Electioneers have no more than sixty-eight heats to their credit, a difference of thirty-nine in favor of Harry Wilkes.

By this method of presenting the matter it is made to appear that the thirteen sons and daughters of Electioneer have averaged no better than 2:18, while Harry Wilkes alone has made the average in sixty-eight heats in better than 2:17.

Following this comparison of Harry Wilkes with all the Electioneers, is the statement that the sons and daughters of George Wilkes won in twenty-two races in which they had trotted three heats in 2:20 or better, while there were only four races won by the sons and daughters of Electioneer in which those heats were made in 2:20 or better, a difference of eighteen races in favor of the Wilkeses. Also it is stated that the sons and daughters of George Wilkes won sixty-eight races in which they made two heats in 2:20 or better, while the sons and daughters of Electioneer had won in all thirty-two races in which they made two heats in 2:20 or better, a difference of thirty-six races, in favor of the Wilkeses. All these figures are up to December 30, 1889.

The method of these statements is ingenious, but the manner of these is disingenuous, and their "purpose is to mislead. It is the craft by which, while "figures won't lie," they are so distorted from their proper realities as to put truth on the defensive; as involved in the intricacies of cunning statement of the records; by artful manipulation, as to cloud the true facts and delude the reader. But no clear-minded horseman, at all informed in the matter, will be deceived, or will fail to detect the hocus-pocus. Omitted from the reckoning are the facts that to the credit of the sons and daughters of Electioneer are records of 2:10½; 2:12¼; and 2:12½, while the best record of the sons and daughters of George Wilkes are 2:13½; 2:14¾ and 2:15. Further, the records are used in the circular to show that in twelve heats in four races won by the Electioneers, the average is not quite 2:18, while in twelve heats in twenty-two races won by the Wilkeses the average was 2:15½, a difference of 2½ seconds in favor of the latter. The average number of heats won by the Wilkeses in the twenty-two races is put down as thirteen and one-fifth, while in the four races won by the Electioneers, the average heats were only three—a difference again in favor of the Wilkeses of ten and one-fifth heats. Summing up, it is made to appear that the average of these races won by the Wilkeses is four and two-fifths, while the average of the Electioneer is only one race, a difference to the credit of the Wilkeses of threeand two-fifths races. The four Electioneers names are Lot Slocum, Palo Alto, Manzanita and Anteeo. The Wilkeses that won the twenty-two heats were Harry Wilkes, Wilson, Rosa Wilkes, Guy Wilkes and Wilton. The device of naming Palo Alto, Anteeo and Manzanita is unworthy a turfmen or breeder. Manzenita was retired after few performances because of disablement. Anteeo was put upon the track only one season, and has been regularly devoted to the stud, and Palo Alto has never been kept to the turf. On the other hand, Harry Wilkes, gelding, was kept exclusively for racing, to say nothing of Guy Wilkes and the others. The entire figuring on the side of the Wilkeses and against the Electioneers, contained in the circular, is to similar effect a distortion of facts to convey a misleading impression.

By similar method of statement and the like process of argument, it could be shown that a campaigner in the 2:20 class with no better record than 2:18, and an average of barely 2:20 in two hundred heats, is superior to the stallion who was kept from the stud one year, for a turf record, and never more figured as a performer after his fourth year, with 2:19 to his average. Goldsmith Maid—an Abdallah, by the way—with a time record of 2:14 at 18 years, again of 2:14½, and twice of 2:15 at 19 years, and at 20 years made forty-one heats in 2:30 or better, and had to her credit 332 heats in 2:30 or better, still her average of time was not equal to that of Harry Wilkes, 2:17. Then, too, is Maud S. speediest of all, the sequent Queen of the Turf, with her 2:08¾ in public, had made no better than 2·26, 2:28, 2:30, 2:31, in some of her races, while Harry Wilkes trotted 107 heats in 2:30 or better, all the way down to 2:13½—his best—and made an average of better than 2:17 in 41 heats. Yet the figuring of the circular pattern would show Harry Wilkes to better advantage than Maud S. It is absurd.

An honest, painstaking and reliable comparison and analysis of the relative merits of Electioneer and George Wilkes, as producers, and of their sons and daughters, with their turf performances, was contributed by J. C. Sibley to the New York Spirit of the Times, some months ago. Every material point sought to be made to the greater advantage of George Wilkes and his get, is clearly set forth by Mr. Sibley to contrary purpose and to the better showing of Electioneer and his progeny. Mr. Sibley makes tabulated statement of all the performances of the Electioneers and of the Wilkeses, and by excellent analysis so clearly presents the whole matter that even the reader inexperienced in relation to the stud or the turf cannot fail to understand and comprehend all that he expresses. After giving the names of the performers, with the number of races won and lost by each, the record and the average, he presents the analysis of the performances to show which is more entitled to rank first. This he awarded to Electioneer upon plain showing in impartial spirit, and awards to George Wilkes the next highest rank. In his statements Mr. Sibley presents the accurate record of performances and his analysis and comparisons are without fault or favor. The Electioneers trotted in 324 races, in which they won 184, and lost 140, a percentage won of 56.79-100, of 43 21-100 lost. The Wilkes trotted in 1124 races, in which they won 387 and lost 735—a per centage of winnings of 34 60 100, of losings of 65.40 100. The average record of the Electioneers was 2:22 43-64; of the Wilkeses, 2:24.14-59. The showing to the credit of Electioneer is too plain to require remark; it is too clear to be clouded by discolored figuring.

In the whole Wilkes family there are none to place with the best of the Electioneers in speed—the 2:10½ of Sunol three years, the 2:12¼ of Palo Alto. The best showing of Harry Wilkes, the fastest of the family, is 2:13½. In many of the races in which the Wilkeses contested, their competitors were of the class, but had not bettered 2:20 lower than one second. In every race the Electioneers contended they had the ranking performers of the class as competitors.

Mr. Sibley, in his closing summary, states his deductions from all that he has cited in support of his opinion that Electioneer holds indisputable rank at the head of the list of trotting stallions and great producers and transmitters. He remarks: "The tables show that to win a race, the Electioneers had to trot nearly three seconds faster than was requisite for the Wilkeses to win their races; yet in spite of this, the Electioneers won 56.77-100 per cent of all theirs," while the Wilkeses won only 34 60-100 per cent. of the races in which they trotted. Then Mr. Sibley, in full candor, concludes: "In comparison with Electioneer, my judgment is that no family of great prominence will stand the test so close as the George Wilkes family." To similar conclusion is Wallace's Monthly of March, in which, without contention as to sires, as producers of speed, the treatment is general as to all of rank. Referring to stallions with record of 2:20 or better, Wallace says, after mention of the entire list by name, without regard to age: "Of these, Alfred G., 2:19½, Allerton, 2:18¾, Antevolo, 2:19½, Axtell, 2:12, Bell Boy, 2:19½, Brown, 2:18¾, Direct, 2:18½, Edgemark, 2:16, Harry Noble, 2:17½, Lord Byron, 2:18, McEwen, 2:18¼, Patron, 2:14½, Repetition, 2:19½, and Sable Wilkes, 2:18, made records below 2:20 at three and four years old, while the ones having the best inheritance as regards colt trotters, particularly in the nearest ancestors, are Bell Boy, Antevolo and Alfred G., representing the first and second generations from Electioneer, Alfred G. being by a full brother to Antevolo."

Now, Mr. Editor, I think the point at which I aim, to show the misleading character of the Kentucky circular, is made and I have no more to remark upon the subject. Anteeo, the noted son of Electioneer, has left splendid token of his own and his great sire's worth in Sonoma county. Here we have Alfred G., G. & M., Sunset, Redwood, and others—the sons of Anteeo, and with these can rest content, on the side of Electioneer. Still, we hold the Wilkes family in high estimation, and have the young stallion Philosopher, son of Pilot Wilkes and a Wilkes dam, as illustration of this. M.

SANTA ROSA, Cal., April 30, 1890.

There is a rumor current that Marvin will try and reduce the two, three and five-mile trotting record with Gertrude Russell, 2:23½. As is well known, this mare is a full sister to Palo Alto, 2:12¼, and she has shown such powers of endurance, that those in charge are satisfied that she can reduce the distance records mentioned above. It is extremely probable that the smashing of records will be attempted in a five-mile dash, so that they will all fall at a single attempt. Those who are supposed to know, state that the mare can accomplish the feat easily, and that she will be reserved for this work alone.

Women Who Raise Horses.

Great Stock Farms Conducted by Women—New York Women Who Drive Regularly, Notwithstanding it is Not Fashionable—Mrs. Rollin M. Squire and Other Country Drivers—Circuit Professionals.

"No, there is no reason why women should not drive trotting horses. I mean no reason based upon hard logic. The trained horse is the gentlest and most intelligent of animals, and most appreciative of delicacy and kindness. Woman's nature is particularly such as to appeal to the high bred horse, and there is no doubt of the fact that she has naturally sufficient physical strength to drive. She would probably acquire much quicker than men that delicacy of touch and handling that goes so far with horses of merit."

This was what Robert Bonner said when he was asked whether there was any reason other than fashion's whim why women should not drive fast horses. He said, however, that he knew of no women who drove or owned fast horses, or who took any but a passing interest in trotters. He did not comment upon this lack of interest in an animal so worthy of woman's attention as he painted. Neither did he attempt to assign a reason for it.

But the trotting horse is not so exclusively a man's animal as Mr. Bonner seemed to suppose. A vast number of women are numbered among its admirers. Women who drive are asserting themselves more strongly every year, and doubling or trebling their numbers with each succeeding season. And, although riding is the prevailing hobby among New York ladies and a dozen riding schools and riding clubs flourish, while there is not a similar institution for driving, nevertheless the fair devotees of the trotter are not a bit discouraged, and boldly prophesy that the logic of the thing, if nothing else, will bring the trotter eventually to the front as the women's horse. To be driven rather than to drive, and to take saddle horses and be densely ignorant of trotters, is fashionable propriety for women to-day. But there are hosts of women who openly defy this dictum, and take their spin in the Park or the highways of the annexed district daily, much to the improvement of health, complexion and good humor. This much can be said of the women devotees of the trotting horse, and it is not always true of those who ride—they do not follow a fad, but a passion. Those who love driving drive in every weather, and because they love it. The saddle horse has followers, the trotter has worshippers. Women, too, are taking an interest in trotting stock, and more than one has made a reputation as a successful horse breeder. The example of Mrs. Lorillard, who carried on, with marked success, her husband's stud farm of runners, is matched by half a dozen women who have put brains and good management into the raising of trotters and have made money out of it. There is another large and growing body of women who, while they drive little and have no taste for breeding horses themselves, are intensely interested in trotters from a semi-scientific standpoint, and take every opportunity they get to see a finely bred or finely trained horse. John Splan says that the reason running races are more popular with women than trotting matches is that the running races are more exciting and spectacular. This quality draws hundreds of women who crave excitement without knowing or caring a straw about a horse. On the other hand, he says every woman who attends a trotting race is very likely an expert, or at least an enthusiast on horses, and if racing crowds were compared, woman for woman, it would be found that the trotting horse, considered as a horse, has a greater following of women than the running horse.

It is impossible to speak of women who love trotting horses to trotting sharps around here without at once hearing of Miss Edith Van Buren. She is the daughter of the late John Van Buren, Consul-General for several years to Japan, and a niece of William Walter Phelps. Though only 26 or 27 years of age, Miss Van Buren has been breeding horses on her father's place at Teaneck, N. J., for a number of years, with the result of having produced some very creditable horses. She has been a student of the trotting horse since a young girl, and, practically, is a thorough horsewoman. On the Van Buren and Phelps places at Teaneck she speeds her horses to her heart's content. Away from home, however, she will not handle the reins. But wherever she is she will lose no chance of inspecting a finely bred horse, and will leave a ballroom any day to talk records and breeding theories with an expert.

Miss Van Buren is described by her friends as very attractive. She is of good figure and very active. Her complexion is fair and she has dark brown hair, and large, dark and thoughtful eyes. In the privacy of her father's and uncle's great grounds at Teaneck she lives an active outdoor life, every hour of which has something to do with a horse. The Van Buren place adjoins William Walter Phelps' place, and the two together contain something like fifteen or twenty miles of drives. This is a very paradise to the young horse lover. There is a half mile trotting track near by under the management of an association, and here she sends her horses at times for timed trials. Not far from her house are large stables, which contain every possible convenience for raising and breaking horses. Miss Van Buren superintends the raising and breaking of her horses herself. She is perfectly capable of doing it. At intervals a veterinary surgeon from the city visits her stables, or comes on her call by telephone.

Miss Van Buren got her first good horse before she was 20 years old. It was a mare of good blood, down in the trotting register as Norma. She bought her at the Waverly State Fair, where she had just got a first prize in her class. Norma has since taken several prizes in the New York horse shows. She has been Miss Van Buren's principal brood mare, having been bred to Idle Gift and several other stallions equally well known. Miss Van Buren has raised five colts from Norma, all of which have proved capital stuff. She owns the Hambletonian black stallion Prosper. Her bay mare Thorndalia by Thorndale, sired by Edwin Thorne, 2:16¼, out of Norma, she is using for breeding purposes. Norma and another mare are at present in foal by Idle Gift in her stables. Two of the get of Prosper, out of Norma, the black gelding Typhoon and the brown mare Pet, are now stabled with John J. Quinn in Harlem for the winter. She has at present eight or nine standard-bred trotters belonging to her stable.

Miss Van Buren's horse breeding is done on thoroughly scientific principles. She knows the literature of the trotters as well as most breeders and can give offhand the pedigree of more good horses than the average expert can. She believes in thoroughbred blood, and is in the habit of analyzing every blooded horse she sees with the idea of tracing its points to their respective origins in strain. In breeding her mares, she studies out with great care the points she wishes to produce in the foals, and selects stallions in accordance. There are two mares now in foal in Miss Van Buren's stables whose foals will be of interest to breeders generally. They will mark the success or failure of any interesting experiment which Miss Van Buren is making in coach horses. Miss Van Buren has long been considering the problem of improving the American coach horse. She has been casting about for some cross to produce a cob made chunky coach, with arch neck, big stride, and great endurance. The American coach horse possessed neither the strength nor the endurance that she wished. Not long ago her attentions was directed to the bronco as a marvel of snap and endurance. The bronco was smaller than she wished and possessed of bad habits to boot. But she determined to try the experiment, believing that if once a strain of horses could be produced with the broncho's endurance and snap, the bad points could be reduced by further breeding. To this end she secured two broncho mares of powerful build and good habit, and put them to a coaching stallion of undoubted blood and unusual size. Her experiment is looked upon with some doubt by some horsemen, who think the broncho will predominate in the get to a degree to spoil a coach horse. But it has never been tried, and conservative horsemen reserve opinions. Miss Van Buren herself is very hopeful of the result. The cross is the result of a good deal of careful study on her part, and she is confident that it will be productive of good.

Nearly every corner of the country has some woman to exhibit who has made a success with breeding trotters. Miss Van Buren's study of trotters is purely a matter of personal enjoyment with her. But there are in other parts of the land women who have entered the field to make money, and who have succeeded. One of the best known of these women is Mrs. John M. Clay of Lexington, Ky., the widow of Henry Clay's son, and the owner of the Ashland thoroughbred stock farm, one of the best known and best equipped stock farms in the blue-grass region. Mrs. Clay's efforts are by no means confined to trotters. She has a number of famous thoroughbred running horses, and raises as good stock as can be had. The whole world knows Henry Clay's love of good horses. His son inherited the taste, and made of his father's stables a great stud farm. John M. Clay died two years ago. Then his wife at once picked up the business, and has been carrying it on since with marked success. She is pushing her way boldly, and is booked by Kentucky horsemen to become a famous horse raiser. She has got out an attractive catalogue of the broodmares at her farm for 1890. In the announcement at the front of the volume she modestly says:

"The management has now fallen into not very competent hands; but the honest effort which sometimes supplies the place of ability will be used to keep the stock, at least approximately, at its standard of excellence."

It is the opinion of horsemen, however, in spite of Mrs Clay's expressions of self-depreciation, that the fine stock in the Ashland farm is in the hands of one who understands it.

Mrs. John Stiner of Detroit is a woman often spoken of as a proof of womans fitness to own and manage and breed trotting horses. She is a very pretty woman of small erect figure, with fair complexion, fair hair, and bright blue eyes. She came by her love of trotting horses through her husband, who is the Secretary of the American Association of Trotting Horse Breeders. Mrs Stiner has a farm at Indianapolis which she visits frequently, and where she personally raises a good many fine trotters. It was she who first brought the great pacer Westmont, whose record is 2:13¾, to the front. She owned Westmont, and rode and drove him. She came to believe he had speed somewhere in him, and set about developing it with a success which enabled her to sell him for a great price.

It is naturally the blue grass region which has produced the largest number of famous horsewomen. One of the best known after Mrs. Clay, is Mrs. Rhodie Patterson of Lexington. It was the death of a husband in her case, as in Mrs. Clay's, that sent her into the business of horse breeding. Her husband made his reputation as the man who brought out Belle Brassfield, who trotted in 2:20, when that was a famous record, and who afterward was Secretary of the Home Driving Park of Pittsburg, Pa. They were a Pittsburg family, lived there always until Mr. Patterson's death, when Mrs. Patterson went to Lexington and began to raise trotters. She now owns a good farm near the city, and is doing a large business. A colt she raised from Belle Brassfield recently sold for $5000 at one of Rose's sales. She is the sole head and brains of her stock farm. Her son Rhodie is growing up under her care, and promises to become a good horseman in his time. She now is intrusting the training of the horses to him, while she looks particularly after the breeding and the general and business management of the farm. One of her horses is the pacer Bessemer, who made 2:15 as a four year old. Mrs. Patterson is making money.

Mrs. Augustus Sharpe is identified with Shady Side Farm three miles from Louisville. This is a prosperous stock farm, where fine trotters are bred. It has an annex of 235 acres on the Taylorsville road, also near Louisville, and puts out voluminous catalogues of stock each year. Augustus Sharpe, the manager and proprietor, is making a fortune out of his business. Mrs Sharpe does not appear as interested. It is well known, however, that she is a thorough horsewoman, and contributes to the success of the farm. So enthusiastic is she that she accompanies her husband around the circuits when their best horses are racing. When their Greenlander, who holds a stallion record of 2:19¼, was beaten at Cleveland recently, Mrs. Sharpe burst into an uncontrollable fit of weeping, and had to be conducted from the grand stands. The occurence made no small sensation, as she is a tall and handsome blonde whose striking appearance had previously attracted widespread attention. Since then she has visited New York with her husband, and seen Greenlander win at the Driving Club races.

Miss Nannie Smith of Lexington, Ky., is generally spoken of as the luckiest women having to do with trotting horses. She was the sole owner of Red Wilkes, the famous son of George Wilkes. She sold a half interest in him to C. W. France for $12,500 several years ago, the understanding being that Mr. France was to manage Red Wilkes in stud. Miss Smith's income from the famous stallion's stud fees has exceeded $10,000 a year since.

Though the women who have gone into raising trotting stock are few and far between, the fair devotees of the fast horse and the light carriage are many. They are little heard of, probably for the reason that fashion has turned its back upon the trotting horse. The ladies who drive, moreover, are generally not seekers for notoriety, and they take their pleasure in a quiet and unassuming way. If one wants to see them for himself, let him go to the Central Park in the early forenoon, and take a seat by a principal driveway. It is generally too crowded for women to venture out in the afternoon, yet some do, and steer their turnouts through the throng of carriages of every sort with great skill. Manager L. T. Curtis of the Winfield stable in fifty eighth street, where a considerable number of ladies keep their horses, says that driving is becoming more popular with ladies every day. Women like fine horses and fast horses, he says, and love to own them. There are many women of standing in the city who take great interest in their horses, enquire about them every day, and give personal direction as to their keep and care. Mr. Curtis is another one of those who believe that women are perfectly able physically to manage thoroughbreds.

The carriage most used by women in the Park and suburbs is the phaeton, rigged either single or double. This is quiet and unassuming, and, with top raised, protects the fair driver from impertinent gaze from sides and back. The fashionably proper thing in phaetons is an extremely heavy vehicle which requires two strong horses. But the enthusiastic snap their fingers at fashion, and purchase as light a phaeton as is made, and this, behind a single horse or pair, is the carriage you most often see driven by ladies in the Park. And very often the expert will pick out some remarkably fine horse hitched to these modern carriages.

But the women who love fast horses do not always confine themselves to phaetons. There is one young woman of striking beauty, who is seen every day in the Park, but is known by none who drive there, whose outfit is, from the horse lover's standpoint, complete. She either drives a pair of browns, which can pull a wagon a mile in 2:40, or a single bay horse, which is the admiration of every horse lover who sees him. She has a black phaeton as a matter of course, which she uses either single or double, but she frequently drives in the afternoon in an airy road wagon of light wood, with light leather finishings and brass guard. A girl who report says is her sister usually accompanies her, and a terrier is generally hid away in the turnout somewhere. When there is snow, she drives out in a green and gold trimmed Stivers cutter which can hardly exceed sixty-five pounds in weight. No day is too rainy or snowy or hot or cold for this young woman to take her spin. She is always accompanied by some one. She drives for the pleasure of the drive, and on pleasant days will speed up Seventh avenue, over the bridge, and often to and beyond Yonkers. Her turnout, with its fine horses, of course attracts no end of attention, but she never looks to right or left, or notices people she meets, except to turn out of their way. Report has it that she lives in Madison avenue near the Park, and is the daughter of a well-known business man.

There is a lady who lives in the Navarro flats, whose husband was a defeated candidate in a recent election, who is seen nearly every day driving in the Park. Her daughter usually accompanies her. Another lady, the wife of a banker, who lives in Sixty-second street, near Fifth avenue, drives a pair of cobs to an English T cart every morning. A red-wheeled road wagon behind a pair of cobs is looked for every morning by the habitues of the park drives. The lady who handles the reins knows how to drive. She is the wife of a Liberty street real estate dealer. Another habitual driver is a brown-haired young woman, who manages a fashion journal. She is usually accompanied by a sister or brother, and drives a black horse to a red-wheeled Brewster wagon. An English woman, who drives a seal brown, bang-tail cob every morning in the Park, is said to be one of the most devoted advocates of driving in this city. Women know much more about horses in England than here, she says. A very stylish turn-out is seen early every morning in the park. It is a spider wheeled buckboard with yellow wheels. The lady who sits in it and drives a pair of black, chunky-built cobs is the wife of a stock broker. On pleasant afternoons she sometimes meets her husband at the elevated station with this rig, and they drive together, the wife handling the reins. Another lady whose face is very familiar in the park on pleasant mornings, is the wife of the manager of a large up-town theatre. She drives a sorrel horse, and likes to drive fast. Miss Fannie Dickinson, the daughter of Col. A. G. Dickinson, is seen almost daily in the park and upper drives of the city. She drives a pair.

The few women here mentioned, any of whom may be recognized in the Park any pleasant day, are only a very few examples of the many ladies who habitually drive in this town, and drive good horses too. The demand for fast horses of good blood for ladies' use is becoming such that horse trainers are making a specialty of training blooded horses to answer to the pull of a ribbon.

To see the woman devotee of the trotter in all her glory, however one must go to the country. At all the resorts during the season the demure city girl, who has been a victim to style for the rest of the year and has sat discontentedly in the back of her brougham while John handled the ribbons, lets herself loose and drives the fast horse at will on country roads over hill and through valley. The country is the trotting horse's paradise all the year round, and country fairs are largely patronized by women who love the speeders. Mrs. Rollin M. Squire is a type of a great many estimable women who delight in a fast horse. The poet ex-Commissioner has a country place in Westchester, and Mrs. Squire delights to drive a superb Kentucky thoroughbred for which her husband paid $5000. She appears at fairs in a dainty country phaeton behind this fine horse, and is so proud of him that she does not miss an opportunity to enter him for the honorary prize for fine blood horses often offered at the larger county fairs. Mrs. Squire has driven her horse herself in such contests, exhibiting his paces and accomplishments.

Philadelphia has a young woman who is well known for her love of fine trotting horses, and sometimes appears, like Mrs. Squire, before a country crowd, if by so doing she can bring laurels to the proud head of a favorite blooded horse. She is Miss Linda Cooper, daughter of James Cooper, once the partner of P. T. Barnum. She is about 20 years old, and an unusually pretty brunette. Her father is very wealthy, and humors his daughter to the utmost in her fancy for fine trotters. Mr. Cooper himself is a natural horseman, and his daughter has inherited his tastes. She drives single or double, and no weather can keep her off the road.

In the field of professionalism, the trotting horse has naturally been the favorite with women. Barring circus horses, whose running is at best nothing more than a desperately slow canter, the running horse is one too many for the professional woman. But there has been no end to the women who have made their living by driving trotters at country fairs and other shows. Every one who has ever attended country fairs with their trotting tracks is familiar enough with the horsy woman, with painted cheeks, gay colored dress, and silk jockey cap who is advertised to drive a trotter with a mile-long pedigree, against time or against a running horse, ridden by Monsieur Somebody, the world-famous jockey. Sometimes these women travel the circuits in pairs and drive against each other in races that are of course more or less "fake," but which throw a country crowd into a state of wild excitement. And very able horsewomen they often are, too. It is not seldom that a woman of this sort is engaged in good faith to drive a favorite trotter in a dash for rich stakes, and often she accomplishes her task and lands her horse a winner in a style that brings her plenty of well-merited applause. There is one woman among these professional horsewomen so far above the rest in accomplishment that she deserves mention. She is Mme. Marroniette. She has been before the public now for nearly fifteen years, has made a comfortable fortune. She has always owned own horses, and has scorned any but the best. She has devoted herself to trotting horses by any means, although trters have naturally occupied most of her attention. She an all-round horsewoman. She originated the idea, which been so popular for years at country fairs, of women dring running horses to light wagons for money prizes, and holds the bona fide record for the fastest work in this li. It was she also who originated the long-distance riding es for women at country fairs, with numerous changes of hses. She comes honestly by her French name, although is an American. She married a Frenchman named Marrotte years ago. As a skillful driver of trotters she is kwn over the circuits from the Atlantic to the Pacific.—N. Y. an.

The Napa Entries.

lthough the entries for the Napa meeting closed on the of last month, it was only this week that we received thn. As sent to us by the secretary, they are as follows:

r District comprising counties of Solano, Napa, Sonoma, Marin, Le, Colusa, Yolo, Mendocino, Butte and Humboldt.

NO. 3—FOR YEARLINGS.

0 guaranteed. District. $40 entrance, payable as follows: $10 Ail 1st, when entries close; $10 June 1st; $10 July 1st; $10 August when colts must be named.

Name.	Residence.
en E. Harris	San Francisco
R. S. Brown	Petaluma
. L. Whitney	Petaluma
. J. Shafter	Olema
Wilfred Page	Penn's Grove
has. Scott	Napa
. B. Starr	Napa
McLees	Vallejo
. C. Holly	Vallejo
. T. Hatch	Suisun
. T. Hatch	Suisun
Brandow	San Francisco
eo E. Guerne	Santa Rosa
. S. Hogoboom	Rohnerville

NO. 4—FOR TWO-YEAR-OLDS.

0 guaranteed. District. $50 entrance, payable as follows: $10 Ail 1st, when entries close: $10 May 1st, $10 June 1st, $10 July 1st, August first, when colts must be named

Name.	Residence.
Frank Drake	Vallejo
en E Harris	San Francisco
. B. Edington	Oakville
. S. Brown	Petaluma
Brughelli	Napa
. De Turk	Santa Rosa
. L. Whitney	Petaluma
. Cookley	Vallejo
Wilfred Page	Penn's Grove
. Kemper	Oakville
. W. Crabb	Oakville
Rufus Murphy	Santa Rosa
. McLees	Vallejo
osedale Breeding Farm	Santa Rosa
. H. White	Lakeville
. C Holly	Vallejo
. Brandow	San Francisco
V. T. Bartlett	Suisun
. S. Hogoboom	Rohnerville

NO. 5—FOR THREE-YEAR-OLDS.

0 guaranteed. District. $50 entrance, payable as follows: $10 Ail 1st, when entries close; $10 May 1st, $10 June 1st, $10 July 1st, August 1st, when colts must be named.

Name.	Residence.
Frank Drake	Vallejo
. J. Budson	Lakeport
. L Whitney	Petaluma
. J. Shafter	Olema
Wilfred Page	Penn's Grove
. W. Crabb	Oakville
Rufus Murphy	Santa Rosa
. H. White	Lakeville
. C. Holly	Vallejo
V. T. Bartlett	Suisun
uy E. Grosse	Santa Rosa

2:20 Class—Trotting; free for all. Purse $1,500.

Name	Residence.
. De Turk	Santa Rosa
rvin Ayers	San Francisco
Pleasanton Stock Farm	Pleasanton
C. Holly	Vallejo
Thos. Smith	Vallejo
. Gonzales	San Francisco
. W. Loeber	St. Helena
. B. Gifford	Los Angeles
. Brandow	San Francisco
San Mateo Stock Farm	San Mateo

2:24 Class—Trotting; free for all. Purse $1,500.

Name.	Residence.
. H. Cooper	Eureka
. L. McCord	Sacramento
Sanborn & Murphy	Santa Rosa
Pleasanton Stock Farm	Pleasanton
. P. Heald	San Francisco
. C. Holly	Vallejo
Frank H. Burke	San Francisco
San Mateo Stock Farm	San Mateo

os. 1 and 2 for two and three-year-olds; free for all, and 2:20 class being not filled.

Merchants and Manufacturer's Stake.

EDITOR BREEDER AND SPORTSMAN.—Herewith I enclose a list of the subscriptions of the Merchants and Manufactur- es Guaranteed Stake of $10,000 to be trotted at the Summer Meting of the Detroit Driving Club, July 22 to 25, 1890.

he list comprises a formable array of noted horsemen, and altogether will give the knowing ones quite an opportunity to guess the winner of this valuable stake, when the horses are named, Monday July 7th.

. T. Foster, Bloomington, Ill.
ames Stimson, Chicago, Ill.
. D. Bills, Tecumseh, Mich.
. Deming, Terre Haute, Ind.
. L. & C. S. Cobb, Eaton Rapids, Mich.
lenview Stock Farm, Louisville, Ky.
ames E. Clay, Paris, Ky.
ickory Grove Stock Farm, Racine, Wis.
. W. Leiby & Son, Chicago, Ill.
add Doble, Chicago, Ill.
. P. Ijams, Terre Haute, Ind.
ohn Lothian, Hamtramck, Mich.
dgewood Stock Farm, Terre Haute, Ind.
eorge H. Hammond, Detroit, Mich.
ames O. Gray, Boston, Mass.
ames Elliott, Philadelphia, Pa.
oh Stewart, Kansas City, Mo.
. S. McGraw, Bay City, Mich.
alo Alto Stock Farm, San Francisco, Cal.

Very truly yours,
P. M. CAMPBELL, Secretary.

ETROIT, Mich, April 21, 1890.

The Coronado Track.

Several times we have had occasion to mention the new track lately finished at Coronado Beach, and are pleased to lay before our readers a letter from an occasional correspondent who shows the advantages of this one over many others of the so-called winter tracks.

EDITOR BREEDER AND SPORTSMAN:—There is probably no place where the horse is found in a higher degree of perfection than in California, and this is especially true in the case of high graded stock. The most of the State is well suited for breeding, raising and training such stock, but the southern portion of it is especially so, and Coronado now enjoys peculiar advantages that entitle it to a foremost rank. Visitors who have spent some few weeks in the locality often remark that the salutary influence of the climate on the state of their health is quite astonishing. The same effect is equally noticeable in the case of horses, and the animals raised in this climate are distinguished for great chest development and increased breathing capacity.

Fully appreciating the rapidly-increasing interest manifested everywhere in the racing and other fast stock of California, the Coronado Beach Company deemed it important to have a first-class race track on their grounds, and that for various reasons: There are but few places in this State where all the requirements of a good race-track can be found, or where the requisite climatic advantages can be had in anything like the same degree as on the peninsula of Coronado. The soil where the track is laid out is a sandy loam, which neither becomes muddy when wet nor cakes in drying. Even after the most drenching rains, the water is soon absorbed, owing to the porous nature of the ground, which is never sloppy or heavy, and requires no artificial drainage. Consequently the horses never cup the soil, but speed onward with clean feet and the easy, elastic bound much appreciated by the riders. For breeding, raising, and training horses of all classes, and especially fast stock, this climate cannot be surpassed; and the superior quality of the water is equally conducive to their health. There are no extremes of heat or cold, no snow or ice, only moderate rains, and no high winds. Fogs are rare, the air is dry and mild, and the days are nearly all fair and sunny. In fact, the climate is all that could be desired. Here the exercising and training of the horses can be carried on with perfect regularity the whole year without intermission, a fact that must be appreciated by distinguished drivers and horsemen, such as Hickok, Marvin, Welch and others.

The racing interests of California are year by year increasing with rapid strides, and will doubtless continue to do so. Hence the necessity for a first-class race track, and it is a fortunate circumstance for horsemen that such a track has been formed in a climate fitted for using it at all seasons. In laying out the track, the services of an eminent railroad engineer were employed, and the work was executed in a scientific manner, special attention being paid to the proper arranging of the stretches and the curves, and also to the due adjusting of the grade of the curves, leaving the outside the higher, with the same precision as on a railway track—a thing of much importance, as an error in this matter would likely cause accidents and much injury both to men and much injury both to men and horses.

The track was located, after mature deliberation, with the advice of that celebrated horseman, Orrin A. Hickok, who visited the ground and designated its location and shape. It is a regulation one mile course with stretches and turns of one-fourth of a mile each. The whole track is so nearly level that there is not three feet of difference in the height of the ground anywhere, and the home stretch comes in with a fall of about a foot and a half.

The grand stand is in a position where it commands a full view of the whole course. There are over one hundred box stalls, each 14 feet square, with ample sheds adjoining, which are rented at $2 per month each. Several of them have already been taken for 1890-91.

This is the only race course in California where weather, soil and climate admit of a race being run almost any day in the year. Yours, etc, JOHN PAUL.

Live Stock Insurance.

The Pacific Coast Live Stock Owners' Mutual Protective Association has been organized under the laws of the State of California for the purpose of preventing the spread of all contagious and infectious disease amongst livestock and to prevent the throwing upon the market of diseased meat animals and the sale of diseased and unwholesome meat for human food, and also by mutual and proportionate subscription to indemnify members for loss of live stock by accident or disease.

This association originated among stockmen in one of the largest stock counties in the State, who, from personal experience, saw the necessity for united action to prevent the disastrous spread of contageous diseases, and after mature deliberation came to the conclusion that an association of this kind, honestly and carefully managed, could not only be made a benefit to its members by securing to them a means of protecting themselves against loss, but be far more powerful and influential to contend with the spread of disease.

The General Manager of the Association is Volney Howard, Room 73, Flood Building, San Francisco, a man of extended experience in the insurance field.

The Secretary is G. W. Gallanar, editor and proprietor of the Pacific Grove Review.

The Actuary is F. D. Howard, proprietor of the Del Monte Drug Store, Monterey.

The Vice-President is Edw. Ingram, ex-Postmaster of Monterey and senior member of the firm of Ingram Bros., wholesale and retail butchers Monterey and Pacific Grove.

The President of the Association is the Hon. B. V. Sargent of Monterey, known throughout the State as one of the largest and wealthiest stockmen in the country. His connection with the association as its President is an assurance of careful and honest management in all its branches.

The President of the association refers to the following well known persons: D. J. Staples of San Francisco, Jesse D. Carr, President of Salinas Bank; A. B. Jackson, Vice-President of Salinas Bank; L. U. Shippee of Stockton, Senator John Boggs of Colusa, Henry Miller of Miller & Lux, San Francisco, Senator Caminetti of Amador, J. H. Gilmore of San Francisco, Dorn & Chapman of San Francisco, Cox & Clark of Sacramento, Marcus D. Borcck of Sacramento, C. F. Ryland of San Jose, Wm. Dunphy of San Francisco, E. and H. Moffatt of San Francisco, M. Brandenstein & Co. of San Francisco, Senator Goucher of Mariposa, Stephen J. Wright of Los Angeles, Senator Steele of San Luis Obispo, L. Worden of San Luis Obispo, and J. B. H. Cooper of San Francisco.

More About Flaxtail 8132.

EDITOR BREEDER AND SPORTSMAN:—I see from your issue of the 26th inst. that some of your exchanges are discussing the breeding of Flaxtail 8132. His stable name when I first knew him was Flaxtail, and he was said to be a "Bull Pup." Just before I came to California, I attempted to trace his breeding. I learned that he was brought to Iowa from Salem, Indiana, by a man by the name of Mitchell. I addressed a letter of inquiry to "Any Leading Horseman, Salem, Indiana." In reply I received a letter, saying in substance, "Our postmaster did me the honor to hand me your letter, and it fell into the right hands. My brother and I broke the horse Flaxtail when he was two years old, and I think he was the fastest pacer in the world, but his breeding is unknown. His dam, a mare that looked like a thoroughbred, was brought to our place in the Fall by a stranger, and sold so cheap, that every one believed she was stolen. In the spring she foaled this colt you are inquiring about." The satchel containing this letter was lost on the way here, and as I considered the pedigree hopeless, I did not charge my memory with the writer's name.

Flaxtail and Blue Bull, from the middle piece forward, bore a most striking resemblance to each other, but Flaxtail had more of the pacing conformation behind. Both were phenominally fast pacers, and there was such a strong resemblance in their produce, that the get of one horse could easily have been passed off for the get of the other. The place of Flaxtail's birth made it possible, and these resemblances made probable that he was sired by the sire of Wilson's Blue Bull. It would have been to my interest to accept the claim that he was of Pilot descent, as Maud S. had made that blood popular. I have never attempted to give his breeding farther than to accept the "said to be" of the Eastern journals, which, for the above reasons, is in accordance with my belief.

M. W. HICKS.

The Race Record—Who Holds it?

EDITOR BREEDER AND SPORTSMAN.—In looking through the table of fastest trotting records, in Wallace's Year Book, I see that Maud S. is credited with the fastest heat made in a race. This honor, I think, belongs to Sunol. Maud S. took her record of 2:13½ in a race against a single competitor, and she, a mare only able to drive Maud S. out in the two previous heats in 2:19 and 2:21½. Sunol's race was for a stake opened two years previous, in which there were twenty-one entries. Most of these made payments up to the last before the race, but in the meantime Sunol had shown such speed that it was useless to go against her, and it would not affect Sunol whether others were in the race or not. It is true that the announcement was informally made that she would go the heat faster than her previous record of 2:13¾, but the fact could not affect the character of the event. No choice could be made of weather or track, and but a single heat could be allowed. Had Trinket been in the race and able to go as fast as she did against Maud S., she would not have got near enough Sunol to be considered as a factor. Had Trinket fallen down immediately after the word was given, Maud S. would still have been given credit for the heat as a race record.

Whether a performance is a race or not, does not depend on the presence of a revival contestant; it needs only be a fixed event, in which competitors can appear, and over which the owner of this trotter has no further right and powers than in any other race. There is no rule of the turf that makes a walk-over anything other than a race. Can it be said that a horse who has been a winner in a walk-over for a regular stake is eligible in a class for horses that have never started in a race? Had a cart-horse been started against Sunol, even Mr. Wallace would not have questioned her race record.

DENVER.

The American Association.

Last week we gave a list of those who are under suspension in the National Association, and herewith follows the persons who are under the ban of the "American." In the expelled list we find

NAME.	RESIDENCE.	DATE.
Chas. E. Picket	Los Angeles	Dec. 3, 1889
Clarence J Richards	Los Angeles	Dec. 3, 1889
Harry Stover	San Francisco	May 13, 1889

The suspensions are more numerous, and as taken from the pamphlet issued by the American Association, are:

Burke, Thos. L	San Diego, Cal	Nov. 9, 1889
Cabara, J. & Co	Fresno, Cal	Oct. 21, 1887
Cochran, Jackson	San Louis Obispo, Cal	Oct. 21, 1889
Cooper, S. A	Sacramento, Cal	Oct 21, 1889
Del Valle, U. F	Camulus, Cal	Nov. 9, 1889
Den, E. R	Santa Barbara, Cal	Nov. 9, 1889
Dietz, A. C	Oakland, Cal	Sept. 7, 1889
Dwyer, Wm	San Jose, Cal	Oct. 21, 1887
Edwards, W. H	Oakland, Cal	Oct. 4, 1884
Eldred, C. H	Sacramento, Cal	Oct. 21, 1887
Emerson, S. B	Mountain View, Cal	Sept. 7, 1889
Erickson, C	Fresno, Cal	Oct. 16, 1879
Green, William	Green Meadows, Cal	Oct. 21, 1887
Horan, Chas	Sacramento, Cal	Nov. 9, 1889
Johnson, Monroe	Sacramento, Cal	July 13, 1889
Johnson, Peter	San Francisco, Cal	Oct. 3, 1885
Kelly, M	Sacramento, Cal	Oct. 6, 1888
Lawrence, H. M	Santa Barbara, Cal	Nov. 9, 1889
Livingstone, Robt	Los Angeles, Cal	Sept. 15, 1888
Maben, O. S	Visalia, Cal	Apr. 26, 1889
McCarty, D	San Francisco, Cal	Oct. 17, 1881
Morine, A. L	Los Angeles, Cal	Apr. 26, 1889
Murphy, Wyman	Santa Rosa, Cal	Sept. 7, 1889
Ray, A. G	Visalia, Cal	Oct. 21, 1889
Reavey, Jno	Sacramento, Cal	Nov. 9, 1889
Rupert, Geo	Stockton, Cal	Oct. 17, 1881
Rose, Harry E	Los Angeles, Cal	Oct. 18, 1889
Thomas, Chas	San Jacinto, Cal	Nov. 9, 1889
Williams, Scott	Oakland, Cal	Sept. 13, 1889

TURF AND TRACK.

Salvator and Firenzi are showing up the best in the Haggin string.

The speedy Reclaire is said to be broken down; if so, Mr. Belmont will get her earlier than he expected.

T. Morton left with the Hearst stable last Saturday, and with average luck should pilot several winners.

Governor Stanford thinks that three of the produce of Beautiful Bells may enter the 2:30 list this year.

An English breeder will send a mare across the water this year to be stinted to Wellington, brother of Sunol.

Ed Geers will handle Virginia Evans, 2:24, this season. Her owner, Mr. Gray, believes that she can beat 2:18.

Only members will be admitted to Beacon Park this season. No spirituous liquors will be sold on the grounds.

W. M. Irvin of Richmond, Ky., had four mares slip their foals recently, entailing a loss of from $7,500 to $15,000.

Among the aristocratic members of the New York Jockey Club is Lord Stanley, the Governor-General of Canada.

Westmont, pacing record 2:13¾, will start against time and with running mate in the southeastern circuit, opening April 29th.

Palm, two-year-old record 2:33, stands 15.3½, and is expected to beat the three-year old stallion record of Maine this year.

B. C. Holly has a nomination in all the closed races given by the 25th Agricultural District, the Solano and Napa Association.

Marcus Daly has nominated his colts in the stakes, both running and trotting, at Deer Lodge, Missoula, Anaconda and Butte.

"The black and gray check" of Budd Doble will probably be behind Houri, 2:17, as she goes down the grand circuit this season.

W. G. Buen, who was ruled off at Saratoga last summer with his horse Ballston, has been reinstated by the Saratoga Association.

The Santa Anita Stable had to leave the two-year old colt Encinado by Rutherford, dam Aritta, at Albuquerque while en route for the East.

Longstreet's dam has just thrown a beautiful colt foal, a full brother to Longstreet. He is her sixth foal, and all of them have been horse colts.

There are thirteen subscribers to the famous Clay Stakes to be trotted at Albany in June. The New England subscribers are George W. Leavitt and John Trout.

Dr. W. S. Webb, who is on a visit to England, has purchased fourteen fillies (probably Hackneys) which are to be shipped at once to his farm at Shelburne, Vt.

Mr. M. F. Dwyer, who has not been enjoying the best of health for some time, is again ailing, and has wisely decided to take a vacation, having gone to Washington.

T. H. Moore of Philadelphia has bought for $3000 of J. B. Perry of Lexington Valley Queen, a four year old bay mare by Red Wilkes, dam Valley Girl by Walkill Chief.

I understand R. Havey, the well known driver, and at one time crack jockey, is going down to Palo Alto to take charge of the trotting department during Marvin's absence.

Tom Stevens has what appears to be another strong stable this year. It is composed of sixteen well bred and good looking horses, with Wary and Florimore at their head.

W. H. Wilson of Cynthiana, Ky., has bought at a price not made public Black Jane, the dam of Simmons 2:28, and Rosa Wilkes 2:18½. She will probably be bred to Sultan 2:24.

Bowerman Brothers of Lexington, Ky., have sold for $3,000 the two year old colt Star McGregor, by Robert McGregor—Lissie, by Aladdin, to J. H. Hartley, of Montgomery, Ala.

Meadowthorpe Stud has lost by death the brood mare Kate Mattingly, by John Morgan-Betsy Hunter, by Oliver. Among her produce were Herbert, Creosote, Matinee and Long Gir .

Stonehenge long ago shrewdly remarked that it is to the tried sire of a fast stallion rather than to the the untried fast stallion himself, that a prudent man will send his valuable mares.

Elkwood, the hero of the Suburban of 1887, has been sold by Mr. Walter Gratz to Maj. Crumbaugh, of Hopkinsville, Ky., for $5,000. Elkwood is by Eolus out of Minnie Andrews

While exercising on the Lexington track the thoroughbred colt Fontenoy, two year old, by Fonso-Sleepy Kate, fell dead from heart disease. He belonged to S. Lucas in the employ of Mr. A. Belmont.

Woodburn Stud has lost by death the broodmare Molly Wood, by Lexington out of Hymenia, by imp. Yorkshire. Among her produce were Falcon, Golden Gate, Woodlark, Mollie Brown, Obelisk, and Altaire.

W. W. Terrell of Denver has bred Pastime by Mambrino Time 1686, dam Fanny K by Hero of Thorndale 549, to William L, and Louise B, by Mambrino Time 1686, dam Mattie D by Blagrave's Paddy Burns to Jay Bird.

Mr. Lee Mantle, while in Helena last week, sold a trotting-bred stallion, a full brother to Raymond's Doncaster, 2:28¼, to a Helena gentleman, who has placed him in Mr. C. Jeffries' hands at the fair grounds for track purposes.

There is some talk of San Diego, Los Angeles and Fresno arranging for three meetings to take place after the circuit. It should be successful if properly arranged, for owners could then afford to attend the Southern meetings.

W. H. Smith has added Duke of Milpitas (Duke of Norfolk—Gypsy) to his stable paying Mr. Boots $2000 for the two year old. Al Farrow, Longshot, Duke of Milpitas and the speedy Susie S should win a good many races, if *well placed*.

Minuet 3, Rayon d'Or—Reel Dance, was sold by W. L. Scott before she ran in her race on the 22d by the Excelsior Stable for $1000 and half the stake if she won. The filly should be worth much more on her breeding alone.

Capt. Sam Brown of Pittsburg, was at the Memphis races. A well known cotton broker was bewailing his losses to him, and the coal king consoled him by saying, "Never mind, old man, next year I will bring a horse down to get you square."

The Memphis Critic says that James G. Sheridan is an excellent starter, only he lines his horses almost a sixteenth behind the starting point, which is hardly right, and increases the distance just that much. Fifty yards beyond the starting point is considered about the proper distance.

Francis D. Kelly died in Philadelphia last week. The deceased was only 15 years of age, yet had gained a good reputation for fearlessness and horsemanship. Among the horses he has ridden are Pope, Leo, Pat Daly, Black Prince, Duke, Maggie A., Nimble Foot, Nat Trimble and others.

Gov. W. R. Merriam of Minnesota on the 21st purchased from W. P. Ijams of Terra Haute, one-fourth owner of Axhis celebrated black mare Reina at a good round price. The figure is not stated. Reina has been one of the greatest attractions at Warren Park Stock Farm, and has a record of 2:22¼.

The declarations in the Decoration Handicap, which is to to be run at Latonia May 30th, are in. Of 57 horses only 10 are declared out. These are Maori, Terra Cotta, Huntress, Bannerette, Sister Geneva, Montrose, Retrieve, Spokane, Maduma and Newcastle. The value of the race is estimated at about $5000.

D. J. McCarty will ship East to-morrow about five carloads of trotting and thoroughbred stock. By the way, Dan says the best spec he made last year was in Chicago where he traded several horses for a town lot and has received ten or twenty letters a week since from would-be purchasers, all offering good prices.

Francis Pope, Secretary of the Helena Fair Association, went over to Anaconda last week to meet, by appointment, the other Secretaries of the racing associations on the west side, with a view of adjusting the conflicting dates existing between Butte and Helena. Mr. Pope has no doubt but that the matter will be amicably adjusted.

The Late General Goodlake who died on April 5th was well known and popular in English Turf circles, and once a prominent patron of coursing, being the nominator of Meg for the Waterloo Cup won by her in 1865. The deceased went all through the Crimea war, and for his distinguished service was decorated with the Victoria Cross.

All the secretaries of the association in the Montana Racing Circuit, with the exception of the Missoula representative, met and arranged the circuit as follows: Missoula, July 14th to July 19th. Deer Lodge, July 22d to July 26th. Anaconda, August 1st to August 9th. Butte, August 12th to August 20th. Helena, August 23d to August 30th.

J. R. Crawford, otherwise "Dick," at the Helena fair grounds, has in training a two-year-old, a full brother to the well known Sunday. Good judges say he is a better built horse than Sunday, and that is saying a good deal. He has another two-year-old in training—Bessie by Regent, also Carrie Lee and Katie Putnam, both three year-olds.

E. Martin, who, it may be remembered, took a number of horses over to Buenos Ayres last year, has returned to Newmarket, bringing with him Hark and Belisarius II. He has been offered a capital berth in Hungary by Baron Rothschild, but prefers, if possible, to ride and train in England, his trip abroad not having impressed him very favorably it would seem.

Seven of the high-bred matrons at Abdallah Park, Ky., have already dropped foals this season, as follows: Chestnut colt, out of Almater, and sired by Ottoman; black colt, out of Lady McDonald, sired by Simmons; bay colt, out of Lottie Thorne, sired by Simmons; bay filly, out of Linda Wilkes, sired by Noonday; black colt, out of Ebony, sired by Simmons; bay colt, out of Marie Rose, sired by Simmons.

The Petaluma Argus says: Fred Haney of this city has the Futurity stake winner. It is a big bright bay colt, by Strathway; first dam by Jackson Temple, second dam by Whipple's Hambletonian, third dam by imported Hercules. Strathway by Steinway, is an inbred Hambletonian, his dam Countess being a daughter of Whipple's Hambletonian, this gives Mr Haney's youngster four Hambletonian crosses.

"Uncle" Frank Harper has a large stable in training at his beautiful home "Nantura." There are eighteen head in the stable, as follows: Long Bow, Unite, Famine, Early Dawn, Long Roll, Sally Byrns, Silver Tip, Corrine Blackburn, Cassella, Corticelli, Linen, Louise Forrest, Bettie Waddell, and the following two year olds: St. August, chestnut colt, by St. Blaise, dam Secret; Milt Young, bay colt, by Jils Johnson, dam Via; Dosta, brown filly, by Silvermine, dam Early Light; and a bay colt by Jils Johnson.

It is not difficult to see that Mr. Lakeland regards one of his most recent purchases with a kindly eye. He says Phœnix, the colt he secured at Mr. A. J. Cassatt's sale, is the biggest three-year-old he ever owned. This colt, which he purchased for $4,000 at the time of Mr. Cassatt's temporary retirement from the turf last October, had only been that gentleman's property a few weeks, he having paid $5,000 for him at the sale of Wm. Walker's horses. Phœnix is by imported Mr. Pickwick—Bonnie Wood.

The improvements in the Kentucky Association track are completed, and it is now one of the handsomest tracks in the West. All the hills have been cut down so that every foot of the going can be seen from the stand. The new building will also be completed shortly, so that this the oldest racing association in the United States, will be up to modern ideas.

Training is progressing slowly, owing to the long continued bad weather, but many of the horses here will be ready to race when the meeting begins May 6th.

The Messrs. Engeman, owners of the Clifton track, announce that the usual thirty days' meeting will be held at the Brighton Beach track, beginning about the first week in July. Purses aggregating $100,000 will be given away during that time. Hurdle races and steeplechases are to be a feature of the meeting, and a new cross-country course is being built according to the rules of the English Grand National Hunt Committee. A long distance steeplechase sweepstake with $1,000 added is being arranged for.

The Sporting World says: A bulletin board ab[out] twenty feet square with the inscription, "No admittan[ce] except for officials," would not be out of place attached to the gate at the entrance of the judg[es'] stand at the Elizabeth course. If the judges and club o[ffi]cials only knew how many people followed the individu[als] from the enclosure to the betting ring or heard the remar[ks] of the occupants of the stand in regard to the unknown ge[n]tlemen who congregate there, they would order the ban[ner] painted at once.

Hanover, the famous son of Hindoo, pulled up lame in [his] work at Gravesend the other day, and a rumor quickly spre[ad] to the effect that he had broken down. Mr. Phil Dwyer w[as] seen at Elizabeth a week ago, and denied that Hanover h[ad] broken down, but said that it was true the horse was ve[ry] lame. Furthermore, Mr. Dwyer says he is afraid that Ha[n]over will not stand the preparation for another race. M[r.] Mike Dwyer was not at the track. He is sufferi[ng] from a slight attack of malaria and has gone to Washingt[on] for a change of air."

At a meeting Saturday of the Directors of the Thirteen[th] District Agricultural Society, the resignation of John Ki[m]ball was accepted, and a vote of thanks was adopted for [his] services to the Society.

The secretary was instructed to request Governor Wat[er]man to appoint C. N. Tharsing, of Sutter County, as a su[c]cessor to Mr. Kimball.

A committee consisting of C. A. Glidden and W. T. El[lis] Jr., was appointed to canvass for subscriptions, and ascerta[in] the disposition of the citizens towards holding the usual a[n]nual fair.

The Board adjourned to meet on Saturday, May 31.

The California Circuit will find Goldsmith the King Pi[n]. Already rumors are flying around about a phenomenal t[wo] year old and an exceptional three year old at San Mate[o]. The next largest stable will probably be Griffins; the la[te] Chicago crack driver has settled down to work in good sha[pe] this spring and has in his string the pacer Little Hope 2:21[;] William E. 2:27½; Patch Allen 2:39; Sol Wilkes, a five year o[ld] brother to Lillian Wilkes, 2:17¾; McGinty, a five year o[ld] green pacer who is showing lots of speed; Wally, a five ye[ar] old gelding barely 14 2 high and about the fastest trotter [on] the track; Little Albert by Albert W. 2:20 has trotted in 2:[..] several times; a speedy Alaska gelding; Alfred D 6206 by R[ob] Roy McGregor 2054 out of Jessie Logan by Logan 521 a[nd] several other promising horses.

The executive board of the Anti-Horse Thief Associatio[n] of St. Louis County met at Clayton last week, and besides o[r]dering necessary blanks printed, authorized the Sheriff [to] offer a reward of $500 for the capture and conviction of a[ny] person who shall steal a horse or other animal from a[ny] member of the association. The Secretary was directed [to] communicate with all county clerks within a radius of 1[..] miles and ascertain the names of all sheriffs, constables, tow[n] marshals or other officers and newspapers within that di[s]trict. He was also directed to establish correspondence wi[th] all organizations of a similar character in Illinois, Arkansa[s,] Kansas, Iowa and other counties in Missouri. The associ[a]tion means business and expects in the next four weeks [to] have at least 4,000 members.

It has been suggested that Prospect Hill Farm, owned [by] Miller & Sibley, ought to be styled "Palo Alto of the Eas[t]." There are five sons of Electioneer in the stud on the far[m]. By the way, it is not generally known that Mr. Sibley a[nd] his partner, Major Miller, made their fortunes in oil. Th[ey] are brothers-in-law, have been partners since both we[re] young, and their friendship rivals that of Damon and Pythi[as]. They are the leading men in the pretty city of Franklin, P[a.,] have built churches and support churches and schools, pa[y]ing preachers' and teachers' salaries, and it is not safe [to] breathe reproach in Franklin against either Joe Sibley [or] Charles Miller. Each is rated in the millionaire class, a[nd] they are forcing Prospect Hill into the front rank of breedi[ng] establishments, having invested upward of $200,000 there[in].

The Weekly Oregonian says: Mr Ed. Hardy, of Bak[er] City, is at The Portland. He is the vice-president of t[he] Baker City Agricultural Association, and is much interest[ed] in the prospects of the Baker City track, and the fall r[ace] meeting there, which opens September 30. There are n[ow] some fifty horses on the race track in training, Mr. Har[dy] says, chiefly from Baker, Union and Grant counties. T[he] track is in fine condition, having been well attended to [all] winter. The association is working it in first-class ord[er,] watering it every day. By the time the races open it is [ex]pected to be the fastest track in Oregon, and the fastest [on] the coast, with the exception of the Sacramento track. T[he] new street car line is expected to be running by that tim[e]. There is already a mile of it completed, and a large force [of] men are daily working on it. It runs from the depot do[wn] Center street, then down Front, across the river and out [to] the race track.

The members of the New York Jockey Club who reside [in] this city have just received their badge of membership for [the] current year. Although an entirely new departure, t[he] badge is thoroughly in keeping with that sumptuousne[ss] that has characterized almost everything connected w[ith] Morris Park from the inception of the enterprise to its co[m]pletion. Instead of the usual ornamentally printed pas[te]board disk the member's badge furnished by the New Yo[rk] Jockey Club is a button of solid silver that is made to fit i[n] the lapel button hole of the coat. The disk, which is d[is]played on the lapel, is about the size of a fifty cent pie[ce,] having a black oxidized ground on which is a grotesque ra[ised] design in burnished silver. This design includes the clu[b] initials, while on a broad raised border of irregular scr[oll] work is engraved the name of the member, while on t[he] button which fits into the buttonhole is engraved the me[m]ber's number, as it stands on the roll of membership.

Kentuckians are not just now as enthusiastic as they mi[ght] be. The greatest source of their next year's lucre has b[een] considerably shortened. They have had, with few exc[ep]tions, universally bad luck with their stock. Their ma[res] have either died or lost their foals, and there will not [be,] either among the trotting or running mares, a one-third c[rop] of foals. At no time in the history of breeding in the St[ate] have their been half so many mares to lose th[eir] foals as now. One of the largest and most extens[ive] breeders of trotters in Kentucky recently remarked about th[e] mares: "Why," said he, "did I not lose another foal I wo[uld] have only six or seven yearlings next year." This bree[der] has about fifty brood mares, and his loss can readily be se[en]. The common opinion among Kentucky horsemen now is t[hat] the great losses to which most of the breeders have b[een] subjected were due principally to the dread Russian inva[der,] *la grippe*. Physicians say that it will disappear with w[arm] weather.

Although some time yet must elapse before the starter for he Twin City Jockey Club will order the racers to the post t Hamline, the management of the club is working hard for he success of the meeting. Secretary Shaw has just returned rom Chicago, where he had a conference with Secretary Brewster, of the Washington Park Club. After the close of Washington Park, there will be a general division of the Western stables. Some will remain at Chicago to race at West Side Park, while others will flock to Saratoga and Hamline. Secretary Shaw has received assurances from the owners of the most prominent stables in the West, that they will hip their strings to Hamline instead of going East. This ssures a brilliant meeting for the Twin City Club.

Chas. Marvin, Superintendent of the Palo Alto trotting epartment, will leave for Terra Haute to-morrow. Among he horses taken on will be the world renowned Sunol, 2:10½; he peerless mare was never better in her life, and though he has had little or no work so far, should go a terrific mile hen keyed up, as she is much stronger and bigger looking han last spring. Palo Alto, 2:12¾, is in grand shape, his et, which troubled him last season, has not shown the lightest indication of soreness so far, and he ought to lower he stallion record, besides accounting for several free for lls. Gertrude Russell, 2:23½, a full sister to Palo Alto, is howing up well and is expected to go low down in the eens. Sport, 2:22¾, is also expected to be very dangerous in ood society. Arol, 2:24, is relied on to lower her mark several notches, as are several of the others, and should reflect redit on Palo Alto and Marvin.

The Hon. Van De Lashmutt, Mayor of Portland, Or., has ad a new race track built in his Witch Hazel Farm, and has n horses there in training Mr. Mosher also has ten head elonging to other parties in training on the track. Mr. De ashmutt has gone extensively into the trotting horses' business, having upwards of a hundred well bred trotters on his nch, and still keeps buying, his latest purchase being the wo year old filly Oregon Belle by Rockwood, son of Fleetwood, by Happy Medium, son of Rysdyk's Hambletonian, am by Dr Lindsay, 2d dam by Snow Storm, 3d dam by Riman, 4th dam by Lummox.

The stallions at Witch Hazel Farm are Hambletonian ambrino 5241, sire of Jane L 2:19½. and others, Portland by illiam L, sire of Axtell 2:12, out of Miss Leggitt by Mamino Star; Blondie, three year old record 2.27, and Pilot hampion by Pilot Medium, sire of Jack, 2:15, etc.

The Hearst sta le in W. L Donathan's care left on the "San meon," which was attached to the 3:30 train, last Saturday r Washington Park, Chicago. They will stop over a day two at Ogden and Council Bluffs, and after a few days' rest Washington Park will re-ship to Westchester. The horses ken on were Almont, b h, 4, Three Cheers—Question, imrted Del Mar, ch b, 4, Somnus—Maid of the Hills, Bagge, ch b, 3, Warwick—Maria F, imported Gertrude, 4, mnus—Geraldine, and five two-year-olds, viz, Primero, c, Powhattan—Speed, Snowball, ch c—brother to Snowop—Joe Hooker—Laura Winston, Anarchist, ch c—brother Dynamite—Joe Hooker—Chestnut Belle, Yosemite, b c, der Ali—Nellie Collier, J. B., b c—brother to Baggage—arwick—Maria F

Donathan took with him two other horses, one being Lord ilkes, who is to be forwarded to J. B. Goodpasture's farm Marian County, Ky., and the other a bay gelding sold by O. Holly.

A special to the Independent from Deer Lodge, Helena, ys: "This morning the ten mile race on the road to Champn took place according to arrangement. The race was ade up some weeks since, and had been extensively adverted. W. H. Higgins bet M S. Parker 2,000 shares of Amern Ruby stock against a mare Belle, belonging to Parker, at the mare Deer Lodge girl could beat Parker's horse to a rtain point on the Champion road at a distance of ten les. The bet was equal to $800 a side. There were about ,000 of side bets. The horses went to buggies, each buggy ntaining two persons. The horses started at 9:56 o'clock m the Kentucky stables in Deer Lodge. Deer Lodge Girl l from the turn loose. She made the ten miles in 49½ nutes, beating the horse 1½ minutes. This is a remarkable cord, as the road is up-hill all the way, with some very avy grades. The finish is 1,300 feet higher than the startg point. Both horses were of course tired, but Deer Lodge irl, after resting an hour, made the return trip in 58 nutes. This race will become as famous as the sixty-mile ce run here in 1869. Another match is talked of.

Orrin A. Hickok left on Thursday for Terra Haute, taking th him Alfred S; 2:18, purchased by him last week for 000, Adonis, pacer 2:14; a chestnut pacer by Guy Wilkes 5¾, out of Lucy 2:14; Monterey, four year old stallion by ectioneer—Minx, Prince Warwick by Alcona 730, out of arwick Maid by Mambrino Almont, and Cubic 2:28½, by ctioneer, out of Cuba by imp, Australia. Mr Hickok took for other parties the pacers Edwin C. 2:15 Racquet 2:20¼ d Roy Wilkes 2:12¾; a mare from L. A Davis and two lo Alto bred colts sold by Kentucky parties. Hickok will obably go from Terra Haute to Detroit, Cleveland, Buffalo d Rochester, and may return in time for the State Fair. He should have a share of the money hung up. Alfred is in good shape, and in the 18 class should prove very ndy, while Adonis will be a tough customer in the pacing green Wilkes Lucy pacer is fast as a ghost; Monterey and ince Warwick are both handy rapid trotters, and Cubic, s Palo Alto trotter, is expected to go very low down. His m Cuba is the dam of Argyle, the sire of the two good o year olds, Fairy and Rinfax.

A Montana horsemen writing from Louisville to the Helena lependent says: Spokane moved for the first time this ring out of an ordinary gallop. He seems to favor his ame leg" considerable and is quite likely to go down in the ner leg in trying to save the one that is already lame. His atest race for this season, I think, will be against his old tagonist, Proctor Knott, and the race will be to see who s tired first. I do not believe that either of them will win y great events this year. King Regent is here, and worked alf mile this morning in 54, which, considering the conion of the track, was very good work. He seems to be all ht, and the weight he has got in the handicaps ought to ke him a sure winner of one or more of the events.

Our horses are doing very well and never looked better.

Nevada is good and will make these Kentucky people wonr what kind of a country Montana is before the season is er.

Ben Kingsberry is a very promising 3 year old, and if he es not win the American Darby, will make the people unrstand that he is a race horse.

Warpeak and X are showing very well and ought to rerm last season's poor work

Old Daniel B. frisks about like a 2 year old and can beat y horse in Kentucky a half mile dash.

"Ah, the race track's full of 'em," said Jack, just as he refused a colored man who had accosted him on West street, a small loan. "Why, you'd scarcely credit it, but there's a gang of them that just make a living borrowing. They'll take from five dollars to a quarter: they'll get you to buy them a badge and then resell it; and, if they can't get anything else, they'll borrow a chew of tobacco. Why, here a little fellow, he was a jockey's valet or stable lad, just about the size of a jockey, bothered me once to pick him three winners. He didn't know much, but he bothered me, and finally I picked him three. Well, as it happened, the three won. Now, what do you suppose that young kid did? He went to a bookmaker and said some trainer or other had said they would win, sure. They were passably long shots, and the bookmaker held them out. Well, to my surprise, every one got there, and the bookmaker staked this kid quite lively. In fact, the kid had a good time until the bookmaker tumbled and got tired. The boy's around now, only he's grown into a big, strapping fellow. They call him Frenchy or something of that sort. Ah, there's lots of schemes on a race track," soliloquized Jack.

At this season of the year when so many two-year olds are being given names, it may not be quite useless to make an appeal to owners and trainers to abstain from giving them such appalling titles as some of our race horses bear. The Weeks Sport, a spicy New York Weekly says: If one looks through racing reports or the pages of the guide, it is hard to reconcile the connection of such magnificent beasts as these thorough reds are, with the outlandish names with which they are weighted. It is not an easy thing to name horses well, I know, though in some stables one notes particularly happy selections, both euphonious and consistent with the breeding, but it is a mistake to give them the names of people, more especially when only initials are used in whole or in part. Every man who keeps posted in racing matters will be able to call to mind a dozen instances of names that are enough to stop horses from showing even decent form, though little good would result from particularizing. It is all very well for half bred plugs destined for bushwhacking round country fairs to be called by names that would appropriately adorn the bar room loafer, but when it comes to giving such soubriquets to high-bred youngsters that quite probably may show stake winning form, it is quite another matter. Some of the two-year-olds that have already made their debuts have been very well named, and perhaps the Hon. W. L. Scott sets a particularly good example in his horses. It is to be hoped that owners will take the trouble to follow such good examples.

The Paris, Ky., News says there has been a loss of probably $50,000 worth of foals in Bourbon county the present season owing to the open winter and the peculiar nature of the grass or other food given to brood mares Stock men have been very reticent about their losses, for fear it will reflect on their stock, and have in most instances requested a suppression of the strictly legitimate news items. The following from the Richmond Register shows the same fatality among the stock men of Madison county, Ky: "Col W. M. Irvine has had the great misfortune recently to have the following mares slip their foals: Mona Wilkes, by George Wilkes, in foal to Lord Russell, full brother of Maud S. 2:08¾; Dictatrix, by Dictator, in foal to Wilton, 2:19, by George Wilkes; Bay mare by Banker, sire of Bermuda, 2:20, in foal to Vatican, 2:29½, by Belmont; Bay mare by Pylas, sire of Susie S., 2.15½, in foal to Umpire, by Dictator; Bay mare by Harold, sire of Maud S, in foal to Belmont Wilkes, by Belmont, dam by George Wilkes. Loss estimated at from $7,500 to $15,000. Col. Irvine has been heretofore particularly fortunate in breeding, never having lost an individual Col. I. S. Irvine has lost fifteen foals from his jennets in foal to his imported jacks, caused, he thinks, by feeding frost bitten corn. He estimates his loss at from $5,000 to $10,000. Eight of these foals were jacks.

Years ago when Alden Goldsmith and Edwin Thorne, two men who lent dignity to the trotting turf, and who are both sleeping under the Orange County sod, bought a colt by Rysdyk's Hambletonian, out of Lady Patriot, daughter of Young Patriot, son of Thoroughbred Patriot, they called him Hambletonian Jr. One day the two fine old Orange County horsemen drove up to Wm. M. Rysdyk's gate at Chester to visit the great father of trotters. When they drove away their conversation was earnest. Mr. Rysdyk resented the naming of the Lady Patriot colt Hambletonian Jr. Being jealous of the name "Hambletonian," the idea of calling Lady Patriot's colts as he was called led the curious old man to rage, and not long after the visitors had left Thorne asked Goldsmith, "What shall we call him?" The rebellion was just then developing from a mere insurrection into a civil war and the patriotic spirit was then rife. Said Goldsmith: "Let us call him 'Volunteer.'" And so the great Volunteer was named.

Volunteer would never have been great but for the hard, intelligent and persistent work of Alden Goldsmith and his sons Mr. Rysdyk lost no opportunity to cast opprobrium upon Volunteer. His dam, he declared, was a mongrel, and he could be nothing. But the Goldsmiths trained and worked with the sons and daughters of Volunteer with perseverance and faith. And when Huntress, the great threemiler, Driver and Gloster, the incomparable trotting racehorses, and St. Julien the record-breaker, came out, there were none to say that Volunteer was a mongrel.

The Volunteers were not young trotters; they took time to develop, and neither were they uniform trotters, like the Electioneers; but that they were race horses of the first water is universally admitted. The family of Volunteer is the only family in trotting history of which it has never been said that any of them were "quitters." The sons of Alden Goldsmith are living up to their name. After Charles Marvin, John A. Goldsmith is easily the star winner of the Pacific Coast. He trained and drove to his record Guy Wilkes 2:15¼, and trained and drove the famous youngsters by Guy Wilkes, viz., Lillian Wilkes, 2:17½, as a three-yearold; Sable Wilkes, 2:18, as a three-year-old; Regal Wilkes, 2:20¾, as a two-year-old; and Hazel Wilkes, 2:20, as a fouryear-old.

Mr. Corbitt the owner of the San Mateo farm, over which John Goldsmith presides, is a rich Californian who has made his money in canned goods. He is an enthusiastic horseman, and has retired from all business except that of breeding trotters (Ed. T. T.) which he has made immensely profitable. J. H Goldsmith, the elder of the Goldsmith boys, was the star driver of the Eastern circuits last season, and probably will be this. He wintered his stable at Washingtonville, N. Y., the old homestead of the Goldsmiths, but has now gone to the one mile track at Paterson, N J., to prepare for the summer campaigns. The great horse of the stable is that good campaigner Gean Smith, record 2:15¼, and he will be a dangerous horse in the free-for-all classes this year.—New York Tribune.

A writer, discussing Capt Sam Brown's 2-year-olds, says: The 2 year old division of seven, all the get of imported Richmond save one, are a fair looking lot of youngsters that look like earning their way this season. They have to the eye many of their famous sire's characteristics, his color, build, etc. The Mayfield colt and the Alabama colt look perhaps the pick of the lot, but then among 2 year olds the turf-world over, "handsome is as handsome does." The Himyar filly, a half sister to the Kentucky Oaks winner, Jewel Ban, looks nearly fit to race now and should be speedy if looks and relationship count for anything. Rogers says that Troubadour's sickness at La Grange farm in Kentucky is not yet over. The Suburban winner has had pinkeye with lung complications, and at last advices was much improved, but not yet out of danger.

We take the following from the anecdote column of the Licensed Victuallers Gazette: It is not generally known that the famous mare Blink Bonny, the winner of the Derby and Oaks of 1857, suffered greatly with her teeth, which prevented her eating and masticating her food Many teeth were extracted, which doubtless gave her some relief; but in the skeleton of the mare, so ably and scientifically preserved and put together by Mr. Tom Bowman, V S, of Sledmere, the presentation of which to the museum of the Yorkshire Philosophical Society in York, was almost the last act of the late Mr. I'Anson's life, there can be seen still remaining in the jaw one of the grinders or back teeth, the blackened and decayed state of which tells of intense suffering and consequent deprivation of food. Many a time, after a morning's exercise in the clear, bracing air of Langton Wold, did she rush with avidity to the corn offered her, and then lay her head on the edge of the manger in despair at being unable to eat it. One day, just before the Derby, Mr. Maw, the respected veterinary surgeon who attended the Spring Cottage and other racing establishments in the district, was asked by several friends about the Epsom race. He answered: "I cannot tell you what will win the Derby, but I can tell you what will not, and that is Blink Bonny, as I took these from her head only a few days ago," at the same time he produced a number of "wolf teeth" from his pocket. How the prediction was verified is known to the merest tyro in racing history.

It will be remembered that for One Thousand Guineas of 1857 Blink Bonny was an immense favorite, which proved the unbounded confidence of Mr. I'Anson, her owner, though without doubt the mare was in very backward condition. Imperiense, who was as rough as a badger, but was full of health and good work, was sent by John Scott, the Wizard of the North, as he was styled, from Whitewall, to take her chance. It was one of Mr. Scott's theories always to run a filly if she was well, as he said, "You never know what may happen." Mr. Scott, a careful man in such matters, as he was not present at Newmarket, gave strict injunctions to his representative, whom he sent with his mare, to hedge his stake, that is to lay the odds to £100 against her. But her rough looks, the prestige of Blink Bonny, and other causes, led to as much as 15 to 1 being offered against Imperiense, and the idea of laying £1,500 to 100 against a filly he knew to be well determined the said representative for once to disobey orders. He therefore had the satisfaction of telegraphing to his principal, "Won easily, and not a sixpence hedged."

Quite a controversy has taken place lately in England as to the use of horse shoes. The Pall Mall Budget says: As the public are being invited to view a collection of horse-shoes at the Animals' Institute, and a series of papers are being read on the art of horseshoeing, the question whether our horses should be shod at all might be raised opportunely. Use and wont have so accustomed us to shod horses that it will appear to many to be as absurd to discuss the practice as it would be to begin a contention as to the wearing of boots. But it is not by any means the first time that the wisdom of nailing an iron shoe on the hoof of horses has been called in question. Some years ago the matter was hotly debated, when the advocates of the shoeless system came in for the abuse usually awarded to the pioneers in any reform. The Royal Society for the Prevention of Cruelty to Animals also gave it out that they would prosecute any man who rode or drove a horse without shoes, being convinced that it would be a piece of cruelty to do so. If they are still of the same mind they need not lack a subject for prosecution, as we know of more than one owner of horses who has converted theory into practice.

A doctor in considerable practice in the north of London has been driving one of his horses for nearly a year past without shoes, and his experience confirms in the fullest degree the views of the Rev. J. G. Wood, as set out in his book on "Horse and Man," a perusal of which induced him to make the experiment. When the shoes were first removed the hoof were soft, and in order that they might harden and so return to their natural condition, the horse was kept on a hard floor in the stable for three months. That is a costly but necessary preparation where shoes have been used, but later economies will more than balance the account. At the close of the period named he was put to work, and, notwithstanding the tear and wear in all weathers and on hard and soft roads indiscriminately, the hoofs are to-day perfectly sound. Frost makes no difference to the surefootedness of the unshod animal, and while the horses of brother practitioners were confined to the stable owing to the slippery condition of the roads, he went his rounds with absolute safety. This is a clear demonstration that a horse can do traction work without shoes with distinct advantage both to the animal and the owner, and the Rev. J G. Wood contends that it can do saddle work also better than when shod on any description of road. Veterinary surgeons, farriers and grooms may be sceptical, but practice is better than theory. The following are the advantages which one of the author's correspondents sets out as the result of his personal experience:—

1. Five or six pounds per annum are saved by non-shoeing, including the frost nails in winter.
2. Can gallop on a road covered with ice, when other horses are not safe even with the use of frost nails.
3. The weight of the shoes is taken off the feet, which is a considerable help to the horse.
4. The foot, being flat from the frog and down to the ground, leaves no receptacle for stones.
6 There is none of the unnecessary jar caused by the shoes, so that the horse travels freer and lighter.

The doctor's groom, who is an enthusiastic convert to the new system, not only confirms these advantages, but claims that the animal is saved from various diseases of the foot caused by shoeing, while its surefootedness is most remarkable. It steps high and goes well, and at the end of a day's work its feet are perfectly cool. If this surefootedness can be secured without detriment to the hoof, it certainly would be an incalculable boon to the horses which are constantly coming to grief in the greasy London streets, and besides it would afford not a little relief to those who have to watch the torture of the animals as they make painful efforts to regain their foothold.

THE FARM.

Stud Books, Herd Books and Pedigree Registers in the United States.

The following is a list compiled by the Breeders' Gazette of the various pedigree registry associations, with the addresses of the Secretaries or other persons to whom application should be made for special information and registration.

HORSES.

American Association of Importers and Breeders of Belgian Draft Horses.—J. D. Connor, Jr., Wabash, Ind., Secretary.

American Association of Jack and Jennet Breeders.—W. H. Goodpasture, Nashville, Tenn., Secretary.

American Cleveland Bay Breeders' Association.—R. P. Stericker, Springfield, Ill., Secretary.

American Clydesdale Association.—Chas. F. Mills, Springfield, Ill., Secretary.

American Percheron Horse Breeders' Association.—S. D. Thompson, Chicago, Ill., Secretary.

American Shetland Pony Club.—J. Murray Hoag, Maquoketa, Ia., Secretary.

American Shire Horse Breeder's Association.—Chas. Burgess, Wenona, Ill., Secretary.

American Stud Book (Thoroughbred).—S. D. Bruce, New York City, Editor.

American Trotting Register.—J. H. Wallace, New York City, Editor.

French Coach Horse Society of America.—S. D. Thompson, Chicago, Ill., Secretary.

National French Draft Horse Association.—C. E. Stubbs, Fairfield, Ia., Secretary.

Select Clydesdale Horse Society of America.—J. B. McLaughlin, Topeka, Kan., Secretary.

American Suffolk Punch Horse Association.—A. B. Galbraith, Janesville, Wis., Secretary.

German Coach Horse Association of America.—A. Oltmanns, Watseka, Ill., Secretary.

The Morgan Register.—Joseph Battell, Middlebury, Vt., Editor.

CATTLE.

American Aberdeen-Angus Breeders' Association.—Thomas McFarlane, Iowa City, Ia., Secretary.

American Branch Association of the North Holland Herd Book.—Fred H. Beach, Dover, N. J., Secretary.

American Devon Cattle Club.—F. W. Reed, Zanesville, O., Secretary.

American Galloway Breeders' Association.—L. P. Muir, Independence, Mo., Secretary.

American Guernsey Cattle Club.—Edward Norton, Farmington, Conn., Secretary.

American Hereford Cattle Breeders' Association.—C. R. Thomas, Independence, Mo., Secretary.

American Jersey Cattle Club.—F. W. Wicks, New York City, Secretary.

American Jersey Herd Book.—O. B. Hadwen, Worcester, Mass., Secretary.

American Shorthorn Breeders' Association.—J. H. Pickrell, Chicago, Ill., Secretary.

American Sussex Association.—Overton Lea, Nashville, Tenn., Secretary.

Ayrshire Breeders' Association.—C. M. Winslow, Brandon, Vt., Secretary.

Brown Swiss Cattle Breeders' Association.—N. S. Fish, Groton, Conn., Secretary.

Dutch Belted Cattle Association.—H. B. Richards, Easton, Pa., Secretary.

Holstein-Friesian Association of America.—Thomas B. Wales, Iowa City, Ia., Secretary.

Holstein-Friesian Register.—S. Hoxie, Yorkville, N. Y., Superintendent.

Maine State Jersey Herd Book.—N. R. Pike, Winthrop, Me., Secretary.

Red Polled Cattle Club of America (incorporated).—J. McLain Smith, Dayton, O., Secretary.

Red Polled Cattle Club of America.—J. C. Murray, Maquoketa, Ia., Secretary.

American Polled Durham Breeders' Association.—A. E. Burleigh, Mazon, Ill., Secretary.

SHEEP.

American Cotswold Association.—George Harding, Waukesha, Wis., Secretary.

American Leicester Breeders' Association.—A. J. Temple, Cameron, Ill., Secretary.

American Lincoln Breeders' Association.—L. C. Graham, Cameron, Ill., Secretary.

American Oxford Down Sheep Association.—W. A. Shafer, Middletown, O., Secretary.

American Southdown Association.—S. E. Prather, Springfield, Ill., Secretary.

American Shropshire Registry Association.—Mortimer Levering, Lafayette, Ind., Secretary.

Hampshire Down Breeders' Association of America.—John I. Gordon, Mercer, Pa., Secretary.

American Rambouillet Sheep-Breeders' Association.—T. F. B. Sotham, Pontiac, Mich., Secretary.

Black-Top Spanish Merino Sheep-Breeders' Association.—W. G. Berry, Houstonville, Pa., Secretary.

Delaine Merino Sheep-Breeders' Association.—J. C. McNary, Houstonville, Pa., Secretary.

Dickinson Merino Sheep Record Company.—H. G. McDowell, Canton, O., Secretary.

Improved Black-Top Merino Sheep Breeders' Association.—L. M. Crothers, Taylorstown, Pa., Secretary.

Improved Delaine Merino Sheep-Breeders' Association.—Geo. W. Poland, Urbana, O., Secretary.

Michigan Merino Sheep-Breeders' Association.—E. N. Ball, Hamburg, Mich., Secretary.

Missouri Merino Sheep-Breeders' Association.—H. V. Pugsley, Plattsburg, Mo., Secretary.

National Improved Saxony Sheep Breeders' Association.—John G. Clark, Toledo, Pa., Secretary.

National Merino Sheep-Breeders' Association.—R. O. Logan, California, Mich., Secretary.

New York State American Merino Sheep-Breeders' Association.—J. Horatio Earll, Skaneateles, N. Y. Secretary.

Ohio Spanish Merino Sheep Breeders' Association.—F. C. Stanley, Cardington, O., Secretary.

Pennsylvania and Ohio Improved Delaine Merino Sheep-Breeders' Association.—R. M. Cleaver, East Bethlehem, Pa., Secretary.

Standard American Merino Register Association.—John P. Ray, Hemlock Lake, N. Y., Secretary.

United States Merino Sheep-Breeders' Registry Association.—A. E. Sprague, Erie, O., Secretary.

Vermont Atwood Club Register.—George Hammond, Middlebury, Vt., Secretary.

Vermont Merino Sheep-Breeders' Association.—Albert Chapman, Middlebury, Vt., Secretary.

Wisconsin Sheep-Breeders' and Wool Growers' Association Merino Sheep Register.—H. J. Wilkinson, Whitewater, Wis., Secretary.

SWINE.

American Berkshire Association.—Phil M. Springer, Springfield, Ill., Secretary.

American Duroc Jersey Swine Breeders' Association.—S. E. Morton, Camden, O., Secretary.

American Essex Association.—W. M. Wiley, New Augusta, Ind., Secretary.

American Small Yorkshire Club.—Geo. W. Harris, New York City, Secretary.

Cheshire Swine Breeders' Association.—G. S. Button, Chittenango, N. Y., Secretary.

Chester White Record Association.—W. H. Morris, Indianapolis, Ind., Secretary.

Todd's Improved Chester White Record Association.—Carl Freigau, Dayton, O., Editor.

Gothland Swine-Breeders' Association.—Grant W. Spear, Aurora, Ill., Secretary.

American Poland-China Record Company.—John Gilmore, Vinton, Ia., Secretary.

Central Poland China Swine Association.—W. H. Morris, Indianapolis, Ind., Secretary.

Northwestern Poland-China Swine Association.—J. O. Young, Washington, Kan., Secretary.

Ohio Poland-China Record Company.—Carl Freigau, Dayton, O., Secretary.

Standard Poland-China Record Company.—Ira K Alderman, Maryville, Mo., Secretary.

Victoria Swine-Breeders' Association.—H. Davis, Dyer, Ind., Secretary.

Store Cattle for Great Britain.

Confirmatory of what has been stated in the Rural World about the desire of the farmers of Great Britain to purchase steers from America and fatten them upon their farms, we publish a portion of the report of Mr. Moreton Frewen, of England, who is thoroughly posted on the subject:

There was one point, he said, of which he had made a close study, and it was worth while to consider whether the legislation which was responsible for the present application of the contagious diseases (animals) act was entirely unwarranted by the circumstances of the time. The result of the rigid exclusion of lean stock from America had been to drive this country more and more into the dead and fat cattle meat trade. As long as the contagious diseases (animals) act precluded the importation of store cattle from the United States to this country, he did not think the conditions of agriculture would be quite healthy. The result of the enforcement of that act had been to prohibit English farmers from buying their store cattle in the one cheap market of the world. He was aware there was a breeders' side to the question. He had no cattle interests to preserve in America, but he was convinced that Ireland could carry one-third more cattle than she had now, and the only chance of her increasing her stock was to buy heifer stock from across the Atlantic and bring it in alive. On this side of the Atlantic there were advantages for fattening cattle which no other country enjoyed. If the cattle trade of which he was speaking was not subjected to the existing restrictions, and if the English farmers had their agents at Chicago who would forward 4,000 or 5,000 head of lean cattle a day, quite a new phase would be put on the agriculture of this country. As to the "bogey" of disease, he pointed out that in dealing with America there were conditions of security which were offered nowhere else. Five or six years ago there was pleuro-pneumonia, but there had never been a single outbreak of foot-and-mouth disease in the United States.

The complete statistics of British imports for the year 1889 have just been issued, and contain some figures in which Americans are highly interested. Great Britain imported in that year no less than 555,221 live cattle against 377,086 in the preceding year, and almost doubling the imports of two years ago. The total of sheep imported was 678,958, that of the preceding year being 956,210. This is the only point in which the imports show a decline. In swine and horses there was a very slight increase, and in fresh beef the total of 657,574 cwt. in 1887 was increased to 1,379,511 cwt. in 1889. These figures are highly significant to the countries which furnish Great Britain with its food supplies. Of the great increase in cattle the United States furnished the bulk, our exports of cattle last year being 294,423 head, against 143,495 head in 1888 and 94,858 head in 1887, the trade of the latter year having been about trebled in 1889. Of the fresh beef which Great Britain imports the United States furnishes about nine-tenths. If as many sagacious observers think our exportation of animal foods should show an increase in 1890, the total report a year hence will be large indeed.—Colman's Rural World.

Qualities of the Cow.

THE GOOD COW.

A good cow when in milking order is neither fleshy nor scrawny, but she is of a happy medium order, that combines muscular symmetry and lacteal voluptuousness. She is represented in all breeds of cattle subject to especial adaptation. She is physically healthy from hoof to horn (provided she hasn't monkeyed with a dehorning chute), and of strong constitution enough to insure vigorous offspring.

While dependent largely on man's care for a substantiation of the term "good," the superiority of her inherited lacteal organism is a marked characteristic peculiarly her own. She is naturally of a sensitive, docile nature, but will stand on the defensive when abused. Her very nature makes her industrious about feeding, and she is never lazy in this regard. When she is in the pasture she grazes assiduously until her stomach is full, then she lies down and ruminates till the food she has absorbed is assimilated, being up and off immediately in search of another repast. Her hair is silky, and she has a refined physical contour. Although a heavy eater, she carries no ill-proportioned "paunch," and she possesses great powers of digestion and assimilation. It matters not whether her name is "Crumpled Horn" or "Muley Jane," she has so many prominent good points that you could spot her for a superior cow in the middle of a ten-acre lot.

THE BAD COW.

She is frequently built like an ox, and her udderine development is either nominal or small. Although cut out by nature solely for beef, she seldom reaches the butcher's block till she has been a costly experiment to some dairyman. She has none of the nervous temperament of her good sister, but is of a coarse, physiological character. Frequently she has fairly good milk traits, and is made bad by the neglect and ignorance of her owner. This is easily accomplished by winter exposure, inadequate feed and general neglect. The cow has no blue-blooded ancestry, and she might be ter[med] "a creature of chance." She will lie lazily in the shade w[hen] she should be up feeding, or she will walk two miles nip[ping] the amount of grass her good relative would have glean[ed from] a rod of ground. I never knew a "tramp cow" to be a p[ro]fitable one. Take it all in all, the bad cow is a most unfo[rtu]nate creature. She is not to blame for being here, yet sh[e is] censured for bringing the records of so many dairies into [dis]repute. Individually she is not to be condemned, but ra[ther] are the men who by lax methods tolerate her in the h[erd]. The best way to open the negligent dairyman's eyes as to [the] real value between the good and the bad cow is by a rela[tive] array of facts. Give him opportunity to note the ac[tual] yield of the former and the actual yield of the latter, [and] then mentally digest the comparison. "Blood will tell," [but] so will feed.

THE MEDIUM COW.

Between the good and the bad of everything there is alw[ays] a medium, and in the American national dairy we find a h[igh] percentage of half way between cows. Many of this c[lass] are evolutions from poorer stock, improving under the [be]nign influence of cross breeding, enhanced care and be[tter] understanding of rationing for milk production. Then ag[ain] there are others, the progeny of dams of good lacteal capa[bil]ities, but by the use of inferior sires the stock has dege[ner]ated until it is below par. We thus have regeneration [and] degeneration blending and producing cows neither hot [nor] cold, but lukewarm, from a lacteal point of view. Altho[ugh] the medium cow is an improvement on the bad one, sh[e is] just the factor that is keeping thousands of dairies un[der] financial distress. So many farmers seem to rest con[tent] with this "passable" stock that is not netting them more t[han] $34 or $40 per head for the milk season. In the great d[airy] section where the writer resides he has knowledge of nu[mer]ous farmers situated as above described, who attribute t[he] low income per bovine capita solely to the produce mar[ket]. When *will* the scales ever fall from their eyes and reve[al to] them their fallacy?

GEO E. NEWELL in Stockman and Farme[r].

The Broad-Tailed Sheep of Western Asia

We have knowledge of but one breeder of this pecu[liar] breed, Col. Jeshington Wates, Laurens, South Carolina; what has been learned of their peculiarities has been by re[ad]ing accounts given by naturalists and visitors to their na[tive] country. Comparatively little has been written about [this] very useful animal in its native clime. This is but a m[ere] mention of it in our English works, and that consisting largely of misrepresentations. The following is from an [ac]count of this sheep written by an Armenian student fr[om] Asiatic Turkey, now at Cornell University:

"From time immemorial this has been the common spe[cies] of sheep existing in Arabia, in Palestine and Syria, in Eg[ypt] and in the Barbary States of Africa, in Asia Minor and western Asia as far as anti-Taurus and the mountains [of] Koordistan. Outside this boundary it gives place to the co[m]mon species.

"Still later we find it mentioned by an Englishman, Jo[hn] Harris, in his book, 'Voyage and Travels," published [in] London, 1705. Mr. Harris' descriptions of monkeys [and] elephants, as well as sheep, are very extraordinary and [sin]gular, and were intended for no other purpose but to sati[sfy] the laudable curiosity of his readers. Unfortunately, m[any] writers, especially religious authors, have exactly cop[ied] this false description, and now it is not uncommon to [see] pictures of this sheep with a tail two or three feet long, a[s in] Cassell's 'Illustrated Bible."

"Where this species first originated is a mystery, but [ac]cording to the most ancient historians, very probably i[t] first came from the peninsula of Modern Arabia.

"The broad tail is highly esteemed in all lands where it [is] found, on account of its caudal appendage, which is co[m]posed of an accumulation of delicate fat—a medium betw[een] lard and butter, but an excellent substitute for the form[er]. The notorious oriental dishes, so well known from the ol[d] times, are wholly prepared with this fat. In localities wh[ere] the climate is cold, this fat is preferred to butter by ma[ny] and is eaten raw after chopping a lump to a compact m[ass]. In warmer climates it can be kept longer than butter with[out] being apt to grow rancid.

"In fact the broad-tail sheep has no separate breed exc[ept] from the changes it has undergone in different climates [and] pastures. There may be specified three different kinds. C[on]sidering Asiatic Turkey as the home of this sheep I sho[uld] say that those found in Koordistan, and in the district aro[und] Mount Ararat, are the largest in flesh and in the size [of] their fatty tails, and are designated by the general name ["]Bayazit" sheep from the city of Bayazit, as the center of [their] home. They are chiefly of a dark brown or light black, w[ith] short and coarse wool. It is in those districts where [the] owners are often obliged to put small carts under the he[avy] tail of the ill-fated animal to relieve him from the pain [and] annoyance of such an incumbrance.

"The shape of the tail is nearly circular, resemblin[g a] chair cushion, and hung on each side of the caudal spi[ne,] while the tail proper extends several inches below at [the] middle. In many cases if the cart is not fixed on in time [the] tail grows fatter and one of the lobes drops off by its o[wn] weight. Those found in Asia Minor, and mainly in the p[ro]vinces of Siva and Angora are smaller in size, of pure wh[ite] or jet black in color, and are noted for the fineness and ab[un]dance of their wool.

"It may be well to note that the form of the tail is inv[ari]ably the same all over.

"Under the hot climate and in the poor pastures of so[uth]ern Mesopotamia we find the species entirely chang[ed,] poorer in flesh, coarser in wool and hardly ever free fr[om] diseases through the careless attention of the noma[d] Arab."

Doubtless in the Mosaic-Law in Leviticus III, 9, "And [the] rump thereof," has reference to this species. This is the [re]motest mention of the existence of this species. At a la[ter] period about twenty-five hundred years ago, Herodotus [has] described it as occurring in Syria and Palestine, and dif[fer]ing from the common Greek sheep by having a tail "[a] cubic in width."—Homestead.

A prominent cattle dealer of Denver discovered the ot[her] day by shipping a trainload of feeders through to Pitts[burgh] instead of stopping them at Chicago, he could realize $[...] more for them. But when he got to the point of billing th[em] through the pooled lines refused to do it. They would s[hip] to Chicago and no farther. In olden times the local bar[ons] levied upon all who passed through their territory. At pr[es]ent missionaries must pay to travel through hostile Afri[ca;] Stanley fought his way through. Chicago is a commer[cial] cut-throat on the way East that must be suppressed, as K[ing] Arthur suppressed the robber barons.

BASE BALL.

[Reviewed by Phil Potts.]

THE WEEK'S GAMES.

Good Ball Being Put Up by the California League Teams.

EXTRA INNING GAMES.

'Frisco Still in the Lead.

The California League teams have completed a week of good, honest base ball before an aggregate assemblage of twenty-five thousand devotees of the sport.

The 'Friscos are still in the lead, with Oakland treading uncomfortably close at her heels. Stockton maintains her third place, and Sacramento, who started off very unluckily at the begining of the season, is now making a great spurt, and intends to keep the leaders hustling. Appended will be found the full scores of all games for the week commencing Thursday, April 24th. This retrospective glance of the happenings of the week on the California diamond, as presented in these columns, will especially commend itself to the many managers and players throughout the entire country, and will be favorably welcomed and appreciated by all admirers of the national game.

Stocktons vs. Oakland, Thursday, April 24, at Haight Street.

The game was a complete surprise to the half thousand persons who saw "steady Pete" Meegan, pitch "gild edged" ball for the Colonels from across the bay. But in the ninth it was a mournful "tale of woe" for the Oaklanders, for the Stocktons opened a fusilade of base hits which went cracking all over the lot, and these, aided by a couple of misplays, gave them seven runs and the game. The score:

STOCKTONS.

	AB.	R.	BH.	SB.	PO	A.	E.
Swan, r f	4	1	0	0	4	1	1
Cahill, l f, 3 b	5	1	2	0	2	0	1
Holliday, c f	5	2	1	1	1	0	0
Fudger, s s	5	3	3	2	0	1	1
Fogarty, 2d b	5	1	3	0	1	3	1
Selna, 1st b	5	1	0	1	9	0	0
Wilson, 3d b, c	4	0	2	1	7	3	0
Borchers, p	5	1	2	0	1	2	0
Fairhurst, c, l f	4	0	0	0	2	3	1
Totals	42	10	13	5	27	11	5

OAKLANDS.

	AB.	R.	BH.	SB.	PO.	A.	E.
C. O'Neill, lf	3	2	2	1	1	0	0
Stickney, s s, 3d b	5	2	2	1	2	3	3
Dungan, r f	4	1	0	2	2	0	0
Farrell, 3d b, s s	4	1	1	0	2	3	1
McDonald, 2d b	4	0	0	0	5	3	3
Lohman, c	4	0	1	1	8	2	1
Hill, c f	4	0	0	0	0	0	0
Isaacson, 1st b	3	1	1	1	7	0	1
Meegan, p	3	1	0	1	0	1	0
Totals	36	8	7	7	27	12	9

SCORE BY INNINGS.

	1	2	3	4	5	6	7	8	9	
Stockton	2	0	1	0	0	0	0	0	7	—10
Oakland	3	2	0	3	0	0	0	0	0	— 8

Earned runs—Oakland, 2. Two-base hits—Stickney, Wilson, Fogarty. Sacrifice hits—Farrell, McDonald, Fairhurst. First base on errors—Oakland, 4; Stockton, 6. First base on called balls—Oakland 1; Stockton 5. Left on bases - Oakland, 6; Stockton, 7. Struck out—By Meegan, 7; by Borchers, 12. Hit by pitcher—Wilson. Double plays—Meegan, McDonald and Isaacson; Swan and Selna. Passed balls—Wilson, 1. Wild pitches—Meegan, 1; Borchers, 1. Umpire—Donohue

Stockton vs. San Francisco, Friday, April 25th, at Oakland.

The grounds at Emery station are yet in poor condition for brilliant ball playing, nevertheless a good game was played there on the above named date, between Stockton and 'Frisco Perrott, a San Joaquin County production, pitched his first game of the season and was touched up lively throughout the game, especially in the ninth, when base hits and errors were as numerous as the holes in the fence. The back stop work of De Pangher and Speer were the features of the game. The score:

SAN FRANCISCO.

	AB.	R.	BH.	SB.	PO.	A.	E.
Shea, 2d b	4	1	1	1	5	0	0
Sweeney, 1st b	4	2	2	0	12	0	0
Hanley, c f	4	2	2	0	0	0	0
Ebright, s s	4	2	2	1	1	1	2
Speer c	5	1	1	0	5	5	0
Levy, l f	3	0	0	0	2	0	0
Stevens, r f	4	1	0	2	2	0	0
Buchan, 3d b	4	1	0	0	0	4	1
Young, p	4	0	0	0	0	5	0
Totals	36	10	8	4	27	15	3

STOCKTONS.

	AB.	R.	BH.	SB.	PO.	A.	E.
Swan, r f	4	0	1	0	0	0	0
Cahill, l f	4	0	1	0	1	0	0
Holliday, c f	4	0	0	1	3	0	2
Fudger, s s	4	1		0	2	3	0
Fogarty, 2d b	4	1		1	3	5	1
Selna, 1st b	4	0		0	12	0	0
Wilson, 3d b	4	0		0	2	0	3
Perrott, p	3	0		0	0	5	1
De Pangher, c	3	0	2	0	5	3	0
Totals	34	2	8	2	17	16	7

SCORE BY INNINGS.

	1	2	3	4	5	6	7	8	9	
San Francisco	3	0	0	0	0	1	0	0	6	—10
Stockton	0	1	0	0	0	0	1	0	0	— 2

Earned runs—San Francisco, 2; Stockton, 1. Two base hits—Sweeney, Hanley Selna. Sacrifice hits—Ebright, Carroll, Levy, Fogarty. First base on errors—San Francisco, 6; Stockton, 3. First base on called balls San Francisco, 3. Left on bases—San Francisco, 7; Stockton, 5. Struck out—By Perrott, 3, by Young, 4. Hit by pitcher - Shea, Ebright, Levy, (2), Buchan. Double plays—Speer and Shea; Wilson (unassisted). Wild pitches—Young, 1. Umpire, Donohue.

Sacramento vs Oakland, Friday, April 25th, at Sacramento.

Cobb pitched a great game for the Colonels but one hit being secured off him. Both Zeigler and Harper were hit out hard and the game ended with the Senators being goose-egged. The score:

OAKLAND.

	AB.	R.	BH.	SB	PO.	A.	E.
C. O'Neill, l f	3	0	1	3	0	0	0
Stickney, 3d b	4	0	1	1	0	1	0
Dungan, r f	3	1	1	1	2	1	1
Farrell, s s	5	1	2	2	1	2	0
McDonald, 2d b	5	1	1	1	4	3	0
Lohman c	4	1	1	0	4	2	0
Hill, c f	2	1	2	1	3	0	0
Isaacson, 1st b	2	1	0	1	10	2	0
Cobb, p	4	1	0	1	3	3	2
Totals	33	7	9	11	27	14	3

SACRAMENTO.

	AB.	R.	BH.	SB.	PO.	A.	E.
Goodenough, c f	3	0	0	0	1	0	0
Daly, s s	3	0	0	1	1	4	0
Godar, 3d b	4	0	0	0	3	1	0
Reitz, 2d b	4	0	0	0	4	0	1
Roberts, l f	4	0	0	1	0	0	0
Smith, 1st b	3	0	1	0	7	0	1
McHale, c	3	0	0	0	7	2	1
Harper, r f & p	2	0	0	1	1	1	0
Zeigler, p and r f	3	0	0	0	0	2	2
Totals	29	0	1	5	24	10	5

SCORE BY INNINGS.

	1	2	3	4	5	6	7	8	9	
Oakland	0	0	0	3	0	1	3	0	0	— 7
Sacramento	0	0	0	1	0	0	0	0	0	— 8

Earned runs—Oakland, 5. Three base hit—Hill. First base on errors—Oakland, 3; Sacramento, 2. First base on called balls—Oakland, 9; Sacramento, 3. Struck out—By Zeigler, 1; Harper, 2; Cobb, 4. Double plays—Smith (unassisted), Dungan and Farrell. Passed balls—Lohman, 1. Wild pitches—Harper, 2. Umpire—Sheridan.

Stockton vs. San Francisco, Saturday, April 26th, at Haight Street.

12 INNINGS.

The best game of the season was played between Stockton and Frisco last Saturday. So said the fifteen hundred cranks who turned out to see Frisco "do" the Gas City's boys.

But while many were disappointed in the result, they were all unanimous in declaring that they more than got their money's worth.

Chase and De Pangher were in the "points" for Stockton, and Lookabough and Speer did the honors for Frisco. Chase, although perceptibly weak toward the end, twirled far the better ball, Lookabough being hit very hard by Holliday, Swan, Fudger and De Pangher. Frisco tied the score in the eighth and then the battle began. Each team scored once in the ninth, but brilliant fielding by both nines prevented runs in the tenth or eleventh. In the twelfth the Friscos were retired in order on infield hits and Swan took the bat for Stockton, making a pretty hit. Cahill flew out to Levy, but Holliday's safety advanced Swan to third. Fudger was next up, and on his beauty to left field the winning run came in amid deafening cheers. The score:

STOCKTON.

	A.B.	R.	B.H.	S.B.	P.O.	A.	E.
Swan, r f	6	1	3	2	1	0	1
Cahill, l f	6	1	1	2	1	0	1
Holliday, c f	6	2	4	2	5	1	3
Fudger, s s	5	0	2	2	1	5	1
Fogarty, 2d b	5	0	1	1	5	4	1
Selna, 1st b	5	0	1	0	17	0	1
Wilson, 3d b	5	1	1	1	3	2	0
Chase, p	4	1	0	0	0	5	0
De Pangher, c	5	1	1	0	2	2	0
Totals	47	7	14	10	36	19	8

SAN FRANCISCO.

	A.B.	R.	B.H.	S.B.	P.O.	A.	E.
Shea, 2d b	7	0	2	0	1	1	0
Sweeney, 1st b	5	1	0	0	14	1	1
Hanley, c f	5	0	1	0	1	0	0
Ebright, s s	3	1	0	0	2	3	0
Speer, c	4	2	1	0	7	1	1
Levy, l f	5	2	2	1	5	0	0
Stevens, r f	6	0	2	1	2	0	0
Buchan, 3d b	5	0	1	1	1	7	0
Lookabough, p	4	0	0	0	1	2	0
Totals	45	6	9	3	34*	14	2

*One out when the winning run was scored.

SCORE BY INNINGS.

	1	2	3	4	5	6	7	8	9	10	11	12	
Stockton	0	0	2	1	2	0	0	0	1	0	0	1	— 7
San Francisco	0	0	0	1	0	2	0	2	1	0	0	0	— 6

Earned runs—Stockton, 6; San Francisco, 1. Three-base hit—Holliday. Two-base hits—Shea (2), De Pangher, Swan, Levy, Stevens, Selna. Sacrifice hits—Fudger, Shea, Sweeney, Selna, Levy, De Pangher, Stevens. Base on errors—Stockton, 1; San Francisco, 5. Base on called balls—Stockton, 2; San Francisco, 6. Left on bases—Stockton, 6; San Francisco, 9. Struck out—By Lookabough 6. Hit by Pitcher - Fogarty, Ebright. Double plays—Buchan Ebright and Sweeney, Buchan, Sweeney and Buchan. Umpire, Donahue.

Sacramento vs. Oakland, Saturday, April 27th at Sacramento.

The Senators evened up on the Colonels in this game, with Reitz in the box. The features Roberts' terrific hitting and Goodenough and Robert's fielding. Bowman made his re-appearance, with Sacramento catching a strong game. Score:

SACRAMENTO.

	AB.	R.	BH.	SB.	PO.	A.	E.
Goodenough, c f	5	1	0	1	4	0	0
Daly, s s	5	1	2	0	0	4	0
Godar, 3d b	4	1	2	0	1	2	1
Reitz, p	4	0	0	0	0	1	0
Roberts, l f	4	2	2	0	5	0	0
Smith, 1st b	4	0	1	1	9	0	2
McHale, r f	4	0	0	0	1	0	0
Zeigler, 2d b	4	0	1	0	2	0	2
Bowman, c	4	0	0	0	5	3	1
Total	38	5	9	2	27	10	6

OAKLAND.

	AB.	R.	BH.	SB.	PO.	A.	E.
C. O'Neill, l f	4	0	1	2	3	0	2
Stickney, 3d b	5	2	1	0	1	1	0
Dungan, r f	3	0	1	1	1	0	0
Farrell, s s	5	0	0	1	4	4	3
McDonald, 2d b	2	2	1	1	1	3	1
Lohman, c	4	0	1	0	4	2	1
Hill, c f	4	0	1	0	3	0	0
Isaacson, 1st b	4	0	0	0	9	0	1
Meegan, p	4	0	0	1	1	2	0
Totals	34	4	5	6	27	12	6

SCORE BY INNINGS.

	1	2	3	4	5	6	7	8	9	
Sacramento	1	0	0	0	1	3	0		0	—5
Oakland	1	0	0	1	1	0	0	1	0	—4

Earned runs—Sacramento, 3; Oakland, 1. Home run—Roberts. Three-base hits—Roberts, Stickney. Sacrafice hit- Reitz. First base on errors—Sacramento, 5; Oakland, 3. First base on called balls—Oakland, 5. Left on bases - Sacramento, 6; Oakland, 8. Struck out—Reitz, 5; Meegan, 3. Hit by pitcher—Isaacson. Passed ball—Bowman, Wild pitch—Meegan, 1. Umpire—Sheridan.

Oakland vs. San Francisco, Sunday, April 27th, at Oakland

Two thousand Oakland enthusiasts saw the "Pets" do up 'Frisco before they got their noonday meal. It was just the kind of a game Oakland's constituents rejoice in seeing, and they gave full vent to their feelings. San Francisco at no "stage of the game was "in it, and no matter where they hit the ball, some big Colonel was always on hand to gather it in. The Oaklands bunched their hits nicely, and to this is due their victory.

SCORE BY INNINGS.

	1	2	3	4	5	6	7	8	9	
Oakland	3	0	3	0	0	0	0	0	0	—9
San Francisco	1	0	2	0	0	0	0	0	0	—3

Oakland vs. San Francisco, Sunday, April 27th, at Haight Street.

Oakland wasn't satisfied with doing 'Frisco up "to the Queens (or rather the Colonels) taste in the morning, for in the afternoon, in the presence of about eight thousand 'Frisco cranks they Just "repeated the dose." It is a sad event to chronicle, but such things happen very often in baseball, and some day (we hope in the very near future) Manager Finn's boys may have "the laugh" on the Athenians, but to do this they will have to improve materially in their hitting and infield work. Cobb was in good form, and kept the hits well scattered but Lookabough curves when they came in contact with the Colonel's bats generally went sailing over the fielder's heads for two or three bases.

SCORE BY INNINGS.

	1	2	3	4	5	6	7	8	9	
Oakland	1	0	3	0	0	2	0	1	*	—7
San Francisco	2	0	1	0	0	1	0	0	0	—4

Professional Pick ups.

Kelly plays on the gate for Stockton.

Dungan has fallen off in his batting.

As a pitcher "Chief" Borchers is "King of them all."

Wilson is a great back stop. He may often be seen in that position this season.

Krehmeyer of last seasons Sacramentos is now covering first bag for Houston of the Texas League.

The Chicago Brotherhood team is well off for pitchers having at its command, King, Baldwin, Dwyer and Barston.

Roberts fielding is perfection itself, and he can justly lay claim to being the "star" fielder of the League.

What a hard earnest worker is Fogarty of the Stocktons. Besides being a great infielder he is a most able captain.

"Pop" Swett is pleasing the Boston Brotherhood people. He is doing fine back-stop work, but his throwing thus far has been somewhat erratic.

To-days game will be between the Sacramentos and the San Franciscos at the Haight Street grounds. On Sunday the Friscos will play the Stocktons.

In the five games for the past week Fudger has made a great batting record, having 9 safe hits and 2 sacrifices to his credit.

New Haven has a player named German; Houston claims one by the name of France; on Wheelings list is another called Ireland and a Mr. England plays with a Pittsburgh team.

San Francisco has a pitcher named Lookabaugh. He is said to be a corker with a man on first. He can Lookabaugh him and fire the ball to the base quicker than a dun mule can switch his fly-brush.—Columbus Press.

Elliff ranked sixth in the batting list of the Texas League last year having a batting average of .288. He was at the "top notch" as a catcher, ranking first with a fielding record of 978.

Roberts made the first home run of the season in last Saturdays game. Fred is keeping the ball rolling pretty lively for in the game Sunday he had three good hits one being another "homer" off Perrott.

Stallings, the new Brooklyn catcher, is a tall, strong, athletic looking fellow, who snaps the ball down to second like a shot. As a back stop he is a star, and his hitting is way up—Sporting Times.

The ball cranks who have joined issues with the Players League have held an indignation meeting, and passed a resolution, to the effect, that the term "crank as applied to them is a misnomer. They now insist on being called "Brotherites."

Jolly Johnny Cooper, the genial but not infallible umpire from Santa Cruz occupied a seat in the Press Box last Sunday. Cooper says that teams from San Jose, Santa Cruz, Salinas and Monterey are contemplating forming a League to be known as the South Central California League.

In the making up of the local team Jack Hayes was "lost in the shuffle". Daddy is nevertheless a very good in or out fielder, a very fair hitter, and a tip top base runner, and would be a valuable acquisition to any of the Northern or interior teams.

Pennsylvania as a base ball State is "out of sight". In fact it is doubtful if as many churches exist in that State as do ball teams. The Philadelphia Press says "In Pennsylvania we have two League, two Players League, and one Association Club. Then we have six clubs in the Inter-state League, two in the New York and Pennsylvania League and not less than 600 A 1 Amateur teams.

The Boston Herald is loud in its praise of Van Heltrans style of pitching. The following is a clipping from that paper:

By the way, is there anything in the brotherhood so graceful as Van Haltren's long sweep of the delivery arm, passing the ball and hand from the right side of the waist high over his head and down to the left side, describing a wide half circle before speeding on its way? Lest we tire of it, he varies it now and then by a straight delivery, but this sweep is the very poetry of motion.

Jim Corbett, Californian's far famed heavy weight and the "Pride of the West" is a ball player of no mean ability. Jim never received gold medals, silver headed canes or elegant diamond scarf pins for his ball playing but he won the highest esteem and eternal friendship of his many associates on the field. Jim as a ball player first came into prominence when pitching for the amateur Shamrocks. He afterwards played with the Olympic Maroons and the Alcazars of the California Amateur League. In this League Corbett was regarded as a star out fielder and base runner, and lead his team in hitting, following close on to Delmas who as a hitter ranked first in the League.

Mr. E. T. Allen of 416 Market Street, City, sends a fine Photograph of the "E. T. Allen's", a ball nine which will make things lively this season.

BILLIARDS.

On Thursday, May 1st, between 8 and. 10 P. M., at the Baldwin billiard room, the balance of the stake money in the great McCleery vs. Schaeffer match of three thousand points for two thousand dollars a side will be put up.

The billiard world of San Francisco is now extremely agitated as the time approaches for the great match game of billiards which is to take place at Metropolitan Temple on May 29th, 30th and 31st between Jacob Schaefer and Professor McCleery of this city. As is well understood, the match is for $2,000 a side at straight rail billiards on a four and a half by nine table of the Brunswick-Balke & Collender Co. make, the Eastern man to discount McCleery. When the match was originally made, a $1,000 a side was deposited, and on the evening of May 1st, the parties interested each put up $1,000 a side more, at the bar of the Baldwin Hotel billiard parlors.

Prof. McCleery has been hard at work for several days preparing himself for the contest, and we understand that Schaefer is on his way West now, in company with Frank C. Ives, the well-known young billiard player of Chicago, the two giving exhibitions en route. As is only natural, McCleery's friends are strong supporters of the theory that no man living can discount him at the straight rail game, and yet we find in looking over the files of our Eastern exchanges that Schaefer has many supporters in the East, and that betting in the match already is 10 to 7 in his favor. The two great tournaments which have lately been finished in the East, the first in New York and the second in Chicago, has tended greatly to enhance the interests of the "gentleman's game," and there are many east of the Rocky Mountains who will watch the result of the contest here with a great deal of interest, as McCleery's prowess is but little known on the other side of the continent. When the match was first made, we were inclined to the belief that McCleery had a little the best of it, owing to the shortness of time that was to elapse between the finishing of the Chicago tournament and the match to take place here, but as the time has been extended which will give Schaefer a longer opportunity to practice than he otherwise would have had, we are now inclined to think that the chances are more even.

It is now some years since we have seen Schaefer nurse the ivories, but the manner in which he has been playing in the East, stamps him conclusively as being one of the greatest players of the present age, and yet with even the bias that must be formed by his friends in his favor, and with his superb playing in Chicago, there are many Californians who will be willing to make many modest little bets that the wizard of the one will be unable to discount the California favorite, McCleery.

THE GUN.

Selby Medal Match.

The Selby Smelting and Lead Company last year offered a handsome medal to be competed for at blue rock targets by residents of Central and Northern California. The medal was won by Mr. Henry A. Bassford. The Selby Company has had another elegant medal made, to be competed for during the present year, and the first match for it was shot at Oakland Trotting Park on Saturday last, eight men shooting under good conditions. All of the matches for the medal will be at thirty single blue rock targets and ten pairs, American Shooting Association rules.

Three of the shooters assumed names for the day. "Brooks" being Mr. C. B. S., of Stockton; "Francis" Mr. William T., of Mountain View; "Lake" Mr. J. O. C., of San Francisco.

The scores were:

Brooks	1	0	1	1	0	1	1	1	1	0	1	1	1	0	1	
	1	1	1	1	1	1	1	1	1	1	1	1	1	1	1	—26
Cadwallader	0	1	1	1	1	1	1	1	1	1	1	0	0	1	1	
	1	1	0	1	1	0	1	1	1	1	1	1	1	0	1	—24
S. I. Kellogg	1	1	1	1	1	1	1	1	1	1	1	1	1	1	1	
	1	1	1	1	1	1	1	0	1	0	1	1	1	1	0	—27
W. Francis	0	1	1	0	0	1	1	1	0	0	1	1	1	1	0	
	1	1	0	1	0	1	1	1	1	1	1	1	1	1	1	—22
Lake	1	1	0	0	1	1	0	0	1	0	1	1	1	0	0	
	0	1	1	1	1	1	1	1	1	0	0	1	0	1	1	—18
C. Cate	1	1	0	0	1	1	1	1	1	1	1	0	1	1	1	
	1	1	0	1	1	1	1	1	1	1	1	1	1	1	1	—26
Eddy	1	0	0	0	1	0	0	1	0	0	0	1	1	0	1	
	0	0	1	0	1	1	0	0	1	1	1	1	0	1	1	—15
Kimble	1	1	1	1	1	1	0	1	0	1	1	1	1	1	1	
	1	1	0	1	0	1	1	0	0	1	0	1	1	1	1	—23

TEN DOUBLE BIRDS.

"Brooks"	01	10	11	10	01	10	11	00	11	11	—13
Cadwallader	10	11	11	11	11	11	01	10	10	00	—14
Kellogg	11	10	11	11	10	11	00	01	10	10	—13
"Francis"	11	11	11	10	11	10	01	17	10	10	—15
"Lake"	10	10	10	11	10	01	11	10	00	10	—11
C. Cate	11	10	10	11	10	10	11	10	11	10	—13
Eddy	10	10	10	11	00	01	10	10	11	11	-12
Kimble	00	01	10	01	11	00	11	00	01	10	— 0

TIES FOR MEDAL AND $70.

Cate	1	1	1	1	1	1	11	11	10	—11
Kellogg	1	0	0	1	0	1	11	10	11	— 8

TIES FOR SECOND MONEY.

Brooks	1	0	1	0	0	0	11	11	10	— 7
Cadwallader	1	0	0	1	1	1	11	11	11	—10

The Traver Fraud.

The Cleveland Target Company, manufacturers of blue rock targets, wrote their agents here, Messrs. Clabrough, Golcher & Co., on April 21st, offering a reward of $25 for evidence that will lead to the conviction of the scoundrels who introduced a "take" target at Traver recently.

The Company offers to make affidavits that it has never made any such bid as that "rung in" at Traver. Incidentally it is mentioned that but one similar fraud has come to notice at which time wooden imitations of blue rock targets were used. Messrs. Clabrough and Golcher and several prominent sportsmen of Traver, are using all diligence to ferret out the guilty persons, and when discovered they will be held up to universal execration.

Mr. N. H. Cadwallader, of San Jose, has challenged Mr. Q. H. Cate to shoot for the Selby Medal won by the latter on Saturday last. The match must take place within a month.

Selby Live Bird Medal.

The conditions of competition for the Selby Smelting and Lead Company's "Standard" Live Bird Challenge Medal for 1890, representing the individual championship Pacific Coast at live birds, are as follows:

The Selby Smelting and Lead Company of San Francisco donates for competition at the trap a medal emblematic of the championship of the Pacific Coast for 1890, at live birds, under the following conditions:

1. This competition is open to all residents of the Pacific Coast.

2. All matches for the above medal shall be shot under the rules of the American Shooting Association, and shall be at forty single live birds.

3. The cartridges used in these matches shall be any of the Standard Shotgun Cartridges, loaded by the Selby Smelting and Lead Co., which shall be taken to the score in original packages, the unbroken seals or labels of which shall be cut by the referee or judge, or in his presence by the contestant.

4. Each time a competitor wins the Standard Live Bird Medal, 1890, he shall be set back one yard in the next match in which he may compete for the same.

5. All matches shall take place under the auspices of some regularly organized gun club, located where the matches occur.

6. Full and accurate scores of all matches shall be sent to the Selby Smelting and Lead Co., with complete details of guns and cartridges used. This condition is imperative.

7. Any competitor violating or attempting to violate any of the conditions and rules provided for these competitions (especially Rule 3), shall forfeit all claim to either the medal or any cash prize.

8. All challenges shall be made in writing to the Selby Smelting and Lead Co.

9. First match for the above medal will be shot at the Oakland Race Track, Oakland, on Saturday, May 17, 1890, commencing at 10 A. M. The entrance fee to which will be $20 00. Birds and trapping extra. Should the number of entries in any match require it, the squad shooting system will be used or the number of birds may be reduced

10. Fifty per cent of the entrance fees in this initial match shall be forwarded to, and will be held by the Selby Smelting and Lead Co., and awarded to the competitor who shall first win the Standard Live Bird Medal, 1890, four times, which shall, however, be done inside of one year from date of first match, failing which the donors reserve the right to otherwise dispose of the medal and entrance fees received from the first match.

11. In the first match the Standard Live Bird Medal, 1890, shall be the first prize. 30 per cent. of the entrance fees shall be the second prize, and 20 per cent the third prize.

12. The competitor winning the first match shall hold the medal, subject to challenge against all comers, one week's time being given him upon being challenged to name time for next match, which shall take place inside of one month from date of challenge, failing which the donors will name time and place for next match.

13. SUBSEQUENT MATCHES. All matches after the first one shall be open to all comers (as per paragraph No. one of these conditions), the entrance fee to which shall be $20, and the total amount of which shall be divided as follows: 1st prize, Standard Medal (40 per cent. of entrance fees shall be given to holder of medal on surrendering it to judge at each match); 2nd prize, 30 per cent.; 3d prize, 20 per cent; and 4th prize, 10 per cent. of entrance fees.

14. In the final match, 1st prize will be the medal; 2d prize, 40 per cent. of the entrance fees; 3d prize, 30 per cent; 4th prize, 20 per cent; 5th prize, 10 per cent.

15. The final winner of the Standard Live Bird Medal, 1890, may claim the Championship of Pacific Coast for 1890 at live birds.

16. The donors reserve the right to so change any of the above conditions as they may deem desirable for the best interests of the competitors.

17. All points arising, are covered by the above conditions, will be decided by the Selby Smelting and Lead Company.

Andrew Baker and Mr. Black, of Fresno, while trout fishing a few days ago on the North Fork of the Middle Tule, put out a large black bear and killed it.

Mr. Chas. Cate, winner of the Selby medal on April 26th, and challenged by Mr. Cadwallader, of San Jose, has named May 25th, 10:30 A. M., at Lincoln Club Grounds, as time and place for the match

Col. Gordon tried the experiment of planting California quails on his plantation, Lochinvar, Mississippi, about thirteen years ago, but it was not successful. The Colonel found that the California birds drove away the native quails, and being such runners, and not lying well to the dog, did not afford the sport to be had with the native quails.

A report comes from Strawberry Valley, high up in the mountains of Yuba County, that the Indians and a few whites are slaughtering deer along the line of the melting snow. It is said that twenty-seven of the animals had been lately killed, ten by one Indian. The past winter was very hard on the deer, and many perished in the snow. Some persons think that to preserve this game from extinction it may be necessary to prohibit killing of any kind of deer for a season or two. The present slaughter is in violation of law, as the close season lasts till July.

John Sanborn was in town from Hay Fork this week and informs us that after the melting of the snow, Jo Smith, of Hay Fork Valley, found within half a mile of his ranch the bodies of forty-five deer piled in a space of ten feet square, says the Trinity Journal. The place where the deer were found was at the foot of a high bluff; last winter the deer came down the ridge of the mountain through the deep snow met the bluff which they could not pass, and, being unable to retrace their steps through weakness and the snow, lay down and died. Mr. Smith skinned the deer and has the hides to show for it If any of our mountain contemporaries have a bigger deer story than this, as a relic of the big winter, let him trot it out and take the persimmon.

ROD.

How to Cook Trout.

A writer in the Sun gives the following direction for cooking trout:

Clean a few trout in the crystal waters of the stream. The trout are buttered, and seasoned with salt and pepper; then wrapped in paper or leaves, and buried in the hot ashes, where they steam in their own fragrant vapor.

The next best mode of cooking small trout is to clean them, rinse quickly in cold spring water, dry with a towel, and rub a little salt on the inside along the bone. Then cut into dice half a pound of the sweetest salt pork obtainable, try it out in the frying pan, and in the pork fat, actively boiling, plunge the delicate fish.

The writer is a firm believer in and a vehement advocate of cooking fish by steaming. Large brook trout, salmon and lake trout are delicious steamed Butter the trout and season with salt and pepper; wrap the fish in muslin, put them in the old fashioned steamer, place it over a pot of boiling water, and the ascending steam will do the rest.

Brook trout are also excellent broiled. Very large trout may be stuffed and baked. Never remove the head, tail or fins of trout; serve them so that they may look as much as possible like their own sweet selves.

If you must veil their native beauty, dredge a little yellow Indian meal, but under no circumstances cover them with batter or a thick layer of crumbs.

Drawn or melted butter, thickened with freshly grated horseradish, forms a harmonious sauce for steamed large trout.

Nothing daintier in the way of trolling tackle has been seen for many a day than the Abalone spoons, manufactured by Mr. E. T. Allen, 416 Market street, city, to whom we are indebted for a sample which will, we hope, get fast in many a big trout this season. The spoons have been tried, and found most killing, the iridesence of the polished shell being just like a glinting minnow.

A very *recherche* bachelor's supper was given at the residence of Dr. A. H. Bailey, on Front Street and Minnesota avenue in Santa Cruz on Thursday evening of last week, one at which genuine enjoyment of a *menu* fit for an epicure was followed by an hour of wit, song and story long to be remembered.

Dr. Bailey entertained, five of his friends, who each contributed something substantial or etherial to the feast. Early in the day, Bootsy—the only Bootsy—had been sent out to a mountain stream for trout. He returned with nearly 100 and these were the main reliance for the feast.

They were cooked by that amateur *cordon bleu*, Howard Coult, who also gave his friends *filets d' abalone* and a capital *salade*, all done by his own fair hands.

W. H. Galbraith brought down some of Kilfasset's famous vintage, so the wines were perfect, while Fred Stevens "set the table" with all the grace of the prettiest of maids.

George H. Ready and LeBaron Olive, having "nothing else to do," were the belles of the evening, and also proved themselves gallant trenchermen.

"Bootsy" was promoted to the office of chief waiter, afterwards acting as *prima donna* with pronounced success. "Aloha" was said regretfully, when the hour grew late.

All of the gentlemen are prominent members of the Santa Cruz Rod and Gun Club of which Mr. E. C. Williams is the efficient Secretary.

THE KENNEL.

Dog owners are requested to send for publication the earliest possible notices of whelps, sales, names claimed, presentations and deaths, in their kennels, in all instances writing plainly names of sire and dam and of grandparents, colors, dates and breed.

Deaths.

Mr. George Bassfords pointer bitch Blossom whelped March 27, 1886, by Glen R.—Josie Bow, died on April 26, 1890. Cause, poison.

Mr. Frank H. Allen has brought from the kennel of Mr. A. H. Moore, Melrose, Mass., a St. Bernard dog puppy, seven weeks old, by Ben Lomond—Saffron. The puppy arrived after its long journey clean and lively. The breeding cannot be beaten.

The death of Mr. Geo. W. Bassford's grand brood bitch Blossom, noted elsewhere is to be deplored, not only because she was the valued companion of her owner, but also because she was of unusual excellence both on the bench and in the field. In sending notice of her death, Mr. Bassford adds a few words which are so eloquent and so touching that we venture, without his permission to use them. Blossom won V. H. C. at the dog show of '86 when only four months old; 2nd at the show of '88 and 1st at the show of '89. She divided third in the field trial derby of '87.

Mr. Bassford writes: My neighbors had put out squirrel poison without notifying me, and she somehow got one of the poisoned squirrels and ate it, and was not discovered until too late to save her though all was done that could be done.

Though I have bred a great many dogs, and make the proud boast of having bred more prize winning pointers both in the field and on the bench, than any other breeder on the coast, I consider Blossom one of the best, combining as she did many of the sterling qualities that go to make a good dog. In the field she was more than an average, as a brood bitch one of the best, as a companion kind affectionate, and obedient. To say I feel her loss keenly, to say that had I lost one of my own flesh and blood I could not feel much more, cannot convey to you any idea of just how I do feel and yet she was only a "Dog".

It is some consolation to know that I have two bitches of her get, one by Point, and one by Scout Croxteth, yet I feel that they will never attain the high estimation that I had of their mother. She was due to whelps to Point the day after she died.

A local light in pointer breeding circles sends us a few notes in relation to the management of the Pacific Coast Field trials, which may be read and carefully considered with profit. He writes:

"As to a certain handler controlling the Pacific Coast Field Trials Club, and running it for his personal benefit, that is an open secret, and it is needless for me to go into detail for you know the facts as well as I. Neither do I wish to be put down as a kicker, for if I or any one else does not like the way the club conducts its trials we have our remedy in withdrawing our entries, and if it is to be a one *man's* club the entries will be light, notwithstanding the fact that contracts are made with parties who receive *presents* of pups to run them in trials for three years.

We all have our hobbies; to raise pointer pups and put them to the front is mine, for I am afraid of no man's pups be they pointers or setters, but when a breeder and handler controls the judges and club it gives him an advantage, and it is a combination that is hard to down."

Whelps.

Echo Cocher Kennel (Stockton) dark red Cocker, Senora, A. K. S. B. 17063, whipped April 20, 1890, three puppies to owners Bronta, A. K. S. B. 17064.

Same owners, liver and white ticked Cocher, Pet. H, whelped April 22, 1890, five puppies, to owners Bronta, A. S. K. B. 17064.

Arsenic for Chorea.

EDITOR BREEDER AND SPORTSMAN.—A young man, a friend of mine, has a small dog puppy, when grown, will weigh twenty or twenty five pounds, and a short time ago it was taken with the jerks in the left fore shoulder, I advised him to give him some Fowler's Arsenic.

He commenced with four drops twice a day, went up to fifteen drops twice a day, then dropped off one drop a day until four drops twice a day from starting point. I saw him yesterday, and he said he didn't think he was any better.

The puppy is five or six months old and fine and healthy—grows finer—good appetite, etc. Please prescribe for it.

STOCKTON, April 28, 1890. A. C. SAVENPORT.

[It is with diffidence that we differ with so sound an authority in canine ills as Dr. Davenport, but accepting his belief that the puppy is choreaic, it is suggested that some emulsion of Cod Liver Oil and the hypophosphites, together with sulphate of strychnia and a little iron would probably induce a more perfect assimilation of food, and a general tonicity of the nervous tract which is the seat of the trouble. Together with the remidies mentioned, we believe in the feeding of bones in plenty; preferably the soft bones of calves. Dogs very much enjoy gnawing them, and will crush, swallow and digest them to an astonishing extent; the result being increased strength, sound bony parts, clean teeth and more than average good health and ability to resist disease.—KEN. ED.]

Treatment of the Patient in Distemper.

As distinguished from the exhibition of remedial agents prescribed by a competent medical adviser which might be termed treatment of the disease, the care of the patient as to food, cleanliness and surroundings may be considered as of the utmost importance in distemper.

The medical aspect of treatment has been so often discussed as to have reached a high development, but the care of the patient is generally but perfectly conducted, and any suggestions on that line should be appreciatively received. The most recent and certainly as sound as any, are offered by an editorial writer in the English Kennel Gazette, Merlin, by signature, who puts in clear and positive language the convictions resultant upon long study and extended experience. He says that isolation is the first thing necessary when distemper is discovered in a kennel.

All dogs attacked must be placed in dry, well-ventilated quarters, which must be warmed artificially if the weather be cold. These quarters must be quite separate from the ordinary kennels, and great care must be taken to prevent those who attend the sick dogs from carrying infection to healthy ones. A special jacket, a large apron, and gloves, should be worn by the attendant while in the "hospital," and should be taken off and left there, to be donned again at every visit to the patients. Mere separation would be useless if the attendant were allowed to pass from diseased to healthy dogs without such precautions as are here indicated. Everything needed for use about the sick dogs, feeding pans, drinking vessels, sponges, etc., should be carefully cleansed after use, and should not be used for any other dogs, being kept in the sick quarters so long as they are needed.

When distemper ends fatally, it is usually because of the extreme exhaustion due to the fever, or because of complications, due to exposure to colds or to other causes. The strengthening of the patient by nourishing food is of the first importance, but there is frequently a great difficulty in administering food, as the disease is accompanied by extreme irritability of the stomach and intestines. Nourishing food must be given regularly, whether the patients like it or not. Beef tea and raw eggs are specially valuable, and a spouted feeding cup should be used for pouring these and other liquids down the patient's throat. Beef jelly is also specially valuable in these cases, and raw beef, minced or scraped, is perhaps still more valuable, for a pill of scraped beef may be given, when the stomach is so irritable as to reject every form of liquid nourishment.

Lime water is especially valuable in correcting the irritability of the stomach and intestines. It may be obtained from any chemist, or may be prepared in a few hours by any person. A piece of unslacked lime the size of a hen's egg should be placed in a large bottle with about three pints of water, and the bottle should be well shaken till the lime is thoroughly broken up. After the lime has settled the clear water should be poured into another bottle and kept for use. Milk should be diluted with an equal proportion of lime water, and the addition of a spoonful of sherry or of brandy to each cupful of milk, and water will be of special value as a stimulant.

For the first day or two the patients will doubtless take broths, etc., pretty freely, but afterward they will probably refuse everything. A cupful of milk and lime water, or of beef tea, should be given, forcibly if necessary, about every four or five hours, and a raw egg might with advantage be added to each cup of beef tea. If there be vomiting, smaller quantities must be given more frequently. If all liquids are rejected by the stomach, beef jelly should be given, a teaspoonful about every two hours, or raw beef scraped and made into pills should be pushed down the throat at similar intervals.

Nothing has been said about medicine, because, as already stated, the treatment of the disease itself is a matter for a properly qualified veterinary surgeon. Some owners treat ordinary cases of distemper without veterinary assistance, relying chiefly on quinine and on careful nursing. It is hoped that these may find something useful in the foregoing notes, although the hints as to feeding are intended chiefly for those who nurse distempered dogs that are under skilled veterinary treatment.

The nose and eyes of a patient must be frequently cleansed with a sponge, which should be rinsed in hot water containing a disinfectant strong enough to destroy disease germs. Food and drinking pans, aprons, gloves, and everything else used in the hospital, should be scalded before being put away, or taken into ordinary use. All woodwork should also be thoroughly scrubbed with hot water, containing a reliable disinfectant in proper strength.

A New Foundland bitch five years old, black, with white star in brisket, and a fine intelligent animal may be found on application to this *office*.

One of the finest and most remarkable coursing matches ever run in the State came off at "Tule,' Johnson's ranch on the Marysville road near Sacramento on Sunday last. It was a match race between Bell Boy, reared and owned in that city by L. Stuart Upson, and Snowball, owned by Mr. O'Connor of Penryn, Placer county. The latter dog has been recognized as one of the best in the State, and bears a high reputation in coursing circles in San Francisco. It was thought that he would surely beat the Sacramento dog, and had backers in plenty. He was run under the management of Major Neary, who has had great experience in coursing.

The match was the best three in five, and was a "corker" from the start. Bell Boy won the first course, making six points to his adversary's three. Snowball won the second, the third and fourth were declared no race; the fifth was won by Snowball; the sixth was no race.

The dogs had been severely punished by these six heats, and Snowball seemed quite distressed, while Bell Boy (in pugilistic parlance) came up for the seventh round in good shape. He won the race handily, Snowball "not being in it."

Bell Boy showed not only great speed, but remarkable staying powers, and by defeating such a true and tried dog as Snowball is entitled to championship honors. He is royally bred, being by Cato, ex-Blue Nell. Cato is by Bradly, and Blue Nell is by Blue Jacket. This breeding shows that Bell Blue comes legitimately by his great racing qualities, as all the dogs named were phenomenals in their day.

Nothwithstanding the fact that it has been proved time and again since the commencement of the world that the dog is man's best friend, a good many cranks would like to see every dog in the country either poisoned and thrown to the buzzards, or converted into the succulent appetizing sausage says an exchange. This is a great mistake, as a dog in its proper place—and it is easy enough to keep them there—is a great benefit to mankind in general, and often save the lives and property of its master.

W. Blake, who lives about a quarter of a mile this *side* of Daunt Tulare County, had a couple of dogs that proved an exception to the rule, but now alas, they are numbered with tho things that have passed. It appears that about 2 A. M. last Monday week, a large Californian lioness accompanied by two cubs wandered down to Blake's place in search of provender, and seeing a plump yearling colt, the property of the aforesaid gentleman nonchalantly roaming about at a short distance from its dam, the lioness concluded that colty was her meat, and straightway made for the unsuspecting quadruped, in that crouching and stealthy manner so peculiar to animals of the leonine species.

Getting within springing distance of her intended victim she was in the act of making the fatal leap, when a couple of sheep dogs, belonging to Blake, and a large white retriever owned by A. J. Doty, evidently smelling something suspicious, appeared upon the scene and attacked the lioness, and a terrible fight ensued. The colt becoming scared ran to its mother; and the noise awakening Blake he rushed out to the scene of the conflict, but only in time to catch a dim glimpse of the lioness and her cubs as they disappeared in the darkness. His two dogs lay torn almost to shreds, and quite dead on the ground, while Doty's dog was badly lacerated that he will probably have to be killed. From the pieces of fur lying about, and the cut up ground where the fight occurred the dogs must have made a terrific stand against their powerful adversary, and the only pity is that they were not victorious. A party of hunters started after the trio, but as we have not heard of their capture or death, the probabilities are that they are on the high road to Modoc or some part of the county.

VETERINARY.

Conducted by W. Henry Jones, M. R. C. V. S.

Subscribers to this paper can have advice through this column in all cases of sick or injured horses or cattle by sending an explicit description of the case. Applicants will send their name and address that they may be identified. Questions requiring answers by mail should be accompanied by two dollars, and addressed to W. Henry Jones, M. R. C. V. S., Olympic Stables, butter Street, San Francisco.

J. O. C.

One of my colts has got a large swelling on both sides of the head and also between the jaw. She feeds well and does not appear to suffer much. What is best to be done to reduce the enlargement?

Answer.—In all probability your colt has strangles. I would advise you to poultice the swellings, till they get soft, then open at the lower part with a sharp knife. Give him good nutritious food and see that he is kept warm and comfortable. Isolate the animal from the rest of your stock, for a time, otherwise the others will be likely to become affected.

C. O. S.

A valuable bitch belonging to me has the mange very badly. I have tried all sorts of remedies but without any good result. Can you assist me with your advice?

Answer.—I would advise you first to well wash the bitch with carbolic soap and warm water, dry thoroughly, then apply olive oil six ounces, oil of tar four ounces, sulphur three ounces, carbolic acid two drams. Rub the mixture well in with the hand or a soft brush, and let it remain on twenty-four hours, then remove with soap and water, and reapply the application. Two dressings will be sufficient. Keep the bowels open, and do not feed on any meat for some time.

WM. HENRY JONES, M. R. C. V. S.

Pacing Records at One Mile.

Johnston, harness, against time, Chicago, Ills., Oct 9, 1884, 2:06¼.

Brown Hal, best stallion record, Cleveland, Ohio, July 31, 1889, 2:12½.

Westmont, July 10, 1884, Chicago, Ills., with running mate, 2:01¾.

Daisy, yearling, Sacramento, Dec. 31, 1885, 2:38¼.

Ed Rosewater, two years old, Council Bluffs, Iowa, Nov. 3, 1889, 2:20¼.

Yolo Maid, 3 years old, San Francisco, Oct. 13, 1889, 2:14.

Gold Leaf, four years old, 2:11¼ on August 17, 1889, at Napa.

Arrow, five years old, 2:13¼, made at Cleveland, Ohio, August 1, 1888

The Standard.

[AS REVISED AND ADOPTED BY THE NATIONAL ASSOCIATION OF TROTTING-HORSE BREEDERS, DECEMBER 14, 1887.]

IN order to define what constitutes a trotting-bred horse and to establish a BREED of trotters on a more intelligent basis, the following rules are adopted to control admission to the records of pedigrees. When an animal meets the requirements of admission and is duly registered, it shall be accepted as a standard trotting-bred animal:—

FIRST.—Any stallion that has himself a record of two minutes and thirty seconds (2:30) or better, provided any of his get has a record of 2:35 or better, or provided his sire or his dam is already a standard animal.

SECOND.—Any mare or gelding that has a record of 2:30 or better.

THIRD.—Any horse that is the sire of two animals with a record of 2:30 or better.

FOURTH.—Any horse that is the sire of one animal with a record of 2:30 or better, provided he has either of the additional qualifications: (1) A record himself of 2:35 or better. (2) Is the sire of two other animals with a record of 2:35 or better. (3) Has a sire or dam that is already a standard animal.

FIFTH.—Any mare that has produced an animal with a record of 2:30 or better.

SIXTH.—The progeny of a standard horse when out of a standard mare.

SEVENTH.—The female progeny of a standard horse when out of a mare by a standard horse.

EIGHTH.—The female progeny of a standard horse when out of mare whose dam is a standard mare.

NINTH.—Any mare that has a record of 2:35 or better, and whose sire or dam is a standard animal.

Best Trotting Records.

1 mile—2:08¾, Maud S., against time, in harness, accompanied the distance by a running horse, Glenville, O., July 30, 1885 ......2:13¾, best time in a race between horses, Maud S., Chicago, Ills., July 24, 1880......2:12, Axtell, against time, accompanied by running horse—fastest stallion time, Terre Haute, Ind., Oct. 11, 1889......2:13¾, Phallas, fastest heat by a stallion against other horses, Chicago, July 14, 1884......2:12¾, Palo Alto, third heat in race at Stockton, Cal., Sept. 26, 1889......2:16¼, Jay-Eye-See, half-mile track, Lincoln, Neb., Sept. 14, 1887......2:15¾, Great Eastern, under saddle, third heat, Morrisania, N. Y., Sept. 22, 1877......2:10¾, Jay-Eye-See, against time, best five-year-old record, Providence, R. I., Sept. 15, 1883......2:16, Manzanita, third heat, best four-year-old record, Lexington, Ky., Sept. 3, 1876......2:16, Edgemark, four-year old stallion record, against time, Lexington, Ky., Oct. 18, 1889......2:10¼, Sunol, in Stanford Stake, accompanied by a runner, best three-year-old record, San Francisco, Nov. 9, 1889, 2:18, Sunol, 2 years, against time, San Francisco, Cal., Oct. 27, 1888......2:20¾, Regal Wilkes, two-year-old stallion record, San Francisco, Nov. 9, 1889......2:31¼, Norlaine, yearling, against time, San Francisco, Cal., Nov. 12, 1887......2:30, Faustino, yearling stallion record, San Francisco, Nov. 9, 1889.

2 miles—4:43 against time, Fanny Witherspoon, Chicago, Ill., Sept. 25, 1885.

3 miles—7:21¼, Huntress, harness, Brooklyn, L. I., Sept. 21, 1872.

4 miles—10:34½, Longfellow, wagon, California, Dec. 31, 1869.

5 miles—13:00, Lady Mac, harness, San Francisco, Cal., April 2, 1874.

10 miles—27:23¼, Controller, harness, San Francisco, Cal., Nov. 23, 1878.

20 miles—58:25, Captain McGowan, harness, half-mile track, Boston, Oct. 31, 1865.

Racing in England.

Reve d'Or Wins the City and Suburban Handicap.

LONDON, April 23.—This was the second and last day of the Epsom Spring meeting. The principal race of the day was for the City and Suburban Handicap, for three-year-olds and upward; about one mile and a quarter (sixty-six subscribers). It was won by the Duke of Beaufort's six-year-old chestnut mare Reve d'Or, by Hampton, out of Queen of the Roses. Baron de Hirsch's four-year-old bay colt Vasistas, by Idus, out of Veranda, was second, and Mr. J. Lowther's four-year-old chestnut colt Workington, by Charibert, out of Hematite, third.

The other starters were Pioneer, Gold, Surbiton, Royal Star, Swift, Bena, St. Kieran, Antibes, Quartus, Kaikoura, Innisheen and Sabrina.

The post odds were 7 to 1 against Reve d'Or, 50 to 1 against Vasistas, 11 to 1 against Workington, 5 to 2 against Pioneer, 8 to 1 against Gold, 14 to 1 against Surbiton, 17 to 1 against Royal Star, 22 to 1 against Swift and Bena, 25 to 1 against St. Kieran, 33 to 1 against Antibes, 40 to 1 each against Quartus, Kaikoura and Innisheen, and 100 to 1 against Sabrina. Royal Star made the play to the straight. Here Reve d'Or and Vasistas headed him and raced home, Reve d'Or winning by a neck. Vasistas was three lengths ahead of Workington. Time, 2:12.

The race for the Hyde Park Plate, for two-year-olds at five furlongs straight was won by Lord Ellesmere's brown filly Sabra, by St. Simon, out of Belinda, by a length. Mr. H. Nixon's chestnut colt Hindebert was second, half a length before Lord Londonderry's gray colt Dereham. Betting—6 to 4 Sabra, 10 to 1 Hildebert and 5 to 2 Dereham.

Grinding Oats.

Grinding oats to a coarse meal for winter food, says The Horse World, is certainly an advantage to the owner as well as the horse. When fed whole, a varying proportion of them pass off unmasticated and undigested. Some people have claimed that the gastric juices of the stomach extracted all the nourishment out of an oat kernel, if passed through in its original form. The folly of this assumption is, however, demonstrated by the fact that chickens and pigs will get fat on such oats, hence they must be rich in nutriment; again, such oats will grow when planted, which is a still stronger proof of their composition having remained unimpaired. The damage sustained when oats are passed undigested is two-fold; first, in the oats themselves, and second, in the loss of energy by the horse, which has gone through the physical efforts of swallowing, salivating and passing them without any compensation therefrom. With high bred horses destined for a career, where absolute superiority is the universal desideratum, this seemingly trifling matter is well worth considering. It has been argued that, when ground oats are fed, the powers of mastication are not properly exercised and that a deficiency results in the amount of saliva given out by the glands. This argument hinges on another wrong assumption. It has been amply demonstrated by modern scientists that a flow of saliva will occur regardless of mastication. Who has not yet experienced the sensation of the saliva coming copiously into the mouth at sight of something good to eat?

Grim's Gossip.

Tenny is now first choice for the Suburban with Raceland and Prince Royal close up.

Jockey Hayward has joined the Hearst Stable at Sheeps-head and is daily in the saddle.

The Fresno meeting is advertised this week, and will receive proper mention in the next issue.

If Kelly & Samuels go East Pliny and Ed McGinnis will be the only two of the string to be taken along.

If there is a heavy track on the day that the Brooklyn Handicap is run, Los Angeles should stand a very good show to win.

A fact not generally known is that the late Aristides Welch was, with Horace Greely and others, one of Jefferson Davis' bondsmen.

Los Angeles, Sorrento, Rico, Flood Tide and Honduras, are the five California horses remaining in the Brooklyn Handicap.

Rico is under the weather sligbtly, and unless he picks up on the journey across the continent it is 2 to 1 that he will not be a starter.

A stable of thoroughbreds from Palo Alto will be on the California Circuit this year. The string will include Pasi, Rinfax, Muta and several others.

It is reported that the programme arranged for the coming fair at Los Angeles includes a subscription purse of $2,000 for all horses eligible to the 2:30 class.

Week before last a stallion show was given at Lexington, Ky., which 5000 persons witnessed. There should be more of these exhibitions given in California.

Lovers of good horses should pay a visit to the Bay District track any morning, and see what the trainers have on hand. There is many a good one being worked out every day.

W. S. McLaughlin, better known as Billy McLaughlin, the veteran jockey, died at Grace Hospital, Detroit, Mich., on Thursday, April 17, from a complication of diseases.

Ross expects to go East with Kitty Van and Oro. Tom Williams made a proposition to have Kitty Van go along in his stable, but it is doubtful if Ross will consent to this.

Ed Bither of Jay-Eye-See and Phallas fame is located at Charter Oak Park, in charge of nineteen head of Allen Farm trotters, some of which will be seen at the front before Fall.

The young stallion, Alex Mc Gregor, 1886, known by many breeders throughout the West, died in Peoria, April 25th He was one of the finest bred and most promising grandsons of Robert McGregor.

Othello is the last Sultan to get a record better than 2:30. In a match race betwen Othello and P. Q. (pacer) at Los Angeles last Friday week, the trotter won in three straight heats the first heat being trotted in 2:28½.

The Sporting World says that "Mr. Thomas Maguire, who was the pioneer of theatricals on the Pacific Coast, now a resident here, is one of the most ardent turf lovers we have. He is rarely missed from the Jersey tracks."

We take pleasure in calling attention to the large advertisement of Gombault's Caustic Balsam which appears on page 399. We hear the remedy highly spoken of by horsemen who have used it, and we think our readers can afford to give it a trial.

Theodore Winters Esq., was represented at the Belle Meade sale and his agent purchased a brown yearling colt by Iroquois, dam Valerian by Vandal. Price $2,000: also the brown yearling colt by Iroquois, dam Toplight by Great Tom. Price, $1,600.

Someone is evidently backing the California horse Floodtide for the Brooklyn Handicap, as several of the "books" have him rubbed off, and the announcement is made that they are "full." Probably his owner, R. Porter Ashe, has sent on a commission.

The Mountain Boy foals which have appeared so far, are all marvels of beauty and the owners of the various ones, each claim that his individual one is the best. By Holly made a wondrous good trade the day that he secured this fine son of Kentucky Prince.

From Eastern exchanges I learn that Bow Bells has been injured and it is not deemed advisable to trot him for a record this year. If the report be true, the Hermitage stud owners will be sadly disappointed as part of their plans were to give the colt a low record this season.

Mr. W. H. Wilson, of Abdallah Park Cynthiana, Ky., has purchased of A. J. Feek, Syracuse, N. Y., the mare Black Jane (dam of Rosa Wilkes 2;18½ and Simmons 2;28, the sire of 9, 2:30 performers at ten years old) by Mambrino Patchen. She will probably be stinted to Sultan 2;24.

Edwin C. 2:15, the pacer lately sold by Mr. Johnston to parties in the East, was not sent on the Hickok car, as the final payment had not been made. Some fifteen hundred dollars is still due on the horse, and Johnston refuses to ship until full settlement is made. Perfectly right to.

In the next issue of the BREEDER AND SPORTSMAN we will try to give the full list of entries for the various races, which closed on May 1st. Secretaries of all associations will please forward lists as soon as possible, and also a list of all second payments on stakes that have closed in the past.

The Eros foals of 1890 are far above the average and happy owners of the promising colts are to be met every day. Mr. Burke will give this son of Electioneer a chance to reduce his record during the present year and those most likely to know, claim that 2:20 is not too low a mark for him.

Mr Davidson, one of the Directors of the new agricultural association that will have headquarters at Modesto, has been visiting the various tracks in this vicinity during the week, for the purpose of gaining all necessary information as to the building of their track, which the members have determined shall be the equal of any in the state. This point is exceedingly desirable as a trotting horse centre, as the breeding interests in that neighborhood are large, and the track will be a desirable one for horsemen when traveling between Stockton and Fresno.

Jack Garrity is moving his chestnut pacer by Sidney, dam Humming Bird along at a lively rate and the visitors to the Bay District track are satisfied that at last Jack has one that will be hard to beat. Old Humming Bird was the fastest pacing mare I ever saw, and it is only natural that from a union with Sidney, that the produce should be of the world beater variety.

Mr. Cyrus Berry one of the administrators of the estate of S. B. Emerson, has determined to settle in California, and to that end has sent in his name as a member of the Trotting Horse Breeders Association. The late Mr. Emerson was devotedly attached to the trotting horse interests, and it is a pleasure to note that his nephew, Mr. Berry, is also inclined the same way.

Governor Waterman has appointed the following Agricultural Directors: John McBeth, of Plumas county, a Director of the Eleventh District Association; C. N. Tharsing, of Sutter county, a Director of the Thirteenth District Association, vice J. H. Kimball, resigned; Wm. H. Hammond and R. E. Hyde, of Tulare county, members of the Fifteenth District Association.

T. D. Meyers, the real estate dealer of Oakland, is at present in Kentucky, picking up the brood mares which he has bought from time to time, and which he proposes to bring out to California within the next few days. While at Lexington he attended the Woodard sale and was fortunate enough to purchase a full sister to Minnehaha, another gem to add to his collection. The price paid was only $800, and a rare good bargain it is.

Some time ago Mr. Valensin was commissioned to buy a good mare that could trot in 2:20 for a gentleman in Italy. He fully intended to procure Wanita 2:20¼. but circumstances prevented him from visiting Mr. Beckwith at Evanston, or he would have bought the young mare. I hear that the Sire Bros. have finally secured her and that John E Turner will have the handling of her on the circuit. Wanita is by Aberdeen, dam Wyoming Belle by Lowe's Pilot, 2nd dam Juanita by Pilot Jr.

"Lucky" Baldwin tells me that he is not training any of his horses for the California Circuit, but will ship another lot East about May 10th, including Laredo and the Emperor of Norfolk. The gentleman claims that the latter is as sound as he ever was and expects good reports from him this year. Baldwin will start East himself in the course of a few weeks and will be in attendance at all the events where his horses are entered.

"Leslie E. Macleod," says the Prince Edward Island Agriculturist, "another brilliant light amongst them, an authority on all that treats and touches of the standard trotter—seems to have the magic touch of pen that captivates the American readers, in telling the never tiring story of how the world beaters are bred. Well, Leslie first saw the light down here by the murmuring sea and we have reason to be proud of him, for he is a 'star performer' in his class, respected and applauded by thousands of his new made American friends."

Pete Woods seems to have caught on, and before another week rolls around, he will have a fine string at work at the Bay District. The Grosvenor colt, owned by E. Topham of Milpitas, is showing up well, as is also the chestnut mare from Del Bosque Rancho. She is a Gibraltar, and will prove one of the fast ones. Dixie by Altamont should add another to the list of his sire, as he can trot better than a "30" gait even this early in the season. Four new ones will be sent to Mr. Woods next week, one of which should prove "good goods."

Throughout the great north-west, the trotting boom is still on the move, and I learn that at many of the tracks throughout Oregon and Washington, the good work has already commenced. At Spokane the beautiful course has been entirely reclayed, making a decided improvement. "Doc" Lindsay has a string already on the move, and he promises to make it warm for those that may have to contend against his flyers this season. Joe Crabb, of Walla Walla, says that their track is in good shape, and expects to see the Washington horses beat all their previous records this year.

The many friends of Dick Havey will be pleased to hear that he will have charge of the Palo Alto horses during the absence of Mr. Mervin, with the Eastern division, and will also drive behind the Palo Alto horses that are to be seen on the California tracks this season. Dick is no stranger at Menlo Park, having worked there years ago, and fully understands the Marvin methods. A good driver, and splendid conditioner, with nerve enough to take advantage of any slip made by his competitors, Dick should prove the necessary sort of man to fill the bill, and we wish him luck in his new position.

A new law in Indiana pertains to the service fee of stallions and requires registry of stock horses with the clerks of circuit courts. One of the requirements of the law is as follows: "That a copy of such license embracing such sworn statements and pedigree, with the fee the owner proposes to charge for service, shall be posted by the owner of such sire in two or more conspicuous places in the vicinity of the place where the sire is kept for service, and should any part of said sworn statement be to the knowledge of the owner of such sire false in any particular, the owner shall not be entitled to collect any fee for such service, and the falsity of such statement, or any part thereof, may be pleaded in the bar to any contract or account for services of such sire."

Baseball is said to be the national sport, but the amount of capital invested in the baseball parks and clubs and players of the United States is trifling compared to that which is represented by the American race-courses, stables, jockeys, trainers and nags, says the World. The Monmouth Park track and improvements will not be valued at less than $700,-000; the New York Jockey Club's new tracks, grand stand and club-house are estimated to have cost $2,000,000; the Coney Island's track is put at $300,000; the Brooklyn at $200,000, the Linden and Elizabeth each at $150,000. The aggregate of these estimates is three and a half million dollars, and many millions more would not represent the value of the horse-flesh that runs on those tracks. Many of the richest men in the United States make money out of race-horses and race-courses. Wm. K. Vanderbilt owns the Coney Island Jockey Club, practically, and Wm. L. Scott and the Dwyers control the Brooklyn Jockey Club.

A. J. Cassatt, who is estimated as a two-millionaire, and Mr. Withers, a tour millionaire, own Monmouth, and John A. Morris, who built the New York Club's new track, is set down at $20,000,000. Senator Hearst is one of the richest millionaire owners of blooded horses. The Goulds and Rockefellers and Flaglers haven't got on the turf yet.

For the sanguine temperament wanted in every horse, th heart and lungs must be large and good. Of these we ca judge something by the frame that contains them. If th chest is small and circular, there will not be room for enoug heart and lung power. If it is large and circular there wi be room for large heart and lungs, but still the lungs will on ly be able to work by pressing on the other vital organs, a a circular chest will resist all efforts to expand it. If th chest is deep and capacious it can expand and contract wit every breath, and can thus meet any extraordinary demand made upon it, provided the lungs are healthy and good, an the heart, air passages, and supplying pipe are all duly pro portioned to them. But all these ifs and buts can only b securely decided by a trial of the horse's wind power unde severe exertion. We cannot look inside, and if fifty thing are right and one wrong, that one will put its limit on th horse's breathing power, and consequently on his capacit for exertion.

It is a pleasure to meet breeders of the type of S. N Straube, and it is very few in the country that can show three such rare good stallions as Clovis 4909, Apex 8935 an Junio 2:22. The last mentioned one has just been purchase by Mr. Straube, so he tells me, from A. M. Gonzalez, and i future that game son of Electioneer will grace the harem a Poplar Grove Breeding Farm, Fresno County. The youn Clovis colts and also those by Apex will be handled this yea by Matt Dwyer, who was understudy at Palo Alto for Mr Marvin, and is thoroughly capable of putting on the finish ing touches to a trotting horse. As will be seen by referenc to the foals of 1890 in this issue, Mr. Straube has a fine lo of youngsters already on the scene of action, and there ar many more of the mares to hear from yet. Mr. Straube ha made a good name for himself among the breeders of Cali fornia, and he is justly entitled to it, for there are none mor conscientious in their dealings with the public.

Redwood 2:24½, the well bred son of Anteeo 2:16½ and Lo Medium by Milton Medium 2:25½, stood during the earl portion of this season at Oakland Trotting Park for servic but the owners have had to remove him to Santa Rosa a there were so many parties in that neighborhood who wishe to breed mares to the horse. Messrs. McFadyen & Murph have any quantity of green pasturage, and will be able t personally superintend the management of the mares a Santa Rosa, so it was deemed expedient to make the change The matrons that were sent to Oakland to receive the em braces of Redwood were all shipped to Santa Rosa free o expense to the owners, and as the change will be beneficial there is no likelihood of complaint. The foals by Redwoo are all of them fine lookers and born trotters, so there i plenty of indication that another Californian horse will ad fresh lustre to the many that have already made the Sta famous.

An old friend, Charles V. Sass, Secretary of the Brighto Beach Association, has sent me a letter in which he says: "A special effort will be made to revive steeplechasing and hurdl racing. Superintendent Clare is now at work laying out th grounds. The jumps and obstacles will be laid out accordin to the rules of the English Grand National Hunt Committe and will be such that only a perfectly trained horse ca enter for or run in them. Assurance have been received tha some sixty horses will be ready for cross country work b the time the meeting opens, and the management now fee so confident of achieving a success with its revival of cros country sport that it will shortly announce a sweepstake with at least $1,000 added, for a grand long-distance steeple chase. The long-distance races on the flat, which prove such a success at Clifton during the winter, will be retaine on the Brighton programme, and other features whic proved popular among horsemen and racegoers will be mai tained and improved on during the ensuing season, whic will open not later than the first week of July."

Orrin A. Hickok has said good-bye to his legion of friend and started for the East taking with him five good campaig ers for use on the "big circuit." Several seasons hav elapsed since Mr. Hickok had any horses on the other sid of the Rockies, but he will be no stranger to the regular tu frequenters as he has always been a decided favorite amon the horsemen of the East. In the stable there is first an foremost Adonis 2:14, a fitting companion for the free-for-a pacers, and one that will take a lot of worrying to beat. Wit ordinary luck he should be able to lower his present recor several seconds and I know that Orrin fancies he can do i Next comes Prince Warwick, a son of Alcona 730, dam Wa wick Maid that is eligible for any event, but with spe enough to stand off any "green" horse that has no recor Monterey is by Electioneer, dam Minx by Don Victor, an he is another of the "unmarked" ones that will puzzle th pool box fiends for a race or two. The 2:25 pacing race one in which there is usually a good deal of guessing, so M Hickok will let the boys fret themselves a trifle abo what speed the son of Guy Wilkes 2:15½ and Lucy 2:14 ca show. This is the fast pacer owned by Ariel Lathrop Esq and he has already shown very fast miles. The last of t lot is Alfred S., already known to fame as his record of 2: shows. This gelding has been purchased from the Seale estate lately, by Mr. Hickok, the price paid being $6,00 With such a string Orrin should make both fame and mone

I received the following note too late for last week's issu but even at this late date it will show what is being done the interests of the pacing horse on the other side of th mountains. "If there are busines reasons why the trotti interests do not admit the pacer to standard rank as a pace there are good business reasons why pacing interests shou organize a National Pacing Horse Breeders' Association. Th Tennessee P. H. B. A. has a first class organization, and good set of rules for standard. It needs the broad domain the United States of America to give it numbers, and cons quent strength and wide influence. A meeting will be he on May 1, 1890, at the Gibson House, Cincinnati, at half pa ten A. M., for the purpose of organizing a National Paci Horse Breeders' Association. The Tennessee Associati sends a strong delegate committee. Pacing interests cities, counties and states are urgently invited to join inte ests and send a delegate. All persons interested in the pac are invited to attend the meeting. Communications as the meeting may be addressed to Thos. C. Parsons, 2 Harkness ave., Cleveland, Ohio, until April 23d, after th date care of the Gibson House, Cincinnati, Ohio; Thos. Parsons, Cleveland, Ohio; Campbell Brown, Spring Hi Tenn.; John W. Morton, Nashville, Tenn.; V. S. Pea Nashville, Tenn.; Titley Bros., Barnharts Mills, Pa.; Arth H. Rice, Oktoc, Miss.; Henry A. Kelly, Mount Clemen Mich.; Reed & Lake, Bloomington, Ill.; D. H. Mast, We Milton, Ohio.

SACRAMENTO SPRING MEETING.

The initial spring meeting under the auspices of the State Agricultural Society began Saturday at the Capital city under the most favorable conditions. The track was in tip-top condition, the weather was perfect, and the racing furnished was first class. The attendance was not quite up to expectation, but this was due to the many counter attractions of the day. The fair sex were well represented, and they lent eclat to the occasion, with their elaborate costumes. Sacramento is noted for its pretty girls, and there was quite a galaxy of the wealth and beauty of the capital city in the grand stand on the opening day. They appeared to evince the greatest interest in the equine struggles for supremacy, and many a pair of daintily gloved hands came in contact when their favorite came under the wire first.

Sacramento has always been famous as a race-horse center, and many a gallant battle has been fought over the Agricultural Park track. It was on this track that the celebrated Norfolk made his great three-mile heat record. This was way back in the sixties, but even yet it is ever a fruitful topic of conversation among old-time racing men. By the way, that record of Norfolk stands to this day. It was over the Sacramento track that the celebrated El Rio Rey was first galloped, and many of the sensational California racehorses first won their spurs at the Capital city.

The phenomenal success of the California bred racehorse on Eastern tracks during the past season, and the increased interest and rapid development of the thoroughbred in the West, induced the Sacramento people to come to the front with big stakes and purses as a further incentive to promote the breeding industry in this State.

The officers of the day were, Judges: Messrs, LaRue, Green and Hancock. Timers: Waterhouse, Wilson and Burns. Starter; W. H. Coombs. The latter gentleman wielded the flag in good style. The opening event on the card was the mile purse. Seven sported silk for this event. Al Farrow was made a red hot favorite. Kitty Van was not without supporters, but the race-goers who mingle a little judgment with their betting, labored under the impression that the Montana mare had a little too much weight to pack. Very little betting was done on the race. Al Farrow justified the confidence reposed in him by winning under a strong pull. Van got the place and Jackson finished third. This colt should not be overlooked in the future. He is a racy looking animal, and is fashionably bred.

SUMMARY.

Purse $400; for three-year-olds and upwards; $15 from starters to go to second horse. A winner this year at this distance to carry three pounds extra. Maidens allowed, if three years old, five lbs.; four or more, ten lbs. Three-quarters of a mile.

W. H. E. Smith's b h Al Farrow, 5, Connor—Della Walker, 124 .... Hill 1
L. J. Rose' b m Kitty Van 4, Vanderbilt—April Fool, 116.... Narvaez 2
Harry Howard's b h Jackson, 5, Luke Blackburn—Ivy Leaf, 114 .... Gannon 3

Time, 1:15.

Mirope, 3, 108, (Casy); Picnic, 4, 116, (Hitchcock), Revolver, 3, 105 (Hennessey) and Carmen 5, 119 (Appleby) also started.

Book betting: Al Farrow 7—10, 1—4, Kitty Van 2½—1, 1 to 2. Picnic 4—1, 8—5; Jackson 10—1, 4—1; Carmen 15—1, 5—1; Revolver 20—1, 6—1; Mirope 30—1, 10 to 1.

Auction pools: Al Farrow $25, Kitty Van $10, Field $8.

THE NORFOLK STAKE.

Out of the twenty three entered, only six faced the starter. Fairy was installed a big favorite. Rinfax was not without supporters, however, and many took advantage of the odds offered to plunge on the chestnut son of Argyle. Minnie B was also fancied little. The youngsters were not at the post very long before Starter Coombs sent them on the journey. Rinfax was the first to show clear of the ruck, but Monaghan sent Fairy to the front, and the race was never afterwards in doubt, the Rose filly winning handily under a strong pull by half a dozen lengths in the excellent time of 1:01. It certainly looked as if Fairy could have run the distance in an even minute if ridden out. Rinfax landed second money for the Palo Alto people while Minnie B finished a good third. It looks as if Mr. Rose has more than a bread winner in Fairy, and the way she romped home with 118 pounds up justifies the opinion that she will be heard from on the Eastern turf.

SUMMARY.

Norfolk Stake.—A sweepstakes for two-year-olds (foals of 1888) of $50 each, half forfeit, or only $10 if declared by January 1st, or $15 by March 1, 1890: with $500 added, of which $100 to second. Winners of a stake to carry three pounds; of two or more five pounds penalty. Beaten maidens allowed, if once, three pounds; if twice, five pounds. Five-eighths of a mile.

L. J. Rose's b f Fairy by Argyle—imp Fairy Rose, 118 ... Monaghan 1
Palo Alto's ch c Rinfax by Argyle—Imp Amelia, 121 .... Narvaez 2
Dennison Bros.' ch f Minnie B by Prince of Norfolk—by Wild Idle .... D. Dennison 3

Time, 1:01.

The Drake, 118 (Hitchcock); Cheerful, 115 (Hill); and Arcade, 113 (Casey) also ran.

Book Betting—Fairy 3 to 5, 1 to 5; Rinfax 3 to 1, 3 to 5; Minnie B 8 to 1, 3 to 1; Drake 6 to 1, 2 to 1; Arcade 30 to 1, 8 to 1; Cheerful 30 to 1, 10 to 1.

Auction Pools—Fairy $25, Field $20.

The next event proved to be the betting race of the day, as every one of the nine starters had friends. It was the selling purse over a mile and a sixteenth course. The betting fluctuated up and down. Oro was probably the real favorite, but just before the race the talent plunged on Jou Jou and the Monday gelding was cut down to 3 to 1. There was quite a Sheridan contingent who also invested at odds of three to one. Applause, Kildare and Welcome were well supported. There were a number of breakaways before the red pennant waved the gentle zephyrs. Welcome cut up as usual, and got decidedly the worst of what was otherwise a splendid start. Applause, Jou Jou and Sheridan passed the stand at the head of the procession. It was a pretty race along the backstretch, but Sheridan managed to keep his nose in front, though hard pressed by Jou Jou. Down the straight whips were brought into free play, but Sheridan was not to be denied and won cleverly by several lengths. Kildare finished second with Applause, Welcome and Oro close up and bunched. The judges awarded the third place to Oro. The Jou Jou crowd looked crestfallen.

SUMMARY.

Selling Purse, $400, of which $50 to second; for all ages. Winners to be sold at auction. Horses entered to be sold for $1500 to carry rule weight. One pound off for each $100 down to $500. Value placed on starters only by 6 P. M., night before race. One mile and a sixteenth

P. Siebenthaler's ch c Sheridan by Young Bazaar—Lost Girl, 3, 106 .... Narvaez 1
Matt Storn's ch g Kildare by Kyrle Daly—Mistake, 5, 116.. Hitchcock 2
J. R. Ross' b g Oro by Norfolk—Golden Gate, a, 120.......... Hill 3

Time, 1:50¼.

Applause, a, 120 (Appleby); Dave Douglass, a, 115 (D. Dennison); Black Pilot, a, 115 (Hazlett); Welcome, 5, 106 (Cook); Jou Jou, a, 115 (Casey), and Jack Brady, a, 115 (Cooper) also ran.

Book betting: Oro 2½—1, 4—5; Sheridan 3—1, 1—1; Black Pilot, Applause and Kildare each 6—1, 2—1; Jou Jou 3—1, 1—1; Dave Douglass and Jack Brady 8—1, 3—1, and Welcome 10—1, 4—1.

Auction pools: Oro $25, Sheridan $10 and field $25.

THE CALIFORNIA OAKS.

This race was considered a cinch for the Palo Alto representative. The filly won the race, but only by a scant nose after a whipping finish It was by long odds the best race of the day, and the Wild Idle filly Raindrop surprised the talent by the wonderfully good showing she made. Appleby rode judiciously, but many held the opinion that if he had come up a little sooner, he might have captured the race. Starter Coombs promises to develop into another Sheridan, for he succeeded in getting the quintette off on very even terms. The colors of Marigold were first distinguished in the front van, with Rettie B. dancing attendance. A blanket would have covered the condidates for the blue ribbon along the backstretch. They were nicely bunched, rounding the bend for the run home, except Raindrop, who was a couple of lengths in the rear. Appleby called upon the filly, and she responded gallantly. A desperate race ensued down the straight. Whips were used in a most determined manner. Cries of "Muta wins," "Look at Raindrop," were heard on all sides as the two leaders rushed up towards the wire. At the distance post Raindrop looks all over a winner, but Narvaez is equal to the occasion, and making a last effort, captured the California Oaks with the Palo Alto representatives.

SUMMARY.

The California Oaks.—A sweepstakes for three-year-old fillies (foals of 1887) of $50 each, $15 forfeit, with $600 added; $100 to second, $50 to third, out of stakes. Winners in 1890 to carry five pounds extra. Beaten maidens allowed five pounds. One mile and an eighth.

Palo Alto Stock Farm's ch f Muta by Wild Idle—imp. Mutiny, 117 .... Narvaez 1
W. L. Appleby's b f Raindrop by Wild Idle—imp. Teardrop, 122 .... Appleby 2
J. B. Chase's ch f Marigold by Milner—Katy Pease....... Monaghan 3

Time, 1:59.

Rettie B., 117 (Dennison) and Eda, 117 (Hennessey) also started.

Book betting: Muta 7—10; Raindrop 6—1, 2—1; Marigold 2—1, 2—5; Rettie B. 8—1, 3—1, and Eda 12—1, 4—1.

Auction pools: Muta $20, field $20.

THE SECOND DAY.

Tuesday morning opened up cloudy but old Sol asserted his supremacy before noon and the weather was pleasant, notwithstanding the breeze that swept over the grounds. The attendance was larger than on the opening day but not in keeping with the sport offered for the patronage of the public.

Mr. Coombs again handled the flag to the satisfaction of everybody and the BREEDER AND SPORTSMAN representative will take time by the forelock and dub the gentleman from Napa, "the Sheridan of the West." Messrs. Storn Green and Hancock were in the judges' stand and their decisions were never questioned. Altogether it was a field day for the backers of the favorites. The festivities were inaugurated with the Matadero Stake for two-year-olds. L. J. Rose telegraphed trainer Bridges not to start Fairy and in consequence it developed upon Conrad to uphold the prestige of the new stable. The four to contest for this stake were Rinfax, Conrad, The Drake and Minnie B. The Palo Alto entry was a decided favorite in the betting and went to the post at three to five. Conrad was backed to some extent. A capital start was effected without much difficulty. Rinfax set out to make the pace and was soon a length and a half ahead of the other two who raced locked along the backstretch. The gap was lessened between the leader and the field before turning into the straight, but Rinfax came away at every stride when called upon. Conrad finished second but the judges very properly gave second money to Minnie B. Half way down the straight, Monaghan plied his cat gut on Conrad, who swerved across the track and interfered, with Minnie B. throwing her out of her stride.

SUMMARY.

The Matadero Stake—A sweepstakes for two year olds (foals of 1888) of $100 each, half forfeit, or only $10 if declared by January 1st, or $25 March 1, 1890, with $600 added, $100 to second, $50 to third. Winners of any event of the value of $800 to carry three pounds; of $1,000, five pounds; of two of any value, seven pounds extra. Beaten maidens allowed five pounds. Three-quarters of a mile.

Palo Alto Stock Farm's ch c Rinfax by Argyle—Imp Amelia, 118 1
Dennison Bros' ch f Minnie B. by Prince of Norfolk, dam by Wild Idle, '10 .... Hazlett 2
L. U. Shippee's b c The Drake, Leonatus—The Teal, 113.. Hitchcock 3

Time, 1:16½.

Conrad, 113 (Monaghan) disqualified for fouling.

Book Betting—Rinfax, 13 to 5; Conrad, 2½ to 1, ½ to 1; The Drake 15 to 1, 4 to 1; Minnie B, 6 to 1, 6 to 5.

Auction pools—Rinfax $20, field $12.

The second event on the card was the Chris Green Handicap. Seven horses saddled up at the signal of bugle the and betting began in a lively manner. Al Farrow was first choice but just before the race the stock of Ed McGinnis rose very considerably. He jumped from $12 to $19 in the pools with lightning rapidity, owing to the over anxiety of several to get on a pool on the son of Grinstead. Then again there were those who couldn't see where Raindrop could lose with only 98 pounds to pack. So to make a long story short, the flag was dropped to a splendid start. The Dennison entries were sent in the lead and the order passing the stand was, Hotspur, G. W. Mikado and Ed McGinnis. It was a pretty race along the backstretch. The whole field was bunched at the half mile pole. Soon after the shout went up 'Look at Al Farrow coming' and he came with a big rush such as only a great racehorse can make, and turning into the straight with a slight lead the Chris Green Handicap was all over but the shouting. There was a great fight for second place, Longstreet snatching the victory from Mikado in the last half a dozen strides by the shortest of heads. The victory of Al Farrow was a popular one and the speedy son of Conner was given an ovation when the Jockey returned to be weighed in. Ed. McGinnis failed to show up as well as his backers anticipated. In fact, his running was a disappointment to many. Mikado ran a good race, especially when it is remembered that it was his first appearance this year. Longshot demonstrated the fact that he can stay a distance in good company.

SUMMARY.

The Chris Green Handicap—A sweepstakes for all ages of $50 each, half forfeit, or $10 if declared: with $800 added: second horse to receive $100 out of stakes. Weights announced March 1st. Declarations due by 6 P. M. April 1st. A winner of any race, after publication of weights, of one mile or upwards, to carry 3 lbs. extra; of two races 5 lbs.; of three or more, 7 lbs. This will not apply to horses handicapped at 125 lbs. or over. One and one-quarter miles.

W. H. E. Smith's b h Al Farrow by Connor—Della Walker, 5, 125 .... Hill 1
W. H. E. Smith's ch h Longshot by Duke of Norfolk—by Langford 4, 121 .... Spooner 2
L. J. Rose's b g Mikado by Shiloh—Margery, a 120...... Monaghan 3

Time, 2:10.

Raindrop, 3, 98 (Narvaez); Hotspur, 4, 113 (Hazlett); G. W., 4, 110 (Hennessey); and Ed McGinnis 5, 122 (Cook) also started.

Book Betting—Al Farrow 8 to 5, ½ to 1; Raindrop 6 to 1, 2 to 1; Hotspur 8 to 1, 3 to 1; G. W. 10 to 1, 4 to 1; Ed McGinnis 2 to 1, 7 to 10; Longshot 3 to 1, 1 to 1.

Auction Pools—Smith's stable $25, Ed McGinnis $19, Field $11.

The mile and a sixteenth proved to be a good betting race, and each one of the three starters had a host of supporters. The betting veered round in a most peculiar fashion, and Picnic, Captain Al and Carmen alternated as favorites. In the pools Captain Al was the favorite all the time. Carmen and Picnic led past the stand, but Carmen disputed the honor rounding the bend. At the half Picnic and Carmen were neck and neck with Captain Al two lengths behind. On the home turn Hennessy shook up Captain Al and the race began in earnest. Captain Al with his light weight outstayed his competitors and won comfortably from Picnic.

SUMMARY.

Purse $400; for all ages; $10 from starters to go to second horse. Maiden allowances: if 3 years, 5 lbs.; four and upwards, 10 lbs. Nonwinners this year allowed 5 lbs. Allowances cumulative. One and one-sixteenth miles.

Miller & Owens' blk c Captain Al by Kingston, dam Black Maria, 3, 106 .... Hennessy 1
L. U. Shippee's br m Picnic by imp Mr. Pickwick, dam Countess, 4, 111.......... Hitchcock 2
W. L. Appleby's ch m Carmen by Wildidle, dam Nettie Brown, 5, 116.......... Narvaez 3

Time, 1:53½.

Book Betting—Captain Al, 1 to 1; Carmen, 7 to 5 and Picnic 8 to 5.

Auction pools—Captain Al $20, Field $25.

Only three faced the starter for the Weinstock and Lubin Stake and the lot were all bred at Palo Alto. Of course, Racine was a terrific favorite, the bookies risking one dollar for every eight dollars handed them. Racine was admired on all sides when he made his appearance on the track. He looked in grand fettle. Rico is not a good looker, his neck being too crane like. It was generally expected that either Pliny or Rico would, at least, be able to extend the pride of Palo Alto. Pliny was a little obstreperous at the start, but after a little delay the trio were sent on their journey. Racine soon forged to the front. He led the Brooklyn Handicap candidate a length at the quarter, which he increased to a length and a half before half the journey had been negotiated. Narvaez was pulling double on the Bishop colt and the veriest tyro could see that the race was all over. Racine galloped under the wire an easy winner. Pliny came with a rush near the end and beat Rico home. The opinion is very general that Racine could have made the mile in 1:40½, if he had been extended.

SUMMARY.

The Weinstock, Lubin & Co. Stake.—A sweepstake for three-year-olds (foals of 1887), of $50 each, half forfeit, or only $15 each if declared January 1, 1890, with $600 added, of which $100 to second, and $50 to third. Winners in 1890 of any three-year-old event, when carrying weight for age or more, of the value of $500, to carry three pounds; of $1000, or two of any value, 5 pounds extra. Non-winners allowed 5 pounds. One mile.

Palo Alto's b c Racine by Bishop, dam Fairy Rose, 122...... Narvaez 1
Kelly & Samuels' b g Pliny by Flood, dam Precious, 122........ Cook 2
L. J. Rose's br g Rico by Shannon, dam Fanny Lewis..... Monaghan 3

Time, 1:42½.

Book Betting—Racine 1 to 8, Rico 5 to 1, Pliny 10 to 1.

Auction pools—Racine $50, Field $10.

THIRD DAY.

The races on Thursday were better patronized than on the preceding days. Many of the fair daughters of Sacramento occupied seats in the grand stand and the band rendered excellent selections between races. The day was a delightful one, there being just enough breeze to make it pleasant for the spectators.

The opening event proved to be a capital race. Seven well bred youngsters sported silk and the parade preliminary to the race was watched with considerable interest.

Rover, a slashing looking Wildidle, was the favorite, and the gold rolled in on him. Take Notice and Prince's First were not without admirers. It was Prince's first debut. He is a handsome looker, and old Dan Dennison had his idol gaily decorated with pink ribbon. It took some little time to effect a start, Kiro refusing to come up to the other horses, When the flag was lowered, the Murray duo were in front. with King Hooker in the rear of the procession. At the quarter Leland was in the lead, with the other horses bunched. Prince's First challenged the leader, and was in advance at the half. A slashing race now ensued, and whips were plied vigorously after turning into the straight. Rover began to improve his position, but it was anyone's race half way down the stretch. Half a furlong from home Rover shot out of the crowd and won by a length. Kiro was second and Leland beat Prince's First by the shortest of heads for third place.

Continued on page 398.

THE WEEKLY

Breeder and Sportsman.

JAMES P. KERR, PROPRIETOR.

The Turf and Sporting Authority of the Pacific Coast.

Office, No. 313 Bush St.

P. O. Box 2300.

TERMS—One Year, $5; Six Months, $3; Three Months, $1.50.
STRICTLY IN ADVANCE.

Money should be sent by postal order, draft or by registered letter, addressed to JAMES P. KERR, San Francisco, Cal.

Communications must be accompanied by the writer's name and address, not necessarily for publication, but as a private guarantee of good faith.

NEW YORK OFFICE, Room 15, 181 Broadway.

ALEX. P. WAUGH, . . . Editor.

Advertising Rates

Per Square (half inch)

One time	$1 50
Two times	2 50
Three times	3 25
Four times	4 00

And each subsequent insertion 75c. per square.

Advertisements running six months are entitled to 10 per cent. discount.

Those running twelve months are entitled to 20 per cent. discount.

Reading notices set in same type as body of paper, 50 cents per line each insertion.

To Subscribers.

The date printed on the wrapper of your paper indicates the time to which your subscription is paid.

Should the BREEDER AND SPORTSMAN be received by any subscriber who does not want it, write us direct to stop it. A postal card will suffice.

Special Notice to Correspondents.

Letters intended for publication should reach this office not later than Wednesday of each week, to secure a place in the issue of the following Saturday. Such letters to insure immediate attention should be addressed to the BREEDER AND SPORTSMAN, and not to any member of the staff.

San Francisco, Saturday, May 3, 1890.

Dates Claimed.

SACRAMENTO (Running Meeting)	April 26th, 29th, May 1st and 3d
EUREKA JOCKEY CLUB	July 2d to 5th
IONE	Aug. 1th to 4th.
LOS ANGELES (6th District)	Aug. 4th to 9th
SAN JOSE	Aug. 11th to 16th
NAPA	Aug. 18th to 23rd
GLENBROOK PARK, 17th District	August 1th to 22d
PETALUMA	Aug. 25th to 30th
OAKLAND (District No. 1)	Sept. 1st to Sept. 6th
LAKEPORT, 12th District	September 23d to 27th
CALIFORNIA STATE FAIR	Sept. 8th to 20th
STOCKTON	Sept. 23rd to 27th.
FRESNO (Fall Meeting)	Sept. 29th to Oct. 4th
VISALIA	Oct. 7th to 11th

Stallions Advertised

IN THE

BREEDER AND SPORTSMAN.

Thoroughbreds.

DOUGLASDALE—Thoroughbred Clydesdale....Lawn View Farm, Cal.
FRIAR TUCK, Hermit—Romping Girl..........C. W. Aby, Middletown.
GREENBACK, Dollar—Music..........C. W. Aby, Middletown.
REVEILLE, Shiloh—Norfolk..........B. C. Holly, Vallejo.
ST. SAVIOR, Eolus—War Song..........C. W. Aby, Middletown.
THREE CHEERS Imp. Hurrah—Young Fashion..........E. S. Culver, San Francisco.

Trotters.

ADMIRAL, Volunteer—Lady Pierson.......... Frank Drake, Vallejo.
ACTOR Prompter—Dam by Sultan..........Lawn View Farm, Cal.
APEX, Prompter—Mary..........Poplar Grove Breeding Farm, Wildflower.
ALCONA, Almont—Queen Mary.......... Fred W. Loeber, St. Helena
BAY ROSE Sultan—Madam Baldwin..........Thos. Bonner, Santa Rosa
CLOVIS, Sultan—Sweetbriar..........Poplar Grove Breeding Farm, Wildflower.
CUPID, Sidney—Venus.......... C. O. Thornquest, Oakland
CHARLES DERBY, Steinway—by Electioneer. Cook Stock Farm, Contra Costa Co.
CALIFORNIA NUTWOOD, Nutwood—Fanny Patchen....Martin Carter, Alameda Co.
C. DIRECTOR, Director—Brainey..........Pleasanton Stock Farm.
DECORATOR, Director—Chess..........Pleasanton Stock Farm
DEXTER PRINCE, Kentucky Prince—Lady Dexter..........L. M. Morse, Lodi.
DAWN, Nutwood—Countess.......... A. L. Whitney, Petaluma
DIRECTOR, Dictator—Dolly..........Pleasanton Stock Farm, Pleasanton.
DON MARVIN, Fallis—Cora..........F. P. Lowell, Sacramento
EL BENTON, Electioneer—Nellie Benton..........Souther Farm, San Leandro.
ELECTION, Electioneer—Lizzie H..........B. C. Holly, Vallejo.
ECLECTIC, Electioneer—Manette..........Wilfred Page, Sonoma County
EROS, Electioneer—Sontag Mohawk..........W. H. Vioget, Menlo Park
FIGARO, Hambletonian—Emblem..........Souther Farm, San Leandro.
GROVER CLAY, Electioneer—Maggie Norfolk..........Denis Gannon, Oakland.
GRAND MOOR 2374, Moor 870—Vashti..........H. I. Thornton, S. F.
G. & M., Anteeo—Rosa B..........George E. Guerne, Santa Rosa.
GUY WILKES, George Wilkes—Lady Bunker..........San Mateo Stock Farm, San Mateo.
GLEN FORTUNE, Electioneer—Glenna..........Souther Farm, San Leandro.
GEORGE WASHINGTON, Mambrino Chief—Fanny Rose..........Thos. Smith, Vallejo.
GRANDISSIMO, LeGrande—Norma..........Fred W. Loeber, St Helena
JESTER D, Almont—Hortense..........Souther Farm, San Leandro
JUNIO, Electioneer—by Granger..........S. N. Straube, Fresno.
KAFIR, Alcazar—Flower Girl..........B. C. Holly, Vallejo.
KING DAVID, Admiral—Black Flora..........Frank Drake, Vallejo.
LEO WILKES, Guy Wilkes Sable..........San Mateo Stock Farm, San Mateo.
MEMO, Sidney—Flirt.......... John Rowen, Oakland
MOUNTAIN BOY, Kentucky Prince Elsie..........B. C. Holly, Vallejo.
MAMBRINO WILKES, George Wilkes—Lady Chrisman..........San Miguel Stock Farm, Walnut Creek.
MART BOORHEM, Sidney—Towhead..........B. C. Holly, Vallejo.
MAMBRINO CHIEF, McDonald Chief—Venus..........Thos. Smith, Vallejo.
MORTIMER, Electioneer—Marti..........Wilfred Page, Sonoma County
NOONDAY, Wedgewood—Noontide..........F. P. Lowell, Sacramento.
PASHA, Sultan—Madam Baldwin..........D. Bryson, Linden
PHILOSOPHER, Pilot Wilkes—Belle.......... George E. Guerne, Santa Rosa.
REDWOOD, Anteeo—Lou Wilton..........A. McFayden, Oakland.
STEINWAY, Strathmore—Abbess..........Cook Stock Farm, Contra Costa Co
SABLE WILKES, Guy Wilkes—Sable..........San Mateo Stock Farm, San Mateo.
VICTOR, Echo—Daughter of Woodburn..........G. W. Hughes, Napa City
WOODSIDE, Woodnut—Veronica..........B. C. Holly, Vallejo.
YOUNG ELMO, St. Elmo—Dam by Woodburn... Lawn View Farm Cal.

Names Claimed.

Lady Lynwood for filly foaled April 25, 1890, by Lynwood, dam Maggie V by Nephew. Entered in BREEDER AND SPORTSMAN'S Futurity Stake. P. VISHER.

A New Enterprise.

Many times since assuming the editorial control of the BREEDER AND SPORTSMAN we have been asked, "how can we insure first class horses?" and have always had to answer that we knew of no reliable association that would take such risks as the owners required. However, this week we have an advertisement from a newly started enterprise which is called the Pacific Coast Live Stock Owners' Protective Association. A careful perusal of their pamphlets and the many inquiries made from those who have agreed to back the enterprise with their money, leads us to the belief that this one should prove beneficial to all owners of stock who may see fit to join the association.

The President of the Association, Hon. B. V. Sargent of Monterey, a gentleman of wealth and extended acquaintance among the leading stock raisers of the coast, called at this office on Saturday last, and stated that he was satisfied in his own mind that the company was one long needed by stock men and that he was willing to give it his earnest support, that while he did not expect that he would be called upon personally to have to pay any large sums of money, still he was fully prepared to indorse the enterprise with his wealth and he was satisfied that it would not take long to put the association on a paying basis. The only person who will receive a salary is Mr. Volney Howard, who for many years has been well and favorably known to all the Insurance Companies of the Pacific Coast, and he has received the unqualified indorsement in his new position, of all the companies for whom he has ever worked. With Mr. Howard's long experience it will enable him to quickly start reliable agencies wherever the Association may choose to operate.

We are also told that if the losses after a fair trial necessitate burdensome and impracticable rates all losses will be paid any way, and the Association will be disbanded with possible loss only to its wealthy projectors. The Association is not only founded for the purpose of insuring live stock but in its articles of incorporation the fact is stated that the objects of the Association will be suppression and the prevention of the spread of any and all contageous and infectious diseases of live stock and the prevention of the throwing upon the market diseased meat, and to assist in the suppression of any infectious and contagious diseases of live stock, and also by proportionate subscription to indemnify all members owing live stock and holding indemnity certificates from the loss arising from the death of the same by reason of such disease.

We would suggest to those of our readers who may be interested in this matter to send to Mr. Howard at the general business office of the company, which is located at Room 73, Flood Building, Market street, San Francisco, for a copy of the rules, regulations and by-laws of the Association so they may thoroughly understand what the company has been started for, and the benefits that will be derived by those who may join.

At present there is a great field in California for such an Association if properly conducted, and from the gentlemen who are connected with the enterprise it seems to us as though it should be highly successful.

The Year Book.

It is with great pleasure that we acknowledge the receipt of a complimentary copy of Wallace's Year Book covering all the trotting and pacing races which took place during the year 1889, and the trotting and pacing records of all time. As is well known to all who have followed the publication of this work, it improves year by year, and the volume now before us is no exception to the general rule. It could not be more complete than it is, it being full of the best information desirable of all horsemen, and there is hardly anything than one may choose to look up but what can be found within its covers.

The first part of the book, covering 193 pages, is devoted entirely to the trotting and pacing races which took place last year throughout the United States. We also find an alphabetical list of all the horses that trotted slower than 2.40 during 1889. Then follows an alphabetical tabulated list of 3651 trotting horses who have secured records of 2:30 or better; and the pacers have not been forgotten as we find a like table comprising 962 of them.

Part third of the volume is a great table of all 2.30 horses under their sires to the close of 1889, giving the pedigree and history of sires of 2:30 trotters, with such of their sons and daughters as have a representative in the 2.30 list. This is a very full and complete table, and while there may be some errors, as is only likely in such a work, still it is one of the most complete that we have ever seen.

Another section of the work is devoted to a table of all trotting horses with a record of 2:20 or better; while still another table is given of the same performers alphabetically arranged under their sires to the close of 1889.

Part six is a table of horses who are the sires of two more dams of 2:30 performers, but are not the sires any 2:30 trotters themselves. This fills quite a wa that was noticeable in Vol. IV., and is of great service the student.

As usual a table of great brood mares is given, a tal that is intended to include, first: all mares who ha produced two or more performers with records of 2:30 better, one of which being a trotter, Second All ma who have produced one 2:30 trotter and another son daughter that has sired or produced a 2:30 trotter.

Part eight is a table of mares who are the dams of t or more producing sons and daughters, but are not the selves the dams of any 2:30 trotters.

We also find a table of the fastest records includi both trotters and pacers.

The indexes alone take up 46 pages in the work, a by that it will be seen what a very comprehensive wo it is.

The book is a beautiful, large octavo, over 500 pag bound in green and gold. No man who wishes to be i formed on trotting-horses and trotting-blood can affo to be without it. Published at $2.50, post-paid, Wallace Trotting Register Company, 280 Broadwa New York, N. Y.

Eureka Jockey Club.

As will be noticed by referring to the advertising c umns, the Eureka Jockey Club sets before our read this week a four days' programme for their annual Ju meeting, commencing on the second day of that mon For several seasons the horsemen of California ha looked forward with pleasure to their annual visit Humboldt County, as the purses are always liberal, t management of the best, and the hospitality extende unsurpassed. In looking over the list we find that t majority of the races are devoted to the thoroughbre still the trotters have not been neglected, as there i purse for the three-minute class, and also a purse for t 2:40 class. The running races include all sorts, fron half mile and repeat to dashes of a mile and a quart The trotting races are best three in five, with four enter and three to start, but the Board of Directo reserves the right to hold a less number than four to t by the withdrawal of a proportionate amount of t purse in the trotting races; the rules of the Americ Trotting Association to govern, and in the running rac as usual the Pacific Coast Blood Horse rules will be t guide.

The Secretary, J. P. Monroe, Esq., will receive entr up to Thursday, June 20th, at which time the list clos Entry blanks will be furnished upon application.

The Beginning of a New Era.

Many of our readers will remember an exchange compliments that took place during the past winter tween the trotting horse and the thoroughbred men. T gist of the discussion was that while the trotter sold the most money, thoroughbreds had far the greater ea ing capacity. The back bone of the trotting industry the fact that it supplies the light harness horse of Am ica, and for every one horse on the race track there dozens in the hands of pleasure drivers. The usefuln of running horses is of course much less, and they ha not the same adaptability to every day life; neverthel system has made it possible for running horses to e many times the amount that can be earned by trotte

The prospects for trotters could not be better th they are to-day, and this is largely due to the recog tion of the fact that large stakes must be organized trotters as well as for runners. These are begun wi the horses that are to contest in them are mere colts small first payment, with easy payments at differ intervals, enabling an owner to enter all his good co and gradually select out those which promise be These small payments when made by a great many ow ers and trainers, are not felt by the individual, and ma in the aggregate very desirable winnings.

The BREEDER AND SPORTSMAN Futurity Stake the opening wedge for stakes of this class for trotti colts of the Pacific Coast. The great success and tremely large entry list for this event is well know 285 first payments are a strong index of the great int est and belief in such stakes. Another event of t same class, and for foals of 1890, is now offered by Golden Gate Association. Entries close on May 15 the purse is $4000, the entrance but three per cent., a that with a first payment of only $10, the other pa ments coming at intervals of about six months. A m liberal purse could hardly be offered, and the Gold Gate Association deserves great credit for its enterpr and liberality.

Both of the above stakes will be trotted in 1893, wh the colts named therein will be three years of age. T aggregate value of these two stakes will be between $8000 and $10,000, and as other Associations will undoubtedly follow in the footsteps of this journal and the Golden Gate Association; the best three-year-old of the year 1893 will earn a small fortune. Nothing will do more to increase the value of this year's crop of colts; let one that is engaged in this or any other large stakes make a good showing in his or her two-year-old form, and its value will be immensely increased. The fact that so much money is to be won will start every one that possibly can, to begin picking up and training all available material, and those that may be outclassed in the great purses will have so many opportunities to earn money in other events that the very number of prospective competitors will surely bring out.

We send our colts East to be sold now; the Easterners will come to us in '93.

This State can raise better baby trotters than any State in the Union, but if we are to do justice to our natural advantages we must keep things moving and give the colts of this State the best possible opportunity.

Contra Costa Agricultural Association.

Among the many other Associations to offer District Colt Stakes for 1890, the Contra Costa County Agricultural Association, known as District No. 23, announces this week to our readers that they have opened a stake for yearling trotters, for two-year olds and for three-year-olds. The moneys will be divided into 60, 30 and 10 per cent, and as there are so many good stallions and excellently well bred broodmares in the District, there should be a long list of entries for each of the three events. The entries do not close until June 1st, and the payment in each stake has been made, $40, of which $10 is required when the entry is made, $15 on September 1st and $15 on September 22d. The Fair will be held from September 22d to 27th inclusive, and there is no reason to believe but what it will be equally successful with that of former years. Those living in the District should read the advertisement carefully and make entries in this stake.

The Haggin Sale.

Readers of the BREEDER AND SPORTSMAN are requested to read the last announcement of Messrs. Killip & Co., who will manage the annual sale of J. B. Haggin's Stock, which takes place at the railroad stables, corner of Turk and Steiner streets, San Francisco, on Thursday next. Those who desire to purchase will have a chance to examine the horses at the stables on and after to day. The catalogues are now ready, and can be had on application to the auctioneers.

The consignment is an extensive one, and consists of road and harness horses, work and draught horses, and several choice Shetland ponies This is a rare chance to secure bargains, and should not be missed by those who are in need of first class animals.

Eastern Sales.

On Monday next the annual sale of yearlings from Runnymede, Coldstream & Loudoun Stock Farms will take place at Raceland, near Paris, Kentucky. As the youngsters are of the very best breeding and by favorite sires, there should be lively competition for them.

On Wednesday and Thursday of next week Messrs. Bruce & Kidd of Lexington, Kentucky, will also sell the entire produce of the Edgewater & Kingston stud yearlings, comprising thirty-four head, together with a lot of yearlings, two-year-olds, three-year-olds, broodmares, stallions and horses in training consigned by various owners. The advertisement for both of these sales may be found in another column.

Palo Alto.

It was definitely arranged last week that the Palo Alto trotters would leave for Terre Haute on their Eastern campaign on or about the third, and consequently a representative of the BREEDER AND SPORTSMAN visited Palo Alto during the middle of the week to see the equine wonders that are to add to Palo Alto and California's fame, as the favored place in America for horse raising. On our arrival at the trotting department, the first familiar face was Dick Havey's. Dick, who was one of America's famous jockeys, being the rider of Norfolk and other flyers in his youthful days, is not a stranger at Palo Alto, having educated trotters there a few years previously, and during Marvins absence East. Havey will take his place, and should fill it well, for his judgment and capacity as a driver, are far above all doubt, for he ranks among the best Californian drivers. In a few moments Chas. Marvin appeared; the popular superintendent and equally popular driver who has done so much towards placing Palo Alto Stock Farm in the foremost place, was behind Sunol 2:10½, having just jogged her a few miles. The peerless bay mare has thickened out, let down and improved immensely, has lost almost all that tucked up appearance that characterised her last fall, and so far has had no real work, but is strong and healthy and as sound as a bell. If she shows up this year, although she may not lower Maud's record, she will probably be left in Marvin's charge for another year, and be brought back to California for another winter. She is number one—out of nine—on the list to go East to-day; the second, Palo Alto 2:12½ is a brilliant example of Senator Stanford's thoroughbred theory. As a four year old he made an Eastern trip, losing one race against aged horses in 2:19¾, 2:19¼ and 2:20, and winning eight others against aged horses with heats split up, and obtained a record of 2:20½ which he last year lowered to 2:13¾ at Stockton and 2:12½ at the Trotting Horse Breeders meeting, and finally at Napa lowered it to 2:12¾ with two breaks; the phenomenal performances of the stallion fully warrant the belief that the stallion record will assuredly be lowered by him. Palo Alto, has served twenty names this season, and consequently has not been in strict training, but looks the picture of health, and the best news I heard of him, was from Mr. Marvin, who said that his foot has not bothered him in the least since last fall. Gertrude Russell 2:23½, full sister to Palo Alto, is a very neatly turned bay mare with beautiful action and in good trim for a journey, being much fitter than either of the cracks. Marvin says that when he returns people will not be talking altogether of Palo Alto and Sunol, for Gertrude will lower her record at a clip that will astonish everyone, and if looks go for anything she should be go down very low in the teens. Arol 2:24 by Electioneer, out of Aurora 2:27 looking big and fat, is rather lame presumably in her feet, but if she gets to a race all right should readily put in three heats better than 2:20.

Navidad, b g, 5, by Whips 2:27½, out of Lady Thorn Jr. dam of Santa Claus 2:17½, and Mollie Mack 2:30½, has shown lots of speed, and should be a very useful green horse. Amigo, a five year old brown stallion by Electioneer out of Nadine by Wildidle out of Norah, sister to Charley Champlin 2:21½, is a big, powerful horse, with more of the Electioneer than the thoroughbred appearance, and is a very resolute fast trotter. Colma is a neat, shapely, gray mare, 4 years old, by Electioneer out of Sontag Mohawk, dam of Sallie Benton 2:17¾, Sport 2:22¾, and Eros 2:29½. She should improve her famous dam's record by going well inside thirty.

Willmont is a very racy, handsome three year old bay mare with grayish forehead, by Piedmont 2·17¼, out of Wildflower 2:21 at 2 years old. She should prove a phenomenal trotter.

And last, but by no means least, is Electric Bell, a beautiful brown colt, 2 years old, with a slightly Moor back, by Electioneer out of Beautiful Bells 2:29½, and therefore a full brother to Bell Boy 2:19½, Hinda Rose 2:19½, St. Bel 2:24½, and Palo Alto Belle 2:22½. Electric Bell will most decidedly not disgrace his illustrious relatives, and next year will find him enrolled in the list of honor.

Such a brilliant collection of fast and highly bred trotting horses have never left the State before, and the care and skillful handling they will receive from Charles Marvin, who is the peer of any man as a trotting horse educator and campaigner, should make them all more renowned than ever. The stable will go to Terra Haute, thence to Detroit, and if all keeps well they will return home in October.

Foals of 1890.

At Poplar Grove Breeding Farm, Property of S. N. Straube Jan. 3rd; sorrel colt, right hind foot white, by Apex 8935, dam Peggy by Hambletonian 725, 2nd dam by Skenandoah 926.

Feby. 13th—Black filly, both hind pasterns white, by Pasha 2039, dam Ada, s. t. b. by Black Hawk.

March 13th—Black filly, left hind foot white, by Pasha 2039, dam Maud by Steeldust, he by Belmont.

March 14th—Bay colt, left hind foot white, by Clovis 4909, dam Ela by A. W. Richmond 1687.

March 18th—Bay colt, solid color, by Apex 8935, dam Black Lucy by Nephew 1220.

March 19th—Black filly, small star, by Apex 8935, dam Silver Dollar, by Silver Threads.

March 25th—Bay colt, by Pasha 2039, dam Fanny Chapman, by Thad Stevens.

April 2nd—Bay colt, by Clovis 4909, dam Ella, by Red Cloud; 2nd dam Lulu by Skenandoah 926.

April 2nd—Bay colt, both hind pasterns white, by Pasha 2039, dam Polly by Belmont (Williamson's.)

April 4th—Brown colt, both hind feet white, by Clovis 4909, dam Fanny by Romulus.

April 5th—Bay filly, left hind pastern white, by Apex 8935 dam Fanny Nelson by Rosenbergers John Nelson.

April 15th—Bay colt, both hind pasterns white, by Apex 8935, dam Gertrude by Pasha 2039; 2nd dam Gitana by Echo 462.

April 16th—Brown colt, by Clovis 4909, dam Lizzie Thorne, by Nephew 1220; 2nd dam Fanny by Romulus.

April 17th—Brown colt, left hind pastern white, by Pasha 2039, dam Flora by Echo 462.

April 21st—Black colt, both hind pasterns white, by Clovis 4909, dam Mattie Consuela, by Steinway 1808, 2nd dam Mattie by Hambletonian 725.

At Valensin Stock Farm. Property of G Valensin.

April 18th, black colt by Sidney; 1st dam by Buccaneer, 2nd dam by Arthurton, 3rd dam by Highland Mary 2:34, by David Hill.

April 20th, bay filly by Sidney; 1st dam by Buccaneer, 2nd dam Venus, dam of Adonis 2:14, 3rd dam by Jack Hawkins (this is a ½ sister to Adonis).

April 20th, Chestnut colt by Sidney; 1st dam by Wilkes Boy 2:24 (sire of Angelena and Constantine), 2nd dam by Mambrino King, 3rd dam by Consternation Jr., he by imp. Consternation.

April 23rd, bay filly by Sidney; 1st dam by Buccaneer, 2nd dam Fernleaf, dam of Goldleaf 2:11½, Shamrock 2:25, Ivy 2:31½, etc.

April 24th, bay colt by Sidney; 1st dam by Eugene Casserly, 2nd dam by Whipple's Hambletonian, 3rd dam by Volscian, etc., full brother to a two-year-old, sold to Mr. Rob. Bonner for $3,000.

At same place. Property of Mr. J. Morehouse.

April 18th, bay colt by Sidney; 1st dam by Com. Belmont, etc.

At Vacaville. Property of D. G. Hawkins.

Brown filly, both hind feet white, by Mountain Boy, dam by Dietz's St. Clair.

At Oakland, April 26th. Property of Dennis Gannon.

Bay filly, star in forehead, right fore pastern white and left hind pastern white, by Noonday, dam Miss. Sidney by Sidney; 2d dam by Hambletonian 725; 3d dam by Geo. M. Patchen Jr; 4th dam by Bellfounder. The name of Twilight is claimed for this filly.

Answers to Correspondents.

Answers for this department MUST be accompanied by the name and address of the sender, not necessarily for publication, but as proof of good faith. Write the questions distinctly, and on one side of the paper only. Positively no questions will be answered by mail or telegraph.

Who Knows This Horse

April 22, 1890.

EDITOR BREEDER AND SPORTSMAN:—I should be obliged if you could discover the pedigree of a stallion called Ashland that stood at San Bernardino about 14 or 15 years ago. He belonged to Mr. Conn and was, I believe, bought by him at Los Angeles, and supposed to be by Ashland the thoroughbred. Yours, W.

W. S. N., Pomona.

We do not think very highly of the breeding you mention. The horse can not be registered in either the standard or non-standard volumes.

M. H. N.

The horse you write to us about is not in the list of suspended ones.

A. R.

Will you kindly let me know the pedigree of Johnny Hayward?

Answer—Wallace says, said to be by Poscora Hayward. That is all we know of the pedigree.

E. B. G.

Will you please publish or give through the columns of your valuable paper the pedigree of St. Patrick, the pacing horse owned by M. Daly of Montana, and is he a stallion or a gelding?

Answer—Bay stallion, foaled 1885, by Volunteer 55, dam Young Selene by Guy Miller, son of Hambletonian 10.

Coronado.

In your next issue please give me list of members of the National and American Trotting Associations in California.

Answer—The list would take more space than we can spare in this column. Write to M. M. Morse, Secretary National Association, Hartford, Conn., and J. H. Steiner, Secretary American Association, Detroit, Mich.

R. N. C.

Will you kindly publish in the columns of your valuable paper, if any of the get of Sherman Black Hawk mentioned in your last issue became famous by performance.

Answer.—We mentioned two Sherman Black Hawk's last week the one which stood at Knight's Ferry has no performers in the 2:30 list, while the other is the sire of Chicago Jack 2:30 and Panic 2:28.

H. Latham:

EDITOR BREEDER AND SPORTSMAN:—Can you or the readers of the BREEDER AND SPORTSMAN tell anything of the breeding of Lady Zephyr bay mare, star and perhaps one white foot; ran races at Sacramento and other places? She was once owned by George Hancock, Oroville, and also by a Mr. Geiger, of San Luis Obispo.

Answer.—We know the mare but do not think there was ever any pedigree given for her. Can any of our readers furnish any information about her?

A. S. B.

Will you please inform me how to lay out a half mile track?

Answer.—The above question comes to us so frequently, and also the one in reference to a mile-track that we give the measurements for both.

FOR A MILE TRACK.

A field of forty-two acres will do. Draw a line through the oblong centre, 440 yards in length, setting a stake at each end. Then draw a line on either side of the first line, exactly parallel with and 140 yards from it, setting stakes at either end of them. You will then have an oblong square 440 yards long and 280 yards wide. At each end of these three lines you will now set stakes. Now then, fasten a cord or wire 140 yards long to the centre stake of your parallelogram, and then describe a half circle, driving stakes as often as you wish to set a fence post. This half circle commencing at one side and extending to the other, will measure 440 yards. When the circle is made at both ends of your parallelogram, you will have two straight sides that measure 440 yards each, and two circles of exactly the same length, which measured three feet from the line, will be exactly a mile. The turns should be thrown up an inch to the foot.

HALF-MILE TRACK.

Draw two parallel lines of 600 feet long and 452 feet five inches apart. Half way between the extreme ends of the two parallel lines drive a stake, then loop a wire around the stake, long enough to reach to either side. Then, make a true curve with the wire, putting down a stake as often as a fence post is needed. When this operation is finished at both ends of the 600 foot parallel lines, the track is laid out. The inside fence will rest exactly on the line drawn, but the track must measure a half mile three feet from the fence. The turns should be thrown up an inch to the foot. The stretches may be anywhere from 45 to 60 feet wide.

Special Notice.

Any one knowing the whereabouts of the race mare Dew Drop, purchased from me last fall by J. W. Dowell, will confer a favor by writing to me at Genoa, Nev. L. FRAY.

Jimmy Dustin is hard at work at the Bay District track, and already he has five good ones which he hopes to pilot to victory on the circuit this year. It is a reminder of old times to hear Jim's cheerful voice calling to his trotters as they come down the stretch, and I trust it may be many a year before we miss it from the California tracks.

Continued from Page 395.

SUMMARY.

The Spring Stakes.—A sweepstakes for three year olds (foals of 1887 that have not won a race previous to January 1, 1890; $50 entrance) half forfeit, or $15 if declared April 1, 1890; $400 added; second to receive $75 from stakes. Maidens at time of starting allowed five pounds. Closed February 1, 1890, with twelve nominations. One mile.
L J Rose's ch c Rover by Wild Idle—imp Rosetta, 117...Monaghan 1
W. M. Murry's ch c Kiro by Joe Hooker, dam by Foster, 117 ....Narvaez 2
W. M. Murry's b g Leland by Flood—Amelia, 117........Hennessy 3
Time, 1:45½.
Marigold 112 (Casey); Prince's First, 117 (D Dennison); Take Notice 117 (Hitchcock); and King Hooker, 117 (Hill) also started.
Book Betting—Rover 7 to 10; Marigold 6 to 1, 2 to 1; Kiro 5 to 1, 2 to 1; Prince's First 4 to 1, 1½ to 1; Leland 8 to 1, 3 to 1; Take Notice 3 to 1, 1 to 1; and King Hooker 10 to 1, 4 to 1.
Auction Pools—Rover $20, Field $10, and Take Notice $6.

The Western Hotel Stakes resulted in a walk over for the sensational Fairy. There were originally eighteen entries, but they were all withdrawn except Fairy and Peri of the Rose Stable. The former was cantered over the track for the stakes.

SUMMARY.

The Western Hotel Stakes—A sweepstakes for two year old fillies (foals of 1888), of $50 each; $15 forfeit; with $500 added; of which $100 to second; winners to carry five pounds extra. Beaten maidens allowed five pounds. Five-eighths of a mile.
L J, Rose's b f Fairy by Argyle—imp. Fairy Rose, 120....Monaghan 1

Five horses were saddled up for the Hall, Luhr and Co. Handicap. They were Mohawk, Muta, Sheridan, Pliny and Captain Al. Pliny was installed a red hot favorite with Muta second choice. This proved to be the first bad start of the meeting. Muta was virtually left at the post and was fully ten lengths to the bad when the horses got going. Pliny led past the stand with Mohawk and Captain Al dancing attendance. At the half Sheridan had moved up second and Muta had lessened the gap between her and the leader about six lengths. The race was never afterwards in doubt, Pliny winning without any great effort. Sheridan came in second and Muta beat Captain Al by very little to spare for third position. Muta must have run the distance as good as 2:09½ and with a good send off would undoubtedly have secured the place.

SUMMARY.

The Hall, Luhrs & Co. Handicap.—A sweepstakes for three-year-olds (foals of 1887), of $50 each, half forfeit, or only $10 if declared January 1, 1890, or $15 if by 4 P. M., day before the race; with $750 added, of which $100 to second, $50 to third. Weights to be announced by 5 P. M., second day before the race. Closed in 1889 with 28 nominations. One mile and a quarter.
Kelly & Samuel's b g Pliny by Flood, dam Precious, 105.......Casey 1
P. Siebenthaler's ch c Sheridan by Young Bazaar, dam Lost Girl, 95 ....Lawless 2
Palo Alto Stock Farm's ch f Muta by Wild Idle, dam Imp Mutiny, 95....................Narvaez 3
Time, 2:10.
Mohawk, 90, (Evans) and Captain Al 100 (Hennessy) also started.
Book Betting—Pliny 2 to 5, Muta 3 to 1, 2 to 5, Sheridan 4 to 1, 7 to 5, Mohawk 15 to 1, 5 to 1, Captain Al, 5 to 1 7 to 5.
Auction pools—Pliny $25, Field $15.

The starter experienced considerable difficulty in getting the horses off in the selling race. Welcome adopted her usual tactics. Starter Coombs stayed with his contract patiently and after working for an hour, got the big field off to a moderately good start. Passing the stand, Oro led by a clear length, Applause Kildare and Jou Jou racing neck and neck around the first bend. Welcome improved her position very materially and was close up with the leaders. At the half, Douglass, Albatross and Black Pilot were fully half a dozen lengths in the rear, and evidently out of the race. Turning into the straight the order was Oro; Jou Jou, and Kildare with the latter horse coming fast. A slashing struggle took place down the stretch but Kildare was not to be denied and won handily by a couple of lengths to spare. Oro got the place while Applause just beat Welcome who was coming fast on the outside. Dennison, Hennessy, Haslett, Narvaez and Hitchcock were each fined $20 for breaking away in front during the starting of the race.

SUMMARY.

Selling purse, $400, of which $50 to second; for all ages. Horses entered to be sold for $2,500 to carry rule weight. One pound off for each $100 down to $500. Value placed on starters only by six P. M. night before race. One and one-eighth miles.
Matt Storn's ch g Kildare, Kyrie Daly—Mistake, 5, 114....Hitchcock 1
J. R. Rose' b g Oro, Norfolk—April Fool, a, 116....................Kees 2
W. L. Appleby's, b g Applause, Three Cheers—Alice N., a, 107 ....Narvaez 3
Time, 1:57½.
Welcome, 106 (Casey); Dave Douglass, 106 (Bustillo); Albatross, 107 (Spooner); Jack Brady, 107 (Hennessy); Jou Jou, 106 (Haslett) and Black Pilot, 106 (Barger) also ran.
Bookbetting: Kildare, Welcome and Applause 2—1, 4—5; Oro 3—1, 1—1; Brady 6—1, 2—1; Jou Jou 10—1, 4—1; Douglass 20—1, 8—1; Black Pilot and Albatross 30—1, 10—1.
Auction pools: Kildare $25, Oro $20, Jou Jou $8, Welcome $5, field $10.

The special purse brought together Tycoon, Ed McGinnis and G. W. McGinnis was made the favorite, and was backed down to 2 to 5 before the start. Tycoon, although it was her first race this season, had a host of supporters at odds of 2 to 1. The race does not need an extended notice. The trio got the flag on the second essay. McGinnis led past the stand by half a length.

The horses raced well together along the backstretch, and turning into the straight for the finish, G. W. had his nose in front. McGinnis then came away at every stride, and won without any great effort by several lengths, G. W. beating Tycoon in the last few strides for the place after a slashing struggle.

SUMMARY.

Special purse, $350; $50 to second. One and one-eighth miles.
Kelly & Samuels' b h Ed McGinnis by Grinstead—Jennie G, a, 115 ....Casey 1
Dan Dennison's b g G. W. by Kyrle Daly—Elizabeth, 4, 106 ....Dan Dennison 2
L. J. Rose's ch g Tycoon by Reveille—Margery, a, 115....Monaghan 3
Time, 1:58
Book Betting—Ed McGinnis, 2 to 5; Tycoon 11 to 5; and G W 10 to 1.
Auction Pools—Ed McGinnis $30, and Field $13.

QUARTER STRETCH GOSSIP.

Their appears to be a lack of unanimity among the horsemen assembled at the State capital about the merits of Flambeau, Racine and El Rio Rey. The Racine adherents had a big inning on Tuesday, and many were heard to remark that night that the Bishop colt was the greatest three year old on the continent. The writer soon after encountered a Flambeau crowd. They were equally enthusiastic about the Wildidle—Flirt colt. He is the greatest three year old "that ever looked through a bridle," one of the party remarked, "and it is all bosh about him being *hors du combat.*" But is all bosh! The impression is very general that he has bolted a tendon and while he is not yet broken down, that it is only a matter of a little time. At all events, it is to be hoped that these horsemen have missed the mark, and that Flambeau will add laurels to the California bred racehorse. Trainer Walsh gives it as his opinion that Flambeau is a greater colt than the great Racine. He also says that Flambeau is still a sound horse.

Mr. Rose telegraphed his trainer, Dave Bridges, not to start Fairy in the Matedero stake on Tuesday, but if he had seen the Argyle filly canter home on Saturday he would undoubtedly have started her.

Billy McCormick is the trainer selected to go East with the William string (Undine Stable) whose shining stars will be Racine and Homer. They are two of a kind that will be hard to beat.

Kelly and Samuels expect to start in the course of a week for Denver.

Rico does not appear to be partial to weight. He is a speedy gelding, but judging by his run on Tuesday, the Brooklyn Handicap distance is a trifle to far for him

Carmen and Raindrop are both to be bred to the Duke of Norfolk.

Dan Dennison never tires of singing the praises of the Prince of Norfolk.

The Palo Alto bred horses are having a big field day in the stake races.

Matt Storn drives out daily behind the stylish looking Belvidere. This three year old is by Le Grande out of Sunny Slope Belle.

At this writing the bookmakers are away behind on the meeting. The talent is picking out winners at every clatter of the box.

On Saturday and Tuesday, Joe Narvaez rode in every race and landed four winners. Joe will in all probability go East with the Undine Stable.

One over night purse would have filled well every day. As it is, owners of second class horses have had to keep their animals in the stable.

A feature of the spring meeting has been the excellent music furnished by the Hussar band.

The proprietor of the Orange Grove Stable announces that he will shortly leave for Denver, and the West side track at Chicago. The string will include Adam, Jack Brady, Joe Woolman, Rosemeade, Earthquake and Bon Ton.

Mr. Smith will start East with Al Farrow, Longshot, and Susie S on the 15th of this month. Billy Hill will go East to ride these horses.

Steve Stroud has been turned out. While being trained at San Jose he showed a half in 48½ and ¾ in 1:15, but when he struck Sacramento he wouldn't run worth a cent. Steve is a great sulker but is very fast if he could be induced to run in company.

Odette is in very bad condition. She did splendidly in the early part of the year but caught lung fever and is now afflicted with a secondary form of the epizootie.

William Hendrickson will have a string of trotters on the grand circuit this year. John Williams, who has had fifty years experience in the sulky, is training for Mr. Hendrickson. Fanny D. is reported to be showing up well in her work. Mr. Hendrickson recently imported from New Jersey Patchen Medium, a two-year-old stallion by Mansfield Medium.

L. M. Morse, of Lodi, is having Homer T. worked at the Sacramento track. He is a promising trotter, and is by Dexter Prince out of a Santa Claus mare.

Minnie B. is to be turned out, and will not be started again this year.

Blue Bonnet has a handsome suckling filly by Prince of Norfolk.

The work of Longshot will have a tendency to boom up the Duke of Norfolk as a sire. Another fine looking colt up here is the Duke of Milpitas, but he has not been given any fast work yet.

Billy Appleby says: "If there ever was a horse who could beat El Rio Rey it was Flambeau."

L. J. Rose arrived here Thursday from Los Angeles. He informed the BREEDER AND SPORTSMAN representative that Mr Merry would arrive from Australia in June with his Australian purchases.

The Rose string was sent East on Friday. They go direct to Brooklyn.

The victory of Kildare on Thursday was a popular one and Matt Storn was kept busy receiving the congratulations of his friends.

On Thursday morning a representative of the BREEDER AND SPORTSMAN was shown the Prince of Norfolk. He is a splendidly muscled horse and of fine conformation. Judging by Minnie B. and Prince's First, the only two of his get trained, Mr. Todhunter's stallion promises to be a little gold mine in the near future. All the sucklings and yearlings by Prince of Norfolk look shapely and have plenty of substance.

Edwin F. Smith has been doing an indefatigable work for the success of the meeting but his efforts have not been seconded by the populace of the Capital City.

Joe Narvaez will go East with the William's string. Monaghan will ride for L. J. Rose in the East.

The favorites have been winning right straight along. How about some outsider for the last day?

The officers of the day on Thursday were: Messrs. Green, Hancock and Cox; timers, Waterhouse, Burns and Wilson; starter, W. H. Coombs.

The spring meeting will be brought to a close with to-day's races—the California Derby, the Hopeful Handicap, the Golden Eagle Hotel Handicap and a purse of all ages mile beats

Wilbur Smith intends to visit Kentucky and the East this year. At the present time he has no trotter to make the California circuit with.

Cheerful, the Drake, and Prince's First, made their first appearance on the turf during the week.

The victory of Sheridan on the opening day was a very popular one with the residents of the capital city.

In the list of suspended persons published last week, the name of Dan McCarty and A. McFadyen appeared. Mr. McCarty called and stated that he settled the matter at the time, and a letter from Mr. McFadyen informs us that at the time of the Sacramento meeting last year, sickness prevented him from attending, but a short time afterwards he sent his cheque for the amount, and has a receipt for the same. Such being the case, it is a shame that these gentleman's names were allowed to be published, and shows gross negligence on the part of local Secretaries.

ATHLETICS.

Athletic Sports and Other Pastimes.

EDITED BY ARTHIPPUS.

SUMMARY.

The Lean-Kolb wrestling match was the only event of importance that took place during the past week. The Alpine athletes are in good form for their sports which will come off to-morrow afternoon. The Olympian amateurs are still hard at work preparing for the opening of their new grounds on May 30th. The wheelmen are practicing hard for the great two days tournament which will come off at the Garden City in July. Judging from the great interest taken this season in all kinds of amateur sports several of the Pacific Coast records should be beaten during the year.

RUNNERS, WALKERS, JUMPERS, ETC.

We are in receipt of a letter from Joseph Barr Buchanan, the champion all-round athlete of the world who is at present residing at the Hotel Brevoort, Chicago, Ills. Mr. Buchanan will probably take a trip to England before long. He will endeavor to make a match with some of the Eastern cracks before leaving America.

Everard Dowdle will represent the Acme Athletic Club in the running high jump on Decoration Day. He is said to be able to do five feet four inches, and should take a place.

The order for the "Relay Trophy" donated by the President of the University at Berkeley, has been given, and the trophy is being made. The design is that of a heavy shield with embossed filagree work of silver and oak with the words "Relay Trophy," at the top. Beneath in succession will be a U. C. monogram, a picture of the gymnasium and of the cinder track and a figure of two sprinters at work.

The cinder path at Berkeley is at the present time in fair condition and the athletic students are now able to exercise on it. Nearly all of last years team are in training and several new men will make their debut at the U. C. sports on the 17th inst. The Olympic athletes will be able to judge on that day what opposition they may expect to meet with on May 30th.

Foulkes should break the University record of 8m 17sec. for the mile walk on May 17th. He was at the Bay District track on Sunday morning last and received some points from P. N. Gafney. Foulkes has a good easy style and with proper training he should prove a dangerous man next season.

Several of the University athletes were at the Bay District Track last Sunday morning. They seemed to take a great interest in the performances of the Alpine boys, who were practicing at the time. E. Coke Hill ran a mile in company with Phil Moody and a couple of other Alpine athletes

Moffitt of the U. C. team is at the present time in Lower California. He will probably be back in time to get into form for the championship games.

The new grounds of the Olympic Club presented an animated appearance on Sunday morning last. The outdoor team were out in full force Captain George W. Jordan and Peter McIntyre were kept very busy coaching the boys, many of whom remained on the track all day. Each athlete, as he passed out on his way home, was requested to write his name on a large slate (which had been hung up near the entrance gate by Captain Jordan) and the length of time which he exercised. During the day athletes from some of the other clubs visited the grounds and declared themselves highly pleased with the cinder path and its surroundings.

John Purcell is getting into trim for May 30th. He will compete in the broad jump, hammer and shot events, and in both hurdle races. On Sunday he exercised in the hand ball court and on the track for several hours encased in a huge sweater. He appears to be getting back into his old time form again, and will no doubt make his appearance known to the other athletes on the day of the champion games.

Young Foster of the O A C is improving daily, and he will be heard from in the high jump and hurdles.

Cooley is running in great form and should make a fine showing in the three miles to-morrow.

The O'Kane brothers and Billy Kenealey were at the new grounds practicing on Sunday.

Coffin and Jarvis are working hard getting into trim for the walks. It is said that Coffin has wonderfully improved since last season and that he will make the mile inside of 7 minutes on Decoration day.

The University regents have made an appropriation of $1,500 to complete the apparatus of the gymnasium. A portion of the money will be spent in converting the gallery into a running track.

The 440 yard open run at the Alpine games to-morrow will be a hot race between Henderson, Garrison and Little. The latter should win with Garrison close at his heels.

Jarvis has withdrawn his name from the 3-mile walk as he says he is not in condition at present to race three miles. P. N. Gafney will start from scratch and will try to lower the Pacific Coast records for 1½ miles 12 min. 7 sec., held by Horace Coffin, O A C; 2 miles 16 min. 57 sec. and 3 miles 25 min. 51½ secs. held by himself. During the past couple of weeks he has walked 3 miles, 2 minutes under the record. Gafney has given up his old style which was too square to be fast and he now walks with the hip motion as practiced by Jarvis and other fast men.

The games of the Alpine Amateur Athletic Club will take place to-morrow at the Bay District Track, commencing at 1.30 P. M. The admission will be only twenty-five cents, which will include a seat in the grand stand. The Phoenix Military band has been engaged and will perform all the afternoon. It will be seen from the list of names below that nearly all the crack amateurs of the P C A A A will compete, and close and exciting contests must necessarily be the result. The club events were handicapped by P. N. Gafney, the official handicapper of the club, while George W. Jordan the official handicapper of the P C A A A attended to the open events. The following is a correct list of the officers of the Day:—

Superintendent, T. J. Cunningham, A A A C; Referee, E. Coke Hill, V C; Starter, F. M. Howard, A A A C; Judges of track events, J. P. Bean, Dr. C. A. Bonesteli, A A A C; George W Jordan, O A C; Timers, J T Sullivan, P B C; R McArthur, O A C; R J Luttringer, A A A C; Judges of walking, John Purcell, O A C; Charles Voltee and Ed Steinway, A A A C; Clerks of the course, J H Donohue and T J Gallagher; Call Stewards, F J Ralph, W C Bean; Marshals, A M King, J R Collins, Henry Tauk, W C Gifford, T J Quinlan.

The programme will be run in the following order:

1. 100-yard run Novice—(club)—G H Simmons, G W Ambruster, R C Stadts, P J Sheedy, J F Hancock, W F Vollmer, E P Levy, T Kelly, W C Clark, John Mellon, J W Creagh.

2. 120-yard run, handicap (club)—John D Garrison, scratch; E P Moody, 5 yards; T Kelly, scratch; G W Ambruster, 6 yards; C A Eldridge, 3 yds; J W Creagh, 6 yds; R C Staats, 3 yds; A Cooke, 6 yds; H P Coleman, 3 yds; G H Simmons, 6 yds; F N Dodd, 3 yds; E P Levy, 8 yds; F E Holland, 3 yds; J Mellon, 8 yds; J M Whelan, 4 yds; W C Clark, 10 yds.

3. Putting 16lb. shot, handicap (club)—P J Sh·e·'y, scratch; J Hart, 3ft; J F Hancock, 2ft; C A Eldridge, 3f.; J F O'Connor, 2ft; E Goodman, 3ft.

4. 440-yard run, handicap (open)—A S Henderson, O A C; scratch; M L Espinosa, O A C, 16yds; J D Garrison, A A A C, 8yds; C A Eldridge, A A A C, 18yds; C Little, A A A C, 10yds; S L Conlan, A A A C, 25yds· S V. Cassady, O A C, 10yds; W H Toomey, O A C, 25yds; W J Kenealley, O A C, 12yds; F N Dodd, A A A C, 25yds.

5. 3-mile walk, handicap (open)—P N Gafney, A A A C, scratch; A Cooke, A A A C, 45 secs; F C Philips, A A A C, 1 min 15sec P N Gafney will attempt to lower the Pacific Coast records for 1½, 2 and 3 miles.

6. 880-yard run, handicap (club)—C Little, scratch; C W Meyer, 50yds; J D Garrison, 15yds; W F Vollmer, 50yds; H C Cassidy, 25yds; S L Conlan, 50yds; J M Whelan, 30yds; C Armbruster, 60yds; E P Moody, 40yds; G W Armbruster, 70yds; R C Staats, 50yds.

7. Running high jump, handicap (club)—J F O'Connor, scratch; F E Holland, 3 in; P N Gafney, 2 in; C Armbruster, 3 in; J F Hancock, 2 in; C W Meyer, 3 in.

8. 220-yard hurdle, handicap (club)—J D Garrison, scratch; H C Casidy, 7yds; A Cooke, 3yds; J F Hancock, 7 yds; E P Moody, 7yds; C W Meyer, 7yds, J M Whelan, 4 yds; F E Holland, 6 yds· C Armbruster, 10yds; W C Clark, 12yds; J W Creagh, 10yds.

9. Three-mile run, handicap (open)—F L Cooley, O A C, scratch; E P Moody, A A A C, 1 min 10sec; W A Scott, O A C scratch; J W Leubert U C, 1min 10sec; H C Cassidy, A A A C, 5sec; W F Vollmer, A A A C, 1min 20sec, M L Espinosa, O A C, 5secs; S L Conlan, A A A C, 1min 15sec; C Little, A A A C, 15secs; W C Clark, A A A C, 1min 15sec; W H. Toomey, O A C, 1min; F C Philips, A A A C, 1min 20sec.

10 100 yard run handicap (open).—A S Henderson, O A C scratch; C A Eldridge, A A A C 5½yds; S V Casady, O A C, 2 yards; E P Levy 6 yards; F G O'Kane, O A C 2yds; T Kelly, 6 yds; W J Kenealiy, O A C 3yds; M. L. Espinosa, 7yds; J D Garrison, A A A C, 4yds; H P Coleman, A A A C 7yds· R C Staats, A A A C 8yds; G W Armbruster, A A A C 8yds; S L Conlan, A A A C, 7yds; F L Cooley, O A C, 10yds; E P Moody, A A A C, 6½yds.

11. Steeplechase, handicap, (club)—H C Cassidy, scratch; C W Meyer, 60yds; J D Garrison, 20yds; E Goodman, 75yds; A Cook, 50 yards; J W Creagh, 75yds.

Any athlete who breaks a Pacific Coast record will receive a special "record" medal. The sprint races will not be run in heats as the track is wide enough to start the men all together.

The tickets are out for the opening of the Olympic Grounds on May 30th. The price of admission has been fixed at 50 cents. It is expected that the Olympic Club members will dispose of at least 5000 tickets which will insure good prizes for the competitors.

The Alpine Club has on view in the window of Kast's shoe store on Market St., a large frame of medals won by the members at different athletic sports in the past. The prizes to be awarded the winners to-morrow have been on exhibition at Lundy's jewelery store, cor Market and Third streets for the past week.

ON THE WHEELS.

The American Bicycle Club was organized April 8th. The members had a club run to Sausalito last Sunday S. B. Morse who was a prominent member of the San Francisco Bicycle Club is an active member of the new club. Some of the S F B C members have resigned to join the American Bicycle Club.

Six trophies and a number of medals will be awarded the different winners at the coming San Jose tournament.

President George Butler of the Bay City Wheelmen is out again on his wheel. He rode to Belmont on Sunday last in company with Langton, Toll and others.

Messrs. Allen, Spaulding and W. E. Thompsan rode to San Jose on Sunday and back (on train) They intended riding both ways but when they arrived at the Garden City it was considered more judicious and less tiresome travelling home by rail.

On May 17th, there will be a century run given under the auspices of the California Division of the L. A. W. The run will be from Oakland to Hollister, the distance being about 102 miles. Only members of the league will be allowed to take part in the run, and each rider's expenses from the time he leaves Oakland until he returns again, will be paid out of the treasury. It is expected that the number of starters will be very large.

The committee appointed to make preparations for the L A. W. meet at San Jose, Cal., are working hard, and it will be no fault of theirs if everything does not turn out all right.

Plummer, Hammer and Wetmore made a round trip of the bay on Sunday, covering 98½ miles. They visited San Jose during the trip, and report the roads all the way in first-class condition.

Of late there has been considerable discussion about the condition of the San Bruno road. Wheelmen who have been over it within a week or so, say that it is in better condition than it has been in for years. Between Milbrae and San Mateo the road is faultless.

A good many of the local wheelmen rode to San Mateo on Sunday, and not a few continued on to San Jose.

The San Jose wheelmen expect to be able to have a new four-lap track ready for the July meet.

AT THE OARS:

Most of the local oarsmen attended the picnic of the Lurline Club on Sunday.

John Muirhead, the champion light-weight amateur single sculler of the Ariel Rowing Club has ordered a new shell of Ruddick of New York.

The Picnic committee of the Pacific Rowing Association have about completed arrangements for the Fall meeting, to be held at Shellmound Park in October.

The picnic given by the Lurline Club on Sunday last was a grand success. Over 1,000 people paid admission at the gate. The process will net the club several hundred dollars. Two new barges are to be built for the use of the members during the coming season.

E. Kolb, the after waist man in the amateur crew of the Dolphin Club won his match with Lean the wrestler, at the Olympic Club on Tuesday evening. This year he will organize a crew that will represent the Olympic Athletic Club.

The Dolphin Swimming and Boating Club will give their eleventh annual outing on May 12th. The excursion will be to the Big Trees. A good time may be expected, as the committee in charge of the affair are well known as hard workers.

CLUB JOTTINGS.

A general meeting of the Alpine Amateur Athletic Club was held at the club rooms, 706 Powell Street, on Thursday evening. Officers were nominated for the ensuing term. Several new members were elected, and it was decided to purchase several new pieces of apparatus for the gymnasium Final arrangements were made for the field-games, which will take place to-morrow.

Several amateur runners claim not to be aware of the fact that the P C A A A forbids its associate club members from competing in picnic races. It would be a good plan to have the Secretary of the P C A A A mail to each of the associate clubs a copy of the rules which govern the athletes as far as their competing is concerned.

Hereafter the P C A A A will be very strict in acting on the application of athletes who desire reinstatement, and only men who can really prove their ignorance of having transgressed the amateur laws will be taken back.

Lean Defeated by Kolb.

About 1500 sportsmen assembled in the gymnasium of the Olympic Club on Tuesday evening last to witness a wrestling match between E. A. Kolb and A. H. Lean. Kolb is a member of the Olympic Club while Lean is unattached. The President of the Club read a long list of rules defining the definition of an amateur and then the articles of agreement drawn up between Lean and Kolb.

At 8:35 the men stepped on to the mat. Lean's weight was announced as being 159 pounds, while his opponent scaled but 149½ pounds. Eugene Van Court seconded Kolb, while Gus Ungerman stood behind Lean. F F Scanlan of the Acme Athletic Club was chosen as referee, and Walter A. Scott and C. Coleman timekeepers respectively for Kolb and Lean.

Lean looked big and strong enough to crush the life out of his rival, but before many minutes had elapsed the smaller man had proven that he was no slouch. For some minutes after the wrestling began neither athlete gained any advantage over the other. Kolb accidentally rubbed his nose up against Lean's shoulder, and it began to bleed. At the end of sixteen minutes Kolb secured a good hold on Lean's body and stood him on his head. After a short but desperate struggle the Olympian forced Lean's shoulders on to the mat and so won the bout. The applause which followed was deafening. Van Court acted a little bit hasty in rushing over to his man before the referee's decision could be heard. The mat was now rolled up, and a couple of boxing exhibitions were given. The four young men who performed did remarkably well, the last setto between Green and Smythe being particularly interesting.

After a rest of about half an hour the wrestlers reappeared. This time Lean looked a trifle nervous, while his opponent looked confident. At 9:20 the struggle for the second fall began: Lean seemed inclined to act more on the defensive than he did in the first bout, and allowed Kolb to do the heavy work. Quick as a flash the florist made a clutch at the Olympian's leg, but that gentleman was prepared and he quickly turned the tables on his heavier rival. How it was done nobody seemed to know, but in exactly two and a half minutes Lean was flat on the carpet and he had lost the match. It would be impossible to describe the scene that followed. Kolb was lifted on to the shoulders of a crowd of his friends and borne in this style to the dressing room, while Lean remained sitting in his corner staring wildly around him, trying to realize that he had lost the match.

The style of wrestling was catch-as catch can. As Kolb was under the required weight, he won the $200 trophy and the amateur championship of the Pacific Coast. Had Lean won the match he would not have received a cent for his trouble as he was ten pounds over weight, the limit being 158 pounds. It was reported after the match that Lean had thrown the match, but persons who are up in wrestling tactics seem to think differently. At all events Lean made a poor showing, and it is almost certain that Kolb is his match in strength as well as in science.

Lean's friends lost considerable money on their champion, and it was said that Lean late in the afternoon had representatives in the pool rooms who bought up all the tickets they could get on Kolb. If this report be true, Lean must have either made up his mind to throw the match or else he lost confidence in himself at the last moment.

W. H. Day again came to the front by winning the team cross country championship at New York on Saturday last. In a cold and beating rain he ran eight miles over the roughest ground imaginable lowering his own record by almost six minutes and covering the distance in 47 minutes 41 seconds.

Races. Races.

Races  Races

JULY WEEK.

AT

South Park Race Track

Eureka, Cal.

GIVEN BY THE

EUREKA JOCKEY CLUB.

FIRST DAY, JULY 2, 1890.

No. 1. Novelty Running Race. Free for all. Dash of one mile. Purse $25). First quarter, $40. Half, $50. Third quarter, $75. Mile, $90.

No. 2. Running Race. Purse $150. Five-eighths dash, for two-year-olds. $125 to first horse; $25 to second horse.

No. 3. Running. Purse $150. Three-quarters and repeat. $125 to first; $25 to second.

SECOND DAY, JULY 3, 1890.

No. 4. Trotting. Purse $200. Three minute Class. $150 to first; $40 to second. (Covey barred.)

No. 5. Running Stake. Five-eighths of a mile. For Humboldt raised two year-olds. $30 entrance, half forfeit. $150 added. First to receive 60 per cent.; second, 30 per cent., third, 10 per cent.

No. 6. Running Stake. Purse $200. Mile Dash. $150 to first horse; $50 to second horse.

THIRD DAY, JULY 4, 1890.

No. 7. Trotting Stake. 2:40 Class. Purse $250. $200 to first horse; $50 to second horse.

No. 8. Running Stake, 1¼ miles. Free-for-all. $40 entrance, ¼ forfeit, $200 added; second horse $75, third horse to save stake.

No. 9. Running Stake. Purse $150; 1-2 mile and repeat; $125 to first; $25 to second.

FOURTH DAY, JULY 5, 1890.

No. 10. Running Stake, 1-2 mile and repeat; for Humboldt horses owned prior to Jan 1, 1890. $125 to first, $25 to second.

No. 11. Running Stake. Purse $200; 7-8 mile and repeat. $150 to first. $50 to second.

CONDITIONS AND REMARKS.

All trotting races are best three in five, unless otherwise specified. Four to enter and three to start, but the Board reserves the right to hold a less number than four to fill by the withdrawal of a proportionate amount of the purse. Entrance fee, 10 per cent. of purse, to accompany nominations. In all trotting races the rules of the American Trotting Association, and all running races the rules of the Pacific Coast Blood Horse Association to govern, but the Board reserves the right to trot heats of any two classes alternately, if necessary, to finish any day's racing. In all entries not declared out by 8 P. M. of the day preceding the race, shall be required to start.

No added money paid for a walk over. In all races, four or more paid up entries required to fill, and three or more horses to start. Racing Colors to be named in entries. In trotting races drivers will be required to wear caps of distinct colors to be named in entries. Entries in all races to close with the Secretary, Thursday, June 5, 1890. Entry blanks will be furnished upon application to the Secretary.

All trotting races for horses owned and in Humboldt County prior to June 1, 1890.

H. M. DEVOY, President.

J. P. MONROE, Secretary.

Breeders' Directory.

Advertisements under this heading 50c. per line per month.

HORSES AND CATTLE.

W. S. JACOBS, Sacramento, Cal. – Breeder of Thoroughbred Shorthorns and Berkshire Hogs.

J. H. WHITE, Lakeville, Sonoma County—Breeder of Registered Holstein Cattle.

EL ROBLAS RANCHO—Los Alamos, Cal., Francis T. Underhill, proprietor, importer and breeder of thoroughbred Hereford Cattle. Information by mail. C. F. Swan, manager.

PAGE BROTHERS.—Penn's Grove, Sonoma Co. Cal. Breeders of Short-Horn Cattle; Draft, Roadster and Standard Bred Horses.

SETH COOK, breeder of Cleveland Bay Horses, Devon, Durham, Polled Aberdeen-Angus and Galloway Cattle. Young stock of above breeds on hand for sale. Warranted to be pure bred, recorded and average breeders. Address, Geo. A. Wiley, Cook Farm, Danville, Contra Costa Co., Cal.

MAMBRINO WILKES COLTS and FILLIES, full brothers and sisters to Gus. Wilkes 2:22, and Balkan 2:29¾, for Sale. Address SMITH HILL, Walnut Creek, Contra Costa County, Cal.

R. F. RUSH, Suisun, Cal., Shorthorns, Thoroughbred and Grades. Young Bulls and Calves for Sale.

PETER SAXE & SON, Lick House, San Francisco, Cal.—Importers and Breeders for past 18 years of every variety of Cattle, Horses, Sheep and Hogs.

HOLSTEIN THOROUGHBREDS of all the noted strains. Registered Berkshire Swine. Catalogues. F. H. BURKE, 401 Montgomery St., S. F.

FERGUSON & AUSTIN,

FRESNO, CAL.

Registered Polled Angus and Short-Horn Cattle.

The Pacific Coast

Live Stock Owners

MUTUAL PROTECTIVE ASS'N.,

MONTEREY, Monterey Co., Cal.

TRUSTEES:

HON. B. V. SARGENT, President,
G. W. GALLANAR, Secretary,
JAMES B. PALMER, Business Manager,
EDW. INGRAM, Vice-President,
FRED. D. HOWARD, Actuary,
R. H. WILLEY, Attorney.

GENERAL BUSINESS OFFICE, Room 78, Flood Building, corner Market and Fourth Streets, San Francisco, Cal.

VOLNEY HOWARD, General Manager.

ADVERTISE YOUR STALLIONS

—IN THE—

Breeder & Sportsman

For the Season---1890.

We are pleased to announce that we have the best facilities for furnishing

Stallion Pictures,

Stallion Cards,

Pedigrees, Folders,

Contracts, Bills, Etc.

We make a specialty of this department of our business, and have UNRIVALED FACILITIES FOR LOOKING UP PEDIGREES and doing accurate and handsome work.

Promptness, Good Work, Low Prices.

BREEDER AND SPORTSMAN,

313 Bush Street, S. F.

J. J. EVANS

—SELLS—

WALLACE'S YEAR BOOK,
WALLACE'S REGISTER No. 8.
STALLION SERVICE BOOKS,
For Office and Pocket.
—ALL KINDS—
PEDIGREE BLANKS.

J. J. Evans,

Stationer and Printer,

406 California Street, San Francisco, Cal.

Mail orders receive prompt attention.

BERGEZ'S

RESTAURANT.

FIRST-CLASS. Charges Reasonable.

Private Rooms for Families.

332—334 Pine St., below Montgomery St.

JOHN BERGEZ, Propr.

K STREET.

SECOND ST

Singleton & Addington

BANK EXCHANGE,

SACRAMENTO,

Wines, Liquors & Cigars.

JESSE E. MARKS. IKE DEUTCH

Yosemite Billiard Parlors,

ST. ANN'S BUILDING,

No. 8 Eddy Street, S. F.

The Poodle Dog

"Rotisserie,"

FIRST-CLASS IN EVERY RESPECT.

Elegant Family Dining Rooms.

S. E. cor. GRANT AVE. and BUSH STREET.

ANDRE POTENTINI, Proprietor.

FIXED EVENTS, 1890

FRESNO

FAIR GROUNDS

Agricultural District No. 21.

Races. Races.

Sept. 30, Oct. 1. 2 & 3

With an Extra Day on Saturday.

ENTRIES CLOSE MAY 15, 1890.

Programme will be issued later for other running, trotting and pacing races, to take place same week, for which liberal purses will be given.

OPEN TO THE WORLD

Nomination Guarantee Purs $1 000

For Horses that have Never Beaten 2:24 Trotting.

$100 entrance; $25 payable May 15, 1890; $25 payable July 15, 1890; $50 payable August 11, 1890, when horses are to be named. To be trotted September 30, 1890, Fresno, Cal. If entrance money amounts to more than $1,000, it will be added to the purse, and the Association will add 20 per cent of amount of purse.

Four moneys: 50, 25, 15 and 10 per cent. of purse.

Horses eligible at closing of entries May 15, 1890, are eligible the day of the race.

Nomination Guarantee Purse $1,200

For Horses That Never Beat 2:30 Trotting.

$120 entrance; $30 payable May 15, 1890; $30 payable July 15, 1890; $60 payable August 11, 189 , when horses are to be named. To be trotted October 2, 1890, Fresno, Cal. If entrance money amounts to more than $1,200 it will be added to the purse, and the Association will add 20 per cent. of amount of purse.

Four moneys: 50, 25, 15 and 10 per cent. of purse.

Horses eligible at closing of entries May 15, 1890, are eligible the day of the race.

Nomination Guarantee Purse $1,000

For Horses That Never Beat 2:30 Pacing.

$100 entrance; $25 payable May 15, 1890; $50 payable August 11, 1890, when horses are to be named. To be paced at Fall fair, 1890, Fresno, Cal. If entrance money amounts to more than $1,000, it will be added to the purse, and the Association will add 20 per cent. of amount of purse.

Four moneys: 50, 25, 15 and 10 per cent. of purse.

Horses eligible at closing of entries May 15, 1890, are eligible the day of the race.

President Stake.

Guarantee Purse $1,000.

For all ages, weight for age; 1⅛ mile dash; $100 entrance; $10 payable May 15, 1890; $15 payable June 15, 1890; $25 payable July 15, 1890; $50 payable Sept. 6, 1890. To be run October, 2, 1890, Fresno, Cal. If entrance amounts to more than $1,000, it shall be added to the purse, and the Association adds 20 per cent. of purse. Three moneys—70, 20 and 10 per cent. of purse. Horse winning an all-aged race of one mile or over at Sacramento or Stockton, where purse or stake amounts to $800 or over, shall carry ten pounds extra. Horse winning an all-aged race of one mile or over at Sacramento or Stockton, where purse or stake amounts to $500 or over, shall carry five pounds extra. American Association rules to govern.

Raisin Handicap.

Guarantee Purse $1,000.

For all ages, 1¼ mil dash; $100 entrance; $10 May 15th; $15 June 15; $25 July 15th. Weights will be declared August 15th and acceptance on or before September 6th, when the other $50 is to be paid; to be run September 30, 1890, Fresno, Cal. If entrance amounts to more than $1,000 it will be added to the purse, and the Association will add 20 per cent. of the amount of purse. Three moneys—70, 20 and 10 per cent. of purse. Horse winning any purse or stake of one mile or over, at Sacramento or Stockton after weights are declared, where purse or stake amounts to $800 or over, shall carry ten pounds extra. Horse winning any purse or stake of one mile or over at Sacramento or Stockton after weights are declared, when purse or stake amounts to $500 or over, shall carry five pounds extra. Nominations are only held for amount paid in. Weights to be declared through BREEDER AND SPORTSMAN August 15, 1890. American Association rules to govern.

REMARKS.

As to the Handicap, the Handicapping Committee will use due diligence in learning the performance of every horse entered and weighting them fairly to their merits. Each entry must be accompanied by entrance money or be considered no entry. All payments must be made when due, or the nominator forfeits all money paid in. We propose, at the finish of the race, the horse winning the purse gets his money and not forfeit papers.

CONDITIONS AND REMARKS.

Nominators are only held for amount paid in. Nominators failing to make payments when due forfeit all money paid in, and nomination reverts back to Association, who have the privilege of disposing of nomination. All nominations are transferable. Trotting and pacing races, mile heats, best 3 in 5 to harness. Horse distancing the field or any part of field only entitled to first money. American Association rules to govern. These Guarantee Purses for trotters and pacers gives the party making the entry the privilege of naming any horse he sees fit the 11th of August, having no better record than specified in the stake, the 15th day of May, irrespective of the record he gets after that date. You will see by this the nominator has almost a sure thing of getting his money back. Money must accompany entry or will be considered no entry.

The track has been re-clayed the past winter, making it the fastest and best track in the State. The stabling and accommodations are the very best. Hay and straw free. Arrangements will be made with the Railroad Company for transportation of horses and men accompanying them at half fare.

Remember we go according to rule: 3 to enter and 2 to start.

Entries close with the Secretary.

LEWIS LEACH, Pres,

F. B. BALDWIN, Manager.

N. I. BALDWIN, Sec'y,

P. O. Drawer U, Fresno, Cal.

ANNUAL SPRING SALE

—OF—

200 HEAD

Road & Harness Horses

AND

Work and Draft Horses

AND SHETLAND PONIES!

From the Ranchos of J. B. Haggin, Esq.

WILL TAKE PLACE AT

RAILROAD STABLES,

Corner Turk and Steiner Streets, San Francisco,

Tuesday, May 6, 1890,

HORSES MAY BE SEEN AT STABLES ON AND AFTER MAY 3d.

Catalogues now ready, and may be had on application.

KILLIP & CO., Live Stock Auctioneers,
22 Montgomery Street, S. F.

Important Closing Out Sale

—OF—

Trotting bred STOCK,

Comprising the Entire Stud of

JOHN G. HILL, of Ventura, Cal

To be held at 10 A. M., at

RAILROAD STABLES,

Corner STEINER and TURK STS., San Francisco.

Take McAllister or Turk Street Cars.

Thursday, May 15, 1890

It will embrace about 80 head of well bred Stallions, Mares and Geldings, principally the get of that celebrated standard bred sire

A. W. RICHMOND, 1687,

out of thoroughbred mares mostly from that noted horse, Woodburn, sire of Monarch 2:28½, and the dam of Victor 2 22, and others.

This will no doubt be the last opportunity to obtain at public auction the blood of this great sire, that, in part, has made ANTEEO, ANTEVOLO, ARROW, ROMERO, RICHMOND JR., and others famous in the trotting history of our State.

The sale is positive and without reserve, as Mr. Hill will engage in other business.

☞Catalogues now ready.

KILLIP & CO., Auctioneers,
22 Montgomery Street, San Francisco, Cal.

Poplar Grove Breeding FARM.

Standard-bred Trotters, Colts and Fillies.

The get of CLOVIS, 4909; PASHA, 2039; APEX, 2935,

For Sale.

Address S. N. STRAUBE, Poplar Grove Breeding Farm,
Fresno, Cal.

Inspection by intending purchasers invited, and information by mail.

FISHING TACKLE,

WHOLESALE AND RETAIL.

CLABROUGH, GOLCHER & CO.,
630 and 632 Montgomery St.

SAMUEL VALLEAU. JAS. R. BRODIE.

J. R. BRODIE & CO.,

Steam Printers,

—And Dealers in—
Poolseller's and Bookmaker's Supplies.
401—403 *Sansome Street, corner Sacramento, San Francisco.*

Old Hermitage Whiskies

"STEINER'S,"

No. 311 BUSH STREET,
San Francisco.
Under Breeder and Sportsman Office.

"Laurel Palace,"

ROME HARRIS, Proprietor.

N. W. corner Kearny and Bush Streets,
SAN FRANCISCO

HENRY J. COX W. S. JOHNSON

The "EDWIN C."

40 EDDY STREET.

Cor. of Mason, San Francisco.
(Private Entrance Mason Street.)

ENTIRE CHANGE

—OF—

PROGRAMME

—OF THE—

Extra Attractions

To take place at the

Oakland.

Fall Meeting, 1890,

UNDER THE MANAGEMENT OF THE

GOLDEN GATE

Fair Association

NOMINATION PURSES.

In which entries close in the name of owners or trainers on May 15th. All nominations transferable and nominators held only for amounts paid in. Horses must be named five days before first advertised day of the meeting. Eight nominations required to fill, four of which must make last payments.

THE NEW LIST PURSE $1000.

For three-year-olds whose sires up to January 1, 1890, have not produced an animal with a record of 2:30 or better, at three years of age or under. Entrance 10 per cent. payable as follows:

$25 May 15th, when entries close in the names of owners or trainers.
$25 June 15th.
$25 July 15th.
$25 five days before first advertised day of meeting, when horses must be named.

GUARANTEED PURSE $1200.

For three-minute class, entrance 10 per cent, payable as follows:

$30 May 15th, when entries close in names of owners or trainers.
$30 June 15th.
$30 July 15th.
$30 five days before first advertised day of meeting, when horse must be named.

GUARANTEED PURSE $1200.

For 2:40 class, entrance 10 per cent, payable as follows:

$30 May 15th, when entries close in names of owners or trainers.
$30 June 15th.
$30 July 15th.
$30 five days before first advertised day of meeting, when horses must be named.

—ALSO A—

Guaranteed Futurity Purse $4,000.

To take place during the Fall Meeting of 1893.

For foals of 1890. Entrance 3 per cent. payable as follows:

$10 May 15, 1890, when entries close in name of foals or of dams and sires.
$10 Jan. 15, 1891.
$15 June 15, 1891.
$15 Jan. 15, 1892.
$15 June 15, 1892.
$15 Jan. 15, 1893.
$20 June 15, 1893.
$20 fifteen days before advertised day of the race.

If the last payment is made on twelve or more entries the horses shall be started in trial races, in which not more than eleven or less than six shall be allotted to start. The trial races shall be mile heats, three in five, for a purse of $1,000, given by the Association for each race. If two trial races are trotted, the first four horses shall only be entitled to start in the final race. If three such trial races are trotted, only the first three horses in each trial race shall start in the final; and if four or more trial races are necessary, only the first two horses in each trial race shall start in the final race.

These trial races must be started not less than five nor more than ten days previous to the day set for the final race; and if possible all trial races will be trotted on the same day.

CONDITIONS.

Neglect to provide payments on the dates stipulated will incur forfeiture of all previous payments.

The Directors reserve the right to change the hour and day of any race except when it becomes necessary to antedate a race, in which instance the nominator will receive three days notice of change by mail to address of entry.

Entries not declared out by 6 P. M. the day preceding the race, shall be required to start.

Purses will be divided into four moneys viz., 50 per cent. to the winner, 25 per cent. to the second horse, 15 per cent. to the third horse, and 10 per cent. to the fourth horse.

A horse distancing the field shall only be entitled to first and third moneys.

Trotting and racing colors shall be named by six o'clock on the day preceding the race, and MUST be worn upon the track.

All purse races, mile heats, best three in five to harness.

Otherwise than the above, National or American Trotting Association Rules—as this Association may select—will govern the races offered.

Entries to close with the Secretary.

R. T. CARROLL, President.

JOS. I. DIMOND, Sec'y, 306 Market St., S. F.

"DICKEY'S,"

SIXTH AVENUE AND D ST.

Near entrance to Bay District Track.

Choicest Brands of

WINES AND CIGARS.

A Delightful Resort.

Telephone 1485. J. R. DICKEY, Propr.

UTAH

Driving Park

ASSOCIATION,

1890.

JUNE 16 to 20, Inclusive

—AT—

SALT LAKE CITY.

Purses - $7,000

TROTTING, RUNNING & PACING,

Entries for all Races to close May 30, 1890.

This meeting is arranged to accommodate horsemen on way to the Great Racing Circuit of Montana, their purses aggregating $45,000. The meeting at Denver closes June 7th, and our meeting begins June 16th and closes June 20th inclusive, and the Montana meetings commence July 14th, thus giving ample time to rest up here. We expect to give a genuine first-class meeting, and will see that all horsemen have a "square deal." Our city is at present enjoying an era of prosperity never before seen, which justifies our hope for the best meeting ever given in Utah. A cordial invitation is extended to all horsemen to come. The Great Salt Lake bathing season is then on, thus affording all visitors a rare treat and pleasant time.

PROGRAMME

—OF—

Utah Driving Park Spring Race Meeting,

Salt Lake City, Utah.

Spring Racing and Trotting Meeting for Five Days, from June 16 to June 20, inclusive.

PURSES, $7000.

FIRST DAY—MONDAY, JUNE 16.

No. 1—Trotting, 2:27 class $500
No. 2—Pacing, 2:35 class 400
No. 3—Running, ¾ mile heats, all ages 300
No. 4—Running, ½ mile heats, all ages 300

SECOND DAY—TUESDAY, JUNE 17.

No. 5—Pacing, 2:24 class $500
No. 6—Trotting, 2:50 class 400
No. 7—Running, ¾ mile dash, three-year-olds 300
No. 8—Running, ⅝ mile heats, all ages 300

THIRD DAY—WEDNESDAY, JUNE 18.

No. 9—Trotting, 2:26 class $500
No. 10—Trotting, three-year-olds (added money) for Colorado, Wyoming, Montana, and Utah horses 300
No. 11—Running ½ mile heats, all ages 300

FOURTH DAY—THURSDAY, JUNE 19.

No. 12—Pacing, free for all pacers $600
No. 13—Trotting, 2:34 class 400
No. 14—Running, 1¼ mile dash, all ages 300

FIFTH DAY—FRIDAY, JUNE 20.

No. 15—Trotting, free for all $600
No. 16—Trotting, 2:30 class 450
No. 17—Running, ¾ mile heats, for horses that have run and not won a race this meeting 250
No. 18—Running, 1 mile heats, all ages 300

F. H. DYER, Secretary,

J. K. GILLESPIE, Manager. Salt Lake City.

CONTRA COSTA CO.

Agricultural Associat'n

District No. 23.

FAIR OF 1890.

Sept. 22 to 27, inclusive.

District Trotting Colt Stakes for 1890.

$40, payable as follows:

$10 June 1st (when stakes close), $15 Sept. 1st, and $15 Sept. 22d.

FOR ONE-YEAR-OLDS, 1 mile dash.
FOR TWO-YEAR-OLDS, mile heats, 2 in 3
FOR 3-YEAR-OLDS, mile heats, 3 in 5.
} $75 added to each.

All moneys divided as follows: 60, 30 and 10 per cent. In case of only two starting, 60 and 40 per cent, and in case of one horse walking over, the whole amount to go to such horse.

A failure to make any payment when due shall be considered a withdrawal and forfeiture of the amount paid in.

National Rules to govern.

The right reserved to refund the first payment in case the stakes do not fill reasonably well.

Entries close June 1, 1890 with the Secretary.

GEO. P. LOUCKS, President.

H. C. RAAP, Secretary, Martinez, Cal.

SUBSCRIBE FOR THE

Breeder and Sportsman.

SAN DIEGO, 8776.

SAN DIEGO is dark seal brown, three years old, and trotted one-quarter miles in 40 seconds as a two-year old.

This grand young horse, and, barring accidents, will make a fast record next fall.

He will be allowed a limited number of mares, at $50 for the season. Mares not proving in foal to be returned free 1891. Best of pasture for mares at $4 per month, but no liability for accidents or escapes.

He will make the season from February 1st to June 1st at Napa Fair Grounds. For further particulars, address or call on

H. B. STARR, Race Track, Napa, Cal.,

or FRED W. LOEBER, St. Helena

Guenoc Stud Farm, Lake Co., Cal.

Imp. GREENBACK

(Sire of the English winners Greenlight, Greenjacket, Greensbank, Greenwave and Greenhorn)

By Dollar, dam Music, by Stockwell. $100 the Season

ST. SAVIOR,

(FULL BROTHER TO EOLE)

By Eolus, dam War Song, by War Dance. $100 the Season.

PASTURAGE, $5 PER MONTH.

With right to return the following year if mare does not prove with foal. The best of care taken, but no liability for accidents or escapes. Mares shipped to C. W. ABY, care ST. HELENA STABLES, St. Helena Napa County, will be taken in charge by competent men.

For further information write to

DR. C. W. ABY, Middletown, Lake County, Cal.

Bay Rose.

REGISTERED No. 9814.

Record 2:20 1-2 Third Heat.

Will make the season of 1890, ending July 1st, at the SANTA ROSA STOCK FARM, (formerly Santa Rosa Race Track), SANTA ROSA.

DESCRIPTION.

BAY ROSE is a dark bay or brown, with black points, 15¾ hands high and weighs 1150 pounds. He is remarkably intelligent, of good disposition, and a pure-gaited trotter. He was foaled in 1881. His Colts are large, stylish, rangy animals, and inherit the qualities of speed and endurance.

PEDIGREE.

BAY ROSE 9814
Sultan, 2:24. Sire of 19 in the 2:30 list.
The Moor 870, sire of Beautiful Bells 2:29½, Del Sur 2:24½, Inez 2:30, Sir Guy 2:28¼, Sultan 2:24, Tommy Gates 2:24
Sultana.
Madam Baldwin
The Moor 870. Sire of 6 in the 2:30 list.
by Ben Lippincott, by Williamson's Belmont.

TERMS: $100 FOR THE SEASON.

Good pasturage $3 per month. First-class care taken of mares in any manner that owners may desire, but no responsibility assumed for escapes or accidents. Limited to a few approved mares. For further particulars, address

THOS. BONNER,
Santa Rosa Stock Farm, Santa Rosa.

Or apply to
IRA PIERCE.
728 Montgomery Street, S. F., Cal.

GEO. WASHINGTON.

11,623.

RECORD 2:30.

Bay colt, bred by Thomas Smith of Vallejo, Cal. Foaled 1886 by Mambrino Chief, Jr., 11,622, record 2:31 1-4, 1st dam Fanny Rose by Vick's Ethan Allen Jr, 2,903, sire of Prince Allen 2:27 2nd dam Jenny Lind, thoroughbred, dam of Prince Allen 2:27. Will serve a limited number of mares at $50 for the season. Mares not proving with foal may be returned next season free.

Mambrino Chief, Jr.

11,622.

RECORD 2:34 1 2.

Sire of George Washington, record 2 30 at three years old. Bay horse bred by Rufus Ingalls of Helvedere, Ill. By McDonald Chief 3'83. First dam Venus by Mambrino Patchen 58. 2nd dam by Wardlow's Shakespeare. 3rd dam Lone Gold 4th dam by Silver Heels. Has not been in the stud before. He was 8 years old when he served a few mares, and his colts all show good style and form.

Terms for the season $40. For further particulars see or address

THOMAS SMITH,
Vallejo, Cal.

CALIFORNIA

NUTWOOD

Will stand for mares the season of 1890, commencing February 15th, and ending July 15th, at the NUTWOOD STOCK FARM, one mile from Irvington.

DESCRIPTION AND PEDIGREE.

He is a dark chestnut, with star in forehead; foaled September 16th, 1881; is 16 hands 1½ inches high and weighs 1200 pounds. Has a beautiful flowing mane and tail, with remarkable style and lofty carriage, a bold, open movement like his sire, but has never been handled for speed. He moves and looks like his sire, except that he is a larger horse.

CALIFORNIA NUTWOOD by Nutwood, record 2:18¾, has 37 trotters and pacers with records from 2:15 to 2:30, and put 8 in the 2:30 list in 1889. He is the only horse that ever lived with a record under 2:20 that produced five under 2:20. He is now serving mares at Dubuque, Iowa, at $500 for the season, and his colts at yearlings sell from $2500 to $5000 each. He is out of the dam of Maud S., record 2:08¾.

Nutwood, by Alexander's Belmont, sire of 32 with records from 2:15¼ to 2:30. Alexander's Belmont by Alexander's Abdallah, sire of Goldsmiths Maid, record 2:14, and 5 others in 2:30 list. Alexander's Abdallah, by Rysdyk's Hambletonian, sire of 41 with records from 2:17¼ to 2:30, and is the founder of the Hambletonian family.

FANNY PATCHEN, dam of California Nutwood, by George M. Patchen Jr., record 2:27, and sire of Wells Fargo, 2:18½, Sam Purdy 2:20½, Ben Ali 2:20¼, and 7 others from 2:24 to 2:30. He has 7 sons who together produced 12 trotters in 2:30 list, and 6 daughters who together produced 5 trotters and 1 pacer in 2:30 or better. He sired Alexander 2:31½. Alexander sired Alex. Button 2:26½; Alex. Button sired Yolo Maid, pacing record 2:14 at 4 years old, the fastest on record; George M. Patchen Jr., by George M. Patchen 2:23½, is sire of Lucy 2:18¼, and 3 others in the 2:30 list; he has 12 sons who together produced 40 trotters from 2:14¼ to 2:30, and 6 daughters who together produced 6 trotters in 2:30 list or better, he is grand sire of Hopeful 2:14¾, and best wagon record 2:16½, and sire of the granddam of Stamboul 2:12½.

George M. Patchen, by Cassius M. Clay, and he by Henry Clay, founder of the Clay family.

Laura, second dam of California Nutwood, was a fine large bay mare, a very fast roadster brought from Chicago by Wm. Wilson, of San Jose, and is said to have made a record of 2.35 in Chicago. Pedigree not traced.

TERMS.

$40 for the season, payable invariably before the animal is removed. Mares not proving in foal can be returned free next season. Pasturage $4 per month, but no liability for accidents or escapes.

For further particulars address the owner,

MARTIN CARTER,
Newark, Alameda Co., Cal., or Irvington, Alameda County, Cal.

Pedigrees Tabulated

IN THE MOST ARTISTIC MANNER,

Giving speed performers under sires and dams. Catalogues Compiled. Stallion Cards and Circulars written up ready for the press. Pedigree blanks for sale. Prices reasonable. Horses bought and sold on Commission. References furnished.

R. Y. HARDIN.
808 W. Madison St., Chicago, Ill.

Vineland Stock Farm

Alcona 730.

Sire of

FLORA BELLE - - - - Record 2:24
CLAY DUKE - - - - - " 2:31½

ALCONA will be a great sire, but four of his Colts have ever been trained, and all have shown full miles better than 2:30, and two of them as good as 2:20. Two of his first sons each sired a colt as a two-year-old, and last season one as a four-year-old trotted a full mile in 2:23¾, and the other, a three-year-old, a mile in 2:31. With opportunities, Alcona is destined to be one of Almont's best sons. Almont, for his opportunities, is beyond doubt the most prepotent sire of his age. He has 36 representatives in the 2:30 list; 49 sons and 21 daughters that have already produced 2:30 performers. Almont died five years ago at 20 years old. If he lived he would be but 25 years old.

PEDIGREE.

ALCONA sired by the great Almont (sire of Westmont 2:13¾, Fanny Witherspoon 2:16¾, Piedmont 2:17¼, and 31 others with records better than 2:30, and grandsire of Belle Hamlin 2:13¾, etc.); by Alexander's Abdallah (sire of Goldsmith Maid 2:14), he by Rysdyk's Hambletonian. Alcona's dam, Queen Mary, by Mambrino Chief (sire of Lady Thorne 2:18 1-4, and 5 others in the 2:30 list, and sire of the dams of Director 2:17, Piedmont 2:17¼, Onward 2:25 1-4, Red Wilkes Almont, Belmont and many other noted sires).

DESCRIPTION.

Alcona is a beautiful chestnut 16 2 1-2 hands high, and weighs 1300 lbs. His colts possess speed, style, finish and beauty, and if they don't trot they command the highest prices for carriage horses.

$50 for the season. Usual return privilege.

Season of Alcona and Grandissimo ends July 1st, 1890.

Grandissimo,

Full Brother to GRANDEE, 3-year old record 2:23 1-2.

Sired by La Grande (son of Almont, and out of Jessie Pepper by Mambrino Chief; Jessie Pepper is the dam of Iona 2:17 1-2, Alpha 2:23 1-2, Sterling Wilkes 2:31¾, and others) dam Norma, by Arthurton (sire of Arab 2:15, Joe Arthurton 2 2? 1-2, etc.)

Grandam Nourmahal (full sister to A. W. Richmond, sire of Arrow 2:13¾, Romero 2:19, and sire of Columbine, dam of Anteeo 2:16¾, and Antevolo 2:19¾ at four years old).

DESCRIPTION.

Grandissimo is four year old, will make a sixteen hand horse; he is a rich mahogany bay in color and perfect in style and action. $50 for the season. Usual return privileges.

"Grandissimo" with limited training last fall as a three-year-old, trotted quarters in 35 seconds and miles in 2:40.

I feel confident that he will trot fast this season, and will be a great sire as his colts this season are all grand youngsters.

The best of pasturage $4 per month. Mares taken care of in any manner that owners may desire, but no responsibility assumed for escapes or accidents.

For further particulars send for circular or call at stables, one mile south of St. Helena.

FRED W. LOEBER Prop'r.

The Trotting-Bred Stallion

RINGWOOD

THE FINEST SON OF THE NOTED SIDNEY,

Will make a Season at Oakland commencing March 1, and ending June 1, 1890.

DESCRIPTION.

RINGWOOD is a dark, rich colored bay, black points, 15 1-2 hands, weight 1100 lbs., and a pure gaited trotter. Has shown great speed. He is now five years old. As a four year old he showed a trial in 2:19 1-2, and but for an accident would have received a record as a four year old of 2:18 or better.

PEDIGREE.

RINGWOOD is by Sidney, record 2:19 3-4, and a half brother to Gold Leaf 2:11 1-4, Adonis 2:14, Fleet (two year old) 2:24, Longworth 2:19, Sister V. 2:27, Faustino, yearling, 2:36, Fleet, yearling, 2:35 Memo, three year old trial 2:2? 1 2.

Sidney is by Santa Claus, record 2:17 1-2; he by Strathmore, sire of 31 in 2:30 list; he by Hambletonian 10, the greatest of all producers; he by Abdallah. Sidney's dam, Sweetness, record 2:21 1-4; she by Volunteer, the sire of St. Julien 2:11 1-4.

RINGWOOD'S dam Alma; she by Dashway, thoroughbred; he by Belmont, he by American Boy; he by Sea Gull; he by imported Expedition. Alma's 1st dam, Fanny Cobb, was a great road mare, pedigree untraced.

TERMS: $50 for the Season.

Payable June 1st, or sooner if mares are taken away. Address Communications to

A. C. DIETZ,
Oakland, Cal.

The Trotting Stallion

CUPID,

Full Brother to Adonis 2:14,

—Sired by—

The Celebrated SIDNEY 2:19 3-4, and out of Venus.

Will make the season of 1890 at the OAKLAND TROTTING PARK.

PEDIGREE.

CUPID is by Sidney out of Venus by Capt. Webster 10173, record 2:30, and sire of Prestone 2:19. Second dam by Shenandoah 836, sire of Daisy Burns 2 19¾, Erwin Davis (sire of two in the 30 list) and dams of four in the 30 list.

DESCRIPTION.

Cupid is a handsome bright bay 15.2¼ hands high, weighs 1100 lbs.; was foaled in 1886. As a yearling, with very little work he showed quarters in 42 seconds, and at 2 years old, quarters in 38 seconds. As a three year old he has not been worked, but he shows the speed and endurance that must come from his excellent blood lines.

TERMS $50 for the season, with the usual return privilege. Good pasturage near the track at $5 per month. The best of care taken of mares in any way that owners may desire, but no responsibility assumed for accidents or escapes.

For further particulars address

C. O. THORNQUEST,
Oakland Trotting Park, or
C. BAAB, 972 Broadway, Oakland.

FOR SALE.

A Mohawk Chief BROODMAR[E]

and a

Director Colt, 6 months old.

For particulars address or apply to ANCON HOT[EL] 9 and 11 Pacific Street, San Francisco.

Stallions and Colt[s]

For Sale.

The Get of the Celebrated Racing Stalli[on] BAYSWATER, FROM FINELY BRED MARES.

Inquire of

J. HEINLEN,
Lemoore, Tulare County, Cal.

For Sale

A HALF BROTHER TO

ALMONT PATCHEN

(2:15, trial 2:13 3-4).

JUANITO JR. is a beautiful bright bay, bla[ck] points, with no white, foaled 1886. As a colt he h[as] given much more promise than did Almont Patch[en] at the same age. Instead of being a pacer, he is [a] good square trotter, with every indication of gre[at] speed, and is so gentle and kind, that a lady can dri[ve] him. The owner's only reason for selling him [is] that business calls him away from this section [of] the State. He will be sold at a reasonable figur[e]. This is a splendid opportunity for a gentleman [to] secure a first-class trotter at a very low figure.

The pedigree of Juanito Jr. is by Juanito (sire [of] Almont Patchen), dam Nettie Moore by Old To[m] Moore. For further particulars, address

JUANITO JR.,
Santa Clara P. O., Cal

For Sale

A FIRST-CLASS

Napa County Farm

—OR—

STOCK RANCH,

800 Acres Improved,

SITUATED TWO AND A HALF MILES FRO[M] NAPA CITY, with good roads leading thereto, good hard finished house of nine rooms, with all mod[ern] improvements, streams running all summer, great amount of live oak and black oak timber. [It] lies in a fruit belt, surrounded by fine vineyards an[d] orchards growing upon the same quality of soil as originally a part of this tract. About one-half hil[l] and one-half rolling land, but none of it is steep a[nd] all easily cultivated, splendidly situated for the bree[d]ing of fine horses. Price, $65 per acre. Further pa[r]ticulars given at this office.

BREEDER AND SPORTSMAN,
313 Bush St.

Pure Bred Clydesdale Mare[s]

TWO MARES (Full Sisters) Five and Six Years Old, Weighing About 1,900 lbs. Each.

Sire imp. BEN. LOMOND.
Dam's sire imp. GLANCER.

For particulars apply to

H. A. MAYHEW,
Niles, Alameda County.

Stallion for Sale

AT A BARGAIN.

Full Brother to Fairmont.

By Piedmont, dam Queen by Garibaldi—see Sta[te] Fair Edition of BREEDER AND SPORTSMA[N] September 14, 1889, for description of Fairmont—thr[ee] years old, solid bay. Can trot a 2:40 gait or bett[er]. Sound in every particular. Can be seen at Oakla[nd] Trotting Park, Oakland.

P. J. WILLIAMS.

Highland Farm,

LEXINGTON, KY,

Home of Red Wilkes.

Standard-bred Trotting Stoc[k]

For Sale,

Sired by Red Wilkes, Wilton, 2:19¾; Allandorf a[nd] Sentinel Wilkes, out of highly bred Standard Ma[res] of the most fashionable blood of the day.

W. C. FRANCE, Proprietor

HORSES PURCHASED ON COMMISSION.

THOROUGHBREDS A SPECIALTY.

Will select and buy, or buy selected Animals [for] all desiring, for reasonable compensation

KEEPS PROMISING YOUNGSTERS IN VIEW.

L. M. LASLEY, Stanford, Ky

References:—J. W. Guest, Danville, Ky.
B. G. Bruce, Lexington Ky.
S. H. Baughman, Stanford, Ky.
G. A. Lackey, Stanford, Ky.
Geo. McAlister, Stanford, Ky.
First National Bank, Stanford, Ky.

The Thoroughbred Stallion

Three Cheers

Will make the season of 1890 at

Sacramento.

PEDIGREE.

THREE CHEERS		
Imp. Hurrah	Newminster	Touchstone, by Camel
		Beeswing, by Dr. Syntax
	Jovial	Bay Middleton, by Sultan
		Sister to Grey Momus, by Comus
Young Fashion	imp. Monarch	imp. Priam, by Emilius
		imp. Delphine, by Whisker
	Fashion	imp. Trustee, by Catton
		Bonnets o' Blue, by Sir Charles

Hurrah was imported by John Reber, of Lancaster, Ohio, a locality where there were but few breeders of thoroughbreds. Under these disadvantages he sired a long list of winners. His sire Newminster, won the St. Ledger 1851, and his dam, Jovial by Bay Middleton, winner of the Derby 1836. Newminster by Touchstone, winner St. Ledger 1834. Dam Beeswing, winner of 54 races out of 64 starts, by Dr Syntax, winner of the Doncaster Cup. 1837—40—41—42, the only horse that ever accomplished that feat.

On the side of the dam Three Cheers is equally well related. Young Fashion was the dam of Surprise, Scotland (the only horse that ever beat Asteroid a heat), Liverpool. Columbia, and Bonnie Kate, the dam of Little Buttercup, and the flying Bonnie Lizzie. His grandam, Fashion was the greatest race mare of her day and beat Boston in that historical match at four mile heats, which is recorded as one of the greatest events in the annals of the turf.

Horsemen who are qualified to judge, pronounce Three Cheers to be the finest type of the Newminster line in America.

LOCATION.

THREE CHEERS will be located at the Arcade Training Stable, Rancho del Paso. This place has been selected for the reason that first class pasturage has been secured there for the exclusive use of these mares and the other facilities to be obtained there for the care of mares (especially mares in foal) are better than can be found elsewhere in the locality.

TERMS.

$60 for the season with the usual return privileges. Pasturage $6 per month. Mares cared for as owners may desire at bottom rates for grain and hay. All bills payable before the mare is removed.

Mares shipped care of WM. IRVINE, Pacific Stables, Sacramento, will be properly cared for and sent to the ranch without delay.

Three Cheers will be in charge of one of the most experienced and competent stud grooms in the State, who will exercise every care, but no reponsibility assumed for accidents or escapes.

For further particulars apply to Louis Crissler, at the ranch; Wm. Irvine, Pacific Stables, Second St., Sacramento; or to the owner,

E. S. CULVER,
313 Bush St., San Francisco.

Sunny Side Breeding Farm.

Admiral 488.

Foaled 1867—Sired by Volunteer 55. Son of Rysdyk's Hambletonian 10.

First dam Lady Pierson by Cassius M. Clay (Neaves') 20; second dam by Diamond; third dam a running mare said to be thoroughbred. He is fitted in an eminent degree to produce colts that will in all respects justify his patrons in their expectations.

Admiral is the sire of Huntress, record 2:27½, Sister, 2:19½, Perhelion, 2:25, Nona Y., 2:25, and others equally as promising, but have not had the advantage of track work. He will serve a limited number of approved mares at $50 the season, with usual return privilege. Season ending August 1, 1890. No liability for accidents or escapes.

KING DAVID 2576.

Bay Stallion—Foaled 1883.

Sired by Admiral 488, dam Black Flora (the dam of Huntress, 2:27½, Sister, 2:19½, Perhelion, 2:25, Nona Y., 2:25), by Black Prince.

King David is one of the best gets of Admiral. He has a good disposition, kind to drive, smooth and even-gaited, and can speed fast. Barring accidents, he will trot in the twenties this Fall. His colts are large, rangy, and well finished. Will serve a limited number of mares at $30 the season, to end July 1, 1890. Every precaution will be taken to prevent accidents and escapes, but no liability will be assumed. Pasturage $4 per month.

Sunny Side Farm is situated two miles east of Vallejo, on the Sulphur Spring road. For further particulars, address

FRANK DRAKE,
Vallejo, Cal.

LAWN VIEW BREEDING FARM STALLIONS.

ACTOR.

A beautiful bay horse foaled 1887 by Promptor 2305 sire of Apex (four-year-old record) 2:26, Transit 2:28¾, Creole 2:20, Blue Belle 2:32, Daisy (yearling record) 2 36¾, he by Blue Bull 75, 1st dam by Sultan 1513 2:24, sire of Stamboul 2:12 1-4, Ruby 2:19¾, Sweetheart 2:22½, Alcazar 2:20¾, Eva 2:23¾, La Grange 2:28¾, and eleven others in 2:30 list, second dam by Fireman by Langford.

Actor, as his pedigree shows, is as purely bred a young stallion as ever made a season in the stud. Blue Bull stock is much sought after in the East, and Sultan, sire of his first dam will make the season in Kentucky this year at $100 per mare. Actor is a handsome bay colt 16 hands high, clean limbed and possesses all the points of a speedy trotter.

TERMS, $40 FOR THE SEASON, usual return privileges.

DOUGLASDALE 7650.

Thoroughbred Registered Clydesdale Stallion

Imported from Scotland, December, 1889, bay, three years old.

TERMS, $35 FOR THE SEASON.

YOUNG ELMO

Two years old sorrel stallion by St. Elmo 2:27, dam by Woodburn.

TERMS, $20 FOR THE SEASON.

For further particulars, address
MANAGER LAWN VIEW FARM, Auburn, Cal.

2:10¾ 2:13¾ 2:10

DEXTER PRINCE.

This Royally-bred Stallion will make the Season of 1890 at the LIVE OAKS Breeding Farm, 2 miles from Lodi, San Joaquin County, Cal.

DESCRIPTION.

DEXTER PRINCE is a blood bay, 16 hands high, weighs over 1 100 pounds; has great power and substance, and the highest finish. When two years old, at Palo Alto, he was timed quarters by Gov. Stanford in 31¼ seconds, and he was driven eighths by Mr. Marvin at a faster rate of speed than that. He is a sure foal-getter, and invariably sires foals of good size, of fine form and finish, and the highest rate of speed.

PEDIGREE.

By KENTUCKY PRINCE, the sire of Guy, 2:10¾, Spofford, 2:18¾, Company, 2:19¾, Bayonne Prince, 2:21 1-4, Fred Folger, 2:20¾, and a score more in the 2:30 list.

First dam LADY DEXTER, full sister of the great set of trotters, Dexter, and the greatest of sires, Dictator, the sire of Director, 2:17, Phallas, 2:13¾, in a fourth heat, and Jay-Eye-See, 1:10.

Second dam Clara, the dam of Dexter, 2:17 1-4, Dida or, Astoria 2:28 1-4, and Almah, 2:28¾. Clara was by American Star, that has 34 daughters that have produced 2:30 or better trotters.

Third dam the McKinstry mare, the dam of Shark, 2 27¾. HAMBLETONIAN, the grandsire of DEXTER PRINCE, has 40 trotters in the 2:30 list, 44 daughters that have produced 2:30 trotters, and more than 100 sons that have sired 2 30 trotters.

CLARK CHIEF, the grandsire on the sire's side, was the sire of performing and producing sons and daughters.

DEXTER PRINCE has faster blood lines, on both sides, than any other stallion in the world—Guy 2:10¾, and Jay-Eye-See. 2:10.

KENTUCKY PRINCE is one of the best bred and speediest stallions in the world. David Bonner, in the presence of Governor Stanford, timed him when he trotted a 2:18 gait. He is by Clark Chief, one of the great broodmare sires; his first dam is Kentucky Queen by Morgan Eagle, son of Hale's Green Mountain Morgan, 2nd dam by Blythe's Whip. 3rd dam by Martin's Brummier, 4th dam by Quicksilver 880, on through the strongest thoroughbred blood.

TERMS.

$100 for the season, with usual return privileges. Payable before mares are removed. Good pasture, and the best care furnished, but no responsibility assumed for accidents.

PREMIUM.

$250 will be given to the first of the produce of DEXTER PRINCE put in the 2:30 list, and $100 each after the first. Address

L. M. MORSE, Lodi, Cal.

2:10 1-2 ELECTIONEER 2:12 1-4

BAY STALLION	BROWN STALLION
ECLECTIC	**MORTIMER**
11,321	5,346
By Electioneer, dam Manette (full sister to Woodnut 2.16 1-2 Manon 2:21 and Maple, dam of Hattie D., three year-old record 2 26¾) by Nutwood 2:18¾, etc., etc.	Four-year-old Record 2:27. By ELECTIONEER, dam MARTI, by Whipple's Hambletonian (sire of 16 in 2:30, and of dams of eight in 2:30). Second dam Ida Martin by Rifleman (sire of Col. Lewis 2:18¾).
Terms $100 for the Season.	Terms $60 for the Season.

Horses shipped via San Francisco may be consigned to J. W. MORSHEAD, City Front Stables, who will attend to their forwarding.

Season Closes JULY 1st, 1890. Usual return privileges.

For further particulars address owner,

WILFRED PAGE, Penns Grove,
Sonoma County, Cal

The Trotting Stallion

Silver Bow

Will make the season of 1890 at the Oakland Race Track

PEDIGREE.

SILVER BOW 11706, two-year-old record 2:37, is by Robert McGregor 647, 2:17½ (sire of Bonnie McGregor, 2:13¾, Earl McGregor, 2:21¾, Mac D., 2:30, McGregor Boy, 2:29¾, Mark Time, 2:30, Roxie McGregor, 2:20¾) by Major Edsall 2:29, by Alexander's Abdallah 15—sire of Goldsmith Maid, 2:14—by Hambletonian 10—sire of Dexter, 2:17¼.

Robert McGregor's dam was Nancy Whitman by American Star 14, by Stockholm's American Star.

SILVER BOW'S first dam is Sadie by Hambletonian 10, sire of Geo. Wilkes, 2:22—sire of Guy Wilkes, 2:15¼—also Electioneer, sire of Sunol, three-year-old record, 2:10½, and Palo Alto, 2:12¾; second dam Lady Wynne by Wm. Welch 341; third dam Elenora Margrave by imp. Margrave.

DESCRIPTION.

SILVER BOW is a handsome bay, no white; 15-2¼ hands high; weighs 1075 pounds; of fine form, with the best of legs and a clean-cut, intelligent head. Is remarkably level-headed, seldom making a break; wears seven-ounce shoes in front. His record, 2:37, is no mark of his speed; he can beat 30 easy, and with his gilt-edge breeding, he is just what he ought to be, a trotter sired by a trotter whose dam was herself a trotter and his grandam the dam of two trotters. His dam Sadie being by Hambletonian 10, shows him to be bred from the cream of the trotting blood.

TERMS: $100 for the season. Mares not proving in foal returnable for the season of 1891 free of charge. Good pasturage and first-class care taken of mares for $5 per month. No responsibilities assumed for escapes or accidents. For further particulars, address

Limited to 15 approved mares.
Season to end June 1st, 1890.

P. J. WILLIAMS,
Care Race Track, Oakland, Cal.

GRAND MOOR, 2374.

Grand Moor 2374	Moor 870. Sire of Beautiful Bells 2:29½; Sire of Sable (dam of Sable Wilkes) 2:18; Sire of Sultan 2:24; Sire of Tommy Gates 2:24; Sire of Del Sur 2:24¾; Sire of Sir Guy 2:28¾. Beautiful Bells is the dam of Hinda Rose, 2:19½ as a 3-year-old, Palo Alto Belle, 2:22¾, Chimes, St. Bell, 2:24¾, Bell Boy (3 years) 2:19¾. Sultan, 2:24 (sire of Stamboul 2:12¾) has 19 in 2:30 list.	Clay Pilot 93. Sire of 2 in 2:30 list.
		Belle of Wabash.
	Vashti. Dam of Don Tomas, who got a record of 2:30 in 1889.	Mambrino Patchen 58. Sire of 14 in 2:30 list. Sire of the dam of Guy Wilkes, 2:15¼; also sire of 20 stallions and 18 mares with get in 2:30 list.
		Kate Taber. By Mambrino Messenger, he by Mambrino Paymaster.

Foaled 1876. Black. Sixteen hands high. Bred by L. J. Rose

A horse of highest form and quality; of great excellence in every point; a type of his celebrated family: of marked individuality, spirit and endurance; never properly trained or raced, but shows the possession of great speed; perfectly manageable in the stable and on the road and track.

As he is sired by The Moor 870, a son of CLAY PILOT, out of Vashti by MAMBRINO PATCHEN, he is a most valuable cross for mares of other families. THE MOOR sired Beautiful Bells and the dams of Sable Wilkes and Margaret 2:28 (dam of Regal Wilkes, 2-year-old record 2:20½).

MAMBRINO PATCHEN is regarded as the unsurpassed sire of broodmares, having, among many others, sired the dam of Guy Wilkes and of Wm. L (the sire of Axtell), and a son of his sired the dam of Axtell. The public sales this year have demonstrated with renewed emphasis the value of The Moor and Mambrino Patchen strains of blood. For combining particularly with the Hambletonians it may be called "the ready money cross."

GRAND MOOR will make the season of 1890 for a time at the Oakland Race Track and afterwards at my Ranch, fifteen miles from Oakland. Mares can be delivered at the race track to the groom in charge. Pasture at $5 per month. For other food, if requested, an additional charge will be made.

TERMS, $150 for the season, with privileges of return if the horse does not change hands.

Every care exercised, but no liability for escapes or accidents.

H. I. THORNTON, 504 Kearny Street.

Cook STOCK FARM.

Season of 1890.

STEINWAY 1808.

Three-Year-Old Record 2:25 3-4.

Sire of STRATHWAY, three year old record 2:26, and sire of the dam of BOURBON RUSSELL 2:30.

By STRATHMORE 408; sire of 31 in the 2:30 list; sire of 4 dams of 8 in the 2:30 list, and sire of 3 sires of 8 in 2:30 list.

1st dam ABBESS (dam of Solo 2:28, and Soprano, dam of C. F Clay 2:18, Eminence 2:27 and Strathbridge, 3 year old record 2:28½) by ALBION, sire of VANITY FAIR 2:24½, and of the dam of FAVORITE 2:25½.

2nd dam by MARSHALL NEY.

3rd dam by BERTRAND, a son of SIR ARCHY.

TERMS—$100 for the season.

CHARLES DERBY 4907

Brown Horse, Foaled 1885.

By STEINWAY 1808.

1st dam by the great ELECTIONEER, sire of SUNOL 3 year old record 2:10½, Palo Alto 2:12¼, etc., etc.

2nd dam FANNY MALONE, by NIAGARA.

3rd dam FANNY WICKHAM, by HERALD.

4th dam by Imp. TRUSTEE.

TERMS—$100 for the season

Pasturage $6 per month. Accidents and escapes at owner's risk. Mares consigned to the farm should be sent to Fashion Stables, Oakland; Geary & Grindle's Stable, Haywards; or to Bennett's Stable, Martinez; from and to which places they will be delivered, free of charge. Address

COOK STOCK FARM,
Danville, Contra Costa, Co., Cal.

The Trotting Stallion

G & M

FULL BROTHER TO

ALFRED G, 2:19¾.

(Who has been taken to Kentucky to stand at $200)

Will make the season of 1890 from FEBRUARY 1st to JULY 1st, at

SANTA ROSA.

G. & M. is by Anteeo, 2:16¾; was foaled 1886; first dam Rosa B. by Speculation (son of Hambletonian 10); 2d dam Elizabeth by Alexander 477; 3d dam Nora by imp. Glencoe. Anteeo is by Electioneer, out of Columbine by A. W. Richmond 1687.

G. & M. is a handsome dark bay; stands 15-2 1-2 hands high, and weighs 1060 pounds. Gameness, soundness, speed and stamina are indelibly impressed in every line of the pedigree of G. & M. Owners of broodmares in search of these qualities, will do well to patronize this promising colt.

PHILOSOPHER,

Foaled 1886 by Pilot Wilkes 2967; first dam Bella by George Wilkes 519; second dam by Bell Morgan 61.

Philosopher's sire, Pilot Wilkes 2967, is by George Wilkes 519, dam Grace (the dam of Alice Woodburn etc.), by Pilot Jr. 12, grandam by Orphan Boy.

Will make the season of 1890, from FEBRUARY 1st to JULY 1st, at Santa Rosa.

TERMS for the season:

G. & M., $50.

PHILOSOPHER, $30,

with privilege of returning mares that do not prove in foal the next season free of charge, provided the horse bred to remains the property of the present owners. Good pasturage at $3 per month. No responsibility assumed for accidents or escapes. Service fees payable before removal of the mare. For further particulars, address

GEO. E. GUERNE,
Santa Rosa Cal.

PASHA,

Registered No. 2039.

RECORD 2:36.

SIRE OF MORO 2:27.

Will make the present season at Linden, twelve miles east of STOCKTON.

Season commencing FEBRUARY 1st and ending JULY 1, 1890.

DESCRIPTION.

PASHA is a beautiful black; 16½ hands high, and weighs 1,240 pounds. He is a horse of beautiful symmetry and magnificent action.

PEDIGREE.

PASHA was sired by Sultan 1513, sire of Stamboul 2:12½, Ruby 2:19½, Alcazar 2.20½. Bay Rose 2:20½, and sixteen others with records below 2:30. First dam Madam Baldwin by The Moor 870; second dam Ben Lippincott by Belmont. Pasha is a full brother to Bay Rose, record 2:20½.

Sultan, by The Moor, sire of Beautiful Bells, dam of Hinda Rose, 2:19½, Bell Boy 2:19½, and Sable, dam of Sable Wilkes, three-year-old record 2:18. First dam Sultana, by Delmonico, sire of Derby 2:16, by Guy Miller, sire of Whipple's Hambletonian. Second dam by Mambrino Chief. Third dam by Downing's Bay Messenger. Fourth dam Miss Caudle, dam of Ericsson, four-year-old record 2:30½.

Terms for the season, $50

With privilege of returning mares that do not prove in foal next season free of charge.

Good pasturage at $2 per month No responsibility will be assumed for accidents or escapes Service fee payable before the removal of the mare.

For further particulars, address

D. BRYSON,
Linden Cal

MEMO.

The Best Son of SIDNEY

Will Make the Season of 1890 at the OAKLAND RACE TRACK

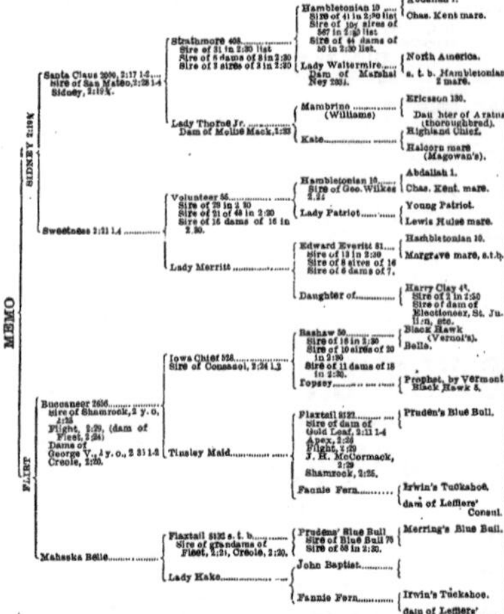

MEMO is, as can be seen at a glance, one of the best bred young stallions in service, having three crosses of Rysdyk's Hambletonian and one of Harry Clay, the sire of Green Mountain Maid (dam of Electioneer, etc.), while Long Island Black Hawk and Flaxtail also contribute to his blood. Sidney (Memo's sire) is universally known as the best young sire in the world, a producer of extreme speed at an early age.

PERFORMANCES.

MEMO trotted in public in his two year-old form, obtaining a record of 2:49, though he was close to Grandee in a race on the Bay District Track, the second heat of which was made in 2:31 1-2, the first in 2:3 . He exhibited phenomenal speed when three years old, and had it not been for a slight strain of his fore fetlock, there is little question the he would have shown in public very close to the best record. On the Oakland track he was timed a mile in 2:29 1-2, and frequently trotted quarters in from 31 1-2 to 34 seconds.

As a four-year-old Memo only started once at Sacramento when, although out of condition, he showed great speed, and improving as he went on, great hopes were entertained of his going well down in the 'teens at the P. C. T. H. B. A. meeting, but after showing several very fast miles his leg filled and he was laid up for the season. He is sixteen hands high, and of powerful build throughout. His color is a glossy black, with both fore-feet white. His disposition is all that could be desired, and his action superb. He is a sure foal getter, only one mare being reported not in foal during his last season.

TERMS, $1?0, with usual return privileges, for a limited number of mares. Season to close JUNE 15th, when he will be prepared for track purposes. Pasturage $4 per month. have leased the cricket ground adjoining the track for pasturage, where there is fine feed. Reasonable charges if fed hay and grain. Best of care taken of mares in any manner owners may desire, but positively no responsibility assumed for accidents or escapes. For further particulars address

J. P. KERR, 313 Bush Street, San Francisco,

or, JOHN ROWEN, Race Track, Oakland, Cal.

HOLLYWOOD BREEDING FARM.

MOUNTAIN BOY 4841.

Br s MOUNTAIN BOY, 4841, bred by Charles Backman, Orange County, New York, foaled 1882, sire Kentucky Prince 2470, dam Elise, sister to Elaine, by Messenger Duroc 106; grandam Green Mountain Maid, 3d dam, Shanghai Mary, will serve a limited number of mares at $100 the season.

ELECTION.

Bay stallion ELECTION, bred at Senator Stanford's Palo Alto Stock farm, foaled 1884, sire Electioneer, dam Lizzie H. by Whipple's Hambletonian 725, grandam Lizzie Harris (by Comus son of Green's Bashaw 50), great grandam by Arnold Harris, thoroughbred.

Election is one of the handsomest bloodlike sons of Electioneer and with his thoroughbred cross through Arnold Harris should prove invaluable as a sire. TERMS, $100 the season.

KAFIR.

B c KAFIR, bred by L. J. Rose, Los Angeles, foaled 1887, sire Alcazar, 2:20½, dam Flower Girl by Arthurton, sire of Arab, 2:15, grandam Flora by General McClellan, 144, sire of three in 2:30 list, great grand dam by Langford, he by Williamson's Belmont, will serve a limited number of mares at $50 the season.

WOODSIDE.

Ch c WOODSIDE, sire Woodnut, 2:16½; 1st dam Veronica by Alcona, 730; 2nd dam Fontana by Almont, 33; 3rd dam Fannie Williams by Alexander's Abdallah, 15. Book full.

MART BOORHEM.

B c MART BOORHEM, by Sydney, 2:19¾; 1st dam Towhead by Echo. This colt is a full brother to St. Nicholas who showed a mile in 2:27½ at three years old. TERMS, $25 the season.

REVEILLE.

The well known thoroughbred stallion REVEILLE, by Shiloh, dam by Norfolk. Reveille is a brother to John Treat and is the sire of Tycoon and Gladstone. TERMS, $25 the season.

Hollywood is nicely situated three miles from Vallejo on the Napa road. Good pasturage and every care will be taken of mares at reasonable rates. For further particulars, apply,

B. C. HOLLY, Vallejo.

Langtry Farms' Stud

Imp. FRIAR TUCK

By the Immortal HERMIT

DAM ROMPING GIRL BY WILD DAYRELL,

AT $50 THE SEASON.

Mares not proving with foal may be returned the following season. Good care taken of mares, but no liabilities for accidents or escapes.

Good Pasturage at $5 per month.

Mares shipped to ST. HELENA, care CHARTES WILLIAM ABY, St. Helena Stables, will be cared for. For further particulars address,

CHAS. WILLIAM ABY,
Middletown, Lake County, Cal.

GROVER CLAY

Bay Stallion, Black Points,

15 3-4 hands high.

Bred by W. W. Traylor, San Francisco.

BY ELECTIONEER.

First dam Maggie Norfolk by Norfolk, son of Lexington, he by Boston. Second dam Tilda Quill by Billy Cheatham he by Cracken, and he by Boston. Third dam by Dorsey's Golddust.

TERMS.

Will make the season of 1890 at the Training Stables of Denis Gannon, near Oakland Trotting Park, at $50 the season, payable at time of service. Season to commence February 1st and ending July 1st. Proper care of mares will be taken, but no responsibility incurred for accidents or escapes. Address,

DENIS GANNON, Oakland, Cal.

Pleasanton Stock Farm Co.'s Stallions.

DIRECTOR, 2:17.

Director's book is open for 15 good mares more than already booked for the season of 1890, at $300 each.

This is the cheapest service fee ever charged for a stallion, taking into consideration his BREEDING and RACE RECORD and the RACE RECORDS OF HIS COLTS.

Season to commence February 15th and close August 1st.

CORRECTOR, Five Years Old.

Sire Director 2:17, dam Brainey, she by Echo. Echo sired by Rysdyk's Hambletonian out of Fanny Felter, by Magnolia he by Seely's American Star. Brainey's dam Lady Dudley, she by Tom Dudley by Blacknose, a son of Medoc, he by American Eclipse. Lady Dudley's dam by Bertrand, Jr., a son of Bertrand.

CORRECTOR is a rich seal brown 16½ hands high, and is the fastest young stallion in the world under the same conditions, never having been off the farm where raised and never been shod or driven for speed before last Christmas, and can trot quarters now in 35 seconds, a 2:20 gait.

He will be allowed to serve ten good mares, at $100 each for the season, which closes June 1st.

DECORATOR, Four Years Old.

Sire Director 2:17, dam Chess, sired by Cardinal 2.37, trial 2:28, he by Gen. Gifford's Morgan, dam of Cardinal, sired by Joe Gales of Ohio, he by Marlborough out of the Duchess of Marlborough by Southern Eclipse; second dam old Duchess of Marlborough by Sir Archy; third dam by imp Diomed. Decorator's second dam a Morgan and Messenger mare.

Decorator is a light bay 16 hands high, and with but little handling for speed has shown eighths in 17½ seconds, a 2:20 gait.

He will be allowed to serve ten good mares at $50 each for the season, which closes June 1st.

Mares not proving with foal may be returned next season free of charge of service fees to the same stallion, if he is still in our possession; however, the company reserves the right to return the fee instead of giving service.

Pasturage $4 per month; hay and grain extra. Accidents and escapes at owner's risk.

Service fees due at time of service, and must be paid, together with pasturage, etc., before mares are taken away, or a good approved note given, payable August 1st, 1890, at which date all bills must be settled.

For further information call or address **M. SALISBURY, 320 Sansome Street, Room 26, San Francisco, or**

PLEASANTON STOCK FARM CO.,
Pleasanton, Alameda Co., Cal.

SOUTHER FARM

P. O. Box 208. San Leandro, Cal.

1½ miles northwest of San Leandro; 8 miles southeast of Oakland. Turn off County road between above places at "Stanley Road," ½ mile north of San Leandro.

Horses boarded at all times in any manner desired. Best of care but no responsibility for accidents. Colts broken and handled for he road or track. Terms reasonable.

Glen Fortune,	Jester D,	El Benton,	Figaro,
By Electioneer.	By Almont.	By Electioneer.	Hambletonian 725
$50 for 1889.	$50 for 1890.	Limited to 5 mares.	Limited to 12 mares
		Book Full.	Book Full.

THE SOUTHER FARM

Has Green Feed the Year Round,

and feeds Hay in connection with the green feed, which a horse must have if he is to thrive. Every animal is given

A Dry, Warm Place to Sleep,

No matter how stormy the weather. All Stock under cover when it rains.

VISITORS WELCOME ANY DAY EXCEPT SUNDAY.

How to Get Stock to the Souther Farm.

The Souther Farm is one and a half miles northeast of San Leandro and eight miles southeast of Oakland. The stables are about one mile east of the county road, which runs between Oakland and San Leandro. The place to turn off is at Stanley Road, where a large signboard of the farm is placed. Guide boards will be found at every cross road. In any ordinary weather the roads are very good, and they are fairly good after the unusually heavy rainfall of the past winter.

All stock sent from San Francisco may be brought over by Gorris's Express, No. 8 Market street, San Francisco. They also have an order box outside of Hawley Bros.' Hardware house on the corner of Market and Beale streets. The express leaves San Francisco on the Creek route boat, which starts at 1:3 , but all orders should be in the order box at Market and Beale streets by 10 o'clock, or at the office, No. 8 Market street, by 11 o'clock at the latest. In the case of very young or very valuable horses, the Souther Farm will send reliable men to lead or drive over any stock that will not lead behind a wagon. A small charge will be made in such cases, to cover the extra expense incurred.

Horses are very easily taken from Oakland to the farm, and where it is inconvenient for owners to bring them or send them, the farm will send after anything that is to come. On horses that stay three months or over there is no charge for getting or delivering. Where a horse stays a short time the actual time and expense only is charged to him.

Horses can be shipped by rail from almost all parts of the State to San Leandro. Always notify the Farm several days before shipping anything, and then men will be on hand to receive stock on arrival. The railroad station is but two miles from the Souther Farm, and the agent invariably gives immediate notice of the arrival of any stock consigned to the above farm, but when word is sent to the farm in good season by letter or telegram, the animals sent are saved waiting a couple of hours in the car.

Passenger trains leave San Francisco (from the broad gauge ferry) and First and Broadway, Oakland, at frequent intervals during the day. There are several trains from San Jose to San Leandro on both the broad and narrow gauge railroads; the broad gauge, by way of Niles, is much more convenient for getting to the farm. There are trains each day from Sacramento, Stockton and Livermore to San Leandro. In ordinary weather it is a short and pleasant drive from Oakland to the Souther Farm or from San Francisco to the Farm by way of the Creek route ferry boat. Always notify the Souther Farm just when you will arrive at San Leandro, and some one will meet you at the station. If you do not recognize the farm conveyance ask the stage driver, who will point it out.

Write to the above address for references, circulars and price lists. Terms reasonable.

GILBERT TOMPKINS, Proprietor.

SAN MATEO STOCK FARM

HOME OF GUY WILKES,

Record, 2:15 1-4.

Guy Wilkes' Book is full for 1890 and 1891, and positively no more mares will be received.

Sable Wilkes, three-year-old record 2:18, will be allowed to serve 25 mares in addition to those already engaged at $250 the season of 1890. SABLE Wilkes, 15½ hands, black horse, by Guy Wilkes, first dam Sable by The Moor; second dam Gretchen by Mambrino Pilot; third dam Kitty Kirkman by Canada Chief; fourth dam by Fanning's Tobe; fifth dam by imp. Leviathan.

Leo Wilkes, brown horse, four years, 16 hands, full brother to Sable Wilkes, will be allowed to serve 30 mares at $100 the season

Mares not proving with foal may be returned the following season free of service fee. Parties engaging the services of any of the above horses must send a deposit of 10 per cent. of service money with engagement. Pasturage $6 per month, and when the condition of the animal requires it, hay or grain, or both, are fed, the charge will be $12 50 per month. Good care will be taken of all mares sent to the Farm, but no liability will be assumed for accidents or escapes.

All bills are due at time of service, but must be paid by August 1st of each year. No stock will be allowed to leave the place until all bills are paid.

WILLIAM CORBITT.
San Mateo Stock Farm.

2:08 3-4 2:10 2:12

MAMBRINO WILKES, 6083.

SIRE OF

GUS WILKES, 2:22; ALPHEUS, 2:27; CLARA P, 2:29½; BALKAN, 2:29½ (3-year-old) and timed separately 2:22½ in 4-year-old Stake, Bay District Track, October 14, 1889.

DESCRIPTION.

Black; sixteen hands; weighs, in exercise, 1,260 lbs. For style, finish, symmetry and proportion, comparison is challenged with any trotting bred horse. His colts follow in size, style and beauty. Balkan, for instance, being "facile princeps" of trotters in these particulars.

PEDIGREE.

Sired by Geo. Wilkes, sire of Harry Wilkes, 2:13¼, Guy Wilkes, 2:15¼, and 60 other trotters in the 2:30 list, in addition to 6 pacers, and of the sire of Axtell, 2:12 (three-year-old) beating all stallions of any age, and the sire of Regal Wilkes, 2:20¾, best two-year-old stallion record.

First dam Lady Chrisman by Mambrino (Todhunter's, son of Mambrino Chief 11; sire of Lady Thorn, 2:18¼; Woodford Mambrino, 2:21½, and four others in 2:30, and of the dams of Director, 2:17, Piedmont, 2:17¼, Onward, 2:25¼, etc.

Second dam by Pilot Jr. 12, sire of nine in the 2:30 list, and of the dams of Maud S., 2:08¾, Jay-Eye-See, 2:10, Nutwood, 2:18¾, Viking, 2:19¼, Pilot Boy, 2:20, Naiad Queen, 2:20¼, etc.

TERMS.

Mares from a distance will be received at the Dexter Stables, Oakland, or Livery Stable, Martinez, the owner notifying Smith Hill, Superintendent at the farm. Good pasture and plenty of water. For the purpose of placing the service of a Wilkes within reach of breeders, the same rate will be maintained as last year, to wit, $75 for the season. Although it is not admitted thereby that this horse is inferior as a producer to the horses whose fees are placed at from $150 to $500. Address

SMITH HILL,
San Miguel Stock Farm,
Walnut Creek, Contra Costa Co., Cal.

2:12¾ 2:13½ 2:15¼

The Trotting Stallion

VICTOR,

Record 2:22.

Will make the season of 1890 at NAPA CITY.

DESCRIPTION.

VICTOR is a handsome dark bay; 15.3 hands high; weighs about 1,100 pounds, and is remarkably intelligent, level-headed of kind disposition, and a magnificent animal in every respect. He is well boned and muscled, of splendid conformation, and possesses the qualities of speed and endurance to an eminent degree—qualities that he imparts to his progeny.

PEDIGREE.

VICTOR, record 2:22
- Echo 462
  - Hambletonian 10, Sire of 42 in the 2:30 list.
    - Abdallah 1
    - Chas. Kent mare
  - Fanny Felter
    - Magnolia 88
    - by Webber's Kentucky Whip
- Daughter of
  - Woodburn
    - Lexington
    - Lulu Horton
  - daughter of
    - Ashland
    - thoroughbred

ECHO is the sire of Belle Echo, 2:20, Senator, 2:21¼, Victor, 2:22, Gibraltar, 2:22¼, Echora, 2:23¼, Tippie, 2:25¼, Lohengrin, 2:27¼, Pasha, 2:27¼, Kiluonte, 2:29, Col. Hawkins, 2:29¼, Annie Laurie, 2.30, Economy, 2:30, Sam Lewis, pacer, 2:25.

TERMS—$60 FOR THE SEASON.

Mares not proving with foal may be returned next season free of charge, provided the horse remains the property of the present proprietor, and stands at the same place, otherwise money will be refunded. The best of care taken of mares in any manner that owners may desire, but no responsibility assumed for accidents or escapes. For further particulars, apply to or address

G. W. HUGHES, Agent,
G. A. DOHERTY, Proprietor. Napa City.

The Fast Trotting Stallion

REDWOOD.

Four-Year-Old Record 2:24 1-2

Will make the season of 1890—February 1st to July 1st—at

SANTA ROSA.

REDWOOD is a dark bay colt, 15.2¼ hands high, weighs 110 lbs. Foaled in 1885 by Anteeo, 2:16¼, sire of Alfred G., 2 19¼. Anteeo is by Electioneer. First dam Lou Milton, by Milton Medium; second dam Old Fly, a thoroughbred mare brought from the East in 1871 by W. C. Ralston, Esq.

Redwood's sire was out of Columbine by A. W. Richmond, the sire of the pacers Arrow 2:13¼, and Elwood 2:23, and the trotters Romero, 2:19¼, and Len Rose, 2:27. Redwood has shown a quarter in 33 seconds

Terms $100

For the season. Mares not proving with foal may be returned next season free of charge, provided Redwood remains the property of the present owners. Good pasturage at reasonable rates. No responsibility assumed for escapes or accidents. Service fees payable before removal of the mare. Limited to 40 approved mares. For further particulars address

A. McFADYEN.
Santa Rosa, Cal.

2:19 NOONDAY $2:20\frac{1}{2}$

STANDARD No. 10,000.

This celebrated trotting bred stallion will make the season of 1890 at the stable of the undersigned at Sacramento, Cal., at $75 for the season and $100 to insure a mare in foal. Payable on or before July 1st, 1890. Money will be refunded on mares bred by insurance as soon as the fact becomes known that they are not in foal.

NOONDAY.
- Wedgewood, 2:19, Sire of Favonia, 2:15, fastest 4th heat for any mare or gelding, and eight others in 2:27 or better.
  - Belmont, Sire of Wedgewood, 2:19, Nutwood, 2:18¾, Viking, 2:19¼, and 29 others in 2:30 list.
    - Alexander's Abdallah, sire of Goldsmith Maid, 2.14; Almont, with 35 horses in 2:30 list, etc.
    - Belle, dam of Hambletonian, 2:26½; B'cara, dam of Pancoast, 2:21¾, the sire of Patron, 2:14¼.
  - Woodbine, Dam of Wedgewood, 2:19, Woodford Mamb., 2:21½, the sire of Pancoast, 2:21¾, the sire of Patron, 2:14¼.
    - Woodford.
    - Singleton Mare.
- Noontide, 2:20½ (Trial, 2:13½).
  - Harold, Sire of Maud S., 2:08¾, and 26 others in 2:30 list.
    - Hambletonian (Rysdyk's), sire of George Wilkes, 2:22, the sire of Guy Wilkes, 2:15¼; Electioneer, the sire of Sunol, 2:10½, and scores of noted trotters and producers.
    - Enchantress, by Abdallah 1.
  - Midnight, Dam of Jay-Eye-See, 2:10, Noontide, 2:20½.
    - Pilot Jr., sire of dams of Maud S., 2:08¾, Jay-Eye-See, 2:10, Nutwood, 2:18¾, etc.
    - Twilight, by Lexington, sire of the dam of Ansel, 2:20.

NOODAY is a dark seal brown, foaled 1884, 16 hands 1¼ inches high. Individually he is equal to his royal breeding. He is all that can be desired in conformation, intelligence, color and trotting action, and no stallion now in public service can show a pedigree with such fast records and royal game trotting blood as Noonday.

DON MARVIN,

Record 2:28 as a five-year-old. Standard by Breeding and Performance

Standard No. 7927.

Don Marvin 2:28.

Don Marvin is a beautiful seal brown, foaled 1884, bred by Hon. Leland Stanford, Palo Alto, Cal., standing 16 hands, and weighs, in ordinary condition, 1200 lbs. He is a fine individual, good style and form, combined with great substance, and good temper. Is very level headed; in his first race the past season he only made one break in five closely contested heats. He has great speed and endurance, with the pure, rapid Electioneer gait. He trots without toe weights, and wears only 8 oz. shoes in front. He gained his record the past season in the third heat, on a slow track, after making a season (serving over 30 mares), with scarcely any preparation. His record is no mark of his speed. He was a natural born trotter, and Mr. Charles Marvin considered him the fastest two year old at Palo Alto that season.

By FALLIS, 2:23, - - by Electioneer, sire of
Sire of Don Marvin, 2:28. — Sunol, three-year-old, 2:10 1-2, Palo Alto, 2:12¾, and 47 others in 2:30 list.

Dam CORA, by Don Victor by Belmont, sire of
Dam of Don Marvin, 2:28. — Ventura, 2:27¼, and sire of the dam of Bell Echo, 2:20, and six others in 2:30 list.

2d dam CLARABEL, - by Abdallah Star,
Dam of Clifton Bell, 2:24 1-2, and grandam of Rexford, three years, 2:24. — Sire of Hattie Maples, 2:28.

3d dam FAIRY, - - by Rysdyk's Hambletonian,
Sister of Sweepstakes, sire of 16 in 2 30 list. — Sire of Electioneer, George Wilkes, and many other noted sires and trotters.

4th dam EMMA MILLS, by Seely's American Star,
Dam of 4 horses that have 2:30 performers. — The great broodmare sire of the world.

The above pedigree should show every intelligent breeder that Don Marvin is "high" bred though very strong in trotting blood. All the comment it is deemed necessary to make as to the value of "thoroughbred blood" in the trotter is simply to refer to the very significant fact that the first and second dams of Maud S., 2 08¾, Jay-Eye-See 2:10, Sunol, three years 2:10 1-2, Palo Alto 2:12¾, Anteeo 2:16¼, Nutwood 2:18¾, Wedgewood 2:19, and many other successful sires and sensational trotters of the day are thoroughbred.

TERMS—Don Marvin will make the ensuing season from February 1st to July 1st, 1890, at $40 the season, with the usual privilege of returning the mare next season if not proving in foal. Mares from a distance met at the cars or boats on notification, and carefully handled, but no responsibility assumed for accidents or escapes.

Good alfalfa pasture furnished (free from barb wire fence) at $4 per month. For further particulars or complete circulars address

F. P. LOWELL,
1520 F Street, Sacramento, Cal.

The Produce of Eros Averaged $2,200 Each at New York Auction Sale in 1889.

THE ELECTIONEER TROTTING STALLION,

5326 EROS 5326

Will make the season of 1890—February 1st to July 1st—at LA SIENTA RANCH, MENLO PARK, adjoining Palo Alto.

PEDIGREE.

EROS (5326)
Standard by his sire
" " dam
" " record
" " produce
" under all rules

EROS (5326)
- Electioneer, Grandsire of Norlaine, 1 yr., 2:31 1-2, Sire of Sunol, 2 yrs., 2.18, Sunol, 3 yrs., 2:10 1-2, Hinda Rose, 4 yrs., 2:16, Palo Alto, 2:12¾.
  - Hambletonian 10, Sire of Dictator, George Wilkes, Happy Medium, and 40 others in 2:30 list, and grandsire of 728 in list.
    - Abdallah 10, Sire of the dams of Goldsmith Maid, 2 14, and 7 other producing dams.
    - Charles Kent mare By imp. Bellfounder.
  - Green Mountain Maid, Dam of Prospero, 2:20, Elaine, 2:20, Dame Trot, 2:22, Elieta, 2:22¼, Storm, 2:26¼, Antonio, 2:28¼, Miranda, 2.31, Mansfield, 2.26.
    - Harry Clay, Sire of the dams of St. Julien, 2:11¼, Bodine, 2 19¼, and 17 more in 2:30 list
    - Shanghai Mary.
- Sontag Mohawk, Dam of Eros, 2:29 1-2, Sport, 2:22¼, Sallie Benton, 2:17¾, Conductor, trial, 2:26, Colma, 3-y-o trial, 2:24.
  - Mohawk Chief, Sire of the dams of Lot Slocum, 2:17½, Sallie Benton, 4 yrs., 2:17¾, Pedlar, 2 yrs., 2 27¾, Stanford, 4 yrs., 2:30, Eros, 6th heat, 2:29 1-2.
    - Hambletonian 10, Sire of the dams of Stamboul, 2:12½, Wilton, 2:19¼, and 20 other trotters.
    - Lady Perrine
  - Sontag Nellie
    - Toronto Sontag By Toronto Chief,
    - Nellie Gray 5-mile record, 13:45.

Produce of Eros
Wanda, 4 yrs., 2 21.
Solita, 3 yrs., 2 41 1-2.
Meriquita, 2yrs., 2:42.
Daylight, 2 yrs., 2:44.
Hiram B., trial, 2:28.

These are the only colts by him that have ever had a harness on except one in New York that went a trial last July in 2:26 1:2.

DESCRIPTION.

EROS is a rich seal brown stallion, bred by Hon. Leland Stanford at Palo Alto, and is the nearest living likeness of his celebrated sire, Electioneer. Stands 15.2 hands high, and weighs 1050 pounds

In breeding to Eros, the owners of mares will strictly follow the great rule of breeding, viz., breed to a stallion by a producer and out of a sure producer of great speed. Eros is by the stallion that has produced more 2:30 trotters that any living horse, and is also the sire of more 2:30 performers than any horse living or dead.

EROS is out of the dam of Sally Benton, four years old, record 2:17¾, Sport 2:22¼, and Eros 2:29½ in the sixth heat, against a field of nine horses. He is from a family that is endowed with great natural speed, trot fast at an early age, train on, throw trotters from all classes of mares, are of good substance, bone, style and action, and breed solid colors.

TERMS.

$100 for the season, with the privilege of return next season should mares not be in foal and horse and mare still remain in the same hands.

Good pasturage can be obtained at $5 per month, but no responsibility for accidents or escapes. There are a large number of box stalls, and animals can be kept up and fed on hay and grain at reasonable rates if required. Mares already in foal can be sent to the ranch for foaling, and will receive all the attention bestowed upon our own mares. Mares left with Mr. Peter Pomyea, Broadway Street Stable, Oakland, or with Mr. F. H. Burke, 401 Montgomery Street, San Francisco, will be forwarded to the ranch free of charge. For further particulars apply to

W. H. VIOGET,
LA SIENTA RANCH, MENLO PARK, CAL.

EROS is the only stallion offered to the public on this Coast that has a dam that has three in the 2:30 list.

POPLAR GROVE

Breeding Farm

STALLIONS.

CLOVIS, 4909,

CLOVIS is a beautiful black, Eight Years Old, 16 1-2 Hands High, and weighs 1260 lbs.

He is a horse of beautiful symmetry and magnificent action.

PEDIGREE.

CLOVIS was sired by Sultan, 2:24, sire of Stamboul, 2:12 1-4, Ruby, 2:19¾, and fifteen others with records of 2.30 or better.

First dam Sweetbriar by Thorndale 2:22 1-2, sire of Edwin Thorne, 2:16 1-2, Daisy Dale, 2.19, and May Thorne, 2.22

Second dam Ulster Queen, dam of Volmer, 2:24¼, by Hambletonian 10. Sire of Dexter, 2 17¼, George Wilkes, 2:22.

Third dam by Thomas Jefferson, a son of Mambrino Paymaster, Jr.

Fourth dam by Mambrino Paymaster, sire of Mambrino Chief.

Sultan, by The Moor, sire of Beautiful Bells, dam of Hinda Rose, 2:19 1-2, and Sable, dam of Sable Wilkes, three year old record 2:18.

First dam of Sultan, Sultana, by Delmonica. Sire of Darby, 2.16 1 2, by Guy Miller, sire of Whipple's Hambletonian.

Second dam by Mambrino Chief.

Third dam by Downing's Bay Messenger.

Fourth dam Mrs. Caudle, dam of Ericsson, four year old record 2.30 1-2.

Clovis will make the season of 1890 at Poplar Grove Breeding Farm, near Wildflower, Fresno County, Commencing February 1st and ending July 1st.

Terms, $75, due at time of service.

Mares cared for in any manner owners may desire; pasturage $2 per month. Every care exercised, but no liability for escapes or accidents. Mares not proving with foal can be returned next season, providing I still own this stallion.

APEX, 8935.

FOUR-YEAR-OLD RECORD, FOURTH HEAT, 2:26.

Will make the present season at the Poplar Grove Breeding Farm, near Wildflower, Fresno Co., season commencing Feb. 1st, and ending July 1, 1890. Terms $50 the season, due at time of service. Apex is eight years old, a beautiful bay, 15 1-2 hands high, and weighs 1140 lbs. He is a horse of fine disposition, and his gait is faultless.

PEDIGREE.

Apex was sired by Promptor 2305, he by Blue Bull 75; first dam Mary by Flaxtail, he by Pruden's Blue Bull Flaxtail being the sire of the dams of Buccaneer, five-year-old record, 2:24 1-2; Pride, yearling record, 2:44 1-2, and Shamrock, two-year old record, 2:25, third heat. Second dam by Bright Eyes, son of Boanarages. Promptor (sire of Apex, record 2:26, and Transit, 2:26 1-2), by Wilson's Blue Bull, by Pruden's Blue Bull, son of Merring's Blue Bull. Promptor's dam Prairie Bird, by Flaxtail; second dam by John the Baptist, son of Tally Ho Morgan, by Sherman Morgan; third dam Fannie Fern by Irwin's Tuckaho

Apex made his appearance in the circuit as a two-year-old, and obtained a record of 2:42. As a three-year-old he reduced this in a race at Santa Rosa against Stamboul to 2:41, it taking six heats to decide the contest, which was won by Apex. As a four year-old he gained his present record of 2:26.

Mares cared for in any manner owners may desire. Pasturage $2 per month. Every care exercised, but no liabilities for escapes or accidents. Mares not proving with foal can be returned next season, providing I still own this stallion.

The Standard Stallion

JUNIO,

RECORD 2:22.

WILL MAKE THE PRESENT SEASON OF AT FRESNO FAIR GROUNDS.

Season Commencing Feb. 1st and ending July 1st.

TERMS—$100 the season, due at time of service.

JUNIO is eight years old, a handsome dark bay 16 hands high, and weighs 1250 pounds. He is the personification of the light harness horse, and his trotting action is superb. At the State Fair of 1886 he took first premium over forty of the finest trotters in the State.

PEDIGREE.

Junio, by Electioneer, premier stallion of Palo Alto (sire of Sunol 2.10 1-2, Palto Alto 2:12 1-4, and 47 others in the 2 30 list. Dam by Granger by imp. Hercules.

Granger, by imp. Hercules, dam Jenny Lind, by Stockbridge Chief, Jr., he by Stockbridge Chief, he by Vermont Black Hawk. Second dam by Kentucky Whip.

Imp. Hercules, by Kingston, first dam daughter of Tuscar, by Bay Middleton, second dam Malvina, by Oscar; 3rd dam Spotless by Walton; 4th dam by Trumpator (see Bruce's American Stud Book, Vol. 1, page 28). Hercules is the sire of the dam of Azmoor 2 20¾; also sire of dam of Menlo 2:21 1-2.

Mares not proving in foal may be returned next year free of charge, providing I still have the horse. Pasturage $2 per month. While every care will be taken of horses, no liability will be assumed for accidents or escapes.

For further particulars address

S. N. STRAUBE, Fresno, Cal
Poplar Grove Breeding Farm.

BOYCE TABLETS.

Leg and Body Wash.

THE BOYCE TABLETS are packed in a nicely decorated metal box with hinged lid—one hundred tablets in each box; directions for use plainly engraved upon the box; therefore, the convenience of the package—no liability to leakage and breakage—economy and ready solubility, together with the absolute certainty of their action, will at once commend the use of BOYCE'S TABLETS to the intelligent horsemen of the country. TABLETS sufficient to make one hundred pints of leg and body wash are conveniently carried in an inside coat pocket or in the hip-pocket of the trousers.

The BOYCE WASH can be applied ALL OVER THE BODY WITHOUT FEAR OF BLISTERING NOR DOES IT AFFECT THE KIDNEYS.

The BOYCE WASH will cure CRACKED HEELS, PUFFS, STOCKINGS, SCRATCHES, INFLAMED TENDONS and FEVERED LEGS.

Price per Box of One Hundred tablets, $2, sent postpaid to any part of the United States; six boxes for $10. A sample of BOYCE'S TABLETS will be mailed to any address on application.

These TABLETS are warranted to keep in any climate. Address

BOYCE TABLET COMPANY,

600 Wabash Avenue, - - - Terre Haute, Indiana.

J. A. McKERRON, Pacific Coast Ag't,

228-230-232 Ellis Street, San Francisco, Cal.

AN UNQUALIFIED ENDORSEMENT.

Peruvian Bitters are made of the purest ingredients and compounded as carefully as any prescription.

Peruvian Bark, one of its principal ingredients, was introduced into Spain by the Countess, wife of Count CINCHON, Spanish Viceroy to Peru in 1630, who was cured of a fever by its use, since which time, no better remedy for Malaria and for Restoring the Natural Tone of the Stomach has been discovered.

On the Atlantic Coast they are used in the principal Hotels, Clubs and Restaurants, and sold by all Grocers and Druggists. We have sold them for the past three years WITHOUT ANY ADVERTISING and sales have constantly increased UPON MERIT ALONE, and we unqualifiedly recommend them to our friends and customers.

ACKER, MERRALL & CONDIT.

New York, Feb. 1st, 1890.

WILMERDING & CO., Agents for Pacific Coast,
216 FRONT ST., SAN FRANCISCO, CAL.

THE IMPROVED NOYES ROAD - CART,

PATENTED JULY 17, 1883, AND JUNE 8, 1886.

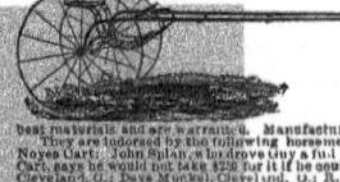

Some of the Advantages of the Noyes Cart Over All Others.

There is no bar for the rider to climb over in getting in or out. The horse can be hitched eighteen inches nearer than any other road-cart made. You can get in or out with perfect safety—no danger of being thrown into the wheel—a great advantage in breaking colts. THE EASIEST CART FOR ROAD OR TRACK. The only cart that a horse can be speeded to within one second as fast as to a sulky. All our carts are made of the very best materials and are warranted. Manufactured by the NOYES CART COMPANY, Kalamazoo, Mich.

They are indorsed by the following horsemen, all of whom are using them. Ask their opinion of the Noyes Cart: John Splan, who drove Guy a full mile in 2:17¾ and Chanter a half-mile in 1:10¾ to a Noyes Cart, says he would not take $25 for it if he could not get another; W. J. Gordon, Glenville, O.; W. B. Fasig, Cleveland, O.; Dave Muckel, Cleveland, O.; R. J. Moorehead, North East, Pa.; W. J. Chamberlain, Cleveland, O.; H. F. Malone, Bradford, Pa.; S. A. Brown & Co., Kalamazoo Stock Farm; Charles Marvin, Menlo Park, Cal.; W. H. Crawford, Lexington, Ky.; S. L. Caton, who gave Bell Boy a mark at Los Angeles, Cal., of 2:19½, and drove Chanter a half mile in 1:08¾ and Lowland Girl a full mile in 2:12 to a Noyes Cart; Mike Bowerman, Lexington, Ky.; James Golden, Medford, Mass.; John E. Turner, Philadelphia, Pa.; T. L. Newton, Beaver Dam, Wis.; P. V. Johnston, Marshall, Mich.; W. H. McCarthy, Los Angeles, Cal.; A. W. Dennison, El Dorado, Kan.; P. O. Shank, Cleveland, O.; Charles Barnard, Boston, Mass.; Johnson Bros., Greenville, Mich.; John G. Avery, Buffalo, N. Y.; General R. L. Howard, Buffalo, N. Y.; Howard Conklin, Buffalo, N. Y.; W. D. Ham, Hennepin, Ill.; R. G. Henry, Waterbury, Conn.; J. E. Hayer, Newburgh, O.; J. C. Hart, Jefferson, Tex.; A. W. Harbison, Rock Point, Pa.; Carl Hodges, Battle Creek, Mich.; Barney Treacy, Lexington, Ky.; George Forbes, Cleveland, O.; Gifford Dudley, Topeka, Kan.; William and J. L. Thompson, Lamont, Pa.; C. F. Emery, Forest City Stock Farm, Cleveland, O.; R. F. Jones, Minneapolis, Minn.; John Forbes, Elyria, O.; D. J. Downs, Battle Creek, Mich.; Frank Caton, Randall Station, O.; Arthur D. Sutton, Ind., Pa.; W. F. Neely, Grand Ridge, Ill.; Walter Clark, owner of Pilot Medium, Battle Creek, Mich.; H. R. Kingman, Battle Creek, Mich.; Dr. Sutton and H. C. Reed, Kalamazoo, Mich.; Budd Doble, Chicago, Ill.

SOLE MANUFACTURERS OF STONE'S PATENT SULKY CASE.

They will more than save their cost in one season, and horsemen campaigning trotters cannot afford to do without them. Would refer to Samuel A. Brown, Kalamazoo Stock Farm, S. L. Caton and W. H. McCarthy. Address

NOYES CART COMPANY, Kalamazoo, Mich.

Office and Factory, corner Rose and Eleanor streets. R. ARTHUR STONE, Manager.

The Park Training Stable.

CHAS. DAVID, PROPRIETOR.

Corner Grove and Baker Streets, near Entrance to Golden Gate Park.

EVERY FACILITY FOR TRAINING COLTS and taking care of Gentlemen's Roadsters.

Finely appointed stable with every convenience and sixteen roomy box stalls.

The best care given all horses by experienced help, under the personal superintendence of the proprietor

Convenient to the Park Speed Drive, and Accessible to Six Lines of Cable Cars.

THE TRAINING OF COLTS AND ROADSTERS A SPECIALTY.

TROTTERS AND ROADSTERS FOR SALE.

HORSES SOLD ON COMMISSION.

The proprietor trained and brought out the following well known horses: "Sister, Huntress," "Perihelion," "Nona Y," and others.

NEW BOOK.

HORSE BREEDING

Seventh Edition, with Appendix,
By J. H. SANDERS,

In which the GENERAL LAWS OF HEREDITY are exhaustively discussed and applied to the PRACTICAL BUSINESS OF BREEDING HORSES, especially with reference to the Selection of Breeding Stock and the Management of Stallions, Brood Mares, Young Foals, and Diseases Peculiar to Breeding Stock.

Price, Post Paid, $2.

BREEDER AND SPORTSMAN,
San Francisco, Cal.
313 Bush Street.

THE HICKS-JUDD CO.

Successors to
HICKS & JUDD, Bookbinders,
and Women's Co-operative Printing Office.

Printers, Bookbinders, Publishers,

23 First St., San Francisco.

BREEDERS' CATALOGUES A SPECIALTY.

JUST OUT. 2d EDITION.

1,000 Receipts

MIXOLOGIST
FOR BARKEEPERS

PRICE $1.00.

All booksellers, and 3 California St., S. F.

GOLDEN EAGLE HOTEL

Corner SEVENTH and K STREETS,
SACRAMENTO.
FIRST CLASS IN EVERY RESPECT.
The LARGEST and FINEST HOTEL in the City.
W. O. BOWERS, Proprietor.
Free 'Buss to and from the Hotel.
Telephone, Telegraph Office and Messenger Service at Hotel

PERRIER-JOUET & Co.

EPERNAY

CHAMPAGNE

W. B. CHAPMAN,

Sole Agent for Pacific Coast.

For sale by all first-Class Wine Merchants and Grocers.

KENNEL ADVERTISEMENTS.

RENTON KENNELS,

SAN FRANCISCO OFFICE, 2922 Pine St

Kennels located at Bolinas, Cal.

Dogs taken to board and broken at reasonable rates.

POINTER PUPPIES FOR SALE.

By Professor—Gracie Bow; Professor—Belle H.; Climax—Drab; Don—Diana.

Thoroughly broken water spaniel, Rock, out of the Prindel stock. Address

W. D. HOWE,
2922 Pine Street, San Francisco.

Puppies for Sale.

ONE GREYHOUND DOG, 14 months old, Saturday Night—Brunette.
ONE GREYHOUND DOG, 14 months old, breeding unknown.
EIGHT GREYHOUNDS (4 Dogs), whelped March 18, 189-, Saturday Night—Brunette.
ONE BLACK AND TAN POINTER, 19 months, and broken; Old Black Joe—Black Bess.
ONE GORDON SETTER BITCH, 12 months old.
ONE GORDON SETTER BITCH, 5 months old.
ONE FOX TERRIER BITCH, 2 months old.
ONE FOX TERRIER BITCH, 2 months old.

Apply to JAMES E. WATSON,
516 Sacramento street,
San Francisco.
P. O. Box 1836.

DOGS---Pointer Pups

FOR SALE.

Sure Bench Show and Field Trial Winners, as they have more bench-show and field-trial blood in them than any that have ever been whelped on the Pacific Coast.

Sire, POINT, double field trial winner; he by Vandevort's Don, great field trial and bench show winner, out of Drab, field trial and bench show winner.

Dam, QUEEN CROXTETH by Rush T., bench show winner, out of Champion Patti Croxteth, field trial and bench show winner. This is the best pointer blood in the world. Breeding and health guaranteed. Address,

A. B. TRUMAN,
1425 Steiner St., near Ellis, S. F., Cal.

FOX TERRIERS--C. A. SUMNER, 7 S. Fort St., Los Angeles, Breeder of Fox Terriers. Blemton Vesuvian (14298), by Champion Lucifer, at stud.

Llewellyn Setter Bitch

GYPSY QUEEN,

Black, White and Tan. Whelped July 24, 1888.

By Hamlet W. 5028—Miss Alice 3763.

Winner First Prize in San Francisco in 1889. Call on or address

SAM. A. WATTSON,
844—854 Harrison Street, City.

CALIFORNIA SPANIEL KENNELS,

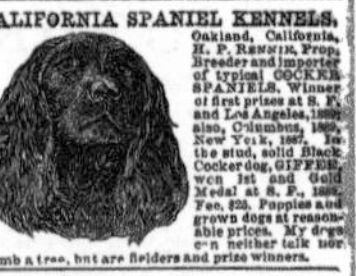

Oakland, California, H. P. RENNIE, Prop., Breeder and importer of typical COCKER SPANIELS. Winner of first prizes at S. F. and Los Angeles, 1889; also, Columbus, 1889, New York, 1887. In the stud, solid Black Cocker dog, GIFFEE, won 1st and Gold Medal at S. F., 1889. Fee, $25. Puppies and grown dogs at reasonable prices. My dogs can neither talk nor climb a tree, but are fielders and prize winners.

Fine Hats,

Latest Styles and Colors.

Meussdorffer & Hubner

8 Kearny Street, San Francisco,
Next to New Chronicle Building

John D. Gall. Jas. P. Dunne

"The Resort,"

No. 1 Stockton Street, cor. Ellis,
San Francisco.

Brushes.

BUCHANAN BROS.,
Brush Manufacturers,

609 Sacramento Street, two doors above Montgomery.

Horse Brushes of every description on hand and made to order. Bristle Body Brushes our Specialty

JOHN FORGIE,

Importing Tailor,

204 Montgomery Street,
N. E. corner Bush, SAN FRANCISCO.

PHIL J. CRIMMINS. JOHN C. MORRISON.

"Silver Palace,"

36 Geary Street,
San Francisco, Cal.

Southern Pacific Co.

(PACIFIC SYSTEM.)

Trains leave and are due to arrive at San Francisco.

LEAVE (FOR)	FROM APRIL 13, 1890.	ARRIVE (FROM)
7.30 A M	Haywards, Niles and San Jose ...	*12.45 P M
7.30 A M	Sacramento and Redding, via Davis	7.15 P M
7.30 A M	Sacramento, Auburn, Colfax	4.45 P M
8.00 A M	Martinez, Vallejo, Calistoga and Santa Rosa	6.15 P M
8.30 A M	Los Angeles Express, Fresno, Bakersfield Mojave and East and Los Angeles	11.15 A M
8.30 A M	Niles, San Jose, Stockton, Ione, Sacramento, Marysville, Oroville and Red Bluff	4.45 P M
10.30 A M	Haywards and Niles	3.45 P M
12.00 M	Haywards, Niles and Livermore	8.45 P M
*1.00 P M	Sacramento River Steamers	**6.00 A M
3.00 P M	Haywards, Niles and San Jose	9.45 A M
3.30 P M	2d Class for Ogden and East	10.45 P M
4.00 P M	Stockton and §Milton; Vallejo, Calistoga and Santa Rosa	9.45 A M
4.30 P M	Niles and Livermore	*8.45 A M
4.30 P M	Niles and San Jose	†6.15 P M
6.00 P M	Shasta Route Express, Sacramento, Marysville, Redding, Portland, Puget Sound, East and Knight's Landing via Davis	10.45 A M
6.00 P M	Haywards and Niles	7.45 A M
7.00 P M	Sunset Route, Atlantic Express Santa Barbara, Los Angeles, Deming, El Paso, New Orleans and East	8.45 P M
6.00 P M	Central Atlantic Express, Ogden and East	9.45 A M

SANTA CRUZ DIVISION.

7.45 A M	Excursion train to Santa Cruz	‡8.05 P M
8.15 A M	Newark, Centerville, San Jose, Felton, Boulder Creek and Santa Cruz	6.20 P M
2.45 P M	Centerville, San Jose, Almaden, Felton, Boulder Creek and Santa Cruz	*11.20 A M
4.45 P M	Centerville, San Jose, and Los Gatos	9.50 A M

Coast Division (Third and Townsend Sts.)

7.25 A M	San Jose, Almaden and Way Stations	2.30 P M
8.30 A M	San Jose, Gilroy, Tres Pinos; Pajaro, Santa Cruz; Monterey; Pacific Grove, Salinas, San Miguel, Paso Robles, Santa Margarita (San Luis Obispo) and principal Way Stations	6.12 P M
10.30 A M	San Jose and Way Stations	5.02 P M
12.01 P M	Cemetery, Menlo Park and Way Stations	3.38 P M
3.30 P M	San Jose, Tres Pinos, Santa Cruz, Salinas, Monterey Pacific Grove and principal Way Stations	*10.00 A M
4.25 P M	Menlo Park and Way Station	*7.58 A M
5.20 P M	San Jose and Way Stations	9.03 A M
6.30 P M	Menlo Park and Way Stations	6.35 A M
11.45 P M	Menlo Park and principal Way Stations	†7.25 P M

A M for Morning. P M for Afternoon.
*Sundays excepted. †Saturdays only. ‡Sundays only.
**Mondays excepted. §Saturdays excepted.

OCEANIC STEAMSHIP CO.

Carrying United States, Hawaiian and Colonial Mails,

WILL LEAVE THE COMPANY'S WHARF, foot of Mission street, No. 1,

For Honolulu, Auckland and Sydney,

WITHOUT CHANGE,

The Splendid New 3,000 ton Iron Steamer,
MARIPOSA ... Saturday, May 3d, 1890, at 12 M.,
Or immediately on arrival of the English mails.

For Honolulu,

S. AUSTRALIA (3,000 tons), May 23, 1890, at 12 M.

For freight or passage, apply at office, 327 Market Street. JOHN D. SPRECKELS & BROS. General Agents.

KILLIP & CO.,

LIVE STOCK AND GENERAL AUCTIONEERS,

22 Montgomery Street, San Francisco

SPECIAL ATTENTION PAID TO SALES OF

High-Bred Horses and Cattle,

At auction and private sale.

Will Sell in All Cities and Counties of the State.

REFERENCES.

HON. C. GREEN, Sacramento. — HON. J. D. CARR, Salinas.
J. P. SARGENT, ESQ., Sargents. — HON. JOHN BOGGS, Colusa.
HON. L. J. ROSE, Los Angeles. — HON. A. WALRATH, Nevada.
J. B. HAGGIN, Esq., San Francisco.

Represented at Sacramento by Edwin F. Smith Secretary State Agricultural Society.
At San Jose by Messrs. Montgomery & Rea, Real Estate Agents.

Being the oldest established firm in the live-stock business on this Coast, and having conducted the important auction sales in this line for the past fifteen years, amounting to one half a million of dollars, we feel justified in claiming unequaled facilities for disposing of live stock of every description, either at auction or private sale. Our list of correspondents embraces every breeder and dealer of prominence upon the Pacific Coast, thus enabling us to give full publicity to animals placed with us for sale. Private purchases and sales of live stock of all descriptions will be made on commission, and stock shipped with the utmost care. Purchases and sales made of land of every description. We are authorized to refer to the gentlemen whose names are appended.

KILLIP & CO., 22 Montgomery Street

HEALD'S

Business College, 24 Post St.

—San Francisco.—

The most popular school on the Coast

E. P. HEALD, President. C. S. HALEY, Sec'y.

Send for Circulars

San Francisco and North Pacific Railway.

THE DONAHUE BROAD-GAUGE ROUTE.

COMMENCING SUNDAY, MARCH 17, 1866, AND until further notice, boats and trains will leave from and arrive at the San Francisco Passenger Depot, Market-street Wharf, as follows:

Leave San Francisco. WEEK DAYS.	Leave San Francisco. SUNDAYS.	DESTINATION	Arrive San Francisco. SUNDAYS.	Arrive San Francisco. WEEK DAYS.
7.40 A M 3.30 P M 5.00 P M	8.00 A M 5.00 P M	Petaluma and Santa Rosa	10.40 A M 6.10 P M	8.50 A M 10.30 A M 6.05 P M
7.40 A M 3.30 P M	8.00 A M	Fulton, Windsor, Healdsburg, Litton Springs, Cloverdale, and way stations.	6.10 P M	10.30 A M 6.05 P M
7.40 A M	8.00 A M	Hopland and Ukiah.	6.10 P M	6.05 P M
7.40 A M	8.00 A M	Guerneville	6.10 P M	6.05 P M
7.40 A M 5.00 P M	8.00 A M	Sonoma and Glen Ellen.	10.40 A M 6.10 P M	8.50 A M 6.05 P M
3.30 P M	8.10 P M	Sebastopol	10.40 A M	10.10 A M

Stage connects at Santa Rosa for White Sulphur Springs, and Mark West Springs; at Geyserville for Skaggs Springs, and at Cloverdale for the Geysers; at Hopland for Highland Springs, Kelseyville, Soda Bay, Lakeport and Bartlett Springs, and at Ukiah for Vichy Springs, Saratoga Springs, Blue Lakes, Willits, Cahto, Calpella, Potter Valley, Sherwood Valley and Mendocino City.

EXCURSION TICKETS from Saturdays to Mondays, to Petaluma, $1.50; to Santa Rosa $2.25; to Healdsburg, $3.40; to Litton Springs, $3.60; to Cloverdale, $4.50; to Hopland, $5.70; to Ukiah, $6.75; to Guerneville, $3.75; to Sonoma, $1.50; to Glen Ellen, $1.80.

EXCURSION TICKETS, good for Sundays only, to Petaluma, $1; to Santa Rosa, $1.50; to Healdsburg, $2.25; to Litton Springs, $2.40; to Cloverdale, $3; to Guerneville, $2.50, to Sonoma, $1; to Glen Ellen, $1.20.

From San Francisco for Point Tiburon and San Rafael: Week Days—7.40, 9.20, 11.20, A. M.; 3.30, 5.00, 6.15 P. M. Sundays—8.10, 9.30, 11.00 A. M.; 1.30, 5.00, 6.30 P. M.

To San Francisco from San Rafael: Week Days—6.20, 7.55, 9.30 A. M.; 12.45, 3.40, 5.05 P. M. Sundays—8.10, 9.40 A. M.; 12.15, 3.40, 5.00 P. M.

To San Francisco from Point Tiburon: Week Days—6.50, 8.20, 9.55 A. M.; 1.10, 4.05, 5.30 P. M.; Sundays—8.40, 10.05 A. M.; 12.40, 4.05, 5.30 P. M.

On Saturdays an extra trip will be made from San Francisco to San Rafael, leaving at 1.40 P. M.

H. C. WHITING, General Manager.

PETER J. McGLYNN, Gen. Pass. & Tkt. Agt.

Ticket Offices at Ferry, 222 Montgomery Street and 2 New Montgomery Street.

CHICAGO, MILWAUKEE AND ST. PAUL RAILWAY,

Steam Heated and Electric Lighted Vestibuled Trains between Chicago, St. Paul and Minneapolis.
Electric Lighted and Steam Heated Vestibuled Trains between Chicago, Council Bluffs and Omaha.
Finest Dining Cars in the world.
Free Reclining Chair Cars between Chicago and Omaha.
Fast Mail Line between Chicago, Milwaukee, St. Paul and Minneapolis.
Transcontinental Route between Chicago, Council Bluffs and Omaha, or St. Paul.
Great National Route between Chicago, Kansas City and St. Joseph, Mo.
5,700 miles of road in Illinois, Wisconsin, Minnesota, Iowa, Missouri, South and North Dakota.
Everything First-Class.
First-Class People patronize First-Class Lines.
Ticket Agents everywhere sell Tickets over the Chicago, Milwaukee and St. Paul Railway.

W. T. ALLEN,
Pacific Coast Passenger Agent
Office, No 138 Montgomery St., San Francisco, Cal.
Under Occidental Hotel

6 DONTS

DON'T own a racehorse.
DON'T be a breeder.
DON'T be a trainer.
DON'T be a jockey.
DON'T bet on the races.
DON'T go to a race track.

WITHOUT HAVING IN YOUR POCKET ONE OF

Goodwin's ANNUAL OFFICIAL TURF GUIDES.

Price, in cloth ... $2.00
Price, in half morocco ... 3.00
Price, in half calf ... 4.00
If sent by mail ... 10 cents extra

SUBSCRIBE TO IT FOR 1890.

It is published semi-monthly during the racing season, and is but $10 per year. Address

GOODWIN BROS.,
241 Broadway, New York City.

OUR IMPROVED. THE BOHANON SULKY! BEST MADE. Perfect Riding Buggies. Breaking Carts.

Bohanon Carriage Co., 161-163 Ogden Ave., CHICAGO.

Send for Catalogue.

THE GREAT

STABLE DISINFECTANT DARBYS FLUID.

Many horses and cattle become diseased and die from the impure atmosphere of their stables, and even though stables may be kept clean and the foul air be unnoticeable, it may still exist.

DARBYS FLUID

IS GOOD FOR CUTS, BRUISES, ETC. WARDS OFF DISEASE, PURIFIES THE AIR AND PREVENTS CONTAGION AMONG ANIMALS

It is cheap and never wasted by free use; should be sprinkled about the stalls and stable as a safeguard against Influenza, Pink-eye, Epizootic, etc.

It you value your horses and stock never be without Darbys Prophylactic Fluid.

J. H. ZEILIN & CO., Philadelphia, Pa.

SOLD BY ALL DRUGGISTS.

HORSE OWNERS TRY GOMBAULT'S

CAUSTIC BALSAM.

A Safe, Speedy and Positive Cure for Curb, Splint, Sweeny, Capped Hock, Strained Tendons, Founder, Wind Puffs, all Skin Diseases or Parasites, Thrush, Diphtheria, Pinkeye, all Lameness from Spavin, Ringbone or other Bony Tumors. Removes all Bunches or Blemishes from Horses and Cattle.
Supersedes all Cautery or Firing.
Impossible to Produce any Scar or Blemish.

Every bottle sold is warranted to give satisfaction. Price $1.50 per bottle. Sold by druggists, or sent by express, charges paid, with full directions for its use. Send for descriptive circulars. Address LAWRENCE, WILLIAMS & CO., Cleveland, O.

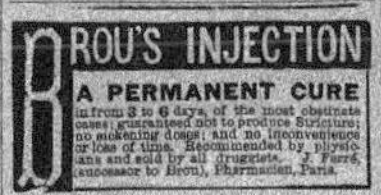
BROU'S INJECTION
A PERMANENT CURE
in from 3 to 6 days, of the most obstinate cases; guaranteed not to produce Stricture; no sickening doses; and no inconvenience or loss of time. Recommended by physicians and sold by all druggists. J. Ferré, (successor to Brou), Pharmacien, Paris.

For any Kind of a

SORE THROAT

USE

McCLELLAN'S DIPHTHERIA REMEDY

An Unfailing Cure.
FOR SALE BY ALL DRUGGISTS

R. LIDDLE & SON

538 Washington St., S. F.,

Wholesale and Retail Dealers in

Guns, Rifles and Pistols.

A Full Line of FISHING TACKLE and SPORTSMAN'S GOODS.

Orders by mail receive prompt attention.

"STANDARD" SHOTGUN CARTRIDGES

By-Laws

—AND—

Rules and Regulations

—OF THE—

NATIONAL

Trotting Association

ALSO THE

AMERICAN

Trotting Association,

AND THE

PACIFIC COAST BLOOD-HORSE ASSOCIATION,

With Betting Rules.

For Sale at the Office of the

Breeder and Sportsman,

313 Bush St., S. F., Cal.

Price, 25c. each.
By Mail, Postage Paid, 30c. each.

VETERINARY.

Dr. Wm. H. Jones, M.R.C.V.S.

Veterinary Surgeon,
(OLYMPIC CLUB STABLES)
503 Sutter Street, San Francisco.
Telephone, No 1404.

Consultations by letter, and cases of URGENT NECESSITY in the Interior will receive prompt attention.

Dr. A. E. BUZARD,

VETERINARY SURGEON,

Member of the Royal College of Veterinary Surgeons, London, England. Graduated April 22d, 1870.

All Operations on the Horse Performed Skillfully.

Special attention given to the Diseases of Dogs. Calls to the country promptly attended to. Advice and prescriptions by mail $2. Office and Residence, No. 11 Seventh street, S. F. (opp. Odd Fellows Hall. Telephone No. 3 69.

W. H. WOODRUFF.

Veterinary Dentist,

AT FASHION STABLES,

221 Ellis Street, San Francisco

Improved Instruments, Humane Methods, First-Class Work.

H. E. CARPENTER,

Veterinary Surgeon,

Graduate of Ontario Veterinary College, Toronto Canada.

RESIDENCE AND VETERINARY INFIRMARY
331 Golden Gate Ave., San Francisco.
Telephone 3069.

OPEN DAY AND NIGHT.

No risk in throwing Horses. Veterinary Operating Table on the premises.

DR. C. MASOERO,

Veterinary Surgeon,

Successor to DR. A. DeTAVEL,

GRADUATE OF ROYAL VETERINARY COLLEGE, TURIN.

OFFICE AND INFIRMARY

No. 811 HOWARD STREET,

Between Fourth and Fifth. SAN FRANCISCO

Telephone, No 457.

R. WATKINS,

Veterinary Dentist,

Office at C. S. Crittendens' Golden Gate Livery and Riding Academy 24 to 28 Golden Gate Avenue.

Refers to Palo Alto Stock Farm; Wm. Corbett, San Mateo Stock Farm; B. C. Holly, Vallejo, and others. Examination Free.

E. J. O'ROUKE.

I have the honor to announce to my old patrons and the general public that I may be found at my old stand, where, as heretofore, the

Shoeing of Horses,

whether for the Track, Drive, or for general work, will receive my personal attention.

Telephone 2011.

E. J. O'ROUKE,
209 Ellis Street

California HorseShoe Co's

I have used in my business the Steel and Iron Shoes made by the above Company, and take great pleasure in saying they are the best I have ever used in twenty-two years' practice. I have never seen anything like the STEEL SHOE made by this Company. I can fully recommend them to every practical Horseshoer in the country.
Yours respectfully,
No. 8 Everett Street. JOHN GRACE.

IF YOU WISH A GOOD REVOLVER PURCHASE ONE OF SMITH & WESSON'S

Finest small arms ever manufactured and the first choice of all experts. In calibres 32, 38 and 44-100. Single or double action, Safety Hammerless and Target models. **Best quality wrought steel**, carefully inspected for workmanship and stock. Unrivaled for **finish, durability and accuracy.** Do not be deceived by cheap *malleable iron imitations* often sold for the genuine article. They are unreliable and dangerous. The SMITH & WESSON REVOLVERS are stamped upon the barrels with firm's name, address and dates of patents, and are **guaranteed** perfect. Insist upon having them, and if your dealer cannot supply you, an order sent to address below will receive prompt attention. Descriptive catalogue and prices upon application.

SMITH & WESSON,
Springfield, Mass.

TWENTY PAGES.

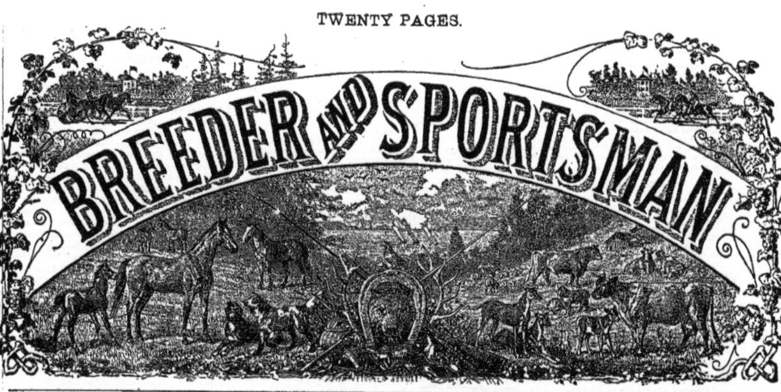

Vol. XVI. No. 19.
No. 313 BUSH STREET.

SAN FRANCISCO, SATURDAY, MAY 10, 1890.

SUBSCRIPTION
FIVE DOLLARS A YEAR.

J. H. WHITE'S TROTTERS.

What the President of the P. C. T. H. B. A. is Doing.

A Fine Lot of Horses in Training.

California is now looked upon as the principal horse breeding State in the Union, and where we have so many choice spots, all of which have their particular advantages for the breeding of race horses, it is a hard matter to decide what particular locality is the best for this industry which has now obtained such great proportions on the Pacific Coast. There is hardly a county in the State but what possesses some individual advantage, but, taken all in all, it will prove a pretty hard matter to show that there is any one county that is superior to Sonoma for this particular branch of business. Less than a year ago Leslie E. Macleod, the assistant editor of Wallace's Monthly in a conversation with the writer stated that from what he had seen of Sonoma County, he was satisfied that it was one of the best places in the United States to raise trotters. A statement such as the above from such authority should have heavy weight with those who are seeking to locate breeding farms, especially in view of the fact that there is not a state in the Union but what has been traversed by Mr. Macleod while seeking information for the articles which he presents to the horse reading public month after month in the Wallace publication.

Among the many prominent breeders located in that chosen spot is J. H. White, the present President of the Pacific Coast Trotting Horse Breeders' Association, a gentleman well versed in everything appertaining to the horse, having been for many years more or less closely interested in turf matters. Mr. White's farm is a small domain in itself, located about six miles south and east of Petaluma, and contains in the neighborhood of 1600 acres. The land is divided into 600 acres of flat land and about 1000 in hilly or rolling land, almost every portion of which is studded with clover and wild oats, a combination that by many is supposed to surpass even the much talked about alfalfa. It is not our object at the present time to discuss the relative merits of the native grasses of California, but there is so much that can be said in favor of clover and wild oats, especially when the horses raised on this succulent food are examined that the spectator is liable to cast a vote in favor of the Sonoma grasses as against the popular alfalfa or alfilleria.

Last Saturday morning was selected for the trip and a more pleasant day it could not have been. While the early morning ocean airs tempted one to wear a spring overcoat, the thoughts of the great valley that we were about to visit made it prudent to take a linen duster instead of a coat of heavier material. As we rolled along through the country compassed by the San Francisco and Northern Pacific Railroad, the beauties seen by the eye surpassed description. From every point there was one continuous carpet of green relieved by the wild flowers and the orchards carrying their loads of blossoms. Verily Sonoma County never looked prettier than it did while we were rushing on toward the quaint old town of Petaluma, where we were met by a carriage and pair to convey us to our destination. The effects of the very bad winter are still to be seen on much of the low land which skirts Petaluma Creek, and the roads are hardly what they might be, still taking everything into consideration, they are not as bad as the many unfavorable reports would have led us to believe.

The proprietor met us with a hearty shake of the hand and welcomed us to his pleasant home. As time was short every advantage had to be taken of each moment, and it was not long before we were on Mr. White's race track, which, by the way, is an exceedingly fast one, and kept in perfect condition. The master reinsman of the place is Steve Crandall, who has for many years been known to all turf frequenters in this State. As we appeared he was sending a beautiful mare through her paces, a mare called Mountain Quail by Hernani, dam Annie by General McClellan; 2nd dam by imp The Lawyer. Steve was joined on the track by one of his assistants who was driving Princess, a beautiful mare by Hernani, dam Susie by Sam McClellan (a son of General McClellan 144), 2nd dam Brownie, the old California mare that was sent East many years ago to contest against the Eastern trotters. It would be hardly fair to tell the times of each mile made by the various horses that we saw, and will simply say that Mountain Quail has a very bright future before her, and it will be some very great accident that will prevent Hernani from having quite a list of 2:30 performers during the present year. As each "work out" was effected new candidates for trotting honors were brought forward, and the scene was a pretty one, for while the usual grand stands and official positions were not to be seen, the clatter of hoofs over the speed track lent a charm to the scene that was singularly striking.

Mr. White has in training altogether about thirty trotters, many of which will no doubt score up for the word during the coming season. Taking the whole lot, it would be a very difficult matter to find on any breeding farm in California, a superior looking stable of horses. Mr. White's two stallions, Hernani (a son of Electioneer) and Marco (a son of Elector, 2:21½, have stamped great individuality on each of their get. It is very rarely that such intelligent heads, finely arched necks, superb bodily conformation and legs which can only be called perfection, are to be found, where such a large number of horses are congregated together.

In addition to the two which have already been mentioned there are a few others that deserve personal notice. One, which is particularly striking to the eye, being Joe by Marco, dam Kate by Milliman's Bellfounder 62. He is a horse of splendid appearance, fine smooth action, and it was intended that he should be sent a very fast mile on the day we were present, but owing to a trifling injury to the foot, it was deemed expedient to give him only slow work, and still it did not require the knowledge of a professional to see that Joe is liable to make a low record for himself this year.

Mabel is a handsome chestnut filly two years old by Hernani, dam Mesquite by Washington (a son of California Smuggler); 2nd dam Fanny (sister to St. Helena); 3rd dam Buttermilk Sal. Mabel is a pacer and shows so much speed at that gait that by many she is looked upon as being another California phenomenon.

Mabel has a full sister, Julia, who gives every evidence of possessing speed and will beyond doubt do honor to both herself and sire.

Ida Franklin is a full sister to Mountain Quail and if looks go for anything, should be able to make the Quail fly very rapidly to beat her.

Alice is still another sister to Ida Franklin and Mountain Quail and was trained last year at Petaluma, she showing, while there, a quarter in 32½ seconds and many in 33½ or better.

A very fine two-year-old colt was seen in Jim Mac by Hernani, dam Mollie Mac, he is of the sturdy improving order and should be heard from in the two year old stakes this year.

Last season Mr. White was fortunate enough to secure a record of 2:22¾ for the handsome brood mare, Kitty Almont and she has as one of her representatives at the farm, a finely put up three-year-old called Dot, this handsome filly is by Hernani and is a typical California trotter. She is a beautifully formed animal, heavily muscled and can show a gait this early in the season that warrants the belief that she will be entitled to a place in the 2:20 list before long.

Marco as stated before is a son of Electioneer 2:21½ and shows the same aptness for the trot as did his well known sire. Marco's dam is by General McClellan 144; his 2nd dam being a sister to St. Helena 2:27½. Owing to stud service he has not been given as much work as some of the others but is an illustration of the often refuted assertion that the Electioneers do not breed on for if Marco does not prove remarkably fast this season, then looks go for nothing.

Another of the promising ones is Henrietta, a four year old by Hernani, dam H. D. by General McClellan; 2nd dam Lady Burgess. This mare gives every indication of being a fast trotter, and backed up as she is in the 2nd dam by the well known Belmont blood should prove a trotter of speed and endurance.

Straitedge is a chestnut colt, three years old, by Marco, dam Fanny by General McClellan 144; his gait is of the best, with that easy, frictionless way of going that always produces high flights of speed. He is a credit to his young sire, and should be one well inside of 2:30 before 1891 is rung in.

A bay gelding, two years old, by Hernani, dam Miss Kohl by Irvington; 2d dam by Speculation, is bred well enough to warrant the belief that he can hold his own against any who are likely to compete with him this year. He is a handsome fellow with extremely fine carriage, nice gaited, and will not require much work to show what he can do.

Mr. White has always been opposed to the early education of trotters, but finding that the other breeders of the State were educating their yearlings, he has taken up several of the youngsters to see what they could do, and one that particularly impressed the writer was a bay colt by Hernani, dam the Ralston mare; this well known mare was used for sometime by the late Wm. Ralston, Esq., for whom she was purchased in Kentucky by one of his agents. While it has not been clearly proven, there is but little reason to doubt that she is a daughter of Alexander's Abdallah, and as we saw her in the paddock, although now twenty-six years old, she shows the traces of grand breeding, and is a superb individual in every way, and to those who have studied the breeding of the Hambletonian family there can be no doubt but that she is richly imbued with that blood; notwithstanding the extreme youth of this colt, he has already shown a number of quarters, beating fifty seconds at every time of asking.

As time was limited, we could not pay the attention to the broodmares that we should like to have done, but a casual glance warrants us in the belief that Mr. White can show as fine a lot of suckling foals, when numbers are considered, as any breeder in the State. They are by Hernani and Marco, and as Mr. White had so many Hernani's on the place, he sent that exceedingly fine stallion to Kentucky this season where he is now standing as a representative of the Electioneer family.

For breeding service this year, Mr. White has secured in addition to his own stallions the handsome bay colt Winwood by Antevolo, dam by Nutwood 600. Winwood is the property of Mr. Requa, of Oakland, and is a typical Antevolo, of splendid carriage and exquisite figure; he would draw attention from his fine appearance from the most fastidious.

From the extremely well bred mares of which Mr. White has many, we can readily believe that Winwood will get a splendid lot of foals.

As time drew near for us to catch the train, the carriage was once more brought into requisition and we were soon rolling back to Petaluma. A glance was made at the race track, which we found in excellent condition, but time would not permit a close examination of the horses, of which there are many now stabled there. General Fine has evidently hit the public taste, and he is the right man in the right place as Superintendent of the track.

We feel assured that we are not transgressing in telling our readers that they will be always welcomed at Mr. White's farm, and the popular owner will ever esteem it a pleasure to show his fellow horsemen of the State what he has at his well arranged stables. A grand entertainer with fund of anecdote that is charming to listen to, Mr. White is one of the most popular horsemen in California, as is evident in the fact that his fellow breeders have made him President of their Association, and the office could not be in better hands. For many years Mr. White has been, like many others in California, endeavoring to raise 2:30 performers, but luck combined with accident has usually presented so many obstacles that his success has not been as great as many of the other breeders: however, from present indications there is every reason to believe that Dame Fortune will smile on him this year, as he has many promising youngsters who are likely to go into the charmed circle.

John Nelson Again.

From Wallace's Monthly.

Mr. Alfred A. Snyder, of Caldwell, has supplied additional information with regard to the stallion John Nelson. Mr. Synder elucidates some hitherto doubtful points in the history of this horse. As part owner of the stallion at one time early in his career, Mr. Synder speaks with authority, and no one is more competent to speak concerning the facts in his possession.

Mr. Synder says that the horse John Nelson was owned by himself and his father, Mr. Halsey Snyder, in 1855. They came into possession of him in the following manner: Mr. Alfred A. Snyder traded a bay mare called Bowery Girl to a Mr. Queolet (or Goslet) for a half interest in the horse. He was then four years old, having been foaled in 1851. He was at that time in the hands of John Nelson, on Long Island for training. Subsequently he came to Newark, and at the earnest solicitation of Mr. Snyder his father purchased Mr. Quoelet's interest, paying therefore $400. Mr. Snyder says that Mr. Queolet either bred the horse himself or purchased him when very young from Mr. Thomas Evans, of New Brunswick. That the horse was bred in New Brunswick by either one of these two men there is no question. John Nelson, Mr. Snyder says, at the time he owned him, was matchless for beauty of conformation. There were very few horses, he says, that could compare with him in style and general finish. There was no appearance of the stallion about him, and any one seeing him traveling along the road would take him for a gelding. Some time during 1855 Mr. Snyder disposed of his interest in the horse to his father. The latter kept him until the spring of 1858, and then sold him to Horace F. Jones, who kept a stable on Mercer street, near Prince, in New York. While Mr. Halsey Snyder owned him he showed a mile in 2:36. Mr. Jones returned the horse to the hands of John Nelson for further training, and during 1859 sold him to parties to go to California. Mr. Jones paid Mr. Snyder $1,800 for the horse and received nearly $6,000 from the California people.

Mr. Alfred Snyder states positively that the dam of John Nelson was by one of the Vermont Morgans, and his sire imp Trustee He says that he told Mr. Bruce several times that the dam of John Nelson was not by Abdallah.

In the year 1855 Mr. Halsey Snyder bought a bay mare from Mr. Queolot, which was in foal to John Nelson. This mare foaled a filly, which was the first of John Nelson's produce. This filly, afterward known as Alice, was bred to John J. Crittenden (by Volunteer), owned by a Mr. Carpenter, living at Woodbridge, and the result was a colt which went by the name of Good Templar. This grandson of John Nelson could trot in 2:40, and was a magnificent roadster. He is now, or was when last heard from, on a stock farm in Colorado. Alfred A. Snyder is firm in his declaration that John Nelson's dam was a Morgan. He says there never was any question about that. Not only did Mr. Queolet say so, but he himself knew the name of her sire when he owned Nelson, although in the long lapse of years the name has escaped his memory.

Mr. Snyder's story corroborates that of Mr. John W. Newell of New Brunswick, in every essential particular. Mr. Newell says that Mr. Evans of New Brunswick raised John Nelson and sold him to Mr. Queolet (Mr. Newell spells that name Geolet, but Mr. Snyder says the name is spelled Queolet on the books), and the latter disposed of him to Mr. Halsey Snyder. As Mr. Halsey Snyder did own the horse, Mr. Newell might easily be mistaken in attributing the sale in the first instance to him, and not to Mr. Alfred A. Snyder, who was really the first purchaser. Mr. Newell also says that the dam of John Nelson came from Vermont. The history of John Nelson in brief is as follows: John Nelson, ch s, tested in 1851, by imp Trustee; dam a Morgan mare. Bred by Thomas Evans of New Brunswick, N. J.; passed through the hands of Messrs. Alfred and Halsey Snyder of Newark, N. J., to Horace F. Jones of New York, and subsequently went to California, where he died in 1871.—Newark (N. J.) Sunday Call.

[Note.—The above agrees substantially with what we have hitherto had about John Nelson, but it does not add much light as to what horse was his sire. Though the presumption is that he was bred by Mr. Thomas Evans of New Brunswick, that fact is not established beyond doubt. If there be uncertainty as to the breeder, there must certainly be uncertainty as to the sire. The only evidence which will put the matter beyond doubt are the books of imp Trustee. —Editor.]

The American Trotting Association.

Two weeks ago we published a list of the persons at present under suspension or that have been expelled by the National, and made a few remarks in reference thereto, which has called out the following letter from the Secretary of the American Association:

Editor Breeder and Sportsman:—Permit me to call your attention to a little error in the heading of "Suspensions and expulsions" published in your issue of April 26th, page 26. Suspensions by the National Trotting Association are not recognized by the American, or *vice versa*; but all persons and horses ruled off by the American Racing Association, or expelled by the National Trotting Association for fraud, are likewise disqualified from competing on tracks of members of the American Trotting Association. But persons and horses expelled by the American Trotting Association for fraud are welcomed by the National Trotting Association. The disqualification on American tracks of persons and horses expelled for fraud by the National Trotting Association was done in order to promote the breeding and trotting interests of the country; as it was deemed by our Congress that a person or horse expelled for fraudulent transactions by any reputable organization was not fit to compete on American tracks.

Yours truly,
J. H. Steiner, Secretary.

Parties having mares that are barren or irregular breeders would do well to consult Dr. G. W. Stimpson, V. S. Office and Hospital 19th Street, near San Pablo Avenue, Oakland, Cal. Best of references.

Entries for the Breeders' Meeting.

We give below a list of the entries received by the Secretary for the P. C. T. H. B. A. Meeting, which will be acted on too late for official notification this week, but in our next issue we will be able to state what action the Directors have taken in regard to them.

TROTTING STAKES.

THREE-YEAR-OLDS—FOALS OF 1887.

Eligible to 2:40 Class. Mile heats, best three in five. Entrance $50, with $300 added. Entrance payable $10 May 1, 1890, $15 July 1, 1890, and $25 on the fifth day preceding the first advertised day of the meeting.

Funk Bros., b f Lizzie, by Elector 2170, dam by Duke McClellan.
Palo Alto Stock Farm's br f Alsifa by Ansel, dam American Girl by Toronto Sontag.
Palo Alto Stock Farm's b c Hugo by Electioneer, dam Helpmate by Planet.
U. S. Gregory's b f Lynette by Lynwood, dam Lady Belle by Kentucky Hunter.
J. A. Goldsmith's ch m Serena by Sidney, dam Blonde by Elmo.
San Mateo Stock Farm's b m Millie Wilkes by Guy Wilkes, dam Rosetta by The Moor.
Geo. W. Woodard's gr h Silver King by Jim Mulvenna.

FOUR-YEAR-OLDS—FOALS OF 1886.

Eligible to 2:30 class. Mile heats, best three in five. Entrance $50, with $400 added. Entrance payable $10 on May 1, 1890, $15 on July 1, 1890, and $25 on the fifth day preceding the first advertised day of the meeting.

Col. H. I. Thornton's br c Valona by Nutwood, Jr., dam Lucy Patchen by Geo. M. Patchen, Jr.
Palo Alto Stock Farm's b f Ariana by Ansel, dam Rebecca by General Benton.
Palo Alto Stock Farm's blk f Ladywell by Electioneer, dam Lady Lowell by Shultz's St. Clair.
W. S. Hobart's ch m Nola by Nutwood, dam Belle Byron by Bowman's Clark Chief.
B. C. Holly's b h Prodigal 6000 by Pancoast, dam Beatrice by Cuyler 100.
Souther Farm's b s Glen Fortune by Electioneer, dam Glenne by Messenger Duroc.
San Mateo Stock Farm's b m Una Wilkes by Guy Wilkes, dam Blanche by Arthurton.
San Mateo Stock Farm's br f Anita by Le Grande, dam Hannah Price by Arthurton.
Pleasanton Stock Farm Co.'s blk f Katie S by Director, dam Alpha Medium by Happy Medium.
Pleasanton Stock Farm Co.'s blk f Lady Director by Director, dam by Hambletonian Jr.
Geo. W. Woodard's b h Alex Button Jr., by Alexander Button, dam by John Nelson.
Wilfred Page's b h Eclectic 11,321 by Electioneer, dam Manette by Nutwood.
Fred W. Loeber's blk m Directa by Director, dam Alida by Admiral.

NOMINATION TROTTING PURSES.

$2,000. Stallion Purse.

Open to stallions eligible to the 2:18 class. Mile heats best three in five. Entrance $200, payable, $40 May 1, 1890, $40 July 1, 1890, $40 August 1, 1890, and $80 on the tenth day preceding the first advertised day of the meeting. Horses to be named at time of last payment.

San Mateo Stock Farm — Pleasanton Stock Farm Co.
E. B. Gifford.

$2,000. Free-for-All.

Mile heats, best three in five. Entrance, $200, payable $40 May 1, 1890, $40 July 1, 1890, $40 August 1, 1890, and $80 on the tenth day preceding the first advertised day of the meeting. Horses to be named at time of last payment.

B. C. Holly. — Cyrus Berry.
San Mateo Stock Farm. — Pleasanton Stock Farm Co.

$1,500. Five-Year-Olds. Foals 1885.

Mile heats, best three in five. Entrance $150, payable $30 May 1, 1890, $30 July 1, 1890, $30 August 1, 1890, and $60 on the tenth day preceding the first advertised day of the meeting. Horses to be named at the time of the last payment.

Palo Alto Stock Farm. — San Mateo Stock Farm.
San Miguel Stock Farm. — Pleasanton Stock Farm Co.

$1,500. 2:22 Class.

Mile heats, best three in five. Entrance, $150, payable $30 May 1, 1890, $30 July 1, 1890, $30 August 1, 1890, and $60 on the tenth day preceding the first advertised day of the meeting. Horses to be named at the time of the last payment.

B. C. Holly. — Palo Alto Stock Farm.
McFayden & Murphy — Souther Farm.
Napa Stock Farm. — San Mateo Stock Farm.
Pleasanton Stock Farm Co. — E. B. Gifford.
H. W. Cooper.

$1,500. 2:27 Class.

Mile heats, best three in five. Entrance $150. Payable, $30 May 1st, 1890, $30 July 1st, 1890, $30 August 1st, 1890, and $60 on the tenth day preceding the first advertised day of the meeting. Horses to be named at time of last payment.

B. C. Holly. — Souther Farm.
C. H. Corey. — San Mateo Stock Farm.
R. T. Carroll. — Pleasanton Stock Farm Co.
A. T. Hatch. — R. Murphy.

NOMINATION PACING PURSES.

$1,500. Free for All.

Mile heats, best three in five. Entrance, 150. Payable, $30 May 1st, 1890, $30 July 1st, 1890, $30 August 1st, 1890, and $60 on the tenth day preceding the first advertised day of the meeting. Horses to be named at time of last payment.

B. C. Holly. — Geo. W. Woodard.
Napa Stock Farm. — C. H. Corey
San Mateo Stock Farm. — J. L. McCord.
Pleasanton Stock Farm Co.

$1,000. 2:25 Class.

Mile heats, best three in five. Entrance, $100. Payable $20 May 1st, 1890, $20 July 1st, 1890, $20 August 1st, 1890, and $40 on the tenth day preceding the first advertised day of the meeting. Horses to be named at time of last payment.

Napa Stock Farm. — Pleasanton Stock Farm Co.
San Mateo Stock Farm. — B. C. Holly.

Guenoc Stock Farm Purchases.

Judge J. McM. Shafter has sold to the Guenoc Stock Farm, five thoroughbred mares and four foals as follows:

Wah-ta-wah, foaled 1876, by War Dance, dam Date Tree by Mickey Free. Wah-ta-Wah has a bay colt by imp Greenback for which the name of "Guenoc" has been claimed.

Prosperine, b m, foaled 1876, by Daniel Boone, dam Anna H. by Lee Paul. This mare has a chestnut filly by imp Greenback, the name of Prostitute being claimed for her.

Una, foaled 1876, by Daniel Boone, dam by Beacon. Una has a brown filly by imp Greenback, for which the name of Leonie is claimed.

Miss Hooker, ch m, foaled 1883, by Joe Hooker, dam Napa Queen by Norfolk. Miss Hooker has a bay filly at her side by St. Savior, and this little lady has been named Itawamba.

Alice T by Haddington, dam Una by Daniel Boone is barren this season.

The price given is not stated.

Mr. Frederick Gebhard and friends started overland on Thursday evening, after a stay of almost a month at the Guenoc Farm. The gentlemen were all pleased with their trip, and Mr. Gebhard is well satisfied with his Lake County investment. He will keep adding from time to time to the brood mare division at Guenoc, hoping in the near future to have a list of matrons that will compare favorably with any establishment of like kind in the Eastern States.

Well Bred Fillies for a California Breeding Farm.

Some weeks ago Mr. Fair's Superintendent, Humphrey Sullivan, started for Wyoming Terrrtory to purchase any well bred mares or fillies that might suit his eye, and at Uinta Stock Farm, the property of A. C. Beckwith, he secured several which are a credit alike to his judgment and good taste. Among those which he has brought back to California with him is Fanny McGregor, a chestnut filly, foaled 1887, by Robert McGreger 647, dam Fanny Patchen by Mambrino Patchen 58; 2nd dam by Mambrino Whalebone; 3rd dam by Tom Crowder: 4th dam by Old Copper Bottom. Fanny McGregor comes from two very fine families, and from her breeding should surely trot and stay for any distance. Her sire is one of the greatest trotting horses that this country has ever seen, while her dam represents the great broodmare family of the present day. Robert McGregor is the sire of eight in the 2:30 list, including the well known Bonnie McGregor, whose record of 2:13½ has stamped him as one of the fastest horses of the present decade. Going into the Mambrino Patchen family, we find this notable sire with fourteen in the list, while twenty-eight of his sons have got fifty-four trotters and three pacers, while thirty-two of his daughters have produced thirty-five trotters and three pacers.

Hattie H. is a bay filly, foaled 1888, by Wyoming Chief 3897, dam Flora Wilkes by Geo. Wilkes 519; 2d dam by Seeley's American Star 14. As Wyoming Chief combines the blood of Strathmore, Woodford Mambrino, Miss Russell and Pilot Jr., this mare should make a very valuable addition to the farm, either for trotting purposes or as an inmate of the harem.

Lizzie H. is a bay filly, foaled 1889, by Wyoming Chief 3897, dam Hilda Rose by Dictator 113; 2d dam Fanny Patchen by Mambrino Patchen 58, etc. This filly is fine, shapely, and trots well, which she should surely do when we consider the combination of great blood lines which flow through her veins.

Annie Kirkwood is a chestnut filly, foaled 1889, by Satinwood 5064, dan Annie Kirksey 408; 2d dam Miss Kirksey by Mambrino Le Grand; 3d dam Nellie by White Mountain; 4th dam Nellie Bly by Rhode's Highlander; 5th dam by Young Sidi Hamet. Here we again find the Hambletonian, Abdallah and Mambrino blood to back up an exquisite filly which is the equal of any yearling ever seen in the country.

Zettie is a bay filly, foaled 1889, by Wyoming Chief 3897, dam Flora Wilkes by Geo. Wilkes 519; 2d dam by Seeley's American Star 14, etc. This is a beautiful little miss, of quality and substance, compact and powerful, very stylish and nicely finished; she is well gaited, and shows nothing but trot. Her dam is one of the finest specimens of the Wilkes family to be found anywhere, and her first foal was sold as a two-year-old for $3,000.

Princess Wilkes is a black filly, foaled 1889, by Ned Wilkes 4775, dam Princess Clay by American Clay 34; 2nd dam Carrie Prince by Black Prince; 3rd dam Gip by Abdallah and thence on through the thoroughbred lines to imp. Diomed; here is another of the grand combinations which should at once produce good game trotters. American Clay with very limited opportunities got three in the 2:30 list, and two of his sons have got six, while seventeen of his daughters have produced eighteen trotters and two pacers. Carrie Prince, the grandam of Princess Wilkes is bred very much like Daniel Lambert, her sire being a son of Hill's Black Hawk, and her dam a daughter of Old Abdallah. The sire of this beautiful little filly is by Baron Wilkes 4758 dam Steinette by Steinway 1808; 2nd dam Ned, the dam of Clemmie G. 2:15¼, Post Boy 2:23, Alice Stoner 2:24½, Mystery 2:25½ and Forest Wilkes 2:24½. With such blood lines emanating from both sire and dam, Princess Wilkes should prove a perfect gem.

We are pleased to see that Mr. Fair has purchased such extremely well-bred mares and fillies, and sincerely trust that the money invested may be well spent.

Inyo Notes.

A few days ago, it was a privilege on my passage up the valley, to call on W. S. Enos, and while there passed a very agreeable hour among the horses owned by him and Mr. McSweeny.

The horse that particularly attracted my attention and admiration was the young horse Falliston, son of Fallis. From his sire he draws some of the bluest of blue trotting blood, that of the justly famous Electioneer; and on the side of his dam he is a great grandson of the thoroughbred Belmont (Williamson's) sire of Venture 2:27¼, and of the dams of some speedy ones; also through his dam he is a grandson of General McClellan, she being sired by Duke McClellan, son of the General.

Falliston is three years old, having been foaled in April, 1887, in Owens Valley, Inyo Co. He is a deep bay with black points, clean limbed and beautiful. He has an intelligent head, kind eye and small well set ears. To my eyes, by no means those of a professional, he is the model of a perfect horse being outlined in every part by Hogarth's line of beauty. In motion he is as near perfection as he looks; he carries himself proudly erect, as if in disdain of his richly endowed companions on the farm, and as he walks, his feet touch the bosom of mother earth as if pavements of gold were none too good for his aristocratic hoofs.

His trotting action is good, but as he has never been trained, the limit of his speed can only be conjectured; however, his ancestors and his own apparent qualifications give promise that when he knocks for admittance at the enchanted portal it will not be denied. Until then he will have to be called a non-standard.

His stable companion is Albenton, son of General Benton and Abbie, by Almont. He is a noble specimen of the equine race, but in many respects not the peer of Falliston.

Being a great lover of a fine horse, I may seem to give a somewhat highly colored picture of this beautiful animal; but other admirers of the same regal race would pardon me if they could have but stood at my side as I feasted my eyes on his symmetrical proportions and graceful movements

We boast of some fine horses here—Thoroughbred, trotting and draft of different breeds, and Inyo with her high altitude, dry climate and good pastures, may, in the near future, begin to make a noise in the world. More anon.

Inyo.

ATHLETICS.

Athletic Sports and Other Pastimes.

EDITED BY ARPHIPPUS.

SUMMARY.

An excellent showing was made by the members of the Alpine Athletic Club on Sunday last, on the occasion of their second out-door meeting, which was held at the Bay District track. Several records were broken and the members of the new organization proved in a substantial manner that their club will be well represented at the championship meeting on Decoration Day.

The outdoor athletes were obliged to stop practice for a couple of days at the beginning of the week owing to the wet weather. The rest, however, will do them more good than harm as many of them have been training hard for several weeks past.

The opening of the Olympic Club's new grounds will be the next event of importance and great preparations are being made for the occasion.

The wheelmen are enthusiastic over the coming century run which promises to bring out an unusually large field of riders.

RUNNERS, WALKERS, JUMPERS, ETC.

It is said that Purcell, of the O. C. team, recently in a private trial broke the Pacific Coast record for pole vaulting.

Judging from the records made by some of the athletes at the sports of the Alpine Club on Sunday last, a good many of the old time Pacific Coast records will be left in the lurch on May 30th.

The members of the Lurline Club will hold a cross country run from Sausalito on May 18th.

The same club will hold a "Ladies' Night" exhibition in about two weeks, when a select programme of athletic sports will be given.

The students at Berkeley will hold a Field-day on Saturday next. The following is a list of the events to be decided:

1. 100 yards run, maiden, closed.
2. 100 yards run, scratch, open.
3. 220 yards run, handicap, closed.
4. 220 yards run, scratch, open.
5. 440 yards run, scratch, open.
6. 880 yards run, scratch, open.
7. 880 yards run, scratch, closed.
8. 1-mile run, handicap, closed.
9. Running broad jump, handicap, op n.
10. Running high jump, handicap, open.
11. Throwing 16-pound hammer, handicap, open.
12. Pole vault, handicap, closed.
13. 1-mile walk, handicap, closed.
14. 120-yard hurdle, handicap, open.
15. High kick, handicap, closed.
16. Consolation race, 440 yards open.
17. Relay race, 1 mile, 5 men, closed.
18. Tug-of-war, teams of 4 men, closed.

These games should be well attended, as all the athletes are now in the pink of condition. The Olympic and Alpine Clubs of this city will send over some of their best men to compete in the open events, which are indeed very numerous. The U. C. men have not been sleeping of late, and will make a good showing against the outside men. Competitors and visitors should take the 12 o'clock boat from this side, as the games will begin promptly at 1 o'clock.

The Alpine Amateur Athletic Club will hold a boxing tournament for members of the club during the month of June. Valuable prizes will be awarded the winners.

Walter Scott of the O C. appears to be getting back into his old form again. He should make a good fight in the five-mile run on May 30th.

Both the Olympic and Alpine tug-of-war teams are practicing hard for the championship struggle.

ON THE WHEEL.

It is expected that the members of the Bay City Wheelmen will carry off the majority of the prizes at the coming two-day tournament to be held at San Jose Cal. Hammer, Plummer and Wetmore should certainly win some of the medals.

A number of the local riders were seen riding in the direction of San Jose on Sunday. The roads are now in first class condition. Four or five years ago it was considered quite a performance for a man to ride fifty miles in one day, but at the present time there are dozens of local riders who think nothing of riding all round the bay, a distance of over one hundred miles, on Sunday.

The membership of the California Division League of American wheelmen has largely increased during the past month. There our several candidates now waiting to be elected.

Runs are being held regulalry every week by the different clubs which keeps the riders in good condition.

AT THE OARS.

The fine weather on Sunday was appreciated by a good number of the North and South end oarsmen who took practise spins on the bay.

The April Club sent out several crews, while the cracks of the Pioneer Club also rowed to the Sugar Refinery and around the city front.

The Lurline Club members were busy on Sunday, and not a single boat remained out of the water. This young club is fast gaining in membership as well as in fame.

CLUB JOTTINGS.

There was no meeting of the P C A A A on Friday evening, May 2nd, as only two delegates were present. It is evident that too many meetings of the Association are held. At present a meeting is held every Friday evening, whereas two meetings a month would be sufficient to transact all the necessary business. Some of the delegates complain of the length of the meetings, which generally drag until about midnight. They say they would willingly attend the meetings if they were held semi-monthly instead of weekly.

The Directors of the California Athletic Club have at last decided to do away with their amateur annex. They made a great mistake when they first started the annex. The men who first suggested the idea were not urged on by their love of pure athletics; it was jealousy and a craving for greatness that prompted them to organize an amateur branch. They thought that by inducing the young members of the Golden Gate Club to come over to them they would cripple that club, but in this idea they were mistaken. On the other hand, they expected to place their club on a level with the Olympic by having under their jurisdiction a body of young amateur athletes. It is true that some of the best amateurs on the Pacific Coast were connected with the California Athletic Club's annex, but the unmanly and ungentlemanly manner in which some of these athletes were treated by the Directors of the club at large is a sufficient proof that the amateur branch was started merely as a bluff at some of the older and more respectable athletic clubs. When the P C A A A refused to recognize the California amateur annex the Directors of the club became demoralized as it were, and finding that their amateurs were of no use to them they started in to get rid of them as quickly and easily as possible.

The second handicap meeting of the California Footracing Association was held at Central Park on Sunday afternoon. Owing to the counter attractions the attendance was only moderate. The sprinting was good, however, and in the majority of the heats fast time was made It was understood that H. M. Johnson the champion all round athlete was to attempt to lower his own record for the 100 yards run, but as Mr. Johnson was ill the trial was not made. The next meeting of the Association will be held at the same place on Sunday, June 8. All the leading professional sprinters in America will take part in the runs.

JOTTINGS FROM ALL OVER.

The annual spring games of the Manhattan Athletic Club will be held at New York City this afternoon.

The individual general athletic championship competition under the auspices of the American Athletic Union will be held at New York City on June 10.

R. C. Chadsy, who rejoices in the title of the champion runner of the National Guard, and claims the best professional indoor record for three miles, has resigned from company E, Ninth Regiment, N G S N Y, and removed to Stamford, Ct., having accepted a position with the Yale & Towne Lock Company. He intends to join Company C, Fourth Regiment, N G C, and will represent said company in future National Guard contests after the Summer is over, as he does not propose to do any running till Fall.

Two fine performances were accomplished at the games of the South London, Eng., Harriers, held at the Kennington Oval, on April 12. The president of the Oxford University Athletic Club, W. Pollock-Hill, had a virtual walk over in the 1,320yds. scratch race, he running out against the watch and making the distance in 3m. 12:3-5s., faster time than was ever previously accomplished on a grass course. In the four mile event the winner, J. Kebblewhite, covered the distance in 20m. 20:3-5s., which also easily beats all previous records on turf. He completely outclassed his field, finishing twenty seconds before Fry, the second man.

The Harvard Cycling Association have decided to accept the challenge for a team race of two miles between three men each of Harvard and Yale Universities, provided that the chairman of the Racing Board of the League of American Wheelmen allows the contest to be governed by other rules than those laid down in track rule 33 of the League

C. G. Psotta will take both a cedar and a paper shell with him to England, and in the race for the Diamond Sculls at Henley will represent the Schuylkill Navy and also wear the colors of his alma mater, Cornell University.

John Teemer, ex-champion sculler of America, has received a license as a saloon keeper at McKeesport, Pa., and it is announced that he will now abandon rowing and give his whole attention to the liquid refreshment business. It is pretty certain, however, that in case Wm. O'Connor returns to the States champion of the world Teemer will have a try for the honors.

The match between Peter Kemp and Neil Matterson, the Australian sculler, for $2,500 a side was rowed over the usual course on the Parramatta River, at Sydney, N. S. W., on April 25th, and resulted in the victory of the former, who led throughout and won by forty lengths. Time, 21m. 13s. It is now in order for the victor to challenge the winner of the race for the championship of the world (which was not included in the issue of the recent race) between Wm. O'Connor and James Stansbury.

The Columbia Athletic Club, of Washington, D. C., opened their new, commodious and elegantly appointed club house on the evening of April 25th, and from the crush within the walls it appeared as though all the youth and beauty of the capital had turned out to celebrate the event. The rooms had been beautifully decorated for the occasion, flowers and tropical plants being here, there and everywhere in the greatest profusion, and the scene ersembling fairyland. The members of the club paid the closest attention to their guests, fair and otherwise, and everybody present managed to derive much real enjoyment from the visit, despite the elbowing they were unavoidably subjected to. The Columbias may well feel proud of their new home, and the inducements now offered should have the effect of adding largely to the membership of the organization.

William Jackson, alias "The American Deer," the veteran runner once famous in sporting circles the world over, is still living in England, and is to take a complimentary benefit at the Royal Albert Music Hall, London, on May 13th.

ALPINE DAY.

A Great Athletic Tournament at the Bay District Track.

Walking and Running Records Broken.

The second out-door athletic meeting of the Alpine Amateur Athletic club was held at the Bay District track on Sunday last under the most favorable auspicies. The weather was warm and delightful, and the surrounding hills and fields looked fresh and green. A more perfect day for field games could not have been selected, the strong winds that generally blow up the home shelter of the Bay District were substituted by gentle zephyrs that soothingly fanned the faces of the spectators as they sat in the grand stands. The attendance was fair, being probably about 1,000, and the track in very good order, especially in front of the club house where the sprint races were decided.

The Phœnix Military Band played choice selections during the progress of the games, and the music certainly encouraged the athletes, for several records were broken. The Alpine Club is a new organization, and we do not care to censure any of its members, but we think the members at large should have taken more interest in last Sunday's games. The management of the meeting was left to half a dozen of the members, most of whom were entered for the games, while the majority stood around or sat up in the grand stands watching the sport. The result was that outsiders had to be called in as judges, timers and measurers. The Alpine Club has now a membership of nearly 200, and in future the members at large should get in and work on an occasion like that of Sunday last, and show the public that they were both willing and able to manage their own games.

The Marshalls failed to do their duty and allowed men and boys to crowd on the track to such an extent that the ladies and their escorts in the Grand Stands were unable to witness the finishes of the races. Several prominent club men were present, including W. Greer Harrison, the ex-President of the Olympic Club, who speaks very highly of the Alpine Club.

The first event on the programme was the 100 yards run (novice) for members of the club. Kelly was the favorite, but J. W. Creagh, a comparatively new man, surprised his club mates by winning the event with perfect ease in 11 3-5 secs. It was said that Creagh had only practiced twice for the race and if the report be correct he should make his mark at sprinting.

A handicap race of 120 yards also for members of the club was next on the programme, and the scratch man John D. Garrison won after a magnificent struggle from E. P. Moody, who had five yards start. Previous to the race many claimed that Garrison was too heavily handicapped, but the handicapper had his time down fine and felt confident that be had a good show to win. Another new man turned up in the shot putting event in the person of P. J. Sheedy, who in his first put covered a distance of 32ft 9½in. Even with big handicaps none of the other contestants could come up to Sheedy, who felt very proud of his victory. With proper practice Sheedy should make a fine showing in the championship games.

The most exciting race of the day was next decided. It was a 440-yard handicap run, open. Many thought that Henderson of the Olympic Club, who was placed at scratch, would have had an easy victory, but Garrison of the Alpines was in too fine a condition to be beaten. He had eight yards start off Henderson and won rather easily in 53 1 5 seconds. The speed and staying powers displayed by the Alpine man in the race caused a good many of the sports present to change their minds as to the respective merits of Henderson and Garrison. Many claimed that Garrison could defeat Henderson from scratch.

A three-mile handicap walk, open, brought out but two starters, P. N. Gafney and A. Cooke, both of the Alpine Club. Gafney was in good condition, having trained faithfully for six weeks before. He broke all the Pacific Coast records. The old records are as follows: One-half mile, 3:31 (Horace Coffin, O. A. C.), one mile, 7:10½ (C. B. Hill, M. C. C.), one and one-half miles, 12:07 (Horace Coffin, O. A. C.), two miles, 16:57, and three miles, 25:51¼ (P. N. Gafney, A. A. A. C.) Gafney's time was as follows: One half mile, 3:26¼; one mile, 7:07; one and one-half miles, 11:03; two miles, 15:13, and three miles, 25:09. It will be seen that all the records were lowered by many seconds. For five days previous to the race, Gafney had been sick, and when he finished the second mile he was obliged to stop through weakness. On coming too, however, he continued on, and although in stopping he lost over one and a half minutes, he managed to break the three-mile record by 42¼ seconds. A couple of prejudiced individuals who were present claimed that Gafney did not walk square during one period of the race, but as the judges who followed the men around the track thought otherwise, Gafney's walking was accepted as square. When C. B. Hill made the mile record of 7:10½ at Oakland six years ago, a good many persons claimed that he had run. It is a hard task to judge walking, and it takes an experienced eye to detect "mixing." Some people imagine that because a man makes very fast time he must be running. They will not take the trouble to watch the performer's movement steadily, preferring to base their opinions on the announced time. Charles Little, of the Alpine Club, surprised the people by winning the Club 880-yard handicap run from scratch in 2m. 7½s., a little over a second slower than the coast record. Little is a very small man, and when in condition weighs only 103 pounds. He has a splendid style, and covers ground in a very graceful manner. Some of the "kickers" present claimed that Little must be a professional on account of the fast time he made. J. F O'Connor, of the Alpine Club, won the running high jump in grand style, clearing 5ft. 3½in. He was the scratch man With steady practice O'Connor should get over 5ft. 6in. Charles Armbruster, who got second, is a very promising young man, and also promises to become famous at this pastime.

Garrison again achieved another victory by winning the 220 yard run from scratch in 24½ secs.

The three mile run brought out all the cracks. Little won in 16min 30sec., breaking the coast record by several seconds. He had 15 seconds handicap. Cooley, of the Olympics, finished second. He was one of the scratch men but Little reversed affairs by gaining on his handicap. Walter Scott also started but had to quit on the second mile. Little can probably beat any amateur on the coast at any distance from a quarter of a mile up to ten miles.

The open hundred yards run was won by J D Garrison, of the Alpines, in 10½ seconds. He had a start of 4 yds.

The final event was a steeplechase which H. C. Cassidy easily won. He made a fine race considering the fact that he was out of form.

Cooke, who participated in the three-mile walk obtained second place. and he, although very tired, made good time.

The following is a summary of the results:

100 yards run Novice (club) J W Creagh, 1 st, Time 11⅗ secs., R C Staats, 2nd by 3 yards.

120 yards run, handicap (club) J D Garrison, scratch, 1st, Time 13 secs., E P Moody, 5yds. 2nd.

Putting 16lb. shot, handicap (club) P J Sheedy scratch, 1st 32ft. 9½in., John Hart 3ft. 2nd.

440 yards run, handicap (open) J D Garrison, 8yds. 1st., A S Henderson, Olympic Club, scratch 2nd. Time 53 1-5sec. won by 3yds.

3-mile handicap walk, (open) P N Gafney scratch, 1st, Time 25min. 9sec., A Cooke, 45secs. 2nd won by 2ft.

880 yards run handicap (club) Charles Little scratch, 1st. Time 2min, 7½secs., E P Moody, 40yds. 2nd., won by a couple of feet.

Running high jump, handicap (club) J F O'Conner, scratch 1st, 5ft. 3½in., Charles Armbruster 3in. 2nd 5ft. 3in.

220 yards run handicap. (club) J D Garrison, scratch, 1st., Time 24½secs., J W Creagh, 8 yds. 2nd won by 2yds.

3 mile run, handicap (open) Charles Little A A A C, 15secs. 1st, F L Cooley O A C scratch, 2nd, Time 16min. 30secs.

100 yard run handicap (open) John D Garrison 4yds, 1st., Time 10½secs, H S Henderson scratch O A C 2nd.

Steeplechase, handicap, (club) H C Cassidy scratch, 1st, A Cooke, 40yds. 2nd., No time taken.

TURF AND TRACK.

Fordham has won eleven races this season.

Mr. Belmont has relegated She to private life.

Gabe Case is in charge of the club house at Fleetwood Park.

The Haggin yearlings will probably be sold this year as Westchester.

A brother to Connemara has been foaled at Mr. Cassatt's Chesterbrook Farm.

Rancho Del Peso's mare Mabel, sister to Beautiful Bells, is stinted to Stamboul 2:12½.

Dan Dennison says: Prince of Norfolk will prove himself the best stallion in California.

Frank Anthony of Denver, Col., has bought a four-year old Red Wilkes colt for $3,700.

C. B. Hawkins recently had a full brother to Longstreet foaled at his farm near Lexington, Ky.

Maud Hampton's filly foal by Sir Modred is as good looking as any the grand old mare has ever produced.

Pancoast has so far recovered from the stroke of lightning received two years ago as to be useful in the stud.

Juno (dam of Earl 2:23½ and Greenlander 2:19¼) by Hambletonian 10 out of Lady Morrison will be bred to Axtell.

Hampden Park, Springfield, Mass., has raised a guarantee fund of $25,000 and will be in the grand circuit as usual.

Messrs. Kelly & Samuels decided to dispense with Cook's services, and have engaged Casey McLaughlin in his place.

Geo. W. Leavitt of Boston has sold the pacing stallion Cohannet, 2:17½, to W. L. Grout of Orange, Mass., for $3,000.

B. C. Holly says Mountain Boy's colts are exceptionally good looking, and he is particularly sweet on one or two of them.

S P. Armstrong, of Juggler fame, has five horses of D. J. McCarty's at the latter's place on the Coney Island plank road.

Messrs Kelly and Samuels last Saturday sold Welcome, br m. 5, Warwick—Aeolia to L. J. Rose, who will breed her to Argyle.

Milton Young has sold his three-year-old filly Helter Skelter, by Pell Mell. Encore, to Edward Corrigan of Kansas City for $5,000.

The two crack broodmares. Explosion and Maud Hampton, have filly foals, the former by Darebin and the latter by Sir Modred.

Small Hopes, Vanderbilt's $10,000 trotter, and afterwards a notorious "ringer," is now hauling an express wagon in New York.

Ed Corrigan has purchased from the Straus Brothers, of Lexington, the yearling colt by Longfellow, dam Latonia by Billet, for $3,000.

Mr. White's Derby candidate, Kirkham, ran third (on the 29th) for the Hastings plate, one mile, Reaume winning and Heckler second.

Col. F. E. Brace, a well known racing man and the breeder of St. Gatien, the dead heater for the Derby in 1884, committed suicide in England.

Messrs. Tucker & Cherry have purchased the brown two year old colt National by Leonatus dam Brandoline. The price is said to be $7,500.

H. D. Miller's Daisy is being stinted to imported Cheviot and if she rounds too, will be raced in the fall instead of going East as was intended.

Judge R. N. Baskin, of Salt Lake City, has bought of S. Herr, the brown two-year-old filly Leora Queen by Emory Boy, dam King Girl, for $1,000.

Henry Walsh returned to Palo Alto last Sunday. He turned over Racine, Homer and Glenlivet to McCormick, who will train them for the Undine Stable.

Two minuses make a plus. A pure-gaited natural trotter is the result of the mating of Roy Wilkes 2.12½, and Jenny Lind 2:17, both pacers, last season.

Since Samuel Emery, the bookmaker, paid $5,000 for Fordham at the Dwyer sale last December, the speedy brown son of Falsetto has won eleven races, worth $3,960.

French Park has been declared out of the Suburban, a fact which would seem to indicate that Mr. Gideon's horse will not be able to undergo the severe work of training.

W. W. Adams of Lexington has bought of R. T. Arnold the two year old colt by Vauxhall-Silken Ban, by King Ban, for $1,000. He will be shipped to Buenos Ayres, where he will race.

The chestnut colt Fontenoy, 2 years, by Fonso, dam Sleepy Kate, dropped dead at Lexington, Ky., while galloping on the 22d. He was well tried and considered a colt of great promise.

One of the handsomest teams in the state is J. L. McCord's two chestnuts, Mary Lou 2:25½ and a four year old gelding full brother to her. Mr. McCord was driving them daily in Sacramento last week.

It is said that Col. McIntyre is having the McCarty white hat renovated after its 17th of March experience, and that it will positively make its reappearance, with a new nap, on Brooklyn Handicap day.

When Donathan left with the Hearst Stable it was intended to go to Washington Park, and after a few days rest go to New York, but while en route Donathan received a telegram and went to St. Louis instead.

"If you stay in the breeding business twenty years longer, I predict that you will make more money than if you worked even a gold mine," was the remark of Senator Stanford to a well known breeder after the close of the Palo Alto sale in New York.

Eclipse by imported Kyrle Daly out of Billow by Longfield was sold at the Haggin sale last year for $325. His owner when asked to put a price on him after his last victory said $25,000, $10,000 was offered for him and refused.

It is of the highest importance that the rule requiring pedigrees of horses to be given with all entries be enforced by managers of trotting associations, and papers reporting trotting races should always pedigree their summaries.

Mr. A. B. Etter, of Amherst, N. S., while on a visit to the United States, a short time ago, purchased the valuable two-year-old filly Highlawn Belle, by Alcantara, 2:23, dam Almonia by Almont 33, out of the dam of Aristomont, 2:27½.

John Reavey bought of Dr. Cutler, the well known Sacramento veterinary surgeon, two colts last week. They are own brothers a yearling and a two-year-old by Joe Hooker out of a mare by Wildidle, grandam Emma Barnes by Norfolk.

Helter Skelter made a show of her company in the Nevada Stakes on May 1st. Ed Corrigan purchased her from Milt Young for $5,000, and by her victory he won more than half of that sum. The filly is by the English stallion Pell Mell.

Messrs. J. A. & A. H. Morris have a two-year-old colt called Glucose. The Castle Stable also rejoices in the possession of a Glucose of the same age. If both stick to the name, the bewildered speculators are apt to get "stuck" on the wrong one.

Charlie Dennison left with the Rose Stable last week. Charlie, who has been very successful this spring, should learn a good deal on the Eastern trip, and as he can ride a handy weight, is quiet and steady, he will reflect credit to his well known sire, the irrepressible Dan.

The well-known broodmare Hettie B died at Capt. Franklin's Kennesaw Stud, Gallatin, Tenn., on the 19th. She was a bay mare, bred by Capt. Franklin in 1876, by imp. Glengarry, dam Kathleen (George Kinney's dam), by Lexington; 2nd dam Maria Innis by imp. Yorkshire.

The May Day races at South Park, Eureka, resulted as follows: Trotting, mile heats, 2 in 3, was won in straight heats by T. F. Rick's bay mare Bessie; time, 2:52, 2:53½. The half mile dash, for two-year-olds, was won by E C. Hunt's Arthur H. Jr. The other trotting race was won in straight heats by Ole Peterson's brown gelding Charlie.

C. B. Hawkins, the breeder of the famous Longstreet, is playing in hard luck. He has six mares, one of whom proved barren, two others slipped their foals, two colts died after living a few weeks, and only one of the lot, Semper Idem, the dam of Longstreet, came out all right with a fine brown colt. He is by the great sire, Longfellow, and therefore a full brother of Longstreet.

The following horses have been shipped by Mr. Ellam of Picadilly, London, with a stud groom and jockey, to Mr. A. Whitehouse of Wyoming: Busy Bee, 8 yrs., bay horse, by Altyre; Queen Bee, by King Tom; Clementia, by Venison; Little Vixen, 5 yrs., mare by Foxhall; Mattie—Astray, by Blair Athol; Iluna, 13 yrs., mare by Blair Athol; Martinique, by Macaroni; Taxation, 6 yrs., mare by Richelieu and a Hackney stallion.

The five-year-old mare Seabreeze, winner of the Oaks and St. Leger in 1888, and many other valuable races has been sent to Welbeck to the Duke of Portland's unbeaten St. Simon by Galopin. Seabreeze is by Isonomy out of St. Marguerite by Hermit out of Devotion by Stockwell. If the result of the mating of two such royally bred race-horses were put up at auction as a yearling the chances are that all yearling prices would be eclipsed.

An Austrian gentleman visiting New York made the journey from his country to induce one of the best of our jockeys to go to Austria and ride for Prince Esterhazy, the principal turfmen in Austria. "Snapper" Garrison was approached by this gentleman, who made a most tempting offer to the "Snapper". It is said to be as high as $30,000 for the season, but Garrison was yet staunch enough to declare that America was good enough for him.

The racing galloway Merry Bells, that died in England about two weeks ago, while being prepared for the Abbey Park meeting, appears to have been a greater performer than old Barnum. She was foaled 1863, sired by Knight of St. Patrick, dam Solitude, and had won one hundred and twenty-two races before she was retired to the paddock at the age of twenty-one. Proving a failure as a matron, she was taken up and put in training at twenty-seven years old, and she was running wonderfully well until a day before her death.

At the Belle Meade sale it was pitiful to see the anxiety of the stud grooms when the stallions were being auctioned off. Old Bob, the venerable head groom, was in a fever of anxiety for fear some of his pets would be sold away from the farm, and when Iroquois was under the hammer and about to be knocked down, the groom, who held the horse's bridle, not knowing where the last bid came from, excitedly called out to Captain Kidd, the auctioneer: "Be shure you close him on de right man."

When a shoe is to be taken off it must not be violently wrenched at the risk of splitting off a large piece of hoof with it. Let the clinched ends of each nail be first turned back. Then the shoe may be carefully raised with the pinchers, far enough to withdraw the nails, so that their heads may be taken hold of by the pinchers and each nail separately drawn. The nails may also be drawn out, one at a time, so as not to alter the position of the tip or shoe, and a fast nail, made to exactly fit the countersink in the shoe and to pass through the same hole in the hoof, may be driven in its place.

Jimmy Dustin is gradually gathering together a select Stable of trotters for the circuit. Dan Dennison's old favorite Rube 2:24 is among the string. Dustin still has room for another good one or two, and as he is well known as one of the best and steadiest drivers in the country; he should soon fill up the vacancies in his stable. Only last week from memory he ran off over twenty horses with records better than 2:20, which he has handled, including Johnston 2:06¼ Maxie Cobb 2:13½, Rowdy Boy 2:13¾, Almont Patchen 2:15, Anteeo 2:16½, Derby 2:10¼, Charley Ford 2:16¾, J Q 2:17¼, Piedmont 2:17½, Ned Winslow 2:17¼, Allan Roy 2:17½, Adelaide 2:18, Monroe Chief 2:18¼, Pickard 2:18½, Keene Jim 2:19¼, Frank 2:19½, Troubador 2:19½, Alfred G 2:19¾, Maggie E 2:19¾, Camors 2:19¾, Deck Wright 2:19¾, besides lowering with Faustino last year the yearling stallion record to 2:35.

The Ione Valley Echo says: Geo. Brown of Plymouth and Elmer Devore of the Consumnes, came to Ione, Wednesday, and while here offered to trot their buggy horse against any horse in town. Alex. Fowler of San Francisco looked at the horse, accepted the proposition, and a bet of $20 a side was made. Mr. Fowler then started out to find a horse, and selected C. F. Bunch's Ajax. The race, one mile dash, took place at the Park in the afternoon. The visitor's horse trotted a lively clip for a half mile, but Ajax was too much for him and won by several lengths. The time, we are informed, was 2:48½.

Several California racing men have been complaining about the dearth of good trainers and yet James Garland, better known as Big Jim, is at present disengaged. Jim, is, as is well known, one of the most successful trainers on the coast, a favorite with all men on account of his kindly nature and good judgment. All race goers recollect the fine shape in which Beaconsfield was brought to the post for his engagements, while only last spring Emotion was in grand form and with ordinary luck could not have lost the six furlong race won by White Cloud. Garland is at present living in Sacramento.

The Undine Stable and W. H. Smith's horses will go to Chicago next week, the former will include Homer, the speedy two year-old who beat Fairy at the Blood Horse meeting; Tycoon, who was very successful last year at Sacramento and other meetings; Racine, who has an untarnished escutcheon, for when he has not won, he has run second to his stable companion; and Glenlivet, a two year-old sister to Guenn. Joe Narvice will ride for the stable, and W. McCormick—than whom there is no better—will train. Mr. Smith will have the sensational Al Farrow, Longshot, the speedy Susie S., and probably Duke of Milpitas with F. De Poister in charge.

Jockeys make a great mistake in bringing the spur into the sides of their horse as the first intimation that he is wanted to jump forward. If daily practiced to walk and to stand a long time in row, and then at some painless signal to start off with companions at no furious pace, and to pull up soon, without any racing, the young horse would come to learn that he need not tear himself to pieces before his race begins, nor be prancing ten yards behind, or with his head the wrong way, when the flag drops. Trainers might often agree together or with any friend on horseback to introduce occasionally the excitement of strange company, which would, no doubt, be an important part of the lesson.

The Kelly & Samuels stable, with Dan Hennessy in charge, will leave for Denver on Monday. Ed McGinnis, Pliny and Lizette will form the stable. The former is well known on the coast, having been a successful performer for three years, while Pliny who was purchased a year ago from Palo Alto, has done well for his owners and should account for the Colorado Derby. Lizette is a two year-old filly by Hyder Ali out of Kate Fletcher. Casey McLaughlin will ride for the stable instead of Cook, whose services have been dispensed with. The Golden Gate Stable and probably the Orange Grove Stable will go at the same date to participate in the racing at the Overland Park meeting.

Last week we noticed that the young Electioneer stallion, Bow Bells, had been severly injured at the Hermitage Stud. "Bon Air" has a paragraph in the Spirit which would tend to show that the colt was not as badly injured as at first supposed; he says

"The great Bow Bells received a slight hurt at the Hermitage Stud the other day, which was at first thought to be serious, but which, I am glad to state, will not result in any permanent injury. The hurt was received while in the act of embracing a mare. In some way all his feet left the earth, and before the attendants could prevent it the horse fell to the ground, striking on his hip. I asked Mr. Overton if the horse was badly hurt, and he replied that he was not; that he would be all right in a few days."

Le Roi Est Mort; Hermit is dead. Most race-goers will recollect the snowstorm year (1867) when Hermit won the Derby at 66—1. He was shortly afterwards relegated to the stud, and has earned undying fame for himself by his sons and daughters, whose racing qualities were so excellent, and the public demand for his services was so great, that Henry Chaplin, the owner of Hermit, had at last to limit him to five approved mares—outside his own—at $1,250 each. Among the best of his get are Shotover, St. Blaise (now Mr. Belmont's property) both Derby winners, Friars Balsam, Thebais, Peter, Tristan, Martini, St. Marguerite (dam of Seabreeze), Lonely, St. Mirin and St. Medard. Hermit mares are invaluable, and as a matter of fact, cannot be purchased for love or money. Flirt, the dam of Gorgo and Flambeau, is one of the few in this country—by the way, Mrs. Langtry's Friar Tuck is a full brother to Flirt. Hermit was foaled in 1864 by Newminster, out of Seclusion by Tadmor, grandam Miss Sellon by Cowl.

The Rose stable left for New York last Saturday morning. Bridges had nine horses on the car, viz., Mikado, ch g, 6, Shiloh, dam Margery; Rico, b g. 3, Shannon, dam Fannie Lewis; Rover, 3, ch c Wildidle, dam imp Rosetta and six 2-year olds; Conrad, br c, Flood, dam imp Goula; Oscar, br c, Wildidle, by imp Petroleuse, a brown colt brother to Rico by Shannon out of Fannie Lewis; Fairy, b f, Argyle, dam Fairy Rose—dam of Racine and Shannon Rose; Peri, blk f, a sister to Oreflamme by Flood—Frolic, and Flight, b f, sister to Faustine by Flood dam imp Flirt, dam of Gorgo and Flambeau. Mikado was very successful last year in California and should make a useful plater. Rico was the winner of the Nighthawk Stakes in 1:42, at Sacramento, last fall, and should be more than useful. Fairy is probably one of the speediest two-year-old fillies in America. Flight should be good. Monohan and Charlie Dennison went on with stable. Mr. Rose left this week for New York.

An express agent, speaking of shipping stock by freight, told a story of Sam Bryant. "I had been negotiating last spring with Sam Bryant concerning shipping his horses to Louisville, and was at West Side Park talking to him, having just about completed arrangements, when a red-faced race-horse owner, who seemed to be on excellent terms with the redoubtable Bryant, came up and in a badgering tone remarked: 'Hello, Sam, you've a fool to ship them horses by express when they will be just as safe and won't cost half as much by freight.' I began to be a little uneasy for fear the remark would influence my man not to let me have the shipment, but I was soon reassured. 'Look here,' said Bryant, as he turned a withering glance upon the speaker and scanned him from head to foot, 'I reckon you wouldn't.' Then after a scornful silence of a few seconds, he jerked out: 'When I had hosses like yourn, an' it ain't long ago neither—yes, I used to have 'em—I didn't ship by express neither. I drove 'em through the country.'"

Secretary Brewster of the Washington Park Club, Chicago, is quoted as saying: "I will bet a good round sum now that El Lio Rey will not win the American Derby, and I will go farther than that and wager that he will not even be a starter. I have had twenty-seven years' experience in the racehorse business, and I have never yet seen a horse that had either lung fever or pneumonia that had pulled through and ran a mile and a half at good speed. I do not care whether the horse is a roarer or not. There is one thing, however, that I do know, and that is he was a very sick horse last fall. It took four men to hold him up for hours, and it was their attention that pulled him through. Had he been allowed to lie down the chances are that he would have died. Should he come to the post there may be a lot of fools who will be scared out by his appearance, for there are lots of fools in the racehorse business.

"At a sale of Nelson stock in this city on the 24th inst," says a Boston correspondent of the New York Sun, "Mr. C. H. Nelson, the owner of the celebrated stallion Nelson, 2:14¼, and 'Myrtle' Downing, a well known sporting man, became involved in a hot argument. Downing offered to wager $2,500 that Alcryon could beat Nelson, and characterized the great national stallion race, which was trotted at Beacon Park last September, which was won by Nelson, as a 'job.' Nelson waxed warm and offered to bet $50 that Downing would not make good his offer to bet $2,500. Whereupon Downing put up $50 that he would bet, and went away to get the money. He returned with $2,500, flaunted it in Nelson's face, after which he planked it down on a desk and called upon Nelson to cover it, at the same time claiming the $50 which he said that Nelson wagered that he would not 'put up.' A hot argument followed, which interfered with the sale. At length a policeman cleared the crowd, and the stakeholder, to stop all disputes, returned both Nelson and Downing their money."

The sons of Eolus are in great request as stallions. Eolian has been sold to Mr. Wm. Easton of New York, to Messrs. Kohrs & Beilenberg, Deer Lodge City, Montana. Eolian is a brown horse, bred in 1883 by Mr. R. J. Hancock at the Ellerslie Stud, Albemarle, Va. He is a son of Eolus, dam Calash, by imp Phaeton; 2nd dam Blandina by Lexington; 3d dam My Lady by imp Glencoe; 4th dam Motto by imp Barefoot. As a racehorse, Eolian was very successful. In 1887, as a four-year-old, he won 16 out of 28 races, among them the Woodlawn Handicap, one mile and three sixteenths, in 2:02½, with 115 pounds, beating Eurus, 116 lbs.; Volante, 120 lbs; Quito, Rupert, Richmond, Barnum, Dry Monopole, Ben Ali, etc. He defeated Hanover twice at Baltimore. At Coney Island he did his mile in 1:40¾, beating a field of sixteen and carrying 111½ lbs. The following spring he eclipsed this when, with 115 lbs. up, he beat a field of eight in 1:40¼, the field including Terra Cotta. Eolian is one of the most highly formed horses in the world, and if Montana expects to produce more Spokanes, he is the right horse.

The conference committee appointed by the Vermont State Agricultural Society and the Connecticut River Valley Association met on the 16th inst. at White River Junction and elected the following officers for the joint fair to be held at White River the second week in September next: President, George W. Hooker; Secretary, E J. Wallace; Treasurer, J. C. Parker; Executive Committee, H. G. Root, H. N. McIntyre, Chester Pike, Henry Chase, F B. Kendrick, J. C. Parker, George W. Smith and George W. Hooker. Plans were submitted to the building committee for a fire-proof exhibition building to be 34 by 100 feet, a grand stand with a capacity of 3,000 people, five stables and other buildings necessary. Purses and premiums amounting to $8,000 are offered for competition. In regard to a track, quite a strong sentiment was expressed in favor of the kite-shaped track, the latest fad in mile tracks One has just been completed at Independence, Ia., and Vermonters want to be the first to introduce one into New England. It would be a big attraction, and as to its practiability it has the indorsement of some of the best horsemen in the country. The indications are at present that the kite-shape will be adopted.

R. E. Loft, writing in the *London Live Stock Journal* on the subject of mules' breeding says:

There are a number of well-authenticated instances of the female mule breeding. I think Herodotus makes mention of one instance, it was, of course, regarded as an omen. If I am not mistaken the Jardin d' Acclimation in the Bois de Boulogne has more than one prolific mule, prolific both with the ass and the horse. I went with the idea of purchasing one, but did not find the manager at home. One strain of Barb (North Africa) is supposed to have a cross of the wild ass of the desert, and there is certainly a mulish appearance in some points noticeable in the Barb that is by no means the case in the Syrian. And the interbreeding of animals in a state of nature is different from that of animals in a state of domestication. I believe a cross between the fowl and pigeon has been produced, but not in a state of nature. I saw the Paris prolific mules, but did not see the foal, but the whole matter is one of notoriety, though by no means common. The male mule is not often seen entire, is extremely troublesome, attacking horses (entire) with great fury. I have never heard of a stud mule getting stock, but there may have been instances.

It is really surprising to note the change among Kentucky breeders in their estimate of Clay blood in a trotting pedigree. But a few years ago it was "No Clay in mine;" now, a horse bearing the name of Clay alone, without prefix or annex, attracts to his embrace the best bred mares in Kentucky, writes Mambrino in the Spirit.

The changed sentiment is probably as gratifying to Col. Strader as anyone in America, excepting always Mr Randolph Huntington. The Colonel relates a pleasant conversation he had with Mr. Bonner after his Electioneer purchases that is at this time quite apropos. He, after congratulating Mr. Bonner upon his liberal investments in Clay blood, remarked to him: "Mr. Bonner, you owe me forty thousand dollars." To a man considering himself no man's debtor financially this was rather a startling announcement to make. "How is that?" inquired Mr. Bonner. "Why," said the Colonel, "when you, several years ago, compared the Clay blood in a trotting pedigree as 'sawdust in oats' it cost me forty thousand dollars. My horse, Cassius M Clay, became valueless to me from that time as a public stallion and just about broke up Bob Strader." Mr. Bonner, after feelingly expressing his deep regret that he should have been the innocent cause of pecuniary loss to the Colonel, turned to his brother David, in his ready way, saying, "Draw the Colonel a check for forty thousand." The Colonel replied, "You draw it; I'll take it." A person fully posted upon the turf performances of some of the Clay families at the time Mr. Bonner was credited with the "sawdust" expression might conscientiously have endorsed Mr. Bonner's views and commended his discernment.

S. R. Crumbaugh has purchased from Walter Gratz, of Philadelphia, the celebrated thoroughbred stallion, Elkwood, for $5,000, says an exchange. During Elkwood's racing career he defeated "The Bard," Hanover, Kingston, Raceland, Firenzi, Dry Monopole, Terra Cotta, Eolian, Exile, Dewdrop, Volante, and a host of other first class horses. Perhaps the two last races ever run by Elkwood were the Kenner Stakes at Saratoga, in which he ran two miles with 118 pounds up in 3:34¼ as a three-year-old. This time has never been beaten on this track by a three-year-old, and the Great Suburban, Coney Island, in 1888, in which he ran one and one-fourth miles with a hundred and twenty pounds up in 2:07¼, this being the fastest Suburban on record. That Elkwood is a great horse, and will make a great sire, there can be little doubt. He was sired by Eolus out of Minnie Andrews, by Victory; 2d dam Nannie Harper by Glencoe; 3d dam Fannie Hill by Monarch; 4th dam Allegrante by Young Truffle; 5th dam imp Phantomia by Phantom, and so on fifteen or twenty crosses to Old Vintner Mare, thus combining the Leamington, Lexington, Glencoe, Revenue, Boston, Eclipse and Emeline blood. Major Crumbaugh has named his breeding establishment "Elkwood Stud Farm," in honor of his famous stallion.

"Yes, gentlemen, Small Hopes, Vanderbilt's $10,000 trotter, is now hauling an express wagon in New York, and it's a shame. He was the greatest 'ringer' on the American turf, made fortunes for more than one man. I ought to know, for I was his rubber."

There were a number of gentlemen in the reading room of the Leland hotel, and they were all admirers of the trotter. A discussion arose about Vanderbilt's and Bonner's possessions of horseflesh, when the "rubber" or groom of Small Hopes opened their eyes about the horse whose name was on the lips of members of every trotting association in America fourteen years ago. After a successful career of five years, the gang who handled him were detected in Boston, and after considerable trouble had been experienced, the greatest turf scandal of modern times was exposed.

The horse was forever barred at the meeting of the National Turf Congress, and his driver, Bill McGuigan, was also barred from ever driving a trotting horse for a purse or stake over an association course. After much litigation the famous horse was sold to Vanderbilt. With Lady Mac he annihilated all team records, and in his old age is compelled to draw an express wagon. He was bought by his present owner for $64.

"He must be about nineteen years old now," said the former groom, who is now in the real estate business, "but when he was five years old he trotted many a mile in 2:15. He was the cleanest trotter that ever looked through blinkers; no boots, braces, check reins or any modern trotting paraphernalia for him. And when it came to heats, he was the greatest stayer I ever heard of."—Horse Review.

Kicking horses are a dangerous nuisance, says a horse exchange, but they can be frequently cured of the habit by the use of expedients and exercise of patience. One lesson that may take a good deal of time with a young horse, and especially with a young mare, is allowing articles of any kind to be placed between its tail and its body. First put on a common crupper, and fasten it moderately tight to the surcingle. The foreleg may be strapped up if necessary for this purpose, and let down again as soon as all is secure. Let the colt move round you, and you will soon see if it is going to be ticklish about its tail. If it kicks let it kick as long as it will, and when it will not kick any longer slacken the crupper, so that it will drop three inches down its tail, and try the colt round at that. When it will no longer kick at a tight or slack crupper, tie a piece of stout string as long as your lounging line to the crupper midway between the tail and the surcingle, and taking the loose end of the string in your hand tighten and slacken the crupper with it as the colt passes round you. When reconciled to this, strap up the foreleg and take off the crupper. Fold and secure a duster or some such fabric round it so as to make the part that goes under the tail three or four inches in diameter. Then put the crupper on again, and try the colt round with it. If it kicks keep it going until it kicks no longer. See that it is not too tight, and that there is nothing about it to make very tender skin under the tail sore, so that it may be kept on several days and nights if necessary. It will have a greater effect, and be less likely to produce any soreness or tenderness if the materials under the tail, as well as its size and position, are varied every day. The crupper can be shortened and lengthened so as to touch different parts of the tail. On the second day a piece of wooly sheepskin may take the place of the duster; on the third day a hay band, on the fourth a loose cloth or a wide piece of leather or sacking, and thus continue something new until the colt will take no notice of any harmless thing, and will not pinch any of them when placed under his tail.—Exchange.

The Times Democrat says: A look of renewed interest was visible on the faces of every one present when the last broodmare at Belle Meade was knocked down and the sale of the stallions began.

There was a storm of enthusiastic applause as Uncle Bob reluctantly led Luke Blackburn into the ring. "You have before you, gentlemen," said Capt. Kidd, "a horse known and admired from Maine to California. He is the most even and beautiful breeder in America, and is regarded as the greatest horse. How much to start him—$20,000?" There was no answer for a minute, when Ed Applegate of New York broke the silence by offering $5000.

Uncle Bob's eyes rolled anxiously in the direction of his master, who had already said $6000. Van Kirkman then bid $10,000 for R. S. Hayne of Knoxville. Thousand dollar bids were then made until the price reached $20,000. It hung fire fully five minutes, and Capt. Kidd raised both hands and announced that when they touched the horse was sold. There was an impressive silence as he slowly brought them together and when they touched and Luke Blackburn was to remain at Belle Meade a great yell went up and Uncle Bob's eyes were raining tears of joy.

Iroquois was started at $15 000 by Wm. Easton, of New York. Gen. Jackson immediately said $16,000. Easton quit, but Geo. Wheelock, for "Lucky" Baldwin, entered into the bidding with $1,000 raises. Gen. Jackson promptly responded. There was a pause after Jackson's bid of $32,000, but finally Wheelock came again with $33,000. Gen. Jackson went him $1,000 better, and after another painful suspense, Iroquois was knocked down to the owner of Belle Meade.

Enquirer did not bring a bid of as much as $1,000, and Gen. Jackson said he should not be started at less, and he was led back to the paddock.

Great Tom met the same fate, Capt. Kidd saying that he had been selling Tom's get ever since he had been in the business.

Bramble was started at $1 000, and run up to $2,500, where he was knocked down to Gen. Jackson.

The Times Democrat of the 2d says: Those who have backed Hanover for any of the early handicaps will not get a start for their money, as the great race horse was fired and blistered on the right foreleg yesterday morning by Dr. Shepherd, and will consequently be thrown out of training. While this does not mean that Hanover retires permanently from the turf, it will be sometime before he will start in a race again. The leg treated has been troublesome for the past week, and sooner than risk breaking him down by continuing his work in that condition, the trip to the veterinary was resorted to. He looks well bodily, and was within three weeks or a month of a race. Sir Dixon will be the Dwyer's reliance in the Brooklyn. With Hanover out of the way Raceland bobs up serenely, and that the gelding is meant for the event is clear from the support he is receiving, $200 having been placed on him yesterday morning in one book. Mr. Belmont's horses will arrive at Sheepshead Bay on Tuesday next. It is generally understood that Gorgo, Senator Hearst's splendid daughter of Isonomy, will also be an absentee from the Brooklyn. The fact of the matter is that the mare is on the shelf at present, the old trouble in the shoulder having shown itself once more. Diablo is doing well in his work for the race, and so is Come-to-Taw.

The New York Jockey Club is pushing with giant strides to the foremost rank as the most powerful jockey club in the world. Its membership, which two months ago was but 800 is now at the 2500 mark. Where in the annals of clubdom can such a record of membership be found. It almost seems beyond belief, but it is an absolute fact, and I have no hesitation in saying that by the fall meeting of 1891 this club will have a list of members in excess, in point of number, of any four jockey clubs in the world. Mr. Koch, the courteous and gentlemanly Secretary of this great association, has done nearly everything in connection with its advancement. It was due to his untiring energy and hard work that the vast membership it now enjoys was secured. He has introduced many features in the new club that will prove of great benefit to horsemen, and the programme that will shortly be issued, will prove a revelation to owners, trainers and racing people generally. It is so far ahead of any of the programmes formerly issued by the various racing associations, and contains so much data information, an important memoranda outside of its entry lists that it will be eagerly sought for by all interested in racing. The books is handsomely gotten up, and no expense has been spared in making it the finest thing of the kind ever sent out by a racing association. Mr. Koch has labored long and earnestly on the book, and to him will be due all the thanks of horsemen for the most complete and magnificent programme we have yet seen. It is the purpose of the New York Jockey Club to allow members of all recognized clubs in United States, Great Britain, France, etc., of good standing, socially and financially, to become members. The new and magnificent club house now being erected at Morris Park at a cost of over a half million dollars, will soon be ready for occupancy, and will be kept open the year round just like any of the other great club houses in this vicinity (such as The Union, Union League, etc.) It will be sumptuously furnished and equipped. Magnificent roads and driveways leading to it are contemplated and will soon be constructed. And when one thinks of how reasonable it all is, to be members of this great club, it seems almost improbable. The initiation fee and dues for the first year, $25, seem ridiculously small, in fact no initiation fee is charged, the dues being only $25 a year to resident members, and $15 per year to non-resident members. The club has a great future before it, and started off successfully by having secured so efficient and hard working Secretary as it has.—The New York Saturday Globe.

Mr. W. B. Jennings, the well-known Maryland turfmen, has a somewhat peculiar lawsuit on his hands just now, being in the nature of an action for damages brought by Miranda Lane of Memphis for depriving her of the services of her son Alexander, says the Sportsman.

It appears that the plaintiff was once a slave, and the boy is her son by a second marriage.

"My client in 1872 married a man named Lane, and this boy was virtually her only child" said Mr. Ottis. "She lived in a little house of her own and worked out. About May 1, 1884—in fact, to-morrow is the sixth anniversary of that event—her boy did not come home for his supper. The mother, distracted and broken-hearted, believed he had fallen into the Mississippi. Not for a week did she obtain the slightest inkling of his whereabouts. Then his playmates spoke of his having frequented the racetrack. Finally she received a communication of Jennings, apprising her of her boys whereabouts.

"She caused letters to be written demanding his return. They were ignored. After this suffering for four years she applied to a lawyer in Memphis, and he sent the case to me. I do not suppose there ever was a case, excepting those of abduction for ransom, so unfeeling and outrageous as this; There never was a case where a man who claims to be respectable, perpetrated and persisted in such an outrage. I can only account for it on the supposition that Mr. Jennings has entirely neglected to put himself in this bereaved old mother's place. If there was no remedy at common law for such a wrong I would want to go out of my profession."

Mr D. F. McDonald of No. 167 Broadway, is attorney to Mr. Jennings. When asked for his side of the story: "In April, 1884," he said, "Mr. Jennings, who has a stable of horses, was with them in Memphis. Day after day this little fellow came about the track importuning the trainer to give him a job. Finally the trainer called his employer's attention to the boy, who said that his mother sent him. He sent word to the mother that he was soon going away. Nevertheless, the boy brought a written agreement which was read by one of his brothers to the mother, and to which he appended her name by her request, wherein she agreed to let him go with Mr. Jennings for three years for his board and clothes, he to have all moneys that he might earn riding horses for other owners than Mr. Jennings.

"You see, he was then a little ragamuffin, and Mr. Jennings thought he was doing an unspeakable service to both mother and boy in thus providing for him. After a year or so she wrote to the boy to come home. Mr. Jennings tried to get him to do so, and offered to give him the money to go with. The boy was doing first rate and wouldn't go. A year or so ago this woman sued him for $2500 wages of the boy and $2500 for loss of his society. This suit is an outrage on the boy, and more especially an outrage on a reputable, generous gentleman like Mr. Jennings, who supposed he was doing both mother and boy a great service in giving the latter employment."

Racing men will understand what a hardship this case must be on the Maryland turfmen. It is bad enough to take one of these urchins and try to make something out of him, but when you can be sued for damages for doing so it is one of those legal peculiarities which men are thinking sadly.

THE GUN.

"Real Sport" in France.

Charles Macalester. a rare shot, and as keen a sportsman as shoots, writes most interestingly of the French manner of seeking sport with the gun. He says:

"Would you like a day's shooting?" was the question put to me one afternoon in Paris by one of the dearest and best Frenchmen that ever lived. I had not fired a gun for nearly three months, and having heard a great deal about a "Battue," but never had a chance to take part in one, it is needless to say I accepted on the spot.

We parted with the understanding of meeting at the *Gare du Nord* next morning at 7:30 sharp.

The next thing was to get a gun My French friend offered me one of his, but they were pin fire with very short and crooked stocks.

Fortunately, I ran across a German-American, who told me he had a beauty of English make and kindly offered it to me.

When it reached home I found a nice No. 16. Having ordered my cartridges, which arrived in due season, with my natural curiosity, and always having a little hesitation about shooting shells unless I know what is in them, I cut one open.

The powder was all right, but the wads! Two, heavy; thick felt over powder, and a good size hair wad over shot. It was too late to change them or order new ones, so I packed them up.

On my arrival at the station next morning I found my friend, with five others, where they had been waiting for me about half an hour. It is characteristic of the Frenchman, when he goes anywhere—no matter how unimportant his object—to start about an hour ahead of time, and wait in the crowd for the gates and ticket office to open. Well, we were fortunate enough to get a compartment to ourselves. As soon as we started a pack of cards was brought out, a game of ecarte began, and we played until we reached our destination.

What card players the French are! They always have their game at night. Father, mother and children all join in and always play for something. I have seen three generations represented at one table, the grand-parents taking as much interest as the children.

On our arrival we found one of the party had won the large sum of twenty francs.

After having a fine luncheon with plenty of red and white wine to wash it down, a stage arrived to take us to the shooting grounds. It was a lovely drive of about four miles. Arriving at the lodge we were met by the head keeper and fifteen beaters, each armed with two sticks about five feet long. After putting our guns together and getting cartridges out, my friend, who happened to be the head man of the club, blew his horn. I fully expected to see some hounds come out, but no, it was to call the party together. He led the way, and stationed us along a narrow road about fifty yards apart. In the meantime the keeper and beaters had gone way around the piece of woods we were to shoot first. Two more blasts from the horn, answered by the keeper a quarter of a mile away, and then perfect stillness, every one on the lookout for rabbits, woodcock, partridges and hares, in fact, anything that should show itself. After a few minutes you hear the beaters hitting the bushes and trees with their sticks, driving everything in front of them. The next minute the bunnies are up to us, and such a cannonading! It is very exciting for a few minutes, but one is in fear of being shot by his neighbor as a rabbit jumps across the road and bang goes the gun of the man next to you.

My gun was so hot I could hardly hold it. We gathered two woodcock (my, what fine birds they are; nearly twice the size of ours), one partridge, fifty-two rabbits; eight owls, two ducks and five hares.

After this we went to another bit of woods, and the same performance was gone through, but this time we did not have quite such good luck, but numbered all about the same amount of game, many of the counts being blackbirds and thrushes.

We then started back for the lodge; after changing clothes, shoes, etc., etc., we had a cup of tea, drove back to the village, took the train and began ecarte again. Before we arrived in Paris our friend had lost the twenty francs he had won in the morning, and when we settled up we found all stood about square, as usual.

They have two kinds of partridges in France—"Perdrix Rouge," or red-legged partridges, are considered the best, and give fine shooting, as they are very fast flyers. "Perdix Grise," gray-legged, are nearly the same in size as the red-legged; they are twice the size of our quail.

Their *Caille*, or quail, are very small; about the size of a marsh blackbird, but broader.

Rabbits are the same size as ours, but much lighter in color; rather a bluish gray.

The hares are the same color as our rabbits, about twice the size. By the way, have we any rabbits in this country, or are they hares? Rabbits burrow. Hares do not; what we call rabbits live entirely above ground.

Two Notes from Shooting Times.

It was not until the beginning of the present century that double-barrelled guns came into favor, and they were at first considered unsportsmanlike. Why? Because *two* birds could be killed at each point!

AN EPITAPH.

Beneath this stone sleeps William Farrel,
Whose earthly dream exploded
When he looked down the shotgun barrel,
Not thinking it was loaded.

The Gun Club has adopted a very neat uniform to wear on occasion of their shoots. It consists of a navy blue "Norfolk" jacket, with a braiding around the collar and cuffs of an inch wide same color, a very genteel, stylish garment, and a navy blue soft felt hat to match. The club hope, at least the members in great part, to wear its new uniforms at the picnic on "Memorial Day," 30th of May, at Ross Valley.

We should like to have the opinion of Dr. S. E. Knowles, Mr. D. J. Haas and Mr. Crittenden Robinson about the subject matter of the following paragraph, touching the headache which in the gentlemen mentioned, too often follows a hard race at the traps.

"How my head aches!" said a beginner at the Wellington traps the other day, to a Boston reporter.

"Merely a gun headache," answered an old trap shot: "you'll soon get used to the noise, and will not be troubled by it."

The reporter cornered one of the oldest trap shots on the grounds and propounded the question:

"What is the cause of gun headache? Is it due to the noise, the recoil, or both?"

"Well," said he, "I think it is due mainly to the noise, though the excitement consequent on the shooting helps as much as anything in the men it attacks. You very seldom hear of it in an old shot, unless his system is out of order. The constant banging soon gets one accustomed to it. Gun headache attacks a man who has never been accustomed to sharp ringing noises, and some are more sensitive than others."

"Is shooting with Shultze or white powder any preventative?"

"Yes, if every one uses it, but at the traps the proportion of black powders is 29 to 1. I think the ache is produced as much by the other reports as by that of one's own gun."

"Have you known men who never have had the trouble?"

"Certainly, just as there are men who go through life without disease. I don't think there is any protection against it, and the cure depends on the conditions."

ROD.

The Fish Commission.

The May meeting of the Board was held on Tuesday at 220 Sutter st, City, both the Honorable Joseph Routier and Honorable J. Downey Harvey being present.

The minutes were read and approved.

The report of the Chief of Patrol was submitted in these words:

THE HONORABLE THE BOARD OF FISH COMMISSIONERS, GENTLEMEN;—The monthly report of the Chief of Patrol for April is submitted with a degree of satisfaction because a very considerable amount of work has been done, both in relation to fish and game. Your Deputies have been active and have been rewarded by the appreciation of all who know of their proceedings.

The cases of Chinese arrested for fishing with bag nets and for having small fish in possession which were pending in the Police Courts of San Francisco at the time of the last report, have all been disposed of. That of Yan Ching was dismissed by Judge Rix because the evidence tended to show that the small fish were caught five miles from shore in the Pacific Ocean, and Judge Rix held that his Court had no jurisdiction. An effort was made to show the absurdity of the Chinaman's claim to have fished with a bagnet and caught the very small fish found in his possession, so far at sea but the opinion of the Judge could not be shaken. Before Judge Lawler on April 14th, five Chinese were tried for having the young of fish in possession and the evidence seemed clear and conclusive, but Judge Lawler professed to be in doubt as to whether the five men found in the boat with the fish were actually owners of the boat and in possession of the fish. The Judge dismissed the case. On April 9th, at Martinez, Judge Jones, of the Superior Court, denied new trials to the nine Chinese convicted before by Judge Bailhache and who appealed from the decision of the Justice. The men are at liberty on bail but will soon be compelled either to undergo imprisonment or to pay their fines. On the 15th, Deputy Curley was compelled to arrest an Italian fisherman who refused to submit to authority and to pay the fishing license. The man was tried by Judge Lawler and dismissed upon agreeing to pay his license at once.

On the 19th Deputy Tunstead discovered and took possession of a lot of deer skins from which evidence of sex had been removed. The skins belonged to L. Lobree of Covelo, Mendocino Co., and were consigned by him to the Sawyer Tanning Co. at Napa. Lobree is the man from whom the Sawyer Tanning Co. received the hides which were the subject of action against the Tannery Co. by your Honorable Board a few months ago. At that time the Sawyer Co. professed to be in sympathy with your Commission and disavowed all desire to antagonize your honorable body, the law and public sentiment. It was hoped at that time that the Sawyer Co. and other Tanning Companies would instruct their agents throughout the mountain regions, not to receive doe skins or skins from which evidence of sex had been removed, but it appears that the confidence was misplaced since Lobree now ships many objectionable hides to the Sawyer people. The hides are in the premises of the San Francisco and North Pacific Railway Co. where they will remain subject to the order of your Honorable Board. There seems to be justification for prosecuting Lobree, and your instructions in relation to the matter are requested.

On the 19th I went to Benicia by direction of Commissioner Harvey to ascertain the condition of affairs among the salmon and shad fishermen there. I found the fishermen on a strike because the canneries refused to pay five cents per pound for salmon delivered to them; three hundred and fifty men and half that number of boats were idle. No fishing was being done nor is it probable that much will be done for some time to come, since the markets of the world are glutted with packed salmon and the canners prefer to suspend operations rather than to run at a loss. From Benicia I went up the Sacramento river, finding no nets with meshes smaller than are allowed by law. A large portion of the month has been passed by Deputies Innes and Curley in collecting licenses from fishermen along the Sacramento, they were compelled to use a row boat, a slow, tedious, ineffective method of progression when the distances to be covered and the necessity for rapid transit are considered; if the Board could secure the use of a steam launch for a few days the whole fishing interests of the Sacramento and San Joaquin rivers and tributaries, as well as the fishing stations about San Francisco Bay, could be visited, and a much larger sum secured from sale of licenses than has ever accrued heretofore. The attorney for the Board, Mr. Ramon E Wilson, in accordance with the request of the Board, drafted an ordinance prohibiting the offering for sale of striped bass less than eight pounds in weight.

The ordinance has been presented to the Supervisors, considered in committee, and received the support of the Board and has become the law for this city and county. The Fisherman's Union at Benicia requests the appointment of a Deputy Fish Commissioner from among the residents of that city, a request which I gladly second. The brown quails distributed by your Honorable Board have in several sections paired, and it seems probable that they will become acclimated readily and do well. Respectfully submitted,

F. P. CALLUNDAN, Chief of Patrol.

SAN FRANCISCO, May, 1890.

Deputy Fish Commissioner A. Googens, of Santa Cruz, in his monthly report to Chief of Patrol Callundan, says:

As requested, I make you a report from my district. I have succeeded in making the fishermen in the bay respect the laws as to Setnets and Bagnets, and as far as I know, the laws are now being observed, unless the night fishermen violate the law, which cannot very well be prevented, as it is difficult to detect them, and the only way to determine that, would be to make a raid on them in the night with a boat. I cannot devote all my time to looking after the law-breakers, as it does not pay me, but will do all I can to see that the law is enforced.

As to trout fishing, I am sorry to say that there is none hardly to be had; the streams, which a few years ago were full of trout are now depleted. Was up on the San Vicente Creek two weeks ago; went up for two miles above the old saw mill, and could not get a bite, and there were no signs of young fish in the stream. This is a beautiful stream of water, and once was a fishing stream; also fished at Mill Creek, which empties into the San Vicente, and that too is cleaned out. Reports from other streams are the same, and unless these streams are re-stocked, trout fishing is done for in Santa Cruz County. The Rod and Gun Club has done good work this last close season in protecting the streams, and expected with the long winter, to have good fishing, but they are much disappointed and discouraged, and declare that the streams are depleted and must be re-stocked, (notwithstanding the report of the Academy of Sciences, saying that our trout are the off-spring of salmon).

I am satisfied that salmon exist in the streams, but they are not, and were never very numerous.

Hoping some time in the near future of seeing you in person and discussing the matter more fully, I am,

Yours truly,

A. GOOGENS, Deputy Fish Commissioner.

J. G. Woodbury, Superintendent of Hatcheries, reported that since the last meeting of the board he had been to Lake Tahoe to begin the spring work there. He found the snow still very deep, the house being entirely buried. The flume was badly damaged and extensive repairs were found necessary. Some delay was caused by the roads being blocked, and a steamer and scow were chartered to take the outfit up to the mouth of Taylor Creek. After providing for the comfort of the expedition, the seines were drawn for several nights, but only a few fish were caught. The streams were low, the water cold and the season was backward. What spawn was obtained was sent to the hatchery at Tahoe. The assistants of Mr. Woodbury—Messrs Hunt and Benton—will continue fishing until the hatchery is full of eggs

Mr. Woodbury went to Sisson and found the 400,000 young salmon in good order. At Shovel Creek 1,200,000 trout egg were taken. Arrangements have been made with the North Pacific Game and Fish Club to receive 100,000 trout eggs from Shovel Creek and hatch them out at Glen Ellen and distribute the young trout into Sonoma Creek and the Russian River and its branches. The club will do this free of cost to the State. Arrangements have also been made with Mr. Knox and Mr. Green to have them receive 50,000 eyed trout eggs from Shovel Creek, which they will send to the hatchery on Los Gatos Creek. They will hatch out these eggs and distribute the young fish, one-half into the headwaters of Los Gatos creek and one-half into the waters of San Lorenzo Creek. Fifty thousand trout eggs will be shipped to Alexander Badlam's new hatchery near Mount St. Helena. These eggs will be a good addition to the streams and cost but little to the State. Four hundred thousand trout eggs will be shipped this week from Shovel Creek to the hatchery at Sisson. As soon as the roads are open to McCloud the Eastern trout will be shipped there and to Senator Stanford's at Vina; also to the west fork of the Sacramento River, Shasta and Big Springs in Siskiyou County.

Mr. Woodbury's energy was favorably commented on by the Commissioners.

Up or Down.

A correspondent has begged an explanation of what the floating fly and dry fly fishing for trout is; and as the topic is one especially seasonable, I will explain briefly says a particularly knowing exchange: It has been found in Europe, and particularly on the clear chalk streams (so called because they arise from the chalk strata), that the wily salmo fario, or brown trout, will not take the fly unless it is almost an exact copy of the natural insect, and also unless it is presented in the most exactly imitated manner of the natural fly. This is the case also on some streams I wot of in this country and hence my correspondent's query.

Such being the state of affairs, what does the angler do? He watches for the rise of the natural insect and captures one and takes it to his fly dresser, or if he can do it himself he sets to work and as nearly as the resources of fur and silk and feathers will allow, he fabricates a counterfeit presentment. A large amount of wing is necessary—sometimes a double pair—and he then proceeds to the river side. Does he go up stream and fish down—oh, no! No such dilettante work—he would never catch a fish. He knows that the trout always heads up-stream, and he wants to get the blind side of him. As Seth Green once said to me about bass fishing, "to catch lots of bass you don't want to let them known you're in the same county," and so is it with our trout fisher. Hence he fishes up; but the fly is delivered with the greatest delicacy, and the leader must be of the finest gossamer gut, and the fly must float on the water without movement of any sort. That is precisely what the water born insect does. He just sails down; he does not struggle like a fly in a milk bowl. Of course the top of the rod is gently lifted to pick up the slack line, and the space fished is very short, but it is in that space that Piscator expects his quarry to be, and if he does not find him in the spot he can comfortably command he tries somewhere else. Perfectly simple!

But, of course the fly gets wet after the second or third cast or throw, and to dry it he makes several false casts—that is, he brings the rod back and forth, but does not allow the lure to fall on the water until he thinks the air has sufficiently dried it to allow of its floating: The floating is a *sine qua non*, and several devices are resorted to to secure the floating prises, especially in the larger flies. One is to use colored straw in the composition of the body; another, to increase the number of wings, and another is to waterproof the wings—which latter is a very good plan, and one I adopt myself, and that with a novel waterproofing. This consists of the oil from the oil sac under the tail of all the duck family—mine is procured from the little oleaginous "dipper" of the eastern and northern counties of New York, but I am not sure the grease from the ordinary domestic duck would not do as well. I boil the feather in this fat, and it is astonishing how the water will run off it. The application of a solution of rubber in peroxide of hydrogen is another way, but it is only applicable to large bass flies and lake trout flies, and its odor is—well, simply appalling.

"The California Fish Commissioners are doing work in the right vein this year. This body was formerly one of the most efficient in the country, and meted out stern punishment to offenders. Then it fell into idle ways and had a triangular quarrel among its members, which long impaired its efficiency. These difficulties, however, seem now to be of the past, and if the Commission continues to work as hard and as intelligently as it has lately, a new era is opening before anglers and sportsmen. California has four large hatcheries—one at Lake Tahoe, with a capacity of twenty-four troughs; one at Sisson's, of forty-four troughs, one of the largest in the United States; a small one at Shovel Creek, used for "eyeing" the trout eggs for distribution over other parts of the State, and a large salmon hatchery on Hat Creek near its mouth, where it empties into the Pit River in Shasta County. The Eastern trout that were put into Placer Creek, Lake Tahoe, and into the headwaters of the American River and Soda Springs, and the South Fork of the Yuba River, have maintained their characteristics and reproduced themselves in large numbers. The striped bass introduced in 1883 have evidently made themselves at home in San Francisco Bay, one weighing thirty-five pounds being caught in Benicia a short time ago. The Commissioners have discovered that the Chinese have been netting young bass of perhaps a quarter of a pound weight, and selling them in Chinatown and elsewhere. The penalty is a fine of one hundred dollars, or one hundred days in the county jail. The city supervisors are expected to pass an additional ordinance for the protection of the bass."

[Those who have followed the labors of our Fish Commission will feel grateful to our skilled and discriminating contemporary. "The Weeks Sport" published in New York for the paragraph clipped. All that can be said for the Commission is inadequate. The places are honorary, but the Commissioners are gentlemen *sans peur et sans reproche.*—Ang. Ed.]

BASE BALL.

[Reviewed by Phil. Potts.]

A Week of Good, Bad and Indifferent Ball Playing.

Games Played.—Standing of the Clubs and Notes.

The past week of baseball has been characterized by the fluctuation of the different terms in the percentage column. Frisco, by a hard struggle, still retains the lead, and Oakland has advanced to second place. Stockton has gravitated down to third position, and the plucky little Senators, though still at the "bottom of the heap," have advanced a trifle in the percentage of games won. The record:

Clubs.	San Franciscos	Oaklands	Stocktons	Sacramentos	Games Won	Games Played	Percentage
San Franciscos	..	2	3	5	10	17	588
Oaklands	3	..	4	5	12	22	545
Stocktons	3	4	..	1	8	18	4
Sacramentos	1	4	3	..	8	19	421
Games Lost	7	10	10	11	..	..	..

San Francisco vs. Sacramento, Friday, May 2nd at Oakland.

About eight hundred rabid Oakland cranks assembled at the grounds at Emery Station in the hope that San Francisco would meet her Waterloo in the game with the Senators. But the Frisco boys just "fooled 'em," although it took eleven innings to do it. The Senators had the best of it as regards hitting, but their infield errors were very costly, and to this may be attributed their defeat. The features were the back stop work of Bowman and Speare, and the pretty fielding of Roberts, Levy, Godar and Reitz.

SCORE BY INNINGS.

San Francisco	1	0	1	0	2	2	0	0	0	0	4	—10
Oakland	3	0	1	0	1	1	0	0	0	0	1	— 7

Base hits San Francisco, 8; Sacramento, 21. Errors, San Francisco. Batteries, Young and Speer, Harper and Bowman.

Stockton vs. Oakland, Friday, May 2nd, at Stockton.

Although outplayed both in the field and at the bat, Oakland was victorious in this game by reason of clever hitting in the first four innings. A brilliant triple in the first inning in which O'Neill, McDonald and Isaacson figured, was the principal feature.

SCORE BY INNINGS.

	1	2	3	4	5	6	7	8	9	
Oakland	1	1	1	2	0	0	0	0	*	—5
Stockton	0	0	0	0	0	0	2	0	0	—2

Base hits—Oakland 9, Stockton, 10. Errors—Oakland 2, Stockton 1. Batteries—Meegan and Lohman, Borchers and Wilson.

San Francisco vs. Sacramento, Saturday, May 3rd, at Haight Street.

The Senators won their first game from San Francisco and their first game on the Haight street grounds by making four runs in the fifth inning, which together with three secured in the second, gave them the lead which they maintained to the close. Zeigler gave way to "Toreador" Harper in the fifth, who pitched out a good game. Reitz, Goodenough and Hanley excelled in fielding, while Daley, who makes marvellous pick ups, was way off in throwing.

SCORE BY INNINGS.

	1	2	3	4	5	6	7	8	9	
Sacramento	0	3	0	0	4	0	0	0	*	—7
San Francisco	2	0	3	0	0	1	0	0	0	—6

Base hits—Sacramento 6, San Francisco 9. Errors—Sacramento 7, San Francisco 5. Batteries—Harper, Zeigler and Bowman; Lookabaugh and Stevens.

Stockton vs. Oakland, ..., May 3rd, at Stockton.

The Stocktons resurrected Dan Flynn from "innocuous desuetude" and put him in to pitch against the Colonels. This he did right well, there being but seven hits secured off his delivery. He was, however, wild, and the nine bases on balls given by him are largely responsible for the Oaklands victory. The battery work of the Oaklands was very effective, and Wilson's Fogarty's and Holliday's fielding was much appreciated. Many of Donohue's decisions did not find favor with the Stocktonians.

SCORE BY INNINGS.

	1	2	3	4	5	6	7	8	9	
Oakland	0	2	3	0	2	1	0	0	*	—8
Stocktons	0	0	0	2	0	0	0	0	0	—2

Base hits—Oaklands 7, Stocktons 4. Errors—Oaklands 1, Stocktons 2. Batteries—Cobb and Lohman; Flynn and De Pangher.

San Francisco vs. Stockton, Sunday May 4th, at Haight Street.

ELEVEN INNINGS.

The second eleven winning game of the week was played last Sunday before some 5,000 people. As a game it was a combination of heavy hitting on one side and miserable blunders on the other. Borchers did not pitch the game he is capable of and Wilson's back stop work was faulty. Kelly playing at third was also very ragged. Buchan and Hanley both played their positions "out of sight" and their hitting was very clever. The score was tied in the seventh and the following three innings were non-productive of runs. In the eleventh Spear led off with a single and stole second. Levy struck out but on Stevens double Spear tallied which was the winning run.

SCORE BY INNINGS.

Base hits—Sacramento, 13; Oakland, 4. Errors—Sacramento, 1; Oakland, 3. Batteries—Harper and Bowman; Meegan and Lohman.

	1	2	3	4	5	6	7	8	9	10	11	
San Francisco	0	5	0	1	0	1	0	0	0	0	1	— 8
Stocktons	1	0	0	0	1	0	5	0	0	0	0	— 7

Base hits—San Francisco, 12; Stockton, 6. Errors—San Francisco, 5; Stockton, 10. Batteries—Young and Stevens; Borchers and Wilson.

Sacramento vs. Oakland, May 5th, at Sacramento.

Meegan was hit unmercifully in the game with the Senators, home runs, triples and safety shots being the order of the day and of their ten runs eight were earned. Harper pitched pennant winning ball from the start and received excellent support. A very disagreeable feature was the quarrel between umpire Chipman and player O'Neill, which resulted in O'Neill who appears to have been the aggressor being arrested.

SCORE BY INNINGS.

	1	2	3	4	5	6	7	8	9	
Sacramento	2	0	2	0	2	0	1	3	0	—10
Oakland	0	0	0	0	0	0	0	2	0	— 2

PROFESSIONAL PICK-UPS.

Where is Hen Moore?

Buchan is improving in hitting.

Borchers did not exert himself in last Sundays game.

Salna is playing an admirable first base for Stockton.

Good news continues to come over the wires concerning "Pap" Swett.

Nick Smith is playing a great short field for Kansas City.

The second base ball play of little Reitz is a revelation to California base ball patrons.

The Sunday crowds seem to be diminishing which may be attributed to the picnic season being now inaugurated.

Daley is the only weak spot in the infield of the Sacramento team. There is much room for improvement in his throwing.

Fudgers salary will be reduced five dollars this month for not running on his fair hit last Sunday.

A new league to be called the Inter Mountain league is being formed by teams from Helena and Butte City Mountain and Salt Lake City and Ogden Utah.

Smalley is more than holding his end up with Cleveland. Reports from that city pronounce him to be the best player ever seen there in that position.

The jewelry firm of Nat Raphael & Co. has offered a trophy to the team winning the championship of the California league. It consists of a silver plated bat and ball, regulation size, and is handsomely engraved. It is now on exhibition in their show windows on Kearney Street.

The friendship existing between Ed Stapleton and Fred Roberts, of the Sacramentos, is of the Damon and Pythias type. Stapleton thinks there is no better fielder in the business than the Oakland boy, and Roberts is of the opinion that as a gentlemanly ball player, Stapleton is at the "top of the heap."

The Sacramento players guy Zeigler for his weakness in hitting. The other day after he had struck out, Capt. Stapleton said: "George, why don't you get your eye on the ball?" to which the pitcher replied: "I can get my eye on the ball all right, but the trouble is I can't get my bat on it."

The Friday games at Emery are graced by several of the Catholic clergy, who take a deep interest in the sport. Base ball since its incipiency has always been recognized by the clergy as a healthful and invigorating pastime, and one which is highly conducive to good morals, and consequently it has received the encouragement and co-operation of "the faculties" of every college throughout the land.

THE AMATEURS.

E. T. Allens vs. Burlington, Sunday 11 a. m. May 4th, at Haight Street.

The Burlingtons won their first game of the season by defeating the Allens "just by a scratch." It was a prettily played game throughout, and the errors made were principal poor throws. The battery work of McDonald and Stanley of the Allens was excellent, and the fielding of Dunn Reilly and McCarthy was of a high order. The Allens out-batted and out-fielded their opponents, but lost the game by the Burlingtons bunching their hits in the ninth inning. The score:

BURLINGTONS.

	AB	R	BH	SB	PO	A	E
Forster, l f	5	0	1	0	1	0	2
Sheridan, r f	5	1	2	2	0	1	0
Shincler, s s	3	1	0	1	0	5	1
Levy, c	3	0	0	2	5	1	0
Curtis, 1st b	3	0	0	0	14	1	2
Bradley, 2d b	3	2	1	2	3	1	1
Dunn, 3d b	4	1	0	1	3	4	1
Deane, c f	3	2	1	1	1	0	0
Sullivan, p	3	0	0	0	0	5	1
Totals	32	7	5	9	27	18	8

ALLENS

	AB	R	BH	SB	PO	A	E
Riley, 2d b	5	1	2	1	1	1	1
McCarthy, l f	5	0	1	0	4	0	1
Evatt, 1st b	4	1	1	0	5	0	0
Geishaker, c f	4	1	1	0	1	0	0
Tribon, r f	3	1	0	0	0	0	0
Lewis, 3d b	4	1	2	0	3	2	1
Murdock, s s	3	1	0	0	2	3	2
McDonald, p	4	0	1	0	0	0	0
Stanley, c	4	0	0	0	11	3	1
Totals	36	6	8	1	27	9	6

SCORE BY INNINGS.

Burlingtons	0	1	3	1	0	0	0	0	2	—7
All-n-	0	2	2	0	0	0	0	1	1	—6

Earned runs—Burlingtons, 2. Three-base hits—McDonald, Reilly. Two base hit—Geishaker. Sacrifice hits—Forster, Sullivan, R illy, McCarthy, Tribon. First base on errors—Burlingtons, 5; Allens, 5. First base on called balls—Burlingtons, 5; Allens, 1. Left on bases—Burlingtons, 8; Allens, 1. Struck out—By McDonald, 9; by Sullivan, 4. First base on hit by pitcher—Tribon, Deane. Triple play—Stanley, Lewis and Evatt. Double play—Bradley to Curtis. Umpire—Sheridan.

AMATEUR SHORT HITS.

Cook is quite a hitter.

Lewis, of the Allens, is on the sick list.

Dick Nagle captains the Woodland team.

Gene Brodericks error was a very costly one.

The E T Allens have been photographed.

Santa Rosa has five left hand hitters.

Haylock and Elwell form the battery for Ventura.

Frank Warren is the veteran manager of the league.

Finnigan is doing fine work in the box for Merced.

Tillson is playing the game of his life at short this season.

Strand, of the Will & Fincks, is the best long distance thrower in the league.

Dave Creamer, of last season's Stocktons, is a valuable acquisition to the ranks of the Allens.

Little Gimmel, of the Santa Rosa's, is referred to as the Hughey Nicol, of the Amateur League.

Leveque has found his position in the field and is playing it "out of sight." There are "no skates" on Joe.

Dave Levy has become quite a coacher. He is said to even rival "Long John Riley" in his palmiest days.

Callen, the blonde pitcher of Santa Rosa, is a most graceful man in the box. He has good speed, curves and drops and best of all possesses a good clear head.

We regret to announce the serious illness of that popular and clever young player John Cooney. John lies very sick at the residence of his parents and it is to be earnestly hoped that he will soon be convalescent.

Matt Stanley is showing a marked improvement in his backstop work. He has effectually remedied his only weakness—that of throwing to bases—and now his good right arm asserts its power at every opportunity.

The Vallejos are still in the League, the differences between Manager Campbell and the other managers of the League being amicably settled. It is stated that under the new arrangement the visiting teams will receive twenty-five dollars and expenses or an option of taking forty per cent. of the gross gate receipts.

THE KENNEL.

Dog owners are requested to send for publication the earliest possible notices of whelps, sales, names claimed, presentations and deaths, in their kennels, in all instances writing plainly names of sire and dam and of grandparents, colors, dates and breed.

A Counter-Blast.

EDITOR BREEDER AND SPORTSMAN.—Permit me, on behalf of the Bakersfield members of the Field Trial Club, to criticise the unfair comments made in your last issue, by a "local light in pointer breeding circles" about one of our brother members, the judges at the last trials, and your endorsement of the views of the growler.

It is to be regretted that the Bakersfield members of the club will make no entries for the trials next January, and having made none this year, we are in a position to judge as to the fairness of the manner in which they were conducted, and as a unit, we agree that any reflection cast upon any member of the club, so far as our observation went, and we were present at all meetings held here, is unjust. When the "pointer man" suggests that any one man controls the club, we consider that his prejudices overcome his good judgment, and when he claims that any decision of the judge was influenced by anyone, we maintain that he makes a wilfull, malicious and unwarranted statement.

The petty dissentions which have cropped out in our club during this year are unworthy of its gentlemanly and whole-souled members; let us bury such sentiments, gentlemen, and join hands with the good will which characterizes the true sportsman, and you, Mr. Editor, never again admit that such views as appeared in your last issue, can "be carefully considered with profit." W. E. HOUGHTON.

BAKERSFIELD, April 4, 1890.

[Our esteemed friend, Mr. Houghton, seems in error when suggesting that we either endorsed or repudiated the opinions expressed by a correspondent last week. His views were given in his own words, and are to be taken for what they are worth. The same desire to be fair which prompts us to present Mr. Houghton's rather severe letter, actuated us in publishing the other, and we can see nothing in the presentation of either, likely to work harm. If a lively rattling of the dryish bones of the field trial association results in increased activity, the end is to be desired. If other readers care to send their views, we shall be glad to publish them.—KEN. ED.]

A large pointer dog, white and lemon in color, obedient to ordinary words of command, and which answers to the name Point (Don—Drab) was lost several days ago. An advertisement in another column offers a liberal reward, without questions, for his return.

Field trialers and sportsmen generally will recognize the dog and we hope will send word if they chance to see him.

The attention of foxterrier fanciers is called to the advertisement of pups for sale from the well known kennels of J. B. Martin, 1323 Page street, this city. The sire and dam of the pups, Blemton Vesuvian and Beatrice, were brought from the kennels of Mr. August Belmont, Jr., New York, and are from the best winning blood.

Mr. Martin also offers a mastiff pup for sale, whose breeding is very good, and which will make a good sized useful dog.

H. H. Briggs, the Kennel Editor, is at present in Los Angeles attending the dog show which is being given under the auspices of the Southern California Club. The entry list has been a large one, and there is every indication that it will far surpass the one given last year. In the next issue of the BREEDER AND SPORTSMAN, a full account of the show will be given.

THE FARM.

The Shorthorn.

At the recent convention of the Wisconsin Farmers' Association, reported in the Southern Gazette, Hon. H. C. Thom made an address to the breeders of Shorthorns, in which he said:

"The trouble with the cattle business at present is not so much the low price they bring as the kind of cattle that are thrown upon the market. Good stock is bringing better than $5 per 100 pounds to-day, while most cattle are changing hands at from $1.75 to $2.50. Beef can be made on Wisconsin farms at $4 per 100 pounds at a fair profit. Lower prices than $3.25 are ruinous to most breeders. As near as I can estimate, beef can be produced at $3 per 200 pounds. That this can be done can be figured as absolutely as that butter can be produced at 13½ cents per pound, or that calico can be manufactured for 3½ cents per yard. Three conditions are essential in order that meat can be produced at this figure: first, good stock; second, economical feeding and handling; third, early maturity. In some respects cattle are like men; the lean and hungry ones, although great consumers, are rarely fat ones. Your attention is respectfully called to the president of this association. It makes some men tired to carry around what they eat; others of closer build and more quiet consciences are content with what they get, and ruminate over the out of the eternal fitness of things and grow fat. The racer is the result of long years of careful breeding. The bullock, although of greater bulk, represents just as much skill as the courser. There is a strong sentiment in many minds against inbreeding. In a broad sense the tide may set the right way. Many of us undoubtedly need training to know just what to do. It might be well to say here, however, that the Shorthorn breed was best developed and perfected in the hands of a man who brought this about by the severest practice of inbreeding. The animals grew under his careful eye in grace and beauty. Desirable points were strengthened and developed; the weak ones eliminated and destroyed. An abiding faith that skill would win brought about the grandest results, made the name of the man immortal and left a race of cattle that lovers of graceful lines and colors will fall down and worship, for verily they were golden calves whose mothers would sniff at the sacred cow. The feeding and handling can best be brought out in the discussion, perhaps, because I can then call to my aid men of greater age and experience. My experience has given me radical ideas on these matters; they may not be progressive; surely they are honest.

"The question of maturity next demands attention. Three and 4-year-old cattle are unprofitable. Thirty months is an extreme age to turn off. The first 600 pounds is cheapest. I know of a 5-year-old steer that was kept 365 days, eating as many pounds of grain and hay as when 4 years old, and gained never a pound. Feeding experiments at our Wisconsin station give ample data to clinch the statement that the quicker the maturity the greater the profit. That feeders complain is not to be wondered at. The stock yards evidence criminal bungling. Matched clear flooring is worth more than cull lumber. A poor ax helve finds a customer only in a plug chopper, who splits kindling wood for his wife at the back door, and does that little under protest. Yet Mr Jones, of Dane county, sends a steer to Chicago that makes the average Texan stare, and kicks because he does not get the top of the market. The steer is not to blame; oh, no! Jones made him and he pays the freight. Jones would not expect a big price for poor eggs, but he does for poor meat. Experience is not quite so strong in the latter business. When he 'goes broke' Jones will wake up. It is all folly to talk of going out of the stock business. It is the true foundation of rotation. Without stock, farms will rapidly deplete in fertility. Wisconsin farmers have had a bitter experience, and will not be caught again. It takes as much time and costs as much money to restore a lost fertility as it does to clear and break the original homestead.

"I would suggest that the general market might be improved if more attention could be given by our foreign consulates to this great industry. With much regret I am constrained to say that few of them know or care how much could be done in this direction. Nothing but flimsy excuses stand in the way of heavy exportation. Many of the so-called rulings are in direct violation of the existing treaties. The thousands who are in the business of beef production, the millions of money invested, should demand recognition and a channel paved to good foreign markets. That herdsmen may not become discouraged, I beg to call attention to the fact that we are growing faster in our demands than we our in skill in breeding and feeding. It is but a few short years since steers were changing hands at $12 per head, just such cattle as we think ought to bring $5 per hundred. What right have we to ask this? This right—that we wish to ride in a carriage. A wagon used to answer. Wheat, so we say, can not be raised for 75 cents per bushel. My father used to raise it for 25 cents, and haul it to Milwaukee with a team, and kept up a cheerful whistle and raised a lusty boy with a good appetite. Ah, yes. Luxuries of those days are necessities now. We are fighting the battle of life against greater odds. Our wants are growing faster than means for supplying them, and we kick the 'big four' the steed, the market, and scold our wives because things are awry.

"A good animal, well matured and finished with a sleek coat, with a good distribution of muscle and fat, will bring more money, more content, and smooth more wrinkles and keep back more gray hairs than all the petulant fault-finding that ever rose to heaven. 'The eye of the master makes the animal.' Keep the old saying in mind; bind your fortune to the Shorthorn. They have had a glorious past; they are steady in the present, and the future is full to repletion of bright promises. It is a popular fallacy that because a pure bred costs a large sum that he will fatten on ragweed and water. Profit comes to no man by shirking responsibility and labor. Give the animal care, treat him kindly, shelter him; feed him; then he will grow under the master's eyes and conform to the measure of an ideal. Out of all of this labor and love will spring a result that will be a credit and an honor to all these years of line breeding, to the men who have fashioned the Shorthorn by a long term of study to be a thing of beauty and a profit forever."

In reply to the questions which were put at the close of his paper, Mr. Thom stated that there are probably as many Shorthorn cows in Wisconsin that are paying their owners in milk production as all other breeds combined. He explained his method of handling steers when in feeding, which is to keep them in a box stall liberally bedded with straw, leaving the boxes uncleaned until the cattle are turned on grass or marketed. In response to questions he submitted figures of the cost of production, showing that he could make a pound of beef by the aid of silage for three cents. A scattering cross fire ensued, and Mr. Thom closed his contribution to the discussion by declaring that in his opinion the present outlook for the beef grower was the brightest he had seen in ten years.

Value of Shorthorns.

W. H. Jacobs, Jr., president of the Wisconsin Shorthorn Association, said the Shorthorns stood in the front rank in the march of progress for half a century, and was now firmly established as the beef breed of America, and also the general purpose cow. He did not claim that the Shorthorn cow would equal in accomplishments at the churn or the milk pail, the best specimens of the special dairy breeds, but she would give most excellent results in dairy products, and produce a calf each year which would promptly contribute a good quantity of cheaply-produced beef of the best quality for the market. "Can beef be produced in Wisconsin for a profit?" was answered in the affirmative by Dairy Commissioner H. C. Thom. To raise beef at a profit requires skill in breeding and feeding, and good judgment in marketing. Experience has proved that with well bred beef animals, properly cared for from the day of their birth until they are ready for the block, there is a good profit for producing beef in Wisconsin at the present prices for a finished article of beef. The silo comes to the relief of the beef producer and renders profit possible. The beef producers of the northwest are now in competition with the whole country. Our herdsmen must down this competition with an article of superior excellence.—*O. J. Farmer.*

Berkshire Pigs the Best in the World.

How many times I have heard visitors at my farm remark, when looking over the swine, "I don't like those nasty black pigs," and at the exhibition shows the same remark is often heard. Probably these people forget for the moment that color is only skin deep, or rather in this case, it is only a light coat of bristles deep. They undoubtedly never had any experience in keeping Berkshires, for if they had such thoughts would lose themselves, in the many attractive qualities they would discover in this breed of swine.

In the first place, the Berkshire is one of the oldest breeds in existence. Having been bred so many years, every characteristic feature about them has become thoroughly established and any one who is breeding the pure stock is as sure of every point showing itself in every litter that is farrowed, as he is that he exists. The Berkshires breed true every time, and a spot or "off" pig is as rare as green peas at Christmas. One of their strongest features is a disposition to grow from the start, and to take on flesh and fat. Another very important point in any breed of animals is possessed to a marked degree by the Berkshire, and that is a decided power or constitution to resist diseases of all kinds. When properly fed and cared for, they are seldom if ever sick, or off their feed, and while breeders of other varieties around me are in constant trouble with a sick sow, or weak or ailing litter of pigs, my herd of Berkshires go right along in perfect health, producing big, strong, vigorous litters of pigs, all of which grow and thrive.

The pure bred Berkshires make the best of mothers, are very gentle with their young, and have an abundance of milk, which continues to flow for a long period when desired. Having been bred in all climates for so many years, they withstand the heat of summers and the cold of our long winters, and are but little affected by either. From this fact fall litters from the Berkshires grow and thrive, while other breeds become stunted and weak from the cold of approaching winter. This feature alone places them far ahead of all other breeds. This fact should overcome any prejudice one has against their color, for all breeders want and expect two litters of pigs a year from their sows, one of which from necessity must farrow in cold weather, and to have the latter grow and thrive is absolutely essential to success. This the Berkshire will do.

Another thing that all careful breeders and farmers try to do, is to produce the largest and best animal, the most meat, for the least amount of money expended for feed, and right here is where the Berkshire pig excels all other kinds in the world. I have bred all of the leading kinds of swine, and made many careful experiments in feeding the same and noting results, and my experience teaches me that whether I am after fat, pork, or meat in a herd of pigs or hogs, I can obtain the same with a herd of Berkshires at three-quarters the expense, or less, for feed and half the expense for care and trouble over any other breed of hogs, and I will not have to fight disease or sickness in producing the same, and I see no more objection in the color black in swine than in any other animal or fowl. That is why I like the Berkshire pig.—G. L. Dow, in the Poultry.

Spangled Hamburghs.

There is no more beautiful variety of the domestic fowl than the Spangled Hamburgh. The clear, rich golden bay of the Golden variety, and the clear, silvery white of the Silvers, with their respective large round black moons or spangles, and the small, neat head, with shapely rose comb, offer a combination which is to be met with in no other breed. And they have also the merit—in which respect they are unlike the Penciled variety, which are purely ornamental—that they are also economical fowls to keep, for they are the most prolific of all layers, and with the Black Hamburgh, easily stand at the head for fecundity. Were it not that their eggs are rather small in size, they would be far more popular with those who have to produce for sale, but at present their eggs are, as a rule, rather below the requirements of the market. So far as the producer is concerned, they are best of all, for they are very small eaters, and hence they are most profitable to keep. By the exercise of a little care, the size of the egg could be enlarged, and selection would go far to remedy this one defect. There are some families which lay larger eggs than do others, and if attention were given to this point, it would soon be improved.

Spangled or Mooney Hamburghs are really the old Lancashire or Yorkshire pheasant breed, and owe all their perfection to the careful way in which they have been bred in these two counties. Long before the era of modern shows, there were small village exhibitions at which the colliers, hand-loom weavers, and others of the industrial population competed with each other's fowls. In those days only the hens were shown, for the cocks were regarded as too ugly, and it was only by the introduction of a cross between the Yorkshire and a Mooney cock that the gentlemen were made fit for the show pen. I have already told, but the story will bear repetition, how it was the custom for the exhibitors to take their birds under their arms and show them in a room on a table, each exhibitor arguing for the good points of his birds, while his rivals pointed out their defects. The judge stood at one side of the table and heard all that was said *pro* and *con*, for each bird, of which two were on the table at one time. The worse of these was taken away, the one left having to face the next competitor, and so on. That left at the conclusion of the contest was declared the winner. This system, which would be utterly impracticable nowadays, doubtless had much to do with the perfection to which the breed was brought; for each breeder learned just in what way his breed was deficient, and he could seek to remedy the defect. In the show-pen at the present time, in this country at least, he has usually to be content with the fact that he is beaten, and must find for himself in what way.

Before giving the standard for this breed as adopted by the Hamburgh Club, I may be permitted to quote from an article on the "Matching and Breeding of Spangled Hamburghs," published about two years ago from the pen of that well known breeder and judge Mr. Henry Beldon of Bingley, Yorks, who has done more to popularise Hamburghs than any living man, and who may safely be called the father of the Hamburgh fancy. On this point Mr. Beldon wrote:

"The spangling of this variety is very bold and very rich in color, the black almost green (the metallic sheen is to be avoided), broad backs that give plenty of room to show off the spangling. The combs of these pure Mooneys are often coarse and the ear lobes reddish, but to the old fanciers these were only minor faults, perfection of feather and size of body being the points sought for. For a further description see my description in Wright's Poultry Book. In breeding, therefore, care must be taken to get hold of the proper article to begin with, and if the amateur has not sufficient knowledge to start with, to put himself into the hands of some well known and experienced breeder. These Mooneys, however, can be recognized by the size of their bodies and richness of spangling. To breed from, get these large birds with broad backs, spangle rich and bold and free from pepperiness, neck well striped up to the head. I prefer a dark bird to one too light, as the tendency is to breed lighter. Combs are, as a rule, coarse, and should be selected not too ugly; the cocks must be hen-feathered and correctly marked, intensely rich in color; defects of any kind to be avoided, such as humpbacks, squirrel or wry tail. Ear lobes are of secondary importance; of course, it does not follow that all hen-feathered cocks are the proper thing, as this hen feathering can be easily got, but a little experience will suffice for the amateur to recognize the proper thing.

"For cock breeding another set is required, the cocks being very profuse and full in feathering, but the fancy is now so very far improved that even these cocks must be spangled or marked at the tip of every feather—I can scarcely call it spangling—the elongated nature of the neck hackle, back and saddle hackle clearly spotted (not cloudy, or brassy, or brown—great defects. The comb should be long, with plenty of work in it, the ear-lobes round and not too large, as these very large lobed birds further develop in their offspring the white face, which is a grevious fault; besides, these neat-lobed cocks look better, and we must never forget that Hamburghs are, of all breeds, birds of feather; he should have nice carriage, carry his tail well, and be free from any marked defect. Some birds are naturally very tractable, and show themselves in a pen, and this property is often hereditary; so of course, cocks possessing it are much to be preferred. With such a bird the beginner should have a fair chance of producing something good; but he must have hens from a reliable source, as these hens cannot always be distinguished by their appearance. Care, however, must be taken to have the hens clearly spangled, with nice carriage and fair size, and with good, long comb, evenly set on the head, and clear lobes. Such birds ought to breed well, but experience is the great teacher. Of course, if you cannot always get perfect birds in all points, care must be taken not to match those with the same faults. As, for instance, if the male has a short comb the hens should have long ones; if he is a little light in marking, the hens should be darker, and so on. Once having got a set of birds that produced good chickens, to stick to them, and not be led away by introducing fresh crosses, as the work of years may be spoiled by this injudicious proceeding."

The following is the standard for Spangled Hamburghs adopted by the Hamburgh Club:

Comb square at front, tapering nicely into a long spike, full of points (by no means plain), firmly and evenly set on the head; face red; ears moderate in size, round as possible, and clear white; legs leaden blue; carriage graceful; plumage very profuse. *Color*—Cocks; Silver spangled, clear silvery white ground, every feather tipped or spangled, the breast bold as possible, but showing the spangle, the bars of the wing regular and bold; neck, back and saddle nicely tipped; bow well marked (by no means cloudy, brown or brassy), back as green as possible. Golden Spangled—color very bright and rich, and black glossy green; the neck, back and saddle nicely striped; bow of wing well marked. Hens: Silver Spangled—the white clear and silvery; the spangles large, green as possible, distinct and clear. Golden Spangled—ground rich, clear spangles, large and distinct.

STEPHEN BEALE, in Cultivator and County Centeman.

Goslins—How to Manage Them.

While the geese are sitting, they should be thoroughly dusted with dry Sulphur once or twice, to cleanse them from vermin. After the twenty-eight day the eggs should be put in milk-warm water a few moments each day. This softens the shell, and enables one to throw away the rotten, and to count the goslins before they are hatched. Have the nest tight, and keep the goslins in over one night after all are out. Make a triangular pen with three long boards, where the grass is short but fresh and green, and move to a new place every day. A shallow dish of water must be placed so they can get into it, and be re-filled as often as it gets foul. Feed a little at a time, but often, while they are small, and at the end of a week they will have gained strength so they may be turned into their pasture, if sheltered at night. If a goslin gets wet so as to look drenched, and it begins to droop, it must be carried to the fire and dried.

Feed corn meal ground with the cob, mixed into dough, rather dry, with an occasional sprinkling of salt. Care must be used to teach them to eat regularly. Throw the dough, a morsel at a time, in the midst of a flock, or the old geese will get the most of it. The goslins soon become tame, and will eat about as long as one will feed them. At the end of the third week feed them only twice a day, and after the sixth not at all, till ready to fatten them for market. A little poultry food and cream for a chilled gosling is about the only remedy I know of for sick ones, nor do I think they will be often sick if they have good care, and poisonous herbs are kept out of their reach. If goslins are taught to eat, then well fed, and kept dry till well feathered, success is almost certain.—Poultry Journal.

Grim's Gossip.

Terra Cotta has been retired to stud duties.

Inspector B. will be taken from the Esdenholm stud by the Dwyer brothers, and put in training for the summer races.

The BREEDER AND SPORTSMAN contains each week more reading matter than any weekly sporting paper in the country.

L. E. Clawson's Brunette, dropped a slashing bay filly by Memo last Saturday. It is entered in the BREEDER AND SPORTSMAN'S Futurity.

Mr. Frost has at the Petaluma Race Track two full sisters to Nellie R 2:17½, which for beauty and stepping qualities should be hard to beat.

W. F. Cutler, the veterinary surgeon of Sacramento warns cattle owners to be prepared for a siege of black-leg this summer, as he anticipates there will be a great deal of it in California this year.

Quite a number of friends have forwarded to me, pedigrees of horses that stood in California during the early days, but, there are many more to hear from. Send along any old pedigrees you may have.

The accuracy observed by writers on turf matters is well exemplified by the fact that Western papers tipped Blarney Stone extensively for the Kentucky Derby, for which the colt is not even entered.

A large breeding establishment is being organized at Martin, Tenn., with a cash capital of $100,000. This enterprise will be organized on the plan of a bank and conducted on business principles.

There is a rumor current that Ruby, 2:19¾, the property of the San Mateo Stock Farm, died a day or two ago, but I have not had time to verify the rumor. If the story is true, the loss will be a serious loss to Mr. Corbitt.

By the time that this issue of the BREEDER AND SPORTSMAN reaches our readers, the Palo Alto and Hickok stables will have reached Terre Haute. No word has been received relative to accident or sickness so it can be presumed that the two stables arrived in good shape.

At the Bruce & Kidd Combination Sale held lately in Kentucky, Casey Winchell, jockey for Mr. Winters, sold his bay colt, Senor, by Bersan, dam Sister by imported Australian. The colt was sold to the Harlan Bros. for $1100, which leaves "Case" a fair margin of profit, he purchasing the colt last fall for a little over $400.

The race for the Sydney Gold Cup, a handicap sweepstake over a course of two miles, run April 7th, resulted in the easy victory of D. S. Wallace's Carbine, Mantilla being second and Muriel third. Fifteen ran. Time, 3:37. Carbine won the same race last year, with 126 pounds up, in 3:32.

The Australian stallion Abercorn, by Chester, dam Cinnamon, has broken down. Some weeks ago his owner, Hon. James White, was offered $40,000 for the horse by Captain Machell, the well known English turfite, with the stipulation that he should not run again. Mr. White refused to sell at any price,

The sale of roadster and carriage horses from the farms of J. B. Haggin Esq , took place at the Railroad Stables on Tuesday and Wednesday. The consignment was far above the average, and each of the lots brought fairly good prices. Messrs. Killip & Co. were the managers of the sale and carried it to a successful conclusion.

Snapper Garrison is not as natty appearing these days as when he was king of them all. He loiters about the grandstand, not having much to say to anyone, and his friends wonder what has come over him. It is a very fair assumption that his late troubles have been a lesson to him, and that before the season is over he will be seen riding in his old brilliant form.

Our thanks are due to B. G. Bruce and J. K. Stringfield of Lexington, Ky., for a neat little book entitled "Thoroughbreds in training in the South and West." It is a very comprehensive work, containing much data that will be useful to all sporting men. The book can be obtained for the small price of ten cents, and should be in the possession of every horseman in the country.

Dan McCarty before leaving for the Atlantic States called on me and stated that he would have a few good "bang-tails" to carry the McCarty colors this season, nothwithstanding he had such a host of trotters to look after. Dan makes money with the long tail horses, but manages to drop a fat slice on the thoroughbreds each season.

Lee Shaner has a wonderfully large string of horses at the Petaluma track, several of the number being of the "promising" kind. They are of all sorts and descriptions, and Lee has his hands full in giving them all the nece sary amount of work; however, he keeps at it from morning to night, persevering in the labor, and feels that he will be amply repaid by bringing several good ones to the front.

The match between Cleon and Charley Gibbons is on for a certainty, and will be trotted at Waverly Park, Newark, on May 30. They are both 2:20 horses and will make a fine race. The stake is said to be $5,000. Cleon is training at Morristown and Charley Gibbons is being worked by his owner. There will be a race meet at Waverly Park on May 30 and 31. This race will be the chief feature.

Paramatta, an Australian bred horse, managed to win a race at Linden Park on Thursday last. A telegram from New York says that "Paramatta is by Senator Hearst's Cheviot." He is nothing of the kind; the horse is one of the Newton importation, and is not by the Cheviot that is in this country. By the way, I should think that Dr. Ross was becoming tired of hearing his stallion always spoken of as Senator Hearst's.

It is a little singular that as late as this in the season not a solitary new-comer to the 2:30 list has been reported. They will come with a rush, probably, when they do come. W. T. Chester in the Turf, Field and Farm.

Why my dear Walter, Sultan has two new representatives in the list already this season. Semi Tropic 2:24 and Othello 2:28½, both of these records were made at Los Angeles.

I. DeTurk of Santa Rosa was in town several days during the week and he reports the trotters in his locality as being ready for the fray. Some fifty horses, not including those owned by the Pierce Bros., are being exercised at the track there, and all of them are doing well.

A. W. Burrell of Petaluma has lately purchased the horse known as The Asbeat Hambletonian Stallion. He is a dark bay, with black points, stands 16 hands, and weighs about 1200 pounds. His pedigree, as given, is by Hambletonian Jr., dam Topsy by Black Pilot, 2nd dam Peggy, a Messenger mare. Mr. Burrell's new stallion has fine action, very stylish, and is a beautiful animal. The price given is not stated.

I wonder if some of the old horsemen of Santa Clara County can tell me how many "David Hills" have stood in their neighborhood. It is necessary that a full history of the David Hills and Black Hawks that have stood in California be published, as many mistakes in pedigrees have already been made by confounding these horses. I shall be glad to receive information from any who will take the trouble to forward it.

Harry J. Agnew writes me that he has taken possession of his new purchase, "The Agnew Stock Farm," and is hard at work getting things in apple pie order. The large barn, which has at present twelve single stalls, will be remodeled and twenty roomy box stalls put up for the accommodation of the royally bred stock, which will be quartered there. Mr. Agnew has an experience extending over almost a quarter of a century, and that the new undertaking will prove successful is the heartfelt wish of many friends.

A little meal mixed with other feed is especially valuable in spring for both cattle and horses. It promotes digestion and helps loosen the old coat of hair, as well as to make the new one come on glossy and beautiful. It is often said that fattening food must not be given to horses at work, but oil meal is strength giving as well as fattening. Mixed with oat meal it is a better ration than the one commonly given of corn and oats, but it is not advisable to feed so large a ration of it as is often given of corn when that is fed with oats.

Last week the Board of Review of the National Trotting Association met at Chicago and investigated quite a number of cases among others being the Roy Wilkes affair. It will be remembered that last season, at Lexington, L. A. Davies, the owner of Roy Wilkes was fined $1 000 and Robens the driver fined $500. Mr. Davies claimed that the fine was unjust and asked for a review of the case, and he presented a lot of affidavits in support of his appeal. The board, however, saw fit to uphold the fine, so Davies will have to pay $1,000 if he wants to pace his horse again.

J. H. Kock, Secretary of the New York Jockey Club, has forwarded to this office an elegant programme book containing a full list of all the fixed events and the entries thereto. In a short preface we find the following:

It will be the endeavor of the New York Jockey Club to make Morris Park, in all its details, the most attractive sporting centre of this continent. There is no form of reputable and popular sport which will not find a home on its grounds. They will never be closed.

From all sections of the country comes the news that tracks are being put in condition for the summer campaign. Owing to the severe winter, many of them will require more than the usual amount of work, but they will all be in shape before long. The track at Greenville, Plumas County is being attended to by W. H. Killeby for Charles H. Lawrence, who will have his stable ready for exercise in a few days. As there are many trotters through the Plumas Valleys, the Greenville track should be well patronized by the local horsemen.

"John Thomas," the purchaser of Edwin C, 2:15, came on from the East during the early part of the week and paid the balance of the amount due. The fast pacer was at once shipped by express over the Southern route, and he is now on his way to his new home. The circumstances attending the sale of this horse would almost warrant us in the belief that he is intended for a "ringer" on the other side of the Rocky Mountains. If any of our Eastern contemporaries hear of a pacer kicking his driver out of the sulky, then they will know that Edwin C. has been heard from.

It often happens that full brothers and sisters to noted trotters and successful stock horses are very indifferent animals. Imported Diomed was one of the most distinguished progenitors of race horses ever brought across the water. His full brother Admiral, foaled in 1779, was also brought to this country, but his name is not found in the pedigree of any distinguished animal, whether racers, trotters or pacers. Fearnaught (2:23¼) was the best son of Young Morrill, by all odds both as a trotter and a sire, yet he had several brothers that were not distinguished either upon the turf or in the stud.

The attendance at the Petaluma race track two weeks ago, was rather small when the bell was rang for the race for named horses, and the sport not very exciting as the grey gelding Chapo, although having but little work was too fast for the balance of his field. The summary was as follows:

B. Boman's g g Chapo	3	1	1	1
A. J. Robinson's b g Fat Boy	1	3	3	2
T. Hoppe's ch m Annie Laurie	2	2	2	3
A. Burrell's b f Daisy S	4	4	4	5
W. P. Fine's b g Wizzard	5	5	5	4

Time, 2:11½, 2:15½, 2:18¼, 2 08½.

"One has to go away from home for news", was never more aptly illustrated than the following item cut from the New York sun. In speaking of Orrin A. Hickok that paper says:

"The fastest trotter in his string is the bay stallion Alfred G , by Anteeo, 2:16½, to whom Hickok gave a record of 2:19½ last November in his four-year-old form."

The racing reporter of the Sun is only on a par with the ordinary, or rather, I should say the extraordinary reporters to be found on the daily papers of this city.

The misunderstanding existing between the Montana Associations, has at last been amicably settled and the dates as now arranged, are as follows:

Missoula, July 14, 15, 16, 17. 18, 19.
Deer Lodge, 22, 23, 24, 25, 26.
Anaconda, August 1, 2, 4, 5, 6, 7. 8, 9.
Butte, August 12, 13, 14, 15, 16, 18, 19, 20.
Helena, August 23, 25, 26. 27, 28, 29, 39.

There is no change in the Missoula and Deer Ridge dates. The Helena visitors to Anaconda speak in highest terms of the outlook for the unusually successful season. All horsemen are looking forward to a splendid circuit.

Several of the sporting papers of the country have a standing paragraph in their composition rooms now-a-days which reads as follows: "Andy McCarthy has been set down for the remainder of the season." This item can usually be inserted six times a year.

Two colt stakes were lately instituted in Yolo County by local horsemen, but they did not fill. The two-year-old stake had one entry, Dixie, by Clay Duke, while the three-year-old stake had also one entry, Riley by Clay Duke. There can be only one of two reasons for this apathy, first because the managers did not advertise in the BREEDER AND SPORTSMAN, or, the local horse owners are afraid of the Clay Duke's. If the latter is the cause, then I am pleased for the sake of Mr. Martin, his owner, as I saw Clay Duke on the circuit last season and was prepossessed in his favor. There is a strong prospect that all of the Alconas will be heard from during 1890.

There are many reasons why the spur is preferable to the whip. In the first place it is far more effectual; it comes without warning, and the horse cannot watch it, or swerve from it, as from a whip. In the second place the whip should be used as a guiding monitor rather than an instrument of punishment, and, for many obvious reasons, the colt is best not to feel much of it. Thirdly, the spur, though more dreaded by the colt, inflicts far less pain upon him. The most superficial spick answers the purpose far better than anything more, and even the deepest prick that a properly made spur would inflict, would not carry so much future pain as a whip used hard enough to produce a weal.

Messrs. Page & Aiken, of Newman, Stanislaus County, have purchased the well known Morgan stallion, Frank Morgan, which has been much admired by the friends of C. W. Welby, his later owner. Frank Morgan is perhaps the handsomest specimen of the Morgan family that ever crossed the Rocky Mountains, and as his get are all of them beautiful, showy horses, he should prove a desirable sire for roadster and carriage horses. Page & Aiken have a number of well bred trotting mares which, when crossed with Frank Morgan, should produce roadsters second to none. Frank Morgan is by a son of Morgan General Jr., he by Morgan General, he by Billy Root, he by Sherman, he by Justin Morgan. The dam is by Romeo, he by Green Mountain, he by Gifford, he by Woodbury, he by Justin Morgan. The price paid for this horse was $1,500.

Tom Murphy, lately Hickock's able lieutenant, has located at the Petaluma track, and starts in with a good string of horses, among which are A. F. Hatch's Lenmer by Admar (son of Admiral); M. T. Tarpey's five-year-old mare by Anteeo, and Wilfred Page's stallion Gran Moro by LeGrande, dam by The Moor; three-year-old filly Leoline by Clovis (son of Sultan). dam by Woodford Mambrino; yearling filly Mortrica by Mortimer, 2:27, dam by Alexander 490, and other equally well-bred youngsters. As Tom drove Arab. 2:15, Elector, 2:21½, Conde, 2:20, and other fast ones in their work on the Petaluma track two years ago in the presence of the Petaluma public, his abilities as a driver and trainer require no commendation at our hands, and his tuition under the "prince of conditioners" should certainly make him the peer of any other trainer in ordering his horses. We bespeak for Tom a hearty reception.

Some of our trainers are beginning to repeat their horses already, says the Rushville Graphic. Last year we knew of several promising colts ruined for all time to come just because they were repeated twice a week as fast as the whip could send them. Some drivers seem to have come to themselves as it were, and learned to harden their horses by short flights of speed. Some argue that if the horse has not his mettle and endurance tested he is not ready for a race, and that he must have two repeats a week. It would be a Godsend to all horses as well as trainers, if no visitors were allowed during "working up" days. Every trainer has a pride in his "string," and his ability as a driver is being reviewed. So he is inclined to let his horse go faster and faster on account of all this as well as to entertain his friends. In this business as much if not more we need men with strong minds, quick perception, well-balanced, and those whose whole soul is in their business.

Every Vermonter knows of the horse, Ethan Allen, says Vision in Wallace's Monthly, and could give a very intelligent account of his history, and at least one version of his pedigree, but not one in a hundred knows anything about the famous general of the Revolutionary War, that died and was buried at Burlington in 1789, and for whom, sixty years later, the horse was named. Whatever the connection, it is practically impossible for a resident of the Green Mountain State to have any conception of this name except as belonging solely to the horse. The grave of the famous general is in a very sightly and beautiful spot, and the monument is surmounted by an excellent life size statue, which strongly shows the characteristics of a great general. One 4th of July many persons were standing around his grave, when a man from the rural districts rather astonished the others by exclaiming, "Well, I never did see old Ethan, but I have seen lots of his colts."

There are quite a number of my readers who imagine that all of Theo Winters thoroughbreds are in the East preparatory to undergoing a severe contest for supremacy as between the Eastern and Californian horses, but in addition to those owned by Mr. Winter's on the other side of the Rocky Mountains, he also has in training at the Reno track a small contigent which although few in numbers are able to cope with any now on this coast. There is a slight possibility that the stable's colors will be seen on the California tracks during the circuit, but the horses now in training in the adjoining State will surely be seen at the meetings held across the divide. An occasional correspondent sends me a list of those now going through their preparations, and also states that Maurice Peppers has charge of the string. Maurice has had lots of experience in this sort of work, and should be able to bring his charges to the postfit to run against any thoroughbreds in the land.

Chas. Haskill is a representative of the well known Norfolk family, being by that great horse, dam Addie O'Neil by Leinster.

The next is a four-year-old gelding, Leb, by Joe Hooker, dam Illusion. Princess Norfolk is a four-year-old filly by the Duke of the same name.

One of the promising ones and one which was originally intended for Eastern campaign work is Black Bart, a son of Three Cheers, while another of the two-year-old lot is the filly Blizzard by Blazes. In addition to the above there are several trotters being speeded at the Reno track, and everything looks prosperous for a splendid season of sport in Nevada this year.

THE WEEKLY

Breeder and Sportsman.

JAMES P. KERR, PROPRIETOR.

The Turf and Sporting Authority of the Pacific Coast.

Office, No. 313 Bush St.
P. O. Box 2300.

TERMS—*One Year, $5; Six Months, $3; Three Months, $1.50.*
STRICTLY IN ADVANCE.

Money should be sent by postal order, draft or by registered letter, addressed to JAMES P. KERR, San Francisco, Cal.

Communications must be accompanied by the writer's name and address, not necessarily for publication, but as a private guarantee of good faith.

NEW YORK OFFICE, Room 15, 181 Broadway.

ALEX. P. WAUGH, - - - - - - Editor.

Advertising Rates

Per Square (half inch)

One time	$1 50
Two times	2 50
Three times	3 25
Four times	4 00

And each subsequent insertion 75c. per square.

Advertisements running six months are entitled to 10 per cent. discount.

Those running twelve months are entitled to 20 per cent. discount.

Reading notices set in same type as body of paper, 50 cents per line each insertion.

To Subscribers.

The date printed on the wrapper of your paper indicates the time to which your subscription is paid.

Should the BREEDER AND SPORTSMAN be received by any subscriber who does not want it, write us direct to stop it. A postal card will suffice.

Special Notice to Correspondents.

Letters intended for publication should reach this office not later than Wednesday of each week, to secure a place in the issue of the following Saturday. Such letters to insure immediate attention should be addressed to the BREEDER AND SPORTSMAN, and not to any member of the staff.

San Francisco, Saturday, May 10, 1890.

Dates Claimed.

EUREKA JOCKEY CLUB....July 2d to 5th
IONE....Aug 1th to 5th.
LOS ANGELES (6th District)....Aug. 4th to 9th
SAN JOSE....Aug. 11th to 16th
NAPA....Aug. 18th to 23rd
GLENBROOK PARK, 17th District....August 19th to 23d
PETALUMA....Aug. 25th to 30th
OAKLAND (District No. 1)....Sept. 1st to Sept. 6th
LAKEPORT, 12th District....September 23d to 27th
CALIFORNIA STATE FAIR....Sept 8th to 20th
STOCKTON....Sept. 23rd to 27th.
FRESNO (Fall Meeting)....Sept. 29th to Oct. 4th
VISALIA....Oct. 7th to 11th

Stallions Advertised

IN THE

BREEDER AND SPORTSMAN.

Thoroughbreds.

DOUGLASDALE—Thoroughbred Clydesdale....Lawn View Farm, Cal.
FRIAR TUCK, Hermit—Romping Girl....C. W. Aby, Middletown.
GREENBACK, Dollar—Music....C. W. Aby, Middletown.
ST. SAVIOR, Eolus—War Song....C. W. Aby, Middletown.
THREE CHEERS, Imp. Hurrah—Young Fashion....E. S. Culver, San Francisco.

Trotters.

ADMIRAL, Volunteer—Lady Pierson....Frank Drake, Vallejo.
ACTOR, Prompter—Dam by Sultan....Lawn View Farm, Cal.
APEX, Prompter—Mary....Poplar Grove Breeding Farm, Wildflower.
ALCONA, Almont—Queen Mary....Fred W. Loeber, St. Helena
BAY ROSE, Sultan—Madam Baldwin....Thos. Bonner, Santa Rosa
CLOVIS, Sultan—Sweetbriar....Poplar Grove Breeding Farm, Wildflower.
CUPID, Sidney—Venus....C. O. Thornquest, Oakland
CHARLES DERBY, Steinway—by Electioneer....Cook Stock Farm, Contra Costa Co.
CORRECTOR, Director—Brainey....Pleasanton Stock Farm.
DECORATOR, Director—Chess....Pleasanton Stock Farm.
DEXTER PRINCE, Kentucky Prince—Lady Dexter....L. M. Morse, Lodi.
DIRECTOR, Dictator—Dolly....Pleasanton Stock Farm, Pleasanton.
EL BENTON, Electioneer—Nellie Benton....Souther Farm, San Leandro.
ECLECTIC, Electioneer—Manette....Wilfred Page, Sonoma County
EROS, Electioneer—Sontag Mohawk....W. H. Vioget, Menlo Park
FIGARO, Hambletonian—Emblem....Souther Farm, San Leandro.
GROVER CLAY, Electioneer—Maggie Norfolk....Denis Gannon, Oakland.
GRAND MOOR 2374, Moor 870—Vashti....H. I. Thornton, S. F.
G. & M., Anteeo—Rosa B....George E. Guerne, Santa Rosa.
GUY WILKES, George Wilkes—Lady Bunker....San Mateo Stock Farm, San Mateo.
GLEN FORTUNE, Electioneer—Glenna....Souther Farm, San Leandro.
GEORGE WASHINGTON, Mambrino Chief—Fanny Rose....Thos. Smith, Vallejo.
GRANDISSIMO, LeGrande—Norma....Fred W. Loeber, St Helena
JESTER D., Almont—Hortense....Souther Farm, San Leandro
JUNIO, Electioneer—by Granger....S. N. Straube, Fresno.
KING DAVID, Admiral—Black Flora....Frank Drake, Vallejo.
LEO WILKES, Guy Wilkes Sable....San Mateo Stock Farm, San Mateo.
MEMO, Sidney—Flirt....John Rowen, Oakland
MAMBRINO WILKES, George Wilkes—Lady Chrisman....San Miguel Stock Farm, Walnut Creek.
MAMBRINO CHIEF, McDonald Chief—Venus....Thos. Smith, Vallejo.
MORTIMER, Electioneer—Marti....Wilfred Page, Sonoma County
PASHA, Sultan—Madam Baldwin....D. Bryson, Linden
PHILOSOPHER, Pilot Wilkes—Belle....George E. Guerne, Santa Rosa.
REDWOOD, Anteeo—Lou Wilton....A. McFayden, Oakland.
STEINWAY, Strathmore—Abbess....Cook Stock Farm, Contra Costa Co
SABLE WILKES, Guy Wilkes—Sable....San Mateo Stock Farm, San Mateo.
VICTOR, Echo—Daughter of Woodburn....G. W. Hughes, Napa City
YOUNG ELMO, St. Elmo—Dam by Woodburn....Lawn View Farm Cal.

Mabel, full sister to Beautiful Bells 2:29½, has been sent from the Rancho Del Paso to receive the embraces of the mighty Stamboul 2:12½. This union should produce good results, and it is the opinion of Mr. Rose that the progeny will far surpass anything ever foaled.

The Story of John Nelson.

In another column of this week's issue will be found an article on "John Nelson Again" which was copied in the current number of Wallace's Monthly, and taken from the Newark (New Jersey) Sunday Call. The following foot-note is also given under the Call article, which, as it is signed "Editor," is supposed to emanate from the pen of Jno. H. Wallace. While we are willing to concede that Bro. Wallace has done more for the trotting horse interests of the United States than any other one man in them, still he has a nack of sticking to a point after he has made an assertion, that becomes annoying, especially when his readers know that he is mistaken. The foot note is as follows:

[NOTE.—The above agrees substantially with what we have hitherto had about John Nelson, but it does not add much light as to what horse was his sire. Though the presumption is that he was bred by Mr. Thomas Evans of New Brunswick, that fact is not established beyond doubt. If there be uncertainty as to the breeder, there must certainly be uncertainty as to the sire. The only evidence which will put the matter beyond doubt are the books of imp. Trustee.—EDITOR.]

The first time we find the name of John Nelson mentioned in any of the registers is in Vol. IV., wherein it states: "John Nelson 187, ch h foaled 1851, got by a son of imp. Trustee, dam the Redmond mare by Abdallah 1; bred on Long Island; taken to California." Now in the editorial note we find that full concurrence is given to the pedigree as stated by the writer in the Sunday Call, and Mr. Wallace even uses the words: "The above agrees substantially with what we have hitherto had about John Nelson." Now if such really is the case, and Mr. Wallace has had the same information before, why is it that even as late as the Year Book, published presumably about the 15th of last month, we still find "John Nelson 187, ch h foaled 1851, got by a son of imp. Trustee, dam the Redmond mare by Abdallah 1; bred on Long Island; taken to California; died 1871." If Mr. Wallace has had any doubts in his own mind as to the breeding of John Nelson, why is it that he still claims the sire as being a son of imp. Trustee and not by Trustee himself; he still sticks to the Redmond mare, and yet confesses in the editorial note that his previous information was that the dam of John Nelson was by one of the Morgan horses; but the more particular point which we wish to claim is, that it is extremely doubtful whether anyone can positively tell John Nelson's breeding. Some one must evidently have shown Mr. Wallace pretty conclusive proofs that he was by a son of imp. Trustee, or the horse would not have been originally registered in that way. And again, Mr. Wallace has in the Year Book, "Died in 1871," whereas, we know positively that the horse was alive in 1876, and for some time Mr. Wallace has refused to register mares which were foaled after 1872. It is only a short time ago that Mr. Shippee, of Stockton, wished to register some John Nelson mares, but Mr. Wallace refused on the grounds that he had information showing that John Nelson died in 1871. When the answer to Mr. Shippee's application was shown in and around Stockton, it caused many of the old horsemen to smile, because it is a well known fact in that city that John Nelson stood there in the Centennial year under the management of Mr. Potter; it was sometime after that before the horse was sold to Messrs. Miller & Lux, and we are only awaiting answers to inquiries sent out to prove positively when the old horse did die.

This is written more to show that the history of John Nelson is somewhat clouded as far as Eastern writers are concerned. When the horse was bought by the California parties alluded to, a certificate of his breeding was given by Mr. Horace F. Jones, which read as follows. "John Nelson is by imp Trustee, out of the Redmond mare (who trotted in 3:35), by Abdallah, he by Mambrino, and he by imp Messenger." That certificate was seen by scores of persons now alive, and the first advertisement that was written for the horse in this State was written by a gentleman who had that certificate in front of him as he wrote the advertisement. The owner of John Nelson was Mr. Edwin M. Pitcher, a dairyman, who lived on the old Auburn road, a few miles out of Sacramento. Mr. Pitcher was an honest man, respected by all who knew him, and it is unnecessary at this late day to state that he was not a man who would have given a false pedigree to any horse. Black Hawks and Morgans were then thought a great deal more of than any other strains of blood here in California. The Abdallah and Hambletonian fever had not set in. Abdallah was, comparatively speaking, an unknown quantity; therefore, if a false pedigree had been given, a much better one could have been advertised than the one that was originally written by Mr. Merry. It is extremely to be regretted that the correct pedigree of John Nelson cannot be obtained, for he has left in this State a name that will endure for many generations. The name of John Nelson, when it occurs in any pedigree, is ample assurance to the horsemen of California that stamina and endurance are part of the composite parts of the animal under consideration. Mr. Wallace finishes up his editorial note very well by saying. "The only evidence which will put the matter beyond doubt is the books of imp Trustee."

The Fresno Fall Meeting.

The Directors of Agricultural District No. 21, located at Fresno, present their annual fall programme to our readers this week, or at least such part of it as requires early entries. As usual the purses are large, and as Mr. Baldwin, the Secretary, states in a letter: "There are no strings to any of them." This Association has seen fit for some time to throw their purses open to all, and district stakes are relegated to other associations. From the inception of this organization, the policy of the Directors has been to do all that could be done for horsemen in the State, feeling assured that they would receive a generous support from those who own horses in training, and consequently would receive a liberal return from the public at the gate, who are always desirous of seeing the best contests possible.

Among the guaranteed purses which the Association offers this year is one of a $1,000 for the 2:24 class, the entrance fee being $100, of which $25 is payable May 15th, $25 payable July 15th and $50 payable August 11th, when horses are to be named.

The second is a guaranteed purse of $1,200 for the 2:20 class, 10 per cent entrance payable, $30 on May 15th, $30 on July 15th and the balance, $60 on August 11th, when horses are to be named.

The third is a nomination guaranteed purse of $1,000 for the 2:30 pacing class, with $1000 entrance, $25 payable May 15th. $25 on July 15th and $50 August 11th when horses are to be named.

In all the above purses, if the entrance money amounts to more than the $1,000 guaranteed by the Association, it will be added to the purse, and the Directors in addition will also add a bonus of 20 per cent of the amount of the purse.

The thoroughbreds are also taken good care of as we find in the announcement, the President stake with a guarantee of $1000 for all ages, weight for age, one and three-eights of a mile dash, $100 entrance, $10 payable May 15th, $15 on June 12th, $25 payable July 15th and $50 payable September 6th.

The second guaranteed purse for the runners is called the Raisin Handicap of $1,000 for all ages, a dash of one mile and a quarter. The entrance money and the payments are the same as the President Stakes. Weights for the handicap will be announced on August 15th, through the columns of the BREEDER AND SPORTSMAN.

The two running races have the same additions annexed to them as have the pacing and trotting races. If the entrance money amounts to more than $1,000, it will be added to the purse and the Association will still further add 20 per cent. of the amount of the purse.

The programme with all the conditions will be found in the appropriate column and we would urge all owners who have horses that are eligible for any of these races, to enter, as Fresno is noted for its well finished track, splendid stabling, magnificent climate and the hospitable character of its inhabitants. Those who attended the fall meeting at that point last year, are all loud in their praises of the management and as Mr. Baldwin has had many years of experience he understands fully the wants of horsemen and is always willing to do whatever lies in his power for the comfort of their horses and themselves. We fully expect that Fresno will have an entry list second to none, and as the number of entries asked for is in accordance with the American Association's rules, they are all bound to fill.

Golden Gate Association.

One of the most prosperous Agricultural Associations within the confines of this State is the one called Golden Gate No. 1. The Directors are all well known horsemen and they are ever ready to accept any suggestions which will add to the pleasure of their meetings. For the present season they have adopted the nomination purses which are now so general throughout the East and have also offered two guaranteed purses for the slower classes in addition to a stake which they call "The New List." Seeing the success of the BREEDER AND SPORTSMAN Futurity Stake, they have taken time by the forelock, as it is the first association in California to offer a large guaranteed purse for foals of 1890; the race to be trotted at the fall meeting of 1893. The subscriptions to each of the purses offered are on the installment plan, so that the payments are easy which enables those who are not over and above well-to-do, a chance to enter in one or more of the stakes. The entries for the races already advertised close on May 15th. so that those who are desirous of making entries should read the announcement at once and not defer it until too late.

The first event in the programme is called "The New List" purse of $1000 for three-year-olds whose sires up to January 1, 1890, have not produced an animal with a record of 2:30 or better at three years of age or under. The entrance fee is 10 per cent., payable $25 on May 15th when entries will close in the name of owners or trainers; $25 is payable on June 15th, $25 on July 15th, $25 five days before the first advertised day of the meeting. When the last payment is made, horses must be named.

The second is a guaranteed purse of $1200 for the three-minute class, entrance 10 per cent., payable $30 on May 15th, $30 on June 15th, $30 July 15th, and $30 five days before the first advertised day of the meeting at which time horses must be named.

A guaranteed purse of $1200 is also offered for the 2.40 class, entrance 10 per cent. of which $30 is payable when the entries close, May 15th, $30 on June 15th, $30 on July 15th and $30 five days before the first advertised day of meeting.

A guaranteed Futurity Purse of $4000 is also offered, the entrance to which is only three per cent., payable in such small installments that any one can afford to enter foals of the present year; entries also close on May 15th for this Futurity Purse, at which time $10 must accompany the entry, $10 on January 15, 1891, $15 on June 15, 1891, $15 January 15, 1892, $15 on June 15, 1892, $15 on January 15, 1893, $20 June 15, 1893, with a last payment of $20 fifteen days before the advertised day of the race. If the last payment is made on twelve or more entries, the horses shall be started in trial races in which not more than eleven nor less than six shall be allotted to start; the trial races shall be mile heats, three in five, for a purse of $1000, given by the Association for each race. If two trial races are trotted, the first four horses shall only be entitled to start in the final race; if three such trial races are trotted, only the first three horses in each trial race shall start in the final; and if four or more trial races are necessary, only the first two horses in each trial race shall start in the final race. These trial races must be trotted not less than five nor more than ten days previous to the day set for the final race, and if possible all trial races will be trotted on the same day. We have no doubt from the success of the BREEDER AND SPORTSMAN Futurity Stake that this one will also receive a generous support from the horsemen of California. The race will be trotted in the same year as the BREEDER AND SPORTSMAN Futurity Stake, and therefore the champion three-year-old of 1893 should be able to win for his owner many thousands of dollars.

Remember entries for all these races close, as stated before, on May 15th, and we therefore urge our readers to carefully scan the advertisement in the appropriate column.

Races at Los Alamos.

The races at Los Alamos on 1st of May were intereresting, and they gave universal satisfaction. The judges were anxious to give all their dues, and each race was watched closely by them. The first race was the 3:00 class, mile heats 2 in 3.

Harry held the inside, Neva second and Don Ramon outside. The horses behaved well and were sent away to a splendid start. Don Ramon took the lead immediately, and was never headed. He won handily in 3:07. Harry 2nd, Neva 3rd.

In the second heat Don Ramon acted badly, he being rank, and wanted to run, but the three horses were soon started. Harry and Don Ramon trotting together till they reached the half. Don Ramon broke and Harry got a lead of five lengths, but on the homestretch Don Ramon trotted fast and overtook Harry, and both horses passed under the wire together. It was declared a dead heat, time 3:02.

Third heat was a walk-over for Don Ramon, who immediately took the lead, and was never headed. He won handily in 3:07.

SUMMARY.

3:00 class purse $60. 75 per cent to first, 25 to second.
Rochin's Stock Farm, Don Ramon, s g 8 by Antioch, dam Angelo P. by Newry............Pete Doyle 1 0 1
Bell's Farm, Harry, b g 16 years old, breeding unknown ....Menchaca 2 0 2
Rucker's, Neva, b m 8—by Bashaw............Rucker 3 3 3
Time 3:07. 3:02. 3:07.

Running race. Half mile and repeat. Purse $50.

Three horses came to face the starter in this race. There was lively betting on this event, Arab being the favorite, with Mercedes and Sportime in the field. The horses were soon started; Mercedes had the rail, Arab 2nd, Sportime 3rd. The horses ran all together around the turn. When they straightened out Sportime fell behind and Arab and Mercedes made a driving finish, the mare Mercedes winning by half a length in 53 seconds. Although the mare won, Arab was still the favorite and when they were called out to run the next heat Arab looked still a winner. As the trio were quiet, the starter had no difficulty in getting them off to a good start. From the beginning Arab and Mercedes ran close together. A large blanket would have covered both all the way around. A hard finish again, and the mare won the heat and race, the talent getting left.

SUMMARY.

Hill's farm b c Mercedes, 5, by Comanche, 108............Ayala 1
Harris' b g Arab, 8, by Dan Rice, 120............Romero 2
Smith's b g Sportime, 6, Unknown, 115............Pico 3
Time, :53, :53½.

After this race Harris matched Arab against Mercedes, half mile and repeat for $250 a side to run in 30 days. The race will come off on May 31st, when there will be two days racing.

ONE-QUARTER MILE DASH. PURSE $40.

The third race was a black eye for the talent. It was so certain that Captain Martinez would win that any bet was good. The odds made no difference. Three horses started. There was little delay in the start and when they got off they were all in a bunch. To the great surprise of all Arata's bay colt won, Lightfoot 2nd and Captain Martinez 3rd. Time, :23¼.

SUMMARY.

Arata's b c, 3, by Robbery, 120............Pico 1
Smith's b c Lightfoot, dam unknown, 110............Rice 2
Rochin's s, 5, Capt. Martinez by Newry, 120............Romero 3
Time, :23¼.

This ended the racing. The judges were John Murry Jr., of Santa Maria, Sherman, of Lompoc and Dr. Graham of Los Alamos.

The Last Day at Sacramento.

The attendance at the Sacramento track on Saturday of last week, was in no wise larger than the average of the preceding days and it seems a shame that the residents of the Capital City should have neglected to patronize the sport so generously offered by the Directors of the State Agricultural Society. A better programme was never arranged, the horses were known to be the equal of any that California has ever produced. The purses were large yet still the public would not attend; we are pleased to say, however, that the Directors do not feel disheartened by their lack of support but will continue in their good work and next spring another running meeting be given, in hope that the public may gradually become educated to the sport of the kings.

The weather was all that could be desired and the racing equal to any seen during the week. The first race on the card was the Golden Eagle Hotel Handicap for two-year olds, the only two coming to the wire being Col. Harry I. Thornton's ch c Arcade and J. E. Smith's ch c Bon Ton. Whether the name of Smith's was a fictitious one or not we do not know, but the colt has been trained in a stable that has a rather unsavory reputation, in fact the owner or at least the principal owner was expelled only last year from the Fresno course, and so stands to-day. Owing to the remarkable and peculiar betting indulged in by those who were eager to place their money on the winner, suspicion was aroused that the race was not to be run on the merits of the horses alone, and therefore the judges took a hand in the matter and made diligent inquiry as to the suspicious circumstances that had caused the betting to change so materially. When the pools first opened Bon Ton was the favorite at $20 to $14 for his opponent but gradually it got down to even money, and finally changed to $20 for Arcade and $13 for Bon Ton, the pools selling like hot cakes. After the judges had taken the matter under consideration for some time, Lawless, the jockey, who was on Bon Ton was taken down and Joe Narvaez selected to fill his place. Joe cantered Bon Ton up and down for some time and finally gave it as his opinion that the colt was "stuffed." At this point the judges who were Messrs. La Rue, Greene and Cox announced that they would defer the running of the initial event until later on in the afternoon to give Bon Ton a more equal chance. The colt was turned over to Henry Walsh, trainer of the Palo Alto stable, who watched his charge carefully until the time came for the race to start.

In the meanwhile the second event on the card, the Hopeful Handicap for all ages, was called. Four horses faced the starter, the favorite being Pliny who sold in the books at 2 to 5, Longshot 2½ to 1, Sheridan 4 to 1 and Oro 6 to 1. After quite a number of false starts the field was sent away to a straggling start with the favorite the last of the quartette. W. H. E Smith's new purchase, Longshot, took the lead at once with Oro a good second and in these positions they passed under the wire the first time; at the quarter Longshot was still leading with the others well bunched close up; the same relative positions were maintained to the half where Oro fell back behind his field, Sheridan and Pliny improving their positions just a trifle, Longshot still leading around the turn and into the homestretch, Pliny having his nose almost even with Longshot as they turned into the straight to come home. Casey, the jockey, on Pliny here plied the bat at a vigorous rate and ultimately showed in front but for a moment only, as Longshot was given his head and he came away winning easily by two lengths, Pliny second, Sheridan third and Oro beaten off.

SUMMARY.

The Hopeful Handicap.—A sweepstakes for all ages of $25 each, $15 forfeit, or $10 if declared, with $400 added, second to receive $100. Weights announced at 10 P. M. day before race. Declarations due by 5 P. M. same day. One and one-eighth miles.
W. H. E. Smith's ch h (4) Longshot, Duke of Norfolk, dam by Langford, 118............Hill 1
Kelly & Samuels' b c (3) Pliny by Flood, dam Precious, 108....Casey 2
P. Siebenthaler's ch c (3) Sheridan by Young Bazaar, dam Lost Girl 108............Narvaez 3
Time, 1:55¾
Oro 105 (Hennessey) ran unplaced.

The California Derby, which earlier in the season promised to prove one of the most interesting races of the meeting, was bereft of the semblance of a contest, as the only horse that came to the post was Muta, the Palo Alto filly, the well known Racine being allowed to stay in the stable, so his companion had a walk over.

SUMMARY.

The California Derby—A sweepstakes for three-year-olds (foals of 1887) of $100 each, half forfeit, or only $10 if declared January 1st, or $25 March 1, 1890, with $1000 added; of which $150 to second and $100 to third. A winner in 1890 of any three-year-old event, when carrying weight for age or more of the value of $500, to carry three pounds; of $1000, or two races of any value, five pounds extra. Non-winners of a sweepstakes allowed five pounds; maidens allowed seven pounds. One mile and a half.
Palo Alto's ch f Muta, Wild Idle—imp Mutiny, 118............ w o 1

The third race of the day was the Handicap for all ages, and it proved the biggest betting race of the day, Guido being installed favorite in the pools, he selling at $25, Ida Glenn at $15 and the field $11. Again there was some little delay, as at least a half dozen scores were made before the flag fell; when Starter Coombs sent them off, the favorite and Kildare started off to make the running, leading the balance of the ruck by two lengths. The same positions were kept up until the homestretch was reached, where Kildare fell back a little and Jackson took second place, the heat resulting in favor of Guido by a length, Jackson being second and Kildare third. For the second heat pools sold, Guido $25, field $14. Again the starter had a great deal of trouble in getting the horses away, as each of the jockeys seemed determined to delay the others and prevent an equitable send off. After an hour had been consumed in this unsatisfactory manner the flag fell, with Guido leading. Casey, the jockey, who, by the way, has stamped himself as a long-headed rider, again made the running with his mount and was never headed. Coming down the stretch Louisa M gave him a little brush, but the filly was not equal to the task and Guido won by a neck, Jackson being third.

SUMMARY.

Purse $400 for all ages; $10 from starters to go to second horse. Non-winners this year at the time of starting allowed, if three years old, five pounds; four years, ten pounds, five and upwards, twelve pounds. Entries close with Clerk of Course at 5 P. M. day before the race. Mile heats.
W. H. Babb's ch. c. (3) Guido—Double Cross—Aurora, 104 ....Casey 1 1
J. McM. Shafter's b. m. (4) Louise M—Kyrle Daly, Nighthawk 103 ....Hazlett 3 2
H. Howard's b. h. Jackson, Luke Blackburn—Ivy Leaf, 109, ...Gannon 2 3
Time 1:44, 1:43.
Kildare 121 (Hitchcock), Ida Glenn, 104 (Hennessy), Hotspur, 107 (Bustellos) and Jack Brady 121 (Cooper) ran unplaced.

After the conclusion of the above race, event No. 1 was called, and the pools now sold, Arcade $20, Bon Ton $15. The race was very uninteresting, for although Bon Ton seemed to have an easy victory, he leading for a half mile by at least two lengths, still when the proper moment came Casey gave Arcade his head and the Thornton colt won very easily by three lengths.

SUMMARY.

Golden Eagle Hotel Handicap—A sweepstake for two year olds (foals of 1888), of $100 each, half forfeit, or only $10 if declared January 1st, 1890, or $25 if by 4 P. M. day before the race; with $700 added, of which $150 to Second. Weights to be announced by 6 o'clock P. M. second day before the day. Three-quarter of a mile.
H. I. Thornton's ch. c. Arcade, Milner—Nannie Hubbard 100 ....Casey 1
J. E. Smith's ch. c. Bon Ton, Flood—May D. 100............Narvaez 2
Time 1:18½.

Petaluma Stakes.

Secretary Maclay of the Sonoma and Marin Agricultural Society sends in the following list of second payments.

Second payments have been made on the following entries under conditions as advertised:

YEARLING DISTRICT.

B f Sidena by Sydney, dam Lena Bowles by Vick's Ethan Allen; Ben E. Harris, San Francisco.

B f Mortvica by Mortimer 5346, dam Reka Patchen by Alexander 490; Wilfred Page, Penn's Grove.

B c Columbus by McDonald Chief 3581, dam Fannie Rose by Ethan Allen Jr., 2903; Thos. Smith, Vallejo.

B f Lady Thorn by Thornhill, dam Lady Nutwood by Nutwood; E. McLees, Vallejo.

B c Rustic King by Rustic, dam Gazelle by General McClellan; P. J. Shafter, Olema.

Br f Rayanetta by Anteeo, dam Debonair by Sultan; Robt. S. Brown, Petaluma.

Br c Nonpareil by Dawn 6407, dam Jennie Offut by Gen. McClellan; A. L. Whitney, Petaluma.

Blk f Antelula by Anteeo, dam Nelly by Belle Alta Jr.; Jos. Wise. Carver, Geyserville.

Br c Zouave by Daly, dam Zaga by Berlin; J. F. Mulgrew, Santa Rosa.

B c Hollywood by Woodnut, dam Aurella by Albert W.; B. C. Holly, Vallejo.

Second payments have been made on the following entries under conditions as advertised; two-year-olds. District.

Ch f Starlight, Dawn—Lena Bowles, Vicks' Ethan Allen; Ben E. Harris, San Francisco.

Blk c Gran Moro, Le Grande 2868—Sunny Slope Belle, The Moor 870; Wilfred Page, Penn's Grove.

Br f Myrtle, Anteeo—Lucella, Nutwood; I. DeTurk, Santa Rosa.

Ch c Walnut, Woodnut—Pinkie, Admiral; P. McLees, Vallejo.

B f Allie B., Alcona—Mollie, Edwin Booth; Harry Rimebauch, Petaluma.

Ch f Nelly K. by Dawn, by Brown's McClellan; Robt. S. Brown, Petaluma.

Sl f Annabelle, Dawn—Pacheco, Hubbard; A. L. Whitney, Petaluma.

B f Tamarack, Carr's Mambrino Jr.—Belle, Belle Alta Jr.; Thos. Donohue, Lytton Springs.

B c Chaldean, Mambrino Wilkes—Fredolia, Fred Arnold; San Miguel Stock Farm, Walnut Creek.

B f Mylitta, Mambrino Wilkes—Mollie Fern, Capt. Kohl, San Miguel Stock Farm, Walnut Creek.

Sl c Charlie Dodge, Daly—Lady S., Smuggler; W. B. Sanborn, Santa Rosa.

B f Ella H., Anteeo—Daisy, Nutwood; Rufus Murphy, Santa Rosa.

B f Tillie Almont, Hernani—Kitty Almont, Tilton Almont; J. H. White, Lakeville.

B f Donia, Dawn—Kitty, Don Juan; Dan McGovern, Petaluma.

Blk c Almonitor, Alcona 730—Pansy, Cassius M. Clay Jr. 22; F. W. Loeber, St. Helena.

Second payments have been made on the following entries under conditions as advertised.

TWO-YEAR-OLDS, FREE-FOR-ALL.

Ch f Starlight, by Dawn, dam Lena Rowles by Vick's Ethan Allen; Ben E. Harris, San Francisco.

B f Duchess by Sidney, dam Young Countess by Sam Patchen; A. L. Whitney, Petaluma.

Ch f Vida Wilkes by Guy Wilkes, dam Vixen by Nutwood; San Mateo Stock Farm, San Mateo.

B f Volita by Antevolo, dam Ruby by Winthrop; Jos. Cairn Simpson, Oakland.

Br c Almoneer by Alban, dam America by Rysdyk's Hambletonian; Palo Alto Stock Farm, Menlo Park.

B f Elleneer by Electioneer, dam Lady Ellen by Carr's Mambrino; Palo Alto Stock Farm, Menlo Park.

Br f Linnet by Electioneer, dam Lizzie Whips by Enquirer; Palo Alto Stock Farm, Menlo Park.

Second payments have been made on the following entries under conditions as advertised.

THREE-YEAR-OLDS, FREE-FOR-ALL.

B c Regal Wilkes by Guy Wilkes, dam Margaret by Sultan; San Mateo Stock Farm, San Mateo.

B c Hugo by Electioneer, dam Helpmate by Planet; Palo Alto Stock Farm, Menlo Park.

Br f Alzira by Ansel, dam American Girl by Toronto Sontag; Palo Alto Stock Farm, Menlo Park.

Answers to Correspondents.

Answers for this department must be accompanied by the name and address of the sender, not necessarily for publication, but as proof of good faith. Write the questions distinctly, and on one side of the paper only. Positively no questions will be answered by mail or telegraph.

W. R. B.

Please let me know in your next issue if a horse called Frank, with running mate, got a record of 2:08½ at Prospect Park, Long Island, Nov. 15, 1883, driven by John Murphy, and is Frank still alive?

Answer.—Frank, with running mate, made a record in 1883 of 2:08½, but the authorities do not give the place or date of meeting. We do not know whether the horse is alive or not.

Dan Voorhees 2nd.

A few weeks ago a correspondent asked for the pedigree of Dan Voorhees 2nd, and a correspondent gives it as follows:

Dan Voorhees 2nd: Brown stallion, foaled April, 1885; bred at McLaughlin's Ranch, Banta Station. Got by Dan Voorhees 2:23½, he by General McClellan, he by North Star, he by Bulrush Morgan; dam Black Swan 2:28½, got by Case's David Hill, son of Vermont Black Hawk.

Names Claimed.

Rinaldo, for dark sorrel colt, sired by Ferndale, dam Kitty Richmond by A. W. Richmond. Property of H. W. Peck, Healdsburg. Colt foaled Apr. 23, 1890.

Fay, for dark bay or brown filly, foaled March 19, 1890, sired by Ferndale dam Gertie, by Belle Alta Jr. Property of J. F. Seaman, Healdsburg, Cal.

VETERINARY.

Conducted by W. Henry Jones, M. R. C. V. S.

Subscribers to this paper can have advice through this column in all cases of sick or injured horses or cattle by sending an explicit description of the case. Applicants will send their name and address that they may be identified. Questions requiring answers by mail should be accompanied by two dollars, and addressed to W. Henry Jones, M. R. C. V. S., Olympic Stables, Sutter Street, San Francisco.

Subscriber.

I have a valuable animal that strained a tendon on his front leg; the tendon is enlarged and he cannot walk on the leg at all. Please prescribe for the same through the columns of your valuable paper and oblige.

Answer.—I would advise you to foment with warm water, three or four daily until such time as the heat and pain are removed; then apply a strong blister, once or twice, and give some three months' rest. In the meanwhile, I would keep an eye on the sound leg and keep it cool with cold water bandages, as it will no doubt swell with the undue pressure placed upon it while the affected limb remains painful. Administer a dose of cathartic medicine, and feed on a low diet.

Foals of 1890.

At Stockton. Property of G. W. Trabern:

March 26th, chestnut filly, three white feet, strip in face by Prince of Norfolk, dam Blue Bonnet by Joe Hooker.

At Vallejo. Property of B C. Holly.

May 1st, black filly by Happy Prince, dam by Alaska.

At Santa Rosa. Property of A. McFadyen:

Bay colt by Redwood, dam Zulu Maid by Zulu Chief, for which the name of Telephone is claimed.

At Vallejo. Property of A. McFadyen:

Bay filly by Mountain Boy, dam Lou Medium by Milton Medium, the name claimed being Edith Mc.

Both of the above foals are entered in the BREEDER AND SPORTSMAN Futurity Stake.

At San Mateo Stock Farm, March 1st. The property of Wm. Corbitt:

Bay colt by Sable Wilkes 2:18, dam Minnie Princess by Nutwood 600. This is another candidate for the BREEDER AND SPORTSMAN Futurity Stake.

At Palo Alto Stock Farm. Property of Hon. Leland Stanford.

B c by Beverly—Lady Agnes by Electioneer.
B c by Electioneer—Lizzie by Wildidle.
B c by Electioneer—Amrah by Nutwood.
B f by Azmoor—Alice by Almont.
B f by Clay—Fidelia by Volunteer.
B f by Nephew—Celina by Electioneer.
Ch c by Liberty—Mollie Cobb by General Benton.
B f by Benefit—Amlet by Fallis.
B f by Wild Boy—Emeline by Electioneer.
Ch f by Piedmont—Cecil by General Benton.
B f by Nephew—Fannie Lewis by Imp. Buckden.
B c by Piedmont—Emma by Electioneer.
B c by Benefit—Evangeline by Longfellow.
B f by Wild Boy—Violet by Electioneer.
B c by Alban—Katherion by Harry of the West.
Br f by Wild Boy—Sontag Mohawk by Mohawk Chief.
B c by Wild Boy—Grisette by Wildidle.

THOROUGHBREDS.

Br c by Flood—Imp. Patilla by Pero Gomez.
Ch c by Imp. Cheviot—Bessie Hooker by Joe Hooker.

At Vina, Tehema Co., Cal.

B c by Clay—Maria Pilot by Mambrino Pilot.
B c by Clay Monte Belle by Mohawk Chief.
Br f by Liberty—Florida by Robt. E. Lee.
B c by Liberty—Martha by Mohawk Chief.
B c by Benefit—Lizzie H by Whipple's Hambletonian.
B f by Benefit—Millie by Milton Medium.
B c by Liberty—Rivulet by Rivoli.
Br f by Liberty—Lady Rhoads by General Taylor.
B f by Benefit—Bertie by Piedmont.
B c by Azmoor—Amy by Messenger Duroc.

Thoroughbred in the Trotter.

Much discussion has been going on in horse papers, the past year or two, respecting the value of thorough blood in the trotter, without any apparent conversion or argument between the parties starting out with opposite views, writes L. Farnham in the Horse and Stable. The reading public have been somewhat instructed by these discussions, but are still at sea as to the real merits of the question.

It is a matter of considerable importance to the extensive breeding interests of this country, whether the union of thorough blood with trotting blood is beneficial to the latter or not; and, as it is a matter of fact determined by experiment, it seems to me that a summing up of the results already obtained should settle the question with approximate correctness. Men do not differ essentially upon the relative value of other strains of blood when properly united with Hambletonian—the great trotting blood of the land.

Is there any more evidence to show the effect of Mambrino Patchen, American Star, Pilot Jr., Black Hawk or Clay blood than there is to show the effect of thoroughbred blood. I cannot avoid the feeling that many writers upon the subject exhibit more or less prejudice according to the side of the house they occupy. One writer says: "If a little thorough blood is good, a good deal is better." If then, a little Clay or Black Hawk is good with Hambletonian, why is not 100 per cent. of it better?

If 50 per cent. of the ass is good to cross with the horse, why isn't the pure blood of either better than the combination?

The logic does not hold. Every one conversant with the horse history knows that the highest types of the horse have been produced by the judicious crossing of entirely distinct families' the idea being to so cross them that whatever deficiencies exist on one side will be made up on the other, without a corresponding loss on other points.

The objection made to thoroughbred is that it lessens the instinct to trot. This is logically and probably in fact true; but does not the infusion of 15 or 25 per cent. of it add enough of nerve force and organic quality to more than balance the damage to trotting instinct?

Let us see if there is any evidence to support the presumption.

The fastest record by any trotter is the 2:08¾ of Maud S.; second fastest 2:10, by Jay-Eye See; and third 2:10½, by Sunol. The fastest five heats in a race was by Oliver K., 2:15¾, 2:15½, 2:16½, 2:16½, and 2:18; the fastest twenty mile heat was 58 25, by Sovereign; the fastest 50 miles 4:55 40½ by Ariel, and the fastest 100 miles 8.56.01, by Conqueror.

A daughter of the thoroughbred Boston produced Maud S. A daughter of Lexington, son of Boston, produced Jay-Eye-See, and he was also the sire of the grandam of Sunol. Oliver K's dam was by a son of Lexington. I am quite certain that Sovereign and Ariel were strongly tinctured with thoroughbred, and the great Conqueror was by Bellfounder. The blood of Duroc is in Dexter 2:17¼, and Phallis 2:13¾. A daughter of Lexington produced Clingstone 2:14, and a son of Wagoner got the dam of Fanny Witherspoon 2:16½. So we might go on.

Now are these facts mere incidents and valueless in determining the importance of thorough blood in the trotter? If so, will some disbeliever in thorough blood explain how so many of the greatest feats on record have been performed by horses burdened with 10 to 25 per cent. of it or more, while those with less have not got there so soon? I will ask him also to explain the probable effect of the 25 per cent. of the blood of Bellfounder on the greatest speed progenitor that ever lived—Rysdyk's Hambletonian.

I lay no claims whatever to being an expounder of the principles of horse breeding, but claim to be able to discriminate between a one-sided argument and one aiming at facts. I would like to see this article criticised, if the ideas it contains are not well grounded, for I am willing to learn the facts and not persist in being the servant of prejudice.

Management of Stallions.

The entire horse in common with all male animals, during the act of copulation, injects into the female what is commonly called the seed. If a drop of this seed is examined under the microscope, it will be found to contain a number of living bodies as evidenced by their ability to move. They have oval shaped heads and many thread-like tails. In order that the coming together of the stallion and mare may bear fruit, it is essential that some of these bodies come in contact with the egg—ovum of the mare, in some portion of the womb, otherwise the egg perishes after a time. The wavy, thread-like tails endow these bodies (spermatozoa) with powers of locomotion, so that on being injected into the passage of the mare (vagina) at copulation, they by degree work themselves into all parts of the womb, and thus come in contact with the ovum of the female.

It is through the medium of these minute fertilizing bodies that the qualities and characteristics of the sire are transmitted to the progeny. Although the general characteristics of the progeny may not be affected by the vigor, or lack of vigor, of the sire at the time of, and shortly prior to copulation, still the strength and vital power of the foal, so essential to tide it over that critical portion of its life—the first few weeks—and enable it to grow, thrive, and strengthen into an animal possessed of constitutional vigor and stamina, depends on the condition of the sire. Taking a shorter sighted view of the matter, and considering the ability of a sire to get mares in foal, and to maintain his health and strength, during the season in which there is such a drain upon his vital powers, it is absolutely essential that he should commence the season in good condition.

We very frequently hear the statement made that such and such stallions are overfed. This, in the majority of instances, is incorrect. We cannot, if we feed rationally, or afford all the nutritious matter that the system can properly assimilate, over-feed a stallion about to commence, or during the season, but we can very easily under-exercise and impair an animal's assimilative power thereby.

A horse is an actively constituted animal, and you cannot produce condition, in the true sense of the word, without sufficient amount of exercise. Condition does not simply mean the presentation of a good appearance, but it signifies the ability to do work and maintain health. The two latter abilities cannot be possessed without liberal feeling and plenty of exercise. Good condition require time to produce. The work of conditioning ought to begin fully two months before the season. The daily exercise and quantity of food should be increased in like ratio; until five miles a day is given a draught, and eight or ten a light horse.

A great invigorator of the horse is rubbing, nothing next to good feeding gives him more vim. A plentiful supply of good, clear, cotton rubbers should be on hand, and the horse should be vigorously rubbed after his exercise, until he is perfectly dry. Groom while the circulation of the skin is active, as after exercise is far more beneficial than at any other time. Have nothing to do with drugs or nostrum, for they do more harm than good if the animal is well, and if sick they should only be used under the guidance of one who understands their action, and the nature of the malady to be cured. Drugs are in no way essential; in fact they are detrimental to the process of conditioning.

It is advisable that the season should begin early and extend over as long a period as possible, so that at no time the stallion's powers shall be unduly taxed. If it is possible to procure the services of a few mares before the enervating effects of the very warm weather come on, so much the better, as the animals powers are gradually stimulated and strengthened thereby.

The death rate amongst heavy stallions during the season is much higher than it need be, which is largely the result of abruptly putting horses into the trying ordeal of heavy service and constant excitement, without building up the system in the manner indicated. Breeders blame stallion owners for having their horses abnormally fat, and consequently lacking in vigor necessary to get good, strong colts. Few, however, have the courage or judgment to allow the animal that looks like a stall-fed ox to pass by, and select one that does not require to be patched up with adipose tissue to conceal his defects.

Many flat-sided, long-backed, slack-loined horses are receiving patronage on account of their defects being considerably masked by layers of fat and flabby muscle.—F. C. Grenside, V. S., in Canadian Live Stock and Farm Journal.

Jealous Mothers.

Will Gocher says: "Some mares, particularly those of sensitive organizations, are excessively jealous of their offspring. Goldsmith Maid was one of that kind. It is related of her that when her first foal was brought forth she would allow no one to come near it. One day Charlie, her old attendant when she was in Budd Doble's stable, visited Fashion Farm. Charlie and the Maid were once firm friends, and to test the endurance of that friendship Charley concealed himself near the doughty old mare and allowed her to hear his voice. The Maid was browsing in a paddock with her colt by her side. On hearing Charley's voice she raised her head, gave a whimmy of delight, and with that bold, free, sweeping stride that in years gone by electrified thousands dashed about the paddock in search of her old friend. When Charley appeared she went to the fence over which he leaned, and showed her joy in every action. Not only did she welcome him, but invited him to fondle her baby. Round about the two she circled, uttering a low whimmy which expressed a mother's pride and love. She pushed the colt up to Charley, smoothing its coat with her tongue, and asked him in the plainest horse language to admire it. It was a beautiful picture of confidence between man and beast. She knew Charlie well and had no fears for her youngster, but let anyone else go near her and a pair of twingling heels warned him to keep his distance."

BILLIARDS.

Mrs. Langtry is very fond of billiards, and wields the cue cleverly.

PATTI'S BILLIARD PLAYING.

"Why," said Mr. Williams, manager for the Brunswick, Balke, Collender Co., I know some women who are fairly crazy about the game. Take for instance Mme. Patti, the noted songstress. She is what you would call a "crank" on the game. She plays a pretty stiff game, too. How it is she became interested in the pastime I do not know, but I do know that I have never yet seen a man or woman who equals her in enthusiasm. You know that when in this city she stops at the Palace Hotel. Well, I remember a few years ago when she was here, she sent an order for a table. Mr. Williams picked the handsomest he had in the house and sent it to the hotel, where it was put up in her private parlor; there, every afternoon and at night, after performances, she and Sig Nicolini played. Slosson is a great favorite with her, and under his instruction she has made rapid progress. She is a poor loser, though, and I just tell you it's fun to see her when she makes a mis cue or fails to effect a carrom; then she scowls and stamps her pretty little foot and does not regain her usual frame of mind until an easy shot is offered her, then she is happy, and ticks off point after point in great style. Why, do you know she is so much in love with billiards, that a couple of years ago she invited Slosson to go over to her castle in Wales so that she could see him play. Her billiard room there is a grand one. The Palace is called Craig-y-Nos, and she has spent a fortune on it, but she spent more on the billiard parlor than on any other room.

Mme. Patti and Sig. Nicolini occupied a box at the Metropolitan Opera House during the late Billiard Tournament in New York.

The coming Schaefer—McCleery Billiard match is much discussed in the different Billiard Rooms and there is considerable speculation as to the outcome. Prof. McCleery is practicing daily and is getting himself in excellent trim, during the week in the presence of a large number of spectators he made runs of 1016, 1000, 602, 478 and several runs of over 200. In making the above runs he made several difficult Masse shots which were loudly applauded. The above run of 1016 was made on a small wager, McCleery betting an outsider that he would make a run of 1000 before Mr. Merrifield, who is a good amateur player, would make a total of 100. He made 94 when McCleery made the required run.

Schaefer was in Kansas City when last heard from giving exhibitions with Frank Ives. He is expected here some time next week.

Additional Rod and Gun.

At the regular monthly meeting of the Fish Commission last Tuesday afternoon, Superintendent of Hatcheries, J. G. Woodbury, reported that since the last meeting of the Board he had visited Sisson and found the 400,000 young salmon in good order. Over 1,200,000 trout eggs had been taken at Shovel Creek. The North Pacific Grove and Fish Club had agreed to receive 100,000 trout eggs from this place and hatch them out at Glen Ellen for the purpose of distributing the young trout in Sonoma Creek and Russian River and its branches without cost to the Commission.

Mr. Knox and Mr. Green have also arranged to take 50,000 eyed trout eggs from Shovel Creek which will be sent to the Los Gatos creek hatchery. The young trout from these eggs will be distributed in Los Gatos Creek at its head waters and San Lorenzo Creek.

Alexander Badlam's hatchery near Mount St. Helena, will also receive 50,000 eggs from Shovel Creek, to be shipped this week from Sisson.

The Eastern trout will be shipped to McCloud as soon as the roads are opened to that point, and like shipments will also be made to the west fork of the Sacramento, Shasta, Big Springs in Siskiyou Co., and Senator Stanford's Vina Ranch as soon as circumstances permit.

Chief of Patrol F. B. Collundan reported the results of his labors during the month. Lack of court jurisdiction had acquitted You Ching, charged with fishing within the five mile limit.

The Fishermen's Union of Benicia sent a request that a deputy Fish commissioner be appointed from the citizens of that vicinity.

License collector J. F. Curley reported that he had collected $1100 since April 1st. Owing to the fishermen's strike along the Sacramento river collections were smaller than expected.

One dollar a year will cover your doctor's bill if you take Simmons Liver Regulator.

No harm ever done by the use of Simmons Liver Regulator.

Drunkenness and the craving for liquor banished by a dose of Simmons Liver Regulator.

FIXED EVENTS, 1890

FRESNO FAIR GROUNDS

Agricultural District No. 21.

Races. Races.

Sept. 30, Oct. 1. 2 & 3

With an Extra Day on Saturday.

ENTRIES CLOSE MAY 15, 1890.

Programme will be issued later for other running, trotting and pacing races to take place same week, for which liberal purses will be given.

OPEN TO THE WORLD

Nomination Guarantee Purse $1,000

For Horses that have Never Beaten 2:24 Trotting.

$100 entrance; $25 payable May 15, 1890; $25 payable July 15, 1890; $50 payable August 11, 1890, when horses are to be named. To be trotted September 30, 1890, Fresno, Cal. If entrance money amounts to more than $1,000, it will be added to the purse, and the Association will add 20 per cent of amount of purse.

Four moneys: 50, 25, 15 and 10 per cent. of purse.

Horses eligible at closing of entries May 15, 1890, are eligible the day of the race.

Nomination Guarantee Purse $1,200

For Horses That Never Beat 2:30 Trotting.

$120 entrance; $30 payable May 15, 1890; $30 payable July 15, 1890; $60 payable August 11, 189 , when horses are to be named. To be trotted October 3, 1890, Fresno, Cal. If entrance money amounts to more than $1,200 it will be added to the purse, and the Association will add 20 per cent of amount of purse.

Four moneys: 50, 25, 15 and 10 per cent. of purse.

Horses eligible at closing of entries May 15, 1890, are eligible the day of the race.

Nomination Guarantee Purse $1,000

For Horses That Never Beat 2:30 Pacing.

$100 entrance; $25 payable May 15, 1890; $25 payable July 15th, $50 payable August 11, 1890, when horses are to be named. To be paced at Fall fair, 1890. Fresno, Cal. If entrance money amounts to more than $1,000, it will be added to the purse, and the Association will add 20 per cent. of amount of purse.

Four moneys: 50, 25, 15 and 10 per cent. of purse.

Horses eligible at closing of entries May 15, 1890, are eligible the day of the race.

President Stake.

Guarantee Purse $1,000.

For all ages: weight for age; 1⅛ mile dash; $100 entrance; $10 payable May 15, 1890; $15 payable June 15, 1890; $25 payable July 15, 1890; $50 payable Sept. 8, 1890. To be run October, 3, 1890, Fresno, Cal. If entrance amounts to more than $1,000, it shall be added to the purse, and the Association adds 20 per cent. of purse. Three moneys—70, 20 and 10 per cent. of purse. Horse winning an all-aged race of one mile or over at Sacramento or Stockton, where purse or stake amounts to $800 or over, shall carry ten pounds extra. Horse winning an all-aged race of one mile or over at Sacramento or Stockton, where purse or stake amounts to $500 or over, shall carry five pounds extra. American Association rules to govern.

Raisin Handicap.

Guarantee Purse $1,000.

For all ages, 1⅛ mile dash; $100 entrance; $10 May 15th; $15 June 15; $25 July 15th. Weights will be declared August 15th and acceptance on or before September 8th, when the other $50 is to be paid; to be run September 30, 1890, Fresno, Cal. If entrance amounts to more than $1,000 it will be added to the purse, and the Association will add 20 per cent. of the amount of purse. Three moneys—70, 20 and 10 per cent. of purse. Horse winning any purse or stake of one mile or over, at Sacramento or Stockton after weights are declared, where purse or stake amounts to $800 or over, shall carry ten pounds extra. Horse winning any purse or stake of one mile or over at Sacramento or Stockton after weights are declared, when purse or stake amounts to $500 or over, shall carry five pounds extra. Nominations are only held for amount paid in. Weights to be declared through BREEDER AND SPORTSMAN August 15, 1890. American Association rules to govern.

REMARKS.

As to the Handicap, the Handicapping Committee will use due diligence in learning the performance of every horse entered and weighting them fairly to their merits. Each entry must be accompanied by entrance money or be considered no entry. All payments must be made when due, or the nominator forfeits all money paid in. We propose, at the finish of the race, the horse winning the purse gets his money and not forfeit papers.

CONDITIONS AND REMARKS.

Nominators are only held for amount paid in. Nominators failing to make payments when due forfeit all money paid in, and nomination reverts back to Association, who have the privilege of disposing of nomination. All nominations are transferable. Trotting and pacing races, mile heats, best 3 in 5 to harness. Horse distancing the field or any part of field only entitled to first money. American Association rules to govern. These Guarantee Purses for trotters and pacers gives the party making the entry the privilege of naming any horse he sees fit the 11th of August, having no better record than specified in the stake, the 15th day of May, irrespective of the record he gets after that date. You will see by this the nominator has almost a sure thing of getting his money back. Money must accompany entry or will be considered no entry.

The track has been re-clayed the past winter, making it the fastest and best track in the State. The stabling and accommodations are the very best. Hay and straw free. Arrangements will be made with the Railroad Company for transportation of horses and men accompanying them at half fare.

Remember we go according to rule: 3 to enter and 2 to start.

Entries close with the Secretary.

LEWIS LEACH, Pres.

F. B. BALDWIN, Manager.

N. I. BALDWIN, Sec'y,
P. O. Drawer U. Fresno Cal.

ENTIRE CHANGE

—OF—

PROGRAMME

—OF THE—

Extra Attractions

To take place at the

Oakland.

Fall Meeting, 1890,

UNDER THE MANAGEMENT OF THE

GOLDEN GATE Fair Association

NOMINATION PURSES.

In which entries close in the name of owners or trainers on May 15th. All nominations transferable and nominators held only for amounts paid in. Horses must be named five days before first advertised day of the meeting. Eight nominations required to fill, four of which must make last payments.

THE NEW LIST PURSE $1000.

For three-year-olds whose sires up to January 1, 1890, have not produced an animal with a record of 2:30 or better at three years of age or under. Entrance 10 per cent. payable as follows:

$25 May 15th, when entries close in the names of owners or trainers.
$25 June 15th.
$25 July 15th.
$25 five days before first advertised day of meeting, when horses must be named.

GUARANTEED PURSE $1200.

For three-minute class, entrance 10 per cent, payable as follows:

$30 May 15th, when entries close in names of owners or trainers.
$30 June 15th.
$30 July 15th.
$30 five days before first advertised day of meeting, when horse must be named.

GUARANTEED PURSE $1200.

For 2:40 class, entrance 10 per cent. payable as follows:

$30 May 15th, when entries close in names of owners or trainers.
$30 June 15th.
$30 July 15th.
$30 five days before first advertised day of meeting, when horses must be named.

—ALSO A—

Guaranteed Futurity Purse $4,000.

To take place during the Fall Meeting of 4893.

For foals of 1890. Entrance 5 per cent. payable as follows:

$10 May 15, 1890, when entries close in name of foals or of dams and sires.

$10 Jan. 15, 1891.
$15, June 15, 1891.
$15, Jan. 15, 1892.
$15 June 15, 1892.
$ 5 Jan. 15, 1893.
$20 June 15, 1893.

$20 fifteen days before advertised day of the race.

If the last payment is made on twelve or more entries the horses shall be started in trial races, in which not more than eleven or less than six shall be allotted to start. The trial races shall be mile heats, three in five, for a purse of $1,000, given by the Association for each race. If two trial races are trotted, the first four horses shall only be entitled to start in the final race. If three such trial races are trotted, only the first three horses in each trial race shall start in the final; and if four or more trial races are necessary, only the first two horses in each trial race shall start in the final race.

These trial races must be started not less than five nor more than ten days previous to the day set for the final race; and if possible all trial races will be trotted on the same day.

CONDITIONS.

Neglect to provide payments on the dates stipulated will incur forfeiture of all previous payments.

The Directors reserve the right to change the hour and day of any race except when it becomes necessary to ante-date a race, in which instance the nominator will receive three days notice of change by mail to address of entry.

Entries not declared out by 6 P. M. the day preceding the race, shall be required to start.

Purses will be divided into four moneys viz., 50 per cent. to the winner, 25 per cent. to the second horse, 15 per cent. to the third horse, and 10 per cent. to the fourth horse.

A horse distancing the field shall only be entitled to first and third moneys.

Trotting and Pacing Colors shall be named by six o'clock on the day preceding the race, and MUST be worn upon the track.

All purse races, mile heats, best three in five to harness.

Otherwise than the above, National or American Trotting Association Rules—as this Association may select—will govern the races offered.

Entries to Close with the Secretary.

R. T. CARROLL, President.

JOS. I. DIMOND, Sec'y, 306 Market St., S. F.

"DICKEY'S,"

SIXTH AVENUE AND D ST.

Near entrance to Bay District Track.

Choicest Brands of

WINES AND CIGARS.

A Delightful Resort.

Telephone 1485. J. R. DICKEY, Propr.

UTAH Driving Park ASSOCIATION, 1890.

JUNE 16 to 20, Inclusive

—AT—

SALT LAKE CITY.

Purses - $7,000

TROTTING, RUNNING & PACING,

Entries for all Races to close May 30, 1890.

This meeting is arranged to accommodate horsemen on way to the Great Racing Circuit of Montana, their purses aggregating $44,000. The meeting at Denver closes June 7th, and our meeting begins June 16th and closes June 20th inclusive, and the Montana meetings commence July 14th, thus giving ample time to rest up here. We expect to give a genuine first-class meeting, and will see that all horsemen have a "square deal." Our city is at present enjoying an era of prosperity never before seen, which justifies our hope for the best meeting ever given in Utah. A cordial invitation is extended to all horsemen to come. The Great Salt Lake bathing season is then on thus affording all visitors a rare treat and pleasant time.

PROGRAMME

—OF—

Utah Driving Park Spring Race Meeting,

Salt Lake City, Utah.

Spring Racing and Trotting Meeting for Five Days, from June 16 to June 20, inclusive.

PURSES, $7000.

FIRST DAY—MONDAY, JUNE 16.

No. 1—Trotting, 2:27 class	$
No. 2—Pacing, 2:35 class	
No. 3—Running, ¾ mile heats, all ages	300
No. 4—Running, ½ mile heats, all ages	300

SECOND DAY—TUESDAY, JUNE 17.

No. 5—Pacing, 2:24 class	$701
No. 6—Trotting, 2:50 class	4 0
No. 7—Running, ¾ mile dash, three-year-olds	200
No. 8—Running, ¾ mile heats, all ages	300

THIRD DAY—WEDNESDAY, JUNE 18.

No. 9—Trotting, 2:26 class	$500
No. 10—Trotting, three-year-olds (added money) for Colorado, Wyoming, Montana, and Utah horses	300
No. 11—Running, ¾ mile heats, all ages	300

FOURTH DAY—THURSDAY, JUNE 19.

No. 12—Pacing, free for all pacers	$600
No. 13—Trotting, 2:34 class	400
No. 14—Running, 1¼ mile dash, all ages	300

FIFTH DAY—FRIDAY, JUNE 20.

No. 15—Trotting, free for all	$600
No. 16—Trotting, 2:30 class	450
No. 17—Running, ¾ mile heats, for horses that have run and not won a race this meeting	250
No. 18—Running, 1 mile heats, all ages	300

F. H. DYER, Secretary.

J. K. GILLESPIE, Manager. Salt Lake City.

CONTRA COSTA CO, Agricultural Associat'n

District No. 23.

FAIR OF 1890.

Sept. 22 to 27, inclusive.

District Trotting Colt Stakes for 1890.

$40, payable as follows:

$10 June 1st (when stakes close), $15 Sept. 1st, and $15 Sept. 22d.

FOR ONE-YEAR-OLDS, 1 mile dash.
FOR TWO-YEAR-OLDS, mile heats, 2 in 3
FOR 3-YEAR-OLDS, mile heats, 3 in 5.
} $75 added to each.

All moneys divided as follows: 60, 30 and 10 per cent. In case of only two starting, 60 and 40 per cent., and in case of one horse walking over, the whole amount to go to such horse.

A failure to make any payment when due shall be considered a withdrawal and forfeiture of the amount paid in.

National Rules to govern.

The right reserved to refund the first payment in case the stakes do not fill reasonably well.

Entries close June 1, 1890 with the Secretary.

GEO. P. LOUCKS, President.

H. C. RAAP, Secretary, Martinez, Cal.

SUBSCRIBE FOR THE

Breeder and Sportsman.

Races, Races,

JULY WEEK.

AT

South Park Race Track

Eureka, Cal.

GIVEN BY THE

EUREKA JOCKEY CLUB.

FIRST DAY JULY 3, 1890.

No. 1. Novelty Running Race. Free for all. Dash of one mile. Purse $250. First quarter, $40. Half, $50. Third quarter, $75. Mile, $90.

No. 2. Running race. Purse $150. Five-eighths dash, for two-year-olds. $125 to first horse; $25 to second horse.

No. 3. Running. Purse $150. Three-quarters and repeat. $125 to first; $25 to second.

SECOND DAY, JULY 3, 1890.

No. 4. Trotting. Purse $200. Three minute Class. $150 to first; $50 to second. (Covey barred.)

No. 5. Running Stake. Five-eighths of a mile. For Humboldt raised two year-olds. $20 entrance, half forfeit. $150 added. First to receive 60 per cent.; second, 30 per cent., third, 10 per cent.

No. 6. Running Stake. Purse $200. Mile Dash. $150 to first horse; $50 to second horse.

THIRD DAY, JULY 4, 1890.

No. 7. Trotting Stake. 2:40 Class. Purse $250. $200 to first horse; $50 to second horse.

No. 8. Running Stake. 1¼ miles. Free-for-all. $40 entrance, ½ forfeit, $200 added; second horse $75, third horse to save stake.

No. 9. Running Stake. Purse $150; 1-2 mile and repeat; $125 to first; $25 to second.

FOURTH DAY, JULY 5, 1890.

No. 10. Running Stake. 1-2 mile and repeat; for Humboldt horses owned prior to Jan 1, 1890. $125 to first, $25 to second.

No. 11. Running Stake. Purse $200; 7-8 mile and repeat. $150 to first. $50 to second.

CONDITIONS AND REMARKS.

All trotting races are best three in five, unless otherwise specified. Four to enter and three to start, but the Board reserves the right to hold a less number than four to fill by the withdrawal of a proportionate amount of the purse. Entrance fee, 10 per cent. of purse, to accompany nominations. In all trotting races the rules of the American Trotting Association, and all running races the rules of the Pacific Coast Blood Horse Association to govern, but the Board reserves the right to trot heats of any two classes alternately, if necessary, to finish any day's racing. In all entries not declared out by 6 p. m. of the day preceding the race, shall be required to start.

No added money paid for a walk over. In all races, four or more paid up entries required to fill, and three or more horses to start. Racing colors to be named in entries. In trotting races drivers will be required to wear caps of distinct colors to be named in entries. Entries in all races to close with the Secretary, Thursday, June 5, 1890. Entry blanks will be furnished upon application to the Secretary.

All trotting races for horses owned and in Humboldt County prior to June 1, 1890.

H. M. DEVOY, President.

J. P. MONROE, Secretary.

C. C. LINIMENT.

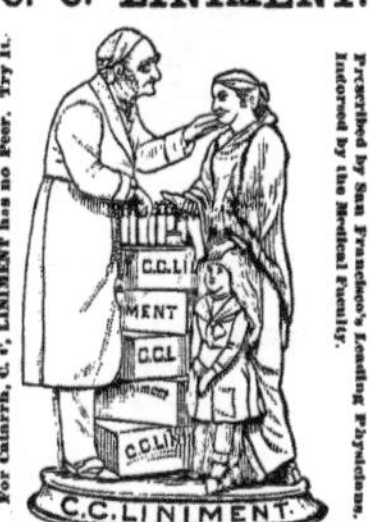

The Great Pain Conqueror for Man and Beast.

For Horsemen and Stockmen this Liniment is Invaluable

OWNERS OF FINE STOCK CANNOT AFFORD TO BE WITHOUT IT.

A remedy for every home, giving instant relief in pain and PERFORMING PERMANENT CURES.

To get the full benefit of the C. C. Liniment in chronic cases, in connection with C. C. Liniment use Compound Sulphur Powder, the "Great Blood Purifier," put up ONLY by The W. H. Bone Co., 17 Bush St., San Francisco. For Habitual Constipation, Indigestion, Piles, etc., it is the greatest remedy known to medical science.

If your druggist does not keep it, we will send direct, post paid, on receipt of price. COMPOUND SULPHUR POWDER is $1 per bottle, 6 for $5. Small bottles, 25c.

The C. C. Liniment Co

12 BUSH STREET, S. F.

W. H. BONE, - - General Manager.

FOR SALE BY ALL DRUGGISTS.

Breeders' Directory.

Advertisements under this heading 50c. per line per month.

HORSES AND CATTLE.

W. S. JACOBS, Sacramento, Cal. — Breeder of Thoroughbred Shorthorns and Berkshire Hogs.

J. H. WHITE, Lakeville, Sonoma County—Breeder of Registered Holstein Cattle.

EL ROBLAS RANCHO—Los Alamos, Cal., Francis T. Underhill, proprietor, importer and breeder of thoroughbred Hereford Cattle. Information by mail. C. F. Swan, manager.

PAGE BROTHERS.—Penn's Grove, Sonoma Co. Cal. Breeders of Short-Horn Cattle; Draft, Roadster and Standard Bred Horses.

SETH COOK, breeder of Cleveland Bay Horses, Devon, Durham, Polled Aberdeen-Angus and Galloway Cattle. Young stock of above breeds on hand for sale. Warranted to be pure bred, recorded and average breeders. Address, Geo. A. Wiley, Cook Farm, Danville, Contra Costa Co., Cal.

HAMBRINO WILKES COLTS and FILLIES, full brothers and sisters to Gus. Wilkes 2:22, and Balkan 2:29¼, for Sale. Address SMITH HILL, Walnut Creek, Contra Costa County, Cal.

PETER SAXE & SON, Lick House, San Francisco, Cal.—Importers and Breeders for past 18 years of every variety of Cattle, Horses, Sheep and Hogs.

HOLSTEIN THOROUGHBREDS of all the noted strains. Registered Berkshire Swine. Catalogues. F. H. BURKE, 401 Montgomery St., S. F.

FERGUSON & AUSTIN,
FRESNO, CAL.
Registered Polled Angus and Short-Horn Cattle.

K STREET.

SECOND ST.

Singleton & Addington
BANK EXCHANGE,
SACRAMENTO.
Wines, Liquors & Cigars.

JESSE E. MARKS. IKE DEUTCH

Yosemite Billiard Parlors,

ST. ANN'S BUILDING,
No. 8 Eddy Street, S. F.

J. J. EVANS
—SELLS—
WALLACE'S YEAR BOOK,
WALLACE'S REGISTER No. 8,
STALLION SERVICE BOOKS,
For Office and Pocket.
—ALL KINDS—
PEDIGREE BLANKS.
NEW STAKE ENTRY BOOK,
PEDIGREE BOOK,
HERD BOOK.

J. J. Evans,
Stationer and Printer,
406 California Street, San Francisco, Cal.
Mail orders receive prompt attention.

The Poodle Dog
"Rotisserie,"
FIRST-CLASS IN EVERY RESPECT.
Elegant Family Dining Rooms.
S. E. cor. GRANT AVE. and BUSH STREET.
ANDRE POTENTINI, Proprietor.

BERGEZ'S
RESTAURANT.
FIRST-CLASS. *Charges Reasonable.*
Private Rooms for Families,
332—334 Pine St., below Montgomery St.
JOHN BERGEZ, Propr

The "EDWIN C."
W. S. JOHNSON, Proprietor.
340 EDDY STREET.
Cor. of Mason. San Francisco.
(Private Entrance Mason Street.)

SAMUEL VALLEAU. JAS. R. BRODIE.
J. R. BRODIE & CO.,
Steam Printers,
—And Dealers in—
Poolseller's and Bookmaker's Supplies.
401—403 *Sansome Street, corner Sacramento, San Francisco.*

The Pacific Coast
Live Stock Owners
MUTUAL PROTECTIVE ASS'N.,
MONTEREY, Monterey Co., Cal.

TRUSTEES:

HON. B. V. SARGENT, President.
G. W. GALLANAR, Secretary.
JAMES E. PALMER, Business Manager.
EDW. INGRAM, Vice-President.
FRED. D. HOWARD, Actuary,
R. R. WILLEY, Attorney.

GENERAL BUSINESS OFFICE, Room 73, Flood Building, corner Market and Fourth Streets, San Francisco, Cal.

VOLNEY HOWARD, General Manager.

FISHING TACKLE,
WHOLESALE AND RETAIL.
CLABROUGH, GOLCHER & CO.,
630 and 632 Montgomery St.

Important Closing Out Sale
—OF—
Trotting bred STOCK,

Comprising the Entire Stud of
JOHN G. HILL, of Ventura, Cal
To be held at 10 A. M., at
RAILROAD STABLES,
Corner STEINER and TURK STS.,
San Francisco.
Take McAllister or Turk Street Cars.

Thursday, May 15, 1890

It will embrace about 80 head of well bred Stallions, Mares and Geldings, principally the get of that celebrated standard bred sire

A. W. RICHMOND, 1687,

out of thoroughbred mares mostly from that noted horse, Woodburn, sire of Monarch 2:28½, and the dam of Victor 2 22, and others.

This will no doubt be the last opportunity to obtain at public auction the blood of this great sire, that, in part, has made ANTEEO, ANTEVOLO, ARROW, ROMERO, RICHMOND JR., and others famous in the trotting history of our State.

The sale is positive and without reserve, as Mr. Hill will engage in other business.

☞ Catalogues now ready.

KILLIP & CO., Auctioneers,
22 Montgomery Street, San Francisco, Cal.

Poplar Grove Breeding FARM.
Standard-bred Trotters, Colts and Fillies.
The get of CLOVIS, 4909; PASHA, 2039; APEX, 2935,
For Sale.
Address S. N. STRAUBE, Poplar Grove Breeding Farm,
Fresno, Cal.
Inspection by intending purchasers invited, and information by mail.

Stallion for Sale
AT A BARGAIN.
Full Brother to Fairmont.

By Piedmont, dam Queen by Garibaldi—see State Fair Edition of BREEDER AND SPORTSMAN, September 14, 1889, for description of Fairmont—three years old, solid bay. Can trot a 2:40 gait or better. Sound in every particular. Can be seen at Oakland Trotting Park, Oakland.

P. J. WILLIAMS.

Highland Farm,
LEXINGTON, KY.,
Home of Red Wilkes.
Standard-bred Trotting Stock
For Sale,
Sired by Red Wilkes, Wilton, 2:19¼; Allandorf and Sentinel Wilkes, out of highly bred Standard Mares of the most fashionable blood of the day.

W. C. FRANCE, Proprietor.

Stallions and Colts
For Sale.
The Get of the Celebrated Racing Stallion
BAYSWATER,
FROM FINELY BRED MARES.
Inquire of
J. HEINLEN,
Lemoore, Tulare County, Cal.

For Sale
A HALF BROTHER TO
ALMONT PATCHEN,
(2:15, trial 2:13 3-4).

JUANITO JR. is a beautiful bright bay, black points, with no white, foaled 1886. As a colt he has given much more promise than did Almont Patchen at the same age. Instead of being a pacer, he is a good square trotter, with every indication of great speed, and is so gentle and kind, that a lady can drive him. The owner's only reason for selling him is that business calls him away from this section of the State. He will be sold at a reasonable figure. This is a splendid opportunity for a gentleman to secure a first-class trotter at a very low figure.

The pedigree of Juanito Jr. is by Juanito (sire of Almont Patchen), dam Nettie Moore by Old Tom Moore. For further particulars, address

JUANITO JR.,
Santa Clara P. O., Cal.

The Trotting-Bred Stallion
RINGWOOD
THE FINEST SON OF THE NOTED SIDNEY,

Will make a Season at Oakland commencing March 1, and ending June 1, 1890.

DESCRIPTION.

RINGWOOD is a dark, rich colored bay, black points, 15 1-2 hands, weight 1100 lbs., and a pure gaited trotter. Has shown great speed. He is now five years old. As a four year old he showed a trial in 2:19 1-2, and but for an accident would have received a record as a four year old of 2:18 or better.

PEDIGREE.

RINGWOOD is by Sidney, record 2:19 3-4, and a half brother to Gold Leaf 2:11 1-4, Adonis 2:11, Fleet (two year old) 2:24, Longworth 2:19, Sister V. 2:27, Faustino, yearling, 2:35, Fleet, yearling, 2:35 Memo, three year old trial 2:13 1-2.

Sidney is by Santa Claus, record 2:17 1-2; he by Strathmore, sire of 21 in 2:30 list; he by Hambletonian 10, the greatest of all producers; he by Abdallah. Sidney's dam, Sweetness, record 2:21 1-4; she by Volunteer, the sire of St. Julien 2:11 1-4.

RINGWOOD'S dam Alma; she by Dashway, thoroughbred; he by Belmont, he by American Boy; he by Sea Gull; he by imported Expedition. Alma's 1st dam, Fanny Cobb, was a great road mare, pedigree untraced.

TERMS: $50 for the Season.

Payable June 1st, or sooner if mares are taken away. Address communications to

A. C. DIETZ,
Oakland, Cal.

The Trotting Stallion
G & M
FULL BROTHER TO
ALFRED G, 2:19¾.

(Who has been taken to Kentucky to stand at $200)

Will make the season of 1890 from FEBRUARY 1st to JULY 1st, at

SANTA ROSA.

G. & M. is by Anteeo, 2:16¼; was foaled 1886; first dam Rosa B. by Speculation (son of Hambletonian 10); 2d dam Elizabeth by Alexander 490; 3d dam Nora by imp. Glencoe. Anteeo is by Electioneer, out of Columbine by A. W. Richmond 1687.

G. & M. is a handsome dark bay; stands 15-3 1-2 hands high, and weighs 1060 pounds. Gameness, stoutness, speed and stamina are indelibly impressed in every line of the pedigree of G. & M. Owners of broodmares in search of these qualities, will do well to patronize this promising colt.

PHILOSOPHER,

Foaled 1886 by Pilot Wilkes 2987; first dam Bella by George Wilkes 519; second dam by Bell Morgan 61.

Philosopher's sire, Pilot Wilkes 2987, is by George Wilkes 519, dam Grace (the dam of Alice Woodburn etc.), by Pilot Jr. 12, grandam by Orphan Boy.

Will make the season of 1890, from FEBRUARY 1st to JULY 1st, at Santa Rosa.

TERMS for the season:

G. & M., $50.

PHILOSOPHER, $30,

with privilege of returning mares that do not prove in foal the next season free of charge, provided the horse bred to remains the property of the present owners. Good pasturage at $3 per month. No responsibility assumed for accidents or escapes. Service fees payable before removal of the mare. For further particulars, address

GEO. E. GUERNE,
Santa Rosa Cal.

HORSES PURCHASED ON COMMISSION.
THOROUGHBREDS A SPECIALTY.

Will select and buy, or buy selected Animals for all desiring, for reasonable compensation

KEEPS PROMISING YOUNGSTERS IN VIEW.

L. M. LASLEY, Stanford, Ky.

References:—J. W. Guest, Danville, Ky.
B. G Bruce, Lexington Ky.
S. H. Baughman, Stanford, Ky.
G. A. Lackey, Stanford, Ky.
Geo. McAlister, Stanford, Ky.
First National Bank, Stanford, Ky.

For Sale
A FIRST-CLASS
Napa County Farm
—OR—
STOCK RANCH,
800 Acres Improved,

SITUATED TWO AND A HALF MILES FROM NAPA CITY, with good roads leading thereto, a good hard finished house of nine rooms, with all modern improvements, streams running all summer, a great amount of live oak and black oak timber. It lies in a fruit belt, surrounded by fine vineyards and orchards growing upon the same quality of soil and originally a part of this tract. About one-half hill, and one-half rolling land, but none of it is steep and all easily cultivated, splendidly situated for the breeding of fine horses. Price, $65 per acre. Further particulars given at this office.

BREEDER AND SPORTSMAN,
313 Bush St.

Pedigrees Tabulated
IN THE MOST ARTISTIC MANNER.

Giving speed performers under sires and dams. Catalogues compiled. Stallion cards and circulars written up ready for the press. Pedigree blanks for sale. Prices reasonable. Horses bought and sold on commission. References furnished.

R. Y. HARDIN.
806 W. Madison St., Chicago, Ill.

The Thoroughbred Stallion

Three Cheers

Will make the season of 1890 at

Sacramento.

PEDIGREE.

THREE CHEERS
- Imp. Hurrah
  - Newminster
    - Touchstone, by Camel
    - Beeswing, by Dr. Syntax
  - Jovial
    - Bay Middleton, by Sultan
    - Sister to Grey Momus, by Comus
- Young Fashion
  - Imp. Monarch
    - Imp. Priam, by Emilius
    - Imp. Delphine, by Whisker
  - Fashion
    - Imp. Trustee, by Catton
    - Bonnets o' Blue, by Sir Charles

Hurrah was imported by John Reber, of Lancaster, Ohio, a locality where there were but few breeders of thoroughbreds. Under these disadvantages he sired a long list of winners. His sire Newminster, won the St. Ledger 1851, and his dam, Jovial by Bay Middleton, winner of the Derby 1836. Newminster by Touchstone, winner St. Ledger 1834. Dam Beeswing, winner of 54 races out of 64 starts, by Dr Syntax, winner of the Doncaster Cup. 1877—40—41—42, the only horse that ever accomplished that feat.

On the side of the dam Three Cheers is equally well related. Young Fashion was the dam of Surprise, Scotland (the only horse that ever beat Asteroid a heat), Liverpool. Columbia, and Bonnie Kate, the dam of Little Buttercup, and the flying Bonnie Lizzie. His grandam, Fashion was the greatest race mare of her day and beat Boston in that historical match at four mile heats, which is recorded as one of the greatest events in the annals of the turf.

Horsemen who are qualified to judge, pronounce Three Cheers to be the finest type of the Newminster line in America.

LOCATION.

THREE CHEERS will be located at the Arcade Training Stable, Rancho del Paso. This place has been selected for the reason that first class pasturage has been secured there for the exclusive use of these mares, and the other facilities to be obtained there for the care of mares (especially mares in foal) are better than can be found elsewhere in the locality.

TERMS.

$60 for the season with the usual return privileges. Pasturage $5 per month. Mares cared for as owners may desire at bottom rates for grain and hay. All bills payable before the mare is removed.

Mares shipped care of WM. IRVINE, Pacific Stables, Sacramento, will be properly cared for and sent to the ranch without delay.

Three Cheers will be in charge of one of the most experienced and competent stud grooms in the State, who will exercise every care, but no reponsibility assumed for accidents or escapes.

For further particulars apply to Louis Crissler, at the ranch; Wm. Irvine, Pacific Stables, Second St., Sacramento; or to the owner,

E. S. CULVER,
313 Bush St., San Francisco.

Sunny Side Breeding Farm.

Admiral 488.

Foaled 1867—Sired by Volunteer 55, Son of Rysdyk's Hambletonian 10.

First dam Lady Pierson by Cassius M. Clay (Neaves') 20; second dam by Diamond; third dam a running mare said to be thoroughbred. He is fitted in an eminent degree to produce colts that will in all respects justify his patrons in their expectations.

Admiral is the sire of Huntress, record 2:27¼, Sister, 2:19½, Perhelion, 2:25, Nona Y., 2:26, and others equally as promising, but have not had the advantage of track work. He will serve a limited number of approved mares at $50 the season, with usual return privilege. Season ending August 1, 1890. No liability for accidents or escapes.

KING DAVID 2576.

Bay Stallion—Foaled 1883.

Sired by Admiral 488, dam Black Flora (the dam of Huntress, 2:27¼, Sister, 2:19½, Perhelion, 2:25, Nona Y., 2:25), by Black Prince.

King David is one of the best gets of Admiral. He has a good disposition, kind to drive, smooth and even-gaited, and can speed fast. Barring accidents, he will trot in the twenties this Fall. His colts are large, rangy, and well finished. Will serve a limited number of mares at $30 the season, to end July 1, 1890. Every precaution will be taken to prevent accidents and escapes, but no liability will be assumed. Pasturage $4 per month.

Sunny Side Farm is situated two miles east of Vallejo, on the Sulphur Spring road. For further particulars, address

FRANK DRAKE,
Vallejo, Cal.

Lawn View Breeding Farm Stallions.

ACTOR.

A beautiful bay horse foaled 1887 by Promptor 2308 sire of Apex (four-year-old record) 2:26, Transit 2:28½, Creole 2:20, Blue Belle 2:32, Daisy (yearling record) 36½, he by Blue Bull 75. 1st dam by Sultan 1513 2:24, sire of Stamboul 2:12 1-4, Ruby 2:19¾, Sweetheart 22¼, Alcazar 2:20½, Eva 2:23½, La Grange 2:23½, and seven others in 2:30 list, second dam by Fireman by Langford.

Actor, as his pedigree shows, is as purely bred a young stallion as ever made a season in the stud. The Bull stock is much sought after in the East, and Sultan, sire of his first dam will make the season in Kentucky this year at $400 per mare. Actor is a handsome bay colt 16 hands high, clean limbed and possess all the points of a speedy trotter.

TERMS, $40 FOR THE SEASON, usual return privileges.

DOUGLASDALE 7650.

Thoroughbred Registered Clydesdale Stallion

Imported from Scotland, December, 1888, bay, three years old.

TERMS, $35 FOR THE SEASON.

YOUNG ELMO

Two years old sorrel stallion by St. Elmo 2:27, dam by Woodburn.

TERMS, $20 FOR THE SEASON.

For further particulars, address
MANAGER LAWN VIEW FARM, Auburn, Cal.

Guenoc Stud Farm, Lake Co., Cal.

Imp. GREENBACK

(Sire of the English winners Greenlight, Greenjacket, Greensbank, Greenwave and Greenhorn)

By Dollar, dam Music, by Stockwell. $100 the Season

ST. SAVIOR,

(FULL BROTHER TO EOLE)

By Eolus, dam War Song, by War Dance. $100 the Season.

PASTURAGE, $5 PER MONTH.

With right to return the following year if mare does not prove with foal. The best of care taken, but no liability for accidents or escapes. Mares shipped to C. W. ABY, care ST. HELENA STABLES, St. Helena Napa County, will be taken in charge by competent men.

For further information write to

DR. C. W. ABY, Middletown, Lake County, Cal.

SAN DIEGO, 8776.

SAN DIEGO 8776
- Alcona Clay 2756
  - Alcona 730. Sire of Flora Belle, 2:24, Clay Duke, 2:31½, etc.
    - Almont 33. Sire of Westmont, 2:15¾, Piedmont, 2:17¼, Puritan, 2:16, and 33 others in 2:30 list.
    - by Mambrino Chief 11. Sire of Lady Thorne, 2:18½.
  - Madonna. Dam of Del Rey, trial 2:31, Alcona Jr., 2:41, sire of Silas Skinner, trial 2:23½.
    - Cassius M Clay Jr. 22. Sire of Durango, 2:23½, Harry Clay, 2:23½, and sire of dam of Happy Thought, 2:22½, and others.
    - by Joe Downing 710. Sire of Abe Downing, 2:20½, Dick Jamison, 2:26, and sire of dams of Kentucky Hambletonian, 2:27, Lorena, 2:15, and others.
- Fontana. Dam of Flora Belle, 2:24, Silas Skinner, trial 2:23½.
  - Almont 33. Sire of 36 in 2:30 list, 49 sons and 23 daughters that have produced 2:30 performers.
  - Fanny Williams. Dam of Bay Chieftain, 2:28½.
    - Abdallah 15. Sire of Goldsmith Maid, 2:14, Thorndale, 2:22¼, also Almont, Belmont, Jim Monroe, etc.
    - by Denmark (thoroughbred).

SAN DIEGO is dark seal brown, three years old, and trotted one-quarter miles in 40 seconds as a two-year old.

This grand young horse, and, barring accidents, will make a fast record next fall.

He will be allowed a limited number of mares, at $50 for the season. Mares not proving in foal to be returned free 1891. Best of pasture for mares at $4 per month, but no liability for accidents or escapes.

He will make the season from February 1st to June 1st at Napa Fair Grounds. For further particulars, address or call on

H. B. STARR, Race Track, Napa, Cal.,
or FRED W. LOEBER, St. Helena

Bay Rose.

REGISTERED No. 9814.

Record 2:20 1-2 Third Heat.

Will make the season of 1890, ending July 1st, at the SANTA ROSA STOCK FARM, (formerly Santa Rosa Race Track), SANTA ROSA.

DESCRIPTION.

BAY ROSE is a dark bay or brown, with black points, 16¼ hands high, and weighs 1150 pounds. He is remarkably intelligent, of good disposition, and a pure-gaited trotter. He was foaled in 1881. His colts are large, stylish, rangy animals, and inherit the qualities of speed and endurance.

PEDIGREE.

BAY ROSE 9814
- Sultan, 2:24. Sire of 19 in the 2:30 list.
  - The Moor 870. Sire of:
    - Beautiful Bells ... 2:29½
    - Del Sur ... 2:24½
    - Inez ... 2:30
    - Sir Guy ... 2:28½
    - Sultan ... 2:24
    - Tommy Gates ... 2:24
  - Sultana.
- Madam Baldwin
  - The Moor 870. Sire of 6 in the 2:30 list.
  - by Ben Lippincott, by Williamson's Belmont.

TERMS: $100 FOR THE SEASON.

Good pasturage $3 per month. First-class care taken of mares in any manner that owners may desire, but no responsibility assumed for escapes or accidents.

Limited to a few approved mares.

For further particulars, address

THOS. BONNER,
Santa Rosa Stock Farm, Santa Rosa.

Or apply to
IRA PIERCE,
728 Montgomery Street, S. F., Cal.

GEO. WASHINGTON.

11,623.

RECORD 2:30.

Bay colt, bred by Thomas Smith of Vallejo, Cal. Foaled 1886 by Mambrino Chief, Jr., 11,622, record 2:34 1-4. 1st dam Fanny Rose by Vick's Ethan Allen Jr. 2,903, sire of Prince Allen 2:27. 2nd dam Jenny Lind, thoroughbred, dam of Prince Allen 2:27. Will serve a limited number of mares at $50 for the season. Mares not proving with foal may be returned next season free.

Mambrino Chief, Jr.

11,622.

RECORD 2:34 1-4.

Sire of George Washington, record 2 30 at three years old. Bay horse bred by Rufus Ingalls of Belvedere, Ill. By McDonald Chief 3583. First dam Venus by Mambrino Patchen 58. 2nd dam by Wardlow's Shakespeare. 3rd dam Lone Gold 4th dam by Silver Heels. Has not been in the stud before. He was 5 years old when he served a few mares, and his colts all show good style and form.

Terms for the season $40. For further particulars see or address

THOMAS SMITH,
Vallejo, Cal.

The Trotting Stallion

CUPID,

Full Brother to Adonis 2:14,

—Sired by—

The Celebrated SIDNEY 2:19 3-4, and out of Venus.

Will make the season of 1890 at the OAKLAND TROTTING PARK.

PEDIGREE.

CUPID is by Sidney out of Venus by Capt. Webster 10173, record 2:30, and sire of Freestone 2:29. Second dam by Skenandoah 855, sire of Daisy Burns 2:29½, Erwin Davis (sire of two in the 30 list) and dams of four in the 30 list.

DESCRIPTION.

Cupid is a handsome bright bay 15.2½ hands high, weighs 1100 lbs.; was foaled in 1885. As a yearling, with very little work he showed quarters in 42 seconds, and at 2 years old, quarters in 36 seconds. As a three year old he has not been worked, but he shows the speed and endurance that must come from his excellent blood lines.

TERMS $50 for the season, with the usual return privilege. Good pasturage near the track at $5 per month. The best of care taken of mares in any way that owners may desire, but no responsibility assumed for accidents or escapes.

For further particulars address

C. O. THORNQUEST,
Oakland Trotting Park, or
C. BAAB, 972 Broadway, Oakland.

Langtry Farms' Stud

Imp. FRIAR TUCK

By the Immortal HERMIT.

DAM ROMPING GIRL BY WILD DAYRELL,

AT $50 THE SEASON.

Mares not proving with foal may be returned the following season. Good care taken of mares, but no liabilities for accidents or escapes.

Good Pasturage at $5 per month.

Mares shipped to ST. HELENA, care CHARLES WILLIAM ABY, St. Helena Stables, will be cared for. For further particulars address.

CHAS. WILLIAM ABY,
Middletown, Lake County, Cal.

Cook STOCK FARM,

Season of 1890.

STEINWAY 1808.

Three-Year-Old Record 2:25 3-4.

Sire of STRATHWAY, three year old record 2:26, and sire of the dam of BOURBON RUSSELL 2:30.

By STRATHMORE 408; sire of 31 in the 2:30 list; sire of 6 dams of 8 in the 2:30 list, and sire of 3 sires of 8 in 2:30 list.

1st dam ABBESS (dam of Solo 2:28, and Soprano, dam of C. F Clay 2:18, Eminence 2:27 and Strathbridge, 3 year old record 2:28½) by ALBION, sire of VANITY FAIR 2:24½, and of the dam of FAVORITE 2:25½.

2nd dam by MARSHALL NEY.

3rd dam by BERTRAND, a son of SIR ARCHY.

TERMS—$100 for the season.

CHARLES DERBY 4907

Brown Horse, Foaled 1885.

By STEINWAY 1808.

1st dam by the great ELECTIONEER, sire of SUNOL 3 year old record 2:10½, Palo Alto 2:12¼, etc, etc.

2nd dam FANNY MALONE, by NIAGARA.

3rd dam FANNY WICKHAM, by HERALD.

4th dam by Imp. TRUSTEE.

TERMS—$100 for the season.

Pasturage $5 per month. Accidents and escapes at owner's risk. Mares consigned to the farm should be sent to Fashion Stables, Oakland; Geary & Grindle's Stable, Haywards; or to Bennett's, Stable, Martinez; from and to which places they will be delivered free of charge. Address

COOK STOCK FARM,
Danville, Contra Costa, Con Cal.

Vineland Stock Farm

Alcona 730.

Sire of

FLORA BELLE - - - - Record 2:24
CLAY DUKE - - - - - " 2:31½

ALCONA will be a great sire, but four of his colts have ever been trained, and all have shown full miles better than 2:30, and two of them as good as 2:20. Two of his first sons each sired a colt as a two-year-old, and last season one as a four-year-old trotted a full mile in 2:23½, and the other, a three-year-old, a mile in 2:31. With opportunities, Alcona is destined to be one of Almont's best sons Almont, for his opportunities, is beyond doubt the most prepotent sire of his age. He has 36 representatives in the 2:30 list; 49 sons and 22 daughters that have already produced 2:30 performers. Almont died five years ago at 20 years old. If he lived he would be but 25 years old.

PEDIGREE.

ALCONA sired by the great Almont (sire of Westmont 2:13½, Fanny Witherspoon 2:16¼, Piedmont 2:17½, and 31 others with records better than 2:30, and grandsire of Belle Hamlin 2:12½, etc.); by Alexander's Abdallah (sire of Goldsmith Maid 2:14), he by Rysdyk's Hambletonian. Alcona's dam, Queen Mary, by Mambrino Chief (sire of Lady Thorne 2 18 1-4, and 5 others in the 2:30 list, and sire of the dams of Director 2:17, Piedmont 2:17½, Onward 2:25 1-4, Red Wilkes Almont, Belmont and many other noted sires).

DESCRIPTION.

Alcona is a beautiful chestnut 16 3 1-2 hands high, and weighs 1300 lbs. His colts possess speed, style, finish and beauty, and if they don't trot they command the highest prices for carriage horses.

$40 for the season. Usual return privilege.

Season of Alcona and Grandissimo ends July 1st, 1890.

Grandissimo,

Full Brother to GRANDEE, 3-year old record 2:23 1-2.

Sired by La Grande (son of Almont, and out of Jessie Pepper by Mambrino Chief; Jessie Pepper is the dam of Ione 2:17 1-2, Alpha 2:23 1-2, Sterling Wilkes 2:31½, and others) dam Norma, by Arthurton (sire of Arab 2:15, Joe Arthurton 2 2: 1-2, etc.)

Grandam Nourmahal, (full sister to A. W. Richmond, sire of Arrow 2:13½, Romero 2:19, and sire of Columbine, dam of Anteeo 2:16¼, and Antevolo 2:19½ at four years old).

DESCRIPTION.

Grandissimo is four years old, will make a sixteen hand horse; he is a rich mahogany bay in color and perfect in style and action. $50 for the season. Usual return privileges.

"Grandissimo" with limited training last fall as a three-year-old, trotted quarters in 35 seconds and miles in 2:40.

I feel confident that he will trot fast this season, and will be a great sire as his colts this season are all grand youngsters.

The best of pasturage $4 per month. Mares taken care of in any manner that owners may desire, but no responsibility assurred for escapes or accidents.

For further particulars send for circular or call at stables, one mile south of St. Helena.

FRED W. LOEBER Prop'r.

GROVER CLAY

Bay Stallion, Black Points,

15 3-4 hands high.

Bred by W. W. Traylor, San Francisco.

BY ELECTIONEER.

First dam Maggie Norfolk by Norfolk, son of Lexington, he by Boston. Second dam Tilda Quill by Billy Cheatham he by Cracken, and he by Boston. Third dam by Dorsey's Golddust.

TERMS.

Will make the season of 1890 at the Training Stables of Denis Gannon, near Oakland Trotting Park, at $60 the season, payable at time of service. Season to commence February 1st and ending July 1st. Proper care of mares will be taken, but no responsibility incurred for accidents or escapes. Address,

DENIS GANNON, Oakland, Cal.

MEMO.

The Best Son of SIDNEY

Will Make the Season of 1890 at the OAKLAND RACE TRACK

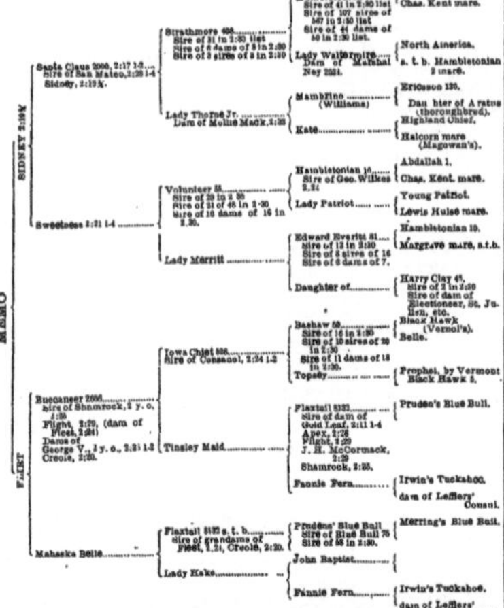

MEMO is, as can be seen at a glance, one of the best bred young stallions in service, having three crosses of Rysdyk's Hambletonian and one of Harry Clay, the sire of Green Mountain Maid (dam of Electioneer, etc.), while Long Island Black Hawk and Flaxtail also contribute to his blood. Sidney (Memo's sire) is universally known as the best young sire in the world, a producer of extreme speed at an early age.

PERFORMANCES.

MEMO trotted in public in his two-year-old form, obtaining a record of 2:49, though he was close to Grandee in a race on the Bay District Track, the second heat of which was made in 2:34 1-2, the first in 2:37. He exhibited phenomenal speed when three years old, and had it not been for a slight strain of his fore fetlock, there is little question that he would have shown in public very close to the best record. On the Oakland track he was timed a mile in 2:30 1-2, and frequently trotted quarters in from 32 1-2 to 31 seconds.

As a four-year-old Memo only started once—at Sacramento—when, although out of condition, he showed great speed, and improving as he went on, great hopes were entertained of his going well down in the 'teens at the P. C. T. H. B. A. meeting, but after showing several very fast miles his leg filled and he was laid up for the season. He is sixteen hands high, and of powerful build throughout. His color is a glossy black, with both fore-feet white. His disposition is all that could be desired, and his action superb. He is a sure foal getter, only one mare being reported not in foal during his last season.

TERMS, $100, with usual return privileges, for a limited number of mares. Season to close JUNE 15th, when he will be prepared for track purposes. Pasturage $4 per month. Have leased the cricket ground adjoining the track for pasturage, where there is fine feed. Reasonable charges if fed hay and grain. Best of care taken of mares in any manner owners may desire, but positively no responsibility assumed for accidents or escapes. For further particulars address

J. P. KERR, 313 Bush Street, San Francisco,

or, JOHN ROWEN, Race Track, Oakland, Cal.

2:10 1-2 ELECTIONEER 2:12 1-4

BAY STALLION	BROWN STALLION
ECLECTIC	**MORTIMER**
11,321	5,346
By Electioneer, dam Manette (full sister to Woodnut 2.16 1-2 Manon 2:21 and Maple, dam of Hattie D., three year-old record 2:26½) by Nutwood 2:18¾, etc., etc.	Four-year-old Record 2:27. By ELECTIONEER, dam MARTI, by Whipple's Hambletonian (sire of 15 in 2:30, and of dams of eight in 2:30). Second dam Ida Martin by Rifeman (sire of Col. Lewis 2:18½).
Terms $100 for the Season.	Terms $60 for the Season.

Horses shipped via San Francisco may be consigned to J. W. MORSHEAD, City Front Stables, who will attend to their forwarding.

Season closes JULY 1st, 1890. Usual return privileges.

For further particulars address owner,

WILFRED PAGE, Penns Grove,
Sonoma County, Cal

The Trotting Stallion

Silver Bow

Will make the season of 1890 at the Oakland Race Track.

PEDIGREE.

SILVER BOW 11706, two-year-old record 2:37, is by Robert McGregor 647, 2:17½ (sire of Bonnie McGregor, 2:13½, Earl McGregor, 2:21½, Mac D., 2:30, McGregor Boy, 2:29½, Mark Time, 2:30, Roxie McGregor, 2:29½) by Major Edsall 2:29, by Alexander's Abdallah 15—sire of Goldsmith Maid, 2:14—by Hambletonian 10—sire of Dexter, 2:17¼.

Robert McGregor's dam was Nancy Whitman by American Star 14, by Stockholm's American Star.

SILVER BOW'S first dam is Sadie by Hambletonian 10, sire of Geo. Wilkes, 2:22—sire of Guy Wilkes, 2:15¼—also Electioneer, sire of Sunol, three-year-old record, 2:10½, and Palo Alto, 2:12¾; second dam Lady Wynne by Wm. Welch 341; third dam Elenora Margrave by imp. Margrave.

DESCRIPTION.

SILVER BOW is a handsome bay, no white; 15-2¼ hands high; weighs 1075 pounds; of fine form, with the best of legs and a clean-cut, intelligent head. Is remarkably level-headed, seldom making a break; wears seven-ounce shoes in front. His record, 2:37, is no mark of his speed; he can beat 30 easy, and with his gilt-edge breeding, he is just what he ought to be, a trotter sired by a trotter whose dam was herself a trotter and his grandam the dam of two trotters. His dam Sadie being by Hambletonian 10, shows him to be bred from the cream of the trotting blood.

TERMS: $100 for the season. Mares not proving in foal returnable for the season of 1891 free of charge. Good pasturage and first-class care taken of mares for $5 per month. No responsibilities assumed for escapes or accidents. For further particulars, address

Limited to 15 approved mares.
Season to end June 1st, 1890.

P. J. WILLIAMS,
Care Race Track, Oakland, Cal.

Pleasanton Stock Farm Co.'s Stallions,

DIRECTOR, 2:17.

Director's book is open for 15 good mares more than already booked for the season of 1890, at $[illegible] each.

This is the cheapest service fee ever charged for a stallion, taking into consideration his BREEDING and RACE RECORD and the RACE RECORDS OF HIS COLTS.

Season to commence February 15th and close August 1st.

CORRECTOR, Five Years Old.

Sire Director 2:17, dam Brainey, she by Echo. Echo sired by Rysdyk's Hambletonian out of Fan Felter, by Magnolia, he by Seely's American Star. Brainey's dam Lady Dudley, she by Tom Dudley Blacknose, a son of Medoc, he by American Eclipse. Lady Dudley's dam by Bertrand, Jr., a son of Bertrand.

CORRECTOR is a rich seal brown 15½ hands high, and is the fastest young stallion in the world under the same conditions, never having been off the farm where raised and never been shod or driven for speed before last Christmas, and can trot quarters now in 35 seconds, a 2:20 gait.

He will be allowed to serve ten good mares, at $100 each for the season, which closes June 1st.

DECORATOR, Four Years Old.

Sire Director 2:17, dam Chess, sired by Cardinal 2.37, trial 2:28, he by Gen. Gifford's Morgan, dam Cardinal, sired by Joe Gales of Ohio, he by Marlborough out of the Duchess of Marlborough by Southern Eclipse; second dam old Duchess of Marlborough by Sir Archy; third dam by imp Diomed. Decorator's second dam a Morgan and Messenger mare.

Decorator is a light bay 16 hands high, and with but little handling for speed has shown eighths in 17½ seconds, a 2:20 gait.

He will be allowed to serve ten good mares at $50 each for the season, which closes June 1st.

Mares not proving with foal may be returned next season free of charge of service fees to the same stallion, if he is still in our possession; however, the company reserves the right to return the fee instead of giving service.

Pasturage $4 per month; hay and grain extra. Accidents and escapes at owner's risk.

Service fees due at time of service, and must be paid, together with pasturage, etc., before mares are taken away, or a good approved note given, payable August 1st, 1890, at which date all bills must be settled.

For further information call or address **M. SALISBURY, 320 Sansome Street, Room 9, San Francisco, or**

PLEASANTON STOCK FARM CO.,
Pleasanton, Alameda Co., Cal.

SOUTHER FARM

P. O. Box 208. San Leandro, Cal.

1½ miles northwest of San Leandro; 8 miles southeast of Oakland. Turn off County road between above places at "Stanley Road," ¾ mile north of San Leandro.

Horses boarded at all times in any manner desired. Best of care but no responsibility for accidents. Colts broken and handled for road or track. Terms reasonable.

Glen Fortune,	Jester D,	El Benton,	Figaro,
By Electioneer.	By Almont.	By Electioneer.	Hambletonian 7[illegible]
$50 for 1889.	$50 for 1890.	Limited to 5 mares.	Limited to 12 mares.
		Book Full.	Book Full.

THE SOUTHER FARM

Has Green Feed the Year Round

and feeds Hay in connection with the green feed, which a horse must have if he is to thrive. Every animal is given

A Dry, Warm Place to Sleep,

No matter how stormy the weather. All Stock under cover when it rains.

VISITORS WELCOME ANY DAY EXCEPT SUNDAY.

How to Get Stock to the Souther Farm.

The Souther Farm is one and a half miles northeast of San Leandro and eight miles southeast of Oakland. The stables are about one mile east of the county road, which runs between Oakland and San Leandro. The place to turn off is at Stanley Road, where a large signboard of the farm is placed. Guide boards will be found at every cross road. In any ordinary weather the roads are very good, and they are fairly good after the unusually heavy rainfall of the past winter.

All stock sent from San Francisco may be brought over by Grole's Express, No. 3 Market street, San Francisco. They also have an order box outside of Hawley Bros.' Hardware house on the corner of Market and Beale streets. The express leaves San Francisco on the Creek route boat, which starts at 1:30, but all orders should be in the order box at Market and Beale streets by 10 o'clock, or at the office, No. 3 Market street, by 11 o'clock at the latest. In the case of very young or very valuable horses, the Souther Farm will send reliable men to lead or drive over any stock that will not lead behind a wagon. A small charge will be made in such cases, to cover the extra expense incurred.

Horses are very easily taken from Oakland to the farm, and where it is inconvenient for owners to bring them or send them, the farm will send after anything that is to come. On horses that stay three months or over there is no charge for getting or delivering. Where a horse stays a short time the actual time and expense only is charged to him.

Horses can be shipped by rail from almost all parts of the State to San Leandro. Always notify the Farm several days before shipping anything, and then men will be on hand to receive stock on arrival. The railroad station is but two miles from the Souther Farm, and the agent invariably gives immediate notice of the arrival of any stock consigned to the above farm, but when word is sent to the farm in good season by letter or telegram, the animals sent are saved waiting a couple of hours in the car.

Passenger trains leave San Francisco (from the broad gauge ferry) and First and Broadway, Oakland, at frequent intervals during the day. There are several trains from San Jose to San Leandro on both the broad and narrow gauge railroads; the broad gauge, by way of Niles, is much more convenient for getting to the farm. There are trains each day from Sacramento, Stockton and Livermore to San Leandro. In ordinary weather it is a short and pleasant drive from Oakland to the Souther Farm or from San Francisco to the Farm by way of the Creek route ferry boat. Always notify the Souther Farm just when you will arrive at San Leandro, and some one will meet you at the station. If you do not recognize the farm conveyance ask the stage driver, who will point it out.

Write to the above address for references, circulars and price lists. Terms reasonable.

GILBERT TOMPKINS, Proprietor.

SAN MATEO STOCK FARM

HOME OF GUY WILKES,
Record, 2:15 1-4.

Guy Wilkes' Book is full for 1890 and 1891, and positively no more mares will be received.

Sable Wilkes, three-year-old record 2:18, will be allowed to serve [illegible] mares in addition to those already engaged at $250 the season of 1890. SABLE Wilkes, 15½ hands, black horse, by Guy Wilkes, first dam Sable by The Moor; second dam Gretchen by Mambrino Pilot; third dam Kitty Kirkman by Canada Chief; fourth dam by Fanning's Tobe; fifth dam by imp. Leviathan.

Leo Wilkes, brown horse, four years, 16 hands, full brother to Sable Wilkes, will be allowed to serve 30 mares at $100 the season.

Mares not proving with foal may be returned the following season free of service fee. Parties engaging the services of any of the above horses must send a deposit of 10 per cent. of service money with engagement. Pasturage $6 per month, and when the condition of the animal requires it, hay or grain, or both, are fed, the charge will be $12 50 per month. Good care will be taken of all mares sent to the Farm, but no liability will be assumed for accidents or escapes.

All bills are due at time of service, but must be paid by August 1st of each year. No stock will be allowed to leave the place until all bills are paid.

WILLIAM CORBITT.
San Mateo Stock Farm.

2:08 3-4 2:10 2:12

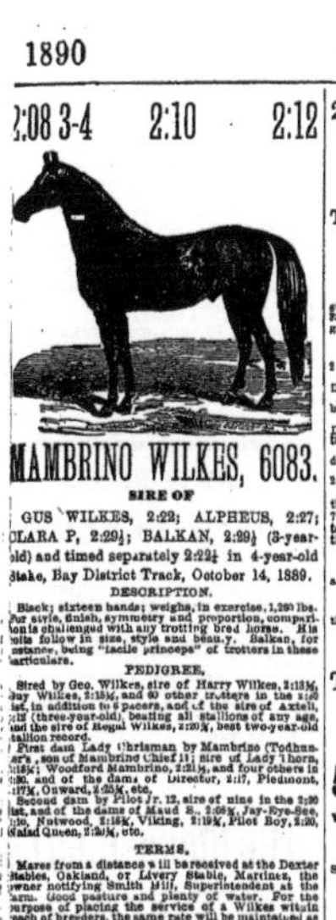

MAMBRINO WILKES, 6083.

SIRE OF

GUS WILKES, 2:22; ALPHEUS, 2:27; CLARA P, 2:29½; BALKAN, 2:29½ (3-year-old) and timed separately 2:22¼ in 4-year-old Stake, Bay District Track, October 14, 1889.

DESCRIPTION.

Black; sixteen hands; weighs, in exercise, 1,260 lbs. For style, finish, symmetry and proportion, comparison is challenged with any trotting bred horse. His colts follow in size, style and beauty. Balkan, for instance, being "facile princeps" of trotters in these particulars.

PEDIGREE.

Sired by Geo. Wilkes, sire of Harry Wilkes, 2:13½, Guy Wilkes, 2:15¼, and 60 other trotters in the 2:30 list, in addition to 6 pacers, and of the sire of Axtell, 2:12 (three-year-old), beating all stallions of any age, and the sire of Regal Wilkes, 2:20¾, best two-year-old stallion record.

First dam Lady Chrisman by Mambrino (Todhunter's, son of Mambrino Chief 11; sire of Lady Thorn, 2:18¼; Woodford Mambrino, 2:21½, and four others in 2:30, and of the dams of Director, 2:17, Piedmont, 2:17¼, Onward, 2:25¼, etc.

Second dam by Pilot Jr. 12, sire of nine in the 2:30 list, and of the dams of Maud S., 2:08¾, Jay-Eye-See, 2:10, Nutwood, 2:18¾, Viking, 2:19¼, Pilot Boy, 2:20, Naiad Queen, 2:20¾, etc.

TERMS.

Mares from a distance will be received at the Dexter Stables, Oakland, or Livery Stable, Martinez, the owner notifying Smith Hill, Superintendent at the farm. Good pasture and plenty of water. For the purpose of placing the service of a Wilkes within reach of breeders, the same rate will be maintained as last year, to wit, $75 for the season. Although it is not admitted thereby that this horse is inferior as a producer to the horses whose fees are placed at from $150 to $500. Address

SMITH HILL,
San Miguel Stock Farm,
Walnut Creek, Contra Costa Co., Cal.

2:12¾ 2:13½ 2:15¼

The Trotting Stallion

VICTOR,

Record 2:22.

Will make the season of 1890 at NAPA CITY.

DESCRIPTION.

VICTOR is a handsome dark bay; 15½ hands high; weighs about 1,100 pounds, and is remarkably intelligent, level-headed, of kind disposition, and a magnificent animal in every respect. He is well boned and muscled, of splendid conformation, and possesses the qualities of speed and endurance to an eminent degree—qualities that he imparts to his progeny.

PEDIGREE.

VICTOR, record 2:22
- Echo 462
  - Hambletonian 10, Sire of 42 in the 2:30 list.
    - Abdallah 1
    - Chas. Kent mare
  - Fanny Felter
    - Magnolia 58
    - by Webber's Kentucky Whip
- Daughter of
  - Woodburn
    - Lexington
    - Lulu Horton
  - daughter of
    - Ashland
    - thoroughbred

ECHO is the sire of Belle Echo, 2:20, Senator, 2:21¼, Victor, 2:22, Gibraltar, 2:22¼, Echora, 2:23¼, Tippie, 2:25¼, Lohengrin, 2:27¼, Pasha, 2:27¼, Elmonte, 2:29, Col. Hawkins, 2:29¼, Annie Laurie, 2:30, Economy, 2:30, Sam Lewis, pacer, 2:25.

TERMS—$60 FOR THE SEASON.

Mares not proving with foal may be returned next season free of charge, provided the horse remains the property of the present proprietor, and stands at the same place, otherwise money will be refunded. The best of care taken of mares in any manner that owners may desire, but no responsibility assumed for accidents or escapes. For further particulars, apply to or address

G. W. HUGHES, Agent,
G. A. DOHERTY, Proprietor. Napa City.

The Fast Trotting Stallion

REDWOOD.

Four-Year-Old Record 2:24 1-2

Will make the season of 1890—February 1st to July 1st—at

SANTA ROSA.

REDWOOD is a dark bay colt, 15.2½ hands high, weighs 1100 lbs. Foaled in 1885 by Anteeo, 2:16¼, sire of Alfred G., 2:19¼. Anteeo is by Electioneer. First dam Lou Milton, by Milton Medium; second dam Old Fly, a thoroughbred mare brought from the East in 1871 by W. C. Ralston, Esq.

Redwood's sire was out of Columbine by A. W. Richmond, the sire of the pacers Arrow 2:13½, and Elwood 2:23, and the trotters Romero, 2:19¼, and Len Rose, 2:27. Redwood has shown a quarter in 33 seconds.

Terms $100

For the season. Mares not proving with foal may be returned next season free of charge, provided Redwood remains the property of the present owners. Good pasturage at reasonable rates. No responsibility assumed for escapes or accidents. Service fees payable before removal of the mare. Limited to 40 approved mares. For further particulars address

A. McFADYEN.
Santa Rosa, Cal.

2:10¾ 2:13¾ 2:10

DEXTER PRINCE.

This Royally-bred Stallion will make the Season of 1890 at the LIVE OAKS Breeding Farm, 2 miles from Lodi, San Joaquin County, Cal.

DESCRIPTION.

DEXTER PRINCE is a blood bay, 16 hands high, weighs over 1100 pounds; has great power and substance, and the highest finish. When two years old, at Palo Alto, he was timed quarters by Gov. Stanford in 37¼ seconds, and he was driven eighths by Mr. Marvin at a faster rate of speed than that. He is a sure foal-getter, and invariably sires foals of good size, of fine form and finish, and the highest rate of speed.

PEDIGREE.

By KENTUCKY PRINCE, the sire of Guy, 2:10¾, Spofford, 2:18¾, Company, 2:19¾, Bayonne Prince, 2:21 1-4, Fred Folger, 2:20¾, and a score more in the 2:30 list.

First dam LADY DEXTER, full sister of the greatest of trotters, Dexter, and the greatest of sires, Dictator, the sire of Director, 2:17, Phallas, 2:13¾, in a fourth heat, and Jay-Eye-See, 2:10.

Second dam Clara, the dam of Dexter, 2:17 1-4, Dicta or Astoria 2:29 1-4, and Almah, 2:28¾. Clara was by American Star, that has 34 daughters that have produced 2:30 or better trotters.

Third dam the McKinstry mare, the dam of Shark, 2:27¾. HAMBLETONIAN, the grandsire of DEXTER PRINCE, has 40 trotters in the 2:30 list, 44 daughters that have produced 2:30 trotters, and more than 100 sons that have sired 2:30 trotters.

CLARK CHIEF, the grandsire on the sire's side, was the sire of performing and producing sons and daughters.

DEXTER PRINCE has faster blood lines, on both sides, than any other stallion in the world—Guy 2:10¾, and Jay-Eye-See, 2:10.

KENTUCKY PRINCE is one of the best bred and speediest stallions in the world. David Bonner, in the presence of Governor Stanford, timed him when he trotted a 2:18 gait. He is by Clark Chief, one of the great broodmare sires; his first dam is Kentucky Queen by Morgan Eagle, son of Hale's Green Mountain Morgan, 2nd dam by Blythe's Whip, 3rd dam by Martin's Brummier, 4th dam by Quicksilver 880, on through the strongest thoroughbred blood.

TERMS.

$100 for the season, with usual return privileges. Payable before mares are removed. Good pasture, and the best care furnished, but no responsibility assumed for accidents.

PREMIUM.

$250 will be given to the first of the produce of DEXTER PRINCE put in the 2:30 list, and $100 each after the first. Address

L. M. MORSE, Lodi, Cal.

The Produce of Eros Averaged $2,200 Each at New York Auction Sale in 1889.

THE ELECTIONEER TROTTING STALLION,

5326 EROS 5326

Will make the season of 1890—February 1st to July 1st—at LA SIESTA RANCH, MENLO PARK, adjoining Palo Alto.

PEDIGREE.

EROS (5326)
Standard by his sire
" " dam
" " record
" " produce
" under all rules

EROS (5326)
- Electioneer — Grandsire of Norlaine, 1 yr., 2:31 1-2, Sire of Sunol, 2 yrs., 2:18, Sunol, 3 yrs., 2:10 1-2, Hinda Rose, 4 yrs., 2:16, Palo Alto, 2:12¾.
  - Hambletonian 10 — Sire of Dictator, George Wilkes, Happy Medium, and 40 others in 2:30 list, and grandsire of 728 in list.
    - Abdallah 1 — Sire of the dams of Goldsmith Maid, 2:14, and 7 other producing dams.
    - Charles Kent mare — By imp. Bellfounder.
  - Green Mountain Maid — Dam of Prospero, 2:20, Elaine, 2:20, Dame Trot, 2:22, Elista, 2:22½, Storm, 2:26¾, Antonio, 2:28¾, Miranda, 2:31, Mansfield, 2:26.
    - Harry Clay — Sire of the dams of St. Julien, 2:11¼, Bodine, 2:19¼, and 17 more in 2:30 list
    - Shanghai Mary.
- Sontag Mohawk — Dam of Eros, 2:29 1-2, Sport, 2:24¾, Sallie Benton, 2:17¾, Conductor, trial, 2:28, Colma, 3-y-o trial, 2:24.
  - Mohawk Chief — Sire of the dams of Lot Slocum, 2:17¼, Sallie Benton, 4 yrs., 2:17¾, Pedlar, 2 yrs., 2:27¾, Stanford, 4 yrs., 2:30, Eros, 6th heat, 2:29 1-2.
    - Hambletonian 10 — Sire of the dams of Stamboul, 2:12¼, Wilton, 2:19¼, and 20 other trotters.
    - Lady Perrine
  - Sontag Nellie
    - Toronto Sontag — By Toronto Chief,
    - Nellie Gray — 5-mile record, 13:45.

Produce of Eros
Wanda, 4 yrs., 2:21.
Solita, 2 yrs., 2:41 1-2.
Meriquita, 3 yrs., 2:42.
Daylight, 3 yrs., 2:54.
Hiram B., trial, 2:28.

These are the only colts by him that have ever had a harness on except one in New York that went a trial last July in 2:36 1-2.

DESCRIPTION.

EROS is a rich seal brown stallion, bred by Hon. Leland Stanford at Palo Alto, and is the nearest living likeness of his celebrated sire, Electioneer. Stands 15.2 hands high, and weighs 1050 pounds.

In breeding to Eros, the owners of mares will strictly follow the great rule of breeding, viz., breed to a stallion by a producer and out of a sure producer of great speed. Eros is by the stallion that has produced more 2:30 trotters that any living horse, and is also the sire of more 2:20 performers than any horse living or dead.

EROS is out of the dam of Sally Benton, four years old, record 2:17¾, Sport 2:22½, and Eros 2:29½ in the sixth heat, against a field of nine horses. He is from a family that is endowed with great natural speed, trot fast at an early age, train on, throw trotters from all classes of mares, are of good substance, bone, style and action, and breed solid colors.

TERMS.

$100 for the season, with the privilege of return next season should mares not be in foal and horse and mare still remain in the same hands.

Good pasturage can be obtained at $5 per month, but no responsibility for accidents or escapes. There are a large number of box stalls, and animals can be kept up and fed on hay and grain at reasonable rates if required. Mares already in foal can be sent to the ranch for foaling, and will receive all the attention bestowed upon our own mares. Mares left with Mr. Peter Pomyea, Broadway Street Stable, Oakland, or with Mr. F. H. Burke, 401 Montgomery Street, San Francisco, will be forwarded to the ranch free of charge. For further particulars apply to

W. H. VIOGET,
LA SIESTA RANCH, MENLO PARK, CAL.

EROS is the only stallion offered to the public on this Coast that has a dam that has three in the 2:30 list.

GRAND MOOR, 2374.

Grand Moor 2374.
- Moor 870 — Sire of Beautiful Bells 2:29½; Sire of Sable (dam of Sable Wilkes) 2:18; Sire of Sultan 2:24; Sire of Tommy Gates 2:24; Sire of Del Sur 2:24½; Sire of Sir Guy 2:28½. Beautiful Bells is the dam of Hinda Rose, 2:19½ as a 3-year-old, Palo Alto Belle, 2:22½, Chimes, St. Bell, 2:24½, Bell Boy (3 years) 2:19½. Sultan, 2:24 (sire of Stamboul 2:12½) has 16 in 2:30 list.
  - Clay Pilot 92 — Sire of 2 in 2:30 list.
  - Belle of Wabash.
- Vashti — Dam of Don Tomas, who got a record of 2:30 in 1889.
  - Mambrino Patchen 58 — Sire of 14 in 2:30 list. Sire of the dam of Guy Wilkes, 2:15¼; also sire of 20 stallions and 18 mares with get in 2:30 list.
  - Kate Taber — By Mambrino Messenger, he by Mambrino Paymaster.

Foaled 1876. Black. Sixteen hands high. Bred by L. J. Rose

A horse of highest form and quality; of great excellence in every point; a type of his celebrated family; of marked individuality, spirit and endurance; never properly trained or raced, but shows the possession of great speed; perfectly manageable in the stable and on the road and track.

As he is sired by The Moor 870, a son of CLAY PILOT, out of Vashti by MAMBRINO PATCHEN, he is a most valuable cross for mares of other families. THE MOOR sired Beautiful Bells and the dams of Sable Wilkes and Margaret 2:28 (dam of Regal Wilkes, 2-year-old record 2:20¾).

MAMBRINO PATCHEN is regarded as the unsurpassed sire of broodmares, having, among many others, sired the dam of Guy Wilkes and of Wm. L. (the sire of Axtell), and a son of his sired the dam of Axtell. The public sales this year have demonstrated with renewed emphasis the value of The Moor and Mambrino Patchen strains of blood. For combining particularly with the Hambletonians it may be called "the ready-money cross."

GRAND MOOR will make the season of 1890 for a time at the Oakland Race Track and afterwards at my Ranch, fifteen miles from Oakland. Mares can be delivered at the race track to the groom in charge. Pasture at $5 per month. For other food, if requested, an additional charge will be made.

TERMS, $150 for the season, with privileges of return if the horse does not change hands.

Every care exercised, but no liability for escapes or accidents.

H. I. THORNTON, 504 Kearny Street.

POPLAR GROVE

Breeding Farm

STALLIONS.

CLOVIS, 4909,

CLOVIS is a beautiful black, Eight Years Old, 16 1-2 Hands High, and weighs 1260 lbs.

He is a horse of beautiful symmetry and magnificent action.

PEDIGREE.

CLOVIS was sired by Sultan, 2:24, sire of Stamboul, 2:12 1-4, Ruby, 2:19¾, and fifteen others with records of 2.30 or better.

First dam Sweetbriar by Thorndale 2:22 1-2, sire of Edwin Thorne, 2:16 1-2, Daisy Dale, 2.19, and May Thorne, 2.28

Second dam Ulster Queen, dam of Volmer, 2:24¾, by Hambletonian 10. Sire of Dexter, 2.17¼, George Wilkes, 2:22.

Third dam by Thomas Jefferson, a son of Mambrino Paymaster, Jr.

Fourth dam by Mambrino Paymaster, sire of Mambrino Chief.

Sultan, by The Moor, sire of Beautiful Bells, dam of Hinda Rose, 2:19 1-2, and Sable, dam of Sable Wilkes, three year old record 2:18.

First dam of Sultan, Sultana, by Delmonico. Sire of Darby, 2:16 1-2, by Guy Miller, sire of Whipple's Hambletonian.

Second dam by Mambrino Chief.

Third dam by Downing's Bay Messenger.

Fourth dam Mrs. Caudle, dam of Ericsson, four year old record 2.30 1-2.

Clovis will make the season of 1890 at Poplar Grove Breeding Farm, near Wildflower, Fresno County, Commencing February 1st and ending July 1st.

Terms, $75, due at time of service.

Mares cared for in any manner owners may desire; pasturage $2 per month. Every care exercised, but no liability for escapes or accidents. Mares not proving with foal can be returned next season, providing I still own this stallion.

APEX, 8935.

FOUR-YEAR-OLD RECORD, FOURTH HEAT, 2:26.

Will make the present season at the Poplar Grove Breeding Farm, near Wildflower, Fresno Co., season commencing Feb. 1st, and ending July 1, 1890. Terms, $50 the season, due at time of service. Apex is eight years old, a beautiful bay, 15 1-4 hands high, and weighs 1150 lbs. He is a horse of fine disposition, and his gait is faultless.

PEDIGREE.

Apex was sired by Promptor 2305, he by Blue Bull 75; first dam Mary by Flaxtail, he by Pruden's Blue Bull, Flaxtail being the sire of the dams of Buccaneer, five-year-old record, 2:24 1-2; Pride, yearling record, 2:44 1-2, and Shamrock, two-year old record, 2:26, third heat. Second dam by Bright Eyes, son of Boanarages. Promptor (sire of Apex, record 2:26, and Transit, 2:26 1-2), by Wilson's Blue Bull, by Pruden's Blue Bull, son of Merring's Blue Bull. Promptor's dam Prairie Bird, by Flaxtail; second dam by John the Baptist, son of Tally Ho Morgan, by Sherman Morgan; third dam Fannie Fern by Irwin's Tuckaho

Apex made his appearance in the circuit as a two-year-old, and obtained a record of 2:42. As a three-year-old he reduced this in a race at Santa Rosa against Stamboul to 2:31, it taking six heats to decide the contest, which was won by Apex. As a four year-old he gained his present record of 2:26.

Mares cared for in any manner owners may desire. Pasturage $2 per month. Every care exercised, but no liabilities for escapes or accidents. Mares not proving with foal can be returned next season, providing I still own this stallion.

The Standard Stallion

JUNIO;

RECORD 2:22.

WILL MAKE THE PRESENT SEASON OF 1890 AT FRESNO FAIR GROUNDS.

Season Commencing Feb. 1st and ending July 1st.

TERMS—$100 the season, due at time of service.

JUNIO is eight years old, a handsome dark bay 16 hands high, and weighs 1250 pounds. He is the personification of the light harness horse, and his trotting action is superb. At the State Fair of 1886 he took first premium over forty of the finest trotters in the State.

PEDIGREE.

Junio, by Electioneer, premier stallion of Palo Alto (sire of Sunol 2:10 1-2, Palo Alto 2:12 1-4, and 47 others in the 2:30 list. Dam by Granger by imp. Hercules.

Granger, by imp. Hercules, dam Jenny Lind, by Stockbridge Chief, Jr., he by Stockbridge Chief, he by Vermont Black Hawk. Second dam by Kentucky Whip.

Imp. Hercules, by Kingston, first dam daughter of Tuscar, by Hay Middleton, second dam Malvina, by Oscar; 3rd dam Spotless by Walton; 4th dam by Trumpator (see Bruce's American Stud Book, Vol. I, page 26). Hercules is the sire of the dam of Atmoor 2:24½; also sire of dam of Menlo 2:21 1-2.

Mares not proving in foal may be returned next year free of charge, providing I still have the horse. Pasturage $3 per month. While every care will be taken of horses, no liability will be assumed for accidents or escapes.

For further particulars address

S. N. STRAUBE, Fresno, Cal

Poplar Grove Breeding Farm.

KENNEL ADVERTISEMENTS.

LOST.

A White Pointer Dog

With lemon spots. Answers to the name of "Point." A liberal reward and no questions asked on delivery of same at

SWAIN'S STABLE,
417 Folsom St.

Fox Terrier Pups for Sale

Sire BLEMTON VESUVIAN (Champion Lucifer—Blemton—Vesta), dam BEATRICE (Champion Bacchanal—Blemton Arrow). This is the best winning blood. Beautifully marked. Will make handsome and game ones.

—Also an—

ENGLISH MASTIFF DOG PUP. Will develop into a good one. Apply or address,

J. B. MARTIN,
No. 1328 Page Street, near Lyon St., S. F., Cal.

RENTON KENNELS,

SAN FRANCISCO OFFICE. 2922 Pine St

Kennels located at Bolinas, Cal.

Dogs taken to board and broken at reasonable rates.

POINTER PUPPIES FOR SALE.

By Professor—Gracie Bow; Professor—Belle H.; Climax—Drab; Don—Diana.

Thoroughly broken water spaniel, Rock, out of the Prinder stock. Address

W. D. HOWE,
2922 Pine Street, San Francisco.

Puppies for Sale.

ONE GREYHOUND DOG, 14 months old, Saturday Night—Brunette.
ONE GREYHOUND DOG, 14 months old, breeding unknown.
EIGHT GREYHOUNDS (4 Dogs), whelped March 18, 1890, Saturday Night—Brunette.
ONE BLACK AND TAN POINTER, 19 months, and broken; Old Black Joe—Black Bess.
ONE GORDON SETTER BITCH, 12 months old.
ONE GORDON SETTER BITCH, 5 months old.
ONE FOX TERRIER BITCH, 2 months old.
ONE FOX TERRIER BITCH, 2 months old.

Apply to JAMES E. WATSON,
516 Sacramento street.
P. O. Box 1836. San Francisco.

DOGS---Pointer Pups FOR SALE.

Sure Bench Show and Field Trial Winners, as they have more bench-show and field-trial blood in them than any that have ever been whelped on the Pacific Coast.

Sire, POINT, double field trial winner; he by Vandevort's Don, great field trial and bench show winner, out of Drab, field trial and bench show winner.

Dam, QUEEN CROXTETH by Rush T., bench show winner, out of Champion Patti Croxteth, field trial and bench show winner. This is the best pointer blood in the world. Breeding and health guaranteed. Address,

A. B. TRUMAN,
1426 Steiner St., near Ellis, S. F., Cal.

CALIFORNIA SPANIEL KENNELS,

Oakland, California, H. P. RENNIE, Prop. Breeder and importer of typical COCKER SPANIELS. Winner of first prizes at S. F. and Los Angeles, 1889; also, Columbus, 1889, New York, 1887. In the stud, solid Black Cocker dog, GIFFEE, won 1st and Gold Medal at S. F., 1888. Fee, $25. Puppies and grown dogs at reasonable prices. My dogs can neither talk nor climb a tree, but are fielders and prize winners.

John D. Gall. Jas. P. Dunne

"The Resort,"

No. 1 Stockton Street, cor. Ellis,
San Francisco.

Brushes.

BUCHANAN BROS.,
Brush Manufacturers,
609 Sacramento Street, two doors above Montgomery.

Horse Brushes of every description on hand and made to order. Bristle Body Brushes our Specialty

JOHN FORGIE,

Importing Tailor,

204 Montgomery Street,
N. E. corner Bush. SAN FRANCISCO.

PHIL J. CRIMMINS. JOHN C. MORRISON.

"Silver Palace,"

36 Geary Street,
San Francisco, Cal.

Old Hermitage Whiskies

"STEINER'S,"
No. 311 BUSH STREET,
San Francisco.
Under Breeder and Sportsman Office.

AN UNQUALIFIED ENDORSEMENT.

Peruvian Bitters are made of the purest ingredients and compounded as carefully as any prescription.

Peruvian Bark, one of its principal ingredients, was introduced into Spain by the Countess, wife of Count CINCHON, Spanish Viceroy to Peru in 1630, who was cured of a fever by its use, since which time, no better remedy for Malaria and for Restoring the Natural Tone of the Stomach has been discovered.

On the Atlantic Coast they are used in the principal Hotels, Clubs and Restaurants, and sold by all Grocers and Druggists. We have sold them for the past three years WITHOUT ANY ADVERTISING and sales have constantly increased UPON MERIT ALONE, and we unqualifiedly recommend them to our friends and customers.

ACKER, MERRALL & CONDIT.

New York, Feb. 1st, 1890.

WILMERDING & CO., Agents for Pacific Coast,
216 FRONT ST., SAN FRANCISCO, CAL.

THE IMPROVED NOYES ROAD - CART,

PATENTED JULY 17, 1883, *AND JUNE* 8, 1886.

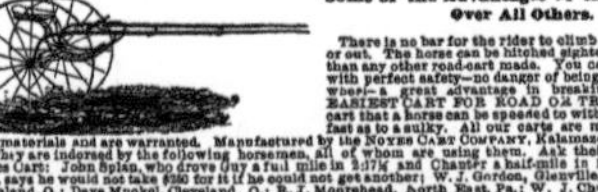

Some of the Advantages of the Noyes Cart Over All Others.

There is no bar for the rider to climb over in getting in or out. The horse can be hitched eighteen inches nearer than any other road-cart made. You can get in or out with perfect safety—no danger of being thrown into the wheel—a great advantage in breaking colts. THE EASIEST CART FOR ROAD OR TRACK. The only cart that a horse can be speeded to within one second as fast as to a sulky. All our carts are made of the very best materials and are warranted. Manufactured by the NOYES CART COMPANY, Kalamazoo, Mich.

They are indorsed by the following horsemen, all of whom are using them. Ask their opinion of the Noyes Cart: John Splan, who drove Guy a full mile in 2:17¾ and Chanter a half-mile in 1 10¾ to a Noyes Cart, says he would not take $250 for it if he could not get another; W. J. Gordon, Glenville, O.; W. B. Fasig, Cleveland, O.; Dave Muckel, Cleveland, O.; R. J. Moorehead, North East, Pa.; W. J. Chamberlain, Cleveland, O.; H. F. Malone, Bradford, Pa.; S. A. Brown & Co., Kalamazoo Stock Farm; Charles Marvin, Menlo Park, Cal.; W. H. Crawford, Lexington, Ky.; S. L. Caton, who gave Bell Boy a mark at Los Angeles, Cal., of 2:19¾, and drove Chanter a half mile in 1:06¼ and Lowland Girl a full mile in 2:22 to a Noyes Cart; Mike Bowerman, Lexington, Ky.; James Golden, Medford, Mass.; John E. Turner, Philadelphia, Pa.; T. L. Newton, Beaver Dam, Wis.; F. V. Johnston, Marshall, Mich.; W. H. McCarthy, Los Angeles, Cal.; A. W. Dennison, El Dorado, Kan.; P. O. Shank, Cleveland, O.; Charles Barnard, Boston, Mass.; Johnson Bros., Greenville, Mich.; John G. Avery, Buffalo, N. Y.; General R. L. Howard, Buffalo, N. Y.; Howard Conklin, Buffalo, N. Y.; W. D. Ham, Hennepin, Ill.; R. G. Henry, Waterbury, Conn; J. E. Hayer, Newburgh, O.; J. C. Hart, Jefferson, Tex.; A. W. Harbison, Rock Point, Pa.; Carl Hodges, Battle Creek, Mich.; Barney Treacy, Lexington, Ky.; George Forbes, Cleveland, O.; Gifford Dudley, Topeka, Kan.; William and J. L. Thompson Lamont, Pa.; C. F. Emery, Forest City Stock Farm, Cleveland, O.; H. F. Jones, Minneapolis, Minn.; John Forbes, Elyria, O.; D. J. Downs Battle Creek, Mich; Frank Caton, Randall Station, O.; Arthur D. Sutton, Ind., Pa.; W. F. Neely, Grand Ridge, Ill.; Walter Clark, owner of Pilot Medium, Battle Creek, Mich.; H. R. Kingman, Battle Creek, Mich.; Dr. Sutton and H. C. Reed, Kalamazoo, Mich.; Budd Doble, Chicago, Ill.

SOLE MANUFACTURERS OF STONE'S PATENT SULKY CASE.

They will more than save their cost in one season, and horsemen campaigning trotters cannot afford to do without them. Would refer to Samuel A. Brown, Kalamazoo Stock Farm, S. L. Caton and W. H. McCarthy. Address

NOYES CART COMPANY, Kalamazoo, Mich.

Office and Factory, corner Rose and Eleanor streets. H. ARTHUR STONE, Manager.

ADVERTISE YOUR STALLIONS

—IN THE—

Breeder & Sportsman

For the Season---1890.

We are pleased to announce that we have the best facilities for furnishing

Stallion Pictures,

Stallion Cards,

Pedigrees, Folders,

Contracts, Bills, Etc.

We make a specialty of this department of our business, and have UNRIVALED FACILITIES FOR LOOKING UP PEDIGREES and doing accurate and handsome work.

Promptness, Good Work, Low Prices.

BREEDER AND SPORTSMAN,
313 Bush Street, S. F.

The Park Training Stable.

CHAS. DAVID, PROPRIETOR.

Corner Grove and Baker Streets, near Entrance to Golden Gate Park.

EVERY FACILITY FOR TRAINING COLTS and taking care of Gentlemen's Roadsters.

Finely appointed stable with every convenience and sixteen roomy box stalls.

The best care given all horses by experienced help, under the personal superintendence of the proprietor

Convenient to the Park Speed Drive, and Accessible to Six Lines of Cable Cars.

THE TRAINING OF COLTS AND ROADSTERS A SPECIALTY.

TROTTERS AND ROADSTERS FOR SALE.

HORSES SOLD ON COMMISSION.

The proprietor trained and brought out the following well known horses: "Sister, Huntress," "Perihelion," "Nona Y," and others.

NEW BOOK.

HORSE BREEDING

Seventh Edition, with Appendix,
By J. H. SANDERS,

In which the GENERAL LAWS OF HEREDITY are exhaustively discussed and applied to the PRACTICAL BUSINESS OF BREEDING HORSES, especially with reference to the Selection of Breeding Stock and the Management of Stallions, Brood Mares, Young Foals, and Diseases Peculiar to Breeding Stock.

Price, Post Paid, $2.

BREEDER AND SPORTSMAN,
San Francisco, Cal.
313 Bush Street.

THE HICKS-JUDD CO.

Successors to
HICKS & JUDD, Bookbinders,
and Women's Co-operative Printing Office,
Printers, Bookbinders, Publishers,
23 First St., San Francisco.

BREEDERS' CATALOGUES A SPECIALTY.

JUST OUT, 2d EDITION.

1,000 Receipts

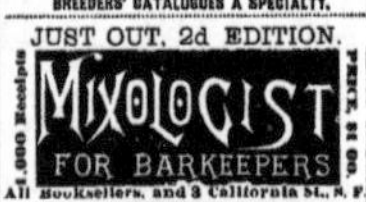

PRICE, $1 00.

All Booksellers, and 3 California St., S. F.

GOLDEN EAGLE HOTEL

Corner SEVENTH and K STREETS,
SACRAMENTO.
FIRST CLASS IN EVERY RESPECT.
The LARGEST and FINEST HOTEL in the City.
W. O. BOWERS, Proprietor.
Free 'Buss to and from the Hotel.
Telephone, Telegraph Office and Messenger Service at Hotel

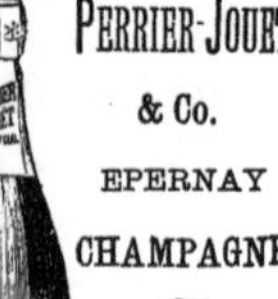

PERRIER-JOUET & Co.

EPERNAY

CHAMPAGNE

W. B. CHAPMAN

Sole Agent for Pacific Coast.

For sale by all first-class Wine Merchants and Grocers.

Southern Pacific Co.

(PACIFIC SYSTEM.)

Trains leave and are due to arrive at San Francisco.

LEAVE (FOR)	FROM APRIL 13, 1890.	ARRIVE (FROM)
7.30 A M	Haywards, Niles and San Jose ...	*12.45 P M
7.30 A M	Sacramento and Redding, via Davis	7.15 P M
7.30 A M	Sacramento, Auburn, Colfax	4.45 P M
8.00 A M	Martinez, Vallejo, Calistoga and Santa Rosa	6.15 P M
8.30 A M	Los Angeles Express, Fresno, Bakersfield, Mojave and East and Los Angeles	11.15 A M
8.30 A M	Niles, San Jose, Stockton, Ione, Sacramento, Marysville, Oroville and Red Bluff	4.45 P M
10.30 A M	Haywards and Niles	2.45 P M
12.00 M	Haywards, Niles and Livermore	8.45 P M
*1.00 P M	Sacramento River Steamers	**6.00 A M
3.00 P M	Haywards, Niles and San Jose	9.45 A M
3.30 P M	2d Class for Ogden and East	10.45 P M
4.00 P M	Stockton and Milton; Vallejo, Calistoga and Santa Rosa	9.45 A M
*4.30 P M	Niles and Livermore	*8.45 A M
*4.30 P M	Niles and San Jose	‡6.15 P M
5.00 P M	Shasta Route Express, Sacramento, Marysville, Redding, Portland, Puget Sound, East and Knight's Landing via Davis	10.45 A M
5.30 P M	Haywards and Niles	7.45 A M
6.00 P M	Sunset Route, Atlantic Express, Santa Barbara, Los Angeles, Deming, El Paso, New Orleans and East	8.45 P M
8.00 P M	Central Atlantic Express, Ogden and East	9.45 A M

SANTA CRUZ DIVISION.

LEAVE		ARRIVE
‡7.45 A M	Excursion train to Santa Cruz	‡8.05 P M
8.15 A M	Newark, Centerville, San Jose, Felton, Boulder Creek and Santa Cruz	6.20 P M
*2.15 P M	Centerville, San Jose, Almaden, Felton, Boulder Creek and Santa Cruz	*11.20 A M
4.45 P M	Centerville, San Jose, and Los Gatos	9.50 A M

Coast Division (Third and Townsend Sts.)

LEAVE		ARRIVE
7.25 A M	San Jose, Almaden and Way Stations	2.30 P M
8.30 A M	San Jose, Gilroy, Tres Pinos; Pajaro, Santa Cruz; Monterey; Pacific Grove, Salinas, San Miguel, Paso Robles, Santa Margarita (San Luis Obispo) and principal Way Stations	6.12 P M
10.30 A M	San Jose and Way Stations	5.02 P M
12.01 P M	Cemetery, Menlo Park and Way Stations	3.38 P M
*3.30 P M	San Jose, Tres Pinos, Santa Cruz, Salinas, Monterey Pacific Grove and principal Way Stations	*10.00 A M
*4.20 P M	Menlo Park and Way Station	*7.58 A M
5.20 P M	San Jose and Way Stations	9.03 A M
6.30 P M	Menlo Park and Way Stations	6.35 A M
†11.45 P M	Menlo Park and principal Way Stations	†7.28 P M

A M for Morning. P M for Afternoon.
*Sundays excepted. †Saturdays only. ‡Sundays only.
**Mondays excepted. ‖Saturdays excepted.

OCEANIC STEAMSHIP CO.

Carrying United States, Hawaiian and Colonial Mails.

WILL LEAVE THE COMPANY'S WHARF, foot of Mission street, No. 1,

For Honolulu, Auckland and Sydney,

WITHOUT CHANGE,

The Splendid New 3,000-ton Iron Steamer.
ZEALANDIA ... Saturday, May 31st, 1890, at 12 M., Or immediately on arrival of the English mails.

For Honolulu.

SS. AUSTRALIA (3,000 tons), May 28, 1890, at 12 M

For freight or passage, apply at office, 327 Market Street. JOHN D. SPRECKELS & BROS. General Agents.

KILLIP & CO.,

LIVE STOCK AND GENERAL AUCTIONEERS,

22 Montgomery Street, San Francisco

SPECIAL ATTENTION PAID TO SALES OF

High-Bred Horses and Cattle,

At auction and private sale.

Will Sell in All Cities and Counties of the State.

REFERENCES.

HON. C. GREEN, Sacramento. HON. J. D. CARR Salinas.
J. P. SARGENT, ESQ., Sargents, HON. JOHN BOGGS Colusa.
HON. L. J. ROSE, Los Angeles. HON. A. WALRATH Nevada.
J. B. HAGGIN, ESQ., San Francisco.

Represented at Sacramento by Edwin F. Smith Secretary State Agricultural Society.
At San Jose by Messrs. Montgomery & Rea, Real Estate Agents.

Being the oldest established firm in the live-stock business on this Coast, and having conducted the important auction sales in this line for the past fifteen years, amounting to one half a million of dollars, we feel justified in claiming unequaled facilities for disposing of live stock of every description, either at auction or private sale. Our list of correspondents embraces every breeder and dealer of prominence upon the Pacific Coast, thus enabling us to give full publicity to animals placed with us for sale. Private purchases and sales of live stock of all descriptions will be made on commission, and stock shipped with the utmost care. Purchases and sales made of land of every description. We are authorized to refer to the gentlemen whose names are appended.

KILLIP & CO., 22 Montgomery Street

HEALDS

Business College, 24 Post St.

—San Francisco.—

The most popular school on the Coast

E. P. HEALD, President. C. S. HALEY, Sec'y.
Send for circulars

San Francisco and North Pacific Railway.

THE DONAHUE BROAD-GAUGE ROUTE.

COMMENCING SUNDAY, APRIL 27, 1889, AND until further notice, boats and trains will leave from and arrive at the San Francisco Passenger Depot, Market-street Wharf, as follows:

FROM SAN FRANCISCO FOR POINT TIBURON AND SAN RAFAEL.
Week Days—7.40, 9.20, 11.20, A. M.; 1.30, 3.30, 5.00, 6.15 P. M.
Sundays—8.00, 9.30, 11.00 A. M.; 1.30, 3.30, 5.00, 6.15 P. M.

FROM SAN RAFAEL FOR SAN FRANCISCO.
Week Days—6.30, 7.55, 9.30, 11:40 A. M.; 1.40, 3.40, 5.05, 6:25 P. M.
Sundays—8.10, 9.40, 11:10 A. M.; 1.40, 3.40, 5.00, 6:25 P. M.

FROM POINT TIBURON FOR SAN FRANCISCO
Week Days—7.15, 8.20, 9.55 A. M.; 12.05, 2.05, 4.05, 5.30, 6.50 P. M.
Sundays—8.35, 10.05, 11:35 A. M.; 2.05, 4.05, 5.30, 6:50 P. M.

Leave San Francisco. WEEK DAYS.	SUNDAYS.	DESTINATION	Arrive San Francisco. SUNDAYS.	WEEK DAYS.
7.40 A M, 3.30 P M, 5.00 P M	8.00 A M, 5.00 P M	Petaluma and Santa Rosa	10.40 A M, 7.25 P M	8.50 A M, 10.30 A M, 7.25 P M
7.40 A M, 3.30 P M	8.00 A M	Fulton, Windsor, Healdsburg, Litton Springs, Cloverdale, and way stations.	7.25 P M	10.30 A M, 7.25 P M
7.40 A M	8.00 A M	Hopland and Ukiah.	7.25 P M	7.25 P M
7.40 A M, 3.30 P M	8.00 A M	Guerneville	7.25 P M	7.25 P M, 10.30 A M
7.40 A M, 5.00 P M	8.00 A M, 5.00 P M	Sonoma and Glen Ellen	10.40 A M, 6.05 P M	8.50 A M, 6.05 P M
7.40 A M, 3.30 P M	8.00 A M, 5.00 P M	Sebastopol	10.40 A M, 7.25 P M	10.30 A M, 7.25 P M

Stage connects at Santa Rosa for White Sulphur Springs, and Mark West Springs; at Geyserville for Skaggs Springs, and at Cloverdale for the Geysers; at Hopland for Highland Springs, Kelseyville, Soda Bay, Lakeport and Bartlett Springs, and at Ukiah for Vichy Springs, Saratoga Springs, Blue Lakes, Willits, Cahto, Calpella, Potter Valley, Sherwood Valley and Mendocino City.

EXCURSION TICKETS from Saturdays to Mondays, to Petaluma, $1.50; to Santa Rosa, $2.25; to Healdsburg, $3.40; to Litton Springs, $3.60; to Cloverdale, $4.50; to Hopland, $5.70; to Ukiah, $6.75; to Guerneville, $3.75; to Sonoma, $1.50; to Glen Ellen, $1.80.

EXCURSION TICKETS, good for Sundays only, to Petaluma, $1; to Santa Rosa, $1.50; to Healdsburg, $2.25; to Litton Springs, $2.40; to Cloverdale, $3; to Guerneville, $2.50, to Sonoma, $1; to Glen Ellen, $1.20.

H. C. WHITING, General Manager.

PETER J. McGLYNN, Gen. Pass. & Tkt. Agt.

Ticket Offices at Ferry, 222 Montgomery Street and 2 New Montgomery Street.

CHICAGO, MILWAUKEE AND ST. PAUL RAILWAY.

Steam Heated and Electric Lighted Vestibuled Trains between Chicago, St. Paul and Minneapolis.
Electric Lighted and Steam Heated Vestibuled Trains between Chicago, Council Bluffs and Omaha.
Finest Dining Cars in the World.
Free Reclining Chair Cars between Chicago and Omaha.
Fast Mail Line between Chicago, Milwaukee, St. Paul and Minneapolis.
Transcontinental Route between Chicago, Council Bluffs and Omaha, or St. Paul.
Great National Route between Chicago, Kansas City and St. Joseph, Mo.
5,700 miles of road in Illinois, Wisconsin, Minnesota, Iowa, Missouri, South and North Dakota.
Everything First-Class.
First-Class People patronize First-Class Lines.
Ticket Agents everywhere sell Tickets over the Chicago, Milwaukee and St. Paul Railway.

W. T. ALLEN,
Pacific Coast Passenger Agent
Office, No 138 Montgomery St., San Francisco, Cal.
Under Occidental Hotel.

6 DONTS

DON'T own a racehorse.
DON'T be a breeder.
DON'T be a trainer.
DON'T be a jockey.
DON'T bet on the races.
DON'T go to a race track.
WITHOUT
HAVING IN YOUR POCKET ONE OF

Goodwin's
ANNUAL
OFFICIAL TURF GUIDES.

Price, in cloth $2.00
Price, in half morocco 3.00
Price, in half calf 4.00
If sent by mail .... 10 Cents extra

SUBSCRIBE TO IT FOR 1890.

It is published semi-monthly during the racing season, and is but $10 per year. Address

GOODWIN BROS.,
241 Broadway, New York City.

OUR IMPROVED. ALL SIZES FOR WEIGHTS. G.W. BOHANON. ESTAB. 1866.

THE BOHANON
SULKY!
BEST MADE.
Perfect Riding Buggies.
Breaking Carts.
Fine Repairing. Reasonable Prices.

Bohanon Carriage Co., 161-168 Ogden Ave., CHICAGO.
Send for Catalogue.

TAKE SIMMONS LIVER REGULATOR

FOR HORSES, DOGS AND CATTLE.

Simmons Liver Regulator, a strictly vegetable compound and general Condition Powder, is

A SAFE AND SURE REMEDY FOR

COLIC,
GRUBS,
LUNG FEVER,
HIDE-BOUND.

No Stable or Kennel should be without it: it gives new life to a lazy or drooping horse, and is a positive preventive and cure for Distemper or Mange in Dogs.

J. H. ZEILIN & CO.,
Proprietors, Philadelphia, Pa

HORSE OWNERS!

TRY GOMBAULT'S

CAUSTIC BALSAM.

A Safe, Speedy and Positive Cure for Curb, Splint, Sweeny, Capped Hock, Strained Tendons, Founder, Wind Puffs, all Skin Diseases or Parasites, Thrush, Diphtheria, Pinkeye, all Lameness from Spavin, Ringbone or other Bony Tumors. Removes all Bunches or Blemishes from Horses and Cattle.
Supersedes all Cautery or Firing.
Impossible to Produce any Scar or Blemish.

Every bottle sold is warranted to give satisfaction. Price $1.50 per bottle. Sold by druggists, or sent by express, charges paid, with full directions for its use. Send for descriptive circulars. Address LAWRENCE, WILLIAMS & CO., Cleveland, O.

BROU'S INJECTION

A PERMANENT CURE in from 3 to 6 days, of the most obstinate cases; guaranteed not to produce Stricture; no sickening doses; and no inconvenience or loss of time. Recommended by physicians and sold by all druggists. J. Ferré, (successor to Brou), Pharmacien, Paris.

For any Kind of a

SORE THROAT

USE

McCLELLAN'S

DIPHTHERIA REMEDY

An Unfailing Cure.
FOR SALE BY ALL DRUGGISTS

R. LIDDLE & SON

538 Washington St., S. F.,

Wholesale and Retail Dealers in

Guns, Rifles and Pistols.

A Full Line of FISHING TACKLE and SPORTSMAN'S GOODS.

Orders by mail receive prompt attention.

SELBY STANDARD THE BEST IS THE CHEAPEST "STANDARD" SHOTGUN CARTRIDGES

By-Laws

—AND—

Rules and Regulations

—OF THE—

NATIONAL

Trotting Association

ALSO THE

AMERICAN

Trotting Association,

AND THE

PACIFIC COAST BLOOD-HORSE ASSOCIATION.

With Betting Rules.

For Sale at the Office of the

Breeder and Sportsman,

313 Bush St., S. F., Cal.

Price, 25c. each.
By Mail, Postage Paid, 30c. each.

VETERINARY.

Dr. Wm. H. Jones, M.R.C.V.S.

Veterinary Surgeon,

(OLYMPIC CLUB STABLES)

503 Sutter Street, San Francisco.

Telephone, No 1404.

Consultations by letter, and cases of URGENT NECESSITY in the interior will receive prompt attention.

Dr. A. E. BUZARD,

VETERINARY SURGEON,

Member of the Royal College of Veterinary Surgeons, London, England. Graduated April 22d, 1870.

All Operations on the Horse Performed Skillfully.

Special attention given to the Diseases of Dogs. Calls to the country promptly attended to. Advice and prescriptions by mail $2. Office and Residence, No. 11 Seventh street, S. F. (opp. Odd Fellows Hall. Telephone No. 3 69.

W. H. WOODRUFF.

Veterinary Dentist,

AT FASHION STABLES,

221 Ellis Street, San Francisco

Improved Instruments, Humane Methods, First-Class Work.

H. E. CARPENTER,

Veterinary Surgeon,

Graduate of Ontario Veterinary College, Toronto Canada.

RESIDENCE AND VETERINARY INFIRMARY
331 Golden Gate Ave., San Francisco.
Telephone 3069.
OPEN DAY AND NIGHT.

No risk in throwing Horses. Veterinary Operating Table on the premises.

DR. C. MASOERO,

Veterinary Surgeon,

Successor to DR. A. DeTAVEL,

GRADUATE OF ROYAL VETERINARY COLLEGE, TURIN.

OFFICE AND INFIRMARY

No. 811 HOWARD STREET.

Between Fourth and Fifth. SAN FRANCISCO

Telephone, No 457.

R. WATKINS,

Veterinary Dentist,

Office at C. S. Crittendens' Golden Gate Livery and Riding Academy 24 to 28 Golden Gate Avenue.

Refers to Palo Alto Stock Farm: Wm. Corbett, San Mateo Stock Farm: B. C. Holly, Vallejo, and others. Examination Free

E. J. O'ROUKE.

I have the honor to announce to my old patrons and the general public that I may be found at my old stand, where, as heretofore, the

shoeing of Horses,

whether for the Track, Drive, or for general work, will receive my personal attention.

Telephone 2011.

E. J. O'ROUKE,
209 Ellis Street

ST. JULIEN

Horse Shoeing

SHOP,

126 Geary Street, S. F.

MARTIN O'DEA, - - PROPRIETOR.

California Horse Shoe Co's

STEEL SHOE
Light, Strong and Perfect.
Superior to all others for Speed Horses.
ALSO
The Celebrated
GOODENOUGH
Pattern Shoe.
OFFICE:
202 Market St.,
San Francisco, Cal.

I have used in my business the Steel and Iron Shoes made by the above Company, and take great pleasure in saying they are the best I have ever used in twenty-two years' practice. I have never seen anything like the STEEL SHOE made by this Company. I can fully recommend them to every practical Horseshoer in the Country. Yours respectfully,

No. 8 Everett Street. JOHN GRACE.

Fine Hats,

Latest Styles and Colors.

Meussdorffer & Hubner

8 Kearny Street, San Francisco.

Next to New Chronicle Building.

Everything for Trotter or Runner,

At J. A. McKERRON'S,

228, 230 and 232 Ellis St., San Francisco

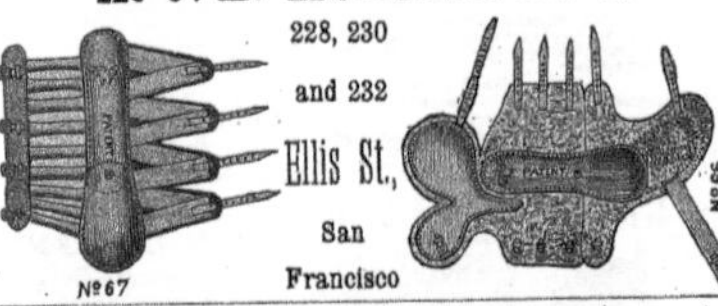

J. O'KANE, Horse Boots, Clothing and Furnishings, For Track, Driving Training and Stable. Every requisite for Horsemen. **Harness, Medicines,** Etc.

The PARKER Hammerless Shot Gun.

At the Annual Tournament of 1889, held at Cannes, France, the grand prize, consisting of 2000 Francs and a Valuable Cup was won by The Parker Hammerless.

The first Parker Hammerless Gun made won the championship of America at Decatur Illinois.

SEND FOR ILLUSTRATED CIRCULAR.

PARKER BROS., Makers,

New York Salesroom, 97 Chambers St. Meriden Conn.

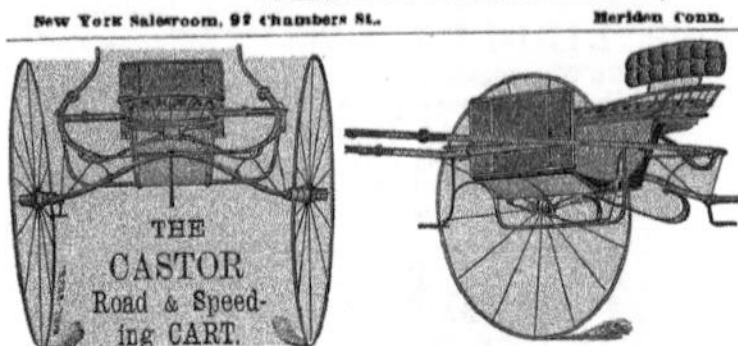

ALWAYS GIVES SATISFACTION.

Combining perfect riding qualities, proportions and balance, with genteel appearance.

No Vehicle exhibits a horse to better advantage, and no Cart approaches them for speeding or training purposes.

A stylish vehicle for exercising or pleasure driving, at one-fourth the cost of a carriage. Have none of the horse jockey or objectionable features of other Road Carts.

They are the Leading Cart wherever introduced, and are in use by the most prominent breeders and pleasure drivers everywhere.

Elegant Shifting Top Carts.

Perfectly Balanced Stylish Pole Carts.

For Illustrated Catalogue, with Prices, address,

LEWIS F. CASTOR,

Frankford, Philadelphia, Pa.

JOHN SPLAN, General Agent.

keeps horses healthy, promotes digestion, fattens horses, loosens the hide, assists the appetite, prevents leg swelling, strengthens the kidneys, regulates the bowels and destroys worms. $7.50 per 100 lbs. Ask your dealer for it or send to

MANHATTAN FOOD CO., 206 Clay St., S. F.

The Brunswick Balke Collender Co.

MANUFACTURERS OF

Standard Billiard and Pool Tables, Saloon and Bank Fixtures,

653--655 Market Street, San Francisco, Cal.

Brothers of the Angle,

Our NEW EIGHT-STRIP SPLIT BAMBOO is the "King" of all fishing-rods. Chubb's New Catalogue for 1890 is now ready. In addition to a complete list of anglers' supplies, it contains articles from the pens of Dr. James A. Henshall, Petronella, W. H. Murray, Geo. B. Goff, Norman, Brother Gardner, and others.

These papers are by the best writers on angling subjects, and are very interesting.

Send 25 cents, and receive Catalogue, post-paid. This amount will be deducted from first order (if accompanied with Coupon in book) for one dollar's worth or more of our goods.

Address

THOS. H. CHUBB.

Fishing-Rod Manufacturer,

POST MILLS, VT.

Please mention BREEDER AND SPORTSMAN.

The Automatic Reel.

Advantages:

It will wind up the line a hundred times as fast as any other reel in the world. It will wind up the line slowly if the angler chooses. No fish can ever get slack line with it. It will save more fish than any other reel. It will prevent tips, lines and snells from being broken by large fish. The reel is manipulated entirely by the hand that holds the rod. It enables the angler, and makes it desirable, to use lighter tackle.

Send for Circular, and mention Breeder and Sportsman.

E. T. ALLEN,

AGENT FOR PACIFIC COAST.

416 Market Street, - - - San Francisco, Cal.

SHAW CARTS and SULKIES

For light road or track use, manufactured from the best selected material. Combines lightness with elegance and ease to riders. Weights 70 to 100 lbs. Used by the best horsemen on this coast. Inspection invited.

ONE CAFFREY SULKY FOR SALE AT A BARGAIN.

CARRIAGES & Light VEHICLES

Manufactured to Order and Kept on Hand.

W. E. SHAW,

1621 MARKET STREET, SAN FRANCISCO, CAL.

REPAIRING DONE—ALL WORK WARRANTED.

Studebaker Bros. Manufact'g Co.

Sole Agents for

FRAZIER

(OF CHICAGO)

Carts

AND

Sulkies,

201--203 Market Street,

SAN FRANCISCO, CAL.

BOYCE TABLETS.

Leg and Body Wash.

THE BOYCE TABLETS are packed in a nicely decorated metal box with hinged lid—one hundred tablets in each box; directions for use plainly engraved upon the box: therefore, the convenience of the package—no liability to leakage and breakage—economy and ready solubility, together with the absolute certainty of their action, will at once commend the use of BOYCE'S TABLETS to the intelligent horsemen of the country. TABLETS sufficient to make one hundred pints of leg and body wash are conveniently carried in an inside coat pocket or in the hip-pocket of the trousers.

The BOYCE WASH can be applied ALL OVER THE BODY WITHOUT FEAR OF BLISTERING NOR DOES IT AFFECT THE KIDNEYS.

The BOYCE WASH will cure CRACKED HEELS, PUFFS, STOCKINGS, SCRATCHES, INFLAMED TENDONS and FEVERED LEGS.

Price per Box of One Hundred Tablets, $2, sent postpaid to any part of the United States, six boxes for $10. A sample of BOYCE'S TABLETS will be mailed to any address on application. These TABLETS are warranted to keep in any climate. Address

BOYCE TABLET COMPANY,

600 Wabash Avenue, - - - Terre Haute, Indiana.

J. A. McKERRON, Pacific Coast Ag't,

228-230-232 Ellis Street, San Francisco, Cal.

TWENTY-FOUR PAGES.

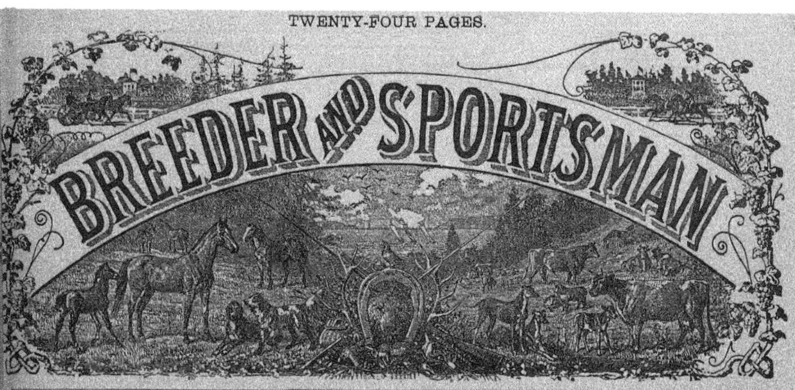

Vol. XVI. No. 20.
No. 313 BUSH STREET.

SAN FRANCISCO, SATURDAY, MAY 17, 1890.

SUBSCRIPTION
FIVE DOLLARS A YEAR.

Our Tennessee Letter.

GALLATIN, TENN., May 4th.

BREEDER AND SPORTSMAN:—The Nashville meeting closed yesterday afternoon after seven days of excellent racing. The opening day was one of the worst imaginable, it having rained several days previous, and that morning it seemed as if some one had turned on the Atlantic Ocean from some place above. The Two Thousand was the race of the day and while it was run on a track ankle deep in mud, it was a splendid race, run in good time, and a good horse won. Robespeirre was a 6 to 5 favorite, and he won almost as he pleased Prince Fonso, a grand horse, gave him a brush in the stretch, but Bob Francis gave the distinguished Frenchman his head and he came away from his field as though they were tied to the furlong pole.

The mud did not suit Prince Fonso, and I hardly think the best horse won. Then, too, Robespeirre had had a race this Spring, and he was much more seasoned. Blarneystone seemed to wear a dark and stubborn coat, and, I hardly believe he was as good as when he ran at Memphis. I think he likes a long distance, and at a mile and a quarter, or a mile and a half he would be a cracker.

E. S. Gardner is having a great run of luck this spring with his Avondale Stables. He has eight head in training now, and his two-year-olds, Ida Pickwick, Monte Rosa and Kaiuna, are about the best trio of youngsters to be found in any of the Western stables. Ida Pickwick had two stakes to her credit at the Nashville, one of which she won carrying 118 pounds. She is by imported Mr. Pickwick—Ida K by King Alfonso. At the Kennesaw sale at Nashville last week, Mr. Gardner purchased the yearling half sister to Monte Rosa for $2200. The yearling is by Mr. Reed's stallion Forester, a son of The Ill-Used, and looks like she could give her half sister weight and a beating now.

The Belle Meade sale will go into history as the biggest sale of thoroughbred horses ever held in this country. It was truly a pleasure to watch the bidding when a choice youngster was led into the ring, or when Great Tom or Bonnie Scotland broodmare was brought under the auctioneer's notice. All was excitement when the stallions were put under the hammer. When Captain Kidd had told the record of Luke Blackburn and Iroquois, and when he had asked, "What am I offered to start this great horse?" everything was as still as death. But not for long, as soon there were bids from almost every seat that surrounded the ring, and the bidding was kept up until Gen. Jackson was forced to pay respectively $20,000 and $34,000 for Luke Blackburn and Iroquois, the latter being the highest price a thoroughbred ever sold for in America. When Captain Kidd wielded his gavel and said, "Luke Blackburn goes to Gen. Jackson for $20,000, old Uncle Bob, the colored character at Belle Meade broke forth with three cheers for Tennessee! Luke has always been Uncle Bob's favorite pet at Belle Meade. The crowd responded with cheers, and Blackburn, with his head erect and ears pricked back, standing before a representative gathering of America's great turfmen, seemed possessed of a dignity that was equal to the occasion, and as he stood in that position many an old turfman's thoughts wandered back to the season of 1880, when the gallant son of hardy old Bonnie Scotland and Jimmy McLaughlin took the field and swept everything before them. I too, had happy thoughts of days gone by, and July 3, 1880, quickly came back into my mind, for was it not on that day that I saw Luke Blackburn lead the great Duke of Montrose and Harold to the win in the Ocean Stakes at Long Branch! I felt like throwing up my hat as I did on that day in doing honor to the greatest horse upon the continent. It was a great day for Tennessee, and thanks to Gen. Jackson for keeping him within the bounds of his native State.

One of the best jockeys now sporting silk in the West is Bob Francis, and he is a young fellow that surely deserves success. This year he is riding for George Hawkin's Chicago Stable, and his work in the saddle can not be criticised. On Thursday he rode four of the five winners at Nashville, and had he not gotten off very badly in the last race he would have most likely landed the winners of the entire programme. It was surely Francis' day, and those who follow his mounts made quite a killing

The sale on the opening day of the meeting at Nashville was largely attended, and with but few instances, I believe the prices realized were satisfactory. Several of the youngsters by Blazes were sold at a sacrifice, I might say, and Mr. Shafer tells me he will never offer another yearling of his for sale at that place. Auctioneer, Wm. Easton was a large purchaser at the sale, and I am inclined to think he will sell his purchases in New York some time later in the season. If he does they will bring double the amount he paid for any of them, which would make the New York market be in demand next season. Horses will bring as much here in Tennessee as they will any where, but breeders and salesmen, you cannot sell your colts unless you advertise your sales. A sale in Tennessee judiciously advertised would draw as many buyers as would the same sale in New York, or any other place, and when you get buyers upon the ground the horses are going to bring good prices. Suppose this be tried next season. Catalogue and advertise your sales, and if you do not get good prices and plenty of buyers, there is nothing in actual experience.

A note from Major Campbell Brown tells me that he will hold his annual spring sale of trotting and pacing horses on May 28th, at Ewell Farm, Spring Hill, Tenn. Major Brown is the pioneer breeder of Tennessee, and the crack trotters and pacers that have left Ewell Farm in the last few years are legion. The stallions at Ewell Farm are Brown Hal (pacer) 2:12½, Talisman, (pacer) Tennessee Wilkes (trial 2:25) by George Wilkes, and McEwen 2:18½, the champion four-year-old race stallion. This is a quartette of trotting and pacing stallions that is hard to beat, and as all mares at Ewell Farm are of the most approved strains, the public will have an opportunity to secure something phenomenal at the coming sale.

I saw Riley, Ed Corrigan's Derby candidate, a few days ago. He is now pretty high in flesh, looks very lusty, and has the build of a great race horse. He does not move along with that free and easy action that denotes health, and I fear his illness at Memphis was of a more serious nature than reported. He was entered in the Two Thousand at Nashville, but the morning of the race Mr. Corrigan decided not to start him, as the track was a sea of mud, and was not suggestive of doing an ailing horse any good. Jake Saunders Riley's stable companion, is a much better looking colt now than the latter, and he strikes me as having more speed than the Kentucky Derby favorite. I did not see Riley extended, but a trainer who has had his eye on the colt for sometime, tells me that he has lost that great burst of speed which he possessed last fall.

And this reminds me of El Rio Rey, who many say is a great "roarer," and of whom much has been written lately. I took a look at him a few mornings ago, and, while he was not moving, I could not see anything indicative to his having turned short-winded, or a roarer. He carries a good deal of surplus flesh just now, but I presume that Courtney will strip him of this before he comes to the post. All the horses in the El Arrayo stable are high in flesh, and those that have started at Nashville have not shown up very well. Joe Courtney ran on the opening day, as did the two-year-olds Average and Oletia, the latter finishing last, while Courtney was no better than third. Average is a smart looking youngster, and will do well later up the line. Don Jose is reported as being ailing, and as far as I can learn, his illness is nothing serious.

I have seen Proctor Knott taking his work several times during the last few weeks, and, no doubt, but what many will be surprised to hear that the big gelding is all right. His limbs are as smooth as a yearlings, and there is absolutely nothing to make one believe he is not sound on his pins. He is in even better condition now then when I saw him run at Nashville and in the Derby last year, and just what right any one has to say that he is mercifully broken down, I cannot tell. He will not come to the post before about the middle of June, when he will start in the Suburban Handicap. His price in that race now stands at 20 to 1, while I notice many books—very wisely so—are holding him out entirely. When he starts, look out for him, and if nothing goes wrong with him, he will take a world of beating in the Suburban.

Maori, another Suburban candidate, will do to watch. She ran a good race at Memphis, and did a fast second to Robespeirre at Nashville. Last Tuesday, in the Duncan Hotel Stakes, and on a heavy track, she ran Robespeirre to a short heat in 1:43. The race was at a mile, and considering the difference in the days and conditions of the two tracks, her race for the Duncan Hotel Stakes was a much better performance than when she led Little Minch, Laura Davidson and Alaho from wire to wire at Washington Park (Chicago), last summer in 1:39 4-5. She is owned by Nick Finzer, the Kentucky turfman, who has great faith in her chances to capture the Suburban, and if she is in condition when that race is run she will be a certain starter. If she is ridden properly in that race, and is fit, she will be dangerous. She has a wonderful burst of speed, and I would not be surprised to see her fighting out the finish with such good ones as Raceland, Knott, Salvator and others of that ilk.

English Lady and Dollikins, two suburban candidates and stable companions of Proctor Knott, are hardly suggestive of being by that class of horses that win the big handicaps. The latter was a winner at Memphis, and while both fillies are very speedy, I am not inclined to think Scoggans will start either if they start Proctor Knott.

Mr. H. C. Shafer of this place tells me that he is negotiating with B. J. Johnson anent the forming of a partnership for the purpose of breeding thoroughbreds. Mr. Shafer now owns that good stallion Blazes, sire of Barney, Gray Rock and Kitty Cheathan, and besides the large number of mares now upon his farm, they will import about twenty-five from England. B. J. Johnson trained the Chicago Stable horses last season, and as he and Mr. Shafer are experienced horsemen, they will only buy the best. I suppose it will be necessary for them to buy another stallion, as it would be taxing the physical powers of one stallion too much to have him serve so many mares. It was currently reported a few months since that Johnson owned the horse Once Again by Onondaga—Black Maria, and if he does it is probable that he will be returned to the new stud. He was a good racehorse, and with his breeding he should be a success in the stud.

Farmer Jere Baxter, now a prominent candidate for Gubernatorial honors in Tennessee, holds his annual sale of trotting horses and Jersey cattle on May 15th. He has a fine collection of trotters catalogued for his sale, and they should realize good prices. His farm, Maplewood, is one of the finest and best arranged stock farms in Tennessee.

KENNESAW.

By reference to our Australian letters it will be seen that Mr. Merry has purchased some exceedingly good brood mares for L. J. Rose, and they will come to California by the next steamer. The breeding of all the mares is of the best, several of them being closely related to the best of the race horses now in training in Oceanica. It is to be regretted that E. J. Baldwin did not give Mr. Merry a commission to purchase a stallion, as there is one badly needed at Santa Anita as an outcross for the fine mares now at that breeding farm.

TWO AUSTRALIAN LETTERS.

The Mighty Carbine—A Great Sale—What Mr. Merry Has Purchased.

CONNOR WANTS THE CHAMPIONSHIP—DEATH OF BARNEY THOMPSON.

SYDNEY, N. S. Wales, April 16, 1889.

EDITOR BREEDER AND SPORTSMAN:—The Hon. James White, having decided to give racing a spell for a couple of seasons, his horses in training were, on the 11th instant, brought under the hammer. The prices in many cases must have proved beyond Mr. White's most sanguine expectations, for good horses as many of them undoubtedly are, they would not have brought such prices had they come out of any other stable. The top price was given for a gelding named Titan, which fell for the fabulous price of 4,600 guineas, to Mr. E. G. Brodribb. Mr. Brodribb is the son of a well known New South Wales squatter, deceased, and in addition to squatting interests, the son made a pile out of the Broken Hill Silver Mines. Mr. Brodribb, however, will want all he has made at the silver mines, to keep up the pace he has started with, he being a veritable Colonial Jubilee Juggins. He went down heavily over Moorbank, about which I spoke in a previous letter, and at the recent A. J. C. Autumn meeting, the writer heard him offer to lay a big Colonial owner and bookmaker £5,000 to £1,000 on Carbine in one of the races afterwards won by the Moari giant.

To a man of Mr. Brodribb's betting proclivities, the sum of 4,600 guineas is not so enormous when it is taken into consideration it gives him command over the wonderfully speedy two-year-old, who has his two Derbeys, New South Wales and Melbourne before him. However, I did not think there was another man in the Colonials who would give a bona fide bid of anything near the price, and I cannot but surmise that the Broken Hill plunger was "run" up to the price he gave. Titan is by Mr. White's favorite sire Chester from Tempe.

The next best in price was a two-year-old filly by Martini-Henry from Phillina, named Prelude, which brought $2,750 guineas. The colt Dreadnought by Chester—Trafalgar, three years, is a good animal undoubtedly, and fell to the nod of Lord Kesteven, who is now on a visit to the Colonials, for 2,100 guineas. so the colt may yet run on English turf.

A bay colt by Martini Henry—Malacca, named Singapore, brought 2,000 guineas. altogether beyond his value as a racer, whatever he may ultimately do at the stud. The next best price was 1,550 guineas for a filly called Litigant, and then the prices tailed off from 820 to 100 guineas, the thirteen horses sold, amongst them being seven geldings, making the handsome total of 16,765 guineas. The following is the full list and prices obtained:

Ch g Sinecure by Martini-Henry—The Solent (imp.) by Favonius—Lady Newby, 3 years; Mr. C. M. Lloyd, 700 guineas.

Ch c Dreadnought by Chester—Trafalgar (imp.) by Blair Athol—Mosquito, 3 years—Lord Kesteven, 2,100 guineas.

B c Singapore by Martini-Henry—Malacca (imp.) by King of the Forest—Catinka, 3 years—Mr. M. O'Shanassy, 2,000 guineas.

Br g Rudolph by Martini-Henry—Rusk (imp.) by Brown Bread—Lady Sophia, 3 years; Mr. W. R. Wilson, 820 guineas.

B g Tribune by Martini-Henry—Wheel of Fortune by Goldsbrough—Brown Duchess, 3 years; Mr. L. Oakley, 100 guineas.

Ch g Titan by Chester—Tempe, by Somnus (imp.)—White and Blue (imp.), 2 years; Mr. E. G. Brodribb, 4,600 guineas.

Ch g Marco by Martini-Henry—Melania, by The Marquis (imp.)—Art Union, 2 years; Mr. A. Johnston, 625 guineas.

Br g Carlist by Chester—Copra, by Robinson Crusoe—Cocoanut (imp.) 2 years; Hon. H. C. Dangar, 550 guineas.

Ch g Denman by Chester—Goldfinch by Kingston (imp.)—Daughter of Little John, 3 years; Mr. J. Woods, 250 guineas.

B f Prelude by Martini Henry—Phillina (imp.) by Bonnyfield—Menandrea, 2 years; Mr. V. J. Dowling, 2,750 guineas.

Br f Ultimate by Martini-Henry—Ultima, by Yattenden—Remnant, 2 years; Mr. T. Sanders, 220 guineas.

B f Utter by Martini-Henry—Uralla, by Chester—Moonstone, 2 years; Mr. H. Oxenham, 500 guineas.

B f Litigant by Martini-Henry—Leonie, by Yattendon—Thyra, 2 years—Mr. C. M. Lloyd, 1,550 guineas.

At the Australian Jockey Club Autumn Meeting, held at Randwick on April 5th, 7th, 10th and 12th, the Hon. D. S. Wallace's four-year-old Carbine by the defunct Musket, from Mersey, proved the hero of the four days, winning the autumn stakes, 1½ miles, the Sydney Cup, 2 miles, the all aged stakes, 1 mile, the A. J. C. Plate, 3 miles, and the Cumberland Stakes, 2 miles. The principal horses he had to beat were Melos, owned by Mr. William Gannon, and the then Hon. Jas. White's Dreadnought. On the first day Titan beat the Hon. D. S. Wallace's filly Wilga, without an effort for the A. J. C. Sire's Produce Stakes, 7 furlongs, but later on in the meeting, when the pair met on the Champagne Stakes, 6 furlongs, the tables were turned, owing to a mistake of judgment by the crack jockey Hales, who allowed Wilga to get too big a lead, and he was unable to bring Titan within more than half a length of the filly at the finish, greatly to the chagrin of the backers of the gelding, on whom they had laid 7 to 2. And it is at a juncture of this sort that a clean reputation stands to owner and rider, for what in the clean potato is looked upon as an error of judgment in the doubtful spud is at once jumped at by the crowd as a "cross." In a former letter I planked in favor of Titan for the Doncaster Handicap, but he was scratched, and the winner turned up in a horse of more interest to you people across the Herring Pond—Sir William, the colt by your Sir Modred from Vesper, who won with 8 stone 6 lb., the second highest weight, from a really good field. Sir Modred still further distinguished himself as a sire on the last day with Antaeus, a colt from Millie, who won the Rous Handicap, 1 mile, 3 furlongs, with 8 st. 7 lb., beating amongst others the speedy gelding Rudolph, 8st. 5lb., who the day before had brought at the White sale 820 guineas. You may remember my speaking of a very fractious colt called Daniel, owned by the Hon. W. A. Long, saying that he would one day be in the humor and run like a racehorse. Well, my remarks were verified on the third day of the meeting, when he won the Welter Handicap, 1½ miles, from rather a large field, with 7st 9lb. in the saddle.

Since Abercorn's breakdown the people out here have "turned up" their old idol and gone in "bald headed" for Carbine as "the best horse Australasia ever saw." I am not altogether of the same way of thinking, and both fit and well would pin my faith to my old horse Abercorn. Carbine certainly has the best showing on paper, as the following tables attest:

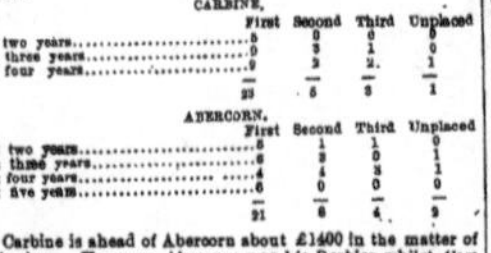

CARBINE.

	First	Second	Third	Unplaced
At two years	5	0	0	0
At three years	9	3	1	0
At four years	9	2	2	1
	23	5	3	1

ABERCORN.

	First	Second	Third	Unplaced
At two years	5	1	1	0
At three years	6	3	0	1
At four years	4	4	3	1
At five years	6	0	0	0
	21	8	4	2

Carbine is ahead of Abercorn about £1400 in the matter of winnings. However, Abercorn won his Derbies whilst Carbine failed in the attempt, and whilst Carbine took 3 minutes 37 seconds to run his two miles in the Sydney Cup on a fine day and a firm course, Abercorn won the Metropolitan Stakes on a heavy course in 3:33, under which circumstances I am loth to transfer my allegiance from Mr. White's erstwhile crack.

Jack Thompson, a very popular Sydney bookmaker, brother to Joe and Barney Thompson, who are now in London and likely shortly to try their luck in America, died in Sydney last week. Poor Jack went through the American war, and many an idle but pleasant hour have I passed listening to yarns of his experiences, both humorous and pathetic. He was at one time in a partnership with the English fighter Jem Mace in Melbourne, and Mace made a very scientific fighter of Thompson, who stood some six feet two in height. Thompson's only fight in the ring, if I recollect aright, was with Christie, a big lump of a man, a Victorian detective and a fair sculler, in addition to his bruising proclivities, whom Thompson defeated in a round. "THE JUNGLE."

Another Letter from the Antipodes.

EDITOR OF THE BREEDER AND SPORTSMAN.—I send by this mail the papers which contain accounts of our autumn race meeting just over.

You will note that the only Sir Modred colts we have running down here were both returned as witness, viz., Sir William, 3 years, in the Doncaster Handicap of 1,000 sovs. 1 mile with 118 lbs. on his back; 29 starters, the distance being covered in 1 03½, which was fast, considering the big field and heavy going. He is a muscular brown colt, short in the back, strong loined, with hind legs well under him, and stands over very little ground. Without being actually first class, he is both fast and constant. Antaeus, the other representative of your handsome exile, is a much longer horse, with unusually powerful thighs, and it is thought by good judges down here that if he had not gone through such a severe preparation as a young three-year-old, for the Melbourne Cup, he would have developed into a much finer horse. He appropriated a race on the last day of the meeting, after a slashing set to and under a big weight, and with a spell may prove a dangerous horse in our next Melbourne Cup in November next, when the rich stake of $10,000 will be run for.

The hero of the meeting of this occasion, however, was the gallant son of the defunct "Musket," "Carbine," who won every race he started for (5) at the meeting, including the Sydney Cup of 1,500 sovs, 2 miles (a handicap), carrying the steadier of 9 s. 9 lbs. He is undoubtedly the most brilliant horse we have ever seen in the colonies, and his great pace enables him to make every post a winning post from 4 furlongs to 3 miles.

His breeding is worth the study by your stud men, and reads by Musket (imp.) from. The Mersey (imp.) by Knowsley, from Clemence by Newminster, from Eulogy by Euclid, from Martha Linn the dam of Voltigeur. Musket is by Toxophilite from a daughter of West Australian from Brown Bess by Camel. Knowsley is by Stokwell from daughter of Maudo from Brown Bess by Camel.

This is one of a large number of pedigees of phenomenal horses put together in the same fashion, and it confirms what we have long extended for, viz, that one of the conditions of success lies in mating strongly the blood of the second and third dam of your sire. A glance at the pedigee of Barcaldine will reveal a similar niching of these elements I cannot call to mind others, but that wonderful sprinter Peter, if I mistake not, is another instance, though the nick of Belchazzer is further away. In each of these three cases it will be remarked that the return is to Blacklock a strain of blood that to my mind responds more powerfully at long distances than any other in the stud book.

Up to the present O'Conner has been unable to get a match on with any of our scullers who are all so busy matching one another to find the best man, that he will probably have to cool his heels for some months to come. It is partly his own fault, as I am told he will only pull for the championship of the world, and as none of our men except Kemp (who is probably our third best man) have any fair claim to hold it, it would be nothing more than a farce to seriously make any such match.

While we all regret the situation, it is impossible to help it, and if he is in real earnest he can get plenty of off matches to fill in the time and aclimatize himself.

I have had many pleasant visits from your old friend Thos. B. Merry, Esq. He came amongst us in a very quiet, unostentations manner and really before I knew it he had secured from me two of my best mares. He has also purchased five or six others from other gentleman and I learn that he is negotiating for our Melbourne cup winner, Dunlop. As near as I can learn, Mr. Merry has bought the following:

Bay mare Lady Alice by Musket, dam Eryeen by Sledmere and therefore own sister to Mitralleuse; this mare is six years old.

The brown mare Ricochet, five years old, sister to the above.

Chestnut mare Hester by Derby, son of Kingsborough, six years old. This mare carried 142 pounds and run second for the Murimbidgee Handicap; she is 15½ and puts me very much in mind of Mr. Haggin's Firenzi.

Chestnut mare Elsie by Grand Flaneur, dam Daughter of the Regiment. Her second dam being the dam of Melos which gives her a double cross of Yattendon, the sire of Chester.

Bay mare Phoebe Marks by Kingsborough, dam Lady Audley, (dam of The Secret). She is 16 hands high and has been trained. She is now in foal to Othello, son of The Barb and is the only one of the mares, so I understand, which Mr. Merry has bought that will foal to the Australian dates.

Brown mare Princess Royal by Goldsborough, dam Queen's Head by Yattendon. I heard Mr. Peyton, trainer for the Hon. Jas. White, say that Mr. Merry had secured two of the best mares in Australia when he bought Princess Royal and Phoebe Marks.

Chestnut mare Montalto by Neckersgat, dam Romola (dam of Menotti and other good ones) This is a very grand mare and as a two-year-old was very speedy but the handicapper made her carry such terrific weights that she was usually beaten before she started.

Mr. Merry is at present negotiating for Laughter, a brown filly, sister to Sweet Anchor, being by St. Albans out of Queen Mary. This filly is at present in training and shows considerable speed. Her owner asks four hundred guineas for her, but Mr. Merry, like all you Americans, is trying to beat him down in price. Laughter is 15½ hands and very heavy bodied. It is altogether likely that if she should be bought by the Californian that she will not be bred but reserved for racing purposes in your country. Yours,

CENTAUR.

American Trotting Association.

CHICAGO, Ill., May 6, 1890.

The Board of Appeals of the American Trotting Association met at the Sherman House pursuant to call with the following members present:

Chas. Green, St. Louis, Mo., Chairman; D. C Beaman, Denver, Col.; W. P. Ijams, Terre Haute, Indiana; C. L. Benjamin, Saginaw, Michigan; G. B. McFall, Oskaloosa, Iowa; John Farley, Toledo, Ohio: J. H. Steiner, Detroit, Mich., Secretary.

The Secretary submitted the following causes which were disposed of, as noted:

No. 229.
American Trotting Association, vs. Wm. G. Cody, Watertown, Wis., and the b g Silverton, alias Farmer Boy. | For fraudulent entry and performance at Marinette, Wis., in the 2:36 Class, May 18, 1889.

It was conclusively proved that the horse entered by said Wm. G. Cody as Farmer Boy was the b g Silverton, by Blue Bull, 2:20½.

Ordered: That Wm G. Cody, Watertown, Wis., and the b g Silverton alias Farmer Boy, be and are hereby expelled from the tracks of ll members of the American Trotting Association.

No. 258.
H. C. Beckwith, vs. Overland Park Club Ass'n, Denver, Colorado. | Appeal from decision of expulsion.

The appeal in above case having been heard and the decision of the judges of the race having been affirmed by the Board at its meeting, December 6, 1889, and the appellant having afterwards been temporarily reinstated by the President pending the action at its May meeting, 1890, and the appellant not having made an application for permanent reinstatemint or a rehearing of the case, and the temporary reinstatement having expired by its terms, it is

Ordered: That the action of the Board at its December meeting be and remain in full force and effect

No 263.
R. W. Sherman, Crete, Neb., vs. H. W. Brown, Fremont, Neb., | For falsely protesting the ch g Charles J. at Grand Island, Neb., Sept., 1889, in violation of rule 39

The evidence offered to the Board by the parties to the action was in direct conflict, and being of apparent equal value, it was held, that the case was not proved, and it was

Ordered: That the action against said H. W. Brown be dismissed.

No. 276.
The American Trotting Association. vs. Richard Roche, Seaforth, Ont., and the blk g Byron Cole, alias Black Bird. | An order for distribution of protested winnings in 2:30 Class at Port Huron, Mich., in October, 1889.

It was shown to the satisfaction of the Board that the horse entered as Black Bird was the blk g Byron Cole; but that Richard Roche had been imposed upon in the purchase of the horse, and had no knowledge of his identity.

Ordered: That the action against Richard Roche be dismissed, and that the protested winnings be redistributed under the rules.

No. 279.
F. H. Cory, Shelbyville, Ind. — Application for re-hearing.

Ordered: Continued.

No. 281.
Sire Bros., New York, N. Y., vs. St. Louis Jockey Club, St. Louis, Mo | Application for an order for return of entrance paid in 2:10 class, 1888.

It was shown that the entrance fee had been paid by the applicants, and that the 2:10 class was declared of on account of bad weather, and could not take place within a week of the meeting.

Ordered: Continued.

No. 277.
The American Trotting Association, vs. John A. F. Fletcher, Waverly, Ill., and ch g Tom Criswell, | Fraudulent entry and performance in the 3:00 class at Rushville, Illinois, August 20, 1889.

It was shown that the horse was entered out of his proper class, and that the defendent had full knowledge of the record of the horse, and it is

Ordered: That John A. Fletcher, Waverly, Ill., and the ch g Tom Criswell be and are hereby expelled from the tracks of all members of the American Trotting Association.

(Note—It is represented that the horse Tom Criswell is now dead, but not authenticated.)

No. 291.
F.N. Fancher, Jonesville, Mich., vs. Alex. Lewis, Salt Lake City, Utah Ter. | Application for order for unpaid premiums in 1888.

The defendant Alex Lewis was Lessee of the Jordan River Park, Salt Lake City, Utah Territory, in 1888, and offered premiums for various classes. The applicant makes affidavit that premiums won by him at said meeting have not been paid. Defendant denies the allegation, and asks for a continuance of the case on account of the late date of receiving notice of action and his inability to present evidence and attend the meeting.

Ordered.

No. 292.
Stanford Soverhil, Janesville, Wis., and b g Ben H. (pacer). | Application for relief from disqualification on account of suppressed time at Evansville, Wis., and Stoughton, Wis., in 1889, and return of $100 fine paid under protest.

It was shown that the b g Ben H. (pacer) had performed under suppressed time at the above named points, without any intentional fraud on the part of his owner or driver.

Ordered: That the disqualification of the horse, owner and driver be and is hereby removed, and that the application for return of the $100 fine for violation of the rules in performing under suppressed time be and is hereby refused.

No. 293.
Pueblo State Fair Association, Pueblo, Colo. | Application for removal of fine imposed by the judge of the race on J. Sandkuhl, Pueblo, Col., and br h Jack O'Hearts in May, 1889.

The Board of Directors of the member met and passed a resolution requesting the American Trotting Association to remove the penalty imposed by the judges of the race. No reason or cause was shown why the fine should be removed, and it is

Ordered: That the application be refused.

No. 294.
The American Trotting Association vs. W. E. Everhart; E. L Hart Maitland, Mo., and the b g Davy Crocket. | For fraudulently entering and performing in the 3:00 class at Shenandoah, Iowa, 1880, and failure to return unlawful winnings.

It was shown that the b g Davy Crocket obtained a record of 2:29¼ at Hiawatha, Kan., September 7, 1888. The evidence submitted shows that the horse was entered at Shenandoah, Iowa, in the 3:00 class in the name of E. L. Hart by said W. E. Everhart, without the knowledge or consent of said Hart; and that said Hart had no interest, absolute contingent, or otherwise, in the horse at the time of the entry, or at any time since.

Ordered: That the case against E. L. Hart, Maitland, Mo., be dismissed, and that W. E. Everhart, Maitland, Mo., and the b g Davy Crocket be and are hereby expelled from the tracks of all members of the American Trotting Association.

No. 295.

The American Trotting Association, vs. C. P. McClure and Philo Sweet, St. Cloud, Minn., and the b g Alkali,	An order for disposal of protested winnings in 2:30 Class, Hamline, Minn., Sept. 9, 1889, and $100 fine imposed.

Ordered: That the protest be overruled and the fine of $100 imposed be refunded to defendants.

No. 296.

John Fairley, Rushville, Ind., vs. Telford Dickerson and John H. Dickerson, Greensburg, Ind., and gr m Jenny B, and gr m Blanche Grant,	For fraudulently performing with two horses in the 2:35 Class in violation of Rule 36 at Cambridge City, Ind., Sept. 13, 1889.

It was shown that the gr m Jennie B and gr m Blanche Grant were both controlled and driven by Telford Dickerson at Rushville, Ind., on September 11, 1889; that on the 13th day of September the gr m Jenny B, entered by John Dickerson, and the gr m Blanche Grant entered by Telford Dickerson, started in the 2:35 class at Cambridge City, Indiana, and that John H. Dickerson drove the mare entered by Telford Dickerson, and Telford Dickerson drove the mare entered by John H. Dickerson, the gr m Jenny B winning third money in said race, and the gr m Blanche Grant winning second money in said race.

Ordered: That the said John H. Dickerson and the said Telford Dickerson be and are hereby ordered to return the winnings of said mares for redistribution under the rules, and that a fine of $50 be imposed upon them for violation of the rules; and that they, together with the horses, be and are hereby suspended until the fine is paid and the money returned to the American Trotting Association for redistribution under the rules.

No. 297.

The American Trotting Association vs. D. Hickman & Son, Reynoldsburg, Ohio, and the b h Brod Walnut.	For entering and performing in the 3:00 class at Columbus, O., Sept. 3, 1889, and failure to return unlawful winnings.

It was conclusively shown that the b h Brod Walnut obtained a record of 2:46¼ at Pataskala, Ohio, August 20, 1888. It was also shown that the defendants had knowledge of the record, the same being published in their catalogue for 1889. The defendants claim that the race at Columbus, O., was a made up race for named horses; but this is positively denied by the Secretary, who says the race was for horses with records not better than 3:00, without any conditions.

Ordered: That D. Hickman & Son, Reynoldsburg, O., and the b h Brod Walnut be suspended until the unlawful winnings ($150) are returned, and a fine of $100 is paid for entering and performing out of class.

No. 298.

The American Trotting Association and M. E. McHenry, Independence, Iowa, vs. Fred S. Shaft, St. Paul, Minn., and ch m French Girl.	Protested first money, $250, in the 2:27 class, Minneapolis, Minn., August 28, 1889.

Protest was filed against the ch m French Girl, starting in the above named class on account of not being entered in her proper and lawful name. It was shown to the satisfaction of the Board that the ch m French Girl had previously started at Langford, South Dakota, in May, 1889, under the name of Dolly, and that the defendant, Fred Shaft, was present when she so performed.

Ordered: That the protest be sustained and the money be redistributed under the rules. That the ch m French Girl be required to pay a recording fee of $50 for change of name, and be suspended until paid.

No. 299.

The American Trotting Association, vs. A. W. Mihills, Merrill, Wisconsin, and b g Harry Drake.	For entering and performing out of class at Merrill, Wis., Sept. 14, 1889, and failure to return $50 unlawful winnings.

It was shown that the b g Harry Drake obtained a record of 2:44 in September, 1887.

Held: That it was the business of the nominator to know the true record of his horse, before entering and starting him in a public race, and it is

Ordered: That A. W. Mihills, Merrill, Wisconsin, and the b g Harry Drake be fined $50, and be suspended until the same is paid, and the $50 unlawful winnings is returned to the American Trotting Association for redistribution under the rules.

No. 300.

The American Trotting Association, vs. Allen Crows, Charleston, Ill., and b g McFadden (pacer) alias Cloverleaf.	For fraudulent entry at Hilford, Illinois, Aug. 23, 1889.

It was shown that the defendant entered the b g McFadden (pacer) in the Free-for-all pace at Hilford, Illinois, Aug 23rd, 1889, under the name of Cloverleaf; that said horse McFadden was under suspension in the American Trotting Association for unlawful winnings at that time, and that said defendant Crows had knowledge of the true name of the horse, and directed his driver to enter him under a fictitious name.

Ordered: That the defendant Allen Crows, Charleston, Ill., and the b g McFadden, alias Cloverleaf, be and are hereby fined $100, and suspended until paid.

No. 301.

C. S. Corning, Peoria, Ill., and blk g Leslie vs. The Lake View Driving Park Association, Peoria, Ill., and the American Trotting Association.	Application for removal of fine of $100 paid under protest.

It was shown that the defendant started the blk g Leslie in the 2:45 trot at Peoria, Ill., September 17, 1889. That he filed a written protest against C. B. Allaire, acting as judge in said race on the ground that he did not believe he was fair or that his horse would receive justice at his hands. This protest seems to have been filed because the judges of the race set the blk g Leslie back from second to third place on account of gaining by a break. The protest was not sustained by the judges of the race, whereupon the protestant, C. S. Corning, withdrew his horse from the race without permission of the judges. It was also shown that Mr. Allaire retired from the stand during the consideration by the judges of the violation of the rules by protestant in withdrawing his horse without permission. The judges imposed a fine of $100 on protestant and his horse, and ordered both suspended until paid.

Held: That the judges of the race properly determined and imposed a penalty, and it is

Ordered: That the protest be over-ruled.

No. 302.

The American Trotting Association vs. Henry Stephenson, Emporia, Kan., and the gr g Billy Hasley, alias Gray Billy.	For return of unlawful winnings and change of name.

It was shown that the defendant purchased the gr g Billy Hasley alias Gray Billy, from O. G. Athey, Columbus, Kan., as a horse without a record and named Gray Billy, and started him over tracks of the American Trotting Association in slow classes under the name of Gray Billy. The true name of the horse was Billy Hasley, record 2:40½; that the defendant had no knowledge of the true name and record of the horse until after the campaign of 1889 was over, when he reported the facts to the Secretary of the American Trotting Association.

Ordered: That the defendant and the gr g Billy Hasley alias Gray Billy be suspended until his unlawful winning out of class on American tracks, and a recording fee of $50 for change of name is paid.

No. 303.

Frank McKean, Terre Haute, Ind.	Application for order for change of record of ch m Laurabel.

The ch m Laurabel won the fifth heat in the Four-year-old Trot at Terre Haute, Indiana, October 14, 1889, and the time recorded against her in the Judge's Book was 2:27. The sworn statement of the Judges and Timers of the race show that the recording of the record was an error, and that the true time which was publicly announced from the stand was 2:27¾.

Ordered: That the record of the ch m Laurabel be changed to 2:27¾.

No. 304.

Robert Thompson, Goderich, Ont.	Application for order for change of record of ch g Baldwin.

The ch g Baldwin performed over the grounds of a non-association track at New Hamburg, Ontario, September 10, 1889, obtaining a record of 2:34½, which was publicly announced from the judges' stand; but has been erroneously published in various turf publications as 2:34.

The affidavits of the Secretary of the meeting and officials of the race were presented showing the correct time and its announcement was 2:34½.

Ordered: That the record of the ch g Baldwin be changed to 2:34½.

J. H. Steiner, Sec'y.

Fresno Notes.

Editor Breeder and Sportsman:—Happening in Fresno City on a rambling tour, I utilized a favorable day in the matter of weather to visit the Fresno Fair grounds and the race track, two and a half miles distant from the city. The ride is made easy by the street railway, running round trips every hour from Hughes' Hotel, which is, by the way, one of the handsomest buildings in the modern style of architecture, with elaborate finish in California, and in internal arrangement, elegance, completeness and decoration, very few hotel buildings equal the Hughes'. Its furnishment is costly and luxurious, in exquisite taste, and the cuisine is sumptuous. It is in full sense a first class hotel.

In less than half an hour the trip to the Fair grounds is made, with fine views of the surrounding fruit orchards, vineyards of wine and raisin grapes, native shade trees and magnificent landscapes extending in every direction to the distant mountain ranges. In all California are no more attractive surroundings to delight the eye, no location better adapted to the purposes of husbandry, viticulture, breeding and the turf.

A local stock company own the grounds and buildings. The tract is one hundred acres in extent, and is in every part as level nearly as a floor. The soil is a light and lively sandy loam, solid to wheel and springy to hoof, free from deep wind and dense dust in wettest and dryest seasons. Abundant water is supplied by three large artesian wells and fifty wells of ordinary bore, which never fail in flow and volume. The track is one foot in excess of a mile three feet from the inside, and in its preparation, thorough means were studied and applied. Upon the hard part a few feet below the surface sand was laid, and upon this quick loam spread and worked in to ensure ease and elasticity, to guard against possible injury to horses in the severest trials of racing performance. It is said to be the best track in California for speed to the comfort and safety of the horse. In quality of soil it much resembles the old Union course on Long Island—the memorable scene of the feats of Eclipse and Sir Henry, of Fashion and Boston, and of Peytona and Fashion, many years agone. In appointments it is much superior to that famous old sporting ground, as the genius of the period surpasses the art of the early turfmen in the management of racing grounds, and the many accessories in late days wrought to a degree that stamps it as perfection, with nothing beyond to devise or accomplish. The Fresno track is laid out after the best approved models, with clear starting way and first rate homestretch from the turn to the finish to enable judges and spectators to witness the concluding struggle for the mastery under the wire. From the straight of the homestretch to the judges' stand, there is an imperceptible decline of twelve inches, which assures utmost speed without possible injury, and heightens the excitement of the race. This is the only departure from complete level all the way around the track, which is maintained in thorough order in every season.

The grand stand is well placed, with shade during afternoons to the occupants, and the view of the track free from obstacle or obstruction. The structure is 130 feet in length, raised to two high stories, with comfortable seats and clear look to everyone, and its capacity is 3 000 grown persons—1,500 on each floor. At each front corner is a lofty tower, of hexagon form, projecting and constructed in trussel manner, so as not to obstruct the view of any in the main stand. On each tier floor is room for thirty persons, seated with comfort. In these are reserved places for press representatives. The entire structure is built with chief regard to strength and safety. The foundation, supports and walls and roofing are assuring against possible accident, from the giving away of any part under the utmost pressure. The judge's stand and the box-like bow structure for the timers both need remodelling and improvement. The track appointments, for weighing, for trainers and grooms, riders and drivers and horses, for placing at the score, for announcing results, and all else, are quite complete. The fences, gates and entrance to the track show the skill of a master hand in arrangement and manner.

Near the track, with fine views of it from the broad and extended balconies of the lower and upper stories, is the club house, a capacious building, fully adapted to its uses and enjoyments, with commodious parlors elegantly furnished, members' rooms, offices and apartments, all appropriately fitted and furnished. The choice portion of the upper balcony is reserved for ladies and their escorts, and proper care is observed in the admission to the building and balconies.

Within the tract are fields of alfalfa and nutritious grasses choicest for pasturing, and these supply abundant feed during every month of the year. In the severest winters there is no trouble from inclement weather, and with the bounteous supply of water by artificial means, the perils of drouth are no more to be dreaded. Budd Doble, with his wide experience in such matters, selected Fresno Fair Grounds last winter for the care of his valuable horses, and those committed to his charge, and in the spring he started eastward with them all in prime condition. It was, too, on Fresno track, that Marvin reduced the record of Sunol to 2:13½, and at the time he was in doubt of her ability to meet the issue because of the condition of the peerless filly of Palo Alto.

Nearer to the principal entrance of the Fair Ground is the pavilion for agricultural and kindred exhibitions of the products of the farm, the orchard, the vineyard, of the skill and handicraft of the housewife, and the fair of the household, of the mechanical art, of everything which goes to make up the grand aggregate of the accustomed Annual Fair which attract multitudes from afar, and in the great holiday festival event of the year to the producers and residents of the locality. It is a large building, of unique architecture, a capacious octagon, with entrance to every side, and one side the equal of every other in the choice of place of exhibition and display. It rises to the quivalent of two lofty stories and a dome or cupola. The roofing is of corrugated iron and to that degree fireproof and preventive of rain pour or tricklings. The lower floor is devoted to the more cumbersome exhibits, with the great central space held for visitors, and on occasions cleaned for dancing if required. The second floor is a kind of gallery for visitors and a place for the display of the more delicate and attractive articles of the artifices and from the realm of femininity, paintings, feathers, flowers, needle-work, etc. Above is the cupola, giving light to the graceful finish which it gives the structure from outside view. The whole building is amply lighted with great windows above and below on every side. Adjacent are the sheds and stalls and pens, for farm animals of every kind; the farms and coops and "contraptions" for poultry, fowls, and every species of the domestic creation. In all the appointments of our Agricultural Fair, up to the advanced condition of the agriculturists of the country, the Fresno Fair Grounds are up to the best examples.

There is still more to add in reference to the excellence of the Grounds in another and kindred relation. The stables specially built for the accommodation of horses with their trainers, grooms, handlers, riders, drivers, and others, are superior to almost any others in the State, in plan, structure, furnishment, space, comfort, food and water, and other important accessions. The care and condition of the horse has evidently been the mindful study and consideration of the owners and managers of the Grounds. It is difficult to suggest improvement upon what has been done so very well. To be seen and to be copied is the consequence of the visit of which I write.

At the stables, during my too brief visit, I was shown many valuable, fine and attractive horses. Of these were Electioneers, Sultans, Wilkes, Nutwoods, Alexanders, and others. Junio and Clovis, each the property of Mr. Straube of Fresno, are paramount in qualities and magnificent in appearance. Junio is the best son of Electioneer, judged by look, that I have seen. A two year old colt, an Electioneer, also owned by Mr. Straube, is a perfect type of the great sire, and a beauty to look at. Clovis, a Sultan, is likewise a noble horse to view.

I have seen and ascertained enough to be convinced that, Fresno is high in the line toward foremost place in trotters in California—and what state equals this? Here they have got the soil, the climate, the grass. Further, they have got the men who have got the money too; men who know a good horse when they see one, and don't haggle as to the price. They want him, they will have him, if he is for sale.

Lewis Leach, a pioneer of Fresno of the Fifties, and President of a Bank here, is president of the Fair Grounds Company. Mr. F. B. Baldwin, an old and experienced breeder and turf man, from New York formerly, is the superintendent and manager in charge. His son is Secretary. The institution is prospering. All the time improvements are pushed onward. Landscape gardening is the latest step to beautification of the grounds. A master artist is employed for the tasteful work. Shade trees, fruit trees, everything to be obtained that will grow and ornament, and choice flowers are cultivated. Fresno has not leaped from a population of 1100 in 1880 to 15,000 now, without recognition of the duties incumbent upon citizens to exert themselves further, and keep up their rapidly growing city to the standard of the consequent prosperity. Here are the finest buildings of splendid architecture, only one, two and three years old. The kind are multiplying. By 1900, Fresno will cover miles of site and display her many hundred of grand edifices to the pride of the 50,000 inhabitants. She is accumulatively raising the progressive wealth of her raisins, now enjoying the top of the market.

M.

May 10, 1890.

Entries for the Stockton Stakes.

DISTRICT TWO-YEAR-OLD STAKES.

$50 each; $150 added.

J. E. Moore's blk f by Hawthorne—a Silverthread mare.
T. J. Crais' b c Farmington Boy by Dexter Prince—by Chieftain.
D. Young's b c Pilot Prince by Dexter Prince—by Nutwood.
R. G. Brush's b c Elastic by Election—by Romulus.
Geo. Kneler's b f Eda by Harry Gear—Mollie by Gen. McClellan.
N. B. Whittaker's b g Arnot.
L. A. Richard's b f Ella M by Elector—Becky by Yorktown.
L. A. Richard's br c L. A. by Elector.
J. A. McCloud's br f Daisy Vernon by Mount Vernon—by Berkeley.

DISTRICT THREE-YEAR-OLD STAKES.

$50 each; $150 added.

J. E. Moore's b c Elect Moore by Elect—Fanny by Bonner.
Funck Bros.' b c Lottery Ticket by Dexter Prince—by Nutwood.
Funck Bros.' b f Lizzie F by Elector—by Duke McClellan.
Geo. French's b f by Mount Vernon—by Chieftain.
L. U. Shippee's br c Brownthorne by Hawthorne—by Priam.

Foals at Du Bois Farm.

Denver, May 7, '90.

Editor Breeder and Sportsman:—We append herewith a partial list of the foals of 1890, at the Du Bois Farm, Denver, Colo:

March 9th, a chestnut filly by Superior 4012, dam Magdalene by Magnet 1328.

March 26th, bay colt by Superior 4012, dam Knoxie by Knox Boy 840.

April 1st, bay filly by Superior 4012, dam Alice Marshall by Pocahontas Boy 1790.

April 17th, bay filly by Superior 4012, dam Ina by Dictator 113.

April 18th, bay filly by Hambletonian Wilkes 1679, dam Ida Niles (dam of Middleway 2.22¼ and Clara Belle 2:31½) by Mambrino Chief Jr. 214.

Of the above, Magdalene, Knoxie and Ina are entered in your Futurity Stake of 1893.

The other Denver entry belonging to Mr. W. R. Rust: April 27th, bay filly by Superior 4012, dam Countess by Admiral.

We will send you other foals later. Resp'y yours,

Du Bois Bros.

When a man starts out with a "ringer", he starts out to steal. He has the courage to do it because the civil law will not reach him if caught, and the penalty imposed by the National or American Associations will not prevent him from doing it over again. The man who does this is hardly as honorable as the burglar who cracks a bank. Both want to get away with the spoils not honestly obtained, and the bank cracker has the courage to risk the punishment of the state. Now to make the identification of the horse and driver more complete, both should have a license from the association over whose track they are trotting.

The driver should file a certificate giving his name, residence, age, height and complexion, attested by three witnesses; a fee of $5 should be paid and a license issued to him. Every horse also should be registered in like manner, giving age, height, breeding, marks and record, it should be renewed every year. An owner should have the right to drive his own horse, but no other, unless he has paid the fee of $5, which would constitute him a professional driver. These fees should constitute a fund from which a judge should be hired to visit every track in a given circuit. If an owner or driver has a complaint or protest to make, it should be lodged with the circuit judge, who should present it to the American or National Association.—Spirit of the Hub.

Parties having mares that are barren or irregular breeders would do well to consult Dr. G. W. Stimpson, V. S. Office and Hospital 19th Street, near San Pablo Avenue, Oakland, Cal. Best of references.

TURF AND TRACK.

Susie S., 2:15, will be trained by her former owner, Henry Traynor.

Inspector B., after a short season in the stud, will be taken up and trained.

A bookmaker in Victoria advertises that he will not be responsible for his sons debts.

The Golden Gate Stables and the Kelly and Samuel's Stable left for Denver last Monday.

Orrin A. Hickok arrived all safe at Terra Haute a week ago yesterday with his horses.

Ex-Governor Oden Bowie has engaged George Black to train the Maryland stable this year.

The stallion Nelson was jogged from five to fifteen miles each day except Sundays during the past winter.

During the winter meeting Clifton disbursed $226 645, of which sum the entrance money amounted to $29,645.

The Palo Alto trotting stable will, in all probability, make their first public appearance at the Detroit meeting.

Jay-Eye-See, the little black gelding whose record of 2:10 stood for a day, is said to have out-grown his lameness.

Ed. Corrigan has a small string this season, but all are clinkers: Riley, Helter Skelter, Ethel and Cornie Buckingham.

The $26,000 Mascot, who ran into a barbed wire fence on Mr. Marcus Daly's Bitter Root Farm, is said to be all right again.

Maud S., Sunol, Axtell, Palo Alto, Gene Smith, Susie S. and Stamboul are all named as candidates for faster marks than 2:08¾.

Isaac Murphy, who was the premier jockey for Santa Anita for several seasons, has been engaged by J. B. Haggin Esq., for the season.

Old Hiram Drew, the man who raised the famous trotting stallion, Hiram Drew, is living in Bangor, and is about 73 years of age.

Beaconsfield is at Denver. The old horse is said to be in fair trim again and is expected to show up in winning form at the coming meeting.

W. L. Appleby is working White Cloud, Applause, Carmen, Wild Oats and several colts at Laurelwood, on Mr. P. J. Donahue's private track.

Mr. Butler, Butte, has engaged Doc Wiande to train Col. Bradshaw and Charley Hilton. Wiande was previous to this trainer for A. C. Beckwith.

Simonian, by St. Simon, winner of the Brocklesby stakes for two-year-olds in England, recently, cost Col. North, his owner, $25,000 as a yearling.

The most heats won by a trotter were captured by Goldsmith Maid, she having 332 heats better than 2:30 to her credit. She won during her career $500,000.

The first of Edgemark's foals is out of a mare by Smuggler, 2:15¼, grandam Madam Powell, the dam of Monroe Chief, 2:18¼. In 1889 Edgemark got a record of 2:16.

Henry Chambers, who formerly took care of Prince Wilkes, 2:14¾, and afterward drove him in his races at Buenos Ayres, is now training horses at Elizabethtown, Ky.

Fitzpatrick has been engaged by Mr. Pierre Lorillard. Ten years ago Fitz was learning his profession in the Lorillard Stable and rode his first race in the cherry and black.

J. D. Prentice has gone from Milwaukee to Helena, Montana, to train Messrs. Huntley and Clarke's trotters, most of which are by either Maxim Bishop or Kentucky Volunteer.

The Dwyers say that whenever Longstreet and Salvator meet they will have a lot of money to bet on Longstreet. They meet in the Suburban at a difference of 10 pounds in Longstreet's favor.

Three English thoroughbreds recently imported to Switzerland have been placed at the covering stations at Tramlingen, Einsiedeln, and Lausanne, where they stand at a fee of only twenty francs (about $3:80.

The highest price paid for a yearling in America this season was $5625 for a bay colt by Longfellow out of Encore, (dam of Helter Skelter). Ed Corrigan was the purchaser, at the sale of the Kingston yearlings.

Diavolo, who was successful in several races in Montana last season, is again in training at Missoula. He is a half brother to Palo Alto, Gertrude Russell and Big Jim, being by Shannon out of Dame Winnie by Planet.

On April 23d, Edgewater Belle dropped a fine bay filly by Lancelot, youngest son of Green Mountain Maid. Edgewater Belle is 11 years old, and her first foal, dropped in 1885, is the unbeaten Edgemark, four-year-old record, 2:16.

An old turfman, speaking the other day of the crowds which now regularly attend Eastern and Western races, said that 20 years ago 500 was considered a big crowd at Monmouth. He ascribes the great interest due to speculation in pools.

J. Williamson of Montana, a part owner and trainer of the Speedy Red Elm, was stricken with a fatal illness a fortnight ago last Friday at the Dwyer racetrack. He was removed to the Elizabeth Hospital, where he died on the following morning.

Grand old Electioneer is slowly but surely dying. After lying down he has to be lifted up. The almost certainty that he will never see another season is probably the reason that Senator Stanford has withdrawn all the Electioneers from the market.

The Directors of the Monterey Agricultural Association have let the contract for enlarging the pavilion to W. P. Mauldin, his bid of $2 005 being the lowest. The pavilion, when finished, is expected to compare favorably with any in the State.

All the first class race tracks in the United States employ a doctor by the year, or rather the season. They pay a liberal price, from $10 a day upward, and expect him to report for duty a half hour before the races begin, and to remain on hand till all the visitors have left.

W. M. Murry left Sacramento for Washington Park, Chicago, last Tuesday, taking with him Lord of the Harem, Kiro, Leland, Oakdale, Lady Ali, Parapet, Power, and several others. J. B. Rose took Oro and Kitty Van on the same car but will reship to Westchester.

A. C. Beckwith, of Utica stock farm Evanston, Wyo., has sold to Sire Bros. of New York City, the iron roan five-year-old mare Wanita, 2:20¼ by Aberdeen, dam Wyoming Belle by Lowe's Pilot, second dam Juanita, dam of Eula Lee, 2:29¼ by Pilot Jr. The price paid was $10,000.

J. I. Case of Racine, Wis., visited Bloomington on the 6th, and offered Capt. Foster, owner of Carrie Walton, $10,000 cash for the mare. The offer was refused. Carrie Walton is 7 years old, has a record of 2:23½, made at Washington Park, Chicago, last June, and has shown a trial in 2:18.

Major H. C. McDowell, Lexington, has sold to Fred Achute of Dusseldorf, Germany, the trotting mare Illusion. She is a brown, three years old, and is by Director out of a mare by Princeps. The price paid was $2500, and this was said to be after a trial in which the mare trotted a half mile in 1:12½.

Almost every American sporting paper, weekly and daily, states that Hermit had for years been covering 100 mares at 250 guineas each. Any man with sense would know that it was impossible at his time of life, and—irrespective of age, no valuable thoroughbred should have more than about 30 mares.

Several New York sporting men are said to be corresponding with the many broncho riders of Mexico, Arizona and Texas in regard to holding an international tournament in Gotham on one of the race tracks. It is expected that the distance of the race will be from 50 to 300 miles, with relays of horses.

A trotting meeting was held at Alexandria Park, London, on May 5th, and was conducted on the American plan—mile heats, three in five. Harry Walkie beat Little Sioux and Boston Boy in straight heats, best time 2:37. It is rumored that several tracks will be built on the American plan and made as fast as possible.

The Undine and Smith Stables will leave to-morrow; the former will go on to Westchester while the latter will stay in Chicago. Homer, Racine, Glenlevit and probably Tycoon will be taken on by the proprietors of the Undine Stable under W. McCormick's charge. Mr. Smith will have Al Farrow, Longshot and Susie S.

Gregory has shown by his work that he has improved, while his old rival, Reclare, has gone back. Burlington begins to show up to advantage, and if he continues to thrive he will rank close up with the first class three-year-olds Not more than half a dozen trials have been run as yet by the horses at work on the various New York tracks, and but few of that number were beyond a mile.

Judge Van Sickle, at the opening of the May term of the Union Court this morning, desired the grand jury to bring in indictments against all bookmakers doing business at the race tracks of the New Jersey Jockey Club and the Linden Blood Horse Association. "Horse racing," he said, "is not against the law of New Jersey, but bookmaking is."

The dam of Reno's baby, the famous Texas colt which last year was campaigned the season through, finally getting a trotting record of 2:25½ and a pacing record of 2:24½ as a two year old, was got by a pacing horse taken to Texas from New York years ago, that was called a Morgan at the time. All attempts to get at the facts of his breeding have proved futile.

Riley won the Kentucky Derby last Wednesday in 2:45, the slowest time since the race was started, but the track was very heavy, and in Murphy's hands Riley romped home five lengths in front, despite the fact that he was said not to be a good mud-horse; he is by Longfellow, out of Geneva by War Dance; probably it was the latter cross that gave him mud-sense.

E. J. Baldwin, the Santa Anita millionaire, has a remarkably stylish five-year-old black brown mare by Sultan 1513, out of Kitty Wink by Corning's Harry Clay. The mare was sent to Chas. David's training stables last week to be broken to harness. Her dam Kitty Wink was brought out as a mate for Volney 2:23, and was very speedy but never was driven for a record being used double by Mr. Baldwin.

Lord Durham, a London correspondent has been told by a racing authority, is determined to sustain his character as a turf reformer, and, undeterred by the trouble and loss to which he was put in regard to his difference with Sir George Chetwynd, is now engaged upon an elaborate statement, which he will shortly publish, and which is intended still further to expose certain abuses of the racing world.

Dan Dennison Sr., and young Dan left Sacramento last Monday for Portland, Ore. Dan wrote me that he would take in the mountain circuit with Hotspur, Dave Douglass, G. W. and Mohawk. On the same car were Coloma and Guido—the latter has not been sold to W. H Smith. Dan should pick up a little money with game old Dave and the useful four-year-old Hotspur, while the speedy but erratic G. W. may account for a race or too.

The Umpire (England) says: There is no Donovan this year, Curiously enough, nearly every 'bad year' has admitted of one horse standing out vigorously from his contemporaries. Will the time ever come when the relative merits of racehorses will be decided by any other test than that at present in vogue? It is yet only a matter of opinion whether Ormonde was the horse of the century. Many people would at the present moment vote Donovan that honor.

Jas. E. Watson informs me that his mare Nellie by McClellan, foaled on April 18th, a splendid black filly by Memo, the foal is entered in the BREEDER AND SPORTSMAN'S Futurity stake, and Mr. Watson says will prove as invincible as Black Joe, his wonderful, ill-fated, black pointer, was—by the way, Mr. Watson has another black pointer recently imported, which is showing up very well, and also an imported black bitch which last week had eight young puppies.

The World says: "On his general reputation this man McCormick ought to go. He has been running his horses in and out for months. Look at Early Blossom. Who knows when she is going to win? Who knows when she will lose? Who knows when Sparling will win? McCormick may be unfortunate. So is the man who has yellow fever or small pox, but that does not keep him from being put into a safe seclusion. The public has had enough of this kind of work. It is about time to stop it."

Owners or trainers who did not, or neglected to, furnish their jockies with their proper colors have been having a hard time of it at Elizabeth. A system of fines was inaugurated which should have a wholesome effect upon delinquents in this regard. A fortnight ago C. J. Donovan & Co., Charlie Littlefield and O. H. Stebbins were fined $10 each for not having their representative colors at the track. The Jockey Club has rightly determined to put a stop to this sort of thing, which has become very troublesome to the officials and annoying to the public.

The Manchester Umpire says: It is always pleasant to note improvements at Newmarket, as a certain section of the public had begun to think, from the continual grumbling of the scribes, that such things were almost unknown at headquarters. One of the latest is that the exercise grounds are now all mapped out with posts placed a furlong apart so that the lads who ride can make no mistake with their charges, but can send them along exactly the distance their trainers instruct them to go. It is also a boon to the amateur tout, of whom there were plenty on the heath during the three days of the Craven Meeting.

The following jockeys are now under suspension: Horton, suspended until June 1st; Murtha, until the end of the present year; A. McCarthy, until the end of the present season; Bender, Croker's rider, until June 26th; Sampson, until the end of the present year; Ross, until the end of the present year; D. Watson, suspended until June 1st; Winslow, until the end of summer meetings; Trainor, until the end of the present year; Johnson, suspended until June 12th; Kelly, until the end of the present year; Murray, until June 25th; Vincent, suspended until June 1st; Tabor, suspended until June 1st; Camp, suspended indefinitely; Van Keuren until he makes satisfactory excuses.

The Poule d'Essai races were run at Paris May 4th. The race for fillies had only three starters, and was won easily by a length and a half by M. Pierre Donon's Wandora, by Bruce out of Windfall. Alicante was second, fifteen lengths in front of Berenice. The last betting was 2 to 1 on Wandora, 4 to 3 against Alicante, and 50 to 1 against Berenice.

In the race for colts there were seven starters. Baron Rothschild's English bred colt Heaume by Hermit, out of Bella, was an easy winner, finishing a length and a half ahead of Pourpoint, who was eight lengths in front of Yellow. The last odds were 6 to 4 against Heaume, 5 to 1 against Pourpoint, and 6 to 1 against Yellow.

The death of Silvio, who has for some years been regarded as one of the leading thoroughbred stallions in France, has followed very closely upon that of his breeder, Lord Falmouth, for whom he won the Derby and St. Leger of 1877, and many other valuable races. Silvio's success at Epsom was more largely due, however, to the mediocrity of his opponents and to the accident which befel Chamant, the French bred son of Mortemer, who had beaten him in the Two Thousand, than to his own merits as a race horse. The late Duc de Castres purchased him of Lord Falmouth for 7,000gs, in 1881, for his stud near Moulins, where he had every chance of distinguishing himself.

The troubles of a light-weight are admirably rendered in the Sydney Bulletin, which has a sketch of a corpulent owner and his emaciated light-weight with the following dialogue:

Jockey to Owner—Very sorry, sir, but I can't quite manage it.

Owner—Been eating anything?

Jockey—No, sir; not tasted anything since yesterday.

Owner—Were you weighed with the pound saddle?

Jockey—Yes, sir.

Owner—Got your lightest jacket on?

Jockey—Yes, sir.

Owner—Oh! D—n it! go and have a shave.

The first Electioneer to enter the 2:30 list this season was Suisun, previous record 2:31½, by Electioneer out of Susie 2:26½ by Geo. M. Patchen Jr. 31. At Washington, D. C. on May 1st, after laying up two heats John E. Turner was called to the stand and after some argument allowed to continue driving the mare who readily took the next heat in 2:25½ and wound up the race in 2:31 and 2:31. Turner was very sore as he did not have a dollar on the mare, and he said afterwards that the Association was much to blame especially, as on the preceding day in the 2:23 pacing Victor and J K made a dead heat in the second heat and the time was given 2:22¾ to keep them in the 2:23 class, while in reality the time was 2:21½.

A new law in Indiana pertains to the service fee of stallions and requires registry of stock horses with the clerks of circuit courts. One of the requirements of the law is as follows: "That a copy of such license, embracing such sworn statements and pedigree, with the fee the owner proposes to charge for service, shall be posted by the owner of such sire in two or more conspicuous places in the vicinity of the place where the sire is kept for service; and should any part of said sworn statement be, to the knowledge of the owner of such sire, false in any particular, the owner shall not be entitled to collect any fee for such service; and the falsity of such statement, or any part thereof, may be pleaded in the bar to any contract or account for services of such sire."

The latest English news of the Derby says Surefoot (Wisdom—by Galopin) proved himself so much in advance of all other competitors in the race for the 2,000 guineas that he has been installed a hot favorite for the Derby at 6 to 4 on. One gentleman this week endeavored to lay £3,000 to £2,000 on him, but without finding any takers at the price. Lord Rothschild's LeNord was so decisively beaten that all hopes of his turning the tables on the favorite in the Derby have been abandoned. The fielders have this week had a good time, as nearly all have a favorite on their books, while scarcely anything was backed for the one thousand guinea beyond Semolina, the winner. The Duke of Portland owns both Semolina and the second mare, Memoir, and all competent judges are of the opinion that Memoir could have won. The Duke, however, had his money on Semolina, who is more than a half sister to Donovan, by St. Simon, out of Mowerina by Scottish Chief, while Donovan is by Galopin, the sire of St. Simon.

The foreleg for speed can hardly be too light at the bottom, but it is never too heavy at the top. There are no muscles below the knee. Not an ounce of superfluous weight is permitted where it would have to be lifted at such a great mechanical disadvantage, so that the muscles on the arm have not only to lift and carry the leg on, but to work every joint below the knee by a beautiful system of polished, well oiled pullies, and smooth strong cords. No strength elsewhere can compensate for weakness in the muscles of the arm. Where great speed is required the arm bone should be long in proportion to the shank bone below it. No horse can be safe, strong and enduring unless the upper portion of this bone exhibits a full supply of well developed muscles.

The Sporting World says, speaking of Hermit and his sensational career:

Perhaps the most marvellous instance of iron nerve evinced over a severe betting loss was when Hermit came to weigh in. Lord Hastings, whom the victory had irretrievably ruined, descended from the stewards' stand, and, without the slightest touch of bravado, patted the horse on the neck. On his death bed, referring to the circumstances, he observed, "I said nothing, but people did not know how I felt." Hermit's career on the turf was not a long one, and he has ever since been located at Blankney serving 100 mares every season, latterly at 250 guineas each. (He was for several years limited to 5 OUTSIDE MARES, and never served anything like 100 in any one season.—Ed. T. T.)

The ups and downs of turf speculators are very like the history of Wall street frequenters. Take the case of Sam Emery as an example. A few years ago he was a rich man. Shortly after he won a fortune with Dry Monopole in the first Brooklyn Handicap he had to sell out his racing stable and retire from the turf. He was "sold out under the rule," to use a Wall street term, to satisfy his creditors. Again, shortly after, he counted his profits by tens of thousands of dollars. Last week he was unable to make a book, as he hadn't the necessary capital to buy a seat in the Bookmakers' Exchange. So he stood on the ground. On Saturday he put the last $50 he had on Ross in the fourth race and won $5000. This week he will probably be bulling the market from his usual stand in the betting exchange at the race tracks.

The outlook for the spring meeting at City View, Portland, continues to grow brighter day by day, says the Oregonian. Recent importations of blooded horses have increased the interest and prospects of horse breeding in the State, and it is generally understood that Oregon, Washington and Montana breeders will have a larger representation here than ever before.

The efforts of the association in improving the track and grounds have evidently created a favorable impression among horsemen hereabouts, and the entries promise to be unusually large. There is no great probability, so far as appears, of any extensive representation of California, and on this account home breeders will undoubtedly feel a greater freedom to enter in all the races.

The Secretary of Charter Oak Park announces 311 entries for the $10,000 colt race for foals of 1889, mile heats, best three in five, to be trotted during August. This list is beyond all anticipations, having entries from twenty-one States and the British provinces. Kentucky leads with 69, New York 44, California 33 Massachusetts 27, Connecticut 27, Pennsylvania 19 and Ohio 18, The others are from 1 to 9 each. The entries include the get of the speediest and greatest stallions in America, viz: Nelson 2:14¼, Paton 2:14½, Stamboul 2:12½, Woodnut 2:16½, Nutwood 2:18¾, Director 2:17, Guy Wilkes 2:15¼ and Electioneer. Palo Alto farm names ten, among which are Belle Flower, Hinda Rose, Palo Alto Belle. The La Siesta Ranch names eight and L. J. Rose of Los Angeles names one by Stamboul and three by Alcazar.

The Helena Independent says: Near by the Montana stable at Louisville is that of H. R. Baker, also of Montana. In this stable there is a large chestnut gelding that attracts a good deal of attention on account of the loud, roaring noise he makes while at work on the track. The horse is Daniel B., by Glen Elm, out of Nettles, a short-bred mare. He was born and reared on the plains of Montana, and on his left shoulder bears the brand of the ranch to which he belonged. Daniel was a powerful race horse when he first went on the turf, and he won nearly every race in the northwest in which he started. Two winters ago he had the distemper, which left the muscles of his throat paralyzed. To enable him to make a race at all, a slit was cut in his throat and a silver tube inserted, through which he breathes. The tube is used only when he makes a race and is exercising; without it a roaring noise is made caused by his breathing through the hole in his throat.

In the spring of 1869, Harry Bassett was sold as a yearling for $345, and the draft made on Col. D. McDaniel for him went to protest. Mr. C. J. Alloway finally took up this draft and the colt passed into possession of the McDaniel confederacy. As a three-year-old Harry Bassett was without a rival, winning thousands of dollars, and as a four-year-old he was the sensation of the East. In 1872 he met Longfellow in the Monmouth Cup at Long Branch, and the whole country went wild over the race. Harry Bassett was beaten, but he turned the tables on the magnificent son of Leamington at Saratoga in the cup contest at the Springs, and he was again the idol of the public. The Turf, Field and Farm also says: Although the chestnut son of Lexington and Canary Bird brought so much wealth to the confederacy, the draft on Col. McDaniel for $345 taken up by Mr. Alloway was never paid. That gentleman still has it. The unwritten history of the turf is full of curious things.

Work upon the new race track for the Stanislaus Stock Breeders' Association is progressing rapidly, says the Stanislaus County News. The track for the entire mile has been plowed up, and considerable grading already done. From the grand stand to the first quarter turn the track is eighty feet wide, and for the rest of the distance sixty feet wide. On the turns the outer edge will be five feet higher than the inside, or one foot to the ten rise that being universally conceded by horsemen to be much better for the horses, as level turns on a track have been found to tend to strain the horses' feet. The track will be completed in about two weeks, and will be one of the fastest and best winter tracks in the State. Four four-horse scrapers are kept constantly at work, and in two weeks it is expected that the track will be graded and rolled and ready for use. Work upon the grand-stand and other buildings will not be commenced until after the next meeting of the Board of Directors, which will be held some time during the present month.

The various reports in the daily papers of the Arcade Bon Ton race at Sacramento, a fortnight ago stated that both boys were taken down. Casey was not taken down but rode and won on Arcade against whose owner and trainer no complaint was made. Reporters should be careful and not make such grave errors.

Many of the nobility—or at least the younger members of that class—now look at trade in one form or another, either for support or as a means of investment, and various are the ways adopted. Some take to stockbroking in the City, others to banking, whilst a few are now engaged in ranching in the Wild West. The Umpire says: A few years back society was startled by the announcement that Lord Marcus Beresford had accepted the position of starter to the Jockey Club—a position at that time considered rather inconsistent with a title. However, his Lordship entered upon his new duties with heart and soul, and has done much during the short time he wielded the red flag to abolish abuses which at times previous were often too frequent. We now learn that he has resigned the position which he lately held so creditably, and has joined the army of trainers. He has taken a large establishment at Newmarket, and will train for the Prince of Wales, Baron Hirsch, and Lord Randolph Churchill.

No Steward of the English Jockey Club within recent times has done so much to make his term of office famous as Mr. James Lowther, and it was the wish of a large number of the racing fraternity that he would allow himself to be re-elected The last three years may justly be described as a critical time for the club, and it is in a very great measure owing to the exertions of the retiring Steward that they have come through it so satisfactorily. The Manchester Umpire says: While regret accompanied the retirement of Mr. Lowther, satisfaction is general at the choice of his successor, Mr. J. H. Houldsworth. The latter gentleman was elected a member of the club in 1874, but previous to that time he had confined his attention in the racing line mainly to the Northern steeplechase meetings. The best horse he has ever owned is undoubtedly Springfield, though that celebrated horse's descendants have not been so successful as might have been expected. As Mr. Houldsworth is practically a non-betting man his green and gold jacket is popular on every race course, but nowhere more so than in the north of England. His accession to office was marked fitly enough by the success of his colors on Evergreen in the Babraham Plate, and that this may be the precursor of many more successes is the wish of all lovers of racing.

The Jacksonville Democratic Times of the 9th says: The annual meeting of stockholders of the Jacksonville county agricultural association was held at the town hall in Jacksonville last Monday afternoon. More than one-half of the capital stock were represented, in person or by proxy, and the following directors were elected unanimously to serve for the ensuing year: I. B. Williams, C. C. Beekham, W. C. Leever, Geo. T. Hershberger, Geo. DeBar, F. T. Downing and J. W. Merritt. The association has at last been able to get its affairs into good shape financially, and will doubtless prove of vast benefit to the country in encouraging fruit culture and fine stock raising. A welcome despatch was received before the meeting adjourned, from F. T. Downing, the association's representative on the Southern Oregon State Board of Agricultural in session at Grant's Pass at the same hour, stating that the district fair will be held on the grounds of the Jackson county fair association next fall. After the adjournment of the stockholders' meeting the newly-elected directors qualified and held a business meeting at which they re-elected I. B. Williams president, Wm. M. Holmes secretary and C. Magruder treasurer for the ensuing year. The following executive committee was appointed: F. T. Downing, J. W. Merritt and Dr. Geo. DeBar.

The Board of Review of the National Association finished its docket on the first of May at Chicago. The following cases were disposed of: James Allen of Kingston, Ontario, and his b. g F. O. P. were expelled; Noah Walker of Baltimore was granted release of himself and Delaware Dude from suspension; W. H. H. Achuff of Philadelphia was granted his request to be reinstated; G. W. Smith of Binghamton, N. Y., was expelled; G. I. Young, East Boston. Mass., was expelled for fraud; C. L. Kood and J. Mayor of Picton, N. Y. and Mattie B., alias Little Eva, were expelled; H. H. Nye, Wellsville, N. Y., his blk. g Jack, alias Duster, were reinstated on payment of claims; Spencer Owens of Taber, N. Y., was expelled; J. A. Juveval of Upper Sandusky, Ohio, Michael Brannigan of Mount Vernon, Ohio, and the b c Dorgan, alleged to be Freddy J., were expelled; L. L. Howe, Geneva, N. Y., as to alleged record of 2:29¼ of Longfellow; obtained at Rochester, N. Y, Aug. 21, 1888—Ordered that the record stand; J. B. C. Barlow, F. A. Cole, Jersey City, and b m Mamie B., alleged to be Fanny C.—Ordered that Barlow, Cole, and the mare be expelled; E. Stoddard of Portsmouth, N. Y.; and ch g Hazard—Horse and man suspended until the case can be further examined; A. P. Burkhart, Dansville, N. Y., relief of b m Confederate Maid from the effect of an alleged "no time" race at Penn Yan, May 28, 1889—Case not proved and dismissed; Thomas Canary, New Brunswick, N. Y., and the b f Mercy C—Ordered that suspension be continued until entrance money is paid; A. J. Libby, Gardiner, Me., removal of expulsion—Denied.

John Reavey's seven-year-old mare Vedette, foaled on the 28th of April, a slashing looking chestnut colt by Duke of Norfolk and has been bred back to him. The youngster should be a race horse sure, as he is full of the best blood in America, his pedigree showing at a glance four crosses of imported Glencoe, three of Lexington, two each of imported Sovereign and imported Yorkshire with crosses of (imp) Bonnie Scotland and (imp) Leamington close up. The pedigree is so rich and rare that I give it below;

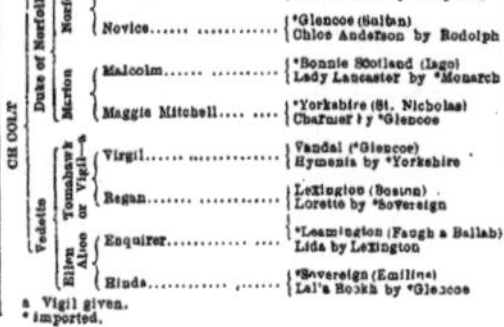

CH COLT	Duke of Norfolk	Norfolk	Lexington	Boston (Timoleon) Alice Carneal by *Sarpedon
			Novice	*Glencoe (Sultan) Chloe Anderson by Rodolph
		Marion	Malcolm	*Bonnie Scotland (Iago) Lady Lancaster by *Monarch
			Maggie Mitchell	*Yorkshire (St. Nicholas) Charmer by *Glencoe
	Vedette	Tomahawk or Vigil—a	Virgil	Vandal (*Glencoe) Hymenia by *Yorkshire
			Regan	Lexington (Boston) Lorette by *Sovereign
		Ellen Alice	Enquirer	*Leamington (Faugh a Ballah) Lida by Lexington
			Hinda	*Sovereign (Emilius) Lal'a Rookh by *Glencoe

a Vigil given.
* imported.

An interesting letter, covering a lot of ground, appears in an English sporting contemporary on racing and its surrounding in Buenos Ayres. It is from the pen of Mr. Brett, one of the leading trainers in the Argentine. He refers to Ormonde, who is in his charge, as being a perfect picture, and says that he gave him good, healthy exercise for about two months, in which he was ridden daily by Kellett.

He continues:—The reason why I gave Ormonde so much exercise was to prevent him from becoming too fresh, and hence prevent an accident, as I was obliged to take him daily through crowds of traffic of all sorts on my way to the exercise grounds. Often you might have seen me leading him by the side of my pony, going through crowds of carts carting sand from the river. The horse at the present time is in charge of my head man, John North, who lived with me when at Kennett, Newmarket, and latterly with Mr. T. Cannon, at Stockbridge. Ormonde takes his daily exercise by the side of a hack, leading him. He has got most comfortable quarters, and is well cared for in every way, and I think when you know that I was engaged as far back as last March twelve months to manage Ormonde I surely know a little more than most people do about the horse.

"The annexed resolutions embody the results accepted at the conference on horse-shoeing, held in connection with the Animals' Institute on Saturday: 1. The foot should have only so much horn removed from it at each shoeing as is necessary for the proper fitting of the shoe, and no more. 2. The frog should have a bearing on the ground, but no other part of the hoof should be weakened to give this healthy action. 3. Shoes cannot be too light if they give sufficient wear. 4. The width of a shoe need be no more than is necessary to cover the bearing surface. 5. Nails are the most secure and simple fastenings for horse-shoes, and a properly driven nail never does any harm. 6. The most important requisite in horse-shoeing is the adoption of a correct system, not the use of any special form of shoe. 7. All shoes should have a level bearing on the foot, extending from the toe to the heel. 8. The ground surface of a shoe should follow the form of the ground surface of an unshod foot which has traveled on a level road. 9. No better form of shoe exists than a narrow one, made rather thicker at the quarters than at the heel and toe. 10. The recent proposal to affix shoes on feet (without nails) by broad projections into the hoof and by pressure round the wall is impraticable and injurious. 11. No advantage follows the retention of shoes on a foot for more than four weeks, as the growth of the horn in that time produces a disproportionate hoof. If in this time the shoe is not worn out it should be removed.—London Live Stock Journal.

There are in the possession of Mr. Wm. Robinson, Danville Ky., several antique documents giving the pedigrees of thoroughbred horses in ye ancient days. The following excerpts will prove attractive to those interested in the genealogy of the blue-blooded racers: "The pedigree of Vampire—The bay colt was by Regulus; his dam by Steady, his grand dam by Partner, his great-grand dam by Greyhound, and bred by the late Craftz Banforth; as witness my hand, this 14th day of April. 1765, [signed] Thomas Hutchinson, Wallier street, London." This certificate then follows: "This colt I sold to Lord Waldegrave for Wm. Avon. This is to certify that the above horse called Vampire was bought as above mentioned by the late Earl Waldegrave, and was sold by order of his Lordship's executors, after his death, by Wm. Pond, at New Market, the 28th day of April, 1763, unto the Rt. Hon'ble Lord Farnhaus, for His Grace, the Duke of Bridgewater, for 400 guineas. James Underhill, Steward to the late Earl Waldegrave. The above mentioned horse, Vampire, I sold in July, 1764. [Signed.] Mr. Thomas Hodgkin." Col. Hodgkin was then living in King and Queens county, Virginia. In another memorandum he mentions Minerva, foaled in 1794, and notes her success in four races run in 1799 in which her total winnings were £372 8s. 0d. The first race was two mile heats, and the other three four-mile heats. One of the latter was run over the Richmond course, the 16th of October. In a note the owner says: "On the morning of this run Mr. John Randolph, now a member of Congress, offered me £2,000 for said mare Minerva." The offer was evidently declined, as a memorandum of a race at Petersburg follows and contains this note: "This is the last race run with success, being injured in her run at Petersburg."—Danville Advocate.

The New York Times referring to the recent arrests at the Brooklyn Jockey Club says: One of the strangest things known in the history of horse racing is "Pete" De Lacy, the proprietor of closed poolrooms in Barclay Street, Park Row and North William Street and the reputed backer of a faro game in the Bowery, posing as a reformer, and advocate of law and order, and an agent for the suppression of gambling. De Lacy is the man whose two clerks, Wynn and Skahill, have caused the arrest of officers of the Brooklyn Jockey Club and the bookmakers at the track. The men first tried to accomplish their object by an appeal to the Union County officers at Elizabeth. They knew who De Lacy was, and that his purpose was merely a matter of retaliation upon the jockey club people for refusing to furnish him information necessary to the running of his city pool rooms. Appeals to them having proved faultless, De Lacy's agents went to Rahway, and there secured from Justice Frazee the necessary warrants. It is only fair to Mr. Frazee to suppose that he knew nothing of the character of the men who swore out the eighty or more warrants, or of their motive for so doing. They represented to him that their action was solely in the interest of law and order! A fine trio indeed to make such representation. As a matter of fact, De Lacy is one of the worst of the proprietors of the city pool rooms. His North William Street place was commonly called "the dollar room" because bets of that amount were taken from clerks, messenger boys, and others who could not afford either to go to a rack track or to play the races. He also allowed combination bets at 25 and 50 cents to be made, this system, as every one knows, being little better than highway robbery, as such a thing as winning one of these bets when extremely long odds were offered is well nigh an impossibility. The city rooms at best are the curse of the whole racing business, and it is in them that the petty embezzlers and thieving employes cast away their earnings. As a rule, the men who go to the race track are close students of the sport and can afford to lose when they do so. They are men who have left the other speculative games at the Stock, Produce and other Exchanges down town for a game where they believe there is a better chance to win, or where at least no half dozen men can control the market and make every one lose when they see fit. There is no public form in stock, oil, grain, cotton, or coffee speculation. The city pool rooms bear exactly the same relation to the race tracks that the bucket shops do to the Exchanges. The first two are four men and boys who cannot afford to speculate at all, the last two for capitalists to indulge their speculative spirit to its full bent.

THE KENNEL.

Dog owners are requested to send for publication the earliest possible notices of whelps, sales, names claimed, presentations and deaths in their kennels, in all instances writing plainly names of sire and dam and of grandparents, colors, dates and breed.

SOUTHERN CALIFORNIA KENNEL CLUB.

Second Annual Bench Show.

A SPLENDID EXHIBIT.

The second bench show of the Southern California Kennel Club began at Los Angeles on Tuesday, April 6th, at 140 and 142 North Main Street, in a well-situated hall, opening directly from a thoroughfare. The hall was of ample size, with convenient annexes in which to cook the necessary food for the dogs, and an ample yard wherein to exercise them. The only criticism to be made upon the hall was that the light might have been better. The club was organized on May 7, 1889; was made a member of the American Kennel Club on September 18, 1889, and is officered as follows: President, H. T. Payne; vice-Presidents, J. F. Holbrook, J. E. Preston; Secretary, E. K. Benchley; Treasurer, E. B. Tufts; Bench Show Committee, J. F. Holbrook, J. E. Preston, C. E. Fout, J. H. Keller, Tony Bright; Superintendent, H. W. Wilson; Veterinary Surgeon, J. A. Edmonds.

The first show given by the club in 1889 was given in conjunction with a poultry association, and it was observed at that time that the dogs attracted the crowds, and were the main source of revenue, as is usually the case in such combination affairs. This year it was resolved to give an independent dog show, and the first day already passed gave assurance that the idea was a wise one. The receipts on Tuesday were $150. On Wednesday nearly twice that amount. All departments of the show have been managed with the utmost discretion, and the success of bench shows in Los Angeles is assured. Several prominent San Franciscans had animals on exhibition, among them Mr. A. B. Truman, Mr. Eugene J. Roy and Mr. J. B. Martin. The show was attended by the fashionable people of the city and vicinity, and was *the thing* of the day, even to the extent of attracting visitors from such ultra suburbs as Pasadena and San Gabriel, Mr. Robert T. Vandevort coming from the former and Capt. A. B. Anderson and lady from the latter.

The officers of the club were all on hand and alert to meet all possible inquiries and needs. The Superintendent was Mr. H. W. Wilson, and a fine one he was; courteous, prompt and firm. President H. T. Payne, vice-President J. F. Holbrook, Secretary Benchley, Directors Tony Bright and C. E. Fout and Veterinary J. A. Edmonds must all be praised for effective service and constant attention.

Of the average quality of the dogs shown, too much can hardly be said, when the conditions under which the show was given are considered. Excepting the six or seven San Francisco entries, the exhibit was purely a local one, and it speaks loudly for the local fanciers, that one hundred and thirty dogs of good breeding and points can be gathered in a city of only one hundred thousand inhabitants, while San Francisco, with its three hundred and fifty thousand dwellers, drawing upon all sources, can bench but two hundred and fifty dogs.

The leading exhibitor is Capt. A. B. Anderson, whose dogs are all of excellent quality and well shown. He has mastiffs, St. Bernards, pointers, collies, fox-terriers and pugs on show.

First in mastiffs was won by Mrs. Dorothea Lummis, of Los Angeles, with Amado (Chino Lion—Chino Beauty), a dog of fair size, good points and able.

In bitches, Capt. A. B. Anderson took first with Atella A. (Imperial Arno—Zella M.), a small beast, but very typical and good.

The greyhounds were strong, both in numbers and quality, first in dogs going to J. W. Gordon's Leo, a handsome fawn. In bitches, Mr. C. F. Holder, of Pasadena, had an easy win with Dina, also a fawn.

Some splendid fox hounds were benched, the best yet seen at a show in California. The Valley Hunt Club of Pasadena getting first in dogs with Melody, a b w and t flecked dog, very nice.

In bitches, first also went to that club for Queen, a properly marked and typical animal.

The pointers, heavy weights, were Mr. E. K. Benchley's Kan Koo, getting first. In light-weight good dogs, Mr. R. T. Vandevort had an easy win with Billy V. (Don—Drab) despite his washed-out color.

Heavy weight bitches brought a new and good one to the front in Mr. A. B. Truman's Queen Croxteth T., a clean, well framed and handsomely marked animal.

Light weight bitches made lively competition between Mr. A. B. Truman's Patti Croxteth T. and Dr. M. E. Taber's Babbetta (Mainspring—Dell). The latter is a recent importation, and is a clinker, clean, upstanding, of high quality, beautiful liver and white markings and excellent points, although not quite the equal of Patti Croxteth.

In pointer dog pups, Capt. A. B. Anderson had things his own way, winning with El Rio Rey (Climax—Roberta) He also won in pointer bitch pups with Susie Post, a litter sister to El Rio Rey.

English setters were very good, first in dogs going to Mr. J. F. Holbrook's Tom Payne, winner last year. In bitches, Mr. Harry Rose's Princess Nellie Elgin got first.

The Irish setter dog class gave the blue ribbon to Mr. A. B. Truman's Mike T., perfectly shown, and in bitches the same gentleman won first with plenty to spare, Lady Elcho T. looking better than ever, although Mr. E. J. Roy had fine entries. The Gordon setters were excellent, first in dogs being given to B. A. Breakey Jr.'s Duke, winner last year, and in bitches to Mrs. Edwin Cawston's Lady Lufton.

SUMMARY.

MASTIFFS—DOGS.

Mrs. Dorothea Lummis, Los Angeles.
Amado, fawn; whelped May 7th, 1888; breeder Richard Gird; sire Chino Lion, (13799), dam Chino Beauty, (13800); first.

Captain A. B. Anderson, Grange Kennels, San Gabriel.
Richland Commodore, light fawn; whelped Sept. 24, 1888; Richland Kennels; sire McCormick, dam Princess Dolly; second.

A. J. Ellis, Los Angeles.
Turk, fawn; whelped Oct. 14, 1888, breeder, Richard Gird; sire Chino Lion (13799) dam Chino Beauty, (13800); third.

MASTIFF—BITCHES.

Capt. A. B. Anderson, Grange Kennels, San Gabriel.
Atella A. (13707), fawn; whelped March 12, 1889, breeder, G. A. Swartout; sire Imperial Arno, (13014); dam Zella M., (6555); first.

Monroe Short, Los Angeles.
Daisy, fawn; whelped Jan. 8, 1889, breeders, Fisher & Atkinson; sire Wellington, dam Cassandra, (15099). Not for sale.

MASTIFF—DOG PUPPIES

Chas D. Willard, Los Angeles.
Wodan, fawn; whelped Dec. 4, 1889; breeder, Dan McFarland, sire Amado, dam Taffy; first.

ST. BERNARD—BITCHES.

Capt. A. B. Anderson, Grange Kennels, San Gabriel.
Dido II, orange white, whelped Aug. 21, 1885; imported. Sire Scotch Barry, dam Dido I; first.

NEWFOUNDLAND DOGS.

E. L. Medler, Los Angeles.
Ponto, black; whelped April, 1886; breeder and pedigree unknown; second.

GREAT DANES—DOGS.

Miss Keyes, Los Angeles.
Kaiser Wilhelm, brown, whelped Feb. 1888; breeder and pedigree unknown; second.

GREAT DANES—BITCHES.

Chas. Schmidt, Los Angeles.
Christiana, blue; whelped Sept. 10, 1888; breeder, Nelson, imported; pedigree unknown; second.

HARLEQUIN GREAT DANES—DOGS.

Dr W LeMoyne Wills, Los Angeles.
Tiger mottled; whelped June, 1888; breeder, owner; sire Bosko, dam Clio. Winnings, 1st. Los Angeles, 1889.

HARLEQUIN DANES—BITCHES.

Dr. W. Le Moyne Wills, Los Angeles.
Clio, mottled; whelped June, 1886; breeder, Wm. Silbey; sire unknown; dam Princess II. Winnings, 1st, 1889; first.

DEERHOUNDS—DOGS.

Mrs. James McLoughlin, Calegrove.
Captain, grey; breeder, Captain Hutchinson; sire Hector, dam Gruagach; first.

GREYHOUNDS—DOGS.

J. W. Gordon, Los Angeles.
Leo, fawn; whelped September 10, 1888; breeder, M. Boone; sire unknown, dam Nita. Value $55. Winnings 1st, Los Angeles, 1889; first.

H. Preston, Los Angeles.
King, brindle; whelped July 10, 1881; breeder, owner; sire Jack, dam Fleet; second.

Robert Heaney, Los Angeles.
Spring brindle; whelped February 10, 1885; breeder, Bella Castle Kennels, Ireland; sire Limerick Pat, dam Norna. Leased to West Coast Kennels; third.

Valley Hunt Club, Pasadena.
Victor, blue. Date of birth, breeder and pedigree unknown. V. H. C., res.

Dr. I. W. Hazelett, San Bernardino.
Dash, fawn; breeder, L. J. Rose. Date of birth and pedigree unknown. V. H. C.

Valley Hunt Club, Pasadena.
Raymond, fawn; breeder, J. De Barth Shorb. Date of birth and pedigree unknown. H. C.

Valley Hunt Club, Pasadena.
Flash, fawn; breeder, date of birth and pedigree unknown.

Valley Hunt Club, Pasadena.
Fleet, fawn. Date of birth, breeder and pedigree unknown.

GREYHOUND—BITCHES.

C. F. Holder, Valley Hunt Club, Pasadena.
Dina, fawn; whelped July, 1887. Breeder and pedigree unknown; first.

Dr. I. W. Hazelett, San Bernardino.
Topsy, fawn. Date of birth pedigree and breeder unknown; second.

GREYHOUND—BITCH PUPPIES.

J. W. Gordon, Los Angeles.
Deno, fawn; whelped July 23, 1889; breeder, M. Boone; sire unknown, dam Nita; first.

FOXHOUND—DOGS.

Valley Hunt Club, Pasadena.
Melody, black, white and tan; whelped March 6, 1889; breeders, owners; sire Byron, dam Echo; first.

Ben Davis, Orange.
Moro, red and white; whelped June 10, 1886; breeder, Cannon Ball Kennels, Ala. Pedigree unknown; second.

Ben Davis, Orange.
Chase, red; whelped Jan. 18, 1889; breeder, W. H. Bowers; sire unknown, dam Mollie, third.

FOXHOUNDS—BITCHES.

Valley Hunt Club, Pasadena.
Queen, black, white and tan; whelped March, 1889; breeders, owners; sire Byron, dam Echo; first.

Ben Davis, Orange.
Mollie, with litters, red and white; whelped March 18 1885; breeders, Cannon Ball Kennels, Ala. Pedigree unknown; second.

Valley Hunt Club, Pasadena.
Music, black, white and tan; whelped March, 1889; breeders, owners. Sire Byron, dam Echo; third.

POINTER DOGS—OVER 55 POUNDS.

R. T. Vandevort, Pasadena.
Billy V, lemon and white; whelped May 3, 1886; breeder, R. T. Vandevort; sire Vandevort's Don (Price's Bang—Peg), dam Drab (Dan—Arrow); first.

J. B. Mason, Los Angeles.
Rush II (10068), liver and white; whelped May 3, 1886; breeder, R. T. Vandevort; sire Don (2878), dam Drab; second.

POINTERS, DOGS, UNDER 55 LBS.

E. K. Benchley, Los Angeles.
Kan Koo, (13437), liver and white; whelped Aug. 5, 1888; breeder, A. B. Truman. Sire Rush T. 10069, (Sensation—Seph G); dam Patti Croxteth T 10128, (Croxteth—Patti M.) Winnings 1st and specials, Los Angeles 1889; first.

I. W. Hazelett, M. D., San Bernardino.
Strictly Business, lemon and white; whelped Aug. 9, 1889; breeder, Geo. W. Bassford; sire Scout Croxteth, 6277, (Croxteth 2801—Frank 7992;) dam Blossom, 10085 (Glen R.—Josie Bow,) second.

John H. Schumacher, Los Angeles.
Shot, liver and white; breeder, date of birth and pedigree unknown; third.

POINTERS, BITCHES, OVER 50 LBS.

A. B. Truman, San Francisco.
Queen Croxteth T., liver and white; whelped Aug. 5, 1888; breeder, A. B. Truman; sire Rush T., 10069, (Champion Sensation—Seph G), dam Patti Croxteth T, 10128, (Champion Croxteth—Champion Patti M); first.

S. D. Sanborne, West Coast Kennel.
Gypsy and litter, lemon and white; breeder, date of birth and pedigree unknown; second.

S A. Bennett, Long Beach.
Zanetta II, (3770) liver and white; whelped Aug. 14, 1886; breeder, R. G. Hall; sire Croxteth 2871, dam Van (Bang Bang 4012—Zanetta 8130) third.

POINTERS, BITCHES, UNDER 50 LBS.

A. B. Truman, San Francisco.
Patti Croxteth T. 10128, liver and white; whelped Dec. 28, 1886; breeder, C. M. Munhall; sire Champion Croxteth. (Champion Young Bang—Jane) dam Champion Patti M., (Champion Donald—Devonshire Lass). Winnings 1st and special San Francisco, 1888, 1st and specials San Francisco, 1889, 1st and specials Los Angeles, 1889; first.

M. E. Taber, San Bernardino.
Babbetta, (11034) liver and white ticked; breeder, E. A. Sterling; sire Mainspring (Mike—Romp), dam Dell (Croxteth 2871—Trinket 3116); second.

E. K. Benchley, Los Angeles.
Amie, lemon and white, whelped May 3, 1886; leased to West Coast Kennels; breeder, R. T. Vandevort; sire, Don, (2878), dam Drab.

POINTER DOG PUPPIES.

A. B. Anderson, San Gabriel.
El Rio Rey, lemon and white; whelped June 7, 1889; breeder, P. D. Linville; sire Climax, (Bang Bang—Bellona), dam Roberta, (Robert Le Diable—Young Beulah); first.

I. W. Hazelett, San Bernardino.
Strictly Business, lemon and white; whelped Aug. 9, 1889; breeder, Geo. W. Bassford; sire Scout Croxteth 6277, (Croxteth—Frank), dam Blossom 10085, (Glen R—Josie Bow); second.

C. E. Fout, Los Angeles.
Young Scout, 10886, liver and white; whelped Aug. 9, 1889; breeder, Geo. W. Bassford; sire Scout Croxteth 6279, (Champion Croxteth 2871—Frank 7992), dam Blossom 10085—(Glen R—Josie Bow); third.

POINTERS, BITCH PUPPIES.

A. B. Anderson, San Gabriel.
Susie Post, lemon and white; whelped June 7, 1889; breeder, P. D. Linville; sire Climax (Bang Bang—Bellona), dam Roberta (Robert le Diable—Young Beulah); first.

CLASS 30.—ENGLISH SETTERS—DOGS.

J. F. Holbrook, Los Angeles.
Tom Payne, 16890, black and white; whelped March 19, 1887; breeder, H. T. Payne; sire Grouse II, (Maybery's Dan—Sybil) dam Princess Claude 8369, (Bergundthal's Rake—Iowa Queen. Winnings 1st and specials, Los Angeles, 1889; first.

Godfrey Fritz, Los Angeles.
Prince Charles, black, white and tan; whelped April 25, 1889; breeder, owner; sire Payne's Jolly Planter 8219, (Champion Plantagenet—Countess Flirt), dam Nellie; second.

Mrs. J. A. Edmonds, West Coast Kennels, Los Angeles.
Prince Albe, 8241, black and white; whelped March 19, 1887; breeder, H. T. Payne. Sire Grouse II (Maybury's Dan—Sybil.) dam Princess Claude 8169, (Bergundthal's Rake—Iowa Queen); third.

ENGLISH SETTER—BITCHES.

Harry Rose, Los Angeles. (Leased to West Coast Kennels).
Princess Nellie Elgin (4843), black, white and tan; whelped June 12, 1885; breeder, H. B. Vondersmith; Sire Harry Elgin (Zanzibar—Lady Elgin); dam Nettie II (Harry Elgin—Princess Nettie; first.

H. T. Payne, Los Angeles. (Leased to West Coast Kennels).
Los Angeles, 8340, black, white and tan; whelped March 19, 1887; breeder, owner. Sire Grouse II, (Mayberry's Dan—Sybil); dam Princess Claude, 8369, (Bergundthal's Rake—Iowa Queen); second.

Tom Keefe, Los Angeles. (Leased to West Coast Kennels).
Nellie K., whelped Feb. 12, 1887; breeder, Harry Rose. Sire Chispa (Rock—Dora); dam Princess Nellie Elgin (Harry Elgin—Nettie II); third.

J. B. Mason, Los Angeles.
Sybil II, black and white; whelped Sept. 6, 1882; breeder, E. L. Maybury. Sire Maybury's Dan (Llewellin's Prince—Dora) dam Sybil (Leicester—Doll; V. H. C.

ENGLISH SETTERS—PUPPIES.

Tony Bright, Los Angeles
Prince Theo, 16888, black and white; whelped Oct. 10, 1889; breeder, Mr. Ruschaupt. Sire Royal Sport (Grouse II—Princess Claud); dam Daisy (Bartlett's Rob Roy—Ola); first.

ENGLISH SETTER—BITCH PUPPIES.

H. T. Payne, Los Angeles.
Jolly Fay, 16136, black and white, whelped May 12, 1889; breeder, owner Sire Jolly Planter, 8219, (Champion Plantagenet—Countess Flirt), dam Los Angeles, 8440, (Grouse II—Princess Claud); first.

IRISH SETTER DOGS.

A. B. Truman, San Francisco.
Mike T, 6435, red; whelped Feb. 17, 1884; breeder, E. Leavesley. Sire Nemo T, (Lany—Quail III); dam Nida (Larry—Red Bess). Winnings 1st and special San Francisco, 1886, 1st and specials San Francisco, 1888, 1st and specials Los Angeles, 1889; first

W. R. Davis, Los Angeles.
Don D, red; whelped July 1887; breeder and pedigree unknown; second.

E. B. Tufts, Los Angeles.
Duke Alexis, red; whelped Feb. 20, 1885, breeder, owner. Sire Jack; dam Bess (Ranger—Kate). Winnings 2nd, Los Angeles, 1889, third.

IRISH SETTER BITCHES.

A. B. Truman, San Francisco.
Lady Elcho, 6451, red; whelped April 3, 1885; breeder, Dr. Wm. Jarvis; sire Champion Elcho (Charlie—Nell), dam Champion Noreen (Champion Garryowen—Bell) Winnings, 1st and specials San Francisco, 1886, 1st and specials San Francisco 1888, 1st and specials San Francisco, 1889; 1st and specials Los Angeles, 1889; first.

Eng. J. Roy, San Francisco.
Rosabelle, red; whelped Nov. 24, 1888; breeder, L. L. Campbell; sire Pat O'More (Rory O'More—Nora O'More), dam Belle C (Mike T—Lady Elcho T). Winnings H. C. puppy class, San Francisco, 1889; second.

IRISH SETTER DOG PUPPIES.

Eug. J. Roy, San Francisco.
Shaun Rhue, red; whelped May 18, 1889; breeder, J. C. Nattrass; sire Nat Glencho, 6436 (Champion Glencho—Maid), dam Red Fanny, 10379 (Smutt—Meg); first.

GORDON SETTER DOGS.

B. A. Breakey, Jr., Los Angeles.
Duke, black and tan; breeder, Associated Fanciers; whelped Sept. 14, 1886; sire Royal Duke, dam Rudolpha. Winnings, 1st and special Los Angeles, 1889; first.

L. R. Darrow, San Diego.
Rover, black and tan; whelped 1884; breeder and pedigree unknown; second.

West Coast Kennels, Los Angeles.
Santa Anna, black and tan; date of birth unknown; breeder Jacob Willets, sire unknown, dam Judy; third.

GORDON SETTER BITCHES.

Mrs. Edwin Cawston, Norwalk.
Lady Lufton, black and tan; whelped April 13, 1885; breeder, G. Proctor, England; sire Stoke, dam Bess. Winnings 1st Los Angeles, 1889; first.

Homer C. Katz, Los Angeles.
Princess Nell and litter, black and tan; whelped 1884; breeder, owner; sire Vignolo's Cæsar, dam Princess Flora; V. H. C. at Los Angeles, 1889; second.

J. J. Hanford, Coronado.
Burton Lass, black and tan; whelped April, 1885; breeder, unknown; sire Stakeshot, dam Bess. Winnings 2nd Los Angeles, 1888; third.

John Machell, Oregon.
Nun, black and tan; whelped July 29, 1886; breeder, J. B. Proctor; sire Glen I, dam Lady Lufton. Winnings 3rd Los Angeles, 1889, V. H. C.

GORDON SETTER PUPPIES.

Jack Rush, Coronado
Belle, black and tan; whelped Oct. 30, 1889; breeder unknown; sire unknown, dam Burton Lass; first.

WATER SPANIEL DOGS.

Geo. Kloiz, Los Angeles.
Barney, seal brown; whelped 1879; breeder and pedigree unknown; second.

Theodore Friese, Los Angeles.
Dick; whelped June, 1888; breeder and pedigree unknown; third.

WATER SPANIEL—BITCHES.

John C. Cline, Los Angeles.
Rose, dark liver; whelped 1882; breeder and pedigree unknown; first.

IRISH WATER SPANIEL—DOGS.

L. W. Roberts, Albuquerque, N. M.
Captain Muldoon, 4897, liver; whelped July 14, 1886; breeder, Geo. Waddington; sire Hall's Dan (Mike, 31 5—Norah), dam Brant (Champion Barney, 3160—Cricket, 3173). Winnings 1st and special Buffalo, N. Y., 1887, 1st and special Kansas City, Mo., 1880, 1st and special Elmira, N. Y., 1889, 2nd Pittsburgh, Pa., 2nd Utica, N. Y., 1889, 2nd Rochester, N. Y., 1889, 2nd Philadelphia, Pa., 1889, 2nd Boston, April 9, 1890; first.

COCKER SPANIELS—BITCHES.

G. H. Hamstadt, San Bernardino.
Snowball, black, whelped Dec. 10, 1888; breeder, Charles Lemon; pedigree unknown. Second.

COCKER SPANIEL—PUPPIES.

Jno. Machell, Orange.
Lad, liver and white, whelped Aug. 27, 1889; breeder, E. Knight, sire, Prince; dam, Belle. First.

Jno. Machell, Orange.
Lass, liver and white; whelped Aug. 27, 1889; breeder, E. Knight, Sire, Prince; dam, Belle. Second.

FIELD SPANIEL—BITCHES.

Capt D. D. Wheeler, Los Angeles.
Chick, solid black; whelped 1886; breeder unknown; from Woodstock kennels. First.

B. B. Heineman, Los Angeles.
Queen, black; whelped Oct 1886; breeder, Mr. Ray. Sire, Rowdy; dam, Topsy. Winnings 2d Los Angeles, 1889. Second.

RETRIEVERS—DOGS OR BITCHES.

C. Milligan, Los Angeles.
Roy, black; whelped Jan. 1886. Breeder unknown. Sire unknown, dam Beauty. First.

W. F. Nordholt, Los Angeles.
Major, black; date of birth, breeder and pedigree unknown. Third.

COLLIE DOGS.

Capt. A. B. Anderson, San Gabriel.
Laddie, sable; whelped July 1, 1889. Breeder, Wood Wattles. Pedigree unknown. First.

COLLIE BITCHES.

Mrs. E. B. MacVine, Sunderlands, Los Angeles Co.
Juno. sable; whelped July 1886. Breeder, R. J. Walker. Pedigree unknown. First.

BULL TERRIERS—BITCHES—CHALLENGE.

Clarence A. Barnes, Los Angeles.
Little Nell. white; whelped April, 1883; breeder, E. Hood. Sire Little Victor; dam, Hood's Daisy Winnings 2d Warwick, England 1885; 1st Wolverhampton, 1885; 1st New York Fanciers, 1886; 1st Philadelphia, 1886; 1st Newark, 1886; 1st Boston, 1886; 1st New Haven 1886; 1st Pittsburg, 1886; 1st challenge class Los Angeles, 1889. First.

FOX-TERRIER DOGS.

C. A. Sumner, Los Angeles.
Blemton Vesuvian 14290, white, black and tan; whelped Aug. 13, 1888; breeder, August Belmont. Sire, Champion Lucifer; dam, Blemton Vesta. First.

Capt. A. B. Anderson, Grange Kennels, San Gabriel.
Regent Jock 10889, white; whelped April 30, 1889. Breeder, August Belmont Sire, Regent Vox (Tucker—Sandy Vic): dam, Blemton Saffron (Belgrave Primrose—Flirt). Winnings 2d San Francisco, 1889. Second.

J. B. Martin, San Francisco.
Blemton Shiner 14277, white and black; whelped July 14, 1889, breeder, August Belmont. Sire, Blemton Rubicon (Champion Regent—Champion Rachel); dam, Blemton Brilliant (The Moonstone—Media). Third.

Bolton & Chadwick, Los Angeles
Rags, black and tan: whelped Sept. 1888; breeder, E Malim, sire Tally, dam Finette II. Winnings 1s, puppy class Los Angeles, 1889; V. H. C. res.

Bolton & Chadwick, Los Angeles.
Tatters, black and white, whelped Sept 1888; breeder E. Malim; sire Tally. dam Finette II. Winnings V. H. C. puppy class, Los Angeles, '89; V. H. C.

FOX TERRIER BITCHES.

Capt. A. B. Anderson, Grange Kennels, San Gabriel.
Golden Patch, black, white and tan, whelped June 23, 1888; breeder, J. B. Martin; sire Sly Mixture (Mixture—Shone), dam Beatrice (Bacchanal—Blemton Arrow). Winnings 1st, Los Angeles, 1889, first.

Edward Malim, Los Angeles.
Folly, white, black and tan; whelped Aug. 15, 1889; breeder, owner; sire Tally (Warren Jim—Dance), dam Finette II (Bela—Finette); second.

Captain A. B. Anderson Grand Kennels, San Gabriel,
Tricksey, white, black and tan; whelped April 18, 1889, breeder, Jas. E. Watson; sire Teddy. dam Gyp 9937, third.

Roswell Hart, Riverside.
Hart's Nannie, white, black and tan; whelped March 25, 1888; breeder, G. L. Warring; sire Laddy (Figaro—Daisy), dam Oxford Milly (Ratter—Norma). V. H. C. res.

FOX TERRIER DOG PUPPIES.

J. B. Martin, San Francisco.
Blemton Shiner. 14277, white and black; whelped July 14. 1889, breeder, August Belmont; sire Blemton Rubicon. 8954, (Champion Regent—Champion Rachel), dam Blemton Brilliant (The Moonstone—Media), first.

FOX TERRIER BITCH PUPPIES.

J. B. Martin, San Francisco.
Golden Lily, white; whelped July 14 1889; breeder, owner; sire Clover Turk (Mixture—Spite); dom Beatrice, 13830, (Champion Bacchanal—Blemton Arrow), first.

C, A. Sumner, Los Angeles.
Warren Truthful, white, black and tan; whelped Aug. 18, 1889; breeder, S. W. Rutherford; sire Warren Jim (Diamond Joe—Diapar) dam Warren Torment (Resolute—Warren Leda), second.

Dan McFarland, Los Angeles.
Clochette, white and tan, whelped July 4, 1889: breeder and pedigree, unknown, third.

BLACK AND TAN TERRIERS OVER SEVEN POUNDS.

Charles F. Manning, Los Angeles.
McGinty, black and tan; whelped Oct. 27, 1887; breeder, owner: sire Jack, dam Chippie; first.

SCOTCH TERRIERS.

Capt. Janes, Los Angeles.
Monkey, red: whelped 1885: breeder, owner: pedigree not known: first.

C. S. Campbell-Johnston, Garavanza.
Tatters, tan: whelped April. 1888; breeder, S Tyler. Sire Scotia, dam Biz. Winning 1st Los Angeles, 1889: second.

S. Tyler, Pasadena.
Pepper, blue and Fawn: whelped September 1, 1889: breeder, owner: sire Scotia, dam Biz: third.

SCOTCH TERRIER PUPPIES.

Captain Janes, Los Angeles.
Shorty, blue: whelped Sept. 1, 1889: breeder, owner: pedigree unknown: first.

TOY TERRIERS UNDER SEVEN POUNDS.

John Horner, Los Angeles.
Midget, black; whelped 1887: breeder and pedigree unknown: first.

JAPANESE SPANIELS—DOGS OR BITCHES

Mrs Alex McBear, Oakland, Cal.
Frou Frou: date of birth, breeder and pedigree unknown. Winnings 1st San Francisco, 1889: first

PUG DOGS.

A. B Anderson, San Gabriel.
Bobby, fawn; date of birth, breeder and pedigree unknown: first.

Chris Krempel, Los Angeles.
Mops, fawn: whelped March, 1884; breeder unknown: sire Mops, dam unknown: second.

PUG BITCHES.

Mrs. H. E. Biewend, Los Angeles.
Patti. fawn: whelped April 30, 1887: breeder, Mrs. Comings: pedigree unknown: first.

Chris Krempel, Los Angeles.
Bella. fawn: whelped October, 1888: breeder, owner: sire Mops, dam Topsy: second.

SPITZ.

Morris Fitzgerald, Los Angeles.
Fany and litter, white: whelped May, 1889; breeder, owner; pedigree unknown: second.

Mrs. K. Short, Los Angeles.
Flossy, white; whelped, 1888: breeder, Mr. Grant; sire Ned: dam unknown: third.

FOX HOUND KENNELS.

Valley Hunt Club, Pasadena, first.

GREYHOUND KENNELS.

Valley Hunt Club, Pasadena, first.

ENGLISH SETTER KENNELS.

West Coast Kennels, Los Angeles, first.

MISCELLANEOUS.

James W Warren, Los Angeles.
Belle, liver and white: whelped 1888: breeder and pedigree unknown; first.

SPECIALS.

Best Pointer Bitch, A. B. Truman's Patti Croxteth T.
Best Scotch Terrier, two specials. Capt Jane's Monkey.
Best Pointer puppy, three specials, Captain A. B. Anderson's El Rio Rey.
Best Cocker Spaniel, two specials, John Machell's Lad
Best Irish setter, best dog in the show, best sporting dog or bitch, best dog and bitch same breed, best breeding kennel, six specials, A. B. Truman's Lady Elcho T.
Best Grey Hound, J. W. Gordon's Leo.
Best Newfoundland dog or bitch, heaviest dog in show, E. O. Medlar's Ponto.
Best Great Dane, Dr. W. L. Will's Tiger.
Best English setter dog. J. F. Holbrook's Tom Payne.
Best Mastiff dog and best Mastiff, three specials, Mrs. Dorothea Lummis' Amado.
Best Water Spaniel, John C. Cline's Rose.
Best English Setter puppy. H. T. Payne's Jolly Fay.
Best dog or bitch of any breed exhibited by a lady, best Deerhound, Mrs. James McLoughlin's Deerhound Captain.
Best exhibit of dogs for one kennel. Capt. A. B. Anderson.
Best greyhound puppy, J. W Gordon's Deno.
Best fox-hound, two specials, Valley Hunt Club's Queen.
Best fox-terrier, one of best kennels of fox-terriers, Capt. A. B. Anderson's Golden Patch.
Best Gordon setter bitch and best Gordon in show, three specials, Mrs. Edwin Cawston's Lady Lufton.
Best fox-terrier dog, C. A. Sumner's Blemton Vesuvian.
Best pointer dog, two specials, E. K. Benchley's Kan Koo.
Best retriever, two specials, C. Milligan's Roy.
Best English setter dog puppy. Tony Bright's Prince Theo.
Best bull terrier, best dog or bitch in Challenged classes, best non-sporting dog or bitch, Clarence A. Barnes' Little Nell.
Best pug. best bred dog exhibited by a lady, three specials, Mrs. A. B. Anderson's Bobby.
Best dog and bitch, same breed, exhibited by one exhibitor, A. B. Truman's Irish setters Mike T., Lady Elcho T.
Best bitch with litter of puppies. E. K. Benchley's Amie.
Best English setter bitch, Harry Rose's Princess Nellie Elgin.
Best collie, two specials, Capt. A. B. Anderson's Laddie.
Best breeding kennel by one exhibitor, A. B. Truman's Mike T., Lady Elcho T., Patti Croxteth T., and Queen Croxteth T.
Best kennel of fox-terriers, Capt. A. B. Anderson's Regent Jock, Tricksey and Golden Patch.
Best spitz. Morris Fitzgerald's Fanny.
Bitch with most puppies, Mrs. Frank Hanley's Nell.
Best black and tan terrier, Chas F. Manning's McGinty.
Best fox-terrier only twelve months old, J. B. Martin's Golden Lilly.
Best greyhound bitch, C. F. Holder's Dina.

Visits.

Mr. Martin Forrest's fox-terrier Fawn to Mr. C. A. Sumner's Blemton Vesuvian (14290), Los Angeles, May 11th.

Mr. J J Kerrigan's English setter, Beezy (Regent—Wildflower) to Mr. W. S. Kittle's Luke (Carl R—Bessie) May 13th at San Francisco.

Whelps.

EDITOR BREEDER AND SPORTSMAN:—I report to you the whelping of two more of my Cocker Spaniel bitches.

Woodstock Ada whelped on 21st April 1890, nine to my cocker dog Kate.

Cherry A K C S B 13056, whelped April 24th 1890—eight to my blk. dog Bropta A K C S B 17064.

A. C. DAVENPORT.

EDITOR BREEDER AND SPORTSMAN:—Last Sunday (May 11th) my Fox Hound bitch, "Jill" just imported, whelped 9—2 dogs and 7 bitches to my Fox Hound dog "Jack."

This pair of dogs "Jack and Jill" arrived here on March 19th direct from the West Kent (England) Kennels, and are a very fine pair.

JAMES E. WATSON.

Notes.

Mr. Geo. T. Allender writes that his dogs are all well, and the Derby entries doing nicely.

If the subscriber who recently expressed a desire to have a Newfoundland-dog, will again send his address, we can perhaps assist him.

The dog show at Los Angeles during last week, was judged in all classes by the Kennel Editor of this paper, which may excuse seeming over sight to correspondents.

The San Francisco visitors to the Los Angeles dog show were invited by Mr. T. E. Walker to his delightful home "The Toltec" and given the freedom of the place.

Owners should not forget that entries to the Field Trials' Derby close on June 1st, and that no entry will be received without the forfeit, $5. Seven have already been made, and the stake should number at least thirty.

A bit of news that will be generally relished, is that Mr. Henry Wormington, of this city, who has been abroad for some months, has returned. A keener courser, kinder man or more likeable companion cannot be found.

Mr. William Schreiber has purchased from Mr. A. B. Truman, a pointer dog puppy by Point (Don—Drab)—Queen Croxteth T. (Rush T.—Patti Croxteth T.) The puppy is said by Mr. Schreiber to be very bright and nice.

The successful outcome of the Los Angeles dog show has caused some little talk among San Franciscans about giving a show here in the fall. It does seem that a show might be given and managed so judiciously as to clear expenses, even if, it does not result in profit. We hope the agitation will continue.

Mr. J. M. Kilgarif, Treasurer of the Pacific Coast Field Trial Club, on Wednesday last embarked upon the sea of Monterey and the train for Los Angeles. We have known "Kil," man and boy, for these many years, and can recall no joining of futures in which both parties could more heartily or confidently be congratulated.

A story comes to us that Mr. Geo. Rainey of Napa County recently killed some deer hounds belonging to Mr. Andrew Jackson of the Napa Soda Springs. It is stated that Mr. Rainey knew the dogs, and that they had been raised with sheep, and were absolutely harmless, but finding them near a band of sheep, he deliberately shot them. If the facts are as stated, no condemnation can be severe enough to meet the gravity of the offence. Even if taken in the act of worrying sheep, the law gives no one a right to kill a dog. There is another remedy and an adequate one. It the temptation to kill a dog is so overpowering, could the owner of the dog be blamed if his resentment led him to summary revenge against the dog slayer? We would like to hear the Rainey side of the affair.

The Prince Regent really the King of Bavaria has presented W F Cody with a diamond ring and Miss Annie Oakley with a diamond bracelet. Each has the Kings crown and monogram engraved on it and are very valuable presents of which they are both very proud.

THE GUN.

The Fourth Shooting Tournament for the Peters Cartridge Company's medal, emblematic of the championship of California at artificial targets, will take place at Coronado Beach, San Diego Co., Cal., May 25, 1890. The conditions will be the same as in previous matches. Shoot 1, at 6 singles and 3 pair Blue Rocks; entrance $2, birds included. Purse to be divided into 40, 30, 20 and 10 per cent. Medal shoot, at 26 single and 12 pair Blue Rocks; entrance $3, birds extra. 40, 30, 20 and 10 per cent., with the additional prizes, donated by the San Diego merchants.

Silver water service ....donated by St. James Hotel, value $40 00
One pair boots or shoes ....donated by F. Wright & Co., " 10 00
Split bamboo rod ....donated by F. S Ecker, " 7
One set of carvers ....donated by F. N. Hamilton, " 7
One years subscription to Daily Sun donated by W. E. Simpson " 7
One gallon best whiskey ....donated by V. Jones, " 6
One fine hat ....donated by J. G. Gaffagan, " 5 50
One dozen photos, cabinet ....donated by J. Lenz, " 5 50
One pearl handle pocket knife...donated by Todd & Hawley, " 4 00

Box of cigars and bottle monogram by C. S. Chase, to be awarded to the contestant making the lowest score during the entire shoots for the day. First prize, Peters medal and a pair of boots or shoes. Contestants making highest scores to have choice of remaining prizes. Merit shooting will be applied in this shoot. Shoot 3, at 20 single Blue Rocks; entrance $3, birds included. Shoot 4, at 6 single and 3 pair Blue Rocks; entrance $200, birds included. Shoot 5, at 15 single Blue Rocks, 28 yds. for 12 g., 30 yds. for 10-gauge guns, Hurlingham rules; entrance $250, birds included. American Association rules to govern. All money to be divided into 40, 30, 20 and 10 per cent. unless otherwise agreed upon.

Alameda County Club.

The May meeting of the club was held at Oakland Trotting Park on Saturday afternoon last, fourteen members participating, despite the wet weather. The birds were poor, but the strong wind made them rather hard to stop. Mr. J. O. Cadman missed the April shoot and was allowed to shoot up his score.

The match was at twelve birds, American Shooting Association rules. The scores were:

F. B Norton	1	1	1	0	1	0	0	0	1	1	1	1	8
W. E Mayhew	1	1	0	1	0	1	1	0	1	0	1	2	9
Dr. Slade	1	1	0	0	1	1	1	1	1	1	0	1	9
C. M. Randall	1	1	0	0	2	0	1	0	1	2	1	1	9
H. Schroeder	2	0	2	0	0	1	1	1	1	2	1	2	8
J. e. Cadman	2	1	1	2	1	1	1	1	0	1	1	1	11
C. Morrison	2	0	1	1	1	1	2	0	0	2	0	0	7
C. Lainer	1	1	1	2	2	2	1	2	1	1	0	1	11
Harry Golcher	1	2	1	2	2	1	0	0	2	1	2	2	10
C. B. Smith	1	1	1	0	1	2	1	1	1	1	1	2	11
J. O. Cadman	1	1	0	0	0	0	2	2	1	1	0	1	7
H McMurchy	2	1	1	1	1	0	2	0	1	1	0	2	9
S. I. Kellogg	0	0	0	2	1	2	2	2	1	1	1	2	9
George Moore	0	2	2	1	1	2	1	1	1	2	0	2	10
G. F. Plummer	0	2	0	0	1	2	2	0	1	0	2	2	7
R. Bell	0	1	0	0	2	1	1	1	0	1	0	1	7
C. T. Boardman	1	1	0	1	1	0	1	1	1	2	0	0	9

ROD.

The "Call" Scored.

EDITOR BREEDER AND SPORTSMAN:—Among the sporting items of the Call in Sunday's issue, the 11th inst., appears another false statement regarding the work now being done by the North Pacific Land and Improvement Company at the Glen Ellen Fishery. As this is not the first uncalled for slur on the work being done here, the Call had better seek a more reliable source for its information, if it wishes its utterances to have any weight with the public.

The following is a statement of facts:

Every fish hatched here this season from eggs taken from Sonoma Creek was put back into Sonoma Creek, and not one was sent to Lake or any other county, as misstated in the Call. The North Pacific Land and Improvement Company purchased in the State of Nevada a large lot of fish eggs, and hatched them here, and when ready placed them in Robinson Creek, a stream emptying into Russian River.

The lot of eggs now hatching here are to be placed when ready in Sonoma Creek and Russian River and its tributaries, unless the ceaseless whinings of the sore-heads cause the Company to leave Sonoma Creek out entirely. As all this work is done free of expense to the sportsmen or the State, one would naturally think they would accept the gratuity with thanks, instead of filling the Call's sporting columns with false statements.

The statement that the streams hereabout are decimated is true, and the cause is equally palpable. The fish that laid the golden egg has been killed during its breeding season by poachers who followed them persistently to their destruction, until the Fish Commissioners made some healthy examples.

The benefit of the work now being done here cannot of course appear until next season or the season following, as your attention is called to the fact that the fish are not hatched fully grown.

As to the matter of "salmon" and "salmon trout" and "steel head salmon trout," etc., etc., the question has been fully settled upon the highest authority, and the only persons who still call our brook trout by these false names are possibly those pseudonym sportsmen who seek to destroy them while spawning. ALFRED V. LAMOTTE.

GLEN ELLEN, May 12, 1890.

EDITOR BREEDER AND SPORTSMAN:—I have recently sold to Mr. George J. Harley, of your city, the Field Trial winning dog Dan Gladstone, (Gladstone—Sue). Mr. Harley leaves here to-night for Frisco accompanied by his dog, as Dan is to be returned East in September. His services should be secured for some of your good bitches. I have seen the dog and some of his get run recently and can recommend him. I have sold that corking good dog Gath's Mark to Mr. Henry Hulman, of Terre Haute, Ind, whom I also sold, Fannie M, Nannie S, Olivette, Rods Gal, I. X. L., all of which are familiar to your readers, besides several others yet to be heard from. Such a really good string of field dogs I have never selected for any one man before. The attached lines, which are undoubtedly original with Dr. Maclin, were tacked on Gath's box when shipped. Am glad to report that I am doing very well with my dog business and its encouraging to know my efforts are appreciated.

PERCY C. OHL.

[The "lines" by Dr. Maclin are as follows:

"Please handle with care and water and feed
This noted dog of range and speed:
Cruelty to animals is the unpardonable sin,
Avoid it if you wish heaven to win.
There is another place that is known full well
In the unrevised book, it's name is hell;
So if you would avoid this and win the other.
Treat "Gaths Mark" as you would a brother."

JAS. N. MACLIN.]

THE FARM.

The Silver Grey Dorking.

No doubt the Dorking is one of the oldest of our domestic fowls, if not the oldest. There are no definite records to show when it was first bred in this country, or whence it came, except in the latter case the supposition that it came to us by the Romans, who evidently possessed a fowl with somewhat similar characteristics. On this point Mowbray says:

"Is undoubtedly a breed of great antiquity, having been noticed and described in the first century of the Christian era by Columella and Pliny; and there seems fair grounds for supposing that these birds were introduced into this country by the Romans, among whom they had attained at that early period, some celebrity, and were much esteemed; with us but few fowls can boast such high and long continued reputation as the Dorkings. It has been suggested that Shakespeare was acquainted with the superior qualities of these fowls, and that he alludes to them in his Henry IV., when he makes Justice Shallow, of Glos'ter, order 'a couple of short legged hens' for his guest's repast. The chief distinctive mark or characteristic of the breed is the presence of a fifth, or supernumerary toe, springing behind, a little above the foot, and below the spur. It has been sought by various writers to deprive Dorking of the honor of being the original and principal rearing place of this justly celebrated variety; and it is asserted that the true Dorking fowls are raised at Horsham, Cuckfield, and other places in the Weald of Surrey; and that the ancient and superior white fowls from Dorking are a degenerated race compared with the 'improved' Sussex breed."

It has also been claimed that the Dorking does not owe its origination to Surrey or Sussex at all, but comes to us from the north of England, for in Wingfield and Johnson's Poultry Book, published early in the fifties, we find it stated that "some writers have even ventured to assert that the native place of the Dorking is among the Cumberland Hills. It is certain that in that region is a race of fowls, five-toed, and bearing other points of resemblance to the Dorking. These are known in Cumberland as the 'Jew breed;' but it appears to be called still farther north, 'the silver pheasant kind,' and at Edinburgh, 'the old Scotch breed.'" In the same work a quotation is made from the Gardener's Chronicle of 1848, which says:

"This Jew kind is said to be very ancient in Cumberland; and it is still very usual for the Lancashire men to carry off any fine birds of this race which they see among the mountain cottagers. However, it would be a vain attempt to trace the origin of a breed which was accurately described 2,000 years ago by a Roman writer; and, as Roman stations abound in Cumberland, it is quite possible that a poultry-fancying prætor, 1,500 years since, might send or carry in the same year the first couple of Dorking fowls to the banks of the Thames, and to the old camp at Ambleside or Castle Hill near Keswick."

Both the colored and the Silver Grey Dorkings have undoubtedly sprung from the old gray variety, the colored being brought to their present form by a cross made by Mr. John Douglass, while the Silver Greys have been produced by careful selection of the light-colored and soundest silver-plumaged birds. That being so, the claim that the Silver Greys are the purer Dorking cannot be denied. It is certainly a very handsome fowl, having that square box shape which is so characteristic of the Dorking race, and in good specimens the plumage is rich in color. It is thought that as a rule the Silver Grey does not attain the same size as the colored, but I have often seen birds of one variety just as large as the other, and there can be no doubt as to the capacity for fattening of these fowls. It is often said that the Dorking is not a hardy fowl. This is, however, misleading. The Dorking cannot certainly be kept on any soil, or in any place, and damp, cold ground is fatal to it. But the fact that it is so largely bred in the north of Scotland, away in the extreme north of Ireland among the Cumberland hills, and in numberless places which are cold and exposed, shows that it is a hardy fowl in all respects save one—that it is unable to withstand damp, clay soils. No matter how cold the place may be so long as it is dry and free from clay; it will do well, at least that is the experience in this country. It is a fair layer, as good as are any of the Dorking family, makes a capital sitter and an attentive "biddy," and, of course, is one of the finest fowls that can be found on the table. This is partially due to the readiness with which it will fatten, for without this quality it would be impossible to ripen the flesh as is now done. The flesh is exquisitely white, and very delicate in its texture. In fact, it is difficult to imagine a finer fowl on the table than the Dorking, and it is equal to nearly all the best French varieties, though I am inclined to think that the La Bresse and La Fleche sometimes surpass it, though they would never do so if the same system of fattening was adopted here as in the districts of France where these two varieties of fowl are so largely bred. Nowadays there are vast multitudes of fowls sold in London as Surrey or Sussex, which have simply been fattened in those counties, but were never bred there and have not a trace of Dorking blood in their veins. But the system of fattening is so excellent that they may make fair birds, though of course, not to be compared with the splendid fat Dorkings which the best poulterers supply.

The advice which must be tendered to those who think of keeping Dorkings is that they should first consider whether the place they have is suitable, for unless this the case, they are better left alone. Then second, the demands of the market or the needs of the poultry-keeper must be regarded. If the demand is for table fowls nothing could be better, provided that anything like a fair price can be obtained for them, as it would not pay to breed Dorkings to sell at three shillings a couple. If eggs are chiefly in demand, Dorkings would be of no use, as they are only moderate layers. The egg is large in size, and very fine in flavor, the shell being pure white. As a proof of the value of this variety of the Dorking it may be mentioned that it is growing rapidly in favor in France, where it is highly esteemed for its economic qualities. The other varieties of the Dorking are scarcely to be met with across the English channel.

The following are the points of color in Silver Grey Dorkings:

Cock.—Head, silvery white; hackle, pure silvery white, as free from stripes as possible; comb, face, earlobes and wattles, bright coral red; beak, horn or white; eye, orange; breast thighs and underparts, black; Back, shoulder coverts, saddle and wing bow, pure silvery white; coverts, greenish black; primaries black, edged with white; secondaries, part of outer web forming "wing bay," white; remainder of feathers forming wing butt, black; tail, greenish, glossy black; legs, feet and toe nails, white.

Hen.—Eye, beak, comb, face, wattles, legs, feet and toe nails, same as in the cock; head, silvery white, with slight grey marking; hackle, silvery white, clearly striped with black breast, rich robin red or salmon red, shading off to grey on lower parts, back, shoulder coverts, saddle, wing bow and wing coverts, bright silvery grey, with minute pencilling of darker grey on each feather; the shafts of the feathers white; primaries, grey or black; secondaries, grey; tail, grey, of a darker shade than body; quill feathers, black.—Stephen Beale in Am Cultivator.

Does Raising Poultry Pay?

We have often been asked, Does it pay to raise poultry? It is just as reasonable to ask us, Does it pay to engage in business pursuits? Some men fail and some succeed. If asked this question, Jay Gould or Russell Sage would say that it did pay, while the ninety-five per cent of all the advertisers who annually fall by the wayside would report discouragingly. If one has adaptability, perseverance, intelligence, and a proper sense of the value of the details, success will follow effort; but slipshod, inexperienced experimenters will unquestionably fail. Too much is expected from slight investments and indifferent attention to minor duties of the business. The tendency of the age is the desire to do a big business and reap large profits on small investments. Men who imagine that they can grow amazingly rich in a few years in raising fancy poultry without much effort should stay out of the business entirely, unless it is treated as an exclusive business with appropriate investment of money and time. We need only address the class who wish to engage in it in a moderate way. To such persons we would say poultry can be made to pay a handsome percentage of profit. Boys and girls on the farm where but slight expense is needed to procure houses, and where feed can be obtained cheaply, may surely expect success if they start with the right kind of stock. But in order to know just what is gained, a strict account of everything that is consumed—every hour's work performed—should be kept; the eggs and meat whether eaten by the family or sent to the market, should be credited to the stock at ruling prices; in short, book accounts must be opened, and the business be conducted on business principles. Experience of that character will be beneficial in more ways than one —Jason Ellais, in Southern Farmer.

The Angora Goat.

Though we find indications in the old testament which make it appear that the Angora goat had already existed in Asia and Asia Minor at and before King Solomon's time and as the Golden Fleece of the ancient Greeks most likely was nothing else but an Angora goat skin of a bright yellowish color, yet the first positive knowledge of this valuable animal's existence was not received in Europe before the middle of the sixteenth century, from a description of Father Belon, then traveling in Asia Minor.

The Angora goat, however, does not appear to have been indigenous to Asia Minor; but according to traditions in the goat districts of that country, it came from Central Asia. This seems very probable, as the very tribe who are now principally carrying on the mohair goat husbandry came, according to the most prominent Orientalist, originally from the southern border of Siberia. Be this as it may, the animal, as it presents itself to us to-day was first found by Europeans in the Asiatic peninsula, had existed there in large numbers for thousands of years, and we may therefore consider that country as its proper home.

The shape of a perfect Angora goat, when in full fleece, should appear like a right-angled square (parallelogram). The body should be full and long, and of straight build. It should be densely and evenly covered with fine, curly and lustrous silky hair, appearing from a distance as if it had been trimmed off below the body. The chest and shoulders, especially with the male animal, should be broad and strong; the legs straight and chunky; the head clean cut and trim, not coarse like that of the common goat. The horns of the buck are long and strong, inclined towards the back, and of spiral-like shape, some almost perfect spirals· the horns of the ewes, short and thin and curved backward. Hornless Angoras exist but are rare. The ears are almost always what are commonly called "lop-ears," and differ very much in size; those of some animals are over a foot long and about four inches wide. However, the existence of so-called "fox ears" or "mouse ears" is by no means an evidence of impurity of blood.

When first born the kid is covered with short, curly, white hair, looking very much like Astrachan fur only coarser. This hair, however, grows but little, and the kid begins to lose it shortly after the mohair has made its appearance, and in its stead a very short straight hair begins to grow between the mohair, which only rarely grows long enough to be touched by the shears at clipping time.—Stock Grower.

Swine Raising.

Management of Pigs After Weaning Time.

After the sow has had her young she should be given food that she can easily digest. At first it is best to feed her lightly, and then gradually increase the amount of food she gets as the strain becomes greater on her. Sickness should be guarded against both in the mother and her young, and the best protections against disease are pure air and sunshine. They should have a good warm pen with a yard attached. The young pigs should be taught to feed themselves as soon as possible. The trough should be a shallow, flat bottomed one, so arranged that the sow cannot get to it. The food of the young pigs should consist first of milk, then of middlings, oats, or barley meal mixed with warm milk. They may be weaned gradually at the end of six or eight weeks, and a little oil meal, and also corn and pea meal, may be added to their food. Their growth should now be pushed along as fast as possible, and they should be fed regularly, say about five times a day, but only given as much as they will eat up clean each time. A little salt may be added. Care should be taken that they are fed regularly as much as they will eat. Green oats pulled up by the roots is a good form of green food for them, as is also green clover, and it is well to have a pasture field or yard provided for the pigs to run in. They should not be fed on foods too fattening in their nature, such as corn, when growing, as a young pig will not grow well if too fat; but they should be given green food principally, as this will supply materials for the building of bone and growing of muscle.—Montana Farming and Stock Journal.

Fat Saps Vitality.

W. E. Pendleton says: Showmen of hogs at the fairs hurt their stock by excessive fattening. Should an exhibition of breeding stock be turned into a fat stock show? A breeder anxious to make a fine display frequently fattens his swine for weeks in advance, and it takes months to reduce them again to good breeding condition. I lost more than I gained by this error last year. Two of my sows shown last year lost their litters of pigs. The pigs were small, weak and puny. The sows had no room to grow and mature pigs; they were too fat. Farrowing caused great pain, the sows were clumsy had little milk and were faulty in many ways, while usually these very animals have done well. The boars were lazy and their offspring weakened. But how are breeders to give up the foolish practice? At the fairs, the judges demand fat breeding hogs. One of my boars at a fair scored high, but was severely cut by the judges because he lacked flesh. I had taken special pains to keep him from being fat, because I wanted good pigs. There is a happy medium between showing for fat stock and for breeders, and the quicker we get there the better. Showing in fair working condition, not too fat, nor by any means too poor, is better for all. This would be just as fair for one breeder as another and would not ruin stock. If it be necessary to show what the breed will produce for the pork barrel, let us have a little side show for fat animals at each fair.—Montana Farming Stock Journal.

Protectionists Tire of the Sheep and Turn to Poultry.

The sheep has perversely refused to respond to the nurturing hand of protection. His fleece has been heavily "protected" for the past quarter of a century, but the obdurate animal has refused to keep pace with increased population and increased demand for his wool. Forty years ago there was a sheep a piece in the country for everyone. Now we are short 20,000,000 sheep of enough to go round.

There is evidence that the incapacity of the sheep to demonstrate the efficacy of protection is turning the minds of protectionists against him and in an other direction. The Committee on Ways and Means have their eyes on the hen. It is a well known fact that this unpretending creature adds every year more to the wealth of the country than do all the sheep in it. She has done this thing in complaining competition with foreign hens. Instead of bleating lament over the injustice done her, she has gone about her task with cackling complacence. This fact is no longer to go unrecognized. There is to be a tariff imposed upon eggs. The hen is to be cherished as she well deserves, and her eggs are to be added to the list of things made dearer and more precious by protection. Republics are not ungrateful.—Philadelphia Record.

Treatment of Milk Fever.

The fear of milk fever in cows creates much anxiety with some dairymen. It can generally be avoided by diet before parturition and for a few days after, but not many take this precaution. It is only when confronted with actual cases that many owners bestir themselves to do anything for the animals. Then unless a veterinary practitioner is convenient the cow usually dies; and when the disease has progressed far it is an even chance with his assistance that the patient recovered. Formerly when managing cows I kept certain remedies on hand. I have treated successfully three cases, one of them almost hopeless. The remedies I used, and how, I give below: Homœopathic tinctures of aconite, belladonna, nux vomica, arsenicum album and ammonium causticum. These were given in ten drop doses, each put in a tablespoonful of water and placed far back on the tongue. At first aconite and belladonna were administered in alternation every two hours as long as symptoms of pain were exhibited. If the animal bloated, and they generally do, I discontinued these for a time and gave one dose of ammonium, which relieved the bloat every time, and then returned to the former treatment if there was still evidence of pain. When that had ceased I gave arsenicum once an hour for five hours, and followed this with nux vomica in two, three, four, five and six hours. The treatment should be varied according to the "ensemble" of the symptoms, bearing in mind that aconite tends to allay fever, belladonna the secretion of milk, ammonium to reduce bloat, and arsenicum and nux vomica have a tendency to strengthen, each to be given as the symptoms indicate. While it is advisable to call a veterinary practitioner it is well to keep these remedies on hand for use when one cannot be had. The Homœophatic physician can furnish the remedies, and while he might advise additional curatives in some cases he will know these are proper to be given as recommended. A further thought is, they can do no harm.—Galen Wilson, in Stockman and Farmer.

The Trail in Texas Stopped by Stockmen.

The day of the Texas trail is about over. The stockmen of southeastern Colorado have taken their Winchester rifles in hand to inform the drovers of the sea lion district that they are well and hope that these few lines will find them the same. They go on to say that they object to having their ranches made a road of, and discuss the side matter of disease germs, bacilli, microbes and distempers. In other words the Colorado cattlemen say that sanitary law or no sanitary law the Texas cattle shall not pass through their ranches if several hundred men with lead and dynamite can head them off. This would be most discouraging to the gentle drover from Texas were it not for the consolation that cattle can be shipped by rail according to law, and arrive at their destination quicker and in better shape. Considering the trouble, delay and opposition it is really better and cheaper to ship than to trail. The trail is gone, the rail is here.—Las Vegas Stock Grower.

Grim's Gossip.

"I told you so; a mare cannot win the Brooklyn Handicap."

Next week we will present a list of the entries to the Oakland Association.

Almont Eagle, 2:27, full brother to Piedmont, 2:17½, will be sent to reduce his record this season.

All reports to the contrary, notwithstanding, the fastest full mile that Direct has made this year is 2:25.

Senator Stanford has fully determined to sell no more Electioneers at present. This should send the market still higher.

"Big Jim" Garland Matt Storn, E F. Smith, Ab Stemler Isadore Townsend, Wilbur F. Smith and General Hart, were all down from Sacramento on Thursday.

It is now claimed in Indiana that Roy Wilkes will make his last season East this year, and that henceforth the pacing stallion will have California as a home.

The A. W. Richmond fillies at the Hill sale averaged $427. The day is not far distant when Richmond mares will be worth many times what they brought at the sale.

Mr. F. D. Meyers of Oakland, who has purchased a number of brood mares in the East, will ship them to their California home, toward the latter part of this month.

Owners of pacers should bear in mind the $1000 offered by the Breeders' Association for the 2:20 sidewheelers. This will be a great contest, and it will be a hard matter to pick the winner.

The Kentucky Derby was run on Wednesday last, and the winner turned up in Ed Corrigan's Riley. Thomas Francis Meagher was heard to observe to Matt Storn, "This is a great day for the Irish."

Mr. William Ashby, of Oakland, reports that his Almont stallion, Ashland Almont 3491, has received a fine lot of mares and that this will be the last season for him to stand at the present price.

Electioneer has still another of his get to bring him honor, as on May 1st Suisun, made her first mark of 2:25½. This makes the first three horses to enter the 2:30 list in 1890, all of California birth.

It is rumored that Mr. Wm. Russell Allen, one of the owners of the Southern Hotel, St. Louis, is considering the idea of erecting a new hotel at Lexington, Ky., where additional hotel accommodations are badly needed.

Many complaints have been heard because the Brooklyn programme books can not be had in San Francisco, but the reason is, Secretary McIntyre has been seriously ill, and the Pacific slope has been overlooked in the distribution.

Guenoc Stock Farm is again in luck as a full brother to St. Savior has lowered the victorious colors of Badge, the mighty sprinter. Eon is the name of the new candidate for turf honors, and he promises to keep up the great reputation of his family.

A gentleman who was present at the recent sale of Nelson stock in Boston says that the yarn printed in a New York paper regarding a heated argument between C. H. Nelson and Myrtle Downing over the Balch stallion race did not contain one truthful statement.

Sam Bryant thinks more attention should be paid to breeding jockies. He says the cross should be sire Irish, dam English to stay, and Jew for cunning. All the dare devil riders are Irish, the English are bull dogs for hanging on, and Providence favors the Jews.

Fannie Witherspoon, 2:16½, has had a fine horse colt by Nutwood 600, and the little fellow, on looks, promises to be as fast as either his sire or his dam. Marcus Daly only needs a first class trainer and driver to make his Bitter Root Farm as well known as any in the country.

When Scott Quintin was out on the coast a few months ago, he told me that Yolo Maid was under the weather, and might not be seen on any track this year. Information now comes from Anaconda that the celebrated mare is once more all right, and Dr. Bovett says "she is as fine as silk."

The Brooklyn Handicap for 1890, has been run and a rank outsider, Castaway II proved the winner. One well known gentleman in San Francisco won about $2,500 on the result. Almost all the talent backed Los Angeles on account of the heavy track, but she failed to come up to expectations.

Speaking of the statement that Emperor of Norfolk was to be brought East later in the season. Bob Thomas, his former trainer, said: "I will bet $5,000 to $250 that Emperor of Norfolk will never win another public race, and another hundred that he is never shipped out of California to run in one."

On May 10th, at Pleasanton, Maude 2:20 gave birth to a black horse colt by Director 2:17. This little gentleman has the proper kind of breeding behind him to warrant the belief that he should be a grand addition to the promising family of young Directors that have made their appearance this season.

A letter from Gravesend says that D. L. McCarty's Pandora did her first work on the track a week ago Thursday morning. She showed somewhat of a sulkiness of temper. A good looking bay filly, by Stanford—Lady Glasgow, also in the same stable, made her first appearance in company with Pandora.

Mr. C. C. Seaman of San Diego has, so it is claimed, the only living stallion foal by Bell Boy, foaled in 1889. The little fellow has been named Ding Dong. His dam is by Walkill Chief, (sire of Dick Swiveller 2:18) 2nd dam by Henry Clay. Report speaks very highly of this well bred youngster, and his owner is justly proud of him.

Frank Baldwin, Manager of the Fresno Track, has paid a visit to San Diego, to assist in arranging a programme, for the opening of the Coronado Beach track in July. It would be a good plan for the owners to secure the services of Mr. Baldwin as manager for the occasion, as he would materially assist in making the opening a success.

Mr. Hamlin of Village Farm is evidently prepared to put more thoroughbred blood yet into his trotting stock. At the Belle Meade sale he bought a two-year-old filly by Iroquois, a mare by Glenelg, and another by Planet. These he will doubtless breed to Chimes by Electioneer, in hopes of emulating the success attained at Palo Alto.

Just before going to press, word was received from our Nashville correspondent that he considers it extremely doubtful if El Rio Rey will ever start in a race again. This is bad news indeed, and it is to be hoped that "Kennesaw" is mistaken in his belief. Throat trouble is at the bottom of this, so it would appear that his last winter's ailment was worse than at first supposed.

A well known driver, while in the office a few days ago, stated that if Norlaine's yearling record was to be broken this season, that there is a strong probability that Sidena owned by Capt. B. E. Harris will be the one to do it. Report speaks very highly of this little lady and she is known to be fast, however 2:31½ is a low mark to aim for, but then one can never tell what each new generation will do.

Race goers are apt to complain of what is known as "race track whisky" and there is often good grounds for the grumbling. However if the lessees of bar rooms will keep a stock of "Jesse Moore" on hand the discontent will soon be a thing of the past, for that well known brand always gives satisfaction. Moore Hunt & Co., have an advertisement in this issue, so retailers can find out where to send in orders.

Mr. Valensin has sent two fine Sidney yearlings to the educational college of James A. Dustin at the Bay District Track. They are both of them very fast, one of them having shown quarters in 40 seconds before leaving the farm. These candidates for honors are named Deana by Sidney, dam Miss Helen by Geo. Benton, 2nd dam Nettie George by Norfolk; the other being called Sid Fleet, she being a full sister to Fleet 2:24.

Mrs. Isabelle Coombs, mother of Frank L, Nathan and William H. Coombs died May 1st, on the steamship New York, while returning from a trip to Panama. The lady had been in bad health for some time, and it was thought that a sea voyage would be beneficial. The body was enbalmed and brought to this port, from whence it was sent to Napa. The family have the sincere sympathy of all freinds in their sad bereavement.

Chas. R Hoppin, former owner of Yolo Maid, writes me that the young stock in his neighborhood are all looking and doing well. Geo. Woodard is exercising Bell Button, 2:20, Button Jr., and several other good ones. The two mentioned are moving nicely, and the mare has improved considerably since last year. As the free-for-all pacing race has been declared off, there is a probability that Belle will be entered in the 2:20 class.

The various agricultural associations are competing with each other in offering liberal purses for the trotting fraternity this year. San Jose, not to be outdone by its rivals, has sent a lot of entry blanks to this office, and by them, it may be seen that the Directors offer $1,200 for the three minute class, $1,200 for the 2:30 class, and $600 for the 2:30 class of pacers. If you have an animal fit for any of these purses send to this office for an entry blank.

Mr. L. A. Richards of Grayson, Stanislaus County, is always on the lookout for something good, and lately he has added to his stable the chestnut colt, Diablo 11404, by Charles Derby 4907, dam by Alcantara 2:23, 2nd dam by Bayard 53; 3rd dam Blandina by Mambrino Chief II; 4th dam (the dam of Roselind 2:21, and Donald 2:27) by Parker's Brown Pilot. In this colt, Mr. Richards has secured a grand individual, one that should make a good cross for his Elector fillies.

Some time ago I called attention to the age of Sidney 4770, it being argued by those who claimed to know, that the great sire was only eight years old instead of nine, as claimed in Wallace's Register. Col. P. A Finigan has kindly furnished the following information, which puts the disputed point at rest. Sweetness was sent to Santa Claus in 1880, and was served February 5th, 14th, 24th and March 4th. The colt Sidney was foaled in 1881, so the register is right as it at present stands.

Andy McDowell has bought for the Pleasanton Stock Farm Co., from M. Henry of Haywards, one-half interest in the stallion Decorator, by Director 2:17, dam Chess by Cardinal, he by Gen. Gifford's Morgan; dam of Cardinal, sired by Joe Gales of Ohio, he by Marlborough out of the Duchess of Marlborough by Southern Eclipse; second dam old Duchess of Marlborough by Sir Archy; third dam by imp Diomed. Decorator's second dam a Morgan and Messenger mare. The price paid for the interest was $4,500.

The following horses were declared out of the Great Eclipse Stakes (New York Jockey Club) May 1st: Beauty, Oberlin, Krikina, Glucose, Glenbriar, Furlano, Gardelia, Imperieuse, Beata, Corine Buckingham, Hempstead, Great Guns, Envoy, Lyceum, Landscape, Kiawah, Calcium, Key West, Woodcutter, Affection, Persistence, Dunbarton, Happy Day, Torchlight colt, Ashen, Ben's Pet, Austrian and Bessie Barnes. The Great Eclipse Stakes closed August 15, 1889, with 233 entries, of which 46 declared out January 1, 1890, 37 declared out April 1, 1890, 28 declared out May 1, 1890, leaving 112 eligible to start. Value of stake (with 30 starters) $30,535.

Tybalt, the trained moose, owned by Francis Dunlap, of Montpelier, Idaho, has trotted a mile in 3:30. Dunlap is eager to match the moose to trot a race of one mile and repeat against any horse in America in the 3:00 class, the stakes to be from $500 to $1,000 a side. The moose is one of the sporting sensations at Montpelier. Tybalt was lassoed 13,000 ft. above the sea in the Teton Mountains, Wyoming Territory. He is 2 years 6 months old, stands 5 feet 6 inches in height, and weighs 600 pounds. He is well broken to harness, can trot single or double, and has shown great speed. He will drop on his knees at command, jump 5 feet in height or over a mustang, and has been trained 19 months.

In conversation with a prominent breeder from the land east of the Rocky Mountains a few days ago, he incidentally stated that he thought it extremely probable that Axtell's three-year-old stallion record was in danger, as he had seen a phenomenal burst of speed by a three-year-old stallion during his visit to the coast. I tried to make him commit himself by saying that Sunol's time was also liable to be beaten, but he would not go that far, yet still he said it would not surprise him if 2:10½ were lowered by the colt he had seen speeded. This is corroborative of what I stated three weeks ago. The gentleman's name is Mr. Fleming, owner of Strathmore 408, Red Bell, 2:17, and Nil Desperandum 1389.

Impudence and cheek carries many persons long journeys, but for the champion man of "gall" commend me to Noble the owner of Alcryon. He has now sued the National Trotting Association and President P. P. Johnston for $25,000 each, claiming that his reputation has suffered to that extent.

Last week attention was called to the rumor prevalent that Ruby, 2:19½, was dead. I heard the report too late to verify or deny the news, but since then Mr. Corbitt has called and denied the story, but showed how the rumor started. Rubina Wilkes, a yearling daughter of Ruby, by Guy Wilkes, died last week, and the owner tells me he had refused $20,000 for her. She had proved that her speed was remarkable, and Mr. Corbitt was aware that he had a yearling second to none in the country. The filly had been exercised in the new kindergarten track, and the owner thinks she was given so much work that she became dizzy, and fell on her head. At least when an autopsy was held, coagulated blood was found at the base of the brain.

Now there is no use trying to disguise the fact that the country is rapidly becoming overstocked with inferior animals. In many instances these animals have excellent pedigrees. The day is at hand when pedigree, unless accompanied by individual merit, will count for but little. The lesson which young breeders should learn is to breed for quality and individual merit, as well as pedigree. There is more profit in the product of one first-class broodmare than in ten inferior ones. It will not pay to breed from inferior mares, and the man who patronizes second and third-class stallions will find horse-breeding up hill work, no matter how rich a pedigree the owner of the worthless animal may be able to show. Young breeders, heed the lesson! Breed only from first-class mares and to first class stallions. There will be blanks even then.—Horse Breeder.

The Directors of the Stockton Fair have secured special passenger rates for those who may visit the "slough city" during the summer meeting, from September 23rd to October 4th inclusive. As advertised, the prices will be:—

Two-thirds round-trip rates for passengers from all points *between* and *including* Bakersfield, San Jose, San Francisco, Marysville, Ione, Los Banos, Valley Springs, Milton and Oakdale to Stockton.

A special passenger train will leave San Francisco on Saturday, September 27th, at 7:30 A. M.; returning, leaves Stockton at 6:30 P. M.

Tickets will be on sale at all points as above noted, good for passage to Stockton, beginning Monday, September 22d, and to return to point of issuance up to and including Sunday, October 5, 1890.

No stop-over privileges allowed on these tickets.

England has at last "caught on," and the trotting fever is now sweeping over great Britain. At Alexandria Park, London, a trotting meeting was held on May 5th, at which the American system of timing was introduced. The meeting was a great success, and there was a big gathering of spectators. There was some heavy betting in favor the Amb horse Little Sioux, driven by Kelley, and Barnum's Boston Boy, both of whom were badly beaten, the race, which was for a challenge cup, run in mile heats, being won by Harry Walker in 2:37, three seconds ahead of the previous English record.

Tom Kirby, as an inducement to Americans, has offered £100 to the owner of any horse who trots a mile in 2:30, either in harness or under the saddle, and guarantees the sale of the horse for a big price.

The Kensal Green Driving Club proposes to construct a new track, which will be the first specially constructed one in England.

George has broken down completely, and it is probable she will never be trained again, says Vigilant in the Spirit. Mr. Frank Clark brought the news to us at Elizabeth on Saturday last, he having come direct from Coney Island, where the black mare is trained. From all we have since learned the mare began hanging out signals of distress a fortnight ago, and has not been at exercise since the 26 ult., but, like all trainers, Allen hated to be convinced that there was no hope. We think it probable that the black Anglo-Californian was one of the speediest mares up to a mile and a furlong we have seen in some time. Her stamina is doubted by many, but she was badly ridden several times when she might have established it. She is bred much like Seabreeze, the English St. Leger winner of 1888, being by Isonomy from a Hermit mare, and all horsemen pray that Gov. Stanford will not waste her in experiments of breeding her to trotting stallions, as she is a mare fit to woo the lovers of kings, such as Longfellow, Iroquois or Hindoo.

The annual sale of yearlings from Rancho Del Paso, are looked forward to with a great deal of interest by racing men and the catalogues are eagerly scanned by prospective buyers. This year the sale will take at Hunts Point and one hundred yearling thoroughbreds; will pass under the hammer. The lot this year will consist of a full sister to Dewdrop, a full sister to Madge L., a half sister to Morristown, a half sister to Bonnie Lizzie, a half brother to Ban Fox and King Fox (by imp St. Blaise), a half brother to Kempland, a half-brother to Bavarian, a half brother to Geronimo, a half brother to Ingleside, a half sister to Pearl L. and Wanderoo, a full brother to Sir John, a full sister to Monsoon and Mucilage, a full sister to Marie Lovell and Milton, a half sister to Ninena, a full brother to Tournament, a half brother to C. H, Todd and Sorrento, a full brother to Fanny J., a half sister to So So, a half brother to Priscilla, a half sister to Starlight, Hiawassee and Housatonic, a full sister to Major Daly, a half sister to Masterlode, a half brother to Cruiser, a half sister to Ballarat, a full sister to Wyndham, a half sister to Hotspur and a half sister to Trade Mark.

One good thing has been gained by our publishing the list of those who are under suspension by the two trotting associations. Names of persons have been sent broadcast as being under a ban, when in reality quite a number of those whose names have been published, have had settlement long ago. In addition to those already spoken of who claim that they have clean records, W. H. E. Smith states that he was suspended at Oakland for non-payment of entrance money, his horse, Ralph Bugbee, having been taken sick, so that he could not start. The horse recovered, and was about to be started at Rohnerville, when objection was made that owner and horse was under suspension. The wires were brought into requisition, and Secretary Vail telegraphed to the 9th District Agricultural Association that if Smith paid three hundred and some odd dollars, the horse might start. Mr. Smith paid the money to Seth Crabtree, the Secretary of the Association, and was allowed to start. Mr. Vail has never taken Mr. Smith's name off the black list, notwithstanding the money was paid. The present Secretary, Mr. M. M. Morse, should inquire into this matter.

THE WEEKLY

Breeder and Sportsman.

JAMES P. KERR, PROPRIETOR.

The Turf and Sporting Authority of the Pacific Coast.

Office, No. 313 Bush St.

P. O. Box 2300.

TERMS—*One Year, $5; Six Months, $3; Three Months, $1.50.*
STRICTLY IN ADVANCE.

Money should be sent by postal order, draft or by registered letter, addressed to JAMES P. KERR, San Francisco, Cal.

Communications must be accompanied by the writer's name and address, not necessarily for publication, but as a private guarantee of good faith.

NEW YORK OFFICE, Room 15, 181 BROADWAY.

ALEX. P. WAUGH, - - - - - Editor.

Advertising Rates

Per Square (half inch)

One time	$1 50
Two times	2 50
Three times	3 25
Four times	4 00

And each subsequent insertion 75c. per square.

Advertisements running six months are entitled to 10 per cent. discount.

Those running twelve months are entitled to 20 per cent. discount.

Reading notices set in same type as body of paper, 50 cents per line each insertion.

To Subscribers.

The date printed on the wrapper of your paper indicates the time to which your subscription is paid.

Should the BREEDER AND SPORTSMAN be received by any subscriber who does not want it, write us direct to stop it. A postal card will suffice.

Special Notice to Correspondents.

Letters intended for publication should reach this office not later than Wednesday of each week, to secure a place in the issue of the following Saturday. Such letters to insure immediate attention should be addressed to the BREEDER AND SPORTSMAN, and not to any member of the staff.

San Francisco, Saturday, May 17, 1890.

Dates Claimed.

EUREKA JOCKEY CLUB........July 2d to 5th
IONE........Aug 7th to 9th.
LOS ANGELES (6th District)........Aug. 4th to 9th
SAN JOSE........Aug. 11th to 16th
NAPA........Aug. 18th to 23rd
GLENBROOK PARK, 17th District........August 19th to 23d
PETALUMA........Aug. 25th to 30th
OAKLAND (District No. 1)........Sept. 1st to Sept. 6th
LAKEPORT, 12th District........September 2d to 27th
CALIFORNIA STATE FAIR........Sept 8th to 20th
STOCKTON........Sept. 23rd to 27th.
FRESNO (Fall Meeting)........Sept. 29th to Oct. 4th
VISALIA........Oct. 7th to 11th

Stallions Advertised

IN THE

BREEDER AND SPORTSMAN.

Thoroughbreds.

DOUGLASDALE—Thoroughbred Clydesdale....Lawn View Farm, Cal.
FRIAR TUCK, Hermit—Romping Girl........C. W. Aby, Middletown.
GREENBACK, Dollar—Music........C. W. Aby, Middletown,
ST. SAVIOR, Eolus—War Song........C. W. Aby, Middletown.
THREE CHEERS Imp. Hurrah—Young Fashion........E. S. Culver, San Francisco.

Trotters.

ADMIRAL, Volunteer—Lady Pierson........Frank Drake, Vallejo.
ACTOR Prompter—Dam by Sultan........Lawn View Farm, Cal
APEX, Prompter—Mary........Poplar Grove Breeding Farm, Wildflower.
ALCONA, Almont—Queen Mary........Fred W. Loeber, St. Helena
BAY ROSE Sultan—Madam Baldwin........Thos. Bonner, Santa Rosa
CLOVIS, Sultan—Sweetbriar........Poplar Grove Breeding Farm, Wildflower.
CUPID, Sidney—Venus........C. O. Thornquest, Oakland
CHARLES DERBY, Steinway—by Electioneer. Cook Stock Farm, Contra Costa Co.
CORRECTOR, Director—Brainey........Pleasanton Stock Farm.
DECORATOR, Director—Chess........Pleasanton Stock Farm.
DEXTER PRINCE, Kentucky Prince—Lady Dexter........L. M. Morse, Lodi.
DIRECTOR, Dictator—Dolly........Pleasanton Stock Farm, Pleasanton.
EL BENTON, Electioneer—Nellie Benton........Souther Farm, San Leandro.
ECLECTIC, Electioneer—Manette........Wilfred Page, Sonoma County
EROS, Electioneer—Sontag Mohawk........W. H. Vioget, Menlo Park
FIGARO, Hambletonian—Emblem........Souther Farm, San Leandro.
GROVER CLAY, Electioneer—Maggie Norfolk........Denis Gannon, Oakland.
GRAND MOOR 2374, Moor 870—Vashti........H. I. Thornton, S. F.
G. & M., Anteeo—Rosa B........George E. Guerne, Santa Rosa.
GUY WILKES, George Wilkes—Lady Bunker........San Mateo Stock Farm, San Mateo.
GLEN FORTUNE, Electioneer—Glenna........Souther Farm, San Leandro.
GEORGE WASHINGTON, Mambrino Chief—Fanny Rose........Thos. Smith, Vallejo.
GRANDISSIMO, LeGrande—Norma........Fred W. Loeber, St Helena
JESTER D, Almont—Hortense........Souther Farm, San Leandro
JUNIO, Electioneer—by Granger........S. N. Straube, Fresno.
KING DAVID, Admiral—Black Flora........Frank Drake, Vallejo.
LEO WILKES, Guy Wilkes—Sable........San Mateo Stock Farm, San Mateo.
MEMO, Sidney—Flirt........John Rowen, Oakland
MAMBRINO WILKES, George Wilkes—Lady Chrisman........San Miguel Stock Farm, Walnut Creek.
MAMBRINO CHIEF, McDonald Chief—Venus........Thos. Smith, Vallejo.
MORTIMER, Electioneer—Marti........Wilfred Page, Sonoma County
PASHA, Sultan—Madam Baldwin........D. Bryson, Linden
PHILOSOPHER, Pilot Wilkes—Belle........George E. Guerne, Santa Rosa.
REDWOOD, Anteeo—Lou Wilton........A. McFayden, Oakland.
STEINWAY, Strathmore—Abbess...Cook Stock Farm, Contra Costa Co
SABLE WILKES, Guy Wilkes—Sable........San Mateo Stock Farm, San Mateo.
VICTOR, Echo—Daughter of Woodburn........G. W. Hughes, Napa City
YOUNG ELMO, St. Elmo—Dam by Woodburn... Lawn View Farm Cal.

An adopted son of John H. Wallace, is reported to have absconded with a large sum of money belonging to his benefactor. When the loss was first discovered Leslie E. McLeod, the associate editor of Wallace's Monthly was arrested for complicity in the matter, but he was almost immediately discharged as there was no proof against him. I am heartily glad that my old companion has come out of the matter with an untarnished record, for I verily believe that "Mac" is as honest as the day is long. We have been friends for years, and I always found him the soul of honor. My congratulations Leslie.

Trotting Horse Breeders' Association.

Last Friday afternoon a meeting of the Directors of the Trotting Horse Breeders' Association was held at this office for the purpose of looking over the entries which had been received for the purses, advertised to close on May 1st.

In addition to the President, J. H. White, Esq., there were also present Wilfred Page, F. H. Burke, Gilbert Tompkins, G. Valensin and F. L. Coombs.

On motion, the reading of the minutes of the last meeting was dispensed with; and after looking over the entry list for the various stakes and purses, the following ones were declared filled.

The Trotting Stake for three-year-olds, foals of 1887, eligible to the 2:40 class with $300 added.

The Trotting Stake for four-year-olds, foals of 1886, eligible to the 2:30 class with $400 added.

The Nomination Trotting Purse of $1,500 eligible to the 2:22 class.

The Nomination Trotting Purse of $1,500 eligible to the 2:27 class.

On motion it was also ordered that the following races be declared not filled:

$2,000 Stallion Purse eligible to the 2:18 class.

Free-for-all, purse $2,000.

The Five-year-old Purse, for foals of 1885, for which $1,500 had been offered.

The Nomination Pacing Race, Free-for-all, for which $1,500 had been offered.

The Nomination Pacing Race, for the 2:25 class, for which $1,000 had been offered.

A motion was made by Mr. Coombs, seconded by Mr. Burke, that a Nomination Purse of $1,200 be given for the 2:20 class which was amended on motion by Mr. Page, duly seconded, to read $1,000. Carried on the amendment.

On motion the entrance was made in the above purse, 10 per cent. payable $20 on June 1st, $20 on July 1st, $20 on August 1st and $40 ten days previous to the first advertised day of meeting.

A motion was made by Mr. Page, seconded by Mr. Coombs that a 2:20 Stallion Purse be given, which was lost.

A motion was made by Mr. Burke and seconded by Mr. Page that the next race meeting of the Association be given between the dates of October 7th and October 18th, which was carried.

On motion the Secretary was instructed to ascertain what track association would add the most money to have the annual meeting take place on their grounds.

A motion was made by Mr. Burke and seconded by Mr. Coombs that the Pacific Coast Trotting Horse Breeders' Association join the National Trotting Association, which was carried.

The following list of names were presented as applicants for membership in the Association:

Charles L. Fair, Knights Landing; E. B. Gifford, San Diego; Cyrus Berry, Mountain View; R. Murphy, Santa Rosa; J. L. McCord, Sacramento; H. W. Cooper, Eureka; John F. English, San Francisco; W. E. Deane, San Francisco.

The list was voted upon and applicants elected members of the Association.

On motion the meeting adjourned subject to the call of the Chair.

"Marvin's Book."

We have received by mail a copy of Mr. Marvin's new work, entitled "Training the Trotting Horse," which not only contains all of the best points which experience has brought him, but also contains a full and detailed account of what is known as the Palo Alto method. Time has not allowed a full and complete perusal of the work, but from a hasty glance it warrants the statement that Mr. Marvin has placed on the market a work superior to any hitherto issued. While quite a number of chapters are devoted to historical data, giving full accounts of many now celebrated races, still ample space is allotted to education, veterinary, shoeing and the proper course to pursue in preparing the trotting horse for campaign work.

While the book will prove invaluable to the young student, there is hardly a man engaged in the horse business but what can find something that may prove beneficial in his business. The kindergarten work is fully explained, as is also the common injuries and ailments from which a horse in training is liable to suffer, and many first class remedies for the more ordinary ailments are given.

The question of breeding has not been neglected, as a very readable chapter is given on Mr. Marvin's theory of "thoroughbred in the trotter." As can be surmised, he pays an exceedingly graceful tribute to Electioneer and says that he believes him to be the greatest of all trotting sires. The writer also has a good word for many of the other California sires.

Speaking of what is known as the Palo Alto method, Mr. Marvin says: "Governor Stanford explained to me his ideas of training, fully outlining a theory, the general principles of which are those now followed at Palo Alto, and which is properly called the 'Palo Alto System.' He explained the advantages he saw in the 'brush plan' of teaching a horse to trot fast. He did not believe that the best way to teach a horse speed was by incessant jogging or working mile after mile in a drilling way. On the other hand, he contended that by sending a horse short distances nearly up to his limit but not far enough to tire him, allowing him to get his breath between dashes, he would make speed faster, and do his work with eagerness, a spirit and relish. He saw that speed was the great essential and that the best results would be attained by making speed and then conditioning the horse to carry it, rather than by drilling him into condition without first teaching him to trot at a high rate."

We can conscientiously recommend all horsemen who are readers of the BREEDER AND SPORTSMAN that they will get their money's worth by subscribing for Mr. Marvin's work.

Los Angeles Association.

In former years it has usually been the custom of the Los Angeles Association to finish up the California grand circuit, but this year they have reversed the order of things and claim for their summer meeting August 4th to 9th inclusive. By the time the horses have usually gotten through the section of the circuit which lies with in a circle of one hundred miles of San Francisco, the animals are nearly worn out and require rest, so consequently the City of the Angels has not had as large a representation in entries as they otherwise would have had and it is probable that that is the reason why they have selected an early date and taken the initial position in the circuit for the year 1890.

Fifteen thousand dollars in all will be given in purses, stakes and premiums, and a speed programme has been prepared which will compare favorably with any given by any other Association. Four races a day seems rather a long card, but undoubtedly if time be not wasted between heats there will be ample opportunity to dispose of their lengthy programmes. It would not be surprising if many of the horsemen of California should not only make entries but take their horses down to the Southern city early enough to prepare them for campaign work. The track will be put in the most perfect order, and every facility will be afforded those who wish to go there for the purpose of training.

Entries for the 2:30 purse and District Trotting Stakes close June 16th, and for everything else July 1st. The purses are large and will beyond doubt, receive hearty support from those who will start the circuit at Los Angeles. The following is the list of the races that will take place each day.

MONDAY, AUGUST 4TH.

Trotting, three-minute class, best three in five; district, $500 added.

Trotting, 2:30 class; free for all, $1,500 added.

Running, Los Angeles Derby; one and one-half miles; $300 added.

Running, Hollenbeck Hotel Stakes; one mile; $300 added.

TUESDAY, AUGUST 5TH.

Trotting, two-year-olds, heats best two in three; $250 added.

Pacing, 2:35; district; $500 added.

Running, Edwards and McKnight Stake; two-year-olds, half mile, $150 added.

Nadeau Hotel Handicap; $1,000 purse; one and a quarter miles.

WEDNESDAY, AUGUST 6TH.

Trotting, 3-year-olds, $250 added.

Trotting, 2:25 class; purse, $1,000

Running, selling plate, seven-eighths of a mile, $250 added.

Hurdle, one and one-half miles, six hurdles, $250 added.

THURSDAY, AUGUST 7TH.

Trotting, 2:40 class, heats, three in five; district, $500 added.

Trotting, 2:27 class, heats three in five, $1,000 purse.

Running, sweepstakes, 2 year-olds, five-eighths of a mile, $300 added.

Running, California Handicap, three-quarters of a mile, $1,000 purse.

FRIDAY, AUGUST 8TH.

Trotting, 2:20 class; free for all, $1000 purse.

Trotting, 2:50 class; district, $500 added.

Running, Flyaway stakes, half-mile heats, $200 added.

Running, Santa Catalina Cup, oneand one-eighth miles, sweepstakes, $300 added.

SATURDAY, AUGUST 9TH.

Trotting, 2:35 class, $800 added.

Pacing, 2:25 class, $600 added.

Running, Junior Handicap, 2-year-olds, three-quarters of a mile, $250 added.

Running, 3-year-olds, one and one-sixteenth miles, $250 added.

The judges at the Benning track, Washington, D. C., were evidently "new hands". In two heats where a horse was a head in front they pronounced it a dead heat, and then placed a new driver behind a jaded horse in the seventh heat, when they should have done so earlier in the race. These are the kind of judges that cause so much dissatisfaction to the drivers and spectators.

The San Jose Association.

The Directors of the various Agricultural Societies are fast coming to the conclusion that liberal purses mean liberal entries, and San Jose comes forward this week with three purses which are entitled to consideration from any who own horses eligible for the slower classes.

$1,200 is a good round sum for the three-minute class and yet there is no reason why a race of this sort should not be particularly interesting, and prove as exciting as many of those which are trotted by horses in much faster classes.

The Directors have also seen fit to offer $1,200 for the 2:30 trotters, and as there are any quantity of green horses this year, the natural inference is that this stake will be supported in a generous manner by horse owners.

The pacers are not forgotten as $600 is offered for the side wheelers eligible to the 2:30 class.

These purses are all guaranteed, with conditions formulated much after the style of those issued by the Breeders' Association. The generosity displayed by the association warrants the belief that horsemen will not overlook San Jose in making up their circuit for the season of 1890.

The Souther Farm.

Santa Clara Valley has been written of many times, and it is always claimed that it is one of the most productive in the State of California. It extends for many miles north and south, the upper end of it skirting the eastern edge of San Francisco bay; from the northern line of Santa Clara county, however, this valley is usually spoken of as the Alameda, probably because it is in the county of that name, yet still it is only a continuation of the Santa Clara.

Nestling in the Contra Costa foot-hills, about two miles from the town of San Leandro, the visitor can find the exceedingly well arranged Souther Stock Farm, which was instituted a little more than three years ago by the present proprietor, Mr. Gilbert Tompkins. Although imbued with the enthusiasm of youth, he has made careful selections of all stock which are now catalogued from the ranch, and his preferences have been of the best. The broodmares will stand equal in pedigree and individuality with almost any stock farm in the State, while the stallions cannot be surpassed anywhere in the country.

The farm in its entirety consists of a trifle more than 300 acres, about evenly divided between foot-hill and valley land. The foot-hills are particularly rich in wild oats, while quite a large pasturage has been prepared of the favorite alfalfa, giving a chance to secure for the stock green feed the entire year round.

Last Saturday a visit was paid to Mr. Tompkins' place, but owing to the heavy showers, but few of the horses were seen at exercise. The proprietor has prepared an exceedingly fine speed track, which is the equal of any to be found anywhere; owing to its slippery condition, the speedy ones had to be exercised on the jogging track, which did not give them an opportunity to be seen at their best. Mr. Tompkins has visited the principal stock farms of California, and in bringing his place to its present effectiveness, has taken all the good points to be found at rival establishments and left out all the bad ones, as a consequence there is probably no breeding farm in California that can show so many modern improvements for the care and education of the horse as the Souther Farm.

When Mr. Tompkins first began his experience in breeding trotters he secured the two well known stallions, Jester D. 5796 by Almont 33, dam Hortense by Messenger Duroc 106 and Figaro by Whipple's Hambletonian 725, dam sister to Voltaire 2:20½. Both of these stallions have had considerable work, but as each campaign season came along accident or sickness has prevented them from making the mark which each is justly entitled to; in their work both have shown their ability to enter the charmed circle, and it has only been bad luck that has prevented them from receiving their just dues. The breeding of both these stallions has given reputation to the Southern Farm and many owners of brood mares have sent their favorite animals to the embraces of these splendid sires. Although but a very short time in service they are both represented with exceedingly fine colts, many of which are entered in the trotting colt stakes of this year. A few months ago Mr. Tompkins also added to his stallion list by purchasing from the Palo Alto Stock Farm the bay colt, El Benton, foaled March 25th, 1888, by Electioneer, dam Nellie Benton (out of the dam of Norval 2:17½, sire of Norlaine 2:31½) by General Benton 1755; 2nd dam Norma 2:33½ (dam of Norval 2.17½) by Alexander's Norman 25; 3rd dam by Todhunter's Sir Wallace. It is a hard matter to describe El Benton except by using the word "perfection," for he is one of the most perfect colts that the writer has ever seen, form, substance and disposition cannot be improved upon, he is a perfect little gem and is a typical Electioneer in speed; Mr. Tompkins has decided to train him himself and will no doubt be seen on the circuit this year piloting his handsome colt to victory.

The second of the purchases from Palo Alto is Glen Fortune, a bay colt with hind ankles white, 15.2½ hands high, foaled February 21th, 1886, by Electioneer, dam Glenne by Messenger Duroc 106; 2nd dam Glenella by Woodward's Star, son of Seely's American Star; 3rd dam Shangha Mary. It would be very hard to improve on such breeding and Mr. Tompkins may well be congratulated on having four such grandly bred stallions to represents his interests; it would indeed be a hard matter to go from one end of the State to the other and purchase such a quartette of horses bred in the purple.

Of the broodmares there are thirty or more, but owing to the bad weather it was our misfortune to miss a view of many of them. Among some of the best known are Veronica by Alcona 730, dam Fontana (dam of Flora Belle 2:25) by Almont 33, 2nd dam Fanny Williams (dam of Bay Chieftain 2:28½) by Abdallah 15.

Namora by Almont Mambrino 761, dam the Lackey mare by Blood's Black Hawk.

Rosebud by Gibraltar, 2:22½, dam by A. W. Richmond 1687, 2nd dam by Crichton.

Rosaline by Major Mono; this mare is the dam of Alphaeus 2:27.

Puss by Shenendoah 926. Puss is the dam of Haverly, with a pacing record of 2:25, and Belle Davis, who, as a three year old, made a record of 2:40 almost twenty years ago. 2:40 is not considered much for a horse at the present day, but the little filly was considered the best foal of her year, and there are many who recollect with pleasure how fast the daughter of Puss could go.

Besides the above there are two mares by Whipple's Hambletonian 725, one by Vernon Patchen, two by Erwin Davis, two by Fleetwood (son of Nutwood 600 and Centennial Belle by Woodburn), two by Figaro, one by Thad Stevens one by Reliance, one by Ulster Chief, and one by Tom Benton (sire of Mary Lou 2:25, and Ned Winslow, who has a pacing record of 2:17¼.)

Mr. Tompkins has arranged his paddocks in a most admirable manner with a series of gates so that they can all be thrown into one or divided off into small ones at pleasure.

The service yard has been fitted up with all the modern accessories, and is as perfect as can be devised, there being absolutely no chance for accident. Large barns and stables have been completed, there being in one building alone single stalls for thirty-two horses, while there are also in the other buildings box stalls to accommodate fifty animals.

Already many entries have been made from Souther Farm for the circuit of 1890, and it may be confidently expected that many victories will be credited to Mr. Tompkins before the seasons ends.

The Hill Sale.

The sale of A. W. Richmond, and other stock, the property of John G. Hill Esq., took place at the railroad stables on Thursday last. The prices were good, sixty four head averaging $310. The following are some of the lots sold.

Steve White, br. h., by A. W. Richmond, dam by Ben Wade, thoroughbred; S. M. White, $1,000.

Ulster Wilkes, ch. h., by Guy Wilkes, dam by Ulster Chief; C. G. Clay, $1,050.

Sterlingwood, ch. h., by Sterling, dam by Nutwood; J. M. Bailey, $495.

Indio, gr. h., by A. W. Richmond, dam unknown; Charles Pilcher, $500.

Bay colt, by A. W. Richmond, dam by Ulster Chief; J. M. Bailey, $710.

Dottie Dimple, blk m, thoroughbred, by Ben Wade, dam by Tom Bedford; W. M. Zeller, $425.

Minute, br m, by A. W. Richmond, dam by Ben Wade; D. J. Murphy, $475.

Beauty, gr m, by A. W. Richmond, dam by Traveler; D. J. Murphy, $510.

Lucy, gr m, full sister to Beauty; same, $510.

Lucille, b m, by A. W. Richmond, dam by a son of old Tennessee Traveler; J. M. Bailey, $360.

Black mare by A. W. Richmond, dam by John Morgan; D. J. Murphy, $450.

Irene, b m, by Ben Wade, dam by John Morgan. F. Blanco, $320.

Carrie, gr m, by A. W. Richmond, dam by Ben Wade; D. J. Murphy, $425.

Young Magail, b m by A. W. Richmond, dam by Ben Wade; J. R. Willoughby, $325.

Wren, b m by A. W. Richmond, dam by John Morgan; D. J. Murphy, $380.

Phoebe Hall, br m by Joe Daniels, dam by Woodburn; W. M. Zeller, $360.

Jennie Hall, gr m by A. W. Richmond, dam by Phœbe Hall; O. H. Willoughby, $750.

Jane Hading, blk m by A. W. Richmond, dam by Ben Wade; D. J. Murphy, $425.

Allie Hill, thoroughbred, b m by Wildidler, dam by Woodburn; W. M. Zeller, $380.

Belle Richmond, b m by A. W. Richmond, dam by Ventura; D. J. Murphy, $475.

Jessie D., b f by Wm. Corbett, dam by Ben Wade; J. M. Baily, $330.

Jessie B., b f, same breeding; J. M. Baily, $330.

Jessie M., gr m, same breeding; D. J. Murphy, $525.

Lady Richmond, gr m, by A. W. Richmond, dam by Ben Wade; J. T. Smith, $310.

Betty, gr m, by A. W. Richmond, dam by Ben Wade; O. H. Willoughby, $300.

Maud, gr m, by A. W. Richmond, dam by Ben Wade; J. M. Bailey, $310.

Lady McKelby, gr m by A. W. Richmond, dam by McKelby mare; E. Taggart, $300.

Black filly, by A. W. Richmond, dam by Ben Wade; Wempe Bros., $465.

Bay filly by Wm. Corbett, dam by A. W. Richmond; R. C. Holly, $460.

Harry Gage by A. W. Richmond; dam by Ben Wade; R. L. Clark, $310.

Bay mare by A. W. Richmond, dam by Algerine; J. McKerron, $465.

VETERINARY.

Conducted by W. Henry Jones, M. R. C. V. S.

Subscribers to this paper can have advice through this column in all cases of sick or injured horses or cattle by sending an explicit description of the case. Applicants will send their name and address that they may be identified. Questions requiring answers by mail should be accompanied by two dollars, and addressed to W. Henry Jones, M. R. C. V. S., Olympic Stables, Butler Street, San Francisco.

J. Harvey.

As a reader of your paper, would say I have a horse eight years old that is troubled with his water; he has great trouble urinating, and groans when he does. He suffers most after a long drive. Would you kindly subscribe for him? What is the trouble?

Answer.—Judging by the meagre description given in your letter of 14th, I should judge that your horse, in all probability, is suffering from calculus of the bladder. Get some veterinary surgeon to make an examination of the animal, and follow his advice. It is a hard matter to prescribe for a case of this description without seeing the animal. If you cannot get a veterinary surgeon, please forward to the office of BREEDER AND SPORTSMAN a small portion of the urine, and I will examine it with a microscope, and by that means be able to arrive at some definite conclusion.

A Reader:

Will you please inform me through the columns of the BREEDER AND SPORTSMAN, where the best veterinary schools are in the United States and Canada?

Answer.—In answer to your inquiry regarding veterinary schools, I think it is a matter of opinion, I would advise you to write to the principals of the different schools and get them to forward you their prospectus and by comparing them you may be able to arrive at a satisfactory conclusion.

Answers to Correspondents.

Answers for this department must be accompanied by the name and address of the sender, not necessarily for publication, but as proof of good faith. Write the questions distinctly, and on one side of the paper only. Positively no questions will be answered by mail or telegraph.

P. M.

Can a filly by a standard horse, making a record of 2:35 at a meeting given by a trotting club on a non-association track, be registered in Wallace's register?

Answer.—Yes, provided that all the requirements of what constitutes a "regular meeting" be complied with.

W. W. B.

Will you please give through your valuable paper the breeding of a horse by the name of Tinner, owned at Woodland at one time? Also the pedigree of May Boy, owned at Red Bluff, and record of both?

Answer.—We do not know either horse.

R. C. M.

To give you a list of the horses that are already entered to race in 1892 would take up several pages of this paper. We cannot spare the space. The Blood Horse Association will in all probability open up several stakes this Fall, in which the colt can be entered.

Emma Temple.

Can you let me know the pedigree of Emigrant, sire of the dam of Emma Temple?

Answer.—Emigrant by Billy McCracken, he by Blackhawk 767, dam the Vincent mare by Vincent's Messenger.

Foals of 1890.

At Pleasanton Stock Farm. Property of H. J. Agnew.

Bay horse colt, near hind pastern white, by Antinous (son of Electioneer), dam Nettie Nutwood by Nutwood 600.

At Danville, Contra Costa Co. Property of Cook Stock Farm:

March 26th, filly by Steinway 1808, dam by Almont Rattler 500.

March 26th, filly by Steinway 1808, dam by Alcantara 729.

March 31st, filly by Steinway 1808, dam by Simmons 2744.

April 5th, filly by Steinway 1808, dam by Anteeo 7868.

April 8th, filly by Steinway 1808, dam by Yosemite 4906.

April 8th, colt by Steinway 1808, dam by Triumver 2546.

April 8th, colt by Noonday 10,000, dam by Steinway 1808.

April 10th, colt by Steinway 1808, dam Sister to Inez 2:22½.

April 15th, colt by Charles Derby 4907, dam by Idol Wilkes 512.

April 20th, filly by Noonday 10,000, dam by Steinway, 1808.

April 21st, filly by Steinway 1808, dam by Robt. McGregor 647.

April 29th, colt by Steinway 1808, dam by Allandorf, 7462.

May 4th, colt by Steinway 1808, dam Sister to Phil Thompson 2:16.

Names Claimed.

EDITOR BREEDER AND SPORTSMAN:—I hereby claim the following names:

ACHSA, for sorrel filly, hind ankles white, star in forehead, foaled March 24, 1889, by Albani (son of Algona, dam Contra by Electioneer 125), dam Emma D. by Silverthread, 2nd dam Ellen by Chieftain 721.

ASTELL, for sorrel filly, description and breeding same as above, foaled May 6, 1890.

Yours respectfully,
H. L. DODGE

STOCKTON, May 7, 1890.

I hereby claim the name of Hillsdale for bay colt by Antinous (son of Electioneer), dam Nettie Nutwood by Nutwood 600.

H. J. AGNEW.

Agnew Stock Farm, Hillsdale, Santa Clara Co.

I claim the name Black Bess for black filly, foaled April 18th, by Memo, dam Nellie by McClellan.

J. E. WATSON.

I hereby claim the name "Alcanzar" (to overtake) for bay filly, few white hairs in forehead, and left hind ankle white, foaled April 15th 1890 by Alcazar 2:20½ dam E wood 2:17½. This filly is entered in the BREEDER AND SPORTSMAN Futurity Stake.

J. S. GRIFFIN, LOS ANGELES.

Late News From Tennessee.

GALLATIN, Tenn., May 10th.

EDITOR BREEDER AND SPORTSMAN:—At a meeting of the Executive Committee of the Memphis Jockey Club, Jockey Fox was reinstated. Fox was suspended for the alleged pulling of the three-year-old colt Joe Walton, owned by Tucker & Cherry, but since Fox was suspended, the horse has run several times, and in very mediocre company, and his performance shows him to be a rank duffer. Fox is a pretty fair boy on a horse, and I think he has been too severely censured since he was suspended. Tales have been told about his pulling this and that horse last season, but there are more jockeys riding to-day that need to be criticised in their work in the saddle.

By the way, I notice that a paper is being circulated among the owners and trainers in and around Chicago, praying for the reinstatement of Jockey Tom O'Hara, who was ruled off at Latonia last Fall for pulling Irish Dan in the race won by Clamor. O'Hara is a first rate jockey, but more than once has he been under a cloud of suspicion. When he was ruled off, he had a stable of his own, and was successful as owner, trainer and jockey. In the race which Irish Dan was said to have been pulled, a watchman was sent up the stretch to see if the horse would be pulled, as there were rumors in the betting ring that things were not just right. Irish Dan got second money after an exciting finish with Clamor, but the watchman said that O'Hara pulled the Irish Dan, and the judges' decision was given accordingly. So it was in the Fox-Joe Walton case; some one standing at the head of the stretch said that Fox took Walton back. It is singular that one man was interested in both of these horses, and that after the suspension of both jockeys, neither horse could beat a goat.

The judges officiating at Nashville the closing day and who suspended Golliday, the jocky, and the trainer of Jesse Armstrong, together with the horse, met in Secretary Gillocks office one day this week, and reinstated horse, jocky and trainer. Jesse Armstrong, like nine-tenths of the get of his sire, is an in-and-outer, and I think the judges were justifiable in reinstating all parties concerned.

Ill luck seems to have attended the Lexington Association this year, but with all the drawbacks and mishaps, the present meeting will prove a howling success. Not long since many of the stables at the track were burned, and the thoroughbred horses were running loose through the streets like sheep upon a farm. The stables were immediately rebuilt, and better than before. Bad weather has lasted almost throughout the entire present meeting, but the racing has been good. Close finishes, heavy betting, and most of all, strict and honest judges in the stand, are foreshadows of a successful meeting.

Memphis is to have a four days trotting and pacing meeting next week. There are no Sunols, Axtells, or Jay-Eye-Sees around the Bluff City, but there are many high steppers there, and with the large number of middle Tennessee horses that are going down to take a hand, there should be some pretty fast miles. This is a new feature in Memphis, and if it takes as well as have the runners the meeting should prove successful and profitable to the management. Joe Mooney will take his string of Tennessee horses, which are now at Huntsville, Ala., to the Memphis meeting and with such good ones as Estella and Tosa, he will get his share of the pie. I am told that Memphis will have another trotting meeting this fall, which will take place during the fair held there.

A rumor has been going the rounds that West Side Park has seen its last racing days. It is a well known fact that stockholders in that Club are opposed to having fairs and trotting meetings at the track, while others insist upon having a trotting meeting each summer or fall. Then it is said that the property in its present location is too valuable to be used as a race track, and some of the club members desire to have it cut up and sold out as town lots. If sold out for town lots the property would bring an enormous sum, but with the buildings, and late improvements upon the track and grounds, I cannot see how the management can afford to abandon the course. Some say that the track would be better if located farther out of the city, but by all means let us retain beautiful West Side Park as it now is, and not try to improve upon it by locating farther away from the city, and in not near such a desirable place. For the sake of past victories of champion equine turf performers that we have seen at West Side Park do not crush out the memory of happy events we have seen upon the best of Western tracks.

They do say that the Tennessee pacer Joe Townsend is going to be a terror in the land the coming season. He is a pacer sure, and if he does not stop the watch in the neighborhood of "10" the coming season, he will be a blank disappointment to those who have seen him at work this spring. As a prominent trainer told me last summer at a big meeting on the grand circuit when I asked him, What must I "play" in the next, a pacing race? "Put your money on that brown Tennessee pacer of course; these Tennessee pacers are h—l when it comes to fighting for a finish." I did accordingly and was benefited. I do not think Joe Townsend is an exception to my emphatic friend's idea of the Tennessee pacers, and the ones that "do" him when he starts will have to hustle from wire to wire.

The daily papers and turf journals in giving reports of the sale on the opening day of the Nashville Spring Meeting, do Mr. Shafer an injustice by giving the average of his colts something below $500. Only six colts catalogued as owned by Mr Shafer belonged to him, and these six made an average of $679.20, and one of these was badly crippled. The other colts sold by Blazes were owned by other parties. This speaks well for the attention the youngsters receive at Peytina, as Mr. Shafer's colts averaged almost double as much as did other well bred colts by the same sire. KENNESAW.

E. C. Walker, of the Chicago Horseman, who is a clever and careful trainer and driver of trotting horses, has a stable near Fleetwood track, containing a number of good horses which he is working. If Mr. Walker has as good success with his horses as he had last season with the bay mare Miss Alice, 2:20½, he will be pretty well to the front. There is no reason why he should not do well this year, since he leaves nothing undone. He attends closely to the details of his stable. Mr. Walker was intimate with the late Dan Mace, with whom he frequently talked over the merits of trotters, and the training and driving of them.

ATHLETICS.

Athletic Sports and Other Pastimes.

EDITED BY ARPSIPPUS,

SUMMARY.

This afternoon an interesting and varied programme of athletic sports will be given on the campus at Berkeley. The athletes are putting on the finishing touches for the championship meeting, and on May 30th, those who will be present at the opening of the Olympic grounds will witness one of the best day's sports ever before given on the Pacific Coast.

IN THE SURF.

The warm weather during the past week was the means of increasing business at the surf bathing establishments. The Shelter Cove baths at the foot of Mason Street, and the Terrace Baths at Alameda were crowded morning and afternoon, especially on Sunday and Monday.

The crack swimmers of the Pacific and Lurline Swimming Clubs are practicing hard, and some good contests will no doubt be shortly witnessed between the members of the two clubs.

The old Terrace Club has reorganized under the name of the Pacific Swimming Club. At a swimming exhibition which was given at the Palace Baths on Sunday evening last, some of the Pacific cracks showed up to good advantage, Vollmer and Spiller in particular. Most of the members of the old club are members of the new one, and during the season the Pacific boys will give a good account of themselves in all the contests which they may enter.

The members of the Civil Service Swimming Club will shortly hold a meeting and elect officers for the ensuing term.

The season has opened at Santa Cruz and Capitola, and already the regular summer visitors are flocking into both places. The bath-house men at Santa Cruz anticipate a successful season, as the beach is in much better condition this year than it was last.

The Palace and Crystal baths fell in for their share of patronage during the week, and at times it was impossible to get a room at either place.

The new bath house which is to be constructed on the site of the old Vienna Gardens, will prove a boon to the public.

RUNNERS, WALKERS, JUMPERS, ETC.

In less than two weeks the great athletic battle will have been fought, and the athletes will have laid themselves down to rest after several weeks of hard training. As the eventful day approaches, the interest in the struggle heightens. The entries will close on next Tuesday evening, May 20th, and until after we have perused the list we cannot suggest who the probable winners will be. From the look of things at present, it would appear that the Olympic team were well in it for the banner, with the University second and the Alpine third. We do not know what men the Garden City Athletic Club will enter, but by next Saturday all the athletes will know who their rivals will be. With John Purcell and Victor E. Schifferstein to back them, it is out of the question for the Olympics to be defeated for first place. In addition to these two champions, the club will be represented by Scott, Cooley, Coffin, Jarvis, Henderson, Cassidy, Winslow, O'Kane, Foster, and a few others not so well known in the athletic world. The U. C. Club will place its last year's team in the field, but the Students will be too heavily handicapped by the stronger and more formidable Olympic team. Some of the first prizes, however, will be carried over to Berkeley. The Alpine team will be limited to a few of the best men in the club, and the representatives of this new organization will possibly make a good showing against some of older clubs. According to reports which were published in the daily papers some weeks ago, regarding the ability of the newly formed San Jose, Cal, Club, the Garden City athletes should also make good records. Gov. Waterman will be present at the championship meeting, and a band of thirty pieces will perform during the progress of the games. We hope the Olympic Club will make a good round sum on this occasion, after all the trouble it has gone to in trying to arouse interest in the meeting.

It is to be hoped that Little's standing will be determined before May 30th. If Mr. Little is really a professional, he should not enter his name for the games, as the fact of his being proven a professional after May 30th would reflect heavily on the club which he represents. If he is an amateur, which his friends claim he is, the half, mile and five mile runners will be badly left in the rear, for Little, when in good condition, is certainly a "phenomenal" runner.

The athlete who wins a medal on Decoration Day will certainly be a good man.

Coffin is holding Jarvis well down in the mile walk, and many persons seem to think that Coffin does not walk square at all times during a race, and as he also claims that Gafney does not walk, he should, if his opinion be correct, have a soft thing in both the one and three mile walks. Cooke of the Alpines is training hard for these races, and as he is also booked as a doubtful man, the three judges will be kept busy during the early portions of both races. Eugene Kelly, a pupil of Jarvis, who walks a mile in about 8 minutes 30 seconds, will probably be entered, as he may, in case Gafney, Coffin or Cooke should be ruled out, win second or third prize.

In the absence of Little, Cooley should win the five mile run. The one mile race will be hotly contested between Hill, Cooley and Cassidy. Scott and Sutton, it is expected, will move pretty lively in the half.

The Garden City Club claims to have a man who will win the 220 yards flat. He is a recent arrival from Scotland and is the lucky possessor of ninety-four medals.

The University and Alpine athletes are a little put out because they will be allowed only two days practice on the Olympic cinder track before the championship games. They will petition the officers of the Olympic Club asking them to break the rule for this special occasion and allow them at least a week's practice so that they may get used to the track, the distances, turns, etc.

The members of the Alameda Olympic Club will hold a cross country run from their gymnasium on Lincoln Avenue to-morrow morning. All members of the Pacific Coast Amateur Athletic Association are cordially invited to participate. The pace will be moderate.

Peter Schumacher, a well known local wrestler, was defeated at Buffalo, N. Y., on Monday evening last by Hugh Leonard of that place. The match was Grecco-Roman style and the stakes $200. Leonard won the first and third bouts.

The spring field day of the University Athletic Club will be held to-day on the campus at Berkely. Several representatives for the Olympic and Alpine Clubs of this city will compete and a fine afternoon's sport will be witnessed. As the majority of the open events are scratch the on lookers will have an excellent chance of judging how some of the championship events will turn out.

The warm nights are highly appreciated by the athletes and many of them may be seen on the track long after dark.

Some of the Olympic Club boys are living at the grounds that they may be able to practice morning and evening. Two of the Alpine Club athletes are living at the Bay District track for the same purpose.

After the championship games it is possible that a monster cross country run will be gotten up in which all the clubs will enter.

The Alpine Athletes appear to have deserted the Harbor View Grounds, which they claim are too small for training purposes. The track, eight laps to the mile, is poorly laid out and is in very bad condition, and the boys are afraid of straining their legs should they practice on it.

The Olympic Club will hold a boxing night some time in June.

The U. C. tug-of-war team are all in good condition, having practised faithfully on the cleats in the gymnasium for weeks past.

The emblems of the O A C and Alpine Club are the same and the Directors of the former club have addressed a communication to the Alpine members asking them to adopt some other emblem, as on field days it would be impossible to discover one club member from another. The O. A. C. was the first to adopt the emblem which is the first letter of the club winged with two spread wings, and the Alpines will probably change theirs.

ON THE WHEEL.

The American Bicycle Club is now composed of six members. Sig B. Morse is the captain.

Run No. 4 will be made to-morrow to Piedmont and Jack Hays' canyon.

The Bay City Wheelmen will surely raffle a Rover Safety for the benefit of their treasury.

The San Francisco Bicycle Club has moved to new quarters.

The Century run has been postponed to June 1st. The wheelmen will assemble at the corner of 21st and Mission streets at 5 A. M., on that day from whence the start will take place League members are requested to bring their League tickets along. The run was postponed on account of the muddy state of the roads and in order to give some of the wheelmen a better chance to prepare themselves for the long ride.

A good many of the local riders visited the park on Sunday. The threatening weather prevented several of the boys from going into the country.

The following circular has been issued by R. M. Thompson:

SAN FRANCISCO, May 1st, 1800.

DEAR SIR: There are many wheelmen in our State who are not members of the League of American Wheelmen, and the reason that such is the case is presumed to be that the advantages and benefits derived from such membership have never been made known to them.

Allow me to present for your consideration the following reasons why every wheelman should join this organization:

In the first place "In union there is strength." The League of American Wheelmen is comprised of upwards of 12,000 members, and is the largest and strongest athletic organization in the United States; it is devoted exclusively to the interests of wheeling, and its objects are to ascertain and protect the rights of wheelmen; to secure the improvement of public roads and highways; to provide for amateurs a pure enjoyment of the sport in all its branches, and to bring together men of kindred tastes and interests, by which is promoted fraternal feeling and good followship.

Every member receives a weekly paper, The Bicycling World and L. A. W. Bulletin, free, which alone is worth the amount of his League dues, the subscription price to non-league members being $1 per year. Valuable road-books are issued to members without cost.

Each division has its League hotels where members are given extra attentions at reduced rates. California Division has already upwards of twenty such hotels, and more are being appointed as fast as arrangements can be made and contracts signed.

In every city and town in our Division where there are any League members, there is a local-consul to whom a ticket of membership is an introduction, which insures the possessor a cordial reception and an introduction into the wheeling circles of every part of the Division.

The League protects the rights of its members and will furnish them legal counsel if these are infringed upon. Mr. Geo. H. Strong, 220 Market Street, San Francisco, is Chairman of the Division Rights and Privileges Committee, and all cases where members' rights are infringed upon, if reported to him, will receive immediate attention.

Through the influence of the League of American Wheelmen, bills have been passed in various legislatures throughout the United States granting wheelmen the same rights and privileges in public parks and public roads as are enjoyed by the drivers of any other vehicle. It obtained from the National Government a decision classifying bicycles as "vehicles" instead of "machinery" which has been of no little value to Americans touring in foreign countries, and has established a precedent for all judicial proceedings.

The League has procured from the principal railway companies throughout the United States, free transportation for wheels. Last year a number of railroad companies withdrew this privilege, but the powerful influence of the League enforced its restoration and on a permanent basis. There is no company in our Division which makes a charge for carrying bicycles.

The League is now directing its attention and influence towards the public roads and highways. Already many bills have been introduced into the different legislatures throughout the country and more are being prepared. The movement has become a general one, and is receiving the endorsement not only of the prominent wheelmen of the country, but of the carriage men, horsemen and farmers, and of many statesmen and other prominent citizens.

On this account, alone, every wheelman owes it to himself, and to his fellow wheelmen, to lend his assistance to the League by becoming a member.

Every wheelman who is not a member of the League is in debt to the League; he has received, and is daily receiving benefits which have been procured by the League for which he has not helped to pay. Is he not in honor bound to join the League?

Now is the time to become a member; it is the beginning of the League year; the Division meet is to be held soon [July 4th and 5th] and non-members cannot participate in the races.

This is to be the grandest bicycle tournament ever held in our State.

There will be a League century-run on July 1st, at which the expenses of each member attending will be paid by the Division.

Members are requested to look out for their renewals immediately as their membership expires July 1, 1890.

If you are not a member, fill out the accompanying blank, forward $2 to the Secretary, and become one.

Fraternally, R. M. Thompson.

The following circular has also just been issued:

San Francisco, May 5th, 1890.

Members Cal Division L. A. W:

At the business meeting of the Division instructions were given me to call a century run for members of the Division, it being the sense of the meeting that expenses incurred while on the run, such as meals, etc., be paid by the Division.

It was the original intention to have this run to San Jose, and return; thus making 100 miles, but I have been petitioned by a large number of members to make the run to Hollister, thus avoiding the strong head-wind we would get on the return from San Jose, and also affording a comparatively new ride with a continued change of scenery. Members say they would prefer to pay the railroad fare from Hollister than to ride back from San Jose.

It was necessary, however, to provide a special train from Hollister, in order to get back to San Francisco the same night. This will cost about $150, which would make the ride rather expensive if only a few participated.

The Board of Officers have deemed it a better plan, and one which will make the run much more of a success, to pay for the special train and let each member taking the run pay his own meals and incidental expenses.

The run is hereby called for June 12, 1890, and will meet at 21st and Mission streets at 5 o'clock A. M., sharp. Breakfast has been ordered at Millbrae, dinner at San Jose, and supper at Hollister.

An L. A. W. special train will leave Hollister at our convenience and it will cost members of the Division nothing to return on it. Non-members making the run will be charged $3 for return fare. I have just returned from Hollister; the roads are good and the run will be an easy and very pleasant one. It is to be hoped that members will encourage the efforts of their Board of Officers to make this run a success, by attending it, and thereby advancing the interests of Cal. Division.

Members reasonably certain of attending will confer a favor by notifying

Yours fraternally,
W. M. Meeker,
No. 17 Franklin St. Chairman Touring Board.

AT THE OARS.

The gloomy weather and the rough sea on Sunday caused a good many of the oarsmen to remain in the shelter of their boat houses. Those who did venture out speedily returned.

The different clubs have taken active measures, and are getting their crews into the finest condition for the coming 4th of July regatta.

The challenge which appeared on the slate at the Pioneer Club House on Sunday, it not taken up by the members, will be open to all bona fide crews of the Pacific Coast Rowing Association. The limit of the weight will be 560 pounds for each crew.

H. O. Farrell, Secretary of the Pacific Coast Rowing Association, has received a letter from A. E. Colfar, Secretary of the Harlem Regatta Association of New York, with a programme of the next regatta of that organization, which will be held on May 30th. Mr. Farrell is also in receipt of several entry blanks, which will be duplicated by the P. C. R. A. and used by that body in future.

Dennis Griffin, the local sculler, anticipates going to Portland this summer, with the expectation of making a match. Mr. Griffin is now engaged in making two double scull working boats, which measure 20 feet long, 3 feet 10 inches wide, and 14 inches deep. They are for the Dolphin and Lurline Clubs.

It would not be amiss for the officers of the Pacific Coast Rowing Association to communicate with the Board of Supervisors, requesting their co-operation in arranging matters for the coming 4th of July regatta.

The well known local sculler Charles Long of the Pioneer Rowing Club has opened a sporting house with Joe Eviston for a partner at 17 Turk street. There will be a grand opening to-night, and all the oarsmen are cordially invited to be present. A royal good time is assured.

Captain A. C. Ronard of the Lurline Club has had his canoe, "The Ho bo," overhauled, and is still practicing with the intention of lowering all previous canoe records.

The Alpine crew will go into active training next month, and will give a good account of themselves at the regatta.

CLUB JOTTINGS.

It is only a matter of time until all the professional clubs go under. The Golden Gate Athletic Club, however, stands a good chance of holding its own, for its members favor amateur sports as well as professional. The G. G. A. C. may yet evolve into a strictly amateur club, as its officers have always upheld the amateur members.

A meeting of the P. C. A. A. A. was held at the Olympic Club rooms on Friday evening, May 9th. Walter A. Scott occupied the chair. The following delegates were present: W. A. Scott and G W. Jordan, O A C; W. F. Knoll, A O C, P. N. Gafney, E. P. Moody, A A A C; T. F. Scanlan, A A C. Final preparations were made for the coming championship games. Charges of professionalism against Charles Little, of the Alpine Club, were made by George W. Jordan. It was decided to mail copies of Mr. Little's photographs all over the United States to the different athletic clubs, with the intention of finding out if Little was known as a professional. It was decided that the Secretary, E. P. Moody, be requested to notify A. H. Lean, Gus Ungerman, Mertes, and Mr. Thos. Flynn, of the Chronicle, to appear before the association on Friday evening, May 16th, for the purpose of being questioned in regard to what they know regarding the Lean-Kolb wrestling match.

The Alpine Club will not hold a cross-country run until after May 30th.

On class nights at the Olympic Club, the gymnasium is generally well filled with ambitious athletes. There is a big difference now in the attendance to what it was a couple of years ago. The teachers may be thanked for the change.

Good Wrestling.

The wrestling tournament opened at the Olympic Club on Tuesday evening and the attendance was not remarkably large. The second night, however saw a larger audience. The following is a summary of the results:

FIRST NIGHT.

The style was catch-as-catch can. The tournament was for juvenile and adult members of the club. F. F. Scanlan of the Acme club was chosen referee. E. A. Kolb and E. S. Van Court acted as Judges. Leader J. A Hammersmith was master of ceremonies.

The exercises were commenced by the special class (juveniles), the weight limit being 125 pounds. Thomas Code, 113 pounds, and Otto Westerfield, 112 pounds, were the first pair to wrestle. Code won in the short space of 29 3-5 seconds. F G Phillips, 116 pounds, and George Zeiler, 125 pounds, followed, and despite the difference in weight, Phillips threw his opponent cleverly in 2m 34s.

The next on the carpet were E K Preston, 113½ pounds, and A M Dupero, 124 pounds. As in the preceding bout, the lighter lad won, the time occupied being 7m 33s. H S Russ, 120 pounds, and Sidney Vernon 124½ pounds, then engaged each other, Russ placing the fall to his credit in 25s.

A. M. Dupero, 124 pounds, drew a bye, but was mated with Code, who rolled him over on his shoulders in 2m 38s.

The second part of the special class wrestling was opened Preston and Russ This bout was very exciting. Preston, although having a disadvantage in weight, proving very wiry and agile. He wriggled out of some dangerous positions over and over again, but Russ finally threw him in 10m 32s

Wegener and Phillips then wrestled, and Wegener won the fall in 8m 5s.

The winners in these bouts were then allowed a breathing spell, and two bantam weights—Philip Boule, 113 pounds, and J M Brewer, Jr., 114 pounds—took the carpet. Brewer threw his man in 7m 5s. As these were the only two entries in the bantam class, they wrestled again, and Brewer once more threw Boule, this time in 3m 48s, and won the medal.

The concluding bouts of the special class resulted as follows: Russ threw Wegener in 3m 14s; Code threw Russ in 25s; Russ threw Code in 3m 7s, and again in 1m 23s. The prize winners were: Russ first, Code second and Wegener third.

The feather-weight competition (limit 125 pounds) resulted as follows: W P Henry, 122½ pounds, threw Harry Baker, 123 pounds, in 1m 13s; F A Grim, 123 pounds, threw Henry in 1m 22s; Henry threw Grim in 1m 23s, and again in 22s. Henry therefore won the prize.

Light weights not exceeding 140 pounds—R Y Cole, 140, threw J S J Otto, 137, in 2m 50s; C J Lutgen, 138, threw G H Wigmore, 134, in 3m 55s; Cole threw C C Beck, 135, in 3m 27s.

Cole and Lutgen then engaged in the final bouts. After fifteen minutes' wrestling no falls had been secured and the verdict for first fall was awarded to Lutgen on points.

Middle-weights not exceeding 158 pounds—W T Haberly threw Alexander Pettee, 158½, in 44s; R Y Cole, 140, threw Edward Gros, 157, in 49s.

During the evening, E. A. Kolb, who recently defeated A. Lean for the middle weight catch-as-catch-can championship of the coast, was presented with the trophy, a handsome gold watch, chain and diamond locket.

SECOND NIGHT.

Quite a large gathering of the members of the Olympic Club were present on Wednesday evening in the club's gymnasium to witness the final bouts of the wrestling tournament, which began on Tuesday evening.

Mr. Cole, who had entered in the light and middle weight classes, was so completely tired out after the hard struggle he had engaged in with his opponents on the night previous, that he withdrew from the final of the light weight contests in favor of Lutgen, thereby giving the latter title to first honors.

Cole was to have wrestled Haverly for premier position in the middle weight class, but as both athletes were suffering with sore arms and necks the match was postponed for three weeks, when the championship of the middle weight class will be decided.

Professor Miehling, McLeod and Haverly gave very clever exhibitions of heavy-weight lifting. Meibling raised two dumb bells, each weighing 100 pounds, over his head. The club will have a grand amateur boxing tournament in June.

BILLIARDS.

Hints To Amateurs.

BY MAURICE DALY.

The most important point in billiards is to hit your cue ball where you aim. All beginners cannot draw a ball because they do not strike where they aim.

It is always better to play with an opponent of superior skill.

In making a miscue, do not rest the blame on the cue. It is mostly faulty aim.

Always make a carom with a view to leaving the balls in position. The majority of new beginners are indifferent to the second shot.

Don't forget that at least 60 per cent. of a player's success is due to his execution, which means that it is necessary to practice a great deal.

The best way to improve is to study position playing.

Do not forget to obtain a thorough knowledge of the twists given a ball, for without that it is impossible to play well. It would be wise to consult professionals on this point.

The draw shot is the most important shot as the best results are obtained with it.

The follow shot is also very important for position playing.

Do not bother about nursing until you learn to gather the balls.

Do not turn to the sand paper every time you miss. A great many good tips are ruined in that way.

Chalk is good, but accurate aim is better.

Do not strive for too much at once.

In driving balls try to drive only one, as it is easier to do one thing than two.

Mr. W. A. Spink, representing the Schaefer and Ives combination, arrived in the city on Wednesday, and is attending to the interests of Mr. Schaefer in his forthcoming match with Prof. McCleery. Mr. Spink states that the two brilliant experts will arrive from Ogden either to-day or to-morrow. On the overland trip they have given quite a number of exhibitions, and in every instance the houses have been packed.

Prof. McCleery has been rusticating for several days during the present week, but has returned and buckled down to hard work for his forthcoming match with the champion. When the doors open for the first match, on May 29th, there should be a large crowd at Metropolitan Hall, for this is the most important match that has taken place on the Pacific Coast since the emblem one was played for, between Deery and Rudolph, when the championship of the United States depended on the result. Already considerable money has been wagered on the result of the coming contest, a well known amateur player having given slight odds, to a prominent club-man, that the coast representative will beat the Eastern champion.

The championship billiard match between Jacob Schaefer and George Slosson, set by agreement for June next, in New York City, has been postponed. Desiring to go to San Francisco to play J. F. B. McCleery, Schaefer asked for a postponement of the other match until about July 15. It would be folly to play in that month, as a corporal's guard would not be in town to see the game. Slosson wired back that the contest would have to take place according to contract or be deferred until October next. No answer was received until the next day, when it was settled that Schaefer and Slosson are to play their championship match about the middle of next October.

$15,000. OPENING $15,000.

of the

GRAND CIRCUIT.

The World's Fair goes to Chicago, but the Greatest Fair ever held in the West takes place at

Agricultural Park, Los Angeles, August 4 to 9, 1890.

Fifteen Thousand Dollars in Purses, Stakes and Premiums.

Speed Programme:

FIRST DAY—MONDAY AUGUST 4TH.

No. 1. The Los Angeles Derby.—A sweepstake for three-year-olds (foals of 1887), $50 each, half forfeit, with $300 added, the second to receive $100, and the third $50, out of the stakes; a winner of any three-year-old stake race to carry five (5) pounds, of two or more eight (8) pounds extra; maidens allowed seven (7) pounds. One mile and a half.

No. 2. The Edwards & McKnight stakes.—A sweepstake for all ages; $50 each, half forfeit; $300 added, the second to receive $100 out of the stakes. Non-winners this year allowed seven pounds. Maidens allowed ten pounds. One mile.

No. 3. Trotting.—The Los Angeles Purse, $1,500, open to all horses eligible to the 2:30 Class, June 16th. Entrance ten per cent, payable as follows: $50 June 16th, when entries close; $50 July 1st, and $50 July 22nd, when horses must be named. No subscription will be received unless the first payment shall accompany the same. Subscribers liable only for the amount paid in, but if a subscriber fails to make any of the payments when due, he shall surrender his subscription and payments to the Association with the right of substitution. The Board reserves the right to declare the "Los Angeles Purse" off, in the event of its not filling satisfactorily.

No. 4. Trotting.—Purse $500. 3 minute Class. District.

SECOND DAY—TUESDAY AUGUST 5.

No. 5. A sweepstake for two-year-olds owned in the Southern Counties; $25 each, $15 forfeit; $150 added; the second to receive $75 out of the stakes. The winner of any race to carry four pounds extra. One-half (½) mile.

No. 6. The Nadeau Hotel Handicap.—Purse $1,000, of which $700 to the first; $200 to the second; and $100 to the third horse. Weight announced July 22nd. Twenty-five dollars ($25) to nominate, and fifty dollars ($50) each from all starters. The winner of any race after the announcement of the Weights to carry five (5) pounds extra. One and one quarter mile.

No. 7. Trotting.—Two-year-old stakes, district, $250 added. See special Condition.

No. 8. Pacing.—Purse $600. 2:35 Class. District.

THIRD DAY—WEDNESDAY, AUG. 6TH.

No. 9. Selling Purse—For all ages, $250. Ten Dollars from starters to go to second horse. Fixed Valuation $1000; three pounds allowed for each $100 less down to $700; then one pound for $100 down to $300; selling price to be named through the entry box at 5 P. M. the day before the race. Seven-eighths of a mile.

No. 10. Hurdle Race—A sweepstake for all ages; $25 each, half forfeit; $200 added; second horse to receive $75 out of the stakes. Five hurdles—about one and one half miles.

No. 11. Trotting—Three-year-old Stake. District $250 added. See special Conditions.

No. 12. Trotting.—Purse $1000. 2:25 Class.

FOURTH DAY—THURSDAY AUG. 7TH.

No. 13. The Hollenbeck Hotel Stakes—A sweepstake for two-year-olds (foals of 1888), $50 each, $20 forfeit; with $300 added, the second to receive $100, and the third $50 out of the stakes. A winner of any stake race before August 1st, to carry three pounds; and two or more stake races, five pounds extra; maidens allowed, if beaten once, five pounds; twice or more, eight pounds. Five-eighths of a mile.

No. 14. The California Handicap.—Purse $1000, of which $700 to the first, $200 to the second, and $100 to the third horse. Weights announced July 22nd. $25 to nominate, and $50 more for all starters. The winner of any race at this meeting to carry five pounds extra. Three-quarters of a mile.

No. 15. Trotting—Purse $1000, 2:27 Class.

No. 16. Trotting—Purse $600, 2:40 Class; District.

FIFTH DAY—FRIDAY, AUGUST, 8TH.

No. 17. The Sierra Madre Stakes.—A sweepstake for all ages. $25 each, half forfeit; $200 added, second to receive $75 out of the stakes. Winner of any race this year at three-quarters (¾) of a mile or less to carry six (6) pounds, and of two or more of such races, ten (10) pounds extra. Maiden allowed ten (10) pounds. One-half (½) mile heats.

No. 18. Santa Catalina Cup.—A sweepstake for all ages, $40 each; $20 forfeit; $300 added; the second to receive $100 out of the stakes. Five pounds above scale. Non-winners in 1889 and 1890 allowed ten (10) pounds. Maidens allowed twelve (12) pounds. A winner at this meeting to carry five pounds extra. One and one-eighth (1⅛) mile.

No. 19. Trotting.—Purse, $1,000, 2:20 class, District.

No. 20. Trotting.—Purse, $500. 2:50 class, District.

SIXTH DAY—SATURDAY, AUG. 9TH.

No. 21. The Citrus Handicap.—A sweepstake for three-year-olds; $40, half forfeit, or only $10 if declared by 5 P. M. the day before the race; $250 added; the second to receive $100 out of the stakes. Weights to be announced by 5 o'clock P. M. second day before the race. One and one-sixteenth (1 1-16) of a mile.

No. 22. The Junior Handicap.—A sweepstake for two-year-olds. $30 each, half forfeit, or only $10 if declared by 5 P. M. the day before the race; $250 added; the second to receive $100, and the third $50 out of the stakes. Weights to be announced by 5 o'clock P. M. the second day before the race. Three-quarters (¾) of a mile.

No. 23. Trotting.—Purse $800, 2:35 Class.

No. 24. Pacing.—Purse, $600, 2:25 Class.

TROTTING STAKES—To close June 16th, 1890.

To be Trotted at the Annual Fair, to be held in Los Angeles in 1890--91.

TROTTING STAKES, 1890.

FOALS OF 1888. Mile and repeat, $250, added by the Association. Entrance, $50, payable in the following forfeits: $10 to accompany the nomination, $20 July 1st, and $20 August 11, 1890.

FOALS OF 1887. Mile heats, three in five. $250 added by the Association. $50 entrance, payable in the following forfeits; $10 to accompany the nomination, $20 July 1st, and $20 August 11, 1890.

TROTTING STAKES, 1891.

FOALS OF 1889. Mile and repeat, $250 added by the Association. $50 entrance, payable in the following forfeits: $5 to accompany nomination, $10 August 1st, 1890; $10 May 1st, 1891, and $25 on the first day of the Fair of 1891.

FOALS OF 1888. Mile heats, three in five. $250 added by the Association. Entrance, $50, payable in the following forfeits: $5 to accompany the nomination; $10 August 1st, 1890; $10 May 1st, 1891, and $25 on the first day of the Fair of 1891.

CONDITIONS.

All nominations to be made on or before June 16th. American Association rules to govern. Nominators liable only for the amount paid in, which becomes forfeit if subsequent payments are not made. All forfeits and entrance fees will be contributed to the stake, the whole divided where there are three or more starters as follows: sixty per cent. to the first, thirty per cent. to the second and ten per cent. to the third. If no more than two horses start, only first and second money shall be awarded, and in case of a walk over, only the first money shall be awarded. A horse distancing the field shall only be entitled to so much of the money as the starters in the race could have won. A nominator in making an entry in any of the above stakes shall give the name of owner, name of breeder and where foaled, the age, color, sex, dam and sire if known. Colts owned in the counties of San Luis Obispo, Fresno, Tulare, Kern, Santa Barbara, Ventura, Los Angeles, San Bernardino, Orange and San Diego shall be eligible to entry.

REMARKS AND CONDITIONS.

All trotting and pacing races to be to harness, mile heats, best three in five, except otherwise specified. Entrance 10 per cent on amount of purse. Trotting and pacing divided as follows: 50 per cent. to first horse; 25 per cent. to second; 15 per cent. to third, and 10 per cent. to fourth. Entries not declared out by 5 P. M. of the day before the race must start. In all trotting and pacing races, five to enter and three to start. The Board reserves the right to hold a less number than five to fill. Horses owned in Fresno, Tulare, Kern, San Luis Obispo Santa Barbara, Ventura, Los Angeles, San Bernardino, Orange and San Diego Counties, are eligible for entry in district races. A horse distancing the field is entitled to first and fourth money. The Directors reserve the right to change the hour and day of any race, if deemed necessary. Races shall commence each day at 1 o'clock. American Association rules to govern, unless otherwise specified. Hay and straw free.

Running—The Pacific Coast Blood Horse rules to govern running races. Colonial-bred horses, foaled on Colonial time, allowed as follows: Two and three-year-olds, eight pounds; four-year-olds five pounds, and five-year-olds, three pounds. In all stakes, starters must be named to the Secretary or through the entry box at the track, on or before 5 P. M. of the day before the race. In all stakes, the right to forfeit ceases at 10 o'clock of the day on which the race is run. Racing colors to be named with the entry. Entries close with the Secretary July 1st.

Remember, entries for the 2:30 Trot and District Trotting Stakes close June 16th, and for everything else July 1st.

L. LICHTENBERGER, President. BEN BENJAMIN, Secretary.

Guaranteed Purses

—Given by the—

San Mateo

AND

Santa Clara Co.

AGRICULTURAL ASSOCIATION

No. 5,

SAN JOSE, CAL.

Fall Meeting, 1890,

August 11th to 15th.

Trotting Purse, $1,200, 3-Minute Class.

Trotting Purse, $1,200, 2:30 Class.

Entrance fee 10 per cent., payable as follows: $10 on June 1st, when entries close; $40 on July 1st, and $40 on August 1st.

Pacing Purse, $800, 2:30 Class.

Entrance fee 10 per cent., payable as follows: $30 on June 1st when entries close; $20 on July 1st, and $30 on August 1st.

CONDITIONS.

Mile heats, three in five. Money must accompany nominations, otherwise the entry will not be considered. Neglect to make payments when due forfeits previous payments.

Eight entries required to fill, four to make last payment and three to start.

Purse will be divided, 50 per cent. to first horse, 25 per cent. to second 15 per cent. to third, and 10 per cent. to fourth. A horse distancing the field will get the 1st and 3rd money.

In case of a walk-over the horse will get the entrance money paid in only; otherwise National Trotting Association rules to govern.

WM. BUCKLEY, President,

G. H. BRAGG, Secretary.

CONTRA COSTA CO,

Agricultural Associat'n

District No. 23.

FAIR OF 1890.

Sept. 22 to 27, inclusive.

District Trotting Colt Stakes for 1890.

$40, payable as follows:

$10 June 1st (when stakes close), $15 Sept. 1st, and $15 Sept. 22d.

FOR ONE-YEAR-OLDS, 1 mile dash.	$75 added to each.
FOR TWO-YEAR-OLDS, mile heats, 2 in 3	
FOR 3-YEAR-OLDS, mile heats, 3 in 5.	

All moneys divided as follows: 60, 30 and 10 per cent. In case of only two starting, 60 and 40 per cent., and in case of one horse walking over, the whole amount to go to such horse.

A failure to make any payment when due shall be considered a withdrawal and forfeiture of the amount paid in.

National Rules to govern.

The right reserved to refund the first payment in case the stakes do not fill reasonably well.

Entries close June 1, 1890 with the Secretary.

GEO. P. LOUCKS, President,

H. C. RAAP, Secretary, Martinez, Cal.

The Trotting Stallion

G & M

FULL BROTHER TO

ALFRED G, 2:19¾.

(Who has been taken to Kentucky to stand at $200)

Will make the season of 1890 from FEBRUARY 1st to JULY 1st, at

SANTA ROSA.

G. & M. is by Anteeo, 2:16¼; was foaled 1886; first dam Rosa B. by Speculation (son of Hambletonian 10); 2d dam Elizabeth by Alexander 490; 3d dam Nora by imp. Glencoe. Anteeo is by Electioneer, out of Columbine by A. W. Richmond 1687.

G. & M. is a handsome dark bay; stands 15-3 1-2 hands high, and weighs 1060 pounds. Gameness, stoutness, speed and stamina are indelibly impressed in every line of the pedigree of G. & M. Owners of brood-mares in search of these qualities, will do well to patronize this promising colt.

PHILOSOPHER,

Foaled 1886 by Pilot Wilkes 2987; first dam Bella by George Wilkes 519; second dam by Bell Morgan 61.

Philosopher's sire, Pilot Wilkes 2987, is by George Wilkes 519, dam Grace (the dam of Alice Woodburn etc.), by Pilot Jr. 12, grandam by Orphan Boy.

Will make the season of 1890, from FEBRUARY 1st to JULY 1st, at Santa Rosa.

TERMS for the season:

G. & M., $50,

PHILOSOPHER, $30,

with privilege of returning mares that do not prove in foal the next season free of charge, provided the horse bred to remains the property of the present owners. Good pasturage at $3 per month. No responsibility assumed for accidents or escapes. Service fees payable before removal of the mare. For further particulars, address

GEO. E. GUERNE,

Santa Rosa Cal.

Stallions and Colts

For Sale.

The Get of the Celebrated Racing Stallion BAYSWATER,

FROM FINELY BRED MARES.

Inquire of

J. HEINLEN,

Lemoore, Tulare County, Cal.

LAWN VIEW BREEDING FARM STALLIONS.

ACTOR.

A beautiful bay horse foaled 1887 by Promptor 2305 sire of Apex (four-year-old record) 2:26, Transit 2:28¾, Creole 2:20, Blue Belle 2:32, Daisy (yearling record) 2:38¾, he by Blue Bull 75, 1st dam by Sultan 1513 2:24, sire of Stamboul 2:12 1-4, Ruby 2:19¾, Sweetheart 2:22¾, Alcazar 2:20¾, Eva 2:23¾, La Grange 2:23¾, and eleven others in 2:30 list, second dam by Fireman by Langford.

Actor, as his pedigree shows, is as purely bred a young stallion as ever made a season in the stud. Blue Bull stock is much sought after in the East, and Sultan, sire of his first dam will make the season in Kentucky this year at $100 per mare. Actor is a handsome bay colt 16 hands high, clean limbed and possesses all the points of a speedy trotter.

TERMS, $40 FOR THE SEASON, usual return privileges.

DOUGLASDALE 7650.

Thoroughbred Registered Clydesdale Stallion

Imported from Scotland, December, 1889, bay, three years old.

TERMS, $35 FOR THE SEASON.

YOUNG ELMO

Two years old sorrel stallion by St. Elmo 2:27, dam by Woodburn.

TERMS, $20 FOR THE SEASON.

For further particulars, address

MANAGER LAWN VIEW FARM, Auburn, Cal.

For Sale

A HALF BROTHER TO

ALMONT PATCHEN,

(2:15, trial 2:13 3-4).

JUANITO JR. is a beautiful bright bay, black points, with no white, foaled 1886. As a colt he has given much more promise than did Almont Patchen at the same age. Instead of being a pacer, he is a good square trotter, with every indication of great speed, and is so gentle and kind, that a lady can drive him. The owner's only reason for selling him is that business calls him away from this section of the State. He will be sold at a reasonable figure. This is a splendid opportunity for a gentleman to secure a first-class trotter at a very low figure.

The pedigree of Juanito Jr. is by Juanito (sire of Almont Patchen), dem Nettie Moore by Old Tom Moore. For further particulars, address

JUANITO JR.,

Santa Clara P. O., Cal.

Races. Races.

JULY WEEK.

AT

South Park Race Track

Eureka, Cal.

GIVEN BY THE

EUREKA JOCKEY CLUB.

FIRST DAY, JULY 2, 1890.

No. 1. Novelty Running Race. Free for all. Dash of one mile. Purse $250. First quarter, $40. Half, $50. Third quarter, $70. Mile, $90.

No. 2. Running Race. Purse $150. Five-eighths dash for two-year-olds. $125 to first horse; $25 to second horse.

No. 3. Running. Purse $150. Three-quarters and repeat. $125 to first; $25 to second.

SECOND DAY, JULY 3, 1890.

No. 4. Trotting. Purse $200. Three minute Class. $150 to first; $50 to second. (Covey barred.)

No. 5. Running Stake. Five-eighths of a mile. For Humboldt raised two year-olds. $30 entrance, half forfeit, $150 added. First to receive 60 per cent.; second, 30 per cent., third, 10 per cent.

No. 6. Running Stake. Purse $200. Mile Dash. $150 to first horse; $50 to second horse.

THIRD DAY, JULY 4, 1890.

No. 7. Trotting Stake. 2:40 Class. Purse $250. $200 to first horse; $50 to second horse.

No. 8. Running Stake, 1¼ miles. Free-for-all, $40 entrance, ½ forfeit, $200 added; second horse $75, third horse to save stake.

No. 9. Running Stake. Purse $150; 1-2 mile and repeat; $125 to first; $25 to second.

FOURTH DAY, JULY 5, 1890.

No. 10. Running Stake, 1-2 mile and repeat; for Humboldt horses owned prior to Jan. 1, 1890. $125 to first, $25 to second.

No. 11. Running Stake. Purse $200; 7-8 mile and repeat. $150 to first, $50 to second.

CONDITIONS AND REMARKS.

All trotting races are best three in five, unless otherwise specified. Four to enter and three to start, but the Board reserves the right to hold a less number than four to fill by the withdrawal of a proportionate amount of the purse. Entrance fee, 10 per cent. of purse, to accompany nominations. In all trotting races the rules of the American Trotting Association, and all running races the rules of the Pacific Coast Blood Horse Association to govern, but the Board reserves the right to trot heats of any two classes alternately, if necessary, to finish any day's racing. In all entries not declared out by 6 P. M. of the day preceding the race, shall be required to start.

No added money paid for a walk over. In all races, four or more paid up entries required to fill, and three or more horses to start. Racing colors to be named in entries. In trotting races drivers will be required to wear caps of distinct colors to be named in entries. Entries in all races to close with the Secretary, Thursday, June 26, 1890. Entry blanks will be furnished upon application to the Secretary.

All trotting races for horses owned and in Humboldt County prior to June 1, 1890.

H. M. DEVOY, President.

J. P. MONROE, Secretary.

GOLDEN GATE

Fair Association

Oakland.

Guaranteed Futurity Purse

$4,000.

To take place during the Fall Meeting of 1893.

For foals of 1890. Entrance 2 per cent. payable as follows:

$10 May 15, 1890, when entries close in name of foals or of dams and sires.

$10, Jan. 15, 1891.
$15, June 15, 1891.
$15, Jan. 15, 1892.
$15 June 15, 1892.
$ 5 Jan. 15, 1893.
$20 June 15, 1893.

$20 fifteen days before advertised day of the race.

If the last payment is made on twelve or more entries the horses shall be started in trial races, in which not more than eleven or less than six shall be allotted to start. The trial races shall be mile heats, three in five, for a purse of $1,000, given by the Association for each race. If two trial races are trotted, the first four horses shall only be entitled to start in the final race. If three such trial races are trotted, only the first three horses in each trial race shall start in the final; and if four or more trial races are necessary, only the first two horses in each trial race shall start in the final race.

These trial races must be started not less than five nor more than ten days previous to the day set for the final race; and if possible all trial races will be trotted on the same day.

CONDITIONS.

Neglect to provide payments on the dates stipulated will incur forfeiture of all previous payments.

The Directors reserve the right to change the hour and day of any race except when it becomes necessary to ante-date a race, in which instance the nominator will receive three days notice of change by mail to address of entry.

Entries not declared out by 6 P. M. the day preceding the race, shall be required to start.

Purses will be divided into four moneys viz., 50 per cent. to the winner, 25 per cent. to the second horse, 15 per cent. to the third horse, and 10 per cent. to the fourth horse.

A horse distancing the field shall only be entitled to first and third moneys.

Trotting and racing colors shall be named by six o'clock on the day preceding the race, and MUST be worn upon the track.

All purse races, mile heats, best three in five in harness.

Otherwise than the above, National or American Trotting Association Rules—as this Association may elect—will govern the races offered.

Entries to close with the Secretary.

R. T. CARROLL, President.

JOS. I. DIMOND, Sec'y, 208 Market St., S. F.

Guenoc Stud Farm, Lake Co., Cal.

Imp. GREENBACK

(Sire of the English winners Greenlight, Greenjacket, Greenshank, Greenwave and Greenhorn)

By Dollar, dam Music, by Stockwell. $100 the Season

ST. SAVIOR,

(FULL BROTHER TO EOLE)

By Eolus, dam War Song, by War Dance. $100 the Season.

PASTURAGE, $5 PER MONTH.

With right to return the following year if mare does not prove with foal. The best of care taken, but no liability for accidents or escapes. Mares shipped to C. W. ABY, care ST. HELENA STABLES, St. Helena Napa County, will be taken in charge by competent men.

For further information write to

DR. C. W. ABY, Middletown, Lake County, Cal.

SAN DIEGO, 8776.

- Alcona Clay 2756
  - Alcona 730. Sire of Flora Belle, 2:24, Clay Duke, 2:31½, etc.
    - Almont 33. Sire of Westmont, 2:13¾, Piedmont, 2:17¼, Puritan, 2:16, and 33 others in 2:30 list.
    - by Mambrino Chief 11. Sire of Lady Thorne, 2:18¼.
  - Madonna. Dam of Del Rey, trial 2:31, Alcona Jr., 2:41, sire of Silas Skinner, trial 2:23¼.
    - Cassius M. Clay Jr. 22. Sire of Durango, 2:23¾, Harry Clay, 2:29¾, and sire of dam of Happy Thought, 2:22¼, and others.
    - by Joe Downing 710. Sire of Abe Downing, 2:20¾, Dick Jamison, 2:26, and sire of dams of Kentucky Hambletonian, 2:27, Lorena, 2:15, and others.
- Fontana. Dam of Flora Belle, 2:24, Silas Skinner, trial 2:23¼.
  - Almont 33. Sire of 36 in 2:30 list, 49 sons and 22 daughters that have produced 2:30 performers.
  - Fanny Williams. Dam of Bay Chieftain, 2:28¼.
    - Abdallah 15. Sire of Goldsmith Maid, 2:14, Thorndale, 2:21¼, also Almont, Belmont, Jim Monroe, etc.
    - by Denmark (thoroughbred).

SAN DIEGO is dark seal brown, three years old, and trotted one-quarter miles in 40 seconds as a two-year old.

This grand young horse, and, barring accidents, will make a fast record next fall.

He will be allowed a limited number of mares, at $50 for the season. Mares not proving in foal to be returned free 1891. Best of pasture for mares at $4 per month, but no liability for accidents or escapes.

He will make the season from February 1st to June 1st at Napa Fair Grounds. For further particulars, address or call on

H. B. STARR, Race Track, Napa, Cal.,

or FRED W. LOEBER, St. Helena

Bay Rose.

REGISTERED No. 9814.

Record 2:20 1-2 Third Heat

Will make the season of 1890, ending July 1st, at the SANTA ROSA STOCK FARM, (formerly Santa Rosa Race Track), SANTA ROSA.

DESCRIPTION.

BAY ROSE is a dark bay or brown, with black points, 16¼ hands high, and weighs 1150 pounds. He is remarkably intelligent, of good disposition, and a pure-gaited trotter. He was foaled in 1881. His colts are large, stylish, rangy animals, and inherit the qualities of speed and endurance.

PEDIGREE.

BAY ROSE 9814

- Sultan, 2:24. Sire of 19 in the 2:30 list.
  - The Moor 870. SIRE OF
    - Beautiful Bells 2:29½
    - Del Sur 2:24½
    - Inez 2:30
    - Sir Guy 2:28½
    - Sultan 2:24
    - Tommy Gates 2:24
  - Sultana.
- Madam Baldwin
  - The Moor 870. Sire of 5 in the 2:30 list.
  - by Ben Lippincott, by Williamson's Belmont.

TERMS: $200 FOR THE SEASON.

Good pasturage $3 per month. First-class care taken of mares in any manner that owners may desire, but no responsibility assumed for escapes or accidents.

Limited to a few approved mares.

For further particulars, address

THOS. BONNER,

Santa Rosa Stock Farm, Santa Rosa.

Or apply to

IRA PIERCE,

728 Montgomery Street, S. F., Cal.

Highland Farm,

LEXINGTON, KY.,

Home of Red Wilkes.

Standard-bred Trotting Stock

For Sale,

Sired by Red Wilkes, Wilton, 2:19¼; Allandorf and Sentinel Wilkes, out of highly bred Standard Mares of the most fashionable blood of the day.

W. C. FRANCE, Proprietor.

Pedigrees Tabulated

IN THE MOST ARTISTIC MANNER.

Giving speed performers under sires and dams. Catalogues compiled. Stallion cards and circulars written up ready for the press. Pedigree blanks for sale. Prices reasonable. Horses bought and sold on commission. References furnished.

R. Y. HARDIN.

809 W. Madison St., Chicago, Ill.

The Trotting Stallion

CUPID,

Full Brother to Adonis 2:14,

—Sired by—

The Celebrated SIDNEY 2:19 3-4, and out of Venus.

Will make the season of 1890 at the OAKLAND TROTTING PARK.

PEDIGREE.

CUPID is by Sidney out of Venus by Capt. Webster 10173, record 2:30, and sire of Freestone 2:19. Second dam by Skenandoah 926, sire of Daisy Burns 2:29½, Erwin Davis (sire of two in the 30 list) and dams of four in the 30 list.

DESCRIPTION.

Cupid is a handsome bright bay 15.3¼ hands high, weighs 1100 lbs.; was foaled in 1886. As a yearling, with very little work he showed quarters in 41 seconds, and at 2 years old, quarters in 36 seconds. As a three year old he has not been worked, but he shows the speed and endurance that must come from his excellent blood lines.

TERMS $50 for the season, with the usual return privileges. Good pasturage near the track at $4 per month. The best of care taken of mares in any way that owners may desire, but no responsibility assumed for accidents or escapes.

For further particulars address

C. O. THORNQUEST,

Oakland Trotting Park, or

C. BAAR, 972 Broadway, Oakland.

Langtry Farms' Stud

Imp. FRIAR TUCK

By the Immortal HERMIT

DAM ROMPING GIRL BY WILD DAYRELL.

AT $50 THE SEASON.

Mares not proving with foal may be returned the following season. Good care taken of mares, but no liabilities for accidents or escapes.

Good Pasturage at $5 per month.

Mares shipped to ST. HELENA, care CHARLES WILLIAM ABY, St. Helena Stables, will be cared for. For further particulars address,

CHAS. WILLIAM ABY,

Middletown, Lake County, Cal.

Cook

STOCK FARM.

Season of 1890.

STEINWAY 1808.

Three-Year-Old Record 2:25 3-4.

Sire of STRATHWAY, three year old record 2:26, and sire of the dam of BOURBON RUSSELL 2:30.

By STRATHMORE 408; sire of 31 in the 2:30 list; sire of 6 dams of 8 in the 2:30 list, and sire of 9 sires of 3 in 2:30 list.

1st dam ABBESS (dam of Solo 2:28, and Soprano, dam of C. F. Clay 2:18, Eminence 2:27 and Strathbridge, 3 year old record 2:28½) by ALBION, sire of VANITY FAIR 2:24½, and of the dam of FAVORITE 2:25½.

2nd dam by MARSHALL NEY.

3rd dam by BERTRAND, a son of SIR ARCHY.

TERMS—$100 for the season.

CHARLES DERBY 4907

Brown Horse, Foaled 1885.

By STEINWAY 1808.

1st dam by the great ELECTIONEER, sire of SUNOL 3 year old record 2:10½, Palo Alto 2:12¼, etc., etc.

2nd dam FANNY MALONE, by NIAGARA.

3rd dam FANNY WICKHAM, by HERALD,

4th dam by Imp. TRUSTEE.

TERMS—$100 for the season

Pasturage $5 per month. Accidents and escapes at owner's risk. Mares consigned to the farm should be sent to Fashion Stables, Oakland; Geary & Grindle's Stable, Haywards; or to Bennett's Stable, Martinez; from and to which places they will be delivered free of charge. Address

COOK STOCK FARM,

Danville, Contra Costa, Co., Cal.

Vineland Stock Farm

Alcona 730.

Sire of

FLORA BELLE - - - Record 2:24
CLAY DUKE - - - - - " 2:31½

ALCONA will be a great sire, but four of his colts have ever been trained, and all have shown full miles better than 2:35, and two of them as good as 2:30. Two of his first sons each sired a colt as a two-year-old, and last season one as a four-year-old trotted a full mile in 2:29½, and the other, a three-year-old, a mile in 2:31. With opportunities, Alcona is destined to be one of Almont's best sons. Almont, for his opportunities, is beyond doubt the most prepotent sire of his age. He has 36 representatives in the 2:30 list; 49 sons and 22 daughters that have already produced 2:30 performers. Almont died five years ago at 20 years old. If he lived he would be but 25 years old.

PEDIGREE.

ALCONA sired by the great Almont (sire of Westmont 2:13¼, Fanny Witherspoon 2:16¼, Piedmont 2:17¼, and 33 others with records better than 2:30, and grandsire of Belle Hamlin 2:13¼, etc.); by Alexander's Abdallah (sire of Goldsmith Maid 2:14), he by Rysdyk's Hambletonian. Alcona's dam, Queen Mary, by Mambrino Chief (sire of Lady Thorne 2:18 1-4, and 5 others in the 2:30 list, and sire of the dams of Director 2:17, Piedmont 2:17¼, Onward 2:25 1-4, Red Wilkes Almont, Belmont and many other noted sires).

DESCRIPTION.

Alcona is a beautiful chestnut 15 3 1-2 hands high, and weighs 1200 lbs. His colts possess speed, style, finish and beauty, and if they don't trot they command the highest prices for carriage horses.

$40 for the season. Usual return privilege.

Season of Alcona and Grandissimo ends July 1st, 1890.

Grandissimo,

Full Brother to GRANDEE, 3-year old record 2:23 1-2.

Sired by La Grande (son of Almont and out of Jessie Pepper by Mambrino Chief; Jessie Pepper is the dam of Ione 2:17 1-2, Alpha 2:23 1-2, Sterling Wilkes 2:31¼, and others) dam Norma, by Arthurton (sire of Arab 2:15, Joe Arthurton 2:20 1-2, etc.)

Grandam Nourmahal, (full sister to A. W. Richmond, sire of Arrow 2:13½, Romero 2:19, and sire of Columbine, dam of Anteeo 2:16¼, and Antevolo 2:19¼ at four years old).

DESCRIPTION.

Grandissimo is four years old, will make a sixteen hand horse; he is a rich mahogany bay in color and perfect in style and action. $50 for the season. Usual return privileges.

"Grandissimo" with limited training last fall as a three-year-old, trotted quarters in 36 seconds and miles in 2:40.

I feel confident that he will trot fast this season, and will be a great sire as his colts this season are all grand youngsters.

The best of pasturage $4 per month. Mares taken care of in any manner that owners may desire, but no responsibility assumed for escapes or accidents.

For further particulars send for circular or call at stables, one mile south of St. Helena.

FRED W. LOEBER Prop'r.

GROVER CLAY

Bay Stallion, Black Points,

15 3-4 hands high.

Bred by W. W. Traylor, San Francisco.

BY ELECTIONEER.

First dam Maggie Norfolk by Norfolk, son of Lexington, he by Boston. Second dam Tilda Quill by Billy Cheatham he by Cracken, and he by Boston. Third dam by Dorsey's Golddust.

TERMS.

Will make the season of 1890 at the Training Stables of Denis Gannon, near Oakland Trotting Park, at $60 the season, payable at time of service. Season to commence February 1st and ending July 1st. Proper care of mares will be taken, but no responsibility incurred for accidents or escapes. Address,

DENIS GANNON, Oakland, Cal.

Memo.

The Best Son of SIDNEY

Will Make the Season of 1890 at the OAKLAND RACE TRACK

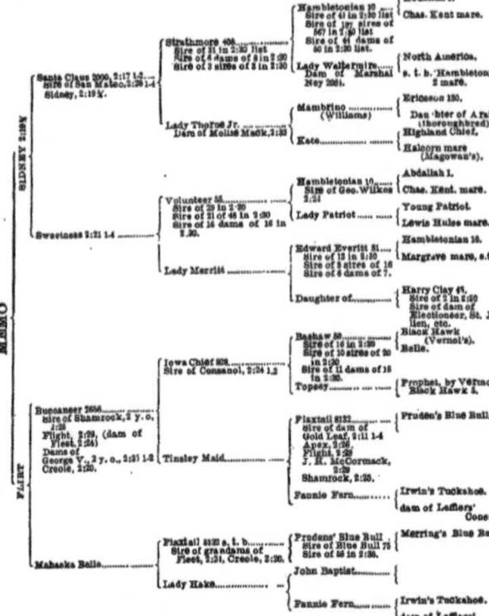

MEMO is, as can be seen at a glance, one of the best bred young stallions in service, having three crosses of Rysdyk's Hambletonian and one of Harry Clay, the sire of Green Mountain Maid (dam of Electioneer, etc.), while Long Island Black Hawk and Flaxtail also contribute to his blood. Sidney (Memo's sire) is universally known as the best young sire in the world, a producer of extreme speed at an early age.

PERFORMANCES.

MEMO trotted in public in his two year-old form, obtaining a record of 2:49, though he was close to Grandee in a race on the Bay District Track, the second heat of which was made in 2:31 1-2, the first in 2:32. He exhibited phenomenal speed when three years old, and had it not been for a slight strain of his fore fetlock, there is little question that he would have shown in public very close to the best record. On the Oakland track he was timed a mile in 2:30 1-2, and frequently trotted quarters in from 33 1-2 to 34 seconds.

As a four-year-old Memo only started once—at Sacramento—when, although out of condition, he showed great speed, and improving as he went on, great hopes were entertained of his going well down in the 'teens at the P. C. T. H. B. A. meeting, but after showing several very fast miles his leg filled and he was laid up for the season. He is sixteen hands high, and of powerful build throughout. His color is a glossy black, with both fore-feet white. His disposition is all that could be desired, and his action superb. He is a sure foal getter, only one mare being reported not in foal during his last season.

TERMS, $100, with usual return privileges, for a limited number of mares. Season to close JUNE 15th, when he will be prepared for track purposes. Pasturage $4 per month. Have leased the cricket ground adjoining the track for pasturage, where there is fine feed. Reasonable charges if fed hay and grain. Best of care taken of mares in any manner owners may desire, but positively no responsibility assumed for accidents or escapes. For further particulars address

J. P. KERR, 313 Bush Street, San Francisco,

or, JOHN ROWEN, Race Track, Oakland, Cal.

2:10 1-2 ELECTIONEER 2:12 1-4

BAY STALLION	BROWN STALLION
ECLECTIC	**MORTIMER**
11,321	5,346
By Electioneer, dam Manette (full sister to Woodnut 2.16 1-2 Manon 2:21 and Maple, dam of Hattie D., three-year-old record 2:28¾) by Nutwood 2:18¾, etc., etc.	Four-year-old Record 2:27. By ELECTIONEER, dam MARTI, by Whipple's Hambletonian (sire of 18 in 2:30, and of dams of eight in 2:30). Second dam Ida Martin by Rifleman (sire of Col. Lewis 2:18¾).
Terms $100 for the Season.	Terms $60 for the Season.

Horses shipped via San Francisco may be consigned to J. W. MORSHEAD, City Front Stables, who will attend to their forwarding.

Season closes JULY 1st, 1890. Usual return privileges.

For urther particulars address owner,

WILFRED PAGE, Penns Grove,
Sonoma County, Cal

The Trotting Stallion

Silver Bow

Will make the season of 1890 at the Oakland Race Track.

PEDIGREE.

SILVER BOW 11706, two-year-old record 2:37, is by Robert McGregor 647, 2:17½ (sire of Bonnie McGregor, 2:13½, Earl McGregor, 2:21¼, Mac D., 2:30, McGregor Boy, 2:20½, Mark Time, 2:30, Roxie McGregor, 2:30¾) by Major Edsall 2:11, 2:29, by Alexander's Abdallah 15—sire of Goldsmith Maid, 2:14—by Hambletonian 10—sire of Dexter, 2:17¼.

Robert McGregor's dam was Nancy Whitman by American Star 14, by Stockholm's American Star.

SILVER BOW'S first dam is Sadie by Hambletonian 10, sire of Geo. Wilkes, 2:22—sire of Guy Wilkes, 2:15¼—also Electioneer, sire of Sunol, three-year-old record, 2:10½, and Palo Alto, 2:12¾; second dam Lady Wynne by Wm. Welch 341; third dam Elenora Margrave by imp. Margrave.

DESCRIPTION.

SILVER BOW is a handsome bay, no white; 15-2¾ hands high; weighs 1075 pounds; of fine form, with the best of legs and a clean-cut, intelligent head. Is remarkably level-headed, seldom making a break; wears seven-ounce shoes in front. His record, 2:37, is no mark of his speed; he can beat 30 easy, and with his gilt-edge breeding, he is just what he ought to be, a trotter sired by a trotter whose dam was herself a trotter and his grandam the dam of two trotters. His dam Sadie being by Hambletonian 10, shows him to be bred from the cream of the trotting blood.

TERMS: $100 for the season. Mares not proving in foal returnable for the season of 1891 free of charge. Good pasturage and first-class care taken of mares for $5 per month. No responsibilities assumed for escapes or accidents. For further particulars, address

Limited to 15 approved mares.
Season to end June 1st, 1890.

P. J. WILLIAMS,
Care Race Track, Oakland, Cal.

Pleasanton Stock Farm Co.'s Stallions,

DIRECTOR, 2:17.

Director's book is open for 15 good mares more than already booked for the season of 1890, at $3[illegible] each.

This is the cheapest service fee ever charged for a stallion, taking into consideration his BREEDIN[G] and RACE RECORD and the RACE RECORDS OF HIS COLTS.

Season to commence February 15th and close August 1st.

CORRECTOR, Five Years Old.

Sire Director 2:17, dam Brainey, she by Echo. Echo sired by Rysdyk's Hambletonian, out of Fan[ny] Felter, by Magnolia, he by Seely's American Star. Brainey's dam Lady Dudley, she by Tom Dudley [by] Blacknose, a son of Medoc, he by American Eclipse. Lady Dudley's dam by Bertrand, Jr., a son of Bertran[d].

CORRECTOR is a rich seal brown 15½ hands high, and is the fastest young stallion in the world und[er] the same conditions, never having been off the farm where raised and never been shod or driven [for] speed before last Christmas, and can trot quarters now in 35 seconds, a 2:20 gait.

He will be allowed to serve ten good mares, at $100 each for the season, which closes June 1st.

DECORATOR, Four Years Old.

Sire Director 2:17, dam Chess, sired by Cardinal 2.37, trial 2:28, he by Gen. Gifford's Morgan, dam [of] Cardinal, sired by Joe Gales of Ohio, he by Marlborough out of the Duchess of Marlborough by Southe[rn] Eclipse; second dam old Duchess of Marlborough by Sir Archy; third dam by imp Diomed. Decorator's second dam a Morgan and Messenger mare.

Decorator is a light bay 16 hands high, and with but little handling for speed has shown eighths [in] 17½ seconds, a 2:20 gait.

He will be allowed to serve ten good mares at $50 each for the season, which closes June 1st.

Mares not proving with foal may be returned next season free of charge of service fees to the sam[e] stallion, if he is still in our possession; however, the company reserves the right to return the fee instea[d] of giving service.

Pasturage $4 per month; hay and grain extra. Accidents and escapes at owner's risk.

Service fees due at time of service, and must be paid, together with pasturage, etc., before mares a[re] taken away, or a good approved note given, payable August 1st, 1890, at which date all bills must [be] settled.

For further information call or address M. SALISBURY, 320 Sansome Street, Room 2[illegible] San Francisco, or

PLEASANTON STOCK FARM CO.,
Pleasanton, Alameda Co., Cal.

SOUTHER FARM

P. O. Box 208. San Leandro, Cal

1½ miles northwest of San Leandro; 8 miles southeast of Oakland. Turn off county road between above places at "Stanley Road," ¾ mile north of San Leandro.

Horses boarded at all times in any manne[r] desired. Best of care but no responsibility fo[r] accidents. Colts broken and handled for [the] road or track. Terms reasonable.

Glen Fortune,	Jester D,	El Benton,	Figaro,
By Electioneer.	By Almont.	By Electioneer.	Hambletonian 72
$50 for 1889.	$50 for 1890.	Limited to 5 mares.	Limited to 12 mare[s]
		Book Full.	Book Full.

THE SOUTHER FARM

Has Green Feed the Year Round

and feeds Hay in connection with the green feed, which a hors[e] must have if he is to thrive. Every animal is given

A Dry, Warm Place to Sleep,

No matter how stormy the weather. All Stock under cover when it rains.

VISITORS WELCOME ANY DAY EXCEPT SUNDAY.

How to Get Stock to the Souther Farm.

The Souther Farm is one and a half miles northeast of San Leandro and eight miles southeast of Oakland. The stables are about one mile east of the county road, which runs between Oakland and San Leandro. The place to turn off is at Stanley Road, where a large signboard of the farm is placed. Guide board[s] will be found at every cross road. In any ordinary weather the roads are very good, and they are fairly goo[d] after the unusually heavy rainfall of the past winter.

All stock sent from San Francisco may be brought over by Garcia's Express, No. 3 Market street, San Francisco. They also have an order box outside of Hawley Bros.' Hardware house on the corner of Mark[et] and Beale streets. The express leaves San Francisco on the Creek route boat, which starts at 1:3[illegible], but a[ll] orders should be in the order box at Market and Beale streets by 10 o'clock, or at the office, No. 3 Marke[t] street, by 11 o'clock at the latest. In the case of very young or very valuable horses, the Souther Farm wi[ll] send reliable men to lead or drive over any stock that will not lead behind a wagon. A small charge will b[e] made in such cases, to cover the extra expense incurred.

Horses are very easily taken from Oakland to the farm, and where it is inconvenient for owners t[o] bring them or send them, the farm will send after anything that is to come. On horses that stay thre[e] months or over there is no charge for getting or delivering. Where a horse stays a short time the actu[al] time and expense only is charged to him.

Horses can be shipped by rail from almost all parts of the State to San Leandro. Always notify th[e] Farm several days before shipping anything, and then men will be on hand to receive stock on arrival. Th[e] railroad station is but two miles from the Souther Farm, and the agent invariably gives immediate notic[e] of the arrival of any stock consigned to the above farm, but when word is sent to the farm in good seaso[n] by letter or telegram, the animals sent are saved waiting a couple of hours in the car.

Passenger trains leave San Francisco (from the broad gauge ferry) and First and Broadway, Oakland at frequent intervals during the day. There are several trains from San Jose to San Leandro on both th[e] broad and narrow gauge railroads; the broad gauge, by way of Niles, is much more convenient for getting t[o] the farm. There are trains each day from Sacramento, Stockton and Livermore to San Leandro. In ordi[nary] weather it is a short and pleasant drive from Oakland to the Souther Farm or from San Francisco t[o] the Farm by way of the Creek route ferry boat. Always notify the Souther Farm just when you will arriv[e] at San Leandro, and some one will meet you at the station. If you do not recognize the farm conveyance as[k] the stage driver, who will point it out.

Write to the above address for references, circulars and price lists. Term[s] reasonable.

GILBERT TOMPKINS, Proprietor.

SAN MATEO STOCK FARM

HOME OF GUY WILKES,

Record, 2:15 1-4.

Guy Wilkes' Book is full for 1890 and 1891, and positively no mor[e] mares will be received.

Sable Wilkes, three-year-old record 2:18, will be allowed to serve 2[illegible] mares in addition to those already engaged at $250 th[e] season of 1890. SABLE Wilkes, 15½ hands, black horse, by Guy Wilkes, first dam Sable by The Moor; second dam Gretchen by Mambrino Pilot; third dam Kitty Kirkman by Canad[a] Chief; fourth dam by Fanning's Tobe; fifth dam by imp. Leviathan.

Leo Wilkes, brown horse, four years, 16 hands, full brother to Sabl[e] Wilkes, will be allowed to serve 30 mares at $100 the seaso[n].

Mares not proving with foal may be returned the following season free of service fee. Parties engaging the services of any of the above horses must send a deposit of 10 per cent. o[f] service money with engagement. Pasturage $6 per month, and when the condition of th[e] animal requires it, hay or grain, or both, are fed, the charge will be $12 50 per month. Good care will be taken of all mares sent to the Farm, but no liability will be assumed fo[r] accidents or escapes.

All bills are due at time of service, but must be paid by August 1st of each year. No stoc[k] will be allowed to leave the place until all bills are paid.

WILLIAM CORBITT.
San Mateo Stock Farm.

2:08 3-4 2:10 2:12

MAMBRINO WILKES, 6083.

SIRE OF

GUS WILKES, 2:22; ALPHEUS, 2:27; CLARA P, 2:29½; BALKAN, 2:29½ (3-year-old) and timed separately 2:22½ in 4-year-old Stake, Bay District Track, October 14, 1889.

DESCRIPTION.

Black; sixteen hands; weighs, in exercise, 1,260 lbs. For style, finish, symmetry and proportion, comparison is challenged with any trotting bred horse. His colts follow in size, style and beauty. Balkan, for instance, being "facile princeps" of trotters in these particulars.

PEDIGREE.

Sired by Geo. Wilkes, sire of Harry Wilkes, 2:13½, Jay Wilkes, 2:18½, and 80 other trotters in the 2:30 list, in addition to 8 pacers, and of the sire of Axtell, 2:12 (three-year-old), beating all stallions of any age, and the sire of Regal Wilkes, 2:20¾, best two-year-old stallion record.

First dam Lady Chrisman by Mambrino (Todhunter), son of Mambrino Chief 11; sire of Lady Thorn, 2:18¼; Woodford Mambrino, 2:21½, and four others in 2:30 and of the dams of Director, 2:17, Piedmont, 2:17¼, Onward, 2:25¼, etc.

Second dam by Pilot Jr. 12, sire of nine in the 2:30 list, and of the dams of Maud S., 2:08¾, Jay-Eye-See, 2:10, Nutwood, 2:18¾, Viking, 2:19¾, Pilot Boy, 2:20, Naiad Queen, 2:20¼, etc.

TERMS.

Mares from a distance will be received at the Dexter Stables, Oakland, or Livery Stable, Martinez, the owner notifying Smith Hill, Superintendent at the farm. Good pasture and plenty of water. For the purpose of placing the service of a Wilkes within reach of breeders, the same rate will be maintained as last year, to wit, $75 for the season. Although it is not admitted thereby that this horse is inferior as a producer to the horses whose fees are placed at from $150 to $500. Address

SMITH HILL,
San Miguel Stock Farm,
Walnut Creek, Contra Costa Co., Cal.

2:12¾ 2:13½ 2:15¼

The Trotting Stallion

VICTOR,

Record 2:22

Will make the season of 1890 at NAPA CITY.

DESCRIPTION.

VICTOR is a handsome dark bay; 15-3 hands high; weighs about 1,150 pounds, and is remarkably intelligent, level-headed, of kind disposition, and a magnificent animal in every respect. He is well boned and muscled, of splendid conformation, and possesses the qualities of speed and endurance to an eminent degree—qualities that he imparts to his progeny.

PEDIGREE.

- Echo 462
  - Hambletonian 10, Sire of 42 in the 2:30 list — Abdallah 1; Chas. Kent mare
  - Fanny Felter — Magnolia 68; by Webber's Kentucky Whip
- Daughter of
  - Woodburn — Lexington; Lulu Horton
  - daughter of — Ashland; thoroughbred

ECHO is the sire of Belle Echo, 2:20, Senator, 2:21¼, Victor, 2:22, Gibraltar, 2:22¼, Echora, 2:23¼, Tippie, 2:25¼, Lohengrin, 2:27¼, Pasha, 2:27¼, Elmonte, 2:29, Del Hawkins, 2:29¼, Annie Laurie, 2:30, Economy, 2:30, Sam Lewis, pacer, 2:30.

TERMS—$60 FOR THE SEASON.

Mares not proving with foal may be returned next season free of charge, provided the horse remains the property of the present proprietor, and stands at the same place, otherwise money will be refunded. The best of care taken of mares in any manner that owners may desire, but no responsibility assumed for accidents or escapes. For further particulars, apply to or address

G. W. HUGHES, Agent,
G. A. DOHERTY, Proprietor. Napa City.

The Fast Trotting Stallion

REDWOOD.

Four-Year-Old Record 2:24 1-2

Will make the season of 1890—February 1st to July 1st—at

SANTA ROSA.

REDWOOD is a dark bay colt, 15.2½ hands high, weighs 1100 lbs. Foaled in 1885 by Anteeo, 2:16¼, sire of Alfred G, 2:19¾. Anteeo is by Electioneer. First dam Lou Milton, by Milton Medium; second dam Old Sally, a thoroughbred mare brought from the East to Cal by W. C. Ralston, Esq.

Redwood's sire was out of Columbine by A. W. Richmond the sire of the pacers Arrow 2:13¼, and Yellowood 2:23, and the trotters Romero, 2:19¼, and Len Rose, 2:27. Redwood has shown a quarter in 33 seconds.

Terms $100

for the season. Mares not proving with foal may be returned next season free of charge, provided Redwood remains the property of the present owners. Good pasturage at reasonable rates. No responsibility assumed for escapes or accidents. Service fees payable before removal of the mare. Limited to 40 approved mares. For further particulars address

A. McFADYEN.
Santa Rosa, Cal.

2:10¾ 2:13¾ 2:10

DEXTER PRINCE.

This Royally-bred Stallion will make the Season of 1890 at the LIVE OAKS Breeding Farm, 2 miles from Lodi, San Joaquin County, Cal.

DESCRIPTION.

DEXTER PRINCE is a blood bay, 16 hands high, weighs over 1,100 pounds; has great power and substance, and the highest finish. When two years old, at Palo Alto, he was timed quarters by Gov. Stanford in 32½ seconds, and he was driven eights by Mr. Marvin at a faster rate of speed than that. He is a sure foal-getter, and invariably sires foals of good size, of fine form and finish, and the highest rate of speed.

PEDIGREE.

By KENTUCKY PRINCE, the sire of Guy, 2:10¾, Spofford, 2:18¾, Company, 2:19¾, Bayonne Prince, 2:21 1-4, Fred Folger, 2:20¾, and a score more in the 2:30 list.

First dam LADY DEXTER, full sister of the greatest of trotters, Dexter, and the greatest of sires, Dictator, the sire of Director, 2:17, Phallas, 2:13¾, in a fourth heat, and Jay-Eye-See, 2:10.

Second dam Clara, the dam of Dexter, 2:17 1-4, Dictator, Astoria 2:29 1-4, and Almah, 2:26¾. Clara was by American Star, that has 34 daughters that have produced 2:30 or better trotters.

Third dam the McKinstry mare, the dam of Shark, 2:27¾. HAMBLETONIAN, the grandsire of DEXTER PRINCE, has 40 trotters in the 2:30 list, 44 daughters that have produced 2:30 trotters, and more than 100 sons that have sired 2:30 trotters.

CLARK CHIEF, the grandsire on the sire's side, was the sire of performing and producing sons and daughters.

DEXTER PRINCE has faster blood lines, on both sides, than any other stallion in the world—Guy 2:10¾, and Jay-Eye-See, 2:10.

KENTUCKY PRINCE is one of the best bred and speediest stallions in the world. David Bonner, in the presence of Governor Stanford, timed him when he trotted a 2:10 gait. He is by Clark Chief, one of the great broodmare sires; his first dam is Kentucky Queen by Morgan Eagle, son of Hale's Green Mountain Morgan, 2nd dam by Blythe's Whip, 3rd dam by Martin's Brummier, 4th dam by Quicksilver 880, on through the strongest thoroughbred blood.

TERMS.

$100 for the season, with usual return privileges. Payable before mares are removed. Good pasture, and the best care furnished, but no responsibility assumed for accidents.

PREMIUM.

$200 will be given to the first of the produce of DEXTER PRINCE put in the 2:30 list, and $100 each after the first. Address

L. M. MORSE, Lodi, Cal.

The Produce of Eros Averaged $2,200 Each at New York Auction Sale in 1889.

THE ELECTIONEER TROTTING STALLION,

5326 EROS 5326

Will make the season of 1890—February 1st to July 1st—at LA SIESTA RANCH, MENLO PARK, adjoining Palo Alto.

PEDIGREE.

EROS (5326)
Standard by his sire
" " dam
" " record
" " produce
" under all rules

- EROS (5326)
  - Electioneer — Grandsire of Norlaine, 1 yr., 2:31 1-2, Sire of Sunol, 2 yrs., 2:18, Sunol, 3 yrs., 2:10 1-2, Hinda Rose, 4 yrs., 2:16, Palo Alto, 2:12¾.
    - Hambletonian 10 — Sire of Dictator, George Wilkes, Happy Medium, and 40 others in 2:30 list, and grandsire of 728 in list.
      - Abdallah 1 — Sire of the dams of Goldsmith Maid, 2:14, and 7 other producing dams.
      - Charles Kent mare — By imp. Bellfounder.
    - Green Mountain Maid — Dam of Prospero, 2:20, Elaine, 2:20, Dame Trot, 2:22, Elista, 2:22½, Storm, 2:26¾, Antonio, 2:28¾, Miranda, 2:31, Mansfield, 2:26.
      - Harry Clay — Sire of the dams of St. Julian, 2:11¼, Bodine, 2:19¼, and 17 more in 2:30 list
      - Shanghai Mary.
  - Sontag Mohawk — Dam of Eros, 2:29 1-2, Sport, 2:22¾, Sallie Benton, 2:17¾, Conductor, trial, 2:26, Colma, 3-y-o trial, 2:24.
    - Mohawk Chief — Sire of the dams of Lot Slocum, 2:17¼, Sallie Benton, 4 yrs., 2:17¾, Pedlar, 2 yrs., 2:27¾, Stanford, 4 yrs., 2:30, Eros, 6th heat, 2:29 1-2.
      - Hambletonian 10 — Sire of the dams of Stamboul, 2:12½, Wilton, 2:19¼, and 20 other trotters.
      - Lady Perrine
    - Sontag Nellie
      - Toronto Sontag — By Toronto Chief,
      - Nellie Gray — 5-mile record, 13:45.

Produce of Eros
Wanda, 4 yrs., 2:21,
Sollita, 2 yrs., 2:41 1-2,
Merignita, 2 yrs., 2:42,
Daylight, 2 yrs., 2:34,
Hiram B., trial, 2:28.

These are the only colts by him that have ever had a harness on except one in New York that went a trial last July in 2:26 1-2.

DESCRIPTION.

EROS is a rich seal brown stallion, bred by Hon. Leland Stanford at Palo Alto, and is the nearest living likeness of his celebrated sire, Electioneer. Stands 15.2 hands high, and weighs 1050 pounds.

In breeding to Eros, the owners of mares will strictly follow the great rule of breeding, viz., breed to a stallion by a producer and out of a sure producer of great speed. Eros is by the stallion that has produced more 2:30 trotters that any living horse, and is also the sire of more 2:20 performers than any horse living or dead.

EROS is out of the dam of Sally Benton, four years old, record 2:17¾, Sport 2:22¾, and Eros 2:29½ in the sixth heat, against a field of nine horses. He is from a family that is endowed with great natural speed, trot fast at an early age, train on, throw trotters from all classes of mares, are of good substance, bone, style and action, and breed solid colors.

TERMS.

$100 for the season, with the privilege of return next season should mares not be in foal and horse and mare still remain in the same hands.

Good pasturage can be obtained at $5 per month, but no responsibility for accidents or escapes. There are a large number of box stalls, and animals can be kept up and fed on hay and grain at reasonable rates if required. Mares already in foal can be sent to the ranch for foaling, and will receive all the attention bestowed upon our own mares. Mares left with Mr. Peter Pomyea, Broadway Street Stable, Oakland, or with Mr. F. H. Burke, 401 Montgomery Street, San Francisco, will be forwarded to the ranch free of charge. For further particulars apply to

W. H. VIOGET.
LA SIESTA RANCH, MENLO PARK, CAL.

EROS is the only stallion offered to the public on this Coast that has a dam that has three in the 2:30 list.

GRAND MOOR, 2374.

- Grand Moor 2374
  - Moor 870 — Sire of Beautiful Bells 2:29½; Sire of Sable (dam of Sable Wilkes) 2:18; Sire of Sultan 2:24; Sire of Tommy Gates 2:24; Sire of Del Sur 2:24½; Sire of Sir Guy 2:28¾. Beautiful Bells is the dam of Hinda Rose, 2:19½ as a 3-year-old, Palo Alto Belle, 2:22½, Chimes, St. Bell, 2:21½, Bell Boy (3 years) 2:19¼. Sultan, 2:24 (sire of Stamboul 2:12½) has 19 in 2:30 list.
    - Clay Pilot 93 — Sire of 2 in 2:30 list.
    - Belle of Wabash.
  - Vashti — Dam of Don Tomas, who got a record of 2:10 in 1889.
    - Mambrino Patchen 58 — Sire of 14 in 2:30 list. Sire of the dam of Guy Wilkes, 2:15¼; also sire of 20 stallions and 18 mares with get in 2:30 list.
    - Kate Taber — By Mambrino Messenger, he by Mambrino Paymaster.

Foaled 1876. Black. Sixteen hands high. Bred by L. J. Rose

A horse of highest form and quality; of great excellence in every point; a type of his celebrated family; of marked individuality, spirit and endurance; never properly trained or raced, but shows the possession of great speed; perfectly manageable in the stable and on the road and track.

As he is sired by The Moor 870, a son of CLAY PILOT, out of Vashti by MAMBRINO PATCHEN, he is a most valuable cross for mares of other families. THE MOOR sired Beautiful Bells and the dams of Sable Wilkes and Margaret 2:26 (dam of Regal Wilkes, 2-year-old record 2:20¾).

MAMBRINO PATCHEN is regarded as the unsurpassed sire of broodmares, having, among many others, sired the dam of Guy Wilkes and of Wm. L. (the sire of Axtell), and a son of his sired the dam of Axtell. The public sales this year have demonstrated with renewed emphasis the value of The Moor and Mambrino Patchen strains of blood. For combining particularly with the Hambletonians it may be called "the ready money cross."

GRAND MOOR will make the season of 1890 for a time at the Oakland Race Track and afterwards at my Ranch, fifteen miles from Oakland. Mares can be delivered at the race track to the groom in charge. Pasture at $5 per month. For other food, if requested, an additional charge will be made.

TERMS, $150 for the season, with privileges of return if the horse does not change hands.

Every care exercised, but no liability for escapes or accidents.

H. I. THORNTON, 504 Kearny Street.

POPLAR GROVE

Breeding Farm

STALLIONS.

CLOVIS, 4909,

CLOVIS is a beautiful black, Eight Years Old, 16 1-2 Hands High, and weighs 1260 lbs.

He is a horse of beautiful symmetry and magnificent action.

PEDIGREE.

CLOVIS was sired by Sultan, 2:24, sire of Stamboul, 2:12 1-4, Ruby, 2:19¾, and fifteen others with records of 2:30 or better.

First dam Sweetbriar by Thorndale 2:22 1-2, sire of Edwin Thorne, 2:16 1-2, Daisy Dale, 2:19, and May Thorne, 2:22.

Second dam Ulster Queen, dam of Volmer, 2:24¾, by Hambletonian 10. Sire of Dexter, 2:17¼, George Wilkes, 2:22.

Third dam by Thomas Jefferson, a son of Mambrino Paymaster, Jr.

Fourth dam by Mambrino Paymaster, sire of Mambrino Chief.

Sultan, by The Moor, sire of Beautiful Bells, dam of Hinda Rose, 2:19 1-2, and Sable, dam of Sable Wilkes, three year old record 2:18.

First dam of Sultan, Sultana, by Delmonico. Sire of Darby, 2:16 1-2, by Guy Miller, sire of Whipple's Hambletonian.

Second dam by Mambrino Chief.

Third dam by Downing's Bay Messenger.

Fourth dam Mrs. Caudle, dam of Ericsson, four year old record 2:30 1-2.

Clovis will make the season of 1890 at Poplar Grove Breeding Farm, near Wildflower, Fresno County, commencing February 1st and ending July 1st.

Terms, $75, due at time of service.

Mares cared for in any manner owners may desire; pasturage $2 per month. Every care exercised, but no liability for escapes or accidents. Mares not proving with foal can be returned next season, providing I still own this stallion.

APEX, 8935.

FOUR-YEAR-OLD RECORD, FOURTH HEAT, 2:26.

Will make the present season at the Poplar Grove Breeding Farm, near Wildflower, Fresno Co., season commencing Feb. 1st, and ending July 1, 1890. Terms $50 the season, due at time of service. Apex is eight years old, a beautiful bay, 15 1-2 hands high, and weighs 1100 lbs. He is a horse of fine disposition, and his gait is faultless.

PEDIGREE.

Apex was sired by Prompter 2305, he by Blue Bull 75; first dam Mary by Flaxtail, he by Pruden's Blue Bull, Flaxtail being the sire of the dams of Buccaneer, five-year-old record, 2:24 1-2; Pride, yearling record, 2:44 1-2, and Shamrock, two-year old record, 2:28, third heat. Second dam by Bright Eyes, son of Boanarages. Prompter (sire of Apex, record 2:26, and Transit, 2:26 1-2), by Wilson's Blue Bull, by Pruden's Blue Bull, son of Merring's Blue Bull. Prompter's dam Prairie Bird, by Flaxtail; second dam by John the Baptist, son of Tally Ho Morgan, by Sherman Morgan; third dam Fannie Fern by Irwin's Tuckahoe.

Apex made his appearance in the circuit as a two-year-old, and obtained a record of 2:42. As a three-year-old he reduced this in a race at Santa Rosa against Stamboul to 2:31, it taking six heats to decide the contest, which was won by Apex. As a four year-old he gained his present record of 2:26.

Mares cared for in any manner owners may desire. Pasturage $2 per month. Every care exercised, but no liabilities for escapes or accidents. Mares not proving with foal can be returned next season, providing I still own this stallion.

The Standard Stallion

JUNIO,

RECORD 2:22.

WILL MAKE THE PRESENT SEASON OF 1890 AT FRESNO FAIR GROUNDS.

Season Commencing Feb. 1st and ending July 1st.

TERMS—$100 the season, due at time of service.

JUNIO is eight years old, a handsome dark bay 16 hands high, and weighs 1200 pounds. He is the personification of the light harness horse, and his trotting action is superb. At the State Fair of 1886 he took first premium over forty of the finest trotters in the State.

PEDIGREE.

Junio, by Electioneer, premier stallion of Palo Alto (sire of Sunol 2:10 1-2, Palo Alto 2:12 1-4, and 47 others in the 2:30 list). Dam by Granger by imp. Hercules.

Granger, by imp. Hercules, dam Jenny Lind, by Stockbridge Chief, Jr., he by Stockbridge Chief, he by Vermont Black Hawk. Second dam by Kentucky Whip.

Imp. Hercules, by Kingston, first dam daughter of Tuscar, by Bay Middleton, second dam Malvina, by Oscar; 3rd dam Spotless by Walton; 4th dam by Trumpator (see Bruce's American Stud Book, Vol. 1, page 20). Hercules is the sire of the dam of Azmoor 2:20½; also sire of dam of Menlo 2:21 1-2.

Mares not proving in foal may be returned next year free of charge, providing I still have the horse. Pasturage $2 per month. While every care will be taken of horses, no liability will be assumed for accidents or escapes.

For further particulars address

S. N. STRAUBE, Fresno, Cal.
Poplar Grove Breeding Farm.

Breeders' Directory.

Advertisements under this heading 50c. per line per month.

HORSES AND CATTLE.

W. S. JACOBS, Sacramento, Cal. — Breeder of Thoroughbred Shorthorns and Berkshire Hogs.

J. H. WHITE, Lakeville, Sonoma County—Breeder of Registered Holstein Cattle.

EL ROBLAS RANCHO—Los Alamos, Cal., Francis T. Underhill, proprietor, importer and breeder of thoroughbred Hereford Cattle. Information by mail. C. F. Swan, manager.

PAGE BROTHERS.—Penn's Grove, Sonoma Co. Cal. Breeders of Short-Horn Cattle; Draft, Roadster and Standard Bred Horses.

SETH COOK, breeder of Cleveland Bay Horses, Devon, Durham, Polled Aberdeen-Angus and Galloway Cattle. Young stock of above breeds on hand for sale. Warranted to be pure bred, recorded and average breeders. Address, Geo. A. Wiley, Cook Farm, Danville, Contra Costa Co., Cal.

MAMBRINO WILKES COLTS and FILLIES, full brothers and sisters to Gus. Wilkes 2:22, and Balkan 2:29¼, for sale. Address SMITH HILL, Walnut Creek, Contra Costa County, Cal.

PETER SAXE & SON, Lick House, San Francisco, Cal.—Importers and Breeders for past 18 years of every variety of Cattle, Horses, Sheep and Hogs.

HOLSTEIN THOROUGHBREDS of all the noted strains. Registered Berkshire Swine. Catalogues. F. H. BURKE, 401 Montgomery St., S. F.

The Thoroughbred Stallion

Three Cheers

Will make the season of 1890 at

Sacramento.

PEDIGREE.

THREE CHEERS
- imp. Hurrah
  - Newminster
    - Touchstone, by Camel
    - Beeswing, by Dr. Syntax
  - Jovial
    - Bay Middleton, by Sultan
    - Sister to Grey Momus, by Comus
- Young Fashion
  - imp. Monarch
    - imp. Priam, by Emilius
    - imp. Delphine, by Whisker
  - Fashion
    - imp. Trustee, by Catton
    - Bonnets o' Blue, by Sir Charles

Hurrah was imported by John Reber, of Lancaster, Ohio, a locality where there were but few breeders of thoroughbreds. Under these disadvantages he sired a long list of winners. His sire Newminster, won the St. Ledger 1851, and his dam, Jovial by Bay Middleton, winner of the Derby 1836. Newminster by Touchstone, winner St. Ledger 1834. Dam Beeswing, winner of 54 races out of 64 starts, by Dr. Syntax, winner of the Doncaster Cup, 1837—40—41—42, the only horse that ever accomplished that feat.

On the side of the dam Three Cheers is equally well related. Young Fashion was the dam of Surprise, Scotland (the only horse that ever beat Asteroid a heat), Liverpool, Columbia, and Bonnie Kate, the dam of Little Buttercup, and the flying Bonnie Lizzie. His grandam, Fashion was the greatest race mare of her day and beat Boston in that historical match at four mile heats, which is recorded as one of the greatest events in the annals of the turf.

Horsemen who are qualified to judge, pronounce Three Cheers to be the finest type of the Newminster line in America.

LOCATION.

THREE CHEERS will be located at the Arcade Training Stable, Rancho del Paso. This place has been selected for the reason that first class pasturage has been secured there for the exclusive use of these mares, and the other facilities to be obtained there for the care of mares (especially mares in foal) are better than can be found elsewhere in the locality.

TERMS.

$60 for the season with the usual return privilege. Pasturage $5 per month. Mares cared for as owners may desire at bottom rates for grain and hay. All bills payable before the mare is removed.

Mares shipped care of WM. IRVINE, Pacific Stables, Sacramento, will be properly cared for and sent to the ranch without delay.

Three Cheers will be in charge of one of the most experienced and competent stud grooms in the State, who will exercise every care, but no reponsibility assumed for accidents or escapes.

For further particulars apply to Louis Crissler, at the ranch; Wm. Irvine, Pacific Stables, Second St., Sacramento; or to the owner,

E. S. CULVER,
313 Bush St., San Francisco.

Sunny Side Breeding Farm.

Admiral 488.

Foaled 1867—Sired by Volunteer 55. Son of Rysdyk's Hambletonian 10.

First dam Lady Pierson by Cassius M. Clay (Neaves') 20; second dam by Diamond; third dam a running mare said to be thoroughbred. He is fitted in an eminent degree to produce colts that will in all respects justify his patrons in their expectations.

Admiral is the sire of Huntress, record 2:27¼, Sister, 2:19½, Perhelion, 2:25, Nona Y., 2:26, and others equally as promising, but have not had the advantage of track work. He will serve a limited number of approved mares at $50 the season, with usual return privilege. Season ending August 1, 1890. No liability for accidents or escapes.

KING DAVID 2576.

Bay Stallion—Foaled 1883.

Sired by Admiral 488, dam Black Flora (the dam of Huntress, 2:27¼, Sister, 2:19½, Perhelion, 2:25, Nona Y., 2:25), by Black Prince.

King David is one of the best gets of Admiral. He has a good disposition, kind to drive, smooth and even-gaited, and can speed fast. Barring accidents, he will trot in the twenties this Fall. His colts are large, rangy, and well finished. Will serve a limited number of mares at $30 the season, to end July 1, 1890. Every precaution will be taken to prevent accidents and escapes, but no liability will be assumed. Pasturage $4 per month.

Sunny Side Farm is situated two miles east of Vallejo, on the Sulphur Spring road. For further particulars, address

FRANK DRAKE,
Vallejo, Cal.

The Pacific Coast

Live Stock Owners

MUTUAL PROTECTIVE ASS'N.,

MONTEREY, Monterey Co., Cal.

TRUSTEES:

HON. R. V. SARGENT, President,
G. W. GALLANAR, Secretary,
JAMES E. PALMER, Business Manager,
EDW. INGRAM, Vice-President,
FRED. D. HOWARD, Actuary,
R. H. WILLEY, Attorney.

GENERAL BUSINESS OFFICE, Room 73, Flood Building, corner Market and Fourth Streets, San Francisco, Cal.

VOLNEY HOWARD, General Manager.

FISHING TACKLE,

WHOLESALE AND RETAIL.

CLABROUGH, GOLCHER & CO.,

630 and 632 Montgomery St.

AN UNQUALIFIED ENDORSEMENT.

Peruvian Bitters are made of the purest ingredients and compounded as carefully as any prescription.

Peruvian Bark, one of its principal ingredients, was introduced into Spain by the Countess, wife of Count CINCHON, Spanish Viceroy to Peru in 1630, who was cured of a fever by its use, since which time, no better remedy for Malaria and for Restoring the Natural Tone of the Stomach has been discovered.

On the Atlantic Coast they are used in the principal Hotels, Clubs and Restaurants, and sold by all Grocers and Druggists. We have sold them for the past three years WITHOUT ANY ADVERTISING and sales have constantly increased UPON MERIT ALONE, and we unqualifiedly recommend them to our friends and customers.

ACKER, MERRALL & CONDIT.

New York, Feb. 1st, 1890.

WILMERDING & CO., Agents for Pacific Coast,
216 FRONT ST., SAN FRANCISCO, CAL.

THE IMPROVED NOYES ROAD-CART,

PATENTED JULY 17, 1883, AND JUNE 8, 1886.

Some of the Advantages of the Noyes Cart Over All Others.

There is no bar for the rider to climb over in getting in or out. The horse can be hitched eighteen inches nearer than any other road-cart made. You can get in or out with perfect safety—no danger of being thrown into the wheel—a great advantage in breaking colts. THE EASIEST CART FOR ROAD OR TRACK. The only cart that a horse can be speeded to within one second as fast as to a sulky. All our carts are made of the very best materials and are warranted. Manufactured by the NOYES CART COMPANY, Kalamazoo, Mich.

They are indorsed by the following horsemen, all of whom are using them. Ask their opinion of the Noyes Cart: John Splan, who drove Guy a full mile in 2:17¾ and Chanter a half-mile in 1:10¾ to a Noyes Cart, says he would not take $250 for it if he could not get another; W. J. Gordon, Glenville, O.; W. B. Fasig, Cleveland, O.; Dave Muckel, Cleveland, O.; R. J. Moorehead, North East, Pa.; W. J. Chamberlain, Cleveland, O.; H. F. Malone, Bradford, Pa.; S. A. Brown & Co., Kalamazoo Stock Farm; Charles Marvin, Menlo Park, Cal.; W. H. Crawford, Lexington, Ky.; S. L. Caton, who gave Bell Boy a mark at Los Angeles, Cal., of 2:19¼, and drove Chanter a half mile in 1:06¾ and Lowland Girl a full mile in 2:12 to a Noyes Cart; Mike Bowerman, Lexington, Ky.; James Golden, Medford, Mass.; John E. Turner, Philadelphia, Pa.; T. L. Newton, Beaver Dam, Wis.; P. V. Johnston, Marshall, Mich.; W. H. McCarthy, Los Angeles, Cal.; A. W. Dennison, El Dorado, Kan.; P. O. Shank, Cleveland, O.; Charles Barnard, Boston, Mass.; Johnson Bros., Greenville, Mich.; John G. Avery, Buffalo, N. Y.; General R. L. Howard, Buffalo, N. Y.; Howard Conklin, Buffalo, N. Y.; W. D. Sam, Hennepin, Ill.; R. G. Henry, Waterbury, Conn; J. E. Hayer, Newburgh, O.; J. O. Mart, Jefferson, Tex.; A. W. Harbison, Rock Point, Pa.; Carl Hodges, Battle Creek, Mich.; Barney Treacy, Lexington, Ky.; George Forbes, Cleveland, O.; Gifford Dudley, Topeka, Kan.; William and J. L. Thompson Lamont, Pa.; C. F. Emery, Forest City Stock Farm, Cleveland, O.; H. F. Jones, Minneapolis, Minn.; John Forbes, Elyria, O.; D. J. Downs Battle Creek, Mich; Frank Caton, Randall Station, O.; Arthur D. Sutton, Ind., Pa.; W. F. Neely, Grand Ridge, Ill.; Walter Clark, owner of Pilot Medium, Battle Creek, Mich.; H. R. Kingman, Battle Creek, Mich.; Dr. Sutton and H. C. Reed, Kalamazoo, Mich.; Budd Doble, Chicago, Ill.

SOLE MANUFACTURERS OF STONE'S PATENT SULKY CASE.

They will more than save their cost in one season, and horsemen campaigning trotters cannot afford to do without them. Would refer to Samuel A. Brown, Kalamazoo Stock Farm, S. L. Caton and W. H. McCarthy. Address

NOYES CART COMPANY, Kalamazoo, Mich.

Office and Factory, corner Rose and Eleanor streets. H. ARTHUR STONE, Manager.

Poplar Grove Breeding FARM.

Standard-bred Trotters, Colts and Fillies.

The get of CLOVIS, 4909; PASHA, 2039; APEX, 2935,

For Sale.

Address S. N. STRAUBE, Poplar Grove Breeding Farm,

Fresno, Cal.

Inspection by intending purchasers invited, and information by mail.

KENNEL ADVERTISEMENTS.

LOST.

A White Pointer Dog

With lemon spots. Answers to the name of "Point." A liberal reward and no questions asked on delivery of same at

SWAIN'S STABLE,
417 Folsom St.

Fox Terrier Pups for Sale

Sire BLEMTON VESUVIAN (Champion Lucifer—Blemton—Vesta), dam BEATRICE (Champion Bacchanal—Blemton Arrow). This is the best winning blood. Beautifully marked. Will make handsome and game ones.

—Also an—

ENGLISH MASTIFF DOG PUP. Will develop into a good one. Apply or address,

J. B. MARTIN,
No. 1321 age Street, near Lyon St., S. F., Cal.

RENTON KENNELS,

SAN FRANCISCO OFFICE, 2922 Pine St.

Kennels located at Bolinas, Cal.

Dogs taken to board and broken at reasonable rates.

POINTER PUPPIES FOR SALE.

By Professor—Gracie Bow; Professor—Belle H.; Climax—Drab; Don—Diana.

Thoroughly broken water spaniel, Rock, out of the Prinder stock. Address

W. D. HOWE,
2922 Pine Street, San Francisco.

DOGS---Pointer Pups

FOR SALE.

Sure Bench Show and Field Trial Winners, as they have more bench-show and field-trial blood in them than any that have ever been whelped on the Pacific Coast.

Sire, POINT, double field trial winner; he by Vandevort's Don, great field trial and bench show winner, out of Drab, field trial and bench show winner.

Dam, QUEEN CROXTETH by Bush T., bench show winner, out of Champion Patti Croxteth, field trial and bench show winner. This is the best pointer blood in the world. Breeding and health guaranteed. Address,

A. B. TRUMAN,
1425 Steiner St., near Ellis, S. F., Cal.

CALIFORNIA SPANIEL KENNELS,

Oakland, California, H. P. RENNIE, Prop. Breeder and importer of typical COCKER SPANIELS. Winner of first prizes at S. F. and Los Angeles, 1889; also, Columbus, 1889, New York, 1887. In the stud, solid Black Cocker dog, GIFFER, won 1st and Gold Medal at S. F., 1889. Fee, $25. Puppies and grown dogs at reasonable prices. My dogs can neither talk nor climb a tree, but are fielders and prize winners.

The Trotting-Bred Stallion

RINGWOOD

THE FINEST SON OF THE NOTED SIDNEY,

Will make a Season at Oakland commencing March 1, and ending June 1, 1890.

DESCRIPTION.

RINGWOOD is a dark, rich colored bay, black points, 15 1-2 hands, weight 1100 lbs., and a pure gaited trotter. Has shown great speed. He is now five years old. As a four year old he showed a trial in 2:23 1-2, and but for an accident would have received a record as a four year old of 2:15 or better.

PEDIGREE.

RINGWOOD is by Sidney, record 2:19 3-4, and a half brother to Gold Leaf 2:11 1-4, Adonis 2:11, Flee (two year old) 2:24, Longworth 2:19, Sister V. 2:21, Fanstine, yearling, 2:35, Fleet, yearling, 2:35 Memo, three year old trial 2:2- 1 2.

Sidney is by Santa Claus, record 2:17 1-2; he by Strathmore, sire of 31 in 2:30 list; he by Hambletonian 10, the greatest of all producers; he by Abdallah. Sidney's dam, Sweetness, record 2:21 1-4; she by Volunteer, the sire of St. Julien 2:11 1 4.

RINGWOOD'S dam Alma; she by Dashway, thoroughbred; he by Belmont, he by American Boy; he by Sea Gull; he by imported Expedition. Alma's 1st dam, Fanny Cobb, was a great road mare, pedigree untraced.

TERMS: $50 for the Season.

Payable June 1st, or sooner if mares are taken away. Address communications to

A. C. DIETZ,
Oakland, Cal.

GEO. WASHINGTON,

11,623.

RECORD 2:30.

Bay colt, bred by Thomas Smith of Vallejo, Cal. Foaled 1886 by Mambrino Chief, Jr., 11,622, record 2:34 1-4, 1st dam Fanny Rose by Vick's Ethan Allen Jr. 2,903, sire of Prince Allen 2:27, 2nd dam Jenny Lind, thoroughbred, dam of Prince Allen 2:27. Will serve a limited number of mares at $50 for the season. Mares not proving with foal may be returned next season free.

Mambrino Chief, Jr.

11,622.

RECORD 2:34 1 2.

Sire of George Washington, record 2:30 at three years old. Bay horse bred by Rufus Ingalls of Belvedere, Ill. By McDonald Chief 3583. First dam Venus by Mambrino Patchen 58. 2nd dam by Wardlow's Shakespeare. 3rd dam Lone Gold 4th dam by Silver Heels. Has not been in the stud before. He was 3 years old when he served a few mares, and his colts all show good style and form.

Terms for the season $40. For further particulars see or address

THOMAS SMITH,
Vallejo, Cal.

Southern Pacific Co.

(PACIFIC SYSTEM.)

Trains leave and are due to arrive at San Francisco.

LEAVE (FOR)	FROM APRIL 13, 1890.	ARRIVE (FROM)
7.30 A M	Haywards, Niles and San Jose ...	*12.45 P M
7.30 A M	Sacramento and Redding, via Davis	7.15 P M
7.30 A M	Sacramento, Auburn, Colfax	4.45 P M
9.00 A M	Martinez, Vallejo, Calistoga and Santa Rosa	6.15 P M
8.30 A M	Los Angeles Express, Fresno, Bakersfield, Mojave and East and Los Angeles	11.15 A M
8.30 A M	Niles, San Jose, Stockton, Ione, Sacramento, Marysville, Oroville and Red Bluff	4.45 P M
10.30 A M	Haywards and Niles	3.45 P M
12.00 M	Haywards, Niles and Livermore.	8.45 P M
*1.00 P M	Sacramento River Steamers	**6.00 A M
3.00 P M	Haywards, Niles and San Jose	9.45 A M
3.30 P M	2d Class for Ogden and East	10.45 P M
4.00 P M	Stockton and ‡Milton; Vallejo, Calistoga and Santa Rosa	9.45 A M
*4.30 P M	Niles and Livermore	*8.45 A M
*4.30 P M	Niles and San Jose	‡6.15 P M
6.00 P M	Shasta Route Express, Sacramento, Marysville, Redding, Portland, Puget Sound, East and Knight's Landing via Davis	10.45 A M
5.00 P M	Haywards and Niles	7.45 A M
6.00 P M	Sunset Route, Atlantic Express, Santa Barbara, Los Angeles, Deming, El Paso, New Orleans and East	8.45 P M
8.00 P M	Central Atlantic Express, Ogden and East	9.45 A M

SANTA CRUZ DIVISION.

LEAVE (FOR)		ARRIVE (FROM)
‡7.45 A M	Excursion train to Santa Cruz	‡8.05 P M
8.15 A M	Newark, Centerville, San Jose, Felton, Boulder Creek and Santa Cruz	6.20 P M
*2.45 P M	Centerville, San Jose, Almaden, Felton, Boulder Creek and Santa Cruz	*11.20 A M
4.45 P M	Centerville, San Jose, and Los Gatos	9.50 A M

Coast Division (Third and Townsend Sts.)

LEAVE (FOR)		ARRIVE (FROM)
7.25 A M	San Jose, Almaden and Way Stations	2.30 P M
8.30 A M	San Jose, Gilroy, Tres Pinos; Pajaro, Santa Cruz; Monterey; Pacific Grove, Salinas, San Miguel, Paso Robles, Santa Margarita (San Luis Obispo) and principal Way Stations	6.12 P M
10.30 A M	San Jose and Way Stations	5.02 P M
12.01 P M	Cemetery, Menlo Park and Way Stations	3.38 P M
*3.30 P M	San Jose, Tres Pinos, Santa Cruz, Salinas, Monterey, Pacific Grove and principal Way Stations	*10.00 A M
*4.20 P M	Menlo Park and Way Station	*7.58 A M
5.20 P M	San Jose and Way Stations	9.03 A M
6.30 P M	Menlo Park and Way Stations	6.35 A M
†11.45 P M	Menlo Park and principal Way Stations	†7.28 P M

A M for Morning. P M for Afternoon.
*Sundays excepted. †Saturdays only. ‡Sundays only.
**Mondays excepted. §Saturdays excepted.

OCEANIC STEAMSHIP CO.

Carrying United States, Hawaiian and Colonial Mails.

WILL LEAVE THE COMPANY'S WHARF, foot of Mission Street, No. 1,

For Honolulu, Auckland and Sydney,

WITHOUT CHANGE,

The Splendid New 3,000-ton Iron Steamer.
SS ZEALANDIA... Saturday, May 31st, 1890, at 12 M., Or immediately on arrival of the English mails.

For Honolulu,

SS AUSTRALIA (3,000 tons), May 23, 1890, at 12 M

☞ For freight or passage, apply at office, 327 Market Street. JOHN D. SPRECKELS & BROS. General Agents.

KILLIP & CO.,

LIVE STOCK AND GENERAL AUCTIONEERS,

22 Montgomery Street, San Francisco

SPECIAL ATTENTION PAID TO SALES OF

High-Bred Horses and Cattle.

At auction and private sale.

Will Sell in All Cities and Counties of the State.

REFERENCES.

HON. C. GREEN, Sacramento.	HON. J. D. CARR Salinas.
J. P. SARGENT, ESQ., Sargents.	HON. JOHN BOGGS Colusa.
HON. L. J. ROSE, Los Angeles.	HON. A. WALRATH Nevada.

J. B. HAGGIN, ESQ., San Francisco.

Represented at Sacramento by Edwin F. Smith Secretary State Agricultural Society.
At San Jose by Messrs. Montgomery & Rea, Real Estate Agents.
Being the oldest established firm in the live-stock business on this Coast, and having conducted the important auction sales in this line for the past fifteen years, amounting to one half a million of dollars, we feel justified in claiming unequaled facilities for disposing of live stock of every description, either at auction or private sale. Our list of correspondents embraces every breeder and dealer of prominence upon the Pacific Coast, thus enabling us to give full publicity to animals placed with us for sale. Private purchases and sales of live stock of all descriptions will be made on commission, and stock shipped with the utmost care. Purchases and sales made of land of every description. We are authorized to refer to the gentlemen whose names are appended.

KILLIP & CO., 22 Montgomery Street

HEALD'S

Business College, 24 Post St.

—San Francisco.—

The most popular school on the Coast

P. HEALD, President. C. S. HALEY, Sec'y.

☞ Send for Circulars.

San Francisco and North Pacific Railway.

THE DONAHUE BROAD-GAUGE ROUTE.

COMMENCING SUNDAY, APRIL 27, 1889, AND until further notice, boats and trains will leave from and arrive at the San Francisco Passenger Depot, Market-street Wharf, as follows:

FROM SAN FRANCISCO FOR POINT TIBURON AND SAN RAFAEL.
Week Days—7.40, 9.20, 11.20, A. M.; 1:30, 3.30, 5.05, 6.15 P. M.
Sundays—8.00, 9.30, 11.00 A. M; 1.30, 3:30, 5.00, 6.15 P. M.

FROM SAN RAFAEL FOR SAN FRANCISCO.
Week Days—6.50, 7.55, 9.30, 11:40 A. M.; 1.40, 3.40, 5.05, 6:25 P. M.
Sundays—8.10, 9.40, 11:10 A. M.; 1.40, 3.40, 5.00, 6:25 P. M.

FROM POINT TIBURON FOR SAN FRANCISCO
Week Days—7.15, 8.20, 9.55 A. M.; 12.05, 2.05, 4 05, 5 30, 6.50 P. M.
Sundays—8.35, 10.05, 11:35 A. M.; 2.05, 4.05, 5.30, 6:50 P. M.

Leave San Francisco. WEEK DAYS.	SUNDAYS.	DESTINATION	Arrive San Francisco. SUNDAYS.	WEEK DAYS.
7.40 A M 9.20 A M 3.30 P M 5.00 P M	8.00 A M 5.00 P M	Petaluma and Santa Rosa	10.40 A M 7.25 P M	8.50 A M 10.30 A M 4.40 P M 7.25 P M
7.40 A M 3.30 P M	8.00 A M	Fulton, Windsor, Healdsburg, Litton Springs, Cloverdale, and way stations.	7.25 P M	10.20 A M 7.26 P M
7.40 A M	8.00 A M	Hopland and Ukiah.	7.25 P M	7.25 P M
7.40 A M 3.30 P M	8.00 A M	Guerneville	7.25 P M	7.25 P M 10.30 A M
7.40 A M 5.00 P M	8.00 A M 5.00 P M	Sonoma and Glen Ellen	10.40 A M 6.05 P M	8.50 A M 6.05 P M
7.40 A M 3.30 P M	8.00 A M 5.00 P M	Sebastopol	10.40 A M 7.25 P M	10.20 A M 7.25 P M

Stage connects at Santa Rosa for White Sulphur Springs, and Mark West Springs; at Geyserville for Skaggs Springs, and at Cloverdale for the Geysers; at Hopland for Highland Springs, Kelseyville, Soda Bay, Lakeport and Bartlett Springs, and at Ukiah for Vichy Springs, Saratoga Springs, Blue Lakes, Willits, Cahto, Calpella, Potter Valley, Sherwood Valley and Mendocino City.

EXCURSION TICKETS from Saturdays to Mondays, to Petaluma, $1.50; to Santa Rosa, $2.25; to Healdsburg, $3.40; to Litton Springs, $3.60; to Cloverdale, $4.50; to Hopland, $5.70; to Ukiah, $6.75; to Guerneville, $3.75; to Sonoma, $1.50; to Glen Ellen, $1.80.

EXCURSION TICKETS, good for Sundays only, to Petaluma, $1; to Santa Rosa, $1.50; to Healdsburg, $2.25; to Litton Springs, $2.40; to Cloverdale, $3; to Guerneville, $2.50, to Sonoma, $1; to Glen Ellen, $1.20.

H. C. WHITING, General Manager.

PETER J. McGLYNN, Gen. Pass. & Tkt. Agt.

Ticket Offices at Ferry, 222 Montgomery Street and 2 New Montgomery Street.

CHICAGO, MILWAUKEE AND ST. PAUL RAILWAY.

Steam Heated and Electric Lighted Vestibuled Trains between Chicago, St. Paul and Minneapolis.
Electric Lighted and Steam Heated Vestibuled Trains between Chicago, Council Bluffs and Omaha.
Finest Dining Cars in the world.
Free Reclining Chair Cars between Chicago and Omaha.
Fast Mail Line between Chicago, Milwaukee, St. Paul and Minneapolis.
Transcontinental Route between Chicago, Council Bluffs and Omaha, or St. Paul.
Great National Route between Chicago, Kansas City and St. Joseph, Mo.
5,700 miles of road in Illinois, Wisconsin, Minnesota, Iowa, Missouri, South and North Dakota.
Everything First-Class.
First-Class People patronize First-Class Lines.
Ticket Agents everywhere sell Tickets over the Chicago, Milwaukee and St. Paul Railway.

W. T. ALLEN,
Pacific Coast Passenger Agent
Office, No 138 Montgomery St., San Francisco, Cal.
Under Occidental Hotel

6 DONTS

DON'T own a racehorse.
DON'T be a breeder.
DON'T be a trainer.
DON'T be a jockey.
DON'T bet on the races.
DON'T go to a race track.

WITHOUT

HAVING IN YOUR POCKET ONE OF

Goodwin's

ANNUAL

OFFICIAL TURF GUIDES.

Price, in cloth........................$2.00
Price, in half morocco.................3.00
Price, in half calf....................4.00
If sent by mail.............10 cents extra

SUBSCRIBE TO IT FOR 1890.

It is published semi-monthly during the racing season; and is but $10 per year. Address

GOODWIN BROS.,
241 Broadway, New York City.

OUR IMPROVED. ALL SIZES AND WEIGHTS. G. W. BOHANON, ESTAB. 1869.

THE BOHANON **SULKY!** BEST MADE.
Perfect Riding Buggies. Breaking Carts.
Fine Repairing, Reasonable Prices

Bohanon Carriage Co., 161-163 Ogden Ave., CHICAGO.

Send for Catalogue.

RUB YOUR HORSES

In cases of SWELLING or STIFFNESS OF THE JOINTS, with

DARBYS FLUID.

If you value your Horses, Dogs and Cattle always keep it on hand.

IT HAS NO EQUAL

For Cuts, Scratches, Bruises, Bites, Sores, Etc.

It gives immediate relief, and prevents Poison, Gangrene and Proud Flesh.

J. H. ZEILIN & CO., - Philadelphia, Pa

SOLD BY ALL DRUGGISTS.

HORSE OWNERS

TRY GOMBAULT'S

CAUSTIC BALSAM.

A Safe, Speedy and Positive Cure for Curb, Splint, Sweeny, Capped Hock, Strained Tendons, Founder, Wind Puffs, all Skin Diseases or Parasites, Thrush, Diphtheria, Pinkeye, all Lameness from Spavin, Ringbone or other Bony Tumors. Removes all Bunches or Blemishes from Horses and Cattle.
Supersedes all Cautery or Firing.
Impossible to Produce any Scar or Blemish.
Every bottle sold is warranted to give satisfaction. Price $1.50 per bottle. Sold by druggists, or sent by express, charges paid, with full directions for its use. Send for descriptive circulars. Address
LAWRENCE, WILLIAMS & CO., Cleveland, O.

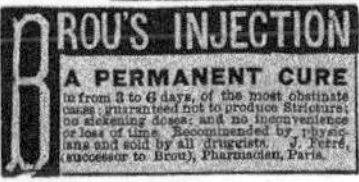

For any Kind of a

SORE THROAT

USE

McCLELLAN'S

DIPHTHERIA REMEDY

An Unfailing Cure.

FOR SALE BY ALL DRUGGISTS

R. LIDDLE & SON

538 Washington St., S. F.,

Wholesale and Retail Dealers in

Guns, Rifles and Pistols.

A Full Line of FISHING TACKLE and SPORTSMAN'S GOODS.

Orders by mail receive prompt attention.

SELBY STANDARD "STANDARD" THE BEST IS THE CHEAPEST SHOTGUN CARTRIDGES

By-Laws

—AND—

Rules and Regulations

—OF THE—

NATIONAL

Trotting Association

ALSO THE

AMERICAN

Trotting Association,

AND THE

PACIFIC COAST BLOOD-HORSE ASSOCIATION.

With Betting Rules.

For Sale at the Office of the

Breeder and Sportsman,

313 Bush St., S. F., Cal.

Price, 25c. each.
By Mail, Postage Paid, 30c. each.

VETERINARY.

Dr. Wm. H. Jones, M.R.C.V.S.

Veterinary Surgeon,

(OLYMPIC CLUB STABLES)

503 Sutter Street, San Francisco.

Telephone, No. 1404.

Consultations by letter, and cases of URGENT NECESSITY in the interior will receive prompt attention.

Dr. A. E. BUZARD,

VETERINARY SURGEON,

Member of the Royal College of Veterinary Surgeons, London, England. Graduated April 22d, 1870.

All Operations on the Horse Performed Skillfully.

Special attention given to the Diseases of Dogs. Calls to the country promptly attended to. Advice and prescriptions by mail $2. Office and Residence, No. 11 Seventh street, S. F. (opp. Odd Fellows Hall. Telephone No. 3 69.

W. H. WOODRUFF.

Veterinary Dentist,

AT FASHION STABLES,

221 Ellis Street, San Francisco

Improved Instruments, Humane Methods, First-Class Work.

H. E. CARPENTER,

Veterinary Surgeon,

Graduate of Ontario Veterinary College, Toronto Canada.

RESIDENCE AND VETERINARY INFIRMARY

331 Golden Gate Ave., San Francisco.

Telephone 3069.

☞ OPEN DAY AND NIGHT. ☜

No risk in throwing Horses. Veterinary Operating Table on the premises.

DR. C. MASOERO,

Veterinary Surgeon,

Successor to DR. A. DeTAVEL,

GRADUATE OF ROYAL VETERINARY COLLEGE, TURIN.

OFFICE AND INFIRMARY

No. 811 HOWARD STREET,

Between Fourth and Fifth. SAN FRANCISCO

Telephone, No. 457.

R. WATKINS,

Veterinary Dentist,

Office at C. S. Crittendens' Golden Gate Livery and Riding Academy, 24 to 28 Golden Gate Avenue.

Refers to Palo Alto Stock Farm; Wm. Corbett, San Mateo Stock Farm; B. C. Holly, Vallejo, and others. Examination Free.

E. J. O'ROUKE.

I have the honor to announce to my old patrons and the general public that I may be found at my old stand, where, as heretofore, the

Shoeing of Horses,

whether for the Track, Drive, or for general work, will receive my personal attention.

Telephone 2011.

E. J. O'ROUKE,
209 Ellis Street

ST. JULIEN

Horse Shoeing SHOP,

126 Geary Street, S. F.

MARTIN O'DEA, - - PROPRIETOR.

California Horse Shoe Co's

I have used in my business the Steel and Iron Shoes made by the above Company, and take great pleasure in saying they are the best I have ever used in twenty-two years' practice. I have never seen anything like the STEEL SHOE made by this Company. I can fully recommend them to every practical Horseshoer in the country. Yours respectfully,

No. 8 Everett Street. JOHN GRACE.

Old Hermitage Whiskies

"STEINER'S,"

No. 311 BUSH STREET,

San Francisco.

Under Breeder and Sportsman Office.

Everything for

Trotter or Runner,

At J. A. McKERRON'S,

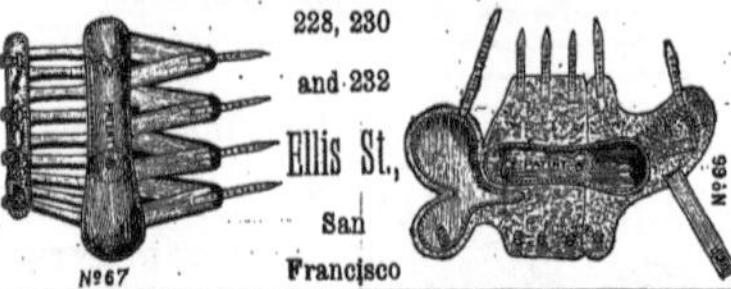

No 67

228, 230 and 232 Ellis St., San Francisco

No 96

J. O'KANE, Horse Boots, Clothing and Furnishings, For Track, Driving Training and Stable. Every requisite for Horsemen. Harness, Medicines, Etc.

The PARKER Hammerless Shot Gun.

At the Annual Tournament of 1889, held at Cannes, France, the grand prize, consisting of 2000 Francs and a Valuable Cup, was won by The Parker Hammerless.

The first Parker Hammerless Gun made won the championship of America at Decatur Illinois.

SEND FOR ILLUSTRATED CIRCULAR.

PARKER BROS., Makers,

New York Salesroom, 97 Chambers St. Meriden Conn.

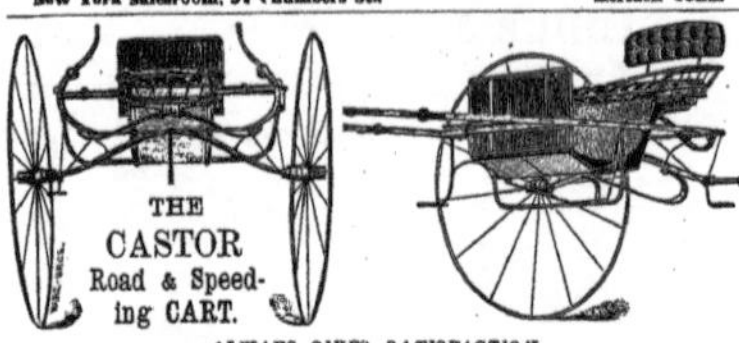

THE CASTOR Road & Speeding CART.

ALWAYS GIVES SATISFACTION.

Combining perfect riding qualities, proportions and balance, with genteel appearance.

No vehicle exhibits a horse to better advantage, and no Cart approaches them for speeding or training purposes.

A stylish vehicle for exercising or pleasure driving, at one-fourth the cost of a carriage. Have none of the horse jockey or objectionable features of other Road Carts.

They are the Leading Cart wherever introduced, and are in use by the most prominent breeders and pleasure drivers everywhere.

Elegant Shifting Top Carts.

Perfectly Balanced Stylish Pole Carts.

For Illustrated Catalogue, with Prices, address,

LEWIS F. CASTOR,
Frankford, Philadelphia, Pa.

JOHN SPLAN, General Agent.

keeps horses healthy, promotes digestion, fattens horses, loosens the hide, assists the appetite, prevents leg swelling, strengthens the kidneys, regulates the bowels and destroys worms. $2.50 per 100 lbs. Ask your dealer for it or send to

MANHATTAN FOOD CO., 206 Clay St., S. F.

The Brunswick Balke Collender Co.

MANUFACTURERS OF

Standard Billiard and Pool Tables, Saloon and Bank Fixtures,
653--655 Market Street, San Francisco, Cal.

ORVIS TROUT FLIES.

Superb in Material, Make and Killing Quality.

E. T. ALLEN,

SOLE AGENT FOR PACIFIC COAST.

Importer of Fine Fishing Tackle & Sporting Goods

416 Market Street, - - San Francisco, Cal.

Brothers of the Angle,

Our NEW EIGHT-STRIP SPLIT BAMBOO is the "King" of all fishing-rods. Chubb's New Catalogue for 1890 is now ready. In addition to a complete list of anglers' supplies, it contains articles from the pens of Dr. James A. Henshall, Petronella, W. H. Murray, Geo. P. Goff, Norman, Brother Gardner, and others.

These papers are by the best writers on angling subjects, and are very interesting.

Send 25 cents, and receive Catalogue, postpaid. This amount will be deducted from first order (if accompanied with COUPON in book) for one dollar's worth or more of our goods.

Address

THOS. H. CHUBB,
Fishing-Rod Manufacturer,
POST MILLS, VT.

Please mention BREEDER AND SPORTSMAN.

SHAW CARTS and SULKIES

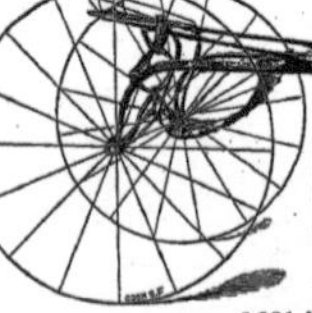

For light road or track use, manufactured from the best selected material. Combines lightness with elegance and ease to riders. Weights 70 to 100 lbs. Used by the best horsemen on this coast. Inspection invited.

ONE CAFFREY SULKY FOR SALE AT A BARGAIN.

CARRIAGES & Light VEHICLES

Manufactured to Order and Kept on Hand.

W. E. SHAW,
1621 MARKET STREET, SAN FRANCISCO, CAL.

REPAIRING DONE—ALL WORK WARRANTED.

Studebaker Bros. Manufact'g Co.

Sole Agents for

FRAZIER

(OR CHICAGO)

Carts

AND

Sulkies,

201--203 Market Street,

SAN FRANCISCO, CAL.

BOYCE TABLETS.

Leg and Body Wash.

THE BOYCE TABLETS are packed in a nicely decorated metal box with hinged lid—one hundred tablets in each box; directions for use plainly engraved upon the box; therefore, the convenience of the package—no liability to leakage and breakage—economy and ready solubility, together with the absolute certainty of their action, will at once commend the use of BOYCE'S TABLETS to the intelligent horsemen of the country. TABLETS sufficient to make one hundred pints of leg and body wash are conveniently carried in an inside coat pocket or in the hip-pocket of the trousers.

The BOYCE WASH can be applied ALL OVER THE BODY WITHOUT FEAR OF BLISTERING NOR DOES IT AFFECT THE KIDNEYS.

The BOYCE WASH will cure CRACKED HEELS, PUFFS, STOCKINGS, SCRATCHES, INFLAMED TENDONS and FEVERED LEGS.

Price per Box of One Hundred Tablets, $2, sent postpaid to any part of the United States; six boxes for $10. A sample of BOYCE'S TABLETS will be mailed to any address on application.

These TABLETS are warranted to keep in any climate. Address

BOYCE TABLET COMPANY,
600 Wabash Avenue, - - - Terre Haute, Indiana.

J. A. McKERRON, Pacific Coast Ag't,
228-230-232 Ellis Street, San Francisco, Cal.

TWENTY-FOUR PAGES.

Vol. XVI. No. 21.
No. 313 BUSH STREET.

SAN FRANCISCO, SATURDAY, MAY 24, 1890.

SUBSCRIPTION
FIVE DOLLARS A YEAR.

RAMBLING NOTES.

A Visit to Fresno—Some of the Horses in Training—The Bernhard Stock Farm—Oregon Boy 5515—Princess Alice—The Shippee Trotters.

I hardly know where to begin as I have called at so many tracks and stock farms within the past ten days that I am afraid my notes have got terribly jumbled; however, I will do the best I can, so your readers may know what is being done on the lines over which I have traveled,

At Fresno, although I arrived there at an early hour in the morning, I found driver Hahn, who was handling the ribbons over a three-year-old Bay Rose filly, who showed a nice turn of speed, she being accompanied on her journey by Doc Williams, who was handling a green horse, whose name I did not learn, but from Doc's talk I fancy he thinks he has a good one.

At 8 o'clock the first of Mr. Straube's string of babies appeared; one proved to be the ladylike and racy two-year-old filly Elise by Clovis, dam Ida Davis by Belnor. As you already know, Mr. Straube has secured the services, as trainer and driver, of Matt Dwyer, who was so long at Palo Alto, and whose experience there has well fitted him for the valuable charges which are now under his care. Elise showed herself in her preliminary work to be a smooth and very even gaited trotter, and bore out the good opinion which I formed of her many months ago, when I saw her for the first time; she showed a very nice eighth of a mile in 19½ seconds, which for this early season and her youthfulness, was considered by all who saw her perform, a capital piece of work.

Poplar Girl was also given a few sharp brushing eighths, one of which was timed in 23 seconds, while other eighths varied from 24 to 25½ seconds.

Valley Girl Maid did not accomplish any of her eighths in better than 24 seconds, but I am told that she has shown much better time.

Mr. Dwyer has quite a number of Mr. Staube's colts at the track, they include the get of Clovis, Apex, Pasha and Anteeo; Mr. Dwyer is fast bringing them to that point necessary for a race, and when the bell rings at any of the points where they are entered the public may rest assured that the Poplar Grove Stock Farm entries will be ready for a contest.

On returning to the hotel we had luncheon, and were then driven to the farm of Mr. Geo. Bernhard, where we were shown the magnificent stallion Oregon Boy 5515. Oregon Boy was bred by Mr. A. C. Goodrich, of Jordan Valley, Ore; he is seventeen hands high and weighs almost 1,400 pounds; he is a beautiful bay with black points, heavy mane and tail, excellent feet and legs, and a great deal of substance; he has a lofty, light carriage and a pure gait, with rather high knee and hock action. Although he has never been regularly worked, Oregon Boy can show quarters in forty seconds: he is by Alcona 730 (son of Almont 33), dam Livonia by Almont 33; 2d dam by Mambrino Champion; 3d dam by Wake-Up Jake, son of Downing's Bay Messenger. Alcona, sire of Oregon Boy, has never had the opportunities that he deserves, for notwithstanding the limited number of good mares which have been sent to him, he shows speed in all of his get, and it will not be surprising if several of his sons and daughters enter the charmed circle this year. The artist of the BREEDER AND SPORTSMAN who accompanied the party, secured some excellent pictures of this well-bred horse, and it is to be presumed that your readers will have the chance to see for themselves before long what he looks like.

The stock farm of Mr. Bernhard is under the management of Mr. Henry McHugh, a careful and painstaking trainer and driver who is constantly looking after the needs of the many well-bred horses which are on the farm. Mac is working quite a number of the mares and colts, and is also giving the big horse a few miles of exercise every day, breaking the monotony at times by making him show some good eighths and quarters. After the season's service is over, Mr. Bernhard intends to try Oregon Boy at his best, and obtain a record for him if possible. Among the get of Oregon Boy which we noticed at the farm, was a strapping big colt out of a Belmont mare. This lordly little fellow is a yearling, and already shows considerable speed; he is entered in the Hughs' Hotel Stakes for yearlings, to be trotted at Fresno Fair this Fall, and should give a good account of himself.

A black filly also by Oregon Boy was next shown, and under inspection proved a very pleasing subject for the critical eye; she looks a trotter all over, and although low in flesh, after the severe winter, will doubtless prove herself a good one when called upon in the Fall.

Among the brood mares we noticed Nell by Black Ralph, bred by G. Valensin. Nell's dam is Humming Bird, a fast pacing mare by Tecumseh; at her side is a fine colt by the premier stallion of the farm.

Jessie is by Western Boy, a son of Chieftain 721, dam Nell by Black Ralph as above. She is accountable for a topping bay colt also by Oregon Boy.

Gipsey is a bright chestnut from the old Belmont stock and she also has a bay colt by Oregon Boy.

Ravielle by Woodburn, dam Minnie Weaver by Langford is stinted to the same horse.

Mag Donahoo, record 2:44 has an exquisitely formed and an exceptionally good colt by the son of Alcona.

Cherry Ripe is a three-year-old bay filly by a son of Geo. M. Patchen Jr., dam Mag Donahoo.

Mattie Vickers by Pasha, dam by Hock Hocking has a handsome bay filly foal at her side by Apex.

Matilda is also by Pasha 2:36 out of a mare by Hock Hocking; 2nd dam by Redmond's Sorrel.

Capulet is by Sea Breeze, a son of Piedmont 2:17¼, dam Nell spoken of before; 2nd dam Humming Bird. Capulet is stinted to Oregon Boy.

In an adjoining pasture were a large number of well bred mares, the property of many owners, who are here on a visit to the lord of the harem.

Adjoining Mr. Bernhard's ranch is the beautifully improved place of Mr. M. F. Tarpey, so well and favorably known to all horsemen throughout California. He has 160 acres of five year-old vines loaded down with luscious grapes; an immense fig avenue runs through the entire place from end to end, while walnut trees encircle the neat and commodious homestead and barns; 640 acres of grain and 60 of alfalfa complete this very valuable property. Mr. Tarpey intends shortly to place the 640 acres in alfalfa and in the near future will move his entire stud of horses to this ranch.

From the lower end of the San Joaquin Valley I travelled away to the north and finally brought up at the Stockton track, our main object being to take a look at the black filly so highly spoken off last year before the circuit opened, and from whom was expected a very low mark during the season, however, she disappointed both owner and friends, but having heard that Princess Alice had again shown high speed, we determined to take a look at her in her work; she is still under the care and guidance of Geo. Kusier who handled her last year; as usual George is very sanguine of being able to give his black pet a very low record during 1890, but whether he will be able to do it or not, time alone will tell. I must confess that last year I very strongly wished that Hickok, Goldsmith or Marvin had this mare in charge, for I am more than satisfied that she would have made a low mark for herself. In the early part of last season it was no trouble for her to go quarters in 32½ seconds, and it was very rarely that she could not go to the half in 1:06. However, George claims that he can beat all former records with her, and does not hesitate to say that if she is fit to go to the wire, Johnson's record will not be too low for the mare to aim at.

In an adjoining stall is Crown Prince, another of Georgie's day dreams. He is a chestnut colt with considerable white markings by Dexter Prince' dam Clara by Chieftain 721.

On asking Kueier for the pedigee of Princess Alice he gave it as follows: by Dexter Prince, dam Mollie by General McClellan; 2nd dam Fanny by McCracken's David Hill, Jr.

There is also in the stable a two-year-old, called Eda by Harry Gear, a son of Echo.

Revive is a two-year-old stallion by Reliance, dam Flora by George M. Patchen, Jr. 2nd dam Lulu by Speculation.

I am rather inclined to the belief that if Princess Alice is well handled this year that she should cause all of the pacers considerable trouble, she is looking more robust and in better condition than when last seen, and I think if anything, a little faster. I timed her from wire to wire at Sacramento last season after nineteen scores in 2:17, and I fancy she can beat that a trifle this year.

Mr. Shippee's stable is under the charge of Harry Whiting and all of the horses look first-rate and show up well for this season of the year. He has in the string Kilrain, a son of Hawthorne, dam by Whipple's Hambletonian. Moses S. who is well known on the tracks of California is looking superb and fit to go with the best of them; if Mr. Shippee does not give this horse a mark far below 2:20 on the circuit this year it will be because accident prevents it.

Harry also has Petro, a bay gelding by Hawthorne, dam Daisy by Chieftain. Chief Thorne is by the same sire and out of the same dam as Petro.

Princewood is by Dexter Prince, dam by Nutwood 600.

Captain Thorne is by Hawthorne, dam an inbred Lambert mare.

Beauty, Lady Pet and one or two others whose names we did not learn are also in the string, Harry has his hands full in looking after this very promising lot,

The journey would not have been complete if we had failed to pay a visit to the establishment of Mr. Morse at Lodi where we were shown that exceedingly good stallion, Dexter Prince; the old horse, if he may be so called, is now at his very best; notwithstanding the heavy strain on his producing powers he seems as fresh as a lark and shows his condition in the brightness of his eye and the glossy health look on his coat; seldom a week passes but what some encourageing report comes from some of Dexter Princess' colts, and there is no reason to doubt that in the near future he will have a long list enumerated among the 2:30 performers.

We were also shown Hero, a dark brown son of Director, dam by Santa Claus; 2nd dam by Bull Pup, 3rd dam by California Patchen; this horse will take his place as second fiddle to Dexter Prince next season and will undoubtedly be well patronized.

We were also shown a fine lot of brood mares but as time was limited we could not get a list of them, however, suffice it to say that Mr. Morse is on the high road to success and we fully expect to get encouraging news from Lodi before long.

The track at this place has been put in good shape and already several contests have taken place, giving much enjoyment to those who live in the neighborhood. The soil is of such a character that I am inclined to the belief that for winter purposes it cannot be excelled in the State, in fact is almost a counterpart of Mr. Salisbury's track at Pleasanton, and we all know what a grand place to exercise that is, when water prevents work at other places.

As I have already taken so much of your valuable space, will give you further particulars of my journey in another letter.

Yours, SAN FRANCISCO.

A Letter from Terre Haute.

EDITOR BREEDER AND SPORTSMAN:—I feel assured that a few lines from this place will be of interest to you and your readers, especially in view of the fact that all the principal trotting horses in this great western country are now centered at Terre Haute.

Much care has been exercised in preparing the track here for preliminary work, and Mr. Jeffries, the able superintendent has had a six-inch coating of yellow clay put over the course, and it now looks very much as did the Bay District Track during the fall of last year; I am certain that it will be very fast, the only fear being that it may get too hard, however, I am satisfied that every care will be taken to prevent that.

As so many trainers and drivers have made application for stall room, it was deemed necessary to increase the number of stalls and this has been done by building two immense barns 150 feet by 50 feet, the buildings being two and a half stories high. These immense structures have just been completed and there are twelve box stalls 12 X 14 on each side with a space between of about twenty feet. All the wood work inside the barns is of Indiana Poplar, with the exception of the gratings in front of the stalls, which are of oak; the ventilation is of the best and the space from the floor to the comb of the roof is fully fifty feet; each stall has a window in it and a large door leading into the open, and in case of fire the latter would prove a very desirable adjunct.

I am pleased to state that the Hickok car arrived all right and all of the horses were in exceedingly good condition, Roy Wilkes looking particularly well, there was not a scratch or a cough among the entire number: it is too bad that the same cannot be said of the Palo Alto string, as several of the horses have colds and a number of them are skinned, one in particular, Arol 2:24 evidently had a genuine attack of horse hysterics; she fell down in the car and was badly bruised and barked, however, I do not think the injury is serious and I fully expect to see her at work before long. Mr. Marvin is quite worn out with the trip, having to be up day and night looking after his charges, but a little rest here will soon set him all right.

Rain has interfered with our working the horses this month, as is always the case in May and we could hardly expect good weather at this season.

The Palo Alto string occupies one entire side of one of the barns while the Hickok string with the necessary feed stalls occupies the other side of the same barn; the other large building is occupied in its entirety by Budd Doble who has an overflow, in addition to the twenty-four large stalls which he uses. Budd is a big favorite with gentlemen who own trotting horses, and that he is a great trainer and pilot can not be gainsaid. However, he could not be otherwise, as he has a good pedigree and is well bred.

I almost wish that the managers of your California race tracks could see the way things are managed here; every thing is in tip top shape and every convenience for horses and horsemen are at hand. I take it that the guiding spirit here is Mr. Ijams, one of the owners of the great Axtell, as he is constantly on the lookout to see that the trainers and drivers are satisfied. There are here now probably three hundred and fifty horses, all of whom are being worked when the track will permit of it and more are coming in every day. Tink Hill is here with Hendryx 2:18½, Tariff 2:21½ and eight or ten more good ones. Tariff is a big black gelding, 16½ hands, and built in proportion, and if he does not have trouble or accident is liable to get a mark of about 2:17; when I say trouble, I mean muscular rheumatism, as the gelding was sorely tried last year with that complaint. His full brother, Free Trade, is learning to trot very fast, and will likely add to the reputation of his sire Young Wilkes by entering the list this year. There is no use talking this Wilkes blood is great stuff and makes horses trot from almost any cross.

The well known Billy Maloney may be seen out almost daily with Jersey Boy and Kitty Grey, and their owner Al Post, of Chicago, aspires to overthrow the great double team pacing record of Silvertail and Daisy D. with this pair of fast ones. "Happy Joe" Rhea when he drove the team to the record of 2:18½ made a mark for the boys that will require a deal of speed to lower. However, if Jersey Boy and Kitty Grey can show any sort of pace, Billy Maloney is surely the man to lower the record. In addition to the two mentioned Maloney has several other good ones that are going very glibly, and it will not surprise me to see some of their names at the top of the summaries during the season's work.

John Dickerson, the "champion kid driver and trainer," is here with a legion; Johnnie has had to refuse business, and from the immense string that he has at present under him, will not have to chew snow-balls next winter. Among the good ones, he has Faustino, 2:35, the champion stallion yearling, of which all Californians naturally feel proud. Geo. Starr brought this trotting phenomenon from Fresno to this place, and turned him over to the care of Dickerson, who will do some driving for Frank Waters of the Genoa Junction Stock Farm this year.

I understand that Mr. Valensin wants to have this magnificent colt get a mark of 2:20 in his two-year-old form, but Dickerson informs me that he has no such orders from Mr. Waters, and that he will feel satisfied if the youngster touches 2:25; however, I am inclined to think from the way the colt looks at present, that Regal Wilkes may possibly have his two-year-old stallion record lowered. This would not surprise me, for Mr. Waters is one of the luckiest men alive; in fact, he is about the only one I know of who could land a whale with a trout line.

I feel confident that Roy Wilkes will beat 2:10 this year before the "pumpkins turn yaller;" if the low mark is made for him, he shall never pace again, as I am satisfied that he will make as good a trotter as he is a pacer; he will only be allowed to serve ten mares outside of our own, as he will begin campaign work about August 1st. I have about made up my mind that California is the place to winter horses, and you may rest assured that, barring accidents, I shall be on the Pacific Slope before the snow falls here. More anon.

Yours respectfully, L. A. DAVIES.

Santa Rosa.

On Saturday last a visit was paid to what is now known as the Santa Rosa Stock Farm, formerly the Santa Rosa race track. Since its purchase by the Pierce Bros. many improvements have been put under way and the place already shows a decided improvement since the change of ownership. Mr. Thos. Bonner is general manager and superintendent of the farm; he has his hands full in looking after not only the large number of mares which have been bred to Bay Rose, but also in seeing that the track is kept in perfect order for the fifty or more horses now in training there. We had but little better than an hour to spend at the track, and consequently there was not the attention given to detail that should have been, but we are pleased to note that many of the horses there are in the best of condition and are all improving in speed.

Under the guidance of Mr. Murphy, it took but a short time to drive from the livery stable of Messrs. McFadyen & Underhill to the track, where we were heartily received by Mr. De Turk, Mart Rollins, William McGraw, W. B. Sanborn, Geo. Kennedy and many others who have horses there. After a look was taken at a few of the best of them, Mr. Bonner outlined his plans for the future, and if carried out in their entirety, it will make the Santa Rosa Stock Farm a favorite winter resort for those who have first class race horses. There is already being prepared and well under way a covered in winter track, which will be over one-eighth of a mile in length, made on the conventional shape with thrown up turns and everything requisite for the proper speeding of horses during the winter months. The track will be finished in the very best style, and already an exceedingly fine quality of loam is being brought in wherewith to finish the track under the sheds. The two stretches will be much longer than the turns as the location of the awnings prevent as wide curves as Mr. Bonner would have liked, still when finished his winter track will far surpass anything at present in the State.

A look was taken at the pavilion, and Mr. Bonner informed us that the entire ground floor will be devoted to the use of large box stalls, of which there will be eighteen in all; the upper floor, or promenade, as it was formerly called, will be used for the storing of hay and grain.

While all these improvements have been going on, the outside track has not been forgotten, as men are constantly at work keeping it in the most perfect condition.

Only a few of the horses were speeded while we were present, the better known ones being the Anteeo filly, Maud Dee; this is a very promising three-year-old owned by Mr. Murphy.

Ned Lock was also given a fast quarter, and he proved himself competent to travel with any of the 2:27 class where ever he may meet them.

Silas Skinner, the black colt owned by Mr. DeTurk, was brought out for inspection, and from what we were told, should judge he might be able to get a piece of the purses in all the 2:30 races in which he may start.

Mr. McGraw also brought out and jogged The Dane by Stamboul. This is a colt formerly called Coronado and owned by the Coombs Bros. of Napa. He has filled out wonderfully since last year and shows himself a trotter of no mean order.

The Pierce Bros. have a large number of well bred mares, many of whom are being stinted to Bay Rose. George Kennedy is looking after one or two thoroughbreds and he only requires a chance to be able to ship a two-year-old back East to take part in the Coney Island Futurity Stake. This is a fine youngster by Three Cheers and George feels pretty confident that he would have a slice of the big plum if he could get the filly across the mountains in as good condition as she is at present.

Many of the gentlemen whom we met at the Santa Rosa track favored the idea of the Trotting Horse Breeders' Meeting being held at that point, and several of them thought that a goodly sum of money might be contributed in the town toward that object if the matter were taken in hand by a good committee.

As train time was approaching we had to leave, not, however, without a strong and abiding faith that when the circuit opens many of the horses now in training at the Santa Rosa Track will give a good account of themselves.

From Kelseyville.

EDITOR BREEDER AND SPORTSMAN:—While rambling through this section of the State a few days ago, I paid a visit to the race track to take a look at the horses in training. The weather has been delightful and as there is no better climate in California in which to train, the horses are all looking in splendid condition. When the track at Lakeport is fit for work, which will be within a few days, those who are here will in all probability be taken over there.

Our old friend Jas. Corcoran is located here and has five which he thinks very highly of; I rather fancy that the best of the lot is Advocate 6544 by Attorney 1005, dam Minta by Bashaw 50, grandam the Dr. McAllister mare by Sampson, son of Sampson Canadian. This horse is now five years old and is the property of Mr. A. B. Rodman, of Lakeport. From the way in which Atto Rex went down the line last season, it should be presumed that this half brother of his will also make a good fair trotter, and it would not surprise me if Corcoran gets a low record for him. Advocate is a remarkably fine looking horse and is not unlike Atto Rex in conformation. He will be given every chance to show his ability and will be sent for a record before the season ends. Corcoran also has two colts, the property of Mr. L. H. Boggs, one is a yearling by Advocate, dam Bent B.; this is a fine rangy looking youngster and presents far more the appearance of a thoroughbred than he does a trotter; the other one is a two-year-old by Oakland Boy from the same dam as the yearling. She is a very handsome bay, and from the peculiar manner in which she is built is apt to give the visitor an opinion of what Sunol looks like, for they are built on almost the same lines. Jim also has a good looking three-year-old brown mare by Anteeo 2:16½, dam by Abbottsford 2:19½. This is a big looking filly and she should most assuredly be heard from in the races this year, as I understand Mr. Boggs will have her entered at several places on the circuit.

The old Petaluma driver also has a very fast pacer which he was exercising while we were present, and a right merry clip was shown us; Jim was very reticent about what the pacer could do, but speed enough was shown us to warrant the belief that he could get a slice of the money, if entered in the 2:20 purse of the Breeders' Association.

H. Tracy is here with the stallion Alwood and two other colts, all of which are showing the benefit of the consistent work which they are receiving.

Charles Piener has four of Mr. Starr's horses here, one of which is a colt by Anteeo out of Old Countess, the dam of Dawn. This one I rather liked, and if well seasoned, there should be another of Countess' colts to enter the 2:30 list.

Before leaving this section, I took a drive over to the farm of Mr. J. W. Boggs, and had the pleasure of viewing several very handsome colts. Mr. Boggs has a very fine place, with any quantity of feed, and something that I always particularly like—plenty of shade. The young stallion Daniel Deronda by Black Ralph, dam Bessie B. by Milton Medium; 2d dam Mollie Higby by Billy Cheatham, is a rare good looker; he has a fine head and neck, well set on his shoulders, a magnificent back and loin, with great driving power. Mr. Boggs naturally feels very proud in the possession of this handsome colt, and within a few weeks will turn him over to some capable driver for the purpose of getting a record for the colt if possible. He also has quite a taking two-year-old by Oakland Boy, dam Bessie B., which is on a par, as far as appearances are concerned, with the balance of the trotters in this neighborhood. He also has a yearling by Advocate out of the same mare, that is as fine a looking colt as one could find anywhere.

From here I shall go to Lakeport, and let you know what alterations and additions are being made to the track at that place.

Yours, TRAVELER.

Fresno Entries.

Secretary Baldwin has forwarded the following list of entries, for the purses which closed on May 15th.

2:30 class, pacing, guarantee purse $1,000—Owen Bros. of Fresno, B. C. Holly of Vallejo, George Hinds of Wilmington, James Linden of Sacramento, E. B. Gifford of San Diego, John Patterson of Linden, H. H. Helman of Visalia, S. C. Tryon of Sacramento, Napa Stock Farm, John Garrity, Griffin & Moran of San Francisco, San Mateo Stock Farm of San Mateo, Agnew Stock Farm of Hillsdale, Howard Bros., Hanford, Cal.

2:20 class, trotting, guarantee purse, $1,200—S. N. Straube of Fresno, B. C. Holly of Vallejo, H. H. Helman of Visalia, E. B. Gifford of San Diego, Palo Alto Stock Farm of Menlo Park, James Dustin of San Francisco, Charles Durfee of Los Angeles, San Mateo Stock Farm of San Mateo, Agnew Stock Farm of Hillsdale.

2:24 class, trotting, guarantee purse, $1,000—B. C. Holly of Vallejo, James Dustin of San Francisco, P. W. Cooper of Fortuna, K. D. Wise, M. D., of Los Angeles, Napa Stock Farm of San Francisco, H. H. Helman of Visalia, Palo Alto Stock Farm of Menlo Park, E. B. Gifford of San Diego, Griffin & Moran of San Francisco, San Mateo Stock Farm of San Mateo, Thomas L. Burke of San Diego, S. N. Straube of Fresno, Charles Durfee of Los Angeles.

President Stake, 1⅛ miles dash, guarantee purse $1,000—For all ages. Maltese Villa stables of Merced b g Mozart, Owen Brothers of Fresno, blk. s Captain Al; Owen Brothers of Fresno, b m Daisy D; Charles Kerr of Bakersfield, s s Apache; F. Bustillos of Fresno, s s Bronco; W. L Appleby of Santa Clara, c m Odette, W. L. Appleby of Santa Clara, b m Raindrop.

Raisin Handicap, 1½ miles dash, guarantee purse $1,000—C. Kerr of Bakersfield, s s Apache; Owen Brothers of Fresno, b m Daisy D.; Owen Brothers of Fresno blk. s Captain Al; Maltese Villa stables of Merced, b g Mozart; F. Bustillos of Fresno, s s Bronco; W. L. Appleby of San Clara, c m Odette; W. L. Appleby of Santa Clara, b m Raindrop; N. Covorrubias of Los Angeles, c c Gold Dust; Ed Ryan of Los Angeles, c c Four Aces.

Marcus Daly's Ranches.

The famous ranch of Mr. Marcus Daly is in the Bitter Root Valley about forty-five miles south of Missoula. The Home ranch lies on the east side of the river, but does not touch it, and contains about three hundred acres, says the Montana Farming and Stock Journal. There is a good mansion upon it fitted for the summer residence of his family, houses for his workmen and stables for his horses, and reservoirs for supplying the horses and stables with water. It seemed to us that the buildings, with the exception of the mansion, were not first class, nor well arranged, but they were better than the houses of farmers in the States. The whole is well fenced, and good gates were found wherever needed, but the arrangements of the fields might have been better.

There is a fine track on the ranch three-quarters of a mile round for training the horses, but owing to the rains, was not in a condition to be used the day we visited the ranch.

The horses Mr. Daly has purchased are of course the chief attraction to visitors, and too much cannot be said in praise of them or of the manner in which they are kept. The thoroughbreds and trotters are kept separate, and a trainer is in charge of each. There are but thirteen thoroughbreds, each two years old, and all, if we remember rightly, from Mr. J. B. Haggin's stables in California. They are:

Brown Fox, b c, by Ban Fox, dam Illusion.
Josephine, b f, by Joe Daniels, dam Nonage.
Dora, b f, by the celebrated Australian Darebin, dam Kate Darling.
Virgin, b f, by Milner, dam Virgie.
Bandana, b f, by Darebin, dam Bessie Peyton.
Governor, b c, by John Happy, dam Susan.
Palfina, b f, by Hyder Ali, sire of Spokane, dam Pandora.
Yoland, ch f, by Joe Daniels, dam Unit.
Walnut, b f, by Sir Modred, dam Wonder.
Edorsada, b f, by Darebin, dam Sozodont.
Bay filly by The Illused, dam Flower Girl.
Chestnut filly by Warwick, dam Eliza.
Chestnut filly by Hyder Ali, dam Assyria.

The weather was bad and the horses were not put upon the track, but we are sure all will give a good account of themselves. If they show up well they will probably be sent to Chicago within a few weeks. They are under charge of Mr. Joseph Nelson, whom we judge to be a competent, careful man, who is not at all given to boasting—about his horses or himself.

The standard or trotting stock are more numerous, and occupy two large stables and several smaller ones. They are under the charge of Mr. S. G. Larimore, a life-long horseman. The appearance of the horses shows the care he gives them. The horses are all kindly treated and they respond to their treatment so well that there is not a vicious one among them. They can be easily handled and touched on any part of their bodies without exhibiting the least displeasure. They are kept in box stalls, where it is impossible for them to injure themselves. All the appliances and dressings known to horsemen are furnished. In this particular, as in every other, the stables are superbly equipped. The following is the record and pedigree or breeding of the trotters:

Lord Lyon, 2:18, b s 5 years old, by General Benton, dam May Day; bred at Palo Alto.

Mascot, b s by Stamboul 2:12½, dam Minnehaha; bred at Rosemeade stock farm.

Prodigal, b s by Pancoast, dam Beatrice; bred at Glenview stock farm, Kentucky.

St. Patrick, 2:19½, b s, by Volunteer, dam Young Seline; bred by Guy Miller, Chester, New York.

Belle Evans, br m, by Echo, dam daughter of Lodi.

Belle F., 2:15½, b m, by Masterlode, dam Belle Hastings.

Brown Silk, b f, by Baron Wilkes, dam Nannie Etticoat.

Easel, b m, by Commodore Belmont, dam daughter of Dictator.

Deputy, 2:41½, b s, by Echo, dam Maria Rose.

Dolly Dimple, 2:40, b m, by New York, dam Kate, by Jim Monroe.

Euclid, ch m, by Commodore Belmont, dam daughter of Cannon's Dillard.

Fannie Witherspoon, 2:16½, ch m, by Almont, dam Lizzie Witherspoon.

Favonia, 2:15, b m by Wedgewood, dam Fadette; bred at Woodburn Stock Farm, Kentucky.

Fannie Bicknell, b m by Hambletoninn, 725, dam daughter of Imported Hercules; bred by A. Hayward, San Mateo, Cal.

Gertie Arnold, b m by Arnold, dam daughter of Almont; bred by Mr. Offut, Scott County, Ky.

Governess, b m by Echo, dam Jones' mare; bred at Rancho del Paso, California.

Hattie D, 2:26½ by Electioneer, dam Maple by Nutwood; bred by Palo Alto Stock Farm, California.

Lightning Bug, b m by General Washington, dam May Bug; bred by Fashion Stud Farm, Trenton, N. J.

Montana Maid, b m by Algona, dam Flora; bred by Rancho del Paso, California.

Maude D, b m by Petoskey, dam Maude.

Maudine, dark b m by Jay Gould, dam Lady Maud; bred by Fashion Stud Farm.

Queen Wilkes, b m by William L., dam Illwind; bred by Wm. L. Simmons, Lexington, Ky.

Sallie Wilkes, b m by Clay Wilkes, dam Novelty.

The Baroness, b f by Baron Wilkes, dam Effie; bred by Col. R. G. Stoner, Paris, Ky.

Thoughtless, b m by Le Grand, dam daughter of Electioneer.

Vixen, b m, by New York, dam Mischief; bred by H. P. Wade, Jefferson, Ohio.

Vesolia, b m, 2:29½ at two years old, by Stamboul, dam Inez; bred at Rosemeade Stock Farm.

Virginia Wilkes, b m, by Denver Wilkes, dam Lady Cassell.

Clara D. b f, by Woodnut, dam Clara Whippleton; bred by E. Wilson, San Francisco, Cal.

Guelda, ch f, by Guy Wilkes, dam Fanny Bicknell.

Griselda, blk f, by Woodnut, dam daughter of Henry Clay.

Helen T, b f, by Electioneer, dam Manette; bred at Palo Alto Stock Farm.

Mountain Lass, ch f, by Woodnut, dam Irish Lass; bred by B. C. Holly, Vallejo, Cal.

Nan, b f, by Princeps, dam Vixen.

Stambella, b f, by Stamboul, dam Fanny Belmont; bred at Rosemeade Stock Farm.

Vera, b f, by Stamboul, dam Zinfandel; bred at Rosemeade Stock Farm.

Yolo Maid, 2:12½, by Alexander Button, dam Mollie by St. Clair.

Frisco, b s, 2:52 at two years old, by Echo, dam by Almont.

St. Patrick and Yolo Maid are pacers.

Besides these there were ten yearlings, all finely bred, the best being a black filly by Director, dam Belle Evans by Echo.

Mr. Daly also has a fine string of thoroughbreds in New York which are expected to give fame to his stable the coming season.

Mr. Daly expects to make this a breeding farm where great horses may be bred, and he will not be satisfied with less results than have been achieved by the breeding farms of California.

This year he is breeding to Lord Byron: Lightning Bug, Easel, Fannie Witherspoon, Lulu B., Vesolia, Hattie D., Lady Byron, Favonia, and Queen Wilkes.

To Prodigal: Fanny Bicknell, The Baroness, Brown Silk, Vera, Mountain Lass, Griselda, Clara D., Helen F., Nan and Irish Lass.

To St. Patrick: Gertie Arnold, Maudine, Maggie C., Maud D., Belle Evans, Governess, Flora, Yolo Maid, Montana Maid and Stambella.

To Mascot: Vixen, Dolly Dimple, Sally Wilkes and Fantasie.

To Deputy: Cora Belle: Virginia Wilkes and Guelda.

Any one who looks up the pedigrees of these and sees the horses and their work will expect some famous horses from this year's breeding.

Which are the best of these would be hard to say. Mascot cost $26,000, and there are others which Mr. Daly would not sell for less than $40,000. While there are many pretty horses, Mascot is par excellence, the perfect horse, with spirit and grace that add to the perfection of his form. Mr. Daly was offered $30,000 for Mascot from a man he did not like to refuse, and he said to Mr. Larimore, "I guess I'll have to let him go. Bring him out till I look at him." He was brought out and looked over, when Mr. Daly said "Put him up; I won't part with him."

Mr. Joseph Cox, recently from Pennsylvania, has charge of the farm. He is an active, energetic, capable man, and has the ability and industry to conduct large farming operations. Next spring will see great improvement in the ranch, if we are not mistaken.

Mr. Daly has two other ranches, a hay ranch of 160 acres and a ranch in Gurge creek valley of about 1600 acres. He has some stock on each. The small grain he uses is principally raised on this ranch, which shows that it is in good hands.

Mr. Daly has some fine Holstein-Friesian cattle, one of which was imported, and a fine herd of two-year-old and yearling Shorthorns, all of which are registered.

Unfortunately Mr. Daly was not at the ranch while we were there, but it is evident that he bought his ranches less than two years ago for the purpose of breeding fine horses and cattle in Montana. He has a love for farm life, and horses and cattle, and while the business of breeding and farming is in the line of his taste, he did not establish this place for profit. If it pays expenses it is all he asks; but he wants to show to the world that fine stock can be raised in Montana as well as in Kentucky or California. In this is shown the public spirit of the man, and his pride in Montana. It seems to us he could not have chosen a better or wiser means to carry out his great ideas, and every citizen of the state will rejoice in the success that is sure to come to him.

Navicular Disease in the Horse.

By Dr. A. E. Buzard, M. R. C. V. S. L.

I have been requested to treat on this important lameness in the column of the BREEDER AND SPORTSMAN.

Fifty years ago navicular disease was unknown, not because it did not exist, for probably it has been a source of lameness since the horse's domestication, but because it was not recoganized until Prof. Turner of the London Veterinary College made the discovery that the mischief lay in the deep-seated structure of the foot. Prior to this, any obscure lameness, for which there was no appearance, was relegated to "the shoulder," especially when the foot was good and open, and presented noappearance of disease, as is frequently the case, while when small and misshapen it was referred to as "contraction." Now we know that contraction is rather the effect than the cause of navicular disease, but "the shoulder" is still a favorite spot for fixing the seat for lameness, and many are the rubbings and blisterings that the unfortunate animal is subjected to before some one a little wiser points to the foot as the correct situation of the disease. The foot of the horse is something more than a lump of horn to which an iron shoe may be nailed. This horney box is nature's shoe, and the true foot structures are contained within it, the principal one being the coffin bone. Behind this a small wedge-shaped bone, called the navicular or "shuttle" bone, and over it the tendon plays as it runs to its insertion into the inferior surface of the coffin-bone. Navicular disease commences in an inflammatory process in this bone, or in the cartilage lining the inner surface. The disease is progressive, caries of the bone takes place, the tendon playing over it becomes involved, and in extreme cases upturned, so that the toe of the animal is cocked up, and the back part of the fetlock touches the ground.

CAUSES.

1.—HEREDITARY.—When we say a disease is hereditary, it is not necessary that it should be congenital, or present at birth; what is meant is that certain structures are predisposed to take on the diseased state, and only require exposure to favorable conditions to insure its development, i. e., the feet of an animal bred from parents, or a parent, lame from navicular disease, would not stand the "'ammer, 'ammer, 'ammer, on the 'ard, 'igh road," like those of an animal that had not the hereditary taint. The feet might remain healthy doing slow work on the soft ground, but fail when fast work on hard roads is demanded. There is no surer way of propagating this disease than breeding from unsound parents. There is a greater tendency to this, perhaps, where navicular disease is concerned than there is with other hereditary unsoundnesses, and for this reason it is rare to find a bad horse suffering from this form of lameness. They are generally good all round, well-bred, well-shaped, good-hearted, good workers and fast; they get lamer and lamer, change owners, until they fall into the hands of some one with an "eye for the beautiful," so far as a mare is concerned, and he perhaps thinks she would throw a good foal. She is cheap, because unless for work, being incurably lame, she is, therefore, put to the horse to earn her keep, and the result is a good looking colt, but one with a predisposition to the same disease.

2.—STABLE MANAGEMENT has something to do with it. Horses are frequently kept standing in the stall for days together. During these periods of rest there is a deficiency of synovial secretions; then the animal is taken out, put to hard fast work, which, but for its irregular character, it could have done very well, and the result is bruising or injury, inflammation and navicular disease.

3.—WORK.—Light horses are more subject to navicular disease than the heavy breeds used in slow draught, although it is sometimes found in those that are "high steppers" and work on stone-paved roads, but the rule is that draught animals are more prone to laminitis than to navicular lameness. A very large proportion of horses suffering from lameness in front in San Francisco and other large cities, are lame from this disease.

The forefeet receive the whole weight of the body, or rather of the head, neck and half the trunk; behind, the hocks receive the greater portion of this weight. Therefore we look principally for foot lameness in front, and hock lameness behind. Added to this weight on the fore feet we have the dashing and banging on hard roads, and it is reasonable to expect that inflammation of structures on which this stress is laid would be excited. Occasionally it may occur suddenly without reference to work, from a slip or stumble, or from concussion in jumping. The horse may be ridden from home sound enough, and fall dead lame so suddenly as to cause one to think it had picked up a stone, but no stone is to be found, or indeed any other apparent cause of lameness, and then the usual tale is that the horse has "sprained its shoulder."

SYMPTOMS.

The first symptoms is generally "pointing", an almost infallible test for navicular disease, although there may occasionally occur a case that does not point. It is often possible to foretell it from this symptom alone, when to all appearance the horse is quite sound, and certainly works so. Horses sometimes point from habit or weariness, but this differs from the pointing of navicular disease. In the former there is a careless, lounging attitude, one hind and one fore foot being rested simultaneously. In the latter only one foot is pointed at a time, and that in a manner that shows the horse is in earnest about it; when both feet are affected he will advance them alternately. The next symptom, and, from want of observation on the part of the owner often the first noticed, is a shortness of step, perhaps without positive lameness, the animal going worse down hill from the weight being thrown on the heels, thus placing the stress on the affected parts. In coming out of the stable the horse seems stiff and disinclined to move, but when he has gone some distance, especially if the ground is soft, the movement is freer and the step longer. A look at the shoes will show a deal. The horse lame from navicular disease always throws as much weight as possible on his toes, thus the shoe is worn at the toe. When both feet are affected the step is short and stilty, and the muscles of the shoulders seem stiff and rigid, giving rise to the ridiculous term "chest founder". This is easily accounted for, the step is short because the pain in the foot on the ground causes the horse to bring the other up quickly to relieve it, and the stiffness arises because the flexion of the foot causes pain in the joint, and he does not pick up his feet freely because he knows that the further they have to come down again the greater will be the shock of the concussion; hence the painful "dot", "dot", of groggy horses. There is negative evidence of navicular disease when no other possible cause of lameness can be found, but the pointing, the peculiar joint, the wear of the shoe, and the varied temperature of the foot, are generally positive, enough to enable an experienced veterinary surgeon to pronounce on the seat of disorder.

TREATMENT.

For navicular disease, there is no cure. A measure of relief may be given in the early stages, and the horse kept working for a time, but sooner or later the lameness becomes so great as to render this out of the question. Frog setons, blisters, and firing at the coronet, and bleeding at the toe, have all been tried, but in vain. Sometimes the treatment adopted for contraction, viz., a dose of physic, cold poultices, a blister to the coronet, and a run at grass seems to give relief, but it is only temporary; the lameness grows gradually worse, there is ulceration of the navicular bone or adhesion, and presently rupture of the flexor tendon, and the horse becomes useless. Rest does not seem to help the animal, indeed, it has been frequently remarked that "The longer they stand in the worse they come out." If the lame animal is put to slow work on soft ground, the disease is found to make slower progress than if it is retained at road work.

UN-NERVING.

The grand remedy in cases of navicular disease is the operation of neurotomy. This does not cure the diseased structure, but it takes away all pain and consequent lameness, and makes the horse useful for a period, depending on the care in selection of cases, and the carefulness of the shoeing smith. Neurotomy is an operation that requires scientific training on the part of the operator. It consists in removing about an inch of the nerves that supply the foot with sensation. The horse is cast, the foot to be operated upon released from the hobbles, the hair closely clipped, and a transverse incision made through the skin just above the pastern, the nerve searched for, freed from connective tissue, cut through, and about an inch removed from the side most remote from the nerve-centre.

There are several ways of performing the operation which need not be entered into. The high operation just described is the best; the nerve being divided above its bifurcation, *all* sensation is then removed from the foot. The want of judgment in selecting subjects for the operation has brought it into disrepute. But for horses incurably lame, either from ringbone, side-bone, or navicular disease, it becomes a question of this sort:

I have an animal that is absolutely worthless, because it is cruel to work it. If I have it unnerved, and it only lasts six months, its labors will have repaid me for the cost of the operation. But, instead of only lasting six months, it may, with judicious treatment, last eight or ten years, or until the horse meets its end from some other cause, so that, instead of being passed from hand to hand until it goes from bad to worse, not only in disease, but as to owner, the animal is usefully performing all the work that we can ask a horse to do. The success of the operation is immediate. The horse *gets up* sound, but about three weeks, often less, are necessary for the wounds to heal. Instead of a cripple, we have an animal that steps as freely as on the day it was foaled, no blundering or stumbling, as some suppose. It may be ridden down hill, over rough roads, with perfect security. I have seen unnerved horses used for every purpose, and out of some scores of cases which I have operated upon have only known two that went wrong from causes other than preventable ones, and these were from disintegration of the tendon, which causes the heel to bulge out and the toe to turn up.

Sometimes nerve-tumors form on the cut end of the nerve, and this happens when taken too soon to work after the operation is performed, but the removing of a neuroma is a simple affair. Pricks from shoeing or other injuries that with feeling in the foot would cause the animal to go lame, and so receive treatment, in the unnerved animal pass unnoticed, there being no sensation; these suppurate and cause the hoof to drop off. This is one of the drawbacks to the operation, but in everything connected with horseflesh luck is a great element. In any case, we have an incurably lame horse; with neurotomy we have a possibly useful servant.

TURF AND TRACK.

It is now said that John E. Turner will campaign Wanita 2:20½.

Lexington, Ky., has started a boom for a new big hotel. It needs one.

Montana Regent has had a highly successful stud season at Denver, Colorado.

It is said that Dick Roche has been "Dave" Johnson's financial backer until recently.

Barnum, the great showman, is building a mile track near his residence at Bridgeport, Ct.

The Dwyer Bros. paid $3,000 for a brother to the race horse Longstreet the other day.

S. J. Trask, Prescott, Wash., has unfortunately lost (dead) a full sister to the speedy Rolly Bolly.

An offer of $30,000 for Campbell's Electioneer, 2:22½, was recently wired by an Austrian company.

It is mighty hard to beat a good Longfellow over a distance, and they ran one, two, in the Derby.

The New York Jockey Club, will name a stake Santa Anita in honor of Lucky Baldwins celebrated stock farm.

W. L. Scott has sold to M. T. Downing the Oliver colt and Cutalong; to W. C. Daly, Seashore, by Wanderer.

Robert Bonner is expected at Terre Haute early next month to take a look at Sunol before she goes to Detroit.

Matt Allen has not been very unfortunate so far this season, Philander and Golden Horn, both getting second place.

John Huggins has offered $4,000 for the two-year-old Lord Harry, who six months ago cost only $225 as a yearling

A former sheriff of Knox county, Mo., has been sentenced to two years from Sedalia for stealing a $100 mule.

It is reported that J. I. Case has offered $10,000 for the seven-year-old mare Carrie Walton, 2:23½, by Gov. Sprague.

Wellington, the six-year-old brother to Sunol 2:10½, is said to be showing the Macy Bros. an exceptional turn of speed.

Yolo Maid 2:12½, the queen of pacers, has been bred to St. Patrick 2;19½ by Volunteer 55 out of Young Selene by Guy Miller.

J H. Shults has booked two mares to Wm. L., sire of Axtell, 2:12, at $500 each. One is by Voltaire and the other by Harold.

A consignment of 100 Shetland ponies arrived in New York recently. One of them was 31 inches high and weighed 180 pounds.

The entries in the Montana Circuit are very promising, sixty at Anaconda, sixty four at Deer Lodge, and sixty six at Butte.

Mr. Quimby, of Portland, Or., the owner of Phalmont Boy, Priesmont and other well known horses, says he will take them East next season.

Mr. Arthur Coventry who was for years the crack gentleman Jock is now wielding Lord Marcus Beresford's flag as official starter in England.

The Cerise colt, who ran a good race with Highland Lass some time ago, has since been purchased by Maj. J. L. Robertson, New York, for $3,000.

The four-year-old horse Spectator by Springbok, dam Hattie Harris, has been sold by O. O. West Jr., of Louisville, to Jockey Isaac Murphy for $1,200.

The Undine Stable left last Sunday for Washington Park, Chicago. After a few days rest they will go to Westchester, Homer being entered in the Eclipse Stake.

There are upwards of one hundred trotters and pacers now at the Exposition Driving Park, Kansas City, in training for the races which take place there May 27th to 30th.

Secretary J. T. Gregg, of the Oregon State Fair Association, says there are eighteen entries for the three-year-old stake race. Mr. Quimby's Phalmont Boy is not entered.

James McKee, a well known horseman of Goshen, has bought the Orange Hotel property there. The purchase includes a lease of the Goshen Driving Park track and stables.

W. H. Coombs, who has been in the race horse business from his boyhood up, and has lately acted so efficiently as starter, says that if ever a horse could beat El Rio Rey and 1:39½, it is Racine.

The Board of Directors of the Minnesota Driving Club have awarded the contract for building its new club house at Hamline. When finished it will cost something in the neighborhood of $10,000.

The man who docked the tails of twenty ponies belonging to John D. Cheever of New York, was sentenced to imprisonment for twenty days and fined $50, while his assistants were fined $40 each.

Texas owns more horses than any other State, the Department of Agriculture crediting to her 1,350,344; Illinois is second on the list, with about 200,000 less, whose value is estimated at $83,301,612.

The catalogue of the Rancho Del Paso yearlings to be sold on June 30th in New York is one of the most perfect ever issued. The particular feature is the handy, carefully arranged pedigree of each of the youngsters.

D. A. McAllister (La Grande, Ore) has sold to William Cushman, the two year old filly by Lemont (by Almont 33) out of Molly by Frank Chapman. The filly is a full sister to Blondie, three year old record 2:27½.

John Splan says "My experience tells me there are two kinds of game horses; the first and very much the most numerous are the ones who plod along and try as long as their drivers force them. The other, which is scarce, are the ones that have the disposition born in them to make an everlasting struggle at the critical moment."

On the strength of the passage of the bill in the New Jersey Senate legalizing betting on race tracks, work was commenced on a three-quarter-mile track at Gloucester City, on which running races will be held as soon as finished.

The Port Jervis Driving Park property, including track, stables and hotel, has been sold by Isaac B. Gurney to James Murphy of Port Jervis. Mr. Gurney goes to Lexington, Ky., where he will engage in training trotting-horses.

"A wise man changes his mind, but a fool never does," reads an old Spanish proverb. "The breeder of horses who has got upon the wrong track might profit by the idea conveyed in this adage," remarks the National Stockman.

Dr. L. Herr, Forest Park Farm, has sold to Judge R. N. Baskin, Salt Lake City, Utah, the brown filly Leonora Queen, two years old by Emory Boy; 1st dam King Girl by Mambrino King; 2d dam Leah by Blue Bull. Price, $1,000.

Budd Doble has a pacer called St. Cloud by Kentucky Prince. He has no record but before being purchased showed a mile in 2:22½, and came back in 2:17½. He probably gets his pacing inclination from his dam who is by Tom Hal.

M. T. Danaher has sold, through Col. S. D. Bruce, to the Melbourne Stud, the bay horse Oneko, foaled 1884, by Uncas, dam imp. Faverdale by The Palmer, her dam Georgiana by Touchstone, out of Lady Emily by Muley Moloch.

Silver Bow, Pete Williams' regally-bred three-year-old, will leave on the 1st for Salt Lake, and will take in the Montana circuit. He has had a highly successful season, and had his owner wished, could have booked many more mares.

B. J. Johnson, trainer last season of the Chicago stables, it is stated, has gone into partnership with H. C. Shafer, Peytona Stock Farm, Gallatin, Tenn. The new firm we are informed will purchase a number of mares and go into breeding on a large scale.

At Cincinnati, May 12th, the Latonia Jockey Club held its annual meeting. Col. R. W. Nelson, of New York, was elected President in the place of the late T. J. Megibben. Judge George G. Perkins was chosen Vice President and Edward C. Hopper Secretary.

R. P. Ashe's Geraldine disappointed the pool room habitues on Wednesday last when Civil Service and Fordham beat her a half mile sprint in :48½. Father William Daly keeps winning with Civil Service, and strange to say he never goes to the post less than eight or ten to one.

That gifted author, Em Pierce, has eclipsed himself in his daintily bound collection of racing verses which he calls "Poems of the Turf." The poems are full of true poetical feeling, and every racing and sporting man, should have them on his table—they will grace any and every.

Wilber F. Smith has among his string the speedy pacer Creole, 2.20. The black son of Prompter has had a fair stud season, and should be very handy round the circuit this season, for Wilber is well known as a quiet, careful, painstaking, experienced educator of either trotters or pacers.

Eon was not in the Brooklyn Handicap, or in any other stake engagement at the meeting. Phil Dwyer said that he had tired of paying forfeits on Eon for the past two years. The horse is the property of Col. R. J. Hancock of Virginia, but the Dwyer Bros. have his running qualities until the end of his six-year-old career.

James Quinn, who is charged with an attempt to bribe the jockey M. Lewis to pull Ballyhoo in the second race on the first day of the Lexington Meeting, has been found guilty. The judges on the 12th ruled Quinn off the track for twelve months. Quinn is a brother-in-law to P. A. Brady, President of the Bookmakers' Association.

The Driving Park Association of Goshen and Warwick, N. Y., and Newton, N. J., will hold a June circuit of three days' trotting meetings. The meetings will open at Newton, June 10, 11, and 12, and will be continued at Warwick June 17, 18 and 19, and at Goshen June 24, 25 and 26. The programme for each day will include purses for running horses.

Farfaletta, bay mare 23 years old, by imported Australian dam Elkhorna, by Lexington, is dead at Fleetwood Farm, near Frankfort. Among other good ones she produced the well known horse Falsetto. Buchu, chestnut mare, 20 years old by Planet dam Lavender, by Wagner, grand dam Alice Carneal (dam of Lexington) by imported Sarpedon, is also dead at the same place. She produced Mr. Tarlton's stallion, Blue Eyes, and others.

L. F. Herrick, Worcester, is the owner of an inbred Electioneer, i. e a foal (colt) dropped a fortnight ago by Whipster, he by Whips 2:27½ (Electioneer out of Lizzie Whips thoroughbred) out of May Bird, half sister to Manzanita 2:16 and Wildflower 2 years 2:21. The colt's dam is by Ansel 2:20 he by Electioneer out of Annette by Lexington. The youngster is therefore full of Electioneer and thoroughbred and should add renown to Palo Alto.

Lucy R. by Sultan, dam Lady Mackey, the dam of Thor, trotted a mile at Rosemeade, Cal., the other day in 2:23½. She had a record as a three-year-old of 2:30. Semi-Tropic out of the same dam, Mr. Rose says, can trot in 2:20. Mr. G. M. Fogg of Nashville purchased Thor, two years old at New York at the Rosemeade sale for $9,000, and he is now being jogged at Melrose. Mr. Rose says he was the fastest yearling ever raised at Rosemeade.

Charles Marvin says, for a two-year-old stallion, I think three or four mares are really beneficial. I would not give him more than six and they should be well distributed over the season. For a three-year-old stallion 20 mares should be the outside limit; and they should be well distributed, too. A four year old stallion can comfortably cover 30 to 35 mares; and at five years old he should take a full season. I believe 50 mares furnish a heavy enough season for any horse to make.

The English Derby now looks as though it would be Surefoot or Sanfoin. Surefoot is a bay colt by Wisdom, dam by Galopin—winner of Derby in 1875, out of Miss Foote; he is the property of Mr. W. A. Merry, and easily accounted for The Two Thousand. Sanfoin is said by a well known writer on turf matters, to be a bright chestnut, blaze face, off hind shank white half-way to hocks, and near white hind fetlock; exquisite shoulders, grandly arched loins, deep and powerful quarters, clean hocks, and stands true on good legs and feet; he is by Springfield out of Sanda, and was bred by "Her Majesty," being bought by John Porter for 550 guineas as a yearling, since then his owner has refused £6,500 for him.

A. J. Cassatt, Chesterbrook Stud, Berwyn, Pa., has purchased from A. Finkle, Woodstock, Canada, the brood mares Simoon, bay, foaled 1874, by War Dance, dam Saratoga by imp. Knight of St. George, her dam Sister to Pryor by imp. Glencoe, and the bay mare Moonlight, foaled 1883, by Princeton, dam Simoon, above, with their foals by imp. Dandie Dinmont (son of Silvio and Meg Merrilies by Macgregor).

St. George in the Denver Horse, says: I had a talk with Frank Harper yesterday about his stallions. He thinks that Longfellow is the greatest stallion in America, and that Jils Johnson is the worst. In reply I told him that he would find Rossington to be equal if not superior to either. His answer was "Maybe so." He intends to breed Belle Knight, the dam of Freeland and other good ones, to Longfellow as long as the old horse lives, and then he would give Rossington a chance at the great matron.

King Solomon of old was a large importer of horses from Egypt, says an exchange, and with his wealth, wisdom and power he is likely to have secured the best, so that there is something very credible in the Arab tradition that their best horses descend from the stud of Solomon. Mahomet appears to have severely tested the powers of the Arabian mare, and as he would be able to obtain the best, mares that had endured such tests from him would naturally become celebrated and thus the Arabs get another starting point in the pedigree of their best horses more than 1,600 years later than the reign of Solomon.

The Beverwyck stable (owner of Castaway II.) is composed of ex-Mayor Nolan of Albany and Johnny Campbell of trotting horse fame. Campbell is known as one of the smoothest men on the turf, and his winnings on the race, in bets alone, are stated on reliable authority to be $27,000. Next to Campbell, Dan DeNoyelles, owner of the trotter Fred Folger, brother of the famous Guy, is the biggest winner, his profits being placed at $17,000. E A. Buck of the Spirit of the Times, who is another of Campbell's friends, is said to have won $10,000.

An exchange says Castaway II., the winner of the Brooklyn, is a plain-looking bay colt by Outcast, out of Lucy Lisle, 15 3 hands high. He has always been a fair performer in sloppy going, but a mile and a quarter was always considered beyond the limits of his powers. He ran this spring at the New Jersey tracks with varying success. The result of the race proved one thing, that seasoned horses are the ones to back, the first three horses in the handicap having been running for a month or more.

Mr. Sampson, or Charlie Sampson as he is better known, left for Denver last Monday. Denver has had several visitors on the coast this season, viz., Mayor DuBois, genial Luke DuBois and Clifton Bell, but none were *more* popular than Mr. Sampson, whose easy, unassuming manner and general all-round knowledge made him a great favorite with all. His place in the Palace coterie of well informed racing men will be hard to fill, and a seat will always be vacant at the round table where he, Hickok, and the rest of the boys most do congregate. After our last conversation with Mr. Sampson, we only said adieu, as he promises to return in the Fall.

The Oregonian says: Superintendent E. W. Allen, of the Industrial Exposition Association, is busy with the prospectus of the fair this fall. The fat stock department is to receive very prominent attention at the hands of the association. The premiums in this department will aggregate $5,500, practically doubling up on last year. A good portion of the first week of the fair will be devoted to the fat stock department, including the horse and cattle day, sheep and wool day, and the barbecue day, when an old fashioned barbecue will be held, and toasts proposed by W. M. Ladd, chairman of the committee, and responded to by leading stockmen. The fair will devote its second day to the press and will extend many courtesies in the way of suburban excursions, a banquet, etc., to the newspaper men of the Pacific Northwest.

A suit, of interest to horsemen, was tried on May 12th, says the N. Y. Times, before Chief Justice Mercer Beasley. It was one brought by Joseph Reilly, a lawyer of Red Bank, against Augustus W. Weingardt of New York, the owner of a stable of race horses. Reilly's suit was based upon a breach of contract. An attachment had been secured against Weingardt by Stephen B. Billings for wages due his son, John Billings, the jockey, for mounts on Wellington, the race horse. Reilly acted as Weingardt's counsel and was victorious in the case, and as Weingardt did not pay the amount due him he attached Weingardt's horses. Charles Littlefield, the trainer, and Harris Onley, the jockey, became Weingardt's bondsmen. The jury rendered a verdict this afternoon against Weingardt for the full amount claimed, $300, with costs and interest added.

One of the most prominent breeders, in conversation a short time since with a gentleman who was about to embark in the business, let fall these words of truth and wisdom: "Begin at the top and breed up. Remember the fact that it is the largest and most prominent of our breeders who are now doing this. You cannot begin below the scale and breed beyond it, and, besides, you consume valuable time in the attempt. If you begin at the top, every generation which is added to your stock is a step in advance, but if you commence at the other end you have to reach the standard of excellence as it now exists, and by the time you have reached what is now regarded as the standard, it has in the meantime advanced also, and you are as far away from the goal for which you are striving as when you began.—Massachusetts Plowman.

The Kentucky Stock Farm says: The farrier too often makes a horse his patient for life by ruthlessly cutting away the elastic cushion, called the frog, which is nature's natural support for the great flexor tendon. This cushion is nature's provision to support the center of the horse's foot, to take off the strain from the sensitive laminæ with which the hoof is connected with the foot, to prevent the extreme depression and consequent strain on the flexor tendon, and to break the concussion caused by the horse's great weight coming so rapidly to the ground. When once severely cut away the frog never entirely recovers its original efficiency, and will be a very long time before it will be even moderately useful. At the same time the enamel, like the enamel covering our finger nails, which covers the whole of the outside of the colt's hoof, and effectually retains its moisture and suppleness, is rasped away to make his foot fit the shoe, and to give it a a round and uniform shape. Thus two of nature's most important provisions to secure an elastic tread are ruthlessly destroyed, and the horse compelled henceforth to stump and jar away with his sensitive foot and loaded sinews resting entirely on the dried and unyielding crust of his hoof, made still more unyielding by being nailed to an iron ring.

E. J. Baldwin, the Santa Anita millionaire went to Sacramento last Sunday to see his mares which have been stinted to imported Cheviot. Mr Baldwin, while over to the Bottom and was particularly impressed with the Rancho Del Paso yearlings He said they were big, strong and very good looking; his favorite among the stallions was Darebin for whom he has a very great liking.

The Rancho Del Paso colts of 1889 are showing up well already. Arcade, Eclipse, Madge L, Priscilla and others have won races. Eclipse, who has proved such a lucky purchase, was bought at the last Haggin sale for $325 by J. Sennett. He is by imp Kyrle Daly out of Billow by Longfield, granddam Medea by Norfolk. Eclipse's dam Billow was a good race mare, winning the California Stake in 1885, and after foaling Eclipse was sold in the fall of 1888 to R. E Bybee for $420, and proving barren was raced last year, and bred, I think, to Leon by Leinster out of Ada by Asteroid. Last Monday, Eclipse, in a five furlong at Brooklyn, carried 121 pounds, and won by a head from Russell, 113, and Lord Harry, 118. Time, 1:02½. Eclipse's owner was asked to put a price on him, as I mentioned some few weeks ago, and said $25,000, but would rather not sell. One never knows when selecting youngsters which will prove the best *if equally well bred*, and this year the Rancho Del Paso youngsters are so exceptionally well formed that all should be good, and the only way to get the best is to buy them all. Kentuckians will be astonished at the sight of so many clinkers.

The newly formed Oakland Driving Association promises to be a decided success. Already upwards of seventy members are enrolled. The intention is to hold matinees on each Wednesday and Saturday at the Trotting Park until a correct idea of the form of the members' horses can be arrived at, and then hold a series of races for members only—owners to drive. Last Saturday several members were speeding their road horses, but only two races were held. The first was for pacers, one mile, two heats. The entries were: Dr. Walker's Woodchuck, W. Coleman's Haverly, J. Birmingham's Oregon Boy, C. W. Knox's Minnie R, O. Emery's Sam Washington. The first heat was won by Haverly in 2:42, Washington second. In the second heat, Haverly who has a record of 2:25, was withdrawn, and Sam Washington won in 2:45, with Oregon Boy second.

The next race was trotting to buggies, one mile. The entries were: J. C. Kimball's Jim Blaine, John T. Jordan's Mary J, Dr. Woolsey's Doctor, J. Brown's Jim, Colonel Ashby's Blackbird. The first heat was won by Jim Blaine in 2:49½, with Mary J second. The second heat was won by Doctor in 2:58, with Jim Blaine second.

The following are the leading North Pacific dates for race meetings:

Oregon State Fair, Salem, Sept. 15—six days.

Eastern Oregon Second District Agricultural Association, The Dalles, Sept. 23—five days.

Montana Agricultural, Mineral and Mechanical Association Helena, July 2—four days; August 20—ten days.

Baker County Agricultural Association, Baker City, Sept. 30—five days.

Portland Speed Association, City View Park (Portland), spring meeting June 11—four days, fall meeting September 9—five days.

Deer Lodge Fair and Racing Association, Deer Lodge, Mon., July 14—six days.

Yamhill County Fair Association, McMinnville, September 2—four days.

Washington County Agricultural Society, Hillsboro, September 23—four days.

Walla Walla Valley Consolidated Agricultural Society, Walla Walla, June 19—three days, October 6—six days,

Latah County Agricultural Fair Association, Moscow, Idaho, September 30—five days.

The Executive Committee of the Southern Oregon State Board of Agriculture assure us, says the Democrat Times, that the coming district fair at Central Point, will be made one of the leading fairs of the northwest. Upwards of $2,000 will be expended in the speed ring alone, possibly as much as $3,000, and all races after Wednesday will be free for all horses on the coast. The fair will continue for an entire week, six days, including a free fruit exhibition on Monday. The event of the week in the speed ring will be a $500 free-for-all trot on Thursday or Friday, and several other good purses will be hung up. Premiums will be advanced in all classes, and especially in the live-stock departments where sweepstakes and herd premiums will be offered, and other important changes made. As the success of the fair is no longer a doubtful matter, the board feels justified in making the premiums in all departments commensurate with the importance that should attach to a district or state enterprise. Their course cannot be too highly commended, as they have no desire to accumulate a surplus in future, and the liberal patronage sure to be bestowed by the citizens of this valley and the district at large insures the financial success of the fair, even though larger premiums be offered than are given at Salem, A magnificent exhibit is assured for next fall, and the whole county will derive benefit from the holding of the fair.

A. L. Hinds is working an exceptionally useful looking lot of horses at the Oakland Trotting Park. They are of course, the property of the San Miguel Stock Farm (with the exception of the pacer) and the nine all look exceptionally well. In the string are three five year-olds. Balkan 2:29½ who is looking better and stronger than ever in his life is expected to—and should, lower his record a good many notches. Yolland, a good looking bay gelding, is a full brother to Gus Wilkes 2:22 and can trot now in about 2:30 and is expected to give Mambrino Wilkes one more in the 2:30 list; the other five-year old is a bay mare by Mambrino Wilkes, out of a John Nelson mare. The only three-year-old Mr. Hinds has is a pacing mare by Mambrino Wilkes, dam by Chieftain. She was raised near Stockton and after showing several quarters in 35½ and 35 was purchased by a gentleman for $1,000 last week and will be left with Mr. Hinds. The two-year-olds are the bay stallion Kodiac, full brother to Gus Wilkes 2:22. Kodiac is the pride of the stable and is expected to make a good showing in the Occident Stake. Chaldean is a neat black colt, an in-bred horse, as his sire is Mambrino Wilkes and his dam Fredolia is by Fred Arnold, her dam by Mambrino Wilkes; he is also entered in the Occident. Mylitta the other two-year-old is a very trim filly by Mambrino Wilkes out of Mollie Fern by Captain Cole, grandam Fannie Fern, dam of Mollie Drew 2:27. Balkan 2:29½, she looks as though she will not disgrace her distinguished relatives. The two yearlings are Sargon, a splendidly shaped yearling by Mambrino Wilkes out of Contra by Electioneer, she out of a thoroughbred mare. The colt shows a good deal of quality being neatly turned and well finished; a Wilkes all over and has an easy pure gait. The other two-year-old is a leggy bay filly by Mambrino Wilkes out of Kitty by Conductor.

A similar race having proved so attractive last season, the Twin City Jockey Club has decided to open a sweepstake for gentlemen riders, the race to be run at its impending summer meeting. The first prize will be piece of silver plate, emblematic of racing, valued at $500. The entrance will be $10 each, play or pay, to accompany the nomination, and to go to the second horse. Horses named must be owned by the nominator at the time of closing the entries, five or more to enter and three to start, or the race may be declared off. The distance will be one mile, weights 28 pounds above the scale, and extra weight will be allowed. The standard scale of weight for age for July, 1890, is as follows, and prospective nominators can figure the weight at which they will start: One mile, two years, 79; 3 years, 109; 4 years, 122; 5, 6 and aged, 124. No conditions interposing, fillies, 2 years old, allowed 3 pounds; mares, 3 years old and upwards, allowed 5 pounds; gelding allowed 3 pounds. Secretary Shaw has received assurances from a number of owners that there will be a large field.

A good story, the truth of which is vouched for, says the Buffalo Commercial, is told of a certain dealer in horses in this city (Buffalo). The dealer in question had been endeavoring for some time to secure a fast pacer. He finally succeeded in purchasing, for a long price, one that had shown a mile in 2:27. The horse was taken to the stable and comfortably domiciled in a box stall. The head salesman was absent when the horse was brought in, and when he returned the proprietor, with an assumption of pride and importance, showed him the pacer and asked him in a joking way, if he thought any one would give a hundred dollars for him. The salesman replied that he thought he could get that much for him. Nothing more was said at the time, but during the day the salesman, while driving on the avenue, met a gentleman who was in search of a pacer. The latter asked the salesman if he knew where he could get one cheap. The salesman replied that he thought the identical animal was at that time in the stable. They both repaired to the stable, and finding the proprietor absent, the pacer was brought out and put through his paces up and down the boulevard. The time was satisfactory and the price asked, $150 promptly paid and the horse delivered. In the evening when the dealer returned the salesman informed him, with a good deal of satisfaction, that he had sold the pacer at fifty dollars advance. "What did you get for him?" queried the dealer. "One hundred and fifty dollars," said the salesman, unable to account for the sudden pallor which overspread the countenance of the other. "One hundred and fifty dollars," moaned the dealer; "why I paid $500 for him this morning."

There should be some one to enlighten the amateur horsemen in the use of the check rein, says the Sporting World, from the fact of there being a number that have a tendency to imitate their neighbors. When any of these people see a horse hitched they go home and try the same plan, frequently checking a colt up as high as they can, and start in to break him. The result is that nine out of ten are partially spoiled and develop a dislike for the check, and it is years before they are cured of the habit of tossing their head. If the beginner would use a little forethought and check a colt up gradually, he would soon find the natural position and avoid future trouble. Under such treatment the colt will soon learn to drive pleasantly and speed without pulling. One colt likes an overdraw, another a side check, and so on; therefore the driver should endeavor to get a kind that will suit. It is never safe to check a colt up until such a point is reached, as he will do his work easier and with more determination. This is especially true of the trotter and road horse. Get him where he trots steady and easy, after his feet are balanced, and do not try to drive him in 2:20 the first week. Wait patiently and find where he likes his head and what kind of check or bit makes him feel most comfortable. In nearly every town an observing man sees horses speed up the streets, over cross walks with their heads stuck up in the air as if they were taking astronomical lessons. Such a method is not the best way to make a good track horse, or even a safe roadster, as he has not liberty enough to see his way or what is going on around him. Give the horse a little freedom in harness, treat him kindly and speak to him when he is doing his work. It does not cost anything, and it wins his confidence.

An old turfman writes the following (to the Turf, Field and Farm), which gives subject for reflection to those contemplating breeding enterprises: "Dr. Merritt, the Virginia turfman, importer of Priam, Margrave and Luzborough, once remarked that if he were (after his observation and experience) to establish a stock farm he would purchase one on which race horses had been bred and no other; not an adjoining one, even, for there were differences in soil, water and grasses not to be detected or discovered by the eye. He declared that Mr. Brodnax, the breeder of Virginian and Virginia Lafayette (incestuously bred, by the way) was the most successful breeder in Virginia, and that his farm in Brunswick County, where the lands were poor and not attractive in appearance, had succeeded, while his neighbors, stimulated by his success, had failed, and that there must have been something in the grasses and water on his that their farms did not possess.

To support this view, note the difference in success between the stud farms of Erdenheim and Chesterbrook, near Philadelphia. One produces racers like Iroquois, Sensation, Pardee and Rataplan, the other a few second rate winners. When Sir L. Newman, a young English turfman, determined many years ago to establish a large stud farm in Devonshire County, a writer in Bell's Life in London predicted his failure on the ground that several previous attempts had failed, and that there was something unknown which would defeat his aims. The prediction became true, for with Gemma di Vergy as the head stallion, and the American mare Prioress as one of the matrons, the enterprise was abandoned after several years' trial.

Recently in The Field, a writer from France about the stud farms there, in commenting on the success of one and the ill-success of another, states that they are similar in every respect, soil, surface, climate and water, and are but eight miles apart, and that the proximity of the non-successful farm to the ocean is the probable reason for the failure. Now, will the baneful effects of the ocean winds account for Glen Cove, on Long Island, sheltered from winds, rearing the racers American Eclipse, Treasurer and Dove: and Babylon, exposed to the ocean breezes, being abandoned by Mr. Belmont, who has removed his mares to Kentucky? Perhaps Mr. Wither's partial success may be attributed to this proximity to old ocean as compared to that achieved where Fashion, Mariner and Clarion were bred, not far from his stud farm.

Referring to the fifth race at Brooklyn on the 16th, in which Anderson had such a narrow escape, the St. Louis Republic says:

Mr. Pierre Lorrillard was on hand to back his filly, but third was the best she could do, while William Daly or Father Bill, if you choose, gave the boys an eye opener in the fifth by winning with Dalayrian. Rancocas was the favorite, and while at the post in a break away the colt was knocked to his knees. Spider Anderson, who had the mount, was thrown to the track and two horses ran over him. The Spider staggered to his feet and reeling would have fallen had not Jim, the starter's assistant caught him.

"Oh, Jim," sobbed the boy, "I'm killed sure; take me to the stand quick." Jim picked the boy up in his arms and placing him in the starter's wagon the team were whipped into a gallop. Nine-tenths of those in the stud thought the colored lad was dead when he was placed on a stretcher and lay motionless. His jacket was torn to rags He was hurriedly carried to the jocky's room and a doctor summoned. After a time he revived, and the doctor asking him how he felt remarked:

"I guess you are all right now; you were more scared than hurt."

The renowned crap-player from Maryland resented this slur on his pluck by retorting:

"D—d if I don't ride that horse yet," and getting on his feet he walked out and, Rancocas having been caught and brought to the paddock, the Spider remounted amid the cheers of the crowd He did not win, but did the next best thing, ran second. Anderson is a nervy boy. A year ago Juggler seized him by the leg and pulled him out of the saddle when he was up on Fides and shook him as a terrier would a rat. Anderson fainted with the pain, but remounted Fides and won the race.

That well known authority, J. G. Truman says. The hackney horse is, without contradiction, the oldest breed of coach horse in existence—tracing back, registered, to Shales (699), foaled in the year 1755. They originated as far back as 200 years, when the Norfolk trotting mares were crossed with Arabian and thoroughbred stallions. The Norfolk trotters have always been noted for their very high knee-action.

In the first volume of the hackney stud, I find Bellfounder (55) foaled in the year 1816, sired by Bellfounder (52), dam, Velocity. The horse was imported into the United States by James Booth, of Boston, July 11, 1822. When at six years old, he trotted nine miles in twenty-nine minutes and thirty-eight seconds, his owner challenging to perform 17½ miles in one hour, but was not accepted. Bellfounder (55), while under control of Col. Jacques, was leased by him to Mr. Timothy T. Kissam, of New York, he described him as follows:

Imported Bellfounder had a small head and ears; full prominent eyes, and wide apart; neck, medium length, set well up from the withers; shoulders deep and oblique; deep girth and full chested; fore legs wide apart; short back, round ribbed, and very broad on the loins; hips wide and well gathered in; full quarters to hocks, and short to fetlocks; limbs strong and well muscled, broad and flat below the knees and hocks; pasterns, rather short; concave hoofs and open heels; tail and mane full-haired; had a large star on forehead, with a diamond strip on end of nose or lip, one hind pastern white, and a little white on the opposite fore foot at the heel. Bellfounder's dam, Velocity, trotted in the year 1808, 28 miles in one hour and 47 minutes. I find that the dam of Rysdyk's Hambletonian (10) is sired by Bellfounder (55). The trotting horses of America to-day are noted not only for their speed but their power of endurance, which they certainly owe chiefly to the infusion of hackney blood through Bellfounder.

The Terre Haute Express says: It was a genial party that gathered in the smoking-room of the Terre Haute House last Saturday evening. The veteran Orrin Hickok, who brought out St. Julien, Arab and a host of other good ones; John Splan, the developer of Rarus, and who set Guy to going; Budd Doble, the taciturn but able horseman who brought out the mighty Dexter, the queen of all campaigners—Goldsmith Maid, and now part owner and trainer of Axtell; the "Kid Drivers," Dickerson and Patterson, pre-eminent among the young horsemen of the country; W. G. Pollock, one of Cleveland's wealthiest citizens and an admirer of horseflesh; Mr. W. P. Ijams and Mr. Frank McKeen. Talk turned upon the fast Cleveland track, and naturally shifted to the mighty deeds done over it. The story of the triumph of the trotting queen, Maud S, was told in Splan's inimitable style. How Bair gave her a warming up mile of 2:12½ and a repeat of 2:11½, how Splan said to the darky Swipe, "Get out the sulky for the runner and if Maud S beats her record I will give you half the stuff." "Smoke who had seen the two hard drives said, "Boss, I guess I won't take that offer, but will sell you my share for five bright dollars." The drive was made from the wire at a killing pace, and when the third quarter was passed, the mare swerved, Splan yelling to Bair, "See, she can never make it." Just then Bair made for the whip, and Splan thought the mare was done for. With a telling force the gad was used. She being too close to the fence to break, collected all her energies, shot forward, the runner hugging close, and the mile was done in 2:08¾, which has stood to the present day.

"I know of no animal," said Hickok reminiscently, "that is in many respects her equal. I used to think she was driven too hard, but I now believe she required all that work to bring her to an edge."

Doble was interrogated, "if in his opinion, the horses twenty years ago were as good as now." The answer was, "Yes; George M. Patchen and Dexter were the equal of any horses now living, when we take into consideration the crude tracks, appliances and the manner of blanketing, and drawing fine then in vogue. There were not so many of them, but the few good ones were as good as the best nowadays."

"You will have to except one," said Splan, "for I believe Axtell will come nearer touching Maud S's record than any horse that I have ever seen. I saw him at Cedar Rapids as a two-year-old, and I then wrote Mr. Bonner, whose interest in the colt was even then aroused, that he was as pure a gaited horse as I had ever seen I believe the day of the two-minute trotter is not so far off as a great many people think. When you get a horse with the pure gait of Axtell and the stamina of Maud S doing quarters in 28½ or 29 seconds, the 2:00 minute trotter will be due."

"How fast do you think Axtell was going under the wire Mr. Doble, when he made his record?"

"It was hard to judge with so smooth a going animal. I should have said at the time not better than a 2:30 gait, and he surely was not going faster than 2:25."

The bright and interesting talk kept on until well into the evening. Such a gathering of brainy men interested in the light harness horse is rare, and one takes no note of time while listening to their fund of experience.

THE KENNEL.

Dog owners are requested to send for publication the earliest possible notices of whelps, sales, names claimed, presentations and deaths, in their kennels, in all instances writing plainly names of sire and dam and of grandparents, colors, dates and breed.

Occidental Coursing Club.

The regular monthly meeting of the Occidental Coursing Club was held at 21 Kearny St., Tuesday evening, May 13th, Col. Gregory in the chair.

After transacting the usual club business the club made final arrangements for the coursing meeting to be held at Newark, on May 30, 1890.

The following gentlemen will officiate as officers of the day for the above meeting:

Field stewards—Col. S. O. Gregory, T. J. O'Keeffe, H. E. Deane.

Slip stewards—J. F. Carroll.

Flag steward—H. Boyd.

Judge—J. R. Dixon; slipper—Jas. Wren.

There will be two stakes, one for the All Aged and one for the puppy class. Entrance fee $5. Entries will close and the draw take place on Tuesday evening May 27th, at 21 Kearny St.

No greyhound can compete at any meeting of the club unless it is registered on the club's stud book.

The proprietor of Newark Coursing Park kindly offered the club all the game required to run off the meeting free of charge, and on motion a vote of thanks was tendered Mr. Shea for his generosity, but the club most respectfully declined to accept the game free of charge, preferring to pay for all hares used.

Charges were preferred against a member for recording his name in the Stud Book and running at the last meeting greyhounds not his own property, and he will be cited to appear at the next monthly meeting of the club and show cause why he should not be found guilty.

J. F. Carroll, Sec.

[In explanation to Secretary Carroll, to whom we are indebted for the excellent report, we may say that it reached the office too late for insertion under the "Kennel" head last week.—Ken. Ed.]

Old Black Joe.

Our readers will be interested in the excellent picture of that great pointer Old Black Joe, owned by Mr. Jas. E. Watson. Joe won the Derby and the all aged stake of his year in grand style, and was one of the best dogs ever whelped. He died soon after his return from the field trial, of distemper.

The picture is of the dog as he appeared when making his last point in the trial. It shows the nerviness of the dog but not his first rate form. But one of his puppies is alive, we believe and whether that is being trained we do not know.

More Pointers.

Editor Breeder and Sportsman:—In sending notice of the visit of my Pointer Patti Croxteth T. to Rush T. I desire if permissible to make a comment or two. Rush T. is the only dog I have ever used as sire with Patti. Patti's first litter of eight all proved to be good ones. Two of them will start in the all-aged stakes of the Pacific Coast Field Trial Club in January next and I confidently expect each of them to be placed. Only four of the litter have been exhibited at bench shows and the following wins are credited to them; Mr. R. K. Gardener's Tennis won second, and my Rab T. won third at the Pacific Kennel Club show in 1889. Mr. E. K. Benchley's Kan Koo, one of the litter when ten months old won first in the open class and a special for the best sporting dog or bitch under a year old at Los Angeles in 1889; also first in the open class for light weight Pointers and a special for the best Pointer dog in the show at Los Angeles a few weeks ago; a third of the litter my Queen Croxteth T. won first in heavy bitches and a special as one of the best breeding kennel on exhibition at Los Angelas recently. I claim the title champion under the American Kennel Club Rules for my Pointer bitch Champion Patti Croxteth T. winner of four first and ten special prizes. For my Irish Red Setter dog Champion Mike T. winner of five first and fourteen special prizes. For my Irish Red Setter bitch Champion Lady Elcho T. winner of five first and twenty six special prizes. The rules as adopted by the American Kennel Club December 19, 1889 to take effect on Feb. 1st 1890 say at article 17, rule 6. "The challenge class shall be for all dogs having won four first prizes in the open class. A dog having won three first prizes in this class shall have the privilege of the title of champion without further competition." It was indeed a pleasure to note at Los Angeles a few weeks ago that Pointers were coming into vogue. The general opinion of the sportsmen gathered at the dog show there was that the short haired nervy, thoroughbred looking, heat-enduring Pointer was the dog of all dogs for use in California and I think it is not untrue to say that San Francisco sportsmen agree with their southern brethren in the belief. Since Mr. Wm. Schreiber, Mr. Will Kittle, Mr. P. D. Linville, Mr. E. W. Briggs and others have actively taken up Pointer culture, the average quality of the breed on this coast has improved marvellously, until now dogs may be had here of as high type, fine quality and great excellence in field attributes as anywhere in the world. The pioneer work in Pointers done by Mr. G. W. Bassford will never be forgotten and if the Pointer men will only breed judiciously, train their dogs systematically and give them an opportunity to get to the front there seems to be no reasons why the Pointer should not be the special dog of the Pacific Slope.

A. B. Truman.

San Francisco, May 22, 1890.

Names Claimed.

Mr. A. B. Truman claims the following names for pointers by Point—Queen Croxteth T. whelped February 17th, 1890.

Don Croxteth for white and lemon dog.

Queen Point for white and lemon bitch.

Visits.

Mr. C. L. Brown's cocker spaniel bitch Bessie by Echo Cocker Kennels stud dog Kate (Carlo x Beauty) ex Jessie Jet ex Fanny to same kennels, blk stud dog Bronte A. K. C. S. B. 17564, May 18, 1890, Stockton, Cal.

Sale.

H. P. Burket has sold Rita E. A. K. C. S. B. 15679 blk cocker Spaniel bitch (Echo Cocker Kennels breeder) whelped March 22, 1889 by Capt. Stubbs ex Vivie 13193 to F. J. Viebrock, Feb. 25, 1890, Stockton.

The Pacific Coast Field Trial Derby closes on June 1st. Entries, with $5 forfeit for each should be sent before that date.

Mr. William Schreiber received by the last steamer from Japan, the skin of a cock pheasant of the "Copper" variety. He will have it nicely mounted.

Baron von Schroders pointer dog Point, loss of which was noted a few weeks since has been found and returned to his owner, who is now at his ranch near Templeton.

We have to acknowledge receipt of a delightful letter from Mr. Edward Dexter full of interesting notes about Mainspring, King of Kent, Rip Rap, and the other famous pointers of his kennel. Next week we may present a resume of his pointer notions.

The draw for the coming meeting of the Occidental Coursing Club will be made on the evening of Tuesday May 27th, at Mr. William Schreibers, 21 Kearney St., City. After the draw the club will be entertained at dinner by Secretary J. F. Carroll.

We are indebted to some careless proof reader for, the opportunity to again mention the recent benedictine indulgence of Mr. J. M. Kilgarif. In last weeks paper he was made to embark upon the sea of "Monterey" instead of "Matrimony". Upon any sea he is sure to sail serenely.

J. M. Bassford, Jr., was in town on Monday last to make his field trial entries and discuss the matter of judges for the next trials. He insists upon fair, unprejudiced men who will watch the work of both dogs in each heat, and who will decide in accord with honest convictions without temporizing.

Dan Gladstone by Gladstone—Sue is at the service of Californian English setter owners as advertised in another column. Every well bred English setter bitch that comes in use during his stay should be sent to him. The blood is invaluable and the fee is a very moderate one. The address of his owner. Mr. Geo. J. Harley, is 844 Harrison St., San Francisco.

Wonders will never cease. The latest freak is in a bitch owned by Mr. E. W. Briggs at 630 Market street, which was confined closely while in season and not bred. After the usual time she was allowed liberty, and it was then noticed that lactation was active. A tabby in the store chanced to have kittens about her and the dog drove away the cat, appropriated the kittens, and is now suckling them as contentedly as though the order of nature had not been reversed.

THE GUN.

The North Pacific Game and Fish Club.

Upon invitation of Mr. Alfred V. LaMotte, manager of the club, two days of last week were passed at the preserves near Ukiah, in company with Mr. LaMotte and Mr. Will Rix. Leaving the city at 7:40, by way of the San Francisco and North Pacific Railway, five hours are consumed most quickly riding through peerless Sonoma County, where everything now is luxuriant—fat orchards, fragrant vineyards, wide expanses of flower starred plain, emerald mountains, tumbling trout streams, and Mr. LaMotte's huge hamper full of glass ware and Hamburg pate combined to induce a beatific frame of mind and to prepare one for the excellent entertainment of mine host Hirsch of the Grand Hotel in Ukiah. Mr. Rix cracked three jokes and a half on the way up, while Mr. LaMotte killed over again the hundreds of deer, antelope, elk and bear which fell to his rifle in Sonoma and Lake Counties during pioneer days. Ukiah reached, a few hours passed in driving about through the country adjacent to the city, some lively chat with Col. Jerry Donohoe and his very courteous partner in business, Mr. Johnson, then a dreamless night and a 5 o'clock start for the preserve. Six miles behind a lively span in the crisp air of the morning through a canyon surpassingly beautiful, and the preserve of 8,000 acres was reached. After driving up through its center so that some general idea of the ground, the streams and the cover could be obtained, it appeared that a more perfectly adapted plot of ground for a game and fish preserve could not be imagined. The preserve is not unlike a huge amphitheater walled in by thickly covered chemise mountains, and traversed by Robinson Creek and its branches, as grand a trout brook as one could wish. Along the floor of the canyon are many little flats of two or three or four acres, upon which buckwheat and other suitable seeds will be planted to sustain the Bob Whites, Grouse, Pheasants and other game with which the preserve is soon to to be heavily stocked. The six miles of Robinson Creek, which also is to be stocked and replenished annually from the hatcheries now in course of construction, will afford the finest of fishing for a large number of rods. A comfortable, commodious and handsome club house is to be erected at once. Robinson Creek will be cleaned of the drift wood and low hanging branches which now make fishing in parts of it rather tasking sport. The stream runs winter and summer an ample head of water, is full of food, running throughout its whole extent under arching and overhanging limbs and foliage. Mr. LaMotte and Mr. Johnson, who accompanied the party, were quite sure that Robinson Creek trout would not take the fly, but in consonance with our practice for years a small fly and a gossamer leader were rigged, soaked and tossed into the first pool. Immediately a lusty half-pounder smashed at the fly as though he wanted it pretty badly, and thenceforth we found no trouble in raising fish with our little dark grouse hackle. By noon several pounds of nice brook fish were in the bag, a halt was called, a goodly frying pan produced, with sufficient store of sweet corned pork and a little bag of cracker dust, a handful of fire, and soon a fragrance went up out of that canyon more delectable by far than any odor to be sniffed about Delmonico's. Mr. LaMotte, Mr. Johnson and Mr. Rix did the eating, another person did the cooking, and it must be admitted that the cooking was superbly done, if the quanties of fish devoured by the non-active members was a guide. After luncheon an hour or two of rest, then four or five more hours of fishing, the result being fifty or sixty very handsome fish, and then a return to town and business. Mr. LaMotte's plan is to induce the joining of fifty men, the yearly fee to be $100, the Directors of the S. F. and N. P. Railway to retain control of the ground, to keep up the stand of game and fish and do the managing generally. The place is perfectly adapted to the uses suggested, and is besides a very beautiful site for a summer resting place—fine springs of sulphur and other mineral waters abound. When the list is open for signatures there will undoubtedly be many applicants, and a hint to those who might care to join, to see Mr. LaMotte soon might not be amiss.

Lincoln Gun Club.

The Lincoln Gun Club held its second monthly medal shoot at Alameda Point on Sunday last, beginning at 10 A. M. and lasting until late in the afternoon.

The club has two medals—the first class and second-class—and the conditions are twenty Blue rocks, eighteen yards rise for ten bores and sixteen for twelves, American Association rules to govern.

Sixteen members shot for the first-class medal, which was won by Parks with sixteen brakes, Potter being next with fourteen. Below are the scores:

First class—Holmes, 8; Cate, 13; Mellish, 9; Campbell, 13; Pretzell, 4; Potter, 14; Kearney, 13; Bruns, 10; Scovern, 13; Parks, 16; Ford, 13; Fisher, 9; Franzen, 12; White, 12; Maillot, 4; Allen, 9.

Second class—Venker, 12; Quinton, 8; Hollings, 8; Brown, 9.

A pool at six singles and six double birds, $1 entrance with twelve entries, was won by Bruns with a score of eight, H. Golden being second with seven.

Selby Live Bird Championship.

On Saturday last, at Oakland Trotting Park, the first contest for the Selby medal for live bird shooting, was brought off. It was expected that Mr. Crittenden Robinson, Mr. Ned Fay, Mr. Henry Bassford and many others, would enter, but only four contestants participated.

Shooting commenced at 10 o'clock, and though the hour was rather early for a full attendance of sportsmen, outside of those directly interested, the number of those present gradually increased as the day wore on.

The medal given is open for competition to all residents of the Pacific Coast, and is emblematic of the Coast championship. All matches are to be shot under the rules of the American Shooting Association, at forty single live birds. Each time a competitor wins the medal he will be set back one yard in the next match in which he may again compete for it.

The birds were average, with now and then a driver, and the shooting was very fine. Mr. C. B. Smith's score of 37 stamps him the peer of any local shot. He used an L. C. Smith gun, and killed his birds cleanly, as did Mr. Eddy. Both Mr. "Randall" and Mr. Haas were clear "off."

In the afternoon Capt. Brewer, the champion trap-shot of the world, paid his first visit to the gun grounds. "As yet," he said, in answer to inquiries, "nothing has been signed, sealed or delivered in the matter of matches here, but three or four are on the cards that are likely to prove somewhat exciting. Anyway, I mean to stay right here for a while yet in the hopes of making some matches."

After the medal match had been shot off, $5 pool-shooting was indulged in, C. J. Haas and "Randall" dividing the first, R. A. Eddy winning the second, with C. B. Smith next, C. J. Haas again winning the third.

Following is the official score of the medal match.

Name	Score	Total
C. J. Haas	1 2 2 1 2 2 2 2 1 1 2 2 1 0 1 1 1 2 0 1	
	2 0 1 0 2 1 1 0 1 2 1 0 1 0 1 1 2 1 2 2	33
C. B. Smith	2 2 2 1 2 0 2 2 0 2 1 1 2 2 1 2 1 1 1 2	
	2 1 1 2 1 1 2 1 2 1 1 2 1 1 2 0 2 1 1 2	37
"Randall"	2 1 1 2 0 1 1 1 1 0 2 1 2 0 1 1 2 1 0 1	
	1 2 0 0 2 1 2 2 1 1 0 2 1 0 2 1 1 1 1 1	32
R. A. Eddy	0 0 1 1 1 1 1 2 2 1 0 2 1 1 1 1 1 2 1 1	
	1 1 2 1 1 0 2 1 0 1 2 1 1 1 1 2 2 1 2 2	35

Notes.

The Blue Rock Club meets at Oakland Trotting Park this afternoon.

The California Wing Shooting Club meets to-morrow at Oakland Trotting Park, taking the 9 A. M. boat.

Henry Seebold, the hunter of San Diego, is now bagging curlew and the frisky cotton-tail rabbit; the latter species of game, he reports, now being found by thousands.

Mr. C. B. Smith, who won the Selby Live Bird Medal on Saturday last has been challenged for it by Mr. R. A. Eddy, and the match will be shot at Oakland Trotting Park on Saturday, June 7th. The shooting is open to all residents of California, and we hope may attract more entries than on Saturday last.

EDITOR BREEDER AND SPORTSMAN:—I hope before a great while to have the pleasure of again meeting you. I am now on my way to the Pacific Coast, and unless something happens, shall certainly be there. I am now with the American Arms Co. of Boston, and am introducing their new Hammerless Shot Gun and Safety Hammerless Revolver, which is meeting with good sales. We shall move our factory to Bluffton, Ala, in about three months. The company has been re-organized.

I saw Major Hammond, of Forest and Stream, yesterday, and hope to meet Mr. Ed Hough also in Chicago.

PHILADELPHIA, May 15, 1890. T. T. CARTWRIGHT.

The sixth annual tournament of the Sportsman's Association of the Northwest will be held in Portland, Oregon, June 12, 13 and 14. It will be conducted under the auspices of the Multnomah Rod and Gun Club, which has been reorganized with T. Muir President, and Buell Lamberson Secretary and Treasurer. Prizes aggregating $6,000 will be offered. There will be the usual medal for the best average. It was won two years ago by A. W. Eberly of Tacoma, and last year by Zeno Doty of Whatcom. Then there will be the Association gold badge valued at $250, and the Tacoma Globe diamond trophy to shoot for.

"It will be the biggest meeting of the association ever held," said Secretary Lamberson recently. "When we were in Tacoma last year we were treated well, and we told the South people that Portland was a great town, and when they come here in June we want to make our word good. San Francisco has promised to send a team and Helena and Butte are corresponding with us with that object in view."

One of the most distressing accidents that has happened in this community for a long time occurred in the hills north of Hot Springs, about eighteen miles from Ukiah, last Sunday evening says the Ukiah Dispatch Democrat. Wm. T. Hollingsworth and Pomery Field were spending the day hunting in the hills, and along the evening they wounded a deer, which ran into a thicket close by. In order to make surer of their game the two boys separated, and in a few minutes Hollingsworth shot at what he supposed was the deer, but which proved to be his companion. The deadly bullet struck Field in the back and went clear through his body, splintering the back bone and hip, and cutting in two the large intestines. Fields was still conscious when Hollingsworth reached him, and upon considering matters it was decided that the latter had better go to Hot Springs—five miles—to procure assistance. It was a terrible trip over the rough, broken country, and at midnight, when the rescuing party arrived at the scene of the tragedy, the poor victim was cold in death.

His body was brought to Ukiah on Monday, and a Coroner,s inquest was held by Dr. Bond, the verdict wholly exonerating Mr. Hollingsworth.

[Moralizing is worthless to the victim of such terrible misfortune, nor can it intensify the grief of the man who fired the fatal shot, but the item may serve to impress caution upon those who will soon go into the brush to shoot deer. It might be suggested that the persons mentioned were breaking the law in shooting deer in May, the season not opening until July 1st.—ED.]

ROD.

How High Will a Salmon Leap?

This is a question at present agitating the experts representing respectively a well known angling paper of Gotham and a fishing and shooting weekly of the "Hub." The latter representative quotes one of the New York Commissioners as saying, "I saw myself at Mechanicsville last summer a salmon that jumped vertically ten feet at least" The former rather inclines to the belief that six feet is the limit says The Week's Sport. Without doubt the swiftness of the current against which the fish is contending is a prime factor in the result. I have seen a large brown trout (s. fario) leap up from comparatively still water over a dam that measured eight feet, the fish being probably ten pounds; but though I have watched salmon trying a similar feat, I cannot state as a fact that so great a height was accomplished. Still, if a trout can do it, doubtless the "lordly" salmon can, also. There are many noted leaps of this fish on record in the works of the European fishermen. "Ephemera" (Mr. Fitzgibbon, long the angling editor of Bell's Life in London), says, in his splendid book on the salmon: "I have seen a grilse, and not a very large one, jump upwards and forwards, somewhat obliquely, the length—I and another calculated—of my fishing rod, that is, seventeen feet." Mr. Young (Inspector of Salmon Fisheries, Scotland), also told Fitzgibbon that before "a portion of the mass of rock in the course of the large skin waterfall was blasted, its first ledge was 16 feet from the surface of the water when the river was at its average height, and salmon could spring into the water on the ledge at a bound, and then, stemming the arch-formed cataract, they would ascend to the upper pools." These are the exact words of an unimpeachable authority, and as such should be conclusive. A certain Dr. Fleming, who gave evidence before a committee of the House of Commons, I am not so sure about. He stated that he had seen a salmon spring over a fall of 30 feet. To which one may retort, *credat judaeus apella*.

Some other curious stories of this leaping power of the salmon are to be found in angling literature, and each one appears to be so authoritative in the light of both internal and external evidence that one may fairly ask if he is warranted in rejecting them. One jotted down from the British Naturalist is to the effect that the Frasers of Lovat—real blue blood of "bonnie" Scotland—were wont to astonish their guests with the voluntary cooking of a salmon, self-caught, self-cooked. A kettle of water was set over a fire at the side of a fall selected, and the company waited until the leaping salmon fell into the cauldron and was thus boiled in their presence. Mr. Cholmondeley Pennell also speaks of a salmon leaping over the heads of two young ladies who were seeking to prevent its escape from a *cul de sac* in the river. It fell on dry ground, and was duly carried home in triumph. By the way, in Brown Goode's "American Fishes," there is a reproduction of an instantaneous photograph of a salmon leaping up a cataract. It appears in mid-air, and is particularly well defined.

How does the salmon leap? This is what Ansonius, the fourth century poet of the Moselle, says, being interpreted:

Nor will I pass the glittering salmon by,
With crimson flesh within of sparkling dye.

A hidden impulse first disturbs the stream
That silent flows; then upward darts the gleam
At middle water; and the bounding fish
Strikes with his quivering tail, in earnest wish
To dart aloft.

The salmon certainly strikes the water beneath the surface with its tail, and so far our poet is an accurate observer. It has since his time been gravely asserted that it takes its tail in its mouth, and bounds like a piece of whalebone bent in a similar fashion; but this is a view not at all justifiable. The following is probable, "and, as far as observation goes, the true *modus operandi:* In making its spring it first sinks rapidly by an upward action of the fins, and then, suddenly reversing their action, and finding a *point d'appui* in the volume of water under it, and bringing the saltant power of its muscles into requisition, it bounds beyond the water's surface in an obliquely vertical direction. The greatest power is furnished by its propeller, the caudal fin of tail."

American Fisheries Society.

The nineteenth annual meeting of the American Fisheries Society opened at Put-in-Bay, Ohio, on May 14th. The society is the largest and most important of its kind in the world, and consists of scientific gentlemen interested in ichthyology and members of various State fish and game commissions. The society was this year entertained by the Ohio commission, and the gathering was called for Put-in Bay, the location of the largest fresh-water hatchery in the world.

The meeting was called to order by President Eugene G. Blackford. The following members were present: New York, Eugene Blackford, Fred Mather, E. P. Doyle; Minnesota, Robert Ormsby Sweeney; Georgia, Dr. H. H. Cary; Pennsylvania, Henry C. C. Ford, W. L. Powell, James Vernon Long; Michigan, Hoyt Post, Hancell Whitaker, L. T. Spencer, J. K. Webster; Wisconsin, James Nevin; Ohio, John H. Low, Dr. J. A. Fenshall, C. N. Osborn, Emery D. Potter; Nebraska, W. L. May. President Blackford delivered the opening address, recalling the society's history and directing attention to the bill introduced in Congress placing the United States Fish Commissioner under the control of the Department of Agriculture. Mr. Blackford strongly argued against the proposition to hand the commission over to the politicians and advised taking some action. The great work of the New York Commission was then explained. "Reports from the regions of streams," said Mr. Blackford, "indicate that, wherever we have placed our fry, trout are unprecedentedly numerous. The success of our shad in the Hudson River alone recompenses the State for its fishery outlay." The stocking of salmon in rivers wherein it had never existed was mentioned as a positive success. The support given the commission by the courts in vigorously prosecuting violators of the law was given as another encouraging indication.

Treasurer Henry C. Ford of Philadelphia, submitted the society's financial statement. A communication from Superintendent F. N. Clark of the Michigan station of the United States Fish Commission was read, in which he referred to fish culture as being in its infancy. The question of hatching eggs, he said, is thoroughly understood, but that of distributing fish at the proper time and in proper places is one of very great importance. I am thoroughly convinced of the practicability of rearing fish to be planted in new waters. Mr. Clark stated that 5,000,000 trout will be distributed the coming winter in the streams of the Northwest

Mr. Whitaker of Michigan moved that a committee of three be appointed to draw up resolutions expressing the sentiment of the society on the proposition to incorporate the Fish Commission with the Bureau of Agriculture. The motion was carried and the committee was announced as follows: Mr. Whitaker, Mr. Osborne of Ohio, and Mr. Powell of Pennsylvania. On motion of Dr. Sweeney of Minnesota, it was decided to hold the next meeting in Washington, D. C. The hearing of papers from members of the society was then begun. They were as follows:

First—"Past and Present Aspect of Fish Culture, with an Inquiry as to What May be Done Further to Promote and Develop the Science," by John F. Gay and William P. Seat of the United States Fish Commission.

Second—"A History of American Fisheries Societies and an Index," by Fred Mather, Superintendent Cold Spring Hatchery, New York.

Third—"The Sturgeon, and Experiments in its Hatching," by Hoyt Post of Michigan.

Fourth—"The Ciscoette," by R. O'Sweeney of Minnesota.

Fifth—"Experiment in Impregnation of Pike Perch Eggs," by Herschel Whitaker.

Sixth—"Remarks on Fish Eggs," by Fred Mather of Michigan.

Seventh—"Origin of Artificial Hatching of Fish in the United States," by Judge E. D. Potter of Ohio.

Eighth—"Measurements of Fish Eggs," by Fred Mather.

Ninth—"Fish Protection," by Dr. J. A. Henshall of Ohio.

Tenth—"The Grayling," by J. H. Bissell of Michigan.

Eleventh—"The Growth of Trout," by S. A. Heinman.

Twelfth—"Michigan White Fish Hatcheries," by S. A. Bissell.

At the evening session a tariff debate was precipitated by Commissioner Osborne of Ohio, who introduced a memorial to Congress asking that a tariff on Canadian fish be exacted during the season when fishing is prohibited in the States. Secretary Doyle of New York and Judge Potter of Ohio spoke strongly against such a policy. During the debate the fact developed that nine-tenths of the society are free traders. Mr. Osborne finally withdrew his resolution.

Boat-Outfit for Bay Fishing.

So many hundreds of our readers go weekly during the season to points about San Francisco and other bays to fish, that these suggestions from an old-time bay-angler may not come amiss:

It may safely be said that a fifteen to sixteen-foot boat built like a skiff, and capable if necessary of holding two men, is best for all practical uses in the bays, rivers and estuaries hereabouts. If one be wise there is seldom or never any necessity for very hard or long pulling in such boats. The trip can generally be timed so that advantage of the tide or wind, or both, can be taken from and to the club house or fishing station. Just a hint or two as to the appliances necessary in a boat of this size and character: The plainer the furniture of such a boat, the better; a mushroom anchor, not too heavy, with a light cotton line braided or plaited of seventy-five to eighty feet in length, is sufficient for the bow of the said boat, and, if it be necessary to anchor midway in a stream or channel, which is a bad thing to do if it can be avoided, as the boat in that case will catch all the drift or seaweed that may be going with the tide, then a light line of twenty-five or thirty feet in length attached to a smaller mushroom anchor is generally sufficient to keep the boat stationary, or nearly so, either as against the tide or wind. If a boat of this description, even if it be shorter than fifteen feet, is rowed and managed by one man, the best plan is to have the bearing or weight in the boat on the third of the boat astern. It will be always found in pulling a boat of skiff shape that it will pull much easier and can be managed very much better if its bow or nose is a trifle out of the water instead of being on an even keel.

It will be found very convenient in the stern of the boat to have a locker that can be kept dry in case any water should get in the boat, and to accomplish this it will be necessary to hang a shelf underneath where the top of the locker is, and by that means provisions and everything else can be kept dry as long as one does not have to put them down on the bottom of the boat. The best plan to keep fishing tackle and all the appliances used during a trip where angling is intended, dry, and to preserve them from the sea water and the dampness of the atmosphere, is to have a little drawer under the seat on which the oarsman sits, which he can pull out without moving, and in which he can have little compartments to keep his hooks, sinkers, floats, reels, and everything else he wants.

A man to fish neatly should also take with him a small gaff hook—it need not be expensive—and also a sharp case knife, not too long in the blade, and he will find also that if he has the gaff hook handle made heavier than they generally are made in the stores—in fact, as thick as a policeman's club is for six inches of the extreme part of the handle end of the gaff hook—it will be a most successful instrument with which to kill dogfish, sharks or any other fish that he does not want to retain. In fact, it should be known that the best plan is to kill fish as soon as they are caught, even if it be in the hottest weather—that is, provided of course that the fish can be brought ashore before they spoil, otherwise it may be necessary to pack them alive into a basket, covered with damp seaweed, and in this way they may be preserved longer perhaps than if killed on the spot as soon as they are caught, but if one wants to retain the flavor of a delicate fish like the weakfish it should be caught, killed at once and eaten within half an hour of the time that it has been taken out of the water.

All professional fishermen carry a club for thumping obstreperous fish. Usually the club is made of the end of an oar. There is no better tool for the purpose. Rubber coat, overcoat and lunch should be kept in a dry locker. A cup should not be forgotten, though it is possible to drink out of the old stone jug in an emergency. A pair of easy old shoes are the correct things to wear in a boat, and a fore-and-aft steamer cap is quite as essential to carry as a broadbrim straw. Keep your boat clear of hamper and lay your line Bristol fashion when you haul it in, so that it will not kink when you pay it out. Never spit in the boat; spit overboard.

Iowa has just passed a new fish law, of which the following is a synopsis:

It is unlawful to take any fish from the waters of this State at any time except with hook and line, with one exception. Suckers and buffalo can be speared between the 1st day of November and the 1st day of March following.

Catching trout is prohibited between the 1st of November and the 1st day of April following, and bass from November 1st to May 15th following. Minnows may be taken for bait with a net, provided all young bass, pike, croppies, trout and salmon are at once returned to the waters from whence taken.

Shooting fish or using medicated bait, or using any other means to stupefy the fish, is absolutely prohibited.

All obstruction of rivers to prevent the free passage of the fish up or down is prohibited, even to the placing of a trot line.

Fishing in streams that have been stocked with trout within one year prior thereto, is prohibited, provided notice of such stocking is posted, by authority of the State Fish Commissioner, wherever a public highway crosses such streams.

The person filing information where the law is violated is entitled to a fee of from $5 to $10, which shall be taxed as a part of the costs.

A person convicted of violation of this law shall be fined not less than $10, nor more than $100, and stand committed to jail until the fine is paid.

This law does not apply to the Mississippi or Missouri rivers.

Under the old law, the trout season was February 1st to November 1st, and for bass June 1st to April 1st.

A new sounding machine is about to make its appearance which has for its object not only the taking of a single sounding, but in thick weather and in uncertain positions the sinker can be let to a safety limit, according to locality, and thus become a continuous sounder, so that the vessel cannot get into a shoal water without a warning being instantly given, says a contemporary. The sinker is practically a kite inverted; it is made of wood loaded with metal, and is so constructed that variations of speed do not effect the vertical depths at which it tows. While the vessel is going at any rate of speed this sinker can be let down to a known depth, and will tow at that depth until the bottom shallows to such limit of safety, when the sinker, upon striking the bottom, frees itself and rises to the surface, simultaneously giving a warning on board the vessel. The dial plate of the counter on deck is graduated to register the vertical soundings attained by the sinker concurrently as the line is paid out; consequently the sounding is known instantly on board without waiting for the sinker to be hauled in, thereby allowing sufficient time to change the course and avoid dangers.

THE FARM.

Hardiness.

The majority of those who write on poultry for agricultural papers recommend the large breeds to farmers. In one sense they are right, because the large breeds are more robust and can stand the rough usage of the barn-yard much better than small birds. Again, it is claimed in their favor that they weigh much heavier, and that one breed can be kept and bred to uniformity, while with the small breed it necessitates other hens to do the hatching. These advantages are worth thoughtful consideration; and yet there are many cases where a small breed, such as Leghorns, would pay more.

Heretofore the Dorking, Leghorn and Houdan have borne the reputation of being too delicate for farm life, in comparison with Asiatic and American classes. Recently Dorking breeders assert that this fowl will compare favorably with any foreign breed, and the Leghorns, as all know, have been tested on farms and village lots in cold and warm climates, and their hardiness and vigor established beyond doubt: and nothing in the line of delicacy can be brought against them except that their combs and wattles will readily freeze if exposed to cold weather and out-of door foraging in winter, which is usually the case on farms.

The large combs and appendages of the Mediterranean breeds are not adapted to our frigid climate if exposed to winter's frost. Neither are the combs of Cochins, Langshans, Javas or Plymouth Rocks. The much-vaunted hardiness claimed for the common fowls is all fudge. They were forced through neglect and indifference to stand all storms and exposure. The dung-hill served them for a standing and scratching place in the midst of winter, and the fence, plow handle, wagon box, or old cheery tree over the woodpile for a roosting place. What was the result? Their combs and wattles fell off with mild weather, their toes were frozen, and the sufferings which they endured put them back so that they did not begin to lay before Easter, and many families in autumn packed eggs for that special occasion, as they were not accustomed to get eggs before grass and vegetation had fairly started. We remember those days well and the sorrowful looking pictures of those dunghills. We kept common fowls many years and know all about their hardiness; we know that frost will not exempt the common fowl any more than the improved fowl. But raise that breed from chickenhood to all kinds of weather and exposure, and it will be as hardy as any dunghill in a few generations.

At Toronto, where the writer was raised, the boys made fun of the colored fowls which had just arrived from the South. When their first winter in Canada begun, they could not bear the cold at first, but after some years they appeared to enjoy the winter as well as the native. It is the same with our thoroughbred fowls; they are accustomed to comfortable quarters and good care, and if they are exposed on the farm to frost and snow they will show greater delicacy in the beginning than do the common fowls, and this has given rise to the belief among some farmers that the improved breeds are not so hardy and robust as the old fashioned common fowls.—JOSEPH WALLACE, in Stockman and Farmer.

Berkshire Pigs the Best in the World.

How many times I have heard visitors at my farm remark, when looking over the swine, "I don't like those nasty black pigs," and at the exhibition shows the same remark is often heard. Probably these people forget for the moment that color is only skin deep, or rather in this case, it is only a light coat of bristles deep. They undoubtedly never had any experience in keeping Berkshires, for if they had, such thoughts would lose themselves, in the many attractive qualities they would discover in this breed of swine.

In the first place, the Berkshire is one of the oldest breeds in existence. Having been bred so many years, every characteristic feature about them has become thoroughly established, and any one who is breeding the pure stock is as sure of every point showing itself in every litter that is farrowed, as he is that he exists. The Berkshires breed true every time, and a spot or "off" pig is as rare as green peas at Christmas. One of their strongest features is a disposition to grow from the start, and to take on flesh and fat. Another very important point in any breed of animals is possessed to a marked degree by the Berkshires, and that is a decided power or constitution to resist diseases of all kinds When properly fed and cared for, they are seldom if ever sick, or off their feed, and while breeders of other varieties around me are in constant trouble with a sick sow, or weak or ailing litter of pigs, my herd of Berkshires go right along in perfect health, producing big, strong, vigorous litters of pigs, all of which grow and thrive.

The pure bred Berkshires make the best mothers, are very gentle with their young, and have an abundance of milk, which continues to flow for a long period when desired. Having been bred in all climates for so many years, they withstand the heat of summers and cold of our long winters, and are but little affected by either. From this fact fall litters from the Berkshires grow and thrive, while other breeds become stunted and weak from the cold of approaching winter. This feature alone places them far ahead of all other breeds. This fact should overcome any prejudice one has against their color, for all breeders want and expect two litters of pigs a year from their sows, one of which from necessity must farrow in cold weather, and to have the latter grow and thrive is absolutely essential to success. This the Berkshire will do.

Another thing that all careful breeders and farmers try to do is to produce the largest and best animals, the most meat, for the least amount of money expended for feed, and right here is where the Berkshire pig excels all other kinds in the world. I have bred all of the leading kinds of swine, and made many careful experiments in feeding the same and noting results, and my experience teaches me that whether I am after fat, pork or meat in a herd of pigs or hogs, I can obtain the same with a herd of Berkshires at three-quarters the expense, or less, for feed, and half the expense for care and trouble over any other breed of hogs, and I will not have to fight disease or sickness in producing the same, and I see no more objection in the black color in swine, than in any other animal or fowl. That is why I like the Berkshire pig.—G. L. Dow, in the Poultry.

Live Sheep Shipments.

From the Argentine Republic to Great Britain.

The fact that over 300 live sheep from Buenos Ayres have been landed at Liverpool, and have been sold at double the price of frozen mutton from the same quarter, is of great importance both to the owners and the consumers of mutton in this country; for in the course of the last year or two there have been pretty clear indications that the supply of sheep in this country is not equal to the demand, and that the import of dead mutton could not make up the want of live sheep. And the Argentine Confederation can give us practically unlimited supplies of sheep if they could be brought here alive. It takes rank next to New Zealand in the weight of frozen mutton which it sends to us. In 1887 we imported from the Argentine Confederation 251,273 cwts. of fresh mutton, and in 1888, the last year for which we have complete returns, we received 345,392 cwts. of mutton. Now that a few of the many millions of live sheep there have found their way to us, and have sold well, we may be certain there are more to follow.—Mark Lane Express (London).

The Suffolk Sheep.

The Suffolk sheep, as its name implies, had its origin in Suffolk. The foundation of the breed was laid about one hundred years ago by a cross between the original Norfolk horned ewe and improved Southdown rams. The Norfolk sheep (now extinct) were noted for their activity, longevity, prolific breeding and success as nurses; the Southdown for its good type and early maturity. The amalgamation of the form and fattening properties of the Southdown with the hardy, prolific and highly-bred Norfolk resulted in the production of a valuable type of animal, combining the best qualities of its progenitors and now recognized as the Suffolk sheep. The breed has been cultivated with great care. Some of the existing flocks date back to 1810. The Suffolk Sheep Society was established in the spring of 1886 for the promotion of the purity of the breed; at the present date about ninety registered flocks are established in Suffolk, Norfolk, Essex, Cambridgeshire and Bedfordshire. Flock prizes are competed for yearly for the best and most uniform flocks of ewes, rams and ewe lambs, the property of one owner.

The Suffolk sheep may be described as about thirty per cent. larger than the Southdown, with black, glossy face, hornless, and clean black legs, long back, with well developed legs and loins; wool of fine texture, thick and of moderate length. In the report of the judges of wool exhibited at Windsor, 1889. R. A. S. Journal, Vol. 25, page 2, it states: "Class 18, Suffolk. It is a pity there were not more entries in this class, which is likely to take an important place in the wool trade of the future. The breed is noted for its fecundity; thirty to thirty-five lambs for every twenty ewes being a frequent average. The ewes are excellent nurses, and live longer than other breeds. Ewes frequently remain in the breeding flock until they are ten and eleven years of age. They are extremely hardy. Their comparative freedom from foot-rot enables them to travel over large tracts of heath land, where they have to roam for their food, but they thrive equally in the enclosed and more productive country where they are confined in hurdles. The mutton is of the finest quality and commands a ready sale. It is of high value, consequent on its venison like flavor and the small percentage of fat, compared with some of the other heavy breeds. They mature early, if well grazed and fed, and are fit for the butcher at ten or twelve months old. In competition with other breeds they have on several occasions been awarded by the first prize at the meeting of the Royal Agricultural Society. In the Report on the Exhibition of Live Stock, at Newcastle (R. A. S. Journal, Vol. 23, page 12), Mr. J. Macdonald states: "The Suffolk breed makes an important addition to the recognized English breeds of sheep. They possess properties which are sure to gain a good name." Suffolk ewes and rams have been exported to Austria, France, Germany, Russia, North and South America, and the English Colonies.—Cor. Am. Agriculturalist.

A Small Flock of Southdowns.

It is a good idea, that should be fostered, to have sheep on every farm, even though the number must from necessity be limited. A few animals of the best breed will be found valuable and profitable, and no breed can be more highly recommended for this purpose than the celebrated Southdowns. American breeders, as a rule, do not go to England for their system of keeping their flocks, and so we find a system of breeding and feeding that is peculiarly American. From the nature of our country and business methods, especial interest is laid upon early maturity, while in England the breeding and feeding are conducted with a view to producing the heaviest and ripest carcass possible. The question of two or three years extra feeding is an important one here, and it may rob the farmer of all his profits. The best success has been obtained when the sheep have been reared with the idea in view of producing first class mutton at two years old or less.

In a general way, it is more expensive to keep a small flock than a large one, other things being equal. Better care, as a rule, is given to the small flocks, because the farmer can look after each individual sheep; but the profits per head are likewise proportionately different. The number that did or do not properly develop, owing to crowding and other causes, in a large flock is not always included in the profits and loss of a large sheep ranch. The whole flock could have been reduced to the number of those which died or failed to improve any during the year, and the profits would have been as large. The food and care given to the unprofitable bones were sheer loss. As the flocks are reduced in size the number of poor sheep is also reduced, until the lowest minimum possible is reached. This is reached on the small farm, where only a limited number of sheep are kept. Few, if any, need die here from cold, lack of food or shelter, and none need fail to increase in weight and quality through lack of attention. The Southdowns show very markedly the effects of good or bad treatment, and for this reason also they are especially good for small farms, where each individual member of the flock can be looked after to a reasonable extent.—J. D. MORROW, in American Cultivator.

The Shorthorn Sales of 1889.

With the sale of the famous Glanatore herd, the sales of Shorthorns for the year were brought to a close, and we, therefore, give a table showing the details of the various public auctions at which the red, white and roan have been offered. On the whole, the year has been a fairly good one, where really well-bred stock has been offered, though for ordinary animals, prices have ruled—as for so many years past—low. As compared with previous years, the average price for the year is as follows:

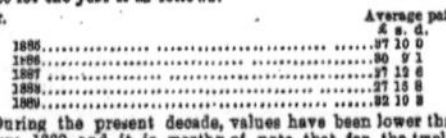

Year.	Average paid. £ s. d.
1885	37 10 0
1886	30 9 1
1887	27 12 6
1888	27 15 8
1889	32 10 8

During the present decade, values have been lower than before 1880, and it is worthy of note that, for the twelve years preceding 1879, the average at the whole of the sales was no less than $54 7s. 7½d. It is exceedingly satisfactory to note that, although values have not reached this average, they are better this year than in any since 1885.

So far as numbers are concerned, it will be seen that at forty-three sales, 2,323 head have been sold for a total of £76,570 14s. 6d. Last year 1,596 head were sold for a total of £44,013 13s. 6d. at thirty-nine sales, and in 1887 there were thirty seven sales, of which 1,353 head were disposed of. It will thus be seen that there is a great increase in the numbers sold, as well as a very satisfactory rise in the average price.—Mark Lane Express.

Angora Goats.

Will They Prove More Profitable Than Sheep?

Statements have been received from all the leading American manufacturers of mohair goods. From these it seems clear that the use of mohair is increasing rapidly; in fact, the demand for mohair dress goods was never better than at present. All the manufacturers seem to agree that the American-grown fleeces are, as a rule, inferior to those brought from Asia Minor or Africa. Whether the Angora goat can reach its highest perfection in our climate is as yet an unsolved problem. Of course, these manufacturers know nothing about breeding the goats; they merely know what they want in their manufacturing. It would seem, then, that a farmer may safely depend upon selling all the mohair he can produce at a price somewhat above that obtained for wool. It is by no means certain that the best quality of mohair can be grown here. The grades that can be grown here are, however, worth as much as the best wool, and in regions where sheep-killing dogs abound, the goats will undoubtedly prove most valuable.—Rural New Yorker.

Food for Hens.

Keeping food before the hens all the time is both wasteful and unprofitable. It is wasteful for the reason that as long as the hens have a plentiful supply before them all the time they will give themselves but little trouble to look for food elsewhere, which is detrimental in not inducing to exercise. It is extravagant, because the hens will not only eat more than they require for healthy digestion, but will scratch and waste a large portion. These objections are small matters, however, compared with the injury occasioned by over feeding, which causes hens to become excessively fat, when they will lay but few eggs, some of which will have no shells, while others will be double-yolked. Instead of keeping food before them constantly, the hens should only be fed when they are hungry, and even then they should be made to hunt and search for what they receive. We do not recommend stinting them of their food, but it should never be placed where they can eat their fill and mope around. Active exercise conduces to prolificacy. The best layers are those that are constantly doing something. The hen that takes matters easy and seldom stirs about will be an excellent subject for the table, but her productive organs will be too much clogged with fat to allow her to lay her quota of eggs.—N. E. Fancier.

Moore's Advice to Beginners.

The following "Suggestions to Purchasers" from the catalogue of Mr. M. E. Moore, Cameron, Mo., are reproduced as being well worthy of study. As an illustration of *multum in parvo* it is excellent:

It is my ambition to breed, to import, and to sell superior cattle only. A disappointment to any one of my patrons would be a greater disappointment to me. I therefore make the following suggestions in reference to selection and management:

1st. Every man who desires to purchase cattle of this breed should post himself upon their history and characteristics.

2nd. Study some standard work upon the principles of selection of milch cows without reference to any particular breed.

3rd. In selecting a herd endeavor to secure general uniformity in size, build, and color. Such uniformity is very pleasing to the eye, besides it gives special character to the herd.

4th. As regards color, the evenly varigated and the black predominating are generally preferred In Europe the lighter colors are thought to be less hardy.

5th. Avoid animals with heads unsymmetrical in form ("mullet heads") or with coarse Roman noses. Such are generally of questionable breeding.

6th. Avoid animals with harsh hair and unmellow skins; such qualities indicate a lack of thrift.

7th. Avoid animals with extremely sloping rumps. There are many objections to this form besides the lack of symmetry.

8th. In breeding do not couple animals together that largely show a similar deficiency in form of character. Those that do not show such deficiency may be inbred for a few generations to establish the especial character of the herd, but always with much watchfulness of results.

9th. Keep breeding animals in good condition. Avoid extremes of leanness or fleshiness, as both these conditions tend to produce degeneracy in the offspring.

10th. Train young cows to large yields and long periods of milking. In order to get the best results in growth, in milk production, and in the developement of offspring, heifers that drop their first calves at two years of age should not be required to bear a second calf in less than 18 months from the first.—Holstein Friesian Register.

Grim's Gossip.

Hanford is particularly blest in the possession of four half mile tracks, all of them owned on private places.

The New York Jockey Club are about to honor E. J. Baldwin by calling one of their fixed events the Santa Anita Stake.

A telegram of Rancho Del Paso notifies me that the great sale of yearlings will take place in New York on June 16th and not on June 30th as heretofore advertised.

What a shaking up of old bones there will be when the circuit opens, for there are so many sure things bottled up for use that a general explosion is likely to occur.

From all who visit J. H. White's place at Lakesville, comes the same story, "Sih has the best lookers in the State." The story is true, and Mr. White should have a lot of trotters this year.

Do not forget to make entries in the stakes of the Contra Costa County Agricultural Association if you have anything that is good for the purses offered. The entries close on June 1st.

Oaknut, the Dawn stallion owned by Mr. Overhelser, trotted a mile during the past week on the Petaluma Track, in 2:28½, which should warrant the belief that 2:20 will be about his mark before the season ends.

In the list of declarations to the Great Eclipse Stake, New York Jockey Club, on May 1st, the name of Sextus was unintentionally omitted. This leaves one hundred and eleven eligible, instead of one hundred and twelve, as stated.

The San Jose Associatian are offering very liberal purses to the horsemen of the State, and those who intend to compete for the large money prizes should not forget the Garden City in making up their circuit. Entries close June 1st.

On Tuesday, June 3rd, Terre Haute will have a great field day, and many of the noted trotters and pacers now congregated there, will be exhibited. Sunol 2:10½, Axtell 2:12, and Palo Alto 2:12¾ are among those advertised to be shown.

From present indications J. H. Shults Esq. will have a small string on the "Big" circuit, among which will be Gold Leaf 2:11½, Arrow 2:13¾ and Thistle the pacer that was purchased at the late sale in New York of the Salisbury horses.

Zoraya, by Guy Wilkes, dam Neluska, by Sultan, the $13,500 purchase of Messrs. Stoner & Clay, is now enjoying the luxuriant bluegrass at Marchmont. Her colt by the great Stamboul is doing nicely. She will be bred to Anteeo 2:16¼.

It does not seem so very long ago that people were impressed with the idea that Director was not a sure foal getter. Last year he got 72 per cent. of his mares with foal, and this year, from the reports already received at Pleasanton, even a larger percentage can be shown.

The old timer Tom Smith of Vallejo has secured a fine lot of mares this year for his stallions, George Washington 11,623 and Mambrino Chief Jr., 11,622, and Tom is about to get the first named ready for track work as his present mark of 2:30 is no measure of his speed.

Wilfred Page reports that Tom Murphy has "caught on" at Petaluma, and already has a fair sized stable under his care. Tom was so long with O. A. Hickok that he should be up to all the tricks of the trade, and will undoubtedly give satisfaction to those who employ him.

Mr. S. S. Howland's horse Ontario, which raised a sensation last year by his wonderful jumping, has surpassed his former efforts by clearing seven feet. This is far in advance of any other authenticated jump, although there is a tradition that seven feet six inches has been cleared in Ireland.

Mr. T. B. Cooper of Adin, Modoc County, advertises that he wishes to sell the sire of Almont Patchen 2:15. In a note accompanying the "ad." Mr. Cooper says that he is willing to dispose of the stallion at an extremely liberal figure, so this is a rare opportunity for some one to secure a first class horse at a low price.

"Good goods" always find a ready market, as Mr. Benton found out when he sent his pacer by Mambrino Wilkes, dam by Chieftain, to Oakland week before last, for the horse was no sooner given his preliminary exercise than Mr. W. Coleman asked for a price on him, and a few days ago the fast pacer changed ownership, the consideration being $1000.

Mr. M. T. Grattan writes me that Jessie, by Bates Emperor, was foaled in 1860, and is therefore thirty years old. She was bred to Herod April 26, 1889, and at no other time during the year. No other stallion had access to her. On the third day of May, 1890, she gave birth to a black pacing colt, the image of its sire, a strong, active, healthy colt.

Mr. A. Hecox, formerly of Gilroy, has taken charge of Capt. Harris' string of trotters for the coming campaign in California. Capt. Harris is to be congratulated upon the acquisition of so good an artist, and Mr. Hecox may be proud of his charge, as among the youngsters he has the promising two-year old filly by Dawn—Lena Bowles, and Acorn, the half brother of the lamented Lorena.

Mr. George Theuerkauf, of Gonzalez, has placed in the hands of Peter Woods for training, the chestnut gelding Lee, five years old by General Lee, dam by General Taylor. Lee has a record of 2:31½ made at the Salinas Fair last fall, he winning the fourth, fifth and sixth heats in the 2:35 class. Mr. Theuerkauf's trotter is a good one and the chances are favorable that he will make a low mark in the 2:30 class this year.

Some exceedingly bright young pirate connected with one of the Press Associations has seen fit to telegraph all over the United States, a list of the horses that Captain Tom Merry purchased in Australia. It is needless to say that he did not give the BREEDER AND SPORTSMAN credit, notwithstanding this was the only paper to receive the news, from our regular Australian correspondent.

Senator George Hearst has at last purchased the Valentine Ranch at Pleasanton, the land was deeded to the new owner by Charles C. McIver, who acquired the property from W. D. and Mary Valentine. The Senator being in the East, it is impossible to find out to what use the farm will be put, but it is presumable, that it will be fitted up as a first class stock farm. With the many fine brood mares now owned by Senator Hearst, the Valentine place should prove a first class establishment, for the raising of thoroughbreds and trotters.

Last week, B. C. Holly, of Vallejo, paid a flying visit to Santa Rosa and took a look at the good stock in that neighborhood. While there he purchased from Mr. Frazier, of that city, a yearling bay filly by Anteeo 7868, dam by Whippleton 1883, 2nd dam by Sam Purdy 918, third dam by Rifleman, fourth dam Lady Crum, the dam of Alexander 400. I have not heard the price that was given for this young miss, but it must have been a long one, bred as she is.

Dr. J. P. H. Dunn, of Oakland, has sold the broodmare Madonna, bred by Gen. W. T. Withers, Kentucky, sired by Cassius M. Clay Jr. 22, dam by Joe Downing 710, with fine large colt by her side by Noonday, to Mrs. Silas Skinner, of Jordan Valley, Oregon; price $2,500. Madonna is the dam of Alcona Jr., 2:41, sire of Silas Skinner, trial 2:23½. She is also the dam of Del Rey, 2:31, and others. Madonna is one of the coming broodmares, and is a serious loss to California.

The directors of the Napa track have secured the services of John True, and he will in future have sole management of their track. Already the new superintendent has set to work, and the noted course is daily the scenes of fast brushes, as the different trainers send their charges down the home stretch. There is some talk of having the grand stand moved back about forty feet, which will be of great convenience to the spectators, for as at present situated it is too close to the stretch. Many other improvements will be made.

Margaret S. 2:19½, was never in better fettle than she is at present, and her work shows that she is faster than ever. Andy McDowell has received a telegram; so I am informed, that he will have to get the mare ready for a trip across the mountains, as she is entered in the Horseman's Stake, for foals of 1886, and the race has been set for July 12th to take place at Detroit. Mr. Salisbury is at present in the East, but on his return arrangements will be made to send the game daughter of Director back East. That she may be successful in her next effort, with the noted trotters of the East, is the heart felt wish of every Californian.

A well known horseman in writing to me about old pedigrees says, "I have kept a pedigree book for the last forty years and at various times I have written down my personal opinion of the animal when writing down the pedigree. In looking up one of my old books, I find the following, written many years ago: Abdallah, a bad headed, ugly dispositioned brute, of ungainly shape and a stain in any pedigree. Of late years my opinion of Abdallah has so changed that I attribute the well known and invariable gameness of the many decendents of John Nelson, as much to the Abdallah as to the Trustee Cross."

From a gentleman who has been visiting Palo Alto during the past week I learn that the reported indisposition of Electioneer resulted from an injury that he received, when dismounting after service. He was strained across the back, and the result was chronicled to the world as a "serious illness" by the gossip mongers. The old horse is once more able to move about but he will not be stinted to any more mares this season, he having already covered twenty five. Next week I will endeavor to give my readers a word picture of this noted stallion, which has added so much to the fame of Palo Alto, and done so much for the good name of California.

On Monday, April 18th, Mr. C. F. D. Hastings sustained a severe loss in the death of the brood mare Juno by Pat Malloy (son of Geo. M. Patchen Jr. 31) dam by Ethel Allen. Juno was a fast and game mare, and her endurance was unlimited. These same characteristics she imparted to her progeny, the best known of which is Como 2:26¾ by Elmo. He was a good game trotter, being always able to win whenever heats were split. He was the first of Juno's foals, the second being Ethel H. by Sultan 2:24. She was never trained and is now used as a brood mare. The third foal was by Anteeo 2:16¼, but he died from the result of an accident. Her fourth foal is now 2 years old, by Fallis 2:23, while the foal of 1889 is a chestnut filly by Woodnut 2:16½. Juno died giving birth to a bay colt by Noonday, and the little fellow will be brought up by hand.

In speaking of the Wallace defalcation, the New York Times says: Leslie E. McLeod, formerly associate editor of Wallace's Monthly, who was arrested Sunday night on a charge of grand larceny in connection with the robbery of certain bonds valued at $35,000, the property of Mr. John Wallace, was yesterday honorably discharged by Justice McMahon at the Tombs Police Court. There was no evidence to show that Mr. McLeod had in any way been connected with Robert C. Wallace in his thefts from Mr. Wallace, amounting to some $50,000.

Assistant District Attorney Lindsay telegraphed the State Department yesterday, requesting that measures be taken for the arrest and extradition of young Wallace and Bookmaker Louitz, who sailed for Havana last week Wednesday on the steamer Saratogo.

The sale of the Auburndale Racing Stable, owned by Mr. J. F. Donnell, took place in the saddling paddocks at the Linden track on the 10th. The pick of the lot, King Hazem, was knocked down to Mr. L. L. Lloyd for $5,600, Mr. Lloyd also purchased the three-year-old filly Unadaga by Onondaga—Una, and that good little colt Jay F. Dee, for the sum of $575 and $1,600, respectively. William Easton, the auctioneer, after some spirited bidding, secured the gelding Kosciusko Kay for $4,800. P. Brady bought the two-year-old filly Enola for $1,000, and G. Walbaum bought the two-year-old chestnut colt by Jils Johnson—Sue Finnie for the same amount, and a bay colt by imported Tympanum out of Creda, by Harry Bassett, for $3,800. The rest brought small prices, J. L. Lubio getting Duke John for $825; E. W. Phillips a two-year-old by Ten Broeck—Belle of Nantura, by Longfellow, for $325; J. R. Dean a three-year-old colt by Dalnacardoch—Blue Lodge for $200, and A. Lakeland buying Saracen for $130.

The county of Sonoma and particularly that portion of it lying between Petaluma and Santa Rosa is so strongly imbued with trotting horse lore that it even occasionally breaks out among the young ladies attending the district schools in that section. A few days ago during the examination in English history, the schoolteacher (who is not very well up in 'records') asked one of the young ladies to name the leader in the great conspiracy that attempted to blow up the houses of Parliament; like a flash came the reply "Guy Wilkes." A titter from her equally well 'posted' classmates called the replicant's attention to her slip of the tongue and she promptly added, "I should have said Guy Fawkes." "And who, I should like to know was Guy Wilkes? asked the teacher. Chorus from the class: "Why! Guy Wilkes 2:15½, of course!" There are rumors that the horsemen in the neighborhood have contributed Wallace's Year Book to the school library for the teachers benefit.

At the last meeting of the San Joaquin Valley Agricultural District Association, held at Stockton, a dispute arose over the right of John A. Goldsmith to return to the wire, after the word was given to start, in a walk over with Regal Wilkes for the two-year-old trotting stake. At the late meeting of the Board of Review the following question was submitted.

"Copy of Minutes:

STOCKTON, Cal., Sept. 24, 1889.

Upon call of the Judges of the races of the day, the Board met at 8 P. M. at the Pavilion office, Directors Sargent and Shepherd absent.

The Judges submitted the following statement:

Mr. John A. Goldsmith started for a walk-over in the two (2) year old Pacific Trotting Stake of Stockton Fair, of this year, with "Regal Wilkes."

Having been tapped off and receiving the signal "go", Goldsmith drove his colt half around the first turn. "Regal Wilkes" made a serious break and Goldsmith returned for another start, claiming the right to start as many times as he saw fit. That afternoon, before Goldsmith reached the wire on his return, the Judges notified him he would not be permitted to start twice for a walk-over. Goldsmith did return, cross the wire and demanded another start. The Judges refused to start him the second time, as the N. T. A. Rules give no rule concerning such cases. The Judges, with Goldsmith will ask the Board of Appeals to establish rules concerning such case.

A true copy from record.

Attest! (Signed) J. M. LA RUE,
Sec'y S. J. V. Agr'l Asso'n, Dist. No. 2, Cal."

It is [illegible]ld that when the word is given a horse must go the full mile.

THE HAPPY FRENCHMAN.

Wells, Fargo's Bank Paid Him a Big Stack of Twenties.

A Laundryman Suddenly Enriched—He Will Invest a Part of His Money in Real Estate.

Dame Fortune never smiled on a more worthy subject than M. Anathase Robert, an old resident of this city, whose parents were born in La Belle, France, and were adherants to the house of Bourbon. M. Roberts awoke a few mornings ago to find himself a wealthy man, for while he was going about his business on the day before, an intervenor of the Mexican Government was inspecting the semi-annual extraordinary drawing of the "Loteria de la Beneficencia Publica" of the City of Mexico, and as a result of that drawing, M. Roberts secured a fortune of $15,000, he holding ticket No. 54700, entitling him to one-eighth of the grand capital prize of $120,000.

The lucky Oaklander had no trouble at all in securing his easily gotten fortune, for presentation of the ticket at the counter of Wells, Fargo & Co's Bank in San Francisco had the same effect as all gilt edged securities, and 750 shining twenty dollar gold pieces were stacked up before the fortunate holder of the ticket as soon as a telegram was received announcing the number of the ticket. In the coolest manner possible M. Robert deliberately shoved the shining pile of gold back at the cashier, after satisfying himself as to the amount, and took a certificate of deposit on that bank. He came back to work in Oakland with a light heart, and the pleasant expression on his face told better than words that something unusual had occurred. This morning a Tribune man called on M. Roberts at his residence, 1579 New Broadway, where everything was in disorder outside. The grade of the street is being raised, and as a consequence it is not in the best condition. Within everything was bright and cheery, a busy little woman was singing merrily at her work, and M. Robert greeted the reporter with a hearty shake of the hand. He was dressed in a manner fitting to his sudden rise in life, and takes his good fortune very gracefully.

He was not disposed to say much about his lucky investment. M. Robert is in the prime of life, and is a single man, and up to the present he has been employed as a laundryman in the French laundry of P. Calon, at Twenty-ninth street and San Pablo avenue. He has often invested in lottery tickets before, buying a number in several companies each month. He has often been warned against the Mexican lottery, but explained that he had resided in the city of Mexico, and knew that the "Loteria de la Benificencia Publica" was the best of all, and so it proved to be for him.

His parents came from sunny France before he was born, and located in the City of Mexico, where he grew into manhood, and had an opportunity to see for himself how the lottery was conducted. He explained that it is under the direct supervision of the Federal Government of Mexico, through an officer duly appointed for that purpose. His relation to the company is somewhat like that of the Comptroller of the United States Treasury to the National banks of this country.

"There are too many dead tickets in these other lotteries," explained M. Robert, "while in the Mexican lottery there are only 80,000 all told and the same number of prizes as any other concern, so you can see the more chances one has of winning."

Several years ago M. Robert came to California with his sister and located in Oakland, where he has been working hard to lay up a little money to carry him through his declining days, but now he has enough to keep him and his sister in regal style without the necessity of hard work.

"I suppose you will marry?" asked the reporter.

"Oh, no, I won't," replied M. Robert, with a broad smile. "I have been an old bach too long now to give it up. I shall move from this house shortly, and will invest some of my money in good real estate, so that it will bring me in something. I have no idea of going into business at present. The laundry business is overdone, and a person must select an opening in which he will not have too much competition. I think I shall buy some property, and that will be all. The money could not come to a more worthy person than I, and I am always glad to hear of any hard working man making a fortune. It is the only chance most of them have, and they should take advantage of it. I may pay a visit to Mexico shortly, to see the scenes of my childhood, and I may go to France, but these things are merely suggestions now," and the man of sudden wealth retired from the room.

THE WEEKLY

Breeder and Sportsman.

JAMES P. KERR, PROPRIETOR.

The Turf and Sporting Authority of the Pacific Coast.

Office, No. 313 Bush St.
P. O. Box 2300.

TERMS—*One Year, $5; Six Months, $3; Three Months, $1.50.*
STRICTLY IN ADVANCE.

Money should be sent by postal order, draft or by registered letter, addressed to JAMES P. KERR, San Francisco, Cal.

Communications must be accompanied by the writer's name and address, not necessarily for publication, but as a private guarantee of good faith.

NEW YORK OFFICE, ROOM 15, 181 BROADWAY.

ALEX. P. WAUGH, - - - - - Editor.

To Subscribers.

The date printed on the wrapper of your paper indicates the time to which your subscription is paid.

Should the BREEDER AND SPORTSMAN be received by any subscriber who does not want it, write us direct to stop it. A postal card will suffice.

Special Notice to Correspondents.

Letters intended for publication should reach this office not later than Wednesday of each week, to secure a place in the issue of the following Saturday. Such letters to insure immediate attention should be addressed to the BREEDER AND SPORTSMAN, and not to any member of the staff.

San Francisco, Saturday, May 24, 1890.

Dates Claimed.

EUREKA JOCKEY CLUB	July 2d to 5th
IONE	Aug 5th to 9th.
LOS ANGELES [6th District]	Aug. 4th to 9th
SAN JOSE	Aug. 11th to 16th
NAPA	Aug. 18th to 23rd
GLENBROOK PARK, 17th District	August 19th to 22d
PETALUMA	Aug. 25th to 30th
OAKLAND (District No. 1)	Sept. 1st to Sept. 6th
LAKEPORT, 12th District	September 23d to 27th
CALIFORNIA STATE FAIR	Sept 8th to 20th
STOCKTON	Sept. 23rd to 27th.
FRESNO (Fall Meeting)	Sept. 29th to Oct. 4th
VISALIA	Oct. 7th to 11th

Stallions Advertised
IN THE
BREEDER AND SPORTSMAN.

Thoroughbreds.

DOUGLASDALE—Thoroughbred Clydesdale....Lawn View Farm, Cal.
FRIAR TUCK, Hermit—Romping Girl.........C. W. Aby, Middletown.
GREENBACK, Dollar—Music.........C. W. Aby, Middletown,
ST. SAVIOR, Eolus—War Song.........C. W. Aby, Middletown.
THREE CHEERS Imp. Hurrah—Young Fashion.........E. S. Culver, San Francisco.

Trotters.

ADMIRAL, Volunteer—Lady Pierson.......... Frank Drake, Vallejo.
ACTOR Prompter—Dam by Sultan.........Lawn View Farm, Cal
ALDONA, Almont—Queen Mary.........Fred W. Loeber, St. Helena
BAY ROSE Sultan—Madam Baldwin.........Thos. Bonner, Santa Rosa
CUPID, Sidney—Venus.........C. O. Thornquest, Oakland
CHARLES DERBY, Steinway—by Electioneer. Cook Stock Farm, Contra Costa Co.
CORRECTOR, Director—Brainey.........Pleasanton Stock Farm.
DECORATOR, Director—Chess.........Pleasanton Stock Farm.
DEXTER PRINCE, Kentucky Prince—Lady Dexter.........L. M. Morse, Lodi.
DIRECTOR, Dictator—Dolly.........Pleasanton Stock Farm, Pleasanton.
EL BENTON, Electioneer—Nellie Benton.........Souther Farm, San Leandro.
ECLECTIC, Electioneer—Manette.........Wilfred Page, Sonoma County
EROS, Electioneer—Sontag Mohawk.........W. H. Vioget, Menlo Park
FIGARO, Hambletonian—Emblem.........Souther Farm, San Leandro.
GROVER CLAY, Electioneer—Maggie Norfolk.........Denis Gannon, Oakland.
GRAND MOOR 2374, Moor 870—Vashti.........H. I. Thornton, S. F.
G. & M., Anteeo—Rosa B.........George E. Guerne, Santa Rosa.
GUY WILKES, George Wilkes—Lady Bunker.........San Mateo Stock Farm, San Mateo.
GLEN FORTUNE, Electioneer—Glenna.........Souther Farm, San Leandro.
GEORGE WASHINGTON, Mambrino Chief—Fanny Rose.........Thos. Smith, Vallejo.
GRANDISSIMO, LeGrande—Norma.........Fred W. Loeber, St Helena
JESTER D, Almont—Hortense.........Souther Farm, San Leandro
KING DAVID, Admiral—Black Flora.........Frank Drake, Vallejo.
LEO WILKES, Guy Wilkes Sable.........San Mateo Stock Farm, San Mateo.
MEMO, Sidney—Flirt.........John Rowen, Oakland
MAMBRINO WILKES, George Wilkes—Lady Chrisman.........San Miguel Stock Farm, Walnut Creek.
MAMBRINO CHIEF, McDonald Chief—Venus.........Thos. Smith, Vallejo.
MORTIMER, Electioneer—Marti.........Wilfred Page, Sonoma County
PASHA, Sultan—Madam Baldwin.........D. Bryson, Linden
PHILOSOPHER, Pilot Wilkes—Bella.........George E. Guerne, Santa Rosa.
REDWOOD, Anteeo—Lou Wilton.........A. McFayden, Oakland.
STEINWAY, Strathmore—Abbess.........Cook Stock Farm, Contra Costa Co
SABLE WILKES, Guy Wilkes—Sable.........San Mateo Stock Farm, San Mateo.
VICTOR, Echo—Daughter of Woodburn.........G. W. Hughes, Napa City
YOUNG ELMO, St. Elmo—Dam by Woodburn....Lawn View Farm Cal.

Horses racing in Italy has taken a firm hold upon the popular imagination. At Milan, which holds two meetings each year, a handicap, with £2,000 added, will be run for at the end of May, while meetings have already been held this year at Pisa, Palermo and Naples, to be followed by Florence, Lazeo, Milan, Turin, Alessandria. All together, there will be more than twenty meetings of one kind and another, and the value of the stakes to be run for, entries included, will fall little, if anything, short of £30,000. This may seem small by comparison with what is to be won in England, but represents an increase of at least one hundred per cent. upon the figures of 1887, and it is this constant increase which shows what strides racing is making in that country.

The Oakland and Fresno Entries.

It must be a source of extreme satisfaction to the Directors of the Oakland and Fresno Associations to see how generously the horsemen of California have subscribed to the stakes and purses advertised by them. There has been a feeling of annoyance expressed by many horsemen in the State who have been under the belief that with the withdrawal of the Hickok and Palo Alto stables that there would not be enough of horses in training to fill the many purses which have been and will be offered; however, that feeling can now be dispelled as the large number of entries made are guaranty enough that not only a large number of horses will come to the wire but that the sport will be of an exciting nature. It is true that the slower classed purses havefilled the best, but from an intimate knowledge of many of the horses at present in training, we can confidently assert that there are many surprises in store for those who may patronize the various fairs during the coming summer and fall. From all sections of the State favorable reports have been received, and there are any quantity of green horses even at this early date which are competent to enter the 2:30 list, while not a few have already been mentioned that are fit to trot with ordinary 2:20 performers. As the season advances undoubtedly many of the horses will improve and those that are at present a trifle slow will show up well enough to warrant their owners in making a bid for part of the purses. Never has a season opened more auspiciously and notwithstanding the absence of many of the most noted horses, the season of 1890 will, beyond doubt, prove as memorable in the horse history of California as any year that has ever preceded it. The Directors of both of these Associations are to be congratulated. Fresno, while situated many miles from the Bay City, has always received a large attendance from here, and it is more than probable that when the bell rings for the first race on September 30th, there will be more strangers in the Raisin City than ever before. Oakland always has a liberal attendance, their fairs receiving a generous support from both sides of the Bay, and with the advanced steps they have taken this year to start a Futurity Stake, it should tend to advertise them more than ever and consequently show an increased amount of profit at at the end of the season. From all sections of the State horsemen have entered their suckling foals for the purse which is to be trotted in 1893, and lucky indeed will be the man who has a colt that can win both the Oakland Futurity Stake as well as the BREEDER AND SPORTSMAN one.

Something to Ponder Over.

A few days ago a number of prominent horsemen congregated in the office of the BREEDER AND SPORTSMAN, when the conversation turned as to the speed that might be expected from the foal of Manzanita 2:16 and Stamboul 2:12½; the handsome little filly by Stamboul, dam Trinket 2:14 was also a subject of discussion, and it seemed to be the concensus of opinion that two very fast horses might be looked for, from these two mares. The large stallion service fee asked by the owners of Axtell and also the enormous prices asked for service by owners of all stallions which have a very low mark, took up considerable of the conversation. There was hardly one present but what was willing to acknowledge that the best results could be obtained by breeding to horses who have low records, but Mr. Wm. Ashby, former owner of Chitwood, upset all this theory by picking up the Year Book and calling attention to the following horses who have low records.

Westmont, pacer, 2:01¼. Minnie R., pacer, 2:05 1-4, You Bet, pacer, 2:05¾, Johnston, pacer, 2:06¼, Maud S., 2:08¾, Jay-Eye-See 2:10, Sunol 2:10½, Guy 2:10¾, St. Julien 2:11¼, Little Brown Jug, pacer, 2:11¾, Axtell 2:12, Fanny Witherspoon two-mile record 4:43, Huntress three-mile record 7:21¼ and Satellite four-mile record 10.52½.

Among the fast trotters and pacers, the only one that is left out, with a record below 2:12 is Goldleaf 2:11¼ by Sidney, yet still of all the others mentioned there is not a sire of any one of them that ever entered the 2:30 list. Now it naturally occurs to the student to ponder over these facts as it is evident that the great problem of breeding speed is still a secret; while it is suspectible of belief that fast horses can be more readily produced by and from fast horses, still the above figures would lead to the belief that there is a great undeveloped secret in the breeding business. Only a few days ago we saw at the Bay District Track a gelding which will in all probability make a mark of 2:20 or better for himself this year, and yet his sire is now running loose on an immense grazing farm away up in Modoc County and his dam has no pedigree whatever. While we would like to believe that some of the very fast and elegantly bred mares that have been served to Axtell might produce the trotter of the future, still the records would almost make us believe that it is too much to expect and that the future record breaker will be sired by a horse that has not the honor to be in the "charmed circle."

Billiards.

As was stated in the BREEDER AND SPORTSMAN in its issue of last week, Messrs. Schaefer & Ives arrived on Saturday. Their advent was the cause of an increased interest in matters billiardistic in the haunts that are most frequented by the knights of the cue. As yet there has been but little money wagered on the result of the forthcoming contest between Schaefer and McCleery, but as the time draws near for the game to take place, undoubtedly all friends of the two men will be eager to back their opinions. McCleery is practicing constantly in a room which has been specially fitted up for him in the Baldwin Hotel; while Schaefer is taking exercise with his companion in a room fitted up for him by Mr. Orndorff in the Flood Building. It is now many years since a first-class contest has taken place in San Francisco, and beyond doubt the three nights' match which occurs on May 29th, 30th and 31st, will cause an increased revival in this gentleman's game.

Both of the principals have secured managers to represent their interests, and it need hardly be stated that everything will be done that is possible for the comfort of those who may go to Metropolitan Hall to witness the game. Especial care will be taken that nothing will be said or done to offend the most fastidious, and gentlemen who wish to take ladies are assured that they may do so without running the risk of giving offense. Already in this city are many ladies who have displayed great aptness for the game, and in many of the larger private residences, a room is devoted especially to this purpose. It is not so very long ago that it would have been considered unwomanly to acknowledge that a lady was familiar with the game, but nowadays it is considered one of the accomplishments, and there are many in San Francisco who wield the cue in not only a graceful but very expert manner. We expect to find many of the fair sex present at the opening of the game between the two great professors of this beautiful game.

Another Futurity Stake.

The Directors of the Sonoma and Marin Agricultural Society are nothing if not progressive, and not to be overshadowed and outdone by others, they this week announce a Futurity Stake for foals owned in their district comprising Sonoma, Marin, Napa, Lake, Mendocino, Solano, Yolo, Colusa and Contra Costa Counties. The stake is for foals of 1890, and the race will be trotted at their annual summer meeting in 1893: the conditions are much the same as those advertised in the BREEDER AND SPORTSMAN Futurity Stake and in the Oakland Futurity Stake. The payments are small and on the installment plan which will enable those who are not well-to-do in this world's goods to enter for what promises to be a valuable stake. The entries will close on July 1st with the Secretary, Dr. Thos. Maclay of Petaluma; the advertisement will be found in another column.

Poems on the Horse.

We have received from the Wenborne-Sumner Co. of Buffalo, New York, an elegant volume of poems relating to the turf, and other ballads written by Emmons S. Pierce. The writer is well known to the turfmen of America from his exquisite work in verse, and having published them in a neat and handy form, they should, and do deserve, a large sale.

The author's dedication is as follows.

To him who loves the noble steed
  And gives him proper care and feed,
Admires his beauty, power and speed,
  And is the horse's friend indeed,
Whose warm heart beams in word and look—
  To him I dedicate this book.

The price of the work is only $2, and those who would like to purchase can do so by sending to the publishers as above.

Foals of 1890.

At Petaluma Race Track, Property of H. J. Agnew:
On May 6th, a horse colt by Billy Thornhill, dam Violet by Jack Patchen, son of Geo. M. Patchen Jr. 31.

At Hollywood Farm. Property of B. C. Holly.
Hattie W, bay mare by Alaska, dam Sally Coward by May Boy, foaled ch filly by Happy Prince, May 15th.

At Chico, Property of F. L. Duncan.
January 21st 1890, bay colt, black points, small star in forehead, small white stripe, around coronet of right hind foot; by Signal Wilkes, dam Gold Elsie; by Sam Purdy. This colt is entered in the BREEDER AND SPORTSMAN Futurity Stake.

At Napa. Property of H. B. Starr.
On May 19th, a dark bay filly foal, by Noonday, dam Lillie C by Alcona Clay, 2nd dam Flora Belle. This foal is entered in the BREEDER AND SPORTSMAN Futurity Stake.

Oakland Entries.

As was to be expected, the entries for the Nomination Purses offered by the Oakland Association filled well. The Futurity Stake was especially well patronized as the list shows.

NEW LIST PURSE $1,000.

For three-year-olds whose sires up to Jan. 1, 1890, have not produced an animal with a record of 2:30 or better at three years of age or under; entrance 10 per cent. payable as follows: May 15th $25, June 15th $25, July 15th $25 and $25 five days before first advertised day of meeting when horses must be named.

Nominations.

A. Weske....San Francisco
A. T. Hatch....San Francisco
Rufus Murphy....Santa Rosa
P. W. Murphy....Santa Margarita
Palo Alto Stock Farm....Menlo Park
U. S. Gregory....Ione

GUARANTEED PURSE $1200.

For three minute class, entrance 10 per cent. payable as follows: May 15th, $30; June 15th, $30; July 15th, $30 and $30 five days before first advertised day of meeting when horses must be named.

Nominations.

A. T. Hatch....San Francisco
J. D. Carr....Salinas City
Pleasanton Stock Farm Co....Pleasanton
B. C. Holly....Vallejo
P. Pumyea....Oakland
Thos. J. Powers....San Francisco
Alex. S. Crawford....Alameda
W. P. Lambert....San Francisco
Sam'l Gamble....San Mateo
Griffin & Moran....San Francisco
Palo Alto Stock Farm....Menlo Park
M. F. Tarpey....Alameda
San Mateo Stock Farm....San Mateo
E. B. Gifford....San Diego
R. F. Simpson....Oakland

GUARANTEED PURSE $1200.

For the 2:40 class, same conditions as the three minute class.

Nominations.

A. T. Hatch....San Francisco
J. D. Carr....Salinas City
I. DeTurk....Santa Rosa
Pleasanton Stock Farm Co....Pleasanton
B. C. Holly....Vallejo
P. Pumyea....Oakland
Alex. S. Crawford....Alameda
W. P. Lambert....San Francisco
Samuel Gamble....San Mateo
Griffin & Moran....San Francisco
Palo Alto Stock Farm....Menlo Park
La Siesta Ranch....Menlo Park
M. F. Tarpey....Alameda
San Mateo Stock Farm....San Mateo
Souther Farm....San Leandro
E. B. Gifford....San Diego
R. F. Simpson....Oakland

FUTURITY PURSE $4000.

For foals of 1890 to trot in 1893, entrance 3 per cent. payable as follows:

1st payment	$10	payable	May 15, 1890.
2nd	"	$10	" January 15, 1891.
3rd	"	$15	" June 15, 1891.
4th	"	$15	" January 15, 1892.
5th	"	$15	" June 15, 1892
6th	"	$15	" January 15, 1893.
7th	"	$20	" June 15, 1893,
8th	"	$20	" 15 days before the advertised day of race.

Name	Sire	Dam	Sire of Dam.
H. I. Agnew	Guy Wilkes	Baby Mine	Nephew
Robt. S. Brown	Secretary	Bebonair	Sultan
J. D. Carr			
Wm. J. Casey	Billy Thornhill	Golden Girl	Cyrus R
L. Funk	Dexter Prince	Lady Emma	Nutwood
Samuel Gamble	Stamboul	Trinket	Princeps
"	Simmons	Kopbta	Mambrino Boy
"	Bell Boy	Four Corners	Mambrino Time
"	Stamboul	Bon Ton	Simmons
"	Alcazar	Eprevous	Alcantara
"	Dictator	Nancy Lee	Onward
"	Stamboul	Kittie Wilkes	Geo. Wilkes
"	Alcyon	Astrione	Stamboul
"	Stamboul	Alta Bell	Electioneer
"	Director	Fontana	Almont
J. Garrity	Gossiper	Sunrise	Regent
D. Gannon	Noonday	Miss Sidney	Sidney
W. E. Greene	Director	Aldane	Wissahickon
J. A. Goldsmith	Guy Wilkes	Manon	Nutwood
"	Sidney	Blonde	Elmo
Wm. Galloway	Altamont	Hollywood	Ham. Mambrino
Chas. Greene	Sidney	Queen	Sultan
A. T. Hatch	Guide	Mollie	Admar
"	Director	Ida	Irvington
"	My Guy	Ida Lee	Le Grande
"	Victor	Lolita	Altamont
B. C. Holly	Woodnut	Economy	Echo
Ben E. Harris	Jim Mulvena	Frona Freeman	Adventure
"	Leland Stanford	Echola	Echo
"	"	Rose Abbot	Abbotsford
Free Haney	Strathway	Eveline Temple	Jackson Temple
M. W. Hicks	Sterling	Empress	Flaxtail
H. H. Helman	Strathway	Scalette	A. W. Richmond
H. S. Hogoboom	Waldstein	Gertrude	The Moor
Jno. B. Hill	Lafayette King	Jennie Hall	Richmond
Rudolph Jordan	Alex Button	Adelina Patti	Effingham
J. W. Knox	Anteeo	Eva	Geo. Wilkes
"	Florida	Patience	Young Jim
"	"	Emily	Geo. Wilkes
"	Anteeo	Angla	"
La Siesta Ranch	Eros	Nerea	John Nelson
"	"	Mona	Brigadier
H. Latham	Dexter Prince	Bellita	Belle Alta
A. Lathrop	Palo Alto	Miss Gift	Gen'l Benton
Oscar Mansfeldt	Guy Wilkes	Amy Fay	Anteeo
D. J. Murphy	"	Carrie Malone	Steinway
"	Soudan	Signa	Sidney
H. A. Mayhew	Son of Director		
J. B. McDonald	Hark	Lassie Jean	Brigadier
Rufus Murphy	Anteeo	Snip	Dan Voorhees
R. O. Newman	Strathway	Richmoor	Pasha
R. L. Patterson	Strathway	Anita	Anteros
"	"	Nell	
J. P. Patery	Alex Button	Lucy	Hercules
Pleasanton Stock Farm	Director	May Day	Ballard's Cassius M. Clay.
"	"	Romana	Gibraltar
Palo Alto Stock Farm	Electioneer	Beautiful Bells	The Moor
"	"	Belle Campbell	Gen'l Benton
"	"	Tellie	"
"	"	Dame Winnie	Planet
"	"	Waxana	Gen'l Benton
"	"	Lady Ellen Carr's	Mambrino
"	"	Sallie Benton	Gen'l Benton
"	Nephew	Wildflower	Electioneer
"	"	America	Rysdyk's Hambletonian
"	"	Lorinne	Gen'l Benton
"	Piedmont	Thalia	Electioneer
"	"	Celia	Fallis
"	"	Lola	Gen'l Benton
"	Azmoor	Bonnie	"
"	"	Emma Robson	Woodburn
"	"	Sprite	Alex. Belmont
"	Palo Alto	Jennie Benton	Gen'l Benton
"	"	Wicket	"
"	Wild Boy	Sontag Mohawk	Mohawk Chief
"	Wildnut	Julia Benton	Gen'l Benton
Wilfred Page	Eclectic	Minnie Allen	Arthurton
"	"	Reinetee	Dexter Prince
"	Mortimer	Lady Del Sur	Del Sur
"	"	Clara B	Nutwood
L. J. Rose	Stamboul	Almeh	Sultan
"	"	Minnehaha	Bald Chief
"	"	Judy	Bob Mason
"	Alcazar	Garrett	Junius
H. T. Rudisell	"	Molly	Pilot of Temple Jr
Thos. Smith	Geo. Washington	Nancy Rose	Admiral
M. F. Tarpey	Clovis	Eurynome	Nutwood
J. W. Robinson	Alcazar	Zoe M	Sultan
"	Stamboul	Jessie Ballard	Archye Hambletonian
A. B. Spreckles	Chris. S	Jennie	Bull Pup
"	Aptos Wilkes	Ashcat's Daughter	Speculation
"	"	Erminie	Abbotsford
W. F. Smith	Albert W	Belle Blanche	The Moor
R. F. Simpson	Director	Belle King	Paddy Magee
"	Jim Madison	Kit Kellogg	Venture
San Miguel Stock Farm	Mambrino Wilkes	Fanny Fern	Jack Hawkins
"	"	Contra	Electioneer
"	"	Satsuma	Grand Moor
"	"	Annie Laurie	Echo
"	Balkan	Belle	Mamb'o Wilkes
"	Mambrino Wilkes	Fredolia	Fred Arnold
San Mateo Stock Farm	Guy Wilkes	Sister	Admiral
"	"	Blanche	Arthurton
"	"	Sable	The Moor
"	Sable Wilkes	Vixen	Nutwood
"	"	Hettie	Tilton Almont
"	Guy Wilkes	Ruby	Sultan
"	Sable Wilkes	Gina Wilkes	Grey Wilkes
"	Guy Wilkes	Margaret	Sultan
Souther Farm	Wilanut	Veronica	Alcono
"	Figaro	Bermood	Fleetwood
"	"	The Driver	"
"	Figaro	Pinkie	Reliance
"	"	Strawberry	Newland's Hamb
"	"	Puss	Kentucky Hunt'r
"	"	Roberta	Vernon Patchen
"	"	Susie Gratton	Johnathan
"	"	Meyers Brown	Erwin Davis
"	Jester D	Bernarda	
"	"	Rosaline	Major Mono
"	"	Mary	
"	"	Effie Deans	Whipple's Ham'
"	"	Kitty Collier	Collier
"	"	Hathaway Mare	Otis Hill's Horse
L. H Titus	Director	Belle Echo	Echo
H. I. Thornton	Jas. Madison	Coquette	
"	Director	Oriole	Monroe Chief
C. O. Thornquest	Cupid	——	Tom Benton
Underhill & McFadden	Redwood	Puss	Dietz St. Clair
Valensin Stock F'.	Sidney	Faustina	Crown Point
"	"	Venus	Capt. Webster
"	"	Flight	Buccaneer
"	"	Ellen Tomlinson	Dictator
"	"	Florence Wilkes	Red Wilkes
"	"	Flirt	Buccaneer
"	Semicolon	Ivy	"
"	"	Fernleaf	Flaxtail
"	"	Santa Rita	Sidney
A. Weeks	Prince Imperial	Amelia	Gray McClellan
G. W. Woodward	Alex. Button	Viola	Flaxtail
"	"	Sybil	
H. Westphal	Cupid	——	Stanford

Our Los Angeles Letter.

The impression is very general that the August meeting of the Sixth District Agricultural Association will eclipse all former meetings of the association. The directors are sparing no expense in booming the meeting, and the Los Angeles public can always be relied on to turn out in force when anything good is offered for their patronage. The owners of colts intend to enter in the trotting stakes, as they appreciate the fact that, the breeders in Southern-California should stand together in order to foster and develop the breeding industry, and the best way to do this is by entering in these stake races.

Many improvements are being made at the Agricultural Park, and when the bell rings for the opening of the grand circuit in 1890, Los Angeles will have a track second to none in the State. By the way, at a meeting of the Directors of the Association, held last Saturday night, it was decided to hold a second meeting in October, when the agriculture and horticulture display will be made. Your readers will see that everything in the way of running and trotting will have a big inning in Los Angeles in 1890. It will not cost a fortune to get there, either with stock, as the railroad people intend to make an unusually liberal rate—possibly $100 a car load.

I still hear favorable accounts from Santa Anita about the Emperor of Norfolk. Manager Unruh, in conversation with the BREEDER AND SPORTSMAN representative, expressed himself confidently in regard to the Emperor standing a campaign. I sincerely hope that the Emperor will live up to the expectations of the Santa Anita people, but I am afraid that it will prove a repetition of the Sir Dixon case.

Last Saturday there was a trot at the Agricultural Park. The time made was not as fast as expected, but Gale was clearly not herself, and suffered from a sore mouth.

SUMMARY.

J. W. Robinson's b m Gale by Commodore Belmont, dam Irene by Dictator	West	3	1	1	1
N. Covarrubias' ch g Tono by Salisbury, dam Hermina	Walters	1	3	3	3
C. Durfee's b m Leonor by Dashwood, dam Geraldine	Durfee	2	2	2	2

Time, 2:45½, 2:47, 2:36, 2:37½.

The judges who officiated were L. Lichtenberger, Hank McGregor and George Vignolo

Jimmy Mack was in town this week. Mack has a string of promising trotters at Santa Paula. This thriving little town is rapidly coming to the front as a trotting center. W. L. Harbison the Ventura Oil King, has started a breeding farm. He has a number of A. W. Richmond mares who are in foal to Alcazar, Gossiper, Bob Mason and Black Pilot. The latter is a most promising four-year-old Sultan stallion. His dam is Highland Maid by Arthurton. He was purchased by a syndicate from L. J. Rose about a year ago. Another stallion that is much sought after by the owners of good mares in that part of the country is the A. W. Richmond stallion out of Bridget by Kentucky Hunter.

There are several promising colts in training at the Santa Paula track for the colt stake, to be trotted at the Los Angeles meeting in August.

QUARTER STRETCH GOSSIP.

What Ho pulled up lame several days since. What Ho is to trotting, what Inspector B. is to the running turf.

Manager Baldwin was here during the past week booming up the Fresno meeting. He got several enteries here.

The new track at Corondo will be dedicated on the Fourth of July.

The Escondido Fair is to be held in October.

The San Diegan recently published an interesting article on the horse interests of San Diego County. That paper says that there are fifteen horses in training at the Corondo track.

Nick Covarrubias has a promising three-year-old in his string of runners.

DAGWORTH.

VETERINARY.

Conducted by W. Henry Jones, M. R. C. V. S.

Subscribers to this paper can have advice through this column in all cases of sick or injured horses or cattle by sending an explicit description of the case. Applicants will send their name and address that they may be identified. Questions requiring answers by mail should be accompanied by two dollars, and addressed to W. Henry Jones, M. R. C. V. S., Olympic Stables, Butler Street, San Francisco.

A Subscriber.

My colts eye has improved a little by the use of Nit. of Silver and distilled water, etc., but think that if you can suggest some other treatment it would improve more. The eyeball is a little blurred under the swollen and inflamed membrane.

Answer.—With reference to your communication *Re* your colt's eye, I am afraid I cannot do much for it under the circumstances. It would be almost impossible to prescribe for such a case, without first seeing the patient. In the meantime apply acetates of lead twenty grains, distilled water one ounce. Keep the eye covered, and cool with the swab I recommended before. Try for one week, and then communicate with the BREEDER AND SPORTSMAN as to the result.

E. D.

What is the best treatment for a two-year-old filly that has soft swelling on inside of leg near hock. Looks very much like a blood spavin, but am not certain that it is. There seems to be considerable fever, but not much lameness. She was hurt while in pasture.

Answer.—Judging by your description of the swelling near hock, I do not consider it a blood spavin. In all probability it is the result of a somewhat severe sprain. As there is considerable fever I would advise you to foment with hot water for several hours daily. Administer a small dose of cathartic medicine, say five drams aloes, and keep the animal quiet. After the fever has subsided, paint the enlargement with Tinct Iodine three times a week. If this does not reduce the swelling apply Biniodide Mercury two drams, Vaseline one ounce. When this is applied it will be necessary to keep the colt tied up for a few days. The tail must be tied up, otherwise, the blister will get all over the abdomen. If no good result follows, write again to BREEDER AND SPORTSMAN.

Answers to Correspondents.

Answers for this department must be accompanied by the name and address of the sender, not necessarily for publication, but as proof of good faith. Write the questions distinctly, and on one side of the paper only. Positively no questions will be answered by mail or telegraph.

W. W. B.

This gentleman asked last week for the breeding of Tinner, and Mr. Ruland, of Woodland, has kindly forwarded it. Tinner ch h, bred by Washington Lambert of Yolo County, was by John Nelson 187; dam Ogburn mare by Old St. Clair; 2nd dam a mare of Hambletonian stock, owned by one McPherson, of Solano or Napa County. Mr Ruland also says that Tinner left a great many colts in Yolo County, but he was burned to death in a livery stable fire, at Knights Landing, just as his value was beginning to be appreciated.

A. E. B.

Can you tell me whether my stallion "Belmont Chief" which I lately purchased of J. F. Houghton of the Home Mutual Insurance Co., is eligible to registration.

He is sired by Mohawk Chief out of Queen—she by Old Belmont. Queen is out of Crimms Black Bess she by Sir James.

Answer.—He is not eligible to registration.

C. L. N.

Would you tell me through your valuable paper the pedigree of Buccaneer, also of Ethan Allen.

Answer.—Buccaneer, by Iowa Chief, dam Tinsley Maid by Flaxtail; 2nd dam Fanny Fern by Irwin's Tuckahoe. (2) Which Ethan Allen do you mean?

J. H.

Please answer the following questions through the columns of your valuable paper: 1.—What is the breeding of Reliance 2:19½, who owns him and where is he now? 2.—What is the breeding of Jim Lick? 3.—Is my mare sired by Reliance, dam by Jim Lick standard bred? 4.—Is Leland Stanford by Electioneer, standard bred, has he a record and who owns him? 5.—Is my mare, sired by Leland Stanford, dam by McCracken's Dave Hill Jr. standard bred?

Answer.—1.—Reliance 969, (2:22½) by Alexander 490, dam Maud by Mambrino Rattler, etc. He is at present owned by S. E. Laribee, Deer Lodge, Montana. 2.—James Lick by Homer, dam Springer mare by Harker's Buster. 3.—No. 4.—Leland Stanford by Electioneer, dam Annie Laurie by Dave Hill Jr, 2nd dam by Owen Dale is not standard bred. He has no record. He is owned by C. P. Harris & Co., Stanislaus Co. 5.—No.

C. H. B.

I entered my horse in a race of one-half mile heats 2 in 3. My horse won the first heat and lost the second. Now did the third horse have a right to start in the third heat, or did only the horses that won a heat each have a right to start? I contend that the third horse was out of the race after the second heat. If you will answer this in your paper, I will be greatly obliged.

Answer.—Only the two horses, which had a heat each to their credit, should start in the third heat.

B. G. M.

(1) "A" shakes the dice and throws a pair of sixes. B bets the cigars for the party that he beats A's throw, and ties him; who wins? (2) A owns a mare with a record of 2:30. Her owner, A, bets B that she can lower her record on a certain day, and the mare on that day does no better than thirty (her previous record); who wins?

Answer.—(1) A. wins. (2) B. wins.

Names Claimed.

I wish to claim the name Melbourne for my horse colt by Sidney out of Bonnibelle. Bonnibelle by the Grand Moor out of Wanda by Cassius M. Clay Jr., third dam by Harry Clay. Born May 12, 1890. Bay colt, solid color.

Very Truly, E. NEWLAND.

I hereby claim the name "Sidka" for bay filly, few white hairs in forehead; foaled May 12, 1890. By Sidney, dam May by John Nelson, Jr; this filly is entered in the BREEDER AND SPORTSMAN Futurity Stake.

I also claim the name of "Kiffel" for dark mahogany bay filly, star in forehead, foaled May 8, 1889. By Antevolo, dam May by John Nelson, Jr. L. VILLEGIA.

2102 Elm Street, Oakland.

State Association.

Last Monday the Directors of the State Agricultural Society met at Sacramento and arranged the speed programme for the annual Fair. Secretary Smith has been kind enough to forward a copy of the proposed speed "menu."

FIRST DAY—THURSDAY, SEPT. 11.

First Race—The Occident Stake. A trotting stake for foals of 1887, Entries closed January 1, 1888. $100 entrance, of which $10 must accompany nomination; $15 to be paid January 1, 1889; $25 to be paid January 1, 1890, and $50 thirty days before the race. The Occident Gold Cup, of the value of $400 to be added by the society. First colt, Cup and six-tenths; second colt, three-tenths, and third colt one-tenth of stakes. Five to enter, three to start; otherwise, N. T. A. rules. Mile heats, three in five to harness. Closed in 1888 with 63 nominations. Value of stake January 1, 1890, $1,8'6.

Second Race—Trotting; Purse $1,200; 2:27 class.

Third Race—Pacing; Purse $600; 2:25 class.

SECOND DAY—FRIDAY, SEPT. 12.

First Race—Opening Scramble. For two-year-olds; a sweepstakes of $25 each; $15 forfeit, or only $10 if declared on or before September 1st, with $250 added, of which $50 to second. Winners at this distance in 1890, once, to carry three pounds; twice, five pounds. Maidens allowed five pounds. Three-quarters of a mile.

Second Race—The California Breeders' Stake; $600 added. One mile and a quarter. Closed in 1889 with 39 nominations.

Third Race—The Rosemeade Handicap. For all ages; of $50 each; half forfeit; $15 declaration, with $400 added; second to receive $100; third, $50 from the stakes. Weights announced by 10 o'clock A. M., and declarations due at 6 P. M., September 11th. One mile and an eighth.

Fourth Race—Selling purse, $300, of which $50 to second; for all ages. Horses entered to be sold for $1,500, to carry rule weights. Two pounds off for each $100 less down to $1,000; then one pound for each $100 less down to $600. Horses entered, not to be sold, to carry five pounds above the scale. Valuation to be placed on starters only by 6 P. M the day preceding the race. Mile heats.

THIRD DAY—SATURDAY, SEPT. 13th:

First Race.—Two-year-old Trotting Stake. $300 added. Closed March 15, 1890, with 14 nominations Mile heats.

Second Race.—The Pacific Stallion Stake. A sweepstakes for trotting stallions 2:18 Class: of $250 each, of which $100 must accompany nominations: $150 payable Sept. 1st, $250 added for each starter up to four, or $1,000 for four or more starters. Stakes divided four-sevenths two-sevenths and one-seventh; added money divided 50, 25, 15 and 10 per cent. A stallion making a walk over, gets all stakes but no added money. Mile heats, three in five.

Third Race.—Trotting Purse $1,000; 2:30 Class.

FOURTH DAY—MONDAY, SEPT. 15th:

First Race.—The Daisy D. Stake for all ages; of $50 each, half forfeit, or only $15 if declared on or before Sept. 1st, with $300 added; of which $75 to second, third to save stake. Maidens if three years old, allowed five pounds; if four or more, seven pounds. Three-quarters of a mile.

Second Race.—The Capital City Stake. A handicap for three-year-olds, of $100 each, half forfeit; $20 declaration with $400 added; second horse $100; weights announced 10 o'clock A. M., Saturday, Sept. 13th. Declarations due at 6 P. M. same day. One and one-sixteenth miles.

Third Race.—The Sunny Slope Stake. A sweepstakes for two-year-old fillies (foals of 1888) of $50 half forfeit, or only $10 if declared on or before January 1st, or $15 by May 1, 1890; declarations without money are void; with $350 added, of which $50 to second. Non-winners allowed five pounds. Five-eighths of a mile. Closed in 1889 with 20 nominations.

Fourth Race.—Selling Purse $350, of which $50 to second; for all ages. Horses entered to be sold for $2,000 to carry rule weights. One pound off for each $100 down to $1,000; then two pounds for each $100 down to $500. Horses entered, not to be sold, to carry five pounds above the scale. Valuations to be placed on starters only by 6 P. M., Saturday, Sept. 13th. One mile and an eighth.

FIFTH DAY—TUESDAY, SEPT. 16th.

First Race.—Trotting Purse $800 for three-year-olds, eligible to 2:40 class.

Second Race.—Trotting Purse $800, for four-year-olds, eligible to 2:30 class.

Third Race—Trotting: purse $1,000; 2:20 Class.

SIXTH DAY—WEDNESDAY, SEPT. 17.

First Race—The California Autumn Stake. $500 added. Closed in 1889 with 33 nominations. Three-quarters of a mile.

Second Race—The Fall Stakes. A handicap sweepstakes for all ages; of $50 each; half forfeit; $15 declaration, with $500 added; second to receive $100; third, $50 from the stakes. Weights announced by 10 A. M. Tuesday, September 16th. Declarations due at 6 P. M. same day. One mile and a quarter.

Third Race—The Palo Alto Stake. A handicap for two-year-olds, of $50 each; half forfeit, or $10 declaration, with $250 added; second to save stake. Weights announced Tuesday, September 16th, at 10 o'clock A. M. Declarations due at 6 o'clock P. M., same day. Three quarters of a mile.

Fourth Race—Purse $400, for three-year-olds and upwards; $15 from starters to go to second horse. Winners at this distance in 1890 to carry, if once, three pounds; twice, five pounds extra. Horses that have started twice in a race one mile or over and not won, in 1890, allowed five pounds. Maidens allowed, if three years old, seven pounds; if four, ten pounds; five or upwards, fifteen pounds. One mile.

Fifth Race—Free Purse, $300, of which $50 to second. For all ages. To close at 6 o'clock P. M. the night before. One mile.

SEVENTH DAY—THURSDAY, SEPT. 18.

First Race—Pacing Stake. For two-year-olds; of $50 each; $25 to accompany nomination, $25 payable day of race; $250 added. Stakes and added money divided 60, 30 and 10 per cent. Mile heats.

Second Race—Trotting; Purse $1,200; 2:24 Class.

Third Race—Pacing purse $600; free for all.

EIGHTH DAY—FRIDAY, SEPT. 19.

First Race—The California Annual Stake; $600 added. Closed in 1889 with 29 nominations. One mile.

Second Race—The President Stake; $750 added. Closed in 1888 with 23 nominations. One mile and a half.

Third Race—The Rico Stake; for all ages; of $50 each, $15 forfeit; $300 added, of which $100 to second, third to save stake; $200 additional if 1:41½ is beaten. Stake to be named after the winner if Rico's time (1:42) is beaten. One mile.

Fourth Race—The La Rue Stake. A handicap for all ages of $100 half forfeit, $20 declaration, with $500 added, of which $100 to second and $50 to third. Weights announced at 10 o'clock A. M. Thursday, September 18th. Declarations due at 6 o'clock P. M. same day. One mile and a half.

Fifth Race—Free purse $300, of which $50 to second; for all ages. Horses that have started twice at this meeting and beaten once allowed five pounds; twice, seven pounds; three times, ten pounds. To name and close at 6 P. M the day before. One and one sixteenth miles.

NINTH DAY, SATURDAY, SEPT. 20TH.

First Race—Trotting Purse $1500. Free for all.

Second Race—Trotting Purse $1000. 2.35 Class.

Third Race—Four-year-old trotting Stake. $400 added. Closed in 1889 with six nominations.

Fourth Race—Three-year-old Trotting Stake. $400 added. Closed March 16th, with six nominations.

"Bon Air," in the New York Spirit, says: I spent the day at Melrose yesterday. J. A. Stevens, the trainer, tells me that he expects to take Thor, Benton, Esmond, Garnet, Almer, Glen Mary and Renwood to St. Louis, Terre Haute and Lexington. He lays "great store" by Renwood, his two year old dependence. Garnet is three, and he says she can trot better than 2:30. She is by Pancoast. As for Renwood, Stevens says, "he is a sure trotter." The half-mile track has been completed and is now being used. Thor is being jogged every day. He is a grand looking horse and a grand goer. What a turning out of the masses there would be if he and Bow Bells could be brought together in a race! Thor is about an inch higher than Bow Bells, though the former is only two years old. Two grander looking horses would be hard to find. In the show ring judges would have a difficult task in awarding the blue ribbon.

ATHLETICS.

Athletic Sports and Other Pastimes.

EDITED BY 'ARYEIPPUS,

SUMMARY.

In our columns will be found a full list of the entries for the great championship meet which will be held on Friday next, Decoration Day. The athletes are all in the pink of condition and the beaten aspirants for championship honors will have no excuse to offer except that the men who finished in front of them were their superiors.

The wheelmen are getting ready for the century run. The oarsmen are commencing to train in earnest for the coming regatta.

RUNNERS, WALKERS, JUMPERS, ETC.

Under the above heading in our last issue appeared an article which referred to Mr. Horace Coffin of the Olympic Club as having said that Gafney did not walk square. Through an error on the part of the printer the sense of the article was entirely changed and a great injustice was done Mr. Coffin. We hasten to make the correction and hope that Mr. Coffin will, under the circumstances, excuse the mistake. The article should have read as follows:

"Coffin is holding Jarvis well down in the mile walk and a good many persons seem to think that Coffin will win that event.

Jarvis seems to think that Coffin does not walk square at all times during a race, and as he also claims that Gafney does not walk square, he should, if his opinion be correct, have a soft thing in both the one and three mile walks."

About 75 persons were present at the Bay District track on Sunday last to witness a match race of one hundred yards between Frank Sheerin and Jack Egan. H. M. Johnson the champion sprinter was appointed starter. After making several false starts the men were sent off even. The heat resulted in a tie, both athletes touching the tape together. Time 11 2-5 seconds.

The referee decided that the race should be run over again. After resting half an hour the men again appeared at the scratch, and after a couple of false starts were sent off. The excitement was intense. Egan led for the first sixty yards, when he was overhauled by Sheerin who rushed past him and won easily in 11 seconds. The prize was valued at $20.

The members of the Alameda Olympic Club will hold another cross country run on Sunday June 1st. All athletes belonging to the associate clubs of the P. C. A. A. A. are invited to attend.

It will be with surprise that amateur athletes and the many friends of Mr. Joseph Barr Buchanan the admitted Prince of Amateur Champions learn that he has positively retired from all outside athletic circles, and is now undergoing a strict course of study for the "entrance" examination to the Chicago Medical University. Expert Phrenologists claim that this young hercules has mental ability quite equal to that of his well known physical strength, and that together with cultivation and a strong nerve, he is the making of an admirable member in that great science of medicine, and more particularly in its branches of surgery and dentistry.

Acting upon the advice of many, Mr. Buchanan has decided to devote the remainder of his life to this study, and will in all probability enter as a student in the above well known Medical College in September next.

A rather peculiar joke was played on the good natured antipodean the other day. It appears when being shown around the college he was, by utter surprise, led into that chamber of horrors—the dissecting room. Buchanan's nerves can perhaps be imagined when (unlike every 99 out of 100) he watched with enraptured interest the students at that remarkable study of cutting and slicing the dead.

Those who have had the pleasure of meeting this handsome young gladiator intimately must admit him to be not only an athlete of the first standing but also an exceptionally shrewd and intelligent fellow. As a lad he was educated at the Auckland College and Grammar School, New Zealand, in which country he was born of Scotch parents on May 18th, 1867. Mr Buchanan's many admirers in this city will watch with interest his future progress, and will hope his mental abilities will prove as great if not greater than his famous physical powers. Mr. Buchanan expects to secure his diploma in 1894.

The amateur athletes are waiting with bated breath for the approach of Decoration Day. Already they have given up severe exercise and are now contenting themselves with jogging. Friday next will certainly prove a red letter day in the history of athletics on the Pacific Coast and it is possible that the championship meet of 1890 will excite more real interest than any other athletic meeting which may take place for years to come. A few records will no doubt be broken, and if the cinder path at the Olympic grounds was not quite so soft, the majority of the Pacific Coast records would be knocked on the head.

The following records will, we feel certain, go under: half, mile and five mile runs, three mile walk, throwing 16lb. hammer. The pennant should be easily won by the Olympic men who have everything in their favor.

With first class training grounds and a large number of athletes to draw from the Olympic Club could not be otherwise than strongly represented. The University team will stand no show whatever for first place. Moffet is out of condition, and Magee will not compete. Somehow or other this year the Students do not seem to take a genuine interest in training, and they can scarcely be blamed. The cinder path at Berkeley has been neglected and the boys have had no place to practice. The Alpines are in the same boat with the Students for they, too, have had to rely on the old Bay District track for training quarters.

The U. C. men on account of their numbers should take second place and as the Garden City Club, after all the newspaper bombast in its favor has sent in only two entries, the Alpine Club will easily win third place.

The next handicap meet of the California Foot-racing Association will be held at Central Park on Sunday, June 8.

A special "Ladies Night" exhibition was given at the Olympic Club rooms on Thursday evening. As we had already gone to press we are unable to present our readers with an account of the entertainment in the present issue.

The boxing contest of six, eight and ten rounds will be given at the Olympic Club in June, for which valuable prizes will be awarded.

Apropos of the half mile race which was run at the new grounds of the Olympic Club on Sunday last, the question arises, Will the P C A A A allow Walter A Scott a record or not? The entries were: W A Scott, scratch, S V Winslow, 29 yds; S V Cassiday, 30yds; J M Whelan, 25yds; J O'Kane, 35yds; C Jellineak, 40yds; J Kortick, 40yds; J W Flynn, 55 yds, and W H Toomy, 55yds. Toomy led for the first quarter, when Flynn took the lead. About 150 yards from the finish Cassidy and Scott closed up with Flynn, and a grand struggle began. Cassidy broke the tape in 2:05 2-5. Scott finished about a foot behind, with Flynn close at his heels. It is claimed that the watches were stopped on Cassidy, which, if true, would deprive Scott of his record. There is no doubt, however, but that Scott broke the record of 2:06 2-5, held by J G Sutton of the U C, and on Decoration Day he should again improve the record.

Jarvis states that he will undertake to lower the one-quarter, one-half and one mile walking records on May 30th. He feels confident that the man who beats him in the mile will have to do better than 6:50.

There will be a handicap one quarter of a mile run at the Olympic grounds to-morrow for members of the club only.

Cooley should win the five mile run on May 30th, with a couple of hundred yards to spare.

McArthur has retired from the cinder path. Had he gone into strict training for the championship games he might have carried off the mile.

Foster stands an excellent chance of winning both hurdle events.

We understand that the Alpine Club has refused the application of Rankin, the runner, for membership on the ground that he is a professional.

"Honest" John Purcell, when asked if he was going to break any of the records on May 30th, answered, "I will try to come within my *measurable* distances." If his business would permit, Purcell could, with a month's practice, lower the hurdle, shot putting and pole vault records.

The Alpine Club has changed the color of its emblem from red to blue.

The Olympic Club has decided that the Lean-Kolb wrestling match was not a fake.

The Occident in a recent issue censured the students for not paying their assessments towards the Athletic fund. The article ended as follows: "The Olympic Club men are working very hard and the Alpines are going to make it warm in several directions. Meantime the boys are taking things pretty easy and will get seriously fooled."

Several new runners will make their appearance in the members races on Friday next. Since the new grounds have been opened a good many young Olympians have discovered that they are runners.

The Acme Athletic Club will give a "Ladies Night" exhibition at the club rooms, 305 14th St., Oakland, on Thursday evening, May 27th. A fine programme of sport has been arranged.

ON THE WHEEL.

H. Lichtenstein and H. Posner will start for Monterey on June 1st. They will possibly remain over a week and then return by another route.

Several members of the Oakland Bicycle Club started from Fruitvale on Sunday last for San Jose, in charge of Captain G. F. Drake. The run turned out to be a very enjoyable one. The start was made at 7:30 A. M. and Captain Drake, J. Revalk, H. J. Gage, S. K. Irish and G. Gibon reached the Garden City at 1:30 P. M. The team returned home by rail.

Capt. Richardson of the Bay City Wheelmen has called a club run to Lake Pilarcitos for to-morrow morning. The start will be made from the cor of 21st and Mission Sts.

AT THE OARS.

Although the bay was rather rough for sculling the few oarsmen who remained home from the Dolphin's Club picnic took their regular spin on Sunday.

Much rivalry exists between the average light weight amateurs of the Pioneer Club. A match race for a trophy will be rowed to-morrow and the same crew will change boats and compete again on the following Sunday. Should each crew be successful in winning a trial then the Captain of each crew will toss up for choice of boats and row the deciding race on the 8th of June. Already several dinners and hats have been wagered that the Hamaban crew will win two straight heats.

There is some talk among the members of the Alpine Amateur Club of making an effort to consolidate with the Columbia Amateur Club of Oakland. The move would certainly be a good one and if carried out would materially help to boom aquatics this season,

It is to be hoped that the Board of Supervisors will accept the services of the Pacific Rowing Association tendered them at their last meeting thereby doing away with the illfeeling existing in past years amongst the oarsmen.

Charley Long and Joe Eirston desire to return their thanks to their many friends for the large and brilliant reception tendered them on last Saturday at the opening of the new sporting resort. The rowing men will at all times receive a very hearty welcome. Mr. Long states that he has retired from match racing but will compete in regattas just for the sake of keeping company with his old partner Billey Growney.

The Triton Club has resumed its former activity and it is to be hoped will be strongly represented at the coming Fourth of July regatta. The Triton crew should make the pace very warm for the Ariels.

The picnic of the Dolphin Club on Sunday last was well attended, and a general good time was had all round.

JOTTINGS FROM ALL OVER.

At the games of the Berkeley Athletic Club held at New York on Saturday last C. H. Sherrill of Yale, won the 100 yards in 10 seconds; L Robinson of the Y A C won the 150 yard run in 14 4 5secs; W C Dohms of the N Y A C equalled the record of 1min 11 2-5 secs in the 600-yard run. The two-mile run was captured by W D Day of New Jersey, in 9min 32 1-5secs beating the American record of 9min 38sec. J P Lee broke the record in the 220-yard hurdle, making the distance in 25 3-5secs.

ASPIRING CHAMPIONS.

The following are the entries for the championship games which will commence at 1 P. M. sharp on Friday next at the new out-door grounds of the Olympic Club, near Golden Gate Park.

100 yard run—V E Schifferstein, O A C, F G O'Kane, O A C, S V Cassey, O A C, C A Jellelek, O A C, M J Kevealley, O A C, S V Winslow, O A C, J O'Kane, O A C—Mays, U C—Gallagher, U C, Ainsworth, U C, McNear, U C, Lakeman, U C, Melone, U C, Winter, U C.

220-yard run—Schifferstem, O A C, Winslow, O A C, Keneally, O A C, Casady, O A C, J D Haires, G C A C, Mays, U C, Ainsworth, U C, Gallagher, U C.

440 yard run—Henderson, O A C, Kenealey, O A C, Casady, O A C, Winslow O A C, R J Wright, Y C A C, McNear, U C, Sutton, U C, Mays U C, Gallagher, U C, Garrison, A A A C, A Mahovey, A A A C.

Half mile run—Scott, O A C, Henderson, O A C, Winslow, O A C, Code, O A C, Sutton, U C, Lakeman, U C, Hill, U C, Winter, U C, Moody, A A A C, Garrison, A A A C

One mile run—Scott, O A C, Cooley, O A C, Dode, O A C, Sapinosa, O A C, Hill, U C, Wearer, U C, Burk, U C, Moody, A A A C, Little, A A A C, Casity, A A A C.

One mile walk—Jarvis, O A C, Coffin, O A C, Laudemann, O A C, Cooke, A A A C, Foulkes, U C.

Putting 16-lb shot—Purcell, O A C, Winslow, O A C, Pringle, O A C, Bouse, U C, Hunt, U C, Roberts, U C, Sheedy, A A A C.

Throwing 16-lb hammer—Pringle, O A C, Bouse, U C, Morrow, U C, Dubbens, U C, Roberts, U C, McKinnon, A A A C.

Broad jump—Schifferstein and Purcell, O A C, Moffitt, McNear, Winter, Wright and Whiting, U C.

High jump—Schifferstein, O A C, Moffit, U C. Whiting, U C, O'Connor, A A A C, Armbruster, A A A C.

Pole vault—Purcell, Schuster Bros. and Kelter, O A C, Van Dyke, Titus, Head and Clarke, U C, Sexsmith, A A A C.

120-yard hurdle race—Foster, Purcell and Whelan, O A C, Moffit, McNear and Wright, U C.

220-yard hurdle race—Purcell, Foster, Cassidy, Winslow, Whelan and Schifferstein, O A C, Moffit, McNear and Bouse, U C.

5-mile run—Scott, Cooley, Espinosa, Collins, Toomey and Middleton, O A C; Little, Vollmer and Casidy, A A A C; Hill, Weaver, Head, U C.

Tug-of-war—Kolb, Gros, Denhard, Helmer, Kerrill, Bruden, Donnolley, Haberly, Hammersley and Boyd, O A C; Roberts, Hunt, Morrow and Bouse, U C.

It will be seen that the Alpine Club is not represented in the sprint races, the hurdles, the tug-of-war or in the broad jump.

The entries for the Olympic special races, open only to members of the club, are:

100-yard run novice—C A Jellineak, J Kortick, E N Francis, T M Wend, F J Meekfessel and J F McDonald.

Half-mile novice—W H Toomey, H M Collins, E N Francis, D B Crane, J B Cos, A C Thoronton and J F McDonald.

440-yard handicap run—W J Kenealley, J O Kane, H M Collins, F G O'Kane, D B Crane, A C Thoronton, J Korteck, P M Waud, C A Jellineak, J. F. McDonald.

P. C. A. A. A.

New Rules Adopted by the Association.

The attention of all amateur athletic organizations and athletes is directed to the following General and Athletic Rules adopted by the Pacific Coast Amateur Athletic Association, March 21, 1890.

RULE I.

RECOGNIZED MEETINGS.

On and after the adoption of these rules anyone competing at open sports held by any club or managing body which is not a member of P. C A. A. A., Amateur Athletic Union Western Association of Amateur Athletics, National Cross-Country Association of America, Inter-Collegiate Association of Amateur Athletics, or any body not registered and approved as provided in the rules of the Amateur Athletic Union, shall thereby disqualify himself from competing in any sports given by organizations members of the P. C. A. A. A. The Association shall have power to reinstate anyone so disqualified if it shall see fit.

RULE II.

UNRECOGNIZED MEETINGS.

Athletic meetings, promoted by companies, incorporated bodies, individuals, or associations of individuals, as private speculations, or in conjunction with a benefit, social or picnic entertainment, are not, unless with the sanction of the P. C. A. A. A., recognized by the P. C. A. A. A., and an athlete competing at an unrecognized meeting shall thereby disqualify himself from all games held under P. C. A. A. A. rules.

RULE III.

SUSPENSION OR DISQUALIFICATION OF INDIVIDUALS.

No person shall be allowed to compete at any meeting held under P C A A A rules while disqualified or under a sentence of suspension passed by either the Amateur Athletic Union, Inter-Collegiate Association of Amateur Athletes, National Cross-Country Association, Pacific Coast Amateur Athletic Association, Western Association of Amateur Athletes. National Amateur Skating Association, League of American Wheelmen, National Association of Amateur Oarsmen, National Lawn Tennis Association, and such other associations as the P C A A A may approve of hereafter. Any person knowingly competing against any one who is disqualified or under sentence of suspension by the P C A A A, or any of the aforementioned associations, shall be himself suspended until the expiration of such sentence, or for such period as the P C A A A may deem proper.

RULE IV.

THE OFFICIAL HANDICAPPER.

An official handicapper shall be employed by the Association, who, during his term of office, shall be ineligible to compete in amateur athletic sport. All club members of the P C A A A must employ the Official Handicapper to handicap their open handicap events unless otherwise authorized by the Association, and for this privilege said clubs shall pay to the Official Handicapper as follows: For handicapping less than 50 entries, $5; for handicapping over 50 entries, $10. In figuring the number of entries each contestant's name shall be counted each time it appears in the entry list.

RULE V.

PRIZES.

Any athlete found guilty of pawning, or using his prizes in any way for a pecuniary gain, shall be at once suspended from all competitions by the P C A A A.

RULE VI.

CHAMPIONSHIP EVENTS.

SECTION 1. The annual championship events shall be as follows, unless changed by authority of the Association:

SEC. 2. Out-door field meeting: 100-yard run; 220-yard run; 440-yard run; 880-yard run; 1-mile run; 5-mile run; 1-mile walk; 3-mile walk; Pole vault for height; Running high jump; Running broad jump; Throwing 16 lb. hammer; Throwing 56-lb. hammer; Putting 16-lb. shot; 120-yard hurdle, 10 flights, 3 ft. 6 in. high; 220-yard hurdle, 10 flights, 2 ft. 6 in. high; Tug-of-war, 4 men, unlimited weight.

SEC 3. Indoor supplementary meeting: 75-yard run; 150-yard run; 300-yard run; 600 yard run; 1000-yard run, 2-mile run; Three-quarter-mile walk; 4 mile walk; Standing broad jump; Standing high jump; Three standing broad jumps; Running, hop, step and jump; Pole-vault for distance; Throwing 56-lb. weight for height; Putting 24-lb. shot; 200-yard hurdle, 10 flights, 3 ft. 6 in. high; 300-yard hurdle, 10 flights, 2 ft. 6 in. high.

SEC. 4. Individual general athletic competition, including standards and order of events:

1. 100-yard run; standard, 11½.
2. Putting 16-lb. shot; standard, 32ft.
3. Running high jump; standard, 5ft.
4. 880-yard walk; standard, 4m 30s.
5. Throwing 16-lb. hammer; standard, 75ft.
6. Pole vault for height; standard, 8½ft.
7. 140-yard hurdle (10 flights, 3ft. 6in. high); standard, 20½.
8. Throwing 56-lb. weight for distance; standard, 18ft.
9. Running broad jump; standard, 18ft.
10. One mile run; standard, 5m 40s.

SEC. 5. The swimming championship events shall be as follows:

100 yards swim, straightaway.
One mile swim, straightaway.

RULE VII.

RECORDS.

A new record at any distance in swimming, walking, running or hurdling, in order to stand, shall be timed by at least three Timekeepers, and a new record at jumping, pole vaulting, or in the weight competitions, shall be measured by at least three Field Judges.

The P. C. A. A. A. will not recognize any new record, unless a report of it is made to the Secretary of the Association, properly supported by the affidavits of the Referee, Timekeepers, Scorers, Starter or Field Judges, as the case may be, as to the correctness of the time, measurement, weather, hour of day and place, with signatures of at least six witnesses, including officials.

RULE VIII.

ELIGIBILITY TO LIMITED EVENTS.

The eligibility to compete in events that are limited to men who have never accomplished a certain time, distance or height in a given event, shall be determined by the competitor's record when the entries for such event closed.

RULE IX.

DEFINITION OF A NOVICE.

A "novice" is one who has never won a prize in any athletic competition open to the members of two or more clubs, and his status shall be determined by his record when the entries for such event closed.

RULE X.

ENTRY FORMS.

All entries for competitions held under P. C. A. A. A. rules must be made on the entry forms adopted by the Association. They shall consist of two forms, one for organizations, clubs and associations, members, and one for individuals, clubs, associations and organizations not members of the P. C. A. A. A. These forms, or sample copies, can be obtained of the Secretary of the Association.

In our next issue we will continue the athletic rules and will, as space affords, continue to publish them until complete.

Willows Athletic Club.

The second exhibition of the Willows Athletic Club was given at Star Hall, Willows, on Friday evening of last week. The club engaged for this exhibition two members of the Olympic Club, of San Francisco, Messrs. Stack and Espinosa. They left the city on Friday morning for Willows, but failed to change cars at Davisville and went into Sacramento, where they telegraphed the club. The managers did not propose to disappoint the people, so they chartered a special train at Sacramento to bring the two performers to Willows. The special left Sacramento at six o'clock and arrived in Willows ten minutes of eight, which is the fastest time ever made between Sacramento and Willows. The performance by the local gymnast boys was far ahead of what was expected.

The tumbling and bar exercise by the Davis and Barns Brothers, Ed. Killebrew, Ed and Bert McMath, Ira Hochheimer, Myron Kyes, Tom O'Brien, Roy Marshall and Mudget, the Clown, were exceptionally good and showed that the boys have made wonderful improvement since their last exhibition. The glove contest between Porter and Ajax showed marked improvement since the last appearance before the public. Duncan McCullam's slack wire walking was far beyond what one would expect from an amateur. Professor Leandro astonished the audience by his wonderful feats in tumbling and on the bar.

Messrs. Espinosa and Stack performed a number of very difficult feats on the bar and in their brother acts of tumbling they were simply wonderful. They also gave the best glove contest ever witnessed in Willows. The performance was a grand success and a credit to the Willows Athletic Club and their excellent teacher, Professor Leandro.

The singing by Messrs. O'Connell, Ajax, Hughes, Waddington and Apperson was "great." O'Connell has a wonderful bass voice and completely captivated the house.

After the performance a social dance was given. Professor Apperson's orchestra furnished the music, and all enjoyed themselves for several hours.

University Athletes.

Good sport at Berkeley witnessed by a large audience.

The University Athletes held their 16th Field-Day on the Cinder track at Berkeley on Saturday last. At least 2,500 people, many of whom were ladies were present. The weather was fine but the track was in very bad condition. The medals were given out to the winners at the close of the sports. The following is a summary of the results:—

220-yard hurdle race:—S W McNear, U C 1st. Time 29 4-5 secs.

120-yard run:—R Gallagher, U C, 2 yards, 1st; E Mays, U C, scratch, 2nd. Time 12½ seconds.

100-yard run, Maiden:—H B Denson, U C, 1st. Time 11½ secs.

1-mile run:—P L Weaver, U C, scratch, 1st. Time 4 min. 56¼ secs.

Pole Vault:—E C Van Dyke, scratch, 1st. Height 8 ft. 8½ in.

100-yard run, final heat—Edwin Mays, U C, 1st. Time 10 3-5 seconds.

120-yard hurdle race—F F Foster, O A C, 1st. Time, 19 1 5 seconds.

880-yard run—Walter A Scott, O A C, 1st; E C Hill, U C, Time, 2m 7¼s.

Running high jump—R V Whitney, U C, 1st; H C Moffit, U C, 2nd. Height, 5ft 4in.

One mile walk—George Foulkes, U C, 1st. Time 8min. 17sec.

Running broad jump—D Winter, U C, 1½ft, 1st. Distance, 20ft 7½in.

220-yard run—V E Schiffenstein, O A C, 1st. Time, 23½ sec.

Putting 16-lb. shot—L E Hunt, U C, scratch, 1st; Distance, 35ft 6in.

High kick—R V Whitney, U C, scratch, 1st. Height, 8ft 5½in.

Throwing 16-lb. hammer—A G Roberts, U C, 8ft, 1st; J J McKinnon, A A A C, scratch 2nd. Distance, 97ft.

880 yard run—C B Lakeman, U C, 1st. Time, 2min 16 1-5 secs.

440 yard run—A S Henderson, O A C, 1st; J D Garrison, A A A C, 2d. Time, 53 2 5 secs.

Hop, step and jump—H C Baldwin, U C, 3½ft, 1st; distance, 43ft 5½in.

440 yard run (consolation) and tug of-war were not given.

The mile relay race was won by the class of '93, the other classes not appearing.

Athletic committee—C E Townsend, '90; C B Lakenan, '90; A F Allen, '91; D Winter, '92; D E Perkins, '93.

Officers of the day—Referee, Lieut G F E Harrison, U S A. Judges—Prof Soule, Walter Magee, T F Scanlon, A A A C. Timers—Prof F Slate, G H Strong, Col Geo C Edwards, J A Hammersmith, Peter McIntyre. Starter—G F Davidson. Judge of walking—J Purcell, O A C. Measurers—J A Brewer, '91, H B Ainsworth, '91, Leslie Simson, '91. Clerk of course—Henry Bailey. Assistant clerks of course—E Bunnell, '91, P Thompkins, '92. Marshals—A D Stoney, '90, J H White, '91, E A Byler, '92.

$15,000. OPENING $15,000.

of the

GRAND CIRCUIT.

The World's Fair goes to Chicago, but the Greatest Fair ever held in the West takes place at

Agricultural Park, Los Angeles, August 4 to 9, 1890.

Fifteen Thousand Dollars in Purses, Stakes and Premiums.

Speed Programme:

FIRST DAY—MONDAY AUGUST 4TH.

No. 1. The Los Angeles Derby.—A sweepstake for three-year-olds (foals of 1887), $10 each, half forfeit, with $300 added, the second to receive $100, and the third $50, out of the stakes; a winner of any three-year-old stake race to carry five (5) pounds, of two or more, eight (8) pounds extra; maidens allowed seven (7) pounds. One mile and a half.

No. 2. The Edwards & McKnight stakes.—A sweepstake for all ages; $50 each, half forfeit; $300 added, the second to receive $100 out of the stakes. Non-winners this year allowed seven pounds. Maidens allowed ten pounds. One mile.

No. 3. Trotting.—The Los Angeles Purse, $1,500, open to all horses eligible to the 2:30 class, June 16th. Entrance, ten per cent, payable as follows: $50 June 16th, when entries close; $50 July 1st, and $50 July 22nd, when horses must be named. No subscription will be received unless the first payment shall accompany the same. Subscribers liable only for the amount paid in, but if a subscriber fails to make any of the payments when due, he shall surrender his subscription and payments to the Association with the right of substitution. The Board reserves the right to declare the "Los Angeles Purse" off, in the event of its not filling satisfactorily.

No. 4. Trotting.—Purse $500. 3 minute class. District.

SECOND DAY—TUESDAY AUGUST 5.

No. 5. A sweepstake for two-year-olds owned in the Southern Counties; $25 each, $10 forfeit; $150 added; the second to receive $75 out of the stakes. The winner of any race to carry four pounds extra. One-half (½) mile.

No. 6. The Nadeau Hotel Handicap.—Purse $1,000, of which $700 to the first; $200 to the second, and $100 to the third horse. Weight announced July 22nd. Twenty-five dollars ($25) to nominate, and fifty dollars ($50) each from all starters. The winner of any race after the announcement of the weights to carry five (5) pounds extra. One and one quarter mile.

No. 7. Trotting.—Two-year-old stakes, district, $250 added. See special condition.

No. 8. Pacing.—Purse $500. 2:35 class. District.

THIRD DAY—WEDNESDAY, AUG. 6TH.

No. 9. Selling Purse—For all ages, $350. Ten Dollars from starters to go to second horse. Fixed valuation $1000; three pounds allowed for each $100 less down to $700; then one pound for $100 down to $300; selling price to be named through the entry box at 5 P. M. the day before the race. Seven-eighths of a mile.

No. 10. Hurdle Race—A sweepstake for all ages; $30 each, half forfeit; $200 added; second horse to receive $75 out of the stakes. Five hurdles—about one and one half miles.

No. 11. Trotting—Three-year-old Stake. District $250 added. See special conditions.

No. 12. Trotting.—Purse $1000. 2:25 class.

FOURTH DAY—THURSDAY AUG. 7TH.

No. 13. The Hollenbeck Hotel Stakes—A sweepstake for two-year-olds (foals of 1888), $50 each, $20 forfeit; with $300 added, the second to receive $100, and the third $50 out of the stakes. A winner of any stake race before August 1st, to carry three pounds; and two or more stake races, five pounds extra; maidens allowed, if beaten once, five pounds; twice or more, eight pounds. Five-eighths of a mile.

No. 14. The California Handicap.—Purse $1000, of which $700 to the first, $200 to the second, and $100 to the third horse. Weights announced July 22nd. $25 to nominate, and $50 more for all starters. The winner of any race at this meeting to carry five pounds extra. Three-quarters of a mile.

No. 15. Trotting—Purse $1000, 2:27 class.

No. 16. Trotting—Purse $500, 2:40 class; District.

FIFTH DAY—FRIDAY, AUGUST, 8TH.

No. 17. The Sierra Madre Stakes.—A sweepstake for all ages. $25 each, half forfeit; $200 added, second to receive $75 out of the stakes. Winner of any race this year at three-quarters (¾) of a mile or less to carry six (6) pounds, and of two or more of such races, ten (10) pounds extra. Maiden allowed ten (10) pounds. One-half (½) mile heats.

No. 18. Santa Catalina Cup.—A sweepstake for all ages. $40 each; $20 forfeit; $300 added; the second to receive $100 out of the stakes. Five pounds above scale. Non-winners in 1889 and 1890 allowed ten (10) pounds. Maidens allowed twelve (12) pounds. A winner at this meeting to carry five pounds extra. One and one-eighth (1⅛) mile.

No. 19. Trotting.—Purse, $1,000, 2:20 class, District.

No. 20. Trotting.—Purse, $500. 2:5

SIXTH DAY—SATURDAY, AUG. 9TH.

No. 21. The Citrus Handicap.—A sweepstake for three-year-olds; $40, half forfeit, or only $10 if declared by 5 P. M. the day before the race; $250 added; the second to receive $100 out of the stakes. Weights to be announced by 5 o'clock P. M. second day before the race. One and one-sixteenth (1 1-16) of a mile.

No. 22. The Junior Handicap.—A sweepstake for two-year-olds. $30 each, half forfeit, or only $15 if declared by 5 P. M. the day before the race; $250 added; the second to receive $100, and the third $50 out of the stakes. Weights to be announced by 5 o'clock P. M. the second day before the race. Three-quarters (¾) of a mile.

No. 23. Trotting.—Purse $800, 2:35 class.

No. 24. Pacing.—Purse, $600, 2:25 class.

TROTTING STAKES—To close June 16th, 1890.

To be Trotted at the Annual Fair, to be held in Los Angeles in 1890—91.

TROTTING STAKES, 1890.

FOALS OF 1888. Mile and repeat. $250, added by the Association. Entrance, $50, payable in the following forfeits: $10 to accompany the nomination, $20 July 1st, and $20 August 11, 1890.

FOALS OF 1887. Mile heats, three in five. $250 added by the Association. $50 entrance, payable in the following forfeits; $10 to accompany the nomination, $20 July 1st, and $20 August 11, 1890.

TROTTING STAKES, 1891.

FOALS OF 1889. Mile and repeat. $250 added by the Association. $50 entrance, payable in the following forfeits: $5 to accompany nomination, $10 August 1st, 1890; $10 May 1st, 1891, and $25 on the first day of the Fair of 1891.

FOALS OF 1888. Mile heats, three in five. $250 added by the Association. Entrance, $50, payable in the following forfeits; $5 to accompany the nomination; $10 August 1st, 1890; $10 May 1st, 1891, and $25 on the first day of the Fair of 1891.

CONDITIONS.

All nominations to be made on or before June 16th. American Association rules to govern. Nominators liable only for the amount paid in, which becomes forfeit if subsequent payments are not made. All forfeits and entrance fees will be contributed to the stake, the whole divided where there are three or more starters as follows: sixty per cent. to the first, thirty per cent. to the second and ten per cent. to the third. If no more than two horses start, only first and second money shall be awarded, and in case of a walk over, only the first money shall be awarded. A horse distancing the field shall only be entitled to so much of the money as the starters in the race could have won. A nominator in making an entry in any of the above stakes shall give the name of owner, name of breeder and where foaled, the age, color, sex, dam and sire if known. Colts owned in the counties of San Luis Obispo, Fresno, Tulare, Kern, Santa Barbara, Ventura, Los Angeles, San Bernardino, Orange and San Diego shall be eligible to entry.

REMARKS AND CONDITIONS.

All trotting and pacing races to be to harness, mile heats, best three in five, except otherwise specified. Entrance 10 per cent on amount of purse. Trotting and pacing divided as follows: 50 per cent. to first horse; 25 per cent. to second; 15 per cent. to third, and 10 per cent. to fourth. Entries not declared out by 6 P. M. of the day before the race must start. In all trotting and pacing races, five to enter and three to start. The Board reserves the right to hold a less number than five to fill. Horses owned in Fresno, Tulare, Kern, San Luis Obispo, Santa Barbara, Ventura, Los Angeles, San Bernardino, Orange and San Diego Counties, are eligible for entry in district races. A horse distancing the field is entitled to first and fourth money. The Directors reserve the right to change the hour and day of any race, if deemed necessary. Races shall commence each day at 1 o'clock. American Association rules to govern, unless otherwise specified. Hay and straw free.

Running—The Pacific Coast Blood Horse rules to govern running races. Colonial-bred horses, foaled on Colonial time, allowed as follows: Two and three-year-olds, eight pounds; four-year-olds five pounds, and five-year-olds, three pounds. In all stakes, starters must be named to the Secretary or through the entry box at the track, on or before 6 P. M. of the day before the race. In all stakes, the right to forfeit ceases at 10 o'clock of the day on which the race is run. Racing colors to be named with the entry. Entries close with the Secretary July 1st.

Remember, entries for the 2:30 Trot and District Trotting Stakes close June 16th, and for everything else July 1st.

BEN BENJAMIN, Secretary.

L. LICHTENBERGER, President.

Guaranteed Purses

—Given by the—

San Mateo

AND

Santa Clara Co.

AGRICULTURAL ASSOCIATION

No. 5,

SAN JOSE, CAL.

Fall Meeting, 1890,

August 11th to 15th.

Trotting Purse, $1,200, 3-Minute Class.

Trotting Purse, $1,200, 2:30 Class.

Entrance fee 10 per cent., payable as follows: $10 on June 1st, when entries close; $10 on July 1st, and $10 on August 1st.

Pacing Purse, $600, 2:30 Class.

Entrance fee 10 per cent., payable as follows: $20 on June 1st, when entries close; $30 on July 1st, and $20 on August 1st.

CONDITIONS.

Mile heats, three in five. Money must accompany nominations, otherwise the entry will not be considered. Neglect to make payments when due forfeits previous payments.

Eight entries required to fill, four to make last payment and three to start.

Purse will be divided, 50 per cent. to first horse, 25 per cent. to second, 15 per cent. to third, and 10 per cent. to fourth. A horse distancing the field will get the 1st and 3rd money.

In case of a walk-over the horse will get the entrance money paid in only; otherwise National Trotting Association rules to govern.

WM. BUCKLEY, President,

G. H. BRAGG, Secretary.

CONTRA COSTA CO.

Agricultural Associat'n

District No. 23.

FAIR OF 1890.

Sept. 22 to 27, inclusive.

District Trotting Colt Stakes for 1890.

$40, payable as follows:

$10 June 1st (when stakes close), $15 Sept. 1st, and $15 Sept. 22d.

FOR ONE-YEAR-OLDS, 1 mile dash.
FOR TWO-YEAR-OLDS, mile heats, 2 in 3
FOR 3-YEAR-OLDS, mile heats, 3 in 5.
} $75 added to each.

All moneys divided as follows: 60, 30 and 10 per cent. In case of only two starting, 60 and 40 per cent., and in case of one horse walking over, the whole amount to go to such horse.

A failure to make any payment when due shall be considered a withdrawal and forfeiture of the amount paid in.

National Rules to govern.

The right reserved to refund the first payment in case the stakes do not fill reasonably well.

Entries close June 1, 1890 with the Secretary.

GEO. P. LOUCKS, President.

H. C. RAAP, Secretary, Martinez, Cal.

The Trotting Stallion

G & M

FULL BROTHER TO

ALFRED G, 2:19¾.

(Who has been taken to Kentucky to stand at $200)

Will make the season of 1890 from FEBRUARY 1st to JULY 1st, at

SANTA ROSA.

G. & M. is by Anteeo, 2:16¼; was foaled 1886; first dam Rosa B. by Speculation (son of Hambletonian 10); 2d dam Elizabeth by Alexander 490; 3d dam Nora by imp. Glencoe. Anteeo is by Electioneer, out of Columbine by A. W. Richmond 1687.

G. & M. is a handsome dark bay; stands 15-2 1-4 hands high, and weighs 1060 pounds. Gameness, stoutness, speed and stamina are indelibly impressed in every line of the pedigree of G. & M. Owners of brood-mares in search of these qualities, will do well to patronize this promising colt.

PHILOSOPHER,

Foaled 1886 by Pilot Wilkes 2887; first dam Bella by George Wilkes 519; second dam by Bell Morgan 61.

Philosopher's sire, Pilot Wilkes 2887, is by George Wilkes 519, dam Grace (the dam of Alice Woodburn etc.), by Pilot Jr. 12, grandam by Orphan Boy.

Will make the season of 1890, from FEBRUARY 1st to JULY 1st, at Santa Rosa.

TERMS for the season:

G. & M., $50,

PHILOSOPHER, $30,

with privilege of returning mares that do not prove in foal the next season free of charge, provided the horse bred to remains the property of the present owners. Good pasturage at $3 per month. No responsibility assumed for accidents or escapes. Service fees payable before removal of the mare. For further particulars, address

GEO. E. GUERNE,

Santa Rosa Cal.

Stallions and Colts

For Sale.

The Get of the Celebrated Racing Stallion

BAYSWATER,

FROM FINELY BRED MARES.

Inquire of

J. HEINLEN,

Lemoore, Tulare County, Cal.

LAWN VIEW BREEDING FARM STALLIONS.

ACTOR.

A beautiful bay horse foaled 1887 by Promptor 2305 sire of Apex (four-year-old record) 2:26, Transit 2:28½, Creole 2:20, Blue Belle 2:32, Daisy (yearling record) 2:38½, he by Blue Bull 75, 1st dam by Sultan 1513 2:24, sire of Stamboul 2:12 1-4, Ruby 2:19¾, Sweetheart 2:22½, Alcazar 2:20½, Eva 2:23½, La Grange 2:28½, and eleven others in 2:30 list, second dam by Fireman by Langford.

Actor, as his pedigree shows, is as purely bred a young stallion as ever made a season in the stud. Blue Bull stock is much sought after in the East, and Sultan, sire of his first dam will make the season in Kentucky this year at $100 per mare. Actor is a handsome bay colt 16 hands high, clean limbed and possesses all the points of a speedy trotter.

TERMS, $40 FOR THE SEASON, usual return privileges.

DOUGLASDALE 7650.

Thoroughbred Registered Clydesdale Stallion

Imported from Scotland, December, 1889, bay, three years old.

TERMS, $35 FOR THE SEASON.

YOUNG ELMO

Two years old sorrel stallion by St. Elmo 2:27, dam by Woodburn.

TERMS, $30 FOR THE SEASON.

For further particulars, address

MANAGER LAWN VIEW FARM, Auburn, Cal.

GROVER CLAY

Bay Stallion, Black Points,

15 3-4 hands high.

Bred by W. W. Traylor, San Francisco.

BY ELECTIONEER.

First dam Maggie Norfolk by Norfolk, son of Lexington, he by Boston. Second dam Tilda Quill by Billy Cheatham he by Cracken, and he by Boston. Third dam by Dorsey's Golddust.

TERMS.

Will make the season of 1890 at the Training Stables of Denis Gannon, near Oakland Trotting Park, at $50 the season, payable at time of service. Season to commence February 1st and ending July 1st. Proper care of mares will be taken, but no responsibility incurred for accidents or escapes. Address,

DENIS GANNON, Oakland, Cal.

GOLDEN GATE

Fair Association

Oakland.

Guaranteed Futurity Purse

$4.000.

To take place during the Fall Meeting of 1893.

For foals of 1890. Entrance 3 per cent. payable as follows:

$10 May 15, 1890, when entries close in name of foals or of dams and sires.

$10 Jan. 15, 1891.
$15, June 15, 1891.
$15, Jan 15, 1892.
$15 June 15, 1892.
$15 Jan. 15, 1893.
$20 June 15, 1893.

$20 fifteen days before advertised day of the race.

If the last payment is made on twelve or more entries the horses shall be started in trial races, in which not more than eleven or less than six shall be allotted to start. The trial races shall be mile heats, three in five, for a purse of $1,000, given by the Association for each race. If two trial races are trotted, the first four horses shall only be entitled to start in the final race. If three such trial races are trotted, only the first three horses in each trial race shall start in the final; and if four or more trial races are necessary, only the first two horses in each trial race shall start in the final race.

These trial races must be started not less than five nor more than ten days previous to the day set for the final race; and if possible all trial races will be trotted on the same day.

CONDITIONS.

Neglect to provide payments on the dates stipulated will incur forfeiture of all previous payments.

The Directors reserve the right to change the hour and day of any race except when it becomes necessary to ante-date a race, in which instance the nominator will receive three days notice of change by mail to address of entry.

Entries not declared out by 5 P. M. the day preceding the race, shall be required to start.

Purses will be divided into four moneys viz., 50 per cent. to the winner, 25 per cent. to the second horse, 15 per cent. to the third horse, and 10 per cent. to the fourth horse.

A horse distancing the field shall only be entitled to first and third moneys.

Trotting and racing colors shall be named by six o'clock on the day preceding the race, and MUST be worn upon the track.

All purse races, mile heats, best three in five to harness.

Otherwise than the above, National or American Trotting Association Rules—as this Association may select—will govern the races offered.

Entries to close with the Secretary.

R. T. CARROLL, President.

JOS. I. DIMOND, Sec'y, 306 Market St., S. F.

$1,000.

The Pacific Coast

Trotting-Horse Breeders' Ass'n,

Fall Meeting 1890.

Offer an Additional

Nomination Pacing Purse

$1,000 for 2:30 class Mile heats, best three in five Entrance $100, payable $20 June 10, 1890, $20 July 1, 1890, $20 August 1, 1890, and $40 on the tenth day preceding the first advertised day of the meeting. Horses to be named at time of last payment.

Entries to close with the Secretary June 10, 1890.

Conditions.

First payment MUST ACCOMPANY NOMINATIONS, or they will not be considered.

Neglect to make payments on the day stipulated will incur forfeiture of all previous payments.

No horses and colts owned on the Pacific Coast by others than members of the P. C. T. H. B. A. are eligible to the above purse, but horses and colts OWNED outside of the Pacific Coast are eligible thereto regardless of membership.

All States and Territories lying in whole or in part west of the Rocky Mountains are held to be part of the Pacific Coast.

The Directors reserve the right to change the hour and day of any race except when it becomes necessary to ante-date a race, in which instance the nominator will receive three days notice of change by mail to address of entry.

Entries not declared out by 5 P. M. of the day preceding the race, shall be required to start.

This Purse will be divided into four moneys, viz., [illegible] per cent. to the winner, 25 per cent to the second horse, [illegible] per cent. to the third horse, and [illegible] per cent. to the fourth horse.

A horse distancing the field shall only be entitled to first and third moneys.

The Board of Directors reserve the right to declare any purse or stake filled or not filled without binding itself to any specified number of entries.

In all nomination purses, eight entries will be required to fill, and four to make the last payment.

Trotting and racing colors shall be named by 5 o'clock on the day preceding the race, and MUST be worn upon the track.

Horses eligible on records standing at time of entry.

Otherwise than the above National Trotting Association Rules will govern.

Persons desirous of making entries in the above purse, and who have not as yet joined the P. C. T. H. B. A., should make application for membership to the Secretary, and remit the sum of $25 to cover membership fee before June [illegible], 1890.

J. H. WHITE, President,

JAS. P. KERR, Secretary, 313 Bush Street, S. F.

Guenoc Stud Farm, Lake Co., Cal.

Imp. GREENBACK

(Sire of the English winners Greenlight, Greenjacket, Greensbank, Greenwave and Greenhorn)

By Dollar, dam Music, by Stockwell. $100 the Season

ST. SAVIOR,

(FULL BROTHER TO EOLE)

By Eolus, dam War Song, by War Dance. $100 the Season.

PASTURAGE, $5 PER MONTH.

With right to return the following year if mare does not prove with foal. The best of care taken, but no liability for accidents or escapes. Mares shipped to C. W. ABY, care ST. HELENA STABLES, St. Helena Napa County, will be taken in charge by competent men.

For further information write to

DR. C. W. ABY, Middletown, Lake County, Cal.

SAN DIEGO, 8776.

SAN DIEGO 8776

- Alcona Clay 2756
  - Alcona 730. Sire of Flora Belle, 2:24, Clay Duke, 2:31½, etc.
    - Almont 33. Sire of Westmont, 2:13¾, Piedmont, 2:17¼, Puritan, 2:16, and 33 others in 2:30 list.
    - by Mambrino Chief 11. Sire of Lady Thorne, 2:18¼.
  - Madonna. Dam of Del Rey, trial 2:31, Alcona Jr., 2:41, sire of Silas Skinner, trial 2:23¼.
    - Cassius M. Clay Jr. 22. Sire of Durango, 2:23¾, Harry Clay, 2:23½, and sire of dam of Happy Thought, 2:22¼, and others.
    - by Joe Downing 710. Sire of Abe Downing, 2:20¼, Dick Jamison, 2:26, and sire of dams of Kentucky Hambletonian, 2:27, Lorena, 2:15, and others.
- Fontana. Dam of Flora Belle, 2:24, Silas Skinner, trial 2:23¼.
  - Almont 33. Sire of 36 in 2:30 list, 49 sons and 22 daughters that have produced 2:30 performers.
  - Fanny Williams. Dam of Bay Chieftain, 2:28¼.
    - Abdallah 15. Sire of Goldsmith Maid, 2:14, Thorndale, 2:21¼, also Almont, Belmont, Jim Monroe, etc
    - by Denmark (thoroughbred).

SAN DIEGO is dark seal brown, three years old, and trotted one-quarter miles in 40 seconds as a two-year old.

This grand young horse, and, barring accidents, will make a fast record next fall.

He will be allowed a limited number of mares, at $50 for the season. Mares not proving in foal to be returned free 1891. Best of pasture for mares at $4 per month, but no liability for accidents or escapes.

He will make the season from February 1st to June 1st at Napa Fair Grounds. For further particulars, address or call on

H. B. STARR, Race Track, Napa, Cal.,

or FRED W. LOEBER, St. Helena

Bay Rose.

REGISTERED No. 9814.

Record 2:20 1-2 Third Heat.

Will make the season of 1890, ending July 1st, at the SANTA ROSA STOCK FARM, (formerly Santa Rosa Race Track), SANTA ROSA.

DESCRIPTION.

BAY ROSE is a dark bay or brown, with black points, 15¾ hands high, and weighs 1150 pounds. He is remarkably intelligent, of good disposition, and a pure-gaited trotter. He was foaled in 1881. His colts are large, stylish, rangy animals, and inherit the qualities of speed and endurance.

PEDIGREE.

BAY ROSE 9814

- Sultan, 2:24. Sire of 18 in the 2:30 list.
  - The Moor 870. SIRE OF Beautiful Bells 2:29½, Del Sur 2:24¼, Inez 2:30, Sir Guy 2:28¼, Sultan 2:24, Tommy Gates 2:24
  - Sultana.
- Madam Baldwin
  - The Moor 870. Sire of 8 in the 2:30 list.
  - by Ben Lippincott, by Williamson's Belmont.

TERMS: $200 FOR THE SEASON.

Good pasturage $3 per month. First-class care taken of mares in any manner that owners may desire, but no responsibility assumed for escapes or accidents.

Limited to a few approved mares.

For further particulars, address

THOS. BONNER,

Santa Rosa Stock Farm, Santa Rosa.

Or apply to

IRA PIERCE,

728 Montgomery Street, S. F., Cal.

The Trotting Stallion

CUPID,

Full Brother to Adonis 2:14,

—Sired by—

The Celebrated SIDNEY 2:19 3-4, and out of Venus.

Will make the season of 1890 at the OAKLAND TROTTING PARK.

PEDIGREE.

CUPID is by Sidney out of Venus by Capt. Webster 10173, record 2:30, and sire of Freestone 2:19. Second dam by Skenandoah 936, sire of Daisy Burns 2:29¾, Erwin Davis (sire of two in the 30 list) and dams of four in the 30 list.

DESCRIPTION.

Cupid is a handsome bright bay 15.2½ hands high, weighs 1100 lbs.; was foaled in 1886. As a yearling, with very little work he showed quarters in 42 seconds, and at 2 years old, quarters in 38 seconds. As a three year old he has not been worked, but he shows the speed and endurance that must come from his excellent blood lines.

TERMS $50 for the season, with the usual return privileges. Good pasturage near the track at $5 per month. The best of care taken of mares in any way that owners may desire, but no responsibility assumed for accidents or escapes.

For further particulars address

C. O. THORNQUEST,

Oakland Trotting Park, or

C. BAAB, 972 Broadway, Oakland.

GEO. WASHINGTON,

11,623.

RECORD 2:30.

Bay colt, bred by Thomas Smith of Vallejo, Cal. Foaled 1888 by Mambrino Chief, Jr., 11,622, record 2:34 1-4. 1st dam Fanny Rose by Vick's Ethan Allen Jr, 2,903, sire of Prince Allen 2:27. 2nd dam Jenny Lind, thoroughbred, dam of Prince Allen 2:27. Will serve a limited number of mares at $50 for the season. Mares not proving with foal may be returned next season free.

Mambrino Chief, Jr.

11,622.

RECORD 2:34 1-2.

Sire of George Washington, record 2:30 at three years old. Bay horse bred by Rufus Ingalls of Belvedere, Ill. By McDonald Chief 3583. First dam Venus by Mambrino Patchen 58. 2nd dam by Wardlow's Shakespeare. 3rd dam Lone Gold. 4th dam by Silver Heels. Has not been in the stud before. He was 5 years old when he served a few mares, and his colts all show good style and form.

Terms for the season $40. For further particulars see or address

THOMAS SMITH,

Vallejo, Cal.

Langtry Farms' Stud

Imp. FRIAR TUCK

By the Immortal HERMIT

DAM ROMPING GIRL BY WILD DAYRELL.

AT $50 THE SEASON.

Mares not proving with foal may be returned the following season. Good care taken of mares, but no liabilities for accidents or escapes.

Good Pastorage at $5 per month.

Mares shipped to ST. HELENA, care CHARTES WILLIAM ABY, St. Helena Stables, will be cared for. For further particulars address.

CHAS. WILLIAM ABY,

Middletown, Lake County, Cal.

Races, Races,

JULY WEEK.

AT

South Park Race Track

Eureka, Cal.

GIVEN BY THE

EUREKA JOCKEY CLUB.

FIRST DAY, JULY 2, 1890.

No. 1. Novelty Running Race. Free for all. Dash of one mile. Purse $250. First quarter, $40. Half, $50. Third quarter, $70. Mile, $90.

No. 2. Running Race. Purse $150. Five-eighths dash, for two-year-olds. $125 to first horse; $25 to second horse.

No. 3. Running. Purse $150. Three-quarters and repeat. $125 to first; $25 to second.

SECOND DAY, JULY 3, 1890.

No. 4. Trotting. Purse $200. Three minute Class. $150 to first; $50 to second. (Covey barred.)

No. 5. Running Stake. Five-eighths of a mile. For Humboldt raised two year-olds. $30 entrance, half forfeit. $150 added. First to receive 60 per cent.; second, 30 per cent. third, 10 per cent.

No. 6. Running Stake. Purse $200. Mile Dash. $150 to first horse; $50 to second horse.

THIRD DAY, JULY 4, 1890.

No. 7. Trotting Stake. 2:40 Class. Purse $250. $200 to first horse; $50 to second horse.

No. 8. Running Stake, 1¼ miles. Free-for-all. $40 entrance, ½ forfeit, $200 added; second horse $75, third horse to save stake.

No. 9. Running Stake. Purse $150; 1-2 mile and repeat; $125 to first; $25 to second.

FOURTH DAY, JULY 5, 1890.

No. 10. Running Stake, 1-2 mile and repeat; for Humboldt horses owned prior to Jan. 1, 1890. $125 to first, $25 to second.

No. 11. Running Stake. Purse $200; 7-8 mile and repeat. $150 to first, $50 to second.

CONDITIONS AND REMARKS.

All trotting races are best three in five, unless otherwise specified. Four to enter and three to start, but the Board reserves the right to hold a less number than four to fill by the withdrawal of a proportionate amount of the purse. Entrance fee, 10 per cent. of purse, to accompany nominations. In all trotting races the rules of the American Trotting Association, and all running races the rules of the Pacific Coast Blood Horse Association to govern, but the Board reserves the right to trot heats of any two classes alternately, if necessary, to finish any day's racing. In all entries not declared out by 6 P. M. of the day preceding the race, shall be required to start.

No added money paid for a walk over. In all races, four or more paid up entries required to fill, and three or more horses to start. Racing colors to be named in entries. In trotting races drivers will be required to wear caps of distinct colors to be named in entries. Entries in all races to close with the Secretary, Thursday, June 20, 1890. Entry blanks will be furnished upon application to the Secretary.

All trotting races for horses owned and in Humboldt County prior to June 1, 1890.

H. M. DEVOY, President.

J. P. MONROE, Secretary.

SONOMA and MARIN

Futurity Stake,

To take place during the

FALL MEETING

OF THE

Sonoma and Marin Agricultural Society,

1893.

For Foals of 1890.

Open to the get of stallions owned in the district which is comprised of the following counties: Sonoma, Marin, Napa, Lake, Mendocino, Solano, Yolo, Colusa and Contra Costa.

Mile heats, 3 in 5; entrance $75, with $25 added for each starter over two and up to five head, and $10 for each additional starter up to ten head.

Payments: $5 must accompany the nomination on July 1, 1890; $5 on January 2, 1891; $5 on July 1, 1891; $10 on January 2, 1892; $10 on July 1, 1892; $15 on January 2, 1893; $25 on July 1, 1893.

CONDITIONS.

1—Neglect to provide payments on the dates stipulated will incur forfeiture of all previous payments.

2—When there is more than one entry to this stake by one person or in one interest, the horse to be started must be named by 6 P. M. of the day preceding the race.

3. The stake will be divided into four moneys, viz., [illegible] per cent. to the first, 25 per cent. to the second, 15 per cent. to the third and 10 per cent. to the fourth horse.

4. If only three horses start in this stake, only the first, second and third money shall be paid; if but two start, there will be no added money, the stake money paid in will be divided—two-thirds to the first and one third to the second horse.

5. A horse distancing the field shall only be entitled to first and third moneys.

6. The Board of Directors reserve the right to declare the stake filled or not filled without binding itself to any specified number of entries.

7. Otherwise than the above, National or American Trotting Association Rules—as this Society may select—will govern the stake.

Entries to close on July 1st with the Secretary.

J. H. WHITE, President.

DR. THOMAS MACLAY, Secretary, Petaluma.

Memo.

The Best Son of SIDNEY

Will Make the Season of 1890 at the OAKLAND RACE TRACK

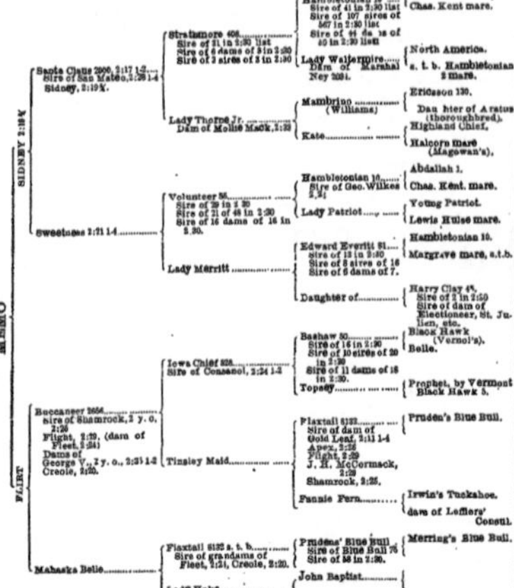

MEMO is, as can be seen at a glance, one of the best bred young stallions in service, having three crosses of Rysdyk's Hambletonian and one of Harry Clay, the sire of Green Mountain Maid (dam of Electioneer, etc.), while Long Island Black Hawk and Flaxtail also contribute to his blood. Sidney (Memo's sire) is universally known as the best young sire in the world, a producer of extreme speed at an early age.

PERFORMANCES.

MEMO trotted in public in his two year-old form, obtaining a record of 2:49, though he was close to Grandee in a race on the Bay District Track, the second heat of which was made in 2:31 1-2, the first in 2:31. He exhibited phenomenal speed when three years old, and had it not been for a slight strain of his fore fetlock, there is little question that he would have shown in public very close to the best record. On the Oakland track he was timed a mile in 2:20 1-2, and frequently trotted quarters in from 32 1-2 to 34 seconds.

As a four-year-old Memo only started once—at Sacramento—when, although out of condition, he showed great speed, and improving as he went on, great hopes were entertained of his going well down in the 'teens at the P. C. T. H. B. A. meeting, but after showing several very fast miles his leg filled and he was laid up for the season. He is sixteen hands high, and of powerful build throughout. His color is a glossy black, with both fore-feet white. His disposition is all that could be desired, and his action superb. He is a sure foal getter, only one mare being reported not in foal during his last season.

TERMS, $100, with usual return privileges, for a limited number of mares. Season to close JUNE 15th, when he will be prepared for track purposes. Pasturage $4 per month. Have leased the cricket ground adjoining the track for pasturage, where there is fine feed. Reasonable charges if fed hay and grain. Best of care taken of mares in any manner owners may desire, but positively no responsibility assumed for accidents or escapes. For further particulars address

J. P. KERR, 313 Bush Street, San Francisco,

or, JOHN ROWEN, Race Track, Oakland, Cal.

2:10 1-2 ELECTIONEER 2:12 1-4

BAY STALLION	BROWN STALLION
ECLECTIC	**MORTIMER**
11,321	5,346
By Electioneer, dam Manette (full sister to Woodnut 2.16 1-2 Manon 2:21 and Maple, dam of Hattie D., three-year-old record 2:26½) by Nutwood 2:18¾, etc., etc.	Four-year-old Record 2:27 By ELECTIONEER, dam MARTI, by Whipple's Hambletonian (sire of 15 in 2:30, and of dams of eight in 2:30). Second dam Ida Martin by Rifleman (sire of Col. Lewis 2:18½).
Terms $100 for the Season.	**Terms $60 for the Season.**

Horses shipped via San Francisco may be consigned to J. W. MORSHEAD, City Front Stables, who will attend to their forwarding.

Season closes JULY 1st, 1890. Usual return privileges.

For further particulars address owner,

WILFRED PAGE, Penns Grove,
Sonoma County, Cal

The Trotting Stallion

Silver Bow

Will make the season of 1890 at the Oakland Race Track.

PEDIGREE.

SILVER BOW 11708, two-year-old record 2:37, is by Robert McGregor 647, 2:17½ (sire of Bonnie McGregor, 2:13½, Earl McGregor, 2:21½, Mac D., 2:30, McGregor Boy, 2:29½, Mark Time, 2:30, Roxie McGregor, 2:30½) by Major Edsall 2:11, 2:29, by Alexander's Abdallah 15—sire of Goldsmith Maid, 2:14—by Hambletonian 10—sire of Dexter, 2:17¼.

Robert McGregor's dam was Nancy Whitman by American Star 14, by Stockholm's American Star.

SILVER BOW'S first dam is Sadie by Hambletonian 10, sire of Geo. Wilkes, 2:22—sire of Guy Wilkes, 2:15¼—also Electioneer, sire of Sunol, three-year-old record, 2:10½, and Palo Alto, 2:12¼; second dam Lady Wynne by Wm. Welch 341; third dam Elenora Margrave by imp. Margrave.

DESCRIPTION.

SILVER BOW is a handsome bay, no white; 15-2½ hands high; weighs 1075 pounds; of fine form, with the best of legs and a clean-cut, intelligent head. Is remarkably level-headed, seldom making a break; wears seven-ounce shoes in front. His record, 2:37, is no mark of his speed; he can beat 30 easy, and with his gilt-edge breeding, he is just what he ought to be, a trotter sired by a trotter whose dam was herself a trotter and his grandam the dam of two trotters. His dam Sadie being by Hambletonian 10, shows him to be bred from the cream of the trotting blood.

TERMS: $100 for the season. Mares not proving in foal returnable for the season of 1891 free of charge. Good pasturage and first-class care taken of mares for $5 per month. No responsibilities assumed for escapes or accidents. For further particulars, address

Limited to 15 approved mares.
Season to end June 1st, 1890.

P. J. WILLIAMS,
Care Race Track, Oakland, Cal.

Pleasanton Stock Farm Co.'s Stallions.

DIRECTOR, 2:17.

Director's book is open for 15 good mares more than already booked for the season of 1890, at $300 each.

This is the cheapest service fee ever charged for a stallion, taking into consideration his BREEDING and RACE RECORD and the RACE RECORDS OF HIS COLTS.

Season to commence February 15th and close August 1st.

CORRECTOR, Five Years Old.

Sire Director 2:17, dam Brainey, she by Echo. Echo sired by Rysdyk's Hambletonian out of Fanny Felter, by Magnolia, he by Seely's American Star. Brainey's dam Lady Dudley, she by Tom Dudley by Blacknose, a son of Medoc, he by American Eclipse. Lady Dudley's dam by Bertrand, Jr., a son of Bertrand.

CORRECTOR is a rich seal brown 15½ hands high, and is the fastest young stallion in the world under the same conditions, never having been off the farm where raised and never been shod or driven for speed before last Christmas, and can trot quarters now in 35 seconds, a 2:20 gait.

He will be allowed to serve ten good mares, at $100 each for the season, which closes June 1st.

DECORATOR, Four Years Old.

Sire Director 2:17, dam Chess, sired by Cardinal 2.37, trial 2:28, he by Gen. Gifford's Morgan, dam of Cardinal, sired by Joe Gales of Ohio, he by Marlborough out of the Duchess of Marlborough by Southern Eclipse; second dam old Duchess of Marlborough by Sir Archy; third dam by imp Diomed. Decorator's second dam a Morgan and Messenger mare.

Decorator is a light bay 16 hands high, and with but little handling for speed has shown eighths in 17½ seconds, a 2:20 gait.

He will be allowed to serve ten good mares at $50 each for the season, which closes June 1st.

Mares not proving with foal may be returned next season free of charge of service fees to the same stallion, if he is still in our possession; however, the company reserves the right to return the fee instead of giving service.

Pasturage $4 per month; hay and grain extra. Accidents and escapes at owner's risk.

Service fees due at time of service, and must be paid, together with pasturage, etc., before mares are taken away, or a good approved note given, payable August 1st, 1890, at which date all bills must be settled.

For further information call or address **M. SALISBURY, 320 Sansome Street, Room 26, San Francisco,** or

PLEASANTON STOCK FARM CO.,
Pleasanton, Alameda Co., Cal.

SOUTHER FARM

P. O. Box 208.	San Leandro, Cal.
1½ miles northwest of San Leandro; 8 miles southeast of Oakland. Turn off County road between above places at "Stanley Road," ½ mile north of San Leandro.	Horses boarded at all times in any manner desired. Best of care but no responsibility for accidents. Colts broken and handled for the road or track. Terms reasonable.

Glen Fortune,	Jester D,	El Benton,	Figaro,
By Electioneer.	By Almont.	By Electioneer.	Hambletonian 725
$50 for 1889.	$50 for 1890.	Limited to 5 mares.	Limited to 12 mares
		Book Full.	Book Full.

THE SOUTHER FARM

Has Green Feed the Year Round,

and feeds Hay in connection with the green feed, which a horse must have if he is to thrive. Every animal is given

A Dry, Warm Place to Sleep,

No matter how stormy the weather. All Stock under cover when it rains.

VISITORS WELCOME ANY DAY EXCEPT SUNDAY.

How to Get Stock to the Souther Farm.

The Souther Farm is one and a half miles northeast of San Leandro and eight miles southeast of Oakland. The stables are about one mile east of the county road, which runs between Oakland and San Leandro. The place to turn off is at Stapley Road, where a large signboard of the farm is placed. Guide boards will be found at every cross road. In any ordinary weather the roads are very good, and they are fairly good after the unusually heavy rainfall of the past winter.

All stock sent from San Francisco may be brought over by Garcia's Express, No. 3 Market street, San Francisco. They also have an order box outside of Hawley Bros.' Hardware house on the corner of Market and Beale streets. The express leaves San Francisco on the Creek route boat, which starts at 1:15, but all orders should be in the order box at Market and Beale streets by 10 o'clock, or at the office, No. 3 Market street, by 11 o'clock at the latest. In the case of very young or very valuable horses, the Souther Farm will send reliable men to lead or drive over any stock that will not lead behind a wagon. A small charge will be made in such cases, to cover the extra expense incurred.

Horses are very easily taken from Oakland to the farm, and where it is inconvenient for owners to bring them, or send them, the farm will send after anything that is to come. On horses that stay three months or over there is no charge for getting or delivering. Where a horse stays a short time the actual time and expense only is charged to him.

Horses can be shipped by rail from almost all parts of the State to San Leandro. Always notify the Farm several days before shipping anything, and then men will be on hand to receive stock on arrival. The railroad station is but two miles from the Souther Farm, and the agent invariably gives immediate notice of the arrival of any stock consigned to the above farm, but when word is sent to the farm in good season by letter or telegram, the animals sent are saved waiting a couple of hours in the car.

Passenger trains leave San Francisco (from the broad gauge ferry) and First and Broadway, Oakland, at frequent intervals during the day. There are several trains from San Jose to San Leandro on both the broad and narrow gauge railroads; the broad gauge, by way of Niles, is much more convenient for getting to the farm. There are trains each day from Sacramento, Stockton and Livermore to San Leandro. In ordinary weather it is a short and pleasant drive from Oakland to the Souther Farm or from San Francisco to the Farm by way of the Creek route ferry boat. Always notify the Souther Farm just when you will arrive at San Leandro, and some one will meet you at the station. If you do not recognize the farm conveyance ask the stage driver, who will point it out.

Write to the above address for references, circulars and price lists. Terms reasonable.

GILBERT TOMPKINS, Proprietor.

SAN MATEO STOCK FARM

HOME OF GUY WILKES,

Record, 2:15 1-4.

Guy Wilkes' Book is full for 1890 and 1891, and positively no more mares will be received.

Sable Wilkes, three-year-old record 2:18, will be allowed to serve 25 mares in addition to those already engaged at $250 the season of 1890. SABLE Wilkes, 15½ hands, black horse, by Guy Wilkes, first dam Sable by The Moor; second dam Gretchen by Mambrino Pilot; third dam Kitty Kirkman by Canada Chief; fourth dam by Fanning's Tobe; fifth dam by imp. Leviathan.

Leo Wilkes, brown horse, four years, 16 hands, full brother to Sable Wilkes, will be allowed to serve 30 mares at $100 the season

Mares not proving with foal may be returned the following season free of service fee. Parties engaging the services of any of the above horses must send a deposit of 10 per cent. of service money with engagement. Pasturage $6 per month, and when the condition of the animal requires it, hay or grain, or both, are fed, the charge will be $12 50 per month. Good care will be taken of all mares sent to the Farm, but no liability will be assumed for accidents or escapes.

All bills are due at time of service, but must be paid by August 1st of each year. No stock will be allowed to leave the place until all bills are paid.

WILLIAM CORBITT.
San Mateo Stock Farm.

Vineland Stock Farm

Alcona 730.

Sire of

FLORA BELLE - - - - Record 2:24
CLAY DUKE - - - - - " 2:31½

ALCONA will be a great sire, but four of his colts have ever been trained, and all have shown full miles better than 2:30, and two of them as good as 2:20. Two of his first sons each sired a colt as a two-year-old, and last season one as a four-year-old trotted a full mile in 2:23¾, and the other, a three-year-old, a mile in 2:31. With opportunities, Alcona is destined to be one of Almont's best sons. Almont, for his opportunities, is beyond doubt the most prepotent sire of his age. He has 36 representatives in the 2:30 list; 49 sons and 32 daughters that have already produced 2:30 performers. Almont died five years ago at 20 years old. If he lived he would be but 25 years old.

PEDIGREE.

ALCONA sired by the great Almont (sire of Westmont 2:13¾, Fanny Witherspoon 2:16¾, Piedmont 2:17¾, and 33 others with records better than 2:30, and grandsire of Belle Hamlin 2:12¾, etc.); by Alexander's Abdallah (sire of Goldsmith Maid 2:14), he by Rysdyk's Hambletonian. Alcona's dam, Queen Mary, by Mambrino Chief (sire of Lady Thorne 2:18 1-4, and 5 others in the 2:30 list, and sire of the dams of Director 2:17, Piedmont 2:17¾, Onward 2:25 1-4, Red Wilkes Almont, Belmont and many other noted sires).

DESCRIPTION.

Alcona is a beautiful chestnut 16 3 1-2 hands high, and weighs 1300 lbs. His colts possess speed, style, finish and beauty, and if they don't trot they command the highest prices for carriage horses.

$40 for the season. Usual return privilege.

Season of Alcona and Grandissimo ends July 1st, 1890.

Grandissimo,

Full Brother to GRANDEE, 3-year old record 2:23 1-2.

Sired by La Grande (son of Almont, and out of Jessie Pepper by Mambrino Chief; Jessie Pepper is the dam of Ione 2:17 1-2, Alpha 2:23 1-2, Sterling Wilkes 2:21¾, and others) dam Norma, by Arthurton (sire of Arab 2:15, Joe Arthurton 2:20 1-2, etc.)

Grandam Nourmahal (full sister to A. W. Richmond, sire of Arrow 2:13¾, Romero 2:19, and sire of Columbine, dam of Anteeo 2:16¾, and Antevolo 2:19¾ at four years old).

DESCRIPTION.

Grandissimo is four years old, will make a sixteen hand horse; he is a rich mahogany bay in color and perfect in style and action. $50 for the season. Usual return privileges.

"Grandissimo" with limited training last fall as a three-year-old, trotted quarters in 35 seconds and miles in 2:40.

I feel confident that he will trot fast this season, and will be a great sire as his colts this season are all grand youngsters.

The best of pasturage $4 per month. Mares taken care of in any manner that owners may desire, but no responsibility assumed for escapes or accidents.

For further particulars send for circular or call at stables, one mile south of St. Helena.

FRED W. LOEBER Prop'r.

The Trotting Stallion

VICTOR,

Record 2:22.

Will make the season of 1890 at NAPA CITY.

DESCRIPTION.

VICTOR is a handsome dark bay; 15.3 hands high; weighs about 1,150 pounds, and is remarkably intelligent, level-headed, of kind disposition, and a magnificent animal in every respect. He is well boned and muscled, of splendid conformation, and possesses the qualities of speed and endurance to an eminent degree—qualities that he imparts to his progeny.

PEDIGREE.

VICTOR, record 2:22.
- Echo 462
  - Hambletonian 10, Sire of 41 in the 2:30 list.
    - Abdallah 1
    - Chas. Kent mare
  - Fanny Felter
    - Magnolia 68
    - by Webber's Kentucky Whip
- Daughter of
  - Woodburn
    - Lexington
    - Lulu Horton
  - daughter of
    - Ashland
    - thoroughbred

ECHO is the sire of Belle Echo, 2:20, Senator, 2:21¾, Victor, 2:22, Gibraltar, 2:22¾, Echora, 2:23¾, Tippie, 2:25¾, Lohengrin, 2:27¾, Pasha, 2:27½, Elmonte, 2:29, Col. Hawkins, 2:29¾, Annie Laurie, 2:30, Economy, 2:30, Sam Lewis, pacer, 2:25.

TERMS—$60 FOR THE SEASON.

Mares not proving with foal may be returned next season free of charge, provided the horse remains the property of the present proprietor, and stands at the same place, otherwise money will be refunded. The best of care taken of mares in any manner that owners may desire, but no responsibility assumed for accidents or escapes. For further particulars, apply to or address

G. W. HUGHES, Agent,

G. A. DOHERTY, Proprietor. Napa City.

The Trotting-Bred Stallion

RINGWOOD

THE FINEST SON OF THE NOTED SIDNEY,

Will make a Season at Oakland, commencing March 1, and ending June 1, 1890.

DESCRIPTION.

RINGWOOD is a dark, rich colored bay, black points, 15 1-2 hands, weight 1100 lbs., and a pure gaited trotter. Has shown great speed. He is now five years old. As a four year old he showed a trial in 2:19 1-2, and but for an accident would have received a record as a four year old of 2:18 or better.

PEDIGREE.

RINGWOOD is by Sidney, record 2:19 3-4, and a half brother to Gold Leaf 2:11 1-4, Adonis 2:11, Fleet (two year old) 2:24, Longworth 2:19, Sister V. 2:27, Faustino, yearling, 2:35, Fleet, yearling, 2:35. Memo, three year old trial 2:20 1-2.

Sidney is by Santa Claus, record 2:17 1-2; he by Strathmore, sire of 31 in 2:30 list; he by Hambletonian 10, the greatest of all producers; he by Abdallah. Sidney's dam, Sweetness, record 2:21 1-4; she by Volunteer, the sire of St. Julien 2:11 1-4.

RINGWOOD'S dam Alma; she by Dashway, thoroughbred; he by Belmont, he by American Boy; he by Sea Gull; he by imported Expedition. Alma's 1st dam, Fanny Cobb, was a great road mare, pedigree untraced.

TERMS: $50 for the Season.

Payable June 1st, or sooner if mares are taken away. Address communications to

A. C. DIETZ,

Oakland, Cal.

2:10¾ 2:13¾ 2:10

DEXTER PRINCE.

This Royally-bred Stallion will make the Season of 1890 at the LIVE OAKS Breeding Farm, 2 miles from Lodi, San Joaquin County, Cal.

DESCRIPTION.

DEXTER PRINCE is a blood bay, 16 hands high, weighs over 1,100 pounds; has great power and substance, and the highest finish. When two years old, at Palo Alto, he was timed quarters by Gov. Stanford in 33¼ seconds, and he was driven eighths by Mr. Marvin at a faster rate of speed than that. He is a sure foal-getter, and invariably sires foals of good size, of fine form and finish, and the highest rate of speed.

PEDIGREE.

By KENTUCKY PRINCE, the sire of Guy, 2:10¾, Spofford, 2:18½, Company, 2:19¾, Bayonne Prince, 2:21 1-4, Fred Folger, 2:20¾, and a score more in the 2:30 list.

First dam LADY DEXTER, full sister of the greatest of trotters, Dexter, and the greatest of sires, Dictator, the sire of Director, 2:17, Phallas, 2:13¾, in a fourth heat, and Jay-Eye-See, 2:10.

Second dam Clara, the dam of Dexter, 2:17 1-4, Dicta or, Astoria 2:29 1-4, and Alma, 2:28¾. Clara was by American Star, that has 34 daughters that have produced 2:30 or better trotters.

Third dam the McKinstry mare, the dam of Shark, 2:27¾. HAMBLETONIAN, the grandsire of DEXTER PRINCE, has 40 trotters in the 2:30 list, 44 daughters that have produced 2:30 trotters, and more than 100 sons that have sired 2:30 trotters.

CLARK CHIEF, the grandsire on the sire's side, was the sire of performing and producing sons and daughters.

DEXTER PRINCE has faster blood lines, on both sides, than any other stallion in the world—Guy 2:10¾, and Jay-Eye-See, 2:10.

KENTUCKY PRINCE is one of the best bred and speediest stallions in the world. David Bonner, in the presence of Governor Stanford, timed him when he trotted a 2:10 gait. He is by Clark Chief, one of the great broodmare sires; his first dam is Kentucky Queen by Morgan Eagle, son of Hale's Green Mountain Morgan, 2nd dam by Blythe's Whip, 3rd dam by Martin's Brummer, 4th dam by Quicksilver 880, on through the strongest thoroughbred blood.

TERMS.

$100 for the season, with usual return privileges. Payable before mares are removed. Good pasture, and the best care furnished, but no responsibility assumed for accidents.

PREMIUM.

$250 will be given to the first of the produce of DEXTER PRINCE put in the 2:30 list, and $100 each after the first. Address

L. M. MORSE, Lodi, Cal.

The Produce of Eros Averaged $2,200 Each at New York Auction Sale in 1889.

THE ELECTIONEER TROTTING STALLION,

5326 EROS 5326

Will make the season of 1890—February 1st to July 1st—at LA SIESTA RANCH, MENLO PARK, adjoining Palo Alto.

PEDIGREE.

EROS (5326)
Standard by his sire
" " dam
" " record
" " produce
" under all rules

EROS (5326)
- Electioneer, Grandsire of Norlaine, 1 yr., 2:31 1-2, Sire of Sunol, 2 yrs., 2:18, Sunol, 3 yrs., 2:10 1-2, Hinda Rose, 4 yrs., 2:16, Palo Alto, 2:12¾.
  - Hambletonian 10, Sire of Dictator, George Wilkes, Happy Medium, and 40 others in 2:30 list, and grandsire of 728 in list.
    - Abdallah 10, Sire of the dams of Goldsmith Maid, 2:14, and 7 other producing dams.
    - Charles Kent mare, By imp. Bellfounder.
  - Green Mountain Maid, Dam of Prospero, 2:20, Elaine, 2:20, Dame Trot, 2:22, Elista, 2:22¾, Storm, 2:26¾, Antonio, 2:28¾, Miranda, 2:31, Mansfield, 2:26.
    - Harry Clay, Sire of the dams of St. Julian, 2:11¾, Bodine, 2:19¾, and 17 more in 2:30 list
    - Shanghai Mary.
- Sontag Mohawk, Dam of Eros, 2:29 1-2, Sport, 2:29¾, Sallie Benton, 2:17¾, Conductor, trial, 2:26, Colma, 3-y-o trial, 2:24.
  - Mohawk Chief, Sire of the dams of Lot Slocum, 2:17¾, Sallie Benton, 4 yrs., 2:17¾, Pediar, 3 yrs., 2:27¾, Stanford, 4 yrs., 2:30, Eros, 6th heat, 2:29 1-2.
    - Hambletonian 10, Sire of the dams of Stamboul, 2:12¾, Wilton, 2:19¾, and 29 other trotters.
    - Lady Perrine
  - Sontag Nellie
    - Toronto Sontag, By Toronto Chief,
    - Nellie Gray, 3-mile record, 12:45.

Produce of Eros
Wanda, 4 yrs., 2:31,
Solita, 2 yrs., 2:41 1-2,
Meriquita, 2 yrs., 2:42,
Daylight, 2 yrs., 2:44,
Hiram B., trial, 2:28.

These are the only colts by him that have ever had a harness on except one in New York that went a trial last July in 2:26 1-2.

DESCRIPTION.

EROS is a rich seal brown stallion, bred by Hon. Leland Stanford at Palo Alto, and is the nearest living likeness of his celebrated sire, Electioneer. Stands 15.2 hands high, and weighs 1050 pounds.

In breeding to Eros, the owners of mares will strictly follow the great rule of breeding, viz., breed to a stallion by a producer and out of a sure producer of great speed. Eros is by the stallion that has produced more 2:30 trotters that any living horse, and is also the sire of more 2:20 performers than any horse living or dead.

EROS is out of the dam of Sally Benton, four years old, record 2:17¾, Sport 2:22¼, and Eros 2:29½ in the sixth heat, against a field of nine horses. He is from a family that is endowed with great natural speed, trot fast at an early age, train on, throw trotters from all classes of mares, are of good substance, bone, style and action, and breed solid colors.

TERMS.

$100 for the season, with the privilege of return next season should mares not be in foal and horse and mare still remain in the same hands.

Good pasturage can be obtained at $5 per month, but no responsibility for accidents or escapes. There are a large number of box stalls, and animals can be kept up and fed on hay and grain at reasonable rates if required. Mares already in foal can be sent to the ranch for foaling, and will receive all the attention bestowed upon our own mares. Mares left with Mr. Peter Pomyea, Broadway Street Stable, Oakland, or with Mr. F. H. Burke, 401 Montgomery Street, San Francisco, will be forwarded to the ranch free of charge. For further particulars apply to

W. H. VIOGET.

LA SIESTA RANCH, MENLO PARK, CAL.

EROS is the only stallion offered to the public on this Coast that has a dam that has three in the 2:30 list.

GRAND MOOR, 2374.

Grand Moor 2374
- Moor 870
  - Sire of Beautiful Bells 2:29½
  - Sire of Sable (dam of Sable Wilkes) 2:18
  - Sire of Sultan 2:24
  - Sire of Tommy Gates 2:24
  - Sire of Del Sur 2:24¾
  - Sire of Sir Guy 2:28¾
  - Beautiful Bells is the dam of Hinda Rose, 2:19½ as a 3-year-old, Palo Alto Belle, 2:22¾, Chimes, St. Bell, 2:21¾, Bell Boy (3 years) 2:19¾.
  - Sultan, 2:24 (sire of Stamboul 2:12¾) has 16 in 2:30 list.
    - Clay Pilot 93, Sire of 2 in 2:30 list.
    - Belle of Wabash.
- Vashti, Dam of Don Tomas, who got a record of 2:20 in 1889.
  - Mambrino Patchen 58, Sire of 14 in 2:30 list, Sire of the dam of Guy Wilkes, 2:15¼; also sire of 20 stallions and 18 mares with get in 2:30 list.
  - Kate Taber, By Mambrino Messenger, he by Mambrino Paymaster.

Foaled 1876. Black. Sixteen hands high. Bred by L. J. Rose

A horse of highest form and quality; of great excellence in every point; a type of his celebrated family; of marked individuality, spirit and endurance; never properly trained or raced, but shows the possession of great speed: perfectly manageable in the stable and on the road and track.

As he is sired by The Moor 870, a son of CLAY PILOT, out of Vashti by MAMBRINO PATCHEN, he is a most valuable cross for mares of other families. THE MOOR sired Beautiful Bells and the dams of Sable Wilkes and Margaret 2:28 (dam of Regal Wilkes, 2-year-old record 2:20½).

MAMBRINO PATCHEN is regarded as the unsurpassed sire of broodmares, having, among many others, sired the dam of Guy Wilkes and of Wm. L. (the sire of Axtell), and a son of his sired the dam of Axtell. The public sales this year have demonstrated with renewed emphasis the value of The Moor and Mambrino Patchen strains of blood. For combining particularly with the Hambletonians it may be called "the ready money cross."

GRAND MOOR will make the season of 1890 for a time at the Oakland Race Track and afterwards at my Ranch, fifteen miles from Oakland. Mares can be delivered at the race track to the groom in charge. Pasturage at $5 per month. For other food, if requested, an additional charge will be made.

TERMS, $150 for the season, with privileges of return if the horse does not change hands.

Every care exercised, but no liability for escapes or accidents.

H. I. THORNTON, 504 Kearny Street.

Cook STOCK FARM.

Season of 1890.

STEINWAY 1808.

Three-Year Old Record 2:25 3-4.

Sire of STRATHWAY, three year old record 2:26, and sire of the dam of BOURBON RUSSELL 2:30.

By STRATHMORE 408; sire of 31 in the 2:30 list; sire of 6 dams of 8 in the 2:30 list, and sire of 3 sires of 3 in 2:30 list.

1st dam ABBESS (dam of Solo 2:28, and Soprano, dam of C. F. Clay 2:18, Eminence 2:27 and Strathbridge, 3 year old record 2:28½) by ALBION, sire of VANITY FAIR 2:24½, and of the dam of FAVORITE 2:25½.

2nd dam by MARSHALL NEY.

3rd dam by BERTRAND, a son of SIR ARCHY.

TERMS—$100 for the season.

CHARLES DERBY 4907

Brown Horse. Foaled 1885.

By STEINWAY 1808.

1st dam by the great ELECTIONEER, sire of SUNOL 3 year old record 2:10½, Palo Alto 2:12¼, etc., etc.

2nd dam FANNY MALONE, by NIAGARA.

3rd dam FANNY WICKHAM, by HERALD.

4th dam by Imp. TRUSTEE.

TERMS—$100 for the season

Pasturage $5 per month. Accidents and escapes at owner's risk. Mares consigned to the farm should be sent to Fashion Stables, Oakland; Geary & Grindle's Stable, Haywards; or to Bennett's Stable, Martinez; from and to which places they will be delivered free of charge. Address

COOK STOCK FARM,

Danville, Contra Costa, Co., Cal.

Sunny Side Breeding Farm.

Admiral 488.

Foaled 1867—Sired by Volunteer 55, Son of Rysdyk's Hambletonian 10.

First dam Lady Pierson by Cassius M. Clay (Neaves') 20; second dam by Diamond; third dam a running mare said to be thoroughbred. He is fitted in an eminent degree to produce colts that will in all respects justify his patrons in their expectations.

Admiral is the sire of Huntress, record 2:27¼, Sister, 2:19¼, Perhelion, 2:25, Nona Y., 2:25, and others equally as promising, but have not had the advantage of track work. He will serve a limited number of approved mares at $50 the season, with usual return privilege. Season ending August 1, 1890. No liability for accidents or escapes.

KING DAVID 2576.

Bay Stallion—Foaled 1883.

Sired by Admiral 488, dam Black Flora (the dam of Huntress, 2:27¼, Sister, 2:19¼, Perhelion, 2:25, Nona Y., 2:25), by Black Prince.

King David is one of the best gets of Admiral. He has a good disposition, kind to drive, smooth and even-gaited, and can speed fast. Barring accidents, he will trot in the twenties this Fall. His colts are large, rangy, and well finished. Will serve a limited number of mares at $30 the season, to end July 1, 1890. Every precaution will be taken to prevent accidents and escapes, but no liability will be assumed. Pasturage $4 per month.

Sunny Side Farm is situated two miles east of Vallejo, on the Sulphur Spring road. For further particulars, address

FRANK DRAKE,

Vallejo, Cal.

The Fast Trotting Stallion

REDWOOD.

Four-Year-Old Record 2:24 1-2

Will make the season of 1890—February 1st to July 1st—at

SANTA ROSA.

REDWOOD is a dark bay colt, 15.2¾ hands high, weighs 1100 lbs. Foaled in 1885 by Anteeo, 2:16¾, sire of Alfred G., 2:19¾. Anteeo is by Electioneer. First dam Lou Milton, by Milton Medium; second dam Old Fly, a thoroughbred mare brought from the East in 1871 by W. C. Ralston, Esq.

Redwood's sire was out of Columbine by A. W. Richmond, the sire of the pacers Arrow 2:13¾, and Elwood 2:23, and the trotters Romero, 2:19¾, and Len Rose, 2:27. Redwood has shown a quarter in 33 seconds.

Terms $100

For the season. Mares not proving with foal may be returned next season free of charge, provided Redwood remains the property of the present owners. Good pasturage at reasonable rates. No responsibility assumed for escapes or accidents. Service fees payable before removal of the mare. Limited to 40 approved mares. For further particulars address

A. McFADYEN.

Santa Rosa, Cal.

For Sale.

JUANITO ALMONT,

Sire of Almont Patchen, 2:15.

JUANITO ALMONT is a bright bay, 16-1 hands in height, and weighs 1,200 pounds.

PEDIGREE.

By Tilton Almont, 2:26, he by the great Almont 33; dam by Signal 3327; he by Bunday's Rob Roy.

JUANITO ALMONT, if given a chance would undoubtedly prove a great sire, and should prove a desirable acquisition to any stock farm in the State.

For further particulars address

T. B. COOPER,

Adin, Modoc County, Cal.

Breeders' Directory.

Advertisements under this heading 50c. per line per month.

HORSES AND CATTLE.

W. S. JACOBS, Sacramento, Cal. – Breeder of Thoroughbred Shorthorns and Berkshire Hogs.

J. H. WHITE, Lakeville, Sonoma County—Breeder of Registered Holstein Cattle.

EL ROBLAS RANCHO—Los Alamos, Cal., Francis T. Underhill, proprietor, importer and breeder of thoroughbred Hereford Cattle. Information by mail. C. F. Swan, manager.

PAGE BROTHERS.—Penn's Grove, Sonoma Co. Cal. Breeders of Short Horn Cattle; Draft, Roadster and Standard Bred Horses.

SETH COOK, breeder of Cleveland Bay Horses, Devon, Durham, Polled Aberdeen-Angus and Galloway Cattle. Young stock of above breeds on hand for sale. Warranted to be pure bred, recorded and average breeders. Address, Geo. A. Wiley, Cook Farm, Danville, Contra Costa Co., Cal.

MAMBRINO WILKES COLTS and FILLIES, full brothers and sisters to Gus. Wilkes 2:22, and Balkan 2:29¾, for Sale. Address SMITH HILL, Walnut Creek, Contra Costa County, Cal.

PETER SAXE & SON, Lick House, San Francisco, Cal.—Importers and Breeders for past 18 years of every variety of Cattle, Horses, Sheep and Hogs.

HOLSTEIN THOROUGHBREDS of all the noted strains. Registered Berkshire Swine. Catalogues. F. H. BURKE, 401 Montgomery St., S. F.

Situation Wanted.

By an Experienced and Successful Trainer of Racehorses.

Address,

S. J. MILLER,

103 South Desplaines Street, Chicago, Ill.

J. J. EVANS

—SELLS—

WALLACE'S YEAR BOOK,
WALLACE'S REGISTER No. 8.
STALLION SERVICE BOOKS,
For Office and Pocket.
—ALL KINDS—
PEDIGREE BLANKS.
NEW STAKE ENTRY BOOK,
PEDIGREE BOOK.
HERD BOOK.

J. J. Evans,
Stationer and Printer,
406 California Street, San Francisco, Cal.
Mail orders receive prompt attention.

C. C. LINIMENT.

The Great Pain Conqueror for Man and Beast.

For Horsemen and Stockmen this Liniment is Invaluable

OWNERS OF FINE STOCK CANNOT AFFORD TO BE WITHOUT IT.

A remedy for every home, giving instant relief in pain and PERFORMING PERMANENT CURES.

To get the full benefit of the C. C. Liniment in chronic cases, in connection with C. C. Liniment use Compound Sulphur Powder, the "Great Blood Purifier," put up ONLY by The W. H. Bone Co., 12 Bush St., San Francisco. For Habitual Constipation, Indigestion, Piles, etc., it is the greatest remedy known to medical science.

If your druggist does not keep it, we will send direct, post paid, on receipt of price. COMPOUND SULPHUR POWDER is $1 per bottle, 6 for $5. Small bottles, 25c.

The C. C. Liniment Co

12 BUSH STREET, S. F.

W. H. BONE, - - General Manager.

FOR SALE BY ALL DRUGGISTS.

The Pacific Coast

Live Stock Owners

MUTUAL PROTECTIVE ASS'N.,

MONTEREY, Monterey Co., Cal.

TRUSTEES:

HON. B. V. SARGENT, President,
G. W. GALLANAR, Secretary,
JAMES E. PALMER, Business Manager,
EDW. INGRAM, Vice-President,
FRED. D. HOWARD, Actuary,
R. H. WILLEY, Attorney.

GENERAL BUSINESS OFFICE, Room 73, Flood Building, corner Market and Fourth Streets, San Francisco, Cal.

VOLNEY HOWARD, General Manager.

FISHING TACKLE,

WHOLESALE AND RETAIL.

CLABROUGH, GOLCHER & CO.,

630 and 632 Montgomery St.

AN UNQUALIFIED ENDORSEMENT.

Peruvian Bitters are made of the purest ingredients and compounded as carefully as any prescription.

Peruvian Bark, one of its principal ingredients, was introduced into Spain by the Countess, wife of Count CINCHON, Spanish Viceroy to Peru in 1630, who was cured of a fever by its use, since which time, no better remedy for Malaria and for Restoring the Natural Tone of the Stomach has been discovered.

On the Atlantic Coast they are used in the principal Hotels, Clubs and Restaurants, and sold by all Grocers and Druggists. We have sold them for the past three years WITHOUT ANY ADVERTISING and sales have constantly increased UPON MERIT ALONE, and we unqualifiedly recommend them to our friends and customers.

ACKER, MERRALL & CONDIT.

New York, Feb. 1st, 1890.

WILMERDING & CO., Agents for Pacific Coast,
216 FRONT ST., SAN FRANCISCO, CAL.

THE IMPROVED NOYES ROAD-CART,

PATENTED JULY 17, 1883, AND JUNE 8, 1886.

Some of the Advantages of the Noyes Cart Over All Others.

There is no bar for the rider to climb over in getting in or out. The horse can be hitched eighteen inches nearer than any other road-cart made. You can get in or out with perfect safety—no danger of being thrown into the wheel—a great advantage in breaking colts. THE EASIEST CART FOR ROAD OR TRACK. The only cart that a horse can be speeded to within one second as fast as to a sulky. All our carts are made of the very best materials and are warranted. Manufactured by the NOYES CART COMPANY, Kalamazoo, Mich.

They are indorsed by the following horsemen, all of whom are using them. Ask their opinion of the Noyes Cart: John Splan, who drove Guy a full mile in 2:17¼ and Chanter a half-mile in 1:10¼ to a Noyes Cart, says he would not take $250 for it if he could not get another; W. J. Gordon, Glenville, O.; W. B. Fasig, Cleveland, O.; Dave Muckel, Cleveland, O.; R. J. Moorehead, North East, Pa.; W. J. Chamberlain, Cleveland, O.; H. F. Malone, Bradford, Pa.; S. A. Brown & Co., Kalamazoo Stock Farm; Charles Marvin, Menlo Park, Cal.; W. H. Crawford, Lexington, Ky.; S. L. Caton, who gave Bell Boy a mark at Los Angeles, Cal., of 2:19¼, and drove Chanter a half mile in 1:06¼ and Lowland Girl a full mile in 2:22 to a Noyes Cart; Mike Bowerman, Lexington, Ky.; James Golden, Medford, Mass.; John E. Turner, Philadelphia, Pa.; T. L. Newton, Beaver Dam, Wis.; F. V. Johnston, Marshall, Mich.; W. H. McCarthy, Los Angeles, Cal.; A. W. Dennison, El Dorado, Kan.; P. O. Shank, Cleveland, O.; Charles Barnard, Boston, Mass.; Johnson Bros., Greenville, Mich.; John G. Avery, Buffalo, N. Y.; General R. L. Howard, Buffalo, N. Y.; Howard Conklin, Buffalo, N. Y.; W. D. Ham, Hennepin, Ill.; R. G. Henry, Waterbury, Conn.; J. E. Hayes, Newburgh, O.; J. C. Hart, Jefferson, Tex.; A. W. Harbison, Rock Point, Pa.; Carl Hodges, Battle Creek, Mich.; Barney Treacy, Lexington, Ky.; George Forbes, Cleveland, O.; Gifford Dudley, Topeka, Kan.; William and J. L. Thompson, Lamont, Pa.; C. P. Emery, Forest City Stock Farm, Cleveland, O.; H. F. Jones, Minneapolis, Minn.; John Forbes, Elyria, O.; D. J. Downs, Battle Creek, Mich.; Frank Caton, Randall Station, O.; Arthur D. Sutton, Ind., Pa.; W. F. Neely, Grand Ridge, Ill.; Walter Clark, owner of Pilot Medium, Battle Creek, Mich.; H. R. Kingman, Battle Creek, Mich.; Dr. Sutton and H. C. Reed, Kalamazoo, Mich.; Budd Doble, Chicago, Ill.

SOLE MANUFACTURERS OF STONE'S PATENT SULKY CASE.

They will more than save their cost in one season, and horsemen campaigning trotters cannot afford to do without them. Would refer to Samuel A. Brown, Kalamazoo Stock Farm, S. L. Caton and W. H. McCarthy. Address

NOYES CART COMPANY, Kalamazoo, Mich.

Office and Factory, corner Rose and Eleanor streets. H. ARTHUR STONE, Manager.

Poplar Grove Breeding FARM.

Standard-bred Trotters, Colts and Fillies.

The get of CLOVIS, 4909; PASHA, 2039; APEX, 2935,

For Sale.

Address S. N. STRAUBE, Poplar Grove Breeding Farm,
Fresno, Cal.

Inspection by intending purchasers invited, and information by mail.

KENNEL ADVERTISEMENTS.

LOST.

A White Pointer Dog

With lemon spots. Answers to the name of "Point. A liberal reward and no questions asked on delivery of same at

SWAIN'S STABLE,
417 Folsom St.

In the Stud.

"DAN GLADSTONE,"

3377 A. K. C. S. B

BY CH. GLADSTONE—CH. SUE.

Winnings—Southern Trials, 1889, Divided Third.
Indiana Trials, 1889, Divided Third.
Southern Trials, 1889, Second.

Will be at Stud in San Francisco until Sept 15, 1890. Fee, $25.

GEO. J. HARLEY, 844 Harrison St., S. F.

DOGS—Pointer Pups

FOR SALE.

Sure Bench Show and Field Trial Winners, as they have more bench-show and field-trial blood in them than any that have ever been whelped on the Pacific Coast.

Sire, POINT, double field trial winner; he by Vandevort's Don, great field trial and bench show winner, out of Drab, field trial and bench show winner.

Dam, QUEEN CROXTETH by Rush T., bench show winner, out of Champion Patti Croxteth, field trial and bench show winner. This is the best pointer blood in the world. Breeding and health guaranteed. Address,

A. B. TRUMAN,
1426 Steiner St., near Ellis, S. F., Cal.

CALIFORNIA SPANIEL KENNELS,

Oakland, California, H. P. RENNIE, Prop; Breeder and importer of typical COCKER SPANIELS. Winner of first prizes at S. F. and Los Angeles, 1889; also, Columbus, 1889, New York, 1887. In the stud, solid Black Cocker dog, GIFFEE, won 1st and Gold Medal at S. F., 1889. Fee, $25. Puppies and grown dogs at reasonable prices. My dogs can neither talk nor climb a tree, but are fielders and prize winners.

Highland Farm,

LEXINGTON, KY.,

Home of Red Wilkes.

Standard-bred Trotting Stock

For Sale,

Sired by Red Wilkes, Wilton, 2:19¼; Allandorf and Sentinel Wilkes, out of highly bred Standard Mares of the most fashionable blood of the day.

W. C. FRANCE, Proprietor.

For Sale

A HALF BROTHER TO

ALMONT PATCHEN,

(2:15, trial 2:13 3-4).

JUANITO JR. is a beautiful bright bay, black points, with no white, foaled 1886. As a colt he has given much more promise than did Almont Patchen at the same age. Instead of being a pacer, he is a good square trotter, with every indication of great speed, and is so gentle and kind, that a lady can drive him. The owner's only reason for selling him is that business calls him away from this section of the State. He will be sold at a reasonable figure. This is a splendid opportunity for a gentleman to secure a first-class trotter at a very low figure.

The pedigree of Juanito Jr. is by Juanito (sire of Almont Patchen), dam Nettie Moore by Old Tom Moore. For further particulars, address

JUANITO JR.,
Santa Clara P. O., Cal

For Sale

A FIRST-CLASS

Napa County Farm

—OR—

STOCK RANCH,

800 Acres Improved,

SITUATED TWO AND A HALF MILES FROM NAPA CITY, with good roads leading thereto, a good hard finished house of nine rooms, with all modern improvements, streams running all summer, a great amount of live oak and black oak timber. It lies in a fruit belt, surrounded by fine vineyards and orchards growing upon the same quality of soil, and originally a part of this tract. About one-half hill, and one-half rolling land, but none of it is steep and all easily cultivated, splendidly situated for the breeding of fine horses. Price, $65 per acre. Further particulars given at this office.

BREEDER AND SPORTSMAN,
313 Bush St.

Stallion for Sale

AT A BARGAIN.

Full Brother to Fairmont.

By Piedmont, dam Queen by Garibaldi—see State Fair Edition of BREEDER AND SPORTSMAN, September 14, 1889, for description of Fairmont—three years old, solid bay. Can trot a 2:40 gait or better. Sound in every particular. Can be seen at Oakland Trotting Park, Oakland.

P. J. WILLIAMS.

Southern Pacific Co.

(PACIFIC SYSTEM.)

rains leave and are due to arrive at San Francisco.

LEAVE (FOR)	FROM APRIL 13, 1890.	ARRIVE (FROM)
7.30 A M	Haywards, Niles and San Jose ...	*12.45 P M
7.30 A M	Sacramento and Redding, via Davis	7.15 P M
7.30 A M	Sacramento, Auburn, Colfax	4.45 P M
9.00 A M	Martinez, Vallejo, Calistoga and Santa Rosa	6.15 P M
8.30 A M	Los Angeles Express, Fresno, Bakersfield, Mojave and East and Los Angeles	11.15 A M
8.30 A M	Niles, San Jose, Stockton, Ione, Sacramento, Marysville, Oroville and Red Bluff	4.45 P M
0.30 A M	Haywards and Niles	3.45 P M
2.00 M	Haywards, Niles and Livermore	8.45 P M
1.00 P M	Sacramento River Steamers	**6.00 A M
3.00 P M	Haywards, Niles and San Jose	9.45 A M
3.30 P M	2d Class for Ogden and East	10.45 P M
4.00 P M	Stockton and ‡Milton; Vallejo, Calistoga and Santa Rosa	9.45 A M
4.30 P M	Niles and Livermore	* 8.45 A M
4.30 P M	Niles and San Jose	‡ 6.15 P M
6.00 P M	Shasta Route Express, Sacramento, Marysville, Redding, Portland, Puget Sound, East and Knight's Landing via Davis	10.45 A M
6.00 P M	Haywards and Niles	7.45 A M
6.00 P M	Sunset Route, Atlantic Express. Santa Barbara, Los Angeles, Deming, El Paso, New Orleans and East	8.45 P M
6.00 P M	Central Atlantic Express, Ogden and East	9.45 A M

SANTA CRUZ DIVISION.

7.45 A M	Excursion train to Santa Cruz	‡ 8.05 P M
8.15 A M	Newark, Centerville, San Jose, Felton, Boulder Creek and Santa Cruz	6.20 P M
2.45 P M	Centerville, San Jose, Almaden, Felton, Boulder Creek and Santa Cruz	*11.20 A M
4.45 P M	Centerville, San Jose, and Los Gatos	9. 0 A M

oast Division (Third and Townsend Sts.)

7.25 A M	San Jose, Almaden and Way Stations	2.30 P M
8.30 A M	San Jose, Gilroy, Tres Pinos; Pajaro, Santa Cruz; Monterey; Pacific Grove, Salinas, San Miguel, Paso Robles, Santa Margarita (San Luis Obispo) and principal Way Stations	6.12 P M
0.30 A M	San Jose and Way Stations	5.02 P M
2.01 P M	Cemetery, Menlo Park and Way Stations	3.38 P M
3.30 P M	San Jose, Tres Pinos, Santa Cruz, Salinas, Monterey Pacific Grove and principal Way Stations	*10.00 A M
4.20 P M	Menlo Park and Way Station	* 7.58 A M
5.20 P M	San Jose and Way Stations	9.03 A M
6.30 P M	Menlo Park and Way Stations	6.35 A M
1.45 P M	Menlo Park and principal Way Stations	†7.28 P M

A M for Morning. P M for Afternoon.
Sundays excepted. †Saturdays only. ‡Sundays only.
**Mondays excepted. §Saturdays excepted.

OCEANIC STEAMSHIP CO.

arrying United States, Hawaiian and Colonial Mails.

WILL LEAVE THE COMPANY'S WHARF, foot of Mission street, No. 1,

For Honolulu, Auckland and Sydney,

WITHOUT CHANGE,

The Splendid New 3,000-ton Iron Steamer.
ZEALANDIA ... Saturday, May 31st, 1890, at 12 M.,
Or immediately on arrival of the English mails.

For Honolulu,

S. AUSTRALIA (3,000 tons), May 23, 1890, at 12 M

For freight or passage, apply at office, 327 Market Street. JOHN D. SPRECKELS & BROS. General Agents.

KILLIP & CO.,

LIVE STOCK AND GENERAL AUCTIONEERS,

22 Montgomery Street, San Francisco

SPECIAL ATTENTION PAID TO SALES OF

High-Bred Horses and Cattle.

At auction and private sale.

Will Sell in All Cities and Counties of the State.

REFERENCES.

Hon. C. Green, Sacramento. — Hon. J. D. Carr, Salinas.
J. P. Sargent, Esq., Sargents. — Hon. John Boggs, Colusa.
Hon. L. J. Rose, Los Angeles. — Hon. A. Walrath, Nevada.
J. B. Haggin, Esq., San Francisco.

Represented at Sacramento by Edwin F. Smith Secretary State Agricultural Society.
At San Jose by Messrs. Montgomery & Rea, Real Estate Agents.

Being the oldest established firm in the live-stock business on this Coast, and having conducted the important auction sales in this line for the past fifteen years, amounting to one half a million of dollars, we feel justified in claiming unequaled facilities for disposing of live stock of every description, either at auction or private sale. Our list of correspondents embraces every breeder and dealer of prominence upon the Pacific Coast, thus enabling us to give full publicity to animals placed with us for sale. Private purchases and sales of live stock of all descriptions will be made on commission, and stock shipped with the utmost care. Purchases and sales made of land of every description. We are authorized to refer to the gentlemen whose names are appended.

KILLIP & CO., 22 Montgomery Street

HEALD'S

Business College, 24 Post St.

—San Francisco.—

The most popular school on the Coast

E. P. HEALD, President. C. S. HALEY, Sec'y.

Send for Circulars.

San Francisco and North Pacific Railway.

THE DONAHUE BROAD-GAUGE ROUTE.

COMMENCING SUNDAY, APRIL 27, 1889, AND until further notice, boats and trains will leave from and arrive at the San Francisco Passenger Depot, Market-street Wharf, as follows:

FROM SAN FRANCISCO FOR POINT TIBURON AND SAN RAFAEL.

Week Days—7.40, 9.20, 11.20, A. M.; 1:30, 3.30, 5.00, 6.15 P. M.
Sundays—8.00, 9.30, 11.00 A. M.; 1.30, 3:30, 5.00, 6.15 P. M.

FROM SAN RAFAEL FOR SAN FRANCISCO.

Week Days—6.50, 7.55, 9.30, 11:40 A. M.; 1.40, 3.40, 5.05, 6:25 P. M.
Sundays—8.10, 9.40, 11:10 A. M.; 1.40, 3.40, 5.00, 6:25 P. M.

FROM POINT TIBURON FOR SAN FRANCISCO

Week Days—7.15, 8.20, 9.55 A. M.; 12.05, 2.05, 4.05, 5.30, 6.50 P. M.
Sundays—8.35, 10.05, 11:35 A. M.; 2.05, 4.05, 5.30, 6:50 P. M.

Leave San Francisco. Week Days.	Leave San Francisco. Sun-Days.	Destination	Arrive San Francisco. Sun-Days.	Arrive San Francisco. Week Days.
7.40 A M 9.20 A M 3.30 P M §5.00 P M	8.00 A M 5.00 P M	Petaluma and Santa Rosa	10.40 A M 7.25 P M	8.50 A M 10.30 A M 4.40 P M 7 25 P M
7.40 A M 3.30 P M	8.00 A M	Fulton, Windsor, Healdsburg, Litton Springs, Cloverdale, and way stations.	7.25 P M	10.20 A M 7.25 P M
7.40 A M	8.00 A M	Hopland and Ukiah.	7.25 P M	7.25 P M
7.40 A M 3.30 P M	8.00 A M	Guerneville	7.25 P M	7.25 P M 10.30 A M
7.40 A M 5.00 P M	8.00 A M 5.00 P M	Sonoma and Glen Ellen	10.40 A M 6.05 P M	8.50 A M 6.05 P M
7.40 A M 3.30 P M	8.00 A M 5.00 P M	Sebastopol	10.40 A M 7.25 P M	10.20 A M 7.25 P M

Stage connects at Santa Rosa for White Sulphur Springs, and Mark West Springs; at Geyserville for Skaggs Springs, and at Cloverdale for the Geysers; at Hopland for Highland Springs, Kelseyville, Soda Bay, Lakeport and Bartlett Springs, and at Ukiah for Vichy Springs, Saratoga Springs, Blue Lakes, Willits, Cahto, Calpella, Potter Valley, Sherwood Valley and Mendocino City.

EXCURSION TICKETS from Saturdays to Mondays, to Petaluma, $1.50; to Santa Rosa, $2.25; to Healdsburg, $3.40; to Litton Springs, $3.60; to Cloverdale, $4.50; to Hopland, $5.70; to Ukiah, $6.75; to Guerneville, $3.75; to Sonoma, $1.50; to Glen Ellen, $1.80.

EXCURSION TICKETS, good for Sundays only, to Petaluma, $1; to Santa Rosa, $1.50; to Healdsburg, $2.25; to Litton Springs, $2.40; to Cloverdale, $3; to Guerneville, $2.50, to Sonoma, $1; to Glen Ellen, $1.20.

H. C. WHITING, General Manager.

PETER J. McGLYNN, Gen. Pass. & Tkt. Agt.

Ticket Offices at Ferry, 222 Montgomery Street and 2 New Montgomery Street.

6 DONTS

DON'T own a racehorse.
DON'T be a breeder.
DON'T be a trainer.
DON'T be a jockey.
DON'T bet on the races.
DON'T go to a race track.

WITHOUT HAVING IN YOUR POCKET ONE OF

Goodwin's

ANNUAL OFFICIAL TURF GUIDES.

Price, in cloth $2.00
Price, in half morocco 3.00
Price, in half calf 4.00
If sent by mail .... 10 cents extra

SUBSCRIBE TO IT FOR 1890.

It is published semi-monthly during the racing season, and is but $10 per year. Address

GOODWIN BROS.,
241 Broadway, New York City.

OUR IMPROVED. ALL SIZES AND WEIGHTS. G. W. BOHANON. ESTB. 1858.

THE BOHANON SULKY! BEST MADE. Perfect Riding Buggies. Breaking Carts. Fine Repairing, Reasonable Prices

Bohanon Carriage Co., 161-163 Ogden Ave., CHICAGO.

Send for Catalogue.

Dairyman's Account Book FREE.

The Dairyman's Account Book is the most practical thing of the kind ever seen. It gives ruled pages for daily record of milk yield, butter made, and sales, for 12 months; convenient size, nicely printed and bound. Wells, Richardson & Co., Burlington, Vt., manufacturers of the celebrated Improved Butter Color, the purest, strongest, and brightest color made, will send a copy free to any butter maker who writes enclosing stamp. Also sample of their Butter Color to those who have never used it, and a pretty birthday card for the baby, if you ask.

FOR STOCK.

COLIC AND GRUBS.

I have used Simmons' Liver Regulator in Colic and Grubs with my mules and horses, giving them about half a bottle at a time, and have not lost one that I gave it to. You can recommend it to every one who has stock as the best medicine known for all complaints that horseflesh is heir to.

E. T. TAYLOR, Ag't for Grangers of Ga

FOR CHICKENS.

In using Simmons' Liver Regulator (Powder) with my chickens for Cholera, I take and mix it with the dough and feed it to them once a day. By this treatment I have never lost a single chicken in the last five years from either Chicken Cholera or Gapes.

T. G. BACON, Edgefield, S. C.

HOG CHOLERA.

A reliable gentleman who raises every year about one hundred head of hogs told me he never lost one from Cholera, although the disease had often appeared among his herd. His remedy is Simmons' Liver Regulator given in drenching—about double that given to a man. I give this information for the benefit of those whose hogs may be attacked with Cholera.—PROF. F. P. HOPGOOD, OXFORD, N. C.

SIMMONS LIVER REGULATOR

is so conveniently given. The Powder mixed with the feed will be eaten by horses, cattle hogs, and chickens readily, while the Liquid (prepared) is easily given as a drench.

—ONLY GENUINE.—

Manufactured by J. H. ZEILIN & CO., Philadelphia, Pa. Price $1.00.

HORSE OWNERS!

TRY GOMBAULT'S

CAUSTIC BALSAM.

A Safe, Speedy and Positive Cure for Curb, Splint, Sweeny, Capped Hock, Strained Tendons, Founder, Wind Puffs, all Skin Diseases or Parasites, Thrush, Diphtheria, Pinkeye, all Lameness from Spavin, Ringbone or other Bony Tumors. Removes all Bunches or Blemishes from Horses and Cattle.

Supersedes all Cautery or Firing.

Impossible to Produce any Scar or Blemish.

Every bottle sold is warranted to give satisfaction. Price $1.50 per bottle. Sold by druggists, or sent by express, charges paid, with full directions for its use. Send for descriptive circulars. Address LAWRENCE, WILLIAMS & CO., Cleveland, O.

BROU'S INJECTION

A PERMANENT CURE in from 3 to 6 days, of the most obstinate cases; guaranteed not to produce Stricture; no sickening doses; and no inconvenience or loss of time. Recommended by physicians and sold by all druggists. J. Ferré, (successor to Brou), Pharmacien, Paris.

For any Kind of a

SORE THROAT

USE

McCLELLAN'S

DIPHTHERIA REMEDY

An Unfailing Cure.

FOR SALE BY ALL DRUGGISTS

R. LIDDLE & SON

538 Washington St., S. F.,

Wholesale and Retail Dealers in

Guns, Rifles and Pistols.

A Full Line of FISHING TACKLE and SPORTSMAN'S GOODS.

Orders by mail receive prompt attention.

"STANDARD" SHOTGUN CARTRIDGES — SELBY STANDARD — THE BEST IS THE CHEAPEST

By-Laws

—AND—

Rules and Regulations

—OF THE—

NATIONAL

Trotting Association

REVISED FOR 1890,

ALSO THE

AMERICAN

Trotting Association,

AND THE

PACIFIC COAST BLOOD-HORSE ASSOCIATION.

With Betting Rules.

For Sale at the Office of the

Breeder and Sportsman,

313 Bush St., S. F., Cal.

Price, 25c. each.

By Mail, Postage Paid, 30c. each.

VETERINARY.

Dr. Wm. H. Jones, M.R.C.V.S.

Veterinary Surgeon,

(OLYMPIC CLUB STABLES)

503 Sutter Street, San Francisco.

Telephone, No. 1404.

Consultations by letter, and cases of URGENT NECESSITY in the interior will receive prompt attention.

Dr. A. E. BUZARD,

VETERINARY SURGEON,

Member of the Royal College of Veterinary Surgeons, London, England. Graduated April 22d, 1870.

All Operations on the Horse Performed Skillfully.

Special attention given to the Diseases of Dogs. Calls to the country promptly attended to. Advice and prescriptions by mail $2. Office and Residence, No. 11 Seventh street, S. F. (opp. Odd Fellows Hall. Telephone No. 3 69.

W. H. WOODRUFF.

Veterinary Dentist,

AT FASHION STABLES,

221 Ellis Street, San Francisco

Improved Instruments, Humane Methods, First-Class Work.

H. E. CARPENTER,

Veterinary Surgeon,

Graduate of Ontario Veterinary College, Toronto Canada.

RESIDENCE AND VETERINARY INFIRMARY

331 Golden Gate Ave., San Francisco.

Telephone 3069.

OPEN DAY AND NIGHT.

No risk in throwing Horses. Veterinary Operating Table on the premises.

DR. C. MASOERO,

Veterinary Surgeon,

Successor to DR. A. DeTAVEL,

GRADUATE OF ROYAL VETERINARY COLLEGE, TURIN.

OFFICE AND INFIRMARY

No. 811 HOWARD STREET,

Between Fourth and Fifth. SAN FRANCISCO

Telephone, No. 457.

R. WATKINS,

Veterinary Dentist,

Office at C. S. Crittendens' Golden Gate Livery and Riding Academy, 24 to 28 Golden Gate Avenue.

Refers to Palo Alto Stock Farm; Wm. Corbett, San Mateo Stock Farm; B. C. Holly, Vallejo, and others. Examination Free.

E. J. O'ROUKE.

I have the honor to announce to my old patrons and the general public that I may be found at my old stand, where, as heretofore, the

Shoeing of Horses,

whether for the Track, Drive, or for general work, will receive my personal attention.

Telephone 2011.

E. J. O'ROUKE,
209 Ellis Street

ST. JULIEN

Horse Shoeing SHOP,

126 Geary Street, S. F.

MARTIN O'DEA, - - PROPRIETOR.

California Horse Shoe Co's

STEEL SHOE

Light, Strong and Perfect.

Superior to all others for Speed Horses.

ALSO

The Celebrated GOODENOUGH Pattern Shoe.

OFFICE: 203 Market St., San Francisco, Cal.

I have used in my business the Steel and Iron Shoes made by the above Company, and take great pleasure in saying they are the best I have ever used in twenty-two years' practice. I have never seen anything like the STEEL SHOE made by this Company. I can fully recommend them to every practical Horseshoer in the country. Yours respectfully,

No. 8 Everett Street. JOHN GRACE.

Old Hermitage Whiskies

"STEINER'S,"

No. 311 BUSH STREET,

San Francisco.

Under Breeder and Sportsman Office.

Everything for Trotter or Runner,

At J. A. McKERRON'S,

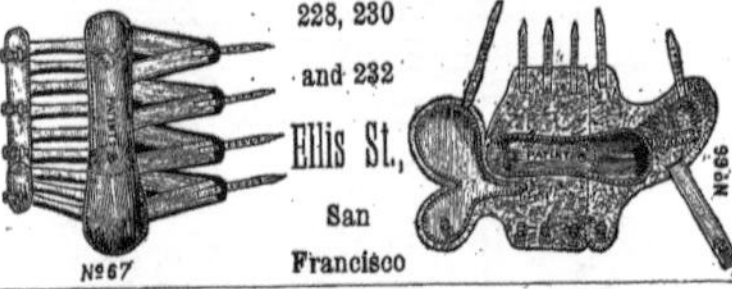

228, 230 and 232 Ellis St., San Francisco

Nº67

The PARKER Hammerless Shot Gun.

At the Annual Tournament of 1889, held at Cannes, France, the grand prize, consisting of 2000 Francs and a Valuable Cup. was won by The Parker Hammerless.

The first Parker Hammerless Gun made won the championship of America at Decatur Illinois.

SEND FOR ILLUSTRATED CIRCULAR.

PARKER BROS., Makers,

New York Salesroom, 97 Chambers St., Meriden Conn.

THE CASTOR Road & Speeding CART.

ALWAYS GIVES SATISFACTION.

Combining perfect riding qualities, proportions and balance, with genteel appearance.

No vehicle exhibits a horse to better advantage, and no Cart approaches them for speeding or training purposes.

A stylish vehicle for exercising or pleasure driving, at one-fourth the cost of a carriage. Have none of the horse jockey or objectionable features of other Road Carts.

They are the Leading Cart wherever introduced, and are in use by the most prominent breeders and pleasure drivers everywhere.

Elegant Shifting Top Carts.

Perfectly Balanced Stylish Pole Carts.

For Illustrated Catalogue, with Prices, address,

LEWIS F. CASTOR,

Frankford, Philadelphia, Pa.

JOHN SPLAN, General Agent.

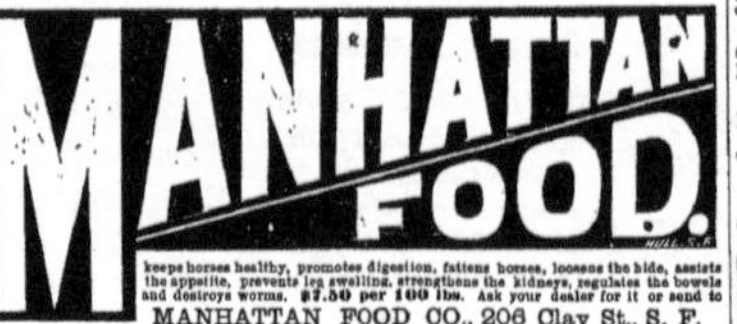

keeps horses healthy, promotes digestion, fattens horses, loosens the hide, assists the appetite, prevents leg swelling, strengthens the kidneys, regulates the bowels and destroys worms. $7.50 per 100 lbs. Ask your dealer for it or send to

MANHATTAN FOOD CO., 206 Clay St., S. F.

The Brunswick Balke Collender Co.

MANUFACTURERS OF

Standard Billiard and Pool Tables, Saloon and Bank Fixtures,

653--655 Market Street, San Francisco, Cal.

ORVIS TROUT FLIES.

Superb in Material, Make and Killing Quality.

E. T. ALLEN,

SOLE AGENT FOR PACIFIC COAST.

Importer of Fine Fishing Tackle & Sporting Goods

416 Market Street, - - San Francisco, Cal.

Brothers of the Angle.

Our NEW EIGHT-STRIP SPLIT BAMBOO is the "King" of all fishing-rods. Chubb's New Catalogue for 1890 is now ready. In addition to a complete list of anglers' supplies, it contains articles from the pens of Dr. James A. Henshall, Petronella, W. H. Murray, Geo. P. Goff, Norman, Brother Gardner, and others.

These papers are by the best writers on angling subjects, and are very interesting.

Send 25 cents, and receive Catalogue, postpaid. This amount will be deducted from first order (if accompanied with Coupon in book) for one dollar's worth or more of our goods.

Address

THOS. H. CHUBB.

Fishing-Rod Manufacturer,

POST MILLS, VT.

Please mention BREEDER AND SPORTSMAN.

SHAW CARTS and SULKIES

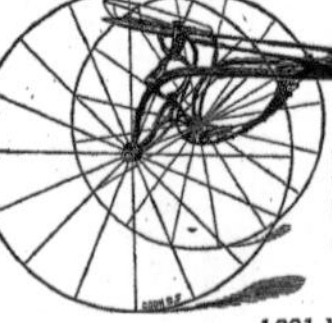

For light road or track use, manufactured from the best selected material. Combines lightness with elegance and ease to riders. Weights 70 to 110 lbs. Used by the best horsemen on this coast. Inspection invited.

ONE CAFFREY SULKY FOR SALE AT A BARGAIN.

CARRIAGES & Light VEHICLES

Manufactured to Order and Kept on Hand.

W. E. SHAW,

1621 MARKET STREET, SAN FRANCISCO, CAL.

REPAIRING DONE—ALL WORK WARRANTED.

Studebaker Bros. Manufact'g Co.

Sole Agents for

FRAZIER

(OR CHICAGO)

Carts

AND

Sulkies,

201--203 Market Street,

SAN FRANCISCO, CAL

BOYCE TABLETS.

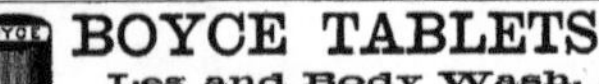

Leg and Body Wash.

THE BOYCE TABLETS are packed in a nicely decorated metal box with hinged lid—one hundred tablets in each box; directions for use plainly engraved upon the box; therefore, the convenience of the package—no liability to leakage and breakage—economy and ready solubility, together with the absolute certainty of their action, will at once commend the use of BOYCE'S TABLETS to the intelligent horsemen of the country. TABLETS sufficient to make one hundred pints of leg and body wash are conveniently carried in an inside coat pocket or in the hip-pocket of the trousers.

The BOYCE WASH can be applied ALL OVER THE BODY WITHOUT FEAR OF BLISTERING NOR DOES IT AFFECT THE KIDNEYS.

The BOYCE WASH will cure CRACKED HEELS, PUFFS, STOCKINGS, SCRATCHES, INFLAMED TENDONS and FEVERED LEGS.

Price per Box of One Hundred Tablets, $2, sent, postpaid to any part of the United States; six boxes for $10. A sample of BOYCE'S TABLETS will be mailed to any address on application.

These TABLETS are warranted to keep in any climate. Address

BOYCE TABLET COMPANY,

600 Wabash Avenue, - - - Terre Haute, Indiana.

J. A. McKERRON, Pacific Coast Ag't,

228-230-232 Ellis Street, San Francisco, Cal.

TWENTY-FOUR PAGES.

BREEDER AND SPORTSMAN

Vol XVI. No 22.
No. 313 BUSH STREET.

SAN FRANCISCO, SATURDAY, MAY 31, 1890.

SUBSCRIPTION
FIVE DOLLARS A YEAR.

PALO ALTO.

Electioneer Recovering—Beautiful Bells and Her Foal—The Palo Alto String—The Thoroughbred Foals—The University Grounds.

For several weeks stories have been rife relating to a serious illness of Electioneer. The rumors have been so varied and contradictory that a representative of the BREEDER AND SPORTSMAN visited Palo Alto Stock Farm on Friday last to determine what truth there was in the many stories which have been circulated anent the grand old horse. More than ordinary pleasure was expected to be derived from the trip, as our companion was to have been Jno. S. McCormick (Macon), the well known sporting writer, who is at present on the Pacific Coast. However, we were denied that pleasure, as a telegram from the East called Mr. McCormick off in another direction, and the trip was to have been made presumably alone, however, on our arrival at Fourth and Townsend streets we were gratified at meeting Mr. L J. Bradbury, the well known traveller and man of the world, whose face is as well known in the Strand, in London, and Broadway, New York, as it is on Market Street in San Francisco. Accompanying Mr. Bradbury was "Nick" Steiner of Bush street, equally well at home when welcoming his guests or driving behind a fast horse on the speed track. The ride to Menlo Park in such pleasant company was accomplished in short order, and on our arrival we found a carriage awaiting us to take the party to Senator Stanford's celebrating breeding establishment. Although the morning was oppressive, and the heat and dust just a trifle disagreeable, the pair of Bentons behind which we sat were but a very short time in conveying us to the farm. On alighting from the carriage we found S. C. Ferguson, Henry Walsh and Richard Havey ready to welcome us.

As was natural the first inquiries were in reference to the health of Electioneer, and the party were more then pleased on learning that a decided improvement was manifest in his condition. It was our extreme good fortune to meet there Dr. Harry E. Carpenter, who for at least a week had been making daily calls on the premier stallion of Palo Alto. Many of the stories which were prevalent in San Francisco in regard to Electioneer were narrated to those in attendance, and each and everyone declared that the stories about a sprain or injury were not grounded on truth. It seems that last year Electioneer was troubled with sciatic rheumatism; the attack was very slight and he readily recovered, but this year the old complaint again returned, leaving him in a rather precarious condition. Veterinary advice was at once sought, and owing to the great care bestowed there is every prospect that Electioneer may still survive for many years. It must be confessed that the horse has been in eminent danger, and for two days his life was despaired of, but Dr. Carpenter feels that the crisis has passed, and there is every reason to believe that Electioneer is on a fair way to recovery. For several days he was fed but milk and eggs, which, with the aid of Pepsine, was easily digested, but now he has so far improved that stronger food is being given him, and he relishes his meals in a manner that shows no signs of weakness inside. The spasmodic twitchings incidental to sciatica are still observable but not nearly so bad, so we were told, as when the horse was first taken ill; owing to weakness, it was found necessary to hoist him with a band and block and tackle, but his legs have recovered so much of their strength that he can now rise without artificial aid. Electioneer, as many of our readers are aware, is now in his twenty-second year and shows the signs of advancing age but still his eye is as bright and his coat as glossy as it was when the writer first saw him in 1879; the back has fallen in a trifle, and the fore legs are bent just enough to show that this great son of Hambletonian is fast approaching the sear and yellow leaf; yet still he has served twenty-eight mares this season, and it is to be hoped that he may live long enough and have the requisite vital strength to leave many more of his progeny behind him before his days of usefulness are over.

A visit was paid to a paddock where Beautiful Bells is located, with her suckling foal by Electioneer. The writer had the pleasure of seeing Beautiful Bells start in the first race she was ever entered in, and although she has taken on the matronly appearance of a broodmare, she still looks as young and vigorous as she did in the latter part of the '70's. Her foal is a handsome bay filly with small star, off hind foot and inside of ankle white, near hind foot white, to ankle with black spots around the coronets; she is apt to put the spectator very much in mind of Hinda Rose, in fact more so than any of the other foals which this prolific mare has ever had.

After viewing the two most celebrated horses on the place a walk was taken to the race track where everything was full of life and animation. Fourteen drivers on a track at one and the same time is a sight hardly to be seen on any public track in the country, let alone a private one, yet still we had this pleasure at Palo Alto, and many were the fast ones brought out and speeded while we were present.

"Dick" Havey, as is well known, has charge of the trotting division during the absence of Mr. Marvin in the East. Havey is no stranger at Palo Alto, having trained horses for Senator Stanford in the years gone by. There are at present in the neighborhood of eighty trotters undergoing the requisite amount of work to enable them to stand a campaign this year. When the season opens up, some ten or a dozen of the best of these will be sent to uphold the supermacy of Palo Alto. Among those which Mr. Havey is handling himself are Electricity 5844 by Electioneer, dam Midnight (dam of Jay Eye See 2:10 and Noontide 2:20½) by Pilot, Jr. 12. Electricity is a large brown horse with rear hind foot white, 16½ hands high, foaled 1884; he has always had a great amount of speed but has never been able to come to the wire owing to an unfortunate habit of interfering, a habit which has caused one of his legs to badly swell, no matter what boots or other appliances have been put on to prevent it. Mr. Havey is under the impression that this sort of annoyance can be obviated, and already there are decided signs of improvement; whether Electioneer will still remain in good fettle or not is impossible to say at present, but if he does there is no cause to doubt but what there will be another of the Electioneer family to go in 2:20 or better.

Express 2:21 is by Electioneer, dam Ester by Express, grandam Colosseum by Colossus, son of imp. Sovereign. This bay gelding is, as can be seen by the pedigree, one-half thoroughbred, and as his head is much more level than it was last year he may be fully expected to lower his present mark considerably.

One of the most graceful horses to be seen at Palo Alto is Sport 2:22¾ by Piedmont 2:17¼, dam Sontag Mohawk (also dam of Sallie Benton 2:17¾ and Eros 2:29½); he is a fine, big, strapping fellow, a beautiful dapple gray in color and is as handsome a horse as one could wish to see, although not in the catalogue as one of the stallions of the ranch, he has served quite a number of mares this year and later on will be driven to reduce his present record.

Almoneer is a bay colt, two years old by Alban 5332, dam America (dam of Bonnie, 2:25, and Benton 2:27½) by Hambletonian 10. This is a handsome little fellow and gives promise of great speed.

Another of the two year-olds from which much is expected this year in the way of speed, is a bay filly by Electioneer, dam Lady Ellen by Mambrino 1739. This elegant young lady is of splendid appearance with a smooth easy way of going that convinces the beholder that she is able to keep up the reputation of the farm. Elleneer was able to trot very fast as a yearling and she will undoubtedly be another of the phenominal productions of Palo Alto.

Rebecca, the dam of Rexford whose three-year-old record of 2:24 made him famous, was bred in 1885 to Ansel 2:20, her production in 1886 being the bay filly Ariane, and bar accident she should be able to give another fast record for a California trotter. She is of handsome appearance, very taking in her gait, and goes her quarters already fast enough to warrant the belief that she is entitled to a place in the stable which will represent the Senator on the circuit.

Another of the Havey string which is showing up very well is Susette by Electioneer, dam Susie (dam of Suisun 2:25) by George M. Patchen Jr. Susette is a full sister to Suisun and has shown speed enough to convince Mr. Havey that he has a first class mare in charge. Susette is one of the brood mares of the farm and already has a brown colt by Nephew but it was deemed expedient to try and get a record for her as she has shown so much speed at the trot.

Of course there were scores of other horses seen going through their work, but the sight presented was more of a moving panorama than anything else. And while pedigrees were given without number, it was a hard matter, in the short time we had at command, to take notes of all the fast ones that were exhibited.

After luncheon a visit was paid to that part of the domain which is ruled over by Henry Walsh, the section where the thoroughbreds are at home and to be seen. Here a legion of boys were found, and it took but a very short time for all the noted broodmares and their foals to be paraded before us. Without fear of contradiction, the assertion is boldly made that on no farm in the world can a finer lot of suckling thoroughbred foals be seen in proportion to their number, than at present are, at Palo Alto. With a pride that was perfectly justifiable, Mr. Walsh called the attention of the party to the many good points of each that were brought forward, and for good strong backs and loins, perfect shape, and stout sturdy legs, these little lads and lasses will take a lot of beating. The old trainer pointed out an exquisite filly which Senator Stanford has selected in his own mind as being the best of the year, and without a doubt she well deserves the compliment, but Henry could not resist the temptation to point out a big, lusty colt to which he has pinned his faith, and if the two ever meet in track work, it would be a hard matter to guess before hand the winner.

The broodmares all looked well, the two to which especial attention was paid being imp. Fairy Rose, dam of Racine, and imp. Flirt, dam of Flambeau; both of them looked well, the first having a foal at her side by imp. Cheviot, while the latter had a handsome foal by Flood.

The stallions were next brought out, and caused favorable comment from their handsome looks. Flood, Shannon, imp. Cyrus, Flambeau, imp. Bruce, Peel and Rinfax were all seen, and although they all have their good points, fancy leads us to believe that the young stallion Cyrus will leave an indelible mark at Palo Alto; he is by Wenlock, dam Teardrop by Scottish Chief, with a pedigree that takes in the more prominent of the celebrated stallions to be found in the English stud book; possibly a little under size to the critical eye, still with power enough to warrant the belief that his progeny should each of them be able to carry "a house and lot."

After bidding Mr. Walsh good-day, our party was driven to the magnificent buildings now being erected by Mr. and Mrs. Stanford, which will in the future be known as the Leland Stanford Jr. University. One cannot conceive the vastness and magnificence of this great donation to the people of the State of California without going to see it themselves. Acre upon acre of ground is covered with mammoth stone buildings which will stand as monuments for all time to come of the generosity of Mr. and Mrs. Stanford to the future generations, of this, their adopted State. From a casual glance it seemed as though a perfect army of men were at work finishing these grand edifices, and outside of the donors, no one will possibly ever know how much has been expended on these mammoth buildings. California will indeed owe a debt of gratitude to the Stanfords for this their great work, and it is safe to say that their honored names will be revered in ages to come for their munificence in this direction.

From the grounds of the University a visit was paid to the magnificent avenues and carriage drives which surround the private residence of the Senator, drives which are lined with trees on either hand, shrubbery and flowers, lending an ambrosial fragrance to the air that is hard to be met with anywhere. Gardners and their assistants were laying out beds of flowers in a most artistic manner, and beautiful scenes of landscape work were being arranged by those having the matter in charge. It is hard for the mind to conceive such a fairy place, for on every hand were such visions of loveliness that is is impossible for the pen of mortal to describe it. One of the celebrated trees after which the place takes its name, is still standing on the San Francesquita Creek, which flows through this great domain. Up to within a very short time ago, two "Palo Altos" stood on the banks, but lately owing to high waters, one has been carried away, leaving only the one sentinel to be pointed out in future, why it was that Senator Stanford's farm got its name.

For the benefit of those who have been unable to visit Palo Alto, we will say there are 540 stalls, three kindergarten tracks, a mile track and a three-quarter mile track for the trotters, and a mile track for the runners. Over eighty men are at present employed looking after the trotting horse division, while about twenty-five men and boys are attending to the thoroughbreds. For the boys who work at the lower end of the ranch under Mr. Walch's charge, a night school has been arranged, and each evening two teachers are on duty so that the little fellows may not suffer for lack of education.

We can hardly close without returning our thanks to Mr. Ferguson, Mr. Reynolds, Mr. Walsh and Mr. Havey for the kindness shown us, and we hope the day may not be far distant when time will allow a repetition of the visit.

Imported Diomed.

As the name of imported Diomed is about as intimately connected with the foundation of the American trotter as that of imported Messenger, the following history of the first winner of the English Derby will be read with interest:

Diomed, by Florizel, son of Herod, bred by Sir Charles Bunbury, foaled 1777, dam sister to Juno, by Spectator, son of Crab, out of Horatia, by Blank. 1789—Newmarket second spring meeting, won a sweepstake, Ditch-in beating Antagonist, Diadem and Savannae; Epsom won the Derby stakes, last mile of the course, defeating Budrow, Spitfire and six others; Newmarket July Meeting, walked over for sweepstakes across the flat; Tuesday, First October Meeting, received forfeit from four others; Ditch-in next day won the Perram Plate, Ditch-in beating Rover, Marygold and eight others; Friday received forfeit from Catalpa, Rowley mile; Second October Meeting, won a subscription of 20 guineas each, eight subscribers, B. M. beating Teetotum, Duchess and two others. 1781—Newmarket Craven Meeting, Diomed received 250 guineas forfeit for Savannah in a match over the Beacon course; First Spring Meeting won the Fortesque stakes, Ditch-in beating Spitfire, King William and three others; Second Spring Meeting, won Claret stakes, Becon course, beating Antagonist, Arake and four others; Nottingham met his first defeat, running second to Fortitude, by Herod, in the Nottingham stakes, twice round the course, Bay Bolton by Matchem, and one other behind him, Newmarket First October Meeting was beaten by Budrow, by Eclipse, Beacon course. 1782—Newmarket First October Meeting, paid forfeit to Crop in sweepstakes, D. C. 1783—Newmarket was unplaced in the Craven stakes, from the ditch to the turn of the lands, won by Alaric; Newmarket First Spring Meeting, was third to Labuenam and Drone, over the R. C. course, six others behind him; same meeting ran second to Drone for the King's Plate, R. C. course, Grasshopper, Buccaneer and Nottingham behind him; Ascot Heath was third to Soldier and Oliver Cromwell, four miles, beating Truth and Guildford; won Her Majesty's Plate, four mile heats, beating Mercury; Lewes was beaten by Mercury and Diadem for Her Majesty's Plate, four mile heats, beating Lottery who won the first heat; Winchester was second to Anvil in Her Majesty's Plate, four mile heats, beating Mercury; Lewes was beaten by Mercury and Diadem for Her Majesty's Plate, four mile heats; Diomed fell lame in the race, and was retired from the turf.

After the season of 1798 Diomed, then in his twenty-second year, was sold for 50 guineas, and afterwards resold to Col. John Hoomes of Virginia, for 1,000 guineas. He was a successful sire in England, the most noted of his get were Glaucus, Lais, Playfellow, Robin Grey, Grayhound, Wrangler, Cedar, Victor, Valiant, Montesuma, Sir Cecil, Anthony, Whisker, Champion, Little Pickle, Fanny, Laurentina, Egham, Agamemnon, Frolic, Lord Fitzwilliam's mare, the dam of Wonder, Miracle, Caleb, Quotem, Cossack, etc., Young Noisette, the dam of Navigator, Clermont, Marmion, etc., Young Giantess, the dam of Sorcerer, and Eleanor, the first mare which ever won the Oaks and Derby, and the dam of Muley, sire of imp. Leviathian, Margrave, etc., Julia, the dam of Phantom, Lydia, dam of Corporal; Cressida, the dam of imp. Priam. There is scarcely a good horse in England of this day but what has some of his blood. In America he sired Sir Archy, called the Godolphin Arabian of America; Ball's Florizel, Duroc, sire of American Eclipse; Tom Gallant, Potomac, Stump the Dealer, Vingt'um; the dams of Henry, Shylock, Cicero, Lady of the Lake, Richmond, Diomed Eagle, Duchess of Marlborough, Maria Archy, Fanny Hill. He also sired Lady Chesterfield, Wringjaw, Miss Jefferson, Peacemaker Hambletonian, Hanie's Maria the best mare of her day; Wonder, Virginius, St. Tammany, Truxton, Herod, Madison, Sting and a host of others. Diomed was a solid chestnut, without white, except on the heel of the right hind foot; 15¾ hands high, with great substance and muscular power, which he transmitted to his stock. He died in Virginia in 1808, aged thirty-one years. He left behind him a name and fame which will endure to the end of all time, and crowned with laurels of the two great racing countries of the world.—England and America.

The Alcryon Case.

Judge Corlett of the Superior Court of Erie County, N. Y., in deciding the injunction suit of F. L. Noble and George Robens vs. The National Trotting Association said:

It appears that the corporation has five judicial districts which include Canada and the Uniten States; that tribunals exist which are a part of the machinery of the corporatian to try and determine questions which may arise, impose penalties and inflict punishment; that this court or tribunal consisted of four members. It also appears that there is within the corporation a congress which represents not only the corporation, but the numerous local organizations which are members. No question is made but that the injunction was obtained for the purpose of preventing the defendants from trying the plaintiffs on the charges of fraud and punish them in case of conviction. The action was brought for that purpose. The structure of the complaint, the form of the prayer for relief, the rules and by-laws, all of which are made a part of the complaint, clearly show the relief sought by this action The numerous allegations in the complaint alleging want of power and jurisdiction in the tribunal to try and determine show that the pleader proceeds upon the assumption that if the tribunal was not regular or lacked jurisdiction, its decision would be null.

The plaintiffs sought before the tribunal to obtain an adjudication in their favor of the jurisdictional questions by way of preliminary objection. It was not until after a ruling against them on those questions that this action was brought and the injunction obtained. It is not alleged, and nowhere appears, that the congress as such has any power or jurisdiction to try and determine charges or inflict punishments. Its functions seem to be legislative and executive, not judicial. The primary object and purposes of the congress seem to be to secure the rights and privileges of the local organizations and produce uniformity and harmonious action between the central corporation and the numerous race-courses which are members. Those local associations appear to be owned by private individuals, the central corporation having no legal title to the property, but for the purpose of furthering the objects for which the corporation was formed, to secure equality, uniformity and harmony, in short, for the interests of the central corporation and all its branch members, a congress was created so that all branches of the corporation should be fully represented and its business harmoniously carried on.

Construing the injunction order and the resolution of the congress in the light of these suggestions it is very clear that the parties charged are not guilty of contempt.

No steps were taken by the tribunal enjoined or any of its members to proceed with the trial after service of the injunction order. On the other hand, the body adjourned, the term for which its members were elected expired, new persons were chosen to perform judicial duties, and then the congress assembled.

It is entirely immaterial whether the individuals composing the congress, or whether the President of the corporation or the members of the judicial tribunal formed a part of that body. It was a different organization, and created for other purposes.

A reference to the preamble of the resolution complained of shows that the injunction order is treated by the Congress as applying to and restraining the Board of Review. There is nothing in the peramble or body of the resolution indicating any intention or purpose to disregard or in any way violate the injunction. Its resolution was to suspend the plaintiffs and their horses from all benefits of the local organizations until after the trial and determination of the question of fraud by the judicial tribunal. So long as grave questions remained undecided, the congress proceeded upon the assumption that the interest of the corporation and its branches would be advanced by preventing the plaintiffs or their horses from participating in its benefits until the accusations were tried and judicially determined according to the rules of the corporation.

Interest, progress, fair dealing and reputation often require action during the pendency of proceedings, in order to preserve reputation and advance the usefulness of the corporation. It may be true that personal animosities and bitter partisanship had arisen between the parties to this controversy, and that in the action taken those considerations produced prompt and extreme action. It also may be true that the practical effect of the resolution, if carried into execution will inflict great injury and loss upon the plaintiffs. But those considerations throw no light upon the question whether its adoption was a violation of the injunction. Those passing the resolution did not assume any right or power to take the place of the trial tribunal, or to adjudge upon any of the questions involved in the action, or as a body representing the corporation and its branches, it did not assume to have the right to pass any resolution it saw fit which in its judgment would be a benefit to the corporation in case it did not violate the injunction. If the passage of the resolution resulted in inflicting injury upon the plaintiffs wrongfully, no reasons are seen why the plaintiffs have not a remedy at law to recover damages against those unlawfully interfering with their rights. But an injunction order granted upon specific grounds to restrain the performance of certain alleged acts cannot be treated as violated because other action may be taken, even though those acts may inflict as much injury as a performance of those restrained by the injunction; assuming it does not embrace the acts restrained.

Every wrong has its appropriate remedy, but a precise remedy applicable to peculiar acts cannot be invoked in support of different acts, though they may be wrongful if not within the scope or compass of the original remedy. The fact that the obtaining of the injunction may be the sole cause of the passing of the resolution is unimportant. Suppose the congress had said in so many words: "Because you brought your action and obtained the injunction and prevented a trial, we will resort to another remedy which will inflict quite as much injury upon you as if you had allowed us to proceed in the matter unrestrained." It is obvious that that act, no matter what motives inspired it, could not be treated as a violation of the injunction order or a contempt of court unless it was a direct or indirect attack upon the order or its effect.

The test is not what injury the proposed action will inflict, but whether it is a violation of the court. A resolution by a body not judicial to deprive a person of rights and privileges cannot be treated as a violation of an order of the court unless it in some way interferes with it or prevents its execution. In this case the congress had power to pass the resolution adopted, provided it in no way interfered or infringed upon the injunction order.

The fallacy of the plaintiffs' position is in assuming that the injunction is broad enough to include all the actions and doings of the corporation or its branches which may tend to injure the plaintiffs.

In Rapelje on Contempts, 57, the rule is stated that an injunction prohibiting use as a tow-path would not be violated by its use for other purposes. Bosley vs. Sus. Canal, 3 Bland (Md.) 63–68.

There is no obscurity or ambiguity about the order or its purposes, and the matters to which it related. It is not perceived that the passage in any way tends to impair its sufficiency or detract from its force.

In Laurie vs. Laurie, 9 Paige's Chan. Rep., 233, it was held that "an injunction should be clear and explicit in its terms, and should not deprive the defendant of any right which the case made by the bill does not require he should be restrained from exercising it."

So in Sullivan vs. Judah, 4 Paige's Chan., Rep., 44, it was decided that "an injunction should upon its face contain sufficient to apprise the party upon whom it is served what he is restrained from doing, without the necessity of his resorting to the complainant's bill to ascertain what the injunction means."

In the Porous Plaster Company vs. Seabury, 16 N. Y. St. Rep. 35, it was held that "in order to punish for a violation of an injunction, the act complained of must be clearly within the inhibited acts." In the Court of Appeals, German Savings Bank vs. Haybrook, 58 How. Prac. Rep. 336, it was held that "in order to punish for a violation of an injunction the order should clearly embrace the act complained of."

It is a familiar rule that an injunction in no way interferes with the posession or exercise of control over property, unless such acts are prohibited in the order.

Hemmingway vs. Preston (Walker), Mich. 528.

People vs. Simonson, 10 Mich. 335.

Applying the doctrine of these cases to the one at bar, it is very clear that the resolution is no violation of the injunction. The complaint, injunction, order and all the objections on the part of the plaintiffs were framed for the purpose of presenting a trial and adjudication. The numerous authorities cited by the learned counsel for the plaintiffs have been carefully examined, but none of them conflict with the doctrine of the above cases.

The application must be denied, and in view of the novelty of the questions, without costs.

The Management of the Stable.

Much has been written on this subject, and much more will have to be written before it can be passed as not needing further consideration. To understand why and wherefore a thing should be done or left undone will result, with kind and well meaning people, in more rational treatment of the horse in the stable than is the general rule.

Pure air is as essential to the blood as sound food is to the sustenance of the body. Consumed air is vitiated air, the volume of oxygen is reduced, carbonic acid is in excess. The stable is full of organic impurities given off by the skin and lungs. Ventilation is found in all well regulated stables, and draughts are unknown, or ought to be. But these are matters for individual consideration, and are best settled by the builder.

Horses drink once or twice a day, and the horse may be trusted to gauge his thirst, except on occasions of extreme exertion, such as a hunting morning. That all horses are the better for being watered before being fed is an admitted fact with all veterinary surgeons and intelligent grooms. Colic and gripes are thus avoided. The explanation given is this: When the stomach is full, water passing rapidly through the stomach, on the way is very apt to carry with it, into the small intestines, undigested corn, and this produces local irritation. There is less danger in watering a horse actively warm than when the system is somewhat lowered. In the latter case there is not sufficient vitality to raise any considerable quantity of cold water up to the temperature of the body; hence so many chills supervene, bowels are deranged, and the coat of such horses looks unthrifty, or, as we call it, "stares." Soft water is better for all stock, and on no account let horses drink dirty water; it is most objectionable.

Horses have small stomachs. We divide the corn into three daily portions, the hay into two. We never give hay just prior to work; it distends the stomach, and causes the horse inconvenience.

Delicate feeders must be tempted to take their rations, and such should never be fed too strongly at one time. A little linseed boiled to a jelly and mixed with the corn is seductive. Hay damped and salted will tempt others.

Tick beans, a double handful, are a relish in weakly subjects; pale malt for the convalescent or indisposed; damp bran oats are engaging for others. Some feeders give carrots and tares in small quantities. Carrots superinduce diabetes if given in excessive quantities. The peculiar habits of horses demand the attention of all horse owners and grooms. A sufficiency of flesh is all that is required, and not "hog fat," or "beastly fat," as some phrase it.

Clover, vetches and trifolium are laxative and cooling, and excellent for the invalid horse or the youngster. They should be given sparingly, at the early part of the season. Green forage should never be given to horses in fast work except on Saturday nights.

Good grooming is demanded under stable management and in fast work. The brush, as a rule, should follow the direction of the hair except when dirt and sweat are caked into the coat; then you require to go against the lie of the coat—the set of the coat. Good grooming shortens the coat, gives a gloss and develops physical force. When a good gloss is present we know the effects of the body—dirt, stall sweat—have been removed by friction and that the sweat and oil glands have been stimulated. Of course warmth shortens a coat, and moderate warmth in a stable, say 60 degrees, is desirable. A hot stable is contrary to all sound practice, and renders bronchial attacks imminent. Horses should always be groomed after exercise, and, if washed should be thoroughly dried. Washing horses, except as a refresher in very hot weather, is bad; it makes the coat harsh. Of course mud is usually removed, for the sake of expedition, by water, but unless well dried after it, grease, cracked heels, mud fever, etc., are sure to set up.

After washing feet and legs, and drying them, the legs should be neatly bandaged. Nostrils are, of course, sponged out twice a day, the dock likewise. White legs must be treated to soap and water. Good grooming, feeding and exercise—i. e., stable management—will put any horse into working condition, and keep him there, with the occasional use of an asperient or diuretic ball, as occasion may demand. —Kentucky Stock Farm.

THE FARM.

Store Cattle For Great Britain.

Confirmatory of what has been stated in the Rural World about the desire of the farmers of Great Britain to purchase steers from America and fatten them upon their farms, we publish a portion of the report of Moreton Frewen, of England, who is thoroughly posted on the subject:

There was one point, he said, of which he made a close study, and it was worth while to consider whether the legislation which was responsible for the present application of the contagious diseases (animals) act was entirely unwarranted by the circumstances of the time. The result of the rigid exclusion of lean stock from America has been to drive this country more and more into the dead and fat cattle trade. As long as the contagious diseases (animal) act precluded the importation of store cattle from the United States to this country, he did not think the conditions of agriculture would be quite healthy. The result of the enforcement of that act had been to prohibit English farmers from buying their store cattle in the one cheap market of the world. He was aware that there was a breeders' side to the question. He had no cattle interests to preserve in America, but was convinced that Ireland could carry one-third more cattle than she had now, and the only chance for her increasing her stock was to buy heifer stock from across the Atlantic and bring it in alive. On this side of the Atlantic there were advantages for fattening cattle which no other country enjoyed. If the cattle trade of which he was speaking was not subjected to the existing restrictions, and if the English farmers had their agents at Chicago who would forward 4,000 or 5,000 head of lean cattle a day, quite a new phase would be put on the agriculture of this country. As to the "bogey" of disease, he pointed out that in dealing with America there were conditions of security which were offered nowhere else. Five or six years ago there was pleuro-pneumonia, but there had never been a single outbreak of foot-and-mouth disease in the United States.

The complete statistics of British imports for the year 1889 have just been issued, and contain some figures in which Americans are highly interested. Great Britain imported in the year no less than 555,221 live cattle against 377,086 in the preceding year, and almost doubling the imports of two years ago. The total of sheep imported was 678,958, that of the preceding year being 956,210. This is the only point in which the imports show a decline. In swine and horses there was a very slight increase, and in fresh beef the total of 657,574 cwt. in 1887 was increased to 1,379,511 cwt. in 1889. These figures are highly significant to the countries which furnish Great Britain with its food supplies. Of the great increase in cattle the United States furnished the bulk, our exports of cattle last year being 294,423 head, against 143,495 head in 1888 and 94,858 head in 1887, the trade of the latter year having been about trebled in 1889. Of the fresh beef which Great Britain imports the United States furnishes about nine-tenths. If as many sagacious observers think our exportation of animal food should show an increase in 1890, the total report a year hence will be large indeed.—Colman's Rural World.

Questions in Dairying.

A new subscriber to The Gazette writes from Southern Dakota that he has been engaged in the unprofitable business of wheat-growing, but having his eyes opened proposes to start into dairying. He has spring water in the pastures, good well water at the buildings, large barns, and contemplates a silo. He wishes to know what breed of cattle to choose for dairying, desiring animals that have beef qualifications as well.

Realising the dangerous character of the ground on which I am treading I will hasten by this interrogation as rapidly as possible. Herfords and Polled Angus are beef breeds in which the production of milk has been practically ignored, and no claims are advanced for them at this time. The Short-horns are descended from excellent dairy stock, and many of the breed in England and this country still retain the milk-giving function to a large degree. It is not common at this time to find pure-bred herds where the cows are regularly and carefully milked, it being considered more profitable to let the calves suck the cows. In spite of this abuse of the milk-giving function, the breed still shows a strong tendency in that direction, and a herd of grade Short-horns can easily be established that will do quite well at the pail, and make good beef. The Red Poll is gaining friends as a general-purpose animal. A step further down from beef and up in milk, is the Holstein-Friesian, with a coarser frame than the Short-horn and a greater tendency to milk. Unfortunately many of the owners of these cattle have been working for a large quantity of milk, ignoring its quality, and a large amount of milk with a low percentage of fat is the result. A large milk yield, even with a low percent of fat, may make the net amount of butter quite large. In selecting these animals insist on a fat test. The Guernsey is a specific butter cow, producing a rich, yellow cream. The Jersey, a little smaller than the Guernsey, stands at the other end of the line from the Hereford, with a bony frame entirely unsatisfactory to the stock-buyer. She yields a moderate amount of milk of high quality for butter production; the milk flow, however, is so well kept up that when the year closes, the total production is entirely satisfactory. The last two are specific butter breeds. Our correspondent can take his choice.

He next inquires regrading methods of manufacturing butter.

This cannot be put down in a brief reply like this. Visit intelligent dairymen and learn from them. Briefly, however, for a small herd adopt the deep setting system, which is simpler and more satisfactory than shallow pans. Run spring water into the dairy house and submerge the milk in Cooley cans, or set it in deep "shot-gun" cans. For churns, beware of patents, using a revolving churn of the barrel or box pattern. Avoid all churns with inside fixtures, and have nothing to do with those wonderful churns that bring the butter in two minutes. At first send the butter to reliable commission men, asking for criticisms on color, salting, grain, etc. Let no personal preferences decide, but make such butter as the market demands. When the art has been learned, and a uniformly high grade of butter can be made, then seek to deal directly with the consumer.

"F. W. I., Garden Ranch, Colorado Springs, Colo.," asks which is preferable for cream separation—the centrifuge separator or the Cooley system.

Each system has its advantage and place. In the Cooley system the milk is submerged in cold water in a deep can. If the water is held not higher than 45 deg Fahr. all of the fat of the milk except something like one-half of one per cent will be raised to the top of the can between milkings, where it can be removed by skimming. Careful experiments with this system show that the cream does not always rise equally well; the milk of some cows will cream so thoroughly that only one or two-tenths of a per cent of fat will remain in the skim-milk, while the milk of other cows on the same feed will leave several times as much fat in the skim-milk. The season of the year or length of time from calving also affect the efficiency of the creaming, but in spite of these disadvantages the system will remain in favor with many dairymen, and is one of the best in many cases. Where cold water or ice can be cheaply secured it is the system to be adopted until the herd numbers 100 cows or over. Where a large amount of milk is to be handled the centrifugal separator is more satisfactory, since with careful management it skims the milk a little closer, on the average, than any other system, and works uniformerly with all breeds and at all seasons.

W. A. HENRY.

Wisconsin Agricultural Experiment Station in Breeders Gazette.

The New Oleo Law in Ohio.

The Legislature of Ohio, March 7th, 1890, passed a law in regard to oleomargarine, which is reported as follows in the Ohio Farmer:

No person, by himself or his agent, or his employe, shall render or manufacture for sale out of any animal or vegetables oil, not produced from unadulterated milk or cream from the same, any article in imitation or semblance of natural butter of cheese produced from pure unadulterated milk or cream from the same, nor compound with, or add to milk; cream, or butter, any acids or other deleterious substance, or animal fats or animal or vegetable oils not produced from milk or cream, so as to produce any article or substance, or any human food, in imitation or semblance of butter or cheese, nor shall sell, keep for sale or offer for sale any article, substance, or compound made, manufactured or produced in violation of the provisions of this section, whether such article, substance, or compound shall be made or produced in this state or elsewhere.

Section 2 defines the terms "natural butter or cheese" to mean butter made from pure, unadulterated milk or cream, with the addition of salt and with or without harmless coloring matter; and cheese made from pure milk or cream, with salt and rennets and with or without harmless coloring matter. It also provides that "nothing in this act shall be constructed to prohibit the manufacture or sale of oleomargarine, in a separate and distinct form, and in such manner as will advise the consumer of its real character, free from any coloring matter or other ingredient, causing it to look like or appear to be butter, as above defined.

Section 3 provides a penalty of $500 to $1,000 fine, or six to twelve months' imprisonment or both, for first violation of this law, and one year's imprisonment for each subsequent offense.

It appears from the same paper that some of the rich oleo makers are disposed to contest the law before the Superior Court.

We live in the hope of seeing a House and Senate in the Massachusetts State House that will enact a similar law.

Sheep Breeding in South America.

There is likely to be a great revolution in the system of sheep breeding in the Argentine, says the London Live Stock Journal: Experts have come to the conclusion that the climate of the province of Buenos Ayres is much too damp for the Merinos, and their conclusions are doubtless well founded, since thousands of these sheep succumbed during the past winter to diseases brought about by the humidity of the atmosphere. Long wooled sheep, especially Lincolns, thrive much better in Buenos Ayres, and the great stretch of thinly populated territory between the province and the Cordilleras offers magnificent pasture for fine wool breeds.

Argentine Sheep in England.

The importations of live sheep into the United Kingdom, which reached a total of 178,354 head in the first quarter of 1888 and 209,029 in the same part of 1889, fell off to 27,345 head in the first three months of the present year. The wonderful change is due to the scheduling of German sheep, which have for a long time formed the bulk of British importations of this stock. This apparently opens up a field for supplies from some other quarter, and advantage of this fact is already being taken by exporters from the Argentine Republic. Over 300 live sheep from Buenos Ayres lately arrived at Liverpool, and proved so attractive to buyers that their flesh brought twice the price of the frozen mutton from the same country. Two or three of our English exchanges say (in the same words, for we often find the same editorial appearing in several of them at once): "In the course of the last year or two there have been unmistakable indications that the supply of sheep in this country is not equal to the demand, and that the imports of dead mutton could not make up the want of live sheep. And the Argentine Confederation can give us practically unlimited supplies of sheep if they could be brought here alive. It takes rank next to New Zealand in the weight of frozen mutton which it sends to us. In 1887 we imported from the Argentine Confederation 251,273 cwt. of fresh mutton, and in '88, the last year for which we have complete returns, we received 345,391 cwt. of mutton. Now that a few of the many millions of live sheep there have found their way to us, and have sold well, we may be certain there are more to follow." British importations of mutton in the first quarter of this year were 401,174 cwt., against 296,249 cwt. in 1889, and 227,090 in 1888.—Sportsman and Farmer.

A Large Poultry Yard.

A correspondent wishes to know where the big farms are, but wants nothing to do with the fancy breeding chaps. I contend that the day is coming when buyers of improved stock will look to the farms to find what they want, i. e., a good constitution, coupled with fine plumage. To use a personal example, I will say I live on a ninety-acre farm, and breed for both utility and fancy points, making specialties of pure bred fowls and eggs, new laid eggs, eggs for incubators, broilers, market poultry, stocking the village poultry houses with laying pullets, etc. The question is, why should I give up selling fancy fowls and eggs because I carry on the other branches of the business? Surely not because I live on a farm, for the village breeder will boast of his farm-raised chicks. Possibly the party who carries on his operations in a village back yard would say I might make a mistake and ship a customer some bird I was getting ready for market. In many cases it could be turned around and read the other way, to the satisfaction of the buyer at least.

I will admit that fowls can be made to pay without selling at fancy prices. In fact, the market business is the surer of the two, but all will admit that pure bred stock will pay the largest profit also, for to cross with success one has to use pure bred males. It strikes me that where one can make a success of keeping fowls in large numbers for poultry and eggs, he will make a successful breeder. While writing I will tell how I have arranged my buildings and care for the stock. My hatching and brooding house is built the same as shown in cuts of the Hammonton farms. My incubator is a 1000 egg hatcher. I can turn out 2000 chicks in three months. I never let the heat get above 102 degrees, and think 100 degrees would do as well. I turn eggs twice a day. My brooders are fourteen in number, and are heated by hot water pipes underneath. We could never get the chicks to stay under the mother of their own accord, as in a lamp brooder, but have now constructed, for trial, false bottoms, with an air space between, and think it will obviate the difficulty. I use the Silver Wyandotte as a business foundation, so to speak, to get the most chicks from 100 eggs. I cross the males on Leghorn hens, to get the earliest layers. I keep the Leghorn pure. The cross lays a little lighter and larger eggs. For the finest and largest eggs we keep the Wyandotte pure. While attending the New York show, the party to whom I ship my eggs told me he compared my eggs with those of one of his other shippers of entirely White Leghorn, and found mine to be superior in both quality and appearance. To get large eggs I feed liberally. My feed for the morning consists of wheat middlings, buckwheat middlings and bran, scalded, and mixed together. At noon, boiled oats, or turnips or cut hay, thickened with bran, with meat once a week. My breeding pens are 10x10 feet, with a yard 10 x 50 feet. I give as many as I can free range.—G. W. Howell, in Poultry Keeper.

Best Breeds of Chickens.

An exchange thus sums up the leading points of preference in the various breeds of the fowls:

The Langshans lay the best in winter. They give a goodly number of eggs, and are excellent table birds.

The Brahmas come next—the light variety of this class excelling the dark.

The Partridge Cochins are the best layers of the Cochin class. The buffs the best table fowls; the whites, blacks and patridge fellow the buffs for meat.

The Plymouth Rocks are good layers and capital table fowls. So are the Wyandottes, but they will lay more eggs than the Rocks. All the American birds are good, and come near being all purpose fowls.

The Houdans, and the whole French class, are excellent layers and grand market birds.

The Leghorns, Minorcas, Spanish Andalusians, and Hamburgs are the fowls with big egg records, but they are not worth much for eating.

The Dorkings are non-superior for flesh qualities.

The white Leghorns, Minorcas, Spanish and Houdans lay the largest eggs.

The brown Leghorns lay the most eggs of the Leghorn family, but they are smaller.

The Javas recommend themselves as table birds, and very readily assume fat.

The Jersey blues are not highly recommended, either as egg producers or table birds.

The Polish are the handsomest of fowls, excellent layers, but not recommended for the table.

The Hamburgs are persistent layers, but of no account for the table.

The American Dominiques are the original American fowl. They are good layers and table birds, and just the farmer's fowls.

The game class are second to none for table use, and also possess a creditable egg record.

Wild Oats.

San Marcos Farmers Will Cultivate Them.

Some experiments that have just been made with wild oats at San Marcos will lead the farmers there to cultivate that crop quite extensively in the future, says the San Diegen.

For years it has been known that wild oats hay, when properly cured, made the very best fodder for either horses or cattle. J. B. Haggin, the horseman, prefers it above all other dry feed for his thoroughbred horses, and when his stock is sent East annually it is usually accompanied by a large consignment of wild oats.

In certain localities where the conditions are favorable, the wild oats grow in a way that amazes a stranger who sees them for the first time. They appear to require a soil which is retentive of moisture, and do extraordinary well in Spring Valley and other places where the soil remains damp until late in the season. And under those conditions thousands of acres of entirely wild land, which has never seen a plow, may be seen bearing crops of these wild oats, the heads of the grain waving above the backs of the horses, and the ground covered thicker than any field of timothy that ever grew in the East.

But until very lately no effort has ever been made to harvest this crop for the grain. D. P. Hale, who has just returned from San Marcos, states that a successful effort has been made there, and the result is surprising. While ordinary oats weighs thirty-two pounds to the bushel, the wild oats are found to weigh thirty-eight pounds to the bushel.

This fact has attracted some attention, as stated, and there is already considerable inquiry for the seed. It is believed that wild oats can be made a most valuable cultivated crop.

The two highest priced cows at the world-famous New York Mills sale of Bates-Duchess Short-horn, viz., the 8th and 10th Duchess of Geneva, brought the amazing sums of $40,600 and $35,000, the highest prices ever paid for cows. The Montana Farming and Stock Journal says: Although it is now generally conceded that the fabulous values reached upon that occasion—when the long-pursed nobility of England and plucky syndicates of western-American breepers met in fierce competition for Duchess cattle—were the result rather of the fever engendered by the excitement of the moment than conservative estimates of actual worth, the event will always stand as the most extraordinary in agricultural history. "Doom the poonds! Gae an wi' the biddin'!"—the late Simon Beattie's quick reply to the query of the British buyer who paused in the thirty thousands to ask how much English money was represented by his bid—sounded the key note of the day. It was "plunging," wild and wonderful such as will probably never be seen again about an auction sale of blooded cattle.

TURF AND TRACK.

Surefoot, the Derby favorite, is the first foal of his dam.

Frigate, the grand National heroine, has been bred to Gallinule.

Lucy R. 2:30 by Sultan 2·24, promises wonderful things for 1890.

The western contingent of the Hearst stable are now at the Westchester track.

Rancho Del Paso yearlings leave on Monday. The sale will take place on the 16th.

Ex-Secretary McGowan of Clifton has been appointed to a position with the New York Jockey Club.

The grey gelding Geriflue, 2:28½, by Pilot Medium, dam Ida by Golden Dawn, has been placed in Doble's stable.

Bailys Magazine for this month has an excellent portrait of the well known sportsman and advocate Sir Chas. Russell.

The chestnut colt by imported Woodlands out of Maggie B B, dam of Iroquois, etc., was sold for $3600 at the Erdenheim sale.

Queen Emma, a full sister to Cousin Peggy—the dam of Geraldine, dropped a fine filly by Thistle, brother to Gold Leaf.

Mr. Henry Howse, the veterinary surgeon in charge, reported Hermit's death as attributable as much to old age as anything.

C. J. Lefevre, the famous French turfmen, gave his daughter a dowry of 6,000,000 francs ($1,200,000) on her marriage a few weeks ago.

W. A. Merry, the owner of Surefoot, has the nice. bet of £10,000 to £100 taken two years ago in Sir John Willoughby's Yearling Book.

The Undine Stable—Homer, Glenlivet and Racine—arrived at Washington Park last week, and will leave on Tuesday for Westchester.

Senator Hearst's speedy pacer Homestake 2:16½ who was through the California Circuit in '87, and has since been on the shelf is now in P. Farrell's hands.

Arol 2:24, by Electioneer, dam Aurora, 2:27, by John Nelson, in Marvin's string, is recovering rapidly from injuries received in transit across the continent.

Daisy Rose, full sister to Alcazar 2:20½; Sweetheart 2:22½; Eva 2:23½; and San Gabriel 2:29¾, property of Edgewood Farm, foaled a bay colt recently, by Jersey Wilkes.

Dan Dennison has unfortunately lost G. W. (Old Sport). On his way to Portland, Oregon, he contracted a severe cold which settled on his lungs, and last Monday he died.

The Chicago stable headed the list of winners at the spring meeting at Nashville; their entries having won $6,490. The Avondale string coming next with a total of $3,607.

Suisun, the Electioneer mare which John Turner gave a record at Washington, continued her victorious career at Baltimore, winning the 2:27 class in straight heats 2:26; 2:29; 2:31.

Maplewood, the fourteen hundred acre farm near Gallatin, Tenn., has been sold by Colonel Jere Baxter to Boston Mass., parties for $300,000. The farm will be cut up into lots for suburban residences.

G. M. Fogg, President of the Tennessee Fair Association has resigned. Mr. Fogg, it is said takes this step because of the opposition of the majority of the stockholders to give a trotting meeting in the fall.

If suitable arrangements can be made with the Tennessee Fair Association, there will be an annual trotting meeting held at Nashville in September. If to the contrary, a trotting track will be constructed.

Whitestockings 2.16, is the fastest trotter of unknown breeding. Guy 2:10¾, is the fastest trotter without any Hambletonian blood. Palo Alto, record 2:12¼, is the fastest trotter out of a thoroughbred mare.

When Hermit went to the Stud in 1870 his fee was 20 guineas; in 1875 it was increased to a hundred; in 1880 to $150, and in 1886 250 guineas was readily paid. Hermit will be succeeded by his son Friars Balsam.

Mr. J. H. Shults' string on the circuit will be a large one, but what it lacks in numbers it mades up in quality. It will probably consist of Gold Leaf 2:11¼, Arrow 2:13¼, Issaquena 2:23½, Thistle, Sally Graham and Daisy D.

Mr. Burdett—Couts has sold from his Brookfield Stud several hackey mares for importation to America. The pedigrees are all unexceptionable, and the prices are said to be in excess of any ever paid for that class of horse before.

C. X. Larabie, Portland, Ore., has purchased from Volney Giddings, Mason City, Iowa, the brown colt Imperialist, three years, by Woodford Wilkes, dam Topsy, by Swigert; granddam Lady Jane, by Goldsmith's Abdallah; great granddam by Richards' Bellfounder.

C. X. Larabie, Portland, Or., has purchased Commodore Belmont 4340 (by Belmont 64) from W. H. Raymond, Belmont Park, the price paid is said to be $10,000. Mr. Raymond will put Doncaster 2:28½ by Commodore Belmont 4340 in his sire's place as premier stallion.

Col Mackey will leave to-morrow for New York with the Rancho Del Paso, thoroughbred yearlings. A better looking lot never left the famous Sacramento stud farm, and Eastern race-goers and breeders will be astonished at the magnificent proportions of the youngsters.

A race meeting at Moree, Australia was brought to a strange conclusion. The river rose rapidly and submerged a portion of the course, and the horses in the last race had to plunge through two hundred yards of water breast high. One was drowned, his rider escaping.

That the American trotter is moving some in Europe, is shown in the time of Blue Belle, who won the race for 6,000 florins at Vienna, May 10th; having trotted the mile without skip or break in 2:26. Blue Belle,s record prior to this event was 2:29¼, made at Kingston, N. Y., in 1885.

Rancho Del Paso has repurchased Billow (the dam of the flying two year old Eclipse) from Mr. Bybee, Oregon, paying $1500 for her. Her filly foal by Leon was not included in the sale, she had been bred back to Leon.

Mr. L. A. Ragsdale of Clarksville, Tenn., has purchased of Mr. B. W. Ford, Lexington, Ky., the gray filly Midsummer, by Lord Russell, dam Noonday, by St. Elmo 2:30, second dam Midnight (dam of Jay-Eye-See 2.10, and Noontide 2:20½), by Pilot, Jr., The filly is at Warren Park safe in foal to Axtell.

It is quite evident that J. I. Case still has a warm spot in his heart for his first love, Governor Sprague, 2:20½. It is stated on good authority that he recently offered Captain Fowler, the owner of Carrie Walton, 2:28½, $10,000 for her. She is seven years old and is by Governor Sprague, dam by Sentinel.

The New Louisiana Jockey Club has re-elected the following Directors; Albert Baldwin, H. W. Connor, G. W. Nott, R. W. Simmons, S. Hernsheim, R. Milliken, C. W. Miltenberger, R, E. Rivers, George H. Dunbar, F. T. Howard, F. P. Poche, James S. Richardson, John A. Morris, C. A. Conard, John Henderson, Jr.

Mr. Samuel Flemming has sold to Mr. James Stinson of Chicago the bay pacing mare Creeping Kate 2:30, and Little Lassie (dam of M'Liss 2:21½), by Outlaw, dam by C. M. Clay 22. Creeping Kate is very fast, having shown a full mile over the Terre Haute track in 2:19. Little Lassie is destined to become one of the great broodmares.

Fred Thomas, an American horse, won a 3075-yard trotting race at the Neuilly-Levallois meeting last month in 5:14½, or at the rate of 2:47½ per mile. Mollie Wilkes won third prize in a two and a half mile trotting race at the same meeting, and thereby won $55. The first horse, a Russian stallion, won $230, and the second horse got $75.

A big petition was circulated by the clergymen and citizens of Elizabeth who are opposed to horse racing, and was presented to the New Jersey Assembly on the 19th, It requests that body to defeat the Senate bill legalizing bookmaking. A prominent opponent of the race track says that it is the intention of the agitators to put on record either for or against the issue every leading citizen of Elizabeth.

The Board of Directors of the Ninth Distict Agricultural Association met at Rohnerville last Saturday and considered the programme for the Autumn fair. The premium list is not yet completed, but the speed premiums are fixed upon. The following officers were elected for the ensuing year; President G. C. Barber; Treasurer, Louis Feigenbaum; Secretary, Geo. Underwood.

Messrs. Miller and Sibley sold last week to Messrs Schumlbach and Parker two yearling colts, Gold Coast and Golden Slope: both were bred at Palo Alto, Gold Coast being by Electioneer out of Edith Carr (dam of Campbell's Electioneer 3. y. o. 2:22½) by Clark Chief 89. Golden Slope is by Electioneer out of Addie (dam of Woodnut 2:16½ and Manon 2:21) by Hambletonian Chief. $12,000 is the reported price.

A number of gentlemen were joking good, faithful old Bob the venerable stud groom at Belle Meade, the other day, One of them remarked to him; "You came very near losing Iroquois out at the sale the other day." "Not a bit uv it, not a bit uv it," replied Bob. "You see, me'n General Jackson had dat thing fixed. De 'greement was dat de Genr'l would bid till de horse went ter $50,000 an' den he wus ter stop short off an' I wus gwine ter lope right in and buy him.

The Directors of the Eleventh Agricultural District met at Quincy last Saturday. Bids for the fair were put in by both Quincy and Susanville. The former gave decidedly the best bid, offering $5,144 in cash and the race track, with stands, etc., in good order. The fair will therefore be held at Quincy. The following officers were then elected: J. W. Thompson, President; J, D. Byers, Vice-President; E. Huskinson, Sec.; J. E. Pardee, Ass't Sec.; J. H. Whitlock, Treas.

In the returns of the sale of the yearlings from Bundoora Park, Australia, it was stated in one that she was out of a mare called Device, which, while galloping about the paddock, broke her leg badly above the knee. Her owner determined to try and save her for breeding, and had her at once slung to a tree. Eventually a wooden crutch was made for the mare, and she recovered sufficiently to walk about and gather her food, and since then she has produced and reared several good foals.

At a meeting of representative men held in Chicago, May 7th, a grand western fall circuit was formed, and the following officers were elected: W. P. Ijams, President; H. D. McKinney, Secretary. The members of the new circuit are Chicago, Independence, Ia ; Kansas City and St. Louis, Mo.; Terre Haute, Ind.; Cincinnati, O ; Lexington, Ky , and Nashville, Tenn. This make a continuous campaign of eight weeks, and no purse will be less than $1,000.

The Montana Farming and Stock Journal publishes the following letter:

ALZADA, Mont, May 14, 1890.

Editor Journal:

Dear Sir:—I have a mare that has had two colts this spring, foaled twenty-five days apart. The first was foaled April 15, and the second was foaled May 10. They are both stout and healthy. Yours respectfully, GEO. K. SHELDON.

The St. Louis Republic says: A remarkable surgical operation to preserve a horse for the stud will be tried this week on the colt Jess Armstrong. The colt is a 3 year old by Glengarry—Myrtle, and has shown this spring to be a crack. He won one race at Memphis and one at Nashville in fast company and was valued at $7,000 by his owner. In an accident at the local track a week ago his right fore leg was fractured and his owner has decided to have the leg amputated and save the colt if possible for the stud. Dr. Crawley has the colt in charge,

In the last number of Belford's Magazine Dr. Higbee has the following on the Kentuckian and his horse: "Were heaven an interminable boulevard, and the transportation of horses assured, no Kentuckian would miss it, though convinced that it lay through a prohibition district. Other men own horses, drive them, admire their beauty, glory in their speed, but nowhere outside of an Arabian legend is a horse the object of so much affectionate solicitude, so nearly a part of its owner's being, as in Kentucky. A Kentuckian may be conceived of without his title? He may exist without an imposing pedigree. A bold flight of imagination may even picture him without his morning toddy—but without a horse he is impossible."

Senator Hearst's Ballarat, says the Sporting World, was more admired by the paddock visitors yesterday than any of the horses seen within the inclosure. He looked very fit, and on his appearance many people backed him. Those who lost their money on him did not regret it, as they no doubt felt that they would get it back again some day, as the colt will be started with a light weight up, and then a young jockey who has vim and courage will ride, and the colt must prove successful.

The Shah of Persia is probably one of the best and most experienced horsemen in the world. The royal stables of Persia have always been stocked with hundreds and thousands of picked steeds, fit for state pageants, hunting and war. The importance attached to this branch of the Shah's household brought about the custom, which existed from time immemorial, until within the present reign, that a fugitive from the wrath of the Shah could find a sanctuary in the royal stables. So long as he remained there he was safe.

Senator Stanford in a recent interview said: "My attention in the future shall be given more to individuality than in the past. I want a trotter with a good head, an intelligent animal. Let a horse have a good head, with all that quality implies, and you will note that self-possession does much to send him first under the wire in a cracking race, a race that all down the stretch may have been fought inch by inch. Such I have tried and will in the future try to produce at Palo Alto in addition to speed, and is what I mean by the individuality of the animal."

An effort is being made in Lexington to establish the Bluegrass Derby, to be run annually at the spring meetings at the Kentucky Association course. Leading merchants have signified their intention of contributing toward the added money, which will not be less than $2,500. The race will be for three year-olds, but as the Lexington spring meetings are held so early in the season, the distance may not be over one and a quarter miles. And as this is the oldest association in active operation in the United States, it is believed that the proposed stake will be liberally assisted by public-spirited turfmen in other States.

There was never a time when good jockeys were so scarce as they are at present. Of the score or more riders who figure as stars, not one of them gives satisfaction to owners. To the public it is evident that races are lost time and again because of the inability of the pilots of the horses to keep their mounts straight, not to speak of riding them out to the best advantage at the finish. As none of the jockeys show improvement, the only consolation that owners can fall back upon just now is that all receive about the same treatment, and the ability of the horses alone, without the aid of their riders, must win the races.

Mr. Hull, the judicious and successful trainer at Woodburn, says the Harrodsburg Democrat, is getting Pistachio, the brother to Nutwood, in shape to trot some this year. Under the Woodburn plan of slow development Pistachio, although four years this spring, has never had any work for speed, but enough has been seen of his gait to induce Mr. Brodhead to believe that he will likely make a very fast horse. After his season this spring Mr. Hull will begin to "feel" him a little, and we predict that the son of Belmont and Miss Russell will respond nobly to training.

C. J. Hamlin has decided to follow Miller & Sibley's lead and bred a few thoroughbred mares to St. Bel's big brother Chimes. His name appears as a purchaser in the Tennessee market last week, and if Buffalo's most successful breeder can teach the results of the union to keep on their feet as well as Mocking Bird or Prince Regent, there will be no more best two-in-three challenges dated from the Village Farm. By the way, Chimes is to be campaigned this year, and in that event it will be doubly interesting to see what the developed sire will get for the most zealous advocate of the undeveloped sire theory from fillies that were dropped at Belle Meade and other Tennessee farms.

America has a lot yet to learn in large attendances at the races. According to the Cheshire (Eng) Observer "No fewer than 60,000 passengers arrived at the Chester General Railway-station on the Cup day, which is stated to be by far the largest number ever recorded on any similar occasion. They were conveyed in 52 specials and 228 ordinary trains. The Cheshire Lines Railway Company brought 12,000 passengers into the city, bringing up the total to 72,000 passengers on both systems, and it requires very little stretch of the imagination to compute that double that number, or close upon 150,000 people, were in attendance at the races on the Cup day."

Fires still continue. An exchange says—speaking of the Oxford stable fire. At Cambridge, Mass., May 10th, a fire broke out in the Oxford stables, the property of Stearns R. Ellis. The stables were very extensive, and contained some valuable trotting and other horses. Of these only seven were saved, among those rescued being the white gelding Charley Thorne, 2:25½, owned by J. H. Davis. By far the larger number were unfortunately destroyed, including the trotters Lady Mack and Lookout, 2:28½, two valuable roadsters owned by J. W. Hazeh, and the pacer Topsy, the property of F. Washbourne. The loss is estimated at $30,000. Mr. Ellis had $4,000 insurance on his property.

There remain two colts with whom the Lambourne crack Surefoot, will have to measure swords on June 4, these being Right Away and Sainfoin. The first named, as a two year old, could hardly lay claim to first class form, but Sainfoin has done all that has been asked of him. His success in the Astley Stakes at Lewes was not a very brilliant performance, but that his more recent display in the Esher Stakes at Sandown is considered by some judges to be quite good enough for Derby form is shown by the fact that Sir James Miller, on May 2nd, concluded the purchase of the colt for $7500, one of the contingencies of the bargain being that, should the colt win the Derby, one-half of the stakes should go to the vendor.

The Montana Agricultural Mineral and Mechanical Association hope to have an exceptional meeting this year particularly in the fall. The officers are A. J. Davidson, president; T. C. Power, vice-president; B. H. Tatem, treasurer; Francis Pope, secretary.

The Directors are W. A. Chessman, L. H. Hershfield, A. J. Davidson, Wm. Muth, B. H. Tatem, C. D. Hard, W. B. Hundley, Francis Pope, T. C. Power.

The rules of the American Trotting Association, and the rules of the American Turf Congress, will govern the races.

The association reserves the right to alter, amend or postpone any or all of these races should the Board of Directors in their judgment and for cause deem it expedient so to do.

John Campbell says he is going to preserve the enormous floral horseshoe, which formed the usual trophy of the race for the Brooklyn Handicap. He says he intends having the natural flowers replaced by artificial ones, and a large picture of the winner, Castaway II., in the center. This is similar to the plan pursued by Willie Martin, the jockey, who preserved the floral horseshoe emblem of Elkwood's Suburban and is very proud of it.

E. Hunter arrived in San Diego last evening from Denver with a carload of pure bred Clydesdale and Cleveland Bay stallions. The San Diegan says:—The car contained twelve animals, which were taken to Levi's stables on H street, where they will be offered at private sale. San Diego is already well supplied with the draft Clydesdales but it is believed this is the first importation of the thoroughbred (pure-bred) Cleveland Bays. Cleveland Bays are becoming the most fashionable of carriage horses, and would make an excellent cross on native stock.

Some of the greatest turf performers the world has known sold for the most insignificant prices previous to their development, says the Newark Sunday Call. Some very wise horsemen think they can tell how fast an untrained colt will go by simply looking it over. No horseman that ever lived can tell absolutely by looking at a horse how fast he will go. That is beyond the kin of horsemen of any type. The appended list will show the prices at which some of the very greatest performers were sold before their greatness was suspected. Would any one of them have been sold for any such sum had their owners been gifted with prescience?

Maud S., 2:08¾, $250; Director, 2:17, $200; King Almont, 2:21½, $200; Epaulet, 2:19, $480; Tucker, 2:19½, $235; Noontide, 2:20¼, $100; Rosa Wilkes, 2:18¼, $400; John W., 2:23¾, $78; Flora Temple, 2:19¾, $13 50; Majolica, 2:15, $400; Princeton, 2:23, $245; Guy, 2:10¾, $460. The list might be increased to great length.

Riley, by Longfellow, won the Kentucky Derby on the 14th inst. in 2:45, the slowest time on record. Following is a complete list of winners and their sires since the race was established in 1875:

Year.	Name and Sire.	Time.
1875	Aristides by imp Leamington	2:39¾
1876	Vagrant by Virgil	2:38¼
1877	Baden-Baden by imp. Australian	2:38
1878	Day Star by Star Davis	2:37¼
1879	Lord Murphy by Pat Malloy	2:37
1880	Fonso by King Alfonso	2:37½
1881	Hindoo by Virgil	2:40
1882	Apollo by imp. Ashtead or Lever	2:40
1883	Leonatus by Longfellow	2:43
1884	Buchanan by Buckden	2:40¼
1885	Joe Cotton by King Alfonso	2:37¼
1886	Ben Ali by Virgil	2:36½
1887	Montrose by Duke of Montrose	2:39¼
1888	Macbeth II by MacDuff	2:38¼
1889	Spokane by Hyder Ali	2:34½
1890	Riley by Longfellow	2:45

Of the half-dozen candidates for the position of starter to the English Jockey Club, choice has fallen upon Mr. A. Coventry, of whose abilities we had a sample during the week just past. The Manchester Umpire says: That he performed his duties satisfactorily goes without saying, and in selecting him to fill the office the Stewards have made a happy choice. The fixed amount of salary paid to the official starter by the Jockey Club is exactly £350 a year. Extra work, however, he is allowed to take, and is paid usually at first-class meetings £5 a day, which brings the emolument up to probably £1500 a year. The promoters of race meetings are not obliged to retain the official starter, as they can engage any other of the duly qualified starters who hold licenses for this duty from the Jockey Club. *Apropos* of this official, the Earl of Suffolk and Mr. W. G. Craven, in their volume on "Racing" in the "Badminton Library," say,—"The starter should be a cool, resolute man, with nerve equal to the strain of moral responsibility and of actual physical danger. He must be firm, even to severity, yet strictly just to the jockeys, who are sharp enough to note any sign of faltering resolution. If the jockeys once lose their confidence in, or their fear of, the starter, chaos quickly ensues."

In the neighborhood of the fetlock there are occasionally found considerable enlargements, oftener on the hind leg than the fore one, which are denominated windgalls. Between the tendons and other parts, and wherever the tendons are exposed to pressure or friction, and particularly about their extremities, little bags or sacs are placed, containing and suffering to ooze slowly from them a mucous fluid to lubricate the parts. From undue pressure, and that most frequently caused by violent action and straining of the tendons, or, often, from some predisposition about the horse, these little sacs are injured. They take on inflammation and sometimes become large and indurated. There are few horses perfectly free from them. When they first appear, and until the inflammation subsides, they may be accompanied by some degree of lameness; but otherwise, except when they attain a great size, they do not interfere with the action of the animal or cause any considerable unsoundness. The farriers used to suppose that they contained wind, hence their name, windgalls; and hence the practice of opening them, by which dreadful inflammation was often produced, and many a valuable horse destroyed. It is not uncommon for windgalls entirely to disappear in aged horses.

Le Sport recently published some very valuable information with regard to horse breeding in Russia. The writer of the article states that the total number of horses in Russia is over 21,000 000, of which 15,000 000, or one for every adult inhabitant, are fit for work. But there is a considerable difficulty in obtaining the number of horses required for the army, the reason being that the Remount Commissions pay such a low price. The creation of stallions depots by the State is designed to remedy this condition of things, and in addition to 3,964 private studs, which comprise about 11,600 stallions and over 100,000 mares, there are now eighteen of these state depots, which contain about 1,500 stallions, all placed at the disposal of local breeders at fees ranging from one to ten roubles, the value of a rouble being now about half a crown. The administration of the Haras also endeavors to encourage breeding by distributing about 100,000 roubles in prizes for shows and races. The most valuable prizes are those named after the Emperor, the Empress, the Czarewitch, and other distinguished personages who have rendered services to the breeding interest, while the weights are fixed according to the English scale. But the distances are not the same, for the flat races range from two and a half miles to four furlongs, while some of the steeple chases are more than twelve miles.

Lieutenant Von Barby, of the Twelfth Hussar Regiment, Germany, has taken the most interesting ride of late. He was riding with the troops in the neighborhood of Merseburg, when his horse took fright and bolted. All efforts to restrain him being fruitless, he gave him the rein and waited his opportunity to jump off. To his dismay the animal swerved suddenly in the direction of a plateau overhanging a broad expanse of water. A few moments and both horse and rider would be over the edge. A bright flash was seen for a moment, the saber of the officer fell upon the head of his steed, and they both came to the ground, the man safe.

Mr. W. G. Craven, the well known English racing man, has written an article in a contemporary, in which he refers to the want of staying powers in the present breed of racehorses. Writers, he says, are continually expatiating on this subject, and their theory seems generally to be that we breed entirely for speed, and that, consequently, it is impossible that our horses should stay. Now there are several causes why we should be careful not to assert that our horses cannot stay. The first is the enormous amount of money that is at the mercy of two-year-olds over short courses, and the comparatively small stakes that are open for competition for older horses over courses of two miles and upwards. The second is the system of breaking and training horses from early youth to jump into their bridles and start with all their speed necessary for two-year-old racing, and thirdly the immense quantity of races which two-year-olds and three year-olds are run in. The upshot of these three causes is that we have no idea how many of our thoroughbreds might stay were their early education that of Eclipse and such horses as are everlastingly quoted. Many of the greatest breeders of modern times believe that our horses can stay as well as their ancestors did, and justly laugh at the idea of extraordinary speed preventing a horse from doing so.

The Chicago Times says: "George V. Hankins, the owner of Robespierre, and his immediate followers, had 'a dead sure thing' yesterday, and they played the brown son of Jils Johnson and Agnes as though the race were all over but the shouting From the general manager of the Hankins' establishment down to the colored porter there was but one feeling and that was that Robespierre would win, and they bet their money accordingly.

"'I am booked for the poor house,' said the veteran Charlie Matthews after the result was made known, and the picture of Robespierre that stood upon an easel in the saloon was draped in mourning.

"In connection with the race a good story is told upon Hankins. So sure was he of winning that he had prepared a canvas four feet square, picturing his horse Robespierre winning the Derby, and this was to have been exhibited in the saloon the moment the race was over. The picture was completed, and all was in readiness for its exhibition, but, alas! 'the best laid plans of mice and men gang aft aglee.' Robespierre was lost in the shuffle, and after the positions of the horses have been changed on the canvas Mr. Corrigan can purchase a good picture of the Derby finish of 1890 very cheaply."

Racing in England seems to be hampered by the very sanctimonious people just as much as it is in the Eastern States, for an Exchange says: The Nottingham Town Council have, after a solemn conclave, passed a resolution that no fresh race committee be appointed after next November, when the present committee will be at an end. This extraordinary action of the Council means practically that the races will cease to exist, for if this august body hold such strong opinions on the subject it is hardly likely they will let the ground—which belongs to them—to anyone else to hold races. Nottingham meetings have always been well conducted, and although that good sportsman, Mr. John Robinson, who is quite well again, used every endeavor to combat this proposition, the white chokers and tea-drinkers outvoted the opposition to this motion. In striking contrast to this feeble policy of the Nottingham people, the Commoners at Warwick have determined to lengthen their course, make a new paddock, and extend the grand stand, and the work is to be taken in hand as soon as possible. The straight run-in will now be six furlongs, and with these improvements Warwick should again take a high place amongst Midland fixtures.

Germany will hold this year, for the first time, a great national horse show, where all the different horse-breeding districts of the country will be well represented. The Horse World says: The arrangements are in the hands of the Union Club, a similar authority to the English Jockey Club, which gives a full guarantee that the matter will be carried through properly. There will be a large number of prizes for the 128 classes, the latter being divided into three great divisions: A, breeding horses; B, luxury and working horses; C, auxiliary branches in connection with horse breeding, etc., as modes of stables, coaches, veterinary requisites, literature (pictures, stud books, etc). The royal stud will send a large collection of thoroughbreds (not competing for prizes). Hanover, Oldenburg, Prussia, etc., will excel in coach horses, Saxony and Silesia in Shires and Clydesdales, etc. Programmes in English as well as in the French language will be issued daily for the convenience of foreign visitors. Interpreters will be in attendance. Foreign breeders and others will have a good opportunity to obtain a thorough knowledge of horse breeding in Germany, as the show will represent a complete picture of German horse-breeding. A special feature will be the draft trials, driving, and riding competitions. The date of the show is June 11th to 22nd.

Horses have curious fancies, likes and dislikes, and are at times as unreasonable as women. Squire Osbaldeston, the well known English turfmen, had a horse called Grimaldi, who for some reason, would not face running water. In consequence of which caprice, he lost the Squire two races; but he had a third on hand, against Col. Charritus' Napoleon for 500 guineas. The course was over the Dunchurch country, so Osbaldeston went to the famous rough rider, old Dick Christian, and consulted with this equine oracle as to what was to be done to get Grimaldi over a stiffish brook that lay in the line of the country. Dick had a wonderful power over horses, his great secret being coaxing and kindness. He agreed to meet the Squire and his horse the next morning at Brixworth, and there, having allowed Grimaldi to smell at a small stream, and patted and coaxed him, at last induced him to cross quite easily. He was then led to the brook. "He'll never cross this, Dick," said the Squire. "I'll bet you a guinea he will, Squire," answered Christian. Dick then waded into the stream, and finding a place where he could stand, he arranged with Osbaldeston to be in that place when the match took place. "I'll be here," he said, "with my hat on the top of a stick; gallop right for me, and keep him going." The Squire carried out these instructions to the letter, and Grimaldi leapt clean over Christian, hat and all, cleared the brook, and won the match for his owner, because he had confidence in the man who coaxed him.

The Umpire says: In the columns of the well-known paper, the "Chester Courant," appeared on Wednesday morning, *apropos* of the race meeting, an extract from the "Courant" of 1790, giving the programme of the May meeting of that year. The worthy citizens, it appears, made the most of the sport, spreading it over five days, commencing on Monday, giving only one race for each day, but, all the events were heats, and some were four mile ones, probably; but what with cocking in the morning "between the gentlemen of Cheshire and Denbighshire," the ordinaries at the various hotels, presumably at the early hour of four or five o'clock, and no doubt some hard drinking and a little dicing in the evening, the day would not prove too long. "The Earl Grosvenor of that day," we quote the "Courant," was an owner of racehorses, his entries being frequently met with:" and later on in the year we stumble across the paragraph: "Lord Grosvenor has not been so successful for many years, as up to the late October meetings at Newmarket his winnings exceed £20,000." This was not bad for the days when added money consisted of very trifling sums, so we must conclude that wagering formed an important portion of that twenty thousand.

In reply to a letter from Joseph Battell, Mr. Joseph Harker, of New York, recently writes that the only mare except Dexter's dam that produced three 2:30 performers by Rysdyk's Hambletonian was Old Kate. "Kate was purchased about 1856 in Canada by an Irishman by the name of Gourley, now dead, who had a small stock farm a short distance from Newburgh, on the Hudson River. He raised Brunette as a three-year-old for $500. He sold Bruno and Daniel Boone at one and two years, I think, for $350 for the two. He then sold Old Kate to Major Morton, a neighbor, for $50. The Major raised Young Bruno, Miss Brunette and Breeze, and then I think he gave the old mare to Mr. Backman. I bought Brunette and Bruno from Mr. Monot, now dead, as four and five-year-olds for $30,000. They trotted in 1867 to my road-wagon, weighing 180 pounds, in 2:25½. If Bruno had been as steady as the mare, they would have trotted in 2:15. They trotted a half mile four days previous to their trial on the Fashion track in 1:06, first quarter in 0:34, second in 0:32. I bought Young Bruno at five years old and Miss Brunette and Breeze when two and three years old. I owned Lulu, Gazelle and May Queen (formerly Nashville Girl), half sister to Lulu, Mattie and Maud S. I bought Maud S. as a four-year-old, and let Mr. Vanderbilt have her as a special favor. I paid $20,000 for her. In 1886, the year after William H. Vanderbilt sold her to Mr Bonner, I offered the latter for a friend of mine $100,000 for her. I sold my brood mares and four of their colts to Governor Stanford. I have been driving on the road but very little for the past five years."—Dunton's Spirit.

"Lord Durham said that racing is the only possible means of obtaining a true test of a horse's speed and courage," and the County Gentleman, apropos of the irrepressible Lord's remarks, says:

"Handsome is as handsome does," is a perfectly unassailable motto from a racing point of view, but when we come to questions of breeding it is only fair to remember that many a famous racer, beautiful and otherwise, has proved a failure at the stud. So that, after all, though success on the turf is an absolute proof of the possession of desirable qualities by the winner himself, it does not demonstrate with equal certainty his power to transmit his own excellencies to his posterity. Again, with regard to the tests of the show ring, these are by no means limited to the points of the horse's physical conformation. His soundness of wind and limb are completely established by a veterinary examination, which some exhibitors consider only too severe, before he is adjudged any of the honors of victory. He is, moreover, "put through his paces," and though a good "action" is not an infallible sign of quality—either as racer, hunter, or hack—it is surely something to the point. * * * At the same time, we quite concur in the dictum that "most practical breeders would prefer to have the services of horses who have distinguished themselves by winning good races at all distances on the turf." We are willing to admit that the race course is by far the best—we simply submit that it is not the only—test of quality in the thoroughbred as regards breeding purposes. We are here brought back to the incontestable and incomparable value of the turf as an institution for maintaining the quality of our British breeds of horses. For the race horse is only one factor in the account. The thoroughbred is the keystone of the whole racing edifice. His strain of blood it is which runs the feebler or fuller volume through hunters, hackneys, army horses, and even the cobs and cart horses of commerce.

Speaking of gentlemen riders, "Rapier," in a recent issue of the Illustrated Sporting and Dramatic News says: "Gentlemen riders are of various kinds—very various. They must not accept payment, but some of them think they may have a tenner or pony on their mount, and forget to pay if it is beaten, not to mention a more or less liberal profit under the head of expenses. But all are, of course, not like this. Some time ago, for instance, a gentleman rider—I must not mention names, I suppose, but the new starter could add some details to the story, I believe—was asked to ride a horse, and was told it would most likely win. He fancied it himself from what he had seen it do, and, asked if he would like to back it, replied that he would have a tenner on. He was beaten, and to the astonishment of the person who managed the horse for the gentleman to whom it belonged, a cheque for the lost bet was sent on the Monday. Soon after he was asked to ride the horse again, and consented. "You'll win to-day," he was told; "what shall I put on for you?" "I won't back him," the gentleman replied. "He disappointed me last time, and I'm afraid Belted Earl will just beat me." "Oh, no, he won't," the manager replied, "I shall put your tenner on; you'll win to-day." "No, I shall not back him to-day. Please understand," he added, checking a remonstrance he saw coming, "I won't have a shilling on." The race was run; Belted Earl, a red-hot favorite was beaten, and the gentleman rider—for it will be seen that he was a gentleman—won his race. His mount started at 5 to 1, and on the Monday he received a cheque for £50, signed by the owner of the horse, with whom he did not chance to be acquainted. I happen to know that £50 would have been exceedingly useful to him that morning, but he had not won it, and disdained to accept it, so, tearing off the signature, he sent back the cheque with an explanation of the circumstances. I think I have heard tales of gentlemen riders which make me think they would not have acted thus." We cannot see that there is anything very remarkable in the above. No man deserves to be lauded for mere honesty of purpose; it is only what we naturally expect of him.

ROD.

An Olla from the Fishing Gazette.

Ballad of the Boots.

Out spake an ancient angler—
"My boy, you've quit of school,
And, well I ween,
With ardours keen
Burn for the banks of Avon green
And Breamore's haunted pool;
Yet sooth," quote he,
"Tho' hot you be,
You'll find the water's cool!

"Wherefore, my son, take this, and this,—
(Nay, never for a clout!)
For twenty years—
Excuse my tears!—
They've served me, turn about;
Take them, my boy,
I wish you joy—
These Waders true and stout,
These Boots, so long
The theme of song—
You'll find the comfort out.

"Up, rods and baits! the train awaits—
Walk back, my son," he said . . .
Down to the Old Mill's tumbling tail,
Where Avon shakes her lilies pale,
The eager angler sped—
And on his feet
The Boots felt sweet,
Tho' ponderous of tread.

There gloomed the broad bay's darkling depth,
There wav'ring water shoots,
There glides the stream
With golden gleam
Beneath the alder roots;
And down he dasht and in he splasht
Amongst the reeds and coots—
"A fool might get
His ankles wet,
But I've got on the Boots!'

Yon shelving beach I now may reach,
Far out in the middle mere;
A lusty trout
Lies thereabout,
Where the stream runs sharp and clear,
And a silv'ry side
Makes a glint in the tide,
For the grayling loves it dear;
I'll drop a cast on their nose at last,
Tho' I've tried for many a year!"

"Oh, the Wader's a free and fetterless thing
The elements formed to flout—
But what's this feel
Trickles cold to my heel?
Are thêre any icebergs about?
I say, hullo!
It's got to my toe—
Perhaps it's a twinge of gout? . . .
It can't be —— *Water!* —— in the *BOOTS!!*
"Those boots 'so true and stout?'
The theme'" . . . . Oh, bosh!
Home, home, squish, squosh,
Thro' a league of dust and drought!

* * * * *

A stretcher met
Him breathing yet:
He'd found the comfort out.

MORAL.

O Sons that would a fishing go,
How thoughtful Fathers are, you know. PUCK.

Eels.

[From Report of the Fish Commission of N. Y., for 1889.]

These fish have been our greatest pests, kingfishes, minks and turtles coming next in the order named. The eels would come up from the salt water at night, through the wet grass, and get into our rearing ponds and burrow into the sandy bottom, with only their protractile nostrils above the sand, and there live and forage by night. At times we would be able to locate one by the clean sand which it had turned over in burrowing; but if the eel was killed it only prevented further damage and did not restore the fry which had been devoured. Our new rearing ponds, just completed, have plank bottoms, in which an eel will find it hard to hide. Some years ago the Fish Commissioners of Michigan came East and took a lot of young eels for planting in the great lakes, above the falls of Niagara. For the sake of fish culture at large, I hope that these fish went to sea and never returned, because they are so very destructive and so persistent in going where ever water goes. Near the salt water, the eel is a great nuisance in the trout ponds, and its keen sense of smell leads it to a deposit of trout eggs, on which it *gorges*.

Few people know what obstacles an eel can surmount in order to reach waters above. At this place there is a mill dam with a fall of a dozen feet or more, but the eels go around it at night, through the wet grass, and cross the road to get into the mill-pond. I have seen them in the grass, and their tracks across the road are sometimes plainly seen. I have seen them in the morning stuck in the dry sand about our ponds, trying to get into them, and in digging for the foundation for our new building, they were shoveled out of the muck twenty feet from the pond. I have seen young eels from two to three inches in length, climb up the boards on the side of a flume near a dam, to the height of three or more feet, in their attempts to surmount the obstacle, and once saw them travel in the moss which grew on the top of an arch, through which the water flowed too swift for them to stem; a full report of this circumstance will be found in the Ninth Annual Report of the American Fishcultural Association, page 20, related by a man who was with me at the time. They clung in the moss as do flies on a ceiling.

As the main damage done by eels is among the fry which are under a year old, it may be possible to prevent it by planking the bottom of the rearing-ponds.

In this connection I may be pardoned for introducing a flattering notice from the New York Sun of November 16, 1888, which shows the remarkable fecundity of the eel. It is headed "Nine Million Eggs in an Eel," and although the subject-matter was published years ago, the Sun makes some editorial additions to it, and says:

"Scientists have known that the eel is an egg-producing fish for a dozen years or more, the Russian naturalist, Syrski, having first figured the ovaries of the female and the spermaries of the male, but how and where these minute eggs are laid is still unknown. In October the eels run down to salt water to breed, and in the spring the young eels ascend the brooks and rivers in swarms. As they are then some two inches long, and of the size of a darning needle, it is evident that they must have been hatched several weeks before, perhaps in February, to have grown so much from so small an egg.

Mr. Fred Mather, the well-known fish culturist, has been estimating the number of eggs in a six pound eel in November (in what is known to fishermen as 'eel fat' but which are really the ovaries), and credits that eel with fully 9,000,000. Under the microscope he found that they measured eighty to the linear inch, and taking one ovary and dividing it by means of the most delicate scales known to science, he halved, quartered, and further divided the mass seventeen times, until he had a section small enough to count the eggs in it.

This section represented 1-131,072 of the total number, and three sections were laboriously counted under the microscope. One of the sections contained sixty-eight eggs, making the total 8,912,896 eggs. The second held seventy-seven eggs, or 10,092,544 in the whole. The third section consisted of seventy-one, from which it would appear that there were 9,306,112 eggs in the eel. Taking the last as the medium number, Mr. Mather figures, in round numbers, that a six pound eel contained 9,000,000 eggs.

There have been many theories about the reproduction of the eel, some of them being wildly absurd, such as their being hatched by fresh water mussels, or that the lamprey was the female and the so called silver eel the male, etc. The fact is that the lamprey, miscalled 'lamper eel,' is a form of life lower than that of the true fishes, to which the eel belongs, and is a vertebrate with a cartilaginous skeleton instead of a bony one, has its skull imperfectly developed, and has no lower jaw. Superficially it appears like an eel, but is not nearly related to it. Mr. Mather has done a service with his microscope in computing the eggs in a fish about whose breeding habits the majority of fishermen are in doubt."

Fecundity.

According to naturalists, a scorpion will produce 65 young, a common fly will lay 144 eggs, a leech 150, and a spider 170. A hydrachna produces 600 eggs, and a frog 1,100. A female moth will produce 1,100 eggs, and a tortoise 1,000. A gall insect has laid 50,000, a shrimp, 6,000, and 10 000 have been found in the ovary of an ascaris. One naturalist found more than 12,000 eggs in a lobster, and another more than 21,000. An insect very similar to an ant (*Mutilla*) has produced 80,000 eggs in a single day. Leuwenhoeck seems to compute 4,000,000 as the crab's share. Many fishes produce an incredible number of eggs. More than 36,000 have been counted in a herring, 38,000 in a smelt, 1,000,000 in a sole, 1,130,000 in a roach, 3,000,000 in a sturgeon, 342,000 in a carp, 383,000 in a tench, 546,000 in a mackerel, 992,000 in a perch, and 1,350,000 in a flounder. But of all the fishes hitherto discovered, the cod seems to be the most prolific. One naturalist computes that this fish produces more than 3,686,000 eggs, and another as many as 9,444,000. A rough calculation shows that, were one per cent of the eggs of the salmon to result in full grown fish, and were they and their progeny to continue to increase in the same ratio, they would in about sixty years amount in bulk to many times the size of the earth. Nor is the salmon the most prolific species. In a yellow perch weighing 3½ ounces have been counted 9943 eggs and in a smelt ten inches and a half in length, 25,141. An interesting experiment was made in Sweden in 1761, by Charles F. Lund. He obtained from fifty female breams 3,100,000 young, from 100 female perch 3,215,000 young, and from 100 female mullets 4,000,000 young.—American Analyst.

The Nepigon Trout.

This name is also spelled Nipigon and Neepigon, but Nepigon is the usual form, that being the name of the station near the river and on the Canadian Pacific Railway 65 miles east of Port Arthur. The river, the lake it flows from and the bay it flows into are named alike. The lake lies northwest of Lake Superior, and was surveyed by Prof Bell in 1868, who considers it the most beautiful of all the great lakes. It contains a great many islands from two to fifteen miles long, the water being clear and cold. The lake is the sixth and last in the chain of Great Lakes, being about as large as Lake Ontario, having a coast line of 500 miles. It is nearly 75 miles long from north to south, and 50 miles wide, with deep bays. Some 16 rivers enter it, one the Kabitotiquaik, has 30 miles averaging 15 feet deep for the first four miles.

At the head of the lake the Hudson's Bay Co. have had a fur post for about a century, as it is a rich fur country. The country bears a variety of timber, and the mineral wealth is varied and great, while extensive tracts of cultivatable soil exist.

Another member then described how once, when lunching in a windy spot, he stuck a fly on gut into a bit of cake to anchor it and mark the spot, and then inadvertently ate the bit of cake! It was agreed his story took the cake for that evening.

Piscatorial Scotch professor, to piscatorial minister, whose guest he is, and who has a fine stream in front of his manse: 'Dae ye never feel tempted, when ye see a fine wimple on the burn there on a Sunday morning, just to go and ha'e a bit quiet throw?" Piscatorial minister: "No, I never feel tempted; I just gang."

At the Flyfishers' Club the other night the question arose as to what would be the effect of accidentally swallowing a fly on gut or on an eyed hook; and one member related how he had placed a hook on gut, when barbel fishing in the Thames, in a glass tumbler; that several of the party had sundry glasses of beer out of the glass, and that they each expect to get a bite inside some day, or find the point coming out of their great toe.

The Buffalo Echo advises its readers to try as far as lies in their power to check the wanton destruction of trout that is going on daily during the irrigating season. It is no mere sentiment that prompts the thinking person to seek to perpetuate this species of fish which makes doubly attractive the mountain regions of the west. There is money in it. Our trout streams in themselves form one of the most tempting attractions to the summer tourist, and the tourist is a money-spender.

"Mary," said one fair creature to another, "is your husband a fisherman?" "Yes, my dear; why do you ask?" "Do you believe him when he tells you he has been fishing?" "Why, certainly, my dear—sometimes." "Yes, I am sure of it." "But he brought no fish home with him." "Now that is why I am so sure he went, for when he has not been he invariably buys a couple of fish at the fishmonger's, and tells me they are trout; he buys all kinds of fish, and thinks I don't know the difference. The varieties of trout he has brought home within the past twelve months are astonishing; I know my business too well to say anything."

The Montana Live Stock Journal sensibly says: and the remarks are applicable to all states: "The game and fish laws of the state, we believe, are being violated almost daily; but we have been unable to procure any testimony whereby a conviction could be made." Such is the report of the grand jury of Cascade county. The same may be said of every county in the state. The people will come to know when it is too late the value of the fish in our streams. The government would stock our streams with fish, but what is the use when men will violate the law for the preservation of the fish, and will not screen the heads of their irrigation ditches to keep out the young fish.

Even if it cannot be said of "Uncle Bob" Liddle at 538 Washington street, City, as it is sometimes said of "Pike", the old time Yosemite guide that he "packed" the dirt to make them hills", it can still be said that he has been longer in the fishing tackle trade than anyone doing business in San Francisco. Beginning modestly with the rude appliances necessary for bay fishing in pioneer days he has gone along through thirty-seven years of trade, always the same accommodating, painstaking good man, popular with all sportsmen and in demand whenever the guild meets either to discuss some public measure or to while away an hour in social relaxation. Mr. Liddle's store and stock are an epitome of the inventions in guns and tackle of all the years since his name was first painted upon the sign which he still uses. Assisted at present by his energetic and popular son George, the firm has taken new lease of life and is rapidly reaching out for preeminence in many lines particularly in the handling of standard fishing tackle.

Just as men differ in tastes, so it seems different firms drift into peculiarities and build up specialities which mark them distinctively. Beginning perhaps with a small stock and finding their goods in a particular line in demand, business grows until it is known of all men that certain things can be had at certain places; as for instance when one fancies the exquisite patterns in trout flies of Mr. Chas. F. Orvis, he at once wends his way to the establishment of that most genial of dealers, Mr. E T. Allen at 416 Market street, City, where Mr. Skinner seems to find real pleasure in showing and praising not only the Orvis flies but also the thousand and one other useful and beautiful creations of the manufacturers represented by Mr. Allen. Such for instance as the Abalone spoons, and the Allcock tackle. One may visit Mr. Allen's and consume almost any amount of time in studying his stock, and go away without feeling embarrassed because of lack of desire to purchase immediately. Such a policy cannot but make for the permanent prosperity of the firm.

Among the questions seemingly never to be answered conclusively is that from the angler who bobs up serenely season after season, to know what flies he shall take in order to insure success. A hundred times in these columns suggestions have been offered, embodying the experience of persons whose success is warrant for reliance upon their judgment. The day has long since gone by when it could be said that any one fly could invariably be relied upon, but it is nevertheless true that beyond a few colors there is little need to load the fly book. An inspection of the patterns and colors offered by that leading firm in fine tackle, Clabrough, Golcher & Co., at 630 Montgomery street, City, and consultation with the members of the firm will enable any novice to prepare himself perfectly for sport in any of the waters of the coast, or for that matter in any waters where trout and salmon abound. To the wise old hand whose judgment has been ripened by years of toilsome study on the streams, it may be suggested that in the store mentioned may be found the longest and finest of gut, either drawn or undrawn, the most perfect of rods of all actions, the lightest and most workmanlike of reels and a varied assortment of the other necessaries which go to complete the outfit of him who would go fishing healthfully and comfortably.

Anglers who draw their inspiration from the dailies may have settled into the belief that the trout fishing during the summer months will not be good, but those who know the peculiarities of the fish and whose experience extends over more than a very few seasons, are persuaded that the season of '90 will be one of the very best known for many years. In ordinary years those rather selfish individuals who go about the country using salmon roe, shrimp, worms, and fleas and other baits, and whose greatest pleasure it is to sit beside roily pools and bottom fish during the earlier weeks of the season, find it possible to clear the streams of about all the good fish which they contain, but this season the individuals mentioned have not been "in it" for the reason that the usually heavy rains have kept all the streams at flood height and all of the fish so glutted with natural food as to make them indifferent to the most skillfully baited hook. Even such streams as the Sonoma, the Purissima, the Lagunitas and the others which run but a short course before emptying into the salt water, have been practicably unfordable and unfishable; they are just now running at fair fishing height, and as the days are at hand when the vacations of business men are permitted, it will cheer all those who love to angle to know that there is a good store of fish finning about in all waters, ready to rise to any fit tackle and to fight the good fight which every trout makes, to the great joy of him who fishes legitimately.

The army of anglers who, prefer the ease of lake fishing at Crystal Springs, for bass, may find many useful hints in these lines from an exchange which says:

Deep holes, large or small, under the shadow of rocks, trees or high banks, are the favorite retreats of black bass. The approach must be made cautiously, for you might as well try to coax a robin to eat your hand as to persuade a black bass to take your bait if he gets a sight of you. He is the most cunning, prudent and suspicious fish that lives, excepting the trout.

Make your cast quietly, and keep as far as possible from the spot where the bait is to be thrown. Then let the minnow dart about, the crab squirm, the hellgramite wriggle, the frog swim, or the grasshopper kick, as the case may be. Unless the bass is unusually hungry, he will rather deliberate about taking the bait. You may have to wait awhile, but be patient. The bass is a food searcher, and is constantly moving about.

The first warning of a bite will be a slow moving away of the line. Let it move. The bass on seizing his prey, does not immediately swallow it. He swims a short distance before beginning that operation. Therefore, keep your line slack and let your victim carry it along 10 or 20 feet. Then give a short, sharp pull. But do not be in a hurry. A lively battle is in store, which will require coolness, skill and patience. The bass will fight for his life, he will display astonishing strength, strategy and pluck. If you attempt to haul him in suddenly, something will break and your capture will escape. Therefore, be firm, but gentle. Temper determination with deliberation. Let your nerves be of steel, albeit sensitive as a magnetic needle. Watch the moods of your fish. He will rush this way and that, he will pull like a draft horse, he will alternately attempt to escape by main strength and try to fool you. You must humor him, without letting him get an advantage

The battle will be an exciting one. The spring of your light elastic rod will tell terribly on the strength and endurance of the noble fellow who frantically endeavors to escape, but he will not give up until completely exhausted. To tire him out will take from five to ten minutes, possibly longer. When he finally surrenders, draw him toward you and get him on land as quickly as possible, for you can never be sure that he has not a final "flop" in reserve. When the victory is won you will have an exhilarating sense of triumph, and will be eager for another fray.

THE GUN.

Fine Rifle Shooting.

A team match was shot at Shell Mound on Saturday afternoon last between Col. J. H. Dickinson and Officer P. D. Linville on one side and Col. Sam E. Beaver and Lieut. L. R. Townsend on the other. The conditions were forty shots per man, 200 yards, off hand, any military rifle, for a dinner.

The weather was most disadvantageous, a belt of thick fog blowing across the range, and for a large portion of the time quite obscuring the target. That such fine scoring should have been done reflects the highest credit upon the skill of the participants.

It was particularly gratifying to note that Col. Dickinson, who is in active command of a regiment of militia, could not only talk rifle-shooting, but could also take his gun and demonstrate his ability on the range.

The gusty wind and a little carelessness in leveling his sights, gave Lieut. Townsend two 3's in his final score, just when he was good for 4's at least, and lost him the match.

Col. Beaver and Mr. Linville shot as usual, in sure style. The scoring was done by H. H. Briggs. The scores were:

DICKINSON TEAM.

Col. J. H. Dickinson	4	4	4	5	3	3	4	5	3	4	39
	4	4	4	4	3	3	4	4	4	4	38
	5	4	3	3	5	4	4	4	4	4	40
	3	4	4	3	4	4	4	5	5	3	39
Total											156
P. D. Linville	4	4	4	5	4	4	4	4	4	4	41
	4	5	5	4	4	5	4	4	5	5	45
	5	4	4	4	4	4	4	4	4	4	41
	5	4	5	4	4	3	5	5	4	4	43
Total											170
Grand total											326

BEAVER TEAM.

Col. Beaver	5	5	4	3	4	5	4	5	5	4	44
	3	4	3	5	4	3	4	4	5	5	40
	4	4	4	5	4	5	4	4	4	5	43
	5	5	5	4	4	5	3	4	4	4	43
Total											170
Lieut. L. R. Townsend	4	4	4	3	4	2	5	5	4	3	38
	4	4	4	5	2	4	4	4	3	4	38
	3	3	5	4	4	4	5	3	3	4	39
	4	4	5	4	5	4	4	3	3	4	40
Total											155
Grand total											325

The Portland Oregonian gives this "line" on Mongolian pheasants:

"Quite a number of persons in this city and East Portland have secured a lot of the eggs of the Mongolian pheasant from parties in the country, paying at the rate of about 10 cents each for them, and have hens sitting on them. The success of Mr. Ferry Henshaw in raising pheasants last year has led others to try their luck, but it is safe to say that although the chicks are hardy, there will be more hatched than will be raised. Mr. Henshaw has two pair of pheasants and the hens have produced forty-six eggs and show no signs of wanting to sit. He placed nineteen under a hen and seventeen of them are now hatched and the chickens are hammering away at the shells of the other two. He says the cocks are such fighters that no poultry can be kept in the same yard with them. They knock out any ordinary chicken without half trying."

Trap at Novato.

A bulls-head breakfast, given by Barney Galindo at Novato, was the motive which induced several shot-gun enthusiasts to go there on May 25th. Mr. Galindo kindly placed his home and grounds at the disposal of the particular little party mentioned. Officer P. D. Linville sent over a barrel of blue rock targets and a trap, and Mr. William Schreiber contributed a Macomber trap and a supply of the "tin pigeons." The members of the party were Col. S. E. Beaver, William Schreiber, William Dormer, James Sanderson, P. D. Linville, Mr. C. McCrea and this reporter.

Of such a crowd, little could be expected except what they chanced to wish to do, and as the day was warm, all of them were especially eccentric. After reaching Galindo's, the traps were soon set, and match shooting began. Mr. Schreiber had never shot over traps, but put his field skill into use.

It was a "find and trap" match, each trapping for the others. Pretty soon the arm of the blue rock trap broke, and the birds were then thrown by hand with most extraordinary results. Some went straight up, others barely skimming the grass, others in coming, and still others to any and every quarter of the compass.

About noon Senator F. C. DeLong drove by, and was invited to take a hand, which he did most effectively. The regular scores of the teams were at 30 blue rocks per man, as follows:

SANDERSON TEAM.

Jos. Sanderson...101001110011100100000000010111—19
P. D. Linville....011101111110011101010111100111—21
Dormer..........110111011001011011111101011111—22
Total...56

SCHREIBER TEAM.

Schreiber.........000110111111000110111000010001—16
Beaver...........000111001110100100111111010101—17
Briggs...........110110101010101011110001001011—17
Total...50

Selby Standard Medal Match.

A match for the Selby medal, emblematic of the championship of Central California, at artificial targets, was shot at Alameda Point on May 25th. Mr. N. H. Cadwallader of San Jose being the challenger, and Mr. C. H. Cate of this city the then holder. Sixteen men entered, and a lively day's sport resulted, the medal being won by Mr. Cadwallader, 30 per cent. of the entrance money by Col. S. I. "Harvey," 20 per cent. by Mr. F. Parks, and 10 per cent. being divided by Messrs. C. H. Cate, Frank E. Coykendall and H. C. Golcher.

The shot was at thirty single blue rocks and ten pairs, American Association rules. Mr. Cadwallader was at once challenged by Mr. C. H. Cate, and the medal will be again shot for at Oakland Point to-morrow, beginning at 10 o'clock A. M. The match is open to all residents of Central California. Entrance $5. The scores were:

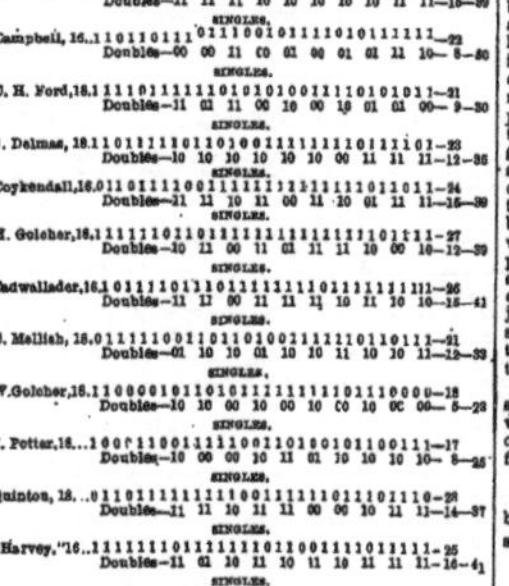

SINGLES.
C. Cate, 19....111111111011111111111110001110 0—24
Doubles—11 11 11 10 10 10 10 10 11 11—15—39
SINGLES.
Campbell, 16..110110111011100101111010111111—22
Doubles—00 00 11 00 01 00 01 01 11 10— 8—30
SINGLES.
C. H. Ford, 18.111101111110101010011110101011—21
Doubles—11 01 11 00 10 00 10 01 01 00— 9—30
SINGLES.
J. Delmas, 18.110111110110100111111110111101—23
Doubles—10 10 10 10 10 10 00 11 11 11—12—35
SINGLES.
Coykendall, 16.011011110011111111111110110111—24
Doubles—11 11 10 11 00 11 10 01 11 11—15—39
SINGLES.
H. Golcher, 18.111111011011111111111111101111—27
Doubles—10 11 00 11 01 11 11 10 00 10—12—39
SINGLES.
Cadwallader, 16.101111011101111111110111111111—26
Doubles—11 11 00 11 11 11 10 11 10 10—15—41
SINGLES.
C. Mellish, 18.011111001101101001111110110111—21
Doubles—01 10 10 01 10 10 11 10 10 11—12—33
SINGLES.
W. Golcher, 18.110000101101011111111101110000—18
Doubles—10 10 00 10 00 10 00 10 00 00— 5—23
SINGLES.
J. Potter, 18...100111001111100110100101100111—17
Doubles—10 00 00 10 11 01 10 10 10 10— 8—25
SINGLES.
Quinton, 18...011011111111110011111101110111 0—28
Doubles—11 11 10 11 11 00 00 10 11 11—14—37
SINGLES.
"Harvey," 16..111111101111111101100111101111 1—25
Doubles—11 01 10 11 10 11 10 11 11 11—16—41
SINGLES.
F. Parks, 18..101010111101111110011111111111—24
Doubles—11 11 10 11 11 10 10 11 10 11—16—40
SINGLES.
H. White, 16..101111001111101011111001101110—21
Doubles—10 10 01 01 00 00 00 01 10 00— 6—27
SINGLES.
A. Allen, 16..111101110100111010110110001001—18
Doubles—11 10 11 00 10 10 10 10 10 10—10—28
SINGLES.
"Lake," 18....111111111111110111111111101011—27
Doubles—10 10 10 00 11 11 00 10 00 10— 9—36

A Correction.

EDITOR BREEDER AND SPORTSMAN.—The next shoot for the Selby Live Bird Trophy comes off on Sunday June 8th, instead of the 7th. Please correct in next issue, as more entries will be made if it is understood that the contest takes place on Sunday. C. B. S.

The Pacific Gun Club of Sacramento will entertain the State Sportsman's Association in October at the annual meeting.

Harvey McMurchy, agent for the L. C. Smith gun, is in the city getting rested after his long trip with Col. Dimick, Incidentally, he is attending to his orders for the Fall trade, and is doing a fine business.

Blue Rock Club.

May 24th was the regular day of the club, and ten members met at Oakland Trotting Park to shoot blue rock targets.

President J. O. Cadman set a good example to his merry men, making the score 20 out of 25. Seventeen was the next figure reached, four of the best men of the club getting into that hole, including the Secretary, Mr. C. B. Stone, to whom we are indebted for these scores. Mr. Sam. Golcher broke ten in nice style for a novice. He comes of shooting stock, already has acquired a graceful, easy position at the traps, and will soon be noted among the winners. The scores were made at 15 singles and 5 pairs of blue rock targets, American Association rules, and follows:

Name	Singles	Doubles	Total
Cadman	1 1 0 0 1 1 1 1 1 1 0 1 1 1 1	11 00 11 11 11	20
Slade	1 1 1 1 1 0 0 1 1 1 0 1 1 1 1	10 11 00 10 10	17
Bell	1 1 1 0 1 0 0 1 0 0 0 1 1 1 1	10 00 11 11 00	14
Adams	1 1 1 1 0 1 1 1 0 1 0 0 1 1 1	00 01 11 00 00	14
Stone	1 1 1 1 1 1 1 0 1 1 0 0 0 1 0	11 10 10 10 01	17
Maynard	0 0 1 1 1 0 1 0 1 0 1 0 1 0 1	01 11 11 11 11	17
W. J. Golcher	1 1 0 0 1 1 1 1 1 0 1 0 1 0 1	10 10 11 10 01	16
Mayhew	1 0 1 0 0 0 1 1 1 0 1 1 1 1 1	10 10 11 11 10	17
S. Golcher	1 0 0 0 0 1 1 0 0 1 0 0 1 0 0	10 00 10 11 10	10
Abbot	1 0 0 0 1 1 0 0 1 1 0 1 1 0 1	10 00 00 10 01	11

A Californian Opinion.

Mr. Edwin Goodall of this city has been going up and down through the earth sight-seeing for some months, and as he uses his eyes to see things as they are, his observations have great value. Last week he sent us the following note, dated at Nice, France, May 3rd., about some shooting done near Cairo in Egypt by Prince Albert Victor, son of the Prince of Wales.

"On the following day the Royal party drove eight miles to the Mena Hotel, and were entertained at luncheon and dinner by Mr. and Mrs. Locke-King. The after-noon was occupied by a ride to the Pyramids of Sakhara, where the "Tombs of the Sacred Bulls" gave shelter from an exaggerated form of Scotch mist which prevailed more or less till sunset, and though wet jackets instead of dusty ones were the order of the day, it was pronounced by all the party to be rather an agreeable change. When the Prince and Sir Evelyn Baring started for the return journey to Cairo, about midnight, the road from the hotel was lined with a double row of Sheikhs, all dressed in their long white gowns and each holding a lantern, a novel, picturesque, but rather ghostly looking spectacle.

The next day a quail shoot on a large scale took place, and nine guns produced nearly five hundred birds, to which total His Royal Highness contributed no less than one hundred and four, and as the fussy little quail is no respecter of persons, and offers no royal road for his own destruction, England's future King must have had his eye and hand in unison to some purpose. A small dinner at Sir Francis Grenfell's and a small reception afterwards were a pleasant wind up to perhaps the most successful day's sport ever known in the neighborhood, and the cuisine, illuminations and general arrangements of the evening were worthy even of Lady Grenfell's well known and unusual ability for entertaining.

Two or three days visiting museums, bazaars, palaces and barracks (which to ordinary mortals would be considered absolute toil, but is looked upon as comparative rest for the limbs of Royalty), and then another "contest" with the quail is organized; but energy on behalf of duty or pleasure, or a combination of the two is not always rewarded according to mortals' desire, and after performing many duties for the public good under a broiling sun, our Royal guest had partially to succumb when anticipated pleasure was within his grasp, for though he commenced shooting with the other sportsmen, a headache (which most travelers to the East become, some time or other, acquainted with) compelled rest in the tent for most of the day, and though at night he went bravely through a dinner at General Sir James Dormer's, when a large reception commenced, afterwards he was wisely persuaded by Sir Evelyn Baring (with whom he has been staying for the week) to retire and prepare himself for his early departure the next morning, and though he still looked jaded and suffering, when the special left for Alexandria a short time on H. M. S. Scout and a breath of sea air seemed to do him the good that everyone in Cairo wished might be the case."

Mr. Goodall adds: "Unless the Prince is an extra good shot the birds must have been pretty thick. I suppose he would not 'ground-sluice' them. One hundred and four in one outing would be a big bag for the best shot in the best fields of California."

Captain Brewer offers $10,000 to $4,000, he to use a twelve bore and any other man on the coast a ten. Long odds it seems for a 100 bird match.

C. W. Long, of Eureka, Humboldt Co., who is always awake to the best interests of his city and county, is making an effort to have the Mongolian pheasant introduced and propagated there. He is trying to procure a brace of the birds from Oregon, where they have become so plentiful, but owing to the stringency of laws and other causes he has not yet been able to secure them. His son, however, promises him some specimens as soon as they can be obtained. While speaking of game why not mention the wild turkey? An effort is being made now to introduce the wild turkey west of the Sierras, and 100 of the birds have been contracted for. May not Humboldt get a few wild turkeys, the noblest game bird of all, to stock our mountain oak orchards, and feed upon our grasshoppers and other insects? We believe that the wild turkey is just the game for our mountains. What say our sportsmen?

[The Humboldt Times does well when it gives space to such spirited appeals as that excerpted. Just what the value of the Mongolian pheasant is, does not yet appear but the preponderance of evidence is against its quality as a game-bird. The Japanese or Copper pheasant is, however, free from the objectionable qualities of the other bird, and is in every way desirable if it can be acclimated. If any one of our readers who is well acquainted with Humboldt County, and who also knows the habits and habitat of the wild turkey, can tell us what prospects are for its successful introduction to that section, we shall be grateful.—Ed.]

California Wing Shooting Club.

The May meeting held on Sunday last at Oakland Trotting Park was the largest of the season, both in number of shooters and of spectators. The day was fit and the birds good. but many of the scores were absurdly poor, notably those of Dr. Slade, Mr. Will DeVaull, Mr. Heeth and Mr. Lewis, Mr. C. J. Haas shot in perfect style and with first rate judgment, as did a guest, Mr. "Johns". Four members scored eleven each, and in the shoot off Mr. Schroeder won second medal and Mr. Robinson third. Mr. Robert Liddle did some extraordinary work with the second barrel, repeatedly killing at fifty to sixty yards. The scores were:

Slade	0	1	1	1	0	1	1	1	1	0	0	0—7
Haas	1	1	1	1	1	1	1	1	1	1	1	1—12
Eddy	1	0	1	1	1	1	0	1	1	1	1	1—10
Heeth	0	0	1	0	1	0	0	0	1	0	0	1—4
Slade	1	0	1	1	1	1	1	1	0	0	0	1—8
Schroder	1	1	1	1	1	1	1	1	1	1	1	0—11
DeVaull	0	0	0	0	1	0	1	1	1	0	0	0—4
Sharp	0	1	0	0	0	1	1	0	0	1	1	1—6
Liddle	1	1	1	1	0	1	1	1	1	0	1	1—10
Chace	1	1	1	1	1	1	1	1	1	1	1	0—11
"Johns"	1	1	1	1	1	1	1	1	1	1	1	1—12
Fay	1	1	1	1	1	1	1	1	1	1	0	1—11
Robinson	1	1	1	1	1	1	1	1	1	1	0	1—11
Lewis	1	0	0	0	0	0	0	0	1	0	0	1—3

Which Is The Most Effective Calibre?

The general rule seems to be that heavy muscular men prefer the 10-bore, while others of lighter build choose the 12-bore, but have any very exhaustive experiments been undertaken to settle the value of Nos. 7, 7-trap, 8 and 8-trap out of 10 and 12-bore guns at all ranges from 25 to 60 yards says a writer in Shooting and Fishing. If so the results are not generally known. The published records of European experiments do not help us much, as they were made with larger shot than we use and more of it into the bargain. At Hurlingham, Cercle des Patineurs and Monte Carlo, unless I am incorrectly informed, 1¼ ounces of shot is allowed and no bigger bore than 12 sanctioned. I also believe that nine-tenths of the winners avail themselves of the privilege and use the full 1¼ ounces No. 5 or 6 (218 and 270 pellets respectively to the ounce), driven by 3½ to 4 drams powder. If this practice is right, ours is wrong. Probably one of the reasons that made the American Shooting Association fix such limits was that 12-bore guns, as a rule, cannot do as well in the way of pattern and penetration combined with 1¼ ounces as they can with 1⅛ ounces when they are shooting No. 7 trap or smaller, but perhaps if the 12-bores were permitted to use more shot they might find a size or two larger a distinct advantage.

It would appear preferable to limit the 12-bores to 1¼ ounces and the 10s to 1½ ounces, as then the best shooting could undoubtedly be brought out of any particular gun. It is my conviction that if properly bored to carry such loads, a 12-bore can shoot 1¼ ounces and 3½ drams, and a 10-bore 1½ ounces and 4½ drams to advantage. I also believe that there is just three yards difference between the two, and that at present the 10-bore has a trifle the best of the odds—supposing the man behind the butt-plate powerful enough to do it justice. As many men are not so built it is, if I am correct in my assumption, a premium in favor of muscle. I may possibly be wrong, and there is the other side to be heard from, and all should allow there is ample room for experimenting.

Many live-bird shots believe that they cannot obtain penetration enough by using more than 1⅛ ounces shot—this, I think, is an entire mistake—additional penetration can better be got by using larger shot. Suppose, for instance, one man to be using 1½ ounces No. 7 (317 pellets) and another loading with 1¼ ounces No. 6 (274 pellets), the latter would, according to my judgment, have by all odds the most killing load. 1½ ounces No. 7 would mean increased recoil and less penetration, and 1⅛ ounces No. 6 rather a sparse pattern, but 1¼ ounces No. 6 should prove to be both thick enough and strong enough.

At inanimate targets of course much less penetration is necessary, the main point being to get a large and well-filled killing circle. In conclusion, what is gained by restricting us to such small loads of shot?

Public Hunting and Fishing and Private Leases.

Within a few years, protests have been becoming more and more frequent against the custom of leasing the fishing and shooting privileges on various tracts of lands. Many of the disgruntled ones argue that it is an injustice to those who are thus deprived of their fishing and shooting. It would not be worth while to discuss this subject here were it not that these protesters have many followers. I think followers a correct designation, inasmuch as I cannot see after their arguments are carefully analyzed, that they have claims to other consideration. It is an undeniable right, moral and legal, that every man can use his property as he chooses, always providing he does not injure his neighbors most sensibly says the Week's Sport. Is it not acting upon this theory that the man with the means and the desire leases certain privileges on the property of one who is willing to part with it? True, he deprives some one, perhaps, from enjoying a like privilege on the leased property, but that is a resultant of ownership always, and, in fact, ownership is only valuable from the right of exclusion. It would be quite as sensible for one to object and denounce another who with more leisure was able to spend greater time in search of sport in the woods, or because possessing more means who could purchase grouse and venison at a price beyond their reach. That those who possess leisure and wealth shall enjoy more luxury than others with less, is an incident of our social condition from which there is no escape, and applies equally to fishing and hunting.

There is one point in their objections that, as regards fishing, is well taken in theory and partly in practice, namely, the State's supplying its hatcheries fry to stock what may be termed private waters. These hatcheries are maintained at public expense, and their product should go only into public streams, where all have an equal right, if theory is carried out. Public streams, are however, limited. Legally they are only those in which the tide ebbs and flows. To confine distribution of the state's fry to these waters would leave many quasi public waters without attention. What seems just, however, is that in large rivers or streams, where exclusive leasing or control is practically impossible, and the public is likely to have an undisputed privilege, the State should distribute the fry. This also, may apply to the large lakes to which the public have access. In the smaller brooks and ponds, however, that are exclusively controlled, the lessees or owners, if they exclude the public, should purchase the fry. This will be the practical outcome of the present issue regarding fishing contracts. We shall find the State maintaining hatcheries to supply the necessary fry for the public waters, and private enterprise supplying private streams and ponds.

It is not calculated to engender good fellowship to be suddenly deprived of the privilege of fishing and shooting on ground that you have long been in the habit of frequenting, and the present outburst is neither novel nor unprecedented with anglers and hunters. Many cases are printed in the law reports of both English and American courts, where those that have fished in a stream for "time almost beyond the memory of man," and been finally ejected, have sought with injured feelings to establish unsuccessfully their cause in the courts. The right to catch and carry away fish in unnavigable waters—that is, in those rivers beyond tidal waters—is not an easement, but a profit a pendre, that proof of custom will not sustain.

Dove shooting begins on June 1st, with prospects for poor sport, because of the late rains, which have chilled and destroyed many hatchings both of doves and quail.

Matches between Mr. Martinez Chick of San Diego, and Capt. Brewer, will be shot at the Haight Street ball ground, on Sunday June 1st., Tuesday June 3rd., and Friday June 6th. Mr. George Carroll makes the match for Mr. Chick, the latter receiving a stipulated sum, win or lose, said sum being just fair recompense for the time, trouble and expense incident to practice, the trip and the time consumed. The matches are for $250 a side each, at 100 live birds per man, each match, London Gun Club rules to govern. It is probable Mr. Ed Fay will referee, he being agreeable to Capt. Brewer. The birds for the first match are to be furnished by Capt Brewer, and the match will begin at about three o'clock, after the ball game, the grounds being cleared, and a seperate entrance fee of 50 cents being charged. Mr. Lawrence, backer of Capt. Brewer, states that the whole of the gate less expenses, goes to the winner. We are told by Mr. Chick that he will shoot to win, and see no reason to doubt his intention to do so. Under the governing rules, the only limitations are upon weight of gun, not to exceed eight pounds, bore 12, shot load not to exceed 1¼ ounces, any position, ground trap.

THE KENNEL.

Dog owners are requested to send for publication the earliest possible notices of whelps, sales, names claimed, presentations and deaths, in their kennels, in all instances writing plainly names of sire and dam and of grandparents, colors, dates and breed.

The Pacific Coast Spaniel Club.

EDITOR BREEDER AND SPORTSMAN:—Permit me to inform you that a club has been formed under the above caption. The officers of the club are as follows: President, Dr. A. C. Davenport, Stockton; Vice-President, Jas. Kerlin, Oakland; Secretary and Treasurer, H. P. Rennie, Oakland; Executive Committee, Joseph B. McVay, San Francisco; George W. Rennie, San Francisco; F. W. Howlett, Oakland; Dr. Davenport, Stockton; H. P. Rennie, Oakland. H. H. Briggs, Kennel Editor BREEDER AND SPORTSMAN, San Francisco, was elected an honorary member of the club and the Secretary instructed to notify Mr. Briggs of the fact.

The members of the club have decided to publish a paper to be called The Spaniel Fancier, a monthly, solely in the interest of Cocker, Field, and other standard bred spaniels. H. P. Rennie, Oakland, has been selected editor and manager, and Dr. Davenport of Stockton associate editor. Spaniel fanciers are requested to at once join the club.

May 27, 1890.

H. P. RENNIE, Secretary,
37 Sixth street, Oakland, Cal.

[Election to the club is gratefully acknowledged. It appears unwise for the club to issue a special publication. It is welcome to all needed space in this journal, and can reach manyfold more readers by utilizing the BREEDER AND SPORTSMAN.—ED.]

English Pointer Club Winners.

The third annual field trials of the English Pointer Club were run near Wrexham May 6 to 8. There were 25 that filled for the Pointer Puppy Stake and 15 for the All Aged Stakes. The winning puppies were,

First, Col. C. J. Cotes's lemon and white bitch Polly Jones 16 mos. (Carlo—Jenny Jones).

Second, Mr. F. Warde's liver and white dog King Pear, 14 mos (Taw—Kent Fairy).

Third, Mr. Barclay Field's liver and white bitch Fordcombe Daisy, 1 yr. (Lake—Dingle.)

Fourth, Mr. A. Richard's liver and white dog Rarid Bang, 16 mos. (Amer—Belle des Bordes.)

ALL-AGED STAKES.

First, Mr. A. P. Heywood Londale's liver, white and ticked bitch Clio, January, 1887 (Plum—Cassandra.

Second, Mr. A. P. Heywood-Lonsdale's liver and white dog Ightfield Estod, June, 1889 (Ightfield Dick—Bess).

Third, Baron Oscar Dickson's liver and white dog Rustem, March, 1889 (Sussex Don—Ringlet).

Fourth, Messrs. F. C. Lowe and A. Bertrand's liver and white bitch Belle des Bordes, 6 yrs. 2 mos. (Young Bang Polly.)

Occidental Club Draw.

The draw for yesterdays meeting of the Club at Newark was made on Tuesday evening at 21 Kearney Street. After the draw the Club was invited by Secretary J. F. Carroll to a spread at the Delmonico on O'Farrell street. Sixteen men were at table, President Gregory at one end and Mr. Carroll at the other. The guests were such well known coursers as Caryl C. Wilkinson, Henry Wormington, Doctor Sharkey, Mr. J. R. Dickson, Mr. Pat Lyman, Mr. Gallagher, Mr. F. P. Callundan, Mr. Thos. J. O'Keeffe, Mr. S. L. Abbot Jr. and Mr. H. Boyd. After demolishing the dainty viands together with certain choice vintages, a lot of little speeches were made, most of them by Mr. O'Keeffe, who also warbled a few warbles about Cruiskeen Lawn and other foreign inventions. Mr. Carroll was particularly felicitous in his remarks about the earlier history of the Club, and in what he said as to its future he became really eloquent.

Mr. O'Keefe entered upon a psychological disquisition that soon carried his hearers into deep water, from which they were rescued by the orator who quit talking to pour forth his welling emotions in unique songs. Considerable money was booked between members about the meeting of yesterday. The dinner initiated a series of similar entertainments to occur after each draw. After expressions of thanks to Mr. Carroll and a little mild chaff between the guests, the party broke up just in time to get the last cars for home.

A full report of yesterdays coursing is necessarily deferred until the next issue.

Several good specimens of cocker spaniels have lately been brought to this state, and this breed bids fair to become very popular.

Dr. Davenport, owner of the Echo Cocker Kennel, offers through the advertising columns, some fine Cocker puppies of unexceptionable breeding, at prices that are most reasonable.

Mr. H. P. Rennie, whose advertisement of Cocker Spaniels appears in another column, now has two nice dog puppies for sale, one liver and one black. They can be seen at No. 37 Sixth St., Oak St. Station, Oakland. Mr. Rennie's stock is all that it should be.

Mr. S. G. Wilder left last week for his home at Honolulu. He left his pointer Roberta (Robert le Diable—Young Beulah) with Mr. M. D. Walter at Galt to be bred to Mr. A. B. Sperry" Count Dick. The cross should prove a good one. Roberta will be sent to the islands as soon as in whelp.

Dr. A. C. Davenport, of Stockton, has lost by death his cocker spaniel, Red Robin. This was the only dog puppy out of that well known prize winner Woodstock Belle, sired by Giffee, owned in California, and the loss is regretted by all spaniel lovers.

Mrs. Folger, of 1308 Jackton Street, Oakland, was unfortunate enough to have a nice little black and tan cocker puppy stolen from her yard a few days ago. The puppy was sired by H. P. Rennies "Giffee", and was a beauty. Dog thieves are very numerous in the vicinity of Oakland just now.

A meeting of the Board of Governors of the Eastern Field Trials Club was held, on May 13th, at the office of Mr. F. R. Hitchcock, 44 Broadway, New York: A communication was read from Mr. F. I. Stone, Chattanooga, Tenn., in which he accepted the invitation of the club to judge at the next field trials. The Secretary was instructed to communicate with Mr. H. B. Duryea and Col. A. Merriman with the views of securing their services as judges at the November trials. It was announced that the Derby, which closed May 1st, has eighty-four entries, six of which were made from England, by Mr. Heywood-Lonsdale. These are composed of three pointers and three setters. This large Derby entry is an excess of twenty-three over that of last year. Messrs Geo. W. Ewing, Fort Wayne, Ind., and W. Hay Bockes, Saratoga Springs, N. Y. were elected members.

Mr. Geo. T. Allender, well known as a trainer of hunting dogs has had unusual success at the Pacific Coast Field Trials as the following table of winnings will show. In '85 he won first in the Derby with Tom Pinch and first in the All-Aged with Mountain Boy both pointers. In '86, he won first in the Derby with Shot an English setter and second with Climax a pointer. In the All-Aged of that year he won second with Lassie and third with Tom Pinch, both pointers.

No trial was held in '87, the date having been postponed to January '88, when Mr. Allender won second in the Derby with the pointer Point and first in the All Aged with Point. In '89 he won first and third in the Derby with Old Black Joe and Nestor respectively, both pointers. In the All-Aged he won first with Old Black Joe. In '90 he won first in the Derby with the English setter Salina and second in the All-Aged Stake with Patti Croxteth T. Some of the wins were without much competition but so many were made in hot company as to stamp Mr. Allender a skillful handler.

Grim's Gossip.

ating on the turf is as bad and as dishonorable as ng in the counting-room.

Saturday, the 31st, there will be several trotting and g races at the Bay District track.

m our exchanges we learn that glanders is quite preva- n the southern portion of the State.

b 2:15 will be seen once more on the Eastern tracks. Golden will have him in charge this season.

P. Rodehaver, of Petaluma, has left his fine horses for me being, and gone on a trip to Oregon and Washing-

. Valensin has been very ill for almost two weeks, but st accounts he was improving as fast as his friends wish.

my Goldsmith has Simmocoloo well in hand, and already hestnut colt is showing miles in 2:26 and 2:28. If all later in the season his present record of 2;29½ should wered.

ere is a quartet of colored jockeys whose mounts seldom the post without having received substantial support. y are Hamilton, Barnes, Anderson and Jones, and for work in the saddle and integrity they are hard to beat.

June 3rd Terre Haute will start the ball rolling for the ing contingent, and the California horses will have a ce to show what they can do. Quite a number of them ntered for the meeting and I hope to have a good account hem.

e Governor has appointed the following Directors of rict Agricultural Associations: E. S. Denn'son, Alameda nty, District No. 1, vice Samuel Gamble, resigned; J. H. uant and R. G. Dean, of Contra Costa County, District 23, vice themselves, terms expired.

few weeks ago, Sid Sperry of Petaluma, came to San ncisco with a couple of fast trotting horses, which he of- d for sale cheap. One of them has been sold to a gentle- from Australia for $1,250. The one sold was Lelia by tic, dam by Eclipse and she could trot full miles better n 2:27.

r. Latham has added another brood mare to his already e list, having purchased from L. D. Wakefield of San quin Valley, the three-year-old ch. f. Princess Dexter, by ter Prince 11363 dam by Mambrino Wilkes 6083' 2nd. by David Hill 857, 3rd dam by Jack Hawkins. This dsome filly will be bred to Director 2:17.

Ex-Senator J. G. Fair has lately had a large barn and sta- combined, erected at the Knight's Ferry Farm It is x 40 feet, and contains ten box stalls 16 x 20 each, in ition to which are the harness room, office and trainers' rtments. A mile track has also been laid out, and . Sullivan is exercising the trotters daily.

The sons of Alden Goldsmith bring honor to the name. hn A. Goldsmith is one of the star drivers of the Pacific ast. He trained and drove to his record Guy Wilkes 2:15½. d Lillian Wilkes 2:17½ as a three-year-old; Sable Wilkes 8 as a three-year-old; Regal Wilkes 2:20½ as a two-year old d Hazel Wilkes 2;20 as a four-year-old —Mirror and rmer.

The Dennison Bros of Sacramento have arrived at Port- d with their string of thoroughbreds, including Dave uglass, Hotspur, Prince's First, Mohawk and G. W. e latter has been under the weather, and it is doubtful ether the Kyrle Daly colt will start at the City View Park eting. Since the above was written, news of his death ve been received.

Before this paragraph reaches my readers, Mr. Valensin l have a new superintendent at his stock farm. On May t Chandler Quinton V. S, brother to Scott of that ilk, rted for California to assume the management of the Val- sin breeding establishment at Pleasanton. "Doc" Quin- is well versed in all that appertains to the horse and ould prove a valuable man for the owner of Sidney.

If there was ever a breeder of horses who purchased a py of "Horse-Breeding," by J. H. Sanders, that did not nk he got more than his money's worth, we have yet to ar of him. It is the only work treating especially of the ngement of stallions and brood mares during the breed- g season, and its thoroughly practical character especially ommends it. Send $2 to this office for a copy of it.

Jim Dustin is kept hard at work at the Bay District Track, ving now a dozen head of trotters that take his constant ention. While there are many "green" ones, Rabe 2:24 probably as far advanced as any of them. This gelding l have a chance to show what he can do this year, and as stin has him already moving as fast as his record, there every reason to suppose that he will be able to race much ter. Rabe is by Strader 673, dam Rose, by Bashaw, 50.

Mr Salisbury returned from his Eastern trip on Monday ght and at once began his arrangements to send the mare rgaret S back east to compete in the Horseman's Stake four-year-olds. She will trot for this rich Stake at De- it between July 22nd and 25th, and not on July 12th as ted last week. The owner feels confidant the Director y will give a good account of herself, and has every hope carrying away the first money.

It is not often that a race is lost by a bite, but the large owd which witnessed the running of the Chicago Derby on nday of this week, at the West Side Driving Park, were ated to such a spectacle, says The Breeders Gazette. The okers of Pilgrim were congratulating themselves on their od judgment as the horses came down the stretch, but t as the race was nearly won Pilgrim turned his head to e at Prince Fonso with whom he was running neck and ck, thereby letting the latter push his nose under the re first.

The following are the declarations out of handicaps re- ived May 1st by the Washington Park Club:

The Oakwood Handicap—Terra Cotta, Santalene, Little nch, Brandolette, Spokane, Somerset, Cynthia, Ballyhoe, wcastle and May O.

The Great Western Handicap—Carnot, Wheeler T, Sports- n, Spokane, Don Jose and Longside.

Alfred S, 2:18, now in the Hickok Stable at Terre Haute is down in all the authorities as dam untraced. The dam was always known in this State as Nora Marshall, but in Poughkeepsie she was known as the Doty Mare, having been bred and raised by a man called John Doty, who sold her to the agent of J. C. Flood in 1874.

Near Eminence Ky. Monday night, the barn of H. G. Moody containing nine head of valuable trotting stock, valued at $10,000, was totally destroyed by fire. The most noted of the animals lost was the fine stallion Senator, by Volunteer, first dam by Woburn, second dam Lady Sears, dam of three in 2:30 list, by Seely's American Star, property of T. J. Jackson, Perryman, Md.; value $5,000. The barn was fired by lightning.

A visitor to Terre Haute writes us that one of the grandest individuals and cleanest gaited colts he ever saw is the two-year-old Sidney Faustino, who holds the stallion yearling record of the world, 2.35 He is here in the stable of John Dickerson, who is very much pleased with him and with his promise for this year. Faustino is owned by Waters Stock Farm, and it is expected that he will next season be in the stud at that farm.—Horse Review.

Some time during the summer, two large brick stables will be erected at the Pleasanton Stock Farm. One of these will be for the exclusive use of Director 2:17, while the other will be occupied by Direct 2:18½ These buildings will lie some distance apart, so that in case of fire, at least one of the stables may be saved. This is a much needed improvement, and there should be similar buildings on all breeding farms, where there are valuable stallions.

At the annual meeting of the Thirteenth District Agricultural Society held in Marysville last Saturday evening says the Appeal, officers for the ensuing year were chosen as follows: W. T. Ellis Jr., President; C. A. Glidden, Vice-President; A. D. Cutts, Treasurer; G R. Eckart, Secretary. It was decided to hold the coming fair on September 2nd to 6th, both days inclusive. The necessary funds have been subscribed and it is expected that the event will be the most successful held for years.

Messrs. Hutchinson & Fisher have completed a good half-mile track on their Lone Oak Stock Farm, situated four miles south of Hanford, says the Fresno Turf. They have at the head of their stud the stallion Lone Oak, by Sam Purdy, 918, record 2:20½ (the sire of Charlie C., 2:24½), by George M. Patchen, 31. They own a number of well-bred mares and fillies, a few of which are standard bred. A 2-year-old colt by Anteeo is very promising, and shows every indication of being a fast and reliable trotter.

Probably the largest owner of pacing horses in California is John Garrity, he having no less than ten in his string, yet even with this number he manages to find time to look after a trotter or two. One of the side wheel division that gives evidence of great promise is an unnamed son of Sidney and Humming Bird. For a green horse he moves his miles like an old hand at the business, and he should play a prominent part in many of the pacing events to be determined this season. Last Saturday he was sent three easy miles, the time of the best one being 2:24½.

One of the questions agitating the minds of many horsemen is the following, how fast will Margaret S. have to trot to win the Horseman's Stake in three straight heats? Very few of them put the first heat at faster than 2:18, although there are a few that think she will have to go in 2:16. Direct has the record of the three fastest heats ever trotted by a four year old in a race, but it is just possible that the great mare will have to lower her stable companion's time, to win the rich stake. I know she can do it.

"To stop the bleeding of a horse or other stock from a snag or wound," says a correspondent of the National Stockman, "make an application of dry manure, and it will stop the bleeding of a wound every time. This information may be worth a good deal to many of your readers, so I send it. While away from home recently a weanling colt of mine broke through a barbed-wire fence and cut his fore leg badly. It had been bleeding for eight hours when I got home. I took dry horse manure and held it on the wound for one minute, and the blood stopped flowing at once."

John Dillard, son of Indian Chief, is the sire of more dams of 2:30 performers than any other horse to date that never sired a 2:30 trotter or pacer. He has thirteen grand daughters and grand-sons in the 2:30 list. Kentucky Clay 194, ranks second with eleven; then Brignoli, Berkeley's Edwin Forrest and Mohawk Chief with seven each; Capt. Walker and Gen. Taylor with six each; Stevens' Bald Chief, Eureka, Hamlin Patchen, Octoroon, Stubtail, Toronto and Vermont Hambletonian with five each. Strange to say, not one of these stallions ever sired a 2:30 trotter, but their daughters, nicked with other horses, have produced most beneficial results.

Mr. John Judson in writing to the Escondido Times says: "There is no place in Southern California where the climate is more even or better calculated for the perfect development of horseflesh than Escondido, which has been proven by the fine condition of the horses kept at the Escondido driving park this last winter. It has been the remark of Eastern horsemen that they never saw horses in better condition than they were at the Escondido track the last winter, and this to a great extent is owing to climate influences. I am satisfied that by keeping our track in good order it can be made the great wintering track of California."

The Cook Stock Farm has sold to Mr. B. C, Holly of Vallejo the three standard fillies mentioned below:

Sunlight by Steinway, 1st dam Katy G by Electioneer, 2nd dam Fanny Malone by Niagara, 3rd dam Fanny Wickham by imp Herald.

Alamo by Steinway, 1st dam Inex, sister to Inez 2:22½, by Sweepstakes, 2nd dam Dolly Bull by Kentucky Bertrand, 3rd dam Nancy by American Star.

Firefly by Director, 1st dam Steinola by Steinway, 2d dam Phaccola by Silverthreads, 3d dam Minnehaha, dam of Beautiful Bells, etc.

The arrival of the California "Cracker-Jacks" with the good weather of the last week has fanned the trotting interests to a white heat. The stream of visitors to the ground keeps up, and every day is a gala-day. Sunol and Palo Alto are the center of attraction. The filly, whose formation is like nothing that roams the earth or swims the seas, is to all a new type. The trainers are at their horses early and late, and the work of conditioning for the contests of the year goes marching on. Fast quarters and eighths still continue to be the rule.—Terre Haute Express, May 18th.

As is well known, Theodore Winters started East immediately on the conclusion of the Sacramento Meeting, and since then has kept a careful eye on his horses. It has been decided that all of the string that are at Nashville will start for Monmouth Park next week, so it may be presumed that all of the Western engagements will be cancelled. The move goes to show that El Rio Rey will not start for some time to come, and there is a strong probability that our Nashville correspondent was right when he said the great colt would never face the starter again.

As we go to press on Thursday of this week, some of our readers will receive the BREEDER AND SPORTSMAN in time to take advantage of the announcement that the Oakland Driving Club will have a matinee at the Oakland Park on Decoration Day. The officers of this Association are: J. C. Kimball, President; Dr. C. H. Walter, Vice President. Directors—W. R Birmingham, P. W. Bellingall, Dr. C. H. Walter, J. C Kimball, W. Coleman, R. F. Simpson, Capt. Ashby, Dr. Woolsey, D. S Brown, and S. J. Smith, Committee on Rules and Regulations—L. J. Smith, Captain Ashby, Myron T. Whidden. L. A. EMLAY, Sec. and Treas.

Keep an eye on the get of Guy Wilkes (2:15¼) this season says the Horse Breeder. Mr Emerson Brooks, who formerly owned the king of wagon trotters, Hopeful 2:14¾ wagon record 2:16½), and visited California a few months since, writes the following in a private letter from which we trust he will pardon us for extracting as follows: "I read the other day the prophecy of some one as to some wonderful trotting to be done this year by the Guy Wilkes tribe. Look out for Regal Wilkes (2:20½). He is a magnificent horse, and has the material to carry any clip. Lillian Wilkes will be there too, but whispers of Vida Wilkes, as yet unknown to fame, promise things I don't dare mention.

The tale of the candidature of the Falkirk Burghs by J. Merry, the father of the owner of Surefoot, the crack favorite for the English Derby, may bear repetition. The gentleman in question took occasion to mention in the course of his speech to the electors that, apart from any question of politics, he desired to do them a good turn, and as his horse Thormanby was sure to win the Blue Riband they must not omit to back it. Falkirk Burghs was "on to a man" after this intimation, and when after Thormanby's success the wealthy ironmaster sent an intimation to the Mayor of the town, "Thormanby has won;" he received the characteristic reply: "Falkirk Burghs is drunk." (Horseman.)

F. Camendzindt has commenced suit in Justice Henry's Court for the possession of a horse says the Record-Union. The suit is a peculiar one, and involves a legal conundrum which is not explained in the law books.

Camendzindt was the owner of a horse which he purchased for $300. He drove the animal for quite a while and became very much attached to it. Some time ago the horse got foundered, and was rendered unfit for work Camendzindt thought he might as well end the poor animal's suffering by killing it, and he gave a man $5 to shoot the animal. The equine executioner offered another man $1 to take the horse to the bone yard and have it killed there.

The offer was accepted and the animal turned over to Daniel Heally at the bone yard. The latter took the horse and resolved to try and cure it. He succeeded, and now has the animal and values it at $150. Camendzindt now wants the horse back, and has brought suit for the possession of the animal, claiming that he never relinquished his title to it. His attorney is F. Estabrook.

There has been quite a spirit of rivalry existing between the towns of Susanville and Quincy as to where the Annual Fair of Agricultural District No. 11 should be held. At a meeting of the Board of Directors held last week, Quincy proved too much for the opposition, and it was decided to hold the fair of 1890 at that place. The bid made by the citizens of Quincy is as follows.

We, the undersigned, in consideration for the holding of the annual Fair of the Eleventh District Fair Association, for the year 1890, at the town of Quincy, in the County of Plumas, State of California, guarantee to the Directors of said Fair Association, the sum of $5,144, which sum to be paid to them for the use of said Association, on the first day of said Annual Fair, as may be demanded by them. We further guarantee to furnish for the use of said Association, during said Fair, free of all costs to said Association, the Race Track in order, fenced with solid board fence eight feet high, the Grand Stand, Judges' Stand, Bar Room, Kitchen and Boarding house, and all other privileges connected with said Track, also sixty-five Box Stalls for horses, fifty-two Single Stalls thirty-five Double Stalls, four water-closets. Also free water for all the purposes of said Association in its use on said track, buildings and other privileges, and also the free use of a hall for Pavilion and Ball. As to the race-track, the above guarantee is that it shall be in good order on the first day of the Fair and thereafter it is to be kept in good order at the expense of the Association.

The mode of training horses is a threadbare question, says the Buffalo Commercial. It has been discussed over and over again, still no definite rules have been laid down. The great Palo Alto Farm will not use toe weights under any consideration. Thousands do, however, and with great success. One thing is certain, the less weight a horse has to carry and be properly balanced the better. It stands to reason that a horse wearing a six-ounce shoe can go more fast miles than he could with a fifteen-ounce shoe. It has been argued, and by eminent breeders too, that one ounce on the toe is equal to ten pounds on the back of a horse. The equine family is not unlike the human family in this respect. An athlete will soon tire of carrying a pound weight in his hand and swinging it all the time, while ten pounds on the back would scarcely be felt. Patience will frequently accomplish more than toe weights in learning the colt how to trot, still there are instances, and many of them too, where toe weights must be used. Out of several hundred horses it is no trouble for Palo Alto Farm to pick out a number of good ones each year that will go very fast without weights, but had toe weights been used sparingly, perhaps, does any one think but what other nags, unheard to-day, might not have been developed more successfully? Horses must be educated in various ways, according to their disposition and natural gait, the same as a wee sma' urchin at school. Whip one boy and it will do him good, whip another, and he will sulk and become more and more unmanageable. Colt trainers should remember that kindness will go farther than abuse; that great care should be taken in shoeing and developing the youngster. It is easy to make a failure, and nothing succeeds like success, but education is the keystone of success. It is just as essential for a trainer of trotting horses to have a good education as it is for the successful business man. Education enlarges the brain and will distance muscle and whip in every class.

THE WEEKLY

Breeder and Sportsman.

JAMES P. KERR, PROPRIETOR.

The Turf and Sporting Authority of the Pacific Coast.

Office, No. 313 Bush St.

P. O. Box 2300.

TERMS—*One Year, $5; Six Months, $3; Three Months, $1.50.* STRICTLY IN ADVANCE.

Money should be sent by postal order, draft or by registered letter, addressed to JAMES P. KERR, San Francisco, Cal.

Communications must be accompanied by the writer's name and address, not necessarily for publication, but as a private guarantee of good faith.

NEW YORK OFFICE, Room 15, 181 Broadway.

ALEX. P. WAUGH, - - - - - Editor.

To Subscribers.

The date printed on the wrapper of your paper indicates the time to which your subscription is paid.

Should the Breeder and Sportsman be received by any subscriber who does not want it, write us direct to stop it. A postal card will suffice.

Special Notice to Correspondents.

Letters intended for publication should reach this office not later than Wednesday of each week, to secure a place in the issue of the following Saturday. Such letters to insure immediate attention should be addressed to the Breeder and Sportsman, and not to any member of the staff.

San Francisco, Saturday, May 31, 1890.

Dates Claimed.

EUREKA JOCKEY CLUB	July 2d to 5th
IONE	Aug 1th to 5th.
LOS ANGELES (6th District)	Aug. 4th to 9th
SAN JOSE	Aug. 11th to 16th
NAPA	Aug. 18th to 23rd
GLENBROOK PARK, 17th District	August 17th to 23d
PETALUMA	Aug. 25th to 30th
OAKLAND (District No. 1)	Sept. 1st to Sept. 6th
LAKEPORT, 12th District	September 23d to 27th
CALIFORNIA STATE FAIR	Sept 8th to 20th
STOCKTON	Sept. 23rd to 27th.
FRESNO (Fall Meeting)	Sept. 29th to Oct. 4th
VISALIA	Oct. 7th to 11th

Another Auction Sale.

Messrs. Killip & Co. will sell next Wednesday an assortment of personal property, the effects of the late J. Mervyn Donahue, including horses, jacks and cattle. Some of the animals are very choice, including Baby by Carr's Mambrino, dam by Owen Dale. Belle by Frank Malone (son of Ethan Allen Jr. and daughter of Langford); 1st dam by Paul's Abdallah (son of Rysdyk's Hambletonian); 2d dam by Owen Dale. Dolly by Bonner. A three-year-old filly by Abbotsford, and also a two-year-old filly by Guy Wilkes.

Baby and Belle have been bred to Dawn this year, which will unquestionably enhance their value.

The advertisement will show the time and place of sale.

Farmers and the Census.

As can be readily understood, many of the readers of the Breeder and Sportsman belong to the farming class, and as the census will be taken this year, all of them are interested in knowing exactly what questions they will have to answer when the supervisors call upon them. Already many inquiries have been sent to the census department in Washington, asking for information in regard to these questions, and for the aid of the farmers throughout the country, a list has been prepared so they may readily understand what the nature of the questions will be. From a pamphlet sent to this office, we have collated the following questions and put them in a concise form so that our readers may understand exactly what is expected of them in the way of information. It will no doubt be of great assistance to those who have this work in hand, if the farmers can have all the information necessary when called upon for their answers; therefore, if the farmers who are readers of this paper will carefully go over the following questions, they can save the enumerators a great deal of time by having the information ready at hand. The following questions are those sent out by the bureau:

(1) Your name as occupant of the farm. (2) Are you owner, renter for money, or for share of the crops of the farm? (3) Are you white or black? (4) Number of acres of land, improved and unimproved. (5) Acres irrigated. (6) Number of artesian wells flowing. (7) Value of farm, buildings, implements, machinery, and live stock. (8) Fences—Cost of building and repairing. (9) Cost of fertilizers. (10) Labor—Amounts paid for labor, including board; weeks of hired labor, white or black. (11) Products—Estimated value of all farm productions sold, consumed, or on hand for 1889. (12) Forestry—Amount of wood cut, and value of all forest products sold. (13) Grasslands—Acres of each kind of grassland cut for hay or pastured; tons of hay and straw sold; clover and grass seeds produced and sold; silos and their capacity. (14) Sugar—Cane, sorghum, maple and beet; sugar and molasses; acres, product and value of each (15) Castor Beans—Acres. (16) Cereals—Barley, buckwheat, Indian corn, oats, rye, wheat; acres, crop, amount of each sold and consumed, and value. (17) Rice—Acres, crop and value. (18) Tobacco—Acres, crop, amount sold and value. (19) Peas and Beans—Bushels and value of crop sold. (20) Peanuts—Acres, bushels and value. (21) Hops—Acres, pounds and value. (22) Fibers—Cotton, flax and hemp; acres, crop and value. (23) Broom corn—Acres, pounds and value. (24) Live Stock—Horses, mules and asses; number on hand June 1, 1890; number foaled in 1889; number sold in 1889; number died in 1889. (25) Sheep—Number on hand June 1, 1890, of "fine wool," "long wool," and "all other;" number of lambs dropped in 1889; "spring lambs" sold in 1889; sold in 1889 other than "spring lambs;" slaughtered for use on farm in 1889; killed by dogs in 1889; died from other causes in 1889. (26) Wool—Shorn spring of 1890 and fall of 1889. (27) Goats—Number of Angora and common. (28) Dogs—On farm June 1, 1890. (29) Neat Cattle—Working oxen, milch cows, and other cattle on hand June 1, 1890; number of pure bred, grade and common; calves dropped in 1889; cattle sold in 1889, slaughtered for use on the farm, and died in 1889. (30) Dairy—Milk, total gallons produced on farm; sold for use in families; sent to creamery or factory; used on farm, including for butter or cheese; used on farm in raising cream for sale, including for creamery or factory. Butter—pounds made on farm and sold in 1889. Cream—quarts sent to creamery or factory; sold other than to creamery or factory. Cheese—pounds made on farm and sold in 1889. (31) Swine—Number on hand June 1, 1890; sold in 1889; consumed on farm and died in 1889. (32) Poultry—Number each of chickens, turkeys, geese and ducks on hand June 1, 1889; value of all poultry products sold; eggs produced, sold, and value in 1889. (33) Bees—Number of stands, pounds of honey and wax produced, and value. (34) Onions—Field crop, number of acres, bushels produced and sold, and value. (35) Potatoes—Sweet and Irish, bushels produced and sold. (36) Market Gardens and Small Fruits—Number of acres in vegetables, blackberries, cranberries, raspberries, strawberries, and other small fruits, and total value of products in 1889. (47) Vegetables and Fruits for Canning—Number of acres, and products, in bushels, of peas and beans, green corn, tomatoes, other vegetables and fruits. (38) Orchards—Apples; apricots, cherries, peaches, pears, plums and prunes, and other orchard fruits; in each the number of acres, crop in 1889, number of bearing trees, number of young trees not bearing, and value of all orchard products sold. (39) Vineyards—Number of acres in vines bearing and in young vines not bearing; products of grapes and raisins, and value in 1889.

Besides these questions on the regular Agricultural Schedule No. 2, Superintendent Robert P. Porter has ordered several special investigations in the interests of agriculture, among which are viticulture, nurseries, florists, seed and truck farms, semi-tropic fruits, oranges, etc., live-stock on the great ranges, and in cities and villages; also the names and number of all the various farmers' organizations, such as Agricultural and Horticultural Societies, Poultry and Bee Associations, Farmers' Clubs, Granges, Alliances, Wheels, Unions, Leagues, etc.

In no part of the census work have the lines been extended more than in the direction of agriculture, and if farmers will now cheerfully co-operate with the enumerators and other officials in promptly furnishing the correct figures, more comprehensive returns regarding our greatest industry will be obtained than ever before.

The Stake Book.

Editor Breeder and Sportsman:—Will you kindly notify horse owners, breeders, etc., through the columns of your paper, that next week we shall have ready for distribution our official stake or nomination book, which will contain the names of all horses entered in every stake that has closed for this year, also for 1891 and 1892, to be run at the Monmouth Park and Saratoga Associations, the American, Coney Island and New York Jockey Clubs; also the Brooklyn Jockey Club for 1891. In addition to the above, there will be a voluminous index, comprising the age, color, sex, sire and dam of every horse entered, by which the engagement of any particular animal in any stake can be found at a glance. The stakes of each club are inserted in alphabetical order, so that any particular one is very easy of search.

This publication will give dates upon which races will close for the future, also dates of declarations and the scale of weight for age now in force. Col. S. D. Bruce has kindly prepared a list of yearlings for 1890, which will form part of this publication.

In order to overcome, if possible, past apathy on the part of horse owners, etc., with regard to this valuable work, which necessitated our charging in previous years $10 per copy, we have decided, as an experiment, to reduce the price of this book just one-half, viz., $5 for the recent volume. Yours truly, Goodwin Bros.

Guaranteed Purses.

Once more we wish to call the attention of our readers to the races advertised by the San Mateo and Santa Clara Country Agricultural District No. 5 for their fall meeting, which takes place from August 11th to 15th. There are two $1200 purses, the first being for the three minute class, while the second is for 2:30 horses. The entrance fee in each is 10 per cent. payable as follows: $40 on June 1st, when entries close, $40 on July 1st, and $40 on August 1st. There is also a $600 purse offered for the pacing division for those eligible to the 2:30 class, the entrance fee is also 10 per cent., payable $20 on June 1st, $20 on July 1st, and $20 on August 1st. These races are, all of them, mile heats, best three in five; a neglect to make payments when due forfeits previous payments. From present appearances, San Jose will have the most successful meeting this year that it has ever held, and as the Directors have seen fit to keep up with the other Associations and offer large and liberal purses, there is no reason to doubt but that they will receive plenty of patronage in return.

The Los Angeles Meeting.

The large and prominent advertisement in the Breeder and Sportsman of the Los Angeles races has caused favorable comment from many of the northern horsemen who have in the past considered the distance to Los Angeles too far for them to take their horses, but the large amount of money offered by the Southern California people is enough to tempt many of them to visit the Angel city and secure a few of the rich plums which have so generously been hung in sight by that association. The trotting stakes close on June 16th, but the balance of the races are left open for entries until July 1st. Already the directors have seen fit to announce that in addition to opening the circuit on August 4th, they will also give another meeting later in the season after the Fresno and Breeders' Association have held their meetings. Unquestionably the Los Angeles people have gone to work right this year, and as their purses are larger than ever, they will receive the unqualified indorsement of all horsemen throughout the State.

One Day Earlier.

Owing to Friday, the 30th of May, being a public holiday, the Breeder and Sportsman appears this week one day in advance of its usual time, so as to enable the employes of this paper to enjoy with the balance of their fellow creatures, a day of rest, which is something rarely accorded to those who are engaged in newspaper work.

District Colt Stakes.

The Contra Costa County Agricultural Association, District No. 23, has three colt stakes advertised in the present issue of the BREEDER AND SPORTSMAN, all of which are of interest to those living in the county. The races are, for one year old, one mile dash, for two year olds, mile heats, two in three, and for three year olds, mile heats, three in five. The Association adds $75 to each of these races, and the payment is $40 in each, divided in installments of $10, payable June 1st, when the stakes close, $15 September 1st, and $15 September 22d. These races will take place at the annual Fair, and will be trotted between September 22d and September 27th, both days inclusive. As Contra Costa County has advanced considerably within the past few years in the breeding industry, it is more than probable that these stakes will receive a generous support from the local horsemen.

The Eureka Jockey Club.

We desire to call the attention of all whom it may concern to the races advertised in this issue by the well managed Association which has its headquarters at Eureka in Humboldt County. The races extend over a period of four days, beginning on July 2d, and from the character of the programme, they should receive the support of all horsemen. Eureka is well known as a racing center, and its anual meetings have always been successfully conducted; the pool box is always liberally patronized, so that those who wish to invest money on their favorites can find plenty of opportunity to do so. The entries do not close until June 20th, but it would be well for those who contemplate a visit to the Coast City to send in their entries in time; so that they may not be overlooked or perhaps forgotten entirely.

2:20 Pacing Purse.

In the advertisement of the Pacific Coast Trotting Horse Breeders' Association which appeared last week asking for entries for a pacing race, a typographical mistake made the announcement read a Nomination Pacing Purse of $1,000 for the 2:30 class whereas it should have read for the 2:20 class. While mention had already been made of what was intended there may have been some who read the advertisement and did not read the remarks thereon and their attention is called to this mistake. There are a large number of pacing horses in the State who are eligible to this purse and undoubtedly when it closes on June 10th, there will be a fine lot of entries. As the mistake has been corrected it is only necessary to call the attention of our readers to the advertisement which appears in another column.

Judge Corlett's Decision.

As will be seen by referring to the decision of Judge Corlett published in another column, he has decided in favor of the National Trotting Association and declares that the Congress did not step outside of their bounds in passing the resolution referring to Noble, Robens and the gray stallion Alcryon. From the present state of affairs it would seem that Noble has very much the worst of the case, and the better thing for him to do, would be to let the Board of Review try his case at once, provided he feels that he is innocent of the charges laid at his door. The association only did what was expected of them and cannot be blamed in the premises. The good name of the trotting turf must be upheld at all hazards or the public will refuse to extend its patronage.

A Good Rule.

At almost every meeting held within our knowledge, people who have lost money have been only to anxious to cry "fraud" when the horses which they had backed failed to win. Of late there has been so much of this sort of business going on that the Brooklyn Jockey Club last week posted up on their grounds at Gravesend, the following notice:

"Any person on or off the track using language detrimental to the interest of racing, such as asserting that a horse has been pulled, or that a race has been 'fixed,' will be promptly ruled off the grounds of this club unless he can substantiate his assertion." By order of the Executive Committee.

It is about time that this idle talk should be done away with and we are pleased to see that the Brooklyn Association has taken the initiative in this matter.

Mr. Wallace's nephew, who is accused of robbing his uncle of over $50,000, has been arrested in Havana, and he will be brought back to New York for trial.

Our Tennessee Letter.

GALLATIN, Tenn., May 24th.

EDITOR BREEDER AND SPORTSMAN:—The racing season of 1890 is now on in full blast, and each day adds more turf events to the history of American racing. One by one the meetings at different points are left behind, and with the close of each we find new names among the list of star turf performers. The two-year-olds more especially are coming out, and since the Memphis meeting began the woods have been full of good two-year-olds. On the Western racing circuit there are more good two-year-olds than have appeared in any previous year. Of the crack colts I may mention Dundee, Georgetown, Allan Bane, Rosseland, Hueneme and probably a few others that have shown themselves to be nearly first class. What is expected to be the great two-year-old of the year, Rey del Rey, has not started yet, and as he does not start before the St. Louis meeting, we can not tell whether he is going to be the equal of his great brothers. In looks he is their superior, and one would think that no road was too long nor any weight too heavy for him to carry any distance successfully.

Of the two-year-old fillies that have started this season Ida Pickwick, Monte Rosa, Annie Brown and Lady Washington are the pick of the lot, and, singularly, it is, all were bred in Tennessee. This lot of colts and fillies have held a monopoly on all the stake races for their age, as they have won every one run in the West since the New Orleans Spring Meeting began.

Isaac Murphy has signed to ride this season for Mr. Haggin, the California turfman. Isaac has several good colts himself, and after this season he will retire from the pigskin and hereafter appear in the role of owner and trainer. Murphy is shoes to pla'es the best jockey that rides in the West, and whenever he appears in the silks upon any Western race course he receives an ovation. He will land the horses of the Haggin string under the wire winners of many events the coming season, and with his guiding hand Firenzi should be well nigh invincible, as should the great Salvator, the Lorillard winner.

It was sad news to hear that the speedy Gorgo had broken down, and to those who had backed her for the Suburban it was fearful. Many trainers have told me that the black daughter of Isonomy would handle Firenzi the coming season, and that when just right she could smash any previous record up to a mile and a quarter. She was the equal of any mare of her age last season and it did look very much like Senator Hearst would take the next Suburban honors to his California home.

A bill has been introduce in the Senate against winter racing at the New Jersey tracks. This bill was most probably introduced by some Senator who had lost his "wad" on the Jersey skates, and who now felt it his duty to ask for the prevention of such cruelty as "racing plug horses in mid winter." I, for one, do not uphold winter racing as a gambling scheme for touts, pickpockets and these, but winter racing conducted as was the latter part of the Clifton Winter Meeting, will neither injure the popularity of American racing nor will it be barbarous. The horses raced at these tracks are not owned by such men as the Dwyers, Baldwin, Hearst, Haggin, Belmont or the Morrises, but they are owned by men who must make them win their feed if possible, and this is their chance. Clifton did more to increase the popularity of racing than any of the more aristocratic summer tracks will do this entire season. That club gave added money to long distance races, and hundreds of people flocked out to see them, that had not in years been upon a race course. If Clifton still keeps up as it ended by all means let it continue to hold its winter meeting. We would refrain from doing anything that this big hearted Senator would call "cruel and barbarous," and we feel a sympathy for his feelings when the bill is brought up for a vote and his brother Senators sit down upon his bill. May they do so.

KENNESAW.

Langford Stock Farm.

On the banks of the Mokelumne, in the shadow of the Sierras, on the richest of native grasses, is the Langford Stock Farm. There Senator Langford has gathered together a large number of gilt edged mares and fillies. In the olden days Senator Langford was a devoted follower of the thoroughbreds. Then he had the best and hottest blood that ever looked through bridles. In that way he has backed up his trotting pedigrees by the stoutest running blood. From "Bessie Sedgwick" by Joe Daniels, dam by Starlight, son of Owen Dale, he has three fillies by Dexter Prince and Hawthorne. The oldest one is a bay, 4 years old, by Dexter Prince. She is large and strong, with plenty of facility and finish. She is being bred to L. M. Morse's Hero, a son of Director.

The next of the Bessie Sedgwick produce is a black, 3-year old filly by Hawthorne, the son of Nutwood and the sire of Tempest 2:19. She has fine trotting action and promises to be prominent in the three year old classes this fall.

The Bessie Sedgwick two year old is a sorrel filly by Hawthorne and with proper handling will be a trotter. The yearling from this mare is a bay filly by Hawthorne, and is owned by N. J. Stone of Mountain View, who also has a suckling at the mare's side by Hawthorne.

From Bessie Sedgwick Senator Langford had a filly foal from the cover of Bayswater, the son of Lexington, and Bay Leaf by imp Yorkshire. From this Bayswater mare the Senator has a four year old mare by Dexter Prince, a three year old filly by the same horse, and a two year old stallion colt. All these are a credit to Dexter Prince and the granddaughter of Lexington and Bay Leaf.

The Bayswater mare has produced two more—a colt and a filly to the cover of Dexter Prince. They are owned by Mr. Stone of Mountain View, and show the royal blood of their sire and dam.

The next of the Senator's mares is a bay, 9 years old, by Tom Vernon, by Hambletonian Chief, 1st dam by Stockbridge Chief. Jr., 2nd dam by Royal George, 3d dam by Grey Eagle. This mare is a great road mare, and is being bred to Hero, Morse's Director—Santa Claus colt. She has a four-year by Dexter Prince that moves well, and is being trained at the Lodi track.

Another broodmare is a grey by Wine Creek, son of McCracken's Black Hawk, with breeding on the dam's side the same as the Tom Vernon mare above. This mare has a grey two-year-old filly by Dexter Prince, which has been broken and jogged, and gives great promise. Her yearling—a bay filly—is as fine a Dexter Prince as there is, and that is high praise, for he is a uniform producer of large, fine looking colts and fillies. By her side this grey mare has a suckling filly by Shippee and Parker's Campaign, son of Electioneer and a daughter of Homer, a son of Mambrino Patchen. She has the size and powerful form of Electioneer and the high finish and quality of the Mambrino Patchens. By the way, I want to say here that Campaign has a number of as fine looking sucklings as I have ever seen.

There is also a brown Mambrino Wilkes mare, 4 years old, dam by LeRock, brother to Priam, son of Whipple's Hambletonian, granddam by Odd Fellow, son of imp Chloroform. She is stinted to Dexter Prince. There is a bay mare by Chieftain, dam a thoroughbred, stinted to Dexter Prince.

Another broodmare is Reliance 2:22, being bred to Morse's Director—Santa Claus colt.

Last but not least is Hazel Kirke, the game and fast daughter of Brigadier. She never looked better than now. She is being bred to Hawthorne and should have a great youngster from this son of Nutwood and the daughter of Volunteer.

In all, Senator Langford has sixteen mares, which will produce foals that will sell well in the Eastern market, and he is constantly adding to his list by purchasing the best blood. He has entered the list of California breeders to stay, and he will train as well as breed.

Answers to Correspondents.

Answers for this department MUST be accompanied by the name and address of the sender, not necessarily for publication, but as proof of good faith. Write the questions distinctly, and on one side of the paper only. Positively no questions will be answered by mail or telegraph.

Subscriber.

Will you please tell me through your valuable paper the fastest time made running by two-year-old colts a quarter and half mile?

Answer.—There are no authentic records by which to decide the time made in a quarter mile race by a two-year-old; for half a mile, Olitipa, 47½.

J. G.

Your horse is not eligible to the 3 minute class.

T. S.

Please let me know in your next issue the record of Hardman by Echo, and is he eligible to registration?

Answer.—2:31½. He is not eligible to registration.

Foals of 1890.

At Palo Alto Stock Farm, property of Hon. Leland Stanford:

B f by Wild Boy—Piney by Electioneer.
B f by Benefit—Irene by Mohawk Chief.
B c by Electioneer—Miss Beecher by Piedmont.
B f by Electioneer—Ashby by General Benton.
B f by Azmoor—Bonnie by General Benton.
B c by Palo Alto—Virtue by General Benton.
B f by Nephew—Monora by Fallis.
B f by Electioneer—Lora by Piedmont.
B f by Benefit—Satanella by Leveller.
B c by Electioneer—Penelope by Mohawk Chief.
B c by Electioneer—Aragon by General Benton.
B c by Palo Alto—Lizzie Collins by Stanseler's Woful.
B c by Benefit—Lady Sealley by Joseph.
B c by Palo Alto—Genie by General Benton.
B c by Clay—Miss Campbell by Endorser.
B f by Nephew—Planetia by Planet.

At Vina Ranch, Tehama County, Cal.:

B c by Beverly—Elle by Sultan or Del Sur.
B c by Nephew—Lilly by Electioneer.
Ch f by Ansel—Barnes by Whipple's Hambletonian.
B c by Ansel—Norah by Messenger Duroc.
B f by Electioneer—Sontag Dixie by Toronto Sontag.
B c by Clay—Wilna by General Benton.
Ch f by Wild Boy—Victress by Baird's Hambletonian Prince.
B c by Benefit—Sultana by Sultan.
Br c by Clay—Josie by Whipple's Hambletonian.
B c by Wild Boy—Nova Zembla by imp Glengarry.

Yours truly, S. FERGUSON, Clk.

At Napa. Property of F. L. and N. Coombs.

May 26th a claimant for the BREEDER AND SPORTSMAN Futurity Stake came into the world, being a bay colt by Director 2:17 dam Lillie Stanley 2:17½. This youngster bred in the purple should be able to sustain the reputation of both sire and dam.

At Sacramento. Property of L. B. Hicks:

On March 28, '90 bay colt, with star by Prompter 2305, dam Valley Belle by Privateer 8135. This foal is entered in the BREEDER AND SPORTSMAN Futurity Stake.

At Rosedale Breeding Farm. Property of the same.

On May 21st, Cygnet, by Steinway 1808, foaled a bay filly with black points, by Daly 5341; 2d dam Leah by Woodford Mambrino 345; 3d dam Maud (dam of King Jim, pacer, 2:20½, and Attorney 1005) by Abdallah 15; 4th dam by Robert Bruce, son of Clinton. This filly is in the BREEDER AND SPORTSMAN Futurity Stake.

Property of Alexander Waugh, San Francisco:

April 20th, a dark bay filly by Almont Patchen, dam said to be thoroughbred.

Names Claimed.

Palo Alto Stock Farm entries to the BREEDER AND SPORTSMAN'S Futurity Stakes. Guaranteed $3,000; to trot in 1893, foals of 1890:

Bell Bird, br f, small star, off hind foot and inside of ankle white; near hind foot white to ankle; black spots around coronets; by Electioneer—Beautiful Bells by The Moor.

Claudio, b c, off hind foot white to ankle; by Electioneer—Belle Campbell by General Benton.

Teazle, b c, inside of near hind coronet and heel white; by Electioneer—Telle by General Benton.

Pacolet, b c, near fore heel white; off hind foot and ankle white; by Electioneer—Dame Winnie by Planet.

Lochinvar, b c, near hind foot and back of ankle white; outside of off hind foot and heel white; by Nephew—Lorinne by General Benton.

Titania, b f, small star, by Piedmont—Thalia by Electioneer.

Bonnibel, b f, large star, by Azmoor—Bonnie by General Benton.

Rowena, b f, off hind heel white, by Azmoor—Emma Robson by Woodburn.

Jessica, ch f, star, by Palo Alto—Jennie Benton by General Benton.

Flower Boy, b c, by Nephew—Wildflower by Electioneer.

I hereby claim the name Jack Nelson Junior for my light bay colt, star in forehead, hind ankles white—foaled April 19th 1890, by Jack Nelson by John Nelson, 1st dam Lottie F. by Newland's Hambletonian; 2nd dam by California Patchen. JOHN FRICK.

LIVERMORE, CAL.

I hereby claim the name of Pilgrim for bay colt, with star by Prompter 2305, dam Valley Belle by Privateer 8135.

L. B. RICKS, Sacramento.

Stallions.

The question is often asked "How many mares should a stallion be allowed in a season?" says the London Live Stock Journal.

This question is so broad that an answer cannot be given except at length; but even when I have done so the reply will still appear vague, and it must be left so for people of common sense to weigh and adapt to the special stallion in whose interests the information is sought. From the way the question is invariably put it appears to be the opinion of many that there is such a thing as a regulation number of mares to a horse, which, if once fixed, will put an end to all thought on the subject: but this number will entirely depend upon circumstances.

In the first place, a young horse should not have as many mares as a horse in the prime of life, neither should an aged horse in his first year have as many mares as one that has got seasoned; secondly, it depends on whether the mares are thoroughbred or half-bred; thirdly, it depends on the temperament and powers of the horse; fourthly, it depends on the knowledge and experience of whoever has charge of the horse: and there are, fifthly, various other facts that materially alter the regulation number of mares that a horse should be allowed in a season.

Now, as to my first query: It must be borne in mind that, as far as the horse is concerned, it is not a question to be considered of how many mares may be allowed him, but it is entirely a question of how many services he is required to give during the season: and a horse young at his work may have to give a larger number of services to produce the same results than would be necessary with a seasoned horse, and each service might, through excessive excitement, take more out of him than it would do when the horse had steadied to his work. This is the case with most horses the first season, and, of course, it is only common sense to consider that a three-year-old unmatured horse should not be subjected to the same exertions as an aged one.

Secondly, as to the difference it makes to a horse whether the mares are thoroughbred or not is an idea that seems to have occurred to but few, yet the difference is very material. Thoroughbred mares come earlier in season than half-bred ones, and owing to the weather being cold they sometimes remain in season only a short time—a day or two; therefore, when the mare is seen to be in season, it becomes necessary to serve her to make sure of her. Then, if she happens to keep in season for several days after, it is evident that she was served too early, and she should be served again. This makes two services in the one pride, whereas, were she a half bred mare coming later in the year, when she first appeared in use it would have been safe to wait a few days and then serve her, and so do with the one service instead of two. Then, again, half bred mares are more spread over the season. Some come late, when a horse's work would be slackening, and that would not cause the same strain as if all the mares came with a rush on the horse at about the same time, as thoroughbred mares mostly do.

Thirdly, horses vary very much in their powers of fruitfulness, and if a horse be specially gifted he can take a great many more mares in a season than a horse that is deficient in this respect, because the latter will miss his mare several times before he stops her, whereas the former horse would stop a large majority of his mares with the one first service, so that a horse of this sort would be able to take a far greater number of mares to a given number of services than another horse who was not such a sure foal-getter. It must be borne in mind that horses frequently vary one year from another. They do not always do the same, and how a horse happens to be doing in a particular year should regulate the number of mares put to him for that year.

Fourthly, much depends on the management of a stallion: he may be got too fat from over-feeding and want of exercise, and this would cause him to miss a great number of his mares, which would return to him and prevent him taking so many with ease to himself. Then, again, the man who has perfect knowledge of the right time to serve a mare and when not to do so, can save his horse much extra work, and prove in the end to be more successful with his mares. I speak from experience in this matter, because I now see the errors that used to be committed in the management of our stallions when we first commenced the stud which I now manage. I am sure that stallions are frequently made to serve mares that are in foal, and had better be left alone, and that from want of knowledge stallions are put on mares when they are not quite ready, and that service is one thrown away. All these little circumstances make a lot of difference in the number of mares a horse should be limited to in a season.

One thing I am convinced of, viz., that one service at the right time, if the horse serves his mare satisfactorily, is as good as two or more services in the same pride, and I consider that a horse worked by an experienced man on this system will get a larger proportion of mares in foal than a stallion worked on the principle of two services better than one, because a horse worked on the latter lines, if given the same number of mares as the former, would have double work, and through being overdone, might fail more or less, whereas the other horse would be fresh all through the season.

Fifthly, I will refer to a few other circumstances not dealt with above. For instance, much depends on the number of mares that come late in the season, say in June. You might count three of these mares to cause no more distress to a horse than one mare coming at the commencement, because the latter may take the horse once every three weeks all the season through, whereas the mares that come late have only one or two chances at most. Then again, one horse may be unlucky in getting several very obstinate old mares, that may be each of them as bad as half a dozen others; while another horse may get a larger proportion of foaling mares which are not so much trouble to get in foal; and, in fact, the whole thing depends on circumstances, and an owner can see as the season goes on when a horse has got as many mares on his list as he should have, and he can close the list until he sees the bulk of the mares promise to be in foal, when, towards the end of the season, he can take a few more.

Systems in Betting.

The experience of most men, who have for any long period been in the habit of risking their money on chance, whether at the racehorse and gambling table, is that systems are a snare and a delusion, says the Week's Sport. Better even then to use such misleading methods of pursuing the "oof bird," is to adopt the eminently unsportsmanlike system of backing jockeys and not their mounts. Of course, it is rediculous to say that one ought not to back a crack jockey's mount against a stable lad's, but not even a Jimmy McLaughlin or a Fred Archer can get out of a horse more than their is in him; but yet one sees absurdly short prices against a horse oftentimes simply because the jocky is the best rider in the race, and the unthinking herd piles on its cash. Some systems have been found to work moderately well, but only such as must necessarily be conducted on the "slow but sure" principle, so that small winnings only can be made. Such a method as that extensively adopted during last season, of which the principle is to back the second favorite for the place, is as good as any.

Men will, of course, bet when they go to the races—more's the pity—but the casual race-goer who has never followed up the form of horses and is in no degree "posted," I do not mean that it is necessary to ferret around all the while to getwind of "robberies." Some frauds are certainly perpetrated, but there is very little substance in all the fuss about "stiffs," etc. At any rate, you may take it for granted that when a job is to be brought off, uncommonly few people are let into the secret, and it is time wasted to attempt to fathom such dark stable secrets. Those that wish to follow the races right along must study public form, learn to judge a horse's condition, gather what information is to be had about private work, carefully noting while at the race course how the horses move in their preliminary work—follow this advise, and you will have more chance to win the bookmaker's dust than by any "system."

Sometimes one discovers an animal, especially in the selling plater class, that has shown good private form, but failed to justify it in public. Prices rule very long against it when it goes to the post, and as time goes on, and it has only succeeded in whipping in the fields it has started with, they become even longer. Follow it right up along and some day, when the horse is feeling just right, it will jump out with perhap 50 to 1 against it, and score brackets. There have been plenty of such instances of late, and one could well have afforded to lose a small sheaf of ten-dollar bills for the sake of the harvest that it would have reaped eventually. To a shrewd judge two-year-old racing can be made a most fruitful source of profit, but it is necessary to bestow careful consideration on the private form, breeding, and handling of the youngsters.

The pith of the whole matter is that on the turf as elsewhere there is no "royal road" to wealth, and those believing they can jump in and make a small fortune, unless by a fleeting stroke of luck, are sorely mistaken. Careful and persistent study and methods are necessary, and even then a man may be unable to keep ahead of the books. For any but the professional racing men betting is a mistake, unless it be to add additional zest to a day's holiday.

Fastest Time on Record.

RUNNING.

Miles.		Time
¼	Jim Miller, 2, Deer Lodge (Mont.), Aug. 15, 1888 / †Sleepy Dick, a, Kiowa (Kan.), Nov. 24, 1888	0:21¼
⅜	Cyclone, a, 120 lbs., Helena (Mont.), Aug. 28, 1889	0:34½
½	Geraldine, 4, 122 lbs., Westchester Course, Aug. 30, 1889	0:46
⅝	Britannic, 5, 122 lbs., Westchester Course, Aug. 31, 1889	0:59
⅝	Fordham, a, 115 lbs., Westchester Course, Oct. 4, 1889	0:56
¾	El Rio Rey, 2, 126 lbs., Westchester Course, Aug. 31, 1889	1:11
¾	Tipstaff, 3, 107, Westchester Course, Oct. 4, 1889	1:11
⅞	Britannic, 5, 110 lbs., Sheepshead Bay, Sept. 5, 1889	1:25 2-5
	Ten Broeck, 5, 110 lbs., Louisville, May 24, 1877 (against time)	1:39¾
1	Maori 4, 108 lbs., Chicago, July 12, 1889, (in a race)	1:39 4-5
1 1-16	Wheeler T., 3, 98 lbs., St. Louis, June 1, 1888	1:47¾
1 1-16	Eyton 4, 108, Chicago, Ill., June 28, 1888	1:47¾
1⅛	Terra Cotta, 4, 134 lbs., Sheepshead Bay, June 23, 1888	1:52
1 3-16	Joe Cotton, 5, 109½ lbs., Sheepshead Bay, Sept. 7, 1887	2:00¾
1¼	Kingston, 5, 122 lbs., Gravesend, Sept. 24, 1889	2:06¼
1 m 500 yds.	Bend'Or, 4, 115 lbs., Saratoga, July 25, 1882	2:10¾
1⅜	Triboulet, 4, 117 lbs., San Francisco, April 26, 1888 / Richmond, 3, 122 lbs., Sheepshead Bay, June 27, 1888	2:21¾
1½	Firenzi, 4, 113 lbs., Monmouth Park, Aug. 2, 1888 / Luke Blackburn, 3, 102 lbs., Monmouth Park, Aug. 17, '80 / Jim Guest, 4, 98 lbs., Chicago, (Washington Park, July 2) '88	2:34
1⅝	Hindoocraft, 3, 75 lbs., Westchester, Aug. 27, 1889	2:48
1¾	Glidelia, 5, 116 lbs., Saratoga, Aug. 5, 1882	3:01
1⅞	Enigma, 4, 90 lbs., Sheepshead Bay, Sept. 15, 1885	3:20
2	Ten Broeck, 5, 110 lbs., Louisville, May 29, 1877	3:27½
2¼	Monitor, 4, 110 lbs., Baltimore, Oct. 20, 1880	3:41½
2½	Springbok, 5, 114 lbs. / Preakness, a, 114 lbs., Saratoga, July 29, 1875	3:56¼
2¾	Aristides, 4, 104 lbs., Lexington, May 13, 1876	4:27½
2⅞	Ten Broeck, 4, 104 lbs., Lexington, Sept. 16, 1876	4:58½
3	Hubbard, 4, 107 lbs., Saratoga, Aug. 9, 1873	4:58¾
3	Drake Carter 4, 115 lbs., Sheepshead Bay, Sept. 6, 1884	5:24
4	Ten Broeck, 4, 104 lbs., Louisville, Sept. 27, 1876	7:15¾

HEAT RACES.

Miles.		Time
¼	Sleepy Dick, a, Kiowa (Kan.), Nov. 24, 1888	0:21½—0:22¼
½	Bogus, a, 113 lbs., Helena (Mont.), Aug. 21, 1888	0:48 —0:48
⅝	Kittie Pease, 4, Dallas (Tex.), Nov. 2, 1887	1:00 —1:00
⅝	Sudie McNairy, 3, 98 lbs., Chicago, July 2, 1888	1:03¼—1:03
¾	Lizzie S., 5, 118 lbs., Louisville, Sept. 28, 1883	1:13½—1:13¾
1	Bounce, 4, 90 lbs., Sheepshead Bay, Sept. 7, 1881	1:42 —1:41½
1	3 in 5. L'Argentine, 6, 115 lbs., St. Louis, June 14, 1879	1:43—1:44 —1:47½
1 1-16	Slipalong, 5, 115 lbs., Chicago (Wash. Park), Sept. 2, 1885	1:50½—1:48
1⅛	Gabriel, 4, 112 lbs., Sheepshead Bay, Sept. 28, 1880	1:56 —1:56
1¼	Glenmore, 5, 114 lbs., Sheepshead Bay, Sept. 25, 1880	2:10 —2:14
1½	Keno, 6, Toledo, Sept. 16, 1881 (1st and 3d heats)	2:43½—2:45
2	Miss Woodford, 4, 107½ lbs., Sheepshead Bay, Sept. 20, 1884	3:33 —3:31¾
3	Norfolk, 4, 100 lbs., Sacramento, Sept. 23, 1865	5:27½—5:29¾
	Ferida, 4, 105 lbs., Sheepshead Bay, Sept. 18, 1880	7:23½—7:41

†Made in a heat race.

*Doubtful, and made in a heat race.

Detroit Stake Subscribers.

The following subscribers to the Detroit Driving Club's Merchants' and Manufacturers' $10,000 Stake for the 2:24 class, to be trotted at the summer meeting, July 22 to 25, made the second payment:

D. T. Foster, Bloomington, Ill.
James Stinson, Chicago, Ill.
C. D. Bills, Tecumseh, Mich.
D. Deming, Terre Haute, Ind.
R. L. & C. S. Cobb, Eaton Rapids, Mich.
Glenview Stock Farm, Louisville, Ky.
James F. Clay, Paris, Ky.
Hickory Grove Stock Farm, Racine, Wis.
G. W. Leiby & Son, Chicago, Ill.
Budd Doble, Chicago, Ill.
W. P. Injams, Terre Haute, Ind.
John Lothian, Hamtramck, Mich.
Edgewood Stock Farm, Terre Haute, Ind.
George H. Hammond, Detroit, Mich.
James O. Gray, Boston, Mass.
James Elliott, Philadelphia, Pa.
Bob Stewart, Kansas City, Mo.
Palo Alto Stock Farm, Menlo Park, Cal.

Flower City Stake.

Secretary Collins of the Rochester Driving Park Association writes that the following subscribers to the Flower City $10,000 Guarantee Stake for the 2:30 class have made the second payment:

C. E. Mosher, Lawrence, Mass.
Leslie W. Russell, New York City.
D. B. Herrington, Poughkeepsie, N. Y.
H. G. Smith, Harlem, N. Y.
Allen Farm, Pittsfield, Mass.
Elm City Stock Farm, New Haven, Conn.
Village Farm, C. J. Hamlin, proprietor, East Aurora, N. Y.
Rensselaer Stock Farm, Rensselaer, Ind.
A. C. Redfield, Galesburg, Ill.
Glenview Stock Farm, Louisville, Ky.
Patchen Farm, J. W. Day, proprietor, Waterloo, N. Y.
Charles Nolan, Philadelphia, Pa.
O. A. Hickok, San Francisco, Cal.
J. W. Quimby, Scranton, Pa.
W. R. Armstrong, Romeo, Mich.
Budd Doble, Chicago, Ill.
John E. Turner, Ambler, Pa.
George W. Eckstein, Philadelphia, Pa.
D. S. Hammond, New York City.
G. W. Archer, Rochester, N. Y.

Best Trotting Records.

1 mile—2:08¾, Maud S., against time, in harness, accompanied the distance by a running horse, Glenville, O., July 30, 1885 ....2:13¼, best time in a race between horses, Maud S., Chicago, Ills., July 24, 1880 ......2:12, Axtell, against time, accompanied by running horse—fastest stallion time, Terre Haute, Ind., Oct. 11, 1889...... 2:13¾, Phallas, fastest heat by a stallion against other horses, Chicago, July 14, 1884......2:13¾, Palo Alto, third heat in race at Stockton, Cal., Sept. 26, 1889......2:15½, Jay-Eye-See, half-mile track, Lincoln, Neb., Sept. 14, 1887......2:15¾, Great Eastern, under saddle, third heat, Morrisania, N. Y., Sept. 22, 1877......2:10¾, Jay-Eye-See, against time, best five-year-old record, Providence, R. I., Sept. 15, 1883......2:16, Manzanita, third heat, best four-year-old record, Lexington, Ky., Sept. 3, 1876 ..... 2:16, Edgemark, four-year old stallion record, against time, Lexington, Ky., Oct. 18, 1889......2:10½, Sunol, in Stanford Stake, accompanied by a runner, best three-year-old record, San Francisco, Nov. 9, 1889..2:18, Sunol 2 years, against time, San Francisco, Cal., Oct. 27, 1888......2:20½, Regal Wilkes, two-year-old stallion record, San Francisco, Nov. 2, 1889...... 2:31½, Norlaine, yearling, against time, San Francisco, Cal., Nov. 12, 1887...... 2:35, Faustino, yearling stallion record, San Francisco, Nov. 9, 1889.

2 miles—4:43 against time, Fanny Witherspoon, Chicago, Ill., Sept 25, 1885.

3 miles—7:21¼, Huntress, harness, Brooklyn, L. I., Sept. 21, 1872.

4 miles—10:34½, Longfellow, wagon, California, Dec. 31, 1869.

5 miles—13:00, Lady Mac, harness, San Francisco, Cal., April 2, 1874.

10 miles—27:23½, Controller, harness, San Francisco, Cal., Nov. 23, 1878.

20 miles—58:25, Captain McGowan, harness, half-mile track, Boston, Oct. 31, 1865.

Pacing Records at One Mile.

Johnston, harness, against time, Chicago, Ills., Oct. 9, 1884, 2:06¼.

Brown Hal, best stallion record, Cleveland, Ohio, July 31, 1889, 2:12½.

Westmont, July 10, 1884, Chicago, Ills., with running mate, 2:01¾.

Daisy, yearling, Sacramento, Dec. 31, 1885, 2:38½.

Ed Rosewater, two years old, Council Bluffs, Iowa, Nov. 8, 1888, 2:20½.

Yolo Maid, 3 years old, San Francisco, Oct. 13, 1888, 2:14.

Gold Leaf, four years old, 2:11½ on August 17, 1889, at Napa.

Arrow, five years old, 2:13½, made at Cleveland, Ohio, August 1, 1889.

ATHLETICS.

Athletic Sports and Other Pastimes.

EDITED BY ARPHIPPUS.

SUMMARY.

During the early part of the week the athletes were busy putting on the finishing touches for the great championship meeting which was held yesterday. After yesterday's work it is probable that the boys will need a couple of weeks rest. Complete arrangements have been for the century run of the California Division, L. A. W., which will commence to-morrow morning.

IN THE SURF.

The different surf-bathing establishments were crowded on Sunday last. The managers of the Terrace Baths at Alameda were kept unusually busy serving out suits, many ladies being noticed amongst the crowd of bathers.

It is estimated that over five thousand people were present in the spectators' gallery at the Terrace baths on Sunday.

Captain Volliner and several other well known swimmers donned their bathing suits and gave fine exhibitions of high and fancy diving during the afternoon.

Several members of the Civil Service swimming Club visited the Sheltered Cove Baths on Sunday and entertained the spectators with good exhibitions of diving and fast swimming.

The Palace and Crystal Baths did a fair business during the week, notwithstanding the fact that the warm weather has a tendency to attract the majority of the bathers to the open sea bathing resorts.

The Pacific Swimming Club will open its season of 1890 at the Terrace Swimming baths, Alameda, to-morrow. A good programme of sports will be given, and Captain Jack Volliner, George W. Spiller and other members of the club will contest in diving and swimming events.

Reports from Santa Cruz say that large crowds daily enjoy the surf bathing at that place. The season has also opened at Monterey and Capitola and promises to turn out well for the bath-house owners at both resorts.

RUNNERS, WALKERS, JUMPERS, ETC.

During the past couple of months several good amateur runners have arrived on the Pacific Coast, the majority of them being from Ireland. Now that the championship games are over, it is more than probable that some of them will join the Olympic Club.

In our next issue we will present our readers with a full and graphic account of the annual championship games of the Pacific Coast Amateur Athletic Association, which were held at the new grounds of the Olympic Club yesterday afternoon.

There has been considerable trouble amongst the athletes on account of the charges of professionalism brought against Charles Little of the Alpine Club. We think all the trouble might have been avoided if Captain Jordan of the Olympic Club, who made the charges, had notified Mr. Little to attend a meeting of the P. C. A. A. A., and in presence of delegates, give an account of all his previous records on the cinder track. Mr. Little was never officially notified to appear at a meeting of the Association, and, in consequence, had no chance to answer the charges brought against him. He was condemned without a hearing, and in refusing his entry when first presented, Mr. Jordan certainly showed a very bad spirit, and he also violated the rules of the Association in which he apparently takes so much pride. Such conduct on the part of a delegate of the P. C. A. A. A., if permitted to continue unchecked, will naturally cause discontent amongst the athletes, and discontent amongst the athletes will most undoubtedly cause a speedy dissolution of the Pacific Coast Amateur Athletic Association. As the outcome of Mr. Jordan's rather premature decision, we have already heard some of the athletes say that if the clubs which they represent do not withdraw from the P. C. A. A. A. they will tender their resignations as members. The officers of the Alpine Club say that it was never their intention to try and shield Little. On the contrary, they were only too anxious to have the charges brought against him, either substantiated or else proven false, but as the P. C. A. A. A. did not seem inclined to give Little a chance to either clear or condemn himself, the Alpine Club will possibly withdraw from the Association.

The Acme Athletic Club held a very enjoyable "Ladies' Night" exhibition on Tuesday evening at the club rooms, 305 Fourteenth street, Oakland.

The members of the Lurline Club gave their first cross-country run from Jackson's Villa, Sausalito, on Sunday last. Mr. Stutz was the first runner home. After the run the boys sat down to a fine lunch which had been prepared by Mrs. Ross Jackson. The club will hold another run from the same place on Sunday, June 8th.

It is said that a new five lap track will be built at Central Park for the use of the athletes who are not members of the Olympic Club. We think the project would pay, as there are several good athletic clubs in the city that would only be too glad to secure the privilege of using the grounds for their members. Go ahead, Mr. McNeill. *On vous attend.*

Walter A. Scott, President of the P. C. A. A. A.; has been elected to the Board of Managers of the Amateur Athletic Union of the United States.

There was a quarter mile run for members of the club only at the Olympic Club grounds on Sunday last. The day was rather windy and was, therefore, dead against fast time. The record, however, under the circumstances, was creditable. The following men started: V E Schifferstein, scratch; S V Cassady, scratch; J O'Kane, 10yds; J Kortick, 13yds; F G O'Kane, 14yds; J A Code, 18yds; C W H Toomey, 20 yds; Frank O'Kane finished first in 53 2-5 sec. Cassady was second by five yards, Schifferstein third by four yards. After the race W. A. Scott made a successful attempt to lower the Pacific Coast 1000 yard running record, held by J. G. Sutton of the University Athletic Club. Mr. Scott beat the record by one-quarter of a second.

The Alpine Amateur Athletic Club will hold a grand two-day boxing tournament on June 18th and 19th at the club rooms, 706 Powell street. Valuable prizes will be given.

M. C Giry and C. C. Johnson are trying to revive the defunct Pacific Athletic Club.

JOTTINGS FROM ALL OVER.

Willie Day, the champion distance runner of America, will be sent to England to participate in the regular championship games.

It is claimed that there are over 200 lawn tennis clubs in New York City and Brooklyn.

Travers Island has been opened for the season, and already several of the New York Athletic Club members are beginning to move over there for the summer months.

At Boston, on Saturday last, Downs ran 440 yards in 49 seconds, and Fearing cleared 6ft. 0¼ in. in the running high jump, both breaking the college records.

AT THE OARS.

The fine weather on Sunday was highly appreciated by a number of the local Oarsmen, who spent the greater portion of the day on the bay.

Several new men will make their debut at the coming Fourth of July regatta, and some of the old oarsmen will have to work hard to hold their laurels.

As in athletics, greater interest will be taken in rowing this season than has been for many years past, on account of the large number of new clubs that have lately sprung into existence.

ON THE WHEEL.

Only one member of the San Francisco Bicycle Club rode to Haywards on Sunday. A regular run of the club was called, but the members were evidently too lazy to obey the mandate.

Captain Manning and his associates have just returned from their eight day run through the Napa Valley. They travelled over 300 miles during the trip, and report the roads in good condition. The weather, however, was rather too hot and somewhat marred the enjoyment of the run.

The members of the Outing 'Cycle Club had a run to Haywards on Sunday.

Messrs. Doane, Plummer, Hammer and Wetmore rode to San Jose on Sunday. They made arrangements with the League Hotels for the reception of the wheelmen who intend starting on the century run to-morrow morning.

The postponed century run will take place to-morrow morning. The start will be made from the corner of 21st and Mission streets, at 5 o'clock sharp. It is expected that at least 75 wheelmen will show up. A schedule has been prepared to govern the riders on their long journey. The first stop will be made at Milbrae, where forty minutes will be allowed for breakfast. San Jose will be reached at 11 A. M. and 45 minutes will be allowed for lunch. It is expected that the riders will reach Hollister at 6 o'clock, making a total of thirteen hours from San Francisco, a distance of one hundred and two miles.

The San Jose Wheelmen are determined to have a four-lap track in readiness for the coming two-day tournament. It is expected that several records will be broken. Some of the Garden City boys are already in training and expect to carry off a good many prizes.

P. C A. A. A. Athletic Rules.

RULE I.

OFFICIALS.

SECTION 1. All amateur meetings shall be under the direction of

One Referee.
Two or more Inspectors.
Three Judges at finish.
Three or more Field Judges.
Three Timekeepers.
One Judge of walking.
One Starter.
One Clerk of the Course.
One Scorer.
One Marshal.

SEC 2. If deemed necessary, assistants may be provided for the Judge of walking, the Clerk of the Course, the Scorer and the Marshal, and an Official Announcer may be appointed.

RULE II.

CHAMPIONSHIP PENNANT.

At the Annual Championship Field Day a championship pennant or banner shall be given to the Association club winning the greatest number of points, which shall be scored as follows: first in each event, five points; second, three points; third, one point.

RULE III.

THE REFEREE.

The Referee shall decide all questions in dispute not otherwise covered in these rules.

He alone shall have power to change the order of events as laid down in the official programme.

When in any but the final heat of a race, a claim of foul or interference is made, he shall have the power to disqualify the competitor who was at fault, if he considers the foul intentional, and shall also have the power to allow the hindered competitor to start in the next round of heats, just as if he had been placed in his trial.

When in a final heat a claim of foul or interference is made he shall have the power to disqualify the competitor who was at fault, if he considers the foul intentional, and he shall also have the power to order a new race between such of the competitors as he thinks entitled to such a privilege.

It shall be the duty of the Referee at any games where an athlete is protested, to immediately notify, in writing, the Secretary of the Association of such protest.

RULE IV.

THE INSPECTORS.

It shall be the duty of an Inspector to stand at such point as the referee may designate; to watch the competitors closely, and in case of a claim of foul to report to the referee what he saw of the incident. Such inspectors are merely assistants to the referee, to whom they shall report, and have no power to make any decisions.

RULE V.

THE JUDGES AT FINISH.

The Judges at Finish shall determine the order of finishing of contestants, and shall arrange among themselves as to noting the winner, second, third, fourth, etc., as the case may require.

Their decision in this respect shall be without appeal, and in case of disagreement a majority shall govern.

RULE VI.

THE FIELD JUDGES.

The Field Judges shall make an accurate measurement and keep a tally of trials of competitors in the high and broad jumps, the pole vault, the weight competitions and the tug of war.

They shall act as judges of these events, and their decision shall likewise be without appeal. In case of disagreement a majority shall govern. In all weight competitions and jumps for distance, a small flag, placed in the ground, shall indicate the best throw or jump as the contest progresses.

RULE VII.

THE TIMEKEEPERS.

The timekeepers shall individually time all events where time record is called for. Should two of the three watches mark the same time and the third disagree, the time marked by the two watches shall be accepted. Should all three disagree, the time marked by the intermediate watch shall be accepted.

The flash of the pistol shall denote the actual time of starting.

In case only two watches are held on an event, and they fail to agree, the longer time of the two shall be accepted.

NOTE.—For record, however, three watches must be held on an event. See Rule VII, General Rules.

RULE VIII.

THE STARTER.

The starter shall have sole jurisdiction over the competitors after the Clerk of the Course has properly placed them in their positions for the start.

The method of starting shall be by pistol report, except that in time handicap races the word "go" shall be used.

An actual start shall not be effected until the pistol has been purposely discharged after the competitors have been warned to get ready.

When any part of the person of a competitor shall touch the ground in front of his mark before the starting signal is given, it shall be considered a false start.

Penalties for false starting shall be inflicted by the starter as follows:

In races up to and including 300 yards, the competitor shall be put back one yard for the first and another yard for the second attempt; in races over 300 yards and including 600 yards, two yards for the first and two more for the second attempt; in races over 600 yards and including 1,000 yds, three yards for the first and three more for the second attempt; in races over 1,000 yards and including one mile, five yards for the first and five more for the second attempt; in all races over one mile, ten yards for the first and ten more for the second attempt. In all cases the third start shall prevent the offender competing in that event.

The starter shall also rule out of that event any competitor who attempts to advance himself from his mark as prescribed in the official programme, after he has been given the warning to "get ready."

RULE IX.

THE CLERK OF THE COURSE.

The Clerk of the Course shall be provided with the names and numbers of all entered competitors, and he shall notify them to appear at the starting line before the start in each event in which they are entered.

In case of handicap events from marks, he shall place each competitor behind his proper mark; shall immediately notify the starter should any competitor attempt to advance himself after the starter has warned them to "get ready," and in time allowance handicaps shall furnish the starter with the number and time allowance of each actual competitor.

He shall control his assistants and assign to them such duties as he may require.

RULE X.

THE JUDGE OF WALKING.

The Judge of Walking shall have sole power to determine the fairness or unfairness of walking, and his rulings thereon shall be final and without appeal.

He shall caution any competitor whenever walking unfairly; the third caution to disqualify, except that he shall immediately disqualify any competitor when walking unfairly during the last 220 yards of a race.

He shall control his assistants and assign to them such of his duties as he may deem proper.

RULE XI.

THE SCORER.

The Scorer shall record the order in which each competitor finishes his event, together with the time furnished him by the timekeepers.

He shall keep a tally of the laps made by each competitor in races covering more than one lap, and shall announce by means of a bell or otherwise when the leading man enters the last lap.

He shall control his assistants and assign to them such of his duties as he may deem best.

RULE XII.

THE MARSHAL.

The Marshall shall have full police charge of the enclosure and shall prevent any but officials and actual competitors from entering or remaining therein.

He shall control his assistants and assign them their duties.

RULE XIII.

THE OFFICIAL ANNOUNCER.

The Official Announcer shall receive from the Scorer and Field Judges their record of each event, and announce the same by voice or by means of a bulletin board.

RULE XIV.

COMPETITORS.

Competitors shall report to the Clerk of the Course immediately upon their arrival at the place of meeting, and shall be provided by that official with their proper numbers, which must be worn conspicuously by the competitors when competing, and without which they shall not be allowed to start.

Each competitor shall inform himself of the time of starting, and shall be promptly at the starting point of each competition in which he is entered, and there report to the Clerk of the Course.

Under no condition shall the attendants be allowed to accompany competitors at the start or during any competition, except in match races, where special agreement may be made.

RULE XV.

PROTESTS.

Protests against any entered competitor may be made verbally to the Referee before or during the meeting. Such protests shall, if possible, be decided immediately by the Referee. If same cannot so be decided, the protested competitor shall compete under protest, and such protest shall be decided by the Association within one week, unless its subject be the amateur standing of the competitor, in which case the Referee must report such protest in writing within forty-eight hours to the Secretary of the P. C. A. A. A.

RULE XVI.

TRACK MEASUREMENT.

All distances run or walked shall be measured upon a line eighteen inches outward from the inner edge of the track, except that in races on straightaway tracks the distance shall be measured in a direct line from the starting mark to the finishing line.

$15,000. **OPENING** $15,000.

of the

GRAND CIRCUIT.

The World's Fair goes to Chicago, but the Greatest Fair ever held in the West takes place at

Agricultural Park, Los Angeles, August 4 to 9, 1890.

Fifteen Thousand Dollars in Purses, Stakes and Premiums.

Speed Programme:

FIRST DAY—MONDAY AUGUST 4TH.

No. 1. The Los Angeles Derby—A sweepstake for three-year-olds (foals of 1887), $10 each, half forfeit, with $300 added, the second to receive $100, and the third $50, out of the stakes; a winner of any three-year-old stake race to carry five (5) pounds, of two or more, eight (8) pounds extra; maidens allowed seven (7) pounds. One mile and a half.

No. 2. The Edwards & McKnight stakes—A sweepstake for all ages; $70 each, half forfeit; $200 added, the second to receive $100 out of the stakes. Non-winners this year allowed seven pounds. Maidens allowed ten pounds. One mile.

No. 3. Trotting—The Los Angeles Purse, $1,500, open to all horses eligible to the 2:30 Class, June 16th. Entrance, ten per cent, payable as follows: $50 June 16th, when entries close; $50 July 1st, and $50 July 22nd, when horses must be named. No subscription will be received unless the first payment shall accompany the same. Subscribers liable only for the amount paid in, but if a subscriber fails to make any of the payments when due, he shall surrender his subscription and payments to the Association with the right of substitution. The Board reserves the right to declare the "Los Angeles Purse" off, in the event of its not filling satisfactorily.

No. 4. Trotting.—Purse $500. 3 minute class. District.

SECOND DAY—TUESDAY AUGUST 5.

No. 5. A sweepstake for two-year-olds owned in the Southern Counties; $25 each, $15 forfeit; $150 added; the second to receive $75 out of the stakes. The winner of any race to carry four pounds extra. One-half (½) mile.

No. 6. The Nadeau Hotel Handicap.—Purse $1,000, of which $700 to the first; $200 to the second, and $100 to the third horse. Weight announced July 22nd. Twenty-five dollars ($25) to nominate, and fifty dollars ($50) each from all starters. The winner of any race after the announcement of the weights to carry five (5) pounds extra. One and one quarter mile.

No. 7. Trotting.—Two-year-old stakes, district, $350 added. See special Condition.

No. 8. Pacing.—Purse $500. 2:30 class. District.

THIRD DAY—WEDNESDAY, AUG. 6TH.

No. 9. Selling Purse—For all ages. $250. Ten Dollars from starters to go to second horse. Fixed valuation $1000; three pounds allowed for each $100 less down to $700; then one pound for $100 down to $300; selling price to be named through the entry box at 5 P. M. the day before the race. Seven-eighths of a mile.

No. 10. Hurdle Race—A sweepstake for all ages; $30 each, half forfeit; $200 added; second horse to receive $75 out of the stakes. Five hurdles—about one and one half miles.

No. 11. Trotting—Three-year-old Stake. District $250 added. See special Conditions.

No. 12. Trotting.—Purse $1000. 2:25 class.

FOURTH DAY—THURSDAY AUG. 7TH.

No. 13. The Hollenbeck Hotel Stakes—A sweepstake for two-year-olds (foals of 1888), $50 each, $25 forfeit; with $300 added, the second to receive $100, and the third $50 out of the stakes. A winner of any stake race before August 1st, to carry three pounds; and two or more stake races, five pounds extra; maidens allowed, if beaten once, five pounds; twice or more, eight pounds. Five-eighths of a mile.

No. 14. The California Handicap.—Purse $1000, of which $700 to the first, $200 to the second, and $100 to the third horse. Weights announced July 22nd. $25 to nominate, and $50 more for all starters. The winner of any race at this meeting to carry five pounds extra. Three-quarters of a mile.

No. 15. Trotting—Purse $1000, 2:27 class.

No. 16. Trotting—Purse $500, 2:40 class; District.

FIFTH DAY—FRIDAY, AUGUST, 8TH.

No. 17. The Sierra Madre Stakes.—A sweepstake for all ages. $25 each, half forfeit; $200 added, second to receive $75 out of the stakes. Winner of any race this year at three quarters (¾) of a mile or less to carry six (6) pounds, and of two or more of such races, ten (10) pounds extra. Maiden allowed ten (10) pounds. One-half (½) mile heats.

No. 18. Santa Catalina Cup.—A sweepstake for all ages, $40 each; $20 forfeit; $300 added; the second to receive $100 out of the stakes. Five pounds above scale. Non-winners in 1889 and 1890 allowed ten (10) pounds. Maidens allowed twelve (12) pounds. A winner at this meeting to carry five pounds extra. One and one-eighth (1⅛) mile.

No. 19. Trotting.—Purse, $1,000, 2:20 class, District.

No. 20. Trotting.—Purse, $500.

SIXTH DAY—SATURDAY, AUG. 9TH.

No. 21. The Citrus Handicap.—A sweepstake for three-year-olds; $40, half forfeit, or only $10 if declared by 5 P. M. the day before the race; $250 added; the second to receive $100 out of the stakes. Weights to be announced by 5 o'clock P. M. second day before the race. One and one-sixteenth (1 1-16) of a mile.

No. 22. The Junior Handicap.—A sweepstake for two-year-olds. $15 each, half forfeit, or only $15 if declared by 5 P. M. the day before the race; $250 added; the second to receive $100, and the third $50 out of the stakes. Weights to be announced by 5 o'clock P. M. the second day before the race. Three-quarters (¾) of a mile.

No. 23. Trotting.—Purse $800, 2:35 class.

No. 24. Pacing.—Purse, $800, 2:25 class.

TROTTING STAKES—To close June 16th, 1890.

To be Trotted at the Annual Fair, to be held in Los Angeles in 1890–91.

TROTTING STAKES, 1890.

FOALS OF 1888. Mile and repeat, $250, added by the Association. Entrance, $50, payable in the following forfeits: $10 to accompany the nomination, $20 July 1st, and $20 August 11, 1890.

FOALS OF 1887. Mile heats, three in five. $250 added by the Association. $50 entrance, payable in the following forfeits; $10 to accompany the nomination, $20 July 1st, and $20 August 11, 1890.

TROTTING STAKES, 1891.

FOALS OF 1889. Mile and repeat. $250 added by the Association. $50 entrance, payable in the following forfeits: $5 to accompany nomination, $10 August 1st, 1890; $10 May 1st, 1891, and $25 on the first day of the Fair of 1891.

FOALS OF 1888. Mile heats, three in five. $250 added by the Association. Entrance, $50, payable in the following forfeits; $5 to accompany the nomination; $10 August 1st, 1890; $10 May 1st, 1891, and $25 on the first day of the Fair of 1891.

CONDITIONS.

All nominations to be made on or before June 16th. American Association rules to govern. Nominators liable only for the amount paid in, which becomes forfeit if subsequent payments are not made. All forfeits and entrance fees will be contributed to the stake, the whole divided where there are three or more starters as follows: sixty per cent. to the first, thirty per cent. to the second and ten per cent. to the third. If no more than two horses start, only first and second money shall be awarded, and in case of a walk over, only the first money shall be awarded. A horse distancing the field shall only be entitled to so much of the money as the starters in the race could have won. A nominator in making an entry in any of the above stakes shall give the name of owner, name of breeder and where foaled, the age, color, sex, dam and sire if known. Colts owned in the counties of San Luis Obispo, Fresno, Tulare, Kern, Santa Barbara, Ventura, Los Angeles, San Bernardino, Orange and San Diego shall be eligible to entry.

REMARKS AND CONDITIONS.

All trotting and pacing races to be to harness, mile heats, best three in five, except otherwise specified. Entrance 10 per cent on amount of purse. Trotting and pacing divided as follows: 50 per cent. to first horse; 25 per cent. to second; 15 per cent. to third, and 10 per cent. to fourth. Entries not declared out by 5 P. M. of the day before the race must start. In all trotting and pacing races, five to enter and three to start. The Board reserves the right to hold a less number than five to fill. Horses owned in Fresno, Tulare, Kern, San Luis Obispo, Santa Barbara, Ventura, Los Angeles, San Bernardino, Orange and San Diego Counties, are eligible for entry in district races. A horse distancing the field is entitled to first and fourth money. The Directors reserve the right to change the hour and day of any race, if deemed necessary. Races shall commence each day at 1 o'clock. American Association rules to govern, unless otherwise specified. Hay and straw free.

Running—The Pacific Coast Blood Horse rules to govern running races. Colonial-bred horses, foaled on Colonial time, allowed as follows: Two and three-year-olds, eight pounds; four-year-olds five pounds, and five-year-olds, three pounds. In all stakes, starters must be named to the Secretary or through the entry box at the track, on or before 5 P. M. of the day before the race. In all stakes, the right to forfeit ceases at 10 o'clock of the day on which the race is run. Racing colors to be named with the entry. Entries close with the Secretary July 1st.

Remember, entries for the 2:30 Trot and District Trotting Stakes close June 16th, and for everything else July 1st.

L. LICHTENBERGER, President.

BEN BENJAMIN, Secretary.

Ontario's Great Jump.

Having gotten away from the officious interference of the Society of the Prevention of Cruelty to Animals, Ontario, Mr. S. S. Howland's remarkable horse, cleverly demonstrated his right to championship honors by jumping seven feet on Saturday afternoon at Washington, and simultaneously establishing a world's record. It is likely to be many a long day ere another horse equals this superb performance.

The bar was first placed at 4 feet 6 inches, and raised four inches at a time until 6 feet 8 inches were reached. Ontario cleared each of the respective heights without effort on the first trial. The bar was then raised to seven feet, and Judge Davis, of the Court of Claims, Col. Carpenter, U. S. A., commander at Fort Meyer, Count Sala of the French Legation, Mr. Sevelyn Brown, Chief Clerk of the State Department, and Mr. Neilson Brown, of Philadelphia, invited to measure it. This they did with a spirit level, and pronounced a full 7 feet. In his first effort Ontario got over in front but pulled off the two top bars. At the second, amid the greatest excitement, with a bound he scored the heretofore considered impossible jump of 7 feet. He was ridden by his usual rider, James Freling, who with his saddle and bridle weighed 159 pounds. The jump was made off the clay floor of the riding academy with a very poor take off and no spring whatever.

All high jumps heretofore have been made off board floors covered with tan bark, which afforded more or less spring

This feat undoubtedly stamps Ontario as the most remarkable jumper the world has ever seen. Under favorable conditions another six inches is within his possibilities: The record of this jump has been attested to in writing by the gentlemen of the committee, whose names are enough to guarantee the performance.—Week's Sport.

The Age of a Horse.

The following, quoted by the Lancet Clinic from the Dublin Farmer's Gazette, is valuable to every one who owns a horse:

The foal is born with twelve grinders. When four front teeth have made their appearance the foal is twelve days old, and when the next four assert themselves its age will be about twenty-eight days. The corner teeth make their appearance when the foal is eight months old, and these latter attain the height of the front teeth at the age of a year. The two-year-olds have the kernel—the dark substance in the middle of the tooth's crown—ground out of all the front teeth. In the third year the middle front of teeth are shifted, and when three years old these are substituted by the permanent (or horse) teeth, which are larger and more yellow than their predecessors. The next teeth are shifted in the fourth year, and the corner teeth in the fifth, giving place to the permanent nippers.

At five years of age a horse has forty teeth, of which twenty-four are grinders, far back in the jaw, with which we have little to do. But, be it remembered, horses invariably have tushes which mares very rarely do. Before the age of six is arrived at the tush is full grown, and has a slight groove on its internal surface (which generally disappears with age, the tusk itself becoming more round and blunt), and at six the kernel or mark is worn out of the middle front teeth. There will still be a difference of color in the center of the tooth.

The tushes have now attained their full growth, being nearly or quite an inch in length, convex without, concave within, tending to a point, and the extremity somewhat curved. Now, or perhaps some months before, the horse may be said to have a perfect mouth.

At seven years the mark, as described, is very nearly worn out of the four center nippers, and fast wearing away in the corner teeth, especially in mares, but the black mark still remains in the center of the tooth, and is not completely filled up until the animal is eight years old. As he gets on past seven the bridle teeth begin to wear away.

At eight the kernel has entirely disappeared from all the lower nippers. It is said to be "past mark of mouth." There are indications, however, after this age which will enable a very shrewd observer to guess very closely at a horse's age, but none that can be relied upon by observers.

CONTRA COSTA CO. Agricultural Associat'n District No. 23.

FAIR OF 1890

Sept. 22 to 27, inclusive.

District Trotting Colt Stakes for 1890.

$40, payable as follows:

$10 June 1st (when stakes close), $15 Sept. 1st, and $15 Sept. 22d.

FOR ONE-YEAR-OLDS, 1 mile dash.
FOR TWO-YEAR-OLDS, mile heats, 2 in 3
FOR 3-YEAR-OLDS, mile heats, 3 in 5.
} $75 added to each.

All moneys divided as follows: 50, 30 and 10 per cent. In case of only two starting, 60 and 40 per cent., and in case of one horse walking over, the whole amount to go to such horse.

A failure to make any payment when due shall be considered a withdrawal and forfeiture of the amount paid in.

National Rules to govern.

The right reserved to refund the first payment in case the stakes do not fill reasonably well.

Entries close June 1, 1890 with the Secretary.

GEO. P. LOUCKS, President.

H. C. RAAP, Secretary, Martinez, Cal.

Bay Rose.

REGISTERED No. 9814.

Record 2:20 1-2 Third Heat.

Will make the season of 1890, ending July 1st, at the SANTA ROSA STOCK FARM, (formerly Santa Rosa Race Track), SANTA ROSA.

DESCRIPTION.

BAY ROSE is a dark bay or brown, with black points, 15¾ hands high, and weighs 1150 pounds. He is remarkably intelligent, of good disposition, and a pure-gaited trotter. He was foaled in 1881. His colts are large, stylish, rangy animals, and inherit the qualities of speed and endurance.

PEDIGREE.

BAY ROSE 9814
- Sultan, 2:24. Sire of 10 in the 2:30 list.
  - The Moor 870, SIRE OF Beautiful Bells 2:29½, Del Sur 2:24½, Ines 2:30, Sir Guy 2:28¼, Sultan 2:24, Tommy Gates 2:24
  - Sultana.
- Madam Baldwin
  - The Moor 870, Sire of 6 in the 2:30 list.
  - by Ben Lippincott, by Williamson's Belmont.

TERMS: $200 FOR THE SEASON.

Good pasturage $3 per month. First-class care taken of mares in any manner that owners may desire, but no responsibility assumed for escapes or accidents. Limited to a few approved mares. For further particulars, address

THOS. BONNER,
Santa Rosa Stock Farm, Santa Rosa.

Or apply to
IRA PIERCE,
728 Montgomery Street, S. F., Cal.

The Trotting Stallion

G & M

FULL BROTHER TO

ALFRED G, 2:19¾.

(Who has been taken to Kentucky to stand at $200)

Will make the season of 1890 from FEBRUARY 1st to JULY 1st, at

SANTA ROSA.

G. & M. is by Anteeo, 2:16¼; was foaled 1886; first dam Rosa B. by Speculation (son of Hambletonian 10); 2d dam Elizabeth by Alexander 490; 3d dam Nora by imp. Glencoe. Anteeo is by Electioneer, out of Columbine by A. W. Richmond 1687.

G. & M. is a handsome dark bay; stands 15-2 1-2 hands high, and weighs 1060 pounds. Gameness, stoutness, speed and stamina are indelibly impressed in every line of the pedigree of G. & M. Owners of broodmares in search of these qualities, will do well to patronize this promising colt.

PHILOSOPHER,

Foaled 1888 by Pilot Wilkes 2987; first dam Bella by George Wilkes 519; second dam by Bell Morgan 61.

Philosopher's sire, Pilot Wilkes 2987, is by George Wilkes 519, dam Grace (the dam of Alice Woodburn etc.), by Pilot Jr. 12, grandam by Orphan Boy.

Will make the season of 1890, from FEBRUARY 1st to JULY 1st, at Santa Rosa.

TERMS for the season:

G. & M., $50,
PHILOSOPHER, $30,

with privilege of returning mares that do not prove in foal the next season free of charge, provided the horse bred to remains the property of the present owners. Good pasturage at $3 per month. No responsibility assumed for accidents or escapes. Service fees payable before removal of the mare. For further particulars, address

GEO. E. GUERNE,
Santa Rosa, Cal.

$1,000.

The Pacific Coast Trotting-Horse Breeders' Ass'n.

Fall Meeting 1890.

Offer an Additional

Nomination Pacing Purse

$1,000 for 2:20 class. Mile heats, best three in five. Entrance $100, payable $20 June 10, 1890, $20 July 1, 1890, $20 August 1, 1890, and $40 on the tenth day preceding the first advertised day of the meeting. Horses to be named at time of last payment.

Entries to close with the Secretary June 10, 1890.

Conditions.

First payment MUST ACCOMPANY NOMINATIONS, or they will not be considered.

Neglect to make payments on the day stipulated will incur forfeiture of all previous payments.

No horses and Colts owned on the Pacific Coast by others than members of the P. C. T. H. B. A. are eligible to the above purse, but horses and Colts OWNED outside of the Pacific Coast are eligible thereto regardless of membership.

All States and Territories lying in whole or in part west of the Rocky Mountains are held to be part of the Pacific Coast.

The Directors reserve the right to change the hour and day of any race except when it becomes necessary to antedate a race, in which instance the nominator will receive three days notice of change by mail to address of entry.

Entries not declared out by 6 P. M. of the day preceding the race, shall be required to start.

This Purse will be divided into four moneys, viz., 50 per cent. to the winner, 25 per cent to the second horse, 15 per cent. to the third horse, and 10 per cent. to the fourth horse.

A horse distancing the field shall only be entitled to first and third moneys.

The Board of Directors reserve the right to declare any purse or stake filled or not filled without binding itself to any specified number of entries.

In all nomination purses, eight entries will be required to fill, and four to make the last payment.

Trotting and racing colors shall be named by 5 o'clock on the day preceding the race, and MUST be worn upon the track.

Horses eligible on records standing at time of entry.

Otherwise than the above National Trotting Association Rules will govern.

Persons desirous of making entries in the above purse, and who have not as yet joined the P. C. T. H. B. A., should make application for membership to the Secretary, and remit the sum of $25 to cover membership fee before June 10, 1890.

J. H. WHITE, President,

JAS. P. KERR, Secretary, 313 Bush Street, S. F.

GEO. WASHINGTON.

11,623.

RECORD 2:30.

Bay Colt, bred by Thomas Smith of Vallejo, Cal. Foaled 1886 by Mambrino Chief, Jr., 11,622, record 2:34 1-2, 1st dam Fanny Rose by Vick's Ethan Allen Jr, 2,903, sire of Prince Allen 2:27. 2nd dam Jenny Lind, thoroughbred, dam of Prince Allen 2:27. Will serve a limited number of mares at $50 for the season. Mares not proving with foal may be returned next season free.

Mambrino Chief, Jr.

11,622.

RECORD 2:34 1 2.

Sire of George Washington, record 2:30 at three years old. Bay horse bred by Rufus Ingalls of Belvedere, Ill. By McDonald Chief 3583. First dam Venus by Mambrino Patchen 58. 2nd dam by Wardlow's Shakespeare. 3rd dam Lone Gold. 4th dam by Silver Heels. Has not been in the stud before. He was 5 years old when he served a few mares, and his colts all show good style and form.

Terms for the season $40. For further particulars see or address

THOMAS SMITH,
Vallejo, Cal.

Langtry Farms' Stud

Imp. FRIAR TUCK

By the Immortal HERMIT.

DAM ROMPING GIRL BY WILD DAYRELL.

AT $50 THE SEASON.

Mares not proving with foal may be returned the following season. Good care taken of mares, but no liabilities for accidents or escapes.

Good Pasturage at $5 per month.

Mares shipped to ST. HELENA, care CHARLES WILLIAM ABY, St. Helena Stables, will be cared for. For further particulars address,

CHAS. WILLIAM ABY,
Middletown, Lake County, Cal.

Guaranteed Purses

—Given by the—

San Mateo AND Santa Clara Co. AGRICULTURAL ASSOCIATION No. 5, SAN JOSE, CAL.

Fall Meeting, 1890,

August 11th to 15th.

Trotting Purse, $1,200, 3-Minute Class.
Trotting Purse, $1,200, 2:30 Class.

Entrance fee 10 per cent., payable as follows: $10 on June 1st, when entries close; $10 on July 1st, and $40 on August 1st.

Pacing Purse, $600, 2:30 Class.

Entrance fee 10 per cent., payable as follows: $20 on June 1st, when entries close; $20 on July 1st, and $20 on August 1st.

CONDITIONS.

Mile heats, three in five. Money must accompany nominations, otherwise the entry will not be considered. Neglect to make payments when due forfeits previous payments.

Eight entries required to fill, four to make last payment and three to start.

Purse will be divided, 50 per cent. to first horse, 25 per cent. to second 15 per cent. to third, and 10 per cent. to fourth. A horse distancing the field will get the 1st and 3rd money.

In case of a walk-over the horse will get the entrance money paid in only; otherwise National Trotting Association rules to govern.

WM. BUCKLEY, President,

G. H. BRAGG, Secretary.

The Thoroughbred Stallion

Three Cheers

Will make the season of 1890 at

Sacramento.

PEDIGREE.

THREE CHEERS
- imp. Hurrah
  - Newminster
    - Touchstone, by Camel
    - Beeswing, by Dr. Syntax
  - Jovial
    - Bay Middleton, by Sultan
    - Sister to Grey Momus, by Comus
- Young Fashion
  - imp. Monarch
    - imp. Priam, by Emilius
    - imp. Delphine, by Whisker
  - Fashion
    - imp. Trustee, by Catton
    - Bonnets o' Blue, by Sir Charles

Hurrah was imported by John Reber, of Lancaster, Ohio, a locality where there were but few breeders of thoroughbreds. Under these disadvantages he sired a long list of winners. His sire Newminster, won the St. Ledger 1851, and his dam, Jovial by Bay Middleton, winner of the Derby 1836. Newminster by Touchstone, winner St. Ledger 1834. Dam Beeswing, winner of 54 races out of 64 starts, by Dr. Syntax, winner of the Doncaster Cup, 1837—40—41—42, the only horse that ever accomplished that feat.

On the side of the dam Three Cheers is equally well related. Young Fashion was the dam of Surprise, Scotland (the only horse that ever beat Asteroid a heat), Liverpool, Columbia, and Bonnie Kate, the dam of Little Buttercup, and the flying Bonnie Lizzie. His grandam, Fashion was the greatest race mare of her day and beat Boston in that historical match at four mile heats, which is recorded as one of the greatest events in the annals of the turf.

Horsemen who are qualified to judge, pronounce Three Cheers to be the finest type of the Newminster line in America.

LOCATION.

THREE CHEERS will be located at the Arcade Training Stable, Rancho del Paso. This place has been selected for the reason that first class pasturage has been secured there for the exclusive use of these mares, and the other facilities to be obtained there for the care of mares (especially mares in foal) are better than can be found elsewhere in the locality.

TERMS.

$60 for the season with the usual return privileges. Pasturage $5 per month. Mares cared for as owners may desire at bottom rates for grain and hay. All bills payable before the mare is removed.

Mares shipped care of WM. IRVINE, Pacific Stables, Sacramento, will be properly cared for and sent to the ranch without delay.

Three Cheers will be in charge of one of the most experienced and competent stud grooms in the State, who will exercise every care, but no reponsibility assumed for accidents or escapes.

For further particulars apply to Louis Crissler, at the ranch; Wm. Irvine, Pacific Stables, Second St., Sacramento; or to the owner,

E. S. CULVER,
313 Bush St., San Francisco.

Highland Farm,

LEXINGTON, KY.,

Home of Red Wilkes.

Standard-bred Trotting Stock

For Sale,

Sired by Red Wilkes, Wilton, 2:19¼; Allandorf and Sentinel Wilkes, out of highly bred Standard Mares of the most fashionable blood of the day.

W. C. FRANCE, Proprietor.

Races, Races,

JULY WEEK.

AT

South Park Race Track Eureka, Cal.

GIVEN BY THE

EUREKA JOCKEY CLUB.

FIRST DAY, JULY 2, 1890.

No. 1. Novelty Running Race. Free for all. Dash of one mile. Purse $250. First quarter, $40. Half, $50. Third quarter, $70. Mile, $90.

No. 2. Running Race. Purse $150. Five-eighths dash for two-year-olds. $125 to first horse; $25 to second horse.

No. 3. Running. Purse $150. Three-quarters and repeat. $125 to first; $25 to second.

SECOND DAY, JULY 3, 1890.

No. 4. Trotting. Purse $200. Three minute Class. $150 to first; $50 to second. (Covey barred.)

No. 5. Running Stake. Five-eighths of a mile. For Humboldt raised two year-olds. $30 entrance, half forfeit. $150 added. First to receive 60 per cent.; second, 30 per cent., third, 10 per cent.

No. 6. Running Stake. Purse $200. Mile Dash. $150 to first horse; $50 to second horse.

THIRD DAY, JULY 4, 1890.

No. 7. Trotting Stake. 2:40 Class. Purse $250. $200 to first horse; $50 to second horse.

No. 8. Running Stake, 1¼ miles. Free-for-all. $40 entrance. ½ forfeit, $200 added; second horse $75, third horse to save stake.

No. 9. Running Stake. Purse $150; 1-2 mile and repeat; $125 to first; $25 to second.

FOURTH DAY, JULY 5, 1890.

No. 10. Running Stake, 1-2 mile and repeat; for Humboldt horses owned prior to Jan. 1, 1890. $125 to first, $25 to second.

No. 11. Running Stake. Purse $200; 7-8 mile and repeat. $150 to first. $50 to second.

CONDITIONS AND REMARKS.

All trotting races are best three in five, unless otherwise specified. Four to enter and three to start, but the Board reserves the right to hold a less number than four to fill by the withdrawal of a proportionate amount of the purse. Entrance fee, 10 per cent. of purse, to accompany nominations. In all trotting races the rules of the American Trotting Association, and all running races the rules of the Pacific Coast Blood Horse Association to govern, but the Board reserves the right to trot heats of any two classes alternately, if necessary, to finish any day's racing. In all entries not declared out by 6 P. M. of the day preceding the race, shall be required to start.

No added money paid for a walk over. In all races, four or more paid up entries required to fill, and three or more horses to start. Racing colors to be named in entries. In trotting races drivers will be required to wear caps of distinct colors to be named in entries. Entries in all races to close with the Secretary, Thursday, June 20, 1890. Entry blanks will be furnished upon application to the Secretary.

All trotting races for horses owned and in Humboldt County prior to June 1, 1890.

H. M. DEVOY, President.

J. P. MONROE, Secretary.

SONOMA and MARIN Futurity Stake,

To take place during the

FALL MEETING

OF THE

Sonoma and Marin Agricultural Society,

1893.

For Foals of 1890.

Open to the get of stallions owned in the district which is comprised of the following counties: Sonoma, Marin, Napa, Lake, Mendocino, Solano, Yolo, Colusa and Contra Costa.

Mile heats, 3 in 5; entrance $75, with $25 added for each starter over two and up to five head, and $10 for each additional starter up to ten head.

Payments: $5 must accompany the nomination on July 1, 1890; $5 on January 2, 1891; $5 on July 1, 1891; $10 on January 2, 1892; $10 on July 1, 1892; $15 on January 2, 1893; $25 on July 1, 1893.

CONDITIONS.

1—Neglect to provide payments on the dates stipulated will incur forfeiture of all previous payments.

2—When there is more than one entry to this stake by one person or in one interest, the horse to be started must be named by 6 P. M. of the day preceding the race.

3. The stake will be divided into four moneys, viz., 50 per cent. to the first, 25 per cent to the second, 15 per cent. to the third and 10 per cent. to the fourth horse.

4. If only three horses start in this stake, only the first, second and third money shall be paid; if but two start, there will be no added money, the stake money paid in will be divided—two-thirds to the first and one third to the second horse.

5. A horse distancing the field shall only be entitled to first and third moneys.

6. The Board of Directors reserve the right to declare the stake filled or not filled without binding itself to any specified number of entries.

7. Otherwise than the above, National or American Trotting Association Rules—as this Society may select—will govern the stake.

Entries to close on July 1st with the Secretary.

J. H. WHITE, President,

DR. THOMAS MACLAY, Secretary, Petaluma.

Memo.

The Best Son of SIDNEY

Will Make the Season of 1890 at the OAKLAND RACE TRACK

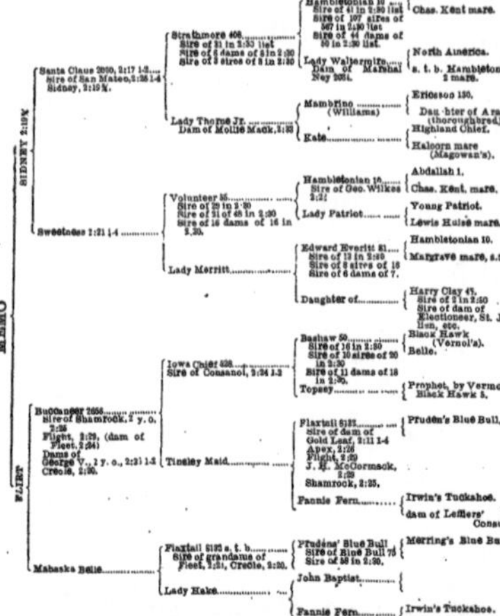

MEMO is, as can be seen at a glance, one of the best bred young stallions in service, having three crosses of Rysdyk's Hambletonian and one of Harry Clay, the sire of Green Mountain Maid (dam of Electioneer, etc.), while Long Island Black Hawk and Flaxtail also contribute to his blood. Sidney (Memo's sire) is universally known as the best young sire in the world, a producer of extreme speed at an early age.

PERFORMANCES.

MEMO trotted in public in his two year-old form, obtaining a record of 2:49, though he was close to Grandee in a race on the Bay District Track, the second heat of which was made in 2:31 1-2, the first in 2:32. He exhibited phenomenal speed when three years old, and had it not been for a slight strain of his fore fetlock, there is little question that he would have shown in public very close to the best record. On the Oakland track he was timed a mile in 2:30 1-2, and frequently trotted quarters in from 33 1-2 to 34 seconds.

As a four-year-old Memo only started once - at Sacramento - when, although out of condition, he showed great speed, and improving as he went on, great hopes were entertained of his going well down in the 'teens at the P. C. T. H. B. A. meeting, but after showing several very fast miles his leg filled and he was laid up for the season. He is sixteen hands high, and of powerful build throughout. His color is a glossy black, with both fore-feet white. His disposition is all that could be desired, and his action superb. He is a sure foal getter, only one mare being reported not in foal during his last season.

TERMS, $100, with usual return privileges, for a limited number of mares. Season to close JUNE 15th, when he will be prepared for track purposes. Pasturage $4 per month. Have leased the cricket ground adjoining the track for pasturage, where there is fine feed. Reasonable charges if fed hay and grain. Best of care taken of mares in any manner owners may desire, but positively no responsibility assumed for accidents or escapes. For further particulars address

J. P. KERR, 313 Bush Street, San Francisco,

or, JOHN ROWEN, Race Track, Oakland, Cal.

2:10 1-2 ELECTIONEER 2:12 1-4

BAY STALLION	BROWN STALLION
ECLECTIC	**MORTIMER**
11,321	5,346
By Electioneer, dam Manette (full sister to Woodnut 2.16 1-2 Manon 2:21 and Maple, dam of Hattie D., three-year-old record 2:26½) by Nutwood 2:18¾, etc., etc.	Four-year-old Record 2:27. By ELECTIONEER, dam MARTI, by Whipple's Hambletonian (sire of 15 in 2:30, and of dams of eight in 2:30). Second dam Ida Martin by Rifleman (sire of Col. Lewis 2:18¾).
Terms $100 for the Season.	Terms $60 for the Season.

Horses shipped via San Francisco may be consigned to J. W. MORSHEAD, City Front Stables, who will attend to their forwarding.

Season closes JULY 1st, 18 Usual return privileges.

For further particulars address owner,

WILFRED PAGE, Penns Grove,
Sonoma County, Cal

The Trotting Stallion

Silver Bow

Will make the season of 1890 at the Oakland Race Track.

PEDIGREE.

SILVER BOW 11708, two-year-old record 2:37, is by Robert McGregor 647, 2:17½ (sire of Bonnie McGregor, 2:13½, Earl McGregor, 2:21½, Mac D., 2:20, McGregor Boy, 2:29½, Mark Time, 2:30, Roxie McGregor, 2:30½) by Major Edsall 2:1, 2:29, by Alexander's Abdallah 15—sire of Goldsmith Maid, 2:14—by Hambletonian 10—sire of Dexter, 2:17¼.

Robert McGregor's dam was Nancy Whitman by American Star 14, by Stockholm's American Star.

SILVER BOW's first dam is Sadie by Hambletonian 10, sire of Geo. Wilkes, 2:22—sire of Guy Wilkes, 2:15¼—also Electioneer, sire of Sunol, three-year-old record, 2:10½, and Palo Alto, 2:12¾; second dam Lady Wynne by Wm. Welch 241; third dam Elenora Margrave by imp. Margrave.

DESCRIPTION.

SILVER BOW is a handsome bay, no white; 15-2¾ hands high; weighs 1075 pounds; of fine form, with the best of legs and a clean-cut, intelligent head. Is remarkably level-headed, seldom making a break; wears seven-ounce shoes in front. His record, 2:37, is no mark of his speed; he can beat 30 easy, and with his gilt-edge breeding, he is just what he ought to be, a trotter sired by a trotter whose dam was herself a trotter and his grandam the dam of two trotters. His dam Sadie being by Hambletonian 10, shows him to be bred from the cream of the trotting blood.

TERMS: $100 for the season. Mares not proving in foal returnable for the season of 1891 free of charge. Good pasturage and first-class care taken of mares for $5 per month. No responsibilities assumed for escapes or accidents. For further particulars, address

Limited to 15 approved mares.
Season to end June 1st, 1890.

P. J. WILLIAMS,
Care Race Track, Oakland, Cal.

Pleasanton Stock Farm Co.'s Stallions,

DIRECTOR, 2:17.

Director's book is open for 15 good mares more than already booked for the season of 1890, at each.

This is the cheapest service fee ever charged for a stallion, taking into consideration his BREED and RACE RECORD and the RACE RECORDS OF HIS COLTS.

Season to Commence February 15th and Close August 1st.

CORRECTOR, Five Years Old.

Sire Director 2:17, dam Brainey, she by Echo, Echo sired by Rysdyk's Hambletonian, out of Fa Felter, by Magnolia, he by Seely's American Star. Brainey's dam Lady Dudley, she by Tom Dudley Blacknose, a son of Medoc, he by American Eclipse. Lady Dudley's dam by Bertrand, Jr., a son of Bertr

CORRECTOR is a rich seal brown 15½ hands high, and is the fastest young stallion in the world u the same conditions, never having been off the farm where raised and never been shod or driven speed before last Christmas, and can trot quarters now in 36 seconds, a 2:20 gait.

He will be allowed to serve ten good mares, at $100 each for the season, which closes June 1st.

DECORATOR, Four Years Old.

Sire Director 2:17, dam Chess, sired by Cardinal 2.37, trial 2:28, he by Gen. Gifford's Morgan, dan Cardinal, sired by Joe Gales of Ohio, he by Marlborough out of the Duchess of Marlborough by Sout Eclipse; second dam old Duchess of Marlborough by Sir Archy; third dam by imp Diomed. Decorat second dam a Morgan and Messenger mare.

Decorator is a light bay 16 hands high, and with but little handling for speed has shown eighth 17½ seconds, a 2:20 gait.

He will be allowed to serve ten good mares at $60 each for the season, which closes June 1st.

Mares not proving with foal may be returned next season free of charge of service fees to the s stallion, if he is still in our possession; however, the company reserves the right to return the fee inst of giving service.

Pasturage $4 per month; hay and grain extra. Accidents and escapes at owner's risk.

Service fees due at time of service, and must be paid, together with pasturage, etc., before mares taken away, or a good approved note given, payable August 1st, 1890, at which date all bills must settled.

For further information call or address M. SALISBURY, 320 Sansome Street, Room San Francisco, or

PLEASANTON STOCK FARM CO.,
Pleasanton, Alameda Co., Cal

SOUTHER FARM

P. O. Box 208. San Leandro, Ca

1½ miles northwest of San Leandro; 8 miles southeast of Oakland. Turn off County road between above places at "Stanley Road," ¼ mile north of San Leandro.

Horses boarded at all times in any man desired. Best of care but no responsibility accidents. Colts broken and handled for road or track. Terms reasonable.

Glen Fortune,	Jester D,	El Benton,	Figaro,
By Electioneer.	By Almont.	By Electioneer.	Hambletonian
$50 for 1889.	$50 for 1890.	Limited to 5 mares.	Limited to 12 ma
		Book Full.	Book Full.

THE SOUTHER FARM

Has Green Feed the Year Round

and feeds Hay in connection with the green feed, which a hor must have if he is to thrive. Every animal is given

A Dry, Warm Place to Sleep,

No matter how stormy the weather, All Stock under cover when it rains.

VISITORS WELCOME ANY DAY EXCEPT SUNDAY.

How to Get Stock to the Souther Farm.

The Souther Farm is one and a half miles northeast of San Leandro and eight miles southeast of O land. The stables are about one mile east of the county road, which runs between Oakland and San Le dro. The place to turn off is at Stanley Road, where a large signboard of the farm is placed. Guide bo will be found at every cross road. In any ordinary weather the roads are very good, and they are fairly g after the unusually heavy rainfall of the past winter.

All stock sent from San Francisco may be brought over by Garcia's Express, No. 3 Market street, Francisco. They also have an order box outside of Hawley Bros.' Hardware house on the corner of Mar and Beale streets. The express leaves San Francisco on the Creek route boat, which starts at 1:30, but orders should be in the order box at Market and Beale streets by 10 o'clock, or at the office, No. 3 Mar street, by 11 o'clock at the latest. In the case of very young or very valuable horses, the Souther Farm send reliable men to lead or drive over any stock that will not lead behind a wagon. A small charge will made in such cases, to cover the extra expense incurred.

Horses are very easily taken from Oakland to the farm, and where it is inconvenient for owners bring them or send them, the farm will send after anything that is to come. On horses that stay th months or over there is no charge for getting or delivering. Where a horse stays a short time the act time and expense only is charged to him.

Horses can be shipped by rail from almost all parts of the State to San Leandro. Always notify Farm several days before shipping anything, and then men will be on hand to receive stock on arrival. railroad station is but two miles from the Souther Farm, and the agent invariably gives immediate not of the arrival of any stock consigned to the above farm, but when word is sent to the farm in good sea by letter or telegram, the animals sent are saved waiting a couple of hours in the car.

Passenger trains leave San Francisco (from the broad gauge ferry) and First and Broadway, Oakla at frequent intervals during the day. There are several trains from San Jose to San Leandro on both broad and narrow gauge railroads; the broad gauge, by way of Niles, is much more convenient for get ina the farm. There are trains each day from Sacramento, Stockton and Livermore to San Leandro. In o nary weather it is a short and pleasant drive from Oakland to the Souther Farm or from San Francisco the Farm by way of the Creek route ferry boat. Always notify the Souther Farm just when you will arr at San Leandro, and some one will meet you at the station. If you do not recognize the farm conveyance the stage driver, who will point it out.

Write to the above address for references, circulars and price lists. Terr reasonable.

GILBERT TOMPKINS, Proprietor.

SANMATEO STOCKFARM

HOME OF GUY WILKES,

Record, 2:15 1-4.

Guy Wilkes' Book is full for 1890 and 1891, and positively no mo mares will be received.

Sable Wilkes, three-year-old record 2:18, will be allowed to serve mares in addition to those already engaged at $250 t season of 1890. SABLE Wilkes, 15½ hands, black horse, by Guy Wilkes, first dam Sable The Moor; second dam Gretchen by Mambrino Pilot; third dam Kitty Kirkman by Cana Chief; fourth dam by Fanning's Tobe; fifth dam by imp. Leviathan.

Leo Wilkes, brown horse, four years, 16 hands, full brother to Sab Wilkes, will be allowed to serve 30 mares at $100 the seas

Mares not proving with foal may be returned the following season free of service fee. Pa ties engaging the services of any of the above horses must send a deposit of 10 per cent. service money with engagement. Pasturage $6 per month, and when the condition of t animal requires it, hay or grain, or both, are fed, the charge will be $12 50 per mont Good care will be taken of all mares sent to the Farm, but no liability will be assumed f accidents or escapes.

All bills are due at time of service, but must be paid by August 1st of each year. No sto will be allowed to leave the place until all bills are paid.

WILLIAM CORBITT.
San Mateo Stock Farm.

inelandStock Farm

Alcona 730.

Sire of

ORA BELLE - - - Record 2:24
AY DUKE - - - - - " 2:31½

LCONA will be a great sire, but four of his colts e ever been trained, and all have shown full miles er than 2:3½, and two of them as good as 2:30. Two is first sons each sired a colt as a two-year-old, last season one as a four-year-old trotted a full in 2:23¼, and the other, a three-year-old, a mile 31. With opportunities, Alcona is destined to be of Almont's best sons. Almont, for his opportu-es, is beyond doubt the most prepotent sire of his He has 36 representatives in the 2:30 list; 46 sons 22 daughters that have already produced 2:30 per-mers. Almont died five years ago at 20 years old, s lived he would be but 26 years old.

PEDIGREE.

LCONA sired by the great Almont (sire of West-t 2:13¾, Fanny Witherspoon 2:16¼, Piedmont ¼, and 35 others with records better than 2:30, and ndsire of Belle Hamlin 2:12¾, etc.); by Alexander's allah (sire of Goldsmith Maid 2:14), he by Rys-'s Hambletonian. Alcona's dam, Queen Mary, Mambrino Chief (sire of Lady Thorne 2:18 1-4, and here in the 2:30 list, and sire of the dams of Direc-2:17, Piedmont 2:17¼, Onward 2:25 1-4, Red Wilkes mont, Belmont and many other noted sires).

DESCRIPTION.

lcona is a beautiful chestnut 16 3 1-2 hands high, and ighs 1200 lbs. His colts possess speed, style, finish beauty, and if they don't trot they command the hest prices for carriage horses.
) for the season. Usual return privilege.
ason of Alcona and Grandissimo ends July 1st,
8.

Grandissimo,

ull Brother to GRANDEE, 3-year old record 2:23 1-2.

red by La Grande (son of Almont, and out of Jes-Pepper by Mambrino Chief; Jessie Pepper is the of Ione 2:17 1-2, Alpha 2:23 1-2, Sterling Wilkes ¾, and others) dam Norma, by Arthurton (sire of b 2:15, Joe Arthurton 2 2[illegible] 1-2, etc.) randam Nourmahal, (full sister to A. W. Rich-d, sire of Arrow 2:13¾, Romero 2:19, and sire of mbine, dam of Anteeo 2:16¼, and Antevolo 2:19¼ ur years old).

DESCRIPTION.

randissimo is four years old, will make a sixteen d horse; he is a rich mahogany bay in color and ect in style and action. $50 for the season. al return privileges.
randissimo" with limited training last fall as a e-year-old, trotted quarters in 35 seconds and s in 2:40.
feel confident that he will trot fast this season, will be a great sire as his colts this season are rand youngsters.
e best of pasturage $4 per month. Mares taken of in any manner that owners may desire, but esponsibility assured for escapes or accidents.
r further particulars send for circular or call at les, one mile south of St. Helena.

FRED W. LOEBER Prop'r.

The Trotting Stallion

VICTOR,

Record 2:22.

ll make the season of 1890 at NAPA CITY.

DESCRIPTION.

ICTOR is a handsome dark bay; 15.3 hands high; ghs about 1,150 pounds, and is remarkably intelli, level-headed, of kind disposition, and a magnifi-t animal in every respect. He is well boned and cled, of splendid conformation, and possesses the lities of speed and endurance to an eminent ree—qualities that he imparts to his progeny.

PEDIGREE.

Echo 462 — Hambletonian 10 (Sire of 42 in the 2:30 list.): Abdallah 1; Chas. Kent mare. Fanny Felter: Magnolia 88; by Webber's Kentucky Whip.
Daughter of — Woodburn: Lexington; Lulu Horton. daughter of: Ashland; thoroughbred.

CHO is the sire of Belle Echo, 2:20, Senator, 2:21¼, tor, 2:22, Gibraltar, 2:22¼, Echora, 2:23¼, Tippie, ¾, Lohengrin, 2:27¼, Pasha, 2:27¾, Kimonte, 2:29, Hawkins, 2:29¼, Annie Laurie, 2:30, Economy, ham Lewis, pacer, 2:2[illegible].

TERMS—$60 FOR THE SEASON.

ares not proving with foal may be returned next son free of charge, provided the horse remains the perty of the present proprietor, and stands at the e place, otherwise money will be refunded. The of care taken of mares in any manner that own-may desire, but no responsibility assumed for idents or escapes. For further particulars, apply r address

G. W. HUGHES, Agent,
A. DOHERTY, Proprietor. Napa City.

The Trotting-Bred Stallion

RINGWOOD

THE FINEST SON OF THE NOTED SIDNEY,

ill make a Season at Oakland, commencing March 1, and ending June 1, 1890.

DESCRIPTION.

INGWOOD is a dark, rich colored bay, black nts, 15 1-2 hands, weight 1100 lbs., and a pure gaited ter. Has shown great speed. He is now five rs old. As a four year old he showed a trial in 2:19 and but for an accident would have received a rec-as a four year old of 2:18 or better.

PEDIGREE.

INGWOOD is by Sidney, record 2:19 3-4, and 's half ther to Gold Leaf 2:11 1-4, Adonis 2:14, Fleet (two r old) 2:24, Longworth 2:19, Sister V. 2:21, Faustino, rling, 2:35, Fleet, yearling, 2:35 Memo, three year trial 2:2[illegible] 1-2.
dney is by Santa Claus, record 2:17 1-2; he by thmore, sire of 31 in 2:30 list; he by Hambletonian he greatest of all producers; he by Abdallah. Sid-'s dam, Sweetness, record 2:21 1-4; she by Volun-, the sire of St. Julien 2:11 1-4.
INGWOOD'S dam Alma; she by Dashway, thor-hbred; he by Belmont, he by American Boy; he ea Gull; he by imported Expedition. Alma's 1st , Fanny Cobb, was a great road mare, pedigree raced.

TERMS; $50 for the Season.

yable June 1st, or sooner if mares are taken away dress communications to

A. C. DIETZ,
Oakland, Cal.

2:10¾ 2:13¾ 2:10

DEXTER PRINCE.

This Royally-bred Stallion will make the Season of 1890 at the LIVE OAKS Breeding Farm, 2 miles from Lodi, San Joaquin County, Cal.

DESCRIPTION.

DEXTER PRINCE is a blood bay, 16 hands high, weighs over 1,100 pounds; has great power and substance, and the highest finish. When two years old, at Palo Alto, he was timed quarters by Gov. Stanford in 33½ seconds, and he was driven eights by Mr. Marvin at a faster rate of speed than that. He is a sure foal-getter, and invariably sires foals of good size, of fine form and finish, and the highest rate of speed.

PEDIGREE.

By KENTUCKY PRINCE, the sire of Guy, 2:10¾, Spofford, 2:18¾, Company, 2:19¾, Bayonne Prince, 2:21 1-4, Fred Folger, 2:20¾, and a score more in the 2:30 list.
First dam LADY DEXTER, full sister of the greatest of trotters, Dexter, and the greatest of sires, Dictator, the sire of Director, 2:17, Phallas, 2:13¾, in a fourth heat, and Jay-Eye-See, 2:10.
Second dam Clara, the dam of Dexter, 2:17 1-4, Dicta or, Astoria 2:29 1-4, and Almah, 2:29¾. Clara was by American Star, that has 34 daughters that have produced 2:30 or better trotters.
Third dam the McKinstry mare, the dam of Shark, 2:27¾. HAMBLETONIAN, the grandsire of DEXTER PRINCE, has 40 trotters in the 2:30 list, 44 daughters that have produced 2:30 trotters, and more than 100 sons that have sired 2:30 trotters.
CLARK CHIEF, the grandsire on the sire's side, was the sire of performing and producing sons and daughters.
DEXTER PRINCE has faster blood lines, on both sides, than any other stallion in the world—Guy 2:10¾, and Jay-Eye-See, 2:10.
KENTUCKY PRINCE is one of the best bred and speediest stallions in the world. David Bonner, in the presence of Governor Stanford, timed him when he trotted a 2:10 gait. He is by Clark Chief, one of the great broodmare sires; his first dam is Kentucky Queen by Morgan Eagle, son of Hale's Green Mountain Morgan, 2nd dam by Blythe's Whip, 3rd dam by Martin's Brummier, 4th dam by Quicksilver 880, on through the strongest thoroughbred blood.

TERMS.

$100 for the season, with usual return privileges. Payable before mares are removed. Good pasture, and the best care furnished, but no responsibility assumed for accidents.

PREMIUM.

$250 will be given to the first of the produce of DEXTER PRINCE put in the 2:30 list; and $100 each after the first. Address

L. M. MORSE, Lodi, Cal.

The Produce of Eros Averaged $2,200 Each at New York Auction Sale in 1889.

THE ELECTIONEER TROTTING STALLION,

5326 EROS 5326

Will make the season of 1890—February 1st to July 1st—at LA SIESTA RANCH, MENLO PARK, adjoining Palo Alto.

PEDIGREE.

These are the only colts by him that have ever had a harness on except one in New York that went a trial last July in 2:26 1-2.

DESCRIPTION.

EROS is a rich seal brown stallion, bred by Hon. Leland Stanford at Palo Alto, and is the nearest living likeness of his celebrated sire, Electioneer. Stands 15.2 hands high, and weighs 1060 pounds

In breeding to Eros, the owners of mares will strictly follow the great rule of breeding, viz., breed to a stallion by a producer and out of a sure producer of great speed. Eros is by the stallion that has produced more 2:30 trotters that any living horse, and is also the sire of more 2:20 performers than any horse living or dead.

EROS is out of the dam of Sally Benton, four years old, record 2:17¾, Sport 2:22¾, and Eros 2:29½ in the sixth heat, against a field of nine horses. He is from a family that is endowed with great natural speed, trot fast at an early age, train on, throw trotters from all classes of mares, are of good substance, bone, style and action, and breed solid colors.

TERMS.

$100 for the season, with the privilege of return next season should mares not be in foal and horse and mare still remain in the same hands.

Good pasturage can be obtained at $5 per month, but no responsibility for accidents or escapes. There are a large number of box stalls, and animals can be kept up and fed on hay and grain at reasonable rates if required. Mares already in foal can be sent to the ranch for foaling, and will receive all the attention bestowed upon our own mares. Mares left with Mr. Peter Pomyea, Broadway Street Stable, Oakland, or with Mr. F. H. Burke, 401 Montgomery Street, San Francisco, will be forwarded to the ranch free of charge. For further particulars apply to

W. H. VIOGET,
LA SIESTA RANCH, MENLO PARK, CAL.

EROS is the only stallion offered to the public on this Coast that has a dam that has three in the 2:30 list.

GRAND MOOR, 2374.

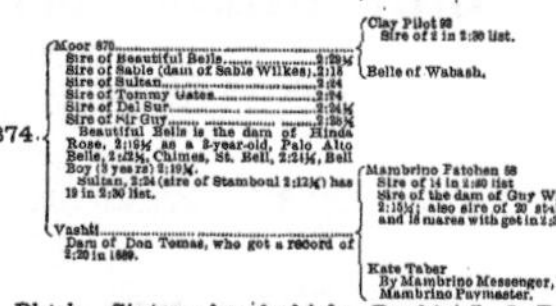

Foaled 1876. Black. Sixteen hands high. Bred by L. J. Rose

A horse of highest form and quality; of great excellence in every point; a type of his celebrated family; of marked individuality, spirit and endurance; never properly trained or raced, but shows the possession of great speed; perfectly manageable in the stable and on the road and track.

As he is sired by The Moor 870, a son of CLAY PILOT, out of Vashti by MAMBRINO PATCHEN, he is a most valuable cross for mares of other families. THE MOOR sired Beautiful Bells and the dams of Sable Wilkes and Margaret 2:26 (dam of Regal Wilkes, 2-year-old record 2:20½).

MAMBRINO PATCHEN is regarded as the unsurpassed sire of broodmares, having, among many others, sired the dam of Guy Wilkes and of Wm. L (the sire of Axtell), and a son of his sired the dam of Axtell. The public sales this year have demonstrated with renewed emphasis the value of The Moor and Mambrino Patchen strains of blood. For combining particularly with the Hambletonians it may be called "the ready money cross."

GRAND MOOR will make the season of 1890 for a time at the Oakland Race Track and afterwards at my Ranch, fifteen miles from Oakland. Mares can be delivered at the race track to the groom in charge. Pasture at $5 per month. For other food, if requested, an additional charge will be made.

TERMS, $150 for the season, with privileges of return if the horse does not change hands.

Every care exercised, but no liability for escapes or accidents.

H. I. THORNTON, 504 Kearny Street.

Cook STOCK FARM.

Season of 1890.

STEINWAY 1808.

Three-Year-Old Record 2:25 3-4.

Sire of STRATHWAY, three year old record 2:26, and sire of the dam of BOURBON RUSSELL 2:30.

By STRATHMORE 408; sire of 31 in the 2:30 list; sire of 6 dams of 8 in the 2:30 list, and sire of 3 sires of 3 in 2:30 list.

1st dam ABBESS (dam of Solo 2:28, and Soprano, dam of C. F. Clay 2:18, Eminence 2:27 and Strathbridge, 3 year old record 2:28½) by ALBION, sire of VANITY FAIR 2:24½, and of the dam of FAVORITE 2:25½.

2nd dam by MARSHALL NEY.

3rd dam by BERTRAND, a son of SIR ARCHY.

TERMS—$100 for the season.

CHARLES DERBY 4907

Brown Horse, Foaled 1885.

By STEINWAY 1808,

1st dam by the great ELECTIONEER, sire of SUNOL 3 year old record 2:10½, Palo Alto 2:12¼, etc., etc.

2nd dam FANNY MALONE, by NIAGARA.

3rd dam FANNY WICKHAM, by HERALD.

4th dam by Imp. TRUSTEE.

TERMS—$100 for the season.

Pasturage $5 per month. Accidents and escapes at owner's risk. Mares consigned to the farm should be sent to Fashion Stables, Oakland; Geary & Grindle's Stable, Haywards; or to Bennett's Stable, Martinez; from and to which places they will be delivered free of charge. Address

COOK STOCK FARM,
Danville, Contra Costa, Co., Cal.

Sunny Side Breeding Farm.

Admiral 488.

Foaled 1867—Sired by Volunteer 55, Son of Rysdyk's Hambletonian 10.

First dam Lady Pierson by Cassius M. Clay (Neaves') 20; second dam by Diamond; third dam a running mare said to be thoroughbred. He is fitted in an eminent degree to produce colts that will in all respects justify his patrons in their expectations.

Admiral is the sire of Huntress, record 2:27½, Sister, 2:19½, Perhelion, 2:25, Nona Y., 2:25, and others equally as promising, but have not had the advantage of track work. He will serve a limited number of approved mares at $50 the season, with usual return privilege. Season ending August 1, 1890. No liability for accidents or escapes.

KING DAVID 2576.

Bay Stallion—Foaled 1883.

Sired by Admiral 488, dam Black Flora (the dam of Huntress, 2:27½, Sister, 2:19½, Perhelion, 2:25, Nona Y., 2:26), by Black Prince.

King David is one of the best gets of Admiral. He has a good disposition, kind to drive, smooth and even-gaited, and can speed fast. Barring accidents, he will trot in the twenties this Fall. His colts are large, rangy, and well finished. Will serve a limited number of mares at $30 the season, to end July 1, 1890. Every precaution will be taken to prevent accidents and escapes, but no liability will be assumed. Pasturage $4 per month.

Sunny Side Farm is situated two miles east of Vallejo, on the Sulphur Spring road. For further particulars, address

FRANK DRAKE,
Vallejo, Cal.

The Fast Trotting Stallion

REDWOOD.

Four-Year-Old Record 2:24 1-2

Will make the season of 1890—February 1st to July 1st—at

SANTA ROSA.

REDWOOD is a dark bay colt, 15.2¾ hands high, weighs 1100 lbs. Foaled in 1885 by Anteeo, 2:16¼, sire of Alfred G., 2:19¾. Anteeo is by Electioneer. First dam Lou Milton, by Milton Medium; second dam Old Sly, a thoroughbred mare brought from the East in 1871 by W. C. Ralston, Esq.

Redwood's sire was out of Columbine by A. W. Richmond, the sire of the pacers Arrow 2:13¾, and Elwood 2:23, and the trotters Romero, 2:19¾, and Len Rose, 2:27. Redwood has shown a quarter in 35 seconds.

Terms $100

For the season. Mares not proving with foal may be returned next season free of charge, provided Redwood remains the property of the present owners. Good pasturage at reasonable rates. No responsibility assumed for escapes or accidents. Service fees payable before removal of the mare. Limited to 40 approved mares. For further particulars address

A. McFADYEN,
Santa Rosa, Cal.

For Sale.

JUANITO ALMONT

Sire of Almont Patchen, 2:15.

JUANITO ALMONT is a bright bay, 16-1 hands in height, and weighs 1,200 pounds.

PEDIGREE.

By Tilton Almont, 2:28, he by the great Almont 33; dam by Signal 3327; he by Bunday's Rob Roy.

JUANITO ALMONT, if given a chance would undoubtedly prove a great sire, and should prove a desirable acquisition to any stock farm in the State.

For further particulars address

T. B. COOPER,
Adin, Modoc County, Cal.

Breeders' Directory.

Advertisements under this heading 50c. per line per month.

HORSES AND CATTLE.

W. S. JACOBS, Sacramento, Cal. – Breeder of Thoroughbred Shorthorns and Berkshire Hogs.

J. H. WHITE, Lakeville, Sonoma County—Breeder of Registered Holstein Cattle.

EL ROBLAS RANCHO—Los Alamos, Cal., Francis T. Underhill, proprietor, importer and breeder of thoroughbred Hereford Cattle. Information by mail. C. F. Swan, manager.

PAGE BROTHERS.—Penn's Grove, Sonoma Co. Cal. Breeders of Short Horn Cattle; Draft, Roadster and Standard Bred Horses.

SETH COOK, breeder of Cleveland Bay Horses, Devon, Durham, Polled Aberdeen-Angus and Galloway Cattle. Young stock of above breeds on hand for sale. Warranted to be pure bred, recorded and average breeders. Address, Geo. A. Wiley, Cook Farm, Danville, Contra Costa Co., Cal.

MAMBRINO WILKES COLTS and FILLIES, full brothers and sisters to Gus. Wilkes 2:22, and Balkan 2:29¾, for Sale. Address SMITH HILL, Walnut Creek, Contra Costa County, Cal.

PETER SAXE & SON, Lick House, San Francisco, Cal.—Importers and Breeders for past 18 years of every variety of Cattle, Horses, Sheep and Hogs.

HOLSTEIN THOROUGHBREDS of all the noted strains. Registered Berkshire Swine. Catalogues. F. H. BURKE, 401 Montgomery St., S. F.

ECHO COCKER KENNELS,

STOCKTON, CAL.

A. C. DAVENPORT, - - - - Proprietor.

Has some fine Cocker Puppies for Sale now, by his solid black Cocker Spaniel, Prize Winning Stud Dog Bronta, A. K. C. S. B., 17,064, (Brant—Mollie) out of registered bitches, for $10 and $20. Stud fee $20.

Situation Wanted.

By an Experienced and Successful Trainer of Racehorses.

Address,

S. J. MILLER,

103 South Desplaines Street, Chicago, Ill.

GOLDEN EAGLE HOTEL

Corner SEVENTH and K STREETS, SACRAMENTO.

FIRST CLASS IN EVERY RESPECT.

The LARGEST and FINEST HOTEL in the City.

W. O. BOWERS, Proprietor.

Free 'Buss to and from the Hotel.

Telephone, Telegraph Office and Messenger Service at Hotel

GROVER CLAY

Bay Stallion, Black Points,

15 3-4 hands high.

Bred by W. W. Traylor, San Francisco.

BY ELECTIONEER.

First dam Maggie Norfolk by Norfolk, son of Lexington, he by Boston. Second dam Tilda Quill by Billy Cheatham he by Cracken, and he by Boston. Third dam by Dorsey's Golddust.

TERMS.

Will make the season of 1890 at the Training Stables of Denis Gannon, near Oakland Trotting Park, at $50 the season, payable at time of service. Season to commence February 1st and ending July 1st. Proper care of mares will be taken, but no responsibility incurred for accidents or escapes. Address,

DENIS GANNON, Oakland, Cal.

NOW IN THE LEAD.

J. O'KANE,

Harness and Turf Goods,

767 MARKET STREET, S. F.

Largest Stock. Lowest Prices.

Send for New Catalogue.

The Pacific Coast Live Stock Owners MUTUAL PROTECTIVE ASS'N.,

MONTEREY, Monterey Co., Cal.

TRUSTEES:

HON. B. V. SARGENT, President,
G. W. GALLANAR, Secretary,
JAMES E. PALMER, Business Manager,
EDW. INGRAM, Vice-President,
FRED. D. HOWARD, Actuary,
B. H. WILLEY, Attorney.

GENERAL BUSINESS OFFICE, Room 73, Flood Building, corner Market and Fourth Streets, San Francisco, Cal.

VOLNEY HOWARD, General Manager.

AN UNQUALIFIED ENDORSEMENT.

Peruvian Bitters are made of the purest ingredients and compounded as carefully as any prescription.

Peruvian Bark, one of its principal ingredients, was introduced into Spain by the Countess, wife of Count CINCHON, Spanish Viceroy to Peru in 1630, who was cured of a fever by its use, since which time, no better remedy for Malaria and for Restoring the Natural Tone of the Stomach has been discovered.

On the Atlantic Coast they are used in the principal Hotels, Clubs and Restaurants, and sold by all Grocers and Druggists. We have sold them for the past three years WITHOUT ANY ADVERTISING and sales have constantly increased UPON MERIT ALONE, and we unqualifiedly recommend them to our friends and customers.

ACKER, MERRALL & CONDIT.

New York, Feb. 1st, 1890.

WILMERDING & CO., Agents for Pacific Coast,
216 FRONT ST., SAN FRANCISCO, CAL.

Guenoc Stud Farm, Lake Co., Cal.

Imp. GREENBACK

(Sire of the English winners Greenlight, Greenjacket, Greensbank, Greenwave and Greenhorn)

By Dollar, dam Music, by Stockwell. $100 the Season

ST. SAVIOR,

(FULL BROTHER TO EOLE)

By Eolus, dam War Song, by War Dance. $100 the Season.

PASTURAGE, $5 PER MONTH.

With right to return the following year if mare does not prove with foal. The best of care taken, but no liability for accidents or escapes. Mares shipped to C. W. ABY, care ST. HELENA STABLES, St. Helena Napa County, will be taken in charge by competent men.

For further information write to

DR. C. W. ABY, Middletown, Lake County, Cal.

SAN DIEGO, 8776.

SAN DIEGO is dark seal brown, three years old, and trotted one-quarter miles in 40 seconds as a two-year old.

This grand young horse, and, barring accidents, will make a fast record next fall.

He will be allowed a limited number of mares, at $50 for the season. Mares not proving in foal to be returned free 1891. Best of pasture for mares at $4 per month, but no liability for accidents or escapes.

He will make the season from February 1st to June 1st at Napa Fair Grounds. For further particulars, address or call on

H. B. STARR, Race Track, Napa, Cal.,

or FRED W. LOEBER, St. Helena.

KENNEL ADVERTISEMENTS.

In the Stud.

"DAN GLADSTONE,"

3377 A. K. C. S. B

BY CH. GLADSTONE—CH. SUE.

Winnings—Southern Trials, 1888, Divided Third.
Indiana Trials, 1889, Divided Third.
Southern Trials, 1889, Second.

Will be at Stud in San Francisco until Sept 15, 1890. Fee, $35.

GEO. J. HARLEY, 844 Harrison St., S. F.

DOGS---Pointer Pups

FOR SALE.

Sure Bench Show and Field Trial Winners, as they have more bench-show and field-trial blood in them than any that have ever been whelped on the Pacific Coast.

Sire, POINT, double field trial winner; he by Vandevort's Don, great field trial and bench show winner, out of Drab, field trial and bench show winner.

Dam, QUEEN CROXTETH by Rush T., bench show winner, out of Champion Patti Croxteth, field trial and bench show winner. This is the best pointer blood in the world. Breeding and health guaranteed. Address,

A. B. TRUMAN,

1425 Steiner St., near Ellis, S. F., Cal.

CALIFORNIA SPANIEL KENNELS,

Oakland, California, H. P. RENNIE, Prop. Breeder and importer of typical COCKER SPANIELS. Winner of first prizes at S. F. and Los Angeles, 18‥ also, Columbus, 18‥ New York, 1887. In the stud, solid Black Cocker dog, GIFFEE, won 1st and Gold Medal at S. F., 18‥ Fee, $25. Puppies and grown dogs at reasonable prices. My dogs can neither talk nor climb a tree, but are fielders and prize winners.

THE HICKS-JUDD CO.

Successors to

HICKS & JUDD, Bookbinders,

and Women's Co-operative Printing Office.

Printers, Bookbinders, Publishers,

23 First St., San Francisco.

BREEDERS' CATALOGUES A SPECIALTY.

JUST OUT, 2d EDITION.

1,000 Receipts

MIXOLOGIST FOR BARKEEPERS

All Booksellers, and 3 California St., S. F.

For Sale

A HALF BROTHER TO

ALMONT PATCHEN

(2:15, trial 2:13 3-4).

JUANITO JR. is a beautiful bright bay, black points, with no white, foaled 1886. As a colt he has given much more promise than did Almont Patchen at the same age. Instead of being a pacer, he is a good square trotter, with every indication of great speed, and is so gentle and kind, that a lady can drive him. The owner's only reason for selling him is that business calls him away from this section of the State. He will be sold at a reasonable figure. This is a splendid opportunity for a gentleman to secure a first-class trotter at a very low figure.

The pedigree of Juanito Jr. is by Juanito (sire of Almont Patchen), dam Nettie Moore by Old Tom Moore. For further particulars, address

JUANITO JR.,

Santa Clara P. O., Cal.

For Sale

A FIRST-CLASS

Napa County Farm

—OR—

STOCK RANCH,

800 Acres Improved,

SITUATED TWO AND A HALF MILES FROM NAPA CITY, with good roads leading thereto, a good hard finished house of nine rooms, with all modern improvements, streams running all summer, a great amount of live oak and black oak timber. It lies in a fruit belt, surrounded by fine vineyards and orchards growing upon the same quality of soil, and originally a part of this tract. About one-half hill and one-half rolling land, but none of it is steep and all easily cultivated, splendidly situated for the breeding of fine horses. Price, $65 per acre. Further particulars given at this office.

BREEDER AND SPORTSMAN,

313 Bush St.

Stallion for Sale

AT A BARGAIN.

Full Brother to Fairmont.

By Piedmont, dam Queen by Garibaldi—see State Fair Edition of BREEDER AND SPORTSMAN September 14, 1889, for description of Fairmont—three years old, solid bay. Can trot a 2:40 gait or better. Sound in every particular. Can be seen at Oakland Trotting Park, Oakland.

P. J. WILLIAMS.

Southern Pacific Co.

(PACIFIC SYSTEM.)

Trains leave and are due to arrive at San Francisco.

LEAVE (FOR)	FROM MAY 25, 1890.	ARRIVE (FROM)
7.30 A M	Haywards, Niles and San Jose...	*12.45 P M
7.30 A M	Sacramento and Redding, via Davis	7.15 P M
7.30 A M	Sacramento, Auburn, Colfax...	4.45 P M
8.00 A M	Martinez, Vallejo, Calistoga and Santa Rosa	6.15 P M
8.30 A M	Los Angeles Express, Fresno, Bakersfield, Mojave and East and Los Angeles	11.15 A M
8.30 A M	Niles, San Jose, Stockton, Ione, Sacramento, Marysville, Oroville and Red Bluff	4.45 P M
10.30 A M	Haywards and Niles	3.45 P M
12.00 M	Haywards, Niles and Livermore.	8.45 P M
*1.00 P M	Sacramento River Steamers	**6.00 A M
3.00 P M	Haywards, Niles and San Jose....	9.45 A M
3.30 P M	2d Class for Ogden and East.	10.45 P M
4.00 P M	Stockton and Milton; Vallejo, Calistoga and Santa Rosa.	9.45 A M
*4.30 P M	Niles and Livermore.	*8.45 A M
*4.30 P M	Niles and San Jose	‡ 6.15 P M
5.00 P M	Shasta Route Express, Sacramento, Marysville, Redding, Portland, Puget Sound, East and Knight's Landing via Davis	10.45 A M
6.00 P M	Haywards and Niles	7.45 A M
6.30 P M	Sunset Route, Atlantic Express Santa Barbara, Los Angeles, Deming, El Paso, New Orleans and East	8.45 P M
6.00 P M	Central Atlantic Express, Ogden and East	9.45 A M

SANTA CRUZ DIVISION.

‡ 7.45 A M	Excursion train to Santa Cruz...	‡ 8.05 P M
8.15 A M	Newark, Centerville, San Jose, Felton, Boulder Creek and Santa Cruz	6.20 P M
* 2.45 P M	Centerville, San Jose, Almaden, Felton, Boulder Creek and Santa Cruz	*11.20 A M
4.45 P M	Centerville, San Jose, and Los Gatos	9. 0 A M

Coast Division (Third and Townsend Sts.)

7.25 A M	San Jose, Almaden and Way Stations	2.30 P M
‡ 7.50 A M	Monterey and Santa Cruz—Sunday Excursion	‡ 8.25 P M
8.20 A M	San Jose, Gilroy, Tres Pinos; Pajaro, Santa Cruz; Monterey; Pacific Grove, Salinas, San Miguel, Paso Robles, Santa Margarita (San Luis Obispo) and principal Way Stations	6.12 P M
10.30 A M	San Jose and Way Stations.	7.31 P M
11.05 A M	Emanuel Cemetery and Baden...	12.32 P M
12.01 P M	Cemetery, Menlo Park and Way Stations	5.12 P M
* 2.30 P M	Del Monte Limited, Menlo Park, San Jose, Gilroy, Pajaro, Castroville, Monterey and Pacific Grove	*11.15 A M
* 3.30 P M	San Jose, Tres Pinos, Santa Cruz, Salinas, Monterey, Pacific Grove and principal Way Stations	*10.00 A M
* 4.30 P M	Menlo Park and Way Stations...	* 7.56 A M
5.20 P M	San Jose and Way Stations.	9.03 A M
6.30 P M	Menlo Park and Way Stations.	6.35 A M
†11.45 P M	San Jose and principal Way Stations	†4.28 P M

A M for Morning. P M for Afternoon.
*Sundays excepted. †Saturdays only. ‡Sundays only.
**Mondays excepted. §Saturdays excepted.

OCEANIC STEAMSHIP CO.

Carrying United States, Hawaiian and Colonial Mails.

WILL LEAVE THE COMPANY'S WHARF, foot of Mission street, No. 1.

For Honolulu, Auckland and Sydney,

WITHOUT CHANGE,

The Splendid New 3,000-ton Iron Steamer,
ZEALANDIA... Saturday, May 31st, 1890, at 12 M., Or immediately on arrival of the English mails.

For Honolulu,

SS. AUSTRALIA (3,000 tons), June 20, 1890, at 12 M

For freight or passage, apply at office, 327 Market Street. JOHN D. SPRECKELS & BROS., General Agents.

By-Laws

—AND—

Rules and Regulations

—OF THE—

NATIONAL

Trotting Association

REVISED FOR 1890,

ALSO THE

AMERICAN

Trotting Association,

AND THE

PACIFIC COAST BLOOD-HORSE ASSOCIATION.

With Betting Rules.

For Sale at the Office of the

Breeder and Sportsman,

313 Bush St., S. F., Cal.

Price, 25c. each.

By Mail, Postage Paid, 30c. each.

"STANDARD" SHOTGUN CARTRIDGES

San Francisco and North Pacific Railway.

THE DONAHUE BROAD-GAUGE ROUTE.

COMMENCING SUNDAY, APRIL 27, 1890, AND until further notice, boats and trains will leave from and arrive at the San Francisco Passenger Depot, Market-street Wharf, as follows:

FROM SAN FRANCISCO FOR POINT TIBURON AND SAN RAFAEL.

Week Days—7.40, 9.20, 11.20, A. M.; 1.30, 3.30, 5.00, 6.15 P. M.

Sundays—8.00, 9.30, 11.00 A. M.; 1.30, 3.30, 5.00, 6.15 P. M.

FROM SAN RAFAEL FOR SAN FRANCISCO.

Week Days—6.50, 7.55, 9.30, 11.40 A. M.; 1.40, 3.40, 5.05, 6.25 P. M.

Sundays—8.10, 9.40, 11:10 A. M.; 1.40, 3.40, 5.00, 6.25 P. M.

FROM POINT TIBURON FOR SAN FRANCISCO

Week Days—7.15, 8.20, 9.55 A. M.; 12.05, 2.05, 4.05, 5.30, 6.50 P. M.

Sundays—8.35, 10.05, 11:35 A. M.; 2.05, 4.05, 5.30, 6.50 P. M.

Leave San Francisco. Week Days.	Leave San Francisco. Sundays.	Destination	Arrive San Francisco. Sundays.	Arrive San Francisco. Week Days.
7.40 A M 9.20 A M 3.30 P M 5.00 P M	8.00 A M 5.00 P M	Petaluma and Santa Rosa	10.40 A M 7.25 P M	8.50 A M 10.30 A M 4.40 P M 7.25 P M
7.40 A M 3.30 P M	8.00 A M	Fulton, Windsor, Healdsburg, Litton Springs, Cloverdale, and way stations.	7.25 P M	10.30 A M 7.25 P M
7.40 A M	8.00 A M	Hopland and Ukiah.	7.25 P M	7.25 P M
7.40 A M 3.30 P M	8.00 A M	Guerneville	7.25 P M	7.25 P M 10.30 A M
7.40 A M 5.00 P M	8.00 A M 5.10 P M	Sonoma and Glen Ellen	10.40 A M 6.05 P M	8.50 A M 6.05 P M
7.40 A M 3.30 P M	8.00 A M 5.00 P M	Sebastopol	10.40 A M 7.25 P M	10.30 A M 7.25 P M

Stage connects at Santa Rosa for White Sulphur Springs, and Mark West Springs; at Geyserville for Skaggs Springs, and at Cloverdale for the Geysers; at Hopland for Highland Springs, Kelseyville, Soda Bay, Lakeport and Bartlett Springs, and at Ukiah for Vichy Springs, Saratoga Springs, Blue Lakes, Willits, Cahto, Calpella, Potter Valley, Sherwood Valley and Mendocino City.

EXCURSION TICKETS from Saturdays to Mondays, to Petaluma, $1.50; to Santa Rosa, $2.25; to Healdsburg, $3.40; to Litton Springs, $3.60; to Cloverdale, $4.50; to Hopland, $5.70; to Ukiah, $6.75; to Guerneville, $3.75; to Sonoma, $1.50; to Glen Ellen, $1.80.

EXCURSION TICKETS, good for Sundays only, to Petaluma, $1; to Santa Rosa, $1.50; to Healdsburg, $2.25; to Litton Springs, $2.40; to Cloverdale, $3; to Guerneville, $2.50, to Sonoma, $1; to Glen Ellen, $1.20.

H. C. WHITING, General Manager.

PETER J. McGLYNN, Gen. Pass. & Tkt. Agt.

Ticket Offices at Ferry, 222 Montgomery Street and 2 New Montgomery Street.

THE BOHANON **SULKY!** BEST MADE.

Perfect Riding Buggies. Breaking Carts.

Fine Repairing. Reasonable Prices

Bohanon Carriage Co., 161-163 Ogden Ave., CHICAGO.

Send for Catalogue.

HEALD'S

Business College, 24 Post St.

—San Francisco.—

The most popular school on the Coast

F. HEALD, President. C. S. HALEY, Sec'y.

Send for Circulars.

KILLIP & CO.,

LIVE STOCK AND GENERAL AUCTIONEERS,

22 Montgomery Street, San Francisco

SPECIAL ATTENTION PAID TO SALES OF

High-Bred Horses and Cattle.

At auction and private sale.

Will Sell in All Cities and Counties of the State.

REFERENCES.

HON. C. GREEN, Sacramento.	HON. J. D. CARR Salinas.
J. P. SARGENT, Esq., Sargents.	HON. JOHN BOGGS Colusa.
HON. L. J. ROSE, Los Angeles.	HON. A. WALRATH Nevada.
J. B. HAGGIN, Esq., San Francisco.	

Represented at Sacramento by Edwin F. Smith secretary State Agricultural Society.

At San Jose by Messrs. Montgomery & Rea, Real Estate Agents.

Being the oldest established firm in the live-stock business on this Coast, and having conducted the important auction sales in this line for the past fifteen years, amounting to one half a million of dollars, we feel justified in claiming unequaled facilities for disposing of live stock of every description, either at auction or private sale. Our list of correspondents embraces every breeder and dealer of prominence upon the Pacific Coast, thus enabling us to give full publicity to animals placed with us for sale. Private purchases and sales of live stock of all descriptions will be made on commission, and stock shipped with the utmost care. Purchases and sales made of land of every description. We are authorized to refer to the gentlemen whose names are appended.

KILLIP & CO., 22 Montgomery Street

Unfailing Specific for Liver Disease.

It acts with extraordinary efficacy on the

LIVER, KIDNEYS, and BOWELS.

AN EFFECTUAL SPECIFIC FOR

Malaria, Bowel Complaints, Dyspepsia, Sick Headache, Constipation, Billiousness, Kidney Affections, Jaundice, Mental Depression, Colic.

If you are a miserable sufferer with Constipation, Dyspepsia, Billiousness or Kidney Affections, seek relief at once in Simmons Liver Regulator. It does not require continual dosing and costs but a trifle. It will cure you.

ONLY GENUINE

Has our Z stamp in red on front of Wrapper.

J. H. ZEILIN & CO., - Philadelphia, Pa., Sole Proprietors. Price, $1.00.

HORSE OWNERS!

TRY GOMBAULT'S

CAUSTIC BALSAM.

A Safe, Speedy and Positive Cure for Curb, Splint, Sweeny, Capped Hock, Strained Tendons, Founder, Wind Puffs, all Skin Diseases or Parasites, Thrush, Diphtheria Pinkeye, all Lameness from Spavin, Ringbone or other Bony Tumors. Removes all Bunches or Blemishes from Horses and Cattle.

Supersedes all Cautery or Firing.

Impossible to Produce any Scar or Blemish.

Every bottle sold is warranted to give satisfaction. Price $1.50 per bottle. Sold by druggists, or sent by express, charges paid, with full directions for its use. Send for descriptive circulars. Address LAWRENCE, WILLIAMS & CO., Cleveland, O.

BROU'S INJECTION

A PERMANENT CURE

in from 3 to 6 days, of the most obstinate cases; guaranteed not to produce Stricture; no sickening doses; and no inconvenience or loss of time. Recommended by physicians and sold by all druggists. J. Ferré, (successor to Brou), Pharmacien, Paris.

For any Kind of a

SORE THROAT

USE

McCLELLAN'S

DIPHTHERIA REMEDY

An Unfailing Cure.

FOR SALE BY ALL DRUGGISTS

R. LIDDLE & SON

538 Washington St., S. F.,

Wholesale and Retail Dealers in

Guns, Rifles and Pistols.

A Full Line of FISHING TACKLE and SPORTSMAN'S GOODS.

Orders by mail receive prompt attention.

6 DONTS

DON'T own a racehorse.
DON'T be a breeder.
DON'T be a trainer.
DON'T be a jockey.
DON'T bet on the races.
DON'T go to a race track.

WITHOUT

HAVING IN YOUR POCKET ONE OF

Goodwin's

ANNUAL

OFFICIAL TURF GUIDES.

Price, in cloth....................$2.00
Price, in half morocco.............3.00
Price, in half calf................4.00
If sent by mail..........10 cents extra

SUBSCRIBE TO IT FOR 1890.

It is published semi-monthly during the racing season, and is but $10 per year. Address

GOODWIN BROS.,

241 Broadway, New York City.

VETERINARY.

Dr. Wm. H. Jones, M.R.C.V.S.

Veterinary Surgeon,

(OLYMPIC CLUB STABLES)

502 Sutter Street, San Francisco.

Telephone, No. 1404.

Consultations by letter, and cases of URGENT NECESSITY in the interior will receive prompt attention.

Dr. A. E. BUZARD,

VETERINARY SURGEON,

Member of the Royal College of Veterinary Surgeons, London, England. Graduated April 22d, 1870.

All Operations on the Horse Performed Skillfully.

Special attention given to the Diseases of Dogs. Calls to the country promptly attended to. Advice and prescriptions by mail $2. Office and Residence, No. 11 Seventh street, S. F. (opp. Odd Fellows Hall. Telephone No. 3 69.

W. H. WOODRUFF.

Veterinary Dentist,

AT FASHION STABLES,

221 Ellis Street, San Francisco

Improved Instruments, Humane Methods, First-Class Work.

H. E. CARPENTER,

Veterinary Surgeon,

Graduate of Ontario Veterinary College, Toronto Canada.

RESIDENCE AND VETERINARY INFIRMARY

331 Golden Gate Ave., San Francisco.

Telephone 2069.

OPEN DAY AND NIGHT.

No risk in throwing Horses. Veterinary Operating Table on the premises.

DR. C. MASOERO,

Veterinary Surgeon,

Successor to DR. A. DeTAVEL,

GRADUATE OF ROYAL VETERINARY COLLEGE, TURIN.

OFFICE AND INFIRMARY

No. 811 HOWARD STREET,

Between Fourth and Fifth. SAN FRANCISCO

Telephone, No. 457.

R. WATKINS,

Veterinary Dentist,

Office at C. S. Crittendens' Golden Gate Livery and Riding Academy. 24 to 28 Golden Gate Avenue.

Refers to Palo Alto Stock Farm; Wm. Corbett, San Mateo Stock Farm; B. C. Holly, Vallejo, and others. Examination Free.

E. J. O'ROUKE.

I have the honor to announce to my old patrons and the general public that I may be found at my old stand, where, as heretofore, the

Shoeing of Horses,

whether for the Track, Drive, or for general work, will receive my personal attention.

Telephone 2011.

E. J. O'ROUKE,
209 Ellis Street

ST. JULIEN Horse Shoeing SHOP,

126 Geary Street, S. F.

MARTIN O'DEA, - - PROPRIETOR.

California Horse Shoe Co's

I have used in my business the Steel and Iron Shoes made by the above Company, and take great pleasure in saying they are the best I have ever used in twenty-two years' practice. I have never seen anything like the STEEL SHOE made by this Company. I can fully recommend them to every practical Horseshoer in the country. Yours respectfully,

No. 8 Everett Street. JOHN GRACE.

Old Hermitage Whiskies

"STEINER'S,"

No. 311 BUSH STREET,

San Francisco.

Under Breeder and Sportsman Office.

Everything for Trotter or Runner.

At J. A. McKERRON'S,

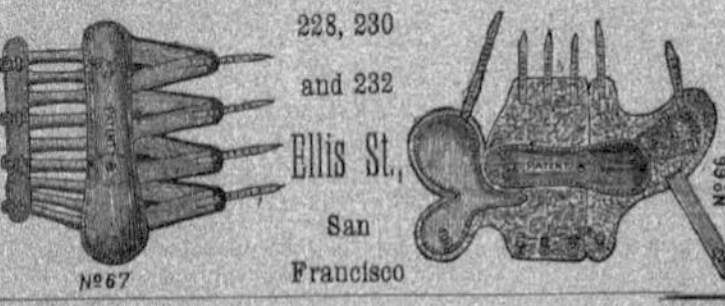

228, 230 and 232 Ellis St., San Francisco

Abell & Priest PHOTOGRAPHERS,
[illegible]23 Market Street, S. F.
Our View is unsurpassed by any Studio in the United States.

The PARKER Hammerless Shot Gun.

At the Annual Tournament of 1889, held at Cannes, France, the grand prize, consisting of 2000 Francs and a Valuable Cup, was won by The Parker Hammerless.

The first Parker Hammerless Gun made won the championship of America at Decatur Illinois.

SEND FOR ILLUSTRATED CIRCULAR.

PARKER BROS., Makers,

New York Salesroom, 97 Chambers St. Meriden Conn.

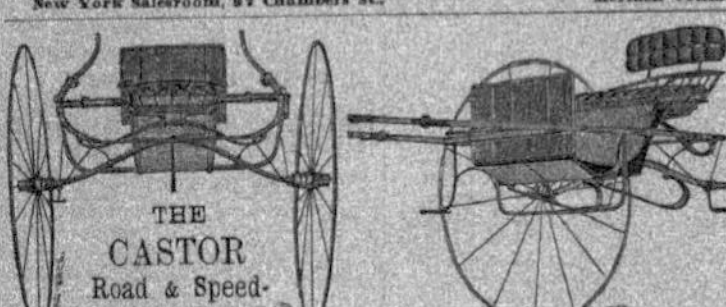

THE CASTOR Road & Speeding CART.

ALWAYS GIVES SATISFACTION.

Combining perfect riding qualities, proportions and balance, with genteel appearance.

No vehicle exhibits a horse to better advantage, and no Cart approaches them for speeding or training purposes.

A stylish vehicle for exercising or pleasure driving, at one-fourth the cost of a carriage. Have none of the horse jockey or objectionable features of other Road Carts.

They are the Leading Cart wherever introduced, and are in use by the most prominent breeders and pleasure drivers everywhere.

Elegant Shifting Top Carts.

Perfectly Balanced Stylish Pole Carts.

or Illustrated Catalogue, with Prices, address,

LEWIS F. CASTOR,
Frankford, Philadelphia, Pa.

JOHN SPLAN, General Agent.

keeps horses healthy, promotes digestion, fattens horses, loosens the hide, assists the appetite, prevents leg swelling, strengthens the kidneys, regulates the bowels and destroys worms, $2.50 per 100 lbs. Ask your dealer for it or send to

MANHATTAN FOOD CO., 206 Clay St., S. F.

The Brunswick Balke Collender Co.

MANUFACTURERS OF

Standard Billiard and Pool Tables, Saloon and Bank Fixtures,
653--655 Market Street, San Francisco, Cal.

ORVIS TROUT FLIES.

Superb in Material, Make and Killing Quality.

E. T. ALLEN,

SOLE AGENT FOR PACIFIC COAST.

Importer of Fine Fishing Tackle & Sporting Goods

416 Market Street, - - San Francisco, Cal.

Brothers of the Angle.

Our NEW EIGHT-STRIP SPLIT BAMBOO is the "King" of all fishing-rods. Chubb's New Catalogue for 1890 is now ready. In addition to a complete list of anglers' supplies, it contains articles from the pens of Dr. James A. Henshall, Petronella, W. H. Murray, Geo. F. Goff, Norman, Brother Gardner, and others.

These papers are by the best writers on angling subjects, and are very interesting.

Send 25 cents, and receive Catalogue, postpaid. This amount will be deducted from first order (if accompanied with Coupon in book) for one dollar's worth or more of our goods.

Address

THOS. H. CHUBB.
Fishing-Rod Manufacturer,
POST MILLS, VT.

Please mention BREEDER AND SPORTSMAN.

Poplar Grove Breeding FARM.

Standard-bred Trotters, Colts and Fillies.

The get of CLOVIS, 4909; PASHA, 2039; APEX, 2935,

For Sale.

Address S. N. STRAUBE, Poplar Grove Breeding Farm,
Fresno, Cal.

Inspection by intending purchasers invited, and information by mail.

Studebaker Bros. Manufact'g Co.

Sole Agents for

FRAZIER (OR CHICAGO) Carts AND Sulkies,

201--203 Market Street,
SAN FRANCISCO, CAL.

BOYCE TABLETS.

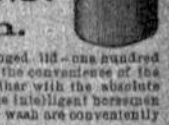

Leg and Body Wash.

THE BOYCE TABLETS are packed in a nicely decorated metal box with hinged lid—one hundred tablets in each box; directions for use plainly engraved upon the box; therefore, the convenience of the package—no liability to leakage and breakage—economy and ready solubility, together with the absolute certainty of their action, will at once command the use of BOYCE'S TABLETS to the intelligent horsemen of the country. TABLETS sufficient to make one hundred pints of leg and body wash are conveniently carried in an inside coat pocket or in the hip-pocket of the trousers.

The BOYCE WASH can be applied ALL OVER THE BODY WITHOUT FEAR OF BLISTERING NOR DOES IT AFFECT THE KIDNEYS.

The BOYCE WASH will cure CRACKED HEELS, PUFFS, STOCKINGS, SCRATCHES, INFLAMED TENDONS and FEVERED LEGS.

Price per Box of One Hundred Tablets, $2, sent postpaid to any part of the United States; **six boxes for $10.** A sample of BOYCE'S TABLETS will be mailed to any address on application. These TABLETS are warranted to keep in any climate. Address

BOYCE TABLET COMPANY,
600 Wabash Avenue, - - - Terre Haute, Indiana.

J. A. McKERRON, Pacific Coast Ag't,
228-230-232 Ellis Street, San Francisco, Cal.

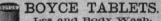

TWENTY-FOUR PAGES.

BREEDER AND SPORTSMAN

Vol XVI. No 23
No. 313 BUSH STREET.

SAN FRANCISCO, SATURDAY, JUNE 7, 1890.

SUBSCRIPTION
FIVE DOLLARS A YEAR.

AUSTRALIAN WILD HORSES.

The Pleasures and Perils of their Capture.

In the year 1868, New South Wales and the greater portion of Victoria suffered from a prolonged draught, and stock, especially cattle died by the thousands from want of feed and from thirst. In the Maquarrie River, some fifty miles from the town of Dubbo, where the present sketch is located, water in 68 was very scarce and grass in proportion. The cattle came from miles in the interior to drink at the stagnant pools which here and there at long intervals marked where the Maquarrie once poured along In the mud and mire round these pools hundreds of cattle got bogged and starved to death being too weak from want of food to make an effort to save themselves. For a mile or two in from the river the plains were as bare of feed as the high road, and were strewn with carcasses of cattle. In the cattle "station" (as the ranches are called in Australia) of Mullah, on which the writer was there gaining "colonial experience", (which means working for no pay) there were upwards of fifteen thousand head of good cattle before the two years draught set in. A "muster" after it was over only produced eleven thousand head of wretched apologies for beef.

Under these conditions water was highly valued and carefully guarded. Eight miles from the main station was a large natural water hole, known for what reason, I cannot tell, as the Four Mile Hole. Here we had to station a man with a rifle to drive off the large mobs of wild horses which each day watered there, and drive off the weak and thirsty cattle, besides using up a vast amount of the precious fluid. It was his business to wait until a mob of horses came in and then to shoot the entires and scare off the rest.

One evening the stockman from the Four Mile House came in for provisions, and told us that two large mobs of wild horses, among which were some fine ones, had lately been coming around the water-hole. He had fired at the stallions several times but so far as he knew had never hit them.

What do you say boys said superintendent K——, if we go out to the Four Mile Hole to-morrow night and take a turn at the "clearskins" — (unbranded horses)?

Of course we were only too willing, for our life for sometime past had been dull and uneventful as the cattle were too weak to disturb and "mustering" for fat stock or calves was out of the question.

The next day we each of us—there were four—got our favorite horses up and fed them bountiful measures of Indian corn, driving the rest of the home horses into the stock-yard, so as to be handy to take with us in the evening, and hungry enough to feed quietly when we got them out to the plain where they were to wait until we drove the wild horses into them, and started the lot for home..

It was about an hour from sunset when we started out for our hunting ground, with the band of tame horses numbering some eighty in front of us and a couple of pack-horses carrying our blankets and pots and pans, for we intended to camp at the water hole, and wait the arrival of the wild horses which usually came in to drink at night.

In about two hours we arrived at the Four Mile Hole and lost no time in making some tea and eating a hearty supper of "damper" and beef. After supper we sent off one of our number to herd the horses on a small plain close to the water hole, then lit our pipes, wrapped ourselves in our blankets and awaited developments, leaving our horses saddled and bridled ready for mounting at a moment's notice.

We had smoked away for half an hour or so, when K said "no more smoking now, or we sha'nt see a horse to-night." And he was strictly obeyed, for we well knew what a keen sense of smell the wild horse has and how suspicious he is of danger.

It was a lovely moonlight night in December, the hottest month in Australia, and all was still as death except for the occasional chirp of an opossum or the howl of a "dingo" (a species of wild dog very like our coyote).

I was just dozing off to sleep when I heard a rustling among the dry leaves close to my head. I gently raised myself up on one elbow and looked for its cause, when to my horror I saw a black snake some four feet long, coiled up close to where my head had lain. I jumped up and killed it with a few blows from my stock whip handle, but there was no more sleep or thought of it for me that night, as I had a horror of snakes and the black snake is one of the most deadly in Australia.

It must have been well on into the night, when I heard one of our horses give a low whinny, and at the same time K clutched my arm and whispered, "Hush! here they come." He was correct, for I could hear the distant tread of hoofs. In a second we were all on the alert though still lying down. "Don't one of you move until I give the signal," said K, and then you E go to the right, you F to the left and I'll get right behind the horses, and we'll rush them out through that thin tea tree scrub onto the plain where P has our quiet horses."

We all held our breaths and watched eagerly for the horses, the dust which they raised being now plainly seen in the moonlight. At last with a loud neigh up trotted a large black stallion. He must have stood nearly seventeen hands. His coat shone like satin and his long tail swept the ground. The waterhole was surrounded by a dense growth of gum trees, but the ground was bare for some ten yards or so around the water. The noble stallion paused for a half minute or so, when he reached the open, threw his head in the air and catching what little wind there was sniffed for danger. Fortunately, we were to leeward of him, and not scenting danger, he soon gave the signal for the rest of the mob to approach.

In a minute there was a wild rush and amidst a cloud of dust we could hear the splashing of some hundred head of horses in the water. When the dust cleared away we saw them all. There were mares and foals, yearlings, two-year-olds, and mares and horses of various sizes and colors. It was a grand sight to see the thirsty and tired brutes disport themselves in the muddy water.

K was just about to give the signal for us all to mount and after them, when a loud neigh was heard to our right, and a heavy cloud of dust was seen rising above the tree tops.

The old stallion heard it as soon or sooner than we did, and he evidently knew what it meant, for he dashed into the water and soon had his startled harem closely herded together in the open space to the left of the water-hole.

Then slowly and majestically we saw a heavy bay stallion emerge from the brush. With distended nostrils and fiercely bulging eyeballs, he seemed to take in the situation at once. Turning half round he gave a low signal to his herd, and then advanced to meet the black horse, who by this time had singled himself out from the other horses, and stood some five yards away, a picture of equine beauty and defiance.

With a wild, half human scream of rage, the two rushed at each other.

In the meantime the bay's band had come into the open, and the two mobs of horses stood perfectly still while their lords and masters fought it out in the arena between them.

They reared and struck at each other like human prize fighters, and bit each other, holding on with bull-dog tenacity, while the hair from their long manes was torn out in handfulls. It was one of the finest struggles of any description I ever saw, and I felt unspeakably disgusted when K gave the signal "to horse."

In a minute we were mounted, and before the startled animals had recovered from the fright of our shouts and the excitement of the fight, we had the two mobs in full gallop towards the plain where our tame horses were, with all three of us behind them riding for dear life.

I have ridden to hounds through many a hard run, in all sorts of countries, from the grasslands of Leicestershire to the dikes of Holderness—but a wilder, fiercer ride than that midnight gallop I never experienced.

Fortunately, I knew enough to give my horse, an old and experienced stock animal, his head, but still I several times narrowly escaped hitting my knees against the tree trunks through which we were going at full speed. Moonlight is very deceiving, and three or four times the only intimation I got that there was any obstruction in our way was a bound that my horse gave as he cleared some fallen tree or leapt over some deep hole where the roots of some giant gum tree had been torn from the ground.

About ten minutes of this dangerous riding brought us to the plain, where our own horses were, and I hailed the sight of the open with joy.

A few of our prey had slipped away in the thick brush, but we had still most of them rushed into the quiet horses, and the whole mob heading for home at a breakneck pace.

In going over the two miles of plain, K got an ugly fall which put him out of the race, and came nearly killing both man and horse.

The intense heat had cracked the ground so, that there were countless fissures at short intervals from each other. Into one of these K's horse put both forefeet and rolled over like a shot rabbit, sending K five yards ahead of him. We were all too excited to stop to see how much damage was done, but as we saw man and horse up again, concluded it was not serious.

Again we were among the dense brush, this time tea and wattle trees, with our horses in a compact band in front of us and so far well under command, with our own going strong and well under as I got terribly scratched about the face and neck, and was heartily glad when we struck the large open plain which lay before us and the stockyard.

In this plain we closed in on our horses and rushed the pace. When, however, within sight of the stockyard a wild stampede ensued, and the old wild horses seeing danger ahead made desperate breaks for liberty. I made after the black stallion but could not turn him as he would sooner run over me than go the way I wanted, besides he had the foot of my now tired bay. However we succeeded in yarding some twenty head of mares, foals and two and three-year-olds.

When K. came limping up two hours later leading his lamed horse, he of course told us that had he been there he would have had every horse in the yard; but we took what he said with a liberal allowance of salt.

These clearskins are seldom of any account, are hard to break and will years after return, if they have a chance, to their old haunts and horses. They are the progeny of horses that have years ago escaped into the bush and in breeding has demoralized them to such an extent that but few of them are even decent specimens of horses. Some are weedy leggy brutes with heads like coffins, and legs like tooth-picks. Others are as long in the back as a boat, slack in the loins and generally weak.

W. L. Eyre.

San Francisco, April 1890.

The man who won most heavily over the Brooklyn was generally supposed to be Johnny Campbell, but it has since been stated that Bookmaker Pearsall, popularly known as "Eole," had landed $75,000. He not only backed Castaway II in the winter books at long odds, but landed over $20,000 at the track on the day of the race. Pearsall is a smooth-faced quiet man of thirty-three or thereabouts, who doesn't say much, but, like the owl, he does a heap of thinking at times.

Our Tennessee Letter.

EDITOR BREEDER AND SPORTSMAN:—Another week draws us nearer to the renewal of the Suburban Handicap, and as the day draws nearer, the interest in the race increases. Many of the candidates are now receiving special preparations for that event, and reports from many sound as if each one is good enough to win. Tenny is being touted to death, as is Longstreet, Fides, Sir Dixon, Salvator, and, although Senator Hearst's Gorgo was said to be broken down, reports from "the stable" say that Allen has her going well, and that after suffering for some time with something like rheumatism, she is now moving in a manner that makes the California turfman's hopes brighten, and even all the stable-hands are said to be moving about with an air of "Gorgo will surely win the Suburban." Well, maybe she will; but I doubt it.

Pulsifer has engaged Jimmy McLaughlin to pilot Tenny in the Toboggan Slide and Suburban Handicaps, in the former carrying 130 and the latter 124 pounds. The great jockey now weighs 153 pounds, and I doubt if he can reduce to the proper weight in time for the Toboggan Slide, which will be run before this has reached the readers of the BREEDER AND SPORTSMAN. Everyone knows that Tenny has a world of speed, but can he carry 124 pounds to victory against the many speedy horses of his own calibre that he will meet at less weights, to say nothing of the dozen or more good horses that have slipped into the big handicap with from 90 to 110 pounds as an impost? Tenny is now favorite at 4 to 1—the shortest odds ever offered against any Suburban candidate this long before the race.

Longstreet has not had a race yet, and no one except his trainer and a few friends of the Dwyer's, know anything about the horse that walked away from Proctor Knott and Salvator at Monmouth last season. He is a Longfellow, and as they improve each season, he may carry the silks of the Brooklyn turfmen across the plate winner.

Badge's form of late would lead one to think that the little son of the Ill-Used was completely out of the race, and while he now seems to be "stale" or "track-sore," he may be resurrected in time to fight out the finish with the best of them.

On the Western circuit, only Maori, Sportsman and English Lady suggest consideration as having a chance at the big all-aged plum. If it be a heavy track, and he starts, I doubt if there is a single horse engaged in the race can beat Sportsman, as his impost is very light at 102 pounds.

Maori's race in the Duncan Hotel Stakes at Nashville, where she drove Robespeirre out a mile in 1:43, and on a slow track, has given her a world of following, and as her owner, Nick Finzer, has his heart set on winning the Suburban, her chances are not to be hooted at.

English Lady's two races at Louisville has caused her being backed from 100 to 1 down to 25 to 1, and her performance in these two races was of such high class, I would think her chances exceedingly rosy, and those who got their money on her at 100 to 1, should feel very lucky. At Louisville she won two good races, one at 1½ miles, and the other the Kentucky Oaks, 1¼ miles, both of which were won in a canter and from good horses. At Lexington she won at a mile in 1:42¼, and her race there was won in the same manner. In these three races she lead all the way under a pull, and won without flourish of whip. She will carry 94 pounds in the Suburban, and with her great turn of speed, she should be able to run away from her field. Then it is said the Scoggans are keeping her for that event, and they think so much of her chances, that Proctor Knott will remain in his stable while other great horses are battling against the Scoggan mare for the big prize.

Los Angeles is now said to be getting into fine form, and if she is the Los Angeles of 1888 and 1889, she will be "there or there abouts." All to start, I look for them to finish in this order: English Lady, Los Angeles and Tenny, while Maori or Salvator may interfere, and one of the other furnish the place horses.

Latonia is now probably holding the best spring meeting ever held at that course. Throughout the entire meeting the racing has been good, the betting spirited, and the attendance large. The race of the meeting, the Derby, saw Riley, Ed Corrigan's Kentucky Derby and Clark Stakes winner, easily beaten by Bill Letcher, a Tennessee-bred colt.

By the way, this reminds me of the great approaching opening of the Washington Park (Chicago) meeting, on the first day of which the Great American Derby is run. California-bred horses have been singularly successful in capturing this race, and a few weeks from now another Californian may be added to the list of American Derby winners, Silver Cloud, C. H. Todd, Emperor of Norfolk and Volante, all hailed from the golden-haired State on the Pacific, and only twice—when Modesty and Spokane won—have horses from other States carried off the Derby honors at Washington Park. Isaac Murphy rode each of the four California colts when they won this race, and it seems as if it is an agreement for Murphy and California to win this event. This year, however, it may be different. El Rio Rey, the pride of the Pacific Slope, and who it was once thought had a moral cinch on winning the Derby, is not the magnificent, strong and great horse he once was, and now, I fear, he will never hear another starter's drum tap. Still many say "Oh! that is all bosh about his wind being affected, and he is as good as ever." Well, there is one thing sure, if El Rio Rey ever wins another race—I mean a race that tests a horse's mind and staying powers—it will be a miracle, and something never performed in this country or upon the English turf before. Johnny Campbell, good trainer and jockey that he is, I heard say once: "Well, if you don't believe old Jim Gray can win, he will show you when he starts." Jim Gray started, but what could he do? Another like case is that of the great English horse Ormonde. He suffered as did El Rio Rey, and he turned a "roarer." El Rio Rey is still at Nashville, as are all of Mr. Winter's horses. I only hope that I may be wrong in my opinion of his condition, but after seeing and hearing that grunting, peculiar noise of his when working, I am led to believe that the greatest two-year-old that ever faced the flag will not be seen upon the turf at three years old.

Other horses of the Winter string are doing well, and they should be able to carry off many a good stake before they are returned to winter quarters. Joe Courtney is a superb trainer, and in him the Winter's stable has a master hand.

The New York plunger, Botay, is the heaviest bettor upon the races in the West, and from his winnings of the last few days, I judge the most successful. He plunged on Bill Letcher in the Latonia Derby, and won upwards of $6,000 on that colt's defeat of Riley. He wound up that day by winning $15,000 on four races, having back Melenie to win $5,000, also. Botay is a professor of languages, and only a short time ago held a lucrative position in a noted New York college. He gave up his class, however, for the charms of the race course, and his advent as a plunger has been followed by success. He is the "Pittsburg *Phil*" of the Western racing circuit. He is very cool and calculated, and gets information from some source that has nearly always put him on the right horse.

KENNESAW.

The Home of Mambrino Wilkes.

A Fine Crop of Foals—The San Miguel Brood Mares.

With all the conveniences that at present exist in regard to railroad service, it is rather a difficult matter to pick out a stock form which is not handy and close to a railroad and yet there is a certain amount of pleasure in a long buggy drive, especially when behind a pair of good trotters, that cannot be derived in any other way.

Last Friday morning an early start was made for Oakland where at the Webster street station the writer was met by Irvin Ayres, Esq., and we were soon on our way toward the Contra Costa hills, our destination being the San Miguel Stock Farm. Although there was a very heavy north wind blowing, there were so many beautiful sights to witness that the unpleasantness of the morning was entirely overlooked. Mr. Ayres has been for so many years closely connected with the horse interests of this State that his many reminiscences tended to make the time roll pleasantly by, and although the up grade was considerable and the distance fully twenty miles, we were little more than two and a half hours in covering the distance.

Smith J. Hill is the superintendent and general manager of Mr. Ayres' Farm and no better man could be had for the place, he is ably assisted by quite a number of hands among whom we found the old and well known horseman "Lige" Downer whose face for many years has been a familiar one on almost every track in the State.

As was to be expected, in the inspection of the stock that followed, the first shown was the well known Mambrino Wilkes 6083, sire of Gus Wilkes 2:22, Alpheus 2:27, Balkan three-year-old record 2:29½ and Clara P. 2:29½. There can be no question of doubt but what if Mambrino Wilkes had received the same class of mares that are accorded to the other members of the Wilkes family in Kentucky, that his name would stand pre-eminent to-day as one of the leading sires of the country; individually he cannot be beaten and it is but little wonder that frequently eastern visitors to this State make the long trip to the San Miguel Farm to take a look at what was generally considered one of the best sons of Old George Wilkes. The dam of Mambrino Wilkes was *Lady* Chrisman by Todhunter's Mambrino out of a daughter of Pilot, Jr. 12, the dam was brought to this State by young Rufus Ingalls, nephew of Gen. Rufus Ingalls at the same time that he brought her son Mambrino Wilkes; the horse was ultimately sold to Mr. A. L. Hinds of Oakland, who in turn transferred him to the present owner. Mambrino Wilkes was bred by Mr. B. J. Tracey of Ashland Park, Lexington, Kentucky, and was brought to this State when very young, he stood for one or more seasons at Stockton where his get is thought highly of and there can be no reasonable doubt but what the fillies he left there behind him will play a prominent part in the future breeding industries of this State. It is fully a year since the writer saw the beautiful black horse prior to this visit, and if anything he has improved in appearance, having filled out well under the good care which he receives. Quite a large number of his get were shown us, and each and every one shows the strong and marked characteristics of the sire, all having fine shoulders, good arms and splendidly finished legs. Gus Wilkes, his son has just been taken East by Dan. McCarthy, where probably he will be sold as a gentleman's roadster with a strong probability that the last has been seen of him for turf use.

Balkan who as a three-year-old made his present record, will be campaigned this your, and although he has been very ill with the prevailing epizootic that troubled all horses last year and the year before, he is better to-day than ever he was in his life, and good judges do not hesitate to assert that he will surely beat 2:20 this season. At a race at the Bay District Track in the fall of last year at the P. C. T. H. B. A. meeting he was separately timed in a race with Direct and Hazel Wilkes, he completing the mile in 2:22 which would have been a splendid mark for a four-year-old, yet still with the two performers he had against him it was impossible to get a record commensurate with his merits. It is not long ago that the BREEDER AND SPORTSMAN called attention to the exceedingly fine lot of brood mares owned by Mr. Ayres. It is true there are many of them which would not be considered gilt edged by those who believe in fashion, yet still the strong and marked individuality in each is apt to strike the spectator; it seems as though each and every one had been selected for its own strong points irrespective of pedigree, and yet there are many of them that are producing mares, and Mr. Ayres fully believes in the theory of S. A. Brown, of Kalamazoo, who in an interview a short time ago stated that he wasn't very much stuck on pedigrees but did like producing mares.

One of the best of the mares to be seen was Annie Laurie, three-year-old record 2:30, who was formerly owned by Wm. Smith of San Gabriel Mission, California. She is by Echo, dam Black Swan by California Ten Broeck, is a handsome bay, 15:3 in height, and was foaled in 1877; she has a magnificent foal at her side by Mambrino Wilkes, who for looks can compare favorably with any suckling in the State, a great big fine fellow, he is a credit alike to sire and dam, and should make a good name for both.

Contra is a bay mare eleven years old formerly owned by Gen. D. D. Colton, she is by Electioneer, dam Mrs. Newby by Billy Cheatham, son of Cracker by Boston; this well bred matron is proud in the possession of a handsome foal by Mambrino Wilkes, it is as beautiful as a picture and combining the Wilkes and Electioneer blood should prove able to go any distance and be as fast as the best.

Fanny Fern is noted as being the dam of Mollie Drew 2:27, Balkan who has been spoken of before, Fred Arnold 2:33½ and Onyx who has a trial record of 2:40, all of her foals have proven speedy and if Balkan does not seriously disappoint all who know him, she will be much more noted before the season passes than she is now; Fanny Fern is by the old thoroughbred, Jack Hawkins who was the sire of the dam of Echora 2:23½ (dam of Direct 2:18¼,) Fanny Fern's dam was one of the Jim Crow mares brought to this State many years ago from Tennessee, and while all of her progeny have been fast and successful trotters, she cannot show a drop of anything but thoroughbred blood.

Another of the mares to command attention was Narka with a handsome foal at foot by Mambrino Wilkes; Narka is by Nephew 1220, dam Baby by Chieftain 721, Narka is one of the individually good mares, in addition to her exquisite breeding, and the strong, stout trotting lines which flow through her, should make her successful as a brood mare.

Fredolia is a handsome black mare 15½ hands high, six years old bred by Henry Beech of San Joaquin County, California, her sire is Fred Arnold and her dam was by Mambrino Wilkes, out of the Beech mare, although by some it might be considered inbreeding, Fredolia was bred to Mambrino Wilkes and has a very handsome foal by that horse, the little thing is jet black, strong and powerfully built and is a "sure enough" trotter now.

Old Fancy has not proved in foal this year and she yet carries her fourteen years as gracefully as could be wished; the beholder is apt to be reminded of Old Belmont when looking at Fancy, as she bears a very strong imprint of the Williamson horse; Fancy is by Bonner, a son of Whipple's Hambletonian, dam Sophia by Belmont; Fancy is noted as being the dam of Gus Wilkes 2:22, who has it in him to go much faster than his record.

Fan is the dam of Patchwork, trial 2:30 and Cricket with a public record of 2:32 and a public trial of 2:27.

Piracy is a beautiful bay mare six years old by Buccaneer, dam Louise by Geo. M. Patchen, Jr.

Satsuma is by The Grand Moor, dam by Wisshickom (sire of the dam of Lord Byron 2:18,) and is as handsome a mare as one could find on any farm in the country; combining as she does the blood of The Moor, Mambrino Patchen and Hambletonian, is it any wonder that she should throw a handsome foal to the cover of Mambrino Wilkes? There are many visitors who are inclined to the belief that the foal of this year out of Annie Laurie is the best on the place but after a critical examination the writer is tempted to declare in favor of Satsuma's foal which is one of the handsomest sucklings seen this year, a large intelligent head well set on a splendidly arched neck, a good set of shoulders, back and loins that cannot be beaten, coupled extremely well, a good set of legs and it is a handsome all-round foal this mare is the mother of.

The yearlings at San Miguel are a fine hardy looking lot and are being worked each day on the track under the guidance of Mr. Hill; there are about a half dozen of them altogether and it will be extremely hard luck if some of them do not become noted in days to come. Many of Mr. Ayres' youngsters are entered in the Occident, Stanford, BREEDER AND SPORTSMAN Futurity and the Oakland Futurity and with such a rare lot of good ones in the crop of this year, there is no question but what some of them will add additional luster to the name of Mambrino Wilkes.

Daylight in the morning found us ready to start back, having made careful note of all the improvements which have been made since our last visit, notes of which advantage will be taken in the future when additional articles are written about this farm. To those who are interested in the trotting horse industry we tender invitation to visit this well laid out Stock Farm. Mr. Ayres will be glad at any time to meet those who are devotees of the light harness horse and we can assure our readers that it would be a hard matter to suggest a more pleasant visit than one to the home of Mambrino Wilkes.

THE FARM.

Can We Grow Beef Profitably on High-priced Land?

Slip-Shod Handlers of Scrubs.—So long as the beef market needs a float, and Wisconsin owns men who hope to foster a profit dollar, slip-shod handlers of scrub stock may join hands and fortunes with Milwaukee's almon-eyed citizens and "take a walk". It is with fear and trembling that I pronounce the fatal word "scrub." It is like unfurling a red rag before Mexico's idol. Some wise individual is wont to spring to his feet and carry an assemblage from the winding paths of the sage-brush plains to the Arabian sands in a vain and inglorious search for a thoroughbred. This blooded solon who is idigenous to the stamping grounds of agricultural societies and state institutes, feels keenly that if he can command the attention of one man in an audience of 2,000 for ten minutes, he has the unbounded gratitude of the remaining 1,999, whose ten minutes each represent about three days'time. Suffice it to say that we mean a class of cattle that does not grow poor from dragging about what they eat.

A Lesson from Low Markets.—In our opinion the low market referred to is of value to Wisconsin feeders who are not driven from the business. The man who jumps from one line to another when he sees a red flag flaunted over his market, deserves but little sympathy. It is well that the eternal fitness of things gives him a low price in his new venture just when he gets ready to turn off the largest product. When the low market does come, the intelligent feeder and business man does not waste his vitality in trying to raise prices by grumbling about the times, but immediately turns his attention to producing an article at less cost.

Wasting Forage.—The severe drought of two years since drove the truth home that Wisconsin farmers had been wasting nearly enough forage to carry the stock through the winter. Men of straitened circumstances fell down on their knees to a corn stalk, and lifted their hats respectfully when they saw a straw stack.

Feeding Steers for the Block.—One who contemplates feeding steers for the block need go to no great expense. We venture a maxim here. When no one wants an article, buy. When people are tumbling over each other to get it, sell. A thoroughbred sire, a registered animal of the beef type, is the only change that need be made. This will place you in possession, in a little time, of grades that will get more of a bushel of corn on the outside of the ribs, than would stick under the pelts of a dozen scrubs. (A humble bow to the man who says, "what is a scrub?"

Hints on Feeding Calves.—A calf should be taken from the dam at two days of age. It is unwise to withhold the first milk of the mother from the calf. The calf should get whole milk for one week, and then skim-milk may be introduced by degrees, thus getting him on skim-milk entirely when two weeks old, and none the wiser for the change. Some may say that wiser is not applicable to a calf. Calves have been known to play with a feeder, and take every trick. The trouble is, we try to feed calves when they are not hungry. Then, too, many have a blind idea that a calf can draw milk through a finger. It is an easier operation to probe the finger. Give the calf two fingers, and we have a machine, as good for the purpose as a nursing tube.

About the time the calf is on skim-milk entirely, whole oats placed before him will stick to his nose, and he unconsciously learns to eat. The ration of oats should be increased to keep pace with the assimilation. Another advantage in feeding oats is that, in eating them, saliva is absorbed, and he never gets that pernicious habit of pulling another calf's ear. A calf shows best treatment when fed three times a day. Two or three quarts of milk will answer.

Fresh water should be within easy reach. A calf will do better turned in a lot without a blade of grass, than he will in the freshest of pasture. A shed from the sun and a lock of dry hay are essential to rapid development. Milk should not be fed sour or cold. The finger is a good thing with which to point out neighbors' faults, but does not serve well for a thermometer. One can get along with his wife much better by heating water than he can by burning milk to the bottom of a kettle. A kettle of boiling water will raise enough milk to blood heat to feed twenty-five calves. More calves are spoiled by over-feeding than by starving.

The oat ration should be continued until the calves are a year old and turned to grass. Feed milk as long as you have it in the fall. Calves that are intended for the block, should never be introduced to a stanchion.

Sheds—Dehorning - Stables.—A good shed, liberal bedding and liberty, make a good match for fat calves. Ensilage, cut straw and bran or oats make a growing ration for yearlings. Horns should be taken off before turning to grass, in spring, when one year old. Upon reaching eighteen months, steers should be fed in barn or shed with no floor. If the manger is raised two and one half feet above the floor, it is not good economy to clean the stables from fall to spring. More straw can be converted into manure in this manner than by any other process. One need not fret about how much evaporates or how much leaks. All, both liquid and solid is saved. Stables can be kept sweet by the use of land plaster. Steers that are coming two, can be kept gaining on ensilage and straw.

Finishing for Market.—When warm weather comes, the cattle can be finished for the June market on corn and grass or corn and ensilage. Too much trouble? Do you know of anything that is too much trouble for your acquaintances, if they can see money in it? If treated as suggested, these steers will weigh twelve hundred pounds, and are just what buyers want.

Cost.—What is the cost? A calf will drink twenty hundred of milk, which, at twenty cents, is four dollars. He will eat fourteen bushels of oats, which, at thirty cents, is four dollars and twenty cents, and one dollar and eighty cents of dry forage, making a cost of ten dollars. A ton of ensilage in the silo costs one dollar. The calf will eat two tons or two dollars worth. He will eat ten bushels of oats, or three dollars, making a total cost, at one year, of fifteen dollars. The rent of a good acre of pasture is five dollars, which will support two yearlings, or two dollars and fifty cents. A steer coming two years will eat six tons of ensilage, or six dollars, making a total cost when he goes on grass, at two years, of seventeen dollars and fifty cents. A steer of two years, on grass, will eat ten cents worth of corn, per day, for ninety days, or nine dollars. An acre of good pasture will support two steers, fed on corn at the same time, for ninety days, which, at five dollars per acre rental, is one dollar and twenty-five cents, making a total cost of thirty-three dollars and seventy-five cents. One hundred and sixty acres of good land will carry twenty milch cows and turn off fifty steers a year.

Swine—Shorthorns.—Steers should be fed whole corn to finish them. While fed on corn the cattle should always be followed by shotes or breeding sows. By careful selection and good treatment, cows can be readily found among the Shorthorns that will give two hundred to two hundred and fifty pounds of butter; and although I have seen raving maniacs among Jersey, Guernsey and Holstein men, I have never found one who was so thoroughly demented as to advocate throwing that amount of butter away, even if it did come from the patient Shorthorn, that animal which has done more to educate and enrich the English speaking people than all other breeds combined.—H. C. Thorn, in Shorthorn Gazette.

A New Zealand Mode of Making Butter.

When some time ago it was discovered in New Zealand that cream buried in the ground for 25 hours was converted into butter without the trouble of churning, the discovery was heartily welcomed, more particularly by cow-keepers in a small way with one or two milkers, as saving a large amount of labor which generally fell on the shoulders of housewives, already sufficiently burdened. That any one, however, suspected the rationale of the change did not appear in the public prints at the time, nor, as far as I am aware, since; most persons who thought at all on the subject imagining, I fancy, a correspondent of the British Mail remarks, that temperature had something to do with it. Mr. James W. Graham, of Waiorongamai, like the rest, buried his cream to save the trouble of churning it, but being naturally disposed to pry into the wherefore of things was led to question the temperature theory. Pressure seemed the only other condition of change present, and by repeated experiments with various degrees of pressure, and at various temperatures, from a cool room to out in the December sun, pressure was fully proved the only condition. Not only so, but constant pressure was found to bring the butter in an hour instead of the 24 required by the burial process, and as in it all the cream is converted into butter, there is thus no less of butter-milk, while the quality of the butter is remarkably good. Mr. Graham has just patented his invention, and will in a short time be prepared to supply his buttermakers at a low figure—the holidays having delayed their manufacture for the present. As the machine can be practically of any reasonable capacity, and may be worked by hand, horse, steam, or any other power, it is equally suitable for the factory, and for the owner of a single cow. As it is simple and inexpensive, and reduces the time of buttermaking to an hour, while the application of the pressure, washing and working the butter, require in all but a few minutes' work, the inventor will no doubt reap a rich reward for cultivating a habit of not taking things as granted.

Montana Cattle Brands.

Rules and regulations for recording brands and marks in the state of Montana, and by the board of stock commissioners, March 22, 1887, under authority conferred upon them by law, approved March 9th, 1887:

1. For the purpose of recording brands and marks, animals shall be divided into the following classes:
   1. Cattle.
   2. Horses, mules and asses.
   3. Sheep, swine and goats.
2. All persons making application for recordings, brands and marks shall designate the class or classes for which said mark or brand is to be used.
3. No mark or brand shall be recorded that in any manner conflicts with any other brand or mark on record.
4. A person recording a brand will be permitted to use the brand on one side only of the animal, and only one place for original brand, and one place for vent of same.
5. In order to transfer title to animals bearing recorded brands, the party selling shall vent, or cause to be vented, the brand same as original brand, but may be the same brand reduced not more than one-half in size and on the same side of the animal as original brand,
6. The addition of a bar, a letter, a figure, or a character to an existing recorded brand, in the same position and same side of animal, shall be considered an infringement on the priority of said brand, and shall not be recorded.
7. No individual or corporation shall be allowed to record for use upon the Montana ranges more than one brand for horses.

Preventing Trouble at Calving.

We often read directions how to prevent milk fever, says the Stockman and Farmer, retention of the placenta, etc. Some advise the giving of drugs of various kinds, while others advise a special line of feeding; the latter we think the only correct way of obviating trouble. As to what shall be fed, opinions differ; one old farmer said he always fed short corn to his cows for a few weeks before calving, and never had any cases of milk fever or other disease to contend with. Others feed whole oats, others bran, and so on. Our own practice has been to feed bran and linseed meal for three or four weeks before the cows are due to calve, and we attribute our freedom from trouble at calving in great part to this course of feeding. In summer when on grass, no grain feed is required, provided the cow's bowels are in a healthy condition. Here is where the danger lies, according to our observation—in constipation or a tendency to that condition. Keep the bowels in a healthy state, give sufficient feed to keep up the strength of the cow, feed lightly and with laxative feed for a few days after calving, and there will rarely be occasion to doctor a sick cow.

Make Your Head Save Your Heels.

"Judicious laziness" is what most farmers want a little more of: Not time for loafing and idle talk, but rest from hard work, that their brains may be rested and clear to think and plan better. I suppose some of the old people will think that I am preaching a bad doctrine to our boys, but I know from personal experience that it is true. Not many years ago, and with a mortgage on the farm, I borrowed money to pay my expenses to horticultural meetings and those of our State Board of Agriculture, and even to go off and visit other farms. I used the opportunities I got for my money. I remembered what I saw and heard, and the farm is improved the mortgage is paid, and I am able to live comfortably and well. To-morrow I intend to visit an intelligent fruit grower, of whom I think I can learn something more. I still practice what I preach, "judicious laziness."—N. E. Homestead.

Clydesdales are Pure Bred.

Breeders are Making Preparations for an Exhibit at the World's Fair.

At a meeting of the American Clydesdale Association, which was held recently, the following resolutions were adopted:

Whereas, The prime object of the American Clydesdale Association is to preserve accurate records of the pedigrees of well bred Clydesdale horses, as well as to encourage the improvement in quality and breeding of the same; and

Whereas, There is every probability that the World's Fair of 1892 will be held at Chicago, conceded to be the most accessible point for the great majority of the prominent breeders of Clydesdale horses to exhibit their stock; and

Whereas, An exhibition of Clydesdale horses held in connection with the World's Fair of 1892 will enable breeders to widely advertise the superiority of this breed of draft horses, and

Whereas, The members of this association have resolved to make the exhibition of Clydesdale horses to be held in connection with the World's Fair of 1892, both in extent and superior quality of the display, most creditable to the breed and of the greatest possible benefit to all interested in the same; therefore be it

Resolved, That it is the sense of the Executive Committee of the American Clydesdale Association that $5,000 in cash prizes be offered by this organization in addition to the premiums offered the breed by the general managers of the World's Fair of 1892, said $5,000 to be awarded to members of this association exhibiting at said show the best specimens of Clydesdale horses of their own breeding.

Resolved, That a committee of three be appointed to devise and report to this association at the next annual meeting the classification of prizes, the conditions that should govern the awards of this association and other matters in connection with the Clydesdale exhibit at the World's Fair of 1892.

Resolved, That the Secretary of this association be and is hereby instructed to transmit a copy of the foregoing resolutions to each member of this organization, with a request for such suggestions as will tend to make the proposed exhibition of the greatest possible benefit to the Clydesdale interest in America.

Breeding Mares.

The failure to get mares with foal is becoming a serious question, says the Western Farm Journal, with the small farmer who keeps only mares to do his work. As a mare can almost as easily raise a colt as not, her failure to breed is a direct loss, and often quite a considerable one. It is the nature of a mare to breed, and if she does not, the failure is usually from one of three reasons: First, she is not healthy; second, proper care has not been exercised in taking her to and from the horse; third, the horse is either impotent, or is poorly fed and cared for. Probably three-fourths of the failures may be attributed to the second reason given. Not many farmers desire to have colts come in March; most of them prefer April or May. This throws the breeding of the mare in May and June, during the pressing work of the year, when every moment is valuable, and when the mare is discovered to be in heat, the idea is to get her to the horse and be back in the field as quickly as possible. The horse is allowed to serve her while she is still warm from trotting to the stand, and immediately after service she is driven home and worked the rest of the day. It is very difficult to get a mare in foal in this way. After the service she should be tied away by herself for an hour or two, then driven home at a slow walk and left alone in the stable until the next day. A little care the first trip will save many other trips. It seems as if it would be better to begin breeding early in April, when work does not push so, and when the horse does not have so much work to do. To be sure, a colt coming in March must have a warm place, but after it is a day or two old it is as hardy as a calf, and will grow right along.

It sometimes happens that a horse is not a reasonably sure foal getter, and in this case the only remedy is to withdraw and breed to another horse. It is more frequently the owner's fault than the horse's. Patrons of a horse should insist that he be regularly exercised. Some mares will breed only every other year, suckling affecting the reproductive organs, and some mares will not come in heat at all while suckling a colt. In some cases this cannot be remedied, and the only thing to do is to get rid of the mare. With other mares the carelessness of the owner in not trying to get her with foal, and persistent breeding will sometimes overcome it. With shy breeders a very good plan is to allow the horse to give two services at an interval of two or three hours, and at the latter part of the heat. The owner of the stallion will usually rather do this than have the mare coming back during the entire season. It frequently happens that old mares will "close up," sometimes within three or four weeks after foaling. In such a case an operation should be performed by the keeper of the stallion before allowing the horse to serve. In case a mare fails to get in foal after one or two services, it is well to have her examined and see if the passage is closed. It is usually better to breed old mares to a two-year-old horse. In rare cases a mare will take the horses after being safe in foal, but usually no damage results from this. The safest plan is to breed on the ninth day after foaling, and try again about the twenty-eighth day after foaling; passing this interval without taking the horse, a mare may usually be considered safe in foal.

A Stallion Club.

In unity there is profit as well as strength. What better plan for the improvement of horse stock could be taken than to form a horse club in your community? This is done in some places with gratifying results. A number of farmers form a co-operative association, advance enough money to pay for a first-class stallion, and charge a reasonable fee for his service. This fee is paid the same as if the horse belonged to an outsider, and non-members are allowed to breed, if the club is not too large, on payment of the regular fee. The keeping of the horse generally costs little cash outlay, some member being willing to care for him in consideration of services rendered for keeper. It is a good plan to have the stallion insured, so that there will be no danger of loss. A recent English paper gave an account of an association of this kind whose club horse, during a period of four years, paid for himself and gave a dividend to the members of the club of about 30 per cent. on the money originally advanced—all this without counting the improvement made in the stock in that community. There is no reason why this cannot be done in many sections where good horses do not abound or held above the reach of the average breeder.—Stockman and Farmer.

TURF AND TRACK.

Benzon or Jubilee Juggings is out again.

Jessica by Enquirer has been sent to Terra Cotta.

Pittsburg Phil is said to be $100,000 ahead this season.

Fannie Witherspoon 2:16½ has a colt foal by Nutwood 2:18¾

J. F. Caldwell will start at Guttenberg during the summer meeting.

The $40,000 King Thomas seems to be a deceiver of the worst kind.

Budd Doble says he bought Lady Bullion for himself—not Governor Merriam.

Brittanic, the crack sprinter, served 20 mares before leaving Bowling Brook.

Sinaloa II is full sister to Bonita, Goliah, Cleopatra, and a half sister to Lucky B.

Hot Springs, Arkansas, purposes having a winter meeting from January to May.

Marcus Daly, the Montana millionaire declined to be a World's Fair Commissioner.

Arol 2:24 will, 'says the Chicago Horseman' probably be saved but she will never race again.

It is expected that the invincible—so far, El Rio Rey will start for the St. Louis Derby to-day.

Johnston 2:06¼, the king of pacers, has been recently sold by John W. Conley to E. C. Long, St. Paul.

W. S. Vosburg, better known as Vigilant, is the official handicapper for the New York Jockey Club.

Dr. W. G. Rose, the well known owner of imported Cheviot, contemplates a trip to England this summer.

Westchester is having the best meeting of the season and the Morris two-year-olds are still almost invincible.

Johnny Dickerson has twenty-seven head in his stable. His campaigning string will consist of about fifteen.

Belle Rene, 2:26½, in Dickerson's string, was shipped this week to her owner, Dr. W. A. Gibson, Jackson, Mich.

Messrs. A. C. Brice, Minneapolis, and George Middleton, Chicago, owner of Jack 2:15, were in Terra Haute last week.

Mr. Loates, the father of the three well known English jockeys Tommy, Sammy and Charley Loates, died last month.

When Wilfred won the second race a Gravesend on the 27th there was not a single mutual ticket on him, his starting price was 50-1.

Russia 2:28 (sister to Maud S 2:08¾) has a colt by King Wilkes; Russia and Jeanne (Kentucky Prince—Suisun) will be bred to Axtell 2:12.

The first Californian to win in the East was Santa Anita's, Sinaloa II, who won the Ladies Stake at Westchester last Tuesday in good style.

Alfred S was kicked on the foreleg last week while being grassed. It is hoped the injury will only be slight so that he will be in trim for Rochester.

Flyaway 3 by Geo. Kinney out of Sunbeam by imp Leamington won three races as a two-year-old, and has been sent this year to be bred to Jim Gore.

J. M. Johnson's fine mare, Folle Farine, by Post Boy, 2:23½, dam by Clark Chief, sire of dam of Phallas, 2.13¾, has foaled a bay colt Chichester, 2:25½.

Mr. Belmonts' Lady Roseberry who died of colic last week was by Kingfisher out of Lady Blessington, she was the dam of Lady Primrose and Lady Margaret.

C. J. Hamlin's string this year includes Belle Hamlin, 2:12¾; Mocking Bird, 2:17½; Globe, 2:19½; Prince Regent, 2:21½; Justina, 2:23½, and W. H. Nichols, 2:23½.

Mr. Oehschlager, a racing man well know all over Europe, died at Berlin on May 12th. Mr. Oehschlager owned some good chasers in his time including Johnny Longtail.

The agricultural pavilion at Salinas has been enlarged and there is now an elegant commodious structure capable of accommodating innumerable sight-seers and exhibitors.

There are sixteen colored jockeys in the country who are paid from $2,500 to $8,000 a year, but not a colored minister in the United States receives one-half of the lesser of these sums.

Green B. Morris last week sold to G. R. Tompkins the chestnut horse Taragon, aged 5 years, by Stratford, out of Tara. The price is stated to be in the neighborhood of $5,000 or $6,000.

Imp Hearst by Fergus 1st out of Romping Girl, who was imported by J. K. Newton and sold last year in New York, was killed in a collision with Gallus Dan and Gyda at Brighton Beach, on May 30th.

John Mackey, Rancho Del Paso's Superintendent, left last Monday at 12:30, with a special train containing 96 yearlings for New York. They will go to Hunt's Point and be sold on the 16th, in the city.

Messrs. Kelly & Samuels' Pliny is doing well in Denver. In addition to winning the Colorado Derby he carried a penalty and readily won the Mountain Stakes, running the mile with 124 lbs. up in 1:44½.

Mr. John Madden's black mare by Kentucky Prince, dam Suisun, 2:25½, by Electioneer, foaled a fine colt foal by Stamboul 2:12½, at Warren Park last week. This one is surely "in it" as to the purple.

The report that Gov. Merriam of Minnesota had purchased Lady Bullion, 5-year-old, record 2:18½, is a mistake. She has been bought by Bud Doble from R. Kingman, Battle Creek, Mich., and will be campaigned by him.

Mr. F. S. Waters, of Chicago, was making the rounds last week. If we owned such a horse as Faustino, we would want to look at him all the time says the Terre Haute Express. Faustino was Count Valensin's crack yearling.

Zoraya, by Guy Wilkes, dam Neluska by Sultan, the $13,000 purchase of Messrs. Stoner & Clay, is now enjoying the luxuriant bluegrass at Marchmont. Her colt by the great Stamboul is doing nicely. She will be bred to Anteo 2:16½.

At the next meeting of the English Jockey Club to be held at Newmarket on the first of July, Lord Lascelles will move to add to rule 47: "Not more than one handicap per day for three-year-olds and over, of less than one mile shall be run.

Timothy Anglin of Glenervon Farm, Lexington, Ky., has sold to Gerhard Lang of Baffalo, N. Y., the bay yearling colt by Wilkes Boy, dam Josie, by the King, for $6,000. Mr. Lang also bought a suckling brother to the yearling for $2,000.

Billy Dowling, of Decatur Ill., has arrived at Terre Haute with Carrie Walton, 2:22½, by Governor Sprague. This is the mare J. I. Case recently offered $10,000 for. Rumor has it she is very fast and that 2:16 will be near her mark before that the season is over.

Each week shows notable improvement in the condition of the Helena track. Horsemen are well pleased with the progress made, and are daily showing more speed to those who visit the grounds in the mornings. The inside pole around the track is about completed.

Gillette, "the black whirlwind" of the Blue Grass region, wears only 14 ounce shoes forward and 3½ ounces behind; Dr. Sparks 2:25½, at two years, wears 6½ ounces forward and 3 ounces back, and the fast two-year-old Snip Nose wears 8 ounces forward and 3 ounces back.

Bonita keeps winning every now and again in good company in the West as she has for several years. Mr. Baldwin probably regrets the day he sold the more than useful half sister to Lucky B. and observing "a la William Daly" that she would make a good buggy mare.

Reina and Betsy Brown, were driven last week at Terra Haute by Budd Doble to a skeleton wagon a half mile in 1:08½, last quarter in 33½ seconds, a 2.14 clip. This is remarkable speed for this season of the year. The trial mile record of Maud S. and Aldine, made in 1883, was 2:15½.

A blind man, guided by a boy, is a daily attendant at the Eastern races. He was quite successful in his speculations one day, and was heard to remark on the way to the train that he never "saw" such good racing. Evidently he viewed the contests through a pair of dollars and cents glasses.

John E. Turner's stable of trotters and pacers this year includes Harry Wilkes 2:13½; Rosaline Wilkes 2:14½; Seymour Belle 2:19¾; Wanita 2:20½; Fred Folger 2:20½; Annie Wilkes 2:21½; Shipman 2:24½; Suisun 2:25; San Mateo 2:28½; Happy Bee 2:29¾; Gossip Jr, 2:13½; and Mambrino Hannis 2:16½.

Hugh Kirkendall's trotting stallion, Procrastination, reached Helena yesterday from Spokane, where he has been in training. Ed. Lafferty with the rest of Mr. Kirkendall's stable leaves Spokane next week and goes direct to Helena. He will not stay over for the Portland meeting as previously announced.

Dr. Aby, the Guenoc Stock Farm's Manager, says that their Agricultural District Association will have a whooping fair this year. By the way the genial Doctor is still more impressed with his grand stallion St. Saviour since his brother Eon's good form and Russell's good races. Both horses are by Eolus—the king of the mud.

"I consider Axtell to be the best-gaited horse living," recently observed John Splan. "His gait is the poetry of trotting action. The man who could ever watch the bend of his knees, the fold of his fetlocks, without being awakened to a sense of perfection of movement unsurpassed has no preception of the beauty in art or nature."

The Rancho del Paso catalogues of the yearling sale arrived last Wednesday evening and are remarkable for the plain, straightforward account of each of the youngster's ancestors, and the carefully arranged tabulated pedigrees of each of the dams. The stallions are all tabulated in the front of the pamphlet which is the most complete ever got up in America.

A wild horse, or what appears to be one, was recently captured at Horse Landing, Fla. A stockmen was herding cattle and drove the pony among them, and so got him into a pen. A faint brand mark is visible, but otherwise the animal appears to be perfectly wild, as much so as a deer, and it is probable that it has been herding with the cattle for a number of years.

The first State Fair of the Montana Agricultural, Mineral and Mechanical Association will be held in Helena next August. Secretary Pope says that the mineral exhibit will be exceptionally fine, and that the horse and cattle exhibits will be up to the usual standard of excellence. The entries in the colt races have been very large, and it is expected that all Montana will be there.

Alcazar 2:20½, purchased this spring by the Uihlien Bros. of Milwaukee, Wis., has held one uninterrupted reception since his arrival, and several times over one hundred horsemen from various parts of the country have paid their respects to the son of Sultan and Minnehaha in one day. His book for this season was immediately filled, and that of next year is rapidly becoming so.

English turfites, in the shape of bookmakers, jockeys, etc., are clearing out from Buenos Ayres, as not being the El Dorado it at first promised to horsemen. The native hidalgos pay big prices for foreign bred horses; but there is little enthusiasm in their sporting proclivities generally; indeed, pigeon shooting, cockfighting and bull fighting have all been put down by the strong hand of the law.

Last week Mr. Dave Cox secured, at Terre Haute photographs of Sunol, Palo Alto, Johnston, Adonis, Jack, Faustino, Fred Arthur, Hendryx, So Long, Gertrude Russel, M'liss, Nutrell and a group consisting of Nutmeg and five of his colts. Those of Sunol, Palo Alto, Johnston, Adonis, and Faustino, were for Artist Cory, of Clark's Horse Review staff, who intends getting up a full page cut of these flyers, grouped around Axtell.

The newly formed Oakland Driving Park Club held thei usual weekly meeting at the Trotting Park last week o Thursday, instead of Saturday. In the future they wil meet every Saturday, and judging from the style in whic they turned out last week and on previous occasions, th club is an un-doubted success.

The Rose fever has, says The Terre Haute Express, com pelled President Ijams to seek the rarified air of Colorad His absence during the race week is much to be regretted as the association not only loses his services as a starte at which he is unexcelled, but his many qualities which a of such valuable assistance toward a success. He has, how ever, secured a first-class starter, Mr. T. Woodmartin, fro Philadelphia, and will leave the other duties in capabl hands.

Speaking of one of the latest recruits to the English Turf i Baron Hirsch, the owner of Vasistas, The sporting man o "Truth" says this "worthy financier was very astute in hi dealings with the Turkish Government, but on the Turf h is as much out of his element as a trout on a gravel walk and the wrongs of the Porte appear likely to be thoroughl avenged on what Lord Beaconsfield described as the "plain of Newmarket."

The clubs of the Manitoba and Northwestern Racing Ci cuit have arranged the following dates for the various rac meetings: Winnipeg, June 30th, July 1st, 2nd; Portage l Prairie, July 8th, 9th; Carberry, July 14th, 15th; Brando July 18th, 19th; Mossomin, July 22d, 23d; Qu 'Appelle, Jul 28th, 29th; Regina, August 1st, 2nd; Morse Jaw, August 6th 7th; Calgary, August 13th, 14th, 15th. The prizes for th race meetings will be $20,000.

The Morris' two-year-olds are almost invincible. Russell i running in tremendous form, and after his race in the mud fo the great American stake Phil. Dwyer said: "There's the be colt I've seen in many a day," Mr. Dwyer don't usually e thuse, and his opinion goes for something. The winner i a dark bay colt, 15.3 hands high, without white, by Eol out of Tillie Russell, and is a full brother to Harry Russell an Charlie Russell. He was bred by Mr. Doswell of Virgini and sold as a yearling to Messrs. J. A. and A. H. Morris.

"The blanketing, drawing fine, and work which Geor M. Patchen had to undergo was terrible" was the recent r mark of John Splan in conversation with Budd Doble. "A one time matched to go under saddle, he was reduced fort pounds in one week, and on the day of the race did not hav as much flesh as a canary bird carries. You rode him in th race, Budd; he was drawn so fine that his sides were glue together. He was on fire at the end of the first heat, an was much distressed, but he had wonderful recuperativ powers."

An exchange says: The ringing business has begun early At Holyoke, May 17th, the bay gelding was protested, ma claiming that it was old Driver. That was a mean thin to do; we do not believe the old fellow ever did a me thing in his life. At the very minute the protest was mad Driver stood in his owners stable in Winchester. If th men who made the kick had been posted, they would hav called the suspected horse Iron Age, but not the famous o roan of that name who was sired by Jules Jurgensen.

An extraordinary incident took place during a race wi Mexican mustangs at Guatemala the latter part of Apri The favorite was winning easily by nearly three lengt amid the loud cheers of the spectators, when suddenly t sharp crack of a rifle was heard from a small wood adjace to the course, and the mustang dropped dead, shot throug the head. A scene of extraordinary excitement ensued, a if the firer of the shot had been captured he would have be lynched, as a large amount of money was invested on t race. The search which followed, however, was unsucces ful, and the miscreant got clean away.

The English Jockey Club appear to have taken a very fi stand against the granting of licences for new race course They announce that, owing to the difficulty in providi days for meetings already in existence, applications for lice ces for additional race courses will only be entertained und very exceptional circumstances, and in no case without straight mile and proper provision for long courses, and th in order to avoid risk of pecuniary loss or disappointme such proposals should be submitted to them in a prelimina shape before any expenditure is incurred.

C. T. Patterson, brother of Rody Patterson, the superi tendent of Edgewood Stock Farm, arrived at Terra Ha last week from Kentucky with a string of horses. They w be given some work there and then go to Janesville, W The stable includes Bessemer, 2:13½ (driven to that mark Rody Patterson last season); Twist, a four year old roan m who obtained a three year old record of 2:29½ in the ni heat of a race; Happy Wanderer, 6 year old horse, 2:37½, Happy Medium. In the same car were Rutledge, gray ho 2:27½, by Onward and Godelia, b m, 2:29½, by Aberde They are owned by Leonard Bros., of Kentucky, and h joined Doble's string.

Such is the rush for the Galopin blood that the you English stallion, King Galop, imported by Mr. Howland, now at Mr. Clay's Iroquois Stud in Kentucky, has his bo full. Mr. Clay says he has been compelled to refuse qui number of mares. King Galop is the only Galopin stalli in Kentucky, and his breeding on the side of his dam is v high, tracing directly to Sunbeam, the mare who won the Leger for Mr. Merry in 1858. In fact, he and Galore are only Galopin stallions in the country, and St. Simon's s cess with Signorina, Semolina and Memoir, as well as G liard's success, shows that the sons of Galopin are likely continue the stud triumphs of the old hero.

Nearly all of the Eastern turf journals have been rep sented at Terre Haute within the past two weeks, and seems to be the concensus of opinion that Palo Alto most surely lower the stallion record this year; in fact, writer claims that it is within the bounds of possibility Senator Stanford's horse may beat the record of Maud Each and all declare that Roy Wilkes is in good shape moving nicely, yet still we have information that leads u believe that the game stallion has a very bad "leg." Su has received the praise she so richly merits, and one and speak of her in the highest terms. In the Hickok lot favorite with the writers seems to be Prince Warwick, many of them are inclined to believe that Orrin has a sec St. Julien. I trust it may be so,

I see the New York Spirit says that on May 15th at Louisville, T. Hazlitt's b f Louise 4 by Kyrle Daly—Nighthawk 100, Allen, won the Finzer Bros. purse, $400, for maidens all ages. Louise M b m (4 Kyrle Daly—Nighthawk) on January 9th and January 14th this year won races at Los Angeles, while last year she won the Vestal stakes at the Blood Horse Fall Meeting. Probably the Spirit is mistaken in the mare, for Goodwin's Guide says it was F. B. Harper's Louisa Forest.

Mr. Lowther is, says a writer in England, much exercised in his mind because certain black sheep who have been warned off the Turf have gone out to Buenos Ayres, where they have succeeded in obtaining lucrative engagements. The trainer of the famous Ormonds is one of these, and Kellett, who rode Acme when he was killed, is warned off both the French and English Turf. I think that Mr. Lowther desires a sort of extradition treaty with the Republic of the Argentine. There is so much jealousy of the English out there that I doubt whether the Jockey Club of that country will enter into working arrangements with the Jockey Club here.

Speaking of big horses, says the New York Sun, that other young giant, King Thomas, has fined down into a noble looking racer. Last year he was, perhaps, a trifle gross for the critics, but now no such fault can be found. And, in addition to that, he is going great guns in his work, his disposition being much improved since he and Hamilton parted company. With Hayward, whose hands are marvellous, to handle him, King Thomas will give a good account of himself this year. Tournament, Ballarat and Anaconda in the same string are all doing well and taking their work regularly under Mr. Allen's careful eye. Anaconda is a maiden, and a nice time a man would have hunting up a maiden able to give him a race.

The Terre Haute Express says:—The Doble, Hicock, Marvin, Hill, Shuler, etc., stables not having early engagements, are still at slow work, repeating in from 2:40 to an occasional "pipe opener" for an eighth or quarter. The visitors from abroad and the city continue to be many. Mr. Marvin is a little early with Sunol, and not many have got to see her worked. He is not doing much with any of his stable, and it will be some little time before a fifth second watch will be needed to catch the quarters. Monterey, in Hickok's stable, by his way of going, is doing much to confirm the belief that when he is turned loose, it will take more than a green horse to head him. Prince Warwick, in the same stable, is about the thing we are all trying to get, "a rare good one."

The Aberdeen line steamship Damascus left Sydney on March 29th for London, via the Cape, with the Australian candidates for the English classic races of 1891 and 1892. The youngsters are Wentworth, a brown colt; Nepean, a bay colt; Mons. Meg, a bay filly; and a bay colt, half brother to Cranbrook and Kirkham, by Martini-Henry from La Princesse. Nepean and Wentworth are engaged in the Two Thousand Guineas, the Derby, and the St. Leger of 1891. Mons. Meg's engagements include the One Thousand Guineas, the Oaks, and the St. Leger for the same season, and the Martini-Henry—La Princesse colt is to appear among the entries for the classic races of 1892. Should the Damascus have fine weather she would most probably reach Plymouth last Monday.

Gorgo, Senator Hearst's fine imported five year old mare, will probably not be seen at the post very soon if ever again. The cause of her lameness cannot be ascertained by the best veterinarians. Conflicting statements have been published regarding her condition; first she would be broken down and the next report would say she was all right and moving well. Last week Senator Hearst was asked about the recent report that she was all right, and said: "It was correct for the day, but that is the funny part of the affair One day she is taken out on the track looking in prime condition and runs like a deer. My trainer is delighted and sends for me and a lot of horsemen to see the mare go. I am delighted and gather a lot of friends together and we visit the track, and as soon as the mare comes out she limps. I guess Gorgo is off the list."

There was an accident in the fourth heat of the first race at Philadelphia during the trotting by which Ed. Odell, the driver of Golddust Prince narrowly escaped serious injury. H. W. Banks, with Carrie C. bumped against Odell's sulky in going round the first turn, and Odell's foot was knocked out of the stirrup. Odell toppled over but hung on to the shaft and tried hard to regain his seat. The horse turned toward the outside of the track carrying out the horses behind him, and when Odell's sulky finally turned over Carrie C. ran into him again. For a moment sulkies, drivers and men were mixed up together. Odell came out of it with a cut over his left eye. One of Golddust Prince's legs was scratched, while Banks and Carrie C. escaped without injury. The judges decided that the accident was not censurable, and allowed the horses to start in the next heat. Golddust Prince trotted gamely in the three succeeding heats, getting second place in each. He finished first by a head in the last heat, but was set back for running. The judges were J. A. Wendroth, Harry Webster and J. A. Munday.

The Coney Island Jockey Club announces the following as list of the days on which the several stakes will be run for during the June meeting:

Tuesday, June 17th—The Double Event, the Equinoctial Stakes, the Suburban Handicap.

Wednesday, June 18th—The Daisy Stakes.

Thursday, June 19th—The Foam Stakes, the Sheepshead Bay Handicap, the Volunteer Handicap.

Friday, June 20th—The Pansy Stakes.

Saturday, June 21st—The Surf Stakes, the Tidal Stakes, the Bay Ridge Handicap.

Monday, June 23d—The Dandelion Stakes.

Tuesday, June 24th—The Zephyr Stakes, the Mermaid Stakes, the Coney Island Stakes.

Thursday, June 26th—The Spring Stakes, the Swift Stakes, the Coney Island Cup.

Friday, June 27th—The Spring Turf Stakes.

Saturday, June 28th—The June Stakes, the Spendthrift Stakes, the Knickerbocker Handicap.

Monday, June 30th—The Thistle Stakes.

Tuesday, July 1st—The Grass Selling Stakes.

Wednesday, July 2d—The Double Event, the Realization Stakes, the Stirrup Cup.

Although no stake race is announced for Wednesday, June 25th, there will be racing on that day, and at least six races on each day of the meeting, which will last fourteen days. The Suburban and Realization days, the two sensational days of the meeting, will be the opening and closing days.

R. E. Bybee, Portland, Ore., writes me that he has not sold Billow (the dam of Eclipse) to Mr. Haggin. "He says: I still own her; she has a very fine filly foal, bay with small star, right forefoot white; it is by St. Paul, he by Alarm, dam Lady Salyers by Longfellow. She has been bred this year to Oregon, he by Monday, dam Planetia by Planet; 2d dam La Henderson." My informant understood Mr. Haggin had bought her, but the sale evidently did not come off.

The St. Louis Republic, describing the race for the Toboggan Slide, says: The race almost from the start lay between Fides and Geraldine, the last named showing her heels to the field until the end of half a mile. Then Hamilton sent Fides along and collaring Geraldine opposite the lower portion of the stand, a desperate race ensued. Geraldine stopped perceptibly when McCarthy struck her with the whip, and Fides won the prize by a length. Blue Rock easily vanquished the others, and was a very close third. Strideaway got off last, but was one of the dangerous elements at the dip by the elm tree. The pace, however, killed him, as it did the others, Sunday, the horse from the West that was said to be a world-beater at the distance, and worth another trick from the uncurried territory, never being able to keep up the merry clip Geraldine and Fides set from the drop of the flag. Tormentor ran a good race, finishing fourth, and imported Delmar will do to remember, the Australian colt showing a rare burst of speed at the half. We all know how good Fides is now, and old turfmen may well shake their heads and look sage when they look at the time she made in to-day's race. It is little short of phenomenal, even on Morris' toboggan slide.

The death of Hermit has revived an interest in the sensational surroundings which marked his Derby triumph of 1867. The Sporting Chronicle says the following are a few of the cross and other bets on the race: £40,000 even on The Palmer against Hermit, which Sir Joseph Hawley laid Mr. Chaplin, in addition to £10,000 even to Sir F. Johnston, when the horses were two-years-old, besides an even £5,000 between Hermit and Marksman laid by their owners at the Middle Park sale, when the colts realized 1,000 guineas each as they followed each other into the ring, as was the case with Kettledrum and Dundee at Doncaster, who also ran first and second in the Derby. A bet of £180,000 to £6,000 laid by the Duke of Hamilton to Captain Machell, who considered that the horse had progressed so satisfactorily on resuming gentle work as to inspire him with fresh confidence, and he backed him to win £10,000 at 1,000 to 15 within the last hour, when it "rained cats and dogs," although his true starting price was 1,000 to 10, which was currently offered afterwards. In his early days Hermit was in William Goater's stable, but subsequently left Michel Grove for Newmarket, with the remainder of Mr. Chaplin's horses, to be trained by the late George Bloss under Captain Machell's management.

The English Derby was run last Wednesday, Surefoot, a red hot favorite was unable to get a place, finishing fourth, the winner being Sainfoin, who was purchased by Sir James Miller for $7,000—with contingencies to Mr. J. Porter, who trained him for his engagements. Sainfoin is said by a well known writer on turf matters, to be a bright chestnut, blaze face, off hind shank white half way to hocks, and near white hind fetlock; exquisite shoulders, grandly arched loins, deep and powerful quarters, clean hocks, and stands true on good legs and feet; he is by Springfield out of Sanda, and was bred by "Her Majesty," being bought by John Porter for 550 guineas as a yearling. The winner was ridden by Watts, who was up on Merry Hampton in 1887, he had since his victory in the Dee Stakes, one and a half miles at Chester, on May 8th, been steadily backed at good odds. Baron Rothschild's Le Nord by Tristan—a son of Hermit, out of La Noce was second—as he was in the Two Thousand—Fred Barrett rode and Hayhoe trained him. The Duke of Westminster's Orwell by Bend Or—the 1880 winner, out of Lily Agnes and therefore own brother to the mighty Ormonde, the winner in 1886—obtained third place. Surefoot, a scorching favorite, ridden by Liddiard was a good fourth.

The New York Tribune says:

Naomi, the Keheilan Arab mare, of the Maneghi-Hedrudj (bred by the Gomussa Bedouins, of the great Anazeh tribes, and brought from the Euphrates Valley to England by the late Capt. Roger D. Upton, of the Ninth Royal Lancers, after whose death she became the property of the Rev. F. F. Vidal, of Creeting Rectory, Needham Market, Suffolk, England) which was sent over in August, 1888, to Randolph Huntington, of Rochester, N. Y., to be bred to Gen. Grant's Seglawi-Jedran Arab, Leopard, gave birth to a colt on the night of May 10. Mr. Huntington describes the youngster as absolutely perfect, and has named him Anezeh. Naomi is said to be the only pure Arabian mare ever brought to America. Leopard, it will be remembered, was presented to Gen. Grant by Abdul Hamid II (successor of Murad V), Sultan of Turkey. "The American people," says Mr. Huntington, "know absolutely nothing of the Arabian horse. What they believe to be Arabs are only Moorish mongrels, or possibly Egyptian, or even Persian mongrel bred animals. Naomi is the only positively pure-bred Arab mare that has come at any time to America. In forty year's breeding I have never seen so perfect, strong and active a foal, immediately from birth, as Anazeh."

The Clear Lake Press says:—A large and enthusiastic meeting was held in Gould & Wood's Club Room on Monday last for the purpose of inaugurating a Jockey Club.

L. H. Gruwell was appointed President of the evening, and I. S. Alexander, Secretary.

At the request of the President, B. F. Gould explained that the object for which the meeting was called was the formation of a Lower Lake Jockey Club, to encourage the breeding and training of trotting stock, and maintaining a racing track known as Clayton Park.

At the conclusion of B. F. Gould's remarks, the following signified their intention of becoming members:

L. H. Gruwell, W. C. Goldsmith, W. H. Turner, R. Keatinge, O. E. Parker, A. Wood, Geo. Wood, C. A. Barker, G. R. Webber, G. S. Hertelet, T. Turner, P. Baylis, B. F. Gould and F. Lynch.

The election of officers was next proceeded with when L. H. Gruwell was appointed President, W. C. Goldsmith Vice President, G. S. Hertslet Secretary, I. S. Alexander Treasurer, and A. Wood, G. R. Webber, T. G. Turner, C. Barker, and B. F. Gould, Directors.

The President having named G. S. Hertslet, G. R. Webber, and B. F. Gould a Committee to draft rules on the basis of those governing the State Agricultural Society.

The meeting adjourned to next week, when the report of the committee will be submitted.

Mr Kennedy, the well known mesmerist, told us a sporting story says Rapier, which—well, we will say contained an amusing coincidence. He was in Australia at the time when Cranbrook, one of the best horses that ever ran in the Antipodes, was carrying all before him. The ring stood to lose heavily over him (I think the race in question was the Melbourne Cup), and one of them, after ruefully looking at his book, said to Mr. Kennedy, "I wish you would mesmerise that horse and prevent him from winning, for it will hit me hard if he takes the cup." The mesmerist replied that he would have a look at the animal, went into the paddock, and presently came across the favorite. "Is that Cranbrook?" he said to the boy leading the horse around, and was answered in the affirmative. "Ah, he's sure to win to-day!" Mr. Kennedy continued, and the lad replied, "Of course he'll win; he'll win this and whatever else he runs for. There's nothing that can ever beat Carnbrook!" Mr. Kennedy made some complimentary rejoinder, and passed his hands before the horse's face. Whether that had anything to do with what happened he does not pretend to say, but, as a matter of fact, the race was run and Cranbrook suffered what, if I remember the tale rightly, was the only defeat he ever met with, a mare called Lady Betty upsetting the good thing.

Singular ignorance has, says a well-known writer, been shown by persons commenting on the result of the One Thousand Guineas, in which the Duke of Portland's Semolina and Memoir ran one two, as to the right possessed by owners in case of two or more horses running for them in any stake. The law is very plain: "An owner running two or more horses in a race may declare to win with one of them, and such declaration must be made at scale. A jockey riding a horse with which the owner has not declared to win must on no account stop such horse, except in favor of the stable companion on whose behalf declaration to win has been made." A curious case in connection with the law to which allusion has just been made, occurred in the Doncaster St. Leger of 1840. The then Lord Westminster started Launcelot and Maroon, the former an own brother to the renowned Touchstone. Launcelot had run second to Little Wonder in a memorable Derby. His owner declared to win the St. Leger with him, and the colt had for his jockey William Scott, whose many St. Leger successes included four successive victories. Maroon was entrusted to John Holmes, who had no pleasant task. Gibraltar, ridden by "Nat" Flatman, threatened such danger to Launcelot, who started favorite, that Holmes had to be ready to come to the rescue at a moment's notice in case of the crack failing. Launcelot managed to win. An old Yorkshire friend, spectator of the contest, used to tell me of the agony of a titled spectator who had backed Launcelot when he saw that Maroon could beat him if necessary. He was a puny voiced man, and yet shrieked an entreaty to Holmes to "hold" Maroon, as if his cry could have availed at all, even had it been heard above the din of Doncaster, when the pinch of the St. Leger had come.

The Monmouth Park Association announces this year an innovation says the N. Y. Sun, which every race goer will thoroughly appreciate. It is the opening in this city, Brooklyn and Philadelphia of ticket offices where tickets of admission to the race course and railroad tickets by any of the routes to the track may be purchased, thus saving to the public the discomfort and annoyance too often experienced in securing these very necessary bits of pasteboard at the ferryhouses. These offices will be opened a couple of weeks before the opening meeting at the new track on the Fourth of July, and they will be kept open during the season. This is a long step in the right direction and one that the great army of race goers will certainly appreciate.

Work at the new track has progressed so rapidly and has been carried on so systematically that there is no doubt but that everything will be in ship shape some time before the date set for the opening of the meeting. It was a prodigious undertaking to build and equip the the new track in something less than a year, yet it has been successfully accomplished, thanks to the push and energy of Mr. Withers, who has personally surpervised the work. The track is nearly ready for horses to work on it, and it will be in prime condition by July. Mr. Withers' new set of racing rules is now in the hands of the printer, and they will be put to a practical test at the coming meeting. This meeting is announced by a thoroughly original and very handsome lithographic picture of the start of a race. The veteran starter, Mr. Caldwell, stands in his box, flag in hand, ready to start a field of racers whose jockeys are represented in the colors of famous American stables. Among these are the silks and satins of the Messrs. Haggin, Withers, Cassatt, Belmont, Dwyer, Lorillard, Morris, Pulsifer, Galway, Scott, Hearst and Brown, and pictures of McLaughlin, Garrison, Hayward, Hamilton, Murphy, Littlefield, Day and other jockeys. Taken altogether, it is decidedly unique and Mr. Croft has eclipsed his previous record for originality in its design.

"Dear Rapier," S. Shirley kindly writes to me from Kimberley. "It may interest you and the numerous readers of your notes to hear of the latest performances of some of the more or less illustrious exiles at present in this part of the world. At the Kimberley Autumn Meeting, of which I enclose programme, the principal races were won by imported horses, and, as you will see, the handicappers did not forget the fact that they were imported. The Trial Stakes six furlongs, was won by Bloodhound, 3 years, 8st 1lb, by Trappist—Blood Red by Lord Lyon. Candelmas, aged, 11st 4lb, by Hermit—Fusee, was second for the big race, the Autumn Handicap, one mile, but could have won easily, his owner declaring to win with his second string—Valhalla, 3 years, 8st 1lb, Colonial bred, by Whackum—Helen Mannering, by Carnival—Miss Mannering. Bloodhound, 7st 11lb, was second for Flying Stakes the same day. On the second day the Criterion, six furlongs was won by Overveen, 3 years, 10st 9lb by Energy—Wild Hyacinth; Bloodhound 3 years, 8st 9lb second. In the Newton Handicap, 1½ miles, Candlemas with the crusher of 11st 7lb was beaten off, his wind stopping him up the hill. On the last day, Loophole, 2 years 9st, by Hagioscope—Victress, who was manifestly short of work, ran unplaced in the Juvenile Stakes, and Overveen scored another victory in the Beaconsfield Handicap, carrying 8st 5lb over a mile in a heavy storm of wind and rain, the course being like a ploughed field." Of these, Bloodhound never won a race in England—the last time he was seen out was at Kempton, the day Dearest beat Reviera for the £6,000 Stakes. Candlemas—own brother to St. Blaise, now the property of A. Belmont, we all remember at Kingsclere; and Overveen looked like making a good colt the day he won the Westminster Stakes at Epsom, for he came down the hill at a tremendous pace, and had all the best of Lactantius, on whom odds were laid; but this was his last success, nine subsequent attempts having been made in vain.—Sporting and Dramatic.

THE KENNEL.

Dog owners are requested to send for publication the earliest possible notices of whelps, sales, names claimed, presentations and deaths, in their kennels, in all instances writing plainly names of sire and dam and of grandparents, colors, dates and breed.

Special Meeting of the American Kennel Club, Held May 22nd, 1890.

President Belmont, Jr., in the chair.

PRESENT.

Associate Members, J. L. Anthony; A. P. Vredenburgh.
American Beagle Club, H. F. Schellhass.
American Pet Dogs Club, Dr. M. H. Cryer.
American Spaniel Club, J. Watson.
Massachusetts Kennel Club, R. Leslie.
Mascoutah Kennel Club, J. Mortimer.
Pointer Club of America, C. W. LaRue.
Virginia Field Sport's As'sn, J. S. Wise.
Westminster Kennel Club, T. H. Terry.
St. Bernard Club of America, J. Lohman.
Collie Club of America, H. B; Cromwell.

Mr. Peshall:—I desire to move that no quorum appearing, this club do now adjourn.

The President:—I rule the motion out of order as Mr. Peshall has not been admitted as a delegate, and is not now a delegate of the club.

Mr. Peshall:—I am here representing the Maryland Kennel Club. This is a meeting of the club. I rise as representing the Maryland Kennel Club, and I move you now that the meeting be adjourned.

The President:—I refuse to entertain the motion.

Mr. Watson:—I move that the club adjourn in order to call a meeting of the executive committee to take action upon the credentials presented to the American Kennel Club.

Mr. Peshall:—Mr. President—

The President:—I cannot recognize you as a delegate.

Mr. Watson's motion seconded and carried.

MEETING OF THE EXECUTIVE COMMITTEE.

President Belmont, Jr., in the chair.

Same clubs represented as recorded at special meeting.

The President:—The chair rules that the delegates of the associate membership do not come under Section II. of the Constitution, Article IV., and recognizes Mr. Anthony as a delegate.

The minutes of the last meeting of the executive commitee read and approved.

The Secretary's quarterly report was read as follows:

MAY 21, 1890.

GENTLEMEN: I have to submit, applications for admission to the American Kennel Club, from the following clubs and associations: Youngstown Kennel Club, of Youngstone, O.; the Louisiana Poultry and Pet Stock Association of New Orleans, La; Northern Illinois Poultry and Pet Stock Association of Rockford, Ill.; Wilmington Agricultural and Industrial Association of Wilmington, Del; the Chesapeake Bay Dog Club of Baltimore, Md.; the Eastern Greyhound and Coursing Club of New York. The applications of these clubs were received in due form and time, as provided for in our Constitution, and action at this meeting is desired. The application of the Eastern Greyhound and Coursing Club was withdrawn, and an application from the National Greyhound Club has been substituted.

The application of the California Kennel Club, which has been in abeyance since August 15, 1889, has been renewed, and action at this meeting is urged. The facts in this matter can be briefly stated as follows: At the September meeting of this club, the application was laid over, until the next meeting, with instruction that your secretary should put himself in correspondence with the Pacific Kennel Club, one of the members of the American Kennel Club, requesting it to advise this club, its opinion as to the expediency of two clubs from the same city being admitted to membership. The reply from the Pacific Kennel Club was that negotiations were pending towards a consolidation of the two clubs, and asked that action might be delayed until the matter should be finally settled. In this the California Kennel Club acquiesced. February 27, 1890, notice was given your secretary that the Pacific Kennel Club would consolidate only upon the following terms:

1st. The name Pacific Kennel Club should be retained.

2d. That the money now in the California Kennel Club (about $100) should be placed to the credit of the Pacific Kennel Club, and used for the purpose of paying off a portion of their debt.

3d. That the members of the California Kennel Club upon entering the Pacific Kennel Club, should assume their pro-rata of the debt of the Pacific Kennel Club. Those terms were rejected, and the application for admission was renewed. Your secretary advised the California Kennel Club that he would notify the Pacific Kennel Club of the renewal of the application, and thus afford it an opportunity to lodge any objection. This he did, and received a reply protesting the admission of another club from San Francisco, a copy of this protest was duly mailed to the applicant, and a reply to the protest signed individually by the five officers and twelve members of the Executive Committee of the California Kennel Club has been received, in which they state that they have fifty members in good standing, they desire to hold annual bench shows, and earnestly ask for admission. All the correspondence in this matter is here on file, and will be read if desired.

The Southern California Kennel Club of Los Angeles, Cal., has held its second bench show, and promptly complied with all the requirements of the American Kennel Club, by sending marked catalogue and registration, with fees to cover same, within ten days of the close of the show. Under date of March 12, 1890, the President of this club informed your Secretary, for the first time, that the letter and rules sent at the time of its first show did not arrive until two days after the show had been open, otherwise there would have been no misunderstanding, and the show would have been strictly under American Kennel Club rules. Under these circumstances, and also in view of the prompt business-like way that they have conducted the second show your Secretary would respectfully recommend that the wins of the show of 1889 be recognized by this club.

The American English Beagle Club notifies this club of its change of name to the American Beagle Club; the Cincinnati Sportsman's Club of its change of name to the Cincinnati Kennel Club, with requests to make such changes upon our records. As such changes are made by resolution, such action is solicited at this meeting.

A communication was received dated March 11, '90 from Mr. Robert Leslie, calling attention to a violation of Rule 31, by the New England Kennel Club in neglecting to publish in its premium list, the list of Recognized Shows, and asking immediate action by the American Kennel Club to have such a serious error rectified. A copy of this letter was forwarded to the Bench Show Committee of the New England Kennel Club, asking an explanation, which was complied with by Mr. H. H. Moore, he assuming all blame in the matter, and satisfactorily explaining the omission, by stating that upon receipt of the electrotype plates of the rules from this office, they were taken to the printers, he supposing that said list of recognized shows were included in the plates, and he did not discover the error until after the premium lists had been printed and mailed, when his attention was called to it by the President of his club. As the plan of the American Kennel Club supplying the rules in plates was something entirely new, the oversight on the part of the New England Kennel Club was natural. The catalogue was published correctly in this respect. Your attention is called to an entry in the catalogue of the Mascoutah Kennel Club, of Mr. Wm. C. Hudson's Kenmore (Irish setter). Your Secretary asked said club to explain why it had accepted the entry of a disqualified man, and received a reply that their entries closed Feb. 17th, and that after the catalogue had been printed, Mr. Hudson wired the Superintendent of his disqualification and asked for the return of his entries and fees. This was done and the dogs consequently did not compete, but it was too late to change the catalogue. The entry in the judge's book was marked disqualified. The matter being thus satisfactorily explained, there was no blame whatever attached to the Mascoutah Kennel Club, and this reference to the matter is simply to explain, what may have been considered by some, as a direct violation of the rules. By the action of the Advisory Committee at its meeting, April 7th, the case of Graham vs Daniels was settled, and your Secretary was directed to forward to Mr Graham the amount of his claim, $50.10, held by this club since January 18, '90. A bill of exchange was mailed to Graham, April 8th, and Mr. Daniels was notified, to which he replied that he desired to be put on record as considering the action of your committee an injustice, and a shield to dishonest and sharp dog dealers.

The Albany Kennel Club had not paid Mr. A. W. Smith the prize awarded his black and tan terrier Buffalo General up to the 30th inst; said club has been notified of this arrearage, to which no reply has yet come to hand. No other claim has been filed against this club.

Mr. W. T. Levering of Baltimore, Md, filed a claim for the use of the prefix "Dundee" for his Chesapeake Bay dogs; the same was published in the April Gazette, and a protest has been filed by Mr. H. T. Drake, of St. Paul, Minn., against allowing said prefix. This correspondence will be read, and your action at this meeting is requested. At the Westminster Kennel Club Show, a special prize of $50 was offered for the best setter with a field trial record, which was awarded to Mr. L. Gardner's English setter dog Roger. The award was protested by Mr. Max Wenzel, he claiming that his Irish setter dog Tim was eligible to compete. This protest was allowed, and the prize was awarded to Tim. Mr. Gardner appealed from this decision to his club, under date of Feb. 18, '90, and deposited $10, as required by the rules. The case is now before you to decide. It is suggested that this club should adopt a list of "recognized field trials," a win at any one of which shall be considered and accepted as a field trial record. The Buffalo Kennel Club has served this club with a notice of the suspension by it, of Mr. Edwin H. Morris, under Rule XXV for the following reason: Said Morris entered four dogs at said Buffalo Kennel Club Show, sending his check for $12 to cover entry fees, said check was protested, and returned with $1.40 charges. The amount has never been made good by Morris. The suspension has been confirmed, pending your action by President Belmont Jr. and notice to that effect has been sent to Morris' address.

(Signed) A. P. VREDENBURGH, Secretary.

Adopted.

Mr. Wise: I move we go into this matter of credentials of delegates.

Motion seconded and carried.

The Secretary stated that credentials were presented by Mr. Lohman, of the St. Bernard Kennel Club; by Mr. Watson, of the Southern California Kennel Club, and Mr. Peshall, of the Maryland Kennel Club.

The credentials presented by Mr. Watson to represent the Southern California Kennel Club were then read, and Mr. Wise moved that Mr. Watson be accepted as representative of the Southern California Kennel Club, provided his credentials were amended so as to conform with the rules.

Mr. Watson: For the present I will withdraw the credentials of the Southern California Kennel Club, and represent the Spaniel Club.

On motion, Mr. Lohman's credentials being regular, were accepted.

The credentials of C. J. Peshall to represent the Maryland Kennel Club were read.

Mr. Leslie:—I move those credentials be accepted.

Mr. Anthony:—I rise to a point of order that the club having appointed Mr. Malcom for the year 1890, had no right in the absence of the resignation of Mr. Malcom, to send another delegate.

Mr. Leslie:—Mr. Peshall responded to the roll-call for the Maryland Kennel Club, and he was recognized.

The President:—He was not recognized. He chose to occupy the floor in spite of my refusal to recognize him.

Mr. Wise:—This is a question of power with me. On the 5th of April, 1890, this Maryland Kennel Club met, and it elected a delegate and duly authorized him for 12 months to represent it as a delegate, and his name is H. Malcom, and he stands here as the duly authorized representative of that club for 12 months. Of course, if there is a resignation there is a vacancy, but it is the principle of law that a delegate has no power to delegate his authority.

The President:—I desire to state for the information of the meeting, that that was the ground on which I ruled. When I first saw the certificate, if such it can be called—I had not heard of it before—I saw that Mr. Peshall had no authority to represent any club here. I did not have an opportunity of stating so when I ruled, because Mr. Peshall did not wish to take my ruling, and to silence his interruption, I was obliged to go on with another motion in order that the meeting might proceed. I think it is very indelicate that Mr Peshall should remain in the room during this discussion, so long as the Chair has ruled that he is not a member or delegate. It is clear that the certificate that he presents is not a valid one in any sense. It states clearly that it is but a substitution, and the constitution does not recognize the possibility of a substitution. If nothing had been said about Mr. Malcom in the certificate, I certainly should have been obliged to recognize Mr. Peshall, no matter whether the regular delegate previously appointed had resigned or not. In this case he is not sent here as a delegate but as a substitute. It is so distinctly stated in the so called certificate.

Mr. Watson:—I very much regret that this discussion has come up in this shape. I think we all know what this means. This is personal animosity to Mr. Peshall.

Mr. Anthony:—In order to cut short all discussion I withdraw my point of order, and I now move that as Mr. Peshall is not a "persona gratia" to the members of this club for a reason you all know, he be not accepted as a delegate to the American Kennel Club.

Mr. Watson—I object with regard to myself to any such motion being put to the meeting.

Motion seconded.

The president (resigning the chair to Mr. Terry)—Concerning Mr. Watson's statement that this action is the result of personal animosity. I think perhaps I am the one to reply to that, as my feelings on the subject would probably be interpreted as personal. They are not at all. I readily believe that the party is not worthy of my personal feeling on the subject. Mr. Peshall has written all sorts of letters and articles in the papers against the American Kennel Club. What his motives were is for you to decide. It was in the main an attack upon the financial conduct of the club, and after an investigation of the books was made, and after the financial condition of the club, as reported by your officers was endorsed by a committee appointed to investigate and report, he did not accept that, and accused the club of so manipulating its accounts as to make it appear that it was in a better financial condition than it really was, and accused me of having come to the assistance of the club with money, which the accounts show I did not, although I offered to do so in the event of its becoming necessary. The statement, made by the American Kennel Club through its officers, that such assistance had not been given, was not believed, and every effort was made on the part of Mr Peshall to have the public, and the dog men in particular, believe the financial statement of the American Kennel Club was a false one, and that the accounts were open to the accusation of mismanagement. I consider on this ground that no one taking that position should be received here as a delegate, because it is saying practically "I don't believe in your club." That is one ground. There is another ground, and that is that it was published in all the papers that a suit was going to be brought against the American Kennel Club to take it into court in order to prove these false entries, as it was claimed. That was published everywhere. Some of the delegates being frightened went so far as to write and ask all sorts of details, etc., until it became such a nuisance that we consulted counsel on the subject, and were advised that even delegates had no right to inspect the books, and I had occasion to write a letter to the delegate of the Massachusetts Club saying that the books could not remain open to inspection longer after the committee had passed upon their accuracy. We are willing to do anything and answer any question that anybody may reasonably ask, but this incessant pecking became not only tiresome but insulting. For instance, if I as your President should make a statement here that I did not give any money to the club I should expect to be believed, and if I am not to be believed I am not fit to be your President. Those statements were made. That suit referred to was never brought, was never intended to be brought, and never could be brought under any process of law. The parties intending to engage in it would have been shown up in a ridiculous light. On the two grounds I have stated I maintain say that Mr. Peshall is not fit to represent any club, nor fit to sit in this room after the accusation he has made, excepting as a private individual. The statement that there is personal animosity here is all nonsense, but if we have any respect for ourselves as an organization we should not receive anybody in it who speaks and writes against it in such a manner.

Mr. Peshall—I ask to be heard:

The Chairman—I cannot recognize you.

Mr. Leslie—I move the delegates grant to Mr. Peshall the privilege of being heard.

Mr. Logan—I have never met the gentleman, nor do I know anything about him, but I believe we have by-laws and a constitution to govern us at these meetings, and I don't think we should depart from them now.

Mr. Anthony's motion that Mr. Peshall be not recognized or admitted as a delegate on the ground that he is not a persona gratia (under Art. XII. Sec. 2) to the majority of the delegates was then put and carried by the following vote:

Ayes, 9—Am. Pet Dog Club, Associate Delegates (2 votes), Mascoutah Kennel Club, Pointer Club of America, Virginia Field Sports Ass'n, Westminster Kennel Club, St. Bernard Club of America.

Nays, 3—Am. Beagle Club, Am. Spaniel Club, Massachusetts Club.

The Treasurer's quarterly report was read as follows:

May 21, 1890.

GENTLEMEN:—I beg to submit to following report:

Receipts from all sources from Jan. 1st to date.............$5,317,32
Expense for same period.............3,317,16

Balance on hand.............$2,041.'6

The following clubs have as yet not paid their annual dues for the following year:

Chattahoochee Valley Exposition Company.
Connecticut State Kennel Club.
Elmira Poultry and Pet Stock Association.
German Mastiff or Great Dane Club.
Hartford Kennel Club.
Syracuse Kennel Club.

By resolution at the last meeting these clubs were given thirty days in which to pay their year's dues, under the penalty of being dropped from the roll of membership. They were duly notified of this resolution and have failed to respond. Exception is made in the case of the German Mastiff or Great Dane Club, which by an oversight I neglected to include in my report at the last meeting and consequently did not communicate with. (Signed) A. P. VREDENBURGH, Treasurer.

Adopted.

The minutes of the last meeting of the Advisory Committee was read, and motion made to accept them.

Mr. Watson moved that section 6 and 7 be stricken from the minutes of the meeting of the Advisory Committee held April 7, 1890.

Motion seconded and lost.

The motion to accept was then put and carried.

Mr. Watson—I give notice that I will make a motion at the next meeting which will give the Advisory Committee the power of suspension which they have not at present.

The following clubs, candidates for membership in the American Kennel Club, were elected, their applications being in proper form: Youngstown Kennel Club of Youngstown, Ohio; the Louisiana Poultry and Pet Stock Association of New Orleans, La.; Northern Illinois Poultry and Pet Stock Association of Rockford, Ill.; Wilmington Agricultural and Industrial Association of Wilmington, Del.; the Chesapeake Bay Dog Club of Baltimore, Md.; the National Greyhound Club of New York, and the California Kennel Club of San Francisco, Cal.

The question of recognizing the wins of the Southern California Kennel Club of Los Angeles, Cal., was then brought up, and Mr. Anthony moved that as the rules and the Secretary's letter did not reach the club until two days after their show of 1889, and as they complied as near as possible with those rules, that those wins be recognized by the American Kennel Club.

Motion seconded and carried.

The requests of the American English Beagle Club and the Cincinnati Sportsman's Club to have their names changed upon the records to "The American Beagle Club," and "The Cincinnati Kennel Club" were on motion granted, and the Secretary instructed to make the changes desired.

On motion, Mr. W. T. Levering, of Baltimore, was granted the prefix "Dundee" for his Chesapeake Bay dogs, against which a protest had been filed by Mr. H. T. Drake, of St. Paul, Minn.

Concerning the special prize of $50, awarded by the Westminster Kennel Club to Mr. L. Gardner's English setter dog Roger, which was protested by Mr. Max Wenzel on the ground that his Irish setter dog Tim was eligible to compete, and which protest was allowed, and the prize awarded to Tim, from which decision Mr. Gardner appealed, Mr. Watson offered the following resolution:

Resolved, that it is the opinion of this committee that the term "Field Trial Record" applies only to public trials for competition open to all, and that the appeal by Mr. L. Gardner in the case of the special prize for the best setter with a field trial record be sustained, and the prize awarded to his English setter dog Roger.

Resolution seconded and carried.

In regard to the suspension of Mr. Edwin H. Morris, under Rule XXV, of which notice was received by the American Kennel Club, the Secretary stated that Morris had deposited with the club $14, which covered entry fees and protest fees on protested check. That he had wired the Buffalo Kennel Club to withdraw the suspension, and he had left extra money to pay wire charges on return. He further stated that under the rules there was one of two things to be done; either the suspension had to be removed, or Mr. Morris would have to be disqualified.

On motion of Mr. Watson, the suspension was removed.

The Secretary—At our last meeting a resolution was adopted giving clubs in arrears 30 days to settle their accounts, otherwise they would be dropped from the roll. I have sent notices to that effect to the following clubs: Chattahoochee Valley Exposition Company, Connecticut State Kennel Club, Elmira Poultry and Pet Stock Association, Hartford Kennel Club and Syracuse Kennel Club. The German Mastiff or Great Dane Club I overlooked, so I do not think that club comes under the resolution.

On motion of Mr. Watson, the clubs named were dropped from the roll.

On request of Mr. Leslie the Secretary read the charges brought by Mr. Leslie against the New England Kennel Club.

Mr. Leslie—I think this is a serious breach of the rules, and something should be done to punish them for such a breach. I move that the New England Club be suspended for the term of one year for non compliance with the rules in not publishing the rules of the Bench Show.

The Secretary—I think that would be very unjust. This is the first year that we have attempted to furnish the rules for the different clubs. After the rules were amended I got them up with all the latest amendments. I had electrotype plates made of them the proper size for catalogues and premium lists, but I did not include the list of recognized shows for the reason that they are changing all the time. In sending these plates to the Boston Club, Mr. Moore very naturally supposed they were included, and did not know of their absence until after the premium lists were printed. To penalize the Boston Club for an error of that kind I think would be a great mistake.

Mr. Leslie's motion seconded.

Mr. Anthony—I move to lay it in the table.

Motion seconded and carried.

Mr. Leslie—I would like an explanation from the Secretary why one delegate should be refused to investigate the report of the Treasurer or the books, and another delegate in a few weeks afterwards be permitted to do so. I should like to know if there is any distinction, whether one man is favored over another.

The Secretary—If you will be kind enough to state the particulars I will answer you.

Mr. Leslie—I made inquiries about the Treasurer's report, etc., and I was refused permission to investigate it. Mr. Watson, a few weeks afterwards, comes from the Forest and Stream and he investigated the Treasurer's report, and the books were thrown open to him.

The Secretary stated that considerable correspondence had passed between them in which he stated in substance he had invited Mr. Leslie to call at the office at any time and the books were at his disposal, and that he was ready to answer any question he asked. That in reply he had received an insulting letter from Mr Leslie. He then wrote to Mr. Leslie that he asked the President of the club about the matter, and that he had received positive instructions from him to positively decline to make any further statement of the finances other than the published ones which were duly examined and audited by the committee appointed by the American Kennel Club for that purpose. That he should strictly carry out the instructions of the President.

The Secretary (continuing): Mr. Watson had written me about the same kind of a letter as Mr Leslie's first letter, asking for certain amounts in my accounts. I wrote Mr. Watson to the same effect as I did to Mr. Leslie, that I had no time to do it. I was very busy at the time. I invited Mr. Watson to come here at the office and look at the books. Mr. Watson sent another letter in which he wrote three or four questions, which I answered, and again invited him to come here and look at the books. He sent me word he would come in the first time he was in town. Mr. Watson did come in after I had written to Mr. Leslie. Mr. Watson had been in the meantime elected a member of the Stud Book Committee. He had a perfect right to those books just as I had or any other officer. Mr. Watson will bear me out in what I say, that he responded to my invitation and looked at the books.

The Secretary called attention to a communication in reference to a special prize offered by the St. Bernard Kennel Club for the best smooth coated St. Bernard dog. An entry was made by Mr. T. B. Lee. It came out subsequently that Mr. Lee did not own the dog entered by him, which was awarded the prize, but that the dog belonged to his wife. Therefore the dog was disqualified. The question now is what is to be done with the cups which were offered as the prize.

Mr. Anthony moved that there being no reserve number and that the Judge not having been requested to re-judge the class, the American Kennel Club consider the cups the property of the St. Bernard Club of America.

Motion seconded and carried.

A communication was read from the Gordon Setter Club asking that the percentage of blood be raised from 62½ to 87½ per cent.

On motion the matter was referred to the Stud Book Committee

Adjourned.

(Signed). A. P. VREDENBURGH.

Occidental Coursing Club.

A coursing meeting of the club was held on May 30th at Newark Park, two stakes being on the card, an all-aged for eight dogs at $5 each, winner $25, runner up $15, and a puppy stake for six puppies at $5 each, winner $20, runner up $10. The day was well suited, but the ground was too villainously hard to make anything like good coursing possible. Stock had been pastured in it during the early spring, and the foot-marks left by the cattle formed innumerable little pits with sharp hard-baked edges which ripped away the nails whenever a dog chanced to step into one. Hares were rather scarce, and some delay was caused by the fact. The attendance was small, not more than fifty persons being present, but those who were there were the jolly sort, and made the day pass in a lively fashion. The officers of the day were S. O. Gregory, T. J. O'Keeffe and H. E. Deane; slip steward, J. F. Carroll; flag steward, H. Boyd; judge, J. R. Dickson; slipper, Jas. Wren.

Most of the courses were very short, and close work was practically impossible, because of the character of the ground. As to several of the courses, there seemed to be room for a difference of opinion after the judgments were rendered, but as was remarked by an old courser, the judge has the best chance to see, and is most likely to be right. A detailed report of the meeting would not, under the circumstances, be of especial value, and as space is limited, a summary must suffice.

SUMMARY.

ALL-AGED STAKE.

H. Boyd's w bk Bo-Peep beat J. F. Carroll's w blk d Scout W.
W. Ball's f w b Princess, a bye.
S. Milliken's w br d Laurelwood beat T. J. Cronin's blk w d Dan B.
J. E. Watson's bk w d Saturday Night beat M. Curtis' br b Mosquito.

II.

Princess beat Bo-Peep; Laurelwood beat Saturday Night.

III.

Princess beat Laurelwood.

Winner—Princess.
Runner up—Laurelwood.

PUPPY STAKES.

T. Cooney's blk w d Dandy Jim beat J. F. Carroll's w blk b Nora.
T. Cooney's w blk d Valley Queen beat H. Boyd's w blk b Bo-Peep.
T. Cooney's blk w d Jim Corbett beat S. Tracy's w bk b May Boy.

All of the winners in the first series being owned by Mr. Cooney, and that gentleman being guarded under the rules, the stake was divided equally between his dogs.

Pacific Coast Field Trial Derby.

The Pacific Coast Field Trial Derby closed on June 1st, with twenty-six entries, seven pointers, fifteen English setters, two Irish setters, one Gordon setter and one dog whose owner did not state the breed in making his entry. The entries are:

POINTERS.

MABLE B., liver and white and ticked bitch by Professor—Gracie Bow, whelped Aug. 20, '89; breeder and owner, Geo. W. Bassford, Suisun City.

RENA B, liver and white, pointer bitch by Scout Croxteth—Blossom, whelped August 8, '89; breeder and owner, Geo. W. Bassford, Suisun City.

NICK WHITE, white and lemon, pointer dog by Scout Croxteth—Blossom, whelped August 8, '89; breeder Geo. W. Bassford; owner, J. M. Bassford Jr., Vacaville.

QUEEN'S LAST, liver and white, pointer bitch by Mountain Boy—Beautiful Queen, whelped July 18, '89; breeder and owner J. M. Bassford Jr., Vacaville.

LADY L., pointer bitch by Professor—Gracie Bow, whelped Aug. 20, '89; breeder, Geo. W. Bassford; owner, D. A. Leonard, Bakersfield.

NED, lemon and white, pointer dog by Roscoe—California, whelped Sept. 4, '89; breeder, Geo. T. Allender; owner, R. E. Wilson, San Francisco.

OLD BLACK JOE II, black pointer dog by ————, whelped June 11, '89; breeder, W. R. Pape; owner, J. E. Watson, San Francisco.

ENGLISH SETTERS.

DASHING BROLLA B., black and white setter dog by Jasper B Pride, whelped Oct. 9, '89; breeder and owner, Albert Peri, Marysville.

PRIMROSE B., litter sister to preceding, orange and white; breeder and owner, Albert Peri, Marysville.

LEO R., white, black and tan, setter dog by Rodney—Phyllis II, whelped Sept. 1, '80; breeder and owner, M. D. Walter, Galt.

DANDY R., litter brother to preceding, white, black and tan; breeder and owner, M. D. Walter, Galt.

FRANCE R., litter brother to preceding, white, black and tan; breeder, M. D. Walter; owner, J. S. Dunham, Stockton.

EL REY, orange and white Setter dog by Loadstone-Euid, whelped May 8, 1889, breeder California Kennels; owner F. B. Dexter, Fresno.

ELITE, orange and white, litter brother to preceding; owner G. G. Goucher, Fresno.

SUBRET, orange and white, Setter bitch by Loadstone-Sweetheart, whelped June 16th 1889, breeder California Kennels, owner D. M. Pyle, Bakersfield.

SUNBURST, orange and white, Setter bitch, litter sister to preceding owners H. C. Chipman and California Kennels, Sacramento.

SARABAND, orange and white, Setter bitch, litter sister to preceding, breeders and owners, California Kennels, Sacramento.

SIREN, orange and white, Setter bitch, litter sister to preceding; breeders and owners California Kennels, Sacramento.

PIERRE, orange belton, Setter dog by Harold-Sunlit, whelped May 15, 1889, breeder California Kennels; owner J. W. Harper, Suisun.

PETRONELLA, orange and white, Setter bitch, litter sister to preceding; breeders and owners; California Kennels, Sacramento.

LORD CHUMLEY, blue belton and tan, Setter dog by Loadstone Janet, whelped May 7, 1889; breeder California Kennel; owner Norman Rideout, Marysville.

MANFRED, black, white and tan, Setter dog by Harold-Miss Druid, whelped July 16, 1889; breeder and owner California Kennel, Sacramento.

IRISH RED SETTERS.

RIO, Red Setter dog by Mike T.—Lady Elcho T., whelped July 30, 1889; breeder A. B. Truman, owner E. G. Schmiedell, San Francisco.

SHAUN RHUE, Red Setter dog by Nat Glencho-Red Fanny, whelped May 18, 1889; breeder J. C. Natirass, owner E. J. Roy, San Francisco.

GORDON SETTERS.

FANNY, black and tan Setter bitch, breeding unknown, whelped December 1889; owner Robert Liddle, San Francisco.

UNCLASSIFIED.

AL FARROW, whelped November 20, 1889; owner Chas. Studarus, Routiers Station.

Consolation Dead.

Mr. Luke W. White writes: "Consolation has just died. He was without exception the best dog I ever handled. I never expect to get a better, and if I get as good again I will be lucky. I have one bitch by him living, presented to me by Col. O'Dell some time ago."

[The gamest field trial race we have ever seen was run at High Point in '86 by Consolation. The dog was sick, some dysenteric trouble ailing him, and it was plainly to be seen that every movement caused acute pain, while the frequent stops necessitated by the peculiar character of his disease strongly militated against his chances in the race, but despite adversities the game little fellow ran a brilliant nervy race, with excellent pace, judgment, level-headedness and obedience. A grander dog than Consolation is rarely seen, and his owner, Colonel C. H. O'Dell will feel the loss keenly.—KEN. ED.]

Whelps.

Capt. Geo. C. Rieter, U. S. S. Ranger, English setter Fannie (Alaska—Countess) whelped, May 16th 1890, four, two dogs, to C. A. Louds, Romeo.

Visits.

Mr. C. A. Chewning's English setter, Lily to C. A. Louds Romeo, on May 14th 1890.

Mr. B. Doherty had his fine greyhound, California Boy by Ben Ali—Daisy, poisoned on May 15th. The dog was a good hound, and the loss is a great one.

We regret to learn that Mr. C. A. Loud has been very ill since reaching his new home at Oceanside, San Diego County. He is now convalescent and we hope will soon be quite well. His illness makes it impossible for him to handle his fine English setter, Rural Nellie. A. K. S.B., 13,944, and he desires to place her in the hands of some one who would value such a dog.

It was a pleasure to receive a call last week from Dr. A. C. Heffenger of the U. S. Navy, who came bearing an introductory note from that prince of co-laborers in the journalistic field, Dr. N. Rowe of the American Field. Dr Heffanger is Vice President of the Brunswick Fur Club of Maine, and is an enthusiast about fox hounds and fox hunting. He is also a keen angler, and all around sportsman whose accession to the guild in these parts is reason for elation. We commend him to all readers to whom he may become known.

Mr. C. J. Peshall has prepared the papers and will present them some day this week to the United States Circuit Court asking for a mandamus compelling Mr. Vredenburgh, the Secretary, to submit the papers and books of the American Kennel Club to Mr. Peshall for his examination, and to answer any questions touching the same. Mr. Peshall bases his action on the ground that the American Kennel Club is a voluntary association, and every member of it is a partner. Another suit is to be commenced asking for an accounting, dissolution and winding up of the partnership, in other words to terminate the existence of the American Kennel Club.—American Field.

[Is there not danger that Judge Peshall will become a nuisance, and forfeit that general esteem which he has gained during the ten years last passed? As we understand the matter, the Judge is moving to gratify petty personal spite, rather than to correct real errors. Go slow, Judge Peshall, the "sun had risen upon the earth before Lot entered into Zoar."—KEN. ED.]

It has been found that when an elongated projectile is fired from a smooth-bore, the head of the bullet is gradually lifted until it is thrown completely over, after which the flight is very uncertain. A judiciously rifled barrel overcomes this defect. It has long been a disputed point as to whether the longer axis of a bullet preserves its original direction or whether the point droops and follows the trajectory curve. It is now believed by the best authorities that the latter obtains, as otherwise projectiles fixed at a high angle would strike nearly lengthways, which has not been observed. An attempt has even been made by constructing a model bullet, mounted on a gyroscope facing a powerful fan, to demonstrate the effect of the air resistance upon a bullet. "As soon as the revolving projectile is put in position, the fan is set in rapid motion; the current of air first causes the point of the bullet to lift slightly, then it moves to the right or left (according to the direction of the spin), and eventually it makes a strong dip down toward the ground." While this is probably true with regard to the motions of a bullet discharged from a rifle barrel, it can hardly be regarded as proved, as the conditions are not the same.

THE GUN.

The Gun Club.

Editor Breeder and Sportsman:—The annual picnic match of the Gun Club was held on Friday of last week in Ross Valley, not far from San Rafael. The day was simply splendid, just breezy enough to give an impetus to the flight of the *best all round* lot of birds it has been my good fortune to look and shoot at for many a day.

The company was delightful, just the kind you generally have met at the Gun Club meeting, and a few ladies were also present. It was a pleasant sight to see old timers like Mr. Thos. Ewing and Mr. C. D. Laing, who made their first appearance in almost two years, and neither of them have forgotten how "to do it." A bountiful and well spread luncheon was set out by the club, and, briefly speaking, it was, as a whole, one of the "red letter" days in the existence of the Gun Club.

The Gun Club is about to issue a challenge to the Alameda Sportsmen's Club at an early day, and as soon as the preliminaries can be arranged. Ten men will probably contest on each side, for a trophy or dinner.

The birds used were very good, and the scores indicate excellent form on the part of the participants. All of the shooting was under American Association Rules, and the scores were:

Club match at 10 birds, handicap.										
Jellett, at 30 yds	1	1	1	2	1	1	1	2	1	1
Butler, 28 yds	1	2	1	2	1	1	1	0	1	0
Laing, 30 yds	0	0	2	2	1	2	0	1	1	2
Golcher, 28 yds	1	2	1	0	2	2	2	0	1	0
Ewing, 28 yds	2	1	1	2	1	1	0	0	2	2
Chapin, 28	0	0	2	1	2	0	0	1	1	0
Hardey, 30	2	1	0	0	0	1	0	2	2	2
Gillette, 28	2	0	2	2	1	1	2	2	1	0
Black, 30	0	0	2	1	1	0	0	2	2	0
Webster, 28	0	1	1	0	1	2	2	1	1	1
Liebenor, 28	2	2	0	1	0	0	1	0	2	0
Swett, 30	0	2	2	1	1	2	0	1	0	2
Wooster, 30	2	2	1	1	2	2	1	1	0	1
Donohoe, 28	0	0	0	2	2	0	0	0	2	0
Sanborn, 28	1	1	2	1	1	2	0	2	2	1
Stone, 28	1	1	0	2	0	2	0	1	2	0
Orr, 30	1	1	0	1	1	2	1	1	1	1
H. W. Woodward, 28	0	0	1	1	0	0	2	2	0	0
Eddy, 28	2	1	2	2	1	2	1	1	2	2
Harcus, 28	2	2	1	1	2	1	0	0	0	0
H. Babcock, 28	2	1	0	1	1	1	1	1	2	0
W. B. Bourne, 30	1	1	1	2	1	0	0	1	1	0
Levinston	1	1	0	2	0	2	1	0	0	0

Three-bird match.			
Jellett, 30	2	2	1
Eddy, 28	2	1	2
Butler, 28	2	0	2
Gillette, 28	1	1	0
W. C. Mabew, 28	1	1	1
C. A. Kone, 28	2	2	1
Donny Harvey, 30	0	0	1
H. Ward Black, 30	1	0	1
E. F. Liebenor, 28	2	1	1
Ed. Donohoe, 28	0	0	0
Wm. Levinston, 28	1	1	1
Orr, 30	1	1	1
Ewing, 28	1	2	0
Babcock, 28	0	2	1
Wooster, 30	1	1	0
Sanborn, 28	2	2	0
F. R. Webster, 28	2	1	1
F. Gallant, 28	2	1	2
W. B. Bowen, 30	0	1	0
A. C. Marcus, 29	1	0	0
E. W. Chapin, 28	0	2	
H. W. Woodward, 28	2	0	

J. K. Orr, Secretary.

Chick vs. Brewer.

On Sunday last at Haight Street base ball grounds, a very interesting match was shot between Capt J. L. Brewer, who has been traveling about the world, shooting, professionally, and Mr. Martinez Chick of San Diego. The match was made by Mr. Geo. Carroll, of this city, who backed Mr. Chick, and Mr. Lawrence, who backed Mr. Brewer. By agreement the men were to shoot three matches, 100 birds to the man in each match, for $250 a side each event; London Gun Club rules.

The first match resulted in favor of Mr. Chick, who scored 95 of his 100 birds against 92 killed by Capt. Brewer. The birds were only ordinary, the most of them being rather slow, with now and then a lightning driver. Gate money was charged, and but very few attended. After the ball game the grounds were cleared, except of those who purchased tickets for the shoot, and perhaps 300 men were present.

Mr. Ed. Fay acted as referee, and not having either a knowledge of the London Gun Club rules or a copy of them, he was in doubt as to many points during the progress of the match. He reversed his decisions, and allowed one of the contestants to do pretty much as he pleased. In style, accuracy with the first barrel, and general pleasantness of manner throughout the match, Mr. Chick had all the best of it; the birds were about equally hard for both. Mr. Chick shot 3¼ drams of Schultze's powder, 1¼ ounces chilled 7's from each barrel, using a 12-bore under eight pounds. Capt. Brewer shot 4 drams of Schultze, and 1¼ ounces of 6's in each barrel, also using a twelve. The score was:

J. L. Brewer.....1111111111222272221222202222702222101222120220120—44
22222222212220222202121222222211212212222212222222—48

Total.....92

M. Chick.........11110111112222112222120222222202222122221012222123—46
22022222221111121121122222222222112212212712222222—49

Total.....95

SECOND MATCH.

On Wednesday the second match of the series was shot, Mr. Chick again winning by a score of 95 to 89. The birds were better, and all of them had their tails clipped. Capt. Brewer got a few birds harder than any of Mr. Chicks, but the latter fairly out-shot his noted competitor at all points. Not more than a hundred spectators were present. The scores were:

Chick.........22101212221122122212211121111111212212121222212010—47
21021222221112121221221122211202222222222222122222—48

Total.....95

Brewer.........20222721212222107121010222211011022222222220121212122—44
112212220221122122222021022222222122222021102224—45

Total.....89

A team match has been made between Messrs. C. B. Smith and C. J. Haas on one side, and Crittenden Robinson and Ed. Fay on the other, for $200 a side; at 100 birds per man, American Association rules; match to be shot within thirty days, probably on June 27th, each side to find birds for the other. Capt. Eddy holds a forfeit for the match, and there is every probability that it will be shot.

Hunting in Modoc.

Fort Bidwell, Modock Co., Cal., May 29, 1890.

Editor Breeder and Sportsman:—What our mutual friend may have said to you concerning the game of this section I know not, but infer from the tone of your letter that life in Modoc was pictured in very rosy tints. Eight years have wrought many changes in this country, and when I remember that he came here in 1880 and left in 1882, and also recall the immense flocks of geese, ducks, sage hens, etc. that we hunted together, I can but believe that he has confined himself to facts. When we took our memorable hunt at Old Camp Warner across the line in Oregon, we got thirteen deer in three days, and no day did I see less than eighteen or twenty in a five mile tramp. But at that time the Indians, who in 1878 committed depredations on Wilson and Alexanders range, where the Old Camp is located, were religiously excluded from that section, and deer had flocked there and multiplied in astonishing numbers, but within two years of that time the Indians were allowed the freedom of the range and they made short work of the deer. There are yet many left, but not one can be found now where ten were then.

Large bands of antelope still roam over the plains of that section, and on the mountains a few big horns are to be found, and I am told an occasional ibex, though this last I have never seen. The Old Camp is fifty miles north-east of Bidwell.

Concerning trout fishing would say that the streams which flow into this (Surprise) valley contain very few trout and these were planted there by the State. This is accounted for by the fact that the lakes in the valley are all very shallow and every few years go dry. To the west of us just across the mountains is the big Goose Lake well filled with trout, and all streams running into it as well as the Pitt River which rises near the lake, afford good sport for the angler.

In the little Chewaucan Valley about 30 miles north of Lakeview is to be found magnificent trout fishing. A letter just received from Hon. John F. Swift, U. S. Minister to Tokio with whom writer had pleasure of a fishing trip to that region in 1885, expressed the belief that the best trout fishing in the world is to be found there.

It is certainly grand sport as is the salmon fishing on the Sprague River west of there. Near Bidwell there are but few sharp tails. They are more numerous in the Goose Lake Valley, where they afforded me good sport in the fall of '88. With a good dog a man could have made good bags.

The strychnine fiend don't allow us to keep a dog in this country many months.

I have heard of some bands of mule deer being seen this spring. Whether this fearful winter has killed many or not we can only surmise, but when from 50 to 90 per cent. of cattle that were left on the range perish it looks dubious for deer.

There are no elk in this section. Immense numbers of swan, geese and ducks called on us as they went north this spring. The swan came in large numbers just after the thaw, Feb. 1st, and the boys had a picnic with them bringing in dozens upon dozens.

Before the writer was sufficiently recovered from the grip to risk exposure to etherial mildness they had become educated and were much too far advanced for him. I hope, however, to have my lamp trimmed and burning by the time they come this way next fall.

Many Canada geese nest in this section and rear their young here; especially is this true of the beautiful Goose Lake Valley. This valley is appropriately named, for when the native flocks of honkers are joined by their cousins from the north accompanied by the snow geese, hundreds of acres of stubble are literally covered with them.

Ask Col. D. S. Gordon, now stopping at the Grand or Palace Hotel, what he knows about goose shooting in Modoc County. He has been there, and can give you some points.

Yes, we have snipe, also curlew and avocets, and a few years ago thousands of quail, but these latter have been nearly or quite exterminated by the last three winters. Deep snow, when accompanied by 24° below zero, has distanced the breech loader in wiping out this boss bird.

Dusky grouse are numerous in the timber. Doves are very plenty, and in August afford splendid sport.

Pelicans and sand-hill cranes are often met here, and the lynx, cougar and grizzly occasionally surrender to the sagacious hunter.

This is an isolated post, perhaps the most so of any in the United States, it being 160 miles from the nearest railroad station (Liegan, the terminus of the Nevada and California R. R., running out from Reno), but if anyone wants a taste of frontier life, and can rough it, if he will spend the month of October or November in this vicinity, my word for it, smashing clay saucers will ever after be deemed tame sport by that individual. As I do not keep a hotel, I have no pecuniary interest in the visits of sportsmen.

A. C. Lowell.

The property holders along Dry Creek, from Oak Knoll, Napa County, to the Sonoma line, have unanimously agreed to stop all fishing, hunting or trespassing of any kind. Notices to that effect will be posted all along the creeks.

Together with a package of glorious cherries Mr. Henry A. Bassford sent from his Vacaville ranch this note: "I just finished packing cherries to-day, had a very good crop. Have had about 75 boys, girls and Chinamen working for the last month. I see quite a good many doves around the last few days. I will have a little spare time now for awhile and I think I will give Mr. Smith a brush for the medal."

Mr. W. E. Perry, who will be pleasantly remembered as one of Colonel Dimick's experts has associated himself with the sterling old gun house of Wm. R. Schaefer & Son in Boston where we hope his attractive personality and his great knowledge of guns and sportsmen's wants may meet a deserved reward.

At Bakersfield on Sunday of last week Messrs. I. L. Miller and C. N. Reed marshalled the trap shots of that game little city into teams and scored at blue rock targets, Captain Millers team breaking 93 and Captain Reed's 87. The best individual score was made by Mr. Henry Borgwardt, the next by Charles Gay and the third by Charley Day. Mr. Ed. Lechner broke 18 out of 21; a very fine performance indeed. Where were Mr. Houghton, Mr. Seymour, Mr. Leonard, Mr. T. L. Briggs and all the other cracks?

The regular monthly shoot of the Blue Rock Club will take place Saturday, June 7th, at Oakland Race Track. Take 1 P. M. Berkeley train.

The London Shooting Times comments upon the recent Traver fraud as follows:

"This novel kind of fraud had better be borne in mind, as clay pigeon matches are pretty frequent on this side of the herring pond. But that such a bare faced imposition could have, at all, succeeded, baffles us. Had we been shooting and heard the shot strike, we would, of course have wanted to know why the birds did not break, of course.

ROD.

The Fish Commission.

The regular meeting hour for the June meeting was 1:30 P. M. on Tuesday last, but as Commissioner Harvey found it impossible to be present at that hour, the Board convened at 8:30 A. M. and transacted the usual routine business. The monthly report of Chief of Patrol Callundan was presented as follows:

The Honorable The Board of Fish Commissioners:—Gentlemen:—The report of the Chief of Patrol and such Deputies as have made their proceedings known to him is submitted herewith. The lack of necessity for watching the trout streams has made it possible to devote more attention to the markets and to the fisheries along the Bay shores. If the views of your Honorable Board are rightly understood it is the desire to preserve the young of fish by such constant and close oversight as will prevent their capture rather than to make an occasional conviction with accompanying fine after the fisherman has worked devastation for a time. It is believed that comparatively few small fish are now being destroyed, the daily patrol of the markets prevents their being offered for sale and the occasional trips of the Deputies to the fishing stations when unexpected makes it hardly worth while for the fishermen to dry the fish for export. Since the passage of the ordinance in San Francisco prohibiting the selling or offering for sale of striped bass less than eight lbs. in weight, your Deputies have been especially vigilant in relation to bass and can report that no small fish of the species have been marketed, although many have been placed on the slabs weighing from twelve to twenty-two and a half lbs.

The traffic in deer skins from which the evidence of sex has been removed seems to be about broken up, the skins consigned by L. Lobree to the Sawyer Tanning Co. some weeks ago still remain under seizure subject to the order of your Honorable Board where it is recommended that they remain until such time as someone attempts to force ownership of them, when a successful prosecution can be initiated. Deputy Tunstead has the matter specially in charge and may be relied upon to perform his duty with the utmost faithfulness. Deputy Innes has devoted his time largely to market inspection and to watching the fish wharves at which the cargoes from the fishing stations are landed. The fishermen report generally poor success, light catches and consequent hardship and inability to pay their licenses promptly although Deputy and License Collector Curley is gradually reaching them all.

Deputies have been sent to various points about the country adjacent to San Francisco in answer to complaints that explosives are being used in the streams. In no case has anyone been detected in the act of using such explosives but it is believed that the trips made by the Deputies have exerted a salutary influence in the way of preventing future like outrages. The Sonoma River at Glen Ellen and near that town was one of the spots visited, Russian River another, the Los Gatos a third and the San Lorenzo a fourth. About the middle of the month a Deputy visited Ukiah and traversed a portion of the Russian River near that City where in former seasons Indian fish traps by hundreds have been set; it is a source of gratification to report that the efforts of your Honorable Commission have entirely put a stop to the Indian way of fishing in that stream and it is hoped that with the increase in the food supply which is destroyed by the poisons used by the Indians in fishing, Russian River will soon become what it formerly was, one of the greatest trout streams of this or any other State. Several inquiries have come about the intention of your Honorable Board as to establishing small hatcheries at various points near suitable public waters, such inquiries are referred for the action of the Board.

On May 3rd and 4th a run was made down the Sacramento River without finding any fishermen violating the law.

The 8th and 9th were spent at Monterey examining the Chinese and Italian fishing stations there. A large number of boats were found though but few of them were in active use most of the fishermen preferring to wait until a little later when greater returns for their work are insured. The Constables and the Justice of the Peace at Monterey promised to interest themselves actively in the enforcing of the law and to sustain your Commission whenever opportunity offers.

May 15th was passed in Martinez settling the cases of the Chinese arrested some months since for illegal fishing. Of the nine cases pending, four paid fines of $85 each and four of $50 each, one of the defendants having died shortly after leaving jail on bail. The total amount $540 was subdivided of which one-third has been paid to the State Board of Fish Commissioners as provided by law.

Some weeks since in Monterey County three Italians were arrested and fined for fishing with too small meshes and the whole amount of the fines, $150 was paid into the County treasury. When the fact became known steps were immediately taken to secure to this Board the portion of the fines to which the State was entitled. A formal claim was made upon the Board of Supervisors at Monterey County for the amount due, which claim will be acted upon at the next meeting. Complaints have come to hand that deer were being killed in Marin County and investigation justifies belief in the rumors, the persons whose names have come to hand have all been notified not to continue their illegal hunting. Deer hunting at present is done with hounds which find the weakened does and young fawns an easy prey. Hunting them is an outrage from any standpoint and prosecutions will be vigorously pushed all against all as to whom evidence of guilt can be secured.

Respectfully submitted,
F. P. Callundan, Chief of Patrol.

Fish Commissioner Geo. Mills of Nevada has distributed 1,000,000 trout already this season and has nearly as many more which will be placed in various streams during June. He is proving the best officer that the state has ever had, being alert, enthusiastic and practical.

Grim's Gossip.

Electioneer continues to improve.

John Green is moving Melrose 2:26½ in a quiet manner, but the Sultan gelding is improving every day.

At the Bay District Track everything is booming and there are always more or less horsemen present to witness the "work outs."

W. H. Wilson, of Cynthiana, Ky., has promised James Goldsmith a new sulky when Simmocolon trots in 2:20. Jimmy will get that sulky sure.

More horsemen will visit Los Angeles in August than ever before. They are going to have a bang up meeting and all visitors can rely upon being hospitably entertained.

The Kentucky Trotting Horse Breeders' Association contemplates opening a stallion representative stake to close January 1, 1891, guaranteeing it to be worth not less than $15,000.

At Glenbrook Park, there are quite a number of horses in training, and as the programme is better than ever before, it is confidently predicted that all former fairs will be surpassed in brilliancy.

J. H. White, president of the Breeders' Association, has been in town during the week, and reports his string as doing well. Ten or a dozen of the best ones have been removed to the Petaluma track.

Wm. Hogoboom is located at the Walla Walla track where he has a fine stable of horses. Billy has been long enough at the business to warrant the belief that he can give satisfaction to those that employ him.

The sale of the J. M. Donohoe horses in this city on Wednesday last by Killip & Co., was productive of good prices. The principal sale was a Guy Wilkes filly which fell to the bid of F. H. Burke, owner of Eros.

And now comes the news that a mare belonging to Wm. Barnes of Elmwood, Mo., has given birth to triplets. Strange to say, all three of the foals are doing well and it is deemed extremely probable that they will survive.

At a meeting of the Willows Agricultural Association it was determined to hold the annual fair of 1890, from Aug. 12 to 16th inclusive. Last year a highly successful meeting was held and a better one is anticipated for this yeor

Programmes and entry blanks for the Sixth District Agricultural Association Meeting to be held at Los Angeles in August, can be obtained at this office. The directors have made a move in the right direction by offering liberal purses.

We have had many calls for the Haggin catalogues of yearling thoroughbreds; but only having one, could not comply with the repeated requests. It is just possible that many possible purchasers have been kept away owing to the neglect.

The question now arises what track will offer the best advantages to the Breeders Association for the fall meeting. Sacramento, Napa, Santa Rosa and Petaluma are all talked of, but there is no telling at present where the honor will fall.

Mr. A. T. Hatch has been asked to name a price on Guide 2:28½ by Director, dam Imogene by Norwood. The gentleman, however, positively refuses to sell his promising young stallion and the colt will remain at the Hatch breeding establishment.

At Terre Haute last Wednesday Budd Doble drove Houri 2:17, and Lady Bullion 2:18¼, in double harness a half mile in 1:08¾—the first quarter in 34¼, and the second in 34. Doble said he thought by Friday or Saturday he could drive the team a half in 1:07.

The trotting meeting at Terre Haute has had the unqualified endorsement of the public as thousands upon thousands were present each day. Sunol, Palo Alto and Axtell have been the great source of attraction, the California filly being pronounced by all an ideal trotter.

Messrs. Miller & Sibley have sold to Schmulback & Park, Wheeling, W. Va., the yearling colt Gold Coast by Electioneer, dam Edith Carr by Clark Chief and the yearling colt Golden Slope by Electioneer, dam Addie, the dam of Woodnut 2:16½. The price for the pair was $12,000.

Mr. Fred W. Loeber, one of the Directors of the P. C. T. H. B. A., has been confined to his bed for a week or two, but is once more able to be around. He reports the young Alconas as being equal to anything in the land, but his first love compels him to state that there are several Whippletons that will enter the list this year.

Many times lately I have heard the remark, "things will be quiet here this year as Marvin and Hickock have gone East". From present appearances it is susceptable of belief that the present Season will surpass all former years in surprises and sensational performers, there being many a "good thing" stowed away on various of the breeding farms of the State

The Southern California Handicap promises to be as popular with the horsemen of California as the Toboggan Slide Handicap was with the Eastern horseowners. The Directors of the Sixth District Agricultural Association made no mistake in giving a thousand dollar purse for a (¾)mile race. The best sprinters in the state will be sent to Los Angeles to have a try for the money.

It would seem as if the California horses are coming rapidly to the front this year, as I see by our Eastern exchanges that a great deal of money has been placed on Salvator for the Suberban. The colt is a good one, the distance suits him well, and if Mr. Haggin is fortunate enough to have his colors pass under the wire first, his many California friends will feel highly elated thereat.

Very nearly all of the Eastern "Hoss" journals have had accounts of the wonderful performances of Blue Belle on the continent, but not one of them have stated that Blue Belle is identical with Mila C., 2:26½, a mare that is in bad odor at present, owing to sharp practices played with her by unscrupulous owners. Her American record of 2:26½ was made at Chicago, Ill., October 25, 1873. She is now one of the most noted trotting horses in Europe, and it is to be hoped that she is in better hands than formerly.

Mr. Valensin has almost recovered from his late illness and is able to be around once more. He has been requested to act as the California representative for the Pacing Association that is now being completed in the East, and while he cannot possibly attend a meeting of delegates which will take place shortly, still it is altogether likely that he will retain the position of committeeman from this State.

DeLong's Ethan Allen, son of Ethan Allen, was killed the other day at the farm of his owner, Mr. Henry J. DeLong of Shoreham, Vt. The old horse had become so infirm that it was thought to be the part of mercy to put an end to his sufferings. He was foaled June 26th, 1856, and was the last of the sons of the famous Ethan Allen. Holabird's Ethan died last summer in Shelburn, Vt.

Mr. S. C. Ferguson, clerk at the Palo Alto Stock Farm, has gotten up a book to enable horse owners to keep a correct and accurate account of the horses which they may have entered in stake races. The book is very complete in its way and will be of great assistance to all owners throughout the country. I understand that Mr. Ferguson has copyrighted the work and will be glad to receive orders for them from any one who may desire to purchase.

We have had a very pleasant call this week from Dr. Aby the superintendent of the Guenoc Stock Farm. He reports that in two weeks at least, work will have commenced on the new race track which is about to be completed at that farm. No expense will be spared to make it one of the most complete and attractive in the State, and it is to be hoped that in the near future, many youngsters may emanate from Guenoc, to do justice to that noted place.

W. H. Wilson of Cynthiana Ky., proprietor of Abdallah Park has added another choice mare to his collection in purchasing of Mrs. A. P. Dills, Hopkinsville Ky. The mare Colon (dam of Simmocolon, 5 years old, rec. 2:23¼) by Strathmore No. 408; 2nd dam Coral, (dam of Coralloid, 3 years old, rec. 2:29½) by Clark Chief 89; 3d dam (dam of Caliban rec. 2:34, sire of C. F. Clay 2:18, Coaster 2:26½, and Cylone 2:23¼ he the sire of Dr. Sparks 2 year old rec. 2:25½, and Gillette 2:25), by C. M. Clay Jr. 22. This mare is in foal to Simmons 2:28.

To-day (Saturday) the Australian steamer will in all probability arrive with a large consignment of thoroughbred mares which have been purchased by Mr. Merry in the antipodes for Mr. L. J. Rose; a list of them has already been printed in our columns and on their arrival a personal inspection will be made so that we may be able to give our readers next week a full account of what they look like. From the breeding, the mares are everything that could be desired and if their individuality is one-half as good, Mr. Rose will have secured many fine brood animals for his establishment.

White Hat Dan McCarthy has left Chicago with his string of California trotters and is now located at Fleetwood Park, New York. Already he has had quite a number of them out for inspection, showing up fast quarters and halves, and Dan always has an enthusiastic crowd around him when he commences to talk of the merits of the horses from the Pacific Slope. W. W. Mendenhall of Livermore is acting as manager for Dan, and between the two, no doubt they will make many profitable sales.

On Wednesday afternoon there was probably no happier man in San Francisco than Mr. Valensin of Pleasanton. As stated in the gossip column a few weeks ago, Simmocolon has been sent back East to the stables of Jas. Goldsmith of Dundee Park, New Jersey; on Wednesday afternoon Mr. Valensin received a telegram from Goldsmith stating that Simmocolon had won a race in three straight heats and received a record of 2:23¼. There were originally ten entries for the purse but whether they all started or not it will be impossible to tell until the Eastern papers arrive with an account of the race.

A letter from Secretary Sproul of the Chico Association informs me that the Directors have decided to hold their fair from August 26th to 30th inclusive. Five days' racing will be given in which there will be many trotting, pacing and running events. $6,000 will be hung up in purses, and there will be for trotters a three-minute 2:40; 2:35; 2:30 and 2:27, and four-year-old classes, for pacers, a class for untried horses, and a 2:25 purse; in the running events there will be a mile dash, three quarters and repeat, half mile and repeat and a mile and repeat; this is a good programme and should warrant a large attendance.

The following clipping from the columns of a Cheshire (England) newspaper will give an idea of the big crowds which turn out to the races in that country: "No fewer than 60,000 passengers arrived at the Chester General Railway station on the Cup day, which is stated to be by far the largest number ever recorded on any similar occasion. They were conveyed in 52 special and 228 ordinary trains. The Cheshire Lines Railway Company brought 12,000 passengers into the city, bringing up the total to 72,000 passengers on both systems, and it requires very little stretch of the imagination to compute that double that number, or close upon 150,000 people, were in attendance at the races on the Cup day."

In a letter which I received this week from Terre Haute, the bad news comes that Alfred. S. was kicked by another horse one day last week, and Hickok has had to let up on him. The letter was sent too soon after the injury for my informant to be able positively to say what the effect of the injury would be. It is to be hoped that Alfred S. is not permanently disabled, for his present mark would have been reduced this year barring accident. Arol, in the Marvin string, of which mention has already been made in reference to her injuries, will probably be saved but will never be able to race again. This is too bad, for Arol gave promise of much speed, and her record of 2.25 is no where near what she could have done.

I am sorry to have to announce the death of Fontana which occurred at Mr. W. S. Hobart's Breeding Farm early in the week. Fontana was a brown mare, foaled in 1879 by Almont 33, dam Fanny Williams by Alexander's Abdallah 15; 2nd dam by Denmark; 3rd dam by Robert Bruce. Fontana was bred by Gen. W. T. Withers of Lexington, Kentucky, who sold her some years ago to the late Silas Skinner; all of her produce have been remarkably speedy, notably Flora Belle by Alcona 730. Flora Belle made a record at Napa last year of 2:25, and was shortly afterwards sold to Mr. Corbitt of the San Mateo Stock Farm. At the late sale of brood mares owned by Mrs. Silas Skinner, Fontana was sold to Mr. Hobart for $4,400; she was in foal to Director which makes the loss still greater; the cause of death is said to be colic.

My correspondent at Santa Barbara sends me word that Carrie B. has foaled a bay filly with left hind foot marked white and small star in forehead by Alcazar. Carrie B. is by A. W. Richmond; her foal is entered in the BREEDER AND SPORTSMAN Futurity Stake; the filly is a most handsome one, active, large and intelligent.

At the track Geo. Sherman's two-year-old by Accident, dam by Newry is doing excellent work, although exercised but a dozen times he ran a quarter last week in twenty-four and a half seconds; quite a number of gentlemen were present and held watches on the colt while the feat was being performed; a sport remarked after the run "that colt can eat his oats out of a silver bowl and drink out of a golden bucket now.' I am glad that George has a good one. Fergusson has the youngster in training.

For sometime it has been a mooted question as to which of the two mares, Minnie Lee or Queen of the West had the most speed, so a match race for $250 a side was made between T. J. Powers and Jno. D. Spreckles, the respective owners of the mares. The race took place on Wednesday afternoon at the Bay District Track, there being a large attendance of prominent horsemen. The judges for the occasion were Messrs. Matthews, Perry and Gonzalez while the timers were Messrs. Farrell, Dickey and Griffin. Jimmy Dustin handled Mr. Spreckle's Minnie Lee, while Jno. Green held the ribbons over Queen of the West. The match was won in three straight heats Minnie Lee winning in 2:32¼ 2:29½ and 2:31½. Queen of the West proved herself a good mare but is yet a little rank, however, if she keeps on improving, the day is not far distant when her owner will be able to say that he has a mare in the 2:30 list.

The race for the Jockey Club prize (the French Derby) was run Sunday, June 1st, at Chantilly, and was won by Baron Rothschild's chestnut colt Heaume, by Hermit, out of Bella. P. Aumont's chestnut colt Mirabeau, by Saxifrage, out of Marionnette, was second, and Baron A. DeShickler's bay colt Fitz-Roya, by Atlantic, out of Perplexite, third. The last betting was 5 to 4 against Heaume, 4 to 1 against Mirabeau and 6 to 1 against Fitz Roya. The other starters and the odds laid against them were: Pour Point, 20 to 1; Chalet, 14 to 1; Le Glorieux, 25 to 1; Reville, 50 to 1; Cedi, 100 to 1. Twelve horses were entered. The absentees were Alicante and LeNord. The field made an excellent start. Chalet and Reville took the start, closely followed by Heaume and Fitz-Roya. At the rise Heaume forged ahead, followed by Mirabeau, Fitz-Roya and Pour Point in the order named. In the home stretch there was a lively struggle, Heaume winning by one length, with Mirabeau half a length in front of Fitz-Roya.

The dam of Darebin is dead. She was found dead in one of the Bundoora Park paddocks a few days ago, and upon examination it was discovered that she had been shot, three or four leaden pellets having passed through the skin into the intestines. Mr. Gardiner thinks the death of the mare was caused through some boys accidentally shooting her while they were after parrots. Lurline was undoubtedly one of the best mares that ever trod the Australian turf. She was bred by Mr. S. Nosworthy in New Zealand in 1869, and was by the imported horse Traducer, from the imported mare Mermaid, by King Tom. In New Zealand she proved the champion mare of her day, and amongst other races she won the Canterbury Cup and Canterbury Plate twice. In 1874 she became the property of Mr. H. Redwood and another, and with her relative Calumny she was brought to Victoria, and ran at the V. R. C. Spring Meeting, but being altogether out of sorts, she did not cut a very respectful figure. Shortly afterwards she was purchased by Mr. Samuel Gardiner for 700 guineas, Mr. W. E. Dakin having her placed in his hands, and in her new owner's colours, she carried 8st 1lb, and won the Australian Cup. In the Sydney Cup, with 9st up, she ran a good third to Imperial, 7st 9lb. At the same meeting she beat Llama, Kingsborough and Redwood in the All-Aged Stakes, and on the following day she defeated The Diver, Melbourne and Goldsborough in the A. J. C. Plate. In May of the same year she journeyed to South Australia, and with 9st 1lb on her back, won the Adelaide Cup very easily, and on the third day of the meeting won the Queen's Plate. Mr. Gardiner put her to the stud in 1876, and The Peer was selected as her mate, the produce being a chestnut colt, who was subsequently named Motes, but he did not shine as a racehorse. In the following year she produced Darebin to the same sire, and he proved himself one of the best horses in Australia.

Norwich (Eng.) Mercury, May 10: "Mr. William Flanders' brown four-year-old Hackney stallion Star of Mepal (1920) was bought on Tuesday for £2,000 by Mr. H. L. Bloodgood of Bloodgood stock farm, New Marlboro Mass., and is to be shipped from London on 22d inst, with several other Hackney—stallions and mares—which Mr. Bloodgood has bought in the Eastern district. Star of Mepel was the reserve to Mr. H. Moore's Rufus for the second Elsenham challenge cup at the great London show in March last, and was deemed the most likely candidate for champion honors at next show. His breeding, as fully set forth in the Hackney Society's report of the show just issued, shows that he traces back to the very best Hackney blood in Norfolk and Yorkshire. His dam, Sunbeam, (337), is full sister of Mr. Flanders' Reality—champion of 1885' 1887 and 1888. His sire, Star o the North (1185), which has lately been exported to America was first-prize winner in the two-year-old class of the 1885 Hackney Horse Society's Show. Much regret will be felt that these horses, and Star of Mepal especially, should have been lost to the country. There were offers of £1,500 for the Star of Mepal, but these were refused. We congratulate Mr. Flanders on his good fortune in breeding so valuable a horse, and the Americans on having won such a prize. A few months ago an American was desirous of buying Mr. C. E. Cook's Cadet at £1,500 and Mr. Henry Moore is reported to have refused an offer of £2,500 for the champion horse Rufus. There can hardly be better evidence required of the rise in the value of good Hackneys. Those who are keenly watching the signs of the times say that the American demand is going to be large and sharp. Such a purchase as this of Star of Mepal, will add considerably to the curiosity of the American mind as to the worth and origin of the Hackney horse. That there is yet a great deal of ignorance in America in regard to this variety of trotting horse is evident from a foot-note to an article on "Road Horses" in the Atlantic Monthly for April. The writer, who would appear to be an authority on trotting horse, informs his readers that the Norfolk trotter is almost, if not wholely extinct (!); and he further demonstrates how very little knowledge he has by a speculation as to the breeding of Jary's Bellfounder on which he asserts that little or nothing is known—as though the Hackney Stud Book had no existence.

THE WEEKLY

Breeder and Sportsman.

JAMES P. KERR, PROPRIETOR.

The Turf and Sporting Authority of the Pacific Coast.

Office, No. 313 Bush St.

P. O. Box 2300.

TERMS—One Year, $5; Six Months, $3; Three Months, $1.50.
STRICTLY IN ADVANCE.

Money should be sent by postal order, draft or by registered letter, addressed to JAMES P. KERR, San Francisco, Cal.

Communications must be accompanied by the writer's name and address, not necessarily for publication, but as a private guarantee of good faith.

NEW YORK OFFICE, Room 15, 181 BROADWAY.

ALEX. P. WAUGH, - - - - - - Editor.

Advertising Rates

Per Square (half inch)

One time	$1 50
Two times	2 50
Three times	3 25
Four times	4 00

And each subsequent insertion 75c. per square.

Advertisements running six months are entitled to 10 per cent. discount.

Those running twelve months are entitled to 20 per cent. discount.

Reading notices set in same type as body of paper, 50 cents per line each insertion.

To Subscribers.

The date printed on the wrapper of your paper indicates the time to which your subscription is paid.

Should the BREEDER AND SPORTSMAN be received by any subscriber who does not want it, write us direct to stop it. A postal card will suffice.

Special Notice to Correspondents.

Letters intended for publication should reach this office not later than Wednesday of each week, to secure a place in the issue of the following Saturday. Such letters to insure immediate attention should be addressed to the BREEDER AND SPORTSMAN, and not to any member of the staff.

San Francisco, Saturday, June 7, 1890.

Dates Claimed.

EUREKA JOCKEY CLUB	July 2d to 5th
IONE	Aug 7th to 9th.
LOS ANGELES [6th District]	Aug. 4th to 9th
SAN JOSE	Aug. 11th to 16th
WILLOWS	August 12th to 16th
NAPA	Aug. 18th to 23rd
GLENBROOK PARK, 17th District	August 19th to 23d
PETALUMA	Aug. 25th to 30th
CHICO	August 26th to 30th
OAKLAND (District No. 1)	Sept. 1st to Sept. 6th
LAKEPORT, 13th District	September 23d to 27th
CALIFORNIA STATE FAIR	Sept 8th to 20th
STOCKTON	Sept. 23rd to 27th.
FRESNO (Fall Meeting)	Sept. 29th to Oct. 4th
VISALIA	Oct. 7th to 11th

Stallions Advertised

IN THE

BREEDER AND SPORTSMAN.

Thoroughbreds.

FRIAR TUCK, Hermit—Romping Girl.........C. W. Aby, Middletown.
GREENBACK, Dollar—Music.........C. W. Aby, Middletown
ST. SAVIOR, Eolus—War Song.........C. W. Aby, Middletown.
THREE CHEERS, Imp. Hurrah—Young Fashion.........E. S. Culver, San Francisco.

Trotters.

ADMIRAL, Volunteer—Lady Pierson.........Frank Drake, Vallejo.
ALCONA, Almont—Queen Mary.........Fred W. Loeber, St. Helena
BAY ROSE, Sultan—Madam Baldwin.........Thos. Bonner, Santa Rosa
CHARLES DERBY, Steinway—by Electioneer. Cook Stock Farm, Contra Costa Co.
CORRECTOR, Director—Brainey.........Pleasanton Stock Farm.
DECORATOR, Director—Chess.........Pleasanton Stock Farm.
DEXTER PRINCE, Kentucky Prince—Lady Dexter.........L. M. Morse, Lodi.
DIRECTOR, Dictator—Dolly.........Pleasanton Stock Farm, Pleasanton.
EL BENTON, Electioneer—Nellie Benton.........Souther Farm, San Leandro.
ECLECTIC, Electioneer—Manette.........Wilfred Page, Sonoma County
EROS, Electioneer—Sontag Mohawk.........W. H. Vioget, Menlo Park
FIGARO, Hambletonian—Emblem.........Souther Farm, San Leandro.
GROVER CLAY, Electioneer—Maggie Norfolk.........Denis Gannon, Oakland.
GRAND MOOR 2374, Moor 870—Vashti.........H. I. Thornton, S. F.
G. & M., Anteeo—Rosa B.........George E. Guerne, Santa Rosa.
GUY WILKES, George Wilkes—Lady Bunker.........San Mateo Stock Farm, San Mateo.
GLEN FORTUNE, Electioneer—Glenna.........Souther Farm, San Leandro.
GEORGE WASHINGTON, Mambrino Chief—Fanny Rose.........Thos. Smith, Vallejo.
GRANDISSIMO, LeGrande—Norma.........Fred W. Loeber, St Helena
JESTER D, Almont—Hortense.........Souther Farm, San Leandro
KING DAVID, Admiral—Black Flora.........Frank Drake, Vallejo.
LEO WILKES, Guy Wilkes Sable.........San Mateo Stock Farm, San Mateo.
MEMO, Sidney—Flirt.........John Rowen, Oakland
MAMBRINO WILKES, George Wilkes—Lady Chrisman.........San Miguel Stock Farm, Walnut Creek.
MAMBRINO CHIEF, McDonald Chief—Venus.........Thos. Smith, Vallejo.
MORTIMER, Electioneer—Marti.........Wilfred Page, Sonoma County
PASHA, Sultan—Madam Baldwin.........D. Bryson, Linden
PHILOSOPHER, Pilot Wilkes—Belle.........George E. Guerne, Santa Rosa.
REDWOOD, Anteeo—Lou Wilton.........A. McFayden, Oakland.
STEINWAY, Strathmore—Abbess.........Cook Stock Farm, Contra Costa Co
SABLE WILKES, Guy Wilkes—Sable.........San Mateo Stock Farm, San Mateo.
VICTOR, Echo—Daughter of Woodburn.........G. W. Hughes, Napa City

The State Fair.

The Secretary of the State Board of Agriculture has sent us a note stating that the Executive Committee have decided to make a number of changes in the programme from the way in which it has been already advertised. They have substituted for the free-for-all trotters a purse of $1,500 for the 2:20 class, and have also changed the 2:25 pacing race to a purse of $800 for the 2:30 class, and the purse for the free-for-all pacers has been increased to $1,000. In the course of a few days, in all probability by next week, the entire programme in its amended form will be advertised in the BREEDER AND SPORTSMAN, so that the horsemen of the State may know exactly what the programme will be at Sacramento this year.

The Story of John Nelson.

Some weeks ago we promised the readers of the BREEDER AND SPORTSMAN that we were on the trail of the persons who owned John Nelson at the time of his death. It will be remembered that Wallace in his Year Books states that John Nelson 187 died in 1871; where he could possibly have gotten his information is hard to tell, for there are hundreds and probably thousands in this State to-day who know that the old horse was alive many years after that. Only a few months ago Mr. L U. Shippee of Stockton sent back a large number of mares to be registered, and among them were several for which the sire's parentage was claimed as John Nelson; the Wallace Publishing Co. at once returned the registration certificates and stated that it was impossible for Mr. Shippee to have any mares by John Nelson born after 1872 as they had positive information in the office that John Nelson had died in 1871.

Mr. Henry Gore of Reno was the first person to send to this office any data by which the true time of the horse's death could be found out, his letter was as follows:

EDITOR BREEDER AND SPORTSMAN:—Being an old subscriber of your paper and reading it regularly every week I find that there is a controversy on hand relative to the time of the death of John Nelson. In 1877 I lived in Colusa and had as a neighbor a man by the name of Nathan Price, he went down to San Francisco and bought from Jas. Eoff, the horse John Nelson who was at that time on a ranch owned by Messrs. Miller & Lux. Price told me when he got him he was running out with a band of mares and looked very bad; Price brought him to Colusa, as near as I can remember, about the first week in March of that same year; Price did not keep the horse but about three weeks and then sold him to T. B. Cooper who now lives in Adin, Modoc County, but at that time lived in Colusa. My impression is that the horse only lived a few months after Cooper bought him and he died on Cooper's ranch about one and a half miles from the Town of Colusa.

Yours respectfully, HENRY GORE.

A letter was at once sent to Mr. Cooper who is a well known horseman, he being at present the owner of Juanito, the sire of Almont Patchen 2:15. It could hardly be expected that without books to refer to, that one can remember the exact date of things that happened over a decade ago. The answer to our letter to Mr. Cooper is as follows:

EDITOR BREEDER AND SPORTSMAN:—Your favor of the 26th inst duly received and contents noted.

In reply will say that I purchased the horse John Nelson 187 from a man by the name of Price sometime during the spring of 1877. I at present know nothing about the man Price, where he is or whether dead or alive. I do not remember the exact date of the purchase of John Nelson or the exact date of his death but know that he died in the fall of 1878. Yours respectfully,

T. B. COOPER.

These letters are at the office of the BREEDER AND SPORTSMAN and can be seen by any and all who are interested in the John Nelson stock, and it is to be hoped that in Wallace's future publications that he will correct the error which he has printed for so many years, and give the exact year of the death of John Nelson and not claim, as at present, the year 1871.

Speed! Speed! Speed!

The marvelous results attained by the trotting fraternity in 1889, has led many to suppose that it would be impossible to surpass them this season. However, from the present outlook we feel every confidence that 1890 will prove as sensational a year as was that of the one preceding it. Already from all quarters of the country come reports of fast quarters, halves and miles, each new report surpassing its predecessor in sensation. California will be well represented not only on our own circuit but also in the East and there is no breeder in this State but what feels that California will as usual head the list with sensational performers during the coming racing season. The runners are also doing well to uphold the glory of our State, Geraldine having acquitted herself with glory in the Toboggan Slide Handicap, for although beaten by half a length she was not disgraced, as the three-quarters of a mile was compassed in the remarkably fast time of 1:10½; the difference in weight carried between herself and Fides, who proved the victor, was enough to account for her defeat. The Santa Anita stable, the Hearst stable and the Haggin stable will be heard from before long. Already two or three victories have been secured by them and their representative horses will soon be in fettle to assert themselves as the superiors of all comers

Philosopher.

In the advertisement to be found in another column it will be seen that Geo. E. Guerne, of Santa Rosa, offers for sale the exquisitely bred stallion Philosopher. This representative of the Wilkes family was brought to California some two years ago by Mr. J. W. Knox, and has since that remained in the neighborhood of Santa Rosa, where he stood during the present season receiving many high class mares. Philosopher should prove a valuable horse for any of the many breeders throughout this State. He is only four years old, his sire being Pilot Wilkes 2987, 1st dam Bella by George Wilkes 519, 2nd dam by Bell Morgan 61; Philosopher's sire, Pilot Wilkes is by George Wilkes, dam Grace by Pilot Jr. 12. With the contention that at present exists between the believers in the Wilkes family and the many who are partial to the Electioneers, it can be readily imagined that there will be many of the former who will try to secure possession of this finely bred young horse.

A Pacing Purse.

The Breeders' Association offers this week a purse of $1000 for pacers eligible to the 2:20 class; the race to be mile heats best three in five and to take place at their meeting this fall. Entrance to the purse is made on the installment plan, the conditions being $100 entrance, payable $20 on June 10th, $20 on July 1st, $20 on August 1st and $40 ten days preceding the first advertised day of the meeting. Horses need not be named until the final payment. There are a large number of the side wheel brigade in California at present, eligible to and qualified to pace for this handsome purse and as the breeders are all now taking an active interest in the organization, we can believe that the entries will be large. It should be understood by those who own horses eligible for this purse that the nominator must be a member of the Association, this is readily accomplished by sending to the Secretary, whose address will be found in the advertisement, the membership fee.

Billiards.

The long expected billiard match between champion Jacob Schaefer and Professor McCleery of this city took place on Thursday, Friday and Saturday of last week, and it must be confessed that the result was a source of surprise to the friends of the Pacific Coast champion. Schafer fairly outdone himself, and after getting the balls together on the first evening McCleery was never allowed another shot. The extraordinary run, 3,000 points, is a record, as that amount has never been made before in a public match. The second contest took place between "Napoleon" Ives and McCleery which also resulted in the defeat of the California representative. The two Eastern players have stamped themselves masters of the game and the exhibitions were witnessed by many who take an active interest in this beautiful pastime. We understand that there are two or three matches on the tapis which will be brought to a conclusion sometime during the coming week.

Hurstbourne Stud Farm.

We have received from N. T. Harris, proprietor of the Hurstbourne Farm the most handsome catalogue that has ever been sent to this office. As is well known the principal stallion is George Kinney who stamped himself as one of the best race horses of his day. The book contains a full and complete list of all of Kinney's performances and a very favorably mention is also made of his full brother John Happy, now standing in Mr. Haggins stud at Rancho del Paso. There is also enumerated a list of thirty seven brood mares, than which there is no better in the country, all of the principal brood lines represented in the English and American stud books can be found permeating the veins of the mares catalogued in the Hurstbourne book. The proprietor, Mr. Harris, is known as one of the most progressive brooders in the country; in addition to Kinney he has Neptune, son of imp. Mortemer, dam imp. Highland Lassie by Blair Athol; the third of the stallions is Saracen, son of imp. Lemington, dam imp. Lurline by Gemmi di Vergy. It cannot be wondered at that such royal brooding produces royal results, and the Hurstbourne yearlings always command a ready sale in the market.

The Sonoma and Marin Futurity Stake.

There is every reason to believe that the Futurity Stake lately opened by the Sonoma and Marin Agricultural Society will have a generous support from those who are in the district comprising Sonoma, Marin, Napa, Lake, Mendocino, Solano, Yolo, Colusa and Contra Costa. There is no section of the State where so many highly bred horses are raised as in the counties enumerated, and as Petaluma is one of the favorite places on the circuit for horsemen to attend, we can believe that all breeders living in the district will heartily support this new stake. Entrance does not close until July 1st, but we are informed that already quite a number of entries have been made which is an assurance that the Futurity will be a pronounced success. The payments are easy and as follows: $5 on July 1, 1890, $5 on January 2, 1891, $5 on July 1, 1891, $10 January 2, 1892, $10 on July 1, 1892, $15 on January 2, 1893, the last and final payment being $25 on July 1, 1893, in which year the trot will take place. We fully expect to receive an extremely large list of entries for this valuable stake from Secretary Maclay when it closes.

Pleasanton Notes.

A telegram was sent to the office of the BREEDER AND SPORTSMAN on last Friday evening containing the information that on the following day many of the fast trotters now at Pleasanton Stock Farm would be worked out. A visit was accordingly paid the next day to the home of Director, and everything was found in a state of activity.

Mr. Salisbury has fully determined to start back East on or about the 10th of this month; it is extremely probable that the horses to be sent East will go by way of Jackson, Grand Rapids and Saginaw, as that will enable Andy McDowell to drive each of the horses a race or two prior to the Detroit meeting. We were requested as a particular favor not to tell the time that was made by the several performers, yet would very much like, as a matter of information, to let our readers know how fast we saw a few of the good ones go, still in deference to the wishes of the proprietor, that part of the information gained will not be given, suffice it to say that Direct is faster to-day than he ever was in his life, and there is every reason to believe that before the end of the present season, Margaret S. will have a record lower by several seconds than she has now.

Another of the speedy ones which will be heard from later on is Katie S., by Director, dam Alpha Medium by Happy Medium; this is a very fast mare, and it will be no trouble for her to beat "twenty." The writer thought it was a grand sight to see Stamboul when he made his record of 2:12½ make his last quarter in 32¼ seconds, and we do not think that we are betraying confidence in stating that we saw an animal worked out a full mile at a very high rate of speed, the last quarter of which was negotiated in faster time than Stamboul made his last quarter in his memorable trial. This will naturally put horsemen guessing as to which of the Salisbury contingent is the fastest, but the proprietor of the Pleasanton Stock Farm has so many good ones this year, that many surprises may be expected from that quarter.

After the Detroit meeting, Mr. Salisbury will in all likelihood ship his horses to Buffalo, and has already entries in the 2:18 and 2:20 classes for trotters, and likewise has made an entry in the pacing race there.

On Tuesday of this week Ed. Lafferty, trainer and driver for Mr. Hugh Kirkendall of Montana, left Pleasanton, where he has been wintering his horses, for Helena, where they will take part in the Montana circuit. Those he took with him were Erect, a two-year-old brother to Direct; Miss J. I. C., two years old, by Director, dam by Wilson's Blue Bull; Homestake by Gibraltar, dam Kate by Old Volunteer; Lady Maxim, 2:26½, by Maxim, dam Lady Graves by Smuggler; Maud J. by Western Lad, dam by Golddust; Dolly by Mambrino Diamond, dam by Live Oak, and also a gelding by Harvester. As most of these are in good racing condition at present, it is only fair to assume that they will earn their oats in the Montana circuit.

Dagworth's Letter.

At the present writing the meeting at Westchester is attracting considerable attention in the horse world and wonderful performances are crowding one another with a rapidity that is truly astounding. It certainly looks as if Geraldine should have captured the Toboggan Slide Handicap. McCarthy made a serious blunder in not breaking away with the leaders. I hardly think that Mr. Belmont would agree to match Fides against Geraldine under the same conditions as these horse met in the Toboggan.

I heard a pool room frequenter remark the other day that Russell is a greater two-year-old than El Rio Rey was. I replied that it was rather early in the year to express such an opinion. His answer was that El Rio Rey never met such high class two years as Russell has. It is remarkable how quickly the general public forget a brilliant performer. It was certainly a great performance for a two-year-old to run half a mile in 46¾ seconds, but it should not be forgotten that when El Rio Rey struck Westchester last season that he was called upon to pack a small sized house. If my memory is not at fault, Cayuga was considered the invincible two-year-old in the East about this time last year, but before the end of the season there were a number who showed their heels to the Iroquois colt. Therefore I think it rather premature to dub Russell a greater two-year-old than El Rio Rey. The season is quite young and a number of gilt edged two year olds have not yet faced the starter,

Esperanza ran third in the Debutante Stakes, five-eighths of a mile, which was won in the record time of 59 seconds. A race between the California fillies, Fairy and Esperanza, would be worth going a long way to see. It would be no easy matter to pick the winner.

The Eastern turfites will find out before another moon that Racine is a worthy substitute for El Rio Rey if the reports now in circulation about Mr. Winters' colt are straight. It is to be hoped, however, that El Rio Rey will be himself again when he next comes to the post.

By the way, what a pity it is that Racine is not entered in the American Derby and some of the other big three year old events. Racine could win that Derby to a certainty. The failure to enter many of the big stakes has robbed California of at least two hundred thousand dollars in the past two years. What was to prevent El Rio Rey from winning the Junior Championship and the Futurity in 1889? There will be a gnashing of teeth along the line because Racine has not entered in some of the big money events, before we are all three months older.

The Los Angeles Derby gives promise of being hotly contested. The event will be decided on the opening day of the grand circuit at Los Angeles on August 4th, and several horses are now in training for the Derby in different parts of the State. I think that it was a very judicious move on the part of the Directors of the Sixth District Agricultural Association to have twelve running races on the programme. It was also wise on their part to give more money than heretofore. The Southern California Handicap for a purse of $1,000 promises to catch a big entry. The distance is to the liking of the majority of horse owners, and many of California's crack sprinters will, no doubt, meet in this ¾ mile race. The directors are negotating with the railroad people and expect to get a liberal rate for the transportation of horses and the men connected with the stables. It is the intention of the association to offer every inducement for horseowners to visit Los Angeles in August.

The knights of the sulky should bear in mind that nominations for the 2:30 class for a purse of $1,500, must be made on or before next Monday week, June 16th. The conditions of the event are most liberal. The readers of this letter, who reside in the Sixth Congressional district, should also remember that nominations for the district trotting stakes for 1890 and 1891 also close on June 16th. It might not be out of place to remark that horses owned in Fresno, San Luis Obispo, Tulare, Kern, Santa Barbara, Ventura, Los Angeles, San Bernardino, Orange and San Diego counties, are eligible to entry. This is a big district, and a creditable list of entries should be obtained. Southern California is, and has been, the home of many well bred sires who will, no doubt, be well represented in the colt stakes. The progeny of several recent importations are not old enough to trot this year, but the owners of colts should not fail to enter them before next Monday week in the stakes of 1891.

QUARTER STRETCH GOSSIP.

L. J. Rose is domiciled at the Hoffman House, New York.

E. B. Gifford was up from San Diego last week.

What Ho was sent a half in 1:09 the other day. He pulled up lame, and his owner thinks that he will never again start in a race.

Ed Smith has commenced to jog Radical.

E Dupuy is the latest addition to the ranks of the breeders of Southern California. He has purchased a farm near Los Angeles, and will breed trotters.

Mr. Rudisil, another gentleman interested in raising trotters, has purchased Orphan Girl. He will start the mare in the slow classes at the coming meeting. The same gentleman has bred four mares to Atto Rex.

DAGWORTH.

Rysdyk's Hambletonian

The following we clip from The Horse Breeder, and feel that it will be of much interest to our readers, as it is from the pen of an eminent writer, and one who fully knows what he is writing.

In answer to an inquiry of mine, the famous New York auctioneer, Peter C. Kellogg recently sent me the following highly interesting letter. I have his permission to make it public.

Hannibal.

"On Nov. 18, 1873, when the horse was twenty-four years old, I made a very careful measurement of Hambletonian. I was assisted by Mr. Guy Miller. In measuring his height at the withers, I was astonished to find that he was only fifteen hands and one fourth inch, whereas measured at the highest point behind he was fifteen hand 2½ inches.

It must not be inferred, however, that because Hambletonian measured so low at the withers he was an under-sized horse He was very peculiarly formed. The tops of his shoulder blades were so far apart that his withers rather sank between than mounted above them. The withers were very low and thick. It must be remembered, too, that apart from his natural formation, which would make him measure 'low for his size,' two other matters had possibly contributed to reduce his normal measurement. He was very old and had covered excessively.

"Whether by reason of covering or for whatever cause, his fore legs were much wider apart at the brisket than when he was in his prime. Possibly with this widening of the fore legs his chest had settled somewhat between them, and consequently the structure above had settled with it, causing him to measure less at the withers.

"Again, some years previous he had been attacked with an inflammation which settled in his front feet causing such agony that his owner believed he would die. An expert named Dunbar, of somewhat sensational repute in those days, asked Mr. Rysdyke to let him operate on the horse's feet, assuring him that he could relieve the pain and save the horse, but it would ruin his feet for anything but moderate use.

"At the last moment Mr. Rysdyke consented. Dunbar was as good as his word, and in 15 minutes the horse was walking on the grass free of pain, but the feet were so cut away as to cause the crust to open and the sole to lose its arch, settling on the ground like a pomaced foot. I always thought that he lost something in height of foot at that time which he never recovered. Originally he had a splendid foot, but after the operation the whole sole of the foot pressed on the ground,

"Hambletonian was not an under-sized horse. Except his low withers he was fully a 15.2 horse, of great length, and his other measurements was proportioned to a horse 15.2 or over. He was in high flesh when this measurement was taken; in fact, until he shrunk from age, he always carried full stud condition without reaching the stage of obesity. In that condition he must have weighed 1,100 pounds.

"At the time of his measurement, Hambletonian was still full of animation and vim. His groom, who had been "taking a horn," shouted at him, and he flew around his box like a wild horse. He showed no signs of age except that his back was swayed, and there was a slight enlargement of the glands at the throat.

"In his walk, Hambletonian was the most elastic horse I ever saw, and there was oily litheness to every movement that deprived him of any approach to the stolid appearance which his photographs show. He was the personification of action, suppleness and power, and his excess of these qualities imparted to him a grace of movement such as I have never seen equaled in any other horse. Truly he was the king.

"PETER C. KELLOGG."

Answers to Correspondents.

Answers for this department MUST be accompanied by the name and address of the sender, not necessarily for publication, but as proof of good faith. Write the questions distinctly, and on one side of the paper only. Positively no questions will be answered by mail or telegraph.

J. C. Mangles.

Please let me know the pedigree of McCracken's Black Hawk.

Answer.—By Black Hawk 5; dam not traced, is the way the horse is in the register.

G. S. H.

I will esteem it a favor if you will be kind enough to forward me a copy of the rules governing the State Agricultural Society or informing me where I can obtain the same.

Answer.—Address Edwin F. Smith, Sacramento, for copy of rules.

Playboy.

Please give pedigree of Ohio Boy?; is he standard and registered?; give records, if any of his ancestors.

Answer.—Ohio Boy is standard and registered in A. T. R. as number 4289. He is by Flying Cloud 4095, dam Bay Maggie (dam of Ohio Maid 2:29¾) by Bellfounder; 2nd dam a Duff Green mare, pedigree not traced.

T. H. V.

Will you tell me through the columns of your paper, how many crosses it takes to produce a standard bred mare; commencing with a cold blooded mare and a standard-bred horse?

Answer.—If you mean a thoroughbred, five complete crosses; if a trotting mare, she must be by a standard horse and out of a mare by a standard horse.

A. H. Frasier.

We have not received the letter you refer to. Send another list, the cost is nothing.

H. P. T.

1. Is California Foxhunter (sire of Dirigo, 2:27) the horse that is registered as Jerry Lad (sire of Hunter, 2:25½.) 2. Has California Foxhunter any record, and has he more than one 2:30 performer to his credit. 3. Can you give breeding of California Foxhunter?

Answer.—We do not know. There is absolutely nothing known about Foxhunter. We only had one 2:30 performer.

Subscriber.

Please let me know if possible the pedigree of Arno. (2) What is the pedigree of Rattler, and what is his record. (3) What is the dam of Pocahontas and her breeding.

Answer.—Arno was by Buccaneer, dam by Volscian. (2) If you mean Werner's Rattler, 2:35. (3) The dam of Pocahontas has always been given as by Glencoe. The Coone Bros., of Elk Grove, Sacramento Co., bred her, and from them you can get the information.

I wish to claim through your valuable paper the following names:

Fleetwing, for bay filly, solid color, black points, foaled May 1st by Hawthorn, out of Linnet, she by Linwood out of Lady Budd: foaled May 1, 1890.

Munro, for stallion, bay, with two white hind feet, star in forehead, by Monroe Chief, out of Lucilla, she by Bell Alta; 2d dam by Langford; 3d dam by Belmont; foaled May 1, 1886.

Melody, sorrel colt, large star in forehead, small snip on nose, by Munro out of Zelica, she by the Grand Moor; 2d dam by Owen Dale; 3d dam by Chloroform; foaled May 8, 1890.

E. NEWLAND.

Names Claimed.

I hereby claim the following names:

BIRDCATCHER FLYAWAY; for sorrel filly, foaled Feb. 8th, 1890, by Birdcatcher, dam Skipaway by Wildidle.

FAIRLAWN, for sorrel colt, blaze in face, two white stockings on right side, foaled April 3rd 1890, by Birdcatcher, dam Taluda by Engineer.

WILDFLOWER, dark bay filly, foaled April 5th 1890, by Birdcatcher, dam Lottie C. by Wildidle.

MANHATTAN, sorrel colt, blaze in face, white stocking on left hind foot, foaled April 23rd 1890, by Birdcatcher, dam Ursula by Duke of Montrose.

SIR EDWARD, dark brown colt, two hind feet tipped with white, by Birdcatcher, dam Harriet by Flood.

E. F. FALLEN,
Fairlawn Farm, Hollister.

Pacing Records at One Mile.

Johnston, harness, against time, Chicago, Ills., Oct 8, 1884, 2:06¼.
Brown Hal, best stallion record, Cleveland, Ohio, July 31, 1889, 2:12½.
Westmont, July 10, 1884, Chicago, Ills., with running mate, 2:01¾.
Daisy, yearling, Sacramento, Dec. 31, 1885, 2:38¼.
Ed Rosewater, two years old, Council Bluffs, Iowa, Nov. 3, 1888, 2:20¼.
Yolo Maid, 3 years old, San Francisco, Oct. 13, 1888, 2:14.
Gold Leaf, four years old, 2:11¼ on August 17, 1889, at Napa.
Arrow, five years old, 2:13¼, made at Cleveland, Ohio, August 1, 1888.

THE CENTURY RUN.

53 Wheelmen Ride to Hollister.

The great century run of the California Division L. A. W. took place on Sunday last, and from every point of view was a glorious success. The start was to take place from the corner of 21st and Mission street at 5 o'clock in the morning. At the appointed hour sixty wheelmen were at the rendezvous and each and every man seemed anxious for the fray. It was twenty minutes past five when the bugle announced the start, and the men shot away at a very rapid pace. Breakfast was partaken of at Milbrae, the wheelmen reaching there at 6.45 A. M. San Jose was reached at 12, and the tired riders enjoyed a fine lunch which had been specially prepared for them. With the exception of a few wheelmen who grew tired or whose wheels broke down, the company reached their destination, Hollister, at 7 P. M., thus covering the entire distance, 100 miles, in thirteen and one-half hours, averaging 10¼ miles per hour riding time. Fifty-three wheelmen reached Hollister. The roads were not in good condition and unfavorable for record breaking. The world's record for the League Century run including time, number of starters, etc, were broken. The men from the Bay City wheelmen furnished and made a world record for their club.

The wheelmen took supper at Hollister and after resting a short time started on to view the town. A special train, which was paid for by the L A W, left there at 9 P. M, and on it the fatigued knights of the wheel returned, reaching San Francisco next morning at 1 o'clock. The run was a decided success, and will be the means of booming cycling during the present year.

VETERINARY.

Conducted by W. Henry Jones, M. R. C. V. S.

Subscribers to this paper can have advice through this column in all cases of sick or injured horses or cattle by sending an explicit description of the case. Applicants will send their name and address that they may be identified. Questions requiring answers by mail should be accompanied by two dollars, and addressed to W. Henry Jones, M. R. C. V. S., Olympic Stables, Sutter Street, San Francisco.

M. G. W:

I have a bay colt four years old, that has been lame for some time in one of his hind legs. People say that he has got a bone spavin forming. If so can you advise me what is the best thing to be done. He has been broken now, two years and has shown signs of lameness for about twelve months.

Answer.—If you take my advise, I would have your colt examined by a qualified veterinary surgeon, and abide by his decision. In the event of you not being able to do so, I will advise you to blister the hock with biniodide of mercury 2 drams, vaseline one ounce. Be careful to tie up the colt by the head for about four days, and also the tail. At the expiration of four days, dress the hock with olive oil and give a little exercise. Keep on low diet and give a small dose of carthartic medicine. Write again in two weeks, stating if there is any improvement.

Laminitis or "Founder in Horses."

[By Dr. W. Henry Jones, M. R. C. V. S.]

Many enquiries relative to this disease have recently been made through the medium of the BREEDER AND SPORTSMAN. I deem it advisable, under the circumstances, to give our readers a short article on the causes of the disease, and also the treatment. The disease may arise from a variety of causes, among them being the common cause, namely, overdriving, and then allowing the animal to stand in a draught, and in all probability giving the horse a large quantity of cold water.

Another prevalent cause is when the animal is in a heated condition, giving, or allowing to be given, a large quantity of food, such as barley, wheat, and other highly nitrogenous material.

I have frequently seen horses in England which have broken loose at night, and when found in the morning, suffering the most intense agony, and quite unable to stand. Recently a case came under my notice, where a valuable horse was driven into town, a distance of about three miles, his shoes removed, and then driven back, but unfortunately for the owner, the driver sent him along fast in the park, and the result was that laminitis supervened, and the probability is that the horse is permanently injured.

It frequently happens that an owner may have the misfortune to have a horse "foundered," and the services of a veterinery surgeon cannot be obtained, it becomes a question as what is best to be done. In all cases I would advise the removal of the shoes, and if possible, get the soles pared down; put the feet in hot water or poultices, and continue the treatment for several days. Administer a strong cathartic, say six to seven drams of aloes, combined with about one dram of ginger, the latter to avoid griping. Keep the horse on a soft, low diet, such as bran mashes and linseed. The horse must be kept perfectly quiet, and on no account should exercise be given. It has been recommended by some veterinary surgeons that heavy bar shoes be put on, and the patient exercised constantly, but this theory is not borne out by such high authorities as Dr. George Fleming, Professors Williams and Pritchard, who are entirely opposed to that course of treatment, and from my own personal experience of over fifteen years, I have found it a failure.

After the treatment I have recommended, if there is no bulging of the sole or any serous effusion round the coronary region, I would suggest that the animal be turned out to pasture for three or four months, the pasture to be soft and murshy if available.

The disease may manifest itself again in the event of a fast drive, and I would advise any owner who has the misfortune to possess a horse that has been foundered, to sell or trade the animal away to the best advantage.

One of the common results of laminitis is to see the horse traveling on his heels, and I have frequently seen cases where disintegration of the fibres of the tendons had taken place, and the poor, unfortunate beast going with the fetlock on the ground.

In all such cases the animal should be destroyed at once, but I regret to state that I saw a case of this sort, within six weeks, in this city, the animal being driven by a Chinaman.

Mares Bred to Silver Bow 11708.

P. J. Williams is the first of the stallion owners of California to send in a list of mares bred to their horses. If only as a matter of future reference all owners should do so, and we trust that breeders throughout the State will follow the example of Mr. Williams.

F. F. Moulton, bay mare by Arthurton, dam Fanny Malone by Niagara.

Ira Pierce's c m Ida May (dam of Lady Ellen 2:28) by Owen Dale.

Ira Pierce's bl m by Mambrino Wilkes, dam by Ethan Allen Jr.

W. E. Greene's g m by Winthrop 505, dam by Belmont.

C. R. Lewis' bay mare by Winthrop 505, dam by Chieftan 721.

Josiah Session's br m by Rustic, dam by Dave Hill Jr.

E. A. Haines' b m by Grand Moor, dam by Erwin Davis.

E. A. Haines' b m by Grand Moor, dam by Erwin Davis.

C. A. Sessions' b m by John M. Botts Jr. dam by John Clay.

W. O. Bowers' b m by Ensign Golddust Jr., dam by Belmont 64.

Theo. Lamourux's br m by Jack Roberts, dam by Belmont.

F. Simpson's b m by Anteeo 2:16¼.

F. Simpson's gr m by Paddy McGee.

W. H. Cade's s m by Red Boy, dam by Norfall.

Wm. Gamble's b m by Echo, dam thoroughbred.

E. Newland's b m by Alcona 730, dam by Owen Dale.

E. Newland's b m Linwood, dam by Ethan Allen Jr.

Mr. Dietz's gr m by Sidney 2:19¾, dam by Del Sur 2:24.

J. A. Carlton's b m by Wormwood, dam by John Nelson.

P. W. Ballingall, b m by Nutwood, dam by Ethan Allen Jr.

Trot and Run.

BY HORACE M. DARLING, M. D.

"I am of the opinion that the mechanical structure most desirable in the trotter is also the most desirable in the runner and *vice versa*.

"There does not appear to me to be any logical reason for supposing that a horse's heart, lungs, arteries, veins, perform their functions any differently when he trots than when he runs."

It is true that the muscles, arteries, veins, nerves, bones and vital organs are similar in all horses, and by the dissection of them and learning the structure, we can possibly say they have identical parts and wholes, yet we will find the same parts differently developed in individuals.

This fact is so well known to anatomists that in the dissecting room a skilled anatomist can, with almost an exactitude, tell the trade, art (and I was nearly saying the profession; if I had, it would be not far erroneous) that the cadaver in life pursued.

Man and woman, although to the laity apparently different in construction, are identical in parts. This seems to my non-professional readers false, still the very parts of the female that distinguish her from the male are possessed by him; and the parts of the male that distinguish him from the female are possessed by her. The only difference is their development and function. Yet by all the human processes known, male cannot be developed into female, nor the female into the male, although each can be approximated somewhat, changed in appearance and function to the other—the hairy woman, the nursing man, the hermaphrodite and other observed conformations.

The trotter and the runner and the pacer are also identical of parts, differing in individual development and function, as the subsequent needs and uses of the animal require. A runner cannot trot any more than a trotter can run (understand me, I am speaking of pure, fast gaits). To an anatomist and physiologist, the function and the development of the trotting muscle from an original running muscle is as impossible during the life of one animal, as it is impossible to develop the mammæ of the man into the breasts of the woman. It can be and has been done, but the results is not commensurate with the effort ordinarily. The natural function and development of the female mamma is consistent, continuous, beautiful, symmetrical and useful; the development of the male's is laborious, intermittent, requiring continued exercise, and once in a life time useful, interrupt the excitant and the function and the organ relapse into innocuous desuetude. The experiment, like developing the trotter from the runner, may be interesting and instructive, but few anatomists and physiologists would advocate leaving the mother's breast and developing the father's because it may be or has been done a few times when necessity compelled. Nor would they advise that such changed function and advanced development were more prolific and beneficial than the harmony of function and the symmetry of development—the utile results of procreative forces of nature. Palo Alto may trot, and the slave may have furnished milk from his own breast for his baby master; still experience, science or utility would hesitatingly imitate such isolated samples of experiment or necessity, unless other and better methods were unknown or unavailable, and if adopting them, they would not ignore the fact that *nolens volens*, the milk gland and milk tube, gave the milk, and the trotting organs made the trot, and the running machine made the run, wherever found, whether from natural or artificial causes.

The scientific law—the law of conformity to type—teaches that there is one kind of life of man, another life of beasts, another of fishes, and another of birds, each distinct, each forming its own finished being, but always in conformity to a specific type It is as Hammond says: "The potter who segments the worm, the potter who forms the horse, and the potter who molds the man." Not the same potter, but each individual potter molds his matter in exact conformity to his pre-existent type, and to no other and in no combination—the same to-day, to-morrow and forever. He molds the muscle, the artery, the nerve, in accordance with the predetermined type, and the result is conformity—trot with trot, run with run, leap with leap, cry with cry, *et al.*

The second generation by judicious breeding—pottering—may approximate the average or the unity of characteristics and parts of the parents, but it is not a combination or division; each potter molds his own, the most potent crowding out the weaker and usurping the place. The scientist does not say, "changed" but "dominant." Our dissecting rooms and the experience and observation of medical men in every day practice of their profession furnish proofs—a simple instance, the right arm, hand and fingers compared with the left; the heredity of the syphilitic, the consumptive, or the scrofulous; and yet I recall not an instance where the inherent function and action of a muscle, or nerve, or artery, ect., has been converted into something other than its natural function, or natural expression of action. We often find complexity ingrafted to simplicity, development and growth of material and function by the ingrafting of similar but more potent. The movements of walking, throwing, running, jumping, lifting, trotting, pulling, kicking, pacing, stricking, vaulting, rolling and other action are simple and easily distinguishable by an anatomist and physiologist. I think you would receive a unanimous response from them that each of these movements are intrinsically and exhaustingly differentiated from another of them; if walking, how pleasantly the child rests by a skip, hop and jump; if lifting, to rest by a pull; if running, to rest by a short gallop; if trotting, to rest by a jump or two, etc. This rest tells us naturally and forcibly that these muscles, arteries, nerves, etc, act in their own way—possess their own function and are rested by self quietude and by another set in motion. It is the mere numerously accepted idea that each motion, each part has its own special nerve fiber. While one is at work the other is at rest, when the motion is changed the fiber is changed.

Every part and parcel of the animal body rests in varying intervals, long or short, or ordinary imperceptibly. The heart, arteries and nerves, by all my lay readers, are supposed to be restless; to them a period of rest for the heart means death; its stopping ends life; yet these organs absolutely rest a long time during the twenty-four hours, and this rest is as essential to their well being and to the continuance of health, and for our own preserve, as rest to the eye, to the brain, to the stomach, to the limbs, etc., is required by our sensibilities to fatigue and by our sensations of comfort. Place your finger on the radical pulse, or lay your ear to the chest of your friend (not the lady's, of course), and you hear the heart beat, beat, beating—lub, dub and repeat; each stroke is work, each silence is rest, thus the heart works alternately and rests alternately in the same manner that the eye, the liver, the brain, the stomach and the muscles do, differing by the intervals. Arteries, nerves and every organ, and the conduits, have periods of rest likewise; work is performed by all under their respective stimulus, pabulum, vital force, blood, food, etc.

Remark: This fact is important and confronts the primery basis of development, of performance, and of endurance; each organ, nerve, muscle, etc., must be worked and rested after its own kind and not inconsistent to its structure or function; if you work or rest the heart, the great cardiac muscle, as you do the hip, the great gluteal muscle; if you work and rest the arterial system as you do the portal system; if you rest the extensor muscles as you do the flexor muscles; or the arterial system as you do the nervous system; or, to exemplify more minutely, if you work and rest the jumping muscles as you do the running muscles—were were any of these instances possible under the present structure of the horse—you would produce death or deterioration of function or substance.

The bearing of all these militates positively against the position that "there does not appear any logical reason for supposing that a horse's lungs, arteries, veins and nerves perform their functions any differently when he trots than when he runs."

Now turn to the movements of the runner and the trotter; the runner rests his muscles, his nerves, his arteries, his heart, and all his body on the jump; his rest is altogether and at once; his work is the propulsion of his body all together and at once; his rest is the time he is passing over and on, and at the moment of contact with the track; it may be short, and it matters not how short, it is the natural way of rest and recuperation during the supreme efforts, for his muscles, heart, nerves, etc.; rest them some other way and something fails—speed or endurance or life.

The trotter, on the other hand, propels his body by the action of first one side, then the other—half at rest, half at work; alternately the muscles of one side work and rest with the other side, and it is the natural inherent way. Of course the alternate action may not be entire and perfect, but the distinction from the jump is; change his rest any other way and, provided the extreme effort continues, something fails—speed or endurance or life. In both these instances the same action must continue, running or trotting; of course this is impossible, for if the rest is in another way, the action will not be identical, but something else; still it enforces the idea that the trotter cannot run by the same action, the same function, or the same instrumentalities with which he trots, and likewise the runner cannot trot with the same action, or function, or instrumentalities with which he runs.

If the foregoing reasoning from anatomy, physiology and science is correct and applicable, the horse's heart, lungs, nerves, arteries, veins perform their functions entirely different when he trots than when he runs.

'Tis true the heart beats and rests when the horse trots and when he runs; the arteries carry the blood and the veins return it; the lungs receive it, either forced by muscular action from all parts of the body as once, or half and half from one side, then the other; the nerves incite contraction and expansion of muscles; the vital force plays its part, but all is done under different impulses and with different concomitants dependent upon the objects desired—one the trotting, the other the running, and the other pacing.—Wallace's Monthly.

ATHLETICS.

Athletic Sports and Other Pastimes.

EDITED BY ARPHIPPUS.

SUMMARY.

Owing to the extended account of the Championship Meeting which we publish in the present issue we are unavoidably compelled to omit our regular weekly notes. We also print reports of the caledonian games, the Napa College spor's and the great century bicycle run to Hollister.

CALEDONIAN GAMES.

Gathering of the Clans at Shell Mound Park.

Peter McIntyre Defeats Little in the Short Race.

About six thousand persons attended the 24th grand gathering and games of the San Francisco Caledonian Club which were held at Shell Mound Park, Berkeley, on Saturday last, May 31st. The track on which the running events were decided was in fair condition and measured ten laps to the mile. The most exciting event of the day was the short race for members of the club. Two of the best runners in America were among the contestants, Peter McIntyre and J. C. Little. It was almost an assured fact that Little would win, as lately he has made some very extraordinary time in private trials. There were a good many present, however, who were willing to back "old reliable" Peter and their expectations were fully realized for he won by about two feet. The performances on the whole were up to the average. The following is a list of the games with the names of the winners and the value of the prizes: (club members only)

Race for boys (under 13 years) handicap—1st prize $3. 2nd prize $2, 3rd prize $1. Won by J Purdie, J Davidson 2nd, Willie Finn 3d,

Race for members' daughters (under 15 years) handicap—1st prize, pair of ladies boots; 2nd prize, one dozen handkerchiefs; 3rd prize, pair vases; won by Jessie Finnie; Lottie Wilson, 2nd; Hattie Wilson, 3d.

Putting heavy stone—1st prize, $10; 2nd prize, $7; 3d prize, $5; won by Charles Reid; W. Morgan, 2nd; R S Duncan, 3d.

Putting heavy stone for competitors whose record is 28 ft. and over—1st prize, $10; 2nd prize, $7; 3d prize, $5; won by Tom Carroll; A Coutts, 2nd.

Putting light stone—1st prize, $7; 2nd prize, $5; 3d prize, $3; won by Charles Reid, R S Duncan, 2nd; J S McIntosh, 3d.

Putting light stone for competitors whose record is over 36 ft—1st prize, $7; 2nd prize, $5; 3rd prize, $3; won by Tom Carroll; A Coutts, 2nd; D G McLeod, 3d.

Throwing heavy hammer—1st prize, $10; 2nd prize, $7; 3d prize, $5; won by A Coutts; Chas. Reid, 2nd; R S Duncan, 3d.

Throwing heavy hammer for competitors whose record is 77 feet and over—1st prize, $10; 2nd prize, $7; 3d prize, $5; won by Tom Carroll; D. G. McLeod, 2nd; J. F. Urquhart, 3d.

Throwing light hammer for competitors whose record is 90 feet and over—1st prize, $7; 2nd prize, $5; 3d prize, $3; won by Tom Carroll; D. J. McLeod, 2nd; J. F. Urquhart, 3d.

Race for men (twice around the track)—1ts prize, $7; 2nd prize, $5; 3d prize, $3; won by Peter McIntyre; J C Little, 2nd; W Morgan, 3d.

Throwing light hammer—1st prize, $7; 2nd prize, $5; 3d prize, 3; won by A. Coutts.

Race for men (50 years and over) once around the track. 1st prize, gold medal, donated by Philo Jacoby; 2nd prize, $7 pair of pants; 3rd prize, Maltese coat, won by D H Finnie; 2nd, R Sutherland; 3rd, J M Duncan.

Tossing the caber. 1st prize, $10; 2nd prize, $7; 3rd prize, $5. Won by Tom Carroll; E S McLeod, 2nd; J A Carmichael, 3rd.

Grand Highland Reel for men in costume. 1st prize, $7; 2nd prize, $5; 3rd prize $3. Won by John McIntosh; A W Matherson, 2nd; Edward Ross, 3rd.

Vaulting with pole. 1st prize, $7; 2nd prize, $5; 3rd prize, $3. Won by Charles Reed; Bert Abner, 2nd; W Morgan, 3rd.

Young ladies race (15 years and over). 1st prize, silk morning gown; 2nd prize, handsome parasol; 3rd prize, case of perfumery. Won by Kitty Weir; Sadie Robertson, 2nd; Etta Hunton, 3rd.

Race for members of the S F Cal. Club (five times around the track). 1st prize, Champion Gold Medal (value $200), donated by Gen. J G Wall, (to be won three times in succession by the same competitor) and $7; 2nd, $7; 3rd, $5. The medal to remain in possession of the club until finally won. Won by J T Urquhart; W Morgan, 2nd; C McCormick, 3rd.

Three-legged race (once around the track). 1st prize, $8; 2nd prize, $6; 3rd prize $4. Won by J S Urquhart and Ed. Ross; W. Finnie and D Finnie, 2nd; F. Wilson and D Paul, 3rd.

Boys race (open to all comers under 15 years) handicap. 1st prize, $3; 2nd prize, $2; 3rd prize, $1. Won by A Corbett; George Scannell, 2nd; W Picton, 3rd.

Girls race (under 15) handicap. 1st prize, pair of opera glasses; 2nd prize, fan; 3rd prize, 1 dozen hankerchiefs. Won by Tessie Finnie; Annie Crowley, 2nd; Lottie Nelson, 3rd.

Young ladies race (over 15 years) handicap. 1st prize, pair of $7 shoes; 2nd prize, silver cup; 3rd prize, satchel. Won by Lillie Garces; Saadie Dancie, 2nd; Pauline Keizer, 3rd.

Married ladies race. 1st prize, silver bread casket; 2nd prize, pair of vases; 3rd prize, box of tea. Won by Mrs. McGuerry; Mrs. Winn, 2nd; Mrs. J Baxter, 3rd.

Race for men (twice around the track). 1st prize, $7; 2nd prize, $5; 3d prize, $3. Won by Tom Kendall; S Burns, 2nd; W Archer, 3d.

Race for men (55 years and over) twice around the track. 1st prize, $7; 2nd prize $5; 3rd prize $3. Won by W A Kendrick; J McGuerry 2nd; C M Burr, 3d.

Hop, step and jump. 1st prize, $7; 2nd prize, $5; 3d prize, $3. Won by T Twaddle; W Curley, 2nd; T Burns, 3d.

1 mile race for men. 1st prize, $15; 2nd prize, $10; 3d prize, $5. Won by J C Little; Tom Kendall, 2nd; T Burns; 3d.

Running high jump. 1st prize, $7; 2nd prize, $5; 3d prize, $3. Won by C Reid; T A Twaddle, 2nd; Tom Carroll, 3d.

Hurdle race (twice around the track). First prize, $7, 2nd prize, $5; 3d prize, $3. Won by Tom Kendall; W Archer, 2nd; N Morgan, 3d.

Standing jump. 1st prize, $7; 2nd prize, $5; 3d prize, $3. Won by T Twaddle; H M Johnson, 2nd; N Curley, 3d.

Running Jump. 1st prize, $7; 2nd prize, $5; 3d prize, $3. Won by H M Johnson; J W Geoghan, 2nd; T A Twaddle, 3d.

Standing high leap. 1st prize, $7; 2nd prize, $5; 3d prize, $3. Won by F J Leary; W Morgan 2nd; Tom Carroll, 3d.

Hitch and Kick. 1st prize, $7; 2nd prize, $5; 3d prize, $3. Won by Charles Reid; W Curley, 2nd; W Morgan, 3d.

Although there were fifty events on the programme, everything went on smoothly, and not one of the contestants had cause to complain owing to the excellent management. Owing to the new rules adapted by the P C A A A, there were no amateur races on the programme.

The prizes will be distributed at the annual ball which will be held in the Mechanic's Pavilion on the evening of June 27th. The following rules govern the games:

Each game will be announced by a bugle call, and competators must enter their names with the Secretary without delay. The last name entered will open the competition. No entries will be received after the game has commenced.

Only two prizes awarded if no more than three competitors enter in any event. None but Caledonians, in good standing in their respective clubs, allowed to compete.

Competators in the handicap races will be allowed one yard for each year under or above the standard.

Handicap, 10 feet for each year for boys between the ages of 12 and 18 yrs.

JUDGES ON GAMES.—R. S. Duncan, Peter McIntyre, Alex. Copeland, Richard Burnett, John Donaldson, W. W. Reid, Peter Ellis, John Spence, Alex. Stewart, David Paul, A. Foreman Jr., Jno. Abrooks, Thos. Ross, Vernon Campbell, James McNab, Duncan McCallum, Chas. D. Reid, Albert J. McKinnon, Wm. McDougald, J. H. McInnes, John McLaren, Jas. Aitken.

COMMITTEE ON Games.—W. C. Burnett, D. A. Macdonald, Angus McLeod, Thomas Wilson, D. G. Chisholm, John M. Duncan, G. W. Elder, Neil Carmichael, John Reid, James A. McKay, Col. Chas. L. Taylor, David Paul, Archie Lauriston, John F. Kennedy, Thomas McGregor, Neil Beaton, M. P. Forbes, Geo. Purdie, Donald McKay, George Davidson, William Urquhart, James Miller, William Mitchell, Alex. N. McDonald, D. R McNeill, Colin M. Boyd, R. S. Falconer, Dr. D. Maclean, Norman Beaton, John A. Ross, James Mearns, Richard Gratto, J. J. McKinnon, David H. Finnie, Dan. A. McDonald, David McKay.

Napa College Students at Play.

The second annual field-day of Napa College was held May 27th at the Napa fair grounds, and was very successful. The following is a summary:

100-yard maiden run—L Springmeyer, 1st; L C Tuck 2d. Time, 11½ secs.

60-yard dash—G B Kutzenstein, 1st; L Springmeyer, 2d. Time, 6¾ secs.

100-yard hurdle race—M S Wilson, 1st; L B Scranton, 2d. Time, 17½ secs.

Standing wide jump—J C Hatch, 1st; H Tillman, 2d; W H Turner, 3; distance, 9ft 1in.

Running hop, step and jump—L N Peck, 1st; R D Hunt, 2d; distance, 39ft 5in.

100-yard run (handicap)—M S Wilson (scratch) 1st; W E Greene (scratch) 2d; B H Andrews (5 yds) 3d; time, 11secs.

Baseball throw—J L Reith, 1st; R D Hunt, 2d; O A Tredway, 3d; distance, 311 ft.

100-yard run—O W Tredway, 1st; L Springmeyer, 2d; time, 10 1-5 secs.

1-mile run—J A Morris; 1st; H S Davis, 2d. Time, 5 min. 45 secs.

Standing hop, step and jump—J L Keith, 1st; distance, 26 feet.

220-yard run—O W Tredway, 1st. Time, 23 secs.

Running long jump—O W Tredway, 1st; distance, 18 feet 10½ inches.

440-yard run—M S Wilson, 1st; H F Coyle, 2d. Time, 57½ seconds.

Putting 16 lb shot—M S Wilson, 1st; distance, 33 feet.

Running high jump—O W Tredway, 1st; height, 4ft 11in.

100-yard (three-legged race)—M S Wilson and W E Green, 1st; O W Tredway and G B Kutzenstein, 2d. Time, 12 secs.

Pole vault—R D Hunt, 1st; height, 7ft 7in.

Tug-of-war College vs. Commercials—Won by Commercials.

Alpine Amateur Athletic Club.

A general meeting of the above club was held on Thursday evening last, when the following officers were elected to serve for the ensuing term of six months:

President, Harry O Farrell; 1st vice-president, John T Sullivan; 2d vice-president, F M Howard; treasurer, John D Garrison; recording secretary, Charles Vultee; financial secretary, A M King; cor. secretary, E P Moody; executive committee, E Steinway, R J Luttringer, T J Cunningham; sergeant at arms, J R Collins; field captain, A Cooke; delegates to the P C A A A, E Steinway, T J Cunningham and E P Moody.

VICTORIOUS OLYMPIANS.

They Easily Win the Much-Coveted Pennant.

GRAND OPENING OF THE NEW OLYMPIC GROUNDS.

A Large Audience and Fine Sport—John Purcell and James Jarvis Lowers Some of the Coast Records.

The new out-door grounds of the Olympic Club were formally thrown open to the public on Friday, May 30th (Decoration Day) and an unusually large crowd of people were present on the occasion. The grounds were opened with the annual championship games of the Pacific Coast Amateur Athletic Association, which this year were held under the auspices of the Olympic Athletic Club. The games were announced to take place at 1 P. M. sharp, and long before that hour the park and Cliff House train brought hundreds of people to the scene of the great contest for supremacy. Owing to some misunderstanding, however, the sports did not begin until nearly two o'clock. At half past one o'clock the flag, which hung at half mast over the grand stand, was hoisted, and the gentleman who hoisted it announced that the new out-door grounds of the Olympic Athletic Club were now formally opened.

A loud cheer went up from the audience when the flag was hoisted and immediately afterwards the officials began to take their positions and the contestants were ordered to get ready. It was 1 45 when the first race was started. It is unnecessary to describe the new grounds as full description of the track, dressing rooms, etc. have appeared in these columns already. The reporters stand is situated in one of the most unsheltered parts of the ground directly opposite the grand stand. It occupies a position where the men of the press cannot fail to catch the full force of the ocean breeze, which on the opening day was rather too strong to be appreciated. The day reminded one of the "raw and gusty day" when Caesar and Cassius plunged into the troubled Tiber. The wind was alarmingly strong and rendered fast time impossible. Had the weather been favorable many coast records might have been broken. The reporters were obliged to strap themselves down to the benches in order to avoid being blown out to sea. Their reporting sheets were cast on the wind and carried away out of sight and many of them were tempted to give up in despair. It seemed as if Boreas had some special wrong to avenge, so furious was he in his efforts to move the entire grounds farther cityward. The loose cinders on the track were blown in all directions and men had to be placed at each set of hurdles to stop them from being blown away. The management of the games were perfect and the audience had no complaints to make, except towards the close of the programme when things began to lag. The programme was rather too long, owing to the introduction of some special non-championship events for members of the Olympic Club only. These races might have been left out on the occasion of a championship meeting.

Thanks to Captain George W. Jordan, the Olympic boys showed up in grand form and each man as he stepped within the enclosure had a look of confidence stamped on his face. The Berkeley students looked determined rather than confident while the few representatives from the Alpine Club walked around with an air of indifference. Little and Gafney of the latter club did not compete and their absence probably lost some points to their club. When the games began at the lowest calculation there were 3,000 people on the grounds, the grand stand being fairly packed. It was perhaps one of the most unenthusiastic audiences that ever assembled at an athletic meeting. It was fashionable, but cold; in fact painfully so, and except when the College boys sent up their war hoop of "Ha! ha! Cal if-or-nia. U C. U C. Ziz, boom; bah!" and the Olympians used their fish horns announcing victory on either side not a sound could be heard save the howling of the wind through the fences. Each time Schefferstein made his appearance a buz of admiration went through the audience and when S. V. Cassady on his way back to the dressing room passed in front of the grand stand the ladies bowed and smiled and waved their tiny handkerchiefs at that promising young sprinter. A Field captain is everything to a club and some of the other clubs should follow the examples of the Olympic Club in selecting an active and energetic man for that position. Captain Jordan deserves praise for the great interest which he took in every member of his team. The official announcer, J. F. Larkin also deserves a word of praise for the brave manner in which he stuck to his post by the black board in the face of a cyclone. The Marshal's were not called upon to perform any extra duty for the reason that the enclosure is an angle so that outsiders cannot enter without permission. Several handsome flags floated over the Grand Stand and all around the grounds, and a handsome flower bed with the letters O. A. C. in the middle appeared on the slope opposite the Grand Stand.

THE FIRST EVENT.

The first event was the one hundred yards run. There were four heats. V E Schifferstein, O A C, won the first heat easily by 6 yards in 10 3-5 seconds. F G O'Kane, O A C, was second and J C Ainsworth, U C 3d by 2 yards. The second heat was won by S V Cassidy, O A C, by 1½ yards in 10 4-5 seconds. R Gallagher, U C was second, De Winter, U C, third. This was a close and exciting race and the winner proved himself to be a strong finisher. Heat No. 3 was won by J D Harris, G C A C by 6yds in 10 4-5secs; E Mays, U C, 2nd, F W McNear, U C, 3rd. The fourth heat was very tame. J O'Kane and J Kortick, both of the O A C, simply cantered over the course. They arranged to run a dead heat which they did. No time given.

JARVIS BREAKS THE RECORD.

The next event was the one mile walk. There were five starters. Jarvis, the ex-English champion, at once cut out the pace and astonished the audience with his wonderful stride. He is a small man in comparison with Coffin and Cook but nevertheless he can take a long stride. Jarvis walked as unconcerned as if he was walking alone, and never once turned his head to look at the men who were struggling behind him. He walked a good steady gait and proved that he is one of the fastest as well as squarest heel and toe artists in America to-day. He made the mile in 7:08 breaking the coast record of 7:10½ held by C. B Hill. Had the wind been less severe Jarvis might have done five seconds better. Coffin walked good but rather loose. He finished second in 7:21. Cook, of the Alpine Club, took third place and promises to do better in the future. He has a fine square gait but needs experience. He walked under 8 minutes. Landmann, O A C, gave up and the U C man Foulkes got fourth place. Foulkes, who is a novice, should improve with practice as he has a fine style. The following is the time which Jarvis made: 1 lap, 1:01; 2 laps, 2:10; half mile, 3:19; 4 laps, 4:34; 5 laps, 5:52; 1 mile, 7min 8secs,

MORE SPRINTING.

100 yard run, second trials—1st heat, Schifferstein, O A C, 1st by 4yds; Gallagher, U C, 2nd; Cassidy, O A C, 3rd. Time, 10 2-5 secs. Second heat, Mays, U C, 1st; Harris, G C A C, 2nd; F O'Kane, O A C, 3rd Time, 10 3-5secs.

120 yard hurdle—John Purcell, O A C, 1st by 2ft; H C Moffitt, U C, 2nd; W Wright, U C, 3d. Time, 18 3-5secs. This was an exciting race and Moffit's friends were sadly disappointed at his defeat. Had he been in good condition he would most unquestionably have won.

SCHIFFERSTEIN WINS.

The final heat of the one hundred yard run was next decided. The champion Victor E Schifferstein, of the O A C, had no trouble in winning, his time being 10 2-5secs; Mays, U C 2nd; Gallagher, U C, third.

A half mile run for Olympic novices was next called. H M Collins led all the way and won handily by 15yds in 2min 17¾secs: E M Francis, 2nd; W H Toomey, 3d.

John Purcell, O A C, put the 16 lb shot 37ft and won that event; L E Hunt, U C, was 2nd with 36 ft; A G Roberts put the ball 32ft 9in and got third place.

A FAST QUARTER.

Only five men toed the scratch for the quarter mile run although there were twelve entered.

Winslow, of the O A C, the favorite, was unable to start, owing to illness, and it was thought that the race would lay between Garrison of the Alpine and Henderson of the O A C. A surprise was in store, however, for the spectators, and the Olympic fraternity were astonished when Steve Cassady went to the front and won a grand race by several feet in the fast time of 52 4-5 seconds. Garrison was pocketed early in the race, and so lost all chance of winning. F W McNear, U C, was second, and A S Henderson, O A C, third. Cassady ran in great style, and promises to turn out an American champion. He is a very strong runner.

JARVIS AGAIN TO THE FRONT.

Only four out of six entries appeared at the starting post when the three-mile walk was called. The men all looked fresh after their previous race. At the crack of the gun Jarvis again took the lead, and before the first half mile was finished, his opponents were hopelessly in the rear. In this race he walked even better than he did in the one mile race, and his style was so easy that a person could look at him walk all day and not tire of the task. Jarvis would certainly make the pace hot for Lange or Nicholl, and the O A C should send him in company with Schifferstein to Washington, D. C., to compete in the American championship meeting, he would bring credit upon his club. Coffin and Cook walked side by side, and at any stage of the race the two men were never more than a yard apart. Coffin was a little too confident, and narrowly escaped defeat at the hands of the Alpine man, whom he beat for second place by only six inches. Cook should beat Coffin next year at this distance. Coffin's time was 25 min. 31½ secs. Foulkes, of the U. C., should have retired on the first mile, as he was sadly in the rear. He finished the entire distance and amused the spectators with an exhibition of fair, but very slow walking. Jarvis made the three-miles as follows: ½ mile, 3m 33s; 1 mile, 7 min. 26 secs; 1½ miles, 11:26; 2 miles, 15:28 3-5; 2½ miles, 19:33, and 3 miles in 23 min. 31 1-5 secs.

PURCELL BREAKS THE POLE VAULT RECORD.

Purcell, O A C, vaulted 9ft 4½in with the pole, and broke the previous Pacific Coast record of 9ft 3½in, held by J. Sexsmith. A. Kelter, O A C, vaulted 9 feet, and took second prize. L. Titus, U C, was third, with 8 feet 9 inches.

220-yard run—1st heat: Schifferstein, O A C, 1st. Time, 23 1-5 secs. Mays, U C, 2d; S V Cassady, O A C, 3d. The second heat was not run, as the men agreed to consolidate the two heats.

SUTTON WINS THE HALF.

Scott, of the O A C, the present record holder of the half-mile run, was unable to fight for his club when that race was announced. He lost his mother-in-law the day previous, and was compelled to remain a silent spectator. His record was not beaten, however, and he breathes freely once more. Sutton, of the U C, won the race in 2min 7 2 5 secs. Henderson, O A C, 2d; E Coke Hill, U C, 3d. Moody, of the Alpine Club, cut out the pace, but at the end of the second lap was content with a back place.

A RECORD FOR THE ALPINE CLUB

S J McKinnon, of the Alpine Club, threw the 16-lb hammer 95ft 4in., and broke his own (coast) record of 94ft 5in. Morrow, U C, was second, with a throw of 90ft 5in. A G Roberts, U C, made a record of 87ft 8in and obtained third place.

100-yard novice run for members of the O A C. There were supposed to be two heats, but as some of the entries failed to show up, one heat decided the event. C A Jellineak and J. Korteck ran a dead heat, with P. M Wand 3d. Time, 11 1-5 seconds. In the run off Korteck won easily by 6 yards in 11 1-5 secs.

220-yard hurdle race—1st heat, H C Moffit, U C, 1st; J M Whelan, O A C, 2d. E, Mays, U C, 3d. Time, 30 4-5 secs. This was an excellent race between the first and second man, the U C representative winning by only one foot.

A LILIPUT RACE.

The most amusing race of the whole day was the juvenile run of one lap. Some of the contestants were not more than two feet high, and did not appear to weigh over twenty pounds. After the pistol was fired, one could imagine that a troop of frightened Liliputs were running away from Gulliver. The winners of first and second place were the smallest kids of the lot, and considering their sizes and ages, ran remarkably well. The scratch man, or rather child, made the lap in 46 seconds.

HILL BEATS COOLEY.

The one mile run was an exciting contest. Hill, of the University, and Cooley, of the O A C, had a hard battle, and the former won in 4min 51 2-5 secs. Casady, of the A A A C, earned a good third. The other men were nowhere.

MOFFIT HOLDS HIS OWN.

Young Moffit won the final heat of the 220-Yard hurdle, with Casady, O A C, a close second. Time, 29 1-5 seconds Whelan, O A C, slipped shortly after the start, and so lost all chance of winning first or second place. He was a good third.

540-yard run, special for O A C members. J Korteck, 1st. Time, 54 2-5 secs. He had an allowance of 12 yards. F G O'Kane, 10 yds, 2d; P M Wand, 15 yds, 3d.

A LONG RUN.

Ten men essayed to run five miles but at the end of 1½ miles only half of that number were left. Espinosa of the O. A. C cut out the pace in the race and up to the end of the second mile was leading by about 30 yards with Cooley, Cassidy and Vollmer running in the order named. At 3½ miles Cooley was leading Epinosa by two yards with Hill of the U C 3d, and Cassidy A A A C 4th. Vollmer was over a lap behind. Hill gave up before finishing his third mile. At 4½ miles Cassidy led Cooley by a couple of yards. Espinosa was one lap behind. On the last lap Cooley put on a great spurt and seemed to run away from Cassidy whom he beat home by 40 yards in 29 min. 34 1-5 secs. Cassidy ran a game race and deserves credit for his grit and perseverance. Espinosa was 1½ laps behind at the finish. He got 3d place.

Running high jump. This contest resulted in a dead heat between Schefferstin, O A C and Whitney, V C, each man clearing 5ft. 5in, They agreed to toss for first place and the Olympic man came out ahead. Moffit of the U C did not jump up to his old form and could do only 5ft. 4in. thus taking only 3d place.

The tug of war proved highly exciting, the U C team winning in three straight pulls. They were again challenged by the Captain of the O A C team and another struggle is sure to take place.

The running broad jump wound up the days sport. Schifferstein cannot be beaten at this game and he won with a jump of 22ft. 3in. McNear U C was second with 20ft. 7½in. and Moffit 3d, with 19ft, 10½ in. Purcell was tired and did not make any effort to win.

The championship flag was won by the Olympic Athletic Club with a score of 78 points. The University Athletic Club made 55 points and the Alpine Amateur Athletic Club 11. The Garden City Athletic Club failed to score a single point.

SCORE OF POINTS FOR CHAMPIONSHIP.

1st place, 5 points; 2d place, 3 points; 3d place 1 point. 9 points, total of each event.

16 Championship Events, total points, 144.

Events.	O. A. C.	U. C.	A. A. A. C
100 yards run	5	4	
1 mile walk	8		1
120 yards hurdle	6	3	
Putting 16lb shot	5	4	
440 yards run	6	3	
3 mile walk	8		1
Pole Nault	8	1	
220 yards run	6	3	
Half mile run	3	6	
Throwing 6lb hammer		4	5
220 yards hurdle	4	5	
1 mile run	3	5	1
5 mile run	6		3
Running high jump	5	4	
Tug of war		9	
Running broad jump	5	4	
Totals	78	55	11

Winner championship Olympic Athletic Club.

The following is a summary of the events:

100 yard run—V E Schifferstein, O A C, 1st: E Mays, U C, second: R Gallagher, U C, 3d. Time, 10 2-5secs.

American record, 10 secs; English record, 10 seconds: Pacific Coast record, 10secs.

One mile walk—James Jarvis, O A C, 1st: Horace Coffin, O A C, 2nd; A Cooke, A A A C, 3d. Time, 7 minutes, 8 seconds.

American record, 6min 29 3-5secs; English record, 6 min 32 1-5secs; Pacific Coast record, 7 min 10½secs,

120 yard hurdle (10 flights, 3ft 6in each)—John Purcell, O A C, 1st; H C Moffit, U C, 2nd; W Wright, U C, 3d. Time, 18 3-5 sec.

American record, 16 1-5 secs; English records, 16secs; Pacific Coast, 17 1-5secs.

Half mile run (Novice) Olympic club members—H M Collins, 1st; E M Francis, 2nd; W H Toomy, 3d. Time, 2min. 17½secs.

Putting 16 lb shot—John Purcell, O A C, 1st, 37ft; L E Hunt, U C, 2nd, 36ft; A G Roberts, U C, 3d, 31 feet, 9in.

American record, 45ft, 2in; English record, 44ft 10½in, Pacific Coast, 38ft 7in.

440-yard run—S V Cassidy, O A C, 1st; F W McNear, U C, 2nd, A S Henderson, O A C, 3rd. Time, 52 4-5sec.

American record, 47½secs, English record, 48 3-5 secs, Pacific Coast record 50 3-5secs.

Three-mile walk—James Jarvis, O A C, 1st; Horace Coffin, O A C, 2nd; A Cooke, A A A C, 3d. Time, 23 minutes, 31 1-5secs.

American record, 21min 9 1-5secs; English record, 21min 25 1-5secs; Pacific Coast record 25min 51½sec.

Pole Vault—John Purcell O A C, 1st; A Kelter, O A C, 2d; L. Titus, U C, 3d; height, 9ft 7in.

American record 11ft 5in; English record 11ft 5in; English record 11ft 7 in; Pacific Coast record 9ft 3½in.

220-yard run—V E Schifferstein, O A C, 1st; E. Mays, U C, 2nd; S V Cassidy, O A C, 3d. Time 23 1-5secs.

American record 22secs; English record 21 4-5sec; Pacific Coast record 22½secs.

880-yard run—J G Sutton, U C, 1st; A S Henderson, O A C, 2nd; E Coke Hill, U C, 3d. Time, 2min, 7 2-5secs.

American record, 1min, 53½secs; English record, 1min 54 2-5secs; Pacific Coast record 2 min 5½secs.

Throwing 16 lb hammer—J J McKinnon, A A A C, 1st; W Morrow, U C, 2nd; A G Roberts, U C, 3rd. Distance, 95 ft 4in.

American record 133ft 8in; English record 126ft 4in; Pacific Coast record 94ft 5in.

100-yard run (novice) for Olpmpic club members—J Kortick, 1st; C A Jellinck, 2nd; P M Wand, 3d. Time, 11 1-5 secs.

220 yard hurdle: H C Moffitt, U C, 1st; S V Casady, O A C, 3rd. Time 29 1-5 seconds.

American record 26 2-5 sec. Pacific Coast 29 4-5 sec.

Juvenile race. 1 lap, handicap members of O A C. W Hogg in 1st; M Carr, 2nd; L. Brown, 3rd. Time 43 2-5.

1 mile run. E Coke Hill, U C 1st; F L Cooley, O A C 2nd; H C Casidy, A A A C 3rd. Time 4 minutes 51 2-5 seconds.

American record 4 min. 21 2-5 sec.

English record 4 min 2-2 sec.

Pacific Coast record 4 min. 43 1-5 sec.

440 yard run, handicap, for members of the O. A. C. J. Korteck, 1st, F. G, O'Kane, 2nd, P. M. Wand, 3d. Time 54 2-5 secs.

5 mile run. F L Cooley, O A C, 1st; H C Cassidy, A A A C 2nd; M L Espinosa, O A C 2d. Time 29min. 34 1-5 secs.

American record 25 min. 23 secs. English 25 secs. 7 4-5 secs. Pacific Coast record 32 min. 6 secs.

Running high jump. V E Schifferstein O A C, 1st; R V Whitney, U C, 2nd; H C Moffitt, U C 3d. Height 5ft. 3 in. American record 6ft. 4in. English record 6ft. 3½in. Pacific Coast 5ft. 8½ in.

Pacific Swimming Club.

The members of the Pacific Swimming Club opened their season at the Terrace Baths, Alameda, on Sunday last. Several members of the club including the Dall Bros., Spiller, Vollmer and Greenebaum, gave fine exhibitions of long and short distance swimming, plain and fancy diving, etc. A large crowd of people witnessed the exhibition.

Bay Rose.

REGISTERED No. 9814.

Record 2:20 1-2 Third Heat.

Will make the season of 1890, ending July 1st, at the SANTA ROSA STOCK FARM, (formerly Santa Rosa Race Track), SANTA ROSA.

DESCRIPTION.

BAY ROSE is a dark bay or brown, with black points, 16¼ hands high, and weighs 1150 pounds. He is remarkably intelligent, of good disposition, and a pure-gaited trotter. He was foaled in 1881. His colts are large, stylish, rangy animals, and inherit the qualities of speed and endurance.

PEDIGREE.

BAY ROSE 9814
- Sultan, 2:24. Sire of 19 in the 2:30 list.
  - The Moor 870, sire of Beautiful Bells ... 2:29½; Del Sur ... 2:24½; Inez ... 2:30; Sir Guy ... 2:28½; Sultan ... 2:24; Tommy Gates ... 2:24
  - Sultana.
- Madam Baldwin
  - The Moor 870. Sire of 6 in the 2:30 list.
  - by Ben Lippincott, by Williamson's Belmont.

TERMS: $200 FOR THE SEASON.

Good pasturage $3 per month. First-class care taken of mares in any manner that owners may desire, but no responsibility assumed for escapes or accidents. Limited to a few approved mares. For further particulars, address

THOS. BONNER,
Santa Rosa Stock Farm, Santa Rosa.

Or apply to
IRA PIERCE,
728 Montgomery Street, S. F., Cal.

The Trotting Stallion

G & M

FULL BROTHER TO

ALFRED G, 2:19¾.

(Who has been taken to Kentucky to stand at $200)

Will make the season of 1890 from FEBRUARY 1st to JULY 1st, at

SANTA ROSA.

G. & M. is by Anteeo, 2:16¼; was foaled 1886; first dam Rosa B. by Speculation (son of Hambletonian 10); 2d dam Elizabeth by Alexander 497; 3d dam Nora by imp. Glencoe. Anteeo is by Electioneer, out of Columbine by A. W. Richmond 1687.

G. & M. is a handsome dark bay; stands 15-2 1-2 hands high, and weighs 1060 pounds. Gameness, stoutness, speed and stamina are indelibly impressed in every line of the pedigree of G. & M. Owners of broodmares in search of these qualities, will do well to patronize this promising colt.

PHILOSOPHER,

Foaled 1886 by Pilot Wilkes 2987; first dam Bella by George Wilkes 519; second dam by Bell Morgan 61.

Philosopher's sire, Pilot Wilkes 2987, is by George Wilkes 519, dam Grace (the dam of Alice Woodburn etc.), by Pilot Jr. 12, grandam by Orphan Boy.

Will make the season of 1890, from FEBRUARY 1st to JULY 1st, at Santa Rosa.

TERMS for the season:

G. & M., $50,

PHILOSOPHER, $30,

with privilege of returning mares that do not prove in foal the next season free of charge, provided the horse bred to remains the property of the present owners. Good pasturage at $3 per month. No responsibility assumed for accidents or escapes. Service fees payable before removal of the mare. For further particulars, address

GEO. E. GUERNE,
Santa Rosa Cal.

GROVER CLAY

Bay Stallion, Black Points,

15 3-4 hands high.

Bred by W. W. Traylor, San Francisco.

BY ELECTIONEER.

First dam Maggie Norfolk by Norfolk, son of Lexington, he by Boston. Second dam Tilda Quill by Billy Cheatham he by Cracker, and he by Boston. Third dam by Dorsey's Golddust.

TERMS.

Will make the season of 1890 at the Training Stables of Denis Gannon, near Oakland Trotting Park, at $50 the season, payable at time of service. Season to commence February 1st and ending July 1st. Proper care of mares will be taken, but no responsibility incurred for accidents or escapes. Address,

DENIS GANNON, Oakland, Cal.

GOLDEN EAGLE HOTEL

Corner SEVENTH and K STREETS, SACRAMENTO.

FIRST CLASS IN EVERY RESPECT.

The LARGEST and FINEST HOTEL in the City.

W. O. BOWERS, Proprietor.

Free 'Buss to and from the Hotel.

Telephone, Telegraph Office and Messenger Service at Hotel

The Thoroughbred Stallion

Three Cheers

Will make the season of 1890 at

Sacramento.

PEDIGREE.

THREE CHEERS
- Imp. Hurrah
  - Newminster: Touchstone, by Camel; Beeswing, by Dr. Syntax
  - Jovial: Bay Middleton, by Sultan; Sister to Grey Momus, by Comus
- Young Fashion
  - Imp. Monarch: Imp. Priam, by Emilius; Imp. Delphine, by Whisker
  - Fashion: Imp. Trustee, by Catton; Bonnets o' Blue, by Sir Charles

Hurrah was imported by John Reber, of Lancaster, Ohio, a locality where there were but few breeders of thoroughbreds. Under these disadvantages he sired a long list of winners. His sire Newminster, won the St. Ledger 1851, and his dam, Jovial by Bay Middleton, winner of the Derby 1836. Newminster by Touchstone, winner St. Ledger 1834. Dam Beeswing, winner of 64 races out of 64 starts, by Dr. Syntax, winner of the Doncaster Cup, 1837—40—41—42, the only horse that ever accomplished that feat.

On the side of the dam Three Cheers is equally well related. Young Fashion was the dam of Surprise, Scotland (the only horse that ever beat Asteroid a heat), Liverpool, Columbia, and Bonnie Kate, the dam of Little Buttercup, and the flying Bonnie Lizzie. His grandam, Fashion was the greatest race mare of her day and beat Boston in that historical match at four mile heats, which is recorded as one of the greatest events in the annals of the turf.

Horsemen who are qualified to judge, pronounce Three Cheers to be the finest type of the Newminster line in America.

LOCATION.

THREE CHEERS will be located at the Arcade Training Stable, Rancho del Paso. This place has been selected for the reason that first class pasturage has been secured there for the exclusive use of these mares, and the other facilities to be obtained there for the care of mares (especially mares in foal) are better than can be found elsewhere in the locality.

TERMS.

$60 for the season with the usual return privileges. Pasturage $5 per month. Mares cared for as owners may desire at bottom rates for grain and hay. All bills payable before the mare is removed.

Mares shipped care of WM. IRVINE, Pacific Stables, Sacramento, will be properly cared for and sent to the ranch without delay.

Three Cheers will be in charge of one of the most experienced and competent stud grooms in the State, who will exercise every care, but no reponsibility assumed for accidents or escapes.

For further particulars apply to Louis Crissler, at the ranch; Wm. Irvine, Pacific Stables, Second St., Sacramento; or to the owner,

E. S. CULVER,
313 Bush St., San Francisco.

C. C. LINIMENT.

For Catarrh, C. C. LINIMENT has no Peer. Try it.

C.C.LINIMENT.

Prescribed by San Francisco's Leading Physicians. Indorsed by the Medical Faculty.

The Great Pain Conqueror for Man and Beast.

For Horsemen and Stockmen this Liniment is Inval).)

OWNERS OF FINE STOCK CANNOT AFFORD TO BE WITHOUT IT.

A remedy for every home, giving instant relief in pain and PERFORMING PERMANENT CURES.

To get the full benefit of the C. C. Liniment in chronic cases, in connection with C. C. Liniment use Compound Sulphur Powder, the "Great Blood Purifier," put up ONLY by The W. H. Bone Co., 12 Bush St., San Francisco. For Habitual Constipation, Indigestion, Piles, etc., it is the greatest remedy known to medical science.

If your druggist does not keep it, we will send direct, post paid, on receipt of price. COMPOUND SULPHUR POWDER is $1 per bottle, 6 for $5. Small bottles, 25c.

The C. C. Liniment Co

12 BUSH STREET, S. F.

W. H. BONE, - - General Manager.

FOR SALE BY ALL DRUGGISTS.

SUBSCRIBE FOR THE

Breeder and Sportsman.

$1,000.

The Pacific Coast

Trotting-Horse

Breeders' Ass'n.

Fall Meeting 1890.

Offer an Additional

Nomination Pacing Purse

$1,000 for 2:20 class. Mile heats, best three in five. Entrance $100, payable $20 June 10, 1890, $20 July 1, 1890, $20 August 1, 1890, and $40 on the tenth day preceding the first advertised day of the meeting. Horses to be named at time of last payment.

Entries to close with the Secretary June 10, 1890.

Conditions.

First payment MUST ACCOMPANY NOMINATIONS, or they will not be considered.

Neglect to make payments on the day stipulated will incur forfeiture of all previous payments.

No horses and colts owned on the Pacific Coast by others than members of the P. C. T. H. B. A. are eligible to the above purse, but horses and colts OWNED outside of the Pacific Coast are eligible thereto regardless of membership.

All States and Territories lying in whole or in part west of the Rocky Mountains are held to be part of the Pacific Coast.

The Directors reserve the right to change the hour and day of any race except when it becomes necessary to ante-date a race, in which instance the nominator will receive three days notice of change by mail to address of entry.

Entries not declared out by 6 P. M. of the day preceding the race, shall be required to start.

This Purse will be divided into four moneys, viz., 50 per cent. to the winner, 25 per cent to the second horse, 15 per cent. to the third horse, and 10 per cent. to the fourth horse.

A horse distancing the field shall only be entitled to first and third moneys.

The Board of Directors reserve the right to declare any purse or stake filled or not filled without binding itself to any specified number of entries.

In all nomination purses, eight entries will be required to fill, and four to make the last payment.

Trotting and racing colors shall be named by 6 o'clock on the day preceding the race, and MUST be worn upon the track.

Horses eligible on records standing at time of entry.

Otherwise than the above National Trotting Association Rules will govern.

Persons desirous of making entries in the above purse, and who have not as yet joined the P. C. T. H. B. A., should make application for membership to the Secretary, and remit the sum of $25 to cover membership fee before June 10, 1890.

J. H. WHITE, President,
JAS. P. KERR, Secretary, 313 Bush Street, S. F.

Langtry Farms' Stud

Imp. FRIAR TUCK

By the Immortal HERMIT.

DAM ROMPING GIRL BY WILD DAYRELL,

AT $50 THE SEASON.

Mares not proving with foal may be returned the following season. Good care taken of mares, but no liabilities for accidents or escapes.

Good Pasturage at $5 per month.

Mares shipped to ST. HELENA, care CHARLES WILLIAM ABY, St. Helena Stables, will be cared for. For further particulars address,

CHAS. WILLIAM ABY,
Middletown, Lake County, Cal.

GEO. WASHINGTON.

11,623.

RECORD 2:30.

Bay colt, bred by Thomas Smith of Vallejo, Cal. Foaled 1886 by Mambrino Chief, Jr., 11,622, record 2:24 1-4, 1st dam Fanny Rose by Vick's Ethan Allen Jr. 2,903, sire of Prince Allen 2:27, 2nd dam Jenny Lind, thoroughbred, dam of Prince Allen 2:27. Will serve a limited number of mares at $50 for the season. Mares not proving with foal may be returned next season free.

Mambrino Chief, Jr.

11,622.

RECORD 2:24 1 2.

Sire of George Washington, record 2:30 at three years old. Bay horse bred by Rufus Ingalls of Belvedere, Ill. By McDonald Chief 3583. First dam Venus by Mambrino Patchen 58. 2nd dam by Wardlow's Shakespeare. 3rd dam Lone Gold 4th dam by Silver Heels. Has not been in the stud before. He was 6 years old when he served a few mares, and his colts all show good style and form.

Terms for the season $40. For further particulars see or address

THOMAS SMITH,
Vallejo, Cal.

Races, Races,

JULY WEEK

AT

South Park Race Track

Eureka, Cal.

GIVEN BY THE

EUREKA JOCKEY CLUB.

FIRST DAY, JULY 2, 1890.

No. 1. Novelty Running Race. Free for all. Dash of one mile. Purse $200. First quarter, $40. Half, $50. Third quarter, $70. Mile, $90.

No. 2. Running race. Purse $150. Five-eighths dash, for two-year-olds. $125 to first horse; $25 to second horse.

No. 3. Running. Purse $150. Three-quarters and repeat. $125 to first; $25 to second.

SECOND DAY, JULY 3, 1890.

No. 4. Trotting. Purse $200. Three minute Class. $160 to first; $40 to second. (Covey barred.)

No. 5. Running stake. Five-eighths of a mile. For Humboldt raised two year-olds. $30 entrance, half forfeit. $150 added. First to receive 60 per cent.; second, 30 per cent., third, 10 per cent.

No. 6. Running Stake. Purse $200. Mile Dash. $150 to first horse; $50 to second horse.

THIRD DAY, JULY 4, 1890.

No. 7. Trotting Stake, 2:40 Class. Purse $250. $200 to first horse; $50 to second horse.

No. 8. Running stake, 1¼ miles. Free-for-all. $40 entrance, ½ forfeit, $200 added; second horse $75, third horse to save stake.

No. 9. Running Stake. Purse $150; 1-2 mile and repeat; $125 to first; $25 to second.

FOURTH DAY, JULY 5, 1890.

No. 10. Running Stake, 1-2 mile and repeat; for Humboldt horses owned prior to Jan. 1, 1890. $125 to first, $25 to second.

No. 11. Running Stake. Purse $200; 7-8 mile and repeat. $150 to first, $50 to second.

CONDITIONS AND REMARKS.

All trotting races are best three in five, unless otherwise specified. Four to enter and three to start, but the Board reserves the right to hold a less number than four to fill by the withdrawal of a proportionate amount of the purse. Entrance fee, 10 per cent. of purse, to accompany nominations. In all trotting races the rules of the American Trotting Association, and all running races the rules of the Pacific Coast Blood Horse Association to govern, but the Board reserves the right to trot heats of any two classes alternately, if necessary, to finish any day's racing. In all entries not declared out by 6 P. M. of the day preceding the race, shall be required to start.

No added money paid for a walk over. In all races, four or more paid up entries required to fill, and three or more horses to start. Racing colors to be named in entries. In trotting races drivers will be required to wear cape of distinct colors to be named in entries. Entries in all races to close with the Secretary, Thursday, June 20, 1890. Entry blanks will be furnished upon application to the Secretary.

All trotting races for horses owned and in Humboldt County prior to June 1, 1890.

H. M. DEVOY, President.
J. P. MONROE, Secretary.

SONOMA and MARIN

Futurity Stake,

To take place during the

FALL MEETING

OF THE

Sonoma and Marin Agricultural Society,

1893.

For Foals of 1890.

Open to the get of stallions owned in the district which is comprised of the following counties: Sonoma, Marin, Napa, Lake, Mendocino, Solano, Yolo, Colusa and Contra Costa.

Mile heats, 3 in 5; entrance $75, with $25 added for each starter over two and up to five head, and $10 for each additional starter up to ten head.

Payments: $5 must accompany the nomination on July 1, 1890; $5 on January 2, 1891; $5 on July 1, 1891; $10 on January 2, 1892; $10 on July 1, 1892; $15 on January 2, 1893; $25 on July 1, 1893.

CONDITIONS.

1—Neglect to provide payments on the dates stipulated will incur forfeiture of all previous payments.

2—When there is more than one entry to this stake by one person or in one interest, the horse to be started must be named by 6 P. M. of the day preceding the race.

3. The stake will be divided into four moneys, viz., 50 per cent. to the first, 25 per cent to the second, 15 per cent. to the third and 10 per cent. to the fourth horse.

4. If only three horses start in this stake, only the first, second and third money shall be paid; if but two start, there will be no added money, the stake money paid in will be divided—two-thirds to the first and one third to the second horse.

5. A horse distancing the field shall only be entitled to first and third moneys.

6. The Board of Directors reserve the right to declare the stake filled or not filled without binding itself to any specified number of entries.

7. Otherwise than the above, National or American Trotting Association Rules—as this Society may select—will govern the stake.

Entries to close on July 1st with the Secretary.

J. H. WHITE, President,
DR. THOMAS MACLAY, Secretary, Petaluma.

Memo.

The Best Son of SIDNEY

Will Make the Season of 1890 at the OAKLAND RACE TRACK

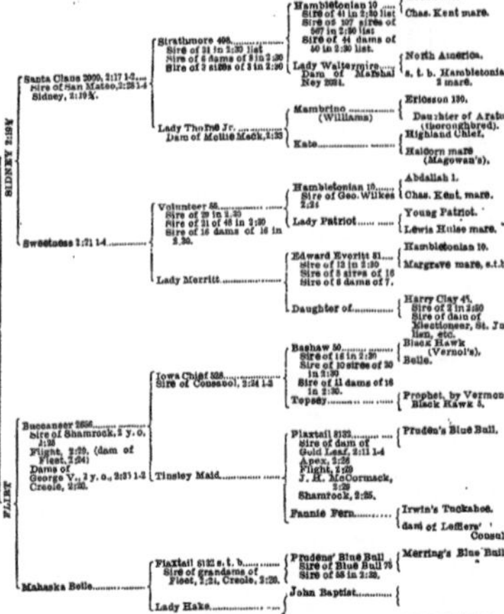

MEMO is, as can be seen at a glance, one of the best bred young stallions in service, having three crosses of Rysdyk's Hambletonian and one of Harry Clay, the sire of Green Mountain Maid (dam of Electioneer, etc.), while Long Island Black Hawk and Flaxtail also contribute to his blood. Sidney (Memo's sire) is universally known as the best young sire in the world, a producer of extreme speed at an early age.

PERFORMANCES.

MEMO trotted in public in his two-year-old form, obtaining a record of 2:49, though he was close to Grandee in a race on the Bay District Track, the second heat of which was made in 2:31 1-2, the first in 2:34. He exhibited phenomenal speed when three years old, and had it not been for a slight strain of his fore fetlock, there is little question that he would have shown in public very close to the best record. On the Oakland track he was timed a mile in 2:29 1-2, and frequently trotted quarters in from 32 1-2 to 34 seconds.

As a four-year-old Memo only started once—at Sacramento—when, although out of condition, he showed great speed, and improving as he went on, great hopes were entertained of his going well down in the 'teens at the P. C. T. H. S. A. meeting, but after showing several very fast miles his leg filled and he was laid up for the season. He is sixteen hands high, and of powerful build throughout. His color is a glossy black, with both fore-feet white. His disposition is all that could be desired, and his action superb. He is a sure foal getter, only one mare being reported not in foal during his last season.

TERMS, $100, with usual return privileges, for a limited number of mares. Season to close JUNE 15th, when he will be prepared for track purposes. Pasturage $5 per month. Have leased the cricket ground adjoining the track for pasturage, where there is fine feed. Reasonable charges if fed hay and grain. Best of care taken of mares in any manner owners may desire, but positively no responsibility assumed for accidents or escapes. For further particulars address

J. P. KERR, 313 Bush Street, San Francisco,

or, JOHN ROWEN, Race Track, Oakland, Cal.

2:10 1-2 ELECTIONEER 2:12 1-4

BAY STALLION	BROWN STALLION
ECLECTIC	**MORTIMER**
11,321	5,346
By Electioneer, dam Manette (full sister to Woodnut 2.16 1-2 Manon 2:21 and Maple, dam of Hattie D., three-year-old record 2:28½) by Nutwood 2:18¾, etc., etc.	Four-year-old Record 2:27 By ELECTIONEER, dam MARTI, by Whipple's Hambletonian (sire of 15 in 2:30, and of dams of eight in 2:30). Second dam Ida Martin by Rifleman (sire of Col. Lewis 2:18¾).
Terms $100 for the Season.	Terms $60 for the Season.

Horses shipped via San Francisco may be consigned to J. W. MORSHEAD, City Front Stables, who will attend to their forwarding.

Season closes JULY 1st, 18 Usual return privileges.

For further particulars address owner,

WILFRED PAGE, Penns Grove,
Sonoma County, Cal

The Trotting Stallion

Silver Bow

Will make the season of 1890 at the Oakland Race Track.

PEDIGREE.

SILVER BOW 11708, two-year-old record 2:37, is by Robert McGregor 647, 2:17¼ (sire of Bonnie McGregor, 2:13½, Earl McGregor, 2:21¼, Mac D., 2:30, McGregor Boy, 2:20¼, Mark Time, 2:30, Roxie McGregor, 2:20¾) by Major Edsall 2:1, 2:29, by Alexander's Abdallah 15—sire of Goldsmith Maid, 2:14—by Hambletonian 10—sire of Dexter, 2:17¼.

Robert McGregor's dam was Nancy Whitman by American Star 14, by Stockholm's American Star.

SILVER BOW'S first dam is Sadie by Hambletonian 10, sire of Geo. Wilkes, 2:22—sire of Guy Wilkes, 2:15¼—also Electioneer, sire of Sunol, three-year-old record, 2:10½, and Palo Alto, 2:12¾; second dam Lady Wynne by Wm. Welch 941; third dam Elenora Margrave by imp. Margrave.

DESCRIPTION.

SILVER BOW is a handsome bay, no white; 15-2½ hands high; weighs 1075 pounds; of fine form, with the best of legs and a clean-cut, intelligent head. Is remarkably level-headed, seldom making a break; wears seven-ounce shoes in front. His record, 2:37, is no mark of his speed; he can beat 30 easy, and with his gilt-edge breeding, he is just what he ought to be, a trotter sired by a trotter whose dam was herself a trotter and his grandam the dam of two trotters. His dam Sadie being by Hambletonian 10, shows him to be bred from the cream of the trotting blood.

TERMS: $100 for the season. Mares not proving in foal returnable for the season of 1891 free of charge. Good pasturage and first-class care taken of mares for $5 per month. No responsibilities assumed for escapes or accidents. For further particulars, address

Limited to 15 approved mares.
Season to end June 1st, 1890.

P. J. WILLIAMS,
Care Race Track, Oakland, Cal.

Pleasanton Stock Farm Co.'s Stallions.

DIRECTOR, 2:17.

Director's book is open for 15 good mares more than already booked for the season of 1890, at $300 each.

This is the cheapest service fee ever charged for a stallion, taking into consideration his BREEDING and RACE RECORD and the RACE RECORDS OF HIS COLTS.

Season to commence February 15th and close August 1st.

CORRECTOR, Five Years Old.

Sire Director 2:17, dam Brainey, she by Echo. Echo sired by Rysdyk's Hambletonian, out of Fanny Felter, by Magnolia, he by Seely's American Star. Brainey's dam Lady Dudley, she by Tom Dudley by Blacknose, a son of Medoc, he by American Eclipse. Lady Dudley's dam by Bertrand, Jr., a son of Bertrand.

CORRECTOR is a rich seal brown 15½ hands high, and is the fastest young stallion in the world under the same conditions, never having been off the farm where raised and never been shod or driven for speed before last Christmas, and can trot quarters now in 35 seconds, a 2:20 gait.

He will be allowed to serve ten good mares, at $100 each for the season, which closes June 1st.

DECORATOR, Four Years Old.

Sire Director 2:17, dam Chess, sired by Cardinal 2.37, trial 2:28, he by Gen. Gifford's Morgan, dam of Cardinal, sired by Joe Gales of Ohio, he by Marlborough out of the Duchess of Marlborough by Southern Eclipse; second dam old Duchess of Marlborough by Sir Archy; third dam by imp Diomed. Decorator's second dam a Morgan and Messenger mare.

Decorator is a light bay 16 hands high, and with but little handling for speed has shown eighths in 17½ seconds, a 2:20 gait.

He will be allowed to serve ten good mares at $50 each for the season, which closes June 1st.

Mares not proving with foal may be returned next season free of charge of service fees to the same stallion, if he is still in our possession; however, the company reserves the right to return the fee instead of giving service.

Pasturage $4 per month; hay and grain extra. Accidents and escapes at owner's risk.

Service fees due at time of service, and must be paid, together with pasturage, etc., before mares are taken away, or a good approved note given, payable August 1st, 1890, at which date all bills must be settled.

For further information call or address M. SALISBURY, 320 Sansome Street, Room 26, San Francisco, or

PLEASANTON STOCK FARM CO.,
Pleasanton, Alameda Co., Cal.

SOUTHER FARM

P. O. Box 208. San Leandro, Cal.

1½ miles northwest of San Leandro; 8 miles southeast of Oakland. Turn off County road between above places at "Stanley Road," ½ mile north of San Leandro.

Horses boarded at all times in any manner desired. Best of care but no responsibility for accidents. Colts broken and handled for the road or track. Terms reasonable.

Glen Fortune,	Jester D,	El Benton,	Figaro,
By Electioneer.	By Almont.	By Electioneer.	Hambletonian 725
$50 for 1889.	$50 for 1890.	Limited to 5 mares.	Limited to 12 mares
		Book Full.	Book Full.

THE SOUTHER FARM

Has Green Feed the Year Round,

and feeds Hay in connection with the green feed, which a horse must have if he is to thrive. Every animal is given

A Dry, Warm Place to Sleep,

No matter how stormy the weather. All Stock under cover when it rains.

VISITORS WELCOME ANY DAY EXCEPT SUNDAY.

How to Get Stock to the Souther Farm.

The Souther Farm is one and a half miles northeast of San Leandro and eight miles southeast of Oakland. The stables are about one mile east of the county road, which runs between Oakland and San Leandro. The place to turn off is at Stanley Road, where a large signboard of the farm is placed. Guide boards will be found at every cross road. In any ordinary weather the roads are very good, and they are fairly good after the unusually heavy rainfall of the past winter.

All stock sent from San Francisco may be brought over by Garcia's Express, No. 3 Market street, San Francisco. They also have an order box outside of Hawley Bros.' Hardware house on the corner of Market and Beale streets. The express leaves San Francisco on the Creek route boat, which starts at 1:3·, but all orders should be in the order box at Market and Beale streets by 10 o'clock, or at the office, No. 3 Market street, by 11 o'clock at the latest. In the case of very young or very valuable horses, the Souther Farm will send reliable men to lead or drive over any stock that will not lead behind a wagon. A small charge will be made in such cases, to cover the extra expense incurred.

Horses are very easily taken from Oakland to the farm, and where it is inconvenient for owners to bring them or send them, the farm will send after anything that is to come. On horses that stay three months or over there is no charge for getting or delivering. Where a horse stays a short time the actual time and expense only is charged to him.

Horses can be shipped by rail from almost all parts of the State to San Leandro. Always notify the Farm several days before shipping anything, and then men will be on hand to receive stock on arrival. The railroad station is but two miles from the Souther Farm, and the agent invariably gives immediate notice of the arrival of any stock consigned to the above farm, but when word is sent to the farm in good season by letter or telegram, the animals sent are saved waiting a couple of hours in the car.

Passenger trains leave San Francisco (from the broad gauge ferry) and First and Broadway, Oakland, at frequent intervals during the day. There are several trains from San José to San Leandro on both the broad and narrow gauge railroads; the broad gauge, by way of Niles, is much more convenient for getting to the farm. There are trains each day from Sacramento, Stockton and Livermore to San Leandro. In ordinary weather it is a short and pleasant drive from Oakland to the Souther Farm or from San Francisco to the Farm by way of the Creek route ferry boat. Always notify the Souther Farm just when you will arrive at San Leandro, and some one will meet you at the station. If you do not recognize the farm conveyance ask the stage driver, who will point it out.

Write to the above address for references, circulars and price lists. Terms reasonable.

GILBERT TOMPKINS, Proprietor.

SAN MATEO STOCK FARM

HOME OF GUY WILKES,

Record, 2:15 1-4.

Guy Wilkes' Book is full for 1890 and 1891, and positively no more mares will be received.

Sable Wilkes, three-year-old record 2:18, will be allowed to serve 25 mares in addition to those already engaged at $250 the season of 1890. SABLE Wilkes, 15½ hands, black horse, by Guy Wilkes, first dam Sable by The Moor; second dam Gretchen by Mambrino Pilot; third dam Kitty Kirkman by Canada Chief; fourth dam by Fanning's Tobe; fifth dam by imp. Leviathan.

Leo Wilkes, brown horse, four years, 16 hands, full brother to Sable Wilkes, will be allowed to serve 30 mares at $100 the season

Mares not proving with foal may be returned the following season free of service fee. Parties engaging the services of any of the above horses must send a deposit of 10 per cent. of service money with engagement. Pasturage $6 per month, and when the condition of the animal requires it, hay or grain, or both, are fed, the charge will be $12 50 per month. Good care will be taken of all mares sent to the Farm, but no liability will be assumed for accidents or escapes.

All bills are due at time of service, but must be paid by August 1st of each year. No stock will be allowed to leave the place until all bills are paid.

WILLIAM CORBITT.
San Mateo Stock Farm.

Vineland Stock Farm
Alcona 730.

Sire of

FLORA BELLE - - - - Record 2:24
CLAY DUKE - - - - - " 2:31½

ALCONA will be a great sire, but four of his colts have ever been trained, and all have shown full miles better than 2:30, and two of them as good as 2:20. Two of his first sons each sired a colt as a two-year-old, and last season one as a four-year-old trotted a full mile in 2:22¾, and the other, a three-year-old, a mile in 2:31. With opportunities, Alcona is destined to be one of Almont's best sons. Almont, for his opportunities, is beyond doubt the most prepotent sire of his age. He has 38 representatives in the 2:30 list; 49 sons and 22 daughters that have already produced 2:30 performers. Almont died five years ago at 20 years old. If he lived he would be but 25 years old.

PEDIGREE.

ALCONA sired by the great Almont (sire of Westmont 2:13¾, Fanny Witherspoon 2:16¼, Piedmont 2:17¼, and 35 others with records better than 2:30, and grandsire of Belle Hamlin 2:12¾, etc.); by Alexander's Abdallah (sire of Goldsmith Maid 2:14), he by Rysdyk's Hambletonian. Alcona's dam, Queen Mary, by Mambrino Chief (sire of Lady Thorne 2:18 1-4, and 5 others in the 2:30 list, and sire of the dams of Director 2:17, Piedmont 2:17¼, Onward 2:25 1-4, Red Wilkes, Almont, Belmont and many other noted sires).

DESCRIPTION.

Alcona is a beautiful chestnut 16 3 1-2 hands high, and weighs 1300 lbs. His colts possess speed, style, finish and beauty, and if they don't trot they command the highest prices for carriage horses.

$40 for the season. Usual return privilege.

Season of Alcona and Grandissimo ends July 1st, 1890.

Grandissimo,

Full Brother to GRANDEE, 3-year old record 2:23 1-2.

Sired by La Grande (son of Almont, and out of Jessie Pepper by Mambrino Chief; Jessie Pepper is the dam of Iona 2:17 1-2, Alpha 2:23 1-2, Sterling Wilkes 2:31¾, and others) dam Norma, by Arthurton (sire of Arab 2:15, Joe Arthurton 2 2: 1.2, etc.)

Grandam Nourmahal, (full) sister to A. W. Richmond, sire of Arrow 2:13¾, Romero 2:19, and sire of Columbine, dam of Anteeo 2:16¾, and Antevolo 2:19¾ at four years old).

DESCRIPTION.

Grandissimo is four years old, will make a sixteen hand horse; he is a rich mahogany bay in color and perfect in style and action. $50 for the season. Usual return privileges.

"Grandissimo" with limited training last fall as a three-year-old, trotted quarters in 36 seconds and miles in 2:40.

I feel confident that he will trot fast this season, and will be a great sire as his colts this season are all grand youngsters.

The best of pasturage $4 per month. Mares taken care of in any manner that owners may desire, but no responsibility assumed for escapes or accidents.

For further particulars send for circular or call at stables, one mile south of St. Helena.

FRED W. LOEBER Prop'r.

The Trotting Stallion
VICTOR,
Record 2:22.

Will make the season of 1890 at NAPA CITY.

DESCRIPTION.

VICTOR is a handsome dark bay; 15-3 hands high; weighs about 1,100 pounds, and is remarkably intelligent, level-headed, of kind disposition, and a magnificent animal in every respect. He is well boned and muscled, of splendid conformation, and possesses the qualities of speed and endurance to an eminent degree—qualities that he imparts to his progeny.

PEDIGREE.

VICTOR, record 2:22
- Echo 462
  - Hambletonian 10 — Sire of 42 in the 2:30 list.
    - Abdallah 1
    - Chas. Kent mare
  - Fanny Felter
    - Magnolia 68
    - by Webber's Kentucky Whip
- Daughter of
  - Woodburn
    - Lexington
    - Lulu Horton
  - daughter of
    - Ashland
    - thoroughbred

ECHO is the sire of Belle Echo 2:20, Senator, 2:21¾, Victor, 2:22, Gibraltar, 2:22¾, Echora, 2:23¾, Tippie, 2:25¾, Lohengrin, 2:27¾, Pasha, 2:27¾, Elmonte, 2:29, Col. Hawkins, 2:29¾, Annie Laurie, 2:30, Economy, 2:30, Sam Lewis, pacer, 2:25.

TERMS—$60 FOR THE SEASON.

Mares not proving with foal may be returned next season free of charge provided the horse remains the property of the present proprietor, and stands at the same place, otherwise money will be refunded. The best of care taken of mares in any manner that owners may desire, but no responsibility assumed for accidents or escapes. For further particulars, apply to or address

G. W. HUGHES, Agent,
G. A. DOHERTY, Proprietor. Napa City.

The Trotting-Bred Stallion
RINGWOOD

THE FINEST SON OF THE NOTED SIDNEY,

Will make a Season at Oakland, commencing March 1, and ending June 1, 1890.

DESCRIPTION.

RINGWOOD is a dark, rich colored bay, black points, 15 1-2 hands, weight 1100 lbs., and a pure gaited trotter. Has shown great speed. He is now five years old. As a four year old he showed a trial in 2:19 1-2, and but for an accident would have received a record as a four year old of 2:18 or better.

PEDIGREE.

RINGWOOD is by Sidney, record 2:19 1-4, and 's half brother to Gold Leaf 2:11 1-4, Adonis 2:11, Fleet (two year old) 2:24, Longworth 2:19, Sister V. 2:21, Fanstino, yearling, 2:35. Fleet, yearling, 2:33. Memo, three year old trial 2:20 1-2.

Sidney is by Santa Claus, record 2:17 1-2; he by Strathmore, sire of 31 in 2:30 list; he by Hambletonian 10, the greatest of all producers; he by Abdallah. Sidney's dam, Sweetness, record 2:21 1-4; she by Volunteer, the sire of St. Julien 2:11 1-4.

RINGWOOD'S dam Alma; she by Dashway, thoroughbred; he by Belmont, he by American Boy; he by Sea Gull; he by imported Expedition. Alma's 1st dam, Fanny Cobb, was a great road mare, pedigree untraced.

TERMS: $50 for the Season.

Payable June 1st, or sooner if mares are taken away. Address Communications to

A. C. DIETZ,
Oakland, Cal.

2:10¾ 2:13¾ 2:10

DEXTER PRINCE.

This Royally-bred Stallion will make the Season of 1890 at the LIVE OAKS Breeding Farm, 2 miles from Lodi, San Joaquin County, Cal.

DESCRIPTION.

DEXTER PRINCE is a blood bay, 16 hands high, weighs over 1 100 pounds; has great power and substance, and the highest finish. When two years old, at Palo Alto, he was timed quarters by Gov. Stanford in 31¾ seconds, and he was driven eights by Mr. Marvin at a faster rate of speed than that. He is a sure foal-getter, and invariably sires foals of good size, of fine form and finish, and the highest rate of speed.

PEDIGREE.

By KENTUCKY PRINCE, the sire of Guy, 2:10¾, Spofford, 2:18¾, Company, 2:19¾, Bayonne Prince, 2:21 1-4, Fred Folger, 2:20¾, and a score more in the 2:30 list.

First dam LADY DEXTER, full sister of the greatest of trotters, Dexter, and the greatest of sires, Dictator, the sire of Director, 2:17, Phallas, 2:13¾, in a fourth heat, and Jay-Eye-See, 2:10.

Second dam Clara, the dam of Dexter, 2:17 1-4, Dicta or, Astoria 2:28 1-4, and Almah, 2:29¾. Clara was by American Star, that has 34 daughters that have produced 2:30 or better trotters.

Third dam the McKinstry mare, the dam of Shark, 2:27¾. HAMBLETONIAN, the grandsire of DEXTER PRINCE, has 40 trotters in the 2:30 list, 44 daughters that have produced 2:30 trotters, and more than 100 sons that have sired 2 30 trotters.

CLARK CHIEF, the grandsire on the sire's side, was the sire of performing and producing sons and daughters.

DEXTER PRINCE has faster blood lines, on both sides, than any other stallion in the world—Guy 2:10¾, and Jay-Eye-See, 2:10.

KENTUCKY PRINCE is one of the best bred and speediest stallions in the world. David Bonner, in the presence of Governor Stanford, timed him when he trotted a 2:10 gait. He is by Clark Chief, one of the great broodmare sires; his first dam is Kentucky Queen by Morgan Eagle, son of Hale's Green Mountain Morgan, 2nd dam by Blythe's Whip, 3rd dam by Martin's Brummier, 4th dam by Quicksilver 880, on through the strongest thoroughbred blood.

TERMS.

$100 for the season, with usual return privileges. Payable before mares are removed. Good pasture, and the best care furnished, but no responsibility assumed for accidents.

PREMIUM.

$250 will be given to the first of the produce of DEXTER PRINCE put in the 2:30 list, and $100 each after the first. Address

L M. MORSE, Lodi, Cal.

The Produce of Eros Averaged $2,200 Each at New York Auction Sale in 1889.

THE ELECTIONEER TROTTING STALLION,

5326 EROS 5326

Will make the season of 1890—February 1st to July 1st—at LA SIESTA RANCH, MENLO PARK, adjoining Palo Alto.

PEDIGREE.

EROS (5326)
Standard by his sire
" " dam
" " record
" " produce
" under all rules

EROS (5326)
- Electioneer — Grandsire of Norlaine, 1 yr., 2:31 1-2, Sire of Sunol, 2 yrs., 2:18, Sunol, 3 yrs., 2:10 1-2, Hinda Rose, 4 yrs., 2:16, Palo Alto, 2:12¾.
  - Hambletonian 10 — Sire of Dictator, George Wilkes, Happy Medium, and 40 others in 2:30 list, and grandsire of 726 in list.
    - Abdallah 10 — Sire of the dams of Goldsmith Maid, 2:14, and 7 other producing dams.
    - Charles Kent mare — By imp. Bellfounder.
  - Green Mountain Maid — Dam of Prospero, 2:20, Elaine, 2:20, Dame Trot, 2:22, Elista, 2:22¾, Storm, 2:26¾, Antonio, 2:28¾, Miranda, 2:31, Mansfield, 2:26.
    - Harry Clay — Sire of the dams of St. Julian, 2:11¾, Bodine, 2:19¾, and 17 more in 2:30 list
    - Shanghai Mary.
- Sontag Mohawk — Dam of Eros, 2:29 1-2, Sport, 2:22¾, Sallie Benton, 2:17¾, Conductor, trial, 2:26, Colma, 3-y-o trial, 2:24.
  - Mohawk Chief — Sire of the dams of Lot Slocum, 2:17¾, Sallie Benton, 4 yrs., 2:17¾, Pedlar, 2 yrs., 2:27¾, Stanford, 4 yrs., 2:30, Eros, 6th heat, 2:29 1-2.
    - Hambletonian 10 — Sire of the dams of Stamboul, 2:12¾, Wilton, 2:19¾, and 20 other trotters.
    - Lady Perrine.
  - Sontag Nellie
    - Toronto Sontag — By Toronto Chief.
    - Nellie Gray — 5-mile record, 13:45.

Produce of Eros
Wanda, 4 yrs., 2 21.
Sollita, 2 yrs., 2 41 1-2.
Meriquita, 2 yrs., 2:42.
Daylight, 2 yrs., 2:44.
Hiram B., trial, 2:38.

These are the only colts by him that have ever had a harness on except one in New York that went a trial last July in 2:36 1-2.

DESCRIPTION.

EROS is a rich seal brown stallion, bred by Hon. Leland Stanford at Palo Alto, and is the nearest living likeness of his celebrated sire, Electioneer. Stands 15.2 hands high, and weighs 1050 pounds

In breeding to Eros, the owners of mares will strictly follow the great rule of breeding, viz., breed to a stallion by a producer and out of a sure producer of great speed. Eros is by the stallion that has produced more 2:30 trotters that any living horse, and is also the sire of more 2:30 performers than any horse living or dead.

EROS is out of the dam of Sally Benton, four years old, record 2:17¾, Sport 2:22¾, and Eros 2:29½ in the sixth heat, against a field of nine horses. He is from a family that is endowed with great natural speed, trot fast at an early age, train on, throw trotters from all classes of mares, are of good substance, bone, style and action, and breed solid colors.

TERMS.

$100 for the season, with the privilege of return next season should mares not be in foal and horse and mare still remain in the same hands.

Good pasturage can be obtained at $5 per month, but no responsibility for accidents or escapes. There are a large number of box stalls, and animals can be kept up and fed on hay and grain at reasonable rates if required. Mares already in foal can be sent to the ranch for foaling, and will receive all the attention bestowed upon our own mares. Mares left with Mr. Peter Pomyea, Broadway Street Stable, Oakland, or with Mr. F. H. Burke, 401 Montgomery Street, San Francisco, will be forwarded to the ranch free of charge. For further particulars apply to

W. H. VIOGET,
LA SIESTA RANCH, MENLO PARK, CAL.

EROS is the only stallion offered to the public on this Coast that has a dam that has three in the 2:30 list.

GRAND MOOR, 2374.

Grand Moor 2374
- Moor 870
  - Sire of Beautiful Bells ... 2:29¾
  - Sire of Sable (dam of Sable Wilkes) ... 2:18
  - Sire of Sultan ... 2:24
  - Sire of Tommy Gates ... 2:24
  - Sire of Del Sur ... 2:24¾
  - Sire of Sir Guy ... 2:28¾
  - Beautiful Bells is the dam of Hinda Rose, 2:19½ as a 3-year-old, Palo Alto Belle, 2:22¾, Chimes, St. Bell, 2:24½, Bell Boy (3 years) 2:19¾.
  - Sultan, 2:24 (sire of Stamboul 2:12½) has 19 in 2:30 list.
    - Clay Pilot 93 — Sire of 2 in 2:30 list.
    - Belle of Wabash.
- Vashti — Dam of Don Tomas, who got a record of 2:30 in 1889.
  - Mambrino Patchen 58 — Sire of 14 in 2:30 list. Sire of the dam of Guy Wilkes, 2:15¼; also sire of 20 stallions and 18 mares with get in 2:30 list.
  - Kate Taber — By Mambrino Messenger, he by Mambrino Paymaster.

Foaled 1876. Black. Sixteen hands high. Bred by L. J. Rose

A horse of highest form and quality; of great excellence in every point; a type of his celebrated family; of marked individuality, spirit and endurance; never properly trained or raced, but shows the possession of great speed; perfectly manageable in the stable and on the road and track.

As he is sired by The Moor 870, a son of CLAY PILOT, out of Vashti by MAMBRINO PATCHEN, he is a most valuable cross for mares of other families. THE MOOR sired Beautiful Bells and the dams of Sable Wilkes and Margaret 2:28 (dam of Regal Wilkes, 2-year-old record 2:20½).

MAMBRINO PATCHEN is regarded as the unsurpassed sire of broodmares, having, among many others, sired the dam of Guy Wilkes and of Wm. L. (the sire of Axtell), and a son of his sired the dam of Axtell. The public sales this year have demonstrated with renewed emphasis the value of The Moor and Mambrino Patchen strains of blood. For combining particularly with the Hambletonians it may be called "the ready money cross."

GRAND MOOR will make the season of 1890 for a time at the Oakland Race Track and afterwards at my Ranch, fifteen miles from Oakland. Mares can be delivered at the race track to the groom in charge. Pasture at $5 per month. For other food, if requested, an additional charge will be made.

TERMS, $150 for the season, with privileges of return if the horse does not change hands.

Every care exercised, but no liability for escapes or accidents.

H. I. THORNTON, 504 Kearny Street.

Cook STOCK FARM,

Season of 1890.

STEINWAY 1808.

Three-Year-Old Record 2:25 3-4.

Sire of STRATHWAY, three year old record 2:26, and sire of the dam of BOURBON RUSSELL 2:30.

By STRATHMORE 408; sire of 31 in the 2:30 list; sire of 6 dams of 8 in the 2:30 list, and sire of 3 sires of 3 in 2:30 list.

1st dam ABBESS (dam of Solo 2:28, and Soprano, dam of C. F Clay 2:18, Eminence 2:27 and Strathbridge, 3 year old record 2:28½) by ALBION, sire of VANITY FAIR 2:24½, and of the dam of FAVORITE 2:25½.

2nd dam by MARSHALL NEY.

3rd dam by BERTRAND, a son of SIR ARCHY.

TERMS—$100 for the season.

CHARLES DERBY 4907

Brown Horse, Foaled 1885.

By STEINWAY 1808,

1st dam by the great ELECTIONEER, sire of SUNOL 3 year old record 2:10½, Palo Alto 2:12¼, etc., etc.

2nd dam FANNY MALONE, by NIAGARA.

3rd dam FANNY WICKHAM, by HERALD.

4th dam by Imp. TRUSTEE.

TERMS—$100 for the season.

Pasturage $5 per month. Accidents and escapes at owner's risk. Mares consigned to the farm should be sent to Fashion Stables, Oakland; Geary & Grindle's Stable, Haywards; or to Bennett's Stable, Martinez; from and to which places they will be delivered free of charge. Address

COOK STOCK FARM,
Danville, Contra Costa, Co., Cal.

Sunny Side Breeding Farm.
Admiral 488.

Foaled 1867—Sired by Volunteer 55, Son of Rysdyk's Hambletonian 10.

First dam Lady Pierson by Cassius M. Clay (Neaves') 20; second dam by Diamond; third dam a running mare said to be thoroughbred. He is fitted in an eminent degree to produce colts that will in all respects justify his patrons in their expectations.

Admiral is the sire of Huntress, record 2:27¼, Sister, 2:19½, Perhelion, 2:25, Nona Y., 2:26, and others equally as promising, but have not had the advantage of track work. He will serve a limited number of approved mares at $50 the season, with usual return privilege. Season ending August 1, 1890. No liability for accidents or escapes.

KING DAVID 2576.

Bay Stallion—Foaled 1883.

Sired by Admiral 488, dam black Flora (the dam of Huntress, 2:27¼, Sister, 2:19½, Perhelion, 2:25, Nona Y., 2:26), by Black Prince.

King David is one of the best gets of Admiral. He has a good disposition, kind to drive, smooth and even-gaited, and can speed fast. Barring accidents, he will trot in the twenties this Fall. His colts are large, rangy, and well finished. Will serve a limited number of mares at $30 the season, to end July 1, 1890. Every precaution will be taken to prevent accidents and escapes, but no liability will be assumed. Pasturage $4 per month.

Sunny Side Farm is situated two miles east of Vallejo, on the Sulphur Spring road. For further particulars, address

FRANK DRAKE,
Vallejo, Cal.

The Fast Trotting Stallion
REDWOOD.

Four-Year-Old Record 2:24 1-2

Will make the season of 1890—February 1st to July 1st—at

SANTA ROSA.

REDWOOD is a dark bay colt, 15.2¾ hands high, weighs 1150 lbs. Foaled in 1885 by Anteeo, 2:16¼, sire of Alfred G., 2 19¾. Anteeo is by Electioneer. First dam Lou Milton, by Milton Medium; second dam Old Sly, a thoroughbred mare brought from the East in 1871 by W. C. Ralston, Esq.

Redwood's sire was out of Columbine by A. W. Richmond, the sire of the pacers Arrow 2:13¾, and Elwood 2:22, and the trotters Romero, 2:19¾, and Len Rose, 2:27. Redwood has shown a quarter in 33 seconds.

Terms $100

For the season. Mares not proving with foal may be returned next season free of charge, provided Redwood remains the property of the present owners. Good pasturage at reasonable rates. No responsibility assumed for escapes or accidents. Service fees payable before removal of the mare. Limited to 40 approved mares. For further particulars address

A. McFADYEN.
Santa Rosa, Cal.

For Sale.
JUANITO ALMONT

Sire of Almont Patchen, 2:15.

JUANITO ALMONT is a bright bay, 16-1 hands in height, and weighs 1,200 pounds.

PEDIGREE.

By Tilton Almont, 2 26, he by the great Almont 33; dam by Signal 3327; he by Bunday's Rob Roy.

JUANITO ALMONT, if given a chance would undoubtedly prove a great sire, and should prove a desirable acquisition to any stock farm in the State.

For further particulars address

T. B. COOPER,
Adin, Modoc County, Cal.

$15,000. OPENING $15,000.

of the

GRAND CIRCUIT.

The World's Fair goes to Chicago, but the Greatest Fair ever held in the West takes place at

Agricultural Park, Los Angeles, August 4 to 9, 1890.

Fifteen Thousand Dollars in Purses, Stakes and Premiums.

Speed Programme:

FIRST DAY—MONDAY AUGUST 4TH.

No. 1. The Los Angeles Derby.—A sweepstake for three-year-olds (foals of 1887), $50 each, half forfeit, with $500 added, the second to receive $100, and the third $50, out of the stakes; a winner of any three-year-old stake race to carry five (5) pounds, of two or more, eight (8) pounds extra; maidens allowed seven (7) pounds. One mile and a half.

No. 2. The Edwards & McKnight stakes.—A sweepstake for all ages; $20 each, half forfeit; $200 added, the second to receive $100 out of the stakes. Non-winners this year allowed seven pounds. Maidens allowed ten pounds. One mile.

No. 3. Trotting.—The Los Angeles Purse, $1,500, open to all horses eligible to the 2:30 Class, June 16th. Entrance, ten per cent, payable as follows: $50 June 16th, when entries close; $50 July 1st, and $50 July 22nd, when horses must be named. No subscription will be received unless the first payment shall accompany the same. Subscribers liable only for the amount paid in, but if a subscriber fails to make any of the payments when due, he shall surrender his subscription and payments to the Association with the right of substitution. The Board reserves the right to declare the "Los Angeles Purse" off, in the event of its not filling satisfactorily.

No. 4. Trotting.—Purse $500. 3 minute Class. District.

SECOND DAY—TUESDAY AUGUST 5.

No. 5. A sweepstake for two-year-olds owned in the Southern Counties; $25 each, $15 forfeit; $150 added; the second to receive $75 out of the stakes. The winner of any race to carry four pounds extra. One-half (½) mile.

No. 6. The Nadeau Hotel Handicap.—Purse $1,000, of which $700 to the first; $200 to the second; and $100 to the third horse. Weight announced July 22nd. Twenty-five dollars ($25) to nominate, and fifty dollars ($50) each from all starters. The winner of any race after the announcement of the weights to carry five (5) pounds extra. One and one quarter mile.

No. 7. Trotting.—Two-year-old stakes, district, $250 added. See special condition.

No. 8. Pacing.—Purse $500. 2:25 Class. District.

THIRD DAY—WEDNESDAY, AUG. 6TH.

No. 9. Selling Purse—For all ages. $250. Ten Dollars from starters to go to second horse. Fixed valuation $1500; three pounds allowed for each $100 less down to $700; then one pound for $100 down to $300; selling price to be named through the entry box at 6 P. M. the day before the race. Seven-eighths of a mile.

No. 10. Hurdle Race—A sweepstake for all ages; $20 each, half forfeit; $200 added; second horse to receive $75 out of the stakes. Five hurdles—about one and one half miles.

No. 11. Trotting—Three-year-old Stake, District $250 added. See special Conditions.

No. 12. Trotting.—Purse $1000. 2:25 Class.

FOURTH DAY—THURSDAY AUG. 7TH.

No. 13. The Hollenbeck Hotel Stakes—A sweepstake for two-year-olds (foals of 1888), $50 each, $20 forfeit; with $300 added, the second to receive $100, and the third $50 out of the stakes. A winner of any stake race before August 1st, to carry three pounds; and two or more stake races, five pounds extra; maidens allowed, if beaten once, five pounds; twice or more, eight pounds. Five-eighths of a mile.

No. 14. The Southern California Handicap.—Purse $1000, of which $700 to the first, $200 to the second, and $100 to the third horse. Weights announced July 22nd. $25 to nominate, and $50 more for all starters. The winner of any race at this meeting to carry five pounds extra. Three-quarters of a mile.

No. 15. Trotting—Purse $1000, 2:27 Class.

No. 16. Trotting—Purse $500, 2:40 Class; District.

FIFTH DAY—FRIDAY, AUGUST, 8TH.

No. 17. The Sierra Madre Stakes.—A sweepstake for all ages. $25 each, half forfeit; $200 added, second to receive $75 out of the stakes. Winner of any race this year at three-quarters (¾) of a mile or less to carry six (6) pounds, and of two or more of such races, ten (10) pounds extra. Maiden allowed ten (10) pounds. One-half (½) mile heats.

No. 18. Santa Catalina Cup.—A sweepstake for all ages, $40 each; $20 forfeit; $300 added; the second to receive $100 out of the stakes. Five pounds above scale. Non-winners in 1889 and 1890 allowed ten (10) pounds. Maidens allowed twelve (12) pounds. A winner at this meeting to carry five pounds extra. One and one-eighth (1⅛) mile.

No. 19. Trotting.—Purse, $1,000, 2:20 Class.

No. 20. Trotting.—Purse, $500. 2:50. District.

SIXTH DAY—SATURDAY, AUG. 9TH.

No. 21. The Citrus Handicap.—A sweepstake for three-year-olds; $50, half forfeit, or only $10 if declared by 5 P. M. the day before the race; $250 added; the second to receive $100 out of the stakes. Weights to be announced by 5 o'clock P. M. second day before the race. One and one-sixteenth (1 1-16) of a mile.

No. 22. The Junior Handicap.—A sweepstake for two-year-olds. $50 each, half forfeit, or only $15 if declared by 5 P. M. the day before the race; $250 added; the second to receive $100, and the third $50 out of the stakes. Weights to be announced by 5 o'clock P. M. the second day before the race. Three-quarters (¾) of a mile.

No. 23. Trotting.—Purse $800, 2:35 Class.

No. 24. Pacing.—Purse, $800, 2:25 class.

TROTTING STAKES—To close June 16th, 1890.

To be Trotted at the Annual Fair, to be held in Los Angeles in 1890--91.

TROTTING STAKES, 1890.

FOALS OF 1888. Mile and repeat, $250, added by the Association. Entrance, $50, payable in the following forfeits: $10 to accompany the nomination, $20 July 1st, and $20 August 11, 1890.
FOALS OF 1887. Mile heats, three in five. $300 added by the Association. $60 entrance, payable in the following forfeits; $10 to accompany the nomination, $20 July 1st, and $30 August 11, 1890.

TROTTING STAKES, 1891.

FOALS OF 1889. Mile and repeat. $250 added by the Association. $50 entrance, payable in the following forfeits: $5 to accompany nomination, $10 August 1st, 1890; $10 May 1st, 1891, and $25 on the first day of the Fair of 1891.

FOALS OF 1888. Mile heats, three in five. $300 added by the Association. Entrance, $50, payable in the following forfeits: $5 to accompany the nomination; $10 August 1st, 1890; $10 May 1st, 1891, and $25 on the first day of the Fair of 1891.

CONDITIONS.

All nominations to be made on or before June 16th. American Association rules to govern. Nominators liable only for the amount paid in, which becomes forfeit if subsequent payments are not made. All forfeits and entrance fees will be contributed to the stake, the whole divided where there are three or more starters as follows: sixty per cent. to the first, thirty per cent. to the second and ten per cent. to the third. If no more than two horses start, only first and second money shall be awarded, and in case of a walk over, only the first money shall be awarded. A horse distancing the field shall only be entitled to so much of the money as the starters in the race could have won. A nominator in making an entry in any of the above stakes shall give the name of owner, name of breeder and where foaled, the age, color, sex, dam and sire if known. Colts owned in the Counties of San Luis Obispo, Fresno, Tulare, Kern, Santa Barbara, Ventura, Los Angeles, San Bernardino, Orange and San Diego shall be eligible to entry.

REMARKS AND CONDITIONS.

All trotting and pacing races to be to harness, mile heats, best three in five, except otherwise specified. Entrance 10 per cent on amount of purse. Trotting and pacing divided as follows: 50 per cent. to first horse; 25 per cent. to second; 15 per cent. to third, and 10 per cent. to fourth. Entries not declared out by 6 P. M. of the day before the race must start. In all trotting and pacing races, five to enter and three to start. The Board reserves the right to hold a less number than five to fill. Horses owned in Fresno, Tulare, Kern, San Luis Obispo Santa Barbara, Ventura, Los Angeles, San Bernardino, Orange and San Diego Counties, are eligible for entry in district races. A horse distancing the field is entitled to first and fourth money. The Directors reserve the right to change the hour and day of any race, if deemed necessary. Races shall commence each day at 1 o'clock. American Association rules to govern, unless otherwise specified. Hay and straw free.

Running—The Pacific Coast Blood Horse rules to govern running races. Colonial-bred horses, foaled on Colonial time, allowed as follows: Two and three-year-olds, eight pounds; four-year-olds five pounds, and five-year-olds, three pounds. In all stakes, starters must be named to the Secretary or through the entry box at the track, on or before 6 P. M. of the day before the race. In all stakes, the right to forfeit ceases at 10 o'clock of the day on which the race is run. Racing colors to be named with the entry. Entries close with the Secretary July 1st.

Remember, entries for the 2:30 Trot and District Trotting Stakes close June 16th, and for everything else July 1st.

BEN BENJAMIN, Secretary.

L. LICHTENBERGER, President.

SAN DIEGO, 8776.

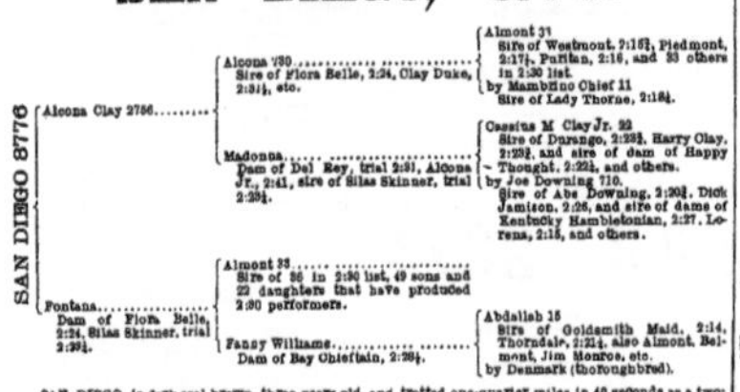

SAN DIEGO is dark seal brown, three years old, and trotted one-quarter miles in 40 seconds as a two-year old.

This grand young horse, and, barring accidents, will make a fast record next fall.

He will be allowed a limited number of mares, at $50 for the season. Mares not proving in foal to be returned free 1891. Best of pasture for mares at $4 per month, but no liability for accidents or escapes.

He will make the season from February 1st to June 1st at Napa Fair Grounds. For further particulars, address or call on

H. B. STARR, Race Track, Napa, Cal.,

or FRED W. LOEBER, St. Helena

Guenoc Stud Farm, Lake Co., Cal.

Imp. GREENBACK

(Sire of the English winners Greenlight, Greenjacket, Greensbank, Greenwave and Greenhorn)

By Dollar, dam Music, by Stockwell. $100 the Season

ST. SAVIOR,

(FULL BROTHER TO EOLE)

By Eolus, dam War Song, by War Dance. $100 the Season.

PASTURAGE, $5 PER MONTH.

With right to return the following year if mare does not prove with foal. The best of care taken, but no liability for accidents or escapes. Mares shipped to C. W. ABY, care ST. HELENA STABLES, St. Helena Napa County, will be taken in charge by competent men.

For further information write to

DR. C. W. ABY, Middletown, Lake County, Cal.

Highland Farm,

LEXINGTON, KY.,

Home of Red Wilkes.

Standard-bred Trotting Stock

For Sale,

Sired by Red Wilkes, Wilton, 2:19¼; Allandorf and Sentinel Wilkes, out of highly bred Standard Mares of the most fashionable blood of the day.

W. C. FRANCE, Proprietor.

HORSES PURCHASED ON COMMISSION.

THOROUGHBREDS A SPECIALTY.

Will select and buy, or buy selected Animals for all desiring, for reasonable compensation.

KEEPS PROMISING YOUNGSTERS IN VIEW.

L. M. LASLEY, Stanford, Ky.

References:—J. W. Guest, Danville, Ky.
B. G. Bruce, Lexington, Ky.
S. H. Baughman, Stanford, Ky.
G. A. Lackey, Stanford, Ky.
Geo. McAlister, Stanford, Ky.
First National Bank, Stanford, Ky.

For Sale

A FIRST-CLASS

Napa County Farm

—OR—

STOCK RANCH,

800 Acres Improved,

SITUATED TWO AND A HALF MILES FROM NAPA CITY, with good roads leading thereto, a good hard finished house of nine rooms, with all modern improvements, streams running all summer, a great amount of live oak and black oak timber. It lies in a fruit belt, surrounded by fine vineyards and orchards growing upon the same quality of soil, and originally a part of this tract. About one-half hill, and one-half rolling land, but none of it is steep and all easily cultivated, splendidly situated for the breeding of fine horses. Price, $65 per acre. Further particulars given at this office.

BREEDER AND SPORTSMAN,

313 Bush St.

For Sale

A HALF BROTHER TO

ALMONT PATCHEN,

(2:15, trial 2:13 3-4).

JUANITO JR. is a beautiful bright bay, black points, with no white, foaled 1886. As a colt he has given much more promise than did Almont Patchen at the same age. Instead of being a pacer, he is a good square trotter, with every indication of great speed, and is so gentle and kind, that a lady can drive him. The owner's only reason for selling him is that business calls him away from this section of the State. He will be sold at a reasonable figure. This is a splendid opportunity for a gentleman to secure a first-class trotter at a very low figure.

The pedigree of Juanito Jr. is by Juanito (sire of Almont Patchen), dam Nettie Moore by Old Tom Moore. For further particulars, address

JUANITO JR.,

Santa Clara P. O., Cal.

FERGUSON & AUSTIN,

FRESNO, CAL.

Registered Polled Angus and Short-Horn Cattle.

Southern Pacific Co.

(PACIFIC SYSTEM.)

Trains leave and are due to arrive at San Francisco.

LEAVE (FOR)	FROM JUNE 1, 1890.	ARRIVE (FROM)
7.30 A M	Haywards, Niles and San Jose ...	*12.45 P M
7.30 A M	Sacramento and Redding, via Davis ...	7.15 P M
7.30 A M	Sacramento, Auburn, Colfax...	4.45 P M
8.00 A M	Martinez, Vallejo, Calistoga and Santa Rosa...	6.15 P M
8.30 A M	Los Angeles Express, Fresno, Bakersfield, Mojave and East and Los Angeles ...	11.15 A M
8.30 A M	Niles, San Jose, Stockton, Ione, Sacramento, Marysville, Oroville and Red Bluff...	4.45 P M
10.30 A M	Haywards and Niles...	3.45 P M
12.00 M	Haywards, Niles and Livermore	8.45 P M
*1.00 P M	Sacramento River Steamers ...	**6.00 A M
3.00 P M	Haywards, Niles and San Jose....	9.45 A M
3.30 P M	2d Class for Ogden and East...	10.45 P M
4.00 P M	Stockton and Milton; Vallejo, Calistoga and Santa Rosa...	9.45 A M
*4.30 P M	Niles and Livermore...	*8.45 A M
*4.30 P M	Niles and San Jose ...	‡6.15 P M
5.00 P M	Shasta Route Express, Sacramento, Marysville, Redding, Portland, Puget Sound, East and Knight's Landing via Davis	10.45 A M
6.00 P M	Haywards and Niles...	7.45 A M
6.00 P M	Sunset Route, Atlantic Express. Santa Barbara, Los Angeles, Deming, El Paso, New Orleans and East...	8.45 P M
8.00 P M	Central Atlantic Express, Ogden and East...	9.45 A M

SANTA CRUZ DIVISION.

LEAVE		ARRIVE
‡7.45 A M	Excursion train to Santa Cruz...	‡8.05 P M
8.15 A M	Newark, Centerville, San Jose, Felton, Boulder Creek and Santa Cruz...	6.20 P M
*2.45 P M	Centerville, San Jose, Almaden, Felton, Boulder Creek and Santa Cruz ...	*11.20 A M
4.45 P M	Centerville, San Jose, and Los Gatos, and Saturday and Sunday to Santa Cruz...	9. 0 A M

Coast Division (Third and Townsend Sts.)

LEAVE		ARRIVE
7.25 A M	San Jose, Almaden and Way Stations...	2.30 P M
‡7.50 A M	Monterey and Santa Cruz—Sunday Excursion...	‡8.25 P M
8.30 A M	San Jose, Gilroy, Tres Pinos; Pajaro, Santa Cruz; Monterey; Pacific Grove, Salinas, San Miguel, Paso Robles, Santa Margarita (San Luis Obispo) and principal Way Stations...	6.12 P M
10.30 A M	San Jose and Way Stations...	7.30 P M
11.05 A M	Emanuel Cemetery and Baden...	12.32 P M
12.01 P M	Cemetery, Menlo Park and Way Stations...	5.13 P M
*2.30 P M	Del Monte Limited, Menlo Park, San Jose, Gilroy, Pajaro, Castroville, Monterey and Pacific Grove...	*11.15 A M
*3.30 P M	San Jose, Tres Pinos, Santa Cruz, Salinas, Monterey Pacific Grove and principal Way Stations...	*10.00 A M
*4.20 P M	Menlo Park and Way Stations....	*7.56 A M
5.20 P M	San Jose and Way Stations...	9.03 A M
6.30 P M	Menlo Park and Way Stations...	6.35 A M
†11.45 P M	San Jose and principal Way Stations ...	†4.28 P M

A M for Morning. P M for Afternoon.
*Sundays excepted. †Saturdays only. ‡Sundays only.
**Mondays excepted. §Saturdays excepted.

San Francisco and North Pacific Railway.

THE DONAHUE BROAD-GAUGE ROUTE.

COMMENCING SUNDAY, APRIL 27, 1890, AND until further notice, boats and trains will leave from and arrive at the San Francisco Passenger Depot, Market-street Wharf, as follows:

FROM SAN FRANCISCO FOR POINT TIBURON AND SAN RAFAEL.
Week Days—7.40, 9.20, 11.20, A. M.; 1:30, 3.30, 5.00, 6.15 P. M.
Sundays—8.00, 9.30, 11.00 A. M.; 1.30, 3:30, 5.00, 6.15 P. M.

FROM SAN RAFAEL FOR SAN FRANCISCO.
Week Days—6.50, 7.55, 9.30, 11:40 A. M.; 1.40, 3.40, 5.05, 6:25 P. M.
Sundays—8.10, 9.40, 11:10 A. M.; 1.40, 3.40, 5.00, 6:25 P. M.

FROM POINT TIBURON FOR SAN FRANCISCO
Week Days—7.15, 8.20, 9.55 A. M.; 12.05, 2.05, 4.05, 5.30, 6 50 P. M.
Sundays—8.25, 10.05, 11:35 A. M.; 2.05, 4.05, 5.30, 6:50 P. M.

Leave San Francisco. WEEK DAYS.	Leave San Francisco. SUNDAYS.	DESTINATION	Arrive San Francisco. SUNDAYS.	Arrive San Francisco. WEEK DAYS.
7.40 A M 9.20 A M 3.30 P M §5.00 P M	8.00 A M 5.00 P M	Petaluma and Santa Rosa	10.40 A M 7.25 P M	8.50 A M 10.30 A M 4.40 P M 7 25 P M
7.40 A M 3.30 P M	8.00 A M	Fulton, Windsor, Healdsburg, Litton Springs, Cloverdale, and way stations.	7.25 P M	10.30 A M 7.25 P M
7.40 A M	8.00 A M	Hopland and Ukiah.	7.25 P M	7.25 P M
7.40 A M 6.30 P M	8.00 A M	Guerneville	7.25 P M	7.25 P M 10.30 A M
7.40 A M 5.00 P M	8.00 A M 5.10 P M	Sonoma and Glen Ellen	10.40 A M 6.05 P M	8.50 A M 6.05 P M
7 40 A M 3.30 P M	8.00 A M 5.00 P M	Sebastopol	10.40 A M 7.25 P M	10.20 A M 7.25 P M

Stage connects at Santa Rosa for White Sulphur Springs, and Mark West Springs; at Geyserville for Skaggs Springs, and at Cloverdale for the Geysers; at Hopland for Highland Springs, Kelseyville, Soda Bay, Lakeport and Bartlett Springs, and at Ukiah for Vichy Springs, Saratoga Springs, Blue Lakes, Willits, Cahto, Calpella, Potter Valley, Sherwood Valley and Mendocino City.

EXCURSION TICKETS from Saturdays to Mondays, to Petaluma, $1.50; to Santa Rosa, $2.25; to Healdsburg, $3.40; to Litton Springs, $3.60; to Cloverdale, $4.50; to Hopland, $5.70; to Ukiah, $6.75; to Guerneville, $3.75; to Sonoma, $1.50; to Glen Ellen, $1.80.

EXCURSION TICKETS, good for Sundays only, to Petaluma, $1; to Santa Rosa, $1.50; to Healdsburg, $2.25; to Litton Springs, $2.40; to Cloverdale, $3; to Guerneville, $2.50, to Sonoma, $1; to Glen Ellen, $1.20.

H. C. WHITING, General Manager.

PETER J. McGLYNN, Gen. Pass. & Tkt. Agt.
Ticket Offices at Ferry, 222 Montgomery Street and 2 New Montgomery Street.

TWENTY-FOUR PAGES.

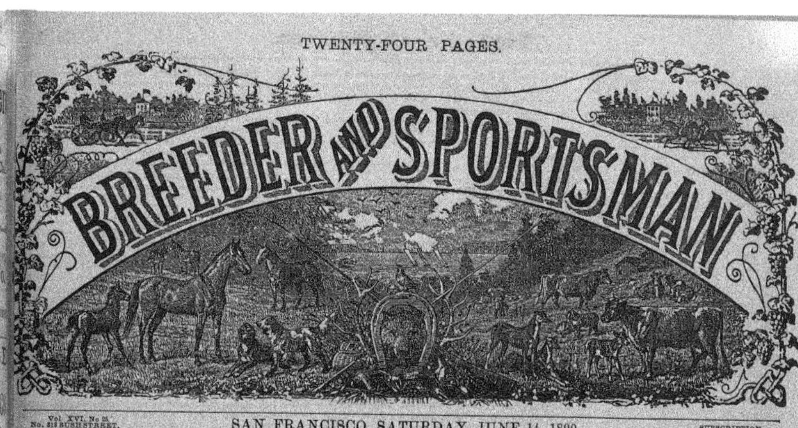

Vol. XVI. No 25.
No. 313 BUSH STREET.

SAN FRANCISCO, SATURDAY, JUNE 14, 1890.

SUBSCRIPTION
FIVE DOLLARS A YEAR.

GUIDE, 2:28½.

The property of A. T. Hatch, Esq., Pleasanton, Cal.

Pleasanton is fast becoming one of the horse-breeding centers of California. For many years it has been noted for its salubrious climate, the effect of which has been to induce owners of large establishments to locate there when land could be had on advantageous terms. The great trouble with the Livermore Valley is that the vast acreage is better adapted for fruit lands than anything else, and as the viticulturists and orchardists have taken almost entire possession of the valley, it is now a very hard matter to secure any land without paying an enormous price therefor. Only lately Senator Hearst has been able to secure a large holding extending over many acres which was formerly known as the Valentine Ranch, and it is understood that he will in the near future bring up all of his thoroughbred mares from the San Simeon ranch to locate a new establishment near Pleasanton. In addition to the noted Pleasanton Stock Farm and the Valensin Stock Farm there is also a great deal of land devoted to the stock belonging to A. T. Hatch, Esq., the President of the State Board of Trade. Mr. Hatch has been interested more or less for many years in stock raising, in fact as he says himself the first money he ever made in his life he took to purchase a horse with. Since 1860 or thereabouts he has owned many horses, and last year came into prominent notice on account of his celebrated young stallion, Guide who made a record of 2:28½ as a four year old last year at Santa Rosa. The handsome brown horse had already won his spurs at Napa, winning there in three straight heats later on in the season was troubled with the prevailing complaint, epizootic, and c not do himself justice during the remainder of the circuit. Wishing to give our readers a picture of this notable horse a visit was paid to the farm last week and an inspection made of him.

Mr. Sutherland, well and favorably known to the residents of Northern California and Oregon as an old driver and trainer, has the horse in charge, and at the request of Mr. Hatch, he was driven around the half-mile track, completing the two circuits in 2:31½, one quarter of which was speeded at a "twenty" gait. Guide is in the best of condition, although he will require a little more work to fit him for an arduous campaign, but as the stallion season is about over, there will be ample opportunity for him to become conditioned before he faces the judges' stand for the first time this year. He has improved wonderfully on h's last year's form; has filled out to a marked degree, and stands to-day, as can be seen by the picture, as handsome a trotter as there is in the State. His breeding is of the best, and being by that well known sire, Director, 2:17, cannot fail to reproduce speed; his dam was Imogene by Norwood 522 (sire of Tommy Norwood, 2:26½); 2d dam by American Star 14; 3d dam daughter of Harry Clay 45. There is no necessity to speak of Guide's sire, as Director and his ancestors are too well known to require comment, but it may not be out of place to say that Norwood was by Hambletonian 10, dam Lady Fallis (dam of Kisbar, 2:27¾. Pickering, 2:30, and Gretchen, dam of Clingstone, 2:14). Lady Fallis was by American Star 14, which, with Clara, the dam of Dictator, gives Guide three crosses of that noted blood. Beyond peradventure, his chances to-day look exceedingly rosy for making a very fast record this year, and as Mr. Hatch has entered him in quite a number of events, we confidently predict that he will add fresh lustre to the name of Director. Mr. Hatch has lately been asked to set a price on this handsome young horse, and although many thousands were offered, absolutely refused to part with him. He has been liberally patronized by those owning good mares, and already two of his yearlings show wonderful trotting action, one especially, owned by Mr. Hatch, being able to show quarters even now in forty seconds. That he will make a famous sire in the days to come, no one can doubt, and as his breeding is of the best, he should add both fame and fortune to his lucky owner.

In addition to Guide Mr. Hatch owns a number of other stallions, one of which, Lenmar, is at present in training at Petaluma. He was a very fast horse in the early portion of '89, but as he was likewise effected with epizootic, was unable to show what he could do. However, his owner thinks that there is a possibility this year of his coming to the wire all right and has turned him over to the careful trainer, Tom Murphy, who will undoubtedly bring him up in good shape when the bell rings. Lenmar is a b s by Admar, dam Lenore by Gladiator 8336; 2nd dam Betty Morgan by Grafton, he a son of Vermont Morgan; 3rd dam Betsey Morgan by Vermont Morgan. As will be seen, Lenmar has nothing to be ashamed of in his pedigree and good luck is all that is necessary to bring him forward as one of the fast horses of the year.

Admiro is a handsome bay horse, eight years old, and stands 17¼ hands high, weighing almost 1400 lbs. He is very speedy for a large horse and can show quarters in 40 seconds without any trouble. Admiro is a son of Admiral 488, dam Zoo Zoo by San Bruno, he a son of Easton's David Hill.

El Rey is a sorrel stallion by Admer, dam Polly Lincoln by a son of Argyle.

Morales is a six-year-old bay horse by Le Grand, dam Mora by Admiral.

My Guy is a bay horse, five years old, by Guy Wilkes 2:15½, dam Gracie by Arthurton 365; 2nd dam Old Lady by David Hill Jr.; 3rd dam by Williamson's Belmont (sire of Venture 2:27¼). We saw several of the colts by My Guy and can vouch for their being as handsome as one can want to see. His breeding is of the best and speed should surely follow.

Omar is a sorrel horse, four years old, by Admar, dam Imogene by Nutwood. Here again we find good breeding as Admar was sired by Admiral, he by Goldsmith's Volunteer (sire of St. Julian 2:11¼). Admar's dam is Bruna by Hathaway's San Bruno, he by Eastons David Hill; 2nd dam Truckee Jane by Grafton.

A handsome little fellow, only a yearling in age, but one to catch the eye at once from his very dignified and intelligent appearance, is Correct, a handsome bay by Morales, dam Imona by Steinway 1808. The above constitutes the stallions at Santa Rita Ranch, and taken all in all, they are a handsome and desirable lot.

Among the geldings, one that struck the writer as being very much of a trotter was Montague, dam Imogene by Norwood. Montague is the exact counterpart of St. Julian, resembles him very much in size, color and conformation. He will be put to work at once to prepare him for circuit purposes, and Mr. Sutherland has confidence that Montague can make a name for himself.

Steindale is a chestnut, six years old, by Steinway, dam the Tiffany mare, dam of Gibraltar 2:22½.

Select is a bay, three years old, by Derby, dam Cigale by Admiral, 2nd dam Betty Morgan by Vermont Morgan; 3d dam, Betsey Morgan by Vermont Morgan. Derby, the sire of Select, is responsible for the parentage of quite a number of animals at Santa Rita, so his pedigree is given here. Derby, by Newland's Hambletonian, dam Phaceola by Silverthreads, he a son of The Moor; 2nd dam, Minnehaha, by Bell Chief; 3d dam Nettie Clay by Strader's Cassius M. Clay, 4th dam by Abdallah. This is royal good breeding, and Select should be able to trot very fast with his combined blood lines, given as above.

Election is three years old, bay, by Admer, dam Electe by Frank Malone's son of Electioneer.

Admon is another bay, three years old, by Derby, dam Admira by Admar.

Melnotte is a sorrel, two years old, by Admar, dam Lenore by Gladiator.

Tancred, bay, two years old, by Derby, dam Admira by Admiral.

Miron, bay yearling by Derby, dam Lenmira by Lenmar.

Lenidon is a sorrel, two years old, by Lenmar, dam Ida by Irvington.

Leonard, sorrel yearling by Admar, dam Lenore by Gladiator.

After inspection of the many horses which are at present being given gentle exercise by Mr. Sutherland, a visit was paid to the large paddocks where the brood mares were eating the rich and succulent grasses. For many years Mr. Hatch has had the major portion of his stock located at Montague, Siskiyou County, and only lately a large number of them were brought down to the Pleasanton Farm. The severe winter had evidently played serious havoc with many of the highly bred animals, but the nutritious pasturage which they are now enjoying is apt before long to bring them up to their normal condition. It must not be understood that the matrons were a bad looking lot, for taken all in all they are far above the average, it was only lack of proper food during thewinter, that has caused them to appear low in flesh. Many of them have suckling foals at their side and the youngsters are all doing well. Among the large number which were to be seen it was a hard matter to get notes about them all but the breeding of some of them will give our readers an idea of the class of trotters that Mr. Hatch has at present.

Gladdie, b m by Gladiator 8336, dam Kate by Hornbeck's Davy Crockett, son of Billy Cheatham.

Gladine, s m by Gladiator, dam Kitty by Davy Crockett.

Lenore, b m by Gladiator, dam Betty Morgan by Grafton, he a son of Vermont Morgan; 2nd dam Betsey Morgan by Vermont Morgan.

Lady Jane, b m by Gladiator, dam Truckee Jane by Grafton; 2nd dam Betsy Morgan.

Lura, b m, by Admiral 488, dam Polly Lincoln by San Bruno; 2d dam by a son of Argyle.

Cigale, b m, by Admiral, dam Betty Morgan by Vermont Morgan; 2d dam Betsy Morgan by Vermont Morgan.

Admira, s m, by Admiral, dam Kitty by Davy Crockett.

Electe, br m, by Frank Malone's Electioneer colt; the dam of the Malone colt was Kishemcower by Hamlet, dam Jennie by Star Davis; the dam of Electe was Jennie Lind, formerly called the Dillon mare, dam of Prince Allen, 2:27.

Lena, b m, by Admiral, dam Lenore by Gladiator; 2d dam Betty Morgan, etc.

Primera, b m, by Admar, dam Lady Jane by Gladiator; 2d dam Truckee Jane by Grafton, etc.

Pauline, br m, by Admar, dam Polly Lincoln by San Bruno; 2d dam by a son of Argy'e.

Trecera, b m, by Admar, dam Lady Jane by Gladiator.

Lady Gamble, blk m, by Steinway 1808, dam the Tiffany mare, the dam of Gibraltar, 2:22½.

Slim Hope, s m, by Admar, dam Admira; 2d dam Kitty by Davy Crockett.

Linda, br m, by Admar, dam Dolly Lincoln; 2d dam Polly Lincoln by San Bruno.

Imona, br m, by Steinway 1808, dam Imogene, the dam of Guide, 2:28½, by Norwood, etc.

La Reina, s m, by Admar, dam Gladine by Gladiator; 2d dam Kitty by Davy Crockett.

Delile, b m, by Admar, dam Delilah.

Bonnie Jean, br m, by Admar, dam Lady Jane by Gladiator; 2d dam Truckee Jane by Grafton, etc.

Bastante, br m, by Admer, dam Gladdie by Gladiator; 2d dam Kate by Davy Crockett, etc.

Colleen, b m, by Arthurton 365 (sire of four in the 2:30 list) dam Cigale by Admiral; 2nd dam Betty Morgam, etc.

Ida, s m, by Irvington 379, dam Young Peanuts (dam of Sweetbriar 2:26½) by George M. Patchen, Jr., 31; 2d dam old Peanuts, said to be by the Morse Horse.

Lenita, b m, by Lenmar, dam Gladdie by Gladiator.

Lenmira, b m, by Lenmar, dam Admira by Admiral.

Electra; blk m, by Admar, dam Electe, a son of Electioneer.

Egypt, a three-year-old filly by Admar, dam Polly Lincoln by San Bruno.

Geraldine, three-year-old, b f, by Admar, dam Gladdie by Gladiator.

Patience, b f, three-year-old by Admar, dam Lady Jane by Admiral.

Derbra, b f, three-year-old by Derby, dam Lura by Admiral.

Dagomar, b f, two year-old by Admar, dam Gladine by Gladiator.

Sybil, two-year-old, blk f, by Derby, dam Lura by Admiral.

Lady Edith, is two-year-old, by Admar, dam Electe by a son of Electioneer.

Jane Porter, two-year-old, b f, by Derby, dam Bonnie Jean by Admar.

La Signa is a handsome bay mare by Le Grand, dam Lady Signal.

Ida Lee, s m, by Le Grand, dam Ida by Irvington.

There is a perfect host of yearlings, all of them looking in first class condition, some of the best of the lot being Night a blk f, by Guide 2:28½, dam Mollie by Admar.

Light is the little miss by Sidney 2:19¾, dam Ida by Irvington.

Mr. Hatch is fairly "in the swim" with this large and well-bred lot of trotters, and there can be no reasonable doubt but what he will be successful in the undertaking of a mammoth breeding establishment. He will have quite a number in training during the season, and that he may meet with his full measure of success, is the earnest wish of his many friends.

Meeting at Albuquerque.

The Spring meeting of the Gentlemen's Driving Association of Albuquerque, New Mexico, was held at the fair grounds in that city on May 15th, 16th and 17th. The programme as arranged was a very interesting one, and the attendance amply repaid the promoters, from which fact it may be confidently predicted that another meeting on a larger scale will be given before very long. The races were interspersed with several events for the runners, but our correspondent failed to send us a report of what the bang tails did. On the first day there was a trot for the four-year-olds and under, May Queen, b f, three years old, by St. Cloud, proving an easy victor in three straight heats, the best time being 3:25, although the filly could undoubtedly have gone fully ten seconds faster. On the same afternoon there was a purse of $75 given for double teams, both horses to be owned by the same party; 75 per cent. of purse going to winner and 25 per cent. to the second. Dandy and Broncho, owned by R. H. Greenleaf, won an easy victory in straight heats, they not being pushed at all. The winners have a record of 3:16 to the pole.

On May 16th, a purse of $50 was offered for green horses, those having no record of any kind, and was won by W. L. Trimble's Babe in three straight heats, the best time being 3:16: Mr. Horne's Kitty Cogan was distanced in the first heat and Grey Eagle owned by J. Eiseman was distanced by the judges in the third heat for running. On the same afternoon a purse of $200 was hung up by the association for the 2:55 class with the condition that the horse had to be owned in Bernalillo County; there were three starters for this event, the winner turning up in the b g Lancet, owned by W. L. Trimble who won the second, third and fourth heats. Bronco owned by Mr. Greenleaf taking the first heat; the best time of the winner was 2:57½. Daniel Boone owned by D. Armstrong was distanced in the first heat; in this race Mr. V. A Greenleaf drove Broncho the fourth heat and was fined $25 for loud shouting and improper use of the whip.

For Saturday, May 17th, the association offered a purse of $300 for Free-For-All trotters, the horses coming to the post being Faro, b g by Mambrino Gift; Roan Dick, r g, and Miss Ruby a roan mare: Faro, who was owned by Dr. Carter, won easily in three straight heats, the best time being 2;39½ in third heat, in which Roan Dick finished at Faro's wheel.

On the same afternoon the 3;15 class had an outing, the entries being Daniel Boone owned by D. Armstrong and Bay Fanny owned by O. R. Cassels Daniel Boone won the second and third heats, Dandy winning the first. The race was given to Daniel Boone as in the third heat Dandy was ruled out for foul driving of his owner; Bay Fanny was distanced in the second heat. The best time made was 3;09.

An extra day was given on May 18th, on which day there was a race which was really the best of the entire meeting, the entries being Lancet, Broncho and Ethan Allen Jr. Broncho is only a $30 Mexican horse, but in the three heats he won, showed himself to be a fair trotter, his powers of endurance being much more than that of his competitors, and in the heats which he won he never made a skip or left his feet once. Lancet won the first two heats, Broncho the third and fourth, and Ethan Allen Jr., the fifth, while Broncho outlasted the others and won the sixth heat, the best time in the race being 2:55. The following are the

SUMMARIES.

May 15th.—Purse $150; trotting, for four-year-olds and under.

James T. Johnson's b f May Queen, 3, by St. Cloud	1	1	1
J. J. Phelan's g m Silver Tail, 4, breeding unknown	2	3	2
C. Barger's r g Richard L, 4, breeding unknown	3	2	3

Time, 3:34, 3:29½, 3:25.

Same Day.—Purse $75; trotting, double teams, both horses to be owned by the same party.

R. H. Greenleaf's Dandy and Broncho	1	1
Thompson and Armstrong's Dan Boone Jr, and Ethan Allen Jr.	2	2
Trimble & Robinson's Lancet and John	3	3

Time, 3:24, 3:27½.

May 16th.—Purse $50: open to green horses only.

W. L. Trimble's Babe, breeding unknown	1	1	1
J. Eiseman's Grey Eagle, breeding unknown	2	2	dis
A. Horne's Kitty Cogan, breeding unknown	Dis.		

Time, 3:20½, 3:31, 3:16.

May 17th. Purse $200. Trotting, 2:55 class. For horses owned in Bernalillo County only.

W. C. Trimble's Lancet, b g, breeding unknown	2	1	1	1
R. H. Greenleaf's Broncho, c g, breeding unknown	1	2	2	2
D. Armstrong's Daniel Boone, Jr., b g, breeding unknown	dis			

Time, 3:04, 2:59½, 2:57½, 2:58.

Same day. Purse $300. Trotting, free for all.

Dr. Carter's Faro, b g, by Mambrino Gift, dam unknown	1	1	1
J. W. Ollinger's Roan Dick, breeding unknown	2	2	2
J. W. Malette's Miss Ruby, r m, breeding unknown	3	3wd	

Time, 2:41, 2:46½, 2:39½.

Same day. Purse $50. Trotting, 3:15 class.

D. Armstrong's Daniel Boone, b g, breeding unknown	2	1	1
R. H. Greenleaf's Dandy, b g, breeding unknown	1	2 ro	
O. R. Cassell's Bay Fanny, b m, breeding unknown	3	dis	

Time 3:11, 3.11, 3:09.

May 18th. Trotting. Special purse.

R. H. Greenleaf's Broncho	3	2	1	1	2	1
W. L. Trimble's Lancet	1	1	2	2	3	2
Mr. Thompson's Ethan Allen, Jr.	2	3	3	3	1	3

Time, 3:01, 2:59, 2:57½, 2:55, 3:00, 2:57.

As sure as fire will burn Darbys Fluid will destroy disease-germs and save your cattle from contagious diseases.

THE FARM.

The Bronze Turkey.

It is claimed by most writers on domestic poultry that the turkey is the only valuable fowl contributed by North America to the table of the world. His native habitat extends from the Northwest Territory to the Isthmus of Panama. South of that he is not found. This is the real and only original bronze turkey. He attains great size, even to 40 and 50 pounds for the male and from 30 to 35 pounds for the hen, But at this size he is no great treat for the epicure. My preference is a fat, young hen weighing from 10 to 12 pounds.

When young, the chicks are quite tender and need much care. Another rather precarious time is when they are feathering out. The courtship of the gobbler commences in February, and when once the hen begins to lay, the whole of that litter is fecundated. She could safely be removed from the flock, and, under normal conditions, every egg would hatch. A turkey hen will lay from seven to eleven eggs at a litter, and will produce three broods if she is not required to hatch but one.

An illustration: A neighbor of mine by the name of Evarts bought one pair of bronze turkeys. In due time the hen laid nine eggs. These were set under a common hen. Again, in about 10 days, the turkey hen laid another litter of 11 eggs; these again were placed under a common hen; a third repetition resulted in seven eggs, and these the turkey hen was allowed to hatch, and if my memory is not greatly at fault, Mr. E. raised the whole twenty-seven turkeys to maturity.

Young turkeys should be placed in a board pen; they cannot get over a board 12 or 14 inches wide. If hatched by a common hen she must be confined, because she is a rambler and the ordinary chick is quite spry when but a week old. The young turkeys should be fed at first on hard boiled eggs chopped very fine. In a few days wheat or cornbread crumbs may be given. They will thrive on this feed. When a greater quantity of food becomes necessary curds and fine chopped onions may be added.

There is no fowl more destructive to insects than the turkey. A flock will spread out over a meadow or grain field like an army with banners, and when they go for grasshoppers they waste no time and never need make a second peck to secure mister hopper.

The poultry dealers of almost every considerable city in our land have their own approved methods in which poultry shall be dressed and placed upon the market. One way approved by self and satisfactory to Chicago and Boston dealers, is this:

When all ready cut off the turkey's head, pick off the feathers dry, being careful not to lacerate the skin. When thoroughly cleaned hang up by the neck and pour over the body a dash of boiling water. The whole fowl will swell up like dough when placed in a hot oven. Draw all the entrails, and these should be nearly empty at the time of killing, but do not draw out the crop. Use no water, but wipe the inside as clean as possible, and place the heart, liver and gizzard back and close up with a few stiches. In this condition when once thoroughly cooled (not frozen) you can send them from here to Boston or San Francisco and have them arrive in the best condition, and they will find a ready sale and bring good prices.—CHAS. W. MURTFELDT, in the Republic.

La Fleche.

La Fleche, the Black Spanish of France, is a veritable nightmare among fowls. Its tall legs, its bold carriage, its inky suit and its strange comb give it a very peculiar appearance. And yet, I fancy, despite the contradictions of many that the comb after all is what gives this fowl its strange look. Because the comb is but a small part of the fowl a great many people who would be wearied with the carriage of one solid idea have protested that the change in comb was not enough to separate two varieties otherwise similar. It so happens that there used to be and perhaps still is a red-faced Black Spanish fowl with a single comb, which in everything but comb bore a very close resemblance to La Fleche, and yet La Fleche and Red Faced Spanish were very different looking fowls—there would be no danger of confounding them. The two upright horns of Red or La Fleche make a wonderful change in the whole appearance of the fowl. If any one doubts that the change in comb makes a great change in the appearance let him take a leghorn cockerel and with a pair of shears cut off the comb and wattles and then place the fowl by the side of an unclipped bird and note the difference. The two birds look as if they belonged to two different breeds.

La Fleche is a composite fowl, produced by the skillful crossing of French poultrymen. That one of the breeds was the Black Spanish there is every reason to believe; that the Polish or some other crested breed was also used is apparent from the peculiar comb, the cavernous nostrils and the small crests that the early specimens used to show.

A good many years ago Mr. Philander Williams imported some of this breed into the United States. The fowls, after a time, passed out of his hands, were scattered through many towns and states, and have practically disappeared. I remember discovering at one time in the town of East Providence, R. I., a small flock of La Fleche, a remnant of the importations of Mr. Williams. These birds had been inbred generation after generation until they were little larger than the Black Hamburghs which were kept by the same man. The first really good La Fleche shown in America in recent years were exhibited at Buffalo, in 1888, by Mr. Owen Scotten, of Detroit, Mich. These birds had been recently imported, and their large size and meaty bodies explained why the French people prize the fowls for the table. At the New York show in 1890 a New Jersey gentlemen exhibited some fine specimens, which I suspect were either the Scotten birds or descendants from them. If not, they must have been a recent importation.

La Fleche have never been popular in this country. Whether this has been due to close inbreeing, caused by the impossibility of obtaining fresh blood when required, or whether it has been the result of the change of climate conditions, or whether it has been owing to prejudice, I cannot say. The fact is obvious, whatever its cause. La Fleche are very good summer layers of large, white eggs, are fairly hardy as fowls, somewhat tender as chickens, and when bred from good stock are excellent for the table. Their black legs, black pin feathers and white skin are objectionable when sold in the markets, but do not affect the quality when served upon the table. The French prize La Fleche much more than the American do, but with better birds it is possible that there will be a greater appreciation of this fowl.

H. S. BABCOCK, in Stockman and Farmer.

Hints From the Greatest Poultry Country.

The Chinese prize the droppings of fowls as the best of manure, carefully collecting those of the geese, ducks, chickens and pigeons. Goose-dung brings very high prices. In the use of such material, they often dilute with water, and they manure the plants rather than the earth squirting the liquid article out of watering pots at the roots of the plants.

They have many ingenious methods to save their fowls from being caught by the hawk. The pigeons in North China have tied to their tails whistles which make a whirring noise as they fly through the air and which frighten hawks away. I was a long time at a loss to know what this sound was. I heard it many times a day in every city of North China. The goose-herder protects his charge in much the same way. He has a sort of bamboo whistle or tube fastened to the end of a rope whip which he swings from time to time around his head to scare away the hawks. Inasmuch as some of the goose-herds number as many as a thousand birds, and as the hawks are numerous and bold, it will be seen that this is not an unnecessary precaution.

The Chinese are very fond of eggs, but they never eat them soft-boiled, and they believe that an egg grows better with age. Preserved eggs are one of the daintiest of China and it takes forty days to pickle them for use. The eggs are covered with a mixture of tea leaves, lime, salt, and wood ashes, made into a paste, and are then packed away in wood ashes, which, all over China, are sold to the egg-packers for this purpose. The older an egg grows after packing the better it is supposed to be. There are methods of pickling which turn the eggs as black as jet. In some cases they are steeped in water in which the leaves of fir or cedar trees have been boiled. The Chinese also pickle eggs in salt water, and they regard these salted eggs as good for medicinal purposes. They have certain festivals at which they give presents of hard boiled, dyed eggs, and when a child is born the family and friends celebrate the event by a feast of dyed eggs. All told, the egg industry of China gives employment to many thousand people, and forms one of the important specialties of this very busy nation.—Frank G. Carpenter.

Store Cattle from America.

Sir Jacob Wilson's speech is a purely selfish one in regard to the importance of store states cattle. His argument is, clear this country of pleuro-pneumonia at whatever cost, in order that we may sell our pure-bred stock to our American buyer; but on no account admit the produce of such stock to this country again, on account of the so-called risk of disease. Sir Jacob Wilson admits that there is at present no pleuro-pneumonia in the western states, but he says it is impossible to get these clean cattle into this country without running the risk of importing disease. Then he holds up the bugbear of Texan fever, which is a climatic disease, and would not live in this country. Moreover this disease is confined within well-defined limits of country, which could easily be scheduled. Besides, we have the ten days' voyage acting as a quarantine; and if any cargo should at any time show symptoms of disease, such cattle could be slaughtered at point of landing. Sir Jacob Wilson says the scarcity of store cattle is only temporary; but where will the price of fat cattle go to if we breed twice the quantity we do at present and also receive all the fat cattle America can send? The success which has attended the feeding of Canadians this season is a strong proof of the great impetus which would be given to agriculture were we to get an unlimited supply of the raw material cheap. The interest of the feeder is also the interest of the consumer, and these interests cannot be wholly set aside to please and help the breeder of pure-bred stock. Sir Jacob Wilson speaks hopefully of stamping out pleuro-pneumonia in this country, but many think this will never be accomplished. In a country such as ours, and necessarily importing largely, there must always be a certain amount of risk of disease; and the question comes to this: Give us the largest supply of store stock possible with the minimum amount of risk. This question of store states cattle is rapidly taking hold of the Scotish agricultural mind, and will be an accomplished fact ere long. Does it not look strange to admit store stock from Ireland where there is always more or less disease, and forbid their importation from the western states of America, where friends and foes alike admit there is no pleuro-pneumonia?—A. Hutcheson, in North British Agriculturist.

What Red Polled Cattle Are.

Hon. S. A. Converse gives the folowing description of Red Polled cattle:

Many make a mistake in calling them the "Red Angus cattle." The word Angus is not properly used in speaking of this breed. They are no more related to the Polled Angus than they are to the Shorthorn or Holstein. The origin is traced in another direction entirely. From the remotest time there has been in Suffolk county, England, the red-muley breed called the Suffolk Dun," and, from the earliest time until the present, always known as a superior dairy breed. Twenty-five years ago this breed was nearly lost by the sweeping ravages of a disease known as the rinderpest. Their scarcity since then accounts for their having been little heard of.

Color is always a solid, beautiful dark red, which is transmitted to all their offspring, and even when crossed with breeds of a different color 90 percent of the grades will be red.

They are absolutely hornless, and when crossed with horned breeds they impart this quality so strongly that out of 250 half-bloods that I have bred not one has horns, only a few have even had loose knobs.

In size they are very good. Most of the bulls at maturity weigh from 1,800 to 2,200 pounds, and cows smaller in proportion.

They mature very early, keep easy, and are smooth, fine bone and muscle.

They are very gentle and easy to handle; and rarely that ever one of the bulls ever gets cross.

Their milking qualities are first class. They usually give a good large mess of very rich milk; and a very valuable characteristic of the breed is that most of them will milk a whole year, and from one calving to another, thus making a long season in milk.

They leave their impression strongly on any breed they are crossed with, and their grade and full blood steers are as fine, pony-built fellows as ever went to market, and are quick sellers.

They will huddle in a shed like sheep and ship with the least possible injury.

Dairying, East and West.

Eastern farmers are not a little disgusted to learn that in the towns nearest them, Iowa creamery butter is retailing at thirty-one and thirty-two cents per pound, while the best Home-Made is retailing at twenty eight cents. The first is made from hay worth from three to five dollars per ton, and corn from eighteen to twenty three cents per bushel, and the second from hay worth in the market nine dollars per ton, and corn worth forty cents per bushel. There is nothing very consoling in this to the Eastern farmer,

While it is true he receives the total amount, less the retailer's profit, and the Western farmer pays that profit and in addition freights and the cost of gathering the cream or milk and that of manufacture, yet his cheap land, together with the ease of cultivating, far more than compensates for this. He has, too, in his large herds, a far better chance of grading up his cows and developing a uniform herd of heavy milkers.

Dairying, whether East or West, to be profitable must be engaged in as a business, and one of the essential features of that business must be a dairy cow that will be a heavy milker. This cannot be obtained by haphazard breeding, or by using one breed and then another, mingling bloods till the herd is all colors and forms. It is difficult to do this on a farm where half a dozen cows are kept and in a neighborhood where four-fifths of the farmers are grain raisers by birth and education. The difficulty is increased where one farmer has moderately level land and can grow good sized cattle, and his neighbor has a hilly farm where the land slides from the hillsides after heavy rains, and he dare not stock it with large cattle.

The Western dairyman therefore, has the advantage, and can always hold the Eastern butter market if he will. To do it, however, he must increase the butter capacity of his cows, must give greater attention to all the details of the business, and must furnish the raw material for a first-class article of butter. The demand for good butter is constantly increasing, and will continue to do so, and there is little danger of the market becoming overstocked. The best will always sell at good prices.—Iowa Homestead.

Argentine Mutton.

London, May 10 —The importations of live sheep into the United Kingdom which reached a total of 178,354 head in the first quarter of 1888 and 209,029 in the same part of 1889, fell off to 27,345 head in the first three months of the present year. This wonderful change is due to scheduling of German sheep, which have for a long time formed the bulk of British importations of this stock. This apparently opens up a field for supplies from some other quarter, and advantage of this fact is already being taken by exporters from the Argentine Republic. Over 300 live sheep from Buenos Ayres lately arrived at Liverpool, and proved so attractive to buyers that their flesh brought twice the price of the frozen mutton from the same country. In the course of the last year or two there have been unmistakable indications that the supply of sheep in this country is not equal to the demand, and that the imports of dead mutton could not make up the want of live sheep. And the Argentine Confederation can give England practically unlimited supplies of sheep if they could be brought here alive. It takes rank next to New Zeland in the weight of frozen mutton which it sends to us. In 1887 England imported from the Argentine Confederation 251,273 cwt. of fresh mutton, and in 1888, the last year for which complete returns are recorded, received 345,395 cwt. of mutton. Now that a few of the many millions of live sheep there have found their way here and have sold well, there are more to follow. British importations of mutton in the first quarter of this year were 401,174 cwt. against 296,289 cwt. in 1889 and 227,090 in 1888.

Which is Best?

No one will claim much profit in 2 or 3-year-old stall-fed steers at 2½ cents a pound, says a correspondent of Farm, Stock and Home; but when they sell for 3 cents and weigh 800 at one year old, it is not so bad; and it is not misleading to say that there are yearlings in this county that weigh 800 and will sell quick at 3 to 3½ cents a pound. One of my neighbors is feeding a calf that he expects to make weigh 1,000 pounds when he is one year old in July next. Quality and early maturity are the points to attain. To illustrate: I saw a few weeks ago a 2-year-old heifer sell for $10; later I saw a heifer of the same age sell for $15; afterward, I heard a man offer $40 for a good grade heifer of same age. Now, on which was there a profit, and what made the difference? Nothing but good quality and early maturity. Another: A neighbor sold some high grade—last fall calves, a few days ago for $20 each. In the same town are yearlings that will not bring $6 each; why the difference? The first were good stock, and had good care; the latter, scrub stock and had scrub care. Is it misleading to recommend the former as the most profitable in times of depression, like the present?

A Long Milking Cow.

One exhibit most likely to arrest the attention of the public in general and farmers in particular at the South Franklin Agricultural Show, held at Bukekohe on March 17, was a well-bred Shorthorn cow, exhibited by Mr. J. Allen, Hillside, Pukekohe (but not for competition), says the Auckland (New Zealand) Weekly. The cow was bred by Mr. Edward Allen, of Mount Albert, calved second and last time September 21, 1882. She then gave five gallons of milk daily, has been milked twice daily ever since, and is now giving a fair quantity. We have never heard of a dairy cow milking so continuously (a period of nearly eight years) without having a calf in the interval, and question very much if it could be beaten even on the large continent of America, where all the unlikely things happen, and the big things grow. We may add that the cow has not been spayed.

Articles of incorporation of the Chicago and Montana Sheep Company have been filed says the Livingston Post with the county clerk. The incorporators are Chas. C. Rice, of Myersburg, Erve G. Blair, of White Sulphur Springs, and Henry E. Rohs, of Chicago, Ill. The capital stock is $25,000 divided into 250 shares of $100 each. Operations will be carried on Myersburg, Mont., where the offices will be located. The object of the company is the buying, selling, feeding and dealing in mutton sheep.

Base Ball and Athletic Department.

Professional Pick-Ups.

Frisco is swimming in honey.

Joe Shea leads the base running.

Buchanan is playing more steadily.

Isaacson is daily expecting his release.

Charley O'Neill is certainly a great fielder.

Fogarty has fallen off somewhat in his fielding.

"Chick" Speer is the smallest man in the League.

Cooney rejoined the Portlands at Seattle Sunday.

"Daddy" Hayes is playing with the Port Townsends.

Ed Stapleton now manages and captains the Senators.

Pokey Chase has been given another trial by Sacramento.

Harper's wildness lost last Sunday's game for the Senators.

It is reported that Hen Moore has been signed by Denver.

Stackwell has done very little catching for Cleveland so far.

Smalley has been doing most wonderful work for Cleveland.

The Oakland clergy are great admirers of the Colonel's team.

"Old man" Perrier running bases is Portland's latest sensation.

Lohman is undoubtedly the slowest base runner in the League.

Selna has been making some circus catches of high foul flys lately.

McHale is played in right field on account of his hitting abilities.

"Giraffe" Stewart is no longer connected with the Gas City aggregation.

Reports say that left fielder Swan will soon be released from Stockton.

Van Haltran has made a great success with the Brooklyn Brotherhood.

Farrell's arm is not sufficiently strong for him to pitch a full game out.

Won't Harper please shake that time honored scarlet cardigan Jacket.

Stapleton has regained his batting eye and oh, my! how he is lining them out.

Norman Baker has been doing some of his gilt edged pitching for Baltimore.

It is quite an unusual thing for Johnny Godar to drop two fly balls in one game.

In the past few games Buck Ebright has been doing some very clever work at short.

Young is not the great "phenom" he was cracked up to be in the fore part of the season.

The Stocktons have released DePangher. Reason: same old gag—to reduce expenses.

Hughey Smith has at last caught on in the East. He is playing second for the Hartfords.

Just as soon as the warm weather sets in, notice the improvement in Meegans pitching.

Goodenough gave a sample of foolish base running in the the ninth inning last Thursday.

When, oh! when, is the Colonel going to pad the front of the Emery grounds press stand.

Hank Reitz's head has not been affected by the exalted praise bestowed on his playing by the press.

Of the first twenty batters, Stockton can claim seven, Sacramento five, Oakland three and Frisco four.

Stapleton leads the League in home runs, having four to his credit, and Daley and Roberts have two each.

In Stockton they refer to Kilroy as the "Irish Indian" and his side partner Vogt is called the "Dutch Indian."

Last week pitcher Cobb of the Oaklands was married, and this week scorer Will H. Young became a Benedick. Next!

Shortstop Daly's work is much improved, in fact it looks now as though this player will lead the players in this position.

Jack Wilson, as a third baseman is a "clinker". Next season will undoubtedly see Jack East with one of the big teams.

Subscriber.—We believe that the Donovan in question is now playing center field for the Boston, National League team.

If the grass surrounding the field at Haight St. grounds would be kept nicely clipped and watered, there would be less dust.

On Decoration Day Pete Sweeney, in two games accepted twenty chances without an error at second base for St. Louis.

The Sacramento players say they can't play their usual brilliant game on the Haight St. grounds on account of the prevailing high winds.

On Decoration Day the total attendance at the games of the three major leagues in the East was almost two hundred thousand people.

The Breeder and Sportsman would be pleased to receive communications from all local and interior teams professional oramateur.

Fred Carroll is not catching the game he is capable of. Reports of an uncomplementary nature are current about his poor work this season.

Before starting East Zeigler boasted that he would have half the Sacramento team in Cincinnati before the month is over. Wonder if he will?

Pitcher Wherle of last season's Oaklands and who was wanted by Sacramento, has been signed by the Wilmingtons, of the Atlantic Association.

Andy Smith of the Stocktons is almost a perfect counterpart of Jack Davis who was recently defeated at the Occidental Club by Joe Coyinski.

It is positively a treat to watch the Sacramento infield play together. Their work doubly discounts that of any of the other infields on the coast.

A Seattle contemporary says that "Hen Harris as a trumpeter can give all the managers of the Pacific North-west League cards and spades and win."

The noisy man from Oakland got just a little too fresh on the coaching line Thursday, and was very promptly suppressed by Sheridan, much to the delight of the audience.

In the Santa Rosa Will and Finck game Sunday, Jim Cusick demonstrated the fact that he can play ball just as good as many players in the big teams who the managers think are his superiors.

First base is being played "out of sight" this year and Charley Sweeney heads the list. If he continues his good work their will be a big demand for his services East next year, for Sweeney is "quite a hitter, you know."

"Dicky" Johnson was released from the Bostons to play with the New York Brotherhood team. Johnson is one of the prize outfielders of the country and is also considered an excellent batsman. He replaces Slattery in the New Yorks.

Cahill has been "lining them out" at great speed this season. Last year Patsy was tie with Gagus and ranked thirty eighth in hitting, with a percentage of 224 and this year he heads the list so far with a percentage of 317 to his credit. Quite a difference.

The magnates made a big mistake in not having John Thompson in one of the big teams. Look at his record in the Vallejo—Report game Sunday. Two hits (one a three bagger off Baltz) five put-outs, three assists and one error. He also figured in two lightning double plays.

The baseball reporters in the Pacific North West League are not very lenient. In the account of the Portland—Seattle game last Saturday two hits were secured off Borchers in the first inning and the Tacoma Ledger comes out with a big head line "Borchers knocked out of the box."

The Texas League is in hard luck this year, being robbed of two of its best players by the "grim reaper" Death. The latest player in that League to join the "silent majority" was William Shockamp, better known as Billy Mussey. Shockamp was a very clever and popular player and left a wife and three young children.

This is the way an Eastern writer speaks of Pete Sweeney in the Sporting Life:

"My, oh! my! Pete Sweeney, he from the land of oranges, grapes, gold mines and Chinese, is putting up as good ball as any man in the profession. Pete will no doubt be kept on bag No. 2."

Pickett played with the Philadelphia Players' Club yesterday, as the Kansas City Club have relinquish all claim on him in consideration of the payment of legal services incurred in the suit which restrained him from playing with any club other than the Kansas Citys and the return of the money advanced to him on account of his salary.—Exchange.

There have been no less than seven professional players by the name of Smith seen on the California diamond within the last four seasons. They are "Phenomenal" Smith now with Philadelphia, Jimmy Smith who played third for the Californias, Hughey, Jack and Nick Smith, formerly of the Pioneers, Pop Smith of the Bostons and Andy Smith now with Stockton.

The idea of a young man playing ball for money is not nearly as abhorrent now as it was some years ago, when a ball tosser and a loafer were synonymous terms to many minds. There is nothing at all derogatory now-a-days in a young man playing base ball for the return it brings him. In fact, it must be considered in the highest degree commendable if a young man has the requisite skill to play ball so that it will command a financial return, and he is thus enabled to defray, in whole or in part, his expenses.—Life.

Shelly as yet has not fully strengthened the Stocktons in their weakest point—the catching department. Vogt is fastidious, and cares only to catch Kilroy, claiming he can't afford to have his hands banged up by working with every pitcher; and Smith is entirely too slow to do effective work at his end when receiving Hapeman. What the Stockton team needs is a catcher who is capable of handling any of them, and such a one is Matt Stanley. Stanley is anxious to be identified with some of the professional teams, and if given a chance, will more than hold his end up. His work with the amateurs this season has been of the very highest order both in catching and throwing. Lately he has improved wonderfully in hitting, and we have no hesitancy in proclaiming him a valuable player.

Digby Bell once officiated as an umpire. It was in a game between Philadelphia nines called the Leans and the Fats. The left-fielder of the Fats was an enormous party who had contracted the habit of staying out late every night and riding home in a cab, after all of the street cars had stopped running. This man did not get to first base until the ninth inning, and then he reached there on a muffed third strike. Through a series of awful muffs on the part of the infield of the Leans, he finally reached third. The next batter made a three-bagger and the big man started to toddle home. He was stopped by willing hands, however, a cab was brought into the field, he was fired into it and drawn home. "We couldn't allow you to break your record, my boy," said the captain of the Fats. "You have always been driven home in a cab."—Review.

Manager Robinson gives evidence of possessing as many erroneous ideas about running a ball team as he has suits of clothes, and they are numberless. His latest is to take McDonald off second and play him in the field. What a piece of stupidity, and where is he going to get Jims equal, outside of the Major Leagues. According to a recent computation McDonald leads the Oaklands in hitting and has had and accepted more chances than any other second base player in the League, ranking close on to the "star" of the position—Reitz. If the Colonel wants to strengthen his infield, why don't he displace the noisy man at short, "who brays loudest and does least." He can certainly find any number of amateurs who can discount this "high-roller" player in the position and its "dollars to doughnuts" that Mr. O'Neill wont have any better percentage this year than he had last, when as a shortstop Wilson, Whitehead, Stickney, Ebright and Newbert ranked ahead of him.

One of the promising ball twirlers of the profession is Knell, of the Philadelphia Brotherhood Club. He has the elements of a good ball player, but he is possessed of two weaknesses, which he must overcome before he can be classed as a winning pitcher. One is his attempt to fool batsmen on balls that do not go over the plate, and the other is his impatience. Veteran batsmen like those who compose the Players' League are trained in hitting, and the ball must come over the plate before they will hit at it. Knell's wildness is mainly due to the fact that he works like a machine, firing one ball after another as rapidly as the catcher returns it to him; and, in consequence, he never stops long enough to steady himself and pick out a mark to throw at. Then, also, a batsman becomes nervous and impatient when the pitcher stands in the box and faces him for a few moments after delivering the ball, and he is less apt to hit it under those circumstances than when one ball after another is sent in rapid succession. Knell is young and this is one of the tricks he has not yet learned in his business.—Sporting News.

THURSDAY'S GAME.
OAKLAND vs. SACRAMENTO.
JUNE 12th, AT HAIGHT ST.

The white stockinged Senators and the black jerseyed Colonels came together before a very fair sized audience on Thursday. The sympathy of the crowd was evidently with Stapleton's men, and loudly applauded their every brilliant play. It was a game, if minus the first inning Sacramento would have won. Pokey Chase, who is brought to the front every time either Stockton or Sacramento is in a hole for a twirler, pitched for Sacramento. His first inning was a most disastrous one, the Oaklands making four runs through his wildness and Bowmans error.

The Senators played a hard up hill game, but their hits were not closely bunched. Their fielding was almost perfection, Stapleton, Reitz, Daly and Godar playing the infield in a most finished style, and Roberts and Goodenough did some marvellous fielding. Bowman worked like a Trojan, and with the exception of his error in the first inning, his playing was in accord with the remainder of the team. Chase, after the first inning worked like a beaver, and was very effective, allowing but seven hits to be made by the Colonels is a very creditable performance for this youngster.

The Oaklands, having been presented with four runs, did not have a hard time winning. Their fielding game was of a yellowish tint in places, the errors being mostly made on easy chances. Stickney and McDonald's work were features, and their outfield played a strong game.

Stapleton did great work at the bat, hitting the ball out hard every time and getting three pretty safe shots. Chase, O'Neill and Hill also hit well. The score:

OAKLAND.	AB.	R.	BH.	SB.	PO.	A.	E.
C. O'Neill, l f	3	2	2	2	1	0	0
Stickney, 3d b	4	0	1	0	2	3	0
Dungan, r f	3	1	0	0	2	0	0
N. O'Neill	4	1	0	0	2	3	1
McDonald, 2d b	4	0	0	0	3	3	1
Lohman, c	3	1	0	1	2	2	2
Hill, c f	4	0	2	0	5	0	0
Isaacson, 1st b	2	1	1	0	9	1	1
Cobb, p	3	0	1	0	1	2	1
Totals	30	6	7	3	27	14	8

SACRAMENTO.	AB.	R.	BH.	SB.	PO.	A.	E.
Goodenough, c f	5	0	0	2	2	0	0
Daly, s s	5	0	1	0	0	6	1
Godar, 3d b	4	0	0	0	0	4	0
Stapleton, 1st b	3	2	3	0	12	1	0
Bowman, c	4	1	0	0	5	4	1
Roberts, l f	4	0	0	0	3	1	0
Reitz, 2d b	4	0	1	0	3	1	1
McHale, r f	4	1	1	1	0	0	1
Chase, p	3	1	2	0	0	3	1
Totals	36	4	8	1	24	18	5

SCORE BY INNINGS.

	1	2	3	4	5	6	7	8	9	
Oakland	4	1	0	0	0	0	0	0	*	—6
Sacramento	0	2	0	0	0	1	0	0	1	—4

Earned runs—Sacramento 1. Two base hits—Isaacson, Hill. Sacrifice hits—Godar, Stickney, Goodenough. First base on errors—Oakland 2, Sacramento 5. First base on called balls—Oakland 4, Sacramento 2. Left on bases—Oakland 4, Sacramento 9. Struck out—By Cobb, 4; by Chase 3. Double plays—Chase, Bowman and Stapleton (2). Passed balls—Lohman 2, Bowman 1. Wild pitches—Cobb 1, Chase 1. Umpire, John Sheridan.

The California League.

GAMES PLAYED AT HOME, OAKLAND SACRAMENTO AND STOCKTON.

THE STANDING OF TH- LUBS.

San Francisco is in advance, Sacramento following second, and Oakland a close third. Stockton is still last.

THE RECORD:—(to June 12, inclusive).

CLUBS.	San Francisco	Oakland	Stockton	Sacramento	Games Won	Games Played	Percentage
San Francisco	....		o	7	28	37	.621
Oakland	6	....	[illegible]	7	21	42	.500
Stockton	4	6	....	4	14	39	.359
Sacramento	4	7	9	....	20	38	.526
Games Lost	14	21	5	18	....	....	....

SUMMARY.	Played	Won	Lost	Percentage
San Francisco	27	23	14	.621
Oakland	38	20	18	.526
Sacramento	42	21	21	.500
Stockton	39	14	25	.359

OAKLAND vs. STOCKTON.

FRIDAY, JUNE 6TH, AT OAKLAND.

About fifteen hundred people, many of whom were decorated with a badge of pearl gray and black ribbons, which are the colors of the Oakland team, viewed this game at Emeryville. It was a very pretty exhibition, full of life and some hard hitting, as the score will attest. The errors made by the Oaklands were of a costly nature however, and were it not for the great General O'Neill's overthrow of Fogarty's sharp grounder in the first inning, and Colonel Hill's misjudgment of Wilson's high fly, the score would certainly have been much different.

Parrott pitched a wonderful game, allowing only three safe hits, and was very steady throughout. Big Andy Smith caught and threw to bases very cleverly. The Stocktons' fielding was much superior to that of their opponents.

THE SCORE.

STOCKTON.	AB	R	BH	SB	PO	A	E
Cahill, r f	4	0	1	0	1	6	0
Swan, l f	4	1	1	1	1	0	1
Holliday, c f	4	0	0	0	1	0	0
Fudger, s s	3	1	1	0	0	4	1
Fogarty, 2d b	4	1	1	0	4	4	1
Selna, 1st b	3	1	1	0	13	1	2
Wilson, 3d b	3	0	1	0	3	3	0
Smith, c	3	0	0	0	4	2	0
Perrott, p	3	0	0	0	0	3	0
Totals	31	4	6	1	27	18	5

OAKLAND.	AB	R	BH	SB	PO	A	E
C. O'Neill, l f	3	1	1	1	0	0	0
Stickney, 3d b	4	0	1	0	0	1	0
Dungan, r f	4	0	1	0	1	0	0
N. O'Neill, s s	4	0	0	0	1	5	2
McDonald, 2d b	4	0	0	1	1	3	1
Lohman, c	3	0	0	0	5	2	0
Hill, c f	3	0	0	1	3	0	1
Isaacson, 1st b	3	0	0	0	12	0	0
Meegan, p	3	1	0	0	1	1	0
Totals	31	2	3	3	24	12	4

SCORE BY INNINGS.

	1	2	3	4	5	6	7	8	9	
Stockton	1	1	0	1	0	1	0	0	*	—4
Oakland	0	0	0	0	0	2	0	0	0	—2

Earned runs—Oakland 1, Stockton 2. Two-base hits—Selna, Dungan, C. O'Neill, Cahill, Fogarty. Sacrifice hits—Selna (2). First base on errors—Oakland 4, Stockton 2. First base on called balls—Stockton, 1. Left on bases—Oakland, 3; Stockton, 4. Struck out—By Perrott, 2; by Meegan 5. First base on hit by Pitcher—C. O'Neill. Double plays—McDonald and Isaacson; Selna and Fogarty. Passed ball—Smith, 1. Umpire, John Donahue.

SAN FRANCISCO vs. SACRAMENTO.

FRIDAY, JUNE 6TH, AT SACRAMENTO.

Lookabaugh pitched great ball in this game keeping the nine hits made off him so widely scattered that they were non-productive of runs till the ninth inning when Reitz and Roberts scored. The Friscos batted Harper freely from the start and won easily. Sweeney, Hanley and Ebright played brilliantly and hit very hard and Stevens caught nicely. The Sacramentos fielded neatly and run bases well, but when runs were needed Lookabaugh was an enigma. Following is the score:

SAN FRANCISCO.	AB.	R.	BH.	SB.	PO.	A.	E.
Shea, 2d b	5	2	1	2	1	2	1
Sweeney, 1st b	5	2	2	1	7	0	0
Hanley, c f	5	1	2	0	2	0	0
Ebright, s s	5	3	1	1	4	6	2
Levy, l f	5	1	2	2	1	0	0
Speer, r f	3	0	0	0	0	1	0
Stevens, c	4	1	2	0	12	2	1
Buchan, 3d b	5	0	1	0	0	2	1
Lookabaugh p	5	1	2	0	0	1	1
Totals	40	11	13	6	27	14	7

SACRAMENTO.	AB	R.	BH.	SB.	PO.	A.	E.
Goodenough, c f	4	0	1	0	4	0	0
Bowman, c	5	0	0	0	4	0	0
Daly, s s	4	0	0	1	1	2	1
Stapleton, 1st b	3	0	1	1	8	0	0
Godar, 3d b	4	0	0	0	2	2	1
Reitz, 2d b	4	1	2	2	3	1	2
Roberts, l f	4	1	2	2	1	0	0
Farrell, r f	4	0	2	1	1	0	1
Harper, p	3	0	1	0	0	3	0
Totals	35	2	9	7	24	8	5

SCORE BY INNINGS.

	1	2	3	4	5	6	7	8	9	
San Francisco	1	0	2	4	1	0	0	3	*	—11
Sacramento	0	0	0	0	0	0	0	0	2	— 2

Earned runs—Sacramento, 1; San Francisco, 5. Two base hits—Stevens, Lookabaugh. Sacrifice hits—Sweeney (2), Stevens, Spear. First base on errors—Sacramento, 4; San Francisco, 4. First base on called balls—Sacramento, 4; San Francisco, 3 Left on bases—Sacramento, 10; San Francisco, 11. Struck out—By Harper, 4; by Lookabaugh, 7. Hit by pitcher—Ebright (2). Double plays—Ebright and Shea. Passed balls—Stevens, 1. Umpire—Sheridan.

OAKLAND vs. STOCKTONS.

SATURDAY, JUNE 7TH, AT HAIGHT STREET.

The game was exceedingly dull, the Stocktons playing very poorly. Carsey and Hapeman were the opposing pitchers, and both were hit hard. Hapeman did not have the best support in Smith's backstop work, the big fellow being slow in recovering, and often falling short in throwing. Fogarty was in miserable form, making three bad errors. McDonald's finger was severely injured in the fourth inning, but, notwithstanding, Jim played a good game, accepting some very difficult chances.

Shickney, Isaacson, Cahill, Wilson and Selna played well, and the hitting honors were about evenly divided between Carsey, Lohman, Charley O'Neill, Cahill, Swan, Holliday and Fudger. The score:

OAKLAND.	AB.	R.	BH.	SB.	PO.	A.	E.
C. O'Neill, l f	5	2	2	2	0	0	1
Stickney, 3b	3	1	1	2	1	5	0
Dungan, r f	4	2	2	1	1	0	0
N. O'Neill, s s	5	2	1	2	1	3	1
McDonald, 2d b	5	1	1	1	4	3	2
Lohman, c	5	1	2	2	3	0	0
Hill, c f	5	0	1	1	2	1	1
Isaacson, 1st b	4	1	1	0	15	0	1
Carsey, p	4	0	1	0	0	4	0
Totals	40	10	12	11	27	16	6

STOCKTONS.	AB.	R.	BH.	SB.	PO.	A.	E.
Cahill, r f	5	3	2	0	2	0	0
Swan, l f	4	1	2	0	0	0	0
Holliday, c f	5	0	2	0	1	1	1
Fudger, s s	5	0	2	0	0	2	0
Fogarty, 2d b	4	0	0	0	1	4	3
Selna, 1st b	4	0	1	0	14	1	0
Wilson, 3d b	4	1	1	1	1	3	1
Smith, c	5	1	0	0	5	3	1
Hapeman, p	3	0	0	0	2	2	0
Totals	39	6	10	1	27	16	6

SCORE BY INNINGS.

	1	2	3	4	5	6	7	8	9	
Oakland	4	0	0	0	5	0	0	1	0	—10
Stockton	0	0	1	0	2	0	0	3	0	— 6

Earned runs—Oakland, 4; Stockton, 2. Three-base hit—Carsey. Two-base hit—Isaacson. Sacrifice hits—Lohman, Fudger (2), Holliday, Stickney, Hill, Selna. First base on errors—Oakland, 5; Stockton, 3. First base on called balls—Oakland, 3; Stockton, 3. Left on bases—Oakland, 6; Stockton, 10. Struck out—By Hapeman, 5. Hit by pitcher—Swan, Wilson. Double play—Hapeman and Selna. Passed balls—Smith, 1. Umpire, John Donahue.

SACRAMENTO vs. SAN FRANCISCO.

SATURDAY, JUNE 7TH, AT SACRAMENTO.

The fifth inning saw the Senators tie the score and then in the sixth with two out they jumped on Young viciously and the result was that in four innings they added seventeen runs to their string. Every ball Young pitched was just "pie" for the heavy hitting Sacramentans, and home runs triples and safe ties were the kind of hitting they were dealing in. The 'Frisco's got badly rattled as they witnessed the wholesale slaughtering and piled up the neat sum of twelve errors of which Captain Ebright took three and the balance were distributed through the remainder of the nine. The Sacramentos had Farrell, Reitz and Harper in the box at different times and but seven hits were secured off them. The score:

SACRAMENTO.	AB	R	BH	SB	PO	A	E
Gooden'gh, c. f	6	1	3	0	1	1	1
Bowman, c	6	1	0	0	6	1	0
Daly, s. s	7	3	3	0	3	7	0
Stapleton, 1st b	5	5	4	0	9	0	0
Godar, 3d b	7	2	2	1	1	1	0
Reitz, 2b & p	6	3	0	0	2	3	0
Roberts, l. f	6	3	4	1	1	1	0
McHale, r. f	5	2	5	1	0	0	0
Farrell, p. & 2b	1	0	0	0	4	1	2
Harper, p	2	1	0	0	0	0	0
Totals	52	21	21	2	27	18	4

SAN FRANCISCO.	AB	R	BH	SB	PO	A	E
Shea, 2d b	4	1	0	2	3	2	1
Sweeney, 1st b	4	0	1	0	9	0	0
Hanley, c. f	5	0	1	0	5	1	2
Ebright, s. s	5	0	1	1	1	5	3
Levy, l. f	3	1	1	0	2	0	1
Speer, c	5	0	0	0	7	2	1
Stevens, r. f	3	1	0	0	1	0	0
Buchan, 3d b	3	2	2	2	0	3	2
Young, p	1	1	0	0	0	1	2
Totals	33	6	7	5	26	14	12

SCORE BY INNINGS.

	1	2	3	4	5	6	7	8	9	
Sacramento	0	0	1	2	1	6	6	3	2	—21
San Francisco	6	1	0	3	0	0	2	0	0	—26

Earned runs—Sacramento, 5; San Francisco, 0. Home runs—Daly and Stapleton. Three-base hits—Roberts, Goodenough and Levy. Two-base hit—Buchan. Sacrifice hits—Sweeney, Hanley and Godar. First base on errors—Sacramento, 10; San Francisco 2. First base on called balls—Sacramento, 5; San Francisco, 7. Left on bases—Sacramento, 11; San Francisco, 10. Struck out—By Farrell, 0; by Young, 8; by Reitz, 1; by Harper, 2. First base on hit by pitcher—Levy, Young and Stapleton. Double plays—Reitz, Daly and Stapleton; Ebright and Shea; Shea, Ebright and Sweeney. Passed balls—Bowman, 0; Speer 2. Wild pitches—Farrell, 1; Young, 0. Time of game 2 hours and 15 minutes. Umpire, Sheridan. Official scorer, Will H. Young

OAKLAND vs. SACRAMENTO.

SUNDAY, JUNE 8TH, AT HAIGHT ST.

Harper was wild as a "Texas Steer" and this with a great many errors and an inability to hit safely when hits were needed, was the cause of Sacramentos crushing defeat last Sunday. The game was interesting till the sixth inning, when the Oaklands piled up five runs on three bases on balls, Lohmans single and ONeills triple. This robbed the contest of all pleasure as the Sacramentos could do but little better than going out in one, two, three order. The fielding on both sides was of a very ordinary character, errors being numerous throughout the game. O'Neill had his usual two and Hill, Daley, Stapleton, Godar and Roberts were each credited with the same number.

Bowmans work was exceptionally clever, having to contend against some very ragged pitching by Harper. Donohue's decisions on balls and strikes were erratic and were decidely unfavorable to the Sacramento team.

THE SCORE.

OAKLAND.	AB	R	BH	SB	PO	A	E
C O'Neill, l f	3	3	0	0	2	0	0
Stickney, 3d b	2	1	1	0	1	1	0
Dungan, r f	4	1	0	1	0	0	0
N. O'Neill, s s	6	1	2	0	2	4	2
McDonald, 2d b	5	1	2	1	4	3	1
Lohman, c	4	3	3	1	5	0	0
Hill, c f	3	1	1	0	0	0	2
Isaacson, 1st b	4	1	1	6	10	3	1
Cobb, p	5	1	0	0	2	4	1
Totals	37	13	10	8	27	15	7

SACRAMENTO.	AB	R	BH	SB	PO	A	E
Goodenough, c f	4	2	0	2	2	0	0
Bowman, c	5	2	2	1	9	2	1
Daly, s s	4	0	1	0	1	3	2
Stapleton, 1st b	4	0	0	0	3	2	2
Godar, 3d b	4	0	0	0	3	0	2
Reitz, 2d b	4	0	0	0	4	2	0
Roberts, l f	4	0	0	0	1	1	2
McHale, r f	4	1	1	0	1	0	0
Harper p	4	0	1	0	0	0	0
Totals	37	5	5	3	24	10	9

SCORE BY INNINGS.

	1	2	3	4	5	6	7	8	9	
Oakland	0	3	0	0	0	5	0	5	*	—13
Sacramento	0	0	2	0	0	0	3	0	0	—5

Earned runs—Oakland, 2. Three-base hit—N. O'Neill. Two-base hits—Stickney, Lohman, McDonald. Sacrifice hits—Roberts, Stapleton. First base on errors—Oakland, 6; Sacramento, 6. First base on called balls—Oakland, 13; Sacramento, 1. Left on bases—Oakland, 13, Sacramento, 6. Struck out—By Harper, 4; by Cobb, 5. Double play—Harper, Bowman and Godar. Passed ball—Lohman, 1. Wild pitch—Harper, 1. Umpire, John Donohue.

SAN FRANCISCO vs. STOCKTON.

SUNDAY, JUNE 8TH, AT STOCKTON.

It was a great game twelve hundred excited Stocktonians witnessed last Sunday. Runs, base hits and errors were scarce and consequently the exhibition was a pretty one. Neither side scored till the fourth inning when Sweeney got his base on balls and Ebrights three baser brought him home. The Stocktons tied the score in the first of the ninth when Selna tallied on his hit and Steal and Vogts single.

Ebright then won the game on his second magnificent three bagger, and Fudgers error. All through the field playing was brilliant.

Both Lookabough and Kilroy did especially well, being very steady and effective. Ebrights work at short was truly wonderful and his hitting was simply terrific.

THE SCORE.

SAN FRANCISCO.	AB.	R.	BH.	SB.	PO.	A.	E.
Shea, 2d b	4	0	0	0	1	2	1
Sweeney, 1st b	3	1	0	0	10	2	0
Hanley, c f	4	0	1	0	2	0	0
Ebright, s s	4	1	0	0	2	8	0
Levy, l f	3	0	0	0	2	0	0
Speer, c	3	0	1	0	8	1	0
Stevens, r f	3	0	0	0	1	0	0
Buchan, 3 b	2	0	0	1	1	1	1
Lookabaugh, p	3	0	0	0	0	2	0
Totals	29	2	4	1	27	16	2

STOCKTON.	AB.	R.	BH	SB.	PO.	A.	E.
Swan, l f	3	0	0	0	2	0	0
Cahill, r f	4	0	1	0	2	0	1
Holliday, c f	4	0	2	0	2	0	0
Fudger, s s	3	0	0	0	2	2	1
Fogarty, 2d b	4	0	0	0	3	4	0
Selna, 1st b	3	1	2	2	7	1	2
Wilson, 3d b	4	0	0	0	1	2	0
Vogt, c	4	0	2	1	4	0	0
Kilroy, p	4	0	1	0	1	2	1
Totals	33	1	7	3	24	11	5

SCORE BY INNINGS.

	1	2	3	4	5	6	7	8	9	
San Francisco	0	0	0	1	0	0	0	0	1	— 2
Stockton	0	0	0	0	0	0	0	0	1	— 1

Earned runs—Stockton, 1. Three-base hits—Ebright (2), Selna. Two-base hits—Vogt, Speer. Base on errors—San Francisco, 2; Stockton, 2. Base on balls—San Francisco, 2; Stockton, 4. Left on bases—San Francisco, 5; Stockton, 9. Struck out—By Lookabaugh, 6; by Kilroy, 4. Double plays—Buchan to Sweeney to Buchan. Umpire, Sheridan.

The Pacific Northwest League.

STANDING OF THE CLUBS.

During the past week Tacoma and Seattle have been getting in their deadly work, and both have passed Spokane, which team had been the leader for the season.

The Spokanes are now third and Portland continues to hold last place.

PORTLAND vs. SEATTLE.

SATURDAY, JUNE 7TH, AT SEATTLE.

The Seattles took a big lead of four runs in the first inning on two safe hits, a base on balls and some costly misplays by the Portlands. In the fourth inning they added three more to their score, while the Web foot boys were goose-egged till the sixth. In that inning, however, they came to time, nimbly knocking out five runs and scored another in the seventh. This was the last of the run getting on either side, and the game ended in favor of the Seattles. Borchers started in to pitch, but retired after the first inning in favor of Munday. The score.

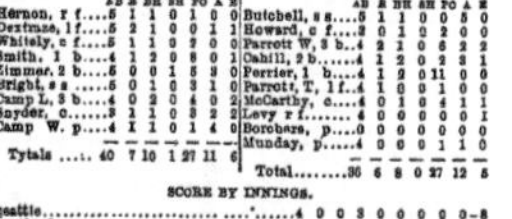

SEATTLE.	AB	R	BH	SH	PO	A	E
Hernon, r f	5	1	1	0	1	0	0
Dextraze, l f	5	2	1	0	0	1	1
Whitely, c f	5	1	1	0	2	0	0
Smith, 1 b	4	1	2	0	8	0	1
Zimmer, 2 b	5	0	0	1	5	3	0
Bright, s s	5	0	1	0	3	1	0
Camp L, 3 b	4	0	2	0	4	0	2
Snyder, c	3	1	1	0	3	2	2
Camp W. p	4	1	1	0	1	4	0
Tytals	40	7	10	1	27	11	6

PORTLAND.	AB	R	BH	SH	PO	A	E
Butchell, s s	5	1	1	0	0	5	0
Howard, c f	3	0	1	2	2	0	0
Parrott W, 3 b	4	2	1	0	6	2	2
Cahill, 2 b	4	1	2	0	2	3	1
Perrier, 1 b	4	1	2	0	11	0	0
Parrott, T, l f	4	1	0	0	1	0	0
McCarthy, c	4	0	1	0	4	1	1
Levy r f	4	0	0	0	0	0	1
Borchers, p	0	0	0	0	0	0	0
Munday, p	4	0	0	0	1	1	0
Total	36	6	8	0	27	12	5

SCORE BY INNINGS.

	1	2	3	4	5	6	7	8	9	
Seattle	4	0	0	3	0	0	0	0	0	—8
Portland	0	0	0	0	0	5	1	0	0	—6

Earned runs—Seattle 3. Two base hits—Hermon, Whiteley and Smith. Double plays—W. Camp, Zimmer and Smith. Bases on balls—Camp 4, Borchers 1, Munday 8. Hits off pitchers—W. Camp 8, Borchers 2. Munday 3. Struck out—By Camp 1, Munday 2. Wild pitches—Borchers 1. Umpire—Ben Young. Time of game, one hour and fifty minutes.

PORTLAND vs. SEATTLE.

Sunday, June 8th, at Seattle.

Parrott was batted all over the lot, and this was the principal reason of Portland's overwhelming defeat. On the other hand, Seattle's star twirler, Fitzgerald, was very effective, keeping the hits well scattered, and giving but one base on balls. The Seattles scored six runs in the first inning, making seven hits off Parrott. In the second they hit him for four more safe shots, adding two runs to their scores. Then they let up till the ninth, when they slaughtered the elongated pitcher again, getting four more "safeties," including a home run by Camp. Notwithstanding the one-sidedness of the score, the fielding was generally good, and at times brilliant. Levy caught an excellent game, barring two passed balls, and "oldman" Perrier did good work at the initial. Billy Cooney made his re-appearance with the team but had no chances. The score:

SEATTLE.	AB.	R.	BH.	SB.	PO.	A.	E.
Hernon, r f	6	2	3	0	1	0	0
Dextraze, l f	6	3	1	0	1	0	0
Whitley, c f	5	3	2	0	1	0	0
Smith, 1st b	6	2	1	0	14	1	0
Zimmer, 2d b	3	2	1	0	1	4	1
Bright, s s	5	2	3	0	1	2	1
L. Camp, 3d b	6	2	4	0	1	5	1
Snyder, c	6	1	2	1	6	0	0
Fitzgerald, p	6	0	1	0	1	2	0
Totals	44	17	18	1	27	14	3

PORTLANDS.	AB.	R.	BH	SB.	PO.	A.	E.
Buchtel, ss	4	0	1	1	2	3	1
Howard, c f	4	0	0	1	1	0	0
W. Parrott, 3b	4	0	0	0	3	1	1
Cooney, r f	4	0	0	0	0	0	0
Cahill, 2b	5	0	0	0	1	2	1
Perrier, 1b	3	0	0	1	11	0	1
T. Parrott, p	4	1	2	0	0	6	1
McCarthy, l f	4	1	3	0	0	0	0
Levy, c	3	1	1	0	8	2	1
Totals	34	3	9	3	27	14	6

SCORE BY INNINGS.

	1	2	3	4	5	6	7	8	9	
Seattles	5	2	0	1	0	1	0	0	7	—17
Portlands	0	0	0	0	1	0	0	2	0	— 3

Earned runs—Seattles 3, Portlands 3.
Two-base hits—Hernon, Whitley, T. Parrott.
Home run—L. Camp.
Stolen bases—Hernon 3 Dextraze 2, Smith, Zimmer.
Double plays—Bright, Zimmer and Smith; Zimmer, Smith and Snyder.
Bases on balls—Off Fitzgerald 1, Parrott 6.
Struck out—By Fitzgerald 4, Parrott 8.
Passed balls—Levy 2.
Wild pitch—Parrott 1.
Time of game—One hour forty minutes.
Umpire—Ben Young.
Scorer—Baxter.

The Amateurs.

Games Played by the California Amateur League and the Pacific Coast Amateur Association.

The Santa Rosas have kept up their winning gait and are now very firm in first position. The Fincks by losing two straight have dropped to third place and the Reports are now second. Vallejo lost another game and the Burlingtons having defeated the Allens last Sunday are now tied with the Marines for fourth place. The Allens are at present the tail enders. The record to date:

Clubs.	Will & Fincks	E. T. Allens	Report	Burlington	Vallejo	Santa Rosa	Games Won	Games Played	Percentage
Will & Fincks	....	2	....	1	2	....	5	8	.625
E. T. Allens	....	....	1	1	....	....	2	10	.200
Reports	2	....	....	2	3	....	7	10	.700
Burlingtons	....	2	....	....	1	....	3	10	.300
Vallejos	....	1	....	1	....	1	3	10	.300
Santa Rosa	1	3	2	2	1	....	9	10	.900
Games Lost	3	8	3	7	7	1	....	....	....

Summary.	Played.	Won.	Lost.	Per C't.
Santa Rosa	10	9	1	.900
Will & Finck	8	5	3	.625
Reports	10	7	3	.700
Vallejo	10	3	7	.300
E. T. Allens	10	2	8	.200
Burlingtons	10	3	7	.300

BURLINGTONS vs. E. T. ALLENS

SUNDAY, JUNE 8TH, AT HAIGHT STREET.

The "Railroaders" and "Sports" came together last Sunday morning, and although errors were numerous, there was plenty of excitement in the game. Both teams presented a rejuverenated appearance, and a good word must be spoken for the new "finds"—Johnson, Walcott, Mulvey and Keily. They are all ball players and will certainly do well.

The Burlingtons took a good lead at the start, and kept adding to their score in nearly every inning.

The Allens, although they hit the ball just as hard, were less fortunate in their run getting. In the ninth inning, however, they made matters very uncomfortable for the Burlingtons. With one man out, Geishaker was safe on Dunn's error of his hard grounder; he promptly stole second and scored on Johnson's pretty drive to left; Reilly then hit safely, and both he and Johnson scored on Evatt's beautiful double to right. Buckley took first on another error by Dunn and Stanley's sacrifice scored Evatt. Five runs and only one more needed to tie the score, but they didn't do it. McCarthy was nervous and retired the side on Dunns assist to Fleming. Both pitchers did well, Walcott being as steady as an old timer. Johnson showed some splendid curves, but was nervous in the fore part of the game and gave eight bases on balls. Stanley and Mulvey were in fine form, and handled their pitchers perfectly. Bradley, Evatt, Buckley and Stanley led in hitting. The score:

Burlingtons.	AB.	R.	BH.	SB.	PO.	A.	E.
Forster, l f	4	4	1	2	0	0	0
Bradley, 2d b	6	2	3	0	0	2	2
Coughlin, s s	5	1	1	0	0	5	1
Dean, c f	6	1	1	0	2	0	0
Mulvey, b	3	0	1	1	7	4	0
Dunn, 3d b	3	0	1	0	2	5	4
Fleming, 1st b	5	0	0	0	14	0	0
Sheridan, r f	3	1	1	0	1	0	0
Walcott, p	4	0	0	0	1	3	0
Totals	38	9	9	3	27	17	7

E. T. Allens.	AB.	R.	BH.	SB.	PO.	A.	E.
Reilly, s s	5	1	1	1	1	5	1
Evatt, 3d b	5	1	2	1	3	3	1
Lewis, 1st b	4	1	1	1	10	0	1
Buckley, 2d b	5	3	2	1	3	3	1
Stanley, c	5	1	1	1	9	3	0
McCarthy, l f	5	0	1	2	0	0	0
Kelly, r f	4	0	1	0	0	1	0
Geishaker, c f	3	1	0	2	0	0	4
Johnson, p	3	1	1	0	1	3	0
Totals	38	8	10	8	27	18	8

SCORE BY INNINGS.

	1	2	3	4	5	6	7	8	9	
Burlingtons	3	1	0	1	1	0	0	1	2	—9
Allens	0	2	0	0	0	0	0	1	5	—8

Earned runs—Allens 3. Three-base hit—Bradley. Two-base hit—Stanley, Evatt. Sacrifice hit—Dean, Stanley (2), Coughlin. First base on errors—Burlingtons, 5; Allens, 5. First base on called balls—Burlingtons, 8; Allens, 1. Left on bases—Burlingtons, 11; Allens 6. Struck out—By Johnson, 7; by Walcott, 8. First base on hit by pitcher—Foster, Lewis. Passed ball—Mulvey. Umpire, John Donohue.

SANTA ROSA vs. WILL & FINCKS.

SATURDAY, JUNE 8TH, AT SANTA ROSA.

The "Young Giants" tackled the "leaders" last Sunday and came off second best. It was a game of the most vital importance to the "Giants" because if they won they would be very close on to the Santa Rosas for first place and by losing they relinquished their hold on second, allowing the Reports to supercede them in that position. Both teams fielded beautifully but the Santa Rosas were stronger at the bat and in running bases. Callen was in fine condition and pitched a great game. The Santa Rosas played superbly but one error being made on their side. Howell also pitched well, but the Sonoma boys developed a hitting streak in the fourth and sixth innings and scored five runs. The Finks had been goose-egged until the ninth, when they also did a little timely hitting. Cusick, Strand and Tillson each hit safely and Billings home run drive cleared the bases, making four earned runs. The excitement at this point was intense but the Fincks couldn't score again and so lost one of the hardest games they ever played. The score.

Santa Rosas.	AB.	R.	BH.	SB.	PO.	A.	E.
Gimmell, l f	4	0	1	0	0	0	0
Cook, 3d b	4	0	1	2	1	2	0
Hulen, 2d b	4	1	2	0	3	3	0
Pace, c	4	1	1	0	6	4	0
Arlett, s s	4	1	2	3	3	3	1
Stultz, 1st b	4	1	1	0	13	0	0
Utt, r f	3	1	2	1	1	0	0
Brown, c f	1	0	0	0	0	0	0
Callen, p	4	0	1	0	0	3	0
Totals	35	5	11	6	27	15	1

Will & Finks.	AB.	R.	BH.	SB.	PO.	A.	E.
Cusick, 1st b	4	1	2	0	12	0	0
Strand, l f	4	1	1	0	1	0	0
Conway, 2d b	4	0	0	0	1	4	0
Tillson, s s	4	1	0	0	1	1	1
Billings, c	5	1	1	0	7	1	1
L. Delmas, 3d b	4	0	0	0	1	4	0
Leveque, c f	4	0	0	0	0	0	0
Twitchell, r f	3	0	0	2	0	0	0
Howell, p	3	0	0	0	1	4	2
Totals	33	4	4	2	24	14	2

SCORE BY INNINGS.

	1	2	3	4	5	6	7	8	9	
Santa Rosas	0	0	0	2	0	3	0	0	*	—5
Will & Fincks	0	0	0	0	0	0	0	0	4	—4

Earned runs—Santa Rosas, 3; Will and Fincks, 4. Home run—Billings. Two-base hits—Gimmell, Hulen (2), Pace, Stultz. Sacrifice hits—Gimmell, Brown, Pace. First base on errors—Santa Rosas, 1; Will & Fincks, 1. Struck out—By Callen, 5; by Howell, 7. Umpire, McConville.

VALLEJOS vs. REPORTS.

SUNDAY, JUNE 8TH, AT VALLEJO.

The Reports won this game in the eleventh inning. They had a slight lead all through till the ninth when the Marines tied the score. Neither side tallied in the tenth and the excitement was great. In the eleventh the Reports hit out three runs and won the game. The batting of the city boys was very heavy, Thompson and Maguire leading. There was also some clever fielding, Farrell, Monet, Hughes, McGuire, McIntyre, Thompson and Sharp excelling in this department. Baltz pitched his usual steady game striking out eleven of the Reports and Farrell rendered him excellent support. The score:

Reports.	AB.	R.	BH.	SB.	PO.	A.	E.
Monet, 1st b	5	0	0	0	18	0	2
McGuire, s s	6	2	2	0	1	5	0
McIntyre, c f	5	3	1	3	2	2	1
Thompson, 2d b	5	1	2	0	5	3	1
Dunphy, 3d b	5	1	1	1	0	5	2
Sharp, l f	5	1	0	0	3	0	0
Gromley, r f	4	2	1	1	0	0	1
Williams, p	5	0	1	1	0	3	1
Green, c	4	0	1	0	8	0	1
Totals	45	10	9	6	*32	18	9

Vallejos.	AB.	R.	BH.	SB.	PO.	A.	E.
Wise, s s	5	2	1	0	2	2	4
Farrell, c	6	2	2	2	10	2	0
Broderick, 3d b	5	0	1	0	1	3	2
Gehrman, r f	5	0	0	0	0	0	0
Stanford, l f	4	0	0	1	2	0	1
Lee, 2d b	5	1	0	1	4	5	1
Bogle, c f	4	1	1	2	1	0	1
Hughes, 1st b	5	1	1	0	13	0	1
Balsz, p	4	0	0	1	0	3	1
Totals	44	7	6	7	33	16	11

*Broderick out for not touching first.

SCORE BY INNINGS.

	1	2	3	4	5	6	7	8	9	10	11	
Reports	1	2	0	3	1	0	0	0	0	0	3	—10
Vallejo	2	0	0	0	0	0	2	0	3	0	0	—7

Earned runs—Reports, 4; Vallejos, 1. Three-base hit—Thompson. Two-base hit—McGuire. First base on errors—Reports, 9; Vallejos, 10. First base on called balls—Reports, 5; Vallejos, 3. Left on bases—Reports, 9; Vallejos, 7. Struck out—By Balsz, 11; Williams, 4. Hit by pitched ball—Dunphy. Wild pitch—Balsz, 1. Passed balls—Farrell, 3. Double plays—Dunphy, Thompson and Monet; McIntyre and Thompson; Wise, Lee and Hughes; Hughes (unassisted). Umpire—Cate.

Amateur Short Hits.

The Burlingtons are doing better.

Jimmy Geishaker had an "off day" last Sunday.

Leveque has not resigned from the Young Giants.

The Vallejos and Burlingtons are now tied for first place.

Gimmel, of the Santa Rosas, leads the amateurs in fielding.

The M. J. Flavins play the San Rafaels Sunday, for $50 a side.

Crackbon of the C. A. Murdochs is said to be a promising twirler.

Stocky Billy Kelly, of the Allens, has the actions of a good ball player.

Twitchell, an old timer, played right field for the Fincks last Sunday.

First base is Hen Stultz's position and he should be kept on that bag.

Dick Nagle has left Marysville, and is now playing first base for Merced.

Extra inning games are quite frequent with the California Amateur League.

The Antiochs defeated the Wilsons of Vallejo last Sunday by a score of nine to eight.

Donovan of the old Greenhoods would be a fine player for some of the amateur teams.

Cusick will play right field for the "Giants" Sunday. Frank Delmas will occupy his old position at first.

Sharp is chasing Gimmel pretty close for fielding honors. The managers of the big league want to keep their eye on this player.

The Rosedales beat the Young Stars last Sunday and Manager Murphy would like to hear from the Shamrocks.—Address 411 Clemintina St.

In Johnson, the Allens have another good pitcher. It is true he is not as speedy as McDonald, but his curves are just as deceiving, and he possesses a cool head when men are on bases.

The Vallejos are just now without a manager, Campbell having resigned. It is said that Broderick and Hughes are without engagements, the team being unable to keep paying them salaries.

In the Amateur League there are several players who have been often seen wearing professional uniforms. They are Buckley, Baltz, Cusick, Williams, Thompson, Monet, Stanley, Lewis and Evatt.

The Fultons will hereafter be known as the M. J. Flavins. The team is open to challenges from any club in the State and communications may be address to F. A. Griffing, Manager, 928 Market St.

Young Mulvey, the Burlington's new catcher, is a "clinker." He has a neat style in catching, and throws strongly to bases. With a little more experience with his pitcher, he will be reckoned one of the best back-stops in the league.

Genial Jim Cusick played a great game at first last Sunday for the "Young Giants". He filled Delmas' position to perfection accepting twelve difficult chances. His hitting was also a feature. In the first inning Jim led off with a hit—the only one secured by the team till the ninth, when he came first to bat again and started the ball rolling with another safe shot.

The standing of the teams of the Pacific Amateur League as computed by scorer Knowles, is:

	Won	Lost	Play'd	Per ct
E. & O. E	3	2	5	.600
Reliance	3	2	5	.600
U. C.	2	3	5	.400
A. N. A. C.	1	2	3	.333

Frank S. Sheridan is now the acting manager of the Burlington team, Gage being unable to attend to the duties on account of other business.

The local amateurs complain that the scorers in the interior towns are continually giving the visiting teams the "worst of it." A prominent amateur said the other day "We can't expect a square deal" from the scorers up country, having never received any thing like a fair show yet. They seem only too willing to give us an error on the slightest pretext and never considerer the adverse circumstances under which some plays are attempted. Then we are often robbed of base hits, sacrifices, base steals and accepted chances, while the home teams always get full credit for every thing they do and a great deal they don't do."

If Loughran could be induced to play again in the Amateur League what an excellent addition he would be to Warrens "Young Giants." They need a change pitcher to relieve Howell and Frank could fill the bill to the Queen's taste. His fielding is of the Roberts style and it is doubtful if any amateur on the coast can touch him. His batting lately is said to be of a very high order also.

No game was played by the Pacific Amateur League last Saturday, the E & O E's being without a full nine. Umpire Van Court declared the game forfeited to the Reliance team score 9 to 0.

Next Saturday the schedule will be completed, the competing teams to be the Reliance and Anglo-Nevadas. Murphy will pitch for the Relience team and either Downey or Rosborough will catch, Clements arm being in poor condition.

The statement published in last Saturday's issue of the BREEDER AND SPORTSMAN that Dave Creamer, the well known second baseman, had been released from the E. T. Allens, did not create much of a surprise. For some time it has been whispered and rumored in private circles, especially among the members of the Raquet Club, that since Dave quit playing with the Stockton team, he has fallen desperately in love with a charming young lady residing near the classic precincts of Seventh and Bryant streets, and, as a result, has neglected ball playing for more congenial amusement. He has also secured a good position with a wholesale cigar firm, and is saving his money with an eye to the future. When questioned as to whether he personally intends to solve that all absorbing question, "Is marriage a failure?" Dave becomes very conservative, and prefers to talk on the success of Tom Powers in Baltimore, but before you leave him he generally finds opportunity to innocently inquire, "How much do you think it would cost to furnish a house of about five rooms?"

The Allens are now in great shape to do some tall ball playing, and they must be counted as "very much in the race", even though they are at the "bottom of the heap" just at present. Manager Keller has been indefatigable in his efforts to have a winning nine, and it must be admitted that his team has played in very "hard luck." But with his new timber we expect to see a big change in the team's playing, and would not be at all surprised to find the "Sports" holding at least second or third place when the season closes. The pitching department is very strong now and by giving both McDonald and Johnson plenty of practice, their only defect—wildness, will be overcome. Stanley is the "star" back stop of the league, and his throwing to bases is a feature of every game he plays in. The infield is somewhat different from the way we stated it last week, and the present arrangement is undoubtedly the best that could be conceived. Lewis is physically fitted to be a fine first baseman, having a long reach and being a sure catcher of hard thrown balls. Tom Buckleys abilities are too well known to need any extended mention in these columns, and Evatt is better placed at third than on first, being lively in pickups and a strong accurate thrower. Josh Reilly is in his element at short, or more properly speaking, all over the field, for we have never seen in any amateur team a harder worker; one who never loses sight of the ball and who is always on the alert backing basemen, than this rising young player. The out field also shows increased strength; McCarthy, Geishaker and Kelly being able to care for everything coming their way. As a hitting team, the Allens ought from this on do some powerful work, for Buckley, Evatt, Lewis, Reilly, Stanley and Kelly are clever, hard strikers. With judicious coaching and good captaining the team ought to push its way rapidly to the front.

SCHEDULE OF GAMES

—OF THE—

CALIFORNIA

Base Ball League,

SEASON 1890.

June 14th to June 21st Inclusive

AT SAN FRANCISCO.

JUNE 14 ......San Francisco vs. Sacramento
JUNE 15 ......San Francisco vs. Oakland
JUNE 19 ......Oakland vs. Stockton
JUNE 21 ......San Francisco vs. Stockton

AT SACRAMENTO.

JUNE 15 ......Sacramento vs. Stockton
JUNE 20 ......Sacramento vs. Oakland
JUNE 21 ......Sacramento vs. Oakland

AT OAKLAND.

JUNE 15 ......San Francisco vs. Oakland
JUNE 20 ......San Francisco vs. Stockton

AT STOCKTON.

JUNE 14 ......Stockton vs. Oakland
JUNE 15 ......Stockton vs. Sacramento, A. M.

Official Schedule California Amateur League.

AT HAIGHT STREET GROUNDS.

JUNE 15 ......Will and Fincks vs. E. T. Allens

AT VALLEJO.

JUNE 15 ......Vallejo vs. Santa Rosa

AT SANTA ROSA.

JUNE 15 ......Burlingtons vs. Daily Reports

The official schedule of the California Base Ball League and Amateur League will be published weekly in this space.

ATHLETICS.

Athletic Sports and Other Pastimes.

EDITED BY ARISTIPPUS,

SUMMARY.

The great athletic event of 1890 is passed and a general quietness now prevails in amateur athletic circles. The new Olympic grounds will in a way help to keep up the interest in athletics, but it is very probable that the majority of the crack amateurs will go out of training, now that they have ended their duty of representing their clubs at the annual championship meeting. There is a great boom in cycling, but a general dullness prevails in the aquatic world.

IN THE SURF.

There is an increased attendance at the different surf baths along the coast. At Santa Cruz, Capitola and Monterey especially the number of bathers for this time of the year is unusually large. Quite a number of our local society ladies who are summering at Santa Cruz swim to the rafts daily, and their daring feats in the ocean never fail to excite admiration from the spectators on shore.

The Terrace Baths at Alameda were packed on Sunday. It was the best day of the season so far. The Pacific Club boys were out in full force as usual, and some of their exhibitions gained considerable applause.

The members of the Lurline Club took the customary practice spins on Sunday, and are getting into trim for the swimming and diving contests which will shortly take place under the auspices of their club. Their club house is admirably situated and the athletes can get up a sweat in the gymnasium and afterwards take a plunge in the open sea.

The Olympic Club will probably in the course of time follow the examples of some of the leading Eastern Amateur Clubs by building a boating and bathing establishment for the use of its members. There are several fine oarsmen and swimmers amongst the members of the O. A. C. and such an addition would most unquestionably prove a great boom.

A sad accident happened at the Terrace Baths, Alameda, on Sunday afternoon last. A young man from Stockton was in bathing in the surf and not being acquainted with the depths of the water, he essayed to dive head foremost from a height of ten feet into eighteen inches of water. The result of his mistake was an injured spine and several bad bruises. The Doctors who attended him were of the opinion that he could not recover. During the past couple of years similar accidents have occurred at both houses in this city resulting fatally in some instances. Bathers have been cautioned time and time again about the folly of diving into water without having first ascertained its depth. We hope Sundays unfortunate accident will influence bathers to be more cautious in future.

CLUB JOTTINGS.

The University athletes are much disheartened over their late defeat by the Olympic Club. Had the students trained as faithfully as the Olympic boys the result would have been more even. It is exceedingly doubtful if the Berkeley men will ever make as good a fight again for the championship pennant, for, while their team may remain just as it is the O. A. C. team will continue to grow larger and stronger so that by next Decoration Day several more men like Schifferstein, Jarvis, Purcell, Cassady, Cooley and Scott are likely to wear the flying O on their shirts.

Lieutenant Donnelly of the O. A. C. has called a cross country run for Sunday June 22. The rendezvous will probably be Sausalito. It is expected that a large number of novices will make their debut and that this will be the most successful run of the year so far

The cross country run of the Lurline Club which was to have taken place last Sunday has been indefinitely postponed.

The Acme and Alameda Olympic Clubs propose to hold several cross country runs during the season. All associate clubs of the P. C. A. A. A. will be invited to attend.

Captain John D. Garrison, of the Alpine Club, has called a run for to-morrow from Jackson's Villa, Sausalito. The run will be to Blythedale and return, a distance of about ten miles. Members are requested to take the 10 A. M. Sausalito boat from this side.

P. C. A. A. A.

RULE XVII.

THE COURSE.

Each competitor shall keep in his respective position from start to finish in all races on straightaway tracks, and in all races on tracks with one or more turns he shall not cross to the inner edge of the track, except when he is at least six feet in advance of his nearest competitor.

The Referee shall disqualify from that event any competitor who wilfully pushes against, impedes, crosses the course of, or in any way interferes with another competitor.

The Referee shall disqualify from further participation in the games any contestant competing to lose, to coach, or in any way impede the chances of another competitor, either in a trial or final contest.

RULE XVIII.

FINISH.

The finish of the course shall be represented by a line between two finishing posts, drawn across and at right angles to the sides of the track, and three feet above which line shall be placed a tape, attached at either end to the finishing posts.

The tape is to be considered the finishing line for the winner, but the order of finishing across the track line shall determine the positions of the other competitors.

A finish shall be counted when any part of the contestant's body, except his hands or arms, shall touch the tape at the finish line.

RULE XIX.

HURDLES.

Different heights, distances and number of hurdles may be selected for hurdle races.

In the 120-yard hurdle race, ten hurdles shall be used, each hurdle to be three feet six inches high. They shall be placed ten yards apart, with the first hurdle fifteen yards distant from the starting mark, and the last hurdle fifteen yards before the finishing line. In the 220-yard hurdle race, ten hurdles shall be used, each hurdle to be two feet six inches high. They shall be placed twenty yards apart, with the first hurdle twenty yards distant from the starting mark and the last hurdle twenty yards before the finishing line.

In hurdle races of other distances and with different numbers of hurdles, the hurdles shall be placed at equal intervals, with the same space between the first hurdle and the starting point and the last hurdle and the finishing line as between each of the hurdles.

In making a record it shall be necessary for the competitor to jump over every hurdle in its proper position.

RULE XX.

JUMPING.

SECTION 1. All jumping shall be made without any assisting devices.

A fair jump shall be one that is made without the assistance of weights, diving, somersets, or handsprings of any kind.

In all handicap jumps the scratch man shall be entitled to try last.

SEC. 2. The Running High Jump.—The Field Judges shall decide the height, at which the jump shall commence, and shall regulate the succeeding elevations.

Each competitor shall be allowed three trial jumps at each height, and if on the third trial he shall fail he shall be declared out of the competition.

Competitors shall jump in order as placed in the programme; then those failing, if any, shall have their second jump trial in like order; after which those having failed twice shall make their third trial jump.

The jump shall be made over a bar resting on pins, projecting not more than three inches from the uprights, and when this bar is removed from its place it shall be counted as a trial jump.

Running under the bar in making an attempt to jump shall be counted as a "balk," and three successive "balks" shall be counted as a trial jump.

The distance of the run before the jump shall be unlimited.

A competitor may decline to jump at any height in his turn, and by so doing forfeits his right to again jump at the height he declined.

SEC. 3. The Standing High Jump.—The feet of the competitor may be placed in any position, but shall leave the ground only once in making an attempt to jump. When the feet are lifted from the ground twice, or two springs are made in making the attempt, it shall count as a trial jump without result.

With this exception the rules governing the high jump shall also govern the standing high jump.

SEC. 4. The Running Broad Jump.—When jumped on earth, a joist five inches wide shall be sunk flush with the earth. The outer edge of the joist shall be called the scratch line, and the measurement of all jumps shall be made from it at right angles to the nearest break in the ground made by any part of the person of the competitor.

In front of the scratch line the ground shall be removed to the depth of three and the width of twelve inches outward.

A foul jump shall be one where the competitor, in jumping off the scratch line, makes a mark on the ground immediately in front of it, and shall count as a trial jump without result.

Each competitor shall have three trial jumps, and the best three shall each have three more trial jumps.

The competition shall be decided by the best of all the trial jumps of the competitors.

The distance of the run before the scratch lines shall be unlimited.

SEC. 5 The Pole Vault.—Poles shall be furnished by the club giving the games, but contestants may use their private poles if they so desire, in which case the other contestants shall also be allowed to use them if they wish. The poles shall be unlimited as to size and weight, but shall have no assisting devices excepting one prong at the end.

The rules governing the running high jump shall also govern the pole vault for hight, and the rules governing the running broad jump shall also govern the pole vault for distance.

SEC. 6. The Standing Broad Jump.—The feet of the competitor may be placed in any position, but shall leave the ground only once in making an attempt to jump. When the feet are lifted from the ground twice, or two springs are made in making the attempt, it shall count as a trial jump without result.

In all other respects the rule governing the running broad jumps shall also govern the standing broad jump.

SEC. 7. The Three Standing Broad Jumps.—The feet of the competitor shall leave the ground only once in making an attempt for each of the three jumps, and no stoppage between jumps shall be allowed.

In all other respects the rules governing the standing broad jump shall also govern the three standing broad jumps.

SEC. 8. Running, Hop, Step and Jump.—The competitor shall first land upon the same foot with which he shall have taken off. The reverse foot shall be used for the second landing, and both feet shall be used for the third landing.

In all other respects the rules governing the running broad jump shall also govern the running hop, step and jump.

RULE XXI.

PUTTING THE SHOT.

The shot shall be a solid sphere, made of metal, of the requisite weight.

It shall be put with one hand, and in making the attempt it shall be above and not behind the shoulder.

The competitor shall stand in a circle seven feet in diameter, on four feet of the circumference of which shall be placed a board four inches high, at which the competitor must stand when the shot leaves his hand.

A fair put shall be one in which no part of the person of the competitor shall touch in front of the circle or on the board in making the attempt.

A put shall be counted as foul if the competitor steps over the front half of the circle or on the board before the measurement of his put is made.

Foul puts and letting go the shot in making an attempt shall be counted as trial puts without result.

The measurement of all puts shall be made from the nearest mark made by the shot to a point on the circumference of the circle, on a line with the object mark and the center of the circle.

A board similar to the one in front may also be used at the back of the circle. The order of competing and number of trials shall be the same as for the running broad jump. Shots shall be furnished by the club giving the games. Any contestant may use his private shot if correct in weight and shape, in which case the other contestants must also be allowed to use it if they wish.

AT THE OARS.

The coming regatta will hardly be as successful as expected. Somehow or other the oarsmen do not seem inclined to settle down to hard work, and in consequence, no brilliant performances may be looked forward to. We do not understand the dullness which at present prevails in rowing circles, unless it be that people are losing interest in aquatic sports. The bay of San Francisco contains some of the finest courses in the United States, and it is a great pity that rowing is not more extensively practiced and fostered.

The annual single scull race at Victoria, B. C., was rowed on May 30th for $30 and a cup presented by R. C. Davis. William Cotsford, C. Bush and J. Seely entered. Cotsford and Bush got away together, Seely following close after them, but falling behind at every stroke. After the first half mile Cotsford showed his friends that he had not forgotten his old-time business and he pulled a good race, being about five lengths ahead of Bush when he showed up. Bush came in second, Seely having no place in the race.

Owing to the low tide on Sunday the South End men were unable to launch their boats and very few crews were out.

J. B. Barber has challenged Joseph S. Nyland, of the Ariel Club, for a three-mile race with a turn, over a course near Tiburon, for a purse of $250.

The Columbia Rowing Club of Oakland is considering the advisability of sending a crew to compete for the Amateur championship at the Victoria (B. C.) regatta, which will be held on Dominion Day, July 1st.

The Lurline canoe fleet and several shells were out on Sunday. The Lurline boys are hard workers, and will make a good showing before the close of the season.

THE WHEELMEN.

The following notice has been issued to all California L. A. W. members:

SAN JOSE, Cal., June 6, 1890.

DEAR SIR: If you will attend the 5th annual meet of the Cal. Division L. A. W. at San Jose, please notify the committee at once whom you wish to invite to the Division party, to be held on Saturday evening, July 5th, at the Hotel Vendome. The hotel will accommodate but a limited number, and we shall give every visiting member an opportunity to invite a few friends. Fraternally yours,

O. GRANICHER.

The following is a complete list of the wheelmen who rode all the way to Hollister on June 1st: W. M. Meeker, in charge of the run—A M Thompson, George P Wetmore, F R Cook, T. L. Hill, E C Landis, F W Ray, A E McKinney, J L Miller, J F C Holroyd, C Elmer, G A Morrill, T E Bullevant, G Sheller, H A Pogue, W I Gilmour, T W Gilmour, C H Bliss, E S Broadwater, R Fairbanks, W W Needham, G L Kessling, J A Delmas, H Smith, J Smith, F Larder, A Rivett, E D Woodmen, O Granicher, Y D Hensiel, A A Deesing, W R Lipsett, R R Martin, L G Hodgkins, A E J Nye, H C Hyde, E C Tole, H W Spaulding, L A Connoy, W G Watchers, F A Leadbettle, J A McNamara, C Lapson, J B Lamb, C N Langton, S Lubin, C W Hammer, Sanford Plummer, A D Allen, J G Cox, W E Thompson, T H Doane, T Stevenson, H F Wyne, L S Stewart, F A McGrew, R A Smyth. Of the wheels ridden, forty-three were "ordinary" and ten were safeties.

The San Jose wheelmen are making great preparations for the coming two day's meet. They will do all in their power to make things pleasant and comfortable for the visiting riders, and are sparing no pains to have the new four-lap track in good order and suitable for record breaking. The local wheelmen have been training faithfully for some weeks past and a good many of the existing coast records will probably go under on July 4 and 5.

PROFESSIONAL SPRINTING.

A moderate crowd of people, many of whom were ladies, was present at Central Park on Sunday afternoon to witness the third Sheffield Handicap. Although a good many well known sprinters were entered the betting was tame.

Captain Jordan of the Olympic Club and several other delegates of the P. C. A. A. A. were noticed amongst the audience, and any amateur who took part in the heats will be summarily dealt with should he attempt to hoodwink any of the amateur clubs in future by posing as an amateur.

The following is a summary of the heats. 135 yard run

1st heat, E. Tiers, 13 yards, 1st. Time 14 1-5 seconds, W. Little, 17 yards, 2nd.

2nd heat: A. D. Leighton, 24 yards, 1st. Time, 13 2-5. J. P. Haughn, 13 yards, 2nd.

3d heat: J. F. Heenan, 21½ yards, 1st. Time, 14 secs. D. B. Thomas, 21 yards, 2nd.

4th heat: L. A. Clinton, 21 yards, 1st. Time, 13 4-5 secs. W. A. Hendrick, 26 yards, 2nd.

5th heat: C. Morrow, 12 yards, 1st. Time, 13 1-5 secs. C. A. Eldridge, 10 yards, 2nd.

6th heat: B Campbell, 19½ yards, 1st. Time, 13 2-5 secs. T. J. Riley, 19 yards, 2nd.

7th heat: Tom Kendal, 18½ yards, 1st. Time, 14 secs. G. Bartels, 21 yards, 2nd.

8th heat: H. M. Johnson, 8½ yards, 1st. Time, 13 secs. W. J. Farmer, 16 yards, 2nd.

1st Final heat: Kendal 1st. Time, 13 1-5 secs. Tiers, 2nd.

2nd Final heat: Clinton 1st. Time 12 2-5 secs. Campbell, 2nd.

The concluding heat was won by Clinton; Campbell, 2nd, Tiers, 3rd.

The purse of $100 was distibuted proportionately to the first three.

The officers of the day were. Official Handicapper, Jos. Acton; Judge, Billy Jordan; Timekeeper, Ed. Eratt.

The next Sheffield handicap will take place on July 4th, when $250 will be given to the winners.

RUNNERS, WALKERS, JUMPERS, ETC.

In consequence of the Little trouble, P. N. Gafney of the Alpine Amateur Athletic Club has declined to serve another term as delegate to the P. C. A. A. A. Owing to business matters, Mr. Gafney has been unable to accept any office in his club for the next term.

George W. Jordan of the O. A. C. has also resigned as a delegate, and will be succeeded by James H. Gilhuly. Mr. Jordan states that his reason for resigning is because some of the other clubs' delegates opposed his action in barring Little of the Alpine Club from the championship games.

Commencing at 2 P. M. on July 4th, the Olympic Athletic Club will hold a handicap meeting at its new grounds. The following programme has been decided upon,

1. 100-yard, handicap (open).
2. 220-yards, Hammersmith medal (open).
3. 1 mile walk, handicap (open).
4. Running broad jump (club) handicap.
5. 1,000-yard run handicap (club).
6. 2-mile run, handicap (open).
7. 100-yard partnership race (club).
8. 300-yard handicap (club).

Entries will close at 8 P. M. June 28th, at the Olympic club rooms.

The club events are open to members of the Olympic Club only. The open events are open to members of clubs belonging to the P. C. A. A. A.

The Directors of the Alpine Club have decided to postpone the boxing tournament until next month. A fine exhibition however, will be given towards the end of June. Next month the prizes won at the late Field Day will be distributed to the winners.

TURF AND TRACK.

W. H. McCarthy does not work the Brookdale horses on Sundays.

Belle Hamlin 2:12½ is receiving a special preparation for a fashionable record.

Addie Bell 2:22¼ has been sent to Ewell Farm to be bred to Brown Hal 2:12½.

The dam of Maud Messenger 2:16¾ has been bred to Lord Wilkes by Guy Wilkes.

The colored ring are said to have scooped in a big pile on Sinoloa II last week.

James Stinson of Chicago has bought from Samuel Fleming two sisters of M'liss 2:21.

Daisy D. has returned to Fresno, having been stinted to Cheviot since the Sacramento races.

Bow Bells has so far recovered that he will be taken through the Southern Circuit by Thomas.

Brown Hal is said to be moving quarters at an amazing gait, and Johnston's record is said to be in danger.

An offer of $10,000 for Miss Alice 2:20½ by Alcantara, dam Thorndale Maid was refused and $15,000 asked.

Sunol is the pride of Terre Haute. Never a stage nor professional beauty's photograph sold as here has in the last few weeks.

Proctor Knott picked up a nail last week, which necessitated a let up in his work for a few days, or he would have been out ere this.

Bruce Cockrill says that the yearling colt, (half brother to Capt. Al) by Ironclad out of Black Maria, is the most racy looking colt he has ever seen.

George Land has sold for $1,200 to R. S. Strader, Lexington, Kentucky, the three-year-old blk. c. Anglan Boy, by Wilkes Boy-Lady West, by Allie West.

A. L. Whitney's two year old filly 'Anna Bell' by Dawn dam by Hubbard beat her solitary opponent in the two year old stake at Sacramento in 2.53 and 3.01.

Tycoon, who was purchased by L. J. Rose from J. Hill, will probably be seen on the circuit again this year instead of being sent east as was at first intended.

The Willows Agricultural Association is building a number of new stalls on the race course to accomodate the many racing men who participate in their annual races.

Jess Armstrong (the horse who broke his leg at St. Louis) had to be killed. His leg was amputated, but afterwards it was decided to kill him as he was in such misery.

Mr. C. O. Seaman of San Diego, the former owner of Bell Boy, has a gold mounted tooth of the unfortunate horse, the only substantial portion of him remaining after his death.

The Kentucky Stock Farm had as a frontis-piece last week a group of free-for-all pacers; Johnston in the center, and heads of Budd Doble, Roy Wilkes, Lillian and Ed Annan.

Kelseyville is rapidly coming into favor among the trotting talent in Lake County. Corcoran is there with a string of five; Hiram Tracy has two, and C. S. Piner is working four.

The Owens brothers are working Capt. Al, Mero, 2—Wildidle—Precious and several youngsters on their track near Fresno. Daisy D. will be put in training for the fall races.

The State of Maine values the horses within her lines at over $10,000,000, without putting on any fancy values. Such being the case, this industry alone is of much value to the State.

The purest gaited and most promising youngster under Bither's care at the Allen Farm is Experta, a two year sister to Express 2:21 by Electioneer out of Esther a thoroughbred mare,

Ella Hopkins, the dam of Geneva S. 2:19½, Quinine S 2:28½ and Mattie H 2:24½, was bred to a jack for two seasons and had that valuable animal been living she would probably having been raising mules yet.

Fides, the winner of the Toboggan Slide, is exceptionally highly bred, by imported Ill Used out of imported Filagree by Stockwell, out of Extasy by Touchstone, thus having a double Stockwell strain.

J. H. Goldsmith made a good start at Dundee Park last week winning the three minute class with Dawson in straight heats 2:31½, 2:26½, 2:28¾, and the 2:20 with (Mr. Valensin's) Simmocolon 2:25½, 2:24½ 2:23½.

John Splan now has about twenty five head of trotters and pacers in training at Cleveland. Among the string is Charley Friel 2:15½. Jas. McLaughlin, a son of Red Bill McLaughlin is Splan's understudy.

Tirailleur, who after Corunna, is the boss New Zealand three year old this year is called "Tra-la-la" by the stable boys. A New Zealand jockey loves French names as much as the gaily dressed bookmaker does.

We have had exceptionally flattering accounts of Lucy Abbott, who obtained a record of 2:26½ at Denver. Pete Brandow's erstwhile pet is now the *Du* Bois brothers' pride, and a mark below 20 is confidently expected.

Mr. McMillan has made an offer to trot Governor Stanford 2.23¾, by Electioneer, out of Barnes by Whipple's Hambletonian against Mr. Hamlin's Chimes by Electioneer out of Beautiful Bells for $1,000 or $5,000 a side.

Palo Alto will have a useful stable for the fall, despite their many sales. Peel is doing fair work and is expected to stand up, while Faustine, Muta and several of the youngsters will be in good trim when required.

Sir William the three year old son of Sir Modred and Vesper, who ran so well in Australia this season over all distances is sire of about fifteen foals, having been turned loose with a band of mares prior to being put into training.

W. H. Wilson Cynthiana has purchased Colon, the dam of Simmocolon, and Patchmore, by Strathmore, from Mrs. A. P. Dills, Hopkinsville, Ky. Colon is in foal to Simmons. Mr. Wilson also bought a yearling by Gordon 3127 out of Colon.

A. Smith McCann of Lexington has sold to Schmulbach & Park of Wheeling, West Va., for $4,500, two yearling fillies by Red Wilkes, dams by Star Almont, and the two year old bay filly Lady McGregor, by Red Wilkes, dam by Robert McGregor.

Soprano, by Strathmore, 408, dam Abbess, by Albion, was foaled in 1875, and she is the youngest broodmare that has three representatives in the 2:30 list. She is the dam of C. F. Clay, 2:18; Eminence. 2:18¾, and Strathbridge, 2:28½, all by different horses.

Prince Royal, carrying 116 lbs. last Wednesday at Westchester, ran one and one-sixteenth miles in 1:46½, the last mile in 1:40, beating all previous records by three-quarters of a second. Evidently the Prince has a good chance for the Suburban yet.

Horses run in all shapes. Tirailleur, the New Zealand crack race horse is said to be a slab-sided, three-cornered kind of a horse, while Tenny, Dave Pulsifer's pet, would not be taken as a model by a sculptor, *mais n'importe*, they race in all shapes.

The Valentine Ranch near Pleasanton, which was purchased a few weeks ago for Senator Hearst, will be used principally for training purposes, a mile track will soon be built and the youngsters from the San Simeon and Cambria ranchos will be sent up as soon as they are broken.

Messrs. W. R. Hearst and J. Follansbee have gone to their ranch in Chihuahua, Mexico. Mr. Follansbee will put in training there Lovelace 3 by Kyrle Daly out of My Love and Kingmaker by Warwick out of Sister to Jim Douglass, and if they show up well will bring them here for the fall meeting of the Blood Horse.

T. H. Williams Jr. last week purchased from Palo Alto Stock Farm the two-year-old Rinfax by Argyle, out of imp. Amelia. Rinfax won a sweepstake for two-year-olds at San Jose, and the Matadero Stakes at Sacramento. He will join the Undine stable, which is at present at Washington Park, Chicago.

W. M. Murry started out in winning form on the opening day last Tuesday at Kansas City. Lord of the Harem; Wildidle—Frolic ran a good second for the Derby, while Parapet Bulwark—Nelly Brady won a five furlong for two year olds and Kiro .3. Hooker—by Foster easily accounted for the six furlong and repeat.

The often quoted veteran racing reformer, Admiral Rous—than whom there was no firmer believer in the progress of the thoroughbred, wrote: "The form of Flying Childers might win a £30 plate, winner to be sold for £40; Highflyer and Eclipse might pull through in a £50 plate, winner to be sold for £200.

Representatives of the Willows, Red Bluff, Chico and Marysville district fairs held a meeting in Marysville last Monday and formed a circuit commencing at Willows August 12th–16th, thence to Red Bluff, 19th–25th and Chico, 26th–30th, winding up with Marysville Sept. 2nd to 6th. Upwards of $20,000 will be offered in purse and stakes.

Andy McDowell left Pleasanton last Wednesday with Direct, 2:18½, Margaret S., 2:19½, Cricket and Katy S. for the Eastern campaign. All of them have been showing great form in their work this season, and great things are expected from them. T. H. Williams sent his recent purchase, Rinfax, in the same car; he will be turned over at Chicago to McCormick.

W. J. Gordon has found a mate for the great Guy, as far as matching in regard to color, size and appearance. The two sons of Kentucky Prince are so much alike that half the people seeing them hitched double for the first time were unable to tell which was Guy and which was Prince Hogarth. Mr. Gordon made his purchase at the recent Fasig sale, and paid $2,150 for the Prince.

Among the purchasers at the Dixiana sale were Messrs. Haggin, Rose and Daly. Marcus Daly paid $4100 for a colt by Alarm out of Adonia and $650 for a colt by Alarm out of Queechy. J. B. Haggin paid $1,500 for the Himyar—Hearsay filly, $1,500 for a colt by Alarm—Haz'em and $1,400 for two others. L. J. Rose gave $650 for a Himyar filly. The 29 head sold for $32,575.

Bravo, the winner of the last Melbourne Cup, has been purchased by Mr. Southall for Messrs. Apcar & Gasper, two prominent Indian turfites. Thirteen hundred guineas was the price paid for Grand Flaneur's son, and, as Mr. Cripps, who purchased him under the hammer last November, only gave 975 guineas for him, he has cleared about 30 per cent, on his five months' investment.

In the House of Commons on May 15th, Mr. Matthews, in answer to Mr. Samuel Smith, said, that every telegram with respect to betting, was not illegal, but only those inviting bets, or advertising special information or advice, with a view to betting. Mr. Matthews said there would be a great difficulty in having such a complete examination of all telegrams as would be necessary to detect those contravening the act.

The English horse Trappist—in his day one of the crack sprinters, has joined the majority. He was by the recently defunct Hermit out of Bunch, by Muscovite out of Diomedia, and when in the zenith of his racing career was the property of Captain Prime, for whom he won the Stewards' Cup at Goodwood in 1875. The best of his produce is probably L'Abbesse de Jouarre, last year's Oaks victress. He was latterly owned by the Duke of Hamilton.

Australians follow the old English plan in dealing with Welshers, an exchange says: A disturbance occurred on the centre of the course at Randwick shortly after the race for the Sydney Cup. One of the speculative gentry, who had evidently overlaid Carbine in his book, was about to make an unostentatious exit from the course, but his victims intercepted him, and treated him to such rough usage that when he escaped his clothing presented a scene of wreckage rarely witnessed on a racecourse.

Jimmie McLaughlin's little nine year old son is already quite a horseman. He exercises a few of the Lorillard string every morning, and it is said that he sits his saddle like a veteran. In face and figure he is remarkably like his father.

"Lucky" Baldwin is as lucky on the turf as in dealings with mining stocks and real estate says a New York daily. He is about five feet nine inches tall, thin and of dark complexion. His hair is gray, and so are his mustache and goatee. He does not bet much. If he has a good thing he will put up $500, and he is nervous and excited all the time until he has won or lost. He places his money himself, and is usually to be found in the betting ring watching the odds of the bookmakers, waiting to get the best of the odds.

Mr. Tom Merry, acting on behalf of Mr. L. J. Rose, has purchased the following thoroughbred mares in Victoria: Catherine's Wheel (full sister to Tantallon), 6 yrs., by Wellington from Phizgig (imported—dam of Suwarrow); Harmony, 5 years, by The Drummer (imported), from Maritana, by New Warrior from Mermaid (grandam of Melos and The Broker); also Spinach, 2 yrs., by Atlantic, from Seakale by Ladykirk, from Saucepan (imported, dam of Haricot, Fryingpan, etc.) Catherine's Wheel is in foal to Dunlop, and Harmony and Spinach are to be served by him at once to foal to American time

It is said that Mr. Abington (Baird) has already run through £500,000 in his short and stormy career on the turf. Mr. Abington started out badly, being ruled off for fixing a race—at Derby, I think, in which he rode the winner. In those days he was one of the worst riders among the so-called gentlemen jocks, but he has shown great improvement in style, seat and finish since his return to the turf, and is now a fairly good rider. One of his first purchases on his being re-instated was the mare Busybody for 8,800 guineas at the Falmouth sale in the spring of 1884, in which year she won the One Thousand and Oaks before breaking down.

The S. S. Alameda which arrived from Australia had on board six mares purchased for Mr. L. J. Rose by T. B. Merry, and a two year old colt. Seven mares were shipped, but one, a full sister to the renowned Sheet Anchor, died en route. The six which arrived were all very healthy but in poor condition evidently having been shipped lean and seem very weedy specimens to be by such horses as Darebin, Musket and The Drummer. What their dams were I could not find out as Mr. Merry's men knew next to nothing about them. Mr. Merry will come on the next trip with the other eight mares which are being bred.

The following horses have recently been purchased in Montana for Senator Fair's breeding farm, close to Knight's landing, near Sacramento: Fanny McGregor, chestnut filly, by Robert McGregor, dam Fanny Patchen by Mambrino Patchen; Hattie H., bay filly, by Wyoming Chief, dam Flora Wilkes by George Wilkes; Lizzie H., bay filly, by Wyoming Chief, dam by Dictator, second dam by Fanny Patchen; Annie Kirkwood, chestnut filly, by Satinwood, dam Annie Kirksey; Zettie, bay filly by Wyoming Chief, dam Flora Wilkes by George Wilkes, and Princess Wilkes, black filly, by Ned Wilkes, dam by American Clay.

Although the racing season of 1889–90 will not actually close for over a month, the Hon. J. White has broken all previous records concerning the amount of stakes won, his total being over £20,000. This (writes the Leader) is a substantial increase on the largest suur ever previously won by one owner in a season in Australia, the highest sum in former seasons (all to Mr. White's credit) being £16,728 for 1887–8; £15,027 for 1885–6; £14,496 for 1888–9; and £13,783 for 1887–7. The Hon. D. S. Wallace will again be second on the list of winning owners, having up to date won about £9,400 in stakes. Last year the contest between the two most popular owners in New South Wales and Victoria respectively was much closer, Mr. White winning £14,496, and Mr. Wallace £10,327.

Phaeton, the well known racing correspondent of the Auckland Weekly News, says: "Since the mighty deeds of Carbine at the recent A. J. C. Meeting I have heard many arguments as to his height and measurements with those of his sire. In order to settle a dispute on the point, I have looked up the question, and the following is the result:

MUSKET.		CARBINE.	
Height,	16h. 1½ in.	Height,	16h. ½in.
Girth,	6ft. 1 in.	Girth,	5 ft. 7½in.
Forearm,	21½ in.	Forearm,	17in.
Below knee,	8½ in.	Below knee,	7½in.

It should be stated, however, that Musket was measured at sixteen years old, while Carbine's measurement was taken when he was rising four years old."

Muzzles are still used by many trainers, particularly race horse men, whose horses often look as though a good feed would have done them good. Charles Marvin whose career as a trainer and educator of horses is phenomenal says in his book on Training the Trotting Horse, that muzzles are an invention in horsewear that are an unmitigated evil, and if every trainer were of my mind the harness-makers would soon forget how to make them. They will drive their heads to the bottom of the bucket of water, and take chances of breathing through their ears rather than draw back; they will try to swallow three quarts of oats in one gulp, will gorge on all the hay, straw or anything eatable in sight, and even in their sleep will dream of hay-stacks. With such a horse I would far rather regulate his feed carefully, bed him with something he cannot eat, or even tie him up. In a rare case the muzzle might be used on a gluttonous colt, but they are hardly ever necessary, and their use hardly ever excusable.

Before the racing began at Morris Park on the 4th, several individuals were to be seen moving about at a lively rate buttonholing every visitor as he arrived at the course. These same individuals talked with horsemen, and in fact everybody at the track whom they could reach. After they had interviewed several hundred people, they retired to one of the cigar stands with the crowd following in the betting ring, and exhibited a petition which stated that the said parties were authorized to represent the undersigned to sue the New York and New Haven Railroad for overcharges of fare, which was paid by said parties last year when 50 cents was paid for excursion tickets to the course. It was claimed that the railroad overcharged its patrons in violation of law, and that the sum, together with damages, would be recovered. When the movements of the lawyers became known to the track officials the sheets were ordered removed from the cigar cases, and the parties warned not to continue to work on their scheme under penalty of ejectment. The whole business created quite some excitement as long as it lasted.

"Some horses, like some men, have greatness thrust upon them," says an exchange, "but pacers have always been an exception to this truism. The side wheeler has always been looked upon as of plebian origin, and any honors enjoyed were dearly earned. Gibson's or Moore's Tom Hal stood the greater part of his life at a fee of $5, and Little Brown Jug was sold for $25. The great Brown Hal, whose present value is almost beyond price, was sold for $56 50, part of the sum being paid in wheat and peas. Wilson's Sam, 15, was at one time kept as a teaser for a jack, and his owner was glad to get $5—for a service when the colt should stand and suck.

So long ago as 1869, the late Lord Derby, in writing of the Turf, suggested that its then deterioration was brought about—"(1) by the premature running of two-year-olds; (2) by the multiplication of short races, which enables horses to be brought out oftener, and so affords more frequent opportunities of gambling; and (3) by the great preponderance of handicaps. These last are a necessary evil, but their avowed tendency is to place the best and worst horses on an equal footing, and thus to encourage the breed of the latter at least equally with the former." It is not a little curious that after an interval of more than thirty years the Jockey Club should be contemplating a change in the direction Lord Derby hinted at in the second of his reasons for a deterioration, which was then, as it is now, more apparent than real.

Up to the present time there are but ten great brood mares that have a record of 2:30 or better. They are as follows: Beautiful Bells, 2:29½, dam of four with records from 2:19¼ to 2:24½, Daisy Burns, 2:29½, dam of two with records of 2:28 and 2:28½; Dixie, 2:30, dam of one, and second dam of one; Lady Franklin, 2:29½, dam of one, and second dam of one; Mary A. Whitney, 2:28, dam of two with records of 2:22¾ and 2:29½; Mollie 2:27, dam of one trotter and one pacer; Pocahontas (pacer) 2:17½, dam of one, second dam of two, and second dam of two speed-producing stallions; Prairie Bird, 2:28½, dam of one, second dam of one, and second dam of one speed-producing stallion; Tackey, 2:26, dam of three from 2:20 to 2:22½, second dam of one (pacer) and second dam of one speed-producing stallion; Lucille Golddust, 2:26¼ dam of two with records of 2:19¼ and 2:20½.

The ten pool room keepers in St. Louis, says the Times-Democrat, were tricked out of a sum estimated between $5,000 and $7,000 by the old wire-tapping scheme. The killing was made by the conspirators on the last race at Latonia. The race wire from Latonia was in trouble after the second race, and there were long delays between the fourth and fifth races. The race was the Harold stake for two-year-olds. Palestine was the favorite at 3 to 1, but the talent in St. Louis selected Gascon and Allan Bane. The gang got the winner, Georgetown, who was 8 to 1, and held the race back fifteen minutes. Such a flood of money came in on Georgetown that the rooms all wiped out the race before the message announcing "off" came." The money was paid on Georgetown and the conspirators were later caught dividing the spoils and talking over the trick. They had the winner, Daisy F, in the fourth race, but as she was an even money shot they could not make much.

Mr. W. G. Craven, referring to racing of thoroughbreds, in an article contributed to a contemporary, seems to doubt whether any benefit would be derived from three-year-olds being trained for long courses. "It must be remembered," he remarks, "that in the old days of long races the horses frequently did not appear in public till four, five and six years of age. Nowadays, two-year-old racing commences in March, when many of the competitors are really not of full age, many having been born in April and May, and there is no clear proof that any harm has come from this system; and certainly the size and quality of our horses have in no way deteriorated, whilst their performances are quite equal to those of their ancestors for the distances over which they are asked to race. Besides which, the system of not running two-year-olds till August exists in France, and twenty years ago people who raised a cry against two-year-old racing prophesied that the French would eventually beat us. Has this come to pass?"

"Ribbleden," the Sydney correspondent of the Australasian, says, speaking of the phenomenal Carbine—"It is a most difficult thing for even the most experienced racing man to tell when Carbine is beaten. He possesses the knack, somehow, of doing exactly what is wanted of him, irrespective of distance, weight, or the quality of his adversaries. The expenditure of his forces is regulated by circumstances. If he were pitted against a hack, he would not try to bring disgrace upon his opponent by finishing the length of a street in front. He would probably win by a head or so; and any but the most practised eye might be deceived as to the horse's real capabilities. No matter under what disadvantages he runs a race, Carbine gets there all the same. What difficulties were presented in the All-Aged Stakes may be gauged from the fact that men who have been racing all their lives betted hundreds and hundreds of pounds at evens that Carbine would not win when Prelude and Correze swept into the straight with four or five lengths the best of it; but the result shows that it is almost impossible for any one to determine when Carbine is beaten. A more honest horse or a more courageous horse was never seen. Mick O'Brien says that the two-year-olds took Carbine off his legs at the start, and never gave him an opportunity of steadying him or of pulling him together."

A Buffalo Commercial representative said to Mr. C. J. Hamlin: "You recently purchased a few thoroughbred mares down in Tennessee to mate with your trotting-bred horses; now, why wouldn't it have been just as wise to have sent some of your trotting-bred mares to be mated to some of the great race horses?" "I maintain," said Mr. Hamlin, "that the sire controls the action more than the dam, because he is stronger. This is true, also in the human family. In nine cases out of ten, children take more after their father than their mother, especially as to gait and disposition." "Would you, a breeder of long experience, advise a young man of limited means to buy a thoroughbred mare to mate with a trotting-bred horse, in hopes of raising a 2:20 nag, in preference to buying an equally good trotting mare?" "No sir. A man with limited means cannot afford to experiment. It is different in the case of Senator Stanford, myself, and perhaps others. If I fail to get good results from my thoroughbred mares from the first cross, I can outcross them again, and get trotting instinct sufficient to overcome the thoroughbred desire to run. Thoroughbred blood, as all know, gives finish and staying qualities. I have been careful in my selection of running mares to secure daughters of thoroughbreds that possessed as much trotting action as possible, so it would be necessary to make but one outcross. Whether I will succeed or not time alone will tell."

The St. Louis Republic of last Saturday says: "Ed Corrigan was the maddest man in town yesterday. He arrived from Latonia yesterday morning with his great 3-year-old, Riley, for the purpose of starting him in the Derby. About 11 o'clock he marched into the Fair Grounds office on Chestnut street, and after a pleasant greeting to Mr. Bruce, who is acting secretary during the meeting, tendered the requisite amount to make Riley a starter in the Derby. When Mr. Bruce informed him that the Jockey Club held a letter from his clerk, in which Riley was ordered declared last April, the big horseman almost dropped to the floor. His face took on several colors and when he had regained control of his voice he demanded that the letter be shown him, which was done. This satisfied him, but it did not cool his temper. Had Riley been in the race yesterday he would certainly have made Bill Letcher stretch his neck to have won the juicy plum at the end of the course.

There are several different speculations as to the form the proposals of the Stewards of the Jockey Club will take as to the supposed preponderance of short distance races, says the Sporting Chronicle. One authority says they will be of "a very stringent character, and will place races of a mile and upwards, on a equal footing with those run over a less distance, so that those managers of meetings who have been contributing large sums of money for short distance races will be compelled in future to frame their programme so that at least as much money must be given away for races of a mile and upwards as for shorter ones. It is very likely that considerable hostility will be found to this proposal from a section of the club, but I have no doubt at all that in the end the Stewards will be successful." Another correspondent thinks that the "Stewards of the Jockey Club can be depended upon, however, to introduce reform in a temperate manner, and will surely turn a deaf ear to some of the suggestions that have been advanced. Handicaps or weight-for-age races decided over long courses must remain in the minority, and the principal object that should be held in view is to strike a blow at the present hurry-scurry system." How the reform can be "stringent" and "temperate" at one and the same time remains to be seen.

The inaugural meeting of the Gridley Trotting Association held last week was highly successful. The Gridley Herald says: The attendance was between 1,000 and 1,500. Henry Block Sr., and C. N. Reed were chosen as judges; Wm. Elliott Sr., timer. The first event was a mile heat for $250 a side, between Elliott's Cyclone and Carstenbrook's Wonder. Cyclone was a favorite in the pools, selling at $8 to $5 for Wonder. The result corroborated the pool box, Cyclone winning with ease, in 2:52½. Next on the programme was a two in three contest between Rhoton's Singleton Jr., and Wm. Sligar's Eclipse. This was a surprise for the sports, the mare Eclipse being unknown so far as speed was concerned. She took the first heat in 2:34. Singleton won the second in 2:39. In the third and deciding heat Singleton held the pole until entering the second quarter when the little mare captured that position and "dusted" him all the way around, winning the heat and race in the remarkably good time of 2:32½. H. Block's Crazy Jane, J. G. Lewis' John G. and F. C. Haack's Lightning Stricker then entered into a two in three contest; purse, $350. Lightning Striker won the first two heats and race. Time, 2:56½ and 2:41½. The sports lost heavily on this race, Crazy Jane being the favorite at odds of 3 to 1 on. W. S. Harkey's Belle and Lightning Striker trotted a single mile for a purse of $250, the latter winning in 2:32¾. John G. and Crazy Jane trotted a mile for $100 a side, owners driving. It was a dead heat. Time, 2:43. The match was declared off.

A meeting was held in Susanville, Lassen County, at which the following resolutions were passed.

"It is proposed to hold a County Fair at the Fair Grounds near Susanville in the month of September or October, 1890, and, if a sufficient sum of money shall be subscribed, it can be made a great success.

"The program, as understood, is to make it strictly a County Fair! No purses or premiums will be given for exhibits from any other locality, or for horses, except those which have been owned and kept within Lassen County for at least six months before the first day of the Fair.

"By this method all money subscribed for the Fair will be distributed among farmers and stock-raisers of the county, and the main objection raised against the District Fair be obviated.

"It will be strictly a Farmers' and Stock-raisers' Fair, as all the money subscribed will be given in premiums and purses for Lassen County products and stock.

"We therefore expect that farmers and stock-raisers will contribute liberally toward the exhibition of our products and advertisement of our county. This is a prosperous season, and it is a great opportunity to show what Lassen county can produce.

"We cannot be loser, for all the money subscribed will be kept at home.

"Let us all put together, and have a grand exhibition."

Evidently Lassen Co. believes in protection, in fact is a good old Tory county.

A prominent English sporting journal says that next to the champion horse of the century (Ormonde), Petrarch was most probably the highest priced animal that ever changed hands. (Petrarch was, I think, the handsomest horse I ever saw.—Ed. T. T.) With Petrarch having won the Middle Park Plate, beating all the best horses in training, and seeming to have stakes to the value of £25,000—including the Guineas, Derby, Grand Prize, St. Leger, and Prince of Wales' Stakes—at his mercy, it is no wonder that he was worth a lot of money. The "cash down" paid by Lord Dupplin was the extremely moderate sum of £11,000, but, in addition to this, Mr. Gosden, who bred and owned the horse, was to receive one-fourth of such races as the horse might win in which, at the time of the sale, he was engaged. Mr. Gosden, not forgetting his jockey, secured for Goater in the agreement £200 in case the horse won the Two Thousand, and £300 for the Derby. Goater did very well by this, as, though Luke rode him when he won the Two Thousand, the £200 was paid all the same, and Lord Dupplin, who was no niggard, gave him £500 when he won the St. Leger. The races Petrarch won under the agreement were: The Two Thousand Guineas, value £4,100; the Prince of Wales' Stakes, value £2,750, and the St. Leger, value, £4,850. This gives a total of £11,700. One-fourth of the above amount represents £2,925, which, added to the £11,000, paid in the first instance, gives a total of £13,925, or £75 less than the Duke of Westminster is reported to have paid for Doncaster. Taking into consideration the £200, however, to which Goater became entitled under the conditions, the purchase money was increased to £14,125—the largest sum that has ever been paid, with the exception of the big sum that is said to have been given for Ormonde.

Judge Morton of the Circuit Court on June 5th appointed E. A. Tipton receiver for the trotting stallion Red Wilkes. He is owned jointly by Miss Nannie Smith and W. C. France. The latter has kept him at his place for more than three years, and Miss Smith brought suit for a receiver, claiming that the books were not kept right, and that the horse's fees should be raised to $500. In granting the receiver the court ordered that the horse should remain at France's farm, but that the receiver should have entire control of him.

The Sporting World speaking of the Tenny race says: While the big handicap was being run, Col. Pulsifer sat up in the grand stand serenely smoking a cigar, and Trainer Donovan looked a little thoughtful as he sat under the shade of the trees in the paddock, but there was one member of the stable that was fully alive to all the excitement and importance of the occasion.

He was a diminutive urchin, with about as cute and mischievous a little black face as one can well imagine, and when the horses were at the post he perched himself monkey-like on the backstretch fence the better to watch the proceeding.

"Dat white boy can't ride, I knowed he nebber couldn't ride that hoss," muttered the youngster as the horses made a break away and Snapper pulled up Tenny fighting for his head.

"Now dat hoss am mad an he ain't again ter try. I know him better dan any ob dem. Doan' I ride him all de time?" And the little scamp's eyes fairly leaped out of their sockets in his intense excitement.

"Look at him now, jes look at him," he screamed. "Dar he's off last and dar der hev shut him off. Pull out dar men and gib that hoss a show. Pull out an he'll beat every body."

As the horse turned into the stretch, and Tenny commenced to close up, he lost all control of his emotions and yelled till he was hoarse, but when the horses had passed the winning post he became as docile as a lamb, and a quiet smile overspread his features as he softly ejaculated:

"I knowed it all de time. I knowed dey couldn't nebber beat dat little bay hoss;" and then he climbed off the fence and wended his way back to the stable, stopping occasionally on the journey to execute an impromptu breakdown; but mainly he confined himself to murmuring through his smiles: "I knowed it all de time."

The venerable Judge Barry, of Gallatin Tenn., who with General Andrew Jackson, used to be active supporters of the turf, gives a correspondent of the Tennessee Farmer a brief description of one of ye olden times races as follows:

The Judge, speaking of old-time racing, described a race he saw when the jockey (who was a slave) won the race and his freedom. It was on the old Nashville course, and the horse was Tennessee Oscar, son of Wonder. He was a runaway horse and dangerous to ride. The rider was Simon, the best jockey of his day. The proprietor of Edgefield, Dr. John Shelby was a generous man, and one of superior judgment. He had great confidence in Oscar, and knew if he was well ridden he would reach any goal aimed at. He bet a large sum of money on him, and told Simon he had bet $250 for him, and that if Oscar won, he could buy himself. Simon belonged to a widow lady who only asked $400 for him, as he was lazy and impudent and only fit for the saddle. In those days jockeys were not in such demand as they are now, nor did they receive half the pay. It was a four-mile heat race, and when the horses were brought to the post, (there were several started) Oscar was in the wildest mood and got a bad start, but in a few rounds, it seemed, he passed one, then another, and by the time he reached the half-mile post where I stood, he was going like the wind. Here Dr. Shelby yelled to Simon: "Why don't you pull that horse?" Simon replied, as he flew on: "Look at his mouth; what more can I do?" His mouth was wide open and he was running away, and such a burst of speed I never saw before nor since. He distanced all the field except a fine Whip horse owned by an excellent man and trainer, Berry Williams, and it was with difficulty he could be stopped. The next heat was but a repetion of the first. Simon was again instructed to pull him, and not to distance Mr. Williams' horse. Simon said: "I will do all I can, gentlemen, but I am riding a crazy horse to-day." Oscar took the bit and ran away. He ran eight miles in all, the Whip horse barely saving his distance. He was the gamest horse I ever saw, and did as much to improve the stock of Tennessee as any horse that ever lived. I was in Gallatin long enough to learn that.

The Gymkhana races of the Rockaway Hunting Club, in which ponies not exceeding 14 hands 1 inch high will compete, will take place at Cedarhurst, Saturday, July 5th, on the arrival of the 1:30 train from Long Island City. The Times says: There will be six races—the first a "dressing race," in which the ponies are to be brought to the starting point with only a bridle on. The saddle and the coat and waistcoat of the rider will be on the ground. After the starting signal is given, each competitor must saddle and girth his pony, put on his coat and waistcoat, and make for the winning post, when the first man to arrive with coat and waistcoat all buttoned will be the winner.

There will also be a "manikin race," each competitor riding to a point in which manikins will be placed, picking up one and carrying it to the winning post; a "polo ball and bucket" race, in which each competitor will have to put three balls in as many buckets, and then come in first; a "cigar and umbrella" race, in which the competitors are provided at the start with a cigar, matches and an umbrella, and must light the cigar, open the umbrella, mount and reach the winning post with cigar alight, and umbrella in good order.

The fifth race, open only to members of the American Pony Racing Association, will be very amusing, and is called the "egg and spoon" race. Each rider must carry an egg in a wooden spoon held in one hand, and must arrive at the winning post with the egg unbroken and in the spoon. If the egg fall, the competitor must replace it without outside assistance, and start again from the point where it fell or he may return to the starting post for another egg. The last will be a "turning race," the start being made midway between two two posts. The riders must run around the two posts twice and finish on the second round at the point at which they started.

First and second prizes will be offered for all races, and the rules of the American Pony Racing Association will govern. Members of any recognized club may compete, except in the fifth race. Entries should be addressed to the Executive Committee of the Gymkhana Races, at Cedarhurst, stating riding colors, on or before Monday, June 30th. Entrance fees are $1 for each race. The judges are V. A. Blacque, Jenkins Van Schaick, and E. C. La Montagne; the clerk of the course is Capt. R. J. Blake, and the Executive Committee is composed of E. C. La Montagne, Leonard Jacob, Jr., and J. D. Cheever.

Overland Park Summaries.

FIRST DAY.

DENVER, Col , May 30th, 1890.—Running; purse, $250, of which $50 to second horse; for all ages; maidens allowed, if three years old, 5 lbs.; if four years old, 8 lbs.; if five years old or upward, 12 lbs. One mile.

Carlile & Shields' br g Lew Charlie, 3, by Nathan Oaks—Frulina, 106 lbs. .... Weaver 1
Golden Gate Stable's br g Jubilee, 4, by Kyrle Daly—Joy, 122 lbs. .... Hazlitt 2
Orange Grove Stable's b f Rosemeade, 3, by Wildidle—Duchess, 101 lbs .... Ward 3

Time, 1:41.

Miss Dolores, 117 lbs., also ran.

Betting: 3 to 5 Lew Carlile, 3 to 1 Jubilee, 10 to 1 each the others.

Won by 3 lengths; 10 lengths between second and third.

Same Day—Colorado Derby, a sweepstake for three-year-olds (foals of 1887); $10 entrance to accompany the nomination, $15 additional to start, with $600 added by the club, of which $100 to second horse and $50 to the third; winners of any stake to carry 3 lbs. extra; of any three-year-old stake, 5 lbs. extra; maidens allowed 5 lbs.; if maidens at time of starting, allowed 7 lbs.; closed with twenty one nominations One mile and a quarter.

Golden Gate Stable's b g Pliny by Flood—Precious, 127 lbs. .... McLaughlin 1
Carlile & Shields' b c Governor Adams by Nathan Oaks—Alleta, 125 lbs. .... Weaver 2
Carlile & Shields' b g Ollie Benjamin by Springbok—Minnie, 122 lb .... Easly 3

Time, 2:12½.

Zufola, 117 lbs., and Blue Rock, 115 lbs., also ran.

Betting: 2 to 1 Pliny, 7 to 10 Carlile & Shields' entry, 8 to 1 Zufola, 15 to 1 Blue Rock.

Won by a head; half a length between second and third.

Same day—Selling purse $200; hors s entered to be sold $2 000 to carry weight for age; for $1,500 allowed 5 lbs; then 1 lb. allowed for each $100 down to $300. One mile and a sixteenth.

Albert Shore's b g B. T., 4, by Trumps—Ten Broeck, $400; 107 lbs. .... Graham 1
Denver Racing Club Association's ch h Kismet, 5, by St. Patrick, Fannie Platte, 114 lbs .... Easly 2
Joseph Werlen's b g Mart Walden, 6, by Clifton Bell—Lucille, 116 lbs .... Gruell 3

Parnell 111 lbs., Patricia 112 lbs., Jou Jou 113 lbs., and Jack Brady, 113 lbs. also ran.

Betting; 3 to 1 Mart Walden, 5 to 1 Kismet, 5 to 1 B. T., even money Patrica, 3 to 1 Jou Jou, 19 to 1 each Parnell and Jack Brady.

Won by length; three-quarters of a length between second and third.

Same day—2.22 class, trotting; purse $500.

George Mosher, ch g, by Strathmore; Charles Dutt	3	1	1	3	1
Bismark, ch st by Hirsch Belmont; Marshall Farm	1	2	3	1	2
Carl, ch g; George W. Cook	2	3	2	2	3

Time, 2:22½, 2:23½, 2:25½, 2:24½, 2:25½.

Same day—3:00 class, trotting; purse $500.

Lucy Abbott, ch m, by Abbottsford; DuBois Bros	1	1	1
Red Bird, ch m; H. L. Camp	3	2	2
Rosita, ch m; Denver Stable	4	3	3
Uncle Toby, br g; H. Hitchcock	2	4	4

Time, 2:29, 2:28½, 2:29½.

SECOND DAY.

DENVER, Col., May 31, 1890.—Purse $250, of which $50 to the second horse; for all ages; horses not having won a race of any kind this year allowed 5 lbs.; maidens, if three years old, allowed 7 lbs.; if four years old and over, 10 lbs. Winners in 1889 of $1,000 or more to carry three lbs. extra. One mile and an eighth.

SUMMARY.

Pierson & Welsh's br m Hindoo Rose, 6, by Hindoo—Delight, 116 .... Fisk 1
Palmer & Key's ch c Bob Ingersoll, 3, by J. W. Norton—Nancy B., 99 .... King 2
E. V. R. Pomeroy's ro g Hark, 6, by Harkaway—Mollie Powers, 121 .... Easly 3

Time, 1:59.

Betting—1 to 3 Hindoo Rose, 4 to 1 Ingersoll, 10 to 1 Hark.

Won by a length and a half; a distance between second and Third.

Same Day—Prairie Stake, a sweepstake for two-year-olds (foals of 1888); $15 entrance to accompany the nomination, $15 additional to start, with $500 added by the club, of which $100 to the second horse. $50 to third; winners of any race of the value of $50 or more to carry three pounds extra; of two or more such races 5 lbs. extra; maidens at time of starting allowed 5 lbs. Five furlongs. Value to winner, $735.

SUMMARY.

Charles Feeney's ch f Celia by Day Star—imp Miss McGregor, 110 .... Feeney 1
Orange Grove Stable's b c Joe Woolman by imp Sizus—Ella Dow, 118 .... McLaughlin 2
O'Brien Bros.' b f Minnie Elkins by Duke of Montrose—Badge 115 .... Graham 3

Time, 1:04½.

Alamosa, 119 lbs; Francesca, 110 lbs; John Winfield, 118 lbs; Bon Ton, 118 lbs, and Clara G., 110 lbs., also ran.

Betting—3 to 5 Minnie Elkins, 5 to 2 Joe Woolman and Bon Ton coupled, 5 to 1 Celia, 6 to 1 Alamosa and Francesca coupled, 10 to 1 John Winfield, 25 to 1 Clara G.

Won by a length and a half; same distance between second and third.

Same Day—Handicap, purse $250, of which $50 to the second horse; for three-year olds and upward. One mile.

Ed Gaylord's b c Billy Duncan, 3, by Fairplay—Lucille, 105 lbs. .... Graham 1
Ed Gaylord's b c Sympathetic's Last, 4, by Fairplay—Sympathetic, 112 lbs .... Weaver 2
John Winfield's ch h Luke Du Bois, 5, by J. W. Norton—Maud, 102 lbs .... Crump 3

Time, 1:45½.

Betting: 1 to 3 Sympathetic's Last and Bill Duncan coupled, 5 to 1 each Dan Meeks, Advent and Du Bois.

Won by a length and a half; same distance between second and third.

Same Day—The Denver Trotting Stake, for colts and fillies three years old or under that have never beaten 2:30; $30 entrance, with $500 added by the club.

Le Roy, blk c, by Joe Young; C. E. Westbrook	1	1	2	1
Murtha, blk f, by Stamboul; Denver Stable	2	2	1	2
Darz'a, blk f; Du Bois Bros	3	4	3	3
Effie Rene, blk f; Millett Bros	4	3	dr	

Time, 2:34½, 2:32½, 2:30, 2:30.

Same Day—2:34 class, trotting; purse $500.

Prince McMahon, blk g, by McMahon; Theodore Bauersach	4	3	2	1	1
Minnie's Almont, br s; George W Cook	6	4	3	2	2
Monarch, br g; W. W. Anderson	5	6	4	3	d
J. C., b h; Charles Dutt	2	1	1	dis	
Sierra La Salle, ch m; Ed Connelly	1	2	dis		
Hailstorm, br g; H. Hitchcock	3	5	dis		

Time, 2.28, 2:29, 2:26½, 2:29½, 2:31.

THIRD DAY.

June 2nd—First race, running—The Phil Zang Brewing Company's purse of $250, of which $50 to the second. For all ages. Owners handicap; owners to fix their own weight; in making the entry and must start with the weight assigned; seven furlongs.

SUMMARY.

G. L. Richardson's b h Painkiller, 5, by Joe Hooker—Betsy McGuire 80 lbs .... Ward 1
Pierson & Welch's br m Hindoo Rose, 6, by Hindoo—Delight 105 lbs .... King 2
Joseph Werlen's b g Mart Walden, 6, by Clifton Bell—Lucille, 100 lbs .... Enos 3

Time, 1:29½.

Hark, 108 lbs.; Miss Dolores, 82, and Zufola 100, unplaced.

Betting—Painkiller 6 to 5, Hindoo Rose, 6 to 5, Mart Warden and Zufola 8 to 1 each, Hark 75 to 1.

Same Day—Second race, running—For a purse of $250, of which $50 to second. For all ages. Maidens allowed, if three years old, 5 pounds; four years old, 8 pounds; 5 years old and upwards, 12 lbs. One mile and an eighth.

SUMMARY.

Ed Gaylord's b c Sympathetic's Last, 4, by Fairplay—Sympathetic, 122 .... Weaver 1
Pierson & Welch's br m Hindoo Rose, 6, by Hindoo—Delight, 121, ... King 2

Time, 2:00.

Betting—Sympathetic's Last 3 to 5, Hindoo Rose 6 to 5.

Same Day—Third race, running—Purse, $200; $10 to accompany nomination and go to second horse. For all ages. Weights for ages. Heats of five furlongs.

Thomas Hazlett's b g Jou Jou (a) by Monday—Plaything, 119 pounds .... Hazlett 3 1 1
H. Coombs' ch h Leadville (4) by Barry O'Fallen—Easter Bell, 117 pounds .... Early 1 2 2
Adsit and Robbins' ch h Sorrel Jim (5) by Sleepy Jim—Sorrel Nell, 119 pounds .... Graham 2 3 0

Time, 1:02½, 1:05, 1:06½.

Cotton Tail, 106 pounds, unplaced.

Betting—Jou Jou 6 to 5, Sorrel Jim 8 to 5, Leadville 6 to 1; Cotton Tail 12 to 1.

Second heat—Jou Jou 4 to 5, Leadville 2 to 1, Sorrel Jim 6 to 1.

Third heat—Leadville 12 to 1.

Fourth race, selling for all ages.—Purse $200; horses to be sold for $1,500 to carry weight for age; if for $1,200 allowed five pounds; if for $1,000 allowed eight pounds, then one pound for each $100 down to $300; one mile.

Denver Racing Association's ch h Kismet (5) by St. Patrick—Fannie Platte, 118 pounds .... Easly 1
Orange Grove Stable's b h Jack Brady (6) by Wildidle—Sour Grapes 118 pounds .... McLaughlin 2
Joseph Werlen's b g Mart Walden (6) by Clifton Belle—Lucille, 117 pounds .... Enos 3

Time, 1:44½.

Marquis Depero, 111 pounds, Black Pilot 112, Mart Walden 117, Blue Rock 94, Patricia 109, Dan Meek 111, unplaced.

Betting—Kismet even money, Blue Rock 5 to 2, Patricia 3 to 1, Mart Walden and Black Pilot 5 to 1 each. Others from 10 to 25 to 1.

Fifth race, special trotting for named horses. Purse $200.

Dora W.	2	1	1	1
Norton McGregor	1	3	4	3
Gig	3	2	3	2
Clara B.	4	4	2	4

Time, 2:42½, 2:42½, 2:38½, 2:36.

Pooling—First heat: Dora W $30, Norton McGregor $15, Gig $6, Clara B $3.

Second heat—Norton McGregor $25, field $10.

Third heat—Dora W $25, field $10.

Fourth heat—Dora W $32, field $10.

FOURTH DAY.

First race, the Merchant's stakes—A sweepstake for all ages; $10 entrance, to accompany the nomination; $15 additional to start, with $500 added by the club, of which $100 to the second horse, $50 to the third. Winners of any race of the value of $1,000, or more, to carry three pounds extra; of two or more such races, five pounds extra. Non-winners in 1890 allowed three pounds. Maidens on February 15th, allowed five pounds. If maidens at time of starting, allowed seven pounds. One mile and a half.

Carlile & Shields, b g Ollie Benjamin (3) by Springbok out of Minnie, 102 lbs .... Hazlitt 1
Carlile & Shields, ch g Justus (4) by Alarm out of Equity, 119 lbs. .... Weaver 2
Clifton Bell, b h. Beaconsfield (a) by Hock Hocking out of Aileen Allanah, 124 lbs .... Feeney 3

Time, 2:41½.

Betting, Carlile & Shields' entry, 1 to 2; Beaconsfield 8 to 5.

Second race, running for a purse of $200, of which $50 goes to second. For all ages, maidens allowed, if 3 years old, 7 pounds, if 4 years old 12 pounds, if older 18 pounds, six furlong heats.

Golden Gate Stable, b m Louisa M (4) by Kyrle Daly, Night Hawk, 112 lbs .... Hazlitt 1 1
Ed. Gaylord, b c Billy Duncan (3) by Fairplay, Lucille, 106 lbs. .... Weaver 2 2
Palmer & Keys, blk g, McBowling (a) by Tom Bowling, Larenta, 119 lbs .... Gruell 3 3

Time, 1:17½, 1:19½.

Jeff. Harrington, 119, ran, unplaced. Betting; Louisa M. 2 to 3, Billy Duncan 8 to 5.

Second heat, no betting.

Third race, selling purse of $200; for all ages; if entered to be sold for $2,000, to carry proper weight; 1 lb. off for every $100 down to $1,000, then 2 lbs. off for every $100 down to $500. One and one-sixteenth miles.

Denver Racing Association, ch h Kismet (5) by St. Patrick—Fannie Platte, 112 lbs .... Early 1
Albert Shore's b g B. T. (4), Trumps—Ten Broeck mare, 109 lbs. .... Graham 2
L. Ogilvy's br c Receiver (4), Regent—Minnie Holton, 108 lbs. .... Weaver 3

Time, 1:51½.

Dan Meek, 106 lbs.; Jack Brady, 112, unplaced.

Betting—B. T., even money; Kismet, 8 to 5; Jack Brady, 4 to 1; Receiver, 6 to 1; Dan Meek, 12 to 1.

Fourth race, trotting, purse $600; for the 2:26 class.

Marquis	1	1	3	1
George Moshier	2	3	1	3
Magnet	3	2	2	2

Time, 2:26½, 2:26½, 2:27, 2:26.

Pools—First heat: George Moshier $25, field $10; second heat—George Moshier $25, field $10; third heat—George Moshier $25, field $20; fourth heat—George Moshier, $25, field $25.

Fifth race, pacing, for a purse of $500, for the 2:24 class.

Uncle Jack	1	1	1
Flossie Reed	2	2	4
C. W. L.	3	3	2
George Gould	4	4	3
Blonde	5	5	0

Time, 2:21½, 2:26½, 2:28½.

Pools—First heat: Uncle Jack $55, Flossie Reed $55, field $14; second heat—Uncle Jack $25, field $5; third heat—Uncle Jack $50, field $5.

FIFTH DAY.

Clifton Bell's ch g, Bugle (3) by Fairplay—Mary F., 106 lbs .... Kelley 1
John Winfield's ch c Luke Dubois (5) by J. W. Norton—Maud, 107 lbs .... Weaver 2
Charles Johnson's br c King Faro III (3) by King Faro—Theodosia, 106 lbs .... Jack 3

Time, 1:32½.

Alla, 109 pounds, Bob Ingersoll, 106, unplaced.

Betting—Bob Ingersoll, 3 to 5; Luke Dubois, 4 to 1; King Faro III, 4 to 1; others 10 to 1.

Second race, selling, for all aged, purse $200; horses entered to be sold for $2,000, weight for age.

Thos. Hazlitt's b g Jou Jou, 2, Monday—Playtime, 110 lbs .... Hazlitt 1
Chas. Dutt's ch g Chickasaw, a, Quartermaster—Mary Wynne, 104 lbs .... Graham 2
L. Ogilvy's br f Zufola, 3, Falsetto—Mintdrop, 106 lbs .... Weaver 3

Time, 1:17½.

Jou Jou 1 to 3, Zufola 4 to 1, Chickasaw 7 to 1.

Third race, purse $250, for all ages, $50 to second horse; all horses to carry 105 lbs. Seven furlongs.

G. L. Richardson's b s Painkiller, 5, Joe Hooker—Betsy McGuire, 105 lbs .... Hazlitt 1
Kelly & Samuel's b g Pliny, 3, Flood—Precious, 105 lbs. McLaughlin 2
Charles Dutt's b g Dick Wright, 5, Quartermaster—unknown, 105 lbs .... Anderson 3

Time, 1:30½.

Louisa M., 105 pounds, unplaced.

Betting—Pliny 3 to 5; Painkiller 6 to 5; Louise M. 8 to 1; Dick Wright 15 to 1.

Fourth race, selling for a purse of $200, for two year olds; if entered to be sold for $1,500, to carry weight for age, then one pound off for each $100 down to $800, then two lbs. off for each $100 to $300; half a mile.

SUMMARY.

Denver Racing Association's ch f Naomi, 2, by Faustus—Alma Lamar, 106 lbs .... Easly 1
John Winfield's b c John Winfield, 2, by John K. Norton—Attribute, 101 lbs .... Weaver 2
M. M. Sage's b c Ben Carlile, 2, by B. G. Bruce—Gypsy, 105 lbs. .... Graham 3

Time, 0:50½.

A. S. Took, 105 lbs. and Clara G., 105, unplaced.

Betting—Naomi, 3 to 5; Ben Carlile, 3 to 1; others, 6 to 1 each.

Fifth race—Trotting, for a purse of $200; 2:25 class.

SUMMARY.

J. C.	4	4	1	1	1
First Call	1	1	3	3	3
Louis S.	2	2	2	2	2
Jasper	3	3	0	0	0

Time, 2:20½, 2:27½, 2:29½, 2:32.

Pools: First heat—J. C., $25, field, $10; second heat—First Call, $25, field, $15; third heat—First Call, $25; field, $15; fourth heat—J. C.; $25; field, $20; fifth heat—J. C., $25; field, $5.

National Trotting Association.

The following penalties have been inflicted by the National Association:

By order of the Board of Review, the following named persons and horses have been expelled, under authority of Rules 6 and 14, to-wit:

Case No. 1887.
J. F. C. Barlow, F. A. Cole, } Jersey City, N. J.; and the b m Fanny C. (pacer), alias Mamie B.

Case No. 1938.
Calvin Predmore, Youngstown, Ohio.

Case No. 1949.
James Allen, Kingston, Ont., Can., and the b g F. O. P., alias Tom Allen.

Case No. 1946.
Geo. W. Smith, Binghamton, N. Y.
Henry Hendricks, Milwaukee, Wis.

Case No. 1965.
C. T. Homewood, Westfield, N. Y., Ira Ryerson, Goshen, N. Y., } and the gr g Taylorson, alias Tryon.

Case No. 1968.
C. L. Rood, J. Maher, } Pictou, N. S., Can., { and the b m Mattie B., alias Little Eva.

Case No. 1977.
Spencer Owens, Taberg, N. Y.

Case No. 1979.
J. A. Juvenall, Upper Sandusky, Ohio, Michael Brannagan, Mount Vernon, O., } and the b g Freddy J., alias Doctor Gordon.

By order of the Board of Review, case No. 1967, George I. Young, East Boston, Mass., has been expelled under authority of Rule 14.

By order of the Board of Review, case No. 1890, Ed Stoddard, Portsmouth, N. H., and the ch g Hazzard, have been suspended under authority of Rule 7.

By order of the Board of Review, case No. 1942, J B Woodbury, Boston, Mass., has been suspended until the further order of the Board, under authority of Rule 14.

By order of the Board of Review, case No. 1942, the b m Victoria has been suspended under authority of Rule 14.

By order of the Board of Review, case No. 1946, R. M. Biggerstaff, Edina, Mo., and the bl g Ralph, have been suspended until the further order of the Board, under authority of Rule 7 and Rule 51.

By order of the Gentlemen's Driving Park, Martin & McAndrews, Proprietors, Baltimore, Md., Ed. S. Zell, Preston, Md., and the b m Lady Hannis, have been suspended for non-payment of entrance money.

By order of the Philadelphia Driving Park Association, Philadelphia, Pa., Thomas Morgan, Bay City, Mich., and the blk g Pat Legg (pacer), have been suspended for non-payment of entrance money.

By order of the Driving Club of New York, New York, the b g Billy was expelled under authority of Rule 14, as notified May 20, 1889. Said penalty was temporarily removed (erroneously) Dec. 7, 1889, but is now revived and remains in force.

M. M. MORSE, Secretary.

Grim's Gossip.

There are seventeen yearling trotters at Rosemeade.

Harry Rose, a son of Senator L. J. Rose, was married on Monday to Miss Currier of San Francisco.

It is now believed that Laredo will not go East. It is reported that he did not show up as well as expected in his work at Santa Anita.

I want every horseman in the state to send me all the news obtainable. We are anxious to hear from all sections, and letters will be always acceptable.

John Watts, the successful rider of Sainfoin in the English Derby received a cheque for £500 from the plucky owner—Sir Jas. Miller.

W. C. Jones, Columbia, has bought from Major Campbell Brown, a half interest in the five-year-old stallion McEwen, 2:18½, for $12,500. Ed Geers will still train him.

Senator Rose is not satisfied with his already large string of thoroughbreds, and has purchased from the Dwyer Bros., of New York, a yearling filly by Reform, dam Megara.

Entry blanks for the Los Angeles meeting can be secured at this office, a liberal supply having been received from the Secretary of the Sixth District Agricultural Association.

Balgowan, who won the Southern Hotel Stakes at St. Louis, is owned by Lieutenant Clay of Los Angeles. He is by Strathmore, and was bred by George Clay of Kentucky.

Sixteen trotters and pacers have this early entered the 2:30 list of 1890, with records ranging from 2:24 to 2:30. Sultan and Jim Wilson are the only sires so far with two to their credit.

Bruce Cockrill,s mare Marvin by Kyrle Daly, dam Marian by Hubbard has had a filly foal by Ironclad and has been sent to Sacramento to receive the embraces of Prince of Norfolk.

L. J. Rose's gorgeous jacket was seen in front at Westchester last Thursday, the speedy filly Fairy beating Blithe, Eclipse and others, running the five furlongs in 1:01¼ on a dead slow track.

When is the great tumbling of records going to cease? Ten Broeck's mile was made in 1:39¾, and yet Fides, in the Toboggan handicap, ran three quarters in 1:10½, at the rate of about 1:33½ for the mile.

It is now said that Major B. G. Thomas has made W. Lakeland an offer for Exile, and that when the horse is retired from the turf he will fall into the Major's hands. I think he will go to Rancho del Paso.

Mr. J. M. Smith of Contra Costa County, has lost a fine filly, by Anteeo Jr. The youngster was being halter broken, and threw herself backward, causing an artery to burst, and the filly only survived a few moments.

J. W. Robinson, one of the directors of the Sixth District Agricultural Association, was in the city this week from Los Angeles. He reports that the meeting to be held in Los Angeles will eclipse all previous efforts.

Bow Bells has recovered from his accident of a few weeks since, and he is now sound and well. Bow Bells, Bonnie Wood, and several Wedgewood two-year-olds will be taken through the Southern Circuit by Johnny Thomas.

H. H. Bancroft of San Diego County, has sold to H S. Richards of El Cajon, the stallion Alert, by Arthurton 365, dam by Geo. M. Patchen Jr. 31. Alert has several promising young colts that should bring him to the front.

There have been many enquiries for the San Jose entries but Secretary Bragg has evidently overlooked this matter and neglected to send them. Horsemen on making entries to purses and stakes want to hear as soon as possible what they have to contend against.

There are many who expect to see the record for a mile and a quarter beaten in the Suburban, if it be good day and track. Kingston made a low mark to shoot at but the extraordinary speed shown by several of the candidates, is enough to cause the assumption.

Although Balkan 2:29½ was withdrawn from the service this year, it was not on account of his foals, as the sucklings by him are much admired by all that have seen them. He will be sent for a low record this year and it will take better than a "twenty" horse to beat him.

Andy McDowell is rolling onward toward the great Eastern circuit having the Pleasanton horses in charge. I asked him before he started what the prospects were but he refused to answer. One of the stable boys said they expected to hire another car to bring back the winnings.

A full brother to Yolo Maid is at present being worked at the track by Mr. Nolan, object being to show two miles in 5:00, which if accomplished will cause the gelding to change hands as a Mr. Foster, from Australia, has an option on him if he accomplishes the distance in the time mentioned.

Gen. Turner was not satisfied with the record he made for Suisun, 2:25½, so to see what he could do with the mare, gave her a gentle "breather" on Saturday last over the Belmont Park track, and negotiated the distance in 2:19½. From present appearances, the Electioneer boom will still continue.

The Los Angeles programme meets with popular approval this year, and in consequence the Southern citrus belt will secure a liberal entry from all over the State. The directors are also booming their meeting, such as it was never boomed before, and are bound to have one of the best meetings on the circuit.

On Thursday afternoon, the Australian mares, sent over for Mr. Rose, were shipped by rail to the breeding establishment of that gentleman in Los Angeles county. The young colt which was brought over for another party was also sent down, and will be kept there until the arrival of Captain Tom Merry.

B. Benjamin, Secretary of the Los Angeles Association, sends me a telegram that the railroad officials have made arrangements to carry horses to the Los Angeles meeting at the rate of $100 per car load. This is a generous reduction and will be appreciated by those who wish to ship their stock to the southern city.

Horsemen intending to enter at Los Angeles are reminded that nominations for the 2:30 trot for $1,500 and the district trotting stakes for 1890 and 1891 close on Monday. Los Angeles sets the ball rolling on the grand circuit this year and it will pay all owners and drivers to carefully read over the programme and conditions published on another page.

The English Oaks was won this year by the Duke of Portland's Memoir, St. Simon—Quiver; Chevalier Ginistrelli's Signorina, St Simon—Star of Portici second, and Mr. J. H. Houldsworth's Pussea, Springfield—Nepoli, third. Memoir ran second (hard held) to her stable companion Semolina in the One Thousand, while Signorina was last year's crack two-year-old.

Stamboul closed the year 1889 with two in the 2:30 list, Vesolia (2 years) 2:29½, and Nehusta 2:30. Already for the present year he has added another, the black filly Martha, her dam being by Flaxtall. With the large number of Stamboul youngsters that are now scattered from the Atlantic to the Pacific, there should be many more enter the circle before the trotting closes for the year.

Last week mention was made of the death of Fontana, and I stated that death was said to be by colic. That was the street rumor, and was given as received. Sam Gamble has sent me a note in which he says that the mare's death was caused by a large tumor in the pylorus of the stomach, as was demonstrated when an autopsy was held. Fontana was within two weeks of fealing, and had her little one come into life, a filly would have been the result.

A peculiar case has just come to light from the Aptos ranch. Mr. Adolph Spreckles reports that last year two youngsters were turned loose in a paddock, one a filly ten months old, and the other a horse colt eleven months old. The result is s own in the fact that the filly has a foal at her side and she is only a little over twenty one months old. The foal is a fine one, perfect in all ways, and is a natural trotter. Who can beat this for extreme youthfulness in both sire and dam.

R. B. Cockrill and Eugene Breen of Salinas Valley made a visit to this office on Thursday morning and reported the horse interests in their section as being booming. Mr. Cockrill has a colt out of Dairy D, from whom "Bruce" expects much as the youngster is full of promise. Mr. Breen thinks well of a yearling that he has by Ironclad, out of a Billy Walker mare. Both of these youngsters will be heard from at the Blood Horse Meeting next year

Mr. Ferguson, the clerk of Palo Alto ranch has an advertisement in this issue, calling the attention of horsemen to his new stake book, which is placed in the market for the first time. With the experience that the author has had, there is no one more competent to construct a book of the kind and those who purchase will find themselves amply repaid by the saving in time and convenience. Sample sheets will be forwarded on the remittance of a two cent stamp.

Miller & Sibley of Franklin, Pa., seem determined to capture all the Electioneer colts that they can get their hands on. A telegram informs me that they have bought from G. H. Hopper of Unionville, Ohio, the four year old stallion Connoisseur by Electioneer, dam Consolation by Dictator 113, 2nd dam Belle (dam of Mary, the dam of Superior 2:19½, and Benefactor 2:28), by Alexander's Norman 25, sire of Lula 2:14¾. The consideration paid was $10,000.

"There is one fact that cannot be obliterated," says the Kentucky Stock Farm. "It is that the trotting bred horse is to be the future roadster of America. Four minute plugs are no longer in demand. Men in cities, towns and villages will be buying more largely every year trotting bred horses for their buggies, phaetons and barouches. This is encouraging to the breeder of trotting horses to the farmer who is patronizing trotting stallions, as he will be sure to get more than double for such produce that he would for ordinary farm horses."

When Major Du Bois was here during the past winter, he purchased from C. W. Smith, of this city, the mare Lucy Abbott by Abbottsford, and took her back to Denver, where she made her first appearance at the Overland Park, and won the three-minute purse in straight heats in 2:29, 2:28¼ and 2:26½. By the way, the following cut from a Denver paper will be full of interest to those who have known the mare for a year or two: "There were four starters. The winner, Lucy Abbott, is owned by the well known Du Bois Bros, who purchased her some time since and relieved her of her duty of hauling a milk wagon." Pete, how much is milk a quart?

"How will the betting be on that pair in the Suburban?" asked a well known trainer of another as he watched Salvator and Frienze canter past one morning at Westchester.

"Well, it's hard to say. Tenny is in there and so is Raceland, and both of them will go all the journey, but I think you will see a big change in opinion after that big chestnut is worked a mile and a quarter for the race, and the horse that beats him will get all the money."

"Then I don't know," responded trainer No. 1. "I like the mare, and don't you overlook her when you put down your money."

W. H. E. Smith of Humboldt County lately started East with a string of thoroughbreds, accompanied by the well known Frank Dupoyster as trainer. My Chicago correspondent has failed to let me know of any disagreement in the stable out the following I clip from the Woodland Democrat which speaks for itself: "George Lambert has reached a high position as a trainer. He has been appointed at a salary of $2,500 per annum to take charge of Al Farrow, Long Shot and Susie S, belonging to W. H. E. Smith, of Humboldt county. These horses are in Chicago, and George leaves Woodland Sunday morning for that city. He has been in Mr. Smith's employ for several years. The horses have already made a fine record."

The Directors of the Oakland, Napa, San Jose and Petaluma Associations will each send a representative to the office of the BREEDER AND SPORTSMAN on Saturday, (to-day) to consult together in reference to a programme for the various meetings. This is a good move, and a step in the right direction, for it would be very inconvenient for Mr. Corbett to trot Hazel Wilkes in the 2:20 class at San Jose on Saturday, and then to have her trot in the same class on Monday at Napa. This personal allusion is made, as it explains the situation and is liable to happen to any horseman. However, a meeting of the representatives will tend to prevent any such a jar, and many other matters can be talked over that will be to the mutual interests of all concerned.

Breeding trotting stock is a very fascinating pursuit, so much so, in fact, that it is attracting the attention of Englishmen to this country. Mr. Cox, of London, England, who lately came to America, intends to embark in the trotting horse breeding business. He also expects to campaign one or two good trotters through the Grand Circuit.

My old friend, Dr. M. W. Hicks of Sacramento, sends me a letter in which he complains, "that not one of the Turf papers of the country have mentioned the fact that Blue Belle 2:26½ (Mila C) was by Blue Bull, not even so fair a paper as the BREEDER AND SPORTSMAN." My dear doctor one would naturally suppose that every person in the country knew the paternal ancestor of "Blue Belle" after the expose that was made when she was ruled off, but you must feel assured that this paper has always been a friend of the Blue Bull family and said what was just and right about them. However that feeling is only what we have for any other great family of producers and as an impartial paper we try to treat all alike.

Last week mention was made of a telegram received from James Goldsmith announcing that Mr. Valensin's Simmocolon had won a race at Dundee Park, N. J. The mail brings information that there were five starters for the $500 purse, but the chestnut horse proved too speedy for his competitors. It will be seen from the summary given below that he improved his time in each heat.

DUNDEE DRIVING PARK, June 3rd.—Purse $500; 2:30 class.

J. H. Goldsmith's ch h Simmocolon, by Simmons	1	1	1
J. Plimley's b m Lady Douglass	2	3	2
M. Demarest's br g Prince A	4	2	3
Rice & Jobe's b g Maurice S	3	4	4
C. A. Horner's rn m Verona	5	5	5

Time, 2:25½, 2:24¼, 2:23¼.

Many months ago the BREEDER AND SPORTSMAN urged the necessity of a meeting of representatives from the different Fair Associations, in the Northern portion of the State, to fix dates for the Fairs of 1890, so that there might be no clashing between them in reference to the times selected. Acting on that suggestion a call was made for last Monday, and the delegates met at Marysville, and the following telegram was sent to this office: "The meeting of Chico and Marysville District Fairs was held here last evening, and it was decided to organize a great northern racing circuit, embracing these districts. The dates of the races and time for the fairs are as follows: Willows, August 12th to 16th; Red Bluff, 19th to 23rd; Chico, 26th to 30th; Marysville, September 2d to 6th. Eighteen thousand dollars in purses and stakes will be offered.

In the June number of Wallace's Monthly just published, the editor, John H. Wallace, gives the explanation of his recent robbery. He states the amount of the robbery at $18,835. The checks were drawn on the funds of the Wallace Trotting Register Company, and signed by Robert L. Wallace, assistant treasurer, except one for $2,500, which was signed by him and raised from $2 to $2,500 and drawn on his personal account. The balance left in the bank is a little rising $4,000. With this sum, Mr. Wallace says, to the credit of the Trotting Register Company, he does not despair of being able to pay the stockholders a dividend of five or six per cent. at the close of the year. Owing to the forged check for $2,500, his personal account was left with a balance of $18 and a few cents. Mr. Wallace gives a plausible explanation of why Leslie E. Macleod became a victim of circumstances in the affair. In conclusion he says: "There is plenty of marrow in the old bones yet and plenty of courage to build anew."

A prominent breeder of New York once told the writer that he had no use for pacers, and what was more, he would not breed them; but, when he coupled a trotting and trotting-bred daughter of Electioneer with a pure-gaited trotting-bred son of George Wilkes, the result was a foal that was a natural pacer, says the Horse World. This brings to mind the fact that Jennie Lind, with a pacing record of 2:17, has given birth to a foal by Roy Wilkes, pacing record 2:12½, and the foal is a natural trotter. It is a very puzzling problem for breeders to solve, how it comes, when after coupling pure-gaited trotting-bred parents, the produce will possess the pacing gait. Take Pocahontas Boy for an example: A pacing bred horse and the sire of more pacers than trotters, one would naturally think that when bred to daughters of the pacing-bred pacer Blue Bull, the produce would surely have the pacing gait. But a look at Pocahontas Boy's 2:30 list shows that while he has sired many pacers and but four trotters, three of his trotters are out of daughters of Blue Bull. Will some one who knows kindly tell why this is?

My correspondent at Franklin, Pa., sends an account of a great fire that occurred in the training and horse barn of Miller and Sibley at Prospect Hill near that city on the afternoon of Tuesday, June 3d. In spite of the most strenuous efforts of the men, the fire was soon beyond control and when the fire department arrived from the city the place was a mass of ruins. In addition to the main building a lot of sheds and stalls to the east of it were also consumed. The main horse barn was 385 feet in length by 160 feet in width, and was one of the most complete structures of its kind in the country. In the heart of the barn was a kindergarten track for colts, and outside of that was a driving track. The outer portion of the building was used as stalls for the horses in training. The heat was so intense that part of the fence around the training track was consumed. At the time the fire broke out the stalls were filled with horses, but owing to the daring and heroic work of Mr. Stinson and his associates not one was lost. The cause of the fire is supposed to be spontaneous combustion. The building was insured for about two thirds its value.

The Horse World says: "Many are the predictions as to what the four year olds will do this season and in nearly every case it is either Sunol or Axtell that is placed at the head. There are, however, three or four colts of that age that have a license to trot as fast as either of those remarkable colts, and there are some astute judges that will not be surprised if one of the unnamed ones should go a faster mile this season than either Sunol or Axtell.

A couple of great young things that may be seen in the East this season are Margaret S., 2:19½, and Direct 2:18½, two game young race goers by a sire of the same kind, Director, 2:17. Director was one of the steadiest racing and gamest race goers ever seen on the grand circuit tracks, and it is a significant fact that no sire was ever represented, the same season, by as good a three year old as Margaret S. and as good a four year old as Direct. There is something more about this pair of young race goers that should set the advocates of non-development in the parents to thinking, and that is that not only are they sired by a developed and campaigned sire, but the dam of Direct is Echora 2:23½, and Margaret S. is out of May Day 2:30."

THE WEEKLY

Breeder and Sportsman.

JAMES P. KERR, PROPRIETOR.

The Turf and Sporting Authority of the Pacific Coast.

Office, No. 313 Bush St.

P. O. Box 2300.

TERMS—*One Year, $5; Six Months, $3; Three Months, $1.50.*

STRICTLY IN ADVANCE.

Money should be sent by postal order, draft or by registered letter, addressed to JAMES P. KERR, San Francisco, Cal.

Communications must be accompanied by the writer's name and address, not necessarily for publication, but as a private guarantee of good faith.

NEW YORK OFFICE, ROOM 15, 181 BROADWAY.

ALEX. P. WAUGH, - - - - - Editor.

Advertising Rates

Per Square (half inch)
One time $1 50
Two times.. 2 50
Three times 3 25
Four times 4 00

And each subsequent insertion 75c. per square.

Advertisements running six months are entitled to 10 per cent. discount.

Those running twelve months are entitled to 20 per cent. discount.

Reading notices set in same type as body of paper, 50 cents per line each insertion.

To Subscribers.

The date printed on the wrapper of your paper indicates the time to which your subscription is paid.

Should the BREEDER AND SPORTSMAN be received by any subscriber who does not want it, write us direct to stop it. A postal card will suffice.

Special Notice to Correspondents.

Letters intended for publication should reach this office not later than Wednesday of each week, to secure a place in the issue of the following Saturday. Such letters to insure immediate attention should be addressed to the BREEDER AND SPORTSMAN, and not to any member of the staff.

San Francisco, Saturday, June 14, 1890.

Dates Claimed.

EUREKA JOCKEY CLUB..........................July 2d to 5th
IONE..Aug 7th to 9th.
LOS ANGELES (6th District) ....Aug. 4th to 9th
SAN JOSE......................................Aug. 11th to 16th
WILLOWS.......................................August 12th to 15th
NAPA..Aug. 18th to 23rd
RED BLUFF.....................................August 19th to 23rd.
GLENBROOK PARK, 17th District.................August 19th to 23d
PETALUMA......................................Aug. 25th to 30th
CHICO...August 26th to 30th
OAKLAND (District No. 1)......................Sept. 1st to Sept. 6th
MARYSVILLE....................................Sept. 2nd to 6th
LAKEPORT, 12th District.......................September 22d to 27th
CALIFORNIA STATE FAIR.........................Sept 8th to 20th
STOCKTON......................................Sept. 23rd to 27th.
FRESNO (Fall Meeting).........................Sept. 29th to Oct. 4th
VISALIA.......................................Oct. 7th to 11th

Stallions Advertised.

IN THE

BREEDER AND SPORTSMAN.

Thoroughbreds.

FRIAR TUCK, Hermit—Romping Girl..........C. W. Aby, Middletown.
GREENBACK, Dollar—Music...................C. W. Aby, Middletown.
ST. SAVIOR, Eolus—War Song................C. W. Aby, Middletown
THREE CHEERS, Imp. Hurrah—Young Fashion........E. S. Culver San Francisco.

Trotters.

ADMIRAL, Volunteer—Lady Pierson........... Frank Drake, Vallejo.
ALCONA, Almont—Queen Mary.............Fred W. Loeber, St. Helena
BAY ROSE Sultan—Madam Baldwin..........Thos. Bonner, Santa Rosa
CHARLES DERBY, Steinway—by Electioneer. Cook Stock Farm, Contra Costa Co.
CORRECTOR, Director—Brainey..................Pleasanton Stock Farm.
DECORATOR, Director—Chess....................Pleasanton Stock Farm.
DEXTER PRINCE, Kentucky Prince—Lady Dexter........L. M. Morse, Lodi.
DIRECTOR, Dictator—Dolly........Pleasanton Stock Farm, Pleasanton.
EL BENTON, Electioneer—Nellie Benton........Souther Farm, San Leandro.
ECLECTIC, Electioneer—Manette........Wilfred Page, Sonoma County
EROS, Electioneer—Sontag Mohawk.........W. H. Vioget, Menlo Park
FIGARO, Hambletonian—Emblem ....Souther Farm, San Leandro.
GROVER CLAY, Electioneer—Maggie Norfolk..........Denis Gannon, Oakland.
GRAND MOOR 2374, Moor 870—Vashti...............H. I. Thornton, S. F.
G. A. M., Anteeo—Rosa B.................George E. Guerne, Santa Rosa.
GUY WILKES, George Wilkes—Lady Bunker ....San Mateo Stock Farm, San Mateo.
GLEN FORTUNE, Electioneer—Glenna...........Souther Farm, San Leandro.
GEORGE WASHINGTON, Mambrino Chief—Fanny Rose........Thos. Smith, Vallejo.
GRANDISSIMO, LeGrande—Norma..........Fred W. Loeber, St Helena
JESTER D, Almont—Hortense..............Souther Farm, San Leandro
KING DAVID, Admiral—Black Flora..............Frank Drake, Vallejo.
LEO WILKES, Guy Wilkes Sable........San Mateo Stock Farm, San Mateo.
MEMO, Sidney—Flirt................................ John Rowen, Oakland
MAMBRINO WILKES, George Wilkes—Lady Chrisman........San Miguel Stock Farm, Walnut Creek.
MAMBRINO CHIEF, McDonald Chief—Venus........Thos. Smith, Vallejo.
MORTIMER, Electioneer—Marti ....Wilfred Page, Sonoma County
PASHA, Sultan—Madam Baldwin......................D. Bryson, Linden
PHILOSOPHER, Pilot Wilkes—Belle......... George E. Guerne, Santa Rosa.
REDWOOD, Anteeo—Lou Wilton...................A. McFayden, Oakland.
STEINWAY, Strathmore—Abbess ....Cook Stock Farm, Contra Costa Co
SABLE WILKES, Guy Wilkes—Sable.........San Mateo Stock Farm, San Mateo.
VICTOR, Echo—Daughter of Woodburn........G. W. Hughes, Napa City

The Tacoma Meeting.

The Secretary of the Morgan Memorial Speeding Track has forwarded to this office a programme of the races for a five days' meeting which it is proposed to hold on July 1st, 2nd, 3rd, 4th and 5th. There are about $6,000 offered in purses, there being altogether five running events, seven purses for the trotting brigade, while the pacers have not been neglected as there are three purses to be divided among the side wheel division: The programme is a good one and will undoubtedly receive the unqualified support of all horsemen throughout the northwest.

2:30 Records.

It would seem that at last the National Trotting Horse Breeders' Association, which formulates the rules by which horses may be enrolled in the American Trotting Register, have determined to try and prevent the oft repeated trials against time and bogus matches by which horses obtain records, and are classed as "in the list." At a late meeting action was taken in the matter, and a set of rules was drawn up by the committee appointed for the purpose, which will be revised, if deemed necessary, before they are given to the public as "the law." Of course it must be understood that these rules only apply to those not already in the charmed circle, and if once a member of that august body, he can then be sent against the watch to lower his record. The rules as given below are not in their entirety, but summarized so that the Directors of the various agricultural associations may understand what is required to obtain a record that will be accepted at headquarters.

1. All performances carrying an animal into the 2.30 list for the first time, must be made at a regular meeting of a reputable association.

2. These performances must be made under the control of the National Association of Trotting Horse Breeders, or of an association in membership and good standing with the American Trotting Association or the National Trotting Association.

3. The meaning of the phrase "regular meeting" is fully defined, and is used in contradiction from what might be really a special meeting, called for the single purpose of giving an animal a record.

4. Under there rules there can be no more bogus matches, gotten up privately, for all performances must be made at a regular meeting in order to secure the benefit of a 2:30 performance.

5. Stakes may be opened by any association, as restricted above, for all animals seeking admission to the 2:30 list, to be called the "Standard Stakes" the terms of entrance to be fixed by the Association, but not less than ten dollars. The entries will be divided into groups of three and so started. In the race, if the leading horse trots in 2:30 or better, he takes his record and goes to the stable. If in the next heat the leading horse trots in 2.30 or better, he also goes to the stable, leaving the third horse to trot the third heat alone, and this is the only case, under the system, in which a horse trots alone and that after he has trotted two heats against others.

6. The one-half of the stakes of the winners in a group or division will go to the horse making the fastest record in the group, the balance to the Association, and the stakes of all failures will revert to the Association.

There may be some amendments or additions to the above, but not enough to materially alter them.

The Australian Importations.

On last Saturday morning the S. S. Alameda arrived with the first consignment of horses sent over by Mr. T. B. Merry for ex-senator L. J. Rose of Los Angeles. It would be very unfair to give a description of the mares in their present condition as the hurried manner in which they were shipped from the antipodes prevented the preparation which they should have received for the long sea voyage. The animals were sent over in charge of Mr. Chas. Wilson who is well known to the racing men of Australia, as the owner and trainer of Gardenia, the only mare that ever beat Mentor. Mr. Wilson informs us that within a day or two of the shipment the mares were running loose in the paddocks and had not been taken up in time to properly fit them for the journey.

The daily papers have all mentioned the arrival of the stock, but as usual got them all mixed up, for by the list published in the BREEDER AND SPORTSMAN some three weeks ago, it was anticipated that several others would be sent, but at the last moment changes were made, the animals sent being as follows: Lady Alice, b m, by Musket out of Erycina by Sledmere and therefore a sister to Mitrailleuse.

Hester, ch m by Derby son of Kingsborough, this was a noted mare and carried 142 pounds and ran second for the Murrimbidgee Handicap; she was a good performer and purchased by Mr. Merry on account of the brackets which stand opposite her name in the racing register.

Elsie, ch m, by Grand Flaneur out of Daughter of the Regiment; 2nd dam the dam of Melos which gives her a double cross of Yattendon, the sire of Chester.

Pheobe Marks, b m, by Kingsborough out of Lady Audley, dam of the Secret. This mare was thought very highly of when in training, but broke down early in her engagements. She is in foal to Othello, son of the Barb and is the only one of the mares purchased by Mr. Merry that will foal to Australian dates.

Keziah, by Darebin out of Lady Fanny, is in foal to Hastings, winner of the Hawkesbury Handicap; Keziah has been stinted to foal according to American time.

Rose of Arizona, formerly called Amber, is by the Drummer, but in the papers sent the 1st and 2nd dams were omitted, the 3rd dam, however, is the dam of Melos.

San Pedro, br c, by Waxlight, dam sister to Calamia, winner of the Melbourne cup.

There was also sent a br f Heiress full sister to Sheet Anchor, she by St. Albans out of Queen Mary; unfortunately this mare died on the voyage over, leaving only seven of the eight to arrive here. Mr. Merry has purchased eight others for Mr. Rose which will arrive on the next steamer. One of the mares which was originally intended to be sent in this first consignment was the br m Ricochet, five years old, full sister to the mare Lady Alice mentioned above, but she received a severe kick from one of the horses and it was deemed expedient to leave her until the second lot was sent.

Another Departure.

It is a fact susceptible of proof that we are all more or less engendered with a feeling of selfishness. Many times within the past few weeks we have heard horsemen deploring the fact that Palo Alto sent the pick of their horses East, and that Hickok had also traveled in the same direction to try and gain honor with those under his charge. It has been a source of grumbling, because many have been of the opinion that their absence would detract from the interest of our local racing circuit, but there is another side to look at in this question, and that is this: California for quite a number of years has been the Mecca to which Eastern horsemen wended their way for the purpose of picking up fast and enduring trotters. The fame of Electioneer, Stamboul, Guy Wilkes, Director, Sidney, Piedmont, and many others has gone broadcast throughout the land, and as a natural consequence breeders in the East have endeavored to secure the speedy sons and daughters of these noted sires. This has been brought about on account of what California bred horses have done on the Eastern tracks, and the residents of this State must bear in mind that every race won by a Californian representative in the East is only adding fresh glory to the Golden State. When the two stables mentioned above started on the eastward journey the BREEDER AND SPORTSMAN wished them Godspeed, and now we have to say a few parting words to still another stable which started on Wednesday morning last. Mr. Salisbury of the Pleasanton Stock Farm has already won golden opinions for his noted sire because he campaigned him throughout the Eastern circuit, meeting the many mighty horses of the day, and beating them all with his speedy black horse. To show the people of the East that Director reproduces his marvelous speed in his progeny, Mr. Salisbury has shipped back for trotting purposes Direct 2:18½, Margaret S 2:19½, and Katie S, with no record at all, all of which are the progeny of Director. There is also in the same car a mare by Steinway called Cricket, a pacer who gives every evidence of being very fast when brought in contact with those of the lateral division. These horses will be campaigned throughout the East until the first of August, and perhaps a week or two later, when they will be brought back to California for the purpose of taking part in the latter end of the circuit here.

The owner takes back with him the good wishes of a legion of friends, and we sincerely trust that victory may perch upon his banner whenever any of his stable start. If he should prove able to beat many of the cracks against whom, no doubt, he will have to contend, there will be fresh laurels to add to the already large wreath of Old Director.

The Northern Circuit.

Attention is called on another page to the Northern Circuit which has just been completed. A correspondent at Chico who was present at the meeting of delegates from the different associations throughout the northern section informs us that $3900 will be offered in purses at the Willows; $3500 at Red Bluff; nearly $6000 at Chico and $5500 at Marysville. We are glad to see that these associations are acting together in harmony, the only regret being that the Directors of Glenbrook Park cannot stand in with the circuit, for the distance between there and the Willows is so short that many who would like to attend both places can only go to one and thus one association must lose some of its expected patronage.

While the Northern Circuit is being made horsemen further south will be busy at San Jose, Napa, Petaluma and Oakland, but there are plenty of horses in training to-day to insure full entries for both of these circuits and we do not doubt but what both of them will show up well as far as entries are concerned. In the course of a week or two we shall be able to offer our readers a full programme for each meeting of the northern circuit and horsemen who desire to make entries up there can find entry blanks at this office.

Los Angeles Entries.

This is the last opportunity we shall have for calling the attention of our readers but more particularly the horse owners throughout the State, to the fact that on Monday next, the 16th inst., the entries will close for a purse of $1,500 for the 2:30 class at Los Angeles, and also close for the District two-year-old trotting stakes for 1890 and 1891. It is unnecessary for us to speak of the liberal manner in which the Directors of this Association have acted towards the horsemen of the State by offering large and generous purses. There is no one who cannot afford to go from the central portion of the State to Los Angeles to compete for the large purses offered, and we fully expect to see many an entry from within a radius of a hundred miles of Sacramento. The Secretary has used his utmost endeavors to make the forthcoming meeting a great success and as the principal portion of this labor consists in trying to get entries for the purses, we feel assured that he will not be disappointed in the work he has done. Read the advertisement in the appropriate column and make entries for the first meeting of the circuit.

Ione Meeting.

The Directors of the 27th Agricultural District comprising Amador and Sacramento Counties will hold their 4th annual fair at Ione on August 5th, 6th, 7th and 8th next. With two exceptions the entire programme consists of running races, there being three or four each day. Handsome amounts have been added to each of the stakes, and the races comprise all distances from a quarter of a mile and repeat up to one and three-eights miles. There will also be during the meeting two match trotting races between stallions owned in the district. The rules of the State Agricultural Society will govern the races except when the conditions named are otherwise. The entries are due on July 15th, and from the highly successful meeting that was held at Ione last year, there are good grounds for the belief that another successful meeting will be held this year. The track, as we are told, is in the best of condition, and those who attend as spectators may rest assured that they will witness grand contests.

Our Tennessee Letter.

GALLATIN, TENN., June 5th.

EDITOR BREEDER AND SPORTSMAN:—By the time this is in print, the BREEDER AND SPORTSMAN's many readers will most probably be able to form some idea anent El Rio Rey's alleged loss of wind, or a "roarer" as some may term it. The Winters' stable of horses left Nashville last Monday for St. Louis, where El Rio Rey is engaged, as are Rey del Rey and other horses of the stable.

It has been given out that El Rio Rey will start in the St. Louis Derby next Saturday, providing the track is good. As that race will be an event of past turf history ere this has reached the printer's case, I will not dwell upon the outcome and probabilities of that race, but will say that any owner with a pretty fair sort of a colt should not let El Rio Rey's presence keep him from starting. True it is that El Rio Rey did an "easy mile" in 1:44 (?) before they left Nashville, but a trial mile is not an actual race of a mile and a half, or the other distances that three-year-olds have to run in the stake races now.

Rey del Rey, without an exception, is the grandest looking horse that ever wore plates, and Courtney has him in the pink of condition. Before leaving Tennessee for St. Louis, he did a trial three-quarters fast enough to assure all connected with him that he can out-run any youngster that has appeared this season, and when he makes his bow to the public, it will only be a repetition of his elder brother's performance last year, when he won every race in which he started.

Don Jose, of the Winter's string, has an ailing limb, and with the possible exception of El Rio Rey being effected, their is not another unsound horse in the string. Average and Joe Courtney will beat more horses than will beat them.

Outside the departure of the Winters horses, there has been no happenings of more than passing importance among the runners. Among the trotters and sidewheelers the same can not be said for from Ewell Farm comes the news of a gait never known to have been accomplished before. Some how or other it sounds like a big Tennessee story with a Mulhattan flavor, but in this fast age we must not look upon anything as an impossibility. I have just received a note from reliable sources at Ewell Farm, which bears the sensational news that Brown Hal 2:12½ had that day paced a quarter in 28 seconds, a 1:52 gait. This can hardly be true, yet under the existing circumstances I must believe that it is. It is one of the most remarkable feats ever accomplished by a trotter or pacer. Brown Hal is a full brother to Little Brown Jug 2:11¾, and is himself the sire of Prince Hal, that obtained a mark last season of 2:16½. Brown Hal has never met defeat upon the race course, and his record of 2:12½ he made last season in the third heat of a winning race, after Roy Wilkes had paced the second heat in 2:13. Considering that he has just made a heavy season in the stud the performance is the more remarkable. Ed Geers will go down the Grand Circuit with him, and it is expected of him to eclipse Johnston's record.

Come over the Rockies, California, with your Adonis, Roy Wilkes and others of that ilk, and Tennessee will try to make it interesting for you with Brown Hal 2:12½, and Hal Pointer 2:13.

Huntress had quite an easy time winning the three Jackpot races at Lexington, Louisville and Latonia. The result of the race this year was hardly what the management of the three Kentucky clubs expected, and I would not be surprised at seeing this race dropped out of the entry books next fall.

Since coming East, Fairy and Rico of the Rose string have both started, but neither have earned brackets. Fairy started in the Great American Stakes at Brooklyn, and while she did not win, she ran a very creditable race, finishing in fourth place, with several crack two year olds strung out behind her. Rico is in the Suburban at a light impost, and after he fully recovers from his long trip across the continent he may be able to show something like Suburban form.

Fide's victory in the Toboggan Slide Handicap has made her price in the Suburban move downward several points. There is quite a difference in six furlongs and a mile and a quarter, and I am inclined to think the Belmont filly much better suited at the former distance. She completely smashed the record in her race for the big Westchester event, and, with her smart turn of speed, she may be a dangerous mare in the Suburban.

By the way; This seems to remind me how fast the 3-year old filly English Lady has loomed up as a formidable suburban candidate. A few weeks ago I spoke of her as not being "suggestive of a Surburan winner? but in this one particular I have changed my opinion considerably. She is shoes to plates, the best three year old in the West, not barring Robespeirre, Riley or Bill Letcher, the three Derby winners. Her four consecutive victories at Lexington, Louisville and Latonia have been the cause of her being backed from 100 to 1, down to 15 to 1 in The Surburban. Her Latonia Oaks one and a quarter miles, 113 pounds up in 2:08¾ is the best race run in the West this season, and in point of time, is equal to 2:07 over the Sheephead Bay Course. She only carries 94 pounds in the Surburban, and if she does not go amiss before Suburban day, her stable companion Proctor Knott, will remain in his stable while The Lady wins Sheepsheads Bay's big race. She is my choice, and if she wins that race, the hottest air-tight cinch ever seen upon an Eastern race course, is going to be uncorked.

Since writing the above I learn, reliably, some sensational news regarding the Winter's Stable, which is to this effect; Three days before the California horses were shipped from Nashville to St. Louis, B. J. Johnson, trainer for the Chicago Stable last season, was in Nashville, and most of the time had business at West Side Park. Whenever the Winter's horses were at work, Johnson was upon the track, watch in hand, noting every movement of the California cracks. Finally he approached Mr. Winters, asking him to put a price upon his entire stable. Mr. Winters told him that El Rio Rey he would not sell, and that the mare Florence A. he would leave at Belle Meade to be bred to Imp. Great Tom, but that he would sell Rey del Rey, Don Juan, Don Jose, Judge Post, Average, Loretta, Blizzard, Atelia, Joe Courtney and the other horses of the stable for $55,000. Johnson then asked Mr. Winters if he would take $45,000 and give him three days' option upon the horses, Mr. Winters responded "I will not give you three minutes. I will sell now, but in three minutes I might not. Give me $55,000 cash and I will turn my stable of horses over to you." Johnson replied that he was not prepared to do so, immediately, but would like to talk to him at the end of the time he asked for. Johnson is now in Louisville, and is supposed to be trying to arrange for the purchase of the horses.

In the Winter Stable is a colt—Rey del Rey—that is worth all of what Johnston offered for the entire string. Before leaving Nashville, as stated above, he showed the fastest six furlongs ever run over that track, and there are several Nashville turfmen who will bet dollars to apples that Rey del Rey can simply loose Russell, the crack colt of the East at any distance. As a prominent Nashville horseman told me to-day, "There are some two-year-olds in the Winters Stable that have shown better work here than have any three-year-olds." The colts alluded to are Don Juano, Rey del Rey and Judge Post, a trio of youngsters that will show their heels to the cracker jacks of the aristocratic Belmont, Dwyer, Morris and Withers Stables when they are taken East.

People who are in a position to know, say that El Rio Rey is effected with something like catarrh, and the peculiar noise made by him when at work is from this, and not caused by being broken-winded. As this is a peculiar disease among horses it is not known to what extent it effects the horse.

KENNESSAW.

Foals of Abdallah Park.

Abdallah Park's second report in 1890, at Cynthiana, Ky.

April 13th, b f by George Simmons 8694, dam Nellie K, pacing record 2:38.

April 20th, b f Jubilee De Jarnette 5705, dam Belva by Indianapolis 2:21.

April 23d, br c by Simmons 2:28, dam Genie by Sultan 2:24, second dam Lady Graves by Nutwood 2:18¾, third dam Lady Babcock, dam of Elector 2:21½ and Soudan 2:27¾ by Hambletonian 725.

April 24th, blk c by Sultan 2:24, dam Linnie, four-year-old record 2:25 by Egbert 1136, 2nd dam by Mambrino Time 1686, 3rd dam by Ward's Flying Cloud.

April 27th, b f by Simmons 2:28, dam Nell by Abdallah Mambrino 3715, 2nd dam by Edwin Forrest.

March 22nd, b c by Simmons 2:28, dam Wasbash Maid by Steven's Bald Chief, 2nd dam Belle of Wabash, 2:40, dam of The Moor 2:37.

April 20th, b f by Simmons, dam Bessie R. by Magic, 2nd dam by Jno. Dillard.

April 27th, b c by Geo. Simmons, dam Pennamite by Geo. D. Prentice, 2nd dam dam of Belle Wilkes 2:27 and Grey Prince 2:39½.

May 4th, b f by Simmons, dam Smuggler's Daughter 2:24¾ by Smuggler, second dam Mollie D. by Mambrino Chief 11.

May 8th, bl c by Geo. Simmons, dam Grey Moll, dam of Belle Wilkes 2:37 and Grey Prince 2:39½.

May 14th, b f by Jubilee De Jarnette, dam Mary Veach by Indian Chief.

May 9th, b c by Geo. Simmons 8694, dam Helen Collins by Indianapolis 2:21, 2nd dam by Stockbridge Chief Jr.

May 10th, b c by Simmons 2744, dam Belle Brassfield, rec. 2.20 by Viley's Cripple, second dam Sally Chorister, dam of Proteine 2:18 and Belle Patchen, dam of Baron Wilkes 2:18, etc.

May 13th, bl f by Simmons, dam Corine by Ravenswood, 2nd dam by Scott's Thomas 2:21.

May 23rd, ch f by Simmons, dam Katie Eastman by Enfield, record 2:29.

May 24th, b f by Simmons 2:28, dam Adelaide 2:18 by Milwaukee 603, second dam Minnie B., dam of Milo 2:21 by Bay Mambrino, son of Alex's Bay Chief.

May 25th, bl c by Geo. Simmons, dam Lillie H. by Clay son of Strader's Clay, second dam Lucy Marshall, dam of Mamie M. 2:22½, Pattie Cooper 2:30 and Mambrino Templar Jr., sire of Long John 2:28½ by Daniel Boone.

Answers to Correspondents.

Answers for this department must be accompanied by the name and address of the sender, not necessarily for publication, but as proof of good faith. Write the questions distinctly, and on one side of the paper only. Positively no questions will be answered by mail or telegraph.

Subscriber.

Will you give in the next number of the paper the address of the owner of Axtell.

Answer.—Axtell is owned by five persons. A letter addressed to W. P. Ijams, Terre Haute, Indiana, will reach the owners.

Reader.

Will you please publish the pedigree of "Paddy Magee" and any noteworthy performances or other qualifications and oblige.

Answer.—Paddy Magee, was by Gen. Taylor, dam a Canadian mare, pedigree untraced. He is registered as Capt. Hanford 804. There are records of nineteen races that he won, but to give an outline of them all, would take more room than we can spare!

Names Claimed.

I hereby claim the following name *Conde* for chestnut colt white stripe on forehead, right fore leg white, foaled April 14th, 1890, by Duke of Norfolk, dam May D. by Wildidle; also;

Estrella for chestnut filly, two hind feet white and one fore foot white, foaled March 22nd, 1890, by Duke of Norfolk dam Belle W.

THOMAS N. FISHER, Coyote, Cal.

VETERINARY.

Conducted by W. Henry Jones, M. R. C. V. S.

Subscribers to this paper can have advice through this column in all cases of sick or injured horses or cattle by sending an explicit description of the case. Applicants will send their name and address that they may be identified. Questions requiring answers by mail should be accompanied by two dollars, and addressed to W. Henry Jones, M. R. C. V. S., Olympic Stables, Sutter Street, San Francisco.

A Correction.

Two weeks ago we published an excellent article on Navicular disease from the pen of Dr. A. E Buzard, and it has been extensively copied throughout the United States. The author calls attention to a couple of mistakes which occurred in it as printed, the proof reader having slighted the "copy." In the sentence, "The disease is progressive, caries of the bone takes place, the tendon playing over it becomes involved, and in extreme cases *upturned*." The word in italics should read ruptured, to make it read correct. Under the headings of symptoms, "the peculiar *joint*" should read the peculiar gait.

Glanders in Horses.

WRITTEN FOR THE BREEDER AND SPORTSMAN

As this disease is becoming very prevalent in this State, I consider that a short article on the disease may be of some utility to the readers of the BREEDER AND SPORTSMAN in assisting them to detect the disease, and also to prevent the spreading of the same.

The causes of this disease are various, but the majority of cases doubtless arise from contagion, that is, coming in actual contact with a diseased animal, or by inhaling the same atmosphere, drinking out of the same bucket, or even cases have been known from wearing the same harness.

It is frequently generated by horses in a low, emaciated condition, being kept in some dark, unventilated and undrained stable, and being allowed to remain for days, or perhaps weeks, on the manure which has accumulated behind them, and then being obliged to continually breathe the vitiated atmosphere, which will necessarily be generated in such cases.

The symptoms of this loathsome disease are frequently very deceptive; many a horse has been destroyed for glanders when the disease did not exist, it being confounded with nasal gleet. To an experienced person such a mistake should not be made, as the symptoms between the two affections, although alike, differ materially, on a close and minute examination. In a case of glanders the discharge from the nostrils is scanty, yellowish in color and frequently streaked with blood, and is very glutinous in character, having a tendency to adhere to the edge of the nostrils. The lining mucous membrane of the nostrils, will, in the majority of cases, be of a leaden hue, and on careful examination, a few ulcers will be found on its surface, these ulcers presenting a very distinct and characteristic appearance. The glands between the lower jaw will be found somewhat enlarged, hard and indurated, and adherent to the bone. The animal will have a cough but not of a very distressing nature, and the general appearance will indicate that the animal is not in perfect health, although I have seen cases where the horses looked the picture of health. Now in ozena or nasal gleet the discharge from the nostrils in the majority of cases will be copious and come away in big white clots, the membrane may not present quite a natural color, the glands will be enlarged but will be soft, and do not adhere to the jaw. In a few cases there may be a soft cough, but the general appearance of the horse will be healthy.

In cases where a horse is found to be glandered, it should be immediately destroyed, and if there be any other horses in the same stable they should be strictly examined, and not allowed to come in contact with any other horses, should not be allowed to drink out of any bucket or trough, which may be used to water other horses. The stable should be thoroughly fumigated and whitewashed as a preventative. In some cases in London, which came under my notice, the entire stable was pulled down and rebuilt with new material. The harness used by the diseased horse or horses, should be scalded with boiling water, and often thoroughly scrubbed with hot water, soap and carbolic acid. In fact, in a bad case, it is advisable to destroy the harness and the stable equipment which has been in use for, or on the diseased animals.

The remainder of the horses should be examined frequently, and on the slightest symptoms the animals should be destroyed and the proper authorities notified.

In few cases, as far as I can ascertain, the health authorities never receive any notification when any animal has been destroyed with glanders. In England it is a criminal offence to possess, knowingly, a horse with glanders, and punishable by fine or imprisonment. Such an arrangement in this State, more especially when this disease is on the increase, would be beneficial to horse owners and the public generally.

It would also be advisable to appoint one or more qualified veterinary surgeons as inspectors, and give them unlimited power, as to entrance to stables and inspection of such stock as they should think fit. There are at present numerous stables in this city which are unfit for occupation, and should the disease get a hold in such places, it will be a most difficult task to eradicate it, much less prevent the spread of the affection.

One word about public water-troughs. In London at one time, they were considered a blessing and a boon to horses, and their owners, but after a time they proved to be a damnably cause. The reason of this was that glandered horses were worked in late night cabs, and the animals were watered at these troughs, the discharge dropped from the nostrils into the water, and the consequence was, that some sound horse was allowed to drink at the same place later on, and in all probability swallowed the discharge, and in a few days the animal would present symptoms of glanders, and then came the question: "Where did the horse get it from?" From numerous experiments on horses made by the Royal Veterinary College in 1874-75, it was proved beyond doubt that glanderous discharge, given to a sound horse, would generate glanders in a short time.

I would advise all horse-owners working horses in this city, or even in the country, to carry a bucket with them and draw the necessary water themselves, and not allow their animals to partake of water at any of the numerous public horse troughs.

Our Terre Haute Letter.

Terre Haute at the present writing is one of the busiest towns in the United States when looked at from the trotting horseman's point of view. There are congregated here at present a large majority of the best known horses in the country, and on Monday when I arrived it seemed as though there were representatives here from all the principal breeding farms in the United States. Special trains were run from a great many points, and advantage was taken of low rates by those who are lovers of the light harness horse.

On Monday evening I called in at the pool rooms to see what sort of betting the Eastern people indulged in, and much to my astonishment, as I entered the door, I heard the auctioneer saying, "How much am I offered for first choice?" You can conceive my astonishment when I heard it knocked down for $7, the second choice sold for $5, and the third for $3. I had always labored under the impression that betting in the Eastern States on trotting races was far and away above anything that Californians indulged in, but this sample of what I saw for the 2:23 purse was so small and insignificant in comparison with what can be seen at Oakland, Napa, Petaluma or Fresno that I am impressed with the belief that Sam Whitehead and his corps of men can do better at the small meetings in your State than they could do if here.

I can readily understand that the doings of the Golden State horses is what will more directly interest your readers, and therefore will not devote much space to the races in which only Eastern horses were engaged. On the opening day, Tuesday, June 3rd, there was a very fair attendance, considering the attractions, and yet it is safe to assert that of the 4,000 people who were in attendance nine-tenths of them paid their admission fee on purpose to witness the matchless Sunol. The day was a beautiful one, and if made to order could not have been surpassed, a day in which one finds relief from the cares of business and the multitude of small annoyances which are bound to compass any one engaged in pursuits of any sort, and it is probable that the fine weather had as much to do with the large attendance as the very ordinary racing which ensued. Since the arrival of the Palo Alto string here hundreds, and probably thousands, have attended the race track, and many had become more or less familiar with the appearance of Sunol and the face of Charlie Marvin; at any rate, when he appeared upon the track with his little bay beauty, they were received with a great deal of cheering and clapping of hands; in answer to the reception the Palo Alto reinsman doffed his cap and started down the reverse way of the track, jogging slowly. When a short distance past the three-quarter pole Sunol was turned around, and from that point home was given what Budd Doble declared to be a "little exercise." It was really marvelous to see the game filly covering the ground at a 2:13 gait, the quarter being completed in 33¼ seconds, and yet those who saw her on your California circuit last year knew she was not being extended even a little bit. I like her much better than I did last year, and that is saying a great deal, and I am inclined to the belief that what Ed. Bither said to me at the Bay District Track on the day when she made her record is true: "That mare can beat Maud S's time whenever she is started for it."

Fred Authur, the pacer, had a record of 2:15½ and that made on a half mile track. I said "had" because before I finish my letter I will show you how he has lowered it. However, the fast son of Belmont was then brought out for exhibition and Mr. Grimes, his driver, was also as cordially received as Marvin. The three races which followed resulted in Nutmeg, a son of Nutwood, winning the 2:23 trot, the fastest time made being 2:22½ which goes to the credit of Frank B., a br g, by Bog oak who won the first heat in that time, the winner's best time being 2:26. In the 2:32 trot which followed, Katie B., owned by L. A. Davies, owner of Roy Wilkes sold favorite over the field, but notwithstanding a strong and vigorous support from the betting men she only won the first heat gaining a record of 2:28½, Joe Eastman winning the next three and gaining a record of 2:29½. The last race of the day was for the 2:50 class, in which there were four starters, Called Back winning in three straight heats, the best time being 2:36½.

On Wednesday the 2:28 trot brought out Twist, a roan filly by Jay Bird; Cubic, a b g, by Electioneer, and Constantine, the Egbert youngster, which was sold for such a long price last year. Twist sold for $10 and the field $10; the roan had things all her own way in three straight heats, and was never troubled in the least by either of her two competitors, winning as she pleased in 2:26½, 2:26½ and 2:27. The papers on the following day saw fit to state that this was the battle royal between Kentucky and California, to sustain their pet theories of breeding the trotters. Such consummate nonsense could only emanate from scribblers who do not know what they are writing about. One of the papers had the following:

"The Palo Alto theory that for speed and endurance at the trot, the thoroughbred cross must be close up, was maintained by Cubic, son of Electioneer, dam Cuba by imported Australian. The roan descendant from the loins of the mighty Wilkes had the best of the argument, and to-night the scalp of Sibley is hung in the Simmon's wigwam."

The 2:35 pacer had four starters and it proved an easy victory for Catherine, a descendant of Dictator, the best time made being 2:32½. During the day Budd Doble appeared behind Jack 2:15, and Harry Starr who is Doble's right hand man, also exhibited Houri 2:17. Johnnie Dickerson also speeded the two-year-old Faustino, who as every one knows has the yearling stallion record of the world.

Friday morning opened up bright and suspiciously, the city being crowded to its utmost capacity, for in addition to the attractions of the race track, Barnum's monster circus also put in an appearance. However, my business called me to the stables with no time to spare for the circus. When the bell was rung it must be confessed that things looked rather home like for there sat Orrin Hickok in the timers' stand as large as life and twice as natural. Johnston 2:06¼ was given a slow mile by George Starr and Palo Alto was driven by Mr. Marvin a slow half. The great feat of the day was the exhibition of the pole team Reina and Betsy Brown driven by Doble who started to beat the half mile record of 1:08½, and it must be confessed that the feat was easily performed, Doble sending them a merry clip and completing the distance in 1.07½, the first quarter being consummated in 32½ seconds. Truly it is wonderful time and Mr. Doble proposes when they are both just right to send them against the double team mile record of the world. The first race of the day was for the 2:40 trotters which was easily won by Hussar, a brown colt by Jersey Wilkes, three straight heats falling to him the fastest mile being 2:26½. The sport of the day finished up with the Free-for-all pacing race, the entries to which were Fred Arthur, Gray Harry and Bessemer. Fred Arthur was the favorite in the pool box bringing $10 to $8 for the field. In the first heat he beat Bessemer by a head only in the really good time for this season of the year, of 2:14½; he easily took the second and third heats, Grey Harry being his runner up in 2:17½ and 2:20½. It could easily be seen that Bessemer was not in condition for a hard race, but as he is of the improving sort you will hear from him later on.

The fourth and last day of the meeting was characterized by having the largest attendance of any preceding day. It seems almost requisite to require a stretch of the imagination to conceive that the following horses were all on the track at one and the same time: Sunol, 2:10½; Axtell, 2:12; Palo Alto, 2:12½; Houri, 2:17; Johnston, 2:06¼; Roy Wilkes, 2:12½ and Adonis, 2:14; such an exhibition of noted horses has never been seen at one time before on any track in the world. Mr. Marvin made himself a great favorite by speeding Sunol a quarter in 32¼ seconds, a 2:09 gait; Johnston, the pacer was sent three heats in 2:27, 2:23 and 2:20, the last quarter of one of the miles being completed in 31½ seconds; the other cracks were only shown to bridle with the exception of Adonis whom Hickok sent a very slow mile. The 2:23 pacing race proved a strong incentive for the betting fraternity who piled in their money quite liberally on Frank, he selling for $10 while the field brought $3, it proved quite an exciting race as Frank won the first heat, Findley the 2nd, Frank the 3rd, Findley taking the 4th and 5th; Frank's best time was 2:26½, Findley's best time, 2:24½.

The sport of the day was brought to a conclusion by the race for the 2:19 class of trotters but only two starters appeared, Almont and the old favorite Kit Curry; Almont won as he pleased in straight heats, the fastest time being 2:20½.

SACRAMENTO.

Horse's Sense of Smell.

The horse will leave musty hay untouched in his bin, however hungry. He will not drink of water objectionable to his questioning sniff, or from a bucket which some odor makes objectionable, however thirsty. His intelligent nostril will widen, quiver and query over the daintiest bit offered by the fairest of hands with coaxings that would make a mortal shut his eyes and swallow a nauseous mouthful at a gulp.

A mare is never satisfied by either sight or whinny that her colt is really her own until she has a certified nasal certificate of the fact. A blind horse now living will not allow the approach of any stranger without showing signs of anger not safely to be disregarded. The distinction is evidently made by his sense of smell, and at a considerable distance. Blind horses as a rule will gallop wildly around a pasture without striking the surrounding fence. The sense informs them of its proximity. Others will, when loosed from the stables go directly to the gate or bars opened to their accustomed feeding grounds, and when desiring to return, after hours of careless wandering, will distinguish one outlet and patiently await its opening. The odor of that particular part of the fence is their pilot to it.

The horse in browsing, or while gathering herbage with his lips, is guided in its choice of proper food entirely by its nostrils. Blind horses do not make mistakes in their diet. In the temple of Olympus a bronze horse was exhibited at the sight of which six real horses exhibited the most violent emotions. Aelian judiciously observes that the most perfect art could not imitate nature sufficiently well to produce so strong an illusion. The scent alone of a buffalo robe will cause many horses to evince lively terror, and the floating scent of a railroad train will frighten some long after the locomotive is out of sight and hearing.

Breeding Fillies.

There is quite a difference of opinion among breeders as to the proper time to commence breeding fillies.

We have had considerable experience during the past fifteen years in breeding mares, having bred a large number during that time, both for ourselves and those who patronized the stallions we kept for public service.

We have always advocated breeding the fillies at two years old, if it is the intention to breed them at all, as it is our opinion they will foal their first colt when three years old with less danger to themselves than when four or five years old, for the following reasons: the mare not being so fully matured as at four or five years old her bones and muscles are not so firmly knit, hence will give more readily, also the foal of the three-year old mare will generally be smaller at birth, thereby lessening the danger of the mare having trouble.

We have never known a three-year old mare to have trouble in foaling, although we have known of quite a number of fine mares being lost by not being able to foal their first colt when five to seven years old.

Two-year old fillies should not be bred too early in the season; it would be better to have them foaled in July than before grass comes in the spring, as they will do far better if they can have a run on grass for a month or more before foaling.

We believe that mares that have their first colts at three years make better and more regular breeders, and in our opinion, the breeder who allows a good two-year old filly to run over without being stinted to a well-bred, matured stallion is losing valuable time.

We say breed the fillies to matured stallions, for in breeding horses, as with all other kinds of stock, if young immature females are bred to young immature males, the stock will rapidly degenerate into mere scrubs.—National Horse Breeder.

THE KENNEL.

Dog owners are requested to send for publication the earliest possible notices of whelps, sales, names claimed, presentations and deaths, in their kennels, in all instances writing plainly names of sire and dam and of grandparents, colors, dates and breed.

Wheles.

Mr. A. B. Truman's Irish red setter dog, Lady Elcho T. (Elcho—Noreen) whelped June 1st, 1890, eight, four dogs to owners, Mike T. (Nemo T.—Nida).

Ben O. Bush, Kalamazoo, Mich., pointer bitch Lady Wallace 12768 A. K. C. S. B., May 26th, whelped three dogs by Jack of Nasso 7044 A. K. C. S. B.

H. Waruf, Kalamazoo, Mich., English setter Fly Noble 11399, A. K. C. S. B., May 15th, whelped ten (three dogs) by Champion Toledo Blade, one dog and two bitches since dead.

Visits.

H. Waruf, Kalamazoo, Mich., pointer bitch Devonshire Kit 11142 A K C S B (Devonshire Sam—Lottie) to Kalamazoo Kennel's Wonder Lad 12767 A K C S B (Champion Lad of Bow x Lady Belle), on May 5th.

California Kennel Club.

The California Kennel Club held its regular monthly meeting on Wednesday last, at the office of J. B. Lewis, corner of Montgomery and Sacramento streets. Those present were Mr. Lewis, A. E. Post, Thomas Higgs, J. B. Martin, A. B. Truman and two others.

Thomas F. Casey ann Jeremiah Noonan were elected members.

A communication was received from A. P. Vredenburgh, Secretary of the American Kennel Club, notifying the California Club that it had been elected to membership.

Max Wenzel of Hoboken, New Jersey, a prominent member of the Irish Setter Club, was unanimously elected a delegate to the American Club to represent the California Kennel Club.

A. E. Post was elected a member of the Executive Committee of the California Kennel Club.

A. B. Truman, Thomas Higgs and J. B. Martin were elected a committee to consider the advisability of giving a bench show in the near future. It is likely that the show will be held.

Some discussion occurred on the proposition to bar Mr. Truman's dogs from competition, but the owner stated that they would be entered in the challenge class, and would therefore not interfere with the entries in other classes.

Interstate Coursing.

The movement towards giving a great coursing meeting at Merced in the Fall, and hanging up purses so great as to make it worth while for some of the Eastern and English dogs to compete, is likely to be successful. A large and enthusiastic meeting of coursing men was held at 539 California street, city, on Wednesday evening last.

The following were elected permanent officers of the association: President, Dominick Shannon; vice-president, Henry Wormington; treasurer, J. C. Nealon; Secretary, J. R. Dickson.

The following committees were appointed to collect subscriptions for the necessary purse required by the Eastern sportsmen who intend to compete in the interstate match:

San Francisco—William Stout, John Grace, James Douglas, Matthew Nunan, John Hammill.

Redwood City—P. Foley and J. Hand.

Petaluma—D. J. Healy and Patrick Carroll.

Oakland—P. Gallagher and P. Miller.

Newark—John Dugan.

San Jose—William McCormick, A. Tracey, T. Cooney.

Santa Clara—Dr. Wadams, Mr. Curtiss, Mr. Portal,

Rockland—Edward O'Connell.

Sacramento—William Hanrahan, Thomas Waite and Patrick Kenny.

Bloomfield—P. Carroll.

Los Angeles—Walter Moore, Thomas Rice.

San Quentin—W. D. Berry.

The President was authorized to appoint any one else whom he may deem worthy.

The president announced that the association had received a guaranty of $500 from Merced. About $3000 will be sufficient to insure the match, and that amount is already assured,

The next meeting will be held on Wednesday, June 25th

The Kennel Club Muddle.

The action of the American Kennel Club in admitting the California Club to membership is being harshly criticized by some members of the Pacific Kennel Club; those who object to its admission insist that it is not a club except in name, that it has no bona fide membership nor any officers who are performing or have performed any services in connection with it for four years last past. The discontented ones persist in saying that the animus of the California Kennel Club is to subvert the purposes of the Pacific Kennel Club; to belittle what has been done by members of that Club and generally to harrass and hamper rather than to move on in good faith for the interest of dogs and their owners. It is urged that after such representations as to the extent of the Kennel field in San Francisco as were made to the American Kennel Club, it was unwise and unfair to the Pacific Kennel Club to admit a competing organization even though that organization existed only nominally. It is proposed by some of the more quick tempered members of the P. K. C. to withdraw that club from the A. K. C., but it is not probable that such action will be taken. We hope that the utmost circumspection will govern all proceedings in this matter. It is worse than folly for any single Club to presume to dictate to the general Kennel organization of America. Any attempt to override the action of the general body can only result in disaster to the club which makes the effort. That mistakes may have been made by the A. K. C. is likely but it is a poor remedy for errors in the working of a grand institution such as the A. K. C. to demolish the body or to weaken it by lessening its membership. We are not prepared to say that the California Kennel Club has any members or that there is in fact any such institution in existence nor can we deny the existence of the club, if anybody acquainted states that it is in operation. A Kennel Club amounts to nothing anyhow except at about the time when a show is to be given. Then the mossbacks swarm about, jabber and bustle as though they had been in it all the time. One thing is sure, viz: that no show in San Francisco can be made to clear its way which is not conducted more economically than those given by the Pacific Club. If the admission of the California Kennel Club to the A. K. C. operates to make the Pacific Club more careful it would be a good thing. At all events it is nonsensical to think of taking the Pacific Club out of the A. K. C., because if the former ever desires to give a show it must necessarily apply for re-admission. A little time would temper the acerbity of those who are now cross firing in relation to the clubs.

Muzzling Greyhounds at Coursing Meetings.

In your valuable journal of May 23 we notice a comment on muzzling greyhounds at inclosed meetings, and to entirely set aside any and all questions in regard to this subject will fully explain the *modus operandi* of the muzz'ing process. The muzzling is done, of course, to protect the rabbit from being killed, and this is done, not for the sake of economy, but to do away with the least shadow of objection to coursing on the score of cruelty. The universal sentiment of those who saw the trials at Hutchinson last Fall with the greyhounds without muzzles was in favor of muzzling; and when the second stake was opened the association decided to use the muzzles on every occasion where the running was on inclosed grounds.

The muzzles used are of very light steel wire and are capacious enough so that the dog can have perfect freedom in the use of his jaws. He can open his mouth to the fullest extent desired.

After each course an attendant secures the dogs at once and the muzzles are taken from them. The straps around the neck are not tight, and in reality the dog is not in any sense distressed or even annoyed by the muzzles; every owner of the greyhounds that competed at the meeting will tell you that there was no appreciable difference in the running of the dogs with the muzzles on, and should those with whom you have conversed witness a course they would be thoroughly convinced of muzzling the dogs.

The muzzle is a sort of basket work covering the nose to the eyes, with three long wires reaching to the neck back of the ears, through he ends of which the strap is fastened, and while it does not prevent his breathing in full, he is unable to close his jaws on the hare. We have now run four meetings with the dogs muzzled and in no one case has a dog suffered in the least and it has proved so universally successful that it will be understood that under no circumstances will a course be run on incl sed grounds without the dogs are muzzled.

When the subject of coursing was broached to the officers of the Humane Society at St. Louis and an explanation was given of the protection given the rabbits by using the muzzle they at once said, "why, of course there can be no objection to the sport if the dogs are muzzled and an escape is made for the hares," and they were out in force and enthusiastic observers of the sport, made harmless and devoid of cruelty by the use of the muzzle. Who knows a better way. —G. Irwin Royce, in Turf, Field and Farm.

[Confess, now, Dr. Royce that you felt uncomfortable in knowing that you could not course to rule with muzzled dogs, because so many points were prevented by their inability to use their jaws freely. Why not make a stand against the mawkish sentimentality which would hamper and practically destroy one of the grandest of sports? What thoroughbred courser would consent to load his dog with wire masks and heavy collars? Ed.]

Occidental Coursing Club.

The Occidental Club held its regular monthly meeting on Tuesday evening last, at 21 Kearny St., city. Those present were Messrs. Gregory. O'Keeffe, Abbott, W. S. Kittle, Dickson, Wormington, Boyd, Nolan and Carroll. Treasurer Abbot reported $48.35 in the treasury. It was suggested by Mr. Abbot that a trophy be added to the regular coin prizes at the Thanksgiving Day meeting of the club, and the suggestion met general approval, some $40, being subscribed on the spot. The club then went into executive session.

Mr. R. E Culbreth has lost his fine St. Bernard Rex. The dog was poisoned on June 9.h by some miscreant. Rex stood 32 inches at the shoulder and in condition weighed 210 pound3.

Mr. W. J. Golcher has become the owner of that very handsome white and liver pointer bitch Jessie Ranger (Ranger Croxteth—Fannie Faust) which was brought by Mr. A. B. Elford from the Dilley Kennel to this city. Jessie Range should bear fine progeny if judiciously bred.

Mr. Watson's Field Trial Derby entry he calls Old Black Joe II but why it is not easy to see since there can be no direct relationship between the dogs. This later importation is like that famous Old Black Joe. a dog of unknown breeding. We hope it may develope the extraordinary excellence of the winner two years ago.

Kennel matters are quiet although the dog days are near at hand. About the only activity noticeable is at the training grounds of Mr. M. D. Walter near Galt, and of Mr. Allender near Watsonville. At these places fine strings of young pointers and setters are being handled in preparation for next January's Trials at Bakersfield. Those who did not send full particulars when sending their Derby entries should do so at once. There is a reason for insisting upon this which will be readily understood by all dog men.

The attention of such of our readers as are interested in coursing is called to the effort being made to give a monster coursing meeting during the coming fall. The citizens of Merced have subscribed $500 toward such an event and other subscriptions are being freely offered. A little vigorous action will insure stake money amounting to several thousands of dollars and will bring to the State the crack dogs of America and probably some from abroad. Those who care to do so may send their subscriptions to the Breeder and Sportsman.

THE GUN.

Some Practice Scores.

Some very fine work was done at Bird's Point a few days ago by Messrs. Robinson, Eddy and Fay. The shooting was strictly to American Association rules. On May 23d the following scores were made:

Robinson.............. 1 0 2 1 1 1 2 1 1 1 1 0 1 0 1 1 0 1 1 1 1 0—17
Eddy..................... 1 1 1 1 0 1 1 1 1 1 1 1 1 1 1 1 1 1 1 1 1 0—20
Fay....................... 1 1 1 0 1 1 1 1 1 1 1 1 1 1 1 1 1 1 1 1 1 1—20

On May 27th, the scores were:

E. Fay..[illegible]—58
E. Eddy [illegible]—47

New Game Birds.

There is something of interest to sportsmen in the report just received at the State Department by Minister Thomas, at Stockholm. The minister proposes to introduce into this country the capercailzie and the black game. These are the two most important birds of Sweden and Norway. In the fall and the winter they are to be seen hanging on branches at the market places of Stockholm.

The capercailzie is the largest and noblest member of the grouse family. The full grown male weighs from ten to twelve pounds. He is an extremely hardy bird. In Sweden and Norway he is found in large numbers up to and beyond the arctic circle, as far as the 70th parallel of north latitude. He can endure the severest cold and deepest snows of the longest winters. He often avoids the bitterest cold by burrowing into the snow, thus obtaining warmth and shelter.

This bird subsists upon the coarsest and commonest food. He feeds upon the buds and leaves of trees, the needles of leaves of the pine and spruce, young pine cones, clover and grass, berries of all sorts, seeds and grain, and insects of every kind. In the depth of winter a capercailzie has been known to live for more than a week in the same pine trees, subsisting entirely upon pine leaves and young pine cones.

The capercailzie is pre-eminently a bird of the pine woods, or pine mixed with birch, spruce, maple and other growths. He loves wooded hillsides better than wooded plains, and he must have fresh water near by—either a brook or pond or piece of swampy ground.

He is a local, not a migratory bird, though sometimes lack of food or other causes may drive him to extensive wanderings. In his habits he much resembles the American ruffed grouse—though in size he is nearly ten times as large.

The black game inhabits nearly the same kind of region as the capercailzie. He is equally hardy and can withstand the cold and snows of the most rigorous northern winters. His weight is about three pounds—about the same as our prairie chicken. The male bird is a lustrous, metallic black in color; hence the name. He has, however, a white strip in his wings, and his jet black, outward-curving tail feathers are much prized as a hat ornament in the Tyrol.

The black game is also a grouse, and he is often found in company with the capercailzie, or at least in close proximity. The black game is also a bird of the woods, but the birch is pre-eminently his tree, though he is met with in mixed growths of almost every variety. He does not frequent the deep woods as the capercailzie; he loves better the borders of the forests and woods and groves with frequent openings. He is also fond of cranberry swamps, and in swampy lands is often found miles away from any forest.

His food is much the same as the capercailzie, though not quite so coarse. It consists chiefly of the buds and leaves of trees, berries and insects. In summer the black game is very fond of blueberries, raspberries and cranberries; in winter he feeds principally upon the buds of the birch, hazel, alder willow and beech, and when pressed for food will eat the young green cones of the pine. This bird seems to be equally fond of animal food, and readily eats snails, worms, the larvæ of ants, flies, beetles, etc.

He is a more social bird than the capercailzie, and comes out more into the fields and clearings, and nearer the abodes of man.

"Hundreds of times," Minister Thomas writes, "when traveling through the forests of Scandinavia, I could scarcely resist the conviction that I must be back again in the woods of New England. Here in Sweden are the same hill sides and mountains, the same swift, clear brooks, foaming in their rocky beds, and the same forest trees—the pine and spruce, the birch, maple and beech, and oak and ash. Here are the same wild berries too, and in Sweden you may pick wild strawberries, raspberries, blueberries and blackberries, just as with us in America.

Then take the two grandest and most useful of the wild animals of Scandinavia. The reindeer of the fields is almost identical with our own caribou, and the most expert naturalists have been unable to distinguish any substantial difference between the Swedish elk and the moose of America. The fact is that a great portion of the United States—at least one third, perhaps one-half—is fitted to be the home of the capercailzie and the black game. for there is a suitable climate, a suitable broken country of hill and dale, well watered and covered with a suitable forest growth, and this forest growth together with its underbrush and bushes, will not only provide shelter for these birds, but will furnish them with all the food they require until they become as plenty as European sparrows now are in our streets and public parks. It is my firm conviction that these valuable birds will thrive throughout all the wooded districts of New England, New York and Pennsylvania, and westward through the greater portion of the states of Michigan, Wisconsin and Minnesota. They will also find a congenial home along the wooded slopes of the Rocky Mountains for their entire length as well as in all the wooded ravines and declivities of the mountain ranges of California, Oregon and Washington,

The fact that these birds are found among the hills and mountains of Europe as far south as Greece, Italy and Spain renders it almost certain that they will find a congenial climate and nature throughout the entire ranges of the Alleghanies, the Blue Ridge and the Cumberland mountains, together with their spurs, side hills and outlying forest districts and may thus be easily acclimated over large sections of the states of Virginia, West Virginia, Kentucky, Tennessee, North Carolina, South Carolina, Georgia and Alabama. And beside the districts above enumerated, there are doubtless many other portions of the United States well fitted to be the home of these magnificent game birds.

The minister explains that it will not be worth while to attempt to try the transportation of the eggs. That method is usually a failure. But he believes it is feasible to ship the full-grown birds, and says that the forests of Scotland and various localities in Hungary, Austria and Germany, where these birds had been exterminated by the hunters, had been restocked in this way. He believes that a hundred capercailzie and a hundred black game can be obtained and put down in this country at a cost of $3,000.

From Austin B. Sperry.

Editor Breeder and Sportsman:—As you were particularly anxious in regard to my appearance when I returned from my journey abroad, I conceived the idea of dropping you a line to prepare you for the real changes in my general appearance. You may expect to see a wind splitter with a suit composed of two plaids, a tall silk hat, and the usual single eye glass. It really takes the American to ape the customs of the old country, and I am just the one to do it. In regard to my travels so far I will not attempt to describe them, as everything is such a change to what they have at home. I am endeavoring to find some one who will invite me to witness the shooting of the London Gun Club, and think I have sufficient cheek to succeed. At Monte Carlo I intend also to witness the shooting. In Corry, Penn., U. S. A., I met a Mr. H. A. Penrose, (who I believe is considered one of the crack shots of the East, and is interested in the manufacture of the Keystone argets.)

He was very kind to me, and invited me to participate in the Club Shoot, which took place while I was there, and which I accepted, but did not distinguish myself. The Keystone targets and traps I consider far superior to the Blue Rocks, and I saw them worked to the best advantage. The birds are much superior, and the traps throw the birds with greater speed and more accuracy than any I have ever seen. I believe them to be the coming artificial bird. They are all packed very carefully, insuring a less percentage of breakage. The Blue Rock manufactory at Cleveland I saw also, but it does not begin to compare with the other.

I wanted to say one thing in regard to the enthusiasm of the Eastern sportsmen over ours. At Corry where I visited, (which is a town of only about 7,000 inhabitants) they have a club of over 70 members, a nice club house on the grounds and all of which is entirely owned by the members, and club day they all turn out. The day I had the pleasure of shooting with them it snowed quite hard, but nearly all were present and participated in the shooting. They shoot very rapidly, over 40 shot this day at 25 birds apiece. We began about half past two and were through before five.

Kindly remember me to all of my friends, and hoping to meet you at the meeting in October. A. B. Sperry.

London, Eng., May 18th.

At a regular meeting of the Pacific Sportsmen's Club of Sacramento last Sunday night, it was decided to hold the next medal shoot at the Gerber grounds on Sunday, June 15th. The club has joined the State Sportsman's Association, and will entertain all visiting clubs in October.

Major S. I. Kellogg, of the Selby Standard Cartridge Company, is visiting Portland, Or., for health and business combined. We hope he may soon return sound in body, and encouraged in his efforts to push the sale of his excellent ammunition.

A very graphic and interesting letter is that from Mr. Austin Sperry. We can clearly picture the man in the moon and without great mental strain can describe Heaven as we understand it, but to conjure Austin Sperry in the character of an Anglo—Ape is too much. We congratulate England, the continent and all those parts, upon the opportunity to meet Mr. Sperry than whom we know no clearer headed or more typical American. We hope that persistent sportsman editor of the Shooting Times Mr. Lewis Clement, may meet Sperry and take him down into the Shires for some sport.

It is well worth noting that Mr. Martinez Chick in making his brilliant shooting against Captain Brewer used Selby Standard Cartridges. The scores were the best ever made at a like number of birds in consecutive matches. Captain Brewer loaded his own cartridges but Mr. Chick simply went into the Selby Company's office and selected his ammunition from the supply in store, not even thinking it worth while to have them specially loaded, so near perfection have the cartridges been brought by Major S. I. Kellogg and his co-laborers in the loading plant. Those who saw the shooting will admit that more even, harder hitting ammunition never was let go from a shot gun.

The fear that the late rains had chilled many nests and destroyed most of the young quails does not appear to be well founded. Reports from many portions of the State agree that not for many years have young birds been so abundant. In Marin, Sonoma, Napa, Solano, Contra Costa, Alameda and San Mateo Counties, those which are most frequented by San Francisco sportsmen, the stand of quails is greater than any since 1883. It is to be regretted that the southern portion of the State, particularly about San Diego, is being swept of its game to meet the never ceasing demand of the great hotels of that section. The San Diego club does not seem to be able to cope with the owners of the Coronado Hotel, which institution we are informed is seldom or never without freshly killed game in its larders.

The sixth annual trap shooting tournament of the Sportsman's Association of the Northwest, will be held at Portland, Ore., on Thursday, Friday and Saturday, June 19th, 20th and 21st. Twelve matches are listed, some at Peoria blackbirds and some at live birds. In the blackbird matches the entrance is $3, at live birds entrance is $5 except in one of the matches on Friday, when the entrance will be $25. The special prizes are very many and of great value, ranging from $150 down to $8. But few of the matches, in fact, only two are limited to residents of the Northwest. Californians can shoot in ten of the twelve events, and if they have not lost all their money by the time they get through with those, they can make special sweeps and get rid of the rest of it. The conditions are these:

All shooting will be class shooting. Prices for inanimate targets will be 5 cents. Prices of live birds will not exceed 40 cents. All matches will be shot under the American Shooting Association rules, subject to the approval of the Association.

Entries in each match will close at the firing of the first gun.

No badge or medal offered in this programme (except the Selby best average badge which is open to all comers), can be won by other than a bona fide member of the Sportsman's Association of the Northwest.

Refreshments and Ammunition can be procured on the club grounds.

The officers of the Assocation are: W. T. Muir, President M. R. and G. C.; H. T. Hudson, Secretary S. A. N. W.; Buell Lamberson, Secretary M. R. and G. C.

Dr. S. E Knowles, Dentist, removed his office from the corner of Post and Dupont Sts. to the S. E. corner Post and Stockton Sts. June 9th, 1890, and students in guns and gunnery should note the change.

Mr. W. G. Steele, President of the Exploration Department of the Oregon Alpine Club of Portland is trying to stop the sending of skins of deer killed out of season from Oregon to this state and we hope will have the sympathy and assistance of all sportsmen.

A very handsome advertisement is that of the Golcher Hunting Boots and Shoes which appears in another column and it can truly be said of these goods that "handsome is as handsome does." If we have a reader who wishes to own a pair of boots or shoes suitable for walking in over quail ground, through the mountains for deer, about summering resorts, as fishing waders, on pedestrian tours or anywhere else where a sensibly shaped thoroughly made shoe of lasting material is needed then we unreservedly advise him to go or write to Clabrough, Golcher & Co., at 630 and 632 Montgomery St., for the Golcher Hunting Shoes. This advice is resultant upon the severest possible test of the shoes for the purposes suggested. A few days ago we visited the store and purchased a pair of the shoes, put them on in the shop, tramped off in them and for two days did hard walking over the mountain roads and along fishing streams, without the slightest discomfort or inconvenience. There are noseams on the inside of the shoes or boots. The leather is alum-tan and oil-tan; there are good stiff counters and firm shanks and tough soles. The shoes weigh 2½ lbs. per pair, the boots 3 lbs, and while seemingly very low in price they are yet strong, well made and cannot but be durable. Nothing approaching them in excellence has ever come to our notice and they will undoubtedly be worn universally by sportsmen, anglers, field trialers, campers and all others who need delightfully easy, light and strong foot wear.

Major S. I. Kellogg writes from Portland as follows;

"I am trying to get up an inter-State match at inanimates. California will have here for her team Cadwallader, of San Jose, Dr. Taber, of San Bernardino, Cadman, of San Francisco and Yours Truly. Can't you stir up H. A. Bassford or Mr. Chick or Frank Coykendall, or a few more to be here and strengthen our team. Mind you the proposition is embryo as yet and may not culminate. Sorry to have missed the Chick-Brewer affair. Regards to all enquirers.'

ROD.

A Trout Pest.

Editor Breeder and Sportsman:—I am sorry to inform you of the fact that a fly is beginning to attack the trout in these waters. It is a black fly with a rather large body for the size of the wings. I send you a specimen of fly with four large trout that they killed last Sunday. Wish you would show the fly to the Fish Commissioners, and get them to inform us as to the best means of exterminating them. What are fruit pests to this? What is an orchard to a brook full of trout as large as these? Hope you will get them in good shape. This is the best I can do so early in the season.

Sierra City. Joe E. Carney.

[We failed to find the fly spoken of, and must ask Judge Carney to send us more, when they will be submitted to the Academy of Sciences. They should be sent in a bottle.—Ed.]

Game Fish of British Columbia.

An exchange published in the far north gives these interesting items about the game fish of that section.

If there is one more than another, thing that will attract the attention of the stranger on his arrival here, it is the excellence and variety of our food fish, while the gameness of some of them will especially commend them to the sportsmen. There are five varieties of salmon in British Columbian waters, to which extended reference has already been made in these columns. Three of them may be spoken of as game fish, viz, the Cohoe, the Sockeye and the Tyhee, or spring salmon. These are emphatically angling fish, and are plentiful in their respective seasons, notably in March and April, and when the rivers are full. They may be taken with the fly, minnow or spoon bait, in the sea, almost at all times. Frequently the rivers are too muddy for them, and they can only be caught at certain times and when there are freshets.

The trout of British Columbia are of two kinds, the ordinary common (salmo purpuratus) having black spots, and the steel head (salmo Gairdneri). The ordinary trout occasionally attains the weight of ten pounds, but three or four pounds may be considered the weight of a good fish. The steel head attains from 25 to 30 pounds. Both species are plentiful in all the rivers, some specimens of common trout being found in the lakes, which are never frequented by the steel head. Both fish afford lively sport for anglers, all through the summer months.

In this province there are two varieties of char, the Salvelinus malma and the Salvelinus Namaycush. The former have red spots and the latter are brown with yellow stripes. It is not often that either of these fish are caught with the fly, the last named variety having a fancy for the spoon bait, the minnow or a piece of bacon; but it is scarcely what may be described as a game fish. They can be caught all summer, and also through the ice in winter. The Salvelinus malma seldom reaches over five or six pounds, while the other is not known to attain over ten pounds, although in Eastern Canada it has been taken at as high as 120 pounds.

The grayling is seldom seen in British Columbia, it being only found, so far as known, in the Cassiar district. On the other side of the Rockies, notably in the tributories of the Peace River and streams having their outlet in the Arctic Ocean it is comparatively common. Although its average weight is from a half to three quarters of a pound, it sometimes reaches from three to four pounds. It takes the fly well, and is full of fight. It is in the best condition in winter.

It is said that "giant powder friends" are at work on the streams of Lake County.

Mr. Ben O. Bush writes from Kalamazoo, Mich., that trout fishing is at its zenith, and that prospects for the coming shooting season are good, young birds being plenty.

A wrinkle to anglers about repairing a broken rod is to split a quill after soaking it, lay a piece or two pieces of watch spring along the break, cover it with the quill and bind the whole tackle with waxed silk.

Mr. Geo. Heazleton left for Webber lake on Monday last to be gone ten days. Mr. S. B. Whitehead, better known as a bookmaker, although a rare angler and owner of as choice a lot of rods as anyone we know goes to Webber next week. We fear both gentlemen will fail to have such sport as they desire because of the lateness of the season at Webber. The snow is barely off the ground now.

The Klamath is the objective point this year for the leading fly casters. Mr. Ramon Wilson intends to visit Shovel Creek, and may be accompanied by Mr. Will Golcher and Jno. M. Adams. What chance has a trout against such a trio? There is one consolation, however, that all of the gentlemen named use the fly and nothing else.

As was foretold, the fishing nowadays is something worthy of remark. The trout streams are just about right, flies are plenty, fish in countless numbers and rising freely. Dr. Heffenger killed something over a hundred in Sonoma Creek on one day of last week. Mr. Will Rix brought a beautiful basket of trout from Maria County last Saturday; the fish were unusually large, none of them being smaller than three to the pound and many weighing three-quarters.

Lagunitas Lake is full of beautiful trout at present, although no stocking has been done for several years. The use of anything but the fly is prohibited there, and we know no more charming spot to visit; whether for fish or merely for an outing. Permission must be secured from the San Rafael Water Co. to visit the premises. The Menlo Water Works Lake is said to be overstocked with bass. The body of water is small, although very favorable for bass; they multiply there astonishingly.

The fishing on the Carmel is superb at present. The first storm last fall washed out the fish ladder, and the fish are huddled below the dam, waiting with their ascension robes to go up. The road has been so that the company could not get lumber up the river to replace the ladder as required by law, but it is reported that it will be done in a week or two, and the Isaac Waltons who want to get in before the fish hegira should not procrastinate in getting there.

For some time past matters have not been going smoothly with the fishermen in the neighborhood of Sacramento of whom there are about twenty-five, exclusive of those operating below Freeport. They had been receiving about 3½ cents per pound for their salmon, which did not pay them as the boats about there average only about 10 fish per night.

On Tuesday last the fishermen met and formed a branch union among themselves. They called on W. R. Jones, proprietor of the Sacramento fish market, and made a satisfactory arrangement with him, by which he is to handle all fish caught by them, and of the net proceeds he is to have 10 per cent commission. If the fish brings 7, 10 or more cents per pound the fishermen will receive the benefit.

Under this agreement made, if any fisherman violates his contract he is to forfeit his boat and outfit to Mr. Jones; and if the latter does not live up to the terms he forfeits his fish market to the fishermen.

The latter were in good humor on Tuesday, and returned to their boats for their night's arduous work, feeling that life was at least worth the living.

The manner in which fish—especially trout—come on to feed during the early stage of a rainy day and "go off" as the volume of descending water increases, is an interesting item for the attentive naturalist-angler, says an exchange. It would seem that the increased volume at first sets free all kinds of hitherto quiescent larvæ, and that some tonic effect comes of the pure soft water of the skies. Later the effect is reversed, and the swarming myriads of water creatures are lost in the preponderating mud and vegetable debris, and the water itself becomes nauseating to the fish. One can quite understand also, how the multitudinous particles of foreign matter in a soiled stream may, after a while, mechanically irritate the delicate bronchiæ of the trout. Some fish will live comfortably in liquid mud (par example, the mud fish of Ceylon, described by Sir Emerson Tennant in his "Fishes of Ceylon"), but not so the patrician trout. His most delightful habitat is the icy and limpid spring gushing from some rock bound mountain glen or grotto. But of course he does not disdain the rain swollen river, providing there is not too much of it, but just enough. At such times he gorges himself on all the varied lower life of the stream, and retires to digest in somnolent complacency, ignoring sublimely the feathered lure of every kind whatsoever.

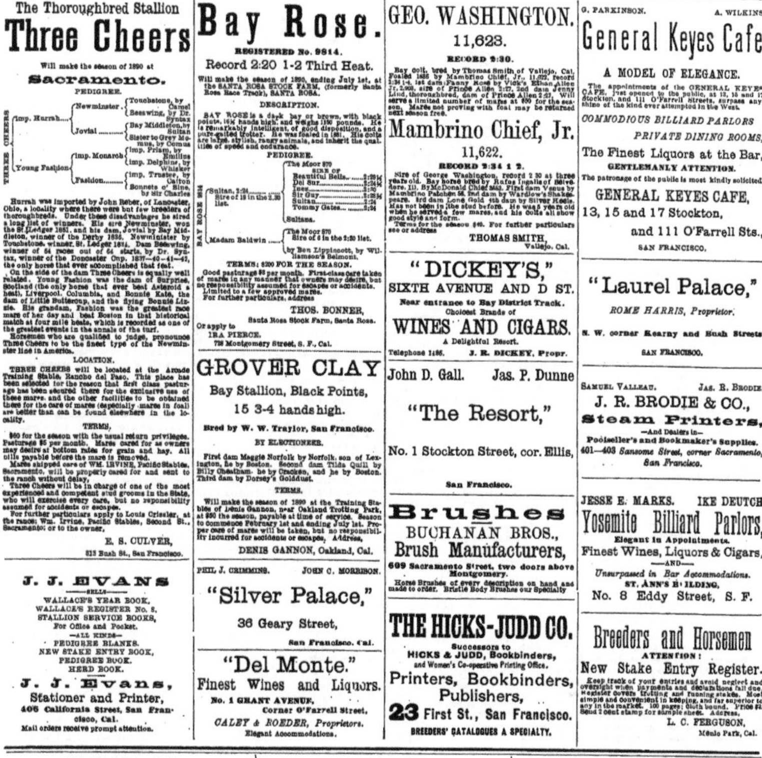

Our Australian Letter.

SYDNEY, New South Wales, May 14, 1890.

DEAR BREEDER AND SPORTSMAN:—The owner of that well performed colt Sir William, by your Sir Modred, has had the doubtful honor conferred upon him of having his horse placed top weight, 9 stone 5 pounds, in the Royal Stakes, a six furlong flutter to be run at Randwick on the 24th of May. Sir William was asked to give 2 pounds to Sedition, which Sir William's owner thought so unfair that he scratched the colt's name out of the race. Sedition, an aged mare by Neckersgat from Irish Queen, is a sterling performer, who last year won the Newmarket Handicap, the champion sprint race of the colonies, and she won the Royal Stakes last year with the same weight in the saddle as she is alloted this year, so that the owner of Sir William may well feel dissatisfied at having to concede such an animal 2 pounds.

Pony racing has been carried to such a pitch in the colonies that the Australian Jockey Club, the premier racing authority in New South Wales has taken the matter up in the interest of legitimate sport, and passed the most stringent rules on the subject. No trainer or jockey is now allowed to own a racing pony under pain of disqualification, and no programme that contains a pony race will be recognized by the Australian Jockey Club. Pony racing is now carried on night and day, the Lillie Bridge grounds, situated in one of the suburbs of Sydney, being fixed up with the electric lights. The Auckland, New Zealand racing Club, have followed the suit of the A. J. C., and placed their ban upon the sport of the lilliputions.

The Hon. James White's career on the English turf has not opened very auspiciously, what with the indifferent running of Kirkham and the bursting of the blood vessel of Plutarch. Kirkham and Narellan are big horses and come of a stock that require plenty of work, and many Australian horsemen are of opinion that if a colonial trainer had gone to England with the animals they would have given a better account of themselves. However, a colonial trainer will in all probability take Mr. White's string in hand next season, and when Kirkham and Narellan mature, I shall expect them to show the Britishers something in the way of weight carrying and staying powers.

Lurline, the dam of Darebin is dead. Lurline won a Melbourne Cup and foaled Darebin, a brace of events the like of which fall to very few mares.

Your Mr. Tom Merry, who is at present here purchasing brood mares, has evolved a scheme which on the face of it looks as though there might be lots of money in the transaction for all concerned. He proposes to promote a company for the purpose of buying at least a half dozen of the principal steeple-chase horses of this country and take them to America for your coming great exposition, where they will be exhibited on the various tracks so that Americans can see what wonderful weights the Australian horses can carry and what enormous jumps it is possible for them to make. Sir Roderick Cameron, who is at present in New York, has been communicated with in reference to the matter and he gives it his earnest support. In his letter Sir Roderick writes: "You would receive a cordial welcome from all sporting men here and they are many and influential. You also should feel encouragement from the success of Buffalo Bill's Wild West Show that proved a great success. If the Sporting Clubs of Melbourne or Sydney should take the matter up and look to the public for subscriptions, I would willingly give a fifty-pound note towards the fund and I would rejoice to see your horses clearing five feet of stiff timber and thus showing to our American cousins how to do it; Jumping here has so far been a farce and I think I am safe in saying that four feet of timber has been the maximum and more frequently it is three feet six of brush that is attempted." There are many here who feel inclined to go into the speculation and I am pretty certain that Mr. Merry will have the company completed before he returns with his brood mares on the next steamer.

This month has been a remarkably quiet one on the Australian turf, so I shall take the opportunity of giving your readers some notion of the most prominent Australian oarsmen which may prove of interest to you Yankees, by reason of our having amongst us your crack sculler, O'Connor. O'Connor is well liked in Australia, and his practice shows the knowing ones that he is amongst the first flight, and it is the general opinion that he is far and away a better man than Ned Hanlon ever showed himself to be in Australia, whatever he may have been before he reached our shores. O'Connor considered himself rather badly treated at first in not at once getting on a match for the championship, which Kemp was supposed to hold, but Australian sportsmen are of rather a suspicious nature, and they thought that if O'Connor met and defeated Kemp for the championship, the Yankee would at once travel for his native shores in company with the coveted honor.

Another point was that Sydney possessed four men, with money at their backs, who considered themselves fit to row for the championship: Stansbury, McLean, Kemp and Matterson, so that it really resolved itself into rowing a series of races in "heats," to find out the best man, but O'Connor wanted the others to "row off," and he to meet the ultimate winner for the championship. This was manifestly unfair, as O'Connor would have started fresh for the final event, whilst his opponent might have been compelled to keep in training for two or three races and then row, a stale man, against O'Connor. Matterson, whose ability to raise the stake money alone put him alongside the other three, has now been defeated with the greatest ease by both Kemp and McLean. Kemp and McLean meet to-morrow afternoon, and your O'Connor is matched against Stansbury, so that it will be between the winners of these two events as to who is the champion of the world.

Before I proceed further I may state that you Yankees may lay the flattering unction to your hearts that we have not another Henry Ernest Searle in Australia. Searle was a phenomenan and his like may never crop up again in the aquatic world. Kemp I expect to see beat to-morrow by McLean, but in Stansbury and McLean, O'Connor will meet men of great pace, and men who possess the physical and mental power to stay out a gruelling race. In Australia, O'Connor is looked upon as a sculler whose races are decided on the first mile, as were Edward Hanlon's until Beach's dogged determination enabled him to wear down the hitherto invincible Canadian, but if such be the case, O'Connor need look for no respite until the judge's flag falls, for both Stansbury and McLean are as tenacious as a couple of bull dogs. It is a peculiarity of Colonial sculling that no other Colony but New South Wales can raise an even moderate professional sculler. The Colonial champions, Green, Hickey, Trickett, Laycock, Rush, Beach, Kemp, in addition to a host of second classers better than anything raised in the other colonies, all hailed from New South Wales. It is one of those things that cannot be understood by Yours, "THE JUNGLE."

When you are hurt you use Darbys Fluid. Do the same for your horses and dogs.

Save your cattle by using Darbys Fluid—the best air purifier and preventative of disease.

Breeders' Directory.

Advertisements under this heading 50c. per line per month.

HORSES AND CATTLE.

W. S. JACOBS, Sacramento, Cal. – Breeder of Thoroughbred Shorthorns and Berkshire Hogs.

J. H. WHITE, Lakeville, Sonoma County—Breeder of Registered Holstein Cattle.

EL ROBLAS RANCHO—Los Alamos, Cal., Francis T. Underhill, proprietor, importer and breeder of thoroughbred Hereford Cattle. Information by mail. C. F. Swan, manager.

PAGE BROTHERS.—Penn's Grove, Sonoma Co. Cal. Breeders of Short Horn Cattle; Draft, Roadster and Standard Bred Horses.

SETH COOK, breeder of Cleveland Bay Horses, Devon, Durham, Polled Aberdeen-Angus and Galloway Cattle. Young stock of above breeds on hand for sale. Warranted to be pure bred, recorded and average breeders. Address, Geo. A. Wiley, Cook Farm, Danville, Contra Costa Co., Cal.

MAMBRINO WILKES COLTS and FILLIES, full brothers and sisters to Gus. Wilkes 2:22, and Balkan 2:29½, for Sale. Address SMITH HILL, Walnut Creek, Contra Costa County, Cal.

PETER SAXE & SON. Lick House, San Francisco, Cal.—Importers and Breeders for past 18 years of every variety of Cattle, Horses, Sheep and Hogs.

HOLSTEIN THOROUGHBREDS of all the noted strains. Registered Berkshire Swine. Catalogues. F. H. BURKE, 401 Montgomery St., S. F.

Situation Wanted.

By an Experienced and Successful Trainer of Racehorses.

Address,

S. J. MILLER,

102 South Desplaines Street, Chicago, Ill.

Stallions and Colts

For Sale.

The Get of the Celebrated Racing Stallion

BAYSWATER.

FROM FINELY BRED MARES.

Inquire of

J. HEINLEN,

Lemoore, Tulare County, Cal.

VISIT GETTYSBURG

And MUSEUM.

MARKET AND TENTH STREETS,

SAN FRANCISCO, CAL.

For Sale.

PHILOSOPHER,

BAY COLT; FOALED 1886; BRED BY Z. E. SIMMONS, LEXINGTON, KY.

Sired By Pilot Wilkes 2987.

SON OF GEORGE WILKES, 2:22.

WHOSE SONS HAVE SIRED

Axtell (3 y. o)	2:12	Allerton (3 y. o.)	2:18¼
Roy Wilkes	2:12¾	William H.	2:18¼
Rosalind Wilkes	2:14¼	Garnet	2:19
Prince Wilkes	2:14¾	Repetition (4 y. o)	2:19¼
Alcryon	2:15¼	J. B. Shedd	2:19¼
Oliver K.	2:16¼	David Wilkes	2:19½
Phil Thompson	2:16½	Sharper	2:19¾
Houri	2:17	Georgiette	2:19¾
Iona	2:17½	Butterfly	2:19¾
Lillian Wilkes (3 y. o.)	2:17¾	Silverone	2:19¾
Sable Wilkes (3 y. o.)	2:18	Veritas	2:20

Regal Wilkes (2 y. o.) ....2:25¾.

1st dam Bella........by George Wilkes 519, record 2:22, sire of Harry Wilkes, 2:13½, Guy Wilkes, 2:15¼, Mike Wilkes, pacer, 2:15¾, Wilcox, pacer, 2.16, Wilson, 2:16¼, So So, 2:17¼, J. B. Richardson, 2:17½, etc.

2d dam Fly............by Bell Morgan 61, sire of Lady Turpin, 2:23, and the dam of Onslaught, 2:28¼.

Pilot Wilkes, by George Wilkes, 2:22, sire of 60 from 2:13¼ to 2:30, and the dams of 21 from 2:21¼ to 2:30.

First dam Grace by Pilot Jr., sire of the dams of Maud S., 2:08, Jay-Eye-See, 2:10, etc.; 2d dam by Orphan Boy, pacer.

NOTE.—Here is another inbred Wilkes with superb out-crosses through both sire and dam. Has never been trained. Price $1,000. SOUND. To be seen at

GEO. E. GUERNE,

Santa Rosa, Cal.

For Sale.

Brood Mare Corinne.

By Geo. C. Gorham; 1st dam Annie McCloud by Jack Hawkins Jr., son of Jack Hawkins thoroughbred 2nd dam by Belmont; will be sold with horse colt foaled June 1st, "De Corne Wilkes" by MAMBRINO WILKES 6083.

—ALSO—

Two-Year-old Brown Filly

AGNES F. WILKES,

And Yearling Black Colt

FERGUS WILKES,

By MAMBRINO WILKES, out of Corinne as above. Mare and colts can be seen at Oakland. For further particulars apply or address,

BREEDER AND SPORTSMAN

313 BUSH STREET S. F.

Poplar Grove Breeding FARM.

Standard-bred Trotters, Colts and Fillies.

The get of CLOVIS, 4909; PASHA, 2039; APEX, 2935,

For Sale.

Address S. N. STRAUBE, Poplar Grove Breeding Farm,

Fresno, Cal.

Inspection by intending purchasers invited, and information by mail.

ALWAYS GIVES SATISFACTION.

Combining perfect riding qualities, proportions and balance, with genteel appearance.

No vehicle exhibits a horse to better advantage, and no Cart approaches them for speeding or training purposes.

A stylish vehicle for exercising or pleasure driving, at one-fourth the cost of a carriage. Have none of the horse jockey or objectionable features of other Road Carts.

They are the Leading Cart wherever introduced, and are in use by the most prominent breeders and pleasure drivers everywhere.

Elegant Shifting Top Carts.

Perfectly Balanced Stylish Pole Carts.

or Illustrated Catalogue, with Prices, address,

LEWIS F. CASTOR,

Frankford, Philadelphia, Pa.

JOHN SPLAN, General Agent.

BOYCE TABLETS.

Leg and Body Wash.

THE BOYCE TABLETS are packed in a nicely decorated metal box with hinged lid—one hundred tablets in each box; directions for use plainly engraved upon the box; therefore, the convenience of the package—no liability to leakage and breakage—economy and ready solubility, together with the absolute certainty of their action, will at once commend the use of BOYCE'S TABLETS to the intelligent horsemen of the country. TABLETS sufficient to make one hundred pints of leg and body wash are conveniently carried in an inside coat pocket or in the hip-pocket of the trousers.

The BOYCE WASH can be applied ALL OVER THE BODY WITHOUT FEAR OF BLISTERING NOR DOES IT AFFECT THE KIDNEYS.

The BOYCE WASH will cure CRACKED HEELS, PUFFS, STOCKINGS, SCRATCHES, INFLAMED TENDONS and FEVERED LEGS.

Price per Box of One Hundred Tablets, $2, sent postpaid to any part of the United States; six boxes for $10. A sample of BOYCE'S TABLETS will be mailed to any address on application. These TABLETS are warranted to keep in any climate. Address

BOYCE TABLET COMPANY,

600 Wabash Avenue, - - - - Terre Haute, Indiana.

J. A. McKERRON, Pacific Coast Ag't,

228-230-232 Ellis Street, San Francisco, Cal.

"BERTON SEC,"

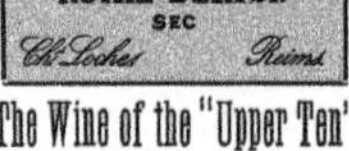

The Wine of the "Upper Ten"

Is used EXCLUSIVELY at the "White House" by both the President and vice-President, Messrs. Harrison & Morton, and the members of the Cabinet, and most Senators in Washington serve it at their receptions, and such gentlemen as Hon. Chauncey M. Depew, Hon. Andrew Carnegie, Cornelius N. Bliss, and others of equal note use it, and declare it to be the best WINE they ever drank.

EM. MEYER & CO., AGENTS,

415—417 Pine Street.

NEW BOOK.

HORSE BREEDING

Seventh Edition, with Appendix,

By J. H. SANDERS,

In which the GENERAL LAWS OF HEREDITY are exhaustively discussed and applied to the PRACTICAL BUSINESS OF BREEDING HORSES, especially with reference to the Selection of Breeding Stock and the Management of Stallions, Brood Mares, Young Foals, and Diseases Peculiar to Breeding Stock.

Price, Post Paid, $2.

BREEDER AND SPORTSMAN,

313 Bush Street. San Francisco, Cal

GOLDEN EAGLE HOTEL

Corner SEVENTH and K STREETS,

SACRAMENTO.

FIRST CLASS IN EVERY RESPECT.

The LARGEST and FINEST HOTEL in the City.

W. O. BOWERS, Proprietor.

Free 'Buss to and from the Hotel.

Telephone, Telegraph Office and Messenger Service at Hotel

Fine Hats,

Latest Styles and Colors.

Meussdorffer & Hubner

8 Kearny Street, San Francisco.

Next to New Chronicle Building.

KENNEL ADVERTISEMENTS.

In the Stud.

"DAN GLADSTONE,"

3377 A. K. C. S. B.

BY CH. GLADSTONE—CH. SUE.

Winnings—Southern Trials, 1888, Divided Third.
Indiana Trials, 1889, Divided Third.
Southern Trials, 1889, Second.

Will be at Stud in San Francisco until Sept. 15, 1890. Fee, $75.

GEO. J. HARLEY, 844 Harrison St., S. F.

DOGS---Pointer Pups

FOR SALE.

Sure Bench Show and Field Trial Winners, as they have more bench-show and field-trial blood in them than any that have ever been whelped on the Pacific Coast.

Sire, POINT, double field trial winner; he by Vandevort's Don, great field trial and bench show winner, out of Drab, field trial and bench show winner.

Dam, QUEEN CROXTETH by Rush T., bench show winner, out of Champion Patti Croxteth, field trial and bench show winner. This is the best pointer blood in the world. Breeding and health guaranteed. Address,

A. B. TRUMAN,

1425 Steiner St., near Ellis, S. F., Cal.

CALIFORNIA SPANIEL KENNELS.

Oakland, California, H. P. RENNIE, Prop. Breeder and importer of typical COCKER SPANIELS. Winner of first prizes at S. F. and Los Angeles, 1889; also, Columbus, 1889, New York, 1887. In the stud, solid Black Cocker dog, GIFFEE, won 1st and Gold Medal at S. F., 1889. Fee, $25. Puppies and grown dogs at reasonable prices. My dogs can neither talk nor climb a tree, but are fielders and prize winners.

37 Sixth St., Oak Street Station.

ECHO COCKER KENNELS,

STOCKTON, CAL.

A. C. DAVENPORT, - - - Proprietor.

Has some fine Cocker Puppies for Sale now, by his solid black Cocker Spaniel, Prize Winning Stud Dog Bronta, A. K. C. S. B., 17,081, (Brant—Mollie) out of registered bitches, for $10 and $20. Stud fee $20.

THE BOHANON SULKY!

BEST MADE.

Perfect Riding Buggies.

Breaking Carts.

Fine Repairing. Reasonable Prices

Bohanon Carriage Co., 161-163 Ogden Ave., CHICAGO.

Send for Catalogue.

NOW IN THE LEAD.

J. O'KANE,

Harness and Turf Goods,

767 MARKET STREET, S. F.

Largest Stock. Lowest Prices.

Send for New Catalogue.

JOHN FORGIE,

Importing Tailor,

204 Montgomery Street,

N. E. corner Bush, SAN FRANCISCO.

BERGEZ'S RESTAURANT.

FIRST-CLASS. – Charges Reasonable.

Private Rooms for Families.

332—334 Pine St., below Montgomery St.

JOHN BERGEZ, Propr.

"Tobey's,"

214 POST STREET,

Adjoining New Hamman Baths.

LARGEST COLLECTION OF THEATRICAL PHOTOGRAPHS IN SAN FRANCISCO.

Has been newly fitted up to the accommodation of the public.

QUIET AND INTERESTING PRIVATE READING ROOMS.

AT Ione.

Fourth Annual Fair

—OF THE—

26th District,

Amador & Sacramento,

August 5, 6, 7 and 8, 1890.

RACE PROGRAMME.

Following is the Race Programme, as adopted by the Board. It is a splendid one and will doubtless call together a grand array of horses:

FIRST DAY—TUESDAY, AUGUST 5, 1890.

No. 1—RUNNING STAKE—Free-for-all, $10 entrance, $15 forfeit, $175 added, of which $50 to second. One and one-eighth miles.

No. 2—RUNNING STAKE—Free-for-all two-year-olds, $25 entrance, $10 forfeit, $125 added, of which $40 to second. Five-eighths dash.

No. 3—RUNNING STAKE—$10 entrance, $5 forfeit, $50 added, of which $10 to second. One-fourth of a mile and repeat. Free for all saddle horses owned in Amador County.

SECOND DAY—WEDNESDAY AUG. 6, 1890.

No. 4—RUNNING STAKE—Free-for-all. $25 entrance, $10 forfeit, $150 added, of which $50 to second. Nine sixteenth dash.

No. 5—RUNNING STAKE—Free-for-all. $30 entrance, $15 forfeit, $175 added, of which $50 to second. Three-fourths repeat.

No. 6—RUNNING STAKE—Free for-all. $40 entrance, $15 forfeit, $200 added, of which $75 to second. One and one-fourth dash.

THIRD DAY—THURSDAY, AUG. 7, 1890.

No. 7—RUNNING STAKE—$15 entrance, half forfeit, $75 added, of which $25 to second. 600 yards and repeat. Free for all horses owned in Amador County.

No. 8—RUNNING STAKE—Free-for-all two-year-olds $25 entrance, $10 forfeit, $100 added of which $50 to second. Three-fourths dash.

No. 9—RUNNING STAKE—Free-for-all. $40 entrance, $20 forfeit, $200 added, of which $75 to second. One mile and repeat.

FOURTH DAY—FRIDAY, AUG. 8, 1890.

No. 10—RUNNING STAKE—$20 entrance, $10 forfeit, $100 added, of which $30 to second. Half mile and repeat. Free for all three-year-olds bred and owned in Amador County.

No. 11—RUNNING STAKE—Free-for-all. $25 entrance, $10 forfeit, $150 added, of which $50 to second. Five-eighths repeat.

No. 12—RUNNING STAKE—Handicap. Free-for-all. $50 entrance, half forfeit, $10 declaration, $225 added, of which $75 to second. Weights announced by 8 P. M., Thursday. Declarations at 8 P. M. same day. One and three eighths miles.

No. 13—FREE PURSE—$125, of which $25 to second. For all ages. Horses that have started at this meeting and been beaten once allowed five pounds; twice, seven pounds. To name and close at 6 P. M., the day before. Seven eighths dash.

MATCH TROTTING STALLION RACES.

To take place during the meeting.

C. F. Bunch's "Ajax" and R. W. Hopkins' "Colonel."

C. F. Bunch's "Ajax" and J. W. Owens' "Lottery."

REMARKS AND CONDITIONS.

Extra Races and Attractions Will Be Arranged During the Meeting.

Rules of the State Agricultural Society to govern running races, except when conditions named are otherwise.

Racing Colors to be named in entries.

Entries to the above races, unless otherwise specified, close with the Secretary on July 15, 1890.

In all races entries not declared out by 6 P. M., of the day preceding the race, shall be required to start.

Where there is more than one entry by one person, or in one interest, the particular horse they are to start must be named by 6 P. M., of the day preceding the race. No added money paid for a walk-over.

A horse making a walk-over shall be entitled only to the entrance money paid in. When less than three starters appear, they may contest for the entrance money, to be divided as follows: 66⅔ per cent. to the first, and 33⅓ to the second.

The Board reserves the right to change the above order of races by giving the contestants notice of the same by 6 o'clock P. M., of the day preceding the race.

Stables, hay and straw free to competitors.

Races commence each day at 1 P. M. sharp.

The Ione Track is one of the best and fastest on the Coast.

U. S. GREGORY, President,

CLOVIS T. LA GRAVE, Sec'y Ione.

The Trotting Stallion

G & M

FULL BROTHER TO

ALFRED G, 2:19¾.

(Who has been taken to Kentucky to stand at $200)

Will make the season of 1890 from FEBRUARY 1st to JULY 1st, at

SANTA ROSA.

G. & M. is by Anteeo, 2:16¼; was foaled 1886; first dam Rosa B. by Speculation (son of Hambletonian 10); 2d dam Elizabeth by Alexander 490; 3d dam Nora by imp. Glencoe. Anteeo is by Electioneer, out of Columbine by A. W. Richmond 1687.

G. & M. is a handsome dark bay; stands 15-3 1-2 hands high, and weighs 1060 pounds. Gameness, stoutness, speed and stamina are indelibly impressed in every line of the pedigree of G. & M. Owners of broodmares in search of these qualities, will do well to patronize this promising colt.

PHILOSOPHER,

Foaled 1886 by Pilot Wilkes 2967; first dam Bella by George Wilkes 519; second dam by Bell Morgan 61.

Philosopher's sire, Pilot Wilkes 2967, is by George Wilkes 519, dam Grace (the dam of Alice Woodburn etc.), by Pilot Jr. 12, grandam by Orphan Boy.

Will make the season of 1890, from FEBRUARY 1st to JULY 1st, at Santa Rosa.

TERMS for the season:

G. & M., $50.

PHILOSOPHER, $30,

with privilege of returning mares that do not prove in foal the next season free of charge, provided the horse bred to remains the property of the present owners. Good pasturage at $3 per month. No responsibility assumed for accidents or escapes. Service fees payable before removal of the mare. For further particulars, address

GEO. E. GUERNE,

Santa Rosa Cal.

California State Fair

—AT—

SACRAMENTO,

September 8th to 20th.

Two Weeks' Fair,

Nine Days' Racing.

Races. Races.

Speed Department.

There shall be awarded to the owner of the sire whose get shall make the best average performance in the races for trotting foals, two, three, and four year-olds, in 1890, 1891 and 1892, the Grand Gold Medal of the California State Agricultural Society, the actual cost of which shall not be less than $200.

The first medal under the above conditions was won by DIRECTOR 1989 upon the performances of MARGARET S., 2:19½, and DIRECT, 2:18½.

First Day, Thursday, September 11th.

TROTTING AND PACING.

NO. 1—THE OCCIDENT STAKE—A trotting stake for foals of 1887. Entries closed January 1, 1888 with fifty-three nominations. Value of stake January 1, 1890, $1,835.

NO. 2—TROTTING PURSE, $1,200—2:22 class.

NO. 3—PACING PURSE, $800—2:30 Class.

Second Day, Friday, September 12th.

RUNNING.

NO. 4—OPENING SCRAMBLE—For two-year-olds. A sweepstake of $25 each; $15 forfeit, or only $10 if declared on or before September 1st; with $300 added, of which $50 to second. Winners at this distance in 1890, once, to carry three pounds; twice, five pounds extra. Maidens allowed five pounds. Three-quarters of a mile.

NO. 5—THE CALIFORNIA BREEDERS' STAKE—A sweepstake for three-year-olds (foals of 1887). One mile and a quarter. Closed in 1888 with thirty-nine nominations.

NO. 6—THE ROSEMEADE HANDICAP—For all ages; of $50 each, half forfeit; $15 declaration; with $400 added; second to receive $100, and third $50 from the stakes. Weights announced by 10 A. M., and declarations due by 6 P. M., September 11th. One mile and an eighth.

NO. 7—SELLING PURSE, $300—Of which $50 to second; for all ages. Horses entered to be sold for $1,500 to carry rule weights; two pounds off for each $100 less down to $1,000; then one pound for each $100 less down to $500. Horses entered not to be sold to carry five pounds above the scale. Valuation to be placed on starters only by 6 P. M. the day preceding the race. Mile heats.

Third Day, Saturday, Sept. 13th.

TROTTING.

NO. 8—TWO-YEAR-OLD STAKE—Entrance $50, of which $10 must accompany nomination; $15 payable July 1st, and remaining $25 August 10, 1890; $300 added by the Society. Closed March 15, 1890, with fourteen nominations. Mile heats.

NO. 9.—THE PACIFIC STALLION STAKE—A sweepstake for trotting stallions—2:18 Class—of $250 each, of which $100 must accompany nomination; $150 payable September 1st; $250 added for each starter up to four, or $1000 for four or more starters. Stakes divided, four-sevenths, two-sevenths and one-seventh. Added money divided. 50, 25, 15 and 10 per cent. If but two starters, stakes and added money divided five-sevenths and two-sevenths. A stallion making a walk-over gets all stakes but no added money. Mile heats, three in five.

NO. 10—TROTTING PURSE, $1,000—2:30 Class.

Fourth Day, Monday, Sept. 15th.

RUNNING.

NO. 11—THE DAISY D STAKE—For all ages; of $50 each, half forfeit, or only $15 if declared on or before September 1st; with $350 added, of which $75 to second, third to save stake. Maidens if three years old, allowed five pounds; if four or more, seven pounds. Three-quarters of a mile.

NO. 12—THE CAPITAL CITY STAKE—A handicap for three-year-olds; of $100 each, half forfeit; $20 declaration; with $400 added; of which $100 to second. Weights announced by 10 A. M. Saturday, September 13th. Declarations due by 6 P. M. same day. One and one-sixteenth miles.

NO. 13—THE SUNNY SLOPE STAKE—A sweepstake for two-year-old fillies (foals of 1888). Five eighths of a mile. Closed in 1889 with twenty nominations.

NO. 14—SELLING PURSE; $350—Of which $50 to second; for all ages. Horses entered to be sold for $2000 to carry rule weights; one pound off for each $100 down to $1000; then two pounds for each $100 down to $500. Horses entered not to be sold to carry five pounds above the scale. Valuation to be placed on starters only by 6 P. M. Saturday, September 13th. One and one-eighth miles.

Fifth Day, Tuesday, September 16th.

TROTTING.

NO. 15—TROTTING PURSE, $800—For three year olds eligible to 2:40 Class.

NO. 16—TROTTING PURSE, $800—For four-year-olds eligible to 2:30 Class.

NO. 17—TROTTING PURSE, $1,800—2:00 Class.

Sixth Day, Wednesday, September 17th.

RUNNING.

NO. 18—THE CALIFORNIA AUTUMN STAKE—A sweepstake for two-year-olds (foals of 1888). Three-quarters of a mile. Closed in 1889 with thirty-three nominations.

No. 19—THE FALL STAKE—A handicap sweepstake for all ages; of $50 each, half forfeit; $15 declaration; with $400 added: second to receive $100, and third, $50 from the stakes. Weights announced by ten A. M., Tuesday, September 16th. Declarations due by 6 P. M. same day. One mile and a quarter.

No. 20—THE PALO ALTO STAKE—A handicap for two-year-olds; of $50 each, half forfeit, or $10 declaration; with $250 added; second to save stake. Weights announced Tuesday, September 16th, at 10 A. M. Declarations due at 6 P. M., same day. Three quarters of a mile.

No. 21—PURSE, $400—For three-year-olds and upwards; $ 0 from starters to go to second horse. Winners at this distance in 1890 to carry, if once, three pounds; twice, five pounds extra. Horses that have started twice in a race one mile or over and not won, in 1890, allowed five pounds. Maidens allowed, if three years old, seven pounds; if four, ten pounds; if five years or upwards, fifteen pounds. One mile.

No. 22—FREE PURSE, $300—Of which $50 to second; for all ages. To close at 6 P. M., the day before. One mile.

Seventh Day, Thursday, September 18th.

TROTTING AND PACING.

No. 23—PACING STAKE—For two-year-olds; of $50 each; $25 to accompany nomination; $25 payable by 6 P. M., day before the race; $750 added; stakes and added money divided, 60, 30 and 10 per cent. Mile heats.

No. 24—TROTTING PURSE, $1,200—2:21 Class.

No. 25—PACING PURSE, $1,000—Free-for all.

Eighth Day, Friday, September 19th.

RUNNING.

No. 26—THE CALIFORNIA ANNUAL STAKE—A sweepstake for two-year-olds (foals of 1888). One mile. Closed in 1889 with twenty-three nominations.

No. 27—THE PRESIDENT STAKE—A sweepstake for three-year-olds (foals of 1887). One mile and a half. Closed in 1888 with twenty-nine nominations.

No. 28—THE RICO STAKE—For all ages; of $50 each; $15 forfeit; $300 added; of which $100 to second; third to save stake; $200 additional if 1:41½ is beaten. Stake to be named after the winner if Rico's time (1:41½) is beaten. One mile.

No. 29—THE LA RUE STAKE—A handicap for all ages; of $100 each, half forfeit; $20 declaration, with $500 added; of which $100 to second; $50 to third. Weights announced by 10 A. M. on Thursday, Sept. 18th. Declarations due by 6 P. M. same day. One mile and a half.

No. 30—FREE PURSE, $300—Of which $50 to second; for all ages. Horses that have started at this meeting and beaten once, allowed five pounds; twice, seven pounds; three times, ten pounds. To name and close at 6 P. M. the day before. One and one-sixteenth miles.

Ninth Day, Saturday, September 20th.

TROTTING.

No. 31—TROTTING PURSE, $1,000—2:20 Class.

No. 32—TROTTING PURSE, $1,000—2:35 Class.

No. 33—FOUR-YEAR-OLD STAKE—Closed March 15th, with six nominations.

No. 34—THREE-YEAR-OLD STAKE—Closed March 15th, with six nominations.

Fixed Events.

Send for entry blanks for fixed running events for 1891-2.

To Close Same as Regular Programme.

August 1, 1890.

For Two-Year-Olds in '91.

THE CALIFORNIA ANNUAL STAKE—THREE-QUARTERS OF A MILE.

THE AUTUMN HANDICAP—ONE MILE.

THE SUNNY SLOPE STAKE, FOR FILLIES—FIVE-EIGHTHS OF A MILE.

For Three-Year-Olds in '92.

THE SUNSET STAKE—ONE AND ONE-QUARTER MILES.

THE PRESIDENT STAKE—A HANDICAP—ONE AND ONE-HALF MILES.

REMARKS AND CONDITIONS.

TROTTING AND PACING.

All trotting and pacing races are the best three in five, except the two-year old, unless otherwise specified; five to enter, and three to start, but the Board reserves the right to hold a less number than five to fill, by the deduction of the entrance money from the purse for each horse less than five. Entrance fee, 10 per cent. on purse, to accompany nomination. Trotting and pacing purses divided at the rate of 50 per cent. to first horse, 25 per cent. to second, 15 per cent. to third, and 10 per cent. to fourth.

In the two, three and four-year-old sweepstakes, unless otherwise provided, moneys are divided as follows: To winning colt, all the stakes and 50 per cent. of the added money; second colt, 33⅓ per cent.; third colt, 16⅔ per cent. of added money. In all stakes payments not made as they become due forfeits all money paid in, and declares entry out.

The National Association Rules to govern trotting; but the Board reserves the right to trot heats of any two classes alternately, if necessary to finish any day's racing, or to trot a special race between heats. A horse making a walk-over shall be entitled only to the entrance money paid in. When less than the required number of starters appear, they may contest for the entrance money, to be divided as follows: 66⅔ to the first, and 33⅓ to the second.

In trotting and pacing races, entries not declared out by 6 P. M. day before must start.

In trotting races drivers will be required to wear caps and jackets of distinct colors, WHICH MUST BE NAMED IN THEIR ENTRIES.

RUNNING.

The State Agricultural Society's rules of 1889 to govern running races, except when conditions named are otherwise.

Please observe that in the foregoing stakes declarations are permitted for a small forfeit.

In all the foregoing stakes the declarations are void, unless accompanied by the money.

Starters in stake races must be named on or before 6 P. M. of day before race. All entries in purse races not declared out by 6 P. M. day before must start.

Racing colors to be named in entries.

Final settlement of all purses and stakes won will be made on Saturday morning, September 20th, at the office of the Secretary.

Entry blanks and racing rules will be furnished upon application to the Secretary. Entries in all races, except otherwise stated, to close with the Secretary on Friday, August 1, 1890.

CHRISTOPHER GREEN, Pres.

EDWIN F. SMITH, Secretary.

Langtry Farms' Stud

Imp. FRIAR TUCK

By the Immortal HERMIT.

DAM ROMPING GIRL BY WILD DAYRELL,

AT $50 THE SEASON.

Mares not proving with foal may be returned the following season. Good care taken of mares, but no liabilities for accidents or escapes.

Good Pasturage at $5 per month.

Mares shipped to ST. HELENA, care CHARLES WILLIAM ABY, St. Helena Stables, will be cared for. For further particulars address,

CHAS. WILLIAM ABY,

Middletown, Lake County, Cal.

The Only S. B. Nolan

JOCKEY, BICYCLE AND BASE BALL UNIFORMS.

Mail Orders.

426 Montgomery Street, S. F., Cal.

Races, Races,

JULY WEEK.

AT

South Park Race Track

Eureka, Cal.

GIVEN BY THE

EUREKA JOCKEY CLUB.

FIRST DAY, JULY 2, 1890.

No. 1. Novelty Running Race. Free for all. Dash of one mile. Purse $250. First quarter, $40. Half, $50. Third quarter, $70. Mile, $90.

No. 2. Running Race. Purse $150. Five-eighths dash, for two-year-olds. $125 to first horse; $25 to second horse.

No. 3. Running. Purse $150. Three-quarters and repeat. $125 to first; $25 to second.

SECOND DAY, JULY 3, 1890.

No. 4. Trotting. Purse $200. Three minute Class. $150 to first; $50 to second. (Cover barred.)

No. 5. Running Stake. Five-eighths of a mile. For Humboldt raised two year-olds. $30 entrance, half forfeit. $150 added. First to receive 60 per cent.; second, 30 per cent., third, 10 per cent.

No. 6. Running Stake. Purse $250. Mile Dash. $150 to first horse; $50 to second horse.

THIRD DAY, JULY 4, 1890.

No. 7. Trotting Stake. 2:40 Class. Purse $250. $200 to first horse; $50 to second horse.

No. 8. Running Stake, 1¼ miles. Free-for-all. $40 entrance, ¼ forfeit, $200 added; second horse $75, third horse to save stake.

No. 9. Running Stake. Purse $150; 1-2 mile and repeat; $125 to first; $25 to second.

FOURTH DAY, JULY 5, 1890.

No. 10. Running Stake, 1-2 mile and repeat; for Humboldt horses owned prior to Jan. 1, 1890. $125 to first, $25 to second.

No. 11. Running Stake. Purse $200; 7-8 mile and repeat. $150 to first, $50 to second.

CONDITIONS AND REMARKS.

All trotting races are best three in five, unless otherwise specified. Four to enter and three to start, but the Board reserves the right to hold a less number than four to fill by the withdrawal of a proportionate amount of the purse. Entrance fee, 10 per cent. of purse, to accompany nominations. In all trotting races the rules of the American Trotting Association, and all running races the rules of the Pacific Coast Blood Horse Association to govern, but the Board reserves the right to trot heats of any two classes alternately, if necessary, to finish any day's racing. In all entries not declared out by 6 P. M. of the day preceding the race, shall be required to start.

No added money paid for a walk over. In all races, four or more paid up entries required to fill, and three or more horses to start. Racing Colors to be named in entries. In trotting races drivers will be required to wear caps of distinct colors to be named in entries. Entries in all races to close with the Secretary, Thursday, June 26, 1890. Entry blanks will be furnished upon application to the Secretary.

All trotting races for horses owned and in Humboldt County prior to June 1, 1890.

H. M. DEVOY, President.

J. P. MONROE, Secretary.

SONOMA and MARIN

Futurity Stake,

To take place during the

FALL MEETING

OF THE

Sonoma and Marin Agricultural Society,

1893.

For Foals of 1890.

Open to the get of stallions owned in the district which is comprised of the following counties: Sonoma, Marin, Napa, Lake, Mendocino, Solano, Yolo, Colusa and Contra Costa.

Mile heats, 2 in 3; entrance $75, with $75 added for each starter over two and up to five head, and $10 for each additional starter up to ten head.

Payments: $5 must accompany the nomination on July 1, 1890; $5 on January 2, 1891; $5 on July 1, 1891; $10 on January 2, 1892; $10 on July 1, 1892; $15 on January 2, 1893; $25 on July 1, 1893.

CONDITIONS.

1—Neglect to provide payments on the dates stipulated will incur forfeiture of all previous payments.

2—When there is more than one entry to this stake by one person or in one interest, the horse to be started must be named by 6 P. M. of the day preceding the race.

3. The stake will be divided into four moneys, viz., 50 per cent. to the first, 25 per cent to the second, 15 per cent. to the third and 10 per cent. to the fourth horse.

4. If only three horses start in this stake, only the first, second and third money shall be paid; if but two start, there will be no added money, the stake money paid in will be divided—two-thirds to the first and one third to the second horse.

5. A horse distancing the field shall only be entitled to first and third moneys.

6. The Board of Directors reserve the right to declare the stake filled or not filled without binding itself to any specified number of entries.

7. Otherwise than the above, National or American Trotting Association Rules—as this Society may select—will govern the stake.

Entries to close on July 1st with the Secretary.

J. H. WHITE, President,

DR. THOMAS MACLAY, Secretary, Petaluma.

Memo.

The Best Son of SIDNEY

Will Make the Season of 1890 at the OAKLAND RACE TRACK

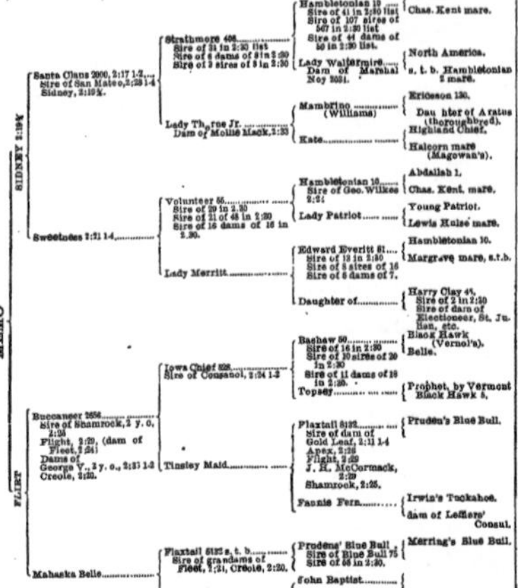

MEMO is, as can be seen at a glance, one of the best bred young stallions in service, having three crosses of Rysdyk's Hambletonian and one of Harry Clay, the sire of Green Mountain Maid (dam of Electioneer, etc.), while Long Island Black Hawk and Flaxtail also contribute to his blood. Sidney (Memo's sire) is universally known as the best young sire in the world, a producer of extreme-speed at an early age.

PERFORMANCES.

MEMO trotted in public in his two year-old form, obtaining a record of 2:49, though he was close to Grandee in a race on the Bay District Track, the second heat of which was made in 2:31 1-2, the first in 2:32. He exhibited phenomenal speed when three years old, and had it not been for a slight strain of his fore fetlock, there is little question that he would have shown in public very close to the best record. On the Oakland track he was timed a mile in 2:20 1-2, and frequently trotted quarters in from 32 1-2 to 31 seconds.

As a four-year-old Memo only started once—at Sacramento—when, although out of condition, he showed great speed, and improving as he went on, great hopes were entertained of his going well down in the 'teens at the P. C. T. H. B. A. meeting, but after showing several very fast miles his leg filled and he was laid up for the season. He is sixteen hands high, and of powerful build throughout. His color is a glossy black, with both fore-feet white. His disposition is all that could be desired, and his action superb. He is a sure foal getter, only one mare being reported not in foal during his last season.

TERMS, $100, with usual return privileges, for a limited number of mares. Season to close JUNE 15th, when he will be prepared for track purposes. Pasturage $4 per month. Have leased the cricket ground adjoining the track for pasturage, where there is fine feed. Reasonable charges if fed hay and grain. Best of care taken of mares in any manner owners may desire, but positively no responsibility assumed for accidents or escapes. For further particulars address

J. P. KERR, 313 Bush Street, San Francisco,

or, JOHN ROWEN, Race Track, Oakland, Cal.

2:10 1-2 ELECTIONEER 2:12 1-4

BAY STALLION **ECLECTIC** 11,321	BROWN STALLION **MORTIMER** 5,346
By Electioneer, dam Manette (full sister to Woodnut 2.16 1-2 Manon 2:21 and Maple, dam of Hattie D., three-year-old record 2:26½) by Nutwood 2:18¾, etc., etc.	Four-year-old Record 2:27. By ELECTIONEER, dam MARTI, by Whipple's Hambletonian (sire of 15 in 2:30, and of dams of eight in 2:30). Second dam Ida Martin by Rifleman (sire of Col. Lewis 2:15½).
Terms $100 for the Season.	**Terms $60 for the Season.**

Horses shipped via San Francisco may be consigned to J. W. MORSHEAD, City Front Stables, who will attend to their forwarding.

Season closes JULY 1st, 18 Usual return privileges.

For further particulars address owner,

WILFRED PAGE, Penns Grove,
Sonoma County, Cal

The Trotting Stallion

Silver Bow

Will make the season of 1890 at the Oakland Race Track.

PEDIGREE.

SILVER BOW 11706, two-year-old record 2:37, is by Robert McGregor 647, 2:17½ (sire of Bonnie McGregor, 2:13½, Earl McGregor, 2:21¼, Mac D., 2:30, McGregor Boy, 2:29¼, Mark Time, 2:30, Roxie McGregor, 2:20¼) by Major Edsall 2:11, 2:29, by Alexander's Abdallah 15—sire of Goldsmith Maid, 2:14—by Hambletonian 10—sire of Dexter, 2:17¼.

Robert McGregor's dam was Nancy Whitman by American Star 14, by Stockholm's American Star.

SILVER BOW'S first dam is Sadie by Hambletonian 10, sire of Geo. Wilkes, 2:22—sire of Guy Wilkes, 2:15¼—also Electioneer, sire of Sunol, three-year-old record, 2:10½, and Palo Alto, 2:12¾; second dam Lady Wynne by Wm. Welch 341; third dam Elenora Margrave by imp. Margrave.

DESCRIPTION.

SILVER BOW is a handsome bay, no white; 15-3¼ hands high; weighs 1075 pounds; of fine form, with the best of legs and a clean-cut, intelligent head. Is remarkably level-headed, seldom making a break; wears seven-ounce shoes in front. His record, 2:37, is no mark of his speed; he can beat 30 easy, and with his gilt-edge breeding, he is just what he ought to be, a trotter sired by a trotter whose dam was herself a trotter and his grandam the dam of two trotters. His dam Sadie being by Hambletonian 10, shows him to be bred from the cream of the trotting blood.

TERMS: $100 for the season. Mares not proving in foal returnable for the season of 1891 free of charge. Good pasturage and first-class care taken of mares for $5 per month. No responsibilities assumed for escapes or accidents. For further particulars, address

Limited to 15 approved mares.
Season to end June 1st, 1890.

P. J. WILLIAMS,
Care Race Track, Oakland, Cal.

Pleasanton Stock Farm Co.'s Stallions.

DIRECTOR, 2:17.

Director's book is open for 15 good mares more than already booked for the season of 1890, at $300 each.

This is the cheapest service fee ever charged for a stallion, taking into consideration his BREEDING and RACE RECORD and the RACE RECORDS OF HIS COLTS.

Season to commence February 15th and close August 1st.

CORRECTOR, Five Years Old.

Sire Director 2:17, dam Brainey, she by Echo. Echo sired by Rysdyk's Hambletonian, out of Fanny Felter, by Magnolia, he by Seely's American Star. Brainey's dam Lady Dudley, she by Tom Dudley by Blacknose, a son of Medoc, he by American Eclipse. Lady Dudley's dam by Bertrand, Jr., a son of Bertrand.

CORRECTOR is a rich seal brown 15½ hands high, and is the fastest young stallion in the world under the same conditions, never having been off the farm where raised and never been shod or driven for speed before last Christmas, and can trot quarters now in 35 seconds, a 2:20 gait.

He will be allowed to serve ten good mares, at $100 each for the season, which closes June 1st.

DECORATOR, Four Years Old.

Sire Director 2:17, dam Chess, sired by Cardinal 2.37, trial 2:28, he by Gen. Gifford's Morgan, dam of Cardinal, sired by Joe Gales of Ohio, he by Marlborough out of the Duchess of Marlborough by Southern Eclipse; second dam old Duchess of Marlborough by Sir Archy; third dam by imp Diomed. Decorator's second dam a Morgan and Messenger mare.

Decorator is a light bay 16 hands high, and with but little handling for speed has shown eighths in 17½ seconds, a 2:20 gait.

He will be allowed to serve ten good mares at $50 each for the season, which closes June 1st.

Mares not proving with foal may be returned next season free of charge of service fees to the same stallion, if he is still in our possession; however, the company reserves the right to return the fee instead of giving service.

Pasturage $4 per month; hay and grain extra. Accidents and escapes at owner's risk.

Service fees due at time of service, and must be paid, together with pasturage, etc., before mares are taken away, or a good approved note given, payable August 1st, 1890, at which date all bills must be settled.

For further information call or address **M. SALISBURY, 320 Sansome Street, Room 26, San Francisco, or**

PLEASANTON STOCK FARM CO.,
Pleasanton, Alameda Co., Cal.

SOUTHER FARM

P. O. Box 208. San Leandro, Cal.

1½ miles northwest of San Leandro; 8 miles southeast of Oakland. Turn off county road between above places at "Stanley Road," ¼ mile north of San Leandro.

Horses boarded at all times in any manner desired. Best of care but no responsibility for accidents. Colts broken and handled for the road or track. Terms reasonable.

Glen Fortune,	Jester D,	El Benton,	Figaro,
By Electioneer.	By Almont.	By Electioneer.	Hambletonian 725
$50 for 1889.	$50 for 1890.	Limited to 5 mares.	Limited to 12 mares
		Book Full.	Book Full.

THE SOUTHER FARM

Has Green Feed the Year Round,

and feeds Hay in connection with the green feed, which a horse must have if he is to thrive. Every animal is given

A Dry, Warm Place to Sleep,

No matter how stormy the weather. All Stock under cover when it rains.

VISITORS WELCOME ANY DAY EXCEPT SUNDAY.

How to Get Stock to the Souther Farm.

The Souther Farm is one and a half miles northeast of San Leandro and eight miles southeast of Oakland. The stables are about one mile east of the county road, which runs between Oakland and San Leandro. The place to turn off is at Stanley Road, where a large signboard of the farm is placed. Guide boards will be found at every cross road. In any ordinary weather the roads are very good, and they are fairly good after the unusually heavy rainfall of the past winter.

All stock sent from San Francisco may be brought over by Garcia's Express, No. 3 Market street, San Francisco. They also have an order box outside of Hawley Bros.' Hardware house on the corner of Market and Beale streets. The express leaves San Francisco on the Creek route boat, which starts at 1:30, but all orders should be in the order box at Market and Beale streets by 10 o'clock, or at the office, No. 3 Market street, by 11 o'clock at the latest. In the case of very young or very valuable horses, the Souther Farm will send reliable men to lead or drive over any stock that will not lead behind a wagon. A small charge will be made in such cases, to cover the extra expense incurred.

Horses are very easily taken from Oakland to the farm, and where it is inconvenient for owners to bring them or send them, the farm will send after anything that is to come. On horses that stay three months or over there is no charge for getting or delivering. Where a horse stays a short time the actual time and expense only is charged to him.

Horses can be shipped by rail from almost all parts of the State to San Leandro. Always notify the Farm several days before shipping anything, and then men will be on hand to receive stock on arrival. The railroad station is but two miles from the Souther Farm, and the agent invariably gives immediate notice of the arrival of any stock consigned to the above farm, but when word is sent to the farm in good season by letter or telegram, the animals sent are saved waiting a couple of hours in the car.

Passenger trains leave San Francisco (from the broad gauge ferry) and First and Broadway, Oakland, at frequent intervals during the day. There are several trains from San Jose to San Leandro on both the broad and narrow gauge railroads; the broad gauge, by way of Niles, is much more convenient for getting to the farm. There are trains each day from Sacramento, Stockton and Livermore to San Leandro. In ordinary weather it is a short and pleasant drive from Oakland to the Souther Farm or from San Francisco to the Farm by way of the Creek route ferry boat. Always notify the Souther Farm just when you will arrive at San Leandro, and some one will meet you at the station. If you do not recognize the farm conveyance ask the stage driver, who will point it out.

Write to the above address for references, circulars and price lists. Terms reasonable.

GILBERT TOMPKINS, Proprietor.

SAN MATEO STOCK FARM

HOME OF GUY WILKES,

Record, 2:15 1-4.

Guy Wilkes' Book is full for 1890 and 1891, and positively no more mares will be received.

Sable Wilkes, three-year-old record 2:18, will be allowed to serve 25 mares in addition to those already engaged at $250 the season of 1890. SABLE Wilkes, 15½ hands, black horse, by Guy Wilkes, first dam Sable by The Moor; second dam Gretchen by Mambrino Pilot; third dam Kitty Kirkman by Canada Chief; fourth dam by Fanning's Tobe; fifth dam by imp. Leviathan.

Leo Wilkes, brown horse, four years, 16 hands, full brother to Sable Wilkes, will be allowed to serve 30 mares at $100 the season

Mares not proving with foal may be returned the following season free of service fee. Parties engaging the services of any of the above horses must send a deposit of 10 per cent. of service money with engagement. Pasturage $6 per month, and when the condition of the animal requires it, hay or grain, or both, are fed, the charge will be $12 50 per month. Good care will be taken of all mares sent to the Farm, but no liability will be assumed for accidents or escapes.

All bills are due at time of service, but must be paid by August 1st of each year. No stock will be allowed to leave the place until all bills are paid.

WILLIAM CORBITT.
San Mateo Stock Farm.

Vineland Stock Farm

Alcona 730.

Sire of

FLORA BELLE - - - - Record 2:24
CLAY DUKE - - - - - " 2:31½

ALCONA will be a great sire, but four of his colts have ever been trained, and all have shown full miles better than 2:30, and two of them as good as 2:20. Two of his first sons each sired a colt as a two-year-old, and last season one as a four-year-old trotted a full mile in 1:23¼, and the other, a three-year-old, a mile in 2:31. With opportunities, Alcona is destined to be one of Almont's best sons. Almont, for his opportunities, is beyond doubt the most prepotent sire of his age. He has 36 representatives in the 2:30 list; 49 sons and 22 daughters that have already produced 2:30 performers. Almont died five y a s ago at 20 years old. If he lived he would be but 28 years old.

PEDIGREE.

ALCONA sired by the great Almont (sire of Westmont 2:13¾, Fanny Witherspoon 2:16¼, Piedmont 2:17¼, and 33 others with records better than 2:30, and grandsire of Belle Hamlin 2:12¾, etc.); by Alexander's Abdallah (sire of Goldsmith Maid 2:14), he by Rysdyk's Hambletonian. Alcona's dam, Queen Mary, by Mambrino Chief (sire of Lady Thorne 2,18 1-4, and 6 others in the 2:30 list, and sire of the dams of Director 2:17, Piedmont 2:17¼, Onward 2:25 1-4, Red Wilkes Almont, Belmont and many other noted sires).

DESCRIPTION.

Alcona is a beautiful chestnut 16 3 1-2 hands high, and weighs 1300 lbs. His colts possess speed, style, finish and beauty, and if they don't trot they command the highest prices for carriage horses.

$40 for the season. Usual return privilege.

Season of Alcona and Grandissimo ends July 1st, 1890.

Grandissimo,

Full Brother to GRANDEE, 3-year old record 2:23 1-2.

Sired by La Grande (son of Almont, and out of Jessie Pepper by Mambrino Chief; Jessie Pepper is the dam of Iene 2:17 1-2, Alpha 2:23 1-2, Sterling Wilkes 2:31¼, and others) dam Norma, by Arthurton (sire of Arab 2:15, Joe Arthurton 2 21 1-2, etc.)

Grandam Nourmahal, (full sister to A. W. Richmond, sire of Arrow 2:13¾, Romero 2:19, and sire of Columbine, dam of Anteeo 2:16¼, and Antevolo 2:19¾ at four years old).

DESCRIPTION.

Grandissimo is four years old, will make a sixteen hand horse; he is a rich mahogany bay in color and perfect in style and action. $50 for the season. Usual return privileges.

"Grandissimo" with limited training last fall as a three-year-old, trotted quarters in 36 seconds and miles in 2:40.

I feel confident that he will trot fast this season, and will be a great sire as his colts this season are all grand youngsters.

The best of pasturage $4 per month. Mares taken care of in any manner that owners may desire, but no responsibility assurred for escapes or accidents.

For further particulars send for circular or call at stables, one mile south of St. Helena.

FRED W. LOEBER Prop'r.

The Trotting Stallion

VICTOR,

Record 2:22.

Will make the season of 1890 at NAPA CITY.

DESCRIPTION.

VICTOR is a handsome dark bay; 15.3 hands high; weighs about 1,100 pounds, and is remarkably intelligent, level-headed, of kind disposition, and a magnificent animal in every respect. He is well boned and muscled, of splendid conformation, and possesses the qualities of speed and endurance to an eminent degree—qualities that he imparts to his progeny.

PEDIGREE.

VICTOR, record 2:22
- Echo 462
  - Hambletonian 10... Sire of 42 in the 2:30 list.
    - Abdallah 1
    - Chas. Kent mare
  - Fanny Felter ....
    - Magnolia 68
    - by Webber's Kentucky Whip
- Daughter of
  - Woodburn ....
    - Lexington
    - Lulu Horton
  - daughter of.........
    - Ashland
    - thoroughbred

ECHO is the sire of Belle Echo, 2:20, Senator, 2:21¼, Victor, 2:22, Gibraltar, 2:22¼, Echora, 2:23¼, Tippie, 2:25¼, Lohengrin, 2:27¼, Pasha, 2:27¼, Elmonte, 2:29, Col. Hawkins, 2:29¼, Annie Laurie, 2.30, Economy, 2:30, Sam Lewis, pacer, 2:25.

TERMS—$60 FOR THE SEASON.

Mares not proving with foal may be returned next season free of charge, provided the horse remains the property of the present proprietor, and stands at the same place, otherwise money will be refunded. The best of care taken of mares in any manner that owners may desire, but no responsibility assumed for accidents or escapes. For further particulars, apply to or address

G. W. HUGHES, Agent,

G. A. DOHERTY, Proprietor. Napa City.

The Trotting-Bred Stallion

RINGWOOD

THE FINEST SON OF THE NOTED SIDNEY,

Will make a Season at Oakland, commencing March 1, and ending June 1, 1890.

DESCRIPTION.

RINGWOOD is a dark, rich colored bay, black points, 15 1-2 hands, weight 1100 lbs., and a pure gaited trotter. Has shown great speed. He is now five years old. As a four year old he showed a trial in 2:19 1-2, and but for an accident would have received a record as a four year old of 2:18 or better.

PEDIGREE.

RINGWOOD is by Sidney, record 2:19 3-4, and 's half brother to Gold Leaf 2:11 1-4, Adonis 2:14, Fleet (two year old) 2:24, Longworth 2:19, Sister V. 2:27, Faustino, yearling, 2:35, Fl , yearling, 2:35. Memo, three year old trial 2:20 1-2. set

Sidney is by Santa Claus, record 2:17 1:2; he by Strathmore, sire of 31 in 2:30 list; he by Hambletonian 10, the greatest of all producers; he by Abdallah. Sidney's dam, Sweetness, record 2:21 1-4; she by Volunteer, the sire of St. Julien 2:11 1-4.

RINGWOOD'S dam Alma; she by Dashway, thoroughbred; he by Belmont, he by American Boy; he by Sea Gull; he by imported Expedition. Alma's 1st dam, Fanny Cobb, was a great road mare, pedigree untraced.

TERMS; $50 for the Season.

Payable June 1st, or sooner if mares are taken away Address communications to

A. C. DIETZ,

Oakland, Cal.

2:10¾ 2:13¾ 2:10

DEXTER PRINCE.

This Royally-bred Stallion will make the Season of 1890 at the LIVE OAKS Breeding Farm, 2 miles from Lodi, San Joaquin County, Cal.

DESCRIPTION.

DEXTER PRINCE is a blood bay, 16 hands high, weighs over 1,100 pounds; has great power and substance, and the highest finish. When two years old, at Palo Alto, he was timed quarters by Gov. Stanford in 32½ seconds, and he was driven eights by Mr. Marvin at a faster rate of speed than that. He is a sure foal-getter, and invariably sires foals of good size, of fine form and finish, and the highest rate of speed.

PEDIGREE.

By KENTUCKY PRINCE, the sire of Guy, 2:10¾, Spofford, 2:18¾, Company, 2:19¾, Bayonne Prince, 2:21 1-4, Fred Folger, 2:20¾, and a score more in the 2:30 list.

First dam LADY DEXTER, full sister of the greatest of trotters, Dexter, and the greatest of sires, Dictator, the sire of Director, 2:17, Phallas, 2:13¾, in a fourth heat, and Jay-Eye-See, 2:10.

Second dam Clara, the dam of Dexter, 2:17 1-4, Dicta or, Astoria 2:29 1-4, and Almah, 2:28¾. Clara was by American Star, that has 34 daughters that have produced 2:30 or better trotters.

Third dam the McKinstry mare, the dam of Shark, 2:27¾. HAMBLETONIAN, the grandsire of DEXTER PRINCE, has 40 trotters in the 2:30 list, 44 daughters that have produced 2:30 trotters, and more than 100 sons that have sired 2 30 trotters.

CLARK CHIEF, the grandsire on the sire's side, was the sire of performing and producing sons and daughters.

DEXTER PRINCE has faster blood lines, on both sides, than any other stallion in the world—Guy 2:10¾, and Jay-Eye-See, 2:10.

KENTUCKY PRINCE is one of the best bred and speediest stallions in the world. David Bonner, in the presence of Governor Stanford, timed him when he trotted a 2:10 gait. He is by Clark Chief, one of the great broodmare sires; his first dam is Kentucky Queen by Morgan Eagle, son of Hale's Green Mountain Morgan, 2nd dam by Blythe's Whip, 3rd dam by Martin's Brummier, 4th dam by Quicksilver 880, on through the strongest thoroughbred blood.

TERMS.

$100 for the season, with usual return privileges. Payable before mares are removed. Good pasture, and the best care furnished, but no responsibility assumed for accidents.

PREMIUM.

$250 will be given to the first of the produce of DEXTER PRINCE put in the 2:30 list, and $100 each after the first. Address

L M. MORSE, Lodi, Cal.

The Produce of Eros Averaged $2,200 Each at New York Auction Sale in 1889.

THE ELECTIONEER TROTTING STALLION,

5326 EROS 5326

Will make the season of 1890—February 1st to July 1st—at LA SIESTA RANCH, MENLO PARK, adjoining Palo Alto.

PEDIGREE.

EROS (5326)
Standard by his sire
" " dam
" " record
" " produce
" under all rules

EROS (5326)..
- Electioneer........ Grandsire of Noriaine, 1 yr., 2:31 1-2, Sire of Sunol, 2 yrs., 2:18, Sunol, 3 yrs., 2:10 1-2, Hinda Rose, 4 yrs., 2:16, Palo Alto, 2:12¾.
  - Hambletonian 10........ Sire of Dictator, George Wilkes, Happy Medium, and 40 others in 2:30 list, and grandsire of 728 in list.
    - Abdallah 10 Sire of the dams of Goldsmith Maid, 2 14, and 7 other producing dams.
    - Charles Kent mare By imp. Bellfounder.
  - Green Mountain Maid........ Dam of Prospero, 2:20, Elaine, 2:20, Dame Trot, 2:22, Elista, 2:22¾, Storm, 2:25¾, Antonio, 2:28¾, Miranda, 2,31, Mansfield, 2:26.
    - Harry Clay Sire of the dams of St. Julien, 2:11¼, Bodine, 2 19¼, and 17 more in 2:30 list
    - Shanghai Mary.
- Sontag Mohawk .... Dam of Eros, 2:29 1-2, Sport, 2:22¾, Sallie Benton, 2:17¾, Conductor, trial, 2:26, Colma, 3-y-o trial, 2:24.
  - Mohawk Chief. .... Sire of the dams of Lot Slocum, 2:17¼, Sallie Benton, 4 yrs., 2:17¾, Pediar, 2 yrs., 2:27¾, Stanford, 4 yrs., 2:30, Eros, 6th heat, 2:29 1-2.
    - Hambletonian 10 Sire of the dams of Stamboul, 2:12¼, Wilton, 2:19¼, and 20 other trotters.
    - Lady Perrine
  - Sontag Nellie........
    - Toronto Sontag By Toronto Chief,
    - Nellie Gray 5-mile record, 13:46.

Produce of Eros
Wanda, 4 yrs., 2 31,
Solita, 2 yrs., 3 41 1-2,
Meriquita, 2yrs., 2:42,
Daylight, 2 yrs., 2:54,
Hiram B., trial, 2.28.

These are the only colts by him that have ever had a harness on except one in New York that went a trial last July in 2:26 1:2.

DESCRIPTION.

EROS is a rich seal brown stallion, bred by Hon, Leland Stanford at Palo Alto, and is the nearest living likeness of his celebrated sire, Electioneer. Stands 15.2 hands high, and weighs 1050 pounds

In breeding to Eros, the owners of mares will strictly follow the great rule of breeding, viz., breed to a stallion by a producer and out of a sure producer of great speed. Eros is by the stallion that has produced more 2:30 trotters that any living horse, and is also the sire of more 2:20 performers than any horse living or dead.

EROS is out of the dam of Sally Benton, four years old, record 2:17¾, Sport 2:22¼, and Eros 2:29½ in the sixth heat, against a field of nine horses. He is from a family that is endowed with great natural speed, trot fast at an early age, train on, throw trotters from all classes of mares, are of good substance, bone, style and action, and breed solid colors.

TERMS.

$100 for the season, with the privilege of return next season should mares not be in foal and horse and mare still remain in the same hands.

Good pasturage can be obtained at $5 per month, but no responsibility for accidents or escapes. There are a large number of box stalls, and animals can be kept up and fed on hay and grain at reasonable rates if required. Mares already in foal can be sent to the ranch for foaling, and will receive all the attention bestowed upon our own mares. Mares left with Mr. Peter Pomyea, Broadway Street Stable, Oakland, or with Mr. F. H. Burke, 401 Montgomery Street, San Francisco, will be forwarded to the ranch free of charge. For further particulars apply to

W. H. VIOGET,

LA SIESTA RANCH, MENLO PARK, CAL.

EROS is the only stallion offered to the public on this Coast that has a dam that has three in the 2:30 list.

GRAND MOOR, 2374.

Grand Moor 2374.
- Moor 870........ Sire of Beautiful Bells........2:29½, Sire of Sable (dam of Sable Wilkes).2:18, Sire of Sultan........2:24, Sire of Tommy Gates........2:24, Sire of Del Sur........2:24½, Sire of Sir Guy........2:28½. Beautiful Bells is the dam of Hinda Rose, 2:19½ as a 3-year-old, Palo Alto Belle, 2:22¾, Chimes, St. Bell, 2:24½, Bell Boy (3 years) 2:19¼. Sultan, 2:24 (sire of Stamboul 2;12¼) has 19 in 2:30 list.
  - Clay Pilot 93 Sire of 2 in 2:30 list.
  - Belle of Wabash.
- Vashti........ Dam of Don Tomas, who got a record of 2:20 in 1889.
  - Mambrino Patchen 58 Sire of 14 in 2:30 list Sire of the dam of Guy Wilkes, 2:15¼; also sire of 30 stallions and 18 mares with get in 2:30 list.
  - Kate Taber By Mambrino Messenger, he by Mambrino Paymaster.

Foaled 1876. Black. Sixteen hands high. Bred by L. J. Rose

A horse of highest form and quality; of great excellence in every point; a type of his celebrated family; of marked individuality, spirit and endurance; never properly trained or raced, but shows the possession of great speed; perfectly manageable in the stable and on the road and track.

As he is sired by The Moor 870, a son of CLAY PILOT, out of Vashti by MAMBRINO PATCHEN, he is a most valuable cross for mares of other families. THE MOOR sired Beautiful Bells and the dams of Sable Wilkes and Margaret 2:28 (dam of Regal Wilkes, 2-year-old record 2:20½).

MAMBRINO PATCHEN is regarded as the unsurpassed sire of broodmares, having, among many others, sired the dam of Guy Wilkes and of Wm. L. (the sire of Axtell), and a son of his sired the dam of Axtell. The public sales this year have demonstrated with renewed emphasis the value of The Moor and Mambrino Patchen strains of blood. For combining particularly with the Hambletonians it may be called "the ready money cross."

GRAND MOOR will make the season of 1890 for a time at the Oakland Race Track and afterwards at my Ranch, fifteen miles from Oakland. Mares can be delivered at the race track to the groom in charge. Pasture at $5 per month. For other food, if requested, an additional charge will be made.

TERMS, $100 for the season, with privileges of return if the horse does not change hands.

Every care exercised, but no liability for escapes or accidents.

H. I. THORNTON, 504 Kearny Street.

Cook STOCK FARM,

Season of 1890.

STEINWAY 1808.

Three-Year-Old Record 2:25 3-4.

Sire of STRATHWAY, three year old record 2:26, and sire of the dam of BOURBON RUSSELL 2:30.

By STRATHMORE 408; sire of 31 in the 2:30 list; sire of 6 dams of 8 in the 2:30 list, and sire of 3 sires of 3 in 2:30 list.

1st dam ABBESS (dam of Solo 2:28, and Soprano, dam of C. F Clay 2:18, Eminence 2:27 and Strathbridge, 3 year old record 2:28½) by ALBION, sire of VANITY FAIR 2:24½, and of the dam of FAVORITE 2:25½.

2nd dam by MARSHALL NEY.

3rd dam by BERTRAND, a son of SIR ARCHY.

TERMS—$100 for the season.

CHARLES DERBY 4907

Brown Horse, Foaled 1885.

By STEINWAY 1808.

1st dam by the great ELECTIONEER, sire of SUNOL 3 year old record 2:10½, Palo Alto 2:12¾, etc., etc.

2nd dam FANNY MALONE, by NIAGARA.

3rd dam FANNY WICKHAM, by HERALD.

4th dam by Imp. TRUSTEE.

TERMS—$100 for the season.

Pasturage $5 per month. Accidents and escapes at owner's risk. Mares consigned to the farm should be sent to Fashion Stables, Oakland; Geary & Grindle's Stable, Haywards; or to Bennett's Stable, Martinez; from and to which places they will be delivered free of charge. Address

COOK STOCK FARM,

Danville, Contra Costa, Co., Cal.

Sunny Side Breeding Farm.

Admiral 488.

Foaled 1867—Sired by Volunteer 55, Son of Rysdyk's Hambletonian 10.

First dam Lady Pierson by Cassius M. Clay (Neaves') 20; second dam by Diamond; third dam a running mare said to be thoroughbred. He is fitted in an eminent degree to produce colts that will in all respects justify his patrons in their expectations.

Admiral is the sire of Huntress, record 2:27½, Sister, 2:19½, Perhelion, 2:25, Nona Y., 2:26, and others equally as promising, but have not had the advantage of track work. He will serve a limited number of approved mares at $50 the season, with usual return privilege. Season ending August 1, 1890. No liability for accidents or escapes.

KING DAVID 2576.

Bay Stallion—Foaled 1883.

Sired by Admiral 488, dam Black Flora (the dam of Huntress, 2:27½, Sister, 2:19½, Perhelion, 2:25, Nona Y., 2:25), by Black Prince.

King David is one of the best gets of Admiral. He has a good disposition, kind to drive, smooth and even-gaited, and can speed fast. Barring accidents, he will trot in the twenties this Fall. His colts are large, rangy, and well finished. Will serve a limited number of mares at $30 the season, to end July 1, 1890. Every precaution will be taken to prevent accidents and escapes, but no liability will be assumed. Pasturage $4 per month.

Sunny Side Farm is situated two miles east of Vallejo, on the Sulphur Spring road. For further particulars, address

FRANK DRAKE,

Vallejo, Cal.

The Fast Trotting Stallion

REDWOOD.

Four-Year-Old Record 2:24 1-2

Will make the season of 1890—February 1st to July 1st—at

SANTA ROSA.

REDWOOD is a dark bay colt, 15.2¾ hands high, weighs 11[illegible] lbs. Foaled in 1 86 by Anteeo, 2:16¼, sire of Alfred G., 2 19¾. Anteeo is by Electioneer. First dam Lou Milton, by Milton Medium; second dam Old Sly, a thoroughbred mare brought from the East in 1871 by W. C. Ralston, Esq.

Redwood's sire was out of Columbine by A. W. Richmond, the sire of the pacers Arrow 2:13¾, and Elwood 2:23, and the trotters Romero, 2:19¾, and Len Rose, 2:27. Redwood has shown a quarter in 33 seconds.

Terms $100

For the season. Mares not proving with foal may be returned next season free of charge, provided Redwood remains the property of the present owners. Good pasturage at reasonable rates. No responsibility assumed for escapes or accidents. Service fees payable before removal of the mare. Limited to 40 approved mares. For further particulars address

A. McFADYEN,

Santa Rosa, Cal.

For Sale.

JUANITO ALMONT

Sire of Almont Patchen, 2:15.

JUANITO ALMONT is a bright bay, 16-1 hands in height, and weighs 1,200 pounds.

PEDIGREE.

By Tilton Almont, 2:26, he by the great Almont 33; dam by Signal 3327; he by Bunday's Rob Roy.

JUANITO ALMONT, if given a chance would undoubtedly prove a great sire, and should prove a desirable acquisition to any stock farm in the State.

For further particulars address

T. B. COOPER,

Adin, Modoc County, Cal.

$15,000. OPENING $15,000.

of the

GRAND CIRCUIT.

The World's Fair goes to Chicago, but the Greatest Fair ever held in the West takes place at

Agricultural Park, Los Angeles, August 4 to 9, 1890.

Fifteen Thousand Dollars in Purses, Stakes and Premiums.

Speed Programme:

FIRST DAY—MONDAY AUGUST 4TH.

No. 1. The Los Angeles Derby.—A sweepstake for three-year-olds (foals of 1887), $50 each, half forfeit, with $500 added, the second to receive $100, and the third $50, out of the stakes; a winner of any three-year-old stake race to carry five (5) pounds, of two or more, eight (8) pounds extra; maidens allowed seven (7) pounds. One mile and a half.

No. 2. The Edwards & McKnight stakes.—A sweepstake for all ages; $50 each, half forfeit; $300 added, the second to receive $100 out of the stakes. Non-winners this year allowed seven pounds. Maidens allowed ten pounds. One mile.

No. 3. Trotting.—The Los Angeles Purse, $1,500, open to all horses eligible to the 2:30 Class, June 16th. Entrance, ten per cent, payable as follows: $50 June 16th, when entries close; $50 July 1st, and $50 July 22nd, when horses must be named. No subscription will be received unless the first payment shall accompany the same, subscribers liable only for the amount paid in, but if a subscriber fails to make any of the payments when due, he shall surrender his subscription and payments to the Association with the right of substitution. The Board reserves the right to declare the "Los Angeles Purse" off, in the event of it s not filling satisfactorily.

No. 4. Trotting.—Purse $500. 3 minute Class. District.

SECOND DAY—TUESDAY AUGUST 5.

No. 5. A sweepstake for two-year-olds owned in the Southern Counties; $25 each, $15 forfeit; $150 added; the second to receive $75 out of the stakes. The winner of any race to carry four pounds extra. One-half (½) mile.

No. 6. The Nadeau Hotel Handicap.—Purse $1,000, of which $700 to the first; $200 to the second; and $100 to the third horse. Weight announced July 22nd. Twenty-five dollars ($25) to nominate, and fifty dollars ($50) each from all starters. The winner of any race after the announcement of the weights to carry five (5) pounds extra. One and one quarter mile.

No. 7. Trotting.—Two-year-old stakes, district, $250 added. See special condition.

No. 8. Pacing.—Purse $500. 2:35 Class. District.

THIRD DAY—WEDNESDAY, AUG. 6TH.

No. 9. Selling Purse—For all ages, $350. Ten Dollars from starters to go to second horse. Fixed valuation $1000; three pounds allowed for each $100 less down to $700; then one pound for $100 down to $300; selling price to be named through the entry box at 5 P. M. the day before the race. Seven-eighths of a mile.

No. 10. Hurdle Race—A sweepstake for all ages; $25 each, half forfeit; $200 added; second horse to receive $75 out of the stakes. Five hurdles—about one and one half miles.

No. 11. Trotting—Three-year-old Stake. District $250 added. See special conditions.

No. 12. Trotting.—Purse $1000. 2:25 class.

FOURTH DAY—THURSDAY AUG. 7TH.

No. 13. The Hollenbeck Hotel Stakes—A sweepstake for two-year-olds (foals of 1888), $50 each, $20 forfeit; with $300 added, the second to receive $100, and the third $50 out of the stakes. A winner of any stake race before August 1st, to carry three pounds; and two or more stake races, five pounds extra; maidens allowed, if beaten once, five pounds; twice or more, eight pounds. Five-eighths of a mile.

No. 14. The Southern California Handicap.—Purse $1000, of which $700 to the first, $200 to the second, and $100 to the third horse. Weights announced July 22nd. $25 to nominate, and $50 more for all starters. The winner of any race at this meeting to carry five pounds extra. Three-quarters of a mile.

No. 15. Trotting—Purse $1000, 2:27 class.

No. 16. Trotting—Purse $500, 2:40 class; District.

FIFTH DAY—FRIDAY, AUGUST, 8TH.

No. 17. The Sierra Madre Stakes.—A sweepstake for all ages. $25 each, half forfeit; $200 added, second to receive $75 out of the stakes. Winner of any race this year at three-quarters (¾) of a mile or less to carry six (6) pounds, and of two or more of such races, ten (10) pounds extra. Maiden allowed ten (10) pounds. One-half (½) mile heats.

No. 18. Santa Catalina Cup.—A sweepstake for all ages. $40 each; $20 forfeit; $300 added; the second to receive $100 out of the stakes. Five pounds above scale. Non-winners in 1889 and 1890 allowed ten (10) pounds. Maidens allowed twelve (12) pounds. A winner at this meeting to carry five pounds extra. One and one-eighth (1⅛) mile.

No. 19. Trotting.—Purse, $1,000, 2:20 class.

No. 20. Trotting.—Purse, $800, 2:50. District.

SIXTH DAY—SATURDAY, AUG. 9TH

No. 21. The Citrus Handicap.—A sweepstake for three-year-olds; $40, half forfeit, or only $10 if declared by 5 P. M. the day before the race; $250 added; the second to receive $100 out of the stakes. Weights to be announced by 5 o'clock P. M. second day before the race. One and one-sixteenth (1 1-16) of a mile.

No. 22. The Junior Handicap.—A sweepstake for two-year-olds. $40 each, half forfeit, or only $15 if declared by 5 P. M. the day before the race; $300 added; the second to receive $100, and the third $50 out of the stakes. Weights to be announced by 5 o'clock P. M. the second day before the race. Three-quarters (¾) of a mile.

No. 23. Trotting.—Purse $800, 2:35 Class.

No. 24. Pacing.—Purse, $800, 2:25 class.

TROTTING STAKES—To close June 16th, 1890.

To be Trotted at the Annual Fair, to be held in Los Angeles in 1890—91.

TROTTING STAKES, 1890.

FOALS OF 1888. Mile and repeat, $250, added by the Association. Entrance, $50, payable in the following forfeits: $10 to accompany the nomination., $20 July 1st, and $20 August 11, 1890.

FOALS OF 1887. Mile heats, three in five. $250 added by the Association. $50 entrance, payable in the following forfeits; $10 to accompany the nomination, $20 July 1st, and $20 August 11, 1890.

TROTTING STAKES, 1891.

FOALS OF 1889. Mile and repeat. $250 added by the Association. $50 entrance, payable in the following forfeits: $5 to accompany nomination, $10 August 1st, 1890; $10 May 1st, 1891, and $25 on the first day of the Fair of 1891.

FOALS OF 1888. Mile heats, three in five. $250 added by the Association. Entrance, $50, payable in the following forfeits; $5 to accompany the nomination; $10 August 1st, 1890; $10 May 1st, 1891, and $35 on the first day of the Fair of 1891.

CONDITIONS.

All nominations to be made on or before June 16th. American Association rules to govern. Nominators liable only for the amount paid in, which becomes forfeit if subsequent payments are not made. All forfeits and entrance fees will be contributed to the stake, the whole divided where there are three or more starters as follows: sixty per cent, to the first, thirty per cent, to the second and ten per cent, to the third. If no more than two horses start, only first and second money shall be awarded, and in case of a walk over, only the first money shall be awarded. A horse distancing the field shall only be entitled to so much of the money as the starters in the race could have won. A nominator in making an entry in any of the above stakes shall give the name of owner, name of breeder and where foaled, the age, color, sex, dam and sire if known. Colts owned in the counties of San Luis Obispo, Fresno, Tulare, Kern, Santa Barbara, Ventura, Los Angeles, San Bernardino, Orange and San Diego shall be eligible to entry.

REMARKS AND CONDITIONS.

All trotting and pacing races to be to harness, mile heats, best three in five, except otherwise specified. Entrance 10 per cent on amount of purse. Trotting and pacing divided as follows: 50 per cent. to first horse; 25 per cent. to second; 15 per cent. to third, and 10 per cent. to fourth. Entries not declared out by 5 P. M. of the day before the race must start. In all trotting and pacing races, five to enter and three to start. The Board reserves the right to hold a less number than five to fill. Horses owned in Fresno, Tulare, Kern, San Luis Obispo, Santa Barbara, Ventura, Los Angeles, San Bernardino, Orange and San Diego Counties, are eligible for entry in district races. A horse distancing the field is entitled to first and fourth money. The Directors reserve the right to change the hour and day of any race, if deemed necessary. Races shall commence each day at 1 o'clock. American Association rules to govern, unless otherwise specified. Hay and straw free.

Running—The Pacific Coast Blood Horse rules to govern running races. Colonial-bred horses, foaled on Colonial time, allowed as follows: Two and three-year-olds, eight pounds; four-year-olds, five pounds, and five-year-olds, three pounds. In all stakes, starters must be named to the Secretary or through the entry box at the track, on or before 5 P. M. of the day before the race. In all stakes, the right to forfeit ceases at 10 o'clock of the day on which the race is run. Racing colors to be named with the entry. Entries close with the Secretary July 1st.

Remember, entries for the 2:30 Trot and District Trotting Stakes close June 16th, and for everything else July 1st.

BEN BENJAMIN, Secretary.

L. LICHTENBERGER, President.

Southern Pacific Co.

(PACIFIC SYSTEM.)

Trains leave and are due to arrive at San Francisco.

LEAVE (FOR)	FROM JUNE 1, 1890.	ARRIVE (FROM)
7.30 A M	Haywards, Niles and San Jose ...	*12.45 P M
7.30 A M	Sacramento and Redding, via Davis	7.15 P M
7.30 A M	Sacramento, Auburn, Colfax	4.45 P M
9.00 A M	Martinez, Vallejo, Calistoga and Santa Rosa	6.15 P M
8.30 A M	Los Angeles Express, Fresno, Bakersfield, Mojave and East and Los Angeles	11.15 A M
8.30 A M	Niles, San Jose, Stockton, Ione, Sacramento, Marysville, Oroville and Red Bluff	4.45 P M
10.30 A M	Haywards and Niles	2.45 P M
12.00 M	Haywards, Niles and Livermore	8.45 P M
*1.00 P M	Sacramento River Steamers	**6.00 A M
3.00 P M	Haywards, Niles and San Jose	9.45 A M
3.30 P M	2d Class for Ogden and East	10.45 P M
4.00 P M	Stockton and Milton; Vallejo, Calistoga and Santa Rosa	9.45 A M
* 4.30 P M	Niles and Livermore	* 8.45 A M
* 4.30 P M	Niles and San Jose	‡ 6.15 P M
5.00 P M	Shasta Route Express, Sacramento, Marysville, Redding, Portland, Puget Sound, East and Knight's Landing via Davis	10.45 A M
6.00 P M	Haywards and Niles	7.45 A M
6.00 P M	Sunset Route, Atlantic Express Santa Barbara, Los Angeles, Deming, El Paso, New Orleans and East	8.45 P M
8.00 P M	Central Atlantic Express, Ogden and East	9.45 A M

SANTA CRUZ DIVISION.

LEAVE		ARRIVE
‡ 7.45 A M	Excursion train to Santa Cruz	‡ 8.05 P M
8.15 A M	Newark, Centerville, San Jose, Felton, Boulder Creek and Santa Cruz	6.20 P M
* 2.45 P M	Centerville, San Jose, Almaden, Felton, Boulder Creek and Santa Cruz	*11.20 A M
4.45 P M	Centerville, San Jose, and Los Gatos, and Saturday and Sunday to Santa Cruz	9. 0 A M

Coast Division (Third and Townsend Sts.)

LEAVE		ARRIVE
7.25 A M	San Jose, Almaden and Way Stations	2.30 P M
‡ 7.30 A M	Monterey and Santa Cruz—Sunday Excursion	‡ 8.25 P M
8.30 A M	San Jose, Gilroy, Tres Pinos; Pajaro, Santa Cruz; Monterey; Pacific Grove, Salinas, San Miguel, Paso Robles, Santa Margarita (San Luis Obispo) and principal Way Stations	6.12 P M
10.30 A M	San Jose and Way Stations	7.31 P M
11.05 A M	Emanuel Cemetery and Baden	12.32 P M
12.01 P M	Cemetery, Menlo Park and Way Stations	5.18 P M
* 2.30 P M	Del Monte Limited, Menlo Park, San Jose, Gilroy, Pajaro, Castroville, Monterey and Pacific Grove	*11.15 A M
* 3.30 P M	San Jose, Tres Pinos, Santa Cruz, Salinas, Monterey Pacific Grove and principal Way Stations	*10.00 A M
* 4.20 P M	Menlo Park and Way Stations	* 7.26 A M
5.20 P M	San Jose and Way Stations	9.03 A M
6.30 P M	Menlo Park and Way Stations	6.35 A M
†11.45 P M	San Jose and principal Way Stations	†4.28 P M

A M for Morning. P M for Afternoon.
*Sundays excepted. †Saturdays only. ‡Sundays only.
**Mondays excepted. §Saturdays excepted.

OCEANIC STEAMSHIP CO.

Carrying United States, Hawaiian and Colonial Mails.

WILL LEAVE THE COMPANY'S WHARF, foot of Mission Street, No. 1,

For Honolulu, Auckland and Sydney,

WITHOUT CHANGE,

The Splendid New 3,000-ton Iron Steamer, ALAMEDA ... Saturday, JUNE 28th, 1890, at 12 M., Or immediately on arrival of the English mails.

For Honolulu,

SS. AUSTRALIA (3,000 tons), June 20, 1890, at 12 M

☞ For freight or passage, apply at office, 327 Market Street. JOHN D. SPRECKELS & BROS. General Agents.

By-Laws

—AND—

Rules and Regulations

—OF THE—

NATIONAL

Trotting Association

REVISED FOR 1890,

ALSO THE

AMERICAN

Trotting Association,

AND THE

PACIFIC COAST BLOOD-HORSE ASSOCIATION.

With Betting Rules.

For Sale at the Office of the

Breeder and Sportsman,

313 Bush St., S. F., Cal.

Price, 25c. each.

By Mail, Postage Paid, 30c. each.

San Francisco and North Pacific Railway.

THE DONAHUE BROAD-GAUGE ROUTE.

COMMENCING SUNDAY, APRIL 27, 1889, AND until further notice, boats and trains will leave from and arrive at the San Francisco Passenger Depot, Market-street Wharf, as follows:

FROM SAN FRANCISCO FOR POINT TIBURON AND SAN RAFAEL.
Week Days—7.40, 9.20, 11.20, A. M.; 1.30, 3.30, 5.00, 6.15 P. M.
Sundays—8.00, 9.30, 11.00 A. M.; 1.30, 3.30, 5.00, 6.15 P. M.

FROM SAN RAFAEL FOR SAN FRANCISCO.
Week Days—6.50, 7.55, 9.30, 11.40 A. M.; 1.40, 3.40, 5.05, 6.25 P. M.
Sundays—8.10, 9.40, 11.10 A. M.; 1.40, 3.40, 5.00, 6.25 P. M.

FROM POINT TIBURON FOR SAN FRANCISCO.
Week Days—7.15, 8.20, 9.55 A. M.; 12.05, 2.05, 4.05, 5.30, 6.50 P. M.
Sundays—8.35, 10.05, 11.35 A. M.; 2.05, 4.05, 5.30, 6.50 P. M.

Leave San Francisco. Week Days.	Leave San Francisco. Sun Days.	Destination	Arrive San Francisco. Sun Days.	Arrive San Francisco. Week Days.
7.40 A M 9.20 A M 3.30 P M §5.00 P M	8.00 A M 5.00 P M	Petaluma and Santa Rosa	10.40 A M 7.25 P M	8.50 A M 10.30 A M 4.40 P M 7.25 P M
7.40 A M 3.30 P M	8.00 A M	Fulton, Windsor, Healdsburg, Litton Spri'gs, Cloverdale, and way stations.	7.25 P M	10.30 A M 7.25 P M
7.40 A M	8.00 A M	Hopland and Ukiah.	7.25 P M	7.25 P M
7.40 A M 6.30 P M	8.00 A M	Guerneville	7.25 P M	7.25 P M 10.30 A M
7.40 A M 5.00 P M	8.00 A M 5.00 P M	Sonoma and Glen Ellen	10.40 A M 6.05 P M	8.50 A M 6.05 P M
7.40 A M 3.30 P M	8.00 A M 5.00 P M	Sebastopol	10.40 A M 7.25 P M	10.30 A M 7.25 P M

Stage connects at Santa Rosa for White Sulphur Springs, and Mark West Springs; at Geyserville for Skaggs Springs, and at Cloverdale for the Geysers; at Hopland for Highland Springs, Kelseyville, Soda Bay, Lakeport and Bartlett Springs, and at Ukiah for Vichy Springs, Saratoga Springs, Blue Lakes, Willits, Cahto, Calpella, Potter Valley, Sherwood Valley and Mendocino City.

EXCURSION TICKETS from Saturdays to Mondays, to Petaluma, $1.50; to Santa Rosa, $2.25; to Healdsburg, $3.40; to Litton Springs, $3.60; to Cloverdale, $4.50; to Hopland, $5.70; to Ukiah, $6.75; to Guerneville, $3.75; to Sonoma, $1.50; to Glen Ellen, $1.80.

EXCURSION TICKETS, good for Sundays only, to Petaluma, $1; to Santa Rosa, $1.50; to Healdsburg, $2.25; to Litton Springs, $2.40; to Cloverdale, $3; to Guerneville, $2.50, to Sonoma, $1; to Glen Ellen, $1.20.

H. C. WHITING, General Manager.

PETER J. McGLYNN, Gen. Pass. & Tkt. Agt.

Ticket Offices at Ferry, 222 Montgomery Street and 2 New Montgomery Street.

The Park Training Stable.

CHAS. DAVID, PROPRIETOR.

Corner Grove and Baker Streets, near Entrance to Golden Gate Park.

EVERY FACILITY FOR TRAINING COLTS and taking care of Gentlemen's Roadsters.

Finely appointed stable with every convenience and sixteen roomy box stalls.

The best care given all horses by experienced help, under the personal superintendence of the proprietor.

Convenient to the Park Speed Drive, and Accessible to Six Lines of Cable Cars.

THE TRAINING OF COLTS AND ROADSTERS A SPECIALTY.

TROTTERS AND ROADSTERS FOR SALE.
HORSES SOLD ON COMMISSION

The proprietor trained and brought out the following well known horses: "Sister, Huntress," "Perihelion," "Nona Y," and others.

HEALD'S

Business College, 24 Post St.

—San Francisco.—

The most popular school on the Coast

P. HEALD, President. C. S. HALEY, Sec'y.

☞ Send for Circulars.

KILLIP & CO.,

LIVE STOCK AND GENERAL AUCTIONEERS,

22 Montgomery Street, San Francisco

SPECIAL ATTENTION PAID TO SALES OF

High-Bred Horses and Cattle.

At auction and private sale.

Will Sell in All Cities and Counties of the State.

REFERENCES.

HON. C. GREEN, Sacramento. — HON. J. D. CARR, Salinas.
J. P. SARGENT, ESQ., Sargents. — HON. JOHN BOGGS, Colusa.
HON. L. J. ROSE, Los Angeles. — HON. A. WALRATH, Nevada.
J. B. HAGGIN, ESQ., San Francisco.

Represented at Sacramento by Edwin F. Smith, Secretary State Agricultural Society.

At San Jose by Messrs. Montgomery & Rea, Real Estate Agents.

Being the oldest established firm in the live-stock business on this Coast, and having conducted the important auction sales in this line for the past fifteen years, amounting to one half a million of dollars, we feel justified in claiming unequaled facilities for disposing of live stock of every description, either at auction or private sale. Our list of correspondents embraces every breeder and dealer of prominence upon the Pacific Coast, thus enabling us to give full publicity to animals placed with us for sale. Private purchases and sales of live stock of all descriptions will be made on commission, and stock shipped with the utmost care. Purchases and sales made of land of every description. We are authorized to refer to the gentlemen whose names are appended.

KILLIP & CO., 22 Montgomery Street.

FOR HORSES, DOGS AND CATTLE.

Simmons Liver Regulator, a strictly vegetable Compound and general Condition Powder, is

A SAFE AND SURE REMEDY FOR

COLIC,
GRUBS,
LUNG FEVER,
HIDE-BOUND.

No Stable or Kennel should be without it: it gives new life to a lazy or drooping horse, and is a positive preventive and cure for **Distemper** or **Mange** in Dogs.

J. H. ZEILIN & CO., Proprietors, Philadelphia, Pa.

HORSE OWNERS!

TRY GOMBAULT'S

CAUSTIC BALSAM.

A Safe, Speedy and Positive Cure for Curb, Splint, Sweeny, Capped Hock, Strained Tendons, Founder, Wind Puffs, all Skin Diseases or Parasites, Thrush, Diphtheria, Pinkeye, all Lameness from Spavin, Ringbone or other Bony Tumors. Removes all Bunches or Blemishes from Horses and Cattle.

Supersedes all Cautery or Firing.

Impossible to Produce any Scar or Blemish.

Every bottle sold is warranted to give satisfaction. Price $1.50 per bottle. Sold by druggists, or sent by express, charges paid, with full directions for its use. Send for descriptive circulars. Address LAWRENCE, WILLIAMS & CO., Cleveland, O.

BROU'S INJECTION

A PERMANENT CURE in from 3 to 6 days, of the most obstinate cases; guaranteed not to produce Stricture; no sickening doses; and no inconvenience or loss of time. Recommended by physicians and sold by all druggists. J. Ferré, (successor to Brou), Pharmacien, Paris.

JUST OUT, 2d EDITION.

MIXOLOGIST FOR BARKEEPERS

1,000 Receipts. PRICE, $1 00.

All Booksellers, and 3 California St., S. F.

R. LIDDLE & SON

538 Washington St., S. F.,

Wholesale and Retail Dealers in

Guns, Rifles and Pistols.

A Full Line of FISHING TACKLE and SPORTSMAN'S GOODS.

Orders by mail receive prompt attention.

6 DONTS

DON'T own a racehorse.
DON'T be a breeder.
DON'T be a trainer.
DON'T be a jockey.
DON'T bet on the races.
DON'T go to a race track.

WITHOUT

HAVING IN YOUR POCKET ONE OF

Goodwin's

ANNUAL

OFFICIAL TURF GUIDES.

Price, in cloth $2.00
Price, in half morocco 3.00
Price, in half calf 4.00
If sent by mail .... 10 cents extra

SUBSCRIBE TO IT FOR 1890.

It is published semi-monthly during the racing season, and is but **$10 per year.** Address

GOODWIN BROS.,
241 Broadway, New York City.

SUBSCRIBE FOR THE

Breeder and Sportsman.

VETERINARY.

Dr. Wm. H. Jones, M.R.C.V.S.

Veterinary Surgeon,

(OLYMPIC CLUB STABLES)

503 Sutter Street, San Francisco.

Telephone, No. 1404.

Consultations by letter, and cases of URGENT NECESSITY in the interior will receive prompt attention.

Dr. A. E. BUZARD,

VETERINARY SURGEON,

Member of the Royal College of Veterinary Surgeons, London, England. Graduated April 22d, 1870.

All Operations on the Horse Performed Skillfully.

Special attention given to the Diseases of Dogs. Calls to the country promptly attended to. Advice and prescriptions by mail $2. Office and Residence, No. 11 Seventh street, S. F. (opp. Odd Fellows Hall. Telephone No. 3 69.

W. H. WOODRUFF.

Veterinary Dentist,

AT FASHION STABLES,

221 Ellis Street, San Francisco

Improved Instruments, Humane Methods, First-Class Work.

H. E. CARPENTER,

Veterinary Surgeon,

Graduate of Ontario Veterinary College; Toronto Canada.

RESIDENCE AND VETERINARY INFIRMARY
331 Golden Gate Ave., San Francisco.

Telephone 2069.

☞ OPEN DAY AND NIGHT. ☜

No risk in throwing Horses. Veterinary Operating Table on the premises.

DR. C. MASOERO,

Veterinary Surgeon,

Successor to **DR. A. DeTAVEL,**

GRADUATE OF ROYAL VETERINARY COLLEGE, TURIN.

OFFICE AND INFIRMARY

No. 811 HOWARD STREET,

Between Fourth and Fifth. SAN FRANCISCO

Telephone, No. 457.

R. WATKINS,

Veterinary Dentist,

Office at C. S. Crittendens' Golden Gate Livery and Riding Academy, 24 to 28 Golden Gate Avenue.

Refers to Palo Alto Stock Farm; Wm. Corbett, San Mateo Stock Farm; B. Q. Holly, Vallejo, and others. Examination Free.

E. J. O'ROUKE.

I have the honor to announce to my old patrons and the general public that I may be found at my old stand, where, as heretofore, the

Shoeing of Horses,

whether for the Track, Drive, or for general work, will receive my personal attention.

Telephone 2011.

E. J. O'ROUKE,
209 Ellis Street

ST. JULIEN

Horse Shoeing SHOP,

126 Geary Street, S. F.

MARTIN O'DEA, - - PROPRIETOR.

California Horse Shoe Co's

I have used in my business the Steel and Iron Shoes made by the above Company, and take great pleasure in saying they are the best I have ever used in twenty-two years' practice. I have never seen anything like the STEEL SHOE made by this Company. I can fully recommend them to every practical Horseshoer in the country.

Yours Respectfully,
No. 8 Everett street. JOHN GRACE.

Old Hermitage Whiskies

"STEINER'S,"

No. 311 BUSH STREET,

San Francisco.

Under Breeder and Sportsman Office.

Everything for Trotter or Runner,

At J. A. McKERRON'S,

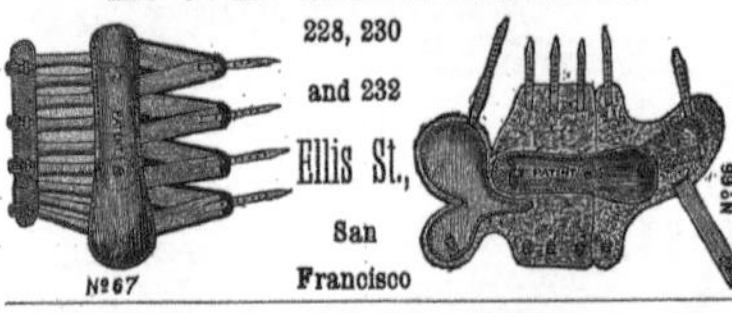

228, 230 and 232 Ellis St., San Francisco

The Brunswick Balke Collender Co.

MANUFACTURERS OF

Standard Billiard and Pool Tables, Saloon and Bank Fixtures,
653--655 Market Street, San Francisco, Cal.

Abell & Priest PHOTOGRAPHERS,
723 Market Street, S. F.
Our View is unsurpassed by any Studio in the United States.

AN UNQUALIFIED ENDORSEMENT.

Peruvian Bitters are made of the purest ingredients and compounded as carefully as any prescription.

Peruvian Bark, one of its principal ingredients, was introduced into Spain by the Countess, wife of Count CINCHON, Spanish Viceroy to Peru in 1630, who was cured of a fever by its use, since which time, no better remedy for Malaria and for Restoring the Natural Tone of the Stomach has been discovered.

On the Atlantic Coast they are used in the principal Hotels, Clubs and Restaurants, and sold by all Grocers and Druggists. We have sold them for the past three years WITHOUT ANY ADVERTISING and sales have constantly increased UPON MERIT ALONE, and we unqualifiedly recommend them to our friends and customers.

ACKER, MERRALL & CONDIT.

New York, Feb. 1st, 1890.

WILMERDING & CO., Agents for Pacific Coast,
216 FRONT ST., SAN FRANCISCO, CAL.

The PARKER Hammerless Shot Gun.

At the Annual Tournament of 1889, held at Cannes, France, the grand prize, consisting of 2000 Francs and a Valuable Cup. was won by The Parker Hammerless.

The first Parker Hammerless Gun made won the championship of America at Decatur Illinois.

SEND FOR ILLUSTRATED CIRCULAR.

PARKER BROS., Makers,

New York Salesroom, 97 Chambers St. Meriden Conn.

The Pacific Coast
Live Stock Owners
MUTUAL PROTECTIVE ASS'N.,
MONTEREY, Monterey Co., Cal.

TRUSTEES:

HON. B. V. SARGENT, President,
G. W. GALLANAR, Secretary,
JAMES B. PALMER, Business Manager,
EDW. INGRAM, Vice-President.
FRED. D. HOWARD, Actuary,
R. H. WILLEY, Attorney.

GENERAL BUSINESS OFFICE, Room 73, Flood Building. corner Market and Fourth Streets, San Francisco, Cal.

VOLNEY HOWARD, General Manager.

Attention.

-:- Campers and Sportsmen -:-

The "GOLCHER" Hunting Boots and Shoes are the only ones in the market that are PRACTICAL, as they combine Lightness, Comfort and Durability. The weight of the boots per pair is 3 lbs.; the shoes, per pair, 2¼ lbs. The uppers are made of alum-tanned leather, and the leg of soft oil-tanned leather. They are provided with good stiff counters and heavy shanks. The seams are all on the outside, which insures comfort. They have a bellows tongue, and lace up the front from instep to top of boot.

Price of Boots, per pair,.......................$5 00
" Shoes, " $3 50

Clabrough, Golcher & Co.,
Guns, Pistols, Fishing Tackle,
Sporting & Athletic Goods,
630 and 632 Montgomery Street, S. F.

MOORE, HUNT & CO.,
404 Front Street, - - - San Francisco.
SOLE AGENTS FOR
Jesse Moore & Co.'s Whiskies.

THOS. KIRKPATRICK, SAN FRANCISCO. G. H. MOORE, H. B. HUNT, SAN FRANCISCO.
Of Jesse Moore & Co., Louisville, Ky.

Studebaker Bros. Manufact'g Co.

Sole Agents for
FRAZIER
(OR CHICAGO)
Carts
AND
Sulkies,
201--203 Market Street,
SAN FRANCISCO, CAL

keeps horses healthy, promotes digestion, fattens horses, loosens the hide, assists the appetite, prevents leg swelling, strengthens the kidneys, regulates the bowels and destroys worms. $7.50 per 100 lbs. Ask your dealer for it or send to

MANHATTAN FOOD CO., 206 Clay St., S. F.

TWENTY-FOUR PAGES.

BREEDER AND SPORTSMAN

Vol. XVI. No. 26.
No. 313 BUSH STREET.

SAN FRANCISCO, SATURDAY, JUNE 21, 1890.

SUBSCRIPTION FIVE DOLLARS A YEAR.

Sam Purdy, 2:20 1-2.

Some time ago we sent a letter to Mr. Foxhall A. Daingerfield, the present owner of Sam Purdy, 2:20½, asking for information relative to the old stallion, as there are so many horses in this country to day that have the blood of Sam Purdy running through their veins. The son of Geo. M. Patchen Jr. has been for many years in the East, and it was not until the year-book for 1889 was published, that we found any of his get enumerated in the 2:30 list; however when that useful publication arrived on the Pacific Coast, it was found that Charlie C., by Sam Purdy, dam Bessie O'Malley by O'Malley, had secured a record of 2:24½ at Baltimore on October 25th, 1889. During the present year, Charlie C. has again started and materially reduced his record, and it was to find out what other sons and daughters, if any, of the old horse could show speed at the trot or pace in addition to the one mentioned, that occasioned the sending of the letter. In answer to the request, the present owner of Sam Purdy has sent us a communication which will be read with interest by all who are interested in the trotting horse:

WREN'S NEST, HARRISONBURG, Virg., June 9, '90.

EDITOR BREEDER AND SPORTSMAN:—Your letter of March 27, 1890, was duly received, but ill health and press of business has so occupied my time as to render more than a bare acknowledgment impossible, and that little has from time to time been postponed in the hope that I should have time for more.

After Sam Purdy left California, he was for some years—or until 1881—the road-horse of Mr. James R. Keene of New York. In the spring of 1881, Mr. Keene (my brother-in-law) sent him to me at this place. Then trotting horses were practically unknown in this valley; the population, largely German farmers, regarding three or four miles per hour fast enough for safety to the bones of the old or the souls of the young, had bred their mares on not the best blood-lines for producing trotters, nevertheless, the size and good looks of Sam Purdy so attracted even these quiet and slow-going farmers, that from the first he had in numbers a liberal patronage. A few of our towns people had saddle or driving mares possessing some running blood, and many of these also were bred to Sam Purdy.

The first foal dropped to him east of the Rockies was a chestnut filly from a mare by Doswell, a son of Planet; she unfortunately got an ankle injured, by breaking through a plank in her stable, and was injured for speed, but even now, having been used as a brood mare, would, I believe, if trained, endanger the 100-mile record.

The second, a gelding (dam a little grey mare used in livery in this town), is now the good horse Charley C., record 2:21¼ in a fourth heat when not in good condition. This is one of the gamest horses now living.

The third, a bay filly (out of a farm mare owned by a German farmer near this town), was purchased on her beauty and natural speed by a gentleman in Missouri, and was sent by him to Mr. J. V. Stryker of Jerseyville, Ill., to be bred to Monon, son of Nutwood. Mr. Stryker regarding her promising for speed, suggested to her owner that she be developed to some extent to give additional value to her foals. Under Mr. Stryker's management, she was trotted trial heats on the St. Louis (Mo.) track in 2:30 and 2:31 as a four-year-old, and she was awarded the first prize at the St. Louis fair as the best roadster, four years or over.

An own brother of the same mare, in a field of eight (all the others standard bred), trotted one-half mile heats, the contest being so close between him and a son of King Rene, as to divide prize and stakes equally between them.

Every foal by Sam Purdy is a natural trotter, regardless of the blood or habit of action of the dam. Many of them pace and show speed at that gait, but they are distinctly double (not mixed) gaited, and the pacing tendency has not, so far as I am informed, in any case interfered with their training for road or track. I know a few that I believe have more pacing than trotting, natural speed.

The owners of these colts, being generally farmers, do not train—or even allow them to exhibit their natural speed—and the fact that their dams are so generally as "common as the town pump" (until some of them had been accidentally allowed to show that they had not only speed but ability to stay an indefinite number of heats), had prevented their being much looked after by persons seeking colts for track purposes. Now, however, they are eagerly sought, and wholly regardless of the want of breeding of their dams, are bought at prices which open the eyes of our farmers to the fact that a trotting horse is not an invention of the Devil, and incline many to the belief that they could give "the aforementioned" more trouble to catch them if behind a fast roadster than a plug.

The result is that the old horse is over-run with mares, such as they are, and gets from them a class of horses with not the smallest impress in quality of their plebian dams. I believe that any candid observer will admit that in purity of action, fine size, style and endurance, the get of Sam Purdy, from all kinds of mares, are as uniform as those of almost any other stallion from mares his equal in breeding.

There are very few recognized tracks in this State, so that very many winners at fairs sired by Sam Purdy have no records. I could name dozens that have won from one to five or six races at fairs and on local tracks in matches, etc., which have no records, but have shown most creditable speed and race-horse qualities.

Since his get from common mares have performed in public, his harem has much improved in quality. Until the day before yesterday none of Sam Purdy's get that was even out of a "mare by a standard horse" had ever faced a starter. On the one-half mile track at Richmond, Va., June 7th, Three Tips, three years old, by Sam Purdy, trotted a match race against a three-year-old Red Wilkes filly, owned by Jo Lasitter of Richmond, Va., on a one-half mile track, defeating her in straight heats in 2:44, 2:42, 2:43¼. The colt Three Tips, the property of Preston Belvin, Esq., of Richmond, Va., is out of Virginia Girl by Hetzel's Hambletonian, and was bred by myself.

The owner of Sam Purdy has bought mares one at a time, until now the old horse has some excellent matrons in his harem, and in the past two or three years, as many as eight States have been represented by the public mares bred to him, so if the "days" of the old horse are "as long in the land" as those of his sire, he may yet see many of his progeny emulating his deeds on the track when in his golden prime.

A colt in my town, which has shown miles in 2:28, has no record, though he has been twice matched for $500 against horses having records better than 2:30, he coming out harnessed for each match and his competitor paying forfeit. A colt (out of a mare not equal to five miles per hour in any gait) has started in two stakes at local fairs, and in three matches, and has not lost a race or a heat.

At Alderson (W. Va.), Lynchburg, Stanton, Lexington, Winchester, Berryville, and many other fairs in Virginia, and at Frederick City and other Maryland tracks, Sam Purdy's colts and fillies have won good races. Many have actual records on regulation tracks in their time for two, three and four-year-olds. Gold Elsie, 2:30½, is just outside "the list." Strontia (a colt that once had his fore legs nearly cut off in trying to get over a stallion fence) has a record of 2:35¾, and last fall trotted in 2:29; Geo. Purdy, record 2:34¼; Frances Purdy, four years old, 2:47½; Stockinette, four years old, 2:46¾, etc., and none of them out of mares with any trotting blood.

Sam Purdy seems to get perfectly level-headed and well-gaited trotters from mares nearly or quite thoroughbred.

I believe I have seen most of the great trotting stallions east of the Rocky Mountains, and have some knowledge of the get of most of the old stallions, and I have never seen one who impressed his gait and individuality upon his offspring to a greater degree than Sam Purdy. He is hale and vigorous, and while dignified in his box, he plays like a five-year-old in his paddock, and frequently has a circus all to himself when his groom goes to catch him and put him in his box. He touches the road as lightly, and enjoys his morning work as fully and with all the gusto of a youngster; his constitutional vigor is wonderful.

In appearance the get of Sam Purdy are exceedingly handsome, showing fine size, shape, style and colors. I enclose a letter from an Englishman who resides at No. 3 Rumford Street, Liverpool, relative to his impressions of a mare (by Sam Purdy, out of a mare by Mambrino Pilot) which I sold him a year ago, and which he had bred to Lord Russell. He had not seen the mare until recently at Woodburn, where she was in good company. You will note his impressions of her.

This same gentleman bought two trotting broodmares in this country a few years ago; he returned with John Splan, and has brought back a filly by Sam Purdy, foaled in England, which he will leave in America to be educated. The other mare he bred to Purdy remains in America.

Two of Sam Purdy's daughters were booked to the ill fated Bell Boy, one by Mr. Wm. Ellison of Richmond, and the other by the English gentleman above referred to.

Nutwood, Lord Russell, Sultan, Nutguard, and other great stallions, are being patronized by owners of good fillies by Sam Purdy, their fine appearance and gait causing their owners to deem them worthy of such mating. In this way the best bred of Sam Purdy's daughters are denied training.

Yours truly, FOXHALL A. DAINGERFIELD.

In addition to the above very interesting letter, we have also received word from Jas. Cox, Esq., of No. 3 Rumford street, Liverpool, England, expressing his high admiration of the Sam Purdy mare which he owns; and he also states that he thought so highly of Nellie Bowyer and her exquisite foal which she now has at her side by Lord Russel that he has bred her back. He also states that when at Woodburn inspecting his mare and filly, that of all the royally bred matrons to be found at Mr. Alexander's Stock Farm, there was not one that excelled the Purdy mare in appearance. He says "she was in high company, and she stood like a queen among the Woodburn mares; I only wish I had a half dozen like her."

Another communication, from Geo. D. McNeill of Moorefield, West Virginia, states that he has a colt called Big Sam by Sam Purdy, which he sent to Baltimore, and in an easy workout showed a mile in 2:39 early in the present season, but unfortunately the horse was ruptured, and Mr. McNeill says he is very much afraid that he will never be able to trot again, although he had every confidence that 2:25 would have been an easy mark for his horse.

On June 7th of the present year a match race for $500 a side for the three year-old trotting championship of Virginia took place at Richmond, in that State, on a half mile track; however, the following communication speaks for itself: "The race for the trotting championship at Richmond, Va., to-day, between Three Tips by Sam Purdy, and Manesh by Red Wilkes, was a complete upset for the betting fraternity, as the filly was a strong favorite at two to one. However, the race turned out a very one-sided affair, for after the first quarter had been trotted it was evident that it was no contest at all, as the filly could never get her nose in from three to five lengths of the colt whose owner ran down the track and motioned to his driver to slow up, the colt jogged under the wire at a five minute gait, reducing the three year old record of the State by fully ten seconds on a half-mile track, which by the way, was 198 feet over length. I may state here that the track was prepared for Buffalo Bill's Wild West Show, and hence the oddity of its length; it would also be as well to notify you that the former three-year-old record of the State was made on a mile track and was in much better condition than the one over which we trotted to-day."

Yours, WM. ELLISON.

Mr. Dangerfield has also tried two experiments, by breeding two daughters of Sam Purdy to their own sire. It was a rather peculiar idea, and has too much the character of incest to be tried by other breeders, yet still the experiment was warrantable, owing to the scarcity of first-class mares. In a supplemental note Captain Dangerfield says: I have in the produce a yearling and a suckling whose gait and speed, age for age, I have never seen equaled, and both are grand, vigorous specimens of the trotter. A look at the weanling in my large pasture field where the foal was standing by the side of her dam makes me almost regret not having bred the mare back again to Sam Purdy, as the suckling filly is such a rare good one. We sincerely trust that in the future Sam Purdy may make a good name for himself in his new home, for most assuredly he has stamped himself while here in California as being one of the greatest trotters that ever appeared on a California track.

At the Denver Overland Park Spring meeting Carlile & Shields won $1,805; Kelly & Samuels, $1,320; Ed Gaylord, $1,000; Charles Feeney, $835; O'Brien Bros., $700; Denver Racing Association, $550; C. L. Richardson, $400; Thomas Hazlitt, $350; Pierson & Welsh, $300; L. Ogilvy, $250; Orange Grove Stable, $250; Golden Gate Stable, $250; Al Shores, $200; Clifton Bell, $200; Charles Johnson, $150; John Werlen, $150; John Winfield, $100; Palmer & Keys, $65; Charles Dutts, $50; John A. Davis, $50; H. Coombs, $50. The Palo Alto bred colt Pliny by Flood out of Precious, owned by Kelly & Samuels, has the largest winnings to his credit, $1,320.

The Bay District Track.

When there are no fogs and but little wind, the Bay District track is always a place of interest for those who take a delight in seeing horses exercised. On last Tuesday morning a visit was paid to the track, word having been received that quite a number of horses would receive work-outs. The rain of the previous night interfered considerably with the programme, as it was not until high noon that a fast mile could be given to any of the trotters at present located there. In addition to the obstacles presented in the way of a slippery track, a very high wind prevented fast time being made, but quite a number of the horses were given moderate exercise, and there is no reason to doubt that there are many surprises in store for track frequenters during the present year.

Jas. A Dustin has a large number under education, several of which show promise of speed; still, there are several in the string that Jimmy has had but a very short time, and consequently no true line could be had on what they are likely to do.

Mr. Clay, of San Francisco, at the late sale of Mr. M. J. Hill, purchased a sorrel stallion named Ulster Wilkes, by Guy Wilkes, 2:15½, dam by Ulster Chief, son of Rysdyk's Hambletonian. This sprightly young gentleman has been turned over to Mr. Dustin, and during the day was given two fairly good quarters; he shows that the noted sire of Guy Wilkes can reproduce speed in any of his get, and it is extremely probable that before the present season ends, that Ulster Wilkes will have a good low mark to the credit of himself and sire.

Rabe is well known to many of the California race-goers; he was last year in the stable of Dan Dennison, who secured for him a record of 2:24. Rabe is owned by Mr. Nixon of Winnemucca, Nevada, who hopes to materially lower his mark this year.

Another in the Dustin string is Mambrino Boy, a handsome bay gelding who takes to his work kindly, and shows every indication of lowering his present record of 2:30.

Gracie S., with a record of 2:22, is liable to have a full sister with a record equally low, as Lillie S. is moving along in splendid shape, and as one of our old drivers used to say, is "threatened with speed."

The old horseman, N. J. Killip, has a pacing team in Dustin's care, one of which was given a mile in 2:29½, while the other negotiated the distance in 2:34.

The Valensin Stock Farm is represented in the same stable by a fine large black gelding whose pedigree was given as being by Black Bird 402, dam by Buccaneer 2656; he was given a mile in 2:28½, and he took to the work so readily, that it is easy to believe that if started in a race he would readily compass the distance in close to 2:20.

California Nutwood, the stallion owned by Martin Carter of Irvington, is represented in the same stable by one of his get, a pacer, who was worked out a nice easy mile in 2:35.

Judge Green, of Oakland, is the fortunate possessor of a Sidney colt who is as yet very rank, still he was able to do a mile in the exceedingly good time, for a green horse, of 2:40½. This gelding has had only a month's handling, but the indications are very strong that he will prove a fast and reliable trotter.

A bay gelding by Nephew was also seen, but as he had only just arrived, no fast time was shown; he is a handsome animal, and will beyond doubt prove fast.

Capt. Frank Drake, of Vallejo, has sent down three to receive their preparatory work at the hands of Mr. Dustin, the first being a bay mare by Director, dam Black Flora (dam of Sister, 2:19½, Nona Y., 2.25, Perihelion, 2:25, and Huntress, 2:28); barring accident, this Director filly should this year add another to Black Flora's already long list of 2:30 performers. She was given a mile in 2:43, and was not pushed in the least. The second one is a full sister to the four named above, being by Admiral out of Black Flora. The third is a two-year-old chestnut stallion by Woodnut, dam by Admiral, who will undoubtedly prove a credit to sire and dam before long.

Mr. Dustin has also one of his own, a bay stallion by Dexter Prince, dam Bessie by General McClellan 144; 2d dam by Belmont; 3d dam by Shiloh. Although only a youngster, he is a good pure-gaited trotter, and his owner has a great deal of confidence in his ultimate speed.

The La Siesta Ranch has a half score of superbly-bred trotting stock at the track, none of which as yet have received any very hard work. Daylight, by Eros, made a name and mark for himself last year at San Jose, and as he is in the pink of condition, should be able to add another to his sire's 2:30 performers.

The bay filly Wanda has filled out and improved wonderfully since last year; she must weigh fully 150 pounds more than when she received her mark of 2:24, and although not given any hard work, seems eager for fast quarters and halves. Mr. Burke, who handled the ribbons over this superb mare, had no trouble in sending her a quarter in 38 seconds, the mare fighting for the bit all the distance.

Clovewood is the daughter of Clovis, dam by Nutwood, who, from a little spurt she made at San Jose early in the present year, deterred many from entering in the two-year-old District Stakes at that place; she is a large-bodied and clean-gaited filly, and if accident does not prevent, should prove her stamina and endurance before the season of 1890 closes.

During the early months of the year, Mr. Burke and his well-known trainer, Wm. Vioget, had many controversies respecting the merits of the best yearlings at the La Siesta Ranch. The many arguments finally closed by Mr. Burke and his trainer, each selecting one to do battle for their opinions; the one selected by the trainer is called Luck of Eros, by Eros, dam by Nutwood; 2d dam the dam of Vanderlynn, 2:21, by Joseph; 3d dam Old Scully by Easton's Black Hawk. The one selected by the proprietor is Donzella by Eros, dam the sister to Lewis D., 2:24½. After a close and critical examination of each of the yearlings, it must be confessed that from present appearances, the Luck of Eros is the better of the two, however, Mr. Burke has great confidence in his own selection, and seems to think that Donzella can beat "Luck" in a contest.

In the same stable we also find Maggie E., 2:19½, by Nutwood, dam by Geo. M. Patchen Jr. This well known mare, like the balance of the string, has received no hard work, but will be gradually prepared for this season's campaign.

Maraquita already has a record of 2:43, and is a handsome, well-disposed miss who, in her present four-year-old form, should considerably reduce her present mark. Maraquita is by Eros, dam by Elmo.

Another promising one in the same stable is Benefactor by General Benton, dam Frolic by Harry Clay 45; 2d dam Maori by imp. Australian; 3d dam by Lexington. Taken all in all, the La Siesta Ranch has a very useful lot of trotters, and from present appearances, there will be quite a number of Eros colts to add to the list this year.

Our Tennessee Letter.

GALLETIN, Tenn., June 13th.

EDITOR BREEDER AND SPORTSMAN:—My worst fears of El Rio Rey's condition have at last become true, and my prediction that he would never win another race has been realized. Upon taking the horse to St. Louis, Mr. Winters had a veterinary surgeon examine him thoroughly, and after a close examination it was deemed best to at once retire him from racing and send him to the stud. It is evident from this fact that the Westchester illness was the commencement of the trouble. While the colt showed a splendid mile at Nashville, he could not go further than that distance, for on a good day and track there his best mile and a quarter was 2:16½.

He will at once be sent to Mr. Winter's breeding farm. His fate is just such as was Sensation's, Tremont's and French Park's, all of whom were unbeaten in their two-year-old form, but were never trained thereafter. As these raced in different years, it will never be positively known which was the best, and almost everybody has different opinions as to their performances, entitling either one of the four to rank as king of two-year-olds. As these four colts met all comers and were never defeated, we must naturally class them superior to those that were good, but still had been beaten.

If the great colt Russell continues to show his heals to his rivals in the East he will probably be the first two-year-old to win as much as $100,000. Besides his already large stake victories he is yet engaged in seventeen of the richest stakes for his age, among which are the Carteret Handicap at Monmouth with $5,000 added, Junior Champion, worth $25,000, Select, Stakes and the rich Double Event, and Futurity Stakes. In all of these races he will meet Rey del Rey, and I look for the Winter's colt to as easily defeat Russell as the latter can a selling plater. Rey del Rey's stake engagements will be worth something over $100,000, and he may be the one to first cross the line. If he fills all his engagements he will, no doubt, come as near securing the $100,000 mark as will the Morris colt.

To-morrow week the seventh renewal of the American Derby will take place at Washington Park, Chicago. It is an open race—not because there are no cracks engaged, but because there are so many of them and they are all so nearly equal. Riley, Protection, Amigo, (His a Californian, and they always win Derbys) Bill Letcher, Prince Fonso, English Lady, Pilgrim, Helter Skelter and a few lesser lights that are engaged will make a hard field to pick from. Good-day and track, I would not be surprised to see them coming in this order, providing all of the above start, English Lady first with Amigo and Bill Letcher for the place horses. The Baldwin string are now quartered at Washington Park, where his horses are well engaged. He has been singularly successful in running this race, and there are a thousand who will back Amigo, thinking there is something in the "Baldwin luck." Bob Campbell, Mr. Baldwin's trainer, expects to win the race with his colt Protection, but I am afraid he will be sorely disappointed with his Junior Champion winner. He is a good colt, however, and he may finish far in the lead of the second horse.

The best played "scoop" of the season was that of the Daisy Woodruff party at Westchester last week; and it was even nicer than shrewd Johnny Campbell's nicely laid plans for the Brooklyn Handicap. Daisy Woodruff is owned by Reuben Payne, who owns a large breeding farm here, and he knows a "dead clinch" when they are about to come off. That day "he went down the line," handling the books a "century" a piece on his little mare at odds of 50 to 1 against, and after she had run the race in 1:13, he found himself winner of $50,000. Every one of his stable boys simply got rich, and his trainer, Major Eliott, is said to have won $10,000. Last year Daisy Woodruff was bred to Asteiro, but owing to her not producing this spring she was again put in training, and very luckily so for Mr. Payne.

After all the Westchester course is not going to be the great thing it was once thought to be. The "straight" track is not what race-goers like to pay their money to see a horse run an eighth of a mile and a quarter race on. The circular track need not feel envious, for the tide of prosperity will soon turn and Sheepshead Bay, Brooklyn and other circular courses will be looked upon as the most aristocratic.

KENNESAW.

Los Angeles News.

The approach of the opening meeting of the Grand Circuit has livened up the horsemen all over Southern California, and the season of 1890 promises to be a memorable one. The entries for the 2:30 trot and the district trotting stake closed on Monday, but at this writing all the entries are not in. The colt stakes have filled splendidly, such sires as Stamboul, Guy Wilkes, Woolsey, Alcazar, Gossiper, Albion, Will Crocker, Wilton, Endymion, Maximilian, Bob Mason and Christmas being represented.

"Lucky" Baldwin has arrived at Santa Anita. The Emperor of Norfolk, La Cienga and Costa Rica were sent East last week. The Emperor is expected to make his debut in the California Stakes at the Saratoga meeting.

The entries for the August meeting close next Tuesday week. A good entry is confidently expected from the Northern end of the State, especially as the railroad company offer to charge but $100 for the transportation of a car load from San Francisco, San Jose, Sacramento, Stockton, Napa, or any point contiguous to the Bay City.

QUARTER STRETCH GOSSIP.

A brown stallion that will be seen on the California circuit this year for the first time is Jud Wilkes by Ira Wilkes. The dam of Jud Wilkes is Champion Maid by Champion Messenger. This stallion was imported from the East by J. W. Robinson.

John D. Young owns the only Monroe Chief stallion in Southern California. He is a three-year-old and his dam is by Young America, who is by Prather's Rattler.

Juan B. Arellanes is training a string of horses at Santa Maria.

Atto Rex and Gossiper are being slowly jogged. Opinion is divided about their standing for more than two or three races.

The only son of Wilton on the coast is entered in the trotting stakes for 1891. He is owned by J. W. Robinson and his dam is Grey Diana by Administrator.

Mr. Sanchez, of Santa Fe Springs, is training Dick Richmond. He expects to take this son of A. W. Richmond on the circuit this year.

Rajah has been thrown out of training.

The local papers are devoting considerable of their valuable space to booming the meeting in August.

DAGWORTH.

The Haggin Sale.

The following prices were received for those mentioned of the Haggin consignment of thoroughbred yearlings, which were disposed of at public auction on Monday last in New York:

Bay colt by Kyrle Daly—Abra, C. Bathgate, $1,350.

Brown filly by Joe Daniels—Alfareta, L. J. Rose, $850.

Bay filly by Darebin—Altitude, L. J. Rose, $1,000.

Chestnut filly by Hyder Ali—Bagatelle, W. C. Rollins, $900.

Brown colt by Darebin—Bavaria, W. I. Rollins, $750.

Bay filly by Darebin—Bessie Peyton, Pierre Lorillard, $800.

Bay colt by Hidalgo—Blue Dress, J. M. Jefferet, $950.

Chestnut filly by Sir Modred—Bonnie Kate, Marcus Daly, $2,000.

Brown colt by Darebin—Carrie, Andrew Thompson, $700.

Brown colt by Sir Modred—Carissima, J. A. & A. H. Morris, $4,200.

Chestnut colt by Sir Modred—Chimera, Marcus Daly, $1,900.

Colt by Sir Modred—Embroidery, Marcus Daly, $2,400.

Bay filly, full sister to Dew Drop, by Falsetto—Explosion, Pierre Lorillard, $3,500.

Chestnut colt by Joe Daniels—Guilia, Marcus Daly, $1,200.

Bay filly by Darebin—Glendive, E. R. Cassidy, $1,050.

Bay filly by Darebin—Glendora, W. Donathan, California, $850.

Chestnut colt, half brother to Kempland, by Hyder Ali—Gloriarme, W. C. Rollins, $750.

Bay colt by John Happy—Gondole, M. A. Hughes, $775.

Bay colt by Sir Modred—Hirondelle, Marcus Daly, $2,000.

Chestnut gelding, half brother to Ingleside, by Warwick Illusion, Pierre Lorillard, $800.

Brown gelding, by Darebin—Katrina; Pierre Lorillard, $6,000.

Brown filly, half sister to Ballarat, by Darebin—La Favorita; M. A. Hughes, $1,050.

Bay filly, by Sir Modred—Lulu by Virgil; Marcus Daly, $5,000.

Brown Colt, by Darebin—Lydia, by Billet; Pierre Lorillard, $2,500.

Bay colt, by Sir Modred—Marian Hubbard; Marcus Daly, $2,600.

Chestnut colt, by St. Blaise—Maude Hampton, by Hunter's Lexington; Marcus Daly, $3,000.

Bay colt, by Joe Daniels-Millie, by Billet; W. C. Rollins, $1,100.

Bay filly, by Sir Modred-Miss Motley, by Billet; John Hunter, $1,050.

Chestnut filly, by Sir Modred-Mottle, by Billet; W. Donathan, $1,050.

Brown filly, by Kyrle Daly—Napa, by Enquirer; Andrew J. Welsh, $1,100.

Bay colt, by Sir Modred-Plaything, by Alarm; Marcus Daly, $4 200.

Chestnut colt, by Sir Modred—Preciosa, by Glenelg; J. A. and A. H. Morris, $2,900.

Bay colt, by Sir Modred-Rosa B., by Norfolk, J. A. and A. H. Morris, $2,550.

Bay colt, by Sir Modred-School Girl, by Pat Malloy, L. J. Rose, $5,800.

Chestnut filly, by Sir Modred-Shasta, by Spendrift, W. Donothan, $1,000.

Brown filly, by Warwick, sister to Jim Douglas-Wild Idle, A. J. Welsh, $1,000.

Bay colt, by Tyrant-Springlike, by Springbok, G. W. Walbum $1,250.

Bay filly, by Sir Modred—Trade Dollar by Norfolk, Marcus Daly, $1,100.

Bay colt, by Darebin—Tulare by Monarchist, Hamilton Smith, England, $5,100.

Bay filly, by Sir Modred—Wanda by Norfolk, Marcus Daly, $1,300.

THE FARM.

DAIRYING.

The New System of Butter Shows in Denmark.

In a report just issued, Mr. Inglis, the consul at Copenhagen, says the Hull, (Eng.) News, who has already published an interesting report on dairy farms in Denmark, describes a new system of state butter shows recently organized in that country by the director of the dairy section of the Danish Agricultural Department. The fault of the old shows was that they were not of much practical benefit in encouraging the production of first class butter or in effectually tracing faults of manufacture to their source. The new plan has the support of a large number of dairies, dairy experts, and leading butter merchants all over the country. Its principal features are: (1) A continuous butter show at the expense of the State during several months of each year. (2) Here fresh samples of butter will be received every fourteen days. Thus there will be two distinct testings, not only of quality but also of weight. (3) The samples are to be sent immediately on the receipt of a letter or telegram, so that the dairymen will not be able to make a special cask for exhibition, and the samples are to be repeated as often as required. (4) Competing dairies must send in a return of the feeding system generally followed on the farm, with special reference to the week during which the samples are sent in. At present the number of dairies entered is 360. Nine judges have been selected, and these act in groups of three each, each group recording an independent opinion on each sample, which is checked by those of the other two groups. Each group will consist of two butter merchants and one dairy expert. The exhibitors are paid the usual market rate for their exhibits. The show will be held at intervals of a fortnight during eight months of the year, and the government grant during the current financial year is £1 350. As the same dairy will send in butter several times in the course of the year, great facilities will be afforded for ascertaining which are the best managed dairies, and it will then be seen where the art of butter making may best be learned. The report concludes by reproducing a series of questions in regard to dairy management put to the managers of competing dairies.

Some Advantages of Dehorning.

Whatever we may think in the matter of removing the horns from cattle when considered from a humane standpoint, we must admit that there are great advantages to be gained, says Field and Farm. First, it disarms the vicious bull of the weapons with which he kills humans. Second, it provides that the quarreling brutes shall live in harmony together. Third, it makes it possible for the weaker ones to live among the stronger ones and to obtain their full share of the feed when in pens or inclosures. There are many reasons in favor of removing the horns, and but a single one against it—that of humanity.

Mr. Morse of the Windsor Farm, with his hundred head of pure-bred dehorned Holsteins, says it has added $50 each to their real value. This from the fact that they dwell in peace together and require much less feed, since none is wasted in fighting and trampling over it. Every cow gets to the water troughs without being gored, and each gets its needed supply. There is peace and harmony in the stables. The management of the Broadmoor dairy dehorned 200 steers to feed for the shambles last fall, and found great benefit from the absence of the horns, since there was a uniform gain in flesh with all of the cattle feeding, and not one maimed or killed, and they went to the market unbruised and unscarred.

The greatest benefit from dehorning we have yet to speak of. With its introduction in the feeding districts of the West it has reduced the labor expense of taking care of cattle fully one-half. Two men will now take care of the number of cattle that, before dehorning, required three or four. Under the modern regime there are no stanchions required or no tying up in the barns. The dehorned brutes can be kept in moderately small pens and under sheds, nor be chained like wild beasts that destroy one another. Stalls in which to fasten and feed cattle will be unnecessary in the future. Close sheds and small corrals will be the style for cattle-feeding.

Proposed Introduction of American Store Cattle Into Scotland.

North British Agriculturist (May 7): A public meeting called by the lord provost was held in Dundee yesterday for the purpose of taking steps toward securing the introduction of United States cattle into this country. There was a large attendance of farmers from the district. After the lord provost opened the proceedings, Mr. Andrew Hutcheson, in moving the first resolution, said that the importation of store cattle from Canada had proved so successful in Glasgow and Aberdeen that he hoped Dundee would get a share of the traffic. It was difficult, however, to make the scheme pay unless they could manage to carry along with them the importation of store cattle from the United States as well as from Canada. These cattle were forbidden because of the existence of pleuro in some of the Eastern States. He did not think there was a sufficient reason for prohibiting these cattle to be sent to this country except under the condition of compulsory slaughter on arrival. Pleuro was not like the cattle plague; it could be controlled. Moreover, many people were skeptical as to the prevalence of pleuro, and he read a letter from Prof. Williams of Edinburg, in which he stated that he had examined thousands of United States cattle, and in no instance did he discover any sign of pleuro-pneumonia contagion. These cases of supposed pleuro were merely cases of lung disease, brought on by exposure, and not of an infectious nature. These testimonies, Mr. Hutcheson added, ought to carry great weight and cause the government to look carefully into the question. Canadian cattle were a limited commodity, but States cattle were practically unlimited, and what they required was free trade in cattle with a reasonable amount of precaution against the introduction and spread of disease. Dundee was deeply interested in this question, because the removal of the restrictions on American cattle would give a great stimulus to the cattle companies and would set them on their feet and add £2 a head to the value of every cattle beast in America. It would do good also to the farmers, for although it would bring down the price of beef, raw material would be cheaper. He was certain the American cattle were freer from disease than Irish cattle. He moved—"That this meeting, representing the town council and harbor trustees of Dundee, and farmers and others in this and neighboring counties interested, are strongly of opinion that it would be in the interests of agriculturists and the community generally that permission should now be granted for the importation of States cattle, on the same conditions as at present exist in regard to Canadian cattle, with such reasonable precautions as may be deemed necessary by the authorities."

Mr. A. Whitton of Couston, said he would go upon the principle of free trade. So long as this country was made the hunting ground not only of the natural but also of the artificial productions of other countries, it was unfair that agriculturists should not have an opportunity of getting raw material on the same terms. It was far from being a fair trade that fat cattle could be brought into this country, and poured, as it were, into the beef market, while they were prevented from going to the like market to supply their legitimate wants in the same way as other countries did. If they had got as many diseased cattle from Canada as they had from Ireland, Canada would have been shut out long ago.

The resolution was then adopted.

Salt Every Day.

Dairy cattle should have access to salt every day, and salt should be added to all their stable feed. A series of experiments has convinced me that when cows are denied salt for a period of even one week they will yield from 14½ to 17½ per cent less milk, and that of an inferior quality. Such milk will on an average turn sour in twenty-four hours less time than milk drawn from the same or similar cows receiving salt, all other conditions of treatment being equal. Comfortable quarters are indispensable to the health and well being of cows. Stables during the winter should have a temperature constantly within the range of from 40 to 55 degrees Fahr. In summer time a shade should be provided in the pasture fields, or adjacent thereto, to protect against the bristle making influence of July and August suns. In all the management of cows such conditions should be provided and such care given as will insure excellent health and apparent contentment. When practicable, milking should be done by the same person with regularity as to time. He only that hath clean hands should be allowed to milk a cow. I say "he" because I think the men of the farm should do all the milking, at least during the winter months. I have exercised the right of changing my mind on that subject since I left the farm. It is no more difficult to milk with dry hands than with them wet. It is certainly more cleanly, and leaves the milk in a much more desirable condition for table use or manufacture. Pure stable atmosphere is indispensable to prevent contamination from that source. Immediate straining will remove impurities which otherwise might be dissolved to the permanent injury of the whole product.—Orange Judd Farmer.

Shorthorns for Milk or Beef.

The handsomest and most showy form for a Shorthorn cow includes a broad as well as deep chest, full crops, fore ribs so round as to leave no depression behind the shoulders; a straight line along the back end of the rump; wide between the huckle bones, and well developed quarters. This is the best shape for making beef. For milk, the chest should be deeper and not so broad, fore ribs rather flat and long, crops less full than for beef, and the quarters quite broad, so that in looking at her in front her body will appear decidedly wedge-shaped, the larger end to the rear. But even thus formed, when dried off, a Shorthorn cow will fatten quickly and cheaply, and make a good carcass of a fine quality of beef. Occasionally one of beef shape—that is, about as full in front as rear, and rather fat—proves a great milker of a highly excellent quality, like some Holstein-Friesians. Many of those latter seem to have changed their nature in America, yielding richer milk generally than in Holland, and yet of a very abundant quality. No doubt this change is owing to the difference of climate and quality of food.

The summers in Holland are cool and wet and in Northern America comparatively hot and dry, with drier and more frosty winters, and the grass of our meadows is less rank and succulent. These have much influence in giving quantity and quality to milk and also in the formation of flesh. Still, the difference in breeds of cattle is paramount, and the animals should be chosen from such as excel in what is most desired by the breeder to produce.—Ex.

Pure bred Cattle for Humbolt.

Peter Saxe & Son have for many years been well known as importers of the purest and best strains of cattle in California. Last year Ira Russ, Humbolt Co., procured through Messrs. Saxe eight head of grandly bred Herefords, and was so pleased with them that under his instructions they sent last Saturday a splendid five year old cow and a ten month old heifer calf to join the herd. On Wednesday the same firm shipped a four year old Jersey Bull—Major Bagstock 18993 A. J. C. C., to Mr. Jas. Roberts of Humbolt.

Characteristics of the Cheshire Hog.

In the admirable articles of Colonel Curtis on "Swine Breeding," he gives quite an extended history of the development of the Cheshire, but does not give their peculiarities; so that one who had never seen them would know little of the difference between them and the other breeds. I give briefly their points of superiority:

1. Early maturity; at nine months or under the Cheshire, on the average, will outweigh any other breed. The best weights I can vouch for are the following: A litter of seven, killed when exactly nine months and one day old, averaged 406 pounds. One pig, from a litter from which the best ones were shipped, butchered when eight months and fourteen days old, dressed, 416 pounds—forty pounds of fat were taken from the entrails, which, if counted, would make dressed weight 456 pounds. Of course, these are exceptional weights, but good pigs, well cared for, should easily average 300 pounds or more at nine months. Half blood pigs from Cheshire boars will grow as well as the full-bloods. It is young pork that pays, considering feed consumed, and it brings a better price.

2. Quality of flesh—The Cheshire gives a larger proportion of lean meat than other hogs. Lean is worth more than fat. To energize the active, nervous Yankee, lean, not fat is needed. The flesh is fine-grained and so of the best quality. The fat meat is solid, not soft and lardy, like that of some breeds. Feed a Cheshire and a small Yorkshire on like food and the Cheshire will give much the larger proportion of lean. These two qualities make the hog for the butcher as well as for home use.

3. Docility—No hog is more easily handled. Children get into the pen with the sow to play with the little pigs. At farrowing time, if weather is cold, a blanket is thrown over the sow, and, as the little fellows arrive, they are put under the blanket by the udders. In a few minutes the pigs are dry, warm and fighting for choice of position. The great loss of pigs at farrowing-time comes from their being chilled before they get dry. I notice some writers claim that hogs with erect ears are not as quiet as those with lopped ears. This rule, if it may be so-called, is utterly refuted by the Cheshire, which is the most docile hog in existence.—E. W. Davis in New York Tribune.

Southdowns.

An influential meeting of Southdown breeders was lately held at the Royal Agricultural Hall, Islington, for the purpose of establishing a society for promoting the interests of the breed; also for conducting some system of registration. There was a unanimous opinion that a society should be established and a register commenced. It was generally allowed that while for the home trade in Southdowns, the reputation of the breed might be sufficient; yet that foreign buyers unacquainted with individual flocks, look for a record. Unless, indeed, a register was established, the foreign trade was found to be seriously curtailed. It appears the movement in the direction alluded to had already produced an influence for good in bringing together many of the leading flockowners, who will find that in union there is strength, and that there are numerous ways in which the interests of the breed can be promoted by combination for that purpose.

Sheep.

No man is qualified for a shepherd who is not gentle in all his ways—a gentleman, remarks Galen Wilson, in N. Y. Tribune. Some are born sheepmen, some acquire skill in handling sheep; others are poison to the race. Grain producing farms grow poorer every year; sheep farms increase in fertility. The sheep crop suffers less by drouth than any other animal or vegetable. Breeding for the most wool to light carcasses is poor policy—there is no reason for sacrificing fleece qualities in carcass improvement. One cross upon pure Merino ewes by compact-bodied, close-wooled rams is usually of advantage, but cross upon cross will deteriorate the flock.

A good constitution combined with mutton and wool qualities, makes the perfect sheep. The breed that can give best return for care and feed is the proper breed to keep, and experience proves the Merino to be the winner in the race for money. The foot disease does not originate on high, dry ground, and animals affected with it recover spontaneously when removed from low to high land. Sheep moved from the limestone soil of the North to the sands of the South generally "die acclimating." Northern crosses upon the natives is the only way to secure desirable flocks there. Some flockmasters in a Western county have adopted heroic treatment of sheep-killing dogs. They feed their sheep pieces of beefsteak sprinkled with a solution of strychnine, and what the sheep leave the dogs consume, "and nobody's to blame." Horns on sheep are in the way all the time. Fewer can be corralled or folded in the same space or fed at the same time; they gouge out each others eyes, and a punch in the abdomen often causes abortion in ewes. Horns are a terror to the shearer, and valuable feed is consumed to produce the worse than useless appendages. Horns on lambs are prevented by excising "the buttons," as with calves, but the humane way is to breed the horns off. There will be muley ram-lambs among most horned breeds, and by use of such a Western shepherd had last season 500 muley ram-lambs out of 800, and he expects to succeed in breeding off all horns horns and establishing a polled Merino breed.

Trials of the Range Sheep Man.

It takes more brain, more energy, more foresight, says Charles Crane, of Utah, to run sheep than any other live stock; they must be constantly under the eye of the shepherd.

Ranges must be looked up, water piped, dug out and troughed, dipping, shearing and lambing looked after and prepared for.

Salt must be packed on the range, pack saddles, wagon and tent repaired; horses shod; supplies purchased; herders looked after; rams taken out and herded and fed, and often purchased; old ewes and poor lambs culled out, and sold; hay and grain looked after, for teams and rams in fall and winter; corrals repaired, etc.

His days are busy, and his nights are restless. The sheep are seldom corraled, and he knows when the moon is up, the flock is apt to move. When the wind blows, they will seek shelter behind a hill if near. He must sleep with one eye and ear open. A constant source of anxiety pervades his soul.

Often during the storms of winter he is up for days and nights, getting his sheep where they will not be snowed in. Often when driving to shelter, he glances around and sees, as far as the eyes can reach, a waste of snow; he struggles on with his flock, until they bunch and refuse to move, he camps, feeds his team, and perhaps without a tree in sight, or brush large enough to burn, goes supperless to bed, or watches his flock all night. In the morning his team is gone, his feet, although well wrapped up, are frozen, the storm continues for days, without a soul in sight; cold, miserable, hungry and wet, he walks around the flock and when the storm ceases, he finds he has lost twenty per cent, perhaps fifty per cent of his entire flock, the result of years of toil, labor and privation.

Is it strange we sometimes hear of a splendid shepherd committing suicide? The constant strain and anxiety, for safety of this flock, weighs heavily upon him, and the splendid physique and active brains give way, and in a moment of despondency, a flash, and a bullet ends a life.

If any one thinks it is lots of fun, and all profits to run sheep, permit me to disabuse his mind.

More failures have occurred than in any other business having the same amount of capital invested.

The causes for this are as numerous as their sheep—drouth, storms, poison weed, low price of wool, floods, etc., are the principal ones; what effects one section, does not another. It is only strong willed, determined, energetic men, who are in the business to stay, who will not be kept down; if they lose fifty per cent this season they keep on hoping to weather the storms next season.—Montana Stock Journal.

TURF AND TRACK.

Freeman has left Dave Pulsifer and will ride in the West.

There is some talk of a match between Palo Alto and Jack.

Mr. Valensin is visiting Bartlett Springs, and his health is rapidly improving.

Charles Ingalls, who has been with Hiram Woodruff some years, has gone to Montana to the Sawyer ranch.

An old man named Tuohy, who once looked after the celebrated Harkaway, died at the Curragh recently.

W. S. Vosburgh has been appointed official handicapper at Monmouth, and will also officiate as third judge.

Hugh Kirkendall, Helena, Montana, lost last week by death a suckling colt, full brother to the speedy Daniel B.

Cassius made all the running in the Suburban and came very near putting off the double event for the Beverwyck stable.

The only standard bred filly by Allerton got caught in a barbed wire fence at Independance, Ia., and had to be destroyed.

Garrison had a close shave when Brother Ban dropped dead on the track last week but luckily the rider was not injured.

Ed. A. Tipton, Secretary of the Kentucky Trotting Horse Breeder's Association, was appointed receiver for the stallion Red Wilkes.

The Directors of the Red Bluff race track will have new stables, fences, and other necessaries completed before the meeting in August.

T. H Williams, Jr., left last Friday for Chicago. The Undine Stable will probably start several horses at the Washington Park meeting.

George Baldwin—Lucky Baldwin's nephew—left last week for Washington Park, Chicago, to take the management of the Santa Anita Stable.

F. B. Baldwin, the Fresno race track manager, is superintending the improvements at the Coronado Beach track, and will be manager of both tracks.

Gen. W. H. Jackson last week purchased from Judge Howell F. Jackson his half interest in the Belle Meade stud, and is now the sole owner of the famous breeding establishment.

Although the New York Jockey Club has a very strict rule in regard to owners carrying their proper colors, yet hardly a day passes but some horses carry the colors of other stables.

It is confidently expected that the half mile and repeat at the Coronado Beach track on the Fourth of July will be very interesting. Already half a dozen horses are in training, including John Treat.

John Williams one of the oldest trotting drivers in the state is educating some of the Rancho Del Paso horses, among others is the Antevolo—Mabel colt who is one of the handsomest in California.

The Morris Bros. seem satisfied with their trial of the Sir Modred's Judging by their purchase of the Carissima and Preciosa colts. We like their display of judgment. Both should prove race horses.

Huntress will never be able to race again. She will be saved for breeding purposes. Among the horses reported killed are Climax, Brown Duke, Little Minnie, Cruiser, Germanic and Banner Bearer.

Isaac Murphy is in great form just now. He rode a grand race on Burlington in the Trial States at Westchester, while last Tuesday he eclipsed himself when he rode his magnificent finish on Salvator.

George Leavitt has sold Early Bird for $10,000, and matched Fanny Slope, a four year old mare, by Florida, against Andy Welch's Directress by Dictator, for $500 a side, over the Mystic Park track in September.

Marcus Daly, who bought the most of the Sir Modreds, should have a good one in Embroidery's son. The Lulu filly which he bought, is the most beautiful creature (a racehorse all over) in the lot. She is the image of Firenzi.

Mr. L. N. Salmon, who has had several years' experience as assistant secretary of several courses, intends to write a book on the management of race tracks. This work will no doubt prove interesting to the public and valuable to officials.

Alex. Sweeton returned to Salinas from San Luis Obispo last week, bringing with him a black yearling filly by Altoona, dam by Venture 2:27. The youngster will be put in training for the yearling trotting race at the Salinas Fair this fall.

Inspector B, after his service in the stud at Erdenheim, where he covered about thirty mares, has been returned to the Dwyers' stables, and will be prepared for races later in the season. He will doubtless make his debut for the season at Monmouth Park.

The Sire Bros., New York, have bought of P. P. Johnston the running qualities of Lady Ban 3 by King Ban—Ladylike and three two year-old fillies—Sunflower by Lelaps—Smilax, Tulip by Powhattan—Hazel Kirke, and an unnamed one by Favor out of Sophy.

Mr. Hamilton Smith bought the Darebin—Tulare colt. This colt will make his bow to the public across the water. In our mind, if there were one colt in the hundred, we would rather choose this as that one. At $5,100 he should be cheap for the English turf.

William Hendrickson of Patchen fame is seriously thinking of taking a stable of trotters to Tacoma and possibly interviewing some of the Montana tracks with his trotters, prominent among which is a son of Nutwood who shows great promise; James Linden will drive.

B. McBride the owner of Major Daly was ordered on June 9th to take all his horses from Morris Park. McBride used very indecent insulting language in front of the club house while denouncing the management for putting up Hamilton in the Major Daly—Watterson race.

Mrs. Barnhardt, the owner of Lou, dam of Axtell, says the name "Can't-Tell" was selected previously to the birth of the sister to Axtell as appropriate to either sex, and a significant answer to the speculative enquiries of visitors as to the future possibilities of the youngster.

Captain Anderson, San Gabriel, Los Angeles, is one of the recent additions to the long list of California racing men. Besides Four Aces and Sir Ladd, he has several youngsters, and it is his intention to purchase some yearlings and two year olds to represent him on the track.

At the Haggin sale, Pierre Lorillard could not let Katrine's colt pass him. The mare's trial with Pontiac before he won the Suburban was enough to convince him about her—she could give him weight and beat him shoes to plates. Mr. Lorillard paid $6,000 for the Darebin colt.

Col. H I Thornton's two-year-old colt Austrian by Darebin out of Bavaria, injured himself in his box stall at Sacramento a few days ago, and it is said he will never be able to race. The youngster was a big overgrown colt, but assuredly would not have disgraced his high lineage.

On Tuesday D. S. Simmons, acting under Dr. Hamlin's instructions will sell at auction seven head of trotting and running bred horses at Agricultural Park, Sacramento. They are pet of such well known stallions as Brigadier 2:21¼, and the well known race horse Joe Hooker.

Soprano, by Strathmore 408, dam Abbess, by Albion, was foaled in 1875, and she is the youngest brood mare that has three representatives in the 2:30 list. She is the dam of C. F. Clay, 2:18; Eminence, 2:18½, and Strathbridge 2:28½, all by different sires. She is the dam of two 2:20 trotters.

People who ought to know say: "The Walton will never bet again. He is an old man now, although he does not look it, and has a large family. It is believed he still has $300,000 he salted away in bonds when he came back from his English triumphs; he should have for he left there in debt.

E. M. Kies, of Cambria, Hillsdale county, Mich., has sold to Dr. W. S. Hull, of Grand Rapids, Mich., for $2,000, the yearling filly by St. Bel, 2:24½, by Electioneer; dam Belle K. by Masterlode. Mr. Kies paid $1,200 for Belle K. as a yearling, and as this is her first foal it was quite a profitable investment.

May 4th, at Allen Farm, Rusina by Belmont, out of Miss Russell, dam of Maud S., 2:08¾, foaled a chestnut colt by Lancelot, brother of Prospero, 2:20; Elaine, 2:20; Dame Trot, 2:22, and Elista, 2:22½. Rusina is a full sister to Nutwood, and Lancelot is the youngest son of Green Mountain Maid, dam of Electioneer.

As Pierre Lorillard bought the best of the Darebins—with one exception—and Marcus Daly and the Morris Bros. the Sir Modreds—in such hands these fine colts should show us what the Australian stallions can do. We can say from observation of the three lots of yearlings sold, that this last is a truly representative one.

Burlington is, says a sporting authority, a perfect gentleman, his color—black—adding to his appearance. He has a small bloodlike head, with beautiful sloping shoulders, grand back ribs, and powerful hindquarters. His forelegs appear light below the knee, but one never saw a black horse yet who did not look lighter than he really was.

There were no sensational prices at the Rancho Del Paso sale in New York, but prices all round were good. The absence of the Dwyers of course made a good deal of difference in some of the sales; Dew Drop's sister, for instance, would most certainly have taken their fancy, and if she does not prove a clinker there is nothing in looks and breeding.

For $4000 cash and $1000 in future winnings W. W. Frazer, of Cynthiana, Ky., sold to J. F. Williams, of Eminence, Ky., and the Bashford Manor stables, Julia Magee, ch. f., three years old, by Springbok, dam Bayadere, by King Alfonso. Julia Magee ran second to English Lady for the Latonia Oaks and is with the exception of the Lady, one of the best 3 year old fillies in the West.

After making a thorough examination of El Rio Rey, a veterinarian advised Mr. Winters to take the unbeaten champion out of training, and it is now understood El Rio Rey will be shipped shortly to California to enter the stud. The authority who pronounced on his ailment says none of his foes need worry over prospective meetings with this great crack—that El Rio Rey has run his last race.

James Golden has twenty five horses in his stables at Mystic. They are unusually good ones, and include the Stamboul filly, who was out of Del Fay, by Del Sur, Fearnaught 2:19½, Arab 2:15, Molly J. 2:22½, Emma E 2:22¾, Daisy R. 2:25½, R. R. H. 2:23¼, Maria Legacy, 2:29¼, Shep Knapp 2:37, by Kentucky Prince, Sweetbriar 2:36½, H. B. Winship 2:20½, and Backman Maid 2:25½. Bard Palmer is there, and the boys are all busy.

The crusade against pool rooms and the bookmakers of New York is said to have driven away hundreds of dollars to Long Island City, as a proof of which merchants, cigar makers, barbers, saloon and restaurant keepers who did business in the vicinity of the pool rooms claim that their business has fallen off 20 per cent, by the closing of the pool rooms in New York.

William Hendrickson who brought Washington and George M. Patchen Jr. to this state, says that all that ever was, or will be, known of the former was that he was by Geo. M. Patchen Jr., dam said to be an Abdallah mare. Washington was raised near him and his dam was well known and said to be an Abdallah but even that was doubtful; she was an exceptionally fine looking mare but *could not* be traced.

Mr. J. D. Sproul, the courteous secretary of the third Agricultural district, has sent us several entry blanks for their fair in Chico beginning on August 26th. Entries close with the secretary on August 1st. Chico is always popular with horsemen—'twas there Goldsmith Maid trotted three heats in 2:19½, 2:14¾ and 2:17¼, and a good entry should result; both runners and trotters are provided for.

Surefoot, the winner of the Two Thousand Guineas, and who was such a red hot favorite for the Derby, has a peculiar pedigree, his sire Wisdom being by Blinkhoolie (*a son of Rataplan*) out of Aline by Stockwell (*brother to Rataplan*). His dam is by Galopin out of Miss Foote by Orlando, out of Gossamer by Birdcatcher, thus giving Surefoot four Birdcatcher crosses and two of Touchstone—through Orlando, a son and Aline's dam a granddaughter of Touchstone.

Byron McClelland won a very popular victory in the Eclipse Stakes at Westchester with his good filly Sallie McClelland. Messrs. Morris started their crack Russell, also Reckon and Dr. Hasbrouck, evidently intending to corral all the money in sight. Russell and Sallie drew away from the field, and after a hard race the mare won by a head. The value of the race to the winner was $23,675. Mutuals paid $59.20 on the winner, who is exceptionally highly bred, being by Hindoo out of Red and Blue, by Alarm out of Maggie B. B., (the dam of Iroquois) by Australian.

The first plunger developed this season on the turf, the racing sharps say, is Jack McDonald the bookmaker, who is reported to have won $50,000 on Daisy Woodruff. "Pittsburg Phil" has gone in for steady profits and is backing at least two books, besides making his own outside ventures. He still follows his peculiar style of betting heavily on long shots, backing a horse with 10 to 1 against him as freely as he would an even chance. He does not seem, indeed, to care to take less than a 10 to 1 chance, but on account of his being in with two bookmakers, he is no longer considered a plunger.

"I went out to Morris Park the day Tenny won his low race," said a gentleman, "and the touts actually made life a burden to me. They swarm about a stranger in the betting ring like carrion crows over a carcass, and they are almost as bold. Most of them borrow a dollar to go out to the track, and there they prey upon the public without a particle of justification. What do you think of having a dozen coarse, ill-smelling fellows, whom you have never seen, slap you on the back and offer confidence in the pure goodness of their hearts to let you in to a good thing? I think the management should have police to look after them."

Hon Charles H. Legrin, Secretary for Agriculture, Province of New Brunswick, states that the government more than once refused $15,000 for Conn's Harry Wilkes, but the horse has more than paid for himself, and is doing most valuable service to the trotting horse breeding interests of the Province. He is also drawing business from the border States. Aurora, brother to Aristos, 2:27¼, which was purchased as a representative Morgan, is satisfying his patrons by imparting style and speed to his colts. The handsomest and fastest juvenile in his class at the Moncton Fair last fall was got by Aurora.

Buyers of pools at the local trotting and pacing meetings near New York complain that they often find it difficult to get a chance to invest their money on an apparently good thing owing to the fact that the poolseller himself has some one outside buying for him. This is altogether wrong and is an imposition upon the public. The poolseller gets 3 per cent. of every bet made, and that is enough. When betting privileges are sold by associations it should be distinctly understood that the men who conduct the business should not buy pools themselves, either directly or by agents. A man in the pool box with the betting sheet before him, and the knowlege of how owners and drivers are placing their money, has a big advantage over the ordinary spectator.

The Little New England pacer Allen Maid, who last season made a record of 2:16½ and equalled it the first time she started this year, was driven on the snow all winter by her owner, who lives in New Hampshire. His system, according to a local paper, was to jog the mare a few miles in the morning, and in the afternoon go out on the drive and clean out the boys. This work seems to have done her good, and indeed it is becoming the general opinion of horsemen that if trotters and pacers are wintered in a section of the country where there is good sleighing for a number of weeks, it does them no harm to indulge in a brush down the road now and then. Of course no horse that is expected to do battle on the turf the following summer wants to be raced on the snow all winter, but there is no harm in a little speeding.

John S. Clark, of New Brunswick, will campaign Sadie D., yearling record 2:35½; Presto, yearling record 2:41½, two-year old 2:25½. The latter has been placed in the hands of Mr. Dickerson, the man who drove him to his record of 2:25½. Crit Davis will have charge of Sadie D. Presto's first engagement is at Chicago, and the first important engagement of Sadie D. will be in the stakes of the Northwestern Breeder's Association, at Detroit. This is a great pair. Mr. Clark affirms with much emphasis that Presto will take a mark of 2:15 this year. "My disposition," Mr. Clark said, "is rather to underestimate the speed of my horses, but I feel enthusiastic over the performances of these two youngsters, having seen them move." Mr. Clark has just returned from Kentucky, and while there was treated to an exhibition with which he was much gratified.

A curious incident happened in the Wickersley Hurdle Race at Rotherham, England, in May. Gladstone was weighed out for by Savage, and his number was hoisted, but subsequently A. Nightingall arrived to ride the horse, and having obtained the permission of one of the stewards he weighed out, and Savage's name was taken down. Gladstone (who had been made favorite) accordingly went to the post, but the stewards then ruled that Nightingall could not ride the horse, as he had not weighed out in time, and a messenger was sent to bring him back to the paddock, when it was then decided that the horse should not run. A meeting of the stewards was then held to consider whether the horse had been under the starter's orders or not, and they decided that Gladstone was not under the starter's orders, and all bets made on the horse were declared off.

The Suburban last Tuesday was productive of a grand race, the nine starters all being well known crack performers. Cassius made all the pace with Strideway, Longstreet and Salvator, three lengths back until the stretch was reached when Murphy on Salvator gradually closed up, and in a close finish beat Cassius by a neck. Time, 2:06 4 5. Salvator's performance may fairly be called phenomenal, 4-years-old and carrying 127 lbs. Kingston who holds the mile and a quarter record 2 06½ carried 122 in September. At weight for age Kingston had therefore nine lbs. the best of the weight compared with Salvator.

Salvator was bred by D. Swigert at Elmendorf, his sire being imported Prince Charlie, the Prince of T. Y. C.

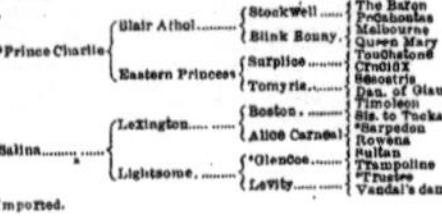

* Imported.

Jimmy Goldsmith is driving as man rarely did before He stole a race with Plush in the 7th heat at Albany, N. Y.—on the 10th from Burke behind Yorktown Belle, the latter being beaten half a length by superior driving.

McCann & Bowman, Fairlawn Farm, Lexington, Ky., have sold to Schmulback & Park, Wheeling, W. Va., the bay filly Lady McGregor, 2 years old, by Red Wilkes, dam by Robert McGregor, for $2 000. Also two yearling fillies by Red Wilkes out of mares by Star Almont, for $1,250 each.

John E. Turner, known as the great strategist of the turf, has his own peculiar way of doing business; and the problem to be solved when he is in a race is not if he is going to lose, but whether he will win. When the "General" is ready to go to the front he puts an order in the pool box on his horse, and the talent are then sure they will get a good drive for their money, but it would nonplus the Delphic oracle to determine just when Turner is ready to cut loose in some instances. As a rule he is silent as the grave about the merits of his flyers and even the owner is frequently kept in the dark as to what the veteran schemer is about to do. The redeeming feature about Turner is that he is manly and straightforward on the track, trusting to his strategic ability to carry him through. If he gets caught with a sleeper it is not necessary to take him out of the sulky for the assurance that he will win if possible is to be relied on.

When C. W. Williams, of Axtell fame, began his career as a breeder, he made a grand coup by sending three mares to Kentucky, one to William L., and Axtell was the result, and he sold the colt last Autumn for $105,000; the second was sent on a visit to Jay Bird, and she dropped Allerton, 2:18¼, who was one of the three-year-old sensations of last year; the third one gave him a son of Onward, who is now doing good work in the stud. This year his luck has been of the opposite character. Out of four mares bred to William L., last season by him he has not a living foal. Two of the mares slipped, one foaled a dead filly, and the last of the quartette, Atoka by Jay Bird, dam by Denver Wilkes, foaled a filly which died two days later. In the great lottery of breeding it was fortunate for the young Iowa breeder that he drew his prizes on the first investment. He can well afford to smile at this year's bad luck.

Goldsmith Maid, to accomplish what she did, had to be "an earnest trotter." She was always driven without blinds and never had her feet loaded with toe weights. Even in her most desperate contests, the bands of music and the cheers from the myriad spectators, and the rush and contention of fields of rivals never disconcerted her. She trotted every inch of the mile to win, and when a throat-latch only was needed to land her a winner she would stretch out her neck like a wild goose to place her nose first across the goal. In her genuine contests with Rhode Island, American Girl, George Wilkes, Occident, George Palmer and many other trotting celebrities, she not only evinced the steadiness of nerves and the strength of her courage, but the remarkable intelligence of her brain. Inbreeding never injured her performances, nor disgraced her behavior under the severest ordeals.

There is no reason at all to doubt that, if some well-known sportsmen were to patronize trotting, that form of amusement would, says the Field, very speedily occupy a more prominent position than it has ever yet done. In England, no less than in America, there is an intimate connection between the trotter and the every-day harness horse; and that is one of the reasons assigned for the popularity of trotting on the other side. The match trotter is to the ordinary harness horse what the steeplechaser is to the hunter; and the Americans take up with the former as readily as with the latter. Hiram Woodruff claimed for his countrymen that they had "a paragon of the animal which is already the wonder of the world, and which, from the familiar, affectionate, and universal use made of him on this continent, has already become an American commercial product of vast importance and proportions. The English have had the stock all along as well as ourselves; but it is our method of cultivation and our perseverance that has made the difference between their fast trotter of a mile in three minutes, and ours of a mile in two minutes and a half"—he might have said 2 min. 8¾ sec. had he been alive at the time the famous Maud S. accomplished her memorable feat.

Said Frank Eames of Bay Ridge: "I remember once when in California in the early days that the legislature adjourned for the purpose of attending the four-mile race between Nathan Coombs' horse, Ashland, and Lathrop's Langford. This was probably the only instance on record in America where a legislative body adjourned for the express and acknowledged purpose of attending a horse-race. Still everybody knows that from a time beyond which the memory of man runneth not to the contrary the English parliament has adjourned every year for the express purpose of attending the Derby. When Lord Palmerston was prime minister he always made the motion himself, and made a nice little speech. It is true he did not call it a horse race, but alluded to it in classic phrase as "our isthmian games," but they knew what games he was up to.

Yes," said Milliard Sanders, "but I can tell you something better than that. During reconstruction days in South Carolina, when there was that famous negro legislation which made history with the bottom rail on top, the legislature not only adjourned for a horse-race, but when the sport was over it appropriated money out of the State treasury to pay the debts lost by the members.—New York Star.

The manner in which the fourth estate is represented in the various jockey clubs is somewhat surprising. The Turf, Field and Farm says "the genial Mr. H. D. McIntyre, Secretary of the Brooklyn and New Jersey clubs, is an old newspaper man of varied experience. Mr. Salmon, who is clerk of the scales for the same clubs, was for many years connected with the local press. Mr H. G. Crickmore, Secretary of the Monmouth, made the World the recognized daily sporting authority for so many years that we cannot begin to remember when "Crick" was not a competent part of that journal. Mr. J. J. Burke, who has presided in the judges' stand at Brighton Beach, Clifton and Guttenburg, and who last week left for the west to occupy a similar position at Kansas City, Washington Park, Chicago and St. Paul, for years ably edited the racing department of a sporting weekly, and is at present connected with a daily. Mr. C. V. Sass, who founded the "pink un" and still finds time to write a column or so of interesting gossip for an afternoon daily, is the secretary at Brighton and Clifton and a right good secretary, too, as is Mr. Samuel Whitehead, of the Hudson County Jockey Club. And now Mr. Vosburgh joins the long list of bright and brainy newspaper men who have found congenial employment with racing institutions.

Inquiry has been made on all sides respecting the status of Fashion Stud Farm for racing material. The Newark Call says: Surprise has been expressed that out of the magnificent contigent herded at the farm none have made their appearance in the classes of the different Spring circuits. The stakes of the State Breeders' Association, it is true, have a large entry list from the farm, but apart from these there have been no entries. Mr. Dunbar attended the Decoration day races at Waverly, and was received very warmly by his host of friends. Good-natured, genial Tom is always interesting, and whenever he sits down for a moment on the quarter-stretch he is sure to be the center of attraction for those who have the greatest respect for his ability in training and treating the trotting horse. Dunbar spoke very encouragingly of the condition of the stock at Fashion. He spoke with great enthusiasm of the work of Beulah (2:19½) particularly, and predicted that when she is cut loose she will beat the great record of Favonia. Most of the racing stock will be campaigned this Fall.

The Clay Stakes was trotted for at Albany on June 12th. The weather was cold, and it rained at intervals throughout the day which prevented a large crowd going out to the track. Six starters turned out for the stakes, value $3,000, which was won in straight heats by Suisun, driven by Turner, was forced out in 2:22¼ twice by Alicante. Mr. Valensin's Simmocolon, driven by J. H. Goldsmith was well backed and made a strong bid for the third heat, showing in front up the back stretch, but left his feet, and when Goldsmith got him straightened out it was too late.

Clay Stakes, $3,000.

Suisun, by Electioneer—Susie	Turner	1	1	1
Alicante	McDonald	2	2	3
Simmocolon	Goldsmith	4	4	2
Maud	O. D. Smith	3	3	5
Jewell	H. G. Smith	5	5	4
Mina	Coville	6	6	6

Time, 2:22¼, 2:22¼, 2:24.

The 2:23 pace on the same day was won by Blanche in 2:26½, 2:22 and 2:24½.

The racing stable most affected by the disastrous wreck on the Wabash at Warrenton, Mo, says the National Horseman, were those of F. J. Keller and Jack Chinn, of Cynthiana, Ky. Not one of Keller's horses escaped. His were in the front car next the engine, and when the collision occurred the car was telescoped, the engine and tender going through it, killing the five horses, father and son who owned them, and four of their employes, colored. The names of the horses were Egypt, Lige P., Spring Dance, Turner, and Ben Ridgely. Of Chinn and Morgan's horses Ganges, Little Prince, St. Bridget, Oklahoma, and Leo were killed outright. Mary McGowan and the fast filly Josie M., were taken out alive, but badly injured and will never race again. Chinn's stable was simply wiped out. Huntress, of the Chicago stable, was in with the Chinn horses and she was buried under the debris for several hours. She was too badly hurt to ever race again, but will do as a brood mare. Hindoocraft, Proctor Knott, Ja Ja, and English Lady were not on the train, as first reported. Good-by, next to Huntress and Josie M., was the most famous racer in the cars, but he was not hurt at all. The train, with its load of eight injured men and the balance of the horses, got into Kansas at three o'clock in the morning.

For some time past, says Sterling in the Melbourne Sportsman, I have urged upon the Victoria Racing Club, the advisability of appointing an officer to act as steward at all meetings within a certain distance of Melbourne, the gentleman so appointed being paid a fixed and liberal salary by the Victoria Racing Club, which could exact a fee for his services from each club for each meeting so attended. Such an officer would, of course, be thoroughly cognisant of the meaning and signification of the rules, and thus would be able to afford the gentlemen he would become associated with most valuable assistance in involved or intricate issues which crop up when least expected. He would at once be able to draw the attention of his brother stewards for the time being to any irregularity of procedure, or to any infraction of the rules of racing taking place at the meeting held under their direction, and at suburban meetings, where it is daily becoming a matter of increasing difficulty to secure the attendance of competent men in the capacity of stewardship, he would be a valuable factor indeed. Recent decisions at Moonee Valley, Elsternwick, and Shepparton are the strongest argument in favor of such an addition to the staff of the Victoria Racing Club, and such an appointment would, while relieving that club's committee from the trouble of everlasting appeal cases, assist the handicapper, and keep the committee fairly informed as to the mode in which the meetings he attended were conducted.

John Splan says: "So many older, smarter, better educated men than myself have written, lectured and said so much about trotting horses that I approach the subject with very little confidence in being able to give it any new light. Theories I find to be all very well in books, newspapers, lectures, etc, but when those same theories are put into actual practice they develop some unlooked for weakness which lets the whole structure fall to the ground. The same I think can truthfully be said in regard to shoeing a trotter. Any knowledge that I have in the matter I have gained from actual practice together with hints and pointers from men like Mr. Robert Bonner and a few others I could name who have made a lifelong study of the matter. The first thing to be decided upon is how little weight you can possibly use in the horse's shoe to protect the foot and at the same time balance the horse so he will be able to go at his highest rate of speed on a trot. What makes it more difficult than anything else to give rules to shoe a horse by is a fact that no two horses can be shod alike. All horses are formed differently, gaited differently, and have different dispositions. In all the great number of horses I have had I cannot now remember of any two that I shod exactly alike. I hardly think that any one outside of an expert ever realizes how much difference it makes to a fast horse to make his shoes a couple of ounces heavier or lighter, but I know plenty of horses with whom to take off or put on two ounces on each forward foot would be enough to change the result of the race. Now if this is true, and I am sure that it is, the shoeing of the horse is of very great importance.

"In this connection toe-weights come in play. I would rather a horse would go without the weights than with them The great trouble with toe weights is that people use them when there is no necessity, and nine times out of ten have them heavier than they need to be. I use toe-weights a great deal; if I have a horse that has to wear over a fourteen ounce shoe, unless he has an extremely large foot, I put on a toe weight. I think there is less strain on a horse's leg with a very light toe weight and a light shoe than there would be with the weight of shoe you would have to put on the horse without the toe weight."

The English Derby.

The following is the telegram sent to the New York papers giving an account of Sainfoin's victory:

LONDON, June 4.—The Derby holiday is over, and to-night sportsmen are wondering how they managed to overlook Sainfoin. Very few knew how good the colt was, and so few indeed shared in the pulling off of the greatest race event in the world. Sir James Miller and his party and the trainer, John Porter, in whose name and colors the winner ran, are credited with having made a grand *coup*, and wonderful stories are told of their winnings.

Derby Day dawned with a leaden sky that was very depressing to the holiday crowd, and light showers of rain fell all the morning. The Derby course was sodden and slippery, the turf holding the water and making the going anything but safe and good. In spite of the weather there was an immense attendance. The crowd looked as if half of London and all the neighborhood people were present, and the nobility were out in force. The betting was tremendous.

There were but eight starters for the Derby, and, as predicted, Surefoot was a top-heavy favorite. His price at the opening was 75 to 40 on, and that was forced to 95 to 40 when they went to the post. Sainfoin was at 7 to 1, Rathbeal and Le Nord 14 to 1 each, Golden Gate and Kirkham each 50 and Martagon and Orwell 100 each.

The field gathered at the High Level starting point. The eight were bunched and sent away at the first effort, but it was with the favorite, Surefoot, behind and standing almost still when the others got in motion. Just before him and behind all the others was Baron de Rothschild's Le Nord. The Duke of Westminster's brother to Ormonde, Orwell, was first away, and he was at once sent on to make the running. The pace was so slow that it was little more than a gallop for a half mile. Sainfoin was second, Watts rating him steadily on. Liddiard, on Surefoot, took a lot out of his horse in closing up the ground he lost at the start, and was at work on the favorite when the distance was half done. Le Nord closed up more slowly. Orwell led at the mile, eight lengths in front of Sainfoin. Golden Gate, Rathbeal and Surefoot next. At the hill, just before Tettenham corner, Sainfoin began to close up. Surefoot was in trouble there, but he gamely kept trying, though Liddiard had alreay made too much use of him. At the corner, where the world-famed Archer had won so often, Watts slipped Sainfoin up. Orwell, Le Nord and Surefoot then set out for him. The finish lasted throughout the straight run. For an instant all were bunched, then Sainfoin drew away, and, with three parts of a length between him and Le Nord, raced home under all Watts' powers of persuasion. He won by a short length, Le Nord second, a neck in front of Orwell, who was a head in front of the favorite, fourth, the others well strung out. The summary follows:

The Epsom Derby Stakes (IIIth renewal) of 5,000 sovs. for the winner, 400 sovs. for the nominator of the winner, 300 sovs. for the owner of the second and 200 sovs. for the owner of the third; for colts, 9 st.; for fillies, 8 st. 9 lbs.; then three years old; by subscription of 50 sovs. each. half forfeit if declared by the first Tuesday in January, 1890, and 10 sovs. only if declared by the first Tuesday in January, 1889, and surplus to be paid to the winner; about one mile and a half, starting from the High Level starting post.

J. Porter's ch c Sainfoin, by Springfield—Sanda............Watts 1
Baron de Rothschild's ch c Le Nord, by Tristan—La Noce ....F. Barrett 2
Duke of Westminster's b c Orwell, by Bend Or—Lizzie Agnes ....G. Barrett 3

A. W. Merry's b c Surefoot (Liddiard), Capt. Machell's b c Rathbeal (Robinson), E. Baird's b c Golden Gate (Cameron), J. White's ch c Kirkham (F. Webb), and J. Snarry's b c Martagon (J. Osborne), ran unplaced.

Betting: 7 to 1 Sainfoin, 1 to 2 place; 14 to 1 Le Nord, 4 to 5 place; 95 to 40 on Surefoot, 14 to 1 Rathbeal, 60 to 1 each Golden Gate and Kirkham, 100 to 1 each Orwell and Martagon.

Sainfoin, the winner, is a son of the Bushy paddock (Hampton Court) sire Springfield, he by St. Albans, dam Viridis, and was bred from Sanda by Sir George Maude, director of Her Majesty's stud. Sanda, Sanfoin's dam, is by Wenlock; his grandsire is Stockwell, and her maternal great grandam was Lady Evelyn, winner of The Oaks in 1849. When a yearling Sainfoin was sold to Sir R. Jardine and Mr. Porter, who raced him as a two year old. Early this spring he was sold to Sir James Miller. As a two year old Sainfoin started but once, then in the Astley Stakes, five furlongs, August 9th, at the Lewes Summer Meeting. With 8st. 8 lbs. he won easily, beating Garter, Springcup, Petrel, Bena, Gosbet, Blondina, Bright Eyes, Rotten Row and Grenadiere. He started for the first time in his three year old form at Sandown Park, April 25th, in the Esher Stakes, one mile, and with 8 st. 11 lbs., won with plenty to spare, beating Dry Toast, Cheroot, Amphion, Wishing Gate, Free Mason, Ingram, Miss Dollar, Ronda, Kaikoura, Teviot and the Strathern Co's filly. He next started in the Dee Stakes, at Kempton Park, his only competitor being the Duke of Beaufort's Bull's Eye. The race was at the Derby distance, a mile and a half, and with Derby weight up Sainfoin won in a common canter. He has never been beaten, and just why he was so overlooked in the Derby until almost the very day of the race it is hard to tell. It had been supposed that Sir R. Jardine and Mr. Porter were dissatisfied with the colt, and on that account sold him to Sir James Miller. But it looks now as if a clever coup had been made, for Sainfoin was backed right and left, and his present owners and the former owners and trainers are known to have pulled off a rare stake over his victory. An immense amount of money was lost over Surefoot, but that won over Sainfoin will made Settling Day (Monday) a rare time for those who laid the odds. Sainfoin has engagements that make him a most valuable horse, now that he has proved himself possessed of quality enough to win a Derby. He is in the Epsom Grand Prize, in which he carries ten lbs. penalty for winning the Derby, and Surefoot will carry the same penalty for the Two Thousand. The great races he is in are the Zetland and Midsummer Plates at the Newmarket first and second July meetings, the Sussex at Goodwood, the Doncaster St. Leger, the Champion at Newmarket, the Roman Grand Prize, the Ascot All Aged and Hardwick, the Stockbridge Biennial and the Knowsley Dinner Stakes at Liverpool.

Base Ball and Athletic Department.

Professional Pick-Ups.

Friso still the people.

Still unsigned—Jack Ryan.

Fogarty is a very timely hitter.

Dungan is improving in his hitting.

Stevens is a silent man when playing.

Scorer Young is said to be very severe.

Jevne still continues his hoodlumish actions.

Swan is now cashier in a large Seattle hotel.

Trick McSorley has been released from Peoria.

Spokane is weak in the pitching department.

Romeo Barry has been released from Portland.

Van Haltran is the Brooklyns winning pitcher.

Hughey Smith is doing well with New Haven.

Tim Keefe has won the last ten games he pitched in.

Goodenough is getting in his fine work base stealing.

Bowman is the hardest worked catcher in the League.

Josh Reilly is a regular member of the San Franciscos.

The Michigan and Texas Leagues have both gone under.

The Californian boys are doing the best work for Portland.

Hen Moore occasionally plays in right field for St. Paul.

The Friscos had thirteen men out practicing Wednesday.

Buchan has recovered and will play at third base this week.

Wonder if Robinson wants to take McDonald off second now?

Speer does not catch Lookabough as perfectly as he does Young.

Cooney and Perrier are both doing some tall hitting for Portland.

The oftener we see Carsey pitch, the more we are impressed with his abilities.

"Now you want to jolly them up a bit" is the latest expression from the coaching lines.

It is estimated that there are four thousand professional ball players in the United States.

Harry O'Day, as a short-stop, ranks third in the fielding averages of the Western Association..

"Mobile" Stickney is fielding his position in elegant fashion, and lately has improved in his hitting.

Wilson, Stickney, Godar, Ebright and Buchan give great exhibitions of throwing from third to first.

In the Philadelphia-New York game of the 9th inst., the New Yorks only got seven hits off Phil Knell.

The Stocktons have not yet struck a winning gait, but they claim they will "get there" before the season is over.

McSorley led the third baseman of the Inter-State League, having a percentage of .913, and still he was released.

People who have seen Pete Sweeney play on first, third and second base say that the latter is his proper position.

Dick Belcher has returned from Tacoma. He sprained his ankle badly in a game and so came home for repairs.

Selna did not play with the Stocktons last Sunday for the reason that he had been on a "tanking" excursion Saturday night.

Reports say that Borchers has been drunk ever since he arrived in Portland. Gratitude is an unknown quantity in Borchers composition.

Charley Dooley's batting is helping Jersey City to victory. Timbs. Oh! if Robinson only had some of his last years Colonels with him now.

Stockton has three good pitchers in Parrott, Kilroy and Hapeman, and with a little assistance from the remainder of the team, ought to win more games.

Nick Smith, O'Day, White, Clark, Moore, Whitehead and Cline, all well known on California diamonds, are doing fine work in the Western Association.

The minister who has undertaken to stop Sunday ball playing, is beginning to realize the fact that he has a pretty big contract upon his hands.—Exchange.

The Friscos are very untidy about their uniforms. To look at Captain Ebright's last Sunday, one would think there was no soap or water within a thousand miles.

Baltimore and New Haven played a great fourteen inning game on Memorial Day, the score being nothing to nothing. Norman Baker, and Doran were the opposing pitchers.

Seattle and Spokane played a great game Sunday, in which the former were victorious—score 3 to 2. Seattle secured but three hits off Klopf and the Spokanes got five off Fitzgerald.

Shea is playing second base better with every succeeding game and is a great run getter. His hitting this season is a marked improvement over his work in this department last year also.

Rube Levy has been doing some terrific work with the stick lately. How the Kindergarten at Height St. would have yelled with delight if they saw his hitting in the Sacramento-Frisco game last Friday at Emeryville.

In the race for the pennant, Tacoma, Seattle and Spokane are very neatly bunched. Tacoma leads, with Seattle just a trifle behind, and Spokane almost treading on Seattle's heels. Portland is as yet way down in in the race.

It must have been a glorious sight to see Latham blush when he was presented with that diamond ring by his Boston friends. It certainly must have been a great surprise as no one on earth suspected that he knew how.

"Reddy" Mack, of the Baltimore Club, it is alleged, appeared in last Sunday's game clad in blue shirt and white trowsers. These two garments, when coupled with his hair, combined the colors of the American flag. Col. Mack is patriotic, if he isn't pretty.—Exchange.

Hen Harris has signed Whittaker, who until recently pitched for the Waco Texas, team. Whittaker's record as a pitcher is a good one, and while in the Texas League he made an excellent showing with the bat, having an average of 240, and ranking twentieth out of sixty-one batsmen.

'Sheridan's thorough knowledge of the science of baseball and of all the tricks and rules of the players, his unerring good judgment, honesty and positive unanswerable 'you're out,' has made him the umpire par excellence of the coast, and the peer of Gaffney, Ferguson and Lynch.—Waller Wallace in Sporting Life.

Billiards captured Patti some years ago, and soon after her arrival in America, Lily Langtry began to "adore" fencing. Mary Anderson, true to the traditions of her native State, loves a running horse as devotedly as she is capable of loving anything, and now Ella Wheeler Wilcox, is writing essays on base ball. Next!

Ed Stapleton is covering first bag for Sacramento in magnificent style. Since his illness his work has improved a hundred per cent. and now he gracefully captures every thing no matter how speedy or awkward the throw. He has also given undeniable evidence of his value as a hitter, having the greatest number of long hits to his credit and often getting as many as three and four safe shots in a game.

There a great many amateurs besides Reilly who only need to be given a chance to prove themselves "desirable acquisitions" to the professional ranks. We have mentioned a number in previous issues, but to refresh the memories of the slumbering managers, will go over the list again. Here's a promising lot of colts to draw from: Tillson, Stanley, Cusick, Thompson, Strand, Monet, Maguire, Leveque, Cook and Frank Delmas.

Robinson is a clever gentleman when making a promise, but like a great many others he evidently believes that "promises are made to be broken" For the past month he has assured members of the press that he would have the front of the stand at the Emery grounds padded, but as yet has failed to do so. The continual driving of the ball against the stand not only promises to ultimately wreck the structure (several of the boards are loose already) but is of constant annoyance to the spectators.

It seems almost inexplicable that the "celebrated, cultivated and underrated" Colonel Tom Robinson, always so tasty and neat in his own personal attire, should select such a homely and mournful costume for his pennant winning team. While the tight fitting jerseys show off the shapely limbs of his men to good advantage, the somberness of the uniform counteracts the other pleasing effect, and instead of a team of happy-go-lucky ball players, one could easily imagine he was looking at a delegation of sorrowful undertakers.

It is not necessary that Joe Noonan (Purcell) should receive the consent of his "academic superiors" before he plays ball again, as stated in one of the morning dailies. Joe is under no restrictions whatever, and is perfectly free to enter into any arrangement he may desire. Of course as he is resolved to study for the priesthood, he prefers acquainting his superiors of his immediate intentions, but this is purely optional on his part. There is no doubt but that if Finn or any other local manager desires Purcell's services, he is in a position to consider any proposition for this season.

The members of the theatrical profession are great sportsmen. Hundreds of them follow the horses and the ball players during the season, while nine out of ten of them would go miles to witness a fight. Senator Billy Crane saw Sullivan whip Ryan at Mississippi City; Horace McVicker saw the big fellow perform the same office for Kilrane at Richburg; Joe Ott, of the Bluebeard Company, is a clever ball player, as is Willie Collier, of The City Directory. The Daly Company, headed by John Drew, always has a ball team in its company. Otis Skinner and Joe Holland are baseball fiends. So are John Russell, Maurice Barrymore, Matt Snyder, Sidney Drew, Frank Moynihan, Jerry Stevens, and a hundred others who might be mentioned.

It must be rather embarrassing to the young player who leaves his minor league club full of ambition, and goes into a major league, where the company is a trifle too speedy for him, and he is crowded out and obliged to sneak back to his home and begin all over again.—Sporting Critic.

California has sent a score or more of young players East, and we have yet to see any of them creeping back home again. In fact, from past and present indications, it looks as though the big leagues are very largely indebted to the Golden State for many of their best talent.—Ed.

Reilly's work in his past few games verifies our statement in the Breeder and Sportsman of the 24th ult. that, "there are a number of amateurs right at home, who, if given a chance would prove themselves as capable as many of their older brethren". Reilly has made a big hit, and his playing Sunday is just a sample of what he can do whenever the same opportunities offer. He certainly fulfills our assertion made in the Amateur Notes of the same date, to wit: "'Josh' Reilley, of the Allens, is a 'comer'. As a second baseman we have never seen his equal in the amateur ranks.. He is as active as a kitten; knows how to play the position for all it is worth; receives a ball, no matter how hard hit, gracefully and easily, and has a clever way of touching a runner. He is one of the hardest hitters in the League, and an earnest and humorous coacher. As a base runner he ranks up with the speediest. Reilly would be a success in any of the big League Clubs on this Coast."

The grounds at Haight Street are anything but pleasant to look upon. Bunches of rank, withered grass here and there, and dust circling in whirlwinds, is all there is to charm the eye of the patient spectator who arrives at the usual time set for the game, and has nothing but this cheerless outlook for a dreary wait of an hour or more, as was the case last Sunday. Dan Mariana, who was most conscientious in his endeavors to have the grounds in good condition, has been dismissed by that "champion releaser," Robinson, and already his absence is felt.. There is no reason whatever why two ground keepers should not be constantly employed; in fact, if the managers care to consider the comforts of the patrons, this is an absolute necessity. With a little expenditure, the grass in the outfield and the plats surrounding the infield could be easily converted into bright, attractive lawns. Then with two men at work with the hose when games are in progress, the dust could be effectually laid, and the comfort of the spectators in this respect insured. This would certainly redound advantageously to the league from a financial standpoint, as increased and less dissatisfied audiences would be the result.

Two lovers went to the base ball game
 One afternoon in May;
He was a crank; she never has seen
 Professional players play.

He faithfully tried to explain it all,
 She tried to understand;
But the more he talked, the less she knew
 While he thought the game was grand.

He cheered, he danced, he yelled "Hi ! hi!"
 She calmly looked about;
And if anyone made a three-base hit
 She asked if the man was out.

She tried her best to keep the score,
 But when the game was done
He found that whenever a foul was hit.
 She had given the man a run.

It dampened his ardor to have her say:
 "Why dose'nt the umpire bat?",
And each question she asked diminished his love,
 Though he wouldn't have owned to that.

Till at last she asked in her guileless way:
 "Which nine is playing now?"
He broke the engagement then and there,
 And now they don't even bow.

—Somerville Journal.

THURSDAY'S GAME.

OAKLAND vs STOCKTON
JUNE 19TH AT HAIGHT STREET.

It was a dull, uninteresting exhibition. There was absolutely nothing in the game aside from a few pretty catches to warrant the most ardent admirer of the sport to give it his attention. Both teams fielded like a lot of wooden men, and balls that should have been caught figured as base hits. The pitchers were in very poor form, and altogether it was a very tame exhibition. Vogt was disabled and Matt Stanley filled his position. Although he was up behind the bat the greater part of the game, he had no chances except a high foul fly which he captured neatly; as Kilroy did not strike out a single Oaklander. But he was strong at the bat, knocking out a number of hard fouls, and securing two hits. The batting generally was heavy, both teams participating. The Oaklands however, bunched their hits, and aided by some good base running and a good deal of error making, won easily. The prominent feature was the fielding of Fogarty, Cahill and Stickney. Fogarty's catch of a hard line drive back of first was a magnificent bit of playing. The score:

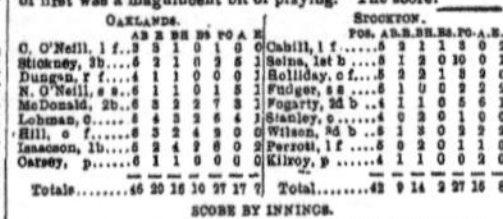

OAKLANDS.

	AB	R	BH	SB	PO	A	E
C. O'Neill, l f..	3	5	1	0	1	0	0
Stickney, 3b....	6	2	1	0	2	5	1
Dungan, r f....	4	1	1	0	0	0	1
N. O'Neill, s s..	6	1	1	0	1	5	1
McDonald, 2b..	6	3	2	2	7	3	1
Lohman, c.....	5	4	3	2	6	4	1
Hill, c f......	6	3	2	4	2	0	0
Isaacson, 1b....	5	2	4	2	8	0	2
Carsey, p......	6	1	1	0	0	0	0
Totals........	46	20	16	10	27	17	7

STOCKTON.

POS.	AB.	R.	BH.	SB.	PO.	A.	E.
Cahill, l f......	5	2	2	1	3	0	2
Selna, 1st b	5	1	2	0	10	0	1
Holliday, c f....	5	2	2	1	3	2	0
Fudger, s s	5	1	0	0	2	2	2
Fogarty, 2d b ..	4	1	1	0	5	6	1
Stanley, c.......	4	0	2	0	1	0	0
Wilson, 3d b ..	5	1	3	0	2	2	2
Perrott, l f	5	0	2	0	1	1	0
Kilroy, p	4	1	1	0	0	2	0
Total........	42	9	14	2	27	15	8

SCORE BY INNINGS.

	1	2	3	4	5	6	7	8	9	
Orkland	7	2	2	0	1	2	2	0	4	—20
Stockton	0	1	1	0	2	3	0	0	2	— 9

Earned runs—Oakland 5; Stockton 4. Three-base hits—Hill, Selna, N. O'Neill. Two-base hits—Isaacson, Stickney, Carsey, Lohman, Holliday (2), Dungan, Wilson. Sacrifice hits—C. O'Neill, Hill, Carsey (2), Fudger, Cahill, Stanley. First base on errors—Oaklands, 7; Stocktons, 4. First base on called balls—Oaklands, 10; Stocktons, 2. Left on bases—Oaklands, 9; Stacktons, 7. Struck out—By Carsey, 4; by Kilroy, 0. Double plays—O'Neill, McDonald; Isaacson, McDonald; Holliday, Fogarty; Carsey and Lohman. Passed balls—Lohman, 1. Wild pitches—Kilroy, 1. Time of game, 2 hours. Umpire, Donohue.

The California League.

GAMES PLAYED AT HOME, OAKLAND, SACRAMENTO AND STOCKTON.

THE STANDING OF THE CLUBS.

The race remains a tight one between the three leaders, although the Friscos have a good advantage. By winning Thursday's game, the Oaklands launched themselves into second place, but Sacramento is such a close third that should Oakland lose a game and Sacramento win, the Sacramentos would assume second position again. Stockton has been steadily retrograding, and still carries the target.

THE RECORD:—(to June 19, inclusive).

Clubs.	San Francisco	Oakland	Stockton	Sacramento	Games Won	Games Played	Percentage
San Francisco	....	8	8	8	24	41	.585
Oakland	8	....	10	7	25	47	.532
Stockton	4	7	....	5	16	44	.363
Sacramento	5	7	10	....	22	42	.524
Games Lost	17	22	28	20	....	....	....

Summary.	Played	Won	Lost	Percentage
San Francisco	41	24	17	.585
Oakland	47	25	22	.532
Sacramento	42	22	20	.524
Stockton	44	16	28	.363

SAN FRANCISCO vs SACRAMENTO.

FRIDAY, JUNE 13TH, AT OAKLAND.

A large attendance welcomed the Friscos and Senators at the Emery grounds and witnessed a lively hard hitting game. In fact it was the greatest batting game of the season. The Friscos presented a patched up appearance, Sweeney being on the sick list, and Young was placed in the outfield, Stevens playing first and Speer catching. Harper was in the box for Sacramento and was hit out merrily. The game opened favorably for the Senators who scored three runs on Daley's single, Buchan's error of Godar's line hit, Stapleton's and Roberts doubles and Bowman's base on balls. The Frisco's were goose egged till the fifth, when they made three on a base on balls, two singles and Levy's double. From the seventh inning Sacramento forged rapidly ahead and won easily. The feature of the day was Levy's terrific hitting. Three doubles and a triple is the best batting Rube has ever done in any one game. Speer, Hanley, Young, Godar, Stapleton and Bowman were also handy with the stick. The score:

SACRAMENTO.

	AB.	R.	BH.	SB.	PO.	A.	E.
Goodenough, c f	4	1	1	2	1	0	0
Daly, s s	6	0	1	2	0	7	2
Godar, 3d b	5	3	3	3	2	3	0
Stapleton, 1st b	4	1	2	0	16	0	0
Bowman, l f	3	3	3	1	2	3	0
Roberts, l f	5	1	1	0	1	0	0
Reitz, 2d b	5	1	1	0	3	4	1
McHale, r f	4	2	1	2	2	0	0
Harper, p	5	1	2	1	0	1	0
Farrell, c f	2	1	0	0	0	0	0
Totals	43	14	15	11	27	18	3

SAN FRANCISCO.

	AB.	R.	BH.	SB.	PO.	A.	E.
Shea, 2d b	4	0	0	0	2	2	1
Young, r f	3	2	1	0	0	0	0
Hanley, c f	5	2	3	0	4	0	1
Ebright, s s	3	1	0	0	0	9	1
Levy, l f	5	2	4	0	3	0	0
Speer, c	5	1	1	1	9	3	0
Stevens, 1st b	4	0	1	0	8	0	1
Buchan, 2d b	4	0	0	0	1	2	2
Lookabaugh, p	4	1	1	0	0	0	0
Totals	37	9	11	1	27	16	6

SCORES BY INNINGS.

	1	2	3	4	5	6	7	8	9	
Sacramento	3	0	0	0	1	3	3	2	2	—14
San Francisco	0	0	0	0	3	0	5	0	1	—9

Earned runs—San Francisco, 3; Sacramento, 2. Three-base hits—Young, Godar, Levy. Two-base hits—Stapleton, Roberts, Stevens, Levy (3), Reitz, Speer. Sacrifice hits—Hanley, Stapleton (2), Daly (2), Roberts, Reitz, Farrell. First base on errors—San Francisco, 2; Sacramento, 2. First base on called balls—San Francisco, 4; Sacramento, 4. Left on bases—San Francisco, 6; Sacramento, 5. Struck out—By Lookabaugh, 5; by Harper, 2. Hit by pitcher—Ebright. Passed balls—Speer, 2. Umpire, Sheridan.

OAKLAND vs STOCKTON.

FRIDAY JUNE 13TH, AT STOCKTON.

The above teams played a great game, the Colonels fielding being perfect while the Gas City boys were credited with only two misplays. Carsey and Kilroy pitched winning ball and were equally steady with men on bases. Stickney and McDonald were in excellent form and played a perfect game in other respective positions. The same may be said of the work of Fudger, Selna, Cahill and Isaacson. Holliday, Cahill, Dungan and Isaacson did some clever and timely hitting. Donahue's decisions were as usual unsatisfactory to the Stocktons. The score:

OAKLAND.

	AB	R	BH	SB	PO	A	E
C. O'Neill, l f	3	1	0	0	0	0	0
Stickney, 3d b	4	1	0	0	3	6	0
Dungan, r f	3	1	2	0	1	0	0
N. O'Neill, s s	4	0	0	0	6	2	0
McDonald, 2d b	4	0	0	0	9	1	0
Lohman, c	4	0	1	0	3	2	0
Hill, c f	3	0	0	0	1	0	0
Isaacson, 1st b	2	0	2	2	8	0	0
Carsey, p	3	0	0	0	1	2	0
Totals	30	3	5	2	27	13	0

STOCKTON.

	AB	R	BH	SB	PO	A	E
Cahill, r f	4	0	2	0	1	0	0
Selna, 1st b	4	0	1	0	14	0	0
Vogt, c	3	0	0	0	3	0	0
Fudger, s s	4	0	1	0	2	4	0
Fogarty, 2d b	3	1	1	0	0	5	1
Swan, l f	3	1	1	0	1	0	0
Holliday, c f	4	0	2	0	2	0	0
Wilson, 3d b	4	0	0	0	0	1	1
Kilroy, p	3	0	1	0	0	3	0
Totals	32	2	9	0	23*	13	2

*Lohman out for being hit by batted ball.

SCORE BY INNINGS.

	1	2	3	4	5	6	7	8	9	
Oakland	1	0	2	0	0	0	0	0	*	—3
Stockton	0	1	0	0	0	0	0	0	1	—2

Earned runs—Stockton, 1. Three base hits—Dungan (3) Cahill. Base on errors—Oakland, 2. Base on balls—Stockton 3, Oakland 2. Left on bases—Stockton 4, Oakland 7. Struck out—By Carsey 2, by Kilroy 3. Hit by pitcher—Dungan. Double plays—Carsey and Isaacson, Stickney and McDonald. Sacrifice hits—McDonald, Wilson. Passed balls—Vogt, 1. Umpire, Donahue.

SAN FRANCISCO vs. SACRAMENTO.

SATURDAY, JUNE 14TH, AT HAIGHT STREET.

The home aggregation and Senators played a wonderfully pretty game last Saturday, with the home team on the winning end. Farrell pitched a masterly game for Sacramento except in the fifth inning, when the 'Friscos almost annihilated him. He began in this inning very wild, giving Young and Shea their base on balls, and then Sweeney, Hanley and Ebright hit safely in rapid succession, making five runs and virtually winning the game. The fielding was of the very highest order, Reitz, Daley, Godar and Stapleton for the Sacramentos, and Hanley, Ebright and Reilly for Frisco, covering themselves with glory. The batting was sharp and heavy, Shea, Sweeney, Hanley, Ebright, Bowman and Reitz doing efficient service with the stick. The score:

SAN FRANCISCO.

	AB	R	BH	SB	PO	A	E
Shea, 2d b	4	4	3	1	0	6	1
Sweeney, 1st b	5	2	2	0	15	0	1
Hanley, c f	5	1	4	1	6	0	0
Ebright, 3d b	5	1	2	1	2	6	0
Levy, l f	5	0	0	1	0	0	0
Speer, c	5	0	0	0	1	0	2
Stevens, r f	2	0	0	0	0	0	0
Riley, s s	4	0	0	1	3	2	1
Young, p	2	2	0	0	0	3	0
Totals	37	10	11	5	27	17	5

SACRAMENTO.

	AB	R	BH	SB	PO	A	E
Goodenough, c f	3	0	0	1	2	0	0
Daly, s s	5	1	0	0	1	3	1
Godar, 3d b	4	2	0	1	0	4	0
Stapleton, 1st b	5	0	0	0	13	0	0
Bowman, c	4	2	2	1	1	1	1
Roberts, l f	3	1	0	2	2	0	0
Reitz, 2d b	5	0	2	0	5	2	0
McHale, r f	4	0	0	0	1	0	0
Farrell, p	2	0	1	0	2	0	0
Totals	35	6	5	5	27	10	2

SCORE BY INNINGS.

	1	2	3	4	5	6	7	8	9	
San Francisco	1	0	1	0	5	2	0	0	1	—10
Sacramento	2	0	2	0	1	0	0	0	1	—6

Earned runs—San Francisco, 4. Three-base hits—Hanley, Ebright, Bowman. Two-base hits—Bowman, Reitz, Shea. Sacrifice hits—Ebright, Goodenough, Daly, Levy, Bowman; McHale. First base on errors—Sacramento, 3. First base on called balls—San Francisco 5, Sacramento 7. Left on bases—San Francisco 5, Sacramento 10. Struck out—By Young, 1. Hit by pitcher—Bowman. Wild pitches—Young 1. Umpire, John Sheridan.

STOCKTON vs. OAKLAND.

SATURDAY, JUNE 14TH, AT STOCKTON.

Hapeman in this game was almost invincible, and Meegan being rapped out for fourteen hits, including three triples, it is scarcely a matter of wonderment that the Stocktons won. Not till the sixth inning, however, was the game in the Stocktonians hands, when with two out Fogarty hit safely and his example was successfully followed by Swan, Holliday, Wilson and Hapeman. This timely hitting netted four runs. Vogt gave Hapeman fine support behind the bat, and Fudger, Fogarty, Selna, Wilson and Cahill also played winning ball. The Oaklands fielding was generally faulty. Fudger's hitting was a principal feature. The score:

STOCKTON.

	AB	R	BH	SB	PO	A	E
Cahill, r f	4	0	1	0	2	0	0
Selna, 1st b	5	0	2	0	13	0	0
Vogt, c	5	0	0	0	4	2	2
Fudger, s s	4	1	2	0	2	2	1
Fogarty, 2d b	4	2	2	0	3	6	1
Swan, l f	4	1	2	0	0	0	0
Holliday, c f	4	2	1	0	1	0	0
Wilson, 3d b	4	1	1	0	1	0	0
Hapeman, p	4	0	1	0	0	2	1
Totals	38	7	13	0	27	14	6

OAKLAND.

	AB	R	BH	SB	PO	A	E
C. O'Neill, l f	3	0	0	0	3	0	1
Stickney, 3d b	4	1	1	0	3	0	0
Dungan, r f	2	1	0	2	0	0	1
N. O'Neill, s s	4	0	0	0	2	4	1
McDonald, 2d b	4	0	1	0	2	4	2
Lohman, c	3	1	0	0	3	1	1
Hill, c f	3	1	1	1	3	0	1
Isaacson, 1st b	4	0	0	0	10	0	0
Meegan, p	3	0	0	0	1	2	0
Totals	30	4	3	3	27	11	7

SCORE BY INNINGS.

	1	2	3	4	5	6	7	8	9	
Stockton	0	2	0	0	1	4	0	0	0	—7
Oakland	1	1	0	0	0	1	0	0	1	—4

Earned runs—Stockton, 3. Three-base hits—Fudger (2), Hapeman. Base on errors—Stockton, 2; Oakland 3. Base on balls—Oakland, 5. Left on bases—Stockton, 6; Oakland, 4. Struck out—By Hapeman, 3; Meegan, 2. Double plays, O'Neill, McDonald and Isaacson. Sacrifice hits—Wilson, N. O'Neill. Passed balls—Vogt, 1. Wild pitch—Hapeman. Umpire, Donahue.

SAN FRANCISCO vs OAKLAND.

SUNDAY, JUNE 15TH AT OAKLAND.

Lookabaugh's curves met with a very warm reception at Emeryville last Sunday morning, and this can be stated as a reason that the Colonels won. It was a good exhibition in which some great hitting and wonderful infield work was displayed. Oakland scored in the fourth, sixth, eight and ninth inning, getting in all twelve runs, five of which were earned. The Frisco's did not hit Cobb hard, and what "safeties" they did get were widely scattered and consequently non-productive. Stickney's hitting was a feature, and McDonald, Lohman, Cobb and Shea shared the batting honors with him. The fielding of N. O'Neill, McDonald, Reilly, Sweeney and Hanley was of a most perfect quality. The audience, which numbered about eight hundred, were very enthusiastic from an Oakland standpoint, and went into ecstacies over every hit and successful play made by the Colonels. Sheridan's decisions as usual, met with favor by players and spectators alike. The score:

OAKLAND.

	AB.	R.	BH.	SB.	PO.	A.	E.
C. O'Neill, l f	5	0	0	0	1	0	0
Stickney, 3d b	5	2	3	0	1	2	1
Dungan, r f	3	2	1	0	0	0	0
N. O'Neill, s s	4	2	0	1	4	5	1
McDonald, 2d b	5	2	2	0	9	5	1
Lohman, c	5	0	2	0	1	4	0
Hill, c f	4	2	1	0	2	0	0
Isaacson, 1st b	4	2	1	0	7	1	0
Cobb, p	4	0	2	0	2	5	1
Totals	39	12	12	1	27	22	6

SAN FRANCISCO.

	AB.	R.	BH.	SB.	PO.	A.	E.
Shea, 2d b	4	1	2	0	3	3	2
Sweeney, 1st b	4	0	0	0	12	0	0
Hanley, c f	4	0	1	0	4	0	0
Ebright, s s	4	0	1	0	2	2	1
Levy, l f	3	0	1	0	1	0	0
Speer, r f	4	0	1	0	1	0	0
Stevens, c	4	0	1	0	3	1	0
Reilley, 3d b	4	0	0	0	1	2	1
Lookabaugh, p	3	1	0	0	0	3	0
Totals	34	2	7	0	27	11	4

SCORE BY INNINGS.

	1	2	3	4	5	6	7	8	9	
Oakland	0	0	0	2	0	5	0	3	2	—12
San Francisco	0	0	0	0	0	1	0	1	0	—2

Earned runs—Oakland, 5. Three-base hits—Hill, Dungan. Two-base hits—Stickney, McDonald. Sacrifice hits—McDonald (2), Isaacson. First-base on errors—Oakland, 2; San Francisco, 5. First base on called balls—Oakland, 5. Left on bases—Oakland, 4; San Francisco, 6. Struck out—By Cobb, 2; by Lookabaugh, 1. Hit by pitcher—Levy. Double plays—N. O'Neill, McDonald and Isaacson; Cobb, McDonald and Isaacson. Passed balls—Lohman, Stevens, 2. Wild pitches—Lookabaugh, 1. Umpire, John Sheridan.

SAN FRANCISCO vs. OAKLAND.

SUNDAY, JUNE 15TH, AT HAIGHT STREET.

The Colonels evidently think they can't have too much of a good thing, for in the afternoon, at the Haight Street grounds, in presence of some six thousand Frisco constituents, they just took the home team into camp as readily as they did on their own grounds in the morning. Oakland is largely indebted to young Mr. Carsey for their victory. He certainly pitched a most masterly game, Frisco's six hits being distributed through five innings. The fourth inning was the only one in which the home team scored, and in that they just earned one little run. Young was hit considerably harder than his more youthful adversary, the third inning being a veritable Waterloo for him. Carsey led off with a pretty single to center, and C. O'Neill did likewise. Stickney's hit forced O'Neill, but Dungan's safety filled the bases again. Then N. O'Neill, for his patience, was awarded first base on balls, and this forced Carsey across the plate; Stickney and Dungan scoring on McDonald's hit, and "Sir" Norris coming home on Lohman's safe drive past third. This gave Oakland four runs and the game.

The fielding honors go to Josh Reilly, just graduated from the amateur ranks. Reilly's playing would do credit to some of the greatest short-stops in the business; in fact, nothing was hit anywhere near him but what he captured with the ease and grace of a most finished player. He received a most hearty ovation for his marvellous exhibition. Shea, Sweeney, Ebright, Stickney, McDonald and N. O'Neill also played a good fielding game. At the bat Dungan, McDonald, Carsey and Levy excelled. The score:

OAKLAND.

	AB.	R.	BH.	SB.	PO.	A.	E.
C. O'Neill, l f	3	0	1	0	0	0	0
Stickney, 3d b	5	1	0	1	3	2	1
Dungan, r f	4	1	3	0	1	0	0
N. O'Neill, s s	4	1	1	0	1	7	0
McDonald, 2d b	4	1	2	0	7	1	1
Lohman, c	4	0	1	0	7	2	1
Hill, c f	4	0	0	0	0	0	0
Isaacson, 1st b	3	0	1	0	7	0	0
Carsey, p	4	1	2	2	1	4	0
Totals	35	5	11	3	27	16	3

SAN FRANCISCO.

	AB.	R.	BH.	SB.	PO.	A.	E.
Shea, 2d b	3	0	0	0	1	[illegible]	[illegible]
Sweeney, 1st b	4	0	1	0	12	[illegible]	[illegible]
Hanley, c f	3	0	1	0	1	[illegible]	[illegible]
Ebright, 3d b	4	1	1	0	1	[illegible]	[illegible]
Levy, l f	4	0	2	0	0	[illegible]	[illegible]
Speer, c	4	0	0	0	2	[illegible]	[illegible]
Stevens, r f	2	0	0	0	2	[illegible]	[illegible]
Riley, s s	4	0	1	0	5	[illegible]	[illegible]
Young, p	2	0	0	0	0	[illegible]	[illegible]
Totals	30	1	6	0	24	[illegible]	[illegible]

SCORE BY INNINGS.

	1	2	3	4	5	6	7	8	9	
Oakland	0	0	4	0	1	0	0	0	[illegible]	[illegible]
San Francisco	0	0	0	1	0	0	0	0	[illegible]	[illegible]

Earned runs—Oakland 3; San Francisco 1. Three-base hit—McDonald. Two-base hit—Ebright. Sacrifice hits—N. O'Neill, Stickney, Young, Dungan. First base on errors—Oakland 2; San Francisco 1. First base on called balls—Oakland 5; San Francisco 3. Left on bases—Oakland 11; San Francisco 7. Struck out—By Carsey, 7; by Young, 2. Hit by pitcher—Shea. Passed balls—Lohman 1; Speer 1. Wild pitches—Carsey, Young. Umpire, Sheridan.

STOCKTON vs. SACRAMENTO.

SUNDAY, JUNE 15TH, AT STOCKTON.

Eight innings was the "game" at Stockton last Sunday morning to enable the teams to catch the Sacramento train. But eight innings was just sufficient to give the Gas City boys eight runs, and as the Senators couldn't make but one-quarter of that number, the Stocktons won with apparent ease. Perrott pitched another good game, being very steady and effective. Chase was hit harder, nine safeties, including a triple and two doubles being secured off him. He also gave four men first on balls. Selna was not on hand and Smith played first base in good form. The infields of both teams put up a very pretty game. Holliday, Fudger, Wilson and Perrott were especially strong at the bat. The score:

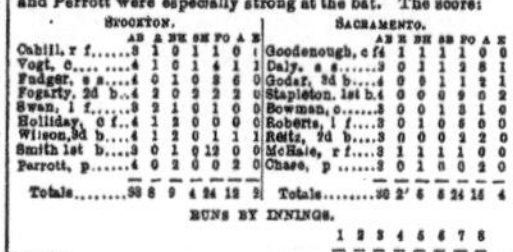

STOCKTON.

	AB	R	BH	SB	PO	A	E
Cahill, r f	3	1	0	1	1	0	0
Vogt, c	4	1	0	1	4	1	1
Fudger, s s	4	0	1	0	3	6	0
Fogarty, 2d b	4	2	0	2	2	2	0
Swan, l f	3	2	1	0	1	0	0
Holliday, c f	4	1	2	0	0	0	0
Wilson, 3d b	4	1	2	0	1	1	1
Smith 1st b	3	0	1	0	12	0	0
Perrott, p	4	0	2	0	0	2	0
Totals	33	8	9	4	24	12	2

SACRAMENTO.

	AB	R	BH	SB	PO	A	E
Goodenough, c f	4	1	1	[illegible]	[illegible]	[illegible]	[illegible]
Daly, s s	3	0	1	1	2	[illegible]	[illegible]
Godar, 3d b	4	0	0	1	1	[illegible]	[illegible]
Stapleton, 1st b	4	0	0	0	9	[illegible]	[illegible]
Bowman, c	3	0	0	1	3	[illegible]	[illegible]
Roberts, l f	3	0	1	0	6	[illegible]	[illegible]
Reitz, 2d b	3	0	0	0	2	[illegible]	[illegible]
McHale, r f	3	1	1	1	1	[illegible]	[illegible]
Chase, p	3	0	1	0	0	[illegible]	[illegible]
Totals	30	2	5	5	24	[illegible]	[illegible]

RUNS BY INNINGS.

	1	2	3	4	5	6	7	8	
Stockton	0	1	0	1	0	0	[illegible]	[illegible]	[illegible]
Sacramento	0	0	1	0	0	0	[illegible]	[illegible]	[illegible]

Earned runs—Stockton 1, Sacramento 1. Three-base hits—Holliday. Two-base hits—Fudger, Perrott. Base on errors—Stockton 4, Sacramento 1. Base on balls—Stockton 3, Sacramento 1. Left on bases—Stockton 4, Sacramento 5. Struck out—By Perrott 3; by Chase, 3. Double plays—Reitz and Daly. Bowman and Godar. Sacrifice hits—Holliday, Cahill, Smith. Umpire—Donahue.

SACRAMENTO vs. STOCKTON.

SUNDAY, JUNE 15TH, AT SACRAMENTO.

The Senators somewhat evened up matters in the afternoon game with the Stocktons, but not without a hard struggle. The game was not called till 4 o'clock, and the sun being low and blazing full in the fielders faces will serve as an excellent excuse for some of the errors made. Harper and Kilroy were the opposing pitchers, and barring their wildness, both did nice work. Stapleton and Daly were indisposed, Bowman playing first and Daly going to right with Farrell at short. Several pretty plays were made, but the hitting was light. Goodenough's work on the paths was a feature. The score:

SACRAMENTO.

	AB	R	BH	SB	PO	A	E
Goodenough, c f	4	3	1	3	2	0	0
Daly, r f	5	0	1	0	2	0	2
Godar, 3d b	3	0	0	1	0	1	0
Farrell, s s	3	0	0	0	0	0	0
Bowman, 1st b	5	1	1	0	6	1	0
Roberts, l f	4	1	1	2	1	0	1
Reitz, 2d b	5	1	0	1	1	3	0
McHale, c	4	0	1	1	14	1	1
Harper, p	4	1	1	0	1	0	0
Totals	37	7	5	8	27	6	4

STOCKTON.

	AB	R	BH	SB	PO	A	E
Cahill, r f	5	1	2	2	1	[illegible]	[illegible]
Vogt, c	5	0	2	1	8	[illegible]	[illegible]
Fudger, s s	5	0	1	1	2	[illegible]	[illegible]
Fogarty, 2d b	3	1	0	0	4	[illegible]	[illegible]
Swan, l f	3	1	0	0	0	[illegible]	[illegible]
Holliday, c f	4	1	0	0	2	[illegible]	[illegible]
Wilson, 3d b	4	0	0	0	2	[illegible]	[illegible]
Smith, 1st b	4	1	1	0	8	[illegible]	[illegible]
Kilroy, p	4	1	1	0	0	[illegible]	[illegible]
Totals	37	6	7	4	27	[illegible]	[illegible]

SCORE BY INNINGS.

	1	2	3	4	5	6	7	8	9	
Sacramento	[illegible]	[illegible]	[illegible]	[illegible]	[illegible]	[illegible]	[illegible]	[illegible]	[illegible]	—7
Stockton	[illegible]	[illegible]	[illegible]	[illegible]	[illegible]	[illegible]	[illegible]	[illegible]	[illegible]	—6

Earned runs—Sacramento 1, Stockton 1. Three-base hits—Daly. Two-base hit—Bowman. Sacrifice hit—Harper. First base on errors—Sacramento 6, Stockton 2. First base on called balls—Sacramento 8, Stockton 4. Left on bases—Sacramento 13, Stockton 9. Struck out—By Harper, 12; by Kilroy, 9. Hit by pitcher—Harper, Swan. Passed balls—Vogt. Wild pitches—Harper (3). Umpire, Donahue.

The Amateurs.

Games Played by the California Amateur League.

The Amateur race is still widely spread out with the Santa Rosa boys having quite a big lead. But as less than one-third of the schedule of games has been completed, the teams at present far down on the list need not feel too badly discouraged, as there is ample opportunity for them to retrieve their losses. The Reports are second and slightly in advance of Warrens "Young Giants." Vallejo is fourth, the Burlingtons fifth, and the Allens are still "in the hole." The record (to date):

Clubs.	Will & Fincks	E. T. Allens	Report	Burlington	Vallejo	Santa Rosa	Games Won	Games Played	Percentage
Will & Fincks	....	3	....	1	2	....	6	9	.666
E. T. Allens	....	....	1	1	....	....	2	11	.181
Reports	2	....	....	2	3	....	7	10	.700
Burlingtons	....	2	....	....	1	....	3	10	.300
Vallejos	....	1	....	1	....	2	4	11	.363
Santa Rosa	1	3	2	2	1	....	9	11	.818
Games Lost	3	9	3	7	7	2	....	....	....

Summary.	Played.	Won.	Lost.	Per C't.
Santa Rosa	11	9	2	.818
Will & Finck	10	7	3	.700
Reports	9	6	3	.666
Vallejo	11	4	7	.363
E. T. Allens	10	3	7	.300
Burlingtons	11	2	9	.181

E. T. ALLENS vs. WILL & FINCKS.

SUNDAY, JUNE 15TH, AT HAIGHT STREET.

It was the "Sports" game up to the sixth inning when the "Giants" did some clever stick work and with the assistance of a few costly errors on the part of the Allens seven runs came in, closing up the score nine to ten. From that inning on it was a great battle in which the "Giants" displayed superior team work and hitting abilities. In the eighth they got three men over the plate. L. Delmas being safe on McDonalds error, Leveque sacrificed him to second and Howells drive to center scored him. Frank Delmas then hit to Evatt who promptly retired the little pitcher at second but Frank scored on Strands hit to left. Conway collided with Lewis at first, who fairly had him out, but being knocked insensible Lewis dropped the ball and Strand scored. Billings ended the inning on his fly out to McCarthy. The Allens failed to score in the seventh, eighth or ninth and the game went to the Fincks. The fielding was at times really brilliant, Tillson F., and L. Delmas, Buckley, Beckett, Geishakher Stanley and McCarthy playing like veterans. Jim Cusick led in hitting having two beautiful doubles and a sacrifice to his credit. Evatt, Lewis, Buckley, Tillson and Howell also did heavy stick work. McConvilles umpiring was not satisfactory. The score:

WILL & FINKS.

	AB.	R.	BH.	SB.	PO.	A.	E.
F. Delmas, 1st b	6	1	0	1	10	0	0
Strand, l f	3	2	1	2	0	1	0
Conway, 2d b	5	0	0	0	3	3	2
Billings, c	5	2	0	0	9	2	1
Cusick, r f	4	1	2	1	2	0	0
Tillson, s s	3	2	2	1	2	4	0
L. Delmas, 3d b	4	2	0	0	1	7	1
Leveque, c f	4	1	1	1	0	0	0
Howell, p	3	1	2	0	0	0	0
Totals	37	12	8	6	27	17	5

E. T. ALLENS.

	AB.	R.	BH.	SB.	PO.	A.	E.
Geishaker, s s	3	3	0	1	2	4	1
Evatt, 3d b	4	2	2	1	4	3	2
Lewis, 1st b	5	1	2	1	5	0	1
Buckley, 2d b	5	1	2	0	3	1	0
Tribou, c f	5	0	1	0	1	0	1
Stanley, c	5	1	0	1	6	2	1
Beckett, r f	3	0	1	0	1	1	0
McCarthy, l f	4	1	0	1	2	0	0
McDonald, p	4	1	0	0	0	4	0
Totals	38	10	8	5	24	15	6

SCORES BY INNINGS.

	1	2	3	4	5	6	7	8	9	
Will & Finks	0	1	0	1	0	7	0	3	*	12
Allens	3	0	1	0	1	5	0	0	0	10

Earned runs—E. T. Allens, 1; Will & Fincks, 2. Two-base hits—Evatt, Cusick (2). Sacrifice hits—Cusick, Strand, Evatt, Tribou, Leveque. First base on errors—Allens, 4; Fincks, 3. First base on called balls—Allens, 3; Fincks, 4. Left on bases—Allens, 2; Fincks, 3. Struck out—By McDonald, 7; by Howell, 6. Hit by pitcher—McDonald, L. Delmas. Double plays—Beckett and Geishaker. Passed balls—Stanley, 1; Billings, 2. Wild pitch—McDonald, 1. Time of game—Two hours. Umpire, McConville.

VALLEJO vs SANTA ROSA.

SUNDAY, JUNE 15, AT VALLEJO.

The Vallejo's and Santa Rosa's played an eleven inning game last Sunday which terminated in favor of the "Marines." In the eighth inning Vallejo forged ahead, making three runs, only to be overtaken and tied in the ninth by Santa Rosa, making the same number. In the eleventh, however, Vallejo settled it, getting two men across the plate, while the Sonoma boys just tallied once. The game, although exciting, was not a good one in any respect, the fielding being miserable and the batting light. Baltz was very effective, striking out sixteen and allowing but three hits, Tufts was in the box for Santa Rosa, and the youngster did fairly well. Callen played center and erred on every chance offered. Maguire made his his first appearance with the "Marines" and acquitted himself creditably. The prominent features of the game were the hard hitting of Farrell McQuire and Lee, and the fielding of Wise, Stultz, Arlett, Cook, Gimmel, Lee and McQuire.

Gimmel, Stultz and Farrell also did some clever and speedy base-running. The score:

VALLEJOS.

	AB.	R.	BH.	SB.	PO.	A.	E.
McGuire, s s	6	1	2	0	4	0	1
Hughes, 3d b	5	2	0	0	2	1	1
Farrell, c	6	3	3	3	1	6	0
Wise c f	5	0	0	0	6	0	1
Stanford, l f	5	1	0	1	1	0	0
Lee, 2d b	4	0	2	1	10	1	1
Mair, 1st b	4	0	0	0	8	1	2
Broderick, r f	5	0	0	0	1	0	1
Balz, p	4	0	1	0	0	3	1
Totals	44	7	8	5	33	12	8

SANTA ROSAS.

	AB.	R.	BH.	SB.	PO.	A.	E.
Gimmell, l f	4	2	1	4	2	0	0
Cook, 3d b	5	1	0	1	4	1	1
Hulen, 2d b	4	1	1	1	3	3	3
Pace, c	5	0	0	0	8	3	1
Arlett, s s	5	0	0	0	3	6	2
Stultz, 1st b	5	0	1	3	12	0	0
Brown, r f	5	0	0	0	1	2	0
Callen, c f	4	0	0	2	0	0	3
Tufts, p	3	2	0	1	0	2	3
Totals	39	6	3	12	33	17	13

SCORE BY INNINGS.

	1	2	3	4	5	6	7	8	9	10	11	
Vallejos	[illegible]	[illegible]	[illegible]	[illegible]	[illegible]	[illegible]	[illegible]	[illegible]	[illegible]	[illegible]	[illegible]	7
Santa Rosas	[illegible]	[illegible]	[illegible]	[illegible]	[illegible]	[illegible]	[illegible]	[illegible]	[illegible]	[illegible]	[illegible]	6

Earned runs—Vallejo 2. Three-base hit—Farrell. Two-base hit—Farrell. First base on errors—Santa Rosa 5; Vallejo 10. First base on called balls—Santa Rosa 3; Vallejo 4. Left on bases—Santa Rosa 3; Vallejo 11. Struck out—By Balsz 16; by Tufts 3. Hit by pitched ball—Lee. Wild pitch—Balsz 1. Passed balls—Farrell 2; Pace 3. Double plays—Brown and Cook, McGuire (unassisted). Umpire, Cate.

The Pacific Northwest League.

PORTLAND vs. TACOMA.

SUNDAY, JUNE 15TH AT PORTLAND.

In this game Portland got there in great shape. Their victory is principally due to some excellent stick work in the first inning. It happened this way. Howard took first on balls, and J. Parrott's line drive scored Howard; a passed ball and error placed Parrott at third, and then Cooney lifted one to short right, Parrott scoring. Cahill hit to short, but McCabe fumbled, and Cooney was safe at second with Cahill at first. "Old man Perrier" scored both men on his double to deep right. Four runs and a brilliant beginning. Portland added one in the second and another in the seventh, while Tacoma only tallied one in each, the first, fourth and ninth, the game ending six to three in favor of the Web-feet. The features were the hard hitting of Cooney, Parrott, Perrier and Hoffman, and the general brilliant fielding of the Portlands. The score:

PORTLANDS.

	AB.	R.	BH.	SB.	PO.	A.	E.
Buchtel, s s	5	1	1	0	0	7	0
Howard, cf	4	1	0	0	2	0	0
W. Parrott, 3b	5	2	2	0	1	2	0
Cooney, r f	4	1	2	0	0	0	0
Cahill, 2b	5	1	0	0	3	3	1
Perrier, 1b	3	0	2	0	16	0	0
T. Parrott, p	4	0	0	0	0	8	0
McCarthy, lf	3	0	0	0	2	0	0
Levy, c	3	0	1	0	3	2	0
Total	36	6	8	0	27	17	1

TACOMA.

	AB.	R.	BH.	SB.	PO.	A.	E.
Mannassau, cf	3	1	0	0	0	0	0
Hoffman, l f	5	0	3	0	2	0	0
McCabe, 2b	4	0	1	1	2	2	1
Strouthers, 1b	4	0	1	0	14	0	0
Pope, 3b	4	1	1	0	1	3	1
Chrisman, rf	3	0	0	1	0	0	0
Ward, c	4	0	0	0	4	3	1
Brittain, ss	4	1	1	0	4	2	1
March, p	4	0	0	1	0	3	1
Totals	35	3	7	3	27	13	5

SCORE BY INNINGS.

	1	2	3	4	5	6	7	8	9	
Portlands	4	1	0	0	0	0	1	0	0	6
Tacomas	1	0	0	1	0	0	0	0	1	3

Earned runs—Tacoma 1. Two-base hits—Buchtel, W. Parrott, Cooney, Perrier, Hoffman 2, Strouthers. Three-base hits—Pope, Brittain. Bases stolen—Cooney, Cahill, Mannasau. Bases on called balls—Off Parrott 3, off March, 3. Hit by pitched balls—Cooney, Levy. Struck out—By March 5, by Parrott 4. Passed balls—Levy 1, Ward 1. Wild pitches—Parrott 2, March 2. Time of game—One hour forty-five minutes. Umpire—Ben. F. Young.

Amateur Short Hits.

Santa Rosa still leads.

Pace is a very accurate thrower.

McCarthy is fielding in fine form.

The Allens missed Reilly Sunday.

The Allens are "jonahed" somewhere.

Santa Rosa has lost two games to Vallejo.

"Blondie" Callen is not a success as a fielder.

Tribou has been re-signed by manager Keller.

The Burlingtons play at Santa Rosa to-morrow.

Jim Cusick's two doubles Sunday were "corkers".

Frank Delmas has fallen off considerably in his hitting.

The Suisuns defeated the Vacavilles last Sunday. Score, 11 to 2.

The "Young Giants" are fast crowding the Reports for second place,

Cate is the most successful umpire the Amateur League has ever had.

Billy Gimmel continues playing his usual brilliant game for Santa Rosa.

Strand's throwing would put many of the professional fielders in the shade.

Jimmy Geishaker was himself last Sunday, and put up a first class game at short.

The Vallejo "Marines" will meet Warrens "Young Giants" at the Haight St. Grounds, Sunday.

The "pony battery" Howell and Billings have been doing some exceptional good work this season.

Jack Cook is Santa Rosa's third baseman now and Stulz will be kept in his proper position—first base.

The players of the Report and Burlington teams were highly interested in the Allen—Finck game last Sunday.

Reed Beckett, the latest addition to the Allen team is a fast fielder and thrower. His double play Sunday proved his value to the team,

The Santa Rosas did not annihilate Baltz last Sunday as they expected. Three little hits by such a heavy team of hitters as the Santa Rosas claim to be is a very poor showing for them, but puts Baltz's stock up at a high standard.

If Cusick continues the way he has been hitting for the last two games he played, he will be at the head of the list when the season closes.

The Allens have sustained an irreparable loss in Josh Reilly going to the San Franciscos. Reilly was the best player in the team and last Sunday his work at the bat was greatly missed. Besides he was a "star" coacher and when the team was in a hole there was no player who could "jolly them up" better than he.

Left field is the position that is being played almost to perfection in the Amateur League. The records of Gimmel, McCarthy, Sharp, Forster and Strand will verify this statement, and it is quite probable that the Amateurs' averages will bear a very favorable comparison with that of the more experienced professionals.

Jack McConville did not have a very sociable time umpiring last Sunday mornings game. He certainly failed to command the respect the autocrat of the field is supposed to receive and in fact several of the Fincks were very much inclined to "josh" his decisions. Fines were certainly in order, and if McConville wishes to preserve decorum he must not be too delicate in placing plasters where they are deserved.

Jim Corbett, the "nimble professor," has a young brother named Joe who, of all promising youngsters, must be put down as a "comer." Joe has been covering second base in such a clever style for a St. Mary's College team, that his youthful breast is now adorned with a handsome gold medal presented by some admiring collegians. The other day Jim had the youngster out to the Olympic Club grounds, and with some others, indulged in a little practice. After Jim had wearied himself pitching all kind of balls, only to be batted all over the lot by the little fellow, he said: "Why, I was never 'in it at all' with the 'two-year-old"; you know I was no slouch of a player myself, but he can double discount me playing now."

We have noticed that the greater part of the errors made by the amateurs are attributable to wild throwing. This is a fault that could easily be remedied. The amateurs like the professionals know that nothing aside from hard hitting brings them more favorably to the notice of managers, press and spectators than clever sharp fielding. Consequently they have become imbued with a desire to figure in rapid and double plays as often as the barest possibility will permit. In this respect they frequently overreach their abilities, for without taking time to guage the distance they must throw, and the desperate chances they are taking to make the play effective, they just bang the ball anywhere to get it out of their hands and the result is, that most generally every men on bases gets home or at least advances a bag. An inning or two of this kind of work is sure to rattle any team, no matter how capable they are in other departments of the game, and defeat is almost inevitable.

The Will & Fincks, or as they have been more familiarly called Warrens "Young Giants", as now constituted, are a team that ought to do some great battling for the pennant. In the Amateur League, they are what the Sacramentos are to the big League. In fact their playing, bearing in mind that they are amateurs, very forcibly reminds one of the gild-edged work of the Senatorial aggregation. Warren from quite an extended experience knows a good player when he sees him, and is always on the alert to strengthen his team in any weak spot. His team to-day is undoubtedly the most formidable in every respect in the League. Howell has proven himself equally as efficient in the box as several pitchers many years his senior, and Billings has been giving him the most encouraging support. The infield is a very clever one; the two Delmas brothers on first and third and Charley Tillson at short having played together for the past few seasons know how to play their positions to the best possible advantage. With Conway they are "four of a kind" and hard to beat. Then the outfield is the most evenly balanced one ever seen on a amateur diamond. Strand, Leveque and Cusick are very fast fielders and accurate throwers. In hitting and base running they will undoubtedly lead the League as Frank Delmas, Cusick, Strand, Leveque. Billings and Tillson are exceptionally strong at the bat. They will probably excel in base running also, Tillson, Leveque, Howell, Strand and Cusick each having already made an enviable reputation in this department. All together they are a very strong team and ought to capture almost "everything in sight."

SCHEDULE OF GAMES

—OF THE—

CALIFORNIA Base Ball League,

SEASON 1890.

June 21st to June 28th Inclusive

AT SAN FRANCISCO.

JUNE 21 .... San Francisco vs. Stockton
JUNE 22 .... San Francisco vs. Sacramento
JUNE 25 .... San Francisco vs. Sacramento
JUNE 28 .... Oakland vs. Sacramento

AT SACRAMENTO.

JUNE 21 .... Sacramento vs. Oakland

AT OAKLAND.

JUNE 27 .... Oakland vs. Sacramento

AT STOCKTON.

JUNE 22 .... Stockton vs. Oakland
JUNE 27 .... Stockton vs. San Francisco
JUNE 28 .... Stockton vs. San Francisco

Official Schedule California Amateur League.

AT HAIGHT STREET GROUNDS.

JUNE 22 .... Will and Fincks vs. Vallejos

AT VALLEJO.

JUNE 22 .... E. T. Allens vs. Daily Reports

AT SANTA ROSA.

JUNE 22 .... Burlingtons vs. Santa Rosa

The official schedule of the California Base Ball League and Amateur League will be published weekly in this space.

ATHLETICS.

Athletic Sports and Other Pastimes.

EDITED BY ARTHIPPUS,

SUMMARY.

A large number of novices are preparing themselves for the coming handicap out door meeting of the Olympic Athletic Club, which will be held at the new grounds on Friday, July 4th. The wheelmen are bestirring themselves and are getting into good condition for their coming two-day tournament. Owing to the liberal prizes which will be offered by the Fourth of July Regatta Committee several of the local professional oarsmen have gone into training and will enter the professional single shell races. Several cross country runs are on the tapis and a boom in that line of sport may be expected.

AT THE OARS.

Sunday last was a good day for the oarsmen and many of them were out in their shells. There was an unusual activity in the neighborhood of Long Bridge, consequent upon the favorable condition of the tide.

The South End Rowing Club has elected the following officers for the ensuing term of one year: J. J. McCarthy, President; J. Traynor, Financial Secretary; W. Richards, Recording Secretary; A. J. Melletz, Treasurer; C Burns, D. Bassett and P. Reardon, trustees. The initiation fee has been reduced to $1, and the monthly dues to 50 cts. Hereafter the club will meet twice a month.

Stokes of the Pioneer Rowing Club is in good condition and his club will expect him to win the amateur shell championship on the 4th of July. A good many of the pioneer scullers were out for practice spins on Sunday.

The amateur crew of the Ariel Club are determined to show up in great shape at the regatta.

The members of the Dolphin Club are losing no time and were out in full force on Sunday.

The oarsmen are in a happy mood because John T Sullivan has been elected Chairman of the Fourth of July Regatta Committee. He is the right man in the right place and will see that the lovers of aqtatic sports get all that is coming to them.

The Lurline Club will be represented by the following crew at the coming regatta: F. H. Taufenbach, bow; J. Ringen, forward waist; P. Gay, after waist; W. Schwartz, stroke; G. Gay, coxswain. Several of the boys were on the bay on Sunday and many of them exercise daily.

About $1,200 will be spent for prizes by the Regatta Committee and this fact alone will help to draw out some of the crack oarsmen who have remained on the shelf for a year or so. The programme will be made out about the middle of next week. It is almost an assured fact that Peterson, Henchman (of Stockton) Growney, Griffin, Van Gulphin, Stokes, Doherty and Deane, (of Stockton) will all enter for the professional events. Such an entry list would make the single shell race highly interesting.

Edward Hanlan has returned to Toronto. He will row in the Duluth regatta on July 22 to 26.

Psotta, the American amateur champion oarsman should win the diamond sculls at the Royal Henley Regatta on the Thames, England, this year. Guy Nicholls, the English amateur champion will not compete in the race. H. Gardner, the stroke of the Cambridge, will row in the race.

The Aldermen of Boston, Mass., have decided on the following programme for the annual professional and amateur rowing regatta on the Charles river. Here it is: 1st race—For professional scullers, 3 miles. 1st prize, $175; 2nd, $100; 3rd, $75. 2nd race—For local professional scullers, 3 miles. 1st prize, $75; 2nd, $50; 3rd, $25. 3rd race—For amateur junior scullers, 3 miles. 1st prize, City of Boston Cup, value $50; 2nd, gold medal, value $25. 4th race—For eight oared shells, amateurs, 1½ miles, straightaway. 1st prize, nine gold medals and flag, value $125; 2nd, nine silver medals, value, $75 5th race—For four oared working boats, professional, 3 miles. 1st prize, $200; 2nd, $100; 3rd, $50. Total value of prizes, $1,125. The entries are free and may be made personally or by letter at the office of the clerk of committees, at the City Hall, until 2 P. M. of July 2, after which time none will be received. The Committee for the city is composed of Aldermen Wooley, Cove and Leary, and Councilmen Burlen, Shaw, Sprague, Pierce, Harrison, Sullivan, Clark and Robinson.

RUNNERS, WALKERS, JUMPERS, ETC.

The athletes do not seem to be taking much interest in the coming field games of the O. A. C., announced to come off on July 4th. Certainly none of the running or walking records will be broken, for the majority of the crack athletes have gone out of training, completely worn out by their exertions trying to get into good trim for the late championship meeting. Several Olympic novices, however, will make their appearances, and it will be interesting to watch their performances.

Kortick, Jellineak, Wheelan, Foster and Crane, all new men, will enter, and good records may be expected from them. Without exception, they are all promising sprinters, and by next year may be able to make bids for championship honors.

Steve Casady has been feeling very pleased since May 30th, and he expects to do some record breaking next year. With proper handling he should leave 50 seconds in the shade for the quarter.

Cooley feels disgusted because of his defeat by Hill in the mile. It is doubtful if he could down the U. C. man in a mile or under, but it is dollars to cents that he could lead Hill all the way from one and a half miles up.

Casady, of the Alpine Club, will continue to practice distance running, and as he is quite a novice compared with Cooley, the young Englishman should improve considerably during the next couple of months.

With a liberal handicap, A. Cook should make it interesting for Coffin in a mile walk. He is an improving man both in style and speed, and may stand a fair chance for a medal on July 4th.

V. P. White, of the California Athletic Club, and W. M. Schwartz, of the Lurline Club, will wrestle a mixed match, catch-as-catch-can and Græco-Roman, before the former club some night in July for a $25 medal.

Leader John Hammersmith, of the Olympic Club, has leased the Grand Opera House for September 3d, on which date the grandest gymnastic exhibition ever witnessed in San Francisco will be given All the prominent athletes in the club will be billed to appear.

It is said that Harry M. Johnson, the professional sprinter, has left town.

There will be two amateur running races at the Scottish Thistle Club picnic at Shell Mound Park, Berkeley, on July 4th, under the auspices of the P C A A A. Three medals, costing respectfully $35, $25 and $15 will be given for each race. The distances will be five laps, or about half a mile, and two laps, or about a fifth of a mile. Several of the leading amateur runners will compete.

The Alpine Club members will take a long walk on Sunday July 6. The journey will be from San Mateo to this city. The athletes will leave on the first train for San Mateo where they will eat lunch. After walking around town for an hour or so they will start for San Francisco, the distance being 21 miles. The pace will be a slow walk averaging about three and a half miles a hour, and Captain John D. Garrison will insist that no sparting shall take place at the close of the walk. The tramp is intended as a pleasure trip as well as an exercise, by which the muscles of the body may be hardened without violent effort.

All associate members of the Pacific Coast Amateur Athletic Association are invited to take part. All information of the walk can be obtained from Captain John D. Harrison, 706 Powell Street. The following men have signified their intention of starting: A Cooke, R Lettringer, J R Collins, J D Garrison (captain) P N Gafney, R Staats, D Vultee, Ed. Steinway, Charles Armbruster, George W Armbruster, A Davis, A M King, F E Holland, W Bowen, H C Casidy, P J Sheedy, A Choynski, E P Levy, C W Meyer, W F Vollmer and T H McCarthy. Judging from the interest taken in the affair, which is an original introduction among the athletic clubs on the Pacific Coast, it is safe to say that fifty athletes will undertake the journey.

About a dozen members of the Alpine Amateur Athletic Club crossed over to Sausalito on Sunday last, where they enjoyed their third cross country run from Jackson's Villa. The run, which was under the direction of Captain John D. Garrison, was to Lime Point and return. All the starters had been over the course before and were familiar with its ins and outs. The outward run was very slow, Garrison arriving at the Fog Station first, with Meyer second and Vollmer third, the rest being close up. After resting five minutes the boys started homeward, Captain Garrison allowing his club mates a start of about 300 yards. The run in was fast, but Garrison, despite his handicap, got home first by a couple of feet in 49 minutes, Meyer was second, Vollmer third, Choynski fourth and King fifth. The following men started: Captain J. D. Garrison, C. W. Meyer, A. M. King, G. H. Simmonds, R. C Staats, Ed Steinway, E. Steinway, Jr., A. Choynski, W. F. Vollmer, C. H. Larkey. After enjoying a refreshing dip in the briny ocean, the tired athletes sat down to a toothsome repast which had been specially prepared for them by Mrs. Ross Jackson. The club photographer, Ed Steinway, took an excellent photograph of the men in their running costumes.

The victorious Olympic team which captured the pennant on May 30th, will shortly hold a banquet. Songs, recitations, and speeches will follow the feast. The exercises will probably close with a grand wine rub down.

An excellent photograph of the O A C championship team was recently taken at the Elite Photograph Gallery. All the men who competed for the O A C in the games on May 30th are included in the group.

M. C. Giry, the ex-President of the Alpine Club, is now clerking at the I X L on Market street.

We understand that Captain G. W. Jordan, the ex-delegate of the O A C to the P C A A A wrote to the Directors of his club informing them if the Alpine Club was allowed to remain in the P C A A A he would resign as a delegate, The Directors accepted his resignation.

The following are the winners of the Olympic athletic games held at St. Louis, on June 7th:

One hundred yard run, scratch—A J Helmuth, O A C, won; time, 10 2-5secs.

One hundred yard run, handicap—L H Aftenkemp, Belleville A C won; time, 19 4 5secs.

One mile walk—H A Hentricks, M A A C, scratch, won in 7min 42secs.

Pole vaulting—Herman Wieneke, M A A C, scratch, broke the Western Association record in a vault of 10ft.

Four hundred and forty yard run—Won by Otto Wareskopsy in 53secs.

The 16-pound hammer was thrown 87ft 4in by Miles Mc Donough, of the Shamrocks, and he won.

The 220 yard walk for members were taken by Phil Hartman in 25 3-5secs.

The one mile run was won by Gus Wagner, Belleville A C, 60yds, in 4min 47secs.

George P. Powell, the Western champion, won the high jump with 5ft 10in. St. Louis will send two teams to the Detroit championships.

During the games of the Interscholastic Association on Holmes' Field, Cambridge, Mass., June 7th, W. C. Downes, the Harvard medium distance runner, made an attempt to excel the best time ever made on that track for half a mile. He had A. M. White, '92, for pacemaker, and succeeded in his effort, breasting the tape in 1min 57 2-5s. The best previous record for the track was 1min 59⅕secs, made by G. P. Coggeshall, '88, in the year '88.

More than three thousand persons were present at the open games of the New York AthleticClub, held at their beautiful country home at Travers Island, on Long Island Sound, on Saturday afternoon, June 7. It was also "ladies day" with the club, and therefore there was even a larger representation of the fair relatives and friends of the members than customary at the sports of this influential organization. Better weather could not have been desired by those bent upon having an enjoyable outing, but the fresh wind that was so welcome to the spectators was not conducive to superior performances on the running path. The grounds were in capital condition, the management was as faultless as ever, and, although there were many absentees among the entries, the sport was excellent, while that phenomenal shot putter, George Gray, distinguished himself by creating four world's records with missiles of different weights, and W. L. Condon added to his reputation by throwing the 16lb, hammer, standing, with one hand, a distance of 123ft. 6¼in. The absence of W C Dohm and W C Downes from races for which their names were down on the programme occasioned much disappointment. The former was reported to be sick, while the representative of Harvard was busy with his examinations and could not attend. The race in which Sherrill, the Yale crack, and Cary, from Princeton, appeared, at one hundred yards, resulted unsatisfactorily, owing to the former, who had easily won his trial heat, straining a tendon in his foot and falling near the finish in the final. A summary:

One hundred yards run—Final heat: Luther H Cary, Manhattan Athletic Club and Princeton College, first, in 10 1-5 s.; F I Lee, New York Athletic Club, second; P Vredenburgh, New York A C and Princeton, third.

Six hundred yards run—J S Roddy, Manhattan Athletic Club and Princeton College, first, in 1m. 20 1-5s; L R Sharp, New York Athletic Club' second.

Hurdle race, 120 yds.—Final heat: H L Williams, New York Athletic Club and Yale College, first, in 16 4-5s; George Schwegler, New York Athletic Club, second; F C Puffer, New Jersey Athletic Club, third.

One mile run—A B George, Manhattan Athletic Club, first, in 4m. 35 4-5s.; W McCarthy, Manhattan Athletic Club, second; W T Young, Manhattan Athletic Club, third.

Putting the 16lb. shot—George R Gray, New York Athletic Club, first, 44ft. 6¾in.; F L Lambrecht, Manhattan Athletic Club, second, 40ft. 11⅝in.; E J Giannini, New York Athletic Club, third, 37ft. 1in.

Pole vault—E D Ryher, New York Athletic Club and Yale College, first, 10ft. 4in.; J Crane Jr., Boston Athletic Association and Harvard College, and R F Curry, Boston Athletic Association and Harvard, tied at 10ft. 1in.

Half mile run—J S Roddy, Manhattan Athletic Club, first, in 2m. 10 2-5s.; W H Wright, New York Athletic Club and Harvard, second; H E Billings Jr., New York Athletic Club, third.

One furlong run—L H Cary, Manhattan Athletic Club, first, in 23 2-5s; T I Lee, New York Athletic Club, second; P Vredenburgh, New York A C and Princeton College, third.

Running high jump—R K Pritchard, Manhattan Athletic Club, first, 5ft. 10in.; H L Hallock, Manhattan Athletic Club, and F C Hooper, Berkeley Athletic Club, tied for second place, 5ft. 6in. and the former won the toss.

Hurdle race, 220yds—George Schwegler, New York Athletic Club, first, in 27 1 5s.; H L Williams, New York Athletic Club and Yale College, second, C E Lentilhon, New York Athletic Club, third.

Quarter mile run—L H Cary, Manhattan Athletic Club and Princeton College, first, in 53s.; J C Devereaux, Manhattan Athletic Club, second; F M Hartshorn, New York Athletic Club, third.

Obstacle race—J H Bell, New York Athletic Club, first, B G Woodruff, New Jersey Athletic Club, second; W B Miles, New York Athletic Club, third.

Throwing the 16lb. hammer—W L Condon, New York Athletic Club, first, 119ft. 9½in. F L Lambrecht, Manhattan Athletic Club, second, 112ft. 8½in.: M O'Sullivan, Pastime Athletic Club, third, 88ft. 2in.

Running long jump—E B Barnes, New York Athletic Club, first, 21ft. 9½in.; Victor Mapes, Berkeley Athletic Club, second, 20ft. 12½in.; C T Weigand, New York Athletic Club, third, 20ft. 4in.

Putting shots—In trials against the record George R Gray, New York Athletic Club, created the following new records; 14lb. shot, 47ft. 7½in.; 16lb. shot, 46ft.; 18lb. shot, 41ft. 9½in.; 21lb. shot, 38ft. 8½in.

Referee, William B Curtis; track judges, A C Stevens, Ed. Milligan, Will Wood, and A G Mills; field judges, B C Williams, S J Cornell and James E Sullivan; timekeepers, J H Abeel Jr., John F. Sterd, George Taylor and Evert Wendell; starter, George Goldie, clerk of the course, A A Jordan; announcer, A C Palmer.

The different lodges of the Sons of St. George in New York City will hold a picnic at Jones Wood, New York, on August 13, the chief feature of which will be the sports in the afternoon, including the following events for which the prizes will consist of gold and silver watches and silver cups: 100 yards run: 220 yards run; 440 yards run: 880 yards run: 1 mile run, open to all amateurs, and a tug of war, and races for men over 200 lbs. in weight and for men over 45 years of age open only to members of the order.

The Board of Governors of the Manhattan Athletic Club, at a meeting held on June 6, adopted a resolution to the effect that the club would not consider the application for membership of any athlete, a member of any club belonging to the Amateur Athletic Union unless he presented with the application his release from the club to which he had belonged.

W. G. George, the ex-champion amateur runner, has assumed the entire management of the Molineux Grounds, Wolverhampton, England, a favorite racing path for 'cyclers.

CLUB JOTTINGS.

Some of the members of the Lurline Club are anxious that the club withdraw its application for admission into the P. C. A. A. A. They seem to have an idea that the Association does not care very much to elect a North Beach club to membership. The Secretary of the Lurline Club received a letter from the Association in regard to the amateur standing of one of its members, William Schwartz, the wrestling instructor, who was said to be receiving a salary. The following reply was mailed to the Association: I beg leave to say for the benefit of the club that we are a new organization heartily endorsing the sentiments of the association in its good work in bringing together strictly amateur clubs to the front, and will not this late day make ourselves liable for any breaking of the rules of the association.

At present we have three boxing teachers, and two in wrestling, and I am desirious of informing the association that there is not one of our teachers under pay or being compensated for services rendered, but strictly voluntary on their part, which was the understanding when they were elected honorary members of the Lurline Club.

The Alpine Club will not hold any exhibition this month, but next month a fine entertainment will be given.

A meeting of the P C A A A was held at the Olympic club rooms on Wednesday evening, June 11th. At 8 o'clock, the hour at which the meeting should have been called to order, there were present over a dozen delegates, but as the night advanced and 10 o'clock resounded through the halls only half that number remained in the waiting room. There was considerable kicking done by the delegates who were compelled to wait, and they had just cause for kicking. It seems inconsistent that meetings of the Association should be called at such a late hour, and the sooner this state of things is remedied the better for the welfare of the P C A A A. At 11 o'clock, when the election of officers took place, only four delegates were present: Messrs. Scott, Steinway, Gilhuly and Moody. The other delegates were obliged to leave, owing to the lateness of the hour. All the old officers were elected. J. H. Gilhuly was accepted as a delegate to succeed George W. Jordan of the O A C, who had resigned. Several records were accepted.

The next meeting of the Association will be held at the same place on June 25th.

THE WHEELMEN.

The programme for the League meeting has not as yet been issued. The new four lap track at San Jose is nearing completion, and will be in tip top condition by the Fourth of July. The grand stand has already been erected, and all the other arrangements are nearly perfected. The ball which will take place on Saturday evening, July 5th, at the Hotel Vendome, promises to be one of the events of the season at San Jose. Several hundred invitations will be issued.

A complete list of the prizes to be awarded the winners will be published on Monday. The prizes will be handsome and costly and will include watches, bicycles, jewelry, etc.

Several Los Angeles wheelmen are in training at San Jose, and doubtless some of the trophies will find their way to the City of Angels.

A good many of the Garden City Wheelmen are also in training and the local riders will need to exert themselves.

The Oakland Bicycle Club has called a run for July 3d. The men will be divided into two teams, a fast one and a slow one. The slow team will leave the cor of 12th and Broadway streets, Oakland, at 4:30 p m. The Scorchers will follow at 7:30. The run will be to San Jose.

The lantern parade on the evening of the 4th, will be an interesting sight to witness.

Chief Consul R. M. Thompson's handbook is about ready and will shortly be issued. It will be one of the largest and best books of the kind ever issued. Every member of the Cal. division L A W will receive a copy free and it will be impossible for outsiders to procure a copy of the book as it will not be for sale.

At a meeting of the Bay City Wheelmen held June 16th, the two following gentlemen were nominated for delegates at large: Dr. T L Hill of San Francisco, and C C Moore of Stockton.

Chief Consul Thompson, George P. Wetmore and Sanford Plummer rode to Santa Cruz on Sunday, going by way of Boulder Creek and Saratoga.

The B C W will hold a road race in September with time handicaps. The race will be on the principle of the great Pullman road races. The race will probably be open to all members of the Cal. Division L A W. Valuable prizes, consisting of bicycles, watches, etc., will be given.

At a meeting of the Bay City Wheelmen held June 9th, a committee was appointed to see what could be done in regard to the issuing of bonds for building purposes.

It is the intention of the Bay City Wheelmen to build a club house of their own in some convenient part of the city. The rooms will be finely furnished, and no doubt many wheelmen who are at present unattached will be only too glad to join a club that will shortly be able to boast of having a finer club house than any other bicycle organization on the Pacific Coast.

Chief Consul Thompson and W. M. Meeker intend going to the Yosemite Valley next month.

A club run of the San Francisco Bicycle Club, occupying a week, is to be taken through Lake and Sonoma counties.

The board of officers of California Division met last week and nominated the committee whose duty is to make nominations for chief consul, vice-consul and secretary-treasurer, for the coming term. C. C. Moore of Stockton, Fred Russ Cook of San Francisco, H. C. F. Smith of Los Angeles, Dr. Van Norden of Alameda and A. C. McKenney of San Jose are the committee. The election will be conducted under the Australian plan, according to the new constitution. Each member of this committee will send his nominees to the secretary-treasurer, and all the names received by him will be placed on one ticket and the ticket sent to each member of the division, who will cross off the names which he does not wish to vote, and then return the ticket to the secretary-treasurer. Any other names received by the secretary-treasurer indorsed by the members in good standing will also be placed on the ticket.

The nominations for representatives at large will be made by the league clubs of the division, of which there are five—Bay City Wheelmen, Los Angeles Wheelmen, Garden City Wheelmen, Vineyard Valley Wheelmen and Palm Leaf Wheelmen. Chief Consul Thompson has notified the secretaries of these clubs to make nominations for five representatives on or before July 1st, 1890.

"Hexameter," the Los Angeles correspondent of the L. A. W. Bulletin, is strongly advocating the re instatement of S. W. Speirs into the amateur ranks. The fact of Mr. Speirs having competed in the Morgan "fake" races at the Mechanics Pavilion some months ago, after having been duly cautioned that any wheelmen who took part in these races would be disqualified as an amateur, is a barrier strong enough to prevent his re-instatement. There are plenty of good wheelmen now in the State, and the loss of one amateur who was hot-headed enough to violate the rules of the L. A. W. will make but little difference to the amateur bicycling world.

Unique Racing.

PHILADELPHIA, PA., June 5.—Milkmen from all sections of the city, after serving their customers with dispatch, to-day turned out in holiday attire, accompanied by their wives or best girls, and wended their way to Belmont Course to witness the third annual races of the Philadelphia Milk Exchange. The Lancaster turnpike and all roads leading to the track were crowded by the jolliest crowd imaginable. All sorts of vehicles, from the genuine buckboard to the dilapidated milk wagon, conveyed over 4,000 spectators to the grounds. The weather was hot and the roads dusty, but everybody enjoyed the day hugely. Honest racing was the order, everybody trying to win. Frank Bower, Joshua Evans, John T. Strickland and Dr. J. A. Marshall were in the judges' stand.

The milk wagon race created considerable amusement for the spectators. Each contestant was stationed at the wire, the driver to load two thirty-quart milk cans, shut up the tail-board, and get in his wagon and drive a mile, the first horse in to be declared the winner. T. Fogarty loaded first, with Siney second, but Lady Forrest took the lead and won the race in 3:21½.

The 2:35 pacing race was hotly contested between the three starters, the bay gelding Eli winning. Best time, 2:34½.

The second Milk Wagon class was a repetition of the first race, Smiling Jimmy getting the start and keeping the lead to the three-quarter pole, when Jersey Boy passed him and won the race in 2:39½.

The 2:50 class was the race of the day, with Stone Cutter the favorite. Stone Cutter won the first heat by a neck. In the second heat Frank had the race in hand to the stretch, when he quit badly, and Stone Cutter passed him a length from the wire. In the third heat all endeavored to beat Stone Cutter. Frank and Butcher Boy made the pace hot, but Stone Cutter outfooted the field and won by a short length. Best time, 2:43.

THE HISTORY OF TROTTING.

Phenomenal Progress Since the Days of the First Three Minute Trotter.

Some little idea may be obtained of the rapid growth of trotting and the phenominal progress made in this rate of speed by a comparison of a few events happening in different decades during the present century. It was in the year 1818 that a horse first trotted in three minutes. It was accomplished at Jamaica, N. Y., by a horse called Boston Blue, and was regarded as a notable performance. Nothing else of importance transpired during that decade. In 1844 Lady Suffolk trotted in 2:26½, and the world wondered. In 1845 Moscow trotted in 2:30, in 1849 Pelham trotted in 2:28, and Lady Sutton in 2:30, and with a notation of these praise worthy performances the history of that decade is written.

In 1853 Highland Maid and Tacony each trotted in 2:27. In '59 George M. Patchen trotted in 2:26½, and Brown Dick in 2.25½, and in 1859 the sun of that decade set in a blaze of glory on account of the world famed performance of Flora Temple, when she trotted in 2:19¾. The news was flashed to the uttermost parts of the earth, horsemen marveled and predicted the end had come, the sturdy little mare was proclaimed the Queen, and conservative men shook their heads and indulged in melancholy musings over the fact that it was a fast age, and men and women were going to the dogs because of their love and admiration for a healthful, pleasant sport which many good men and true, believed immoral.

During the next decade trotting assumed some sort of form, and 2:20 was frequently beaten. In '67, '68 and '69 Dexter earned lasting fame by trotting in 2:17¼. Lady Thorne trotted in 2:18½, American Girl in 2:19½. In '78 Rarus trotted in 2:13¼, in '74 Goldsmith Maid in 2:14, in '78 St. Julien trotted in 2:12¾, in '78 Hopeful trotted in 2:14¾, in '75 Lula trotted in 2:14¾, and in 1876 Smuggler trotted in 2:15¼, and in '74 American Girl obtained a record of 2:16½. By this time trotting had become a recognized sport and a good part of the stigma or odium attached to it had been removed, while the business of breeding the trotter was assuming a practical form and becoming reduced to a system.

In 1885 Maud S. trotted in 2:08¾. 1884 Jay-eye-see trotted in 2:10, in 1881-2 Trinket trotted in 2:14, in 1882 Clingstone went a mile in 2:14, in 1880 St. Julien trotted in 2:11¼, in 1884 Phallas trotted in 2:13¾ and the same year Maxie Cobb was credited with a record of 2:13¼. In 1887 Harry Wilkes trotted a mile in 2:13½, in 1888 Prince Wilkes trotted in 2:14¾, and Rosaline Wilkes in 2:14¼, in 1887 Patron trotted in 2:14¼, in 1889 Guy trotted in 2:10¾, Sunol, a three year old in 2:10½, Axtell, a three year old, in 2:12, Stamboul in 2:12½ Palo Alto in 2:12¾, Belle Hamlin in 2:12¾, and Bonnie McGregor in 2:13½.

It was in 1876 that Smuggler obtained the stallion record of 2:15¼, and that stood against all competition for eight years until Phallas trotted in 2:13¾, and Maxie Cobb in 2:13¼ These records defied all competition for five years, when the record was beaten by three stallions, one of them a three year old. It was in the year 1844 that 2:30 was first beaten, and in the year 1889 there were nearly six hundred accessions to the list. It was in 1883 that Hinda Rose astonished the world by trotting to a three year old record of 2:19½. That record stood unchallenged until 1887, when Sable Wilkes trotted in 2:18, and since then it has been beaten by seven other three year olds, and in 1889 was reduced by Sunol to 2:10½. There are twelve three year olds that have trotted in 2.20 or better. In 1886 Manzanita trotted in 2.16 as a four year old. That record has never been beaten, and only once equaled, and that was in 1889 by Edgemark. It was in 1881 that Wildflower, a two year old, trotted in 2:21. That record was never even approached until 1888, when Sunol trotted in 2:18 and Axtel in 2:23, while in 1889 Regal Wilkes trotted in 2:20¾. Only one two year old has beaten 2:20. In 1881 Hinda Rose, a yearling, trotted in 2:36½. That record was considered invincible until 1887, when Norlaine trotted in 2.31¾ and Susie D. trotted in 2.35½. In 1888 Faustino trotted a mile in 2:35, and this closes the list of fast yearlings. This shows a most remarkable rate of progress.

There occurs occasionally a phenomenal performance, made perhaps under advantageous circumstances by a supreme effort; with everything, including nature and the ingenuity of man in its favor. This performance is rarely equaled until a certain combination of forces or fortunate circumstances afford opportunity, and then the attempt is made. The die is cast, some speculative or daring individual risks all upon one grand supreme effort; all circumstances are favorable, and at once, almost as by an electric spark, records are broken and smashed to atoms, a great victory over time and almost over nature is won, and applauding thousands witness, without fully appreciating its full significance, a phenomenal event. Perhaps the grandest struggle against the old man with the scythe was the battle royal last year between the great 3-year olds, Sunol and Axtell. In all its conditions it was an unequal contest. On the one side was the prestige of wealth, recognized breeding, a famous sire and one of the most competent trainers and handlers of colt trotters the world has ever seen. On the other hand was a poor, obscure young man, a colt by a sire "to fortune and to fame unknown," very little money and presumably very little judgment in training and handling. The record is, as it reads to-day: Axtell, 2:12, king of stallions; Sunol, 2:10½, queen of 3-year-olds.

The grand filly, almost unapproachable, in the marvelous splendor of her supreme performance, has earned the laurel she so proudly wears; earned it by tention of nerves and muscle, by one grand, glorious, series of great deeds that have placed her away beyond her kind, and made her name throughout the length and breadth of this great land a household word. The wonderful colt, born in a little country town, educated, trained and driven by an amateur whom all the world laughed at, shipped from town to town, from State to State, from track to track, wherever there was a dollar in sight; trotted under all sorts of disadvantegeous circumstances, and finally by one grand, unexpected, unlooked-for great effort, crowned king of stallions. The great filly, 2:10½, the superb stallion, 2:12; which is the greater do you say? That's for you to decide, gentle reader. We don't know or don't care. We knew them both as babies, and watched them both in their grand career. One thing we do know, and it is this: Their dams were each by sires almost unknown, entirely without reputation, among men as brood mare sires. One thing we don't know is this, and that is why their dams were not one or the other some far famed mare of great renown, a queen mother in some great brood-mare family. From absolute obscurity two mares have been raised to the highest pinnacle of fame by the performance of two of the greatest youngsters ever born, and it is the very irony of fate that these self-same mares were by sires unknown to fame.

Why is it, do you say? Quien Sabe; who knows? Who can tell? Who, among all the wise mem, the eminent creators and formulators of beautiful theories, will rise and explain? The people are anxiously waiting. Let the scientist who has fathomed the awful mysteries of life and death, or the flippant theorist who knows all about it, solve the problem and instruct the people. As for us, we have passed that point in the study of the science of breeding, and honestly and humbly proclaim ourselves a mere student of the mysteries of the great mother nature, and be it understood, the more we study, the more we observe, the less competent we feel to instruct; the more humble we feel as to our absolute knowledge of the great science. More and more, as we observe and study are we inclined to be humble, and be satisfied to be a recorder of facts and events, leaving to abler and more astute minds and to men who have studied and observed less, the task of elucidating the great problem and of explaining it to the people. Some one will criticise this article, and we will be glad of it, for as the great premier of England wrote, "Critics are the men who have failed," and again a great poet said: "To every trade man serves apprenticeship save to the trade of censure. Critics all are ready made." What we would like to see and what the people demand is that some estimable gentleman who has never bred a mare or owned a trotter, and who could scarely tell whether a horse had a spavin or the glanders should explain these so-called mysteries.—Clark's Horse Review.

Have Mercy on the Horses.

As the spring work begins, writes a farmer in the Michigan Farmer, remember horses feel the heat as much or more than we do, as, if we become burdened, we can easily lay aside our heavy clothing and substitute that which is lighter. The horse cannot always do this, for although nature proclaims that animals "shed their coat" in the spring, yet it is often the case that the horse does not part with his heavy coat of hair until late in the season. Then, too, do not hurry him too much. How would you relish being urged continually at your work? when limbs are growing weary and exercise and sunshine combine to bring the perspiration starting from every pore, to have a whip flourished around your ears, while some one who holds the reins shouts "Get up!" How good it would seem to stop and rest a minute to get your breath! Perhaps when that corner is reached you will hear the welcome "whoa". As the corner is neared you involuntarily slacken your pace, expecting to be allowed to stop. But no, instead is heard the command to go on, enforced quite likely by a whiz of the whip.

How a good drink of water would taste, your mouth is so hot! But you know better than to expect that; and when at last, tired and panting, you are allowed to rest a few minutes the driver drops his lines, and if it be not too far from the pump, you soon hear the sound of gushing water, and as he drains cup after cup of the refreshing fluid you can only hope he will perhaps remember that you are thirsty too, and bring you some. But no; back he comes empty-handed, when only one pail of water would have been so refreshing to you and your mate. For you know quite well that the idea that a drink of water will injure a horse when warm any more than it will a man is utterly false, unless it be used immoderately.

Then there is the check-rein. What it was ever invented for is more than you or I know. It is nothing but a torture when at work to have your head drawn up, and do what you will you cannot get rid of it. You turn your head this way and that, trying to get a little relief, and have the whip applied for your pains. Then, when you have to start a load, how much easier it is if you can get your head down.

Blinders are another thing often annoying to a horse. How often we see them so close to the eye that they impede the free action of the eye-lashes, which would be very annoying to us, and why is it not to the horse? Look over that work harness, and if there is any tendency on the part of the blinders to "flop" over the horse's eyes, cut them off, and you will never have cause to regret it. A horse soon becomes accustomed to their absence, and I am sure if he had a voice in the matter, would much prefer to have them removed.

Then when you hitch up to go to town don't expect to make a first-class carriage horse out of one that has been working in the plow all week, and pull his head in the air and expect him to trot off as lively as a colt.

Much of the cruelty practiced upon farm horses (and it is nothing less) is the result of thoughtlessness, and pages might be written on the subject. How often are the horses jerked and yelled at in cultivating, only making them excited and incapable of performing their work as well as they would if handled quietly and gently!

I have in mind a horse of nervous temperament, which with quiet treatment is an excellent horse to cultivate with, scarcely ever stepping out of place, apparently as careful to keep off the hills of corn or potatoes as a person would be. At a blow or harsh word or jerk of the reins she is fairly wild, jumping into the next row, taking the cultivator too in her excitement.

Don't urge the slow-walking team to keep up with one that walks faster. Note the difference in people as to gait. Some men will with perfect ease walk twice as fast as others; and ought the slow horse be blamed because he cannot keep up with another?

Particular attention should be given to the collar that it does not cause a gall. A well fitting collar, kept smooth and clean, will rarely give trouble in that direction.

Grim's Gossip.

The new stake book arranged by Mr. Ferguson is meeting with great sale.

The Horse World, formerly issued as a monthly, now appears as a weekly. It is a readable paper and deserves success.

Mr. Walter S. Vosburgh, official handicapper of the New York Jockey Club, has been appointed to the same position by the Monmouth Park Association.

Mohawk Chief was seen not long since at Palo Alto pulling a barrow on the Kindergarten track. He is as handsome a horse as ever, and took to his work kindly.

The well known horseman, Lee Mantle of Butte, Mont., was crushed by the explosion of a boiler in the Silver Bow Electric Light Works, in Butte, on Friday, June 13th.

Seconds and thirds seems to be as near as the Malte e Villa Stable can get to the front in the East. Everyone would be pleased to see Porter Ashe's pretty cherry jacket in the van once or twice.

Mr. Valensin has not quite recovered from his late illness. although he has been able to be around once more. At present he is rusticating at Bartlett Springs, taking advantage of the health giving waters.

Geraldine has been unfortunate enough to run second quite a number of times in very fast time, but those who have pinned their faith to the mare have reason to believe that she will shortly show her heels to the best of them.

W. B. Sanborn of Santa Rosa was in town Monday, and he reports favorably in regard to the horses in training at the track there. He says that Sonoma County is prepared to spring a surprise or two on the trotting world when the season opens.

The Hills Bros. of Lompoc, Santa Barbara Co. have lately purchased the bay stallion Commodore Nutwood by Nutwood, the consideration paid being $1,000 and a valuable mare. The horse has a record of 2:32 and has shown a trial in 2:28.

The famous Green Mountain Maid's youngest son, Lancelot, is three years old, and those who have seen him recently say he is the best of his wonderful family, and he will probably enter the 2:30 list this season. Ed Bither is training him.

H. Silverman of 1016 Golden Gate Avenue has for sale, the mare Elaine by Bonner (son of Chieftain 721) dam by McCrackens Black Hawk. Elaine is only nine years old and should prove a valuable brood mare for those that are looking for bargains.

Victor 2:22 who has stood during the season at Napa, has been taken to Indian Valley, where his owner Mr. Doherty will prepare him for another campaign. Victor is one of the favorites on the circuit and race goers always look for a sensation whenever he appears.

The good people of San Luis Obispo are going to have a one day's meeting on July 5th. Mr. Lew Warden reports that the track is in superb condition being both fast and safe; he also says that the regular fall races will commence on Sept. 2nd and end on the 6th.

Robert Bonner and a party of friends have paid a visit to Terre Haute to inspect Sunol and everything is satisfactory. The great four-year-old moved a quarter in 31 1-5 seconds, at which Mr. Bonner was much pleased. The query of the day among horsemen is, how fast can Sunol go?

The Tennessee correspondent of this paper was the first to announce that Brown Hal 2:12½ had paced a quarter in 28 seconds. Considerable discredit was thrown on the statement, but now Major Campbell Brown comes forward and verifies the report, which settles the disputed point.

The horse loving people of Los Angeles are confident that they will have one of the best meetings of the circuit and that the entry list will be very large. The Directors are already assured of patronage enough from horse owners to feel that that they were warranted in offering large purses.

The Greenville (Plumas County) Driving Park Association has been organized with a cash capital of $400, and land has been leased in the neighborhood of the city from Frank Kruger. The Directors of the Association are D. McIntyre, G. S, Bransford, C. H. Lawrence, D. McKinley and D. L. Haun.

We are under many obligations to Edwin F. Smith, Secretary of the State Agricultural Society, for a copy of the published report of the society for the year 1889. In addition to a complete record of all the races which took place at the State Capitol, there are also full reports of the contests that took place at the other Agricultural Meetings throughout the State.

R. L. Carroll tells me he will have the Oakland programme out next week in the Breeder and Sportsman. Four days trotting and pacing will be provided for the talent, while the thoroughbred element will not be neglected, as three days will be devoted to their mode of progression, and probably five races a day, for which free purses on a liberal scale will be hung up.

If the telegraphed accounts are true, Judge Green, President of the St. Louis Jockey Club, is in very bad odor, owing to a decision given on Thursday last, he naming a wrong horse as winner. Mr. Green has always held a high place among the patrons of the turf and I should be loath to believe that he was guilty of intentional wrong, unless the testimony against him was overwhelming.

Wm. Napier of Pleasanton was in the city on Wednesday, and from him I learn that the Three Cheers—Queen Emma filly, owned by Schweere & Napier has been sent to the stable of Matt Storn at Sacramento to receive preparatory work for a fall campaign. She has been well entered in all the stakes of this year, and "Billy" seems to think that he has got a "show in" for at least a part of the money.

Before another issue of this paper the ball will have started rolling at Chicago, and many Californian horses will have shown to the world what they are capable of doing. The Smith Stable, as well as one belonging to T. H. Williams, have been quartered at Washington Park for some time, and those who fancy the runners have every reason to believe that both of these strings will give good accounts of themselves.

Two well known horsemen met in the office of the Breeder and Sportsman a few days ago and a controversy arose as to how fast Sunol was likely to trot during the year 1890. The wordy war finally finished by a wager being made that the peerless queen would show a mile sometime during the year in 2:06. This may seem rather a low mark to set for the great mare, yet still there are scores who expect to see her perform the marvelous feat.

Major Campbell Brown, Ewell Farm, Spring Hill, Tenn., has sold to W. C. Jones, Columbia, Tenn., a half interest in the chestnut horse McEwen, 4 yr. old record 2:18½, foaled 1885, by McCurdy's Hambletonian 1644, record 2:26½ (son of Harold 413 and Belle, dam of Belmont by Mambrino Chief) dam Mary M. by Bassinger. This is the young horse that many Eastern turfmen think can beat Direct.

A big hunt for wild horses ended successfully at Casper, Wyoming, last Monday. Three weeks ago a party of four cowboys started for Salt creek to try and capture a herd of wild horses which have ranged in the vicinity for several years. The wild herd was sighted and circled into a narrow canyon, where thirty of them were captured. They were all magnificent animals. Seven of them were branded, the remainder were "slicks," or horses which had run wild from birth.

Mr. J. H. Walters, proprietor of the Lakeport track will have a one day meeting on Saturday, June 27th. Six events are on the programme, three being for trotters and a like number for the "bang tails." This is the season of the year when life is enjoyable in Lake County and as the famous summer resorts of that section are already extensively patronized, the day's sport should be generously supported by both the local residents, and those who are at present up there for recreation and pleasure.

Mr. Irvin Ayres, owner of Alpheus 2:27, has leased that stallion to H. D. Albright of San Luis Obispo, who will in all probability have him trained and trotted in the southern part of the state during the present year. Alpheus is by Mambrino Wilkes 6083, dam by Major Mono. Mr. Albright will also make the season of 1891 with the horse at or near his home, and it will be a splendid opportunity for those owning well bred mares in that neighborhood, to secure the services of a well bred and dead game horse.

Matt Storn has eight thoroughbreds in training at the Sacramento track, and they are all doing well. Lurline has been bred to imp Cheviot, but will be seen in races this fall. Marigold is moving nicely, and Matt expects to win with her on the circuit. A two year old filly by Three Cheers, dam Mistake (dam of Kildare) is a beauty, closely resembling in looks Mr. Haggin's mare Firenzi. The stable boys are very sweet on her, and she has been named Mystery. Mr Storn also has his trotter Belvidere doing slow work, and threatens to give him a record this fall.

There can be no reason to doubt the ultimate success of the Pacing Horse Breeders Association, which will meet at the Gibson House, Cincinnati on Thursday of next week. The gentlemen having the matter in hand are enthusiastic in the cause and will carry the matter to a successful conclusion. The interests of horse breeding demands a strong organization for registery purposes, and it is proposed that the committee appointed for the purpose will have a good set of rules to lay before the association to regulate the pacers of America.

"There is no quality that exerts a greater influence on the selling value of road horses, family horses and coach horses than the quality of beauty. A horse of symmetrical form, with gracefully curved neck, clean limbs, fine head and proud demeanor, pleasing color and silky coat, will almost always sell readily for all he is worth, whether he is large or small, fast or slow. Other horses that are rough coated, homely colored, and of ungainly form will have to go begging for a customer, even though they may be far more serviceable animals than the beauties.

A telegram was received June 2 by District Attorney Fellows, New York City, from the United States Consul at Havana, stating that Robert L. Wallace, the defaulting cashier of the Wallace Register Company, had voluntarily surrendered to him $18,000 in United States bonds, and $3 000 in cash, being, it is presumed, all he had left of the $52,000 which he abstracted. Although there was no treaty of extradition between the United States and Spain, it is quite possible that young Wallace and his companion, I. B. Lowitz, may be brought back and punished for their crime.

Secretary F. P. Lowell, of the Sacramento Colt Stake Association, writes me to say that at the annual meeting held at the race track, Sacramento, on June 10th, only two competitors came forward to do battle for the two-year-old trotting stake. The first was T. J. Draice's Farmington Boy, by Dexter Prince, and the other A. L. Whitney's Anna Bell by Dawn. The latter won easily in straight heats, the time made being 2:53 and 3:01. Those who saw the race are under the impression that the winner could have trotted in 2:40 or better if necessity had required.

The news had no sooner been received of Salvator's victory in the Suburban than the New York Herald telegraphed to the San Francisco representative to send on a message as to the manner in which the "win" was received by local horsemen. As was only natural the correspondent at once visited the Breeder and Sportsman office, where a large number of prominent horsemen had congregated to discuss the good work done by Mr. Haggin's colt. It was the generally expressed belief that Salvator is the best horse of the year, as he beat the best cracks of the East carrying lumps of weight.

Two races are announced for July 4th at Petaluma. The first one is for a purse of $200, mile heats, three in five, with the following horses: Lee Shaner names b s Poco Tempo by Anteeo; A. N. Burrell names b m Lillie Mac by Auctioneer Johnnie; J. B. Hinkle names b s Whalebone by Inca; Steve Crandall names b m Mountain Quail by Hernanni. The second race will be contested for by C. Futroe's g m Nellie Rustic by Rustic; A. N. Burrell's b m Annie L by Alexander; R. S. Brown's b g Robbin and Dan Misners g g Chappo by Rustic.

Peter Woods, who has had a large stable of horses at the Bay District Track in training, has been engaged by Gilbert Tompkins, Esq., owner of the Souther Stock Farm, to prepare the promising horses on the Farm for the fall circuit. Mr. Woods will have the grand young stallion El Benton under his charge and also the four year old Glen Fortune. I consider the first named one of the best two year olds in the State to-day, and under "Pete's" able management should make a sure enough trotter.

It is likely that Bess, by Fadladeen, out of Betsy, has run her last race. She ran away the other day, and covered three miles before she could be pulled up. While she suffered no apparent harm, it is probable that she will be put out of training.

One of the noticeable features at Palo Alto is the quietness with which everything is conducted. There is never any loud or boisterous language, and swearing in and around the stables is never heard. This is in contradistinction to many of the tracks and farms in the State, where most of the rubbers and grooms seem to think it essential and necessary to use rough and coarse language to the animals under their charge, yet still there is not a stable in the country where trotting horses are more quiet and gentle than they are at Senator Stanford's.

"Kennesaw," the well known collector of news for the Breeder and Sportsman, in Tennessee, has from the first proclaimed that Rio Rey would never face the starter again, and now his prognostications turn out to be true, for Mr. Winters has had his suburb colt thrown out of training, and the son of Norfolk and Marion will be sent back to Nevada to take the place of his sire in the stud. He was the great colt of his year, and it only remains to be seen whether his younger brother can follow in El Rio Rey's illustrious footsteps.

A match race, half a mile and repeat, took place at Los Alamos, Santa Barbara Co., last week between Harris' Pinto stallion and Hill's bay mare, the amount run for being $500. Our correspondent writes and says: "It is astonishing how some horses will run slower the more they train on, but perhaps it is not always the fault of the horse, the trainer has much to do with it and the riders often make a horse run faster one day than they can another. Hill's bay mare one month ago could negotiate a half mile in 52 seconds, yet still, on the day of the race she was easily beaten by Pinto in 57 and 57½."

Attention is called to the programme of the 17th Agricultural District, the races of which will take place at Glenbrook Park, commencing August 19th, when $6,500 in purses will be distributed among those fortunate enough to own the winners. There are three races each day, and as the purses are more than liberal, it may be expected that the entry list will be a large one. Last year the fair at Glenbrook Park was one of the most successful held in the northern portion of the State, and we confidently believe that the fair of 1890 will be even more so than the one of last year.

Reports from the southern portion of the State confirms the rumor that Nick Covorrubias has a grand race horse this year in Dan Murphy. He has been given a couple of "pipe openers," the first being a half mile in 49 seconds, while a mile was made in the fast time of 1:42½. The well known trainer Gus Walters is handling all of Nick's horses and has them in the pink of condition; they will no doubt be heard from when the southern circuit opens. In the same string is a very large, handsome three-year-old by Hock-Hocking who runs just as fast as he pleases, no company is too speedy for him and he is expected to show his heels to many during the circuit races.

One of the most important sales that has taken place in California for many a day, was consumated on Tuesday last; B. C. Holly of Vallejo, purchasing from J. A. Goldsmith of San Mateo, the chestnut mare Manon 2:21, by Nutwood, dam Addie (dam of Woodnut 2:16½) by Hasbrouck's Hambletonian Chief, son of Hambletonian 10. With the mare, goes her three living foals; the first a ch. f. foaled 1888, the second a blk colt foaled 1889, and a ch. colt foaled 1890, all of the three being by Guy Wilkes 2:15¼, and the mare is bred back to the same horse. The price paid was $20,000, and from the way prices go at present, the sum is not exorbitant. In buying Manon, Mr. Holly has returned to his early love, for that good mare is a full sister to his celebrated stallion Woodnut, which he sold last year to Mr. Steele of Cedar Farm. If the colt of last year is in good condition twelve months from now, Mr. Holly should be able to sell him for an amount equal to what he paid for the lot.

In the current number will be found an advertisement from the Directors of the Stockton Fair Association in which they announce the opening of five stakes and purses which will be trotted for during their meeting, commencing September 23rd. The 1st is a guarantee purse of $1,000 for the three-minute class; the 2nd is a guarantee purse of $1,000 for the 2:25 class; the 3rd for four-year-olds or under with a purse of $500, open to the district only; the 4th is for the 2:30 class and the 5th for the 2:40 class, both of the latter being for a guaranteed purse of $1,000 each. They also announce the opening of the Amador Stake for the running division open to horses of all ages. This stake is for animals owned in Amador, Calaveras, San Joaquin and Stanislaus counties. The entrance is $20 each for all starters with $150 added; the 2nd horse to receive half the entrance money, the distance being one mile. For the guaranteed trotting purses, the entrance is 10 per cent., payable as follows: $30 on July 1st, when nominations close; $35 on August 1st, and $35 on September 1st, when horse must be named. As is usual in all nomination purses, neglect to make payments forfeits all previous amounts paid in.

A meeting of the representatives of the fair associations of Napa, Petaluma, San Jose and Oakland was held in the Breeder and Sportsman offices last Saturday. F L. Coombs represented Napa; G. H. Bragg, San Jose; J. H. White and B. Brown, Petaluma; R. T. Carrol, Dr. Lathem and George Bement, Oakland. A lengthy discussion took place in regard to having the same class of races at each of the meetings and thus make it an inducement for horse owners to enter with a chance of earning a respectable amount of money through the circuit, it being conceded that it was not worth an owner's while to go to the trouble and expense of training a horse for only one race and it is confidently expected that by giving a series of races of one pattern at four of the most prominent meetings, a larger and more uniform class of horses would enter and better contests would ensue. With this object it was ultimately decided to give at San Jose, Napa, Petaluma and Oakland a 2:20 trot and 2:27 trot the opening day, on the third day of the meeting a 3:00 trot and a 2:30 pace, and on another day a 2:24 trot and a free-for-all pace. The first day at Napa, San Jose and Petaluma will be on a Tuesday. Oakland will commence on Monday, September 1st and continue to Tuesday, Sept. 9th, and will include three days for runners and four for trotters and pacers.

THE WEEKLY

Breeder and Sportsman.

JAMES P. KERR, PROPRIETOR.

The Turf and Sporting Auth rity of the Pacific Coast.

Office, No. 313 Bush St.

P. O. Box 2300.

TERMS—*One Year, $5; Six Months, $3; Three Months, $1.50.*
STRICTLY IN ADVANCE.

Money should be sent by postal order, draft or by registered letter, addressed to JAMES P. KERR, San Francisco, Cal.

Communications must be accompanied by the writer's name and address, not necessarily for publication, but as a private guarantee of good faith.

NEW YORK OFFICE, ROOM 15, 181 BROADWAY.

ALEX. P. WAUGH, - - - - - - Editor.

Advertising Rates

Per Square (half inch)

One time	$1 50
Two times	2 50
Three times	3 25
Four times	4 00

And each subsequent insertion 75c. per square.

Advertisements running six months are entitled to 10 per cent. discount.

Those running twelve months are entitled to 20 per cent. discount.

Reading notices set in same type as body of paper, 50 cents per line each insertion.

To Subscribers.

The date printed on the wrapper of your paper indicates the time to which your subscription is paid.

Should the BREEDER AND SPORTSMAN be received by any subscriber who does not want it, write us direct to stop it. A postal card will suffice.

Special Notice to Correspondents.

Letters intended for publication should reach this office not later than Wednesday of each week, to secure a place in the issue of the following Saturday. Such letters to insure immediate attention should be addressed to the BREEDER AND SPORTSMAN, and not to any member of the staff.

San Francisco, Saturday, June 21, 1890.

Dates Claimed.

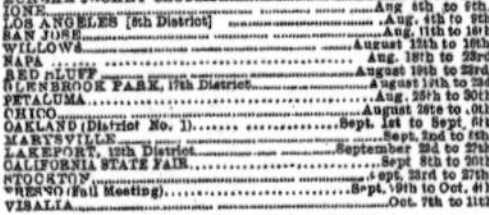

EUREKA JOCKEY CLUB	July 2d to 5th
IONE	Aug 6th to 9th.
LOS ANGELES [6th District]	Aug. 4th to 9th
SAN JOSE	Aug. 11th to 16th
WILLOWS	August 12th to 16th
NAPA	Aug. 18th to 23rd
RED BLUFF	August 19th to 23rd.
GLENBROOK PARK, 17th District	August 19th to 23d
PETALUMA	Aug. 25th to 30th
CHICO	August 26th to 30th
OAKLAND (District No. 1)	Sept. 1st to Sept. 6th
MARYSVILLE	Sept. 2nd to 5th
LAKEPORT, 12th District	September 23d to 27th
CALIFORNIA STATE FAIR	Sept 8th to 20th
STOCKTON	Sept. 23rd to 27th.
FRESNO (Fall Meeting)	Sept. 29th to Oct. 4th
VISALIA	Oct. 7th to 11th

Stallions Advertised

IN THE

BREEDER AND SPORTSMAN.

Thoroughbreds.

THREE CHEERS Imp. Hurrah—Young Fashion......R. S. Culver. San Francisco.

Trotters.

ADMIRAL, Volunteer—Lady Pierson..........Frank Drake, Vallejo.
ALCONA, Almont—Queen Mary..........Fred W. Loeber, St. Helena
BAY ROSE Sultan—Madam Baldwin..........Thos. Bonner, Santa Rosa
CHARLES DERBY, Steinway—by Electioneer..Cook Stock Farm, Contra Costa Co.
DEXTER PRINCE, Kentucky Prince—Lady Dexter.........L. M. Morse, Lodi.
EL BENTON, Electioneer—Nellie Benton..........Souther Farm, San Leandro.
ECLECTIC, Electioneer—Manette.........Wilfred Page, Sonoma County
EROS, Electioneer—Sontag Mohawk..........W. H. Vioget, Menlo Park
FIGARO, Hambletonian—Emblem..........Souther Farm, San Leandro.
GROVER CLAY, Electioneer—Maggie Norfolk..........Denis Gannon, Oakland.
GRAND MOOR 2374, Moor 870—Vashti..........H. I. Thornton, S. F.
G. & M., Anteeo—Rosa B..........George E. Guerne, Santa Rosa.
GLEN FORTUNE, Electioneer—Glenna..........Souther Farm, San Leandro.
GEORGE WASHINGTON, Mambrino Chief—Fanny Rose..........Thos. Smith, Vallejo.
GRANDISSIMO, LeGrande—Norma..........Fred W. Loeber, St Helena
JESTER D, Almont—Hortense..........Souther Farm, San Leandro.
KING DAVID, Admiral—Black Flora..........Frank Drake, Vallejo.
MEMO, Sidney—Flirt..........John Rowen, Oakland
MAMBRINO WILKES, George Wilkes—Lady Chrisman..........San Miguel Stock Farm, Walnut Creek.
MAMBRINO CHIEF, McDonald Chief—Venus..........Thos. Smith, Vallejo.
MORTIMER, Electioneer—Marti..........Wilfred Page, Sonoma County
PHILOSOPHER, Pilot Wilkes—Belle..........George E. Guerne, Santa Rosa.
REDWOOD, Anteeo—Lou Wilton..........A. McFayden, Oakland.
STEINWAY, Strathmore—Abbess ...Cook Stock Farm, Contra Costa Co
VICTOR, Echo—Daughter of Woodburn..........G. W. Hughes, Napa City

A Convert.

One of the best known and most popular of writers on the trotting horse is "Iconoclast," whose able articles in each successive issue of the Kentucky Stock Farm are read with much interest by all who have a fondness for the trotter. For a long, long time he has made strong and aggressive war against the thoroughbred theory in trotters, and has hit many heavy blows in defense of his pet theory; however, he undoubtedly finds that at least a little thoroughbred is a good thing in the present day, as in the current number of his valued paper he makes use of the following remark: "There is no breeder who is not glad to have the blood of Miss Russell on his farm; it is the very *giltest* of gilt edged crosses." We are only too glad to see that the Judge has come around a little bit to our way of thinking, and sincerely trust that before many days he may see fit to become a strong advocate of Senator Stanford's theory.

The Haggin Sale.

It must be a source of great satisfaction to Mr. Haggin and Jno. Mackey, his superintendent, to know that the stock which is bred at Rancho del Paso is so highly thought of by Eastern buyers. The telegraph has not as yet given us full particulars as to the average made at the great sale on Monday last, but enough has been wired over to warrant the belief that all former averages have been beaten at this great sale. When the stock left Sacramento some few weeks ago, it was the concensus of opinion that never before had such a grand lot of yearlings ever left this State, and this opinion has been borne out by the purchasers as in many instances the large prices obtained were not on account of the breeding alone but of the magnificent individuality of the animals offered for sale, and it can hardly be wondered at, that buyers are plenty and eager in their efforts to obtain the thoroughbreds annually offered for sale by Mr. Haggin, for at each of the Eastern sales which he has had, there have been many noted horses sold and many stake winners secured. The extremely large average attained in 1888 was due in a measure to the price obtained for King Thomas, $38,000 being the figure at which he was purchased by Mr. Appleby, who in turn disposed of him for $40,000 to Senator Hearst; and last year the average was still kept up by the St. Blaze colt, which was bought by Mr. Daly for $22,000 and the Explosion yearling which brought the handsome sum of $10,000. This year we find, however, that there have been no sensational prices paid for any of the yearlings, but taken all in all the prices are higher than those obtained at the former sales. This encouraging outlook is enough to warrant the extension of breeding establishments in this State and is enough to force one to the belief that in the very near future Eastern buyers will be apt to visit California to attend annual sales, instead of California breeders having to send their horses back to the Eastern market.

Napa Aroused.

The communication which appears in another column signed "Napa Sportsman" is like scores of others which reach us month after month, year out and year in. It need not be said that the BREEDER AND SPORTSMAN deprecates illegal fishing, the consistent course of this paper for many years is well known and has always made for the strictest observance of the game and fish laws.

Our repeated utterances in relation to the matter have often times been reproduced in our exchanges, and we hope have contributed to the creation and growth of a right popular sentiment with regard to game and fish. At times it seems advisable to use severe phrases in characterizing the vandals who persist in destroying breeding fish and game and the young, and when such language has been used we have made no reservation, nor have we regretted its use, but it is apparent that the BREEDER AND SPORTSMAN without the active co-operation of the officials in the various counties and the intelligent assistance of sportsmen everywhere can accomplish but little. We know the hesitancy natural when it is proposed to impeach a neighbor and can hardly blame individuals for refusing to proceed actively against their fellow townsmen, even though it is notorious that they are violating the law as to fish and game. In theory no citizen can be excused who shuts his eyes in the presence of such violations, but in operation the police supervision of streams and shooting grounds rests with the paid officers of the law who are charged with a thousand other duties and who are seemingly prone to wink at fish cases and game cases anyhow. District attorneys as a rule let such matters go by default. When prosecutions are vigorously pushed it is generally at the instance of some one other than the regular County officials and the fund necessary must be contributed either by the State or by private persons. The residents of Napa are the persons most interested in maintaining a stand of food fish close at hand and we would suggest that they bring pressure to bear upon their District Attorney, their Sheriff and law officers generally and make a few examples. If the poaching vandals once see that the sentiment of the community is averse to the continuance of their nefarious practices there is every reason to suppose that illegal fishing will cease. Meantime it might not be unwise for the sportsmen and anglers of Napa City to take some concerted action as to the matters mentioned by our correspondent. The Board of Fish Commissioners has done very much and is now willing to do all that it can in behalf of protection, but funds are not at hand, and it is really asking too much to ask that gentlemen holding purely honorary positions shall open their private purses for the general welfare. One point in relation to our correspondent's letter we dislike; that is, he does not mention the name of the persons he accuses. When it is known absolutely that men are violating the law, it has a good corrective effect to hold them up to ignominy and to make their names by words.

Colt Stakes.

There can be no question but what Colt Stakes are becoming more popular every year, and under the exceedingly low entrance fees required, breeders have no hesitancy in making a large number of entries in all stakes offered either East or West. The great success of the BREEDER AND SPORTSMAN Futurity Stake in which of the two hundred and eighty-four entries, all but eleven were from the State of California, has warranted others in opening up other Futurity Stakes. Oakland with its usual characteristic enterprise followed suit and received large and abundant entries. Petaluma is already advertising a District Futurity Stake which will close on July 1st. And now comes the Chicago Horsemen offering a guaranteed stake that will be worth more money at futurity than a field of colt trotters ever contended for. This stake is for foals of 1890, and will be trotted between July 1 and October 15, 1894. The Horsemen guarantees a main stake of $11,000, divided, $5,000 to the first horse, $2,500 to the second, $1,500 to the third, $1,000 to the fourth, with plate to the actual value of $1,000 to the breeder of the winner, and a consolation stake of $1,500, to be trotted within four days from the date of the decision of the first race, open to horses that start and win no part of the main stake. The entrance of $200 is payable as follows. $10 with the nomination, on or before July 1, 1890, $10 on January 1, 1891, $10 July 1, 1891, $10 January 1, 1892, $10 July 1, 1892, $10 January 1, 1893, $10 July 1, 1893, $25 July 1, 1892, $25 January 1, 1894, and $100 for those declaring to start on July 1, 1894.

Bad Luck.

Last year the phenomenal luck of C. W. Williams, of Independence, Iowa, was in the mouths of everyone interested in any way in horse breeding. Starting as a poor man he bred two mares, one to William L. and the other to Jay Bird and from these two unions produced the wonderful colt Axtell 2:12 and Allerton 2:18¼, both records being made at three years of age. From these two mares has be secured an ample fortue, selling Axtell as he did, for the enormous sum of $105,000 yet still retaining Allerton for his own use and benefit. It would seem that lightning does not strike twice in the same place for we are sorry to have to announce that last year four mares were bred to William L., the sire of Axtell and Mr. Williams has been unfortunate enough to have nothing to show from the connections; two of the mares did not get in foal; a third one dropped a dead colt and the last of the quartette had a foal which only lived two days. Mr. Williams is a clear headed young man who will not take seriously to heart these sad losses but will undoubtedly breed back again, to see if there is still another Axtell in the loins of William L.

Goodwin's Official Stake Book.

We take much pleasure in acknowledging the receipt of a copy of Goodwin's Official Stake Entries for 1890, '91 and '92 containing the entries for all stakes which have closed from Monmouth Park and Saratoga Associations, and American, Coney Island, New York and Brooklyn Jockey Clubs, together with a complete and carefully compiled index, so that any horse whose name is mentioned in the book may be found very readily. Among the other valuable data, we find dates of declarations, closing of stakes, scale of weights, dates of meeting and list of yearlings of 1890, which has been compiled expressly for this work by Col. S. D. Bruce, compiler of the American Stud Book. It is a very valuable work for all horsemen, and should be in the hands of every breeder and thoroughbred owner in the country. Last year the price of the work was $10, but this year it has been reduced to $5, at which price it may be obtained from Messrs. Goodwin Bros., 241 Broadway, New York.

Nevada State Agricultural Society.

Taking time by the forelock the Directors of the Nevada State Agricultural Society advertise their programme for the annual fair to be held at Reno commencing Monday, September 22nd. The card, as will be seen by reference to the advertisement is a good one, there being liberal purses offered for the trotting, pacing and thoroughbred divisions. Entries do not close until the 15th day of August next, by which time owners of horses eligible for the various classes will be able to determine whether their animals are fit to start or not. We shall have occasion to speak more fully of this event as the time draws nearer for the entries to close.

The Guenoc Stock Farm.

A trip into Lake County at this season of the year is a pleasure that is always looked forward to by those who either from business or pleasure are required to cross the mountains. Last Friday morning a representative of the BREEDER AND SPORTSMAN left this city for the purpose of visiting the celebrated stock farm of Fredrick Gebhard Esq. It had been determined that the trip should be made via Calistoga, and on the train the time passed delightfully as we met those two well known horsemen, Hon. Jno. Boggs and Professor Heald. As is natural to infer, the conversation was on equine matters only; Mr. Boggs, just as enthusiastic as in the days of yore when he owned Old Langford, and the Professor confident in the thought that he has several trotters now in training with which he expects to win many first monies.

On arriving at the end of the railroad line, Mr. Palmer, representing the Middletown and Harbin Springs stage Company was on hand to receive us with two reserved outside seats, and after a hearty luncheon at the Magnolia Hotel we were soon on our way, crossing the St. Helena Mountains. The air was perfumed from the rich scents arising from the buckeyes and laurel which are to be found on both sides of the road for almost the entire drive of eighteen miles; while the day was warm, still the heat was not oppressive and as the ponderous coach slowly traveled up the side of the mountains a delightful breeze was experienced which was a relief from the sun's rays, and tended to make the grand panoramic effects, which are seen from the mountains, more enjoyable.

At 3.15 the stage pulled up in front of the Middletown Hotel and we found in waiting Dr. C. W. Aby, Superintendent of the Guenoc & Langtry Farms, with a carriage and four ready to take us the balance of the journey, some eight or nine miles. In very short order we arrived at the handsome residence of Mr. Gebhard, but owing to the fatigue from the journey, it was deemed expedient to postpone the object of our visit until the following morning.

Already much has been written in these columns in reference to the stock owned at Guenoc, but now we wish to see what class of foals has arrived since our last visit to the place. After an evening delightfully spent in talking over old reminiscences, many good stories being told by the genial doctor of things he had heard and seen while at old Nantura, the stallions were brought out the following morning for inspection. They are under the charge of Mr. Chas. Drew, a young Englishman of extended knowledge in matters equine. It was with pardonable pride that he brought out horse after horse for our inspection; the first one shown being the well bred imported Greenback; the extraordinary good care which this horse has received since his importation to Guenoc has considerably improved his appearance, and as we had not seen him since shortly after his arrival, the improvement was easily noticed. From his lordly appearance and exquisite breeding it is little wonder that he received the first premium at the State Fair last September.

St. Savior was the next horse shown and he looked as full of fire and courage as he did on that memorable day when led out to do battle for the Emporium Stakes in which he was cut down, and yet with the gameness characteristic of his family finished second to the celebrated Rataplan, on three legs only. The old scar is still observable, but in his exercise he shows no evil effects from the wound, and when being cantered back to the stable it was all the boy could do to hold him back.

Friar Tuck, the noted son of a noted sire, by Hermit, dam Romping Girl, by Wild Dayrell, is a most beautifully formed horse and one that should nick with the grand American mares that are to be found at the Gebhard Farm. He is a handsome animal and typical of the Hermit family, his services have been in great demand and it is not to be wondered at, for his breeding entitles him to a place with the best.

Several other entires were also shown, but as they were not of as high order as those spoken of, it is hardly necessary to mention them.

We now come to the primary object of our visit, viz., the foals of the year, and it is a hard matter to describe them individually where each of them are so near perfection. Glen Queen has a bay colt by St. Savior for which the name "St. Peter" has been claimed, he is a handsome well behaved youngster and shows his grand breeding in every step he takes.

Leverette has a handsome chestnut filly called "Lake County" by imp. Greenback who gives every evidence of proving a thorough race horse, she is a finely finished little thing and is a credit alike to sire and dam.

We saw also the old and well known race mare Night Hawk, proud and happy in the possession of a bay colt with a blazed face by St. Savior. This elegant young gentleman, from the performances of his parents should prove a racehorse of no mean ability.

Imp. Restless, a bay colt by St. Savior, a grand looking foal well put up, with strong sturdy legs and good back. The word little can hardly be applied to him, for he seems to be farther advanced, considering his age, than any suckling we have seen this year.

Her Ladyship has a grey or brown filly by Greenback, who is worthy of mention as she is a very handsome animal. In fact, more so than her dam who will be remembered by the patrons of the turf, as she ran only a few year ago.

We also had the pleasure of seeing Mistake, Mr. J. B. Chase's mare, who has a handsome bay colt by imp. Friar Tuck. This is one of the best looking foals on the farm, and Mr. Chase may be congratulated on having such a fine foal from the daughter of Katy Pease.

We also saw Priscilla who is the mother of a chestnut colt by imp. Mariner, she having been sent up to the farm to be bred to imp. Greenback.

Glen Ellen was also seen, she having been sent to the farm to be bred to St. Savior.

The largest foal on the place is called "Guenoc" in honor of the farm name. He is by imp. Greenback and out of Wah-ta-Wah. If size and appearance are criterions, Guenoc should prove a world beater.

The old Daniel Boone mare Prosperine has a very fine chestnut filly by Greenback. This is a beautiful animal, and one from whom much is expected.

Another of the Daniel Boone mares, Una, formerly owned by Judge Shafter of this city, has a brown filly by imp. Greenback, Leonie being the name claimed for her.

Miss Hooker has a very nice bay filly at her side by St. Savior, the name for which is claimed being "Itawamba."

These are a few of the many that were seen at this great farm, and it was with pleasure that Dr. Aby informed us that late in the summer he will start East to bring out another carload of especially selected mares for Guenoc.

To those who take this trip for the first time it may seem a long distance to go, but on arrival one is amply repaid for all the trouble and bother that it may have cost, for beyond doubt there is no place in California that is the superior to the Guenoc Farm for the purposes for which it is intended.

The rich native grasses were so thick and heavy that quantities have fallen from its own weight, one field especially of red top clover being thicker than any ever seen before by the writer. Fully a year has elapsed since the last visit was paid there, and the additions and improvements made by Dr. Aby have completely changed the look of the farm; paddocks have been laid out, fences rebuilt, stallion barns erected, with stables and other necessary buildings in profusion. A race track has been surveyed in the large field directly in front of Mr. Gebhard's residence, and when finished will be the equal of any training track in the State; it will be a full mile in length and forty feet in width, with the usual grade on the turns. It would hardly do for a public track, as in the center is a large field of oaks, which on a private track simply adds to the beauty of the place and does not detract but very little from the sight seeing. Thirty-eight men are now engaged on the place and more will be added to their number as it becomes necessary to finish up the vast and extensive improvements which are contemplated by the proprietor.

In starting for our return to the city, instead of coming back via Middleton, the trip was made homeward over Howell Mountain, we arriving in St. Helena in ample time to catch the afternoon train for San Francisco, where we duly arrived in ample time for an early dinner.

The McCarty String.

From letters received from New York we learn that the "irrepressible Dan" has arrived at Fleetwood Park with a very large number of California horses which he proposes to sell, raffle or dicker off before the snow flies in the Eastern States during the coming fall. He started from San Francisco during the first week in May and arrived in Chicago with his four carloads all in good condition, not one having even the most trifling ailment.

McCarty is as well known in the Windy City as he is in either New York or San Francisco, and it was not long before he had an enthusiastic crowd of horsemen around him to examine the consignment of California horses which he had brought on with him. To Mr. Stinson, the owner of Nutmeg 2:22½, Dan sold eight finely bred mares, viz: Susie B. by Sargent's Brown Jug; Daisy McVernon by Mt. Vernon; Lida S. by Fred Hull; Rosalie by Bay Rose 2:20½; Alzina by Nephew; Lady Waterford by Waterford; Queen of Santa Maria by Brigadier 2:21¼, and Loretta 2:29½. He also sold Grayson by Elector (sire of J. R. 2:24), to a party living in Wilton, Maine, for $5000. Three road horses were also disposed of to different parties for $1500, $1000 and $800, the entire sales just completing a carload. A week ago last Friday the outfit arrived at Fleetwood, and during the week Dan has been busy at work trying to dispose of the other three carloads. On last Sunday McCarty electrified the spectators by giving the brown gelding, Milton, a half mile in 1:09½, the best time made for the distance on the track so far this year. Wesley, a four year old green horse by Mr. Richard's Elector, was sent a mile in 2:33¼, the last half being completed in 1:14½. Wesley is a very promising young horse, and will surely make a fast one as he has had but two workouts since Dan bought him.

Of course it would not be "White Hat" if he did not patronize the running tracks, and already he has made two very large winnings figuring up in the thousands. Our correspondent says that while the party was in Chicago they were shown two handsome Director colts, one a brother to Margaret S. called Pleasanton, and the other out of Sweetness (the dam of Sidney) who will undoubtedly make a good mark for himself under the appropriate name of Saccharine. They looked so well and moved so nicely that the McCarty party were all pleased with the beautiful animals, especially as they were California productions. Sidney stands very high in the East as a sire, so our correspondent writes, and he furthermore says "We will have a chance to see one of his get start for first money at Fleetwood as the Parkville Stock Farm has Sidney Smith entered in the slow class, and he is well spoken of by those who have seen him move. Will write and tell you what he does. More anon."

VETERINARY.

Conducted by W. Henry Jones, M. R. C. V. S.

Subscribers to this paper can have advice through this column in all cases of sick or injured horses or cattle by sending an explicit description of the case. Applicants will send their name and address that they may be identified. Questions requiring answers by mail should be accompanied by two dollars, and addressed to W. Henry Jones, M. R. C. V. S., Olympic Stables, Sutter Street, San Francisco.

W. T. W.

I have an aged gelding which has shown signs of lameness for about six or seven months. There is no swelling on the fore legs and I cannot detect any sore spot. He rests one front foot and then the other, as if the pain was in the feet. Will you please inform me what is the cause of lameness, and the best remedy to apply.

Answer.—Judging from the description of your lame horse I have no hesitation in pronouncing the animal to be lame from navicular disease. The remedy I would suggest, is to have the operation of neurotomy performed, and I have no doubt that if the operation is properly and skillfully performed that the horse with care will last you some time.

Cruelty to Animals.

I consider that it is necessary that attention be drawn to the large amount of cruelty that is practiced in this city. It may be safely said that it prevails to a greater extent than in any other city in the States. One has only to observe the poor wretches that are used by fruit and fish peddlars, and notice the large piece of old sacking that is placed under the saddle and withers. If this be removed, a large suppurating wound will be brought to sight, and the sacking, in some cases, stick fast to the wound.

It would be a great boon to these animals, if some influential persons would interest themselves on their behalf, and bring a few of the owners before the police judge, and no doubt the cruelty would quickly decrease, at least for a time.

The milk ranches should also have some inspection as regards cruelty, to say nothing of the sanitary arrangements. The transportation of poultry in over-crowded boxes from the East is a too frequent cause of cruelty, many of the birds dying in transit from want of room and water.

The Deadly Glanders.

The following clipping has been sent to this office, but without the name of the paper being mentioned, so we can not give proper credit.

A number of horses have died in the vicinity of Madera during the past few weeks from a mysterious disease. The following excerpetd from a communication to the Fresno Republican may throw some light on the subject, and should be read by every owner of stock: "Every reader of your estimable journal who owns or has horses or mules in his possession ought to know that scores of animals in the valley are affected and dying with glanders or farcy. It is no stretch of imagination to say that these fatal diseases are so prevalent that it is at a risk that one waters his horse at any of the hundreds of inviting watering troughs in the county, the glanders being far more easily contracted from nasal droppings than from inhalation of the breath of diseased animals. In fact, we have known horses thus diseased to be worked with and run in the same pasture with sound horses for months that did not contract the disease, whereas a single drop of the virus did the deadly work. Hence watering places are where the disease is most generally carried from one animal to another, especially standing water, as in troughs. It may not be generally known that the glanders is a blood disease and can easily be contracted by the human family, especially by a person troubled by catarrh or lung trouble inhaling the breath of diseased animals, or by the virus getting into any embrasure of the skin. Leprosy and cancer are the only diseases to be equally dreaded and compared with the glanders when once in the system."

Answers to Correspondents.

Answers for this department must be accompanied by the name and address of the sender, not necessarily for publication, but as proof of good faith. Write the questions distinctly, and on one side of the paper only. Positively no questions will be answered by mail or telegraph.

W. K. B.

Your inquiry in reference to *Fish's Comet* we have been unable to answer. A letter was sent to the former owner, but as yet no answer has been received.

G. J., San Jose.

The dam of Dictator was Clara, by American Star Jr.; the dam of Director 1989 was Dolly by Mambrino Chief 11.

H. H. J.

There has only been one "Joe Daniels," and he is still alive at Rancho Del Paso. This is the same one that you term the "old four-mile horse." He is by imp. Australian, dam Dolly Carter by imp. Glencoe. He is chestnut in color, and is 21 years of age.

SIGN YOUR LETTERS.

There are several communications remain unanswered this week, as the writers have failed to send their names. Hereafter no queries will be answered unless this rule is complied with.

J. R. M.

Can you tell me where the famous mare Flore Temple was raised? Did she ever come as far west as Chicago?

Answer—Flora Temple, 2:19¾, was bred by Samuel Welch, Oneida County, N. Y. She trotted several times in Chicago.

Foals of 1890.

At Palo Alto Stock Farm: *Property of Hon. Leland Stanford.*

B f by Azmoor—Edith Carr by Clark Chief.
Ch f by Allie Wilkes—Kitty by Exchequer.
B c by Clay—Ramona by Bentonian.

At Vina Ranch, Tehama Co., Cal.

B f by Beverly—Patti by Don Victor.
B f by Benefit—Flora by Whipple's Hambletonian.
B f by Benefit—Wildred by Mohawk Chief.
B c by Benefit—Wilmina by Mohawk Chief.
B c by Benefit—Addie W. by Whips.
B c by Benefit—Susie by Geo. M. Patchen J.

Property of Alex. Waugh.

Bay filly, foaled May 23, 1890, by Lottery, dam Lucy W.

Names Claimed.

I hereby claim to the name of BEN MA CHREE for a sorrell colt, white star in the face, foaled March 8th 1890, by Three Cheers dam Jaunita Lee, by Joe Daniels. Also,

MISS NELSON for a sorrell filly, no marks, foaled March 6th, 1890 by Three Cheers, dam Bonita Lee by Joe Daniels.

STOCKTON. FRED WALKER.

I hereby claim the name of EARLY WILKES for bay filly, with star in forehead, also diamond on nose, foaled March 1st, 1890, by Wilkes Moor, son of Guy Wilkes, dam Dolly by California Plow-Boy. I. W. DIXON.

Colonia Farm, Ventura Co.

Owing to errors in a former publication of the following, the list is again given, with the necessary corrections.

FLYAWAY, for sorrel filly, blaze in face, foaled February 8th, 1890, by Birdcatcher, dam Skipaway by Wildidle.

FAIRLAWN, for sorrel colt, blaze in face, two white stockings on right side, foaled April 3rd, 1890, by Birdcatcher, dam Talluda by Enquirer.

WILDFLOWER, for dark bay filly, foaled April 5th, 1890, by Birdcatcher dam Lottie L. by Wildidle.

MANHATTAN, for sorrel colt, blaze in face, white stockings on left hind foot, foaled April 23rd, 1890, by Birdcatcher, dam Ursula by Duke of Montrose.

SIR EDWARD, for dark brown colt, two hind feet tipped with white, by Birdcatcher, dam Harriet by Flood.

E. F. FALLON, Fairlawn Farm, Hollister.

The Portland Races.

It is very evident that there is something the matter with the mails or there is something the matter with our Portland correspondent, as we have failed to receive the full reports of the races at that point which we fully expected in time for the current issue of the BREEDER AND SPORTSMAN. The following synopsis of the events have been culled from the brief reports received in this city but which for some unaccountable reason have been spoken of very rarely by the daily papers:

On the first day the well known chestnut colt Guido by Double Cross, dam Aurora by Thad Stevens, won a good race beating the Dennison Bros.' Princesses' First, Witmore's Coloma, Green's J. M. R. and Sear's Carrie M., the horses running in the order given. Time for the seven-eighths of a mile 1:31. Mutual pools on Guido paid $20.50. J. H. McDonough was fortunate enough with his roan horse Tim Murphy to win the half mile dash in 50 seconds, beating such good ones as Daily Oregonian, Sunday, Cyclone and Ben L.

The 2:26 class for trotters brought out Kitty Ham, Alta, Lady Beach and Blondie; Kitty Ham won the first, 5th and 6th heats, the 2nd heat being a dead one between her and Alta; Lady Beach captured the 3rd heat while Blondie was fortunate enough to take the 4th. The best time made in the race was 2:32.

On the second day Sunday won the five-eighths dash in the very good time of 1:03½.

The second race of the day, a mile-dash, fell to Guido with Tom Daly, a good 2nd. Time 1:44½.

The race for the 2:50 class for trotters was rather uninteresting, the winner turning by in Hannibal, Jr.

The third day brought Sinfax to the front. The Cy Mulkey colt managed to beat R. E. Bybee's Rain Drop, Dennison's Princess' First, Green's J. M. R. and Sears's Carrie M., the time being 1:16½ for three-fourths. In the trotting race Susie S. had no difficulty in beating her opponents, winning in straight heats, time being 2:29½, 2:29½ and 2:31½.

There was also a three-eighths of a mile and repeat race, the entries for which were Sunday, Cyclone, Red Dick, Little Dick and Ben L., Sunday winning the 1st and 3rd heats while Cyclone took the 2nd. The time was 36, 36½ and 35½ seconds.

The last day's races showed up Guido as a winner in the mile and repeat, Guido winning handily in 1:44½ and 1:44. In the first heat Tom Daly was second and Coloma third, but in the final heat the positions were reversed, Coloma being 2nd and Daly 3rd.

In the 2.40 trotting race Mozier's Joe Kinney had no difficulty in defeating the field, the best time made being 2:32½.

The free-of-all trotters was productive of a great surprise, Lady Beach winning the first heat in 2:35, while Alta won the 2nd in 2:32½. Alta also won the 3rd heat in exactly the same time, but becoming lame was easily beaten in the next three heats by Little Joe, who took the 4th, 5th and 6th heats, his best time being 2:32.

Breeding Trotters.

The majority of professional trainers, those which rank among the best, have probably had but little experience in breeding trotters. By far the greater portion of them have given the subject but comparatively little thought. There are exceptions, however, and among these is the well known trainer Charles Marvin, who, it is safe to assert, has broken a greater number of records with trotters that he has developed than any other trainer living or dead.

During the past twelve years Mr. Marvin has been located at Palo Alto, the most successful trotting breeding establishment in the world. This has given him a better opportunity than any other trainer ever enjoyed to study from a practical standpoint the science of breeding trotters. His views upon the subject should prove both interesting and profitable to young breeders. The following is an extract from Marvin's recent work, "Training the Trotting Horse":

"On no other subject connected with the trotting horse has so much been written as on breeding, and on no other do opinions so widely differ. I do not propose to theorize on the subject, nor to treat it exhaustively, as my main subject is how to train the trotter rather than how to breed him; but I may briefly throw together the conclusions that have formed in my mind from extended observations with trotters.

"First, I hold that there has been wide error, not, perhaps, in giving too much attention to blood to the exclusion of everything else. Form and action, I believe, have been too generally neglected, and especially is this true of action. Although it may seem paradoxical to say so, the gait I would consider perfection in a campaigner would not exactly suit me for a stock horse. I would perfer for a sire a horse with abundant and exuberant action, both before and behind, [illegible]e with perfectly true and square stroke, and without a touch of mixing.

"I do not object to a horse starting on an amble, but when he trots let it be a trot. I do not care how a horse is bred, nor how good he is individually, if his action is faulty he would not suit me for a sire. A foul-gaited horse will get foul gaited progeny, and that kind can never hold their own with evenly balanced trotters. Action is not the only thing in a sire, but it is an essential for the absence of which nothing can atone.

"I believe that the chief reason why Smuggler has not been a greater success than he is as a sire is because he has not the proper order of action. I would expect of course the best results from Smuggler when bred to mares with excessive action.

"The truest kind of action is what we may call line trotting. The horse does not sprawl to get his hind feet outside of the front ones. The hind foot goes low, and the fore foot is lifted just high enough to let the hind one go under, not outside of the front one.

"I like a horse with a fairly wide chest, and the legs to stand well apart, and fall straight to the ground (not "both come out of one hole" like a sawhorse), and they should be especially well muscled. The idea that a narrow chest is favorable for speed arose, I suppose, from the idea that a horse's hind feet must necessarily go outside of his front ones in trotting. It is certainly an error.

"I need not go into a lengthy description of what the form of an ideal stallion ought to be; you all know it. He should be of fair size, with a good, brainy, intelligent head, a strong, sloping shoulder, a round barrel, with a strong, springy loin, quarters of great power, muscled well inside and out, strong gaskins and forearms, square set hocks and knees, short cannons, strong pasterns of medium angle and good feet.

"Some will argue that long cannons are just as good as short ones; that a horse with a long cannon will stride just as far as a short cannoned horse. That may be true, but I hold that all the driving power is above the hock, and all the muscles run from that point upward, and the horse with the longest thigh has the greatest driving power, and more leverage to handle the leg and foot.

"In the dam I want also good action, but I would not be quite as exacting in her case as to have plenty of it, for, right or wrong, it is my belief that the sire generally controls the action. Sallie Benton's dam had very little action; Dame Winnie, the dam of Palo Alto (2:12¾), and Annette, the dam of Ansel (2:20), had not any to speak of, but they were mated with Electioneer, a horse of superabundant action. I would avoid a brood mare with faulty action, just as I would a sire. Let what they have be square, true and good.

"I like a broodmare of moderate size. The dam of Manzanita stood only 14.3; the dam of Bonita, 14.2. Beautiful Bells and Dame Winnie are 15.2; May Queen fifteen hands. I prefer mares of rather blocky build, and that they should have good heads, tempers and dispositions. I need not say that soundness should be exacted in a broodmare, and of course the more perfect the general form the better. The idea that anything will do for a broodmare is a fallacy of bygone days. If I were breeding trotters I would have good mares or none.

"In conclusion, I like the sire and dam to be developed trotters, and the faster they can go the better. If they are natural trotters, and have in training shown great speed, together with good form and balance, from mating them you are almost sure to get a trotter. As for the trotting blood you have, of course the richer the better. The best test of trotting blood is how fast and how much it has trotted, and how many and how fast trotters it has produced. Any kind of blood is better than unknown blood."

Preserve your horses' health by sprinkling Darbys Fluid freely about their stables.

A Curious Craze in Horse-Breeding.

Even the most casual student of human nature must admit that he was not deserving of the epithet "cynic" who first declared that men are like sheep—where one leads others follow pell-mell. The most superficial observer of the affairs of men knows this to be the most patent fact of human history. In a multitude of forms it finds manifestation. It is not difficult to read a bit of evidence of the decent of man from the ape in the actions of the imitative monkey. In every line of human thought, in every field of human action the vast majority of men are imitators, each following a lead which appeals to his fancy, his ambition or his cupidity. In politics, religion, society or business, men tread in the footsteps of predecessors so closely that, like the band of indians marching single file over the snow-covered prairie, each moccasined foot falling unerringly into the track before it, they leave but a single trail behind.

These reflections are awakened by the fact that all agricultural Iowa has turned its attention to trying to breed Axtells and Allertons. Williams' wonderful luck has driven Iowa well nigh daft, and nearly every dung-hill old mare in the State has been stinted this season to a trotting-bred stallion at stud fees exhorbitantly, ridiculously, appallingly high. Especially is this craze manifested for stallions of Wilkes blood—whence probably comes the phenomenal speed of the two Iowa wonders—but the book of every stallion which carries a drop of trotting blood, fashionable or unfashionable, in his veins has been crowded with mares at stud fees heretofore scarcely dreamed of. The surpassing absurdity of this craze—for it is worthy of no higher term—is seen in the character of the mares thus bred from which it is fondly hoped fortunes will be dropped in the shape of record-breaking foals. Such singularly grotesque mismating has never before been seen in the history of horse breeding on this continent. Instead of seeking a stallion fitted in form and character to mate with a given mare, her owner puts her to the first standard-bred stallion he comes upon, be the two never so incongruous in character. What the harvest will be is not difficult to foretell. It is not the first time that Bohemian oats have been bought by the farmer greedy for undue gain. Seeds have many times been sown the cost of which the crop did not realize. The Gazette suggests the possibility that there will be more paid out in trotting stallion fees this season in Iowa than the entire crop of colts from the misfit unions now being made will bring when put upon the market. There is food for thought in this suggestion.

The Gazette of all papers is the least apt to object to the use of high-class, high-priced stallions when properly chosen to mate with the mares to be bred. No journal has more persistantly taught the necessity of patronizing first class sires, even at increased service fees; but there are limits to all things—save space and eternity. It now seems as if we should have to revise our philosophy to include among these things without limits, the Iowa trotting-bred stallion service fees. Surely the farmers of the "Hawkeye" State overlooked the fact that Axtells and Allertons are the produce of a half century. The labor of parturition necessary to produce such phenomenons seems to exhaust Dame Nature as to render her incapable for decades of another such birth. And yet the Mountain of agricultural Iowa is in costly labor; when the mouse is brought forth there will be many a wiser—and sadder—Man.—Breeders' Gazette.

Gen. Fine has the Petaluma track in good condition, and the many horses in training there are doing well. Lee Shaner is beginning to "move up" a few of his good ones, although as yet no extraordinary time has been made.

THE KENNEL.

Dog owners are requested to send for publication the earliest possible notices of whelps, sales, names claimed, presentations and deaths, in their kennels, in all instances writing plainly names of sire and dam and of grandparents, colors, dates and breed.

Names Claimed.

J. B. Martin, San Francisco Cal, claims the names:

GOLDEN FAIRY, for white, with ticked ear, fox terrier bitch pup, whelped April 3rd 1890, by Blemton Vesuvian, (Champion Lucifer—Blemton Vesta) out of Beatrice, (Champion Bacchanal—Blemton Arrow).

GOLDEN FLEECE. for white fox terrier dog pup, same litter.

GOLDEN DUST, for white, black and tan fox terrier pup, same litter.

Sales.

J. B. Martin, San Francisco, Cal., has sold Golden Lilly, white foxterrier bitch, whelped July 24, 1889, by Clover Turk (Mixture—Spite), out of Beatrice (Champion Bacchanal—Blemton Arrow), to Mr. Lowden, San Francisco, Cal.

——, white, black and tan foxterrier bitch pup, whelped April 3, 1890, by Blemton Vesuvian (Champion Lucifer—Blemton Vesta), out of Beatrice (Champion Bacchanal—Blemton Arrow), to Mr. I. N. Isaac, Tulare, Cal.

——, white, black and tan foxterrier bitch, same litter, to Captain A. B Anderson, San Gabriel, Cal.

——, white, black and tan foxterrier dog, same litter, to Captain A. B. Anderson, San Gabriel, Cal.

——, fawn, black mask mastiff dog pup, whelped March, 1890, by Leo (Neno 2d—Gypsey), out of Bess, to Mrs. Treadwell, San Francisco, Cal.

A Pointer With a Wooden Leg.

There is a man now in the north of France who lives in an out-of-the-way village on the coast, and shoots for the market, who has a most extraordinary pointer, one with a wooden leg—says an exchange. This is the near hind leg, which, it appears, was run over by a cart two or three years ago, and had to be amputated. The dog was then six years old, and rather than destroy his faithful and invaluable companion the owner appealed to the local doctor, who fitted a wooden leg to the stump.

At first the dog wanted to gnaw the wound, but eventually he recovered and now takes no notice of his unusual appendage. He goes at a trot with a very slight limp, so slight as to be hardly noticeable. The bottom of the artificial leg is fitted with a round mushroom head-shaped iron ferrule, rather broader than the wood, and so far as work is concerned the dog, who is a *Braque*, is in no way impeded.

He is as firm as a rock on his points and retrieves marvelously well.

The American Beagle Club.

EDITOR BREEDER AND SPORTSMAN:—The American Beagle Club desires, through your columns, to call attention to its organization and the benefits to the breed arising from such club.

The club has been in existence for some seven years, and has done a great deal of good in perfecting the breed and bringing order out of chaos then existing when the club was arranged. At bench shows at the time mentioned one judge would award prizes to the large species, and another would fancy the smaller ones, which created dissension by clashing of opinions, and exhibitors were all at sea. After the Beagle Club was formed, it centralized ideas in regard to merit and demerit of the ideal dog, and filled a long felt want. It was gotten up with the intention of including all Beagle breeders and owners in the United States, and the club heartily extends an invitation to join to all such that reside on the Pacific slope, and all readers of your valuable journal. Follow in are the standard and scale of points which will prove gof interest to all who have any welfare in this favorite of breeds.

STANDARD—HEAD.

The skull should be moderately domed at the occiput. with the cranium broad and full. The ears set on low, long and fine in texture, the forward or front edge closely framing and inturned to the cheek, rather broad and rounded at the tips, with an almost entire absence of erectile power at their origin.

The eyes full and prominent, rather wide apart, soft and lustrous, brown or hazel in color. The orbital processes well developed. The expression gentle, subdued and pleading.

The muzzle of medium length, squarely cut, the stop well defined. The jaws should be level. Lips either free from or with moderate flews. Nostrils large, moist and open.

DEFECTS.—A flat skull narrow across the top of the head, absence of dome. Ears short, set on too high, or when the dog is excited rising above the line of the skull at their points of origin due to an excess of erectile power. Ears pointed at the tips, thick or boardy in substancel or carried out from cheek showing a space between. Eyes of a light or yellow color. Muzzle long and snipey. Pig jaws or the reverse known as under shot. Lips showing deep *pendulous* flews.

DISQUALIFICATIONS.—*Eyes close together, small, beady and terrier-like.*

NECK AND THROAT.

Neck rising free and light from the shoulders, strong in substance, yet not loaded, of medium length. The throat clean and free from folds of skin, a slight wrinkle below the angle of the jaw, however, may be allowable.

DEFECTS.—A thick, short, cloddy neck, carried on a line with the top of the shoulder. Throat showing dewlap and folds of skin to a degree termed "throatiness."

SHOULDERS AND CHEST.

Shoulders somewhat declining, muscular, but not loaded, conveying the idea of freedom of action, with lightness, activity and strength. Chest moderately broad and full.

DEFECTS.—Upright shoulders and a disproportionately wide chest.

BACK, LOIN AND RIBS.

Back short, muscular and strong. Loin broad and slightly arched, and the ribs well sprung, giving abundant lung room.

DEFECTS.—A long or swayed back, a flat, narrow loin, or a flat constricted rib.

FORELEGS AND FEET.

Forelegs straight with plenty of bone. Feet close, firm, and either round or harelike in form.

DEFECTS.—Out elbows. Knees knuckled over or forward, or bent backward. Feet open and spreading.

HIPS, THIGHS, HIND-LEGS AND FEET.

Hips strongly muscled, giving abundant propelling power. Stifles strong and well let down. Hocks firm, symmetrical and moderately bent. Feet close and firm.

DEFECTS.—Cow hocks and open feet.

TAIL.

The tail should be carried gaily, well up and with medium curve, rather short as compared with size of the dog, and clothed with a decided brush.

DEFECTS.—A long tail, with a tea pot curve.

DISQUALIFICATIONS.—A thinly haired rattish tail, with entire absence of brush.

COAT.

Moderately coarse in texture, and of good length.

DISQUALIFICATIONS.—A short, close and nappy coat.

HEIGHT.

The meaning of the term "Beagle," (a word of Celtic origin and in old English begele) is small, little. The dog was so named from his diminutive size. Your committee therefore for the sake of consistency, and that the Beagle shall be in fact what his name implies, strongly recommends that the height line be sharply drawn at fifteen inches, and that all dogs exceeding that height shall be disqualified as over grown, and outside the pale of recognition.

COLOR.

All hound colors are admissable. Perhaps the most popular is black, white and tan. Next in color is the lemon and white, then blue and lemon mottles, then follow the solid colors, such as black and tan, tan, lemon, fawn, etc.

This arrangement is of course arbitrary, the question being one governed entirely by fancy. The colors first named form the most lively contrast and blend better in the pack, the solid colors being sombre and monotonous to the eye.

It is not intended to give a point value to color in the scale for judging, as before said all true hounds being correct. The foregoing remarks on the subject are therefore simply suggestive.

GENERAL APPEARANCE.

A miniature fox hound, solid and big for his inches, with the wear and tear look of the dog that can last in the chase and follow his quarry to the death.

NOTE.—Dogs possessing such serious faults as are enumerated under the heading of "Disqualifications" are under the grave suspicion of being of impure blood.

Under the heading of "Defects" objectionable features are indicated; such departures from the standard not, however, impugning the purity of the breeding.

SCALE OF POINTS.

	POINTS.
HEAD—	
Skull	5
Ears	15
Eyes	10
Muzzle, Jaws and Lips	5
BODY—	
Neck	5
Shoulders and Chest	10
Back and Loins	15
Ribs	5
RUNNING GEAR—	
Forelegs and Feet	10
Hips, Thighs and Hind-Legs	10
COAT AND STERN—	
Tail	5
Coat	5
Total	100

Beagle breeders are aware of the fact that a Standard and Scale of Points are an absolute necessity, so that an authorized type of the Beagle Hound is made apparent for Bench Show Judges to base their decisions upon, as no two are similar in opinion, as to quality and the breed marks of the race. With an accepted standard, a Judge has a guide to lead him through the difficulties of his position, and the breeder if a novice will be enabled with its assistance to discard those animals that are deficient in quality, and recognize merit where it exists, thus elevating the status of his kennel.

The present officers of the club are: President—Herman F. Schellhass, No. 6 Brevoort Place, Brooklyn, N. Y; Secretary and Treasurer—Louis Smith, East Saginaw Mich., care of Evening News; Executive Committe—George Laick, Tarrytown N. Y; Wm. H. Child, 613 Commerce St. Philadelphia Pa.; J. M. Fronefield Jr., Wayne Pa.

If any readers of this article are desirous of joining the American Beagle Club, they are respectfully invited to send their names to the Secretary.

LOUIS C. SMITH, Sec. A. B. C.

Sport at Coronado.

A party of fourteen riders was made up at Coronado on June 12th for an afternoon with hounds and hares. The party was made up at the hotel about 3 o'clock, and the horsemen and horsewomen, of whom there were half a dozen, were followed to the hunting ground by a number of the hotel guests in carriages.

Of the 1,000 acres comprising North Island fully one-half has been plowed this season, by the Beach Company and planted to barley. The crop was off, and only the stubble was left. It was over this stubble that most of the chasing was made. The surrounding thickets were found to be full of rabbits, which the dogs uncovered and chased to the clearing, and then came the horsemen. The chase on several occasions was a long and exciting one, and the sport was rarely enjoyed by all.

Ernie Babcock, Mr. Babcock's eldest son, was the successful captor of the first rabbit, Miss Siebrin securing the second, and Miss Huntington the third. E. S. Babcock was himself among the foremost riders, but he can take lessons from his boys in rabbit-hunting, his younger son being in for the "brush" of two jacks before his father had captured one.

Patterson Sprigg, J. Callen, W. O. Gassoway, Budd Story, W. H. Doud, Mr. Simmons, Mr. Shaffer, Dr. Yeaman, Dr. Morton, and a number of other San Diego riders were among the party, and all were led by J. T. Fisher, of the Beach, who was master of the hounds.

The hounds used were gaze-hounds, and were secured from the Valley Hunt Club of Pasadena. They have been too well kept by somebody and were over fat for heavy work in soft soil. The result was that they tired easily. Proper training and frequent hunts will remedy all that, however.

The sport has been entered into with enthusaism by the Beach people, and a club is to be organized for holding meets once or twice a week during the summer. Mr. Babcock will secure several more dogs, and there is talk of diversifying the sport occasionally by introducing a fox or a coyote.

Mr. Allender's Kennels.

EDITOR BREEDER AND SPORTSMAN:—As requested I will give you a slight description of George Allender's new quarters.

It is about five miles from Watsonville and can be reached from this city by the 8.30 A. M. train, having the train stopped at Vega, a flag station, 3 miles this side of Pajaro, and a walk of a short mile lands one at the best location for the purpose I ever saw. It is in a nice nook sheltered from both North and East winds. He has leased about twenty acres—part in orchards, about two acres of lake—some in vegetables and the rest pasturage.

On the left as you enter is the yard where he can turn a batch (four) of dogs to play about until he cleans out their, I may say stalls, because they are more like stalls than kennels. Then they are returned to their kennels and another batch are turned out. After the yard comes a nest of four stalls or kennels the arrangement of which I like very much. They are airy but still warm. They stand about a foot or 15 inches above the ground. The floor has a slope of 2 inches from the rear towards the door. The bed is made at the rear by simply putting a loose piece of board across which is removed when it is required to wash out the kennels. A little distance from this comes another batch, then 20 yards further along is an outbuilding where he has his caldron for cooking, and on the wall are hooks for collars and chains, etc, all in apple-pie order. Another portion of this building is used as a store room. Then directly across the drive stands his cottage. Further along are more nests of kennels—only four in each nest and sufficiently far apart to prevent dogs in one nest contracting any contagious disease from dogs in the next nest. Another good thing is the security of the dogs never being either drowned or burned up—misfortunes which George has had to pass through. Had he been at this pots last January I should never have suffered the loss of the finest bitch I ever owned. He has sown a patch near the house with rye grass for the dogs to eat—another good thing. I may say I never saw his dogs looking better. There are lots of quail all around even in his orchard.

Dog owners may place their dogs in Allender's hands with perfect confidence of their being safe and well cared for.

JAMES E. WATSON.

A valuable dog belonging to S. Sellers of Livermore was poisoned last Saturday by some scoundrel. Mr. Sellers offers a reward of $100 for the arrest and conviction of the miscreant.

Mr. Stubenrauch's pointer Diana, (Professor—Belle H.) whelped May 26th, eight, three dogs, to W. D. Howe's Don (Climax—Drab D.)

Membership in the American Beagle Club, described in another column, may be acquired by sending the name of the applicant together with two dollars to the Secretary, Mr. Louis Smith, East Saginaw, Mich., Care of Evening News.

Attention is again called to the presence of Dan Gladstone (Gladstone—Sue) at 844 Harrison St., City, and to the fact that he can be utilized at stud.

Mr. H. T. Payne of Los Angeles is breeding to him and others should do so.

Mr. C. M. Osborn's grand pointer, Professor, is surrounding himself with fine representatives, the last lot being grand-descendants which are advertised for sale in another column by "V. S." The blood is superior, and the youngsters, combining the excellencies of Professor, Diana, Belle H., Don, Climax and Drab D. should be clinkers. Intending buyers should examine them.

THE GUN.

Blue Rock Club.

Secretary Charles F. Stone very kindly sent the scores of the last meeting in time for our last issue but they were accidentally obscured, and are now presented with an apology to the efficient executive officer and the members.

The Club met at Oakland Trotting Park on June 7th, ten members being present. The day was warm and the breeze materially helped the targets.

The shooting is done under American Association rules. The scores were, at 15 singles and 5 pairs of Blue Rock Targets.

SINGLES.

J. O. Cadman	1	1	0	1	0	1	1	0	1	0	1	1	1	0	1
Slade	0	0	1	1	1	1	1	0	1	1	0	1	1	1	0
Maynard	1	0	1	0	0	1	1	1	1	1	0	0	0	0	0
Moore	1	0	1	0	0	1	1	1	1	1	1	1	1	1	0
H. Golcher	1	0	1	0	1	1	1	1	1	1	1	1	1	1	1
Mayhew	0	1	0	0	0	0	0	1	0	1	1	0	1	1	1
Swane	0	1	1	0	1	1	0	0	0	1	1	1	0	0	1
Boardman	0	1	0	0	0	1	0	1	1	1	1	0	0	1	1
Abbot	0	0	0	1	0	1	1	0	1	1	1	0	1	1	0

PAIRS.

J. O. Cadman	10	11	11	11	10—18
Slade	10	00	10	11	10—15
Maynard	11	10	10	00	10—11
Moore	10	10	01	01	10—16
H. Golcher	11	10	01	11	11—21
Mayhew	00	00	10	01	10—11
Swane	00	10	10	10	11—13
Boardman	11	11	11	10	01—16
Abbot	00	10	11	10	11—13
Bell	01	10	10	00	11—(5)

Suisun Gun Club.

The members comprising the above named club met at the Arlington Hotel, Suisun, last Sunday evening and elected the following officers to serve for the ensuing year: W. G. Downing, M D, president; J. W. Harper, treasurer; Wm. H. Bryant secretary. The club has secured the privilege of shooting on the Stables tract of land adjoining the town on the north, where the railroad crosses Main street, and have had built suitable sheds, benches, etc, for the comfort of its members. The first regular shoot of the club will take place to-morrow afternoon, June 22. Several impromptu matches have taken place during the week between the members, in all of which Dr. Downing, carried off the laurels. He made a remarkable score on Tuesday, of four out of a possible twelve, with the advantage however of the wind blowing 30 miles an hour against the traps, causing the birds to remain almost stationary in the air. The club extends an invitation to all lovers of the gun to attend any of its meetings.

Selby Live Bird Medal Contest.

The second match for the live-bird medal offered by the Selby Smelting and Lead Company was shot off at Oakland Trotting Park on Sunday last. The birds were good, and the day propitious, but only a handful of spectators attended, and just four entries were made. The shooting was not very good, many birds dying out of bounds. The medal was first won by Mr. C. B. Smith, and now passes into the hands of Mr. C. J. Haas. The scores were:

At 25 birds; American Shooting Association rules:

R. A. Eddy	2	1	1	1	2	0	1	0	0	0	2	2	2	0	1	2	1	1	1	1	2	0	0	1	1—18
C. B. Smith	0	2	0	1	2	0	0	0	2	2	2	1	1	1	0	1	0	1	1	2	1	1	0	2	1—17
C. J. Haas	0	2	2	1	2	2	1	2	0	2	1	1	1	1	1	1	1	1	0	1	0	1	0	1	0—19
F. "Randall"	2	1	2	1	2	0	2	0	0	1	1	0	2	0	1	1	0	1	2	1	2	1	1	1	1—18

Pools, into which each man who entered put $5, were shot for in the afternoon. Six birds were shot at in each case, with about the following results from all entries:

E. Fay	1	2	1	2	2	2—6
C. Robinson	1	1	1	2	2	1—6
C. J. Haas	2	1	1	2	2	0—5
C. B. Smith	1	0	2	2	1	2—5
"Randall"	2	1	0	1	2	1—5

In the other pools the money was about equally divided by the gentlemen named, and by Messrs. "Randall," Haas and Smith.

Pacific Sportsmen's Club.

The June meeting of the club was held at the Gerber grounds in the suburbs of Sacramento, on Sunday last. The birds were strong flyers, and the fresh breeze carried them away from the traps in a manner to severely test the shooters' abilities. The gold medal was won by Frank Ruhstaller with a score of 11 out of 12

After the medal shoot several pool matches were shot, in which Messrs. Damm and Gerber were the winners. The medal scores were:

Ruhstaller	1	1	1	1	1	1	1	0	1	1	1	1—11
Gerber	1	1	1	1	1	1	1	1	1	0	1	0—10
Gotobed	0	1	1	1	1	1	1	0	1	1	1	1—10
Bennett	1	0	1	1	1	1	0	1	0	1	1	1—9
Dwyer	1	1	0	1	1	0	1	1	0	1	0	1—9
George	0	0	1	1	1	1	1	1	0	1	1	1—9
Damm	1	1	0	1	1	1	1	1	1	0	1	0—9
Chapman	1	1	1	1	1	0	1	0	1	1	1	0—9
Kuns	1	1	1	1	1	0	1	0	0	1	1	1—9
Talman	0	1	1	1	1	1	1	1	0	0	1	1—9
Nicolaus	1	0	1	0	1	0	1	0	1	1	1	1—8
Sims	0	1	1	1	1	0	0	1	1	1	1	0—1
Grubler	1	0	0	1	0	1	1	0	1	1	1	1—8
Flohr	1	1	1	0	0	1	1	1	0	1	0	1—7
Maddux	0	1	1	0	1	0	1	1	1	1	1	0—7
Wittenbrock	1	1	0	1	0	0	1	1	1	0	0	0—6
Wenke	1	1	0	1	0	1	0	0	0	0	1	0—5

Alameda County Club.

The Alameda County Sportsman's Club held its fourth shoot of the season at the Oakland Trotting Park Sunday afternoon. Although the birds were old and strong, they flew from the trap badly on account of the warm weather. The scores were as follows:

S. E. Knowles	1	0	1	1	1	1	1	1	1	1	0	1—10
W. W Haskell	1	1	1	1	1	1	1	1	1	1	0	1—11
C. M. Osborn	1	1	1	1	1	1	1	1	1	1	1	1—12
R. E. Bell	1	0	1	1	1	1	1	0	1	1	1	1—10
C. B. Smith	1	1	0	1	0	0	1	1	1	1	1	1—9
Charles Lainer	0	0	1	0	1	0	0	1	1	1	1	1—7
C. T. Morrison	1	1	0	1	1	1	1	0	0	1	0	1—8
C. Schroder	1	0	1	1	1	1	0	1	1	0	1	1—9
Boardman	1	1	1	1	1	1	1	1	1	1	1	1—12
W. E. Mayhew	1	1	1	1	1	1	0	1	1	1	1	1—11
Cadman	1	1	0	1	1	1	1	0	1	1	0	*—9

Mr. Haskell not being present at the May shoot, he was allowed 12 extra birds, of which he killed 11. The tie was then shot off between Osborn and Boardman for first prize, resulting as follows:

Osborn	1	1	1	1	0	1—5
Boardman	1	1	1	0	0	0—3

The next event was a pool shoot, $2.50 entrance, 6 birds, resulting as follows:

"Randall"	1	1	1	1	0	1—5
Smith	1	1	0	1	1	1—5
Schroeder	0	1	1	1	1	1—5
Pixley	1	1	0	1	1	1—5
Swett	1	1	1	0	1	1—5
Lainer	1	0	1	1	1	1—5
Lake	0	1	0	1	1	1—4
Boardman	1	1	1	0	0	*—3
Moses	1	0	0	1	1	*—3

A New Club.

A Sportsman's club was organized last week in Yreka, Mendocino Co., by about twenty of the lovers of hunting and fishing. The object of the club is to procure game birds and fish that are foreign to the county and that would be the means of furnishing sport to all who are fond of hunting and fishing, also to see that the game laws of the State and county are strictly enforced. It has been a well known fact for years past that parties are in the habit of killing deer and antelope out of season, and particularly in the winter season, when they are killed for their pelts, and their carcasses left to rot. If this is allowed to continue, it will be only a few years before it would be almost impossible to find any game at all in our mountains, where in early days, it was no unusual sight to see deer and antelope in bands of hundreds, while now very seldom more than three or four can be seen at once. The introduction of a lot of fine fish for food will also receive their attention, and they have been promised 70,000 Eastern trout and Lake Tahoe trout to begin with. These could not be obtained before the State Commissioners were assured that the fish would be prevented from leaving the main streams and entering the irrigation ditches, which would be guarded against by the use of screens, probably placed at the head of all irrigating ditches. After some time and trouble, the Board of Supervisors passed a screen law with this object in view, and it is now the firm determination of the members of the club to see that the law is strictly enforced. It does not work any hardship on any one to obey the law, and it will be wise for all who have ditches of any size, to place screens at their heads and save themselves trouble and expense. This movement on the part of the sportsmen is certainly a good one, and it is hoped that all will do what they can to make it a success. The regular officers of the year have been elected, their by-laws and constitution adopted, and they are now ready for business or pleasure. During the year they will hold both rifle and shotgun shooting tournaments, to be participated in by members of the club, and at the annual meeting of the State Sportsman's Association, the club will have its representatives selected from those who have the best scores for the year. They will hold monthly meetings, or oftener as business may require.

In another portion of the paper Mr. E. T. Allen, sole agent for the Pacific Coast, whose store is at 416 Market St., city, advertises the original and only genuine Canadian Hunting Boots of the original high quality but at reduced prices. The original Canadian Hunting Boots were introduced by Mr. Allen nearly four years ago. They are made of oil tanned material. The leg is made of select alum tanned calf skin with bellows tongue, to lace. The bottom and uppers are in one piece like a moccasin. The boots and shoes are hand-sewed, neat, light and most comfortable; a man's boots weighing but 2½ lbs. per pair, ladies' but 1½ lbs. per pair. The shoes weigh but 2 lbs. per pair. They are very highly recommended by the sportsmen and campers who have used them, and are most popular where they are best known. Mr. Allen has in stock many hundreds of pairs of new and improved styles, and those who wish a light, easy and practically indestructible boot or shoe of the sort will find their profit in examining the Canadian. At this season of the year when all the world goes abroad, a well-shaped shoe is a *sine qua non*, and those who use the Canadian will find that after a summering in the mountains where protracted pedestrian exercise is taken, their feet are in perfect condition. For children especially the shoes are most admirable since they can be laced around the ankle affording firm support while the youngsters are climbing about under unusual conditions and more than commonly exposed to sprains or wrenches of the extremities.

J. H. Philip, E B. Batchelder and C. J. McDonald are building a house-boat at Hayward's landing near San Mateo for use this fall when hunting on the marshes. It is a scow eight feet wide, upon which a small house, 12x8 feet, is built with a four foot platform at each end. Inside are two double bunks affording sleeping accommodations for four men besides a stove and a table. The purpose of the boat is to furnish a rendezvous for the owners after a day's sport. It will be towed about the marsh by means of row boats. Similer boats are in use upon the Sacramento river and are known as "arks" The cost is about $60.

The other day Lum Mulkey, Geo. Grubb, Bobby Re·s and Albert Amonsen visited Agency creek near Salem City, Or., for the purpose of capturing a wild horse that had been running there for some time. They were all well mounted and equipped for the trip, and as they were riding carelessly along they came upon a young grizzly, who ran from them at the first glimpse. They gave chase and soon overhauled and lassoed him, and after dragging him for some distance got him into the creek, where he was finally captured and placed in a sack and conveyed to George Yearian's ranch, where he was put into a small enclosure for safe keeping. He would fight anybody or anything that went into the pen. The boys intend to keep and train him.

In response to our request for information about the suitability of Humboldt County as a habitat for wild turkeys, the Humboldt Times says:

"We can inform our contemporary that we are somewhat familiar with the habits and habitat of the wild turkey, or at least, were in the days of our blissful childhood, and also claim some acquaintance with Humboldt county. We can therefore venture the opinion that the prospects for its successful introduction here are good. It is not probable that the turkey would multiply so rapidly here as in Michigan or some of the wooded districts of the East, because there are so many enemies in the animal kingdom that would set about its extermination. But it would flourish in a fair degree, and the country abounds in food adapted to the needs of the wild turkey. A wild turkey that doesn't grow enthusiastic and become enthused with gratitude when placed among Humboldt acorns, grasshoppers, wild berries and cow peas, is certainly devoid of the true American spirit.

There may be some danger that the turkey would die from sheer gluttony if placed in the midst of Humboldt abundance, but of that our readers in the hill regions can better judge. Will some of them write us their opinion of the real chances of the wild turkey to run the gauntlet of coyotes, coons, wild-cats and poor marksmen in the oak forests of the back country?

ROD.

Virtuous Indignation.

EDITOR BREEDER AND SPORTSMAN:—There are several persons in this city who violate the fish laws to such an extent that some action must be taken now or it will be too late to accomplish any good. For the last three or four years, shad have been coming up Napa River, sometimes called Napa Creek, to spawn in large numbers. The fish up here including shad, pike, carp, trout and striped bass have suffered disastrously this season. There are four or five men who go netting daily with a large net which reaches from one side of the creek to the other, and as I said they have been netting almost daily since about the first of May. Although they claim to go out for shad they also get the other varieties of fish I have mentioned. There is strong talk against them, but nothing is being done to stop them or to punish them severely as they ought to be punished since they are common every-day vagrants and catch anywhere from fifty to three-hundred fishes daily, many of them being fish which are now spawning. One would probably be surprised to learn what they do with so many fish, and it is said with regret that they find a market for about all they can catch, even when they have no permission to catch or net them or any license to sell them. Hoping this rascally work may reach the ears of the Fish Commissioners and that the BREEDER AND SPORTSMAN may denounce them in strong terms.

NAPA, June 13, 1890. NAPA SPORTSMAN.

Silkworm Gut.

In a private letter one of the chief English gut importers tells me there is likely to be a "corner" on this indispensable material this next season. The new crop has just been gathered in Spain (Murcia), and is one of the smallest on record, * * * certainly the smallest since the dire cholera year, 1885, when one-third the population of the gut-producing districts either died or were mortally sick with the cholera scourge. It is said to be not equal to one-fourth of the crop of '88 or one-third of that of '89. Two months or thereabouts will elapse before any of it will reach the American market, and it is fortunate in one sense that salmon fishing will then be virtually over, for there is not more than about 20,000 strands *in all* of the best salmon gut. This means that next season the best salmon gut will be at least three times dearer than it was in 1889, and I presume I need not tell my readers that the pick of this gut will be retained over the water, notwithstanding the picturesque references of some of our home tackle-makers to "our gut factory in Spain." This anxiety and uncertainty about the "gut" crop should speedily have an end. Where is American enterprise? Why cannot it be made in this country? California has an ideal climate for it, and some of those thousands of "unspeakable" heathen Chinese could be pressed into congenial service in tending the worms and drawing the gut. Why not?—The Week's Sport.

[The suggestion as to establishing gut factories in California is one which was considered several years ago, at which time an exhaustive discussion of the methods of raising the worms and manufacturing the gut was presented in these columns. Our contemporary is quite right in believing that the climate of this State is suitable both for the growing of the mulberry and the worms. The tree flourishes wherever planted, and the experiments of the State Society for the fostering of the silk industry have proven that the worms grow to a large size, develope large silk sacs, and produce a fine, strong, lively gut when properly handled. There is a fortune in the scheme.]

To Fishermen.

EDITOR BREEDER AND SPORTSMAN:—In accordance with the provisions of the act of Congress for taking the Eleventh and subsequent censuses, it is purposed to secure statistics concerning fish and fisheries. Mr. Charles W. Smiley has been appointed a special agent to take charge of this work. The special agent thus appointed has all the authority of a census enumerator under the act of March 1, 1889, and is empowered to conduct in his own name correspondence relative to this subject.

Obtaining statistics concerning the fishing that is carried on by people who devote only a small portion of their time thereto, and upon the various inland rivers and lakes of the country, is very difficult; but the subject is altogether too important to be entirely neglected. This office cannot, however, undertake to include fishing which is merely for sport or recreation, and which yields but small returns, nor yet those rare and occasional days of fishing which men indulge in to get *a few* pounds for immediate home consumption. It does, however, desire to obtain certain statistics concerning every one who, as an actual part of his daily toil, resorts to fishing as the best means of obtaining food or money. There are cases where farmers leave their farming, and, with horse and wagon, go to fishing places in order to obtain whole loads of fish, which they carry home and salt for use throughout the year. Such fishing should be included in our inquiry. Less than seven days per year devoted to fishing, and a total catch of less than 140 or 150 pounds, is hardly worth considering in the present inquiry.

The objects of fishing which are comprehended in this inquiry include not only fish used for food, but for all other purposes, such as making oil, fertilizers, etc., as well as, clams, oysters, turtles, terrapins, etc.

If there is *any part* of this circular to which you feel inclined to return a reply, your kind attention will be greatly appreciated. If you would regard it as any return for your courtesy to have copies of the Fishery Bulletins sent to you when issued, your name will be placed upon the list.

ROBERT P. PORTER, Superintendent of Census.

WASHINGTON, April 10, 1890.

Fish Commissioners Criticized.

There are always men who are willing to carp at those in public office and to decry the endeavors of all, as to whose motives and actual labors they know nothing, and the members of the State Board of Fish Commissioners do not fail to receive their share of the adverse criticism. Nor are the gentlemen of the California Board the only ones who have to meet quibblers, as is evidenced by the following notes from an exchange. The Albany Journal contained the following letter:

"The fish commissioners seem to have overlooked the highest interests of our citizens in the line of wholesome food and recreation at the same time; for they succeed in stocking our waters only too slowly, both for the lack of public spirit in raising the necessary money to pay the expressage. If our State were divided up into seven districts and a fish commissioner appointed for each and a hatching house was at his service, he might restock all the waters in his district once in three or five years, and so all our streams would abound with fish adapted to the location. The Legislature should provide for replenishing the fish in our streams, which in many sections are well nigh extinct."

The Journal comments upon it, saying: "Of what advantage is the wholesale stocking of the streams of New York if it only benefits the market fisher, the poacher and the trout hog? It would appear as if the authorities were doing all they could to stock our streams and the people not doing a single thing to protect them."

Our exchange adds, and its observations should be weighed by many of our own readers:

'It is much easier to find fault with the acts of the New York Fish Commissioners than it is to improve upon their methods of conducting the Commission. The letter quoted above is a fair sample of the kicks at the Commissioners made by well-meaning people who really are not well informed about the subject of the kick. There is yet a vast army of fishermen who have an idea that in order to stock or restock a water it only requires that a large quantity of young fish shall be turned into it and the object is accomplished.

In the first place it should be understood that the New York Fish Commissioners give a lot of valuable time to the State, and to those who are benefited by their acts, without any return, except the consciousness of well doing, the approval of the majority of fishermen, and the kicks of the minority, for they serve the people without pay in dollars and cents. As fish rearing and fish planting is their business—a business to which they devote much thought, and to which they bring the best talent obtainable—it can be imagined that they know more about it, and the methods of conducting it to obtain the best results, than those who do not make it their business, and have but an imperfect knowledge of it.

The letter writer thinks the Commissioners lack system, and public spirit in raising money to pay express charges on the fish sent out. As to the first charge, we will say that the Commissioners are progressive men, constantly seeking to improve the service of the Commission, and if the letter writer will suggest to them an improvement upon their present excellent system—the outgrowth of twenty years' experience—we guarantee they will adopt the improvement; for that is what they all labor for. As to the second charge, is it not rather too much to ask of a business man to give his services to the people, and then ask him to pass his hat around that the people may be further benefited? Now, "honest Injun," could any sane man expect them to do it?

They have said, over and over, that the fish hatched by the State should be distributed by the State free. They have asked the State that furnishes money to hatch the fish to furnish, also, the money to plant them, claiming justly that the State had not finished its work until the fish were planted. The State has not seen fit to furnish the money to plant the fish, and, very properly, the Commissioners decline to pass their hats. They hatch millions of fish, doing the work as cheaply as possible that the State may get a good return for its money, and say to the fishermen: "We would send out these fish free to you to be planted in suitable waters, but we regret that the State has not furnished us with the means to do it; we know that the State should do so, but until it does we must ask you to pay the bare transportation expenses."

It was for the purpose of furnishing free transportation for fish fry that the Commissioners asked for a fish car last winter.

If there were seven Commissioners, one of them "might restock all the waters in his district once in three or five years, and so all our streams would abound with fish adapted to the location."

Then the millennium and ascension robes! What a simple affair it is to stock all the streams once in three to five years—on paper!

And the only place that we know of that it can be done is on paper. To stock a stream properly it should be planted annually for a number of years, and food must be provided for the fish, if it is lacking, and then the remark of the Albany Journal comes in very properly; for if the fish are not protected during infancy and, later, during the spawning seasons, the mere planting of the fish fry is money and labor wasted.

Fish protection is a matter of education and if it was in our power to influence the Fish Commissioners, we would say to them: In communities opposed to fish protection let this education go on while the streams are barren; send out not a single fish to a district where the fish laws are openly and persistently violated—where the sentiment of the people is opposed to protection. The Legislature and the Fish Commissioners may do their utmost to stock streams with fish, and their efforts will be utterly futile unless there is a determined effort on the part of the people to do their share of the work and protect the fish at times and seasons when they require protection to thrive and multiply.

$15,000. OPENING $15,000.

of the

GRAND CIRCUIT.

The World's Fair goes to Chicago, but the Greatest Fair ever held in the West takes place at

Agricultural Park, Los Angeles, August 4 to 9, 1890.

Fifteen Thousand Dollars in Purses, Stakes and Premiums.

Speed Programme:

FIRST DAY—MONDAY AUGUST 4TH.

No. 1. The Los Angeles Derby.—A sweepstake for three-year-olds (foals of 1887), $50 each, half forfeit, with $500 added, the second to receive $100, and the third $50, out of the stakes; a winner of any three-year-old stake race to carry five (5) pounds, of two or more, eight (8) pounds extra; maidens allowed seven (7) pounds. One mile and a half.

No. 2. The Edwards & McKnight stakes.—A sweepstake for all ages; $10 each, half forfeit; $200 added, the second to receive $100 out of the stakes. Non-winners this year allowed seven pounds. Maidens allowed ten pounds. One mile.

No. 3. Trotting.—The Los Angeles Purse, $1,500, open to all horses eligible to the 2:30 Class, June 16th. Entrance, ten per cent, payable as follows: $50 June 16th, when entries close; $50 July 1st, and $50 July 22nd, when horses must be named. No subscription will be received unless the first payment shall accompany the same. Subscribers liable only for the amount paid in, but if a subscriber fails to make any of the payments when due, he shall surrender his subscription and payments to the Association with the right of substitution. The Board reserves the right to declare the "Los Angeles Purse" off, in the event of its not filling satisfactorily.

No. 4. Trotting.—Purse $500. 3 minute class. District.

SECOND DAY—TUESDAY AUGUST 5.

No. 5. A sweepstake for two-year-olds owned in the Southern Counties; $25 each, $15 forfeit; $150 added; the second to receive $75 out of the stakes. The winner of any race to carry four pounds extra. One-half (½) mile.

No. 6. The Nadeau Hotel Handicap.—Purse $1,000, of which $700 to the first; $200 to the second; and $100 to the third horse. Weight announced July 22nd. Twenty-five dollars ($25) to nominate, and fifty dollars ($50) each from all starters. The winner of any race after the announcement of the weights to carry five (5) pounds extra. One and one quarter mile.

No. 7. Trotting.—Two-year-old stakes, district, $250 added. See special condition.

No. 8. Pacing.—Purse $500. 2:35 class. District.

THIRD DAY—WEDNESDAY, AUG. 6TH.

No. 9. Selling Purse—For all ages, $350. Ten Dollars from starters to go to second horse. Fixed valuation $1000; three pounds allowed for each $100 less down to $700; then one pound for $100 down to $300; selling price to be named through the entry box at 5 P. M. the day before the race. Seven-eighths of a mile.

No. 10. Hurdle Race—A sweepstake for all ages; $30 each, half forfeit; $200 added; second horse to receive $75 out of the stakes. Five hurdles—about one and one half miles.

No. 11. Trotting—Three-year-old Stake. District $250 added. See special conditions.

No. 12. Trotting.—Purse $1000. 2:25 class.

FOURTH DAY—THURSDAY AUG. 7TH.

No. 13. The Hollenbeck Hotel Stakes—A sweepstake for two-year-olds (foals of 1888), $50 each, $20 forfeit; with $300 added, the second to receive $100, and the third $50 out of the stakes. A winner of any stake race before August 1st, to carry three pounds; and two or more stake races, five pounds extra; maidens allowed, if beaten once, five pounds; twice or more, eight pounds. Five-eighths of a mile.

No. 14. The Southern California Handicap.—Purse $1000, of which $700 to the first, $200 to the second, and $100 to the third horse. Weights announced July 22nd. $25 to nominate, and $70 more for all starters. The winner of any race at this meeting to carry five pounds extra. Three-quarters of a mile.

No. 15. Trotting—Purse $1000, 2:27 Class.

No. 16. Trotting—Purse $500, 2:40 class; District.

FIFTH DAY—FRIDAY, AUGUST, 8TH.

No. 17. The Sierra Madre Stakes.—A sweepstake for all ages. $25 each, half forfeit; $200 added, second to receive $75 out of the stakes. Winner of any race this year at three-quarters (¾) of a mile or less to carry six (6) pounds, and of two or more of such races, ten (10) pounds extra. Maiden allowed ten (10) pounds. One-half (½) mile heats.

No. 18. Santa Catalina Cup.—A sweepstake for all ages, $40 each; $20 forfeit; $300 added; the second to receive $100 out of the stakes. Five pounds above scale. Non-winners in 1889 and 1890 allowed ten (10) pounds. Maidens allowed twelve (12) pounds. A winner at this meeting to carry five pounds extra. One and one-eighth (1⅛) mile.

No. 19. Trotting.—Purse, $1,000, 2:20 class.

No. 20. Trotting.—Purse, $500, 2:50. District.

SIXTH DAY—SATURDAY, AUG. 9TH

No. 21. The Citrus Handicap.—A sweepstake for three-year-olds; $40, half forfeit, or only $15 if declared by 5 P. M. the day before the race; $250 added; the second to receive $100 out of the stakes. Weights to be announced by 5 o'clock P. M., second day before the race. One and one-sixteenth (1 1-16) of a mile.

No. 22. The Junior Handicap.—A sweepstake for two-year-olds. $40 each, half forfeit, or only $15 if declared by 5 P. M. the day before the race; $250 added; the second to receive $100, and the third $50 out of the stakes. Weights to be announced by 5 o'clock P. M. the second day before the race. Three-quarters (¾) of a mile.

No. 23. Trotting.—Purse $800, 2:35 Class.

No. 24. Pacing.—Purse, $600, 2:25 Class.

TROTTING STAKES—To close June 16th, 1890.

To be Trotted at the Annual Fair, to be held in Los Angeles in 1890--91.

TROTTING STAKES, 1890.

FOALS OF 1888. Mile and repeat. $250, added by the Association. Entrance, $50, payable in the following forfeits: $10 to accompany the nomination, $20 July 1st, and $20 August 11, 1890.

FOALS OF 1887. Mile heats, three in five. $250 added by the Association. $50 entrance, payable in the following forfeits; $10 to accompany the nomination, $20 July 1st, and $20 August 11, 1890.

TROTTING STAKES, 1891.

FOALS OF 1889. Mile and repeat. $250 added by the Association. $50 entrance, payable in the following forfeits: $5 to accompany nomination, $10 August 1st, 1890; $10 May 1st, 1891, and $25 on the first day of the Fair of 1891.

FOALS OF 1888. Mile heats, three in five. $250 added by the Association. Entrance, $60, payable in the following forfeits; $5 to accompany the nomination; $10 August 1st, 1890; $10 May 1st, 1891, and $35 on the first day of the Fair of 1891.

CONDITIONS.

All nominations to be made on or before June 16th. American Association rules to govern. Nominators liable only for the amount paid in, which becomes forfeit if subsequent payments are not made. All forfeits and entrance fees will be contributed to the stake, the whole divided where there are three or more starters as follows: sixty per cent. to the first, thirty per cent. to the second and ten per cent. to the third. If no more than two horses start, only first and second money shall be awarded, and in case of a walk over, only the first money shall be awarded. A horse distancing the field shall only be entitled to so much of the money as the starters in the race could have won. A nominator in making an entry in any of the above stakes shall give the name of owner, name of breeder and where foaled, the age, color, sex, dam and sire if known. Colts owned in the Counties of San Luis Obispo, Fresno, Tulare, Kern, Santa Barbara, Ventura, Los Angeles, San Bernardino, Orange and San Diego shall be eligible to entry.

REMARKS AND CONDITIONS.

All trotting and pacing races to be to harness, mile heats, best three in five, except otherwise specified. Entrance 10 per cent on amount of purse. Trotting and pacing divided as follows: 50 per cent. to first horse; 25 per cent. to second; 15 per cent. to third, and 10 per cent. to fourth. Entries not declared out by 6 P. M. of the day before the race must start. In all trotting and pacing races, five to enter and three to start. The Board reserves the right to hold a less number than five to fill. Horses owned in Fresno, Tulare, Kern, San Luis Obispo, Santa Barbara, Ventura, Los Angeles, San Bernardino, Orange and San Diego Counties, are eligible for entry in district races. A horse distancing the field is entitled to first and fourth money. The Directors reserve the right to change the hour and day of any race, if deemed necessary. Races shall commence each day at 1 o'clock. American Association rules to govern, unless otherwise specified. Hay and straw free.

Running—The Pacific Coast Blood Horse rules to govern running races. Colonial-bred horses, foaled on Colonial time, allowed as follows: Two and three-year-olds, eight pounds; four-year-olds five pounds, and five-year-olds, three pounds. In all stakes, starters must be named to the Secretary or through the entry box at the track, on or before 6 P. M. of the day before the race. In all stakes, the right to forfeit ceases at 10 o'clock of the day on which the race is run. Racing colors to be named with the entry. Entries close with the Secretary July 1st.

Remember, entries for the 2:30 Trot and District Trotting Stakes close June 16th, and for everything else July 1st.

BEN BENJAMIN, Secretary.

L. LICHTENBERGER, President.

SAN DIEGO, 8776.

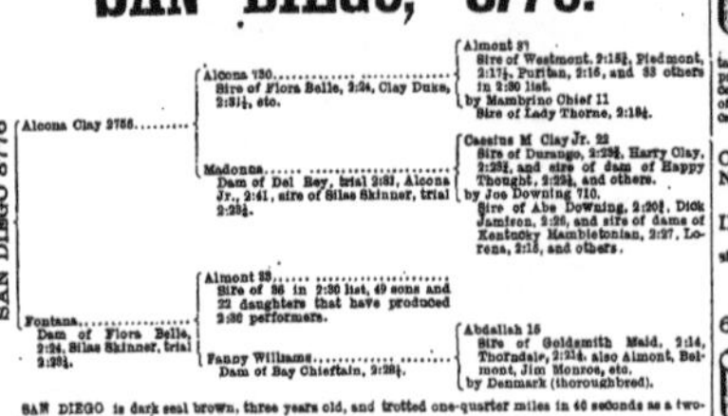

SAN DIEGO is dark seal brown, three years old, and trotted one-quarter miles in 40 seconds as a two-year old.

This grand young horse, and, barring accidents, will make a fast record next fall.

He will be allowed a limited number of mares, at $50 for the season. Mares not proving in foal to be returned free 1891. Best of pasture for mares at $4 per month, but no liability for accidents or escapes.

He will make the season from February 1st to June 1st at Napa Fair Grounds. For further particulars, address or call on

H. B. STARR, Race Track, Napa, Cal.,

or FRED W. LOEBER, St. Helena

Vineland Stock Farm

Alcona 730.

Sire of

FLORA BELLE - - - - Record 2:24
CLAY DUKE - - - - - " 2:31½

ALCONA will be a great sire, but four of his colts have ever been trained, and all h.ve shown full miles better than 2:3½, and two of them as good as 2:20. Two of his first sons each sired a colt as a two-year-old, and last season one as a four-year-old trotted a full mile in 2:22¼, and the other, a three-year-old, a mile in 2:21. With opportunities, Alcona is destined to be one of Almont's best sons. Almont, for his opportunities, is beyond doubt the most prepotent sire of his age. He has 38 representatives in the 2:30 list; 49 sons and 22 daughters that have already produced 2:30 performers. Almont died five years ago at 20 years old. If he lived he would be but 25 years old.

PEDIGREE.

ALCONA sired by the great Almont (sire of Westmont 2:13¾, Fanny Witherspoon 2:16¾, Piedmont 2:17¼, and 34 others with records better than 2:30, and grandsire of Belle Hamlin 2:12¾, etc.); by Alexander's Abdallah (sire of Goldsmith Maid 2:14), he by Rysdyk's Hambletonian. Alcona's dam, Queen Mary, by Mambrino Chief (sire of Lady Thorne 2:18 1-4, and 5 others in the 2:30 list, and sire of the dams of Director 2:17, Piedmont 2:17¼, Onward 2:25 1-4, Red Wilkes Almont, Belmont and many other noted sires).

DESCRIPTION.

Alcona is a beautiful chestnut 16 3 1-2 hands high, and weighs 1300 lbs. His colts possess speed, style, finish and beauty, and if they don't trot they command the highest prices for carriage horses.

$40 for the season. Usual return privilege.

Season of Alcona and Grandissimo ends July 1st, 1890.

Grandissimo,

Full Brother to GRANDEE, 3-year old record 2:23 1-2.

Sired by La Grande (son of Almont and out of Jessie Pepper by Mambrino Chief; Jessie Pepper is the dam of Ione 2:17 1-2, Alpha 2:23 1-2, Sterling Wilkes 2:21¾, and others) dam Norma, by Artherton (sire of Arab 2:15, Joe Arthurton 2:20 1-2, etc.)

Grandam Nourmahal (full sister to A. W. Richmond, sire of Arrow 2:13¾, Romero 2:19, and sire of Columbine, dam of Anteeo 2:16¼, and Antevolo 2:19¾ at four years old).

DESCRIPTION.

Grandissimo is four years old, will make a sixteen hand horse; he is a rich mahogany bay in color and perfect in style and action. $30 for the season. Usual return privileges.

"Grandissimo" with limited training last fall as a three-year-old, trotted quarters in 35 seconds and miles in 2:40.

I feel confident that he will trot fast this season, and will be a great sire as his colts this season are all grand youngsters.

The best of pasturage $4 per month. Mares taken care of in any manner that owners may desire, but no responsibility assumed for escapes or accidents.

For further particulars send for circular or call at stables, one mile south of St. Helena.

FRED W. LOEBER Prop'r.

The Trotting Stallion

VICTOR,

Record 2:22.

Will make the season of 1890 at NAPA CITY.

DESCRIPTION.

VICTOR is a handsome dark bay; 15-3 hands high; weighs about 1,150 pounds, and is remarkably intelligent, level-headed of kind disposition, and a magnificent animal in every respect. He is well boned and muscled, of splendid conformation, and possesses the qualities of speed and endurance to an eminent degree—qualities that he imparts to his progeny.

PEDIGREE.

VICTOR, record 2:22
- Echo 462
  - Hambletonian 10 (Sire of 42 in the 2:30 list.)
    - Abdallah 1
    - Chas. Kent mare
  - Fanny Felter
    - Magnolia 68
    - by Webber's Kentucky Whip
- Daughter of
  - Woodburn
    - Lexington
    - Lulu Horton
  - daughter of
    - Ashland
    - thoroughbred

ECHO is the sire of Belle Echo, 2:20, Senator, 2:21¼, Victor, 2:22, Gibraltar, 2:22¼, Achora, 2:23¾, Tippie, 2:25¾, Lohengrin, 2:27¼, Pasha, 2:27¾, Kimunte, 2:29, Col. Hawkins, 2:29¾, Annie Laurie, 2:30, Economy, 2:30, Sam Lewis, pacer, 2:2½.

TERMS—$60 FOR THE SEASON.

Mares not proving with foal may be returned next season free of charge, provided the horse remains the property of the present proprietor, and stands at the same place, otherwise money will be refunded. The best of care taken of mares in any manner that owners may desire, but no responsibility assumed for accidents or escapes. For further particulars, apply to or address

G. W. HUGHES, Agent,

G. A. DOHERTY, Proprietor. Napa City.

The Trotting-Bred Stallion

RINGWOOD

THE FINEST SON OF THE NOTED SIDNEY,

Will make a Season at Oakland, commencing March 1, and ending June 1, 1890.

DESCRIPTION.

RINGWOOD is a dark, rich colored bay, black points, 15 1-2 hands, weight 1100 lbs., and a pure gaited trotter. Has shown great speed. He is now five years old. As a four year old he showed a trial in 2:19 1-2, and but for an accident would have received a record as a four year old of 2:18 or better.

PEDIGREE.

RINGWOOD is by Sidney, record 2:19 3-4, and is half brother to Gold Leaf 2:11 1-4, Adonis 2:11, Fleet (two year old) 2:24, Longworth 2:19, Sister V. 2:27, Faustino, yearling, 2:35, Fleet, yearling, 2:35, Memo, three year old trial 2:2? 1-2.

Sidney is by Santa Claus, record 2:17 1-2; he by Strathmore, sire of 31 in 2:30 list; he by Hambletonian 10, the greatest of all producers; he by Abdallah. Sidney's dam, Sweetness, record 2:21 1-4; she by Volunteer, the sire of St. Julien 2:11 1-4.

RINGWOOD'S dam Alma; she by Dashway, thoroughbred; he by Belmont, he by American Boy; he by Sea Gull; he by imported Expedition. Alma's 1st dam, Fanny Cobb, was a great road mare, pedigree untraced.

TERMS: $50 for the Season.

Payable June 1st, or sooner if mares are taken away. Address Communications to

A. C. DIETZ,
Oakland, Cal.

2:10¾ 2:13¾ 2:10

DEXTER PRINCE.

This Royally-bred Stallion will make the Season of 1890 at the LIVE OAKS Breeding Farm, 2 miles from Lodi, San Joaquin County, Cal.

DESCRIPTION.

DEXTER PRINCE is a blood bay, 16 hands high, weighs over 1,100 pounds; has great power and substance, and the highest finish. When two years old, at Palo Alto, he was timed quarters by Gov. Stanford in 35¼ seconds, and he was driven eighths by Mr. Marvin at a faster rate of speed than that. He is a sure foal-getter, and invariably sires foals of good size, of fine form and finish, and the highest rate of speed.

PEDIGREE.

By KENTUCKY PRINCE, the sire of Guy, 2:10¾, Spofford, 2:18¾, Company, 2:19¾, Bayonne Prince, 2:21 1-4, Fred Folger, 2:20¾, and a score more in the 2:30 list.

First dam LADY DEXTER, full sister of the greatest of trotters, Dexter, and the greatest of sires, Dictator, the sire of Director, 2:17, Phallas, 2:13¾, in a fourth heat, and Jay-Eye-See, 2:10.

Second dam Clara, the dam of Dexter, 2:17 1-4, Dictator, Astoria 2:29 1-4, and Almah, 2:28¾. Clara was by American Star, that has 34 daughters that have produced 2:30 or better trotters.

Third dam the McKinstry mare, the dam of Shark, 2:27¾. HAMBLETONIAN, the grandsire of DEXTER PRINCE, has 40 trotters in the 2:30 list, 44 daughters that have produced 2:30 trotters, and more than 10 sons that have sired 2:30 trotters.

CLARK CHIEF, the grandsire on the sire's side, was the sire of performing and producing sons and daughters.

DEXTER PRINCE has faster blood lines, on both sides, than any other stallion in the world—Guy 2:10¾, and Jay-Eye-See, 2:10.

KENTUCKY PRINCE is one of the best bred and speediest stallions in the world. David Bonner, in the presence of Governor Stanford, timed him when he trotted a 2:10 gait. He is by Clark Chief, one of the great broodmare sires; his first dam is Kentucky Queen by Morgan Eagle, son of Hale's Green Mountain Morgan, 2nd dam by Blythe's Whip, 3rd dam by Martin's Brummier, 4th dam by Quicksilver 580, on through the strongest thoroughbred blood.

TERMS.

$100 for the season, with usual return privilege. Payable before mares are removed. Good pasture, and the best care furnished, but no responsibility assumed for accidents.

PREMIUM.

$250 will be given to the first of the produce of DEXTER PRINCE put in the 2:30 list, and $100 each after the first. Address

L. M. MORSE, Lodi, Cal.

The Produce of Eros Averaged $2,200 Each at New York Auction Sale in 1889.

THE ELECTIONEER TROTTING STALLION,

5326 EROS 5326

Will make the season of 1890—February 1st to July 1st—at LA SIESTA RANCH, MENLO PARK, adjoining Palo Alto.

PEDIGREE.

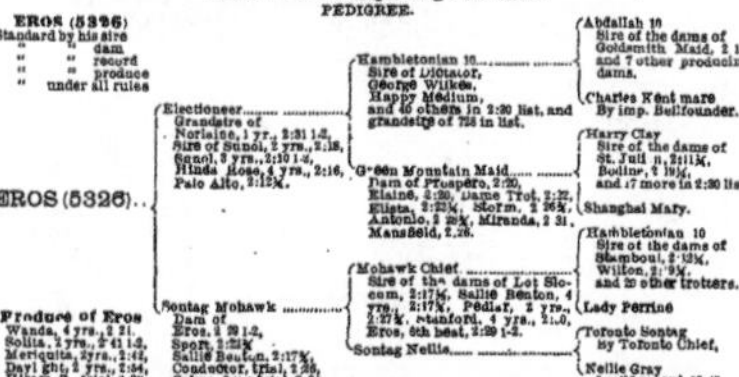

These are the only colts by him that have ever had a harness on except one in New York that went a trial last July in 2:26 1-2.

DESCRIPTION.

EROS is a rich seal brown stallion, bred by Hon. Leland Stanford at Palo Alto, and is the nearest living likeness of his celebrated sire, Electioneer. Stands 15.2 hands high, and weighs 1060 pounds.

In breeding to Eros, the owners of mares will strictly follow the great rule of breeding, viz., breed to a stallion by a producer and out of a sure producer of great speed. Eros is by the stallion that has produced more 2:30 trotters that any living horse, and is also the sire of more 2:30 performers than any horse living or dead.

EROS is out of the dam of Sally Benton, four years old, record 2:17¾, Sport 2:22¾, and Eros 2:29½ in the sixth heat, against a field of nine horses. He is from a family that is endowed with great natural speed, trot fast at an early age, train on, throw trotters from all classes of mares, are of good substance, bone, style and action, and breed solid colors.

TERMS.

$100 for the season, with the privilege of return next season should mares not be in foal and horse and mare still remain in the same hands.

Good pasturage can be obtained at $5 per month, but no responsibility for accidents or escapes. There are a large number of box stalls, and animals can be kept up and fed on hay and grain at reasonable rates if required. Mares already in foal can be sent to the ranch for foaling, and will receive all the attention bestowed upon our own mares. Mares left with Mr. Peter Pomyea, Broadway Street Stable, Oakland, or with Mr. F. H. Burke, 401 Montgomery Street, San Francisco, will be forwarded to the ranch free of charge. For further particulars apply to

W. H. VIOGET.
LA SIESTA RANCH, MENLO PARK, CAL.

EROS is the only stallion offered to the public on this Coast that has a dam that has three in the 2:30 list.

GRAND MOOR, 2374.

Foaled 1876. Black. Sixteen hands high. Bred by L. J. Rose

A horse of highest form and quality; of great excellence in every point; a type of his celebrated family; of marked individuality, spirit and endurance; never properly trained or raced, but shows the possession of great speed; perfectly manageable in the stable and on the road and track.

As he is sired by The Moor 870, a son of CLAY PILOT, out of Vashti by MAMBRINO PATCHEN, he is a most valuable cross for mares of other families. THE MOOR sired Beautiful Bells and the dams of Sable Wilkes and Margaret 2:26 (dam of Regal Wilkes, 2-year-old record 2:20½).

MAMBRINO PATCHEN is regarded as the unsurpassed sire of broodmares, having, among many others, sired the dam of Guy Wilkes and of Wm. L (the sire of Axtell), and a son of his sired the dam of Axtell. The public sales this year have demonstrated with renewed emphasis the value of The Moor and Mambrino Patchen strains of blood. For combining particularly with the Hambletonians it may be called "the ready money cross."

GRAND MOOR will make the season of 1890 for a time at the Oakland Race Track and afterwards at my Ranch, fifteen miles from Oakland. Mares can be delivered at the race track to the groom in charge. Pasture at $5 per month. For other food, if requested, an additional charge will be made.

TERMS, $100 for the season, with privileges of return if the horse does not change hands.

Every care exercised, but no liability for escapes or accidents.

H. I. THORNTON, 504 Kearny Street.

Cook STOCK FARM.

Season of 1890.

STEINWAY 1808.

Three-Year-Old Record 2:25 3-4.

Sire of STRATHWAY, three year old record 2:26, and sire of the dam of BOURBON RUSSELL 2:30.

By STRATHMORE 408; sire of 31 in the 2:30 list; sire of 6 dams of 8 in the 2:30 list, and sire of 3 sires of 3 in 2:30 list.

1st dam ABBESS (dam of Solo 2:28, and Soprano, dam of C. F. Clay 2:18, Eminence 2:27 and Strathbridge, 3 year old record 2:28½) by ALBION, sire of VANITY FAIR 2:24½, and of the dam of FAVORITE 2:26½.

2nd dam by MARSHALL NEY.

3rd dam by BERTRAND, a son of SIR ARCHY.

TERMS—$100 for the season.

CHARLES DERBY 4907

Brown Horse, Foaled 1885.

By STEINWAY 1808.

1st dam by the great ELECTIONEER, sire of SUNOL 3 year old record 2:10½, Palo Alto 2:12¼, etc., etc.

2nd dam FANNY MALONE, by NIAGARA.

3rd dam FANNY WICKHAM, by HERALD.

4th dam by Imp. TRUSTEE.

TERMS—$100 for the season.

Pasturage $5 per month. Accidents and escapes at owner's risk. Mares consigned to the farm should be sent to Fashion Stables, Oakland; Geary & Grindle's Stable, Haywards; or to Bennett's Stable, Martinez; from and to which places they will be delivered free of charge. Address

COOK STOCK FARM,
Danville, Contra Costa, Co., Cal.

Sunny Side Breeding Farm.

Admiral 488.

Foaled 1867—Sired by Volunteer 55. Son of Rysdyk's Hambletonian 10.

First dam Lady Pierson by Cassius M. Clay (Neaves') 20; second dam by Diamond; third dam a running mare said to be thoroughbred. He is fitted in an eminent degree to produce colts that will in all respects justify his patrons in their expectations.

Admiral is the sire of Huntress, record 2:27½, Sister, 2:19½, Perbelion, 2:25, Nona Y., 2:25, and others equally as promising, but have not had the advantage of track work. He will serve a limited number of approved mares at $50 the season, with usual return privilege. Season ending August 1, 1890. No liability for accidents or escapes.

KING DAVID 2576.

Bay Stallion—Foaled 1883.

Sired by Admiral 488, dam black Flora (the dam of Huntress, 2:27½, Sister, 2:19½, Perbelion, 2:25, Nona Y., 2:25), by Black Prince.

King David is one of the best gets of Admiral. He has a good disposition, kind to drive, smooth and even-gaited, and can speed fast. Barring accidents, he will trot in the twenties this Fall. His colts are large, rangy, and well finished. Will serve a limited number of mares at $30 the season, to end July 1, 1890. Every precaution will be taken to prevent accidents and escapes, but no liability will be assumed. Pasturage $4 per month.

Sunny Side Farm is situated two miles east of Vallejo, on the Sulphur Spring road. For further particulars, address

FRANK DRAKE,
Vallejo, Cal.

The Fast Trotting Stallion

REDWOOD.

Four-Year-Old Record 2:24 1-2

Will make the season of 1890—February 1st to July 1st—at

SANTA ROSA.

REDWOOD is a dark bay colt, 15.2¼ hands high, weighs 110· lbs. Foaled in 1885 by Anteeo, 2:16¼, sire of Alfred G., 2 19¾. Anteeo is by Electioneer. First dam Lou Milton, by Milton Medium; second dam Old Fly, a thoroughbred mare brought from the East in 1871 by W. C. Ralston, Esq.

Redwood's sire was out of Columbine by A. W. Richmond, the sire of the pacers Arrow 2:13¾, and Elwood 2:23, and the trotters Romero, 2:19¾, and Len Rose, 2:27. Redwood has shown a quarter in 33 seconds.

Terms $100

For the season. Mares not proving with foal may be returned next season free of charge, provided Redwood remains the property of the present owners. Good pasturage at reasonable rates. No responsibility assumed for escapes or accidents. Service fees payable before removal of the mare. Limited to 40 approved mares. For further particulars address

A. McFADYEN.
Santa Rosa, Cal.

For Sale.

JUANITO ALMONT

Sire of Almont Patchen, 2:15.

JUANITO ALMONT is a bright bay, 16-1 hands in height, and weighs 1,300 pounds.

PEDIGREE.

By Tilton Almont, 2:26, he by the great Almont 33; dam by Signal 3327; he by Bunday's Rob Roy.

JUANITO ALMONT, if given a chance would undoubtedly prove a great sire, and should prove a desirable acquisition to any stock farm in the State.

For further particulars address

T. B. COOPER,
Adin, Modoc County, C

SPEED PROGRAMME OF THE Nevada State Agricultural Society.

Sept. 22nd to 27th inclusive, 1890, at

RENO, NEV.

FIRST DAY, MONDAY, SEPTEMBER 22.

No. 1.—Selling purse, $300, of which $50 to second, $25 to third; for three-year-olds and upwards; horses entered to be sold for $1,500 to carry rule weights; two pounds allowed for each $100 down to $1,000, then one pound for each $100 less down to $400; selling price to be stated through entry box at 6 P. M. the day before the race. One mile.

No. 2.—Running stake; two-year-olds. Five-eighths of a mile; $200 added; $50 entrance; $15 forfeit; second horse to save entrance.

No. 3.—Running; purse $400. One and one-quarter miles; $75 to second, $30 to third.

SECOND DAY, TUESDAY, SEPT. 23.

No. 4.—Running. Half mile and repeat; purse $200, of which $50 to second.

No. 5.—Pacing; class 2:20; purse, $1,200; $700 to first, $300 to second, $150 to third.

No. 6.—Trotting; three-minute class; district horses. Purse $300; $150 to first, $100 to second, $50 to third.

THIRD DAY, WEDNESDAY, SEPT. 24.

No. 7.—Running stake, three-year-olds. One and one-quarter miles; $300 added; entrance $50; forfeit $10; second horse to save entrance.

No. 8.—Running. Seven-eighths of a mile. Purse $300, of which $75 to second, $25 to third.

No. 9.—Trotting, class 2:30; purse $800; $500 to first, $150 to second, $50 to third.

No. 10. Trotting three-year-olds; best two in three; purse $200; $100 to first, $75 to second, $25 to third.

FOURTH DAY, THURSDAY, SEPT. 25th.

No. 11. Running. Five-eighths of a mile; purse $250, of which $50 to second.

No. 12. Trotting, 2:25 class; purse, $1,000; $600 to first, $300 to second, $100 to third.

No. 13. Trotting, 2:40 class, district horses; purse $300; $150 to first, $100 to second, $50 to third.

FIFTH DAY, FRIDAY, SEPT. 26th.

No. 14. Running Stake, two-year-olds, seven-eighths of a mile; $200 added; $50 entrance, $15 forfeit; second horse to save entrance.

No. 15. Running. One mile, for three-year-olds; purse $350, of which $50 to second.

No. 16. Running. Seven-eighths of a mile; purse $300, of which $75 to second, $40 to third.

No. 17. Trotting, 2:17 class; purse, $1,200; $750 to first horse, $300 to second, $150 to third.

SIXTH DAY, SATURDAY, SEPT. 27th.

No. 18. Trotting, 2:30 class; purse, $800; $500 to first, $200 to second, $100 to third.

No. 19. Pacing, 2:30 class; purse, $1,000; $600 to first, $300 to second, $100 to third.

REMARKS AND CONDITIONS.

Nominations and entries to all stakes and purses must be made to the Secretary on or before the 15th day of August, 1890. Entries for the purses must be made two days preceding the race at the regular time for closing entries as designated by the rules. Those who have nominated in stakes must name to the Secretary in writing which they will start the day before the races at 6 P. M. Horses entered in purses can only be drawn by consent of the Judges.

Entries to all trotting races will close September 1st, with the Secretary.

Five or more to enter and three or more to start in all trotting races.

National Trotting Association Rules to govern trotting races. Pacific Coast Blood Horse Association Rules to govern running races.

All trotting and pacing races are the best three in five, unless otherwise specified; five to enter and three to start. But the Board reserves the right to hold a less number than five to fill, by the withdrawal of a proportionate amount of the purse. Purse to be divided pro rata. Entrance fee, 10 per cent. on purse, to accompany nomination.

National Association Rules to govern trotting; but the Board reserves the right to trot heats of any two classes alternately, if necessary to finish any day's racing, or to trot a special race between heats. A horse making a walk over shall be entitled only to the entrance money paid in. When less than the required number of starters appear, they may contest for the entrance money, to be divided as follows: 66⅔ to the first and 33⅓ to the second.

In divided purses no horse shall receive more than one money.

In all the foregoing stakes the declarations are void unless accompanied by the money.

Please observe that, in the above stakes, declarations are permitted for a small forfeit.

In all running races entries not declared out by 6 P. M. of the day preceding the race shall be required to start.

Where there is more than one entry by one person, or in one interest, the particular horse they are to start must be named by 6 P. M. of the day preceding the race. No added money paid for a walk-over.

Racing colors to be named in entries.

In trotting races drivers will be required to wear caps of distinct colors which must be named in their entries.

Each day's races will commence promptly at one o'clock P. M.

All entries must be directed to C. H. Stoddard, Reno, Nevada.

W. H. GOULD, President,

C. H. STODDARD, Secretary.

For Sale.

Brood Mare Corinne.

By Geo. C. Gorham; 1st dam Annie McCloud by Jack Hawkins Jr. son of Jack Hawkins thoroughbred 2nd dam by Belmont; will be sold with horse colt foaled June 1st, "De Corne Wilkes" by MAMBRINO WILKES 5066.

—ALSO—

Two-Year-old Brown Filly

AGNES F. WILKES,

And Yearling Black Colt

FERGUS WILKES,

By MAMBRINO WILKES, out of Corinne as above. Mare and colts can be seen at Oakland. For further particulars apply or address,

BREEDER AND SPORTSMAN

313 BUSH STREET S. F.

"Laurel Palace,"

ROME HARRIS, Proprietor.

N. W. corner Kearny and Bush Streets

SAN FRANCISCO.

PHIL J. CRIMMINS. JOHN C. MORRISON.

"Silver Palace,"

36 Geary Street,

San Francisco, Cal.

Sixth Annual Fair OF THE 17th Agricultural District, AT Glenbrook Park,

NEVADA COUNTY.

$6,500 in Purses.

Commencing August 19th. and continuing five days.

SPEED PROGRAMME.

TUESDAY, AUGUST 19TH.

No. 1.—RUNNING, three-fourths mile and repeat; purse, $400.

No. 2. TROTTING, one mile and repeat, for two year olds, county, $250.

No. 3. TROTTING, for four year olds, District, $500.

WEDNESDAY, AUGUST 20TH,

No. 4. RUNNING, 1¼ mile dash, $400.

No. 5. TROTTING, 2:40 class, $500.

No. 6. TROTTING, one year olds, one mile, for colts owned in the county, $150.

LADIES' TOURNAMENT AT 11 A. M.

THURSDAY, AUGUST 21ST.

No. 7. RUNNING, five-eighths mile and repeat, for horses owned in the County, $150.

No. 8. TROTTING, 2:27 class, $750.

No. 9. TROTTING, three year olds, District, $300.

FRIDAY, AUGUST 22ND.

No. 10. RUNNING, one mile and repeat, $500.

No. 11. Trotting, 2:35 class, $600.

No. 12. TROTTING, four years old, free for all, $500.

SATURDAY, AUGUST 23RD.

No. 13. RUNNING, two miles and repeat, $800.

No. 14. TROTTING, free for all, $1,000.

SADDLE HORSE race (county) for $50, will be given during the week, notice of which will be made on the previous day.

REMARKS AND CONDITIONS

No. 1. All trotting races are the best 3 in 5 (except the two year olds and yearlings) 6 to enter and three to start, but the Board reserves the right to hold a less number than 6 to fill by the deduction of a proportionate amount of the purse.

No. 2. Any races filling with 10 or more paid up entries the Society will add all monies over and also 25 per cent. of the purse.

No. 3. The National Association rules to govern, but the Board reserves the right to trot heats of any two classes alternately, or to trot a special race between heats.

No. 4. A horse making a walk over is entitled only to the entrance money paid in. When less than the required number of starters appear they may contest for the entrance money paid in, to be divided as follows: two-thirds to first, one-third to second.

No. 5. The State Agricultural Society rules of 1890 to govern all running races, except when conditions named are otherwise.

No. 6. Non-starters in running races will be held for entrance.

No. 7. In all of the above races the entrance will be 10 per cent. of purse, and to accompany nominations. Purses will be divided into 60, 30 and 10 per cent.

No. 8. In all races entries not declared out by 6 P. M. of the day preceding the race will be required to start.

No. 9. When there is more than one entry by one person or in one interest, the particular horse they are to start must be named by 6 P. M. of the day preceding the race.

No. 10. In races designated as District all horses are eligible that were owned in the counties of Nevada, Placer, Yuba, Sutter, Colusa, Butte, Sierra, Shasta, Plumas, Tehama and Lassen, and Washoe and Ormsby counties of the State of Nevada, prior to July 1st; also horses training on the Society's track from July 1st.

No. 11. Horses are eligible in county races if owned in the county prior to July 1st, or trained on the Society's track from July 1st.

No. 12. Hay, straw and Feed will not be furnished by the Society, but will be for sale on the grounds at reasonable rates.

Entries close with the Secretary on August 1st.

All purses are free to all unless otherwise designated.

The track at Glenbrook Park is now in first-class condition, and will be kept so and is free to all who wish to train on the course.

M. L. MARSH, President,

I. J. ROLFE, Secretary, Nevada City, Cal.

Training The Trotting Horse

BY CHARLES MARVIN.

This great practical horse book is a handsome, three hundred page octavo, bound in cloth, elegantly printed, superbly illustrated, and explains in every detail the remarkable success of CHARLES MARVIN and the whole plans and methods pursued at Palo Alto as to breaking, training, shoeing, gaiting, driving, keeping, racing and breeding trotters.

Read what J. C. Sibley, the owner of St. Bel, says of this book: "In this work Marvin has let out all the mysteries of the craft, and it is so simple and plain that any breeder, owner, trainer or rubber who has any relish for his business can take a colt as a yearling and develop to the highest and fullest extent that colt's capacity as a trotter. The work impressed me so strongly that I have ordered twenty copies, and shall place one in the hands of every rubber on our farm." Mailed postpaid for $5.50.

Address,

THE BREEDER & SPORTSMAN,

313 Bush St., San Francisco, Cal.

Brushes

BUCHANAN BROS., Brush Manufacturers,

609 Sacramento Street, two doors above Montgomery.

Horse Brushes of every description on hand and made to order. Bristle Body Brushes our Specialty

For Sale.

PHILOSOPHER,

BAY COLT; FOALED 1886; BRED BY Z. E. SIMMONS, LEXINGTON, KY.

Sired By Pilot Wilkes 2987.

SON OF GEORGE WILKES, 2:22,

WHOSE SONS HAVE SIRED

Axtell (3 y. o.)	2:12	Allerton (3 y. o.)	2:18¼
Roy Wilkes	2:12½	William H.	2:18½
Rosalind Wilkes	2:14½	Garnet	2:19
Prince Wilkes	2:14¾	Repetition (4 y. o.)	2:19¼
Alcryon	2:15¼	J. R. Shedd	2:19¼
Oliver K.	2:16¼	David Wilkes	2:19½
Phil Thompson	2:16½	Sharper	2:19
Houri	2:17	Georgiette	2:19¼
Iona	2:17½	Butterfly	2:19¼
Lillian Wilkes (3 y. o.)	2:17½	Silverone	2:19¼
Sable Wilkes (3 y. o.)	2:18	Veritas	2:20

Regal Wilkes (2 y. o.) .....2:20¾.

1st dam Bella.......by George Wilkes 519, record 2:22, sire of Harry Wilkes, 2:13½, Guy Wilkes, 2:15¼, Mike Wilkes, pacer, 2:15¼, Wilcox, pacer, 2:16, Wilson, 2:16½, So So, 2:17¼, J. B. Richardson, 2:17½, etc.

2d dam Fly.........by Bell Morgan 91, sire of Lady Turpin, 2:22, and the dam of Onslaught, 2:28½.

Pilot Wilkes, by George Wilkes, 2:22, sire of 69 from 2:13¾ to 2:30, and the dams of 21 from 2:21¾ to 2:30.

First dam Grace by Pilot Jr., sire of the dams of Maud S., 2:08¾, Jay-Eye-See, 2:10, etc.; 2d dam by Orphan Boy, pacer.

NOTE.—Here is another inbred Wilkes with superb out-crosses through both sire and dam. Has never been trained. Price $1,000. SOUND. To be seen at

GEO. E. GUERNE,

Santa Rosa, Cal.

Stallions and Colts For Sale.

The Get of the Celebrated Racing Stallion BAYSWATER, FROM FINELY BRED MARES.

Inquire of

J. HEINLEN,

Lemoore, Tulare County, Cal.

Breeders and Horsemen

ATTENTION:

New Stake Entry Register.

Keep track of your entries and avoid neglect and oversight when payments and declarations fall due. Register covers trotting and running stakes. Most simple and convenient in keeping, and far superior to any in the market. 100 pages; cloth bound. Price $2. Send 2 cent stamp for sample sheet. Address,

S. C. FERGUSON,

Menlo Park, Cal.

C. C. LINIMENT.

The Great Pain Conqueror for Man and Beast.

For Horsemen and Stockmen this Liniment is Invaluable.

OWNERS OF FINE STOCK CANNOT AFFORD TO BE WITHOUT IT.

A remedy for every home, giving instant relief in pain and PERFORMING PERMANENT CURES.

To get the full benefit of the C. C. Liniment in chronic cases, in connection with C. C. Liniment use Compound Sulphur Powder, the "Great Blood Purifier," put up ONLY by The W. H. Bone Co., 12 Bush St., San Francisco. For Habitual Constipation, Indigestion, Piles, etc., it is the greatest remedy known to medical science.

If your druggist does not keep it, we will send direct, post paid, on receipt of price. COMPOUND SULPHUR POWDER is $1 per bottle, 6 for $5. Small bottles, 25c.

The C. C. Liniment Co

12 BUSH STREET, S. F.

W. H. BONE, - - General Manager.

FOR SALE BY ALL DRUGGISTS.

KENNEL ADVERTISEMENTS.

In the Stud.

"DAN GLADSTONE,"

3372 A. K. C. S. B.

BY CH. GLADSTONE—CH. SUE.

Winnings—Southern Trials, 1888, Divided Third. Indiana Trials, 1889, Divided Third. Southern Trials, 1889, Second.

Will be at Stud in San Francisco until Sept. 15, 1890. Fee, $35.

GEO. J. HARLEY, 844 Harrison St., S. F.

DOGS---Pointer Pups FOR SALE.

Sure Bench Show and Field Trial Winners, as they have more bench-show and field-trial blood in them than any that have ever been whelped on the Pacific Coast.

Sire, POINT, double field trial winner; he by Vandevort's Don, great field trial and bench show winner, out of Drab, field trial and bench show winner.

Dam, QUEEN CROXTETH by Bush T., bench show winner, out of Champion Patti Croxteth, field trial and bench show winner. This is the best pointer blood in the world. Breeding and health guaranteed. Address,

A. B. TRUMAN,

1425 Steiner St., near Ellis, S. F., Cal.

CALIFORNIA SPANIEL KENNELS,

Oakland, California, H. P. RENNIE, Prop. Breeder and importer of typical COCKER SPANIELS. Winner of first prizes at S. F. and Los Angeles, 1889, also, Columbus, 1889, New York, 1887. In the stud, solid Black Cocker dog, GIFFEE, won 1st and Gold Medal at S. F., 1889. Fee, $25. Puppies and grown dogs at reasonable prices. My dogs can neither talk nor climb a tree, but are fielders and prize winners.

37 Sixth St., Oak Street Station.

ECHO COCKER KENNELS,

STOCKTON, CAL.

A. C. DAVENPORT, - - - Proprietor.

Has some fine Cocker Puppies for Sale now, by his solid black Cocker Spaniel, Prize Winning Stud Dog Bronte, A. K. C. S. B., 17,031, (Brant—Mollie) out of registered bitches, for $10 and $20. Stud fee $20.

POINTERS FOR SALE.

FINE POINTERS whelped May 24, 1890, by Don (Climax—Drab D), out of Diana (Professor—Belle H). Correspondence solicited.

V. R.

BREEDER AND SPORTSMAN, 313 Bush street, City.

OUR IMPROVED.

ALL SIZES AND WEIGHTS

G. W. BOHANON.

THE BOHANON SULKY! BEST MADE.

Perfect Riding Buggies. Breaking Carts. Fine Repairing. Reasonable Prices

Bohanon Carriage Co., 161-163 Ogden Ave., CHICAGO.

Send for Catalogue.

NOW IN THE LEAD.

J. O'KANE,

Harness and Turf Goods,

767 MARKET STREET, S. F.

Largest Stock. Lowest Prices.

Send for New Catalogue.

JOHN FORGIE, Importing Tailor,

204 Montgomery Street,

N. E. corner Bush. SAN FRANCISCO.

BERGEZ'S RESTAURANT.

FIRST-CLASS. Charges Reasonable.

Private Rooms for Families,

332—334 Pine St., below Montgomery St.

JOHN BERGEZ, Propr

VISIT GETTYSBURG And MUSEUM,

MARKET AND TENTH STREETS, SAN FRANCISCO, CAL.

Southern Pacific Co.

(PACIFIC SYSTEM.)

Trains leave and are due to arrive at San Francisco.

LEAVE (FOR)	FROM JUNE 15, 1890.	ARRIVE (FROM)
7.30 A M	Haywards, Niles and San Jose	*12.45 P M
7.30 A M	Sacramento and Redding, via Davis	7.15 P M
7.30 A M	Sacramento, Auburn, Colfax	4.45 P M
8.00 A M	Martinez, Vallejo, Calistoga and Santa Rosa	6.15 P M
9.00 A M	Los Angeles Express, Fresno, Bakersfield, Mojave and East and Los Angeles	10.15 A M
8.30 A M	Niles, San Jose, Stockton, Ione, Sacramento, Marysville, Oroville and Red Bluff	4.45 P M
10.30 A M	Haywards and Niles	3.45 P M
12.00 M	Haywards, Niles and Livermore	8.45 P M
*1.00 P M	Sacramento River Steamers	**6.00 A M
2.00 P M	Haywards, Niles and San Jose	8.45 A M
3.30 P M	2d Class for Ogden and East	9.45 P M
4.00 P M	Sunset Route, Atlantic Express, Santa Barbara, Los Angeles, Deming, El Paso, New Orleans and East	8.45 P M
4.00 P M	Martinez, Vallejo, Calistoga and Santa Rosa	9.45 A M
4.00 P M	Lathrop and Stockton	10.15 A M
4.30 P M	Sacramento and Knight's Landing via Davis	10.15 A M
* 4.30 P M	Niles and Livermore	* 8.45 A M
* 4.30 P M	Niles and San Jose	‡ 6.15 P M
5.00 P M	Haywards and Niles	7.45 A M
7.00 P M	Shasta Route Express, Sacramento, Marysville, Redding, Portland, Puget Sound & East	7.45 A M
8.00 P M	Central Atlantic Express, Ogden and East	9.45 A M
	SANTA CRUZ DIVISION.	
‡ 7.45 A M	Excursion train to Santa Cruz	‡ 8.05 P M
8.15 A M	Newark, Centerville, San Jose, Felton, Boulder Creek and Santa Cruz	6.20 P M
* 2.45 P M	Centerville, San Jose, Almaden, Felton, Boulder Creek and Santa Cruz	*11.20 A M
4.45 P M	Centerville, San Jose, and Los Gatos, and Saturday and Sunday to Santa Cruz	9. 0 A M
	Coast Division (Third and Townsend Sts.)	
7.25 A M	San Jose, Almaden and Way Stations	2.30 P M
‡ 7.50 A M	Monterey and Santa Cruz—Sunday Excursion	‡ 8.25 P M
8.30 A M	San Jose, Gilroy, Tres Pinos; Pajaro, Santa Cruz; Monterey; Pacific Grove, Salinas, Soledad San Miguel, Paso Robles, Santa Margarita (San Luis Obispo) & principal Way Stations	6.12 P M
10.30 A M	San Jose and Way Stations	7.30 P M
12.01 P M	Cemetery, Menlo Park and Way Stations	5.15 P M
* 2.30 P M	Del Monte (Limited), Menlo Park, San Jose, Gilroy, Pajaro, Castroville, Monterey and Pacific Grove	*11.15 A M
* 3.30 P M	San Jose, Tres Pinos, Santa Cruz, Salinas, Monterey, Pacific Grove and principal Way Stations	*10.00 A M
* 4.20 P M	Menlo Park and Way Stations	* 7.56 A M
5.20 P M	San Jose and Way Stations	9.03 A M
6.30 P M	Menlo Park and Way Stations	6.35 A M
†11.45 P M	San Jose and principal Way Stations	†4.38 P M

A M for Morning. P M for Afternoon.
*Sundays excepted. †Saturdays only. ‡Sundays only.
**Mondays excepted. §Saturdays excepted.

OCEANIC STEAMSHIP CO.

Carrying United States, Hawaiian and Colonial Mails.

WILL LEAVE THE COMPANY'S WHARF, foot of Mission Street, No. 1.

For Honolulu, Auckland and Sydney,

WITHOUT CHANGE.

The Splendid New 3,000-ton Iron Steamer, ALAMEDA... Saturday, JUNE 28th, 1890, at 12 M., Or immediately on arrival of the English mails.

For Honolulu.

SS. AUSTRALIA (3,000 tons), June 20, 1890, at 12 M.

☞ For freight or passage, apply at office, 327 Market Street. JOHN D. SPRECKELS & BROS, General Agents.

By-Laws

—AND—

Rules and Regulations

—OF THE—

NATIONAL

Trotting Association

REVISED FOR 1890,

ALSO THE

AMERICAN

Trotting Association,

AND THE

PACIFIC COAST BLOOD-HORSE ASSOCIATION.

With Betting Rules.

For Sale at the Office of the

Breeder and Sportsman,

313 Bush St., S. F., Cal.

Price, 25c. each.

By Mail, Postage Paid, 30c. each.

"STANDARD" SHOTGUN CARTRIDGES
THE BEST IS THE CHEAPEST

San Francisco and North Pacific Railway.

THE DONAHUE BROAD-GAUGE ROUTE.

COMMENCING SUNDAY, APRIL 27, 1890, AND until further notice, boats and trains will leave from and arrive at the San Francisco Passenger Depot, Market-street Wharf, as follows:

FROM SAN FRANCISCO FOR POINT TIBURON AND SAN RAFAEL.
Week Days—7.40, 9.20, 11.20, A. M.; 1.30, 3.30, 5.00, 6.15 P. M.
Sundays—8.00, 9.30, 11.00 A. M.; 1.30, 3.30, 5.00, 6.15 P. M.

FROM SAN RAFAEL FOR SAN FRANCISCO.
Week Days—6.50, 7.55, 9.20, 11.10 A. M.; 1.40, 3.40, 5.05 6.25 P. M.
Sundays—8.10, 9.40, 11.10 A. M.; 1.40, 3.40, 5.00, 6.25 P. M.

FROM POINT TIBURON FOR SAN FRANCISCO
Week Days—7.15, 8.20, 9.55 A. M.; 12.05, 2.05, 4.05, 5.30, 6.30 P. M.
Sundays—8.25, 10.05, 11.35 A. M.; 2.05, 4.05, 5.30, 6.50 P. M.

Leave San Francisco. Week Days.	Leave San Francisco. Sundays.	Destination	Arrive San Francisco. Sundays.	Arrive San Francisco. Week Days.
7.40 A M 9.20 A M 3.30 P M 5.00 P M	8.00 A M 5.00 P M	Petaluma and Santa Rosa	10.40 A M 7.25 P M	8.50 A M 10.30 A M 4.40 P M 7.25 P M
7.40 A M 3.30 P M	8.00 A M	Fulton, Windsor, Healdsburg, Litton Springs, Cloverdale, and way stations.	7.25 P M	10.30 A M 7.25 P M
7.40 A M	8.00 A M	Hopland and Ukiah.	7.25 P M	7.25 P M
7.40 A M 3.30 P M	8.00 A M	Guerneville	7.25 P M	7.25 P M 10.30 A M
7.40 A M 5.00 P M	8.00 A M 5.00 P M	Sonoma and Glen Ellen	10.40 A M 6.05 P M	8.50 A M 6.05 P M
7.40 A M 3.30 P M	8.00 A M 5.00 P M	Sebastopol	10.40 A M 7.25 P M	10.30 A M 7.25 P M

Stage connects at Santa Rosa for White Sulphur Springs, and Mark West Springs; at Geyserville for Skaggs Springs, and at Cloverdale for the Geysers; at Hopland for Highland Springs, Kelseyville, Soda Bay, Lakeport and Bartlett Springs, and at Ukiah for Vichy Springs, Saratoga Springs, Blue Lakes, Willits, Cahto, Calpella, Potter Valley, Sherwood Valley and Mendocino City.

EXCURSION TICKETS from Saturdays to Mondays, to Petaluma, $1.50; to Santa Rosa, $2.25; to Healdsburg, $3.40; to Litton Springs, $3.60; to Cloverdale, $4.50; to Hopland, $5.70; to Ukiah, $6.75; to Guerneville, $3.75; to Sonoma, $1.50; to Glen Ellen, $1.80.

EXCURSION TICKETS, good for Sundays only, to Petaluma, $1; to Santa Rosa, $1.50; to Healdsburg, $2.25; to Litton Springs, $2.40; to Cloverdale, $3; to Guerneville, $2.50, to Sonoma, $1; to Glen Ellen, $1.20.

H. C. WHITING, General Manager.

PETER J. McGLYNN, Gen. Pass. & Tkt. Agt.

Ticket Offices at Ferry, 222 Montgomery Street and 2 New Montgomery Street.

The Park Training Stable.

CHAS. DAVID, PROPRIETOR.

Corner Grove and Baker Streets, near Entrance to Golden Gate Park.

EVERY FACILITY FOR TRAINING COLTS and taking care of Gentlemen's Roadsters.

Finely appointed stable with every convenience and sixteen roomy box stalls.

The best care given all horses by experienced help, under the personal superintendence of the proprietor

Convenient to the Park Speed Drive, and Accessible to Six Lines of Cable Cars.

THE TRAINING OF COLTS AND ROADSTERS A SPECIALTY.

TROTTERS AND ROADSTERS FOR SALE.

HORSES SOLD ON COMMISSION

The proprietor trained and brought out the following well known horses: "Sister, Huntress," "Perihelion," "Nona Y," and others.

HEALD'S

Business College, 24 Post St.

—San Francisco.—

The most popular school on the Coast

P. HEALD, President. C. S. HALEY, Sec'y.

☞ Send for Circulars.

KILLIP & CO.,

LIVE STOCK AND GENERAL AUCTIONEERS,

22 Montgomery Street, San Francisco

SPECIAL ATTENTION PAID TO SALES OF

High-Bred Horses and Cattle.

At auction and private sale.

Will Sell in All Cities and Counties of the State.

REFERENCES.

HON. C. GREEN, Sacramento. — HON. J. D. CARR, Salinas.
I. P. SARGENT, ESQ., Sargents. — HON. JOHN BOGGS, Colusa.
HON. L. J. ROSE, Los Angeles. — HON. A. WALRATH, Nevada.
J. B. HAGGIN, ESQ., San Francisco.

Represented at Sacramento by Edwin F. Smith Secretary State Agricultural Society.

At San Jose by Messrs. Montgomery & Rea, Real Estate Agents.

Being the oldest established firm in the live-stock business on this Coast, and having conducted the important auction sales in this line for the past fifteen years, amounting to one half a million of dollars, we feel justified in claiming unequaled facilities for disposing of live stock of every description, either at auction or private sale. Our list of correspondents embraces every breeder and dealer of prominence upon the Pacific Coast, thus enabling us to give full publicity to animals placed with us for sale. Private purchases and sales of live stock of all descriptions will be made on commission, and stock shipped with the utmost care. Purchases and sales made of land of every description. We are authorized to refer to the gentlemen whose names are appended.

KILLIP & CO., 22 Montgomery Street.

TAKE
SIMMONS
LIVER
REGULATOR

It is really surprising how people will suffer month after month and year after year with

CONSTIPATION,

when a regular habit of body can be secured without changing the diet or disorganizing the system, if they will only

A Simple but Effective Vegetable Compound.

"I have used Simmons Liver Regulator for Constipation, and always with decided benefit."—HIRAM WARNER, Late Chief Justice of Ga.

—Prepared by—

J. H. ZEILIN & CO., Philadelphia, Pa.

HORSE OWNERS

TRY GOMBAULT'S

CAUSTIC BALSAM.

A Safe, Speedy and Positive Cure for Curb, Splint, Sweeny, Capped Hock, Strained Tendons, Founder, Wind Puffs, all Skin Diseases or Parasites, Thrush, Diphtheria, Pinkeye, all Lameness from Spavin, Ringbone or other Bony Tumors. Removes all Bunches or Blemishes from Horses and Cattle.

Supersedes all Cautery or Firing. **Impossible to Produce any Scar or Blemish.**

Every bottle sold is warranted to give satisfaction. Price $1.50 per bottle. Sold by druggists, or sent by express, charges paid, with full directions for its use. Send for descriptive circulars. Address

LAWRENCE, WILLIAMS & CO., Cleveland, O.

BROU'S INJECTION

A PERMANENT CURE

in from 3 to 6 days, of the most obstinate cases; guaranteed not to produce Stricture; no sickening doses; and no inconvenience or loss of time. Recommended by physicians and sold by all druggists. J. Ferré, (successor to Brou), Pharmacien, Paris.

JUST OUT, 2d EDITION.

1,000 Receipts — MIXOLOGIST FOR BARKEEPERS — PRICE, $1.00.

All Booksellers, and 3 California St., S. F.

R. LIDDLE & SON

538 Washington St., S. F.,

Wholesale and Retail Dealers in

Guns, Rifles and Pistols.

A Full Line of FISHING TACKLE and SPORTSMAN'S GOODS.

Orders by mail receive prompt attention.

6 DONTS

DON'T own a racehorse.
DON'T be a breeder.
DON'T be a trainer.
DON'T be a jockey.
DON'T bet on the races.
DON'T go to a race track.

WITHOUT

HAVING IN YOUR POCKET ONE OF

Goodwin's

ANNUAL

OFFICIAL TURF GUIDES.

Price, in cloth $2.00
Price, in half morocco 3.00
Price, in half calf 4.00
If sent by mail .... 10 cents extra

SUBSCRIBE TO IT FOR 1890.

It is published semi-monthly during the racing season, and is but **$10 per year.** Address

GOODWIN BROS.,

241 Broadway, New York City

SUBSCRIBE FOR THE

Breeder and Sportsman.

VETERINARY.

Dr. Wm. H. Jones, M.R.C.V.S.

Veterinary Surgeon,

(OLYMPIC CLUB STABLES)

503 Sutter Street, San Francisco.

Telephone, No. 1404.

Consultations by letter, and cases of URGENT NECESSITY in the interior will receive prompt attention.

Dr. A. E. BUZARD,

VETERINARY SURGEON,

Member of the Royal College of Veterinary Surgeons, London, England. Graduated April 22d, 1870.

All Operations on the Horse Performed Skillfully.

Special attention given to the Diseases of Dogs. Calls to the country promptly attended to. Advice and prescriptions by mail $2. Office and Residence, No. 11 Seventh street, S. F. (opp. Odd Fellows Hall. Telephone No. 3 [illegible].

W. H. WOODRUFF.

Veterinary Dentist,

AT FASHION STABLES,

221 Ellis Street, San Francisco

Improved Instruments, Humane Methods, First-Class Work.

H. E. CARPENTER,

Veterinary Surgeon,

Graduate of Ontario Veterinary College, Toronto Canada.

RESIDENCE AND VETERINARY INFIRMARY

331 Golden Gate Ave., San Francisco.

Telephone 3069.

☞ OPEN DAY AND NIGHT. ☜

No risk in throwing Horses. Veterinary Operating Table on the premises.

DR. C. MASOERO,

Veterinary Surgeon,

Successor to **DR. A. DeTAVEL,**

GRADUATE OF ROYAL VETERINARY COLLEGE, TURIN.

OFFICE AND INFIRMARY

No. 811 HOWARD STREET,

Between Fourth and Fifth. SAN FRANCISCO

Telephone, No. 457.

R. WATKINS,

Veterinary Dentist,

Office at **C. S. Crittendens'** Golden Gate Livery and Riding Academy, **24 to 28 Golden Gate Avenue.**

Refers to Palo Alto Stock Farm; Wm. Corbett, San Mateo Stock Farm; B. C. Holly, Vallejo, and others. Examination Free.

E. J. O'ROUKE.

I have the honor to announce to my old patrons and the general public that I may be found at my old stand, where, as heretofore, the

Shoeing of Horses,

whether for the Track, Drive, or for general work will receive my personal attention.

Telephone 2011.

E. J. O'ROUKE,
209 Ellis Street

ST. JULIEN

Horse Shoeing

SHOP,

126 Geary Street, S. F.

MARTIN O'DEA, - - PROPRIETOR.

California Horse Shoe Co's

STEEL SHOE

Light, Strong and Perfect.

Superior to all others for Speed Horses.

ALSO

The Celebrated GOODENOUGH Pattern Shoe.

OFFICE: **203 Market St.,** San Francisco, Cal.

I have used in my business the Steel and Iron Shoes made by the above Company, and take great pleasure in saying they are the best I have ever used in twenty-two years' practice. I have never seen anything like the STEEL SHOE made by this Company. I can fully recommend them to every practical Horseshoer in the country. Yours respectfully,

No. 8 Everett Street. JOHN GRACE.

Old Hermitage Whiskies

"STEINER'S,"

No. 311 BUSH STREET,

San Francisco.

Under Breeder and Sportsman Office.

The Original and Only Genuine
CANADIAN HUNTING BOOTS

Moccasin Style.

New and Improved Styles. All Hand Sewed.

The most Popular Hunting Boot for Ladies and Gents in the Market

Prices Reduced. Quality Maintained.

These are the original Canadian Boots introduced by us nearly four years ago. They are made of waterproofed, oiled tanned material, which is manufactured especially for our Boots. The leg is made of selected alum tanned calfskin, laced up with bellows tongue. The bottom and uppers are one piece like an Indian Moccasin. The sole is sewed on by hand, to the sewed sole is added a tap sole and heel, studded with hunting hob nails. The Canadian Boot is very light. Ladies' and Boys' sizes being extra light and neat, and owing to its moccasin style is the most comfortable boot made. Men's boots weigh 2½ pounds per pair; Ladies' boots, 1½ pounds per pair. Men's high cut hose, 2 pounds per pair. They are recommended by the hundreds of sportsmen and campers who use them. The Canadian Boot is very popular.

Ladies' Sizes, Nos. 1½ to 6.......Per Pair, $5.00
Men's Sizes, Nos. 5 to 11, Single Sole and Tap Sole and Heel....... " " 5.00
Men's Sizes, with Oak Tanned Double Sole, Tap and Heel....... " " 6.00
Canadian Hunting Shoes, high cut, lace, bellows tongue....... " " 5.50

—for sale ONLY by—

E. T. ALLEN, - - Agent for Pacific Coast,

416 Market Street, San Francisco, Cal.

Everything for Trotter or Runner,

At J. A. McKERRON'S,

228, 230 and 232 Ellis St., San Francisco

The Brunswick Balke Collender Co.

MANUFACTURERS OF

Standard Billiard and Pool Tables, Saloon and Bank Fixtures,
653--655 Market Street. San Francisco, Cal.

Abell & Priest PHOTOGRAPHERS,
723 Market Street, S. F.
Our View is unsurpassed by any Studio in the United States.

AN UNQUALIFIED ENDORSEMENT.

Peruvian Bitters are made of the purest ingredients and compounded as carefully as any prescription.

Peruvian Bark, one of its principal ingredients, was introduced into Spain by the Countess, wife of Count CINCHON, Spanish Viceroy to Peru in 1630, who was cured of a fever by its use, since which time, no better remedy for Malaria and for Restoring the Natural Tone of the Stomach has been discovered.

On the Atlantic Coast they are used in the principal Hotels, Clubs and Restaurants, and sold by all Grocers and Druggists. We have sold them for the past three years WITHOUT ANY ADVERTISING, and sales have constantly increased UPON MERIT ALONE, and we unqualifiedly recommend them to our friends and customers.

ACKER, MERRALL & CONDIT.

New York, Feb. 1st, 1890.

WILMERDING & CO., Agents for Pacific Coast,
216 FRONT ST., SAN FRANCISCO, CAL.

The Pacific Coast
Live Stock Owners
MUTUAL PROTECTIVE ASS'N.,

MONTEREY, Monterey Co., Cal.

TRUSTEES:

HON. B. V. SARGENT, President,
G. W. GALLANAR, Secretary,
JAMES E. PALMER, Business Manager,
EDW. INGRAM, Vice-President,
FRED. D. HOWARD, Actuary,
R. R. WILLEY, Attorney.

GENERAL BUSINESS OFFICE, Room 73, Flood Building, corner Market and Fourth Streets, San Francisco, Cal.

VOLNEY HOWARD, General Manager.

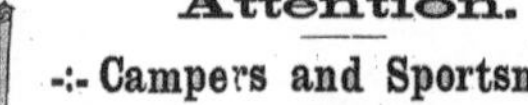

Attention.

-:- Campers and Sportsmen -:-

The "GOLCHER" Hunting Boots and Shoes are the only ones in the market that are PRACTICAL, as they combine Lightness, Comfort and Durability. The weight of the boots per pair is 3 lbs.; the shoes, per pair, 2½ lbs. The uppers are made of alum-tanned leather, and the leg of soft oil-tanned leather. They are provided with good stiff counters and heavy shanks. The seams are all on the outside, which insures comfort. They have a bellows tongue, and lace up the front from instep to top of boot.

Price of Boots, per pair,.......$6 00
" Shoes, ".......$5 50

Clabrough, Golcher & Co.,

Guns, Pistols, Fishing Tackle,
Sporting & Athletic Goods,
630 and 632 Montgomery Street, S. F.

MOORE, HUNT & CO.,
404 Front Street, - - - San Francisco.
SOLE AGENTS FOR
Jesse Moore & Co.'s Whiskies.

THOS. KIRKPATRICK, SAN FRANCISCO. G. H. MOORE, H. B. HUNT, SAN FRANCISCO.
Or Jesse Moore & Co., Louisville, Ky.

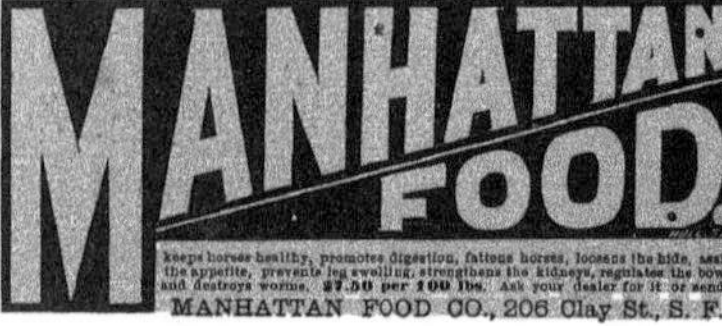

ALWAYS GIVES SATISFACTION.

Combining perfect riding qualities, proportions and balance, with genteel appearance.

No vehicle exhibits a horse to better advantage, and no Cart approaches them for speeding or training purposes.

A stylish vehicle for exercising or pleasure driving, at one-fourth the cost of a carriage. Have none of the horse jockey or objectionable features of other Road Carts.

They are the Leading Cart wherever introduced, and are in use by the most prominent breeders and pleasure drivers everywhere.

Elegant Shifting Top Carts.

Perfectly Balanced Stylish Pole Carts.

or Illustrated Catalogue, with Prices, address

LEWIS F. CASTOR,
Frankford, Philadelphia, Pa.

JOHN SPLAN, General Agent.

MANHATTAN FOOD.

keeps horses healthy, promotes digestion, fattens horses, loosens the hide, assists the appetite, prevents leg swelling, strengthens the kidneys, regulates the bowels and destroys worms. $7.50 per 100 lbs. Ask your dealer for it or send to

MANHATTAN FOOD CO., 206 Clay St., S. F.

TWENTY-FOUR PAGES.

Vol. XVI. No 27.
No. 313 BUSH STREET.

SAN FRANCISCO, SATURDAY, JUNE 28, 1890.

SUBSCRIPTION
FIVE DOLLARS A YEAR.

Our Fresno Letter.

EDITOR BREEDER AND SPORTSMAN:—The late spell of intense warm weather has had its effect upon man and beast alike. Fresno, you are aware, is among the southern tier of valley counties in which the temperature reveals during the summer months that it means business strictly, and still gives the mercury a fair degree of rest, resting between 70 degrees and 90 degrees as good average, although dropping occasionally to 50 degrees, but asserting itself by mounting to 100 degrees. Within the past three weeks the thermometer has rarely shown lower than 65 degrees, and two or three days last week the true reckoning was at midday 102 degrees, and at no hour of the entire day lower than 75 degrees. Still, on account of the natural salubrity of this remarkably healthful section, there has been no actual discomfort and not a single case of illness from overheating. The soil is so light and active and the atmosphere so clear and elastic, that the malarial influences which prevail in sections of adobe soil and heavy damps, with frequent fogs and earthy vapors, are quite unknown in Fresno.

The residents of the valley regulate their labors and ways of life agreeably to the changes of weather, and hence in the heated term of the summer months they neither fatigue themselves nor forget their domestic animals in the lines of every day business and necessary toil. The cautious old dame of Missouri who demurred in early years to emigrate to California because she had learned enough of the Pacific Coast to cause her to believe that it was a "mighty easy country for men and dogs, but awful hard on women and horses," would be converted to the better conviction in Fresno, and come here to pass the remainder of her days in comparative ease and the comforts which promote happy longevity, while her sons and daughters could do better than in Missouri in the refining influences of *dulce et decorum.*

As a matter of course you do not expect much to be said of horses and turf affairs in this warm spell. Still things go on with good promise for the fall meeting at the Fresno Fair grounds in late September and early October; also in the lines of high breeding and the bettering of graded stock. Besides the large and fine breeding farm of Mr. Straube in this county, there is no other fully entitled to be classed in that category, yet increased attention is devoted to stock improvement in the county and throughout this magnificent domain of San Joaquin valley, in some of the expansive grain fields of which Rhode Island and Delaware could be rolled up and hidden beyond the quest of the detectives of the Government to find out in which of the Valley counties the two missing States were concealed.

Out at the Fair grounds are between forty and fifty horses in training and keeping for the Fall races. The lists are already filled to insure excellent sport—pacing, trotting and running. The horses are worked very little this warm weather, and all are in good condition, in fine form, to begin the work when the time comes. Manager Frank Baldwin, the veteran turfman and Fair Superintendent, has everything well arranged, with the determination that the ensuing Fair shall excel in the display of agricultural products and objects of interest of articles which delight the wives and daughters of farmers, of the fanciers of art and adornment which please city dames and belles of society, and of the beauties of Flora's culture, radiant and of delicious perfume, in which all find pleasure and attraction. Landscape gardening, like that at Del Monte, is among the beautifying additions to the capacious grounds, and during the Fair within the handsome Pavilion and about the walks will be the charm of music, the melody of choirs, and the transports of the dance, heightened in effect by the brilliant illumination of myriad incandescent electric lights. Of the sports of the track better opportunity will occur for the definite recital.

Fresno is all the time growing and advancing. Rome was not built in a day, and during centuries continued to decline. As Silas Wagg had it, to the Golden Dustman, it was the decline and fall of the Rooshan Empire. Silas was a little off in his knowledge of history, and had for his display of ignorance the simple, honest Baffin. Fresno is attracting the notice of the entire land, and of Europe besides, with her wealth of soil and luxuriance of products—the choicest of scriptural chronicles and most favored of the luscious fruits of warm and genial climes—as we read of the repose of the patriarchal household in the refreshing shade of the vine and fig tree; and fancy the children of the Holy Land feasting on milk and honey in the famed region of Goshen. The dwellers of Fresno may read the Sacred Book in the midst of his family and friends, and for practical illustration of the integrity of the text, had them all into his own grounds of bounteous supply, to rest and regale after the manner of the patriarchal gatherings.

Nor does the guest, though a wayfarer, have occasion to go without the gratifying comforts and delicious treats of appetite in Fresno, in case he may not visit the teeming vineyards of grapes for wine, for the table or for raisins, or has not the opportunity to pluck the ripe figs or the luscious oranges from the laden tree. Fresno has clear right to become famous for her hotels. In a previous letter, mention of the Hughes Hotel was made. It would be invidious to neglect or omit mention of the Grand Central Hotel of Fresno, of which Mr. Fulton G. Berry is owner and landlord. The term host, in its complete sense, is fitly applicable. A pioneer, of ripe prime years, of large public spirit and great enterprise, conversant with the vicissitudes of life in California, and of the mettle which lifts men superior to depressing circumstances, he has made his permanent home in Fresno; here pressed on from adversity to fortune, and, assured in the possessing substantial we lth, he directs his energies to plans and means that shall further advance the place and establish Fresno as the chief city of the valley of the San Joaquin. The Grand Central is maintained in actually first-class style, not as the classification is in some instances perverted, to the fatigued traveler, the guest accustomed to the comforts of a cosy home and the good things in the way of living, and to the epicure, the uppermost desire and most satisfying realization centre in the entertainment at the table, and in the after contemplation of the delights of rest and refreshing sleep. At Berry's Grand Central, these comforts and luxuries are assured and enjoyed, with the pleasing accessories of excellent attendance at table, courteous treatment in every department of the hotel, and the closing reckoning which better invites the departing guest to come again, than honeyed phrase and excessive politeness can induce.

Fishing and hunting are sports yet to be better cultivated in Fresno. A Sportsman's Club will in time be organized. Fine trout fishing is found in King's river, and over in the San Joaquin I am told of salmon trout, which are probably young salmon. Quail and grouse are in the mountains, and deer are plenty. There are good sportsmen in Fresno and about, but the thing needed is organization. The Pacific Coast Field Club has membership here, and for the trial Derby to come off at Bakersfield, for which entries closed June 1st, two fine dogs owned in Fresno will contest: El Rey, setter, Goodstone—Enid, one-year-old; and Elite, litter brother to El Rey, owned by Senator Goucher. El Rey is owned by Frank B. Dexter, chief clerk of the Grand Central Hotel. He is a genuine sportsman and clever gentleman, foremost in promoting the sports of the field and gun, and of the rod and stream, an expert on the wing, skilled in angling, genial in the qualities of companionship, sturdy in the elements of manhood. As in Pinafore, the song goes by the crew in tribute to Sir Joseph Porter, with all his addenda of titles, it is made very much to his credit that he is an Englishman, similarly it can be underwritten to the credit of Mr. Dexter, that he is a zealous friend and an observant patron of the BREEDER AND SPORTSMAN. He files away the numbers as he finishes the perusal.

Manager Frank Baldwin is absent on a visit to Coronado Beach, where he is preparing the track for racing Fourth of July. He will return in a day or two and from him no doubt I can obtain information which will make another letter interesting reading.

Fresno has an excellent Fire Department. Opportunity to note the skill and courage of the firemen has occurred, and I can conscientiously commend them. They should be better equipped with engines and with hose and apparatus. The fire in the Expositor building two weeks ago was notable demonstration of efficiency of the department. They reserved from apparent certain destruction the large handsome brick building and the more valuable fine printing office of the Evening Expositor, owned by Mr. J. W. Ferguson, the pioneer newspaper man of this section and an estimable leading citizen. Ferguson and his assistants and printers displayed their grit and quality of getting out an extra edition —full size, eight pages—with good account of the fire during the morning. Fire can't destroy this order of newspaper. They will develop the Phœnix quality. J. O. M.

FRESNO, June 9th.

Our Lakeport Letter.

EDITOR BREEDER AND SPORTSMAN:—Since writing my last the track and grounds of the Lakeport Park Association have been undergoing a thorough renovation at the hands of Mr. J. H. Walter, the new proprietor, an energetic, wide-awake, progressive gentleman, who in a very short time has made a place of which Lake County should be proud. A fine drive has been thrown up connecting with the county road, and winds picturesquely along the creek, shaded by broad oaks and graceful willows. A large social hall is in course of construction, club rooms have been put in, a base-ball and cricket-field has been laid off, a steam pump has been purchased for watering purposes, and lastly the track is getting in good shape, and will, before Walter gets through with it, compare favorably with any track in the State. Horses from the outside will find this track and climate just about right, and can ship by railroad to Hopland thence 16 miles over a good road to Lakeport.

There are now at the track 13 trotters and 6 bang tails. The trotters are in the hands of Tracy, Corcoran and Piner. Tracy has two stars, viz., Alwood and a two-year-old Mambrino Wilkes filly. Alwood is showing in great shape, far ahead of expectations, while the filly—well, we have to keep quiet, but when a two-year-old with three weeks driving can beat three minutes far and away we can say safely she is an ordinarily good road animal.

Corcorans string has received an addition from Fred Shafer of Brentwood—a five-year b. s. by Bashaw, which is a very smooth goer and an unusually handsome animal. Lady Armington owned by Superior Judge Hudson, by Anteeo, dam by Abbotsford, is gaining speed slowly and surely, has a powerful, strong gait, and is a worthy representative of her blood lines.

C. S. Piner has in charge Geo. Washington (or Anti-C.) by Anteeo, out of Countess, and four other good ones, some of which will make a good showing before long. Washington has had to be carried along carefully, but as soon as his stud season ends will be given a chance to exert himself.

Among the bang tails P. E. Smith has three, the best of which, and about the best in the State, is Lulu B. The other runners are in various hands, and lively times are expected on the 27th, when the opening races occur.

By the way, speaking of horses and horsemen, there is a good one going the rounds on "Doc" Aby. His friends noticed, on his last visit here, that he was not his being especially sensitive on the subject of trotters and Chinamen. This weakness was freely commented on, but seemed inexplicable until this rumor got out, when everything was made clear. It seems the Doctor was bowling along at a lively rate behind his spanking bays, cheerily humming "Little Annie Rooney," when he observed a cloud of dust ascending the heavens. The afternoon being warm and the genial Aby being likewise, peculiarly susceptible to both heat and dust, he clucked to his team, swayed them gently over to one side and was about to pass. But he knew not what he did, neither did he wot. That is, not till later. The personage was none less than One Lung, our Chinese gardener, and the way his old carcass of a horse can trot is a caution. After One Lung slowed up a little, Abe sung out to him, "Hi! yi! you sabe! Too muches dusty. Gibbes you one dolla, lettes me go by!" Whereupon the thrifty Lung accepted, and Aby came in town tired, covered with dust and dirt, and his voice husky with emotion, but the name of Aby will be long remembered by the various country urchins who watched the race, as the one man who could contest with One Lung and still be victorious. X.

How Salvator Won the Suburban.

When the news came across the wires that Salvator had won the now classic Suburban, Californians were particularly well pleased, and around the racing headquarters the great race was the only thing talked about. So that our readers may learn how the race was lost and won the following excellent report is taken from the Herald;

"Polo Jim," Starter Caldwell's dusky right bower, gives the horses their position, and down the quarter stretch they walk in Indian file. Salvator is in command at the head of the column and steps quietly along like a perfect gentleman.

"That's where he'll finish. Hell be in front all the time!" cries one enthusiast admirer of the Haggin colt, and thousands feel their hearts beat in echo of the sentiment.

Strideway, with Taylor riding, is next in the line and receives some admiration, but the general feeling is that he won't do—that he has no business in such Titanic company. Even his owners have not backed him and thoroughly appreciate the slimness of his chances.

Firenzi, the peerless mare of '89 is close at Strideaway's heels and obtains some applause from those that fail not to remember her triumphs of past years. Ray rides her and is the cause of considerable speculation, as few racegoers are aware of his ability as a jockey.

Montague, Longstreet and Cassius follow in the order named, and then comes Tenny. His thousands of backers are cheerful now that they can see him, and well they may be, for the horse they have chosen is in the pink of condition, full of life and fiery spirit and impatient to go out and run. As of yore he wears the hood and blinkers, but who dares to call them the badge of a rogue?

Raceland and Prince Royal bring up the rear, and after all have passed before the stand a bell clangs, the line is broken and off they gallop, singly and in pairs, up the stretch to the starting post, where Starter Caldwell is in readiness to take them in hand.

As they paraded, so they line up across the track, with Salvator having the best position by the inner rail and Prince Royal last at the outer edge of the track.

This is a crucial moment, and the spectators anxiously await the falling of the little red flag firmly grasped in the starter's hand.

But there is a delay. Longstreet is fractious, Raceland is nervous and Salvator the most restless of all. All of them feel their oats and they give no end of trouble.

They break away, with Raceland, Longstreet and Montague leading, and quick as a wink Mr. Caldwell scans the track to see if all are in motion. Prince Royal is too far behind to have a chance, and it is no start. Back they come, and after a deal of kicking and cavorting they break away again.

"They're off!" yells a man in the grand stand, and he is promptly denominated a falsifier, for the flag has not fallen.

One more trial and this time they're off in earnest.

Who's leading?

Cassius!

Yes, there he goes, like an arrow speeding from the bow, ready, willing and determined to assume the responsibility and brave the dangers of making the pace in the great race. Strideaway is second at the fall of the flag, and after him come Longstreet, Prince Royal, Tenny, Salvator, Firenzi and Raceland in the order named. Montague is in his proper position—last of all the lot. Last he is and last he will be if he can't show more speed than he is exhibiting at present, for the others are running away from him at every stride.

Like a crested wave they move along the initial furlong past the lawn and to the judges' stand. It's a killing pace from the start and more than one will surely fall by the wayside, leg weary and heart broken. Taral has no waiting orders and gives Cassius loose rein till he has command by the pole. Then he steadies his horse and sets out at an even gait on the long journey before him.

It's make or break with the Dwyers, too, for Bergen pushes Longstreet into second place, close at the heels of the flying Caussius, while Strideaway falls back to third position at the head of the plunging cluster of horses that threaten momentarily to run clear over him, so furious are their movements.

Prince Royal is at Strideaway's outer flank, while on the inside are the California team, Salvator and Firenzi, both tugging wildly against their riders' restraining pull. Garrison, strong armed, resists Tenny's impetuous efforts, and keeps Pulsifer's pride well back in the rear, where Raceland keeps him company.

Montague maintains his humble rearward position, and Mr. Galway's smile evaporates.

Cassius has only a length the best of it as they pass the judges' stand, and Taral is not satisfied with this advantage. He is bound to make a runaway race of it if he can and repeat the trick performed by Castaway II. in the Brooklyn Handicap. So, passing the paddock, he loosens rein once more, and in a twinkling there is daylight between Cassius and Longstreet, his nearest opponent.

"Oh, dear! look at Cassius! Tenny will never, never catch him." I hear a vision of female loveliness and lace cry out, close behind me in the grand stand. Nor are her fears groundless, if she has risked her little wager on the son of Rayon d'Or, for Cassius is opening a palpably big gap in front, while Tenny is laying further and further back in the rear.

Now they swing around the paddock turn, having traversed exactly a quarter of a mile. There's a mile still before him, but if Cassius can keep up that soul stirring gait they won't be long in covering it. He's two lengths in the lead and going as easily as if he were out for exercise. Longstreet retains second position, and like Cassius has done something in the way of running away from the others, for he's a length and a half away in front of Strideaway.

They're stringing out, for the pace is already having effect Salvator's nose grazes Strideaway's tail, and Firenzi is a length behind her stable companion. Prince Royal is in difficulty, even at this early stage of the game, for Anderson finds no little difficulty in keeping up with the others. But the Belmont hopes are not centred on the Prince, and as Raceland is close at his side the supporters of the "maroon and scarlet" as yet feel no fear.

But what's the matter with Tenny? He's next to last. Come, Garrison, this will never do. Don't wait too long.

The "Snapper" seems to appreciate this fact, for as Cassius shows the way into the backstretch Tenny begins to move up with his adversaries. There's time yet for him to make up all the lost ground, but his backers would like it better if he was nearer the front:

Faster, faster and faster still, like a flying demon. Cassius continues to increase the pace, and there's a gap of three lengths between him and Longstreet now. The further he goes the greater his advantage, and Isaac Murphy, back in the ruck with Salvator, recognizes that he cannot afford to stay where he is. Isaac is a good judge of pace, and he knows what he is about when he lets out a link of his pull on the great colt's head.

The effect is instantaneous, for the moment they are all well straightened out on the backstretch, Cassius' lead commences to decrease. Not that he is going a bit slower, for he's not. Those behind him are going faster, all impelled by Salvator's movement. Strideaway moves up to Longstreet and he gains visibly on Cassius. Salvator has taken fourth place at Strideaway's side and Firenzi is not far away. Raceland and Tenny have begun to hurry and both are within striking distance of those before them. Prince Royal is no longer a candidate for Suburban honors, and Montague is more out of the race than ever before.

"Longstreet's hurt! What can be the matter?"

Something is, indeed, wrong. The Dwyer's colt is falling back faster than the others are going on.

They are just starting around the long turn for home, and the son of Longfellow is still second, the position he has gallantly maintained from the start. But he's in trouble. See Bergen's whip rise and fall, and almost before we can appreciate Longstreet has fallen back behind Strideaway, Salvator, Raceland and Tenny. That ends the "dark horse." He's a back number, and in a furlong more will surely be disputing with Montague for last place.

It's a gallant race and in deadly earnest now. Cassius continues to monopolize the foremost position, but the giants are overhauling him at every stride. Will they catch him? That's what "Johnny" Campbell, his estate owner, asks himself. Strideaway's race is about run, and he is flying signals of deep distress as Salvator challenges him in the chase after the fleet footed pacemaker. It's an easy task for the Haggin colt to dispose of Strideaway, and Murphy now looks forward to gathering in the scalp of the single one in front of him. Garrison, too, watchful of Murphy, is coming along at a tremendous gait with Tenny, and black visaged Hamilton has Raceland close behind him.

They're the only ones left in the race. The rest are already beaten.

Into the homestretch, with only a quarter of a mile to go, Salvator is at Cassius' saddle skirts, and Tenny, passing Strideaway, takes third place, two lengths behind the leaders. Now for a finish. Look out for that stupendous spurt of Tenny's at the end. Garrison calls on his horse, but Tenny is unmindful of whip or spur, or else unable to respond. He spurts not, neither does he gain an inch. It's all up with him, and "Dave" Pulsifer's half a hundred thousand dollars is already lost. Raceland is no better off, and Hamilton gives up riding him, disgusted and dispairing.

But the leaders, what are they doing? It's a magnificent contest between Salvator and Cassius for the supermany. A furlong from the finish Salvator's nose is on even terms with Cassius, but there he seems to hang. Never a gamer horse than Cassius has ever been seen. True, he is carrying twenty pounds less than the California giant, but it is no mean task to keep up such a tremendous pace. Gamely he does it, too, Taral using his whip and spurs meanwhile with desperate and cruel vigor.

Ride, Murphy, ride, if you want to win.

It's a critical moment, and Murphy thus far has refrained from punishing the kingly Salvator. But Cassius is still on even terms with him, and extreme measures are plainly necessary. Up flashes Murphy's whip and again and again it falls, raising great welts on the magnificent colt's quivering flanks. Nor is this punishing in vain. Fity yards from the goal Salvator puts his head in front, and then slowly increasing his advantage to a neck, dashes past the judges, winner of the Suburban of 1890.

Cassius takes second honors by three lengths from the disappointing Tenny, who pulls up as tired a horse as ever looked through a bridle. Strideaway is fourth, and then Raceland, Firenzi, Prince Royal and Montague, who at the end resigns last place to the fatigued and forlorn Longstreet.

The timer hangs out 2:06 4-5 and a yell greets the performance, for it is the fastest Suburban ever run, and only a fraction of a second behind the record, 2:06½, made by Kingston, five years old, and carrying 122 lbs. Salvator's performance is much the better as he is only four years old and carried 127 lbs. The track was good, but not lightning fast, and turfmen who stood around the stand when the time was displayed said it was the greatest performance on record.

Of course Murphy was seized by the maddening crowd as soon as he had weighed out, and being placed inside the monstrous floral horseshoe, was carried to the jockeys' dressing quarters, where he was congratulated by all his fellow knights of the pigskin.

A detailed summary of the race is as follows;

Fourth Race.—The Suburban; a handicap sweepstakes of $100 each, the association to add the amount necessary to make the value of the race $10,000; the second to receive $2,000 and the third $1,000 out of the money so added; one mile and a quarter.

J. B. Haggin's ch c Salvator, 4, by Prince Charlie, dam Salina, 127 lbs .... I. Murphy 1

Beverwyck Stables' b c Cassius, 4, by Longfellow, dam Southern Belle, 107 lbs .... Taral 2

D. T. Pulsifer's b c Tenny, 4, by Rayon d'Or, dam Belle of Maywood 126 lbs .... Garrison 3

Islip Stable's ch h Strideaway, 6, by Glenmore, dam Spinaway, 116 lbs .... Taylor 4

August Belmont's b g Raceland, 5, by Billet, dam Calomel, 128 lbs, ... Hamilton 5

J. B. Haggin's b m Firenzi, 5, by Glenelg, dam Florida, 126 lbs.. .... Ray 6

August Belmont's ch h Prince Royal, 5, by Kingfisher, dam Princess 123 lbs .... Anderson 7

Preakness Stable's ch g Montague, 6, by Mortemer, dam Evadne, 104 lbs .... Martin 8

Dwyer Bros.' b c Longstreet, 4, by Longfellow, dam Semper Idem, 117 lbs .... Bergen 9

Time, 2:06 4-5.

Won by a neck, three lengths between second and third.

FRACTIONAL TIME.

Quarter mile	0:25 2-5	Mile	1:40 4-5
Three-eighths	0:38 3-5	Mile and an eighth	1:53 4-5
Half	0:50 1-2	Mile and an quarter	2:06 4-5
Three-quarters	1:15 2-5		

Salvator is a handsome chestnut colt, four years old by imported Prince Charlie, dam Salina, and was purchased as a yearling in Kentucky for $4,500. In his two-year-old form he started six times. His maiden effort was the Junior Champion Stakes, when he finished fourth to Proctor Knott. In the Futurity he was beaten half a length by Proctor Knott after a punishing finish. Salvator's first win was the Flatbush Stakes, at Sheepshead, and he followed it up by winning the Maple Stakes at Gravesend and the Tuckahoe and Titan Stakes at Jerome Park. The colt's winnings that year amounted to $17,000.

Last year Salvator started eight times and won seven races, his total winnings amounting to $71,000. His victories included the Tidal and Realization Stakes at Coney Island in the summer, the Lorillard Stakes and Jersey Handicap at Monmouth, the September Stakes at Sheepshead in the fall, and a sweepstakes and purse at Jerome Park.

Including yesterday's Suburban, Salvator has won $95,000 in stakes and purses.

Cheating the Books.

The Third street pool room people are very sore, and all because, in the vernacular of their more regular customers, they have been worked. And the feature of the affair that is most disagreeable to them is that they don't know just exactly how it was done. They are sure, however, that they are out on the little game they went against just $1,700, and that is material proof enough.

The fraud has been going on to the certain knowledge of the pool room proprietors for two days, but the sad discovery was not made until yesterday afternoon, just before the last race at Latonia—The Harold Stake—was run. The telegraph operators in the various pool rooms had each received the message that the horses were at the post when a medium sized, neatly dressed young man of about 26 years of age, wearing a black moustache and closely cropped sideburns, stepped up to Bookmaker Satterwhite, in the turf pool room, and, pulling out a roll of bills, said:

"One hundred dollars on Georgetown."

"I'll take fifty," replied Satterwhite.

"Make it fifty each way," remarked the young man.

"All right," was the reply, and in exchange for $100 the bookmaker handed over a ticket calling for $450 straight and $200 place if the horse won, Georgetown being at odds of 8 to 1 and 3 to 1, first and second respectively. The bookmaker than changed the odds to 3 to 1, and even only to get, almost immediately, another bet of $25 each way from a smaller and lighter complexioned man of about the same age, who, it was afterwards learned, had been seen in company with the larger man and heavier bettor. As soon as the Turf had nibbled the plunger went next door to the Newmarket pool room, and though Mike Flynn, the principal bookmaker had rubbed out his odds, and was in the cashier's office with his money, the stranger approached one of the books where only small bets are received, and said he wanted to bet $100 on Georgetown. The bookmaker called Mr. Waddill, and the latter repeated the matter to his business associate, the famous Joe Burt.

"Take it," said Joe, and at odds of $600 to $100 the bet was made. "Money easy won" may have been Burt's mental comment, while Waddill probably thought "another sucker."

The bet had hardly been recorded, however, before it was learned by an employe of Mr. Waddill that the same man had won $90 under similar circumstances on Ethel, in the last race of the previous day, from his house, and $300 from the Turf Exchange. This at once aroused the suspicions of Mr. Waddill, but like Daniel when the king caught him, "it was too late—the laugh was on him."

"Off!" shouted Joe Burt, and then a few minutes later, "Georgetown first passed the post." The young man stood around until the official result, and then collected his money.

Mr. Waddill, Mr. Burte and the other employes of the house also stood around. They were puzzled and mad. They felt that they had been defrauded, but they were not certain, and besides could not have done anything about it if they were, though it is said that after the man walked coolly out, with a cigar between his lips and the boodle in his pocket, that Mr. Waddill wanted very much to go out and "catch him."

The money won in the turf was collected first. The young man had tried to bet in the Suburban, but they would not take it, as they adhere strictly to the rule not to take a big bet after the horses are at the post. He did not tackle the Climax, Johnny Payne having had too much experience in this line.

That the two men worked together there was no doubt, and the coincidence that both are unknown, and have only made two bets on the last race, under the same unusual circumstances, satisfies the poolroomers that they had obtained the result before the bet was made. How, they cannot guess. Manager Smith, of the Western Union, said that he could offer no theory. The tapping of wires was the only way he could suggest, and that he hardly thought feasible.

But no matter just how the fraud was practiced, the public doesn't care; it is glad some one got ahead of the races. The pool rooms hereafter will take no more bets after the horses have faced the starter.

The men got two $10 bets at 8 to 1 on with the small books in the Turf, thus running their total haul for the two days up to $1,700. The Newmarket lost $690, the Turf; $1,010.—Louisville Commercial.

In regard to horse breeding in France, at present there are in the twenty-two national depots of France 2514 stallions (196 English thoroughbreds, 129 Arab thoroughbreds, 124 Anglo-Arab thoroughbreds, 1765 half breds, 302 train), to whom 180,000 mares are sent during the year. The commission sent last year to Syria returned with six stallions and fifteen mares. Including all expenses, each stallion cost 5324, (£213), each mare 600fr. (£240). The amount annually expended for promoting the breeding of horses in France is 8,000,000fr. (£350,000), of which 1,180,000fr. (£47,200) are for prizes, and 7,000,000fr. (£280,000) are donations for horse racing, of which 5,000,000fr. (£200,000 are given by the companies. In '88 France imported 11,242 horses, and exported 34,558.

THE FARM.

Butter at the New Zealand Exhibition.

The Auckland Weekly News of the 28th of April says: The special representative of the Sydney Mail makes the following remarks upon a Chinaman receiving the grand prize for butter at the Dunedin Exhibition:—This colony of New Zealand prides itself, among other things, upon its ability to turn out really first-class dairy produce. It is justified in entertaining the feeling. On the other hand, if it did not turn out thoroughly good cheese and butter, it would have ample reason for entertaining a feeling the very reverse of pride. This is a land of moist air and frequent rains, of succulent and practically perennial grass. New Zealand, with its fine farming population of old country yeomen from both sides of Tweed, would have to experience another sensation than that of pride if it did not turn out good dairy produce. Yet good farming old country folk and their off spring, though New Zealand does possess, they have had to acknowledge themselves beaten at their own work, on their own ground, by an unconsidered stranger from an alien land.

At the New Zealand and South Seas Exhibition there was an exhibition dairy produce show, open to all the colony. Tons of cheese and tons of butter were sent in. Men who had made butter in Devonshire valleys, and others who had done so in the mountains in Ayrshire, were amongst the competitors. The great exhibit—the great butter competition—was for the best half a ton of butter, suitable for ex port. No one supposed otherwise than that the first award would go to some one who hailed from the British Isles. It did not so go, however. Amongst the half-ton exhibits there came one from a Mr. Chew Chong, of Taranaki, in the Mount Egmont region of the North Island, 500 miles distant up country, and the pluck, enterprise, and good work of this son of the Flowery Land were rewarded by his obtaining the first prize. I think I can see some of my old friends of the Illawarra, the Shoolhaven, the Ulladulla, and the Eden districts opening their eyes at this, and shaking their heads, as did their fellow-countrymen on this side. There is no nationally inherited gift in doing work, and one good result of this defeat will be that the New Zealand farmers will apply themselves with renewed watchfulness and care to every part of their work, to win back the premier position which has been wrested from them. As Mr. Chew Chong's position, as the best buttermaker in New Zealand, is somewhat unique, possibly a brief account of his career and reference to his dairy may prove of interest. Born in the city of Canton, he received a good education, including a knowledge of the English language. From there he went to Singapore, and served eight years in a merchant's office, then emigrated to Victoria, where, in Castlemaine, he was store keeping for 11 years. From there to Otago, N. Z., in 1867, again trading: and in 1870 he went north to the then new district of Taranaki, still as a storekeeper Here, thinking the butter he bought of the farmers should be better than it was, he started a butter factory with such success that he has now 120 milch cows, besides buying large quantities of milk of the surrounding farmers. Mr. Chow Chong ships large quantities of butter to Melbourne and London, packing it in boxes of his own invention. I add the following extract from the report of Mr. R. M'Callum, Government Inspector, on Mr. Chew Chong's Jubilee Farm. He says:—"This is one of the best butter factories I have visited. The machinery is good and in first-rate condition, and everything about is thoroughly clean. The machinery is driven by a water-wheel. There are two Danish cream separators, each capable of putting through 150 gallons of milk per hour, one large box churn, and a level butter worker. The water-wheel is inside of the lower part of the building. The butter, when churned, is taken to a space between the wheel and the outside wall to be made up. When the wheel is in motion it causes a current of cold air in the place, throwing at the same time a spray of cold water in the air, which assists to cool it in hot weather, a method invaluable for buttermaking. The building of a tunnel to bring the water to the wheel and plant cost over £700." Mr. Chew Chong is a naturalized British subject, has married a European lady, and has a large family of sons and daughters.

A correspondent on May 10th writes to the News as follows:—In your last issue of the Weekly News, you reproduce an extract from the Sydney News which has been going the round of the papers, anent the New Zealand Exhibition award for butter going to Mr. Chew Chong's factory. The subject affords exclamations of wonder, etc., at the expense of New Zealand dairy people who are of British descent. To think that Chinamen should beat them at dairying! All this makes a readable paragraph, and is probably a sufficient representation of fact for newspaper purposes. The truth, however, is that, apart from supplying the needful capital and showing judgment, as well as having good fortune in selecting a good dairyman, for which he doubtless merits commendation, Mr. Chew Chong has no more claim to be a competent dairyman than I have to be considered a competent bank manager, because I may happen to hold an interest in a successfully managed bank. The Eltham Factory is a small one, and probably has less output than the smallest of our local ones. Its design and arrangement was the work of an English-born dairyman, Mr. Sydney Morris, and the entire management of it, from beginning to end, has been in Mr. Morris' hands. The reputation of this gentleman as a successful buttermaker was established long prior to the advent in dairy circles of Mr. Chong. Mr. Chong rarely visits his factory, and knows nothing of its manufacturing workings, excepting, which is enough for him, that these are in good hands. I do not know what may be the position of matters in the future. Possibly a time may come when a Chinaman may excel even the best of our butter makers, although, considering the wonderful interest which has been taken in dairying during the last few years, I do not fear the competition. Yet in dairying matters up to the present, and as far as New Zealand is concerned, it is hardly fair to assume, as the paragraphist has done, that "the Caucasian is wiped out."

The immense building which has been in course of construction as an addition to Armour & Co.'s immense establishment at Packingtown, was formally opened last week It is an immense structure and will be used as a beef killing house. It has thirty-two beds and is the largest beef house the firm has, the part known formerly as the new beef house containing only twenty-four beds. Alderman Johnny Kenney, who has been foreman of the old beef house has been placed in charge of the new establishment and will have 500 men under him. The house has a capacity of killing 2,000 head of cattle per diem, but for the present about 1,500 will be killed. It is fitted up with the latest appliances, and is a model house in every respect. This house was built to kill cattle for the export trade, into which line of business the house is now embarking—Chicago Drover's Journal.

Dairying in Sweden.

While in Sweden last year (writes Mr. F. K. Moreland to the American Agriculturist) I had occasion to pay some attention to the most recent practice and methods in the dairying of that country. There are two points in which the people of Sweden are not behind the foremost nations of the world, and these are inventions and dairying. The people of Sweden seem to have a natural talent for making inventions, and some of the most important of those, applied to dairy science, have come to us from almost within the Arctic Circle. These comprise the entire range of utensils and machinery used in the different branches of dairying, and of late years leading dairy teachers have carried their studies still further. It is the objective point with the Swedish dairymen, as with the American, to increase his income. Whether this increase comes from a higher price received in the market or from a cheaper manufacture, from a larger dairy product or a more profitable use of the refuse of the dairy, it is equally welcome.

A Swedish dairy instructor, Mr. Rhenstrom, has successfully dealt with the question of profitably disposing of all refuse material. In fact, under his method there ceases to be such a thing as refuse in the dairy. Whey to be run into the gutter, or skim-milk to be fed at little profit to calves or pigs, are, in Sweden, things of the past. In the most modern method of Swedish dairying, skim-milk, sweet and sour, and whey become valuable raw material, which, properly handled, adds much to the income of the dairymen. The process is as follows: Skim-milk is handled as in the manufacture of "skim-cheese," except more rennet is used and the precipitation is made at a higher temperature in order to be more complete. This product is pressed, dried and ground, and in this form, containing as it does a very large percentage of protein, is used with milk-stuff in making compound feeding-cakes for horses, cattle, dogs, etc. The whey remaining after the curds have been removed, as above described, or in usual cheesemaking, is mixed with an equal quantity of skim-milk and evaporated. When the evaporation is complete the product is dried in cakes, cut in small cubes, roasted and ground, ready for use.

It is hardly the province of a laymen to give the chemical values or elements of the products of the two processes described. It is more satisfactory to state that the product of skim-milk finds a more legitimate and profitable use than if the milk were fed to swine and calves, or turned into "skim-cheese," and offered on a market where there is not nor never will be a demand for it. The process of evaporation makes useful absolutely all the solids of the skim-milk and whey. There is nothing wasted, while the point may be urged that the digestive functions of pigs and calves utilize all the nourishment of skim-milk and whey in its natural form, yet the fact remains that the several products of the processes described are available for more profitable uses. The skim-milk product may be stored up on the farm in the form of feeding-cakes for future use, or shipped at slight expense to any available market.

The product of the evaporation process has a dozen profitable uses. Mixed with coffee or cocoa, it is used with satisfaction by the best Swedish families. It is also used as a body for soups and sauces. The manufacturers of these goods in Sweden pays for the dry pressed curds and the evaporated product a price equivalent to about six cents per gallon for skim milk. When it is understood that as a food for calves and pigs it can hardly be worth more than two cents per gallon, and that the cost of producing the pressed curds or evaporated cakes is at most but trifling, the importance of this innovation will readily be understood. It is quite probable that this new method of disposing of skim-milk will soon become an important factor in American dairy economy.

English Breeds of Sheep.

W. F M. V. asks the Rural New Yorker:—"Would a pure bred Hampshire Down ram make a good cross on pure bred South Down ewes? What is the difference between the Hampshire, Oxford, and Shropshire sheep? Which is the largest of the three? Would the Lincoln sheep be a good breed to raise for wool and mutton? Are sheep of this breed the largest?"

The Hampshire is a larger sheep than the South Down and the cross contemplated would increase the size of the cross bred sheep. As a rule, cross breeds, the progeny of two different pure breeds, gain in size over either of the parents—(see figures below). The difference between the breeds mentioned consists in several points; they are all cross breeds and English in their origin, and all have South Down blood in them. The Hampshire originated 80 or 90 years ago, in a cross between a large white faced horned sheep of the county of Hampshire and the pure South Down. By selection and some crossing with the Cotswold this breed has been brought up to a large size and made to produce a valu. long wooled fleece. The Oxfordshire sheep is a cross between the Hampshire and the Cotswold made sixty years ago. It is a large sheep and has a fleece finer than the Cotswolds, and coarser than the Hampshires. Its fleece is not so black as that of the Hampshires. The Shropshire is of rather mixed progeny. It came from a cross of the Cotswold on the Morfe-Common sheep, a black-faced, horned kind, small, but very hardy. This cross was further mixed with Leicester blood and finally with South Down. The breed is about 100 years old. It is smaller than the other two, but larger than the South Down, and has a longer, somewhat coarser fleece, but of the same class of wool—"medium clothing." The relative sizes may be seen by comparing the following weights of the prize fat wethers and lambs under a year old at the English shows of the past fall months. The common average weights of the sheep mentioned are about two-thirds of those of the fat wethers given below:

Breeds	Sheep	Lambs
Leicester	254	165
Cotswold	277	174
Lincolns	321	191
South Downs	217	163
Hampshire	269	198
Shropshire	241	148
Oxfordshire	293	183
Cross-breeds	288	213

The Lincoln is the largest of all sheep and its fleece is the longest. Fat wethers of this breed have reached a weight of over 400 pounds and the wool a length of 16 inches. The Hampshire, as the weight of the lambs will show, is remarkable for its rapid early growth and the size of the lambs. For the production of early lambs its quick growth and black face give it an advantage over all other breeds. The Lincoln breed has been imported to a small extent, but it has proved quite unsuitable to the American climate and conditions of feeding. It is rapidly retrograding in England and giving way to the Oxfords and Shropshires. If not loaded with fat it is nothing but "a bag of bones," and the taste for excessively fat mutton is disappearing even in England; consequently this breed would not be a good one for any American farmer for any purpose. The Shropshire is hardy, yields the best mutton and a very good fleece of excellent wool, rears its lambs well and is not particular about the climate or locality. In these respects its surpasses all the others named except the South Down, and it surpasses this in its size and the weight of its fleece.

White Rose-Combed Bantams.

It has been said on no less authority than that of Darwin, that white fowls are more delicate than their dark-hued brethren, but the experience of later years has shown that some of our hardier breeds are white, notably the White Leghorn. There can be no question as to the beauty of the white fowl. In this country, where we have so much pasture land, and where the well kept lawn and park is to be found everywhere, their green makes a splendid background for the white plumage of fowls. Hence while white fowls will never become as popular as dark, probably there is no country where so many are kept.

The Bantam family embraces many lovely Varieties, and the two known as the Rose-combed are perhaps about the most perfect in shape and contour Their sprightly carriage, neat beads, and flowing tails are so well balanced that the eye has perfection before it in a good specimen. The black variety has already been dealt with, and now we turn to the white, which in most respects is an exact fac simile, the difference being chiefly in the plumage. Instead of being a metallic black, showing very dark green reflections, the variety under review is of a satiny white, pure and clear, but with that sheen which satin bears. The head is small, and surmounted with a neat rose comb, upon which much stress is laid, for a badly shaped comb will spoil the appearance of any bird however perfect it may be in other respects. Upon the top the comb should be covered with what are known as points, and the more even these are in height and shape the better. Behind, the comb runs to a point, known as a spike, and it should be of a bright red and well fitted on to the head. The wattles are small, and with the face should also be of a bright red, the beak being white. In this country the ear lobe is white also, but it would be better if red as in the American Standard, for the red lobe on the white plumage must be very striking and pleasing. White in the face should not be tolerated under any circumstances, and white ear lobes always have a tendency in that direction. The legs and feet are white, and the entire appearance of the bird is sprightly and active. Of course size is an important consideration, and some of the best birds bred in this country have not weighed more than 12 or 13 oz. In these miniature specimens every point is brought out at its best, for in Bantams it is undoubtedly true that "good stuff goes into little bundles," whereas those larger are very apt to get coarse. We must not omit to mention that the wings should drop somewhat, not enough to touch the ground, but below the line of the body, and the tail must be very full and the sickles large.

The following is the standard of perfection adopted by the English Poultry Club:

COCK—Comb rose, broad in front and tapering into a long spike at the back, pointing slightly upwards, full of separations, flat on top and firmly set on head; head short, lively and smart; beak short and small; eye full; face smooth; ear lobe flat and nearly circular; wattles thin and well rounded; neck moderately long and arched, hackle very long and full, coming well over the shoulders; breast full and round; back moderate in length, looking short owing to length of hackle; wings large, neatly tucked up; tail carried upright, but not squirrel fashion; sickles and coverts broad, plentiful and sweeping; thighs slender, short and neat; legs, small boned, taper and medium length; toes slender and well spread; general shape and carriage lively, graceful and strutting.

HEN—Comb as in cock, but not too large; head, beak, face, eye, wattles, breast, back, wings and thighs as in cock; ear lobe smooth and round, not wrinkled, fitting close to face; tail ample and broad in feather, carried at a medium height; legs short and taper.

COLOR—Cock and hen—Comb, face and wattles rich bright red; ear lobe pure white; eye bright red; beak white; plumage pure white; legs white.

STEPHEN BEALE

Notes.

In the first four months of this year, the United Kingdom imported 124,976 beef cattle, of which 100,010 came from the United States, against 64,743 from this country in the same part of 1889 and 42,585 in 1888.

Australian live stock returns: Horses, numbers returned on January 1 1890, 430,777; on January 1 1899, 411,368; increase, 19,409. Cattle, 1890, 1,741 592; 1889, 1,622,907; increase, 18 685. Sheep, 1890, 50,106,768; 1889, 46,503,499; increase, 3,603,299.

President Thayer, of the Union Stock Yards and Transit company of Chicago, says that the sale of the business to the City of London Contract company, is practically assured; negotiations have been in progress since last February.

During the first five months of 1890 Chicago received over 5,190,000 head of all kinds of live stock, divided as follows; Cattle, 1,321,521; calves, 38,492; hogs, 2,911,296; sheep, 875,-003; horses, 46,100. Compared with receipts for the corresponding period last year these figures exhibit an increase of 217,000 cattle, 584,000 hogs, and 201,000 sheep.

The present Stock Yards bank at Kansas City will go into liquidation on July 1. A new bank, with a capital stock of $1,000,000, will occupy the field, to be known as the Inter-State National bank. The capital is to be loaned in the interest of the live stock trade of Kansas, Missouri and Nebraska. The management will have a special care to foster and build up the live stock interests of these states.

The bonds between the Texas Dressed Beef and Packing company and the Metropolitan Trading association of London, were signed and deposited today. This closes one of the largest and most important contracts ever executed in Texas. To a representative of the Texas afternoon press, Charles Goodnight said: "Suppose the big four do come in here and buy up all the cattle and advance prices so as to defeat the carrying out of this contract, we will then have accomplished more than we hoped to do by the fulfillment of the contract. To advance the cattle market to a point where the contract would not be profitable would mean $25,000,000 in the pockets of the stock raisers of Texas. That is just what we want, and it will enable us to divide handsomely with our English friends, who helped make a mark[illegible] Texas meat."

TURF AND TRACK.

Mr. Hamlin is said to have made a very tempting offer to match Belle Hamlin against Sunol.

Cy Mulkey has purchased Tim Murphy, a roan gelding by Kyrle Daly, bam Maggie R., for $1500.

Rover was sold by L. J. Rose to W. Daly, and almost immediately turned up in winning form.

Col. North, the Nitrate King, is reported to have won upwards of £150,000 at the late Epsom meeting.

Kirkham, the Australian candidate for classic honors in England, finished absolutely last in the Derby.

Beaconsfield and Jim Douglass have both been retired and will be used for stud duties next season in Colorado.

D. A. Honig has purchased from Theodore Winters the chestnut colt Rascal, foaled 1887, Joe Hooker out of Mattie Glenn.

Reference 2:18 has been purchased by Matthew Riley, New York, and has gone to his new home instead of joining Doble's string.

H. C. Airhart, Secretary of the Coronado Beach Race Track Association, proposes to hold particularly interesting races next Friday.

When Father Bill Daly makes up his mind to buy a winner in a selling race the owner will have a hard time of it, especially if Father Bill owns the second horse.

The New York Sportsman of the 14th had on its outer cover a horseshoe encircling Tenny, Salvator, Raceland and Longstreet. There have been worse tips than that.

Guido has proved a very handy horse since Col. H. I. Thornton sold him as a yearling for $95 After winning three races at Portland, W. H. Babb is said to have refused $3500 for him.

The favorite stallion for getting horses, suitable for the army in India, is the Norfolk trotter. The Horse Breeding Department is strongly in favor of them, and all-round they are in great favor.

The weather at Westchester was all through the meeting exasperatingly hot, and the crowds at times so large that many would-be bettors did not care to face the crowd in front of the betting stands.

"How much will the yearling, if there ever is one, by Salvator out of the peerless Firenze bring?" asked a prominent turfmen last Wednesday afternoon. $50,000 was the answer of our sporting editor.

To see George Barrett in breeches and gaiters, riding a bicycle through Newmarket, looking as scared as a stray cat in a strange garret, is one of the sights of the Turf Metropolus, says a London (Eng.) exchange.

Salvator should, according to the late Admiral Rous who is even yet the authority on racing, at least seven pounds better than Tenny, for there is no doubt at all it is a great disadvantage to make your own running.

Secretary Wheatly informs me that the horse Ballston, who was ruled off in 1889, has been reinstated to all the privileges of the turf by the action of the majority of the Board of Stewards of the Saratoga Association.

Guido won $910 for his owner at the Portland meeting. J. Dowd's Sunday won $520; T. H. Tongue's trotters pulled down $800, and the rest of the $5600 was split up in small sums of which the veteran Dan Dennison only obtained $110.

Greenville (Plumas Co.) Park Association have leased for fifteen years a large tract of land on which they will at once build a race track, and buildings necessary to make it the most elegant and complete in the North East of California.

Ed. McGinnis on Wednesday, and Al Farrow on Tuesday did not add much to the renown of California. Ed.(by Grinstead) was beaten by Bonita, (a cast off of E. J. Baldwin's) by Grinstead out of Maggie Emerson dam of Lucky B., one and one half miles.

The English Derby day was the wettest and dreariest since Macaroni won in 1863. Nevertheless it was patronized by the Prince and Princess of Wales, their two married daughters, the Dukes of Cambridge and Clarence and Prince Christian, with Lords innumerable.

Uncle Bob will no doubt be the happiest man in America, as his namesake by his favorite Luke Blackburn readily accounted for the Chicago Derby last Saturday on a worse track than even when Volante won with that good mud horse Favor second, the rest nowhere.

Secretary Kock has made a great success at Westchester, and is now admitted to be the peer of any of the racing secretaries. It is strange that a man with no previous experience should within a year gain such a reputation, and must have been the result of many a day's hard work.

The supreme test of a brood mare is that when bred to any horse, she produces natural trotters, which in turn beget trotters. If in addition to this she happens to be deeply bred in potent and fashionable trotting lines, then indeed is she a pearl of great price, and her value is beyond computation.

Matt Allen, Senator Hearst's trainer, says that he is playing in the toughest kind of luck. His horses appear fit to run for a man's life, but something always happens to cause their defeat. Then his imported Japanese cock was defeated in a battle for $1,000 the other night, and altogether Matt is in doubt as to whether this world is worth living in or not.

W. L. Scott's Bolero by imported Rayon D'Or out of All Hands Around by War Dance, when in receipt of thirteen pounds from Russell, easily beat him in the Zephyr Stakes, six furlongs, last Tuesday. Vagabond, Bolero's stable companion, finished second three lengths back, and two in front of Russell, who was evidently overrated a few weeks ago.

A great brood mare is a mare that produces a 2:30 trotter; a greater one is one that produces two or more trotters; still a greater one is a mare that produces one or more 2:20 trotters; but greater than all these is the mare that universally produces to the embrace of any kind of horse, colts endowed with extreme speed, which, when put in the stud or harness themselves, produce first class trotters with uniformity.

Official statistics as to Russian studs show that in Lula, where horse breeding is chiefly carried on by the Government, there are altogether 103 studs. In fifty-five studs trotters are bred: in twenty-four, draught horses and coachers; and in the other twenty-four, only riding horses. The first category of studs possesses 182 stallions and 926 mares, the second category sixty-seven stallions and 375 mares, and the third class of studs 21 stallions and 158 mares. The total number of horses in all the studs is 336,850.

The one mile rule for races for three-year-olds and upward has been thoroughly tested at Latonia, and has given the amplest satisfaction. It was a failure at Lexington because of the scarcity of horses, and was by no means an entire success at Louisville, for the fields there were meagre in quite a number of races. At St. Louis they have been ample, numerous, as a rule, and a trifle unwieldly at times, but the contests they afforded have been so much more satisfactory than the short scrambles the public had been used to that there is no comparison between them.

Albert Cooper, the veteran colored trainer, had a slight argument on Suburban day with one of the Hough brothers and threw up the stable. Albert had done very will this year with the black three year old Burlington; Come-to-Taw and Drizzle. The probability is the Houghs will not do as well with their stable under different hands for the rest of the season. Cooper will have a public stable and should have lots of patronage, as at one time or another he has handled a host of cracks for J. B. Haggin, Santa Anita, Theodore Winters and other prominent turfmen.

The well known thoroughbred mare Huntress died on the 13th, from injuries received in the railroad accident. She was carefully nursed to the last, and when George Hankins was notified of her death he instantly telegraphed back, 'See a physician and have Huntress' body embalmed; do this at any cost."

Huntress was by Springbok—Edith, and was the greatest handicap mare in the West. As a three-year-old she won both the St. Louis Fair Oaks and Charles Green Stakes. She won all three of the Kentucky Jackpot Stakes at Lexington; Louisville and Latonia this spring

"Tunbridge Wells is justly famous," says a Kentish paper, "for the piety and propriety of its inhabitants, who comprise more than the average number of maiden ladies. The most respectable virtues, however, may be overdone, says the 'Pink Un' which is edited by the versatile J. Corlett. The owner of a well known stud horse (Evolution) in the neighborhood of Tunbridge Wells has been accustomed to send the horse weekly to the market in charge of a groom. The other day, however, the groom was stopped and sent back by the police on the ground that an animal of that character could not be allowed to show itself in the town. I presume that an edict will shortly be issued requiring all horses in Tunbridge Wells to be put into trousers'"

English trotting has produced this scheme of handicap. In the Novelty Stake, at the Alexandra Park Trotting Club, for horses and ponies, the entries start from marks arranged according to the following scale, calculations being made from January 1, 1888:

15 hands or over	Scratch.
14 hands 2 inches and under 15 hands	25 yards start.
14 hands 0 inches and under 14 hands 2 inches	50 yards start.
13 hands 2 inches and under 14 hands 0 inches	75 yards start.
13 hands 0 inches and under 13 hands 2 inches	100 yards start.
12 hands 2 inches and under 13 hands 0 inches	125 yards start.
12 hands 0 inches and under 12 hands 2 inches	150 yards start.
Under 12 hands 0 inches	175 yards start.

In silent, patient, unresisting endurance of suffering from which he has not been allowed to fly, the horse has few equals, says the Sporting World. He plods patiently on from day to day suffering from heat, cold, starvation and thirst, until his bones start through his skin, and his wasted muscles can no longer raise him from the ground. He carries his rider without a groan or a pause with flanks heaving for life until he drops dead. No person can be prepared to deal properly with the horse who starts with the too common impression that he has to deal with a cunning, courageous, obstinate animal. He has usually to deal with an animal simple as a baby, nervous as a lady, and timid as a partridge.

To Mr. Bybee or any other horseman—*Dear Sir:* If any of your friends have any doubt that everything is not all right in regard to our race meeting to be held at Tacoma, commencing July 1, you will do me a great favor by telling them that on account of the short time I had to get the track in condition I could not come over to the meeting at Portland and explain. Now, if you consider my word equal to the occasion, and that I am responsible, tell any horseman there will be $6,000 to race for put up by C. P. Chamberlin, as that amount has been agreed upon by the owners, and I will give security that the same will be forthcoming.

ORGEONIAN. C. P. CHAMBERLIN, Portland.

The third annual Rancho Del Paso sale was highly successful; 95 head were sold for $115,850, an average of $1,219. Last year 95 head were sold for $113,750, while in 1888, 64 head were sold for $112,795. The principal difference is in the Maud Hampton colt, which this year sold for $7,000 as against $22,000 last year, and $38,000 in 1888. Marcus Daly was the largest purchaser, buying twelve head for $31,500; Pierre Lorillard bought nine for $16,300, while L. J. Rose gave $11,375 for nine head. Of the stallions Sir Modred had much the best average, 24 (15 colts and 9 fillies), youngsters averaging $1919. Darebin's eight colts and seven fillies averaged $1533; Tyrant' four averaged $838; Warwick's nine, $761; Kyrle Daly's eight, $753; Joe Daniels, eight, $703; Tyrant four, $838; Hyder Ali, eleven, $568; John Happy, eight, $563; Longfield, two, $600; Talisman two, $555; Milner, one, $450.

There is no doubt in my mind that the character of the colt is largly determined by the condition of the parents at the time of conception, an exchange says. If the sire's vigor be sapped by too much stud service, you can hardly expect the colt to be uniform with one begotten in a state of full vigor. I suppose the reader means, as a breeder, to aim at great results rather than numbers. To that end it is certainly enough to let a horse serve once a day; and, indeed, I would prefer that he is used only on alternate days if practicable. Certainly one good colt is worth ten ordinary ones, and if it be true, as I verily believe, that moderation in the use of stallions will result in better progeny, then it is poor economy to yield to the temptation to overdo it. With all the care that can be exercised you will get enough common ones, but no one will doubt the sapped condition that over service produces must prove detrimental to a stallion's success as a sire.

Joe Courtney has left Mr. Winter's employ. Rascal has been sold, El Rio Rey turned out, and the rest of the stable turned over to John Davis, who at one time trained for Clifton Bell, winning for him, among other races, the Omnibus of 1882 with Harry Gilmore. Little Ruffin and John Davis were among the other more than useful horses trained by Davis for different owners during his long career as a trainer. Davis should soon win a race with the Winters' stable, which so far has been unable to catch the judge's eye first.

The love of sport is early planted in the mind of an English school boy, as the following story shows:

"A clergyman, whose vigorous denunciation of all kinds of racing and betting is well known, called at a school whose teacher he knew, and asked the young scholars several questions in Biblical history. Among other items he inquired: 'Who was Ishmael?' and was rejoiced to see the alacrity with which a bright-faced boy held up his hands indicative that he was brimful of the required information. 'Well, my boy, who was he,' inquired the reverend gentleman. 'A jockey,' replied the youth. The clergyman was much shocked at the 'sporting' character of the answer, but had sufficient presence of mind to ask the reason for such a supposition. The urchin promptly replied that according to the verse 'Ishmael grew and became an Archer.' The examination in Biblical history was at once brought to a close."

Speaking of exercise for stallions, a well known English racing authority says: Although it will always remain matter for doubt in some minds whether Bend Or is Bend Or by Doncaster, out of Rouge Rose, or Tadcaster by Doncaster, out of Clemence, certain it is that Bend Or, as he stands at Eaton, is one of the loveliest specimens of horse flesh that the eye ever looked upon. His career at the stud without being unique, as in the case of St. Simon, has nevertheless been successful enough to be worthy of his great celebrity as a race horse, and most remarkable has it been how very few of the mares that have been sent to him subsequently proved barren, only two such being recorded in his last season. It is well within the bounds of possibility that this excellent record is in the main due to the fact that Bend Or does a hundred and twenty miles of walking exercise every week of his life, averaging twenty miles in each of the six working days, while the seventh is observed as a day of rest.

Messrs. Judson, Latta and the Old brothers have, says the Escondido Times organized the San Pasqua Horse Breeders' Association, for the purpose of improving the stock of horses in this part of the county. The fine imported pure bred Cleveland-bay stallion, Goldfinder, purchased by them last month is the first move. In establishing a breed of fine horses, John Judson and B. B. Rockwood have had up to the present time some fine horses, and experience has proven to them that in no part of the State can be found better conditions, in way of climate, soil and feed, for the successful raising of fine horses, than are to be had in the San Pasqual, Valley Center, Escondido and the country—tributary to this section. Hence at great expense they have organized the present company for the purpose of handling pure bred imported stock, crossed with our native horses. In a few years this section will become noted as producing as fine horses as are raised in any part of the State. It is one of the best signs of the new era of prosperity in this part of the State to find our farmers investing in this class of property.

The annual meeting of the Directors of Agricultural District No. 25, composed of the counties of Napa and Solano, was held in Napa Thursday of last week, the following Directors being present: L. L. James, Nathan Coombs, John Even, Napa; F. W. Loeber, St. Helena; L. G. Harrier, Vallejo; J. Hoyt, Benicia; E. Leake, Dixon. J. T. Hatch, of Suisun, was unavoidably absent.

Napa was again selected as the place for holding the next Fair, and the date was fixed for August 18th to 23rd, inclusive, making Napa second in the Grand circuit, San Jose preceding, Petaluma following, and Oakland succeeding Petaluma.

Officers for the ensuing year were elected as follows: President, L. L. James; Vice President, F. W. Loeber; Treasurer, John Even; Mr. McCullom, Treasurer of the Napa Co. Association, will however, perform the duties, Mr. Even turning over the business to him; Secretary, A. H. Conkling.

The following Committee on Premiums was appointed; Messrs Loeber, Coombs, Even, Harrier, Leake.

The local Association was empowered to receive and expend the State appropriations, and to take entire charge of the Fair.

A well known Eastern gentleman (at present stationed at Mare Island), endowed with sporting proclivities, slightly inclining to fox hunting, but still with a great love for the trotter, writes me in regard to the birthplace of the well known trotter Pilot Knox.

Down on the coast of Maine, in Knox County, there is a rugged little peninsula dear to the sportsmen's heart, known as Bristol Point. This tongue of rocks, birdus and alders affords capital woodcock and ruffed grouse shooting, and when the bird season closes, no better ground for chasing sly reynard can be found. It was for this last sport that I found myself on the point during the frosty mornings of November a few years ago.

While returning one afternoon from a very exciting chase, in which a grand old red fox of sixteen pounds had been deprived of his brush, a young farmer who had joined in the chase, and was returning to the rendezvous with me, called my attention to an exceedingly dilapidated little barn, and marked that it was "in thar" that Pilot Knox first saw the light.

Of course, my curiosity was at once aroused, and a few questions elicited the following facts: Mr. Orville Clark, who owned the rocky little farm, tumble down barn, etc., had been the possessor of a very good road mare of local raising by Col. Elsworth 1709, dam unknown, and as she managed to pass all turnouts on the road, he was emboldened to breed her to a local stallion, Black Pilot 1797, who at that time had no particular reputation otherwise than being considered a strong, clean legged, strong backed horse, with every indication of "getting useful if not speedy" colts. The colt Pilot Knox came in due time, but showed no great form, and Mr. Clark being rather disappointed, sold him for a fair price for what he had shown. In new hands the colt soon developed speed, and promised so well that he was sold to some expert horseman, and eventually proved himself one of the greatest stallions in the country. When Mr. Clark heard how well the colt had shown up, he bred the mare again to the same stallion, and the next colt, Silver Knox, was eagerly sought for and brought a much better price than the first. Silver Knox, however, proved a disappointment, for though a good trotter in Maine, he did not develop speed enough to win any money out of the State, and Mr. Clark, in a fit of disgust, sold the mare, whose subsequent history was unknown to my informant.

Ella B. obtained a record of 2:26½ at Patterson. She is by Guy Wilkes 2:15¼.

Miss Ford, once Santa Anita's crack mare, has foaled a grand looking youngster by ——.

J. H. Goldsmith expects to make a big bid for the Free-for-all at Detroit with Jene Smith 2:15½.

L. A. Davies, the owner of Roy Wilkes, says that the foal by Roy out of Jenny Lind 2:17 has reverted to pacing.

Highland May 2:26 by Pocahontas Boy has been sent from Canada to Terra Haute to be bred to Roy Wilkes 2:12½.

Mr. Long, the new owner of the king of pacers—Johnston, says after this season he will be retired to private life.

Racine, with 107 lbs, fairly romped home from Cecil B and a large field, running the mile in 1:41—never headed. Narvice rode him.

Great things are expected from Faustino, the two-year-old son of Sydney. The colt is showing up remarkably well in Dickerson's hands.

Yet another stable has been burned out. J. C. Rodemer, Gallatin, Tenn., last week lost nine horses valued at $4,500, and a large stable through fire.

"Considering what a demand there is for beauty in horse flesh," says a late writer, "it seems strange that more breeders do no try harder to produce it."

The Elmwood Stable has a large string of horses in training at San Jose, amongst them being the ex-Palo Alto horse, imported Brutus, who is confidently expected to earn his oats this fall.

Theodore Winters had some astounding offers from admiring Kentuckians who wished to breed to El Rio Rey. It is said they did not receive a very favorable answer to their liberal proposition.

Porter Ashe's speedy mare Geraldine showed her heels to the field in a scramble (Futurity course) at Coney Island last Wednesday. Ridden by Taylor she fairly smothered her opponents in 1:10.

The commissioners of German trotting societies have decided to found a central trotting stud from the receipts of trotting races. The Emperor will be asked to appoint a State Commissioner to co-operate with the trotting societies in producing good horseflesh.

The Emperor of Norfolk with two stable companions are now in Chicago. Mr. Baldwin says the big horse never was better. Ensenado, who was left at Albuquerque when the first contingent went East has since died. He was a two-year-old colt by Rutherford out of Aritta.

On July 15th, the Dowager Duchess of Montrose, will send a number of brood mares, yearlings, etc., to Newmarket to be sold by Messrs. Tattersall during the second July meeting. There will be a chance to obtain some regally bred mares if any enterprising Americans wish.

The Missoula Gazette says that Joe Nelson and Barney Mowry came down Tuesday morning of last week from the Marcus Daly's ranch with a carload of fine horses. They consisted of eight two-year-old thoroughbred runners, and the celebrated St. Patrick 2:19½. Mr. Nelson went East with the running horses the same day, and Mr. Lowry left the next evening with St. Patrick for California.

Although the horses Alcryon and Nelson, with their owners and the driver of the former, stand suspended by a resolution passed by the Congress of the National Trotting Association, the members of the Grand Circuit have determined not to be caught napping by any legal trick; they have therefore, by resolution, barred both horses, owners and driver from participating on any of their tracks during the season of 1890.

The board of stewards of the Grand Trotting Circuit met at Rochester, N. Y., and arranged schedules for the coming season. Pittsburg, Cleveland, Buffalo, Rochester, Poughkeepsie, Hartford, Springfield, Albany, New York and Philadelphia will comprise the circuit which will open at Pittsburg July 22nd. F. L. Noble, George Robins and C. H. Nelson, were barred from participation on any circuit track.

The Haggin stable followed up their grand victory of Wednesday, by winning the Coney Island Cup on Thursday with that grand old mare Firenze, who, like her stable companion Salvator, was in record beating form. Carrying 117 lbs., she ran the mile and a-half in 2:33. The previous record of 2:34 had stood since 1880, but had twice been equalled: in 1886 by Jim Guest (Supervisor), and in 1888 by Firenze, who was then four years old.

A New York morning paper says: It is amusing to note the wrapt adoration of Pierre Lorillard for his love, the turf. Once in a while the master of Rancocas writes a letter to the newspapers protesting that he does not bet more than $500 on a race, and doubtless that is true, but it should be remembered that Mr. Lorillard plays what are technically known as "short horses." A "short horse" always has a long price. Mr. Lorillard is nothing if not enthusiastic, and it is due to his unquenchable enthusiasm that he attained his former great figure in the racing world. A sudden fondness for yachting, and later on a complete absorption in Tuxedo caused him some years ago to lose his faith in mankind in general and racing in particular. He left the turf with as much precipitancy as he had gone on it, but it was impossible for him to keep entirely away from his old love. He is the popular idol of a racing man—big, breezy, handsome, well dressed, friendly and strictly reliable. His stable has always been run on principles of absolute integrity. This year Mr. Lorillard has been on the track morning, noon and night. He talks horse until midnight, and is the first man around the following morning. A good many men have tried to get away from the fascination of racing, but the majority of them do not make any more of a success than that which has distinguished Mr. Lorillard's recent effort. The public is to be congratulated upon the return of an old-timer in this instance.

Mr. A. C. Dietz has already sent Ringwood to J. A. Dustin to be campaigned through the circuit. Longsworth 2:19, who has made a highly successful stud season in Ventura County, will be sent up to Dustin next week. Both are confidently expected to get very low marks before next year.

Senator Stanford has purchased from R. S. Strader, Lexington, Ky., Miss Rowett, brown mare, foaled '87 by Hyder Ali; first dam Ella G. by Colossus, second dam Estella (grand dam of Alcantara, 2:23; Alcyone, 2:27; Arbiter, 2:30) by imp Australian, third dam Fanny G. (Endorser's dam and great grandam of Palo Alto, 2:12¾, Gertrude Russell 2:23½, and Big Jim, 2:23) by Imp Margrave, fourth dam Lancess by Lance by American Eclipse. Hyder Ali's dam, Lady Duke by Lexington, is also the dam of Ryadyk, sire of Clingstone, record 2:14.

Also a bay filly, foaled '88 by Duke of Montrose; first dam Kitty Clover by Aristides, second dam Mary Taylor by imp Sovereign, third dam by Grey Eagle, fourth dam by imp Nonplus. Duke of Montrose by Waverly, dam by imp Bonnie Scotland, sire of Scotland, 2:22¼.

The less important betting agencies have yielded to M. Constans' ordinance, which was published in the Journal Officiel to-day, but has not yet been served on those whom it concerns The London Daily News of June 4 says: According to the decree, bets can only be made on race courses, and for sums over 5f. There are 3 000 agencies in Paris, most of which are held at public houses, where drinking and gambling go hand in hand. The great agencies, however, which have offices of their own, intend to fight the Government before the Council of State. They will be represented by Maitre Demange, a Bonapartist advocate. Last night they elected a syndicate of defense. It appears that there is an *arrête* of the Court of Appeal of Rouen declaring betting agencies of the "Pari Mutuel" class to be legal. Fifteen agencies and sporting offices took part in the election of the syndicate. Some advise defiance, others propose simply to continue business in a disguised form as commission merchants, taking 5 per cent. on the bets. A movement is being started to transfer the business of the betting agencies to the race-course companies. The pretext is that the business would in this way be utterly disassociated from drink. But it is probable the public houses would spring up around the new agencies, perhaps, belonging to the racing companies. Racing and tippling in absinthe, beer, and other drinks which are now sold at bars, are brutalizing the male part of the trading classes, and the working population of Paris. I met a Frenchman to-day who has been thirty years in South America. He was at Chantilly last Sunday, and was horrified at the drinking and rowdyism which he witnessed there. In his time, people used to take coffee and *eau sucree* flavored with orange flower water, and never thought of a "nip" unless immediately before dinner. Civilians seldom took absinthe, which was introduced by officers who had served in Algiers.

Secretary Kock of the New York Jockey Club announces the following as the gross winnings of the stables that have raced during the Morris Park meeting. The money was distributed among sixty-seven different owners, Byron McClelland's victory in the Eclipse Stakes lifting him from a position among the small winners up to the second place, next to the owners of the race course. These are the winners:

J. A. & A. H. Morris	$32,100	James Shields	$865
Byron McClelland	28,739	P. J. Flinn	855
D. D. Withers	17,650	Shepardsbush Farm	870
August Belmont	17,255	C. P. Sanders	870
Hough Bros	14,455	J. J. Hyland	860
D. T. Pulsifer	13,390	Hanover Stable	850
Santa Anita Stable	5,870	Sam Emery	815
G. B. Morris	9,160	R. McBride	810
W. C. Daly	9,740	T. W. Shreve	690
G. Walbaum	8,520	P. B. Pollard	650
D. Gideon	2,850	Oakwood Stable	502
George Hearst	4,890	John Hunter	450
Rancocas Stable	2,790	Oden Bowie	450
Preakness Stable	2,455	Labold Bros	400
George Forbes	2,595	S. W. Street	350
L. Stuart & Co	2,460	S. S. Brown	302
Beverwyck Stable	2,390	C. D. McCoy	300
D. W. McCoun	2,275	William Corbett	300
Maltese V. S. F.	2,200	D. Johnson	250
Dwyer Bros	2,120	J. Pincus	250
W. L. Scott	2,015	Madison Stable	250
Edmund Blunt	1,975	Empire Stable	250
O. B. McStea	2,130	J. N. Mulholland	200
Chas. Reed & Sons	1,895	William Donohue	200
— Mehrbach	1,668	Bennett & Warren	200
— Van Brunt	1,665	M. J. Daly	200
Keystone Stable	1,537	J. B. Haggin	100
W. P. Birch	1,460	Sunol Stable	100
J. E. McDonald	1,475	R. McElmeel	100
Excelsior Stable	1,400	Jeter Walden	100
G. S. Tompkins	1,300	J. A. Batchelder	100
William Jennings	1,140	Bradford Stable	100
L. J. Rose	950	McDonald & Corbett	100
C. Jacobs	930	P. Hanner	100

Quite a good story is told of how Isaac Murphy frightened millionaire Baldwin once so as to cause him to swallow a chew of tobacco. It was two years ago, and Murphy had the mount on Baldwin's horse Volante at Saratoga; just before the start he called Murphy into the grand stand and said, "Now Murphy, I don't want any monkeying about this race, none of your sensational finishes. You just cut the old horse loose, and send him from the fall of the flag to the finish. I've got a lot of money on this race, and don't want to be worried about the result." Murphy showed his white teeth in a smile of acquiescence, and then in a low tone impressed the ladies in Baldwin's party that he would make the old man faint away. When the flag fell, Murphy pulled Volante back to fourth place, and held him steady 'round the turn; going up the back stretch the leaders flew, with Murphy trailing along quietly as though out for a pleasure ride. Baldwin began to kick, and bit off a big chunk of tobacco and began to chew at a tremendous rate. As the horse rounded the lower turn and entered the stretch, Murphy began moving up inch by inch; it seemed an impossibility for him to reach the leaders, but he did, and one by one they surrendered, until when within a hundred feet of the wire Volante had disposed of all but one. Then with a magnificent exhibition of horsemanship, Murphy fairly lifted his mount up to even terms, and in the last bound landed Volante a winner by a nose. Before the jockeys dismounted, Baldwin turned to a member of the party and said: "George, I wish you would get these tickets on Volante cashed and bring the money to me at the hotel. I'm going home right away. I don't feel well; some fellow swallowed a chew of tobacco which I had in my mouth, when that black devil made that close finish."

The above story has been published in all—or almost all the Eastern papers, and as no credit is given is given one cannot tell who was the expert who manufactured it. The tale itself is very amusing and does credit to the original writer; unfortunately the most amusing portion of the production is hardly justifiable, for *Mr. Baldwin does not chew.*

The slander action which was some time ago instituted in Australia, in connection with statements m de re Moorbank's running in the Caulfield Cup appears to be coming to a head at last. The Melbourne Sportsman says: The case came before Mr Justice Webb in the Supreme Court, on Friday last, in a preliminary form. The action is brought by Mr. Patrick Kelly against Mr. James B. Gill for the recovery of £5000 for slander, the alleged slander consisting of statements that the plaintiff had "stuffed" and "stiffened" Moorbank for the last Caulfield Cup. The defendant pleads that the words were true, and, furthermore, that they were spoken on a privileged occasion and without malice. Particulars of the defence were asked for, and the defendant then stated that what he had said was true, and that the words were spoken of by him as a member of the Victoria Amateur Turf Club and the Victoria Club, and a person pecuniarily interested in the running of Moorbank in the Caulfield Cup, in the course of an inquiry into the suspicious running of the horse, and for the purpose of carrying out the object of the club in regulating and managing horse racing in Victoria, and to persons interested as owners of horses and employers of the plaintiff in the conduct of the plaintiff as a horse trainer. Mr. Fink applied on Friday for further particulars. Mr. Duffy said that to give further particulars would be in reality furnishing the plaintiff with the evidence in support of the defence. His Honor agreed with this view, and refused the application.

During the past few days I have been, says a member of the Pink Un Staff, an interested listener to a good deal of information concerning the mode and manner of racing in Buenos Ayres, given by a gentleman well qualified to form an opinion, seeing that he gave it a practical trial of six months' duration, and "but for other ties at home would be very glad to have another turn over there." The now familiar tales of foul riding and general thieving amongst the contemporary jockeys over there was confirmed, as also to some extent the poor welcome given to English aspirants to fame and fortune. Extraordinary tales were told and instances cited of gigantic sums being given for horseflesh, young or old, merely through pique or jealousy among the would-be buyers, and this was remarkably so in regard to a yearling sale, when some thirty youngsters were disposed of on an average of a little over or under a "thousand." The demand for European blood was at its height last year, when as much as £24,000 was actually offered for Stuart, and half that sum was similarly rejected in the case of Amphion; and I believe I am right in adding that neither the one nor the other has since won a race.

It is, I believe, the rule, rather than exception—with a view, of course, of advertisement—to give free leaps in Buenos Ayres in a horse's first season, and this will account for the assertion that when Ormonde made his appearance in Buenos Ayres, M. Bocau, his owner, received no less than eight hundred offers of mares to send to the Eaton cast-off, whose plucky owner, however, declined graciously, on the plea that he had given £14,000 for the son of Bend Or and Lily Agnes with the sole aim and purpose of keeping him to serve his own mares exclusively. From all accounts, the Duke of Westminster's colt did not desert these shores without first leaving his mark, and the time may not be far distant when his late owner will wish him back again; for I am told by a competent judge of such matters, that two grander looking yearlings than his colts from Shotover and Angelica respectively have seldom been seen. The former, who will be remembered as winner of the Derby, has grown into a magnificent mare, that is certain to make a big mark, the more so, as I understand she is one of the privileged lot that have visited St. Simon this year. Angelica is the dam of Blue Green, and if the mare could throw such a useful youngster to Cœruleus, she should surely produce something out of the common to so exceptional a horse as Ormonde. There seems now greater reason than ever to regret that Bend Or's best son should be in exile.

There has been as intimated in a previous issue a good deal of kicking anent the 1000 guineas. Vigilant and the Wizard, equally well known racing writers, say in the Sporting Times: "We are much surprised that no one has ventured to accuse the Duke of Portland of not being a sportsman for not having allowed Semolina and Memoir to be ridden out to the last ounce in the One Thousand. 'When a man makes a fool of himself, I always notice that there are plenty of people to cheer,' was the sententious remark of the "Old Castilian" on a memorable occasion, and we have no doubt that if the Duke of Portland had given the jockeys of Semolina and Memoir orders to ride irrespective of each other, loud would have been the cheering. The most remarkable occasions of one horse being pulled in order allow the stable companion to win were the Derby of 1827, when it was said that if the bridle had broken, Glenartney would have beaten Mameluke; in the St. Leger of 1840, when Lord Westminster sacrificed Maroon to Launcelot; and in the Stewards' Cup of 1878, when the Duke of Hamilton's Lollypop had his head almost pulled off in order prevent him from running over Midlothian. At Shrewsbury, when Queen of the Chase beat Blue Beard, and almost broke the owner of Amsterdam, the declaration was made to win with the loser, the jockey of the winner, who, it transpired had a spite against his employer, pretending that he did not know that it was Blue Beard that was running second. This gave rise to a tremendous controversy, Admiral Rous writing letters to the Times declaring that to pull a horse under any circumstances was an act of brutality, and Mr. Chaplin, on the other hand, contending that where a public declaration was made of the owner's intentions, no wrong was done. The common sense of the argument, in our opinion, lay with Mr. Chaplin. We forget when Count Lagrange ran first and second for the Cambridgeshire with Palestro and Gabrielle d'Estries, whether any declaration was made. The most remarkable instance of two horses belonging to the same owner running home together in a great race was when Marie Stuart and Doncaster fought out the St. Leger of 1873, when every yard of the road was contested, and the filly eventually beat the colt by a head. Mr. Merry, who owned these animals, was then getting old, and was contemplating parting with his stud; and, moreover, the two animals had few engagements of any value. Under these circumstances he gave the public some fun for their money with a vengeance. He acted very differently over the St. Leger of 1858, when The Hadji, ridden by Aldcroft, interfered with the deep-laid plain to win with Blanche of Middlebie in preference to Sunbeam. Luke Snowden watched Aldcroft as a cat would a mouse, and when he saw that The Hadji had taken the measure of Blanche of Middlebie, he pounced on him with Sunbeam and won the race, "Blanche" finishing third. The desire was to win with the latter, though financially it made little difference to Mr. Merry which won, he having backed them both. They were trained in different stables.

Base Ball and Athletic Department.

Professional Pick-Ups.

Exit Sheridan.

A promising catcher—Stanley.

Nick Smith is on his way home.

Big Burke is now with Indianapolis.

Goldie has been released from Peoria.

Zeigler has been signed by Pittsburg..

Speer has recovered from his lameness.

Trick McSorley has gone to Indianapolis.

Ebright is the heaviest man in the Frisco team.

Buchan is playing an elegant game at third now.

Pete Meegan is not a startling success as an umpire.

"Peek-a-boo Veach" is playing a grand first base for Cleveland.

It is said that both the O'Niells are devout Church members.

Hassamer is the name of Portland's new first baseman and captain.

Fielder Stewart of the Tacomas is also a school teacher by profession.

Goldie, recently released by Peoria, has been signed by Indianapolis.

Swett's work behind the bat for Boston, has been pronounced excellent.

It was reported that Finn is after Coughlin, who has been released by Chicago.

Josh Reilly has not been regularly signed by the San Franciscos, but should be.

Tacoma has signed a new pitcher named Stuart. He is said to be a good one.

"His Wind-mills" Hanley is hitting the ball out hard and frequently this season.

To reduce expenses, Catcher Stallings has been released from the Brooklyn League team.

The Sporting Life says:—"Peek-a-boo Veach has a voice like a whisper from a saw factory".

George Van Heltran is considered one of the best general players in the Brotherhood ranks.

Duane and Armstrong, Stockton's new catchers and outfielders are expected to arrive this week.

Radbourn says he wants no better backstop than "Pop" Swett, the young Californian.—Exchange.

Perrier, Barry and McCarthy have been released by Portland. Who will be the next to receive a document?

Charley Gagus is to officiate as umpire, and if satisfactory, will be retained by the League for the season.

The chances are that Wherle will be out here before long. Probably there is a greater incentive for the trip than an engagement with a ball team.

The Oaklands attended a German Opera in a body last Tuesday night. We can expect some coaching in classical German from the Colonels now.

Stockwell has not been worked very hard by the Cleveland management. In a letter to a friend he says he will return to the Pacific Slope this winter.

Harry Hulin or Howard who played last season with Stockton, has been released by Detroit, and has once more turned his footsteps toward the Pacific Coast.

Harry O'Day won't be able to resume his position with the Minneapolis team for a month, in consequence of the injury he received to his hand at Kansas City recently.

Pitcher France will undoubtedly be with the Sacramentos before long. His acceptance of the terms practically makes him a member of the Sacramentos, and consequently Louisville can not keep him. His only alternative if he does not come to California, is to join the Brotherhood.

Daly has struck his gait with the Senators and is putting up a wonderful article of ball. For a heavy man he is an exceedingly active one, and the hardest hit ground ball scarcely ever passes him. His throwing lately has been very accurate, and his general clever work and gentlemanly demeanor has made him a prime favorate with Frisco audiences. He also stands high in the batting averages, being considered one of the heaviest and most reliable hitters in the League. Daly is certainly an inestimable treasure to Sacramento.

Base-ball has taken a firm grip upon the inhabitants of the Hawaiian Islands, who now have a four club league of their own. Games are played every Saturday, and large crowds always assemble at the contests. The double-umpire system has been adopted, and the game is enjoying a big boom.

A spectator in the bleachers last Sunday said that "Reilly was so much surprised when he made that hit to right, that he kept on running out to the field to see if it actually was a hit". He certainly could have made second without much exertion, but that he did not we believe was the coacher's fault and not Reilly's.

The Senators have added strength to their pitching department in Hoffman. The new pitcher has showed himself to be a good one and has yet in reserve a few balls that will be puzzlers. In addition to a good out and drop ball he is said to possess one that fairly jumps and which is most deceiving and effective.

In the four games in which Stanley caught, he made an excellent record. He was sixteen times at bat, and made four hits, a percentage of .250. Of twenty-one chances he accepted fourteen put outs and five assists giving him a fielding average of .905. In the four games, he caught Kilroy, Perrott and Hapeman, all strangers to him and had but one passed ball.

The Pittsburg League Club has signed pitcher Zeigler, ex-manager of the Sacramento Club. Shouldn't wonder but what he may turn out to be a good man.—Sporting Life.

Well, if Zeigler can be termed a good man, why, we can just flood the Eastern market with a car load of amateur pitchers who can give the ex manager cards and spades and beat him easily.

Port Townsend is gathering together a strong team, and makes a very good showing in the exhibition games played against the Pacific North West League teams. Daddy Hayes and Dwyer, ex-manager and captain of the Portlands, have already been signed, the former to play at short and the latter second base. Billy Hulin, one of the best infielders in the California Amateur League, has also left to join the same team.

We are very much inclined to believe that the "very knowing, over flowing, easy going" Colonel has made a serious mistake in releasing Meegan. Steady Pete is in the "zenith of his glory" in the sultry days of July August and September, and these are the months in which the actual struggle for the pennant occurs. Possibly before the season is over, Robinson will have occasion to regret his hasty action, but then he has to keep up his reputation as "champion releaser" you know.

The Sacmmentos are called the "Senators", and the Oaklands are generally known as the "Colonels". The Stocktons are referred to as the "Wind Mill", "Gas City" or "Slough City" team, while the San Franciscos have been without any special designation except simply the "Friscos". A baseball writer on a daily paper has, however, dubbed them the "Goblins" which is a very appropriate appellation, goblin blue being the shade of the uniform worn by the team.

With the bases full, Haddock, at New York (P. L.), made a fearfully wild pitch that went clear to the backstop, O'Day on third started for home, but Mack secured the ball on the first rebound from the backstop, and throwing it to Haddock, who was covering the plate, caught the runner, and Umpire Ferguson said he was out. Ewing immediately claimed that the ball had passed the catcher ninety feet, and consequently the runner was entitled to the base. Measureurement showed that it was eighty-nine feet to the backstop. —Pittsburg Chronicle.

Jack Sheridan has tendered tendered his resignation to the California League, and has been appointed on the staff of the Players League umpires. Sheridan was undisputably the best umpire ever seen on the California diamond, and it is doubtful if he has any superiors in the country. He has shown himself to be possessed of excellent judgment, is quick but cautious, and immovably decisive. Honest, fearless and capable he won the admiration of players and public alike, and who now stand as one man in wishing him every success in his new sphere of usefullness.

The following is from the Stockton Independent.—Stanley, the young amateur catcher, made a decided hit and was cheered every time he came to the bat, and the applause was deserved. He may be only an amateur, but so far as ability is concerned, if Sunday's game may be taken as an index, he outranks many professionals. He catches well, but his strong point is throwing to bases. At the commencement of the game, the Oaklands tried the experiment of running from first to second, but they found the ball and the second baseman waiting for them with such unfailing regularity, that they were taught wisdom by experience. Both the O'Neils and Duugan tried to steal second on Stanley, to their sorrow.

Bowman, the catcher of the Sacramentos, is a player that is "up to date". He is one of the prize gems of that constellation of Senatorial stars, and, clever as the remainder of the team are, with an inferior man in his position, the Sacramentos would not occupy the exalted station they hold today. Bowman is a player of the most finished style, knows every point of the game, never loses his head, and has wonderful powers of perception. Add to this his great reach, receiving and throwing abilities, and you have a thorough back stop in the fullest meaning of the term. Bowman is also a strong reliable hitter, is speedy on the paths, and tireless as a coacher. Without being offensive in the least, he can "jolly up" his own team (and "jolly down" the others) better than any coacher we have seen this season.

By the proposed transfer of the Stockton club to San Jose Stocktonians have at last awakened to the fact that they have not been giving the team that represents their city in the League the support it deserves. It was all very well while the team was winning games, but when it experienced a streak of hard luck such as is likely to visit any team, no matter how strongly constituted, the people withdrew their financial aid, and shifted the expenses of the team on the shoulders of the too good natured directors. Stockton has yet an abundance of time in which to recuperate, and if her new timber turns out favorably, good accounts may henceforth be expected. None of the teams are "out of the woods" yet, and Stockton's chances for pennant honors are almost as auspicious as those of any of them.

The following story is told by Frank Lane; actor, journalist and ex-umpire, about Harry Pitt, a Boston actor, formerly of the Daly company. Pitt is an American, but he is awfully "English, you know." There was to be a ball game between theatrical people for the benefit of a deserving charity, and Pitt was asked to add *eclat* to the occasion by officiating as umpire. He knew not the first thing about base ball, but he consented to officiate if it would help the charity. In the first inning a hit was made by the second man at the bat. He reached first, and danced off toward second. The batter knocked a liner to the short stop, who pulled it down and threw it over to catch the man at first. The first baseman touched the runner, who slid back to the bag, but it was a very close decision. "How is it?" he yelled appealing to Pitt for a decision. The latter, lost in admiration of the play, responded with; "Bloody wonderful, my boy!"

An exchange says: "In private life, Anson is one of the most interesting and pleasant companions one can ask for. He is a good talker. There are four subjects on which he will argue with anybody—baseball, politics, billiards, and his trip around the world. He is a fine story teller, and can spin yarns as long as he can keep awake. He has been called 'the Rider Haggard of baseball', and as far as the ability to tell an interesting narrative goes the appellation is correct. On the field, Anson, in spite of his 'kicking', and his bulldozing of umpires, which is quite as notorious as that of Ewing, and oftentimes more to the purpose, is universally popular. His value as a player, captain and manager cannot be overestimated, as may really be judged by the able way in which he has, during the past three years, brought his almost experimental team to the front. His methods are more of the driving than the persuasive kind, and the rigor with which he holds players up to their duty does not make him over popular with them. And yet few men who ever worked for Anson have other feelings toward him than intense admiration and respect.

THURSDAY'S GAME.

SAN FRANCISCO vs SACRAMENTO.

JUNE 26TH AT HAIGHT STREET.

The Sacramentos came down with the determination of winning at least two of the three they play here, and if they play as well as they did Thursday, the chances are they'll come off with flying colors and win all three. Their team was in great form, Daly being back at short and Hoffman in the box. The new pitcher showed himself to be a good man, but did not exert himself to any great extent, relying more on hits in-field than his strike out abilities. His support was absolutely perfect. Young and Stevens were in the points for Frisco, and the strong armed pitcher did good service, barring an occasional wildness. The Senators did not hit him hard, but their hits were very fortunately bunched with out-field errors of the Friscos, and this gave them the game. The Capitol City boys started off well in the first inning, Daley getting his base on balls, and then Godar hit safely to center, the ball passed Hanley and before fielded inside the diamond, both Daley and Godar scored. They tallied again in the fourth inning getting two runs, and in the fifth and sixth one each. The Friscos had been blanked till the sixth, in which inning they earned two runs on Sweeney's double, and Hanley's and Ebrights singles. In the seventh they earned another. Buchan hit safely to center and crossed the plate after two men were out, on Shea's double. This was the extent of the home team's run getting, and the score ended six to three. The principal features were the batting of Ebright, Godar, Shea and Bowman, and the magnificent playing of Stapleton, Daley, Godar, McHale, Reilly and Sweeney. Gagus umpired, and although the audience seemed inclined to guy many of his decisions, his judgment on bases was in every instance correct. On balls and strikes he was a little "off", but favored neither one side nor the other. The score.

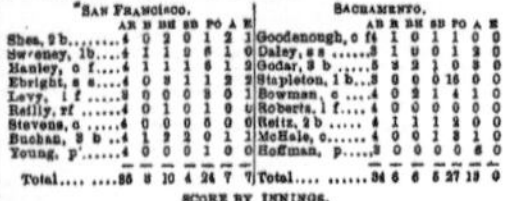

SAN FRANCISCO.	AB	R	BH	SB	PO	A	E	SACRAMENTO.	AB	R	BH	SB	PO	A	E
Shea, 2 b	4	0	2	0	1	2	1	Goodenough, c f	4	1	0	1	1	0	0
Sweeney, 1b	4	1	1	0	6	1	0	Daley, s s	3	1	0	0	1	3	0
Hanley, c f	4	1	1	1	6	1	2	Godar, 3 b	5	3	2	1	0	3	0
Ebright, s s	4	0	3	1	1	2	2	Stapleton, 1 b	3	0	0	0	16	0	0
Levy, l f	3	0	0	0	3	0	1	Bowman, c	4	0	2	1	4	1	0
Reilly, rf	4	0	1	0	1	0	0	Roberts, l f	4	0	0	0	0	0	0
Stevens, c	4	0	0	0	5	0	0	Reitz, 2 b	4	1	1	1	2	0	0
Buchan, 3 b	4	1	2	2	0	1	1	McHale, c	4	0	0	1	3	1	0
Young, p	4	0	0	0	1	0	0	Hoffman, p	3	0	0	0	0	6	0
Total	35	3	10	4	24	7	7	Total	34	6	6	5	27	13	0

SCORE BY INNINGS.

San Francisco	0	0	0	0	0	2	1	0	0	—3
Sacramento	2	0	0	2	1	1	0	0	0	—6

Earned runs—San Francisco, 3; Sacramento, 0. Two base hits—Sweeney, Shea (2), Ebright, Bowman. Sacrifice hits—None. First base on errors—San Franciscos, 0; Sacramentos, 5. First base on called balls—San Franciscos, 1; Sacramentos, 7. Left on bases—San Franciscos, 6; Sacramentos, 11. Struck out—By Young, 4; by Hoffman, 4. Double plays—McHale to Stapleton; Henley to Ebright. Time of game—1 hour, 25 minutes. Umpire—Gagus. Official Scorer—Stapleton.

The California League.

GAMES PLAYED AT HOME, OAKLAND, SACRAMENTO AND STOCKTON.

THE STANDING OF THE CLUBS.

The three leaders are all now nicely bunched, with the Friscos having a slight lead. Sacramento has pulled up wonderfully and has a firm hold on second with the possibility of being in first place before a fortnight. The Oaklands are a good third, and the Stocktons are still at the bottom of the list.

THE RECORD:—(to June 26, inclusive).

Clubs.	San Francisco	Oakland	Stockton	Sacramento	Games Won	Games Played	Percentage
San Francisco	....	8	10	8	26	45	.577
Oakland	8	....	10	8	26	50	.520
Stockton	4	8	....	5	17	47	.361
Sacramento	7	8	10	....	25	46	.543
Games Lost	19	24	30	21	....	....	....

Summary.	Played	Won	Lost	Percentage
San Francisco	45	26	19	.577
Sacramento	46	25	21	.543
Oakland	50	26	24	.520
Stockton	47	17	30	.361

SAN FRANCISCO vs. STOCKTON.

FRIDAY, JUNE 20TH, AT OAKLAND.

Four hundred people were all that witnessed this game which was one of the best ever played on the Emery grounds. There was lots of good hard hitting, and the fielding was sharp and with few exceptions perfect. Both Young and Perrott were exceptionally steady and gave a superb exhibition of their art, neither allowing a base on balls. Frisco started off in the third inning scoring three runs on Steven's hit, Fudger's error of Shea's fly. Sweeney's hit and Hanley's triple. In the eight Stockton who had been playing magnificently got in four runs by hitting Young hard and timely and Ebright's very costly error. In the ninth Frisco tied the score by tallying one on successive singles by Levy, Speer and Stevens. Then in the tenth they won the game. Hanley hit safely again, Ebright ditto and Hanley scored on Levy's sacrifice, Ebright coming home also on a wild pitch. This ended the run getting and the score closed six to four in favor of Frisco. Aside from the heavy hitting the features of the game were base play of Buchan, Selna, Sweeney, Shea and Fogarty, the fielding of Cahill, Holliday and Levy and the splendid backstop work of Stanley. The score:

SAN FRANCISCO.

	AB	R	BH	SB	PO	A	E
Shea, 2 b.	5	1	1	1	3	4	0
Sweeney, 1 b.	5	1	2	0	14	0	0
Hanley, c. f.	5	1	2	0	1	0	0
Ebright, s. s.	5	1	1	0	3	7	2
Levy, l. f.	4	1	1	0	2	0	0
Speer, c.	5	0	1	0	5	1	0
Stevens, r. f.	5	1	2	0	1	0	0
Buchan, 3 b.	4	0	2	0	1	5	0
Young, p.	4	0	0	0	0	1	0
Totals	42	6	12	1	30	18	2

STOCKTONS.

	AB	R	BH	SB	PO	A	E
Cahill, r. f.	5	1	2	0	1	2	0
Selna, 3 b.	5	1	1	0	3	6	1
Holliday, c. f.	5	0	0	0	1	0	0
Fudger, s. s.	5	1	0	0	1	5	1
Fogarty, 2 b.	5	0	2	0	3	6	0
Hapeman, l. f.	5	0	0	0	0	0	1
Stanley, c.	4	0	1	0	4	1	0
Perrott, p.	4	0	2	0	0	2	0
Smith, 1 b.	4	1	2	0	16	0	2
Totals	42	4	10	0	30	22	5

SCORE BY INNINGS.

San Franciscos	0	0	3	0	0	0	0	0	1	2	—6
Stockton	0	0	0	0	0	0	0	4	0	0	—4

Earned runs—San Franciscos 1. Three-base hit—Henley. Two-base hit—Sweeney. Sacrifice hits—Ebright, Levy. Buchan, Holliday. First base on errors—San Franciscos, 4, Stockton, 2. Left on bases—San Franciscos, 7, Stocktons, 8. Struck out—By Young, 4, by Perrott 1. Hit by pitcher—Levy. Double plays—Cahill to Smith; Fudger, Fogarty and Smith. Wild pitch—Perrott. Time of game—I hour, 30 minutes. Umpire—Donohue. Scorer—Stapleton.

OAKLAND vs. SACRAMENTO.

FRIDAY, JUNE 20TH, AT SACRAMENTO.

This was an extra inning day and in the game at Sacramento the Senators lost a twelve inning game just by an "eye brow." It was a great game all through and the Sacramento boys should have won. A close decision by Meegan favoring Oakland gave them the victory. Both pitchers did excellent work, Harper being very effective. Cobb was hit harder but kept the safe shots off him well scattered. At the beginning of the twelvth inning the score stood three to two in favor of Sacramento. For Oakland, C. O'Neill led off with a single. Stickney hit to Harper, who threw to second, and Daly and Reitz, who were both covering the bag, allowed the ball to pass and C. O Neill scored, when there should have been a double play. Stickney went to third on the throw and scored the winning run on N. O'Neill's hit to Reitz. The score:

OAKLANDS.

	AB	R	BH	SB	PO	A	E
C. O'Neill, l f.	5	2	1	1	1	0	0
Stickney, 3 b.	5	2	1	1	1	4	0
Dungan, r f.	5	0	1	0	1	0	0
N. O'Neill, s s.	5	0	1	0	0	2	2
McDonald, 2b.	5	0	1	0	6	2	1
Lohman, c	5	0	1	0	11	2	0
Hill, c f.	5	0	0	0	1	1	0
Isaacson, 1b.	5	0	0	0	15	0	0
Cobb, p.	4	0	0	0	0	8	1
Totals	46	4	6	2	36	19	4

SACRAMENTOS.

	AB	R	BH	SB	PO	A	E
Goodenough, c f	6	1	1	0	1	0	0
Daly, s.	6	0	2	0	3	4	3
Godar, 3 b	6	1	2	1	1	1	1
Stapleton, 1 b.	3	0	1	2	13	0	0
Bowman, c.	5	0	1	0	7	3	0
Roberts, l f.	5	1	1	0	2	0	1
Reitz, 2 b.	5	0	1	0	6	7	0
McHale, r f.	5	0	2	0	0	0	1
Harper, p.	4	0	0	0	1	5	0
Totals	45	3	11	3	36	20	6

SCORE BY INNINGS.

Sacramentos	0	0	0	1	0	0	0	0	1	0	0	1	—3
Oaklands	0	0	0	0	0	0	0	0	0	0	0	2	—4

Earned runs—Sacramentos, 1. Sacrifice hits—Roberts, McDonald, Isaacson, Godar, Stapleton, 2, Goodenough. First base on errors—Sacramento, 2; Oaklands, 4. First base on called balls—Sacramentos 3, Oaklands, 7. Left on bases—Sacramentos, 11: Oaklands, 12. Struck out—By Harper, 7; by Cobb, 8. Double plays—Reitz, Daly and Stapleton. Passed balls—Lehman. Wild pitches—Harper, 3. Time of game—2h. 40m. Umpire—Meegan. Scorer—Young.

SAN FRANCISCO vs. STOCKTON.

SATURDAY, JUNE 21ST, AT HAIGHT STREET.

This was a very one-sided affair, with San Francisco getting the best of it throughout. But it was not a tame game by any means, and although badly worsted, Stockton played a plucky up-hill game. The Friscos certainly won on their merits. They batted heavily, ran the base scientifically, and fielded elegantly. But one error was made on their side, and that was a misplay by Sweeney. The Stocktons did not do near so well. Their hitting was light and their fielding was marred by some serious fumbles at critical moments. Hapeman was touched up very lively, and was wild. Stanley's catching was simply grand, and he saved Hapeman a number of wild pitches. Speer was suffering from a sprained ankle, and gave way in the fourth inning to Young, who did well both at the bat and in the field. The score:

SAN FRANCISCO.

	AB.	R.	BH.	SB.	PO.	A.	E
Shea, 2d b.	4	2	2	2	3	3	0
Sweeney, 1st b.	5	3	2	0	10	0	1
Hanley, c f.	5	2	3	1	2	0	0
Ebright, s s.	3	2	1	1	2	5	0
Levy, l f	5	2	1	0	3	0	0
Speer, r f	2	0	0	0	0	0	0
Stevens, c.	2	0	2	1	2	2	0
Buchan, 3d b.	4	0	0	1	4	3	0
Lookabaugh, p.	4	2	2	0	0	2	0
Young, r f.	3	1	1	1	1	0	0
Totals	37	14	12	7	27	15	1

STOCKTON.

	AB.	R.	BH	SB.	PO.	A.	E.
Cahill, l f.	4	0	1	0	0	0	0
Selna, 3d b	4	1	0	0	2	2	1
Holliday, c f.	4	1	3	1	0	0	0
Fudger, s s.	4	0	0	0	5	2	2
Fogarty, 2d b.	4	1	2	1	2	6	0
Stanley, c.	3	0	0	1	5	1	1
Smith, 1st b.	3	0	0	0	10	1	1
Perrott, r f.	3	0	0	0	3	0	0
Hapeman, p.	2	0	0	0	0	1	0
Totals	31	3	6	3	27	13	5

SCORE BY INNINGS.

	1	2	3	4	5	6	7	8	9	
San Francisco	3	0	4	0	3	3	0	1	0	—14
Stockton	0	0	0	1	0	0	1	1	0	—3

Earned runs—San Francisco 7; Stockton 2. Three base hits—Levy, Holliday (2), Young. Two-base hits—Hanley. Sacrifice hits—Levy, Fudger, Hanley, Ebright, Sweeney. First base on errors—San Francisco 3; Stockton 1. First base on called balls—San Francisco 3; Stockton 3. Left on bases—San Francisco 3; Stockton 4. Struck out—By Lookabaugh 0; by Hapeman 2. Hit by pitcher—Stevens (2), Ebright. Double plays—Fudger (alone), Smith and Fogarty; Fogarty, Fudger and Smith; Ebright Buchan and Shea. Wild pitches—Hapeman 2. Umpire—Donohue.

SACRAMENTO vs OAKLAND

SATURDAY, JUNE 21ST., AT SACRAMENTO.

The Senators took sweet revenge on the Colonels in this game by shutting them out without a run. Hoffman made his first appearance for the Senators, and pitched winning ball. He was admirably supported by Bowman and the remainder of the team. Carsey pitched a nice game for the Colonels, but their fielding was very rocky at times, and this contributed to Sacramento's victory. Stafford, formerly of the Altas, umpired very satisfactorily. The score.

SACRAMENTO.

	AB.	R.	BH	SB.	PO.	A.	E
Goodenough, c f.	4	0	1	2	1	0	0
Farrell, s s	4	1	1	0	1	1	1
Godar, 3d b.	4	0	0	0	0	3	0
Stapleton, 1st b.	4	0	2	1	14	0	0
Bowman, c.	4	0	0	0	7	1	0
Roberts, l f.	4	0	1	0	1	0	0
Reitz, 2d b	4	1	1	0	3	2	0
McHale, r f.	4	0	1	0	0	1	0
Hoffman, p.	4	0	0	0	0	3	1
Totals	36	2	7	3	27	10	2

OAKLAND.

	AB.	R.	BH.	SB.	PO.	A.	E
C. O'Neill, l f.	4	0	2	0	2	0	0
Stickney, 3d b	3	0	0	0	2	2	1
Dungan, r f.	3	0	1	0	0	0	2
N. O'Neill, s s.	4	0	0	0	2	5	0
McDonald, 2d b	4	0	0	0	4	2	2
Lohman, c	3	0	0	1	7	3	2
Hill, c f.	4	0	1	0	1	0	0
Isaacson, 1st b.	3	0	0	0	8	0	1
Carsey, p.	4	0	0	0	1	1	1
Totals	32	0	4	1	27	13	9

SCORE BY INNINGS.

	1	2	3	4	5	6	7	8	9	
Sacramento	0	0	0	0	1	0	0	1	0	—2
Oakland	0	0	0	0	0	0	0	0	0	—0

Three base hit—C. O'Neill. Two-base hit—Hill. Sacrifice hits—Hoffman, N. O'Neill. First base on errors—Sacramento 5; Oakland 2. First base on balls—Oakland 4. Left on bases—Sacramento 7; Oakland 9. Struck out—By Hoffman 4; by Carsey 5. Umpire, Stafford.

SAN FRANCISCO vs SACRAMENTO.

SUNDAY, JUNE 22ND., AT HAIGHT STREET.

This was a superb game. It was full of snap and ginger, and both teams did some wonderful playing. The Senators, inspired by their victory of the day previous were in excellent form, and gave the six thousand people present a sample of pennant winning ball. Harper was a "tower of strength" in himself, and allowed but two singles. The team back of him bunched their hits nicely and fielded like "thoroughbreds". Young was also in excellent condition and pitched a masterly game. The fourth inning was a fatal one for him though. Goodenough cracked out a safe one, and Farrell sent out another. Then the quiet little third baseman—Godar met one squarely, and it sailed over to the right field fence on a line, Goodenough and Farrell scoring, and Godar breathing easily at third. This was two runs and a magnificent lead. Then Stapleton scored in the sixth. Ed took his base on balls, Bowman's hit advanced him to second, and then Roberts hit a hard one to Ebright. The short-stop gathered it in neatly and forced Bowman at second, but in attempting to complete a double he threw wildly to Sweeney and Stapleton scampered home. The Friscos never had a chance to come anywhere near scoring, their two hits being divided between two innings. Their fielding, though, was excellent, and almost on a par with that of the Senators. The score-

SACRAMENTO

	AB.	R	BH.	SB.	PO.	A.	E.
Goodenough, c f.	3	1	1	1	1	0	1
Farrell, s s.	4	1	1	0	4	3	1
Godar, 3d b.	4	0	2	0	1	1	0
Stapleton, 1st b.	2	1	0	0	10	0	0
Bowman, c.	4	0	1	0	8	3	0
Roberts, l f.	4	0	1	0	2	0	0
Reitz, 2d b.	3	0	0	0	2	3	0
McHale, r f.	3	0	0	0	0	1	0
Harper, p.	3	0	0	0	0	1	0
Totals	26	3	6	1	27	12	2

SAN FRANCISCO.

	AB.	R.	BH.	SB.	PO.	A.	E.
Shea, 2d b.	4	0	0	0	0	5	0
Sweeney, 1st b.	3	0	0	0	11	1	0
Hanley, c f	4	0	0	0	2	0	0
Ebright, s s.	3	0	0	0	2	5	1
Levy, l f.	4	0	1	0	1	0	0
Riley, r f.	3	0	1	0	0	0	0
Stevens, c.	3	0	0	0	6	2	0
Buchan, 3d b.	2	0	0	0	0	2	1
Young, p.	2	0	0	0	1	1	0
Totals	28	0	2	0	24	16	2

SCORE BY INNINGS.

	1	2	3	4	5	6	7	8	9	
Sacramento	0	0	0	2	0	1	0	0	*	—3
San Francisco	0	0	0	0	0	0	0	0	0	—0

Earned runs—Sacramento, 2. Three base hit—Godar. Two base hit—Roberts. First base on errors—San Francisco, 2; Sacramento, 1. First base on called balls—San Francisco, 4, Sacramento, 4. Left on bases—San Francisco, 5; Sacramento, 5. Struck out—By Young, 5; by Harper, 4. Passed balls—Stevens, 1; Bowman, 1. Umpire—Donohue.

STOCKTON vs. OAKLAND.

SUNDAY, JUNE 22D AT STOCKTON.

The Stocktons gained a most decisive victory in this game. They had their team rightly placed again, Wilson being on third, Selna at his old position and Stanley behind the bat. Kilroy started off badly but soon steadied down and pitched a fine game. His support was clever. The Oaklands played a good game but did not hit Kilroy hard while Cobb was landed out heavily at opportune moments. Prominent among the features of the game was young Stanley's magnificent work behind the bat. He captured the crowd but throwing out three of the Colonels in the forepart of the game and then they hugged the bases closely. Cahill, Holliday, Fudger, Perrott and C. O'Neill were strong at the bat and McDonald, N. O'Neill, Cahill, Selna and Fogarty excelled in fielding. Meegan's umpiring was very unsatisfactory. The score:

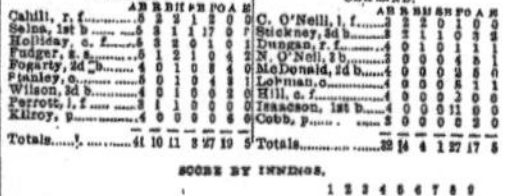

STOCKTON.

	AB	R	BH	SB	PO	A	E
Cahill, r. f.	5	2	2	1	2	0	0
Selna, 1st b	5	3	1	1	17	0	1
Holliday, c. f.	5	3	2	0	1	0	1
Fudger, s. s.	5	1	2	1	0	4	2
Fogarty, 2d b.	4	0	1	0	3	4	0
Stanley, c.	5	0	1	0	4	3	1
Wilson, 3d b.	4	0	1	0	0	2	0
Perrott, l. f.	3	1	1	0	0	0	0
Kilroy, p.	4	0	0	0	0	6	0
Totals	41	10	11	3	27	19	5

OAKLAND.

	AB	R	BH	SB	PO	A	E
C. O'Neill, l. f.	3	2	2	0	1	0	0
Stickney, 3d b.	3	2	1	1	0	3	3
Dungan, r. f.	4	0	1	0	1	1	1
N. O'Neil, 3 b.	3	0	0	0	4	5	1
McDonald, 2d b.	4	0	0	0	2	5	0
Lohman, c.	4	0	0	0	5	1	1
Hill, c. f.	4	0	0	0	2	0	0
Isaacson, 1st b.	4	0	0	0	11	0	0
Cobb, p.	3	0	0	0	0	2	0
Totals	32	4	4	1	27	17	5

SCORE BY INNINGS.

	1	2	3	4	5	6	7	8	9	
Stockton	2	0	2	0	3	1	0	0	2	10
Oakland	2	0	0	0	0	0	0	2	0	—4

Earned runs—Stockton, 2; Oakland, 1. Three-base hits—Fudger, Perrott, Cahill. Base on errors—Stockton, 3; Oakland, 3. Base on balls—Stockton, 1; Oakland, 3. Left on bases—Stockton, 3; Oakland, 3. Struck out—By Cobb, 4; Kilroy, 4 Double play—N. O'Neill, McDonald and Isaacson. Sacrifice hits—Fogarty, N. O'Neill, Isaacson. Passed ball—Stanley, 1. Umpire, Meegan.

The Pacific Northwest League.

SEATTLE vs PORTLAND.

SATURDAY, JUNE 21ST, AT SEATTLE.

Seattle both outbatted and outfielded Harris' Webfooters in this game and won with apparent ease. Munday pitched a good game for Portland, but his support was poor while the Seattles backed up Fitzgerald in winning style. The game was devoid of any specially brilliant plays. Cooney did not play in right field, Whittier taking his place. The score:

SEATTLE.

	AB.	R.	BH.	SB.	PO.	A.	E.
Hernon, r f.	5	1	2	0	0	0	0
Dextraze, l f.	3	1	0	1	0	0	0
Whiteley, c f.	4	0	2	0	4	0	0
Smith, 1 f	5	1	1	1	13	0	0
Zimmer, 2 b.	5	0	1	0	3	1	0
Bright, s s.	5	0	0	0	2	3	2
Camp, L. 3b.	4	1	1	0	2	1	0
Snyder, c.	5	2	1	0	3	0	0
McCormick, p	3	1	0	0	0	4	0
Total	39	7	8	2	27	9	2

PORTLAND.

	AB.	R.	BH.	SB.	PO.	A.	E.
Howard, c f.	5	0	0	1	3	0	0
Rhul, s s.	4	1	1	0	1	2	2
Buchtel, l f.	3	0	0	0	4	0	1
Hassamer, 1 d.	4	1	1	0	11	2	3
Parrott, 3b.	3	0	2	0	2	3	2
Whittier, r f.	4	1	0	0	0	0	0
Cahill, 2b.	4	1	0	0	2	4	1
Levy, c.	4	0	1	0	3	2	0
Munday, p.	4	0	1	0	1	1	0
Total	35	3	6	1	27	14	9

SCORE BY INNINGS.

Seattle	0	0	0	3	1	2	0	1	0	—7
Portland	0	1	0	0	0	2	0	0	0	—3

Earned runs—Portland, 1; Seattle, 1. Two-base hits—Smith, Zimmer, Levy, Parrott. Stolen bases—Dextraze, Whitley, L. Camp. Double plays—Smith unassisted. Bases on called balls—Off McCormick 2, off Mundy 5. Struck out—By McCormick 3, by Mundy 4. Wild pitches—By McCormick 1, by Mundy 1. Time of game, 1:43. Umpire—McCue. Scorer—Baxter.

SEATTLE vs. PORTLAND.

SUNDAY, JUNE 22D AT SEATTLE.

Three thousand enthusiastic spectators saw the Seattleites "do" the Portlands in this game by a score of six to five. The contest was full of ginger from the start and was anybody's game till the last man went out. Whittaker made his first appearance in the box for Portland, and barring wildness pitched an excellent game. Hassamer, the Portlands new captain played short and put up a wonderful exhibition. Rhue filled the first base position in acceptable style. The Portlands had a nice lead till the seventh inning when the Seattles tied the score and went one better. The Portlands failed to get a man across the plate after the third inning. The features of the game were the fielding of Howard, Zimmer's work at second, and Hernon's at first, Parrot's at third, and the remarkable game of Hassamer at short and at the bat. The score:

SEATTLE.

	AB	R	BH	SB	PO	A	E
Hernon, r f 1 b.	4	2	1	0	10	1	0
Dextraze, l f.	5	1	1	0	1	0	0
Whitely, c f.	3	0	1	0	0	0	0
Smith, 1 b.	1	0	1	0	1	0	0
Happold, r f.	4	0	0	0	0	0	1
Zimmer, 2 b.	4	1	1	0	3	2	0
Bright, s s	3	1	1	1	3	3	1
Camp, L. 3b	4	1	1	0	0	0	1
Snyder, c.	4	0	0	1	6	0	2
Fitzgerald, p.	3	0	0	0	3	2	0
Totals	36	6	7	2	27	8	5

PORTLAND.

	AB	R	BH	SB	PO	A	E
Howard, c f.	5	1	1	0	2	0	0
Rhue, 1 b.	5	2	3	0	12	1	1
Buchtel, l f.	5	0	1	1	0	0	0
Hassamer, s s.	5	1	3	0	5	6	1
Parrot, T. 3 b.	4	1	1	1	0	3	0
Cooney, r f.	4	0	1	0	1	0	1
Cahill, 2 b.	4	0	0	0	1	0	0
Whittaker, p.	3	0	1	0	1	2	0
Levy, c.	4	0	0	0	4	0	2
Totals	39	5	11	2	27	12	5

SCORE BY INNINGS.

Seattle	0	0	1	1	0	2	2	0	0	—6
Portland	2	0	3	0	0	0	0	0	0	—5

Runs earned—Seattle, 3, Portland 1.

Two-base hits—Hernon, Smith, Zimmer, Rhue, Parrott and Whittaker;

Three-base hits—L. Camp.

Stolen bases—Harnon 2, Dextraze, Howard, Hassamer.

Double plays—Whittaker, Rhue, Levy.

Base on Balls—Off Whittaker, 4.

Hit by ball—By Fitzgerald, 1.

Struck out—By Fitzgerald, 5; Whittaker, 3.

Wild pitches—Whittaker, 1.

Time of game—One hour and fifty minutes.

Umpire—McCue.

Scorer—Baxter.

The Amateurs.

Games Played by the California Amateur League.

The teams are in the same rank as they were last week, but the averages show considerable change. Santa Rosa still maintains her good lead. The Reports, by doing some good work of late have pulled up very perceptibly. The Fincks are a very safe third, and the Vallejos firm in fourth place. The Burlingtons are still fifth, and the Allens continue to repose undisturbed at the bottom of the ladder. Record to date:

Clubs.	Will & Fincks	E. T. Allens...	Report.......	Burlington.....	Vallejo.......	Santa Rosa.....	Games Won....	Games Played	Percentage....
Will & Fincks	....	3	....	1	2	....	6	10	.600
E. T. Allens	....	....	1	1	....	....	2	12	.166
Reports	2	1	....	2	3	....	8	11	.727
Burlingtons	...	2	....	....	1	....	3	11	.273
Vallejos	1	1	....	1	...	2	5	12	.417
Santa Rosa	1	3	2	3	1	....	10	12	.833
Games Lost	4	10	3	8	7	2	....	....	....

Summary.	Played.	Won.	Lost.	Per C't.
Santa Rosa	12	10	2	.833
Reports	11	8	3	.727
Will & Finck	10	6	4	.600
Vallejo	12	5	7	.417
Burlingtons	11	3	8	.273
E. T. Allens	12	2	10	.166

DAILY REPORTS vs E. T. ALLENS.

SUNDAY, JUNE 22ND AT HAIGHT STREET.

The Allens were not in this game at all, being outplayed at every point. But their being in a very crippled condition, will, to a certain extent, excuse the poor showing they made. They had Johnson in the box and the little fellow worked hard, but he was badly handicapped, Allen being unable to catch him effectively, and besides he faced a team of terriffic sluggers. The Reports lost no time in getting to work, for in the first inning they pounded out four runs, which was one more than the Allens secured in the entire game. Monet was in good form, and the team back of him played splendidly. The Allens presented a zigzag appearance, with the players badly placed, and practically no catcher. Allen retired to right field in the fourth inning, Beckett going behind the bat, and his work was a vast improvement on that of his big predecessor. Monet, McIntyre, Sharp, Gormley, Reilly, Lewis and Evatt swelled their batting records considerably, each doing some powerful work with the stick. The short stop work of Reilly and Thompson, the base play of Evatt, Gormley, Buckley and Lewis, and the catching of Green and Beckett were the features. The score.

Daily Reports.	AB	R	BH	SB	PO	A	E
Monet, p	5	2	3	0	0	4	0
McIntyre, c f	5	0	3	0	0	0	0
Thompson, s s	5	2	1	0	3	8	2
Dunphy, 3d b	5	1	1	0	0	2	0
Creamer, 2d b	5	0	1	0	3	4	1
Sharp, l f	4	3	2	1	0	0	0
Gormley, 1st b	4	1	3	1	16	0	1
Hearty, r f	5	2	0	0	1	0	0
Green, c	5	2	2	2	4	3	0
Totals	43	13	16	4	27	21	4

Allens.	AB	R	BH	SB	PO	A	E
Reilly, s s	5	2	3	2	1	10	2
Evatt, 1st b	5	0	1	0	16	0	1
Lewis, 3d b	4	1	2	1	4	3	1
Buckley, 2d b	5	0	1	2	2	3	1
Geishaker c f, r f	3	0	0	1	1	0	1
Allen, r f & f	4	0	0	0	2	1	0
McCarthy, f f	4	0	1	0	0	1	1
Beckett, c & c f	4	0	0	0	1	8	0
Johnson, p	4	0	0	0	0	2	0
Totals	36	3	5	5	27	25	7

SCORE BY INNINGS.

	1	2	3	4	5	6	7	8	9	
Daily Reports	4	0	0	3	1	3	0	0	2	—13
Allens	1	0	0	0	0	0	0	2	0	—3

Earned runs—Allens, 1; Reports, 2. Two base hit—McCarthy. Sacrifice hits—Evatt (2), Lewis, Thompson. First base on errors—Allens, 4; Reports, 5. First base on called balls—Allens, 1; Reports, 2. Left on bases—Allens, 8; Reports, 5. Struck out—By Johnson, 3; by Monet, 4. First base on hit by pitcher—Lewis. Double play—Reilly to Evatt. Passed balls—Allen, 3; Beckett, 1. Umpire—Finn.

VALLEJO vs. WILL & FINCK.

SUNDAY, JUNE 22D AT VALLEJO.

This game was a most complete walk over for the Marines. The Young Giants were scarcely in it at all and presented a very weak team. In the first inning Vallejo scored six runs which gave them a big lead and which they maintained till the close of the game. The Vallejos under new management, has now a very promising team, and if they can play as well from this on as they did on last Sunday, will surely have a mortgage on the pennant. Howell and Billings were the battery for the Giants and played their customary good game. The two Delmas brothers and Cusick were greatly missed, as their positions had to be filled in by raw material, and had the above named been on hand the base hit column would certainly have had a few more figures added to it. The Vallejos played almost perfectly, Balsz pitching wonderful ball and being accorded great support from Hughes at the receiving end. The fielders had but little to do, all the put outs being confined to Hughes, Ryan, Maguire and Wise. For the Giants the battery, Leveque, Gately and Tillson performed the best work. The score:

Vallejos.	AB	R	BH	SB	PO	A	E
McGuire, s s	5	1	1	0	1	1	0
Hughes, c	3	1	0	1	11	2	0
Ryan, 1st b	4	2	0	0	10	0	0
Wise, c f	4	2	1	0	2	0	0
Stanford, l f	3	1	0	1	0	0	0
Lee, 2d b	4	0	0	0	0	1	0
Kavanaugh, r f	4	2	0	1	0	0	0
Broderick, 3d b	3	1	1	0	0	2	1
Balsz, p	4	0	2	0	0	1	0
Totals	34	10	5	3	27	7	1

Will & Fincks.	AB	R	BH	SB	PO	A	E
Gately, c f	3	1	1	0	2	0	0
Strand, 3d b	4	0	0	1	0	3	2
Conway, 2b	4	0	0	0	3	0	2
Billings, c	4	0	0	0	3	0	1
Heron, 1st b	4	0	0	0	6	1	2
Tillson, s s	4	0	0	0	1	3	1
Pierce, r f	2	0	0	0	0	0	0
Leveque, l f	3	1	1	1	1	0	0
Howell, p	2	1	1	0	1	2	0
Totals	30	3	3	2	24	9	8

SCORE BY INNINGS.

	1	2	3	4	5	6	7	8	9	
Vallejos	6	0	1	2	0	0	0	1	*	—10
Will & Fincks	1	0	0	0	1	0	0	1	0	—3

—Three-base hits—Wise, McGuire. Two-base hits—Broderick, Balsz. First base on errors—Vallejos 5; Will & Fincks, 1. First base on called balls—Will & Fincks, 2; Vallejos, 6. Left on bases—Will & Fincks, 3; Vallejos, 6. Struck out—By Howell, 8; by Balsz, 15. Hit by pitched ball—Pierce. Wild pitch—Balsz, 1. Past balls—Billings, 4; Hughes, 2. Umpire, Cate.

SANTA ROSA vs. BURLINGTONS.

SUNDAY, JUNE 22d, AT SANTA ROSA.

The Sonoma boys did the Rail roaders up in great shape last Sunday to the tune of twelve to five. It was not a brilliant or even an interesting game although witnessed by almost a thousand spectators who remained till the last man was out. The Santa Rosas outbatted the Burlingtons while the opposite was the case in fielding. But the Burlingtons errors were nicely bunched with the hitting of the Santa Rosas in the third inning, and this inning told the tale. Callen pitched his usual strong game but was not well supported. Cook, Gimmel and Stultz did some very pretty fielding and Pace's record barring his error column would have been an exceedingly bright one. The Burlingtons did not score till the fifth when one run came in, and in the seventh and eighth they added four more but they were too far behind to have any chance of catching up. Their fielding was far superior to that of the "country fellers," Bradley, Mulvey, Deane, Dunn and Fleming playing their positions in a finished style. McConville, as umpire, gave good satisfaction. The score:

Santa Rosas.	AB	R	BH	SB	PO	A	E
Gimmell, l f	3	2	0	1	2	0	1
Cook, c f	4	2	2	1	2	2	0
Hulen, 2d b	4	3	1	0	0	0	2
Pace, c	5	2	4	3	10	1	5
G. Arlett, s s	4	1	0	0	1	1	2
Stultz, 1st b	2	1	0	0	9	0	0
Kelly, r f	3	1	0	0	0	0	0
J. Artlett, 3d b	4	0	0	0	1	4	1
Callen, p	4	0	1	0	2	6	0
Totals	37	12	8	5	27	14	12

Burlingtons.	AB	R	BH	SB	PO	A	E
Foster, l f	5	0	0	1	1	0	0
Bradley, 2d b	3	0	0	3	3	2	0
Buick, p	5	0	1	2	1	1	1
Mulvey, c	4	1	1	2	7	1	2
Kennedy, s s	4	0	1	0	1	3	2
Deane, c f	4	0	1	1	1	2	0
Fleming, 1st b	4	2	1	0	8	0	0
Dunn, 3d b	3	2	1	1	2	1	1
McKenzie, r f	3	0	0	0	0	0	0
Totals	35	5	6	10	24	10	6

SCORE BY INNINGS.

	1	2	3	4	5	6	7	8	9	
Santa Rosas	2	0	6	0	1	2	0	1	*	—12
Burlingtons	0	0	0	0	1	0	2	2	0	—5

Two base hits—Pace, Fleming. Sacrifice hits—Hulen, G. Arlett (2), J. Arlett, 2, Dunn. Base on balls—Santa Rosas, 6; Burlingtons, 4. Struck out—By Callen, 7; by Buick, 3; by Walcott, 2. Left on bases—Santa Rosas, 4; Burlingtons, 7. Time of game, 2 hrs. Umpire—McConville.

Amateur Short Hits.

Green is a very clever back stop.

Advancing—Reports and Vallejos.

The Will and Finks need a "bracer."

McDonald has been given quite a rest.

Retrograding—Will & Fincks and Allens.

Strand is not a success as a third baseman.

The Reports are a very heavy hitting team.

When, oh! when will the Allens win a game?

The Merceds are having new uniforms made.

Kelly is now playing right field for Santa Rosa.

McIntyre is the safest hitter in the Report team.

Monet is pitching ball longer than any of the Amateurs.

Pace did some tremendous hitting in last Sunday's game.

McCarthy is as sure a fly catcher as either Gimmell or Sharp.

"Dutch" Allen gave a very rocky exhibition of catching Sunday.

Buick is the fifth pitcher the Burlingtons have had this season.

Evatt, Lewis and Buckley are the tallest men in the Amateur League.

Howell has pitched in every game except one this season, for the Will & Fincks.

Heron, formerly of the Alameda Maroons, and lately with Santa Cruz, played first for the Giants Sunday.

Dunphy has had fewer chances at third base than any other player in the same position in the League.

There was only one chance offered to the outfield of the Reports last Sunday which was accepted by Hearty.

Santa Rosa seems bound to win the championship, but Warren and Ashman say that the Sonoma boys aint going to have a walk over.

Jack Ryan, formerly the first baseman of the Greenhood and Morans, played that position very acceptably for the Vallejos last Sunday.

McGuire was an excellent addition to the Vallejo team. He has always been considered a fine in-fielder and heavy batter, and will be sure to do good service for his new team.

Little Beckett is the utility man for the Allens, and he is a good 'un. He is active, clever and earnest, and although in speedy company, he is not behind any of them in playing.

Ashman has strengthened his infield considerably by securing Dave Creamer to play second, and placing John Thompson at short. Ashman is out for the pennant and intends to keep the leaders hustling.

The following are the Captains of the amateur teams: Will & Fincks—Charley Tillson. E. T. Allens—Scotty Evatt. Burlingtons—Alex Bradley. Daily Reports—Gray Gormley. Santa Rosas—Billy Hulin. Vallejos—Tom McGuire.

Manager Keller has arranged to take the Allens to Merced to play three games with the team of that place on July 3rd, 4th and 5th. The team winning two out of three games will capture the stake amounting to $500 and 60 per cent. of the gate receipts.

A singular coincidence occurred in last Sunday's game. The two short stops, Reilly and Thompson, each had thirteen chances offered, and each accepted eleven; and Gormley and Evatt at first had each seventeen chances and both players accepted sixteen.

Reilly showed he was possessed of good horse sense by playing with the Allens last Sunday. Although he has made a wonderful showing with the professionals, he has not been affected with the swelled head, and says he is quite willing to lend his services to the amateurs until regularly attached to a professional team.

The Young Giants had a badly patched up team to Vallejo last Sunday. First baseman Frank Delmas, third baseman Lonny and right-fielder Cusick were absent, and their places were hurridly filled in by back numbers. As the three players named are among the star hitters of the team it is no wonder the Giants suffered defeat.

Baltz has been making a great record for himself lately. In the game against Santa Rosa, on the 21st inst., he struck out sixteen and allowed only three hits, and last Sunday he struck out the Giants fifteen times, and only allowed the same number of safeties. There is no use of the professional managers looking East for pitchers, when we have players of equal ability right at home in the amateur ranks.

The Burlington team have undergone quite a change, and are practically the old Franklin team now. Billy Buick is pitching again, and last Sunday did some excellent work. McKenzie is placed in right, and is a very strong man in that position, and young Kennedy is also a nice infielder. The team is a much improved one in every respect, and the "Rail roaders" are henceforth expected to give a good account of themselves.

Manager Keller is dissatisfied with his present team, and and intends securing some new talent. Tom Buckley will be made captain, and a new battery signed. Among the players who might be seen wearing one of their expensive uniforms shortly might be mentioned Burt Parker for catcher, and Southpaw Nolan, Rohan or Hyde for pitchers. Frank Loughran might also be induced to play, and will either be placed in the field or on first base. Ed Hammer would be another good man, and Keller wont have much difficulty in transforming his now tottering team into a winning one. With Parker behind the bat, and any of the above named pitchers in the box, Loughran on first, Buckley second, Evatt short, Lewis third and McCarthy, Hammer, Geishaker and Beckett as fielders, the Allens would then be conditioned to beat any team in the League.

Grant Goucher, for several seasons connected with the E. & O. E. team, has temporarilly retired from the diamond, and is now undergoing a severe course of training preparatory to his entering the "paper weight" class of the Sparring tournament at the Olympic Club. The medal for this class has been successively held by Wave Thompson and Fred McWilliams. Thompson however, has now reduced to a "shadow weight", and as no member of the club cares to dispute his claim to this honor, the medal awarded him by his confreres will no doubt gracefully repose on his manly bosom for some time to come. With McWilliams and Goucher it is somewhat different. Both are aspirants for "paper weight" honors, and the outcome of this match is patiently awaited by hundreds of admirers of both parties.

SCHEDULE OF GAMES

—OF THE—

CALIFORNIA

Base Ball League,

SEASON 1890.

June 28th to July 5th Inclusive.

AT SAN FRANCISCO.

JUNE 28........Oakland vs. Sacramento
JUNE 29........Oakland vs. Stockton
JULY 3........San Francisco vs. Oakland
JULY 4........San Francisco vs. Oakland
JULY 5........Oakland vs. Sacramento

AT SACRAMENTO.

JUNE 29........Oakland vs. Stockton
JULY 4........Sacramento vs. Stockton

AT OAKLAND.

JULY 4........Oakland vs. San Francisco, A. M.

AT STOCKTON.

JUNE 28........Stockton vs. San Francisco
JULY 3........Stockton vs. Sacramento
JULY 4........Stockton vs. Sacramento, A. M.
JULY 5........Stockton vs. San Francisco

Official Schedule California Amateur League.

AT HAIGHT STREET GROUNDS.

JUNE 29........Will and Fincks vs. Burlingtons

AT VALLEJO.

JUNE 29........E. T. Allens vs. Vallejos

AT SANTA ROSA.

JUNE 29........Daily Reports vs. Santa Rosa

The official schedule of the California Base Ball League and Amateur League will be published weekly in this space.

ATHLETICS.

Athletic Sports and Other Pastimes.

EDITED BY ARPHIPPUS,

SUMMARY.

Friday next will be a gala day for the runners, wheelmen and oarsmen. The games of the Scottish Thistle Club, which will be held as usual at Shell Mound Park, Berkeley, will draw a very large crowd of people, while the friends of the club whose emblem is the flying O are sure to patronize its sports, which will take place on the afternoon of the same day. The wheelmen are bound to be well treated at San Jose, and as the regatta will be a free show, the oarsmen are certain to attract a large audience.

THE OARSMEN.

The Regatta Committee have finally decided to allow $500 for prizes for the Oarsmen on the Fourth of July. As stated in the BREEDER AND SPORTSMAN some time ago, the regatta will hardly be as successful as in former years. Somehow or other, the Oarsmen this year do not seem to take a genuine interest in their training, and with the exception of the professional shell race, the contests are liable to prove tame. The Ariel crew stands a good chance of winning the amateur championship.

Peterson has been out of training for some months, and Charley Long should be in it at the finish in the professional scull race.

Growney and Sullivan have been taking practice spins right along, and they are also liable to be heard from.

The amateur barge race will probably be confined to the Pioneer and Ariel and the Olympic Club Crews, as the Lurline Club is hardly prepared to send out a crew that would do it full justice.

Sunday forenoon the weather was rather disagreeable and the water choppy, and but very few of the oarsmen mustered up courage enough to launch their shells. In the afternoon, however, there was a change for the better and several crews put out for exercise.

On Monday last, Stansbury of Shoalhaven, New South Wales, the champion oarsman of the world, defeated O'Connor, of Toronto Canada, champion of America. The race was for the championship and £500 a side, and was rowed on the Paramatta river. It was an unusually severe struggle for a mile, but Stansbury outlasted his man and won easily in the finish. The contest was witnessed by 40 000 people, and the betting was very heavy, the winner being a 6-to-5 favorite.

The race was rowed down stream from Ryde to The Brothers, a distance of three miles. The start was by mutual consent, and for the first 600 yards the men rowed on even terms. At this point there is a slight bend in the river and around it the American showed slightly in the lead, at which his friends sent up a joyful shout. The champion, however put on more steam, and at the white beacon, a mile from home, had guaged his opponent and had him practically beaten.

The record for every distance from a mile to three miles was broken. The whole distance was covered in 19:53, the previous record of 20:44 having been made by Beach in his race against Trickett over the same course.

O'Connor's backers feel very sore over his defeat, as they placed great confidence in their man and fully expected to bring the championship back to America.

Thomas Gibon, the veteran amateur oarsman of this city, has entirely recovered from his recent illness and was out in his boat at Tiburon on Sunday last.

The house of the Alameda Boat Club at the foot of Chestnut street has been comfortably fitted up and the club is now on a prosperous basis. It will hold its first regatta the latter part of next month.

C. W. Chauncey, president of the O-Wash-to-nong Boat Club, of Grand Rapids, Mich., has been recently elected president of the North-western Rowing Association.

The great Duluth-Superior regatta will be held on Superior Bay, situated between Duluth and Superior, commencing July 21 and ending July 26. It will undoubtedly be the greatest event of its kind ever held in America. Duluth is situated on the west side of Superior bay in Minnesota, and has a population of nearly fifty thousand. Superior is directly across the bay in Wisconsin, with a population of about twenty thousand. Between the two cities they have raised nearly $20,000, about $15,000 of which will be given away in prizes in the various events. In the professional events the prize money will be as follows:

Singles—1st prize, $1,750; 2d, $800; 3d, $400.
Doubles—1st prize, $1,000; 2d, $550; 3d, $350.
Four-oared—1st prize, $1,250; 2d, $600; 3d, $300.
Single quarter—mile dash—1st prize, $400; 2d, $250; 3d, $100.

The Mississippi Valley Amateur Rowing Association's regatta will be held during the same week. The Duluth Superior Association has subscribed $2,500 toward the prizes, expenses, etc.

It will be decided in a few days if any open amateur events will be added to the programme. If there are some of the Eastern oarsmen will doubtless be attracted to Duluth. The course that the race will be rowed on is situated directly between the two cities and is a fine piece of water, well sheltered from the wind, and even in the roughest weather there is hardly a ripple on its surface. It is undoubtedly the finest rowing course in America.

THE WHEELMEN.

The members of the American Bicycle Club had a run in full uniform to Mill Valley, Sausalito, on Sunday last. This was the sixth run of the club and was under the charge of Captain Sig. B. Morse.

The committee in charge of the League Meet at San Jose, Cal., have issued the following notice to all members of the League:

"DEAR SIR: The League Meet at San Jose on the Fourth will be the grandest one ever held in California. The track is excellent and the grand stand capable of seating 1,400 people. You will miss a rare treat in wheeling if you do not come. The programme will reach you in a few days, it having been unavoidably delayed.

Committee L. A. W."

The following circular recently issued by Chief Consul Ralph M. Thompson will be read with interest by all wheelmen:

OFFICE OF THE CHIEF CONSUL,
SAN FRANCISCO, Cal., June 18, '90.

DEAR SIR: The renewal list of California Division, L. A. W., received June 4th, does not contain your name.

Allow me to call your attention to the fact that your membership expires on July 1st.

California Division is fast moving towards the front and is now in a position to offer far more advantages than ever before. The League meet to be held July 4th, will be the grandest celebration ever known to California wheelmen. Non-members will not be permitted to participate. Enough will be saved on this occasion alone, to far more than defray the cost of renewing your membership.

The Division hand book will be issued July 1st, free to members. It alone will repay you for renewing.

Many plans are being devised by the Division Board of Officers for giving members personal benefits during the coming year, aside from the general advantages with which you are acquainted.

We have just given a century run and it is the intention to give a series of shorter runs during the coming year, the expenses of which will be borne by the Division.

In order to carry out all our plans, however, it is necessary that our membership be kept up.

Applications are being received daily and the membership rapidly increasing, but we shall regret very much losing any of our old members.

Hoping that if you have not already sent your renewal East, you will see that it goes prior to July 1st.

(After that date it will cost $2 instead of $1.)

I am, fraternally yours,
RALPH M. THOMPSON,
Chief Consul, Cal. Div., L. A. W.

C. C. Moore, of the B.C. W., has taken up riding again and can be seen almost any night on his "star."

Burke, of Los Angeles, is training at the Haight Street grounds. He is now in good condition and will show up well on the Fourth of the coming month.

Wheaton, formerly of the San Francisco Bicycle Club and Plummer, of the Bay City Wheelmen, are going to ride in the tandem race on Friday next.

Dr T. L. Hill, C. W. Hammer and C. J. Schuster, of the B. C. W, and several unattached men rode to the Garden City on Sunday.

George P. Wetmore and Sanford Plummer started on their wheels from this city on Saturday morning last at four o'clock with the intention of wheeling to Santa Cruz. They were compelled to walk from Saratoga to the summit on account of the rough state of the road which was covered with six inches of gravel. From Boulder Creek into Santa Cruz they found the roads in better order. They remained over night at Santa Cruz and returned Sunday by way of Sequel, Hotel de Rulo and Alma.

The members of the Bay City Wheelmen are jubilant over the success of the bond scheme, which is now an assured success. Large sums have already been subscribed, and in the course of a couple of weeks the committee expects to be able to surprise the club by producing a long list of subscribers. The B. C. W. boys are deserving of their success for they have always worked hard and faithfully in each others interest.

Chief Consul Thompson rode to San Jose on Sunday to examine the condition of the recently constructed four lap track which is to be used by the wheelmen on Friday and Saturday next. The Consul had the men mix cinders with the loose earth and now the track is in tip top condition for record smashing.

A. D. Allen Jr, H. W. Spalding, W. E. Thompson and E. C. Landis rode from San Mateo to Spanishtown on Sunday. They report the roads in that neighborhood to be in fine condition.

The annual run of the 'cyclists of the Metropolitan District from Newark, N. J., to Philadelphia, came off on Saturday, June 14th, two hundred starting. The roads were found to be in a miserable condition, retarding the progress of the participants, and making them about two hours behind the schedule time. Out of the large number which started, only sixty had the pluck and endurance to complete the journey. The great effort made by the Century Club of Philadelphia, to secure the handsome banner offered for the best attendance, was successful, this club having the greatest number of men in at the finish. Among those who completed the journey were Mrs. Dalsen, captain of the Fairmount Ladies 'Cyclers; Miss L. Frehelberg and Miss G. Welch of the Wissahickon Wheelmen. Among the first ones to arrive were Captain Dalsen and several members of the Century Wheelmen, Dr. Finn, Kings County Wheelmen; F. M. Cossitt, Riverside Wheelmen; Mrs. W. Fuller, W. H. Meeter, H. E. Raymond, C. F. Quimby, N. Rogers, G. Warren, and W. J. Masterson of the Brooklyn Bicycle Club, and members of the Park Avenue and Oxford Wheelmen. The various 'cycling clubs of Philadelphia tendered a reception to their visitors in the evening.

The Elwell European party left New York June 7th on the La Bretagne of the French line. On reaching Havre they will begin a tour through France, spending the remainder of June in that country. Switzerland, Germany and Holland will use up July and part of August, and on August 17th they will sail from Rotterdam for London, where they will disband on August 19th.

The annual Catford race meeting in England was one of the most successful meets ever held, 10,000 people attending. The programme was phenomenal in size, there being 183 entries for the half mile novice's handicap in twenty-four heats, and 147 entries in eighteen heats for the open mile mixed handicap. The latter, the principal event of the day, was won by C. A. Murray in 2m 42 4-5s. The quarter mile scratch race was won by F. J. Osmond in 37 1-5s. and the quarter mile safety was captured by E. Leitch in 36 4-5s. The five mile team race, eight men a side, was won by the Catford team.

One of the latest additions to 'cycling accessories is an instrument looking something like a steam gauge, to be fastened to the front forks of a machine, which indicates at what speed per hour the rider is traveling.

An electric bicycle lamp has been patented in England which will burn for fifteen hours.

A ladies bicycle club, with a membership of 15 has been organized at Bridgeport, Conn.

The annual races of the Connecticut Division of the League of American Wheelmen, held in New Haven, June 9th, was attended by about 500 bicyclists. Four hundred of these took part in the parade at 10 o'clock. David J. Post, of Hartford, was marshal of the parade, and Fred Bailey, of New Haven, was adjutant. The aids were Dr. W. H. Emery, of Boston; Charles S. Davol, of Warran, R. I; L. A Miller, of Meriden; E. A. DeBlois, of Hartford; Fred Atwater, of Bridgeport, and Arthur Munson, of Stamford.

The Hartford Bicycle Club was awarded the prize for the largest number of men in line, and the Colt Club of Hartford won the prize for the best appearance. In the afternoon a tournament was held at the Elm City Driving Park, the races resulting as follows:

One mile novice race—Charles G. Sage, Hartford, 1st, in 3:07½, with Leo. C. Heir, Waterbury, 2d.

Yale Harvard two mile team race—Harvard won by 13 points to 5. W. H. Greenleaf, Harvard, was 1st, in 6:27½, with Philip Davis, Harvard, 2d.

One mile safety for State League companionship—C. E. Larom, New Haven, won in 2:09 4-5, with G. A. Pickett, New Haven, 2d.

One mile handicap, road wheels—A. A. Zimmerman, New Jersey Athletic Club, 1st, in 2:46 2 5; Charles L. Sage, Hartford, 2d.

One mile safety, club championship—C. E. Larom, New Haven, won in 3:10 4-5, with W. C. Palmer, New Haven, 2d.

Two mile safety, First District championship—Hoyland Smith, New Bedford, Mass., won in 6:28 3-5, with P. J. Berlo, South Boston, Mass., 2d.

One mile race, open—W. W. Windle, Millbury, Mass., won in 2:47 3 5, with E. C. Antony, Dorchester, Mass, 2d.

One mile safety, open—Hoyland Smith, New Bedford, Mass, won in 2:59, with R. H. Davis, Harvard and New York Athletic clubs, 2d.

One mile First District championship—W. W. Windle, Millbury, Mass., won in 2:06 1 5, with E. C. Anthony, Dorcester, Mass., 2d.

One mile safety, handicap—Hoyland Smith, New Belford, Mass., 1st, in 2:46, with T. J. Berlo, South Boston, Mass., 2d.

One mile tandem safety, district championship—Hoyland Smith, New Bedford, Mass., 1st, in 3:05, with P. J. Berlo, South Boston, Mass., 2d.

One mile consolation race—W. K. Murphy, Brooklyn, won in 3:05, with F. G. Brown, New Jersey Athletic Club, 2d.

A business meeting was held at noon prior to the races, and these nominations were made, to be voted on by mail:—For chief consul, Arthur Allen Dean, of Danielsonville; vice president, A. G. Froder, of New Haven; secretary and treasurer, E A. DeBlois, of Hartford.

The L. A. W. Meet.

The programme of the coming League meet has just been issued and it is a very neat and artistic piece of work. The following information is given in the book:

"The League of American Wheelmen is an organization to promote the general interests of cycling; to ascertain, defend and protect the rights of wheelmen (which are those of any driver of horse and wagon), to encourage and facilitate touring, and to regulate the government of all amateur sports connected with the use of the wheel.

Officers for 1890—Ralph M. Thompson, Chief Consul, San Francisco; Walter D. Sheldon, Secretary-Treasurer, 128 Davis Street, San Francisco.

Representatives.—At large: C C Moore, Stockton; Dr. J W Gibson, San Francisco; A C McKenney, San Jose.

Of the Bay City Wheelmen—Dr. Thos. L. Hill, Charles C. Moore.

General Committee, California Division, Fifth Annual Meet, of the L. A. W., on July 4th and 5, 1890, at San Jose, Cala.: Chairman, Arthur C. McKenney, 89 N. First St., San Jose; Secretary-Treasurer, Allan C. Wagener, 89 N. First St., San Jose; Assistant Secretary-Treasurer, Oswold Granicher, 15 S. First St., San Jose; Thos. L. Hill, San Francisco; Geo. F. Drake, Oakland; Alfonse Col., San Jose.

Committee of Chairmen—Transportation, Thomas L Hill, Odd Fellows' Building, S. F.; tours, runs and parade, W M Neeker, 713 21st St, S. F.; accomodation, Oswold Granicher, 15 S First St, San Jose; races, A C McKenney, 89 N First St., San Jose; entertainment, Ralph M. Thompson, The Oriel Hotel, S. F.; programme and printing, Allan C Wagener, 89 N. First St., San Jose; reception, Garden City Wheelmen, San Jose.

The General Committee removes a year's accumulated dust from its gold tipped Stylograph to pen a cordial invitation to its fraters in the League, and its friends among the uninitiated, to its Fifth Annual Meet; the former that we may take them by the hand in a healthy L. A. W. grip, and renew the jolly good fellowship of former years—and the latter that we may make the benefits of a membership in our organization apparent to them.

In selecting the "Garden City" for its '90 tournament, the members of the California Division feel that its easy accessibility, its good roads, the numerous pleasant spins in its vicinity, and the well known hospitality of its people, will combine to attract together a large representation of the Division. We would like to greet every devotee of the noblest of sports, "from Del Norte to San Diego, from the Sierras to the Sea," and hope they can all arrange to be with us on the Nation's Birthday. At this early date indications are good for a very successful meet.

Away up in the rocky confines of Milpitas, the rarified atmosphere already resounds with the soul stirring notes of the club bugler, scaring the fleet winged Willfwinkum Occidentalis with a startled wail from her lofty perch, and announcing that the wheelists of the metropolis are preparing to begin the perilous descent of the precipitous declivities to the plains of San Jose; while, with ear to the ground, the anxious chairman of the Gen. Com. hears a rasping sound, as the lone cyclist of Siskiyou saws off the unthawed legs of his winter overalls to make knickerbockers.

A letter just received from an intending "meeter," who evidently resides in the Murchison part of Los Angeles, says: "What is the special booking for cyclists to San Jose, don't you know? And is there a tavern in the beastly village?" "As the secretary has fainted, we will tell you the rest at the party.

The League party will take place at the Hotel Vendome on Saturday evening, July 5th. The grand march is announced for half after eight, and carriages may be ordered for twelve. Wheelmen will appear in uniform, their friends in evening dress. Tickets, admitting gentleman and ladies, $1, to be obtained on presentation of invitation, of A. C. McKenney, 89 North First sreet, or Oswold Granicher, 15 South First street.

The St. James, the League Hotel is centrally located on First street, and prepared to accommodate a goodly number of wheelmen at the League rate, $2 per day. To secure the rate, please present your membership tickets. Further information promptly and cheerfully furnished by the Chairman of the Accommodation Committee, at 15 South First St., Kocher's jewelry store. By invitation of the Garden City wheelmen, the headquarters of the Division will be at club rooms, W. Santa Clara St, between the bridges, where visitors will register.

Saturday, July 5th, owing to the variety of interesting points in the vicinity of San Jose, it has been deemed advisable to give visiting wheelmen their choice of spins, instead of calling a division run to some point which many may have visited before. In consequence, the committee offers the following list of desirable places to visit, with the names of local wheelmen who will act as guides, and to whom visitors will report, after selecting their tour, at the time and place named:

New Almaden Quicksilver Mines, round trip, 24 miles; Wm. R. Lipsett, G. C. W. Club Rooms, 8 A. M.

Los Gatos, Saratoga, Congress Springs, round trip 25 miles; Joseph Desimone, G. C. W. Club Rooms, 9 A. M.

Santa Clara, Mountain View, Mayfield, Stanford University, round trip, 40 miles; Geo. Owen.

Agnews Asylum, Santa Clara, Fredericksburg, round trip, 11 miles; W. Needham, G. C. W. Club Rooms, 9 A. M.

Alum Rock Springs and Penitencia Falls, round trip, 15 miles; S Alley.

Hall's Valley, Smith's Creek, Mt. Hamilton, Lick Observatory, round trip, 54 miles, F. Larder.

Lantern parade. On the evening of July 4th the division will entertain the citizens with a Lantern Parade, the line being formed in front of the G. C. W. Club-room at 8.30 P. M. sharp. The order of parade will be precisely as in the morning. Participants will decorate their mounts with Japanese lanterns and flags; and the division will furnish fireworks. All are requested to turn out and assist in making this a most beautiful pageant.

The division's race tournament will be held on Friday afternoon, July 4th, at two o'clock sharp, on the track built for the occasion, situated on Julian Street, near the Guadaloupe bridge. Entries will close with Chairman McKenney, 89 North First street, San Jose, at 10 P. M. Saturday, June 28. The entrance fee, $1, will be returned to starters.

Our League members can compete in these races, and all League members will be admitted to the grounds free on showing membership tickets. The winner of the District Championship events will be sent East to the National Tournament at the expense of the League. Following is the programme of events:

1. One-mile novice. 2. Quarter-mile dash. 3. One-mile safety, scratch. 4. One-mile district championship. 5. Three-mile handicap. 6. Half-mile state championship. 7. One-mile tandem safety, scratch. 8. Five-mile district championship. 9. One-mile handicap. 10. Two-mile handicap.

RUNNERS, WALKERS, JUMPERS, ETC.

Little, Kendall and McIntyre will meet again at Shell Mound Park on Friday next and one of the best races that has ever taken place in that park will be witnessed. The Scotchmen will back McIntyre while the knowing ones will take chances on Little.

On account of so many counter attractions, the Games Committee of the Olympic Club have decided to give only a small programme of events on the Fourth of July. Five of the events will be for members of the Club, while throwing the hammer, the running broad jump and the two mile run will be open to all associate members of the P C A A A. No special effort will be made to boom the meeting, as it is the intention of the club to hold its first grand outdoor meeting on Admission Day. The meeting on Friday next, however, should attract a fair crowd of sport lovers as some of the crack athletes will appear.

The two amateur races will bring out a fine field of runners, and with such men as Cooley, Scott, Moody, Garrison, Casady, Casidy, Hill and others, the job of capturing ten handsome medals will be a rather difficult one.

The amateur races will be run off in the forenoon in order to give the runners who have entered a chance to recross the bay in time to compete in the Olympic games, which will commence at 2 o'clock P. M.

It would be in order for the Directors of the Alpine Club to drop a couple of names from their membership roll, as the parties we refer to have most outrageously violated the amateur rules by competing in all kinds of professional races.

Last week we received a detailed account of a "fake" foot race which was stated to have taken place on the previous Sunday at San Jose between two well known runners. Apart from the account referred to, we heard so many contradictory statements that we decided to withhold the facts until something more definite is heard in regard to the true nature of the "swindle." Several amateur and professional athletes and oarsmen are involved in the affair, and when we do publish the account our readers can rest assured that it will be authentic.

Captain George W. Jordan of the Olympic Club has returned from a much needed vacation, and will start in to coach his men again.

Coffin and Jarvis will probably not go in the mile walk on Friday, and the club novices will have a chance to win some prizes.

Those who intend taking part in the road walk of the Alpine Club from San Mateo to this city on Sunday July 6th, will take the train which leaves Fourth and Townsend streets at 8:30 A. M. Field Captain John D. Garrison recommends the men to wear canvas shoes, straw hats, woolen shirts and light clothing. All outside amateurs are heartily invited to take part in the walk.

The U. C. athletes are now enjoying a vacation and will not take any active part in athletics until after their return to college.

Albert Perkins, of London, has lowered the roller skating record for one mile 7⅘s. He covered the distance in 2m 59s.

Frank Cooley, the well known athlete, is becoming popular as an amateur reciter. He appears at nearly all the leading entertainments.

V. E. Schifferstein will attempt to lower the American record for the running broad jump at his club's games on Friday next.

CLUB JOTTINGS.

If the application of the Lurline Club is not acted upon at the next meeting of the P. C. A. A. A. the application will probably be withdrawn.

On Wednesday last in this city Mr. DeWitt C. Davis, champion light weight wrestler of the Olympic Club met defeat at the hands of an opponent not so heavy as he by twenty pounds. It was a catch-as-catch-can match best of sixteen thousand two hundred and fifty falls, to be continued from day to day until one or the other quits. The victor up to this writing is Mrs. D. C. Davis, nee Miss Ruby Arey The happy and heartily congratulated pair left on a honeymooning trip to the fashionable resorts immediately after being married, and carried with them the best wishes of half a city full of admirers and friends.

A meeting of the P. C. A. A. A. was to be have been held on Wednesday evening, but owing to the absence of Walter A. Scott, the presiding officer, the meeting was postponed to next Wednesday evening, July 2d at 8 o'clock.

The amateur clubs are in a quandary on account of the law against boxing. If boxing exhibitions are to be prohibited in future some of the amateur clubs are likely to follow in the footsteps of the professional organizations and go under.

A boom is expected in wrestling, but the sporting men who have been used to witnessing bloody battles for the last couple of years will soon grow tired of this tame carpet sport and resign from the clubs to which they belong.

The members of the Alpine Club are complaining against the location of their club rooms and it is not at all improbable that a change will soon be made. There will be a special meeting of the members at 706 Powell St. this evening at 9 o'clock for the purpose of considering an offer made to the club by D. R. McNeill of Central Park. Should the club decide to move to Central Park a club house will be fitted up at once in the park and the members will have the full use of the grounds for training on. As the majority of the members are out door men the chances are that the club will foster only out door sports in the future.

Grim's Gossip.

On Monday next, Marvin and Hickok will leave Terra Haute with their horses and go to Detroit.

Intending competitors are reminded that all entries for the Los Angeles meeting close next Tuesday, July 1st.

The bangtails should be well represented at Los Angeles. The running programme could hardly be improved on.

James Boyd of San Jose will have his stallion Billy Thornhill worked, so as to try and secure a record for him this year.

The time for nominating in the 2:30 trot at Los Angeles has been extended until next Tuesday. The purse for this event is $1,500.

L. A. Davis and Orrin Hickok were interested spectators on Derby day at Chicago, both of them making expenses on the day.

J. A. Dustin has had another addition to his stable. Mr. Theurkauf, of Gonzalez, has turned over to Jimmy the fast gelding Lee.

The Rural Spirit says that Cy Mulkey has purchased the roan gelding Tim Murphy, by Kyrl Daly, dam Maggie R., paying $1,500.

The Ione track is reported to be in splendid condition and the horses now there are all doing well. Ione will have a good meeting this year.

The Governor has appointed E. C. Voorhees of Amador County and E. J. Gregory of Sacramento Directors of Agricultural District 26.

Who will win the 2:30 class trot at Napa? is an open question at present and is a source of much speculation among horsemen throughout the State.

We have received number 5 of Goodwin's Official Turf Guide and as usual it is "chock" full of information for those who patronize the turf.

Mr. A. C. Dietz of Oakland, has sent his trotter. Ringwood to the stable of J. A. Dustin, who will handle the Sydney horse during the fall meetings.

Are you going to Los Angeles for the opening meeting of the grand circuit? If not why not? The purses are liberal. Do not fail to enter on Tuesday.

The Detroit Driving Club will this year again carry out the original feature adopted last year of not charging admission to their grounds on the opening day of the summer meeting.

Dan Honig has purchased from Theodore Winters the three-year-old colt Rascal by Joe Hooker, dam Mattie Glenn. He is a fairly good colt and should earn money for his new owner.

As was predicted in these columns some time ago, Arol, 2:24: will never again come up for the word. The injuries she received in transportation will prevent the mare being ever trained again.

Jack Hallivan has two fine Sidney foals at the ranch of Smith & Sotherland which are perfect beauties He also has a yearling Director which should prove a trotter if there is anything in good looks.

For the great Blue Ribbon stake at Detroit, it is generally conceded that Goldsmith will start Simmocolon. As Turner will have in Suisun and Hickok, Prince Warwick, the contest should be an interesting one.

Jimmy Goldsmith evidently has Richmond Jr. on edge as I see that he has entered him in a number of purses back East. Richmond Jr. is a fast horse and his mark of 2:22¾ should be reduced materially this year.

Fred Taral, by Frogtown dam Caller Ou by imp Leamington, has been bought by R. H. Cole of Los Angeles, from M. Berry of St. Louis. The horse will probably make a first appearance at the Angel city during the coming fair.

Rumor caused me to say last week, that Mr. Albright of San Luis Obispo had leased the services of Alpheus, 2:27. From headquarters I now learn that the horse was sold outright to Mr. Albright, the price paid is said to be $5,000.

Jim L., 2:20, owned by Mr. Linscott of Watsonville, has been taken from the stud, and is now receiving preparatory work at San Jose; C. B. Coffin has him in charge, together with Mr. Montgomery's Boodle, and several other good ones.

Guido has shown such exceedingly good form since leaving California for the north that Mr. Babb, his owner, has refused $3,500 for him. The colt is a good one and should be very valuable for a stock horse when his racing days are over.

F. A. Sprague has been in the city several days during the week working up the interests of the Glenbrook Park, Chico and Marysville meetings. Fred is an active hustler and already many entries have been promised for all of these meetings.

Henry Sears, of Woodland, has sent his trotting stallion Harry Nutwood to Sacramento, where he will be prepared for track work by Worth Ober. The horse is five years old, by Fleetwood (son of Nutwood), dam by Gold Dust. He is right bred, and should prove a trotter.

The piratical journal, Parishs Referee of Chicago, after stealing a copy of Racine's picture from the BREEDER AND SPORTSMAN and running it as Dan Honig's Cartoon, last week republished it as a cut of Salvator. Keep it Friend Referee you may be able to use it again as Firenzi or Cassius.

On the day that Marvin trotted Sunol a quarter in 31 1-5 seconds, Bonner offered Hickok $100, if he would send Adonis a quarter of a mile and beat 32¼. Orrin refused the offer as, by winning the "century" he might lose thousands by giving his horse too fast work at this early stage of the game.

Among the best known to Californian horsemen, of those who won money at the Portland meeting were. W. H. Babb, $910; Cy Mulkey $380; W. Whitmore $180; Dennison Bros. $110; and Jay Beach $50. The Meeting was a glorious success from start to finish, and the Directors are entitled to great credit.

In a letter from Leslie E. Macleod, he states that $25,000 will heal his wounded feelings in the Wallace matter, and that suit will be brought for that amount against the owner of the monthly. If the news telegraphed to this city is correct, Inspector Byrnes and the Safe Deposit officials should also be made parties to the suit.

A drawf among drawfs was foaled recently in the stud of Mr. George Bruce, Secretary of the Northern Agricultural Society in England. It was a Shetland pony, weighing at birth only 16 pounds, and being 21¼ inches high, otherwise complete from tip to tail. The dam stands 38 inches, and the sire, Paris, is 39 inches high.

Much of the cruelty practised upon farm horses (and it is nothing less) is the result of thoughtlessness, and pages might be written on the subject. How often are horses jerked and yelled at in cultivating, only making them excited and incapable of performing their work as well as they would if handled quietly and gently!

Owing to the Fourth of July falling on Friday of next week, the BREEDER AND SPORTSMAN will be issued one day earlier than usual and correspondents must be guided thereby. I am always glad to hear from all sections with regard to horse news, and can always find room to chronicle the doings of trotters or runners in the various portions of the state.

When Marvin started East with the Palo Alto string he took with him the colt Electric Belle, by Electioneer—Beautiful Bells, which had been purchased some time before by Miller & Sibley of Franklin, Pa. The youngster has been inspected by G. H. Hepper, one of the owners of Bell Boy, at the time of his death, and rumor now has it that the colt will surely change hands at the reputed price of $50,000.

On Tuesday, July 1st, entries close for the Spring racing meeting, to be held at Helena, Mont. The programme is a good one, and as many Californian horses are at present in Montana, the racing should prove both exciting and profitable. In another column will be found the advertisement of the association.

G. C. Owen, who was formerly employed at Palo Alto Stock Farm, has opened a public training stable at San Jose. Already he has secured several promising youngsters from gentlemen in the neighborhood, and feels satisfied that when once his merits are known, that he will have all the work he can attend to.

Harry Starr has his hands full at Napa, having almost a score of promising good ones. I have heard favorable reports from more than one about one of his string named Oakville Maid, owned by Mr. Crabb, and if Dame Rumor is correct in her surmises, this filly will be a thorne in the side of more than one owner this season.

W. M. Murray has disposed of two of his thoroughbreds in Kansas City. The first is the two-year-old bay filly, Lady Scoggan, by Little Ruffin, dam Hiawasse, who has been purchased by J. T. Speaks. The second sold, is the two-year-old bay colt Parapet, by Bulwark, dam Nettie Brady. This one was sold to the Paxton Bros.

Mr. Winters has evidently tired of the services of Joe Courtney as trainer, for he has disposed of Joe, and placed Tom Conley in charge of the stable. Rey del Rey has received no hard work since leaving Nashville as he has been under the weather, but is now recovering and he will at once be prepared for his engagements.

C. H. Corey has taken charge of the San Jose race track, and it goes without saying that everything will be attended to in first class shape. A horseman himself, "Charley" thoroughly understands the wants of others, and those who attend the Garden city meeting, will have cause for congratulation that a good man is in charge.

Charles Davids has in training at the Napa track Nona Y., 2:25; Gold Medal (pacer) with no record; Josie S. by Ha-Ha, 2:22½; Capt. Anderson's b m Eva L.; Mountaineer by Whippleton, dam Nona Y., and a couple of green colts. Several of these are above the average, and Charley expects to get a slice of the money at more meetings than one.

One of Hickok's horses is thus spoken of by the Terre Haute Express: Prince Warwick, by Alcona (he by Almont) dam Warwick Maid, by Almont Mambrino, the 5 years old, entire horse owned by Hickok, showed up splendidly in his work. He is a green horse but is sweet gaited and is sure to give some of them an argument before the season is done.

The Directors of Glenbrook Park will spend a large sum of money in prepairing their track and grounds for the annual meeting in August. They have decided to leave no stone unturned toward making the 1890 fair the most successful ever held in Northern California, and if energetic push can accomplish that feat, I do not fear but what they will realize their wish.

Dr. Richards, a homeopathic V. S. of Delavan, Wis., has taken the colts from several mares whose time for foaling had expired and who showed by infallible signs that maturity was nigh. In most cases where the dam had made no efforts to foal, he found the foal out of place. In less than forty minutes he has the colt alive, standing on its feet and nursing.

Matt Storn is a rare guesser, or he has exceedingly good judgment. To all of his friends he imparted the information that Salvator would win the Suburban and Cassius get the place, and for the American Derby, he played Uncle Bob straight and Santiago for place. His winnings will help pay expenses until the Glenwood Park meeting, where his colors will be seen on the opening day.

Frank Baldwin has accepted the management of the Coronado Beach Track, and in a note he states that there will one day's racing given on July 4th. Frank also says that after the Breeder's meeting Coronado will give a big meeting at which there will be liberal purses offered and endeavors made to secure all the best horses in the state to attend. The buildings and track are not as yet completed, but when the finishing touches are placed on, Mr. Baldwin says he will have racing grounds second to none in the State.

B J. Johnson purchased a few days ago from Edward Brown (Brown Dick) the three year old filly Ruperta, by Prince Charlie, dam Marguerite. The price paid was $10,000 a pretty steep figure for a filly, but then Ruperta is one in a hundred. A good many believe she is the equal of English Lady, and that means a good deal. It is a question whether Mr. Johnson has purchased for himself or for somebody else, may be for the latter.

Mr. Gilbert Tompkins, of the Souther Farm, has had patented a new style of foot rasp which should at once spring into popular favor. It is so constructed that the horse-shoer can fill a'e parts of the foot at once without touching the frog thus assuring an evenness of surface for the part that is to receive the shoe. Mr. Tompkins is a close student in matters that pertain to the equine race, and he is convinced that the invention will prove of great benefit to those that try to keep abreast of the times.

"Broadchurch" is nothing if not original, in speaking of the St. Louis Derby he says: "It was not much of a race—the St. Louis Derby. Bill Letcher was not in form and ordinary horses could have beaten him, but the other two horses were not fit to run in a selling race. Bill Letcher is only an ordinary little horse; any good horse ought to give him ten pounds. It is true he beat Riley at Latonia, but that was no true race. Riley was pulled so his neck was almost broken and besides he was carrying a barrel of whiskey."

Talking over the article in last week's issue on Sam Purdy, Frank Malone tells me that after Mr. Keene purchased the Stallion he was given two heats of two miles each, one after-noon at the track, but as there were a large number of persons present, it was deemed expedient to take private time at some other point than from wire to wire. The driver was notified of the change in the timing place, and drove accordingly. The two heats were accomplished in the clever time of 4:41 and 4:41½, although as taken from wire to wire, the time was several seconds more. Purdy was a great horse, and his like may not be seen for many a day.

Did you ever visit a pool-room and watch the faces of the crowd as the caller announced the positions of the horses at the various dividing posts in the mile? A large majority of those present have a "wee bit" on the result, and as their choice happens to be in a favorable position or almost "out of it," the facial expression vary according to the teller's report. The modern pool-room would have been a grand place for Walter Besant or W. M. Thackery to study character, for surely "all sorts and conditions of men" can be found in that "Vanity Fair."

The Oakland folks have arranged a bill of fare for their patrons, which is sure to draw large entries, and is a guarantee of a "big gate." Secretary Diamond has worked indefatigably to secure good entry lists for the stakes already closed, and who can doubt but what the events that close on August 1st will be equally well patronized by the horsemen from all sections of the State when they are arranging their circuits. The Directors are all "old hands" at the business, and their programme is of such a character that there is no chance for them to be distanced in the race of competition.

I had a pleasant call this week from President Kimball and Secretary Hook of the Red Bluff association and they promise to have things in splendid condition prior to the opening up of their new track. Every attention will be given to detail, and those who may elect to visit the Bluff City may be sure of a hearty welcome. It is now many years since first I visited Red Bluff, and no doubt many of the old timers that used to frequent the old track have passed away, yet still there will be some to talk over the reminiscences of early days when money flowed like water on quarter races, and thousands were won or lost on a single event.

In that great French remedy known as Gombault's caustic balsam American horsemen have the king of veterinary remedies for animals suffering from spavin, ringbones, curbs and all kinds of bony enlargements, as well as strains, rheumatism, etc. This balsam is specially prepared by Dr. J. E. Gombault, ex-veterinarian to the French Government stud, and is imported direct by Lawrence, Williams & Co., Cleveland, O., who are the sole American agents. It has been used in American stables for about a dozen years and has relieved thousands of horses from the above mentioned troubles. As a counter-irritant it has the approval of our surgeons, and has the further advantage that it can be used with perfect safety, for it will not leave the slightest blemish on the animal. It is sold by all druggists, $1 50 per bottle. Send to Lawrence, Williams & Co., for circulars, testimonials etc.

When Mr. Winters left St. Louis for Chicago, the intelligent correspondent who is supposed to pick up news for distribution abroad, telegraphed out the following.—"There has been considerable dissatisfaction with the management of the races, which culminated to-day in the semi-officiel announcement that Mr. Theodore Winters will be conspicuous by his absence from the St. Louis track after this, as will also his stable. Mr. Winters claims that Starter Ferguson is deliberately giving his horses the worst of the start at every opportunity. Winters has also had a falling out with President Charles Green. He complained to Mr. Green of Ferguson's poor starting, but his complaint was entirely disregarded. A popular idea prevails out at the Fair Grounds that Winters is "sore" because of the bad showing of his horses. He has not made a cent yet, and El Rio Rey, the most petted animal of his gilt edged stock will not run again this Summer."

Mr. Manly came to town last Friday with a four-horse load of wood, says the Fresno Expositor. He disposed of the wood to Jim Hudson, the north side grocer.

On Saturday afternoon he loaded up with provisions and started for home. Prior to doing so he watered his horses at the trough in front of Jim's store.

With a flourish of whip Manly pulled out homeward bound.

Just before reaching Ferguson's place, about 25 miles out, where he was to camp for the night, Mr. Manly noticed his near leader belching water from its mouth. He thought nothing of the occurance at the time.

Arriving at the station, the horse, a young bay eight years old, standing 16½ hands and weighing 1232 pounds, dropped down in the traces a moment later to be seized with violent convulsion.

Mr. Manly and others labored incessantly to relieve the animal, but without success. At midnight the horse, in a paroxysm of pain, died.

At the post-mortem examination held yesterday morning, Mr. Manly found a squirming catfish in the belly of the horse. Its horn had punctured the covering of the belly, and an aperture fully eleven inches long showed conclusively what had caused the painful death.

"There can be no doubt," said Mr. Manly to an Expositor reporter, "but what the horse swallowed the fish at the trough in front of Hudson's grocery. I did't water my team at any other place. Some time ago I read how Mr. Baker lost a horse in the same way, but I thought, to my sorrow now, that it was a newspaper yarn.

THE WEEKLY

Breeder and Sportsman.

JAMES P. KERR, PROPRIETOR.

The Turf and Sporting Authority of the Pacific Coast.

Office, No. 313 Bush St.

P. O. Box 2300.

TERMS—*One Year, $5; Six Months, $3; Three Months, $1.50.*
STRICTLY IN ADVANCE.

Money should be sent by postal order, draft or by registered letter, addressed to JAMES P. KERR, San Francisco, Cal.

Communications must be accompanied by the writer's name and address, not necessarily for publication, but as a private guarantee of good faith.

NEW YORK OFFICE, Room 15, 181 Broadway.

ALEX. P. WAUGH, - - - - - Editor.

To Subscribers.

The date printed on the wrapper of your paper indicates the time to which your subscription is paid.
Should the Breeder and Sportsman be received by any subscriber who does not want it, write us direct to stop it. A postal card will suffice.

Special Notice to Correspondents.

Letters intended for publication should reach this office not later than Wednesday of each week, to secure a place in the issue of the following Saturday. Such letters to insure immediate attention should be addressed to the Breeder and Sportsman, and not to any member of the staff.

San Francisco, Saturday, June 28, 1890.

Dates Claimed.

EUREKA JOCKEY CLUB	July 2d to 5th
IONE	Aug 5th to 9th.
LOS ANGELES (6th District)	Aug. 4th to 9th
SAN JOSE	Aug. 11th to 16th
WILLOWS	August 12th to 16th
NAPA	Aug. 18th to 23rd
RED BLUFF	August 19th to 23rd.
GLENBROOK PARK, 17th District	August 19th to 23d
PETALUMA	Aug. 25th to 30th
CHICO	August 26th to 30th
OAKLAND (District No. 1)	Sept. 1st to Sept. 6th
MARYSVILLE	Sept. 2nd to 6th
LAKEPORT, 12th District	September 2d to 27th
CALIFORNIA STATE FAIR	Sept 8th to 20th
STOCKTON	Sept. 23rd to 27th.
FRESNO (Fall Meeting)	Sept. 29th to Oct. 4th
VISALIA	Oct. 7th to 11th

Stallions Advertised

IN THE

BREEDER AND SPORTSMAN.

Trotters.

ADMIRAL, Volunteer—Lady Pierson.......... Frank Drake, Vallejo
ALCONA, Almont—Queen Mary.......... Fred W. Loeber, St. Helena
BAY ROSE Sultan—Madam Baldwin.......... Thos. Bonner, Santa Rosa
CHARLES DERBY, Steinway—by Electioneer. Cook Stock Farm, Contra Costa Co.
EL BENTON, Electioneer—Nellie Benton.......... Souther Farm, San Leandro.
FIGARO, Hambletonian—Emblem.......... Souther Farm, San Leandro.
GROVER CLAY, Electioneer—Maggie Norfolk.......... Denis Gannon, Oakland.
GRAND MOOR 2374, Moor 870—Vashti.......... H. I. Thornton, S. F.
G. & M., Anteeo—Rosa B.......... George E. Guerne, Santa Rosa.
GLEN FORTUNE, Electioneer—Glenna.......... Souther Farm, San Leandro.
GEORGE WASHINGTON, Mambrino Chief—Fanny Rose.......... Thos. Smith, Vallejo.
GRANDISSIMO, LeGrande—Norma.......... Fred W. Loeber, St Helena
JESTER D, Almont—Hortense.......... Souther Farm, San Leandro.
KING DAVID, Admiral—Black Flora.......... Frank Drake, Vallejo.
MEMO, Sidney—Flirt.......... John Rowen, Oakland
MAMBRINO WILKES, George Wilkes—Lady Chrisman.......... San Miguel Stock Farm, Walnut Creek.
MAMBRINO CHIEF, McDonald Chief—Venus.......... Thos. Smith, Vallejo.
PHILOSOPHER, Pilot Wilkes—Belle.......... George E. Guerne, Santa Rosa.
REDWOOD, Anteeo—Lou Wilton.......... A. McFayden, Oakland.
STEINWAY, Strathmore—Abbess.......... Cook Stock Farm, Contra Costa Co
VICTOR, Echo—Daughter of Woodburn.......... G. W. Hughes, Napa City

The Ione Meeting.

The first class programme arranged by the Directors of the Amador and Sacramento Association has brought forth favorable comment from all owners of thorough bred horses throughout the State, and as it is the only meeting that is given up almost exclusively to the "bang tails" it can readily be surmised that at this meeting beginning August 5th, there will be representatives present from all the principal stables of the State. Rules of the State Agricultural Society will govern the meeting, except when the conditions named in the advertisement are otherwise.

The Directors also announce that stable room, together with all necessary hay and straw will be free to prospective competitors. The various stakes and purses are so diversified both in regard to distance and for the different aged horses that almost anyone owing a thoroughbred can find some favorable race in which to enter. Entries for this meeting close on July 15th.

The Horseman Guarantee Stake.

The Chicago Horseman, through our columns this week, announce to the readers of the Breeder and Sportsman, that they have opened up the Horseman's Guaranteed Stake for trotting foals of 1890. A stake of $12,500 to be trotted for in 1894. While there have been many stakes instituted for thoroughbreds which far exceed this amount, still it is the largest sum of money ever offered by private individuals or association for trotting foals, and no doubt the breeders throughout the United States will heartily support this great stake. Although the guarantee is a very large one, the entrance is very small, and even then payable on the installment plan. Entries will close on July 1, 1890, at which time $10 must accompany the nomination; $10 is payable January 1, 1891; $10 on July 1, 1891; $10 on January 1, 1892; $10 July 1, 1892; $10 January 1, 1893; $15 on July 1, 1893; $25 on January 1, 1894, and $100 from those declaring to start on July 1, 1894. Like all other produce stakes, mares not having foaled by July 1st may be nominated, and the entry must give the name of the mare and stallion to whom she is bred, and within thirty days after foaling, name and description of foal must be forwarded. In case of a dead foal, the entrance fee will be refunded. Nominators are liable only for the first payment, and failure to make any subsequent payments when due shall be considered a withdrawal from the stake with forfeiture of all former payments.

The Horseman guarantees that the total value of the stake shall be not less than $12,500; the main stake to be $11,000, divided $5,000 to the first horse, $2,500 to second, $1,500 to third, $1,000 to fourth, and a piece of plate of the actual value of $1,000 will be presented to the breeder of the winner.

A Consolation Stake of $1,500 is also offered to be trotted for within four days after the date of decision of first race, over the same track and under the same conditions and rules. This Consolation stake is open only to horses who start and win no part of the main stake. In case the stakes exceed in value, the guaranteed sum of $12,500, the excess shall be added to the Consolation stake, which shall be divided into 50, 25, 15 and 10 per cent.

As there are so many breeding farms in California that depend upon Eastern markets for their sales, it is only natural to suppose that this stake will receive a bountiful support from the large establishments here. Those who are interested will find full particulars in the advertisement.

Guaranteed Purses at Stockton.

On the first day of July the entries will close for the six trotting and running events offered by the Stockton Fair Association. Attention has already been called to these stakes in a former issue, but so that owners of horses eligible for these purses may not overlook them, we deem it expedient to call their attention once more to them. Four guaranteed purses are offered of $1,000 each for the three minute class, 2.25 class, 2:30 class and the 2:40 class; the payment of each of these is the usual 10 per cent., divided in installments into three different payments, the horse having to be named when the final payment is made.

A district trotting race for four-year-olds or under, is open to Amador, Calaveras, Tuolumne and all the San Joaquin Valley Counties. The purse is $500, which will be divided into four moneys. The Amador stake is for the thoroughbred division for all aged horses open to Amador, Calaveras, San Joaquin and Stanislaus Counties. The entrance to this purse is $20 each for all starters, and the Association adds $150, the second horse to receive half of the entrance money, the distance being one mile. In both of these district stakes we anticipate a large number of entries, as the horse breeding industry of that particular district has gone forward with long bounds within the past few years. In the vicinity of Stockton alone there are many first class breeding farms, and the highly representative stallions that are now owned in that immediate neighborhood would be a credit to any breeding farm in the country.

Remember the entries for all of these stakes and purses close on Tuesday, July 1st.

The Los Angeles Association.

A note from the Secretary of the Los Angeles Association notifies us that the 2:30 trotting race, for which entries were to have closed last week, has been, by order of the Board of Directors, kept open until July 1st, as there are many other large purses in addition to this one that also close on the same date; horsemen should read the Los Angeles advertisement over carefully and then make their nominations. The Association this year has surpassed all previous efforts in preparing a first class programme and also in offering very large amounts in added moneys, and they are well worthy the support of all horsemen throughout this and adjoining States.

The Grand Coast Circuit.

San Jose, Napa, Petaluma and Oakland have joined in together, and this week present to the readers of the Breeder and Sportsman a full page advertisement containing each programme for their respective race meetings, which will take place in August and September next. There has never been a time in California when so much money has been offered in purses as the present year, and the horse owners who may be fortunate enough to have winners will be able to recoup themselves for all trouble and expense that they may have gone to in preparing their horses for the season's campaign. The Oakland Association has adopted the novel rule of naming the majority of their stakes after some prominent stallion, and it must not appear strange if a Guy Wilkes should win the Director stake or a Sidney win the Dexter Prince, while a Mambrino Wilkes is liable to carry off the honors in the Hawthorne purse; as Mountain Boy has been such a short time in this State, we can hardly expect him to win the Electioneer purse, but there is a possibility that a young Dawn may carry off the money offered in the Stamboul purse. Taken all in all, the programmes, as presented, are good and arranged in such order that horsemen will have no trouble in filling their dates at the different meetings. There are still a large number of purses which are open for entries so that horse owners in the State should make a careful examination of the programmes and enter accordingly.

For the Honor of California.

The smoke of battle had hardly cleared away from the great contest which occured on Tuesday of last week at Sheepshead Bay, before the wires notified us of the fact that a match race had been made between those great giants of the turf, J. B. Haggin's Salvator and D. T. Pulsifer's Tenny. The excitement in regard to the Suburban had run high and Tenny had been quoted for many days prior to the event as the favorite in the betting, but within the last forty-eight hours prior to the Suburban's being run, Salvator had improved considerably in the minds of the public and as a consequence the two were almost equal in the betting, the Californian representative having many staunch and true friends. The word "Californian" is hardly proper to use in connection with Salvator except that the honor be applied from pride of possession, a Kentucky bred colt, he has never seen the Golden State, for although bought as a yearling he was sent on to the Eastern stable of Mr. Haggin, and as yet has not made the overland trip. However, Mr. Haggin's ownership of the wonderful colt was enough to make all residents of this State pin their faith to what they recognized as their representative in the great contest and when he won the Sururban, as is only natural to suppose, great joy was expressed by all who are interested in horses. For two or three days prior to last Wednesday the principal topic of conversation in all the hotels, clubs and popular places of resort was the great race match that was to determine the merits of the two well bred stallions. That California supported Salvator to a man is only reasonable to believe, for while there may have been a few who believed in the great sprinting ability of Tenny, still Salvator had shown himself such a wonderful colt that it looked useless to place money against him, and that the many friends of the Haggin stable had good grounds for their judgment was evident in the result of the race.

Kingston's remarkable performance of 2:06½ made last year was knocked completely in the shade and from the telegraphic account, it can be readily surmised that there was less than a quarter of a second difference between the two gladiators, although the mile and a quarter was compassed in the remarkable time of 2.05. Mr. Haggin may well be congratulated in the possession of such a horse for we know it has been his intention for some time to add Salvator to the already large stud at Rancho del Paso.

The Undine stable owned by Messrs. Williams & Ramsdell have also cause for congratulation as they have during the week tended to enhance the value of California productions by winning at Chicago with their first class colt Racine. It is true that for the class of company he was in, the Palo Alto bred colt was in at remarkable light weight, having evidently been overlooked by the handicapper; by winning his mile as he did, hands down, in the really excellent time of 1:41 we may presume that hereafter he will have to carry lumps of more weight.

Not to be outdone by other stable the Maltese villa colors were seen first past the winning post on Wednesday last at Sheepshead Bay. The wonderfully good mare, Geraldine, making the short three-quarter track in 1:10, and on the following day L. J. Rose's Fairy was second in a race, the time of which was 1:09 2.5. Following up the successes of her stable companion Firenzi on Thursday defeated a field of good horses at her own special distance, one and a half miles, winning in the record-breaking time of 2:33. This mare has been a good bread winner for several seasons for the Haggin stable, and as she has just come to herself there is every reason to believe that there is plenty of more dollars in sight which she will add to her credit on the right side of the stable ledger. The thoroughbreds have started off all right for California's honor a d glory, we can only trust that our trotting representatives who are now in the East will do fully as well and repay the owners for the great trouble and large expense to which they have gone, in taking their horses to the Eastern States to compete with the best there is in the land.

The Sonoma and Marin Futurity Stakes.

In conversation with several prominent members of the Sonoma and Marin Agricultural Society within the past few days, we find that it is extremely probable that an exceedingly large list of entries will be made in the Futurity Stake recently opened by that progressive association. While it is true that the stake is confined to a limited district, still there can be no doubt but what the counties named contain a larger number of first class horses than can be found in almost any other section of California.

The race will take place in 1893 for foals of 1890 and as the entrance fee is only $75, the payment of which is distributed over almost three years, there is no one but what can afford to enter for this prospectively large stake. As usual neglect to make payment on the dates stipulated incurs a forfeiture of all payments already made. Entries will close on next Tuesday, July 1st., at which time those making nominations must pay $5 for each entry. $5 will also be due on January 2, 1891, $10 on January 2, 1892, $10 on July 1st, 1892, $15 on January 2nd, 1893 and $25 on July 1st 1893. The association will add $25 for each starter over two and up to five, and $10 for each additional starter up to ten.

The district from which entries will be received comprises Sonoma, Marin, Napa, Lake, Mendocino, Solano, Yolo, Colusa and Contra Costa Counties. The Board of Directors reserve the right to declare the stake filled or not without binding themselves to any specified number of entries. We fully expect to see a very large entry list and look forward with great anticipation to a note from Secretary Maclay assuring us that the stake has met with unqualified indosement from all horse breeders throughout the district.

The Northern Circuit.

The Northern California Circuit announces through our columns this week that they have arranged for four consecutive weeks' racing, beginning at The Willows on August 12th, Red Bluff August 19th, at Chico August 26th and at Marysville on September 2nd; $18,000 are offered in stakes and purses, the entries for which will close with the various Secretaries on August 1st at 10 o'clock P. M. The events have been so placed on the different programmes at the four points of meeting that there will be no clashing, and the horses taking part will have ample time for rest between races of a like class at the different points. We shall have occasion in the near future to speak something further of this Northern Circuit, but in the meantime would advise all horsemen to carefully examine the programme as published in this week's issue.

Hugh E. Deane.

A sudden and much to be regretted death was that of Mr. Hugh E. Deane, which occurred last week at his home in Oakland. Mr. Deane was never of pronounced physique, but had been fairly well until about three months ago, when a general failure of vitality began and the courtly man went day by day down to the grave. Mr. Deane was created of fine clay, in the shapeliest mould, and within him moved all those instinctive promptings which make the gentleman par excellence. Modest and retiring, generous alike to all, cleaving to friends through all exigencies, he will be sadly missed at all councils of those who fancy coursing in which sport he found his only recreation.

Change of Entry Date.

The Directors of the Nevada State Agricultural Society have seen fit to change the time of the closing of entries for their annual races from September 1st to August 1st. This is a very good move, as without doubt there are many horses now eligible to the slower classes which will before the 1st of September, have secured records for themselves, and this fact would probably deter many from crossing the mountains to take part in the Nevada races. By closing at an earlier date it will give the owners a better chance to place their horses in the races where they now belong, and will also insure larger fields of horses for the annual meeting at the Nevada Fair.

Our Tennessee Letter.

GALLATIN, TENN., June 21

BREEDER AND SPORTSMAN—It is many weeks yet before the racing season of 1890 draws to a close, but after the running of the Brooklyn and Suburban Handicaps, the races for the older horses do not excite much interest, and the racing seems to lack animation, when it is compared with the enthusaism and speculation that has made the two big handicaps such famous events. True it is there will be a great deal of stakes offered for the aged horses, but after the Brooklyn and Suburban, that part of the racing drama is overshadowed by the big stakes for the two and three year olds; such as the Junior Champion, Matron and Futurity stakes, and the Omnibus, Realization and Lorillard Stakes.

I, for one, believe the Jockey Clubs would make a move in the right direction if they would announce more stakes with more added money for the older division. What can a first-class four-year-old win nowadays compared to the winnings of a two-year-old or a three-year-old? Take the racing season of 1888 as one example. Proctor Knott, as a two-year-old, won upwards of $69,000, while The *Bard*, who won all his races but one, and who started in every big all-aged event of the season except the Suburban, had less than $20,000 to his credit. The same season there were half a dozen three year olds that placed considerably over $20,000 a piece to their credit. Last season El Rio Rey and Chaos—the latter a very ordinary youngster—won $46,480 and $63,180, respectively, while the amount won by the six largest winning 4-year olds and upwards of the season did not amount to as much. So it will be this season, Russell will come near winning $100,000—provided he retains his form, and Salvator, the best horse of the year, will probably stop under $30,000.

Let's give the older horses a chance. Let's do not b:ng up a mint of money for five and six furlong sprint 2-years old races, but divide the thing and see such gallant turf heroes, as Salvator, Tenny, R:celand, Kingston, Firenzi, Prince Royal, Hanover, Lcs Angeles, Proctor Knott and horses of that ilk measuring strides for big money and over a distance of ground. The rapidly increasing amount of added money given each season by the numerous racing clubs forcibly illustrates that we are still on the ascendency in American racing, but pray do not let us ignore the champions of other years and give all to the younger division. I hope to see some club remember the "old guard" when the stakes for another year are opened, and every old turf man of the country would dance with delight to know that we were going to have, say a half a dozen, two-mile races with from $10,000 to $20,000 to the winner.

Mr. Winter's stable of horses are now at Washington Park, where his horses are engaged in all of the stakes. Jo Courtney no longer trains for Mr. Winters, and he has returned to California. The veteran trainer, John Davis, of Missouri, has been engaged by Mr. Winters, and he now has command of all the horses. Mr. Winters has sold to Dan Honig the chestnut three-year old colt, Rascal, by Joe Hooker, dam Mattie Glen, she by Imp. Glen Athol. He has given to some relative in Illinois the bay colt Barrett by Joe Hooker, out of Countess Zicka. Barrett is a full brother to Don Jose, whom Mr. Winters has given to Pat Grogan to train. So far none of the Winters' horses have shown winning form, but under the watchful eye of John Davis I expect the horses to begin to earn brackets.

At the recent Morris Park meeting, which closed last Saturday, the stables of Messrs. Baldwin, Hearst, Ashe, Rose and Haggin captured $14,020 of the money hung up for the bang-tails. The Californians made a good start at Sheepshead Bay the opening day when Porter Ashe was second with Geraldine in the opening scramble, and Mr. Haggin's great Salvator won the Suburban.

Brown Hal truly astonished the world with his remarkable quarter of a mile trial at Ewell Farm, and when it was read in the columns of the daily papers and turf journals of the country many old Grand Circuit followers shook their heads and simply said "it won't do." Well, it will do, and it has been done. To me it seemed an impossibility, but now a note from Mr. Horace Polk, Secretary at Ewell Farm, tells me that it was an absolute fact, and that not only did he pace a quarter in 28 seconds, but that when he did so he was pulling a road cart. Of the performance Mr. Polk writes: "There can be no doubt of Brown Hal's going the quarter in 28 seconds, for there were four watches on him. Ed Geers who drove him caught the time in 28 seconds; Dr. W. E. Henderson of Sardis, Miss., made the time in 27¾; George Thomas made the time 273-5, and Major Brown made it either 28 or 28¼, I have forgotten which. He went a quarter for John Bostick in 27¾ seconds once, but we never mentioned it for no one would believe it." If Brown Hal can pace a quarter in 28 to cart, pray tell me how fast he would go at Cleveland to a sulky?

Mr. Polk also writes: "We had a pretty well bred foal dropped on the 8th inst. in a bay colt by Anteeo, 2.16¼, dam Alice Russell, by Lord Russell, 2nd dam Aline by Allie West, 2:25 (sire of Jewett 2:14), 3rd dam Coquette (dam of Nutmeg 2:23¼ and Col. Stevens 2:28¼) by American Clay. This youngster will be entered in all the big stakes now open, and we expect to be able to get some of the money with him.

Mr. Charles Reed shipped from here to-day to New York 48 head of yearlings, the produce of Long Taw, Miser, Muscovy, Imp. Mr. Pickwick and Forrester, Mr. Reed's own stallion. In the lot is a half sister to the Bard, and a filly by Miser out of the great Thora. There is also a colt out of Henlopen, a filly out of Sarony, a colt out of Bonnie Wood and a filly out of Acquittal.

One would judge that ill luck is now a very close attendant in the Scoggan stable. Early in the season the horses of the Louisville turfmen fairly swept their fields before them, and now they are frequently numbered among the swept. The Scoggan's had great hopes of winning the Suburban with Knott, or English Lady, but when the horses arrived in the East Knott had developed a splint, and after English Lady had been given an easy mile and quarter in 2:15 she pulled up very lame, which necessitated her absence as a starter. Knott was left with Dr. Sheppard, who will fire and and blister the big gelding, and English Lady was taken to Chicago where they hope she will be able to fill her engagements. I am of the opinion that Knott, famous as the first Futurity winner, will never win another race.

KENNESAW.

Answers to Correspondents.

Answers for this department must be accompanied by the name and address of the sender, not necessarily for publication, but as proof of good faith. Write the questions distinctly, and on one side of the paper only. Positively no questions will be answered by mail or telegraph.

Subscriber.

We do not know the particular Anteeo Jr. to which you refer, as there are several named the same way. Write to Mr. Keating at Reno, and he can probably give you the information. Dexter Prince is standard bred, and is registered; his number is 11363.

A. G. A., Chicago.

Will you please give breeding of Lady Tolman or Golman and her record? I understand she paced at Chico or Red Bluff in 2:31½; also, who is she owned by now?

Answer.—Lady Tolman is probably the mare you mean; She has no record, although she has started. She is by Frank Tolman, dam untraced. She is now under the charge of S. Montgomery of Chico.

J. E. W.

Can you inform me through the columns of your paper the name of the horse which ran second to Cremorne for the Derby?

Answer.—J. N. Astley's Pell Mell ran second to Cremorne in 1872.

Subscriber.

The horse which was 3, 4, 3 is the one entitled to third money.

C. W. B.

Will you please give me the breeding of the mare called Fannie Malone owned in Sacramento.

Answer—By Niagara dam Fannie Wickham by Herald.

A reader:

Please give me the pedigree, description and date of death of the standard bred horse A. T. Stewart.

Answer.—Brown horse, foaled 1872 by Mambrino Patchen 58, dam the Harris mare by Mambrino Chief II, second dam by Young's Pilot Jr. He died May 29, 1885.

O. M.

Anteeo is now eleven years old. You had better write to Mr. Simpson to decide the second question, as he is probably the only person that can answer it.

Knight's Landing.

Will you kindly inform me through the columns of your paper whether two colts by the same sire and different dams can be called half brothers or sisters, or should they both be out of the same dam and different horses?

Answer—While it would be proper to call them half brothers, if by the same sire, still common usuage determines that only those out of the same dam shall be so called, when by different horses.

Names Claimed.

I hereby claim the name SABLE CZAR for black colt foaled June 12, 1890, by Sable Wilkes 2:18, dam Olivette by Whipple's Hambletonian; also,

HARVARD for bay colt, foaled April 20th, by Ringwood (by Sidney), dam Sallie Pierce by Whipple's Hambletonian.

A. C. DIETZ.

I hereby claim the name Sydney Jr. for bright bay colt, two hind feet white to just above ankle; star in forehead and small white snip on nose. Foaled May 31, 1890, by Sydney, dam Maye by Newland's Hambletonion, he by Speculation, and he by Hambletonian 10; 2d dam by Langford; 3d dam full sister to Bell Alta. This is my Futurity entry.

OAKLAND, Cal. G. W. STIMPSON, V. S.

Foals of 1890.

At Pleasanton. The property of C. W. Welby.

On June 15th, chestnut filly by Guy Wilkes, dam Bay View Maid by Gen. Benton. The mare has been bred to Director.

Best Trotting Records.

1 mile—2:08¾, Maud S., against time, in harness, accompanied the distance by a running horse, Glenville, O., July 30, 1885.....2:13¾, best time in a race between horses, Maud S., Chicago, Ills., July 24, 1880......2:12, Axtell, against time, accompanied by running horse—fastest stallion time, Terre Haute, Ind., Oct. 11, 1889...... 2:13¾, Phallas, fastest heat by a stallion against other horses, Chicago, July 14, 1884......2:17¾, Palo Alto, third heat in race at Stockton, Cal., Sept. 26, 1889......2:15½, Jay-Eye-See, half-mile track, Lincoln, Neb., Sept. 14, 1887......2:15¾, Great Eastern, under saddle, third heat, Morrisania, N. Y., Sept. 22, 1877......2:10¾, Jay-Eye-See, against time, best five-year-old record, Providence, R. I., Sept. 15, 1883......2:16, Manzanita, third heat, best four-year-old record, Lexington, Ky., Sept. 3, 1876 .... 2:16, Edgemark, four-year old stallion record, against time, Lexington, Ky., Oct. 18, 1889.....2:10½, Sunol, in Stanford Stake, accompanied by a runner, best three-year-old record, San Francisco, Nov. 9, 1889..2:18, Sunol, 2 years, against time, San Francisco, Cal., Oct. 27, 1888..... 2:30¾, Regal Wilkes, two-year-old stallion record, San Francisco, Nov. 9, 1889..... 2:31½, Norlaine, yearling, against time, San Francisco, Cal., Nov. 11, 1887..... 2:35, Faustino, yearling stallion record, San Francisco, Nov. 9, 1889.

2 miles—4:43 against time, Fanny Witherspoon, Chicago, Ill., Sept 25, 1885.

3 miles—7:21¼, Huntress, harness, Brooklyn, L. I., Sept. 21, 1872.

4 miles—10:34½, Longfellow, wagon, California, Dec 31, 1869.

5 miles—13:00, Lady Mac, harness, San Francisco, Cal., April 2, 1874.

10 miles—27:23¼, Controller, harness, San Francisco, Cal., Nov. 23, 1878.

20 miles—58:25, Captain McGowan, harness, half-mile track, Boston, Oct. 31, 1865.

THE GUN.

Annual Meeting—Sportsmen's Association of the Northwest.

The sixth annual meeting of the Association began at Riverview race track, Portland Oregon, Thursday July 19th. The weather was all that could be desired, and the attendance throughout most flattering, very many ladies gracing the grand stand and applauding the more brilliant performances of the notable experts present.

Portland, Seattle, Tacoma, Spokane Falls, Walla Walla, The Dalles and Eugene had representatives at the tournament, all told, there being about fifty shooters in attendance, including Major Kellogg and J. O Cadman of San Francisco.

H. T. Hudson, secretary of the association, and Buell Lamberson, secretary of the Multnomah Rod and Gun Club, had made every preparation in the line of accommodations for the event.

A large tent was utilized as a sort of headquarters room, and also served the further purpose of making a convenient place for the ammunition, gun cases and other traps usually carried by nimrods. Sandwiches and liquid refreshments were served from the grand stand, and the shooting continued the entire day. There was no interruption from the time the first shot was fired until late in the evening, when it became too dark to see.

No live birds could be procured, and the Peoria blackbird was the only target used. The targets flew sharply' but few were broken by the traps, and the targets met with general approval. All shooting was under American Shooting Association rules.

FIRST DAY.

The shooting did not begin on Thursday until half past ten, because of delays in listing the participants, and securing the proper adjustment of one or two of the traps. Mr. Buell Lamberson acted as scorer.

At 10 Peoria blackbirds, four moneys. A. S A. rules.

E. E. Ellis	1	0	1	1	1	1	1	1	1	1— 9
Frank Conley	1	1	1	1	1	1	1	1	1	1—10
Carroll Hughes	1	1	1	1	1	1	1	1	1	1—10
J. O. Cadman	1	1	1	1	1	0	1	1	1	1— 9
S. J. Kellogg	0	1	1	1	1	1	1	1	1	0— 8
A. W. Eberly	1	1	1	1	0	1	1	0	0	1— 7
H. A. Herrick	1	1	0	0	1	1	1	0	1	1— 7
B. S Barlow	1	1	1	1	1	1	1	1	1	1—10
A. J. Fisk	0	1	0	0	0	1	1	1	1	1— 6
T. F Smith	1	1	1	1	1	1	1	1	1	1—10
E. A. McCoy	1	1	0	0	1	1	1	1	1	1— 8
L. E. Brigden	1	1	1	1	1	1	0	1	1	1— 9
D. Cooper	1	1	0	1	1	1	0	1	1	1— 8
B. D. Prine	1	1	1	1	0	0	1	0	0	1— 6
J. Meek	1	0	1	0	1	1	1	0	1	1— 7
J. J. Evans	0	1	1	1	1	1	1	1	0	1— 8
W. A. Story	0	1	0	0	1	0	0	0	1	1— 4
E. W. Stewart	1	1	0	0	1	0	1	1	1	1— 7
J. Doty	1	1	1	1	1	0	1	1	1	1— 9
R. M. Townsend	0	1	0	0	0	0	0	1	1	0— 3
C. H. Mellius	1	0	1	1	0	1	0	1	0	0— 5
F. G. Farrell	1	0	0	1	0	1	1	0	1	0— 5
T. A. Bingham	1	0	1	1	1	1	1	1	1	1— 9
"Hope"	1	1	1	1	1	1	1	1	1	1—10
M Moore	1	1	1	1	1	1	1	1	1	1—10
J. H. Riley	0	1	0	1	1	1	1	1	0	1— 7
J. R. Clarke	1	0	0	0	1	1	0	0	1	1— 5
"Oregon"	1	1	1	1	1	0	1	0	1	1— 8
J. Paquet	0	1	0	0	1	1	1	1	1	1— 7
W. D. Close	1	1	1	1	1	0	1	0	1	1— 8
A. W. DuBray	0	1	0	1	0	1	1	1	1	1— 7
Z. K. Strait	0	1	1	1	1	1	0	1	1	1— 8
E. Long	1	1	1	1	1	1	1	1	1	1—10
W. H. Schan	1	1	1	1	1	0	0	0	1	1— 7
Sam Stein	1	0	1	1	1	1	1	1	1	0— 8
F. Tolles	1	1	0	1	1	0	1	1	1	1— 8
C. A. Hungate	1	1	1	1	1	0	1	1	1	0— 9
Lewis	1	1	0	1	1	1	1	1	1	1— 9
McNorton	1	1	0	1	1	1	1	1	0	1— 8
Dodge	1	1	1	1	1	1	1	1	1	0— 9

By this score it will be seen that Conley, Hughes, Barlow, Smith, "Hope" Moore and Long tried for first prize; Ellis, Cadman, Brigden, Doty, Bingham, Lewis and Dodge for second; Kellogg, McCoy, Cooper, Evans, "Oregon," Close, Strait, Stein, Tolles, Hungate and McNorton for third: and Eberly, Herrick, Meek, Stewart, Riley, Paquet, DuBray and Eckhard for fourth. The money in each class was divided with the exception of the third prize, the winners of that shooting it out in the next match.

The second match was won by Mr. J. J. Evans with a clean score. Mr. Evans will be remembered as the visiting shot who did such fine work at San Jose in October last. While not a graceful man at the traps he has the "get there" quality. Twenty-five Peoria blackbirds per man was the match.

Ellis, Barlow, Conley, Brigdon, Du Bray and Fish, each hit 24 birds; McNaughton, Smith, Long, Eberly and Lang, each scored 23; Hughes, Bingham, Dodge, Stein, Hope, Herrick, Howe, Oregon and Meek got 22; Lewis, Cooper, Mc Coy, Doty and Dowell, each 21; and "Oakland," Fields and Rauert, each made 20.

The others made various scores ranging from 12 to 19. The prizes in this contest were:

First prize—One Colt's rifle, 22-caliber, donated by James Caraher, and $100 cash.

Second prize—One pair shooting shoes, value $7, donated by Eggert, Young & Co., and $50 in cash.

Third prize—One hat, value $5, donated by Stuffum & Pendleton, and $25 cash.

Fourth prize—One banjo, value $25, donated by Hoyt's music store: 100 Standard "A. B" shells, value $3, donated by Selby Smelting and Lead Company.

Fifth prize—Chicago tin pigeons and trap, value $10, donated by W. D Close.

Third was the Ithaca Gun contest, and was more interesting because doubles were sprung as well as singles.

The prizes also were larger, making it worth while for each shooter to do his best. The contest called for ten single and five pairs of blackbirds.

Forty-three contestants entered the match with the following result:

	Single.									Double.					
	1	2	3	4	5	6	7	8	9	10	11	12	13	14	15
Meek	0	1	1	1	1	1	1	1	1	1	11	11	10	0C	10—15
Doty	1	1	1	1	1	1	0	1	0	1	10	11	10	10	10—14
Brigdon	1	1	1	1	1	1	1	1	1	1	11	00	11	11	11—18
Hope	1	1	1	1	1	1	1	1	1	1	10	11	10	10	11—17
Rondall	1	1	0	1	1	0	1	1	1	0	10	11	10	10	11—12
Paquet	0	1	1	0	1	1	1	0	1	1	10	10	10	10	10—12
Close	1	1	0	1	0	1	1	1	0	1	11	10	10	10	10—13
Evans	1	1	1	1	0	1	1	1	1	1	00	11	10	10	10—13
Eckhard	1	1	1	1	0	1	1	1	0	1	00	00	11	10	11—12
Hudson	0	1	1	0	1	1	1	1	0	0	10	11	10	10	10—12
Conley	1	1	1	1	0	1	1	1	1	0	10	11	10	11	11—16
Stewart	1	0	1	0	0	0	1	1	0	1	01	10	11	10	10—14
Lang	1	1	1	1	1	1	1	1	1	1	10	01	10	11	10—16
Lewis	1	0	1	1	1	1	1	1	1	1	10	11	10	00	10—16
"Oregon"	1	1	1	1	1	0	1	1	1	1	00	10	01	00	10—12
Herrick	1	1	1	1	1	1	1	0	0	1	11	10	10	10	11—15
Tolles	1	1	0	1	1	1	1	1	1	1	10	11	10	10	01—15
Du Bray	1	1	0	1	1	1	1	0	1	1	10	11	00	10	00—12
Steins	0	0	1	0	1	1	1	1	0	1	10	10	00	00	10— 9
Eberly	1	1	1	1	1	1	1	1	1	1	10	10	11	10	11—17
Smith	0	0	1	1	1	0	1	1	1	0	11	11	10	10	11—14
"Oakland"	0	1	1	1	1	1	0	1	0	1	11	10	11	11	10—14
McCoy	1	1	1	1	1	0	1	1	1	1	10	10	01	11	11—16
Barlow	1	1	1	0	1	1	1	1	1	0	10	10	01	11	11—16
Cooper	1	1	1	0	1	1	1	1	1	1	01	01	10	11	11—17
D. K. Howe	1	1	1	1	1		1	1	0	0	11	10	11	10	11—18
Fisk	1	1	1	1	1	1	1	1	0	0	01	00	10	11	10—15
Conley	1	1	1	1	1	1	1	1	1	1	10	11	11	10	11—18
Cadman	1	1	1	1	1	1	1	1	1	0	10	11	10	11	10—16
J. H. Fields	0	0	1	1	0	1	1	1	1	1	10	11	10	10	10—13
W. R. Dodge	0	1	1	1	1	1	1	1	0	0	01	11	11	11	11—16
McNaughton	1	1	1	1	1	1	1	1	1	1	11	10	10	11	11—18
Bingham	1	1	1	1	1	1	1	1	1	1	10	10	10	11	10—16
Ellis	1	1	1	1	1	1	1	1	1	1	10	10	10	10	10—14
J. R. Clark	0	1	1	0	0	0	1	1	0	0	11	00	10	00	10— 7
Riley	0	1	1	1	1	1	0	1	1	0	11	11	00	10	11—14
Caraher	0	0	1	0	0	1	1	1	1	1	10	11	11	11	01—14
Hungate	1	1	1	1	1	1	1	1	1	1	11	11	10	00	10—16
Hughes	1	0	1	1	1	1	0	1	1	0	11	10	00	11	01—13
M. Moore	1	1	1	1	1	0	0	1	1	1	11	11	01	01	01—15
Straight	1	0	0	0	1	1	0	1	0	0	11	00	11	10	00— 9
Millins	0	1	1	1	0	0	0	1	1	1	10	11	11	11	00—12
J. Dowell	1	1	0	0	0	0	0	1	0	1	10	10	11	10	10—10

The prizes offered in this contest were:

First prize—One Ithaca hammerless shotgun, to order, value $50; donated by the Ithaca Gun Company, and $35 cash.

Second prize—One road cart, value $25, donated by Staver & Walker, and $20 cash.

Third prize—Six fine shirts, value $15, donated by the Consolidated Shirt Warehouse, made to order; 100 Standard "A. B." shells value $3, donated by the Selby Smelting and Lead Company, and $10 cash.

Fourth prize—One pair cut glass bottles, value $10, donated by Woodard, Clark & Co., druggists, and $5 cash.

Fifth prize—One pair hunting boots, value $9, donated by Protzman & DeFrance; one pair bronze vases, value $10, donated by Forbes & Breeden.

Sixth prize—One hat, donated by A. B. Steinbach, value $10.

Seventh prize—One gallon best gun oil, value $2, donated by D. M. Dunne.

Messrs. Conley & McNaughton, who got eighteen out of twenty possible birds sold the gun on the premises and divided the money. All others who tied for second, third, fourth, fifth, sixth and seventh prizes shot them off in the next match.

SECOND DAY.

The second day's shoot of the Sportsman's Association of the Northwest opened promptly at 10 o'clock. The attendance was larger than on the opening day and the shooting owing to the importance of the matches were more exciting. Match No. 4, postponed from Thursday, was first shot off. The Tolley gun contest and the champion banner matches followed. Match No. 7 was omitted and the Winchester gun contest (shooting at 5 singles and 3 triplets with Winchester guns only) closed the shooting for the day. The last contest was the most exciting. The shooters tried their best to down three birds at a time, but most of them were in big luck in getting two.

The day opened with the match for the individual championship of the Northwest held by Mr. A. W. Du Bray.

At 20 Peoria blackbirds.

E. E. Ellis	0 1 1 1 1 0 0 1 1 1 1 0 1 1 1 1 1 1 0 1 1—15
Straight	1 1 0 1 1 1 1 1 1 1 1 0 1 1 1 1 1 0 1 1 1 1—17
Kellogg	1 1 1 1 1 1 1 1 1 1 1 1 1 1 1 1 1 1 0 1 1—19
Du Bray	1 1 0 0 1 1 1 1 1 0 1 1 1 1 1 1 1 1 1 0 1—16
Lang	1 1 1 1 1 1 0 1 1 1 1 1 1 1 1 0 1 1 1 1 1—18
Smith	0 0 1 1 0 0 0 1 0 1 1 1 1 1 1 1 1 1 1 1 0—13
Carnser	0 0 0 1 0 1 1 0 0 1 0 0 1 1 1 0 1 1 1 1 1—11
Cadman	1 1 1 1 1 0 1 1 1 0 0 1 1 0 1 1 1 1 1 1 1—16
Barlow	1 1 1 1 1 1 1 1 1 1 0 1 1 1 1 1 1 1 1 1 1—19
Lewis	1 1 1 1 1 1 1 1 1 1 1 1 1 1 1 1 1 1 0 0 0—17
Eberly	1 1 1 1 1 1 1 1 1 1 1 0 1 1 1 1 1 1 1 1 1—19
Farrell	0 0 1 1 0 1 1 1 0 1 1 1 0 1 0 0 1 1 1 1 1—13
Oregon	1 1 1 1 1 1 1 1 1 1 0 1 1 1 1 0 1 1 0 1 1—17
Stewart	1 1 1 1 1 0 1 0 0 0 1 0 0 1 1 1 1 1 1 0 1—13
Burgess	1 1 0 1 1 1 1 0 1 1 1 1 1 1 1 1 1 1 1 1 1—18
Steinman	1 1 1 1 1 0 1 0 0 1 0 0 1 1 1 1 1 1 1 1 0—14
Estes	1 0 1 0 0 1 0 0 0 1 1 0 0 0 1 1 1 1 0 1 1—14
Tolles	0 1 0 0 1 1 1 1 0 0 1 1 1 1 1 0 1 1 1 0 1—13
McNaughton	0 1 1 1 0 1 1 1 1 1 1 1 1 1 1 1 1 1 0 1 1—17
J. Collins	1 1 1 0 0 1 0 0 0 0 1 1 1 0 0 1 1 1 1 1 1—12
Doty	1 1 0 1 1 1 1 1 1 0 1 1 1 1 1 1 1 1 1 1 1—20
Cooper	1 1 1 1 1 1 1 1 1 1 1 1 1 1 1 1 1 1 1 1 1—00
Evans	1 1 1 1 0 0 1 1 1 0 1 1 1 1 1 1 1 0 0 1 1—16
Dodge	1 1 1 0 0 1 1 1 1 1 1 1 1 1 1 0 1 1 1 1 1—17
Bingham	1 1 1 1 1 1 1 1 1 1 1 0 1 1 1 1 1 1 1 0 1—13
Eckhardt	0 1 1 0 1 1 1 1 0 1 1 1 1 1 1 1 1 1 1 1 1—17
H. J. Burrell	1 1 0 1 1 1 0 0 1 0 1 1 1 1 1 1 1 1 1 1 1—15
W. F. Burrell	1 1 1 0 0 1 1 1 1 1 1 1 1 1 1 0 1 1 1 1 1—17
Herrick	1 1 1 1 1 1 1 1 1 1 1 1 1 1 1 1 1 1 0 1 1—19
Brigdon	1 1 1 1 1 0 0 1 1 0 0 1 1 1 1 1 1 1 1 1 0—15
Peters	0 0 1 1 0 1 0 0 0 0 0 1 0 1 0 0 0 0 0 0 1— 7
McCoy	1 1 1 0 1 1 1 1 0 1 1 1 1 0 1 0 1 1 1 1 1—16
Fields	1 1 1 0 1 1 1 0 1 1 1 0 1 1 1 0 1 1 1 1 1—15
Conley	0 1 1 1 1 1 1 1 1 1 1 1 1 1 1 1 1 1 0 1 1—17
Hope	1 0 1 1 0 1 1 1 0 1 1 1 1 1 1 1 1 1 1 1 1—17
Fisk	1 1 1 1 0 1 1 1 1 1 1 1 1 1 1 1 1 1 1 1 1—27
Riley	1 1 1 1 1 0 0 0 1 1 0 1 1 1 1 1 0 1 1 0—19
Hungare	1 1 0 1 0 1 1 1 0 1 0 1 1 1 1 0 0 1 1 0—14
Close	1 1 1 1 1 0 1 1 1 1 1 0 1 0 1 1 1 1 0 1—17

First prize—The champion gold medal, valued at $250; presented to the association by the Multnomah Rod and Gun Club, of Portland, and one 18x22 photograph of the winner; value, $15; donated by E. W. Moore, photographer.

Second prize—Fifteen per cent of entrance money.

Third prize—Ten per cent of entrance money.

Fourth prize—One box Schiller cigars; value, $10; donated by Sichel & Mayer; 100 standard "A. B." shells, value, $3, donated by Selby Smelting & Lead Company.

Fifth prize—One hammock, value, $5; donated by Zan Bros.'

Sixth prize—One gallon best gun oil, value $2, donated by D. M. Dunne.

In the match Cooper and Fisk each got twenty birds. They shot the tie off soon after and Cooper bringing down twenty more was the winner. Fisk got eighteen in the shoot. The other prizes were variously divided, some of the ties being shot off, lots being drawn for others, and the remaining ones were divided even.

The next match was the Tolley gun contest at five singles and three pair of blackbirds. There were forty-two entries, and the score was as follows:

	Singles.					Doubles.		
	1	2	3	4	5	8	9	10
Herrick	1	1	1	1	0	10	10	10— 7
Eberly	1	1	1	1	1	10	11	11—10
Barlow	1	1	0	1	1	10	11	11— 9
Ellis	1	1	1	1	1	11	11	10—10
Bringham	1	1	1	1	1	10	11	00— 8
Collins	1	1	1	0	1	11	10	10— 8
Kellogg	1	1	1	0	1	10	10	00— 6
Steinman	0	1	1	1	1	10	01	10— 7
DuBray	1	1	1	1	1	11	11	10—11
Lewis	1	1	1	1	1	10	11	11—10
Brigdon	1	1	1	1	1	11	11	10—10
Fisk	1	1	1	1	1	11	10	10— 9
M'Naughton	1	1	1	1	1	11	11	10—10
W. R. Dodge	1	1	1	1	1	11	10	10— 9
Doty	1	1	1	1	0	01	11	11— 9
Smith	1	1	1	1	1	10	10	00— 7
Close	1	1	1	1	1	10	11	10— 9
Cadman	1	1	0	0	1	11	11	10— 8
Eckhardt	1	1	1	1	1	10	10	10— 8
Millins	0	1	1	1	0	10	10	10— 7
Hope	1	1	1	1	1	11	11	10—10
Randler	1	0	1	1	1	10	10	01— 7
Jones	1	1	1	1	0	11	11	00— 8
Meek	0	1	1	1	0	10	11	10— 7
McCoy	1	1	1	1	1	00	11	10— 8
"Oregon"	1	1	1	1	1	10	10	00— 7
H. J. Burrell	1	1	1	0	1	10	11	10— 8
Lang	0	1	1	0	1	11	10	11— 8
W. F. Burrell	1	0	0	1	0	10	10	11— 5
Caraner	0	1	1	1	1	11	00	10— 8
Sibson	1	1	1	0	1	11	10	11— 9
Estab	1	1	0	0	1	01	10	10— 6
Hungate	1	0	0	1	1	10	10	00— 5
Conley	1	1	1	1	1	11	11	10—10
Cooper	1	1	1	1	1	11	11	10—10
Clark	0	0	1	1	0	00	10	00— 3
Evans	1	1	1	1	1	11	10	01— 8
Peters	1	0	0	0	0	10	10	00— 3
Fields	1	1	1	0	1	11	10	11— 9
Monastes	1	1	0	1	1	10	10	00— 6
Straight	1	0	1	1	0	11	00	11— 6
Riley	0	1	1	1	1	10	11	10— 7

The following are the prizes:

First prize—One Tolley gun, donated by H. T. Hudson; value $50 and $25 cash.

Second prize—One case of birds, value $50, donated by Captain Douglass, and $15 cash.

Third prize—One pointer bitch, value $50, donated by Antione, Three Mile house, and $10 cash.

Fourth prize—One case champagne, value $36, donated by Hotaling & Co., and $5 cash.

Fifth prize—One fancy cake, value $8, donated by Baum & Brandes, and $100 Standard "A. B." shells, value $3, donated by Selby Smelting and Lead Company.

Sixth prize—One box cigars, value $5, donated by J. D. Meyer.

Seventh prize—One hat, value $5, donated by Currier & Co.

The sixth match was between teams of three for the champion banner with the following entries:

Portland Gun Club.—W. F. Burrell, W. S. Sibson and H. J. Burrell; Seattle Club—Collins, Stine and Lewis; Spokane Club—Herrick, Eckhart and Lang; Tacoma Club—Barlow, Ellis and Eberle; Willamette Club—Evans, Riley and Long; Multnomah Club—Monastes, Carabar and Moore; Walla Walla Club—DuBray, Hungate and Strait.

The following was for twenty singles and the following is the result of the shoot:

		Totals for Clubs.
W. F. Burrell	13	
W. S. Sibson	15	
H. J. Burrell	15—43	Portland Club
O Collins	15	
Stine	11	
Lewis	15—41	Seattle Club
Herrick	18	
Lane	14	
Eckert	16—48	Spokane Club
Barlow	19	
Ellis	16	
Eberly	19—54	Tacoma Club
Evans	16	
Riley	17	
Long	19—52	Willamette Club
Monastes	9	
Carabar	9	
Moore	16—34	Multnomah Club
DuBray	18	
Hungate	14	
Straight	11—43	Walla Walla Club

The first prize, "the championship banner of the Northwest, value $100, presented to the Association by Mrs. Pease of Seattle, Wash., and three 16x22 photographs of the winning team, donated by E. W. Moore, photographer," was accordingly won by the Tacoma Club; the second, "sixty per cent. of the entrance money," by the Willamettes; and the third, "forty per cent. of the entrance money," by the Spokane Club. In addition to these prizes, the Selby Smelting and Lead Company donate as a special prize to the winning club 500 Selby Standard "A. B." shells, valued at $15. The lowest team one box Webster cigars, donated by M. A. Gunst & Co., value $5. Highest individual score in any one team, one sportsman's vase, value $20, donated by L. C. Henrichsen.

WINCHESTER GUN CONTEST.

The last match was the Winchester Gun contest, participated in by twenty-four shooters. The following is the score:

Collins	1	1	1	1	1	1	0	0	1	0	0	1	1	0— 9
Rauert	0	1	1	1	0	0	0	0	0	0	0	0	0	0— 3
Brigden	0	1	0	1	1	1	0	0	0	0	0	1	0	0— 5
Stine	1	1	1	1	0	1	0	0	0	1	0	1	0	0— 7
Lewis	1	1	1	1	0	1	0	0	0	0	0	1	0	0— 6
Conley	1	1	0	0	1	1	0	0	1	0	1	1	0	0— 6
Ellis	1	0	1	1	1	1	0	0	0	0	0	0	1	0— 6
McNaught	1	0	1	1	1	1	1	0	1	1	0	0	0	0— 8
Kelly	0	1	0	1	0	1	0	0	1	1	0	1	0	0— 4
Fisk	1	1	1	1	1	1	0	0	1	1	0	1	0	0— 8
Cadman	0	1	1	1	1	1	0	0	0	0	0	1	0	0— 6
Long	1	0	1	0	0	1	1	0	1	0	0	0	1	0— 6
Herrick	1	1	1	1	1	1	0	0	1	1	0	1	0	0—10
Bringham	0	1	1	1	0	1	1	0	1	1	0	1	0	0— 8
Dodge	1	1	1	1	1	1	1	0	1	0	0	1	1	0—10
Carahar	0	0	1	1	0	1	1	0	1	0	0	0	0	0— 5
Evans	1	1	1	0	0	1	1	0	1	0	0	0	0	0— 6
Eberly	1	0	0	0	0	1	0	0	0	0	0	1	0	0— 3
Barlow	0	1	1	1	1	1	0	0	0	0	0	0	0	0— 5
McCoy	0	0	0	1	1	0	0	0	0	0	0	0	0	0— 2
"Oregon"	0	0	1	1	0	1	0	0	1	0	0	0	0	0— 4
Meek	1	0	1	1	0	1	0	0	0	0	0	1	1	0— 6
Eckhardt	1	0	1	1	1	0	0	0	1	1	0	1	0	0— 7
Tolls	0	1	1	1	0	1	0	0	1	0	0	1	0	1

The prizes were:

First prize—Winchester gun, value $60; second, sixty per cent; third, 30 per cent., and fourth, 10 per cent. of the entrance money.

THIRD DAY.

The first match was the Parker gun contest, shooting at five live birds at a rise of thirty yards. There were thirty-seven entries and the following is the score of the shoot:

Ellis	1	1	1	0	0—3
B. McCoy	1	0	1	0	0—2
J. J. Evans	1	1	0	1	1—4
W. J. Riley	0	0	0	0	0—0
"Oregon"	1	1	0	1	1—4
T Bringham	1	1	0	1	1—4
H. H. Lewis	1	1	1	0	1—4
Dr. Smith	0	0	1	1	0—2
"Hope"	1	1	1	1	1—5
E. Long	1	0	1	1	0—3
D. K. Howe	1	0	1	0	1—3
W. R. Dodge	0	0	1	0	0—1
I. E. Brigdon	1	1	1	1	1—5
A. W. DuBray	1	1	1	0	1—4
J. R. Clark	1	1	0	1	0—3
Burgess	1	1	1	1	1—5
Tolles	0	0	1	1	1—3
Lang	0	1	0	1	0—2
W. Muir	1	1	1	1	0—4
J. Collins	1	1	0	0	0—2
W. D. Close	1	1	0	0	1—3
Fields	1	0	1	1	0—3
W. H. Eckhardt	0	0	1	0	0—1
C. E. Hudges	1	1	0	1	0—3
W. A. Eberly	1	1	1	1	1—5
J. O. Cadman	0	1	1	1	1—4
H. A. Herrick	1	1	1	0	1—4
San Stine	1	1	1	0	1—4
T. G. Farrell	1	0	0	0	0—1
J. Fisk	0	1	1	1	1—4
Conley	0	1	0	1	0—2
Z. Doty	1	1	1	1	1—5

L. Cooper	1	1	0	1	0—3
E. Monnastes	1	0	1	0	1—3
A. W. McNaughton	0	1	0	0	1—2
E. Barlow	1	1	1	1	1—5

Eberly, Doty, Barlow, Brigdon and Burgess, killing the full number, divided the first prize. The other prizes were variously divided, some pro rata and the balance were shot off. The prizes were:

First prize—One gun, value $100, donated by Parker Bros., and $50 cash.

Second prize—Three lots in Yaquina, value $125, donated by Charles Sliter, and $20 in cash.

Third prize—One Remington rifle, value $18, donated by Randlaub & Raubert; $10 cash, and one hat, value $5, donated by Arthur Kohn; 100 Selby loaded shells, value $3, donated by Selby Smelting and Lead Co.

Fourth prize—One silk umbrella, value $7, donated by A. Roberts & Co., and one gallon best gun oil, donated by D. M. Dunne, value $2.

Next came a team match participated in by twelve teams of two men each. The shooting was at ten singles instead of ten singles and five doubles as was announced on the programme. The following is the score:

Cooper	1	1	1	1	1	1	1	1	1	1
Doty	1	1	1	1	1	1	1	1	1	1—20
Hope	1	1	1	1	1	1	0	1	1	1
Herrick	0	1	1	1	1	1	1	1	1	1—18
Bingham	1	1	1	1	1	1	1	1	1	1
McNaught	1	1	1	1	1	0	1	1	1	1—19
Smith	1	1	1	1	1	1	1	1	0	1
McCoy	1	0	1	1	1	1	1	1	1	1—18
Dodge	1	1	1	0	1	1	1	1	1	0
Ellis	1	1	1	1	1	1	1	1	1	1—18
Eberly	1	1	1	1	1	1	0	1	1	1
Barlow	1	1	1	1	1	1	1	1	1	1—19
Fisk	1	1	1	1	0	1	1	1	1	1
Conley	1	1	1	1	1	1	1	1	1	1—19
Kellogg	0	0	1	1	1	1	1	1	1	1
Cadman	1	1	1	1	1	1	1	1	1	1—18
Muir	1	1	1	1	1	1	0	1	1	1
Moore	1	1	0	1	1	1	1	0	1	0—16
Riley	1	0	1	1	1	1	1	1	0	1
Evans	1	1	1	1	1	1	1	1	1	1—18
Du Bray	1	1	1	1	1	1	1	1	1	1
Burger	1	1	1	1	0	1	0	1	1	1—18
Close	1	1	1	0	1	1	0	1	1	1
Fields	0	1	1	1	0	0	1	0	0	0—12

Cooper and Doty bringing down twenty birds were awarded first prize, 60 per cent of the entrance money. The second prize was 30 per cent of the entrance money and the third 10 per cent. Besides these prizes there were prizes for the highest individual score—one bronze hunting piece, value $15, donated by A. Feldenheimer, and 100 Selby standard shells, value $3, donated by Selby Smelting and Lead Company—and lowest individual score—one case claret, value $9, donated by Charles Kohn & Co.

All these prizes were divided, with the exception of one or two, which were shot for.

The most important match of the day was the Globe trophy contest. Instead of using ten live birds, the shooters shot at twenty-five Peoria blackbirds. There were twenty-eight entries, and the shooting was lively. The following is the result of the shoot:

Dr. Smith	18	Echardt	21
T. Bringham	24	Collins	20
Herrick	22	Muir	20
Du Bray	17	H. J. Burrell	17
Conley	21	Oregon, Jr	12
Fisk	21	Dolly	20
Eberly	24	Cooper	25
Barlow	22	Evans	23
Lewis	25	Cadman	22
McNaught	24	Howe	10
McCoy	18	Oregon	22
Ellis	24	Long	24
Dodge	21	Briggs	24
Gibson	16		

Lewis and Cooper making a full score, were obliged to shoot off the tie. This gave the victory to Cooper, who brought down twenty more straight, Lewis missing his twentieth bird. The Globe trophy is presented by the Tacoma Globe and is valued at $350.

HIGHEST AVERAGE PRIZES.

The following highest average prizes were awarded at the close of the day's shooting:

First prize—Gold badge—W. A. Eberly.
Second prize—Three lots in Yaquina.—E. S. Barlow.
Third prize—Two gallons of whisky.—F. Conley.
Fourth prize—Silver cup and saucer —D. Cooper.
Fifth prize—Ink stand.—A. W. McNaughton.
Sixth prize—Dressing case.—T. A. Bringham.

On Friday evening the annual election of officers of the Association occurred and the following gentlemen were selected: T. A. Bringham, Tacoma, president; H. H. Lewis, Seattle, first vice-president; H. A. Herrick, Spokane Falls, second vice-president; and Fred McBroom, Spokane Falls, secretary and treasurer. It was decided to hold the next annual tournament in Spokane Falls next June, the exact time to be decided later.

Gun Club.

The Gun Club held its regular monthly meeting at Oakland Trotting Park on Saturday last. The day was cool and the birds lively.

The match was at 12 birds, A. S. A. rules, for club prizes, and the scores were:

B. B. Woodward, 30 yards	2	1	1	2	1	1	2	2	1	2	2	2—12
H. Black, 30 yds	0	0	1	1	2	0	0	2	0	1	1	1— 7
J. D. Harvey, 30 yds	0	0	0	0	0	0	0	0	0	1	1	2— 8
F. S. Butler, 28 yds	0	0	1	1	2	1	1 withdrawn					— 5
D. B. Gillett, 32 yds	1	1	0	0	0	0	1	1	1	0	1	2— 7
George Levison, 30 yds	1	2	1	2	0	1	2	2	0	1	0	1— 9
F. W. Tallant, 28 yds	1	2	0	1	2	1	1	2	1	1	0	1—10
J. H. Jellett, 30 yds	0	1	1	2	1	2	1	2	1	1	0	0— 9
Alex. Hamilton, 28 yds	2	1	1	0	1	0	1	1	0	1	1	0— 8
F. B. Webster, 28 yds	1	2	1	2	1	0	2	1	2	1	2	1—11
J. K. Orr, 28 yds	1	1	0	2	2	1	2	2	1	0	2	0— 9
E W. Chapin, 28yds	1	2	0	1	2	0	2	2	1	2	1	0— 9
Hy Babcock, 28 yds	1	2	1	1	2	2	1	0	1	1	0	2—10
E. F. Tichenor, 28 yds	2	2	1	1	0	0	2	2	1	2	1	0— 9
J. D. Redding, 28 yds	0	0	1	0	0	0	0	1	2	2	0	0— 4
W J. Golcher, 28 yds	0	1	0	2	1	0	1	0	1	1	1	1— 8
F. H. Swett	1	1	2	1	1	2	2	1	0	1	1	2—11

After the regular shoot a pool was made up. The entrance fee was placed at $2.50, and five birds to be shot at, resulting in first prize being won by Mr. Hamilton. Following is the score:

Swett	1	1	1	1	0—4
Woodward	1	1	1	1	0—4
Tallant	1	1	1	1	0—4
Webster	1	1	1	1	0—4
Hamilton	1	1	1	1	1—5

The California Wing Shooting Club is to meet at Oakland Trotting Park to-morrow at 10 o'clock.

Mr. Rolla O. Heikes who shot with the Dimick aggregation here a few months ago is soon to shoot a match with Mr. J. A. R. Elliott at 100 live birds for $100 a side, 30 yards rise, 5 ground traps, use of one barrel only.

Fun at Grass Valley.

The Grass Valley Sportsman's Club, one of the oldest and most firmly knit sportsman's organizations on the coast has for many years held semi-annual reunions in the field. One in June when doves are plenty and one in the fall when quail shooting is at its best. The club throughout its membership is unexceptionable from the sportsmen's standpoint, its members being not only good shots and very fond of sport but also considerate men, alive to all public interests tending to elevate sport and particularly awake to the necessity which exists that men who desire to shoot or fish, either upon public lands or upon the properties of their neighbers should recognize rights of ownership and should practice the amenities, lacking which man is but a savage. On Saturday last the club and its invited guests drove down to Ben. Van Slyke's fine foothill ranch, some fifteen miles below Grass Valley to hold its dove reunion and camp stew for the year. The season of course militates against the presence of many visitors from a distance. Most men who are able to leave for their vacations have already gone to the mountains or to seaside resorts, yet about 100 gathered at Van Slyke's and passed a day in such sport and jollity as only those royal Grass Valley men can afford.

Leaving Grass Valley at 4 o'clock in the morning the party by various roads reached the rendezvous in time for breakfast at 10 o'clock, some of them bringing doves, some cotton tails and one detachment which drove by Mr. Montgomery's having a sack of chickens which that free hearted man insisted were in his way. President Geo. Fletcher was there as usual. He always seems to be there, just why nobody has ever been able to determine. It certainly cannot be to kill game or else he would occasionally hit something. He is not known to be learned in the miscibility of lime juice, sugar and ice and tansy and cold tea and other fluids, although a legend of the neighborhood credits him like the Polar bear with having been known to "eat three tubs of ice, then call for soda water" on the morning after a day at Van Slyke's. Lots of people were there, Hon. Bill D. English and Dr. Matthews from Fresno were ubiquitous, they carried wood, stirred the camp stew, ate all the tid bits and cut up generally. Dr. I. W. Hays and Coon Seaman relaxed a little the stern morality which has held their Sunday-school classes for them for going on a few months. Sweet-faced Charlie Mitchell wandered about showing his familiarity with strange tongues and his newly imported whiskers. There was only one sad man present, Mr. Jim Shoemaker, and his sadness was because the heat was so intense and perspiration so profuse that he found it impossible to raise his spirits even though downing whole pints of the spirits of corn made perfect. Assessor Bond, Capt. Rapp, M. P. Stone and M. L. Elliott formed a guard of honor about a little booth in a shady spot where they seemed to be targeting pistols or something like that, if the popping noises were not misconstrued. That saintly man, Judge Dibble, tried to stand off unregenerate Geo. W. Starr in the matter of stew consumption, but after Starr had called for his fourteenth plate the Judge "smole a ghastly smile," rolled over on his back and was vacuous for the rest of the day. After breakfast Mr. Stokes, the caterer, drove everybody from camp in search of doves, and while they were gone laid the foundation for the thirty gallons of camp stew which suffices to feed the Grass Valley crowd and the special five gallon caldron which is always made for Mr. Tom Bourne. The hunters began straggling in about 2 o'clock, and by 3 all had returned, bringing in in toto some fifteen dozens of doves together with many rabbits. The game was all cleansed and dumped into the caldron which was already simmering. After the seething mess had boiled and bubbled until the peppers and the onions were thoroughly disseminated, the game and chickens cooked just right, the bacon and potatoes done to a toothsomeness, fit for Rev. Mr. Bowman or any other connoisseur, the hundred hungry sportsmen grabbed each his pannikin and set about that stew in a way to recall the King of the Cannibal Islands. An hour of quiet munching and sipping and sighing and smacking and calling for more followed, until there was no more stew nor any bread, nor even tea or anything in the jugs, and a melancholy settled down over the outfit broken only by a consentaneous convulsive sob as Fletcher and two or three other jokers falsely so called attempted to say funny things. The evening shadows gathered and through them sportsman after sportsman stole silently away to assimilate stew until the fall when the club again will gather at Van Slyke's to pour other oblations to Diana.

The match between Messrs. C. B. Smith and C. J. Haas and Crittenden Robinson and Ed Fay is off.

The organization styled the Sportsman's Protective Association of California has issued a pamphlet, the central idea of which is to discourage the formation and maintenance of clubs of sportsmen which shall lease or acquire by purchase and preserve suitable tracts of ground or water upon which to hunt. The pamphlet is a rehash of what has been said from time to time by one or two rather thoughtless and inconsiderate sportsmen's journals. There is no argument in it and the sentiment is rot. The Protective Association has neither sympathy nor support at the hands of sportsmen generally. Its animus is unworthy, its methods are questionable, and it is, altogether, a good thing to let alone severely.

In sending a report of the Portland Tournament, Major S. I. Kellogg, adds these characteristic notes:

"Oregon and Washington full of woods. Woods full of shooters. Shooters full of "get there" and enthusiasm. California boys here, full of "get left" and despair. Cadman shooting like a sky rocket. Your humble servant sampling local mud and soup with a big and varied stock to draw from.

Tournament a success. "Walk around" system used to everyone's satisfaction. No live birds to be had for love or money. Peoria blackbird used exclusively. Everybody asking "Where's that duffer Maynard?" We sympathize with friend Cadwallader in his trouble and miss him. Where's Dr. Taber and all the other California shots who ought to be here? This is a great country. You should be here to sample the strawberries and see the pretty girls. Du Bray says, "Come to breakfast" No more. Yours, ready! pull!!"

The supervisors of Lake County have changed the game law for that county so that the open season for quails is from August 20th to March 1st. For deer, from June 1st to October 15th.

Mr. W. J. Fox, the affable and popular book keeper at Messrs Clabrough, Golcher and & Co's. returned from his first wedding trip on Wednesday last. Seasonable compliments are offered to him and the favored help-meet.

Rarely indeed is it that the same photographic plate imprints the counterfeit presentment of an individual with an interval of fifty years between the pictures, yet such appears upon a photograph recently received by Mr. E. T. Allen of this City from John P. Lovell of the John P. Lovell Arms Co., of Boston. Mr. Lovell was born in Braintree Mass. on July 25th 1820. Commenced business in Dock Square, Boston, on June 13th 1840 on which day he had a daguerreotype made of himself, which shows a pleasant faced, bright-eyed shock headed, chokered young man in decidedly antique costume. He has remained in business in Boston ever since, and on June 13th 1890, just fifty years after beginning business, he was again photographed. The picture showing a portly, slightly bowed, bald-headed., firm jawed, shrewd looking old gentleman of seventy years. The employes of his firm feted him at the Quincy House in Boston, on the fiftieth anniversary of his business life, and presented to him a beautiful, gold-headed, ebony cane. He was then invited to the residence of his son, Col. Ben. S. Lovell, in East Weymouth, where forty or more of his associates of his early business life had gathered to do honor to their old friend. Such an occasion must have been one of great interest. Mr. Lovell is of that sterling type of business men now fast passing away, whose ambition was first to preserve business honor inviolate, second to deal only in articles of excellence, and thirdly to extend business connections only by legitimate means.

THE KENNEL

Dog owners are requested to send for publication the earliest possible notices of whelps, sales, names claimed, presentations and deaths, in their kennels, in all instances writing plainly names of sire and dam and of grandparents, colors, dates and breed.

Muzzling Hounds.

EDITOR BREEDER AND SPORTSMAN:—In your issue of 14th, I read an article on muzzling greyhounds. You are correct. It is just as natural for a hound to pick up a hare as it is for a cat to catch a mouse. Give it to the cranks when they go after legitimate sport. W. GREGG.

KNIGHTS LANDING, Cal.

Chorea.

EDITOR BREEDER AND SPORTSMAN:—Would you kindly in your next issue furnish me a prescription for my eight months old English setter. He has had distemper for the past two weeks and now I notice that his muscles keep twitching most of the time. I believe they call this symptom by the name of Chorea, but I have been unable to find any treatment for it. Would you please furnish me with one through your next issue. J. A. CANFIELD.

[Our correspondent prescribes no easy task when he desires specific instruction for the cure of Chorea. The constitutional condition of which Chorea is a symptom is one that too often has its origin in congenital weakness, excessive mentality, what might be called hyperæsthesia or excessive nervousness, with corresponding weakness of the digestive tract and excretories. It is a truism that a perfectly healthy dog will not be troubled by the twitching styled Chorea, but in a general way it may be suggested, as it has been in these columns from time to time that the feeding of proper food, including meats and bones, access to pure water, with a few doses of cod liver oil and hypophosphites, and perhaps the administration of some alterative and tonic such as strychnia, in combination with iron or quinia, are as likely to correct the general condition of the dog as any other lines of treatment. Success is more probable in the case of young animals than in those which have gone beyond a year in age. If in a litter the Choresic tendency is manifested generally, it is probably the best course to destroy those dogs affected, and in the future breeding, select some other sire. Life is too short to make it worth while to tinker with a twitching, weakly, badly nourished beast that at best is only capable of slight exertion and is liable at any time to fits or utter failure of the vital powers. It seems hardly possible that if our correspondent's dog has been sick only two weeks he should have more than passed the acute stage of his distemper, and we strongly advise that the dog be taken to the infirmary of Dr. Masoero, at 811 Howard street, and left there for treatment.—KEN. ED.]

Mr. B. F. Seitner of the Idstone Kennels, Dayton, Ohio, sends his last catalogue and announcement which may be had on application to him.

Mr. J. Martin Barney still has two Pointer puppies by Tom Pinch—Galatea which he offers for sale. They should be pretty to look at and good ones to go.

Attention is called to an advertisement of native foxhounds which appears in another column. The dogs are young, of the black and tan sort, and very good looking.

The movement in behalf of a inter-state coursing meeting is going along smoothly. Mr. Dominick Shannon reports several hundred dollars already subscribed and is sanguine the amount will reach at least $3,000. The coursing will be done at Merced and if the stake money or purses are large enough, plenty of entries may be looked for from other States and there is little doubt that if invited, Col. North and some of the other leading English coursers would send over dogs. Why does not Mr. Henry Wormington import some of the grand dogs which he saw recently in England? Such an enthusiast is fairly entitled to the best dog to be had any where.

Kennel readers will regret to learn that the pointers expected by Mr J. M. Bassford, Jr., and Wm. Schreiber, from their brood animals, Beautiful Queen and Sal, did not appear. Queen had been bred to Mountain Boy, a nick which had produced Queen's Last, one of the best young dogs ever bred in the State a year ago, and Sal had been sent to Los Angeles to be bred to Mr Vandevort's Billy V. It was hardly expected that Queen would produce another litter, being very old, but Sal was relied upon for some splendid youngsters. Both animals gave every indication of being in whelp.

It is proposed to initiate coursing at Coronado. Mr. F. B. Baldwin, manager of the Coronado Race Track, writes that there are about 5,000 hares on the island and that he proposes to organize a coursing club. He will find active co-operation at the hands of Mr. Babcock, of the Coronado Hotel, and other sport loving gentlemen in the vicinity.

Judge Pushall makes a long and labored statement in his own behalf in the last American Field as to his relations with and views about the American Kennel Club. The statement lacks the accuracy, clearness and convincing quality of most of the writings of that brilliant man. It is to be regretted that he remains at outs with the Kennel world.

The Spaniel Club is increasing its membership rapidly. Those desiring to join may send applications to H. P. Rennie, at 37 Sixth St., Oakland.

A letter from Bakersfield informs us that quails are exceedingly plenty this year; on the Field Trial ground particularly, bevies are large and numerous. Bakersfield is fast resuming its position as the banner town of Central California for energy, public spirit and general attractiveness. Its young business men are of the rarest excellence. One of them, Mr. Henry L. Borgwardt is to be made Sheriff for the coming term barring political mishaps. His determination, thorough acquaintance with Kern Co., absolute integrity and general popularity will go far to secure general support for him. We extend the heartiest wishes for his success.

Mr. F. B. Dexter, manager of the Grand Central Hotel at Fresno and owner of several fine pointers and setters, visited San Francisco last week, partly to attend to business affairs and partly to select a few new songs to be sung at the next Field Trial. One of the most touching sights we remember was Mr. Dexter as he marched up and down through the muddy streets at Bakersfield last January dressed in his best suit of clothes, and warbling Annie Rooney, without regard for the sanitary future of the city, the expostulations from the police or the evident terror of all the inhabitants within hearing. He spent an evening at Mr. Schreiber's while here with Mr. Linville, Mr. Sanderson and a few more, and we have not learned whether his remains have since been identified yet or not.

GRAND COAST CIRCUIT

FOR 1890.

TROTTING, PACINC AND RUNNINC.

Over $50,000 in Purses.

ENTRIES CLOSE AUGUST 1st, 1890.

SAN JOSE, August 12th to 16th.

SPEED PROGRAMME

—OF THE—

San Mateo & Santa Clara County AGRICULTURAL ASSOCIATION No. 5,

—AT—

SAN JOSE, CAL.

TUESDAY, AUG. 12TH.

No. 1. Trotting Purse, $1,000; 2:20 Class.
No. 2. Trotting Purse, $1,000; 2 27 Class.
No 3. Trotting District Infant Stake. Closed.

WEDNESDAY, AUG. 13TH.

No. 4. Running Stakes, a handicap sweepstakes for all ages; $50 entrance, $25 forfeit, $200 added; $75 to second horse, $50 to third. Weights announced Tuesday, Aug. 12th, at 10 A. M. Declarations due at 6 P. M. same day. Three-quarters of a mile.

No. 5. Running Stakes for two-year-olds; $50 entrance, $25 forfeit, $200 added; $75 to second horse, $50 to third. Seven-eighths of a mile.

No. 6. Running Stakes, a sweepstakes for three-year-olds; $50 entrance, $25 forfeit, $250 added, $75 to second horse, $50 to third. One and one-eighth miles.

No. 7. Selling Purse, $300; of which $50 to second horse, for all ages. Horses entered to be sold for $1 500 to carry rule weight, two lbs. for each $100 less down to $1,000, then one lb. for each $100 less down to $500. Horses entered not to be sold to carry five lbs. above the scale. Valuation on the starters only by 6 P. M., the day preceding this race. Mile heats.

THURSDAY, AUGUST 14TH.

No. 8. Trotting Purse, $1,000; three minute Class.
No. 9. Pacing Purse, $600; 2:30 Class.
No. 10. Trotting, Santa Clara County Stake for two-year-olds. Closed.

FRIDAY, AUGUST 15TH.

No. 11. Running Stakes, a handicap sweepstakes for all ages, $50 entrance, $25 forfeit, $250 added; $75 to second horse, $50 to third. Weights announced Thursday Aug. 14th, at 10 A. M. Declarations due at 6 P. M., same day. Two and one-fourth miles.

No. 12. Running Stakes, for all ages; $50 entrance, $25 forfeit, $[illegible] added; $75 to second horse, $50 to third. One mile.

No. 13. Running Stakes, a sweepstakes for three-year-olds; $50 entrance, $25 forfeit, $200 added, $75 to second horse, $50 to third. Winner of No. 6 to carry three pounds extra. One and one-fourth miles.

No. 14. Selling Purse, $300, of which $50 to second horse for all ages. Horses entered to be sold for $1 500, to carry rule weight, two lbs. for each $100, less down to $1,000, then one lb. for each $100 less down to $500. Horses entered not to be sold to carry five lbs. above the scale, valuation to be placed on the starters only by 6 P. M. the day preceding the race. Three-quarter mile heats.

SATURDAY, AUGUST 16TH.

15. Trotting Purse. $1,000; 2:24 Class.
16. Pacing Purse $1,000; free-for-all.
17. Trotting Purse $500; for District named horses. (Send for list.)

Races to begin each day at 2 P. M.

WM. BUCKLEY, President.

G. H. BRAGG, Secretary, San Jose.

NAPA, August 18 to 23.

SPEED PROGRAMME

—OF THE—

SOLANO AND NAPA Agricultural Associa'n

District No. 25.

FOURTH ANNUAL FAIR

—AT—

NAPA CITY.

TUESDAY, AUG. 19TH.

No. 1. Trotting, 2:20 Class; purse $1,000.

No. 2. Trotting, 2:30 class, guaranteed stake, $1,500 closed.

No. 3 Trotting District (Silas Skinner barred); 2:40 Class; purse $600.

No. 4. Trotting District, yearling stake guaranteed; $250; closed.

WEDNESDAY, AUG. 20TH.

No. 5. Running: three-fourths mile and repeat; $200 added.

No. 6. Running: one mile and repeat; $250 added.

No. 7. Running, one and one quarter mile dash; $300 added.

THURSDAY, AUG. 21ST.

No. 8 Trotting: three minute class; purse $1000.

No. 9. Pacing: 2:30 class; purse $600.

No. 10. Trotting District; three year old guaranteed stake $400, closed.

No. 11. Trotting District; two year old guaranteed stake $350; closed.

FRIDAY, AUG. 22ND.

No. 12. Running, one and one-half mile dash: $250 added.

No. 13. Running, one mile dash. Owners handicap; $150 added.

No. 14. Running; one half mile and repeat; $150 added.

SATURDAY, AUG. 23RD.

No. 15. Trotting: 2:24 class; guaranteed stake $1,500; closed.

No. 16. Pacing: Free for all; purse $800.

No. 17. Trotting, District; 2:25 class; purse $800.

REMARKS AND CONDITIONS.

In all running races whole amount of added money to first horse, two thirds entrance to second, balance to third.

In No. 12 weights to be handed to the Secretary by 6 o'clock the night before the race.

L. L. JAMES, President.

A. H. CONKLING, Secretary.

Box 218, Napa City.

PETALUMA, August 25th to 30th.

SPEED PROGRAMME

—OF THE—

SONOMA and MARIN Agricultural Assoc'n,

ANNUAL FAIR AT

PETALUMA.

TUESDAY, SEPT. 26TH.

1.—Two-year-old Trotting Stake. District. Mile and repeat. Closed May 1, 1890, with 24 entries .... $200 added
2.—2:20 Class; Trotting Purse $1200
3.—2:27 Class; Trotting Purse 800

WEDNESDAY, SEPT. 27TH.

4.—Yearling Trotting Stake. District. Mile dash Closed May 1, 1890, with 14 entries .... $100 added
5.—2:40 class Trotting Purse. District 600
6.—Free for all Trotting Purse 1200
7.—Pacing Purse for District Pacers that have never started in a race 400

THURSDAY, SEPT. 28TH.

8. 3.00 class Trotting Purse 800
9.—Three-Year-Olds. Free for all. Trotting. Closed May 1, 1890, with 5 entries 500
10.—Three-Year-Olds. Trotting. District. Closed May 1, 1890, with 9 entries 300
11.—2:30 Class Pacing Purse 800

FRIDAY, SEPT. 29TH.

12.—Running. All Ages. One and one-half mile dash 500
13.—Running. All Ages. One mile dash 400
14.—Running, All Ages. Three-quarter mile dash 300
15.—Running. Two-Year-Olds. Three quarter mile dash 400
16.—2:40 Class Trotting Purse 800

SATURDAY, SEPT. 30TH.

17.—Two-Year-Olds. Free for all. Trotting Purse Mile and repeat. Closed May 1, 1890, with 8 entries 400
18.—2:27 class Trotting Purse. District 500
19.—2.24 Class Trotting Purse 1000
20.—Free for all. Pacing Purse 1000

J. H. WHITE, President,

DR. THOS. MACLAY, Secretary, Petaluma.

OAKLAND, September 1st to 6th.

SPEED PROGRAMME

—OF THE—

GOLDEN GATE FAIR

District No. 1,

Oakland Race Track.

MONDAY, SEPT. 1, 1890.

1—THE DAWN three-year-old purse; 2:40 class; $600.
2—THE STAMBOUL purse; 2:27 class; $1,000.
3—THE ELECTIONEER purse; 2:20 Class; $1,200.

TUESDAY, SEPT. 2, 1890.

4—THE MOUNTAIN BOY Guaranteed Purse; 3:00 Class; Closed with 116 nominations; $1,200.
5—PACING purse; 2:30 Class; $800.

WEDNESDAY, SEPT. 3, 1890.

RUNNING.

6—FIVE-EIGHTHS MILE—THE J. D. CARR free purse; $400; $50 to second, $25 to third; for two-year-olds. Winner of any two-year-old race after August 1st, when carrying weight for age or more, to carry three pounds extra; of two or more such races, five pounds extra.

7—THREE-QUARTER MILE HEATS—Free selling purse, $400; $50 to second, $25 to third; for three-year-olds and over. Horses entered to be sold for $1,200 to carry mile weights; two pounds allowed for each $100 less down to $300. No heat allowances.

8—ONE MILE—Free purse, $400; $50 to second, $25 to third; for three-year-olds and over. Beaten maidens, if three years old, allowed 7 pounds; if four years old or over, allowed 12 pounds.

9—NINE-SIXTEENTHS OF A MILE—Free purse, $300; $50 to second; for all ages.

THURSDAY, SEPT. 4, 1890.

10—THE GRAND MOON three-year-old new list trotting purse. Closed with seven nominations; $1,000.

11—THE HAWTHORNE 2:35 Class; trotting; purse $1,000.

12—THE GUY WILKES two-year-old trotting purse, $500.

FRIDAY, SEPT. 5, 1890.

RUNNING.

13—THREE-QUARTERS OF A MILE—THE GOLDEN GATE RIDING ACADEMY free purse, $400; $50 to second, $25 to third; for two-year-olds. Winner of the J. D. Carr purse at this meeting to carry three pounds extra.

14—ONE-HALF MILE HEATS—Free purse, $350; $50 to second; for three-year-olds and over. Weight for age.

15—ONE AND ONE-SIXTEENTH MILES—Free purse; $400; $50 to second, $25 to third; for all ages. Horses starting in No. 8 and not placed allowed five pounds.

16—FIFTEEN-SIXTEENTHS OF A MILE—Free selling purse, $400; $50 to second, $25 to third; for three-year-olds and over. Horses entered to be sold for $1,000 to carry weights; three pounds allowed for each $100 down to $300.

SATURDAY, SEPT. 6, 1890.

17—THE DIRECTOR 2:24 Class; trotting; purse $1,200.
18—THE SIDNEY Free-for-all pacing; purse $1,000. (Yolo Maid and Adonis barred.)

MONDAY, SEPT. 8, 1890.

RUNNING.

19—SEVEN-EIGHTHS OF A MILE—Free purse, $400; $50 to second, $25 to third; for two-year-olds. Winner of the J. D. Carr purse at this meeting allowed two pounds; of the Golden Gate Riding Academy purse, four pounds. A horse winning both these races allowed nothing; all others allowed seven pounds below the scale.

20—ONE MILE AND 100 YARDS—Free Selling purse, $400; $50 to second, $25 to third. Horses entered to be sold for $1 000, to carry mile weights; three pounds allowed for each $100 down to $300.

21—FIVE-EIGHTHS OF A MILE—Free purse, $300; $50 to second; for three-year-olds and over. Winner of No. 9 to carry five pounds extra.

22—ONE MILE AND A QUARTER—THE LELAND STANFORD free purse, $400; $50 to second, $25 to third. A handicap for all ages. Weights announced Saturday, Sept. 6th, at 10 o'clock A. M. Declarations due at 6 P. M. the same day.

TUESDAY, SEPT. 9, 1890.

23—THE DEXTER PRINCE 2:40 Class Guaranteed Purse, $1,200. Closed.

24—THE MAMBRINO WILKES 2:30 class; for four-year-olds; purse; closed with 17 nominations; $900.

EXHIBITION TROT—For a sulky, set of harness and gold medal for the three-year-old beating Sable Wilkes' record. If two or more start, the one making the fastest time to win.

CONDITIONS.

In the running races, four or more horses to start will be required. The Directors reserve the right to change the order of the events in case any fail to fill, or to substitute other races for such as do not receive the required number of entries.

In selling purses, the selling price must be named through the entry box at 6 o'clock P. M. the day before the race.

R. T. CARROLL, President.

JOS. I. DIMOND, Secretary.

308 Market Street, S. F.

Remarks and Conditions.

The district races for the Napa and Petaluma Fairs are open to the Counties of Sonoma, Marin, Napa, Solano, Mendocino, Lake, Yolo and Colusa. Unless otherwise ordered by the Board no horse is qualified to be entered in any District race that has not been owned by a resident in the District six (6) months prior to the day of the race, and any entry by any person of any disqualified horse shall be held liable for the entrance fee contracted, without any right to compete for a purse, and shall be held liable to penalties prescribed by the American Trotting Association and Rules of the Pacific Coast Blood Horse Association and expulsion from this Association.

All trotting and pacing races mile heats, best three in five, unless otherwise specified; five to enter and three to start; the Board, however reserves the right to hold a less number than five to fill.

Entrance ten per cent. of purse, to accompany nomination.

Purses divided into four moneys, of which fifty per cent. shall go to the first horse, twenty-five per cent. to the second, fifteen per cent. to the third, and ten per cent. to the fourth.

A horse distancing the field entitled only to first and third money.

The Directors reserve the right to change the hour and day of any race, if deemed necessary.

Entries not declared out by 6 P. M. of the day preceding the race shall be required to start.

When there is more than one entry to a purse or stake by one person or in one interest, the horse to be started must be named by 6 P. M. of the day preceding the race.

Any race that cannot in the opinion of the judges, be finished on the last day of the meeting, may, at their option, be continued or declared off.

Trotting and pacing colors shall be named with the entries, and MUST be worn upon the track.

American Trotting Association rules shall govern all trotting and pacing races, and Pacific Coast Blood Horse Association rules all running races. Suspensions from Associations working under American rules recognised.

Colt stakes to be governed by the conditions under which they were advertised.

Races shall commence each day at 1 o'clock P. M. sharp.

Stables, hay and straw free.

ENTRIES CLOSE AUGUST 1, 1890, with the Secretaries.

SPEED PROGRAMME
OF THE
Nevada State Agricultural Society.
Sept. 22nd to 27th inclusive, 1890, at
RENO, NEV.

FIRST DAY, MONDAY, SEPTEMBER 22.

No. 1.—Selling purse, $200, of which $50 to second, $25 to third; for three-year-olds and upwards; horses entered to be sold for $1,500 to carry rule weights; two pounds allowed for each $100 down to $1,000, then one pound for each $100 less down to $400; selling price to be stated through entry box at 6 P. M. the day before the race. One mile.

No. 2.—Running stake; two-year-olds. Five-eighths of a mile; $200 added; $50 entrance; $15 forfeit; second horse to save entrance.

No. 3.—Running; purse $250. One and one-quarter miles; $70 to second, $30 to third.

SECOND DAY, TUESDAY, SEPT. 23.

No. 4.—Running. Half mile and repeat; purse $200, of which $50 to second.

No. 5.—Pacing. Class 2:20; purse, $1,200; $700 to first, $300 to second, $150 to third.

No. 6.—Trotting; three-minute class; district horses. Purse $300; $150 to first, $100 to second, $50 to third.

THIRD DAY, WEDNESDAY, SEPT. 24.

No. 7.—Running stake, three-year-olds. One and one-quarter miles; $250 added; entrance $50; forfeit $10; second horse to save entrance.

No. 8.—Running. Seven-eighths of a mile. Purse $300, of which $70 to second, $30 to third.

No. 9.—Trotting, class 2:30; purse $500; $300 to first, $150 to second, $50 to third.

No. 10.—Trotting, three-year-olds; best two in three; purse $300; $100 to first, $75 to second, $25 to third.

FOURTH DAY, THURSDAY, SEPT. 25th.

No. 11. Running. Five-eighths of a mile; purse $250, of which $50 to second.

No. 12. Trotting, 2:25 Class; purse, $1,000; $600 to first, $300 to second, $100 to third.

No. 13. Trotting. 2:40 Class, district horses; purse $300; $150 to first, $100 to second, $50 to third.

FIFTH DAY, FRIDAY, SEPT. 26th.

No. 14. Running Stake, two-year-olds, seven-eighths of a mile; $200 added; $50 entrance, $15 forfeit; second horse to save entrance.

No. 15. Running. One mile, for three-year-olds; purse $300, of which $50 to second.

No. 16. Running. Seven-eighths of a mile; purse $300 of which $70 to second, $30 to third.

No. 17. Trotting, 2:20 class; purse, $1,200; $750 to first horse, $300 to second, $150 to third.

SIXTH DAY, SATURDAY, SEPT. 27th.

No. 18. Trotting, 2:30 class; purse, $800, $500 to first, $200 to second, $100 to third.

No. 19. Pacing, 2:30 class; purse, $1,000; $600 to first, $300 to second, $100 to third.

REMARKS AND CONDITIONS.

Nominations and entries to all stakes and purses must be made to the Secretary on or before the 15th day of August, 1890. Entries for the purses must be made two days preceding the race at the regular time for closing entries as designated by the rules. Those who have nominated in stakes must name to the Secretary in writing which they will start the day before the races at 6 P. M. Horses entered in purses can only be drawn by consent of the Judges.

Entries to all trotting races will close August 1st, with the Secretary.

Five or more to enter and three or more to start in all trotting races.

National Trotting Association Rules to govern trotting races. Pacific Coast Blood Horse Association Rules to govern running races.

All trotting and pacing races are the best three in five, unless otherwise specified; five to enter and three to start. But the Board reserves the right to hold a less number than five to fill, by the withdrawal of a proportionate amount of the purse. Purse to be divided pro rata. Entrance fee, 10 per cent. on purse, to accompany nomination.

National Association Rules to govern trotting; but the Board reserves the right to trot heats of any two classes alternately, if necessary to finish any day's racing, or to trot a special race between heats. A horse making a walk over shall be entitled only to the entrance money paid in. When less than the required number of starters appear, they may contest for the entrance money, to be divided as follows: 66⅔ to the first and 33⅓ to the second.

In divided purses no horse shall receive more than one money.

In all the foregoing stakes the declarations are void unless accompanied by the money.

Please observe that, in the above stakes, declarations are permitted for a small forfeit.

In all running races entries not declared out by 6 P. M. of the day preceding the race shall be required to start.

Where there is more than one entry by one person, or in one interest, the particular horse they are to start must be named by 6 P. M. of the day preceding the race. No added money paid for a walk-over.

Racing colors to be named in entries.

In trotting races drivers will be required to wear caps of distinct colors which must be named in their entries.

Each day's races will commence promptly at one o'clock P. M.

All entries must be directed to C. H. Stoddard, Reno, Nevada.

W. H. GOULD, President,

C. H. STODDARD, Secretary.

STOCKTON FAIR FOR 1890.

September 23 to 27, 1980
(Inclusive.)

Races Races

Five Days Racing. Eleven Days Fair
CLOSING OCTOBER 4, 1890.

Entries for each race herein named close July 1, '90.

ADDITIONAL PROGRAMME WILL BE ISSUED ABOUT JULY 1ST.

TUESDAY, September 23, 1890.

No. 2—Running, Amador Stake; for all ages; open to Amador, Calaveras, San Joaquin and Stanislaus counties. $20 each for all starters; $150 added. Second horse half of entrance money. One mile.

No. 4—Trotting. 3:00 class. GUARANTEED PURSE........................$1,000

WEDNESDAY, September 24, 1890.

No. 8—Trotting. 2:25 class. GUARANTEED PURSE........................$1,000

THURSDAY, September 25, 1890.

No. 12—Trotting. Four-year-old or under. Purse $500. Open to Amador, Calaveras, Tuolumne, and all San Joaquin Valley counties. Four moneys.

FRIDAY, September 26, 1890.

No. 19—Trotting. 2:30 class. GUARANTEED PURSE........................$1,000

SATURDAY, September 27, 1890.

No. 23—Trotting. 2:40 class. GUARANTEED PURSE........................$1,000

Conditions.

Horses for Races Nos. 2 and 12 must have been owned in the counties named six months prior to the day of the race. *Five or more to enter 3 or more to start.*

Guaranteed Purses—Entrance 10 per cent. of purse, payable as follows: July 1st, 1890, with entry $30; August 1st, $35; September 1st, $35, *when horse must be named.* Neglect of above requirements will forfeit entry and previous payments. Eight entries required, four making final payment; three or more to start. Four moneys.

All other conditions, as appears in National Trotting Association Revised Rules, subject to full conditions of this Association published in our Speed Programme of 1890, will govern.

L. U. SHIPPEE, President.

J. M. LARUE, Secretary, P. O. Box 188, Stockton, Cal.

Races, Races,
JULY WEEK.
AT
South Park Race Track
Eureka, Cal.
GIVEN BY THE
EUREKA JOCKEY CLUB.

FIRST DAY, JULY 2, 1890.

No. 1. Novelty Running Race. Free for all. Dash of one mile. Purse $250. First quarter, $40. Half, $50. Third quarter, $70. Mile, $90.

No. 2. Running Race. Purse $150. Five-eighths dash, for two-year-olds. $125 to first horse; $25 to second horse.

No. 3. Running. Purse $150. Three-quarters and repeat. $125 to first; $25 to second.

SECOND DAY, JULY 3, 1890.

No. 4. Trotting. Purse $200. Three minute Class. $150 to first; $50 to second. (Covey barred.)

No. 5. Running Stake. Five-eighths of a mile. For Humboldt raised two year-olds. $50 entrance, half forfeit. $150 added. First to receive 60 per cent.; second, 30 per cent., third, 10 per cent.

No. 6. Running Stake. Purse $250. Mile Dash. $150 to first horse; $50 to second horse.

THIRD DAY, JULY 4, 1890.

No. 7. Trotting Stake. 2:40 Class. Purse $250. $200 to first horse; $50 to second horse.

No. 8. Running Stake, 1¼ miles. Free-for-all. $40 entrance, ¼ forfeit, $200 added; second horse $75, third horse to save stake.

No. 9. Running Stake. Purse $150; 1-2 mile and repeat; $125 to first; $25 to second.

FOURTH DAY, JULY 5, 1890.

No. 10. Running Stake, 1-2 mile and repeat; for Humboldt horses owned prior to Jan. 1, 1890. $125 to first, $25 to second.

No. 11. Running Stake. Purse $200; 7-8 mile and repeat. $150 to first, $50 to second.

CONDITIONS AND REMARKS.

All trotting races are best three in five, unless otherwise specified. Four to enter and three to start, but the Board reserves the right to hold a less number than four to fill by the withdrawal of a proportionate amount of the purse. Entrance fee, 10 per cent. of purse, to accompany nominations. In all trotting races the rules of the American Trotting Association, and all running races the rules of the Pacific Coast Blood Horse Association to govern, but the Board reserves the right to trot heats of any two classes alternately, if necessary, to finish any day's racing. In all entries not declared out by 6 P. M. of the day preceding the race, shall be required to start.

No added money paid for a walk over. In all races, four or more paid up entries required to fill, and three or more horses to start. Racing colors to be named in entries. In trotting races drivers will be required to wear caps of distinct colors to be named in entries. Entries in all races to close with the Secretary, Thursday, June 26, 1890. Entry blanks will be furnished upon application to the Secretary.

All trotting races for horses owned and in Humboldt County prior to June 1, 1890.

H. M. DEVOY, President.

J. F. MONROE, Secretary.

SONOMA and MARIN
Futurity Stake,
To take place during the
FALL MEETING
OF THE
Sonoma and Marin Agricultural Society,
1893.
For Foals of 1890.

Open to the get of stallions owned in the district which is comprised of the following counties: Sonoma, Marin, Napa, Lake, Mendocino, Solano, Yolo, Colusa and Contra Costa.

Mile heats, 3 in 5; entrance $75, with $25 added for each starter over two and up to five head, and $10 for each additional starter up to ten head.

Payments: $5 must accompany the nomination on July 1, 1890; $5 on January 2, 1891; $5 on July 1, 1891; $10 on January 2, 1892; $10 on July 1, 1892; $15 on January 2, 1893; $25 on July 1, 1893.

CONDITIONS.

1—Neglect to provide payments on the dates stipulated will incur forfeiture of all previous payments.

2—When there is more than one entry to this stake by one person or in one interest, the horse to be started must be named by 6 P. M. of the day preceding the race.

3. The stake will be divided into four moneys, viz., 50 per cent. to the first, 25 per cent to the second, 15 per cent. to the third and 10 per cent. to the fourth horse.

4. If only three horses start in this stake, only the first, second and third money shall be paid; if but two start, there will be no added money, the stake money paid in will be divided—two-thirds to the first and one third to the second horse.

5. A horse distancing the field shall only be entitled to first and third moneys.

6. The Board of Directors reserve the right to declare the stake filled or not filled without binding itself to any specified number of entries.

7. Otherwise than the above, National or American Trotting Association Rules—as this Society may select—will govern the stake.

Entries to close on July 1st with the Secretary.

J. H. WHITE, President,

DR. THOMAS MACLAY, Secretary, Petaluma.

Vineland Stock Farm
Alcona 730.
Sire of

FLORA BELLE - - - - Record 2:24
CLAY DUKE - - - - - " 2:31½

ALCONA will be a great sire, but four of his colts have ever been trained, and all have shown full miles better than 2:35, and two of them as good as 2:30. Two of his first sons each sired a colt as a two-year-old, and last season one as a four-year-old trotted a full mile in 2:22½, and the other, a three-year-old, a mile in 2:31. With opportunities, Alcona is destined to be one of Almont's best sons. Almont, for his opportunities, is beyond doubt the most prepotent sire of his age. He has 36 representatives in the 2:30 list; 49 sons and 22 daughters that have already produced 2:30 performers. Almont died five years ago at 20 years old. If he lived he would be but 25 years old.

PEDIGREE.

ALCONA sired by the great Almont (sire of Westmont 2:13¾, Fanny Witherspoon 2:16¼, Piedmont 2:17¼, and 34 others with records better than 2:30, and grandsire of Belle Hamlin 2:12¾, etc.); by Alexander's Abdallah (sire of Goldsmith Maid 2:14), he by Rysdyk's Hambletonian. Alcona's dam, Queen Mary, by Mambrino Chief (sire of Lady Thorne 2:18 1-4, and 5 others in the 2:30 list, and sire of the dams of Director 2:17, Piedmont 2:17¼, Onward 2:25 1-4, Red Wilkes Almont, Belmont and many other noted sires).

DESCRIPTION.

Alcona is a beautiful chestnut 16 3 1-2 hands high, and weighs 1300 lbs. His colts possess speed, style, finish and beauty, and if they don't trot they command the highest prices for carriage horses.

$40 for the season. Usual return privilege.

Season of Alcona and Grandissimo ends July 1st, 1890.

Grandissimo,
Full Brother to GRANDEE, 3-year old record 2:23 1-2.

Sired by La Grande (son of Almont, and out of Jessie Pepper by Mambrino Chief; Jessie Pepper is the dam of Jone 2:17 1-2, Alpha 2:23 1-2, Sterling Wilkes 2:31¼, and others) dam Norma, by Arthurton (sire of Arab 2:15, Joe Arthurton 2 20 1-2, etc.)

Grandam Nourmahal, (full sister to A. W. Richmond, sire of Arrow 2:13¾, Romero 2:19, and sire of Columbine, dam of Anteeo 2:16¼, and Antevolo 2:19¼ at four years old).

DESCRIPTION.

Grandissimo is four years old, will make a sixteen hand horse; he is a rich mahogany bay in color and perfect in style and action. $60 for the season. Usual return privileges.

"Grandissimo" with limited training last fall as a three-year-old, trotted quarters in 38 seconds and miles in 2:40.

I feel confident that he will trot fast this season, and will be a great sire as his colts this season are all grand youngsters.

The best of pasturage $4 per month. Mares taken care of in any manner that owners may desire, but no responsibility assumed for escapes or accidents.

For further particulars send for circular or call at stables, one mile south of St. Helena.

FRED W. LOEBER Prop'r.

Sunny Side Breeding Farm.
Admiral 488.
Foaled 1867—Sired by Volunteer 55' Son of Rysdyk's Hambletonian 10.

First dam Lady Pierson by Cassius M. Clay (Neaves') 20; second dam by Diamond; third dam a running mare said to be thoroughbred. He is fitted in an eminent degree to produce colts that will in all respects justify his patrons in their expectations.

Admiral is the sire of Huntress, record 2:27¼, Sister, 2:19½, Perhelion, 2:25, Nona Y., 2:25, and others equally as promising, but have not had the advantage of track work. He will serve a limited number of approved mares at $50 the season, with usual return privilege. Season ending August 1, 1890. No liability for accidents or escapes.

KING DAVID 2576.
Bay Stallion—Foaled 1883.

Sired by Admiral 488, dam Black Flora (the dam of Huntress, 2:27¼, Sister, 2:19½, Perhelion, 2:25, Nona Y., 2:25), by Black Prince.

King David is one of the best gets of Admiral. He has a good disposition, kind to drive, smooth and even-gaited, and can speed fast. Barring accidents, he will trot in the twenties this Fall. His colts are large, rangy, and well finished. Will serve a limited number of mares at $30 the season, to end July 1, 1890. Every precaution will be taken to prevent accidents and escapes, but no liability will be assumed. Pasturage $4 per month.

Sunny Side Farm is situated two miles east of Vallejo, on the Sulphur Spring road. For further particulars, address

FRANK DRAKE,
Vallejo, Cal.

For Sale.
Brood Mare Corinne.

By Geo. C. Gorham; 1st dam Annie McCloud by Jack Hawkins Jr. son of Jack Hawkins thoroughbred 2nd dam by Belmont; will be sold with horse colt foaled June 1st. "De Corne Wilkes" by MAMBRINO WILKES 6083.

—ALSO—

Two-Year-old Brown Filly
AGNES F. WILKES,
And Yearling Black Colt
FERGUS WILKES,

By MAMBRINO WILKES, out of Corinne as above. Mare and colts can be seen at Oakland. For further particulars apply or address,

BREEDER AND SPORTSMAN
313 BUSH STREET S. F.

"Laurel Palace,"
ROME HARRIS, Proprietor.

N. W. corner Kearny and Bush Streets

SAN FRANCISCO.

PHIL J. CRIMMINS. JOHN C. MORRISON.

"Silver Palace,"
36 Geary Street,

San Francisco, Cal.

Stallions and Colts
For Sale.
The Get of the Celebrated Racing Stallion BAYSWATER.

FROM FINELY BRED MARES.

Inquire of

J. HEINLEN,
Lemoore, Tulare County, Cal.

The Trotting-Bred Stallion
RINGWOOD
THE FINEST SON OF THE NOTED SIDNEY,

Will make a Season at Oakland, commencing March 1, and ending June 1, 1890.

DESCRIPTION.

RINGWOOD is a dark, rich colored bay, black points, 15 1-2 hands, weight 1100 lbs., and a pure gaited trotter. Has shown great speed. He is now five years old. As a four year old he showed a trial in 2:19 1-2, and but for an accident would have received a record as a four year old of 2:25 or better.

PEDIGREE.

RINGWOOD is by Sidney, record 2:19 3-4, and is half brother to Gold Leaf 2:11 1-4, Adonis 2:11, Flee (two year old) 2:24, Longworth 2:19, Sister V. 2:27, Faustino, yearling, 2:35, Fleet, yearling, 2:35, Memo, three year old trial 2:20 1-2.

Sidney is by Santa Claus, record 2:17 1-2; he by Strathmore, sire of 31 in 2:30 list; he by Hambletonian 10, the greatest of all producers; he by Abdallah. Sidney's dam, Sweetness, record 2:21 1-4; she by Volunteer, the sire of St. Julien 2:11 1-4.

RINGWOOD'S dam Alma; she by Dashway, thoroughbred; he by Belmont, he by American Boy; he by Sea Gull; he by Imported Expedition. Alma's 1st dam, Fanny Cobb, was a great road mare, pedigree untraced.

TERMS: $50 for the Season.

Payable June 1st, or sooner if mares are taken away. Address communications to

A. C. DIETZ,
Oakland, Cal.

$15,000. OPENING $15,000.

of the

GRAND CIRCUIT.

The World's Fair goes to Chicago, but the Greatest Fair ever held in the West takes place at

Agricultural Park, Los Angeles, August 4 to 9, 1890.

Fifteen Thousand Dollars in Purses, Stakes and Premiums.

Speed Programme:

FIRST DAY—MONDAY AUGUST 4TH.

No. 1. The Los Angeles Derby.—A sweepstake for three-year-olds (foals of 1887), $10 each, half forfeit, with $500 added, the second to receive $100, and the third $50, out of the stakes; a winner of any three-year-old stake race to carry five (5) pounds, of two or more, eight (8) pounds extra; maidens allowed seven (7) pounds. One mile and a half.

No. 2. The Edwards & McKnight stakes.—A sweepstake for all ages; $50 each, half forfeit; $300 added, the second to receive $100 out of the stakes. Non-winners this year allowed seven pounds. Maidens allowed ten pounds. One mile.

No. 3. Trotting.—The Los Angeles Purse, $1,500, open to all horses eligible to the 2:30 Class, June 16th. Entrance, ten per cent, payable as follows: $50 June 16th, when entries close; $50 July 1st, and $50 July 22nd, when horses must be named. No subscription will be received unless the first payment shall accompany the same. Subscribers liable only for the amount paid in, but if a subscriber fails to make any of the payments when due, he shall surrender his subscription and payments to the Association with the right of substitution. The Board reserves the right to declare the "Los Angeles Purse" off, in the event of its not filling satisfactorily.

No. 4. Trotting.—Purse $500. 3 minute class. District.

SECOND DAY—TUESDAY AUGUST 5.

No. 5. A sweepstake for two-year-olds owned in the Southern Counties; $25 each, $15 forfeit; $150 added; the second to receive $75 out of the stakes. The winner of any race to carry four pounds extra. One-half (½) mile.

No. 6. The Nadeau Hotel Handicap.—Purse $1,000, of which $700 to the first; $200 to the second; and $100 to the third horse. Weight announced July 22nd. Twenty-five dollars ($25) to nominate, and fifty dollars ($50) each from all starters. The winner of any race after the anouncement of the weights to carry five (5) pounds extra. One and one quarter mile.

No. 7. Trotting.—Two-year-old stakes, district, $250 added. See special condition.

No 8. Pacing.—Purse $500. 2:25 Class. District.

THIRD DAY—WEDNESDAY, AUG. 6TH.

No. 9. Selling Purse—For all ages, $250. Ten Dollars from starters to go to second horse. Fixed valuation $1000; three pounds allowed for each $100 less down to $700; then one pound for $100 down to $300; selling price to be named through the entry box at 5 P. M. the day before the race. Seven-eighths of a mile.

No. 10. Hurdle Race—A sweepstake for all ages: $30 each, half forfeit; $200 added; second horse to receive $75 out of the stakes. Five hurdles—about one and one half miles.

No. 11. Trotting—Three-year-old Stake, District $250 added. See special conditions.

No. 12. Trotting.—Purse $1000. 2:25 class.

FOURTH DAY—THURSDAY AUG. 7TH.

No. 13. The Hollenbeck Hotel Stakes—A sweepstake for two-year-olds (foals of 1888), $50 each, $20 forfeit; with $300 added, the second to receive $100, and the third $50 out of the stakes. A winner of any stake race before August 1st, to carry three pounds; and two or more stake races, five pounds extra; maidens allowed, if beaten once, five pounds; twice or more, eight pounds. Five-eighths of a mile.

No. 14. The Southern California Handicap.—Purse $1000, of which $700 to the first, $200 to the second, and $100 to the third horse. Weights announced July 22nd. $25 to nominate, and $50 more for all starters. The winner of any race at this meeting to carry five pounds extra. Three-quarters of a mile.

No. 15. Trotting—Purse $1000, 2:27 class.

No. 16. Trotting—Purse $500, 2:40 class; District.

FIFTH DAY—FRIDAY, AUGUST, 8TH.

No. 17. The Sierra Madre Stakes.—A sweepstake for all ages. $25 each, half forfeit; $200 added, second to receive $75 out of the stakes. Winner of any race this year at three-quarters (¾) of a mile or less to carry six (6) pounds, and of two or more of such races, ten (10) pounds extra. Maiden allowed ten (10) pounds. One-half (½) mile heats.

No. 18. Santa Catalina Cup.—A sweepstake for all ages. $40 each; $20 forfeit; $300 added; the second to receive $100 out of the stakes. Five pounds above scale. Non-winners in 1889 and 1890 allowed ten (10) pounds. Maidens allowed twelve (12) pounds. A winner at this meeting to carry five pounds extra. One and one-eighth (1⅛) mile.

No. 19. Trotting.—Purse, $1,000, 2:20 class.

No. 20. Trotting.—Purse, $500. 2:50. District.

SIXTH DAY—SATURDAY, AUG. 9TH

No. 21. The Citrus Handicap.—A sweepstake for three-year-olds; $40, half forfeit, or only $10 if declared by 5 P. M. the day before the race; $250 added; the second to receive $100 out of the stakes. Weights to be announced by 5 o'clock P. M., second day before the race. One and one-sixteenth (1 1-16) of a mile.

No. 22. The Junior Handicap.—A sweepstake for two-year-olds. $40 each, half forfeit, or only $15 if declared by 5 P. M. the day before the race; $300 added; the second to receive $100, and the third $50 out of the stakes. Weights to be announced by 5 o'clock P. M. the second day before the race. Three-quarters (¾) of a mile.

No. 23. Trotting.—Purse $800, 2:35 class.

No. 24. Pacing.—Purse, $500, 2:25 Class.

TROTTING STAKES—To close June 16th, 1890.

To be Trotted at the Annual Fair, to be held in Los Angeles in 1890–91.

TROTTING STAKES, 1890.

FOALS OF 1888. Mile and repeat, $250, added by the Association. Entrance, $50, payable in the following forfeits: $10 to accompany the nomination, $20 July 1st, and $20 August 11, 1890.

FOALS OF 1887. Mile heats, three in five. $250 added by the Association. $50 entrance, payable in the following forfeits; $10 to accompany the nomination, $20 July 1st, and $20 August 11, 1890.

TROTTING STAKES, 1891.

FOALS OF 1889. Mile and repeat. $250 added by the Association. $50 entrance, payable in the following forfeits: $5 to accompany nomination, $10 August 1st, 1890; $10 May 1st, 1891, and $25 on the first day of the Fair of 1891.

FOALS OF 1888. Mile heats, three in five. $300 added by the Association. Entrance, $50, payable in the following forfeits; $5 to accompany the nomination; $10 August 1st, 1890; $10 May 1st, 1891, and $25 on the first day of the Fair of 1891.

CONDITIONS.

All nominations to be made on or before June 16th. American Association rules to govern. Nominators liable only for the amount paid in, which becomes forfeit if subsequent payments are not made. All forfeits and entrance fees will be contributed to the stake, the whole divided where there are three or more starters as follows: sixty per cent. to the first, thirty per cent. to the second and ten per cent. to the third. If no more than two horses start, only first and second money shall be awarded, and in case of a walk over, only the first money shall be awarded. A horse distancing the field shall only be entitled to so much of the money as the starters in the race could have won. A nominator in making an entry in any of the above stakes shall give the name of owner, name of breeder and where foaled, the age, color, sex, dam and sire if known. Colts owned in the Counties of San Luis Obispo, Fresno, Tulare, Kern, Santa Barbara, Ventura, Los Angeles, San Bernardino, Orange and San Diego shall be eligible to entry.

REMARKS AND CONDITIONS.

All trotting and pacing races to be to harness, mile heats, best three in five, except otherwise specified. Entrance 10 per cent on amount of purse. Trotting and pacing divided as follows: 50 per cent. to first horse; 25 per cent. to second; 15 per cent. to third, and 10 per cent to fourth. Entries not declared out by 6 P. M. of the day before the race must start. In all trotting and pacing races, five to enter and three to start. The Board reserves the right to hold a less number than five to fill. Horses owned in Fresno, Tulare, Kern, San Luis Obispo, Santa Barbara, Ventura, Los Angeles, San Bernardino, Orange and San Diego Counties, are eligible for entry in district races. A horse distancing the field is entitled to first and fourth money. The Directors reserve the right to change the hour and day of any race, if deemed necessary. Races shall commence each day at 1 o'clock. American Association rules to govern, unless otherwise specified. Hay and straw free.

Running—The Pacific Coast Blood Horse rules to govern running races. Colonial-bred horses, foaled on Colonial time, allowed as follows: Two and three-year-olds, eight pounds; four-year-olds, five pounds, and five-year-olds, three pounds. In all stakes, starters must be named to the Secretary or through the entry box at the track, on or before 6 P. M. of the day before the race. In all stakes, the right to forfeit ceases at 10 o'clock of the day on which the race is run. Racing colors to be named with the entry. Entries close with the Secretary July 1st.

Remember, entries for the 2:30 Trot and District Trotting Stakes close June 16th, and for everything else July 1st.

L. LICHTENBERGER, President.

BEN BENJAMIN, Secretary.

SAN DIEGO, 8776.

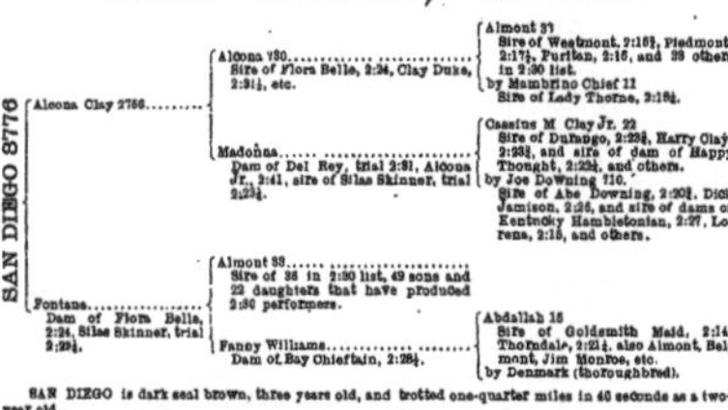

SAN DIEGO is dark seal brown, three years old, and trotted one-quarter miles in 40 seconds as a two-year old.

This grand young horse, and, barring accidents, will make a fast record next fall.

He will be allowed a limited number of mares; at $60 for the season. Mares not proving in foal to be returned free 1891. Best of pasture for mares at $4 per month, but no liability for accidents or escapes.

He will make the season from February 1st to June 1st at Napa Fair Grounds. For further particulars, address or call on

H. B. STARR, Race Track, Napa, Cal.,

or FRED W. LOEBER, St. Helena.

GRAND MOOR, 2374.

Grand Moor 2374	Moor 870 Sire of Beautiful Bells ... 2:29½ Sire of Sable (dam of Sable Wilkes) 2:18 Sire of Sultan ... 2:24 Sire of Tommy Gates ... 2:24 Sire of Del Sur ... 2:24½ Sire of Sir Guy ... 2:28½ Beautiful Bells is the dam of Hinda Rose, 2:19½ as a 3-year-old, Palo Alto Belle, 2:22½, Chimes, St. Bell, 2:24½, Bell Boy (3 years) 2:19½. Sultan, 2:24 (sire of Stamboul 2:12½) has 19 in 2:30 list.	Clay Pilot 93 Sire of 2 in 2:30 list. Belle of Wabash.
	Vashti Dam of Don Tomas, who got a record of 2:20 in 1889.	Mambrino Patchen 58 Sire of 14 in 2:30 list Sire of the dam of Guy Wilkes, 2:15½; also sire of 20 stallions and 18 mares with get in 2:30 list. Kate Taber By Mambrino Messenger, he by Mambrino Paymaster.

Foaled 1876. Black. Sixteen hands high. Bred by L. J. Rose

A horse of highest form and quality; of great excellence in every point; a type of his celebrated family; of marked individuality, spirit and endurance; never properly trained or raced, but shows the possession of great speed; perfectly manageable in the stable and on the road and track.

As he is sired by The Moor 870, a son of CLAY PILOT, out of Vashti by MAMBRINO PATCHEN, he is a most valuable cross for mares of other families. THE MOOR sired Beautiful Bells and the dams of Sable Wilkes and Margaret 2:28 (dam of Regal Wilkes, 2-year-old record 2:20¼).

MAMBRINO PATCHEN is regarded as the unsurpassed sire of broodmares, having, among many others, sired the dam of Guy Wilkes and of Wm. L (the sire of Axtell), and a son of his sired the dam of Axtell. The public sales this year have demonstrated with renewed emphasis the value of The Moor and Mambrino Patchen strains of blood. For combining particularly with the Hambletonians it may be called "the ready money cross."

GRAND MOOR will make the season of 1890 for a time at the Oakland Race Track and afterwards at my Ranch, fifteen miles from Oakland. Mares can be delivered at the race track to the groom in charge. Pasture at $5 per month. For other food, if requested, an additional charge will be made.

TERMS, $150 for the season, with privileges of return if the horse does not change hands.

Every care exercised, but no liability for escapes or accidents.

H. I. THORNTON, 504 Kearny Street.

Highland Farm,

LEXINGTON, KY.,

Home of Red Wilkes.

Standard-bred Trotting Stock

For Sale,

Sired by Red Wilkes. Wilton, 2:19¼; Allandorf and Sentinel Wilkes, out of highly bred Standard Mares of the most fashionable blood of the day.

W. C. FRANCE, Proprietor.

HORSES PURCHASED ON COMMISSION.

THOROUGHBREDS A SPECIALTY.

Will select and buy, or buy selected Animals for all desiring, for reasonable compensation.

KEEPS PROMISING YOUNGSTERS IN VIEW.

L. M. LASLEY, Stanford, Ky.

References:—J. W. Guest, Danville, Ky.
B. G. Bruce, Lexington, Ky.
S. H. Baughman, Stanford, Ky.
G. A. Lackey, Stanford, Ky.
Geo. McAlister, Stanford, Ky.
First National Bank, Stanford, Ky.

For Sale.

JUANITO ALMONT

Sire of Almont Patchen, 2:15.

JUANITO ALMONT is a bright bay, 16-1 hands in height, and weighs 1,200 pounds.

PEDIGREE.

By Tilton Almont, 2:26, he by the great Almont 33; dam by Signal 3327; he by Bunday's Rob Roy.

JUANITO ALMONT, if given a chance would undoubtedly prove a great sire, and should prove a desirable acquisition to any stock farm in the State.

For further particulars address

T. B. COOPER,

Adin, Modoc County, Cal.

FOR SALE.

ALAMEDA LILY

Five Year-Old Pacing Mare.

Record 2:39.

Sired by WASHINGTON, Record 2:21; dam by GENERAL TAYLOR.

CAN SHOW A 2:20 GAIT,

And can be seen at the stables of

C. O. THORNQUEST,

Race Track, Oakland,

Memo.

The Best Son of SIDNEY

Will Make the Season of 1890 at the OAKLAND RACE TRACK

MEMO

- SIDNEY 2:19¾
  - Santa Claus 2000, 2:17 1-2, Sire of San Mateo, 2:28 1-4, Sidney, 2:19¾.
    - Strathmore 408, Sire of 31 in 2:30 list, Sire of 6 dams of 8 in 2:30, Sire of 3 sires of 3 in 2:30
      - Hambletonian 10, Sire of 41 in 2:30 list, Sire of 107 sires of 587 in 2:30 list, Sire of 44 dams of 50 in 2:30 list.
        - Abdallah 1.
        - Chas. Kent mare.
      - Lady Waltermire, Dam of Marshal Ney 2081.
        - North America.
        - s. t. b. Hambletonian 2 mare.
    - Lady Thorne Jr., Dam of Mollie Mack, 2:33
      - Mambrino (Williams)
        - Ericsson 130.
        - Daughter of Aratus (thoroughbred).
      - Kate
        - Highland Chief.
        - Halcorn mare (Magowan's).
  - Sweetness 2:21 1-4
    - Volunteer 55, Sire of 29 in 2:30, Sire of 21 of 48 in 2:30, Sire of 16 dams of 16 in 2:30.
      - Hambletonian 10, Sire of Geo. Wilkes 2:22
        - Abdallah 1.
        - Chas. Kent. mare.
      - Lady Patriot
        - Young Patriot.
        - Lewis Hulse mare.
    - Lady Merritt
      - Edward Everitt 81, Sire of 13 in 2:30, Sire of 8 sires of 16, Sire of 6 dams of 7.
        - Hambletonian 10.
        - Margrave mare, s.t.b.
      - Daughter of
        - Harry Clay 45. Sire of 2 in 2:30, Sire of dam of Electioneer, St. Julien, etc.
- FLIRT
  - Buccaneer 2656, Sire of Shamrock, 2 y. o., 2:25, Flight, 2:29, (dam of Fleet, 2:24), Dams of George V., 3 y. o., 2:31 1-2, Creole, 2:20.
    - Iowa Chief 528, Sire of Consanol, 2:24 1-2
      - Bashaw 50, Sire of 16 in 2:30, Sire of 10 sires of 20 in 2:30, Sire of 11 dams of 15 in 2:30.
        - Black Hawk (Vernol's).
        - Belle.
      - Topsey
        - Prophet, by Vermont Black Hawk 5.
    - Tinsley Maid
      - Flaxtail 8132, Sire of dam of Gold Leaf, 2:11, Apex, 2:26, Flight, 2:29, J. H. McCormack, 2:29, Shamrock, 2:25.
        - Pruden's Blue Bull.
      - Fannie Fern
        - Irwin's Tuckahoe.
        - dam of Leffiers' Consul.
  - Mahaska Belle
    - Flaxtail 8132 s. t. b., Sire of grandams of Fleet, 2:24, Creole, 2:20.
      - Prudens' Blue Bull, Sire of Blue Bull 75, Sire of 58 in 2:30.
        - Merring's Blue Bull.
    - Lady Hake
      - John Baptist
      - Fannie Fern
        - Irwin's Tuckahoe.
        - dam of Leffiers' Consul.

MEMO is, as can be seen at a glance, one of the best bred young stallions in service, having three crosses of Rysdyk's Hambletonian and one of Harry Clay, the sire of Green Mountain Maid (dam of Electioneer, etc.), while Long Island Black Hawk and Flaxtail also contribute to his blood. Sidney (Memo's sire) is universally known as the best young sire in the world, a producer of extreme speed at an early age.

PERFORMANCES.

MEMO trotted in public in his two-year-old form, obtaining a record of 2:49, though he was close to Grandee in a race on the Bay District Track, the second heat of which was made in 2:31 1-2, the first in 2:32. He exhibited phenomenal speed when three years old, and had it not been for a slight strain of his fore fetlock, there is little question that he would have shown in public very close to the best record. On the Oakland track he was timed a mile in 2:20 1-2, and frequently trotted quarters in from 32 1-2 to 34 seconds.

As a four-year-old Memo only started once—at Sacramento—when, although out of condition, he showed great speed, and improving as he went on, great hopes were entertained of his going well down in the 'teens at the P. C. T. H. B. A. meeting, but after showing several very fast miles his leg filled and he was laid up for the season. He is sixteen hands high, and of powerful build throughout. His color is a glossy black, with both fore-feet white. His disposition is all that could be desired, and his action superb. He is a sure foal getter, only one mare being reported not in foal during his last season.

TERMS, $100, with usual return privileges, for a limited number of mares. Season to close JUNE 15th, when he will be prepared for track purposes. Pasturage $4 per month. Have leased the cricket ground adjoining the track for pasturage, where there is fine food. Reasonable charges if fed hay and grain. Best of care taken of mares in any manner owners may desire, but positively no responsibility assumed for accidents or escapes. For further particulars address

J. P. KERR, 313 Bush Street, San Francisco,

or, JOHN ROWEN, Race Track, Oakland, Cal.

The Trotting Stallion

Silver Bow

Will make the season of 1890 at the Oakland Race Track.

PEDIGREE.

SILVER BOW 11706, two-year-old record 2:37, is by Robert McGregor 647, 2:17½ (sire of Bonnie McGregor, 2:13½, Earl McGregor, 2:21½, Mac D., 2:30, McGregor Boy, 2:29¼, Mark Time, 2:30, Roxie McGregor, 2:20½) by Major Edsall 2:21, 2:29, by Alexander's Abdallah 15—sire of Goldsmith Maid, 2:14—by Hambletonian 10—sire of Dexter, 2:17¼.

Robert McGregor's dam was Nancy Whitman by American Star 14, by Stockholm's American Star.

SILVER BOW'S first dam is Sadie by Hambletonian 10, sire of Geo. Wilkes, 2:22—sire of Guy Wilkes, 2:15¼—also Electioneer, sire of Sunol, three-year-old record, 2:10½, and Palo Alto, 2:12¾; second dam Lady Wynne by Wm. Welch 341; third dam Elenora Margrave by imp. Margrave.

DESCRIPTION.

SILVER BOW is a handsome bay, no white; 15-3¼ hands high; weighs 1075 pounds; of fine form, with the best of legs and a clean-cut, intelligent head. Is remarkably level-headed, seldom making a break; wears seven-ounce shoes in front. His record, 2:37, is no mark of his speed; he can beat 30 easy, and with his gilt-edge breeding, he is just what he ought to be, a trotter sired by a trotter whose dam was herself a trotter and his grandam the dam of two trotters. His dam Sadie being by Hambletonian 10, shows him to be bred from the cream of the trotting blood.

TERMS: $100 for the season. Mares not proving in foal returnable for the season of 1891 free of charge. Good pasturage and first-class care taken of mares for $5 per month. No responsibilities assumed for escapes or accidents. For further particulars, address

Limited to 15 approved mares.
Season to end June 1st, 1890.

P. J. WILLIAMS,
Care Race Track, Oakland, Cal.

THE HICKS-JUDD CO.

Successors to
HICKS & JUDD, Bookbinders,
and Women's Co-operative Printing Office.

Printers, Bookbinders,
Publishers,

23 First St., San Francisco.

BREEDERS' CATALOGUES A SPECIALTY.

Samuel Valleau. Jas. R. Brodie.

J. R. BRODIE & CO.,

Steam Printers,

—And Dealers in—

Poolseller's and Bookmaker's Supplies.

401—403 *Sansome Street, corner Sacramento, San Francisco.*

For Sale

A FIRST-CLASS

Napa County Farm

—OR—

STOCK RANCH,

800 Acres Improved,

SITUATED TWO AND A HALF MILES FROM NAPA CITY, with good roads leading thereto, a good hard finished house of nine rooms, with all modern improvements, streams running all summer, a great amount of live oak and black oak timber. It lies in a fruit belt, surrounded by fine vineyards and orchards growing upon the same quality of soil, and originally a part of this tract. About one-half hill, and one-half rolling land, but none of it is steep and all easily cultivated, splendidly situated for the breeding of fine horses. Price, $65 per acre. Further particulars given at this office.

BREEDER AND SPORTSMAN,
313 Bush St.

SOUTHER FARM

P. O. Box 208. San Leandro, Cal.

1½ miles northwest of San Leandro; 8 miles southeast of Oakland. Turn off county road between above places at "Stanley Road," ¼ mile north of San Leandro.

Horses boarded at all times in any manner desired. Best of care but no responsibility for accidents. Colts broken and handled for the road or track. Terms reasonable.

—:o:—

Glen Fortune,	Jester D,	El Benton,	Figaro,
By Electioneer.	By Almont.	By Electioneer.	Hambletonian 725
$50 for 1889.	$50 for 1890.	Limited to 5 mares.	Limited to 12 mares
		Book Full.	Book Full.

THE SOUTHER FARM

Has Green Feed the Year Round,

and feeds Hay in connection with the green feed, which a horse must have if he is to thrive. Every animal is given

A Dry, Warm Place to Sleep,

No matter how stormy the weather. All Stock under cover when it rains.

VISITORS WELCOME ANY DAY EXCEPT SUNDAY.

How to Get Stock to the Souther Farm.

The Souther Farm is one and a half miles northeast of San Leandro and eight miles southeast of Oakland. The stables are about one mile east of the County road, which runs between Oakland and San Leandro. The place to turn off is at Stanley Road, where a large signboard of the farm is placed. Guide boards will be found at every cross road. In any ordinary weather the roads are very good, and they are fairly good after the unusually heavy rainfall of the past winter.

All stock sent from San Francisco may be brought over by Garcia's Express, No. 3 Market street, San Francisco. They also have an order box outside of Hawley Bros.' Hardware house on the corner of Market and Beale streets. The express leaves San Francisco on the Creek route boat, which starts at 1:30, but all orders should be in the order box at Market and Beale streets by 10 o'clock, or at the office, No. 3 Market street, by 11 o'clock at the latest. In the case of very young or very valuable horses, the Souther Farm will send reliable men to lead or drive over any stock that will not lead behind a wagon. A small charge will be made in such cases, to cover the extra expense incurred.

Horses are very easily taken from Oakland to the farm, and where it is inconvenient for owners to bring them or send them, the farm will send after anything that is to come. On horses that stay three months or over there is no charge for getting or delivering. Where a horse stays a short time the actual time and expense only is charged to him.

Horses can be shipped by rail from almost all parts of the State to San Leandro. Always notify the Farm several days before shipping anything, and then men will be on hand to receive stock on arrival. The railroad station is but two miles from the Souther Farm, and the agent invariably gives immediate notice of the arrival of any stock consigned to the above farm, but when word is sent to the farm in good season by letter or telegram, the animals sent are saved waiting a couple of hours in the car.

Passenger trains leave San Francisco (from the broad gauge ferry) and First and Broadway, Oakland, at frequent intervals during the day. There are several trains from San Jose to San Leandro on both the broad and narrow gauge railroads; the broad gauge, by way of Niles, is much more convenient for getting to the farm. There are trains each day from Sacramento, Stockton and Livermore to San Leandro. In ordinary weather it is a short and pleasant drive from Oakland to the Souther Farm or from San Francisco to the Farm by way of the Creek route ferry boat. Always notify the Souther Farm just when you will arrive at San Leandro, and some one will meet you at the station. If you do not recognize the farm conveyance ask the stage driver, who will point it out.

Write to the above address for references, circulars and price lists. Terms reasonable.

GILBERT TOMPKINS, Proprietor.

Bay Rose.

REGISTERED No. 9814.

Record 2:20 1-2 Third Heat.

Will make the season of 1890, ending July 1st, at the SANTA ROSA STOCK FARM, (formerly Santa Rosa Race Track), SANTA ROSA.

DESCRIPTION.

BAY ROSE is a dark bay or brown, with black points, 16¼ hands high, and weighs 1150 pounds. He is remarkably intelligent, of good disposition, and a pure-gaited trotter. He was foaled in 1881. His colts are large, stylish, rangy animals, and inherit the qualities of speed and endurance.

PEDIGREE.

BAY ROSE 9814

- Sultan, 2:24, Sire of 19 in the 2:30 list.
  - The Moor 870, SIRE OF
    - Beautiful Bells 2:29½
    - Del Sur 2:24¼
    - Ines 2:30
    - Sir Guy 2:28¼
    - Sultan 2:24
    - Tommy Gates 2:24
  - Sultana.
- Madam Baldwin
  - The Moor 870, Sire of 6 in the 2:30 list.
  - by Ben Lippincott, by Williamson's Belmont.

TERMS: $200 FOR THE SEASON.

Good pasturage $3 per month. First-class care taken of mares in any manner that owners may desire, but no responsibility assumed for escapes or accidents.

Limited to a few approved mares.

For further particulars, address

THOS. BONNER,
Santa Rosa Stock Farm, Santa Rosa.

Or apply to
IRA PIERCE,
728 Montgomery Street, S. F., Cal.

The Trotting Stallion

VICTOR,

Record 2:22.

Will make the season of 1890 at NAPA CITY.

DESCRIPTION.

VICTOR is a handsome dark bay; 15-3 hands high; weighs about 1,100 pounds, and is remarkably intelligent, level-headed, of kind disposition, and a magnificent animal in every respect. He is well boned and muscled, of splendid conformation, and possesses the qualities of speed and endurance to an eminent degree—qualities that he imparts to his progeny.

PEDIGREE.

VICTOR, record 2:22

- Echo 462
  - Hambletonian 10, Sire of 42 in the 2:30 list.
    - Abdallah 1
    - Chas. Kent mare
  - Fanny Felter
    - Magnolia 68
    - by Webber's Kentucky Whip
- Daughter of
  - Woodburn
    - Lexington
    - Lula Horton
  - daughter of
    - Ashland
    - thoroughbred

ECHO is the sire of Belle Echo, 2:20, Senator, 2:21¼, Victor, 2:22, Gibraltar, 2:22¼, Echora, 2:23¼, Tippie, 2:25¾, Lohengrin, 2:27¼, Pasha, 2:27½, Elmonte, 1:29, Col. Hawkins, 2:29¼, Annie Laurie, 2:30, Economy, 2:30, Sam Lewis, pacer, 2:25.

TERMS—$60 FOR THE SEASON.

Mares not proving with foal may be returned next season free of charge, provided the horse remains the property of the present proprietor, and stands at the same place, otherwise money will be refunded. The best of care taken of mares in any manner that owners may desire, but no responsibility assumed for accidents or escapes. For further particulars, apply to or address

G. W. HUGHES, Agent,
G. A. DOHERTY, Proprietor. Napa City.

GEO. WASHINGTON.

11,623.

RECORD 2:30.

Bay colt, bred by Thomas Smith of Vallejo, Cal. Foaled 1886 by Mambrino Chief, Jr., 11,622, record 2:34 1-4. 1st dam Fanny Rose by Vick's Ethan Allen Jr, 2,903, sire of Prince Allen 2:27. 2nd dam Jenny Lind, thoroughbred, dam of Prince Allen 2:27. Will serve a limited number of mares at $50 for the season. Mares not proving with foal may be returned next season free.

Mambrino Chief, Jr.

11,622.

RECORD 2:34 1-4.

Sire of George Washington, record 2:30 at three years old. Bay horse bred by Rufus Ingalls of Belvadere, Ill. By McDonald Chief 3583. First dam Venus by Mambrino Patchen 58. 2nd dam by Wardlow's Shakespeare. 3rd dam Lone Gold 4th dam by Silver Heels. Has not been in the stud before. He was 8 years old when he served a few mares, and his colts all show good style and form.

Terms for the season $40. For further particulars see or address

THOMAS SMITH,
Vallejo, Cal.

The Fast Trotting Stallion

REDWOOD.

Four-Year-Old Record 2:24 1-2

Will make the season of 1890—February 1st to July 1st—at

SANTA ROSA.

REDWOOD is a dark bay colt, 15.2¼ hands high, weighs 1100 lbs. Foaled in 1885 by Anteeo, 2:16¼, sire of Alfred G., 2:19¾. Anteeo is by Electioneer. First dam Lou Milton, by Milton Medium; second dam Old Fly, a thoroughbred mare brought from the East in 1871 by W. C. Ralston, Esq.

Redwood's sire was out of Columbine by A. W. Richmond, the sire of the pacers Arrow 2:13¾, and Elwood 2:28, and the trotters Romero, 2:19¾, and Len Rose, 2:27. Redwood has shown a quarter in 33 seconds.

Terms $100

For the season. Mares not proving with foal may be returned next season free of charge, provided Redwood remains the property of the present owners. Good pasturage at reasonable rates. No responsibility assumed for escapes or accidents. Service fees payable before removal of the mare. Limited to 40 approved mares. For further particulars address

A. McFADYEN.
Santa Rosa, Cal.

Cook STOCK FARM.

Season of 1890.

STEINWAY 1808.

Three-Year-Old Record 2:25 3-4.

Sire of STRATHWAY, three year old record 2:26, and sire of the dam of BOURBON RUSSELL 2:30.

By STRATHMORE 408; sire of 31 in the 2:30 list; sire of 6 dams of 8 in the 2:30 list, and sire of 3 sires of 3 in 2:30 list.

1st dam ABBESS (dam of Solo 2:28, and Soprano, dam of C. F. Clay 2:18, Eminence 2:27 and Strathbridge, 3 year old record 2:28½) by ALBION, sire of VANITY FAIR 2:26½, and of the dam of FAVORITE 2:25½.

2nd dam by MARSHALL NEY.

3rd dam by BERTRAND, a son of SIR ARCHY.

TERMS—$100 for the season.

CHARLES DERBY 4907

Brown Horse, Foaled 1885.

By STEINWAY 1808.

1st dam by the great ELECTIONEER, sire of SUNOL 3 year old record 2:10½, Palo Alto 2:12¾, etc., etc.

2nd dam FANNY MALONE, by NIAGARA.

3rd dam FANNY WICKHAM, by HERALD.

4th dam by Imp. TRUSTEE.

TERMS—$100 for the season.

Pasturage $5 per month. Accidents and escapes at owner's risk. Mares consigned to the farm should be sent to Fashion Stables, Oakland; Geary & Grindle's Stable, Haywards; or to Bennett's Stable, Martinez; from and to which places they will be delivered free of charge. Address

COOK STOCK FARM,
Danville, Contra Costa, Co., Cal.

For Sale.

PHILOSOPHER,

BAY COLT; FOALED 1886; BRED BY Z. E. SIMMONS, LEXINGTON, KY.

Sired By Pilot Wilkes 2987.

SON OF GEORGE WILKES, 2:22.

WHOSE SONS HAVE SIRED

Axtell (3 y. o.)	2:12	Allerton (3 y. o.)	2:18¼
Roy Wilkes	2:12½	William H.	2:18¼
Rosalind Wilkes	2:14¼	Garnet	2:19
Prince Wilkes	2:14¾	Repetition (4 y. o.)	2:19¼
Alcryon	2:15¼	J. R. Shedd	2:19¾
Oliver K.	2:16¼	David Wilkes	2:19¼
Phil Thompson	2:16¾	Sharper	2:19
Houri	2:17	Georgiette	2:19¾
Ione	2:17¼	Butterfly	2:19¾
Lillian Wilkes (3 y. o.)	2:17¾	Silverone	2:19¾
Mabie Wilkes (3 y. o.)	2:18	Veritas	2:20

Regal Wilkes (2 y. o.) ..... 2:25¾.

1st dam Bella .... by George Wilkes 519, record 2:22, sire of Harry Wilkes, 2:13½, Guy Wilkes, 2:15¼, Mike Wilkes, pacer, 2:15¾, Wilcox, pacer, 2:16, Wilson, 2:16¼, So So, 2:17¼, J. B. Richardson, 2:17½, etc.

2d dam Fly .... by Bell Morgan 61, sire of Lady Turpin, 2:22, and the dam of Onslaught, 2:28¼.

Pilot Wilkes, by George Wilkes, 2:22, sire of 69 from 2:13½ to 2:30, and the dams of 21 from 2:21¾ to 2:30.

First dam Grace by Pilot Jr., sire of the dams of Maud S., 2:08, Jay-Eye-See, 2:10, etc.; 2d dam by Orphan Boy, pacer.

NOTE.—Here is another inbred Wilkes with superb out-crosses through both sire and dam. Has never been trained. Price $1,000. SOUND. To be seen at

GEO. E. GUERNE,
Santa Rosa, Cal.

For Sale

A HALF BROTHER TO

ALMONT PATCHEN,

(2:15, trial 2:13 3-4).

JUANITO JR. is a beautiful bright bay, black points, with no white, foaled 1886. As a colt he has given much more promise than did Almont Patchen at the same age. Instead of being a pacer, he is a good square trotter, with every indication of great speed, and is so gentle and kind, that a lady can drive him. The owner's only reason for selling him is that business calls him away from this section of the State. He will be sold at a reasonable figure. This is a splendid opportunity for a gentleman to secure a first-class trotter at a very low figure.

The pedigree of Juanito Jr. is by Juanito (sire of Almont Patchen), dam Nettie Moore by Old Tom Moore. For further particulars, address

JUANITO JR.,
Santa Clara P. O., Cal.

John D. Gall. Jas. P. Dunne

"The Resort,"

No. 1 Stockton Street, cor. Ellis,

San Francisco.

Poplar Grove Breeding FARM.

Standard-bred Trotters, Colts and Fillies.

The get of CLOVIS, 4909; PASHA, 2039; APEX, 2935,

For Sale.

Address S. N. STRAUBE, Poplar Grove Breeding Farm,
Fresno, Cal.

Inspection by intending purchasers invited, and information by mail.

The PARKER Hammerless Shot Gun.

At the Annual Tournament of 1889, held at Cannes, France the grand prize, consisting of 2000 Francs and a Valuable Cup, was won by The Parker Hammerless.

The first Parker Hammerless Gun made won the championship of America at Decatur Illinois.

SEND FOR ILLUSTRATED CIRCULAR.

PARKER BROS., Makers,

New York Salesroom, 97 Chambers St. Meriden Conn.

BOYCE TABLETS.

Leg and Body Wash.

THE BOYCE TABLETS are packed in a nicely decorated metal box with hinged lid—one hundred tablets in each box; directions for use plainly engraved upon the box; therefore, the convenience of the package—no liability to leakage and breakage—economy and ready solubility, together with the absolute certainty of their action, will at once commend the use of BOYCE'S TABLETS to the intelligent horsemen of the country. TABLETS sufficient to make one hundred pints of leg and body wash are conveniently carried in an inside coat pocket or in the hip-pocket of the trousers.

The BOYCE WASH can be applied ALL OVER THE BODY WITHOUT FEAR OF BLISTERING NOR DOES IT AFFECT THE KIDNEYS.

The BOYCE WASH will cure CRACKED HEELS, PUFFS, STOCKINGS, SCRATCHES, INFLAMED TENDONS and FEVERED LEGS.

Price per Box of One Hundred Tablets, $2, sent postpaid to any part of the United States; six boxes for $10. A sample of BOYCE'S TABLETS will be mailed to any address on application. These TABLETS are warranted to keep in any climate. Address

BOYCE TABLET COMPANY,
600 Wabash Avenue, - - - Terre Haute, Indiana.

J. A. McKERRON, Pacific Coast Ag't,
228-230-232 Ellis Street, San Francisco, Cal.

GOLDEN EAGLE HOTEL

Corner SEVENTH and K STREETS,
SACRAMENTO.

FIRST CLASS IN EVERY RESPECT.

The LARGEST and FINEST HOTEL in the City.

W. O. BOWERS, Proprietor.

Free 'Buss to and from the Hotel.
Telephone, Telegraph Office and Messenger Service at Hotel

Fine Hats,

Latest Styles and Colors.

Meussdorffer & Hubner

8 Kearny Street, San Francisco.

Next to New Chronicle Building

The Only S. B. Nolan

JOCKEY, BICYCLE AND BASE BALL UNIFORMS.

Mail Orders. 426 Montgomery Avenue, S. F., Cal.

"BERTON SEC,"

The Wine of the "Upper Ten"

Is used EXCLUSIVELY at the "White House" by both the President and vice-President, Messrs. Harrison & Morton, and the members of the Cabinet, and most Senators in Washington serve it at their receptions, and such gentlemen as Hon. Chauncey M. Depew, Hon. Andrew Carnegie, Cornelius N. Bliss, and others of equal note use it, and declare it to be the best WINE they ever drank.

EM. MEYER & CO., AGENTS,
415—417 Pine Street.

Breeders and Horsemen

ATTENTION!

New Stake Entry Register.

Keep track of your entries and avoid neglect and oversight when payments and declarations fall due. Register covers trotting and running stakes. Most simple and convenient in keeping, and far superior to any in the market. 100 pages; cloth bound. Price $2. Send 1 cent stamp for sample sheet. Address,

S. C. FERGUSON,
Menlo Park, Cal.

"Del Monte."

Finest Wines and Liquors.

No. 1 GRANT AVENUE,
Corner O'Farrell Street,

CALEY & ROEDER, Proprietors.

Elegant Accommodations.

KENNEL ADVERTISEMENTS.

In the Stud.

"DAN GLADSTONE,"

3377 A. K. C. S. B.

BY CH. GLADSTONE—CH. SUE.

Winnings—Southern Trials, 1888, Divided Third.
Indiana Trials, 1889, Divided Third.
Southern Trials, 1889, Second.

Will be at Stud in San Francisco until Sept 15, 1890. Fee, $75.

GEO. J. HARLEY, 844 Harrison St., S. F.

DOGS---Pointer Pups

FOR SALE.

Sure Bench Show and Field Trial Winners, as they have more bench-show and field-trial blood in them than any that have ever been whelped on the Pacific Coast.

Sire, POINT, double field trial winner; he by Vandevort's Don, great field trial and bench show winner, out of Drab, field trial and bench show winner.

Dam, QUEEN CROXTETH by Bush T., bench show winner, out of Champion Patti Croxteth, field trial and bench show winner. This is the best pointer blood in the world. Breeding and health guaranteed. Address,

A. B. TRUMAN,
1425 Steiner St., near Ellis, S. F., Cal.

CALIFORNIA SPANIEL KENNELS,

Oakland, California, H. P. RENNIE, Prop. Breeder and importer of typical COCKER SPANIELS. Winner of first prizes at S. F. and Los Angeles, 1889; also, Columbus, 1889, New York, 1887. In the stud, solid Black Cocker dog, GIFFEE, won 1st and Gold Medal at S. F., 1889. Fee, $25. Puppies and grown dogs at reasonable prices. My dogs can neither talk nor climb a tree, but are fielders and prize winners.

37 Sixth St., Oak Street Station.

ECHO COCKER KENNELS,

STOCKTON, CAL.

A. C. DAVENPORT, - - - Proprietor.

Has some fine Cocker Puppies for Sale now, by his solid black Cocker Spaniel, Prize Winning Stud Dog Bronte, A. K. C. S. B., 17,081, (Brant—Mollie) out of registered bitches, for $10 and $20. Stud fee $20.

POINTERS FOR SALE.

FINE POINTERS whelped May 26, 1890, by Don (Climax—Drab D), out of Diana (Professor—Belle H). Correspondence solicited.

V. S.

BREEDER AND SPORTSMAN, 313 Bush street, City.

THE BOHANON SULKY!

BEST MADE.

Perfect Riding Buggies.

Breaking Carts.

Fine Repairing. Reasonable Prices.

Bohanon Carriage Co., 161-165 Ogden Ave., CHICAGO.

Send for Catalogue.

NOW IN THE LEAD.

J. O'KANE,
Harness and Turf Goods,
767 MARKET STREET, S. F.

Largest Stock. Lowest Prices.

Send for New Catalogue.

JOHN FORGIE,

Importing Tailor,

204 Montgomery Street,

N. E. corner Bush, SAN FRANCISCO.

BERGEZ'S

RESTAURANT.

FIRST-CLASS. *Charges Reasonable.*

Private Rooms for Families.

332—334 Pine St., below Montgomery St.

JOHN BERGEZ, Propr

VISIT GETTYSBURG
And MUSEUM,
MARKET AND TENTH STREETS,
SAN FRANCISCO, CAL.

Southern Pacific Co.

(PACIFIC SYSTEM.)

Trains leave and are due to arrive at San Francisco.

LEAVE (FOR)	FROM JUNE 15, 1890.	ARRIVE (FROM)
7.30 A M	Haywards, Niles and San Jose	*12.45 P M
7.30 A M	Sacramento and Redding, via Davis	7.15 P M
7.30 A M	Sacramento, Auburn, Colfax	4.40 P M
8.00 A M	Martinez, Vallejo, Calistoga and Santa Rosa	6.15 P M
9.00 A M	Los Angeles Express, Fresno, Bakersfield, Mojave and East and Los Angeles	10.15 A M
8.30 A M	Niles, San Jose, Stockton, Ione, Sacramento, Marysville, Oroville and Red Bluff	4.45 P M
10.30 A M	Haywards and Niles	3.45 P M
12.00 M	Haywards, Niles and Livermore	8.45 P M
*1.00 P M	Sacramento River Steamers	**6.00 A M
3.00 P M	Haywards, Niles and San Jose	9.45 A M
3.30 P M	2d Class for Ogden and East	9.45 P M
4.00 P M	Sunset Route, Atlantic Express Santa Barbara, Los Angeles, Deming, El Paso, New Orleans and East	8.45 P M
4.00 P M	Martinez, Vallejo, Calistoga and Santa Rosa	9.45 A M
4.05 P M	Lathrop and Stockton	10.15 A M
4.30 P M	Sacramento and Knight's Landing via Davis	10.15 A M
* 4.30 P M	Niles and Livermore	* 8.45 A M
* 4.30 P M	Niles and San Jose	‡ 6.15 P M
6.00 P M	Haywards and Niles	7.45 A M
7.00 P M	Shasta Route Express, Sacramento, Marysville, Redding, Portland, Puget Sound & East	7.45 A M
8.00 P M	Central Atlantic Express, Ogden and East	9.45 A M

SANTA CRUZ DIVISION.

LEAVE (FOR)		ARRIVE (FROM)
‡ 7.45 A M	Excursion train to Santa Cruz	‡ 8.05 P M
8.15 A M	Newark, Centerville, San Jose, Felton, Boulder Creek and Santa Cruz	6.20 P M
* 2.45 P M	Centerville, San Jose, Almaden, Felton, Boulder Creek and Santa Cruz	*11.20 A M
4.45 P M	Centerville, San Jose, and Los Gatos, and Saturday and Sunday to Santa Cruz	9. 0 A M

Coast Division (Third and Townsend Sts.)

LEAVE (FOR)		ARRIVE (FROM)
7.25 A M	San Jose, Almaden and Way Stations	2.30 P M
‡ 7.30 A M	Monterey and Santa Cruz—Sunday Excursion	‡ 8.25 P M
8.30 A M	San Jose, Gilroy, Tres Pinos; Pajaro, Santa Cruz; Monterey; Pacific Grove, Salinas, Soledad San Miguel, Paso Robles, Santa Margarita (San Luis Obispo) & principal Way Stations	6.12 P M
10.30 A M	San Jose and Way Stations	7.30 P M
12.01 P M	Cemetery, Menlo Park and Way Stations	5.13 P M
* 2.30 P M	Del Monte (Limited), Menlo Park, San Jose, Gilroy, Pajaro, Castroville, Monterey and Pacific Grove	*11.15 A M
* 3.30 P M	San Jose, Tres Pinos, Santa Cruz, Salinas, Monterey Pacific Grove and principal Way Stations	*10.00 A M
* 4.20 P M	Menlo Park and Way Stations	* 7.56 A M
5.20 P M	San Jose and Way Stations	9.03 A M
6.30 P M	Menlo Park and Way Stations	6.35 A M
†11.45 P M	San Jose and principal Way Stations	†4.25 P M

A M for Morning. P M for Afternoon.
*Sundays excepted. †Saturdays only. ‡Sundays only.
**Mondays excepted. §Saturdays excepted.

OCEANIC STEAMSHIP CO.

Carrying United States, Hawaiian and Colonial Mails.

WILL LEAVE THE COMPANY'S WHARF, foot of Mission Street, No. 1,

For Honolulu, Auckland and Sydney,

WITHOUT CHANGE,

The Splendid New 3,000-ton Iron Steamer.

ALAMEDA... Saturday, JUNE 28th, 1890, at 12 M., Or immediately on arrival of the English mails.

For Honolulu,

SS. AUSTRALIA (3,000 tons), June 20, 1890, at 12 M

☞ For freight or passage, apply at office, 327 Market Street. JOHN D. SPRECKELS & BROS. General Agents.

By-Laws

—AND—

Rules and Regulations

—OF THE—

NATIONAL

Trotting Association

REVISED FOR 1890,

ALSO THE

AMERICAN

Trotting Association,

AND THE

PACIFIC COAST BLOOD-HORSE ASSOCIATION.

With Betting Rules.

For Sale at the Office of the

Breeder and Sportsman,

313 Bush St., S. F., Cal.

Price, 25c. each.

By Mail, Postage Paid, 30c. each.

San Francisco and North Pacific Railway.

THE DONAHUE BROAD-GAUGE ROUTE.

COMMENCING SUNDAY, APRIL 27, 1890, AND until further notice, boats and trains will leave from and arrive at the San Francisco Passenger Depot, Market-street Wharf, as follows:

FROM SAN FRANCISCO FOR POINT TIBURON AND SAN RAFAEL.

Week Days—7.40, 9.20, 11.20, A. M.; 1.30, 3.30, 5.00, 6.15 P. M.

Sundays—8.00, 9.30, 11.00 A. M; 1.30, 3.30, 5.00, 6.15 P. M.

FROM SAN RAFAEL FOR SAN FRANCISCO.

Week Days—6.50, 7.55, 9.30, 11:40 A. M.; 1.40, 3.40, 5.05 6.25 P. M.

Sundays—8.10, 9.40, 11:10 A. M.; 1.40, 3.40, 5.00, 6 25 P. M.

FROM POINT TIBURON FOR SAN FRANCISCO

Week Days—7.15, 8.20, 9.55 A. M.; 12.05, 2.05, 4.05, 5.30, 6 50 P. M.

Sundays—8.35, 10.05, 11:35 A. M.; 2.05, 4.05, 5.30, 6:50 P. M.

Leave San Francisco. Week Days.	Leave San Francisco. Sundays.	Destination	Arrive San Francisco. Sundays.	Arrive San Francisco. Week Days.
7.40 A M 9.20 A M 3.30 P M 5.00 P M	8.00 A M 5.00 P M	Petaluma and Santa Rosa	10.40 A M 7.25 P M	8.50 A M 10.30 A M 4.40 P M 7 25 P M
7.40 A M 3.30 P M	8.00 A M	Fulton, Windsor, Healdsburg, Litton Springs, Cloverdale, and way stations.	7.25 P M	10.20 A M 7.25 P M
7.40 A M	8.00 A M	Hopland and Ukiah.	7.25 P M	7.25 P M
7.40 A M 3.30 P M	8.00 A M	Guerneville	7.25 P M	7.25 P M 10.20 A M
7.40 A M 5.00 P M	8.00 A M 5.00 P M	Sonoma and Glen Ellen	10.40 A M 6.05 P M	8.50 A M 6.05 P M
7.40 A M 3.30 P M	8.00 A M 5.00 P M	Sebastopol	10.40 A M 7.25 P M	10.30 A M 7.25 P M

Stage connects at Santa Rosa for White Sulphur Springs, and Mark West Springs; at Geyserville for Skaggs Springs, and at Cloverdale for the Geysers; at Hopland for Highland Springs, Kelseyville, Soda Bay, Lakeport and Bartlett Springs, and at Ukiah for Vichy Springs, Saratoga Springs, Blue Lakes, Willits, Cahto, Calpella, Potter Valley, Sherwood Valley and Mendocino City.

EXCURSION TICKETS from Saturdays to Mondays, to Petaluma, $1.50; to Santa Rosa, $2.25; to Healdsburg, $3.40; to Litton Springs, $3.60; to Cloverdale, $4.50; to Hopland, $5.70; to Ukiah, $6.75; to Guerneville, $3.75; to Sonoma, $1.50; to Glen Ellen, $1.80.

EXCURSION TICKETS, good for Sundays only, to Petaluma, $1; to Santa Rosa, $1.50; to Healdsburg, $2.25; to Litton Springs, $2.40; to Cloverdale, $3; to Guerneville, $2.50, to Sonoma, $1; to Glen Ellen, $1.20.

H. C. WHITING, General Manager.

PETER J. McGLYNN, Gen. Pass. & Tkt. Agt.

Ticket Offices at Ferry, 222 Montgomery Street and 2 New Montgomery Street.

The Park Training Stable.

CHAS. DAVID, PROPRIETOR.

Corner Grove and Baker Streets, near Entrance to Golden Gate Park.

EVERY FACILITY FOR TRAINING COLTS and taking care of Gentlemen's Roadsters.

Finely appointed stable with every convenience and sixteen roomy box stalls.

The best care given all horses by experienced help, under the personal superintendence of the proprietor.

Convenient to the Park Speed Drive, and Accessible to Six Lines of Cable Cars.

THE TRAINING OF COLTS AND ROADSTERS A SPECIALTY.

TROTTERS AND ROADSTERS FOR SALE.

HORSES SOLD ON COMMISSION

The proprietor trained and brought out the following well known horses: "Sister, Huntress," "Perihelion," "Nona Y," and others.

HEALD'S

Business College, 24 Post St.

—San Francisco.—

The most popular school on the Coast

P. HEALD, President. C. S. HALEY, Sec'y.

☞ Send for Circulars.

KILLIP & CO.,

LIVE STOCK AND GENERAL AUCTIONEERS,

22 Montgomery Street, San Francisco

SPECIAL ATTENTION PAID TO SALES OF

High-Bred Horses and Cattle.

At auction and private sale.

Will Sell in All Cities and Counties of the State.

REFERENCES.

HON. C. GREEN, Sacramento.	HON. J. D. CARR Salinas.
J. P. SARGENT, ESQ., Sargents.	HON. JOHN BOGGS Colusa.
HON. L. J. ROSE, Los Angeles.	HON. A. WALRATH Nevada.

J. B. HAGGIN, ESQ., San Francisco.

Represented at Sacramento by Edwin F. Smith Secretary State Agricultural Society.

At San Jose by Messrs. Montgomery & Rea, Real Estate Agents.

Being the oldest established firm in the live-stock business on this Coast, and having conducted the important auction sales in this line for the past fifteen years, amounting to one half a million of dollars, we feel justified in claiming unequaled facilities for disposing of live stock of every description, either at auction or private sale. Our list of correspondents embraces every breeder and dealer of prominence upon the Pacific Coast, thus enabling us to give full publicity to animals placed with us for sale. Private purchases and sales of live stock of all descriptions will be made on commission, and stock shipped with the utmost care. Purchases and sales made of land of every description. We are authorized to refer to the gentlemen whose names are appended.

KILLIP & CO., 22 Montgomery Street

RUB YOUR HORSES

In cases of **SWELLING** or **STIFFNESS OF THE JOINTS**, with

DARBY'S FLUID.

If you value your Horses, Dogs and Cattle always keep it on hand.

IT HAS NO EQUAL

For Cuts, Scratches, Bruises, Bites, Sores, Etc.

It gives immediate relief, and prevents Poison, Gangrene and Proud Flesh.

J. H. ZEILIN & CO., Philadelphia, Pa

SOLD BY ALL DRUGGISTS.

HORSE OWNERS!

TRY GOMBAULT'S

CAUSTIC BALSAM.

A Safe, Speedy and Positive Cure for Curb, Splint, Sweeny, Capped Hock, Strained Tendons, Founder, Wind Puffs, all Skin Diseases or Parasites, Thrush, Diphtheria Pinkeye, all Lameness from Spavin, Ringbone or other Bony Tumors. Removes all Bunches or Blemishes from Horses and Cattle.

Supersedes all Cautery or Firing. **Impossible to Produce any Scar or Blemish.**

Every bottle sold is warranted to give satisfaction. Price $1.50 per bottle. Sold by druggists, or sent by express, charges paid, with full directions for its use. Send for descriptive circulars. Address LAWRENCE, WILLIAMS & CO., Cleveland, O.

BROU'S INJECTION

A PERMANENT CURE in from 3 to 6 days, of the most obstinate cases; guaranteed not to produce Stricture; no sickening doses; and no inconvenience or loss of time. Recommended by physicians and sold by all druggists. J. Ferré, (successor to Brou), Pharmacien, Paris.

JUST OUT, 2d EDITION.

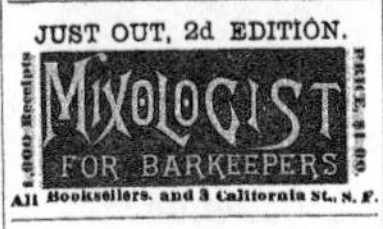

All Booksellers, and 3 California St., S. F.

R. LIDDLE & SON

538 Washington St., S. F.,

Wholesale and Retail Dealers in

Guns, Rifles and Pistols.

A Full Line of FISHING TACKLE and SPORTSMAN'S GOODS.

Orders by mail receive prompt attention.

6 DONTS

DON'T own a racehorse.
DON'T be a breeder.
DON'T be a trainer.
DON'T be a jockey.
DON'T bet on the races.
DON'T go to a race track.

WITHOUT

HAVING IN YOUR POCKET ONE OF

Goodwin's

ANNUAL

OFFICIAL TURF GUIDES.

Price, in cloth $2.00
Price, in half morocco 3.00
Price, in half calf 4.00

If sent by mail .... 10 cents extra

SUBSCRIBE TO IT FOR 1890.

It is published semi-monthly during the racing season, and is but $10 per year. Address

GOODWIN BROS.,

241 Broadway, New York City.

SUBSCRIBE FOR THE

Breeder and Sportsman.

VETERINARY.

Dr. Wm. H. Jones, M.R.C.V.S.

Veterinary Surgeon,

(OLYMPIC CLUB STABLES)

503 Sutter Street, San Francisco.

Telephone, No. 1404.

Consultations by letter, and cases of URGENT NECESSITY in the interior will receive prompt attention.

Dr. A. E. BUZARD,

VETERINARY SURGEON,

Member of the Royal College of Veterinary Surgeons, London, England. Graduated April 22d, 1870.

All Operations on the Horse Performed Skillfully.

Special attention given to the Diseases of Dogs. Calls to the country promptly attended to. Advice and prescriptions by mail $2. Office and Residence, No. 11 Seventh street, S. F. (opp. Odd Fellows Hall. Telephone No. 3 69.

W. H. WOODRUFF.

Veterinary Dentist,

AT FASHION STABLES,

221 Ellis Street, San Francisco

Improved Instruments, Humane Methods, First-Class Work.

H. E. CARPENTER,

Veterinary Surgeon,

Graduate of Ontario Veterinary College, Toronto Canada.

RESIDENCE AND VETERINARY INFIRMARY

331 Golden Gate Ave., San Francisco.

Telephone 3069.

☞ OPEN DAY AND NIGHT. ☜

No risk in throwing Horses. Veterinary Operating Table on the premises.

DR. C. MASOERO,

Veterinary Surgeon,

Successor to **DR. A. DeTAVEL,**

GRADUATE OF ROYAL VETERINARY COLLEGE, TURIN.

OFFICE AND INFIRMARY

No. 811 HOWARD STREET,

Between Fourth and Fifth. SAN FRANCISCO

Telephone, No. 457.

R. WATKINS,

Veterinary Dentist,

Office at C. S. Crittendens' Golden Gate Livery and Riding Academy, 24 to 28 Golden Gate Avenue.

Refers to Palo Alto Stock Farm: Wm. Corbett, San Mateo Stock Farm: B. C. Holly, Vallejo, and others. Examination Free.

E. J. O'ROUKE.

I have the honor to announce to my old patrons and the general public that I may be found at my old stand, where, as heretofore, the

Shoeing of Horses,

whether for the Track, Drive, or for general work will receive my personal attention.

Telephone 2011.

E. J. O'ROUKE,
209 Ellis Street

ST. JULIEN
Horse Shoeing
SHOP,

126 Geary Street, S. F.

MARTIN O'DEA, - - PROPRIETOR.

California Horse Shoe Co's

STEEL SHOE

Light, Strong and Perfect.

Superior to all others for Speed Horses.

ALSO

The Celebrated GOODENOUGH Pattern Shoe.

OFFICE: 203 Market St., San Francisco, Cal.

I have used in my business the Steel and Iron Shoes made by the above Company, and take great pleasure in saying they are the best I have ever used in twenty-two years' practice. I have never seen anything like the STEEL SHOE made by this Company. I can fully recommend them to every practical Horseshoer in the country.

Yours respectfully,

No. 8 Everett street. JOHN GRACE.

Old Hermitage Whiskies

"STEINER'S,"

No. 311 BUSH STREET,

San Francisco.

Under Breeder and Sportsman Office.

The Original and Only Genuine
CANADIAN HUNTING BOOTS

Moccasin Style.

New and Improved Styles. All Hand Sewed.

The most Popular Hunting Boot for Ladies and Gents in the Market

Prices Reduced. Quality Maintained.

These are the original Canadian Boots introduced by us nearly four years ago. They are made of waterproofed, oiled tanned material, which is manufactured especially for our Boots. The leg is made of selected alum tanned calfskin, laced up with bellows tongue. The bottom and uppers are one piece like an Indian Moccasin. The sole is sewed on by hand, to the sewed sole is added a tap sole and heel, studded with hunting hob nails. The Canadian Boot is very light. Ladies' and Boys' sizes being extra light and neat, and owing to its moccasin style is the most comfortable boot made. Men's boots weigh 3½ pounds per pair; Ladies' boots, 1½ pounds per pair. Men's high cut shoes, 2 pounds per pair. They are recommended by the hundreds of sportsmen and campers who use them. The Canadian Boot is very popular.

Ladies' Sizes, Nos. 13 to 6 .... Per Pair, $5.00
Men's Sizes, Nos. 5 to 11, Single Sole and Tap Sole and Heel .... " " 6.00
Men's Sizes, with Oak Tanned Double Sole, Tap and Heel .... " " 6.00
Canadian Hunting Shoes, high cut, lace, bellows tongue .... " " 3.50

——for sale ONLY by——

E. T. ALLEN, - - Agent for Pacific Coast,

416 Market Street, San Francisco, Cal.

Everything for Trotter or Runner.

At J. A. McKERRON'S,

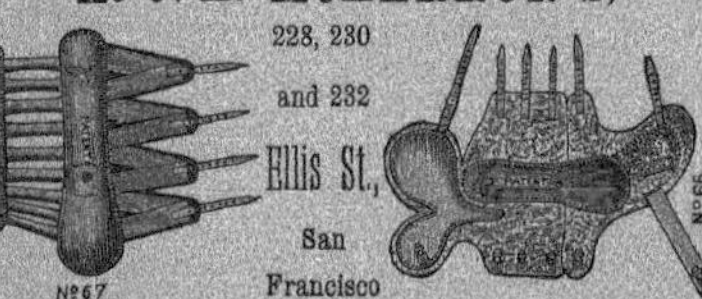

228, 230 and 232 Ellis St., San Francisco

The Brunswick Balke Collender Co.

MANUFACTURERS OF

Standard Billiard and Pool Tables, Saloon and Bank Fixtures,
653--655 Market Street. San Francisco, Cal.

Abell & Priest PHOTOGRAPHERS,
723 Market Street, S. F.
Our View is unsurpassed by any Studio in the United States.

AN UNQUALIFIED ENDORSEMENT.

Peruvian Bitters are made of the purest ingredients and compounded as carefully as any prescription.

Peruvian Bark, one of its principal ingredients, was introduced into Spain by the Countess, wife of Count CINCHON, Spanish Viceroy to Peru in 1630, who was cured of a fever by its use, since which time, no better remedy for Malaria and for Restoring the Natural Tone of the Stomach has been discovered.

On the Atlantic Coast they are used in the principal Hotels, Clubs and Restaurants, and sold by all Grocers and Druggists. We have sold them for the past three years WITHOUT ANY ADVERTISING and sales have constantly increased UPON MERIT ALONE, and we unqualifiedly recommend them to our friends and customers.

ACKER, MERRALL & CONDIT.

New York, Feb. 1st, 1890.

WILMERDING & CO., Agents for Pacific Coast,
216 FRONT ST., SAN FRANCISCO, CAL.

The Pacific Coast

Live Stock Owners
MUTUAL PROTECTIVE ASS'N.,

MONTEREY, Monterey Co., Cal.

TRUSTEES:

HON. B. V. SARGENT, President,
G. W. GALLANAR, Secretary,
JAMES E. PALMER, Business Manager,
EDW. INGRAM, Vice-President,
FRED. D. HOWARD, Actuary,
R. H. WILLEY, Attorney.

GENERAL BUSINESS OFFICE, Room 73, Flood Building, corner Market and Fourth Streets, San Francisco, Cal.

VOLNEY HOWARD, General Manager.

Attention.

-:- Campers and Sportsmen -:-

The "GOLCHER" Hunting Boots and Shoes are the only ones in the market that are PRACTICAL, as they combine Lightness, Comfort and Durability. The weight of the boots per pair is 3 lbs.; the shoes, per pair, 2¼ lbs. The uppers are made of alum-tanned leather, and the leg of soft oil-tanned leather. They are provided with good stiff counters and heavy shanks. The seams are all on the outside, which insures comfort. They have a bellows tongue, and lace up the front from instep to top of boot.

Price of Boots, per pair $5 00
" Shoes " $3 50

Clabrough, Golcher & Co.,

Guns, Pistols, Fishing Tackle,
Sporting & Athletic Goods,
630 and 632 Montgomery Street, S. F.

MOORE, HUNT & CO.,
404 Front Street, - - - San Francisco.
SOLE AGENTS FOR
Jesse Moore & Co.'s Whiskies.

THOS. KIRKPATRICK, SAN FRANCISCO. G. H. MOORE, H. B. HUNT, SAN FRANCISCO.
Of Jesse Moore & Co., Louisville, Ky.

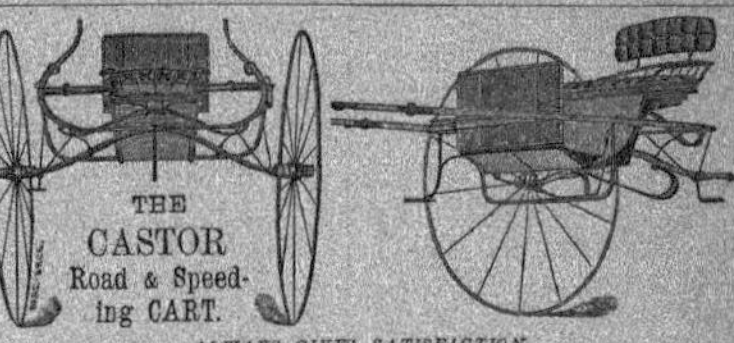

THE CASTOR Road & Speeding CART.

ALWAYS GIVES SATISFACTION.

Combining perfect riding qualities, proportions and balance, with genteel appearance.

No vehicle exhibits a horse to better advantage, and no Cart approaches them for speeding or training purposes.

A stylish vehicle for exercising or pleasure driving, at one-fourth the cost of a carriage. Have none of the horse jockey or objectionable features of other Road Carts.

They are the Leading Cart wherever introduced, and are in use by the most prominent breeders and pleasure drivers everywhere.

Elegant Shifting Top Carts.

Perfectly Balanced Stylish Pole Carts.

For Illustrated Catalogue, with Prices, address,

LEWIS F. CASTOR,
Frankford, Philadelphia, Pa.

JOHN SPLAN, General Agent.

keeps horses healthy, promotes digestion, fattens horses, loosens the hide, assists the appetite, prevents leg swelling, strengthens the kidneys, regulates the bowels and destroys worms. **$7.50 per 100 lbs.** Ask your dealer for it or send to

MANHATTAN FOOD CO., 206 Clay St., S. F.

Lightning Source UK Ltd.
Milton Keynes UK
UKHW010604051218
333419UK00009B/670/P